WHO WAS WHO IN THE USSR

A Biographic Directory
Containing 5,015 Biographies of Prominent Soviet Historical Personalities

Compiled by
THE INSTITUTE FOR THE STUDY OF THE USSR
Munich · Germany

Edited by
Dr. Heinrich E. Schulz,
Paul K. Urban, Andrew I. Lebed

THE SCARECROW PRESS, Inc.
Metuchen, New Jersey, USA
1972

WHO WAS WHO IN THE USSR

Library of Congress Catalog Card No.: 70-161563
ISBN 0-8108-0441-7

Contents

Preface

The Institute for the Study of the USSR now has over thirteen years of experience in compiling and publishing biographies of outstanding persons in the Soviet Union. During this time, it has accumulated detailed biographical information on more than 136,000 Soviet citizens. Its research facilities, including a liberary of some 80,000 volumes and a collection of over 750 Soviet newspapers and periodicals, have made this immense undertaking possible.

Since the project was initiated, the Institute has produced the following series of reference works: *Biographic Directory of the USSR*, The Scarecrow Press, Inc., 1958; *Who's Who in the USSR 1961–1962*, International Book and Publishing Co. Ltd., 1962; *Who's Who in the USSR 1965–1966*, International Book and Publishing Co. Ltd., 1966 (Second Edition); *Prominent Personalities in the USSR*, The Scarecrow Press, Inc., 1968; *Party and Government Officials of the Soviet Union 1917–1967*, The Scarecrow Press, Inc., 1969; *The Soviet Diplomatic Corps 1917–1967*, The Scarecrow Press, Inc., 1970; *Soviet Science 1917–1970. Part I: Academy of Sciences of the USSR*, The Scarecrow Press, Inc., 1971.

Interest shown in these publications by research workers, editors, journalists, politicians and state officials all over the world continues to grow. In collated and easily accessible form these reference works furnish the fullest and most accurate data available on the better known Soviet Party and government officials, the scientific and cultural personalities of the USSR, Party, state and scientific establishments, and so forth. Such data is not to be found in corresponding Soviet reference works and encyclopedias, which present the additional obstacle that they are written in Russian.

The present book, named *Who Was Who in the USSR*, is the eighth reference work in this series. By its nature and purpose it differs somewhat from previous biographical manuals in that it deals with persons no longer living. Moreover, it includes a certain number of biographies of people who actively campaigned against the Soviet regime or were later exiled or put to death by the Soviet authorities. The reference work covers the period from 1917 to 1967 and contains 5,015 biographies of prominent individuals who have made major contributions to the political, intellectual, scientific, social and economic life of the country.

Munich, Germany
April 1971

The Editors

Russian-English Transliteration System

А	=	A, a	П	=	P, p
Б	=	B, b	Р	=	R, r
В	=	V, v	С	=	S, s
Г	=	G, g	Т	=	T, t
Д	=	D, d	У	=	U, u
Е	=	Ye, (e)*	Ф	=	F, f
Ё	=	Yo, yo	Х	=	Kh, kh
Ж	=	Zh, zh	Ц	=	Ts, ts
З	=	Z, z	Ч	=	Ch, ch
И	=		Ш	=	Sh, sh
Й	=	Y, y	Щ	=	Shch, shch
К	=	K, k	Ы	=	Y, y
Л	=	L, l	Ь	=	‘
М	=	M, m	Э	=	E, e
Н	=	N, n	Ю	=	Yu, yu
О	=	O, o	Я	=	Ya, ya

Adjectival Endings

ый	=	yy
ий	=	iy
ые	=	yye
ие	=	iye
ая	=	aya
ое	=	oye

* "e" is used immediately after a consonant; in all other positions "ye" is used.

Abbreviations and Terms

Acad Academy, academician
Admin Administration, administrative
agric agriculture, agricultural
amb ambassador
Apr April
Arm Armenia, Armenian
asst assistant
Assoc Association, associate
ASSR Autonomous Soviet Socialist Republic
Aug August
Azer Azerbaydzhan, Azerbaydzhani

Bash Bashkiria, Bashkir
Bd Board
Bel Belorussia, Belorussian

cand candidate
capt captain
CC Central Committee
centr central
Cheka Extraordinary Commission Against Counter-revolution, Sabotage and Speculation
chm chairman
col colonel
Comecon Council of Mutual Economic Aid
Comintern Communist International
Comr Commissar
Comrt Commissariat
Comt Committee
corresp corresponding, correspondent
CP (CP[B]) Communist Party (Communist Party[Bolsheviks])
CPSU Communist Party of the Soviet Union
CPSU(B) All-Union Communist Party (Bolsheviks)

Dagh Daghestan, Daghestani
Dec December
deleg delegate, delegation
dep deputy
dept department
dipl diplomat, diplomatic
dir director
Distr district
Div Division
DOSAAF Voluntary Society for Cooperation with the Army, Airforce and Navy
Dr Doctor

Econ Economy, economics, economic, economist
ed editor, edition, editorial
ed bd editorial board
electr electricity, electrical
eng engineering, engineer
Est Estonia, Estonian
etc etcetera
Exec Executive

Fac Faculty
Feb February
Fed Federation, federal
For Foreign

GDR German Democratic Republic
gen general
Geo Georgia, Georgian
GFR German Federal Republic
Gosplan State Planning Committee
Gosstroy State Construction Committee
Govt Government
grad graduate

Hon Honored, honorary, honer

ind industry, industrial
Inst Institute
int international

Jan January

Kaz Kazakhstan, Kazakh
Kir Kirghizia, Kirghiz
kolkhoz collective farm
Komsomol Communist Youth League
Kray territorial-administrative unit

Lat Latvia, Latvian
lit literature, literary
Lith Lithuania, Lithuanian
lt lieutenant

mang manager, management
maj major
Mar March
mech mechanics, mechanic, mechanical, mechanized
med medicine, medical
mil military
Min Minister, Ministry
Mold Moldavia, Moldavian
MTS machine and tractor station
MVD Ministry of the Interior

nat national
NKVD People's Commissariat of Internal Affairs
Nov November

Oblast basic territorial-administrative unit
Oct October
OGPU Joint State Political Administration
Okrug subdivision of an oblast or autonomous republic
Org organization, organizational

pedag pedagogics, pedagogic
Petersburg St. Petersburg
plen plenipotentiary
polit political
Politburo Political Bureau
Pop People's, popular
postgrad postgraduate
pres president
prof professor
publ publication, publishing

Rayon small territorial-administrative unit
RCP (B) Russian Communist Party (Bolsheviks)
Regt Regiment, regimental
republ republican
revol revolution, revolutionary

RSDRP	Russian Social-Democratic Workers' Party
RSDRP (B)	Russian Social-Democratic Workers' Party (Bolsheviks)
RSFSR	Russian Soviet Federative Socialist Republic
sci	science, scientific
secr	secretary
Sept	September
Soc	Society, social
Sov	Soviet
sovkhoz	state farm
Sovnarkhoz	Economic Council
SSR	Soviet Socialist Republic
supr	supreme
Supr Sov	Supreme Soviet
Tadzh	Tadzhikistan, Tadzhik
TASS	Telegraphic Agency of the USSR
tech	technical, technician
technol	technology, technological
trans	transport, transportation
Turkm	Turkmenia, Turkmen
UAR	United Arab Republic
Uyezd	former administrative subdivision of a province or oblast
Uk	United Kingdom of Great Britain
Ukr	Ukraine, Ukrainian
UN	United Nations Organization
Univ	University
US	United States (adjective)
USA	United States of America
USSR	Union of Soviet Socialist Republics
Uzbek	Uzbekistan, Uzbek
vil	village
vol	volume
Volost	former small rural district
WW 1	World War 1
WW 2	World War 2
Zemstvo	former local government authority

Biographies

A

ABAGINSKIY (KUDRIN-ABAGINSKIY), Arkhip Georgiyevich (1907-1960) Yakut poet; *Born:* 20 Jan 1907, son of a peasant; *Educ:* studied at Irkutsk Teachers' Training Inst; *Publ:* verse collections: "Verse and Songs" (1927); "Step by Step" (1931); "From Victory to Victory" (1939); poems: "Shanghai" (1933); "I Am a Son of the People" (1938); WW 2 verse cycles: "The West" and "The East"; children's books; in Russian translation: *Izbrannoye* (Selected Works) (1953); *Yakutiyu poyu* (I Sing of Yakutia) (1957); *Died:* 22 Sept 1960.

ABAKUMOV, Sergey Ivanovich (1890-1949) Philologist; Dr of Philological Sci; prof; corresp member, RSFSR Acad of Pedag Sci from 1947; *Born:* 4 June 1890; *Educ:* 1912 grad History and Philology Fac, Kazan' Univ; *Career:* from 1912 taught Russian language and lit at a Kazan' high-school; from 1930 college lecturer; 1943-49 senior assoc, Research Inst of Teaching Methods, RSFSR Acad of Pedag Sci; developed methods of teaching Russian at secondary-school level; *Publ: Na putyakh k novomu uchebniku* (Approaches to a New Textbook) (1925-27); *Uchebnik russkoy grammatiki. Opyt primeneniya printsipov nauchnoy grammatiki v shkol'no-grammaticheskoy praktike* (A Russian Grammar Textbook. Experience in the Use of Scientific Grammatical Principles in School Grammar Practice) (1926); *Material k planirovaniyu uchebnoy raboty po russkomu yazyku v 5-10 klassakh* (Material for Planning Russian Language Tuition in the 5th-10th Grades) (1936); *Sbornik uprazhneniy po pravopisaniyu* (A Collection of Spelling Exercises) (1939); *Sovremennyy russkiy literaturnyy yazyk* (Modern Literary Russian) (1942); *Metodika punktuatsii* (Punctuation Methods) (3rd ed, 1951), etc; *Died:* 7 May 1949.

ABAKUMOV, Viktor Semyonovich (1894-1954) Govt official; USSR Min of State Security; CP member from 1917; *Born:* 1894 in Taganrog; *Career:* 1917 began his career with the All-Russian Cheka and was soon appointed head, operations dept of a Moscow Rayon, then dep chm, Moscow Cheka; May 1920 head, Southeastern Front's Rear Admin, then head, Special Section, All-Ukr Cheka; 1921 head, Special Section, Tambov Mil Distr; helped suppress the Antonov peasant revolt; 1923-27 head, Moscow GPU Admin; 1927 involved in coal ind of the Donets Basin on special orders to increase the coal output; organized the Donbass Coal Trust and, by incredibly ruthless methods, boosted coal output; 1929-38 with NKVD Centr Admin in Moscow, then with the Intelligence Section ot the Gen Staff; Sept 1942 helped organize the Gen Staff for Partisan Warfare and Diversion; from Dec 1942 head, State Security Section of Sov Army *Smersh* (Death to Spies); 1946 appointed USSR Min of State Security; 1951 vanished from the polit scene, Dec 1954 publicly tried in Leningrad on charges of falsifying the so-called "Leningrad Case" and other court cases, also of using "criminal interrogation methods"; sentenced to death; *Died:* executed 12 Dec 1954.

ABASHELI (real name: CHOCHIYA), Aleksandr (Isaki) Vissarionovich (1884-1954) Geo poet; *Born*: 28 Aug 1884 in vil Sachochno, Kutaisi Province; *Career:* took part in 1905 Revol, for which was exiled to Sol'vychegodsk; 1908 returned from exile, began to write; *Publ:* collected verse "Laughter of the Sun" (1913) reflects his symbolism period from 1908 to 1917; verse: "Tbilisi Night" (1926); "To Poets" (1929); "The Lyricist and the Gardener" (1932); "October Thunder" (1937); "The Birth of a Verse"; "Immortality" and "To My Native Land" (1938), etc, glorified the labor of Sov people and urged poets to be in the forefront of the fight for Communism; works expressed firm belief in victory: "In Germany"; "A Letter From Mother"; "Beat Them Off!"; "Stalingrad"; "The Khevsurian Tank Driver," etc; numerous poems were dedicated to the CP, its leaders, and the friendship of the peoples of the USSR: "I Must See Lenin"; "Lenin's Heart"; "To the New Georgia"; "Song of the Homeland"; "The October Star Shines"; "I See the Radiance of Coming Days"; "To the Ukraine"; "The Kremlin Towers"; "The Dove of Peace"; "We Do Not Want War"; "My Dream." etc; promoted publ of Geo lit classics; produced first complete ed of Vazha Pshavely's works; together with poet G. Abashidze composed Geo nat anthem; *Died:* 27 Sept 1954 in Tbilisi.

ABASHIDZE, Anastasiya (Taso) Vasil'yevna (1881-1958) Geo actress; Pop Artiste of Geo SSR from 1943; *Born*: 29 Mar 1881 in Tbilisi; daughter of prominent Geo actors V. Abashidze and M. Saparova-Abashidze; *Career*: 1899 stage debut with Tiflis Drama Company; also appeared in operas and operettas; from 1921 at Rustaveli Theater in Tbilisi; from 1926 at Chiaturi Theater and other Geo theaters; 1934-48 at Mardzhanishvili Theater, Tbilisi; *Roles:* Avandil in Gedevanishvili's "The Light"; Ripsime in Antonov's "Solar Eclipse in Georgia"; Masho in Aziani's "Money and Origin"; *Publ:* "Memoirs" (1954); *Died:* 15 Sept 1958.

ABASHIDZE, Erekle Kitayevich (1906-1956) Psychologist; *Born*: 1906 in Tbilisi; *Career*: from 1930 various posts at research institutes and higher educ establishments; edited works of Inst of Psychology, Geo Acad of Sci; edited and published vol 1 of D. N. Uznadze's works; wrote short dictionary of psychology (1950-51) and translated foreign psychological and pedag works, including Boring's "A History of Psychology," Rousseau's "Emile" and Pestalozzi's "Swangsong"; *Publ:* "The Psychology of the Weaver" (1932); "Methods for a Psychological Study of Fatigue in Weavers" (1932); "Aristotle's Treatise 'On the Soul'" (1939); "Descartes' Psychological Teaching" (1940); "The Relationship and Stability of Experimentally Fixed Ideas" (1940); "The Saturation Factor in the Operation of an Experimentally Fixed Idea" (1945); "The Psychology of Proverbs" (1945); "Some Features of the Historical Development of Human Reason" (1948); "Habit in Stern's Personalistic Psychology" (1942); "The Psychology of Sporting Skills (an Auxiliary Aid for Sport and Physical Training Instructors)" (1951); "The Psychological Essence of Sport and Physical Exercise" (1953); "Figurative Thinking in Modern Speech (the Relationship of Speech and Thinking)" (1952); "A Psychological Analysis of Some Logical Errors" (1953); "The Psychology of Conclusions" (1955); "The Psychology of So-Called Logical Errors" (1956); "The Problem of Personality" (1956), etc; *Died:* 21 Sept 1956.

ABASHIDZE, Vasiliy (Vaso) Alekseyevich (1854-1926) Actor; Pop Artiste of Geo SSR from 1922; *Born*: 1854 in Dusheti (Geo), son of a teacher; *Educ:* grad Tbilisi secondary school; *Career:* from 1879 with Tbilisi Geo Drama Company; *Roles:* Karapet in Eristavi's "The Miser" and Mkrtum in Eristavi's "Partition"; Zimzimov in Sundukyan's *Pepo*; the mayor in Gogol's *Revizor* (The Government Inspektor); Belogubov in Ostrovkiy's *Dokhodnoye mesto* (A Lucrative Post), etc; pioneer of realism in Geo theater; also worked as producer; Tbilisi Musical Comedy Theater was named after him; 1885 founded and edited newspaper *Teatri*; author of several plays; translated and adapted 42 comedies, vaudeville pieces and musical comedies; published *Kratkiye svedeniya o dramaticheskom iskusstve* (A Short Guide to Stagecraft) (1894); *Died:* Oct 1926 in Tbilisi.

ABASOV, Eyub Dzhebrail ogly (1905-1957) Azer writer; Hon Art Worker of Azer SSR; *Born:* 1905 in vil Shaki, now Arm SSR, son of a peasant; *Educ:* grad Azer Teacher's Training Inst; *Career:* 1932 first work published; contributed to Azer newspapers; verse glorified the builders of socialism; *Publ:* poem "A Steamship Under the Red Flag" (1953) dealt with everyday life in India and Sov aid to that country; poem "A Word About Truth" (1953) described heroism of Brazilian woman Elisa Branko; novel Zangezur (vol 1-2, 1956-57; Russian translation 1959) depicted struggle of Azer and Arm people to establish Sov regime; wrote verse and plays for children; translated S. Mikhalkov's play *Ya khochu domoy* (I Want to Go Home), S. Marshak's poem *Byl' i nebylitsa* (Truth and Fable), and Polish poet Julian Tuwim's book "Verse for Children"; *Died:* 18 Dec 1957 in Baku.

ABBASOV, Mirza Ali (1874-1943) Actor; Hon Artiste of Geo SSR from 1924; *Born:* 1874; *Career:* 1898 stage debut; worked for Azer drama company in Tiflis; appeared in Tebriz, Tashkent, etc; 1916 co-founder, actor and stage dir, Tiflis Azer Theater; *Roles:* Kadzhar in Akhverdov's *Aga Mukhammed-shakh Kadzhar*; Othello; Franz Moor in Schiller's "The Robbers"; *Died:* 1943.

ABDULLAYEV, Khabib Mukhamedovich (1912-1962) Uzbek geologist, Party and state functionary; Dr of Geological and Mineralogical Sci from 1946; member, Uzbek Acad of Sci from 1947; corresp member, USSR Acad of Sci form 1958; CP member from 1941; *Born:* 1912; *Educ:* 1935 grad Centr Asian Geological Survey Inst; 1935-39 postgrad work at Moscow Geological Survey Inst; *Career:* 1940-41 at Centr Asian Ind Inst, Tashkent; 1941-48 and 1955-56 dept head, CC, CP Uzbek Council of Min, chm, Uzbek Gosplan; 1943-47 corresp member, 1947-52 vice-pres, 1956-61 pres, Uzbek Acad of Sci; 1956-62 member, CC, CP Uzbek; several times elected dep, Uzbek Supr Sov; dep, USSR Supr Sov of 1958 convocation; chm, Uzbek Sci and Tech Soc; chm, Uzbek Branch, All-Union Mineralogical Soc; chm, Council for Study of Uzbek Productive Resources, Uzbek Acad of Sci; from 1960 Bureau member, Dept of Geological and Geographical Sci, USSR Acad of Sci, and member, Comt for Lenin Prizes for Sci and Technol, USSR Council of Min; specialist in theory of formation of magmatic rocks and ore deposits in Centr Asia; author of over 130 sci works; *Publ: Geologiya sheyelitonosnykh skarnov Sredney Azii* (Geology of the Scheelitic Skarns of Central Asia) (1947); *Geneticheskaya svyaz' orudneniya s granitoidnymi intruziyami* (The Genetic Relationship of Mineralization to Granitoid Intrusions) (1954); *Dayki i orudneniya* (Dikes and Mineralizations) (1957), etc; *Awards:* Lenin Prize (1959); Order of Lenin; two Orders of the Red Banner of Labor; three Orders of the Red Star; Badge of Honor; medals; *Died:* 20 June 1962 after long and severe illness.

ABDULOV, Osip Naumovich (1900-1953) Russian actor; Pop Artiste of RSFSR from 1944; *Born:* 16 Nov 1900; *Career:* amateur acting while studying at Fac of Soc Sci, Moscow Univ; 1918-23 acted at Chaliapin Studio, where his first role was the tramp in Schnitzler's "The Green Parrot" (1919); acted at Komissarzhevskaya Theater, where he played Rasplyuyev in a stage adaptation of Sukhovo-Kobylin's *Otzhitoye vremya* (Past Time), and at Moscow Acad Arts Theater; 1929 joined studio theater managed by Yu. A. Zavadskiy; 1938-42 acted at Moscow Theater of the Revol; 1943-53 at Mossovet Theater; his acting technique was a masterly combination of lush comedy and a fine sense of humor and irony; from 1924 he also performed on radio, producing over 200 radio plays and preparing children's programs; from 1933 he played film roles and taught acting at the Zavadskiy Studio; *Stage Roles:* Krutitskiy in *Na vsyakogo mudretsa dovol'no prostoty* (There's a Simpleton in Every Sage) (1928); Gen Burgoyne in Shaw's "The Devil's Disciple" (1933); Lynyaev in *Volki i ovtsy* (The Wolves and the Sheep) (1934); Knurov in *Bespridannitsa* (Girl Without a Dowry) (1940); Fromanteville in Verneuil's "School for Debtors" (1936); Narzulayev in Voytekhov and Lench's *Pavel Grekov* (1939); Sorin in *Chayka* (The Seagull) (1945); Uncle Vasya in Nushich's *Gospozha ministersha* (Mrs Minister) (1946); Bob Murphy in *Russkiy vopros* (The Russian Question) (1947); Acad Ryzhov in Surov's *Rassvet nad Moskvoy* (Dawn over Moscow) (1950); the old bard in Khikmet's *Rasskaz o Turtsii* (A Tale of Turkey) (1953); *Film Roles:* the prof in *Pokoleniye pobediteley* (A Generation of Conquerors) (1936); the dir in *Svetlyy put'* (The Radiant Path) (1940); Isaacs in *Aleksandr Popov* (1949), etc; *Awards*: Stalin Prize (1951); *Died*: 14 June 1953.

ABEGYAN, Manuk Khachaturovich (1865-1944) Arm folklorist, lit historian and linguist; Hon Sci Worker of Arm SSR; member, Arm Acad of Sci; prof, Yerevan Univ; *Born:* 29 Mar 1865; *Career:* wrote several dozen works on Arm folklore, lit and grammar; prepared acad ed of major folklore and lit works; *Publ:* "Armenian Folk Myths in Movses Khorenskiy's 'A History of Armenia'" (1899); "The Armenian Folk Epic:: (1908); "The Syntax of the New Armenian Literary Language" (1912); "Movses Khorenskiy's 'A History of Armenia'" (1913); "Ancient Gusan Folk Songs" (1931); "The Meter of Armenian Verse" (1933); "Social Motifs in Medieval Armenian Fables" (1935); "A History of Armenian Literature" (2 vol, 1944-46); "David Sasunskiy" (2 vol, 1936-46); "Gusan Folk Songs"; "Folk Ditties" (1940); *Russko-armyanskiy voyennyy slovar'* (A Russian-Armenian Military Dictionary) (1925); *Died:* 25 Sept 1944; the Inst of Lit, Arm Acad of Sci is named after him.

ABELYAN, Ovanes Artyom'yevich (1865-1936) Arm actor; Pop Artiste of Arm and Azer SSR; *Born:* 4 Febr 1865 in Shemakha, now Azer SSR; *Career:* 1882 stage debut at Russian Theater, Baku; 1886 switched to Arm stage; 1925 at Sundukyan Theater, Yerevan; in the course of his 54 years on the stage he performed some 1,200 roles, including: Elizbaron in A. Shirvanzade's "For the Sake of Honor"; Pepo in G. Sundukyan's *Pepo*; Neschastlivtsev in Ostrovskiy's *Les* (The Forest); Bulychyov in Gorky's *Yegor Bulychyov*; Oedipus in Sophocles' "Oedipus Rex"; Lear in Shakespeare's "King Lear"; Stockmann in Ibsen's "Doctor Stockmann"; Osip in Gogol's *Revizor* (The Government Inspector), etc; was a talented, temperamental and dynamic actor and a leading figure of the Arm stage; from 1918 chm, Actors' Union, Tiflis; performed in Turkey, Egypt, Germany, USA and other countries; *Awards:* Hero of Labor (1942); *Died:* 1 July 1936 in Yerevan.

ABOLIN, Ans Kristianovich (1891- ?) Party official; secr, All-Union Centr Trade-Union Council; CP member from 1908; *Born*: 1891, son of a peasant; *Career*: longshoreman, then office worker; club leader and propagandist, Riga Party org; 1913 drafted into the army; after 1917 Oct Revol secr to the comr of a Petrograd bank; comr, Moscow Pop Bank; then trade-union work; from 1919-21 in the Red Army; after his discharge from the army worked for the Agitation and Propaganda Dept, and from May 1922 secr, Kuban'-Black Sea Oblast Party Comt; 1924-26 dep head, Dept of Agitation and Propaganda, CC, CPSU(B); 1926-28 secr, Penza Province and Samara Okrug CPSU(B) Comt; 1929-30 chm, CC, Union of Educ Workers; Presidium member and secr, All-Union Centr Trade-Union Council; member, All-Russian Exec Comt and USSR Exec Comt of several convocations; 1933 Presidium member, All-Russian Exec Comt and member, Profintern Exec Bureau; *Died:* date, place and cause of death unknown.

ABRAMOVICH, Dmitriy Ivanovich (1873-1955) Russian lit historian; corresp member, USSR Acad of Sci from 1921; *Born:* 7 Aug 1873 in vil Gulevichi, Volhynian Province; *Educ:* 1897 grad Petersburg Theological Acad; *Career:* from 1903 head, Chair of Russian and Old Slavonic, Petersburg Theological Acad; 1909 dismissed for "unreliability"; taught history of Russian lit and Russian language, Old Slavonic and paleography at Bestuzhev Higher Women's Courses in Petersburg, Petrograd Univ, etc; prof, Leningrad Univ; prof, Smolensk Teachers' Traning Inst; in his latter years prof, Vilnius Univ; specialized in ancient Russian lit; wrote studies of the Kiev Pechera Paterikon, Nestor the Chronicler, etc; edited the *Paterik Kiyevo-Pecherskogo monastyrya* (The Paterikon of the Kiev Pechera Monastery) (1911); edited *Zhitiye svyatykh muchenikov Borisa i Gleba* (The Life of the Holy Martyrs Boris and Gleb) (1916); compiled model exemplary accounts of a number of manuscript collections, including *Opisaniye rukopisey Sanktpeterburgskoy dukhovnoy akademii. Sofiyskaya biblioteka* (An Account of the Manuscripts of the Saint Petersburg Theological Academy. The Sofia Library) (1905-10); also wrote studies of Gogol, Maykov and other 19th-Century Russian writers; edited *Polnoye sobraniye sochineniy M. Yu. Lermontova* (The Complete Collected Works of M. Yu. Lermontov) (5 vol, 1910-13); 1920 published hitherto unknown work of Goncharov *Neobyknovennaya istoriya* (An Unusual Story); *Publ: Issledovaniye o Kiyevo-Pecherskom paterike kak istoriko-literaturnom pamyatnike* (A Study of the Kiev Pechera Paterikon as a Monument of Literary History) (1902); *K voprosu ob ob'yome i kharaktere literaturnoy deyatel'nosti Nestora Letopistsa* (The Scope and Nature of Nestor the Chronicler's Literary Work) (1902); *Pis'ma russkikh pisateley k A.S. Suvorinu* (Russian Writers' Letters to A.S. Suvorin) (1927); *Died:* 4 Mar 1955 in Vilnius.

ABRAMOVICH, Frants Vikent'yevich (1864-1933) Surgeon and health service official; Dr of Med from 1900; *Born:* 1864 in vil Klessel', Minsk Province; *Educ;* 1883 grad Chernigov High-School; 1833-86 studied at Med Fac, Kiev Univ; 1889 grad Petersburg Mil Med Acad with distinction; *Career:* after grad zemstvo distr physician in Peterhof Uyezd, then dir, Kamenskoye Zemstvo Factory Hospital, Tver' Province; 1900 defended doctor's thesis on the hemastatic effect of steam and hot air on liver wounds; from 1902 senior physician, Tver' Province Zemstvo Hospital; chm, Tver' Soc of Physicians, 1914 senior physician, Gomel' Gynecological Hospital, during WW 1 dir, mil hospital based on Gomel' Gynecological Hospital; after 1917 Oct Revol head, Surgical Dept, Gomel' City Hospital; from 1923 head, Surgical Dept, Mozyr' Okrug Hospital, where he developed a reputation for complex operations for diseases of the abdominal organs and lesions and diseases of the extremities; delivered papers at several All-Union and Bel surgical congresses; chm, Mozyr' Physicians' Soc; dep, chm, 1st Congress of Bel Surgeons, Obstetricians and Gynecologists, wrote 22 works; *Publ:* doctor's thesis *O krovoostanavlivayushchem deystvii vodyanogo para i goryachego vozdukha pri raneniyakh pecheni* (The Hemastatic Effect of Water Vapor and Hot Air on Liver Wounds) (1900); *Ob osumkovannykh kishechnykh khronicheskikh peritonitakh* (Chronic Encapsulated Intestinal Peritonitis) (1925); *Khronicheskiy appenditsit, yego diagnostika, operativnoye lecheniye i otdalyonnyye rezul'taty* (Chronic Appendicitis, Its Diagnosis, Operative Treatment and Long-Term Sequelae) (1929); *Ob obyazatel'noy khirurgicheskoy pomoshchi v rayonakh* (Essential District Surgical Aid) (1929); *Died:* June 1933 in Mozyr' of typhus contracted from a patient.

ABRAMOVICH (real name: REYN), Rafail Abramovich (1880-1963) RSDRP (Mensheviks) leader; chief ed, centr RSDRP organ Sotsialisticheskiy vestnik; *Born*: 21 July 1880 in Dvinsk; *Educ*: studied at Riga Polytech Inst and in Liège (Belgium); *Career*: while still a student took part in the student, then labor polit movement, soon becoming a prominent figure in the Gen Jewish Workers' League in Russia and Poland (Bund); 1902, after suppression of Riga Bund org, left Riga for Liège to complete tech educ; 1903 attended 5th Congress of Bund; 1904 returned to Russia and engaged in underground work as rep, CC, Bund; 1905 co-opted member, CC, Bund; member of Bund deleg at 4th (Amalgamative) Congress of RSDRP; from 1906 member, CC, RSDRP (Mensheviks); for next few years worked with CC, Bund, editing legal and illegal publ; 1911 arrested and exiled to Vologda Province, whence he fled abroad; 1912-14, in Vienna, on ed staff of legal Bund organs: *Leben Frage* (Warsaw), *Zeit, Unser Zeit*, etc (Petersburg); during WW 1 sided with defensists; spring 1917 returned to Russia and became member, CC, Bund, and CC, RSDRP (Mensheviks); 1917-18 active in party and soc orgs (including All-Russian Union of Railroad Workers) trying to form broad socialist coalition govt; arrested in July 1918 at All-Russian Conference of Factory and Works Deleg and spent six months in prison; 1920, at 12th Conference of Bund, vigorously opposed Bundist faction advocating merger with the RCP(B) and led the rightist wing out of the Bund, later forming the Soc-Democratic Bund; late 1920, as member of a for deleg of Mensheviks and the Soc-Democratic Bund, he remained abroad and from 1 Feb 1921, together with Martov, began to publish *Sotsialisticheskiy vestnik*, editing this journal until his death; in 1923 took part in Congress of the Workers' International; for almost 20 years he was a member of the Exec Comt and exec Bureau of this org; 10 Apr 1937 his only son, Mark, was kidnapped in Barcelona; *Died*: Apr 1963 in New York.

ABRAZHANOV, Aleksandr Alekseyevich (1869-1931) Surgeon; Dr of Med; prof from 1922; *Born*: 1869; *Educ*: 1891 grad Med Fac, Warsaw Univ; *Career*: joined revol movement while still a student; after grad intern under chief surgeon Trachtenberg, Maria Hospital, Petersburg; June 1893 arrested for revol activities and exiled to Urals; under permanent police surveillance worked for six years as surgeon-physician at Yuryuzan' Iron Works; chm, Ufa Province Med Soc; from 1897 active member, Ural Med Soc, Yekaterinburg; read papers at Pirogov Russian Surgical Soc congresses; from 1899 head, Surgical Dept, Zlatoust Rural Hospital, where he did research on animals for the doctor's thesis he subsequently defended at Petersburg Mil Med Acad; 1901-02 intern under Prof Borngaupt, 1902-05 assoc prof, Hospital Surgical Clinic, Kiev Univ; 1905-13 head, Surgical Dept, Poltava Province Rural Hospital; from 1913 dir, Khar'kov Red Cross Surgical Clinic; simultaneously assoc prof, Khar'kov Univ, where he lectured on exploratory surgery; from 1922 until death head, Chair of Fac Surgery Clinic, Dnepropetrovsk Med Inst; chm, Ufa and Poltava Physicians' Soc; chm, Dnepropetrovsk Med Sci; chm, Dnepropetrovsk Surgical Soc; dep, Dnepropetrovsk City Sov; co-ed *Dnepropetrovskiy meditsinskiy zhurnal*; wrote over 60 works; *Publ: K voprosu o lechenii gnoynogo plevrita operativnym putyom* (The Operative Treatment of Purulent Pleurisy) (1894); *Kostnoplasticheskiy sposob chrezmyshchelkovoy amputatsii bedra* (An Osteoplastic Method of Transcondylar Amputation of the Thigh) (1897); *Peresadka i plombirovaniye kostey* (The Transplantation and Filling of Bones) (1899); *Chetyre nablyudeniya nad zakrytiyem trepanatsionnykh otverstiy v cherepe* (Four Observations on the Closure of Trepanning Apertures in the Skull) (1900); *Died*: 1931 in Dnepropetrovsk of cardiac arrest while undergoing an operation for bilateral nephrolithiasis.

ABRIKOSOV, Aleksey Ivanovich (1875-1955) Pathoanatomist; prof from 1918; Dr of Med from 1904; member, USSR Acad of Sci from 1939; member, USSR Acad of Med Sci from 1944; Hon Sci Worker of RSFSR from 1929; Hero of Socialist Labor from 1945; CP member from 1939; *Born*: 18 Jan 1875 in Moscow; *Educ*: 1899 grad Med Fac, Moscow Univ, with honors; *Career*: after two years internship in univ infectious diseases clinic specialized in pathological anatomy; 1904 defended doctor's thesis; 1904-18 asst lecturer, Moscow Univ; from 1904 prosector, Morozov Hospital, Moscow; from 1911 also prosector, Botkin City Hospital, Moscow; 1918-20 prof, Dept of Pathological Anatomy, 2nd Moscow Univ; 1920-53 prof, Dept of Pathological Anatomy, 1st Moscow Univ (from early 1930's 1st Moscow Med Inst); from 1920 dir, Inst of Pathological Anatomy, Moscow Univ; from 1924 dean, Med Fac, 1944-51 dir, Inst of Normal and Pathological Morphology, USSR Acad of Med Sci; 1924 Inst of Pathological Anatomy, Botkin City Hospital, Moscow, named for him; from 1927 Bd member, 1st Moscow Univ; also member, State Learned Med Council, Learned Council, RSFSR and USSR Min of Health, Higher Certification Commission and Comt for Award of Stalin Prizes; in his latter years Presidium member and vice-pres, USSR Acad of Med Sci; founder and chm, Moscow Soc of Pathoanatomists; member, many other sci soc in USSR; member, German Soc of Pathologists and Polish Acad of Sci; from 1935 founder and chief ed, journal *Arkhiv patologii*; co-ed, *Bol'shaya meditsinskaya entsiklopediya* (Large Medical Encyclopedia); founded major school of pathological anatomy; more than 500 sci works written under his supervision; wrote 105 works which shed new light on pathological anatomy of tuberculosis, tumors of the muscular tissue, osteodystrophia fibrosa, etc; first accurate description of histogenesis of pulmonary tuberculosis (1914); first proof of histogenetic link between rhabdomyomas and Purkinje's cells of the heart (1909); established affinity of edema neonatorum with fetal cachexia (1910); ascertained origin of primary atrophy of the cerebral cortex (1912); established possibility of ascertaining chemical action of lipoids microchemically (1912); gave histological explanation of calcification (1914); proved identity of bone lesions in adult scurvy with Barlow's disease (1916); first to pay attention to various pathological processes in the sympathetic ganglia (1921); proposed classification of pathoanatomical forms of pulmonary tuberculosis (1923); discovered new type of muscle tumor - myomas from myoblasts (1925, 1931); established pathoanatomical features of oleogranulomas and ascertained their pathogenesis (1927, 1931); confirmed the independence of reticuloendotheliosis (1927); detailed description of the morphology of allergy (1934, 1936, 1940); *Publ*: doctor's thesis *O pervykh anatomicheskikh izmeneniyakh v lyogkikh pri nachale lyogochnogo tuberkulyoza* (First Anatomical Lesions in the Lungs at the Outset of Pulmonary Tuberculosis) (1904); *Materialy k morfologicheskomu izucheniyu zhira kletochnoy protoplazmy* (Materials on the Morphological Study of Fat in Tissue Protoplasm) (1913); *Patologicheskaya anatomiya polosti rta i zubov* (Pathological Anatomy of the Oral Cavity and the Teeth) (1914); *Osnovy patologicheskoy anatomii* (Principles of Pathological Anatomy) (1923, 1925, 1927, 1933; 9th ed, 1949); *Osnovy chastnoy patologicheskoy anatomii* (Principles of Specific Pathological Anatomy) (1939; 3rd ed, 1946); *Chastnaya patologicheskaya anatomiya* (Specific Pathological Anatomy) (3 vol, 1938-53); *Tekhnika patologo-anatomicheskikh trupov* (Pathoanatomical Cadaver Technique) (1925; 4th ed, 1948); his textbooks have been translated into Ukr and other languages; *Awards*: three Orders of Lenin; Order of the Red Banner of Labor; medals; Stalin Prize (1942); *Died*: 9 Apr 1955 in Moscow.

ABROSIMOV, Pavel Vasil'yevich (1900-1961) Architect; member, USSR Acad of Construction and Architecture; exec secr, Bd, USSR Union of Architects from 1955; *Born*: 1900, son of a worker; *Educ*: 1928 grad Leningrad Acad of Arts; *Career*: 1928-35 helped design housing in Leningrad and draft designs for Palace of Soviets in Moscow; 1935-38, together with Acad I.A. Fomin, built Govt House in Kiev; 1941-45 contributed to construction of defense installations and erection of ind plants in Urals; 1945-55 member, USSR Gosstroy; and chm of its Council of Experts; simultaneously helped design Moscow's Lomonosov State Univ and helped direct reconstruction, to his own design, of war-damaged Vakhtangov Theater; member, Exec Comt, Int Union of Architects; 1958 pres, 5th Congress of Int Union of Architects in Moscow; *Awards*: two Stalin Prizes; two Orders of the Red Banner of Labor; medals; *Died*: 21 Mar 1961 after protracted illness.

ABSALYAMOV, Miftakh Shageyevich (1894-1928) Actor; *Born*: 1894; *Educ*: 1920 studied at K. Tinchurin and Z. Sultanov's Tatar Theatrical Studio, Samara; *Career*: from 1921 with Tatar Model Drama Theater, Kazan' (now Kamal Theater); *Roles*: Ivan in A.K. Tolstoy's *Smert' Ioanna Groznogo* (The Death of Ivan the Terrible); the Mullah Gaynetdin in Isanbet's "Resettlement"; *Awards*: Hero of Labor (1926); *Died*: Jan 1928.

ABZHALILOV, Khalil Galeyevich (1896-1963) Actor; Pop Artiste of Tatar ASSR; Pop Artiste of USSR from 1957; CP member from 1944; *Born*: 29 Sept 1896 in vil Mustafa, now Orenburg Oblast; *Career*: from 1916 in Tatar *Shirkat* (Comradeship) drama group; 1919 founded Tatar "Eastern Theater" in Orenburg; 1920-23 helped establish Uzbek nat theaters in Tashkent, Bukhara, Khiva and Khorezm; from 1928 actor, Tatar Kamal State Acad Theater; *Roles*: Osip in Gogol's *Revizor* (The Government Inspector); Luka in Gorky's *Na dne* (The Lower Depths); Lear in Shakespeare's "King Lear"; Pugachev in Fayzi's

Pugachyov v Kazani (Pugachev in Kazan'); Kharitonov in Lavrenev's *Za tekh, kto v more* (For Those at Sea); Ioakim Pino in Virta's *Zagovor obrechyonnykh* (Conspiracy of the Doomed); Biktimor in Gizzat's *Potoki* (Currents); Badri in Fayzi's *Galiyalanu*; title role in Isbanet's *Khuzha Nestretdin*; the bo'sun in Lavrenev's *Razlom* (Break-Up); Pozhelayev in Rakhmanov's *Bespokoynaya starost'* (Restless Old Age), etc; *Awards*: Order of the Red Banner of Labor (1956); *Died*: 20 Mar 1963.

ACHARYAN, Rachiya Akopovich (1876-1954) Arm linguist and lit historian; founder of Arm dialectology; hon corresp member, Czechoslovak Acad of Sci from 1937; member, Arm Acad of Sci from 1943; *Born*: 20 Mar 1876; *Educ*: studied at Sorbonne and Strasbourg Univ; *Career*: from 1922 prof, Yerevan Univ; specialized in general linguistics, history of the Arm linguistics, history of the Arm language, comparative grammar, Arm lexicology and the lexicography of dialects; *Publ: Istoriya novoy armyanskoy literatury* (A History of Modern Armenian Literature) (3 vol, 1906-12); *Armyanskiy slovar' dialektov* (An Armenian Dictionary of Dialects) (1913); *Etimologicheskiy korennoy slovar'* (A Dictionary of Etymological Roots) (7 vol, 1925-35); *Istoriya armyanskogo yazyka* (A History of Armenian) (2 vol, 1940-51); *Slovar' armyanskikh sobstvennykh imyon* (A Dictionary of Armenian Proper Names) (4 vol, 1942-48); *Polnaya grammatika armyanskogo yazyka v sravnenii s 562 yazykami* (A Complete Grammar of Armenian Compared with 562 Other Languages) (4 vol, 1952-59); *Died*: 17 Mar 1954 in Istanbul.

ACHKANOV, Fyodor Pavlovich (1881-1957) Revolutionary; Party official; CP member from 1903; *Born*: 6 Feb 1881 in Odessa, son of a sailor; *Career*: metalworker, Odessa Main Railroad Workshops; from 1900 in revol movement; active in July 1903 gen strike and 1905-07 Revol in Odessa; member, Odessa RSDRP Comt; several times arrested and exiled; May 1917 elected member, Centr Exec Comt of Rumanian Front, Black-Sea Fleet and Odessa Mil Distr; helped organize Red Guards in Odessa; deleg at 2nd All-Russian Congress of Soviets; fought in 1917 Oct revolt in Petrograd; elected member, All-Russian Centr Exec Comt; 1918, during German occupation of Ukr, underground Party work in Khar'kov, Kiev and Odessa; 1919 member, Kiev then Odessa Revol Comt; dep chm, All-Ukr Railroad Revol Comt; from 1920 Party, govt and econ work; *Publ: Pervyye etapy revolyutsii pyatogo goda v Odesse /Vospominaniya/* (First Stages of the 1905 Revolution in Odessa /Memoirs/) (1925); *Nasha rabota v Glavnykh zh.-d. masterskikh* (Our Work in the Main Railroad Workshops) (1926); *Died*: 26 Nov 1957.

ACHKANOV, Grigoriy Pavlovich (1887-1939) Revolutionary; marine eng; dep head, Sov Merchant Fleet; CP member from 1904; *Born*: 1887 in Odessa, son of a sailor; *Career*: from 1906 member, Odessa City RSDRP Comt; from 1917 Presidium member, Odessa Sov; helped organize All-Russian Rivermen and Seamen's Union; Jan 1918 member, Odessa Revol Comt; also member, Revol Comt, Centr Exec Comt of Rumanian Front, Black-Sea Fleet and Odessa Oblast Sov; then Comr of Posts and Telegraphs, Odessa Council of Pop Comr; 1921-23 Bureau member, Don RCP(B) Comt; Collegium member, RSFSR Pop Comrt of Means of Communication; dep chm, CC, Transport Workers' Union; Presidium member, All-Russian Sovnarkhoz; 1926 member, Centr Council, Trade-Union International (Profintern); from 1931 dep head, Sov Merchant Fleet; author of a number of works on revol movement in Odessa; arrested by State Security organs; *Died*: 1939 in imprisonment.

ADAMOV, G. (real name: Grigoriy Borisovich GIBS) (1886-1945) Russian writer; *Born*: 18 May 1886 in Kherson, son of a worker; *Career*: began journalistic work with Soc-Democratic newspaper *Yug*; *Publ*: collected essays *Soyedinyonnyye kolonny* (United Columns); novels: *Pobediteli nedr* (Conquerors of the Depths) (1937); *Tayna dvukh okeanov* (The Secret of Two Oceans) (1939); *Pioner* (The Pioneer) (1946); *Izgnaniye vladyki* (The Ruler's Exile) (1946); *Died*: 14 July 1945 in Moscow.

ADAMOVICH, Iosif Aleksandrovich (1897-1937) Bel politician; former chm, Bel Council of Pop Comr (1923-27); CP member from 1918; *Born*: 7 Jan 1897 in Minsk, son of a worker; *Educ*: 1908 grad parish school in Novoborisovo; 1922-23 studied at Moscow Mil Acad; *Career*: 1908-15 factory worker; 1915-17 in Russian Army on Northwestern Front; late 1917 secr, Borisovo Sov; 1918 commander, 1st Smolensk Battery and uyezd (later province) mil comr; 1918-19 in charge of quelling anti-Sov revolts in Smolensk, Vitebsk, Mogilyov, Chernigov and Minsk Provinces; from July 1920 member, three-man Bel Mil-Revol Comt, mil comr and garrison commander, Minsk Province; late 1920 Bel Pop Comr of Mil Affairs and dep chm, Bel Centr Exec Comt; 1922 Bel Pop Comr of Interior and dep chm, Bel Centr Exec Comt; 1923-27 chm, Bel Council of Pop Comr; support for Bel nat and cultural renaissance brought him into conflict with A. Krinitskiy, first secr, CC, CP(B) Bel, as a result of which in mid-1927 he was removed from all his posts and exiled to a sovkhoz in Ukr; subsequently called to Moscow to direct sugar trust; 1932 exiled to Far East as dir, sugar refinery in Voroshilov (now Ussuriysk); later fishery dir on Kamchatka; 1937 arrested by NKVD; *Died*: 22 Apr 1937 in imprisonment; posthumously rehabilitated.

ADAMOVICH, Yevgeniya Nikolayevna (1872-1938) Revolutionary; CP member from 1903; *Born*: 1872 in Khorol' Uyezd, Poltava Province, daughter of a land-owner; *Educ*: studied at Tartu Univ; *Career*: from 1892 in the revol movement; 1893 first arrest for revol activities; from 1896 revol work in Poltava and Khar'kov; from 1898 worked for RSDRP org in Moscow, then in Kaluga; 1905-10 member of various rayon RSDRP(B) comts in Petersburg; 1912 secr, Khar'kov RSDRP(B) Comt; 1913 exiled to Pechera Kray and 1916 to Yakutsk Province; after 1917 Feb Revol released from jail, worked as secr, Vasiliy Ostrov Rayon Party Comt and in the Cultural and Educ Section, State Duma; during 1917 Oct Revol worked for Petrograd Mil-Revol Comt; later in RSFSR Pop Comrt of Educ; from 1919 in Ukr on govt work; from 1922 with the Commission for Collecting and Studying Material on Party and Oct Revol History, CC, CP Ukr; author of a number of works on history of Ukr Bolshevik org; also wrote recollections of meeting with Lenin. *Died*: 1938.

ADARYUKOV, Vladimir Yakovlevich (1863-1932) Russian book historian, bibliographer and art critic; prof, Chair of Book History, Higher Tech Art Workshops from 1920; *Born*: 19 Dec 1863 in Kursk; *Educ*: grad Konstantin Mil Acad in Petersburg; *Career*: 1884-96 served in army; then art historian and expert on engraving and drawing at museums and galleries; 1909-18 at the Hermitage; 1918-20 at the Russian Museum; 1920-24 at the Rumyantsev Museum; 1924-32 at the Museum of Fine Arts (from 1925 head, Dept of Russian Engraving); 1903 first work published; from 1920 chm, Russian Soc of Bibliophiles; author of works on history of books, theater, engraving and lithography; *Publ: Stepan Filippovich Galaktionov i yego proizvedeniya* (Stepan Filippovich Galaktionov and His Works) (1910); *Ocherk po istorii litografii v Rossii* (An Outline History of Lithography in Russia) (1912); *Slovar' russkikh litografirovannykh portretov* (A Dictionary of Russian Lithographic Portraits) (1916); *Russkiy knizhnyy znak* (The Russian Bookmark) (1922); *A.P. Ostroumova-Lebedeva* (1922); *Bibliografiya russkikh tipograficheskikh shriftov* (A Bibliography of Russian Type Faces) (1924); *Gravyura i litografiya v knige XIX veka* (Engraving and Lithography in the 19th-Century Book) (1925); *Ukazatel' gravirovannykh i litografirovannykh portretov A.S. Pushkina* (Engraved and Lithographed Portraits of A.S. Pushkin) (1926); *Died*: 4 July 1932 in Moscow.

ADEN, Viktor Bogdanovich (1880-1942) Artist; *Born*: 1880; *Educ*: 1903 grad Moscow College of Painting, Sculpture and Architecture; 1908 grad Petersburg Acad of Arts; *Career*: after grad Acad went to Italy, France and Germany, where he worked as cinema artist; worked mainly for German film studios; from 1925 in USSR; *Works*: contributed to films: *Mabul* (1927); *Yad* (Poison) (1927); *Chuzhaya* (The Alien) (1927); *Kruzheva* (Lace) (1927); *Dva druga, model' i podruga* (Two Friends, a Model and the Girl-Friend) (1928); *Sed'moy sputnik* (The Seventh Satellite) (1928); *Priyomysh* (The Foster-Child) (1929); *Privideniye, kotoroye ne vozvrashchayetsya* (The Non-Recurring Vision) (1930); *Gosudarstvennyy chinovnik* (The Civil Servant) (1931); *Dve materi* (Two Mothers) (1931); *Te, kotoryye prozreli* (The Enlightened) (1931); *Dvadtsat' shest' komissarov* (Twenty-Six Commissars) (1933); *Ismet* (1934); *U samogo sinego morya* (Right by the Blue Sea) (1936); *Igra v lyubov'* (The Love Game) (1936); *Bakintsy* (The People of Baku) (1938); *Gornyy marsh* (Mountain March) (1939); *Kendlilyar* (1940); *Died*: 1942.

ADORATSKIY, Vladimir Viktorovich (1878-1945) Party official and Marxist historian; member, USSR Acad of Sci from 1932; CP member from 1904; *Born*: 1878 in Kazan', son of a clerk; *Educ*: Law Fac, Kazan' Univ; *Career*: from 1904 secr, Kazan' (RSDRP(B) Comt; 1905 arrested and exiled to Astrakhan' Province; 1906-07 and 1911-18 abroad after his sentence of exile was commuted to deportation; 1918-20 worked for the RSFSR Pop Comrt of Educ; 1920-29 dep head, RSFSR Centr Records Bd;

1928-31 dep dir, Inst of Lenin, simultaneously dir, Inst of Red Prof and member, Communist Acad; 1931-39 dir, Inst of Marx-Engels-Lenin; simultaneously dir, Inst of Philosophy, USSR Acad of Sci; from 1939 chief ed, Inst of Marx-Engels-Lenin; worked on the history of Marxism; helped prepare Lenin's works for publication; also edited 15 vol of the works of Marx and Engels; deleg at 16th, 17th and 18th CPSU(B) Congresses; *Publ*: *Nauchnyy kommunizm Karla Marksa* (The Scientific Communism of Karl Marx) (1923); *O gosudarstve* (The State) (1923); *Ob izuchenii proizvedeniy V.I. Lenina* (Study of the Works of V.I. Lenin) (1931); *K voprosu o nauchnoy biografii V.I. Lenina* (The Problem of the Scientific Biography of V.I. Lenin) (1933); *K. Marks - osnovopolozhnik nauchnogo kommunizma* (Marx - the Founder of Scientific Communism) (1933), etc; *Died*: 5 June 1945.

ADZHZI (real name: SIDDIKI, Khodzhi Said-Akhmad-Khodzha (1865-1926) Tadzh writer and pedag; *Born*: 1865 in Samarkand; *Career*: ideologist of Centr Asian Djadidism (nationalist movement); wrote in Farsi (Tadzh länguage), Turki (related to Uzbek language) and Arabic; at beginning of 20th Century visited Baku and Tiflis, becoming involved in Azer theater and falling under influence of Azer poet Sabir; 1912-1913 contributed to Djadidist periodical "Noble Bukhara"; 1913-15 contributed to Djadidist periodical "The Mirror"; after Oct Revol active in Union of Moslem Workers - "Ittifok"; taught, published satirical verse, and translated Gogol, Turgenev, etc, into Tadzh; *Publ*: "Mirror of Example" (1913); "Assembly of Souls" (1913); "Treasury of Wisdom" (1914); "The Essence of Education" (1913); *Died*: 1926.

ADZHI-MOLLAYEV, Abdulla Adzhiyevich (1899-1966) Roentgenologist; prof; Dr of Med; sci dir, X-Ray Diagnosis Dept and dep dir, Uzbek Research Inst of Traumatology and Orthopedics, Tashkent from 1946; member, Learned Council, Uzbek Min of Health; *Born*: 1899; *Educ*: 1927 grad Med Fac, Centr Asian Univ, Tashkent; *Career*: 1927-30 intern, Chair of Roentgenology, Centr Asian Univ; 1931-41 roentgenologist, Murmansk and Transcaucasian Railroads; 1942-46 mil roentgenologist, Sov Army; Bd member, Uzbek Soc of Roentgenologists and Uzbek Orthopedic Soc; member, ed council, *Meditsinskiy zhurnal Uzbekistana*; developed an original method for the dynamic clinico-roentgenological and clinico-functional study of patients recovering from penetrating thoracic wounds; devised a method for the pneumographic and roentgenomycographic recording of external respiration in studying the sequelae of thoracic injuries and analysed the pneumograms and respiratory kymograms for a study of respiration; 1949, together with eng N. Nazarov, designed a simplified roentgenotomograph; studied the x-ray diagnosis and therapy of malignant and benign tumors, osteochondropathy, fibrous osteodystrophy, bone injuries and their sequelae, the effects of radiation sickness on consolidation of bone fractures, pain sensation, for bodies in the thoracic cavity, etc; wrote some 50 works; *Publ*: *Kliniko-rentgenologicheskaya kharakteristika slepykh raneniy grudnoy kletki* (Clinico-Roentgenological Characteristics of Blind-Ended Thoracic Wounds) (1961); coauthor, *Klinicheskiye, rentgenologicheskiye i patologicheskiye sopostavleniya pri pervichnykh opukholyakh kostey konechnostey* (Clinical, Roentgenological and Pathological Comparisons in Primary Tumors of the Extremity Bones) (1963), etc; *Awards*: Order of the Red Star; medals; *Died*: 2 May 1966.

AFANAS'YEV, Fyodor Mikhaylovich (1883-1935) Mil commander; lt-col, Russian Army Gen Staff; officer, Red Armv; *Born*: 1883; *Educ*: 1913 grad Gen Staff Acad; *Career*: veteran of the Russo Japanese War (1904) and WW 1 (1914-18); from 1918 in the Red Army; during Civil War chief of staff, 2nd Army on Eastern Front, Special Army Group on Southern Front, then Southeastern Front; 1921-22 asst commander in chief of Sov armed forces in Siberia; 1922-24 asst commandant, Mil Acad; 1924 retired on med grounds; *Awards*: Order of the Red Banner (1921); *Died*: 1935.

AFANAS'YEV, Pyotr Onisimovich (1874-1944) Pedag; Dr of Pedag Sci; prof, Lenin Teachers' Training Inst, Moscow; *Born*: 14 Feb 1874; *Educ*: grad Moscow Theological Acad; *Career*: began teaching in vil school; from 1918 taught at teachers' Training colleges and research institutions in Moscow; studied methods of Russian-language teaching and devised Russian-language program for Sov schools; some of his textbooks and teaching aids have run through 20 ed; *Publ*: *Metodicheskiye ocherki o prepodavanii rodnogo yazyka* (Studies in Methods of Native-Language Teaching) (1914); *Metodika rodnogo yazyka v trudovoy shkole* (Methods of Teaching Native Languages in Workers' Schools) (1923); *Chitay, pishi, schitay* (Read, Write and Count) (1925); coauthor, *Uchebnik russkogo yazyka* (A Russian Language Textbook) (1933); *Metodika russkogo yazyka v sredney shkole* (Methods of Teaching Russian in Secondary Schools) (1944); etc; *Died*: 20 Aug 1944.

AFANAS'YEV, Stepan Ivanovich (1894-1965) Admin worker; CP member from 1912; *Born*: 25 Oct 1894; *Career*: began revol work in Petersburg; 1918 elected dep, Petrograd Sov; then chm, Exec Comt, Petrograd's Peterhof-Narva Rayon Sov; 1920 secr, Nikolayev rayon RCP(B) comt; 1921 dep head, Petrograd Province Polit Educ Bd; 1922-52 exec admin work including dir, Putilov Plant; 1929-30 head, Leningrad Sovnarkhoz; deleg at 16th, 17th and 18th Party Congresses; at 16th Congress elected cand member, CC, CPSU(B); from 1952 pensioner; *Died*: 13 Jan 1965.

AFANAS'YEV, Vladimir Aleksandrovich (1873-1953) Mil historian; maj-gen; *Born*: 1873; *Career*: until 1918 wrote several works on mil history; founded Circle to Commemorate the 1812 Fatherland War; advised artist F.A. Rubo on his painting "The Battle of Borodino"; from 1918 in Red Army; worked for RSFSR Mil Communications Bd; 1923-25 taught history of mil art at Red Army Mil Acad; 1925-30 dep head, Zhukovskiy Air Force Acad; 1930-40 with USSR Pop Comrt of Means of Communication; 1940-50 with Inst of History, USSR Acad of Sci; 1950-53 at State Historical Museum; *Died*: 1953.

AFANAS'YEV, Vyacheslav Alekseyevich (1859-1942) Pathoanatomist; Dr of Med from 1885; prof from 1894; *Born*: 1859; *Educ*: 1882 grad Petersburg Med Surgical Acad; *Career*: after grad retained at acad in Dept of Pathological Anatomy under N.P. Ivanovskiy; 1885 defended doctor's thesis, then mil physician in Kiev where he continued studying pathological anatomy in V.V. Podvysotskiy's laboratory; from 1890 lecturer, Mil Med Acad; during foreign assignment worked with Mechnikov, Virchow and Baumgarten; 1894 appointed prof of gen pathology and pathological anatomy, Derpet (Tartu) Univ; from 1918 prof of pathological anatomy, Voronezh Univ; 1930 retired on pension; 1934 appointed supernumerary prof, Voronezh Med Inst; in later years worked in pathohistological laboratory, Voronezh Inst of Oncology; his efforts to correlate pathoanatomical findings with experimental research permeate all his most important works on histogenesis of experimental tubercles, septicemia, neoplasms (sarcomas of the lungs), endocrinous disorders, Addison's disease and arteriosclerosis; also did research on bacteriology; keen advocate of Mechnikov's phagocyte theory; numerous sci works written under his supervision, including 16 doctor's thesis at Derpet; *Publ*: thesis *O patologoanatomicheskikh izmeneniyakh v tkanyakh zhivotnogo organizma pri otravlenii khlornovatokislym kaliyem (bertoletovoy sol'yu)* (Pathoanatomical Lesions in the Tissues of the Human Body in Potassium Chlorate Poisoning) (1885); *K patologii Addisonovoy bolezni* (Pathology of Addison's Disease) (1888); *Experimentelle Untersuchungen über einige Mikroorganismen aus der Gruppe der sogenannten haemorrhagica* (1892); *Pervichnaya sarkoma lyogkogo i smert' ot khloroforma* (Primary Sarcoma of the Lung and Death from Chloroform) (1929); *O gistogeneze eksperimental'nogo bugorka v tkanyakh krolika* (Histogenesis of an Experimental Tubercle in Rabbit Tissues); *Died*: 1942 in Voronezh.

AFINOGENOV, Aleksandr Nikolayevich (1904-1941 Russian playwright; CP member from 1922; *Born*: 4 Apr 1904 in Skopin, former Ryazan' Province; *Educ*: 1924 grad Moscow Inst of Journalism; *Publ*: 1926 first play produced - *Po tu storony shcheli* (Beyond the Divide after a story by Jack London; plays staged in 1926-29 included *Na perelome (V ryady)* (The Turning Point /Into the Ranks/); *Glyadi v oba* (Keep Your Eyes Peeled!); *Malinovoye varen'ye* (Raspberry Jam); play *Chudak* (The Crank) (1928) marked his break with the "Proletarian Culture" movement; play *Strakh* (Fear), (1930), staged at Moscow Acad Arts Theater, dealt with the class struggle in sci; theoretical study *Tvorcheskiy metod teatra. Dialektika tvorcheskogo protsessa* (The Creative Method of the Theater. The Dialectics of the Creative Process) written in 1931, when author was secr, Russian Assoc of Proletarian Artists; play *Dalyokoye* (The Distant Past) (1935) glorified the everyday labor of ordinary Sov people; drama *Salyut, Ispaniya!* (Salute to Spain!) (1936) dealt with Spanish Civil War; lyrical comedy *Mashen'ka* (1940) gives a poetic portrayal of the Sov schoolgirl; from the outset of WW 2 headed the Lit Dept, Sov Information Office; Sept 1941 completed play *Nakanune* (On the

Eve) dealing with the struggle against the Germans; *P'yesy* (Plays) (1935 and 1940); *Died*: 29 Oct 1941 killed in Moscow in a German air raid.

AFONIN, Grigoriy Ivanovich (1894-1959) Variety artiste; *Born*: 12 Feb 1894; *Educ*: 1913 grad Moscow College of Painting, Sculpture and Architecture; studied at Moscow Arts Theater Studio; *Career*: during Civil War acted with frontline drama brigades; composed rhymed slogans, satirical ditties and mil couplets, etc; from 1920's performed on variety stage, presenting satirical feuilletons; *Works*: feuilletons: "Don't Get Under My Feet"; "Citizen, You've Lost Face"; "Let's Have an Elegant Life"; "Criticism of a Whining Citizen"; "Live, Damn You, Live!" (1933); "About Fools" (1937); "One Minute" (1939); "Not Fitted for Life" (1941); "Thanks for Your Help" (1946); "Does It Bother You? " (1954), etc; *Died*: 14 Apr 1959.

AGABABOV, Sergey Artyom'yevich (1926-1960) Composer; conductor; Bd member, Dag Composers' Union from 1955; *Born*: 25 Oct 1926 in Makhachkala; *Educ*: 1951 grad Dag Med Inst; 1951 grad conducting and choral Dept, Dag Musical College; 1956 grad composition class, Moscow Conservatory; from 1956 postgrad studies, Moscow Conservatory; *Works*: "Daghestani Suite to Lezghin Folk Melodies" (1954); piano works: "A children's Album" (1951); "Toccata" (1955); violin and piano works: "Suite" (1951); "Variations" (1951); some 30 songs, including: "The Song of Khanum" (1948); "To the Izberbash Oil Workers" (1949); "I Glorify Thee, Daghestan" (1952); "To the Pilots of the Country of Soviets" (1953); "A Forest Ball" (1963); children's songs; music for shows; vocal cycle "From the Poetry of the Past" (1958); contatas: "The Ballad of Freedom"; "Labor Day"; "Soviet Daghestan"; arrangements of Lakh folk melodies (1959); *Died*: 196O.

AGABAL'YANTS, Georgiy Gerasimovich (1904-1967) Viticulturist; prof from 1934; Dr of Agric Sci from 1939; prof, Krasnodar Inst of Viticulture and Viniculture from 1937; *Born:* 1904; *Educ:* 1926 grad Don Inst of Agric and Melioration: *Career:* 1930-37 assoc, All-Russian Research Inst of Viticulture and Viniculture; specialist in wine chemistry and technol; helped develop and introduce ind biochemical and physicochemical methods for the automatic continuous production of champagne; *Publ:* coauthor, *Issledovaniye prevrashcheniy organicheskikh kislot pri nepreryvnoy shampanizatsii* (A Study of the Conversions in Organic Acids During the Continuous Champagne Process) (1965); *Issledovaniye protsessa avtoliza drozhzhey pri nepreryvnoy shampanizatsii* (A Study of Yeast Autolysis During the Continuous Champagne Process) (1966), etc; *Died:* Mar 1967.

AGAFANGEL (secular name: PREOBRAZHENSKIY, Aleksandr Lavrent'yevich) (1854-1928) Former Metropolitan of Yaroslavl', Russian Orthodox Church; vicar to Patriarch Tikhon; second vicar of Patriarchal Throne; Cand of Theology from 1881; *Born:* 1854 in Tula Province; *Educ:* 1881 grad Moscow Theological Acad: *Career:* from 1881 teacher, Ranenburg Theological College, then supervisor, Skolo Theological College; 1885 appointed priest-monk and assumed name of Agafangel; 1886-88 inspector and fathersuperior, Tomsk Seminary; 1888 rector and archimandrite, Irkutsk Seminary; 1889-93 Bishop of Kirensk; 1893-97 Bishop of Tobol'sk; 1897-1904 Bishop, 1904-10 Archbishop of Riga; 1910-13 Archbishop of Lith and Vilnius; from 1913 Archbishop, then Metropolitan of Yaroslavl'; 1917-18 attended synod of Russian Orthodox Church; shortly before his trial, Patriarch Tikhon appointed him head of church admin; condemned non-canonical demands of reform clergy and proposals for local self-admin organs; was confined to Yaroslavl' by OGPU and thus prevented from performing admin duties; named vicar of Patriarchal Throne by Patriarch Tikhon's dying behest but could not assume this post because he was under house arrest; rejected attempts of reform clergy to win his cooperation with promise of freedom; Aug-Dec 1925 imprisoned in Lubyanka, then exiled to Narym Kray; 1926 re-imprisoned in Lubyanka; resisted OGPU pressure but renounced vicarship; struggled against subjugation of clergy to Sov authority; uncompromising opponent of Communist ideology; *Died:* Oct 1928 and was buried in Yaroslavl'.

AGAMALY-OGLY, Samed-Aga (1867- ?) Govt official; Azer writer; chm, Azer Centr Exec Comt and Centr Exec Comt, Transcaucasian Sov Fed Socialist Republic; *Born:* 1867 in vil Kyrak-Kesemen, Kaz Uyezd, son of a peasant; *Career:* 1887 began work in Gandzha; from 1888 underground revol work; active in popularizing new Turkic/Latin/alphabet; 1924 prepared and published, with his preamble, famous pamphlet by Mirza-Fetkh-Ali-Akhun-Zade entitled "Kyamaluddovle and Dzhamaluddovle"; wrote for most of newspapers and journals published in Azer at that time; 1929 chm, Azer Centr Exec Comt and Centr Exec Comt, Transcaucasian Sov Fed Socialist Republ; *Publ:* "Where Are We Bound? " about the new Turkic alphabet (1924); "Problems of Culture in the Turkic World" (1924); *Dve kul'tury* (Two Cultures) /in Russian/ (1927); *Died:* date and place of death unknown.

AGANBEKYAN, Artavazd Arshakovich (Arkad'yevich) (1894-1967) Theater historian and drama teacher; Hon Cultural Worker of RSFSR from 1966; *Born:* 15 Dec 1894; *Educ:* 1925 grad Arm Theater Studio, Moscow; *Career:* 1929-30 at Leninakan Arm Theater, where he founded a drama studio; 1933-34 stage dir, Baku Arm Theater, where he also founded a drama studio; 1934-41 drama teacher and stage dir, Arm Theater Studio, Moscow; 1937-43 founder-dir, Bibliographic Section, All-Russian Theatrical Soc; from 1943 dir, Centr Acad Library Theater, All-Russian Theatrical Soc, Moscow; *Publ: Moskovskiy khudozhestvennyy teatr. 1898-1938. Bibliografiya* (The Moscow Arts Theater. 1898-1938. Bibliography) (1939); *K.S. Stanislavskiy. Bibliograficheskiy ukazatel'* (K.S. Stanislavskiy. A Bibliographic Index) (1946); *Letopis' Sovetskogo teatra perioda Velikoy Otechestvennoy voyny: iyun'-dekabr' 1941 goda* (A Chronicle of the Soviet Theater During the Great Fatherland War: June-December 1941) (1944); Ibid: Jan-Dec 1942 (1945); Ibid: Jan-Dec 1943 (1945); Ibid: Jan-Dec 1943 (1946); Ibid: Jan-Dec 1944 (1946); *Died:* 6 Sept 1967.

AGARKOV, Mikhail Mikhaylovich (1890-1947) Lawyer; Dr of Law; prof; *Born:* 1 Apr 1890 in Kazan'; *Career:* from 1917 taught and did research on civil law; head, chair of civil law and lecturer, various higher educ establishments; dep dir, Inst of Law, USSR Acad of Sci; toward end of life worked at Moscow Univ and Acad of Soc Sci, CP, CPSU(B); wrote several works on legal control of the nat econ; *Awards:* Order of the Red Banner of Labor; medals; *Died:* 25 July 1947.

AGASIYEV, Kazi-Magomed (1882-1918) Party officia CP member **from 1904**; *Born:* 1882 in vil Akhty, Dag, son of an artisan; *Career:* worked at Baku oil fields; underground work for Baku RSDRP Comt; 1905 founded "Faruk" Lezghin Bolshevik group; repeatedly arrested and exiled from Baku; 1918 comr for Derbent Rayon and Southern Dag; during Civil War underground work and founded a partisan detachment; *Died:* Oct 1918 killed in action; settlement Adzhikabul renamed Kazi-Magomed and a rayon in Azer SSR was named for him.

AGDAMSKIY (real name: BADALBEYLI), Akhmed Bashir ogly (1884-1954) Azer opera singer (tenor); Hon Art Worker of Azer SSR from 1943; *Born:* 5 Jan 1884; *Career:* helped found Azer musical theater, began stage career with Nidzhat ensemble, Baku; 1911-1920 performed mainly female roles in musicals - Leyli, Asli, Gyul'chokhra, Gyul'naz in Gadzhibekov's "Leyli and Medzhnun," "Asli and Kerem," *Arshin mal alan* and "If Not Her, Then the Other"; Shakhsenem in Gadzhibekov's *Ashik Garib*, etc; also performed dramatic roles; 1921 began teaching; *Died:* 1 Apr 1954.

AGGEYEV, S.P. (1898-1938) Govt official; chm, Ivanovo Oblast Exec Comt; CP member from 1918; *Born:* 1898; *Career:* from 1918 exec govt and Party work in Tula, Yefremov and Tyumen'; 1921-23 secr Voronezh Province RCP(B) Comt; from 1923 chm, Voronezh Province Exec Comt; RSFSR Pop Comr of Domestic Trade; dep chm, Bd, USSR Centr Union of Consumer Soc; dep chm, Moscow Oblast Exec Comt; from 1932 chm, Ivanovo Oblast Exec Comt; arrested by State Security organs; *Died:* 1938 in imprisonment.

AGRANENKO (real name: YERUKHIMOVICH), Zakhar Markovich (1912-1960) Russian dramatist and producer; CP member from 1945; *Born:* 6 July 1912; *Educ:* 1937 grad Production Dept, State Inst of Stagecraft; *Career:* staged plays at Leningrad Theater of Drama and Comedy and Leningrad Bolshoy Drama Theater; Simonov's *Russkiy vopros* (The Russian Question) (1947) and *Chuzhaya ten'* (Alien Shadow) (1949); lit manager and producer, Baltic Fleet Theater; scripted and directed films: *Bessmertnyy garnizon* (Immortal Garrison) (1956) and *Leningradskaya simfoniya* (Leningrad Symphony) (1957); *Publ:* plays: *Dobro pozhalovat* (Welcome); coauthor, *Krestovskiy ostrov* (Krestovskiy Island) (1942); coauthor, *Zemlya podtverzhdayet* (The Earth Confirms) (1943); *Novyy god* (New Year) (1949); *Shest'desyat chasov* (Sixty Hours) (1954); *Bespokoynyye khudozhniki* (Turbulent Artists) (1957); *Pervyy raz v kino. . . Iz rezhissyorskogo dnevnika* (First Time at the Cinema. . . From a Producer's Diary)

(1961), etc; *Died*: 24 Oct 1960.

AGRANOV, Yakov Saulovich (1893-1938) Govt official; USSR First Dep Pop Comr of Internal Affairs; CP member from 1915; *Born:* 1893; *Career:* 1912-1914 member, Socialist-Revol Party; arrested and exiled; 1917-18 secr, Poles'ye Oblast Party Comt; 1918-19 secr RSFSR Council of Pop Comr; 1919 worked for punitive organs; All-Russian Cheka, GPU and NKVD as special plen for important cases; head, Secret Dept; plen for Moscow Oblast; USSR First Dep Pop Comr of Internal Affairs; held the rank Comr of State Security, 1st Class; 1921 conducted the investigation in the following cases: the Nat Center in Moscow; the Tactical Center; the Pop Union for the Defense of the Fatherland and Freedom (1921); the Antonov Revolt's staff; the centr org of the Socialist-Revol Party, the Ind Party, the Peasants' Labor Party (1930); 1934 directed the investigation in the case of the Leningrad Terrorist Center charged with the murder of Kirov, etc; member, CPSU(B) Auditing Commission; member, All-Union Centr Exec Comt; 1937 expelled from the Party for "persistent violation of socialist legality" and later arrested; *Awards:* two Orders of the Red Banner; *Died:* 1938 in imprisonment.

AGRANOVSKIY, L.S. (1890-1937) Trade-union official; CP member from 1917; *Born:* 1890; *Career:* 1910-17 lived abroad; after 1917 Oct Revol exec Party and admin work in Staraya Russa, Novgorod and Ufa; deleg at 8th RCP(B) Congress; later secr, CC, Sewing Ind Workers' Union and head, Sewing Ind Workers Section, Supr Sovnarkhoz; then head, Leningrad Clothes Trust; arrested by State Security organs; *Died*: 1937 in imprisonment.

AGUMAA, Kiazym Karamanovich (1915-1950) Abkhazian writer; *Born*: 1 May 1915 in vil Gvada, now Abkhazian ASSR; *Educ*: 1937 grad Kalinin Teachers' Training Inst; *Career*: worked for Abkhazian newspaper *Apsny kapsh*; during WW 2 fought with Chapayev's Partisan Unit in Bryansk forests; 1934 first work printed; translated into Abkhazian Arm epic "David Sasunskiy," Shevchenko's poem "The Dream" and verse of Geo poets; his works have been translated into Russian and Geo; *Publ*: verse: "Gyd's Family"; "Kolchida"; "In the Garden"; "I Love Kvikvi"; poem "Tariel Rashba"; ballad "The Reed-Pipe"; stories "Unshed Tears" and "Temraz and Tsitsana"; novelette "The Prisoner"; play "The Great Land"; *Died*: 10 Dec 1950.

AKHIKYAN, Vtranes Galustovich (1872-1936) Arm painter and graphic artist; Hon Art Worker of Arm SSR; *Born*: 1872; *Educ*: grad Petersburg Acad of Arts; *Career*: before 1917 Revol worked mainly as a graphic artist and illustrator because he could not afford painting materials; after 1917 specialized in painting small landscapes and still-lifes notable for their simplicity and veracity; in his latter years turned to themes of socialist construction, including "The Building of the People's House" (1928-32), "The Attack of the Red Cavalry" (1933); taught art and worked at museums; *Died*: 1936.

AKHMADIYEV, Shagit (1888-1930) Tatar writer; *Born*: 10 Jan 1888 in vil Tatar Yaltany, son of a peasant; *Educ*: grad Orenburg Tatar Medressah; *Career*: during the 1905 Revol active in Shakirdov movement; active Party work during 1917 Oct Revol; from 1921 Tatar Comr of Educ; *Publ*: 1911 first work published; of particular interest are his realistic stories on soc injustice: "The Drowned Daughter-in-Law" (1912); "God's Man" (1915); "Wealth" (1915); lyric blank verse "The Poet's Fancies" (1913); "Eyes" (1913); "Melancholy" (1914); "To a Tatar Girl" (1914); *Died*: 12 Aug 1930.

AKHMANOV, Aleksandr Sergeyevich (1893-1957) Philosopher and logician; *Born*: 19 Aug 1893; *Educ*: 1916 grad Moscow Univ; *Career*: from 1919 taught philosophy, logic and esthetics at Sov higher educ establishments; specialized in history of logical theory, analysis of the basic concepts and laws of formal logic and the interrelationship of logical and linguistic categories; *Publ*: coauthor, *Istoriya grecheskoy literatury* (A History of Greek Literature) (vol 2, 1955); coauthor, *Voprosy logiki* (Problems of Logic) (1955); coauthor, *Myshleniye i yazyk* (Thought and Language) (1957); coauthor, *Aristotel'. Ob iskusstve poezii* (Aristotle. The Art of Poetry) (1957); *Died*: 5 June 1957.

AKHMATOV, Viktor Viktorovich (1875-1934) Geodesist, gravimetrist and hydrographer; *Born*: 9 Feb 1875; *Career*: helped survey Spitzbergen; took part in hydrographic expeditions 1902 to Lake Baykal, 1907 to Lake Onega and Ladoga, where he determined astronomic points and gravitational forces; helped survey White Sea and directed triangulation of Karelian littoral, establishing a number of triangulation points; 1917-30 asst head, Hydrographic Bd; 1905-34 secr, asst chm, then chm, Russian Astronomical Soc; *Died*: 1934.

AKHMATOVA (real name: GORENKO), Anna Andreyevna (1889-1966) Russian poetess and translator; *Born*: 23 June 1889 in Odessa, daughter of an eng; *Educ*: studied at Law Dept, Kiev Higher Courses for Women; grad Petersburg Higher Courses in History and Lit; *Career*: spent childhood in Tsarskoye Selo and Petersburg; before WW 1 toured Germany, France, Italy and other European countries; 1911 first verse published; 1912 joined Acmeist movement; after the leader of the Acmeists, her husband Gumilyov, was shot by the Cheka in 1921 Sov publ houses refused her work; her verse was published once more during the wars with Japan, Poland, Finland and Germany; during the Leningrad blockade evacuated to Tashkent, where she remained until 1944; Aug 1946 the CC, CPSU(B) declared her work pernicious and expressive of ideas "alien to the Sov people"; accused of still adhering to Acmeism, a movement declared reactionary because it "preached art for art's sake and deviated into mysticism"; 1953 rehabilitated and began to publish in centr press; her post-war work "Poem Without a Hero" appeared only in excerpts in Sov press but was published in full in New York under the title "Air Ways" (1953); 1964 visited Italy to receive Etna-Taormina Prize; 1965 elected Bd member, Leningrad Branch, RSFSR Union of Writers; much of her verse has been translated into English, French, German, Italian, Japanese, etc; *Publ*: first lyric poetry (1911); collected verse: *Vecher* (Evening) (1912); *Chyotki* (The Rosary) (1914); *Belaya staya* (The White Flock) (1917); *U samogo morya* (Right by the Sea) and *Podorozhnik* (The Plantain) (1921); *Anno Domini MCMXXI* (1921); critical article "Pushkin's Last Story" (1933); *Iz shesti knig* (From Six Books) and *Iva* (The Willow) (1940); *Izbrannoye* (Selected Verse) (1943); *Rekviyem* (Requiem); patriotic verse: *Klyatva* (The Oath) (1941); *Muzhestvo* (Courage) (1942); cycle *Tashkentskiye stikhi* (Tashkent Verse) (1944); *Govoryat deti* (Children Speaking) (1950); ed, anthology *Koreyskaya klassicheskaya poeziya* (Korean Classical Poetry) (1958); critical article "Pushkin's 'Stone Guest'" (1958); poem *Tryptych* (1960); anthology *Beg vremeni* (The Course of Time) (1966); translated poetry from Chinese, Korean, French, Polish, etc; *Died*: 5 Mar 1966.

AKHMED DZHAVAD (real name: AKHUNDZADE, Dzhavad Mamedali ogly) (1892-1937) Azer poet; *Born*: 1892 in vil Seyfali, now Azer, son of a peasant; *Career*: 1913 first work printed; translated into Azer Shakespeare's "Othello" (1935) and verse of Pushkin, Shota Rustaveli, etc; *Publ*: verse collections: "Goshma" (1916); "Aren't We Brothers? " (1929); "Kura" (1930); "Cotton" (1931); "Moscow" (1935), etc; *Died*: 1937.

AKHMEDOV, Agamirzali Mirza ogly (1905-1964) Govt and Party official; Azer Min of Trade; CP member from 1928; *Born*: 1905 in vil Angikharen, Shemakha Rayon, son of a peasant; *Educ*: grad High School for Party Organizers, CC, CPSU; *Career*: 1920-27 member, All-Union Komsomol; after grad from above school, spent several years in leading Party posts: secr of various rayon Party comts; secr, Nakhichevan Oblast, and Kirovabad and Baku City Comt, CP Azer; 1941-45 dep head, Polit Dept, Transcaucasian Railroad; then head, polit dept of a mil unit; 1955 dep chm, 1956-58 chm, Exec Comt, Baku City Sov; 1958-1963 Azer Min of Trade, then senior official, Azer Council of Min; 1955-57 Bureau member, Baku City Comt, CP Azer; 1956-61 member, CC, CP Azer; 1961-64 member, Auditing Commission, CC, CP Azer; dep, USSR Supr Sov of 1950 convocation; dep, Azer Supr Sov of 1955 and 1959 convocations; *Awards*: two Orders of the Red Banner of Labor; Badge of Hon; Order of the Fatherland War; medals; *Died*: 13 May 1964 and buried in Baku.

AKHMETELI, Aleksandr (Sandro) Vasil'yevich (1886-1937) Geo stage dir; co-founder, Sov Geo theater; Pop Artiste of USSR from 1933; *Born*: 25 Apr 1886 in vil Anaga, Geo, son of a priest; *Educ*: 1916 grad Law Fac, Petrograd Univ; *Career*: from 1909 theater critic; 1920 began stage career with production of Shanshiashvili's *Berdo Zmaniya*; from 1924 chief stage dir, Rustaveli Theater, Tbilisi; as pupil of Mardzhanishvili co-produced Shanshiashvili's "Ereti the Hero" and Shakespeare's "The Merry Wives of Windsor"; while at Rustaveli Theater produced: Glebov's *Zagmuk* (1926); Shanshiashvili's *Anzor* (1928); Kirshon's "City of the Winds" (1929); Dadiani's *Tetnul'd* (1931); "The Robbers" (1933), etc; at Opera and Ballet Theater produced: Arakishvili's "The Tale of Shota Rustaveli" and Paliashvili's "Latavra"; made major contribution to development of Geo theater, enhancing

Rustaveli Theater's reputation for heroic and romantic productions; his productions were notable for their emotional appeal, impact and dynamism; made effective use of crowd scenes and folk music; *Died*: 29 June 1937.

AKHOSPIRELI (real name: BEGLARIDZE), Beglar Beglarovich (1880-1921) Geo poet and playwright; *Born*: 3 Nov 1880; *Career*: 1900's began stage and lit work; bit parts as actor; translated Gorky's plays into Geo; wrote vaudevilles; *Publ*: plays: "My Song"; "Homeless"; "Awareness and Love," etc; *Died*: 26 Apr 1921.

AKHUNBABAYEV, Yuldash (1885-1943) Govt official; chm, Presidium, Uzbek Supr Sov; CP member from 1921; *Born*: 1885 in settlement Dzhoy Bazar, Fergana Oblast, son of a peasant; *Career*: until 1917 farmhand; during the Civil War in Centr Asia fought against Basmachi; 1918 organized the Dzhoy Bazar Vil Sov; 1919-20 bd chm, Marchelon Branch, Union of Poor Peasantry; 1921-24 Presidium member, Fergana Oblast Exec Comt; organized volost-level branches of the Union of Poor Peasantry; from 1924 Presidium member, Turkestan Centr Exec Comt; 1925-37 chm, Uzbek Centr Exec Comt; 1938-43 chm, Presidium, Uzbek Supr Sov; dep chm, Presidium, USSR Supr Sov; member, USSR Centr Exec Comt of 3rd - 7th convocations; *Awards*: Order of Lenin; two Orders of the Red Banner of Labor; *Died*: 28 Feb 1943.

AKHUNDOV, Rukhulla Ali ogly (1897-1938) Publicist; scholar; CP member from 1919; *Born*: 13 Jan 1897 in vil Shuvelyany, Baku Province, son of a teacher; *Career*: from 1916 worked at a printing-house; 1917 member, Azer Leftist Socialist-Revol Faction; 1918, ed, Baku Sov *Izvestiya*; edited Azer newspapers *Kommunist* (1919; 1922-25); *Khurriyyet* (1919); *Bakinskiy rabochiy*, etc; also ed, lit periodical *Ingilab ve medeniyyet* (1927-28); from 1920 dept head, CC, CP(B) Azer; secr, Baku Party Comt; 1924-30 secr, CC, CP(B) Azer, and Azer Pop Comr of Educ; 1930 elected secr, Transcaucasian Kray CPSU(B) Comt; deleg at loth-17th Party Congresses; during his latter years worked at the Inst of Party History, CC, CP Azer; one of the first to translate Marx, Engels and Lenin into Azer; author of a number of works on theory and history of lit, articles about Firdousi, M.F. Akhundov, Pushkin, etc; also wrote about music and painting; arrested by State Security organs; *Died*: 1938 in imprisonment; posthumously rehabilitated.

AKHUNDOV, Sidgi Rukhulla Fatulla ogly (1886-1959) Azer actor; Pop Artiste of USSR from 1949; stage dir, Meshadi Azizbekov Azer State Drama Theater; *Born*: 21 Mar 1886 near Baku; *Career*: 1906 Azer stage debut; until 1926, producer-dir Azizbekov Theater; played more than 300 roles on Azer stage; during WW 2 toured the Transcaucasian, Crimean and North Caucasian Fronts; *Roles*: in plays by Azer playwrights - Atakishi in Dzh. Dzhabarla's "Seville"; Mukhtar-Bey in S. Vurgun's "Khanlar"; Suleyman in M. Ibragimov's "Khayat"; Musa in S. Rakhman's "The Wedding"; Taras in Zeynala Khalil's "Vengeance," etc; in foreign and Russian classical plays - Lear in Shakespeare's "King Lear"; Escalus in "Romeo and Juliet"; Iago and Othello in "Othello"; Franz Moor in Schiller's "The Robbers"; the Actor in Gorky's *Na dne* (The Lower Depths); the mayor in Gogol's *Revizor* (The Government Inspector), etc; *Awards*: Stalin Prize (1948); Order of Lenin (1956); *Died*: 5 May 1959.

AKHUNDOV, Suleyman Sani (1875-1939) Azer writer; one of the first Azer playwrights; *Born*: 3 Oct 1875 in Shusha, now Nagorno-Karabakh Autonomous Oblast; *Educ*: grad Gori Teachers' Training Seminary; *Publ*: stories: "Star of Freedom" (1905); "The Feast" (1905); "The Blackie" (1913); "Mister Gray's Dog" (1927), etc; first play "The Money-Grubber" (1899) ridicules human cupidity; comedy "Dibdad Bek" (1906) criticises the election of deputies to the State Duma; plays: "The Falcon's Nest" (1921); "The Devil" (1922); "From Darkness to Light" (1921); "A New Life" (1923), etc; drama "Love and Revenge" (1922) depicts the hard lot of the peasantry; *Chernushka* (The Blackie) and *Strashnyye rasskazy* (Dreadful Stories) were published in a Russian translation in 1956 and 1958; Akhundov introduced new themes and images into Azer lit and influenced its development on the basis of the best traditions of nat realistic drama; until his death he engaged in teaching work; author of several textbooks; *Died*: 29 Mar 1939.

AKHUTIN, Mikhail Nikiforovich (1898-1948) Surgeon; corresp member, USSR Acad of Med Sci; lt-gen, med corps; *Born*: 1898; *Educ*: 1920 grad Petrograd Mil Med Acad; *Career*: for 10 years worked under Prof V.A. Oppel'; from 1933 head of surgical clinic in Khabarovsk; 1939 head of surgical clinic in Kuybyshev; 1938-39 took part in mil operations on Lake Khasan and River Khalkin-Gol; 1939-40 army surgeon in Finno-Sov War; 1941-45 chief surgeon of front; from 1945 dep chief surgeon of Sov Army and head, Dept of Fac Surgery, 1st Moscow Med Inst; *Publ*: more than 70 works on surgical experience in Far East, Finland and during WW 2, treatment of combat injuries (of thorax, main vessels and joints), immobilization for travel, wound infections and other aspects of mil surgery: *Khirurgicheskaya rabota vo vremya boyov u ozera Khasan* (Surgery During the Fighting at Lake Khasan) (1939); *Khirurgicheskiy opyt dvukh boyevykh operatsiy* (Surgical Experience in Two Combat Operations) (1940); *Opyt organizatsii khirurgicheskoy raboty v voyskovom rayone* (Experience of Organizing Surgery in a Military Area) (1940); *Nerazreshyonnyye zadachi voyenno-polevoy khirurgii* (Unresolved Problems of Field Surgery) (1941); *Voyenno-polevaya khirurgiya* (Field Surgery) (1942), etc; *Awards*: numerous orders and medals, mainly for war services; *Died*: 1948 in Moscow.

AKHVERDOV, Abdurragim bek Asadbek ogly (1870-1933) Azer writer; Hon Art Worker of Azer SSR; *Born*: 1870 in Shusha, in what is now the Nagorno-Karabakh Autonomous Oblast; *Educ*: 1894 grad Tiflis secondary school; studied at Oriental Fac, Petersburg Univ; *Career*: 1892 first work published; *Publ*: tragedy "The Ravaged Nest" (1896) depicted the soc crisis of a noble family in the late 19th Century; play "An Unfortunate Young Man" (1900) was the first attempt in Azer drama to portray a democrat engaged in fighting the patriarchal and feudal soc order; play *Aga Mukhammed shakh Kadzhar* (1907) depicted a typical Oriental despot; from 1906 wrote for democratic journal *Molla Nasreddin* and published numerous stories, feuilletons and articles such as: "Letters from Hell"; "The Bomb"; "Mozalanbek's Journey"; "My Deer"; post-revol works portrayed the struggle to build a new soc in the Azer vil and criticized survivals of the past; such works included: "In the Shade of a Tree"; "Women's Holiday"; "The Old House"; "Excellent," etc; sketch "From the History of the Azerbaydzhani Theater" (1924); monograph "M.F. Akhundov's Life and Work" (1928); translated Shakespeare, Schiller, Zola, Gorky and Chekhov; *Died*: 12 Dec 1933 in Baku.

AKIMENKO, Il'ya Petrovich (1891-1956) Soc worker; specialist in methods of trade and career training for deaf and retarded children; *Born*: 31 July 1891; *Career*: devised programs and visual aids for teaching carpentry in auxiliary schools and schools for deaf children; helped found first trade college for deaf-mutes in Tula; *Publ: Metodicheskoye rukovodstvo po stolyarnomu delu* (A Manual on Methods of Teaching Carpentry) (1948); *Stolyarnoye delo v shkole glukhonemykh* (Carpentry in Schools for Deaf-Mutes) (1953); *Died*: 19 May 1956.

AKIMOV, Georgiy Vladimirovich (1901-1953) Specialist in physico-chemistry of metals; corresp member, USSR Acad of Sci from 1939; Hon Sci and Tech Worker of RSFSR from 1943; CP member from 1920; *Born*: 23 Apr 1901; *Educ*: 1926 grad Moscow Higher Tech College; *Career*: from 1926 employed in aviation ind; 1927 established first Sov laboratory for corrosion research at Zhukovskiy Centr Inst of Aerodynamics; 1931 established Corrosion Dept at Moscow Inst of Non-ferrous Metals and Gold; from 1947 chm, Anti-Corrosion Commission, USSR Acad of Sci; from 1949 dir, Inst of Physical Chemistry, USSR Acad of Sci; solved several important theoretical problems related to metal corrosion; developed a new heat-resistant alloy for aircraft engine parts and several stainless steels; *Publ: Gazovaya korroziya uglerodistykh staley pri vysokikh temperaturakh* (Gas Corrosion of Carbon Steels at High Temperatures) (1931); *Teoriya i metody issledovaniya korrozii metallov* (Metal Corrosion Theory and Research Methods) (1945); *Osnovy ucheniya o korrozii i zashchite metallov* (Principles of Metal Corrosion Theory and Protection) (1946); coauthor, *Metallovedeniye klapannogo ugla aviatsionnogo motora i novyy printsip uluchsheniya yego raboty v svyazi s problemoy povysheniya moshchnosti* (Research on Metal Used in the Valves of Aircraft Engines and a New Principle for Increasing Its Efficiency in Connection with the Problem of Increased Power) (1946); *Awards*: three Stalin Prizes; Mendeleyev Prize (1952); two Orders of Lenin; *Died*: 23 Jan 1953.

AKOPOV, Stepan Akopovich (1899-1958) Eng; USSR Min of Automobile, Tractor and Agric Machine-Building; CP member from 1919; *Born*: 1899 in Tiflis; *Educ*: Bauman Higher Tech College, Moscow; *Career*: from 1919 leading Komsomol, Party and admin work: secr, Tbilisi Komsomol Comt; instructor, Moscow Bauman

Rayon CPSU(B) Comt; 1931 grad Bauman Higher Tech College in Moscow and worked as chief eng, then dir of the Podol'sk Machine-Building Plant near Moscow; from 1937 dir, Ural Heavy Machine-Building Plant in Sverdlovsk; from 1939 USSR Dep Pop Comr of Machine-Building; 1941-45 USSR Pop Comr of Medium Machine-Building; 1946 USSR Min of Automobile Ind; from 1947 USSR Min of Automobile and Tractor Ind; 1954-55 USSR Min of Automobile, Tractor and Agric Machine-Building; dep, USSR Supr Sov; *Awards*: two Orders of Lenin; Order of Kutuzov, 1st Class; Order of the Red Banner of Labor; Order of the Red Star; three medals; *Died*: 9 Aug 1958.

AKOPYAN, Akop (1866-1937) Arm poet; father of Sov Arm lit; Pop Poet of Arm and Geo from 1923; CP member from 1904; *Born*: 29 May 1866 in Gandzha, now Kirovabad, son of a craftsman; *Educ*: studied at Gandzha High School; *Career*: in his youth worked in Tbilisi and Baku as apprentice pharmacist, gen laborer, timekeeper and bookkeeper; 1899 first collection of verse published; from 1902 active in revol workers' movement in Transcaucasus; searched and arrested several times; philosophical outlook reatly influenced by his friend, the Communist S.G. Shaumyan; after establishment of Sov rule in Geo in 1921, appointed Comr of Geo Banks and elected member, Centr Exec Comt of Transcaucasian Fed; *Publ*: poems "New Morning" (1909); "Red Waves" (1911); fighting songs: "At Dawn" (1910); "The Watch" (1913); poems: "Equality" (1917); "The Gods Spake" (1922); "The Shir Canal" (1924); "Volkhovstroy" (1925); translated "The Internationale" and other revol songs into Arm; poetry glorifies revol; works translated into Russian, Ukr, Geo, French, etc; *Died*: 13 Nov 1937.

AKSEL'ROD, Lyubov' Isaakovna (pseudonym: Orthodox) (1868-1946) Philosopher and lit historian; *Born*: 1868 in vil Bunilovichi, Vilnius Province; *Educ*: 1900 grad Bern Univ; *Career*: 1884 joined revol movement; 1887 emigrated to France, then Switzerland; from 1892 supporter of Marxist "Liberation of Labor" group; Dec 1900 published in the periodical *Nauchnove obozreniye* the article "Experience of Criticizing Criticism"; a follower of Plekhanov, 1901-02 she contributed to the periodical *Zarya* and 1901-05 to the newspaper *Iskra*, opposing economism, philosophical revisionism and especially neo-Kantianism; 1903 joined the Mensheviks; 1906 returned to Russia; in 1907-10 published a number of articles defending materialistic philosophy against empirical criticism; while expounding Marxist philosophy she made concessions to agnosticism and relativism; during WW 1 sided with defensists; early 1917 member, CC, RSDRP (Mensheviks); late 1917 member, Plekhanovite *Yedinstvo* (Unity) group; 1921-23 taught at the Inst of Red Prof, then worked at the Russian Assoc of Soc Sci Research Institutes' Inst of Sci Philosophy and at the State Acad of Arts; in the 1920's favored the mechanistic revision of Marxist philosophy; opposed the Bolsheviks and Lenin's philosophical views; the 1926-30 philosophical debate and the 25 Jan 1931 decision of the CC, CPSU(B) criticized the mechanism that she supported; in her latter years studied the sociology of arts; *Publ*: *Razvitiye mirovozzreniya Tolstogo* (The Development of Tolstoy's Weltanschauung) (1902); collections: *Filosofskiye ocherki. Otvet filosofskim kritikam istoricheskogo materializma* (Philosophic Essays. A Reply to Philosophic Critics of Historical Materialism) (1906); *Protiv idealizma. Kritika nekotorykh idealisticheskikh techeniy filosofskoy mysli* (Against Idealism. Criticism of Some Idealistic Trends in Philosophic Thought) (1922); *Karl Mark kak filosof* (Karl Marx as Philosopher) (1924); *Kritika osnov burzhuaznogo obshchestvovedeniya i materialisticheskoye ponimaniye istorii* (Criticism of the Foundations of Bourgeois Social Science and the Materialistic Conception of History) (1924); *Etyudy i vospominaniya* (Studies and Reminiscences) (1925); *V zashchitu dialekticheskogo materializma. Protiv skholastiki* (In Defense of Dialectical Materialism. Against Scholasticism) (1928); *Lev Tolstoy* (2nd ed, 1928); *Idealisticheskaya dialektika Gegelya i materialisticheskaya dialektika Marksa* (Hegel's Idealistic Dialectics and the Materialistic Dialectics of Marx) (1934); *Died*: 5 Feb 1946.

AKSEL'ROD, Pavel Borisovich (1850-1928) Menshevik leader; *Born*: 1850; *Educ*: studied at Kiev Univ; *Career*: in 1870's sided with Populists; 1874 went abroad, contributed to newspaper *Rabotnik* and helped edit journal *Obshchina*; 1879 returned to Russia; after the split in the *Zemlya i volya* (Land and Freedom) movement joined the *Chyornyy peredel* (Black Redivision) faction; 1880 emigrated to Switzerland; 1880-82 worked for *Vol'noye Slovo*; 1883 helped found the *Osvobozhdeniye truda* (Liberation of Labor) group; 1900 joined ed staff of the newspaper *Iskra*; 1903 after the 2nd RSDRP Congress became a Menshevik leader; ideological founder of "liquidationism"; active in the 2nd International; attended the Zimmerwald and the Kienthal Party Conferences; during WW 1 sided with the centralists; 1917 member, Exec Comt, Petrograd Sov; actively supported the Provisional Govt; after 1917 Oct Revol went abroad; *Publ*: *Die Entwicklung der sozial-revolutionären Bewegung in Russland* (1881); *Pis'mo k tovarishcham* (A Letter to My Comrades) (1884); *Rabocheye dvizheniye i sotsial'naya demokratiya* (The Workers' Movement and Social Democracy) (1885); *Otvet tovarishchu* (Answer to a Comrade) (1887); *Pis'ma k russkim rabochim ob osvoboditel'nom dvizhenii proletariata* (Letters to Russian Workers on the Proletarian Liberation Movement) (1889); *Rabochiy klass i revolyutsionnoye dvizheniye v Rossii* (The Working Class and the Revolutionary Movement in Russia) (1907) (translations of articles published in *Neue Zeit* and *Arbeiter Zeitung*); *Perezhitoye i produmannoye* (Experiences and Reflections) (vol 1, 1923); *Died*: 1928 in Berlin.

AKSEL'ROD, T.L. (1888-1938) Journalist; CP member from 1917; *Born*: 1888; *Career*: until 1917 Bund member; 1910-17 lived in Switzerland; Mar 1917 delivered Lenin's "Parting Letter to Swiss Workers"; Oct 1917-July 1918 head, Press Bureau, Council of Pop Comr; 1920-21 head, Press Dept, Comintern; from 1922 with Pop Comrt of For Affairs; then ed and publ work; *Died*: 1938.

AKSEL'ROD, Zelik Moiseyevich (1904-41) Jewish writer; member, Bel Writers' Union from 1934; *Born*: 30 Dec 1904 in Molodechno, son of an artisan; *Educ*: studied at Bryusov Lit Inst and Lenin Teachers' Training Inst, Moscow; *Career*: worked for several years in a Minsk children's home and then on the Jewish newspaper *Stern*; in his latter years ed work at Bel State Publ House; 1921 first work published; wrote "restrained" lyric poetry, mainly about nature and youth; translated Bel and Russian writers into Yiddish; spring 1941 arrested by State Security organs; *Publ*: collected verse: *Zitter* (Trembling) (1922); *Lieder* (Songs) (1932); *Und wieder Lieder* (More Songs) (1935); *Oyg af Oyg* (Eye to Eye) (1937); *Reutarmeische Lieder* (Songs of the Red Army) (1939); *Died*: 26 July 1941 in imprisonment; posthumously rehabilitated.

AKSYONOV, Aleksey Mikhaylovich (? - 1937) Div eng; dep head, Red Army Signals Bd; 1937 arrested by State Security organs; *Died*: 1937 in imprisonment; posthumously rehabilitated.

AKSYONOV, Vsevolod Nikolayevich (1898-1960) Actor; Hon Artiste of RSFSR from 1947; *Born*: 19 Mar 1898; *Career*: 1920-46 (with intervals) actor, Moscow Maly Theater; from 1935 variety work; gave poetry readings; specialized in renditions of West European literary and musical classics; also did film work; taught dramatic reading at Shchepkin Theatrical College; *Roles*: Glumov in Ostrovskiy's *Na vsyakogo mudretsa dovol'no prostoty* (There's a Simpleton in Every Sage); Mechik in *Razgrom* (Rout), after Fadeyev; film roles: Harry Smith in *Russkiy vopros* (The Russian Question), etc; *Publ*: *Iskusstvo khudozhestvennogo slova* (The Art of Recitation) (1954); *Awards*: Stalin Prize (1948); *Died*: 29 Mar 1960.

AKULOV, Ivan Alekseyevich (1888-1939) Party and govt official; secr, USSR Centr Exec Comt; CP member from 1907; *Born*: 4 Apr 1888 in Petersburg; *Educ*: grad Marxism courses at Communist Acad; *Career*: until 1917 Party work in Petersburg and Samara; arrested and exiled; 1917 worked for Vyborg mil Party org; 1918-22 secr, Ural Oblast, Orenburg, then Kir Kray and Crimean Oblast RCP(B) Comt; fought in Civil War; 1922-27 Presidium member, CC, Miners' Union; chm, Donetsk Province Miners' Union; 1927-29 chm, All-Ukr Trade-Union Council; 1929 secr, All-Union Centr Trade-Union Council; 1930-31 USSR Dep Pop Comr of Workers and Peasants' Inspection and Presidium member, Centr Control Commission; 1931-32 first dep chm, OGPU; 1932-33 secr for Donets Basin affairs, CC, CP(B) Ukr; 1933-35 USSR Prosecutor, then secr, USSR Centr Exec Comt; member, Centr Control Commission of various convocations; arrested by State Security organs; *Died*: 1939 in imprisonment.

AKYYEV, Kalyk (1883-1953) Kir akyn (folk bard); Pop Artiste of Kir SSR; *Born*: 1883 in vil Kuldzhygach, Tyan'-Shan' Oblast, son of a nomadic cattleherder; *Career*: from an early age worked as hired agric laborer; at age 14 began to compose songs; *Works*: folk poems *Kurmanbek* (1938); *Dzhanysh-Bayysh* (1939); *Kedeykan* (1938), etc; *Died*: 3 Nov 1953.

ALABYAN, Karo Semyonovich (1897-1959) Architect; member, USSR Acad of Building and Architecture; CP member from 1917; *Born*: 26 July 1897 in Kirovabad, Arm; *Educ*: 1929 grad Moscow

Higher Inst of Art Technol; *Career*: 1923-31 Party work in Arm as member, Arm Centr Exec Comt and CC, CP Arm; then worked at Moscow Inst for the Planning of Housing Construction, where in his latter years he managed an architectural design dept; co-founder, secr and Presidium member, Sov Architects' Union; for a while vice-pres, USSR Acad of Building and Architecture; 1934-40 co-designed and built Centr Theater of Red Army, Moscow; 1939 co-designed Arm pavilion at All-Union Agric Exhibition, Moscow; 1945 co-planned reconstruction of Stalingrad; 1955 designed Sochi port terminal, etc; *Died*: 5 Jan 1959.

ALADZHALOVA, Nina Nikitichna (1881-1964) Party official; CP member from 1902; *Born*: 1881; *Career*: 1904-06 tech secr, Caucasian Joint RSDRP Comt; Apr 1906 arrested in connection with discovery of Avlabary illegal printing house; 1906-12 underwent med treatment abroad and carried out Party assignments; late 1916 helped establish Sewing Ind Workers' Union; after 1917 Feb Revol elected by this union dep, Bolshevik faction, Sov of Workers and Peasants' Dep; 1917-19 member and secr, Caucasian Kray RCP(B) Comt; 1919 arrested and exiled to Aleksandropol' (now Leninakan), where she founded a Red Cross branch; 1919-21 with Russian, then Arm missions in Geo; 1922-24 dep head, Women's Dept, Transcaucasian Kray RCP(B) Comt; 1924-34 Presidium and Party Collegium member, Transcaucasian Kray CPSU(B) Control Commission; 1934-37 Party Collegium member, Party Control Commission for Transcaucasia, CC, CPSU(B); 1937-40 chm, CC, Geo Branch, Int Org for Aid to Revol Fighters; from 1946 pensioner; *Died*: 17 Oct 1964.

ALAFUZOV, Vladimir Antonovich (1901-1966) Admiral; commandant, USSR Naval Acad; CP member from 1920; *Born*: 1901; *Educ*: 1926 grad Frunze Naval Acad; 1932 grad Operations Fac, Frunze Naval Acad; *Career*: 1918 volunteer in Red Navy, starting as signalman; from 1932 served with the Staff of the Black Sea Fleet; 1937-38 counsellor, then chief naval counsellor to commander of the Spanish Republ Navy; 1939-41 commander, Baltic Naval Base; chief, Operations Bd, Main Headquarters, USSR Navy; 1941-45 dep chief, then chief of Gen Staff, USSR Navy; chief of staff, USSR Pacific Fleet; after WW 2 head, and during last years of his life consulting prof, USSR Naval Acad; fought in Civil Wars in Russia and Spain, in Sov-Finnish, Sov-German Wars and in campaign against Japan; Jan 1947 unwarrantedly charged with divulging mil secrets and sentenced to long-term imprisonment; after Stalin's death rehabilitated and reinstated in USSR Navy; *Publ: Doktrina germanskogo flota* (The Doctrine of the German Navy) (1964); *Awards*: two Orders of Lenin; two Orders of the Red Banner; Order of Ushakov; Order of the Fatherland War; Order of the Red Star; medals; *Died*: May 1966.

ALAMYSHEV, Aman-Durdy (1904-1943) Turkm poet; *Born*: 1904 in vil Geokcha, near Ashkhabad, son of a peasant; *Career*: teacher; 1925 first work printed; translated Yershov's *Konyok-gorbunok* (The Little Hunch-Back Horse), Lermontov's *Pesnya pro kuptsa Kalashnikova* (The Song of Kalashnikov the Merchant), and the verse of Pushkin, Shevchenko, Mayakovski, Navoi and Shota Rustaveli; *Publ*: poems "At the Kyzyl-Arvat Plant" (1928); "Sona" (1928); "The Woman Shock-Worker at Her Post" (1932); "At the Silk Mill" (1932); *Died*: 1943.

ALAZAN (real name: Vagram Martirosovich GARBUZYAN) (1903-1966) Arm writer; CP member from 1925; *Born*: 19 May 1903; *Career*: worked as typesetter; 1921 first work printed; 1923-36 active in Arm Assoc of Proletarian Writers, then Arm Sov Writers' Union; *Publ*: verse collection "The Heart of a Poet" (1954); "Horizons" (1957); novel "The North Star" (1956), etc; *Died*: 17 May 1966.

ALCHEVSKAYA, Khristina Alekseyevna (1882-1931) Ukr poetess and pedag; *Born:* 16 Nov 1882 in Khar'kov, daughter of the celebrated pedag Kh. D. Alchevskaya; *Career:* teacher at a secondary school in Khar'kov; 1903 first work published; works influenced by 1905-07 revol; after 1917 Oct Revol works published in *Kommunarka Ukrainy, Zorga* and other publ; in the 'twenties concentrated on translating Beranger, Victor Hugo, Lev Tolstoy, etc; *Publ:* "Longing for the Sun" (1907); "Song of the Heart and the Fastness" (1914); "Cherry Blossom" (1912); "To My Country" (1914); collected verse *Probuzhdennya* (The Awakening) (1917), reflecting the revol events of 1917; dramatic poem "Louise Michele" (1930); *Died:* 27 Oct 1931 in Khar'kov.

ALCHEVSKAYA, Khristina Danilovna (1843-1920) Pedag; specialist in adult educ; *Born:* 16 Apr 1843 in Borzna, Chernigov Province, daughter of a land-owner; *Career:* 1862 opened in Khar'kov an illegal (from 1870 legal) Sunday school for women, which she directed for over 50 years; devised methods of adult educ; corresponded with other Sunday schools, acting as advisor and displayed the work of her own and other schools at pedag exhibitions in Paris (1889), Moscow and Nizhniy Novgorod (1895-96); member of numerous educ soc and vice-pres, Int League of Educ; wrote many works on methods of adult educ; *Publ:* coauthor, *Chto chitat'narodu?* (What Shall We Read to the People) (3 vol, 1884-1906); *Polgoda iz zhizni voskresnoy shkoly* (Six Months in the Life of a Sunday School) (1895); *Kniga vzroslykh* (The Adults' Book (Nos 1-3, 1899-1900); *Peredumannoye i perezhitoye. Dnevniki, pis'ma, vospominaniya* (Thoughts and Experiences. Diaries, Letters, Reminiscences) (1912), etc; *Died:* 15 Mar 1920.

ALDABERGENOV, Nurmolda (1906-1967) Kolkhoz official; CP member from 1940; *Born:* 20 Dec 1906; *Career:* began work as farmhand; 1927-29 worker, Turkestani-Siberian Railroad; from 1930 helped found and consolidate kolkhoz in vil Chubar, Taldy-Kurgan Rayon; starting as an ordinary kolkhoznik progressed to dir, Large Kolkhoz; fought in WW 2; from 1945 again kolkhoz dir; from 1965 chm, Karl Marx Kolkhoz, Alma-Ata Oblast; deleg, 20th CPSU Congress; dep, USSR Supr Sov of 5th and Kaz Supr Sov of 3rd and 4th convocations; *Awards:* twice Hero of Socialist Labor (1947 and 1958); *Died:* 17 Nov 1967.

ALDANOV (real name: LANDAU), Mark Aleksandrovich (1889-1957) Russian writer and chemical eng; *Born:* 26 Oct 1889 in Kiev; *Career:* 1915 debut as lit critic; 1919 emigrated to France; published cycle of historical novels on themes from Russian and West European 18th- and 19th-Century history; *Publ: L. Tolstoy i Rollan* (Lev Tolstoy and Romain Rolland) (Vol 1, 1915); *Ogon' i dym* (Fire and Smoke) (1922); *tetralogy Myslitel'* (The Thinker), comprising: *Svyataya Yelena, malen'kiy ostrov* (St Helena, the Little Island) (1923), *Devyatoye Termidora* (The 9th of Thermidore) (1923), *Chortov most* (Devil's Bridge) (1925) and *Zagovor* (The Plot) (1927); essays: *Sovremenniki* (Contemporaries) (1928) and *Portrety* (Portraits) (1931); *Sochineniya* (Collected Works) (4 vol, 1937); novels: *Nachalo kontsa* (Beginning of the End) (1942); *Istoki* (The Sources) (1945); *Zhivi kak khochesh'* (Live as You Wish) (1952); *Klyuch* (The Key) (1955); *Bred* (Delirium) (1955); *Samoubiystvo* (Suicide) (1958); *Begstvo* (Flight); *Peshchera* (The Cave); *Died:* 25 Feb 1957 in Nice.

ALEKPEROV, Alekser Gadzhi Aga ogly (1910-1963) Azer actor; Pop Artiste of USSR from 1961; CP member from 1944; *Born:* 1910; *Career:* from 1927 at Azer Workers' Theater, Baku; from 1929 performed film roles; dep USSR Supr Sov of 1962 convocation; *Roles:* Akmed in *Dom na vulkane* (The House on the Volcano) (1929); Kolkhoz Chm in *Lyatif* (1930); Fuad in *Almas* (1936); Goydamir in *Kendlilyar* (1940); CC Organizer in *Novyy gorizont* (The New Horizon) (1941); Ferrero in *Na dal'nikh beregakh* (On Distant Shores) (1958); title role in *Fatali-Khan* (1959); Prof Sardarly in *Teni polzut* (Creeping Shadows) (1959); Padre Agila in *Nasledniki* (The Heirs) (1961); Sheikh Amiri in *Skazaniye o lyubvi* (A Tale of Love) (1961); Rustam in *Velikaya opora* (The Great Bulwark) (1962); *Died:* 31 Jan 1963.

ALEKSANDRA FYODOROVNA(nee: Alix Victoria Helene Luise Beatrix) (1872-1918) Empress of Russia; *Born:* 25 May 1872, daughter of Louis IV, Grand Duke of Hesse-Darmstadt; *Career:* from 14 Nov 1894 Empress of Russia and wife of Tsar Nikolay II, on whom she exercised a strong influence; had five children, including the hemophilic Aleksey; a religious and superstitious women, she surrounded herself with all kinds of faith-healers, including Rasputin, who influenced her on matters of state; Mar 1917 arrested and exiled to Tobol'sk and later to Yekaterinburg; condemned to death along with other members of royal family by Ural Oblast Sov; *Died:* 16 July 1918 executed by firing-squad.

ALEKSANDRENKO, Gleb Vasil'yevich (1899-1963) Lawyer; prof of law; *Born:* 1 Jan 1899 in Petersburg, son of prof of int law; *Educ:* 1925 grad Law Fac, Khar'kov Inst of Nat Econ; *Career:* from 1925 instructor, Khar'kov Inst of Nat Econ, then instructor and prof at various Ukr higher educ establishments; from 1957 senior researcher, Section for State and Law, Ukr Acad of Sci; wrote numerous works on Sov and foreign law; *Publ: Marksizm-leninizm o derzhavnoy federatsii* (Marxism-Leninism on State Federation) (1960); *Burzhuaznyy federalizm* (Bourgeois Federalism) (1962), etc; *Died:* 22 Jan 1963.

ALEKSANDROV, Aleksandr Petrovich (1900-1945) Rear-Admiral; naval theoretician; *Born:* 1900; *Educ:* 1927 grad Naval Acad; 1928 completed postgrad course at Leningrad Branch, Communist Acad; *Career:* fought in Civil War; 1928-34 head, Chair of Strategy and Operations Technique, Naval Acad; advocated equipping Sov Navy with submarines; by start of WW 2 commanded Novorossiysk Naval Base; July-Oct 1941 commander, Azov Flotilla; relieved of this post for errors in his work; 1944-45 commander, Leningrad Naval Base; chief of staff, Baltic Fleet; *Publ: Kritika teorii vladeniyem morem* (A Critique of the Theory of Control of the Sea) (1932); coauthor, *Operatsii podvodnykh lodok* (Submarine Operations) (1933); *Protivodesantnaya operatsiya* (Anti-Landing Operations) (1933); *Operatsiya na morskikh soobshcheniyakh* (Operations on Maritime Routes) (1934); *Died:* 1945

ALEKSANDROV, Aleksandr Vasil'yevich (1883-1946) Composer and choirmaster; Dr of Arts; Pop Artiste of USSR from 1935; maj-gen; prof, Moscow Conservatory from 1922; founder and dir, Sov Army Song and Dance Ensemble from 1928; CP member from 1939; *Born:* 1883 in vil Plakhino, Ryazan' Province; *Educ:* 1913 grad composition and singing classes under Prof Vasilenko and Prof Mazetti, Moscow Conservatory; *Career:* 1913-18 music teacher and choirmaster in Tver', where he organized music school; 1918-22 instructor, Moscow Conservatory; 1922-28 choirmaster, Moscow State Chamber Theater; 1926-30 conductor, State Choir; 1928 founded Red Army Song Ensemble (Subsequently known as the Sov Army Red-Banner Song and Dance Ensemble) at the Centr Club of the Red Army, Moscow; also known as the Aleksandrov Ensemble, this choir sings to the balalaika, the domra and other folk instruments and is extremely popular in the USSR and abroad, where it has made many guest appearances; *Works:* opera *Rusalka* (The Water Nymph); symphonic poem "Life and Death"; musical compositions dealing with the First Cavalry Army, the defense of Tsaritsyn, and Shchors; arragements of songs of the Civil War, including "From Beyond the Forest" and "Chapayev the Hero"; arrangements of old folksongs, including "Kalinka", "The Little Night", "Unharness the Horses, Lads" and "Be Still, Thou Green Grove"; also composed "Cantata to Stalin", "Song of Voroshilov" and "The Holy War"; wrote music for Sov nat anthem (1943); *Awards:* Order of Lenin; two Stalin Prizes (1942, 1946); diploma 1st class and gold medal at World's Fair, Paris (1937); *Died:* 8 July 1946 during guest performance in East Berlin.

ALEKSANDROV, Arshak Semyonovich (1881-1957) Party and govt official; CP member from 1900; *Born:* 1881; *Career:* Party work in Transcaucasia and Ukr; 1902 arrested for underground revol work and sentenced to 10 years at hard labor, followed by two years' exile; 1917 agitator, Odessa's Peresyp' Rayon; 1918 head, Agitation and Propaganda Dept, CC, CP(B) Ukr; 1918-19 chm, Vladimir and Oryol Province (RCP(B) Comt; 1920 secr, Groznyy City RCP(B) Comt; during Civil War dep commander, North Caucasian Mil Distr; then chm of a province sovnarkhoz and dir of various bds, trusts and insts; *Awards:* Order of the Red Banner of Labor; *Died:* Oct 1957.

ALEKSANDROV, Georgiy Fedorovich (1908-61) Philosopher; Dr of Philosophical Sci from 1938; prof from 1938; member, USSR Acad of Sci from 1946; CP member from 1928; *Born:* 7 Apr 1908 in Leningrad, son of worker at the Putilof Plant; *Educ:* 1932 grad Moscow Inst of Hist and Philosophy; completed postgrad studies at same in 1935; *Career:* from 1922 Komsomol and Party propaganda work; 1935-39 at Bel Acad of Sci, lecturer, then prof, Bel State Univ; 1939-46 prof at Party High School, CC, CPSU(B); 1946-55 dept head, Acad of Soc Sci, CC, CPSU; 1947-54 simultaneously dir, Inst of Philosophy, USSR Acad of Sci; also (1953-54) acad secr, Dept of Econ, Philosophy and Law and (1953-55) Presidium member, USSR Acad of Sci; from 1955 senior researcher, Inst of Philosophy, USSR Acad of Sci; author of over 200 works on dialectical and historical materialism, history of philosophy and sociological theory, 1947 drew Party criticism for "deviation from the principle of Party primacy in philosophy" in his book *Istoriya zapadnoyevropeyskoy filosofii* (A History of West European Philosophy); *Publ:* monographs: *Filosofskiye predshestvenniki marksizma* (The Philosophical Precursors of Marxism) (1939); *Marksizm-Leninizm o nauchnom predvidenii* (Marxism-Leninism on Scientific Prediction) (1939); *Aristotel'* (Aristotle) (1940); *Formirovaniye filosofskikh vzglyadov Marksa i Engel'sa* (The Formation of Marx and Engels' Philosophical Views) (1940); coauthor and ed, *Istoriya filosofii* (A History of Philosophy) (3 vol, 1940-42); *O sovremennykh burzhuaznykh teoriyakh ovshchestvennogo razvitiya* (Contemporary Bourgeois Theories of Social Development) (1946); *Istoriya zapadnoyevropeyskoy filosofii* (A History of West European Philosophy) (1946); coauthor, *Dialekticheskiy materializm* (Dialectical Materialism) (1954); *Istoriya sotsiologii kak nauka* (The History of Sociology as a Science) (1958); *Ocherk istorii sotsial'nykh idey v drevney Indii* (An Outline History of Social Concepts in Ancient India) (1959); *Istoriya sotsiologicheskikh ucheniy. Drevniy Vostok* (The History of Sociological Theories. The Ancient East) (1959); coauthor, *O filosofskikh tetradyakh V.I. Lenina* (Lenin's Philosophical Notebooks) (1959); *Awards*: two Stalin Prizes (1943 and 1947); *Died:* 21 July 1961 in Moscow after short but severe illness.

ALEKSANDROV, Ivan Gavrilovich (1875-1936) Eng; specialist in power eng and hydrotechnics; prof; member, USSR Acad of Sci from 1932; *Born:* 1 Sept 1875; *Educ:* 1901 grad Moscow Eng College; *Career:* from 1901 worked for several years on construction of Orenburg-Tashkent Railroad and helped to design bridges in Petrograd and Moscow; from 1921 Presidium member, USSR Gosplan; helped draft plan for electrification of RSFSR; prof, Plekhanov Inst of Nat Econ and Timiryazev Agric Acad, Moscow; Collegium member, USSR Pop Comrt of Agric; 1927-32 designer and chief eng, Dnieper Hydroelectric Plant; drafted gen plan for electrification of Centr Asia, in particular for Chirchik ind power complex; helped plan Baykal-Amur Highway; dir, Lower Volga project involving construction of Kamyshin Hydroelectric Plant and irrigation of the left-bank regions of the Volga; *Publ: Ekonomicheskoye rayonirovaniye Rossii* (The Economic Zoning of Russia) (1921); *Proyekt orosheniya Yugo-Vostochnoy Fergany* (The Southeast Ferghana Irrigation Project) (1924); *Osnovy khozyaystvennogo rayonirovaniya SSSR* (Principles of the Economic Zoning of the USSR) (1924); *Elektrifikatsiya Dnepra* (The Electrification of the Dnieper) (1924); *Dneprostroy. Proyekt* (The Dnieper Development Plan) (2 vol, 1929-35); *Problema Angary* (The Angara River Problem) (1931); *Kamyshinskiy uzel i irrigatsiya Zavolzh'ya v svyazi s resheniyem problemy Bol'shoy Volgi* (The Kamyshin Barrage and the Irrigation of the Left-Bank Volga in Relation to the Solution of the Problem of the Greater Volga) (1934); *Died:* 2 May 1936.

ALEKSANDROV, Nikolay Grigor'yevich (1870-1930– Actor; Hon Artiste of RSFSR from 1928; *Born:* 21 Dec 1870; *Career:* from 1895 performed for Soc of Art and Lit; 1898 founder-member, Moscow Arts Theater; highly esteemed by Stanislavsky as performer of small character roles and as asst producer; 1913 co-founder of a drama school from which developed 2nd Studio of the Moscow Arts Theater; *Roles:* Artyom'yev in *Zhivoy trup* (The Living Corpse); Yasha in *Vishnyovyy sad* (The Cherry Orchard); the Actor in *Na dne* (The Lower Depths); *Died:* 3 Nov 1930

ALEKSANDROV, Vasiliy Aleksandrovich (1877-1956) Therapist and balneologist; Dr of Med from 1905; prof from 1925; Hon Sci Worker of RSFSR; *Born:* 1877; *Educ:* 1901 grad Med Fac, Moscow Univ; *Career:* 1901-14 intern, then asst, Fac Therapy Clinic, Moscow Univ; 1918-20 head, balneology sub-dept, Dept of Health Resorts, RSFSR Pop Comrt of Health; 1921-25 dir, health resort clinic in Moscow; from 1925 prof and head, Dept for Study of Spa Resources, Centr Inst of Spa Treatment, RSFSR Min of Health; propagated extra-spa pelotherapy and demonstrated its efficacy; proposed original classification of resort factors - mineral waters and muds - which won int recognition; headed expeditions to study spa resources which resulted in development of new spas; 1933 responsible for opening of resort at Bayram-Ali in Turkm SSR for climatic therapy of kidney disorders; ed, journal *Voprosy kurortologii*; member, ed bd, manual *Osnovy kurortologii* (Principles of Spa Treatment) 3 vol, 1932-36); various monographs and theses on spa treatment published under his supervision; member, ed bd, journal *Voprosy kurortologii, fizioterapii i lechebnoy fizkul'tury*; chm, Spa Council, Main Bd for Spas and Sanitariums, RSFSR Min of Health; *Publ:* about 150 works mainly on pelotherapy; *Yessentuki kak lechebnaya mestnost'* (Yessentuki as a Health Resort) (1932); *Meteoroterapiya* (Climatic Therapy) (1924); *Peloidy SSSR* (Muds of the USSR) (1940); coauthor, *Osnovy kurortologii* (vol 2, 1934); *Turkmeniya i yeyo kurortnyye bogatstva* (Turkmenia and its Spa Resources) (1930); *Died:* 1956 in Moscow.

ALEKSANDROV (real name: Keller), Vladimir Borisovich (1898-1954) Russian lit critic; *Born:* 21 Aug 1898 in Saratov, son of Acad B.A. Keller; *Educ:* 1923 grad Soc Sci Fac, Voronezh Univ; 1929 completed postgrad course at Moscow Inst of Econ; *Career:* lectured at Bel Univ, Perm' Teachers' Training Inst, etc; 1918 began lit work; *Publ: Pugachyov* and *Narodnost' i realizm Pushkina* (Pushkin's Populism and Realism) (1936-37); study of

Pasternak's poetry *Chastnaya zhizn'* (A Private Life) (1937); *Spassyonnoye serdtse* (A Heart Saved) (1938); *Innokentiy Annenskiy* (1939); *Rasin* (Racine) (1940); *Pis'ma v Moskvu* (Letters to Moscow) (1942); a study of Lozinskiy's translation of the "Divine Comedy" – *Russkiy Dante* (The Russian Dante) (1945); *Idei i obrazy Dostoyevskogo* (The Ideas and Images of Dostoyevsky) (1948); *Tri poemy Tvardovskogo* (Three Poems of Tvardovsky's) (1946-50); *Mikhail Isakovskiy* (1950); *Died:* 21 Sept 1954 in Moscow.

ALEKSANDROVA, Yekaterina Mikhaylovna (nee: DOLGOVA; Pseudonyms: ZHAK; SHTEYN; NATAL'YA IVANOVNA) (1864-1943) Revolutionary; *Born:* 1864; *Career:* in late 1880's joined *Narodnaya Volya* (Poeple's Will) org; 1894 exiled for 5 years to Vologda Province, where she joined the Soc-Democratic Party; after the 2nd RSDRP Congress active Menshevik; 1904 co-opted to CC, RSDRP; secr, Menshevik Org Commission; from 1906 no active polit work; 1910-12 sided with Trotsky's *Pravda* group; after 1917 Oct Revol worked for cultural and educ institutions; from 1924 pensioner; *Died*: 1943.

ALEKSANDROVICH, Andrey Ivanovich (1906-1963) Bel poet; corresp member, Bel Acad of Sci, from 1936; CP member from 1930 and again, after rehabilitation, from 1960; *Born:* 22 Jan 1906 in Minsk, son of a cobbler; *Educ:* 1925 grad Minsk Teachers' Training Technicum; 1930 grad Teachers' Training Dept, Bel State Univ; *Career:* 1923-27 member, *Maladnyak* lit assoc; from late 1937 member, *Polymya* lit assoc; joined Bel Dept of Proletarian Writers; 1925-26 simultaneously ed, *Malady araty* (journal of CC, Bel Komsomol) and Klimovichi newspaper *Nash pratsaunyk*; dep ed, Polotsk newspaper *Chyrvonaya Polachchyna*; from 1932 dep chm, org comt for establishment of Bel Writers' Union; from 1934 dep chm, Bel Writers' Union; for a time dir, Inst of Language, Bel Acad of Sci; secr and member, ed bd, journal *Bal'shavik Belarusi*; ed, journal *Zaklyk*; elected cand member, CC, CP(B) Bel and member, Bel Centr Exec Comt; 1921 first work published; his verse extolled the "happy everyday life" of Sov man and brought him into conflict with nationalist trends in Bel lit; opposed manifestations of Bel "bourgeois nationalism"; helped prepare 1934 Bel orthographic reform, aimed at the rapprochement of Bel to Russian; in this connection edited publications *Pisatel' i yazyk* (The Writer and Language), *Pisateli BSSR o reforme pravopisaniya belorusskogo yazyka* (Belorussian Writers on Belorussian Orthographic Reform) and the *Russko-belorusskiy slovar'* (Russian-Belorussian Dictionary); 1938 arrested and interned in concentration camps; worked on construction of Noril'sk Metallurgical Combine and at lumber camps in Krasnoyarsk Kray; 1955 rehabilitated; *Publ:* verse collections: *Pa belaruskamu bruku* (Along the Belorussian Highway) (1925); *Prozalats'* (1926); *Ugrun'* (1927); *Fabryka smertsi* (The Factory of Death) (1929); *Naradzhenne chalaveka* (Birth of Man) (1931); *Vershy i paemy* (Verse and Poems) (1931); *Uzbroyenyya pesni* (Armed Songs) (1936); *Vybranaye* (Selected Works) (1958); poems - "The Rebels" (1925) "Sunspots" (1930); "Poem for Liberation" (1930); collected short stories: *Sutarenne* (The Underground) (1925); children's books: *Horad ranitsay* (The City at Morn) (1930); *Shchaslivaya daroha* (The Happy Road) (1935); *Padarunak dzetkam-malaletkam* (The Kiddies' Gift) (1936), etc; *Died:* 6 Jan 1963 in Minsk.

ALEKSANDROVICH (pseudonym: DMITRIYEVSKIY), V.A. (1884-1918) Dep chm, All-Russian Cheka; member, Leftist Socialist-Revol Party; *Born:* 1884; *Career:* during WW 1 adopted internationalist stand; after 1917 Feb Revol member, Petrograd Exec Comt; after 1917 Oct Revol appointed by Leftist Socialist-Revol Party dep chm, All-Russian Cheka; on orders from the CC, Leftist Socialist-Revol Party, played an active part in the July 1918 Leftist Socialist-Revol Partyrevolt; arrest; *Died:* 1918 executed.

ALEKSANDROVSKIY, Sergey Sergeyevich (1889-1945) Diplomat; *Born:* 1889; *Career:* from 1923 in dipl service; 1924-25 head, Dept of Centr European Countries, USSR Pop Comrt of For Affairs; 1925-27 USSR plen in Lith; 1927-29 USSR plen in Finland; 1929-31 USSR Pop Comrt of For Affairs plen in the Ukr Council of Pop Comr; 1931-33 counsellor, USSR mission in Germany; 1933-39 USSR plen in Czechoslovakia; *Died:* 1945.

ALEKSANDROVSKIY, Vasiliy Dmitriyevich (1897-1934) Russian poet; CP member from 1917; *Born:* 3 Jan 1897 in vil Baskakovo, Smolensk Province, son of a peasant; *Educ:* completed zemstvo school; *Career:* from age 11 worked as errand-boy in an office and at a leather workshop in Moscow; 1914-18 private at the front, wounded; 1913 first work published; 1918-19 assoc, Lit Studio, Moscow Branch of the Proletarian Culture Org; later joined *Kuznitsa* (The Smithy) lit group; *Publ:* collected verse: *Vosstaniye* (The Revolt) (1919); *Utro* (Morning) (1921); *Solnechnyy put'* (Sunny Path) (1922); *Shagi* (Steps) (1924); *Veter* (Wind) (1925), etc; poems: "The Village" (1921); "Poem of Pakhom" (1923); autobiographical poem "The Blue" (1922) reflected the destruction of the old country way of life and sharp class struggle during the New Econ Policy period; Lyric works influenced by Blok, Yesenin and Mayakovskiy; *Died*: 13 Nov 1934.

ALEKSEYEV, Aleksey Georgiyevich (1888-1950) Protistologist; *Born:* 1888; *Educ:* from 1901 studied at Sorbonne; 1913 grad med fac; *Career:* from 1907 research work under M. Caullery; 1914-21 bacteriologist in Feodosiya; 1921 moved to Leningrad, then Tashkent; prof and dir,Clinic of Protozoal Diseases, Centr Asian Univ, Tashkent; 1928-34 dir or consultant at tropical stations in Tbilisi, Yerevan and Batumi; 1946-50 head, clinic of an ape and monkey breeding station in Sukhumi; studied cytology, development and taxonomy of various pathogenic and freemotile protozoa; made valuable study of cytology of Flagellata and life cycle of Sarcosporidia and blastocysts; also studies amebiasis, leishmaniosis and malaria; did research on hematology; *Publ: Parabazal'noye tel'tse, aksostil' i mitokhondrii u zhgutikovykh* (The Parabasal Body, Axostyle and Mitochondria in Flagellata) (1924); *Matériaux pour servir a l'étude des Protistes coprozoites* (1929); *Sur le métabolisme du glycogène chez les Trichomonas et les Entamibes* (1936); *Awards:* Tsenkovskiy and Gorozhankin Prize of Russian Protistological Soc; *Died:* 1950.

ALEKSEYEV, Mikhail Nikolayevich (1892-1967) Eng; CP member form 1910; *Born:* 22 May 1892; *Educ:* 1924 grad workers' fac, tech inst; 1933 grad Ind Acad; *Career:* 1908-12 laborer, Petersburg's Voronin Textile Factory; for revol activities repeatedly arrested and exiled to Arkhangel'sk and Yeniseysk Provinces; member, then secr, Textile Workers' Union; rep, Petersburg Trade-Union Bureau; contributed to *Zvezda* and *Pravda*; 1916 drafted into Russian Army; Feb 1917, after demobilization, worked at Erikson Plant in Petrograd, where he joined Red Guards; after 1917 Oct Revol with commandant's office at Smol'nyy; Feb 1919 sent to the front as polit officer, balloon detachment on Karelian Sector; 1924-29 worked at "Il'ich" Plant; 1933-41 econ work; 1941 in Sov army; 1942-54 eng, Il'ich Abrasive Products Plant; from 1954 pensioner; *Died:* 6 Oct 1967.

ALEKSEYEV, Mikhail Vasil'yevich (1857-1918)Russian mil commander; infantry gen; one of the chief organizers of the 1917-18 anti-Bolshevik movement; *Born*: 16 Nov 1857, son of a junior capt, a veteran of Sebastopol; *Educ*: 1876 grad Moscow Mil School; 1890 grad Gen Staff Acad; *Career*: from 1876 in Russian Army; 1877-78 ensign in Russo-Turkish War; 1878-87 commands in the army, eventually with the rank of junior capt; 1890-1900 Gen Staff officer and simultaneously instructor at mil schools and acad; 1900-04 head, Operations Dept, Main Staff; 1904-05 as head, Operations Bd, 3rd Army Staff, fought in Russo-Japanese War; 1905-08 first chief-quartermaster, Gen Staff; 1908-12 chief of staff, Kiev Mil Distr; 1912-14 commander, 13th Army Corps; 1914-15 chief of staff, Southwestern Front; played an important role in the success of the Galician campaign; Mar-Aug 1915 commander in chief, Northwestern Front; successfully extricated his troops from the "Polish sack", thus avoiding encirclement by the German army; from Aug 1915 as chief of staff to Supr Commander in Chief Nicholas II, virtually directed all mil operations of the Russian Army on all fronts; in the first days of 1917 Feb Revol played an important part in abdication of Nicholas II; 1917 Supr Commander in Chief and mil adviser to the Provisional Govt; then chief of staff to Supr Commander in Chief Kerenskiy; Nov 1917, after the Oct Revol, mustered in Novocherkassk (Don) from young officers the first Russian anti-Bolshevik mil volunteer formation, the so-called "Alekseyev Org," which became the nucleus of the celebrated Volunteer "White" Army; Jan 1918 transferred the command of the troops to Gen Kornilov, retaining the management of polit and finance affairs; soon after this displaced from polit management by Kornilov; after the death of Kornilov in Apr 1918 acknowledged as commander in chief of the Volunteer Army; headed the so-called "Special Consultation" - the polit organ of the Volunteer Army; *Died*: 25 Nov 1918 in Yekaterinodar of a heart disease.

ALEKSEYEV, Nikolay Aleksandrovich (1873- ?) Party and govt official; Hero of Socialist Labor from 1963; CP member from 1897; *Born*: 17 Nov 1873 in Shostsy, now Sumy Oblast, son of an office worker; *Career*: from 1897 member, League for the

Liberation of the Working Class; 1898 arrested and exiled to Vyatka Province, whence he soon fled; 1898-1905 lived in England and for some time worked on ed staff of newspaper *Iskra*, which was founded by Lenin; participated in the 1905 Revol in Petersburg; 1917 Feb Revol found him in Irkutsk; active in 1917 Oct Revol, headed Exec Comt, Irkutsk Sov of Soldiers' Dep; from 1921 in Moscow, worked for the Main Polit Educ Bd, the Comintern and for the CPSU(B) CC; then with the USSR Pop Comrt, later Min of For Trade; simultaneously teaching and sci work; deleg at 3rd RSDRP Congress and 22nd CPSU Congress; author of memoirs about Lenin *Died*: date and place of death unknown.

ALEKSEYEV, Vasiliy Mikhaylovich (1881-1951) Russian; philologist and sinologist;prof from 1918; member, USSR Acad of Sci, from 1929; *Born*: 14 Jan 1881 in Petersburg; *Educ*: 1902 grad Oriental Studies Fac, Petersburg Univ; *Career*: 1909-18 lecturer, from 1918 prof, Petersburg, then Leningrad Univ; 1923-29 corresp member, Russian Acad of Sci; later senior researcher, Inst of Oriental Studies, USSR Acad of Sci; worked on history of Chinese lit, the ethnography and culture of China and Chinese language; 1907 and 1912 visited China on ethnographical field trips; studied and evaluated archeological finds discovered by P.K. Kozlov in Mongolia in 1910 and 1923-26; prior to and after WW 2 directed compilation of "Chinese-Russian Dictionary" at the Inst of Oriental Studies, USSR Acad of Sci; *Publ: Kitayskaya poema o poete. Stansy Sykun Tu. Perevod i issledovaniye* (A Chinese Poem About a Poet. Stanzas of Sze Kun-tu. Translation and Analysis) (1916); coauthor, *Literatura Vostoka* (Oriental Literature) (1920); coauthor, *Izbrannyye rasskazy Lyao Chzhaya* (Selected Stories of Liao Chai) (1922); *Monakhi-volshebniki* (The Wizard Monks) (1923); *Strannyye istorii* (Strange Tales) (1928); *Kitayskaya iyeroglificheskaya pis'mennost' i yeyo latinizatsiya* (The Chinese Hieroglyphic Script and Its Latinization) (1932); *Rasskazy o lyudyakh neobychaynykh* (Tales of Unusual People) (1937); coauthor, *Kitay* (China) (1940); ed, *Kitaysko-russkiy slovar'* (Chinese-Russian Dictionary) (1947); *V starom Kitaye. Dnevniki puteshestviya 1907g.* (In Old China. Diaries of a 1907 Journey) (1958); *Kitayskaya klassicheskaya proza* (Chinese Classical Prose) (1958); *Died*: 12 May 1951 in Leningrad.

ALEKSEYEV, Vasiliy Petrovich (Vasya Alekseyev) (1896-1919) Co-founder of Communist youth movement in Russia; CP member from 1912; *Born*: 1896 in Petersburg, son of a worker; *Career*: from age 15 employed in ordnance shop, Putilov Plant; organized underground youth org at Putilov Plant and other factories; during 1917 Feb Revol elected member, Narva-Peterhof Rayon RSDRP(B) Comt and member, Petrograd Sov; member, first Petersburg Comt, Young Workers' Union; ed, periodical *Yunyy proletariy*; 1917 deleg at 6th RSDRP(B) Congress where he delivered a speech on the youth unions; participated in storming of Winter Palace; during the Civil War served with crew of an armored train; *Died*: 28 Dec 1919; 1928 monument erected to him in Leningrad.

ALEKSEYEV, Vladimir Sergeyevich (1861-1939) Stage dir; Hon Artiste of RSFSR from 1935; *Born*: 11 Nov 1861, brother of K.S. Stanislavsky; *Career*: 1877 began working with Alekseyev Amateur Club, run by Stanislavsky; club's musical dir; here staged Gilbert and Sullivan's operetta "The Mikado"; staged shows in Moscow for S.I. Mamontov's private opera company, including Gounod's "Philemon and Baucis," etc; 1918-39 producer and instructor, Opera Studio, then Stanislavsky Opera Theater; together with Stanislavsky produced Rimsky-Korsakov's operas *Tsarskaya nevesta* (Bride of the Tsar) (1926); *Mayskaya noch'* (May Night) (1928); *Zolotoy Petushok* (Golden Cockerel) (1932); Puccini's *La Bohème* (1927), etc; *Died*: 8 Feb 1939.

ALEKSEYEVA, Yelizaveta Pavlovna (1879-1967) Pedag; CP member from 1904; *Born*: Oct 1879; *Career*: revol work among sailors in Odessa; 1905 arrested an imprisoned; after 1917 Oct Revol with Irkutsk and Krasnoyarsk Province Health Depts; 1922-26 worked for CC, RCP(B); from 1927 teacher in Moscow schools; 1931-33 head, school of Sov trade mission in London; 1934-41 library work; from 1941 pensioner; *Died*: 22 Jan 1967.

ALEKSI-MESKHISHVILI (ALEKSEYEV-MESKHIYEV, Lado Meshkhishvili), Vladimir Sardionovich (1857-1920) Geo actor and stage dir; Pop Artists of Geo SSR; *Born*: 28 Feb 1857 in Tiflis, son of a physician; *Educ*: studied at Med Fac, Moscow Univ; *Career*: abandoned Moscow Univ studies on med grounds and returned to Geo, where he taught; also acted in Russian amateur dramatic shows; 1881 appeared with Tiflis Geo drama company; 1887-90 and 1906-10 acted at Russian theaters; 1906-07 with Moscow Arts Theater; 1890-96 and 1910 dir, Tiflis Geo Drama Theater; 1897-1906 dir, Kutaisi Drama Theater; from 1890 also worked as stage dir and taught drama; gave dramatic readings on variety stage; also film work; translated several plays into Geo; *Roles*: Levan Khimshiashvili in Eristavi's "Homeland"; Gocha in Tsereteli's "Artful Tamara"; Gayoz Pagava in Guniy's "Brother and Sister"; Yusov in Ostrovskiy's *Dokhodnoye mesto* (A Lucrative Post); *Rasplyuyev in Svad'ba Krechinskogo* (Krechinskiy's Marriage); Franz Moor in Schiller's "The Robbers"; Hamlet; Othello; Edgar in Shakespeare's "King Lear"; Uriel' in Gutskov's *Uriel' Akosta*; Tartuffe in Molière's *Tartuffe*; *Died*: 24 Nov 1920 in Tbilisi; Kutaisi Drama Theater and a Tbilisi street named after him.

ALEKSYUTOVICH, Konstantin Antonovich (1884-1943) Choreographer; *Born*: 20 May 1884; *Educ*: 1907 grad Petersburg Ballet School; *Career*: 1921-37 choreographer, Bel drama theaters; 1937-41 chief choreographer, Bel Song and Dance Ensemble; *Works*: produced ballets: Delibes' "Coppelia" and Drigo's "The Enchanted Forest" (1922-28); *Died*: 26 Feb 1943.

ALEYNIKOV, Moisey Nikiforovich (1885-1964) Film dir; *Born*: 16 Nov 1885; *Educ*: 1914 grad Moscow Tech College (now Bauman Moscow Higher Tech School); *Career*: 1907-17 ed, journals *Sinefono* and *Proyektor*; organizer, *Rus'* artists' collective (1918-23); 1926-30 with *Sovkino* film studio; 1930-33 with *Soyuzkino* studio; 1936-44 ed, *Mosfil'm* studio; from 1945 lit activity; helped to popularize cinematographic techniques and attracted to film work many figures from associated arts and young talent: Ya. Protazanov, V. Pudovkin, A. Golovnya, Yu. Rayzman, B. Barnet, L. Kuleshov, etc; *Publ: Razumnyy kinematograf* (The Intelligent Cinematographer) (1912-14); *Prakticheskoye rukovodstvo po kinematografii* (Practical Guide to Cinematography) (1916); *Puti sovetskogo kino i MKhAT* (Paths of the Soviet Cinema and the Moscow Arts Theater) (1949), etc; *Died*: 30 Apr 1964.

ALGAZIN, Aleksey Sergeyevich (1902-1937) Mil writer and instructor; *Born*: 1902; *Career*: from 1925 in Red Army; chief of staff, air force brigade; lecturer, then head, Chair of Operations Technique, Zhukovskiy Air Force Acad; arrested by State Security organs; *Publ: Obespecheniye vozdushnykh operatsiy* (The Mounting of Air Force Operations) (1928); *Taktika bombardirovochnoy aviatsii* (Bomber Command Tactics) (1934); *Aviatsiya v sovremennoy voyne* (The Air Force in Modern Warfare) (1935); *Died*: 1937 in imprisonment.

ALIBEKOV, Alibek Kulibek ogly (1878-1964) Public health official; Hon Sci Worker of Azer SSR; Hero of Labor of Azer SSR from 1933; *Born*: 1878; *Educ*: from 1911 studied at Med Fac, Kiev Univ; *Career*: active in student revol movement; 1913 arrested; 1916 received doctor's diploma and worked as intern, then senior physician, Red Cross hospital on Southwestern Front; after establishment of Sov regime in Caucasus, worked for Sov public health service; 1923-43 exec work with Azer Pop Comrt of Health; from 1932 head, Chair of Public Health Org and Med History, Azer Med Inst; wrote 61 works; helped combat malaria in Azer; co-founder and for many years chm, Azer Soc of Hygienists and Public Health Doctors; member, Azer Centr Exec Comt; member, Baku Sov; *Publ*: thesis "Malaria, Its Dissemination and Methods of Combatting It in the Azerbaidzhani SSR" (1935); *Died*: 1964.

ALIBEKOV, Serazhutdin Yusupovich (1903-1967) Dermovenereologist; assoc prof from 1940; Cand of Med from 1937; Hon Physician of RSFSR; Hon Physician and Hon Sci Worker of Dag ASSR; *Born*: 1903 in Dag; *Educ*: 1928 grad Med Fac, Azer Univ; *Career*: 1928-33 distr physician in vil Nizhniy Dzhengutay, Dag; physician at Buynaksy Tuberculosis Hospital; lecturer, Makhachkala Med College and physician, Makhachkala Skin and Venereological Outpatients Clinic; 1933-37 postgrad studies at Chair of Skin and Venereal Diseases, 1st Moscow Med Inst; 1937-52 asst prof, then assoc prof, from 1952 head, Chair of Skin and Venereal Diseases, Dag Med Inst; chm, Dag and bd member, All-Union Sci Soc of Dermovenereologists; Presidium member, Dag "Knowledge" Soc; published over 50 works on various aspects of dermatology, venereology, regional pathology, health resort therapy and particularly skin tuberculosis, skin leishmaniosis and fungi diseases; *Awards*: various orders and medals; *Died*: Jan 1967.

ALIKHANYAN, Isaak Semyonovich (1876-1946) Arm actor; Pop Artiste of Arm SSR from1923; *Born*: 7 Feb 1876 in Dusheti (Geo); *Educ*: 1896 grad Norsesyan Theological Seminary, Tiflis;

Career: 1897 stage debut; 1897-1903 and 1907-09; performed in Baku 1903-06 and 1910-21 in Tiflis; 1906-07 in Rostov-on-Don; 1912 with Arm troupes performing in Moscow and Petersburg; 1921 founded 1st State Theater of Arm in Yerevan (now Sundukyan Theater); from 1922 with Tbilisi Arm Theater; *Roles*: 1903 Khlestakov in Gogol's *Revizor* (The Government Inspector); Prince Myshkin in Dostoyevsky's *Idiot*; 191O Fyodor in A.K. Tolstoy's *Tsar' Fyodor Ioannovich*; 1912 Protasov in Lev Tolstoy's *Zhivoy trup* (A Living Corpse); 1943 Princivale in Maeterlinck's "Monna Banna"; 1939 Elizbarov in Shirvanzade's "For Honor's Sake"; 1942 Ashot Yerkat in Muratsanu's "Gevork Marzpetuni," etc; *Died*: 15 Mar 1946 in Tbilisi.

ALIMDZHAN KHAMID (1909-1944) Uzbek poet, journalist and lit critic; CP member from 1942; chm, Uzbek Writers' Union from 1939; corresp member, Uzbek Acad of Sci; *Born*: 12 Dec 1909 in Dzhizak, now Uzbek SSR; *Educ*: 1928-31 studied at Uzbek Teachers' Training Acad, Samarkand; *Career*: 1929 first work published; works influenced by Gorky and Mayakovsky; *Publ*: collected verse: "Springtime" (1929); "Death to the Enemy" (1932), etc; "First Period of Soviet Uzbek Literature" (1935); "Tolstoy and the Uzbek People" (1938); "The Class Nature of Dzhadidist Literature" (1935); poems: "Aygul' and Bakhtiyar" (1938); "Zaynab and Aman" (1938); fairy tales: "Somurg" (1939) "Roxana's Tears" (1944); play "Mukanna" (1942-43) on the Uzbek struggle against the Arab conquerors; collection "Take Up Arms" (1942), etc; translated into Uzbek works of Pushkin, Lermontov, Ostrovskiy and Shevchenko; *Died*: 3 July 1944.

ALISH, Abdulla (real name: ALISHEV, Abdulla Bariyevich (1908-1944) Tatar writer; *Born*: 15 Sept 1908 in vil Kuyuki, now Tatar ASSR; *Educ*: 1938-41 studied at Kazan' Teachers' Training Inst; *Career*: 1931 began lit work; wrote mainly for children; during WW 2 in Sov Army; Oct 1951 taken prisoner by Germans at Bryansk and interned in Moabite Prison, Berlin; *Publ*: collected stories "The Pioneer Squad's Banner" (1931); essay "The Boar Wins" (1932); novelette "At the Bright Lake" (1933); collected stories "Waves" (1934) and "The Oath" (1935); collected verse "Together with Ilgiz" (1940) and "My Brother" (1940); "Mother's Tales"; coauthor, plays "The Little Prisoner," "The Talkative Duck," etc (1934-35); plays "Neighbors" and "The Star"; verse: "Fatherland"; "The Song of Death"; "Native Village"; "The Song of Oneself," etc (written from 1942 onwards in Moabite Prison); *Died*: 1944 executed at Moabite Prison, Berlin.

ALIYEV, Azis Mamedovich (1897-1962) Public health official; Hon Physician of Azer SSR; CP member from 1926; *Born*: 1897; *Educ*: 1927 grad Azer Med Inst; from 1927 intern, asst prof, then assoc prof, Chair of Therapy, Azer Med Inst; 1929-38 dir, Clinical Inst, then dir, Azer Med Inst and head, Baku Public Health Dept; 1937 defended doctor's thesis; 1938-51 exec party and govt work; secr, Presidium, Azer Supr Sov; secr, CC, CP Azer; first secr, Dag Oblast Party Comt; dep chm, Azer Council of Min; 1951-59 dir, Research Inst of Orthopedics and Restorative Surgery; from Oct 1959 dir, Azer Inst of Postgrad Med Training, which now bears his name; wrote 74 works; *Publ*: "Clinical Analysis" (1934); "Allergy" (1936); "Experimental Nephritis" (1937); "Biochemical Shifts in the Blood in the Course of Experimental Nephritis" (1940); *Died*: 1962.

ALIYEV, Makhmud Ismaylovich (1908-1959) Public health official; Hon Physician of Azer SSR; CP member; *Born*: 1908; *Educ*: 1931 grad Azer Med Inst; *Career*: 1937-43 head, Med Educ Bd, Azer Pop Comrt of Health; dir med inst; head, Schools and Sci Dept, CC, CP Azer; from 1943 USSR Dep Pop Comr of For Affairs; from 1944, with formation of Azer Pop Comrt of For Affairs, Azer Pop Comr (then Min) of For Affairs; 1950-53 Azer Min of Health; 1953-59 rector, Azer Inst of Postgrad Med Training; cand member, CC, CP Azer; *Died*: 1959.

ALIYEV, Mirza Aga Ali ogly (1883-1954) Actor; Pop Artiste of USSR from 1949; CP member from 1943 *Born*: 1883 in vil Govsan, son of a peasant; *Career*: 1906 became professional actor; performed with various Azer drama groups; 1910-18 performed in Tiflis, Astrakhan' and Iran; 1921-24 helped run Baku Free Satire and Agitation Theater; from 1920 at Azizbekov Theater, Baku; *Roles*: stage roles: Osip in Gogol's *Revizor* (The Government Inspector) (1908), Sultanbek in Gadzhibekov's *Arshin mal Alan*; Iskender in Mamedkulizade's "The Dead Men" (1916); Meshadi Gulan Gusein in Ibragimov's *Mukhabbet* (1942); film roles: the Mullah in *Vo imya Boga* (In God's Name) (1925); the American worker in *Na raznykh beregakh* (On Different Shores) (1929); Mirza Samandar in *Almas* (1936); Ali-Bala in "The Fires of Baku" (1950), etc; *Publ*: one-act plays "Meshedi Marries" and "This Way and That"; *Awards*: two Stalin Prizes (1943 and 1948); *Died*: 25 Oct 1954 in Baku.

ALKSNIS (ASTROV), Yakov Ivanovich (1897-1938) Lat; army commander, 2nd Class; USSR Dep Pop Comr of Defense; chief, Red Army Air Force; CP member from 1916; *Born*: 1897, son of a farmhand; *Educ*: 1919 grad Odessa ensigns' school; 1924 grad Frunze Mil Acad; 1929 grad mil pilots' school; *Career*: 1917-18 in Russian Army; from 1918 in Red Army; staff comr, Oryol Mil Distr, then 55th Rifle Div; comr, Don Oblast Mil Comt; asst commander, Oryol Mil Distr; 1924-26 asst chief, chief, then comr of admin, Red Army Staff; 1926-31 dep chief, Red Army Air Force; 1931-34 chief, Red Army Air Force and member, Red Army Revol-Mil Council; 1934-37 chief, Red Army Air Force and member, Mil Concil, USSR Pop Comrt of Defense; 1937 USSR Dep Pop Comr of Defense, responsible for the Air Force; deleg at 17th (1934) CPSU(B) Congress; 1937 member, Special Judicial Office, USSR Supr Court, that tried Tukhachevskiy and co; was proposed as dep, USSR Supr Sov of 1937 convocation, but was not elected; Nov 1937 arrested by state Security organs; *Awards*: Order of the Red Banner; *died*: 1938 in imprisonment; posthumously rehabilitated.

ALKSNIS, Yan Yanovich (1895-1938) Lat; div commander; head Chair of Troop Org and Mobilization, Red Army Gen Staff Acad; CP member from 1913; *Born*: 1895, *Career*: from 1918 in the Red Army; fought in Civil War; 1920's and 1930's head, 9th Bd, Red Army Staff; then research and teaching work; arrested by State Security organs; *Publ*: *Militsionnoye stroitel'stvo* (Building up a Militia) (1925); *O kharaktere budushchey mobilizatsii burzhuaznykhh armiy* (The Future Mobilization of Bourgeois Armies) (1927); *Nachal'niy period voyny* (The Initial Stage of War) (1929); *Awards* : Order of the Red Banner; Order of the Red Star; medal "20th anniversary of the Red Army"; *Died*: 1938 in imprisonment; posthumously rehabilitated.

ALLILUYEV, Pavel Sergeyevich (1894-1938) Mil man; div eng; brother of Stalin's wife (Nadezhda Alliluyeva); CP member from 1917; *Born*: 1894, son of a worker; *Career*: fought in Civil War; mil comr, Automobile and Armored Tank Bd, Red Army; 1920 commanded various signal units; then worked for Armored Tank Troops Bd, USSR Pop Comrt of Defense; *Awards*: Order of the Red Star (1936); Order of the Red Banner (1938); medal " 20th Anniversary of the Red Army" (1938); *Died*: after returning from Germany died in 1938 of a heart attack precipitated by the State Security organs' arrest of all the Bd staff.

ALLILUYEV, Sergey Yakovlevich (1866-1945) Russian revolutionary; Cp member from 1896; Stalin's father-in-law; *Born*: 25 Sept 1866 in vil Ramen'ye, Novokhopyorsk Uyezd, Voronezh Province, son of a peasant; *Career*: from 1890 metalworker in Tiflis; 1896 joined Tiflis Soc-Democratic org; until 1907 revol work in Tiflis, Baku, Moscow and Rostov-on-Don; seven times arrested, twice exiled by admin order; 1907-18 worked in a Petersburg printing house and at an electr power plant; 1912-17 his apartment was a regular secret meeting place of the Bolsheviks; during 1917 Feb Revol elected member, electr power plant comt; July 1917 Lenin used his apartment as a hiding place; during Civil War underground work in Ukr and Crimea; 1921 member, Yalta Revol Comt; then exec econ work in Moscow, Leningrad and the Ukr; *Publ*: *Proydennyy put'* (Completed Journey) (1946(; *Died*: 27 July 1945.

ALLILUYEVA, Nadezhda Sergeyevna (1901-1932) Stalin's wife; CP member from 1918; *Born*: 22 Sept 1901, daughter of a worker, an old underground Bolshevik; *Educ*: studied at the Ind Acad; *Career*: from 1919 in Secretariat, RSFSR Council of Pop Comr; during Civil War served on Tsaritsyn Front; later worked for journal *Revolyutsiya i kul'tura* and newspaper *Pravda*, which sent her to Ind Acad; 1 Dec 1932 due to grad Ind Acad and Mendeleyev Inst of Synthetic Fibers; 1921 expelled from CP; it was thanks only to Lenin's personal intervention and his letter to Zalutskiy and Sol'ts on the Centr Commission for Purging the Party that she was reinstated in the CP; the reasons for her expulsion are not known; mother of two children by Stalin: son Vasiliy and daughter Svetlana; *Died*: in the early hours of 9 Nov 1932 committed suicide; buried at Moscow's Novodevich'ye Cemetery.

AL'MEDINGEN, Boris Alekseyevich (1887-1960) Russian stage designer and architect; *Born*: 1887; *Educ*: studied under well-known artist A.Ya. Golovin; *Career*: 1910 began working at Mariinskiy Theater; altough essentially a realist in approach, his designs at the Petrograd Acad Theater of Drama in the 1920's showed his predilection for the "psychological grotesque," e.g., sets for Sukhovo-Kobylin's *Smert' Tarelkina* (Tarelkin's Death) (1918), *Dyadyushkin son* (Uncle's Dream), after Dostoyevsky (1923); designed sets for many other theaters; his works were marked by a graphic approach, clear, calm and expressive composition and a brilliant command of perspective; *Works*: sets for: Gounod's "Romeo and Juliet" (1920, 1955) and Verdi's "La Traviata" (1923, 1952) at Leningrad Maly Opera Theater; for Wagner's "Meistersinger" and Minkus' "Don Quixote" (1926) at Khar'kov Opera and Ballet Theater; *Died*: 19 May 1960.

AL'MEDINGEN-TUMIN (TUMIN-AL'MEDINGEN), Nataliya Alekseyevna (1883-1943) Pedag; specialist in preschool training; *Born*: 1883; *Career*: member, Petersburg Froebel Soc; 1909-17 ed, journal *Vospitaniye i obucheniye*; prof and head, Chair of Preschool Pedag, Herzen Teachers' Training Inst; prof, Leningrad Inst of Preschool Training; wrote definitive analysis of R. Owen's pedag ideas and experience; *Publ*: ed, *Doshkol'noye delo* (Preschooling) (1922); *Chto takoye doshkol'noye vospitaniye?* (What Is Preschooling Training?) (1924); *Doshkol'nyye uchrezhdeniya. Rabota s sem'yoy i naseleniyem* (Preschool Institutions. Working with the Family and the Public) (1923); ed, *V pomoshch' doshkol'nomu rabotniku* (An Aid to the Preschool Worker) (1925); *Istoriya doshkol'noy pedagogiki* (A History of Preschool Pedagogy) (1940); *Pedagogicheskiye opyty i vzglyady R. Quena* (The Pedagogic Experience and Views of R. Owen) (1960); *Died*: 1943.

ALONOV, Yevgeniy Filippovich (1875-1929) Veterinarian; *Born*: 1875; *Educ*: 1903 grad Warsaw Veterinary Inst; *Career*: distr veterinarian in Vitebsk Province; 1911 senior veterinarian, Vitebsk Province; from 1912 head, Vitebsk Province Veterinary Dept; from 1924 head, Veterinary Bd, Bel Pop Comrt of Agric; from 1925 rector, Vitebsk Veterinary Inst; 1913 established Belorussia's first veterinary laboratory; 1918 founded Bel Veterinary Zoological Museum; co-founder and first rector, Vitebsk Veterinary Inst; organized publ of veterinary lit; 1912-15 published journal *Veterinarnaya khronika Vitebskoy gubernii*; until 1929 ed, journal *Belorusskaya veterinariya*; 1925-29 member, Bel Centr Exec Comt; wrote some 60 works; *Publ: Vitebskaya guberniya v veterinarno-sanitarnom otnoshenii (1903-1910)* (Veterinary Health Aspects of Vitebsk Province /1903-1910/) (1912); *Belorusskiy Gosudarstvennyy veterinarnyy institut* (The Belorussian State Veterinary Institute) (1925); *Awards*: Hero of Labor (1924); *Died*: 1929.

ALPATOV, Nikolay Ivanovich (1906-1963) Pedag; Dr of Pedag Sci; prof; CP member from 1946; *Born*: 22 May 1906; *Educ*: 1931 grad Pedag Dept, Herzen Teachers' Training Inst, Leningrad; *Career*: from 1928 worked at a children's home; from 1935 lecturer at various higher educ establishments, then head, Chair of Pedag and Psychology, Voronezh Teachers' Training Inst; also taught in Chelyabinsk specialized in history of pedag and public educ, theory and practice of training and polytech educ; *Publ: Vneklassnaya vospitatel'naya rabota v gorodskoy sredney shkole* (Extracurricular Training Work in the Urban Secondary School) (1949); *Pedagogicheskaya deyatel'nost I.N. Ul'yanova* (The Pedagogic Career of I.N. Ul'yanov) (1956); ed, *Vospitaniye u detey soznatel'noy distsipliny i navykov kul'turnogo povedeniya* (Training Children in Conscious Discipline and Good Behavior) (1956); ed, *Vospitatel'naya rabota v shkolakhinternatakh Yuzhnogo Urala* (Training Work at Boarding Schools in the Southern Urals) (1958); *Shkola-internat. Voprosy organizatsii i opyt vospitatel'noy raboty* (The Boarding School. Problems of Organization and Experience in Training) (1958); *Uchebno-vospitatel'naya rabota v dorevolyutsionnoy shkole internatnogo tipa* (Instruction and Training in Pre-Revolutionary Boarding Schools) (1958); *Vospitaniye i shkola na sovremennom etape* (Modern Training and Schooling) (1961); *Died*: 5 Oct 1963.

AL'SHVANG, Arnol'd Aleksandrovich (1898-1960) Music critic, teacher and historian; Dr of Arts from 1944; *Born*: 19 Sept 1898 in Kiev; *Educ*: 1915-20 studied at Kiev Conservatory, grad from piano, composition and music theory classes; *Career*: 1914-15 exiled to Olonets Province for revol activities; 1917 while still a student engaged in politics and helped to reorganize Kiev Conservatory; 1919 head, 1st Mil Music School, Kiev; from 1920 instructor and dean, Fac of Music Theory, Kiev Conservatory; 1923-32 member, State Acad of Arts; 1930-34 taught history of music at Moscow Conservatory; from 1932 assoc prof; in mid-1930's contracted encephalitis and was unable to continue teaching; *Publ*: "Claude Debussy" (1935); article "Russian Musical Culture" (1938); *A.N. Skryabin. Fortep'yannyye sonaty* (A.N. Skryabin. Piano Sonatas) (1938); *Simfonicheskoye tvorchestvo A.N. Skryabina* (Skryabin's Symphonic Works) (1938); "Richard Wagner" (1938); *Kolokola S. Rakhmaninova* (Rachmaninoff's "Bells") (1940); article "Skryabin's Philosophical System" (1940); *A.N. Skryabin. Zhizn' i tvorchestvo* (Skryabin. His Life and Work) (1945); "M. P. Moussorgsky" (1946); *Sovetskiy simfonizm* (Soviet Symphonic Music) (1946); "Joseph Haydn" (1947); *Opyt analiza tvorchestva P.I. Chaykovskogo 1864-1878* (Experimental Analysis of Tchaikovsky's Works 1864-1878) (1951); "Beethoven" (1952); *Proizvedeniya K. Debyussi i M. Ravelya* (The Works of Claude Debussy and Maurice Ravel) (1963); *Died*: 28 July 1960 in Moscow.

AL'SKIY, Arkadiy Osipovich (1892-1939) Financial official; CP member from 1908; *Born*: 1892; *Career*: propaganda among workers; 1913 arrested; subsequently operated in underground; during 1917 Feb Revol member, Lozovaya Exec Comt and Pavlograd Sov; Oct 1917 - Apr 1919 dep chm, Voronezh Province Exec Comt; chm, Voronezh Province Trade-Union Council and head, Voronezh Province Finance Dept; 1919 Lith and Bel Pop Comr of Finance; from Nov 1919 head, Finance Dept, Moscow Sov; then head, Accounting and Distribution Dept, CC, RCP(B); 1921-27 RSFSR then USSR Dep Pop Comr of Finance; in subsequent years econ posts; published several works on financial problems; from 1923 sympathized with Trotsky; 1927 expelled from the Party; 1930 readmitted to Party; 1933 re-expelled as a Trotskyist, then convicted; *Died*: 1939 in imprisonment.

ALTAUZEN, Yakov (Dzhek) Moiseyevich (1907-1942) Russian poet; *Born*: 14 Dec 1907 in the Lena area, son of a gold-digger; *Educ*: studied at a higher lit art inst and a univ; *Career*: at age 11 ran away from home and lived in Harbin and Shanghai; worked at Irkutsk tannery; 1922 published first verse in Irkutsk; member, *Pereval* (The Pass) lit group; contributed to *Krasnaya nov'*, *Molodaya gvardiya* and other journals; at outset of WW 2 joined Sov Army; wrote a number of war poems; *Publ*: coauthor, verse novelette *Leninskiy nakaz* (Lenin's Instructions) (1925); coauthor, poem *Otpusknik Artyom* (Artyom on Leave), etc; children's verse *Yakutyonok Oles'ka* (Yakut Boy Oles'ka) (1927); *Komsomol'skiye poemy* (Komsomol Poems) (1934); *Izbrannoye* (Selected Works) (1957, posthumously); *Stikhotvoreniya* (Verse) (1959, posthumously); *Died*: May 1942 killed in action near Khar'kov.

ALTAYEV, Al. (real name: YAMSHCHIKOVA, Margarita Vladimirovna; nee: ROKOTOVA) (1872-1959) Children's writer; *Born*: 5 Dec 1872 in Kiev, daughter of an actor; *Educ*: studied at Froebel Teachers' Training Courses and at a drawing school in Petersburg; *Career*: 1889 first work published; wrote mainly for children and young people; described life of painters, composers and writers, such as Raphael, Leonardo da Vinci, Michelangelo, Bryullov, Glinka, Beethoven, Turgenev, Lermontov, Schiller, etc; *Publ*: historical novelettes and novels: *Pod znamenem bashmaka* (Under the Sign of the Shoe') (1906) dealing with T. Muenzer, leader of a peasant revolt; *Trotsnovskiy pan* (The Gentleman of Trocna) (1908) about the Czech nat hero Ja. Zizka; *V velikuyu buryu* (Into the Great Strom) (1913) about the times of Cromwell; *Sten'kina vol'nitsa* (Stenka's Freebooters) (1925) about Stepan Razin; *Vlast' i zoloto* (Power and Gold) (1929) about the conquest of Peru; *Dekabryata* (December Children) (1926); *Semyonovskiy bunt* (The Semyonov Mutiny) (1926) about the Decembrists; *Pamyatnyye vstrechi* (Memorable Encounters) (1946); "Tchaikovsky" (1956), etc; *Died*: 12 Feb 1959 in Moscow.

AL'BITSKIY, Pyotr Mikhaylovich (1853-1922) Pathophysiologist; *Born*: 1853; *Educ*: 1877 grad Med Surgical Acad; *Career*: mil surgeon, Danube Army; from 1880 postgrad student, dissector, then assoc prof, Chair of Gen Pathology, Mil Med Acad; 1890 prof of gen pathology, Tomsk Univ; 1891-1912 prof, Chair of Gen Pathology, Mil Med Acad; 1898-1922 prof of gen pathology, Women's Med Inst (1st Leningrad Med Inst); studied gas metabolism and gen metabolic processes; designed special animal test chamber with facilities for gradually reducing the oxygen content of the gas mixture at normal atmospheric pressure and used this device for studying oxygen starvation on healthy animals; established the importance of the time factor, reduction in urine secretion, the role of foodstuffs and the reaction of the blood's from elements; studied the body's compensatory reactions with shortage of oxygen; extended V.V. Pashutin's classification of oxygen starvation with a form marked by primary disturbances of tissue metabolism; laid the foundation for the study of the effects of toxic substances during their excretion from the body; discovered the phenomenon of the "reverse action, or post-action of carbon dioxide" (intensive motor excitation, tonic convulsions, etc, in an animal brought into the fresh air after carbon dioxide poisoning); hypothesized that this phenomenon originated in the cortex; made a valuable contribution to the study of the role of carbon dioxide and other metabolic products in the autoregulation of metabolic processes; established that slight hypercapnia increases resistance to oxygen starvation; *Publ*: thesis *O vliyanii kislorodnogo golodaniya na azotistyy obmen veshchestv v zhivotnom organizme* (The Effects of Oxygen Starvation on Nitrogen Metabolism in Animals) (1884); *Kratkiy kurs obshchey patologii* (A Short Course in General Pathology) (1897); *Zapiski po obshchey patologii* (Notes on General Pathology) (1905); *Ob obratnom deystvii ili "posledeystvii" uglekistoty i o biologicheskom znachenii CO_2, obychno soderzhashcheysya v organizme* (The Reverse Action, or "Post-Action" of Carbon Dioxide and the Biological Importance of the Body's Normal CO_2 Content) (1911); *Died*: 1922.

AL'TFATER, Vasiliy Mikhaylovich (1883-1919) Mil man; first commander, RSFSR Navy; *Born*: 1883; *Educ*: 1902 grad Naval Cadet Corps; 1908 grad Hydrographic Fac, Naval Acad; *Career*: from 1908 senior posts with Baltic Fleet; from 1910 with Navy Gen Staff; at time of 1917 Feb Revol chief of operations, Baltic Fleet, with rank of rear admiral; after 1917 Oct Revol was one of few who retained their posts; headed Mil Consultation Section at Brest-Litovsk Peace Talks with Germany; spring 1918 Collegium member, RSFSR Pop Comrt of Naval Affairs, and asst chief, Navy Gen Staff; from Oct 1918 commander, RSFSR Navy, and member, RSFSR Revol-Mil Council; after a year's intensive work, put Navy back into shape and reorganized it along new lines; instrumental in org of Volga Flotilla; *Publ: Voyenno-geograficheskoye i voyenno-statisticheskoye opisaniye Chyornogo morya* (A Military-Geographical and Military-Statistical Account of the Black Sea); *O primorskikh krepostyakh* (Naval / Stroughold s); *Died*: 20 Apr 1919 of a heart attack.

ALYAKRITSKIY, Vyacheslav Vasil'yevich (1885-1960) Pathoanatomist; Dr of Med; prof; *Born*: 1885 in Kostroma; *Educ*: 1912 grad Med Fac, Moscow Univ; *Career*: specialized in pathoanatomy and microbiology; 1918-19 dissector, Moscow's Yauza Hospital; from 1920 senior asst, Chair of Microbiology, Ivanovo Polytech Inst; 1922-26 prof of pathoanatomy, Smolensk and 1926-31 Perm' Univ; from 1931 prof, Voronezh Med Inst; also dep dean, Med Fac, Smolensk Unvi; pro-rector of studies, Voronezh Med Inst; during WW 2 directed org of dissection work at Voronezh and Ul'yanovsk Hospitals; wrote some 30 works on epidemic goitre, eosinophilia of the tissues and blood, persistent septic endocarditis, etc; *Awards*: various medals; *Died*: 1960.

ALYMOV, Andrey Yakovlevich (1893-1965) Epidemiologist and microbiologist; prof; Dr of Med from 1939; corresp member, USSR Acad of Med Sci from 1946; CP member from 1945; *Born*: 1893; *Educ*: 1921 grad Khar'kov Med Inst; *Career*: 1922-30 epidemiologist working for USSR Pop Comrt of Health and in mil med institutions; 1930-36 senior assoc and laboratory head, Inst of Normal and Pathological Physiology, Moscow; 1940-48 head, Dept of Epidemiology, Leningrad Naval Acad; 1942-45 chief epidemiologist, Sov Navy; 1948-51 chief epidemiologist, Sov Army; 1948-54 head, Dept of Epidemiology, Mil Fac, Centr Postgrad Med Inst, Moscow; 1953-65 head, laboratory of infectious pathology, Inst of Normal and Pathological Physiology, USSR Acad of Med Sci; 1930-34 studied rickettsiosis in Iran; ascertained role of *Ornithodorus tholozani* in transmission of Persian relapsing fever and demonstrated in experiments on animals the importance of *Salmonella enteritidis* and *Salmonella cholera suis* in the occurrence of complications attending this spirochetosis; 1936-40 studied Marseilles fever and first proved its existence in the Crimea; during study of various infections produced autoinfection with sandfly fever and then brucellosis which enabled him to resolve various important problems of their pathogenesis and to determine their incubation periods; dep chm, Bd, All-Union Soc of Microbiologists, Epidemiologists and Infectionists; member, ed bd, journal *Byulleten' eksperimental'noy biologii i meditsiny*; co-ed, "Microbiology" section, *Bol'shaya meditsinskaya entsiklopediya* (Large Medical Encyclopedia), 2nd ed; *Publ*: more than 70 works; *Persidskiy vozvratnyy tif* (Persian Relapsing Fever) (1935); *Spontannyye oslozhneniya eksperimental'nogo kleshchevogo rekurensa i ikh vliyaniye na techeniye spirokhetoza* (Spontaneous Complications of Experimental Tick-Borne Recurrence and Their Effect on the Course of Spirochetosis) (1937); *Osnovy diagnostiki i profilaktiki parazitarnykh tifov i likhoradok* (Principles of Diagnosis and Prophylaxis of Parasitic Typhus and Fevers) (1939); *Awards*: Order of the Red Banner of Labor; Order of the Red Star; medals; *Died*: 1965 after long and serious illness.

ALYMOV, Sergey Yakovlevich (1892-1948) Russian poet and song writer; *Born*: 5 Apr 1892 in vil Slavgorod, Khar'kov Province; *Career*: 1911 exiled to Siberia for revol activities, but fled from exile and went abroad; 1926 returned to USSR; 1920 first verse collection published in Harbin; *Publ*: songs: "Strike from the Sky, Planes!"; "Vasya-Vasilyok"; "Paths and Roads"; "Song of Russia"; "By Dales and Hills"; "Baltic Glory"; "Song of the Marines," etc; collections: *Pesni* (Songs) (1939); *Stikhi i pesni* (Verse and Songs) (1949); *Izbrannyye stikhi* (Selected Verse) (1953); *Died*: 29 Apr 1948 in Moscow.

ALYOKHIN, Aleksandr Aleksandrovich (1892-1946) Russian chess-player; World Chess Champion from 1927 to 1935 (after defeating Capablanca) and from 1937 to 1946 (after defeating M. Euwe, who was temporarily World Champion); *Born*: 1 Nov 1892 in Moscow; *Career*: 1921 emigrated from Russia; 1924 settled in France, which he from then on represented in int chess tournaments; represented Russian chess school founded by A.D. Petrov and M.I. Chigorin; his best achievements: 1st prize at major int tournaments: Baden-Baden (1925), Kecskemet (1927), San Remo (1930), Bled (1931), Zurich (1934); brilliantly intuitive chess player with a profound grasp of the laws of positional play and perfect technique; world record-holder for blindfold play; author of various works on chess notable for their depth of analysis and clear exposition; developed the "Alyokhin Defense" opening (1. e4, kf6); *Publ: Moi luchshiye partii* (My Best Games) (1927); *Na putyakh k vysshim dostizheniyam* (On the Way to the Top) (1932); *Mezhdunarodnyy shakhmatnyy turnir v N'yu-Yorke 1927* (The 1927 International Chess Tournament in New York) (translated from German) (1930), recounting all the games in the tournament; *Died*: 24 Mar 1946.

ALYOKHIN, Vasiliy Vasil'yevich (1882-1946) Russian geobotanist and phytocoenologist; Dr of Biological Sci from 1935; prof from 1918; founder of Moscow School of Phytocoenology; *Born*: 16 Jan 1882 in Kursk; *Educ*: 1907 grad Dept of Natural History, Physico-Mathematical Fac, Moscow Univ; *Career*: 1907-14 post-grad work, Chair of Botany, Moscow Univ; from 1914 assoc prof, and from 1918 prof, Moscow Univ; 1923-46 founder and head, Chair of Geobotany, Moscow State Univ; taught contemporaneously at Moscow Advanced Courses for Women (1908-18), Moscow Mining Acad (1920-25), Timiryazev Agric Acad (1923-24), Moscow Geodetic Inst (1930-32), etc; led geobotanical expeditions in Tambov Province (1913-15), Kursk Province (1919), Moscow Oblast (1925-31), Gorky Oblast (1925-29), Kalinin Oblast (1936) and Turkmenia (1942); made major contribution to development of phytocoenology (study of plant communities); investigated and developed methods of studying morphology and dynamics of plant communities; classified steppe vegetation; compiled survey maps of vegetation in the European and Asian USSR and maps of contemporary restored flora in Moscow and Gorky Oblasts; wrote over 100 sci works and textbooks on phytocoenology and plant geography, some of them in French and German; *Publ: Ocherk rastitel'nosti i yeyo posledovatel'noy smeny na Streletskoy stepi pod Kurskom* (Summary of the Flora of the Strelets Steppe Near Kursk and Its Successive Replacement) (1909); *Osnovnyye cherty v raspredelenii rastitel'nosti Yevropeyskoy Rossii* (Basic Features in the Distribution of Vegetation in European Russia) (1921); *Chto takoye rastitel'noye soobshchestvo?* (What Is a Plant Community?) (1924); *Nashi poyomnyye luga* (Our Flood Meadows) (1925); *Rastitel'nyy pokrov stepey Tsentral'no-Chernozyomnoy oblasti* (Flora of the Central Black Soil Steppes) (1925); coauthor, *Metodika floristicheskikh i fitotsenologicheskikh issledovaniy* (Methods of Floristic and Phytocoenological Research) (1925); *Karta rastitel'nosti Yevropeyskoy chasti SSSR* (Vegetation Map of the European USSR) (1930); *Karta rastitel'nosti Aziatskoy chasti SSSR* (Vegetation Map of the Asian USSR) (1930); coauthor, *Metodika krayevednogo izucheniya rastitel'nosti* (Methods of Regional Vegetation Study) (1933); *Rastitel'nost SSSR v osnovnykh zonakh* (Basic Vegetation Zones of the USSR) (1936, 2nd ed, 1951); *Osnovy botanicheskoy geografii* (Principles of Botanic

Geography) (1936); *Metodika polevogo izucheniya rastitel'nosti flory* (Methods of Studying Vegetation and Flora in the Field) (1938); *Geografiya rasteniy. Osnovy fitogeografii, ekologii i fitotsenologii* (Plant Geography. Principles of Phytogeography, Ecology and Phytocoenology) (1938); *Rastitel'nost' i geobotanicheskiye rayony Moskovskoy i sopredel'nykh oblastey* (The Vegetation and Geobotanic Regions of Moscow and Adjacent Oblasts) (1947), etc; *Died*: 3 Apr 1946 in Moscow.

ALYOSHIN, Sergey Semyonovich (1886-1963) Sculptor; leading member, Assoc of Artists of Revol Russia; *Born*: 1886; *Educ*: studied under Andreyev at Stroganov College; *Career*: 1913-15 sculptural ornamentation of Kiev Station, Moscow, his most important pre-Revol work; helped implement Lenin's "monumental propaganda" plan;; also taught sculpture; *Works*: model for Marx Monument, Moscow; bust of Frunze; reliefs for Trade-Union Int (Profintern) Club, Sverdlovsk (1930); group sculpture "Greetings to the Komsomol" (1930); "The First Casting at Magnitogorsk" (1937); "For Our Native Fields" (1947); statue of Karl Marx (1947); *Died*: 1963.

ALYUTIN, Aleksey Polikarpovich (1884-1967) Party and govt official; CP member from 1917; *Born*: 1884; *Educ*: 1923-26 studied at Sverdlov Communist Univ; *Career*: from 1902 asst engine-driver, China-Eastern Railroad; later worked in a sulphur mine; 1917-19 chm, Commission for Mil Investigation, Vladivostok Oblast Sov of Workers and Soldiers' Dep; 1919-20 chief of staff and chm, Sov of Ol'ginka and Combined Partisan Detachments; 1921 head, Org Dept, Verkhneudinsk Province RCP(B) Comt; chm, town council; 1922-23 chm, Uyezd Revol Comt; chm, Baykal Exec Comt; 1926-27 secr, Chita City Party Comt; 1930-32 Party work in Khabarovsk; 1933-35 Party work in Alma-Ata; 1935-36 Party work in Moscow; from 1936 admin work in Moscow with Pop Comrt of Defense and Pop Comrt of Electr Ind; 1953-67 pensioner; *Died*: 11 Mar 1967.

AL'BERTON, Meyer Iosifovich (1900-1947) Jewish writer; *Born*: 15 Aug 1900 in Ukr; *Educ*: studied at Dnepropetrovsk Mining Inst; *Career*: member, All-Ukr Assoc of Proletarian Writers; *Publ*: story "Fyodor Zubkov" (1927); novel "Mines" (1929); play "Roman Tsat" (1930); essay collections "Without Invention" (1941 and 1947); travel notes "Birobidzhan" (1929); *Died*: 20 Nov 1947.

AL'TMAN, Iogann L'vovich (1900-1955) Russian lit historian and theater critic; CP member from 1920; *Born*: 1 May 1900; *Educ*: 1926 grad Moscow Univ; 1932 grad Lit Dept, Inst of Red Prof; *Career*: 1936-38 ed, newspaper *Sovetskoye iskusstvo*; 1937-41 ed, journal *Teatr*; wrote works on theory of drama and articles about Lunacharsky, Trenyov, Bill'-Belotserkovskiy, Vishnevskiy, Afinogenov, Kirshon and productions of Moscow, Arm, Geo and Azer theaters; *Publ: Dramaticheskiye printsipy Aristotelya* (The Dramatic Principles of Aristotle) (1936); *Teoriya dramy Lessinga* (The Theory of Lessing's Drama) (1936); *Lessing i drama* (Lessing and Drama) (1939); *Akakiy Alekseyevich Khorava* (1947); *Izbrannyye stat'i* (Selected Articles) (1957, posthumously); *Died*: 26 Feb 1955.

AMAGLOBELI, Sergey Ivanovich (1899-1946) Geo theater critic and stage dir; CP member from 1923; *Born*: 24 May 1899; *Educ*: 1920-24 at Tbilisi Univ; *Career*: while still a student worked for ed bd, newspaper *Tribuna*; 1924-28 lecturer, univ, conservatory and Transcaucasian Communist Univ; 1925 dir, Rustaveli Theater, Tbilisi; 1926-27 dir, Geo State Cinematographic Ind Trust; 1928 worked in Moscow at Acad of Arts, Communist Acad and other institutions of learning; 1931-32 dir and art manager, Novyy Theater; 1933-36 dir and art manager, Maly Theater; *Publ*: plays *Khoroshaya zhizn'* (The Good Life)(1934); *Sbor mandarinov* (Assembly of Mandarins) (1935), etc; *Died*: 12 Apr 1946.

AMANGEL'DY IMANOV (1873-1919) Kaz revol; helped establish Sov rule in Kaz; CP member from 1918; *Born*: 1873; *Career*: worked as farmhand; during 1905-07 Revol fought in peasant revolt; 1908 arrested for armed clash with police; 1916 headed mutiny in Turgay Uyezd; late July 1916 unified most of detachments operating in Turgay, Kustanay, Aktyubinsk and Irgiz Uyezds; drilled and trained revolutionaries and set up arms workshops; Oct 1916 besieged Turgay; 17 Nov 1916, after the arrival of strong relief forces, compelled to raise the siege; Feb 1917 his headquarters in Batnakkar was routed by Tsarist troops; retreated with his men to the steppes and until 1917 Oct Revol fought against punitive detachments; Oct 1917-Jan 1918 helped establish Sov rule in Turgay region; appointed mil comr, Turgay Uyezd; formed first nat Kaz units in Red Army; helped partisans in Kolchak's rear and maintained liaison with Red Army; *Died*: 18 May 1919 killed in Turgay during an anti-Sov revolt.

AMANTAY, Abdulla Gareyevich (1907-1944) Bash poet and folklorist; CP member from 1926; *Born*: 1907 in vil Kunakbay, Orenburg Province, son of a teacher; *Educ*: 1932 grad Leningrad Inst of Philosophy, Lit and History; *Publ*: 1927 first collected verse - "Songs of Struggle" - published; verse dealt with role of youth in the building of socialism, radical changes in the life of people, new human relationships; children's works: "To My Little Friends" (1928); "At the River" (1930); "Tales of a Crow" (1935), etc; textbook on Bash lit (1934); works on Bash folklore; arrested by State Security organs; *Died*: 30 Mar 1944 in imprisonment; posthumously rehabilitated.

AMANZHOLOV, Kasim Rakhimzhanovich (1911-1955) Kaz poet; CP member from 1944; *Born*: 1911 in what is now Karaganda Oblast; *Career*: 1931 first work published; glorified life, heroic deeds and spiritual image of his contemporaries, their courage and staunchness in lyrically—toned collected verse: "Life Confession" (1938); "The Storm" (1948); poems "Mysterious Girl" (1939); "Tale of a Poet's Death" (1944); "Our Homestead" (1947); works were marked by optimism and lyricism; introduced into Kaz verse the ten—syllable line used by Kaz poets in their creative work and in translating; other collected verse and poems: "A Fine Child" (1949); "Verse" (1949); "Radiant World" (1950); translated into Kaz works by Pushkin, Lermontov, Tvardovskiy, ect; *Died*: 17 Jan 1955.

AMBARTSUMYAN, Sarkis (1880— ?) Govt official; CP member from 1917; *Born*: 1880 in Nagornyy Karabakh, son of a peasant; *Educ*: grad univ; *Career*: 1902 arrested for attending a student polit rally; 1903 arrestet in connection with suppression of Moscow Soc—Democratic org, exiled to Baku and placed under police surveillance; joined CP in Baku; after graduating from univ, worked as physician in Shusha and campaigned against Dashnaks; Sept—Oct 1917 openly sided with Bolsheviks; 1918 arrested after rout of Sov regime in Baku; 1921 Arm Pop Comr of Health; 1922 chm, Arm Centr Exec Comt and member, CC, CP Arm; 1926 chm, Arm Council of Pop Comr; *Died*: date, place and cause of death unknown.

AMELIN, Mikhail Petrovich (1896-1937) Russian mil commander; army comr, 2nd class; CP member from 1917; *Born*: 4 Dec 1896 in vil Solomina, Kursk Province, son of a peasant; *Educ*: 1918 grad courses for mil comr; 1920 grad Poltrava infantry officers' courses; 1923 grad Moscow Higher Mil Instructors College; 1930 grad advanced officers' courses; *Career*: 1910-15 carpenter at a Donbass plant, mine timberman, joiner; 1915 drafted into Russian Army, completed mil training and appointed platoon commander; sent to penal company for anti-war propaganda, fled to Urals and worked at a plant there; after 1917 Feb Revol returned to Russian Army and was elected company commander; from 1918 in Red Army, fought against the Germans; 1919-21 comr-extraordinary for supplies to Yekaterinoslav sector of front; dep chm, Odessa Mil-Revol Tribunal; plen, Revol-Mil Council, 3rd Ukr Army; regt comr; chief of a combat sector; comr of a mil cadets detachment; polit officer with a composite cadets div; 1921-28 comr at mil training institutions in Poltava and Kiev; 1928-34 asst commander for polit work, 14th Corps; dep head, Polit Bd, Ukr Mil Distr; from Apr 1934 member, Revol-Mil Council, and head, Polit Bd, Ukr (from Aug 1935 Kiev) Mil Distr; member, Mil Council, USSR Pop Comrt of Defense; during Civil War helped to crush anti-Sov peasant revolts and fought against forces of Ukr anarchist leader Makhno; from 1933 member, Org Bureau, CC, CP(B) Ukr; 1934 deleg at 17th RCP(B) Congress; 1937 arrested by State Securiky organs; *Awards*: Order of the Red Banner (1933); *Died*: June 1937 executed in Moscow; posthumously rehabilitated.

AMFITEATROV, Aleksandr Valentinovich (1862-1938) Russian writer, publicist and essayist; *Born*: 26 Dec 1862 in Kaluga; *Educ*: 1885 grad Moscow Univ; *Career*: early 1880's contributed satirical articles to newpaper *Novoye vremya*; toured Italy and Slavic countries as corresp for Russian newspapers; 1899 co-founder, newspaper *Rossiya*; 1902 exiled to Minusinsk for satirical article on Tsarist family entitled "Messrs Deceivers"; 1900 began publ of *Zver' iz bezdny* (The Beast from the Abyss), a voluminous work on Ist Century AD; 1905 emigrated to Paris, where he published the journal *Krasnoye znamya*; 1916, after his return to Russia, helped found newspaper *Russkaya volya*; 1922 went into emigration; *Publ*: novels: *Vos'midesyatniki* (Men of the Eighties) (2 vol, 1907-08) and *Devyatidesyatniki* (Men of the Nineties) (2 vol, 1910), which formed part of a historical cycle entitled *Kontsy i nachala. Khronika 1880-1910* (Ends and Beginnings. A Chronicle of 1880-1910); *Sobraniya sochineniy* (Collected Works) (vol 1-30, 33-35, 37, 1911); other novels: *Viktoriya Pavlovna* and *Zacharovannaya step'* (The Enchated Steppe) (1921); collected stories *Demonicheskiye povesti XVII veka* (Horrorr Stories of the 17th Century) (1929); *Literatura v izgnanii* (Leterature in Exile) (1929); *Died*: 26 Feb 1938 in Levanto, Italy.

AMIRASLANOV, Ali Agamaly ogly (1900-1962) Geologist; prof from 1950; corresp member, USSR Acad of Sci from 1953; CP member from 1920; *Born*: Dec 1900; *Educ*: 1930 grad Moscow Mining Acad; *Career*: from 1930 at All-Union Inst of Mineral Ores and at Gold Mining Research Inst; 1939-47 chief eng, 1948-53 dir and 1954-57 chief geologist, Main Geological Survey Bd, USSR Min of Non-Ferrous Metals; simultaneously 1931-55 instructor, Moscow Geological Survey Inst; 1955-57 dep acad secr, Dept of Geological and Geographical Sci, USSR Acad of Sci; 1957-62 staff member, Inst of Ore Deposit Geology, Petrography, Mineralogy and Geochemistry, USSR Acad of Sci; Bureau member, Dept of Geological and Geographical Sci, USSR Acad of Sci; from 1960 specialized in study of deposits of non-ferrous and rare metals, especially copper, lead and zinc; *Publ* (The Levikha Group of Pyrite Deposits in the Urals) (1934); *Karpushikhinskoye mestorozhdeniye na Urale i yego perspektivy* (The Karpushikha Deposit in the Urals and its Prospects) (1936); *Mineralogicheskaya kharakteristika kolchedannykh mestorozhdeniy Urala i vtorichnyye protsessy v nikh* (The Mineralogical Characteristics of the Pyrite Deposits of the Urals and Secondary Processes Therein) (1937); *Awards*: two orders; medals; *Died*: 16 Oct 1962.

AMIRKHAN, Fatikh Zarifovich (1886-1926) Tatar writer and publicist; *Born*: 13 Jan 1886; *Educ*: studied at Mukhamediya Medressah; *Career*: expelled from medressah in 1905 for active participation in school refom movement; from 1907 contributed to Tatar-language journal "Child Training"; 1907-09 founded and ran radical newspaper *El Islakh* (Reform); closely associated with Bolshevik Khusain Yamashev, avant garde writers G. Kulakhmetov, G. Tukay, G. Kamal, ect; 1907 first work published – story "Dream Before a Holiday"; lit and publicistic works attacked survivals of feudalism in everyday life, depiced Tatar youth's aspirations for a new mode of life and Russian culture; from 1912 worked for liberal newspaper *Koyash* (Sun) and journal *An* (Consciousness); by advocating realism and adherence to moral principles in criticism, he contributed much to the development of Tatar lit criticism; after 1917 Oct Revol concentrated on journalism; major critical articles dealt with work of Tukay, Kulakhmetov, Kamal, etc; in last decade of his life turned to mysticism under the influence of an incurable illness, the famine in the Volga area, and the horrors of the Civil War; *Publ*: "A Tatar Girl" (1909); *Fatkhulla Khazrat* (1909); "At the Crossroads" (1912); play "Youth" (1910); "The First Flower" (1957); selected works "The Tatar Woman" (1959); *Died*: 9 Mar 1926.

AMIROV, Tatevos Minayevich (1873-1918) Mil commander; *Born*: 1873 in vil Kirk, Geokchay Uyezd; *Career*: 1908 joined terrorist group; member, Dashnak Party; 1918 fought in defense of Baku Commune; 1918 sentenced to death for attempting to use his detachment for the defense of the Baku Commissars at the time of their arrest in Krasnovodsk; *Died*: 1918 executed togehter with the 26 Baku comr.

AMIR'YAN, Arseniy (pseudonyms: AMIROV; ARSEN) (1881-1918) One of the 26 Baku Comr; CP member from 1910; *Born*: 1881; *Career*: 1904, while a student at Kiev Univ, joined revol movement (Dashnaktsutyun Party); 1910 switched to Marxists; during WW 1 worked for Arm newspaper *Naykar*; after 1917 Revol exec ed, Bolshevik organ *Bakinskiy rabochiy*; *Publ*: *Pora ochnut'sya* (Time to Come to Our Senses); *Krizis dashnaktsutyun* (The Dashnaktsutyun Crisis); *Died*: after fall of Sov regime in Baku arrested and shot as one of 26 Baku Comr in night of 19/20 Sept 1918.

AMMOSOV, M.K. (1897-1939) Party official; CP member from 1917; *Born*: 1897; *Career*: during 1917 Feb Revol engaged in agitation and propaganda work; Yakut workers' leader; member, Yakutsk Sov of Workers' Dep; member, Yakutsk Comt for Public Security; 1920-21 chm, Yakutsk Province Revol Comt; head, Yakutsk Section, Yakutsk Province RCP(B) Bureau; from the 8th All-Russian Congress of Soviets member, All-Russian Centr Exec Comt; 1922-32 exec work in Yakutia: with Presidium, All-Russian Centr Exec Comt; then with CPSU(B) CC; 1932-37 first secr, West-Kaz and North-Kaz Oblast Party Comt; secr, CC, CP(B) Kir; arrested by State Security organs; *Died*: 1939 in imprisonment.

AMMOSOV, Sergey Nikolayevich (1897-1943) Russian; col; mil theorist and instructor *Born*: 1897; *Educ*: 1928 grad Frunze Mil Acad; *Career*: from 1918 in Red Army; Civil War veteran; 1921-25 instructor at an artillery school; 1928-36 instructor at mil schools and acad; 1936-38 commander and comr, mech brigade; *Publ*: *Reydy motomekhsoyedineniy* (Raids of Motorized and Mechanized Formations) (1931); *Taktika motomekhsoyedineniy* (Tactics of Motorized and Mechanized Formations) (1932); *Tanki v operatsiyakh proryva* (Tanks in Break-Through Operations) (1932); *Vzaimodeystviye tankov s pekhotoy* (Combined Operations of Tanks and Infantry) (1934); *Taktika i takticheskaya podgotovka* (Tactics and Tactical Training) (1934); 1938 arrested by State Security organs; *Died*: 1943 in imprisonment; posthumously rehabilitated.

AMOSOV, Aleksey Mefod'yevich (1896-1937) Trade-union and govt official; CP member from 1914; *Born*: 1896; *Career*: metalworker; illegal Party work in Moscow workers' clubs and organized Party cells in Sokol'niki Rayon; 1916 arrested and imprisoned for seven months; 1917-21 Party work in Moscow; simultaneously worked for CC, Railroad Workers' Union; 1921-22 chm, CC, Ukr Railroad Workers' Union, Khar'kov; at one time Collegium member, Pop Comrt of Means of Communication; 1928 chm, CC, Railroad Workers' Union; from 1931 USSR Dep Pop Comr of Means of Communication; member, All-Ukr, All-Russian and All-Union Centr Exec Comts of various convocations; Presidium member, All-Union Centr Trade-Union Council of 8th convocation; arrested by State Security organs; *Died*: 1937 in imprisonment.

AMOSOV, Pavel Nikanorovich (1893-?) Party and govt official; CP member from 1917; *Born*: 1893, son of a peasant; *Educ*: grad tech school; *Career*: worked in a Petersburg iron foundry; from 1910 active in RSDRP; during 1905-07 actor, Apollo Theater; from 1908 stage dir and actor, Riga New and Works Comt; Presidium member, Higher Labor Control org; one of Workers' Theater of Sov Lat (now Lat Acad Drama Theater); 1944-49 Soviets elected member, All-Russian Centr Exec Comt; Dec 1917-21 worked for All-Russian Sovnarkhoz; for some time Collegium member, Petrograd Cheka; 1921-23 dep chm, Northwestern Oblast Ind Bureau, All-Russian Sovnarkhoz; 1923-26 member, RCP(B) Centr Control Commission; *Died*: date, place and cause of death unknown.

AMTMAN-BRIYEDIT (real name: AMTMANIS), Al'fred Fritsevich (1885-1966) Lat stage dir and actor; Pop Artiste of USSR from 1953; *Born*: 5 Aug 1885; *Educ*: 1909-12 drama courses in Riga; *Career*: from 1903 actor, New Lat Theater, Riga; 1905-07 actor, Apollo Theater; from 1908 stage dir and actor, Riga New Theater; 1915-18 at the Lat Theater in Petrograd; 1919 joined the Workers'. Theater of Sov Lat (now Lat Acad Drama Theater); 1944-49 artistic dir, from 1949 chief stage dir of this theater; from 1949 prof, Theater Fac, Lat State Conservatory; dep, Lat Supr Sov of 1959 convocation and member, Commission for Culture and Educ; one of the greatest exponents of stagecraft in Lat; *Roles*: Uldis and Indulis in *Vey, veterok* (Blow, Breeze) (1914) and "Indulis and Aria" (1912), Belugin in *Zhenit'ba Belugina* (Belugin's Wedding) (1929); Knurov in *Bespridannitsa* (Girl Without a Dowry) (1948), etc; produced: *Syn rybaka* (The Fisherman's Son), after V.T. Latsis (1949); A. Upit's *Zemlya zelyonaya* (The Green Land) (1950); R. Blauman's *Dni portnykh v Silmachakh* (The Days of the Silmachi Tailors) (1955); Ya. Raynis' *Iosif i yego brat'ya* (Joseph and His Brothers) (1956); *Prosvet v tuchakh* (Break in the Clouds), after A. Upit's novel; *Morskiye vorota* (Gateway of the Sea), after D. Zigmonte's novel (1961); staged plays by Shakespeare, Schiller, Ostrovskiy, Gorky, etc; also taught acting and stagecraft; *Awards*: Stalin Prizes (1948, 1950 and 1951); Order of Lenin (1956); Prize of Lat Theater Soc (1963); Order of the Red Banner of Labor; *Died*: 15 May 1966.

AMTMAN, Teodor, (1884-1938) Lat actor and stage dir; brother of famous Lat stage dir and actor A.F. Amtman-Briyedit; *Born*: 1884; *Career*: 1909-13 at New Riga Theater, where he produced plays: Raynis' "Indulis and Aria" (1912); Upit's "Voice and Echo" (1911); Hebbel's "Living Corpse" (1911); Hebbel's "Judith" (1911), etc; best roles included: Antyn and Ugis in Raynis' "The Golden Horse" and "Indulis and Aria"; Protasov in "Living Corpse," etc; 1911-13 dir, New Riga Theater; 1915-17 staged Lat shows in Tallin; after 1917 Oct Revol worked at Lat theaters in USSR; 1918-19 stage dir, Lat Workers' Theater in Moscow, where he staged "The Enemies"; 1921-22 directed Lat Propaganda Theater in Moscow; also worked at Moscow Realistic Theater; *Died*: 1938.

AMVROSIY (secular name: KHELAIYA) (1860-1927) Catholicos and Patriarch of All-Geo; *Born*: 1860 in Verkhnyaya Mingreliya, Sukhumi Okrug; *Educ*: grad Stavropol' Theological Seminary and Moscow Theological Acad; *Career*: took monastic vows while still a senior student; as priest-monk appointed father-superior, Bediyskiy Monastery, West Geo; as archimandrite and member, Geo-Imeritinskaya Synodal Office was made father-superior of Spaso-Preobrazhensk Monastery, Novgorod Province; censured for open opposition to exarchate admin of Geo Church; after 1917 Oct Revol administered Sukhumi Eparchy as member, Catholicos Council; acquired fame as ecclesiastical archeologist, publishing research results under the pseudonym "Am-Beri"; elected Catholicos and Patriarch of All-Geo at synod in Gelati Monastery a few months after Sov occupation of Geo; this was soon followed by acts of sacrilege at Motsamed Monastery (defilement of relics) and a campaign to expropriate church treasures, leading to ruthless persecution of Amvrosiy along with all other members of Geo clergy; 1922 protested persecution of Church by Sov regime in memorandum to Conference of Genua; was arrested and faced show tria at which he assumed full responsibility; prison sentence commuted to house arrest on med grounds; *Died*: 1927.

ANAN'YEV, V. Ye (Party alias: KUTUZOV) (1882-1937) Party official; CP member from 1903; *Born*: 1882; *Career*: Party work in Yaroslavl', Rybinsk and Nizhniy-Novgorod; several times arrested by Tsarist authorities; after 1917 Oct Revol served in Red Army; from 1922 Party and econ work; deleg at 5th RSDRP Congress; arrested by State Security organs; *Died*: 1937 in imprisonment.

ANDREY (secular name: Count Roman-Marian SHEPTITSKIY) (1865-1944) Metropolitan of Galicia; Archbishop of L'vov and Bishop of Kamenets-Podol'skiy, Greek-Catholic Church; Dr of Divinity, Philosophy and Law; *Born*: 1865 in vil Pril'bichi, Galicia; *Educ*: 1888 grad Law Fac, Breslau Univ; *Career*: from 1883 mil service with Austrian cavalry regt; 1890 entered Vasilian Monastery, Dobromil'; 1892 took monastic vows with name of Andrey; studied theology, philosophy and ancient and modern languages; was fluent in five Slavic languages; 1896-98 father-superior, St Onuphrius Monastery, L'vov, and publ,monthly journal *Missioner*; 1898-1901 Bishop of Stanislav; 1901 elevated to Metropolitan of Galicia, Archbishop of L'vov and Bishop of Kamenets-Podol'skiy; 1913 financed Ukr Nat Museum in L'vov; 1914 arrested during occupation of Galicia by Russian army and banished to Suzdal' Monastery and then to Kursk; 1917 returned to L'vov and supported proclamation of Ukr independence; 1921 went abroad after occupation of Ukr by Poles, seeking support for Ukr independence in USA, Canada and Brazil; 1923 returned to Galicia, was arrested by Polish authorities but soon released; 1941-43 during Nazi occupation defended faith and opposed murder of Jews; his home was frequently searched by Gestapo; built churches, founded religious soc and provided financial support for students and novices; engaged in considerable theological research; *Publ*: three-vol study of Vasiliy the Great; *Died*: 1944; buried in L'vov.

ANDREYEV, Fyodor Andreyevich (1879-1952) Pathophysiologist and clinician; Dr of Med from 1918; prof; Hon Sci Worker of RSFSR; *Born*: 1879; *Educ*: 1906 grad Med Fac, oscow Univ; *Career*: pupil of pathophysiologist A.B. Fokht; gifted teacher, for many years head of dept of pathological physiology and therapy in Moscow, Minsk and Sverdlovsk; studied role of centr nervous system in pathogenesis of internal diseases (ulcers and hypertonia) and introduced method of treating them by means of protracted sleep; did important work on pathology and physiology of the heart and lungs, pathogenesis of anoxia and alimentary dystrophy, and role of human constitution in development of pathological process; contributed to development of restoration of vital bodily functions as new branch of sci med; *Publ*: more than 70 works, of which two awarded Moscow Univ prizes; doctor's thesis *K ucheniyu o diastole serdtsa i yeyo kompensatorn om znachenii pri fiziologicheskikh i patologicheskikh usloviyakh* (A Study of the Cardiac Diastole and its Compensatory Effect in Physiological and Pathological Conditions) (1918); coauthor, *Nervnaya regulyatsiya krovoobrashcheniya i dykhaniya* (Nervous Regulation of Blood Circulation and Respiration) (1952); coauthor, *Problema sna* (The Problem of Sleep) (1954); *Opyty vosstanovleniya deyatel'nosti serdtsa, dykhaniya i funktsiy tsentral'noy nervnoy sistemy* (Experiments in Restoring Heart Action, Respiration and the Functions of the Central Nervous System) (1913); *Died*: 1952.

ANDREYEV, Fyodor Fyodorovich (1900-1950) Mil surgeon; prof; lt-gen, Med Corps; Dr of Med from 1940 *Born*: 1900; *Educ*: 1923 grad Mil Med Acad; *Career*: until 1928 at Kronshtadt naval hospital and on warships of Baltic Fleet; attached as surgeon to Mil Med Acad; from 1930 surgeon, Novocherkassk and Rostov-on-Don Okrug Hospitals; 1939-40 instructor, Kuybyshev Mil Med Acad and Leningrad Naval Acad; 1940-47 head, Naval Med Service; 1947-50 chief surgeon, Sov Navy; simultaneously prof of surgery, lst Moscow Med Inst; specialiced in org of naval med service, particularly ship surgery; made clinical study of trauma of upper extremities; after WW 2 helped to summarize experience of Sov med service; member, ed bureau and co-ed, *Entsiklopedicheskiy slovar' voyennoy meditsiny* (Encyclopedic Dictionary of Military Medicine); *Publ*: *Peredniy vyvikh plecha* (Anterior Dislocation of the Upper Arm) (1943); *Organizatsiya khirurgicheskoy pomoshchi na voyenno-morskom flote* (Organization of Surgery in the Navy) (1947), etc; *Died*: 1950.

ANDREYEV, Leonid Aleksandrovich (1891-1941) Surgeon and physiologist; prof from 1937; *Born*: 1891; *Educ*: 1914 grad Med Fac, Kazan'Univ; *Career*: after grad retained for postgrad studies at N.A. Gerken's surgical laboratory; later worked at Leningrad Inst of Experimental Med in I.P. Pavlov's laboratory and also in S.P. Fyodorov's surgical clinic (1921); in Pavlov's laboratory did research on physiology of the auditory analyser which provided experimental basis for the resonance theory of hearing proposed by Helmholtz; 1931 sent on two-year assignment to Canada by Pavlov to work on principles of the pathogenesis of hardness of hearing; 1934 set up laboratory for physiology of the sensory organs, All-Union Inst of Experimental Med, which he headed till his death and where he did detailed research on physiology of the auditory analyser; from 1937 prof, Dept of Animal Physiology, Moscow Univ, lecturing on physiology of sensory organs; *Publ*: *Sposobnost' razlicheniya tonov vysokoy chastoty u sobak* (Ability of Dogs to Differentiate High-Frequency Tones) (1934); coauthor, *Sbornik dokladov VI s'ezda fiziologov, biokhimikov i farmakologov* (Collected Papers of Sixth Congress of Physiologists, Biochemists an Pharmacologists) (1937); *Fiziologiya organov chuvstv* (Physiology of the Sensory Organs) (1941); coauthor, *Fiziologiya nervnoy sistemy* (Physiology of the Nervous System) (vol 3, book 2, 1952); *Died:* 1941 in Moscow.

ANDREYEV, Mikhail Stepanovich (1873-1948) Ethnographer and linguist; specialist in Iranian languages; corresp member, USSR Acad of Sci from 1929; member, Uzbek Acad of Sci from 1943; Hon Sci Worker of Uzbek and Tadzh SSR; *Born*: 24 Sept 1873 in Tashkent; *Educ*: grad Turkestani Teachers' Seminary; *Career*: 1905-14 lived and worked in India, studying Urdu and Pushtu and collecting ethnographic data on Indian peoples on behalf of Acad of Sci; from 1910 Russian vice-consul in Pondichery; 1914-18 inspector of educ colleges in Centr Asia; from 1918 first rector, Turkestani Oriental Inst (later Oriental Fac, Centr Asian Univ); also taught Persian language and ethnography; led expeditions to Centr Asia; 1925 and 1927 to Yagnob; 1929 and 1943 to the Pamirs and Western Pamirs; 1936 and 1940 to Bukhara, etc; 1926 journeyed through Afghanistan; collected ethnographic data on the Indian and Centr Asian peoples;*Publ*: coauthor, „Ishkashim and Vakhan" (1911); *Po etnologii Afganistana. Dolina Pandzhshir* (The Ethnology of Afghanistan. The Panjshir Valley) (1927); *Ornament gornykh Tadzhikov verkhov'yev Amu-Dar'i i kirgizov Pamira* (The Ornaments of the Tadzhik Highlanders of the Upper Amu-Dar'ya and the Pamir Kirghiz) 1928); *Tadzhiki doliny Khuf* (The Khuf Valley Tadzhiks) (1953), etc; *Died*: 10 Nov 1948.

ANDREYEV, Nikolay Andreyevich (1873-1932) Sculptor; graphic artist and stage designer; Hon Art Worker of RSFSR from 1931; *Born*: 26 Oct 1873 in Moscow, son of an ex-serf; *Educ*: grad Stroganov school and Volnukhin School of Painting, Sculpture and Architecture; *Works*: initially influenced by impressionism and modernism, yet retained a realistic approach; 1906-09 sculpted monument to Gogol (Moscow); from 1913 worked in the theater, painted sets for plays such as Potyomkin's "Cleopatra," Byron's "Cain" (1920), Sukhovo-Kobylin's *Delo* (The Case) (1927), etc; in the early years of Sov rule active in the "Monumental Propaganda" movement; 1918-22 sculpted monuments to Herzen and Ogarev and carved the statue "Liberty"; 1929 monument to Ostrovskiy; created some 100 sculptures of Lenin, Stalin and Kalinin and a series of busts of Stanislavsky, Nemirovich-Danchenko, Kachalov, Yablochkina and other stage figures; graphic works include portraits of Lenin, Stanislavsky, Gorky, etc; *Died*: 24 Dec 1932 in Moscow.

ANDREYEV, Nikolay Petrovich (1892-1942) Lit historian and folklorist; *Born*: 23 Nov 1892; *Career*: prof, Leningrad Teachers' Training Inst; specialized in Russian and Ukr fairy-tales; also studied interaction of lit and folklore; *Publ: Ukazatel' skazochnykh syuzhetov* (An Index of Fairy-Tale Subjects) (1929); *Fol'klor i literatura* (Folklore and Literature) (1936); *Fol'klor v poezii Nekrasova* (Folklore in Nekrasov's Poetry) (1936); *Proizvedeniya Pushkina v fol'klore* (Pushkin's Works in Folklore) (1937); study of the Russian *lubok* genre *Ischezayushchaya literatura* (A Vanishing Literature) (1921); anthology *Russkiy fol'klor* (Russian Folklore) (1936); anthology *Byliny* (Legends) (1938); *Died*: 15 Jan 1942 in Leningrad.

ANDREYEV, Pavel Nikolayevich (1872-1949) Veterinary microbiologist and epizoologist; prof from 1915; Hon Sci Worker of RSFSR from 1946; *Born*: 1872 in Smolensk, son of a mil surgeon; *Educ*: 1897 grad Khar'kov Veterinary Inst; *Career*: from 1897 asst prof, Bacteriological Laboratory, Khar'kov Veterinary Inst; 1900 defended master's thesis; from 1901 toured Germany, Holland, England, France and other European countries to study veterinary supervision of slaughter-houses, meat processing plants and meat storage facilities; 1907-09 studied bacteriology in Berlin, first under Prof Wassermann, at the Koch Inst of Infectious Diseases, then under Prof Uhlenhuth and Prof Neufeld; returned to Russia and directed production of sera; lectured on gen and specialized bacteriology at bacteriology courses for veterinarians; 1915 assoc prof, Chair of Epizoology, Mil Med Acad; from 1916 prof, Novocherkassk Veterinary Inst; from 1922 prof, Moscow Zooveterinary Inst; 1922-25 consultant, Main Veterinary Bd, USSR Pop Comrt of Health; drafted first USSR Veterinary Statutes and drew up rules for the inspection and condemning of meat products, as well as regulations for the opening, operation and content of slaughter-houses; 1927-49 variously dep dir, head, Microbiology Dept, head, Laboratory for Infectious Diseases of Hogs, All-Union Inst of Experimental Veterinary Sci; 1905, 1909 and 1914 attended Int Veterinary Congresses in Budapest, the Hague and London; wrote 100 works; *Publ: K voprosu o londonskom myasnom rynke* (London's Meat Market) (1901); *Zakonodatel'stva, rasporyazheniya, instruktsii i pravila ob osmotre uboynogo skota i myasnykh produktov v Germanii i drugikh yevropeyskikh gosudarstvakh* (Legislation, Regulations, Instructions and Rules Governing the Inspection of Cattle Intended for Slaughter and Meat Products in Germany and other European States) (1902); *Teoriya i praktika otkorma myasnogo skota i torgovlya im v Rossii* (The Theory and Practice of Meat Cattle Fattening and Trading in Russia) (1903); *Trikhinoskopirovaniye s pomoshch'yu Proyektsionnogo apparata* (Trichinoscopy with a Projector) (1904); *Bolezni sviney infektsionnogo kharaktera* (Infectious Diseases of Hogs) (1928); *Died*: 1949.

ANDREYEV, Pavel Zakharovich (1874-1950) Opera singer (bass-baritone); Pop Artiste of USSR from 1939; *Born*: 9 Mar 1874 in vil Os'mino, Petersburg Province; *Educ*: 1903 grad S. Gabel's singing class, Petersburg Conservatory; *Career*: 1903 made opera debut; 1903-04 at Pop Center; 1904-05 Nemetti's Lyric Opera Theater; 1905-06 Tsereteli's New Opera Theater; then performed in Kiev; 1907-ca 1947 at Mariinskiy Theater; also concert work; from 1919 taught singing; from 1926 prof, Leningrad Conservatory; *Roles*: Ruslan in *Ruslan i Lyudmila* (Ruslan and Ludmilla); Igor' in *Knyaz' Igor* (Prince Igor); the Demon in *Demon*; Holofernes and Pyotr in Serov's *Yudif'* (Judith) and *Vrazh'ya sila* (A Hostile Force); Mizgir' in *Snegurochka* (The Snow-Maiden); Tomskiy in *Pikovaya dama* (The Queen of Spades); Mephistopheles in Gounod's "Faust"; Peter I in Lortzing's *Czar und Zimmermann*, etc; *Died*: 15 Sept 1950 in Leningrad.

ANDREYEV, Vasiliy Vasil'yevich (1861-1918) Musician; balalaika virtuoso; *Born*: 26 Jan 1861 on estate in Tver' Province; *Career*: 1886-87 founded first Russian folk instrument orchestra in Petersburg, with which he toured Russia and abroad; in conjunction with S. Nalimov, arranged for construction of balalaikas of various sizes and range; together with F. Passerbskiy, arranged for manufacture of improved domra models; founded numerous Russian folk instrument orchestras; composed concert pieces, waltzes, etc, for balalaika; 1894 founded school of balalaika playing; *Publ*: *K voprosu o russkoy narodnoy muzyke* (Russian Folk Music) (1899); *Les instruments nationaux en Russie, anciens et perfectionnés* (Folk Instruments in Russia, Ancient and Improved) (1916); *Died*: 26 Dec 1918 in Petrograd; Leningrad Radio Folk Orchestra is named after him.

ANDREYEV, Vladimir Andreyevich (1874-1941) Naval hygienist; Dr of Med from 1934; prof from 1940; *Born*: 1874; *Educ*: 1899 grad Imperial Mil Med Acad, Petersburg; *Career*: after grad, naval surgeon on ship and ashore; observed that ventilation, heating and other systems sometimes did not serve their purpose and in certain cases were a health risk; studied sanitary and tech equipment of warships and formulated hygiene standards for them; studied conditions required for prolonged service on board ship; took part in refitting of numerous ships; his work proved importance of hygiene factors in designing warships; appointed to staff of Main Shipbuilding Bd, Min of the Navy, as specialist on shipboard sanitary eng; after 1917 Oct Revol asst, then head, Health Bd, Baltic Fleet; from 1932 permanent rep of Mil Health Bd for Supervising Design and Construction of Ships, Sci and Tech Comt, Sov Navy; also performed teaching duties; from 1938 assoc prof, then prof, Dept of Naval Health Disciplines, Naval Fac, 1st Leningrad Med Inst (later Naval Med Acad); *Publ*: doctor's thesis *Korabel'naya sanitarnaya tekhnika* (Shipboard Sanitary Engineering) (1934); *Died*: 1941 in Leningrad.

ANDREYEV, Vyacheslav Andreyevich (1890-1945) Russian sculptor; *Born*: 1890; *Educ*: Stroganov College, Moscow; *Career*: worked singly and with brother, sculptor N.A. Andreyev; main work - portraits of Stalin (now in Tret'yakov Gallery), Chernyshevskiy, N.V. Stankevich, D. Bednyy, etc; monument to Prof N.Ye. Zhukovskiy, the founder of modern hydro- and aero- mech; his best work is the monumental statue of a worker made for the Sov Pavilion at the 1939 New York World Fair; *Died*: 1945.

ANDREYEVA (real name: YURKOVSKAYA), Mariya Fyodorovna (1868-1953) Russian actress and revol; CP member from 1904; wife of Gorky; *Born*: 1868; *Educ*: 1894 grad Moscow Conservatory; *Career*: took part in 1905 Revol, provided financial support for CP and undertook Party missions for Lenin; 1906-12, as Gorky's secr, toured several European countries and USA; 1912 returned illegally to Russia, where she was arrested but later permitted to resume stage career; after 1917 Oct Revol was comr for theaters and entertainments in Petrograd; 1919 helped found, 1919-26 performed at Bolshoy Drama Theater, Petrograd; from 1894 acted under Stanislavsky at Soc of Art and Lit; from 1898 performed at Moscow Arts Theater; 1931-48 dir, Moscow Scientists and Scholars' Club; *Roles*: Lelya in Ostrovskiy's *Snegurochka* (The Snow-Maiden); Irina in Chekhov's *Tri Sestry* (Three Sisters); Varya in Chekhov's *Vishnyovyy sad* (The Cherry Orchard); Natasha in Gorky's *Na dne* (The Lower Depths); Rautendelein in Gerhart Hauptmann's "The Sunken Bell," etc; *Died*: 8 Dec 1953.

ANDRIANOV, Nikolay Grigor'yevich (1898-1967) Col; served with Cheka and border troops; CP member from 1917; *Born*: 21 Oct 1898; *Educ*: 1924 grad Higher Border School; 1934 grad Mil-Polit Acad; *Career*: Red Guard during Bolshevik 1917 Oct coup, took part in disarming of officer cadets; July 1918 helped to suppress revolt of Leftist Socialist-Revol in Sormovo; 1919 in Red Army; company polit instructor, 38th Infantry Regt on Tsaritsyn Front; 1920 comr, 178th Infantry Regt; plen, Special Dept, 11th Army on Caucasian Front; 1923-24 member, Transcaucasian Cheka; 1925-31 OGPU official in Bel; 1934-38 inspector, Main Bd of Border Troops; 1938-41 polit worker, Bel and Transbaykal Mil Distr; from 1941 NKVD polit worker with mil units on various fronts; from 1950 retired; *Died*: 18 Oct 1967.

ANDRONIKASHVILI, Konstantin Iosifovich (1887-1954) Geo stage dir and drama teacher; prof from 1947; Hon Art Worker of Geo SSR from 1950; *Born*: 20 Dec 1887; *Educ*: 1906-10 studied at Lit Fac of Sorbonne in Paris; *Career*: worked at Odéon Theater in Paris under Antoine; studying producing and directing; 1911-31 stage dir at various Geo theaters; 1931-45 at Russian theaters in Gorky, Kuybyshev, Saratov, etc; from 1945 taught acting at Tbilisi Theatrical INst; simultaneously stage dir at Mardzhanishvili Theater; *Died*: 2 July 1954.

ANDRONOV, Aleksandr Aleksandrovich (1901-1952) Physicist; prof; member, USSR Acad of Sci from 1946 *Born*: 11 Apr 1901; *Educ*: grad and postgrad, Moscow State Univ; *Career*: 1931-52 prof, Groky Univ; worked on oscillation and automatic control theory; solved important non-linear problems in theory of radio eng, clockwork mechanisms and automatic control; founded school of specialists in theory of non-linear oscillation and related problems; dep, USSR Supr Sov of 1946 and 1950 convocations; *Publ*: *Sobraniye trudov* (Collected Works) (1956); *Died*: 31 Oct 1952.

ANDRUSHCHENKO, Andrey Iosifovich (1906-1967) Historian; Cand of Historical Sci from 1947; assoc prof; *Born*: 23 Sept 1906 in vil Zakusilovski, now Zhitomir Oblast, son of a peasant; *Educ*: 1924 grad Volhynian Inst of Educ, Zhitomir; 1939 grad Moscow

Municipal Teachers' Training Inst; 1947 completed postgrad studies at Moscow Univ; *Career*: from 1924 teacher at seven-year schools in Ukr; 1934-41 teacher at secondary schools in Moscow; wounded and shell-shocked in WW 2; from 1947 dean, Fac of Int History, Moscow Inst of Int Relations, USSR Min of For Affairs; from 1957 staff member, Inst of History, USSR Acad of Sci; *Publ*: *Arkhipelagicheskaya ekspeditsiya russkogo flota 1769-1775 gg.* (The 1769-1775 Archipelagic Expedition of the Russian Fleet) (1947); *Krest'yanskaya voyna 1773-1775 gg. /na Yaike, v Priural'ye, na Urale i v Sibiri/* (The Peasant War of 1773-1775 /On the Yaik in the Ural Foothills, the Urals and Siberia/) (1967), etc; *Awards*: Order of the Fatherland War, 2nd Class; medals *Died* : 8 Mar 1967 in Moskow.

ANGARETIS (real name: ALEKSA), Zigmas Ionovich (1882-1940) Lith CP leader; *Born*: 13 June 1882 in vil Obelyupay, Vilkavishk Uyezd, Suvalka Province (Lith), son of a peasant; *Educ*: 1902-04 studied at Warsaw Veterinary Inst; *Career*: 1904 participated in anti-war demonstration; 1906 in Vilnius joined Lith Soc-Demo cratic Party; 1907 at 7th Lith Soc-Democratic Party Congress in Cracow elected member, CC, Lith Soc-Democratic Party; 1908-09 ed, newspaper *Darbininku Zodis* (The Workers' Word); 1909 arrested and sentenced to four years penal servitude at Pskov Prison; 1915 exiled to Siberia (Angara region); there conducted Bolshevik propaganda; wrote a number of articles which were published abroad in Lith Soc-Democratic newspapers under the pseudonym Angaretis; from 1917 in Petrograd, ed, newspaper *Tiesa* (Truth); elected secr, Lith Rayon Comt (Lith Section), Petrograd RSDRP(B) Org; member, Petrograd Bolshevik Comt; deleg at 7th (Apr) All-Russian RSDRP(B) Conference and 6th RSDRP(B) Congress; member, Centr Bureau, Lith Section, CC, RSDRP(B); fought in 1917 Oct Revol in Petrograd; Dec 1917 appointed Dep Comr of Lith Affairs of RSFSR Pop Comrt of Nationalities; during Brest-Litovsk peace talks sided with "Leftist Communists"; Nov 1918 sent to Vilnius on underground Party work; there coopted to CC, CP Lith; late 1918 -early 1919 Pop Comr of Internal Affairs in first Lith Sov govt; deleg at 8th RCP(B) Congress; from 1920 secr, For Bureau, and member, CC, CP Lith (located in Russia); from 1924 Politburo, member, CC, CP Lith; represented CP Lith in Comintern Exec Comt; at the 5th, 6th and 7th Comintern Congresses elected member, Int Control Commission; 1926-35 secr, Int Control Commission; author of 119 books and pamphlets; *Publ*: *Istoriya revolyutsionnogo dvizheniya i bor'by rabochikh Litvy* (History of the Revolutuinary Movement and the Struggle of the Lithuanian Workers) (2 vol, 1921); *Istoriya rabochey partii Litvy* (History of the Lithuanian Workers' Party); *Dela i ucheniye vtoroy sotsial-demokraticheskoy partii Litvy* (The Actions and Doctrine of the 2nd Lithuanian Social-Democratic Party) (1925) and other pamphlets and articles on the history of the workers' and Communist movement; *Died*: 22 May 1940.

ANGARSKIY (real name: KLESTOV), Nikolay Semyonovich (1873-1943) Govt and Party official; lit critic; CP member from 1902; *Born*: 1873 in Smolensk; *Career*: 1902 began revol career abroad with *Iskra* Paris group; 1904 returned to Russia and carried out underground RSDRP work; 1905-12 on various occasions arrested and exiled; published Lenin's books *Za 12 let* (For Twelve Years) and *Agrarnyy vopros* (The Agrarian Problem) (1907) and the Soc-Democrat pamphlet series *Knizhki dlya vsekh* (Booklets For All) via the *Zerno* Press in Petersburg; upon instructions from the Moscow RSDRP(B) Comt, opened *Vesna* bookstore which supplied legal and illegal lit to Moscow Bolsheviks; took part in 1917 Oct Revol in Moscow; member, Moscow RSDRP(B) Comt and Moscow Sov; after 1917 Oct Revol trade rep in Lith and Greece; then research and publ work; 1919-22 ed, lit journal *Tvorchestvo* 1924-32 managed *Nedra* Publ House; *Publ: Legal'nyy marksizm* (Legal Marxism) (1925); *Oktyabr'skoye vosstaniye v Moskve* (The October Uprising in Moscow) (1922); *Zametki o poezii i poetakh* (Notes on Poetry and Poets); *Staryye pisateli i novyy byt* (Old Writers and the New Life); *Novaya poeziya i starye priyomy kritiki*, (New Poetry and Old Techniques of Criticism), etc; *Died*: 1943.

ANGELINA, Praskov'ya Nikitichna (1912-1959) Tractor driver; head of tractor drivers' team, Staro-Beshevo MTS,Ukr SSR; CP member from 1937; *Born*: 12 Jan 1912 in Staro-Beshevo; *Educ*: 1940 grad Timiryazev Agric Acad; *Career*: 1928 joined Staro-Beshevo agric artel; 1929 studied at tractor drivers' school; initiated special courses for training women tractor drivers; 1935 ättended 2nd All-Union Congress of Kolkhoz Shock-Workers, also a Moscow conference of specialists in increasing crop yields; 1938 appealed to Sov women to train as tractor drivers; during WW 2 led a team of female tractor drivers at a MTS in the Kaz SSR; after WW 2 headed a tractor drivers' team at the Staro-Beshevo MTS, Ukr SSR; dep, USSR Supr Sov of 1-5th convocations; elected member, CC, CP(B) Ukr at 14th-19th Ukr Party Congresses; *Publ*: *Lyudi kolkhoznykh poley* (People of the Kolkhoz Fields) (1950); *Awards*: three Orders of Lenin; Order of the Red Banner of Labor; Stalin Prize (1946); twice Hero of Socialist Labor; *Died*: 21 Jan 1959.

ANICHKOV, Nikolay Nikolayevich (1885-1964) Pathologist; prof from 1919; Dr of Med from 1912; member, USSR Acad of Sci from 1939; member, USSR Acad of Med Sci from 1944; Hon Dr, Med Fac, Humboldt Univ, East Berlin, from 1960; corresp member, East German Acad of Sci from 1963; *Born*: 3 Nov 1885 *Educ*: 1909 grad Petersburg Mil Med Acad; *Career*: until 1912 specialized in pathological anatomy at Petersburg Mil Med Acad; 1912 defended doctor's thesis and sent on sci assignment to Germany; 1913-14 postgrad studies in Germany at laboratories of Aschoff, Chiari and others; from 1914 army physician; 1916-19 lecturer, Dept of Pathological Anatomy, Petrograd Mil Med Acad; 1919-39 head, Dept of Gen Pathology, 1939-46 head, Dept of Pathological Anatomy, above acad; 1920-64 head, Dept of Pathological Anatomy, Inst of Experimental Med, USSR Acad of Med Sci, Leningrad; 1946-54 pres, USSR Acad of Med Sci; formed Leningrad school of pathologists; member, Learned Med Council, USSR Min of Health; ed and co-ed of many med publ, including Sov encyclopedias, journal *Arkhiv patologii* and multi-vol *Opyt sovetskoy meditsiny v Velikoy Otechestvennoy voyne 1941-1945 gg.* (Soviet Medical Experience in the 1941-45 Great Fatherland War); member, ed council, journal *Patologicheskaya fiziologiya i eksperimental'naya terapiya*; member, sci ed bd, int journal "Living Conditions and Health"; dep USSR Supr Sov of 1946 convocation; research on vascular pathology (atherosclerosis, atheromatosis, hypertonia), heart diseases, infections, morphology of wound healing, the reticuloendothelial system, interrelation of centers of the medulla oblongata, pattern of functional disorders in connection with anemia of the brain, battle traumas, etc; 1912 described in detail inflammatory lesions in the myocardium of rabbits and was first to reveal unusual cells with chromatin in an infiltrate (Anichkov's myocytes); 1913 in eonjunction with S.S. Khalatov, described experimental model of atherosclerosis and proved that hypercholesterolemia arising from a diet rich in cholesterol causes atherosclerosis in rabbits as a result of infiltration of the intima of the aorta and the arteries by lipoids; with pupils later ascertained role of various factors determining atherosclerotic vascular lesions (nervous and hormonal effects, blood supply of the vascular wall, condition of connective tissue, etc); works on atherosclerosis and the reticuloendothelial system earned him worldwide reputation; in eonjunction with his pupils, gave classic description of wound healing in man and was first to ciscribe role of fat cell in course of wound process; created new trend in study of infectious processes and developed theory of autoinfection; with pupils, also developed and made detailed study of models of experimental appendicitis and pleurisy; *Publ*: more than 150 works; doctor's thesis *K ucheniyu ob eksperimental'nom miokardite* (Study of Experimental Myocarditis) (1912); *Ucheniye o retikuloendotelial'noy sisteme* (Study of the Reticulo-endothelial System) (1930,1939); *Uchebnik patologicheskoy fiziologii* (Textbook of Pathological Physiology) (4th ed, 1938); *Fiziologiya i patologiya serdechno-sosudistoy sistemy* (Physiology and Pathology of the Cardiovascular Sysem) (1941); coauthor, *Ob izmeneniyakh arteriy v starcheskom vozraste i pri ateroskleroze* (Arterial Lesions in Old Age and in Cases of Atherosclerosis) (1941); *Morfologiya zazhivleniya ran* (Morphology of Wound Healing) (1951); *Sovremennoye sostoyaniye voprosa ob eksperimental'nom ateroskleroze* (The Present State of Experimental Atherosclerosis) (1956); *Sosudy* (Vessels) (1947); *Eksperimental'naya autoinfektsiya* (Experimental Autoinfection) (1947) ; *Awards*: Stalin Prize (1942); Mechnikov Prize (1952); two Orders of Lenin; Order of the Red Banner; Order of the Red Banner of Labor; Order of the Fatherland War, 1st Class; Order of the Red Star; medals; *Died*: 7 Dec 1964.

ANIKST, Abram Moiseyevich (1887-1941) Politician; member, RSFSR Gosplan; CP member from 1918; *Born*: 1887 in Kishinyov, son of a worker; *Educ*: partial secondary educ; *Career*: from 1904 in revol movement; 1906 went underground; 1906-07 participated in revol movement as Anarchist-Communist in Southern Russia; 1907-17 polit emigre; worked as electrician in factories and took active part in revol trade-union movement (French Confederation of Labr, syndicalist movement of French Switzerland, etc); also active in for groups of Russian anarchist-syndicalists; 1917 returned to Russia and joined the Bolsheviks; chm, Pavlograd Uyezd (Yekaterinoslav Province) Sov of Workers' Dep; directed 1917 Oct uprising in Pavlograd; 1919-22 Collegium member, RSFSR Pop Comrt of Labor; later RSFSR Dep Pop Comr of Labor; 1920 simultaneously acting dep chm, Main Comt for Gen Labor Conscription; late 1922 dep chm, Ural Oblast Econ Council; 1923 Ukr Pop Comr of Labor; then worked for CC, Miners' Union, and CC, Construction Workers' Union; late 1925-37 Presidium member, RSFSR Gosplan; arrested by State Security organs; *Publ*: *Organizatsiya rabochey sily* (Organization of Manpower) (1920); *Rabochaya sila* (Manpower) (1920); *Etapy razvitiya narodnogo komissariata truda* (Stages in the Development of the People Commissariat of Labor) (1923), etc; *Died*: 1941 in imprisonment.

ANISIMOV, Ivan Ivanovich (1899-1966) Lit historian and critic; Dr of Philology; corresp member, USSR Acad of Sci from 1960; prof from 1959; Bd member, USSR Writers' Union from 1959; CP member 1939; *Born*: 16 Feb 1899 in vil Glotovka, Smolensk Provine; *Career*: 1927 first work published; from 1928 taught history of for lit at Inst of Red Prof and other educ institutions; dir, Gorky Inst of World Lit, USSR Acad of Sci from 1952; 1954 visited Switzerland with deleg of Sov cultural figures; from 1960 ed, journal *Literaturnoye nasledstvo*; member, Lenin Prize Comt for Lit and Art, USSR Council of Min; *Publ: Vsemirnaya literatura i sotsialisticheskaya revolyutsiya* (World Literature and the Socialist Revolution) (1957); *Torzhestvo revolyutsionnoy pravdy /A. Barbyus i sovremennost'/* (The Triumph of Revolutionary Truth /A. Barbus and the Present/) (1960); *Klassicheskoye nasledstvo i sovremennost'* (The Classical Legacy and the Present) (1960); *Lenin i novyye gorizonty vsemirnoy literatury* (Lenin and New Horizons of World Literature) (1961); ed, *Istoriya frantsuzskoy literatury* (History of French Literature) (1963); monograph *Novaya epokha vsemirnoy literatury* (The New Era of World Literature) (1967), etc; author of numerous articles on work of Zweig, Zola, Rolland, Shaw, etc; *Awartds*: Belinskiy Prize (1967, posthumously); *Died*: 11 June 1966.

ANISIMOV, Nikolay Andreyevich (1895-1920) Revolutionary; helped establish Sov regime in Groznyy; Civil WAr veteran; CP member from 1913; *Born*: 1895 *Career*: 1914-17 helped run Groznyy Bolshevik org; 1917 chm, Groznyy Sov of Workers, Soldiers and Cossacks' Dep; deleg at 6th RSDRP(B) Congress and 2nd All-Russian Congress of Soviets in Petrograd; chm, Mil-Revol Comt, Stavropol' Garrison; 1918-19 mil comr, Stavropol' Province; mil polit comr, Bryansk Oblast; member, Mil—Revol Council, 11th and 12th Armies, and Caspian-Caucasian Front; 1919-24 Jan 1920 member, Mil-Revol Council, 9th Army on Caucasian Front; *Died*: 25 Jan 1920.

ANISIMOV, V.A. (1878-1938) Revolutionary; pedag; *Born*: 1878; *Career*: from 1902 in Soc-Democratic movement; Party work in Saratov and Kazan' Provinces; 1907 elected 2nd State Duma; dep, Saratov Province; member, Soc-Democratic Faction Comt, 2nd State Duma; in the trial involving the Soc-Democratic Faction sentenced to hard labor; from 1912 in exile in Irkutsk, where he cotributed to legal Soc-Democratic press; after 1917 Feb Revol returned to Petrograd and joned Defensist-Mensheviks; member, Exec Comt, Petrograd Sov of Workers and Soldiers' Dep; elected member, Centr Exec Comt of 1st convocation; 1918-19 in Siberia; helped publish Socialist-Revol newspaper *Nashe delo* (Our Cause) in Irkutsk; 1921 member, Constituent Assembly, Far Eastern Republ; represented Mensheviks in coalition govt of Far Eastern Republ; later pedag work; as deleg of Soc-Democratic Faction, 2nd State Duma, switched to the Bolsheviks at 5th RSDRP Congress; arrested by State Security organs; *Died*: 1938 in imprisonment.

ANNENKOV, Boris Vladimirovich (1890-1927) Russian mil commander; maj-gen with Admiral Kolchak's forces; prominent in anti-Bolshevik struggle in Centr Asia during Civil War; *Born*: 1890 in Novgorod Province, son of a nobleman; *Career*: until 1914 officer, Siberian Cossack Army; 1914-17 fought in WW 1; 1918-20 organized and led anti-Bolshevik Cossack force which operated in the Semipalatinsk and Semirech'ye area and was notable for its discipline and bravery; ruthlessly suppressed a number of Bolshevik uprisings; May 1920, under pressure from the Red Army, retreated with part of his force into Western China, where he was interned and then imprisoned; 1924 released from prison and went to Mongolia; 1926 returned to Sov territory, but was arrested in Sverdlovsk; Aug 1927 sentenced to death by mil tribunal; *Died*: Aug 1927 executed in Semipalatinsk.

ANNENKOVA-BERNAR, Nina Pavlovna (1864-1933) Actress; *Born*: 1864; *Educ*: studied at V.V. Samoylova's drama classes; *Career*: 1880 stage debut; 1880-88 at theaters in Vilnius, Kazan', Orenburg, Samara, etc; 1889 at Gorevaya Theater, Moscow; 1890-93 at Alexandrine Theater, Petersburg; after 1917 Oct Revol lived in Orenburg and for a while directed a young pop theatrical studio; subsequently abandoned the stage and concentrated on lit work; *Roles*: Negina in *Talanty i poklonniki* (Talents and Admirers); Nina in *Maskarad* (Masquerade); the Queen in "Don Carlos"; Yudif' in Gutskov's *Uriel' Akosta; Publ*: play *Doch' naroda* (A Daughter of the People) (1914); *Died*: 1933.

ANSEROV, Nikolay Ivanovich (1894-1944) Anthropologist and anatomist; prof; *Born*: 10 Jan 1894; *Educ*: 1916 grad Moscow Univ; *Career*: 1923-27 prof, Perm' Med Inst; from 1927 prof, Azer Med Inst in Baku; conducted anthropological research in Azer, several of whose peoples he was the first to study; founded the anthropological classification of Eastern Transcaucasia; devised a method of studying the blood supply of the skeleton with the aid of luminous substances; *Publ: Tyurki sovetskogo Azerbaydzhana* (The Turks of Soviet Azerbaydzhan) (1930); *Talyshi. Mediko-antropologicheskoye issledovaniye* (The Talysh. A Medical and Anthropological Study) (1932); *Arterial'naya sistema skeleta cheloveka* (The Arterial System of the Human Skeleton) (1939); *Died*: 1944.

ANSKIY, (real name: RAPOPORT), Semyon Akimovich (1863-1920) Jewish revol, belletrist and publicist; *Born*: 1863; *Career*: for a long while active in Populist movement; personal secr to P. Lavrov; in Russian published first stories about Jewish life, folk art, studies and articles on sociological themes; later wrote in Yiddish; toward the end of his life quit the revol movement and associated himself with conservative Jewish soc groups; *Publ*: verse "The Oath," which became the anthem of the Bund (Gen Jewish Soc-Democratic League); religious mystic poem "The Jewish Lucifer"; Hasidic drama *Der Dibuk* (Obsessed), which became very popular after it was staged by Vakhtangov at Moscow's Jewish "Habima" Theater'; novelette *V novom rusle* (In a New Channel) (1907), etc; *Died*: 1920.

ANSON, Karl Karlovich (1887-1966) Psychologist; CP member from 1911; *Born*: 1887 in Liflyand Province, son of a blacksmith; *Educ*: grad Pedag Fac, Second Moscow Univ; postgrad studies at Moscow Inst of Psychology; *Career*: 1912 imprisoned for revol activities; early 1917 exiled to Narym Kray; late 1917 helped establish Sov rule in Siberia and the Urals; served with Red Army; secr, Party orgs during studies at Moscow Univ and Inst of Psychology; from 1930 secr, Party org, then laboratory head, Moscow Inst of Psychology; from 1944 rector, Riga Teachers' Training Inst; published works on campaign against idealism in Sov psychology; *Awards*: Order of the Red Banner of Labor; badge "Outstanding Educator of Lat SSR"; *Died*: 1966.

ANTIKAYNEN, Toyvo (1898-1941) Revolutionary; founder and Leader, CP Finland; *Born*: 1898; *Career*: 1915 joined the Finnish Soc-Democratic Workers' Party; early 1918 active in workers' revol in Finland; Aug 1918 attended CP Constituent Congress; 1918-20 in Civil War served in Red Army; 1921 helped crush Kronstadt Mutiny; 1923 elected member, CC, CP Finland, which operated in the underground; 1925 Politburo member, CC, CP Finland; 6 Nov 1934 arrested and sentenced to hard labor for life; 3 May 1940 released with the help of Sov govt; 1940 elected dep, USSR Supr Sov; *Awards*: Order of the Red Banner of Labor (1922); *Died*: 4 Oct 1941 killed in action during WW 2.

ANTIPIN, Pyotr Fyodorovich (1890-1960) Metallurgical eng; prof from 1938; corresp member, USSR Acad of Sci from 1939; *Born*: 25 Dec 1890; *Educ*: 1921 grad Petrograd Inst of Electr Eng; *Career*: 1921-31 instructor, Petrograd Polytech Inst; 1931-36 instructor, Leningrad Inst of Chemical Technol; 1933-38 instructor, from 1938 prof, Leningrad Polytech Inst; worked for various planning org, including All-Union Inst of Aluminum and Magnesium, Leningrad; 1929-32 directed planning of Dnieper Aluminum Plant; 1932-36 directed planning of Ural Aluminum Plant; specialized in aluminum metallurgy and electrochemistry of molten metals; *Publ: Otdel'nyye tsvetnyye metally* (Individual Non-Ferrous Metals) (1934); *Tsvetnyye metally, ferrosplavy* (Non-Ferrous Metals and Ferrous Alloys) (1934); coauthor, *Elektrokhimiya rasplavlennykh soley* (The Electrochemistry of Molten Salts) (1937); *Awards*: two orders; medals; *Died*: 30 Oct 1960.

ANTIPOV, Nikolay Kirillovich (1894-1941) Party and govt official; CP member from 1912; *Born*: 1894, son of a peasant; *Educ*: tech school of maritime dept; *Career*: fitter at Petersburg factories; until 1917 Party work in Petrograd and Moscow; several times arrested, imprisoned and exiled; after 1917 Feb Revol member, Petrograd RSDRP(B) Comt; deleg at 7th (Apr) Party Conference; member, Petrograd Sov; during 1917 Oct Revol member, Petrograd Centr Council of Factory and Plant Comts; after 1917 Oct Revol Presidium member and dep chm, All-Russian Sovnarkhoz; dep chm, then chm, Petrograd Cheka; 1919 secr, Kazan' Province RCP(B) Comt; chm, Kazan' Province Exec Comt and member, Mil–Revol War Council of RSFSR Reserve Army; 1920 Presidium member, All-Union Centr Trade-Union Council; 1923 secr, Moscow RCP(B) Comt; from Aug 1924 head, Distributing Organ, CC, RCP(B); 1925 secr, Ural Oblast Party Comt; 1926 secr, Leningrad Province CPSU(B) Comt and secr, Northwestern Bureau, CC, CPSU(B); member, Sov of Nationalities; 1928-31 USSR Pop Comr of Posts and Telegraphs; from Mar 1931 USSR Dep Pop Comr of Workers and Peasants' Inspection; Presidium member, CPSU(B) Centr Control Commission and chm, Supr Sports Council, Presidium, All-Russian Centr Exec Comt; from 1934 dep chm, Sov Control Commission; from Apr 1935 dep chm, USSR Council of Pop Comr and USSR Labor and Defense Council; chm, Sov Control Commission, USSR Council of Pop Comr; at 13th-17th Party Congresses elected member, CC, CPSU(B); member, All-Russian and All-Union Centr Exec Comts; arrested by State Security organs; *Died*: 1941 in imprisonment; posthumously rehabilitated.

ANTONIY (secular name: PEL'VITSKIY) (1898-1957) Archbishop of Stanislav and Koloma from 1954; Vicar of Samborsk and Drogobych Eparchy, Russian Orthodox Church from 1955; *Born*: 1898; *Career*: for many years priest of Greek Catholic Church; after WW 2 switched to Russian Orthodox Church; 1946 took monastic vows, consecrated bishop and appointed to Eparchy of Stanislav and Koloma; from 1955 Vicar of Samborsk and Drogobych Eparchy; *Died*: 3 Feb 1957.

ANTONOV, Aleksandr Aleksandrovich (1891-1966) Revolutionary; dir, Glass Research Inst; CP member from 1914; *Born*: 1891 in Petersburg, son of a worker; *Educ*: attended factory school; 1912 grad night school for workers in Petersburg; *Career*: worked as messenger-boy, then from 1903 as apprentice foreman, Westinghouse Plant, Petersburg; 1905 joined revol movement; acted as contact man, collected money for Party lit, distributed illegal publ, took part in work of factory clubs run by the *Znaniye-svet* cultural and educ soc; 1912-13 mil service; from 1914 electrician, Obukhov Plant, Petrograd; 1915-16 dep, Petrograd RSDRP(B) Comt, headed Neva Rayon Party Comt; July 1916 transferred to Kronstadt, then to Nikolayev; Feb 1917 returned to Petrograd and headed Obukhov Subrayon RSDRP(B) Comt; simultaneously chm, Presidium, Neva Rayon Party Comt; Oct 1917 dep commandant, Neva Rayon, and comr at Obukhov Plant; headed deleg of workers of this plant at 2nd All-Russian Congress of Soviets; after 1917 Oct Revol became first Communist dir, Obukhov Plant; spring 1919 drafted and sent to the front: comr, then chief, Eng Supplies Bd, Southern Front; later member, Secretariat of Party Cells, Staff of the Southern Front; 1920 chief and mil comr, Supply Bd, 14th Army; 1921 plen for production supplies in the Ukr; 1922-24 Presidium member, Moscow City Trade-Union Council; dep, Moscow Sov and cand member, Moscow Party Comt; 1925 transferred to work in glass ind; duties entailed several visits to Germany, England and USA; from 1930 at USSR trade mission in Germany; from 1933 dir, Glass Research Inst; until 1956 at USSR Min of Light Ind; from 1956 pensioner; helped compile compendia: *Doneseniya komissarov Petrogradskogo voyenno-revolyutsionnogo komiteta* (Reports of the Commissars of the Petrograd Military-Revolutionary Committee) (1957); *Rayony Petrograda v dvukh revolyutsiyakh* (Petrograd Districts in Two Revolutions); *Died*: 6 Jan 1966 in Moscow.

ANTONOV, Aleksandr Pavlovich (1898-1962) Actor; Hon Artiste of RSFSR from 1950; *Born*: 13 Feb 1898; *Career*: 1920-24 performed at Moscow Theater of Proletarian Culture; 1925 played first film role as a worker in *Stachka* (Strike); 1926 played his most important silent role as Vakulinchuk in *Bronenosets "Potyomkin"* (The Battleship "Potyomkin"); specialized in character parts; *Roles*: the Sailor in *Kafe Frankoni* (Franconi's Cafe) (1927); Gleb Grinyov in *Zolotoye runo* (The Golden Fleece) (1928); Fil'ka in *Kogda zatsvetut polya* (When the Fields Flower) (1929); the NCO in *Iuda* (Judas) (1930); the Squadron Comr in *Kryl'ya* (Wings) (1933); Klyuyev in *Lyubov' Alyony* (Alyona's Love) (1934); Tyurin in *Suvorov* (1941); Ignat Fomin in *Molodaya gvardiya* (The Young Guard) (1948); Col Popov in *Stalingradskaya bitva* (The Battle of Stalingrad) (1949); Fyodor Volkov in *Sluchay v tayge* (Taiga Incident) (1954); Antonov in *Matros soshyol na bereg* (The Sailor Went Ashore) (1957), etc; *Died*: 26 Nov 1962.

ANTONOV, Aleksey Innokent'yevich (1895-1962) Army gen; first dep chief, USSR Armed Forces Gen Staff; chief of staff, Warsaw Pact Armed Forces; CP member from 1928; *Born*: 15 Sept 1895 in Grodno (Bel), son of a Russian officer; *Educ*: 1916 grad Pavlovsk Ensigns' School; 1921 grad Frunze Mil Acad; 1933 grad Operations Fac, Frunze Mil Acad; 1938 grad USSR Gen Staff Acad; *Career*: 1916 drafted into Russian Army; fought in WW 1; 1918-19 worked for Petrograd Food Comt; from 1919 in Red Army; during Civil War chief of staff of a brigade, then a div; after the Civil War served on the staff of mil units and distr; 1937-41 chief of staff, Moscow Mil Distr; instructor, Frunze Mil Acad; dep chief of staff, Kiev Mil Distr; 1941-42 chief of staff, Southern, North Caucasian and Transcaucasian Fronts; 1942-45 head, Operations Bd, then dep chief, Gen Staff of Red Army; 1945-46 chief, Gen Staff; 1946-48 first dep chief, Gen Staff; 1948-49 first dep commander, 1949-54 commander, Transcaucasian Mil Distr; 1955-62 chief of staff, Warsaw Pact Armed Forces, and first dep chief, Gen Staff, USSR Armed Forces; attended Yalta (1944) and Potsdam (1945) Conferences; dep, USSR Supr Sov of 1946, 1950, 1954, 1958 and 1962 convocations; dep, Geo Supr Sov of 1951 convocation; *Awards*: three Orders of Lenin; Order of Victory; four Orders of the Red Banner; two Orders of Suvorov, 1st Class; Order of Kutuzov, 1st Class; Order of the Fatherland War; medals and foreign orders; *Died*: 18 June 1962.

ANTONOV, A.S. (? -1922) Mil leader of 1919-21 peasants' revolt in Tambov Province; member, Socialist-Revol Party from 1905; *Born*: in Kirsanov, son of a worker; *Career*: 1907-17 in exile; Mar 1917-Aug 1918 head, Kirsanov Uyezd (Tambov Province) militia; peasants' discontent with the system of compulsory food allotment led to an open uprising under his leadership against Sov rule; Sept 1918 peasants' uprising in the vil Rudovka, Vasil'yevka and Nikol'skoye was swiftly crushed by the Sov regime; by summer 1919 only guerrilla groups were left; uprising proper started in Aug 1920 in Kamenka vil, Kirsanov Uyezd and soon spread to Tambov, Morshansk, Kozlov and Borisoglebsk Uyezds, Tambov Province, and then to Balashov and Serdobsk Uyezds, Saratov Province; by late 1920 the rebels' infantry and cavalry numbered 7,000-8,000 men, and by summer of 1921 almost 50,000 men, organized into two armies, the Kozlov Brigade, the Kolesnikov detachment and several smaller units; org of rebel troops, as with all other peasant forces fighting against Sov regime, was modelled on Red Army; there were also polit depts, revol tribunals and even internal security forces; politically the armed forces were subordinate to the Province Comt, Working Peasants' Union; militarily they were subordinate to Headquarters Staff; troops were recruited on a territorial basis: each army was divided into regts, attached to specific areas which were responsible for replacement of man-power and horses; the rebels' army was also reinforced with Red Army deserters; Aug 1920 Sov govt proclaimed a state of siege in Tambov Province; Jan 1921 Sov regime sent some 30,000 men and special detachments to suppress the peasants' uprising; a mil command (under Tukhachevskiy) was formed in Tambov Province; at the same time there operated a Special Commission of the All-Russian Centr Exec Comt under Antonov-Ovseyenko; by Aug 1921 the uprising had been suppressed; Antonov was killed in June 1922.

ANTONOV, Ivan Zakharovich (1919-1960) Mordvinian writer; *Born*: 13 Jan 1919, son of a peasant in Sigachi, now Chuvash ASSR; *Career*: 1936 first work published in Alatyr Rayon newspaper *Leninskiy put'*; *Publ*: novels *V sem'ye yedinoy* (A United Family) (1954) on the friendship of peoples in WW 1; *Ukhaby na dorogakh* (Bumpy Roads) (1954); *Razliv na Alatyr-reke* (Flood on the Alatyr River) (1955); collected stories *Devich'i glaza* (Maidenly Eyes) (1957); *Trudoden'* (The Workday) (1958); *Zhizn' podskazyvayet* (Life Suggests) (1960), etc; *Died*: 1 Nov 1960.

ANTONOV, Nikolay Semyonovich (1903-1934) Student; CP member; *Born*: 1903; *Career*: 25 Dec 1934 charged with membership of oppositional Zinov'yevite group, an alleged counterrevol terrorist group and part of terrorist and counterrevol "Leningrad Center," the purpose of which was to force CP and Sov regime to change their policies so as to conform to the Zinov'yev-Trotskyist platform; also accused of complicity in 1 Dec 1934 assassination of S. M. Kirov-Presidium member, USSR Centr Exec Comt; Politburo member, CC, CPSU(B); secr, CC, CPSU(B); secr, Leningrad Oblast and Leningrad City CPSU(B) Comt; 29 Dec 1934 sentenced to death by Assizes of Mil Collegium, USSR Supr Court; *Died*: 29 Dec 1934 executed in Leningrad.

ANTONOV, Vasiliy Grigor'yevich (1882-1967) Journalist; CP member from 1903; *Born*: Dec 1882; *Career*: took part in 1905-07 Revol in Voronezh and Moscow; for revol activities repeatedly arrested and exiled; polit émigré in Belgium and Italy; fought for establishment of Sov regime in the Far East; head Food Dept, Vladivostok Province Exec Comt; chm, Maritime Oblast Govt; ed, organ of the Far Eastern Bureau, CC, RCP(B) (Chita); 1923-30 head, TASS Branch in Tokyo, Rome, Paris; subsequently publ work; from 1945 with Sov Information Bureau; until 1952 represented Sov Information Bureau in Italy; 1953-67 pensioner; *Died*: May 1967.

ANTONOV, Vasiliy Ivanovich (1914-1967) Party official; CP member from 1931; *Born*: 1914; *Educ*: 1957 grad Moscow Corresp Teachers' Training Inst; *Career*: 1927-30 modeller's apprentice, then modeller, metal products plant; 1930-37 exec Komsomol work; 1937-39 teacher, then dir, secondary school; head, rayon educ dept, Orenburg Oblast; 1939-41 worked for Orenburg Oblast CPSU(B) Comt; 1941 secr, Orenburg Oblast CPSU(B) Comt; 1941-46 polit work in Sov army; 1947-56 secr, then second secr, Orenburg Oblast CPSU Comt; 1957-61 first secr, Karachayevo-Cherkessk Oblast CPSU Comt, Stavropol' Kray; from 1961 first secr, Astrakhan' Oblast CPSU Comt; from 1961 cand member, CC, CPSU; dep, RSFSR Supr Sov of 1955 and 1959 and USSR Supr Sov of 1962 and 1966 convocations; member, Commission for Public Educ, Sci and Culture, Sov of the Union; *Awards*: medal "For Valiant Labor" (1959); Order of the Red Banner of Labor (1964); *Died*: Aug 1967.

ANTONOV, Vladimir Pavlovich (pseudonym: Saratovskiy) (1884-1965) Party and govt official; CP member from 1902; *Born*: 1 Aug 1884 in Saratov, son of a clerical worker; *Educ*: grad Law Fac and Fac of History and Philology, Moscow Univ; *Career*: active in 1905 Dec uprising in Moscow; member, Saratov Party Comt; 1908 arrested; 1911 sentenced to fortress imprisonment, then exiled; after 1917 Feb Revol member, Saratov RSDRP(B) Comt; chm, Saratov Sov; during 1917 Oct Revol as chm, Saratov Province Exec Comt, helped establish and consolidate Sov regime in Saratov; 1919 Collegium member, RSFSR NKVD; then member, Southern Front Revol Tribunal; organized revol comts on Southern Front; 1920 chm, Donets Basin Province Revol Comt; later Ukr Pop Comr of Internal Affairs and member, Mil-Revol Council, 4th Army; 1921 rector, Sverdlov Communist Univ; 1923-38 chm, Draft Bills Commission, USSR Council of Pop Comr; chm, Criminal Collegium and member, USSR Supr Court; 1939-52 in RSFSR Pop Comrt of Justice; took part in special sessions of USSR Supr Court in the Shakhtinskiy, Ind Party and Union Bureau of Russian Mensheviks trials; deleg, 8th, 9th and 12th CPSU(B) Congresses and 3rd and 4th Congresses of Soviets; Presidium member, All-Russian Centr Exec Comt; from 1941 pensioner; *Publ: Oktyabr' v Saratove* (October in Saratov); *Otbleski besed's Il'ichyom* (Reflections of Discussions with Il'ich); *Pod styagom proletarskoy bor'by* (Under the Banner of the Proletarian Struggle) (1925); *Krasnyy god* (The Red Year) (1927), etc; *Awards*: Order of Lenin; *Died*: 3 Aug 1965.

ANTONOV-OVSEYENKO, Vladimir Aleksandrovich (1884-1938) (Party pseudonym: **SHTYK** pen name: **A. GAL'SKIY**) Party official, diplomat and mil man; CP member from 1917; *Born*: 9 Mar 1884 in Chernigov, son of a lt; *Educ*: 1904 grad Petersburg mil school; *Career*: 1902 joined Mensheviks; 1905 organized Warsaw RSDRP Mil Comt; for propaganda among troops and for organizing 1906 revolt in Sebastopol sentenced to death; verdict commuted to 20 years at hard labor; 1907 escaped, conducted propaganda work in Finland, then in Petersburg and Moscow; 1910 went to France, organized and contributed to internationalist newspapers *Golos*, *Nashe slovo* and *Nachalo*; 1916 broke with Mensheviks and joined leftist Zimmerwald Group; May 1917 returned to Russia and joined RSDRP(B); for his part in 1917 July riots arrested by Provisional Govt and together with Trotsky imprisoned in *Kresty* Prison; during 1917 Oct Revol member, Mil-Revol Comt; directed storming of Winter Palace and arrest of Provisional Govt; 1917 at 2nd All-Russian Congress of Soviets elected member, Comt for Mil and Naval Affairs, RSFSR Council of Pop Comr; from Nov 1918 member, Ukr Revol Mil Council; 1919 commander, Petrograd Mil Distr; later commander, Ukr Front; 1920 Collegium member, RSFSR Pop Comrt of Labor; dep chm, RSFSR Small Council of Pop Comr; Bd member, NKVD; 1921 helped crush Antonov peasant revolt in Tambov Province and Kronstadt Mutiny; Jan-June 1919 commander in chief, Armed Forces of Ukr Republ and Donets Workers' Republ; later Ukr Pop Comr of Mil and Naval Affairs; fall 1922-24 head, Polit Bd, and member, Ukr Revol-Mil Council; 1923-27 sided with Trotskyist opposition, advocated various measures concerning the Red Army, which would have virtually changed the principles of the Army's Party infrastructure; from 1925 USSR plen in Czechoslovakia; from 1928 USSR plen in Lith; from 1930 USSR plen in Poland; for some time RSFSR Prosecuter; 1938 USSR plen in Spain; elected member, All-Russian Centr Exec Comt; arrested by State Security organs; *Publ: Stroitel'stvo Krasnoy armii v revolyutsii* (The Build-Up of the Red Army During Revolution) (1923); *Zapiski o grazhdanskoy voyne* (Notes on the Civil War) (4 vol, 1929); *V semnadtsatom godu* (The Year 1917) (1933); *V revolyutsii /Vospominaniya/* (During the Revolution /Memoirs/) (1957); *Awards*: Order of the Red Banner; *Died*: 1938 in imprisonment; posthumously rehabilitated.

ANTONOVSKAYA, Anna Arnol'dovna (1886-1967) Russian writer; *Born*: 12 Jan 1886 in Tbilisi; *Career*: active in 1905 Revol in Caucasus; 1918 first work printed; wrote verse, essays, plays and novels; *Publ*: novel *Velikiy Mouravi* (Mouravi the Great) (6 vol, 1937-58); coauthor, novel *Angely mira* (Angels of Peace) (1945-46); novelette *Na Batumskom reyde* (In the Batumi Roads) (1948); *Awards*: Stalin Prize (1942); *Died*: 21 Oct 1967.

ANTONS, Rikhard Iokhanovich (1899-1966) Economist; member; Est Acad of Sci from 1961; *Born*: 1899; *Career*: 1940-41 and 1945-51 assoc prof, then head, Chair of Econ and pro-rector, Tartu State Univ; 1951-54 rector, Est Agric Acad; from 1954 dir, Inst of Econ, Est Acad of Sci; 1951-61 corresp member, Est Acad of Sci; from 1961 dep acad secr, Dept of Soc Sci, and chm, Council for the Study of Production Resources, Est Acad of Sci; *Publ: Agrarnyy vopros v Estonii do ustanovleniya sovetskoy vlasti i puti yego razresheniya* (The Agrarian Question in Estonia Before the Establishment of Soviet Rule and Means of Solving It) (1949); *Awards*: Order of the Red Banner of Labor; two Orders of the Red Star; medals "For Victory over Germany in the 1941-45 Great Fatherland War" and "For Valiant Labor in the 1941-45 Great Fatherland War"; Scroll of Hon, Presidium of Est Supr Sov; *Died*: May 1966.

ANTSELOVICH, Naum Markovich (1888-1952) Trade-unionist; CP member from 1905; *Born*: 1888 in Petersburg, son of a worker; *Career*: electrician; Party and trade-union work in Odessa, Petersburg and other towns; often arrested by Tsarist authorities; Oct 1917 member, Petrograd Mil-Revol Comt; after 1917 Oct Revol responsible for internal defense of Petrograd; dep head, Polit Dept, Revol-Mil Council of Southern Front; from 1920 trade-union, Party and govt work; chm, Petrograd Trade-Union Council; 1921-22 member of Sov trade-union deleg abroad; then secr, All-Union Centr Trade-Union Council; 1923-30 chm, CC, Union of Agric and Forestry Workers; from 1931 Presidium member, Centr Control Commission, and RSFSR Dep Pop Comr of Workers and Peasants' Inspection; RSFSR Pop Comr of Forestry; RSFSR Dep Min of Trade; 1941-45 fought in WW 2; member, All-Russian and All-Union Centr Exec Comts; at 15 th and 16th Party Congresses elected cand member, at 18th CP Congress elected member, CC, CPSU(B); *Died*: 1952.

ANTSIFEROV, Nikolay Pavlovich (1889-1958) Lit critic and historian; *Born*: 11 Aug 1889 in vil Sofiyevka, Uman' Uyezd; *Educ*: 1916 grad Fac of History and Philology, Petrograd Univ; *Career*: 1936-56 worked at Moscow State Lit Museum; specialized in lit history of Russian cities, particularly Moscow and Petersburg; did research on life and work of Pushkin, Herzen, Turgenev and Dostoyevskiy; in his latter years helped analyze and annotate the "Prague Collection" of Herzen and Ogarev's papers for publ in journal *Literaturnoye nasledstvo; Publ: Dusha Peterburga* (The Spirit of Petersburg) (1922); *Byl'i mif Peterburga* (Life and Legend in Petersburg) (1924); *Teoriya i praktika literaturnykh ekskursiy* (The Theory and Practice of Literary Excursions) (1926); *Puti izucheniya goroda kak sotsial'nogo organizma* (Ways of Studying Towns as Social Organisms) (1926); coauthor, *Detskoye Selo* (Children's Village) (1927); *Kak izuchat' svoy gorod* (How to Study Your Town) (1929); *Prigorody Leningrada.*

Goroda Pushkin, Pavlovsk, Petrodvorets (The Suburbs of Leningrad. Pushkin, Pavlovsk and Petrodvorets) (1946); *Moskva Pushkina* (Pushkin's Moscow) (1950); *Peterburg Pushkina* (Pushkin's Petersburg) (1950); *Pushkin v Tsarskom Sele* (Pushkin at Tsarskoye Selo) (1950); *Died*: 2 Sept 1958 in Moscow.

ANUCHIN, Dmitriy Nikolayevich (1843-1923) Russian anthropologist, ethnographer, archeologist and geographer; prof from 1884; member, Russian Acad of Sci from 1896; *Born*: 8 Sept 1843 in Petersburg; *Educ*: 1867 grad Moscow Univ; *Career*: from 1880 assoc prof of anthropology, Moscow Univ; 1884-1920 prof of anthropology and ethnography and head, Chair of Geography, Moscow Univ; from 1920 prof, Chair of Anthropology, Moscow Univ; from 1890 life pres, Soc of Friends of Natural Sci, Anthropology and Ethnography, and chm, Geographical Dept of this soc; 1894-1923 founder-ed, journal *Zemlevedeniye*; also founded Anthropological and Ethnographic Museum at Moscow Univ; established school of Russian anthropologists and geographers at Moscow Univ; after 1917 Oct Revol worked for Gosplan, Pop Comrt of Educ and headed Centr Bureau of Regional Studies; specialized in anthropology, combining this with studies on evolution, comparative anatomy, biology and racial theory; wrote a number of historical research works based on ethnological and ethnographical material; *Publ: Materialy dlya antropologii Vostochnoy Azii. Plemya Aynov* (Material on the Anthropology of Eastern Asia. The Ainu Tribe) (1876); *Sani, lad'ya i koni, kak prinadlezhnost' pokhoronnogo obryada* (Sleighs, Boats and Horses as Appurtenances of Funereal Rites) (1890); *K istorii oznakomleniya s Sibir'yu do Yermaka* (The History of the Study of Siberia Prior to Yermak) (1890); *K istorii iskusstva i verovaniy v priural'skoy chudi* (The History of the Art and Beliefs of the Cisural Chud') (1899); *Konspekt lektsiy po fizicheskoy geografii* (A Summary of Lectures on Physical Geography) (1904); *Yaponiya i yapontsy. Geograficheskiy, antropologicheskiy i etnograficheskiy ocherk* (Japan and the Japanese. A Geographical, Anthropological and Ethnographic Study) (1907); *Proiskhozhdeniye cheloveka* (The Origin of Man) (3rd ed, 1927); *Izbrannyye geograficheskiye raboty* (Selected Geographical Works) (1947); *Geograficheskiye raboty* (Geographical Works) (1954), etc; *Died*: 4 June 1923.

ANVEL'T, Yan Yanovich (pen name: EESSAARE AADU) (1884-1938) Professional revol; writer; CP member from 1907; *Born*: 1884 in vil Orgu, Fellin Uyezd, Liflyand Province, son of a peasant; *Educ*: studied at Yur'yev (Tartu) Teachers' Seminary; passed teachers' examinations in Petersburg; from 1907 studied at Law Fac, Petersburg Univ; *Career*: 1905-07 teacher; helped found newspaper *Kiir*; during 1917 Feb Revol head, Narva Revol Comt, then Narva Sov; member, Revel' and North Baltic RSDRP(B) Comt and Exec Comt, Estland Sov; July 1917 arrested by Provisional Govt; from Oct 1917 member, Mil-Revol Comt, then chm, Estland Kray Sov Exec Comt; from Feb 1918 in Petrograd as mil comr, Northwestern Region; from Nov 1918 chm, Estland Labor Commune Govt, and Pop Comr for Mil Affairs; 1919-20 senior posts in Red Army; 1920 elected member, CC, CP Est; 1921-25 underground Party work in Estland; helped lead 1 Dec 1924 uprising; 1925 sent by Party to USSR; 1926-29 comr, Moscow's Zhukovskiy Air Force Acad; 1929-35 dep head, Main Civil Aviation Bd; deleg at 14th, 15th and 16th CPSU(B) Congresses and 6th and 7th Comintern Congresses; 1935-37 member and exec secr, Comintern Control Commission; wrote various works of fiction, including novel *Vne zakona* (Outside the Law), etc; arrested by State Security organs; *Died*: 1938 in imprisonment; posthumously rehabilitated.

APANASENKO, Iosif Rodionovich (1890-1943) Army gen from 1941; Civil War hero; CP member from 1919; *Born*: 16 Apr 1890, son of a farmhand, in vil Mitrofanovskoye (now Apanasenkovskoye), Stavropol' Kray; *Educ*: 1932 grad Special Fac, Frunze Mil Acad; *Career*: until 1911 farmhand for an estateowner; fought in WW 1; 1918-19 organized and led a partisan detachment in Stavropol' Kray, then Stavropol' Cavalry Div; 1919 commander, 6th Cavalry Div, Budyonny's Cavalry Corps; Nov 1919, for failure to execute an order, demoted to brigade commander in same div; Aug 1920 reinstated as commander, 6th Cavalry Div; Sept 1920 sentenced to death by Revol Mil Tribunal for pogroms and looting during move from Polish to Wrangel Front; in consideration of his outstanding mil record sentence commuted; 1920-22 chm, Stavropol' Province Exec Comt; 1922 returned to Red Army; 1924-37 commander, 5th and 4th Leningrad Cavalry Div, corps commander, dep commander (for cavalry), Bel Mil Distr; 1937-41 commander, Centr Asian Mil Distr; 1941-43 commander, Far Eastern Front; 1943 dep commander, Steppe Front, then Voronezh Front; *Awards*: three Orders of the Red Banner; *Died*: 5 Aug 1943 killed in action near Belgorod; monument to him erected in Belgorod.

APIN, Edgar Petrovich (1902-1957) Party and govt official; CP member from 1919; *Born*: 1902, son of a metalworker; *Career*: from 1945 exec Party work in Lat SSR; from 1951 dep, from 1955 chm, Lat Supr Sov; from 1952 first secr, Riga City Comt, CP Lat; member, CC, CP Lat; *Died*: 1957.

APINIS, Robert A. (1892-1937) Lat; helped establish Sov regime in Lat in 1919; Red Army polit worker; Comintern official; CP member from 1912; *Born*: 1892 in vil Dravniyeki, now Lat, son of a peasant; *Career*: 1915-17 private, the NCO in Lat infantry regts, Russian Army; after 1917 Feb Revol member, then chm, Soldiers' Comt, 5th Zemgal'skiy Lat Infantry Regt; from 1918 in Red Army; 1918 mil comr, 2nd Lat Brigade, Eastern Front Headquarters; 1918-21 polit work in various Sov Lat infantry units; Dec 1918-Feb 1919 fought in Riga campaign to liberate Lat from German troops and establish Sov regime; fall 1919 helped defeat Denikin's troops near Oryol; Apr 1920 took part in storming of Perekop; from 1921 mil comr, Bd, All-Russian Gen Staff and Red Army Headquarters; in 1920's and 1930's official, Lat Section, Comintern; Bd member, Lat Club in Moscow; in 1930's journalist in Magadan Oblast; then worked for USSR Soc for Promotion of Defense, Aircraft and Chemical Ind; 1937 arrested by the NKVD; *Died*: 1937 in imrisonment; posthumously rehabilitated.

APOLLONSKIY, Roman Borisovich (1865-1928) Actor; *Born*: 1865; *Educ*: 1881 grad Ballet Dept, Petersburg Theatrical College; *Career*: from 1881 with ballet company of Alexandrine Theater, where he performed until his death in 1928; during the summer seasons performed in Odessa, Kiev, Khar'kov, etc; after 1917 Oct Revol artistic dir, former Alexandrine Theater; then member, Directorate and manager until 1920, former Alexandrine Theater; *Roles*: Hamlet; Protasov in Lev Tolstoy's *Zhivoy trup* (A Living Corpse); Tarelkin in *Delo* (The Case); Storitsyn in Andreyev's *Professor Storitsyn* etc; *Died*: 1928.

APPAKOVA, Darzhiya Seyfullovna (1898-1948), Tatar writer; *Born*: 14 Mar 1898 in vil Baygulovo, Kazan' Province; *Educ*: 1923 grad Drama Studio, Kazan' Drama Theater; *Career*: 1914-19 teacher; 1919-25 reporter for newspaper *Kyzyl Alyam*; 1923-25 actress, Kazan' Polit Dept Theater Company; *Publ*: 1932 first work published in Uzbekistan; novel "Mikhnat" (1933-35) reflects collectivization of agric; story "Mamet and Old Amon" (1934) and noveltte "Lyuli" (1937) dealt with hardships of Turkm and gypsy children; novelette "The Story of Little Banu" (1938) depicts life of Tatar farmhands; wrote children's plays and fairy tales; major works: collected stories "Squeaky Shoes" (1948); "Stories and Plays" (1953); play *Il'dus* (1952) and book *Izbrannyye proizvedeniya* (Selected Works) (1957) were published in Russian; *Died*: 28 May 1948 in Kazan'.

APPOGA, Ernest Frantsevich (1898-1937) Corps commander; CP member from 1917; *Born*: 1898; *Educ*: 1924 grad Higher Acad Courses; 1927 grad Frunze Mil Acad; *Career*: until 1918 worker; from Apr 1918 in Red Army; 1918-30 comr, Staff, Urals Mil Distr; commander and mil comr, Admin Dept, Staff of 10th Army; chief of staff, 37th Div; commander, 9th Don Div; head, Dept of Mil Training for Civilians, USSR Pop Comrt of Navy; head, Signals Bd, Red Army Staff; 1930-37 head, Red Army Signals Corps; member, Mil Council, USSR Pop Comrt of Defense; ed, "Military Transport" section, *Sovetskaya voyennaya entsiklopediya* (Soviet Military Encyclopedia); 1934-35 took part in construction of a bridge over the River Volga at Saratov; 1937 arrested by NKVD; *Awards*: Order of the Red Banner; *Died*: 1937 in imprisonment; posthumously rehabilitated.

APSE, Martyn Yanovich (1892-?) Corps comr; CP member from 1912; *Born*: 1892; *Career*: until 1917 worker; during and after Civil War polit work in Red Army; early 1930's head, polit dept of a div, Leningrad Mil Distr; 1937 member, Mil Council, Transcaucasian Mil Distr; member, CPSU(B) Centr Control Comission; Dec 1937 arrested by State Security organs; *Died*: date, place and manner of death unknown.

APTEKMAN, Osip Vasil'yevich (1849-1926) Populist; prominent functionary and hostorian, *Zemlya i Volya* (Land and Freedom) Soc; *Born*: 18 Mar 1849; *Educ*: studied at Acad of Med and Surgery; completed med training in Munich; *Career*: 1874, within a few months of completing his course at the Acad of Med and

Surgery, "went out among the people," conducted propaganda work in Volga area; until 1879 organizer and member, *Zemlya i Volya* Soc; after *Zemlya i Volya* schism joined *Chyornyy Peredel* (Land Distribution) Group and edited its organ; 1880, after break-up of this org, exiled by admin order for five years to Yakutia; 1885-89 abroad (Germany); 1889 returned to Russia, worked as country physician in Nizhniy-Novgorod; under the influence of "young" Soc-Democrats, broke with remnants of *Narodnaya Volya* Party and joined Soc-Democratic Party; 1905 arrested for incitement to mutiny, organizing a battle group and agitating for replacement of volost admin; 1906-07 lived in Switzerland and until WW 1 sided with Mensheviks; from start of WW 1 adopted internationalist stand; 1919 switched to Sov ideology; from 1917 took no active part in polit life; *Publ*: books: *Obshchestvo Zemlya i Volya 70-kh godov* (The "Land and Freedom" Society in the 1870's) (1905; 1923 revised and expanded ed); *Chyornyy Peredel* (The Land Distribution Movement) (1923); various articles in periodicals; *Died*: 1926.

ARABLINSKIY (real name: KHALAFOV), Gusseyn Mamed ogly (1881-1919) Azer actor and stage dir; founder of Azer professional theater; *Born*: 1881 in Baku; *Career*: trained in realistic tradition of Russian theater; acting marked by romanticism and emotionalism; 1905 began professional acting career; portrayed passionate champions, rebels and staunch-spirited types such as: Farkhad in Akhverdov's "An Unfortunate Youth"; Karl Moor in Schiller's "The Robbers," etc; other roles included: Khlestakov in Gogol's *Revizor* (The Government Inspector); Franz Moor in Schiller's "The Robbers"; Othello in Shakespeare's "Othello"; title role in Akhverdov's "Aga Mamedshakh Kadzhar," etc; first Azer film actor; appeared in film "The Kingdom of Millions and Oil" (1917); staged plays by Akhundov, Vezirov, Gogol, Turgenev, Schiller and others; *Died*: Mar 1919 killed in Baku by a member of Azer "Musavat" nationalist party.

ARAKISHVILI (ARAKCHIYEV), Dimitriy Ignat'yevich (1873-1953) Geo composer and music teacher; Pop Artiste of Geo SSR from 1929; member, Geo Acad of Sci from 1950; Dr of Arts from 1943; *Born*: 23 Feb 1873 in Vladikavkaz; *Educ*: 1901 grad School of Music and Drama, Moscow Philharmonic; 1918 grad Moscow Archeological Inst; *Career*: 1908 founded journal *Muzyka i zhizn'*; founder-member, Moscow Pop Conservatory; collected and popularized Geo folk music; compositions are based on Geo folk song and Geo pop music; in his operas the ballad style predominates; taught from 1902; from 1918 prof, Tiflis (Tbilisi) Conservatory; *Works*: wrote first Geo opera to be performed on professional stage, "The Legend of Shota Rustaveli" (1919); opera "Life Is Joy" (1927); music for film "Dzhurgay's Shield"; many books on folk music, including: "Georgian Folk music" (1916); "A Short Historical Survey of Georgian Music" (1940); "A Review of East Georgian Folk Song" (1948); *Awards*: Stalin Prize (1950); *Died*: 13 Aug 1953 in Tiflis.

ARALOV, Semyon Ivanovich (1880-?) Revolutionary, CP member from 1918; *Born*: 1880 in Moscow; *Career*: from 1902 worked for Mascow Soc-Democratic org; Oct 1905 propaganda among Russian troops in Harbin; 1906 worked for Party mil org; 1917 joined Soc-Democratic Internationalists and served on army comts; from 1918 head, Operations Dept, RSFSR Pop Comrt of Mil Affairs; member, RSFSR Revol-Mil Council; 1919-20 member, Revol-Mil Council, 12th and 14th Armies and Southwestern Front; from 1921 USSR plen in Lith, Turkey and Lat; 1925-27 Collegium member, USSR Pop Comrt of For Affairs; from 1927 worked for USSR Supr Sovnarkhoz; from 1931 Collegium member, USSR Pop Comrt of Finance; 1938-41 dep dir, then dir, State Lit Museum; *Died*: date, place and cause of death unknown.

ARAPOV, Anatoliy Afanas'yevich (1876-1949) Stage designer; *Born*: 3 Dec 1876; *Educ*: 1906 grad Moscow College of Painting, Sculpture and Architecture; *Career*: 1905 began theater work at Povarskaya Street Studio; designed sets and costumes for Nezlobin Theater, Komissarzhevskaya Theater, Free Theater, etc; after 1917 Oct Revol worked for theaters in Moscow, Leningrad, Kiev, etc, and also designed for cinema; *Works*: sets and costumes for: *Rasteryayeva ulitsa* (Rasteryayeva Street), after Uspenskiy (1929); Trenyov's *Na beregu Nevy* (On the Banks of the Neva) (1937); Goldoni's "Women" (1929); *Varvary* (The Barbarians) (1937); Kryukov's *Stantsionnyy smotritel'* (The Station-Master) (1940); etc; painted landscapes: "Mikhaylovskoye Village" (1926); "Kanev" (1929); "Shchyolkovo" (1935) "Istra" (1940), etc; *Died*: 21 Dec 1949.

ARBATOV, Il'ya Il'ich (1894-1967) Arm ballet-dancer and ballet-master; Pop Artiste of Arm SSR from 1967; one of the founders of Arm nat ballet; *Born*: 18 Mar 1894; *Educ*: 1921 grad Perini's Ballet Studio, Tbilisi; *Career*: 1926-38 soloist and ballet-master in Tbilisi, Tashkent, Khar'kov, Kazan', Ufa and Baku opera and ballet theaters, where he performed the roles: Girey in *Bakhchisarayskiy fontan* (The Fountain of Bakhchisaray); Li Fan-fu in *Krasnyy mak* (The Red Poppy); Peter I in *Mednyy vsadnik* (The Bronze Horseman); Gabo in *Schast'ye* (Fortune); Mato in "Sevan"; the Father in "Marmar," etc; here, too, he staged the ballets: *Lebedinoye ozero* (Swan Lake); "Coppelia"; "The Red Poppy"; Arends' "Salambo"; "The Fountain of Bakhchisaray"; "Sheherezade"; Arenskiy's "Gulyandom" (1940), etc; 1938-57 (with intervals) chief ballet-master, Spendiarov Opera and Ballet Theater, where he staged nat ballets such as: Khachaturyan's "Fortune" (1939); Spendiarov's "Khandut" (1945); Yegiazaryan's "Sevan" (1956); Oganesyan's "Marmar" (1957); also staged ballets by Russian composers, such as Morozov's "Doctor Aybolit" (1949); "The Bronze Horseman" (1949); arranged nat dances in operas: Spendiarov's "Almast"; Tigranyan's "Anush," etc; directed nat dances in choreographic ensembles of Geo, Arm, Azer, North Ossetia, etc; *Died*: 29 Sept 1967.

ARBATOV (real name: ARKHIPOV), Nikolay Nikolayevich (1869-1926) Russian stage dir and drama teacher; *Born*: 1869, *Educ*: grad Law Fac, Moscow Univ, and Fedotov Drama School; *Career*: began amateur acting at age 15; actor and stage dir under Stanislavsky at Art and Lit Council, which he took over when Stanislavsky went to Moscow Arts Theater; 1903 embarked on full-time theatrical career; worked at Komissarzhevskaya Theater, Petersburg, where he produced Gorky's *Deti solntsa* (Children of the Sun), etc; 1908-15 chief stage dir, Suvorin Theater (theater of Petersburg Lit and Art Soc), where he staged Russian classics and plays by Ibsen, Hauptmann, etc; after 1917 Oct Revol chief stage dir, Theater of State Pop Center, Petrograd; 1918 invited by Lunacharskiy to work on Arts Bd, Comt for Photography and Cinema; helped organize first Russian school of cinematography and later an inst and college of cinematographic art; 1921-22 chief stage dir, Alexandrine Theater; 1923-24 again chief stage dir, Theater of State Pop Center; also taught acting; his productions were notable for perfect reproduction of the style and atmosphere of the age in which they were set;*Died*: 1926.

ARDAROV (real name: BOGDANOVICH), Grigoriy Pavlovich (1888-1956) Russian actor and stage dir; Pop Artiste of RSFSR from 1954; *Born*: 9 Apr 1888; *Educ*: grad Odessa Drama School; *Career*: 1908 began stage career in Rostov-on-Don; worked at theaters in Khar'kov, Baku and Tiflis; from 1917 stage dir; from 1936 actor and stage dir, Kazan' Drama Theater; possessed of great stage presence, a powerful and expressive voice, and a subtle, gentle sense of humor; *Roles*: Arbenin; Satin; Krechinskiy; Othello; Tsar Ivan in A.K. Tolstoy's *Smert' Ioanna Groznogo* (Death of Ivan the Terrible); Philip in Victor Hugo's "Don Carlos"; Bersenev in *Razlom* (Break-Up); Talanov in *Nashestviye* (Invasion); Macpherson in *Russkiy vopros* (The Russian Question); Stessel in Stepanov and Popov's "Port Arthur"; *Productions*: Rakhmanov's "Professor Polezhayev" and *Bespokoynaya starost'* (Turbulent Old Age); Gogol's *Revizor* (The Government Inspector); *Dvoryanskoye gnezdo* (A Nest of Gentlefolk), after Turgenev, etc; *Died*: 17 Feb 1956.

ARENDS, Andrey (Genrikh) Fyodorovich (1855-1924) Conductor, violinist and composer; Hon Artiste of RSFSR from 1922; *Born*: 14 Mar 1855 in Moscow; *Educ*: 1877 grad Moscow Conservatory; *Career*: 1883-92 violinist, Bolshoy Theater Orchestra, Moscow; 1892-1900 conductor, Moscow Maly Theater; 1900-21 conductor, Ballet Company, Bolshoy Theater; *Works*: conducted first Moscow performances of Tchaikovsky's *Spyashchaya krasavitsa* (Sleeping Beauty) (1899) and Glazunov's "Raymonda" (1900); also conducted new production of Tchaikovsky's *Lebedinoye ozero* (Swan Lake) (1901); composed ballet "Salambo," after Flaubert's novel (1910); wrote music for shows, including Shakespeare's "Cymbeline," etc; symphonic and chamber works; *Died*: 27 Apr 1924 in Moscow.

ARENKOV, Konstantin Mikhaylovich (1894-1946) Composer; *Born*: 13 May 1894 in Odessa; *Educ*: studied piano at Odessa Music School; 1923 grad Sov Law Fac, Petrograd Univ; 1914-20 took composition lessons from A. Sass-Tisovskiy and 1928-33 from R. Mervol'f in Leningrad; *Career*: 1914-17 cinema pianist; 1922-32 cinema conductor; 1933-38 conductor, Music Hall Theater; 1939-40 conductor, Variety Theater; 1935-38 musical dir, Leningrad Oblast Young Playgoers' Theater; 1941-42 musical dir, Leningrad Oblast Philharmonic; 1942-44 musical dir, Leningrad Oblast Operetta Theater; 1944-46 musical dir, Leningrad Variety Theater; 1930-32 secr, Composers' Section, All-Russian Soc of Playwrights and Composers; 1933-41 exec secr, Leningrad City Composers' Comt; *Works*: operettas: *Pauk* (The Spider) (1924); *Mikrob lyubvi* (The Love Microbe) (1925); *Dzhentl'meny* (Gentlemen) (1935); vaudevilles: *Spichka mezhdu dvukh ogney* (A Match Between Two Fires) (1943); *Vesyolaya putanitsa* (Merry Confusion) (1946); pieces for variety orchestra (1944-46); piano pieces; waltz for piano and saxophone (1946); songs "My Dear One, My Small One," to words by V. Dykhovichnyy (1943), etc; music for some 10 shows; circus music; arrangements for variety orchestra; *Awards*: medal "For the Defense of Leningrad"; other medals; *Died*: 15 May 1946 in Leningrad.

ARENSON, Ivan Adamovich (1894-1967) Revolutionary; Civil War veteran; CP member from 1917; *Born*: 23 Dec 1894; *Career*: metalworker at Sveaborg dockyard; from 1917 worked at "Lorents" Plant in Petrograd; 1917 helped organize a Red Guard detachment; as member of this detachment helped crush Kornilov mutiny and during 1917 Oct Revol fought against Provisional Govt; 1918 commander, partisan detachment, Vyatka Special Div on Eastern Front; 1919-24 mechanic at a Moscow plant; subsequently with Moscow Criminal Investigation Dept; from 1927 dept head, "GOMZA" Trust; in subsequent years econ work in Moscow and Khar'kov; from 1944 in Tallinn; dir; paper mill; from 1952 Est Dep Min of Food Ind; from 1954 Est Dep Min of Meat and Dairy Ind; 1956-67 pensioner; *Died*: 25 Apr 1967.

ARGUNOV (VORONOVICH), Andrey Aleksandrovich (1866- ?) Right-wing Socialist-Revol; one of oldest members of Socialist-Revol Party; *Born*: 1866, son of a nobleman; *Educ*: grad Moscow Univ; *Career*: in late 1880's while still at school attended *Narodnaya Volya* (People's Will) club in Tomsk; early 1890's active in Moscow underground student clubs; 1896 set up Socialist-Revol Union in Saratov; helped draft "basic tenets of Socialist-Revol Union programm," published in 1898 as a pamphlet entitled *Nashi zadachi* (Our Tasks), with a brief outline history of revol movement; 1901 founded Russia's first illegal Socialist-Revol journal *Revolyutsionnaya Rossiya*; at 1st Socialist-Revol Party Congress (29 Dec 1905-4 Jan 1906) elected member, Party's first CC; 1907 at 2nd Party Congress co-opted member, CC; subsequently elected to various senior Party posts; 1909, on behalf of CC, negotiated with former chief of police A.A. Lopukhin and obtained from him evidence needed to unmask police informer Azef; 1914 sided with majority Party faction that approved the war; also contributed to *Narodnaya Volya* organs *Za rubezhom* and *Novosti*; Sept 1915, together with G.V. Plekhanov, N.D. Avksent'yev, G.A. Aleksinskiy, etc, signed the "Manifesto of the United Group of Soc-Democrats and Socialist-Revolutionaries, Drafted at the 1915 Geneva Conference" proclaiming that "defeat of Russia in the war against Germany would also entail her defeat in the struggle for freedom"; after 1917 Feb Revol contributed to newspaper *Volya naroda* - organ of right-wing Socialist-Revol faction; 1918 member, Ufa Directory (All-Russian Provisional Govt"); late 1918 emigrated; *Died*: date and cause of death unknown.

ARINKIN, Mikhail Innokent'yevich (1876-1948) Hematologist; prof from 1919; Dr of Med from 1905; member, USSR Acad of Med Sci from 1944; *Born*: 1876; *Educ*: 1902 grad Imperial Mil Med Acad, Petersburg; *Career*: after grad retained for postgrad studies in S.S. Botkin's Fac Therapy Clinic; from 1908 lecturer, after death of S.S. Botkin asst prof, same dept under N. Ya. Chistovich; from 1919 head, Dept of Specific Pathology and Therapy of Internal Diseases, Petrograd Mil Med Acad; clinical views influenced by physiological line of S.P. and S.S. Botkin; co-founder of clinical hematology in USSR; 1927 proposed intravital sternal puncture, important method of diagnosing pathology of the hemopoietic system, particularly acute and aleukemic leukoses; 1935 proposed similar puncture of lymph nodes; more than 100 works written under his supervision, including some on aviation med; from 1908 secr, Leningrad Soc of Russian Physicians; permanent presidium member, and from 1936 founder and head, Hematology Section, Leningrad S.P. Botkin Therapeutic Soc; *Publ: Retikulo-endotelial'naya sistema pri boleznyakh krovi i krovetvornykh organov* (The Reticuloendothelial System in Diseases of the Blood and Hemopoietic Organs); *K patologii nefrita* (Pathology of Nephritis) (1905); *K metodike issledovaniya pri zhizni kostnogo mozga u bol'nykh s zabolevaniyem krovetvornykh organov* (Method of Examining the Bone Marrow *intra vitam* in Persons Suffering from Diseases of the Hemopoietic Organs) (1927); *Klinika bolezney krovi i krovetvornykh organov* (Clinical Aspects of Diseases of the Blood and Hemopoietic Organs) (1928); *Died*: 1948 in Leningrad.

ARISTARKHOV, A.A. (Party pseudonyms: Bagrov; Osetrov; Volgin) (1875-1942) Revolutionary; CP member from 1903; *Born*: 1875; *Career*: Party work in Kursk; after 1917 Feb Revol Major of Kursk; May 1917 left Party in disagreement with Party line on socialist revol; June 1918 rejoined Party; from 1919 govt and teaching work in Kursk, Samara, Arkhangel'sk and Tambov; from 1931 dir, Moscow Textile Technicum; 1934-35 dep dir, Shcherbakov Factory; from 1935 pensioner; deleg at 3rd, 4th and 5th RSDRP Congresses and 11th RCP(B) Congress; *Died*: 1942.

ARISTOV, Fyodor Fyodorovich (1888-1932) Slavist and lit historian; prof; *Born*: 14 Oct 1888 in Varnavino, Kostroma Province; *Educ*: grad Econ Fac, Moscow Business Inst; grad Fac of History and Philology, Moscow Univ; *Career*: while still a student worked for Slavic Philanthropic Comt; 1908 founder and pres, *Slavia* Student Soc; secr, *Slavia* Polit Soc, Moscow; worked for following Slavic org in Moscow: Slavic Auxiliary Soc, Galician-Russian Soc, Stur Slovako-Russian Soc, Jan Hus Russo-Czech Soc, Krizanic Russo-Croatian Soc; head, Slavic section, journal *Russkiy arkhiv*; ed, journal *Slavyanskoye ob'yedineniye*; 1907 founded Carpatho-Russian Museum, which existed until 1917; after grad univ taught at various colleges in Moscow; 1914-17 in Russian Army; 1917-22 in Sov Army; Sept 1918-Sept 1920 taught at secondary schools in Transcaucasus; Oct 1920-Sept 1922 at Feodosiya Pop Univ and Feodosiya Inst of Educ; 1921 taught at 64th Feodosiya command courses, becoming dep head of studies; 1922-32 prof, Moscow State Univ; read lectures at ind and econ courses, at courses for top employees of Moscow Finance Dept, at Lat Inst of Educ, at Moscow Inst of Journalism and at Moscow Inst of Oriental Studies; author of over 200 works, mainly on Slavic studies, many of which were not published; unpublished manuscripts include: *Slovatskaya literatura* (Slovak Literature); *Literaturnoye razvitiye Podkarpatskoy Rusi* (The Literary Development of Subcarpathian Rus); *Istoriya Karpatskoy Rusi* (The History of Carpathian Rus) (3 vol); *Podkarpatskaya Rus' v proshlom i nastoyashchem* (Subcarpathian Rus in the Past and Present); *Istoriya literaturnogo razvitiya Karpatskoy Rusi* (A History of the Literary Development of Carpathian Rus); planned to publish 30-vol annotated "Library of Carpatho-Russian Writers"; *Publ*: coauthor, *Russko-slavyanskiy yezhegodnik na 1908 god* (A Russo-Slavic Yearbook for 1908) (1907); *Obshcheslavyanskiy yazyk* (A Pan-Slavic Language) (1911); *Galitsko-russkiye pisateli V.D. Zalozetskiy, D.N. Vergun, M.F. Glushkevich* (The Galician Russian Writers Zalozetskiy, Vergun and Glushkevich) (1911); *Rossiya i cheshskiy vopros* (Russia and the Czech Question) (1914); ed, *Biblioteka karpato-russkikh pisateley* (A Library of Carpatho-Russian Writers) (4 vol, 1911-16); *Karpato-russkiye pisateli* (Carpatho-Russian Writers) (Vol 1, 1916); *Russkiye natsional'nyye sotsialisty* (The Russian National Socialists) (1917); *Russkiy natsional'nyy vopros i Zakavkaz'ye* (The Russian Nationality Question and the Transcaucasus) (1918); *A.I. Dobryanskiy* (1924); *G.A. Deditskiy* (1927); *Yu.A. Yavorskiy* (1928); *I.I. Sharanevich* (1929); *Karpato-russkiye pisateli. A.V. Dukhnovich* (Carpatho-Russian Writers. A.V. Dukhnovich) (1929); *A.A. Polyanskiy* (1930); *A.F. Kralitskiy* (1930); ed, *Karpato-russkaya bibliografiya. Annotirovannaya biblioteka* (A Carpatho-Russian Bibliography. /An Annotated Library/) (1931); *Died*: 5 Nov 1932.

ARISTOV, Vasiliy Mikhaylovich (1898-1962) Actor and stage dir; Pop Artiste of Ukr SSR from 1946; actor, Pushkin Russian Drama Theater, Khar'kov from 1936; CP member from 1940; *Born*: 1898; *Career*: from 1913 actor in Moscow; 1923-33 founder and actor, Moscow Oblast Trade-Union Council Theater; 1935-36 at Kiev's Russian Drama Theater; *Roles*: Polezhayev in Rakhmanov's *Bespokoynaya starost'* (Restless Old Age); Bezsemyonov in Gorky's *Meshchane* (The Philistines); Shadrin in *Chelovek s ruzh'yom* (The Man with a Gun); Siplyy in *Optimisticheskaya tragediya* (An Optimistic Tragedy), etc; *Productions*: Ivanov's *Bronepoyezd 14-69* (Armored Train 14-69); Gorky's *Vragi* (The Enemy); *Died*: 9 May 1962.

ARISTOVSKIY, Vyacheslav Mikhaylovich (1882-1950) Microbiologist; Dr of Med from 1912; prof from 1920; Hon Sci Worker of RSFSR; member, USSR Acad of Med Sci; *Born*: 1882; *Educ*: 1908 grad Med Fac, Kazan' Univ; *Career*: after grad, received special training in microbiology and immunology from immunologist I.G. Savchenko; 1909-14 worked under Savchenko at Inst of Bacteriology, Kazan' Univ; 1912 defended doctor's thesis; during WW 1 worked in laboratory of Fort Aleksandr I, Kronstadt, where anti-tetanus serum was prepared; 1918 asst prof and dir, Inst of Bacteriology, Kazan'; 1920 organized dept of microbiology at Med Fac, Kazan' Univ; from 1932 till death head, Dept of Microbiology, Leningrad Mil Med Acad; 1921 devised method of culturing *Borrelia recurrentis* on artificial nutrient medium he developed; with R.R. Gel'ttser later produced culture of *Treponema pallidum*; also carried out research on pathogenesis of relapsing fever and immunity to it; formulated new theories on anaerobiosis and pathogenic anaerobes used in diagnosis and prophylaxis of gas gangrene; proposed special device (Aristovskiy's anaerostat) for culturing anaerobes; 1925-32 set up and directed Regional Inst of Microbiology, Tatar Pop Comrt of Health, Kazan'; assisted Kazan' health authorities to draft anti-epidemic measures and acted as co-ed, *Kazanskiy meditsinskiy zhurnal*; about 200 sci works published under his supervision; pupils included N.N. Blagoveshchenskiy, M.I. Mastbaum, R.R. Gel'ttser, A.F. Agafonov and N.V. Sokolov; chm, Soc of Physicians, Kazan' Univ, and later chm, Leningrad Section, All-Union Soc of Epidemiologists, Microbiologists and Infectionists; *Publ*: 74 works mainly on immunology; coauthor, *Uchebnik meditsinskoy mikrobiologii* (Textbook of Medical Microbiology) (1945); doctor's thesis *Vliyaniye reaktsii sredy na spetsificheskiy tsitoliz* (The Effect of the Reaction of a Medium on Specific Cytolysis) (1912); *O kul'tivirovanii spirokhet Obermeyera* (Culturing *Borrelia recurrentis*) (1921); *Nekotoryye nablyudeniya nad kul'tivirovaniyem spirokhet Obermeyera* (Some Observations on Culturing *Borrelia recurrentis*) (1923); *O spirokhetakh i spirokhetozakh* (Spirochetes and Spirochetoses) (1924); *K ucheniyu o spirokhetakh* (The Study of Spirochetes) (1926); *Immunitet pri sifilise* (Immunity to Syphilis) (1930); *K metodike kul'tivirovaniya Sp. pallidae dlya massovogo polucheniya antigennogo materiala* (Methods of Culturing *Treponema pallidum* for Mass Production of Antigen) (1935); *K uproshcheniyu metodiki kul'tivirovaniya patogennykh anaerobov* (Simplifying Methods of Culturing Pathogenic Anaerobes) (1938); *Lektsii po infektsii i immunitetu* (Lectures on Infection and Immunity) (1936); *Apparat dlya vyrashchivaniya anaerobov* (An Apparatus for Culturing Anaerobes)(1940); *Died*: 1950 in Leningrad.

ARKADIN, Ivan Ivanovich (1878-1942) Russian actor; Hon Art Worker of RSFSR from 1935; *Born*: 1878; *Career*: 1908 began acting with Gaydeburov Touring Drama Theater, where his first role was Pavlin in *Volki i ovtsy* (The Wolves and the Sheep); 1914-38 at Moscow Chamber Theater; from 1938 at State Centr Theater of Young Playgoers; specialized in comic and slapstick roles, played in a sincere and simple style bordering at times on the tragic; *Roles*: the Prime-Minister in Lecoq's "Day and Night"; Rosetti in the adaptation of Sobol's "Sirocco"; Theramenes in Racine's "Phaedra"; Herod in Wilde's "Salomé"; Silenus in Annenskiy's "Famira-Kifared"; the Prince of Boulogne in Scribe and Legouve's "Adrienne Lecouvrère"; Famusov in *Gore ot uma* (Woe from Wit); the clerk in Sizovoy's *Mikhaylo Lomonosov*; Prof Shatrov in Del's *U lukomor'ya* (At the Seashore), etc; *Died*: 1942.

ARKAD'YEV, Ivan Petrovich (1872-1946) Russian conductor, violinist and music teacher; *Born*: 19 Jan 1872; *Educ*: 1893 grad Petersburg Conservatory; *Career*: 1896 began conducting at Kononov Opera Theater, Petersburg; 1910-25 conductor, Pop Center; conducted operas in which Chaliapin, Sobinov, Nezhdanova, etc, performed; 1917-19 musical dir and conductor, Performers' Opera and Drama Union, Pyatigorsk; 1920-23 conducted operas at Sibiryakov Theater, Odessa; prof, Odessa Conservatory; from 1923 supported amateur opera and choral groups in Petrograd; at Leningrad's "Red Triangle" Plant produced the operas *Ruslan i Lyudmila* (Ruslan and Ludmilla), *Knyaz' Igor'* (Prince Igor), "Carmen," *Tikhiy Don* (Quiet Flows the Don), etc; *Died*: 30 Dec 1946.

ARKAD'YEV, Vladimir Konstantinovich (1884-1953) Physicist; prof, Moscow Univ from 1930; corresp member, USSR Acad of Sci from 1927; *Born*: 21 Apr 1884 in Moscow; *Educ*: 1907 grad Dept of Physics and Mathematics, Moscow Univ; *Career*: 1907-11 and 1918-30 lecturer, Moscow Univ; 1921-26 also prof, Moscow Inst of Timber Technol; worked for several years at All-Union Electr Eng Inst; chm, Commission for Magnetic and Conductive Materials, USSR Acad of Sci; 1919 founder-head, Laboratory of Magnetism (later Laboratory of Electromagnetism), Moscow Univ; developed basic principles of modern magnetodynamics and methods of magnetic spectroscopy; *Publ: Teoriya elektromagnitnogo polya v ferromagnitnykh metallakh* (Theory of the Electromagnetic Field in Ferromagnetic Metals) (1913); *Nauchno-tekhnicheskiye osnovy gazovoy bor'by* (The Scientific and Technical Principles of Gas Warfare) (1917); *Magnitnaya spektroskopiya* (Magnetic Spectroscopy) (1924); *Elektromagnitnyye protsessy v metallakh* (Electromagnetic Processes in Metals) (2 vol, 1934-46), etc; *Died*: 1 Dec 1953.

ARKHANGEL'SKIY, Aleksandr Andreyevich (1846-1924) Russian choral conductor and composer; Hon Artiste of RSFSR from 1921; *Born*: 23 Oct 1846 in Penza; *Career*: 1880 organized mixed choir in Petersburg, with which he toured Russia and abroad; one of the first to include women in church choirs; composed choral works, arranged folk songs; *Publ: Repertuar kontsertov* (Concert Repertoire); *Died*: 16 Nov 1924 in Prague while touring with his choir.

ARKHANGEL'SKIY, Aleksandr Grigor'yevich (1889-1938) Russian poet; *Born*: 16 Nov 1889 in Yeysk; *Career*: 1922-32 on ed staff, journal *Krokodil*; wrote humorous verse and stories for satirical journals *Lapot'* (pen-name: "Arkhip") *Begemot* and *Krasnyy perets; Publ*: 1919 first work published, collected satire *Chyornyye oblaka* (Black Clouds); first collected verse dealt with country life: *Babiy komissar* (The Women's Commissar) (1925); *Derevenskiye chastushki* (Village Part-Songs) (1928); *Kulak i radio* (The Kulak and the Radio) (1931), etc; best known for his parodies on contemporary writers, compiled in books *Parodii* (Parodies) (1927); *Izbrannoye. Parodii, epigrammy, satira* (Selected Works. Parodies, Epigrams and Satire) (1946); *Parodii* (Parodies) (1958); parodies displayed his acute observation, his knack of "embodiment," his skill in reproducing a writer's stylistic features and his ability to single out and ridicule his most vulnerable points; also wrote feuilletons castigating bigotry, conceit and polit apathy; some of his collected parodies were illustrated by cartoonists Kukryniksy; *Died*: 13 Oct 1938 in Moscow.

ARKHANGEL'SKIY, Aleksandr Semyonovich (1854-1926) Lit historian; Dr of Russian Philology from 1891; corresp member, Russian Acad of Sci from 1904; *Born*: 24 July 1854 in Penza, son of a priest; *Educ*: 1876 grad Fac of History and Philology, Kazan' Univ; *Career*: 1882-1908 prof, Kazan' Univ; then for a time prof, Petersburg Univ; after 1917 Oct Revol co-founder and lecturer, Simbirsk Univ; specialized in history of Russian lit, especially religious lit; work distinguished by meticulous analysis of manuscript material; *Publ: Nil Sorskiy i Vassian Patrikeyev, ikh literaturnyye trudy i idei* (Nil Sorskiy and Vassian Patrikeyev - Their Literary Works and Ideas) (1882); *Teatr dopetrovskoy Rusi. Istoriko-literaturnyy ocherk* (The Theater in Pre-Petrine Rus. A Historical and Literary Study) (1884); *Ocherki iz istorii zapadno-russkoy literatury XVI-XVII vekov* (An Outline History of 16-17th-Century Western Russian Literature) (2 vol, 1887); *Tvoreniya otsov tserkvi v drevnerusskoy pis'mennosti* (The Works of the Church Fathers in Ancient Russian Writings) (5 vol, 1888-91); *Literatura domongol'skoy Rusi* (The Literature of Pre-Mongolian Rus) (1903); *Russkaya literatura XVIII veka* (18th-Century Russian Literature) (1910); *Literatura Moskovskogo gosudarstva s kontsa XV-XVII vekov* (The Literature of Muscovy from the Late 15th to the 17th Century) (1913); *Vvedeniye v istoriyu russkoy literatury* (An Introduction to the History of Russian Literature) (vol 1, 1916); *Died*: 24 Apr 1926.

ARKHANGEL'SKIY, Andrey Dmitriyevich (1879-1940) Russian geologist; Dr of Geological Sci from 1912; member, USSR Acad of Sci from 1929; *Born*: 8 Dec 1879; *Educ*: 1904 grad Fac of Physics and Mathematics, Moscow Univ; *Career*: 1906-13 asst Chair of Geology, Moscow Univ; from 1914 member, Geological Comt; 1919-24 co-directed research on Kursk Magnetic Anomaly with I.M. Gubkin; 1920-32 prof, Moscow Univ; 1924-32 simultaneously prof, Moscow Mining Acad; from 1932 prof, Moscow Geological Survey Inst and Collegium member, RSFSR Pop Comrt of Educ; from 1934 dir, Geological Inst, USSR Acad of Sci; 1936-38 led combined expedition to study geological structure of Kaz; 1939-40 led similar expedition in European USSR; wrote over 180 works on regional geology, on the fauna and stratigraphy of the Paleogene and Upper Cretaceous sedimentations of the Volga, Transvolga and Centr Asian regions, on lithology, paleography and tectonics, and on the relation of gravitational and magnetic anomalies to the geological structure of the USSR; demonstrated the importance of knowing the conditions under which modern sedimentations occurred for understanding the genesis of sedimentary rocks of past geological periods; *Publ: Verkhnemelovyye otlozheniya vostoka Yevropeyskoy Rossii* (Upper Cretaceous Sedimentations in the Eastern Area of European Russia) (1912); *Verkhnemelovyye otlozheniya Turkestana* (Upper Cretaceous Sedimentations in Turkestan) (1916); *Vvedeniye v izucheniye geologii Yevropeyskoy Rossii* (An Introduction to the Study of the Geology of European Russia) (vol 1, 1923); *Usloviya obrazovaniya nefti v Severnom Kavkaze* (The Conditions for Oil Formation in the Northern Caucasus) (1927); *Geologiya i gravimetriya* (Geology and Gravimetry) (1933); *Tipy boksitov SSSR i ikh genezis* (Bauxite Types in the USSR and Their Genesis)(1937); *Geologicheskoye znacheniye anomaliy sily tyazhesti v SSSR* (The Geological Importance of Gravitational Anomalies in the USSR) (1937); coauthor, *Geologicheskoye stroyeniye i istoriya razvitiya Chyornogo morya* (The Geological Structure and Development History of the Black Sea) (1938); *Geologicheskoye stroyeniye i geologicheskaya istoriya SSSR* (The Geological Structure and Geological History of the USSR) (2 vol, 4th ed, 1947-48); *Izbrannyye trudy* (Selected Works) (2 vol, 1952-54); *Awards*: Lenin Prize (1928); *Died*: 16 June 1940.

ARKHANGEL'SKIY, Boris Aleksandrovich (1890-1954) Obstetrician and gynecologist; prof from 1931; Dr of Med; member, USSR Acad of Med Sci; Hon Sci Worker of RSFSR; *Born*: 1890; *Educ*: 1914 grad Med Fac, Moscow Univ; *Career*: from 1921 asst, 1922-30 assoc prof, Obstetrics Clinic, Moscow Univ; 1931-50 head, Dept of Obstetrics and Gynecology, 2nd Moscow Med Inst; developed method of external prophylactic cephalic version in cases of transverse position of the fetus and pelvic presentation; pupils included subsequent dept heads, Professors V.N. Vlasov, S.B. Golubchin, A.Z. Kocherginskiy and O.Ye. Nudol'skaya; for eight years chm, Moscow Soc of Obstetricians and Gynecologists; member, Learned Council, USSR Min of Health; 1947 dep, Moscow City Sov; *Publ*: deal mainly with use of irradiation in obstetrics and gynecology, contracted pelvis, methods of combatting toxicoses in pregnancy and cancer; *Novyy metod prognoza rodov* (A New Method of Forecasting Births) (1926); *Luchi Rentgena i radiya v ginekologii i akusherstve* (X-Rays and Radium in Gynecology and Obstetrics) (1928); *O novykh printsipakh glubokoy rentgenoterapii i o konstruktsii sootvetstvuyushchey apparatury* (New Principles of Deep X-Ray Therapy and Design of Appropriate Apparatus) (1929); *K voprosu o patogeneze eklampsii i yeyo terapii* (Pathogenesis of Eclampsia and its Treatment) (1935); *Uzkiy taz* (Contracted Pelvis) (1935); *Klinika uzkogo taza* (Clinical Aspects of Contracted Pelvis) (1939); *Naruzhnyy profilakticheskiy povorot na golovku v zhenskikh konsul'tatsiyakh* (External Prophylactic Cephalic Version in Gynecological Clinics) (1945); *Died*: 1954.

ARKHANGEL'SKIY, Sergey Ivanovich (1882-1958) Historian; corresp member, USSR Acad of Sci from 1946; *Born*: 22 Jan 1882; *Educ*: 1906 grad Fac of History and Philology, Moscow Univ; *Career*: until 1917 teacher, Nizhniy Novgorod college; from 1917 lecturer, Nizhniy Novgorod Teachers' Training Inst; from 1946 prof, Gorky Univ; specialized in history of the Great Civil War in 17th-Century England, agrarian history and peasant movements in England from 1640-60; *Publ: Agrarnoye zakonodatel'stvo Velikoy angliyskoy revolyutsii 1643-48 godov* (Agrarian Legislation During the Great English Revolution of 1643-48) (1935); *Agrarnoye zakonodatel'stvo angliyskoy revolyutsii 1649-60 godov* (Agrarian Legislation During the English Revolution of 1649-60) (1940); *Angliyskaya burzhuaznaya revolyutsiya XVII veka* (The 17th-Century English Bourgeois Revolution) (2 vol, 1954); *Krest'yanskiye dvizheniya v Anglii v 40-50-ykh godakh XVII veka* (Peasant Movements in England in the 1640's and 1650's) (1960); *Awards*: Order of the Red Banner of Labor (1957); *Died*: 7 Oct 1958.

ARKHIPOV, Abram Yefimovich (1862-1930) Painter; member, Acad of Painting from 1898; Pop Artist of RSFSR from 1927; *Born:* 27 Aug 1862 in vil Yegorovo, Ryazan' Province; *Educ*: 1877-88 (with intervals) studied at Moscow College of Painting, Sculpture and Architecture; 1884-86 at Petersburg Acad of Arts; *Career*: from 1891 itinerant artist; 1892-1918 prof, Moscow College of Painting, Sculpture and Architecture; 1918-23 prof, Higher Tech Art Workshops; from 1904 member, Russian Artists' Union; from 1924 member, Assoc of Artists of Revol Russia; *Works*: paintings: "Visiting a Patient" (ca. 1885); "The Village Icon-Painter" (1889); "Along the River Oka" (1890); "The Ice Has Passed" (1895); "The Returnee" (1896); "Day-Laborers at an Iron Foundry" (1896); "Washerwomen" (1899 and 1901); "A Northern Village" (1903); "The Young Girl" (1919); "A Peasant Woman from Ryazan' Province" (1926); "The Shepherd Boy" (1928), etc; *Died*: 25 Sept 1930.

ARKIN, David Yefimovich (1899-1957) Art and architectural historian and critic; prof from 1934; *Born*: 2 Feb 1899; *Career*: 1932-55 co-founder and leading member, Sov Architects' Union; 1933-41 ed, journal *Arkhitektura SSSR*; 1941-56 corresp member, USSR Acad of Architecture; taught architecture; 1934-38 founder and ed, periodical *Mastera iskusstva ob iskusstve* (Masters of Art About Art); *Publ: Iskusstvo bytovoy veshchi* (The Art of Domestic Objects) (1933); *Obrazy arkhitektury* (Architectural Images) (1941); "Zakharov and Voronikhin" (1953); "Rastrelli" (1954), etc; *Died*: 23 May 1957.

ARKIN, Yefim Aronovich (1873-1948) Pedagogue and physician; Dr of Pedag Sci; member, USSR Acad of Pedag Sci from 1947; helped found Sov system of preschool educ; *Born*: 13 Jan 1873; *Educ*: 1897 grad Med Fac, Kiev Univ; *Career*: 1907-19 lectured on physiology and children's diseases at secondary med schools in Moscow; from 1919 research and teaching work at a high school and research establishments; 1930-45 prof, Lenin State Teachers' Training Inst, Moscow; worked on preschool, family and physical training, human physiology and hygiene; *Publ: Mozg i dusha* (The Brain and the Psyche) (1928); *Chelovek* (Man) (1928); *Fiziologiya cheloveka* (The Physiology of Man) (1929); *Besedy o vospitanii* (Talks on Training) (1945); *Fizicheskoye vospitaniye v detskom sadu* (Physical Training in the Kindergarten) (1946); *Osobennosti shkol'nogo vospitaniya* (Features of School Training) (1947); *Rabota detskogo sada s sem'yoy* (Kindergarten Family Work) (1947); *Doshkol'nyy vozrast* (The Preschool Age) (1948); *Roditelyam o vospitanii. Vospitaniye rebyonka v sem'ye ot goda do zrelosti* (A Parents' Book of Training. Child Training in the Family from the Age of One to Maturity) (1957); *Died*: 31 Jan 1948.

ARMAND, Fyodor Aleksandrovich (1896-1935) Sov Air Force pilot; *Born*: 1896 in vil Pushkino, Moscow Province, of intellectual, Russianized French parents (his mother, Inessa F. Armand was a friend and aide of Lenin from 1919 to 1920); *Educ*: until 1914 studied at a Moscow tech school; 1915 grad Alekseyev Mil School; 1917 grad Gatchin Flying School and flying school in England; *Career*: Dec 1914 drafted into Russian Army; 1915-16 junior officer, company commander in infantry regt; 1917 translator with English Mission at Moscow Centr Depot of Aviation Equipment; last rank in Russian Army - lt; Aug 1918 drafted as reservist into Red Army; 1918-21 pilot-observer, acting commander, adjutant (chief of staff), 38th Air Squadron; 1919 arrested by div comr for suspected treason but released after a telegram from Lenin; 1921 as pilot-observer participated in campaign to crush Antonov Revolt in Tambov Province; 1921-26 instructor, Red Army Air Force; 1926 transferred to reserve on med grounds; 1926-35 worked for Moscow sports orgs; *Died*: 1935 from the effects of war wounds.

ARMAND, Pavel Nikolayevich (1902-1964) Film dir; Hon Art Worker of Lat SSR from 1947; CP member from 1945; *Born*: 23 Apr 1902; *Educ*: 1928 grad Tchaikovsky Cinematography Courses, Moscow; *Career*: from 1928 asst dir, then dir, State War-Film Studios; 1929 co-directed first independent film *Sbornaya eksperimental'naya programma* (Combined Experimental Program); 1931-33 script-writer and dir, Arm Cinema Studios; 1935-42 dir, Lenin Film Studios; directed several pop sci films; wrote music and lyrics for films *Chelovek s ruzh'yom* (The Man with a Gun), *Tanker "Derbent"*, etc; wrote screenplay for *Baltiyskaya simfoniya* (Baltic Symphony); from 1954 at Riga Film Studios; 1955 co-dir, *Vesenniye zamorozki* (Late Frosts), based on classical Lat novella by Blaumann; 1957 dir, *Za lebedinoy stayey oblakov* (Beyond a Swan-Like Flock of Clouds); 1959 dir, *Povest' o latyshskom strelke* (The Tale of a Latvian Gunner); 1961 dir, *Chyortova dyuzhina* (The Devil's Dozen); *Died*: 16 Aug 1964.

ARMAND (nee: STEFFEN), Yelizaveta Fyodorovna (Party pseudonym: INESSA; pen-name: Yelena BLONINA) (1875-1920) Active in int Communist women's movement; close friend and aide of Lenin's; CP member from 1904; *Born*: 26 Apr 1875 in Paris (of an English father and French mother); *Educ*: educated at home; attended Brussels Univ; *Career*: orphaned early in life, she was raised in Moscow, where her aunt was governess to the family of factory-owner Armand; 1893 married A.Ye. Armand, with whom she had been raised; later set up school for children on her husband's estate; also worked for anti-prostitution section of Moscow Soc for Improving the Status of Women; 1904 joined Bolsheviks and worked for Moscow Bolshevik org; several times arrested and exiled; 1909 emigrated; at first lived and studied in Brussels; 1910 moved to Paris, active as Presidium member, Paris Group for the Promotion of the Bolshevik Party; 1911 active at Party School established by Bolsheviks at Longjumeau near Paris; 1912 returned illegally to Russia and worked for Petersburg Bolshevik org; 1912 arrested; 1913, after her release from prison, moved to Krakow; worked for foreign branch of journal *Rabotnitsa*; attended Int Women's Congress and Int Youth Conference; 1915-16 attended Zimmerwald and Kienthal Conferences of Internationalists, assisting Lenin in translation of conference resolution and proceedings; after 1917 Feb Revol, together with Lenin and other Bolsheviks, returned to Russia via Germany and worked in Moscow; after 1917 Oct Revol member, Moscow Province Party Comt; member, Moscow Province Exec Comt, and chm, Moscow Province Sovnarkhoz; 1918 represented RSFSR Red Cross in visit to France; 1918-20 head, Women's Dept, CC, RCP(B); active in 1st (1919) and 2nd (1920) Comintern Congresses; 1949 first publ of Lenin's letters to her, written in late 1916 and 1917; *Died*: 24 Nov 1920 from cholera contracted en route to Caucasus; buried in Moscow's Red Square.

ARNOL'D, Igor' Vladimirovich (1900-1948) Mathematician; Dr of Pedag Sci; prof; corresp member, RSFSR Acad of Pedag Sci from 1947; *Born*: 18 Mar 1900; *Educ*: 1929 grad Physics and Mathematics Fac, Moscow Univ; from 1912 taught mathematics at workers' fac in Odessa; from 1930 taught at college level; 1944-48 senior assoc, Teaching Methods Research Inst, Acad of Pedag Sci; devised methods of teaching mathematics in secondary schools; *Publ: Teoreticheskaya arifmetika* (Theoretical Arithmetic) (1939); *Otritsatel'nyye chisla v kurse al'gebry* (Negative Numbers in an Algebra Course) (1947); *Pokazateli stepeni i logarifmy v kurse elementarnoy algebry* (Power Indices and Logarithms in an Elementary Algebra Course) (1949), etc; *Died*: 20 Oct 1948.

ARNOL'DI, Vladimir Mitrofanovich (1871-1924) Botanist; specialist in plant morphology and Alpine plants; prof from 1909; *Born*: 24 June 1871 in Kozlov; *Educ*: 1893 grad Moscow Univ; *Career*: 1909-19 prof, Khar'kov Univ; 1919-22 prof, Kuban' Univ; 1922-24 prof, Moscow Univ; specialized in morphology of gymnosperms and green algae; *Publ: Ocherk yavleniy istorii individual'nogo razvitiya u nekotorykh predstaviteley gruppy Sequoiaceae* (A Study of the Phenomena in the History of the Individual Development of Some Members of the Sequoiceae Group) (1900); *Morfologicheskiye issledovaniya nad protsessom oplodotvoreniya u nekotorykh golosemyannykh rasteniy* (Morphological Studies of the Fertilization Process in Some Gymnospermous Plants) (1906); *Vvedeniye v izucheniye nizshikh organizmov* (An Introduction to the Study of the Lowest Organisms) (1901); *Po ostrovam Malayskogo Arkhipelaga* (Around the Islands of the Malayan Archipelago) (1911); *Died*: 22 Mar 1924.

ARONSHTAM, Lazar' Naumovich (1896-1937) Mil commander; Jew; army comr, 2nd class; CP member from 1915; *Born*: 1896; *Career*: until 1917 underground revol work; imprisoned for two years by Tsarist authorities; 1918-21 Red Army private, polit worker, regt comr on Western, Eastern, Southern, Southeastern and Caucasian Fronts during Civil War; 1921-24 comr, 14th and 28th Div; comr for inspection of Red Army artillery and armored forces; 1924-28 underground Party Work in Western Bel (Poland); 1928-29 secr, Vitebsk Okrug Comt, CP Bel; 1930-33 member, Revol-Mil Council, and head, Polit Bd, Bel Mil Distr; 1933-37 member, Revol-Mil Council, and from 1934 member, Mil Council and head, Polit Bd, Special Red-Banner Far Eastern Army; member, Mil Council, USSR Pop Comrt of Defense; member, CPSU(B) Centr Control Commission; arrested by State Security organs; *Awards*: Order of the Red Banner (1921); *Died*: 1937 in imprisonment; posthumously rehabilitated.

AROSEV, Aleksandr Yakovlevich (1890-1938) Russian writer; Party and govt functionary; CP member from 1907; *Born*: 25 May 1890 in Kazan'; *Educ*: 1908 grad Kazan' secondary school; 1909-11 studied at Fac of Philosophy and Lit, Liège Univ; *Career*: 1905 began revol work; often subjected to reprisals; Mar 1917 elected chm, Tver' Sov of Workers, Soldiers and Peasants' Dep; during 1917 Oct Revol member, Moscow Mil-Revol Comt, and commander, Moscow Mil Distr; 1918 comr, Main Civil Aviation Bd; 1919 fought at Tsaritsyn; 1920 chm, Ukr Supr Revol Tribunal; 1921 counselor, USSR Mission in Riga; then worked at Lenin Inst, Moscow; 1924 head, Press Dept, USSR Mission in Paris; 1927-28 USSR plen in Lith; 1929-33 USSR plen in Czechoslovakia; from 1934 chm, All-Union Soc for Cultural Relations with For Countries; arrested by State Security organs; 1916 first work published; *Publ*: story *Plotniki* (The Carpenters) (1916); 1920 first collected stories *Revolyutsionnyye nabroski* (Revolutionary Sketches); novelettes: *Strada. Zapiski Terentiya Zabytogo* (Toil. Notes by Terentiy Zabytyy) (1921); *Nedavniye dni* (Recent Times) (1921); *Predsedatel'* (The Chairman) (1921); *Nikita Shornev* (1924); *Ot zhyoltoy reki* (From the Yellow River) (1927); essays *Po sledam Lenina* (In Lenin's Footsteps) (1924); *Materialy k biografii V.I. Lenina* (Material for Lenin's Biography) (1925); *O Vladimire Il'iche* (About Vladimir Il'ich) (1926); *Kak my vstupali v revolyutsionnuyu rabotu* (How We Joined the Revolutionary Effort) (1926); *Kazanskiye ocherki revolyutsii 1905 g.* (Kazan' Notes on the 1905 Revolution) (1925), etc; *Sobraniye sochineniy* (Collected Works) (2 vol, 1929); stories: *Belaya lestnitsa* (The White Staircase) (1923); *Oktyabr'skiye rasskazy* (October Stories) (1925); *Farsitskaya legenda* (A Parsi Legend) (1927); *Na zemle pod solntsem* (On the Land Beneath the Sun) (1928); novel *Senskiye berega* (Banks of the Seine); novel *Korni* (Roots) (1933); *Died*: 1938 in imprisonment; posthumously rehabilitated.

ARSENKO, Arsen Dionisovich (1903-1945) Bel opera singer (baritone); Pop Artiste of Bel SSR from 1944; *Born*: 15 Mar 1903; *Educ*: 1928 grad Khar'kov Inst of Music and Drama; *Career*: 1928 began stage career in Khar'kov with itinerant opera and ballet theater; from 1930 worked at various Sov opera theaters, including USSR Bolshoy Theater (1936-37); from 1937 soloist, Bel Opera and Ballet Theater in Minsk; *Roles*: Kuz'mich in Bogatyryov's *V pushchakh poles'ya* (In the Woods of Polessie); Andrey in Turenkov's *Tsvetok schast'ya* (Flower of Happiness); Yeletskiy in *Pikovaya dama* (Queen of Spades); Figaro in "The Barber of Seville"; Zhermon, Onegin, etc; very pop as singer of chamber works; *Died*: 30 Aug 1945.

ARSEN'YEV, Vladimir Klavdiyevichh (1872-1930) Russian writer; geographer and ethnographer; explorer of the Far East; *Born*: 10 Sept 1872 in Petersburg; *Educ*: grad of a mil school; *Career*: 1902, as officer in mil survey corps, took part in a number of expeditions to study Southern Maritime Region; 1906-10 explored Sikhote Alin' Highlands; 1917 undertook expedition to Byki-Biginen and Yan-de-Yange ranges; 1918-26 explored Kamchatka and Komandorskiye Islands; 1927 undertook major expedition from Sovetskaya Gavan' to Khabarovsk-on-Amur; his works combine sci accounte with descriptions of fauna and flora of explored areas; in addition to sci expeditions engaged in org work and lectured at higher educ institutions of Far East; 1910-18 dir, Khabarovsk museum; *Publ: Po Ussuriyskomu krayu* (In the Ussuri Kray) (1921); *Dersu-Uzala* (1923); *Skvoz' taygu* (Across the Taiga) (1930); *V gorakh Sikhote Alinya* (In the Sikhote Alin' Mountains) (1937); *Sochineniya* (Works) (6 vol, 1947-49); *Died*: 4 Sept 1930 in Vladivostok.

ARSKIY, Pavel Aleksandrovich (1886-1967) Russian writer; CP member from 1918; *Born*: 6 Nov 1886, son of a worker; *Career*: quarry worker, hammerman, legerclerk, miner, then performing artist; active in 1905 Revol; during WW 1 in Russian Army; in 1917 Oct Revol helped storm Winter Palace; 1917 first work printed; *Publ*: verse collections *Pesni bor'by* (Songs of Struggle) (1918); *Serp i Molot* (Hammer and Sickle) (1925); collected stories: *Krov' rabochego* (Worker's Blood) (1919); *Metla revolyutsii* (The Broom of the Revolution) (1921); novel *Chelovek u konveyyera* (The Man at the Conveyor) (1929); plays and stage adaptations: *Za krasnyye Sovety* (For the Red Soviets) (1918); *Osvobozhdyonnyy trud* (Liberated Labor) (1920); *Golgofa* (Golgotha) (1924); *Shturm neba* (Storming the Sky) (1929), etc; *Died*: 20 Apr 1967.

ARTEM'YEV, Nikolay Andreyevich (1870-1948) Electr eng; *Born*: 28 Nov 1870 in Moscow; *Educ*: 1895 grad Moscow Higher Tech College; *Career*: 1900-11 senior instructor, then prof of electr eng, Dept of Mech, Kiev Polytech Inst; 1911-15 planned main power station and supply grid for Women's Med Inst; also taught on advanced courses in pharmaceutics and natural sci for women; Mechanization and Electrification of Agric; designed an electrostatic telephone, a short-impulse synchronizer and a protective suit for work on high-tension cables; *Died*: 5 Aug 1948.

ARTSIKHOVSKIY, Vladimir Martynovich (1876-1931) Botanist and plant physiologist; *Born*: 20 July 1876 in Zhitomir, son of a postal official; *Educ*: 1894-96 studied at Moscow Univ; 1900 grad Petersburg Univ; *Career*: 1900-07 lecturer, Chair of Botany, Petersburg Univ, and Women's Med Inst; also taught on advanced courses in pharmaceutics and natural sci for women; 1907-22 prof of plant physiology and microbiology, Don Polytech Inst, Novocherkassk; 1910-22 founder and rector, Advanced Women's Courses in Natural Sci, later renamed Don Agric Inst; 1923-25 head, Chair of Plant Physiology, Moscow Timber Inst; 1926-27 head, Laboratory of Plant Physiology, Nikita Botanical Gardens, Crimea; from 1928 head, Dept of Biology, Moscow Wood Research Inst, and head, Chair of Botany, Moscow Timber Inst; 1923-27 assoc, then member, USSR Gosplan; research included study of effects of toxic substances on plants, the antagonism of salts as a basis for the chemical improvement of solonetz (a dark, strongly alkaline soil), the water regime in various types of wood, the anatomy of the saxaul, the pigments bacteriopurpurine and zoopurpurine, etc; *Publ: Polucheniye chistykh semyan s pomoshch'yu dezinfektsii* (Obtaining Clean Seeds by Disinfection) (1915); *Botanika. Kurs* (A Botany Course) (1926); *Rost saksaula i anatomicheskoye issledovaniye yego stvola* (The Growth of the Saxaul and an Anatomical Study of Its Trunk) (1928); *Died*: 13 June 1931 in Moscow.

ARTYOM (real name: SERGEYEV), Fyodor Andreyevich (1883-1921) Professional revol; Party and govt official; CP member from 1901; *Born*: 7 Mar 1883 in vil Glebovo, Fatezh Uyezd, Kursk Province, son of a peasant; *Educ*: Yekaterinoslav secondary school; 1901-02 studied at Moscow Tech High School; *Career*: expelled from school and arrested for revol activities; 1902 emigrated to Paris; 1903 *Iskra* (The Spark) agent in Ukr; from early 1905 head, Khar'kov Bolshevik org; Dec 1905 directed armed uprising in Khar'kov; 1906 deleg at 4th RSDRP Congress; 1906 arrested and imprisoned in Khar'kov jail, but soon managed to escape; Party work in Urals; head, Perm' RSDRP Comt; 1907 elected deleg, 5th RSDRP Congress, but in Mar 1907 re-arrested and imprisoned in Perm' jail; 1909 sentenced to exile in Eastern Siberia for life; Aug 1910 fled via Korea and China to Australia, which he reached in 1911; worked there as longshoreman and farmhand; in Queensland (Australia) headed Union of Russian Emigrant Workers; 1912 organizer and ed, Russian Soc-Democratic newspaper *Avstraliyskoye ekho* (Australian Echo); 1917 returned to Russia, headed Bolshevik faction of Khar'kov Sov; July 1917 elected Secr, Bureau, Donetsk Oblast RSDRP(B) Comt; then secr, Khar'kov Oblast Metalworkers' Union; 1917 at 6th RSDRP(B) Congress elected member, CC, RSDRP(B); Nov 1917 chm, Khar'kov Sov; chm, Khar'kov Province Mil—Revol Comt; Dec 1917, at 1st All-Ukr Congress of Soviets, elected member, Ukr Centr Exec Comt and Ukr Pop Secr for Trade and Ind; from Feb 1918 chm, Council of Pop Comr and Comr of Nat Econ, Sov Donetsk- Krivoy Rog Republ; member, CC, CP(B) Ukr (1918, 1919, 1920); fought in Civil War in Ukr; 1919 elected to Ukr Council of Pop Comr as Pop Comr of Agitation and Propaganda; 1919 at 8th RCP(B) Congress elected cand member, CC, RCP(B); summer 1919 Red Army comr for Chuguyev Sector; 1920 chm, Donetsk Province Exec Comt; 1920 at 9th RCP(B) Congress elected member, CC, RCP(B); attended 2nd and 3rd Comintern Congresses and 1st Trade-Union International (Profintern) Congess; 1920 headed Sov trade-union deleg to Norway, Germany and Czechoslovakia; Nov 1920-21 secr, Noscow RCP(B) Comt; then chm, CC, All-Russian Miners' Union; 1920-21 member, RSFSR Labor and Defense Council; member, All-Russian Centr Exec Comt; *Died*: 24 July 1921 killed while testing a flying boxcar; buried in Moscow's Red Square; a town, a number of workers' settlements, schools and streets in RSFSR, Ukr and Azer SSR have been named after him.

ARUTCHYAN, Mikhail Avetovich (1897-1961) Artist;stage designer; Pop Artist of Arm SSR from 1958; CP member from 1939; *Born*: 18 July 1897; *Educ*: 1918-19 studied at Higher Tech Art Workshops, Saratov; then studied in Berlin and Paris; *Career*: from 1919 stage designer; 1928-39 chief stage designer, Sundukyan Theater, Yerevan; 1939-49 chief stage designer, Spendiarov Opera and Ballet Theater; also designed for cinema; designed sets and costumes for some 150 shows; *Works*: sets and costumes for: "Pepo" (1935) and "David Bek" (1944), etc; for films: *Khas-push* (1928); *Shestnadtsatyy* (The Sixteenth) (1929); *Zamallu* (1930); *Severnaya raduga* (The Northern Rainbow) (1961); *Died*: June 1961.

ARUTYUNYAN, Khoren Ovanesovich (1891-1952) Arm actor; Pop Artiste of Azer SSR from 1943; *Born*: 1891; *Career*: from 1911 worked at Arm Theater, Tiflis, acting there (with intervals) until 1931; 1931-49 actor, Arm Theater, Baku; from 1949 at Stepanakert Arm Theater during the prime of his acting career; specialized in heroic and romantic parts; *Roles*: Pepo in Sundukyan's "Pepo"; Rustam in Shirvanzade's "Namus"; Miller in Schiller's *Kabale und Liebe*; Semyon in Akhumyan's "Wrath"; Godun in "Break-Up," etc; *Died*: 1952.

ARVATOV, Boris Ignat'yevich (1896-1940) Russian art historian and critic; CP member from 1918; *Born*: 3 Apr 1896 in Vilkovyshki (now in Poland), son of a lawyer; *Career*: 1912 commenced lit activity in Warsaw; fought in Civil War as comr on Polish front; was theoretician of *Proletkul't* cultural and educ org and *Lef* lit group; propounded concept of "productive art," demanding abolition of easel-painting and merger of art with the production of objects of material value; tried to combine principles of formalism with sociological study of art; championed theory of "leftist art" in painting; nervous illness resulting from war injury forced him to retire from lit activity in late 1920's; *Publ*: analysed poetic form in his articles "Mayakovsky's Syntax. An Attempt at the Formal Sociological Analysis of the Poem 'War and Peace'" (1923) and "Counter-Revolutionary Forms" (1923); *Iskusstvo i klassy* (Art and the Classes) (1923); "Nathan Altman" (1924); *Iskusstvo i proizvodstvo* (Art and Production) (1926); *Sotsiologicheskaya poetika* (Sociological Poetics) (1928); *Ob agitatsionnom i proizvodstvennom iskusstve* (Agitational and Productive Art) (1930); *Died*: 14 June 1940 in Moscow.

ARVATOV, Yuriy Ignat'yevich (1896-1937) Mil pilot; Civil War veteran; *Born*: 1896; *Career*: from 1920 in Red Army; 1920 fought against Pilsudski's army on Western Front as pilot, 9th Reconnaissance Air Detachment, 1924 fought against Basmachi in Turkestan as commander, 4th Air Detachment; 30 Sept 1924 flew from Termez to Kabul to deliver aircraft to Afghanistan; then commander of an air squadron and tech dir, "Deruluft" Sov-German Air Communications Soc; 1937 arrested by State Security organs; *Awards*: three Orders of the Red Banner; Hero of the Civil War; *Died*: 1937 in imprisonment; posthumously rehabilitated.

ARVELADZE, Pyotr Yakovlevich (1888-1919) Revolutionary; CP member from 1906 *Born*: 16 Jan 1888 in vil Chagani, Kutaisi Uyezd, son of a peasant; *Career*: 1906 joined Bolshevik Party and worked with M. Tsakheya, Stalin, Shaumyan, M. Azizbekov, Ordzhonikidze and others; member, Tiflis Bolshevik Comt; 1910 arrested and exiled from Caucasus for three years; 1910-13 revol propaganda among workers in Khar'kov; late 1913 drafted into Russian Army; after 1917 Feb Revol head, Bolshevik Faction, Aleksandropol' Sov of Workers, Soldiers and Peasants' Dep; Feb-July 1917 ed and publisher, newspaper *Rabochiy i soldat*; from Juliy 1917 chm, Aleksandropol' RSDRP(B) Comt; also managed publ of weekly *Pravda zhizni*; early Dec 1917 elected chm, Soldiers' Section, Aleksandropol' Sov of Workers, Soldiers and Peasants' Dep; shortly thereafter sent by Caucasian Kray Bolshevik Party Comt to Baku; from Jan 1918 asst to A. Dzhaparidze, chm, Baku Sov of Workers, Soldiers and Sailors' Dep; then secr to S. Shaumyan, chm, Baku Council of Pop Comr; after suppression of Sov regime in Baku in Aug 1918 evacuated with a group of officials to Astrakhan' and appointed polit comr, Lenin Regt, 2nd Red Army; fought against Gen Denikin at Astrakhan' and in Northern Caucasus; *Died*: 19 Mar 1919 killed in action.

ARYAMOV, Ivan Antonovich (1884-1958) Psycholgist; Dr of Pedag Sci; CP member from 1945; *Born*: 5 Feb 1884; *Educ*: 1912 grad Dept of Natural Sci, Fac of Physics and Mathematics, Moscow Univ; 1914 grad Med Fac, Moscow Univ; *Career*: from 1899 primary school teacher, Penza Province; from 1914 pedag and med work; 1938-57 prof and head, Chair of Psychology, Krupskaya Oblast Teachers' Training Inst; specialized in child psychology, psychology of teaching and school hygiene; *Publ*: coauthor, *Shkol'naya gigiyena* (School Hygiene) (1940); *Osobennosti detskogo vozrasta* (Characteristics of Childhood) (1953); *Died*: 30 Sept 1958.

ARZHANOV, Mikhail Aleksandrovich (1902-1960) Lawyer; Dr of Law from 1938; prof; corresp member, USSR Acad of Sci from 1939; CP member from 1924; *Born*: 14 Aug 1902; *Educ*: univ grad; 1930 completed postgrad studies; *Career*: from 1920 Komsomol and vigilante work against kulaks; then exec Party work in Donbass; from 1930 at Inst of Law, USSR Acad of Sci; prof, Acad of Soc Sci, CC, CPSU; specialized in theory of state and law; adhered to Party line in approach to legal problems;

during WW 2 served in Sov Army; *Publ: Gegel'yanstvo na sluzhbe germanskogo fashizma* (Hegelianism in the Service of German Fascism) (1933); *Nemetskiy fashizm - rezhim bespraviya i bezzakoniya* (German Fascism - A Regime of Lawlessness and Illegality) (1938); *Gosudarstvo i pravo v ikh sootnoshenii* (The Correlation of State and Law) (1960); *Awards*: Order of the Fatherland War, 1st Class; Order of the Red Star; Badge of Hon; medals; *Died*: 22 Oct 1960.

ARZHANOV, M. M. (1873-1941) Railroad eng; non-Party man; *Born*: 1873; *Career*: until 1918 trasport work; from 1918 exec posts with RSFSR Pop Comrt of Means of Communication; 1919-22 head, Centr Bd of Mil Communications, RSFSR Revol-Mil Council; 1921 member, Higher Transport Council; from 1922 chief of supply, Red Army; from 1924 inspector of railroad troops; late 1924 again exec posts with USSR Pop Comrt of Means of Communication; during last years of his life member, Learned Tech Council, USSR Pop Comrt of Means of Communication; *Awards*: Hero of Socialist Labor; *Died*: 1941.

ARZUMANYAN, Anushavan Agafonovich (1904-1965) Arm economist; member and acad secr, Dept of Econ Sci, USSR Acad of Sci from 1962; CP member from 1921; *Born*: 27 Feb 1904 in vil of Kavart, now Kafan Rayon, Arm SSR, son of a peasant; *Educ*: 1936 grad Inst of Red Prof in Moscow; *Career*: 1921-37 Komsomol and Party work in Arm; 1926-37 member, CC, CP Arm; 1937-41 rector, then snior lecturer, Yerevan Univ; 1941-45 polit worker in Sov Army at front; 1946-52 assoc prof and pro-rector, Azer State Univ; 1952-53 section head, 1953-56 dep dir, Inst of Econ, USSR Acad of Sci; from 1956 dir, Inst of World Econ and Int Relations, USSR Acad of Sci; 1958-62 corresp member, USSR Acad of Sci; from 1956 chm, Sov Comt for Solidarity with Afro-Asian Countries; from 1960 dep chm, All-Union Soc for the Dissemination of Polit and Sci Knowledge; dep, USSR Supr Sov of 1962 convocation; specialist on polit econ, world econ and int relations; many of his works, strictly adhering to orthodox Party line, deal with crisis of world capitalist system, struggle and prospects of world revol process, econ competition between two systems, nat liberation movements, etc; *Publ: K voprosu o klassovoy sushchnosti i metode teorii stoimosti angliyskoy klassicheskoy politicheskoy ekonomiki* (The Class Nature and Method of the Theory of Value in British Classical Political Economy) (1940); *Velikaya oktyabr'skaya revolyutsiya i krizis kapitalizma* (The Great October Revolution and the Crisis of Capitalism) (1957); *Sorevnovaniye dvukh mirovykh sistem i Kairskaya koferentsiya* (The Rivalry of the Two World Systems and the Cairo Conference) (1958); *Novyy etap obshchego krizisa kapitalizma* (The New Stage in the Gerneral Crisis of Capitalism) (1961); *Krizis mirovogo kapitalizma na sovremennom etape* (The Crisis of World Capitalism in its Current Stage) (1962); *Vazhnyye voprosy razvitiya mirovoy ekonomiki* (Major Aspects of the Development of the World Economy) (1962); *Problemy sovremennogo kapitalizma* (Problems of Modern Capitalism) (1963), etc; *Awards*: Order of Lenin; Order of the Red Banner of Labor; Order of the Red Banner; Order of the Red Star; Order of the Fatherland War; Badge of Hon; medals; *Died*: 18 July 1965 after a protracted illness.

ASAF'YEV (pen-name: GLEBOV, Igor'), Boris Vladimirovich (1884-1949) Music historian and composer; Dr of Arts; member USSR Acad of Sci from 1943; Pop Artiste of USSR from 1946 *Born*: 29 July 1884 in Petersburg; *Educ*: 1908 grad Fac of History and Philology, Petersburg Univ; 1910 grad composition class, Petersburg Conservatory *Career*: 1906 first compositions, including fairy-tale operas, ballets romances and piano pieces; from 1910 pianist-concertmaster, Ballet Company of Mariinskiy Theater, Petersburg; from 1914 music critic for Moscow weekly *Muzyka*; 1919-30 head, History of Music Section, Leningrad State Inst for History of the Arts; from 1925 prof, Leningrad Conservatory; in 1920's member, Assoc of Modern Music, and chm, "New Music Club," which popularized the works of modernist composers; 1943 moved to Moscow and headed Music Section, Inst for History of the Arts, USSR Acad of Sci; 1948 elected chm, USSR Composers' Union at 1st All-Union Composers' Congress; viewed music as a reflection of soc development processes; used folk themes in compositions; composed 27 ballets, 10 operas and three symphonies; *Publ: Instrumental'noye tvorchestvo Chaykovskogo* (Tchaikovsky's Instrumental Works) (1922); *Simfonicheskiye etyudy* (Symphonic Etudes); *Pyotr Il'ich Chaykovskiy - yego zhizn' i tvorchestvo* (Tchaikovsky, His Life and Works) (1922); "A.G. Rubinstein" (1929); "Glinka" (1947); *Cherez proshloye k budushchemu* (Through the Past to the Future); *Russkaya muzyka i slavyanstvo* (Russian Music and Slavdom); *Muzyka moyey rodiny* (The Music of my Fatherland); *Muzykal'naya forma kak protsess* (The Musical Form as a Process) (1930-47, etc; *Works*: ballets *Plamya Parizha* (The Flame of Paris) (1932); *Bakhchisarayskiy fontan* (The Fountain of Bakhchisaray) (1934); *Baryshnya-krest'yanka* (The Peasant Miss) (1946); operas *Krasnaya shapochka* (Little Red Riding-Hood); *Zolushka* (Cinderella) (1906); *Snezhnaya koroleva* (The Snow Queen) (1908); "Minin and Pozharskiy" (1936); *Kaznacheysha* (The Treasurer) (1937); music for Sophocles' "Oedipus Rex"(1918) and Marshak's *Dvenadtsat' mesyatsev* (A Twelvemonth) (1947); *Awards*: two Orders of Lenin; two Stalin Prizes (1943 and 1948); *Died*: 27 Jan 1949 in Moscow.

ASATIANI, Levan Nikiforovich (1900-1955) Lit historian and critic; *Born*: 12 July 1900 in Tiflis (now Tbilisi); *Educ*: 1927 grad Tbilisi Univ; *Career*: author of studies on classic Geo writers: D. Guramishvili, G. Orbeliani, A. Chavchavadze, etc; one of first historians of Geo lit to explore connections of Geo lit with Ukr, Russian and French lit; *Publ: Poetessy drevney Gruzii* (Poetesses of Ancient Georgia) (1936); *Zhizn' Akakiya Tsereteli* (The LIfe of Akakiy Tsereteli) (1940); *Grigoriy Orbeliani* (1946); *Pushkin i gruzinskaya literatura* (Pushkin and Georgian Literature) (1949); *Mayakovskiy i Gruziya* (Mayakovskiy and Georgia) (1951); *Literaturnyye svyazi gruzinskogo naroda s bratskimi narodami* (Literary Connections of the Georgian and Fraternal Peoples) (1955); *Beranzhe v gruzinkoy literature* (Beranger in Georgian Literature), etc; *Died*: 14 May 1955 in Tbilisi.

ASATIANI, Mikhail Mikhaylovich (1882-1938) Psychiatrist; prof from 1921; co-founder of sci psychiatry in Geo; *Born*: 1882; *Educ*: 1907 grad Med Fac, Moscow Univ; *Career*: after grad, intern at psychiatric clinic, above fac; later worked at neuropsychiatric sanitarium near Moscow and co-ed, journal *Psikhoterapiya*; from 1917 asst, Dept of Psychiatry, Moscow Univ; from 1921 head, Dept of Psychiatry, Tbilisi Univ; 1925 set up Asatiani Psychiatric Research Inst in Geo; supervised writing of more than 300 sci works; used theory of conditioned reflexes in psychiatry; research directed mainly to establishing physiological bases of psychic disorders with ephasis on psychasthenia; considered that phobias and other obsessive states derive from pathological conditioned reflexes and that psychoneuroses are a pure form of "psychic reactions," with the basic constructive link in the formation of any psychoneurotic complex of syptoms being the phenomenon of "psychophysiological plasticity"; being a constitutional type feature, psychophysiological plasticity enables an individual to transform "notions into somatic syptoms"; at any given moment the presence of a psychoneurotic symptom may be due to a unique activation of "traces of the association reflex type"; he reckoned that in psychoneuroses the fixation capacity in a state of emotion and reduced psychic tension has no need of a multiplicity of apposition processes - to form certain psychic links constituting pathological conditioned reflexes a single apposition is sufficient; *Publ*: 40 works on clinical and org psychiatry and psychotherapy; *Metod reproduktivnykh perezhivaniy v lechenii psikhonevrozov i rol' tak nazyva'emykh signal'nykh simptomov psikhonevrozov* (The Reproductive Experience Method in Treatment of Psychoneuroses and the Role of the So-Called Signal Symptoms of Psychoneuroses) (1926); *Uslovnyye refleksy v prilozhenii k simptomam psikhonevrozov* (Conditioned Reflexes in Apposition to Symptoms of Psychoneuroses) (1926); "Psychoneuroses" (in Geo) (1932); *Died*: 1938 in Tbilisi.

ASATKIN–VLADIMIRSKIY, A.N.(Party pseudonyms: Boris; Boris VLADIMIRSKIY) (1885-1937) Party official; CP member from 1904; *Born*: 1885; *Career*: Party work in Kostroma, Saratov and Vladimir; 1906-08 head, Vladimir Okrug RSDRP Comt; subjected to reprisals by Tsarist authorities; from May 1917 leading official, Ivanovo-Voznesensk Textile Workers' Union; from Sept 1917 member, Ivanovo-Voznesensk City RSDRP(B) Comt; 1918-22 exec posts with CC, RCP(B); 1924 instructor, then secr, CC, CP(B) Bel; 1925-28 secr, Vladimir Province CPSU(B) Comt; 1928-29 chm, Bd, All-Union Agric Bank; 1930-31 chm, Far Eastern Kray Exec Comt; from 1931 USSR trade rep in Tokyo; from 1933 exec Party work in Kiev; deleg at 5th RSDRP Congress; arrested by State Security organs; *Died*: 1937 in imprisonment.

ASEYEV, Nikolay Nikolayevich (1889-1963) Russian poet; *Born*: 10 July 1889 in L'gov, now Kursk Oblast, son of an insurance agent; *Educ*: studied at Moscow Business Inst and Philological Fac, Moscow State Univ; *Career*: 1913 had first verse published and met Mayakovskiy, who influenced his work; 1916-17 in Russian Army; 1918-22 worked for Sov org and contributed to underground Bolshevik newspaper in Vladivostok; 1922 founded the "Buffoon" lit soc and joined the "Centrifuge" group, to which Pasternak and Bobrov belonged; 1923 foundedthe "Left Front" lit group and published its journal *LEF*; 1924 fell into disfavor for his poem "Lyrical Digression" and the "gen decadence" of his works; also translated poets of Sov republ; many of his patriotic poems were set to music; *Publ*: collected verse *Nochnaya fleyta* (The Nocturnal Flute) (1914); *Zor* (1914); *Letorey* (1915); *Stal'noy solovey* (The Steel Nightingale) (1922); *Budyonnyy* (1922); *Sovet vetrov* (The Council of the Winds) (1923); *Semyon Proskakov* (1928); *Plamya pobedy* (The Flame of Victory) (1946); *Razdum'ya* (Meditations) (1955); *Stantsiya Vydumka* (Fable Station) (1960); *Awards*: Order of Lenin; Stalin Prize (1940); *Died*: July 1963.

ASFENDIAROV, Sadzhar Dzhafarovich (1889-?) Party and govt official; CP member from 1919; *Born*: 1889 Tashkent; *Educ*: 1912 grad Mil Med Acad; *Career*: in WW 1 captured in Eastern Prussia; returned to Russia after exchange of prisoners; 1917 member, Bukhara Oblast Sov of Workers and Soldiers' Dep; 1918 fought against the Emir of Bukhara; 1919-25 held a number of Party and govt posts in Turkestani Republ (exec secr, CC, CP Turkestan; member, Centr Asian Bureau, CC, CPSU(B), etc); 1926 Presidium member and dep secr, All-Russian Centr Exec Comt; *Died*: date, place and cause of death unknown.

ASHENBRENNER, Mikhail Yul'yevich (1842-1926) Revolutionary; leading functionary, *Narodnaya Volya* (People's Will) Party's mil org; col; *Born*: 1842 in Moscow, son of a mil eng; *Educ*: 1860 grad Moscow mil cadet school; *Career*: 1863 refused assignment to help suppress Polish uprising, resulting in his transfer from unit to unit and finally in his exile to Turkestan; 1870 returned to centr Russia; 1881, while in Odessa, recruited by V.N. Figner to join *Narodnaya Volya* and worked in its mil org; 1883 toured provincial mil-revol groups with the aim of coordinating their activities; task facilitated by his rank of col; 1884 sentenced to death by mil tribunal; sentece subsequently commuted to an indefinite term at hard labor, 20 years of which were spent in Schlisselburg Fortress; Sept 1904 released; until 1917 lived under police surveillance in Smolensk; *Publ: Voyennaya organizatsiya "Narodnoy Voli" i drugiye vospominaniya* (The Military Organization of "Narodnaya Volya" and Other Memoirs) (1924); *Died*: 1926 in Moscow.

ASHKHAMAF, Daud Aliyevich (1897-1946) Linguist and translator; *Born*: 1897; *Career*: specialized in Adyge linguistics; wrote first textbook and orthographic dictionary of the Adyge language; helped devise Cyrillic alphabet for Adyge; translated *Kratkiy kurs istorii VKP(b)* (A Short Course in the History of the CPSU(B); translated Pushkin, Lermontov, Tolstoy and Chekhov into Adyge; *Publ*: coauthor, *Kratkaya grammatika adygeyskogo yazyka* (A Short Grammar of the Adyge Language) (1930); *O printsipakh postroyeniya adygeyskoy ortografii* (The Structural Principles of Adyge Orthography) (1934); *Adygeyskaya ortografiya* (Adyge Orthography) (1938); *Kratkiy obzor adygeyskikh dialektov* (A Short Survey of Adyge Dialects) (1939); coauthor, *Grammatika adygeyskogo literaturnogo yazyka* (A Grammar of Literary Adyge) (1941); *Died*: 1946.

ASHMARIN, Nikolay Ivanovich (1870-1933) Turkologist and folklorist; founder of Chuvash linguistics; corresp member, USSR Acad of Sci from 1929; *Born*: 22 Sept 1870 in Yadrin; *Educ*: 1894 grad Lazarev Inst of Oriental Languages, Moscow; *Career*: specialized in Chuvash language and folklore and Tatar philology; wrote 17-vol Chuvash dictionary; recorded enough Chuvash oral lit to fill 30 vol; *Publ: Ocherk narodnoy poezii u chuvashey* (A Study of Chuvash Folk Poetry) (1892); *Materialy dlya issledovaniya chuvashskogo yazyka* (Research Material on the Chuvash Language) (1898); *Sbornik chuvashskikh pesen* (An Anthology of Chuvash Songs) (1900); *Ocherk literaturnoy deyatel'nosti Kazanskikh tatar-magometan za 1880-1895* (A Study of the Literary Activities of the Mohammedan Tatars of Kazan' in 1880-1895) (1901); *Bulgary i chuvashy* (The Bulgars and the Chuvash) (1902); *Opyt issledovaniya chuvashskogo sintaksisa* (Results of Research on Chuvash Syntax) (vol 1-2, 1903-23); *Slovar' chuvashskogo Yazyka* (A Chuvash Dictionary) (vol 1-17, 1903-50); *Osnovy chuvashskoy mimologii* (The Principles of Cuvash Mime) (1918); *Sbornik chuvashskikh poslovits* (An Anthology of Chuvash Proverbs) (1925); *Podrazhaniye v yaykakh Srednego Povolzh'ya* (Onomatopoeia in the Languages of the Central Volga Region) (1925); *Obshchiy obzor narodnykh tyurkskikh govorov goroda Nukhi* (A General Survey of Turkic Folk Pronunciations in the Town of Nukhi) (1926); *K voprosu o raspolozhenii chastey predlozheniya v tatarskom yazyke* (The Order of Parts of the Sentence in Tatar) (1927); *O morfologicheskikh kategoriyakh podrazhaniy v chuvashskom yazyke* (Morphological Categories of Onomatopoeia in Chuvash) (1928); *Died*: 26 Aug 1933.

ASHURKOV, Yevgeniy Dmitriyevich (1908-1961) Public health official; CP member; *Born*: 1908; *Educ*: 1930 grad Med Fac, Voronezh Univ; *Career*: asst, Chair of Skin and Venereal Diseases; 1935 defended cand thesis; 1941-48 in Sov Army; from 1948 head, Dept of Skin Venereal Diseases, RSFSR Min of Health; then head, Higher Med Institutions Bd, RSFSR Min of Health; 1950-51 RSFSR Dep Min of Health; from 1951 worked at Public Health Org Inst and Semashko Inst of Med History; for a number of years dir, Semashko Inst of Med History; from 1960 chief ed, newspaper *Meditsinskiy rabotnik*; simultaneously head, Chair of Public Health Org, 2nd Moscow Med Inst; wrote over 120 works on org and history of Sov public health organs; co-founder, pop sci journal *Zdorov'ye*; chm, Moscow Sci Soc of Med Historians; *Publ: Voprosy gigiyeny i sanitarii v trudakh V.I. Lenina* (Problems of Hygiene and Publik Health in V.I. Lenin's Works) (1957); *Voprosy zdravookhraneniya na zasedaniyakh Sovnarkoma RSFSR (1917-1922)* (Public Health Problems at RSFSR Council of People's Commissars Meetings /1917-1922/)(1957); *V.I. Lenin o sotsial'noy sushchnosti zdravookhraneniya* (V.I. Lenin's Views on the Social Significance of Public Health Work) (1957); *Voprosy okhrany zdorov'ya naroda v programmnykh dokumentakh partii* (Problems of Public Health Care in the Party's Programme Documents) (1959); *Leninskiye printsipy sovetskogo zdravookhraneniya* (Lenin's Principles in the Soviet Public Health Service) (1961), etc; *Died*: 1961.

ASKNAZIY, Abram Isakovich (1887-1937) Meteorologist and weather forecaster; *Born*: 1887; *Career*: from 1911 worked at Main Physical Observatory, where under B.N. Mul'tanovskiy he helped to develop first long-range weather forecasting system; after 1917 worked in Moscow for Main Mil Meteorological Bd, then at Moscow Weather Bureau, where he compiled and published first Sov weather forecasting manual (1928); one of founders of frontological method of weather forecasting; author of a number of research works on synoptic processes in USSR; *Publ: Sostavleniye sinopticheskikh kart i predskazaniye pogody* (Compilation of Synoptic Maps and Weather Forecasting) (1928); *Oblachnost' Kislovodska i Sedlovoy gory pri razlichnykh troposfericheskikh massakh* (Cloud Formation in the Area of Kislovodsk and Mount Sedlovaya With Various Tropospheric Masses) (1934); *K voprosu o letney tsirkulyatsii vozdukha na yevropeyskoy territorii SSSR* (Summer Air Circulation in the European USSR) (1934); *K voprosu o metodike dolgosrochnykh prognozov pogody* (Long-Range Weather Forecasting) (1936); *Died*: 1937.

ASKOCHENSKIY, Aleksey Konstantinovich (1871-1947) Russian opera singer (tenor) and teacher; *Born*: 3 Apr 1871; *Educ*: 1893 grad Moscow Philharmonic College; 1894-98 further training as a singer in Italy under A. Buzzi (Milan) and V. Vieggine (Naples); *Career*: as opera singer began in Italy where he stayed until 1901; then sang at provincial Russian theaters in Yekaterinoslav, Simbirsk, Tambov, Khar'kov, Odessa, etc; from 1907 in Moscow; Pop Center (1907-13), Zimin Opera Theater (1913-15), Bolshoy Theater (1915-19); his great experience of stagecraft and good schooling enabled him to give successful performances opposite leading European singers such as M. Galvani, Titta Ruffo, etc; from 1905 teaching work in Moscow; from 1940 prof, Moscow Conservatory; *Roles*: German and Vseslav in Verstovskiy's *Askol'dova mogila* (Askold's Grave); the Duke in "Rigoletto"; Almaviva in "The Barber of Sevilla," etc; *Died*: 19 Dec 1947.

ASKOL'DOV, Yakov Lazarevich (1893-1937) Mil commander; Civil War veteran; CP member from 1917; *Born*: 1893; *Career*: fought in WW 1; sentenced to death by field court martial, 1st Army Corps for revol activities among troops; Feb 1917 released from Bobruysk Fortress, where he had been held in solitary confinement; 1917 member, Army Comt, 2nd Army and Front Comt, Western Front; during 1917 Oct Revol member, Slutsk Revol Comt and commander of a revol detachment, 2nd Army; from 1918 in Red Army; 1918-20 mil comr, 1st Lith Rifle Div,

Daugavpils Fortified Region; mil comr, 10th Rifle Div; alternate member, Revol-Mil Sov, 3rd Army; acting commander, 3rd Army; 1920-24 dep commander, Khar'kov Mil Distr; chief inspector, Siberian and Far Eastern Republ Mil Training Establishments Bd; commander and mil comr, Main Mil Eng Bd; 1924 transferred from army to civilian admin work; during 1930's construction manager and dir, Siberian Metal Construction Plant, Novosibirsk, and "Bolshevik" Plant, Kiev; 1937 arrested by NKVD; *Awards*: two Orders of the Red Star; Hero of the Civil War; *Died*: 1937 in imprisonment; posthumously rehabilitated.

ASLANOV, Nikolay Petrovich (1877-1944) Russian actor; *Born*: 1877; *Educ*: 1905 grad Moscow Arts Theater School; *Career*: began stage career in provinces; 1906-09 in Voronezh, Nizhniy Novgorod, etc; then in Moscow: 1909-13 at Nezlobin Theater; 1913-14 at Free Theater; 1914-16 and 1938-43 at Chambo Theater; 1943-44 at Moscow Arts Theater; *Roles*: Polonius in "Hamlet"; Schluck in Hauptmann's "Schluck and Jau"; Petrovich in Ostrovskiy's *Ne bylo ni grosha, da vdrug altyn* (From Rags to Riches); Tokeramo in Lend'yel's *Tayfun* (Typhoon); Prince Myshkin in "The Idiot," based on Dostoyevskiy's novel; Don Rinaldo in Amfiteatrov's *Don Zhuan v Neapole* (Don Juan in Naples); Count di Riccamarina in Goldoni's "The Fan"; Khil' in Kuzmin's *Dukhov den' v Toledo* (Judgment Day in Toledo); Plyushkin in *Myortvyye dushi* (Dead Souls); Kharitonov in *Russkiye lyudi* (Russian People); *Died*: 1944.

ASMIK (real name: AKOPYAN), Takui Stepanovna (1879-1947) Actress; Pop Artiste of Arm SSR from 1935; *Born*: 21 Mar 1879 in Nakhichevan'; *Career*: from 1904 amateur shows in Tiflis; 1906 professional stage debut with Drama Soc; became very pop actress with audiences of workers; 1920 appointed by Revol Comt to head theater group touring rural areas and mil units; 1921 helped found 1st State Theater of Arm in Yerevan (now Sundukyan Theater); henceforth career linked to this theater; dep, Arm Supr Sov of 1938 convocation; *Roles*: Yarovaya in *Lyubov' Yarovaya* (1927); Shushan in Sundukyan's "Pepo" (1929); Anna in Gulakyan's "At Dawn" (1937); Vasilisa in *Na dne* (The Lower Depths) (1932); Melaniya in *Yegor Bulychyov i drugiye* (Yegor Bulychyov and Co) (1933); Shpanik in Shirvanadze's "Namus"; Anna Andreyevna in Gogol's *Revizor* (The Government Inspector) (1923); Kabanikha in *Groza* (The Storm) (1935); Ustian in Demirchyan's "Brave Nazar" (1924); also many film roles: Mariam in "Namus"; Agyul' in "Zangezur," etc; *Awards*: Hero of Labor (1936); *Died*: 23 Aug 1947 in Yerevan.

ASSUR, Leonid Vladimirovich (1878-1920) Mech eng; *Born*: 1878; *Educ*: 1901 grad Fac of Physics and Mathematics, Moscow Univ; 1906 grad Moscow Higher Tech College; *Career*: from 1910 instructor, Petersburg Polytech Inst; from 1918 prof, Petrograd Timber Inst; developed system of classification for plane hinge mechanisms; proposed classification of all mechanisms in phyla, classes, genera and species; developed "Assur group" of kinematically-linked plane mechanisms; *Publ: Analogi uskoreniya i ikh primeneniye k dinamicheskomu raschyotu ploskikh sterzhnevykh sistem* (Analogues of Acceleration and Their Application to the Dynamic Calculation of Plane Pivotal Systems) (1908); *Osnovnyye svoystva analogov uskoreniya v analiticheskom izlozhenii* (The Basic Properties of Analytically Arranged Analogues of Acceleration) (1909); *Issledovaniye ploskikh sterzhnevykh mekhanizmov s nizshimi parami s tochki zreniya ikh struktury i klassifikatsii* (A Study of Base-Coupled Plane Pivotal Mechanisms with Regard to Their Structure and Classification) (2 vol, 1913-15); *Died*: 19 May 1920.

ASTAKHOV, Fyodor Alekseyevich (1892-1966) Marshal of the Air Force; CP member from 1931; *Born*: 1892; *Educ*: 1923 grad mil acad course for senior commanders; 1929 grad advanced tech course for senior commanders at Zhukovskiy Mil Acad; 1939 grad courses for senior commanders, Gen Staff Acad; *Career*: from 1918 in Red Army; 1918-21 airman, squadron commander, commander of army air force, then commander, air force group on Eastern Front; 1923-24 commandant, Orenburg Flying School; 1924-25 commandant, Serpukhov Aerial Warfare School; 1925-41 senior commands in air force units and with the Air Force Training Establishments Bd; air force commander, Kiev Special Mil Distr; 1941 commander, Operational Air Force Group on Southwestern Front; 1942-47 head, Main Civil Aviation Bd, and dep commander, Sov Air Force; *Awards*: two Orders of Lenin; three Orders of the Red Banner; Order of Suvorov, 2nd Class; Order of Kutuzov, 1st Class; Order of the Red Star; medals; *Died*: 12 Oct 1966 after protracted illness; buried at Moscow's Novodevich'ye Cemetery.

ASTAKHOV, Nikolay Aleksandrovich (1875-1941) Stomatologist; Dr of Med from 1908; prof from 1921; *Born*: 1875; *Educ*: 1899 grad Imperial Mil Med Acad; *Career*: after grad, specialized in dentistry; from 1903 taught in dental schools; 1908 received doctor's degree for thesis *K voprosu o patogeneze zubnykh okolokornevykh kist* (The Pathogenesis of Peridental Cysts), a classic piece of research refuting P. Grawitz' theory of the origin of epithelial cells in dental granulomas being due to their penetration through the dental fistulas; 1921 founded Dept of Stomatology, Leningrad Postgrad Med Inst, which he headed until his death; attended all stomatology congresses and conferences; 1938 chm, Leningrad Soc of Stomatologists; wrote more than 40 works; coauthor of manual on orthopedic stomatology; *Died*: 1941 in Leningrad.

ASTAPENKA, Dmitriy Yemel'yanovich (1910-1944) Bel poet; *Born*: 1910 in vil of Kolesniki, Smolensk Province, son of a teacher; *Career*: 1926 first work published; *Publ*: collected poems *Na voskhod solntsa* (To the Sunrise) (1931); *Strane* (To the Country) (1931); *Vozmushchyonnyye* (The Indignant) (1932); cycle of poems on life of people in West Bel "Night on Negarelae Station" (1931); poem "Two Comrades" (1932); sci-fiction novel "Forces Released"; best work: poem "Edem" (1944; publ 1957); *Died*: 1944 killed in action during WW 2.

ASTANGOV (real name: RUZHNIKOV), Mikhail Fyodorovich (1900-1965) Stage and film actor; Pop Artiste of RSFSR from 1950 and of USSR from 1955; *Born*: 3 Nov 1900 in Warsaw; *Educ*: grad A.A. Matveyeva's Theater School; *Career*: 1918 stage debut; from 1920 at Chaliapin Studio; from 1923 at Komissarzhevskaya Theater-Studio; 1925-27 and 1930-41 at Theater of the Revol, Moscow; 1927-30 at Odessa and Kazan' theaters; 1943-45 at Moscow Sov Theater, Moscow; From 1945 member, Arts Council, Vakhtangov State Theater, Moscow; 1960 took part in acad session of Inst of Russian Lit, USSR Acad of Sci; *Roles*: stage roles: Gay in Pogodin's *Moy drug* (My Friend); Fyodor Talanov in Leonov's *Nashestviye* (Invasion); Matthias Klausen in Hauptmann's "Before Dawn"; Hamlet in Shakespeare's "Hamlet"; Chichikov in Gogol's *Myortvyye dushi* (Dead Souls); MacPherson in Simonov's *Russkiy vopros* (The Russian Question), etc; film roles: Prince Sumbatov in *Konveyer smerti* (The Conveyer Belt of Death) (1933); Kostya Kapitan in *Zaklyuchyonnyye* (The Prisoners) (1936); Arakcheyev in "Suvorov" (1941); Gen Ennecke in *Tretiy udar* (The Third Onslaught) (1948); Hitler in *Stalingradskaya bitva* (The Battle of Stalingrad) (1949), etc; *Awards*: three Stalin Prizes (1948, 1950 and 1951); two Orders of the Red Banner of Labor; *Died*: 20 Apr 1965.

ASTREYKA, Sergey Adamovich (1913-1937) Bel poet; *Born*: 1913 in vil Kolosovshchina, now Minsk Oblast, son of a peasant; *Educ*: from 1928 studied at Bel Teachers' Training Technicum and Bel State Univ, Minsk; *Career*: expelled from Bel Univ for "bourgeois nationalism"; worked for Inst of Language, Bel Acad of Sci; verse published in journals *Polymya* and *Chyrvonaya Belarus'*; his long poem "Bengalia" was banned; first verse collection (sent to press in 1933) was taken out of print; 1933 sentenced to five years exile in Irbit, Western Siberia; *Died*: 1937 in imprisonment; posthumously rehabilitated.

ASTVATSATUROV, Mikhail Ivanovich (1877-1936) Neuropathologist; Dr of Med from 1908; prof from 1916; *Born*: 1877; *Educ*: 1900 grad Natural Sci Dept, Petersburg Univ; 1904 grad Imperial Mil Med Acad; *Career*: as student worked in N.Ye. Vvedenskiy's physiology laboratory, where he received gold medal for work *O prodolzhitel'nosti perezhivaniya nerva* (Duration of Nerve Experience); 1904, after grad, retained in Dept of Mental and Nervous Diseases under V.M. Bekhterev; 1908-11 on assignment abroad; 1912 consultant, Warsaw Mil Hospital; 1914 consultant on nervous diseases, Nikolayevskiy Mil Hospital, Petersburg; 1916-36 head, Dept of Nervous Diseases, Leningrad Mil Med Acad; major research on study of motor and reflex disorders in the light of the theory of evolution; main theme of works that many symptoms of disease of the nervous system, including Babinski's sign, Rossolimo's Reflex and Wernicke-Mann's contracture, reflect the past evolution of the nervous system; various works on this problem reflect trend which provided basis for corticovisceral pathology later developed by K.M. Bykov; *Publ*: more than 100 works; *Oshibki v diagnostike i terapii nervnykh bolezney* (Errors in the Diagnosis and Treatment of Nervous Diseases); *Uchebnik po nervnym boleznyam* (Textbook on

Nervous Diseases) (8 ed); thesis *Klinicheskiye i eksperimental'no-psikhologicheskiye issledovaniya rechevoy funktsii* (Clinical and Experimental Psychological Study of the Speech Function) (1903); *Simptomatologiya porazheniya piramidnogo puchka s tochki zreniya ucheniya ob uslovnykh refleksakh* (Symptomatology of Disease of the Corticospinal Tract from the Standpoint of the Theory of Conditioned Reflexes) (1918); *Über biogenetische Grundlagen der Symptomatologie der Pyramidenbahnerkrankung* (1923); *Psikhoterapiya i psikhoanaliz* (Psychotherapy and Psychoanalysis) (1923); "On the Phylogenetic Origin of Deep Reflexes" (1925); coauthor, *Oshibki v terapii i diagnostike* (Errors in Therapy and Diagnosis) (1930); *O reperkussii i yeyo znachenii dlya ob'yasneniya nekotorykh klinicheskikh yavleniy* (Repercussion and Its Importance in Explaining Certain Clinical Phenomena) (1932); *Obzor sovremennogo polozheniya problemy boli* (Review of Carrent Theory on the Problem of Pain) (1935); *O psikhosomaticheskom vzaimootnoshenii pri zabolevaniyakh vnutrennikh organov* (Psychosomatic Correlation in Diseases of the Internal Organs) (1934); *Uchebnik nervnykh bolezney* (Textbook of Nervous Diseases) (1939); *Died*: 1936 in Leningrad.

ATA SALIKH (1908-1964) Turkm poet; Pop Shakhir (improvizing poet); blind from childhood and illiterate; CP member from 1941; *Born*: 1 June 1908 in Shortepe Aul, now in Turkm SSR; *Career*: lost eyesight at age three; 1930 first work published; poems published by mil newspaper *Kyzyl Koshun*, satirical journal *Tokmak*, etc; *Publ*: 1941-45 patriotic verse, "Poem - Orders for Young Warriors Bound for the Front"; "This is Lenin, You Know"; "Long Live the Unity of Peoples!"; "Taras Shevchenko"; "By the Grave of Taras Shevchenko"; "We Shall Defend Our Homeland!": "Moscow"; "Order to My Brother Mamed"; lyrical epic "With All My Heart"; *Izbrannyye stikhi* (Selected Verse) (1954); *Awards*: Order of the Red Banner of Labor; Order of the Red Star; Badge of Hon; *Died*: 26 Dec 1964.

ATABAYEV, Kankhizis Sardarevich (1887- ?) Turkm govt official; CP member from 1919; *Born*: 1887; *Educ*: 1907 grad teachers' seminary; *Career*: 1907-12 teacher; helped establish Sov regime in Centr Asia; asst chm, Transcaucasian Oblast Revol Comt; chm, Turkestani Council of Pop Comr; chm, Turkm Council of Pop Comr and member, Revol-Mil Council, Turkm Front; 1935 elected member and Presidium member, USSR Centr Exec Comt; *Died*: date and place of death unknown.

ATABEKOV, Grigoriy Iosifovich (1908-1966) Electr eng; Dr of Technol from 1942; prof from 1943; *Born*: 20 May 1908 in Yerevan; *Educ*: 1930 grad Electr Eng Fac, Tbilisi Polytech Inst; *Career*: until 1935 senior eng, Transcaucasian Oblast Power Bd; simultaneously instructor, Transcaucasian Inst of Ind; from 1935 senior eng, Moscow Oblast Power Bd, Thermoelectr Power Plant Design Agency, and Centr Electr Eng Research Laboratory; from 1938 assoc prof, Moscow Inst of Power Eng; from 1945 worked for Centr Research Laboratory, USSR Min of Power Plants; from 1946 head, Chair of Theoretical Principles of Electr Eng, Moscow Inst of Aviation; 1955-59 member, Electr Eng Expert Commission, Higher Certification Commission, USSR Min of Higher Educ; author of over 100 sci works and about 40 inventions in the field of electr eng; *Publ*: *Problema sozdaniya maloreleynykh zashchit v elektricheskikh sistemakh* (Problems of Low-Capacity Relay Protection in Electrical Systems) (1942); *Teoreticheskiye osnovy releynoy zashchity vysokovol'tnykh setey* (Theoretical Principles of Relay Protection in High-Voltage Networks) (1958); *Teoriya lineynykh elektricheskikh tsepey* (The Theory of Linear Electrical Circuits) (1960), etc; *Awards*: Stalin Prize (1950); *Died*: 16 June 1966 after a protracted illness.

ATAKHANOV, Ergash Isabayevich (1914-1967) Internist and hematologist; prof from 1951; Dr of Med from 1958; Hon Sci Worker of Uzbek SSR; corresp member, Uzbek Acad of Sci from 1960; corresp member, USSR Acad of Med Sci from 1961; *Born*: 1914 in Namangan; *Educ*: 1936 grad Tashkent Med Inst; *Career*: 1936-39 postgrad student, 1939-43 asst prof, 1943-49 assoc prof, 1949-51 prof, Hospital Therapy Clinic, Tashkent Med Inst; from 1951 head, Chair of Propaedeutics of Internal Diseases, Sanitary-Hygiene and Pediatric Facs, Tashkent Med Inst; sci consultant, Centr Asian Railroad; 1955-62 chm, Learned Med Council, Uzbek Min of Health; Presidium member, Bd, All-Union Soc of Therapists; chm, Uzbek Soc of Therapists; Plenum member, Higher Certification Commission; member, All-Union Problem Commission on the Physiology and Pathology of Digestive Organs; member, ed bd, *Meditsinskiy zhurnal Uzbekistana*; member, ed council, journals *Klinicheskaya meditsina* and *Referativnyy meditsinskiy zhurnal*; co-ed, 2nd ed, *Bol'shaya meditsinskaya entsiklopediya* (Large Medical Encyclopedia); from 1964 Bureau member, Dept of Clinical Med, USSR Acad of Med Sci; attended int med congresses in France, Italy, Japan, East Germany, etc; established the mechanism for the pathogenesis of leucoses, erythremia and pernicious anemia; studied changes in the hemopoietic system with diseases of the digestive organs; studied the pathology of the liver and metabolic processes in hot climates; devised a differential diagnosis for Addison-Burmer's disease; traced the genesis of hyperchrome megalocytic anemia in pregnant women; one of first Sov internists to use lipotropic drugs (choline, lipocaine, Vitamin B_{12} and folic acid) for treating chronic hepatitis, and protein hydrolysates for diseases of the internal organs; wrote some 80 works; *Publ*: cand thesis *Materialy k patogenezu i klinike razlichnykh form anemii* (Material on the Pathogenesis and Clinical Aspects of Various Forms of Anemia); doctor's thesis *Osnovnyye materialy po biofiziologii elementov krovi pri vazhneyshikh zabolevaniyakh krovetvornoy sistemy* (Basic Material on the Biophysiology of Blood Elements with the Main Diseases of the Hemopoietic System) (1948); *K patogenezu vazhneyshikh zabolevaniy krovetvornoy sistemy* (The Pathogenesis of the Main Diseases of the Hemopoietic System) (1952); coauthor, *Voprosy krayevoy patologii* (Problems of Regional Pathology); ed and coauthor, *Pathologiya kishechnika i sistema krovi* (The Blood System and Intestinal Pathology), etc; *Awards*: medal "For Labor Valor," etc; *Died*: 18 Nov 1967.

ATARBEKOV, Georgiy Aleksandrovich (1891-1925) Party and govt official; CP member from 1908; *Born*: 1891 in Echmiadzin, Erevan Province; *Educ*: 1910-11 studied at Moscow Univ; *Career*: 1917 Party work among soldiers in Aleksandropol' (now Leninakan); then member, underground Sukhumi Party Comt; fought to establish Sov regime; during Civil War head, Special Dept, Caspian-Caucasian Front, then Southern Front; 1920 chm, Rostov Revol Comt; head, Special Dept, Revol-Mil Council of Caucasian Front; then All-Russian Cheka plen in Baku; 1921 chm, Arm Provisional Revol Comt; then Transcaucasian Pop Comr of Posts and Telegraphs in Tiflis; Transcaucasian Dep Pop Comr of Workers and Peasants' Inspection; Presidium member, Transcaucasian Party Control Commission; *Died*: 22 Mar 1925 killed in plane crash.

AUEZOV, Mukhtar Omarkhanovich (1897-1961) Kaz writer; prof; Dr of Philolog; member, Kaz Acad of Sci from 1946; Hon Sci Worker of Kaz SSR from 1957; *Born*: 28 Sept 1897 in Chingistay Rayon, Semipalatinsk Uyezd; *Educ*: 1917 grad Semipalatinsk Teachers' Seminary; 1928 grad Leningrad Univ; 1930 completed postgrad studies at Centr Asian Univ; *Career*: from 1946 Inst of Language and Lit, Kaz Acad of Sci; dep, Kaz Supr Sov of 1955 and 1959 convocations; member, Sov Comt for the Defense of Peace; from 1960 Presidium member, Comt for Solidarity with Afro-Asian Peoples; 1960 member, deleg of Sov writers to USA; 1917 began lit career; wrote many research works on Kaz and Kir folklore and Kaz lit; *Publ*: coauthor and co-ed, "History of Kazakh Literature" (1948); plays: "Enlyk Kebek" (1917); "Karakoz" (1926); novelette "Hard Times" (1928); drama "For October" (1932); stories: "Shoulder to Shoulder" (1933); "Traces" (1935); "Steepness"; novels: "Abay" (1942-47); "The Road of Abay" (1952-56); monograph on the epic poem "Manas" (1948); translated into Kaz: Gogol's *Revizor* (The Government Inspector), Shakespeare's "Othello" and "The Taming of the Shrew" and K.A. Trenyo's *Lyubov' Yarovaya* (1936-44) *Awards*: Order of Lenin (1957); Stalin Prize (1949); Lenin Prize (1960); *Died*: 27 June 1961 in Moscow.

AUSSEM (GROMOV), Otto Khristianovich (1875- ?) Revolutionary; diplomat; CP member from 1906; *Born*: 1875, son of a teacher; *Career*: from 1893 in revol movement; active in student movement in Moscow; ran workers' clubs in Kiev; 1898 joined RSDRP; 1899 exiled for threee years to Vologda Province; after release, smuggled illegal lit into Russia; 1904 worked in Yuzovka; 1905 ed, journal *Kolokol* in Poltava; 1905 attended conference of Party mil org in Terioki; 1906-07 worked for RSDRP mil org in Warsaw under alias Aleksandr Sventoslavskiy; 1907 sentenced to hard labor for these activities; after 1917 Oct Revol govt and Party posts in Chita, Blagoveshchensk and Nikolayev-on Amur; fought with partisans in Far East; member, Mil-Revol Staff, Amur-Sakhalin Kray; 1920 chm, Nikolayev-Amur Oblast Comt, RCP(B); 1922 secr, Yalta Okrug Party Comt; from 1923 in Berlin and Prague on work for Ukr Pop Comrt of Educ; 1924 USSR consul-gen in Paris; *Died*: place, cause and date of death unknown.

AUSSEM, Vladimir Khristianovich (1879- ?) Revolutionary; govt official; CP member from 1917; *Born*: 1879, son of a teacher; *Career*: 1899 began revol career; 1899-1901 ran workers' clubs and took part in student movement in Khar'kov; 1901 joined RSDRP; 1901 exiled to Oryol but fled and went abroad, where he remained until 1904; 1904-06 worked for Soc-Democratic Menshevik-leaning org *Spilka* (Union) in Podol'sk Province; 1917 joined CP(B) Ukr; 1918 deleg at 1st Ukr Party Congress; spring 1918 Ukr Pop Secr of Finance; Nov 1918-20 fought in Civil War; during German occupation organized insurgent movement in centr zone; 1919 member, Revol-Mil Council, 8th Army; 1921-25 foreign postings: Ukr plen and counsellor, USSR plen mission in Berlin; then USSR plen in Vienna; from 1925 chm, Ukr Supr Sovnarkhoz; *Died*: place and date of death unknown.

AVANESOV (pseudonyms: Martirosov, Karpych), Varlaam Aleksandrovich (1884-1930) Govt official; RSDRP member from 1903; *Born*: 1884 in Karsk Oblast, son of a peasant; *Educ*: grad Med Fac, Zurich Univ; *Career*: 1901 joined revol movement; at first member, Arm Dashnaktsutyun Party, then Arm Soc-Democratic Party Gnchak; 1905 propaganda work among troops in Northern Caucasus; 1907-13 in Switzerland, secr, Joint RSDRP Group; 1914-17 RSDRP(B) work in Russia; from Mar 1917 member, Bolshevik faction, Moscow Sov, then Presidium member, Moscow Sov; Oct 1917 member, Petrograd Mil-Revol Comt; 1917-19 Presidium member and secr, All-Russian Exec Comt; 1919-30 Presidium member, All-Russian Exec Comt; 1919-20 Collegium member, State Control Commission; 1920-24 RSFSR Dep Pop Comr of Workers and Peasants' Inspection and Collegium member, All-Russian Cheka; 1924-25 USSR Dep Pop Comr of For Trade; from 1925 Presidium member, USSR Sovnarkhoz; 1922-27 member, USSR Centr Exec Comt; *Died*: 16 Mar 1930.

AVDEYEV, Arseniy Dmitriyevich (1901-1966) Theater historian; *Born*: 20 Nov 1901; *Educ*: 1927 grad Higher State Art History Courses, Inst of Art History, Leningrad; *Career*: 1926-38 teacher, actor and stage dir, Leningrad Young Playgoers' Theater, Leningrad Oblast Young Playgoers' Theater and New Young Playgoers' Theater; 1938-39 and 1955-65 assoc, Inst of Ethnography, USSR Acad of Sci; *Publ: Oktyabr' 1924 goda* (October 1924) (1926); *Opyt izucheniya spektaklya dlya detey* (Experience in the Study of Children's Shows) (1932); *Proiskhozhdeniye teatra* (The Origin of Theater) (1959); *Indoneziyskiy teatr "Vayang Kulit"* (The Indonesian "Vayang Kulit" Theater) (1966); *Teatral'noye iskusstvo i kino* (The Theater and the Cinema) (1965); *Teatr i kinematografiya* (Theater and Cinematography) (1966); *Teatral'noye iskusstvo* (The Art of the Theater) (1966); *Died*: 12 Nov 1966.

AVDEYEV, Nikolay Nikolayevich (Party alias: ALEKSEY) (1879-1926) Historian and pedag; CP member from 1905; *Born*: 1879 in Kozlov, son of a merchant; *Career*: from 1900 in revol movement; repeatedly arrested; from Dec 1905 member, Yekaterinoslav RSDRP Comt; Jan 1906 arrested and exiled to Siberia; fled to Moscow; 1906-07 propagandist, Moscow's Railroad Rayon RSDRP Comt; after 1917 Feb Revol member, RSDRP Internationalist Group; dep, Tyumen' Sov; ed, newspaper *Nash put'*; 1919 arrested by Kolchak's mil authorities and shot together with his wife O. Dilevskaya; Dilevskaya was killed but Avdeyev, seriously wounded, managed to escape; subsequently worked for Commission for Collation and Study of Materials on Party History and Oct Revol, CC, CPSU(B); Collegium member, Centr Archives Bd; co-founder and active member, Soc of Marxist Historians; wrote a number of works on Party history; *Publ: Revolyutsiya 1917 goda (Khronika sobytiy)* (1917 Revolution/A Chronicle of Events/) (1923), etc; *Died*: 18 Apr 1926.

AVENARIUS, Georgiy Aleksandrovich (1903-1958) Cinema historian; *Born*: 30 Sept 1903; *Educ*: 1926 grad Odessa Acting Studio, Soc of Russian Cinema Fans; 1929 grad Cameraman Fac, Odessa Film Technicum; *Career*: 1926-27 bit parts in films; from 1929 asst cameraman; 1932-36 lectured on history of Sov and world cinematography at Kiev Film Inst; from 1936 lectured on history of for cinema at All-Union State Inst of Cinematography, Moscow; co-founder, USSR State Film Fund and from 1948 head of its For Dept; for a number of years worked on *Istoriya mirovogo kino* (A History of World Cinema), left unfinished at his death; trained many film historians; gave pop lectures on history of cinema; *Publ: K metodologii opredeleniya kinozhanrov* (Methods of Determining Film Genres); *Montazhnyye teorii Eyzenshteyna* (Eisenstein's Montage Theories); *K istorii razvitiya ukrainskoy komedii* (The History of the Development of Ukrainian Comedy); *Problema khudozhestvennogo obraza v fil'makh A.P. Dovzhenko* (The Artistic Image in A.P. Dovzhenko's Films); *Zhan Renuar* (Jean Renoir) (1939); articles: "An Outline History of Foreign Cinema. Griffiths and Chaplin" (1939); "The Social Film in America" (1940); "What Hollywood Purveys in Europe" (1948); "Gogol on Foreign Screens" (1952); "L.N. Tolstoy's Works on the Foreign Screen" (1953); "The Latin American Cinema in Its Struggle with Hollywood" (1954); "Chaliapin Before the Camera" (1955); "The Modern American Cinema in the Service of the Warmongers" (1955); "English Cinematography and Its Proponent Alexander Korda" (1956); "Bernard Shaw and the Film-Maker" (1956); "The Early Period of Charles Spencer Chaplin's Work" (1956); "Charles Spencer Chaplin. A Study of the Early Period of His Work) (1957), etc; *Died*: 18 July 1958.

AVERBAKH, Mikhail Iosifovich (1872-1944) Ophthalmologist; prof from 1912; Dr of Med from 1900; member, USSR Acad of Sci from 1939; Hon Sci Worker of RSFSR from 1933; *Born*: 29 May 1872 in Mariupol'; *Educ*: 1895 grad Med Fac, Moscow Univ; *Career*: 1895-1900 retained at eye diseases clinic in Moscow Univ, where he worked under Prof A.A. Kryukov; 1900-03 intern, 1904-35 chief physician, Alekseyev City Eye Hospital, Moscow; dir, Gel'mgol'ts Centr Ophthalmological Inst after its formation from above hospital; 1904-11 lecturer, eye clinic, Moscow Univ; from 1912 founder and head, Dept of Eye Diseases, Med Fac, Moscow Higher Women's Courses (from 1918 2nd Moscow Univ), where he continued to head this dept and was dir of eye clinic till his death; 1925 this eye clinic was named for him; 1931-44 founder and head, Dept of Eye Diseases, Centr Postgrad Med Inst, Moscow; co-founder, 1911-24 Presidium member, Moscow Soc of Ophthalmologists; 1924 formed Moscow Ophthalmological Soc, uniting ophthalmologists of Moscow City Dept of Health; took part in congresses of Pirogov Soc, int ophthalmological congresses and work of State Learned Med Council; for many years exec ed, journal *Arkhiv oftal'mologii* later renamed *Vestnik oftal'mologii*; founder and exec ed, journal *Voprosy oftal'mologicheskoy optiki*; chm, All-Union and Moscow Soc of Ophthalmologists; dep, Moscow City Sov; formed own school of ophthalmologists specializing in practical clinical work and its soc importance which produced M.L. Krasnov, N.A. Pletneva, P.Ye. Tikhomirov and others; developed and introduced new eye operations, including operation for detached retina, dacryocystorrhinostomy, opticociliary resection, and operation for pulsating exophthalmus; special prize named for him awarded annually by Presidium of USSR Acad of Med Sci to author of best work on ophthalmology; *Publ*: more than 100 works; doctor's thesis *K dioptrike glaz razlichnykh refraktsiy* (Dioptrics of Eyes with Double Refraction) (1900); *Kon'yunktivit Parinaud* (Parinaud's Conjunctivitis) (1909); *Problema proiskhozhdeniya klinicheskoy refraktsii glaza* (Origin of Clinical Refraction of the Eye) (1925); *Soust'ye mezhdu sleznym meshkom i nosom kak metod radikal'nogo lecheniya dakriotsistitov* (Anastomosis Between the Tear-Sac and the Nose as a Radical Method of Treating Dacryocystitis) (1926); *Promyshlennyye glaznyye povrezhdeniya i osnovy bor'by s nimi* (Industrial Eye Injuries and Principles of Combatting Them) (1928); *Optikotsiliarnaya rezektsiya* (Opticociliary Resection) (1934); *Oftal'mologicheskiye ocherki* (Essays in Ophthalmology) (1940, 1949); *Glavneyshiye formy izmeneniy zritel'nogo nerva* (Major Forms of Lesion of the Optic Nerve) (1944); *Povrezhdeniya glaz i okruzhayushchikh ikh chastey* (Injuries of the Eyes and Surrounding Parts) (1945); *Awards*: Stalin Prize (1943); *Died*: 29 July 1944 in Moscow.

AVERCHENKO, Arkadiy Timofeyevich (1891-1925) Russian writer and humorist; *Born*: 1881, son of a merchant; *Career*: worked as clerk; from 1908 ed, humorous journal *Satirikon*, then *Novyy satirikon*; contributed to journals *Zhurnal dlya vsekh, Utro, Zritel'*, etc; his humorous stories ridiculed everyday life and Philistinism; after 1917 Oct Revol emigrated to Paris, whence he ridiculed the Bolshevik Revol in Russia; *Publ: Rasskazy* (Stories) (3 vol, 1909-10); collected works *Razvorochenny muraveynik* (Anthill Disturbed) (emigre ed entitled *Dyuzhina nozhey v spinu revolutsii* /A Dozen Knives in the Back for the Revolution) (1927); *Yumoristicheskiye rasskazy* (Humorous Stories) (1964), etc; *Died*: 1925.

AVERIN, Vasiliy Kuz'mich (1885-1945) Party and govt official; CP member from 1904; *Born*: 1885, vil Letoshniki, Roslavl' Uyezd, Smolensk Province, son of a peasant; *Career*: worked in Donets

Basin coal mines; from 1900 apprentice molder, casting shop, Bryansk Plant in Yekaterinoslav; 1905 member, plant's Bolshevik Comt; 1914 factory worker in Kamensk and Amur-Nizhnedneprovsk; from 1915 exiled to Verkholensk; from Feb 1917 metalworker at Bryansk Plant in Yekaterinoslav and member, Yekaterinoslav RSDRP(B) Comt; 1917 at 2nd Party Congress elected member, All-Russian Exec Comt; Dec 1917 appointed member, All-Russian Cheka; during Civil War from 1918 chm, Yekaterinoslav Sov; member, Provisional Workers and Peasants' Govt of Sov Ukr and All-Ukr Centr Exec Comt; head, Polit Dept, Kursk Forces Group; member, Revol-Mil Council, 2nd Army and chm, Revol-Mil Council, Yekaterinoslav Fortified Area; drew up special plan of campaign against Denikin and Petlyura's forces for Ukr Labor and Defense Council and CC, CP(B) Ukr; then exec govt, econ and admin work; 1923 chm, Exec Comt, Volhynian, Khar'kov and Odessa Province Sov; from 1923 exec posts in aviation ind, then railroad and water transport; member, CC, CP(B) Ukr; member USSR Centr Exec Comt; wrote his memoirs and a number of articles about revol movement in the Ukr; exiled to Yakutsk; *Died*: 1945 in imprisonment; posthumously rehabilitated.

AVETISYAN, Unan Makichevich (? -1943) Sergeant; Komsomol member; asst platoon leader in an infantry unit; *Born*: Date of birth unknown; *Career*: 16 Sept 1943, while the Sov army was breaking through the German defenses in the Kuban', ordered his platoon to pin down an enemy pillbox while he crawled to its gun port to knock it out with hand grenades; altough wounded, managed to reach the gun port an block it with his body, thus ensuring the success of the attack; 16 May 1944 posthumously proclaimed Hero of the Soviet Union; permanently registered on the roll of the unit's 1st Company in which he was serving at the time of his heroic act; his picture appeared on a postage stamp issued in 1963; *Died*: 16 Sept 1943 killed in action in Verkhne-Bakanskiy Rayon, Krasnodar Kray.

AVETYAN, Grigor Karapetovich (1870-1946) Actor; Pop Artiste of Arm SSR from 1935; *Born*: 20 Jan 1870; *Career*: 1888 stage debut; formed drama companies which toured Russia (Tiflis, Baku and other Transcaucasian towns), Turkey and Rumania; from 1923 actor, 1st Arm State Theater, Yerevan (now Sundukyan Theater); translated a number of plays into Arm, including Gorky's *Na dne* (The Lower Depths); also worked as stage dir; wrote his memoirs "Forty-Five Years on the Armenian Stage"; *Roles*: Giko in Sundukyan's "Pepo"; Sagatel and Tsiplitsatur in Shirvanzade's "For Honor" and "Namus"; Manuk-aga in Paronyan's "Highly Esteemed Beggrs"; Luka in Gorky's *Na dne* (The Lower Depths); Bobchinskiy in Gogol's *Revizor* (The Government Inspector); Bublik in Gorky's *Platon Krechet*; Gornostayev in *Lyubov' Yarovaya*; film roles in: "Pepo"; "Zangezur," etc; *Died*: 15 May 1946.

AVILOVA, Mariya Aristarkhovna (1898-1964) Party official; CP member from 1916; *Born*: 1898; *Career*: Feb 1917 member, Petrograd Side Rayon Party Comt; deleg, 2nd Congress of Petrograd Party Orgs; Sept 1917 secr, Petrograd Side Rayon Party Comt; during 1917 Oct Revol worked for Mil Revol Comt mustering Red Guards units; May 1918-Nov 1919 worked for Lenin's secretariat; 1921-22 with Sov plen mission in Czechoslovakia; 1923 assoc, Acad of Communist Educ; then worked for Small Council of Pop Comr; 1924-39 assoc, Inst of Marx and Lenin, CC, CPSU(B); 1938-41 pensioner; 1941-44 assoc, Inst of History, USSR Acad of Sci; from 1946 again pensioner; *Died*: 19 Sept 1964.

AVILOV, Boris Vasil'yevich (1874-1938) Lawyer; politician; CP member 1904-17; *Born*: 1874 son of an official; *Educ*: grad univ; *Career*: lawyer by profession; as a student, joined revol movement; twice banished from Moscow for participating in student polit movement; after grad univ did revol work in Petersburg, Astrakhan', Kaluga, Baku and Khar'kov, where he played an active part in the local Soc-Democratic org and preached Bolshevik line rallies and assemblies; lit head, Khar'kov *Vperyod* (Forward) Group; Group's rep at 3rd RSDRP Congress, where he took a reconciliationist stand toward the Mensheviks; during 1905 Revol member, Struggle Comt; helped to organize and direct armed revolt in Khar'kov; 1908 acquitted before a court martial on charges of membership of the Bureau of Mil Revol Orgs; 1910 exiled to Vologda Province; then lived in Khar'kov; Council member, Congress of Miners; worked for various periodicals, including newspaper *Pravda*; active in State Duma election campaigns; 1913-14 head, Soc-Democratic faction of Bolshevik students; after 1917 Feb Revol member, Petrograd RSDRP Comt; Apr 1917 quit Bolsheviks and sided with platform of Menshevik newspaper *Novaya zhizn'*; Aug 1917 joined Soc-Democrat Internationalists; early 1918 resigned from Internationalist CC and then completely abandoned politics; until 1928 worked for Centr Statistical Bd; from 1929 with RSFSR Gosplan; then with USSR Pop Comrt of Means of Communication; arrested by State Security organs; *Died*: 1938 in imprisonment.

AVILOV, Mikhail Ivanovich (1882-1954) Russian painter; specialist in battle scenes; Hon Art Worker of RSFSR; Pop Artist of RSFSR from 1953; member, USSR Acad of Arts from 1947; *Born*: 18 Sept 1882; *Educ*: 1904-13 studied battle painting under Rubo and Samokish at Petersburg Acad of Arts; *Career*: during WW 1 contributed to illustrated mil journals; from 1923 active member, Assoc of Artists of Revol Russia; in 1920's painted famous pictures of feats of Red Army and partisans in Civil War, including "Siberian Partisans" (1926), "Surrender of Kolchak's Troops at Krasnoyarsk" (1926), "The First Cavalry Army Penetrating the Polish Front in 1920" (1928), etc; his consistent skill and realism placed him among the foremost Sov battle artists; his painting "Comrade Stalin Visiting the First Cavalry Army in 1919" (1933) became especially famous; painted many pictures of life in Sov army in peacetime, including "On Maneuvers" (1934) and "The Capture of a Diversionary" (1937); during WW 2 painted a vast canvas entitled "The Duel Between Peresvet and Chelubey" (1943), which symbolized struggle of Russian people against Tatars; from 1920 also taught painting; *Awards*: Stalin Prize (1946); *Died*: 14 Apr 1954.

AVILOV, Nikolay Pavlovich (Party pseudonyms: Gleb N; Glebov) (1887-1942) Revolutionary; CP member from 1904; *Born*: 1 Oct 1887, son of a worker; *Career*: Party work in Kaluga, Moscow, Petersburg and the Urals; several times arrested and exiled; studied at Party School in Bologna but did not sympathize with Bolshevik *Vperyod* (Forward) faction; 1913-14 contributed to *Pravda*; 1913 attended "Summer" RSDRP CC Conference with Party representatives in Poronino; after 1917 Feb Revol member, Exec Commission, CC, RSDRP(B); worked for Petrograd Trade-Union Bureau, then with Exec Comt, All-Union Trade-Union Council; Apr 1917 at RSDRP(B) Conference elected cand member, CC; after 1917 Oct Revol RSFSR Pop Comr of Posts and Telegraphs in first Sov govt; May 1918 comr, Black-Sea Fleet; then Presidium member and secr, All-Union Trade-Union Council; Ukr Pop Comr of Labor; from 1922 Party work in Petrograd; 1924-25 chm, Leningrad Province Trade-Union Council and Presidium member, Leningrad Exec Comt; 1925 sided with "New Opposition"; 1927, after 15th Party Congress, recanted his errors; member, Sov trade-union deleg at London talks with Trade-Union Council; elected member, USSR Centr Exec Comt of 6th and 7th convocations; from 1928 construction chief, then dir, agric machine-building plant in Rostov-on-Don; arrested by State Security organs; *Died*: 13 July 1942 in imprisonment; posthumously rehabilitated.

AVINOVITSKIY, Yakov Lazarevich (? -1937) Corps comr; helped to organize Sov chemical troops; *Born*: date of birth unknown; *Career*: 1918-19 mil comr of training establishments for Western Front; 1919-22 mil comr, Red Army training establishments; from 1932 first head of newly-established Red Army Mil Chemical Defense Acad; 1937 arrested by NKVD; *Died*: 1937 in imprisonment; posthumously rehabilitated.

AVKSENT'YEV, Nikolay Dmitriyevich (1878-1943) Politician; leading functionary Socialist-Revol Party; *Born*: 1878; *Career*: 1905 member, Petersburg Sov of Workers' Dep; 1907-17 abroad; right-wing member, CC, Socialist-Revol Party; supported struggle by legal methods and rejected terrorism; during WW 1 contributed to patriotic publ *Za rubezhom* and *Novosti*; co-ed, Paris periodical *Prizyv*; 1917 member, Exec Comt, Petrograd Sov of Workers' Dep; chm, All-Russian Sov of Peasants' Dep; July-Aug 1917 Min of Internal Affairs in Provisional Govt; Oct 1917 chm, Pre-Parliament; opposed 1917 Oct Revol and Sov regime; 1918 helped organize struggle against Sov regime in Volga area and Siberia; member, Ufa Directorate (All-Russian Provisional Govt); from late 1918 emigre; *Died*: 1943.

AVKSENT'YEVSKIY, Konstantin Alekseyevich (1890-1941) Russian mil commander; CP member from 1917; *Born:* 30 Sept 1890 in vil Staryy Kunozh, Vologda Province, son of an office worker; *Educ:* grad Tot'ma Teachers' Training Seminary; 1915 grad Vladimir Infantry School; 1923 grad Red Army advanced commanders' courses; *Career:* until 1914 vil teacher; from 1914 private, then officer in Russian Army; 1917 assisted Bolshevik coup in Torzhok and helped establish Sov rule in Vologda Province; 1918-19 commanded 1st Vologda Communist Company; mil comr, Vologda Oblast, and commandant Vologda Garrison; mil comr, Yaroslavl' Okrug; Apr – Aug 1919 commander, 4th Army on Eastern Front; from Aug 1919 member, Revol-Mil Council of Southern Group on Eastern Front, then of 1st Army; from Jan 1920 dep commander, Turkestani Front; from Apr 1920 commander, Transvolga Mil Distr and commander, 2nd Revol Labor Army; Aug-Oct 1920 commander, 6th Army on Southeastern and Southern Front; from Oct 1920 dep commander, Southern Front; from Dec 1920 dep commander, Ukr and Crimean Armed Forces; 1920 directed suppression of anti-Sov revolt in Volga area; 1921-22 helped crush forces of Ukr anarchist leader Makhno; July-Aug 1922 Min of War and commander in chief, Far Eastern Republ; 1923-25 commander, 8th and 6th Rifle Corps; dep commander, Ukr and Crimean Armed Forces; 1925-28 commander, Turkestani Front; commander, Centr Asian Mil Distr; directed operations against Basmachi; 1928-31 commander, Red-Banner Caucasian Army; Apr 1931 pensioned on med grounds; for a while admin posts with Centr Union of Consumer Soc; *Awards:* two Orders of the Red Banner; Order of the Red Banner of Labor; *Died:* 2 Nov 1941.

AVLOV, Grigoriy Aleksandrovich (1885-1960) Stage dir; theater critic; drama teacher; Hon Artiste of RSFSR from 1941; *Born:* 25 Nov 1885; *Career:* organized amateur dramatic groups; wrote books and articles on amateur dramatics; from 1956 head, Chair of Art History and Amateur Art Work, Leningrad Higher Trade-Union School, All-Union Centr Trade-Union Council; *Publ: Kak postavit' spektakl' v derevne* (How to Stage a Village Show) (1926); *Klubnyy samodeyatel'nyy teatr* (Club Amateur Dramatics) (1930); *Teatral'nyye agit-prop-brigady v klube* (Agitation and Propaganda Theatrical Teams in Clubs) (1931); *Died:* 6 Feb 1960.

AVRAAMOV, Arseniy Mikhaylovich (1886-1944) Musicologist; folklorist; composer; *Born:* 22 June 1886 in Novocherkassk; *Educ*: 1906-09 studied at Musical Drama College, Moscow Philharmonic Soc; *Career*: worked in Novocherkassk; contributed to Petersburg and Moscow music journals; 1914-18 rejected mil service, fled abroad, and worked as ship's stoker, circus artiste, etc; 1918-19 fought in Civil War; worked for Pop Comrt of Educ; 1919 head, Kazan' Art Dept; directed Russian choirs in schools and mil units; 1919 returned to Moscow; 1920-21 taught theory (according to his own 48-tone musical system) at Rostov-an-Don Conservatory; 1922 collected Dag and Kabardian songs and arranged Don Cossack songs; 1923-26 assoc, State Inst of Musical Sci; 1926 defended his thesis on *Universal'naya 48-tonovaya sistema* (A Universal 48-Tone System); 1927 demonstrated his system at Frankfurt-on-Main; 1930-31 conducted an optional course at Rostov Conservatory on his tone system; helped produce sound films: *Plan velikikh rabot* (A Plan of Great Works); *Kem byt'* (Who to Be); *Gibel' sensatsii* (The End of a Sensation); 1932-33 head, Recorded Sound Laboratory, Research Inst of Cinematography Comt; 1935 musical specialist, 1935-41 researcher at above inst; worked for Kabardian nat theater in Nal'chik; helped found Kabardian nat song and dance ensemble; 1941-43 artistic dir, A. Yarkov's Russian Folk Choir; *Works:* symphonic works: "Kabardian Dances" (1936); two fantasias on Kabardian themes; overture "Aul Batyr" (1940); brass band works: "March on Kabardian Themes" (1936); instrumental works on Kabardian themes: "Fantasia," "Uch," "Zhankidesh," etc; unaccompanied Kabardian choral work; music for shows: A. Shogentsukov's "Karigot" (1936); Shavtanov's "Aul Batyr" (1940); choral arrangements of Russian folk songs; recorded songs of North Caucasian peoples, including more than 300 Kabardian songs; *Died:* 19 May 1944 in Moscow.

AVRANEK, Ul'rikh Iosifovich (1853-1937) Czech operatic choirmaster and conductor; Pop Artiste of RSFSR from 1932; *Born:* 26 Dec 1853 in vil Klucence, Bohemia; *Educ:* 1870 grad cello and theory classes, Prague Conservatory; *Career:* played with German opera orchestra in Prague; from 1874 cellist and conductor in Russia; performed with P.M. Medvedev's opera company in Kazan', Nizhniy Novgorod, Saratov, Samara, Yekaterinburg, Khar'kov, etc; from 1882 for more than 50 years conductor and chief choirmaster, Bolshoy Theater, Moscow; from 1883 taught music; *Works:* helped produce and conduct operas: *Knyaz' Igor'* (Prince Igor) (1898); *Noch' pered rozhdestvom* (The Night Before Christmas) (1898); *Motsart i Sal'yeri* (Mozart and Salieri) (1901); Rubinshteyn's *Makavei* (The Maccabaeans) (1889); "The Magic Flute" (1900); Massenet's "Werther" (1907); Verstovskiy's *Askol'dova mogila* (Askold's Grave) (1883), etc; *Awards:* Hero of Labor (1934); *Died:* 12 Aug 1937 in Moscow.

AVRAMOV (ABRAMOV), R.P. (1882-1937) Bulgarian and Russian revolutionary; member, Bulgarian Soc-Democratic Party from 1898; CP member from 1925; *Born:* 1882; *Career:* 1900 member, Marxist club in Geneva; 1901-02 worked for Berlin *Iskra* Promotion Group; after 2nd RSDRP Congress became a Bolshevik; secr, Bolshevik For Org Comt; directed transport of illegal Party lit; 1904 helped organize Berlin Bolshevik group; 1905 foreign agent of CC, RSDRP(B); member, Econ Commission, CC, RSDRP(B); arranged custody of Party records after Lenin's departure for Russia in Oct 1905; after Oct Revol worked for Sov trade establishments abroad; 1930-37 manager, "Khlebostroy"/Grain Trust; arrested by State Security organs; *Died*: 1937 in imprisonment.

AVROV, Dmitriy Nikolayevich (1890-1922) Mil commander; CP member form 1918; *Born*: 1890; *Career*: during WW1 ensign Russian Army; after 1917 Oct Revol helped organize Red Army; comr, 1st Army; 1918 fought on Eastern Front; then commandant, Kazan' and Kursk Fortified Areas; 1919 commander, Petrograd Fortified Area; then chief of Petrograd's internal defenses; 1920-21 commander, Petrograd Mil Distr; helped crush Kronstadt Mutiny; from Aug 1921 civilian work; *Awards:* Order of the Red Banner; *Died:* 1922; buried on Field of Mars, Leningrad.

AVTOKRATOV, Dmitriy Mikhaylovich (1868-1953) Veterinary anatomist; Hon Sci Worker of RSFSR; Dr of Veterinary Sci; prof; *Born:* 1868; *Educ:* grad Kazan' Veterinary Inst; *Career:* 1895-96 veterinarian on Vologda-Arkhangel'sk Railroad; 1896-97 active in campaign against cattle murrain in Transcaucasia; 1898-1907 asst dissector under Prof L.A. Tret'yakov, Chair of Anatomy of Domestic Anamils, Kazan' Veterinary Inst; 1900 defended master's thesis; 1903 attended 1st All-Russian Congress of Veterinarians, Petersburg; from 1905 assoc prof, of ophthalmology, Kazan' Veterinary Inst; 1908-15 assoc prof, Chair of Normal Anatomy of Domestic Animals, Warsaw Veterinary Inst; 1916-35 head and prof, Chair of Normal Anatomy of Domestic Animals, Novocherkassk Zooveterinary Inst; 1935-37 head, Chair of Normal Anatomy of Domestic Animals, Moscow Zootech Inst of Poultry-Raising; 1937-41 head, Chair of Normal Anatomy of Domestic Animals, Red Army Mil Veterinary Acad; 1941-43 head, Chair of Normal Anatomy of Domestic Animals, Moscow Zooveterinary Inst; 1943-52 head, Chair of Normal Anatomy of Domestic Animals, Moscow Chemical Technol Inst of Meat and Dairy Ind (now Moscow Technol Inst of Meat and Dairy Ind); wrote over 100 works on anatomy and histology of domestic animals, pharmacology and ophthalmology; studied variability of arterial system, arterial pattern in extremities, morphology of the vegetative nervous system of domestic animals and poultry, etc; *Publ: K voprosu o deystvii nekotorykh alkaloidov opiya (morfiya, narkotina,. apomorfina) i atropina na ptits* (The Effects of Some Alkaloids of Opium (Morphium, Narcotine, Apomorphine) and Atropine on Poultry) (1900); *Konspekt lektsiy po ekster'yeru* (A Summary of Lectures on Exterior Veterinary Science) (1908-09); *Kurs anatomii sel'skokhozyaystvennykh zhivothnykh* (A Course on the Anatomy of Agricultural Animals) (1926-27); *Anatomiya sel'skokhozyaystvennykh zhivotnykh s osnovami gistologii* (The Anatomy of Agricutural Animals with the Principles of Histology) (1930-31); *Anatomiya domashnikh zhivotnykh* (The Anatomy of Domestic Animals) (1949); *Died:* 1953.

AYANBERGEN MUSAYEV (1880-1936) Kara-Kalpak folk poet; *Born:* 1880; *Publ:* poems "Lenin" and "Song of Stalin" translated into Russian; *Died:* 1936.

AYDAROV (real name: VISHNEVSKIY), Sergey Vasil'yevich (1867-1938) Actor; Hon Art Worker of RSFSR from 1937; *Born:* 1867; *Educ:* 1898 grad drama courses under A.P. Lenskiy, Moscow School of Stagecraft; *Career:* 1898-1938 actor, Moscow Maly Theater; 1925-30 headed Yermolova Studio; from 1904 taught drama; *Roles:* Krutitskiy in Ostrovskiy's *Na vsyakogo mudretsa dovol'no prostoty* (There's a Simpleton in Every Sage); Vishnevskiy in Ostrovskiy's *Dokhodnoye mesto* (A Lucrative Post); Berendey in Ostrovskiy's *Snegurochka* (The Snow-Maiden); Ivan the Terrible in *Vasilisa Melent'yeva*; Caesar in Shakespeare's "Julius Caesar"; Arakcheyev in Platon's *Arakcheyevshchina* (The Arakcheyev Regime), etc; at Maly Theater also staged Ostrovskiy's plays: *Vasilisa Melent'yeva* (1914); *Na boykom meste* (A Lively Spot) (1915); Gnedich's *Pered zaryoy* (Before Daybrak) (1910), etc; *Died:* 16 Aug 1938.

AYDAROV, Sitdik Khanifeyevich (1895-1938) Actor and singer; *Born:* 1895; *Educ:* 1934-38 studied at Tatar Opera Studio, Moscow Conservatory; *Career:* 1912 stage debut with *Sayyar* Tatar touring company; during Civil War acted with frontline theater brigades; from 1921 actor, Tatar Model Drama Theater, Kazan' (now Kamal Theater); *Roles:* Khalil' in Fayzi's "Galiya-banu"; Batyrzhan in Gizzat's "The Hired Laborer"; Bulat in Tinchurin's "The Blue Shawl"; Makhmut in Kamal's "In the Raven's Nest"; *Died:* 13 Sept 1938.

AYDYN (real name: Manzura SABIROVA) (1906-1953) Uzbek writer; *Born:* 1906 in Tashkent; *Educ:* studied at women's educ inst; 1927-33 at Uzbek Teachers' Training Acad, Samarkand; *Career:* ed, journal *Yangi yul; Publ:* play "The Path to a New Life" (1925); verse collection "Songs of Dawn" (1931); "Able Hands" (1932); story "Zumrad, or the Reprimand" (1934); stories: "A Holiday Gift," "Is She Happy, My Friend? " and "Eyes Agog" (1938-41); collected stories "Girls" (1943); "Shirin Has Come" (1944); in Russian translation: *Rasskazy* (Stories) (1955); *Died:* 1953.

AYKAZYAN, Vil'yam Nersesovich (1907-1963) Film dir; Hon Art Worker of Arm SSR from 1963; CP member from 1934; *Born*: 14 Apr 1907; *Educ*: 1932-35 studied at All-Union State Inst of Cinematography; *Career*: chronicle film dir, Arm Film Studios; directed film sketches, documentaries and cinema journals; also directed film dubbing; *Works*: films: "For Copper, Molybdenum and Aluminum" (1948); "Science Serves the People" (1948); "Viticulture in Armenia" (1952); "Avetik Isaakyan" (1956); "Armenia Today" (1957); "The Architecture of Armenia" (1958); "Poem of Armenia" (1961; "In the Embraces of One's Country" (1964); *Died*: 11 Sept 1963.

AYNALOV, Dmitriy Vlas'yevich (1862-1939) Russian art historian; prof from 1903; corresp member, Russian, then USSR Acad of Sci from 1914; *Born*: 20 Feb 1862; *Career*: 1890-1903 lectured at Kazan' Univ; from 1903 prof, Petersburg, then Leningrad Univ; specialist in history of Byzantine art and art of Kievan Rus'; contributed greatly to development of Russian Byzantine studies; *Publ*: coauthor, *Kiyevo-Sofiyskiy sobor* (The Cathedral of St Sophia in Kiev) (1889); *Ellinisticheskiye osnovy vizantiyskogo iskusstva* (The Hellenic Foundations of Byzantine Art) (1900); *Arkhitektura chernigovskikh tserkvey* (Chernigov Church Architecture) (1909); *Vizantiyskaya zhivopis' XIV stoletiya* (14th-Century Byzantine Painting) (1917); *Istoriya russkogo monumental'nogo iskusstva* (A History of Russian Monumental Art) (2 vol, 1923-33); *Etyudy o Leonardo da Vinchi* (Studies on Leonardo da Vinci) (1939); *Died*: 12 Dec 1939.

AYNI (real name: SADRIDDIN SAIDMURADOVICH) (1878-1954) Tadzh writer; founder of Sov Tadzh prose; first pres, Tadzh Acad of Sci from 1951; Hon Sci Worker of Tadzh SSR; hon member, Uzbek Acad of Sci; *Born*: 27 Apr 1878 in vil Soktare (now Uzbek SSR), son of a peasant; *Educ*: grad Bukhara medressah; *Career*: joined lit circle in Bukhara; from 1894 wrote verse; 1905 joined Dzhadidist movement in Bukhara Khanate; from 1909 worked in illegal modern school and compiled textbooks; 1915, because of persecution by the Emir, fled from Bukhara; 1917 arrested; released from jail by Russian soldiers; moved to Samarkand; 1920 broke with Dzhadidism and took part in Bukhara Revol; wrote in Tadzh and Uzbek; *Publ*: "March of Freedom" (1918); elegy "On the Death of a Brother" was an appeal for the overthrow of the emirate; prose works: "Butchers of Bukhara" (1920); "History of the Mangit Dynasty of the Bukhara Emirs" (1921); novelette "Odina" (1924); novels: "The Poor Man" (1927-29); "Slaves" (1934); novelette "Death of a Moneylender" (1939); "Anthology of Tadzhik Literature" (1925); various works on the history, lit and language of Tadzh people; essay " The Hero of the Tadzhik People - Temur-Malik" (1944); autobiographical novelette "Memoirs" (1948), etc; with his works Ayni laid the foundation of modern Tadzh lit; *Awards*: two Orders of Lenin; Stalin Prize (1950); *Died*: 15 July 1954 in Dushanbe.

AYZENSHTADT, I.L. (pseudonym: YUDIN) (1867-1937) Politician; leading functionary, Bund; *Born*: 1867; *Career*: from 1902 member, CC, Bund; worked in Minsk and Odessa; after 2nd RSDRP Congress active Menshevik; hostile to 1917 Oct Revol; 1922 emigrated to Germany, where he headed a Bund group; *Died*: 1937.

AYVAZYAN, Tigran Nikitich (1893-1956) Actor; Hon Artiste of Arm SSR from 1935; *Born*: 6 Jan 1893; *Career*: 1922 stage debut; actor, Sundukyan Theater, Yerevan; from 1926 film work; *Roles*: film roles: Gusakov in "The House on the Volcano" (1929); the Cardinal in "Always Prepared" (1930); the Sheikh in "The Yezid Kurds" (1933); Tigran in "David Bek" (1944); the Guest in "The Showing" (1956); *Died*: 21 Feb 1956.

AZANCHEVSKAYA, S.V. (1874-1951) Revolutionary; member, Socialist-Revol Party, then Leftist Socialist-Revol Party; *Born*: 1874; *Career*: 1908-17 in emigration; 1918 head, Finance Dept, and Collegium member, RSFSR Pop Comrt of Educ; 1920-21 dep head, Finance Dept, and head, Personnel Dept, RSFSR Pop Comrt of For Affairs; subsequently statistician and accountant; *Died*: 1951.

AZARIN (real name: MESSERER), Azariy Mikhaylovich (1897-1937) Actor; Hon Artiste of RSFSR from 1935; *Born*: 30 Mar 1897; *Educ*: 1918 studied at Vakhtangov Studio; 1919 studied at 2nd Studio, Moscow Arts Theater; *Career*: actor, Moscow Arts Theater; 1925-36 at 2nd Moscow Arts Theater, where he also worked as stage dir; from 1936 at Maly Theater, Moscow's Yermolovaya Theater and Centr Theater of the Red Army; *Roles*: the Father in *Skazka ob Ivane-durake* (The Tale of Ivan the Fool), after Lev Tolstoy, adapted for the stage by Chekhov; Kuligin in Ostrovskiy's *Groza* (The Storm); Kosme in Calderon's "The Invisible Womann"; the Cat in Maeterlinkck's "The Blue-Bird"; Bobchinskiy in Gogol's *Revizor* (The Government Inspector); Zagoretskiy in Griboyedov's *Gore ot uma* (Woe from Wit); Tarelkin in Sukhovo-Kobylin's *Delo* (The Case); Volgin in Afinogenov's *Chudak* (The Crank); Malvolio in Shakespeare's "Twelfth Night," etc; *Productions*: Amaglobeli's "The Good Life" (1934); "The Tempest," etc; *Died*: 30 Sept 1937.

AZBUKIN, Dmitriy Ivanovich (1883-1953) Defectologist and psychiatrist; Dr of Pedag; prof; corresp member, RSFSR Acad of Pedag Sci from 1945; Hon Sci Worker of RSFSR from 1947; Cp member from 1942; *Born*: 4 June 1883; *Educ*: 1910 grad Med Fac, Moscow Univ; *Career*: 1911-15 intern, from 1915 asst prof, Psychiatric Clinic, Moscow Univ; 1947-54 dir, Research Inst of Defectology, RSFSR Acad of Pedag Sci; research mainly on teaching of metal defectives and clinical aspects of oligophrenia; organized special training for teachers of mental defectives at higher educ institutions; *Publ: Umstvennaya otstalost' detey i kak s ney borot'sya* (Mental Retardment in Children and How to Deal with It) (1926); *Polovoye vospitaniye i prosveshcheniye detey i podrostkov v shkole* (Sex Education of Children and Adolescents in School) (1928); *Osnovy psikhopatologii i psikhogigiyeny detskogo vozrasta dlya pedagogov* (Principles of Child Psychopathology and Mental Health for Teachers) (1930); co-ed, *Osobennosti obucheniya vo vspomogatel'noy shkole* (Features of Instruction in Auxiliary Schools) (1934); *Klinika oligofreniy* (Clinical Aspects of Oligophrenia) (1936); *Problemy spetsial'noy pedagogiki i psikhologii* (Problems of Special Pedagogics and Psychology) (1948); co-ed, *Kniga dlya uchitelya glukhonemykh* (The Deaf-Mute Teacher's Handbook) (1949); *Died*: 8 June 1953.

AZIN, Vladimir Mikhaylovich (1877-1920) Mil commander; Civil War veteran; CP member from 1918; *Born*: 1887 in Rostov-on-Don; *Educ*: grad Yelizavetgrad (now Kirovograd) cavalry school; *Career*: 1914-17 officer (last rank: Cossack capt), 46th Don Cossack Regt, Russian Army; after 1917 Oct Revol sided with Sov regime; from Dec 1917 comr, then commander, Red Guard detachmetns; from Aug 1918 commanded Arsk Group of Red Guard detachments, 2nd Army on the Eastern Front; commander, 2nd Composite Div; helped crush anti-Sov peasant revolts; his Arsk Group played an important part in the liberation of Kazan'; his div captured Izhevsk and Yekaterinburg and fought at Tsaritsyn; *Awards*: Order of the Red Banner; Hero of the Civil War; *Died*: hanged on 18 Feb 1920 after his div was surrounded and captured the day before by White Army cavalry; a street in Sverdlovsk has been named for him.

AZIZBEKOV, Meshadi Asim-bek-ogly (1876-1918) Professional revolutionary technol eng; Baku Comr; CP member from 1898; *Born*: 6 Jan 1876 in Baku, son of a worker; *Educ*: 1908 grad Petersburg Technol Inst; *Career*: 1890's joined student and gen revol movement; twice arrested; participated in 1905-07 Revol; leading functionary, Baku Soc-Democratic *Gummet* group; taught and took part in various revol org in Baku; 1906 organized "Banner of Freedom" battle squad; dep chm, *Nidzhat* (Salvation) cultural and educ soc; 1910 elected member, Baku City Duma; 1917 elected member, Baku Sov of Workers' Dep; Mar 1918, after establishment of Sov regime in Baku, appointed Baku Province

Comr and Baku Dep Pop Comr of Internal Affairs with Baku Council of Min; from May 1918 simultaneously chm, Exec Comt, Baku Uyezd Sov of Peasants' Dep; *Died*: after collapse of Sov regime in Baku arrested and shot as one of the 26 Baku Comr in the night of 20 Sept 1918; rayons in Azer and Arm SSR named after him.

AZMAYPARASHVILI, Shalva Il'ich (1903-1957) Composer; Hon Art Worker of Geo SSR from 1941; bd member, Geo Composers' Union from 1956; CP member from 1940; *Born*: 7 Jan 1903 in Tiflis (now Tbilisi); *Educ*: 1930 grad Tbilisi Conservatory; 1933 completed postgrad course there; *Career*: 1923-28 played in brass band and symphony orchestra; directed amateur symphony orchestras of Tiflis Railroad and Politech Inst; 1932-38 conductor, 1938-54 chief conductor, Tbilisi Opera and Ballet Theater; 1943-53 also conductor, Tbilisi Radio Symphony Orchestra; artistic manager, Geo Chamber Orchestra; from 1954 conductor, Geo State Symphony Orchestra; from 1927 taught; dep, Geo Supr Sov of 1938, 1947 and 1951 convocations; *Productions*: staged operas: Dzherzhinskiy's *Tikhiy Don* (Quiet Flows the Don) (1938); Kiladze's *Lado Ketskhoveli* (1941); Mshvelidze's *Skazaniye o Tariele* (Tale of Tariel) (1946), etc; *Works*: opera "Elder of Gocha" (1951); musical comedies: *Inyye nynche vremena* (Times Have Changed) (1952); *Zhelannyy zhenikh* (The Desirable Bridgegroom) (1957); vocal-symphonic poem "Kartli" (1946) for symphony orchestra: "Children's Suite" (1933); "Collective Farm Suite" (1939); "Symphony S" (1945); romance "Are You a Violet or a Rose? " (1963), etc; *Awards*: Order of the Red Banner of Labor; two Badges of Hon; medals; Stalin Prize (1947); *Died*: 17 May 1957 in Tbilisi.

B

BAAL-DIM'ON (real name: Nokhim SHTIF) (1879-?) Philologist; specialist in history of Yiddish language and lit; *Born*: 1879 in Rovno, Volhynian Province; *Career*: 1899-1910 organizer, Jewish socialist Zionist workers' groups; after 1903 Kishinev pogrom together with P. Dashevsky, who attempted to assassinate Krushevan, organized one of first Jewish self-defense squads; arrested twice; finally quit socialist Zionist movement and worked for Soc for the Enlightenment of Jews and Soc of Artisan Labor, etc; after Feb Revol organizer, Jewish "Volks-Partei"; from 1920 lived in Germany studying documents relating to origins of Yiddish language; published in Russian and Yiddish "Pogromy na Ukraine pri dobrovol'cheskoy armii" (Progroms in the Ukraine Under the Volunteer Army); 1926 returned to Kiev; headed Dept of Yiddish Language and Lit, Ull-Ukr Acad of Sci; published papers on Yiddish philology and lit; translated into Yiddish monographs on history of Yiddish culture; *Died*: date, place and cause of death unknown.

BAAZOV, Gertsel Davydovich (1904-45) Geo writer and playwright; *Born*: 23 Oct 1904; *Educ*: 1928 grad Tbilisi Univ; *Publ*: stories and novelettes about life of Geo Jews; plays: "The Dumb Spoke" (1932); "Without Respect for Persons" (1935); *Itska Rizhinashvili* (1937) (performed at Mardzhanishvili Theater, Tbilisi); *Died*: 5 June 1945.

BABADZHANOV, Yatim (real name: FYZYL) (1904-56) Stage dir and actor; Pop Artiste of Uzbek SSR from 1943; *Born*: 1904; *Educ*: 1927 grad Uzbek Studio, Moscow; *Career*: one of the founders of Uzbek theater; 1920 at Karl Marx Theater; from 1927 at Khamza Theater, Tashkent; played Tartalia in Gozzi's "Princess Turandot", Brigella in "Servant of Two Masters", Karavayev in Furmanov's *Myatezh* (Mutiny) 1931-32 stage dir, Uzbek Theater, Bukhara, where he staged Fukhtullin's "The Mask Is Off", "The Traitors", etc; 1943-46 artistic dir, Yangi-Yul'sk Uzbek Theater; 1946-48 chief producer, Tashkent Sov Theater, Tashkent; 1948 again at Khamza Theater, where he staged: Yashen's *Razgrom* (The Rout) (1934); "Kabale und Liebe" (1936); Khamza's "The Bey and the Farmhand" (1939); "A Man With a Rifle"' (1940); Safarov's "The Dawn of the East" (1951); taught at Tashkent Theater Inst also at other educ institutions; *Died*: 26 Dec 1956.

BABAREKA, Adam Antonovich (1899-1938) Bel writer and lit critic; *Born*: 15 Oct 1899 in vil Sloboda-Kuchinka, now Minsk Oblast; son of a peasant; *Educ*: studied at Minsk Theological Seminary; 1927 grad Dept of Ethnology and Linguistics, Pedag Fac, Bel State Univ; *Career*: 1919-21 schoolteacher in Sunayevo and Sloboda-Kuchinka; fought with partisans against Poles; for a time member, Puka Volost Revol Comt and head, Puka Volost Dept of Educ; 1921-22 in Red Army; from 1922 lived in Minsk; 1922-27 ed, newspaper *Savetskaya Belarus'*; 1923-26 member, then head, criticism section, *Maladnyak* (Youth) Lit Assoc; from 1925 lecturer in Bel language and lit, Bel Communist Univ; from 1926 secr and ideologist, *Uzvyshsha* (Eminence) Lit Assoc; from 1928 asst prof, Chair of Bel Lit History, Bel State Univ; defended "purity" of Bel lit; rejected Party attacks on writers M. Bahdanovich, Yanka Kupala, Yakub Kolas and Z. Byadula; 1930 exiled for five years as Bel "nat-democrat" and "nationalist" to Slobodskoy Vyatskoy, now Kirov Oblast; 1935 sentenced to two more years in exile; 1937 re-arrested and interned in concentration camp; *Publ*: "Short Stories" (1925); literary criticism: "The Life and Works of Yanka Kupala" (1925); "From the Valleys to the Hills" (1926); "The Concept of Artistic Creativity and Some Questions of Belorussian Literature" (1927); "Literary Notes" (1927); "Literary Evaluations of M. Bahdanovich" (1927); "The Works of Vladimir Dubovka" (1928); "The Poetry of Exaltation" (1929), etc; *Died*: 1938 in concentration camp; posthumously rehabilitated.

BABAYANTS, Ruben Ambartsumovich (1889-1962) Hygienist; prof form 1931; Dr of Med from 1937; corresp member, USSR Acad of Med Sci; *Born*: 1889; *Educ*: 1916 grad Natural Sci Dept, Physics and Mathematics Fac, Petrograd Univ; 1916-20 at Petrograd Mil Med Acad; 1924 grad 1st Leningrad Med Inst; *Pos*: 1925-26 ass prof, 1st Leningrad Med Inst; 1926-31 supernumerary assoc prof, Dept of Hygiene, Leningrad Postgrad Med Inst; 1927-39 head, Dept of Hygiene, Inst of Communal Construction; 1939-41 head, Dept of Communal Hygiene, 1941-62 head, Dept of Gen Hygiene, 1944-51 dean, 1953-62 dep dir for research, Leningrad Health Hygiene Med Inst; *Career*: developed new standards for sanitary evaluation of soil and urban atmosphere, scales for comparative evaluation of air pollution, methods of taking samples and rendering refuse harmless, and methods of evaluating soil mineralization; worked on improving health conditions in Leningrad; co-founder and bd member, Leningrad Section, Soc of Hygienists; bd member, All-Union Soc of Hygienists; co-ed, "Hygiene" section, *Bol'shaya meditsinskaya entsiklopediya* (Large Medical Encyclopedia), 2nd ed; member, ed council, journal "Gigiyena i sanitariya"; *Publ*: more than 130 works; doctor's thesis *Eksperimental'nyye izucheniya sostava i pochvennoy mineralizatsii gorodskikh otbrosov* (Experimental Studies of the Composition and Soil Mineralization of City Refuse) (1937); *Zagryazneniye gorodskogo vozdukha* (Air Pollution in Cities) (1948); *Sanitarnaya okhrana atmosfernogo vozdukha promyshlennykh gorodov* (Prevention of Air Pollution in Industrial Cities) (vol 1, 1949); *Metodika i rezul'taty issledovaniya gorodskikh otbrosov* (Methods and Results of Research on City Refuse) (1950); coauthor, *Spravochnik sanitarnogo vracha* (Handbook for Medical Health Officers) (1961) *Died*: Feb 1962.

BABAYEV, Andrey Avanesovich (1923-64) Composer; Hon Art Worker of Arm SSR from 1958; Pop Artiste of Arm SSR from 1962; *Born*: 27 Dec 1923 in Memna, Nagorno-Karabakh Autonomous Oblast, Azer SSR; *Educ*: 1950 grad K. Karagev's composition class, Baku Conservatory; *Career*: 1941-45 artistic dir, Song and Dance Ensemble, Baku Garrison; 1946-47 artistic dir, Saz Folk Instrument Ensemble, Baku Philharmonic; 1947-50 choirmaster, Song and Dance Ensemble, Baku Philharmonic; *Works*: operas: "Artsvaberd" (1957), dealing with collectivization of agric in Arm; "Old Bagdasar" (1966); music for plays; three rhapsodies (1943, 1949 and 1954); cantata "October" (1947), etc; Suite (1946); overture "Youth" (1948); music for films: *Khitrost' starogo Ashira* (Old Ashir's Guile) (1956); *Alyoshiny skazki* (Alyosha's Tales) (1964), etc; *Awards*: three medals; *Died*: 21 Oct 1964.

BABEL' Isaak Emanuilovich (1894-1941) Russian Jewish writer; *Born*: 13 July 1894 in Odessa, son of a Jewish trader; *Educ*: grad Odessa Business College; *Career*: after grad from Business College lived in Kiev; 1915 moved to Petrograd; 1916 first stories published in Gorky's journal "Letopis'"; 1917 soldier on Rumanian Front; then worked for Odessa Province Comt and Pop Comrt of Educ; 1918 took part in grain procurement expeditions; served with Northern Army against Gen Yudenich; served with Budyonny's Army on Polish Front; after demobilization worked for Petrograd, Odessa and Tiflis newspapers; 1934 at 1st All-Union Writers' Congress dubbed the "Great Silent One," which was a condemnation of him as a writer; 1936 arrested for first time;

1937 re-arrested and exiled; *Publ*: stories "Sol'" (Salt); *Pis'mo* (The Letter); *Smert' Dolgushova* (The Death of Dolgushov) and *Korol'* (The King) (1923); *Konarmiya* (The Cavalry Army) (1926); film script *Bluzhdayushchiye zvyozdy* (Wandering Stars) (1926); collected stories: *Istoriya moyey golubyatni* (The History of My Dove-Cote) (1926); *Benya Krik* (1926); *Konets sv. Ipatiya* (The End of St. Hippatius) (1926); plays: *Zakat* (Sunset) (1928); *Mariya* (Maria) (1935); story *Di-Grasso* (Di Grasso) (1937), etc; *Died*: 17 Mar 1941 in imprisonment; posthumously rehabilitated.

BABENKO, Aleksandr Kalistratovich (1881-1959) Physicist and methods specialist; prof; dept head, Gorky Teachers' Training Inst, Kiev from 1932; CP member from 1946; *Born*: 25 May 1881 in Yasinuvattsy, now Kiev Oblast, son of a peasant; *Educ*: 1907 grad Kiev Univ; *Career*: 1907-29 taught physics at secondary schools in Vinnitsa and Vinnitsa Oblast; 1930-32 lectured at Kiev higher educ institutions; from 1932 at Gorky Teachers' Training Inst, Kiev; *Publ*: *Elektromagnitnaya induktsiya* (Electromagnetic Induction); *Zvuk* (Sound); *Kolebaniya i volny* (Oscillations and Waves); coauther, *Ocherki po metodike prepodavaniya fiziki* (Methods of Teaching Physics, etc; *Awards*: Order of Lenin; *Died*: 30 Sept 1959.

BABIY, Aleksandr Maksimovich (1906-1953) Sound eng; *Born*: 1906; *Educ*: grad Kiev Inst of Cinematography; *Career*: from 1936 at Kiev Feature Films Studio; worked on films *Ivan* (1932), *Posledniy port* (The Last Port). *Gibel' eskadry* (The Loss of a Squadron) (1935); *Khrustal'nyy dvorets* (The Crystal Palace) (1934); *Ya lyublyu* (I love) (1936), *Zaporozhets za Dunayem* (A Dnieper Cossack Beyond the Danube) (1938); *Vsadniki* (The Horsemen) (1939); *Eskadril'ya* (The Squadron), *Voyna nachinayetsya* (The War Begins) (1939); *Kak zakalyalas' stal'* (How the Steel Was Tempered((1942); *Partizany v stepyakh Ukrainy* (Partisans in the Ukrainian Steppes) (1943); *Raduga* (The Rainbow) (1944); *Nepokoryonnyye* (The Unsubdued, (1945); *Ukrainskiye melodii* (Ukrainian Melodies) (1945); *Podvig razvedchika* (The Scout's Feat) (1947); *Tretiy udar* (The Third Thrust) (1948); *Taras Shevchenko* (1951); *Geroi Shipki* (The Heroes of Shipka) (1955); etc; *Died*: 31 Oct 1953.

BABKIN, I. P. (1885-1940) Party and admin official; CP member from 1902; *Born*: 1885; *Career*: Party work in Rostov, Saratov etc; participated in 1905-07 Revol in Rostov; arrested by Tsarist anthorites; 1917 member, Rostov-Nakhichevan Sov; 1918-21 head, Labor Dept, RSFSR Pop Comrt of Food; later in Volga-Caspian Region directing petroleum exports from Astrakhan' for Council of Pop Comr and Labor and Defense Council; from Sept 1921 Presidium member, USSR Centr Union of Consumer Soc; chm, All-Russian Fishery Producers' Co-operative Union; member, Supr Arbitration Commission, Labor and Defense Council; Presidium member, RSFSR Supr Sovnarkhoz; chm, Karelian Council of Pop Comr; dep chm, Main Timber Export Bd; *Died*: 1940.

BABUSHKIN, Mikhail Sergeyevich (1893-1938) Explorer; pilot-officer, Russian Army; Sov Hon Polar Pilot; *Born*: 1893; *Educ*: 1915 grad Gatchina Pilots School; *Career*: fought in Civil War; from 1926 aerial reconnaissance for trapping outfits in the Arctic; 1928 member of expedition to rescue crew of "Italiya" airship; 1933-34 participated in fateful SS *Chelyuskin* expedition (via North Sea Passage); 1935 participated in Arctic expedition on icebreaker *Sadko*; 1937 as second flagship pilot flew to North Pole to land Papanin and other personnel of first polar station; dep, USSR Supr Sov of 1937 convocation; *Awards*: Hero of the Sov Union (1937); Order of Lenin; *Died*: 1938 in a plane crash.

BABUSHKIN, Yefim Adrianovich (Party pseudonyms: TSYBULYA; TSYBUL'SKIY; GRAF (1880-1927) Revolutionary and govt official; CP member from 1902; *Born*: 26 Dec 1880 in Nizhnyaya Toyma, Vyatka Province, son of a worker; from 1899 worked in Perm' railroad workshops; 1900 joined Soc-Democratic circle, emigrating after suffering polit persecution; 1904-05 secr, Bolshevik club in Paris, where he became acquainted with Lenin; from Nov 1905 Party work in various Russian towns; deleg ot 4th RSDRP Congress; from Aug 1917 organizer and head of Bolshevik org in Kokand and chm, Kokand Sov; from Sept 1918 Sov consul-gen in Iran, where in 1919 he was arrested by British Mil Mission an taken first to India then to a London prison; released in 1921; then held senior govt and admin posts; *Died*: 31 July 1927.

BACHINSKIY, Aleksey Iosifovich (1877-1944) Physicist; *Born*: 2 Apr 1877; *Educ*: 1899 grad Moscow Univ; *Career*: after grad retained at Dept of Physics, Moscow Univ; 1900 published first two sci works: *K dinamicheskoy teorii elektrichestva* (The Dynamic Theory of Electricity) and *O zavisimosti vyazkosti rtuti ot temperatury* (The Relationship Between the Viscosity of Mercury and Temperature); 1907-18 lecturer, 1918-44 prof, Moscow Univ; best known for his works on molecular physics and thermodynamics; established that surface tension of a liquid is directly proportional in the fourth degree to the difference between the density of its liquid state and its saturated steam state; several of his works deal with relationship between pressure and temperature of saturated steams; Bachinskiy's law on the viscosity of liquids, founded 1912-13, is particularly well-known, has been confirmed theoretically and experimentally and is widely applied in practice; wrote series of text books on physics for higher and secondary schools and articles on gen physics; *Died*: 31 July 1944.

BADAYEV, Aleksey Yegorovich (1883-1951) Party and govt official; CP member from 1904; *Born*: 4 Feb 1883 in Yur'yev, Orel Province; *Career*: fitter at Aleksandrovskiy Plant; 1912 elected dep to 4th State Duma by workers of Petersburg and Petersburg Province; member, Bolshevik faction, 4th State Duma; 1913 took part in consultations of CC, RSDRP with Party workers in Cracow and Poronin; member, Petersburg RSDRP Comt and Russian Bureau, CC, RSDRP; worked on newspaper *Pravda*; at outset of WW 1 staged anti-war rallies in various towns; Nov 1914 arrested at instigation of Duma's Soc-Democratic faction and exiled to Turukhansk Kray; returning from exile after 1917 Feb Revol, elected Bolshevik cand to Petrograd City Duma; after 1917 Oct Revol chm, Petrograd Food Bd and comr for provisioning Petrograd and Northern Oblast; from 1921 chm, Petrograd Consumers' Union; from 1925 dep chm, Leningrad Province Exec Comt; from 1930 chm, All-Union Consumers' Assoc, Moscow Union of Consumers' Associations, and dep chm, Moscow Sov; from 1936 admin work at Pop Comrt of Food Ind; 1938-43 chm, Presidium, RSFSR Supr Sov and dep chm, Presidium, USSR Supr Sov; from 1943 Collegium member, USSR Min of Food Ind; at 11th-13th Party Congresses elected cand member, and at 14th-18th Congresses full member, CC, RCP(B); *Publ*: *Bol'sheviki v gosudarstvennoy dume. Vospominaniya* (The Bolsheviks in the State Duma. Memoirs.) (1929); *Awards*: two Orders of Lenin; Order of the Red Banner of Labor; *Died*: 3 Nov 1951.

BADIN, Aleksey Lavrent'yevich (1888-1935) Mil commander; cavalry sergeant-maj, Russian Army; Civil War veteran; CP member from 1928; *Born*: 1888; *Educ*: 1934 grad Frunze Mil Acad; *Career*: fought in WW 1; from July 1919 in Red Army; 1919-21 commanded platoon, cavalry regt aide-de-camp, then commanded 7th Cavalry Regt and separate cavalry brigade; after Civil War commanded cavalry brigade; asst cavalry inspector, Transvolga Mil Distr; commanded brigade in 10th Cavalry Div; commander and mil comr, 5th Stavropol' Cavalry Div; 1935 commander and comr, 10th Cavalry Div; 1920 distinguished himself in battles against Gen Wrangel's troops; *Awards*: two Orders of the Red Banner; *Died*: 1935.

BADUYEV, Said Suleymanovich (1904-43) Chechen writer, poet and dramatist; founder of Chechen lit; *Born*: 14 Sept 1904 in Groznyy, now Chechen-Ingush ASSR, son of a tradesman; *Educ*: 1923 grad teachers' courses; *Career*: from 1923 teacher in Chechen schools; 1927 first work published; 1938 arrested by NKVD; *Publ*: stories: "The Well"; "Beshto"; "The Fiery Mountain"; collected stories "Adaty" (1930); novelette "Famine" (1930); plays: "It's Not Always Bayram for the Mullah" (1930); "Red Fortress"; "The Golden Lake"; "Political Section" (1934); comedy "Tsaeby's Wedding"; collected verse "Our Garden" (1935), etc; *Died*: 20 Dec 1943 in imprisonment; posthumously rehabilitated.

BAGADUROV, Vsevolod Alaverdiyevich (1878-1954) Musical historian, teacher and composer; opera singer (tenor); Dr of Arts from 1939; prof from 1940; *Born*: 4 Mar 1878 in Nizhniy Novgorod; *Educ*: 1901 grad Petersburg Univ; studied music theory under G. Konyus and B. Yavorskiy; studied singing in Moscow with N. Speranskiy and N. Miller; *Career*: 1904-05 sang in opera in Tiflis; 1906-14 in Nizhniy Novgorod; from 1914 performed periodically in Moscow (Zimin Opera Theater); in Nizhniy Novgorod worked for Soc of Russian Music-Lovers and Fine Arts Soc, taught and gave concerts, read lectures, conducted an orchestra and wrote musical criticism; 1922-50 at Moscow Conservatory; from 1946 also at Inst of Art Training, RSFSR Acad of Pedag Sci; *Works*: opera *Eros i Psikheya* (Eros and Psyche) (1916); *Dvoryanskoye gnezdo* (A Nest of Gentlefolk), based on Turgenev's novel; helped compose music for drama *Tsar' Maksimilian* (The Emperor Maximilian); *Publ*: *Ocherki po istorii vokal'noy metodologii* (An Outline History of Vocal Methodology) (1929); *O merakh podnyatiya vokal'nogo iskusstva i pedagogiki* (Measures for Improving Vocal Music and Teaching) (1926); *Okhrana i vospitaniye detskogo golosa* (Child Vocal Care and Training) (1947); *Ocherki po istorii vokal'noy pedagogiki* (An Outline History of Vocal Training) (1956), etc; *Died*: 11 Oct 1954 in Moscow.

BAGALEY, Dmitriy Ivanovich (1857-1932) Ukr historian; Dr of Historical Sci from 1887; prof from 1887; member, Ukr Acad of Sci from 1919; *Born*: 1857 in Kiev, son of an artisan; *Educ*: studied at Kiev Univ; 1882 grad Khar'kov Univ; *Career*: 1883-87 assoc prof, from 1887 prof of Russian history, Khar'kov Univ; from 1883 also in charge of Khar'kov Historical Archives; 1906-10 rector, Khar'kov Univ; 1906 and 1910-14 member, State Council; 1914-17 Mayor of Khar'kov; 1919-32 member and vice-pres, Ukr Acad of Sci; prof of Ukr history, Khar'kov and Poltava Inst of Public Educ; simultaneously head, Khar'kov Dept of Research into Ukr History, Inst for History of Ukr Culture, Inst of Shevchenko Studies, and Ukr Centr Archives Bd; twice elected chm, Bureau of Ukr Researchers' Sections; pupil of historian V.B. Antonovich; shared M.S. Grushevskiy's views on Ukr history; specialist in Ukr history of 15th-18th Century; his most valuable work was to put the Khar'kov historical archives in order and publish material from the archives; *Publ*: *Ocherki iz istorii kolonizatsii i byta stepnoy okrainy Moskovskogo gosudarstva* (An Outline History of the Colonization and the Way of Life of the Steppe Regions of the State of Muscovy) (1887); *Kolonizatsiya Novorossiyskogo kraya i perviye shagi yego po puti kul'tury* (The Colonization of the Novorossiysk Region and Its First Steps Along the Path of Culture) (1889); *Opyt istorii Khar'kovskogo universiteta* (The History of Khar'kov University) (2 vol, 1893-1904); coauthor, *Istoriya goroda Khar'kova* (The History of the City of Khar'kov) (2 vol, 1905-12); *Russkaya istoriya* (Russian History) (2 vol, 1909-11); *Istoriya Slobodskoy Ukrainy* (A History of Free Settlements in the Ukraine) (1918); *Ocherk ukrainskoy istoriografii* (An Outline of Ukrainian Historiography) (2 vol, 1923-25); *Ocherk istorii Ukrainy na sotsial'no-ekonomicheskoy pochve* (A Social and Economic Outline History of the Ukraine) (1928); *T.G. Shevchenko - poet prignoblennykh mass* (T.G. Shevchenko - Poet of the Oppressed Masses) (1931); *Died*: 1932.

BAGATUR, Yekaterina Beglarovna (1870-1944) Arm playwright; *Born*: 1870; *Career*: 1905 began lit work; wrote essays, stories, theater reviews, then plays; *Publ*: historical tragedies: "Ara and Shamiram" (1915); *Artavazd* (1923); play "The Trial" (1929); tragedy "The Tondrakiites" (1939), etc; *Died*: 9 Nov 1944.

BAGAYEV, M.A. (1874-1949) Admin and trade-union official; CP member from 1892; *Born*: 1874; *Career*: co-founder and leader, Northern Workers' Union; took part in 1905-07 Revol; deleg, Tammerfors Conference and 4th Congress of RSDRP; several times arrested and exiled; in 1912 gave up active revol work; June 1917-1921 dep chm, Bd of Consumers' Cooperatives in Novonikolayevsk (now Novosibirsk); 1921-23 head of Warehouses Dept, Siberian Branch, All-Union Centr Union of Consumers' Soc; 1924 readmitted to CP; from 1924 active in econ admin and trade-union work; *Died*: 1949.

BAGDASAROV, Andrey Arkad'yevich (1897-1961) Therapist; prof from 1931; Dr of Med from 1939; member, USSR Acad of Med Sci from 1957; Hon Sci Worker of RSFSR from 1957; CP member from 1918; *Born*: 15 Feb 1897; *Educ*: 1923 grad Med Fac, 2nd Moscow Med Inst (formerly 2nd Moscow Univ); *Pos*: 1923-31 asst prof, then assoc prof, 1931-32 prof, Dept of Internal Diseases, 1928-32 dir, 2nd Moscow Med Inst; 1928-32 simultaneously dep dir, 1932-61 dir, Centr Inst of Hematology and Blood Transfusion, USSR Min of Health; 1946-61 head, Dept of Hospital Therapy, Pediatric Fac, 2nd Moscow Med Inst; 1932-61 chief hematologist, USSR Min of Health; *Career*: 1945-57 corresp member, USSR Acad of Med Sci; Bd member and chm, Hematology Section, Moscow Soc of Therapeutists; ed, journal *Problemy gematologii i perelivaniya krovi*; co-ed, "Internal Diseases" section, *Bolshaya meditsinskaya entsiklopediya* (Large Medical Encyclopedia), 2nd ed; 1959-61 member, Learned Med Council, USSR Min of Health; 1958-61 Bd member, Int Soc of Hematologists; 1955 attended 5th European Congress of Hematologists in Freiburg, Germany; *Publ*: about 110 works; coauthor, *Gemoterapiya v klinike vnutrennikh bolezney* (Hematotherapy in the Clinical Treatment of Internal Diseases) (1952); coauthor, *Sostoyaniye krovetvornoy sistemy u bol'nykh, podvergayushchikhsya rezektsii zheludka* (The Condition of the Hematopoietic System in Patients Undergoing Resection of the Stomach) (1956); *Krovetvoreniye pri rakovoy bolezni* (Hematopoiesis in Cancer) (1956); coauthor, *Problemy gematologii i perelivaniya krovi* (Problems of Hematology and Blood Transfusion) (1956); coauthor, *Primeneniye leykotsitarnoy massy pri lechenii khronicheskoy luchevoy bolezni* (The Use of Leukocytic Matter in Treating Chronic Radiation Sickness) (1955); doctor's thesis *Geterogemoterapiya yazvennoy bolezni zheludka i dvenadtsatiperstnoy kishki* (Heterohematotherapy of Gastric and Duodenal Ulcers) (1939); coauthor, *Perelivaniye krovi* (Blood Transfusion) (1939); coauthor, *Perelivaniye krovi* (Blood Transfusion) (1951); coauthor, *Properdinovaya sistema organizma* (The Properdin System of the Body) (1961); *Awards*: two Stalin Prizes (1946 and 1952); *Died*: 26 Aug 1961 in Moscow.

BAGDAT'YEV, S.Ya. (Sergey) (1887-1949) Party and admin worker; CP member from 1903; *Born*: 1887; *Career*: Party work in Baku, Tiflis and Petersburg; frequently arrested by Tsarist authorities; after 1917 Feb Revol member, Petersburg RSDRP(B) Comt; during Apr 1917 demonstrations called for immediate overthrow of Provisional Govt, but was censured by resolution of CC, RSDRP(B) on 5 May 1917; deleg to Petrograd City RSDRP(B) Conference and 7th (Apr) All-Russian RSDRP(B) Conference; after Oct Revol senior admin posts; *Died*: 1949.

BAGIROV, Mir Dzafar Abbasovich (1896-1956) Party functionary and govt official; CP member from 1917; *Born*: 17 Sept 1896 in Kuba, Baku Province; *Educ*: grad teachers' training courses; 1932 grad Marxism-Leninism courses, CC, CPSU(B); *Career*: from 1915 vil teacher, from 1915 participated in revol movement; active in 1917 Oct Revol; 1917 dep chm, Kuba Revol Comt; 1918-20 exec mil-polit work in Civil War; 1919 commanded 290th Regt that took part in suppressing an uprising in Astrakhan' and fought against Gen Mamontov's forces at Millerovo and Liski; 1920 dep chm, Karabakh Oblast Revol Comt; then mil comr and chm, Mil Tribunal, Azer Div and dep chm, Mil Tribunal, 11th Army; 1921-30 chm, Azer Cheka-GPU; Azer Pop Comr for Internal Affairs; dep chm, Azer Council of Pop Comr; 1932-33 chm, Azer Council of Pop Comr; from 1933 first secr, Baku City Comt and CC, CP(B) Azer; 1934 at 17th Party Congress elected cand member, CC, CPSU(B); 1939 at 18th Party Congress elected member, CC, CPSU(B); during WW 1 member, Mil Council, Transcaucasian Front; dep, USSR Supr Sov of 1937, 1946 and 1950 convocations; Presidium member, USSR Supr Sov; July 1953 expelled from Bureau and Jan 1954 from CC, CP Azer for "violating Party principles in personnel selection and for replacing Party methods of leadership. . . with crude arbitrary administration and violating the rights of Bureau and CC members"; Apr 1956 tried and sentenced to death for "treason, acts of terrorism and participation in a counter-revol org"; USSR Supr Sov Presidium rejected his plea for mercy; *Publ*: *Iz istorii bol'shevistskoy organizatsii Baku i Azerbaydzhana* (The History of the Bolshevik Organizations in Baku and in Azerbaydzhan); *Awards*: five Orders of Lenin; two Orders of the Red Banner; two Orders of the Red Banner of Labor; Order of the Fatherland War, 1st Class; Order of the Red Banner of Labor of the Azer SSR; Badge of Hon; two medals; *Died*: May 1956 executed by firing squad.

BAGIROVA, Basti Masim kyzy (1906-1962) Kolkhoz chm; member, CC, CP Azer; CP member from 1937; *Born*: 1906 in vil Abdulla-bek, Azer; *Educ*: completed evening school and two years' preparatory courses at Azer Agric Inst; *Career*: from early youth worked on cotton plantations; 1935-36 attended All-Union Congress of Kolkhoznik Shock-Workers; 1936, as fieldteam leader, achieved record cotton harvest; initiated "hundred centner movement" (picking a hundred centners of cotton per hectare); dep, USSR Supr Sov of 1937, 1946, 1950, 1954 and 1958 convocations; member, Council for Kolkhoz Affairs, USSR Council of Min; deleg, 20th CPSU Congress; 1959 Presidium member, Azer Supr Sov; *Awards*: two Orders of Lenin; Order of the Red Banner of Labor; medals; twice Hero of Socialist Labor; *Died*: Mar 1962.

BAGOTSKIY, Sergey Yustinovich (1879-1953) Physician; *Born*: 1879; *Educ*: studied at Mil Med Acad and Med Fac, Kiev Univ; *Career*: 1912-14 living in Krakow and Poronino, where he met Lenin and carried out Party tasks for him; 1914-17 lived in Switzerland; from Feb 1917 chm, All-Swiss Comt for Repatriation of Russian Political Emigres; took active part in organizing Lenin's return to Russia; 1918 worked for Council of Doctors' Panels and Med Collegium, RSFSR NKVD; 15-18 June 1918 presented paper *Ob osnovnykh printsipakh stroitel'stva mestnykh sovetskikh vrachebnosanitarnykh organizatsiy* (Basic Principles for

Setting Up Local Soviet Medical and Public Health Organizations) at 1st All-Russian Congress of Med and Public Health Dept of Sov of Workers and Soldiers' Dep; fall 1918-37 Russian Red Cross Soc rep with Int Red Cross Comt, Switzerland; Sov rep at numerous int Red Cross conferences; from 1937 consultant on for relations, Exec Comt, Union of Red Cross and Red Crescent Soc, Moscow; in his latter years worked at Mil Med Museum; 1950-55 senior sci ed, med section, *Bol'shaya sovetskaya entsiklopediya* (Large Soviet Encyclopedia); wrote various publications on work of Sov Red Cross during Civil War and period of Allied intervention; *Died*: 1953.

BAGRAYEV, Sozur Kurmanovich (1888-1928) Ossetian poet; *Born*: 18 June 1888; *Career*: from 1908 wrote lyric verse; wrote in Digor dialect; partisan in Civil War; *Publ*: verse "The Door to the Heart" (1905); "To the Leader"; "Our Tree"; "Collectively"; "The Blacksmith"; "Pioneer Campaign"; "The Party of Lenin"; "In Memoriam," etc; *Died*: 9 July 1928.

BAGRITSKIY, Eduard Georgiyevich (real name: DZYUBIN) (1895-1934) Russian Jewish poet; *Born*: 16 Nov 1895 in Odessa; *Career*: 1915 first work published; during Civil War in Red Army; 1919 with All-Russian Centr Exec Comt Special Partisan Detachment; 1926 joined *Pereval* (The Pass) lit group; then member, Lit Center of Constructivists; from 1930, after joining Russian Assoc of Proletarian Writers, worked as poet and painter for Southern Branch, Russian News Agency; until 1925 contributed to newspapers and periodicals in Odessa; from 1925 in Moscow; *Publ*: collected poetry and poems: *Avto v oblakakh* (Car in the Clouds) (1915); *Osvobozhdeniye* (Liberation) (1923); *Frontovik* (The Front-Line Fighter) (1924); *Vesyolyye nishchiye* (Merry Beggars) (1928); *Duma pro Opanasa* (Ballad of Opanas) (1926); *Poslednyaya noch'* (The Last Night) (1932); *Smert' pionerki* (Death of a Pioneer Girl) (1932); translated works of Yanka Kupala, Sosyura, Nazym Kikhmet, etc; *Died*: 16 Feb 1934 in Moscow.

BAGUN, Mikhas' (real name: BLOSHKIN, Mikhail Fedorovich) (1908-1938) Bel poet; *Born*: 8 Nov 1908 in Minsk, son of an office worker; *Educ*: 1927 finished secondary school; 1928 grad Minsk Teachers' Training Technicum; *Career*: 1929-31 village teacher in Rozhna, Begomel Rayon, then worked on road construction; 1931-32 on ed staff, newspaper *Chrvonaya Polachchyna;* 1932-36 at Bel State Publ House, then on ed staff, newspaper *Litaratura i mastatstva;* belonged to group of orthodox Sov poets whose revol romantic works praised Sov way of life; during 1929-30 active in collectivization of agric; was supporter of Sov Bel; arrested by NKVD as "enemy of the people"; *Publ*: verse collections: "Golden Morning" (1933); "Echo of the Storms" (1935); collection of poems "Poems" (1935); "Verse and Tales" (1936); *Died*: 23 Feb 1938 in NKVD prison.

BAKANOV, Ivan Mikhaylovich (1870-1936) Painter; pedagogue; specialist in Palekhian miniatures; Hon Art Worker of RSFSR from 1933; *Born*: 22 Jan 1870; *Career*: from 1914 taught at Palekh art school; one of first Palekh painters to turn to modern themes after successfully overcoming the conventionality of icon-painting; his work included subjects from works of Russian lit classics and Russian folklore; through the application of ancient enameling techniques his works are distinguished by their original coloring and subtle palette; painted on wood, ceramics, enamel, papier-mache; also did book illustrations; *Works*: "The Reading-Room" (1925); "Reconstruction of Agriculture" (1930); "The Iron Stream" (1931); "The Fountain of Bakhchisaray" (1930-32); "The Tale of the Golden Cockerel" (1932); "The Tale of the Dead Princess" (1936), etc; *Died*: 21 Aug 1936.

BAKAYEV, Ivan Petrovich (1887-1936) Party and govt official; CP member from 1906; *Born*: 1887 in Saratov Province, son of a peasant; *Career*: worker; 1905 joined revol movement; worked for Soc Democratic org in Kamyshin; 1906 helped organize and took part in Kamyshin uprising; went underground and did revol work in Baku and Astrakhan; from 1910 revol work in Petersburg; was frequently exiled and spent more than six years in prison; took part in 1917 Feb Revol in Petrograd, where he was working as a lathe operator at Russo-Baltic Aeronautics Plant; took part in 1917 Oct Revol as dep secr, then secr, Petrograd Sov of Workers and Peasants' Dep; from 1917 member, Leningrad Sov and Leningrad Province Exec Comt; after Oct Revol held a succession of other posts, including: comr, 3rd Div on Ural Front; comr, 2nd Div on Petrograd Front; 1919-20 chm, Petrograd Province Cheka with title of Hon Chekist; later Cheka plen in Southeastern Kray; head, Polit Bd and member, Revol-Mil Council, Leningrad Mil Distr; chm, Leningrad Province CPSU(B) Control Commission; plen, Pop Comrt of Workers and Peasants' Inspection; deleg at several All-Russian Party Congresses; at 14th Party Congress was member of Leningrad deleg which opposed CC; after Congress joined Zinov'yev-Kamenev-Trotskyist opposition group; 1926 member, CPSU(B) Centr Control Commission, and USSR Centr Exec Comt; expelled from Party but reinstated after declaring solidarity with Party Program; Jan 1935 sentenced to eight years' imprisonment for alleged complicity in assassination of Kirov; 24 Aug 1936 sentenced to death in trial of "Trotsky-Zinov'yev terrorist center"; *Died*: 1936 executed by firing squad.

BAKH, Aleksey Nikolayevich (1857-1946) Biochemist; member, USSR Acad of Sci from 1929; Hon Sci Worker of RSFSR from 1927; Hero of Socialist Labor from 1945; pioneer of Sov biochemistry; *Born*: 25 Mar 1857 in Zolotonosha, Poltava Province, Ukr, son of a distillery technician; *Educ*: 1875 grad gymnasium; 1875-78 studied at Fac of Physics and Mathematics, Kiev Univ; 1881 resumed studies at Kiev Univ; *Career*: 1878 expelled from Kiev Univ for taking part in student riots and exiled to Belozersk for three years; 1883 joined *Narodnaya volya* (People's Will) Party, engaged in revol activities and wrote book *Tsar Golod* (King Famine); 1885 emigrated to France, where he worked as a biochemist; 1891 travelled to USA with chemist Ephron to introduce improved fermentation method in American distilleries; 1894 moved to Geneva and set up his own laboratory, where he conducted over 70 experiments which brought him recognition in sci circles; 1917 awarded hon doctorate by Lausanne Univ; after 1917 Feb Revol returned to Russia; 1918 established chemical laboratory under the Supr Sovnarkhoz to provide sci and tech services to the chemical ind; he soon reorganized the laboratory as the Karpov Inst of Physics and Chemistry, which he directed until his death; 1920 established Biochemical Inst, Pop Comrt of Health and was its dir for a number of years; from 1937 member, All-Russian Centr Exec Comt; 1927 co-initiator and organizer, from 1928 chm, All-Union Assoc of Sci and Tech Workers for the Promotion of Socialist Construction; 1928 dep chm, Comt for Development of Sov Chemical Ind, USSR Council of Pop Comr; from 1932 until death, pres, All-Union Mendeleyev Chemical Soc; 1935-46 founder-dir, Inst of Biochemistry, USSR Acad of Sci, which now bears his name; 1937 dep, USSR Supreme Sov of 1st convocation; 1939-45 acad secr, Chemical Dept, USSR Acad of Sci; member, Moscow City Sov; ed, journals *Sovetskaya nauka, Biokhimiya,* chemistry series of *Izvestiya Akademii nauk SSSR* and other sci publ; 1893 developed theory of carbon assimilation by chlorophyl plants; 1897 theory of the reduction of nitrates in plants; 1912 theory of auto-oxidation of organic compounds of living cells and catalytic role of this process; after 1917 Oct Revol did major research on reduction fermentation processes which led to rationalization of numerous processes in tobacco, tea, wine-making, baking and other ind using organic raw materials; devised methods of studying enzymes which are now used in clinical, hygiene and agric laboratories; after his death Bakh Prizes and scholarships were instituted for outstanding work in biochemistry and physiochemistry; wrote numerous works on biochemistry, notably on carbon assimilation by chlorophyl plants, nitrogen extraction, oxidation processes, respiration, fermentation processes, etc; *Publ: Sbornik izbrannykh trudov* (Selected Works) (1937); *Sobraniye trudov po khimii i biokhimii* (Collected Works on Chemistry and Biochemistry) (1950), etc; *Awards*: four Orders of Lenin; Lenin Prize (1926); Stalin Prize (1941); Order of the Red Banner of Labor; other orders and medals; *Died*: 13 May 1946 in Moscow.

BAKH, Robert Romanovich (Robertovich) (1859-1932) Sculptor; member, Petersburg Acad of Arts from 1891; *Born*: 1859; *Educ*: grad Petersburg Acad of Arts; *Career*: for many years prof, Acad of Arts; *Works*: statue "The Genius" (1891); Leningrad monuments to Pushkin (1899) and Glinka; busts of Turgenev, Gogol, Krylov, Chistyakov, etc; after 1917 Oct Revol busts of Marx, Engels, Herzen and Frunze; *Died*: 1932.

BAKHMET'YEV, B.A. (Party pseudonyms: N; NIKOL'SKIY) (1880-1951) Prof, Petersburg Polytech Inst; Soc-Democrat (Menshevik); *Born*: 1880; *Career*: 1902-03 member, propagandist's group, Petersbrug RSDRP Comt; during 1905-07 Revol worked in Vasiliy Ostrov Rayon, Petersburg; deleg, 4th (Amalgamative) RSDRP Congress; represented Mensheviks as member, CC, RSDRP; shortly after the above Congress abandoned Party work and eventually broke with workers' movement; after 1917 Feb Revol Asst Min of Trade and Ind; from July 1919 Kolchak govt envoy in USA; *Died*: in 1951.

BAKHMET'YEV, Vladimir Matveyevich (1885-1963) Russian writer; CP member from 1909; *Born*: 14 Aug 1885 in vil Zemlyansk, now Voronezh Oblast; *Career*: as a youth joined revol movement; after Oct Revol member, Tomsk Province Party Comt; member, Tomsk Province Exec Comt; Pop Comr of Educ, West Siberian Okrug; edited Party and lit newspapers and journals; 1905 began journalistic career; 1910 first fiction published; *Publ*: his pre-revol novelettes and stories dealt with life of masses, revol underground and exile: *Sukhoy potop* (The Dry Deluge) (1914); *Alyona* (1915); *Kandal'nik* (Handcuffed) (1916); *Posledniye dni yego prevoskhoditel'stva* (The Last Days of His Excellency) (1918), etc; novel *Prestupleniye Martyna* (Martin's Crime) (1938) about Communists during the Civil War; novel *Nastupleniye* (The Attack) (1933-40); books about V. Ya. Shishkov (1947); *Sobraniye sochineniy* (Collected Works) (1930); *Izbrannoye* (Selected Works) (1953); *Died*: 16 Oct 1963.

BAKHMUTSKIY, Aleksey Ivanovich (1893-1939) Inventor; chief mech, May-Day Mine Bd, Donbas; *Born*: 1893; *Career*: 1932 designed mining combine for cutting, breaking and loading coal at the face, an improved version of which (the B-6-39) was prodeced in 1939 at Kirov Plant in Gorlovka and operated in Donbas mines until 1941; contributed to design of other mining combines; *Died*: 25 Sept 1939 in a mine accident during trials of new coal combine.

BAKHRUSHIN, Aleksandr Mikhaylovich (1900-1938) Div commander; former air force commander, Kiev Mil Distr; CP member from 1919; *Born*: 1900; *Career*: during Civil War polit worker at front; after grad from pilots course assigned commands with Red Army Air Force; 1935-37 commander, Kiev Air Brigade; 1937 air force commander, Kiev Mil Distr; 1937 arrested by NKVD; *Died*: 1938 in imprisonment; posthumously rehabilitated.

BAKHRUSHIN, Aleksey Aleksandrovich (1865-1929) Russian theater figure; *Born*: 31 Jan 1865 in Moscow, son of a merchant; *Career*: from 1890's began to collect material on history of Russian theater; in 1894 founded private lit and theater museum (later exclusively theater museum) on basis of this collection; 1913 turned over museum to Acad of Sci; from 1918 chm, Museum and Archives Section, Theater Dept, Pop Comrt of Educ; 1918 Moscow Theater Museum was named after him and he was appointed its dir for life; a great connoisseur of the theater, especially the Russian theater, he arranged numerous theater exhibitions; *Died*: 7 June 1929 in vil Gorki, Moscow Oblast.

BAKHRUSHIN, Sergey Vladimirovich (1882-1950) Historian; Dr of Historical Sci; prof; corresp member, USSR Acad of Sci from 1939; member, RSFSR Acad of Pedag Sci from 1945; senior sci assoc, Inst of History, USSR Acad of Sci from 1937; Hon Sci Worker of Uzbek SSR from 1943; *Born*: 8 Oct 1882 in Moscow; *Educ*: 1904 grad History and Philosophy Fac, Moscow Univ;*Career*: 1909-50 lecturer, then prof, Moscow Univ; for a number of years worked at Inst of History and State History Museum, Moscow; 1937-40 senior assoc, from 1940 head of section dealing with history of Russia up to 19th Century at Inst of History, USSR Acad of Sci; simultaneously active at RSFSR Acad of Pedag Sci; from 1946 member, Dept of History, USSR Acad of Soc Sci, CC, CPSU; outstanding specialist in Siberian history and soc, econ and polit history of 16th-17th Century Muscovy; pupil of V. O. Klyuchevskiy and a life-long adherent of some of his concepts, especially with regard to history of Kiev Rus'; for this reason he refused for a long time to acknowledge the "feudal" character of Kiev Rus' in 9th and 10th Centuries, considering that up to the end of the 10th Century a "stable state organization" was lacking, thus denying the Sov theory of the presence of a "strong and unified ancient Russian state" in Kiev Rus' in 9th and 10th Centuries; during World War 2 he came to agree to some extent on these questions with the opinion of B. D. Grekov; despite his theories, he played an important role in Sov historiography and in dispute with M. N. Pokrovskiy's school of history; several of his works, including *Ivan Groznyy* (Ivan the Terrible) and *Aleksandr Nevskiy i bor'ba russkogo naroda s nemetskoy agressiyey v XIII v.* (Aleksandr Nevskiy and the Struggle of the Russian People Against German Aggression in the 13th Century), written during the war years are marked by jingoistic Russian patriotism, idealization of the cult of historical personalities and justification of their arbitrary actions; also wrote several textbooks for secondary schools and higher educ institutions; helped write history of Yakut ASSR, Komi ASSR, Tatar ASSR and Kazakh, Uzbek and Turkmen SSRs; *Publ*: *Knyazheskoye khozyaystvo v XIV-XVI vv.* (Principality Economy in the 14th-16th Centuries) (1909); *Moskovskoye vosstaniye 1648* (The 1648 Moscow Uprising) (1917); *Ocherki po istorii kolonizatsii Sibiri v XVI i XVII vv.* (An Outline History of the Colonization of Siberia in the 16th and 17th Centuries) (1927); *Torgovyye krest'yane v XVII v.* (Peasant Traders of the 17th Century) (1928); *Yasak v Sibiri v XVII v.* (Yasak in 17th-Century Siberia) (1927); *Ostyatskiye i vogul'skiye knyazhestva v XVI-XVII vv.* (The Ostyak and Vogul Principalities in the 16th and 17th Centuries) (1935); coauthor, *Istoriya diplomatii* (A History of Diplomacy) (vol 1, 1941); *Ivan Groznyy* (Ivan the Terrible) (1942); *Izbrannaya rada Ivana Groznogo* (Ivan the Terrible's Elected Rada) (1945); ed, *Predposylki 'vserossiyskogo' rynka v XVI v.* (The Prerequisites for an 'All-Russian' Market in the 16th Century) (1946) ed, *Istoriya narodov Uzbekistana* (History of the Peoples of Uzbekistan) (vol 2, 1947); *Ocherki po istorii remesla, torgovli i gorodov Russkogo tsentralizovannogo gosudarstva XVI-nachala XVII v.* (An Outline History of the Crafts, Trade and Towns of the Russian Centralized State of the 16th and Early 17th Century) (1952); coauthor and ed, *Istoriya Moskvy* (The History of Moscow) (2vol, 1952-53) ; coauthor, *Ocherki istorii SSSR. Period feodalizma. IX-XV vv.* (Outline History of the USSR. The Feudal Period. 9th-15th Century) (2vol, 1953); coauthor, *Ocherki istorii SSSR. Period feodalizma. Konets XV-nachalo XVII v.* (An Outline History of the USSR. The Feudal Period. The Late 15th to the Early 17th Century) (1955); coauthor, *Ocherki istorii SSSR. Period feodalizma. XVII v.* (Outline History of the USSR. The Feudal Period. 17th Century) (1955); *Nauchnyye trudy* (Learned Works (4vol, 1952-59); *Ocherki po istorii Krasnoyarskogo uyezda v XVII v.* (Outline History of the Krasnoyarsk Uyezd in the 17th Century) (1959); *Awards*: Order of the Red Banner of Labor; Stalin Prize (1942); *Died*: 8 Mar 1950.

BAKHTUROV, Pavel Nikolyevich (? -1920) Don Cossack; polit worker in Budyonny's 1st Cavalry Army; CP member from 1917; *Career*: before 1917 Revolution, schoolteacher; 1917-18 organizer, Red partisan detachments on Don opposing White forces of Gen Kaledin and Gen Krasnov; from mid-1919 brigade comr, Budyonny's Cavalry Corps; from Nov 1919 Comr 6th and 11th Cavalry Div, Budyonny's 1st Cavalry Army; *Awards*: Order of the Red Banner; *Died*: 31 Oct 1920 killed in action on Wrangel Front.

BAKHURIN, Ivan Mikhaylovich (1880-1940) Sov specialist in mine surveying and geophysics; corresp member, USSR Acad of Sci from 1939; Born: 13 Oct 1880; *Educ*: 1909 grad Petersburg Mining Inst; later prof at this inst; worked out theory for interpreting data obtained by magnetic surveying to determine shape and sitze of magnetic bodies buried deep in the earth and methods of magnetic micro-surveying; his work on methods of mine surveying (theory of equalizing mine surveys, theory of mining polygons, research into accuracy of surveys and fallibility of measurements) is of great practical importance; from 1932 supervised study of mining subsidence and problems of regulating pressure in mines in Dontes, Moscow and Kuznets Basins and Urals; Centr Mine Surveying Research Bureau (now All-Union Mine Surveying Research Inst) was organized on his initiative and he was its sci dir until his death; *Publ*:*Kurs marksheyderskogo iskusstva. Spetsial'naya chast'* (A Course in Mine Surveying. Special Section) (1932); *Voprosy marksheyderskogo iskusstva* (Problems of Mine Surveying) (1936); coauthor, *Kurs magnitnoy razvedki* (A Course in Magnetic Prospecting) (1935); *Sdvizheniye gornykh porod pod vliyaniyem gornykh razrabotok* (Mining Subsidence) (1946); *Died* 2 Oct 1940.

BAKHUTASHVILI-SHUL'GINA, Ol'ga Aleksandrovna (1876-1950) Opera singer (soprano): singing teacher; Pop Artiste of Geo SSR from 1942; *Born*: 13 Mar 1876 in Kutaisi; *Educ*: 1901 grad Petersburg Higher Vocal Courses; 1907 completed singing training in Milan; *Career*: from 1903 with Tbilisi Opera Theater; 1918-21 instructor, from 1921 prof, Tbilisi Conservatory; 1921 dir and ed, State Folk Opera, Pop Comrt of Educ; performed in Moscow, Kiev, Khar'kov, Odessa, etc; *Roles*: Eteri in Paliashvili's "Abesalom and Eteri"; Gul'china in Arakishvili's "The Tale of Shota Rustaveli"; Liza in *Pikovaya dama* (The Queen of Spades); title role in "Madame Butterfly", etc; *Publ: Opyt vokal'noy pedagogiki* (Experience in Voice Training) (1936); aids on methods of teaching singing; coauthor, *Ocherki po istorii vokal'nogo obrazovaniya v Gruzii* (An Outline History of Voice Training in Georgia) (1959); *Died*: 29 May 1950 in Tbilisi.

BAKSHEYEV, Vasiliy Nikolayevich (1862-1958) Landscape painter; member, Acad of Painting from 1913; Pop Artist of USSR from

1956; member, USSR Acad of Arts from 1947; *Born*: 24 Dec 1862 in Moscow; *Educ*: 1888 grad Moscow School of Painting, Sculpture and Architecture; studied under V.Ye. Makovskiy, A.K. Savrasov and V.D. Polenov; *Career*: from 1893 with Assoc of Itinerant Art Exhibitions; from 1894 instructor at higher and secondary art schools in Moscow; from 1922 member, Assoc of Artists of Revol Russia; 1917-19 with Commission for the Preservation of Monuments of Art and the Past, Kremlin; *Works*: "Girl Feeding Pigeons" (1887); "Everyday Prose" (1892-93); landscapes: "The First Greenery" (1900); "Blue Spring" (1930); "Road Into the Forest" (1935); "Zhiguli Mountains" (1946); a number of his works are displayed at the Tret'yakov Gallery; *Awards*: Stalin Prize (1943); *Died*: 28 Sept 1958.

BAKULEV, Aleksandr Nikolayevich (1890-1967) Surgeon; prof from 1939; Dr of Med; member, USSR Acad of Med Sci from 1948 and USSR Acad of Sci from 1958; Hon Sci Worker of RSFSR from 1947; Hero of Socialist Labor from 1960; *Born*: 8 Dec 1890 in Sloboda Rayon, Kirov Oblast, son of a peasant; *Educ*: 1918 grad Med Fac, Saratov Univ; *Pos*: 1915-17 physician in Russian Army; 1918-22 regt physician in Red Army; 1922-26 asst prof, Surgical Clinic, Saratov Univ; 1926-30 asst prof, then assoc prof, 1939-67 prof and dir, Spasokukovskiy Clinic of Fac Surgery, Pirogov 2nd Moscow Med Inst; 1942-43 chief surgeon, evacuation hospitals in Moscow and head, Surgical Dept, 1st Moscow Municipal Hospital; 1953-60 pres, USSR Acad of Med Sci; 1956-59 dir, 1959-67 sci dir, Inst of Cardiovascular Surgery, USSR Acad of Med Sci; *Career*: 1947-58 corresp member, USSR Acad of Med Sci; 1956 founded Inst of Thoracic Surgery, USSR Acad of Sci; dep, USSR Supr Sov of 1950, 1954 and 1958 convocations; ed, journal *Vestnik Akademii meditsinskikh nauk SSSR*; member, ed bd, journal *Grudnaya khirurgiya*; ed, *Bol'shaya meditsinskaya entsiklopediya* (Large Medical Encyclopedia) (2nd ed) and *Populyarnaya meditsinskaya entsiklopediya* (Popular Medical Encyclopedia); member, ed bd, journals *Novyy khirurgicheskiy arkhiv* and *Khirurgiya*; chm, Sci Coordinating Center, USSR Acad of Med Sci; from 1960 hon member, All-Union Soc of Surgeons; 1945 visited San Francisco with Sov deleg for inauguration of UN; 1955 delivered paper on heart surgery at 16th Int Congress of Surgeons, Copenhagen; attended 7th Yugoslav Surgeons Congress, Belgrade; visited Norway and Sweden; 1956 visited England; delivered paper on "The Operative Treatment of Mitral Stenosis" at the 4th Int Congress on Thoracic Diseases, Cologne; 1957 delivered paper on "The Indication of Vascular Anastomoses in Congenital Cyanotic Disorders of the Heart" at Int Congress, Turin: 1960 attended 12th Congress of Surgeons, Rome; from 1959 member, Serbian Acad of Sci; from 1960 hon member, Purkyne Med Soc, Czechoslovakia; from 1961 hon member, Polish Surgeons Soc; 1963 attended 20th Int Congress of Surgeons and 4th Int Congress on Cardiovascular Surgery, Rome; from 1965 Hon Dr of Glasgow Univ; wrote numerous works on brain, chest and heart surgery and on lung diseases; *Publ: Operativnoye lecheniye opukholey spinnogo mozga* (The Operative Treatment of Tumors of the Spinal Cord) (1939); *Konservativnoye lecheniye abstsessov mozga (punktsiyami)* (The Conservative Treatment of Brain Abscesses [Lancing]) (1940); *Glukhoy shov pri pozdnikh obrabotkakh cherepnomozgovykh ran* (Blind Sutures in the Late Treatment of Craniocerebral Wounds) (1942); *K diagnostike i lecheniyu slipchivykh perikarditov* (The Diagnosis and Treatment of Pericarditis adhesiva) (1948); coauthor, *Pnevmonektoniya i lobektomiya (metodika operatsiy)* (Pneumonectomy and Lobectomy [Operation Methods]) (1949); coauthor, *Opyt primeneniya kontrastnoy angiokardiografii v grudnoy khirurgii* (Experience in the Application of Contrast Angiocardiography in Thoracic Surgery) (1951); *Khirugicheskoye lecheniye bolezney serdtsa i magistral'nykh sosudov (raspoznavaniye, opyt i perspektivy)* (The Surgical Treatment of Diseases of the Heart and Main Blood Vessels [Diagnosis, Experience and Prospects]) (1952); *K khirurgii priobretyonnykh zabolevaniy aorty* (Surgery of Acquired Diseases of the Aorta) (1954); coauthor, *Vrozhdyonnyye poroki serdtsa* (Congenital Heart Defects) (1955); coauthor, *Khirurgicheskoye lecheniye gnoynykh zabolevaniy lyogkikh* (The Surgical Treatment of Suppurative Lung Diseases) (1961); coauthor and ed, *Khirurgicheskoye lecheniye koronarnoy bolezni* (The Surgical Treatment of Coronary Disease) (1965); coauthor) *Khirurgicheskoye lecheniye verkhney poloy veny i yeyo protokov* (The Surgical Treatment of the Superior Vena Cava and Its Ducts) (1966); coauthor, *Khirurgicheskoye lecheniye opukholey i kist sredosteniya* (The Surgical Treatment of Tumors and Cysts of the Mediastinum) (1967); *Awards*: Stalin Prize (1949); Lenin Prize (1958); Scroll of Hon of World Peace Council (1959); Order of Lenin (1960); "Hammer and Sickle" gold medal (1960); three Orders of the Red Banner of Labor; medals; Diploma of Hon, 1st Class of USSR Min of Health; *Died*: 31 Mar 1967 in Moscow.

BAKULIN, Ivan Ivanovich (1900-1942) Party official; CP member from 1928; *Born*: 29 July 1900 in vil Khotunok, now Rostov Oblast; *Educ*: 1931 grad Khar'kov Inst of Public Educ; *Career*: from 1931 dir, Rokitnoye Agric Technicum Khar'kov Oblast; then dept head, Ukr Inst of Agric Specialist Extension Training, Khar'kov; lecturer, Khar'kov Agric Inst; from 1938 secr, Party Bureau, Khar'kov Agric Inst; 1941-42 secr, underground Khar'kov Oblast Comt, CP(B) Ukr; May 1942 arrested by German mil authorities; *Awards*: Order of Lenin (posthumously); *Died*: 24 Sept 1942 in German imprisonment.

BAKULIN, Ivan Vasil'yevich (1902-1956) Sov trade rep in Iran; CP member from 1927; *Born*: 1902; *Educ*: studied at workers' fac; 1930 grad Moscow Higher Tech College; *Career*: worked as fitter; 1939-48 USSR trade rep in China, then in Czechoslovakia; 1948-54 various exec posts with USSR Min of For Trade; from 1955 USSR trade rep in Iran; *Awards*: Order of Lenin; medals; *Died*: 11 Apr 1956.

BAKUNTS, Aksel' (1899-1938) Arm writer and scriptwriter; CP member from 1925; *Born*: 25 June 1899 in Goris, now Arm SSR; *Educ*: 1923 grad Khar'kov Agric Inst; *Career*: from 1923 chief agronomist, Zangezur Uyezd; 1918 first work printed; member, Arm Assoc of Proletarian Writers; from 1926 member, "November" lit group; from 1930 wrote scripts for films; translated Gogol's "Taras Bul'ba" into Arm; 1937 arrested by State Security organs; *Publ*: collected novelettes and stories "In a Dark Ravine" (1927); novelette "Ovnatan March" (1927); collected novellas "The Sowers of Black Land" (1933); "Kiores" (1935); unfinished novel *Khachatur Abovyan*; novellas: "Alpine Violet"; "The Pheasant"; "The White Horse"; "The Huntsman's Son," etc; scripts for films: "Under the Black Wing" (1930); "Child of the Sun" (1932); "Zangezur," etc; study of Khachatur Abovyan (1932); *Died*: 1938 in imprisonment; posthumously rehabilitated.

BAKUSHINSKIY, Anatoliy Vasil'yevich (1883-1939) Art historian, teacher and museum curator; *Born*: 1883; *Career*: collected and studied examples of art of peoples of the USSR; promoted revival and development of miniature painting in vil of Palekh and Mstera under Sov rule; assisted Palekh masters in difficult artistic transition from painting icons to painting secular utensils and creation of miniatures on contemporary Sov themes, lit and folk tales; as curator of museum collections, including Tret'yakov Gallery, helped organize art museums; played important role in training Sov art historians and devising methods of art training for children; *Publ: Muzeyno-esteticheskiye ekskursii* (Visits to Art Museums) (1919); *Lineynaya perspektiva v iskusstve i zritel'noye vospriyatiye real'nogo prostranstva* (Linear Perspective in Art and the Perception of Real Space) (1923); *Palekhskiye laki* (Palekh Lacquers) (1925); *Khudozhestvennoye tvorchestvo i vospitaniye* (Art Works and Art Training) (1925); *Iskusstvo Palekha* (Palekh Art) (1934); "N.A. Andreyev, 1873-1939" (1939), etc; *Died*: 1939.

BALABAN, Boris Aleksandrovich (1905-59) Stage dir and playwright; Hon Artiste of Ukr SSR from 1942; *Born*: 21 Dec 1905 in Khar'kov, son of a physician; *Career*: 1922-34 actor and stage dir, Berezil' Theater; worked in theaters in Moscow, Leningrad, Kiev, Khar'kov and L'vov; from 1948 stage dir, Franko Theater in Kiev; *Works*: plays and musical comedies: *Sto millionov* (A Hundred Million); *Zelyonyy lug* (The Green Meadow); "Gabi"; *Solnechnoy dorogoy* (Along the Sunny Road); *Productions*: Irchan's *Platsdarm* (Base of Operations); Korneychuk's *V stepyakh Ukrainy* (In the Ukrainian Steppe); Gusev's *Slava* (Glory); operettas: Offenbach's "Orpheus in the Underworld"; Suppé's "Boccaccio"; Rachmaninov's opera "Aleko," etc; *Died*: 8 Mar 1959.

BALABANOV, Mikhail Solomonovich (1873-?) Historian; member, RSDRP (Mensheviks); *Born*: 1873 in Chernigov; *Career*: 1894 joined RSDRP; after schism sided with Mensheviks; 1903-04 member, Don RSDRP Comt, Rostov-on-Don; 1905-06 worked in Petersburg for newspapers *Nachalo, Nasha zarya, Delo*, etc; from 1909 worked for newspaper *Kiyevskaya mysl'*; 1917 member, Kiev City Duma; 1918 member, Ukr Centr Rada; 1919 Comt member, Kiev Menshevik Org and ed, newspaper *Iskra*; 1920 sentenced by revol tribunal in Kiev and deprived of polit rights until end of Civil War; after Civil War devoted himself to historical research; wrote many books on history of ind, working class and revol movement in Russia; *Publ: Promyshlennost' v 1904-07*

(Industry in 1904-07) (1911); *Ocherki po istorii rabochego klassa v Rossii* (Outline History of the Working Class in Russia) (3 vol, 1926); *Istoriya revolyutsionnogo dvizheniya v Rossii* (A History of the Revolutionary Movement in Russia) (1925); *Ot 1905 k 1917 godu* (From 1905 to 1917) (1927), etc; *Died*: date and place of death unknown.

BALABANOVA, Anzhelika Isaakovna (1877-1965) Politician; active in Russian and Italian socialist movement; *Born*: 1877 in Chernigov, daughter of a rich merchant; *Career*: 1897 left Russia to continue her educ in Belgium, Germany and Italy; 1897, while in Germany, joined Union of Russian Soc-Democrats Abroad; 1903, after schism in RSDRP, sided with Mensheviks; 1912-16 member, CC, Italian Socialist Party; 1912-14 co-ed, newspaper *Avanti*, centr organ of above Party; represented Italian Socialist Party at Basel Congress and Zimmerwald and Kienthal Conferences; at Zimmerwald Conference elected secr, Int Socialist Commission; 1917 returned to Russia and joined RSDRP(B); 1919 Sov Ukr Pop Comr of For Affairs; persuaded by Lenin to attend 1st Comintern Congress, where she was elected secr, Comintern (according to her own account, Lenin wished to profit by her name to raise the Comintern's prestige as an int org); Dec 1921, disillusioned with Bolshevik regime and policy, emigrated from Sov Russia; 1924 expelled from RCP(B) for campaigning against Comintern; 1924-35 lived in Paris and was member, ed bd, *Avanti*; 1925 elected secr, Int Bureau of Revol-Socialist Parties; from 1936 in New York; campaigned against int Communist movement and opposed joint action by Italian Socialist Party and Italian Communist Party; *Died*: 1965, in Rome.

BALAKHONOV, Yakov Filippovich (1892-1935) Civil War veteran; CP member from 1919; *Born*: 23 Mar 1892 in vil Blagodarnenskaya, Stavropol' Province; *Educ*: 1917 grad Tiflis Ensigns' School; 1928 grad Frunze Mil Acad; *Career*: until WW 1 worker; from 1918 in Red Army; 1918-21 commander of a Red Guard detachment, commander of a column, 11th Army, asst brigade commander, brigade commander, commander of 33rd and 5th Cavalry Div, asst commander, 3rd Cavalry Corps; 1920 led successful cavalry raid into rear of Wrangel's army in northern Tavrida; 1921-24 commander, 16th Cavalry Div, mil comr, Karachay-Circassian Autonomous Oblast; 1928-35 exec posts in mil ind; *Awards*: two Orders of the Red Banner; Hon Arms of Revol; *Died*: 3 Mar 1935; 1937 posthumously declared an "enemy of the people" and his grave razed to the ground; 1956 rehabilitated.

BALANCHIVADZE, Meliton Antonovich (1863-1937) Composer; Pop rtiste of Geo SSR from 1933; *Born*: 5 Jan 1863 near Kutaisi (Geo); *Educ*: 1895 grad Petersburg Conservatory; *Career*: sung in choir as a child; from 1880 with chorus of Tiflis Opera Theater; studied theory of composition under Rimsky-Korsakov and harmony under Johannsen; 1895-1917 founded choirs and toured Centr Russia; Ukr, Poland, the Baltic area and Geo; 1918 founded the Kutaisi Music College; from 1921 headed Dept of Music, Geo Pop Comrt of Educ; 1929-31 dir, Batumi Music School; from 1935 dir, Kutaisi Music School; *Works*: romances "When I Gaze at You" and "Lullaby" (1889); opera *Tamara Kovarnaya* (Cunning Tamara) (1926, revised in 1936 and retitled *Daredzhan Kovarnaya*/Cunning Daredzhan/); cantata "Glory to the Zages Power Plant"; duet "Spring"; "Song of the Students" (1928), etc; *Awards*: Order of the Red Banner of Labor (1937); *Died*: 21 Nov 1937 in Kutaisi.

BALANDIN, Aleksey Aleksandrovich (1898-1967) Organic chemist; prof, Moscow State Univ from 1934; laboratory head, Inst of Organic Chemistry, USSR Acad of Sci from 1935; member, USSR Acad of Sci from 1946; CP member from 1949; *Born*: 20 Dec 1898; *Educ*: 1928 grad Moscow Univ; *Career*: from 1927 lecturer, Moscow Univ; 1943-46 corresp member, USSR Acad of Sci; developed multiplet theory of heterogeneous catalysis and applied it to research on kinetics of catalytic hydrogenation and dehydrogenation; *Publ: Sovremennyye problemy kataliza i teorii mul'tipletov* (Modern Catalysis Problems and Multiplet Theory) (1935); *O kataliticheskoy degidrogenizatsii uglevodorodov i yeyo primeneniye k sintezu kauchuka iz gazov* (The Catalytic Dehydrogenation of Hydrocarbons and its Application to the Synthesis of Rubber from Gases) (1942); *Teoriya organicheskogo kataliza* (The Theory of Organic Catalysis) (1947); *Teoriya izbiratel'nogo kataliza* (The Theory of Selective Catalysis) (1956); *K voprosu o kinetike degidrogenizatsii spirtov* (The Kinetics of Alcohol Dehydrogenation) (1957); *Termodinamika reaktsii demetilirovaniya toluola i krezolov vodyanym parom* (The Thermodynamics of the Steam Demethylation Reaction of Toluol and Cresols) (1963); *Skorost' prevrashcheniya M-krezola pod deystviyem vodyanogo para na nikelovykh katalizatorakh* (The Conversion Rate of M-Cresol Under the Influence of Steam on Nickel Catalysts) (1965), etc; *Awards*: Order of Lenin; Mendeleyev Prize (1936); Lebedev Prize (1945); Stalin Prize (1946); two Orders of the Red Banner of Labor (1958); medals; *Died*: 22 May 1967 in Moscow after a long illness.

BALANOVSKAYA, Leonida Nikolayevna (1883-1960) Opera singer (soprano); singing teacher; *Born*: 26 Oct 1883; *Educ*: grad Petersburg Conservatory; *Career*: 1906 opera debut in Petersburg; 1907-08 at opera theaters in Kiev; 1908-19 soloist, Bolshoy Theater; 1919-22 at opera theaters in Sebastopol; 1925-26 again soloist, Bolshoy Theater; 1926-33 at Khar'kov Opera Theater; from 1933 instructor, from 1941 prof, Moscow Conservatory; *Roless*: Marina Mnishek in *Boris Godunov*; Ganna in *Mayskaya noch'* (May Night); Oksana and Mariya in Tchaikovsky's *Cherevichki* and *Mazepa*; Francesca in *Francesca da Rimini*; Musette in "La Bohéme"; Aida and Amneris in "Aida," etc; *Died*: 28 Aug 1960.

BALASHOV (Party pseudonym: STRANNIK), Semyon Ivanovich (1874-1925) Party and govt official; CP member from 1898; *Born*: 1874 in vil Sal'tsevo, Vladimir Province; *Career*: factory worker in Ivanovo-Voznesensk at age 14; helped organize Ivanovo-Voznesensk RSDRP Comt; 1905 one of leaders of Ivanovo-Voznesensk strike; 1906-08 Party work for Orel-Bryansk RSDRP Comt in Ivanovo-Voznesensk; then Party work in Moscow; Nov 1908 arrested; 1910 exiled to Siberia; 1917 chm, Ivanovo-Voznesensk RSDRP(B) Comt; 1918 fought against troops of Gen Kaledin and helped suppress Yaroslavl' uprising; from 1919 Party work in Khar'kov, Poltava and Moscow; *Died*: 1925.

BALITSKIY, Vsevold Apollonovich (1892-?) Party and govt official; CP member from 1915; *Born*: 1892 in Verkhnedneprovsk, Yekaterinoslav Province; *Educ*: studied at Moscow Univ; *Career*: 1913 began revol activities in Moscow student circles; 1915 drafted into army and served in Tavriz, Iran; 1917 during Feb Revol elected chm, regt comt, 114th Infantry Reserve Regt; chm, Sov of Garrisons and member, Sov of Soldiers' Dep; after Oct Revol worked in Ukr as Collegium member, Pop Comrt of the Interior; dep chm, All-Ukr Cheka; member, Kiev and Volhynia Revol Comt; member, Kiev Party Comt; 1923-30 Ukr Pop Comr of the Interior and chm, Ukr OGPU; from 1931 dep chm, USSR OGPU; from 1933 simultaneously chm, Ukr OGPU and commander, Ukr Border and Interior Defense Troops; 1934 appointed Ukr Pop Comr of the Interior; held rank of Comr of State Security, 2nd Class; member, USSR and All-Ukr Centr Exec Comt; member, CC, CP Ukr; elected member, Centr Control Commission at 16th CPSU(B) Congress; elected member, CC, CPSU(B) at 17th Congress; Politburo member, CC, CP Ukr from 11th Congress; arrested by State Security organs; *Awards*: three Orders of the Red Banner; Order of the Red Banner of Labor; *Died*: date and place of death unknown.

BALKASHIN, Yuriy Anatol'yevich (1923-1960) Composer and teacher; *Born*: 18 Oct 1923 in Petrograd; *Educ*: at the age of 12 made first attempts to compose music, began to attend music circle of young composers at Vasiliy Ostrov Rayon Pioneers Club in Leningrad; elder brother was a pianist and studied at Leningrad Conservatory; spring 1941 met composer M. F. Gnesin and showed him his works; at Gnesin's suggestion turned to composition; 1941-42 studied at music school of Leningrad Conservatory; 1948 grad Leningrad Conservatory under Prof B. Arapov; 1951 completed postgrad course under Prof. V. Voloshinov; *Career*: 1950-90 taught composition and instrumentation at Leningrad Conservatory; 1950 became member, Leningrad Branch of Composers' Union; 1957 at 2nd Composers' Congress elected bd member, USSR Composers' Union; *Works*: symphonic suite "Stone Flower" (1949); symphony *Pavlik Morozov* (1953); two choruses "The Sun Rises in the East" to words by M. Dudin and "The Birch"; romances for voice and piano to verse of V. Gusev; sonata for violin and piano; music for films *Nizhe nulya* (Below Zero) and *Goryuchiy kamen'* (The Burning Stone); poem for chorus, bass soloist and orchestra "The Trenches Are O'ergrown With Grass" (1959); string quartet, etc; *Died*: 24 Oct 1960 in Komarovo, Leningrad Oblast.

BALLYUZEK, Vladimir Vladimirovich (1881-1957) Stage desginer; *Born*: 25 Dec 1881; *Educ*: studied at Higher Art College, Petersburg; 1905 exiled for membership of revol circles; emigrated to Germany, received higher art training in Munich; *Career*: worked in Paris in theaters and decorators' studios; after return to

Russia designed sets for various theaters; from 1914 active in cinema; worked at Yermol'yev Film Studio, *Sevzapkino, Azgoskino, VUFKU, Mezhrabpomfilm, Mosfilm* and other studios; *Works*: designed sets for films; *Pikovaya dama* (Queen of Spades) (1916); *Ella* (1917); *Otets Sergiy* (Father Sergiy) (1918); *Komediantka* (The Comedienne) (1923); *Papirosnitsa ot Mossel'proma* (The Cigarette Girl From Mossel'prom) (1924); *Dva-Bul'di-dva* (1930); *Prazdnik svyatogo Iorgena* (The Feast of St. Jorgen) (1930); *Vesenniye dni* (Spring Days) (1934); *Deti kapitana Granta* (Captain Grant's Children) (1936); *Noch' v sentyabre* (A Night in September) (1939), etc; produced films: *Legenda o devich'yey bashne* (The Legend of the Maiden's Tower) (1st and 2nd series, 1924); *Gamburg* (Hamburg) (1926); *Lishyonnyye dnya* (Deprived of Daylight (1927); *Zemlya zovyot* (Earth Calling) (1928), etc; also contributed to films: *Tsarevich Aleksey* (1919); *My zhdyom vas s pobedoy* (Come Back Victoriovs) (1941); *Molodoye vino* (Young Wine) (1942), etc; *Publ: Zhivopisno-malyarnyye raboty na kinoproizvodstve* (Set Designing in the Film Industry) (1948); *Died*: 9 Sept 1957.

BAL'MONT, Konstantin Dmitriyevich (1867-1943) Russian poet; one of first symblists in Russian poetry; *Born*: 15 June 1867 in vil Gumnishche, Vladimir Province; *Publ*: collections: *Pod severnym nebom* (Under the Northern Sky) (1894); *V bezbrezhnosti* (In Boundless Space) (1895); *Tishina* (Silence) (1898); *Goryashchiye zdaniya* (Burning Buildings) (1900); *Budem kak solntse. Kniga simvolov* (Let Us Be Like the Sun. A Book of Symbols) (1903); *Pesni mstitelya* (Songs of the Avenger) (1907); *Svetozvuk v prirode i svetovaya simfoniya Skryabina* (The Sound of Light in Nature and Skryabin's Symphony of Light) (1917); *Slovo o muzyke* (A Word About Music)(1917),etc; expoundet "pure art" in his articles; translated works of Whitman, Poe, Calderon, etc; his lyrics were used for the cantatas: Stanislavsky's *Zvezdolikiy* (The Beamer); Prokofiev's *Semero ikh* (They Were Seven); Rakhmaninov's *Kolokola* (Bells); verse set to music in romances and choruses of Arenskiy, Taneyev, Myaskovskiy, Cherepnin, etc; sympathized with 1905 revol but not with Oct Revol, after which he emigrated; *Died*: 24 Dec 1943 in Paris.

BALODIS, Karl Yakovlevich (1889-1964) Ophthalmologist; Dr of Med from 1933; prof from 1946; Hon Sci Worker of Lat SSR; *Born*: 1889 in Riga, son of a Worker; *Educ*: grad Med Fac, Novorossiysk Univ, Odessa; *Career*: specialized in ophthalmology under Acad V. P. Filatov; from 1924 tainee, Eye Clinic, Lat Univ; from 1929 asst prof, Chair of Eye Disease, Lat Univ; 1933 defended doctor's thesis on comparative observations of mech and chemical tatooing of the cornea; from 1937 assoc prof; 1945-1964 head, Chair of Eye Diseases, Med Fac (now Riga Med Inst), Lat Univ; was also chief ophthalmologist of Lat SSR; from 1947 founder and life-chm, Lat Soc of Ophthalmologists; Presidium member, All-Union Soc of Ophthalmologists; did major research on eve injuries and surgical and conservative treatment of glaucoma; was first Lat eye surgeon to perform corneal transplant; trained numerous ophthalmologists; *Publ*: doctor's thesis *Sravnitel'nyye nablyudeniya nad mekhanicheskim i khimicheskim tatuazhem rogovitsy* (Comparative Observations on Mechanical and Chemical Tatooing of the Cornea) (1933), ect; *Anwards*: Order of Lenin; medals; *Died*: 26 Dec 1964 in Riga.

BALTAGULOV , Tyuregel'dy Baltagulovich (1920-1966) Kir Party and govt official; CP member from 1941; *Born*: 1920; *Educ*: grad Higher Party School, CC, CPSU; *Career*: 1939-43 teacher at seven-year school, school inspector and head, rayon dept of educ; 1943-54 Komsomol, Party and govt work; 1954-55 chm, Osh Oblast Exec Comt, Sov of Workers' Dep; 1955-58 first secr, Dzhamal-Abad Oblast Comt, CP Kir; 1958-60 chm, Osh Oblast Sov of Workers' Dep; 1960-62 first secr, Osh Oblast Comt, CP Kir; 1962-66 chm, Kir Trade-Union Council; 1954-56 cand member, from 1956 member, CC, CP Kir; Presidium member, CC, CP Kir; dep, USSR Supr Sov of 1958 and 1962 convocations; comt member, USSR Parliamentary Group, Interparlimentary Union; *Awards*: Order of Lenin (1957); medal "For Valiant Labor" (1959); Scroll of Hon of Kir Supr Sov (1958); *Died*: Feb 1966.

BALUKHATYY, Sergey Dmitriyevich (1892-1945) Russian lit historian and bibliographer; corresp member, USSR Acad of Sci from 1943; *Born*: 24 Feb 1892 in Feodosiya; *Educ*: grad Fac of History and Philology, Petrograd Univ; *Career*: 1919-23 prof, Samara, then Leningrad Univ; from 1930 head, Dept of 20th-Century Russian Lit, Pushkin Center, USSR Acad of Sci; specialized in folklore, 17th-18th century Russian lit, lit theory, journalism, bibliography and interpretation; most important works were bibliography and interpretation of Gorky and studies of Gorky and Chekhov's plays; *Publ: Sotsial'noye znacheniye pervykh dram Gor'kogo* (The Social Significance of Gorky's Early Dramas) (1933); *Kritika o M.Gor'kom* (A Critique of Maxim Gorky) (1934); *Literaturnaya rabota M.Gor'kogo* Gorky's Literary Works) (1936); *Chekhov – dramaturg* (Chekhov the Dramatist) (1936); *Voprosy izucheniya dramaturgii M.Gor'kogo* (Problems of the Study of Gorky's Dramaturgy) (1938); *Gor'kovskiy seminariy* (A Gorky Seminar) (1946), ect; *Died*: 2 Apr 1945 in Leningrad.

BANAYTIS, Stanlislav Iosifovich (1899-1954) Surgeon; maj-gen, Med Corps; member, Lith Acad of Sci; corresp member, USSR Acad of Med Sci; pupil of V. A. Oppel'; *Born*: 1899; *Educ*: 1923 grad Petrograd Mil Med Acad; *Career*: 1923-33 trained in surgery at various mil hospitals; 1933-37 posted to Kirov Mil Med Acad, Leningrad, where he did research on field surgery and wrote doctor's thesis on wound shock; 1937 posted to Far East, where he was in charge of troop surgery and taught surgery on advanced training courses for mil physicians; 1939-40 chief surgeon of an army on the Finnish Front; 1940-41 head, Chair of Field Surgery, Kuybyshev Mil Acad; during WW 2 surgeon on the Western and Bel Fronts; after WW 2 Lith Min of Health, then head, Chair of Field Surgery, Kirov Mil Med Acad, Leningrad; co-ed, *Opyt sovetskoy meditsiny v Velikoy Otechestvennoy voyne* (The Experience of Soviet Medicine in the Great Fatherland War); wrote over 100 works, mostly on field surgery; specialized in wound shock and its treatment in the case of gunshot wounds; also in first-aid treatment of head wounds and gunshot fractures of the thigh; *Publ*: coauthor, *Kurs voyenno-polevoy khirurgii* (A Course in Field Surgery); *Organizatsiya khirurgicheskoy pomoshchi ranenym v voyskovom i armeyskom tylu* (The Organization of Surgical Aid for the Wounded in the Immediate and Army Rear); *Voyenno-polevaya khirurgiya po opytu Velikoy Otechestvennoy voyny* (Field Surgery During the Great Fatherland War) (1946); *Travmaticheskiy shock* (Traumatic Shock) (1947); *Krovotecheniya i ikh ostanovka v polevykh usloviyakh* (Bleeding and its Staunching in Field Conditions) (1952); coauthor, *Travmaticheskiy shock, yego patogenez, preduprezhdeniye i lecheniye* (Traumatic Shock, Its Pathogenesis, Prevention and Treatment) (1953), etc; *Awards*: nine orders; five medals; *Died*: 1954.

BANAYTIS, Yuozas Augustavovich (1908-1967) Govt official; *Born*: 1908; *Career*: 1954-57 Lith Min of Culture; 1958-67 Lith Min of Culture; dep, Lith Supr Sov of 1955, 1959 and 1963 convocations; member, Commission for For Affairs, Lith Supr Sov of 1959 convocation; 1958-67 member, CC, CP Lith; *Awards*: Order of the Red Banner of Labor; Lith Supr Sov Scroll of Hon (1958); *Died*: Mar 1967.

BANTSAN, Robert Fritsovich (1891-1943) Actor; stage designer, Hon Artiste of RSFSR from 1935; CP member from 1919; *Born*: 11 Dec 1891; *Educ*: 1925 grad *Skatuve* Studio, Moscow; studied at All-Union Tech Art Workshops; *Career*: from 1932 actor and dir, *Skatuve* Theater; 1937 arrested by State Security organs; *Roles*: the Booth Owner in Toller's "Eugen the Unfortunate"; Al'fa in Laytsen's "Al'fa and Avto"; von Stube in "Razlom" (Break-Up); Kruglov in Apin and Iokum's *Avantyura* (The Venture); Myuzenbakh in Kirshon's *Bol'shoy den'* (The Great Day); *Works*: designed sets and costumes for: *Razlom* (Break-Up) (1927); Glebov's *Zoloto i mozg* (Gold and Brain) (1929); *Zhdannyye i nezhdannyye* (The Expected and the Unexpected) (1931), etc; wrote and produced play *Zhdannyye i nezhdannyye* (1931); also produced Goldoni's "An Amusing Incident"(1936), ect; *Died*: 27 Feb 1943 in imprisonment; posthumously rehabilitated.

BARABANOV, Arseniy Yakovlevich (1901-1952) Mil med officer; lt-gen, Med Corps; CP member; *Born*: 1901; *Educ*: 1929 grad Kirov Mil Med Acad; *Career*: 1929-39 rose from junior surgeon to chief of med service of a mil distr; then lectured at Chair of Mil and Mil-Med Disciplines, Kuybyshev Mil Med Acad; during WW 2 chief of med service of an army, then Don, Centr and 1st Bel Fronts; 1945-47 head, Chair of Med Service Org and Tactics, Mil Med Acad; 1947-51 dep chief, Main Mil Med Bd; then fac head, Mil Med Acad; his outstanding organizational talent enabled him to arrange med service for main operations of the war (Battle of the Volga, Kursk Salient operation, Bel campaign, Vistula-Oder operation, Berlin campaign, ect); wrote several works on org of mil med service, summarizing experience of Sov mil med in WW 2; *Publ: Sanitarnoye obespecheniye strel'kovogo batal'ona v* *oborone* (Medical Facilities for an Infantry Battalion on the Defensive) (1940); *Sanitarnoye obespecheniye strel'kovoy roty v oborone* (The Medical Facilities for an Infantry Company on the Defensive) (1941); *Sovetskaya voyennaya meditsina* (Soviet Military Medicine) (1948); *Died*: 1952.

BARAMISHVILI, Ol'ga Ivanovna (1907-1956) Composer; *Born*: 30 Nov 1907 in Tiflis *Educ*: 1930 grad Tbilisi Conservatory; 1931-33 postgrad studies at Leningrad Conservatory; *Career*: 1938-43 asst prof of harmony, Tbilisi Conservatory; from 1943 assoc prof of special and gen solfeggio, Tbilisi Conservatory; wrote music for plays, romances, etc; *Works*: song cycle "Lyric Cycle" (1935); suite "Happy Childhood" (1934); poem "Song of the Stormy Petrel" (1942); symphonic works: "The Story of the Little Doe" (1946); "Cardle Song" (1948); piano piece "Fairy-Tale" (1950); cantata "The Happiness of Peoples Is Peace" (1951); piano piece "Spanish Dance" (1953); suite for "Romeo and Juliet" (1955); *Died*: 25 Sept 1956 in Tbilisi.

BARAN, Mikhail Lukich (1880-1937) Party functionary and govt official; CP member from 1917; *Born*: 1880 in vil Skala Podol'skaya, Tarnopol Province; *Career*: during WW 1 prisoner-of-war in Russia; helped found Communist Party of Eastern Galicia; fought in Civil War; 1920 commander, 1st Brigade, Ukrainian Galician Red Army; dep chm, Galician Revol Comt; Politburo member, CC, CP Galicia; represented Galician Socialist Sov Republ at 1920 Sov-Polish Peace Conference; after Civil War various exec Party and govt posts; arrested by State Security organs; *Died*: 1937 in imprisonment.

BARANNIKOV, Aleksey Petrovich (1890-1952) Expert on Indian languages; prof from 1919; member, USSR Acad of Sci from 1939; founder and head of Sov school of specialists on Indian philology; *Born*: 2 Apr 1890 in Zolotonosha, now Cherkassy Oblast, son of a carpenter; *Educ*: 1914 grad Fac of History and Philology, Kiev Univ; *Career*: from 1919 prof, Samara Univ; from 1920 prof, Saratov Univ; 1922-52 prof, then head, Chair of Indian Philology, 1911-38, simultaneously head, Chair of Indian Languages, Leningrad Inst of Living Oriental Languages; 1921-28 sci curator, Russian Musem; 1936-39 head, Chair of Indian Languages, Moscow Inst of Oriental Studies; 1938-40 dir, Inst of Oriental Studies, USSR Acad of Sci; studied ancient, medieval and modern Indian languages and ancient Indian lit; also studied gypsy dialects among Ukr and Russian gypsies; translated and analysed Indian medieval epics: Lallu ghi Lala's "Prem Sahar" (1937) and Tulsi Dasa's "Ramayany" (1948); *Publ*: some 250 works, including *Kratkaya grammatika khindustani (Urdu)* (A Short Hindustani / Urdu / Grammar) (vol 1, 1926): *Ukrainskiye tsygane* (The Ukrainian Gypsies) (1931); *Ukrainskiye i yuzhnorusskiye tsyganskiye dialekty* (Ukrainian and South Russian Gypsy Dialects) (1933); *Kratkiy ocherk novoindiyskikh literatur* (A Brief Outline of Modern Indian Literatures) (1933); *Khindustani (Urdu i Khindi)* (Hindustani / Urdu and Hindu /) (2 vol, 1934); *Indiyskaya filologiya. Literaturovedeniye* (Indian Philology. Literary Studies) (1959); *Died*: 4 Sept 1952 in Leningrad.

BARANOV, Konstantin Arsen'yevich (1888-1922) Revolutionary, metalworker; CP member from 1917; *Born*: 1888; *Career*: 1903 at railroad car repair shops, Putilov Plant, Petersburg; 1904 joined RSDRP; after 1905 gen strike was fired from Putilov Plant and barred from employment in other plants; 1911 drafted into the Baltic Fleet; imprisoned for 6 months for insubordination; sentenced to service in a penal battalion for refusal to serve in Navy; released on med grounds and resumed revol work among Petersburg workers; 1914 exiled from Petersburg as "unreliable element"; prior to and during 1917 Oct Revol carried out active revol work; organized a Red Guard detachment and led it in July 1917 demonstration on side of Bolsheviks; in same month drove Lenin and Zinov'yev from Petrograd to a secure hideout; deployed his detachment in defense of Petrograd during Gen Yudenich's offensive; later held responsible positions at Russian Renault Plant; *Died*: 1922.

BARANOV, Mikhail Ivanovich (1888-1943) Health service official and army physician; CP member from 1917; *Born*: 1888; *Educ*: 1913 grad Med Fac, Moscow Univ; *Career*: 1914-17 physician at a mil hospital; after 1917 Feb Revol chief of health section, Moscow Garrison, then mil health inspector, Moscow Mil Distr; during Oct Revol dir, Moscow Sov Hospital; 1918-20 head, Main Mil Health Bd; from Feb 1920 Ukr Dep Pop Comr of Health and member, CC, Ukr Red Cross Soc; from 1925 head, West Siberian Kray Health Dept; 1928-37 Head, Mil Health Bd, Red Army, with rank of corps dr; also Collegium member, USSR Pop Comrt of Health; ed, journal *Voyenno-sanitarnoye delo;* wrote numerous articles on public health and mil health service; ed, section on mil health service, *Sovetskaya voyennaya entsiklopediya* (Soviet Military Encyclopedia); *Died*: 1943.

BARANOV, Pavel Aleksandrovich (1892-1962) Botanist; prof from 1928; corresp member, USSR Acad of Sci from 1943; Hon Sci Worker of Uzbek SSR from 1944; *Born*: 28 July 1892; *Educ*: 1917 grad Moscow Univ; *Career*: 1921-28 lecturer, 1928-45 prof, Centr Asian Univ, Tashkent; 1945-54 at Main Botanical Gardens, USSR Acad of Sci; 1949-54 simultaneously Presidium chm, Mold Branch, USSR Acad of Sci; from 1954 dir, Komarov Botanical Inst, USSR Acad of Sci; specialized in embryology of orchids, anatomy of mountain plants, and biology and evolution of grapevine; author of over 80 works; *Publ: Osnovnyye etapy razvitiya botaniki* (Basic Stages in the Development of Botany) (1933); *Istoriya embriologii rasteniy* (The History of Plant Embryology) (1955); *V tropicheskoy Afriki. Zapiski botanika* (In Tropical Africa. A Botanist's Notes) (1956), etc; *Died*: 17 May 1962.

BARANOV, Pyotr Ionovich (1892-1933) One of founders of Sov Air Force and aviation ind; CP member from 1912; *Born*: 23 Aug 1892 in Petersburg (now Leningrad), son of a scrap merchant of peasant origin; *Career*: from age 12 worked as office boy; 1913 arrested in connection with case of the Centr Trade-Union Bureau; 1915 drafted into Russian Army; 1916 sentenced by a field court martial to seven years at hard labor for revol work in army; freed during 1917 Feb Revol and resumed active Bolshevik work in army; from 1918 in Red Army; commanded 4th Donets Army; member, Revol-Mil Council of Southern Group, Eastern Front, 1st and 14th Armies; Mar 1921, as deleg at 10th Party Congress, helpel crush Kronstadt Mutiny; 1921-22 member, Revol Mil Council, Turkestani Front; fought against Basmachi; 1923 chief and comr, RSFSR Armed Forces; 1923-24 polit affairs asst to chief of Air Force; Dec 1924-June 1931 chief, Red Army Air Force; from Mar 1925 also member, USSR Revol Mil Council; from June 1931 Presidium member, USSR Supr Sovnarkhoz and head of its Aviation Assoc; from Jan 1932 USSR Dep Pop Comr of Heavy Ind and head, Main Aviation Ind Bd; 1924-25 member, RCP(B) Centr Control Commission; 1927-33 cand member, CC, CPSU(B); *Awards*: Order of Lenin; Order of the Red Banner; Order of the Red Banner of the Khorezm Republic; Gold Star of the Bukhara Republic; *Died*: 5 Sept 1933 killed in a plane crash; buried on Red Square, Moscow.

BARANOVYKH, Symon (real name: BARANOV, Semyon Yakovlevich) (1900-1942) Bel writer; member, Bel Writers' Union from 1934; *Born*: 1 Sept 1900 in vil Rudkovo, now Minsk Oblast; son of a farm-hand; *Educ*: 1931 grad Dept of Lit and Philology, Pedag Fac, Bel State Univ; *Career*: from 1913 farmhand; 1920-23 in Red Army; 1923-25 vil librarian and member, vil Sov; 1925 went to Minsk and joined *Maladnyak* (Youth) Lit Assoc; 1928 became member, Bel Assoc of Proletarian Writers; 1927 first works published; wrote "revolutionary romances" on class struggle during first years of Soviet rule and collectivization of agric; frequently criticized by Party for sympathizing with kulaks and Bel *natdemocrats*; persecuted for his "nationalist" work *Matchyn syn* (A Mother's Son) which was dedicated to Yanka Kupala; 1934 his book *Marashniki* (Ant-Hills) was taken out of print for the same reason; 1937 arrested by NKVD; *Publ*: collections of short stories: *Zlosts'* (Anger) (1930); *Mezhy* (Limits) (1930); *Chuzhaya zyamlya* (Alien Land) (1930); *Pastka* (The Snare) (1935); *Novaya daroha* (The New Road) (1936); novel *Kali uzykhodzila sontsa* (When the Sun Rose) (1957); *Died*: 10 Nov 1942 in a concentration camp; posthumously rehabilitated.

BARANSKIY, Nikolay Nikolayevich (1881-1963) Geographer; prof from 1921; corresp member, USSR Acad of Sci from 1939; Hon Sci Worker of RSFSR from 1943; CP member from 1920; *Born*: 26 July 1881, in Tomsk, son of a teacher; *Educ*: 1899-1901 studied at Law Fac, Tomsk Univ; 1914 grad Moscow Business Inst; *Career*: 1901 expelled from Tomsk Univ for taking part in students' polit strike; from 1902 helped lead RSDRP orgs in Siberia; several times arrested; in 1920's worked for RSFSR Supr Sovnarkhoz and Pop Comrt of Workers and Peasants' Inspection; simultaneously prof of econ geography at Moscow higher educ establishements; from 1925 dep rector, then rector, Communist Univ for Workers of the East; from 1929 prof and from 1932 dir, Geography Research Inst, Moscow Univ and head, Chair of Econ Geography, Inst of Red Prof; during WW 2 dir, Geography Section, Kaz Branch, USSR Acad of Sci and prof, Alma-Ata Teachers' Training Inst; chief ed, journal *Voprosy geografii* worked on econ geography of USSR and other countries; author of geography textbooks, including *Ekonomicheskaya geografiya SSSR* (Economic Geography of the USSR) (1926-55) for use in secondary schools and which has run to 16 ed; *Publ: Fizicheskaya geografiya SSSR* (Physical Geography of the USSR((7th ed, 1943); *Ekonomicheskaya geografiya SShA* (Economic Geography of the USA) (vol 1, 1946); *Ocherki po shkol'noy metodike ekonomicheskoy geografii* (Outline Methods of Teaching Economic Geography) (1946); *Ekonomicheskaya geografiya v sredney shkole – Ekonomicheskaya geografiya v vysshey shkole* (Secondary-School Economic Geography – High-School Economic Geography) (1957); *Metodika prepodavaniya ekonomicheskoy geografii* (Methods of Teaching Economic Geography) (1960); *Ekonomicheskaya geografiya – Ekonomicheskaya kartografiya* (Economic Geography – Economic Cartography) (2nd ed, 1960), etc; *Awards:* Order of Lenin; Order of the Red Banner of Labor; Badge of Hon; Stalin Prize (1952); Hero of Socialist Labor (1962); *Died:* 29 Nov 1963.

BARANTSEVICH, Zoya Fyodorovna (1896-1953) Film actress and sciptwriter; *Born:* 1896; *Career:* stage debut with Rostov theater; from 1914 film work; in 1920's with Film Factory of All-Ukr Photo and Cinema Bd; *Works*: film roles: Yelena in *Zhizn'yu smyatyye dushi* (Souls Downtrodden by Life) (1916); Agni in *Chyornaya lyubov'* (Black Love) (1917); Irina in *Epizod lyubvi* (An Episode of Love) (1918); Tat'yana in *Gerasim and Mumu* (1919); Klavdiya in *Vikhr' revolyutsii* (The Whirl wind of the Revolution) (1922); the Courtesanne in *Poslednyaya stavka mistera Ennioka* (Mister Enniok's Last Gamble) (1923); the Banker's Wife in *Ne poyman – ne vor* (First Catch Your Thief) (1924); Zhuravtseva in *Troye* (The Three) (1928), etc; wrote scripts for films: *Legenda chyornykh skal* (The Legend of the Black Cliffs); *Marionetki roka* (The Puppets of Fate) (1916); *Umirayushchiy lebed'* (The Dying Swan) (1917);*Died:* 1953.

BARATOV, Leonid Vasil'yevich (1895-1964) Stage dir and actor; prof, State Stagecraft Inst from 1947; Hon Art Worker of RSFSR; Pop Art Worker of RSFSR from 1958; chief stage dir, Moscow's Stanislavsky and Nemirovich-Danchenko Music Theater from 1950; *Born:* 1 Apr 1895; *Educ:* from 1914 studied at Law Fac, Moscow Univ; *Career:* 1918-22 actor, 2nd Studio, Moscow Arts Theater; 1922-23 actor, Music Studio, Moscow Arts Theater; 1923-31 actor and stage dir, Music Studio (later Nemirovich-Danchenko Music Theater); 1931-38 stage dir, Bol'shoy Theater; 1936-38 producer, Lunarcharskiy Opera and Ballet Theater, Sverdlovsk; 1938-43 chief producer, Leningrad's Kirov Opera and Ballet Theater; 1943-50 chief producer, USSR Bolshoy Theater; instructor, school of Moscow Arts Theater, Inst of Cenematography, and Opera Dept, State Stagecraft Inst; *Productions:* Aristophanes' *Lysistrata* (1923); Rimsky-Korsakov's *Pskovityanka* (The Woman from Pskov); Tchaikovsky's *Yevgeniy Onegin* (Eugene Onegin) and *Mazepa* (Mazeppa) (1931-38); Glinka's "Ivan Susanin"; Khrennikov's *V buryu* (Into the Storm); Tchaikovsky's *Charodeyka* (The Sorceress); Koval's *Yemel'yan Pugachyov* (Emelian Pugachev) (1938-43); Mussorgsky's *Boris Godunov* (1949-50) and *Khovanshchina* (1951); Kabalevskiy's *Sem'ya Tarasa* (Taras' Family) (1952); Prokofiev's *Voyna i mir* (War und Peace) (1958), etc; *Awards:* two Orders of the Red Banner of Labor; medals; five Stalin Prizes (1943, 1949, 1950, 1951 and 1952); *Died:* 22 July 1964.

BARBARUS (real name: VARES), Iokhannes Yakovich (1890-1946) Est poet and govt official; Hon Writer of Est SSR from 1945; CP member from 1940; *Born:* 12 Jan 1890, son of a peasant; *Educ:* 1914 grad Med Fac, Kiev Univ; *Career:* from 1914 army physician; 1918 first work published; 1920-39 physician in Pärnu; 1928-35 toured USSR, France, Spain, Hungary, Greece and Albania, organizing aid for republ Spain; 1940 Prime Min of Est; later Presidium chm, Est Supr Sov; his early writings revealed strong symbolist influence; *Publ:* "Fata Morgana" (1918); "Relations" (1922; "The Geometric Man" (1924); "The Multiplied Man" (1927); "Verse" (1930); "The Estonian Republic" (1932); "Culmination" (1932-34); "Memento" (1936); "Fish out of Water" (1937); pamphlet "Spain Is Burning" (1937); "Across the Threshold" (1939); "Armed Verse" (1943); "Front-Line Roads" (1944); "Against the Current" (1946); coauthor, nonfiction book "The Rebirth of Soviet Estonia" (1945); *Died:* 29 Nov 1946 in Tallinn./

BARBASHEV, Nikolay Illarionovich (1889-1962) Educationalist; Dr of Pedag Sci; CP member form 1919; *Born:* 13 May 1889; *Educ:* 1916 grad Shipbuilding Dept, Petrograd Polytech Inst; *Career:* from 1926 dean, Factory and Plant Students Fac, Krupskaya Acad of Communist Training; senior assoc, History of Machine-Building Section, Inst for the History of Natural Sci and Eng, USSR Acad of Sci; specialized in polytech aduc and training of tech personnel; *Publ: Sistema podgotovki kadrov i tekhnicheskoye obrazovaniye v SShA* (The Personnel Training System and Technical Education in the USA) (1932); *K istorii morekhodnogo obrazovaniya v Rossii* (The History of Merchant Marine Training in Russia) (1959), etc; *Died:* 16 Nov 1962.

BARDAKH, Yakov Yul'yevich (1857-1929) Microbiologist; *Born*: 1857 in Odessa, son of a teacher; *Educ*: 1880 grad Dept of Physics and Mathematics, Novorossiysk Univ; 1883 grad Mil Med Acad; *Career*: 1886 together with I. I. Mechnikov and N. F. Gamaleya established first Russian anti-rabies station in Odessa, which later became the Mechnikov Bacterioloical Inst; 1895 introduced first independent Russian course for training assoc prof at Novorossisk Univ; this later became the Chair of Microbiology, which he headed until his death; chm, Odessa Sci Med Soc; hon member, Petersburg Microbiological Soc; one of first to support Mechnikov's phagocyte theory; developed hypothesis that immunity depends on the active reaction of the body's cells, particularly the cellular elements of certain organs (e.g. the spleen), which "learn" to absorb bacteria and produce antidotes; 1891 began research on production of diphtheria vaccine and developed successful techniques independently of Behring and Roux; 1893 published first details of this research; 1894 gave a full account of his studies of diphtheria in doctor's thesis *Issledovaniya po difterii. K ucheniyu o predokhranenii i lechenii difterii krovyanoy syvorotkoy iskusstvenno nevospriimchivykh sobak* (Research on Diphtheria. The Theory of the Prevention and Treatment of Diphtheria with Blood Serum from Artificially Immune Dogs); 1891 perfected method of obtaining tuberculin; 1903 set up first Ukr ambulance service in Odessa; wrote papers on rabies, diphtheria, immunity theory, typhoid, relapsing fever, the protective function of the spleen, etc; *Publ: K voprosu o predokhranitel'nykh privivkakh beshenstva (Preventive Vaccination Against Rabies* (1887); *K ucheniyu o difterii, o sposobakh yego predokhraneniya i lecheniya sobach'yey krovyanoy syvorotkoy* (The Theory of Diphtheria and Methods of Preventing and Curing it with Canine Blood Serum) (1893), etc; *Died*: 17 July 1929 in Odessa.

BARDIN, Ivan Pavlovich (1883-1960) Eng and metallurgist; govt official; dir, Inst of Metallurgy, USSR Acad of Sci from 1939; member (from 1932) and vicepres (from 1942), USSR Acad of Sci; *Born*: 13 Nov 1883 in vil Shirokiy Ustup, now Saratov Oblast, son of a peasant; *Educ*: 1902-05 studied at Novo-Aleksandrovsk Agric and Forestry Inst; 1910 grad Kiev Polytech Inst; *Career*: 1910-11 worked at metallurgical plants in USA; 1911-20 at metallurgical plants in southern Russia and Ukr SSR as draughts-man-designer, superintendent of blast furnaces and chief eng of iron and steel works; 1929-36 in charge of construction then head of Kuznetsk Metallurgical Combine; 1937-41 successively chief eng, Main Bd of Metallurgical Ind, chm, Tech Council, USSR Pop Comrt of Heavy Ind and USSR Dep Pop Comr of Ferrous Metallurgy; during war directed Ural Branch, USSR Acad of Sci and led work of USSR Acad of Sci in mobilizing resources of eastern regions of USSR for war effort; after the war worked on reconstruction of war-damaged factories and helped draw up long-range plans for development of ferrous metal ind; 1939-60 also dir, Inst of Metallurgy, USSR Acad of Sci; 1942-60 vice-pres, USSR Acad of Sci; 1944-60 dir, Centr Research Inst of Ferrous Metallurgy, USSR Min of Metallurgical Ind; designed large iron and steel works and standard metallurgical plant; worked on improvenent of metallurgical processes, especially with the assistance of oxygen, and on discovery and integrated utilization of new types of metllurgical raw materials; dep, USSR Supr Sov of 1st-5th convocations; *Awards*: seven Orders of Lenin; two Stalin Prizes, Ist Class (1941 and 1948); Lenin Prize (1958); Hero of Socialist Labor (1945); *Died*: 7 Jan 1960.

BARI, Nina Karlovna (1901-1962) Mathematician; prof, Moscow Univ from 1934; Dr of Physical and Mathematical Sci from 1935; member, French and Polish Mathematical Soc from 1927; *Born*: 19 Nov 1901 in Moscow; *Educ*: 1921 grad Moscow Univ; 1925 completed postgrad studies at Moscow Univ; *Career*: from 1926 taught at Moscow Univ; did research on theory of functions of true variables and synonymtiy of the definition of the coefficients of a trigonometric series according to the function which it represents; *Publ: Teoriya ryadov* (The Theory of Series) (1938); *Problema yedinstvennosti razlozheniya funktsii v trigonometri-*

cheskiy ryad (The Problem of the Uniqueness of the Expansion of a Function Into a Trigonometric Series) (1949); *O primitivnykh funktsiyakh i trignometricheskikh ryadakh, skhodyashchikhsya pochti vsyudu* (Generally Convergent Primary Functions and Trigonometric Series) (1952); coauthor, *Nailuchshiye priblizheniya i differentsial'nyye svoystva dvukh sopryazhyonnykh funktsiy* (Optimum Approximations and Differential Properties of Two Conjugate Functions) (1956); *O vsyudu skhodyashchikhsya k nulyu podposledovatel'nostyakh chastnykh summtrigonometricheskogo ryada* (Subsequences of the Partial Sums of a Trigonometric Series Which Converge Entirely to Zero) (1960); *Died*: 1962.

BARISOVA, Raisa Borisovna (Party name: Rashel') (1890-1966 Party official; CP member from 1912; *Born:* 1890; *Educ:* 1929-32 at Communist Univ, Leningrad; *Career:* 1912-15 worked for Dvinsk RSDRP group; from 1915 Party work in Ukr; helped organize RSDRP(B) groups in Bakhmut (Artemovsk) and at Konstantinov glass factory; from July 1917 exec Party work in Saratov Province; 1920-29 worked for Samara and Khar'kov Publ Educ Depts; 1934-41 lit work for newspaper *Pravda*; 1941-43 polit officer, evacuation hospital; from 1947 pensioner; *Died:* 21 Sept 1966.

BARKHATOVA, Lidiya Nikolayevna (1874-1966) Party official; CP member from 1903; *Born:* 27 Feb 1874; *Career:* member, Petersburg League for the Liberation of the Working Class; 1901 arrested for membership in *Iskra* org; after 2nd RSDRP Congress member, Petersburg RSDRP(B) Comt; then propagandist, Baku RSDRP(B) Comt; 1905-07 several times arrested; from 1914 Party propaganda among young factory workers in Presnya, Moscow; after 1917 Feb Revol secr, Krasnaya Presnya Sov of Workers' Dep; fought in 1917 Oct Revol; from 1920 with educ organs; *Died:* Jan 1966.

BARKHUDARYAN, Patvakan Andreyevich (1898-1948) Film dir; Hon Artiste of Arm SSR from 1938; *Born:* 1898; *Educ:* 1923 grad theatrical school; 1937 grad All-Union State Inst of Cinematography; *Career*: from 1923 film dir and actor, Arm Film Studio; *Productions:* films: *Zloy dukh* (The Evil Spirit) (1928); *Pyat' v yablochko* (Five in the Bull) (1929); *Shestnadtsatyy* (The Sixteenth) (1929); *Pod chyornym krylom* (Under the Black Wing) (1930); *Kikos* (1931); *Dve nochi* (Two Nights) (1933); *Gornyy potok* (Mountain Flood) (1940); *Vtoroy armyanskiy kinokontsert* (The 2nd Armenian Film Concert) (1946), etc; *Died:* 1948.

BARKOV, Aleksandr Sergeyevich (1873-1953) Geographer; Dr of Geographical Sci; prof from 1931; member, RSFSR Acad of Pedag Sci from 1944; Hon sci Worker of RSFSR from 1945; *Born:* 13 May 1873; *Educ:* 1898 grad Natural Sci, Dept, Fac of Physics and Mathematics, Moscow Univ; *Career:* from 1899 geography teacher, Alexandrine College, Moscow, then instructor, Tikhomirov Women's Courses; 1931-50 prof of geography, Moscow Univ; from 1941 head, Chair of African Physical Geography, 1947-50 senior assoc, Moscow Univ; 1944-47 head, Geographical Methods Section, Inst of Teaching Methods, RSFSR Acad of Pedag Sci; 1922 did field work in Crimea, 1929 in Moscow Oblast and 1930-31 in Samarskaya Luka; wrote works on general and regional geography; 1900-10 together with S. G. Grigor'yev, A. A. Kruber and S. V. Chefranov wrote geography textbooks and primers for schools; also wrote articles on methods of teaching geography; *Publ:* coauthor, *Fizicheskaya geografiya* (Physical Geography) (1935); article "University Geograhpy and the Secondary School" (1940); article "The Tasks of Physical Geography Courses for High Schools" (1946); *Fizicheskaya geografiya chastey sveta. Afrika* (Physical Regional Geography. Africa) (1953); *Slovar'-spravochnik po fizicheskoy geografii* (A Reference Dictionary of Physical Geography) (1940), etc; *Died:* 28 Feb 1953.

BARNET, Boris Vasil'yevich (1902-1965) Film dir; Hon Artiste of RSFSR from 1935; Hon Art Worker of Ukr SSR from 1951; CP member from 1943; *Born:* 18 June 1902 in Moscow; *Educ:* grad Main Mil School for Workers' Physical Training; studied at State Cenematography Technicum; *Career:* from 1920 film actor; from 1927 film dir; also wrote film scripts; *Productions:* films: *Devushka s korobkoy* (The Girl with the Box) (1927); *Na Trubnoy* (On Trubnaya Street) (1928); *Okraina* (The Outskirts) (1933); *U samogo sinego morya* (By the Bluest Sea) (1936); *Noch'v sentyabre* (A Night in September) (1939); *Muzhestvo* (Courage) (1941); *Odnazhdy noch'yu* (Once at Night) (1945); *Podvig razvedchika* (The Scout's Feat) (1947); *Shchedroye leto* (Generous Summer) (1955); *Poet* (1957); *Annushka* (1959); *Alyonka* (1961), etc; film roles: the Cowboy Jeddy in *Neobychaynoye priklyucheniye Mistera Vesta v strane bol'shevikov* (The Unusual Adventure of Mister West in the Land of the Bolsheviks) (1924); the Trick Actor in "Miss Mend" (1926); Gen Kyun in *Podvig razvedchika* (The Scout's Feat) (1947), etc; *Publ: Na podstupakh k sovetskoy komedii* (On the Approaches to Soviet Comedy) (1927); *Kritikovat' v protsese raboty* (Criticizing in the Course of Work) (1935); *Kak ya stal rezhissyorom* (How I Became o Film Director) (1946); *Awards:* Stalin Prize (1948); *Died:* 8 Jan 1965.

BARNOVI, Vasiliy Zakhar'yevich (1856-1934) Geo novelist; *Born:* 3 June 1856; *Career:* wrote historical novels calculated to foster Geo nat pride and protest against for conquest; his novels deal with nat liberation struggle and somewhat idealize the heroic epic and romance of the past; *Publ:* novels "The Dawn of Isani" (1901); "Martyr of Love" (1908); "The Extinguished Fire" (1913); "The Khazar Bride" (1922); "The Fall of Armazi" (1925); "The Great Mouravi Georgiy Saakadze" (1925), etc; *Died:* 4 Nov 1934.

BARONENKOV, Aleksandr Vasil'yevich (1900-1966) Mining eng; Cand of Tech Sci from 1953; assoc prof; CP member; *Born:* 18 Oct 1900 in Aktarsk, Saratov Province, son of a worker; *Educ:* 1928 grad Moscow Mining Acad; *Career:* 1928-38 organized work at mines producing chemical raw materials, then chief eng and shaft mang, Moscow Subway; from 1938 head, Tech Dept, Main Ore Bd, USSR Pop Comrt of Ferrous Metallurgy; from 1944 dep head, Main Nickel and Cobalt Bd, USSR Pop Comrt of Non-Ferrous Metallurgy; from 1948 head, Tech Dept and Collegium member, State Mining Tech Supervision Bd; also taught at Moscow Mining Inst; 1953-66 assoc prof, Chair of Ind Econ and Org, Moscow Mining Inst; also lectured at Moscow Inst of Radio Electronics and Mining Electromech; member, ed bd and dep chief ed, periodical *Gornyy zhurnal; Publ: Organizatsiya i planirovaniye proizvodstva na kar'yerakh* (The Organization and Planning of Quarrying) (1953); *Vybor rezhima raboty gornogo predpriyatiya* (The Selection of Mining Operation Techniques) (1958), etc; *Awards:* Order of the Red Banner of Labor; medals; *Died:* 5 May 1966.

BARSHAUSKAS, Kazimeras Matovich (1904-1964) Physicist; Dr of Physical and Mathematical Sci from 1938; prof from 1941; member, Lith Acad of Sci from 1956; rector, Kaunas Polytech Inst from 1950; Hon Sci Worker of Lith SSR from 1964; CP member from 1950; *Born:* 13 May 1904 in vil Gizhay, Vilkavishkis Uyezd; son of a peasant; *Educ:* 1930 grad Fac of Physics and Mathematics, Kaunas Univ; *Career:* 1930-40 junior laboratory asst, then senior asst prof, Kaunas Univ; 1941 prof and head, Chair of Physics, Kaunas Univ; 1941-44 secondary-school teacher; 1944-50 prof and dean, Fac of Electric Eng, Kaunas Univ; 1950-64 prof and dean, Kaunas Polytech Inst; specialized in the study of cosmic rays, ultrasonics, semiconductors and magnetic nuclear resonance; 1958-64 member, CC, CP Lith; dep, Lith Supr Sov of 1955, 1959 and 1963 convocations; *Publ:* "Beiträge zur Energieverteilung im kosmischen Strahlenschauer" (1937); *Antriniu spinduliu energijos pasiskirstymo klausimu* (1938); *Kosminiai spinduliai* (1946); *Fizika* (4 vol, 1950); coauthor, *Ultragarsinio pastovaus ilgio interferometro taikymas fiziniu ir cheminiu pasikeitimu kontrolei* (1957); coauthor, *Magnetinės garso dispersijos elektrai laidziuose skysciuose klausimu* (1958); coauthor *Vzaimodeystviye yadernykh magnitnykh momentov s avtokolebatel'noy sistemoy, imeyushchey dve stepeni svobody* (The Interaction of Nuclear Magnetic Moments With a Self-Oscillatory System Having Two Degress of Freedom) (1962); *Awards:* Order of Lenin; Order of the Red Banner of Labor; medals; *Died:* 24 May 1964.

BARSKAYA (CHARDYNINA), Margarita Aleksandrovna (1901-1937) Stage dir; *Born*: 1901, *Career:* began film work with serial roles in Ukr silent films; pop scriptwriter and dir for children's films; *Roles:* Dar'ya in *Babiy Log* (Ravine of Women) (1925); the Girl in *Yagodka lyubvi* (The Love Berry) (1926); Yagella in *Taras Tryasilo* (1927), etc; wrote scripts for and produced: *Rvanyye bashmachki* (The Tattered Shoes) (1933), etc; *Died*: 1937.

BARSKIY, Boris Yevseyevich (1890-1937) Mil signals specialist; CP member from 1918; *Born:* 1890; *Career:* from 1918 in Red Army; during Civil War head, Mil Communications Bd, Staff of Revol Mil Council; 1922 head, Mil Communications Dept, 5th Army; from 1924 head and mil comr, Red Army Mil Communications Bd; head, 3rd Dept, Red Army Staff; 1937 arrested by State Security organs; *Died:* 1937 in imprisonment; posthumously rehabilitated.

BARSKIY, Vladimir Grigor'yevich (1889-1936) Geo film actor and dir; *Born:* 1889; *Roles:* Golikov in *Bronenosets Potyomkin* (The Battleship Potyomkin) (1926); Zhan in *Zavodnoy zhuk* (The Clockwork Beetle) (1928); Blanshan in *Torgovtsy slavy* (Merchants of Glory) (1929); Sudarikov in *Nasten'ka Ustinova* (1934); the Chm of the Court in *Pepo* (1935), etc; *Productions:* directed films: *Obezglavlennyy trup* (The Beheaded Corpse) (1919); *Ne spi* (Don't Sleep) (1920); *Skazhi zachem* (Tell Me Why) (1920); *Izgnannik* (The Exile) (1922); *Razboynik Arsen* (Arsen the Brigand) (1924); *Koshmary proshlogo* (Nightmares of the Past) (1925); *Devyatyy val* (The Ninth Wave) (1926); *Knyazhnya Meri* (Princess Meri) (1926); *Bella* (1927); *Kazaki* (Cossacks), after Lev Tolstoy (1928), etc; *Publ: Kak ya snimal 'Devyatyy val'* (How I Shot the "Ninth Wave") (1929); *Died:* 24 Jan 1936.

BARSOVA (real name: VLADIMIROVA), Valeriya Vladimirovna (1892-1967) Russian singer (lyric and coloratura soprano); prof, Chair of Solo Singing, Moscow Conservatory from 1950; Pop Artiste of USSR from 1937; CP member from 1940; *Born:* 13 June 1892 in Astrakhan'; *Educ:* 1919 grad in piano and singing under U. Mazetti, Moscow Conservatory; *Career:* 1915-20 performed at Theater of the Union of Workers' Org, in Baliyev's *Letuchaya Mysh'* (The Bat) and an opera by Zimin; 1920-48 soloist, Bolshoy Theater, Moscow; simultaneously worked at Musical Studio, Moscow Acad Arts Theater; sang at concerts; performed in England, Turkey, Finland and East European countries; 1952 abandoned stage and became teacher; dep, RSFSR Supr Sov of 1938 convocation; dep, Moscow City Sov of first two convocations; pres, Theater Section, All-Union Soc for Cultural Relations With For Countries; Bd chm, Art Workers Center; 1954 member, Sov deleg at Congress of USSR-CSSR Friendship Soc; 1959 jury member, 7th World Festival of Youth and Students, Vienna; *Roles*: Lyudmila in Glinka's "Ruslan and Lyudmila", Antonida in Glinka's "Ivan Susanin"; title role in Rimsky-Korsakov's *Snegurochka* (The Snow-Maiden); Rosina in Rossini's "The Barber of Seville"; Violetta in Verdi's "Traviata"; Gilda in Verdi's "Rigoletto", etc; *Awards:* Order of Lenin; Order of the Red Banner of Labor; medals; Stalin Prize (1941); *Died:* 15 Dec 1967.

BARTOL'D, Vasiliy Vladimirovich (1869-1930) Historian and orientalist; Dr of Historical Sci from 1900; prof, Petersburg (Leningrad) Univ from 1901; member, Russian (USSR) Acad of Sci from 1913; *Born:* 15 Nov 1869; *Educ:* 1891 grad Fac of Oriental Languages, Petersburg Univ; *Career:* from 1896 lecturer, then prof, Petersburg Univ; 1910-13 corresp member, Russian Acad of Sci; 1912 founded and headed journal *Mir islama*; in 1920's chm, Collegium of Orientalists, Acad of Sci; from 1925 ed, journal *Zapiski Kollegii vostokovedev*; 1926-29 asst chm, Acad of History of Material Culture and, from 1928, dir of its Turkological Office; also edited collection *Iran*; helped found Centr Asian Inst in Tashkent and worked on commission for latinizing Arabic scripts of USSR peoples; attended int congresses and conventions of orientalists and read lectures at univ in Britain, Turkey, etc; author of over 400 works on history, geography, culture and religion of peoples of Near and Middle East, including Centr Asia; research distinguished by great erudition; *Publ: Turkestan v epokhu mongol'skogo nashestviya* (Turkestan at the Time of the Mongol Invasion) (2 vol, 1898-1900); *Istoriko-geograficheskiy obzor Irana* (A Historical and Geographical Survey of Iran) (1903); *Khalif i Sultan* (Caliph and Sultan) (1912); *Istoriya izucheniya Vostoka v Yevrope i v Rossii* (History of the Study of the East in Europe and in Russia) (1911); *K istorii orosheniya Turkestana* (History of Irrigation in Turkestan) (1914); *Ulugbek i yego vremya* (Ulug-bek and His Time) (1918); *Islam. Obshchiy ocherk* (Islam. A General Outline) (1918); *Kul'tura musul'manstva* (The Culture of Islam) (1918); *Musul'manskiy mir* (The Moslem World) (1922); *Istoriya Turkestana* (History of Turkestan) (1922); *Mesto prikaspiyskikh oblastey v istorii musul'manskogo mira* (The Place of the Caspian Regions in the History of the Moslem World) (1925); *Museylima* (1926); *Koran i more* (The Koran and the Sea) (1925); *Iran. Istoricheskiy obzor* (Iran. A Historical Survey) (1926); *Istoriya kul'turnoy zhizni Turkestana* (History of the Culture Life of Turkestan) (1927); *Kirgizy. Istoricheskiy ocherk* (The Kirghiz. An Outline History) (1927); *Ocherk istorii Semirech'ya* (An Outline History of Semirech'ye) (1943), etc; *Died:* 19 Aug 1930.

BARTRAM, Nikolay Dmitriyevich (1873-1934) Artist; specialist in decorative art and art ind; *Born:* 1873 in Moscow; *Educ:* grad Moscow College of Painting, Sculpture and Architecture; *Career:* did illustrations for children's books; 1904-16 head of art and crafts work, Moscow Province Zemstvo; founded Patterns Museum at Crfts Museum (now Folk Art Museum); did research on history of children's toys, children's books and children's theater; worked for children's clubs in Moscow and for Free Child Center; from 1918 founder-dir, State Toy Museum, Moscow; 1919 founded Museum of the 'Forties; 1923 agganged crafts side of 1st All-Russian Agric Crafts Ind Exhibition, Moscow; 1925 helped arrange Russian Dept, Int Exhibition of Art Ind and Decorative Art, Paris; displayed his works at art exhibitions in Russia, Paris, London, etc; wrote works on educ theory, art ind, peasant art and crafts; edited various periodicals on these subjects; *Died:* 1934.

BARVINSKIY, Vasiliy Aleksandrovich (1888-1963) Composer and pianist; prof from 1939; *Born:* 20 Feb 1888 in Tarnopol'; *Career:* 1915-39 dir, Lysenko Higher Music Inst; 1939-48 dir, Lvov Conservatory and prof, piano and composition class; arrested by NKVD; returned to Lvov only in 1958; *Works:* chorale "The Testament" (1917); "Nocturne" (1933); "Song of the Homeland" (1940); Piano Concerto (1937); "My Country Famed in Song" (1960); etc; *Died:* 9 June 1963 in Lvov

BARYKIN, Vladimir Aleksandrovich (1879-1942) Microbiologist and epidemiologist; Dr of Med from 1906; prof from 1915; *Born:* 1879; *Educ:* 1900 grad Med Fac, Kazan' Univ; *Career:* 1908-10 asst to Prof I. G. Savchenko; worked under I. I. Mechnikov in Paris and J. Bordet in Brussels; 1910-15 assoc prof, Chair of Microbiology, Kazan' Univ; 1915-21 prof of microbiology, Rostov Univ; 1921-31 founder-dir, Moscow Microbiological Inst; simultaneously head, Chair of Microbiology, 1st Moscow State Univ; from 1931 sci dir, Mechnikov Inst, Moscow; from 1932 sci dir, Microbiological Inst of Kiev and then Baku; 1933-38 sci dir, Centr Inst of Postgrad Med Training; was a staunch supporter of the physiochemical school in immunity theory; propounded "condition theory" to explain basic immunological phenomena, according to which immunity is not stimulated by presence of new substances but by changes in colloidal state of the body's liquids and tissues; did much-publicized research on avidity of immune sera and devised method of determining it; 1909 isolated chronic nodular form of the plague in *Marmota sibirica*; 1921 first Sov sci to describe infectious jaundice; devised method of vaccinotherapy for carriers of diphtheria; taught such famous microbiologists and immunologists as G. V. Vygodchikov, P. F. Zdorovskiy, L. A. Zil'ber, Ye. N. Levkovich, P. V. Smirnov, L. M. Khatenever, V. V. Frize and V. A. Chernokhvostov; from 1921 Presidium member of all Sov congresses of microbiologists and epidemiologists; for several years ed *Zhurnal mikrobiologii, epidemiologii i immunologii*; co-ed *Bolshaya meditsinskaya entsiklopediya* (Large Medical Encyclopedia) (1st ed); wrote 114 papers and four monographs on etiology, pathogenesis, prophylaxis and diagnosis of typhus, cholera, Siberian plague, etc; *Publ*: doctor's thesis *Paratifoznyye zabolevaniya v Macnch'zhurii* (Paratyphoid Diseases in Manchuria) (1906); article "A Nodal Form of the Plague in *Marmota sibirica*" (1909); several papers on typhus in *Trudy 4-ogo Vserossiyskogo s'yezda bakteriologov i epidemiologov* (Proceedings of the 4th All-Russian Congress of Bacteriologists and Epidemiologists) (1921); coauthor, article "The Theory of the Nature of Antigens" (1924); article "Immunity as a Functional Condition" (1927); *Died:* 1942.

BARYSHEV, Nikolay Andreyevich (1907-44) Stage designer; Hon Art Worker of RSFSR from 1940; CP member from 1937; *Born:* 1907; *Educ:* 1929 grad Kazan' Art School; *Career:* from 1929 at Crimean Gorky Theater in Simferopol', later chief stage designer of this theater; during WW 2 on behalf of underground Crimean Party Comt, organized and led in German-occupied Simferopol' a group of patriots, who compiled maps showing disposition of German mil units, distributed Sovinformbyuro leaflets and brought medical supplies to partisans; 1944 arrested by Gestapo; *Works:* Sets for plays *Kak zakalyalas' stal'* (How the Steel was Tempered) (1938), *Chelovek s ruzh'yom* (The Man with the Gun) (1939), *Kremlyovskiye kuranty* (Kremlin Chimes) (1940, etc; *Died:* 1944 executed.

BARYSHNIKOV, Vladimir Arkhipovich (1889-1919) Revolutionary; active in Oct Coup in Moscow; polit official of Red Army during Civil War; CP member from 1905; *Born:* 1889 in Orekhovo-Zuyevo, son of a textile worker; *Career:* 1905 participated in revol in Orekhovo-Zuyevo; member, Orekhovo-Zuyevo Bolshevik Comt and Sov of Workers' Dep; 1906 arrested in connection with 1905 revol and exiled to Narym Kray for four years; 1907 ascaped from exile; 1907-08 illegal Party work in Moscow area; 1908-10 in prison; 1910-12 again illegal Party work in Orekhovo-Zuyevo and Moscow; 1912 arrested and exiled to Turukhan Kray; returned from exile to Moscow; during WW 1 conscripted into Russian Army, from which he was discharged on med grounds after 1917 Feb Revol; from Apr 1917 chm, Orekhovo-Zuyevo City Bolshevik Comt; Bureau member, Moscow Okrug Bolshevik Comt; Aug 1917 deleg at 6th RSDRP(B) Congress; from Aug 1917 chm, Orekhovo-Zuyevo City Sov; Oct 1917 arrived in Moscow at head of a detachment of Red Guards from the Moscow area which played a large role in the Bolshevik victory in Moscow; from Jan 1918 dep chm, Moscow Province Exec Comt and Moscow Province Comr of Labor; member, All-Russian Centr Exec Comt of 1918 convocation; from Oct 1918 head, 9th Army Polit Dept; 1919 member, 8th Army Revol Mil Council; *Died:* Aug 1919 captured by Gen Mamontov's Cossacks and hanged.

BARYSHNIKOVA (nickname: KUPRIYANIKHA), Anna Kupriyanovna (1868-1954) Russian fabulist; member, Union of Writers from 1938; *Born:* 24 Aug 1868 in vil Churikovo, Voronezh Province; *Career:* learned her stories primarily from her father; her varied repertoire included over one hundred fairytales and satirical and animal stories; she narrated in traditional, rhyming manner, using vivid, picturesque language and a fine sense of humor; in 1949 wrote story *Kak nemetskiy general k partizanam v plen popal* (How a German General Fell Into the Hands of the Partisans); *Awards:* Order of the Red Banner of Labor; *Died:* 23 Aug 1954.

BASANGOV (pen-name: Gashuta BAATR), Baatr Badmayevich (1911-44) Kalmyk writer; *Born*: 1911 in vil Pekerta, now in Kalmyk ASSR, son of a peasant; *Educ*: school for peasant children; *Career*: 1928 first work published; contributed to newspaper *Tangchin zyang*; 1940 compiled "Russian-Kalmyk Dictionary"; *Publ*: collected stories "The Truth of Past Years" (1931); plays "Chuche", "The Backward Plutocrat", "Song About a Mother"; novelette "Bulgun"; fairytale play "The Land of Bumba" (1940), etc; *Died*: 1944.

BASHINDZHAGYAN, Gevork Zakharovich (1857-1925) Arm landscape painter; founded Arm school of landscape painting; *Born*: 28 Sept 1857; *Educ*: 1879-83 studied at Petersburg Acad of Arts; *Career*: strongly influenced by I. K. Ayvazovskiy, A. I. Kuindzhi and other Russian landscape painters; his best pictures are faithful renditions of Transcaucasian landscape; *Works*: "Rainy Day at Sevan" (1900); "Perfect Calm" (1901); "The Road Along the Ravine" (1892); "The Alazan' Valley" (1902); "Ararat" (1912), etc; *Publ*: collection of short stories *Iz dnevnika dvoryanina* (From a Noblemean's Diary), honest and accurate descriptions of the daily life of the Armenians and Georgians of Transcaucasia; *Died*: 4 Oct 1925.

BASOV, Mikhail Yakovlevich (1892-1931) Psychologist; specialist in gen and pedag psychology; *Born*: 3 Nov 1892; *Career*: worked on motor-volitional activity under A.F. Lazurskiy at Petrograd Psychoneurological Inst; in his latter years concentrated on pedology; *Publ*: *'Volya, kak predmet funktsional'noy psikhologii* (The Will as a Subject of Functional Psychology) (1922); *Opyt metodiki psikhologicheskikh nablyudeniy i yeyo primeneniye k detyam doshkol'nogo vozrasta* (Experience in Methods of Psychological Observation and Its Application to Preschool Children) (1923); *Lichnost' i professiya* (Personality and Profession) (1926); *Psikhologiya, refeksologiya i fiziologiya* (Psychology, Reflexology and Physiology) (1927); *Obshchiye osnovy pedologii* (The General Principles of Pedology) (1928), etc; *Died*: 6 Oct 1931.

BASOV, Osip Nikolayevich (1892-1934) Actor, producer and teacher; Hon Artiste of RSFSR from 1933; *Born*: 14 Feb 1892; *Career*: 1918 entered Mamontov Studio; 1919 transferred to Vakhtangov Studio (from 1926 Vakhtangov Theater); one of best rep of Vakhtangov school; gifted with keen observation, humor and spontaneity; in 1934 directed Moscow Contemporary Theater; *Roles*: Revunov-Karaulov in Chekhov's *Svad'ba* (The Wedding) (1920); Gustav in Maeterlink's "The Miracle of St Anthony" (1921); Al'toum in Gozzi's "Turandot" (1922); Podkolesin in *Zhenit'ba* (Marriage) (1924); Fedot in Seyfullinaya and Pravdukhin's *Virineya* (1925); Louis XIII in Hugo's "Marion Delorme" (1926); Miller in "Kabale und Liebe" (Guile) (1930); Dostigayev in Gorky's *Yegor Bulychyov i drugiye* (Yegor Bulychyov and Co) (1932) and *Dostigayev i drugiye* (Dostigayev and Co) (1933); assisted in Vakhtangov Theater productions of: "Kabale und Liebe" (1930); Pogodin's *Temp* (Tempo) (1930); Katayev's *Doroga tsvetov* (Road of Flowers) (1934), etc; *Died*: 10 Oct 1934.

BASOV, Viktor Semyonovich (1901-1946) Stage designer; *Born*: 3 Oct 1901; *Educ*: grad Leningrad Stage Designing Workshop; 1926 grad Ind Art Technicum; *Career*: from 1921 stage designer and actor, Ust'-Kamenogorsk Pop Center; then stage designer at Theater Studio, Maly Opera Theater, Musical Comedy Theater, Bolshoy Drama Theater, Leningrad's Kirov Opera and Ballet Theater, Moscow's Maly Theater and Khar'kov Russian Drama Theater, etc; *Works*: designed sets and costumes for: "Romeo and Juliet" (1933); "Othello" (1934); Afinogenov's *Dalyokoye* (The Distant Past) (1936); Shakespeare's "Measure for Measure" (1936); Smetana's "The Bartered Bride" (1937); Aleksandrov's *Svad'ba v Malinovke* (Wedding at Malinovka) (1938); *Chelovek s ruzh'yom* (The Man with a Gun) (1938); "Faust" (1941); Griboyedov's *Gore ot uma* (Woe from Wit) (1946); *Died*: 19 Dec 1946.

BATALOV, Nikolay Petrovich (1899-1937) Actor; Hon Artiste of RSFSR from 1933; *Born*: 6 Dec 1899 in Moscow; *Career*: 1916-24 actor, 2nd Studio, Moscow Arts Theater; from 1924 in company of Moscow Arts Theater, where in 1927 he played Figaro, his first big role; possessed great stage presence and his playing was infused with a keen feeling for modernity, sincerity, popular humor and temperament; *Roles*: stage roles: Petya in Gippius' *Zelyonoye kol'tso* (The Green Ring) (1916); Vas'ka Okorok in *Bronepoezd 14-69* (Armored Train 14-69) (1927); the sailor Rubtsov in Ivanov's *Blokada* (Blockade) (1929); Lup Kleshnin in A.K. Tolstoy's *Tsar' Fydor Ioannovich*; Medvedev in Gorky's *Na dne* (The Lower Depths); Lopakhin in Chekhov's *Vishnyovyy sad* (The Cherry Orchard); Sobakevich in Gogol's *Myortvyye dushi* (Dead Souls) (1933), etc; film roles: Gusev in "Aelita" (1924); Pavel Vlasov in *Mat* (Mother) (1926); Sergeyev in first Sov sound film *Putyovka a zhizn* (Passport to Life) (1931); the husband in *Tret'ya Meshchanskaya* (The Third Meshchanskaya) (1927); Leva in *Gorizont* (Horizon) (1933); Ivanov in *Petukh i Tsar'* (The Rooster and the Tsar) (1935); Latsis in *Tri tovarishcha* (Three Comrades) (1935), ect; *Died*: 10 Nov 1937.

BATKIS, Grigoriy Abramovich (1895-1960) Health service official; hygienist and sanitary statistician; corresp member, USSR Acad of Med Sci; CP member from 1919; *Born*: 1895; *Educ*: 1919 grad Med Fac, Kiev Univ; *Career*: until 1923 helped to organize Ukr health service; from 1923 engaged in pedag work in Moscow, at first under direction of N. A. Semashko and A. V. Mol'kov; from 1931 head, Chair of Soc Hygiene, then Chair of Health Service Org, 2nd Moscow Med Inst; 1938-41 head, Dept of Sanitary Statistics, USSR Pop Comrt of Health; devised new system of post-natal care based on continuous observation, and a questionnaire method of demographic research which proved particularly useful for studying influence of economic and hygienic factors on demographic processes and principles of mass migration statistics; supervised compilation of a history of early Russian sanitary statistics; criticized " pseudo-scientific bourgeois theories" of med and hygiene; read papers on theory and practice of Sov health system at various congresses; wrote over 150 papers on theory of soc hygiene, health service org and sanitary statistics; his *Rukovodstvo po sotsial'noy gigiyene* (Manual of Social Hygiene) (1935-36, 1940) and *Rukovodstvo po organizatsii zdravookhraneniya* (Manual of Health Service Organization) (1948) became prescribed reading in med colleges; 1950-52 latter work was published in Bulgaria, Poland, Hungary, Rumania, Czechoslovakia and China; *Publ*: article "An Outline of Statistical Methodology and the Study of Mortality Rates" (1928); coauthor, *Uchyot, otchyotnost' i statistika zdravookhraneniya* (Record-Keeping, Accounting and Statistics in the Health Service) (1939); *Sotsial'naya gigiyena* (Social Hygiene) (1940); *Aktivnyy patronazh grudnykh detey* (Active Post-Natal Care) (1940); *Sotsial'naya gigiyena* (Social Hygiene) (1940); *Organizatsiya zdravookhraneniya* (The Organization of the Health Service) (1948); *Statistika zdravookhraneniya* (Health Service Statistics) (1951); coauthor, *Teoriya i organizatsiya sovetskogo zdravookhraneniya* (The Theory and Organization of the Soviet Health Service) (1961); selected works *Voprosy sanitarnoy i demograficheskoy statistiki* (Problems of Sanitary and Demographic Statistics) (1964); *Awards*: Semashko Prize of USSR Acad of Med Sci (1961); *Died*: 1960 in Moscow.

BATURIN (real name: ZAMYATIN), Nikolay Nikolayevich (Party pseudonym: "Konstantin") (1877-1927) Professional revol;

propagandist and publicist; historian; CP member form 1901; *Born*: 6 Dec 1877 Chertkovo Railroad Station, Southeastern Railroad; *Educ*: studied at Petersburg Univ; 1899 expelled from univ for participation in student movement, went abroad and continued studies at Berlin, Zurich and Leipzig Univ; *Career*: 1901 returned to Russia; Party work in Kiev, Tula, Petersburg, Voronezh, Moscow and Urals; frequently arrested and exiled; 1901-04 in Geneva, together with V.D. Bonch-Bruyevich founded RSDRP, CC library and records center; contributed to newspapers *Zvezda* and *Pravda*; 1913-18 lived abroad; 1918 returned to Russia and held various exec Party and govt posts; 1918-19 member, ed bd, newspaper *Pravda*; bd member, Commission for Collating and Studying Material on the History of the 1917 Oct Revol and the History of the Communist Party; lecturer, Sverdlov Communist Univ; 1926 lectured on history of Party and Leninism, Voronezh Agric Inst; author of a number of works on CP history; *Publ*: *Ocherk istorii sotsial-demokratii Rossii* (An Outline History of Social-Democracy in Russia) (1906); *Ocherki istorii rabochego dvizheniya 70 i 80 gg* (An Outline History of the Workers' Movement in the 1870's and 1880's) (2nd ed, 1925); *Bor'ba za sovety, kak organy proletarskoy diktatury* (The Struggle for the Soviets as the Organs of Proletarian Dictatorship) (1925), etc; *Died*: 23 Nov 1927.

BATURIN, Vladimir Petrovich (1902-1945) Geologist; Dr of Geological and Mineralogical Sci; prof from 1943; head, Laboratory of Petrography and Paleogeography, Inst of Combustible Minerals, USSR Acad of Sci from 1934; *Born*: 1902; *Educ*: 1927 grad Leningrad Mining Inst; *Career*: led study of geology and oil deposits in Ural-Emba region; from 1938, and especially during WW 2, studied petrography and paleogeography of paleozoic oil deposits in Ural-Volga region; worked on petrography of sedimentary rocks and petroleum, general and historical geology; devised method for study of sedimentary strata poor in residual minerals, based on research into mineralogical composition of fragmentary rocks; first applied this method in 1928 and 1931 while studying productive oil-bearing layer in Apsheron Peninsula; *Publ*: *Paleogeografiya po terrigennym komponentam* (Paleogeography by Terrigenous Components) (1937); *Petrographicheskiy analiz geologicheskogo proshlogo po terrigennym komponentam* (Petrographical Analysis of the Geological Past by Terrigenous Components) (1947); *Awards*: Spendiarov Prize of Int Geological Congress (1937); Stalin Prize (1948); *Died*: 7 Nov 1945.

BATYRMURZAYEV, Zaynalabidin Nukhayevich (1897-1919) Kumyk writer and playwright; *Born*: 1897, son of writer N. Batyrmurzayev; *Career*: worked as teacher; ran "Morning Star" lit and dramatic circle in Khasavyurt; edited Bolshevik newspaper *Rabochiy narod*; 1919 partisan leader in Khasavyurt Okrug (now Dag ASSR); *Publ*: plays *Daniyalbek*, "Contrary to the Mullahs" and "The Mullah Came to the Medressah"; *Died*: 1919 executed as partisan by White forces.

BATYROV, Shadzha Batyrovich (1908-1965) Party and govt official; historian; Dr of Historical Sci from 1962; member and pres, Turkm Acad of Sci from 1959; member, CC, CP Turkm from 1960; CP member from 1930; *Born*: 3 Oct 1908 in vil Desht, now Ashkhabad Oblast, son of a peasant; *Educ*: 1934 grad Ashkhabad Teachers' Training Inst; 1952-54 postgrad studies at Acad of Soc Sci, CC, CPSU; *Career*: 1934-36 postgrad student and instructor, Ashkhabad Teachers' Training Inst; 1936-39 ed, newspaper *Bor'ba za gramotnost'*; head, Party affairs dept, dep ed, then ed, newspaper *Sovetskaya Turkmeniya*; 1939-40 dir, Ashkhabad Research Inst of Language and Lit; 1940-42 head, Bd of Art Affairs, Turkm Council of Pop Comr; 1942-46 secr in charge of propaganda and agitation, CC, CP(B) Turkm; 1946-47 second secr, CC, CP(B) Turkm; 1947-51 first secr, CC, CP Turkm; 1954-59 head, Chair of Marxism-Leninism and dir, Turkm Teachers' Training Inst; dep, USSR Supr Sov of 1950 convocation; dep, Turkm Supr Sov of 1951, 1959 and 1963 convocation; 1961 elected member, Turkm Republ Comt of Solidarity with Afro-Asian Countries; Presidium member, Turkm Supr Sov; member, Comt for Lenin Prizes in Sci and Technol; *Publ*: *Teoriya i programma Kommunisticheskoy partii po natsional'nomu voprosu* (The Communist Party's Theory and Program on the Nationality Question); *K voprosu o formirovanii i razvitii sotsialisticheskikh natsiy v SSSR* (The Formation and Development of Socialist Nations in the USSR); *O rukovodyashchey roli KPSS v obrazovanii i razvitii sotsialisticheskikh natsiy v SSSR* (The Leading Role of the CPSU in the Formation and Development of Socialist Nations in the USSR) (1961); coauthor *Russko-turkmenskiy slovar'* (Russian-Turkmenian Dictionary); *Formirovaniye i razvitiye sotsialisticheskikh natsiy v SSSR* (The Formation and Development of Socialist Nations in the USSR) (1962); *Awards*: two Orders of Lenin; Order of the Red Banner of Labor; Order of the Fatherland War, 1st Class; Badge of Hon; two medals; *Died*: 14 Oct 1965.

BATYUK, Yakov Petrovich (1918-1943) Komsomol official; *Born*: 1918 in Nezhin, Chernigov Oblast; *Career*: during WW 2 carried out underground work despite his blindness; directed Komsomol org which assisted local partisan detachment in Nezhin; arrested by German mil authorities; *Awards*: Hero of the Sov Union (1965, posthumously); *Died*: 6 Aug 1943 executed by German firing squad.

BAUMAN, Karl Yanovich (1892-1937) Party official; CP member from 1907; *Born*: 29 Aug 1892 in vil Lachi, Liflyand Province; son of a peasant; *Educ*: studied at Pskov Agric College and Kiev Business Inst; *Career*: 1907 joined revol movement; frequently arrested by Tsarist authorities; 1916 helped to organize Lat Section, Kiev Soc-Democratic org; after 1917 Oct Revol elected Lat Pop Comr in Kiev and dep, Kiev Sov of Workers' Dep; later appointed Comr of Private Banks, Kiev Revol Comt and dep mang, Pop Bank; 1920 chm, Uyezd Exec Comt, and member, Uyezd Party Comt in Putivl', Kursk, then chm, Grayvoron Uyezd Exec Comt; from Dec 1920 Secr, Kursk Province Party Comt; from summer 1923 dep head, Org Dept, CC, RCP(B); from Sept 1924 head, Org and Distribution Dept, Moscow Oblast Party Comt; 1928 head, Dept of Rural Work, CC, CPSU(B); late 1928 elected second secr, Moscow CPSU(B) Committee; from Apr 1929 first secr, Moscow Oblast CPSU(B) Comt; in same month named cand Politburo member and secr, CC, CPSU(B); from Feb 1931 secr, Centr Asian Bureau, CC, CPSU(B); from 1934 head, Dept of Sci, Discoveries and Inventions, CC, CPSU(B); elected member, CC, CPSU(B) at 14th, 15th, 16th and 17th Party Congresses; elected member, USSR Central Exec Comt of several convocations; arrested by State Security organs; *Died*: 14 Oct 1937 in imprisonment.

BAUMAN, Vladimir Ivanovich (1867-1923) Mine surveying specialist; prof, Dept of Geodesy and Mine Surveying, Petersburg Mining Inst form 1899; *Born*: 21 Apr 1867; *Educ*: 1890 grad Petersburg Mining Inst; *Career*: 1909-13 directed official triangulation of Donets Basin which, during planning of mining operations in pits of Donbas, served as basis for transition to a gen system of coordinates for the whole basin, known as "Baumann System of Coordinates"; devised simple method for determining position of two points in relation to two given points, often used for orientation in mine surveying; worked out geometrical classification of progressive rock displacement; introduced new, simple rules for calculating reserves of useful minerals ("Bauman's Izogips Method" and "Bauman's Formula"); amended and improved magnetometric method of prospecting for magnetic ores; *Publ*: *Kurs marksheyderskogo iskusstva* (A Course in Mine Surveying) (3 vol, 1905-08); *Kurs magnetometrii* (A Course in Magnetometry) (1927); *Died*: 15 Mar 1923.

BAYAN, Nur Galimovich (1905-1945) Tatar poet; *Born*: 15 May 1905 in vil Anyak, now Tatar ASSR, son of a peasant; *Career*: 1925 first work published; works marked by strong patriotic feeling; *Publ*: verse and martial songs "Our Banners" (1937); "Lenin Among the People" (1941); "Spring" (1942); "Lenin Is the Guiding Light that Marks Our Route" (1943), etc; *Died*: 23 Apr 1945 killed in action in Austria in World War 2.

BAYAR, Yelizaveta Martynovna (1879-1967) Party official; CP member from 1904; *Born*: 18 Sept 1879; *Career*: worked for Riga RSDRP org; distributed illegal lit and maintained arms cache; 1916 Party printing press was run in her apartment; helped establish short-lived Sov regime in Riga; then went underground and was later arrested; 1919 member, Riga Party Comt; 1920 re-arrested and turned over to Sov govt in prisoner exchange; worked in Moscow, for Lat Section, Cominter; from 1933 pensioner; *Died*: 16 Oct 1967.

BAYETOV, Musa (1902-1949) Kir singer (tenor) and song-writer; Pop Artiste of Kir SSR from 1946; *Born*: 1902; *Career*: in his early youth sang at Kir folk festivals; 1934 began professional singing career with Kir Musical Drama Theater; *Roles*: Kul'choro and Sergak in Vlasov's *Aychurek* and Maldybayev and Fere's *Manas* etc; performed as concert singer; composed many songs; *Died*: 9 May 1949.

BAYGANIN, Nurpeis (1860-1945) Kaz akyn (improvising folk bard); Hon Art Worker of Kaz SSR from 1939; *Born*: 20 July

1860 in what is now Aktyubinsk Oblast; *Career*: from age 17 composed songs and performed nat heroic epics which he had learned by heart; *Works*: epic poems *Narkyz* and *Akkenzhe*; heroic epic songs: *Koblandy-batyr* and *Yer-Targyn*; improvisations: "The Stalin Age" (1938); "Song of Stalin" (1938); "Lenin" (1939); "Flourishing Life" (1939); "Moscow" (1941); "Song of a Hero" (1942), etc; *Izbrannyye proizvedeniya* (Selected Works) (1946); *Died*: 9 Apr 1945.

BAYKOV, Aleksandr Aleksandrovich (1870-1946) Metallurgist and chemist; prof from 1903; member, USSR Acad of Sci from 1932; Hon Sci and Tech Worker of the RSFSR from 1934; Hero of Socialist Labor from 1945; *Born*: 6 Aug 1870 in Fatezh, now in Kursk Oblast; *Educ*: 1883 grad Physics and Mathematics Fac, Petersburg Univ; *Career*: from 1895 lecturer, Petersburg Inst of Communications; 1899 worked on chemistry and metallurgy in Paris with Le Chatellier; from 1903 prof, Chair of Metallurgy, Petersburg Polytech Inst; lectured at other Leningrad higher educ establishments; 1919-23 rector and prof, Simferopol' Univ; 1927-32 corrsp member, USSR Acad of Sci; worked on transformations in metals and theory of metallurgical processes; 1909 proved existence of austenite by high-temperature etching of iron and steel with dehydrated hydrogen chloride in an atmosphere of nitrogen; determined physical and chemical conditions for transformation of certain iron oxides into others and developed a theory of redox processes; conducted important research into metallurgy of non-ferrous metals and production and application of cement and refractory products; *Publ*: *Issledovaniye splavov medi i sur'my i yavleniy zakalki v nikh nablyudayemykh* (An Analysis of Copper and Antimony Alloys and the Tempering Phenomena Observed in Them) (1902); *Vosstanovaleniye i okisleniye metallov* (The Reduction and Oxidization of Metals) (1927); coauthor, *Putstsolanovyye tsementy* (Puzzuolanic Cements) (1927); *Fiziko-khimicheskiye usloviya proizvodstva ogneupornykh izdeliy* (The Physical and Chemical Conditions for the Manufacture of Refractory Products) (1931); *Sobraniye trudov* (Collected Works) (5 vol, 1948-52); *Awards*: Stalin Prize (1943); *Died*: 6 Apr 1946.

BAYKULOV, Daut Pagoyevich (1902-42) Karachay poet; *Born*: 1902 in vil of Verkhnyaya Mara, now Karachay-Circassian Autonomous Oblast; *Career*: 1925 began to publish in Karachay newspapers; *Publ*: collected verse: "For a New Life" (1931); "Verse" (1935); "New Songs" (1937); "Verse and Tales" (1940); story "Bekmurza's Life" (1931); poems: "Mariyam and Efendi" (1932); "Shamay Then and Now" (1934); "Zalikhat" (1935); latest verse included in anthology of Karachay poets "Forward For the Homeland" (1941); *Died*: Nov 1942.

BAYRAM SHAKIR (MAMEDOV) (1871-1948) Turkm folk poet; *Born*: 1871, son of a nomad; *Career*: from age seven farmhand; from age 16, though illiterate, began to compose verse; *Works*: verse: "Akby bay"; "Bay aga"; "Kyasim's Reply to the Mullah"; "Mountains"; "The Eagles Gather"; "I Would Be"; "Peri the Beauty"; "Let's Go Against the Foe, Brothers!" (1919); "The Offensive"; "Poverty" (1924); "Ashkhabad"; "He Remained"; "Look!" etc; *Died*: 1948.

BAYSEITOVA, Kulyash (1912-1957) Opera singer (lyric soprano); Pop Artiste of USSR from 1936; soloist, Kaz Music Theater, Alma-Ata from 1933; CP member from 1943; *Born*: 2 May 1912 in Vernyy (now Alma-Ata); *Career*: from 1921 folksinger; 1930-33 performed at Kaz Drama Theater, Alma-Ata; from 1933 soloist, Kaz Music Theater, Alma-Ata (later Abay Theater of Opera and Ballet); also performed as concert singer; *Roles*: title role in Brusilovskiy's *Kyz-Zhibek*; Sara in Tulebayev's "Birzhan and Sara"; Tatyana in Tchaikovsky's "Eugene Onegin"; title role in Puccini's "Madame Butterfly", etc; *Awards*: two Stalin Prizes (1948 and 1949); *Died*: 6 June 1957 in Moscow.

BAYTURSUNOV, Akhmet (1873-?) Cossack poet; journalist; linguist; *Born*: 1873; *Career*: 1913 founded first Cossack newspaper *Kazak*; until 1917 Oct Revol ed of this newspaper; after 1917 Feb Revol elected by "Alash" Party to Constituent Assembly; from 1920 worked for RSFSR Pop Comrt of Educ; published a collection of poetry *Masa* (The Gnat), where he sharply criticized Sov colonizing policy and incited Cossacks to rise in protest; in consequence arrested; 1913 compiled first Cossack grammar; translated fables of Krylov; 1930 arrested for publicizing nationalistic views; *Died*: in imprisonment; date of death unknown.

BAZAROV, V. (real name: RUDNEV, Vladimir Aleksandrovich) (1874-1939) Econ, publicist and philosopher; *Born*: 1874 in Tula; *Educ*: 1892-97 studied at Moscow Univ; *Career*: from 1896 revol work for the Social Democrats; from 1901 member, Moscow RSDRP Comt; 1904 joined Bolsheviks; was member, Petersburg RSDRP(B) comt, and Ed Bd, Party centr organ; for some time member, Bolshevik Center, which directed the Bolshevik faction from 1907 to 1912; subsequently quit Bolshevik movement; was repeatedly arrested and exiled; during WW I was a moderate "internationalist", contributing to journal *Sovremmenik* and the newspaper *Novaya zhizn'*; rejected 1917 Oct Revol; during Civil War became a nationalist; contributed to Menshevik journal *Mysl'* and newspaper *Nash golos*; from 1922 worked as econ for Gosplan; 1931 imprisoned for belonging to Menshevik org; wrote numerous philosophical works, including *Avtoritarnaya metafizika i avtonomnaya lichnost'* (Authoritarian Metaphysics and the Autonomous Personality); *Problemy idealizma* (Problems of Idealism); *Mistitsizm i realizm nashego vremeni* (Mysticism and Realism in Our Time), etc; while criticizing mystic idealism, he advocated idealist positions as propounded by Mach and Avenarius; his departure from the materialist Weltanschauung found its strongest expression in his open letter to Russian intellectuals entitled "The Mystical Nature of Patriotism", in which he dissociated himself from his revol past and advocated atonement and humility; his main econ works were *Anarkhicheskiy kommunizm i marksizm* (Anarchic Communism and Marxism); *Na puti k sotsializmu* (On the Path to Socialism); and *Kapitalisticheskiye tsikly i vostanovitel'nyy protsess khozyaystva SSSR* (Capitalist Cycles and the Restorative Process of the Soviet Economy); also wrote numerous articles on econ and finance; co-translated Marx's "Capital"; *Publ*: apart from the above-mentioned works, *Trud proizvoditel'nyy i trud, obrazuyushchiy tsennost* (Productive Labor and Value-Creating Labor) (1899); *Krivyye razvitiya kapitalisticheskogo i sovetskogo khozyayastva* (Development Graphs of the Capitalist and Soviert Economies) (1926), etc; *Died*: 1939 in imprisonment.

BAZHANOV, Vasiliy Mikhaylovich (1889-1939) Mining eng; admin official; CP member from 1910; *Born*: 1889; *Educ*: grad Petersburg Mining Inst; *Career*: Party work among Petrograd workers; member, RSDRP(B) faction's Joint Comt of higher educ establishments; member, Petrograd RSDRP(B) Comt; after 1917 Feb Revol worked in Donbas; member and chm, Makeyevka Rayon Party Comt; late 1917 directed nationalization of Makeyevka mines and factories and appointed chm of their admin; simultaneously chm, Southern Oblast (Khar'kov) Sovnarkhoz; deleg, 2nd All-Russian Congress of Soviets; 1918-22 dep chm, then chm, Main Coal Comt; simultaneously first chm, Donbas Coal Ind Bd; 1922-24 manager, Kuznets Basin Trust; from 1925 Presidium member, RSFSR Gosplan, followed by admin work in coal ind; author of numerous articles in econ periodicals and books on coal ind; *Publ*: *Kamennougol'naya promyshlennost'* (The Coal Industry) (1920); *Kamennougol'naya promyshlennost' SSSR* (The USSR Coal Industry) (1925); *Polozheniye i perspektivy kamennougol'noy promyshlennosti Sibiri* (The Condition and Prospects of the Siberian Coal Industry) (1925), etc; *Died*: 1939.

BAZHENOV, Nikolay Nikolayevich (1857-1923) Psychiatrist; close assoc of S.S. Korsakov; *Born*: 1857; *Educ*: 1881 grad Med Fac, Moscow Univ; *Career*: 1886-89 founder-dir, Ryazan' Psychiatric Hospital; extended and equipped Voronezh Zemstvo Psychiatric Hospital; 1894 defended doctor's thesis on significance of auto-intoxication in the pathogenisis of nervous syndromes; from 1904 chief physician, Preobrazhenskoye Psychiatric Hospital, Moscow; from 1910 prof of psychiatry, Moscow Higher Women's Courses; specialised in metabolic processes in the course of nervous and mental diseases; studied creativity process and its pathological deviations; reorganized psychiatric hospital care and regime; introduce home care for psychiatric patients in Russia; drew up draft bill for defending the interests of mental patients; 1915 appointed Red Cross plen for the supervision of mentally ill soldiers in the Caucasus; 1916 attached to Russian Expeditionary Corps in France and Salonika; 1923, while in Belgium, fell serviously ill and returned to Moscow; *Publ*: *Osnovy ucheniya o likhoradke* (The Principles of Fever Theory) (1883); doctor's thesis *K voprosu o znachenii autointoksikatsii v patogeneze nervnykh simptokompleksov* (The Significance of Auto-Intoxication in the Pathogenesis of Nervous Syndromes) (1894); *Ob organizatsii prizreniya dushevnobol'nykh v Sankt Petersburge* (The Organization of Mental Patients Care in Saint Petersburg) (1896); *Dushevnaya drama Garshina* (Garshin's Mental Drama) (1903); *Istoriya Moskovskogo Dollgauza, nyne Moskovskoy gorodskoy Preobrazhenskoy bol'nitsy dlya dushevnobol'nykh* (The History of the Moscow Dollgauz, now the Moscow City Preobrazhenskoye Hospital for

Mental Patients) (1909); *Proyekt zakonodatel'stva o dushevnobol'nykh* (Draft Legislation on Mental Patients) (1911); *Died*: 23 Mar 1923 in Moscow; buried in Moscow.

BAZHENOV, Pavel Dmitriyevich (1904-41) Painter of Palekh miniature school; *Born*: 1904; *Career*: work characterized by his penetrating, dynamic line, rich decoration and fine gilding; specialized in past and present heroic themes and folk epos; *Works: Aleko* (1931); *Saltychikha* (1932); *Il'ya Muromets* (1932); "Guarding the Frontiers of the USSR" (1933, 1935); *Alyosha Popovich* (1939), etc; designed sets for a number of stage productions, including "Ruslan and Lyudmila" (performed at Leningrad Puppet Theater in 1937) and color cartoon film *Skazka o rybake i rybke* (The Tale of the Fisherman and the Little Fish) (1935-36), etc; *Died*: 1941.

BAZHOV, Pavel Petrovich (1879-1950) Russian writer; CP member from 1918; *Born*: 27 Jan 1879 near Yekaterinburg, now Sverdlovsk, son of a steel worker; *Educ*: 1899 grad Perm' Seminary; *Career*: until 1917 elementary teacher, then volunteer in Red Army; 1923-29 assoc, ed bd, newspaper *Krest'yanskaya gazeta*, Sverdlovsk; dep, USSR Supr Sov of 1946 and 1950 convocations; *Publ*: book of essays *Ural'skiye byli* (True Stories From the Urals) (1924); novelette *Zelyonaya kobylka* (The Green Mare) (1939); collected folk-tales *Malakhitovaya shkatulka* (The Malachite Casket) (1930) based on Ural folklore; *Klyuch-kamen'* (The Keystone) (1942); *Skazy o nemtsakh* (Folk Tales About the Germans) (1943); *Skazy o Lenine* (Folk Tales About Lenin) (1942-45), etc; his stories were taken as the basis for the: film *Kamennyy tsvetok* (The Stone Flower) (1946); Prokoffiev's ballet *Skaz o kamennom tsvetke* (The Tale of the Stone Flower) (1954); Muravlev's symphonic poem "Mount Azov" (1949), etc; *Awards*: Order of Lenin; Stalin Prize (1943); *Died*: 3 Dec 1950 in Moscow; buried in Sverdlovsk.

BAZILEVICH, Georgiy Dmitriyevich (1889-1938) Corps commander from 1935; CP member from 1917; *Born*: 7 Feb 1889 in Chernigov Province, son of a peasant; *Educ*: grad high school; 1910 grad Kiev Mil College; *Career*: 1915 1st lt in active army, wounded seven times; after 1917 Feb Revol elected asst chm, Exec Comt, Special Army; from Mar 1918 in Red Army; during Civil War battalion commander; member, Higher Mil Inspectorate; commander, Kamyshin defense sector; member, Revol Mil Council, 8th Army; commanded various sections of Southeastern Front; commander, Reserve Army, Caucasian Front, and Ukr Reserve Army; 1920-21 chief of supply, Red Army; 1921-24 commanded 4th Turkestani Div against Basmachi; 1924-25 asst commander, 1925-27 commander, Moscow Mil Distr; 1927-31 commander, Volga Mil Distr; 1931-38 secr, Defense Comt, USSR Council of Pop Comr; Nov 1938 arrested by NKVD; *Awards*: Order of the Red Banner; Order of the Red Star; *Died*: 1938 in imprisonment; posthumously rehabilitated.

BAZILEVICH, Konstantin Vasil'yevich (1892-1950) Historian; Dr of Historical Sci; prof from 1935; senior researcher, Inst of History, USSR Acad of Sci from 1936; *Born*: 1892 in Kiev; *Educ*: 1913 grad Mikhaylovskoye Artillery College and Aviation School; 1922 grad Moscow Univ; *Career*: from 1914 in the Tsarist then the Red Army at the front; 1922-29 researcher, State Historical Museum, Moscow; 1929-33 researcher, Inst of Communications, and Eng Tech Communications Acad; simultaneously worked for Russian Assoc of Soc Sci Research Inst; from 1930 instructor, 1935-50 prof, Historical Fac, Moscow Univ; from 1939 simultaneously lecturer, Party High School, CC, CPSU(B); worked on soc, econ and polit history of Muscovy in 15-17th centuries; author of textbooks on history of USSR for secondary schools and higher educ establishments, including univ textbook *Istoriya SSSR ot drevneyshikh vremyon do kontsa XVII veka* (The History of the USSR from the Earliest Times to the Late 17th Century) (1946); active opponent of M.N. Pokrovskiy's historical school; coauthor and ed, collection *Protiv istoricheskoy kontseptsii M.N. Pokrovskogo* (Against M.N. Pokrovskiy's Idea of History) (vol 1,1939); *Publ: V gostyakh u bogdykhana. Puteshestviye russkikh v Kitay v XVII v.* (Guests of the Chinese Emperor. A Journey by Russians to China in the 17th Century) (1927); *Denezhnaya reforma Aleksey Mikhaylovicha i vosstaniye v Moskve v 1648* (The Monetary Reform of Aleksey Mikhaylovich and the 1648 Moscow Revolt) (1936); *Gorodskiye vosstaniya v Moskovskom gosudarstve XVII v.* (Urban Revolts in the 17th-Century Muscovy) (1936); coauthor, *Problemy istochniknovedeniya* (Problems of the Study of Sources) (2 vol, 1933-36); *Russkoye voyennoye iskusstvo* (Russian Military Art) (1945); *Minin i Pozharskiy* (Minin and Pozharskiy) (1946); coauthor, *Istoriya Moskvy* (The History of Moscow) (vol 1, 1952); *Vneshnyaya politika Rossii v period obrazovaniya tsentralizovannogo gosudarstva (2-ya polovina XV v.)* (The Foreign Policy of Russia During the Formation of the Centralized State /The Late 15th Century/) (1952), etc; *Awards*: Badge of Hon; medals; Lomonosov Prize, 1st Class (1950); *Died*: 3 Mar 1950.

BAZYKIN, Vladimir Ivanovich (1908-1965) Diplomat; *Born*: 1908; *Career*: 1940 joined dipl service; 1945-48 dep head, USA Dept, USSR Min of For Affairs; from 1949 counsellor, Sov embassy in USA; 1952-56 dep head, USA Dept, then Dept of American Countries, USSR Min of For Affairs; 1957-62 Sov amb to Mexico; from 1962 head, Dept of American Countries, USSR Min of For Affairs; held rank of amb extraordinary and plen; *Died*: 11 Aug 1965.

BEBURISHVILI, Mikhail Yemil'yanovich (1881-1967) Party and govt official; CP member from 1903; *Born*: 27 Oct 1881; *Career*: from 1898 in revol movement; as hammerman at Transcaucasian Railroad workshops took part in 1904 railroad workers' strike; 1905 member, Bolshevik battle group in Tiflis; arrested for revol activities and exiled to Vyatka Province; 1911-17 worked in Kazan'; 1917 helped form Red Guard squads; 1919-20 comr of a brigade, 10th Army, 1st Mounted Cavalry Div on Southern Front; 1921-51 exec Party and admin work; from 1951 pensioner; *Died*: Dec 1967.

BEDNYAKOV, K.N. (1882-1942) Party and govt functionary; CP member from 1902; *Born*: 1882; *Career*: Party work in Petrograd and Samara; after 1917 Feb Revol member, Vologda Province Sov of Workers' Dep; after 1917 Oct Revol chm, Vologda Province Revol Tribunal; member, Mil-Revol Tribunal, 1st Army, Turkm Front; member, Fergana Oblast Revol Comt and chm, Fergana Oblast CP Comt; later member, Mil Transport Bd Supr Revol Tribunal and Supr Court, Moscow; Presidium member, CC, Int Org for Aid to Revol Fighters; arrested by State Security organs; *Died*: 1942 in imprisonment.

BEDNYY, Dem'yan (real name: PRIDVOROV, Yefim Alekseyevich) (1883-1945) Russian poet; CP member from 1912; *Born*: 13 Apr 1883 in vil Gubovka, Kherson Province, son of a peasant; *Educ*: 1908 grad History and Philology Fac, Petersburg Univ; *Career*: 1909 first work published; 1909-10 contributed to the periodical *Russkoye bogatstvo*; 1910 published his polit verse and fables in Bolshevik newspaper *Zvezda*; 1912-14 worked for newspaper *Pravda*; simultaneously worked from 1912 for periodical *Sovremennyy mir* and from 1913 for Bolshevik periodical *Prosveshcheniye*; 1913 arrested; 1914 drafted into the army; during WW 1 served for 18 months as med asst on Western Front; during Civil War front-line poet-agitator; later worked for newspapers *Izvestiya VTsIK Bednota* and *Pravda;* in early 1920's his status in the USSR and in the CP was considerable: he played a very important role at the Jan 1925 All-Union Conference of Proletarian Writers, which was organized mainly to discredit fellow-traveler writers; during this period he attacked the "Left Arts Front" lit group, the Symbolists, the Chamber Theater and the Revol Russian Painters' Assoc, accusing them of being decadent and influenced by West European Art; at the same time repeatedly and scathingly attacked Mayakovskiy, whom he regarded as a petty bourgeois formalist; 1034, at 1st All-Union Congress of Sov Writers, made a denunciatory speech against Bukharin, his erstwhile friend; in his works invariably lauded the Revol, but even so two of his works — a satirical story and a play under the same title *Kak chetyrnadtsataya diviziya v ray shla* (How the 14th Division Gained Paradise) — were regarded as blasphemous and inadmissible even under the Sov regime; 1936 his play *Bogatyri* (The Heroes) was removed from the repertoire of the Moscow Chamber Theater and confiscated for vulgarization and distortion of the historical past; during WW 2 his works were again published; wrote mainly under the pseudonym D. Boyevoy; worked for publ houses; *Publ*: verse "And a Year Went By" (1909); "Dem'yan Bednyy, the Bad Man"; fable *Kukushka* (The Cuckoo) (1912); *Sbornik proizvedeniy* (Collected Works) (1913); verse novelette *Pro zemlyn, pro volyu, pro rabochuyu dolyu* (Earth, Freedom and the Workers' Fate) (1917); song *Provody* (Seeing People Off) (1918); anti-religious works: *Zemlya obetovannaya* (The Promised Land) (1920); *Novyy zavet bez iz'yana yevangelista Dem'yana* (The Immaculate New Testament of Dem'yan the Evangelist) (1925), etc; works about "socialist construction": *Tempy* (The Pace) (1930); *Shaytan-arba* (The Shaitan-Cart) (1930); Verse: "We'll Pull Through" (1931); "Heroic Memorial" (1937); poetry of WW 2 period: "I Believe in My People" (1941); "The Place" (1943);

"Victory Day" (1945), etc; 1918-20 the following collections of his works were published with an overall printing of 5 million copies: *V ognennom kol'tse* (In the Fiery Ring), *Kainovo nasledstvo* (Cain's Legacy) and *Krasnyy kazak* (Red Cossack); *Awards*: Order of the Red Banner of Combat (1923); Order of Lenin; *Died*: 25 May 1945 in Moscow.

BEDRO, Ivan Prokhorovich (1874-1943) Horticulturist; founder, first Siberian experimental fruit station; *Born*: 1874 in vil Smeloye, now Suma Oblast, son of a peasant of Zaporozhian Cossack stock; *Educ*: grad Uman College of Horticulture and Petrovsko-Razumovskiy Agric Acad (now Timiryazev Agric Acad); *Career*: after grad continued studies in Germany and France; while in France studied fruit-growing and viticulture; after return from France opened fruit nursery at Lokhvitsa, Poltava Province; 1905 sentenced to three years' exile for revol activities but returned to Poltava Province after proclamation of 17 Oct 1905 Manifesto; 1908 sentenced to life exile in Siberia and deported to Minusinsk Uyezd, Yenisey Province; 1910 established fruit nursery and experimental orchard near Minusinsk with money sent by his wife; 1915 amnestied for his work on cultivation of Siberian varieties of rennet and other large apples and the breeding of local varieties by hybridization; by 1918 cultivated several thousand hybrid apple and cherry seedlings; 1927-29 his orchard served as an experimental base of All-Union Horticultural Research Inst, and in 1931 as basis of the Minusinsk Experimental Fruit and Berry Plantation; 1931-34 worked at Narym State Selection Station at Kolpashevo, Tomsk Oblast; 1934-36 planted large fruit and berry orchard at *Sadovoparkovoye* Sovkhoz, Stalinsk, Kemerovo Oblast; 1936-40 cultivated decorative plants at Maykop experimental station, All-Union Horticultural Research Inst; *Publ: Kratkiy otchyot akklimatizatsionnoy pomologicheskoy stantsii v gorode Minusinske Yeniseyskoy gubernii za 1911-yy, 1912-yy i 1913-yy gody* (A Short Report on the Acclimatizational Pomological Station at Minusinsk, Yenisey Province, for 1911, 1912 and 1913) (1915); *Plodovodstvo v Sibiri* (Fruit-Growing in Siberia) (1925); *Died*: 1943 at vil Belorechenskaya, Krasnodar Kray.

BEGICHEV (BIGICHEV), Nikifor Alekseyevich (1874-1927) Explorer and sailor; *Born*: 19 Feb 1874; *Career*: 1895-1905 served in Russian Navy; 1900-02 member, E.V. Toll's polar expedition; during Russo-Japanese war served on torpedo-boat *Besshumnyy*; from 1906 lived mainly in Lower Yenisey region; explored the Taymyr Peninsula; 1908 explored the estuaries of the Khatanga and Anabar, where he discovered a large island which now bears his name; 1921-22 took part in search for members of Amundsen's expedition with the "Maude" stranded on the Taymyr Peninsula; *Died*: 18 May 1927 in winter camp at estuary of Pyasina River.

BEGIMOV, Asan Izimovich (1907-1958) Karakalpak writer and playwright; Hon Art Worker of Uzbek SSR from 1957; *Born*: 30 Aug 1907; *Educ*: 1932 grad Kazakh Teachers' Training Inst; *Career*: 1927 first works published; 1957 took part in festival of Karakalpak art and lit, Tashkent; *Publ*: plays: "Liberation from Oppression" (1928); "Who's That? " (1932); co-author, musical play *Garip Ashyk* (1949); poems: *Sapura* (1938); *Omir* (1951); novel "The Fisherman's Daughter" (1957), etc; *Died*: 6 May 1958 in Nukus, Karakalpak ASSR.

BEGIZOV, Chermen Davidovich (1899-1941) Ossetian writer; CP member form 1918; *Born*: 4 Jan 1899 in Yedis, Tiflis Province; *Educ*: 1928 grad Moscow Inst of Journalism; *Career*: fought with partisans; his works were notable for their local color; *Publ*: diary "Ardent Life" (1930); plays "Who Won? " and "The Banner Waves" (1930-36); collected verse "The Drawn Sabre" (1933); novelette "The Wolves" (1934); novellae "The Talking Towers" (1934); *Died*: 20 Jan 1941.

BEGLYAROV, Sergey Nikitich (1898-1949) Turkm painter of Arm extraction; Hon Art of Turkm SSR; *Born*: 1898; *Educ*: grad Yerevan Art College; *Career*: co-founder and teacher, Turkm Art College; *Works*: "Turkmenian Girls" (1928); "Village Soviet Chairman Kipchak" (1929); "Portrait of a Kurd Worker" (1930); "Baluchistani Dance" (1936); "The Ashkhabad-Moscow Horse Race" (1938); "Turkmen Kolkhoz Workers Delivering Horses to the Red Army" (1942); landscapes and still lifes; *Died*: 1949.

BEGMA, Vasiliy Andreyevich (1906-65) Party functionary; maj-gen; CP member form 1927; *Born*: 1906 in Odessa; *Career*: 1920-28 worker; 1928-38 exec Komsomol, Party and trade union work in Kherson, Dnepropetrovsk and Khar'kov Oblasts; 1938-39 worked for CC, CP(B) Ukr; then secr, Kiev Oblast Comt, CP(B) Ukr; 1939-41 first secr, Rovno Oblast Comt, CP(B) Ukr; 1941-42 member, Mil Council, 2nd Army; 1942-44 commanded partisan detachments in German occupied Rovno Oblast; 1944-49 first secr, Rovno Oblast Comt, CP Ukr; 1950-59 first secr, Khmel'nitskiy Oblast Comt, CP Ukr; 1959-65 chm, Party Commission, CC, CP Ukr; 1940-65 member, CC, CP Ukr; dep, USSR Supr Sov of 1937, 1946, 1950, 1954 and 1958 convocations; member, Budget Commission, Sov of Nationalities, USSR Supr Sov of 1958 convocation; dep, Ukr Supr Sov of 1963 convocation; *Awards*: four Orders of Lenin; other orders and medals; *Died*: 12 Aug 1965.

BEKARYUKOV, Dmitriy Dmitriyevich (1861-1934) Specialist in school hygiene; *Born*: 1 Jan 1861; *Educ*: 1880 entered Med Fac, Khar'kov Univ but expelled for polit activities; 1886 grad Med Fac, Kazan' Univ; *Career*: after graduation worked as intern, Khar'kov Zemstvo Hospital; was active in revol movement; 1889 arrested and exiled for three years to Akmolinsk; 1898 moved to Moscow and worked for journal *Vestnik vospitaniya*; from 1901 worked as school physician in Moscow; 1901 elected secr, Commission of School Physicians in recognition of his knowledge of school hygiene and org talents; from 1907 life chm, Commission of School Physicians; active member, Pirogov Commission for the Popularization of Hygiene; compiled one of first Russian manuals on school hygiene, which was highly praised by F. F. Erisman and became a standard reference work for school hygienists; was a strong supporter of Erisman's view that school hygiene should train children of all ages in hygienic practices both in school and at home; won over Moscow school hygienists to concept of hygiene as a form of prophylaxis; Oct 1917-27 head, Moscow Bureau of School Sanitation; contributed to pedag and med journals; 1926 ed, manual on child welfare in schools; cooperated with pedag in adapting curricula to hygienic requirements; from 1931 until death worked at Erisman Inst; wrote over 60 works; *Publ: Osnovnyye nachala shkol'noy gigiyeny* (The Basic Principles of School Hygiene) (1906); *Shkol'naya gigiyena* (School Hygiene) (1911); *Ostrozaraznyye zabolevaniya v shkolakh* (Highly Infectious Diseases in Schools) (1920); ed, *Okhrana zdorov'ya detey v shkolakh* (Child Health Care at School) (1926); *Ob iskussvtennom osveshchenii v shkole* (Artificial Lighting in Schools) (1932); *K voprosu o ventilyatsii v shkol'nykh zdaniyakh* (The Problem of Ventilation in School Buildings) (1933); *Awards*: Hero of Labor (1926); *Died*: 13 Sept 1934.

BEKAURI, Vladimir Ivanovich (1882-1938) Geo mil eng and inventor; *Born*: 27 Dec 1882 in vil Kitokhi, Tiflis Province; *Educ*: 1903 grad Tiflis Railroad Eng College; *Pos*: 1903-05 technician on construction of Trans-Caucasian Railroad; 1905 technician on railroad at Khashuri; 1907-17 odd jobs in Siberia, then worked in Petersburg; 1919-20 worked in Petrograd for city heating system and railroad; from 1921 headed Special Tech Bureau for Mil Inventions, then various mil design bureaus; *Career*: 1905 took part in revol, making bombs and weapons for revolutionaries in Khashuri; 1905-07 in hiding from police; from 1919 worked on mil inventions; designed many weapons for Red Army, including: "BEMI" radiooperated bomb trigger, designed in conjunction with Academician V. F. Mitkevich and put into service in 1929; devices for slinging motor-cycles, armored cars and light tanks under airplanes; donated his cash awards to public charities: for famine relief in the Volga region (1922), to purchase a tractor for his nativ village (1931) and for the construction of hospitals in Khashuri and in the vil Ali (1934-36); 1937 arrested by NKVD; *Awards*: Order of Lenin; Order of the Red Star; Order of the Red Banner of Labor; *Died*: 8 Feb 1938 in imprisonment; posthumously rehabilitated.

BEKETOV, Aleksey Nikolayevich (1863-1941) Architect; member, Russian Acad of Arts from 1894; member, USSR Acad of Architecture from 1939; prof from 1898; Hon Art Worker of Ukr SSR from 1941; *Born*: 3 Mar 1863 in Khar'kov, son of Acad N. Beketov; *Educ*: 1885 grad Petersburg Acad of Arts: *Works*: constructed over 30 buildings in Khar'kov: Land Bank (1898); Commercial Bank (1899); Volga-Kama Bank (1907); Sholars' Center; Il'ich Club; Korolenko Library; Law Inst; Bacteriological Inst; Electr Eng Inst, etc; built also in Dnepropetrovsk, Simferopol, etc; his best works reflect the traditions of Russian classical architecture; built also in modern style; *Died*: 23 Nov 1941.

BEKHTEREV, Vladimir Mikhaylovich (1857-1927) Neuropathologist, psychiatrist and health service official; Hon Sci Worker of RSFSR; prof from 1885; Dr Med from 1881; *Born*: 1 Feb 1857 in vil Sorali (now Bekhterevo), Vyatsk Province; *Educ*: 1878 grad Petersburg Mil Med Acad; *Career*: after graduation stayed on at

Petersburg Mil Med Acad to prepare for professorship of Chair of Psychiatry; 1881 defended doctor's thesis on *Opyt klinicheskogo issledovaniya temperatury tela pri nekotorykh formakh dushevnykh zabolevaniy* (A Clinical Research Experiment on Body Temperature in Certain Forms of Mental Disease); 1884 went abroad to study experimental psychology under Bundt and methods of research on cerebral neural paths under Flexig in Leipzig; worked in several German clinics and with Charcot in Paris; 1885 appointed prof ordinarius for psychiatry, Kazan' Univ, where he established a neurological and psychiatric clinic, published first Russian neurological journal *Nevrologicheskiy vestnik* and founded first Russian Soc of Neuropathologists and Psychiatrists and world's first psychophysiological laboratory, which did psychosomatic research and studied structure and functions of brain; 1894-1913 prof of neuropathology and psychiatry, Petersburg Mil Med Acad; 1897-1914 simultaneously prof, Petersburg Women's Med Inst; during this period established several special laboratories at the Mil Med Acad and turned his chair into a internationally known sci center which developed new methods of research on nervous and mental disorders; 1895 published in Petersburg journals *Obozreniye psikhiatrii, nevrologii i eksperimental'noy psikhologii* and *Vestnik psikhologii, kriminal'noy antropologii i gipnotizma*; also founded Soc of Normal and Pathological Psychology and Soc of Clinicians for Nervous and Mental Diseases; co-founder, All-Russian Union of Psychiatrists and Neuropathologists; 1903 established Petersburg Psychoneurological Inst with facs of med, law and philology; 1911 with donated money built Psychiatric Inst and Inst for the Study of Alcoholism attached to the Psychoneurological Inst; 1912 built Clinic for Nervous Diseases and Pirogov Neurosurgical Clinic; 1918 founded "University for the People," a school for medical orderlies, the Brain Research Inst (which he directed from 1918 until 1927), the Inst of Character Training, the Inst of the Blind, the Pedag Inst, etc; also published new journal *Voprosy izucheniya i vospitaniya lichnosti*; was member Leningrad Sov of several convocations; made major contributions to world sci; devised and introduced into neuropathological and psychiatric practice a number of instruments for studying nervous system, including an algesimeter, a baresthesiometer, a myosthesiometer, an osteoacusometer, a seismometer, a trychesthesiometer, etc; described numerous normal and pathological reflexes, including acromial, expiratory, hypogastric, tarsophalangeal (Mendel'-Bekhterev reflex), carpophalangeal and deep reflex of lower extremities when the foot and toes are plantar-flexed (which he described before Marie and Foi); detected special form of spondylosis (Bekhterev's disease), choreal epilepsy and syndromes of apoplectic hemihypertonia, acroerythrosis, etc; made important contributions to the study of the structure of the spinal cord and cerebrum; described a number of funiculi and fasciculi, as well as vestibular nucleus (Bekhterev's nucleus), etc; after his death the Leningrad Psychoneurological Inst, RSFSR Min of Health, was named after him and a Bekhterev Museum was set up there; on the 100th anniversary of his birth the street on which the Leningrad Psychoneurological Inst is situated was named after him and a monument was erected opposite the building; member, Italian Acad of Sci and hon member, several foreign sci soc; wrote over 600 works on neuropathology, psychiatry, neuromorphology, physiology of nervous system, psychology, reflexology and pedag; **Publ:** *Provodyashchiye puti spinnogo i golovnogo mozga* (Funiculi of the Spinal Cord and the Cerebrum) (1893, 1896, 1898); *Nervnyye bolezni v otdel'nykh nablyudeniyakh* (Different Observations of Nervous Deseases) (Vol 1-2, 1894-99); *Psikhika i zhizn'* (Psyche and Life) (2nd ed, 1902); *Osnovy ucheniya o funktsiyakh mozga* (Principles of the Theory of Brain Functions) (7 issues, 1903-07); *Ob'yektivnaya psikhologiya* (Objective Psychology) (1907-10); *Nevropatologicheskiye i psikhiatricheskiye nablyudeniya* (Neuropathological and Psychiatric Observations) (1910); *Gipnoz, vnusheniye i psikhioterapiya i ikh lechebnoye znacheniye* (Hypnosis, Suggestion and Psychotherapy and Their Therapeutic Significance) (1911); *Obshchaya diagnostika bolezney nervnoy sistemy* (General Diagnosis of Deseases of the Nervous System) (2 issues, 1911-15); *Kollektivnaya refleksologiya* (Collective Reflexology) (1921); *Obshchiye osnovy refleksologii cheloveka* (General Principles of Human Reflexology) (4th ed, 1928); *Mozg i yego deyatel'nost'* (The Brain and Its Activity) (1928); *Izbrannyye proizvedeniya* (Selected Works) (1954); most of his works have been translated into other languages; *Died*: 24 Dec 1927.

BEKLEMISHEV, Vladimir Aleksandrovich (1861-1920) Sculptor; member, Acad of Arts from 1892; prof from 1894; *Born*: 1861 near Yekaterinoslav; *Educ*: 1887 grad Acad of Arts, Petersburg; *Career*: from 1888 worked in Italy; from 1892 junior prof, Acad of Arts, Petersburg; 1901-11 rector, Higher Art College, Acad of Arts; work was closely connected with late-acad school influenced by realism of the *peredvizhniki* (Itinerants); trained a number of great Sov sculptors of older generation (V.V. Lishev, etc); *Works*: "St. Barbara" (1894); "How Fine and Fresh the Roses" (1895); "Rustic Love" (1896); "P.I. Tchaikovsky" (1898); "V.Ye. Makovskiy" (1906); "A.I. Kuindzhi" (1909), etc; memorials to A.S. Griboyedov in Teheran (1904), to Yermak in Novocherkassk (1904) and to S.P. Botkin in Leningrad (1908); *Died*: 1920.

BEKLEMISHEV, Vladimir Nikolayevich (1890-1962) Zoologist and parasitologist; prof from 1920; Dr of Biological Sci; member, USSR Acad of Med Sci from 1945; Hon Sci Worker of RSFSR from 1947; *Born*: 4 Oct 1890; *Educ*: 1913 grad Natural Sci Dept, Fac of Physics and Mathematics, Petersburg Univ; *Pos*: 1913-18 asst prof, Chair of Invertebrate Zoology, Petersburg Univ; 1918-20 assoc prof, 1920-32 prof of zoology, Perm' Univ; 1924-32 dir, Kama Biological Station and dep dir, Perm' Biological Research Inst; 1932-62 head, Dept of Entomology and Section for Combatting Parasitic Diseases on Land-Reclamation Projects, Moscow Inst of Malaria, Parasitology and Helminthology, USSR Min of Health; 1934-62 prof, Biology Fac, Moscow Univ; *Career*: made major contributions to campaign against ticks in foci of tick-borne encephalitis in Far East and Siberia and campaign against malaria in USSR; one of first chm for med parasitology, Learned Council, USSR Min of Health; from 1959 member, Polish Acad of Sci; foreign member, Finnish Soc for the Study of Fauna and Flora; from 1960 member, Encephalitis Comt, RSFSR Min of Health; dep ed, journal *Meditsinskaya parazitologiya i parazitarnyye bolezni*; consultant on communicable deseases, USSR and RSFSR Min of Health; wrote over 120 papers on invertebrate zoology, biocenology, parasitology, epidemiology, etc; *Publ: O parazitarnykh turbellyariyakh Murmanskogo morya* (The Parasitic Turbellariae of the Sea of Murmansk) (1916); *Organizm i soobshchestvo* (The Organism and the Community) (1928); *Osnovnyye ponyatiya biotsenologii v prilozhenii k zhivotnym komponentam nazemnykh soobshchestv* (The Basic Concepts of Biocenology as Applied to the Animal Components of Ground-Level Communities) (1931); *Turbellyarii* (Turbellariae) (1937); *Ekologiya malyariynogo komara* (The Ecology of the Malarial Msosquito) (1944); *Uchebnik meditsinskoy entomologii* (A Textbook of Medical Entomology) (2 vol, 1949; 2nd ed, 1952); *Osnovy sravnitel'noy entomologii bespozvonochnykh* (The Principles of Comparative Invertebrate Entomology) (1944, 1952), etc; *Awards*: two Stalin Prizes (1944 and 1952); *Died*: 4 Sept 1962.

BEK-NAZAROV, (real name: AMBARTSUM), Amo Ivanovich (1892-1965) Film actor, dir and scriptwriter; Pop Artiste of Arm SSR from 1935; *Born*: 31 May 1892; *Educ*: 1914 grad Moscow Business Inst; *Career*: 1914 actor at K. Libken's Studio, Yaroslavl'; from 1915 actor, A. Khanzhonkov's Film Studio; 1921 organizer, dir and artistic dir, Film Section, Geo Pop Comrt of Educ; 1923 debut as film dir; 1925 appointed by Arm Council of Pop Comr to head Arm film ind; organizer, "Vostok" Film Studio; great influence on development of film ind and directing technique in Arm, Geo and Azer; *Roles*: Krasotin in "My Campfire Shines Through the Mist" (1915); Aleko in "Airplane Drama" (1916); Verigin in "Dance of Grief and Care" (1918); the Count in "The Eternal Fairytale of Life" (1919); Durmish in "The Fortress of Suram" (1922), etc; *Works*: produced films: "Namus" (1926); "Zare" (1927); "Khas-push" (1928); "The House on the Volcano" (1929); "Evil Spirit" (1928); "Seville" (1929); "Man With a Medal" (1933); "Pepo" (1935), after Sundukyan's comedy of the same name; "Zanzegur" (1938); "David Bek" (1944); "The Girl from Ararat Valley" (1950); "The Housewarming" (1955); "Nasreddin in Khodzhent" (1960), etc; *Publ*: "How I Worked on a Picture" (1926); film script "Pepo" (1939); "Cinema in Soviet Armenia" (1950); "Notes of a Film Actor and Director" (1965); many scripts for films produced by himself and others; *Died*: 27 Apr 1965.

BEK-NAZARYAN (pseudonym: GAROSH), Garush Ivanovich (1894-1967) Cameraman; Hon Art Worker of Arm SSR from 1944; *Born*: 23 June 1894; *Career*: from 1923 cameraman, Geo "Goskinoprom" Studio; from 1925 with Arm Film Studio; *Works*: camera work for films: *Pyat' v yablochko* (Five Into an Apple); *Shestnadtsatyy* (The Sixteenth) (1929); documentary films *Strana Nairi* (The Land of Nairi); *Pervyye luchi* (The First

Rays); *Vnimaniye* (Attention) (1930); *Meksikanskiye diplomaty* (Mexican Diplomats) (1932); "Gikor" (1934); "Pepo" (1935); "Zangezur" (1938); "David Bek" (1944); *Sem'ya patriotov* (A Family of Patriots) (1941); *Devushka Araratskoy doliny* (Girl of the Ararat Valley) (1950), etc; *Died*: 2 Sept 1967.

BEKOV, Tembot Dardaganovich (1873-1938) Ingush writer; pioneer of Ingush lit; *Born*: 1873; son of a peasant; *Educ*: 1901 grad Vladikavkaz College; studied at Warsaw Polytech Inst; *Career*: after Oct Revol took active part in Ingush public life; was a teacher and journalist; introduced rhyme and laid foundations of written Ingush poetry; *Publ*: "Two Epochs"; "The Execution of the Workers on the Lena"; "11 and 5", etc; *Died*: 10 Feb 1938.

BEKRENEV V. P. Party functionary; CP member from 1920; *Career*: 1907-18 anarchist-Communist; 1921-22 active member, "Workers' Opposition" group; signed the declaration to Comintern; 1935 expelled from Party for persistently violating Party and state discipline; arrested by State Security organs; *Died*: date and place of death unknown.

BEKRITSKIY, Arkadiy Arkad'yevich (1881-1967) Otolaryngologist; prof from 1939; Dr of Med from 1939; *Born*: 7 July 1881 in Torzhok, Tver' Province (now Kalinin Oblast); *Educ*: 1909 grad Med Fac, Berlin Univ; *Career*: 1909-11 intern and asst prof, various German otolaryngological clinics; 1912-18 intern, Dept of Ear, Nose and Throat Diseases, Staroyekaterinenskaya Hospital, Moscow; 1918-22 physician in Red Army; 1922-38 asst prof, then assoc prof, Chair of Otolaryngology, Centr Inst of Postgrad Med Training; 1938-66 head, Chair of Ear, Nose and Throat Diseases, Moscow Med Stomatological Inst; member, ed bd, journal *Vestnik otorinolaringologii*; active in All-Union and Moscow Soc of Otolaryngologists; elected chm, Auditing Commission, All-Union Learned Soc of Otolaryngologists at 4th and 5th All-Union Congresses of Otolaryngologists; wrote over 50 works on various aspects of otolaryngology; *Publ*: monograph *Meningity ushnogo proiskhozhdeniya* (Meningitis of Aural Origin) (1938), etc; *Died*: 1967.

BEKZADYAN, Aleksandr Artem'yevich (pseudonyms: YURIY, YUR'YEV) (1881-1939) Govt official; RSDRP member from 1901; *Born*: 1881; *Career*: helped run Baku Bolshevik org; repeatedly subjected to reprisals by Tsarist Govt; 1906 emigrated; 1912 member, Bolshevik deleg at Basel Congress; 1915 returned to Caucasus; after 1917 Oct Revol exec govt and dipl work; 1919-20 member, illegal Transcaucasian Kray Party Comt; later member, Arm Council of Pop Comr, and member, Transcaucasian Union Sov; subsequently with USSR trade mission in Berlin; Transcaucasian Pop Comr of Trade and Pop Comr of Finance; dep chm, Transcaucasian Council of Pop Comr, and Presidium member, Transcaucasian Kray Party Comt; from late 1930 USSR plen in Norway; arrested by State Security organs; *Died*: 1939 in imprisonment.

BELEN'KIY, A. Ya. (1883-1941) Govt official; CP member from 1902; *Born*: 1883; *Career*: 1904 emigrated to France; after 1917 Feb Revol returned to Russia; ran printing press for CC, RSDRP(B) in Petrograd, then worked for Cheka and OGPU; 1919-24 chief of Lenin's bodyguard; from 1924 worked for NKVD; arrested by State Security organs; *Died*: 1941 in imprisonment.

BELEN'KIY (Party pseudonym: BELINSKIY), Grigoriy Yakovlevich (1885-1938) Party official; CP member from 1903; *Born*: 1885 in vil Sverzhen', Mogilev Province; *Career*: 1899 joined revol movement; 1901 joined RSDRP, siding with "Iskra" platform; 1901 arrested for membership of Minsk RSDRP org and, after a year in prison, sentenced to three years' exile in Arkhangel'sk Province; 1904, after serving reduced sentence, worked as organizer and propagandist for Minsk Bolshevik org; 1906 worked in Vilnius, then became member, Tech Group, Petersburg Comt (after London Congress this group subordinated to CC); Oct 1907 arrested for membership of Petersburg Comt and spent 11 months in "Kresty" Prison; then sent for four months to barracks of 100th Ostrovskiy Regt in Dvina Fortress, where he set up a mil Party org; became secr, Vilnius RSDRP(B) org; helped to prepare Northwestern Kray Conference; 1908 Northwestern Kray deleg to All-Russian Conference in Paris; after return to Russia became Party organizer in Kovno, then secr, Dvina Party org; 1910 re-arrested and after a year in prison exiled for life to Yenisey Province in Siberia; spent two years in exile helping to organize Soc of Exiled Settlers, then fled to Paris, where he spent four years; as secr, Paris Bolshevik Section corresponded with Comt of For Org, Lenin, Inessa Armand, Zinov'yev, etc; 1917 returned to Russia, where he at first worked for Moscow Okrug Party org and was a member of Moscow Oblast RSDRP(B) Comt; became Party organizer, Presnya Rayon, Moscow, where he helped to prepare Oct Revol; elected member, Moscow RSDRP(B) Comt; 1917-25 secr, Krasnaya Presnya Rayon Comt; member, All-Union Centr Exec Comt of several convocations; 1923 opposed Trotsky in a series of policy debates; 1926 joined Zinov'yev-Kamenev-Trotsky opposition group; 1927 expelled from Party for Trotskyism; arrested by State Security organs; *Died*: 1938 in imprisonment.

BELETSKIY, Aleksandr Ivanovich (1884-1961) Lit historian; prof form 1920; member, Ukr Acad of Sci from 1939; dir, Inst of Lit, Ukr Acad of Sci from 1944; member, USSR Acad of Sci from 1958; Hon Sci Worker of Ukr SSR from 1944; *Born*: 2 Nov 1884 in Kazan', son of an agric teacher; *Educ*: 1907 grad Fac of History and Philology, Khar'kov Univ; *Career*: from 1917 assoc prof, Chair of Russian Lit, Khar'kov Univ; from 1920 prof, from 1926 head, Chair of Lit History, Khar'kov Univ; from 1920 also prof, Acad of Theoretical Disciplines; from 1921 prof, Khar'kov Inst of Public Educ; 1922-26 head, Section of Lit History, Chair of Research on the History of European Lit; after WW 2 prof, Kiev Univ; for a time vice-pres, Ukr Acad of Sci; specialized in Ukr and Russian lit; *Publ: V masterskoy khudozhnika slova* (In the Workshop of the Word Artist) (1923); *Starinnyy teatr v Rossii* (Ancient Theater in Russia) (1923); *Dvadtsat' let novoy ukrainskoy liriki* (Twenty Years of Modern Ukrainian Lyric Poetry) (1924); *Karl Marks, Fridrikh Engel's v istorii literatury* (Karl Marx and Friedrich Engels in the History of Literature) (1934); *Problema sinteza v literaturovedenii* (The Problem of Synthesis in the Study of Literature) (1940); *Khrestomatiya drevney ukrainskoy literatury* (An Anthology of Ancient Ukrainian Literature) (1949); coauthor and chief ed, *Istoriya ukrainskoy literatury* (A History of Ukrainian Literature) (1954-57); coauthor, *Ivan Franko. Zhizn' i tvorchestvo* (Ivan Franko. His Life and Work) (1956); *Ukrainskoye literaturovedeniye za sorok let 1917-57* (Forty Years of the Study of Ukrainian Literature 1917-57) (1957); coauthor, *T.G. Shevchenko* (1958); *Ukrainskaya literatura sredi drugikh slavyanskikh literaturakh* (Ukrainian Literature in Relation to Other Slavic Literatures) (1958); *Ot drevnosti do sovremennosti. Sobraniye proizvodeniy po voprosam ukrainskoy literatury*~~sM,~~ (From the Ancient to the Modern. An Anthology of Works on Ukrainian Literature) (2 vol, 1960); *Died*: 2 Aug 1961 in Kiev.

BEL'GOV, V. P. (1884-1936) Party and govt official; CP member from 1905; *Born*: 1884; *Career*: 1908-13 in emigration; then in Russian Army; after 1917 Oct Revol dipl, econ and Party work in Ukr, Siberia and Far Eastern Republ; deleg, 10th RCP(B) Congress; from 1921 with RSFSR Pop Comrt of For Trade; USSR trade rep in Iran; 1922-24 dir, USSR trade mission in Austria; 1925 rep of USSR Pop Comrt of For Trade in Centr Asia, etc; *Died*: 1936.

BEL'SKAYA, Serafima Aleksandrovna (1846-1933) Russian operetta artiste; *Born*: 1846; *Career*: late 1860's began stage career in provinces; played in comedies and vaudivilles; from 1876 at Lentovskiy, Blumental'-Tamarin and Rodon Theaters in Moscow; *Roles*: Denise in Hervé's "Mademoiselle Nitouche"; Helene and Pericola in Offenbach's "La Belle Hélène" and "Pericola"; Nanon in Genet's "Nanon"; Fatinitsa in Suppé's "Fatinitsa," etc; *Died*: 1933.

BELIASHVILI, Akakiy Ionovich (1903-1961) Geo writer; bd member, Geo Writers' Union; *Born*: 24 Apr 1903 in Chiatura, now Geo SSR; *Educ*: studied at Tbilisi Polytech Inst; *Career*: master of short story writing; 1927 first work published; 1937 published first collection of stories; 1941-49 head, Scenario Section, "Gruziyafil'm" Film Studio; *Publ*: "Novellae" (1939); "Stories" (1956); novels: "Demons" (1947); "The Golden Tent" (1952); "The Pass" (1956); "Rustavi" (1960); scenarios for films: *Lager' v gorakh* (The Camp in the Mountains) (1930); *Nastoayshchiy kavkazets* (A Genuine Caucasian) (1934); *Sokrovishcha Tsenskogo ushchel'ya* (The Treasures of Tsen Canyon) (1941); co-scripted: *Oni spustilis' s gor"* (They Came Down from the Mountains) (1955); *Otarova vdova* (Otar's Widow) (1958), etc; *Died*: 14 Dec 1961.

BELINSKIY, Miron L'vovich (1904-1966) Film dir; Hon Art Worker of Mold SSR from 1947; CP member from 1925; *Born*: 20 Sept 1904 in Odessa; *Career*: from 1924 worked in Ukr; *Productions*: feature films: *Kazn'* (Execution); *Staraya krepost'* (The Old Fortress); *Semnadtsatiletniye* (The Seventeen-Year-Olds); documentary films: *Donbass*; *Gornyaki Krivorozh'ya* (The Miners of Krivoy Rog); *Eskadra povorachivayet na Zapad* (The Squadron

Turns West), etc; *Died*: 30 Apr 1966.

BELITSER, Aleksandr Vasil'yevich (1873-1940) Veterinary epizoologist and protozoologist; prof; *Born*: 1873; *Educ*: 1899 grad Warsaw Veterinary Inst; *Career*: from 1899 veterinarian, Spassk Uyezd Zemstvo, Ryazan' Province; 1901 head, Ryazan' Bacteriological Station; 1903 defended master's thesis at Warsaw Veterinary Inst; head, Veterinary Dept, Ryazan' Province Zemstvo Admin; 1911-12 studied infectious diseases of farm animals in Germany; 1917-19 head, Chair of Epizoology, Don Veterinary Inst, Novocherkassk; 1928-38 head, Chair of Epizoology, Veterinary Fac, Moscow Zootech Inst; also head, Dept of Protozoology, All-Union Inst of Experimental Veterinary Sci; 1906, in cooperation with Ye.I. Martsinovskiy, established causative agent of pyroplasmosis in horses; 1911 discovered causative agent of tupping disease in horses; studied causes of rabies and epizootic abortion in cattle, etc; *Publ: Chakhotka domashnikh zhivotnykh* (Phthisis in Domestic Animals) (1925); *Novaya zlokachestvennaya bolezn' loshadey. Poval'noye zabolevaniye mozga* (A New Malignant Disease of Horses. Epidemic Infection of the Brain) (1924); *Materialy po issledovaniyu piroplazmoza loshadey v Rossii* (Material on the Study of Equine Pyroplasmosis in Russia) (1911); coauthor, *Protozoynyye zabolevaniya domashnikh zhivotnykh* (Protozoal Diseases of Domestic Animals) (1931), etc; *Died*: 1940; Ryazan' Province Veterinary Bacteriological Laboratory is named after him.

BELITSKIY, Semyon Markovich (1889-1937) Mil researcher; Civil War veteran; 1905-17 member, Socialist-Revol Party; CP member from 1920; *Born*: 1889; *Educ*: 1922 grad Frunze Mil Acad; *Career*: 1918-20 various command and staff posts; asst commander of an army; 1924-26 chief, Operations Bd, Red Army Staff; from 1927 postgrad student then instructor, Chair of Strategy and Art of Mil Operations, Red Army Acad; from 1931 chief of staff, North Caucasian Mil Distr; 1932-37 dep chm, Centr Council, USSR Soc for the Promotion of Aviation, Defense and Chemical Ind; 1937 arrested by State Security organs; *Publ: Kharakter sovremennoy voyny* (The Nature of Modern Warfare) (1927); *Strategicheskiye rezervy* (Strategical Reserves) (1930); *Operativnaya razvedka* (Operational Reconnaissance) (1928); *Voyna* (War) (1931); *Awards*: Order of the Red Banner; *Died*: 1937 in imprisonment; posthumously rehabilitated.

BELLYARMINOV, Leonid Georgiyevich (1859-1930) Ophthalmologist; Dr of Med from 1886; prof from 1893; founded important school of ophthalmology; *Born*: 1859; *Educ*: 1883 grad Petersburg Acad of Med and Surgery; *Career*: from 1883 worked under V.I. Dobrovol'skiy at Chair of Eye Diseases, Petersburg Acad of Med and Surgery; 1889-93 assoc prof, from 1893 prof, Chair of Eye Diseases, Petersburg Mil Med Acad; under his dir this chair became one of the best in Russia, issuing over a period of 30 years more than 250 papers and books on various problems of ophthalmology; made major contributions to campaign against blindness in Russia; 1893-1914 organized over 500 mobile ophthalmological units throughout the country, creating a system which was retained under Sov rule and copied in other countries; simultaneously chm, Dept for Prevention of Blindness, Trust for Welfare of Blind; devised new methods of ophthalmoscopy, operations for ptosis and various ophthalmological equipment; organized and attended ophthalmological congresses in Russia and abroad; for many years chm, Petersburg Ophthalmological Soc; after 1917 Oct Revol chm, Leningrad Ophthalmological Soc; taught such well-known ophthalmologists as N. I. Andogskiy, V. N. Dolganov, Ya. V. Zelenkovskiy, S. V. Lobanov, A. S. Savvaitov, Ye. F. Klimovich and A. I. Merts; wrote 36 works, of which some (e.g. a paper on the colorimetric method of studying diffusion in the anterior chamber of the eye [1902]) are still of sci interest; *Publ*: doctor's thesis *Opyt primeneniya graficheskogo metoda k issledovaniyu dvizheniya zrachka i vnutriglaznogo davleniya* (Experimental Use of the Graphic Method for Studying the Motion of the Pupil and Intraocular Pressure) (1886); co-ed, *Rukovodstvo po glaznym boleznyam* (A Manual of Eye Diseases) (3 vol, 1928-30); *Died*: 1930.

BELOBORODOV, Aleksandr Georgiyevich (1891-1938) Party and govt official; CP member from 1907; *Born*: 1891 in Aleksandrovsk, Perm' Province; son of a factory worker; *Educ*: attended primary school; *Career*: from 1905 apprentice, then office worker at a factory in Nadezhdinsk; 1907 electrician, Lun'yevka Mines, Solikamsk Uyezd; 1907 joined local Bolshevik Soc-Democratic org of which he was soon elected comt member; early 1908 received prison sentence for polit activity; from 1912 worked at a factory in Lys'va, Perm' Province; after 1917 Feb Revol member, Ural Oblast RSDRP(B) Comt, and Ural Oblast Sov; Apr 1917 deleg, All-Russian Conference of Bolsheviks; from 1918 chm, Ural Oblast Exec Comt; in same year sided with "leftist Communists" and opposed Brest-Litovsk Peace Treaty; 1919 Labor and Defense Council plen on Southern Front and member, Revol-Mil Council, 9th Army; 1920 dep chm, Revol Council, Caucasian Labor Army; elected member, CC, RCP(B) at 8th Congress; from late 1921 RSFSR Dep Pop Comr of Internal Affairs; from 1923 RSFSR Pop Comr of Internal Affairs; 1927 expelled from Party for membership of Trotskyite opposition; 1930 reinstated and sent on Party work to ' Rostov-on-Don; again expelled from Party and arrested by State Security organs; *Died*: 1938 in imprisonment.

BELOKOSKOV, Vasiliy Yevlampiyevich (1898-1961) Col-gen; logistics specialist; CP member from 1919; *Born*: 25 Apr 1898; *Pos*: from 1918 in Red Army; Civil War veteran; 1921-41 command and staff posts with units and mil distr; 1941-45 chief, Red Army Motor Transport Bd, dep chief of rear areas, USSR Armed Forces; 1955-60 USSR Dep Min of Defense for Construction and Quartering of Troops; from 1960 retired; *Career*: dep, USSR Supr Sov of 1954 convocation; *Died*: 21 Oct 1961.

BELOKUR, Yekaterina Vasil'yevna (1900-1961) Painter; specialist in Ukr decorative folk art; Pop Artist of Ukr SSR from 1956; *Born*: 7 Dec 1900 in vil Bogdanovka, now Kiev Oblast; *Career*: while working on kolkhoz, active in amateur art circle; late 1930's exhibited her work in oblast, republ, all-union and int exhibitions; painted still-lifes in Ukr decorative folk art style; her usual subjects were flowers, fruit, vegetables and fields with golden corn; painted large canvases in minute detail; her paintings are on show at museums throughout the Ukr; *Works*: "The Emperor Grain"; "Kolkhoz Field"; "Lunch"; "Kolkhoz Abundance"; "In the Cherkassy Area," etc; *Died*: 10 June 1961.

BELOPOL'SKIY, Aristarkh Apollonovich (1854-1934) Russian astronomer and astrophysicist; Dr of Astronomy from 1896; astrophysicist, Pulkovo Observatory from 1891; member, Russian (then USSR) Acad of Sci from 1903; *Born*: 13 July 1854 in Moscow; *Educ*: 1877 grad Dept of Physics and Mathematics, Moscow Univ; *Career*: 1879-88 asst, Moscow Observatory; 1888-1934 adjunct, from 1891 astrophysicist, 1917-19 dir, Pulkovo Observatory; chm, Russian Branch, Int Union for Solar Research; at Pulkovo he studied rotation of Sun from motion of solar flares and by measuring numerous photographs of Sun taken at Pulkovo from 1881 to 1888; studied radial velocity of celestial bodies; 1895 used measurement of radial velocity to study structure of rings of Saturn and showed that they consist of a mass of tiny satellites orbiting the planet according to Kepler's Third Law; determined radial velocity of some 200 stars of 2 1/2-4th magnitude in order to plot motion of Sun and examine spectra of variable stars; discovered that periodic variation in radial velocity of Cepheid equals variation in their brilliance and established that maximum brilliance coincided in time with maximum velocity of the star's approach to the Sun; concluded that this variation in radial velocity stemmed from motion of one of the components of a binary star around the center of gravity of the pair; discovered same phenomenon in another Cepheid, η Aquila, and subsequently it was found in all Cepheids; also discovered velocity variations in Algol, β Lyra, Polaris the α Canes Venatici and other stars; did not restrict himself to one set of observations bu repeated them several times; for instance, with ρ Cepheus from 1894 through 1914, and noted variations in their radial velocity graph and also in the intensity and width of individual lines of the spectrum; determined the radial velocity of the individual components of the binary stars γ Virgo and γ Leo; dissatisfied with the proofs of the Doppler Effect based on observing the radial velocity of stars, he constructed an ingenious device for ists laboratory proof; this consisted of mirrors attached to the rim of wheels rapidly rotating toward each other; the reflection of light from the moving mirrors produced the same spectral shift, as though the light source itself had shifted; this proof was constructed without any kind of theoretical basis but proved of crucial significance and placed astrophysics on a firm foundation; with the aid of a stellar spectrograph he also tried to study the rotation of the Sun; in 1912 he ordered a special instrument for this which, however, was only delivered in 1923; with its aid he began to photograph the spectra of the edge of the Sun according to a plan adopted at meetings of the Int Union for Solar Research; in these studies he noticed that the speed of rotation of the Sun diminished slightly between 1925 and 1933, which was also confirmed by the observations of other astronomers; studied the spectra of comets and the physical structure and chemical composition of their tails; published detailed data on spectral lines, so that his articles contain enormous material for future research; *Publ: Pyatna na Solntse i ikh dvizheniye* (Sunspots and Their Motion) (1886); *Issledovaniye spektra peremennoy zvyezdy δ Cephei pri pomoshchi 30-ti dyuymovogo refrektora Observatorii v Pulkove* (Study of the Spectrum of the Variable Star δ Cephei Using the 30-Inch Refractor at the Pulkovo Observatory) (1895); *Issledovaniye luchevykh skorostey peremennoy zvezdy 'Algolya' po nablyudeniyam v Pulkove v 1902-1907 gg* (Study of the Radial Velocity of the Variable Star Algol Using Observations at Pulkovo from 1902 to 1907) (1908); *Issledovaniye luchevykh skorostey i spektra peremennoy zvezdy 'Algolya' po nablyudeniyam v Pulkove v 1907-1911 gg* (Study of the Radial Velocity and Spectrum of the Variable Star Algol Using Observations at Pulkovo from 1907 to 1911) (1912); coauthor, *Astrospektroskopiya* (Astrospectroscopy) (1921); *O dvizhenii materii na poverkhnosti Solntsa* (The Movement of Matter on the Surface of the Sun) (1933); *Vrashcheniye Solntsa po spektrograficheskim nablyudeniyam v Pulkovo v 1931, 1932 i 1933 godakh* (The Rotation of the Sun According to Spectrographic Observations at Pulkovo in 1931, 1932 and 1933) (1933); *Opredeleniye vrashcheniya Solntsa v 1933 adademicheskim spektrografom* (Determining the Rotation of the Sun in 1933 by the Academic Spectrograph) (1934), etc; *Awards*: Jansen Gold Medal (1908); Lalande Prize of the Paris Academy of Sciences (1918); *Died*: 16 May 1934 in Pulkovo.

BELOSTOTSKIY, Yefim Isayevich (1893-1961) Sculptor; *Born*: 1893 in Yelizavetgrad (now Korovograd, Ukr SSR); *Educ*: 1918 grad Secondary Art School; 1920 grad Odessa Art College; *Career*: worked mainly with artists G. Pivovarov and Yu. Fridman; from 1944 worked in Kiev; *Works*: monumental sculpture "Il'ich's Legacy" (1925); sculptural portraits "Lenin and Stalin in Gorki" (1937); groups "Stakhanovites of Industry" and "Stakhanovites of Agriculture" for Ukr pavilion at All-Union Agric Exhibition in Moscow (1938); "Monument to Communist Youths Who Died in Tripol'ye" (1939); designed monument to Amangel'da Imanov for the town of Kustanay (1943); composition "Stalin and Khrushchev" (1944); "Marx and Engels" (1949); bas-relief "Lenin and Stalin" (1949); portraits "The Partisan Woman Kovalenko" (1945); "Bogdan Khmel'nitskiy" (1954); "M. Frunze" (1955); "A. Makarenko" (1957); sculptures "Glory to Labor," "Lamps of Communism," etc; *Died*: 2 Oct 1961.

BELOTSKIY, Morits L'vovich (1895-1944) Mil commander; Civil War veteran; CP member from 1918; *Born*: 1895 in Vinnitsa; *Educ*: 1922 grad Red Army Mil Acad; *Career*: 1918 chm, Lith Revol Comt; took part in revolt against Petlyura govt in Ukr; 1919 secr, Lipovets and Uman Uyezd CP Comt; from Aug 1919 polit worker, 12th Army; dep head, Polit Bd, 1st Mounted Army; comr, 11th Cavalry Div; 1920 fought on Polish and Wrangel Fronts; 1921 helped crush Kronstadt Mutiny; 1922-24 tauhgt sociology and econ at Red Army Mil Acad; asst comr, Mil Acad; 1924-32 secr, uyezd, okrug then oblast Party comt; 1932-37 dep chm, Centr Council, Soc for Furthering the Defense, Aviation and Chemical Ind of USSR; 1937 arrested by NKVD; *Awards*: two Orders of Red Banner; *Died*: 1944 in imprisonment; posthumously rehabilitated.

BELOUSOV, Ivan Alekseyevich (1863-1930) Russian Poet, writer and translator; *Born*: 9 Dec 1863 in Moscow; son of a tailor; *Educ*: grad college in Moscow; *Career*: worked in fahter's tailoring shop; 1882 first verse published; wrote verse and stories for children; translated Robert Burns, Ada Negri, Maria Konopicka, Yanka Kupala, Avetik Isaakyan, etc; after death of I.Z. Surikov helped run his lit and music circle for self-taught writers; his verse eulogized nature and the work of the peasant and crafstman; some of his poems were set to music by Kyui and Rebikov; *Publ: Iz kobzarya T.G. Shevchenko* (Shevchenko the Bard) (1887); *Stikhotvoreniya* (Verse) (1909); *Atava* (1915); memoirs *Literaturnaya Moskva. Pisateli iz naroda. Pisateli-narodniki* (Literary Moscow. Writers from the People. Populist Writers) (1926); *Ushedshaya Moskva* (Bygone Moscow) (1927); *Pisatel'skiye gnezda* (Nests of Writers) (1930); also published reminiscences of "Sreda" writers' club and meetings with Lev Tolstoy, Gorky, Chekhov, etc; *Died*: 7 Jan 1930 in Moscow.

BELOUSOV, Mikhail Mikhaylovich (1905-1960) Actor; Pop Artiste of Ukr SSR from 1948; *Born*: 28 Feb 1905 in Kazan'; *Educ*: 1923 grad Kazan' Theatrical Technicum; *Career*: 1923 stage debut with Kazan' Drama Theater; worked at theaters in Ul'yanovsk, Gorky, Rostov and Tbilisi; from 1939 actor, Kiev Russian Drama Theater; also film work; *Roles*: Chatskiy in Griboyedov's *Gore ot uma* (Woe from Wit); Zhadov in Ostrovskiy's *Dokhodnoye mesto* (A Lucrative Post); Belugin in Ostrovskiy's *Zhenit'ba Belugina* (Belugin's Marriage); Ferdinand in Schiller's *Kabale und Liebe*; Don Juan in Lesya Ukrainka's *Kamennyy vlastelin* (The Stone Sovereign); *Died*: 11 Nov 1960.

BELOV, Grigoriy Akinfovich (1895-1965) Russian actor; Pop Artiste of USSR from 1956; CP member from 1942; *Born*: 18 Dec 1895; *Career*: 1917 stage debut in Cherepovets; 1922-33 at theaters in Tver', Yaroslavl', Vladikavkaz, etc; 1933-40 actor, Arkhangel'sk Theater; from 1945 with Volkov Theater, Yaroslavl'; also did film work; *Roles*: stage roles: Pyotr, Vlas, Cherkun and Somov in Gorky's *Posledniye* (The Last Ones), *Dachniki* (The Summer Villa Residents), *Varvary* (The Barbarians) and *Somov i drugiye* (Somov and Co); Yarovoy and Shvandya in Trenyov's *Lyubov' Yarovaya*; Plakun in Zorin's *Vechniy istochnik* (The Perpetual Spring); Voropayev in Pavlenko's *Schast'ye* (Happiness); Zhadov and Krutitskiy in Ostrovskiy's *Dokhodnoye mesto* (A Lucrative Post) and *Na vsyakogo mudretsa dovol'no prostoty* (There's a Simpleton in Every Sage), etc; film roles: Michurin in *Michurin* (1949); Arsen'yev in *Sel'skiy vrach* (Country Doctor) (1952); Rimsky-Korsakov in *Rimsky-Korsakov*; (1953); Yevseich in *Zemlya i lyudi* (Land and People) (1956); Prof Nikol'skiy in *Prizvaniye* (The Calling) (1957); Chicherin in *Moskva-Genua* (Moscow-Genoa) (1964); *Awards*: Stalin Prize (1949); *Died*: 8 Jan 1965.

BELOV, Ivan Panfilovich (1893-1938) Russian mil commander; army commander, 1st class from 1935; 1917-19 member, Leftist Socialist-Revol Party; CP member from 1919; *Born*: 15 June 1893 in vil Kalinnikovo, now Vologda Oblast, son of a poor peasant; *Educ*: grad as external student from teachers' seminary; 1923 grad Advanced Officer Training Courses, Gen Staff Acad; *Pos*: until 1913 sawmill worker, teacher; 1913 drafted into Russian Army; 1913-16 private, petty officer, 13th Siberian Infantry Regt; fought in WW 1; 1916-17 in a penal battalion; 1917-18 elected commander, 1st Siberian Reserve Infantry Regt; 1918-19 commandant, Tashkent Garrison and Tashkent Fortress; 1919 commander in chief, Armed Forces of Sov Turkestani Republic; 1919-21 commander, 3rd Turkestani Infantry Div in Semirech'ye; commander, forces group, Turkestani Front; 1921-22 commander, 2nd Don, 22nd Krasnodar and 9th Don Infantry Div; 1923-25 commander, 15th, 9th and 2nd Infantry Corps; asst commander, North Caucasian Mil Distr; 1925-27 asst commander, Moscow Mil Distr; 1927-31 commander, North Caucasian Mil Distr; 1931-35 commander, Leningrad Mil Distr; 1935-37 commander, Moscow Mil Distr; 1937-38 commander, Bel Mil Distr; 1934-38 simultaneously member, Mil Council, USSR Pop Comrt of Defense; *Career*: 1917-21 helped to establish and consolidate Sov rule in Turkestan against the forces of the Emir of Bukhara; 1921-22 helped suppress anti-Sov revolts in Caucasus; 1917-19 member, Exec Comt, Tashkent City Sov; 1921 member, Turkestani Centr Exec Comt; member, USSR Centr Exec Comt; deleg at 1934 CPSU(B) Congress; dep, USSR Supr Sov of 1937 convocation; June 1937 member, Special Judicial Office, USSR Supr Court, which sentenced Marshal Tukhachevskiy and other commanders to death; Jan 1938 summoned to Moscow and arrested by State Security organs; *Died*: 1938 in imprisonment; posthumously rehabilitated.

BELOV, Pavel Alekseyevich (1897-1962) Russian mil commander; col-gen from 1944; cavalry commander; CP member from 1925; *Born*: 1897 in Shuya; *Educ*: 1934 grad evening courses at Frunze Mil Acad; *Pos*: until 1916 weighman, office employee; from 1916 private, NCO in a Hussar regt; 1918-21 instructor for basic mil training, Ivanovo-Voznesensk; cavalry platoon leader and squadron commander; 1922-26 commander of a cavalry regt; 1929-34 with Red Army Cavalry Inspectorate; 1934-41 asst commander, then commander, cavalry div; chief of staff, 5th Cavalry Corps; 1941-42 commander, 2nd Cavalry Corps, later reorganized as 1st Guards Cavalry Corps; 1942-45 commander, 61st Army; 1945-55 commanded various mil distr; 1955-60 chm, CC, DOSAAF; from 1960 retired; *Career*: 1941 took part in battle of Moscow; 1942 led his corps in famous raid in Vyaz'ma area; for several months operated in rear of German troops; dep, USSR Supr Sov of 1946, 1950, 1954 and 1958 convocations; deleg at 1952 CPSU Congress; *Awards*: Hero of the Sov Union; four Orders of Lenin; three Orders of the Red Banner; three Orders of Suvorov, 1st Class; Order of Kutuzov, 1st Class; medals;

Died: 3 Dec 1962 in Moscow; buried at Novodevich'ye Cemetery, Moscow.

BELOV, Sergey Andreyevich (1911-1967) Party official; *Born*: 1911 in vil Vorontsovo-Aleksandrovskoye, now Stavropol Kray; *Career*: 1959-62 second secr, Baku City Comt, CP Azer; 1963-67 second secr, Nakhichevan Oblast Comt, CP Azer; dep, Azer Supr Sov of 1963 and 1967 convocation; 1964-67 cand member, CC, CP Azer; *Died*: Oct 1967.

BELYAKOV, Aleksey Aleksandrovich (1870-1927) Econ administrator; CP member from 1903; *Born*: 1870; *Educ*: trained as teacher; *Career*: from 1880's active in revol movement; 1893 worked with Lenin in Samara Marxist circles; 1896 arrested and exiled to Arkhangel'sk Province; as construction technician directed work on Tomsk Technol Inst and other major buildings and bridges in Siberia; 1905 agitation work for newspaper *Novaya zhizn'*; 1906 arranged printing of Bolshevik Centr organ, newspaper *Vperyod*; 1911 again arrested; during 1917 Oct Revol in Geo; 1920 moved to Moscow and held various posts connected with textile ind in Supr Sovnarkhoz; contributed regular feuilletons to newspaper *Izvestiya TsIK SSSR i VTsIK*; member, Auditing Commission, State Publ House; chm, "Red East" Trust; ed work for State Publ House and Publ House of Anti-Illiteracy Soc; *Died*: 16 Oct 1927 in Moscow.

BELYANKIN, Dmitriy Stepanovich (1876-1953) Geologist; prof from 1920; member, USSR Acad of Sci from 1943; *Born*: 23 Aug 1876; *Educ*: 1901 grad Yur'yev (Tartu) Univ; *Career*: 1903-20 lecturer, 1920-35 prof, Leningrad Polytech Inst; from 1930 senior assoc, Petrographic Inst, then Inst of Geological Sci, USSR Acad of Sci; 1933-43 corresp member, USSR Acad of Sci; from 1949 acad secr, Dept of Geological and Geographical Sci, USSR Acad of Sci; member, Main Ed Bd, "BSE" (Large Soviet Encyclopedia); specialized in petrography and mineralogy; did research in Urals, Caucasus and northern part of European USSR; studied composition and structure of rocks in Il'menskiy Mountains in Urals; in Caucasus discovered and studied young intrusive rocks which frequently indicate presence of ore deposits; his observations led him to the conclusion that contact relations (interaction of intrusive magma with solidified magma or sedimentary rocks) are an important factor in formation of various types of rock; his mineralogical research concentrated on main petrogenetic minerals (feldspars, micas, clay minerals) and on rare minerals, for example vishnevites of Centr Urals, hydrogarnets of Transcaucasus, narsarsukites of White Sea area, etc; also did research on ind stone (refractories, ceramic products, slags, binders, abrasives, glass, etc); laid foundations of tech petrography, which plays the same role in silicate technol as does metallography in metallurgy; *Publ*: coauthor, *Geologicheskiye issledovaniya v oblasti Pereval'noy zheleznoy dorogi cherez glavnyy Kavkazskiy khrebet* (Geological Research in the Region of the Pereval Railroad Across the Main Caucasian Range) (1914); coauthor; *Kamennyye stroitel'nyye materialy* (Stone Building Materials) (1924); *Khristallooptika* (Crystal Optics) (3rd ed, 1949); coauthor, *Petrografiya tekhnicheskogo kamnya* (The Petrography of Industrial Stone) (1952); *Izbrannyye trudy* (Selected Works) (vol 1, 1958); *Died*: 20 June 1953.

BELYAYEV, Aleksandr Romanovich (1884-1942) Russian science-fiction writer; lawyer; *Born*: 16 Mar 1884 in Smolensk; *Educ*: studied law and music; *Career*: 1910 first work published; worked as an artiste, a librarian and a warden in a children's home; from 1925 full-time writer; wrote about conquest of space and sci and technol development of future, displaying considerable social awareness, humor and a feeling for sci trends; also wrote on theory of sci-fiction; *Publ: Golova professora Douelya* (Professor Dowell's Head) (1925); *Ostrov pogibshikh korabley* (The Island of Lost Ships) (1926-27); *Nad bezdnoy* (Above the Abyss) (1927); *Chelovek-amfibiya* (The Amphibious Man) (1928); *Bor'ba v efire* (The Battle of the Air Waves) (1928); *Pryzhok v nichto* (The Leap to Nowhere) (1933); *Zvezda Kets* (The Star of Kets) (1936); *Laboratoriya Dubl've* (Laboratory W) (1938); *Pod nebom Arktiki* (Under Arctic Skies) (1938); *Izbrannyye nauchno-fantasticheskiye proizvedeniya* (Selected Science-Fiction Works) (vol 1-2, 1958); *Povesti i rasskazy* (Stories and Tales) (1958); film script for *Kogda pogasnet svet* (When the Light Goes Out), etc; *Died*: 6 Jan 1942 in Pushkin, Leningrad Oblast.

BELYAYEV, Ivan Stepanovich (1907-67) Karelian; govt functionary; Cand of Pedag Sci; CP member from 1944; *Born*: 1907, son of a peasant; *Educ*: grad Kalinin Teachers' Training Inst; *Career*: from 1930 teacher, inspector-methodologist, dir of studies at a teachers' training technicum; 1941-51 bd head, Karelian Pop Comrt of Educ; Karelian Min of Educ; dep chm, Karelian Council of Min; 1955-56 chm, Karelo-Finnish Council of Min; 1956-57 chm, Karelian Council of Min; dep, USSR Supr Sov of 1946, 1950, 1954, 1958, 1962 and 1966 convocations; *Awards*: medal "For Valiant Labor" (1959); *Died*: Mar 1967.

BELYAYEV, Mikhail Fyodorovich (1880-1955) Psychologist; Dr of Pedag Sci; prof; *Born*: 1880; *Educ*: 1922 grad teachers' Training Fac, Yakutsk Univ; *Career*: 1906 began to teach at secondary educ establishments; 1918-20 taught teachers' training courses at Yakutsk Univ; from 1922 research work; 1931-55 head, Chair of Pedag and Psychology, Yakutsk State Teachers' Training Inst; specialized in psychology of secondary school children's interests and labor interests of leading workers and kolkhozniks; *Publ: Sotsial'no-pravovoye povedeniye detey i vzroslykh* (The Social Law Behavior of Children and Adults) (1927); *Sotsial'nyye vyskazyvaniya detey* (Social Comments of Children) (1928); *Osnovnyye polozheniya psikhologii interesa* (The Basic Tenets of the Psychology of Interest) (1940); *D.I. Pisarev ob interese* (D.I. Pisarev on Interest) (1950); etc; *Died*: 10 Nov 1955.

BELYAYEV, Nikolay Il'yich (1903-1966) Party and govt official; CP member from 1921; *Born*: 1903 in vil Kuterem, now Bashkir ASSR; *Educ*: 1925 grad Plekhanov Inst of Nat Econ, Moscow; *Career*: 1919-22 exec secr, Kaleginsk Rayon and Birsk Uyezd Komsomol Comt; 1925-40 agric cooperative posts in Omsk, Tomsk and Novosibirsk; chm, Okrug Cooperative Unions Bd; head, tractor service centers of various agric organs; dep chm, Siberian Kolkhoz Union; 1940-43 secr for food ind, Novosibirsk Oblast CPSU(B) Comt; then first dep chm, Novosibirsk Oblast Exec Comt; 1943-45 chm, Altay Kray Exec Comt; 1945-55 first secr, Altay Kray CPSU(B) Comt; 1955-57 secr, CC, CPSU; 1956-57 simultaneously dep chm, Bureau for RSFSR, CC, CPSU; 1957-Jan 1960 first secr, CC, CP Kaz; Jan 1960-June 1960 first secr, Stavropol' Kray CPSU Comt; 1952-61 member, CC, CPSU; 1957-60 Presidium member, CC, CPSU; dep, USSR Supr Sov of 1946, 1950, 1954 and 1958 convocations; 1958-60 Presidium member, USSR Supr Sov; then Presidium member, dep, RSFSR Supr Sov of 1955 convocation; *Awards*: two Orders of Lenin; two Orders of the Red Banner of Labor; medal "For Valiant Labor" (1959); other medals; *Died*: Oct 1966.

BELYAYEV, Nikolay Mikhaylovich (1890-1944) Eng; specialist in theory of durability; prof from 1924; corresp member, USSR Acad of Sci from 1939; *Born*: 5 Feb 1890; *Educ*: 1916 grad Petrograd Inst of Communications Eng; *Career*: from 1916 lecturer, from 1924 prof, Leningrad Inst of Communications Eng and other higher educ establishments in Leningrad; from 1934 prof, Leningrad Polytech Inst; from 1939 simultaneously senior assoc, Inst of Mech, USSR Acad of Sci; 1924-40, as head of a Leningrad laboratory for research on steel rails, studied theory of contact tensions occurring during compression of bodies in contact; directed development of new rail manufacturing techniques; devised methods of preventing breakage in axles and other parts of locomotives and rolling stock; *Publ*: co-author, *Inzhenernyye sooruzheniya i stroitel'naya mekhanika* (Engineering Structures and Construction Mechanics) (1924); *Metod podbora sostava betona* (A Method of Selecting the Composition of Concrete) (4th ed, 1930); co-author and ed, *Prochnost, uprugost' i polzuchest' betona* (The Strength, Elasticity and Creep of Concrete) (1941); *Soprotivleniye materialov* (The Resistance of Matrials) (5th ed, 1949); *Died*: 25 Apr 1944.

BELYAYEV, Sergey Mikhaylovich (1883-1953) Russian writer; *Born*: 22 Jan 1883; *Educ*: grad Med Fac, Yur'yev Univ; *Career*: 1905 first work printed; after 1917 Oct Revol combined writing with doctor's practice; wrote many children's works; *Publ: Seminarskiye ocherki* (Seminar Studies) (1906); stories *Pozhar* (The Fire) (1926); film scripts and plays; *Zametki sovetskogo vracha* (Notes of a Soviet Doctor) (1926); pop sci works for young readers: *Radiomozg* (The Radio Brain) (1927); *Istrebitel' 2Z* (Destroyer 2Z) (1939); *Vlastelin molnii* (The Master of Lightning) (1947); *Priklyucheniya Samuelya Pinglya* (The Adventures of Samuel Pingle) (1945); *Desyataya planeta* (The Tenth Planet) (1945); *Died*: 11 Feb 1953 in Moscow.

BELYAYEV, Svyatoslav Aleksandrovich (1903-1942) Cameraman; *Born*: 29 Aug 1903; *Career*: 1923 began film work as asst to cameraman F. Verigo-Dorovskiy; for many years worked with film dir Ye. Chervyakov; *Works*: films: *Minaret smerti* (The Minaret of Death) (1925); *Mishka Zvonov* (1925); *Napoleon-gaz* (The Napoleon-Gas) (1925); *Poet i tsar'* (Poet and Tsar) (1927); *Tur-*

bina No. 3 (Turbine No. 3) (1927); *Order na zhizn'* (Life Warrant) (1927); *Devushka s dalyokoy reki* (The Girl from a Distant River) (1928); *Moy syn* (My Son) (1928); *Dzhoy i druzhok* (Joy and Her Friend) (1928); *Ubityy zhiv* (Corpse Alive) (1928); *Zolotoy kiyuv* (The Golden Beak) (1929); *Goroda i gody* (Cities and Years) (1930); *Muzykal'naya olimpiada* (The Musical Olympics) (1932); *Lichnoye delo* (A Private Affair) (1932); *Gorod v stepi* (The City in the Steppes) (1933); *Bal'tiytsy* (The People of the Baltic) (1938); *Stanitsa Dal'nyaya* (Dal'nyaya Station) (1940), etc; *Died*: 22 Feb 1942 killed on Leningrad Front.

BELYAYEV, Vasiliy Afanas'yevich (1904-1957) Diplomat with rank of envoy extraordinary and plen, 2nd class; *Born*: 1904; *Career*: from 1936 in dipl service; 1940-46 dep head, then head, Consular Dept, USSR Pop Comrt of For Affairs; 1946-48 head, Consular Bd, USSR Min of For Affairs; 1948-50 counsellor, USSR embasy in Turkey; 1951-53 USSR envoy in Syria and Lebanon; 1953-56 USSR envoy in Lebanon; *Died*: 1957.

BELYAYEV, Yevgeniy Aleksandrovich (1895-1964) Orientalist; specialist in Arabic languages and Islam; Dr of Historical Sci; Hon Member, UAR Acad of Sci; *Born*: 21 Feb 1895 in Rzhev; *Educ*: 1913-16 studied at Oriental Fac, Petersburg Univ; 1922 grad Moscow Inst of Oriental Studies; *Career*: from 1924 lecturer, Moscow Inst of Oriental Studies; 1929-30 also worked for "Atheist" Publ House; 1931-34 with League of Militant Atheists; 1934-42 assoc prof, 1945-54 head, Chair of History and Econ of Near and Middle East Countries, Moscow Inst of Oriental Studies; 1942-45 assoc prof, Mil Inst of For Languages; also lectured on Oriental Medieval history at Higher Party School, CC, CPSU(B), at Higher Dipl School and at Moscow Univ; 1951-64 senior assoc, Inst of Oriental Studies, then Inst of the Peoples of Asia and Africa, USSR Acad of Sci; wrote over 80 works on the history of the Oriental peoples and Islam; 1954, 1957 and 1960 attended Int Congresses of Orientalists; Presidium member, Sov-Arab Friendship Soc; *Publ: Proiskhozdeniye Islama* (The Origin of Islam) (1931); *Musul'manskoye sektanstvo* (Moslem Sectarianism) (1957); coauthor, *Istoriya stran zarubezhnogo Vostoka v sredniye veka* (A History of Foreign Oriental Countries in the Middle Ages) (1957), etc; *Awards*: Badge of Hon (1953); *Died*: 5 Sept 1964.

BELYAVSKIY, Sergey Ivanovich (1883-1953) Astronomer; corresp member, USSR Acad of Sci from 1939; *Born*: 7 Dec 1883; *Career*: 1909-25 and 1931-32 head, Simeiz Branch, Pulkovo Observatory; 1937-44 dir, Pulkovo Observatory; specialized in astrophotometry and astrophotography; disovered over 37 asteroids and 250 variable stars, including Vladilena, and one comet; *Publ: Katalog fotograficheskikh velichin 2,777 zvyozd* (A Catalog of the Photographic Magnitudes of 2,777 Stars) (1915); *Astrograficheskiy katalog 11,322 zvyozd mezhdu 70° severnogo skloneniya i severnym polyusom* (An Astrographic Catalog of 11,322 Stars Between a Declination of 70° North and the North Pole) (1947); *Died*: 13 Oct 1953.

BELYY, Andrey (real name: BUGAYEV, Boris Nikolayevich) (1880-1934) Russian poet and writer; theorist of symbolism; *Born*: 26 Oct 1880 in Moscow, son of mathematician N. V. Bugayev; *Educ*: 1903 grad Dept of Natural Sci, Fac of Mathematics, Moscow Univ; *Career*: studied Darwinism, positivism, theosophy, occultism, neo-Kantianism and the philosophy of Schopenhauer and Vladimir Solov'yov; along with Blok, Vyacheslav Ivanov, S. Solov'yov and Ellis, belonged to "younger generation" of symbolists; 1910-11 toured Italy, Egypt and Palestine; 1912 visited Switzerland, where he became a pupil of leading anthroposophist Steiner; 1916 returned to Russia; after 1917 Oct Revol gave a course on theory of poetry and prose for Moscow "Proletkul't" org; 1921 went to Berlin, where he contributed to Gorky's journal "Beseda"; two years later returned to Moscow; published journal "Zapiski mechtateley"; *Publ*: mystery play *Antikhrist* (The Antichrist) (1898); collected verse *Zoloto v lazuri* (Gold on Azure) (1904); blank-verse cycle in four parts in the form of musical symphonies: *Geroicheskaya* (Heroic Symphony) (1900), also known as *Severnaya simfoniya* (Northern Symphony); *Dramaticheskaya* (Dramatic Symphony) (1902); *Vozvrat* (The Return) (1905); *Kubok meteley* (The Cup of Snowstorms) (1908); verse collections *Pepel* (Ashes) (1909); *Urna* (The Urn) (1909); *Khristos voskrese* (Christ Is Risen) (1918); *Korolevna i rytsari* (The Princess and the Knights) (1919); *Posle razluki* (After Parting) (1922); novel *Serebryanyy golub'* (The Silver Dove) (1909); novel "Petersburg" (1913-14); autobiographical stories: *Kotik Letayev* (1922); *Kreshchenyy kitayets* (The Baptized Chinaman) (1927); historical epos *Moskva* (Moscow) (2 vol, 1926); *Maski* (Masks) (1932); non-fiction: *Simvolizm* (Symbolism) (1910); *Lug zelyonyy* (The Green Meadow) (1910); *Ritm kak dialektika* (Rhythm as Dialectic) (1929); *Mednyy vsadnik* (The Bronze Horseman) (1929); memoirs *Na rubezhe dvukh stoletiy* (At the Turn of the Century) (1930); *Nachalo veka. Vospominaniya* (The Beginning of the Century. Reminiscences) (1933); *Mezhdu dvukh revolyutsiy* (Between Two Revolutions) (1934); other books *Tragediya tvorchestva. Dostoyevskiy i Tolstoy* (The Tragedy of Creativity. Dostoevsky and Tolstoy) (1912); *Masterstvo Gogolya* (Gogol's Artistry) (1934), etc; *Died*: 8 Jan 1934 in Moscow.

BEN'KOV, Pavel Petrovich (1879-1949) Painter; Hon Art Worker of Uzbek SSR from 1939; *Born*: 20 Dec 1879; *Educ*: 1909 grad Petersburg Acad of Arts; *Career*: 1909-29 lived and worked in Kazan'; from 1922 member, Assoc of Artists of Revol Russia; 1929 moved to Samarkand; from 1930 dir and instructor, Samarkand Art College; *Works*: paintings: "The Covered Bazaar at Bukhara" (1929); "Khiva Girl" (1931); "Water Bearers at the Khauz" (1932); "March 8 in Registan" (1933); "Earthing up Cotton" (1936); "A Hero's Encounter" (1938); "Proclamation of the Uzbek SSR" (1940); "Girl-Friends" (1940); "Girl with a Dutar" (1947), etc; *Died*: 16 Jan 1949.

BENUA, Aleksandr Nikolayevich (1870-1960) Painter, graphic artist, stage designer, art historian, art critic, producer; *Born*: 3 May 1870, son of architect N. L. Benua; *Educ*: 1894 grad Law Faculty, Moscow Univ; attended classes at Acad of Arts; *Career*: ideologist, organizer and theoretician of "World of Art" artists' group; 1900 debut as set designer; after Oct Revol worked at Bolshoy Drama Theater in Petrograd; from mid-1920's lived abroad; worked in French and Italien theaters; *Works*: 1900 designed sets for Taneyev's *Mest' amura* (Cupid's Revenge) at the Hermitage Theater, Petersburg; sets for Wagner's "Goetterdaem merung" (1903), Cherepnin's *Pavil'on Armidy* (Armida's Pavilion) (1907) and *Pikovaya dama* (The Queen of Spades) (1921) at the Mariinskiy Theater, Petersburg; sets for Grillparzer's "Die Ahnfrau" (1908) at the Komissarzhevskaya Theater, Petersburg; did a great deal of work for Diaghilev's theatrical enterprise in Paris; designed sets for: Moussorgsky's *Boris Godunov* (1908); Stravinsky's *Petrushka* (1911); "Le Rossignol" (1914); at Moscow Arts Theater did sets for Molière's "Le Mariage Forcé" and his own production of "Le Malade Imaginaire" (1913); 1915 produced and did sets for Pushkin's *Kamennyy gost* (The Stone Guest), *Motsart i Sal'yeri* (Mozart and Salieri) and *Pir vo vremya chumy* (The Feast During the Plague), and Goldoni's "La Puta Onorata" (1914); designed and produced "The Merchant of Venice" (1920), "Il Servitore di Due Padroni" (1921) and "Le Médecin Malgré Lui" (1921); among his works abroad were his sets for Rimsky-Korsakov's *Zolotoy petushok* (The Golden Cockerel) (1927, Grand Opéra, Paris), *Idiot* (The Idiot) after Dostoevsky (1925 Vaudeville Théatre, Paris), Stravinsky's *Petrushka*, "Eugene Onegin", Prokofiev's *Petya i volk* (Peter and the Wolf) (1946-49 La Scala, Milan); also painted landscapes; illustrated Pushkin's *Mednyy vsadnik* (The Bronze Horseman) (1916), etc; great connoisseur of art, culture and life of various centuries and peoples; paintings: "Louis XIV Out Walking" (1897); "The Chinese Pavilion" (1906); "The King Out Walking" (1906); "The Marquise's Bath" (1906), etc; *Publ: Istoriya zhivopisi vsekh vremyon i narodov* (A History of the Painting of All Times and Peoples) (1913); *Tsarskoye selo* (1910); *Zhizn' khudozhnika. Vospominaniya* (Life of an Artist. Memoirs) (1955), etc; *Died*: 9 Feb 1960.

BENUA, Leontiy Nikolayevich (1856-1928) Russian architect; member, Acad of Architecture from 1882; Hon Art Worker of RSFSR from 1927; *Born*: 23 Aug 1856, son of the architect M.L. Benua; *Educ*: 1879 grad Petersburg Acad of Arts; *Career*: from 1892 prof, from 1893 workshop dir, Petersburg Acad of Arts; continued classical traditions in architecture; taught many leading Sov architects; *Works*: Singing Capella building in Petersburg; Obstetrics and Gynecological Inst, Petersburg; house on Kamennyy Ostrov (now Kirov) Prospekt, Leningrad; exhibition building of Russian Museum, Leningrad; present USSR Min of For Affairs building in Moscow, etc; *Died*: 8 Feb 1928.

BERDNIKOV, Aleksandr Ivanovich (1883-1959) Party and govt official; CP member from 1905; *Born*: 4 Dec 1883 in Shuya, now Ivanovo Oblast, son of a worker; *Career*: Dec 1905 active in armed revolt in Moscow; several times arrested for revol activities; exiled to Siberia; fled from exile and went abroad; fall 1917 returned to Russia; 1918-20 member and cand member, All-Russian Centr Exec Comt; worked for All-Russian Centr Exec Comt's

Commission to Draft First Constitution; 1919-28 admin, govt and Party work; 1919-20 head, Ed and Publ Dept, All-Russian Metalworkers' Union and coordinating ed of its publ house; 1921-23 head, Ed and Publ Dept, All-Russian and USSR Centr Exec Comt; 1923-25 worked for CC, CPSU(B); also dep head, RSFSR State Publ House; 1925-28 chm, All-Union Press Comt; CC, CPSU(B) plen for radio broadcasting; 1928-49 exec posts with USSR Gosplan; pensioner; *Publ*: coauthor, *Kurs politgramoty* (A Political Education Course); *Awards*: Order of Lenin; Badge of Hon; *Died*: 24 July 1949.

BERDNIKOV, Yakov Pavlovich (1889-1940) Russian poet; *Born*: 1889 in vil Vanov'ye, Tambov Province, son of a peasant; *Educ*: grad parish school; *Career*: metalworker at Putilov Plant and other factories; 1905 took part in workers' demonstration; 1908 deported to his place of birth for distributing RSDRP proclamations; 1911 first work printed in workers papers and Bolshevik newspapers *Zvezda* and *Pravda*; then wrote for Petrograd journals *Gryadushcheye* and *Plamya*; *Publ*: verse: "Roar, Furnace, Blow More Strongly"; "To Freedom" (1912); verse collections: *Sonet rabochego* (A Worker's Sonet) (1917); *Tsvety serdtsa* (Flowers of the Heart) (1919); *Proisshestviye* (The Incident) (1921); *V nevole* (In Captivity) (1922); *Na literaturnom fronte* (On the Literary Front) (1924); *Yerema* (1925); *Died*: 5 Mar 1940.

BERDYAYEV, Nikolay Aleksandrovich (1874-1948) Philosopher; *Born*: 6 Mar 1874 in Kiev; *Educ*: studied at Kiev Univ; *Career*: 1900 expelled from univ for participating in revol-democratic movement and exiled to Vologda Province; in early 1900's sided with "Legal Marxists"; 1909 one of principal contributors to periodical *Vekhi* which opposed materialism and atheism and advocated religion and idealism; 1922 expelled from USSR; set up Acad of Philosophy and Religion in Berlin; 1924 moved to Paris and founded journal *Put'* (published 1925-40); *Publ: F.A.Lange i kriticheskaya filosofiya* (F.A. Lange and Critical Philosophy) (1900); *Kritika istoricheskogo materializma* (A Critique of Historical Materialism) (1903); *Katekhizm marksizma* (Catechism of Marxism) (1905); *Oputy filosofskiye, sotsial'nyye i literaturnyye* (Philosophical, social and Literary Experience) (1907); *Novoye religioznoye soznaniye i obschestvennost'* (New Religious Consciousness and Society) (1907); *Dukhovnyy krizis intelligentsii* (The Spiritual Crisis of the Intelligentsia) (1910); *Filosofiya svobody* (The Philosophy of Freedom) (1911); *Sud'ba Rossii. Opyty po psikhologii voyny i natsional'nosti* (The Fate of Russia. Experience in the Psychology of War and Nationality) (1918); *Smysl istorii. Opyt filosofii chelovecheskoy sud'by* (The Sense of History. Experience in the Philosophy of Human Fate) (1923); *Mirosozertsaniye Dostoyevskogo* (Dostoyevsky's Philosophy) (1923); *Filosofiya neravenstva. Pis'ma k nedrugam po sotsial'noy filosofii* (The Philosophy of Inequality. Letters to Adversaries in Social Philosophy) (1923); *Novoye srednevekov'ye. Razmyshleniya o sud'be Rossii i Yevropy* (The New Medieval Era. Contemplations on the Fate of Russia and Europe) (1924); *Russkaya ideya* (The Russian Idea) (1946); *Istoki i smysl russkogo kommunizma* (The Sources and Meaning of Russian Communism) (1946); etc; *Died*: 23 Mar 1948.

BERENDS, Konstantin Georgiyevich (? -1935) Mil instructor; strategy specialist; officer, Russian Army Gen Staff; *Career*: after 1917 Oct Revol sided with Sov regime; commands and staff posts during Civil War; then prof, Chair of Strategy and History of Mil Technique, Frunze Mil Acad; *Publ: Strategicheskiye vekhi* (Strategy Milestones) (1925); *Polevyye rekognostsirovki. Posobiye dlya shtabnykh rabotnikov* (Field Reconnaissance; A Manual for Staff Officers); *Died*: 1935.

BERENS, Yevgeniy Andreyevich (1876-1928) Naval specialist and diplomat; capt, Russian Navy; non-Party man; *Born*: 30 Oct 1876 in Tiflis of a noble seafaring family; *Educ*: 1895 naval cadet school; *Career*: 1904 in Russo-Japanese War as senior navigator of cruiser *Varyag*; 1908 as first officer of battleship *Tsesarevich*, distinguished himself by aid to victims of Sicilian earthquake; taught naval history at cadet school; lectured at Gen Staff Acad; 1910-14 naval attache in Germany; 1914-17 head, For Dept, Naval Gen Staff; after 1917 Oct Revol elected chief, Naval Gen Staff; planned Arctic convoy in which Russian Baltic Fleet vessels escaped from Helsingfors to Kronstadt; suggested scuttling of Black Sea vessels to prevent their capture by Germans; from Apr 1919 commander, Sov Naval Forces and asst commander in chief for Naval Affairs; on his initiative old river and lake flotillas were reinforced and new ones organized; fought at Tsaritsyn; from Feb 1920 special plen of RSFSR Revol-Mil Council; Sov naval expert at int conferences in Genoa (1922), Lausanne (1922-23) and Rome (1924); 1923-24 naval expert with Sov mission in England; from Mar 1924 naval attache in England; from 1925 simultaneously naval attache in France; from late 1926 special emissary for Pop Comrt of the Navy; *Died*: 7 Apr 1928 in Moscow.

BERESNEV, Nikolay Yakovlevich (1893-1965) Film dir and scriptwriter; *Born*: 26 June 1893; *Educ*: 1915 grad directing class, Komissarzhevskiy Theatrical School; *Career*: 1926-33 film dir and scriptwriter, Leningrad Film Studio; 1936-38 film dir and scriptwriter, Bel State Film Studio; from 1949 at Pop Sci Film Studio, Leningrad; also produced plays at Leningrad and Moscow theaters; *Productions*: films: *Zolotoy myod* (Golden Honey) (1928); *Razgrom* (Rout) (1931); *Annenkovshchina* (The Annenkov Movement) (1933); *Pushkin v Petersburge* (Pushkin in Petersburg) (1950); *Tolstoy v Yasnoy Polyane* (Tolstoy at Yasnaya Polyana) (1952); *Maksim Gorky* (1954); *Gosudarstvennyy Ermitazh* (The State Hermitage) (1955); *Sovetskaya batal'naya zhivopis'* (Soviet Battle Painting) (1958); *Gogol' v Peterburge* (Gogol in Petersburg) (1959); *Khudozhnik Vladimir Serov* (The Painter Vladimir Serov) (1961); *Ital'yanskaya skul'ptura Ermitazha* (Italian Sculpture in the Hermitage) (1962), etc; scripts for films: *Romantika grazhdanskoy voyny* (The Romance of the Civil War) and *Konnitsa skachet* (The Gallopping Cavalry) (1929); *Died*: 12 July 1965.

BEREZHKOV, Nikolay Georgiyevich (1886-1956) Historian; *Born*: 12 June 1886; *Educ*: grad Moscow Univ; *Career*: after 1917 Oct Revol taught at Moscow Archeological Inst, Nizhniy Novgorod Univ, etc; 1924-34 at Museum of the Revol; 1934-35 at Penal Servitude and Exile Museum; from 1935 at Inst of History, USSR Acad of Sci; specialized in Lith history; in his latter years traced the chronology of Russian chronicles; *Publ*: doctor's thesis *Litovskaya metrika kak istoricheskiy istochnik* (Lithuanian Metrics as a Historical Source) (vol 1, 1946), etc; *Died*: 12 Mar 1956.

BEREZHNOV, Pyotr Antonovich (1904-1964) Hydraulic eng and meliorationist; Turkm Min of Water Management from 1954; member, CC, CP Turkm from 1954; *Born*: 1904; *Educ*: 1934 grad Centr Asian Inst of Irrigation and Agric Mechanization; *Career*: worked for Turkm water management system; dep, Turkm Supr Sov of 1955, 1959 and 1963 convocation; *Awards*: two Orders of the Red Banner of Labor (1957 and 1961); Badge of Hon; *Died*: 7 Nov 1964.

BEREZIN, Mikhail Yegor'yevich (1864-1933) Politician; statistician; *Born*: 1864; *Educ*: 1889 grad Kazan' Univ; *Career*: shortly after grad Kazan' Univ arrested for revol propaganda among craft and printing workers, exiled to Ivanovo-Voznesensk and placed under police surveillance; 1897, after 14 months' imprisonment, again exiled for three years to Vyatka Province; after his term of exile, worked for Insurance Dept, Saratov Zemstvo Admin; 1905 helped organize and convene Saratov Oblast Congress of Peasant League and established Labor Group; 1907 Saratov dep in 2nd State Duma; elected asst chm, 2nd State Duma; 1918 statistics consultant, Pop Comrt of Labor and Cooperative Insurance League; then consultant, RSFSR State Insurance Bd; *Died*: 1933.

BEREZNEGOVSKIY, Nikolay Ivanovich (1875-1926) Surgeon; *Born*: 1875; *Educ*: 1903 grad Med Fac, Tomsk Univ; *Career*: from 1903 intern, Chair of Hospital Surgical Clinic, Tomsk Univ; 1909 defended doctor's thesis on grafting ureter to intestine; studied advanced med techniques in Moscow, Petersburg and abroad; from 1912 prof, Chair of Surgical Pathology and Therapy, Tomsk Univ; during WW 1 directed Red Cross hospitals in Riga and Kiev; 1918-26 head, Chair of Hospital Surgical Clinic, Tomsk Univ; studied intravenous narcosis, organ and tissue grafts, physiology of gastrointestinal tract after surgery, surgical treatment of some forms of epilepsy, etc; dep chm, 16th Russian Surgeons' Congress; 1918, together with Prof. A.P. Malyshev, founded East Siberian Prosthesis Inst in Tomsk; 1920 organized first physicians' courses on orthopedics and prostheses; wrote 67 works; *Publ: O peresadke mochetochnikov v kishechnik* (Grafting the Ureters to the Intestine) (1908); *Povrezhdeniya i khirurgicheskiye zabolevaniya selezyonki* (Injuries and Surgical Ailments of the Spleen) (1909); *Died*: 1926.

BEREZOVSKIY, Feoktist Alekseyevich (1877-1952) Russian writer; CP member from 1904; *Born*: 13 Jan 1877 in Omsk, son of a worker; *Career*: farm laborer, typesetter and railroad official; active in revol movement; 1906 sentenced to death by firing squad but was saved from death by a lucky chance; interned in Aleksandrov Centr Prison; 1908 exiled to Chinese border; from 1918 underground Bolshevik work in Omsk; then chm, Omsk Province Exec Comt; 1922 helped found journal *Sibirskiye ogni*;

from 1924 lived and worked in Moscow; 1900 first work printed; his works portray revol underground activities and Civil War, mainly in Siberia; *Publ*: novelettes: *Mat'* (Mother) (1923); *Pereput'ya* (Crossroads) (1928); novels: *V stepnykh prostorakh* (In the Expanses of the Steppes) (1924); *Bab'i tropy* (Women's Paths) (1928); essays *Tayezhnyye zastrel'shchiki* (Taiga Pioneers) (1926); *Sobraniye sochineniy* (Collected Works) (3 vol, 1928); *Died*: 6 Apr 1952 in Moscow.

BERG, Lev Semyonovich (1876-1950) Geographer and biologist; Dr of Geography from 1909; prof from 1913; member, USSR Acad of Sci from 1946; senior assoc, Zoological Inst, USSR Acad of Sci from 1934; Hon Sci Worker of RSFSR from 1934; *Born*: 14 Mar 1876 in Bendery, now Mold SSR; *Educ*: 1898 grad Moscow Univ; *Career*: until 1903 mang, Aral Sea Fishery; 1904-13 head, Dept of Ichthyology, Zoological Museum, Russian Acad of Sci; 1913 prof, Moscow Psychoneurological Inst; 1914-18 prof of ichthyology, Moscow Agric Inst; 1916-30 and later prof of geography, Petersburg (Leningrad) Univ and Geographical Inst; 1922-34 head, Dept of Applied Ichthyology, State Inst of Experimental Agronomy (later Fishery Inst); 1930-34 assoc, Geomorphological Inst, USSR Acad of Sci; 1934-50 ichthyologist and head, Dept of Fossil Fish, Zoological Inst, USSR Acad of Sci; 1928-46 corresp member, USSR Acad of Sci; from 1904 member, Russian Geographical Soc; did research on geography, limnology, geomorphology, biogeography, geology, petrography of sedimentary rocks, hydrobiology, paleography, toponymy, ichthyology and gen biology; in geography took up and developed V.V. Dokuchayev's ideas on "nature zones"; developed theory of geographical landscapes according to which the proper subject of geography is landscape - a naturally bounded area of the earth's surface incorporating characteristic features and phenomena; 1922 contributed concept of "nomogenesis" to gen biology which denied creative role of natural selection and monophyletic origin of modern animal and plant species and depicted evolution as a teleological process; this theory was subsequently criticized for being "idealistic" and "anti-Darwinian"; *Publ: Ryby Turkestana* (The Fish of Turkestan) (1905); *Aral'skoye more* (The Aral Sea) (1908); *Ryby basseyna Amura* (The Fish of the Amur Basin) (1909); *Ryby presnykh vod Rossii* (Russian Freshwater Fish) (1916); *Klimat i zhizn'* (Climate and Life) (1922); *Otkrytiye Kamchatki i kamchatskiye ekspeditsii Beringa* (The Discovery of Kamchatka and Bering's Kamchatka Expeditions) (1924); *Osnovy klimatologii* (The Principles of Climatology) (1927); *Ocherk istorii russkoy geograficheskoy nauki* (An Outline History of Russian Geography) (1929); *Landshaftno-geograficheskiye zony SSSR* (Landscape and Geographical Zones of the USSR) (1931); *Priroda SSSR* (Flora and Fauna of the USSR) (1937); *Sistema ryb, nyne zhivushchikh i iskopayemykh* (The Classification of Living and Fossil Fish) (1940); *Ocherki po istorii russkikh geograficheskikh otkrytiy* (An Outline History of Russian Geographical Discoveries) (1946); *Vsesoyuznoye geograficheskoye obshchestvo za 100 let, 1845-1945* (A Hundred Years of the All-Union Geographical Society, 1845-1945) (1946); *Geograficheskiye zony SSSR* (Geographical Zones of the USSR) (2 vol, 1947-52); *Ryby presnykh vod SSSR i sopredel'nykh stran* (Freshwater Fish of the USSR and Contiguous Countries) (2 vol, 1948-49); *Ocherki po fizicheskoy geografii* (Studies in Physical Geography) (1949), etc; *Awards*: Stalin Prize (1951, posthumously); *Died*: 24 Dec 1950.

BERG, Pavel Semyonovich (1883-1966) Govt official; CP member from 1903; *Born*: 30 Dec 1883; *Career*: took part in 1917 Feb and Oct Revol in Petrograd; fought in Civil War; 1919 drafted into Red Army; 1920 member, Rostov, and 1921 Stavropol' City Sov; head, Public Health and Land Depts, Rostov and Stavropol' Sov; from 1922 exec railroad admin work in Moscow; from 1936 pensioner; *Died*: 22 July 1966.

BERGEL'SON, David Rafailovich (1884-1952) Jewish impressionist writer; *Born*: 12 Aug 1884 in vil Orkhimovo, now Cherkassy Oblast; son of wealthy parents; *Career*: 1909 first works published; 1921 left USSR and lived mostly in Berlin; contributed to newspaper "Vorwärts"; 1925 began publishing journal *V upryazhke,* in which he appealed to Jewish intellectuals to serve the Revol; returned to USSR for two visits; 1929 settled down in USSR, where he became one of the leading Jewish writers; *Publ*: novelette "Around the Station" (1909); story "The Deaf Man" (1910); novels: "After All" (1913); "Departure" (1920); "Degree of Severity" (1926-27); collected short stories "Turbulent Days" (1927); novel "By the Law of Justice" (1933), which was adapted for the stage; short stories "The Birobidzhanians" (1934) and "Step by Step," which described the role of Jewish workers in socialist construction and their training in the spirit of socialism, novel "On the Dnieper" (1935), which depicted the social differences among Jews prior to the 1905 Revol; historical play "Prince Reubeini" (1946) on the Jews in Spain; unfinished novella *Aleksandr Barash* (1946); stories of Soviet heroism in WW 2: "New Stories" (1947) and "Two Worlds"; his short story "The Deaf Man" was adapted for the stage and ran at the Piscator Theater in Berlin and the Jewish Theater in Minsk; arrested by State Security organs; *Died*: 12 Aug 1952 in imprisonment.

BERINGOV, Mitrofan Mikhaylovich (1889-1937) Painter; *Born*: 1889; *Educ*: 1913-15 studied under N.K. Rerikh and A.A. Rylov at School of Soc for Promotion of the Arts; *Career*: from 1922 lived and worked in Moscow; member, Assoc of Artists of Revol Russia; from 1925 made annual trips to Far North; 1933 took part in icebreaker "Sedov" Arctic expedition; his paintings deal mainly with the Arctic; in 1920's influenced by Modernists; *Works*: "Red Guard Patrol" (1924); "Murmansk Fishermen" (1925); "The Midnight Sun" (1926); "The Baltic Fleet's Arctic Cruise" (1928); "On a Minesweeper" (1930); "Cape Chelyuskin" (1934), etc; *Died*: 1937.

BERISHVILI, Zakariy Ivanovich (1887-1965) Stage dir and actor; Hon Artiste of Geo SSR from 1945; Hon Art Worker of Geo SSR from 1961; *Born*: 28 Jan 1887; *Career*: 1905-21 actor; 1921 helped found Film Section, Geo Pop Comrt of Educ; asst film dir; also played small parts in films; from 1926 film dir; from 1946 directed dubbing of films into Geo; *Works*: directed films: "Samanishvili's Step-Mother" (1927); "The First and the Last" (1927); "Encountering Life" (1929); "Room No. 79" (1930); "The Trumpet Trumpets the Tocsin" (1931); "Beyond the River" (1935); "The Treasure of Tsen Gorge" (1941); *Died*: 9 May 1965.

BERIYA, Lavrentiy Pavlovich (1899-1953) Party and govt official; CP member from 1917; *Born*: 29 Mar 1899 in vil Merkheuli, Geo; *Educ*: 1915-17 studied at Baku Mech-Construction College; 1919 grad tech college; 1920 studied at Baku Polytech Inst; *Career*: 1917 in Russian Army on Rumanian Front; 1920 illegal revol mission in Geo to prepare the armed uprising; arrested and deported from Geo; from Apr 1921 worked for Cheka; chm, Geo State Pol Bd; chm, Transcaucasian State Pol Bd and OGPU plen in Transcaucasian Socialist Fed Sov Republ; Collegium member, USSR OGPU; from Nov 1931 first secr, CC, CP(B) Geo and secr, Transcaucasian Kray CPSU(B) Comt; from 1932 first secr, Transcaucasian Kray CPSU(B) Comt and secr, CC, CP(B) Geo; at 17th, 18th and 19th Party Congresses elected member, CC, CPSU(B); Politburo (Presidium) member, CC, CPSU; 1935 published book *K voprosu ob istorii bol'shevistskikh organizatsiy v Zakavkaz'ye* (The History of Bolshevik Organizations in the Transcaucasus) which distorted historical facts and falsely presented Stalin as leader and inspirer of revol struggle in Transcaucasus; 1938-45 USSR Comr of Internal Affairs; from Feb 1941 chm, USSR Council of Pop Comr; from June 1941 member, from May 1944 dep chm, USSR State Defense Comt; July 1945 promoted Marshal of the Soviet Union; from Apr 1953 first dep chm, USSR Council of Min and simultaneously USSR Min of Internal Affairs; dep, USSR Supr Sov of 1937, 1946 and 1950 convocations; 10 July 1953 expelled from CC and CPSU at plenary session of CC, CPSU and relieved of posts of first dep chm, USSR Council of Min and USSR Min of Internal Affairs by Presidium of USSR Supr Sov for ". . . criminal anti-state activities . . . designed to undermine the Sov State in the interests of foreign capital . . . manifested in treacherous attempts to place the USSR Min of Internal Affairs above the Sov Govt and the CPSU"; case sent to USSR Supr Court; *Awards*: Hero of Socialist Labor (1943); five Orders of Lenin; Order of Suvorov, 1st Class; two Orders of the Red Banner; seven Sov medals; *Died*: 23 Dec 1954 executed by firing squad by order of USSR Supr Court.

BERKALOV, Ye.A. (1878-1952) Lt-Gen, Eng and Tech Corps; prof; Dr of Tech Sci; member, Acad of Artillery Sci; *Born*: 1878; *Career*: from 1918 in Red Army; helped improve Sov artillery service; *Died*: 1952.

BERKENGEYM, Abram Moiseyevich (1867-1938) Organic chemist; Dr of Chemistry; Hon Sci and Tech Worker of RSFSR from 1934; *Born*: 1867; *Career*: prof, Moscow Inst of Fine Chemical Technol; applied electron theory of atomic structure to organic chemistry; helped found Sov chemico-pharmaceutical ind; devised ind means of producing various drugs and aromatic synthetic compounds (albichthole, atophan, novocaine, dionine, coumarin, saiodine, etc), enabling USSR to end imports of these products; demonstrated that the value of the thermal effects contributed to the gen energetic balance of a chemical reaction by the individual chemical elements is a periodic function of their atomic number; *Publ: Osnovy elektronnoy khimii organicheskikh soyedineniy* (The Principles of the Electron Chemistry of Organic Compounds) (1917); *Osnovy teoreticheskoy khimii* (The Principles of Theoretical Chemistry) (2nd ed, 1926); *Khimiya i tekhnologiya sinteticheskikh lekarstvennykh sredstv* (The Chemistry and Technology of Synthetic Drugs) (1935); *Died*: 1938.

BERKENGEYM, Aleksandr Moiseyevich (1880-1932) Cooperator; member, Socialist-Revol Party; *Born*: 1880; *Educ*: studied at Physics and Mathematics Fac, Moscow Univ but did not grad because of arrest and banishment in 1899 for participation in student actions; grad Dresden Polytech School; *Career*: on return from abroad engaged in polit work; as a member of Socialist-Revol Party repeatedly arrested and exiled; during exile in Arkhangel'sk Province took part in local cooperative movement; on return official, then bd member, Centr Union of Consumers' Soc; after 1917 Feb Revol chm, Moscow Food Comt; elected member, Pre-Parliament and State Conference; broke with Socialist-Revol Party and ran for Constituent Assembly as cand of recently formed Cooperative Block; after 1917 Oct Coup traveled abroad on Centr Union of Consumers' Soc business; headed its foreign branches and concluded deals and commissions; 1922 emigrated; 1926-32 chm, Union of Jewish Cooperative Soc in Poland; *Died*: 1932.

BERLIN, Pavel Abramovich (1877-1962) Econ and journalist; *Born*: 1877 in Rostov-on-Don, son of a sawmill owner; *Educ*: grad Berlin Univ; *Career*: after graduation from a non-classical high school went to Berlin to continue his studies; early 1900's began lit career by contributing to publ *Nauchnoye obozreniye, Zhizn, Obrazovaniye* and *Mir Bozhiy*; after grad univ lived in Paris; 1908 returned to Petersburg where he became a regular contributor to newspaper *Sovremennoye slovo*; during WW 1 and Revol did cooperative work; 1922 went to Berlin where he worked for seven years in Sci and Information Dept, USSR Centr Union of Consumer Soc; 1928 dismissed from this post, moved to Paris and became an emigre; worked for Jewish soc orgs, contributed to Russian and French press; after WW 2 contributed to *Sotsialisticheskiy vestnik; Publ: Germaniya nakanune 1848* (Germany on the Eve of 1848) (1906); *Pervyy nemetskiy parlament* (The First German Parliament) (1907); *Ocherk razvitiya ekonomicheskikh idey v XIX veke* (An Outline of the Development of Economic Ideas in the 19th Century) (1907); *Karl Marks i yego vremya* (Karl Marx and His Time) (1909), twice reprinted in Moscow; *Apostoly anarkhizma Bakunin, Kropotkin, Makhayev* (Apostles of Anarchism – Bakunin, Kropotkin and Makhayev) (1909); *Russkaya burzhuaziya v staroye i novoye vremya* (The Russian Bourgeoisie in Former and Modern Times) (1925); *Died*: 12 Apr 1962 in Paris.

BERNOTAS, Napoleonas Iozo (1914-1959) Lith actor; *Born*: 12 Feb 1914; *Educ*: 1938 grad Klaypeda Teachers' Training Inst; 1939 studied at Kaunas Univ; 1940-41 studied in Theatrical Dept, Philology Fac, Vilnius Univ; *Career*: from 1939 actor and stage dir at theaters in Vilnius and Klaypeda; from 1956 film work; *Roles*: Oloizas in "Before It Is Too Late" (1957); Chief of Police Stryupas in "The Bridge" (1957); the German Officer in "Red Sheets" (1958); Pampikas in "The Blue Horizon" (1959); Stumbras in "Turkeys" (1959); *Died*: 7 Apr 1954.

BERNSHTAM, Aleksandr Natanovich (1910-1956) Historian and archeologist; Dr of History; prof, Leningrad Univ; senior assoc, Inst of Archeology, USSR Acad of Sci; CP member from 1940; *Born*: 1 Oct 1910 in Kerch', son of a professional Bolshevik revol; *Educ*: 1931 grad Ethnography Dept, Leningrad Univ; 1931-35 postgrad student, State Acad of the History of Civilization; *Career*: from 1930 assoc, then senior assoc, State Acad of the History of Civilization (subsequently Inst of the History of Civilization and now Inst of Archeology), USSR Acad of Sci; simultaneously prof, Leningrad Univ; led 20 archeological expeditions to Semirech'ye, Tyan'-Shan', Altay, Pamirs and Fergana Valley; discovered remains of Saka culture in Centr Asia; laid foundations of research on permanent settlements in Semirech'ye, centr Syr-Dar'ya and Fergana; compiled chronology of archeological relics of Centr Asia from 2,000 BC to 15th Century AD; attributed particular importance to Huns in ethnogenesis of Centr Asia; also studied history of Centr Asian art, epigraphy and numismatics; *Publ: Arkheologicheskiy ocherk Severnoy Kirgizii* (An Archeological Study of Northern Kirgizia) (1941); *Pamyatniki stariny Talasskoy doliny* (Ancient Relics of the Talass Valley) (1941); *Istoricheskoye proshloye kirgizskogo naroda* (The Historical Past of the Kirgiz People) (1942); *Sotsial'noekonomicheskiy stroy orkhono-yeniseyskikh tyurok VI-VIII vekov* (The Social and Economic Structure of the Orkhon-Yenisey Turks of the 6th-8th Centuries) (1946); *Epokha vozniknoveniya velikogo kirgizskogo eposa 'Mana'* (The Age of the Emergence of the Great Kirgiz Epic "Manas") (1946); *Drevneyshiye tyurkskiye elementy v etnogeneze Sredney Azii* (Ancient Turkic Elements in the Ethnogenesis of Central Asia) (1947); *Arkheologicheskiye pamyatniki Kirgizii* (The Archeological Relics of Kirgizia) (1950); *Ocherk istorii Semirech'ya* (An Outline History of the Semirech'ye) (1950); *Chuyskaya dolina* (The Chu Valley) (1950); *Drevnyaya Fergana* (Ancient Fergana) (1951); *Ocherk istorii gunnov* (An Outline History of the Huns) (1951); *Istorikoarkheologicheskiye ocherki tsentral'nogo Tyan'-Shanya i Pamiro-Altaya* (Historical and Archeological Studies of Central Tyan'-Shan' and the Pamir-Altay Region) (1952); *K voprosu o proiskhozhdenii kirgizskogo naroda* (The Origin of the Kirgiz People) (1955); *Awards*: Order of the Red Banner of Labor; medal for Valiant Labor; *Died*: 10 Dec 1956.

BERNSHTEYN, Aleksandr Nikolayevich (1870-1922) Psychiatrist; Dr of Med from 1900; assoc prof from 1902; *Born*: 1870; *Educ*: 1893 grad Med Fac, Moscow Univ; *Career*: 1893-1903 intern, then asst prof, Korsakov Psychiatric Clinic; 1899 founder-dir, Centr Admission Ward for Mental Patients, Moscow Municipal Admin; set up patho-anatomical, biochemical and experimental psychology laboratories at which he taught as an assoc prof of Moscow Univ from 1902 until his death; 1901-05 head, Psychology Laboratory, Psychiatric Clinic, Moscow Univ; 1907-12 head, Psychology Laboratory, Pedag Assembly; co-ed and ed, various journals of psychiatry and psychology; 1920-22 dep head, Main Bd for Sci Museums and Sci and Art Institutions, Pop Comrt of Educ; dir, Moscow Psychoneurological Inst; devised a qualitative intelligence test for certain mental disorders; wrote over 50 works on med psychology and psychiatry; *Publ*: doctor's thesis *Materialy k ucheniyu o klinicheskom znachenii myshechnogo valika u dushevno-bol'nykh* (Material on the Theory of the Clinical Significance of the Sarcostyle in Mental Patients) (1900); *Klinicheskiye priyomy psikhologicheskogo issledovaniya dushevno-bol'nykh* (Clinical Methods for the Psychological Examination of Mental Patients) (1911); *Klinicheskiye lektsii o dushevnykh boleznyakh* (Clinical Lectures on Mental Diseases) (1912); *Osnovnyye problemy nauchnoy psikhiatrii* (The Basic Problems of Scientific Psychiatry) (1922); *Died*: 1922.

BERNSHTEYN, Nikolay Aleksandrovich (1896-1966) Physiologist; corresp member, USSR Acad of Med Sci; *Born*: 5 Oct 1896; *Educ*: 1919 grad Med Fac, 1st Moscow Univ; then attended courses at Mathematical Fac, Moscow Univ; *Career*: wrote numerous works on aspects of physiology of movements; improved techniques for recording and analysing movements (kymocyclography, cyclogrammetry, etc); studied biodynamics of striking motions, piano playing and such locomotions as running, walking and jumping; studied dynamics of muscle-power, innervation structure of motor action by detailed biodynamic analysis of motions; influenced the development of biomech studies in the physiology of motion; founded and directed laboratories of physiology of motion at various research establishments; in his latter years concentrated on cybernetics; *Publ: Obshchaya biomekhanika* (General Biomechanics) (1926); *Problema vzaimootnosheniy koordinatsii i lokalizatsii* (The Correlations of Coordination and Localization) (1935); ed, *Issledovaniya po biodinamike khod'by, bega, pryzhka* (Research on the Biodynamics of Walking, Running and Jumping) (1940); *O postroyenii dvizheniy* (The Structure of Motions) (1947); "Die kymocyclographische Methode der Bewegungsuntersuchung" (The Kymocyclographic Method of Motion Studies) (1936); *Died*: 16 Jan 1966.

BEROYAN, Mari Georgiyevna (1892-1960) Arm actress; Pop Artiste of Geo SSR from 1946; *Born*: 8 Feb 1892; *Career*: 1913 stage debut in Tiflis; from 1922 with Arm Drama Theater, Tbilisi; specialized in character and comedy roles; dep, Geo Supr Sov of 2nd-4th convocations; *Roles*: Salome in Sundukyan's "The Ruined Hearth"; Khamperi in Sundukyan's "Khatabala"; Shpanik in Shirvanzade's "Namus"; Zarnishan in Shirvanzade's "The Evil Spirit", etc; *Died*: 22 July 1960.

BERSENEV (real name: PAVLISHCHEV), Ivan Nikolayevich (1889-1951) Actor and stage dir; prof, Moscow Inst of Stagecraft; Pop Artiste of USSR from 1948; CP member from 1947; *Born*:

23 Apr 1889 in Moscow; *Educ*: studied at Law Fac, Kiev Univ and Lepkovsky Drama School; *Career*: from 1907 actor, Solovtsov Theater, Kiev; also performed in Odessa, Vinnitsa and Yekaterinodar; from 1911 actor, Moscow Arts Theater; from 1914 also acted in films; 1924-36 actor, from 1925 stage dir and from 1928 artistic dir, Moscow Acad Arts Theater; 1936-38 actor and stage dir, Theater of Moscow Oblast Trade-Union Council; 1938-51 actor and artistic dir, Lenin Komsomol Theater, Moscow; *Roles*: on stage: Rodet in *Tri sestry* (Three Sisters); Zhadov in *Dokhodnoye mesto* (A Lucrative Post); Mitya in *Bednost' ne porok* (Poverty Is No Vice); Johannes in Hauptmann's "Einsame Menschen"; Malcolm in Shakespeare's "Macbeth"; the Coroner in L. Tolstoy's *Zhivoy trup* (The Living Corpse) (1911); Petr Verkhovenskiy in *Nikolay Stavrogin* (1913), after Dostoevsky; Zagoretskiy in Griboyedov's *Gore ot uma* (Woe from Wit) (1914); Boris Godunov in A. Tolstoy's *Smert' Ioanna Groznogo* (The Death of Ivan the Terrible) (1927); Pierre Massoubre in Deval's "Supplication for Life" (1935), etc; film roles: Tsikhovskiy in *Mech miloserdiya* (The Sword of Mercy) (1918); Kartashov in *Velikiy grazhdanin* (The Grand Citizen) (1939); Marshal Tito in *V gorakh Yugoslavii* (In the Mountains of Yugoslavia) (1946), etc; *Productions*: co-producer, Afinogenov's *Chudak* (The Crank) (1929); producer: Afinogenov's *Salyut Ispanii* (Salute to Spain) (1936); Gergey and Litovskiy's *Moy syn* (My Son) (1939); Simonov's *Paren' iz nashego goroda* (A Lad From Our Town) (1941); Korneychuk's "Front" (The Front Line) (1942); co-producer, Ibsen's "Nora," etc; *Died*: 25 Dec 1951 in Moscow.

BERSHADSKIY, Yuliy Rafailovich (1869-1956) Painter; Hon Art Worker of Ukr SSR from 1941; *Born*: 9 Jan 1869 in Tiraspol'; *Educ*: 1899 grad Petersburg Acad of Arts; *Career*: in his early years sided with itinerant artists movement; from 1900 member, Assoc of Southern Russian Artists; 1907-28 founder-instructor, Odessa Art Studio; 1928-41 contributed to All-Ukr art exhibitions; from 1941 lived and worked in Sverdlovsk; *Works*: paintings: "Widowhood" (1893); "The Secret" (1898); "Southern Bazaar" (1899); "Thoughts" (1906); "Fishermen" (1934); "Kolkhoz Festival" (1937); portraits of Acad Pavlov (1944) and the writer Bazhov (1944), etc; *Died*: 26 Sept 1956.

BERTEL'S Yevgeniy Eduardovich (1890-1957) Orientalist; Dr of Philology from 1935; prof from 1928; corresp member, USSR Acad of Sci from 1939; senior assoc, Inst of Oriental Studies (now Inst of the Peoples of Asia), USSR Acad of Sci from 1930; Hon Sci Worker of Uzbek SSR from 1944; Hon Sci Worker of Tadzh SSR from 1946; *Born*: 25 Dec 1890 in Petersburg, son of a physician; *Educ*: 1914 grad Law Fac, Petersburg Univ; 1920 grad Oriental Dept, Fac of Soc Sci, Petersburg Univ; also studied at Petrograd Conservatory; *Career*: 1920-30 assoc, Asian Museum Russian (USSR) Acad of Sci; from 1921 lecturer, from 1928 prof, Inst of Living Oriental Languages, Leningrad Univ; from 1932 also head, History and Language Section, Tadzh Base, USSR Acad of Sci; specialized in languages and lit of Centr Asia, Azer, Persia and Afghanistan; dean of Sov Iranian studies; compiled grammars of Persian and Pashto; wrote studies of Persian, Tadzh, Uzbek, Turkm and Azer lit; did translations from Sanskrit, Avestan, Arabic, Persian, Pahlavi, Pashto, Turkish, Tajiki, etc; supervised compilation of critical ed of Nizami's poems *The Sharaf-Nama* and *Igbal-Nama* and Firdausi's *Shah-Nama* (Book of Kings), etc; from 1951 hon member, Turkm Acad of Sci; from 1956 hon member, Uzbek Acad of Sci; from 1944 corresp member, Iranian Acad of Sci; from 1955 corresp member, Arabic Acad of Sci, Damascus; *Publ: Grammatika persidskogo yazyka* (A Persian Grammar) (1926); *Bakhtiar-name. Persidskiy tekst i slovar'* (The Bakhtiar-Nama. Persian Text and Vocabulary) (1926); *Ocherk istorii persidskoy literatury* (An Outline History of Persian Literature) (1928); *Uchebnik persidskogo yazyka* (A Persian Textbook) (1932); translated and annotated *Nasir-i Khusrau. Safar-name (Kniga puteshestviya)* (Nasir-i Khusrau. The Safar-Nama (Book of Travels)) (1933); *Abu-l-Kasim Firdousi i yego tvorchestvo* (Abul Qasim Firdausi and His Works) (1935); *Stroy yazyka pushtu* (The Structure of Pashto) (1936); ed, *Iz arkhiva sheykhov Dzhuybari. Materialy po zemel'nym i torgovym otnosheniyam Sredney Azii XVI veka* (From the Archives of the Iubari Sheikhs. Documents on Land and Trade Relations in Central Asia in the 16th Century) (1938); *Velikiy Azerbaydzhanskiy poet Nizami. Epokha, zhizn', tvorchestvo* (The Great Azerbaydzhani Poet Nizami. His Age, Life and Works) (1940); ed translator, *Nizami Gyandzhavi. Iskender-name, chast' 1, Sharaf-name* (Nizami Ganjavi. The Sikandar-Nama, Part 1, The Sharaf-Nama) (1940); *Nizami (Zhizn' zamechatel'nykh lyudey)* (Nizami [The Lives of Outstanding Personalities]') (1947); ed *"Sharaf-name' Nizami* (Nizami's *Sharaf-Nama*) (1947); ed, *'Ikbal-name' Nizami* (Nizami's *Iqbal-Nama*) (1947); *Navoi. Opyt tvorcheskoy biografii* (Novoi. An Attempt at a Creative Biography) (1948); *Roman ob Aleksandre i yego glavnyye versii na Vostoke* (The Book of Alexander the Great and its Main Eastern Versions) (1948); *Dzhami. Epokha, zhizn', tvorchestvo* (Jami. His Age, Life and Works) (1949); chief ed, *Russko-tadzhikskiy slovar'* (A Russian-Tadzhik Dictionary) (1949); *Kabus-name. Issledovaniye, perevod i primechaniye* (The Qabus-Nama [Mirror of Princes]'. A Critical Annotated Translation) (1953); chief ed, *Tadzhiksko-russkiy slovar'* (A Tadzhik-Russian Dictionary) (1954); *Nizami. Tvorcheskiy put' poeta* (Nizami. The Poet's Creative Path) (1956); ed, *Shakhname. Tom 1. Ot nachala poemy do skazaniya o Sokhrabe* (The Shah-Nama. Vol 1. From the Beginning of the Poem to the Tale of Sohrab) (1957); *Istoriya persidsko-tadzhikskoy literatury* (A History of Persian Tadzhik Literature) (1960); *Firdousi. 'Shakhname'. Kriticheskiy tekst* (Firdausi's *Shah-Nama*. An Annotated Text) (vol 1, 2960), etc; *Awards*: Stalin Prize (1948); *Died*: 7 Oct 1957 in Moscow.

BERYOZKIN, Vsevolod Aleksandrovich (1899-1946) Oceanographer; *Born*: 1899; *Educ*: 1924 grad Leningrad Univ; 1928 grad Naval Acad; *Career*: took part in oceanographic expeditions to Barents Sea, Kara Sea, Greenland Sea, etc; taught oceanography at Leningrad Univ, Naval Acad and Leningrad Hydrometeorology Inst; 1925 published details of observations made during 1923 expedition with the *Murman* in book *Prilivy na Novoy Zemle* (Tides at Novaya Zemlya); 1928-29 charted currents of the Gulf of Finland; 1932 took part in expedition to Kara Sea on icebreaker *Taymyr*, during which he observed maelstroms near latitude 78° North; suggested they were caused by presence of shoals further north, a hypothesis which was confirmed in 1935 by discovery of Ushakov Island and shoals in this area; 1934 member, first non-stop voyage from Vladivostok to Murmansk along Great Northern Sea Route with icebreaker *Litka*; 1935 member, highlatitude expedition with *Sadko*; 1939 member, expedition to the northern Atlantic with *Sibiryakov*; *Publ*: coauthor, *Trudy pervoy vysokoshirotnoy ekspeditsii na 'Sadko' v 1935-om godu* (Transactions of the First High-Latitude Expedition on the *Sadko* in 1935) (1939); *Dinamika morya* (The Dynamics of the Sea) (1938); *Died*: 1946.

BERYOZOV, Yefim L'vovich (1895-1958) Surgeon; specialist in gastric surgery and oncology; prof from 1930; Dr of Med; Hon Sci Worker of USSR from 1943; pupil of S. I. Spasokukotskiy and P. A. Gertsen; *Born*: 5 Sept 1895 in Vinnitsa; *Educ*: studiet at Zurich and Petrograd Univ; 1919 grad Med Fac, Saratov Univ; *Career*: while still a student worked in S. I. Spasokukotskiy's Surgical Clinic, where he did his first research on hematological lesions before and after splenectomy; after graduation worked for a short time as a surgeon at Vinnitsa Zemstvo Hospital under Malinovskiy; 1919-21 served in Red Army as head of evacuation stations on various fronts during Civil War; 1921-24 intern, Prof P. A. Gertsen's Surgical Clinic, 1st Moscow State Univ; 1924-26 asst prof, 1927-30 assoc prof, Spasokukotskiy Surgical Clinic, Saratov Med Inst; 1927 studied gastric surgery at Austrian and Czechoslovak hospitals; from 1930 prof, Chair of Surgery, Astrakhan' Med inst, where he established a large experimental laboratory and a branch of the Centr Blood Transfusion Inst; from 1930 spent summers in Zheleznovodsk and Yessentuki, establishing a surgical dept in the former health resort; from 1937 until death head, Chair of Fac Surgery, Gorky Med Inst, which he turned into one of leading Sov surgical centers and where he established an experimental and biochemical laboratory and a branch of Centr Blood Transfusion Inst; during WW 2, also worked as consultant to various hospitals and was chief surgeon, Gorky Evacuation Station; after WW 2 chief surgeon of Gorky; established municipal oncological dispensary which became an extension of Fac Clinic; apart from clinical, research and teaching duties also worked for several med org; bd member, All-Union Soc of Surgeons and dep chm, All-Russian Soc of Surgons; 1930-37 chm, Astrakhan' Sci Surgical Soc; 1937-58 chm, Gorky Sci Surgical Soc; trained many surgeons, twelve of whom hold chairs at various med inst; supervised compilation and defense of over 60 doctor's theses; made major contribution to development of Sov oncology and helped to organize cancer diagnostic service in Gorky Oblast; wrote over 140 works on thoracic surgery, oncology, wound surgery, pathophysiology and surgery, metabolism blood transfusion, etc; *Publ: O funtsiyakh selezyonki* (The Functions of the Spleen) (1924); *O* *posleoperatsionnom atsidoze, yego profilaktike i lechenii insulinom i glukozoy* (Postoperative Acidosis. Its Prevention and Treatment with Insulin and Glucose) (1928); *O total'noy rezektsii zheludka* (Total Resection of the Stomach) (1933); coauthor *Bolezni operirovannogo zheludka* (Postoperative Stomach Ailments) (1940); *Khirurgiya pishchevoda i kardii zheludka pri rake* (Surgery for Cancer of the Oesophagus and the Cardia) (1951; *Rasshiryonnyye i kombinirovannyye rezektsii zheludka pri rake* (Extended and Combined Resection of the Stomach in Cases of Cancer) (1957); ed 11 collections of papers on surgery; *Awards*: two Orders of the Red Star; Acad Burdenko Prize; *Died*: 14 Aug 1958.

BERZARIN, Nikolay Erastovich (1904-1945) Mil commander; col-gen; *Born*: 1904; *Educ*: grad *Vystrel* Higher Tactical and Marksmanship Courses; *Career*: from 1918 in Red Army; 1918-21 fought in Civil War; 1937-41 regt commander, asst chief, Combat Training Dept, Special Far Eastern Army; commander, 21st and 32nd Infantry Div; 1938 his 32nd Infantry Div took part in operations against Japanese at Lake Khason; 1941-45 commander, 27th, 34th and 5th Assault Armies; 1945 Sov troops under his command were first to break into Berlin; first mil commandant of Berlin; *Awards*: Hero of the Sov Union; Order of Lenin; Order of the Red Banner; Order of Suvorov; other orders; *Died*: 16 June 1945 in Berlin in a motorcycle crash.

BERZIN, Reyngol'd Iosifovich (1888-1939) Lat; prominent mil polit figure; Cheka administrator; CP member from 1905; *Born*: 16 July 1888, son of farm laborer on Kinigsgof Estate, former Lifland Province; *Educ*: 1916 grad Pskov Ensigns' School; *Career*: while still a child herded cattle, then worked at *Fortuna* Factory, Rujiena; 1905 joined Lat Soc-Democratic Party; 1905 active in armed uprising of *Rujiena Republic*; 1906-08 underground work; 1908-11 worked in Riga; 1911 arrested for distributing illegal lit and imprisoned; on release worked as stockman; 1914 drafted into Russian Army; 1916-17 junior officer in active army; during 1917 Feb Revol chm, corps comt; deleg, 2nd Congress of Soviets; member, Exec Comt, 2nd Army (Minsk Rayon); after 1917 Oct Coup member, Mil-Revol Comt, old Western Front; commanded detachments responsible for liquidating old Headquarters in Mogilev; comr attached to chief of staff, Sov Supr Commander in Chief; Dec 1917 commanded 1st Minsk Revol Detachment, organized first attack on anti-Bolshevik forces under Gen Kaledin and Polish Legion of Dowbor-Musnicki; from early 1918 commander in chief, Western Front against counter-revol forces; from June 1918 commander in chief, Northern Ural-Siberian Front, commanding 3rd and 9th Armies; from Dec 1918 inspector, Sov Lat Army; from July 1919 member, Revol Mil Council, Western Front; organized defense of Petrograd; 1919-20 member, Revol Mil Council, Southern and Southwestern Fronts; Dec 1923-July 1924 member Revol-Mil Council, Turkestani Front; organized campaign against Basmachi; 1924-26 member, Revol Mil Council, Western Mil Distr; 1927 relieved of duties in army for siding with Trotskyite opposition; transferred to admin work; from 1931 head, OGPU-NKVD Bd, Far North Construction Trust (responsible for gold mining in Kolyma area with prison-camp labor); arrested by NKVD; *Awards*: Golden Arms; RSFSR Order of the Red Banner; Bukhara Order of the Red Banner; Order of the Red Banner of the Khorezm Republic; 1937 arrested by NKVD; *Died*: 11 Sept 1939 in imprisonment; posthumously rehabilitated.

BERZIN', Rudol'f Yanovich (1881-1949) Opera singer (dramatic tenor); Pop Artiste of Lat SSR from 1944; CP member from 1940; *Born*: 21 Sept 1881 in Riga; *Educ*: vocal training in Riga, Copenhagen and Berlin; *Career*: from 1889 chorist and dramatic actor; 1905 participated in revol and spent about a year in jail; 1906-08 founder and manager, Apollo Drama Theater in Riga; from 1908 opera singer abroad, mainly in Germany; from 1919 soloist, from 1944 dir and artistic dir, Riga Opera and Ballet Theater; from 1940 instructor, Lat Conservatory; *Roles*: Buzhut in Kalnyn's *Banyuta*; Grishka Kuter'ma in Rimsky-Korsakov's *Skazaniye o nevidimom grade Kitezhe* (Legend of the Invisible City Kitezh); Title roles in Wagner's "Tannhäuser" and "Lohengrin"; Othello in Verdi's "Othello"; Ramses in Verdi's "Aida", etc; *Died*: 31 Jan 1949 in Riga.

BERZIN, Yan Antonovich (Party pseudonyms: ZIYEMEL; Ya'A.; PAVLOV, Ya.) (1881-1941) Lat revolutionary; Party and govt official; diplomat; CP member from 1902; *Born*: 29 Sept 1881 in Venden Uyezd, former Lifland Province, son of a peasant; *Career*: teacher; repeatedly arrested and exiled; 1906-07 secr, Petersburg RSDRP Comt; 1907 deleg, 5th (London) Party Congress; from 1908 emigré; active in for groups of Lat Soc-Democratic Party; 1915 attended Zimmerwald Conference and helped organize "Zimmerwald Leftist" group; 1917 member, CC, Lat Soc-Democratic Party; 1917 at 6th RSDRP(B) Congress elected member, CC, RSDRP(B); at 7th Congress elected cand member, CC, RCP(B); after 1917 Oct Revol member, All-Russian Centr Exec Comt; 1918 RSFSR plen in Switzerland; 1919 Lat Pop Comr of Educ; 1919-20 secr, Comintern; 1921 RSFSR plen in Finland; 1921-25 with Sov mission in England; from 1925 USSR plen in Austria; from 1927 plen, USSR Pop Comrt of For Affairs with Ukr govt and member, CC, CP(B) Ukr; from 1929 dep chm, Commission for Publ of Dipl Documents; from 1932 head, USSR and RSFSR Centr Records Bd; ed, periodical *Krasnyy arkhiv* (Red Archives); wrote numerous works, mainly in Lat, on subjects ranging from politics to lit criticism; arrested by State Security organs; *Died*: 12 Apr 1941 imprisonment; posthumously rehabilitated.

BERZIN, Yan Karlovich (real name: Peter KYUZIS) (1890-1937) Lat mil commander; army comr, 1st class; former chief, Intelligence Agency, Red Army Gen Staff and member, Mil Council, USSR Pop Comrt of Defense; CP member from 1905; *Born*: 13 Nov 1890 in Volgof Volost, Kurland Province, son of a peasant; *Educ*: until 1905 studied at a teachers' seminary; *Career*: during 1905 revol served with "Forest Brethren" partisan detachments; 1906-09 imprisoned for armed resistance to Cossack punitive squads (sentenced to death, but verdict commuted to imprisonment because he was a minor); 1911 arrested for membership of RSDRP and exiled to Siberia; 1914 fled from exile to Lat; 1915-16 private at front; 1916 deserted to Petrograd, worked as fitter; 1917 took part in Feb Revol and in Bolshevik coup; 1918-19 manager, then Sov Lat Dep Pop Comr of Internal Affairs; from May 1919 in Red Army as head div polit dept, then head, Special Dept, All-Russian Cheka, 15th Army; from Dec 1920 with Red Army Intelligence Agency; 1924-35 head, Red Army Intelligence Agency; 1935-36 asst, then dep commander, Special Far Eastern Army; 1936-37 senior advisor in republ Spain; from June 1937 again head, Red Army Intelligence Agency; late 1937 arrested by NKVD; *Awards*: Order of the Red Banner; *Died*: 1937 in imprisonment; posthumously rehabilitated.

BESPALOV, Ivan Mikhaylovich (1900-1937) Lit critic; CP member from 1919; *Born*: 11 June 1900 in vil Smolino, now Chelyabinsk Oblast; son of a peasant; *Educ*: 1926 grad Inst of Red Prof; *Career*: fought in Civil War; lecturer and dep dir, Inst of Red Professors; worked for Dept of Agitation and Propaganda, CC, CPSU(B); 1929-31 dep ed, journal *Pechat' i revolyutsiya*; ed, journal *Krasnaya nov'*; TASS for correspondent; one of leaders of "Litfront" (Literary Front) group; from 1934 chief ed, State Lit Publ House; 1937 arrested and imprisoned; *Publ: Stil' rannikh rasskazov Gor'kogo* (The Style of Gorky's Early Short Stories) (1928); *Stil' kak zakonomernost'* (Style as a Natural Law) (1929); *Problemy literaturnoy nauki* (Problems of the Science of Literature) (1929); articles on Mayakovsky, Fadeyev, Bagritskiy and Gorky as petty-bourgeois writers (1934-37); *Died*: 1937 in imprisonment; posthumously rehabilitated.

BESSAL'KO, Pavel Karpovich (1887-1920) Russian writer; CP member from 1917; *Born*: 1887 in Yekaterinoslav; *Educ*: grad Yekaterinoslav parish school; *Career*: from 1903 at railroad workshops; 1904 joined Mensheviks; 1907 arrested, imprisoned for two years, then exiled for life to Yeniseysk Province; 1910 fled from exile and went abroad; worked in Vienna, Florence and Paris; Mar 1917 returned to Russia and worked at Yekaterinoslav Railroad Workshops; from late 1917 with Petrograd Proletarian Culture Org; then ed, journal *Gryadushcheye*; in his lit articles analysed worker poets and criticized Futurism; late 1919 drafted into Red Army, sent to Southern Front and appointed ed of an army newspaper; *Publ: Almazy Vostoka* (Diamonds of the East) (1916); play *Kamenshchik* (The Stonemason) (1918); novelette *Detstvo Kuz'ki* (Kuz'ka's Childhood) (1918); novels: *Bessoznatel'nym putyom* (The Subconscious Path) (1918); *Katastrofa* (The Catastrophe) (1918); novelette *K zhizni* (Toward Life) (1919); coauthor, *Problemy proletarskoy kul'tury* (Problems of proletarian culture) (1919); *Pesni sadovnika* (A Gardener's Songs) (1921); *Kuz'ma Darov* (1929); *Died*: Feb 1920 of typhus in Khar'kov.

BETSKIY (real name: KOBETSKIY), Mikhail Aleksandrovich (1883-1937) Actor; Hon Artiste of RSFSR from 1933; *Born*: 2 Oct 1883; *Educ*: 1905 grad V.N. Davydov's class, Petersburg Drama Courses; *Career*: from 1905 actor, V.F. Komissarzheskaya

Theater and "Comedy Theater", Petersburg, etc; from 1910 played provincial theaters; 1917-25 in Astrakhan; 1925-28 in Krasnodar, Kazan' and Novosibirsk; 1928-30 in Chelyabinsk, Perm' and Nizhniy Tagil; 1930-37 actor, Sverdlovsk Theater; also did production work and taught acting; *Roles*: Chatskiy; Prince Myshkin and Raskol'nikov in Dostoevsky's "Idiot" and *Prestupleniye i nakazaniye* (Crime and Punishment); Yarovoy in *Lyubov' Yarovaya*; Nezelasov in *Bronepoyezd 14-69* (Armored Train 14-69); Godun in Lavrenyov's *Razlom* (Break-Up); Gennadiy in Romashov's *Ognennyy most* (The Fire Bridge); *Died*: 18 Apr 1937.

BETYOKHTIN, Anatoliy Georgiyevich (1897-1962) Geologist and mineralogist; prof from 1937; Dr of Geological and Mineralogical Sci from 1937; member, USSR Acad of Sci from 1953; prof, Moscow Inst of Non-Ferrous Metals and Gold from 1949; prof, Chair of Minerals, Leningrad Mining Inst and head, Laboratory of Mineralography, Inst of Ore Deposit Geology, Petrography, Mineralogy and Geochemistry, USSR Acad of Sci from 1937; sci consultant, Ural and Kola Branches, USSR Acad of Sci; chief ed, journal *Geologiya rudnykh mestorozhdeniy* from 1958; *Born*: 1897 in vil Strigino, now Vologda Oblast; *Educ*: 1924 grad Leningrad Mining Inst; *Pos*: 1923-28 ore geologist at "Red Ural" Mine, Nizhniy Tagil' Admin, Ural Platinum Trust; 1928-29 senior asst prof, Chair of Mineralogy, Leningrad Mining Inst; 1939-42 dep dir, Inst of Geological Sci, USSR Acad of Sci; 1953-55 head, Dept of Ore Deposits, Inst of Geological Sci, USSR Acad of Sci; *Career*: 1929-46 did research on Chiatura and other manganese deposits; 1930-36 did research on chrome deposits in Urals and Caucasus; 1937-40 ed and coauthor, various geological publications of USSR Acad of Sci; 1941-44 under wartime program for development of natural resources led manganese prospecting expeditions for Comt on Geology and Ind Org, Pop Comrt of Ferrous Metallurgy; 1946-53 corresp member, USSR Acad of Sci; 1946-48 made trips to Czechoslovakia, East Germany and Poland as a geological consultant; 1955 visited Communist China with Sov geological deleg for conference on formation of ore deposits; 1956 attended Int Geological Congress in Mexico; wrote over 200 works; developed method of studying polished sections of platinum ore in reflected light; compiled mineralography of ore deposits in USSR; advanced several theories of ore deposit formation; *Publ: Odna iz osobennostey struktury korennoy platiny* (A Structural Characteristic of Indigenous Platinum) (1928); *O nekotorykh osobennostyakh ural'skikh korennykh platinovykh rud* (Some Characteristics of Platinum Ores in the Urals) (1930); *K mineralogii Belokanskogo mednogo mestorozhdeniya* (The Mineralogy of the Belokany Copper Deposit) (1931); *Boraty* (Borates) (1932); *Opredeleniye rudnykh mineralov pod mikroskopom* (The Determination of Ore Minerals Under the Microscope) (1933); *K izucheniyu mestorozhdeniy khromistogo zheleznyaka* (The Study of Chromite Deposits); *O teksturakh i strukturakh rud* (The Texture and Structure of Ores); *Napravleniye nauchno-issledovatel'skoy raboty na Chiaturskom margantsevom mestorozhdenii* (The Direction of Research on the Chiatura Manganese Deposit) (1934); *Platina i drugiye mineraly platinovoy gruppy* (Platinum and Other Minerals of the Platinum Group) (1935); *Mineragraficheskoye izucheniye mineral'nykh vidov burykh zheleznyakov iz nekotorykh ural'skikh mestorozhedniy* (The Mineralographic Study of Mineral Varieties of Brown Hematites from Some Ural Deposits) (1936); *Shordzhinskiy khromitonosnyy peridotitovyy massiv v Zakavkaze i genezis mestorozhdeniy khromistogo zheleznyaka voobshche* (The Shordzha Chromite-Bearing Peridotite Massif in the Caucasus and the Genesis of Chromite Deposits in General) (1937); *O mineragrafii* (Mineralography) (1945); *Promyshlennyye margantsevyye rudy SSSR* I(Industrial Manganese Ores of the USSR) (1945); *Mineralogiya* (Mineralogy) (1950); *Kurs mineralogii* (A Course of Mineralogy) (1951, 1956, 1957); *Osadochnyye margantsevyye obrazovaniya* (Sedimentary Manganese Formations) (1958), etc; *Awards*: two Orders of the Red Banner of Labor (1945, 1957); Order of Lenin (1953); Stalin Prize, 2nd Class (1947); Prize of the Presidium of the USSR Acad of Sci; Lenin Prize (1958); *Died*: 20 Apr 1962.

BEYYER, Vladimir Ivanovich (1868-1945) Russian stage designer; Hon Artiste of RSFSR from 1932; *Born*: 1868; *Educ*: 1892 grad Petersburg Acad of Arts; *Career*: after 1917 Oct Revol cofounder, Leningrad Young Playgoers' Theater; from 1921 chief stage designer, Leningrad Young Playgoers' Theater; *Works*: sets and costumes for: *Konyok-gorbunck* (The Little Hunchback Horse), after Yershov (1922); Gorlov's *Pokhititel' ognya* (The Thief of Fire) (1924), etc; *Died*: 29 June 1945.

BEZBORODOV, Mikhail Il'ich (1907-1935) Mordvinian poet and playwright; one of first Moksha-Mordvinian poets; *Born*: 10 Jan 1907 in vil Staryye Pichengushi, now Mordvinian ASSR; *Career*: 1927 first work published; *Publ*: poems "Fact and Fable" (1930); "For Liberty" (1930); "Stifled Anger" (1930); play "Two Camps" (1933); verse "The Poet-Plowman"; "Spring"; "Winter Is Coming", etc; *Died*: 11 Mar 1935.

BEZDOMNYY (real name: PELEKHATYY), Kuz'ma Nikolayevich (1886-1952) Ukr writer, journalist and revolutionary; CP member from 1948; *Born*: 11 Nov 1886 in vil Opory, Galicia; *Educ*: 1908 grad Higher Inst of Journalism, Vienna; *Career*: 1921-27 published newspaper *Volya narodu*; 1927-32 published newspaper *Sel'-Rob*; 1930-32 worked for newspaper *Sila*; these periodicals were run by the West Ukr CP; from 1946 exec govt work; 1949-52 chm, L'vov Oblast Exec Comt; dep chm, Ukr Supr Sov; *Publ*: "What Collectivization Is" (1930); "And the Mother-Land Will Smile" (1959); satirical feuilletons, pamphlets, etc; *Died*: 28 Mar 1952 in L'vov.

BIANKI, Vitaliy Valentinovich (1894-1959) Russian children's writer; *Born*: 11 Feb 1894 in Petersburg; son of a biologist; *Educ*: studied at Dept of Natural Sci, Fac of Physics and Mathematics, Petrograd Univ; *Career*: 1923 began writing; from travels, expeditions and hunting trips accumulated a profound knowledge of animal kingdom which he later used in his writings; contributed to journals *Vorobey* (later *Novyy Robinzon*), *V masterskoy prirody, Druzhnyye rebyata* and *Znaniye - sila*; also contributed to almanach *Sovetskiye rebyata; Publ*: stories and fairytales for young children *Pervaya okhota* (The First Hunt) (1924); *Myshonok Pik* (Pik the Mouse); (1928); *Zayach'ya khitrost* (The Cunning Hare) (1941); *Dve vorony* (The Two Crows) (1955); *Pauchok pilot* (The Pilot Spider) (1956); stories for older children *Odinets* (The Loner) (1927); *Askir* (1927); *Posledniy vystrel* (The Last Shot) (1928); *Dzhul'bars* (1937); *Lesnyye byli i nebylitsy* (Forest Facts and Fables) (1952); calendar of woodland life *Lesnaya gazeta* (The Forest Gazette) (1928); collection *Rasskazy i skazki* (Stories and Fairytales) (1951); *Povesti i rasskazy* (Tales and Stories) (1959), etc; his easy colorful style and amusing animal descriptions appealed directly to the imagination of children; *Died*: 10 June 1959 in Leningrad.

BICHERAKHOV, Georgiy Fyodorovich (? -1920) Ossetian eng; member, RSDRP (Mensheviks); *Career*: summer 1918 organized uprising of Cossacks in Terek region and headed Terek Cossacks and Peasants' Sov; chm, Provisional Pop Govt, Terek Kray; Nov 1918, after uprising was crushed by Sov troops, fled to Petrovsk (now Makhachkala), where he helped his brother L. F. Bicherakhov to set up Caucasian-Caspian Democratic Govt; *Died*: 1920 hanged in Baku by Bolsheviks.

BICHERAKHOV, Lazar' Fyodorovich (? -1952) Ossetian mil commander; Cossack maj-gen; *Career*: 1914 front-line service as staff capt with Gorsko-Mozdok Regt; fought against Germans and Turks; early 1917 led Terek Cossack unit of Persian Expeditionary Corps during march on Kermanshah and Baghdad; July 1918 returned with unit to Baku, helped to liberate town from German and Turkish troops, then fought against Sov regime; late 1918 drove Sov troops out of Petrovsk (now Makhachkala) and set up Caucasian-Caspian democratic govt; 1919 emigrated to England; 1943 joined Vlasov army in Germani, working in North Caucasian Dept until May 1945; *Died*: 22 July 1952 in Dornstadt, Western Germany.

BIKHTER, Mikhail Alekseyevich (1881-1947) Conductor and pianist; Hon Art Worker of RSFSR from 1938; *Born*: 23 Apr 1881 in Moscow; *Educ*: 1910 grad Moscow Conservatory, where he studied under A.N. Yesinova and A.K. Lyadov; *Career*: 1912-17 worked at Petersburg Theater of Music and Drama, where, together with producer I.M. Lapitskiy, he staged following operas: Dargomyzhskiy's *Kamennyy gost'* (The Stone Guest); *Yevgeniy Onegin* (Eugene Onegin); *Boris Godunov; Snegurochka* (The Snow-Maiden); "Die Meistersinger von Nürnberg", etc; from 1934 prof, Leningrad Conservatory; acquired fame as accompanist to N.I. Zabela-Vrubel', F. I. Shaliapin, I.A. Alchevskiy, etc; *Died*: 7 May 1947 in Leningrad.

BILANOVSKIY, Ivan Dmitriyevich (1878-1958) Entomologist; *Born*: 20 Jan 1878 in Lokhvitsa, now Poltava Oblast; *Educ*: 1900 grad Petersburg Forestry Inst; *Career*: prior to 1924 forester and forestry inspector, Khar'kov and Kiev Provinces; from 1924 entomologist at various establishments; 1936-46 assoc, 1946-58 head, Dept of Invertebrate Fauna, Inst of Zoology, Ukr Acad of Sci; wrote over 50 works on agric and forestry insect pests; *Publ: Takhiny USSR* (Tachina Flies of the Ukrainian SSR) (2 vol, 1951-53), etc; *Died*: 15 Apr 1958.

BILIBIN, Ivan Yakovlevich (1876-1942) Graphic artist and stage designer; prof, Acad of Arts; expert on ancient Russian art; *Born*: 16 Aug 1876; *Educ*: 1898 grad Soc for Promotion of the Arts, Petersburg; 1898 studied under A. Azhbe in Munich; studied for three years at Acad of Arts in Repin's studio; *Career*: member, "World of Art" artists' soc; 1907 began designing sets in Petersburg; designed sets and costumes for many plays; contributed to journals *Zhupel* and *Adskaya pochta*; works executed in stylized, graphic, flat decorative manner; after 1918 lived abroad; 1936 returned to USSR; *Works*: illustrated: epics of Dobrynya Nikitich (1904); Il'ya Muromets (1912); Pushkin's *Skazka o tsare Saltane* (Tale of Tsar Saltan) (1905); *Skazka o zolotom petushke* (Tale of the Golden Cockerel); sets and costumes for: *Boris Godunov* (1909); *Zolotoy petushok* (The Golden Cockerel) (1909); "Ruslan and Lyudmila" (1913); *Sadko* (1914); illustrated A. N. Tolstoy's novel *Pyotr I* (Peter I) (1937) and Lermontov's works (1941), etc; *Died*: 7 Feb 1942 during blockade of Leningrad.

BILIBIN, Yuriy Aleksandrovich (1901-1952) Geologist; Dr of Geological and Mineralogical Sci from 1943; corresp member, USSR Acad of Sci from 1946; *Born*: 19 May 1901; *Educ*: 1926 grad Leningrad Mining Inst; *Career*: 1926-28 worked for Aldan Gold Trust, then for Centr Geological Survey Research Inst (All-Union Geological Research Inst); studied metallogeny, petrography, tectonics and geomorphology of deposits; devised theory of tectono-magmatic complexes, linking specific types of ore deposits with concrete stages in the development of the individual zones in the mobile belts of the Earth's crust and marked by specific aspects of intrusive magmatism; discovered several gold deposits in the USSR; *Publ: Osnovy geologii rossypey* (The Principles of Deposit Geology) (1938); *Petrologiya Yllymakhskogo intruziva* (The Petrology of the Yllymakh Intrusive) (1947); *Metallogenicheskiye provintsii i metallogenicheskiy epokhi* (Metallogenic Provinces and Metallogenic Epochs) (1955); *Awards*: Stalin Prize (1946); *Died*: 4 May 1952.

BILYASHEVSKIY, Nikolay Fedotovich (1867-1926) Ukr archeologist, ethnographer and art historian; member, Ukr Acad of Sci from 1919; *Born*: 12 Oct 1867 in Uman'; *Career*: 1902-23 dir, Kiev Museum of History; studied archeological relics of various periods (Mount Knyazheskaya, Borisov Settlement, etc); pioneered establishment of museums in Ukr; wrote works on Ukr ornamentation; *Died*: 21 Apr 1926.

BINASIK, M.S. (Party pseudonyms: NOVOSEDSKIY; NOVODVORSKIY) (1883-1938) Govt official; member, RSDRP (Mensheviks); *Born*: 1883; *Career*: attorney; 1906 deleg, 4th (Amalgamative) RSDRP Congress; after 1906 left Soc-Democratic movement; after 1917 Feb Revol chm, Mil Section, Peotrgrad Sov and member, Petrograd Exec Comt; member, RSFSR Centr Exec Comt of 1st convocation; after 1917 Oct Revol, chm, Coalition Cabinet in Vladivostok; later worked as an econ in Moscow; arrested by State Security organgs; *Died*: 1938 in imprisonment.

BINIYATOV, Bashir Nur Ali Ogly (1895-1967) Party official; CP member from 1917; *Born*: 1895; *Career*: began work at age 15 as laborer in Baku oil fields; arrested many times for revol activities; 1912-15 participated in workers' strikes in Baku; 1917 elected member, Baku Sov; comr of food, Romanino Rayon; secr, Romanino Rayon RSDRP(B) Comt; Mar 1918 helped to suppress uprising in Baku; after fall of Baku Commune continued revol activities in underground; branch organizer, "Gummet" Soc-Democratic group and Union of Oil Workers, Surakhany; dep chm, Surakhany Rayon Exec Comt; after establishment of Sov regime in Azer, Party and govt work; elected member, CC, CP Azer; member, Azer Centr Exec Comt; from 1950 pensioner; *Died*: Apr 1967.

BIRKENFELD, Yan Khristianovich (1894-1967) Lat revol; CP member from 1912; *Born*: 1894; *Career*: worked as a farm-hand; from 1916 teacher; from 1915 member, Vidien Soc-Democratic Comt, Lat Kray; after 1917 Feb Revol member, Vidzeme Sov of Landless Peasants; also member, Valk-Ruya Comt, Lat Soc-Democratic Party; took part in 1917 Oct Revol; elected to Sov of Lat Workers Soldiers and Landless Peasants' Dep; member, Sov Lat Centr Exec Comt; during German occupation worked in underground, first in Vidzeme, then in Kurzeme; from 1920 in Red Army; from 1955 pensioner; *Died*: 9 Feb 1967.

BIRYUKOV, Nikolay Zotovich (1912-1966) Russian writer; CP member from 1951; *Born*: 1912 in Orekhovo-Zuyevo, now Moscow Oblast; *Educ*: studied at evening construction technicum; 1938 completed corresp course at Gorky Lit Studio; corresp studies at Inst of For Languages; *Career*: worked at textile mill; as a result of an ind accident bedridden for life; 1932 first work printed; 1928 deleg, 8th Komsomol Congress; *Publ: Pobed ne schest'* (Victories Uncountable) (1932); *Na khutorakh* (On the Farmsteads) (1939); novelette *Chayka* (The Seagull); novel *Vody Narina* (The Waters of Narin) (1950); collected essays *Na mirnoy zemle* (On the Peaceful Land) (1951); historical novelette *Pervyy grom* (The First Thunder) (1957); trilogy *Skvoz' vikhri vrazhdebnyye* (Through Hostile Whirlwinds) (1963); *Awards*: Stalin Prize (1950); *Died*: 1 Feb 1966.

BIRYUKOV, Pavel Ivanovich (1860-1931) Russian writer and public figure; L.N. Tolstoy's biographer; *Born*: 15 Nov 1860 in vil Ivanovskoye, Kostroma Province; *Career*: 1884 met Lev Tolstoy, adopted and preached his doctrine of "non-resistance to evil"; worked for publ houses in Russia and abroad, including *Posrednik* Press; 1893 together with Tolstoy organized famine relief in Samara Province; 1897 exiled to Kurland Province for signing the "Help" appeal prepared by V. Chertkov to protect the Dukhobor sect; from 1898 lived mostly abroad, where he met Lenin; in his work on Tolstoy used excerpts from Tolstoy's diaries, letters, autobiographical recollections, advice from L. N. Tolstoy himself, etc; his biography of Tolstoy is still valid and factual; *Publ: Biografiya L'va Nikolayevicha Tolstogo* (Biography of Lev Nikolayevich Tolstoy) (vol 1, 1905; vol 2, 1908; vol 3, 1921 in Berlin; vol 4, 1923 in Moscow); short biography of L. N. Tolstoy published by Tolstoy Soc in Moscow (1912); *Died*: 10 Oct 1931 in Geneva.

BIRYUZOV, Sergey Semyonovich (1904-1964) Russian; Marshal of the Sov Union from 1955; chief of Gen Staff and USSR First Dep Min of Defense from 1963; member, CC, CPSU from 1961; CP member from 1926; *Born*: 1904 in Skopin, Ryazan' Province; *Educ*: 1926 grad Mil School; 1937 grad Frunze Mil Acad; *Publ*: until 1922 railroad worker; from 1922 in Red Army; fought anti-Communist partisans in Northern Caucasus; 1926-37 platoon leader, company and battalion commander in Moscow Proletarian Div; from 1937 chief of Operations Dept and dep chief of staff, Khar'kov Mil Distr; from 1939 commander, 132nd Div in same mil distr; 1941-42 commander, same div, now in 13th Army; 1942 chief of staff, 48th Army; Dec 1942-Apr 1943 chief of staff, 2nd Guards Army under Marshal Malinovskiy; 1943-44 chief of staff, Southern, 3rd and 4th Ukr Fronts; from Oct 1944 commander, 37th Army of 3rd Ukr Front in Bulgaria; 1946-47 dep commander in chief, Sov Ground Forces; 1947-53 commanded mil distr in Far East; 1953-54 commander in chief, Centr Army Group (Austria, Hungary and Rumania); 1954-55 first dep commander in chief, and 1955-62 commander in chief, Anti-Aircraft Defense System; 1962-63 commander in chief, Strategic Missile Forces; 1955-63 simultaneously USSR Dep Min of Defense; *Career*: during the first months of WW 2 three times managed to save his 132nd Div from encirclement; as chief of staff, 2nd Guards Army on 3rd and 4th Ukr Fronts, fought at Stalingrad and helped to plan the Miussy, Tavrida, Crimean and Yassy-Kishinev operations; 1944-45 acting chm, Allied Control Commission in Bulgaria; 1956-61 cand member, CC, CPSU: deleg at 20th, 21st and 22nd CPSU Congresses; dep, USSR Supr Sov of 1946, 1954, 1958 and 1962 convocations; dep, RSFSR Supr Sov of 1951 convocation; mil publicist; author of a series of articles on missiles; *Publ: Kogda gremeli pushki. Memuary* (When the Guns Were Thundering. Memoirs) (1961); *Awards*: Hero of the Sov Union; five Orders of Lenin; three Orders of the Red Banner; Order of Suvorov, 1st and 2nd Class; Order of Bogdan Khmel'nitskiy, 1st Class; other orders and medals; *Died*: 19 Oct 1964 in a plane crash near Belgrade.

BIRZNIYEK-UPIT (BIRZNIEKS-UPITIS), Ernest Teodorovich (1871-1960) Lat writer; Pop Writer of Lat SSR from 1947; *Born*: 6 Apr 1871 on Bisniyeki Estate, Lat; *Educ*: 1889 grad Tukums Uyezd College; *Career*: from 1889 private tutor; 1893 moved to the Caucasus, where he worked as teacher, librarian, etc; 1908-21 founder-dir, *Dzirtsiyemniyeki* Book Publ House, which published progressive Lat books and supported such democratic writers as Raynis, Sudrabu Edzhus, etc; 1921 returned to Lat and worked for Riga libraries; 1880's began writing under influence of Lat folklore; 1891 published first story "Mother," then wrote short stories, essays, and tales based mainly on the life of farm laborers and rural artisans; 1920's began to write for children; *Publ*: "Stories of the Grey Stone" (1914); "Caucasian Stories" (1927);

children's books: "The Tales of Nina" (2 vol, 1922-24); "Skaydrite" (1926); "Datse's Granddaughter" (1949); "Mobile Yanitis" (1955); trilogy: "Pastarin's Diary" (1922); "Pastarin at School" (1923); "Pastarin in the World" (1924); "collected Works" (6 vol, 1946-50); in Russian translation: *Rasskazy serogo kamnya* (Stories of the Grey Stone) (1955); *Dnevnik Pastarinya* (Pastarin's Diary) (1951); *Pastarin' v shkole* (Pastarin at School) (1953); *Died*: 30 Dec 1960 in Riga.

BITSENKO (née: KAMERISTAYA), Anastasiya Alekseyevna (1875-?) Party and govt official; CP member from 1918; *Born*: 1875, daughter of a peasant, in Yekaterinoslav Province; *Educ*: teachers' training courses in Moscow; *Career*: 1899 worked for org running communal kitchens for the starving in Kazan' Province; 1901, for anti-govt propaganda, exiled from Moscow, where she had been attending teachers' training courses, and barred from teaching; 1902 joined Soc-Democrat Party; 1902-03 org and propaganda work in Smolensk and Petersburg; Jan 1904 arrested; spring 1905 exiled to Vologda Province; fled to Geneva, but in Aug 1905 returned to work illegally in Moscow; member, Moscow Comt of Socialist-Revol Party and organizer for Moscow's Railroad Rayon; led Oct strike in this rayon; Nov 1905 switched to militant work; 22 Nov 1905, as member, flying squad of Militant Org, assassinated Adjutant-Gen Sakharov who had been putting down peasant revolts in the Volga area; 3 Mar 1906 sentenced by Mil Distr Court to an indefinite term at hard labor (instead of death penalty); served ten years' hard labor at Akatuy and Mal'tsevskoye; Mar 1917 released; joined leftist, internationalist wing of Soc-Democrats; member, Chita, then Moscow Oblast Party Comt; after 1917 Oct Revol served on Presidium of Moscow Sov as member, CC of Leftist Socialist-Revol and member, All-Russian Centr Exec Comt; participated in Brest-Litovsk peace talks as member of 1st and 2nd peace deleg; in sharp opposition to majority opinion of Leftist Socialist-Revol Party CC, supported conclusion of a peace treaty; after 1918 revolt of Leftist Socialist-Revol, disagreed on many points with its CC and left the Party; for a time tried to unite those Leftist Socialist-Revol who accepted policy of CP; Nov 1918 joined RCP(B); exec posts with RSFSR Pop Comrt of Agric connected with establishment of kolkhozes; *Died*: date and place of death unknown.

BITTE, Avgust Martynovich (? -1938) Corps comr from 1935; member, Mil Council and chief, Polit Bd, North Caucasian Mil Distr; CP member from 1911; deleg, 17th CPSU(B) Congress; 1937 arrested by NKVD; *Died*: 1938 in imprisonment; posthumously rehabilitated.

BIZOV, Boris Vasil'yevich (1880-1934) Chemist; specialist in rubber and synthetic rubber chemistry; *Born*: 10 Aug 1880; *Educ*: completed higher educ; *Career*: from 1918 prof, Leningrad 2nd Polytech Inst and Leningrad Teachers' Training Inst; 1923-34 head, Chair of Rubber Technol, Leningrad Technol Inst; developed rubber vulcanization theory and ind means of producing synthetic rubber from petroleum products; *Died*: 27 June 1934.

BLAGONRAVOV, Aleksandr Ivanovich (1906-1962) Mil eng; specialist in tank design; maj-gen; assoc prof; Cand of Tech Sci; CP member from 1929; *Born*: 1 Aug 1906; *Educ*: 1932 grad Dzerzhinskiy Acad of Mil Eng; *Career*: from 1930 in Red Army; 1932-44 lecturer, researcher and designer, Dzerzhinskiy Acad of Mil Eng; 1944-59 exec posts with USSR Min of Defense, and staff officer; 1959-62 head, Main Armor Bd, USSR Min of Defense; wrote numerous works on tank design; *Awards*: Stalin Prize (1943); two Orders of Lenin; Order of the Red Banner; three Orders of the Red Star; Badge of Hon; medals; *Died*: 28 May 1962 in the course of his duties.

BLAGONRAVOV, Georgiy Ivanovich (1896-1938) Revolutionary; active in Oct Coup; veteran of USSR State Security organs; CP member from 1917; *Born*: 1896; *Career*: after Feb Revol, while an ensign in the Russian Army, joined Mil Org, CC, RSDRP(B); on eve of Oct Coup sent by Bolsheviks to Peter and Paul Fortress as its comr; 25 Oct 1917 the guns of the fortress opened fire on the Winter Palace on his orders; after coup appointed commandant, Peter and Paul Fortress; member, All-Russian Centr Exec Comt of 1917 convocation; 1918 member, Mil Council, Eastern Front; Oct 1918-31 worked for All-Russian Cheka, State Polit Bd and OGPU; 1931-34 Dep Pop Comr of Means of Communication; arrested by State Security organs; *Died*: 1938 in imprisonment; posthumously rehabilitated.

BLAGOOBRAZOV, Vladimir Sergeyevich (1896-1967) Russian actor and stage dir; Pop Artiste of RSFSR from 1965; *Born*: 5 Feb 1896; *Educ*: trained in 4th Studio, Moscow Acad Arts Theater; *Career*: 1922-28 actor, 4th Studio and Moscow Acad Arts Theater (from 1927 Realistic Theater); from 1929 with Centr Theater of the Red Army (now Centr Theater of the Sov Army); 1937 made stage dir debut at this theater; *Roles*: Reginald Hornby in Maugham's "The Promised Land"; Baklushin in Ostrovskiy's *Ne bylo ni grosha, da vdrug altyn* (From Rags to Riches); Valère in Molières's "Tartuffe"; Baptista in Shakespeare's "The Taming of the Shrew"; Oberon in Shakespeare's "Midsummer Night's Dream"; Tebano in Lope de Vega's "The Dancing Master"; Krutitskiy in Ostrovskiy's *Na vsyakogo mudretsa dovol'no prostoty* (There's a Simpleton in Every Sage); Old Zhan in Gorky's *Yakov Bogomolov; Productions*: Lenskiy's *Lev Gurych Sinichkin* (1939); Ostrovskiy's *Zhenit'ba Bal'zaminova* (Bal'zaminov's Wedding) (1944); Turgenev's *Kholostyak* (The Bachelor) (1960), etc; *Died*: 28 June 1967.

BLAGOV, Aleksandr Nikolayevich (1883-1961) Russian poet; CP member from 1940; *Born*: 2 Dec 1883 in vil Sorokhta, Kostroma Province; *Career*: from age 14 worked as weaver; active in Ivanovo workers' revol movement; 1909 first work printed; several of his poems ("The Song of the Old Weaver," "The Spinner" and "The Textile Workers' March") have been set to music; *Publ*: "The Woman Weaver's Groan" (1910); "Ballad" (1914); "Ten Letters" (1916); *Trilogiya* (Trilogy) (1943-48); *Nasha fabrika* (Our Factory) (1950); *Slovo tkachikhi* (The Weaver's Word) (1950); *Izbrannoye* (Selected Verse) (1953); *Died*: 16 Sept 1961 in Ivanovo.

BLAKITNYY (real name: YELLANSKIY), Vasiliy Mikhaylovich (1894-1925) Ukr writer, poet, journalist and revol; CP member from 1920; *Born*: 1894 in vil Kozly, Chernigov Province, son of a priest; *Educ*: studied at Chernigov Seminary and at Kiev Business Inst; *Career*: while at school took part in Ukr nationalist circles; from 1917 member, Ukr Socialist-Revol Party, led one of the left-wings of this party (from 1918 Militant Socialist-Revol Party) and was ed, party organ *Borot'ba*; after liquidation of this party in Mar 1920 accepted into CP(B) Ukr and elected member CC, CP(B) Ukr; took part in war against Poland; arrested and imprisoned for several months under Hetman Skoropadskiy's rule in Ukr; after release underground work in Odessa, Nikolayev and Poltava; again arrested and imprisoned under Petlyura regime after abortive coup of Militant Soc-Revolutionaries in Poltava; liberated by Sov troops; led insurgent movement against Gen Denikin's White Army in Right-Bank Ukr; after defeat of White Army member, Revol-Mil Council, 12th Army; chm, Ukr State Publ House and ed, *Visty VUTsVK,* organ of Ukr Centr Exec Comt; Nov 1920 at 5th CP(B) Ukr Congress adopted nationalist stand; 1920-25 member, Ukr and USSR Centr Exec Comt; 1912 first work printed; founded and edited journals *Shlyakhy mystetstva, Vsesvit* and *Chervonyy perets',* etc; founded and directed "Hart" proletarian writers' union; wrote as publicist and lit critic under alias Blakitnyy, as poet under alias V. Yellan, as prosaist under alias A. Ortal', as satirist under alias Valer Pronoza and Markiz Popelyastyy; Proletarian Writers' Center in Khar'kov was named after him; *Publ*: verse "Strokes of the Hammer and Heart" (1920); satire: "Pencil Notes" (1924); "Soviet Mustard" (1924); "The Statesman's Brain" (1925); "Homesickness"; "Ataman Tyutyutinik's Kanossa"; "The Lackeys," etc; also wrote on polit topics, censured the activities of nationalists and the Ukr Autocephalous Church; *Awards*: Order of the Red Banner of Labor (posthumously); *Died*: 4 Dec 1925 in Khar'kov.

BLAZHEVICH, Iosif Frantsevich (1891-1939) Lith mil commander; div commander from 1935; veteran anti-aircraft defense forces; *Born*: 13 Sept 1891 in vil Novoselki, Vilnius Province, son of a peasant; *Educ*: 1913 grad Vilnius Mil College; 1922 grad Higher Acad Courses; *Career*: 1913-14 junior officer, 70th Ryazhsk Infantry Regt on Northern Front; final rank in Russian army – lt-col; from 1918 in Red Army; 1918-20 in Operations Dept, 5th Army Group; commanded regt, then brigade; commander, 27th Infantry Div; 1920-21 commander, 59th Infantry Div; commander, Semipalatinsk Forces Group; commander, 1st Turkestani Div; commander, 1st Army, Turkestani Front; 1922-26 commander, 16th Infantry Corps; 1926-38 on Red Army Staff; chief, 6th Bd, Red Army Staff; inspector of infantry tactics; inspector, then dep head, Anti-Aircraft Defense Bd, Red Army; member, All-Russian Centr Exec Comt; member Bel Centr Exec Comt; 1938 arrested by NKVD; *Awards*: two Orders of the Red Banner; medal "Twenty Years of the Red Army"; *Died*: 16 Mar 1939 in imprisonment; posthumously rehabilitated.

BLAZHEVICH, Vladislav Mikhaylovich (1881-1942) Composer, conductor and trombonist; prof from 1922; *Born*: 15 Aug 1881 in vil Tregubovka, Smolensk Province; *Educ*: grad Moscow Conservatory; *Career*: 1906-28 played in orchestra of Bolshoy Theater, Moscow; 1920-22 instructor, 1922-42 prof, Moscow Conservatory, where he was first to hold Chair for Mil Conductors; 1937 organized USSR State Brass Band, becoming its first conductor; wrote music for brass instruments (concertos, études, quartets, etc,) and brass bands (marches and overtures); *Publ: Shkola kollektivnoy igry na dukhovykh instrumentakh* (A Manual of Group Playing for Wind Instruments) (1935); *Shkola dlya razdvizhnogo trombona* (Slide Trombone Manual) (1939); *Shkola dlya tuby* (Tuba Manual) (1939), etc; *Died*: 10 Apr 1942 in Moscow.

BLAZHKO, Sergey Nikolayevich (1870-1956) Astronomer; prof; corresp member, USSR Acad of Sci from 1929; Hon Sci Worker of RSFSR from 1934; *Born*: 17 Nov 1870; *Educ*: 1892 grad Moscow Univ; *Career*: from 1895 at Moscow Observatory; 1918-31 head of this observatory; 1910-18 assoc prof, from 1918 prof, Moscow Univ; first chm, Moscow Assoc of Research Institutes; for many years chm, Centr Commission for Study of Variable Stars; member, ed bd *Astronomicheskiy zhurnal* and journal *Peremennye zvyozdy*; research on variable stars and practical astronomy; 1895 began systematic photographic charting of stellar sky with wide-angle camera, laying foundation for the rich collection of photographs at the Moscow Observatory; 1904-07 obtained successful photographs of spectra of meteors and gave first correct interpretation of them; 1912 in thesis *O zvyozdakh tipa Algolya* (Stars of the Algol Type) published first general theory of eclipsed variable stars of the Algol type; studied more than 200 variable stars; was first to discover in certain short-periodic cepheids periodic changes in the curvature and duration of brilliance (so-called Blazhko Effect); devised a new method for photographing small planets; invented several original devices: blink microcope, an attachment for evening out the brilliance of stars when viewing them from a meridian circle, etc; *Publ: O zvyozdakh tipa Algolya* (Stars of the Algol Type) (1912); *Kurs prakticheskoy astronomii* (A Course in Practical Astronomy) (2nd ed, 1940); *Kurs obshchey astronomii* (A Course in General Astronomy) (1947); *Kurs sfericheskoy astronomii* (A Course in Spherical Astronomy) (1948), etc; *Awards*: Stalin Prize (1951); Order of Lenin; *Died*: 11 Feb 1956.

BLINOV, Boris Vladimirovich (1909-1943) Actor; Hon Artiste of RSFSR from 1935; *Born*: 19 Apr 1909; *Career*: acted at Leningrad Young Playgoers' Theater; then famous as film actor; *Roles*: Furmanov in *Chapayev* (1943); the wounded comr in *Podrugi* (Friends) (1936); the partisan-sailor Bublik in *Volochayevskie dni* (Volochayevka Days) (1937); the Rayon Comt Secr in *Chlen pravitelstva* (Member of the Government) (1940); the officer Kraynev in *Chetvyortyy periskop* (The Fourth Periscope) (1939); the airman Yermolov in *Zhdi menya* (Wait for Me) (1943); the sailor Zheleznyakov in *Vyborgskaya storona* (Vyborg Side) (1938); the partisan unit commander in *Boevoy kinosbornik No. 12* (Combat Newsreel No. 12) (1942); Bondarets in *Nepobedimyye* (The Invincible) (1943); the infantryman Ostapenko in "Front" (1943); the Colonel in *Vozdushnyy izvozchik* (Air Taximan) (1943), etc; Blinov favored roles which combined strong will with emotion, outward reserve and human compassion; he was also a master of incidental roles and could create an expressive character with just a few touches; *Died*: 1943.

BLINOV, Mikhail Fedoseyevich (?-1919) Civil War veteran; Don Cossack; *Career*: until 1917 private in Cossack troops; during 1917 Oct Revol joined Bolsheviks; Feb 1918 elected member, Ust'-Medveditsa Okrug Revol Comt; spring 1918 organized a Cossack squadron and fought against Gen Krasnov; early 1919 commander, 1st Don Revol Regt, then asst chief, 23rd Infantry Div; Sept 1919, as commander of a cavalry brigade, made successful raid on Filonovo; from Nov 1919 commander of a cavalry group, 9th Army; *Awards*: Order of the Red Banner; *Died*: mortally wounded in action at Buturlinovka died 22 Nov 1919; 22 Feb 1920 the cavalry group he used to command was reorganized as the 5th Blinov Cavalry Div in commemoration of his name.

BLIOKH, Yakov Moiseyevich (1895-1957) Film dir; CP member from 1918; *Born*: 1895; *Career*: fought in Civil War; mil comr, 1st Cavalry Army; 1931-34 organizer and dir with Voroshilov Film Train — a roving film documentary unit which covered building projects of 1st Five-Year Plan; from 1934 admin work; directed film studios: *Soyuzkinokhronika* (1937-39); Odessa Studios (1939-40); Sverdlovsk Studios (1946-48); *Works*: films: *Za frontom front* (The Front Behind the Front) (1931); *XV Oktyabr'* (The 15th of October) (1932); co-directed *Sergo Ordzhonikidze* (1937) and *Kirov* (1934); produced documentary film *Shankhayskiy dokument* (Shanghai Document) (1928), etc; *Publ: Aktyor i stsenariy* (Actor and Scenario) (1926); *Strana sotsializma na ekrane* (The Land of Socialism on the Screen), etc; *Died*: 5 July 1957.

BLIZNYAK, Yevgeniy Varfolomeyevich (1881-1958) Hydrologist; communications engineer; Dr of Tech Sci; prof from 1923; head, Drought Dept, Geographical Fac, Moscow Univ, from 1950; Hon Sci and Tech Worker of RSFSR from 1947; hon member, USSR Geographical Soc; *Born*: 9 Apr 1881 in Mstislavl'; *Educ*: 1899 grad Mogilev Gymnasium; 1904 grad Petersburg Inst of Communications Eng; *Career*: 1907-15 survey of entire Yenisey; at start of WW 1 directed construction of a bridge over Vistula near Warsaw; 1918-28 chief engineer for planning linkage of Volga and Don; chief, Centr Tech Water Bd, Pop Comrt of Means of Communication; dep chm of its Sci and Tech Comt; also active in drafting plan of State Commission for Electrification of Russia; from 1921 lectured at Moscow higher educ institutions, including Moscow Higher Tech College; 1928 founded, 1928-30 directed Hydrological and Hydrotech Research Inst, Pop Comrt of Means of Communication; from 1944 chm, Water Management Section, USSR Acad of Sci; helped compile water survey of USSR; 1947-49 at same time chm, Eng and Construction Section, Hydraulic Eng Council under Presidium of USSR Acad of Architecture; then chm, Hydraulic Eng and Power Section, Moscow House of Sci, USSR Acad of Sci; attended many int hydrological and hydrotech congresses; author of over 200 sci works; *Publ: Rukovodstvo k barometricheskomu nivelirovaniyu* (Handbook on Barometric Calibration) (4th ed, 1939); *Vodnyye issledovaniya* (Hydraulic Research) (5th ed, 1952); *Died*: 21 Oct 1958.

BLIZNICHENKO, Andrey Yemel'yanovich (1888-1938) Govt official; CP member from 1912; *Born*: 1888 in Khar'kov; *Educ*: 1924-28 studied at Columbia Univ (USA) and in Germany; *Career*: turner; Party work in Khar'kov and on Northern-Donetsk Railroad; after 1917 Feb Revol comr, Northern-Donetsk Railroad; member, Khar'kov Sov of Workers, Peasants and Soldiers' Dep; active in 1917 Oct Revol and Civil War; from 1918 comr, Southern Area Communications System; Ukr Dep Pop Comr of Communications; chm, Railroad Workers' Org Bureau, CC, CP Ukr; developed designs for heavy armored trains; 1921-24 rep, USSR Railroad Mission in Germany, then in Canada; from 1928 econ work; at 16th Party Congress elected member, CPSU(B) Central Control Commission; at 2nd CP Ukr Congress elected cand member, CC, CP Ukr; worked for Centr Control Commission, USSR Pop Comrt of Workers' and Peasants' Inspection; Presidium member, USSR Supr Sovnarkhoz; arrested by State Security organs; *Died*: 14 Oct 1938 in imprisonment.

BLOK, Aleksandr Aleksandrovich (1880-1921) Russian symbolist poet and playwright; *Born*: 28 Nov 1880 in Petersburg, son of a law prof of nobiliary rank; *Educ*: 1906 grad Philology Fac, Petersburg Univ; *Career*: spent childhood in the family of his maternal grandfather A. N. Beketov, rector of Petersburg Univ; began to write verse at age 18; 1903 first verse published; in same year married daughter of famous chemist D. I. Mendeleyev; was influenced by poetry of Zhukovskiy, Fet, Polonskiy, Apukhtin, Solov'yov, Belyy and Bryusov; toured Germany, Italy and France; 1907-08 mang, criticism dept, journal *Zolotoye runo*; 1916 drafted into army and served in Union of Zemstvos and Towns; 1917 worked for Extraordinary Investigation Commission of Provisional Govt; after 1917 Oct Revol worked for Commission for Publ of the Classics and for Repertoire Commission, Theater Dept, Pop Comrt of Educ; also worked for "World Lit" Publ House; chm, Petrograd Dept, All-Russian Poets' Union; 1919 co-founder and member, Production Bd, Bolshoy Drama Theater in Petrograd and co-founder, Free Philosophical Assoc; his poetry is notable for its purity of style, philosophical content and emotional drama; he holds a place in Russian lit as a great lyric poet and a verse innovator who developed the potential of Russian verse and influenced the development of 20th-century poetry; many of his works have been translated into other languages and set to music; *Publ*: verse cycle "Ante lucem"; book *Stikhi o Prekrasnoy Dame* (Poems of the Beautiful Lady) (1904); play *Balaganchik* (The Buffoon) (1906); verse collection *Nechayannaya radost'* (Unexpected Joy) (1906); verse cycle *Snezhnaya maska* (The Snow Mask) (1907); drama *Pesnya sud'by* (The Song of Fate) (1908); verse cycle *Vol'nyye mysli* (Free Thoughts) (1907); verse cycle *Na pole Kulikovom* (On Kulikovo Field) (1908); verse *Rossiya* (Russia) (1908); *Ital'yanskiye stikhi* (Italian Poems) (1909); verse collection *Nochnyye chasy* (Nocturnal Hours) (1911); drama *Roza i krest* (The Rose and the Cross) (1913); verse cycle *Strashnyy mir* (The Terrible World) (1909-16); poem *Dvenadtsat'* (The Twelve) (1918); verse *Skify* (The Scythians) (1918); poem *Vozmezdiye* (Retribution) (1921); book *Posledniye dni imperatorskoy vlasti* (The Last Days of Imperial Rule) (1919); translated Ruteboeuf's miracle play "Miracle de Theophile" (1907) and Grillparzer's tragedy "Die Ahnfrau" (1908); *Died*: 7 Aug 1921 in Petrograd.

BLOK, David Semyonovich (1888-1948) Composer; conductor; film worker; Hon Art Worker of Tadzh SSR from 1940; *Born*: 11 Dec 1888; *Educ*: 1918 grad Rostov Conservatory; *Career*: 1905 debut as a orchestra conductor; in silent-film days directed orchestras in large cinemas; his accompaniment, based on the film's musical score, was in marked contrast to the usual amateurish improvisation; from 1930 composed and conducted for talking pictures; wrote and arranged music for more than 200 films; organizer and manager, State Orchestra, USSR Min of Cinematography; *Works*: music for films: *Mat'* (Mother) (1926); *Plenniki morya* (Prisoners of the Sea) (1928); *Varya – kapitan* (Varya the Captain) (1939); *Gibel' 'Orla'* (Wreck of the "Oryol") (1941); *Strana rodnaya* (My Native Land) (1946), etc; *Publ*: coauthor, *Muzykal'noye soprovozhdeniye v kino* (Musical Accompaniment in the Cinema) (1929); *Died*: 4 Oct 1948.

BLOKH, Maks Abramovich (1882-1941) Chemist; chemistry historian and publisher; Dr of Chemical Sci; *Born*: 15 Aug 1882; *Educ*: 1903 grad Riga Polytech Inst; studied at Heidelberg Univ; *Career*: 1917 set up in Petersburg Sci Chemistry and Technol Publ House (now State Sci-Tech Publ House for Chemical Lit) and issued large number of reference books, textbooks and monographs on chemistry and chemical technol; then worked for Comt for the Application of Chemistry in the Nat Econ, USSR Gosplan; also worked for various other publ houses; wrote numerous books on history of chemistry; *Publ: Biograficheskiy spravochnik: Vydayushchiyesya khimiki i uchyoniye XIX i XX stoletiiy* (A Biographical Handbook: Outstanding Chemists and Scientists of the 19th and 20th Centuries) (2 vol, 1929-31); *Khronologiya vazhneyshikh sobytiy v oblasti khimii i smezhnikh distsiplin i bibliografiya po istorii khimii* (A Chronology of Major Events in Chemistry and Allied Disciplines and a Bibliography on the History of Chemistry) (1940); *Died*: 14 Jan 1941.

BLOKHIN, Aleksey Aleksandrovich (1897-1942) Oil geologist; prof from 1937; *Born*: 1897; *Educ*: 1929 grad Moscow Mining Acad; *Career*: geological survey of Kerch Peninsula, western slopes of the Urals and Ural foothills; studies on oil-bearing potential of Bash Ural region culminated in 1932 with discovery of first major Ishimbayev oil deposit; dep chief, Main Geological Bd, USSR Pop Comrt of Heavy Ind; member, org comt for convening 17th Int Geological Congress; member, ed bd *Geologiya SSSR; Publ*: articles: *Neftyanyye mestorozhdeniya Bashkirskoy ASSR* (Oil Deposits of the Bashkir ASSR) (1940); *Stratigrafiya paleozoyskikh otlozheniy basseyna rek Nugusha i Beloy* (Stratigraphic Features of Paleozoic Deposits of the Nugush and Belaya River Basins) (1947); *Died*: 6 Oct 1942.

BLONSKIY, Pavel Petrovich (1884-1941) Educator and psychologist; specialist in pedology; prof; *Born*: 26 May 1884; *Educ*: 1907 grad History and Philology Dept, Kiev Univ; *Career*: from 1907 taught educ theory and psychology at Moscow women's secondary educ institutions; from 1913 lecturer in psychology and philosophy, Moscow Univ; at same time gave courses in pedag and psychology at Shanyavskiy Univ and Higher Women's Teachers' Training Courses; in Sov period lectured at 1st and 2nd Moscow Univ; helped found and run Krupskaya Acad of Communist Educ; supervised team of young psychologists and postgrads at Moscow Inst of Psychology; helped to reform school system and establish labor polytech school; critized standard syllabuses and curricula and class work; 1921 joined Sci Pedag Section, State Learned Council, RSFSR Pop Comrt of Educ; helped draft new programs aimed at gearing school to life and to tasks of socialist construction; opposed idealistic psychology and conducted pedological research; in 1930's, when Sov school system reverted to previous traditions, he was criticized for instilling positivism and biologism in educ and mechanistic concepts in pedology; *Publ: Kurs pedagogiki* (A Pedagogics Course) (1916); *Trudovaya shkola* (The Labor School) (1919); *Ocherk nauchnoy psikhologii* (An Outline of Scientific Psychology) (1921); *Pedagogika* (Pedagogics) (1922); *Osnovy pedagogiki* (Principles of Pedagogics) (1925); *Pedologiya* (Pedology) (1925); *Pamyat' i myshleniye* (Memory and Thinking) (1935); *Razvitiye myshleniya shkol'nika* (The Development of Thought in the Schoolchild) (1935); *Izbrannyye pedagogicheskiye proizvedeniya* (Selected Pedagogical Works) (1961); *Died*: 15 Feb 1941.

BLUMBAKH, Fyodor Ivanovich (1864-1949) Metrologist; hon member, USSR Acad of Sci from 1946; Hon Sci Worker of RSFSR; *Born*: 1864; *Career*: colleague of D. I. Mendeleyev at Main Chamber of Weights and Measures where he worked from the day of its foundation (1893) to 1921; under Mendeleyev's guidance worked on standardization of the *arshin* and established precise correlation between Russian and metric measurements of length; set up a time laboratory at Main Chamber of Weights and Measures; 1896, 1906 and 1914 supervised observation of total solar eclipses; in his latter years headed Dept of Astronomy, Lat State Univ; *Died*: 1949.

BLUMENAU, Leonid Vasil'yevich (1862-1931) Neuropathologist; Dr of Med from 1889; prof from 1903; *Born*: 1862; *Educ*: 1886 grad Petersburg Mil Med Acad; *Career*: after graduation received three years of specialist training at Petersburg Mil Med Acad and worked at I. P. Merzheyevskiy's Clinic; from 1889 worked at Waldeier's Anatomical Inst in Berlin, at Flexig's Laboratories in Leipzig, under Golgi in Pavia and under Charcot in Paris; after return to Russia became assoc prof, Chair of Nervous and Mental Diseases, Petersburg Mil Med Acad, read courses on anatomy and physiology of the brain and conducted seminars on diagnosis of nervous diseases; from 1903 prof, Clinic for Nervous Diseases, Yeleninskiy (now State) Clinical Inst; 1904-12 lectured on teachers' training courses and at Pedag Acad, League of Educ; 1909-14 chm, Soc for Educ and Training of Defective Children; 1913-16 member, Municipal Hospital Comt, Petersburg City Duma; 1918-20 member, Learned Med Council, RSFSR Pop Comrt of Health; from 1920 until death member, Neuropsychiatric Council, Leningrad Province Health Dept; from Nov 1924 founder-member and chm, Soc of Leningrad Neuropathologists; 1887-1926 member, 1926-31 hon member, Soc of Psychiatrists; one of first clinical neuropathologists to use Pavlov's theory to explain pathogenesis of functional disorders of nervous system, particularly hysteria; wrote over 60 papers on anatomy and physiology of brain, neuropathology, balneotherapy of nervous diseases and balneology in gen; *Publ*: doctor's thesis *K ucheniyu o davlenii na mozg* (The Theory of Pressure on the Brain) (1889); *Mozg cheloveka* (The Human Brain) (5 vol, 1907-13); *Isteriya i yeyo patogenez* (Hysteria and Its Pathogenesis) (1926), etc; *Died*: 1931.

BLUMENFEL'D, Feliks Mikhaylovich (1863-1931) Polish pianist, conductor and composer; Hon Art Worker of RSFSR from 1927; prof from 1897; *Born:* 19 Apr 1863 in vil Kovalevka, Kherson Province; *Educ*: 1885 grad Petersburg Conservatory; pupil of Rimsky-Korsakov; *Career*: 1885-97 instructor, 1897-1918 prof of piano and ensemble playing, Petersburg Conservatory; 1918-22 prof and dir, Kiev Conservatory; 1922-31 prof, Moscow Conservatory; 1898-1918 conductor, Mariinskiy Theater; also active as virtuoso pianist and accompanist; directed various operas, including Rimsky-Korsakov's *Skazaniye o nevidimom grade Kitezhe i deve Fevronii* (Legend of the Invisible City Kitezh and the Maiden Fevroniya) (1907 at the Mariinskiy Theater, Petersburg); Moussorgsky's *Boris Godunov* (1908 in Paris); *Publ*: 70 compositions for piano; more than 50 romances; symphony "To the Memory of the Dear Departed"; string quartet, etc; *Died*: 21 Jan 1931 in Moscow.

BLUMENTAL', Fridrikh Leopol'dovich (1896-1937) Mil commander; div comr from 1935; Red Army polit officer and mil-polit writer; CP member from 1919; *Born*: 31 July 1896 in Riga, son of a German physician and his Lat wife; *Educ*: studied at Med Fac, Moscow Univ but prevented from graduating by advent of WW 1; 1920 grad Kiev Infantry Officers Training Courses; *Career*: during WW 1 medic at the front; from 1919 in Red Army; 1920 chm, regt culture and educ comt; regt comr; dep chief, div polit dept; 1921 information officer, head of org and instruction, head of propaganda and agitation, div polit dept; dep head, Polit Dept, 30th Div; 1921-24 head, Propaganda and Agitation Dept, Polit Bd, Khar'kov Mil Distr; 1924-27 chm, Chair of Party and Polit Work, then head, Mil-Polit Fac, Tolmachev Mil Polit Acad; 1927-37 head, Propaganda and Agitation Dept, Red Army Main Polit Bd; 1937 arrested by State Security organs; *Publ: Politicheskaya rabota v voyennoye vremya. Voprosy boyevoy obstanovki* (Political Work During Wartime. Factors of Combat Situation) (1927 and 1929); *Burzhuaznaya politrabota v mirovuyu voynu*

(Bourgeois Political Work During the World War) (1928); *Politicheskaya podgotovka burzhuazii k voyne* (Political Preparation of the Bourgeoisie for War) (1929); *Politicheskoye obespecheniye mobilizatsii* (Political Work During Mobilization) (1928 and 1929); *Kak imperialisty gotovyat voynu* (How the Imperialists Prepare for War) (1930), etc; *Died*: in imprisonment 23 July 1937; posthumously rehabilitated.

BLYAKHIN, Pavel Andreyevich (1887-1961) Russian writer and scriptwriter; CP member from 1903; *Born*: 7 Jan 1887 in vil Verkhodym, now Saratov Oblast, son of a peasant; *Career*: 1919 began lit work as anti-religious publicist; also carried out Party and govt work; from 1926 head, Feature Production Dept, Sov Film Studio; then worked for Main Repertoire Comt; from 1934 chm, CC, Cinema and Photographic Workers' Union; wrote novelettes and film scripts; *Publ*: plays: *Cherez pobedu k miru* (Through Victory to Peace) (1920); *Provozglasheniye kommuny* (The Proclamation of the Commune) (1920); novelettes: *Krasnyye d'yavolyata* (Red Devils) (2 vol, 1923-26); *Na rassvete* (At Dawn) (1950); *Moskva v ogne* (Moscow Burning) (1956); *Dni myatyezhnyye* (Rebellious Days) (1959); last three novelettes comprise a trilogy entitled *Dni myatezhnyye. Povest' o dnyakh moyey yunosti* (Rebellious Days. A Tale of the Days of My Youth) (1961); scripts for films: *Krasnyye d'yavolyata* (Red Devils) (1923); *Vo imya Boga* (In the Name of God) (1925); *Bol'shevik Mamed* (Mamed the Bolshevik) (1925); *Iuda* (Judas) (1930); *Died*: 19 June 1961 in Moscow.

BLYUKHER, Vasiliy Konstantinovich (1890-1938) Russian mil commander; Marshal of the Sov Union from 1935; cand member, CC, CPSU(B) from 1934; CP member from 1916; *Born*: 19 Nov 1890 in vil Borshchinki, Yaroslavl' Province, son of a peasant; *Educ*: completed vil parish school; *Pos*: 1904-05 apprentice in Petersburg shop; 1905-07 apprentice metalworker at Franco-Russian Plant in Petersburg; 1908-09 salesclerk in Petersburg draper's shop; 1909-10 metalworker at *Mytishchi* Car Plant near Moscow; 1910-13 in prison (allegedly for inciting workers to strike); 1914 salesclerk in Moscow shop; 1914-15 private, non-commissioned officer and non-commissioned ensign in Russian Army on Southwestern Front; 1915-16 hospitalized with wounds; 1916-17 salesclerk in Moscow shop; 1917 voluntarily returned to mil service; 1917-18 comr, Red Guard detachment; commanded various Red Guard detachments; commander, Southern Ural Partisan Army; 1918-19 commander, 4th Infantry Div, later renamed 30th Infantry Div; asst commander, 3rd Army on Eastern Front; in charge of defense of Vyatka area; 1919-20 commander, 51st Infantry Div, Eastern Front; 1920 commander, home-guard troops, West Siberian Mil Distr; commander, 51st Infantry Div, Southern Front; 1921-22 Min of War and commander in chief, Far Eastern Pop Republ; 1922-24 commander, 1st Infantry Corps; commander, Leningrad Fortified Distr; 1924-25 chief mil adviser to Sun Yat-sen and Chang Kai-shek in China; 1925-26 worked for USSR Revol Mil Council; 1926-27 again chief mil adviser to Chang Kai-shek; 1927-29 asst commander, Ukr Mil Distr; 1929-38 commander, Far Eastern Army Distr; 1938 commander, Far Eastern Front; 1934-37 member, Mil Sov and 1937-38 member, Main Mil Sov, USSR Pop Comrt of Defense; *Career*: 1918 united and led Red Guard detachments of the Southern Urals (up to 10,000 men) and, after raiding White and Czechoslovak Armies from the rear for three months, joined Red Army with his men; 1920 his 51st Infantry Div played an important role in the storming of Perekop; 1922 commanded troops in battles near Volochayevka; 1924-27, entitled Gen Ka Ling, helped to master and strengthen armed forces of National China; devised and implemented plan for Northern Campaign; 1929-38 did much to boost mil and econ strength of Sov Far East; 1937 member, Special Tribunal of USSR Supr Court which sentenced Marshal Tukhachevskiy and others to death; Presidium member, USSR Supr Sov of 1937 convocation; 22 Oct 1938 arrested by NKVD at Sochi; his second wife Glafira and his brother Pavel, a Red Army pilot, were arrested with him; shortly afterwards his first wife Galina Pavlova was arrested in Leningrad; his children Zoya and Vsevolod from the first marriage and Vaira and Vasilin from the second were sent to orphanages; he was charged with spying for Japan from 1921; *Awards*: two Orders of Lenin; five Orders of the Red Banner; Order of the Red Star, 1st Class; *Died*: 9 Nov 1938 shot in Lefortov Prison in Moscow; posthumously rehabilitated.

BLYUMENTAL'-TAMARINA, Mariya Mikhaylovna (1859-1938) Actress; Pop Artiste of USSR from 1937; wife of well-known producer and actor A. Blyumental'-Tamarin; *Born*: 16 July 1859 in Petersburg; *Educ*: 1875 grad Mariinskaya High School for Girls; *Career*: from 1885 active on amateur stage; 1887 made debut at Letniy Theater, Moscow; 1889 appeared at Theater of Melodrama and Sundry Presentations; 1890-91 at provincial theaters in Tiflis, Vladikavkaz, Rostov-on-Don and Khar'kov; 1901-14 and 1921-33 actress at Moscow's Korsh Theater; 1914-15 at Sukhodol'skiy Theater; 1918-20 at State Playhouse; 1933-38 at Maly Theater in Moscow; *Theater Roles*: Galchikha in *Bez viny vinovatyye* (Guilty Without Guilt) (1891); Anfusa in *Volki i ovtsy* (Wolves and Sheep) (1896); Matryona in L. Tolstoy's *Vlast' t'my* (The Power of Darkness) (1896); Yelizaveta Antonovna in L. Andreyev's *Dni nashey zhizni* (The Days of Our Life) (1909); Motyl'kova in Gusev's *Slava* (Glory) (1936); Knyazeva in Trenyov's *Na beregakh Nevy* (On the Banks of the Neva) (1937), etc; *Film Roles*: Babchikha in *Vstrechnyy* (Encounter) (1915); the priest's wife in *Kombrig Ivanov* (Brigade Leader Ivanov) (1923); Volkov's wife in *Na kryl'yakh vvys'* (Winging Upwards) (1924); Krepysh's mother in *Krepysh*; Luker'ya in *Posledniy vystrel* (The Last Shot) (1928); Marfa in *Doch' Rodiny* (Daughter of the Motherland) (1937), etc; *Died*: 16 Oct 1938 in Moscow.

BLYUMKIN, Yakov Grigor'yevich (1898-1929) Jewish veteran of All-Russian Cheka and OGPU; member, Socialist-Revol Party from 1918; CP member from 1921; *Born*: 1898, son of a salesman; *Educ*: in 1920's grad Red Army Mil Acad; *Pos*: in youth messenger boy in shops and offices; 1917-18 worked for All-Russian Cheka; 1918-21 in Red Army; from 1921 worked for All-Russian Cheka, State Polit Bd and OGPU (For Dept); *Career*: 4 July 1918 attempted to assassinate German ambassador to Moscow Mirbach on orders from Leftist Socialist-Revol Party CC in order to wreck Brest-Litovsk Peace Treaty; was wounded but escaped; after Leftist Socialist-Revol revolt was crushed he gave himself up to Sov authorities, publicly renounced struggle against Sov regime, was pardoned and sent to the front; 1929 secretly visited Trotsky who had been exiled abroad; after returning to the USSR betrayed by Radek; arrested as a Trotsky agent; *Died*: 1929 shot.

BOBINSKIY, S.Ya. (1882-1938) Party official; CP member from 1905; *Born*: 1882; *Career*: did Party work among Polish and Lith Soc-Democrats; 1905-13 in emigration; from 1913 member, Warsaw Comt, Soc-Democratic Party of Poland and Lith; frequently arrested by Tsarist authorities; 1917 worked with Moscow group, Soc-Democratic Party of Poland and Lith; member, Centr Exec Comt, for groups of Soc-Democratic Party of Poland and Lith; from May 1917 member, Moscow Sov; after 1917 Oct Revol did mil and Party work; secr, Polish Bureau, CC, RCP(B); deleg from Moscow org, 6th RSDRP(B) Congress; arrested by State Security organs; *Died*: 1938 in imprisonment.

BOBINSKIY, Vasiliy Petrovich (1898-1938) Ukr poet; *Born*: 11 March 1898 in Kristinopol', Galicia, son of a railroad watchman; *Educ*: attended high schools in Lvov and Vienna; *Career*: from 1923 contributed to Communist press; published weekly *Svitlo* (1925-27) for which he was punished by Polish occupation authorities; 1927-30 ed, journal *Vikna* which united proletarian writers; 1930 took Sov citizenship and settled in Khar'kov; took part in lit life of Sov Ukr; member, "Western Ukraine" lit org and All-Ukr Union of Proletarian Writers; *Publ*: poem "Franko's Death" (1926); "Poems and Pamphlets" (1933); translated into Ukr Blok's *Dvenadtsat'* (The Twelve) and the verse of Rimbaud, Verhaeren, Becher, etc; arrested by State Security organs; *Died*: 2 Jan 1938 in imprisonment; posthumously rehabilitated.

BOBRISHCHEV-PUSHKIN, Aleksandr Vladimirovich (1875-?) Lawyer and politician; *Born*: 1875; *Career*: until 1905 lawyer; belonged to right wing of Russian legal profession; during 1905 Revol joined "Right Order" Party but soon resigned and joined "Union of 17 Oct," being elected member, CC and co-chm; altough reputed to have leftist leanings, he joined the Union majority in supporting Stolypin's policies; after 1917 Feb Revol left politics; after 1917 Oct Revol returned to polit scene, joined Collegium of Counsels for the Defense and defended Purishkevich and others at their trials before Revol tribunals; 1919 fled south, joined Gen Denikin and fought against Sov rule; then emigrated; 1921 in Prague co-published a collection of political essays entitled *Smena vekh* (Changing Landmarks) calling on emigres to endorse the Revol; 1923 amnestied after repeated public recantation and returned to USSR to resume legal practice; became member, Leningrad Collegium of Counsels for the Defense; *Publ: Sudebnyye rechi* (Court Speeches) (2 vol, 1909-12); articles in Octobrist newspapers *Golos Moskvy* and *Golos pravdy* under pseudonym Gromoboy; articles in anthology *Smena vekh* (Changing Landmarks) (1921) and in journal of same name; articles in newspaper *Nakanune*; book *Voyna bez perchatok* (War Without Gloves) (1925); *Died*: date and place of death unknown.

BOBROV, A.N. (1886-1938) Party and govt official; CP member from 1905; *Born*: 1886; *Career*: 1905-07 fought in Revol; 1907-14 in emigration; from 1914 lathe-operator, "Phoenix" factory, Petrograd; 1918-20 plen, Pop Comrt of Food; then worked for NKVD and Pop Comrt of Workers and Peasants' Inspection; 1922-23 chm, Orel Province Exec Comt; 1934-37 worked for Main Admin of Northern Sea Route; arrested by State Security organs; *Died*: 1938 in imprisonment.

BOBROV, Boris Iosifovich (1896-1937) Army gen; div commander from 1935; chief of staff, Bel Mil Distr; CP member from 1919; *Born*: 1896; *Career*: 1918 joined Red Army; during Civil War adjutant, then chief of a staff, operations dept; after Civil War chief of staff, 2nd Caucasian Infantry Div; adjutant, Azer Infantry Div; commandant, 21st Tiflis Infantry School; adjutant, Staff Operations Bd, Red Army; chief, Staff Dept, Moscow Mil Distr; commander of an infantry corps; 1936-37 chief of staff, Bel Mil Distr; 1937 arrested by NKVD; *Died*: 1937 in imprisonment; posthumously rehabilitated.

BOBROVSKAYA (ZELIKSON), Tsetsiliya Samoylovna (1876-1960) Revolutionary; CP member from 1898; *Born*: 19 Sept 1876 in Velizh, Vitebsk Province, daughter of an office worker; *Career*: 1894 began revol activities in Warsaw; later worked in Khar'kov as party organizer and propagandist; 1900 fled abroad; in Zurich joined "Liberation of Labor" group; 1902-03 agent of *Iskra*; Aug 1904 sent by Lenin to work in Tiflis, then in Baku; repeatedly arrested and jailed; participated in 1905-07 Revol and 1917 Feb and Oct Revol; after Oct Revol worked in Moscow as secr, Labor Control Commission; member of commission to organize Moscow Sovnarkhoz; head, Mil Dept, Moscow RCP(B) Comt; asst head, Org Dept, CC, RCP(B); from 1922 worked for Commission for Party History, Sverdlov Communist Univ, Lenin Inst and Comintern Exec Comt; repeatedly elected to Moscow Control Commission; from 1939 pensioner; *Publ: Stranitsy iz revolyutsionnogo proshlogo /1903-1908 gg./* (Pages From the Revolutionary Past /1903-08/) (1955); *Zapiski podpol'shchika 1894-1917* (Notes of an Underground Worker, 1894-1917) (1957), etc; *Awards*: Order of Lenin; *Died*: 6 July 1960.

BOBROVSKIY, Vladimir Semyonovich (1873-1924) Veterinarian; professional revolutionary; pioneer of Sov veterinary med; CP member from 1900; *Born*: 1873; *Educ*: 1898 grad Khar'kov Veterinary Inst; *Career*: during studies worked for Khar'kov RSDRP org; 1898-1913 engaged in revol work for RSDRP in Khar'kov, Kiev, Moscow, Saratov and Transcaucasus; frequently arrested and exiled; 1914-17 senior veterinary surgeon, 1st Reserve Artillery Brigade, Serpukhov, where he agitated among workers and soldiers; 1918-20 head, Veterinary Section, Moscow Health Dept and dir, Moscow municipal slaughterhouses; 1921-23 head, Centr Veterinary Bd, RSFSR Pop Comrt of Agric; 1924 worked at State Inst of Journalism, Moscow; 1923 helped to draw up first Veterinary Regulations; 1920 helped to found Veterinary Training Center, Moscow; also helped to set up such research establishments as the All-Union Inst of Experimental Veterinary Med; recruited old veterinary surgeons for work in Sov establishments; *Died*: 1924.

BOBYNIN, Viktor Viktorovich (1849-1919) Historian; specialist in history of mathematics; *Born*: 8 Nov 1849; *Educ*: 1872 grad Moscow Univ; *Career*: from 1882 lecturer, then prof of mathematics, Moscow Univ; for more than 40 years studied and popularized history of mathematics; wrote two research works on history of mathematics in Russia; 1885-94 founder-publisher, journal *Fiziko-matematicheskiye nauki v ikh nastoyashchem i proshedshem*; published numerous articles and studies on history of mathematics in Russia in this journal and, as a supplement, published still valid *Russkaya fiziko-matematicheskaya bibliografiya* (Russian Physics and Mathematics Bibliography) (3 vol, 1885-1900); 1908 wrote chapter "Elementary Geometry in the Late 18th Century" for vol 4 of M. Kantor's *Istoriya matematiki* (The History of Mathematics); *Publ*: master's thesis *Matematika drevnikh yegiptyan* (The Mathematics of the Ancient Egyptians) (1882); *Sostoyaniye matematicheskikh znaniy v Rossii do 16-go veka* (The State of Mathematical Knowledge in Russia up to the 16th Century) (1884); *Ocherki istorii razvitiya fiziko-matematicheskikh znaniy v Rossii* (An Outline History of the Development of Physical and Mathematical Knowledge in Russia) (2 vol, 1886-93), etc; *Died*: 25 Nov 1919.

BOCHAROV, Aleksandr Il'ich (1886-1956) Ballet dancer and teacher; *Born*: 24 July 1886; *Educ*: 1904 grad Petersburg Theater College; *Career*: from 1904 dancer, Mariinskiy Theater, Petersburg, where he specialized in character and mimic roles; 1908-09 guest appearances in Stockholm, Berlin and Prague; 1910 appeared with A. P. Pavlova's touring company in London; after 1917 Oct Revol worked at Kirov Theater of Opera and Ballet, Leningrad; 1922-23 taught at Volynskiy's School of Russian Ballet, Petrograd; 1930-56 taught character dancing at Leningrad Choreographic College; 1947 retired from stage; *Roles*: Quasimodo in *Esmeralda*; the Marquis in *Plamya Parizha* (The Flame of Paris), etc; *Publ*: coauthor, *Osnovy kharakternogo tantsa* (The Principles of Character Dancing) (1939); *Died*: 21 Jan 1956.

BOCHAROV, Leonid Porfir'yevich (1909-1964) Maj-gen; senior polit worker in Sov Army; *Born*: 1909 in Verkhne-Ural'sk, son of a worker; *Educ*: 1937 grad Mil-Polit Acad; after WW 2 grad Gen Staff Acad; *Career*: from 1931 in Red Army, starting as officer cadet; 1937-41 inspector, Main Polit Bd, Red Army; 1941-45 head, Polit Dept, Separate Maritime Army; member, Mil Council, 57th Army; after grad Gen Staff Acad held various commands; in 1950's retired; fought at Sevastopol, Odessa and Kursk and in operations for the liberation of Rumania, Bulgaria, Yugoslavia and Hungary; *Awards*: Order of Lenin; four Orders of the Red Banner; Orders of Kutuzov, 1st and 2nd Class; Order of Bogdan Khmel'nitskiy, 2nd Class; Order of the Fatherland War, 1st Class; Order of the Red Star; Yugoslav and Bulgarian orders; medals; *Died*: 19 Oct 1964 killed in plane crash near Belgrade.

BOCHVAR, Anatoliy Mikhaylovich (1870-1947) Metallurgist; founder, Moscow school of metallography; prof, Moscow Inst of Non-Ferrous Metals from 1930; Hon Sci and Tech Worker of RSFSR from 1933; *Born*: 28 Aug 1870; *Educ*: 1897 grad Moscow Higher Tech College; *Career*: 1908 established first metallographic laboratory in Moscow at Higher Tech College, where he also read courses on metallography; from 1917 prof, Moscow Higher Tech College; 1919 helped to organize Moscow Mining Inst, where he taught as a prof; from 1930 prof, newly-created Moscow Inst of Non-Ferrous Metals and Gold; did major research on white antifrictional alloys, on cast steel, on the thermal processing of gray cast iron, and on calcium-sodium babbitt alloys; developed babbitt alloy B-16 whichis widely used in the Sov machine-building and automotive ind; also did research on light alloys based on aluminium and magnesium, and on new bronzes and their technol; *Publ: Issledovaniye belykh antifriktsionnykh splavov* (Research on White Antifrictional Alloys) (1918); *Tekhnologiya neorganicheskikh veshchestv* (The Technology of Inorganic Substances) (8th ed, 1927); coauthor, *Tovarovedeniye s neobkhodimymi svedeniyami iz tekhnologii* (Commedity Research with Essential Information from Technology) (vol 1, 1922); *Died*: 11 Sept 1947.

BOGACHYOV, Pavel Mikhaylovich (1902-1962) Party and govt official; CP member from 1928; *Born*: 1902, son of a peasant; *Educ*: grad Acad of Soc Sci, CC, CPSU; *Career*: in 1930's worked for land authority and other govt agencies; from 1939 second, then first secr, Buy Rayon CPSU(B) Comt; Party organizer, Yaroslavl' Tire Plant; secr, Kostroma Oblast CPSU(B) Comt; after grad from Acad of Soc Sci, section head, Dept of Propaganda and Agitation, CC, CPSU; from 1953 dir, USSR Lenin State Library; pensioner; *Awards*: Order of the Red Star; medals; *Died*: Sept 1962.

BOGATYRYOV, Semyon Semyonovich (1890-1960) Sov composer and teacher; Dr of Arts from 1947; Hon Art Worker of RSFSR; *Born*: 15 Feb 1890 in Khar'kov; *Educ*: began to study music at age 14; played French horn in high-school orchestra; 1912 grad Law Fac, Khar'kov Univ; 1912-15 studied at Petersburg Conservatory under Prof Ya. Vitol, V. P. Kalafati and M. O. Shteynberg; 1914 wrote sonata for piano while studying at conservatory; *Career*: 1916-17 taught music theory at Petrograd Conservatory; 1917 moved to Khar'kov, where he composed and taught; 1934 entitled Hon Prof of Ukr SSR; 1941 appointed dir, Khar'kov Conservatory; 1942 managed House of Pop Creative Work in Krasnoyarsk; late 1942 - Nov 1943 instructor, Kiev Conservatory, which had been evacuated to Sverdlovsk; 1943-60 prof, Moscow Conservatory; 1943-48 asst dir, Moscow Conservatory; 1944-48 head, Dept of Composition; 1946 Hon Art Worker of RSFSR; 1955 elected dep, Moscow Oblast Sov; his pupils included: O. M. Gordeli, D. D. Klebanov, E. Lazarev, N. G. Kolyada, V. N. Nakhabin, I. V. Sposobin, I. O. Dunayevskiy, Yu. S. Meytus, S. F.

Tsintsadze and A. Ya. Shtogarenko (last four were Stalin Prizewinners); *Publ: Dvoynoy kanon* (The Double Canon) (1947); *Obratimyy kontrapunkt* (Reversible Counterpoint) (1960); restoration, instrumentation and revision of Tchaikovsky's unfinished symphony, score published in Moscow in 1961 (9 Apr 1958 first performance of symphony in Moscow); *Works*: "Suite for String Quartet" (1955); "Suite and Intermezzo for Small Symphony Orchestra" (1957); *Awards*: Order of the Red Banner of Labor (1946); Order of Lenin (1953); *Died*: 31 Dec 1960 in Moscow.

BOGAYEVSKIY, Afrikan Petrovich (1872-?) Cossack gen and ataman; *Born*: 1872; son of a Cossack sergeant; *Educ*: grad cadet corps and mil acad; *Career*: fought in WW 1; Feb 1919 elected ataman of Don Cossack Army; Jan 1920 appointed chm, South Russian govt; emigrated after Civil War in the Crimea; *Died*: Date and place of death unknown.

BOGAYEVSKIY, Avksentiy Trofimovich (1848-1930) Surgeon; *Born*: 25 Dec 1848 in vil Ustinka, Mirgorod Uyezd, Poltava Province, son of a peasant; *Educ*: 1874 grad Med Fac, Kiev Univ; *Career*: from 1874 distr physician in Mirgorod; from 1883 senior physician, Kremenchug Zemstvo Hospital, where he introduced cavitary operations; performed gastrotomies, operations for hydatid cysts and abdominal dropsy; trained many outstanding surgeons; from 1911 Dr of Med, honoris causa of Kiev Univ; attended all congresses of Pirogov Russian Physicians' Soc, Russian Surgeons' Congresses and various int congresses; established soc causes of disease, campaigned for free med care and helped improve zemstvo med services; wrote 85 works; *Awards*: Hero of Labor; *Died*: 5 Dec 1930.

BOGAYEVSKIY, Boris Leonidovich (1882-1942) Philologist and historian; prof, Leningrad Univ; *Born*: 1882; *Career*: in his early works wrote from a formalistic viewpoint; in 1930's began to study material and intellectual culture from the standpoint of soc class analysis; specialized in soc foundations of Aegean culture; *Publ: Zemledel'cheskaya religiya Afin* (The Agricultural Religion of Athens) (vol 1, 1916); *Krit i Mikeny* (Crete and the Myceneans') (1924); coauthor, *Iz istorii antichnogo obshchestva* (The History of Ancient Society) (1934); coauthor, *Protiv fashistskoy fal'sifikatsii istorii* (Against Fascist Falsification of History) (1939); *Died*: 1942.

BOGAYEVSKIY, Konstantin Fyodorovich (1872-1943) Landscape painter and graphic artist; Hon Art Worker of RSFSR from 1933; *Born*: 24 Jan 1872 in Feodosiya; *Educ*: took first drawing lessons from I. K. Ayvazovskiy and A. I. Fessler; 1897 grad Acad of Arts under A. I. Kuindzhi; *Career*: two periods of art study in Western Europe; 1908 settled in Feodosiya; main theme of pre-revol work was landscape of Eastern Crimea; stylization evident in his departure from reality in imitation of works of old artists; joined "World of Art" group; works marked by decorativeness of composition, tapestry-like muted colors, conventionalized perspective and unrealistic lighting; *Works*: pre-revol period: "The Ancient Fortress" (1902); "The Old City" (1904); "The Country of Giants" and "Credences" (1907-08); "Morning. A Pink Tapestry" (1909); "Recollections of Mantegna" (1910), etc; works of post-revol period: *Dneprostroy* (1930); "Panorama of a Building Giant" (1930); "Landscape Near Moscow" (1931); "City of the Future" (1932); "The Rocky Shore" (1935); *Azovstal'* (1937), etc; in the course of painting these works did many studies at Dneprostroy, Makeyevka, Stalino and Baku; *Died*: 17 Feb 1943.

BOGAYEVSKIY, Mitrofan Petrovich (1882-1918) Don Cossack leader; *Born*: 1882; *Career*: teacher; from June 1917 asst mil ataman, Don Army; stood for inviolability of Cossack lands and class privileges; chm, Supr Army Council; from Jan 1918 member, Don Govt; March 1918 surrendered to Sov troops and appealed to Cossacks to end Civil War; arrested and sentenced to death; *Died*: 1 Apr 1918 shot for counterrevol activities.

BOGDAN, Vasiliy Semyonovich (1865-1939) Plant breeder and experimentalist; prof from 1917; *Born*: 23 Apr 1865 in vil Sosnovka, now Sumy Oblast; *Educ*: 1892 grad Petrovsk Agric and Forestry Acad; from 1892 founder-researcher, Valuyki (Kostychev) Experimental Station, Samara Province; under threat of dismissal for "polit unreliability," moved to Orenburg; 1893-1907 senor agronomist, Turgay-Ural Resettlement Area; 1910 founded Krasnokutsk Experimental Station; 1911 appointed prof, Novo-Aleksandriysk Agric Inst, but Min of Educ refused to confirm his appointment; 1917-21 prof of agric, Saratov, and from 1921 Kuban' Agric Inst; made geobotanical studies of virgin steppe and fallow lands; devised methods for experimental work in steppe conditions; established role of micro-relief in soil formation; refined theory of earlynaturing fallow land and established the importance of grass sowing to increase the cropping of xeric areas; 1898-1900 introduced use of wild crested wheat grass (Agropyron cristatum), later used as basic gramineous component for grass mixtures in steppe areas; *Publ: Otchyot Valuyskoy sel'skokhozyaystvennoy opytnoy stantsii 1895-1896)*(A Report on the Valuyki Argicultural Experimental Station in 1895-1896) (1900); *Rastitel'nost' Turgaysko-U ral'skogo pereselencheskogo rayona* (The Vegetation of the Turgay-Ural Resettlement Area) (1908); *Zhitnyak (pshenitsa)* (Crested Wheat Grass) (1937), etc; *Died*: 3 Oct 1939.

BOGDANKEVICH, Vladimir Ivanovich (1895-1958) Film sound operator; *Born*: 27 May 1895; *Career*: 1928-32 sound operator, Sov Film Studio; 1933-58 sound operator, Moscow Film Studio; 1936-37 at Tech Film Studio; 1956 helped produce first stereophonic feature film *Il'ya Muromets; Works*: sound for films: *Mechtateli* (The Dreamers) (1934); *Lyotchiki* (Pilots) (1935); *Poslednyaya noch'* (The Last Night) (1937); *Aleksandr Nevskiy* (1938); *Lenin v Oktyabre* (Lenin in October) (1937); *Podnyataya tselina* (Virgin Soil Upturned) (1940); *Paren' iz Taygi* (A Lad from the Taiga) (1941); *Delo Artamonovykh* (The Artamonov Affair) (1941); *Ivan Groznyy* (Ivan the Terrible) (two versions, 1945 and 1958); *Sud chesti* (Court of Honor) (1949); *Zagovor obrechyonnykh* (Conspiracy of the Doomed) (1950); *Vozvrashcheniye Vasiliya Bortnikova* (The Return of Vasiliy Bortnikov) (1953); *Ognennyye versty* (Fiery Milestones) (1957); *Died*: 1958.

BOGDANOV (real name: MALINOVSKIY), Aleksandr Aleksandrovich (1873-1928) Philosopher, econ, politician and physician; *Born*: 22 Aug 1873; *Educ*: studied at Moscow Univ; 1899 grad Med Fac, Khar'kov Univ; *Career*: expelled from Moscow Univ for polit activities; 1901 exiled to Vologda, where he worked as an intern in psychiatric dept of a zemstvo hospital; after exile resumed polit activity; 1903 joined Bolsheviks at 2nd RSDRP Congress; elected member, CC, RSDRP at 3rd, 4th and 5th Congresses; member, ed bd, Bolshevik newspapers *Novaya zhizn', Vperyod*, etc; 1905 left Bolsheviks after abortive revol; criticized by Lenin for philosophical views and theory of empiriomonism, a variant of Mach and Avenarius's empiriocriticism; was said by Lenin to be one of those people who wanted to be Marxists but embarked on a "real crusade against the philosophy of Marxism"; 1909 expelled from Party; 1914 drafted to front as a mil surgeon and gave up polit activities; 1917 after Oct Revol worked for Proletkul't org; later resumed med career; from 1926 dir, Inst for Blood Transfusion (now Centr Inst of Hematology and Blood Transfusion), which was founded on his initiative; wrote numerous works on philosophy, econ, med, lit, etc; *Publ: Poznaniye s istoricheskoy tochki zreniya* (Cognition from the Historical Viewpoint) (1901); *Psikhologiya obshchestva* (The Psychology of Society) (2nd ed, 1906); *Revolyutsiya i filosofiya* (Revolution and Philosophy) (1907); sci-fiction novels *Krasnaya zvezda* (The Red Star) (1908) and *Inzhener Menni* (Engineer Menni) (1912); *Nauka ob obshchestvennom soznanii* (The Science of Social Awareness) (1914); *Nauka i rabochiy klass* (Science and the Working Class) (1918); *Elementy proletarskoy kul'tury v razvitii rabochego klassa* (Elements of Proletarian Culture in the Development of the Working Class) (1920); *Ekonomika i kulturnoye razvitiye* (Economics and Cultural Development) (1920); *Filosofiya zhivogo opyta* (The Philosophy of Experience of Life) (3rd ed, 1923); *O proletarskoy kul'tury* (Proletarian Culture) (1924); *Vseobshchaya organizatsionnaya nauka. Tektologiya* (A Universal Organizational Science. Tectology) (3 vol, 3rd ed, 1925-29); *Bor'ba za zhiznesposobnost'* (The Struggle for Survival) (1927); *Died*: 7 Apr 1928 as the result of a blood-transfusion experiment with a student suffering from malaria and tuberculosis.

BOGDANOV, Elliy Anatol'yevich (1872-1931) Zootech; *Born*: 17 May 1872 in Moscow, son of a zoologist; *Educ*: 1895 grad Moscow Univ; *Career*: 1897-1908 lecturer, from 1908 prof, Moscow Agric Inst (now Timiryazev Agric Acad); specialized in biology and physiology of animal feeding; established positive effects of symbiosis of microflora in the macroorganism; established standard Sov fodder unit and tables of nutritive value for various types of fodder; laid down rules for fattening of young livestock; *Publ*: thesis *O pryamom i kosvennom uchastii belkov v obrazovanii zhira* (The Direct and Indirect Participation of

Proteins in the Formation of Fats) (1909); *Kormleniye molochnykh korov, ikh soderzhaniye, doyeniye v svyazi s organizatsiyey stada i vsego molochnogo dela* (The Feeding,Care and Milking of Milch Dows in Connection with the Organization of a Herd and General Dairying) (1910); *Otkarmlivaniye sel'skokhozyaystvennykh zhivotnykh* (The Fattening of Agricultural Animals) (1911); *Tekhnika otkorma krupnogo rogatogo skota* (The Technique of Cattle Fattening) (3rd ed, 1933); *Vyrashchivaniye i otkorm sviney* (Raising and Fattening Hogs) (2nd ed, 1932); *Kak mozhno uskorit' sovershenstvovaniye i sozdaniye plemyonnykh stad i porod* (How to Speed up the Improvement and Establishment of Pedigree Heras and Breeds) (3rd ed, 1938); *Obosnovaniye printsipov vyrashchivaniya molodnyaka krupnogo rogatogo skota* (Basic Principles for Raising Young Cattle) (1947); *Proiskhozhdeniye domashnikh zhivotnykh* (The Origin of Domestic Animals) (1937); *Izbrannyye sochineniya* (Selected Works) (1949); *Died*: 14 Oct 1931.

BOGDANOV, Ivan Anfimovich (1891-1966) Party official; CP member from 1914; *Born*: 25 Oct 1891, son of a peasant; *Career*: worked at Sormovo Plant; 1916 chm, underground Northern Rayon Party Comt and member, Sormovo Plant Party Comt; 1916 arrested and exiled to Irkutsk Province; after 1917 Feb Revol worked for Nizhniy Novgorod Province Trade-Union Secretariat; during 1917 Oct Revol member, Nizhniy Novgorod Province Revol Comt; from 1918 polit work in Red Army; 1921-27 exec govt work in Nizhniy Novgorod, then Sebastopol; 1930 chm, Kazakhstan Kray CPSU(B) Control Commission; from 1936 Sov Control Commission plen for Azov-Black Sea Kray; from 1939 exec posts with USSR Pop Comrt of Automobile and Tractor Machine-Building; dep dir of a research inst; from 1945 pensioner; deleg at 15th-17th Party Congresses; at 15th and 16th Party Congresses elected member, CPSU(B) Centr Control Commission; after 17th Congress member, Sov Control Commission; member, All-Russian and USSR Centr Exec Comt of several convocations; *Died*: 19 Nov 1966.

BOGDANOV, Ivan Petrovich (1855-1932) Painter; *Born*: 1855; *Educ*: 1878-89 studied under Makovskiy and Pryanishnikov at Moscow College of Painting, Sculpture and Architecture; *Career*: exhibitor, then member, Assoc of Itinerant Art Exhibitions; early paintings depict plight of poor peasantry in Tsarist Russia; after 1917 Oct Revol did several paintings on Sov themes; also taught art; *Works*: "The Settlement" (1890); "The Newcomer" (1893); "The Devout" (1899); "Mushroom-Pickers" (1903); "Lenin and the Worker" (1927), etc; *Died*: 1932.

BOGDANOV, Nikolay Nikolayevich (1872-1949) Veterinary surgeon; specialist in dermatology and therapy; Dr of Veterinary Sci from 1937; Hon Sci Worker of USSR from 1946: CP member from 1920; *Born*: 1 Dec 1872 in vil Ilev, Gorky Oblast, son of a land surveyor; *Educ*: 1899 grad Kazan' Veterinary Inst; *Career*: while still a student joined revol movement; after grad worked as a zemstovo veterinary surgeon; 1908 sent to Germany and France by Kursk Zemtsvo authorities to study org of local veterinary services and teaching methods at higher veterinary schools; 1909-12 in charge of clinics, Animal Protection Soc, Kiev; 1912-14 head, Veterinary Dept, Kostroma Province Zemstvo Bd; 1914-16 on active mil service; 1918 head, Epizootic Section, Centr Veterinary Dept, NKVD; 1919-24 worked for Kostroma Province Veterinary Dept; 1921-23 lectured on the anatomy of domestic animals and historical materialism at Kostroma Agric Inst; from 1925 rector, then head, Chair of Regional Pathology and Therapy, Khar'kov Veterinary Inst, where he established a clinic for treatment of small animals with X-ray and physiotherapeutic equipment; was first inst member to experiment in transplanting organs of animals; wrote over 40 works on veterinary subjects, including: natural cycle of Siberian plague; zootech, ophthalmology, obstetrics and infectious diseases; also compiled a gen veterinary manual and a dictionary of veterinary terms, which were not published; *Publ: Glaznyye bolezni domashnikh zhivotnykh* (Eye Diseases in Domostic Animals) (1931); *Dovidnyk veterinarnoho likarya* (A Reference Book for Veterinary Surgeons) (1931); *Nashkirni khvoroby sviys'kykh tvaryn* (Skin Diseases in Domestic Animals) (1923); *Ochni khvoroby sviy'skykh tvaryn* (Eye Diseases in Domestic Animals) (1933); *Kurs kozhnykh bolezney domashnikh zhivotnykh* (A Course on Skin Diseases in Domestic Animals) (3rd ed, 1936); translations: E. Vogel's "The Veterinary Surgeon's Companion"; E. Frener's "Short Course of Regional Surgery for the Veterinary Surgeon"; W. Pfeiffer's "Course of Veterinary Surgical Operations," etc; *Awards*: Badge of Hon; Order of the Red Banner of Labor; *Died*: 30 Apr 1949.

BOGDANOV, Pyotr Alekseyevich (1882-1938) Govt official; CP member from 1905; *Born*: 1882 in Moscow, son of a merchant; *Educ*: 1899 grad business college, started higher tech college; *Career*: from 1900 in revol student movement; 1901 arrested and sentenced to 6 months' imprisonment; 1905 in Finland attended illegal All-Russian Congress of Student Orgs; late 1905 moved to Voronezh and joined local RSDRP(B) Comt and mil org; 1906-08 member, Moscow RSDRP(B) Comt and worked for Moscow mil org; 1909-14 eng, Moscow municipal admin and simultaneously with Moscow RSDRP(B) promotion group; repeatedly arrested; 1914 drafted into the army; during WW 1 sided with defensists; after 1917 Feb Revol chm, mil section, Gomel' Sov of Workers, Peasants and Soldiers' Dep; Presidium member, Gomel' Exec Comt and chm, Gomel' Revol Comt; during 1917 Oct Revol chm, Gomel' Revol Comt; June 1918-21 Collegium member, Chemistry Dept and chm, Council of Mil Ind, RSFSR Supr Sovnarkhoz; later Collegium chm, Main Bd of Metallurgical Ind; 1922-23 as chm, RSFSR Supr Sovnarkhoz, directed application of new econ policy in ind; 1923-25, after the formation of the All-Union Supr Sovnarkhoz, chm, RSFSR Supr Sovnarkhoz and member, RSFSR Council of Pop Comr; from Feb 1926 chm, North Caucasian Kray Exec Comt; chm, American Trade Bd in USA; from 1935 RSFSR Dep Pop Comr of Local Ind; author of a number of articles and reports on the situation and goals of USSR ind, which were published in Supr Sovnarkhoz accounts and in periodicals; arrested by State Security organs; *Died*: 1938 in imprisonment.

BOGDANOV, Semyon Il'ich (1894-1960) Russian; Marshal of Armored Troops from 1945; CP member from 1942; *Born*: 28 Aug 1894 in Petersburg, son of a worker at the Putilov Plant; *Educ*: 1923 grad Moscow Higher Mil-Pedag School; 1930 grad Higher Infantry Tactics Courses; 1936 grad acad courses at Mil Acad for Motorization and Mechanization; *Pos*: 1907-15 apprentice mechanic and mechanic, Putilov Plant; 1915-18 private, then officer, Russian Army; from 1918 in Red Army; 1918-20 platoon, company then battalion commander; from 1923 held teaching, staff and command posts; 1930-38 commanded infantry regt, mechanized brigade of a mechanized corps, Leningrad Mil Distr; 1940-41 taught history at a secondary school in Luga; 1941-42 commander, 30th Tank Div; head, Armored Troops Bd, Moscow Mil Distr; dep commander, 5th Army, Mozhaysk Sector of Moscow Defense System; chief of armored troops, 10th Army; 1943-45 commander, 6th Mechanized Corps; July 1943-47 commander 2nd Tank Army, reformed in 1944 as 2nd Guards Tank Army; 1947-48 dep commander, 1948-54 commander, Armored and Mechanized Troops of Sov Army; 1954-56 commandant, Armored Forces Acad; from May 1956 retired on med grounds; *Career*: WW 1 and Civil War veteran; Apr 1938 arrested by State Security organs and imprisoned until 1940; during imprisonment his family renounced him as an "enemy of the people"; 1941-45 fought at Brest, Moscow and Stalingrad, and in the Korsun'-Shevchenko, Warsaw-Poznan, East-Pomeranian and Berlin operations; as commander of Sov armored and mechanized troops, reequipped them with new material and modernized them; dep, USSR Supr Sov of 1946, 1950 and 1954 convocations; 1952-56 cand member, CC, CPSU; *Awards*: twice Hero of Soviet Union (1944 and 1945); two Orders of Lenin; four Orders of the Red Banner; Orders of Suvorov and Kutuzov, 1st and 2nd Class; other orders and medals; *Died*: 12 Mar 1960; buried at Novo-Devich'ye Cemetery, Moscow.

BOGDANOVA Medina Iskanderovna (1908-1962) Russian lit critic; CP member from 1942; *Born*: 26 Dec 1908 in Bukhara; *Educ*: 1930 grad Oriental Dept, Centr Asian Univ; 1934 completed postgrad studies at Inst of Nationalities, USSR Centr Exec Comt; *Career*: studied lit of Centr Asia and Kaz; helped latinize, then cyrillicize alphabets of Turkic-speaking peoples of USSR; wrote first study of history of Kir lit *Kirgizskaya literatura* (Kirghiz Literature) (1947); articles on folklore and epics of peoples of Centr Asia; *Died*: 6 May 1962 in Moscow.

BOGDANOVICH, Aleksandr Vladimirovich (1874-1950) Opera singer (lyric tenor); Hon Artiste of RSFSR from 1925; *Born*: 3 Nov 1874 in Smolensk; *Educ*: studied med; studied singing under Irina Onore (Petersburg, 1901), A. Broggi (Italy, 1903) and F. Valero; *Career*: 1902 debut as singer; 1906-36 soloist, Bolshoy Theater, Moscow; helped found Opera Studio of Bolshoy Theater and assisted Stanislavsky in running the studio; active member, All-Russian Theatrical Soc; chm, corporation of solo artistes of

Bolshoy Theater; from 1930 artistic manager, Stanislavsky Opera Theater; accomplished exponent of Russian nat repertoire; often appeared in chamber and symphony concerts; *Roles*: Levko in Rimsky-Korsakov's *Mayskaya noch'* (May Night) and *Snegurochka* (The Snow Maiden), etc; *Died*: 6 Apr 1950 in Moscow.

BOGOLEPOV, Aleksandr Aleksandrovich (1874-1941) Dermatologist; prof from 1926; Hon Sci Worker of RSFSR from 1941; *Born*: 22 Oct 1874; *Educ*: 1902 grad Tomsk Univ; specialist training at Ye. S. Obraztsov's Clinic; *Career*: worked and studied under leading French dermatologists; 1917-31 dir, Clinic for Skin and Venereal Diseases, Tomsk Univ; 1928 founded Clinic for Skin and Venereal Diseases, Tomsk State Inst of Postgrad Med Training, which now bears his name; 1931-41 directed this clinic after it moved to Novosibirsk with the inst; 1936 established Clinic for Skin and Venereal Diseases, Novosibirsk Med Inst; life chm, Tomsk and Novosibirsk Sci Soc of Dermatologists; corresp member, French Dermatological Soc; opposed theory of monomorphism and did major research on such skin disease agents as pathogenic fungi and their mutability; devised method of studying spirochetes cultivated from granular forms and a method of staining tissue for studying flora in it; the following fungi bear his name: *Tiachlidium Bogolepovi* (Vuillemin, 1912); *Mydium Bogolepovi* (Jannin, 1913); *Streptothrix Bogolepovi* (Nekachalov, 1930); wrote over 25 papers on: the relation between bacteria and thread fungi; the endogenous development of mycoses; the role of the filtration stage of mycotic excitants; the relationship between certain mycoses, e.g. mycotic stomatitis and tuberculosis; the description of new parasitic fungi in the human organism; the etiology of syphilis; tuberculosis of the skin; leprosy; gonorrhea; soft chancre; the intra-specific mutability of agents of infectious diseases, etc; *Died*: 1941.

BOGOLEPOV, Dmitriy Petrovich (1885-1941) Econ; CP member from 1907; *Born*: 1885; *Educ*: 1909 grad Law Fac, Moscow Univ; postgrad work in Dept of Financial Law, Moscow Univ; *Career*: 1902 began revol work; 1914-15 worked for Bolshevik faction, 4th State Duma and contributed to Bolshevik newspapers and journals; 1917-20 Collegium member, then RSFSR and Ukr Asst Pop Comr of Finances; subsequently worked for Gosplan; during Brest peace talks sided with "leftist Communists"; 1914 lectured at Moscow Univ; from 1918 prof, Moscow State Univ, Timiryazev Agric Acad, etc; 1933 researcher, Int. Agrarian Inst; from 1933 worked at Inst of Nationalities, USSR Centr Exec Comt; as econ specialized in finance; *Publ: Kratkiy kurs finansovoy nauki* (A Short Course of Finance) (1925-29); *Den'gi Sovetskoy Rossii* (The Money of Soviet Russia) (1924); *Populyarnyy finansovo-ekonomicheskiy slovar'* (Popular Dictionary of Finance and Economics) (1925), etc; arrested by State Security organs; *Died*: 1941 in imprisonment.

BOGOLEPOV, Mikhail Aleksandrovich (1875-1933) Geographer and climatologist; prof, Moscow Univ and Shanyavsky Pop Univ; *Born*: 10 Aug 1875; *Educ*: completed higher educ; *Career*: studied ancient Russian chronicles for data on periodic climatic changes; developed theory of "climatic disturbances," caused by the periodic increase or decrease in the intensity of solar radiation; supported continental drift theory; *Publ: O kolebaniyakh klimata Yevropeyskoy Rossii v istoricheskuyu epokhu* (Climatic Varations in European Russia in the Period of Known History) (1907); *Kolebaniya klimata v zapadnoy Yevrope s 1000 do 1500 goda* (Climatic Variations in Western Europe from 1000 to 1500) (1908); *Po povodu odnoy gipotezy gorizontal'nykh peredvizheniy zemnoy kory* (A Hypothesis on Horizonal Shifts in the Earth's Crust) (1931), etc; *Died*: 1933.

BOGOLEPOV, Mikhail Ivanovich (1879-1945) Economist; prof; corresp member USSR Acad of Sci from 1939; *Born* 21 Jan 1879; *Educ*: 1903 grad Law Fac, Tomsk Univ; *Career*: 1902-12 lectured on finance at Tomsk Univ; 1910 joined major expedition to study econ of Mongolia; 1912-17 helped edit Min of Finance publications in Petersburg and lectured on finance and allied disciplines at Petersburg Univ and other higher educ institutions; 1917-22 rector, Inst of Nat Econ; also member of commissions working out measures for nationalization of banks; chm, Ind Geography Dept, Commission for the Study of Natural Production Resources, Russian Acad of Sci; from 1922 over 15 qears' exec work for USSR Gosplan; acting chm, Comt for State Orders, Labor and Defense Council; expert, USSR Gosbank; chm, Econ Section, All-Union Chamber of Trade; at same time lectured at Moscow higher educ institutions; also headed Circulation Section, Inst of Econ, USSR Acad of Sci; *Publ: Finansy, pravitel'stvo i obshchestvennyye interesy* (Finance, the Government and Public Intersts) (1907); *Gosudarstvennyy dolg: K teorii gosudarstvennogo kredita* (State Debt. The Theory of State Credit) (1910); coauthor, *Ocherki russkomongol'skoy torgovli* (An Outline of Russo-Mongolian Trade) (1911); *Osnovnyye prichiny narastaniya gosudarstvennykh dolgov* (The Basic Reasons for the Growth of State Debts) (1910); *Voyna, finansy i narodnoye khozyaystvo* (War, Finance and the National Economy) (1914); *Yevropa posle voyny* (Europe After the War) (1921); *Bumazhnyye den'gi* (Paper Money) (1922); *Valyutnyy khaos. K sovremennomu polozhneniyu Yevropy* (Monetary Chaos. The Present Position of Europe) (1922); *Yevropa vo vlasti krizisa 1920-22* (Europe in the Grip of the 1920-22 Crisis) (1922); *Finansovyy plan pyatiletki 1928/29-1932/33* (The Financial Plan of the 1928/29-1932/33 Five-Year Plan) (1929); *Sovetskaya finansovaya systema* (The Soviet Financial System) (1945); *Awards*: two Orders of the Red Banner of Labor; *Died*: 7 Aug 1945.

BOGOLYOBOV, Veniamin Yakovlevich (1895-1954) Sculptor; *Born*: 7 Dec 1895; *Educ*: 1930 grad Leningrad Acad of Arts; *Career*: lived and worked in Leningrad; from 1929 collaborated with V.I. Ingal on a large number of sculptural portraits and statues of Sov Party leaders; *Works*: statue of G.K. Ordzhonikidze (1937); portrait statues of S.M. Kirov and G.K. Ordzhonikidze (1938); I.V. Stalin and Mamlyakat (1938); I.V. Stalin (1940 and 1943); Lenin Monument in Riga (1947-50); Rimsky-Korsakov Monument in Leningrad (1944-52); individual works: marble portrait of Lenin (1947); statue of Marshal L.A. Govorov (1946); sculptural portrait of Acad A.M. Krylov (1949), etc; *Awards*: Stalin Prize (1941); *Died*: 28 June 1954.

BOGOMOLETS, Aleksandr Aleksandrovich (1881-1946) Pathophysiologist and health service official; member from 1932, vice-pres from 1942, USSR Acad of Sci; member from 1929, pres from 1930, Ukr Acad of Sci; member, USSR Acad of Med Sci from 1944; member, Bel Acad of Sci from 1939; hon member, Geo Academy of Sci from 1944; Hon Sci of Ukr SSR from 1943; Hero of Socialist Labor from 1944; Hon Sci Worker of RSFSR from 1935; *Born*: 24 May 1881 in Luk'yanov Prison, Kiev, where his mother was serving a sentence for revol activities; *Educ*: 1906 grad Med Fac, Novorossiysk Univ, Odessa; *Career*: after grad asst prof, Med Fac, Novorossiysk Univ; 1909 in Petersburg defended doctor's thesis *K voprosu o mikroskopicheskom stroyenii i fiziologicheskom znachenii nadpochechnykh zhelez v zdorovom i bol'nom organizme* (The Microscopic Structure and Physiological Significance of the Suprarenal Glands in the Healthy and Diseased Organism); from 1909 assoc prof, Chair of Gen Pathology, Novorossiysk Univ; for a time continued postgrad studies at Laboratory of Experimental Pathology, Sorbonne; from 1911 prof, Chair of Gen Pathology, Saratov Univ, where he established a pathophysiological laboratory which became an influential center of his school of pathophysiology; 1924 managed to get pathophysiology accepted as a separate discipline at all Sov univ; from 1925 prof, Chair of Pathological Physiology, 2nd Moscow State Univ, now Pirogov 2nd Moscow Med Inst; 1926 co-founder, 1928-31 dir, 1931 until death consultant and sci dir, Centr Inst of Hematology and Blood Transfusion, USSR Min of Health, Moscow; 1931 moved to Kiev; from 1931 founder-dir Inst of Experimental Biology and Inst of Clinical Physiology, Ukr Acad of Sci, both of which now bear his name; during WW 2 directed important research work; dep, USSR Supr Sov of 1942 and 1946 convocations; engaged in a wide range of med research, including pathological physiology, endocrinology, the vegetal nervous system, the human constitution, diathesis, immunity, anaphylaxis, experimental oncology, hematology, blood transfusion, the prolongation of life, neuromuscular fatigue, blood circulation, etc; 1925 produced antireticular cytotoxic serum from animals immunized with cell elements of the spleen and spine, which in small doses stimulates the function of the connective tissue; during WW 2 this serum was used in Sov hospitals to treat ulcerous diseases and to accelerate wound healing; established that the connective tissue also has trophic, plastic and antitumoral functions; wrote numerous works, including many monographs; *Publ: K voprosu o mikroskopicheskom stroyenii nadpochechnikov v svyazi s ikh otdelitel'noy deyatel'nost'yu* (The Microscopic Structure of the Suprarenal Glands in Connection with Teir Secretive Action) (1925); *Krizis endokrinologii* (The Crisis of Endocrinology) (1927); *O vegetal'nykh tsentrakh obmena* (Vegetal Exchange Centers) (1928); *Prodleniye zhizni* (The Prolongation of Life) (1938); *Otyok* (Edema); *Arterial'naya gipertoniya* (Arterial Hypertony); *Rukovodstvo po patologicheskoy fiziologii* (A Manual of Pathological Physiology) (3 vol, 1941), etc; *Awards*: two Orders of Lenin; Order of the Great Fatherland War, 1st Class; Order of the Red Banner of Labor; Stalin Prize (1941); medals; *Died*: 19 July 1946.

BOGORAZ, Nikolay Alekseyevich (1874-1952) Surgeon; specialist in restorative surgery; Dr of Med from 1909; prof from 1912; Hon Sci Worker of RSFSR from 1936; *Born*: 13 Feb 1874 in Tiflis; *Educ*: 1897 grad with distinction Petersburg Mil Med Acad; *Career*: 1897-1906 gen practitioner; 1906-09 asst prof, 1909-12 assoc prof, Chair of Surgery, Med Fac, Tomsk Univ; 1912-18 prof, Chair of Hospital Surgery, Warsaw Univ, which was later transferred to Rostov-on-Don; 1918-41 head, Chair of Hospital Surgery, Med Fac, Rostov-on Don Univ, which was later enlarged to become the Rostov Med Inst; 1941-43 surgeon with evacuation hospitals in Tashkent; 1943-52 head, Chair of Fac Surgery, 2nd Moscow Med Inst; 1944-47 consultant, 1947-52 first surgeon, Burdenko Communist (now Main Mil) Hospital, Moscow; founded influential school of surgery; devised new methods of vessel suturing, operative alterations of the extremities, and the transplantation and restoration of functioning organs; 1912 devised artery-vein suture in gangrene of the extremities; 1913 devised suture of the mesenteric artery to the inferior vena cava to circumvent the liver in cirrhosis; 1925 proposed method of anastomosis of the gall bladder and stomach in ulcerous diseases; 1925 also devised method of lengthening the extremities; 1930 devised method of "replanting" the lower and upper extremities on vessel and nerve tracts; 1936 developed techniques of implanting thyroid and pituitary glands in dwarves to increase their height by 8-16 centimeters and of restoring the penis with Filatov's stem and strips of cartilage; chm, Rostov and Tashkent Sci Surgical Soc; ed, various med journals; a man of great personal courage, he continued his surgical and teaching career even after the loss of both legs; wrote over 100 works on gen, field, restorative, bone and vascular surgery, traumantology, etc; his works include several important manuals and monographs; *Publ*: doctor's thesis *O chatnykh amputatsiyakh stopy v funktsional'nom otnoshenii* (Partial Amputation of the Foot from the Functional Viewpoint) (1909); *K khirurgii pishchevoda* (Surgery of the Oesophagus) (1911); *Povrezhdeniya i zabolevaniya loktevogo sustava i predplech'ya* (Lesions and Diseases of the Elbow Joint and the Forearm) (1914); *O kostnoy plastike melkimi chastyami kostey* (Osteoplasty with Small Pieces of Bone) (1926); *Lektsii po klinicheskoy khirurgii* (Lectures on Clinical Surgery) (1935); *Vosstanovitel'naya khirurgiya* (Restorative Surgery) (2 vol, 2nd ed, 1940-48); *Awards*: Stalin Prize, 1st Class (1950); *Died*: 15 July 1952.

BOGORAZ-TAN (real name: BOGORAZ), Vladimir Germanovich (1865-1936) Russian Jewish ethnographer, writer, folklorist, philologist and public figure; *Born*: 27 Apr 1865 in Ovruch, Volhynian Province; *Educ*: studied at Petersburg Univ; *Career*: 1880, on arrival in Petersburg, joined Populist Revolutionaries; 1886-89 imprisoned in Peter and Paul Fortress; begann sci career in 1890's at Kolyma, whither he was exiled in 1889 for membership of People's Will Party; 1894-96 and 1900-01 participated in expeditions to study peoples of Far Northeast, especially the Chukchi; helped compile orthography for peoples of North; wrote fundamental works on ethnography and folklore of peoples of Northeast Asia; wrote textbooks, dictionaries and grammars of Chukchi language; from 1918 employed at Museum of Anthropology and Ethnography, USSR Acad of Sci; from 1921 prof of ethnography, Geographical Inst, later Leningrad Univ and other higher educ establishments; helped form Comt for North, Presidium of All-Union Centr Exec Comt and Inst of Peoples of the North; founder, and from 1932 dir, Museum of History of Religion, USSR Acad of Sci; *Publ*: poems *Kolymskiye motivy* (Kolyma Motifs) (1896); study *Krivonogiy* (Crooknose) (1896); *Chukotskiye rasskazy* (Chukotsk Tales) (1899); *Vosem' plemyon* (Eight Tribes) (1902); *Zhertva drakona* (The Dragon's Victim) (1909); *Sobraniye sochineniy* (Collected Works) (1911); *Kolymskiye rasskazy* (Kolyma Tales) (1931); novel *Soyuz molodykh* (League of the Young) (1934); novel *Voskressheye plemya* (The Resurrected Tribe) (1935); poems: "Song," "The First of May," *Tsushima*, "Song Before Death," etc; research works: *Materialy po izucheniyu chukotskogo yazyka i fol'klora* (Materials on the Study of the Chukchi Language and Folklore) (1900); *Oblastnoy slovar' Kolymskogo russkogo narechiya* (A Lexicon of the Kolyma Russian Dialect) (1901); *Novyye zadachi russkoy etnografii v polyarnykh oblastyakh* (New Tasks for Russian Ethnography in the Polar Areas) (1921); *Obnovlennaya derevnya* (The Renewed Village) (1925); *Yevreyskoye mestechko* (The Jewish Township) (1926); *Komsomol v derevne* (The Komsomol in the Countryside) (1926); monograph *Chukchi* (The Chukchi) (1934), etc; *Died*: 10 May 1936.

BOGORODITSKIY, Nikolay Petrovich (1902-1967) Electr eng; Dr of Tech Sci from 1940; prof and rector, Leningrad Electr Eng Inst from 1954; CP member from 1948; *Born*: 20 May 1902 in Tashkent; *Educ*: 1929 grad Leningrad Polytech Inst; *Career*: 1930-37 instructor, Leningrad Polytech Inst; 1933-42 instructor, Budyonnyy Mil Electrotech Acad, Leningrad; 1935-42 instructor, later assoc prof, Leningrad Electrotech Inst; during war managed large factory laboratory; from 1945 prof and head, Dept of Electrotech Materials, Leningrad Electr Eng Inst; 1949 at same inst organized and headed new Dept of Dielectrics and Semiconductors, which he directed until his death; also directed in this dept Experimental Laboratory of Electrophysical Processes in Dielectrics and Semiconductors which was founded on his initiative in 1956; 1949-54 pro-rector (for research), from 1954 rector, Leningrad Electr Eng Inst; for a long time senior sci worker, Mathematics Inst, USSR Acad of Sci; did research on physical nature of dielectric loss in various types of electric insulating materials and development of new low-loss materials; 1933-42 developed first Sov radio ceramic materials such as ticond, micalex, high-frequency glass, radio porcelain and ultra-porcelain which have found wide ind use; during his last years various major research projects were conducted by his dept and experimental laboratory: development and study of dielectric amplifiers, high-voltage glass and ceramic compressed-gas condensors, etc; developed new semiconductor ceramics which led to wave-guide load absorbers of various wave-bands, ignitron igniters and nonlinear resistances; helped write textbooks for power eng and electr eng colleges and fac – *Elektrotekhnicheskiye materialy* (Electrotechnical Materials); *Teoriya dielektrikov* (Theory of Dielectrics); *Materialy v radioelektronike* (Materials in Radio Electronics); member, Leningrad City and Oblast CPSU Comt; *Publ: Izoliruyushchiye materialy dlya tekhniki vysokikh chastot* (Insulating Materials for High-Frequency Equipment) (1937); *Vysokochastotnyye dielektriki* (High-Frequency Dielectrics) (1938); ed, *Rukovodstvo k laboratornym zanyatiyam po elektroizoliruyushchim materialam* (Guide to Laboratory Work on Electric Insulating Materials) (1946); coauthor, *Vysokochastotnyye neorganicheskiye dielektriki* (High-Frequency Inorganic Dielectrics) (1948); coauthor, *Elektrofizicheskiye osnovy vysokochastotnoy keramiki* (Electro-Physical Principles of High-Frequency Ceramics) (1958); *Awards*: three Stalin Prizes (1942, 1952); Order of Lenin; Order of the Red Banner of Labor (1961); Badge of Honor; medals; *Died*: 19 June 1967 after a long illness.

BOGORODITSKIY, Vasiliy Alekseyevich (1857-1941) Linguist; Dr of philology; prof; corresp member, Russian (then USSR) Acad of Sci from 1915; *Born*: 6 Apr 1857; *Educ*: 1879 grad Kazan' Univ; *Career*: 1881-88 lecturer, from 1888 prof, Kazan' Univ, later Kazan' Teachers' Training Inst; pupil of Bodyen de Kurtene; Kazan' linguistic school; worked on gen linguistics, phonetics, comparative historical grammar of Indo-European languages, Russian language and Turkic linguistics; at Kazan' Univ founded Russia's first experimental phonetics laboratory; applied experimental phonetic method to study of rhythm of Russian verse; *Publ: Glasnyye bez udareniya v obshcherusskom yazyke* (Unstressed Vowels in Common Russian) (1884); *Ocherki po yazykovedeniyu i russkomu yazyku* (An Outline of Linguistics and the Russian Language) (1901); *Obshchiy kurs russkoy grammatiki* (A General Course of Russian Grammar) (1904); *Lektsii po obshchemu yazykovedeniyu* (Lectures in General Linguistics) (1911); *Kratkiy ocherk sravnitel'noy grammatiki ario-yevropeyskikh yazykov* (A Brief Outline on Comparative Grammar of the Indo-European Languages) (1916); *Kurs eksperimental'noy fonetiki primenitel'no k literaturnomu russkomu proiznosheniyu* (A Course of Experimental Phonetics Applied to Literary Russian Pronunciation) (3 vol, 1917-22); *Russkaya grammatika* (Russian Grammar) (1918); *Zakony singarmonizma v tyurskikh yazykakh* (Laws of Synharmonism in the Turkic Languages) (1927); *Fonetika russkogo yazyka v svete eksperimental'nykh dannykh* (Phonetics of the Russian Language in the Light of Experimental Data) (1930); *Etyudy po tatarskomu i tyurskomu yazykoznaniyu* (Studies in Tatar and Turkic

Linguistics) (1933); *Vvedeniye v tatarskoye yazykoznaniye v svyazi s drugimi tyurskimi yazykami* (An Introduction to Tatar Linguistics in Connection with Other Turkic Languages) (1934); *Vvedeniye v izucheniye sovremennykh romanskikh i germanskikh yazykov* (An Introduction to the Study of Contemporary Romance and Germanic Languages) (1953); *Died*: 22 Dec 1941.

BOGORODSKIY, Aleksey Yakovlevich (1870-1944) Physicochemist; *Born*: 8 Nov 1870; *Educ*: 1894 grad Kazan' Univ; *Career*: from 1912 prof, Kazan' Univ; from 1929 prof, Kazan' Chemical Technol Inst; 1895 demonstrated that cryohydrates, until then regarded as specific chemical compounds, were actually mech mixtures of crystals of ice and salts; made first systematic study of the electrolysis and electr conductivity of molten salts; determined the aqueous solution temperature of various salts and the thermal capacity of solutions; *Publ*: master's thesis *Materialy po elektrokhimii neorganicheskikh soyedineniy v tak nazyvayemom ognennozhidkom sostoyanii* (Material on the Electrochemistry of Inorganic Compounds in a So-Called Fiery-Liquid State) (1905), etc; *Died*: 1944.

BOGORODSKIY, Fyodor Semyonovich (1895-1959) Painter; Hon Art Worker of RSFSR from 1946; corresp member, USSR Acad of Art from 1947; prof from 1938; CP member from 1917; *Born*: 21 May 1895 in Nizhniy Novgorod; *Educ*: 1922-24 studied at Higher State Art Tech Workshops; *Career*: 1916-18 seaman, mil pilot; from 1918 chm, Dept for Special Affairs, Cheka; then worked for Nizhniy-Novgorod Province Cheka; as comr of naval flotilla badly concussed in fighting at Tsaritsyn; then head, Special Dept, Orenburg Province Cheka; from 1920 again with Nizhniy Novgorod Cheka; then head, Investigation Dept, Revol Mil Tribunal of Volga Oblast; from 1922 chm, Art Workers' Union; from 1924 Council member, Assoc of Artists of Revol Russia; 1928-30 in Austria, Germany and Italy; for a while lived and worked with Gorky in Sorrento; during WW 2 war artist in besieged Stalingrad, in Leningrad and in Hungary; from 1938 lecturer, Art Dept, State Inst of Cinematography; one of organizers of this inst; *Works*: series "Waifs and Strays" (1925); "Sailors in Ambush" (1927); "Portrait of Gorky" (1931); "Portrait of a Fisherman's Daughter" (1930); "Construction of a Bridge in Gorky" (1931); "Little Brother" (1932); "Hail to Fallen Heroes" (1945), etc; also painted landscapes and still-lifes; many of his works are hung in Sov museums, including the Tret'yakov Gallery in Moscow; *Awards*: Order of the Red Banner of Labor; Stalin Prize (1946); *Died*: 3 Feb 1959.

BOGOSLOVSKIY, Mikhail Mikhaylovich (1867-1929) Historian; Dr of History from 1909; prof; member, USSR Acad of Sci from 1921; *Born*: 13 Mar 1867; *Educ*: 1891 grad History and Philological Fac, Moscow Univ; *Career*: from 1898 lecturer, 1911-25 prof, Moscow Univ; secr, Moscow Soc of History and Russian Antiquities; chm, Russian Historical Soc; later chm, Russian History Section, Inst of History; pupil and rep, V. O. Klyuchevskiy's historical school and his successor as head of Dept of Russian history, Moscow Univ; specialized in 18th-century Russian history; author of detailed, scholarly biography of Peter I; works notable for thorough analysis of historical sources and wealth of facts; *Publ: Oblastnaya reforma Petra Velikogo. Provintsiya 1719-27 godov* (Peter the Great's Regional Reform. The Provinces in 1719-27) (1902); *Zemskoye samoupravleniye na russkom severe v XVIII v.* (Zemstvo Self-Government in the Russian North in the 18th Century) (2 vol, 1909-12); *Konstitutsionnoye dvizheniye 1730 g.* (The 1730 Constitutional Movement) (1906); *Pyotr Velikiy i yego reforma* (Peter the Great and His Reform) (1920); *Administrativnyye preobrazovaniya Petra Velikogo v 1699-1700 gg.* (Peter the Great's Administrative Changes of 1699-1700) (2 vol, 1928-29); *Pyotr I. Materialy dlya biografii* (Peter I. Material for a Biography) (5 vol, 1940-48), etc; *Died*: 20 Apr 1929.

BOGOSLOVSKIY, Sergey Mikhaylovich (1870-1931) Sanitarian and health statistician; *Born*: 1870; *Educ*: 1896 grad Med Fac, Moscow Univ; *Career*: 1896-97 worked as physician on the Caucasian Black Sea coast; 1898-1900 factory physician, Bogorodskoye Uyezd, Moscow Province; from 1900 health officer, Bogorodskoye Uyezd, then Moscow Province Health Statistics Bureau; 1906 imprisoned for involvement with "Polit Insurance Fund," which provided financial aid for members of the revol movement; after 1917 Oct Revol joined Health Statistics Bureau, Moscow Health Dept; 1918-31 worked for Centr Statistical Bd; 1898 in his first article on public health criticized the working and living conditions of laborers building port facilities in Tuapse; did research on health in domestic industries and on working conditions and occupational diseases in the large textile mills of Bogorodskoye Uyezd and, later, in almost all branches of ind in Moscow Province; 1913 published standard work describing health conditions in 5,284 professions; devised method of statistical research on occupational diseases; regarded as the father of Russian statistics on occupational diseases; 1924-25 established that the physique of workers, particularly young workers, was better than during the period 1879-85 (Erisman's findings); 1927 devised plan for organizing health statistics in the USSR; together with P. I. Kurkin and P. A. Kuvshinnikov compiled uniform regulations and forms for recording med and health statistics; cofounder and assoc, Obukh Inst of Labor Hygiene and Occupational Diseases, Moscow; *Publ: Sanitarnoye sostoyaniye rabochikh Glinkovskoy manufaktury Bogorodskogo uyezda* (The State of Health of Workers at the Glinkov Factory in Bogorodskoye Uyezd) (1900); *Zabolevayemost' rabochikh Bogorodsko-Glukhovskoy i Istomkinskoy fabrik Bogorodskogo uyezda* (The Incidence of Sickness Among Workers of the Bogorodskoye-Glukhovo and Istomka Factories in Bogorodskoye Uyezd) (1902); *Sanitarnoye opisaniye zavedeniy melkoy promyshlennosti Bogorodskogo uyezda* (A Health Survey of Small Industrial Enterprises in Bogorodskoye Uyezd) (1907); article "The Zemstvo Medical Budget of Moscow Province in 1883-1904" (1910); coauthor, article "Methods of Statistical Research on Occupational Diseases" (1911); *Sistema professional'noy klassifikatsii* (A Job Classification System) (1913); *Metody statisticheskogo issledovaniya professional'noy boleznennosti* (Methods of Statistical Research on Occupational Diseases) (1913); article "Insalubrious Industrial Working Conditions and Their Effect on the Workers' Health" (1915); *Boleznennost' fabrichno-zavodskikh rabochikh Moskovskoy gubernii* (The Sick Rate of Factory and Plant Workers in Moscow Province) (1923); *Klassifikatsiya i nomenklatura meditsinskikh professiy* (The Classification and Cataloguing of Medical Professions) (1924); coauthor, *Vvedeniye v professional'nuyu gigiyenu* (An Introduction to Job Hygiene) (1925); *Metodika statisticheskogo issledovaniya professional'noy zabolevayemosti* (Methods for the Statistical Study of Occupational Sick Rates) (1925); *Statistika professional'noy zabolevayemosti* (Statistics on Occupational Diseases) (vol 1, 1926); *Sostoyaniye zdorov'ya rabochikh i sluzhashchikh goroda Moskvy* (The State of Health of Manual and Office Workers in Moscow) (1930); *Fizicheskoye razvitiye i zdorov'ye promyshlennykh rabochikh i sluzhashchikh goroda Moskvy* (The Physical Development and Health of Industrial Manual and Office Workers in Moscow) (1927); *Died*: 1931.

BOGOYAVLENSKIY, Sergey Konstantinovich (1871-1947) Historian and archivist; prof; corresp member, USSR Acad of Sci from 1929; *Born*: 17 Feb 1871; *Educ*: 1895 grad Moscow Univ; *Career*: from 1898 worked in archives, Russian Min of For Affairs; after 1917 Oct Revol worked for Moscow Oblast Archives, then for USSR Centr Archives Bd; helped to plan and implement archives reform; 1922-29 prof, Dept of Archives Management, Moscow State Univ; from 1939 senior researcher, Inst of History, USSR Acad of Sci; worked on history of Moscow and Muscovy of the 16-18th Centuries and history of the 18th-Century Russian Army; published many archive documents; author of many works published in various journals, collections and joint works; *Publ: Sudebnik tsarya Feodora Ioannovicha 1589 g.* (Tsar Feodor Ioannovich's 1589 Legal Codex) (1900); *Novgorodskiye pistsovyye knigi* (The Novgorod Cadastres) (vol 5-6, 1905-10); *Akty vremeni mezhdutsarstviya* (Records from the Interregnum) (1915); coauthor, *Moskovskiy kray v yego proshlom* (The Moscow District in the Past) (Part 2, 1930); *Prikaznyye sud'yi XVII v.* (Departmental Judges of the 17th Century) (1946); coauthor, *Istoriya Moskvy* (A History of Moscow) (vol 1, 1952); coauthor, *Ocherki istorii SSSR. XVII v.* (An Outline History of the USSR. The 17th Century) (1955), etc; *Died*: 31 Aug 1947.

BOGUSLAVSKIY, Konstantin Yevgen'yevich (1895-1937) Ukr composer and choirmaster; *Born*: 1895 in vil Pavlovka, now Lugansk Oblast; *Career*: 1922-33 choirmaster, School of Red Sergeants, Khar'kov; *Works*: mass songs "Twelve Mowers"; "In Praise of Freedom"; "Year After Year"; Red Army songs "The Red Army March"; "The Song of Chapayev"; "The Battleship", etc; quartet *Komarik*; children's opera *Andriykokozak* (Andriyko the Cossack); also arranged Ukr folksongs; *Died*: 1937.

BOGUSLAVSKIY, Mikhail Solomonovich (1888-1937) Party and govt official; CP member from 1917; *Born*: 1888, son of an artisan; *Career*: type-setter; 1904 arrested in Khar'kov for helping organize Printers' Trade Union; 1905 joined Jewish Socialist Party; worked for legal workers' orgs in Nikolayev and Kremenchug; after 1917 Feb Revol exec govt, trade-union and Party work in Kremenchug, Voronezh and Khar'kov; after 1917 Oct Revol member, first Ukr Centr Exec Comt and member, Ukr Govt; 1919 elected secr, Ukr Centr Exec Comt and secr, Ukr Council of Pop Comr; from 1920 in Moscow with Main Communications Polit Bd; later chm, Printers' Trade Union; 1921 with Moscow Sov; 1922-24 asst chm, Moscow Sov; 1924 chm, Main State Insurance Bd; 1924-27 chm, RSFSR Small Council of Pop Comr; 1920-21 sided with anti-Party "democratic centralism" group, and later with Trotskyist opposition; 1927 by decree of 15th CPSU(B) Congress expelled from the Party; arrested by State Security organs; *Died*: 1937 in imprisonment.

BOGUSLAVSKIY, Sergey Anatol'yevich (1883-1923) Physicist; *Born*: 1 Dec 1883; *Educ*: studied at Freiburg Univ; 1913 grad Goettingen Univ; 1917 grad Petersburg Univ; *Career*: 1918 prof, Saratov Univ; from 1919 prof, Moscow Univ; devised methods for calculating thermodynamic values from the standpoint of statistical physics and applied this method to various special problems of molecular physics; did research on pyroelectricity, theory of dielectr crystal structure, the effects of magnetic field and space charges on thermoionic current; outlined motion of electrons in electromagnetic fields; *Publ: Kineticheskaya teoriya izolyatorov. Zavisimost' dielektricheskoy postoyannoy ot temperatury. Piroelektrichestvo* (The Kinetic Theory of Insulators. Ratio of the Dielectric Constant to the Temperature. Pyroelectricity) (1914); *O stroyenii dielektricheskikh kristallov* (The Structure of Dielectric Crystals) (1915); master's thesis *Osnovy molekulyarnoy fiziki i primeneniye statistiki k vychisleniyu termodinamicheskikh potentsialov* (The Principles of Molecular Physics and the Application of Statistics to the Calculation of Thermodynamic Potentials) (1918); *Puti elektronov v elektromagnitnykh polyakh* (Electron Paths in Electromagnetic Fields) (1929), etc; *Died*: 3 Sept 1923.

BOKARIUS, Nikolay Sergeyevich (1869-1931) Specialist in forensic med; pioneer of Sov forensic med; prof from 1910; Dr of Med from 1902; emeritus prof from 1925; *Born*: 1869 in Odessa, son of a high-school teacher; *Educ*: 1895 grad Med Fac, Khar'kov Univ; *Career*: after graduation worked as intern at a surgical clinic in Khar'kov; from 1897 asst dissector, Chair of Forensic Med, Khar'kov Univ, under Prof F. A. Patenko; 1903-10 assoc prof, 1910-31 prof, Chair of Forensic Med, Khar'kov Univ, then Khar'kov Med Inst; developed this chair into one of best-equipped chairs of forensic med in USSR or abroad; 1896-1911 delivered lectures and plastic anatomy at Khar'kov Art School; 1923 founder and life-dir, Office of Forensic Expertise, which became a research inst in 1925 and was named for him after his death; organized Ukr Center of Forensic and Criminological Expertise; analyzed over 5,000 items of material evidence and performed over 3,000 autopsies; trained forensic experts and instructors in forensic med; 1905-30 prof of forensic med, Law Fac, Khar'kov Univ; head, Dept of Higher Med Educ, Ukr Pop Comrt of Educ; head, Dept of Forensic Med, Ukr Pop Comrt of Health; from 1928 until death foremost forensic med expert of Ukr SSR; 1924-31 consultant, Ukr Main Militia and Investigatory Bd; 1926-27 founder-ed, journal *Arkiv kryminolohii i sudebnoy medytsyny*; 1931 founder-ed, journal *Pytannya kryminalistyki ta naukovo-sudebnoy ekspertyzy*; wrote over 130 works, including manuals on forensic medicine and expertise, of which the best-known are *Rukovodstvo po naruzhnomu osmotrv trupov* (Manual on the External Examination of Corpses) (1925, 1929) and *Uchebnik sudebnoy meditsiny dlya medikov i yuristov* (Textbook of Forensic Medicine for Physicians and Lawyers); 1902 wrote doctor's thesis on the chemical nature and the forensic use of Florence's crystals, in which he determined their structure and refuted Florence's findings concerning the specificity of these crystals; devised various techniques of clue evaluation; his sperm test and macroscopic method of examining strangulation marks are to be found in all manuals and textbooks on forensic med; *Publ*: doctor's thesis *Kristally Floransa, ikh khimicheskaya priroda i sudebnomeditsinskoye zhacheniye* (Florence's Crystals, Their Chemical Structure and Significance in Forensic Medicine) (1902); *Sudebnomeditsinskiye mikroskopicheskiye i mikrokhimicheskiye issledovaniya veshchestvennykh dokazatel'stv* (The Forensic Microscopic and Microchemical Examination of Material Evidence) (1910); *Sudebnaya meditsina v izlozhenii dlya yuristov* (Forensic Medicine Interpreted for Lawyers) (vol 1, 1915); *Pervonachal'nyy naruzhnyy osmotr trupa pri militseyskom i rozysknom doznanii* (Preliminary External Examination of the Corpse in Police and Criminal Investigations) (1925); *Naruzhnyy osmotr trupa na meste proisshestviya ili obnaruzheniya yego* (External Examination of the Corpse at the Scene of Death or the Place of Its Discovery) (1929); *Sudebnaya meditsina dlya medikov i yuristov* (Forensic Medicine for Physicians and Lawyers) (2 vol, 1930); *Died*: 1931.

BOKIS, Gustav Gustavovich (? -1938) Div commander; former chief, Red Army Motorized and Armored Troops; *Career*: 1936-37 chief, Red Army Motorized and Armored Troops; Nov 1937 registered as dep, USSR Supr Sov, but was replaced by another cand on account of his arrest by State Security organs; *Died*: 1938 in imprisonment.

BOKIY, Gleb Ivanovich (Party pseudonyms: "Kuz'ma"; "Dyadya"; "Maksim Ivanovich") (1879-1941) Party and govt official; CP member from 1900; *Born*: 1879 in Tiflis, son of a teacher; *Educ*: 1896 grad secondary school; studied at Petersburg Mining Inst; *Career*: from 1897 in student movement; active in Petersburg League for the Liberation of the Working Class; participated in 1905-07 Revol in Petersburg; helped organize fighting groups; repeatedly arrested and exiled; late 1916 co-opted to Russian Bureau, CC, RSDRP(B); 1917 deleg, 7th (Apr) All-Russian RSDRP(B) Conference and 6th RSDRP(B) Congress; Apr 1917-Mar 1918 secr, Petrograd RSDRP(B) Comt; member, Petrograd Mil-Revol Comt; Feb-Mar 1918 member, Comt for Revol Defense of Petrograd; later chm, Petrograd Cheka; 1918 deleg, 7th RCP(B) Congress; sided with Leftist Communists, opposed Brest Peace Treaty; from 1919 head, Special Dept, Turkestani Front; member, Turkestani Commission, All-Russian Centr Exec Comt and CC, RCP(B); from 1921 member, All-Russian Cheka; subsequently Collegium member, OGPU then NKVD; from 1927 simultaneously Collegium member, Main Lit Bd and member, USSR Supr Court; elected cand member and member, RSFSR Centr Exec Comt of 2nd – 12th convocations and USSR Centr Exec Comt of 1st and 2nd convocations; arrested by State Security organs; *Died*: 24 May 1941 in imprisonment.

BOKLEVSKIY, Konstantin Petrovich (1862-1928) Shipbuilding eng; *Born*: 1862; *Educ*: 1884 grad Kronstadt Naval Eng College; 1888 grad Naval Acad; *Career*: from 1888 worked at shipyards on Baltic and Black Seas, then supervised construction of battleship *Tsesarevich* and cruiser *Bayan* in France; later, as asst chief eng, Petersburg Port, and chief eng, Naval Dept Shipyard, supervised construction of ships for Far East; organizer, 1902-23 dean, Russia's first shipbuilding fac opened in 1902 at Petersburg Polytech Inst; on his initiative this fac began training aeronautical engineers; also founded an aerodynamics laboratory at Petersburg Polytech Inst; helpd develop motorships; 1898 suggested using oil-fired internal combustion engines in ships; 1903 presented plans for a motorship with this type of engine; later designed number of naval ships and civilian vessels with such engines as main drive; the tower monitor motorships built on his initiative for the River Amur were highly rated by A. N. Krylov; co-founded Russian Registry Soc aimed at freeing Russian shipbuilding from foreign tutelage; after Oct Revol chm, Tech Council, USSR Registry and ran special bureau for designing merchant vessels; *Publ: O postroyke minonostsev smeshannoy system* (The Construction of Mixed-System Minelayers (1895); *Lektsii proyektirovaniya sudov* (Lectures on Ship Designing) (1904-05); *Korabel'naya arkhitektura* (Ship Architecture) (Part 1, 1914), etc; *Died*: 1. Juni 1928.

BOKONBAYEV, Dzhoomart (1910-1944) Kir poet and playwright; CP member from 1932; *Born*: 16 May 1910 in vil Mazar-Say, now Osh Oblast, Kir SSR; *Educ*: 1933-35 studied at Inst of Journalism, Moscow; *Publ*: 1927 first work published; "To the Poor Peasants Who Have Received Land" (1927); "Kokosh Opens His Eyes" (1928); "Poverty" (1928); "Desert of Life" (1930); "Chuya Valley" (1930); "Along Lenin's Path" (1931); "My Ferghana" (1932); poems: *Kyzyk Kyya* (1932), *Turksib* (1932); collected verse "Labor Initiative" (1933); *Suluktu* (1933); musical drama "The Golden Girl" (1937); libretto for operas: *Aychurek* (1937); "Life in Blossom" (1939); drama *Kargasha* (1939); libretto for opera *Toktogul* (1939); WW 2 poems: "Moscow, The Fortress," "The Spirit of the Great Lenin," "The Red Banner Is My Heart," "Over the Lake," "Death and Honor," etc; *Died*: 1 July 1944 killed in an automobile accident.

BOL', Boris Karlovich (1897-1958) Pathologist and anatomist; prof from 1932; Dr of Veterinary Sci from 1937; *Born*: 1897; *Educ*: 1921 grad Kazan' Veterinary Inst; *Career*: 1921-28 asst prof, Chair of Pathological Anatomy, Kazan' Veterinary Inst, where he worked under his father Prof K. G. Bol'; from 1928 until death head, Chair of Pathological Anatomy, Moscow Zooveterinary Inst (from 1948 Moscow Veterinary Acad); did research on the veterinary pathology of infectious diseases (glanders, infectious encephalomyelitis in horses, hoof-and-mouth disease, etc), on the metabolic pathology of high-yield cows and on the seasonal morphology of reindeer; his doctor's thesis was devoted to the *Patologicheskaya anatomiya i patogenez sapa lyogkikh loshadey* (Pathological Anatomy and Pathogenesis of Glanders in Small Horses); 1932 led an expedition to study glanders in horses in Northern Caucasus; his findings are reflected in instructions for the treatment of this disease; made major contribution to veterinary med with his research on infectious encephalomyelitis in horses, which he conducted in conjunction with Prof K. I. Vertinskiy; their discovery of inclusion bodies in the ganglionic cells of the central nervous system in this disease (Bol'-Vertinskiy bodies) provided morphological proof that the disease is of viral origin, a fact which was confirmed by later research; in the last years of his life studied the pathomorphology and pathogenesis of metabolic disorders in high-yield cows; established that pathological lesions in the organs and tissues of these cows are caused by intoxication of the organism as a result of over feeding with highly-concentrated fodder; helped to coordinate the various schools of veterinary med which existed in pre-Revol Russia; 1935 drew up first program on pathological anatomy based on nosological principles for instruction at veterinary colleges; *Publ*: coauthor, *Osnovy patologicheskoy anatomii sel'skokhozyaystvennykh zhivotnykh* (Principles of the Pathological Anatomy of Farm Animals) (3rd ed, 1961); *Patologoanatomicheskoye vskrytiye sel'skokhozyaystvennykh zhivotnykh* (The Pathological Anatomical Dissection of Farm Animals) (4th ed, 1957); articles "Glanders in Small Horses" (1926); "Infectious Abortion in Swine" (1930); coauthor, "The Pathological Anatomy of the Kidneys in Swine Plague" (1938); coauthor, article "The Diagnostic Significance of Inclusions in the Cerebral Nerve Cells of Horses Infected with Epizootic Encephalomyelitis in the USSR" (1935); articles: "Pathological Anatomical Lesions in the Lungs of Cattle Experimentally Infected with Peripneumonia" (1948); coauthor, "Pathological Anatomical Lesions in the Kidneys of Silver Vixen After Leptospirosis" (1960); coauthor, article "Pathomorphology and Problems of the Pathogenesis of Metabolic Disturbances in High-Yield Cows" (1956); coauthor, "Pathomorphological Changes in Cows Suffering from Metabolic Disturbances" (1957); *Awards*: Order of Lenin; medals; *Died*: 1958.

BOL', Karl Genrikhovich (1871-1959) Veterinary pathologist and anatomist; prof from 1921; Dr of Veterinary Sci from 1934; Hon Sci Worker of RSFSR from 1930; Hon Sci Worker of Tatar ASSR from 1951; *Born*: 1871; *Educ*: 1895 grad Kazan' Veterinary Inst; *Career*: after graduation worked as a zemstvo veterinary surgeon; 1896-99 asst dissector, Chair of Pathological Anatomy, Kazan' Veterinary Inst; 1899 defended master's thesis on *K voprosu o patologoanatomicheskikh izmeneniyakh spinnogo mozga pri chume sobak* (Pathological Anatomical Lesions of the Spine in Canine Plague); from 1900 head, Chair of Pathological Anatomy, Kazan' Veterinary Inst; 1921-24 simultaneously head, Chair of Pathological Anatomy, Med Fac, Kazan' Univ; 1922-30 head, Chair of Pathological Anatomy, State Inst for Postgrad Med Training; 1919-38 dir, Kazan' Veterinary Inst; devised new classification of inflammatory processes and described the cellular forms of foci of inflammation; devised a classification of horse colics; developed theory of a specific pathomorphological syndrome common to many infectious diseases and theory of hemotransudation; proposed new classification of hemorrhage; compiled a collection of color slides on animal pathological anatomy for training purposes; established a museum of pathological anatomy containing over 3,000 exhibits; supervised the writing of 220 papers, including 58 doctor's theses on the pathomorphology and pathogenesis of infectious and infestant diseases; trained 13 dr of sci and 45 cand of sci; organized and attended many veterinary conferences and congresses; member, Tatar Centr Exec Comt; dep, Kazan' City Sov; 1927-37 ed, Kazan' Veterinary Inst journal *Uchyonyye zapiski*; wrote over 60 works on gen pathology and the pathomorphology and pathogenesis of infectious and infestant diseases in animals; compiled textbook on the pathological anatomy of farm animals for use in higher veterinary educ establishments; *Publ: Osnovy patologicheskoy anatomii domashnikh mlekopitayushchikh i ptits* (Principles of the Pathological Anatomy of Domestic Mammals and Birds) (5th ed, 1938); coauthor, *Osnovy patologicheskoy anatomii sel'skokhozyaystvennykh zhivotnykh* (Principles of the Pathological Anatomy of Farm Animals) (3rd ed, 1961); master's thesis *K voprosu o patologoanatomicheskikh izmeneniyakh spinnogo mozga pri chume sobak* (Pathological Anatomical Lesions of the Spine in Canine Plague) (1899); articles: "Hemorrhage, Its Origin and Classification" (1926); "Glanders" (1926); "Inflammation" (1929); "Paratuberculous Enteritis in Cattle" (1927); "The Cellular Elements of Foci of Inflammation and Their Histogenesis" (1945); "Horse Colics" (1947); "The Diagnosis of Infectious Diseases" (1946); "Contemporary Veterinary Education and Its Needs" (1927); *Awards*: Order of Lenin; Order of the Red Banner of Labor; medal "For Valiant Labor in the Great Fatherland War"; Scroll of Hon of Presidium of Tatar Supr Sov; *Died*: 1959.

BOLDYREV, Anatoliy Kapitonovich (1883-1946) Crystallographer and mineralogist; *Born*: 26 Oct 1883; *Educ*: studied at Petersburg Mining Inst; *Career*: expelled from Mining Inst for revol activity and exiled to the Urals, where he engaged in geological research; from 1918 worked for Geological Comt, then for All-Union Geological Research Inst; from 1921 siumultaneously prof, Leningrad Mining Inst; 1925 proposed simplified method of determining the chemical composition of substances by measurement of their crystals on the basis of earlier work performed by Ye. S. Fyodorov; 1937-39 helped compile vol 1 of *Opredelitel' kristallov* (A Crystal Determinant); also proposed new method of determining minerals by X-ray photography and established one of first Russian laboratories for this purpose; 1938-39 supervised compilation of two-part *Ryontgenometricheskiy opredelitel' mineralov* (Roentgenometric Determinant of Minerals); also did research on deposits of iron, copper, tin, tungsten, bismuth and beryllium; this research led to the discovery of new tin deposits; helped to develop generally accepted crystallographic nomenclature; *Publ: Printsipy novogo metoda kristallograficheskogo diagnoza veshchestva* (The Principles of a New Method of Crystallographic Diagnosis) (1924); *Kurs opisatel'noy mineralogii* (A Course in Descriptive Mineralogy) (Parts 1-3, 1926-35); *Kristallografiya* (Crystallography) (3rd ed, 1934); *Khimicheskaya konstitutsiya i kristallicheskaya struktura slyud* (The Chemical Composition and Crystalline Structure of Micas) (1937); *Died*: 25 Mar 1946.

BOLDYREV, Vasiliy Georgiyevich (1875-?) Mil commander and politician; lt-gen, Russian Army; *Born*: 1875, son of a blacksmith; *Educ*: grad Gen Staff Acad; *Career*: 1904-05 fought in Russo-Japanese War; from 1911 instructor, then prof, Gen Staff Acad; during WW 1 commanded army corps, then 5th Army; after 1917 Oct Revol arrested and imprisoned for a while for refusing to carry out orders of Sov supr commander in chief Krylenko; joined anti-Sov groups in Moscow – "Rightist Center, then "League for the Renaissance of Russia"; member, joint mil bd of these two groups (Gen Tsitovich, Admiral Nemtts and Boldyrev himself); Sept 1918 one of five members of anti-Sov Provisional All-Russian Govt (Ufa Directorate) and supr commander in chief of its armed forces; Nov 1918, after Admiral Kolchak's coup, moved to Japan; 1920 returned to Vladivostok and held senior mil posts with anti-Sov govt of Maritime Oblast Land Administration, then with coalition govt of Far Eastern Republ, consisting of Communists and reps of democratic groups; 1921 joined Far Eastern Democratic League, founded under Japanese occupation, and sided with left wing of Maritime Pop Assembly; Nov 1922, after Sov occupation of Vladivostok, arrested and imprisoned in Novo-Nikolaevka Prison; amnestied after professing his willingness to serve Sov regime; 1925 published book *Direktoriya, Kolchak, interventy* (The Directorate, Kolchak and the Interventionists); 1926 worked for Siberian Planning Commission; *Died*: date and place of death unknown.

BOL'SHAKOV, Nikolay Arkad'yevich (1874-1958) Opera singer (tenor); singing teacher; Hon Art Worker of RSFSR from 1938; *Born*: 23 Nov 1874 in Khar'kov; *Educ*: studied singing under I.B. Pryanishnikov; also studied at Petersburg Univ; *Career*: 1899 opera debut in Petersburg; 1905-29 soloist, Mariinskiy Theater; 1923-35 instructor, from 1935 prof, Leningrad Conservatory; performed in Paris, Berlin, Barcelona and other European cities; *Roles*: Finn in Glinka's *Ruslan i Lyudmila* (Ruslan and Ludmilla); Yurodivyy in *Boris Godunov*; Grishka Kuter'ma in Rimsky-

Korsakov's *Skazaniye o nevidimom grade Kitezhe i deve Fevronii* (The Tale of the Invisible City of Kitezh and the Maid Fevroniya); Khlopusha in Pashchenko's *Orlinyy bunt* (Eagles Revolt); Pinkerton in "Madam Butterfly"; Lenskiy in Tchaikovsky's *Yevgeniy Onegin* (Eugene Onegin); German in Tchaikovsky's *Pikovaya dama* (The Queen of Spades); *Died*: 20 Jan 1958 in Leningrad.

BOL'SHINTSOV, Manuel' Vladimirovich (1902-1954) Film scriptwriter and producer; *Born*: 1902; *Career*: 1924 helped found *Kinokomsomol* film studio in Rostov-on-Don; 1927-29 producer, Yalta Film Studio, All-Ukr Film Bd; 1930 active in *Kino-Sibir'* film studio; from 1931 worked mainly as film scriptwriter; during WW 2 chief ed of studio for documentary films; directed camera teams on 1st Bel Front; *Works*: produced films: *Istoriya odnogo avansa* (The Story of an Advance) (1924); *Pokhozhdeniye Van'ki Gvozdya* (The Adventures of Van'ka Gvozd') (1924); *Prikaz No . . .* (Order Number . . .) (1926); *Odna noch'* (One Night) (1927); *Ostrov begletsov* (Island of Fugitives) (1927); wrote screenplay for *Tungus s Khenychara* (Tungus from Khenychar) (1930), etc; wrote screenplays for: *Krest'yane* (The Peasants) (1935); *Velikiy grazhdanin* (The Great Citizen) (1942); coauthor, *Nebo Moskvy* (The Moscow Sky) (1944); *Ot Visly do Odera* (From the Vistula to the Oder) (1945); *Donbass* (1946); *Dneproges* (Dnieper Power Plant) (1948); coauthor, *Oni spustilis' s gor* (They Came Down from the Mountains), etc; *Died*: 1954.

BOL'SKA (real name: SKOMPSKAYA), Adelaida Yulianovna (1864-1930) Polish singer (lyric coloratura soprano); *Born*: 1864 in Moscow; *Educ*: 1888 grad Komissarzhevskiy's class, Moscow Conservatory; *Career*: 1888-89, on assignment in Italy, sang at Milan's La Scala; 1889-93 at Moscow Bolshoy Theater; 1893-97 performed abroad, mainly in Paris; 1897-1918 at Petersburg Mariinskiy Theater; after 1917 Oct Revol performed only sporadically; *Roles*: Tat'yana in Tchaikovsky's *Yevgeniy Onegin* (Eugene Onegin); Gorislava in Glinka's *Ruslan i Lyudmila* (Ruslan and Ludmilla); Volkhova in Rimsky-Korsakov's *Sadko*; Elsa and Elisabeth in Wagner's "Lohengrin" and "Tannhäuser", etc; *Died*: 29 Sept 1930 in Revel.

BOLTUNOV, Aleksandr Pavlovich (1883-1942) Psychologist and pedag; specialist in child psychology; prof from 1917; Dr of Pedag Sci from 1936; *Born*: 23 Aug 1883; *Educ*: 1909 grad Berlin and Moscow univ; *Career*: studied experimental research methods; 1916 published first major work *Metod ankety v pedagogicheskom i psikhologicheskom issledovanii* (The Questionnaire Method in Pedagogic and Psychological Research); 1923 reviewed psychological aspects of problem of establishing labor schools in his book *Trudovaya shkola psikhologicheskom osveshchenii* (The Labor School in the Light of Psychology); towards the end of his life he studied the theory and methods of pedag diagnostics; *Publ: Kak vesti pedagogicheskiy dnevnik* (How to Keep a Pedagogic Journal) (1923); *Pedagogicheskaya kharakteristika rebyonka* (The Pedagogic Characteristics of the Child) (1926); *Pedagogicheskiy eksperiment v massovoy shkole* (A Pedagogic Experiment in a Mass School) (1929); *Praktikum po teorii psikhologicheskikh ispytaniy* (Practical Work on the Theory of Psychological Tests) (1927); *Pedologiya v shkole* (School Pedology) (1930); *Proforientatsiya v shkole* (Career Guidance at School) (1934); *Slushaniye i chitaniye v protsesse obucheniya* (Listening and Reading in the Instruction Process) (1945); *Died*: Feb 1942).

BOLTYANSKIY, Grigoriy Moiseyevich(1885-1953) Film dir and historian; Hon Worker of Sov Cinematography from 1923; *Born*: 24 Feb 1885; *Career*: one of first Sov newsreel producers; 1917 began film work in Social Chronicle Dept, Skobelev Educ Comt; filmed events of Feb and Oct revol; 1918-20 head, Newsreel Dept, Petrograd Film Comt; 1920-22 head, Newsreel Section, All-Russian Photography and Film Dept, Pop Comrt of Educ; 1922-24 head, Newsreel Dept, North Eastern Film Enterprises, Pop Comrt of Educ; 1924-26 head, Newsreel Dept, Centr State Photography and Film Enterprises, Pop Comrt of Educ; filmed Lenin and his fueral; 1926 as head, Film Chamber, USSR Acad of Arts, established sci basis of Sov film research; 1925, 1926 and 1940 organized exhibitions of film posters; 1927 organized the exhibition "The Cinema on the 10th Anniversary of the Oct Revol"; 1929 organized the xhibition "The Rural Cinema"; 1938 organized the exhibition "The Cinema in the Struggle Against Fascism"; 1947 organized the exhibition" The Cinema on the 30th Anniversary of Sov Rule"; co-initiator of amateur film movement in USSR; 1926-31 chm, Amateur Film and Photography Section, Soc of the Friends of the Sov Cinema; from 1931 lecturer, State Inst of Cinematography, where he organized a newsreel dept; from 1943 worked on film chronicle of WW 2; *Publ*: *Lenin i kino* (Lenin and the Cinema) (1925); *Kino v derevne* (The Cinema in the Countryside) (1925); *Kinokhronika i kak yeyo snimat'* (Newsreels and How to Make Them) (1926); *Kul'tura kinooperatora. Opyt issledovaniya, osnovannyy na rabotakh E. K. Tisse* (Camera Technique. The Results of Research Based on the Work of E. K. Tisse) (1927); *Kinospravochnik* (Cinema Guide) (1926, 1927, 1928); *Fotografiya i obshchestvennost'* (Photography and the Public) (1930); *Puti sovetskoy kinokhroniki* (The Soviet Newsreel) (1933); *Ocherki po istorii fotografii SSSR* (An Outline History of Photography in the USSR) (1939), etc; *Died*: 15 June 1953.

BONACHICH, Anton Petrovich (1878-1933) Opera singer (baritone, then dramatic tenor); *Born*: 25 Jan 1878 in Mariupol'; *Educ*: 1901 grad Petersburg Conservatory; *Career*: opera debut in Khar'kov; 1902-04 in Tiflis, Kiev, etc; 1905-20 at Bolshoy Theater; from 1921 opera producer and teacher in Omsk, Tomsk, Saratov and Minsk; 1909 performed in Italy and France; 1911 in Monte Carlo; *Roles*: Zvezdochyot in *Zolotoy petushok* (The Golden Cockerel); Tamino in Mozarts' s "Magic Flute"; Albero and Paulo in Rakchmaninov's *Skupov rytsar'* (The Miserly Knight) and "Francesca da Rimini"; Prince Golitsyn in *Khovanshchina*; Don Juan in Dargomyzhskiy's *Kamennyy gost'* (The Stone Guest); Romeo in Gounod's "Romeo and Juliet"; Tannhäuser in Wagner's "Tannhäuser," etc; wrote operetta *Ostrov nevinnosti* (The Isle of Innocence) (1909); *Died*: 26 Jan 1933 in Minsk.

BONCH-BRUYEVICH, Mikhail Aleksandrovich (1888-1940) Radio eng; prof; corresp member, USSR Acad of Sci from 1931; *Born*: 21 Feb 1888 in Oryol; *Educ*: 1909 grad Eng College; grad Mil Electr Eng School, Petersburg; *Career*: 1919-29 headed Nizhniy Novgorod Radio Laboratory; from 1922 prof, Moscow Higher Tech College; from 1932 prof, Leningrad Inst of Communications Eng; 1916-19 studied electronic tubes and was first to organize Sov production of such tubes; on orders of Lenin, planned and in 1922 built world's first powerful (12-kilowatt) radio transmitter, the "Comintern" Station in Moscow; 1919-25 designed powerful water-cooled generator tubes and circuits for radio-telephone stations; 1927 40-kilowatt transmitter with external-anode tubes designed by Bonch-Bruyevich was built in Moscow; 1924-30 supervised research into short-wave propagation; designet world's first short-wave directional antennas and built short-wave long-distance radio communication lines; studied physical properties of upper layers of atmosphere and conducted ionosphere research by means of radio echo techniques; studied ultra short waves and their use, i.e., for radio location; *Publ: Osnovy radiotekhniki* (Prinicples of Radio Engineering) (2 vol, 1936); *Sobraniye trudov* (Collected Works) (1956), etc; *Died*: 7 Nov 1940.

BONCH-BRUYEVICH, Mikhail Dmitriyevich (1870-1956) Geodesist and mil commander; lt-gen from 1944; brother of V. D. Bonch-Bruyevich; *Born*: 8 Mar 1870 in Moscow, son of a land-surveyor; *Educ*: 1890 grad Moscow Land Survey Inst; 1898 grad Moscow Univ and Gen Staff Acad; *Career*: 1898-1907 staff-officer, Kiev Mil Distr; from 1907 lecturer in tactics, Gen Staff Acad; at outbreak of WW I quartermaster-gen, 3rd Army; from Sept 1914 quartermaster-gen, Northwestern Front; from Mar 1915 chief of staff, Northern Front; Aug-Sept 1917 commander in chief, Northern Front; Sept-Oct 1917 special duties with Kerensky, then garrison-commander in Mogilev; joined Bolsheviks during Oct Revol; from 20 Nov 1917 chief of Staff to Supr Commander Trotsky; from Mar 1918 mil chief, Higher Mil Council; Mar 1919-23 founder and head, Higher Geodetic Bd, Supr Sovnarkhoz; June-Aug 1919 chief of Field Staff, Red Army; from 1925 head, State Aerial Photography Bureau; 1939-49 ed, 9-vol reference book *Geodeziya* (Geodesy); *Publ: Poterya nami Galitsii* (How We Lost Galicia) (2 vol, 1920-26); *Aerofotos'yomka* (Aerial Photography) (1931); *Aerofotos'yomka na sluzhbe sotsialisticheskogo khozyaystva* (Aerial Photography in the Service of the Socialist Economy) (1934); *Spravochnik po aerofotos'yomke* (A Reference Book of Aerial Photography) (1934); *Dragomirov o boyevoy podgotovke ofitserov* (Dragomirof on the Combat Training of Officers) (1944); *Vsya vlast' Sovetam. Vospominaniya* (All Power to the Soviets. Memoirs) (1958); *Died*: 3 Aug 1956.

BONCH-BRUYEVICH (VELICHKINA), Vera Mikhaylovna (1868-1918) Revolutionary; physician; co-founder, Soviet health service; *Born*: 8 Sept 1868 in Moscow; *Educ*: 1899 grad Med Fac, Bern Univ; *Career*: as a student active in Russian Revol movement; on several occasions arrested by police; while living abroad, contributed to Bolshevik newspapers *Vperyod* and *Proletariy*; 1905 returned to Russia and was elected to Petersburg Sov of Workers' Dep; arrested and after release from prison placed under police surveillance; during 1917 Oct Revol helped organize and direct Proletarian Red Cross; closely acquainted with Lenin and his family; with formation of RSFSR Pop Comrt of Educ directed its School Hygiene (School Health) Dept; from Mar 1918 dep chm, Council of Physicians' Collegia; from June 1918 member, 1st Collegium, RSFSR Pop Comrt of Health; helped found Inst of Physical Culture and Moscow's first model child health care establishments - a children's preventive med outpatients clinic, a children's tuberculosis outpatients clinic, a forest school, etc; *Publ: Okhrana zdorov'ya detey i postanovka fizicheskogo obrazovaniya* (Child Health Care and Physical Education Facilities) (1918), etc; *Died*: 1918.

BONCH-BRUYEVICH, Vladimir Dmitriyevich (1873-1955) Party official, historian, ethnographer and writer; Dr of Historical Sci; member USSR Writers' Union; dir, Museum of the History of Religion and Atheism, USSR Acad of Sci from 1945; CP (RSDRP) member from 1895; *Born*: 1o July 1873 in Moscow; son of a land-surveyor; *Educ*: studied at Moscow Land Survey Inst, Kursk Land Survey College and Zurich Univ; *Career*: 1889 expelled from Moscow Land Survey Inst for revol activity and exiled from Moscow; from 1892 in Moscow Marxist groups; 1896-1905 as an emigre in Switzerland worked with the Liberation of Labor group; then worked for RSDRP; 1903 joined Bolshevik faction after 2nd RSDRP Congress; 1903-05 headed RSDRP CC group in Zurich, helped to organize Centr Party Archives and found newspaper *Vperyod*; 1905 helped to prepare 3rd RSDRP Congress; returned to Petersburg and took part in 1905-07 Revol; worked for newspapers *Novaya zhizn'* and *Nasha mysl'* and helped to found Bolshevik newspapers *Volna, Vperyod* and *Ekho*; 1908-18 dir, legal Bolshevik publ house "Life and Knowledge"; 1910-11 worked for the newspaper *Zvezda* and from 1912 for *Pravda* after 1917 Feb Revol member, Ed Bd, *Izvestiya Petrogradskogo soveta* and temporary ed, Bolshevik newspaper *Rabochiy i soldat* Oct 1917-Oct 1920 business mang, Council of Pop Comr; 1920-36 chief ed, cooperative publ house "Life and Knowledge"; 1933-39 org and dir, State Lit Museum, Moscow; 1945-55 dir, Museum of the History of Religion and Atheism, USSR Acad of Sci; specialist in history of Russian revol movement, history of religion and atheism, ethnography and lit; *Publ: Zhivotnaya kniga dukhoborov* (A Bestiary of the Dukhobors) (1909); *Iz mira sektantov* (The Sectarians' World) (1922); *Kak pechatalis' i tayno dostavlyalis' v Rossiyu zapreshchyonnyye izdaniya nashey partii* (How Our Party's Banned Publicantions Were Printed and Smuggled into Russia) (1924); *Na boyevykh postakh Febral'skoy i Oktyabr'skoy revolyutsii. Vospominaniya o V. I. Lenine* (At the Battle Stations of the February and October Revolutions. Reminiscences of Lenin) (1930); *Na zare revolyutsionnoy proletarskoy bor'by. Po lichnym vospominaniyam* (At the Dawn of the Proletarian Revolutionary Struggle. Personal Reminiscences) (1932); *V. I. Lenin v Petrograde i v Moskve 1907-1920. Vospominaniya* (Lenin in Petrograd and Moscow 1907-1920. Reminiscences) (1956); *Lenin i sovkhoz 'Lesnyye polyany'. Vospominaniya* (Lenin and the "Lesnyye Polyany" Sovkhoz. Reminiscences) (1957; *O religii, sektantstve i tserkvi* (Religion, Sectarianism and the Church) (1959); *Izbrannyye sochineniya* (Selected Works) (2 vol, 1959-61), etc; *Died*: 14 July 1955.

BONDARENKO, Aleksey Dmitriyevich (1911-1956) Party official; 1952-55 cand member, CC, CPSU; CP member from 1932; *Born*: 1911 in vil Pogromets, Kursk Oblast, son of a peasant; *Educ*: 1949 grad Higher Party School, CC, CPSU(B); *Career*: 1931-38 Komsomol work in Kursk and Oryol Oblasts; from 1938 Party work; secr, Trubchevsk Rayon CPSU(B) Comt; 1942-44 comr of partisan detachments in Bryansk forests; 1944 first secr, Yelets City CPSU(B) Comt; 1944-47 secr, Bryansk Oblast CPSU(B) Comt; 1949-55 first secr, Bryansk Oblast CPSU(B) Comt; 1955-56 secr, Tambov Oblast CPSU Comt; *Awards*: Hero of the Sov Union (1942); Order of Lenin, etc; *Died*: 14 Dec 1956; unofficially reported to have comitted suicide.

BONDARENKO, Fyodor Pimenovich (1903-1961) Russian stage dir; Hon Art Worker of RSFSR from 1959; CP member from 1954; *Born*: 1903; *Educ*: studied at 1st Moscow Univ and at Meyerhold's Theatrical College; *Career*: Stage dir and actor, Meyerhold Theater; then stage dir, Leningrad sov Theater; 1938-41 dir, Leningrad Opera and Ballet Theater; 1943-48 dir, Bolshoy Theater; 1950-53 and from 1959 dir, Vakhtangov Theater; 1948-50 and 1953-59 head, Research and Creative Dept, All-Russian Theatrical Soc; *Productions*: Goldoni's "A Servant to Two Masters" (1936); *Kak zakalyalas' stal'* (How the Steel Was Tempered) (1937); *Chelovek s ruzh'yom* (The Man with a Gun) (1938); *Snegurochka* (The Snow-Maiden) (1959); *Russkiy les* (Russian Forest), after Leonov (1961), etc; *Died*: 24 Mar 1961.

BONDARENKO, Mikhail Zakharovich (1913-1947) Air Force officer; CP member from 1942; *Born*: 21 Sept 1913 in vil Bogdanovtsy, Poltava Oblast; *Educ*: 1945 grad Air Force Acad; *Pos*: from 1936 in Red Army; 1941-44 mil fighter pilot; 1945-47 commander, air force regt; *Awards*: twice Hero of Sov Union (1941, 1943); Order of Lenin; Order of the Red Banner, etc; bronze bust erected in his native vil; *Died*: 27 July 1947.

BONDI, Yuriy Mikhaylovich (1889-1926) Stage designer and dir, established children's theaters; *Born*: 20 Sept 1889; *Career*: 1912-15 stage designer, Meyerhold Studio, then Meyerhold Directing Workshops; 1923 dir, 1st State Children's Theater, Moscow; *Works*: designed sets and costumes for: Calderon's "Obeissance to the Cross"; (1912); Strindberg's "Guilty-Innocent" (1912), etc; productions: children's plays: Auslender and Solodovnikov's *Kol'ka Stupin* (1924); Nikiforov's *Samolyot* (The Airplane) (1925), etc; *Died*: 9 Mar 1926.

BONDIN, Aleksey Petrovich (1882-1939) Russian writer; *Born*: 17 Aug 1882 in Nizhniy Tagil; *Career*: for more than 30 years locksmith at Ural plants; took part in revol workers' circles; wrote about life of workers; *Publ*: play *Vragi* (The Enemy); (1920); stories *Tabel'shchitsa* (The Timekeeper) (1923); *Strelochnik* (The Switchman) (1925); novel *Loga* (Ravines) (1925); novelette *Moya shkola* (My School) (1934); novel *Ol'ga Yermolayeva* (1939); *Sobraniye sochineniy* (Collected Works) (3 vol, 1948, posthumously); *Izbrannoye* (Selected Works) (2 vol, 1957-58); *Died*: 7 Nov 1939 in Nizhniy Tagil.

BORCHANINOV (Party pseudonym: CHAYKIN), Aleksandr Lukich (1884-1932) Party and govt official; CP member from 1903; *Born*: 1884 in Motovilikha, son of a worker; *Career*: from 1901 in revol movement; 1903 member, Perm' and Motovilikha RSDRP Comt; active in Dec 1905 mutiny in Motovilikha; from Mar 1906 member, Kiev RSDRP Comt; May 1907 arrested, sentenced to four years at hard labor, then exiled to Yakutsk; from June 1917 chm, Motovilikha Sov; member, Perm' RSDRP(B) Comt; deleg, 6th RSDRP(B) Congress; active in 1917 Oct Revol in Petrograd; deleg, 2nd All-Russian Congress of Sov; fought in Civil War on Eastern and Southern Fronts; from Aug 1920 member, Revol Mil Council, 2nd Cavalry Army; from Aug 1921 chm, Perm' Province Cheka; until 1932 govt and Party work in Tyumen', Zlatoust, Perm', Tula, Krasnodar and Rostov; 1926-28 instructor, All-Russian Centr Exec Comt; *Died*: 23 Mar 1932.

BORIN-SHVARTSMAN, Boris Abramovich (1899-1965) Ukr stage dir; Pop Artiste of Ukr SSR from 1960; CP member from 1941; *Born*: 19 Oct 1889; *Career*: 1925-31 asst stage dir, then stage dir, Odessa Ukr Drama Theater; 1931-44 chief stage dir, Oct Revol Theater; from 1941 dir, Chernovtsy Theater; *Productions*: Bezymenskiy's *Vystrel* (The Shot) (1923); Ostrovskiy's *Dokhodnoye mesto* (A Lucrative Post) (1938); Gorky's *Yegor Bulychyov i drugiye* (Yegor Bulychyov and Co) (1941); Gorky's *Platon Krechet* (1939); *Partizany v stepyakh Ukrainy* (Partisans in the Ukrainian Steppes) (1943); *Gibel' eskadry* (The End of a Squadron) (1945); Latsis' *Syn rybaka* (The Fisherman's Son) (1949); Buryakovskiy's *Praga ostayotsya moyey* (Prague Remains Mine) (1951); *Vesenniy potok* (Spring Flood) (1951); *Yaroslava* (1953); Korneychuk's *Kryl'ya* (Wings) (1956); Pogodin's *Kremlyovskiy kuranty* (Kremlin Chimes) (1957); *Optimisticheskaya tragediya* (An Optimistic Tragedy) (1958); Zubar's *Doch' vetra* (Daughter of the Wind) (1963); Fed'kovich's *Dnestrovyye kruchi* (Slopes of the Dniester) (1964), etc; *Died*: 10 Feb 1965.

BORIS (real name: VIK, Boris Ivanovich) (1906-1965) Metropolitan of Odessa and Kherson from 1959; hon member, Moscow Theological Acad; *Born*: 27 Aug 1906 in Saratov; *Pos*: 1923-42 novice, priest-deacon and priest-monk, Saratov Spaso-Perobrazhensk Monastery; 1942-44 priest-monk and dean, Saratov Cathedral; 1944 archimandrite and dean, Saratov Cathedral; in same year ordained Bishop of Nezhin and Vicar of Chernigov Eparchy; 1945-47 Bishop of Chernigov and Nezhin; 1947 Bishop of Saratov and Vol'sk; 1949 Bishop of Chkalov; 1950 Bishop of Berlin and Germany and acting Exarch of Moscow Patriarchy in Western Europe; 1951 elevated to archbishop; 1954 simultaneously in charge of Yaroslavl' Eparchy; 1954-62 Exarch of Moscow Patriarchy in North and South America with title of Archbishop of the Aleutians and North America; 1956-59 simultaneously Archbishop of Odessa and Kherson; until 1956 also in charge of Krasnodar Eparchy; *Career*: until 1962 performed numerous diplomatic missions for Russian Orthodox Church; 1947 organized inauguration of Saratov Theological Seminary; 1950-54 apart from managing parishes of Moscow Patriarchy in Germany also organized parishes in Switzerland, France and England; suggested inviting President of German Evangelical Church, Pastor Niemoeller to USSR; campaigned for re-unification of Orthodox parishes in USA with Moscow Patriarchy and for return of emigres to USSR; accompanied Patriarch Aleksiy on his trips abroad and foreign patriarchs during visits to USSR; led Moscow Patriarchy deleg to Unified Church in Canada; *Awards*: right to wear cross on cowl (1954); Order of St Vladimir, 1st Class (1963); medal "For Valiant Labor in the Great Fatherland War"; *Died*: 16 Apr 1965 in Odessa; buried in cemetery of Spaso-Uspensk Monastery, Odessa.

BORISENKO, Anton Nikolayevich (1889-1937) Corps commander; veteran of Sov armored troops; CP member from 1918; *Born*: 7 July 1889 in vil Gora-Podol, Grayvoron Uyezd, Kursk Province, son of farmhand; *Educ*: 1915 grad Tiflis Ensigns School; 1923 grad Higher Acad Courses; *Pos*: 1897-1900 errand boy at an artisan weaving mill; 1900-06 shepherd; 1906-10 messenger and clerk at volost' office; 1910-15 at exchequer offices of various towns in Transcaucasia; from 1915 in Russian Army; during WW 1 at the Caucasian Front; 1917 chm of a regt comt, elected commander, 22nd Rifle Regt; Mar 1918 in Grayvoron organized Red Guards detachment and fought against Austro-German troops; 1918 commanded company and battalion on Eastern Front and on the Don; 1919 commanded regt on the Southern Front; 1919-21 commander, 26th Brigade, North-Caucasian, Southern and Transcaucasian Fronts; 1921-22 commander, 6th Separate Rifle Brigade; 1924-29 commandant, Ukr Centr Exec Comt Red Officiers' School, Khar'kov; 1929-32 commander, 45th Volhynian Rifle Div; 1932-37 commander of a mechanized corps, Kiev Mil Distr; 1921 helped to establish Sov regime in Geo; 1937 arrested by State Security organs; *Awards*: two Orders of the Red Banner; inscribed gold watch from RSFSR Centr Exec Comt; *Died*: 1937 in imprisonment; posthumously rehabilitated.

BORISEVICH, Ol'ga Mikhaylovna (1903-1947) Bel stage dir; *Born*: 1903; *Educ*: 1923-26 studied at Bel Theatrical Studio; *Career*: 1927-31 stage dir, 2nd Bel Drama Theater; 1931-46 stage dir, Bel Opera Studio and Bel Opera and Ballet Theater; 1937-39 asst stage dir, Bolshoy Theater, Moscow; *Productions*: operas: *Rusalka*; "Madame Butterfly"; "The Barber of Seville"; *Yevgeniy Onegin* (Eugene Onegin), etc; *Died*: 13 Sept 1947.

BORISOGLEBSKAYA, Anna Ivanovna (1868-1939) Actress; Pop Artiste of Ukr SSR from 1936; *Born*: 13 July 1968 in vil (now town) Sebezh, Pskov Oblast; *Educ*: grad Kharkov school of "Philantropic"; 1886 qualified as primary schoolteacher; *Career*: from 1886 schoolteacher in Novoselitsa (Kharkov Province); debut with amateur show in Slavyansk; 1888-1902 with M.L. Kropivnitskiy's company; then in number of major Ukr troupes — 1902-06 P.K. Saksaganskiy's and Karpenko-Kariy's; 1906-07 Kolesnichenko and Shatkovskiy's; 1907-17 N. Sadovskiy's; 1919-25 with Ukr Theater Assoc company; 1925-39 at Kiev's Franko Theater; founded Shevchenko State Ukr Theater, Kiev; artistically convincing and realistic portrayal of characters in classical and Sov drama; *Roles*: Terpelikha in Kotlyarevskiy's *Natalka-Poltavka* (Natalya the Poltavian); Shkandybikha in Mirnyy's *Limerivna*; Khivrya in *Sorochinskaya yarmarka* (Sorochintsy Fair); Tat'yana and Hanna in *Bestallanaya* (The Luckless Woman) and Karpenko-Kariy's *Sueta* (Grief); Lukash's mother in Lesya Ukrainka's *Lesnaya pesnya* (Forest Song); Poshlyopkina and Svakha in Gogol's *Revizor* (The Government-Inspector) and *Zhenit'ba* (The Wedding); Mariya Tarasovna, Ryzhova and Varvara in Korneychuk's *Platon Krechet, Pravda* (Truth) and *Bogdan Khmel'nitskiy*; Odarka in Kvitka-Osnov'yanenko's *Svatan'e na goncharovke* (Goncharovka Wooing), etc; *Died*: 26 Sept 1939 in Kiev.

BORISOGLEBSKIY, Viktor Valer'yanovich (1913-1964) Mil lawyer; lt-gen of Justice Corps; CP member from 1940; *Born*: 28 Jan 1913; *Educ*: 1937 completed higher law training; *Career*: from 1937 worked for Mil Procurator's office; then for seven years exec posts with CC, CPSU; 1954-57 (as col) dep chm, from 1957 chm, Mil Collegium, USSR Supr Court; assisted in trial of Abakumov and other officials of USSR Min of Internal Affairs and USSR Min of State Security; 1960 headed case against USAF U-2 pilot Powers; *Awards*: seven orders; medals; *Died*: 4 Feb 1964.

BORISOV, Aleksandr Alekseyevich (1866-1934) Landscape painter; *Born*: 1866; *Educ*: 1895-97 studied under Shishkin and Kuindzhi at Petersburg Acad of Arts; *Career*: realistic painter; specialized in landscapes of Far North; also wrote travel notes on his trips to the tundra and Novaya Zemlya; *Works*: paintings: "Novaya Zemlya Coastline" (1896); "In the Region of Eternal Ice"; "Spring Polar Night," etc; *Died*: 1934.

BORISOV (real name: GUROVICH), Boris Samoylovich (1873-1939) Actor; Hon Artiste of RSFSR from 1927; *Born*: 1873; *Educ*: higher legal training; *Career*: 1895-97 with Kropivnitskiy's Ukr Drama Company; 1899-1903 worked in Khar'kov, Kiev, etc; 1903-13 and from 1925 at Korsh Theater, Moscow; also acted at Moscow's Bat Theater and gave variety shows; *Roles*: Lyubim Tortsov in *Bednost' ne porok* (Poverty Is No Vice); Grumio in "Taming of the Shrew"; Vanyushin in Naydyonov's *Deti Vanyushina* (Vanyushin's Children); Potash in Montague and Glass' "Potash and Mother-of-Pearl"; Sinichkin in Lenskiy's *Lev Gurych Sinichkin*; Zupan in Strauss' "The Gipsy Baron"; Zhyoltukhin in A.N. Tolstoy's *Kasatka* (The Swallow); Shepshovich in Ash's *Bor Mesti* (God of Vengeance) etc; *Publ: Istoriya moyego smekha* (The Story of My Laughter) (1929); *Died*: 11 Nov 1939.

BORISOV, Ivan Nikolayevich (1860-1928) Railroad eng; *Born*: 1860; *Educ*: 1884 grad Petersburg Inst of Transport Eng; *Career*: from 1884 worked for railroad admin, advancing to dir of a railroad; 1911 transferred to Centr Bd, Min of Means of Communication; as head, Operations Dept, then dir, railroad admin; finally as Asst Min of Means of Communication; 1916 chm, Interdept Commission for Planning Railroad Construction; 1919 member, Financial and Econ Council, Main Comt for State Installations; from 1920 head, Main Means of Communication Bd, Pop Comrt of Means of Communication; helped reorganize railroad admin and restore railroads after WW 1 and Civil War; from 1923 USSR Dep Op Comr of Means of Communication; *Awards*: Scroll of All-Russian Centr Exec Comt; *Died*: 1928.

BORISOV, P.S. (1892-1939) Party and econ official; CP member from 1913; *Born*: 1892; *Career*: Party work in Petersburg, Tula and Samara; repeatedly arrested by Tsarist authorities; after 1917 Feb Revol Party work in Samara; after 1917 Oct Revol econ work in Petrograd and Moscow: dep Bd chm, Low-Tension Plants Trust; Bd chm, later manager, *Soyuzsel'mash* (All-Union Agric Machine-Building) Trust; member, RSFSR Supr Sovnarkhoz; from 1933 head, Main Agric Machine-Building Bd, USSR Pop Comrt of Heavy Ind; 1921-22 member, anti-Party "Workers' Opposition" group; signed the 22-signature Comintern declaration; soon after 9th Congress (1922) withdrew from opposition; arrested by State Security organs; *Died*: 1939 in imprisonment.

BORISOV, Sergey Alekseyevich (1905-1964) Govt official; USSR First Dep Min of For Trade from 1955; *Born*: 1905; *Career*: 1953-55 USSR Dep Min of For Trade; 1955-64 USSR First Dep Min of For Trade; headed many Sov trade delegs on visits to for countries and at sessions of UN econ and trade organs; *Awards*: Order of Lenin (1958); Order of the Red Banner of Labor (1955); *Died*: 1964.

BORISYAK, Aleksey Alekseyevich (1872-1944) Geologist and paleontologist; prof; member, USSR Acad of Sci from 1929; dir, Paleontological Inst, USSR Acad of Sci from 1930; *Born*: 3 Sep 1872 in Romny; *Educ*: 1896 grad Petersburg Mining Inst; *Career*: 1896-1932 served on Geological Comt, directing the paleontological service he founded; 1911-30 lecturer, then prof, Petersburg/Leningrad/Univ; from 1918 at Geological Museum, USSR Acad of Sci; 1923-29 corresp member, USSR Acad of Sci; 1930 founded Paleontological Inst, USSR Acad of Sci and directed it until his death; in geology developed the theory of facies, i.e., conditions for the formation and conversion of geological rocks depending on physical-geographical conditions and their historical evolution; his profound geosynclinal theory contributed to an understanding of the tectonic structure of the earth's core and of its development, regarding the history of the earth as a single regular process in the development of physical-geographical conditions and organic life; studied the geological structure of the Donets Basin and the Crimea the tectonics of the northwestern Donets Ridge; monographs on the fauna of the Jurassic molluscs of European Russia; studied Tertiary mammals; was the first to describe a number of ancient mammal fossils; wrote textbooks on paleontology, historical geology and the geological features of Siberia; wrote pop sci works and biographies of sci personalities; founded specialist periodicals: *Trudy Paleontologicheskogo Instituta AN SSR* (1932); *Paleontologicheskoye obozreniye* (1939); *Paleontologiya SSSR* (1935); organized major paleontological expeditions; *Publ: Kurs paleontologii* (A Course in Paleontology) (3 vol, 1905-19); *Kurs istoricheskoy geologii* (A Course in Historical Geology) (4th ed 1935); *Geologicheskiy ocherk Izyumskogo uyezda* (A Geological Study of Izyum Uyezd) (1905); *Sevastopol'skaya fauna mlekopitayushchikh* (Sebastopol Mammal Fauna) (No. 1-2, 1914-15) etc; *Awards*: Stalin Prize (1943); *Died*: 25 Feb 1944.

BORODIN, Ivan Parfen'yevich (1847-1930) Russian botanist and plant physiologist; Dr of Botany from 1886; prof from 1880; member, Russian (USSR) Acad of Sci from 1902; *Born*: 18 Jan 1847 in Novgorod; *Educ*: 1869 grad Physics and Mathematics Fac, Petersburg Univ; *Career*: 1869-80 lecturer, from 1880 prof, from 1894 hon pof, Petersburg Agric (then Forestry) Inst; also prof, Mil Med Acad; assoc prof, then prof extraordinary, Petersburg Univ; from 1900 chief botanist, Petersburg Botanical Garden and dir, Botanical Museum, Russian Acad of Sci; 1917-19 vice-pres, Acad of Sci; studied plant respiration and chlorophyll; did research on crystalline deposits in cells, distribution of hesperidine, dolcite and other substances in plants; wrote studies of fertilization in plants; 1897 sponsored establishment of freshwater biological station at Lake Bologoy; from 1916 founder and life pres, Russian Botanical Soc; supported some vitalist theories, which drew heavy criticism from A.K. Timiryazev; several species and genera have been named after him; *Publ*: master's thesis *Fizilogicheskiye issledovaniya nad dykhaniyem listonosnykh pobegov* (Physiological Studies of the Respiration of Foliate Suckers) (1876); *Kratkiy uchebnik botaniki* (A Short Botany Textbook) (1888); *Kurs anatomii rasteniy* (A Course in Plant Anatomy) (1888); *Protsess oplodotvoreniya v rastitel'nom tsarstve* (The Process of Fertilization in the Plant Kingdom) (1888); *Kurs dendrologii* (A Dendrology Course) (1891); *Protoplazma i vitalizm* (Protoplasm and Vitalism) (1894); *Kollektory i kollektsii po flore Sibiri* (Siberian Flora Collectors and Collections) (1908), etc; *Died*: 5 Mar 1930.

BORODIN (real name: GRUZENBERG), Mikhail Markovich (Party pseudonym: Kirill) (1884-1951) Govt and Party ovvicial; CP member from 1903; *Born*: 9 July 1884 in settlement Yanovichi, Vitebsk Province; *Educ*: studied at univ; *Career*: early 1900's joined revol movement; member, Bund (Jewish Soc-Democratic Party); 1904-late Jan 1905 emigré in Bern; 1905-06 active in Soc-Democratic org in Riga; 1905 deleg, Tammerfors RSDRP Conference and 1906 deleg, 4th (Amalgamative) RSDRP Congress; late 1906 emigrated to England; early 1907-July 1918 in USA; organized there special school for polit emigrés; active in Russian Polit Prisoners Aid Soc; 1918-22 with Comintern and RSFSR Pop Comrt of For Affairs; early 1923 visited China at invitation of Sun Yat-sen; 8 Sept 1923 – early July 1927 polit adviser, Kuomintang Centr Exec Comt; 1927 returned to USSR; until 1932 USSR Dep Pop Comr of Labor; 1932-34 dep dir, TASS; 1934-49 chief ed, Sov Information Bureau; from late 1949 chief ed, newspaper "Moscow News"; arrested by State Security organs; *Died*: 29 May 1951 in imprisonment; posthumously rehabilitated.

BORONIKHIN, Yevgeniy Aleksandrovich (? -1929) Actor; *Born*: date of birth unknown; *Educ*: 1910 grad Theatrical School, Lit and Art Soc; *Career*: from 1910 actor, Suvorin Theater, Petersburg; 1918-22 actor, Korsh Theater; from 1923 film work; *Roles*: film roles: Mikhail Beydeman in *Dvorets i krepost'*(Palace and Fortress) (1924); the First Husband in *Prostyye serdtsa* (Simple Hearts) (1924); Gapon in *Devyatoye yanvarya* (January 9th) (1925); Ganuimer in *Napoleon-Gaz* (The Napoleon–Gas) (1925); Gromov in *Na zhizn' i na smert'* (For Life and for Death) (1925); Nikol'skiy in *Stephan Khalturin* (1925); Fogel' in *Severnoye siyaniye* (Northern Lights) (1926); Nicholas I in *Dekabristy* (The Decembrists) (1927); Dal' in *Poet i tsar'* (Poet and Tsar) (1927); Pamburley in *Mogila Pamburleya* (Pamburley's Grave) (1928), etc; *Died*: 1929.

BOROVKOV, Aleksandr Konstantinovich (1904-1962) Orientalist and turcologist; Dr of Philological Sci; prof; corresp member, Uzbek Acad of Sci from 1943 and USSR Acad of Sci from 1958; Hon Sci Worker of Uzbek SSR from 1945; CP member; *Born*: 16 Mar 1904 in Tashkent; son of a foreman at Sulyuktin coal mine; *Educ*: 1928 grad Fac Oriental Studies, Centr Asian Univ; 1932 completed postgrad studies at Inst of Language and Logic, USSR Acad of Sci; *Career*: 1928-38 assist prof, then assoc prof, Eastern Inst, Leningrad; later prof, higher educ establishments in Leningrad and Tashkent; from 1934 held posts of senior assoc and head, Centr Asian Office and dep dir, Inst of Oriental Studies; senior assoc, Altay Languages Section and dep dir, Inst of Linguistics, USSR Acad of Sci; from 1958 also Bureau member, Dept of Lit and Language, USSR Acad of Sci; specialized in Turkic languages and lit; helped to devise alphabets and orthographic systems for Uzbek, Uygur, Karachay-Balkar and other Turkic languages; also collaborated on grammatical, lexicological and dialectological textbooks for these languages; compiled and edited Uzbek-Russian and Russian-Uzbek dictionaries; *Pubbl: Uchebnik uygurskogo yazyka* (An Uygur Textbook) (1935); *Ocherki karachayevobalkarskoy grammatiki* (An Outline Grammar of Karachay-Balkar) (1935); *Uzbekskiy literaturnyy yazyk v period 1905-17* (Literary Uzbek from 1905 to 1917) (1941); *Grammatika uzbekskogo yazyka* (An Uzbek Grammar) (1943); *Ocherki po istorii uzbekskogo yazyka* (An Outline History of Uzbek) (2vol, 1948), etc; *Awards*: Badge of Hon (1949); Order of Lenin (1953); *Died*: 12 Nov 1962.

BOROVSKIY, Pyotr Fokich (1863-1932) Med researcher and surgeon; prof from 1920; Dr of Med from 1891; discovered pathogenic agent of skin Leishmaniosis (Borovskiy's disease); *Born*: 1863; *Educ*: 1887 grad Mil Med Acad; *Career*: after graduation trained for professorship at Mil Med Acad; 1891 wrote doctor's thesis on tuberculosis of the bones and joints; from 1892 head, Bacteriological Section and intern, Surgical Dept, Tashkent Mil Hospitals; 1894 began research on the etiology of Oriental sores (Aden ulcer); 23 Sept 1898 delivered paper on the pathogenic agent of this disease to Russian Surgical Soc in Petersburg; Nov 1898 published results of his discovery in the *Voyenno-meditsinskiy zhurnal*; refuted the prevalent theory that Oriental sores were caused by a bacterial agent and provided a key to the propagation, treatment and prophylaxis of Leishmaniosis; his findings had a decisive influence on the research of A. Wright, Leishman and C. Donovan during the next five years; 1932 his discovery received int recognition; from 1920 until death head, Chair of Hospital Surgery, Centr Asian Med Inst, Tashkent; helped to organize public health service in Uzbek SSR; chm, Tashkent Soc of Physicians; his portrait hangs in the gallery of eminent parasitologists at the Molten Inst, Cambridge; wrote some 50 works on hospital surgery, etc; *Publ*: doctor's thesis *Materialy k ucheniyu o bugorchatke kostey i sustavov* (Material on the Theory of Tuberculosis of the Bones and Joints) (1891); article "The Etiology of the Saratov Plague (Oriental Sores)" (1898); article "Oriental Sores" (1899); *Kozhnyy Leishmaniosis* (Leishmaniosis of the Skin) (1949); *Awards*: Hero of Labor (1927); Order of the Red Banner of Labor (1927); *Died*: 1932.

BORTKEVICH, Viktor Mikhaylovich (1875-1944) Forestry specialist; cand of Agric Sci from 1938; *Born*: 10 Mar 1875 in Vitebsk; *Educ*: 1897 grad Petersburg Forestry Inst; *Career*: 1900-02 forestry work in Voronezh and Perm' Provinces; 1903-14 head, Sand and Gully Forestry Section, Poltava Province; 1919-22 with Main Forestry Comt; 1923-24 inspector for forestry conservation, Centr Agronomical Bd, Pop Comrt of Means of Communication; also forester and meliorationist, Centr Forestry Bd; 1925-31 specialist, Naturalization Dept, All-Union Inst of Applied Botany and New Crops, then All-Union Inst of Plant-Growing; 1932-35 with Pop Comrt of Communal Econ and Acad of Communal Econ; 1937-42 engaged in establishment of shrubs and trees at new construction sites in many cities; helped establish Arboreum in Tiberda Nature Preserve; introduced many for varieties of plants and shrubs into Russia and the USSR; made valuable collections of shrubs and trees; *Died*: 30 Nov 1944 in Moscow.

BORUKAYEV, Ramazan Aslanbekovich (1899-1967) Geologist; member, Kaz Acad of Sci from 1954; acad secr, Dept of Celestial and Terrestrial Sci, and Presidium member, Kaz Acad of Sci from 1956; dir, Inst of Geology, Kaz Acad of Sci from 1964; Hon Sci Worker of Kaz SSR from 1944; CP member from 1931; *Born*: 1899; *Educ*: 1931 grad Leningrad Mining Inst; *Career*: 1931-38 led geological survey groups; chief eng, then head, Kaz Geological Bd; from 1938 at various establishments of Kaz Branch, USSR Acad of Sci; from 1940 dep dir, Acad of Geological Sci; led teams which discovered and surveyed chromite deposit in Mugodzhary, phosphorite deposit in Karatau, the Tekeli and Nikolayev mixed metal deposits and the large copper deposit at Boshchekul'; wrote papers on regional geology, stratigraphy, tectonics, vulcanism and metallogeny; helped to compile prognostic metallogenetic maps of the USSR and Kaz; *Publ: Dopaleozoy i nizhniy paleozoy severovostoka Tsentral'nogo Kazakhstana* (The Pre-Paleozoic and the Lower Paleozoic in the Northeast of Central Kazakhstan) (1955); ed, *Soveshchaniye po unifikatsii stratigraficheskikh skhem dopaleozoya i paleozoya Vostochnogo Kazakhstana* (Conference of the Unification of Stratigraphic Charts of the Pre-Paleozoic and the Paleozoic in Eastern Kazakhstan) (1960); *Awards*: Order of the Red Star; Lenin Prize; medals; *Died*: 9 July 1967.

BORUTA, Kazis (1905-1965) Lith poet, writer and translator; *Born*: 6 Jan 1905 in vil Kulokay, now Lith SSR; *Educ*: 1924-26 studied at Kaunas Univ, 1926-30 at Vienna Univ; *Career*: 1921 first work published; 1928 ed, almanach "Storm"; 1932 ed, almanach "Labor"; 1930-31 founder and contributor, journal "The Third Front"; 1932-40 assoc, journal "Culture"; 1940-41 Presidium secr, Lith Acad of Sci; 1941-43 assoc, Inst of Lit, Lith Acad of Sci; translated Schiller, Ibsen, etc into Lith; *Publ*: collected verse "Hello" (1925); "Songs of the Swaying Willows" (1927); "Lithuania of the Crosses" (1927); "Our Daily Bread" (1934); "Verse and Poems" (1939); prose "The Wind on the Plowed Field" (1927); novels "Miracles in Wood" (1938); "Trip to the North" (1939); short story "The Mill of Baltaragis" (1945); fairytale "The Sky Is Falling" (1955); short story "Painful Relics" (1957); *Died*: 9 Mar 1965.

BORZILOV, Semyon Vasil'yevich (1893-1941) Mil commander; maj-gen of armored troops from 1940; Civil War veteran; *Born*: 1893; *Educ*: 1932 grad Red Army Acad of Mechanization and Motorization; *Career*: fought in WW 1; from 1918 in Red Army; 1918-21 squadron commander, then asst commander, 96th Cavalry Regt; 1921-30 regt commander; from 1932 asst div commander, then div commander, All-Union Centr Exec Comt Joint Mil School; 1941 commander, 7th Tank Div; *Awards*: two Orders of the Red Banner; *Died*: 28 Sept 1941 killed in combat against the Germans near Perekop; buried in Simferopol'.

BORZOV, Aleksandr Aleksandrovich (1874-1939) Geographer; prof; Hon Sci Worker of RSFSR from 1935; *Born*: 10 Aug 1874; *Educ*: 1900 grad Moscow Univ; *Career*: 1912 passed master's examinations and two years later began lecturing at Moscow Univ; from 1918 prof, from 1923 head, Dept of Geography, Moscow Univ; concentrated on relief of USSR; led research expedition in Moscow area, southern Bug Basin, southern (Bash) Ural region and elsewhere; determined contemporary features and developmental stages of moraine surfacesof Russian plains, with special attention to the relief of the "secondary moraine plains"; studied development of asymmetry of valleys in plains, rivers and watersheds according to geological, climatic and other conditions (*Borzov's Rule*); also examined the possiblility of determining the age of the relief from the degree of development of the deluvian layers; first to undertake a systematic geomorphological survey of the USSR; using the Moscow area as an example, he established the standard for geomorpholigical maps; published the first monograph on the relief of the European USSR; founded a sci school of geomorphologists; designed methods of mapping remote regions; edited a number of maps, including the "Large Soviet Atlas of the World"; devised first Sov visual aids for the teaching of geography in secondary schools; together with D. N. Anuchnin organized Geographical Research Inst at Moscow Univ and a geographical studies museum; *Publ: Kartiny po geografii Rossii* (Pictures on the Geography of Russia) (2 vol, 1908-17); *Geograficheskiye raboty* (Geographical Works) (2nd ed, 1954); *Died*: 6 Mar 1939.

BOSH, Mariya Petrovna (1899-1967) Party and govt official; CP member from July 1917; *Born*: 1899; *Career*: began work at age of 14; 1917-18 polit work in Red Army units; served with Red Cossack units in Ukraine; Party work in Tambov Province and Moscow; 1919-20 with CC, CP Ukr; secr, Chernigov Province Party Comt; chm, Chernigov Province Court; with Yekaterinoslav Province Party Comt; 1920 polit work in Moscow; 1922-29 research and publ work; 1929-34 exec posts with RSFSR Pop Comrt of Finance; 1932-36 Party work in Vladivostok and Khabarovsk; 1937-41 pensioned on med grounds; during WW 2 helped recruit civil defense for Lenin Rayon, Moscow; from Jan 1942 pensioner; *Died*: Nov 1967.

BOSH (GOTLIBOVNA), Yevgeniya Bogdanovna (1879-1925) Govt official; CP member from 1901; *Born*: 1879 in Ochakov, Nikolayev Province, daughter of a German immigrant mechanic; *Career*: until 1907 Party work in Voznesensk, Kherson Province; played leading role in reconstruction of Kiev Party org, destroyed in 1909; from 1910 to her arrest in 1912 secr, Kiev Party Comt; 1912 exiled to Siberia but managed to escape to USA; 1915 delegated by Party CC to attend Bern Conference In Switzerland; worked on ed bd of Bolshevik jounal *Kommunist*; also worked in Sweden and Norway; during WW 1 sided with Bukharin and Pyatakov on nationality question; 1917 in Petrograd, later in Kiev, where she worked for the Kiev Party Comt and Kiev Sov of Workers' Dep; helped to found Southwestern Oblast Party Union and was elected chm, Southwestern Oblast Party Comt; deleg at 6th Party Congress; active in overthrowing the Provisional Govt by persuading 2nd Guards Corps to move into Kiev; attended 1st All-Ukrainian Congress of Soviets in Khar'kov; was Pop Secr (Comr) of Int Affairs; also Secretariat chm of first Sov Ukr Govt; 1918, when the Germans were advancing into the Ukr, was Collegium member, Ukr Pop Comrt of Mil Affairs; upon the fall of Kiev left the govt and went to the front, leading Red Guards detachments in the areas of Bakhmach, Romny, Akhtyrka and Khar'kov; 1918 Party posts in Penza; 1918-19 special plen on the Caspian-Caucasian Front; simultaneously, member Astrakhan' Province Party Org; 1918 opposed conclusion of the Brest-Litovsk Peace Treaty; 1919 member, Defense Council of Lith-Bel Republic; then special plen, Sov Ukr Govt; active in Party org in Poltava and Chernigov as member, province Party org and member, Defense Council; 1920 chm, Mil-Historical Commission; also Presidium member, CC, All-Russian Agric and Forestry Workers' Union; from 1922 incapacitated by illness; 1923 sided with the Trotskyist oppostion; *Publ: Natsional'noye pravitel' stvo i Sovetskaya vlast' na Ukraine* (The National Government and the Soviet Regime in the Ukraine) (1918); *God bor'by* (A Year of Struggle) (1925); *Died*: 5 Jan 1925 committed suicide because of grave illness.

BOTSIYEV, Boris Timofeyevich (real first name and patronymic: Baron Tatariyyevich) (1901-1944) Ossetian poet, playwright and novelist; one of first Ossetian poets; CP member from 1926; *Born*: 13 Sept 1901 in vil Botsitikau, North Ossetia; *Educ*: 1928 grad Communist Univ of Workers of the East, Moscow; 1934 completed postgrad studies at North Ossetian Research Inst; *Career*: during youth worked as farm-hand, errand boy and newshawk in Vladikavkaz; 1921-22 exec secr, Alagir Gorge Revol Comt; *Publ*: novel "The Broken Chain" (1935); verse "The Kolkhoz Girl"; "Safirat"; "Dance Night"; "Three Girls"; "The Death of the Brave Man"; "The Lay of Ordzhonikidze"; poems "Brave Khadzy-myrza" and "Partisan Bibo" (1942); "October Joy" (1937); children's verse "The Pilots' Song", "The Children's Song"; verse fairytale "The Man and the Lion" (1939); *Died*: 20 Aug 1944.

BOYARSKIY, Yakov Osipovich (1890-1940) Trade-union and theater official; CP member from 1919; *Born*: 13 Mar 1890; *Educ*: studied at Minsk Business College; expelled for revol activities; *Career*: after 1917 Feb Revol chm, company comt, then regt comt, 101st Infantry Regt; 1919-21 in charge of agitation and propaganda, Tver' Party Comt; 1921-24 chm, Smolensk Trade-Union Council; 1924-25 chm, Orenburg and Kaz Trade-Union Council; 1925-29 chm, Tatar Trade-Union Council, Kazan', and Centr Volga Trade-Union Council, Kuybyshev; until 1936 chm, CC, Art Workers' Trade Union; 1936-37 first dep chm, Comt on Art Affairs, USSR Council of Pop Comr; 1937-39 dir, Moscow Arts Theater; 1939 arrested and imprisoned; *Publ: Rabotniki iskusstv v bor'be za kachestvo khudozhestvennoy produktsii* (Art Workers in the Struggle for Quality in Artistic Production) (1931); *Ot VIII k IX s'yezdu profsoyuzov* (From the 8th to the 9th Trade-Union Congress) (1932)); *Obshchestvenopoliticheskoye vospitaniye sovetskogo aktyora* (The Social and Political Training of the Soviet Actor) (1935); *Died*: 1940 in imprisonment; posthumously rehabilitated.

BOYCHENKO, Aleksandr Maksimovich (1903-1950) Ukr writer and Komsomol official; CP member from 1923; *Born*: 22 Sept 1903 in Kiev; *Educ*: grad higher primary school; *Career*: from 1920 member, Ukr Komsomol; from 1923 secr, Rayon Komsomol Comt, Kiev Okrug; 1928-30 secr, CC, Ukr Komsomol; 1930-32 secr-gen, CC, Ukr Komsomol; was Bureau member, CC, All-Union Komsomol and cand member, Org Bureau, CC, CP(B) Ukr; 1930 member, Ukr and USSR Centr Exec Comt; *Publ*: novelette "Youth" (1945); articles "For Lenin's Style in Work" (1931); "Along Lenin's Paths" (1931), etc; *Died*: 30 May 1950.

BOYTSOV, V. I. (1892-1944) Party official; CP member from 1918;

Born: 1892; *Career*: from 1913 sailor, Baltic Fleet; 1917 served with Caspian Naval Flotilla; elected secr, Flotilla CC; Nov 1917, with proclamation of Sov rule in Baku, fought against counter-revol elements; mid-Apr 1918 visited Lenin with sailors' deleg; then comr, Baku raid radio station; after collapse of Baku Commune fought for establishment of Sov regime in Azer; tehn various exec posts; 1939 at 18th Party Congress elected member, CPSU(B) Centr Auditing Commission; *Died*: 1944.

BOZHENKO, Vasiliy Nazarovich (1871-1919) Ukr partisan leader during Civil War; CP member from 1917; *Born*: 1871 in vil Berezhanka, son of a peasant; *Career*: until 1904 worked as a joiner in Odessa; 1904 arrested for distributing socialist leaflets and interned in Odessa Prison; 1904 fought in Russo-Japanese War with rank of sergeant-maj; 1907 arrested for involvement in 1905 Revol and sentenced to three years' imprisonment; 1915-17 worked as joiner in Kiev machine shops; helped to organize Kiev trade-union movement; Oct 1917 commanded a Red Guard unit in Bolshevik uprising in Kiev; 1918 commanded Red Guard and partisan units in struggle against Ukr Nat Centr Rada and against German occupation troops; 1918-19 commander, Tarashcha Partisan Regt, Tarashcha Brigade, 1st Ukr Sov (later 44th) Div; *Awards*: gold sword; *Died*: 19 Aug 1919; buried in Zhitomir.

BOZHKO, Savva Zakharovich (1901-1947) Ukr writer and journalist; *Born*: 1901 in vil Krutoyarovka, now Dnepropetrovsk Oblast; *Educ*: 1923 grad Artem Communist Univ; *Career*: started work as journalist; member, *Plug* (The Plow) lit group; *Publ: Nad kolybel'yu Zaporozh'ya* (Over the Cradle of Zaporozh'ye) (1925); *Chabanskaya zhizn'* (Chaban Life) (1927); *Ukrainskaya shampan'* (Ukrainian Champagne) (1930); novel *V stepyakh* (In the Steppes) (1930), etc; *Died*: 27 Apr 1947.

BRAMSON, Leontiy Moiseyevich (1869- ?) Jewish politician, lawyer and publicist; *Born*: 1869; *Career*: 1905 active member, "Leagne of Unions"; member form Kaunas Province, 1st State Duma; co-founder, Labor Group; 1917 represented Pop Socialists and Laborists (Trudoviki) in Exec Comt, Petrograd Sov of Workers and Soldiers' Dep; after 1917 Oct revol joined "Union of Renaissance"; 1927 emigrated and worked in Paris and Berlin as member, CC, Jewish Soc of Artisan and Agrarian Labor; wrote numerous articles on Jewish question; *Publ*: booklet *K istorii trudovoy partii. Trudovaya gruppa I Gosudarstvennoy dumy* (The History of the Labor Party. The Laborist Group in the 1st State Duma) (2nd ed, 1917); *Died*: date and place of death unknown.

BRAUDO, Yevgeniy Maksimovich (1882-1939) Music historian and critic; Hon Art Worker of RSFSR from 1932; *Born*: 20 Feb 1882 in Riga; *Educ*: 1911 grad Fac of History and Philology, Petersburg Univ; also studiet at Riga Polytech Inst, Riga School of Music and various German univ; *Career*: 1903 began working as a music critic; from 1914 taught history of music; 1916-21 lecturer; from 1921 prof, Inst of Art History; was *Pravda* music critic and edited music section of *BSE* (Large Soviet Encyclopedia); contributed to numerous art and music journals; *Publ: Vseobshchaya istoriya muzyki* (A General History of Music) (1922-27); *Aleksandr Porfir'yevich Borodin. Yego zhizn' i tvorchestvo* (Aleksandr Porfir'yevich Borodin. His Life and Works) (1922); *Nitsshe - muzykant* (Nietzsche the Musician) (1922); *Rikhard Vagner i Rossiya* (Richard Wagner and Russia) (1923); *Plutarkh o muzyke* (Plutarch on Music) (1923); *Svad'ba Figaro. Opyt razbora teksta i muzyki* ("The Mariage of Figaro." An Analysis of the Text and Music) (1926); co-author, *Boris Godunov Musorgskogo* (Moussorgsky's "Boris Godunov") (1927), etc; *Died*: 17 Oct 1939 in Moscow.

BRAUNER, Aleksandr Aleksandrovich (1857-1941) Zoological taxonomist, zootechnician and archeologist; *Born*: 25 Jan 1857 in Simferopol'; *Educ*: 1881 grad Novorossiysk Univ, Odessa; *Career*: worked as a civil servant, studying the fauna of the Ukr and Crimea in his free time; 1884 began publishing his research results; after 1917 Oct Revol became full-time sci and lecturer; 1918 co-founder Odessa Agric Inst, where he was in charge of the Chair of Animal Husbandry; 1923-25 sci dir, Odessa Agric Inst; 1933-35 consultant, All-Union Inst of Animal Hybridization and Acclimatization, Askaniya-Nova; wrote mainly on the mammals, birds, fish and insects of the Ukr and Crimea; in animal husbandry specialized on grey Ukr and red steppe cattle; studied the origins of domestic animals and demonstrated how their entire behavior patterns change under environmental influences; a number of mammalian and insect species and varieties bear his name; *Publ: Zhivotnovodstvo* (Animal Husbandry) (1922); *Porody sel'skokhozyaystvennykh zhivotnykh. 1 - Rogatyy skot* (Breeds of Agricultural Animals. 1 - Cattle) (1922); *Materialy k poznaniyu domashnikh zhivotnykh Rossii. 1 - Loshad' kurgannykh pogrebeniy Tiraspol'skogo uyezda Khersonskoy gubernii* (Material on the Identification of Domestic Animals. 1 - The Horse of the Burial Mounds of the Tiraspol' Uyezd, Kherson Province) (1916); *Sobaki kammenogo veka reki Amura* (Dogs of the Stone Age Along the Amur River) (1923); *Sel'skokhozyaystvennaya zoologiya* (Agricultural Zoology) (1923); *Died*: 5 May 1941.

BRAVIN (real name: VASYATKIN), Nikolay Mikhaylovich (1883-1956) Operetta artiste (baritone); Pop Artiste of RSFSR from 1954; *Born*: 25 Oct 1883 in Astrakhan'; *Educ*: 1906 grad School of Music in Astrakhan'; studied singing at Moscow Conservatory under Mazetti; *Career*: 1906-07 with Struyskiy's company in Astrakhan'; 1908-09 at Blyumental'-Tamarin's Operetta Theater; 1909-10 at the Bouffe Theater; 1910-15 at the Hermitage Theater; 1915-18 at Potopchina's Theater; 1918-22 at various theaters in the Far East; from 1922 appeared in Moscow at Dmitrovskiy Theater and later at Moscow Operetta Theater; *Roles*: Nazar Duma in Aleksandrov's *Svad'ba v Malinovke* (The Wedding at Malinovka); Savchuk in Blanter's *Na beregu Amura* (On the Banks of the Amur); Caesar Gallius in Dunayevskiy's *Vol'nyy veter* (The Free Wind); the General in Milyutin's *Devichiy perepolokh* (Girlish Turmoil); Nikita in Strel'nikov's *Kholopka* (The Bondwoman); Barinkay in Strauss' "Der Zigeunerbaron"; Danilo in Lehar's "Die Lustige Witwe"; Ferri in Kalman's "Silva", etc; *Died*: 10 June 1956 in Moscow.

BRAYTSEV, Vasiliy Romanovich (1878-1964) Surgeon; Dr of Med from 1910; prof from 1919; member, USSR Acad of Med Sci; Hon Sci Worker of RSFSR; *Born*: 1878, son of a peasant; *Educ*: 1906 grad Med Fac, Moscow Univ, summa cum laude; *Career*: after grad worked as intern in Moscow Univ clinics under such leading specialists as P. I. D'yakonov and A. V. Martynov; 1911-20 asst prof, then assoc prof, Hospital Surgery Clinic, Moscow Univ; from 1919 head, Chair of Operative Surgery, from 1920 head, Chair of Fac Surgery, Clinic of Moscow Higher Med School; from 1924 sci dir, Surgical Dept, Semashko Centr Clinical Hospital, USSR Min of Communications; 1937-64 simultaneously head, Chair of Clinical Surgery, Centr Inst of Postgrad Med Training, Moscow; during WW 2 ran a hospital in Moscow; 1946-47 chief surgeon, USSR Min of Health; delivered papers at surgical congresses and conferences of med soc; supervised writing of over 30 doctor's theses; three times dep chm, then chm, hon member and hon chm Moscow and Moscow Oblast Surgical Soc; hon member, All-Union Sov of Surgeons and Bel Surgical Soc; member, Int Soc of Surgeons; dep, Moscow City Sov; chief surgeon, USSR Railroads; devised artificial leather omosternal oesophagus; established principles of proctology in USSR; devised new methods of operating on the liver, gall bladder and mediastinum and surgery for fibrous osteodystrophy, lung cancer and pleurisy; founded pathoanatomical museum; wrote over 100 works on surgical problems, including several monographs; *Publ*: article *Maxillary Cysts* (1907); doctor's thesis *Rak pryamoy kishki, operativnoye yego lecheniye* (Cancer of the Rectum and Its Operative Treatment) (1910); *Funktsional'naya sposobnost' pochek pri khirurgicheskikh zabolevaniyakh* (The Postoperative Functional State of the Kidneys) (1913); *K voprosu o shve i peresadke krovenosnykh sosudov* (The Suturing and Transplantation of Blood Vessels) (1916); article "Gunshot Wounds of the Blood Vessels (Hematomas and Aneurisms)" (1917); article "Experimental Plastic Formation of an Artificial Skin Oesophagus" (1928); article "Some Forms of Abdominal Adhesion" (1929); *Ostryy appenditsit* (Acute Appendicitis) (1946); *Fibroznaya osteodistrofiya* (Fibrous Osteodystrophy) (1947); *Zabolevaniya pryamoy kishki* (Diseases of the Rectum) (1952); *Vrozhdyonnyye (dizontogeneticheskiye) obrazovaniya sredosteniya i lyogkikh* (Congenital [Dysontogenetic] Formations of the Mediastinum and the Lungs) (1960); *Awards*: two Orders of Lenin; Order of the Red Banner of Labor; medals; *Died*: 9 July 1964.

BRENKO, Anna Alekseyevna (1848-1934) Russian actress and theater figure; Hon Artiste of RSFSR from 1934; *Born*: 1848; *Educ*: grad higher pedag courses; drama training in Petersburg under Boborykin, Tarnovskiy, and Vasil'yeva; also studied abroad; *Career*: 1878-82 actress at Malyy Theater; 1879 organized Moscow troupe called "Free Players"; this theater soon ran into financial difficulties, leading to its closure in 1882; subsequently taught in Kiev and Petersburg; 1885-87 acted at Aleksandrinskiy Theater, Petersburg; 1900 organized workers' amateur theater in

Moscow; 1914 from pupils at Prechistenskiy courses in Moscow formed the Workers' Theater which entertained Red Army units during the Civil War; in 1920's ran studio at Mocow Dept of Educ; *Publ*: two plays: *Sovremennyy lyud* (Modern People) (1883) and *Dotayevtsy; Died*: 1934.

BRESHKO-BRESHKOVSKAYA, Yekaterina Konstantinovna (1844-1934) Politician; organizer and leader, Socialist-Revol Party; *Born*: 1844 in Chernigov Province, daughter of rich Verigo family; *Career*: late 1860s married landowner and justice of the peace Breshko-Breshkovskiy; her educ and enlightenment of the peasants dates from this time; came under police surveillance for her cultural activities; 1873 left family and went out "into the people"; toured the Ukr on foot conducting propaganda among the peasants; 1874 organized revol circles in Kiev along with Stefanovich and Fisher; 1874 arrested and after three years in jail tried with 193 others for "revol propaganda in the Empire"; sentenced to five years' hard labor; 1879 hard labor commuted to deportation to Barguzin, Transbaykal Oblast; escaped from settlement but was arrested and sentenced to four years' hard labor in Kara and 40 lashes; latter punishment was not carried out; after serving her term of hard labor in Kara deported to Selenginsk and in early 90's to Irkutsk where she engaged in lit work until 1896; after amnesty returned to Russia; reacted strenuously against budding Soc-Democratic movement here; active in org and work of Socialist-Revol Party; organized circles, helped plan acts of terrorism, wrote pamphlets, appeals and articles; 1903, after destruction of Socialist-Revol org, moved to Switzerland and later to America; 1905 returned to Russia and completely dedicated herself to party work; belonged to extreme right wing of Socialist-Revol Party and maintained very close ties with liberal intellectuals; 1907 betrayed to authorities; 1910 deported to Eastern Siberia for membership of Socialist-Revol Party; despite advanced age again tried to escape but was arrested and confined in Irkutsk Jail; May 1914 deported under escort first to Yakutsk, then Irkutsk and finally Minusinsk; after 1917 Feb Revol returned to Petrograd, was elected to Constituent Assembly and occupied important position in ranks of the extreme right wing of Socialist-Revol Party, giving her backing to Kerensky's Provisional Govt; violently opposed to Oct Revol; 1918 member, Constituent Assembly Comt in Samara; 1919 emigrated to USA; 1923 moved to Czechoslovakia; from 1927 lived in Paris and contributed to Socialist-Revol organ *Dni*; in Russia was nicknamed "Grandmother of the Russian Revol"; *Publ: Avtobiografiya* (Autobiography) (1917); *Died*: 1934.

BREYTERMAN, Aleksandr Davydovich (1883-1967) Econ; Dr of Econ Sci; prof from 1935; head, Chair of Econ Geography, Leningrad Inst of Eng and Econ; *Born*: 1883 in Moscow; *Educ*: 1908 grad Petersburg Polytech Inst; *Career*: from 1908 lecturer in polit econ and econ geography, Petersburg Higher Business College; contributed to various econ publ; during WW 1 econ statistician, Special Food Conference 1918-30 and 1933-34 assoc, then senior specialist, Commission for the Study of Natural Productive Resources, USSR Acad of Sci; 1920-66 consecutively lecturer, prof and head, Chair of Econ Geography, Leningrad Inst of Eng and Econ; specialized in econ history of pre-revol Russia and econ geography of USSR; wrote over 200 works; *Publ: Dorogvizna i vneshniy tovaroobmen* (High Prices and Internal Commodity Circulation) (1922); coauthor and ed, *Potrebleniye sakhara v Rossii* (Sugar Consumption in Russia) (1916); *Tsvetnyye metally* (Non-Ferrous Metals) (1925); *Mednaya promyshlennost SSSR i mirovoy rynok* (The Soviet Copper Industry and the World Market) (3 vol, 1922-30); *Ekonomicheskaya geografiya SSSR. Chast' 1. Geografiya tyazhyoloy promyshlennosti* (The Economic Geography of the USSR. Part 1. The Geography of Heavy Industry) (1958), etc; *Died*: 30 Nov 1967.

BRICHKINA, Sof'ya Borisovna (1883-1967) Revolutionary; Party official; CP member from 1903; *Born*: 15 Mar 1883; *Educ*: 1932 grad Inst of Red Prof; *Career*: began work at age 13; from 1900 in revol movement; 1906 arrested, but soon released; 1917 secr, Moscow Sov; 1919 head, Secretariat, RSFSR Council of Pop Comr and Labor and Defense Council; 1920 dep manager, CC, RCP(B); 1921-29 with Comintern Exec Comt; worked for ed staff of newspaper *Gudok* and for State Publ House; 1929-31 exec econ work; from 1932 dep dir, Inst of Criticism and Bibliography; 1934 with Comintern Exec Comt; 1935-37 with Presidium Secretariat, All-Russian Centr Exec Comt; from 1938 dep dir, Museum of the Peoples of the USSR; 1939-41 worked for RSFSR Pop Comrt of Educ; 1941 dep chm, Oyrot-Tura (Altay Kray) City Exec Comt; later chief ed, Oblast Radio Comt; from 1943 with RSFSR Pop Comrt of Educ; subsequently research work with Inst of Marxism-Leninism, CC, CPSU; from 1949 pensioner; *Died*: 11 Sept 1967.

BRIK, Osip Maksimovich (1888-1945) Russian writer, lit theoretician and dramatist; *Born*: 16 Jan 1888 in Moscow; *Educ*: grad Moscow Univ; *Career*: 1915 first work published; 1914-23 organizer, formalist lit group, Soc for the Study of the Theory of Poetic Language; published *Sborniki po teorii poeticheskogo yazyka* (Anthologies on the Theory of Poetic Language) (1916-17); in collaboration with Mayakovsky edited newspaper *Iskusstvo kommuny* (1918), journal *Lef* (1923-25) and *Novyy Lef* (1927-28); publicized *Lef* theories and "fact lit" and "soc order" slogans; *Publ*: research works: *Zvukovyye povtory* (Assonance) (1917); *Poetika* (Poesy) (1919); *Usluzhlivyy estet* (The Obliging Esthete) (1923); coauthor, play *Radio Oktyabr* (Radio October) (1926); *Ritm i sintaksis* (Rhythm and Syntax) (1927); film scripts *Potomok Chingis-khana* (Descendant of Genghis Khan) (1928); mime *Moskva gorit* (Moscow Is Burning) (1930); libretto for operas: *Kamarinskiy muzhik* "Kamara Peasant" (1933); *Imeniny* (The Name-Day) (1935); "Blok and Mayakovskiy" (1936); *Ivan Groznyy* (Ivan the Terrible) (1941), etc; *Died*: 22 Feb 1945 in Moscow.

BRILL', Yefim Aleksandrovich (1896-1959) Stage dir; Hon Art Worker of RSFSR from 1940; CP member from 1941; *Born*: 1896; *Educ*: 1920 grad Odessa Theatrical School; *Career*: from 1915 stage dir in Kishinev and Odessa; 1928 helped found Khar'kov Young Playgoers' Theater; 1930-36 worked in Moscow at former Korsh Theater, Young Playgoers' Theater and Centr Theater of the Red Army; then at Rostov, Gorky, Sverdlovsk and Chelyabinsk theaters; from 1954 chief stage dir, Chelyabinsk Theater; from 1923 taught drama; *Productions*: Virta's *Zemlya* (Land) (1937); Gorky's *Zykovy* (The Zykovs) (1937); Rakhmanov's *Bespokoynaya starost'* (Turbulent Old Age) (1938); Chekhov's *Chayka* (The Seagull) (1940); Pogodin's *Kremlyovskiye kuranty* (Kremlin Chimes) (1940); Chirskov's *Pobediteli* (The Victors) (1947); Gogol's *Revizor* (The Government Inspector) (1952); Verdi's "Othello" (1945); *Awards*: Stalin Prize (1946); *Died*: 27 July 1959.

BRITAYEV, Yelbyzdyko Tsopanovich (1881-1923) Ossetian playwright; founder of Ossetian dramaturgy and Ossetian nat theater; *Born*: 22 Mar 1881 in vil Dalagkau, Ter'Oblast; *Educ*: 1917 grad Law Fac, Petrograd Univ; *Career*: 1905-07 took part in Revol as a Socialist-Revolutionary; imprisoned and then exiled to Ossetia; 1912 published Ossetian lit and art journal "Sunbeam" in Petersburg; 1917 member, "League of United Highlanders" and ed of its journal "Highland Life" in Vladikavkaz (now Ordzhnikidze); 1918 left politics and became a teacher in vil Dzuarikau; from 1920 worked for educ authorities in Vladikavkaz; *Publ*: plays "The Man Who'd Been in Russia" (1902); "Death Before Dishonor" (1903); historical plays: *Khazbi* (1907); "Two Sisters" (1908); tragedy based on Ossetian folk theme "Amran" (1913), etc; *Died*: 25 Sept 1923 in Vladikavkaz.

BRITSKE, Ergard Viktorovich (1877-1953) Chemist and metallurgist; member, USSR Acad of Sci from 1932; *Born*: 20 Jan 1877 in Riga; *Educ*: 1903 grad Riga Polytech Inst; *Career*: 1906-10 assoc prof, from 1910 prof, Riga Polytech Inst; lectured on chem eng, metallurgy, technol of building materials, and mineral fertilizers; from 1919 prof, Plekhanov Inst of Nat Econ; from 1921 prof, Moscow Higher Tech College; working for All-Russian Sovnarkhoz, helped to develop mineral fertilizer ind, establish major chemical plants and open up chemical deposits; also helped to organize Inst of Applied Mineralogy and, in 1919, Fertilizer Inst (later renamed Sci Inst for Fertilizers and Insectofungicides); 1923-38 dir, Sci Inst for Fertilizers and Insectofungicides; from 1934 member, All-Union Lenin Acad of Agric Sci; 1936-39 vice-pres, USSR acad of Sci and acad secr, Dept of Tech Sci, USSR Acad of Sci; from 1929 Presidium member, USSR Acad of Sci; during WW 2 dep chm, Commission for Mobilizing the Resources of the Urals for Defense Needs, USSR Acad of Sci; 1932 launched specialized journal on chemical analysis *Zavodskaya laboratoriya*; performed basic research in three main fields: the physiochemical and technol problems of processing raw materials in metallurgy; the chemistry and technol of mineral raw materials (phosphates, natural salts, etc); and the development of the Soviet chemical ind; introduced methods for extracting phosphorus with the help of gases and slags, the continuous extraction of phosphoric acid from phosphorites, and applications for titano-magnetites; made important contributions to the theory of metallurgical processes, particulary with regard to the reduction of sulphide ores; *Publ*: coauthor, *Termicheskoye polucheniye fosfornoy kisloty i vysokoprotsentnyy fosfatov* (The Heat Extraction of Phosphoric Acid and High-Grade Phosphates) (1929); coauthor, *Termicheskiye konstanty neorganicheskikh veshchestv* (The Thermal Constants of Inorganic Substances) (1949); *Awards*: Lenin Prize; Stalin Prize (1942); *Died*: 28 Sept 1953.

BRODSKAYA, Sarra Akimova (1887-1967) Party official; CP member from 1909; *Born*: 1887; *Career*: from 1905 in revol movement; 1906-09 lived in Paris; joined in French workers' movement; 1909 in Odessa then Kiev Bolshevik org; arrested for revol activities; 1915, after leaving prison, underground work in Kiev then Moscow; arrested for revol propaganda among soldiers and exiled to Irkutsk Province; after 1917 Feb Revol elected secr, Sokolniki Rayon, Moscow; during 1917 Oct Revol member, Revol Comt; 1918-1919 secr, Basman Rayon Sov; 1919-21 secr, Basman Rayon RCP(B) Comt; then exec Party posts; from 1955 pensioner; *Died*: Mar 1967.

BRODSKIY, Isaak Izrailevich (1884-1939) Painter and graphic artist; Hon Art Worker of RSFSR from 1932; *Born*: 6 Jan 1884 in vil Sofiyevka near Berdyansk; *Educ*: 1902 grad Odessa Art School; 1908 grad Petersburg Acad of Arts under I. Ye. Repin; *Career*: 1903-04 participated in exhibitions of the *Peredvizhniki* and the Union of Russian Artists; later at int exhibitions in Rome, Venice, London and Munich; 1910 visited Gorky on Capri and painted his portrait; after Oct Revol became "court portraitist" and painted a whole gallery of CP figures; member, Assoc of Artists of Revol Russia; 1934-39 prof and dir, All-Russian Acad of Arts; 1930 the Brodskiy Art Museum was founded in Berdyansk and the Brodskiy Apartment Museum in Leningrad; *Works*: sketch "The Beautiful Funeral" (1906); canvases: "Fallen Leaves," "Winter" (1913); "Portrait of L. M. Brodskaya" (1913); "The Summer Garden" (1916); "Lenin and the Demonstration" (1919); "Official Opening of the Second Comintern Congress" (1920-24); "Execution of the 26 Baku Commissars" (1925); "Lenin in Smol'ny" (1930); landscape "Park Alley" (1930); "Lenin's Speech to Red Army Units Leaving for the Polish Front" (1933); portraits of CP figures: Stalin, Voroshilov, Frunze, Menzhinskiy, Molotov, Kirov, Kuybyshev, Zhdanov, Lazar' Kaganovich and Ordzhonikidze, etc; many of his pictures are exhibited at the Tret'yakov Gallery, the Centr Museum of the Sov Army, the Brodskiy Apartment Museum and other galleries; *Publ: Moy tvorcheskiy put'* (My Career) (1940); *Awards*: Order of Lenin (1940); *Died*: 14 Aug 1939 in Leningrad.

BRODSKIY, Nikolay Leont'yevich (1881-1951) Lit historian and pedagogue; prof; member, RSFSR Acad of Pedag Sci; *Born*: 15 Nov 1881 in Yaroslavl'; *Educ*: 1904 grad Moscow Univ; *Career*: from 1918 assoc prof, then prof, Moscow Univ; gave gen courses on Russian lit and special seminars at many higher educ establishments in Moscow and other cities; specialized in methods of teaching lit; long before 1917, as supporter of cultural history school, criticized lack of ideological content in lit works; after 1917 Oct Revol contributed to Marxist lit history studies; did research on 19th-Century Russian lit and its connections with the development of Russian soc thought; wrote numerous studies of Belinskiy, Herzen, the Slavophiles, the Westernizers, Chernyshevskiy, Dostoyevsky and the development of the Russian theater in the 18th-20th Centuries; made a detailed study of Turgenev's papers; edited lit history collections: *Turgenev i yego vremya* (Turgenev and His Time) (1923); *I.S. Turgenev* (1940); *Tvorcheskiy put' Dostoyevskogo* (Dostoyevsky's Creative Career) (1924), etc; *Publ*: articles "Has Belinskiy Been Unmasked?" (1914) and "Chernyshevskiy and His Readers in the 1860's" (1914); studies: *Zamysli I.S. Turgeneva* (Turgenev's Intentions) (1917); *Turgenev i russkiye sektanty* (Turgenev and the Russian Sectarians) (1922); *Belinskiy i Turgenev* (Belinskiy and Turgenev) (1924); *A.S. Pushkin. Biografiya* (A.S. Pushkin. A Biography) (1937); *M.Yu. Lermontov. Biografiya* (M.Yu. Lermontov. A Biography) (1945); *V.G. Belinskiy* (1946); *'Borodino' Lermontova* (Lermontov's "Borodino") (1947); *I.S. Turgenev* (1950); *'Yevgeniy Onegin' roman Pushkina. Kommentariy* (A Commentary on Pushkin's Novel "Eugene Onegin") (1957), etc; *Died*: 5 June 1951 in Moscow.

BRONSKIY, Mechislav Genrikhovich (1882-1941) Govt official; Polish Soc-Democrat, then Bolshevik; *Born*: 1882 in Poland, son of a cotton-mill owner; *Educ*: grad secondary school, then registered at Munich Polytech Inst; 1903 transferred to Econ Fac, Munich Univ; *Career*: from 1900 active in Polish "progressive" student movement, siding with Soc-Democrats; 1902 joined Soc-Democratic Party of Poland and Lith; until 1905 worked mostly abroad; from Feb 1905 in Warsaw as propagandist, then member of Party comt in various towns; several times arrested and detained for short periods; 1906 member, ed bd, centr Party organ *Czerwony Sztandar*, Warsaw; fall 1966 arrested in Lublin and imprisoned until late 1907; upon release went to Switzerland, lived in Zurich, joined Swiss Soc-Democratic Party and worked in its local org; regularly contributed to Swiss Soc-Democratic newspapers; was member, Party Group, Polish Soc-Democratic Party; with the start of WW 1 adoped internationalist stand; deleg of Polish Soc-Democratic Party at Zimmerwald and Kienthal Conferences; summer 1917 returned to Russia; agitator and propagandist, Petrograd RSDRP(B) Comt; member, ed bd, Polish Party newspaper *Trybuna*; after 1917 Oct Revol worked for newspaper *Pravda*; council member, State Bank; until spring 1919 RSFSR Dep Pop Comr of Trade and Ind; council member, Supr Sovnarkhoz; simultaneously member, All-Russian Centr Exec Comt of several convocations; 1918, as "left-wing" Communist, opposed conclusion of Brest Peace Treaty; 1920-22 Sov polit rep in Austria; from 1924 Collegium member, USSR Pop Comrt of Finance; 1927 member, Communist Acad, and prof, Chair of Econ Policy, 1st Moscow Univ; exec ed, journal *Sotsialisticheskoye khozyaystvo*; arrested by State Security organs; *Publ*: "Die gutsherrlichbäuerlichen Verhältnisse und die Bauernfrage in Polen in XVIII Jahrh." (1914); "Wer soll die Kriegsrechnung bezahlen" (1920) (under the pen-name of M.I. Braun); *Voprosy ekonomicheskoy politiki* (Problems of Economic Policy) (1924); *Died*: 1941 in imprisonment.

BROUNOV, Pyotr Ivanovich (1853-1927) Meteorologist; Dr of Meteorology and Physical Geography from 1886; prof from 1891; corresp member, Russian (USSR) Acad of Sci from 1914; *Born*: 2 Jan 1853 in Petersburg; *Educ*: 1875 grad Fac of Physics and Mathematics, Petersburg Univ; *Career*: 1877-80 assoc, Weather Service Dept, Main Physical Observatory; 1891-95 prof, Kiev Univ; 1899-1916 prof of geography, from 1917 head, Chair of Meteorology, Petersburg (Leningrad) Univ; 1917-25 simultaneously lecturer in meteorology, Geographical Inst; 1895 founder-dir, Dnieper meteorological network; from 1897 head, Meteorological Bureau, Learned Comt, Min of Agric; devised rules for predicting the path of cyclones on the basis of rising and falling barometric pressure and the position of isotherms on the synoptic chart; also explained the formation and movement of cyclones; detected "critical periods in the life of crops when they are particularly sensitive to heat or shortage of moisture; 1925 compiled isoclimatic atlas of world; *Publ: Postupatel'noye dvizheniye tsiklonov i antitsiklonov v Yevrope i osobenno v Rossii* (The Gradual Movement of Cyclones and Anticyclones in Europe with Special Reference to Russia) (1882); *Vremennyye barometricheskiye maksimumy v Yevrope* (Temporary Barometric Highs in Europe) (1886); *Sel'skokhozyaystvennaya meteorologiya. Rossiya v kontse XIX veka* (Agricultural Meteorology. Russia at the End of the 19th Century) (1900); *Kurs fizicheskoy geografii* (A Course in Physical Geography) (1910); *Klimaticheskiye usloviya Leningradskogo kraya* (Climatic Conditions in Leningrad Kray) (1923); *Atmosfernaya optika* (Atmospheric Optics) (1924); *Klimaticheskiye i sel'skokhozyaystvennyye rayony Rossii* (The Climatic and Agricultural Zones of Russia) (1924); *Kurs meteorologii* (A Course in Meteorology) (2 vol, 1927); *Died*: 24 Apr 1927 in Leningrad.

BROYDO, Grigoriy Isaakovich (1885-1956) Govt official; CP member from 1918; *Born*: 1885; *Career*: 1903 joined RSDRP and sided with Bolsheviks; 1905 agitation work among troops; ed, newspaper *Soldatskaya gazeta*; during 1917 Feb Revol head, Tashkent Sov; sided with Menshevik defensists; 1918 re-joined Bolshevik Party; 1919 member, Revol Mil Council, 1st Army on Eastern Front; later head, For Relations Dept, Turkestani Commission; 1920 sent to Khiva as plen, Turkestani Commission; 1921-23 RSFSR Dept Pop Comr of Nationality Affairs; helped organize Communist Eastern Workers' Univ; until 1926 rector of this univ; from 1933 first secr, CC, CP Tadzh; 1934-41 RSFSR Dep Pop Comr of Educ; dir, Party Publ House; member, USSR Centr Exec Comt; *Publ: Natsional'no-kolonial'nyy vopros* (The Nationality and Colonial Problem) (1924); *Natsional'nyy vopros i VKP(b)* (The Nationality Problem and the CPSU(B)) (1925), etc; *Died*: 1956.

BRUNO, G.I. (1889-1945) Govt official; CP member from 1906; *Born*: 1889; *Career*: Party work in Riga, Petersburg and Irkutsk; often arrested; after 1917 Feb Revol chm, Minusinsk Okrug Sov; took part in Oct 1917 armed uprising in Petrograd; 1918-19 fought in Civil War; from 1920 govt and admin posts; Collegium member, Main Metal Ind Bd; chm, Ukr Agric Machine-Building Trust; Bd chm, All-Russian Agric Machinery and Implements Syndicate; assoc, Inst for the Designing of Electric Power Plants, RSFSR Pop Comrt of Heavy Ind; 1921-22 sided with "Workers' Opposition" group, but broke with it shortly after 11th Party Congress; arrested by State Security organs; *Died*: 1945 in imprisonment.

BRUSHTEYN, Sergey Aleksandrovich (1873-1947) Physiotherapist and specialist in postgrad med training; prof; Dr of Med from 1910; Hon Sci Worker of RSFSR; *Born*: 1873; *Educ*: 1897 grad Med Fac, Kazan' Univ; *Career*: after grad worked under V. M. Bekhterev in Clinic for Nervous and Mental Diseases, Mil Med Acad; completed specialist training under Prof Gerhardt, Jolly, Mendel, Leiden, Oppenheim, Marie and Babinskiy; for many years dir, Leningrad Inst of Postgrad Med Training; founder-dir, Leningrad State Physiotherapy Inst; member, Learned Med Council, RSFSR Pop Comrt of Health; exec ed, *Zhurnal dlya usovershenstvovaniya vrachey* and journal *Fizioterapiya*; chm, All-Union Assoc of Physiotherapists; hon chm, Leningrad Physiotherapy Soc; hon member, Odessa Balneological Soc; asst chm, All-Union Rheumatism Comt; considered a pioneer of Russian physiotherapy; devised several therapeutic methods; wrote over 200 works on various aspects of physiotherapy and related subjects, notably *O vazomotornom tsentre prodolgovatogo mozga* (The Vasomotoric Center of the Medulla Oblongata) (1901), in which he established that this center is located in the region of the formatio retricularis griseae; ed of a manual on physiotherapeutic methods; *Publ*: doctor's thesis *O vliyanii obshchikh elektrosvetovykh vann na sochetatel'no-dvigatel'nyy refleks u cheloveka* (The Influence of Electrophototherapeutic Baths on the Combinative-Motor Reflex) (1910); *Diatermiya* (Diathermy) (1929); coauthor and ed, *Rukovodstvo po fizicheskim metodam lecheniya* (A Manual of Physical Treatment Methods) (4 vol, 1928-30); *Fizioterapiya detskogo vozrasta* (Child Physiotherapy) (1931); *Fizicheskiye metody lecheniya nervnykh bolezney* (Physical Methods of Treating Nervous Diseases) (1931); articles in German and French med journals; *Died*: 1947.

BRUSILOV, Aleksey Alekseyevich (1853-1926) Russian mil commander; cavalry gen; one of most outstanding Russian Army generals of WW 1; *Born*: 1 Sept 1853 in Tiflis, son of a Russian Army Gen; *Educ*: 1872 grad Cadet School for Sons of the Nobility; *Pos*: from 1872 officer, Russian Army; fought in 1877-78 Russo-Turkish War; 1902-06 commandant, Cavalry Officers School, Petersburg; 1906-12 commander, 2nd Guards Cavalry Div, 14th Army Corps; 1912-13 asst commander, Warsaw Mil Distr; 1913-14 commander, 12th Army Corps; 1914-16 commander, 8th Army; 1916-17 commander in chief, Southwestern Front; May-July 1917 supr commander in chief of Russian Army; July-Oct 1917 special advisor to the Provisional Govt; from May 1920 in Red Army; 1920-23 cavalry advisor to RSFSR Revol Mil Council; chief inspector, RSFSR Main Bd for Horse Breeding and Stud Farming; 1923-24 inspector of cavalry, Red Army; from 1924 retired yet available to RSFSR Revol Mil Council for especially important missions; *Career*: June 1916 while commander in chief of Southwestern Front, broke through Austro-Hungarian defense zone (so called Lutsk break-through); at the beginning of 1917 Feb Revol put pressure on Tsar Nicholas II to abdicate in favor of a more authoritative person; took resolute action against Bolsheviks and Bolshevik propaganda among his troops; as supr commander in chief signed order introducing field courts and death penalty at front as a means of tightening mil discipline; July 1917 relieved of post as supr commander after Russian Army's abortive counter-offensive; May 1920, after Polish troops advanced into Russia, offered his services to Sov Govt; bonded some former generals into the Special Conference under the Sov supr commander in chief which appealed to all former officers to defend Russia against the Polish invaders; *Publ: Moi vospominaniya* (My Memoirs) (1963); *Died*: 17 Mar 1926 in Moscow from pneumonia; interred with mil honors at Novodevich'ye Cemetery.

BRUSILOVSKIY, Lev Yakovlevich (1890-1962) Neuropathologist; prof from 1923; Dr of Med Sci from 1935; co-founder and dep chief ed, *Bol'shaya Meditsinskaya Entsiklopediya* (Large Medical Encyclopedia) (1st and 2nd ed); *Born*: 1890; *Educ*: 1919 grad Med Fac, 1st Moscow State Univ; *Pos*: 1910-33 intern, asst prof, then assoc prof, 1939-41 prof, Clinic for Nervous Diseases, 1st Moscow State Univ; 1941-44 consultant to evacuation hospitals; 1945-62 consultant neuropathologist, Moscow Centr Clinic, USSR Min of Health; *Career*: ed, *Entsiklopedicheskiy slovar' voyennoy meditsiny* (An Encyclopedic Dictionary of Military Medicine); *Entsiklopedicheskiy meditsinskiy spravochnik dlya srednego meditsinkogo personala* (An Encyclopedic Medical Reference Book for Nursing and Technical Personnel); *Entsiklopedicheskiy meditsinskiy spravochnik dlya voyennykh fel'dsherov* (An Encyclopedic Medical Reference Book for Medical Orderlies); suggested that the 2nd ed of the "Large Medical Encyclopedia" include "stereoscopic" illustrations and phonograph records of heartbeats, respiration, etc; wrote over 100 papers on clinical neurology, pathomorphology and clinical anatomical parallels, the prophylaxis of nervous diseases, neurosurgery and the study of the working capacity of mental invalids; *Publ*: coauthor, *Zemlyetryaseniye v Krymu i nevropsikhicheskiy travmatizm* (The Crimean Earthquake and Neuropsychic Traumatism) (1928); article "A Description of Dr L. Ya. Brusilovskiy's Apparatus for Inducing Wassermann's Reaction"; *Serodiagnostika sifilisa, venericheskikh i kozhnykh bolezney i ikh immunoterapiya* (The Serodiagnosis of Syphilis, Venereal and Skin Diseases and Their Immunotherapy) (1930); doctor's thesis *Kompensatornyye mekhanizmy i proizvodstvennaya metodika u nevropsikhicheskikh kontingentov s ostatochnoy trudosposobnost'yu* (Compensatory Mechanisms and Working Techniques in Neuropsychic Groups with Vestigial Working Capacity) (1935); *Yatrogennyye zabolevaniya v gospital'noy obstanovke i bor'ba s nimi* (Iatrogenic Ailments in Hospitals and Countermeasures) (1942); article "How the 'Large Medical Encyclopedia' Was Compiled" (1936); *Died*: 1962 in Moscow.

BRUSILOVSKY, Yefrem Moiseyevich (1854-1933) Rheumatologist and balneotherapist; *Born*: 1854; *Educ*: 1882 grad Acad of Med and Surgery; *Career*: founder-dir, Clinical Dept, All-Ukr Balneological Inst, Odessa; pioneer of natural balneotherapy; made major contributions to the theory of balneotherapy and to the study of gen and specific reactivity; established an arthrological clinic where he developed efficacious methods of mud treatment for diseases of the support and motor apparatus, including the use of mud in combination with specific and non-specific therapy; taught balneology and balneotherapy and took an interest in popularizing these subjects; helped to organize numerous Russian and several int balneological exhibitions; 1919 organized first Russian balneological exhibition in Odessa, which became a permanent museum in 1920; from 1883 bd member, from 1914 life chm, Odessa Balneological Soc; hon member, All-Union Comt for the Study of Rheumatism and Moscow Sci Health Resort Soc; wrote over 70 works on clinical aspects of rheumatic diseases; the theory and practice of balneotherapy and gen med problems; *Publ: Odesskiye limany i ikh lechebnyye sredstva* (The Odessan Estuaries and Their Curative Muds) (1895, 1914); *Khvoroby rukhovoho ta pidtrymnoho apparatu i likuvannya ikh* (Diseases of the Support and Motor Apparatus and Their Tratment) (1934); *Died*: 1933.

BRUSNEV, Mikhail Ivanovich (1864-1937) Revolutionary; organized one of first Soc-Democratic groups in Russia; *Born*: 13 Jan 1864; *Educ*: 1891 grad Petersburg Technol Inst; *Career*: from 1881 in revol movement; 1888 founded some 20 propaganda circles from disbanded groups of D. N. Blagoyev and P. V. Tochisskiy; 1890 member of comt which coorninated all circles in Soc-Democratic org (later known as Brusnev Group); 1891 organized first May Day celebration in Petersburg; moved to Moscow; founded new circles and liaised with other cities; 1892 Brusnev group disbanded by police and he was sentenced to exile in East Siberia; on return from exile abandoned active revol work; from 1901 member, Russian Polar Expedition; 1904 returned to Petersburg; joined Soc-Democratic group, Union of Eng; 1907 one of State Duma electors from leftist bloc (Bolshevik and Socialist-Revol); subsequently withdrew from polit activities; after 1917 Oct Revol worked at Pop Comrt of Labor and Pop Comrt of For Trade; *Publ: Vozniknoveniye pervykh sotsial-demokraticheskikh organizatsiy. Vospominaniya* (The Emergence of the First Social-Democratic Organizations. Memoirs) (1923); *Died*: 1 July 1937 in Leningrad.

BRUTSKUS, Ber Davidovich (1878- ?) Econ and agronomist; *Born*: 1878; *Educ*: 1898 grad New Alexandrine Inst of Agric and

Forestry; *Career*: from 1908 taught at Petersburg Agric Inst; 1922 expelled from USSR for "unorthodox" econ opinions; described P. A. Stolypin's agrarian policy as historically justified and in keeping with the interests of the national econ and, particularly, the peasantry; criticized the Populists (Narodniki); argued that the socialist econ system is untenable because it lacks a market; was an adherent of the econ theories of Menger, Jevons and Walras; explained the rente principle with the marginal utility theory of value; argued that the law of diminishing returns is universally applicable in agric and that profit and rente are logical and not historical econ categories; wrote a number of works on agric and compiled econ statistics on the Jewish population of Russia; *Publ: Professional'nyy sostav yevreyskogo naseleniya Rossii* (The Professional Composition of the Jewish Population of Russia); *Statistika yevreyskogo naseleniya* (Jewish Population Statistics); *Agrarnyy vopros i agrarnaya politika* (The Agrarian Question and Agrarian Policies) (1922); *Ekonomiya sel'skogo khozyaystva* (Agricultural Economy) (1924); *Problemy narodnogo khozyaystva pri sotsialisticheskom stroye* (Problems of the National Economy in the Socialist System) (1922); *Agrarentwicklung und Agrarrevolution in Russland* (Agrarian Development and Agrarian Revolution in Russia) (1925); *Died*: date and place of death unknown.

BRYAGIN, Aleksandr Ivanovich (1888-1948) Painter; master of Mstyora miniature painting; *Born*: 1888; *Educ*: attended icon-painting school in Mstyora; *Career*: painted papier-maché cases, boxes, plates etc; illustrated lit classics; used techniques of ancient Russian painting in his works with predominance of cinnabar and mother-of-pearl tones and uniquely expressive silhouettes; landscape display wide range of subjects and good decorative qualities; restored many ancient Russian paintings; *Works*: "Happy Life"; "Harvest Festival"; "Harvesters in the Field"; "Kolkhoz Meeting"; "The Golden Cockerel"; The Legend of Tsar Saltan," etc; *Died*: 1948.

BRYANTSEV, Aleksandr Aleksandrovich (1883-1961) Stage dir; dir, Leningrad Young Playgoers' Theater; Pop Artiste of USSR from 1956; CP member from 1943; *Born*: 14 Apr 1883 in Petersburg; *Educ*: 1908 grad Fac of History and Philology, Petersburg Univ; *Career*: until 1904 actor and asst stage dir at theaters in Petersburg; 1904 actor, asst stage dir, then stage dir, Gaydeburov's Everyman Theater; 1905 helped to organize the "Mobile Theater"; 1919 together with Gaydeburov founded theatrical dept, Petrograd Inst of Extra-Curricular Activities; 1922-61 founder-dir, Leningrad Young Playgoers' Theater; *Productions*: Sophocles' "Oedipus Rex" (1906) and "Antigone" (1908); Hauptmann's "Einsame Menschen" (1909); Gogol's *Zhenit'ba* (Marriage) (1916); *Konyok-Gorbunok* (The Little Hump-Backed Horse), after Yershov (1922); Ostrovskiy's *Bednost'ne porok* (Poverty Is No Vice) (1923); Makar'yev's *Timoshkin rudnik* (Tim's Mine) (1925); Gogol's *Revizor* (The Government-Inspector) (1936); Katayev's *Syn polka* (Son of the Regiment) (1946); Mikhalkov's *Krasnyy galstuk* (The Red Necktie) (1947), etc; *Roles*: Luka in Gorky's *Na dne* (The Lower Depths); Firs in Chekhov's *Vishnyovyy sad* (The Cherry Orchard); Rasplozhenskiy in *Svoi lyudi sochtyomsya* (Like Father, Like Son), etc; *Publ: Oproshcheniye teatral'noy dekoratsii* (Simplifying Stage Settings) (1917); *Khudozhnik v teatre dlya detey* (The Artist in Children's Theaters) (1927); over 70 articles on the theory and practice of staging plays for children; *Awards*: Stalin Prize (1950); two Orders of the Red Banner of Labor; medals; *Died*: 30 Sept 1961.

BRYKOV, Aleksandr Petrovich (1889-1937) Govt official; CP member from 1917; *Born*: 1889, son of a peasant; leather worker; 1905 began revol work in Moscow; 1907 exiled for two years; after 1917 Feb Revol helped found Moscow Leather Workers' Union; after 1917 Oct Revol member, Exec Comt, and Presidium member, Soldiers' Section, Moscow City Sov; also dep chm, Centr Dept for Mil Procurement, Supr Sovnarkhoz; 1919-24 plen, Labor and Defense Council; also dep chm, Siberian Revol Comt and member, Siberian Bureau, CC, RCP(B); from 1924 dep chm, RSFSR Supr Sovnarkhoz; head, Main Paper Ind Bd; from 1926 simultaneously chm, Council of Potato-Growing Cooperatives and other admin posts; at 12th Party Congress elected member, Centr Control Commission, CC, RCP(B); at 16th Party Congress elected member, Auditing Commission, CC, CPSU(B); member, USSR Centr Exec Comt of 1st and 2nd convocations; arrested by State Security organs; *Died*: 1937 in imprisonment.

BRYUKHANOV, Nikolay Pavlovich (Party pseudonyms: Andrey UFIMSKIY; Stepan; Andrey SIMBIRSKIY) (1878-1942) Party and govt official; CP member from 1902; *Born*: 16 Dec 1878 in Simbirsk (now Ul'yanovsk), son of survey official; *Educ*: studied at Moscow Univ; *Career*: 1899 participated in revol movement while at Moscow Univ; underground work in Vologda, Ufa and Simbirsk; 1903 member, Kazan' Party Comt; 1904 exiled to Vologda Province; deleg, 5th (London) Party Congress (1907) and 7th All-Russian Party Conference (Apr 1917); after 1917 Feb Revol chm, Ufa Sov of Workers' Dep; after 1917 Oct Revol member, Ufa Revol Comt; 1918 Collegium member, RSFSR Pop Comrt of Food; then RSFSR Dep Pop Comr of Food; Dec 1921-24 RSFSR and USSR Pop Comr of Food; 1924-30 USSR Pop Comr of Finance; 1931 USSR Dep Pop Comr of Supply; from Feb 1933 dep chm, Centr Commission for Crop Yields, USSR Council of Pop Comr; at 15th and 16th Party Congresses elected cand member, CC, CPSU(B); arrested by State Security organs; *Died*: 1 July 1942 in imprisonment; posthumously rehabilitated.

BRYUKHONENKO, Sergey Sergeyevich (1890-1960) Pathophysiologist; pioneer in the design of heart-lung machines; prof; Dr of Med Sci from 1935; *Born*: 30 Apr 1890 in Kozlov, now Michurinsk, son of a mech eng; *Educ*: 1914 grad Med Fac, Moscow Univ; *Career*: 1914-17 junior physician in Russian Imperial Army; 1917-19 health officer, Sokol'niki Sov of Workers' Dep, Moscow; 1919-26 asst prof under prof F. A. Andreyev, Clinic of Regional Pathology and Therapy, 2nd Moscow State Univ; 1927-30 head, laboratory of experimental therapy, Chemical-Pharmaceutical Research Inst; 1931-35 head, laboratory of experimental physiology and therapy, Centr Inst of Hematology and Blood Transfusion; 1935-41 dir, Inst of Experimental Physiology and Therapy; 1941-51 senior assoc, Sklifosovskiy First Aid Research Inst, Moscow; 1951-58 dep med dir, dep dir, then head, physiological laboratory, Research Inst of Experimental Surgical Apparatus and Instruments; 1958-60 head, laboratory of artificial blood circulation, Inst of Experimental Biology and Med, Siberian Branch, USSR Acad of Sci; 1920-24 invented and designed artificial blood-circulation apparatus (autojector), which he demonstrated at 2nd All-Russian Congress of Pathologists in 1925; May 1926 together with S. I. Chechulin demonstrated how the isolated brain of a dog could be kept alive with this apparatus; proved the feasibility of maintaining the viability of the isolated centr nervous system for several hours and demonstrated the use of this method for reanimation; did research on the theory of blood coagulation; together with his pupils developed some 120 anticoagulants; devised new method of obtaining antithrombin (heparin) from the lungs of cattle, which was mass-produced in Baku; developed anticoagulant synantrin, which was produced in Khar'kov; used artificial blood circulation for reanimation after clinical death; from 1929 together with Prof N. N. Terebinskiy used this technique in open-heart operations on animals; 1928 and 1930 demonstrated his equipment at 3rd and 4th All-Union Congresses of Physiologists; 1935 gave similar demonstration at 15th Internat Congress of Physiologists, Moscow; from 1931 conducted experiments in hypothermy on dogs, stopping their hearts by freezing and reanimating them by means of artificial blood circulation; from 1941 experimented in reanimating human beings who had died suddenly; 1951 helped to organize Research Inst of Experimental Surgical Apparatus and Instruments; developed methods of stereoscopic drawing based on the physiological laws of three-dimensional vision; trained such eminent physicians as V. D. Yankovskiy, T. S. Fedotov, M. K. Martsinkevich, T. T. Shcherbakova, Yu. M. Gal'perin, S. A. Pronin, N. V. Puchkov, A. G. Lapchinskiy, N. M. Yurman, Ye. D. Zavadovskaya, Ye. I. Strelkov, etc; wrote over 70 works and took out 16 patents on various inventions; *Publ*: coauthor, article "Experiments in Isolating Dogs' Heads" (1928); "Artificial Circulation of the Entire Blood Supply (of a Dog) After the Heart Has Been Stopped" (1928); "A Device for Artificially Maintaining the Blood Circulation of Warm-Blooded Animals" (1928); "The Use of Artificial Blood Circulation in Reanimation" (1937); "Theoretical Problems of Artificial Blood Circulation" (1957); *Awards*: Lenin Prize (1965) posthumously; *Died*: 20 Apr 1960.

BRYUSOV, Valeriy Yakovlevich (1873-1924) Russian symbolist poet, translator and lit historian; Arm folk poet; prof, Moscow Univ from 1921; CP member from 1919; *Born*: 13 Dec 1873 in Moscow, son of a merchant; *Educ*: 1899 grad History Dept, Fac of History and Philology, Moscow Univ; *Career*: 1904-09 ed, journal *Vesy*; 1910-12 head, lit criticism dept, journal *Russkaya mysl'*; 1914 war corresp; during WW 1 collaborated with Gorky;

after 1917 Oct Revol head, Dept of Sci Libraries, head, Lit Dept, head, Dept of Art Educ and member, State Learned Council, Pop Comrt of Educ; 1919 member, Moscow City Sov; 1921 founder-rector, Higher Inst of Lit and Art; edited works of Karolina Pavlova; *Publ*: verse collections: "Chef d'oeuvres" (1895); *Tertia vigilia* (1900); *Kamenshchik* (The Stonemason) (1901); "Urbi et Orbi" (1903); *Kinzhal* (The Dagger) (1903); *Dovol'nym* (To the Satisfied) (1904); *Venok* (The Wreath) (1906); poems "In My Country"; "Grain" (1909); "The Egyptian Slave" (1911); collected verse *Zerkalo teney* (A Mirror of Shadows) (1912); *Polnoye sobraniye sochineniy i perevodov* (Complete Works and Translations) (1914); *Noch'* (Night) (1915); *Tridtsatyy mesyats* (The Thirtieth Month) (1917); *Tret'ya osen'* (The Third Autumn) (1920); *Nam proba* (A Trial for Us) (1920); "Lenin" (1924), etc; lit criticism *Dalyokiye i blizkiye* (The Far and the Near) (1912); *Nauka o stikhe* (The Science of Poetry); translated Emil Verhaeren, Arm poets, etc; a number of his works have been put to music, including *Ognenny angel* (The Fiery Angel), an opera by Prokofiev; *Vrubel'*, a symphony by Gnesin; *Syn zemli* (A Son of the Earth), an oratorio by Veselov; romances by Grechaninov, Kuy, Rachmaninoff, etc; *Awards*: Scroll of Honor of the All-Russian Centr Exec Comt (1923); *Died*: 9 Oct 1924 in Moscow.

BRYUSOVA, Nadezhda Yakovlevna (1881-1951) Musicologist; prof from 1921; CP member from 1938; *Born*: 19 Nov 1881 in Moscow; sister of poet V.Ya. Bryusov; *Educ*: 1904 grad in theory of music under S. I. Taneyev and in piano under K. N. Igumnov, Moscow Conservatory; *Career*: 1921-43 taught theory of music and musical folklore; 1922-28 prorector; 1931-32 head of ed dept, 1940-43 head, Chair of Musical Folklore, Moscow Conservatory; until 1929 headed Gen, then Professional Musical Training Dept, USSR Pop Comrt of Educ; compiled textbooks for amateur performers; took part in folklore research expeditions; edited musical journals; etc; *Publ: Nauka o muzyke* (The Science of Music) (1910); *Zadachi narodnogo muzykal'nogo obrazovaniya* (Tasks of Public Musical Training) (1919), *Russkaya narodnaya pesnya v russkoy klassike i sovetskoy muzyke* (The Russian Folk Song in Russian Classical Music and in Soviet Music) (1948), *Vladimir Zakharov* (1949), etc; *Died*: 28 June 1951 in Moscow.

BRZHOZOVSKIY, Anton Grigor'yevich (1870-1961) Surgeon; Dr of Med from 1921; prof from 1922; *Born*: 1870 in Bobruysk; *Educ*: 1895 grad Med Fac, Moscow Univ; *Career*: after grad zemstvo physician in Vol'sk Uyezd; 1901-18 senior physician, Khvalynsk City Hospital, Saratov Province; during Civil War worked at hospitals in Chelyabinsk, Irkutsk and Saratov; 1920 senior asst to Prof V. I. Razumovskiy, Surgical Clinic, Saratov Univ; from 1922 head, Chair of Fac Surgery, Astrakhan' Med Inst; founder, Astrakhan' Soc of Surgeons; 1935-53 head, Chair of Fac Surgery, Kuybyshev Med Inst; from 1935 also chm, Kuybyshev Branch, All-Russian Surgical Soc; from 1960 hon bd member, All-Union Soc of Surgeons; did research on terminal arteriovenous aneurisms; was first Russian surgeon to use a circular suture on the cephalic artery in an operation for aneurism; devised various original operating techniques; wrote over 50 works; *Publ: Uchebnik po chastnoy khirurgii* (A Textbook on Special Surgery) (1941); *Appenditsit* (Appendicitis) (1960); *Died*: 1961.

BUACHIDZE (pseudonym: NOY), Samuil Grigor'yevich (1882-1918) Professional revol; helped to establish Sov regime in Northern Caucasus; CP member from 1902; *Born*: 17 June 1882 in vil Partskhnali, Kutaisi Province, son of a peasant; *Educ*: 1902 completed Kutaisi Agric College and teachers' courses; *Career*: worked as a teacher; 1905 led armed peasant revolt in Western Geo together with M. Tskhakaya and N. D. Kikinadze; late 1907 arrested, jailed and exiled until 1911; fled from exile and emigrated to Turkey, then Bulgaria where he worked under D. Blagoyev and G. Dimitrov; in Switzerland met Lenin; carried out commissions for Foreign Party Center; Apr 1917 returned to Russia; worked in Vladikavkaz, helping Kirov to run the Bolshevik org; from Mar 1918 chm, Council of Pop Comr, Tersk Pop Republic; *Died*: 20 June 1918 assassinated while addressing a soldiers' rally in Vladikavkaz.

BUBENETS, Ivan Konstantinovich (1897-1926) Mil commander; Civil War veteran; *Born*: 1897; *Educ*: 1925 grad basic training course at Mil Pilot-Observers School; *Career*: fought in WW 1; late 1917 founded Red Guard detachment; 1918 joined V. I. Chapayev's brigade with his detachment; 1918-19 regt commander, Cavalry Brigade, Chapayev's 25th Infantry Div; 1919-21 commander, 219th Infantry Regt; from 1921 brigade commander, Red Cossack Cavalry Div; 1925-26 with 6th "Red Moscow" Air Reconnaissance Detachment; *Awards*: two Orders of the Red Banner; *Died*: 1926 in a plane crash.

BUBLICHENKO, Lazar' Ivanovich (1875-1958) Gynecologist and obstetrician; health service official; prof from 1923; Dr of Med from 1912; *Born*: 1875 in Kursk Province; *Educ*: 1900 grad Med Fac, Khar'kov Univ; *Career*: while still a student won gold medal for research work; 1903-09 distr physician, Khar'kov Province, where he helped to organize the rural midwife service; from 1909 extern, then intern, from 1912 head, Dept of Puerperal Diseases, Petersburg Inst of Midwifery and Gynecology (now Inst of Obstetrics and Gynecology, USSR Acad of Med Sci); 1912 won medal at World Hygiene Exhibition, Dresden, for services to Russian obstetrics; from 1912 also delivered lectures on puerperal diseases at Inst of Postgrad Med Training and helped to organize obstetric services at zemstvo level; from 1923 until death head, Chair of Puerperal Diseases, Centr Research Inst of Obstetrics and Gynecology; active in various med soc; developed system of prophylaxis and treatment of puerperal diseases; devised technique of treating suppurative mastitis without lancing, by draining the pus and injecting penicillin; developed the subsequently proven theory that penicillin not only has a bacteriostatic effect but also imbues the tissues of the organism with resistance to the processes of decomposition and suppurative decay; for many years member, Obstetrics Council, USSR Min of Health; chm, Leningrad Oblast Obstetrics Comt; chm, Leningrad Sci of Obstetricians and Gynecologists; helped to organize All-Union and All-Russian congresses of obstetricians and gynecologists; hon member, various obstetrical and gynecological soc; wrote over 170 works, including several monographs and manuals; *Publ*: doctor's thesis *Blennoreya glaz u novorozhdyonnykh i yeyo preduprezhdeniye* (Ocular Blennorrhea in New-Born Babies and its Prevention) (1912); *Rukovodstvo po izucheniu likhoradochnykh poslerodovykh zabolevaniy* (A Manual for the Study of Febrile Puerperal Diseases) (1923, 1930); *Patologiya poslerodovogo perioda* (The Pathology of the Puerperal Period) (1939); *Poslerodovaya infektsiya* (Puerperal Infection) (3 vol, 1946-49); *Funktsional'naya diagnostika pri poslerodovykh zabolevaniyakh* (Functional Diagnosis in Puerperal Diseases) (1954); *Awards*: Order of Lenin; Stalin Prize; *Died*: 1958.

BUBLIKOV, Nikolay Yevlampiyevich (1871-1942) Painter; specialist in seascapes; *Born*: 1871; *Educ*: 1896 grad Petersburg Acad of Arts; *Works*: "Before the Squall" (1898); "Storm" (1903); "Freshening Wind" (1925); "Squall" (1926); "Evening Before the Storm" (1929); "The Battleship 'Paris Commune' in the Bay of Biscay" (1930); "Yacht Race" (1934); "Finnish Coast" (1935); "The Battleship 'Andrey Pervozvannyy' Crushing the Socialist-Revolutionary Revolt" (1936); "The Icebreaker 'Krasin' Conducting a Convoy" (1937); "In The Column's Wake" (1937); "The Icebreaker 'Yermak' Convoying Ships" (1940), etc; *Died*: 1942.

BUBNOV, Aleksandr Pavlovich (1908-1964) Artist; corresp member, USSR Acad of Arts from 1954; Hon Art Worker of RSFSR from 1954; *Born*: 4 Mar 1908 in Tiflis; *Educ*: 1926-30 studied at Higher State Inst of Art and Draughtsmanship; *Career*: illustrated works of Gogol, Pushkin, Shevchenko, etc; his monumental canvas "Morning on Kulikovo Field" is exhibited in the Tret'yakov Gallery; *Works*: "October Scene" (1936); "Apple" (1942); "Morning on Kulikov Field" (1947); "Taras Bulba" (1954); "Conversation" (1957); *Awards*: Stalin Prize (1948); *Died*: 30 June 1964.

BUBNOV, Andrey Sergeyevicch (Party pseudonyms: "Khimik" and Yakov; lit pseudonyms: A. GLOTOV; S. YAGLOV; A.B., etc) (1883-1940) Party and govt official; historian and publicist; CP member from 1903; *Born*: 23 Mar 1883 in Ivanovo-Voznesensk; *Educ*: studied at Moscow Agric Inst; *Career*: expelled from Moscow Agric Inst for revol activity; 1905 member, Ivanovo-Voznesensk RSDRP(B) Comt; 1906 Bureau member, Ivanovo-Voznesensk RSDRP(B) Union; 1906 and 1907 deleg, 4th and 5th RSDRP Congress; 1907 member, Moscow RSDRP Comt; 1908 member, RSDRP Oblast Bureau, Centr Ind Region; 1909-17 Party work in Nizhniy Novgorod, Sormovo, Petersburg, Samara and other towns; frequently imprisoned and banished; 1910 coopted to Russian Bolshevik Center; 1912 elected cand member, CC, RSDRP at 6th All-Russian Conference in Prague; after 1917 Feb Revol member, Moscow Oblast RSDRP(B) Bureau; elected member, CC, RSDRP(B) at 6th Congress; CC rep with Petrograd RSDRP(B) Comt; Oct 1917 elected Politburo member, CC, RSDRP(B) and to Mil Revol Party Center in Charge of the Oct

Armed Uprising; member, Petrograd Mil Revol Comt and comr in charge of railroad termini; 1917 after 2nd Congress of Sov member, All-Russian Centr Exec Comt and Collegium member, Pop Comrt of Means of Communication; Nov 1917 posted to Southern Russia as railroad comr and fought against Gen Kaledin; 1918 joined "leftist Communists"; 1918 became member, Ukr Sov govt and CC, CP(B) Ukr; Oct 1918 sent to Kiev to work in underground; became member, Kiev Oblast Bureau, CP(B) Ukr; 1919 member, Revol Mil Council, Ukr Front and 14th Army; from late 1919 worked for Main Textile Enterprises Bd, Moscow; simultaneously Bureau member, Moscow RCP(B) Comt; 1921 helped to put down the Kronstadt Muting; 1921-22 member, Revol Mil Council; North Caucasian Mil Distr; 1922-23 head, Dept of Agitation and Propadanga, CC, RCP(B); 1920-21 joined Democratic Centralists opposition group; 1923 joined Trotsky group; subsequently withdrew from opposition; early 1924-Sept 1929 head, Pol Bd, Red Army and member, USSR Revol Mil Council; member, Org Bureau, CC, CPSU(B); 1925 secr, CC, RCP(B); 1929-37 RSFSR Pop Comr of Educ; elected member, CC, CPSU(B) at 13th, 14th, 15th, 16th and 17th Congress; wrote books and articles on history of CP; arrested by State Security organs; *Publ: Osnovnyye momenty v razvitii kommunisticheskoy partii v Rossii* (Basic Factors in the Development of the Communist Party in Russia) (1921); *Osnovnyye voprosy istorii RKP* (Basic Problems of the History of the Russian Communist Party) (4th ed, 1924-26); article on CPSU in 1st ed of "BSE" (Large Soviet Encyclopedia); *1924 god v voyennom stroitel'stve* (Military Construction in 1924) (1925); *Boyevaya podgotovka i politicheskaya rabota* (Military Training and Political Work) (1927); *Grazhdanskaya voyna, partiya i voyennoye delo* (The Civil War, the Party and Military Affairs) (1928); *O Krasnoy Armii* (The Red Army) (1958); autobiography in "Granat" Encyclopedic Dictionary (vol 41); *Awards*: Order of Lenin (1933); Order of Red Banner; *Died*: 12 Jan 1940; posthumously rehabilitated.

BUBNOV, Ivan Grigor'yevich (1872-1919) Naval architect; *Born*: 18 Jan 1872; *Educ*: 1891 grad Kronstadt Naval Eng College; 1896 grad Naval Acad; *Career*: 1904-09 lecturer, from 1909 prof of naval architecture, Petersburg Polytech Inst; from 1910 simultaneously prof, Naval Acad; 1908-12 dir, Petersburg Experimental Shipyard, Min of Marine; outstanding theoretician of naval architecture, especially of structural mech; designed and built the "Del'fin", Russia's first submarine with an internal combustion engine (keel laid in 1902); designed and built "Bars" Class submarines (keel 1912 laid); *Publ: Spusk sudna na vodu* (The Launching of a Ship) (1900); *Napryazheniya v obshivke sudov ot davleniya vody* (Water-Pressure Stresses in Ship's Plates) (1902); *Stroitel'naya mekhanika korablya* (The Structural Mechanics of Ships) (2 vol, 1912-14); *Dopolneniye k kursu 'Stroitel'naya mekhanika korablya'* (Supplement to the Course "The Structural Mechanics of Ships") (1930); *Died*: 13 Mar 1919.

BUBRIK, Samuil Davydovich (1899-1965) Film dir; Hon Art Worker of Lat SSR from 1949; *Born*: 22 June 1899; *Educ*: studied direction under Eisenstein in Moscow; *Career*: from 1929 worked for "Cutural Film" Studios; from 1931 film dir, Centr Documentary Film Studios; 1931-32 with roving film units; 1932-35 film dir, mobile newsreel unit, USSR Newsreel Studios; 1933-36 instructor, Camera Operators Fac, All-Union State Inst of Cinematography; 1937-44 worked on series of documentary films *Sovetskoye iskusstvo* (Soviet Art); wrote screenplay for most of his films; *Films*: co-dir, *Tovarishch prokuror* (Comrade Procurator) (1934); *Bor'ba za Kiyev* (The Battle of Kiev) (1935); *Vozvrashchyonnaya zhizn'* (Life Returned) (1935); *Prazdnik pesni Sovetskoy Latvii* (The Soviet Latvian Song Festival) (1949); co-dir, *Vsesoyuznyy parad fizkul'turnikov 1947* (The 1947 All-Union Parade of Gymnasts) (1947); *Vladimir Mayakovsky* (1940); *Maxim Gorky* (1941); co-dir, *Visarion Belinskiy* (1948); *Pushkin* (1949); *Lev Tolstoy* (1953); *Chekhov* (1954); *Dostoyevsky* (1956); "Bernard Shaw" (1956); *Zdes' zhil Lenin* (Lenin Lived Here) (1957); "Robert Burns" (1958); *N.K. Krupskaya* (1959); *Rabindranath Tagore* (1961); *Stanislavsky* (1963); *Vsesoyuznyy starosta* (The All-Union Elder) (1964); *Mir pobedit voynu* (Peace Shall Conquer War) (1949); *1905 god* (The Year 1905) (1955); *Viva Kuba* (Viva Cuba) (1960); *Geroi ne umirayut* (Heroes Never Die) (1963); *Publ*: articles - co-author, "Experience with Roving Film Units" (1931); "Documentary Film Biographies" (1963); *Awards*: Stalin Prize (1948); *Died*: 18 Oct 1965.

BUBRIKH, Dmitriy Vladimirovich (1890-1949) Linguist; specialist in Finno-Ugrian languages; corresp member, USSR Acad of Sci from 1946; *Born*: 25 July 1890; *Career*: prof, Leningrad and Moscow Univ; from 1925 head, Chair of Finno-Ugrian Philology, Leningrad Univ; studied the phonetics, vocabulary, morphology and historical grammar of the Finno-Ugrian languages, as well as the history of the Finno-Ugrian peoples; *Publ: Zvuki i formy erzyanskoy rechi. Po govoram s. Kozlovki* (The Sounds and Forms of the Eryan Dialect as Spoken in the Village of Kozlovka) (1930); *Proiskhozhdeniye karel'skogo naroda* (The Origin of the Karelian People) (1947); *Istoricheskaya fonetika finskogo-suomi yazyka* (A History of the Phonetics of Finno-Suomi) (1948); *Istoricheskaya fonetika udmurtskogo yazyka* (A History of the Phonetics of Udmurt) (1948); *Grammatika literaturnogo komi yazyka* (A Grammar of Literary Komi) (1949); *Died*: 30 Nov 1949.

BUCHMA, Amvrosiy Maksimilianovich (1891-1957) Actor; stage dir; prof from 1940; Pop Artiste of USSR from 1944; CP member from 1942; *Born*: 14 Mar 1891 in L'vov; *Educ*: studied at Lysenko Musical-Dramatic Inst, Kiev; *Career*: 1905 member of chorus, actor at Ukr Drama Theater of *Rus'ka Besida* Assoc; 1914 drafted into Austrian army; for anti-war agitation sent to penal batallion; 1915 surrendered to Russians; after Oct Revol acted for some time with the Sadovsky and Rubchak theaters; 1919 headed "New L.vov Theater" group; 1920 helped found Franko theater; 1921 helped run Franko Studio in Cherkassy; from 1922 actor at *Berezil'* theater in Kiev; 1926-30 at Odessa Film Studio of All-Ukr Cinematography Bd; 1930-36 at *Berezil'* Theater (from 1933 the Shevchenko Theater), Khar'kov; 1936-57 actor and producer, Franko Theater, Kiev; 1945-48 art dir, Kiev Film Studio; 1936-40 lecturer, from 1940 prof Karpenko-Kariy State Inst of Stagecraft, Kiev; *Roles*: Khlestakov in Gogol's *Revizor* (The Government Inspector); Gurman and Zadorozhnyy in Franko's *Ukradyonnoye schast'ye* (Stolen Happiness); Pyotr, Mikhail and Ivan in Karpenko-Kariy's *Sueta* (Cares); Ivan Kalyayev in Popovskiy's *Nakanune* (On the Eve) (1925); Gayday and Krechet in Korneychuk's *Gibel' eskadry* (Death of the Squadron) and *Platon Krechet* (1933, 1934); Kotko in Katayev's *Shyol soldat s fronta* (A Soldier Came From the Front) (1938); Lenin in Korneychuk's *Pravda* (The Truth) (1937); Dubrava in Korneychuk's *Makar Dubrava* (1948) etc; *Productions*: Halbe's *Molodost* (Youth) (1926); Kheyerman's *Gibel' 'Nadezhdy'* (The End of the "Hope") (1930); Shevchenko's *Nazar Stodolya* (1931); Karpenko-Kariy's *Khozyain* (The Master) (1939); Kotlyarevskiy's *Natalka Poltavka* (Natalya the Poltavian) (1942); Korneychuk's *Missiya mistera Perkinsa v stranu bol'shevikov* (Mister Perkins' Mission to the Land of the Bolsheviks) (1943; opera *Natalka Poltavka* (1954), etc; *Awards*: : Order of Lenin; two Orders of the Red Banner of Labor; Stalin Prizes (1941 and 1949); *Died*: 6 Jan 1957.

BUDKEVICH, Konstantin (1867-1923) Roman Catholic prelate; vicar-gen, Mogilev Eparchy, Roman Catholic Church; *Born*: 1867 in Batic region; *Educ*: grad Petersburg Roman Catholic Seminary and Theological Acad; *Career*: 1903-05 asst vicar, from 1905 vicar, St Catherine Parish, Petersburg; later dean of Petersburg parishes; from 1917, by preaching in Russian at St Catherine's Church, converted many Russians to Catholicism; resisted Bolshevik decrees on confiscation of Church treasures and ban on religious instruction of children; Mar 1923 ordered to Moscow along with Archbishop Tseplyak and other Roman Catholic priests, arrested and imprisoned; charged with counter-revol activities and hostility to Sov regime at show trial and sentenced to death by firing squad; *Died*: 31 Mar 1923 executed; buried in a mass grave in Sokol'niki, Moscow.

BUDNIKOV, Mikhail Sergeyevich (1904-1966) Technol eng; specialist in construction org; Dr of Tech Sci from 1952; Hon Sci and Tech Worker of Ukr SSR from 1964; *Born*: 1904 in Kiev; *Educ*: 1927 grad Kiev Polytech Inst; *Career*: prof and head of a dept, Kiev Civil Eng Inst; 1956-63 member, USSR and Ukr Acad of Construction and Architecture; specialized in prefabricated construction techniques; *Publ: Potochnoye stroitel'stvo sel* (Production-Line Rural Construction) (1949); *Stroitel'stvo mnogoetazhnykh zdaniy potochno-raschlenyonnym metodom* (The Construction of Multi-Story Buildings by the Distributed Production-Line Method) (1952); *Tekhnologicheskoye proyektirovaniye pri stroyenii seriynykh zhilishchnykh zdaniy* (Technological Planning in the Building of Standardized Apartment Houses) (1955); *Normirovaniye zadela v zhilishchnom stroitel'stve* (The Standardization of Masonry Work in Housing Construction) (1960); *Puti razvitiya teorii stroitel'nogo potoka*

(The Developmental Paths of Construction-Line Production Theory) (1962); *Terminologiya v oblasti potochnykh metodov stroitel'stva* (Terminology in Production-Line Construction Methods) (1962); *Awards*: Order of the Red Banner of Labor (1961); *Died*: 4 Mar 1966.

BUDNITSKIY, Yakov Grigor'yevich (1899-1967) Party and govt official; helped to establish Sov rule in Feodosiya; CP member from 1917; *Born*: 1899; *Educ*: 1931-35 studied at 1st Moscow State Univ; *Career*: 1918-19 member, then secr and Bd member, Feodosiya City Party Comt; member Feodosiya Revol Comt; 1920 fought on Southern Front; 1921-23 polit comr of a subdistr, Feodosiya and Sudak Health Resort Admin; 1924-31 worked for Pop Comrt of Finance in Orenburg and Moscow; 1936-41 worked at State Inst for the Planning of Machine-Building Plants and for Bureau, State Inst for the Planning of Heavy Ind Plants; 1941-45 fought in WW 2; 1945-54 worked for State Inst for the Planning of Heavy Ind Plants; from 1954 in retirement; *Died*: 17 June 1967.

BUDYAK, Yuriy (real name: POKOS, Yuriy Yakovlevich) (1879-1938) Ukr writer and poet; *Born*: 1879 in vil Krasnogorka, now Poltava Oblast; *Career*: member, *Plug* (The Plow) lit group; wrote many poems and plays for children, translated into Russian and Bel; *Publ*: poems; "The Ukrainian Prisoner" (1907); "On the Fields of Life" (1910); "Pan Bazaley" (1911); "To Small Children" (1927); "Winter" (1928); "To the Great Gate" (1929), etc; *Died*: 1938.

BUDZYN'SKIY, Stanislav (1894-1937) Party official; leading member, Polish workers' movement; *Born*: 9 Aug 1894 in Warsaw, son of a worker; *Career*: shoemaker; 1912 joined Soc-Democratic Party of Kingdom of Poland and Lith (SDKP&L): 1913 elected member, Warsaw Comt of this Party; 1915 arrested; Nov 1916 released on bail; Mar 1917 joined the RSDRP(B) together with a group of SDKP&L members which he organized; attended April RSDRP(B) Conference; member, Bolshevik Faction, Moscow Sov; during 1917 Oct Revol member, Moscow Mil-Revol Comt; Dec 1917 returned to Poland; member, Main Bd and Warsaw Comt, SDKP&L; Dec 1918 attended Amalgamative Congress, which founded the Communist Workers' Party of Poland (from 1925 - CP Poland); 1919 arrested; Apr 1920, after exchange of polit prisoners, returned to Russian; 1920, during the Sov-Polish War, at the Western Front; helped edit various front publ; 1921-22 with Sov mission in Lat; 1924-27 member, Polish Bureau, CC, CPSU(B); attended 3rd - 6th CP Poland Congresses; from 1929 member, CC, CP Western Bel (part of CP Poland); from 1930 lived in USSR; Bureau member, CC, CP Bel; 1931-36 ed, newspaper *Zvezda* (Star); from 1931 lecturer at Int Lenin School in Moscow; from 1934 prof; head, Chair of Leninism at above school; 1937 arrested by State Security organs; *Died*: 22 Aug 1937 in imprisonment; posthumously rehabilitated.

BUGAYSKIY, Boris Nikolayevich (1889-1961) Opera singer (bass); Hon Artiste of RSFSR from 1933; *Born*: 6 Sept 1889; *Educ*: 1918 grad Moscow Conservatory, where he studied under U. Mazetti; *Career*: 1919 stage debut with Zimin Opera Theater and Opera Studio, Bolshoy Theater; 1920-51 soloist, Bolshoy Theater; *Roles*: Varlaam in *Boris Godunov*; Prince Ivan Khovanskiy in *Khovanshchina*; Ivan the Terrible in *Pskovityanka* (The Woman of Pskov); Nilacantha in *Lakme*; the Standard-Bearer in Pototskiy's *Proryv* (Break-Through); Sashka and Plovtsev in *Tikhiy Don* (Quiet Flows the Don) and *Podnyataya tselina* (Virgin Soil Upturned), etc; *Died*: 3 July 1961.

BUGOSLAVSKIY, Sergey Alekseyevich (1888-1945) Music critic; composer; specialist in history of Russian lit; Dr of Arts; prof, Moscow Univ; *Born*: 2 July 1888 in Chernigov; *Educ*: studied under Prof Peretets of Kiev Univ; *Publ: K voprosu o kharaktere i ob'yome literaturnoy deyatel'nosti Nestora* (The Character and Scope of Nestor's Literary Work) (1915); *Drevne-russkiye proizvedeniya o Borise i Glebe* (Ancient Russian Works About Boris and Gleb) (1916); *Pamyat' i pokhvala knyazyu Vladimiru* (Commemoration and Praise of Prince Vladimir) (1925); *Khudozhestvennaya literatura v shkolakh 2-y stupeni* (Fiction for Grade-Two Schools) (1925); etc; also wrote about 80 songs, choruses, piano pieces, etc; *Died*: 14 Jan 1945 in Moscow.

BUKHARIN, Nikolay Ivanovich (1888-1938) Party official; economist and sociologist; leader of right-wing opposition in CPSU(B); CP member from 1906; *Born*: 27 Sept 1888 in Moscow, son of a teacher; *Educ*: grad high-school; from 1907 studied at Econ Dept, Law Fac, Moscow Univ; *Career*: 1905 joined student revol group; 1906 did Party propaganda work in Zamoskvorech'ye Rayon, Moscow; 1907-08 propagandist and agitator, Khamovniki Rayon, Moscow; 1908 coopted member, Moscow RSDRP(B) Comt; 1909-10 twice arrested; 1911 emigrated to Germany, where he lived in Hanover; fall 1912 met Linin, began to write regularly and contribute articles to *Pravda* and *Prosveshcheniye*; 1912-14 worked among Russian Soc-Democrats in Vienna; 1914 arrested on espionage charges by Austrian police shortly before outbreak of WW 1 and deported to Switzerland after Austrian Soc-Democratic leaders testified on his behalf; attended Berne RSDRP Conference; July 1915 moved to Sweden under the alias Dolgolevskiy; 1916 arrested for anti-war statements and deported to Norway; while living in Scandinavia differed with Lenin on theoretical questions concerning the nationalities problem and the role of the state; Oct 1916 left Norway and entered USA illegally via Denmark; edited newspaper *Novyy mir* in New York and made propaganda tour of American cities; after 1917 Feb Revol returned to Russia via Japan and was elected to Exec Comt, Moscow Sov and Moscow RSDRP(B) Comt; ed, journals *Sotsial-demokrat* and *Spartak*; at 6th Party Congress elected to CC, of which he was a member until 1934 and then a cand member until 1937; from Oct 1917 member, Moscow Mil—Revol Comt and ed, newspaper *Izvestiya Moskovskogo voyenno-revolyutsionnogo komiteta*; from late Dec 1917 until conclusion of Peace of Brest-Litovsk (3 Mar 1918) ed, *Pravda*: as an opponent of a separate peace with Germany became leader of "leftist Communists" group and ed, newspaper *Kommunist*; summer 1918-31 again ed, *Pravda*; 1917-18 and later undertook many trips abroad for CP and Comintern; 1918 met Karl Liebknecht in Germany and established contacts between RCP(B) and the Spartacists, thus exposing German Communists to Bolshevik influende; November 1918 expelled from Germany with Sov embassy staff a few days before the outbrek of the Revol; 1922 deleg, Conference of the Three Internationals, Berlin; 1923 visited Norway; played a leading role in Comintern from its inception; helped to organize 1st Comintern Congress, at which he was elected to the Exec Comt and Presidium; reelected to these organs at all subsequent congresses; at 2nd Comintern Congress delivered paper on parliamentarianism; at 3rd Comintern Congress took part in debate on tactical questions; at 4th and 5th Comintern Congresses delivered papers on Comintern program; 1920-21 during trade-union controversy first adopted a middle-of-the-road position, then sided with Trotsky; from 1928, together with Rykov and Tomsky, led "rightist deviationists" in CP and Comintern; 1929 removed from CC, CPSU(B) and from Presidium, Comintern Exec Comt; 1931 Presidium member, USSR Supreme Sovnarkhoz; for a number of years prof, Moscow Univ; 1934-37 ed, *Izvestia*; member, All-Russian and USSR Centr Exec Comt of various convocations; active in Party congresses and conferences; delivered innumerable speeches at workers' and Party meetings; drafted many Party documents; read several lecture courses; published numerous pamphlets, popular books, articles and several important theoretical works; Mar 1937 expelled from CPSU(B) and sentenced to death at trial of "anti-Soviet rightist Trotskyite center"; *Publ: Klassovaya bor'ba v Rossii* (The Class Struggle in Russia) (1917); *Mirovoye khozyaystvo i imperializm. Ekonomicheskiy ocherk* (The World Economy and Imperialism. An Economic Study) (1918); *Politicheskaya ekonomiya rant'ye. Teoriya tsennosti i pribyli avstriyskoy shkoly* (The Political Economy of the Rentiers. The Austrian School's Theory of Value and Profit) (1919); *Obshchaya teoriya transformatsionnogo protsessa* (The General Theory of the Transformation Process) (1920); *Teoriya istoricheskogo materializma* (The Theory of Historical Materialism) (1920); *Azbuka kommunizma* (The ABC of Communism) (1920); *'Ataka'. Sbornik teoreticheskikh statey* ("Attack". A Collection of Theoretical Articles) (1924); *Imperializm i nakopleniye kapitala* (Imperialism and the Accumulation of Capital) (1925); *Tsezarizm pod maskoy revolyutsii* (Caesarism Under the Guise of Revolution) (1925); *Mezhdunarodnaya burzhuaziya i Karl Kautskiy, yeyo apostol* (The International Bourgeoisie and Its Apostle Karl Kautsky) (1925); *Leninizm i problema kul'turnoy revolyutsii* (Leninism and the Problem of the Cultural Revolution) (1928), etc; *Died*: 15 Mar 1938 executed by firing squad.

BUKHARINA-LUKINA, N.M. (1887-1940) Party and govt official; wife of N. I. Bukharin; CP member from 1906; *Born*: 1887; *Career*: Party work in Moscow and abroad; after 1917 Oct Revol worked for newspapers *Pravda* and *Izvestia*; 1918 sided with "leftist Communists" who opposed Peace of Brest-Litovsk; did Party and govt work; 1937 expelled from Party for "anti-Sov activities"; arrested by State Security organs; *Died*: 1940 in imprisonment.

BUKOVETSKIY, Yevgeniy Iosifovich (1866-1948) Artist; *Born*: 5 Dec 1866 in Odessa; *Educ*: 1890 grad Odessa Drawing School; *Career*: member, Assoc of Southern Russian Artists; displayed his work at exhibitions of itinerant artists; *Works*: "At a Rich Relative's" (1891); "In Court" (1895); portraits: P. Nilus (1902); K. Chukovskiy (1903); I. Bunin (1919); Prof. P. Stolyarovskiy (1937); Acad V. Filatov (1940), etc; *Died*: 27 July 1948.

BUKREYEV, Boris Yakovlevich (1859-1962) Mathematician; prof from 1899; Hon Sci Worker of Ukr SSR from 1941; *Born*: 6 Sept 1859 in L'gov, now Kursk Oblast; *Educ*: completed higher educ; *Career*: from 1889 prof, Kiev Univ; also worked for various research inst; co-founder, Kiev Mathematical Soc; hon member, Moscow Mathematical Soc; specialized in theory of complex variable functions, differential equations and differential geometry, also non-Euclidean geometry; *Publ: Kurs prilozheniy differentsial'nogo i integral'nogo ischisleniya k geometrii* (A Course on the Applications of Differential and Integral Calculus to Geometry) (1900); *Vvedeniye k variatsionnomu ischisleniyu* (An Introduction to Variation Calculus) (3rd ed, 1934); *Neevklidova planimetriya v analaticheskom izlozhenii* (An Analytical Explanation of Non-Euclidean Planimetry) (1947); *Awards*: Order of Lenin; Order of the Red Banner of Labor (1959); *Died*: 2 Oct 1962.

BUKSHA, Mikhail Mikhaylovich (1869-1953) Opera conductor; Hon Art Worker of Lith SSR from 1945; *Born*: 16 Apr 1869; *Educ*: 1900 grad Rimsky-Korsakov, Lyadov and Solov'yov's composition theory class, Petersburg Conservatory; *Career*: 1898 conducting debut in Nizhniy Novgorod; 1899-1927 conducted operas and ballets in Petersburg, Moscow, Tiflis, Samara, Smolensk, Khar'kov, Vladikavkaz, Perm', etc; 1927 returned to Lith; 1927-48 chief conductor, Kaunas Opera Theater; 1948-53 conductor, Vilnius Opera Theater; 1944-48 instructor, from 1948 prof, Kaunas Conservatory; *Works*: conducted operas: *Grazhina* (1933); Karnavichyus' *Radvila Perkunas* (1937); Rachyunas' "Three Talismen" (1936); Shimkus' "Trees on the Estate" (1942), etc; *Died*: 7 Mar 1953 in Kaunas.

BULAK-BALAKHOVICH, Stanislav N. (? - ?) Mil and partisan commander; cavalry capt, Russian Army; maj-gen, Yudenich Army; active in anti-Sov partisan movement, during and after Civil War; *Born*: date and place of birth unknown; *Career*: fought in WW 1; from 1918 in Red Army; spring 1918 commanded Punin Mounted Partisan Unit in fighting near Petrograd; sustained serious chest wounds in clash with German troops; then commanded mounted partisan regt; Aug 1918 ruthlessly crushed anti-Sov peasant revolt in Luga area, burning several vil; Nov 1918 defected with regt to Pskov, held by Germans and White forces; then served with Gen Yudenich's White Army, commanding Pskov Province unit; 1920 linked up with Pilsudski and conducted large-scale partisan operations against Red Army in Bel; Aug 1920 attacked Pinsk and cut Sov communications during Tukhachevskiy's retreat from Warsaw; after RSFSR-Polish armistice linked up with anti-Sov units of Peremykin and Yakovlev and invaded Sov Bel at head of 26,000-man army; Nov 1920 defeated in battle and led remnants of his force back to Poland, where they were interned; 1921 formed sabotage squads which operated in Bel, terrorising Sov authorities; in 1920's lived in Poland; *Died*: date and place of death unknown.

BULAKHOVSKIY, Leonid Arsen'yevich (1888-1961) Slavist; prof from 1917; member, Ukr Acad of Sci from 1939; corresp member, USSR Acad of Sci from 1946; dir, Potebnya Inst of Linguistics, Ukr Acad of Sci from 1944; *Born*: 14 Apr 1888 in Khar'kov; *Educ*: 1910 grad Fac of History and Philology, Khar'kov Univ; *Career*: 1917-21 prof, Perm' Univ; from 1921 prof, Khar'kov Univ; 1943-44 prof, Moscow Univ; 1946-60 prof and head, Chair of Slavic Philology, Kiev Univ; chm, Ukr Slavists' Comt, Ukr Acad of Sci; specialized in history of lit Ukr and Russian, comparative and historical grammar and etymology of Slavic languages and Slavic accentology; reconstructed ancient Slavic accentuation and elucidated historical aspects of stress and quantitative concepts in various Slavic languages; developed modern Ukr orthographic system, which was adopted in 1946; *Publ: Kurs russkogo literaturnogo yazyka* (A Course of Literary Russian) (1935); *Istoricheskiy kommentariy k russkomu literaturnomu yazyku* (A Historical Commentary on Literary Russian) (1936); *Russkiy literaturnyy yazyk pervoy poloviny XIX veka* (Literary Russian in the Early 19th Century) (2 vol, 1941-48); *Ukrainskoye literaturnoye proiznosheniye* (The Pronunciation of Literary Ukrainian) (1943); *Aktsentologicheskiy kommentariy k pol'skomu yazyku* (An Accentological Commentary on Polish) (1950); *Kurs sovremennogo ukrainskogo literaturnogo yazyka* (A Course of Modern Literary Ukrainian) (2 vol, 1951-52); coauthor and ed, *Vvedeniye v yazykoznaniye* (An Introduction to Linguistics) (2 vol, 1953); *Ocherki po obshchemu yazykoznaniyu* (Essays on General Linguistics) (1955); *Voprosy proiskhozhdeniya ukrainskogo yazyka* (Problems of the Origin of Ukrainian) (1956); *Died*: 4 Apr 1961 in Kiev.

BULANKIN, Ivan Nikolayevich (1901-1960) Biochemist; member, Ukr Acad of Sci from 1951; rector, Khar'kov Univ from 1945; Hon Sci Worker of Ukr SSR from 1951; CP member from 1924; *Born*: 3 Feb 1901 in vil Ten'ki, Tatar ASSR; *Educ*: 1926 grad Khar'kov Inst of Publ Educ; *Career*: 1934-45 prof, Khar'kov Univ; specialized in protein chemistry, the chemistry of ageing and comparative biochemistry; *Publ: Zakonomernosti stareniya zoley i studney zhelatiny* (Laws Governing the Ageing of Sols and Gelatines) (1939); *Elektrokhimicheskaya obratimost' i kislotnoshchelochnaya denaturatsiya globulyarnykh belkov* (Electrochemical Reversibility and the Acid-Alkaline Denaturation of Globular Proteins) (1949); *O prirode denaturatsii globulyarnykh belkov* (The Denaturation of Globular Proteins) (1955); *Awards*: three Orders of the Red Banner of Labor; *Died*: 31 Oct 1960.

BULATOV, Dmitriy Aleksandrovich (1889-1941) Party and govt official; CP member from 1912; *Born*: 1889, son of a peasant; *Career*: worker; 1915 arrested for revol activities and exiled to Turukhan Kray; 1917 chm, uyezd sov in Tver' Province; 1918-20 dep chm, Tver' Province Exec Comt; Tver' Province comr for food, then chm, Tver' Province Exec Comt; from 1920 exec Party work: head, Org and Instruction Dept, CC, CPSU(B); from 1931 Collegium member and head, Personnel Dept, OGPU; 1934-37 first secr, Omsk Oblast CPSU(B) Comt; 1930 at the 16th CPSU(B) Congress elected cand member, CC, CPSU(B); arrested by State Security organs; *Died*: 1941 in imprisonment.

BULGAKOV, Aleksandr Sergeyevich (1888-1953) Russian theater historian; *Born*: 1888; *Educ*: 1925 grad Leningrad State Inst of Art History (later State Acad of Art History); *Career*: until 1935 worked for Leningrad State Acad of Art History; *Publ: Angliyskiy teatr pri puritanakh* (The English Theater Under the Puritans) (1927); *Komediya o Tamerlane i Bayazete* (The Comedy of Tamerlan and Bayazet (1928); *Teatr i teatral'naya obshchestvennost' Londona epokhi rassveta torgovogo kapitalizma* (The London Theater and Theater Public in the Heyday of Mercantile Capitalism); (1929); coauthor, *Gosudarstvennyy agitatsionnyy teatr v Leningrade* (The Leningrad State Agitation Theater) (1931); *Ranneye znakomstvo s Shekspirom v Rossii* (Early Acquaintance with Shakespeare in Russia) (1934), etc; *Died*: 1953.

BULGAKOV, Aleksey Dmitriyevich (1872-1954) Ballet dancer and teacher; Hon Art Worker of RSFSR from 1949; *Born*: 24 Mar 1872; *Educ*: 1897 grad Petersburg Ballet College, where he studied under P.A. Gerdt and M.I. Petipa; *Career*: 1897-1909 dancer, Mariinskiy Theater; from 1911 dancer and producer, 1913-17 chief producer, Bolshoy Ballet; 1909-14 made foreign tours with ballet ensembles; 1909-11 taught plastic movements and mime at Suvorin Theater School; 1926-29 taught mime and choreography at Bolshoy Theater; *Roles*: the Ogre in *Spyashchaya krasavitsa* (Sleeping Beauty); Rotbart in *Lebedinoye ozero* (Swan Lake); the Captain in *Krasnyy mak* (*Krasnyy tsvetok*) (The Red Poppy [The Red Flower]); Stepan Razin in Glazunov's *Sten'ka Razin*; Marquis de Beauregard in Asaf'yev's *Plamya Parizha* (The Flame of Paris); Lorenzo in "Romeo and Juliet", etc; *Died*: 14 Jan 1954.

BULGAKOV, Mikhail Afanas'yevich (1891-1940) Russian writer and dramatist; *Born*: 14 May 1891, son of a prof at Kiev Theological Acad; *Educ*: 1916 grad Med fac, Kiev Univ; *Career*: 1916-19 country physician; 1919 first work published; 1920-23 lived abroad; 1920-22 contributed to Russian fin de siècle newspaper *Nakanune* and journal *Rossiya* in Berlin; 1923 returned to USSR and devoted himself full-time to lit; lived in Kiev, Vladikavkaz, then in Moscow; many of his works criticized by Sov official press, plays removed from repertoire and works no longer published; 1930 Sov govt refused him permission to emigrate; play *Dni Turbinykh* (Days of the Turbins) remained in repertoire of Moscow Arts Theater; 1930-36 became asst producer at Moscow Arts Theater; *Publ*: novel *Belaya gvardiya* (The White

Guard) (1924), dramatized as *Dni Turbinykh* (Days of the Turbins) (1926), depicting Civil War years in Ukraine where Whitists perish in fight against advancing Red Army; plays: *Zoykina kvartira* (Zoya's Apartment) (1926); *Beg* (Flight) (1928); *Bagrovyy ostrov* (Crimson Island) (1928); "Molière"; *Posledniye dni* (Pushkin) (The Last Days /Pushkin/); collected stories *D'yavoliada* (Devilment); autobiography *Zapiski na manzhetakh* (Notes on the Cuff) (1923); collected tales *Rokovyye yaytsa* (Fateful Eggs), etc; *Died*: 10 Mar 1940 in Moscow.

BULGAKOV, Sergey Nikolayevich (1871-1944) Economist, philosopher and publicist; *Born*: 16 July 1871; *Career*: in 1890's "Legal Marxist"; 1900 in doctor's thesis *Kapitalizm i zemledeliye* (Capitalism and Agriculture) revised Marxist theory of agrarian question; after 1905-07 revol joined Constitutional Democrats; contributed to anthology *Vekhi*; 1907 elected Oryol Province dep to 2nd State Duma; from 1918 orthodox priest; 1922 expelled from USSR for anti-Sov activities; 1923 organized Soc of St Sophia; 1925-44 prof, Theological Inst in Paris; *Publ: O rynkakh pri kapitalisticheskom proizvodstve* (Markets in Capitalist Production) (1897); *Problemy idealizma* (Problems of Idealism) (1902); *Ot marksizma k idealizmu* (From Marxism to Idealism) (1903); *Svet nevecherniy* "Non-Evening Light" (1917); *Tikhiye dumy* (Quiet Thoughts) (1918); *Died*: 13 July 1944.

BULIN, Anton Stepanovich (1894-1937) Mil commander; army comr, 2nd class from 1935; CP member from 1914; *Born*: 1894 in Moscow Province, son of a peasant; *Career*: before 1917 Revol exiled for organizing a strike of office workers in Petrograd; 1917 was serving in the ranks of the 3rd Infantry Regt, Petrograd Garrison when the Feb Revol began; elected member, Polit Comt, 3rd Infantry Regt; took part in Bolsheviks' July demonstrations against Provisional Govt, was arrested and imprisoned; took part in Oct Revol in Petrograd; as comr of Petrograd Garrison helped to rout Kerensky's troops near Tsarskoye Selo; Aug 1918 put down anti-Bolshevik peasant uprising in Luga; 1919 comr, 6th, 56th and 55th div on Petrograd Front; 1920 comr, 16th Div on Polish Front; fought in Warsaw Campaign; 1921 commandant, Petrograd Fortified Region; 1921-23 secr, Vasiliy Ostrov and Kronstadt Rayon RCP(B) Comts in Petrograd; 1923 staff Comr, Western Front and dep head, Polit Bd, Western Front; summer 1924, in connection with the purge of Trotskyites from the centr organs of the Red Army, transferred to Moscow as polit asst to the commander and head, Polit Bd, Moscow Mil Distr; 1928-35 dep head, Red Army Polit Bd; from 1934 member, Mil Council, Pop Comrt of Defense; 1935-37 polit asst to the commander and head, Polit Bd, Bel Mil Distr; from June 1937 head, Main Personnel Bd, Pop Comrt of Defense and acting head, Red Army Polit Bd; 1926-31 member, Central Control Comt, CPSU(B); 1931-37 cand member, CC, CPSU(B); Nov 1937 arrested by NKVD; *Awards*: Order of the Red Banner; engraved gold watch from Petrograd Sov; *Died*: 1937 in imprisonment; posthumously rehabilitated.

BULYCHEV, Vyacheslav Aleksandrovich (1872-1959) Choirmaster and composer; *Born*: 24 Sept 1872 in Pyatigorsk; *Career*: 1901 organized and headed Moscow Symphony Chorus; 1907 together with S. Tapeyev and others founded Music Theory Library Soc which collected an enormous special library, administered by the Moscow Conservatory since 1924; from 1918 lived in Rumania; *Publ: Orlando Lasso* (1904); *Muzyka strogogo stilya kak predmet deyatel'nosti Moskovskoy simfonicheskoy kapelly* (Strict-Style Music as a Subject for the Moscow Symphony Chorus) (1909); *Khorovoye peniye kak iskusstvo* (The Art of Choral Singing) (1910), etc; *Died*: 10 Apr 1959 in Bucharest.

BUMAZHKOV, Tikhon Pimenovich (1910-1941) Bel partisan organizer and leader; CP member from 1930; *Born*: 1910; *Educ*: 1933 grad Minsk Chemical Technol Technicum; *Pos*: 1933-38 dir, Klimovichi Lime Works and Petrikov Brick Factory; 1938-39 chm, Petrikov Rayon Exec Comt; 1939-41 first secr, Oktyabr' Rayon Comt, CP Bel; *Career*: July-Aug 1941 organized and led in German rear "Red October" partisan unit; *Awards*: Hero of Soviet Union (1941); Order of Lenin; *Died*: 1941 killed in action.

BUNIAT-ZADE, D.Kh. (1888-1938) Party and govt official; CP member from 1908; *Born*: 1888; *Career*: 1917-18 one of leaders, Azer "Gummet" Soc-Democratic group in Baku RSDRP Comt; May-June 1918 member, Exec Comt, Baku Uyezd Sov; from fall 1918 chm, Comrt for Transcaucasian Moslem Affairs, Astrakhan; from 1920 member, CC, CP(B) Azer and member, Azer Revol Comt; from 1921 Azer Pop Comr of Food, Azer Pop Comr of Agric, chm, Azer Gosplan and dep chm, Azer Council of Pop Comr; arrested by State Security organs; *Died*: 1938 in imprisonment.

BUNIN, Ivan Alekseyevich (1870-1953) Russian writer and poet; hon member, Russian Acad of Sci from 1909; *Born*: 22 Oct 1870 in Voronezh, son of a nobleman; *Educ*: 1885 completed four grades at Yelets High-School; then tutored at home by his elder brother Yuliy, who had returned from exile a Populist; *Career*: spent his youth on the family estate at Butyrka, Oryol Province; 1887 published his first poem "At Nadson's Grave"; from 1889 worked as proof-reader, statistician, librarian and journalist; 1891 published first collected verse *Stikhotvoreniya* (Poems) in Oryol; from 1892 also wrote prose; from mid-1890's printed work in periodicals *Russkoye bogatstvo* and *Novoye slovo*; late-1890's involved with *Sreda* (Medium) writers' group, including Maxim Gorky, Leonid Andreyev, Aleksandr Kuprin, etc; then worked for Gorky's *Znaniye* (Knowledge) Publ House; traveled extensively in Europe and visited some Asian and African countries; hostile to 1917 Oct Revol; 1919 edited anti-Sov newspaper *Odesskiye novosti* in Odessa, occupied by White forces and foreign interventionists; 1920 emigrated to France; following traditions of 19th-Century Russian lit, was one of last critical realist writers in 20th-Century Russia; *Publ*: collected verse: *Pod otkrytym nebom* (Under the Open Sky) (1898); *Listopad* (The Fall) (1901); stories: *Sukhodol* (Dry Valley) (1911); *Nochnoy rasskaz* (Night Story) (1911); *Budni* (Workdays) (1913); collected stories: *Tyomnyye allei* (Dark Alleys) (1946); novelettes: *Derevnya* (The Village) (1910); *Brat'ya* (Brethren) (1914); *Gospodin iz San-Frantsisko* (The Gentleman from San Francisco) (1915); *Mitina lyubov'* (Mitya's Love) (1924); *Solnechnyy udar* (Sunstroke) (1927); *Lika* (Faces) (1939); novel *Zhizn' Arsen'yeva* (The Life of Arsen'yev) (1939); *Vospominaniya* (Memoirs) (1950); translated: Longfellow's "The Song of Hiawatha" (1896); Byron's dramas "Manfred" (1904), "Cain" (1905) and "Sky and Earth" (1909), etc; *Awards*: Pushkin Prizes of Russian Acad of Sci; Nobel Prize (1933); *Died*: 8 Nov 1953 in Paris.

BURACHEK, Nikolay Grigor'yevich (1871-1942) Landscape painter; Hon Art Worker of Ukr SSR from 1941; *Born*: 16 Mar 1871 in Letichev, now Khmel'nitskiy Oblast; *Educ*: 1905-10 studied at Krakow Acad of Art; 1910-12 studied in Paris; *Career*: 1925-31 prof, Khar'kov Art Inst; also worked as a set designer; did research on Taras Shevchenko; his early works reveal impressionist influences whereas his later canvases are purely realist; many of his paintings are exhibited in Ukr museums; *Works*: "Morning on the Dnieper" (1934); "Apple Blossom" (1937); "The Kolkhoz Road" (1937), etc; *Publ*: monograph on Shevchenko "The Great National Artist" (1939); *Died*: 12 Aug 1942.

BURDENKO, Nikolay Nilovich (1876-1946) Surgeon; pioneer of Sov neurosurgery; prof from 1912; Dr of Med Sci from 1909; member, USSR Acad of Sci from 1939; member, USSR Acad of Med Sci from 1944; Hon Sci Worker of RSFSR from 1933; Hero of Socialist Labor from 1943; col-gen, Army Med Service; CP member from 1939; *Born*: 8 May 1876 in vil Kamenka, Penza Province; *Educ*: 1906 grad Med Fac, Yur'yev (now Tartu) Univ; *Career*: 1901 expelled from univ for participating in student strike; for a while worked as med orderly, Siberian Railroad Admin; 1904 served in Russo-Japanese War with a Red Cross dressing unit; was wounded in arm and suffered concussion; 1909 defended doctor's thesis on "The Sequelae of Ligation of the Vena Porta"; sent by univ to Germany, France and Switzerland for postgrad training in surgery and neurology; from 1910 assoc prof, from 1912 prof, Chair of Operative Surgery, Yur'yev Univ; during WW 1 asst med chief, Russian Red Cross, then army surgeon, Northwestern Front; after 1917 Feb Revol chief med inspector, Russian Army; from 1917 head, Chair of Fac Surgical Clinic, Yur'yev Univ; 1918 founded Pirogov Surgical Soc in Voronezh; 1920 compiled "Regulations for the Military Medical Service of the Red Army"; from 1920 prof of surgery, 1st Moscow State Univ, member, State Learned Council and member, Russian Surgical Soc; from 1922 head, Chair of Operative Surgery and Topographical Anatomy; 1924-46 head, Chair of Fac Surgical Clinic, Med Fac, 1st Moscow State Univ, where he established a neurosurgical dept; 1929 established a neurosurgical clinic at the Moscow Roentgen Inst; 1934 expanded this clinic into Neurosurgical Inst, of which he became dir; from 1934 consulting surgeon, Main Mil Hospital, USSR Pop Comrt of Defense, which now bears his name; 1935 member, All-Union Centr Exec Comt of 16th convocation and member, Moscow City Sov; from 1937 chief consulting surgeon, Sov Army; during WW 2 chief surgeon of Sov Army; 1944 co-founder, member and (until 1946) pres, USSR Acad of Med Sci; 1945 his Neurosurgical Inst came under the aegis of the USSR Acad of Sci and was named after him; chm, All-Union Assoc of Surgeons; chm, Learned Med Council, USSR Pop Comrt of Health; Bureau chm, All-Union Neurosurgical Council; founder-ed, journal *Voprosy neyrokhirurgii*; member, ed bd, journals *Khirurgiya, Voyenno-sanitarnoye delo*, etc; hon member, Royal Soc (London), American Surgical Assoc, Int Soc of Surgeons, etc; hon dr, Paris Acad of Surgeons; devised numerous surgical and neurosurgical operating methods; founded first maj Sov school of neurosurgery; developed theory of neurosurgery and introduced practical techniques of surgery of the central and peripheral nervous system; made new contributions to surgery of the lungs, abdomen and joints, to the biology of wounds, to field surgery and to the org of the mil med service; memorials or commemorative plaques have been set up in all the institutions which he directed; there are Burdenko Prizes for outstanding contributions to surgery and Burdenko scholarships for outstanding students and postgrad students; *Publ*: over 400 works on field surgery, gen surgery, neurosurgery and the theory and history of med, which are contained in *Sobraniye sochineniy* (Collected Works) (5 vol, 1950); *Awards*: Stalin Prize (1941); threee Orders of Lenin; Order of the Red Banner; Order of the Red Star; Order of the Great Fatherland War, 1st Class; medals; *Died*: 11 Nov 1946.

BURDZHALOV (real name: BURDZHALYAN), Georgiy Sergeyevich (1869-1924) Actor; *Born*: 14 Apr 1869; *Educ*: completed higher tech college; *Career*: while still a student, acted in productions of Art and Lit Soc; 1898-1924 actor, Moscow Arts Theater; from 1921 head, 4th Studio, Moscow Arts Theater and co-founder Moscow Arts Theater Museum; *Roles*: Kostylyov in Gorky's *Na dne* (The Lower Depths); Vasiliy Shuyskiy in A.K. Tolstoy's *Tsar' Fyodor Ioannovich*; the Marquis in Goldoni's "The Innkeeper's Wife"; Pastor Collin in Hauptmann's "Lonely People"; the Grandfather in Ibsen's *Peer Gynt,* etc; *Died*: 10 Dec 1924.

BURDZHALYAN, Arkadiy Sergeyevich (1880-1946) Stage dir; Hon Art Worker of Arm SSR from 1934; *Born*: 7 Jan 1880 in Astrakhan, son of a vintner; *Career*: 1896 joined Stanislavsky's Soc of Art and Lit; from 1908 actor and producer, "Bat" chamber theater; 1913-17 worked at Korsh Theater; 1919-21 producer, Rostov-on-Don Theater; early 1920's mang, Arm Drama Studio, then Arm Theater, Tbilisi; 1924-27 producer, 1st Arm State Theater, Yerevan (now Sundukyan Theater); 1940-43 producer, Mravyan Theater, Leninakan; co-founder and producer, Arm Opera and Ballet Theater, Yerevan; made important contribution to development of Arm nat theater and to reform of production techniques; was one of first producers to apply Stanislavsky method in Arm; *Productions*: "Le Malade Imaginaire" (1923); *Revizor* (The Government Inspector) (1923); Lope da Vega's "The Gardener's Dog" (1925); "The Merchant of Venice" (1926); "Hamlet" (1924); "Othello" (1926); *Shirvanadze's Morgan's Godparent* (1927); Lunacharskiy's *Osvobozhdyonnyy Don Kikhot* (Don Quixote at Large) and *Krasnaya maska* (The Red Mask) (1924); Fayko's *Chelovek s portfelem* (The Man with the Briefcase) (1928), etc; *Died*: 4 Sept 1946.

BURE (real name: NEBEL'SEN), Valeriy Anastas'yevich (1899-1955) Russian actor; Pop Artiste of RSFSR from 1951; *Born*: 5 June 1899; *Career*: 1917 stage debut in Omsk; worked at theaters in Chita, Tobol'sk, Zlatoust, Tula, Khar'kov, Irkutsk and Magnitogorsk; 1932-38 at Sverdlovsk Theater; 1948-54 at Kuybyshev Theater; from 1954 at Stalingrad Theater; *Roles*: Romeo; Cyrano de Bergerac; Rivares in *Ovod* (The Gadfly), after Voynich; Ferdinand in "Kabale und Liebe"; Protasov in Lev Tolstoy's *Zhivoy trup* (The Living Corpse); Semyon Kotko in Katayev's *Shyol soldat s fronta* (A Soldier Came from the Front); Harry Smith in *Russkiy vopros* (The Russian Question); Mayorov in Kron's *Glubokaya razvedka* (Deep Reconnaissance); Napoleon in Solov'yov's *Fel'dmarshal Kutuzov* (Fieldmarshal Kutuzov); Lenin in Pogodin's *Kremlyovskiye kuranty* (Kremlin Chimes); Stalin in Vishnevskiy's *Nezabyvayemyy 1919-y* (The Unforgettable 1919); Ordzhonikidze in Marvich's *Put' v gryadushcheye* (The Path to the Future), etc; *Died*: 31 Oct 1955.

BURLACHENKO, Georgiy Andreyevich (1894-1967) Roentgenologist; prof from 1953; Dr of Med from 1953; *Born*: 1894 in vil Primorskoye, Donetsk Oblast, son of a peasant; *Educ*: 1925 grad Khar'kov Med Inst; *Career*: 1925-29 intern, 1929-41 asst prof, Chair of Roentgenology, Khar'kov Med Inst; 1938-53 Cand of Med Sci; 1941-45 head, x-ray dept, front hostpital; 1945-50 assoc prof, Chair of Roentgenology, Khar'kov Inst of Postgrad Med Training; 1950-67 head, Chair of Roentgenology and Radiology, Khar'kov Med Inst; member, Auditing Commission, All-Union Sci Soc of Roentgenologists and Radiologists; bd member, Ukr and Khar'kov Sci Soc of Roentgenologists and Radiologists; member, Learned Med Council, Ukr Min of Health; consultant at Khar'kov clinics; trained 15 cand of med; wrote over 50 works; *Publ: Rentgenologicheskiy metod opredeleniya obyoma serdtsa* (A Roentgenological Method for Determining the Volume of the Heart) (1938); *Abstsessy lyogkikh* (Lung Abscesses) (1953); *Awards*: Order of the Red Banner of Labor; Order of the Fatherland War, 2nd Class; medal "For Victory Over Germany"; *Died*: 1967.

BURMISTRENKO, Mikhail Alekseyevich (1902-41) Party and govt official; CP member from 1919; *Born*: 1902 in vil Aleksandrovka, Saratov Province; *Educ*: grad Leningrad Communist Univ and Communist Inst of Journalism; *Career*: 1918-22 worked for OGPU in Penza and Engel's; later govt work in Engel's; 1926-32 ed-in-chief of *Trudovaya pravda* in Engel's; 1932-36 second secr, Kalmyk Oblast CPSU(B) Comt; 1936-38 exec posts with CC, CPSU(B); from Jan 1938 second secr, CC, CP(B) Ukr; elected CC member at 14th and 15th Congresses of CP(B) Ukr; Politburo member, CC, CP(B) Ukr; elected member, CC, CPSU(B) at 18th Party Congress; 1938-41 chm, Ukr Supr Sov; during WW 2 member, mil council of a front; *Died*: Sept 1941, killed in action.

BURNASH, Fatkhi (real name: BURNASHEV) Fatkhelislam Zakirovich (1898-1946) Tatar dramatist, poet and publicist; CP member from 1919; *Born*: 13 Jan 1898 in vil Bikshik, now in Chuvash ASSR; *Educ*: studied at Kazan' madressah; *Career*: 1914 first work published; 1916 teacher; during Civil War edited frontline newspapers; 1927-29 dir Tatar Acad Theater, Kazan'; organized and edited many Tatar newspapers and magazines; after formation of Tatar ASSR (1920) elected member, Tatar Centr Exec Comt; *Publ*: anthology "Flowers of the East" (1918); tragedy "Takhir and Zukhra" (1920); drama "Young Hearts" (1920); plays *Husain Mirza* (1922); "Old Kamali" (1925); dramas: "The Prodigal Girl" (1928); "Falcons" (1934); "Aunt Khatira" (1929); "Asma the Weaver" (1932); "Yarulla the Individual Farmer" (1940), etc; also wrote *Poety sovetskoy Tatarii* (Poets of Soviet Tataria) (1936); made first translations of *Yevgeniy Onegin,* N. Ostrovskiy's *Kak zakalyalas' stal'* (How the Steel Was Tempered), Gorky's *Mat'* (Mother), Turgenev's *Otsy i deti* (Fathers and Sons), Tolstoy's *Hadji Murat,* etc; *Died*: 1946.

BUROVTSEV, M.V. (1889-1954) Party and govt official; CP member from 1905; *Born*: 1889; *Career*: after 1917 Oct Revol mang, Moscow Labor Dept and Collegium member, Moscow Public Educ Dept, Moscow Sov; 1921-22 head, National Minorities Dept, CC, RCP(B); 1920-21 in trade-union controversy sided with Ye. Ignatov group, which held the same views as the "workers' opposition"; 1923-24 sided with Trotskyists; 1922-36 worked at intervals for Pop Comrt of For Affairs; arrested by State Security organs; 1937 expelled from Party for Trotskyist sympathies; *Died*: 1954 in imprisonment.

BURTSEV, Vladimir L'vovich (1862-1942) Politician; *Born*: 1862, brought up by his uncle, a rich merchant; *Career*: as a student, in early 1880's sided with *Narodnaya Volya* (People's Will) groups; 1885 arrested for these polit activities and imprisoned in Peter and Paul Fortress; 1886 exiled to Irkutsk Province, fled abroad; 1889 in Geneva financed and published newspaper *Svobodnaya Rossiya,* which he edited with Dragomanov and Debagoriy--Mokriyevich; through *Svobodnaya Rossiya* he championed union of revolutionaries and liberals as "solid anti-govt party" and favored techniques of polit terror; this led to a split with his co-editors; 1891 went to London and studied history of revol movement in Russia, resulting in 1896-97 publ of anthology on history of revol movement *Za Sto Let* (The Past Hundred Years); at same time published journal *Narodovolets*, advocating revol terror and return to Narodnaya Volya methods to achieve polit freedom; arrested by British police and tried for inciting assassination of Nicholas II; sentenced to 18 months' hard labor; 1900, on release, published historical revol journal *Byloye*; altough close to opinions of Socialist-Revolutionaries and keeping contact with them, he did not join the Socialist-Revol Party but instead inclined increasingly to liberal ideas; 1903-04 expelled from France and Switzerland; 1905 wrote letter to Premier Witte promising to speak out against terror if govt would refrain from persecuting revolutionaries; 1905 went to Russia; 1907 again went abroad; gained notoriety by unmasking provocateurs and agents of Russian polit police, especially Garding-Landeyzen and Azef; 1908 resumed publ of emigre journal *Byloye*; 1917 arrived in Russia, started to publish Petrograd newspaper *Obshcheye delo*; following 1917 Oct Revol and after serving short prison sentence moved to South Russia and then to Paris, where he continued to publish *Obshcheye delo*; *Publ: Vospominaniya* (Memoirs) (1923); *V bor'be s bolshevikami i nemtsami* (The Struggle Against the Bolsheviks and Germans) (1923); *Died*: 1942.

BURUNOV, Karadzha (1898-1965) Turkm poet and playwright; Hon Art Worker of Turkm SSR from 1943; *Born*: 1898 in vil Amansha-Kapana, now Ashkhabad Oblast; *Educ*: grad Oriental Fac, Leningrad Univ; *Career*: 1924 first work printed; also translated Russian and for classics into Turkm; *Publ*: play *Dakylma* (1927); poems "The Opium-Smoker" (1927); "Eighteen Drowned" (1929); coauthor, play *Keymir Kyor* (1941); plays: "Cotton"; "Viyuter"; libretto for operas: "Shansenem and Garib" (1943); "Kemine and Kazi" (1944); libretto for ballet "Aldar Kose"; "Selected Works" (1959); translated: Gogol's *Revizor* (The Government Inspector); Pushkin's *Kamennyy gost'* (The Stone Guest); Ostrovskiy's *Groza* (The Storm); Shakespeare's "King Lear" and "Othello"; Korneychuk's "Front"; film scripts: *Lenin v Oktyabre* (Lenin in October); *Velikiy grazhdanin* (The Great Citizen), etc; *Died*: 23 Mar 1965.

BUSH, Nikolay Adol'fovich (1869-1941) Botanist; Dr of Biology; prof; corresp member, USSR Acad of Sci from 1920; senior assoc, Botanical Inst, USSR Acad of Sci from 1931; *Born*: 10 Nov 1869 in Slobodskaya, now Kirov Oblast; *Educ*: 1887-91 studied at Fac of Physics and Mathematics, Kazan' Univ; 1896 grad Petersburg Forestry Inst; *Career*: 1895-1902 asst dir, Botanical Garden; from 1900 assoc prof, Yur'yev Univ; 1902-12 conserver, Petersburg Botanical Garden, simultaneously lectured at various Petersburg higher educ establishments; from 1909 prof, from 1918 head, Chair of Botanical Geography, Petersburg (Leningrad) Univ; 1912-31 simultaneously senior botanist, Botanical Museum, Russian (USSR) Acad of Sci; 1920 founder-dir, Peterhof Biological Inst, Leningrad Univ; 1920-33 also prof, Agronomy (later Agric) Inst; 1931-41 dir, Caucasian Herbarium, Botanical Inst, USSR Acad of Sci; specialized in flora of Caucasus, Siberia and Far East; described numerous new plant varieties and compiled regional botanical maps; suggested new division of Siberia into botanical and geographical zones; wrote textbook on the morphology and taxonomy of higher plants which ran through several ed; *Publ: Obshchiy kurs botaniki. Morfologiya i sistematika rasteniy* (A General Botany Course. Plant Morphology and Taxonomy) (1915); *Botaniko-geograficheskiy ocherk Yevropeyskoy chasti SSSR* (A Botanical and Geographical Study of the European USSR) (1923); coauthor, *Botanicheskoye issledovaniye Yugo-Osetii. 1. Zapadnaya chast'* (A Botanical Study of Southern Ossetia. 1. The West) (1931); *Botaniko--geograficheskiy ocherk Kavkaza* (A Botanical and Geographical Study of the Caucasus) (1935); coauthor, *Rastitel'nyy pokrov vostochnoy Yugo-Osetii i yego dinamika* (The Vegetation of the Eastern Part of Southern Ossetia and Its Dynamics) (1936); *Kurs sistematiki vysshikh rasteniy* (A Course in the Taxonomy of Higher Plants) (1940); *Died*: 7 Aug 1941 in Belozersk.

BUSH, Vladimir Vladimirovich (1888-1934) Lit historian; CP member from 1932; *Born*: 16 Jan 1888 in Petersburg; *Educ*: grad Petersburg Univ; *Career*: from 1915 assoc prof, Petersburg Univ; from 1920 prof, Tashkent Univ; from 1925 prof, Saratov Univ; from 1931 learned secr, Pushkin Center, USSR Acad of Sci, first publ dealt with ancient Russian lit, especially lit of 17th Century; also specialized in Russian populist lit, writing studies of Gleb Uspenskiy, N. Ye. Karonin-Petropavlovskiy, A. I. Ertel, etc, which contained hitherto unknown archive material; also studied the works of self-taught folk writers; *Publ*: *Pamyatniki starinnogo russkogo vospitaniya* (Monuments of Ancient Russian Education) (1918); *Gl. Uspenskiy. V masterskoy khudozhnika slova. Etyudy* (Gleb Uspenskiy. In the Studio of a Master of the Pen. Etudes) (1925); *Literaturnaya deyatel'nost' Gl. Uspenskogo. Ocherki* (The Literary Career of Gleb Uspenskiy. Essays) (1927), etc; *Died*: 14 May 1934 in Leningrad.

BUSHKIN, Aleksandr Ivanovich (1896-1929) Graphic artist and film dir; *Born*: 1 Apr 1896; *Educ*: 1919 grad Kiev Art College; *Career*: 1922 founded cartoon workshop at Moscow State Film Studio; from 1924 artist and dir for cartoon fulms; *Productions*: cartoons; *Yumoreski* (Humoresques); *V mordu II Internatsionalu* (A Slap in the Face for the 2nd International); *Germanskiy dela i delishki* (German Deeds and Doings); *Abort*; *Sluchay v Tokio* (Tokio Incident) (1924); *Kar'yera Makdonal'da* (Mac Donald's Career) and *Durman Dem'yana* (Dem'yan's Trance) (1925); *Chto dolzhen znat' rabochiy i krest'yanin o SSR* (What the Worker and Peasant Should Know About the USSR) (1928), etc; *Publ*: pamphlet *Tryuki i mul'tiplikatsiya* (Tricks and Cartoons) (1926); article "Still Photography" (1926); *Died*: 5 June 1929.

BUTKEVICH, Aleksandr Yakovlevich (1900-1966) Admin official; CP member from 1917; *Born*: Jan 1900; *Career*: helped establish Sov regime in Tomsk; from 1919 in Red Army; after Civil war govt, Party and admin work; fought in WW 2; from 1946 econ admin work; deleg at 14th Party Conference and 17th Party Congress; member, All-Union Centr Exec Comt of 16th convocation; from 1955 pensioner; *Died*: 11 Nov 1966.

BUTKEVICH, Vladimir Stepanovich (1872-1942) Botanist, microbiologist and biochemist; Dr of Biological Sci and Dr of Agric Sci from 1934; corresp member USSR Acad of Sci from 1929; hon member, Russian Botanical Soc from 1926; *Born*: 19 June 1872 on father's estate at vil Rusanovo, Tula Province; *Educ*: 1889 grad Tula Classical Gymnasium; 1894 grad Natural Sci Dept, Fac of Physics and Mathematics, Moscow Univ; 1897 grad Moscow Agric Inst; *Career*: 1898-99 asst prof, Petersburg Agric Laboratory; Russian Min of Agric; 1899-1901 in Switzerland and Germany; 1901-03 prepared for professorship at Moscow Agric Inst; from 1903 assoc prof, Chair of Botany, Moscow Univ; 1903-04 senior asst prof, Chair of Plant Physiology, Novorossiysk Univ; 1904-05 lecturer in plant anatomy and physiology, Warsaw Polytech Inst and lecturer in botany, Warsaw Veterinary Inst; 1905-21 prof, Novo-Aleksandriysk Agric Inst; 1921-25 assoc, Petrovsk Agric Acad; 1925-28 prof, 2nd Moscow State Univ; 1928-42 prof, Timiryazev Agric Acad, Moscow; died major research on the transformation of proteins in plants; determined the function of alpha-aminosuccinamic acid as a reservoir of nitrogenous substances in plants; also did important research on the chemism of the formation and transformation of organic acids in plants--an area of plant physiology which he developed almost singlehanded; developed new theory of plant respiration according to which the basic process consists in the acidification of hydrocarbons without preliminary fission along the lines of spirit fermentation; his work on the formation of citric acid in mould fungi led to the creation of a new branch of the Sov chemical ind--the production of citric acid from sugar; his microbiological method of prospecting for oil and gas is of importance for the oil industry, as is his method of determining how much phosphorus and nitrogenous fertilizer different soils need for agric; did research on the bacteria of the Arctic seas and established the presence of micro-organisms in the formation of ferromanganese deposits on the sea bed; wrote over 110 works; *Publ*: articels "Ammonia as a Product of the Conversion of Albuminous Substances by Mould Fungi and the Conditions of its Formation" (1916); "Acids as an Intermediary Stage of the Acidifying Conversion of Sugar by Fungi" (1925); "The Biochemical Origin of Vegetable Acids" (1932); coauthor, "Microbiological Methods of Determining the Fertilizer Requirements of Soils" (1932); "The Present State of Knowledge on the Chemism of Respiratory Processes in Vegetable Organisms" (1941); *Izbrannyye trudy* (Selected Works) (1957); *Awards*: Order of the Red Banner of Labor (1940); *Died*: 4 Nov 1942 in Moscow.

BUTOMO, Viktor Grigor'yevich (1894-1963) Obstetrician and gynecologist; col, Navy Med Service; Dr of Med; *Born*: 1894 in Mogilev Province; *Educ*: 1919 grad Petrograd Mil Med Acad (now Kirov Mil Med Acad, Leningrad); *Pos*: 1919-45 intern, asst prof, senior asst prof, assoc prof and prof, Chair of Obstetrics and Gynecology, Leningrad Naval Med Acad; 1945-56 head, Chair of Obstetrics and Gynecology, Naval Fac, Leningrad Mil Med Acad; *Career*: in charge of gynecological research and org work for Navy med service; Presidium member, Leningrad Obstetrical and Gynecological Soc; member, Obstetrics Council and Council for Forensic Med Expertise, Leningrad City Health Dept; examiner, Higher Certifying Commission, USSR Min of Higher and Specialized Secondary Educ; member, ed bd, journal *Akusherstvo i ginekologiya*; wrote over 70 works, notably on: clinical and experimental research on protein therapy in obstetrics and gynecology, nitrogen and phosphorus exchange in the parenteral application of protein, the role of the reticulo-endothelial system, the significance of sex hormones in human and animal pregnacy, infertility, the influence of malaeria on pregnancy, the metabolism between mother and fetus, painless childbirth, and physiological processes in the sex life of women within the Arctic Circle; *Publ*: doctor's thesis *Diagnosticheskaya tsennost' metoda produvaniya fallopiyevykh trub pri razlichnykh formakh zhenskogo besplodiya* (The Diagnostic Value of Ventilating the Fallopian Tubes in Various Forms of Female Infertility); *Malariya i beremennnost'* (Malaria and Pregnancy); *Organizatsiya ginekologicheskoy pomoshchi v period Velikoy Otechestvennoy voyny* (The Organization of Gynecological Assistance During the Great Fatherland War); two collections of material on metabolism between mother and fetus; *Awards*: Order of Lenin; two Orders of the Red Banner; medals; *Died*: 26 Apr 1963.

BUTORIN, Nikolay Nikolayevich (1893-1961) Actor, stage dir and teacher; Hon Artiste of RSFSR from 1945; CP member from 1943; *Born*: 23 May 1893; *Career*: 1914-16 at V. E. Meyerhold's studio; from 1915 producer, Petersburg Fine Arts Soc; after 1917 Oct Revol producer, Kuban' Workers' Theater; chief producer, Kuban' Children's and Youth Theater; 1924-26 actor, 1925-26 dir, Meyerhold Theater, Moscow; 1926-29 producer, Shevchenko and Franko Theaters and chief producer, Children's and Youth Theater, Dnepropetrovsk; 1930 co-founder, Siberian Experimental Theater (from 1934 Irkutsk Theater); 1940-43 artistic dir, Krasnoyarsk Theater; 1943-50 artistic dir; Vladivostok Theater; 1950-52 artistic dir, South Sakhalinsk Theater; *Productions:* Kheyermans' *Gibel' 'nadezhdy'* (The End of the "Nadezhda"); *Vzryv Sofiyskogo Sobora* (The Explosion at Sofia Cathedral) (1925); *Karnaval knigi* (The Book Carneval) (1926), etc; *Died*: 1 Sept 1961.

BUTSENKO, Afanasiy Ivanovich (1889-1965) Govt official; CP member from 1909; *Born*: 1889, son of a peasant; *Career*: metalworker at the Dumont Plant in Lugansk; 1909 joined RSDRP(B); in WW 1 taken prisoner by the German army and interned in Ukr pow camp; active in prisoners' socialist group; after 1917 Oct Revol member, first CC, CP Ukr; also elected member, Centr Control Commission, CP(B) Ukr; during the hetman regime did underground work in Ukr; 1923-29 Presidium member, All-Ukr Centr Exec Comt; 1927 secr, All-Ukr Centr Exec Comt; from 1930 chm, Far Eastern Kray Exec Comt; 1933-35 member, RSFSR Council of Pop Comr; head, Main Bd, Road Trans Construction; 1936-37 chm, Tobol'sk Okrug Exec Comt; 1937 arrested by State Security organs; 1955 rehabilitated; from 1955 pensioner; *Died*: 21 Mar 1965.

BUTURLIN, Sergey Aleksandrovich (1872-1938) Zoologist, geographer and hunter; *Born*: 1872; *Career*: expert on northern regions of USSR; explored north of Arkhangel'sk Oblast, Kolguev Island, Novaya Zemlya, Kolyma and the Chukot Peninsula; pioneer of Sov professional hunting techniques; made major contribution to ind exploitation of game and wildfowl reserves; also specialized in taxonomy, ecology and biogeography af birds; wrote over 2,000 works and compiled large ornithological collection, which is now in the Zoological Museum of Moscow Univ; *Publ*: coauthor, *Po severu Rossii* (In the North of Russia) (1901); *Kuliki Rossiyskoy imperii* (The Snipes of the Russian Empire) (1902); *Nastol'naya kniga okhotnika* (The Hunter's Manual) (1930); *Opredelitel' promyslovykh ptits* (A Catalog of Game Birds) (1933); coauthor, *Polnyy opredelitel' ptits SSSR* (A Complete Catalog of the Birds of the USSR) (5 vol, 1934-41); *Died*: 1938.

BUTYAGIN, Pavel Vasil'yevich (1867-1953) Microbiologist; Dr of Med from 1901; prof from 1919; Hon Sci Worker of RSFSR; *Born*: 1867; *Educ*: 1893 grad Med Fac, Tomsk Univ; *Career*: 1895 established first Siberian unit for the production of diphtheria vaccine at Tomsk Univ; 1906 helped to organize Tomsk Bacteriological Inst, which he directed for 25 years and which provided specialist training for microbiologists and physicians from outlying districts; from 1910 assoc prof, from 1919 prof, Tomsk Univ; subsequently prof, Tomsk Inst of Postgrad Med Training, which later moved to Novosibirsk, where he was in charge of the Chair of Microbiology; specialized in the physiology of bacteria and the production of vaccines and sera; did research on antibodies and changes in the blood of immunized animals, for which he found 20 criteria; produced a potent diphtheria vaccine; *Publ: Ob izmenenii krovi u loshadey, immuniziruyemykh protiv difterii* (Blood Change in Horses Immunized Against Diphtheria) (1901); *O gazoobmene bakteriy* (The Gas Metabolism of Bacteria) (1908); *O vliyanii nizkikh temperatur an zhiznesposobnost' bakteriy* (The Effect of Low Temperatures on the Viability of Bacteria) (1909); *O batsillyarnykh vozbuditelyakh dizenterii v svyazi s voprosom ob etiologii dizenterii v Tomske* (The Bacillary Agents of Dysentery in Connection with the Etiology of Dysentery in Tomsk) (1911); *Died*: 1953.

BUTYRSKIY, Vasiliy Petrovich (1898-1938) Mil commander; div commander from 1935; CP member from 1923; *Born*: 1898; *Career*: during Civil War chief, Operations Dept, Staff of 45th Infantry Div; after Civil War held various staff and command posts; 1936-37 chief of staff, Kiev Mil Distr; 1937 arrested by NKVD; *Died*: 1938 in imprisonment; posthumously rehabilitated.

BUYKO, Aleksandr Mikhaylovich (Party pseudonyms: SHURA NARVSKIY, OKRUZHNOY) (1885-1941) Party and govt official; CP member from 1904; *Born*: 1885 in Vilnius Province, son of a peasant; *Career*: 1899-1907 metalworker, Putilov Plant in Petersburg; simultaneously studied at the plant's tech night school; 1904 joined RSDRP(B); 1906 member, Petersburg RSDRP(B) Comt; 1907-09 full-time Party work; 1908 attended All-Russian Party Conference in Paris; 1 Mar 1909 arrested and permanently exiled to Eastern Siberia; stayed there from 1910 to 1917 Feb Revol; in exile worked for the co-operative system and wrote reports for *Zvezda* and *Pravda*; 1917 elected asst chm, Verkhneudinsk Sov of Workers, Peasants and Soldiers' Dep; later town mayor; early 1918 chm, Revol Tribunal in Baykal Region and member, Baykal Oblast Exec Comt; from late 1918, after collapse of Sov regime in Siberia and Far East, emigrated to Mongolia and China; from 1921 worked in the Far Eastern Republ; 1922 chm, Pop Assembly, Far Eastern Republ; 1921-24 member and secr, Far Eastern Bureau, CC RCP; from 1925 RSFSR Dep Pop Comr of Trade; dep chief arbiter, RSFSR Council of Pop Comr; arrested by State Security organs; *Died*: 1941 in imprisonment.

BUYKO, Mariya Stepanovna (1885-1965) Educationist; revol; CP member from 1907; *Born*: 5 Mar 1885 *Educ*: grad Bestuzhev Courses; *Career*: teacher in Petrograd; Oct 1905 first-aid nurse at Putilov Plant, Petrograd; 1910-17 in exile in Irkutsk Province and Verkhneudinsk; propaganda among soldiers' wives and teachers; from 1923 lectured in Chita and Moscow; from 1941 pensioner; *Died*: 12 Mar 1967.

BUYKO, Pyotr Mikhaylovich (1895-1943) Gynecologist and obstetrician; prof from 1938; Dr of Med Sci from 1940; Hero of the Sov Union from 1944 (posthumously); CP member from 1921; *Born*: 19 Oct 1895 in Bel'sk, Grodno Province, Bel; *Educ*: 1922 grad Kiev Med Inst; *Career*: Apr 1917 joined revol movement in Kiev; Jan 1918 took part in uprising against Centr Rada; 1919 med orderly, Turbov Sugar Refinery, near Vinnitsa, where he engaged in underground revol work; 1922-30 gynecologist and obstetrician at various hospitals; 1930 assoc prof, Gynecological and Obstetric Clinic, Kiev Med Inst; from 1931 head, Chair of Gynecology and Obstetrics, Kiev Stomatological Inst; from 1933 dir, Ukr Research Inst of Mother and Child Care, which he helped to found; 1940 defended doctor's thesis on the surgical treatment of colpocystosyrinx using placental tissue as a free transplant; devised method of fistulography for detecting fistules in the early stages; from 1938 prof, Chair of Obstetrics and Gynecology, Kiev Med Inst; 1939 took part in occupation of the Western Ukr as head of a med battalion; at beginning of WW 2 first surgeon in a med battalion; wounded in the shoulder and captured near Uman'; escaped and made his way to Fastov, where he worked in the rayon hospital, treating wounded partisans in the infectious ward during the occupation; on discovery by the Germans fled with medical equipment and personnel; July 1943 joined partisan detachment and took charge of med unit; 13 Oct 1943 captured by Germans in vil Yaroshevka; executed two days later after rejecting chance to escape for fear of reprisals against the villagers; *Publ*: doctor's thesis *Khirurgicheskoye lecheniye puzyrno-vlagalishchnykh svishchey u zhenshchin s primeneniyem platsentarnoy tkani. Kliniko-eksperimental'noye issledovaniye* (The Surgical Treatment of Colpocystosyrinx Using Placental Tissue. Clinical Experimental Research) (1948); *Died*: 15 Oct 1943.

BUYNAKSKIY, Ullubuy Danielovich (1890-1919) Kumyk revolutionary; one of first Bolsheviks among Dagh highlanders; CP member from 1916; *Born*: 19 Nov 1890 in vil Ullu-Buynak; prince by descent; *Educ*: grad Stavropol College; attended Moscow Univ; *Career*: after 1917 Feb Revol worked for Moscow Bolshevik Party org; then moved to Dagh and set up Bolshevik group; Nov 1917 headed Mil Revol Comt in Petrovsk Port (now Makhachkala); Mar 1918, after collapse of Sov regime in city moved to Astrakhan'; Apr - fall 1918 headed Sov regime in Dagh; when highland nationalists took power in Dagh he returned to Astrakhan'; Mar 1919 illegally returned to Dagh with group of Astrakhan' Bolsheviks; established underground Oblast RCP(B) Comt and organized insurgent Red Army; 13 May 1919 entire staff of Dagh Oblast RCP(B) Comt arrested by nationalists; *Died*: 18 Aug 1919 sentenced to death and shot; city of Temir-Khan-Shura renamed Buynaksk in his memory.

BUZESKUL, Vladislav Petrovich (1858-1931) Ancient historian; Dr of Historical Sci from 1895; prof from 1890; member, USSR Acad of Sci from 1922; member, Ukr Acad of Sci from 1925; *Born*: 8 Mar 1858 in vil Popovka, now Donetsk Oblast; *Educ*: completed higher educ; *Career*: 1890-1921 prof, Khar'kov Univ, then worked for USSR Acad of Sci; specialized in history of Ancient Greece; *Publ: Perikl. Istoriko-kriticheskiy etyud* (Pericles. A Critical Historical Study) (1889); *'Afinskaya politika' Aristotelya kak istochnik dlya istorii gosudarstvennogo stroya Afin do kontsa 5 veka* (Aristotle's Poliya" as a Source for Studying the History of the Athenian Political Structure Until then End of the 5th Century) (1895); *Istoriya afinskoy demokratii* (The History of Athenian Democracy) (1909); *Vvedeniye v istoriyu Gretsii* (An Introduction to the History of Greece) (3rd ed, 1915); *Antichnost' i sovremennost'* (The Ancient and the Modern World) (1913); *Otkrytiya XIX i nachala XX vekov v oblasti istorii drevnego mira* (19th- and Early 20th-Century Discoveries in the History of the Ancient World) (2 vol, 1923-24); *Vseobshchaya istoriya i yeyo predstaviteli v Rossii v XIX i nachale XX veka* (General History and Its Exponents in Russia in the 19th and Early 20th Centuries) (2 vol, 1929-31); *Died*: 1 Apr 1931.

BUZ'KO, Dmitriy Ivanovich (1891-1943) Ukr writer; *Born*: 1891 in Kherson; *Educ*: grad Agric Fac, Copenhagen Univ; *Career*: in 1920's began lit work; for a while member, *Novaya generatsiya* (The New Generation) lit assoc; also wrote for children and young people; *Publ*: "The Forest Beast" (1924); "Holland" (1930); "Blast Furnaces" (1932); "Descendants of the Brave" (1933); "The Crystal Land" (1935); "Yadviga and Malka - Polish Partisans" (1936), etc; *Died*: 18 Apr 1943.

BUZUK, Pyotr Afanas'yevich (1891-1933) Bel philologist; *Born*: 1891; *Educ*: 1916 grad Odessa Univ; *Career*: from 1925 chm, Dialectological Commission, Inst of Bel Culture; also prof of gen linguistics, Bel Univ; 1931-33 dir, Inst of Linguistics, Bel Acad of Sci; specialized in Bel and other East Slavic languages; fall 1933 arrested, held for a time by State Security organs and interrogated on charges of "Bel nationalism"; *Publ: Kratkaya istoriya ukrainskogo yazyka* (A Short History of Ukrainian) (1924); *Mesto belorusskogo yazyka sredi drugikh slavyanskikh yazykov* (Belorussian's Place Among the Other Slavic Languages) (1927); *Ocherk istorii doistoricheskoy epokhi slavyanskoy fonetiki* (An Outline History of the Prehistoric Period of Slavic Phonetics) (1928); *Ocherk lingvisticheskoy geografii Belorussii* (A Study in the Linguistic Geography of Belorussia) (1928), etc; *Died*: 1933 committed suicide by self-immolation.

BYADULYA, Zmitrok (Real name: PLAVNIK, Samuil Yefimovich (1886-1941) Bel writer of Jewish extraction; member, Bel Writers' Union from 1934; *Born*: 5 May 1886 in vil Pasadets, Vilnius Province; *Educ*: studied at Jewish theological seminaries in vil Dovginovo and Il'ya; *Career*: 1902-1912 laborer, then overseer for timber floats; 1910 first works published; from 1912 worked for Bel newspaper *Nasha niva* in Vilnius; 1920-26 on ed staff of newspaper *Savetskaya Belarus'*; 1921-23 simultaneously ed, children's magazine, *Zorka*; 1923-26 member, *Maladnyak* (Youth) Lit Assoc; 1926-31 member, *Uzvyshsha* (Eminence) Lit Assoc; from 1927 ed, regional studies journal *Nash kray*, organ of the Inst of Bel Culture, then of the Bel Acad of Sci; 1929-30 subjected to Party criticism for Bel nationalism; 1930 published letter of repentance in order to avoid arrest and exile; during 1930's criticized for "ideological errors" in his short story "The Nightingale" and novel *Yazep Krushyinski*; wrote very little during last decade of life; *Publ*: collected stories *Abrazki* (Scraps) (1913); *Na zacharovanykh gonyakh* (The Enchanted Cornfields) (1923); *Apavyadan'ni* (Short Stories) (1926); *Vybranyya apavyadan'i* (Selected Stories) (1926); *Nezvychaynyya historyi* (Strange Tales) (1931); *Pa proydzenykh stsezhkakh* (The Beaten Track) (1940); novellae *Tanziliya* (1927); collected verse: *Pad rodnym nebam* (Beneath Native Skies) (1922); *Buralom* (Windfallen Wood) (1925); *Paemy* (Poems) (1927); short stories: *Salavey* (The Nightingale) (1928); *Nablizhen'ne* (The Approach) (1935); *U drymuchym lese* (In the Dense Forest) (1939); novel *Yazep Krushynski* (2 vol, 1929-32); children's books: *Kakachka-tstsachka* (The Toy Duckling) (1927); *Vyasnoy* (Springtime) (1928); *Haspadarka* (The Farm) (1930); *Khlopchyk z-pad Hrodna* (The Lad from Grodno) (1940); *Lyutsik* (1941); *Murashka Palashka* (Palashka the Ant) (1948); *Maye zabavy* (My Pastimes) (1949); *Kazki* (Fairytales) (1956); *Syarebranaya tabakerka* (The Silver Snuff-Box) (1958); *Vybranyya tvory* (Selected Works) (1945); *Paemy* (Poems) (1947); *Zbor tvoray* (Collected Works) (4 vol, 1951-53); *Awards*: Order of the Red Banner of Labor (1939); *Died*: 3 Nov 1941 during evacuation near Ural'sk.

BYALYNITSKIY-BIRULYA, Aleksey Andreyevich (1864-1938) Zoologist; prof, Leningrad Univ; senior zoologist and dir, Zoological Museum, USSR Acad of Sci; *Born*: 1864; *Career*: 1899 took part in Spitzbergen expedition of Russian Acad of Sci; 1900-03 took part in polar expedition under E. V. Toll'; helped to found Permanent Comt for the Study of Malarial Mosquitos, Zoological Museum, USSR Acad of Sci; 1928 organized expedition to Centr Asia which marked the beginning of large-scale field research on parasitology in USSR; did research on coelentrates, worms, crustaceans, myriapods, arachnids, birds and mammals; wrote over 120 works, notably on the taxonomy of mammals, Scorpionida and Galeodes arancoides; did his own illustrations; *Publ*: article "Studies of Bird Life on the Polar Littoral of Siberia" (1907); article "Arthropods and Arachnids of the Caucasian Region" (1917); article "Scorpionida" (1917); article "Galeodes arancoides" (1917); *Died*: 1938.

BYALOKOZ, Yevgeniy Lyudvigovich (1861-1919) Hydrographer; lt-gen; founder of Sov hydrography; *Born*: 1861 in Moscow; *Educ*: 1882 grad Naval College; 1888 grad Hydrographic Dept, Naval Acad; *Career*: from 1888 engaged in hydrographic work; from Mar 1917 head, Main Hydrographic Bd; on his initiative time zone system was introduced in the Russian Navy from 1 May 1918 and in the whole country from 1 Apr 1919; 1918-19 organized hydrographic service in the Baltic and Caspian; Apr 1918 suggested that a hydrographic expedition be dispatched to the Arctic to find sea routes for the exploitation of Siberian maritime areas; *Died*: 18 Dec 1919.

BYCHKOV, Aleksandr Ivanovich (1862-1925) Politician; member, People's Will Party; *Born*: 1862, son of an eng; *Educ*: grad Kiev high-school; *Career*: 1879 joined Kiev People's Will org; 1881 arrested for revol propaganda and sentenced to admin banishment from Kiev; then sentenced to death; sentence commuted to indefinite exile; twice fled from exile and prison; while in Siberia, contributed to local newspapers and journals on regional studies; 1906 moved to Moscow; exiled from Russia; returned to Russia, then exiled to Chyornyy Yar, Astrakhan' Province; 1911 edited periodical *Sumskiy vestnik*; spent a total of 29 years in prison and exile; after 1917 Oct Revol member, Khar'kov Sov of Workers' Dep; from 1922 directed Museum of Centr Archives of the Revol, Khar'kov; *Publ*: articles "Revolutionary Circles in Kiev in 1879, 1880 and 1881" (1924); "Two Escapes" (1926); *Died*: 27 Sept 1925.

BYCHKOV, Ivan Afanas'yevich (1858-1944) Archivist and bibliographer; corresp member, Russian (USSR) Acad of Sci from 1903; *Born*: 19 Aug 1858; *Educ*: 1881 grad Law Fac, Petersburg Univ; *Career*: for 63 years custodian, Manuscript Dept, Public Library - a post formerly held by his father A.F. Bychkov; continuing a tradition established by his father, he published annual "Reports" on the library's manuscript collections and accessions; from 1887 member, Archives Commission; after father's death published Vol 5-7 of *Pis'ma i bumagi Petra Velikogo* (Letters and Documents of Peter the Great); published material on 19th-century Russian writers and personalities, including V.A. Zhukovskiy, M.A. Korf, Pushkin, Gogol, etc; apart from being an expert on manuscripts, he was also a specialist in related historical disciplines; during WW 2 stayed in Leningrad during siege to help collect the manuscripts of dead or evacuated scholars and writers; *Died*: 23 March 1944.

BYKHOVSKIY, Grigoriy Borisovich (1861-1936) Surgeon and oncologist; *Born*: 1861; *Educ*: 1889 grad Kiev Univ; *Career*: while still a student, worked at F.K. Borngaupt's Surgical Clinic and after grad worked for a number of years as Borngaupt's asst; co-founder and practitioner, Kiev Free Surgical Clinic; 1922 co-founded Kiev Clinical Inst of Postgrad Med Training; 1922-31 head, Surgical Clinic, above inst; 1932 founded oncological outpatients dept and 1934 an oncological clinic at the Kiev Roentgenological Inst; trained many oncologists; chm, Surgical Section, United Sci Med Soc; bd member, then chm, Med Council, Kiev City Med Aid Soc; from 1930 asst chm, Kiev Surgical Soc; *Publ*: coauthor and co-ed, *Zlokachestvennyye novoobrazovaniya* (Malignant Neoplasms); *K* *voprosu o predelakh probnoy laparotomii* (The Limits of Trial Laparotomy) (1927); *Rak pryamoy kishki* (Cancer of the Rectum) (1934); *Rak tolstykh kishok* (Cancer of the Large Intestine) (1937); *Died*: 1936 in Kiev.

BYKOV, Anatoliy Vladimirovich (1892-1943) Actor, stage dir and playwright; *Born*: 1892; *Educ*: grad Physics and Mathematics Fac, Moscow Univ; *Career*: 1917, together with A.A. Lyovshina, founded a theater studio, reorganized in 1919 into the Semperante Theater; artistic dir, stage dir and actor, Semperante Theater; scripted and produced his own plays; *Roles*: Nabukh-Sagaylo in *Karusel'* (Carousel); Sklipa in *Grimasy* (Grimaces) (1921); Troll' in *Dva* (Two) (1924); Klyuyev in *Golovonogiy chelovek* (The Cephaloped Man) (1929), etc; *Died*: 1943.

BYKOV, Konstantin Mikhaylovich (1886-1959) Physiologist; prof from 1926; Dr of Med; Hon Sci Worker of RSFSR from 1940; maj-gen, Mil Med Service from 1943; member, USSR Acad of Med Sci from 1944; member, USSR Acad of Sci from 1946; corresp member, Int Acad of the History of Sci; *Born*: 20 Jan 1886 in Chukhloma, Kostroma Province; *Educ*: 1906 began studies at Fac of Physics and Mathematics, Kazan' Univ; in same year transferred to Fac of Physics and Mathematics, Geneva Univ; 1908 returned to Kazan' Univ, entered Med Fac and grad 1912; *Career*: 1911-14 did research on physiology under Prof N. A. Mislavskiy; from 1912 asst dissector, from 1920 dissector, Chair of Physiology, Kazan' Univ; also taught physiology on dental courses and at school for med orderlies in Kazan'; 1914-15 wrote doctor's thesis at Kazan' Univ; 1915-17 mil physician; 1921-32 asst prof, Physiology Dept, Leningrad Inst of Experimental Med, where he worked under Pavlov; simultaneously taught physiology at Herzen State Teachers' Training Inst, initially as assoc prof, then, from 1926, as prof; 1923-27 head, physiology section, 1924-28 head, laboratory for the study of higher nervous activity, Red Army Physical Training Courses; 1925-30 co-ed, journal *Trudy fiziologicheskikh laboratoriy akademika Pavlova*; 1927 assoc prof, Chair of Animal Physiology, Leningrad Univ; in same year visited Germany and France to study latest physiological research methods; 1928-40 prof, Chair of the Physiology of Higher Nervous Activity, Leningrad Univ; 1932-33 head, Dept of Applied Physiology, All-Union Inst of Experimental Med; 1932-40 head, Chair of Physiology, 3rd Leningrad Med Inst; 1933-50 head, Dept of Gen Physiology, All-Union Inst of Experimental Med; 1940-51 head, Chair of Physiology, Leningrad Naval Med Acad; 1948-50 founder-dir, Inst of the Physiology of the Centr Nervous System, USSR Acad of Med Sci; 28 June-4 July 1950 as chm, Sci Council on Pavlov's Physiological Theory, USSR Acad of Sci, was one of main speakers at joint session of USSR Acad of Sci and USSR Acad of Med Sci which drafted policy for further development of Sov physiology and repudiated school of physiology represented by L. A. Orbeli and I. S. Beritashvili; from 1950 dir, Pavlov Inst of Physiology, USSR Acad of Sci and chief consultant on physiology, USSR Navy; 1950 dep, Leningrad City Sov; 1951 dep, RSFSR Supr Sov; 1955 dep chm, RSFSR Supr Sov; from 1932 dep chm, Sechenov Soc of Physiologists, Leningrad; from 1950 dep chm, All-Union Soc of Physiologists, Biochemists and Pharmacologists; from 1948 founder and life chm, Leningrad Soc of Med History; chief ed, numerous sci publ; 1947, 1950 and 1956 attended Int Physiological Congresses in England, Copenhagen and Brussels; wrote over 250 works on Pavlov's theory, life and works, the functional relationship between the cerebral cortex and internal organs, the physiology of digestion, the chemical transfer of stimuli, experimental balneology, etc; supervised compilation of 35 doctor's theses, 55 cand theses and 600 papers; *Publ: Lektsii po fiziologii pishchevareniya* (Lectures on the Physiology of Digestion) (1940); *Kora golovnogo mozga i vnutrenniye organy* (The Cerebral Cortex and the Internal Organs) (2nd ed, 1944); *Uchebnik fiziologii dlya meditsinskikh studentov* (A Textbook on Physiology for Medical Students) (2nd ed, 1947); article "The Development of the Ideas of Soviet Theoretical Medicine" (1947); coauthor, *Kortiko-vistseral'naya teoriya patogeneza yazvennoy bolezni* (The Cortico-Visceral Theory of the Pathogenesis of Ulcerous Diseases) (1949); article "Pavlov's Theory in the Light of Dialectical Materialism" (1949); *Razvitiye idey I. P. Pavlova* (The Development of Pavlov's Ideas) (1950); *Izbrannyye proizvedeniya* (Selected Works) (3 vol, 1953-58); *Awards*: Order of Lenin; two Orders of the Red Banner of Labor; Order of the Red Star; Pavlov Prize (1939); Stalin Prize, 1st Class (1946); Pavlov Gold Medal (1951); medals and inscribed dirk; *Died*: 13 May 1959.

BYKOV, Nikolay Alekseyevich (1862-1939) Thermal eng; specialist in internal combusition engines; *Born*: 18 Dec 1862; *Educ*: 1888 grad Med Fac, Kazan' Univ; 1896 grad Petersburg Technol Inst; *Career*: 1899-1910 lecturer, from 1910 prof, Petersburg Technol Inst and Electr Eng Inst; after 1917 Oct Revol prof and head, Chair of Internal Combustion Engine Design, Naval Acad; 1902 gave first Russian course on steam turbines; 1900-30 tested almost all new thermal machinery, isolating teething problems and faults; tested first reversive diesel to be built at Russian Diesel Plant and installed in first Russian diesel vessel; permanent consultant and expert for many enterprises and establishments, such as Russian Registry Office, Diesel Research Inst, etc; *Publ: Termodinamika* (Thermodynamics) (1928); *Dopol'nitel'nyye stat'i po termodinamike* (Additional Articles on Thermodynamics) (1929); *Died*: 23 Apr 1939.

BYKOV, Nikolay Vladimirovich (1909-1945) Cameraman; CP member from 1943; *Born*: 31 Dec 1909; *Educ*: studied at Kiev Inst of Cinematography; *Career*: 1929 began working as film critic, then became a cameraman at Kiev Studios for Pop Sci Films; during WW 2 filmed with frontline documentary unit, accompanying partisans behind the lines; worked on Dovzhenko's film *Osvobozhdeniye* (liberation) about the annexation of the Western Ukr; *Works*: contributions to *Kinoletopis' Velikoy Otechestvennoy voyny* (Film Chronicle of the Great Fatherland War) and *Narodnyye mstiteli* (Avengers of the People); pop sci film *Parazitologiya* (Parasitology) (1931); series *Bor'ba s avariynost'yu* (Accident Prevention) (1932-37); training films *Teoriya polyota* (The Theory of Flight) (1939); *Desantirovaniye vozdushnykh voysk* (Paratroop Drops); *Parashyut* (The Parachute); *Tarannyy udar* (Frontal Assault), etc; *Awards*: Stalin Prize (1946); *Died*: 18 Apr 1945 during capture of Breslau.

BYKOV, Pyotr Vasil'yevich (1843-1930) Russian writer and bibliographer; *Born*: 1 Nov 1843 in Sebastopol; *Educ*: grad Physics and Mathematics Fac, Khar'kov Univ; *Career*: 1861 first work printed; wrote verse, stories and articles; 1881-1900 helped edit journal *Russkoye bogatstvo*; 1911-15 co-ed, journal *Sovremennik*; 1885-86 co-ed newspaper *Step'*; 1904-05 co-ed, newspaper *Slovo*; wrote bibliographical studies of major lit figures such as: A.S. Afanas'yev-Chuzhbinskiy, A.N. Pleshcheyev, M.L. Mikhaylov, I.V. Omulevskiy (Fyodorov), Leskov, Lermontov, Tyutchev, etc; *Publ: L.A. Meya* (1887); *N.S. Leskov* (1889); *Siluety proshlogo* (Silhouettes of the Past) (1930), etc; *Died*: Oct 1930 in Leningrad.

BYSTRYANSKIY, Vadim Aleksandrovich (1885-1940) Historian; and journalist; CP member from 1907; *Born*: 1885; *Educ*: studied at Petersburg Univ; *Career*: 1907-09 Party work in Petersburg; 1909 arrested; spent some eight years in prison and exile; after 1917 Feb Revol worked for Kiev RSDRP(B) Comt and Bolshevik newspaper *Zvezda* in Yekaterinoslav; Oct 1917 returned to Petrograd and did propaganda and agitation work in connection with Oct Revol; 1917 at 2nd All-Russian Congress of Soviets elected member, All-Russian Centr Exec Comt; member, ed staff, *Izvestia*; from 1922 teaching and research work in Leningrad; 1919, 1927 and 1930 deleg at 8th, 15th and 16th Party Congresses; wrote studies of Lenin; compiled systematic index of Lenin's works; in his latter years directed Leningrad Inst of Party History; *Publ: Lenin kak materialist-dialektik* (Lenin as a Dialectical Materialist) (1925); *Leninistorik. Istorizm v Leninizme* (Lenin the Historian. Historicism in Leninism) (1925), etc; *Died*: 13 Dec 1940.

BYUL'-BYUL' (real name: MAMEDOV), Rza-ogly (1897-1961) Opera singer (lyric and dramatic tenor); soloist, Azer Opera Theater, Baku, (later Akhundov Theater of Opera and Ballet) from 1920; prof, Azer State Conservatory, Baku from 1940; Pop Artiste of USSR from 1938; *Born*: 22 June 1897 in vil Khanbagy, now Azer SSR; *Educ*: 1927 grad Azer State Conservatory; *Career*: 1932-40 instructor, Azer State Conservatory; 1932 founded group for research on Azer music; 1938 and 1956 published two anthologies of Azer folksongs; also made concert appearances; dep, Azer Supr Sov of 1947, 1951 and 1955 convocations; *Roles*: leads in Azer operas - Gliere's *Shakhsenem*; Gadzhibekov's *Kyor-ogly* and *Arshin mal alan*; Magomayev's *Nergiz*; Karayev and Gadzhiyev's *Veten*, etc; also sang leads in Verdi's "Rigoletto"; Puccini's "Tosca"; Rachmaninoff's "Aleko", etc; *Awards*: Stalin Prize (1950); Order of Lenin; Order of the Red Banner of Labor; Badge of Hon; medals; *Died*: 26 Sept 1961 in Baku.

BYULER, Vol'demar Aleksandrovich (1896-1938) Mil commander; brigade commander from 1935; CP member from 1915; *Born*: 1896; *Educ*: grad higher pilot-observers school; *Career*: active in 1917 Oct Revol in Kazan'; first Tatar Republ Pop Comr of Posts and Telegraphs; from 1918 in Red Army; polit work in Civil War;

in 1930's commands with Air Force and anti-aircraft defense system; 1938 arrested by NKVD; *Died:* 1938 in imprisonment.

BYVALOV, Yevgeniy Sergeyevich (pseudonym: Yevgeniy ZYUYTVEST) (1875–?), Russian writer; CP member from 1917; *Born:* 1875 in Mariupol'; *Educ:* studied at nautical school; *Career:* from 1891 merchant seaman; also worked as translator in customs office; mil service as helmsman in Russian Navy; deserted in Constantinople and did not return to Russia until 1916; worked as seaman, helmsman, greaser and skipper on sailing ships, mainly in the Pacific; as skipper on small sailing vessels cruised between San Francisco and New Zealand archipelago; 1921 began to write; work printed in journals *Krasnyy flot, Bor'ba mirov, Smena, Na vakhte, Molodaya gvardiya,* etc; *Publ:Morskiye bryzgi* (Sea Spray); *Pod vsemi shirotami* (In All Latitudes); *Deti paluby* (Children of the Deck); *Chelovek s paluby* (The Man from the Deck); stories *Na Potyomkine* (On the Potyomkin); *Polundra; Dvadtsat' chetyre i odin* (Twenty-Four and One) (1928), etc; *Died:* date and place of death unknown.

BYZOV, Boris Vasil'yevich (1880–1934) Chemist; specialist in chemistry of rubber; *Born:* 10 Aug 1880; *Educ:* 1903 grad Petersburg Univ; *Career:* from 1903 laboratory head, *Treugol'nik* Plant; from 1918 prof, 2nd Petrograd Polytech Inst and Petrograd Teachers' Training Inst; from 1923 prof, Leningrad Technol Inst; studied chemical colloidal phenomena in rubber vulcanization theory; studied the effects of vulcanization accelerators; pioneered ind production of synthetic rubber from petroleum products; 1914–16 devised means of obtaining divinyl by the pyrogenetic cracking of oil at a temperature of 700–800°, followed by rapid cooling of the derivates; *Publ: Kratkiy kurs tekhnologii kauchuka v svyazi s izgotovleniyem protivogazovykh masok* (A Short Course on Rubber Technology in Connection with the Manufacture of Gas Masks) (1917); collected articles *O prirode vulkanizatsii kauchuka* (The Nature of Rubber Vulcanization) (1921); *Polucheniye kauchuka iz nefti* (Producing Rubber from Petroleum) (1935), etc; *Died:* 27 June 1934.

C

CHAGIN (real name: BOLDOVKIN), Pyotr Ivanovich (1898–1967) Party official; CP member from July 1917; *Born:* 1898; *Career:* as student joined revol movement; participated in 1917 Oct Coup in Moscow; chm, Zamoskvorech'e Sov; secr Zamoskvorech'e Rayon Party Comt; from Aug 1918 secr, Volga German Oblast Party Comt; from 1921 ran Baku Educ Dept; from 1922 secr, CC, CP Azer; ed, newspaper *Bakinskiy rabochiy;* from 1926 senior admin posts in publ houses and on ed bds of newspapers and journals; *Died:* Oct 1967.

CHAGOVETS, Vasiliy Yur'yevich (1873–1941) Physiologist; member, Ukr Acad of Sci from 1939; pioneer of modern electrophysiology; founded Kiev school of physiology; *Born:* 3 Apr 1873 in hamlet Patichikha, Poltava Province; son of a land surveyor; *Educ:* 1897 grad Petersburg Mil Med Acad; *Career:* 1898–1900 served as army physician with an infantry regt; 1900–03 did research on physiology under Pavlov; 1903 defended doctor's thesis on "A Study of Electrical Phenomena in Living Tissues"; in same year worked as dissector, Chair of Physiology, Women's Med Inst, Petersburg; 1904–09 assoc prof, Petersburg Mil Med Acad; 1909 prof, Chair of Pharmacology, Tomsk then Khar'kov Univ; from 1910 prof, Chair of Physiology, Med Fac, Kiev Univ; 1921–35 head, from 1935 prof, Chair of Physiology, Kiev Med Inst; 1936–41 head, Chair of Physiology, 2nd Kiev Med Inst; specialized in electrophysiology; 1896 published article on applications of theory of electrolytic dissociation proposed by Arrhenius to explain the origin of electrical phenomena in the living organism; made first attempt to explain muscular demarcational currents from the viewpoint of modern physiochemistry and outlined theory of ionic excitation; in his opinion the electrical currents in living tissues (passive and active currents) result from concentrations in the tissue of metabolic products (carbonic, lactic and phosphoric acid); 1903 elaborated this theory and used it to explain electrical phenomena in the glands, in the organs of animals and in plants; 1906 developed condensor theory of electrical stimulation of living tissues and provided a physiochemical explanation of the stimulatory effect of electric current; his ideas were further developed by other physiologists; considerable sci interest was aroused by his work on electrogastrography, which dealt with the electrical phenomena associated with the motor and secretory activity of the stomach; designed numerous electrophysiological instruments which were produced at special workshops in Kiev; *Publ:* article "The Application of Arrhenius' Theory of Dissociation to Electromotor Phenomena in Living Tissues" (1896); doctor's thesis *Ocherk elektricheskikh yavleniy na zhivykh tkanyakh s tochki zreniya noveyshikh fiziokhimicheskikh teoriy* (A Study of Electrical Phenomena in Living Tissues from the Viewpoint of the Latest Physiochemical Theories) (2nd ed, 1903–06); article "Electrogastrograms of Various Functional States of the Gastric Gland" (1935); *Izbrannyye trudy* (Selected Works) (1957); *Awards:* various money prizes of Ukr Pop Comrt of Health; *Died:* 19 May 1941.

CHANBA, Samson Yakovlevich (1886–1937) Abkhazian writer; founder of Abkhazian dramaturgy; Abkhazian govt official and public figure; *Born:* 18 June 1886 in vil Atara, now Abkhazian ASSR; *Career:* 1919 first work published; 1923–30 chm, Abkhazian Centr Exec Comt; *Publ:* plays on historical and revol themes and comedies from life of the people; *Makhadzhiry;* "From Bygone Days"; *Ansny Khanym; Keraz;* novelette *Seydyk* 1934 about the establishment of kolkhozes in Abkhazia; novels "A Stone From Grandfather's Hearth"; "The Old Oak," etc; *Died:* 26 July 1937.

CHAPAYEV, Vasiliy Ivanovich (1887–1919) Red Army officer; Civil War hero; member, Anarchist Party from 1917; CP member from 1918; *Born:* 28 Jan 1887 in vil Buydaki, Cheboksary Uyezd, Kazan' Province, son of a peasant; *Pos:* until 1909 carpenter, then itinerant street musician; 1909–13 private in Russian Army; 1914–17 private and noncommissioned officer in Russian Army at the front; decorated for bravery with four St George Crosses; after 1917 Oct Revol elected commander, 138th Reserve Infantry Regt in Nikolayevsk (now Pugachyovsk); early 1918 appointed mil comr of Nikolayevsk and mustered detachments for Red Army; from May 1918 brigade commander against White Army, Ural Cossacks and Czech Legion; Sept–Nov 1918 head, 2nd Nikolayevsk Div; Feb–Apr 1919 commander, Aleksandro-Gaysk Group, 4th Army; from Apr 1919 commander, 25th Rifle Div; *Career:* 1918 in command of one of his own detachments suppressed a series of anti-Sov peasant revolts in Nikolayevsk Uyezd; Nov 1918 sent to study at Gen Staff Acad but abandoned it in Jan 1919, "refusing to study under former tsarist generals"; 1919 his 25th Rifle Div distinguished itself in the Buguruslan, Belebey and Ufa operations; became famous in USSR after publ of D. Furmanov's book *Chapayev* (1923) and the appearance of a film under same name (1934); *Awards:* Order of the Red Banner; *Died:* in the early hours of 5 Sept 1919 White Cossacks surrounded and attacked his staff at Lbishchensk; Chapayev, already wounded, tried to escape by swimming across the Ural River but was hit again and drowned; monument erected to him in Samara.

CHAPLIN, Nikolay Pavlovich (1902–1938) One of founders and leaders of Komsomol movement; CP member from 1919; *Born:* 1902 in vil Rogpodin, Roslavl' Uyezd, Smolensk Province, son of a vil priest; immediately after 1917 Oct Revol father broke with Church and worked for Polit Bd of Western Front and other Sov orgs, while all his four children became Communists; *Educ:* 1928–29 attended Marxism-Leninism courses; *Career:* while still a schoolboy set up one of the first Komsomol cells in Smolensk; 1919 chm, Smolensk City and Uyezd Komsomol Comt; late 1919 sent by CC, Komsomol to Tyumen', where he set up a number of Komsomol org and was chm, Tyumen' Oblast Komsomol Comt; 1920 returned to Smolensk; elected chm, Smolensk Province Komsomol Comt and member, Smolensk Province RCP(B) Comt; from 1921 member, CC, Russian Komsomol; until 1923 headed Polit Educ Dept, CC, Russian Komsomol; 1922–23 secr, Transcaucasian Kray Komsomol Comt; member, Transcaucasian Kray RCP(B) Comt and member, Centr Exec Comt, Transcaucasian SFSR; 1924–28 secr-gen, CC, All-Union Komsomol; Jan 1924 member, guard of honor at Lenin's coffin; 1928 at 8th Komsomol Congress elected hon Komsomol member; at 13th, 14th and 16th Party Congresses elected cand member, CC, CPSU(B); was cand member, Org Bureau, CC, CPSU(B); 1924–28 member, USSR and All-Russian Centr Exec Comt; 1928–30 second secr, Transcaucasian Kray CPSU(B) Comt; 1931–33 chm, All-Union Section for Public Catering, Centr Union of Consumers' Soc; 1933–36 head, Polit Dept, Kirov Railroad; 1937 dir, Southeastern Railroad; author of numerous articles and works on history of Komsomol and problems of youth movement; arrested by State Security organs; *Awards:* Order of Lenin; *Died:* 22 Sept 1938 in imprisonment; posthumously rehabilitated.

CHAPLIN, Vladimir Mikhaylovich (1859-1931) Eng; heating and ventilation specialist; *Born:* 1859; *Educ:* grad Moscow Higher Tech College; *Career:* from 1898 prof, Moscow Higher Tech College; invented original water heating systems; 1905 built Russia's first forced-circulation water heating system; from 1910 specialized in ventilation of ind enterprises; some of his ventilation systems are still rated among the best available; *Publ: Kurs otopleniya i ventilyatsii* (A Heating and Ventilation Course) (1928); *Died:* 10 Nov 1931.

CHAPLYGIN, Nikolay Nikolayevich (1904-1953) Actor; Hon Artiste of RSFSR from 1945; CP member from 1940; *Born:* 26 Nov 1904; *Educ:* from 1923 studied at Theatrical School, Chamber Theater; *Career:* from 1925, while still a student, acted for Chamber Theater; 1940-51 dir, Chamber Theater; *Roles:* Moris Saksonskiy in Scribe's "Adrienne Lecouvrere"; Aleksey in *Optimisticheskaya tragediya* (An Optimistic Tragedy); the Leader in Nikitin's *Liniya ognya* (Line of Fire); the artist Rice in the operetta' "Sirocco"; Gersh in Yasnovskiy's *Duma o Britanke* (The Ballad of Britanka); Periko in Mdivani's *Alkazar;* the Commissar in Vishnevskiy's *U sten Leningrada* (At the Walls of Leningrad); Fedotov in Maklyarskiy's *Podvig ostayotsya neizvestnym* (An Anonymous Feat); Rodolphe in "Madame Bovary," after Flaubert; Rumel' in Paustovskiy's *Poka ne ostanovitsya serdtse* (As Long as the Heart Beats); *Died:* 31 Oct 1953.

CHAPLYGIN, Sergey Alekseyevich (1869-1942) Mathematician; specialist in theoretical mech, hydromech and aeromech; Dr of Physical and Tech Sci; prof; member, USSR Acad of Sci from 1929; Hon Sci Worker of RSFSR from 1929; *Born*: 5 Apr 1869 in Ranenburg (now Chaplygin, Lipetsk Oblast), son of a salesman; *Educ:* 1890 grad Moscow Univ; *Career:* 1894-1903 assoc prof, from 1903 prof, Chair of Applied Mathematics, Moscow Univ; 1895-1901 simultaneously lecturer, Moscow Land Survey Inst; 1896-1906 lecturer, Moscow Higher Tech College; from 1901 prof of mech, 1905-18 dir, Moscow Higher Women's Courses; 1911 resigned from Moscow Univ in protest against the policies of Educ Min Kasso; 1917 resumed post at Moscow Univ; from 1918 co-founder and assoc, Centr Aero-Hydrodynamics Inst; from 1921 (after death of predecessor N. E. Zhukovskiy) sci dir, 1928-30 dir, Centr Aero-Hydrodynamics Inst; 1922-26 Collegium Member, Sci and Tech Bd, Supr Sovnarkhoz; his first research, performed under the aegis of N. E. Zhukovskiy, was on hydromech; 1894 and 1897 gave an almost classic interpretation of the behavior of solids in liquids; studied important problems of theoretical mech; 1902 wrote doctor's thesis on gas streams throughout the subsonic range, thus laying the foundations of gas dynamics; 1909, in a paper on "The Pressure of a Plane Parallel Stream on Obstructions," was first to give precise definition of the rate of circulation flow around an aerofoil; this hypothesis (the Chaplygin-Zhukovskiy postulate) makes it possible to calculate drag on wings and other bodies, also solved numerous other complex aeromech problems; made an important contribution to mathematics in gen, especially with his studies on the theory of differential equations; *Publ:* doctor's thesis *O gazovykh struyakh* (Gas Streams) (1920); *Sobraniye sochineniy* (Collected Works) (4 vol, 1948-50), etc; *Awards:* two Orders of the Red Banner of Labor (1927, 1931); two Orders of Lenin (1933); Hero of Socialist Labor from 1941; *Died:* 8 Oct 1942.

CHAPYGIN, Aleksey Pavlovich (1870-1937) Writer; *Born:* 17 Oct 1870 in vil Bol'shoy Ugol, Olonets Province, son of a peasant; *Career:* during adolescence workes as a shepherd, then as a house-painter in Petersburg; 1913 first work published; 1918-19 lived in Khar'kov; *Publ:* short stories about the urban poor: *Baryni* (The Ladies), *Igoshka, Makridka* and *Poslednyaya doroga* (The Last Road) (1904-11); novel *Belyy skit* (The White Monastery) (1913); novella *Na lebyazh'ikh ozerakh* (Swan Lakes) (1916); collection of hunting stories *Po zverinoy trope* (Following the Spoor) (1918); trilogy *Razin Stepan* (Stenka Razin) (1927); *Sobraniye sochineniy* (Collected Works) (1928); autobiographic stories: *Zhizn' moya* (My Life) (1929); *Po tropam i dorogam* (Highways and Byways) (1930); *Oskolok togo zhe zerkala* (A Chip off the Old Block) (1933); novel on the peasant movement during the Razin rebellion *Gulyashchiye lyudi* (The Walkers) (1937); screenplays for *Zlatyye gory* (The Golden Hills) (1931) and *Stepan Razin* (1939); *Died:* 21 Oct 1937.

CHARENTS (real name: SOGOMONYAN), Yegishe (1897-1937) Arm poet; CP member from 1918; *Born:* 13 Mar 1897 in Kars, son of a merchant; *Career:* until 1915 teacher; from 1915 volunteer in Russian Army; 1918-19 in Red Army; *Publ:* early works showed strong influence of symbolists; poems: "Dante's Legend" (1915); "The Rainbow" (1917); "Somma" (1918); "Raging Mobs" (1919); "Songs of the People" (1920); autobiography "Charents-name" (1922); novel "Land of Nairi" (1922); comedy "Caucasian Spectacle" (1923); poems: "Lenin and Ali" (1924); "Uncle Lenin" (1925); *Khmbapet Shabarsh* (1928); collected poems "Epic Dawn" (1930) and "Book of the Road" (1933), etc; also wrote theater reviews and translated works of Mayakovsky, Ryl'skiy, Tikhonov, etc, including plays *Myatezh* (Mutiny), *Bronepoyezd* (The Armored Train), etc; *Died:* 28 July 1937 in Yerevan.

CHARNOLUSKIY, Vladimir Ivanovich (1865-1941) Pedag; public educ official; *Born:* 24 Sept 1865; *Educ:* grad Law Fac, Kiev Univ; *Career:* member, CC, Pop Socialist Party; 1905-17 co-founder and leader, All-Russian Teachers' Union; 1905 and 1917 member, Petersburg (Petrograd) Sov of Workers' Dep; 1917 founder-chm, State Comt on Educ, Provisional Govt; from 1921 worked for RSFSR Pop Comrt of Educ; mang, State Library on Public Educ; sci consultant, Dept of Pedag Bibliography, Book Chamber and Lenin State Public Library; prof, pedag Fac, Moscow Univ; wrote many works on history of pedag and public educ, including a reference book on public educ containing a complete summary of educ laws and decrees and reference material on all aspects of scholastic and extra-scholastic educ; *Publ:* coauthor, *Nastol'naya kniga po narodnomu obrazovaniyu* (A Reference Book of Public Education) (4 vol, 1899-1911); *Narodnoye obrazovaniye v Rossii* (Public Education in Russia) (1899); coauthor, *Nachal'noye narodnoye obrazovaniye v Rossii* (Primary Education in Russia) (4 vol, 1900-05); *Osnovnyye voprosy organizatsii shkoly v Rossii* (Basic Problems of School Organization in Russia) (1909); *Osnovnyye voprosy organizatsii vneshkol'nogo obrazovaniya v Rossii* (Basic Problems of the Organization of Extra-Scholastic Education in Russia) (1909); *Zemstvo i narodnoye obrazovaniye* (The Zemstvo and Public Education) (2 vol, 1910-11); *Bibliografiya statey po narodnomu obrazovaniyu* (A Bibliography of Articles on Public Education) (1916); coauthor, *Proyekt klassifikatsii russkoy literatury po voprosam narodnogo prosveshcheniya* (A Preliminary Classification of Russian Literature on Public Education) (1929); *Died:* 2 Nov 1941.

CHARNYY, Abram Markovich (1891-1953) Pathophysiologist; *Born:* 1891; *Educ:* 1923 grad Khar'kov Med Inst; *Career:* 1930 founded Chair of Pathophysiology, Perm' Med Inst; 1935-53 founder-head, Chair of Pathophysiology, Centr Inst of Postgrad Med Training, Moscow; wrote over 80 works; studied anoxia, structure of hemoglobin, lead poisoning, metabolism of lungs and liver; *Publ: Toksicheskiy otyok lyogkikh* (Toxic Edema of the Lungs) (1935); *Patofiziologiya anoksicheskikh sostoyaniy* (The Pathophysiology of Anoxic States) (1947); *Patofiziologiya gipoksicheskikh sostoyaniy* (The Pathophysiology of Hypoxic States) (2nd ed, 1961); *Died:* 1953.

CHARNYAVSKIY, Boleslav Boleslavovich (1898-1961) Mil commander; Pole; col-gen, Sov Army; CP member from 1919; *Born*: 1898, son of a peasant; *Educ:* early 1920's grad artillery courses; 1928 grad Frunze Mil Acad; *Career:* from 1918 in Red Army; fought against Germans, Denikin, Pilsudski and insurgents in Tambov Province; after Civil War various artillery commands; 1941-44 corps artillery chief, then chief of artillery of army; 1944-45 front artillery chief with Polish Armed Forces; 1945-56 mil work in Poland; 1956-61 head, Chair of Artillery, Frunze Mil Acad; *Awards:* Order of Lenin; four Orders of Red Banner; two Orders of Kutuzov, 1st Class; Order of the Read Star; Polish orders and medals; *Died:* 29 Apr 1961 in Moscow.

CHAROT, Mikhas' (real name: KUDEL'KA, Mikhail Semyonovich) (1896-1938)) Bel poet; member, Bel Writers' Union from 1934; CP member from 1920: *Born:* 7 Nov 1896 in vil Rudensk, now Minsk Oblast, son of a peasant; *Educ:* 1917 grad Molodechno Teachers' Seminary; 1921-22 studied at Bel Theatrical Studio, Moscow; *Career:* 1917-18 served in army; 1918-20 studied at Bel Teachers' Training Inst, Minsk and did undercover work for Bel Communist org; 1923-27 chm, *Maladnyak* lit assoc of proletarian writers and ed, newspaper *Savetskaya Belarus'*; 1927 joined *Polymya* lit assoc; joined Bel Assoc of Proletarian Writers; member, Inst of Bel Culture; member, CC, CP(B) Bel and Bel Centr Exec Comt; 1919 first work published; wrote mostly on Sov subjects in "revol romantic" style; also wrote purely nationalist works, the most pop of which, the play *Na Kupale* (On

Kupala) based on Bel folk themes, was banned; 1937 arrested by NKVD and held under investigatory arrest in Minsk Prison; *Publ:* poems "The Barefoot Fire-Walkers" (1921); "The Red-Winged Oracle" (1922); "Bast-Sandalled Belorussia" (1924); *Maryna* (1925); The Ale-House (1925), etc; drama *Na Kupale* (On Kupala) (1921); comedies *Mikitau lapats'* (Nikita's Sandal) and *Slutskaya varona* (The Crow of Slutsk); dramatic poem *Son na bolotse* (The Dream in the Swamp) (1919-21); verse collections: *Zavirukha* (The Blizzard) (1922); *Vybranyya vershy* (Selected Verse) (1925); *Sonechnyy pakhod* (Walk in the Sun) (1929); *Vibranyya vershy i paemy* (Selected Verse and Poems) (1935); collected short stories *Vesnakhod* (Approach of Spring) (1924); collection of children's plays *Pastushki. Danilka i Ales'ka* (The Shepherds. Danny and Alex) (1925); *Zbor tvorau* (Collected Works) (3 vol, 1933-36); *Zbor tvorau* (Collected Works) (2 vol, 1958); *Died*: 14 Dec 1938 in Minsk Prison; posthumously rehabilitated.

CHASOVENNYY, Semyon Ivanovich (1883-1967) Govt official; CP member from 1904; *Born:* 1883; *Career:* began work at Putilov Plant; 1905 drafted into army; 1907 arrested for revol propaganda among soldiers; 1909 sentenced to hard labor; 1917-19 member, Olonets Province Exec Comt and Dep Comr of Food; 1920-21 exec ed, newspaper *Olonetskaya kommuna*; later admin work for Nat Comrt of For Trade, State Trade Org and other institutions; dir, Inst of For Trade, then Sov trade rep in Lat; 1948-49 worked for USSR Museum of Revol; pensioner; *Died*: 1967.

CHAVAYN (real name: GRIGOR'YEV), Sergey Grigor'yevich (1888-1942) Mari poet and playwright; teacher; *Born:* 1888 in vil Mali, now Mari ASSR; *Educ:* 1908 grad Kazan' Teachers' Seminary; *Career:* 1908 began writing; translated several Russian plays into Mari, including *Zhenit'ba* (The Marriage), *Groza* (The Thunderstorm) and *Dokhodnoye mesto* (A Lucrative Post); his plays were staged by the 1st Sov Mari Mobile Theater, the Mari Theater Studio and the Mari Theater; *Publ*: plays "The Wild Duck" (1912); "Autonomy" (1920); "The Sun Rises, the Black Clouds Disperse" (1921); "Yamblat Bridge" (1927); musical "The Bee--Garden" (1928); "The Cougar" (1929); plays "Living Water" (1930); "The Sawmill" (1932); "The Mari Company" (1934); *Akpatyr* (1935); a historical play on the role of the Mari in the Pugachev Rebellion; "The Gleam of Money" (1939); comedies "The Hundred-Ruble Bride-Price" (1927); "The Rustling Forest"; *Died*: 1942.

CHAVDAROV, Savva Khristoforovich (1892-1962) Pedag; prof; corresp member, RSFSR Acad of Pedag Sci from 1947; Hon Sci Worker of Ukr SSR from 1943; *Born:* 9 Aug 1892 in vil Bashalmi, now Mold SSR; son of a teacher; *Educ:* 1917 grad Fac of History and Philology, Kiev Univ; *Career:* 1917-26 taught Ukr and Russian at schools in Kiev Province; 1926-30 school inspector; 1929-39 taught pedag and methods of teaching Ukr and Russian at teachers' training colleges in Kiev; 1939-41 prof of pedag, Kiev Univ; 1941-43 prof, Sukhumi Teachers' Training Inst; 1944-62 prof and head, Chair of Pedag, Kiev Univ; 1944-56 simultaneously dir, Ukr Pedag Research Inst; specialized in polytech educ, methods of teaching Ukr and Russian, educ and training work of schools and the history of pedag; wrote textbooks on Ukr language for use in 1st-4th classes at Ukr schools; *Publ: Metodika prepodavaniya ukrainskogo yazyka v nachal'noy shkole* (Methods of Teaching Ukrainian in Primary Schools) (1939); *Metodika prepodavaniya ukrainskogo yazyka v sredney shkoly* (Methods of Teaching Ukrainian in Secondary Schools) (1946); *Printsipy sovetskoy didaktiki* (The Principles of Soviet Didactics) (1949); *Pedagogicheskiye idei T. G. Shevchenko* (T.G. Shevchenko's Pedagogic Ideas) (1953); *Russko-ukrainskiye svyazi v razvitii otechestvennoy pedagogiki* (Russian-Ukrainian Relations in the Development of Soviet Pedagogies) (1954), etc; *Awards:* Ushinskiy Prize; *Died:* 20 Sept 1962.

CHAYANOV, Aleksandr Vasil'yevich (1888-?) Econ; prof, Inst of Agric Econ and Policy; chm, Timiryazev Agric Acad; *Born:* 1888; *Career:* from 1917 worked for RSFSR Pop Comrt of Agric and Gosplan; headed chair, Econ Fac, Timiryazev Agric Acad; lecturer in econ, Communist Acad; supporter of *neo-populism* in peasant question; opposed collectivization of agric and advocated a cooperative system under which farms should operate individually as public enterprises linked to the state by a cooperative framework; although he subsequently repudiated these ideas and acknowledged the "historical necessity of collectivization" he was accused of belonging to rightist opposition and of founding with Kondrat'yev "counterrevol" Labor and Peasant Party, which had connections with "interventionist" group of Ind Party; 1930 sentenced for counter-revol activities and sabotage of agric in Kondrat'yev-Chayanov-Sukhanov trial; wrote economic textbooks, including *Kurs kooperatsii* (A Course on Cooperation); *Publ: Voyna i krest'yanskoye khozyaystvo* (War and Peasant Economy) (1914); *Nashi napravleniya* (Our Goals) (1917); *Chto takoye agrarnyy vopros* (Essence of the Agrarian Question) (1917); *Puteshestviye moyego brata Alekseya v stranu krest'yanskoy utopii* (My Brother Alex's Voyage to the Peasant Utopia) (1920); *Ob optimal'nykh razmerakh* (Optimum Dimensions) (1922); *Ocherki teorii trudovogo khozyaystva* (Studies in the Theory of Labor Economy) (1924), etc; *Died:* date and place of death unknown.

CHAYKINA, Yelizaveta Ivanovna (1918-1941) Partisan in WW 2; Komsomol official; *Born*: 1918 in vil Runa, Tver' Province, daughter of a peasant; *Career:* 1933 joined All-Russian Komsomol; first Komsomol member in her native vil; ran vil reading room; 1939 elected secr, Pyonev Rayon Komsomol Comt, Velikiye Luki Oblast; after German occupation stayed in Pyonev Rayon and continued as secr, underground Komsomol rayon comt; helped organize partisan detachment and participated in its operations; Nov 1941 conducted discussions on 24th anniversary of Oct Revol in 15 occupied vil; 22 Nov 1941 arrested by German authorities at Krasnoye Pokatishche; *Awards*: Hero of the Sov Union (1942, posthumously); *Died*: 23 Nov 1941 executed by Germans: 11 Dec 1941 partisans buried her with mil hon.

CHAYKOVSKIY, Nikolay Vasil'yevich (1850-1926) Politican; *Born:* 1850 in Vyatka, son of a landowner; *Educ:* 1868 entered Petersburg Univ; *Career:* 1869 in the wake of student unrest joined med students' circle founded by M. A. Natanson, which became known as the "Chaykovskiy Circle"; 1874 gave up revol work after the circle was dissolved; emigrated to USA, where he tried to set up an agric commune with his followers; 1879 returned to Europe after failure of this project; 1880 settled in London, where he helped to organize Fund of the Free Russian Press; became member, Agrarian Socialist League and Socialist-Revol Party; 1905 returned to Russia, broke with Socialist-Revolutionaries, legalized his status and joined cooperative movement, abandoning polit activity; during WW 1 "defensist"; after 1917 Feb Revol elected member, Exec Comt, Sov of Peasants' Dep; member, CC, Joint Pop-Socialist Labor Party; strongly supported coalition with Constitutional Democrats in Democratic Assembly and "Pre-Parliament"; after 1917 Oct Revol member, All-Russian Committee for the Salvation of the Fatherland from Revol; Apr 1918 helped to found Renaissance League in Moscow; from Aug 1918 head, Northern Oblast Supreme Admin, Arkhangel'sk; Jan 1919 fled to Paris; Feb 1920 member, Gen Denikin's South Russian Govt; then supported Gen Wrangel; *Died:* 1926 in emigration.

CHEBAN (real name: CHEBANOV), Aleksandr Ivanovich (1886-1954) Actor and stage dir; Pop Artiste of RSFSR from 1947; *Born:* 30 Aug 1886; *Educ:* from 1907 studied at Moscow Conservatory; *Career:* 1909-11 with Choir, 1911-24 and 1936-54 with Drama Company, Moscow Acad Arts Theater; 1924-35 actor, 2nd Moscow Arts Theater; from 1922 also stage dir; *Roles:* Simon in Kheyyermans' *Gibel' 'Nadezhdy'* (The End of the "Nadezhda"); Friebe in Hauptmann's "World Festival"; Stratton in Berger's *Potop* (The Flood); Mons in Strindberg's "Erik XIV"; Claudius in "Hamlet"; Mendel' Krik in Babal's *Zakat* (The Sunset); Izmaylov in Finn's *Svidaniye* (The Rendezvous); Ivan in A.K. Tolstoy's *Smert' Ioanna Groznogo* (The Death of Ivan the Terrible); the Dog in Maeterlinck's "The Blue-Bird"; Tatarin in Gorky's *Na dne* (The Lower Depths); Koshkin in *Lyubov' Yarovaya*; Ivan Pazukhin in Saltykov-Shchedrin's *Smert' Pazukhina* (Pazukhin's Death); McPherson in Simonov's *Russkiy vopros* (The Russian Question); Vinogradov in Chirskov's *Pobediteli* (The Victors); Paul Dombey in "Dombey and Son," after Dickens; *Productions:* directed or co-directed: "Hamlet" (1924); Belyy's *Peterburg* (St Petersburg); (1925); A.K. Tolstoy's *Smert' Ioanna Groznogo* (The Death of Ivan the Terrible) (1927); Afinogenov's *Chudak* (The Crank) (1929); Finn's *Svidaniye* (The Rendezvous) (1935); *Died:* 8 Oct 1954.

CHEBOTAREV, I.N. (1861-1934) Politican; member, People's Will Party; *Born:* 1861; *Career:* from 1886 in revol movement; arrested on suspicion of involvement with Lenin's brother, A.I. Ul'yanov; close acquaintance of Ul'yanov family from its Simbirsk period; in Petersburg Lenin used his address for correspondence with his family and for dispatch of illegal lit; 1906-22 worked at secondary school, Popovka Station; then bookkeeper with admin of Northwestern Railroead; *Died:* 1934.

CHEBOTARYOV, Nikolay Grigor'yevich (1894-1947) Mathematician; Dr of Mathematical Sci from 1927; prof, Kazan' Univ from 1928; corresp member, USSR Acad of Sci from 1929; Hon Sci Worker of RSFSR from 1943; *Born:* 15 July 1894 in Kamenets-Podol'skiy, Ukr; *Educ:* 1916 grad Kiev Univ; *Career:* 1918-21 lecturer, Kiev Univ; 1921-27 prof, Odessa Inst of Educ; then worked for Ukr Acad of Sci; from 1928 prof, Kazan' Univ; concentrated on contemporary problems of algebra; 1924 solved problem of Frobenius, thereby obtaining more profound generalization of Dirichle theorem on simple numbers in an arithmetical progression; 1930 advanced first general theorem on resolvent theory, etc; *Publ: Sobraniye socheneniy* (Collected Works) (3 vol, 1949-50); *Awards:* Stalin Prize (1948, posthumously); Order of Lenin; two other orders; *Died:* 2 July 1947.

CHECHVYANSKIY (real name: GUBENKO), Vasiliy Mikhaylovich (1888-1938) Ukr satirist; brother of writer Ostap Vyshnya; *Born:* 11 Mar 1888 in vil Chechva, now Sumy Oblast; son of a peasant; *Educ:* grad school for med orderlies; *Career:* until 1917 in Russian Army; during Civil War in Red Army; 1924 first work published; founder and contributor, journal *Chervonyy perets; Publ:* "Lords of Nature" (1928); "Oh, Comrades . . ." (1928); "The Factor" (1929); "By the Way" (1930); "The Republicans" (1930), etc; *Died:* 26 Oct 1938.

CHEKALIN, Aleksandr Pavlovich (1925-1941) Partisan in WW 2; member, Komsomol; *Born:* 17 Mar 1925 in vil Peskovadskoye, Tula Oblast, son of a peasant; *Educ:* 1923-41 at secondary school; *Career:* with start of WW 2 volunteered for annihilation squad; as German troops approached Likhvin, where he was living, remained in enemy rear on orders from rayon Komsomol comt and was assigned to partisan detachment; served as radio operator and schout for partisan detachment; Nov 1941 fell seriously ill and was taken by partisans to his native vil, where he was arrested by German mil authorities; *Awards:* Hero of the Sov Union (1942, posthumously); *Died:* 6 Nov 1941 executed in Likhvin by German mil authorities; Likhvin, a kolkhoz and his old school were renamed after him.

CHEKHOV, Mikhail Aleksandrovich (1891-1955) Actor, stage dir and teacher; Hon Artiste of RSFSR from 1924; nephew of the writer A. P. Chekhov; *Born:* 28 Aug 1891 in Petersburg; *Educ;* 1911 grad Petersburg's Suvorin Theater School; *Career:* 1912 actor, Lit and Art Soc Theater; from 1913 at Moscow Arts Theater; worked for 1st Studio, Moscow Arts Theater and 2nd Moscow Acad Arts Theater; 1919-22 head, Chekhov Studio; from 1924 head, 1st Studio, Moscow Arts Theater (same year converted into 2nd Moscow Acad Arts Theater); 1928 left this theater and went abroad; acted in Paris, Prague, New York, Riga and Kaunas; 1932-34 head, Riga and Kaunas studios; 1935 directed drama courses in New York; 1936-39 head of a theater school in England; 1939-40 head, Chekhov Players Theater; in 1940's head, Hollywood "Actors Laboratory"; among his students were such famed actors as V. Bendin, V. Gromov, M. Knebel', V. Tatarinov, the English actor P. Rogers, American actors Gregory Peck, Yul Brynner, etc; *Roles:* Tsar' Fyodor in A. Tolstoy's *Tsar' Fyodor Ioannovich* (1912); Kobus in Kheyyermans' *Gibel' "Nadezhdy"* (The End of the "Nadezhda") (1913); Caleb in Dickens' "Cricket on the Hearth" (1914); Fraser in Berger's *Potop* (The Flood) (1915); Malvolio in Shakespeare's "Twelfth Night" (1917); Khlestakov in Gogol's *Revizor* (The Government Inspector) (1921); Hamlet in Shakespeare's "Hamlet" (1924); Ableukhov in Belyy's *Peterburg* (1925); Muromskiy in Sukhovo-Kobylin's *Delo* (The Case) (1927); Ivan the Terrible in A. Tolstoy's *Smert' Ioanna Groznogo* (The Death of Ivan the Terrible) (1933); Foma in Dostoyevskiy's *Selo Stepanchikovo* (Stepanchikovo Village) (1933), etc; *Productions*: produced plays: "Twelfth Night" (1930; "Hamlet" (1932); "The Death of Ivan the Terrible" (1933); "Stepanchikovo Village" (1933); "The Government Inspector" (1933); operas: "Parsival" (1934); *Sorochinskaya yarmarka* (Sorochintsy Fair) (1942), etc; directed films: *Chelovek iz restorana* (The Man from the Restaurant) (1927); *Zacharovannyy* (The Bewitched); *Rapsodiya* (Rhapsody), etc; *Publ*: book *Put' aktyora* (The Actor's Path) (1928); *Died:* 30 Sept 1955 in Berverly Hills, California.

CHEKHOV, Mikhail Pavlovich (1865-1936) Russian writer, playwright and theater critic, brother and biographer of A.P. Chekhov; *Born:* 1865; *Career:* theater critic for Yaroslavl' and Petersburg newspapers; 1899-1901 Russian Theatrical Soc rep in Yaroslavl'; *Publ:* farces and vaudevilles: *Za dvadtsat' minut do zvonka* (Twenty Minutes Before the Bell) (1894); *Vaza* (The Vase) (1896); *Goluboy bant* (The Blue Ribbon) (1898); *Anton Chekhov i yego syuzhety* (Anton Chekhov and His Themes) (1923); *Anton Chekhov, teatr, aktyory i 'Tat'yana Repina'* (Anton Chekhov, the Theater, Actors and "Tat'yana Repina") (1924); *Vokrug Chekhova* (Around Chekhov) (1933); *Died:* 14 Nov 1936.

CHEKHOV, Nikolay Vladimirovich (1865-1947) Pedag; specialist in teaching methods; Dr of Pedag Sci; prof; Hon Sci Worker of RSFSR from 1940; member, RSFSR Acad of Pedag Sci from 1944; *Born:* 27 June 1865; *Educ:* 1888 grad History and Philology Fac, Petersburg Univ; *Career:* 1890 began pedag and org work in Bogoroditsa Zemstvo, Tula Province; 1896 co-founder, teachers' mutual aid soc; 1895-96 helped prepare and direct All-Russian Congress of Vocational and Tech Training Teachers; 1897-1902 directed Yekaterinoslav Railroad College and Yekaterinin Railroad schools; helped found Soc for the Promotion of Children's Physical Development; lectured on history of Russian lit at Pop Univ; 1902 moved to Tver' Zemstvo and elected chm, local teachers' soc; 1904 moved to Petersburg; during 1905-07 Revol attended illegal teachers' congresses in Moscow and Finland; member, CC, illegal All-Russian Teachers' Union; chm, Fed of Nat Teachers' Union and Educ Socs; from 1906 taught at Petersburg Zemstvo Teachers' Seminary; 1909 moved to Moscow; from 1910 head, Tikhomirov Women's Teachers Training Courses, Moscow; also contributed to various pedag journals; after 1917 Oct Revol helped train teaching personnel; 1920-27 head, Unified School Dept, then Dept of Model Experimental Establishments, RSFSR Pop Comrt of Educ; Collegium member, Main Soc Training and Polytech Educ Bd, RSFSR Pop Comrt of Educ; from 1923 teaching and research work at Teachers' Training Fac, 2nd Moscow Univ; also taught on Higher Pedag Research courses, at Library Inst, Children's Reading Inst, Inst of Sci Pedag, etc; *Publ:* anthology *Detskaya literatura* (Children's Literature) (1909); collection *Narodnoye obrazovaniye v Rossii 60-kh godov XIX veka* (Public Education in Russia from the 1860's) (1912); *Tipy russkoy shkoly v ikh istoricheskom razvitii* (Types of Russian Schools in their Historical Development) (1923); *Opyt trudovoy shkoly v Rossii* (Experience with the Labor School in Russia) (1924); *Vvedeniye v izucheniye detskoy literatury* (An Introduction to the Study of Children's Literature) (1915); *Materialy po istorii detskoy literatury, 1750-1855* (Material on the History of Russian Children's Literature, 1750-1855); (1927-29); *Kartinnyy slovar' russkogo yazyka. Naglyadnoye uchebnoye posobiye dlya uchashchikhsya nerusskikh nachal'nykh shkol* (A Picture Dictionary of the Russian Language. A Visual Teaching Aid for Pupils in Non-Russian Elementary Schools) (1960); *Awards:* Order of Lenin: *Died:* 8 Nov 1947.

CHEKHOVA, Mariya Pavlovna (1863-1957) Lit Figure; sister of Anton Chekhov; *Born:* 12 Aug 1863 in Taganrog, now Rostov Oblast; *Educ:* 1886 grad Moscow Higher Women's Courses; *Career:* until 1904 taught history and geography at girls' high schools; collected and annotated letters and lit papers of her brother; from 1921 founder-dir, Chekhov Museum, Yalta; *Publ:* six-vol ed of Chekhov's letters; memoirs *Iz dalyokogo proshlogo* (From the Distant Past) (1960); *Died:* 15 Jan 1957.

CHEKHOVSKOY, Vladimir Moiseyevich (1877-?) Public figure and govt official; *Born:* 1877 son of a priest; *Career:* in youth follower of Ukr democrat M. N. Dragomanov, then joined Ukr Soc-Democratic Party; 1917 elected to its CC; 1918-19 as chm, first Council of Nat Ministers, appointed by Ukr Directory, and as Min of For Affairs, took active part in struggle against Sov regime; 1921 organized, then headed Ukr Autocephalous Church; 1926 organizer and dep chm, Ukr Liberation League; 1930 sentenced in Ukr Liberation League trial; *Died:* date and place of death unknown.

CHEKIN, Pavel Osipovich (1917-1967) Party official; member, CC, CP Uzbek from 1966; *Born:* 12 June 1917 in Tula; *Educ:* 1942 grad Timiryazev Agric Acad, Moscow; *Career:* from 1942 exec work on sovkhozes and with Uzbek Min of Agric; from 1954 head, Agric Dept, Samarkand Oblast Comt, CP Uzbek; 1956-61 first dep chm, Bukhara Oblast Exec Comt; 1962-67 second secr, Bukhara Oblast Comt, CP Uzbek; dep, Uzbek Supr Sov of 1959, 1963 and 1967 convocations; 1966 deleg at 22nd CPSU Congress; *Awards:* Order of the Red Banner of Labor; Badge of Hon; medals; *Died:* 25 Aug 1967.

CHEKRYGIN (CHEKRYGIN II), Aleksandr Ivanovich (1884-1942) Ballet dancer, teacher and ballet-master; Hon Art Worker of RSFSR from 1936; *Born:* 5 Aug 1884; *Educ:* 1902 grad Petersburg Theater College under P. K. Karsavina, A. V. Shiryayev and N. G. Legat; *Career:* 1902-28 character dancer, Mariinskiy Theater, Petersburg; from 1904 instructor, Petersburg Theater College; 1914 together with his brother set up his own school; 1918 started work as ballet-master; 1923-28 dir of choreography, Maly Opera Theater and ballet-master, Acad Theater of Drama, Leningrad; 1932-41 instructor at Moscow Choreographic College; from 1937 also artistic dir, Pedag Dept of above college; *Roles:* Conrad in Adane and Pugny's "The Corsair"; Gringoire and Quasimodo in "Esmeralda"; the Fairy Karabos in *Spyashchaya krasavitsa* (Sleeping Beauty), etc; *Productions:* Drigo's "Romance of the Rose" (1919); Kratov's *Kaprizy babochki* (Caprices of the Butterfly) (1922); Arenskiy's *Yegipetskiye nochi* (Egyptian Nights) (1923); dances in opera *Snegurochka* (The Snow Maiden), etc; Gliere's "The Comedians" (1931); *Shchelkunchik* (The Nutcracker) (1932); *Spyashchaya krasavitsa* (Sleeping Beauty) (1936); *Publ:* coauthor, textbook *Metodika klassicheskogo trenazha* (Methods of Classical Ballet Training) (1940); *Died:* 17 Mar 1942.

CHEKUNOV, I.A. (? -1928) Politician; *Born:* date and place of birth unknown; *Career:* agric worker in Vladimir Province; 1906 joined Pop Freedom Party; 1910 zemstvo councillor for Fominki Volost; chm, Fominki Agric Soc; from 1917 worked for newspapers *Golos naroda* and *Trudyashchayasya bednota*; 1919-21 frequent contacts with Lenin on publ, admin and peasant cooperative matters; from 1921 Collegium member, Pop Comrt of Agric; in his latter years contributed to newspapers *Bednota* and *Krest'yanskaya gazeta; Died*: 1928.

CHELINTSEV, Aleksandrlr Nikolayevich (1874-?)Economist; cofounder and theorist, Neo-Populist Movement in agric; *Born*: 1874; *Career*: disputed that soc-hcon differentiation in agric was result of capitalist development; viewed econ inequality of peasant farms as a consequence of demographic (family) differentiation; beginning 1904 wrote a number of works on econ and org of peasant farming, agric distr, agric cooperation, credits and marketing relations of peasant farming based on so-called labor and consumer theory of agric econ; according to this theory, leading element in evolution and org of agric farming is the family and "each combination of the needs of a farming family and its labor resources calculated per unit of arable land corresponds to a certain structure, size and state of agric productive branches, i.e., a certain type of farm org"; opposed 1917 Oct Revol; after defeat of Denikin's army emigrated; 1927 returned to USSR; wrote numerous works on econ problems, farming org and agric policy; elaborated his pre-revol theory of organizing individual peasant farms by econ measures conducive to individual farming; essence of this theory, advocated from 1928 to 1930, was proposal to reorganize policy of prices, credit and processing of agric produce so as to favor and stimulate development of individual farming; opposed CPSU(B) gen policy of industrialization and socialist reorganization of agric; 1928-30 repeatedly attacked establishment of sovkhozes (state farms), demonstrating their unprofitability, and objected to support rendered to kolkhozes; after the 1930 Labor and Peasants' Party trial for "counter-revol and sabotage," he was subjected to Party criticism and was arrested in early 1930's; *Publ: Teoreticheskiye osnovaniya organizatsii krest'yanskogo khozyaystva* (Theoretical Principles of Peasant Farm Organization) (1919), etc; *Died*: date and place of death unknown.

CHELINTSEV, Vladimir Vasil'yevich (1877-1947) Organic chemist; corresp member, USSR Acad of Sci from 1933; Hon Sci Worker of RSFSR from 1935; *Born*: 22 Feb 1877; *Career*: from 1910 prof, Moscow Univ; from 1917 prof, Saratov Univ; his research was of great importance for development of chemistry of organic magnesium compounds; isolated individual organic magnesium compounds, devised theory of their structure, explained mechanism of their formation and showed in 1904 that ether and tertiary amino acids act as catalysts in Grignard's reaction; in reaction of simple ethers, sulphides and tertiary amino acids on individual organic magnesium compounds he established formation of oxone, thionic and ammonium complexes, determined temperature of their formation and temperature of their solution in water; by studying highest valencies in oxygen, sulphuric and nitrous organic compounds he compiled a table of their thermochemical properties; studied chlorophyl and hemin; found methods of synthesizing new pyrrole compounds, Ketonic acids, isomeric and non-saturated acids; studied condensation of furane derivatives; devised methods of determining small quantities of acetone, furfural, formaldehyde, acetaldehyde, etc; *Publ: Teoriya reaktsii Grin'yara i novyy metod polucheniya magniy-organicheskikh soyedineniy* (The Theory of Grignard's Reaction and a New Method of Obtaining Organic Magnesium Compounds) (1905); *Issledovaniye vysshikh atomnostey u kislorodnykh, sernistykh i azotistykh organicheskikh soyedineniy* (A Study of the Higher Atomic Values of Oxygen, Sulphuric and Nitrous Organic Compounds) (1912); *Glavneyshiye momenty iz istorii razvitya khimii pirrol'nykh soyedineniy* (Major Stages in the History of Development of the Chemistry of Pyrrole Compounds) (1917); *Organicheskiye katalizatory i kompleksnyye organicheskiye soyedineniya kak promezhutochnyye veshchestva pri katalize* (Organic Catalysts and Complex Organic Compounds as Intermediary Substances in Catalysis) (1939); *Died*: 3 Apr 1947.

CHELPANOV, Georgiy Ivanovich (1862-1936)Psychologist, logician and idealist philosopher; prof; pioneer of Russian experimental psychology; *Born*: 1862; *Educ*: univ grad; *Career*: 1892-1906 prof of philosophy and psychology, Kiev Univ; 1907-23 prof of philosophy and psychology, Moscow Univ; 1912-23 founder-dir, Moscow Inst of Psychology (later Inst of Psychology, RSFSR Acad of Pedag Sci); was an adherent of Bundt in psychology and Stumpf in philosophy; specialized in experimental psychology, which he interpreted as a discipline based, in the final analysis, on self-observation; 1897 wrote textbook on logic; 1905-06 wrote textbook on psychology for secondary schools, which ran into many ed; 1946 his textbook on logic was republished; *Publ: Problemy vospriyatiya prostranstva v svyazi s ucheniyem ob apriornosti i vrozhdyonnosti* (Problems of Spatial Perception in Relation to the Theory of Apriority and Innateness) (2 vol, 1896-1904); *Mozg i dusha* (The Brain and the Psyche) (1900); *O pamyati i mnemonike* (Memory and Mnemonics) (1900); *Vvedeniye v filosofiyu* (An Introduction to Philosophy) (6th ed, 1916); *Vvedeniye v eksperimental'nuyu psikhologiyu* (An Introduction to Experimental Psychology) (3rd ed, 1924); *Psikhologiya i marksizm* (Psychology and Marxism) (2nd ed, 1925); *Ob'yektivnaya psikhologiya v Rossii i Amerike* (Objective Psychology in Russia and America) (1925); *Psikhologiya ili refleksologiya?* (Psychology or Reflexology?) (1926); *Ocherki psikhologii* (Studies in Psychology) (1926); *Died*: 13 Feb 1936.

CHELYAPOV, Nikolay Ivanovich (1889-?) Specialist in state law; musician; CP member; *Born:* 1889, son of peasant painter; *Educ:* grad Law Fac, Moscow Univ; *Career:* after 1917 Oct Revol worked for Supr Sovnarkhoz, CC of All-Russian Metalworkers' Union, and Main Bd for Professional Educ; 1928 dir, Inst of Sov Law; Presidium member, All-Russian Assoc of Soc Sci Research Institutes; from 1929 head, Sov Construction Section, Inst of Sov Construction and Law, Communist Acad; prof, Inst of Red Prof; until 1931 dir and head, Music Section, State Acad of Arts; 1933 chm, USSR Composers' Union; exec ed of its organ *Sovetskaya muzyka*; ed, "State Law" and "Music" sections of *BSE* (Large Soviet Encyclopedia); wrote numerous articles on state law and Sov construction in journals *Revolyutsiya prava, Sovetskoye gosudarstvo i revolyutsionnoye pravo* and *Vlast' Sovetov*, and "Large Soviet Encyclopedia," "Small Soviet Encyclopedia", etc; ed, "State Law and Sov Construction" section of *Entsiklopediya gosudarstva i prava* (Encyclopedia of State and Law); *Publ:* book *Ucheniye K. Marksa o gosudarstve i prave* (The Teaching of Karl Marx on Problems of State and Law) published for 50th anniversary of Marx's death; edited series of books on state law and state machinery; author of numerous articles on theory and history of music in "Large" and "Small Soviet Encyclopedias" and in periodicals *Muzyka i revolyutsiya, Sovetskaya muzyka* and *Sovetskoye iskusstvo*; *Died*: date and place of death unknown.

CHELYSHEV, M. I. (1888-1937) Govt official; CP member from 1914; *Born:* 1888; *Career:* from 1917 secr, Kanava Rayon RCP(B) Comt; head, Org Dept, then chm, Nizhniy Novgorod City RCP(B) Comt;, 1921-22 sided with "Workers' Opposition"; one of 22 signatories in statement to the Comintern; voting deleg to 11th Party Congress from Centr Auditing Commission; from 1922 chm, Criminal Appeals Division, RSFSR Supr Court; chm, Moscow Oblast Court; dep chm, Amnesty Commission, All-Russian Centr Exec Comt; from 1935 dep chm, Main Court, Dagh ASSR; arrested by State Security organs; *Died:* 1937 in imprisonment.

CHEMENZEMINLI, Yusif Vezir (real name: VEZIROV, Yusif Baba ogly) (1887-1943) Azer writer and scholar; *Born:* 12 Sept 1887 in Shusha, now Azer SSR; *Educ:* grad Kiev Univ; *Career:* worked in Saratov and Odessa; from 1916 lived in Istanbul and Paris; 1925 returned to USSR; wrote studies on lit history and folklore of Azer; translated works of Tolstoy, Turgenev, etc into Azer; *Publ:* story: "Ticket to Paradise" (1907); novelette "Students" (1914);

novel "The Maiden Spring" (1934), etc; *Died:* 3 Jan 1943.

CHENTSOV, I. D. (1885-1937) Party official; CP member from 1904; *Born:* 1885; *Career:* active in 1905-07 Revol in Rostov-on-Don; Party work in Rostov, Novocherkassk and Taganrog; arrested by Tsarist authorities; after 1917 Feb Revol member, Rostov-Nakhichevan Party Comt; member, Mil Revol Comt and chief of staff of Red Guards in Rostov-Nachichevan; after 1917 Oct Revol mil work; from 1919 Party and econ admin work in Khar'kov, Batumi, Kursk, Oryol and Rostov-on-Don; from 1926 Party, govt and admin work in Rostov; at 11th-13th Party Congresses elected member, RCP(B) Centr Control Commission; 1922-25 member, Party Collegium, RCP(B) Centr Control Commission; arrested by State Security organs; *Died:* 1937 in imprisonment.

CHENTSOV, Vladimir Vasil'yevich (1896-1967) Health worker; organizer of psychiatric service; Hon Physician of RSFSR; CP member; *Born:* 1896 in vil Lukonets, Oryol Province, son of a worker; *Educ:* 1917 grad med orderlies school; in 1920's grad Med Fac, Moscow Univ; *Career:* 1914 joined RSDRP and did underground revol work; elected to Bolshevik faction, sov of workers and soldiers' dep; after grad from med orderlies school, worked as doctor's asst at dispensary of "Richard Pol'" and *Stal'* Plants, where he conducted Party propaganda; during Civil War fought with partisan detachments on Southern Front in rear of White armies; then commanded mounted reconnaissance squad; helped crush peasant revolts; after grad univ head, Tambov, then Kostroma Province Health Dept; head, Personnel Bd, Pop Comrt of Health; chief physician, Moscow Oblast's Yakovenko Psychiatric Hospital; founder and dir, specialist med orderlies' school; then dir, Moscow Oblast Inst of Psychoneurology; chief physician, Kursk, then Kalinin Psychiatric Hospital; during WW 2 served with Sov Army and headed specialized mil hospital; 1945, after discharge from the army, returned to Kalinin's Litvinov Psychiatric Hospital; from 1948 chief physician, Moscow Oblast's Yakovenko Psychiatric Hospital; 1959 directed org and construction of Moscow Oblast Psychoneurological Hospital Nr 17 in vil Kurilovo, Podol'sk Rayon, Moscow Oblast; until his death served as chief physician at this hospital; repeatedly elected member, sov of workers' dep; bd member, All-Russian Neuropathologists and Psychiatrists' Soc; *Awards:* Order of Lenin; Order of the Red Banner of Labor; Order of the Fatherland War, 2nd Class; Order of the Red Star; medals; *Died:* 30 Dec 1967.

CHEPTSOV, Yefim Mikhaylovich (1875-1950) Painter; Hon Art Worker of RSFSR from 1946; *Born:* 9 Jan 1875; *Educ:* 1905-11 studied at Petersburg Acad of Arts; *Career:* member, Assoc of Russian Revol Artists; also taught art; *Works:* paintings: "At the Doctor's"; "In the Family"; "They Listen"; "On the Isle of Capri"; "A Village Cell Meeting" (1924); "The Retraining of Teachers" (1925); "Kolkhoz Threshing" (1934); "The Latest News from the Front" (1942); "Leaving for Work" (1947); *Died:* 8 Jan 1950.

CHEPUROV, Mikhail Nikiforovich (1892-1965) Party official; Cp member from 1915; *Born:* 9 July 1892; *Career:* fought in 1917 Oct Revol and Civil War; 1919-21 member, Polit Dept, 47th Div on Southwestern Front; 1921-41 senior Party and govt work; 1941-45 fought in WW 2; 1945-47 instructor, Moscow rayon soc security dept; 1947-59 financial work in Tadzh SSR; from 1959 pensioner; *Died:* 9 Nov 1965.

CHERDANTSEV, Gleb Nikanorovich (1885-1958) Economist and geographer; Dr of Econ Sci from 1936; prof from 1921; corresp member, Uzbek Acad of Sci from 1943; Hon Sci Worker of Uzbek SSR from 1955; *Born:* 4 Aug 1885 in Omsk; *Educ:* 1909 grad Econ Dept, Petersburg Polytech Inst; *Career:* 1918-24 co-founder, first rector, dean, Fac of Soc Sci, and prof of polit econ, Centr Asian Univ, Tashkent; 1924-58 prof, Moscow Inst of Geodesy, Aerial Survey and Cartography, where he was in charge of compiling and editing maps and directed postgrad training; during WW 2 acting dir of this inst after its transfer to Tashkent; at various times worked for: Zoning Section, USSR Gosplan; Power Eng and Electrification Research Inst; Inst for the Org of Land Exploitation and Resettlement; State Planning Inst for Research and Planning of Outdoor Water Conduits, Sewers and Hydrotech Installations; State Waterworks Research and Planning Inst; Inst of Power Eng; Council for the Study of Production Resources; Inst of Geography and Inst of Econ, USSR Acad of Sci; from 1943 worked for part of the year at Inst of Econ, Uzbek Acad of Sci; took part in expeditions to study development prospects of Khorezm, to organize rice sovkhozes in southeastern Kazakhstan, to harness Ili River, to develop agric in Tadzhikistan and to study econ potential of Kara Kum; wrote textbooks on econ geography for cartographic and geodetic schools and teachers' training inst; compiled soc and cultural maps; *Died:* 5 Dec 1958 en route from Tashkent to Moscow.

CHEREMNYKH, Mikhail Mikhaylovich (1890-1962) Graphic artist and cartoonist; member, USSR Acad of Arts from 1958; prof, Surikov Art Inst, Moscow, from 1949; Pop Artiste of RSFSR from 1952; *Born:* 30 Oct 1890 in Tomsk; *Educ:* 1917 grad Moscow College of Painting, Sculpture and Architecture; studied under K.Korovin, S.Malyutin, A.Arkhipov and N.Kasatkin; *Career:* 1919-21 founder and contributor, poster series *Okna ROSTA* (Windows of the Russian News Agency); regular contributor of cartoons to journal *Krokodil*; painted anticlerical posters; 1941-45 again contributed to poster series *Okna ROSTA*; illustrated works of Saltykov-Shchedrin, Chekhov and Krylov; also worked as set designer; head, Poster Studio, Surikov Art Inst; 1954-58 corresp member, USSR Acad of Arts; *Awards:* Stalin Prize (1942); *Died:* 7 Aug 1962.

CHERKASOV, Nikolay Konstantinovich (1903-1966) Actor, Pushkin State Acad Drama Theater, Leningrad, from 1933; member, Lenin Prize Comt for Lit and Art, USSR Council of Min from 1960; member, Org Comt, USSR Film Workers' Union from 1957; member, Sov Peace Comt; Pop Artiste of USSR from 1947; CP member from 1940; *Born:* 27 July 1903 in Petersburg; *Educ:* 1926 grad Leningrad Inst of Stagecraft; *Career:* 1926-27 actor, Leningrad Young Playgoers' Theater; 1927-29 actor, "Komsoglaz" youth ensemble; 1929-31 worked as an entertainer in Moscow and Leningrad; 1931-32 actor, Leningrad Comedy Theater; from 1926 also acted in films; member, Sov actors' deleg to Canada, China, India, France, Italy, Finland, Poland, Czechoslovakia, Rumania, etc; 1957 head, Sov deleg at Int Film Festival in Spain; member, Sov parliamentary deleg to England; 1959 head, Sov deleg at US première of film *Zhuravli letyat* (The Cranes Are Flying); bd chm, Leningrad Dept, All-Russian Theater Soc; dep, RSFSR Supr Sov of 1938 and 1947 convocations; dep, USSR Supr Sov of 1950 and 1954 convocations; *Roles:* stage roles: title role in *Don Kikhot* (Don Quixote) (1927); Varlaam in Pushkin's "Boris Godunov" (1934); title role in A.N. Tolstoy's *Pyotr Pervyy* (Peter I) (1938); Gorky in Kapler and Zlatogorova's *Lenin v 1918-om godu* (Lenin in 1918) (1939); Mayakovskiy in V.A. Katanyan's *Oni znali Mayakovskogo* (They Knew Mayakovskiy) (1954); Gen Khudov in Bulgakov's *Beg* (Flight) (1958), etc; film roles: Prof Polezhayev in *Deputat Baltiki* (The Baltic Deputy) (1937); Tsarevich Aleksey in *Pyotr Pervyy* (Peter I) (1937-39); title role in *Aleksandr Nevskiy* (1938); title role in *Ivan Groznyy* (Ivan the Terrible) (1945); title role in *Don Kikhot* (Don Quixote) (1956); Acad Dronov in *Vsyo ostayotsya lyudyam* (It All Depends on the People) (1963), etc; *Publ:* *Iz zapisok aktyora* (From an Actor's Notes) (1951); *V Indii. Putyevyye zametki* (In India. Travel Notes) (1952); *Zapiski sovetskogo aktyora* (Notes of a Soviet Actor) (1953); *Chetvyortyy Don Kikhot* (The Fourth Don Quixote) (1956); *V teatre i v kino* (On Stage and Screen) (1961), etc; *Awards:* two Orders of Lenin; three Orders of the Red Banner of Labor; four Stalin Prizes (1941, 1946, 1950 and 1951); Prize of Stratford (Canada) Int Film Festival (1958); Lenin Prize (1964); medals; *Died:* 14 Sept 1966.

CHERKASSKIY, Emil' Davydovich (1873-1955) Composer; Hon Art Worker of Tatar ASSR from 1944; *Born:* 16 July 1873 in Kiev; *Educ:* 1893 grad Kiev Musical College; *Career:* 1894-1905 conductor at opera and operetta theaters in Zhitomir, Odessa, Minsk, Kazan' and Saratov; 1908-15 conductor, symphony orchestras in Tambov, Voronezh, Sebastopol, Khar'kov, Poltava and Krasnodar; 1916-48 musical dir, composer and conductor, Drama Theaters in Krasnodar, Kurgan, Bezhitsa, Dnepropetrovsk, Omsk, Kirov, Stalinsk and Kazan'; *Works:* musical comedy *Noch', kotoroy ne bylo* (The Night that Never Was), after Gogol's novelette *Noch' pered rozhdestvom* (The Night Before Christmas); "Dedication to October" for choir, narrators and symphony orchestra; symphonic works: "Eastern Suite"; two Spanish dances; "Dreams"; piano works: "Prelude"; two expromptus; three waltzes, etc; for violin and piano: "Lyric Poem"; "Intermezzo Waltz"; "Chaconne"; "Sarabande", etc; 14 romances, including seven to words by Pushkin; seven songs; music for 98 shows; *Died:* 20 July 1955 in Moscow.

CHERLYUNCHAKEVICH, N.A. (1876-1938) Lawyer; govt official; CP member from 1907; *Born:* 1876; *Educ:* completed legal training; *Career:* Party work in Chernigov, Moscow and Poland; after

1917 Oct Revol worked for Moscow Pop Court, then Collegium member, RSFSR Pop Comrt of Justice; 1922-26 worked in Ukr; from 1927 dep mang, Centr Statistical Bd and Presidium member, RSFSR Gosplan; *Died*: 1938.

CHERNETSKIY, Semyon Aleksandrovich (1881-1950) Conductor and composer; Hon Art Worker of RSFSR from 1936; maj-gen from 1944; instructor, Mil Fac, Moscow Conservatory; *Born*: 24 Oct 1881 in Odessa; *Educ*: 1917 grad N. Cherepnin's conducting class, Petersburg Conservatory; *Career*: 1900-18 mil bandmaster; 1918-24 inspector of mil bands, Petrograd Mil Distr; 1924-48 inspector of mil bands, Sov Army; 1932 founded model wind orchestra, Moscow Mil Distr; for many years led bands at mil parades in Moscow; *Works*: over 70 marches for wind orchestras, including *Krasnoy armii* (To the Red Army) (1922); *Vstrechnyye* (Encounter Marches) (1923, 1924, 1925); *Industrial'nyy* (Industrial March) (1932); *GTO* (Exercise March) (1933); *Krasnaya zarya* (Red Dawn) (1933); *Marsh tankistov* (The Tankmen's March); *Geroi Stalingrada* (The Heroes of Stalingrad); also composed waltzes and fantasias; *Awards*: Order of the Red Star (1933); Order of the Red Banner (1944); Order of the Fatherland War, 2nd Class (1944); Order of Lenin (1946); Stalin Prize (1946); *Died*: 13 Apr 1950 in Moscow.

CHERNOMORDIK (Party pseudonym: P.LARIONOV), Solomon Isayevich (1880-1943) Health service official; professional revolutionary; CP member from 1902; *Born*: 1880 in Smolensk, son of an office worker; *Educ*: from 1899 studied at Fac of Natural Sci and Mathematics, then Med Fac, Moscow Univ with many interruptions because of frequent imprisonment; 1914 grad as physician; *Career*: from 1905 member, Moscow RSDRP(B) Comt; took part in 1905 Dec uprising in Moscow; 1907 deleg, All-Russian Party Conference, Helsinki, and 4th RSDRP Congress, London; during WW 1 served as army physician on Persian Front; after 1917 Oct Revol worked for Pop Comrt of Health and Labor; combined med career with Party work; 1919 army health service chief, Simbirsk, then Samara Fortified Region, Eastern Front; 1919 transferred to Southern Front as polit asst to chief of med admin; contracted typhus and was evacuated to Moscow after recovery; from 1921 head, South Crimean Littoral Health Resort Admin; 1922-24 dir, Moscow Museum of the Revol; 1928-30 Berlin rep for RSFSR Pop Comrt of Health and Exec Comt, USSR Red Cross and Red Crescent Soc; 1932-38 member and Congress deleg, Int Org for Aid to Revol Fighters; 1938-43 senior assoc, Inst of History, USSR Acad of Sci; wrote a number of works on history of CPSU and revol movement; *Died*: 1943.

CHERNOMORDIKOV, David Aronovich (1869-1947) Musician and public figure; pianist; teacher; composer; critic; *Born*: 17 July 1869 in Baku; *Career*: 1905-07 participated in revol; *Works*: "First Collection of Revolutionary Songs"; 10 harmonized songs; workers' anthem "Forward"; military march "Hold High the Red Banner," etc; *Died*: 31 Jan 1947 in Moscow.

CHERNORUTSKIY, Mikhail Vasil'yevich (1884-1957) Therapist; member, USSR Acad of Med Sci from 1948; Hon Sci Worker of RSFSR; *Born:* 26 Feb 1884; *Educ:* 1908 grad Petersburg Mil Med Acad, where he won Bush Prize; *Career:* three years of specialist training under Prof V. N. Sirotinin at Hospital Therapeutic Clinic, Petersburg Mil Med Acad; simultaneously assoc, Prof N.O. Ziber-Shumova's biochemical laboratory, Inst of Experimental Med; 1911 defended doctor's thesis; 1912-13 toured therapeutic clinics in England, Germany and France; 1914-18 chief physician, Field Reserve Hospital No. 304; after WW 1 asst prof, then assoc prof, Hospital Therapeutic Clinic, Petrograd Mil Med Acad; 1922 prof, Petrograd Univ; 1923-57 head, Hospital Therapeutic Clinic, 1st Leningrad Med Inst; during 2 also consultant, various evacuation hospitals, Leningrad Front; 1950-57 head, Therapy Section, Pavlov Inst of Physiology; from 1925 ed, journals *Prakticheskaya meditsina, Sovetskiy vrachebnyy zhurnal, Terapevticheskiy arkhiv* and *Klinicheskaya meditsina* and newspapers *Vrachebnaya gazeta* and *Sovetskaya vrachebnaya gazeta*; co-ed, *Bol'shaya meditsinskaya entsikolpediya* (Large Medical Encyclopedia); member, ed bd, State Med Publ House; did research on the human constitution from the morphological, functional and clinical viewpoints; in the latter area studied the significance and role of the constitutional factor in the pathogenesis and clinical treatment of disease; directed research on the role of heredity, constitution and metabolism in rheumatism and on allergy, acute nephritis, acute hepatitis and serous pleurisy; wrote over 90 works, including studies of alimentary dystrophy, avitaminosis and wartime changes in the clinical treatment of diseases; co-founder, Botkin Soc of Therapists, Leningrad; dep chm, All-Union Soc of Therapists; chm, Leningrad Comt for the Study of Rheumatism; member, All-Union Comt for the Study of Rheumatism; member, learned councils of various med institutions and commissions; trained many specialists in internal med; *Publ:* doctor's thesis *K voprosu o vliyanii nukleinovoy kisloty na zhivotnyy organizm* (The Effects of Nucleic Acid on the Animal Organism') (1911); article "The Theory of Constitution" (1928); *Diagnostika vnutrennikh bolezney* (The Diagnosis of Internal Diseases) (1938); article "Acute Rheumatism" (1941); coauthor and ed, *Alimentarnaya distrofiya v blokirovannom Leningrade* (Alimentary Dystrophy During the Leningrad Blockade) (1947); article "The Theory of Allergy in the Light of Wartime Pathology" (1948); *Awards:* two Orders of Lenin; medal "For the Defense of Leningrad"; medal "For Valiant Labor in the Great Fatherland War"; badge "For Outstanding Health Work"; Prof Netskiy Prize, etc; *Died:* 10 June 1957.

CHERNOV, Mikhail Mikhaylovich (1879-1938) Composer; prof from 1918; Dr of Arts from 1938; *Born:* 22 Apr 1879 in Kronstadt; *Educ:* 1903 grad Natural Sci Dept, Physics and Mathematics Fac, Petersburg Univ; 1906 grad Petersburg Conservatory in composition class of Rimsky-Korsakov and Lyadov; *Career:* from 1910 taught composition and instrumentation at Petersburg (Leningrad) Conservatory; 1930-37 head, chair of Instrumentation, above conservatory; pupils included A. Zhivotov, Kh. Kushnaryov, Ye. Mravinskiy, Ye. Ovchinnikov, P. Ryazanov and Prokofiev; *Works*: cantata *Ioan Damaskin* (St John of Damascus) (1906); collected piano pieces: "Flowers" (1907); "Music for Shows" (1909); "Waltz" and "Gavotte" (1916); three symphonies (1928); "The Komsomol Anthem" (1928); coauthor, musical comedy *Zarnitsy* (Summer Lithtning) (1931); music for films: *Stroyeniye materii* (The Structure of Matter) and *Skorost' i yeyo vragi* (Speed and Its Enemies) (1936); cello concerto (1937); translated and edited Berlioz's "Instrumentation Theory" (1938); *Awards:* First Prize at International Competition for his Third Symphony in Memory of Schubert (1928); *Died:* 1 Aug 1938 in Leningrad.

CHERNOV, Viktor Mikhaylovich (pseudonyms: GARDENIN, VECHEV, TUCHKIN, etc) (1873-1952) Russian politician; leader and theorist, Socialist-Revol Party; *Born:* 1873; *Educ:* studied at Moscow Univ; *Career:* active in student movement; 1894 arrested for his connection with *Narodnoye pravo* (Pop Rights) group and exiled for three years to Tambov; contributed to legal periodicals; from 1899 lived abroad and helped found Agrarian Socialist League; 1905 returned to Russia; permanent member, CC, Socialist-Revol Party and ed, its centr organ *Revolyutsionnaya Rossiya*; leader, Socialist-Revol faction, 2nd State Duma; attended 1915 Zimmerwald and 1916 Kienthal Conferences; 5 May-26 Aug 1917 Min of Agric, 1st and 2nd Provisional Coalition Govt; Jan 1918 elected chm, Constituent Assembly; 1918 helped organize anti-Sov revolts in the Volga region; 1918 headed Ufa Congress of Constituent Assembly members; from 1920 abroad; 1921, in a bid to support Kronstadt Mutiny, came to Tallinn; in his lit and publicistic works opposed Sov regime; *Publ: K voprosu o kapitalizme i krest'yanstve* (Capitalism and the Peasantry) (1905); *Filosofskiye i sotsiologicheskiye etyudy* (Philosophical and Sociological Studies) (1907); *Sotsialisticheskiye etyudy* (Socialist Studies) (1908); *Teoretiki romanskogo sindikalizma* (Theorists of Romanic Syndicalism) (1908); *K voprosu o sotsializatsii zemli* (The Problem of Land Socialization) (1908); *Krest'yanin i rabochiy, kak ekonomicheskiye kategorii* (Peasant and Worker as Economic Categories) (3rd ed, 1917); *Zemel'nyy vopros* (The Land Problem) (1917); *Istinnyye i mnimyye porazhentsy* (Real and Imaginary Defeatists) (2nd ed, 1917); *Konstruktivnyy sotsializm* (Constructive Socialism) (1925), etc; *Died:* 1952.

CHERNYAK (TODORSKAYA), Ruzya Iosifovna (1900-1937) Party official; CP member from Mar 1917; *Born:* 1900 in Lodz, Poland, daughter of an office worker; *Educ:* from 1923 studied at Moscow Higher Tech College; *Career:* from 1914 took part in underground student Marxist circles in Chernigov, then in Moscow; from Mar 1917 tech secr, Moscow Party Comt; helped found Youth League and rally youth in support of Bolsheviks; during 1917 Oct Revol acted as messenger to Red Guard detachments on behalf of Moscow Party Comt and Mil Revol Comt; after 1917 Oct Revol secr, Sokol'niki Rayon Party Comt, Moscow; 1918, together with R. S. Zemlyachka, conducted polit work at front; head, Polit Dept, 38th Infantry Div and 58th Infantry Brigade; dep head, Polit Dept, 20th and 32nd Div and other units; after Civil War continued to work in Red Army; was secr, Baku City Sov, then held exec positions in Pop Comrt of Heavy Ind and Defense Ind; arrested by State Security organs; *Awards:* recommended for an Order of the Red Banner; *Died:* 1937 in imprisonment.

CHERNYAK, Valentin Zakhar'yevich (1893-1963) Veterinarian; Dr of Veterinarian Sci; prof from 1929; head, Chair of Pathoanatomy, Leningrad Veterinary Inst from 1933; *Born:* 1893; *Educ:* 1917 grad Warsaw Veterinary Inst; *Career:* 1917 in Russian Army on Caucasian Front; during Civil War served with Red Army on Western Front; 1921 in Moscow at Centr Microbiological Station of Red Army Main Veterinary Bd; 1927-29 assoc prof, Leningrad Veterinary Inst; 1929-33 head, Chair of Pathoanatomy, Voronezh Veterinary Inst; 1933-38 founder-dir, Laborary of Pathoanatomy, Leningrad Veterinary Research Inst; *Publ: Patologoanatomicheskaya diagnostika glavneyshikh infektsionnykh zabolevaniy sel'skokhozyaystvennykh zhivotnykh* (The Pathoanatomical Diagnosis of the Main Infectious Diseases of Agricultural Animals) (1957); coauthor, book on forensic veterinary expertise (1962); *Died:* 24 June 1963.

CHERNYAKHOVSKIY, Ivan Danilovich (1906-1945) Ukr; army gen from 1944; CP member from 1928; *Born:* 28 June 1906 in vil Oksanina, Cherkassy Oblast, son of a railroad switchman; *Educ:* 1928 grad Kiev Artillery School; 1936 grad Mil Acad for Mechanization and Motorization of the Red Army; *Pos:* 1919-20 herdsman; 1920-24 railroad repairman, apprentice fitter, railroad freight escort, cooper and driver; 1924 joined Red Army via Komsomol draft; 1928-31 platoon leader; head, regt topographical detachment; polit officer of a battery; commander of a reconnaissance training battery; 1937-41 chief of staff of a tank battalion; commander of a separate tank battalion and a separate light-tank regt; dep commander, 2nd Tank Div; 1941-42 commander, 28th Tank Div, which became the 241st Infantry Div after losing its tanks; 1942 commander, 18th Tank Corps; 1942-44 commander, 60th Army; 1944-45 commander, 3rd Bel Front; *Career:* 1941 his div distinguished itself in battles at Novgorod; 1942 his corps fought staunchly at Voronezh; Feb 1943 his army liberated Kursk and in Sept 1943 crossed the Dnieper; 1944 distinguished himself in Bel campaign; Oct 1944 his troops were the first to break into East Prussia; throughout the war displayed great personal valor; *Awards:* twice Hero of the Sov Union (1943 and 1944); Order of Lenin; four Orders of the Red Banner; two Orders of Suvorov, 1st Class; other orders and medals; *Died:* 18 Feb 1945 fatally wounded by shrapnel while inspecting troops; town of Insterburg in East Prussia (now Kaliningrad Oblast) was renamed Chernyakhovsk in his honor; also commemorated by a monument in Vilnius.

CHERNYAVSKIY, Vladimir Il'ich (1893-1939) Party and govt official; CP member from 1911; *Born:* 1893 in Odessa, son of a worker; *Career:* 1910 joined revol movement; underground work in Kiev and Kremenchug; arrested and exiled to Siberia; 1917, after return to Kiev, joined Bolshevik faction, Exec Comt, Kiev Sov of Workers' Dep and Centr Trade-Union Council; Jan 1918 secr, Kiev Revol Comt and member, Strike Comt; fought in Civil War in Ukr; during German occupation worked for underground in Kiev Province; 1919 secr, Kiev Province Party Comt; 1920-23 served in Red Army and did polit work in Kiev, Poltava, Vinnitsa and Yekaterinoslav; 1924-26 Odessa Province Procurator; from Jan 1927 Party work in Kiev and Odessa; Nov 1930-Feb 1932 secr, CC, CP(B) Ukr, then first secr, Dnepropetrovsk Oblast Comt, CP(B) Ukr; from Oct 1932 frist secr, Vinnitsa Oblast Comt, CP(B) Ukr; deleg, 15-17th CPSU(B) Congresses; deleg, 5th and 7th Conferences and 9th-13th Congresses, CP(B) Ukr; elected cand member, Centr Control Commission at 9th Congress, CP(B) Ukr; elected member, CC at 10-13th Congresses, CP(B) Ukr; 1930-Aug 1937 cand Politburo member CC, CP(B) Ukr; member USSR and All-Ukr Centr Exec Comt; 1937 arrested by State Security organs; *Died:* 13 Nov 1939 in imprisonment.

CHERNYAYEV, Il'ya Il'ich (1893-1966) Inorganic chemist; prof from 1932; member, USSR Acad of Sci from 1943; head, Dept of Simple and Complex Inorganic Compounds, Inst of Gen and Inorganic Chemistry, USSR Acad of Sci from 1962; *Born:* 20 Jan 1893; *Educ:* 1915 grad Physics and Mathematics Fac, Petrograd Univ; *Career:* 1918-32 asst prof, 1932-35 prof and head, Dept of Inorganic Chemistry, Leningrad State Univ; 1935-41 prof, Moscow Oil Inst; 1945-66 prof, Moscow State Univ; from 1918 also worked at Inst for Study of Platinum, USSR Acad of Sci; 1934-41 senior assoc, 1941-62 dir, Inst of Gen and Inorganic Chemistry, USSR Acad of Sci; 1933-43 corresp member, USSR Acad of Sci; specialized in chemistry of complex compounds, platinum metals, methods of analysis, refining, etc; discovered shift in rotation of plane of polarization by optically active amino compounds of quadrivalent platinum during their transformation into amido or imido compounds; studied the oxidation reactions of complex platinum compounds; studied the reduction reaction of iridium compounds with the aid of different sugars and demonstrated the connection between the nitro-group and platinum via nitrogen; *Publ: Voprosy khimii kompleksnykh soyedineniy* (The Chemistry of Complex Compounds) (1936); *O geometricheskoy izomerii soyedineniy chetyryokhvalentnoy platiny* (The Geometrical Isomerism of Quadrivalent Platinum Compounds) (1947); *Eksperimental'noye obosnovaniye zakonomernosti transvliyaniya* (Experimental Demonstration of the Laws of Cross-Effect) (1954); *Akvo-karbonatnyye kompleksnyye soyedineniya uranila* (The Hydrocarbonate Complex Compounds of Uranyl) (1956); coauthor, *O reaktsiyakh dinitrodimetilaminovykh soyedineniy chetyryokhvalentnoy platiny* (Reactions of Dinitrodimethylamino Compounds of Quadrivalent Platinum) (1957); *Zadachi khimii kompleksnykh soyedineniy* (The Tasks of Complex Compound Chemistry) (1959), etc; *Awards:* three Orders of Lenin; two Orders of the Red Banner of Labor; medals; two Stalin Prizes (1946 and 1952); two Lenin Prizes; *Died:* 30 Sept 1966.

CHERNYSHEV, Aleksandr Alekseyevich (1882-1940) Electr eng; prof; member, USSR Acad of Sci from 1932; *Born:* 21 Aug 1882 in Lovani, now Chernigov Oblast;*Educ*: 1907 grad Petersburg Polytech Inst; *Career*: retained by Petersburg Polytech Inst to train for professorship and worked at Inst for rest of his life (from 1919 prof, Radio Eng Fac); trained at Göttingen Univ, Germany; 1913-15 posted to USA where he worked at major electr eng plants; from 1918 simultaneously dep dir, Physical Eng Research Inst, Leningrad; from 1929 corresp member, USSR Acad of Sci, and dir of its Electrophysical Research Inst; also head, Dept of High Tension Eng, Physics and Mechanics Inst, Leningrad; later also worked for Power Eng Inst, USSR Acad of Sci and for its Commission on Automation and Telemechanics, etc; specialized in High-tension techniques and radio eng, protection against overloading and a. c. and d. c. long-distance transmission; devised methods of increasing high-tension output capacity (up to one million volts) by means of series of linked transformers; studied problem of protecting lines of communication against interference by elect power lines; studied possibility of communications transmission via high-frequency power cables; studied range of radiotelephonic transmission; developed and studied radio tubes, etc; 1918 designed first Sov electronic tubes with preheated cathodes; also studied television, electrification of railroads, research planning and history of electr eng; *Publ: Absolyutnye izmereniya v vysokovol'tnykh tsepyakh* (The Absolute Measurement of High-Voltage Circuits) (1913); *Fotoelementy* (Photoelectric Cells) (1919); coauthor, *Ustroystvo dlya zashchity ot perenapryazheniy* (A Device for Protection Against Overloading) (1929); *Died*: 18 Apr 1940.

CHERNYSHEV, Andrey Borisovich (1904-1953) Thermal eng; specialist in gasification; corresp member, USSR Acad of Sci from 1939; CP member from 1943; *Born*: 22 Apr 1904; *Educ*: 1929 grad Leningrad Technol Inst; *Career*: from 1930 at Leningrad Branch, Peat Inst; from 1937 with Gasification Commission, USSR Acad of Sci; 1933-35 and from 1942 taught at Moscow Chemical Technol Inst; from 1948 dir, Inst of Combustible Minerals, USSR Acad of Sci; specialized in gasification, including subterranean gasification and thermal cracking of solid fuels; did research on coal gasification under a pressure of 100 athmospheres; devised a method of producing urban gas by the catalytic methane processing of water gas; studied the comprehensive power and chemical utilization of fuels; helped develop and incorporate a method for improving the productivity of coke-chemical plants; *Awards*: three orders; medals; Stalin Prize (1946); *Died*: 22 Nov 1953.

CHERNYSHEV, Boris Isidorovich (1888-1950) Geologist and paleontologist; prof; member, Ukr Acad of Sci from 1939; Hon Sci Worker of Ukr SSR from 1945; *Born*: 27 Jan 1888 at Yasenskaya Station, now Krasnodar Kray; *Educ*: 1916 grad Yekaterinoslav (now Dnepropetrovsk) Mining Inst; *Career*: 1923-26 prof, Dnepropetrovsk Univ and senior geologist, Geological Comt; 1930-39 prof of geology, Leningrad Univ; 1939-50 prof, Kiev Univ and dir, Inst of Geology, Ukr Acad of Sci; from 1945 also vice-pres, Ukr Acad of Sci; specialized in stratigraphy and invertebrate fauna of Donets, Kuznets and other coal-bearing basins; made major contribution to study of litte-knwon group of paleozoic arthropods and molluses; *Publ*: articles "Phyllocarridae from the Devonian Deposits of the Urals" (1928); "Calceola from the Devonian Deposits of the Salair Ridge" (1930); "Carbonicola Anthracomya and Najadites of the Donets Basin" (1931); "Cirripedia from the Donets and Kuznets Basins" (1935); "Before the Taxonomy of Upper Paleozoic Taxodonta" (1943); "The Family of Grammysiidae from the Upper Paleozoic Deposits" (1950); *Died*: 31 Aug 1950.

CHERNYSHEV, Il'ya Semyonovich (1912-1962) Diplomat; amb extraordinary and plen; CP member from 1940; *Born*: 1912 in Tokmak (Kir), son of a peasant; *Educ*: 1940 grad Moscow Univ; *Career*: 1940 began dipl work; 1944-45 counselor, USSR mission in Sweden; 1945-47 Sov minister in Sweden; 1947-49 USSR amb to Sweden; 1949-52 first dep exec mang, USSR Telegraph Agency (TASS); 1953-57 asst, then Dep Secr-Gen of UN; 1957-58 counselor to USSR For Min; 1959-61 first dep chm, State Comt for Radio and Television, USSR Council of Min; Dec 1961-Oct 1962 USSR amb to Brazil; *Awards*: Order of the Red Banner of Labor; Red Star; medals; *Died*: Oct 1962.

CHERNYSHEV, Sergey Yegorovich (1881-1963) Architect; Hon member, USSR Acad of Construction and Architecture from 1956; *Born*: 16 Oct 1881; *Educ*: 1901 grad Moscow School of Painting, Sculpture and Architecture, under L. N. Benua; advanced studies in Greece and Italy; *Career:* 1910-17 built residential houses in Moscow; reconstructed country estate *Gorenki*, built in late 18th Century; 1918-50 instructor, Moscow Inst of Architecture; 1934-41 chief architect, Planning Dept, 1944-48 chief architect, Architectural Planning Bd, Moscow City Exec Comt: 1939 chief architect, All-Union Agric Exhibition: from 1939 member, 1950-55 vice pres, USSR Acad of Architecture; *Works:* designed: Lenin Inst (now Inst of Marxism-Leninism) (1924-27); Ind Acad (1927-28); *Dinamo* complex (1931); Second House of Soviets (1932); co-designed Moscow Univ on Lenin Heights (1949-53), etc; *Awards*: Order of Lenin; Order of the Red Banner of Labor; Badge of Hon; Stalin Prize (1949); *Died*: 26 Apr 1963.

CHERNYSHYOVA, Lyudmila Sergeyevna (1908-1963) Russian actress; Pop Artiste of RSFSR from 1960; CP member from 1951; *Born*: 27 Sept 1908 *Career*: 1922 began career at Young Playgoers' Theater in Ryazan'; 1929-36 at Moscow Music Hall; 1936 joined Centr Children's Theater; played mischievous children, dreamers, frank and honest boys and girls; in mid-50's began playing character roles with greater psychological depth and satirical element; *Roles*: Gavrik in Katayev's *Beleyet parus odinokiy* (The Lone White Sail); Seryozha in *Belyy pudel'* (The White Poodle), after Kuprin; Zhenya Khvat in Mikhalkov's *Osoboye zadaniye* (Special Mission); Timka Zhokhov in Kassil's *Dorogiye moi mal'chishki* (My Dear Lads); Valeriy in Mikhalkov's *Krasnyy galstuk* (The Red Necktie); Klava in Inoshnikova's *Gde-to v Sibiri* (Somewhere in Siberia); Kroshechka-Khavroshechka in Razanov's *Baba-yaga*; Hedgehog in Marshak's *Skazki* (Fairy Tales); Averina and Tamara's aunt, in Rozov's *V dobryy chas* (In the Nick of Time) and *Neravnyy boy* (The Unequal Battle); Novikova in *Drug moy, Kol'ka* (My Friend Kol'ka); Aunt Sasha in Ivanter's *Byvshiye mal'chiki* (Former Boys); also acted in film *V dobryy chas* (In the Nick of Time), etc; *Died*: 15 Aug 1963.

CHERTKOV, Vladimir Grigor'yevich (1854-1936) Journalist; close friend and follower of Lev Tolstoy; *Born*: 1854; *Career*: founded, "Mediator" and ..Free World" Publ Houses; published journals *Svobodnoye slovo* and *Svobodnyye listki* in Britain; 1897 deported from Russia for his appeal to Caucasian Dukhobors; lived 10 years in Britain, where he published and distributed those of Tolstoy's works banned in Russia and material on the history of Russian sectarianism; ed, jubilee ed of Tolstoy's "Works"; 1920-21 chm, United Council of Religious Communities and Groups; chm, Bd, Council of 1st All-Russian Congress of Sectarian Agric Assoc; *Died*: 1936.

CHERVINSKIY, Mikhail Abramovich (1911-1965) Russian poet and playwright; *Born*: 13 June 1911; *Career*: 1944 began lit work; wrote satirical feuilletons and monologues, variety scenes, parodies and humoresques; also wrote libretto for musical comedies and operettas; often worked in collaboration with V.Z. Mass; *Publ*: coauthor, revue *Gde-to v Moskve* (Somewhere in Moscow) (1944); coauthor, political revues *Ikh bylo troye* (They Were Three) and *Chuzhoye delo* (None of Our Business) (1945); coauthor, comedies: *Tshchetnaya predostorozhnost'* (Vain Precaution) (1946); *O druz'yakh-tovarishchakh* (Friends and Comrades) (1947); libretto for operettas: *Trembita* (1949); *Samoye zavetnoye* (The Most Cherished Things) (1952); *Belaka akatsia* (White Acazia) (1955); *Moskva, Cheryomushki* (Moscow, Cheryomushki) (1959);variety programs; *Dobro pozhalovat'* (Welcome); *Lyubov' i tri apel'sina* (Love and Three Oranges) (1959), etc: *Died*: 12 Aug 1965.

CHERVYAKOV, Aleksandr Grigor'yevich (1892-1937) Bel Party and govt official; chm, Bel Centr Exec Comt from 1924; Bureau member, CC, CP Bel from 1924; CP member from 1917; *Born*: 8 Mar 1892 in vil Dukorka, now Minsk Oblast, son of a peasant; *Educ*: attended parish school, Minsk; 1909 grad Minsk high school; 1915 grad Vilnius Teachers' Training Inst; *Career*: from 1909 teacher, Trakai Uyezd, Vilnius Province; from 1915 served in army; attended Alexandrine Mil College, Moscow and Oranienbaum Officers' School; from Feb 1918 chm, Bel Nat Comt, RSFSR Council of Pop Comr; div comr, Southern Front; then comr, Bel Bureau, CC, RCP(B) and head, Cultural and Educ Dept, All-Russian Bureau of Mil Comr; from 1 Jan 1919–Bel Pop Comr of Educ, then member, CC, CP(B) Lith-Bel SSR and Centr Exec Comt Lith-Bel SSR; 1919-20 polit work in Red Army; dept head, Mil-Revol Council, Western Front; chm, Mil-Revol Comt, Minsk Province; member, three-man Bel Mil-Revol Comt; late 1920-23 chm, Bel Centr Exec Comt and Council of Pop Comr; 1924-37 chm, Bel Centr Exec Comt and co-chm, USSR Centr Exec Comt; co-founder of Bel SSR; supported Bel nat and cultural renaissance; *Died*: 16 June 1937 in his Minsk office, committed suicide to escape arrest by NKVD; posthumously rehabilitated.

CHETAYEV, Nikolay Gur'yevich (1902-1959) Physicist; specialist in mech and analytical mech; prof, Moscow Univ from 1940; corresp member, USSR Acad of Sci from 1943; *Born*: 6 Dec 1902; *Educ*: 1924 grad Kazan' Univ; *Career*: 1930-40 prof, Kazan' Univ; in 1930's founded own school of stability of motion; 1934 established gen theorem on instability of motion; 1938 reversed Lagrange's theorem on stability of equilibrium; 1949 proposed effective methods for solving problems of stability of unsettled motion; his works are of practical importance for calculating the flight stability of missiles and for solving a number of other problems of contemporary ballistics; *Publ: O printsipe Gaussa* (Gauss's Principle) (1932-33); *Ob uravnenii Puankare* (Poincaré's Equation) (1941); *Ob odnom svoystve uravneniy Puankare* (A Property of Pointcaré's Equations) (1955); *Ustoychivost' dvizheniy* (Stability of Motion) (2nd ed, 1955), etc; *Awards*: Lenin Prize (1960); Order of Lenin; Order of the Red Banner of Labor: *Died*: 17 Oct 1959.

CHEVERYOV, Aleksandr Mikhaylovich (1889-1921) Mil commander; CP member from 1908; *Born*: 1889, son of a worker; *Career*: from 1914 worked at Simsk Plant, Southern Urals; Apr 1917 Simsk RSDRP org deleg at All-Ural Party Conference; 1917 worked in Ufa; formed battle squad, which he led in fighting for Orenburg; twice wounded; fall 1918 his detachment was expanded into a regt, which he commanded in the storming of Izhevsk; seriously wounded; after convalescence given staff duties with 5th Army and Eastern Front, organizing grain collection in Ufa Province and crushing peasant revolts in Southern Urals; 1920-21 mil comr of brigade in Dag and Transcaucasia; 1921 RSFSR mil rep in Far East; *Awards*: Order of the Red Banner; gold watch (1918); golden arms (1919); *Died*: 1921 of food poisoning.

CHEYSHVILI, Nikolay Simonovich (Semyonovich) (1886-1965) Govt official; CP member from 1905; *Born*: 1886; *Educ*: 1908-10 at Moscow Univ; *Career*: active in student revol movement; 1911 expelled from univ for membership of RSDRP, arrested and exiled to Vologda Province; after 1917 Oct Revol mil work; 1918-19 head, Polit Bd, Western Mil Distr; 1919-20 mil comr with troops guarding Sov railroads; 1921-23 comr for mil supply, Moscow Mil Distr; 1923-25 staff comr, Caucasian Army; from 1926 exec govt work; from 1936 senior econ admin work; deleg at 16th Party Congress; from 1953 pensioner; *Died*: 21 Oct 1965.

CHICHERIN, Georgiy Vasil'yevich (1872-1936) Diplomat; RSDRP member from 1905; CP member from 1918; *Born*: 2 Dec 1872 in Tambov Province, son of a retired diplomat; *Educ*: grad History and Philology Fac, Petersburg Univ; *Career*: from 1897 worked in archives, Russian Min of For Affairs; 1904 joined revol movement for which compelled to emigrate to Germany in same Year; 1905 joined Berlin RSDRP org; 1907 attended RSDRP London Congress; late 1907 expelled from Prussia and moved to Paris; worked for French Socialist Party and int youth movement; during WW 1 lived in London and took part in British Workers' Movement; while abroad drifted away from Mensheviks and finally sided with

Bolsheviks in late 1917; 1917 arrested and interned in Brixton Prison as secr of org for repatriation of polit emigres to Russia; early 1918 was exchanged for British amb to Tsarist Russia Buchanan and returned to Russia; joined RCP(B) and appointed RSFSR Dep Pop Comr of For Affairs; from 30 May 1918 RSFSR Comr of For Affairs; took part in second round of peace negotiations at Brest-Litovsk; 3 Mar 1918 signed Brest-Litovsk Peace Treaty for RSFSR; 1920 negotiated with Turkey, Iran and Afghanistan, resulting in signing of treaties with these countries in 1921; 1922 represented Soviet Union at Genua Conference; 1922-23 led Sov deleg at Lausanne Conference on Middle East; 1922 signed Rapallo Treaty with Germany; 1925 signed treaty of non-aggression and neutrality with Turkey, in 1927 with Iran, etc; member, All-Russian and USSR Centr Comt; elected to CC, CPSU(B) at 14th (1925) and 15th (1927) Party Congresses; 1925 contracted serious illness; 1928-29 underwent treatment in Germany; 1930 returned to USSR; frequently differed with Stalin, Rykov and Bukharin on int policy, especially about relations with Germany and Oriental countries, aid to economically backward countries, etc; 6 Mar 1921 "Pravda" published his article "Against Stalin's Theses"; 1930 relieved of his post as USSR Pop Comr of For Affairs; *Publ: Stat'yi i rechi po voprosam mezhdunarodnoy politiki* (Articles and Speeches on Problems of International Policy) (1961); *Died*: 7 July 1936.

CHICHEROV, Vladimir Ivanovich (1907-1957) Ethnographer and folklorist; Dr of Philology; *Born*: 11 June 1907 in vil Vyazniki, now Vladimir Oblast; *Educ*: 1928 grad Moscow Univ; *Career*: while a student, took part in 1926-28 expedition of Sokolov brothers, retracing the steps of the ethnographers and folklorists Rybnikov and Gil'ferding; took part in many other expeditions and collected a vast fund of folklore material; from 1953 prof, Moscow Univ; *Publ*: coauthor, *Onezhskiye byliny* (Onega Tales) (1948); *Zimniy period russkogo zemledel'cheskogo kalendarya XVI-XIX vekov* (The Winter Period of the Russian Agricultural Calendar in the 16th-19th Centuries) (1957); *Russkoye narodnoye tvorchestvo* (Russian Folk Art) (1959); *Voprosy teorii i istorii narodnogo tvorchestva* (The Theory and History of Folk Art) (1959); *Died*: 11 May 1957.

CHICHIBABIN, Aleksey Yevgen'yevich (1871-1945) Organic chemist; prof; member USSR Acad of Sci from 1928; *Born*: 29 Mar 1871 near Poltava; *Educ*: 1892 grad Moscow Univ; *Career*: from 1900 prof, Moscow Univ; 1926-28 corresp member, USSR Acad of Sci; from 1930 until death in emigration; Dec 1936 deprived of membership of USSR Acad of Sci for refusal to return to USSR; specialized in pyridine and other nitrogenous heterocycles; devised method of obtaining derivatives of pyridine by condensation of aldehydes and ketones with ammonia; 1914 discovered method of obtaining alpha-amino pyridine by the reaction of sodium amide with pyridine (Chichibabin's reaction); applied this reaction to homologues of pyridine, chinoline and isochinoline; did research on the halogenation, sulphuration and nitration of alpha-amino pyridine; obtained alpha-oxypyridine by the reaction of potassium hydroxide on pyridine; studied the tautomerism of amino pyridines and oxypyridines; deciphered structure and synthesized various alkaloids and other vegetable substances (pilocarpine, santonin and bergenin); also did research on free aromatic radicals; devised method of synthesizing aldehydes with organic magnesium compounds;made major contribution to development of chemical and pharmaceutical ind in Russia; *Publ: O produktakh deystviya galoidnykh soyedineniy na piridin i khinolin* (The Products of the Reaction Between Haloid Compounds and Pyrodine and Chinoline) (1902); *Issledovaniya po voprosu o tryokhatomnom uglerode i o stroyenii prosteyshikh okrashennykh trifenilmetana* (Research on Trivalent Carbon and the Structure of the Simplest Colored Derivatives of Triphenyl-Methane) (1912); article "Proteins and How to Synthesize Them" (1912); *Issledovaniya iz oblasti piridinovykh osnovaniy* (Research on Pyridine Bases) (1918); *Osnovnyye nachala organicheskoy khimii* (Basic Principles of Organic Chemistry) (1924); *Awards*: Lenin Prize (1926); *Died*: 15 Aug 1945 in emigration.

CHICHINADZE, N.G. (KARTVELOV) (1875-1921) Menshevik politician; *Born*: 1875; *Career*: journalist; worked for various Geo newspapers; from 1895 in revol movement; 1905 worked in Kutaisi, then Tiflis; Kutaisi Party org deleg at 4th (Amalgamative) RSDRP Congress; after 1917 Feb Revol worked in Rostov; 1918 returned to Geo; Asst Min of Internal Affairs, then Min of War of Geo Republ until Sov coup in Geo; *Died*: 1921.

CHIKOVANI, Simon Ivanovich (1903-1966) Geo poet; translator; Presidium member, Geo Writers' Union; Bd member, USSR Writers' Union from 1959; CP member from 1941; *Born*: 9 Jan 1903 in vil Nayesakao, now Geo SSR; *Career*: 1922 one of founders of Geo left-wing futurist lit group; 1923 first work published; translated into Geo *Slovo o polku Igoreve* (Lay of the Host of Igor) and many works by Pushkin, Shevchenko, Mayakovsky, etc; ed, journal *Mnatobi*; dep, USSR Supr Sov of 1946 and 1950 convocations; dep chm, Sov-Polish Friendship Soc; 1959 at 3rd USSR Writers' Congress appointed member, Commission to Amend the Statutes of the USSR Writers' Union; *Publ*: verse "The Road" (1927); *Ushgul Komsomol* (1929); "Caught by the Evening in Khakhmati" (1932); "For the Masters of Vardziya" and "Lake Tsunda" (1936); "Specters of Armazi" (1941); collection "We Wish Our Homeland Victory" (1942); poem "Song of David Gurashvili" (1944); "Kartli Evenings"; "Victory Celebration"; "Who Said. . . " (1944-47); poetic cycles "On the Polish Road" and "Flowers Beyond the Oder" (1952-53); in Russian translation *Izbrannoye* (Selected Works) and *Novyye stikhi* (New Verse) (1954); "Poems" (1957); "Selected Works" (1958); verse "The Shell" (1960); collection "Under the Canopy of the Mountains" (1961); poem "Return" (1961); "Sixty Poems" (1963); collection "Two Wings" (1964), etc; *Awards*: Stalin Prize (1947); Order of Lenin; two Orders of the Red Banner of Labor (1958 and 1963); medals;*Died*: 24 Apr 1966.

CHIRIKOV, Yevgeniy Nikolayevich (1864-1932) Russian writer and playwright; *Born*: 5 Aug 1864 in Kazan', son of an official of noble rank; *Educ*: 1883-87 studied at Kazan' Univ; *Career*: 1885 first work published; 1887 expelled from univ for polit unreliability; contributed to journals *Nachalo* and *Zhizn'*; worked for *Znaniye* (Knowledge) Publ House; 1902 debut as dramatist; until 1905 sided with left-wing Russian intellectuals; later, especially during WW 1, sympathized with nationalists; after 1917 Oct Revol sided with White forces; 1920 emigrated and wrote articles against the Sov regime; *Publ*: collected stories: *Invalidy* (The Invalids) (1897); *Caligula* (1899); *Chuzhestrantsy* (Foreigners) (1899); "Faust" (1900); *Kapitulyatsiya* (Capitulation) (1901); plays: *Na dvore vo fligele* (In the Annexe Outside) (1902); *Yevrei* (Jews) (1903, prohibited by the censors; staged in Berlin, London and USA; 1905 staged in Petersburg); *Muzhiki* (Muzhiks) (1905); *Ivan Mironych* (1905); *Mariya Ivanovna* (1907); *Lesnyye tayny* (Forest Secrets) (1910); *Tsar' prirody* (The Emperor of Nature) (1909); *Dom Kocherginykh* (The Kochergins' House) (1910); *Shakaly* (Jackals) (1911); trilogy *Zhizn' Tarkhanova* (The Life of Tarkhanov) (1911-14); *Sem'ya* (The Family) (a sequel to the trilogy written while he was living abroad); *Sobraniye sochineniy* (Collected Works) (1910-16), etc; his plays were staged at the Moscow Arts Theater of Art, the Korsh Theater in Moscow, the Comedy and Drama Theater in Petersburg, the Maly Theater in Moscow, the Theater of the Lit and Art Soc in Petersburg, and in theaters abroad; *Awards*: Griboyedov Prize (1909); *Died*: 18 Jan 1932 in Prague.

CHIRKIN, V. G. (1877-1954) Govt official; CP member from 1920; *Born*: 1877; *Career*: worker; 1903 joined revol movement; early 1905 joined Mensheviks; from 1906 active in trade-union movement; Petersburg org deleg at 5th RSDRP Congress; after 1917 Feb Revol deleg, 1st Congress of Soviets and 2nd All-Russian Congress of Soviets; 1918 broke with Mensheviks and in 1920 joined Bolsheviks; 1920-22 Presidium member, Southern Bureau, All-Russian Centr Trade-Union Council; member, All-Ukr Centr Exec Comt; dep chm, then chm, All-Ukr Union of Consumers' Soc; later held exec posts in railroad trans; *Died*: 1954.

CHIRVINSKIY, Pyotr Nikolayevich (1880-1955) Geologist and petrographer; *Born*: 7 Feb 1880; *Educ*: 1902 grad Kiev Univ; *Career*: from 1909 prof, Don Polytech Inst, Novocherkassk; from 1943 prof, Perm' Univ; did extensive research on mineralogy and petrography; studied minerals of Kola Pensinsula, Ukr, Crimea, Transcaucasus and Urals; studied overall chemical composition of rocks; developed method of "geometrochemical" analysis and calculated the percentage of various chemicals in the earth as a whole; wrote papers on chemistry, mineralogy and petrography of meteorites and on laws governing the composition of meteoric matter; also studied formation of meteorites in solar system; published well-known works on experimental mineralogy and petrography, hydrogeology, geochemistry, crystallography and glaciology; described various ore and mineral deposits, including Kedabek copper deposits, Khopyor Rayon iron deposits, centr Russian phosphorite deposits and Transcaucasian pumic deposits;

helped to compile a catalog of minerals in the Northern Caucasus; 1922 wrote textbook on hydrogeology; 1926 wrote *Kurs mestorozhdeniy poleznykh iskopayemykh* (A Course on Mineral Deposits); a mountain near the Tungus meteorite and a mineral (Chirvinskite) discovered by N. Kh. Platonov are named after him; *Died*: 21 June 1955.

CHISTOVICH, Fyodor Yakovlevich (1870-1942) Pathoanatomist and specialist in forensic med; prof from 1908; Dr of Med from 1895; Hon Sci Worker of RSFSR from 1935; *Born*: 1870; *Educ*: 1893 grad Petersburg Mil Med Acad; *Career*: 1893-99 asst prof, 1899-1908 assoc prof, Chair of Pathological Anatomy, Petersburg Mil Med Acad; 1909-1921 prof and head, Chair of Pathological Anatomy, Med Fac, Kazan' Univ; after 1917 Oct Revol rector, Kazan' Univ; 1921-42 prof, Leningrad Inst of Postgrad Med Training and 1st and 2nd Leningrad Med Inst; 1941-42 continued work in Leningrad during blockade; discovered specific precipitins which led to a method of determining blood groups in forensic med (Chistovich-Uhlenhut reaction); did research on blood diseases; 1929 proposed new classification of diseases of hematogenic system; described specific pathology of chemical weapons and inflammatory lesions caused by components of tubercular mycobacteria; wrote 62 works on pathological anatomy and hematology; *Publ*: doctor's thesis *O patologoanatomicheskikh izmeneniyakh golovnogo mozga pri aziatskoy kholere* (Pathoanatomical Lesions of the Cerebrum in Asiatic Cholera) (1895); article "Congenital Rachitis" (1896); article "Changes in the Properties of the Blood After the Injection of Foreign Serum and Blood in Relation to Ehrlich's Theory of Immunity" (1899); *Kurs patologicheskoy anatomii* (A Course of Pathological Anatomy) (2 vol, 1919-20; *Prakticheskiy kurs patologicheskoy gistologii* (A Practical Course of Pathological Histology) (1924); *Died*: 1942 during evacuation from Leningrad.

CHISTYAKOV, Vasiliy Matveyevich (1890-1965) Pedag; specialist in methods of teaching Russian in non-Russian schools; prof; Dr of Pedag; *Born*: 1890; *Educ*: 1912 grad Yaroslavl' Teachers' Inst; *Career*: from 1912 taught in elementary school; then taught Russian at Kineshma and Tver' higher elementary colleges; 1921-30 taught at school, at workers' fac and teachers' inst in Kalinin; 1930-36 head, Chair of Russian, Ferghana Teachers' Training Inst; from 1938 worked in Moscow at Centr Teachers' Training Inst of Nat Minorities, Inst of Schools, and Advanced Training Inst for Educ Workers; 1944-49 at Research Inst of Teaching Methods; 1949-65 at Research Inst of Nat Schools, RSFSR Acad of Pedag Sci; developed original methods of teaching Russian in non-Russian schools; wrote textbooks, teaching aids and Russian-language curricula for Tuva, Uighur, Karakalpak, Lith, Mari, Tatar, Uzbek, Yakut, Khakas and other Sov nationality schools; *Publ*: coauthor, *Ocherki po metodike prepodavaniya russkogo i rodnogo yazykov v tatarskoy shkole* (Studies in Methods of Teaching Russian and the Native Language in Tatar Schools) (1952); coauthor, *Razgovornyye uroki po russkomu yazyku v nerusskoy shkole* (Russian Language Conversation Lessons in Non-Russian Schools) (1956); *Uprazhneniya po razvitiyu russkoy rechi uchashchikhsya 5-7 klassov nerusskoy shkoly* (Exercizes for the Development of Russian Conversation for Pupils in 5th-7th Grades of Non-Russian Schools) (1957); *Uprazhneniya po razvitiyu russkoy rechi uchashchikhsya 8-10 klassov nerusskoy shkoly* (Exercizes for the Development of Russian Conversation in Pupils of 8th-10th Grades of Non-Russian Schools) (1958); *Osnovy metodiki russkogo yazyka v nerusskikh shkolakh* (The Principles of Teaching Russian in Non-Russian Schools) (4th ed, 1958); *Uprazhneniya po razvitiyu russkoy rechi uchashchikhsya nachal'nykh klassov nerusskoy shkoly* (Exercizes for the Development of Russian Conversation for Pupils in the Initial Grades of Non-Russian Schools) (1960); ed, *Metodika prepodavaniya russkogo yazyka v shkolakh tyurko-yazychnoy gruppy* (Methods of Teaching Russian in Turkic-Speaking Schools) (1964); *Died*: 1965.

CHIZHEVSKIY, Nikolay Prokop'yevich (1873-1952) Metallurgist; specialist in coke chemistry; member, USSR Acad of Sci from 1939; *Born*: 8 Apr 1873 in Kazan', son of an office worker; *Educ*: 1899 grad Petersburg Univ; 1902 grad Mining Acad in Leoben, Austria; 1904 grad Kiev Polytech Inst; *Career*: 1910-23 prof, Tomsk Technol Inst; from 1923 prof, Moscow Mining Acad; then Moscow Steel Inst; from 1935 at Inst of Combustible Minerals, USSR Acad of Sci; specialized in metallurgy and coke chemistry; 1910-14 studied effects of nitrogen, carbon, manganese and silicon on mechanical properties of iron and steel; first to discover that nitrogen-saturated iron readily takes tempering; laid foundation for metallography of nitrated iron; proposed method for boron cementation of steel; 1914 devised method for using vacuum in steel production; proposed a method of determining gases in steel; directed first major Sov research on coking coal aimed at extending the raw material base for coke production and at improving coke quality; proposed new coke technol; proved that metallurgical coke can be derived from mixture of gas, coal, waste coal and lignite; demonstrated that iron coke and chrome coke can be obtained by introducing flue dust or chrome ore into coal seam; 1935, together with D. V. Nagorskiy, laid theoretical basis for construction of first Soviet coke furnaces; conducted research on properties of oil coke for production of ind graphite; *Publ: Koksovaniye podmoskovnykh ugley vmeste s donetskimi i v samostoyatel'nom vide* (The Coking of Moscow Coal, Independently or with Donets Coal) (1932); *Problemy izucheniya tvyordykh goryuchikh, iskopayemykh* (Problems of Studying Solid Combustible Minerals) (1948); *Izbrannyye trudy* (Selected Works) Vol 1-2, 1958); *Awards*: Stalin Prize (1943); two orders; medals; *Died*: 22 Apr 1952.

CHKALOV, Valeriy Pavlovich (1904-1938) Russian; brigade commander; outstanding Sov pilot; CP member from 1936; *Born*: 2 Feb 1904 in vil Vasil'yevo, Gorky Oblast, son of a worker; *Educ*: grad Yegor'yevo Flying School (Moscow Oblast); grad Borisoglebsk Flying School, Moscow Advanced Flying School and Serpukhov Higher School of Aerial Gunnery and Bombing; *Pos*: 1918-19 steamship stoker; 1919-21 soldier-worker in an aircraft assembly crew at Nizhniy Novgorod (now Gorky) Aviation Supply Depot; from 1921 cadet at aviation schools; 1924-30 fighter pilot; 1930-33 test pilot, Research Inst, USSR Air Force; 1933-38 test pilot at a Moscow aircraft plant; *Career*: advocated contour flying for attacking ground targets; developed and was the first to perform some new aerobatic flight maneuvers, such as an upward spin and a slow roll; frequently found himself in difficult situations while testing aircraft yet always managed to overcome them with his skill, endurance, self-control, knowledge of aircraft and self-confidence; tested over 70 types of aircraft; 20-22 July 1936, together with pilots G. F. Baydukov and A. V. Belyakov, made a nonstop flight from Moscow via Petropavlovsk-on-Kamchatka to Udd Island, covering 9,374 km in 56 hours and 20 minutes; 18-20 June 1937, with the same pilots, made a nonstop flight in an ANT-25 aircraft from Moscow to Vancouver (USA), via the North Pole, setting a new world nonstop flight record (over 12,000 km in 63 hours and 25 minutes); dep, USSR Supr Sov of 1937 convocation; *Awards*: Hero of the Sov Union (1936); two Orders of Lenin; Order of the Red Banner; *Died*: 15 Dec 1938 killed in a crash, while testing a new high-speed fighter; his native vil, Udd Island and the town of Orenburg were named after him (the latter was renamed Orenburg after Stalin's death).

CHKHEIDZE, Nikolay Semyonovich (1864-1926) Politician and journalist; leader, RSDRP (Mensheviks); *Born*: 1864; *Career*: late 1890's took up polit work in Caucasus; 1907-12 and 1912-17 Tiflis Province dep, 3rd and 4th State Dumas; leader, Menshevik faction, 4th Duma; during WW 1 supported centrist policies; during 1917 Feb Revol member, Provisional Comt, State Duma; sided with defensists; Feb-Aug 1917 chm, Petrograd Sov of Workers and Soldiers' Dep; chm, Centr Exec Comt of 1st convocation; supported Provisional Govt; after 1917 Oct Revol chm, Geo Constituent Assembly; 1921 emigrated to France after establishment of Sov rule in Geo; *Died*: 1926 committed suicide in Paris.

CHKHEIDZE, Nina (Nutsa) Platonovna (1881-1963) Geo actress; Pop Artiste of Geo SSR from 1925; *Born*: 12 Oct 1881, daughter of an actor; *Career*: 1894 stage debut at age 13 as Emma in Giacometti's "La Morte Civile"; was trained in V. S. Aleksi-Meskhishvili and K. Meskhi's heroic-romantic method; had a powerful voice and excellent stage presence; 1896-1922 acted at Kutaisi Theater; 1922-25 and 1938-48 at State Drama Theater, Tbilisi (later Rustaveli Theater); *Roles*: Zeynab, Gayane and Rukayya in Sumbatov-Yuzhin's *Izmena* (Treason); Ketevan in Eristavi's "Homeland"; Marine in Gunia's "Brother and Sister"; Natasha and Lyubov' in Gorky's *Na dne* (The Lower Depths) and *Posledniye* (The Last Men); Kruchinina and Polina in *Bez viny vinovatyye* (Guilty Without Guilt) and *Dokhodnoye mesto* (A Lucrative Post); Ophelia and Desdemona in "Hamlet" and "Othello"; Louise and Amalia in Schiller's "Räuber" and "Kabale und Liebe"; Marguerite Gautier in Dumas-fils' "La Dame aux Camélias"; Magda in Sudermann's "Heimat"; Jocasta in

Sophocles' "Oedipus Rex"; Mekhru in Kaladze's *Khatidzhe*: the Mother in Shanshiashvili's *Georgiy Saakadze*; Tat'yana in *Razlom* (The Beak-Up), etc; also acted in the films "Dariko", "Arsen", etc; *Publ*: Vospominaniya (Reminiscences) (1950, 1956); *Died*: 15 Aug 1963.

CHKHEIDZE, Ushangi Viktorovich (1898-1953) Actor; Pop Artiste of Geo SSR from 1935; *Born*: 27 Nov 1898; *Educ*: attended Kutaisi High School; studied at Agronomic Fac, Tbilisi Univ, and G. Dzhabadari's Studio; *Career*: acted in school plays and during summer vacation with semi-professional Geo troupes; on graduation from studio became member of Avchala Workers' Theater; 1921 actor, Rustaveli Theater; 1928 helped to found theater in Kutaisi; from 1931 in Tbilisi; from 1933 at Mardzhanishvili Theater, where he worked until 1935; *Roles*: Hamlet; Iago; Uriel Akosty in Gutskov's play of the same name; Godun in *Razlom* (Break-Up); Onufriy in Andreyev's *Dni nashey zhizni* (The Days of Our Life); Kvarkvare Tutaberi in Kakabadze's play of the same name; the police officer Chaliani in Dadiani's *Vcherashniye* (Yesterdays), etc; also acted in films; *Works*: historical drama *Georgiy Sakkadze* (produced at Mardzhanishvili Theater); various articles on stagecraft and two books *Kote Mardzhanishvili – rezhissyor i uchitel'* (Kote Mardzhanichvili - Producer and Teacher) (1949) and *Vospominaniya i pis'ma* (Memoirs and Letters) (1956); *Died*: 1 Dec 1953 in Tbilisi.

CHKHIKVADZE, Zakhariy Ivanovich (1862-1930) Geo folklore expert; choral conductor and teacher; *Born*: 5 Dec 1862 in Telavi, now Geo SSR; *Career*: 1905 founded Geo Philharmonic Soc; from 1919 founder-dir, music schools in Signakhi and Telavi; from 1925 curator, Museum of Ancient Geo Art, Tbilisi; *Works*: church concertos; anthology of Geo folk songs *Salamuri* (1906); *Died*: 27 Apr 1930 in Tbilisi.

CHODRISHVILI, Mikhail (Miho) Iosifovich (1853-1929) Party and govt official; CP member from 1896; *Born*: 1853 in Signakh, Tiflis Province, son of an artisan; *Career*: from age nine hired laborer; 1873 began work at Tiflis carpentry factory but was dismissed for organizing a strike; then worked at carpentry shops in Tiflis, Vladikavkaz and Baku; from 1888 at railroad car shop, Tiflis Main Railroad Workshop; 1895-98 helped found first illegal RSDRP workers' circles in Tiflis; several times arrested for revol activities; from 1910 in exile; 1913 returned from exile and engaged in revol work in Tiflis; 1918 founded Bolshevik cell and rayon Party comt in Tiflis; 1919 arrested by Geo authorities; from 1920, after establishment of Sov regime in Geo, member of Centr Control Commission, CP Geo; member, Geo Centr Exec Comt; member, Transcaucasian SFSR Centr Exec Comt; Collegium member, Geo Supr Court; *Publ*: "My Memoirs" (1927); *Died*: 1929.

CHORNYY, Kuz'ma (real name: ROMANOVSKIY, Nikolay Karlovich) (1900-1944) Bel novelist and short-story writer; member, Bel Writers' Union from 1934; CP member from 1943; *Born*: 7 July 1900 on Borki Estate, near Slutsk; son of a farmhand; *Educ*: 1916-19 studied at Nesvizh Teachers' Seminary; 1923-35 studied at Lit Dept, Pedag Fac, Bel State Univ; *Career*: 1920-23 worked for mil dept, Timkovichi Volost Revol Comt, for Slutsk Uyezd Mil Comrt, then as teacher in Timkovichi; 1924-28 worked for Minsk newspaper *Belaruskaya vyoska*; from 1928 devoted himself to lit work; 1923-26 member, *Maladnyak* assoc of proletarian writers; from 1926 co-founder and chm, *Uzvyshsha* lit assoc; 1932 member, Org Comt, Bel Writers' Union; 13 Oct 1938-8 June 1939 in prison for alleged complicity in plot to kill Voroshilov; from 1941 worked for "Soviet Bel" radio and broadsheet *Razdavim fashistskuya gadinu* in Moscow; from Sept 1944 in Minsk; *Publ*: collections of short stories and novellae: *Apavyadan'ni* (Short Stories) (1925); *Srebra zhyts'tsya* (Life's Silver) (1925); *Pa daroze* (On the Way) (1925); *Pachuts'tsi* (Feelings) (1926); *Khvoi havorats'* (The Talking Pines) (1926); *Veras'nyovyya nochy* (September Nights) (1929); short stories: *Lyavon Bushmar* (1929); *Lyuba Luk'yanskaya* (1936); *Skip'yeuski les* (Skip'yevo Forest) (Part 1, 1944); plays *Leta* (Summer) (1932); *Bats'kaushchyna* (The Fatherland) (1939); *Irynka* (1940); novels: *Syastra* (The Sister) (1927); *Zyamlya* (Earth) (1928); *Idzi, idzi* (Begone) (1930); *Bats'kaushchyna* (The Fatherland) (1931); *Trytstsats' hod* (Thirty Years) (1934); *Tretsyay pakalen'ne* (The Third Generation) (1935); *Poshuki buduchyni* (In Search of the Future) (1943); *Mlechny shlyakh* (The Milky Way) (1944); *Vyaliki dzen'* (A Great Day) (1944); *Zbor tvorau* (Collected Works) (6 vol, 1954); *Died*: 22 Nov 1944 in Minsk of heart failure.

CHUBAR', Vlas Yakovlevich (1891-1939) Party and govt official; CP member from 1907; *Born*: 10 Feb 1891 in vil Fedorovka, former Yekaterinoslav Province, son of a peasant; *Educ*: 1911 grad tech college in Aleksandrovsk, now Zaporozh'ye; *Career*: from 1904 in revol movement; after graduating from tech college worked at plants in Kramatorsk, Gulyaypole and Mariupol'; 1911 twice arrested but managed to escape; 1912 imprisoned for participating in strike at Kramatorsk Plant; 1915-17 turner at Artillery Plant, Petrograd; took part in 1917 Feb Revol, then set up factory comt at above plant and was elected its chm; 1917, at first conference of factory comts became member of Exec Commission, Petrograd Council of Factory Comts; until early 1918 dep chm of this commission; after 1917 Oct Revol comr, Main Artillery Bd, then on Workers' Control Council; after reorganization of this body, until 1922 member, Exec Bureau (Presidium), Supr Sovnarkhoz; 1918-19 Bd chm, Nationalized State Plants Trust of Former Sormovo and Kolomna; from 1918 member, All-Russian Centr Exec Council; member and until 1938 Presidium member, USSR Centr Exec Council; dep, USSR Supr Sov of 1937 convocation; from early 1920 member, Ukr Supr Sovnarkhoz; instrumental in reconstruction of Ukr ind; from 1922 managed state coal ind in Donbass; from 1920 member, Ukr Revol Comt; at 4th All-Ukr Congress of Soviets elected member, All-Ukr Centr Exec Comt; reelected member of that body at all subsequent congresses; combined Party, govt and admin posts with trade-union work: for CC, Metal Workers' Union in Moscow; as member, Southern Bureau, All-Russian Centr Trade-Union Council; then as member, Donetsk Province Miners' Union; July 1923-Apr 1934 chm, Ukr Council of Pop Comr; then dep chm USSR Council of Pop Comr; from Sept 1937 simultaneously USSR Pop Comr of Finance; from 1920 member, CC, CP(B) Ukr; May-Nov 1920 cand member, Nov 1920 to 1934 member, Politburo, CC, CP(B) Ukr; 1921 at 10th RCP(B) Congress elected cand member, CC, RCP(B); at 11th Congress and subsequent congresses elected member, CC, RCP(b); from 1927 cand member, Politburo, CC, CPSU(B); arrested by State Security organs; *Awards*: Order of the Red Banner of Labor; *Died*: 26 Feb 1939 in imprisonment; posthumously rehabilitated.

CHUCHIN, F. G. (1883-1942) Party official; CP member from 1904; *Born*: 1883; *Career*: Party work in Orekhovo-Zuyevo, Moscow, Petersburg and other cities; after 1917 Feb Revol member, Tomsk Sov of Soldiers' Dep; comr for Anzhero-Sudzhensk mines; member, Siberian Oblast RSDRP(B) Bureau; 1918-19 underground Party work in territory held by Czechoslovakian Corps and Kolchak's troops; attended 9th Party Congress; from 1923 research and teaching work at Moscow higher educ establishments; *Died*: 1942.

CHUDAKOV, Yevgeniy Alekseyevich (1890-1953) Mech eng; specialist in automotive eng; member, USSR Acad of Sci from 1939; *Born*: 2 Sept 1890; *Educ*: 1916 grad Moscow Higher Tech College; *Career*: from 1916 instructor, from 1926 prof, Moscow Higher Tech College and other higher educ establishments; 1918 helped to found Sci Automotive Laboratory; 1921 co-founder, Sci Automotive Inst; from 1938 co-founder and dir, Inst of Mech Eng, USSR Acad of Sci; 1939-42 vice-pres, USSR Acad of Sci; from 1942 Presidium member, USSR Acad of Sci; specialized in automotive theory; 1928 published *Dinamicheskoye i ekonomicheskoye issledovaniye avtomobilya* (A Dynamic and Economic Study of the Automobile), in which he provided a sci analysis of the relationship between the design features of the automobile and its functions as a means of transport; studied the durability of automobiles and the reliability of automotive parts; solved numerous problems relating to the reliability of machine parts and the theories of friction and metal wear, thus making a major contribution to mech eng in gen; from 1949 member, Main Ed Bd, *BSE* (Large Soviet Encyclopedia); member, Sov Peace Defense Comt; chm, Council of Sci, Eng and Tech Socs, etc; *Publ: Teoriya avtomobilya* (Automotive Theory) (1935); *Raschyot avtomobilya* (Automotive Calculations) (1936); *Ustroystvo avtomobilya* (Automobile Layout) (1941); coauthor, *Atlas konstruktsiy sovetskikh avtomobiley* (An Atlas of Soviet Automobiles Design) (5 vol, 1948-54); *Awards*: two Stalin Prizes (1943 and 1951); two Orders of Lenin; Order of the Red Banner of Labor; medals; *Died*: 19 Sept 1953.

CHUDNOVSKIY, Grigoriy Isaakovich (1894-1918) Party official; CP member from 1917; *Born*: 1894; *Career*: active in revol movement; 1907-10 Menshevik and Plekhanov supporter; 1913 fled from exile and settled in Vienna; during WW 1 adopted centrist stand; from 1916 lived in America; 1917 returned to Russia; joined *Mezhrayontsy* group and together with this group was admitted to RSDRP(B); Oct 1917 member, Petrograd Mil Revol Comt; directed units in storming of Winter Palace; wounded in battle with Kerenskiy's forces at Tsarskoye Selo; after convalescence appointed comr of Southwestern Front; late 1917 arrested in Kiev by Ukr Centr Rada; after Bolshevik occupation of Kiev appointed mil comr of Kiev; *Died*: Apr 1918 killed on Ukr Front.

CHUDOV, Mikhail Semyonovich (1893-1937) Party and govt official; CP member from 1913; *Born*: 1893, son of a peasant; *Career*: revol work among Petersburg printers; Bd member, Printer's Union; arrested for revol activities; after 1917 Feb Revol trade-union and Party work in Petrograd; 1918 chm, Bezhetsk Uyezd Sov Exec Comt; 1920-22 chm, Tver' Province Sov Exec Comt; 1922-25 secr, Tver' Province CPSU(B) Comt; 1925-28 at Rostov-on-Don as secr, Donetsk Oblast and North Caucasian Kray CPSU(B) Comt; from 1928 secr, Leningrad Oblast CPSU(B) Comt; at 12th Party Congress elected cand member, CC, CPSU(B); at 14th-17th Party Congresses elected member, CC, CPSU(B); also elected member, All-Russian Centr Exec Comt from 8th convocation; member USSR Centr Exec Comt from 1st convocation; arrested by State Security organs; *Died*: 1937 in imprisonment.

CHUDOVSKAYA, Mariya Khananovna (Amaliya KLEYNBART) 1882-1967) Revolutionary; CP member from 1907; *Born*: 1882; *Career*: 1898 began revol activity in Bel; 1903-18 in Germany, working at cigarette factories in Munich, Baden-Baden and other cities; 1903-07 member, Munich Group, Bund; 1907-18 member, Soc-Democrat Party of Germany; 1907, after Stuttgart Congress of Second International joined Esslingen (later Stuttgart) Group for Promoting the RSDRP(B); 1909-18 simultaneously Bd member, Stuttgart Tobacco Workers' Union; arrested for revol activities; 1916-18 member, "Spartak" Group; 1918 returned to Russia and did polit work on Western and Eastern Fronts; 1928-30 lived with husband in Poland, polit work among women; 1930 returned to USSR and engaged in Party work; from 1934 pensioner; *Died*: Nov 1967.

CHUDOVSKIY, Nikolay Nikolayevich (1882-1966) Party and govt official; CP member from 1904; *Born*: 13 Mar 1882; *Career*: 1890's joined revol movement; active in 1905-07 Revol in Minsk Province; member, militant squad; several times arrested by tsarist authorities for revol activities; 1907-18 emigre in Germany; member, German Soc-Democrat Party; one of active organizers, "Spartak" Group; Aug 1918, on return to Russia, exec posts with Pop Comrt of For Trade and other institutions; from 1943 pensioner; *Died*: 15 Mar 1966.

CHUGAYEV, Lev Aleksandrovich (1873-1922) Chemist; *Born*: 17 Oct 1873 in Moscow; *Educ*: 1895 grad Moscow Univ; *Career*: after grad head, Dept of Chemistry, Bacteriological Inst, Moscow Univ; 1904-08 prof of chemistry, Moscow Higher Tech College; 1908-22 prof of organic chemistry, Petersburg Univ; 1909-22 prof of organic chemistry, Petersburg Technol Inst; from 1918 founder-dir, Inst for the Study of Platinum and Other Precious Metals, USSR Acad of Sci; did first research on biochemistry and bacteriology; 1900 discovered sensitive luminescent reaction, making it possible to distinguish between the common coliform bacterium and the typhoid bacillus; made major contribution to study of terpenes and camphors; 1899 developed new "xanthogenic" method of synthesizing hydrocarbons which consists in obtaining the ethyl xanthate of the corresponding spirit and then separating the ethyl by heating; 1911 discovered new type of anomalous rotary dispersion caused by the presence in an organic compound molecule of two assymetric centers rotating in different directions and having different dispersion coefficients; made important contribution to chemistry of complex compounds; 1906 established that the most stable complex compounds contain five- or six-membered internal rings (Chugayev's ring rule); 1905 discovered new sensitive reaction of nickel with dimethylglyoxime (Chugayev's reagent); 1918 discovered similar reaction of osmium with thiourea; gave impetus to new trend in analytic chemistry based on use of organic reagents; 1920 in the course of research on complex compounds of platinum group achieved first synthesis of hypothesized pentammine compounds of quadrivalent platinum $[Pt(NH_3)_5Cl]X_3$ (Chugayev salts); 1915 discovered conversion of complex amino-compounds into corresp amido-compounds; established Sov school of inorganic chemists specializing in complex compounds; *Publ: Izbrannyye trudy* (Selected Works) (2 vol, 1954-55), etc; *Awards*: Lenin Prize (1927, posthumously); *Died*: 23 Sept 1922.

CHUGURIN, Ivan Dmitriyevich (1883-1947) Party and govt official; CP member from 1902; *Born*: 15 Aug 1883 in Sormovo, son of a worker; *Educ*: 1894 grad parish church school; 1911 attended course for Party workers; *Career*: from 1895 worked at Sormovo Plant; Mar 1906 arrested for revol activities and imprisoned in Perm' Prison; 1911 attended school organized by Lenin for Party workers at Longjumeau near Paris; late 1911 returned to Russia, but soon arrested and exiled for five years to Narym Kray; 1916 worked as tinsmith at Petrograd *Promet* Plant, then at *Ayvaz* Plant; after 1917 Feb Revol secr, Vyborg Rayon Party Comt, Petrograd; Apr 1917 issued Lenin his Party card upon Lenin's return from emigration to Petersburg; 1918, on Lenin's instructions, organized first workers' food detachment in Vyborg Rayon; 1918-19 chief, Polit Dept, 5th Army on Eastern Front; 1919-20 Presidium member and exec secr, All-Russian Cheka; from 1921 admin work; chm, Bd, Siberian Coal Trust; head, Yuzovka Rayon Coal Bd; from 1924 dir, Northern Shipbuilding Yard; then dir, *Elektropribor* Electr Instruments Plant; retired on pension; *Died*: 1947 near Moscow.

CHUKOVSKIY, Nikolay Korneyevich (1905-1965) Russian writer; *Born*: 2 June 1905 in Odessa, son of the writer K. I. Chukovskiy; *Educ*: 1930 grad Inst of the History of Arts; *Career*: 1930 first work published; prose writer, critic and translator; during Sov-Finnish War and WW 2 corresp for Navy newspapers; *Publ*: story *Tantalena* (1925); novel *Yunost'* (Youth) (1930); story *V solnechnom dome* (In the Sunny House) (1931); novels: *Slava* (Fame) (1935); *Knyazhiy ugol* (The Prince's Corner) (1936); *Yaroslavl'* (1938); *Leto* (Summer) (1941); book about great mariners, sea journeys, geographic discoveries and explorations *Voditeli fregatov* (Frigate Captains) (1941); stories and novelettes: *Devyat' brat'yev* (Nine Brothers) (1943); *Nochi na ostrove* (Nights on the Island) (1945); *Morskoy okhotnik* (The Sea Hunter) (1945); *Domik na reke* (House on the River) (1947); *Ostrov Sukho* (Sukho Island) (1951); *V posledniye dni* (In the Last Days); *Poslednyaya komandirovka* (The Last Mission); *Dvoye* (Two Men) (1957), etc; his story *Morskoy okhotnik* (The Sea Hunter) was screened under the same title in 1954; also well known as translator of Robert Louis Stevenson, Mark Twain, etc; *Died*: 4 Nov 1965.

CHULPAN (real name: SULAYMANOV), Khamid (1896-1938) Uzbek poet, playwright and critic; *Born*: 1896; *Career*: 1914 began career as writer and critic; before 1917 Revol criticized feudalist aspects of life in Turkestan; 1921-32 lit dir, Uzbek Khamzy Drama Theater; his works have a marked nationalistic content; also wrote reviews of plays and articles on the theater; *Publ*: romantic drama *Yarkin-oy* (1920); plays about women's suffrage "The Slave-Girl's Revolt" (1925); coauthor, "The Advance" (1927); other plays "The Kulak", "Comrade Karshibayev", etc; translated a number of plays into Uzbek, including *Revizor* (The Government Inspector) (1925); *Ekho* (The Echo) (1925); Bill'-Belotserkovskiy's *Shtorm* (The Gale) (1927); *Bronepoyezd 14-69* (Armored Train 14-69) (1927); "Hamlet" (1935); *Died*: 1938.

CHUMANDRIN, Mikhail Fyodorovich (1905-1940) Writer; CP member from 1927; *Born*: 1905 in Tula, son of a worker; *Career*: worked at Tula railroad sheds; 1930-32 worked at *Krasnyy putilovets* Plant, Leningrad; 1931 made trip abroad; worked for several years as newspaper corresp; chm, Russian Assoc of Proletarian Writers; defended this org against Party criticism but subsequently acceded to Party line; 1925 first work published; *Publ*: short stories: *Skloka* (The Squabble) (1926); *Rodnya* (Kinsfolk) (1927); novels: *Fabrika Rable* (The Rabelais Factory) (1928); *Byvshiy geroy* (The Erstwhile Hero) (1929); *Moi putilovskiye dnevniki* (my Putilov Diaries) (1931); "Leningrad" (1931); short story *Belyy kamen'* (The White Stone) (1931); essays *Germaniya* (Germany) (1933); *God rozhdeniya 1905* (Year of Birth – 1905) (1938); plays *Bikin vpadaet v Ussuri* (The Bikin Flows Into the Ussuri) and *Stoybishche Mitakheza* (Mitakhez's Camp) (1939), etc; *Awards*: Order of Lenin; *Died*: 4 Feb 1940 on Finnish Front during Sov-Finnish War.

CHUMBURIDZE, Teymuraz Sergeyevich (1882-1937) Pedag and public figure; CP member from 1923; *Born*: 1882; *Educ*: grad History and Philology Fac, Khar'kov Univ; *Career*: taught at colleges in Khashur and Kutaisi; head, Kutaisi Uyezd Educ Dept; ran Kutaisi Branch, Geo Soc of Marxist Teachers; from 1925 worked for State Learned Council, Geo Pop Comrt of Educ; dean, Dept of History, Kutaisi Teachers' Training Inst; arrested by State Security organs; *Publ*: Geo-language "History of Primitive Culture" (1923); textbook for secondary general education schools and technicums *Obshchestvovedeniye* (Social Sciences) (1927); *Died*: in imprisonment 1937.

CHUPRYNKA, Grigoriy Avramovich (1879-1921) Ukr poet; rep of modernism in Ukr poetry; *Born*: 15 Sept 1879 in Gogolevo, now Poltava Oblast; *Educ*: studied in Kiev; *Career*: 1905 arrested and imprisoned for revol activities; 1907 first work published; contributed to journal *Ukrayins'ka khata* and other journals and newspapers; during WW 1 office worker with a forestry admin, Chernigov Province; 1917 founded *Prosvita* Ukr educ circles; 1918 Cossack, 1st Khmel'nitskiy Regt, Ukr Army; 1919 organized revolt against Bolsheviks in Chernigov Province; 1921 member, Centr Insurgent Comt which prepared anti-Bolshevik uprising in Right-Bank Ukr; *Publ*: works dealing with nat liberation included: "My Native Land," "The Poet," "To My Father," "At Night" and "Row, Lads!"; collected verse "The Fiery Flower"; "The Meteor" and "The Hurricane" (1910); "A Vanished Dream" and "The White Tempering" (1911); "Contrasts" (1912); "A Knight Is He"; collection "Works of G. Chuprynka" (1926, in Prague); "Selected Poetry" (1930); *Died*: executed by Bolsheviks on 28 Aug 1921 for his part in preparing an uprising in the Ukr.

CHURKIN, Nikolay Nikolayevich (1869-1964) Composer and folklorist; Pop Artiste of Bel SSR from 1949; *Born*: 21 May 1869 in vil Dzhelal-Ogly, now Tbilisi Oblast; *Educ*: 1892 grad M. Ippolitov-Ivanov's composition class, Tiflis College of Music; *Career*: 1892-1902 music teacher in Baku; 1903-35 taught singing and music theory at educ establishments in Kaunas, Vilnius, Mstislavl' and Mogilev; from 1935 lived in Minsk, where he collected some 3,000 Bel folksongs and dances; during WW 2 collected Tadzh songs and melodies; *Works*: operas "Liberated Labor" (1922) and "The Gauntlet" (1940); musical comedies "Berezina's Song" (1947) and *Koksagyz*; three short symphonies and an overture in memory of Yanka Kupala (1952); six quartets; opera "The Ravaged Nest" (1958), etc; *Publ*: anthology "Belorussian Folksongs and Dances" (1949); *Awards*: two Orders of the Red Banner of Labor (1939 and 1955); Badge of Hon (1940); *Died*: 27 Dec 1964 in Minsk.

CHUTSKAYEV, Sergey Yegorovich (1876-1946) Govt official; CP member from 1903; *Born*: 1876, son of a stationmaster; *Educ*: 1902-03 studied at Heidelberg Univ; *Career*: 1895 joined revol movement; 1896-97 worked for Petersburg League for the Struggle to Liberate the Working Class; revol propaganda among workers at the New Admiralty Plant; imprisoned in Kresty Jail for participation in student movement and demonstration at Kazan' Cathedral; May 1897 re-arrested and jailed for a year, then exiled for two years to his home in Perm Province; 1902 went to Germany and entered Heidelberg Univ, where he studied until 1904; on return from abroad worked for Party orgs of Yekaterinburg (now Sverdlovsk), Orenburg, Ufa and Chelyabinsk; 1905-07 attended Ural Oblast RSDRP Congresses; until 1918 wrote and disseminated Party propaganda, often elected to underground Party comts; member, Ural Oblast Party Comt; 1918-21 Collegium member, RSFSR Pop Comrt of Finance; then RSFSR Dep Pop Comr of Finance; 1921-22 dep chm, then chm, Siberian Revol Comt; 1922 again Collegium member, RSFSR Pop Comrt of Finance; 1923-27, USSR Dep Pop Comr of Workers and Peasants' Inspection; Presidium member, CPSU(B) Centr Control Commission; 1927-29 chm, Far Eastern Kray Exec Comt; member, Far Eastern Kray CPSU(B) Comt, Khabarovsk; 1929-33 chm, Budget Commission, USSR Centr Exec Comt; then worked for Comt for Land Settlement of Working Jews; from 1918 almost continuously member or cand member, All-Russian and USSR Centr Exec Comt; from 1927 cand member, CC, CPSU(B); 1938 expelled from CPSU for "errors" in work of Comt for Land Settlement of Working Jews; arrested by State Security organs; *Died*: 1946 in imprisonment.

CHUVASHEV, Il'ya Vasil'yevich (1893-1963) Teacher; specialist in history of educ; Dr of Pedag; prof; *Born*: 28 July 1893; *Educ*: 1912 grad Arkhangelsk Teachers' Seminary and Higher Pedag Courses at 2nd Moscow Univ; *Career*: from 1912 vil teacher; organizer and teacher, Yarensk (Arkhangel'sk Province) Teachers' Training College; from 1925 lectured at teachers' training college; from 1928 lectured at Moscow higher teachers' training establishments; from 1944 research work and directed training of postgrad students at Inst of Theory and History of Pedag, RSFSR Acad of Pedag Sci; worked on history of Russian and for educ, Sov school system, pre-school educ and family upbringing; in his latter years studied legacy of N. K. Krupskaya at RSFSR Acad of Pedag Sci pedag; *Publ: Ocherki po istorii doshkol'nogo vospitaniya v Rossii* (An Outline History of Pre-School Education in Russia) (1955); *N. K. Krupskaya – teoretik trudovogo i politekhnicheskogo obucheniya* (N. K. Krupskaya – Theoretician of Practical and Polytechnic Education) (1960); *Died*: 30 Mar 1963.

CHUVYRIN, Mikhail Yevdokimovich (1883-1947) Party and trade-union official; CP member from 1903; *Born*: 9 Sept 1883 in Nizhniy Novgorod Province, son of a peasant; *Career*: metalturner by trade; 1902 worked at Sormovo Plant where he was active in workers' Marxist circles; 1904 arrested and exiled to Ussuri Kray; 1909-17 Party work in Nizhniy Novgorod, Petrograd, Kiev, Pskov and other places; 1918-21 Party and mil work in Arzamas, Simbirsk and elsewhere; from 1922 in Ukraine; secr, Kobelyak and Krasnograd Okrug Party Comts; secr, Poltava Province Control Commission; from 1924 secr, Krivoy Rog Okrug Comt, CP(B) Ukr; from 1926 secr, Lugansk Okrug Comt, CP(B) Ukr; from 1929, chm, All-Ukr Trade-Union Council; 1932-36 secr, Donetsk Oblast Comt, CP(B) Ukr; deleg, 13th RCP(B) Congress and 14th-17th CPSU(B) Congresses; at 15th Congress elected cand member, CC, and at 16th and 17th Congresses member, CC, CPSU(B); deleg, 8th Conference and 9th-12th Congresses of CP(B) Ukr; at 9th-12th Congresses elected member, CC, CP(B) Ukr; 1929-37 Politburo member, CC, CP(B) Ukr; 1937 arrested by State Security organs; *Died*: 14 Sept 1947 in imprisonment.

CHYURLENENE-KIMANTAYTE, Sofiya (1886-1958) Lith writer; playwright; *Born*: 13 Mar 1886; *Educ*: studied philosophy at Cracow Univ; *Career*: 1905 began lit career; 1909 married artist and musician K. M. Chyurlyonis; 1935-38 taught Lith at Kaunas Univ; wrote satirical works ridiculing morals of bourgeoisie and lower middle classes; critical works and translations into Lith of classical drama (Moliere, etc); played important role in development of Lith theater; *Publ*: comedies: "Money" (1918) produced at Kaunas Theater in 1921; "Decoration of the Villa" (1932, Kaunas Theater); wrote from Lith folklore motifs fairytale play *Dvenadtsat' brat'yev-chyornykh voronov* (The Twelve Black Raven Brothers) (1931), produced 1934 at Kaunas Theater; "The Grand Fair" (1939), produced 1944 at Kaunas Theater; *Died*: 1 Dec 1958.

D

DADASHEV, Sadykh Alekper-ogly (1905-1946) Architect; prof; architectural historian; Hon Art Worker of Azer SSR; corresp member, USSR Acad of Architecture from 1941; member, Azer Acad of Sci from 1945; *Born*: 15 Apr 1905 in Baku, son of a merchant; *Educ*: 1929 grad Baku Polytech Inst; *Career*: architectural and historical research work in close assoc with architect M. A. Useynov; from 1940 instructor at Azer Ind Inst; *Works*: designed Nizami Museum (1930-40); Nizami Cinema (1934-39); Azer State Conservatory (1937-39); premises of CC, CP Azer (1937-40); pavillion of Azer SSR at All-Union Agric Exhibiton in Moscow (1939); memorials to poet Nizami in Baku and Kirovabad, etc; *Publ*: coauthor of research works: *Azerbaydzhani architectural Relics in Baku* (1938); "Architectural Monuments of Baku" (1946); "Azerbaydzhani Architecture" (1948); "The Architecture of Soviet Azerbaydzhan" (1950), etc; *Awards*: Stalin Prize (1941); Order of Lenin; Order of the Red Banner of Labor; medals; *Died*: 24 Dec 1946.

DADAU MAGOMETOV (pseudonym: Mikayel MIKAYELOV) (1863-1926) Kumyk folk poet; *Born*: 1863; *Career*: metal and wood craftsman; active in peasant movement just prior to 1905 Revol; 1917 elected first chm of a vil sov; during Civil War served in partisan detachment; from 1920, after establishment of Sov rule in Dag, rural corresp for a newspaper; for 20 years composed songs reflecting life of Dag highlanders; *Died*: 1926.

DADENKOV, Nikolay Fyodorovich (1885-1955) Pedag; *Born*: 15 Apr 1885 in Vyatka; *Educ*: grad Nezhin Inst of History and Philology; *Career*: 1910-19 high-school teacher; 1919-27 taught at Kiev Froebel Inst; 1927-41 prof, Dnepropetrovsk, Nezhin and Kiev Teachers' Training Institutes; 1941-44 taught at Kutaisi Teachers' Training Inst; from 1944 head, Dept of History of Pedag, Ukr Pedag Research Inst; also head, Chair of Pedag, Kiev Teachers' Training Inst; wrote several works on history of pedag and esthetic training; *Publ*: coauthor, *K.D. Ushinskiy* (1945); *Istoriya pedagogiki* (A History of Pedagogics) (1947); *Zhizn', deyatel'nost' i pedagogicheskiye idei A.S. Makarenko* (The Life, Career and Pedagogic Ideas of A.S. Makarenko) (1949); *Died*: 19 Jan 1955.

DADIANI, Shalva Nikolayevich (1874-1959) Geo writer, playwright and poet; Pop Artiste of Geo SSR from 1923; CP member from 1945; *Born*: 21 May 1874 in settlement Zestafoni, Geo, son of a writer; *Career*: 1892 first work published; from 1893 actor, Kutaisi Theater; from 1907 stage dir; 1912 founded, 1912-14 directed a touring company in Batumi; toured with this group in Tiflis, Kutaisi, Baku and Novorossiysk; 1921 helped found Geo Actors' Union and Geo Writers' Union; head, Theater Dept, Geo Pop Comrt of Educ; from 1950 chm, Geo Theater Soc; dep, USSR Supr Sov of 1937 and 1946 convocations; exponent of critical realism; *Publ*: collected poetry "Spark" (1892); story "Sincere Tears" (1896); plays: "In the Cave" (1905); "At the Time of the Feast" (1907); *Gegechkori* (1915); "Calamity" (1916); "People of Yesterday" (1917); historical novel *Yuriy Bogolyubskiy* (1926); comedy "Right Through the Heart" (1928); tragedy *Tetnul'd* (1931); plays: "From the Spark" (1937); *Rustaveli* (1938); "Pushkin in Georgia" (1939); "News From the Front" (1943); historical novel "The Gvirgviliani Family" (1956), etc; author of about 100 stories, novelettes, articles on lit and theater; most of his 50 plays were written under the Sov regime; dramatized for the stage: Ninoshvili's *Guriya Ninoshvili* (1934); Chavchavadze's "Broken Bridge" (1935); *Awards*: Order of Lenin; *Died*: 15 Mar 1959 in Tbilisi.

DAKHADAYEV, Magomed-Ali (Makhach) (1882-1918) Dag revolutionary; *Born*: 1882 in vil Untsukul', Dag; son of a blacksmith; *Educ*: 1910 grad Petersburg Inst of Communications Eng; *Career*: 1901-02 took part in student strikes; 1905 returned to Dag; Nov 1906 exiled from Dag and resumed studies in Petersburg; until 1916 eng, Maykop Railroad; after 1917 Feb Revol joined Dag socialist movement as leader of the left wing; member, Dag Oblast Sov, Temir-Khan-Shura; organized vil sovs in Dzhengutay, etc; early 1918 commissioned by Temir-Khan-Shura Mil-Revol Comt and Bolshevik Bureau to organize Red Guard detachments; from May 1918, after capture of Temir-Khan-Shura, member, Oblast Mil-Revol Comt and Mil Comr of Dag; together with U.Buynakskiy formed Dag Volunteer Red Army; from Aug 1918 member, 1st Sov Oblast Exec Comt; member, Dag Extraordinary Mil Council; *Died*: 22 Sept 1918 executed by White Army after Sov defeat in Dag; Port Petrovsk was renamed Makhachkala in his memory.

DALETSKIY, Pavel Leonidovich (1903-1963) Russian writer; CP member from 1955; *Born*: 3 Feb 1903 in Novogeorgiyevsk Fortress; *Educ*: 1924 grad Philology Fac, Far Eastern Univ; *Publ*: 1924 first work published; novels *Nergul'* (1931); *Kontsessiya* (The Concession) (1932); *Torfmeyster* (The Peat Master) (1933); essay *Tikhookeanskiy forpost* (Pacific Outpost) (1931); novels *Takhoma* (1939) (1955 published under title "Takhama"); best-known novel dealt with Russo-Japanese War and first Russian revol - *Na sopkakh Man'chzhurii* (On the Hills of Manchuria) (1951); novel *Na krayu nochi* (On the Edge of Night) (1959); *Rasskazy o starshem lesnichem* (Stories of the Old Forester) (1961); *Iyenes* (1962), etc; *Died*: 8 July 1963 in Leningrad.

DALIN (real name: LEVIN), David Yul'yevich (1889-1962) Econ; member, RSDRP (Mensheviks; *Born*: 1889; *Educ*: studied at Heidelberg Univ in Germany; *Career*: from Aug 1917 member, CC, RSDRP (Menshikovs); edited Printers' Union newspaper *Utro Moskvy* and *Vecher Moskvy*; 1922 deported abroad by decision of Politburo, CC, RCP(B); joined ed staff, centr organ of For Deleg, RSDRP (Menshikovs) *Sotsialisticheskiy vestnik* published in Berlin; 1934-39 in Poland; 1939 moved to Paris; 1940 went to USA, where he continued contributing to journal *Sotsialisticheskiy vestnik* and wrote for American "New Leader"; *Publ: Posle voyn i revolyutsiy* (After Wars and Revolutions) (1922); coauthor, "Forced Labor in Soviet Russia" (1948); "The New Soviet Empire" (1951); "Die Sowjetspionage. Prinzipien und Praktiken" (1956); "From Purge to Coexistence. Essays on Stalin's and Khrushchev's Russia" (1964); *Rossiya i emigratsiya* (Russia and the Emigration); *Died*: 22 Feb 1962.

DAL'NYA, Sofiya (real name: DERMAN, Sof'ya Yakovlevna) (1886-1960) Russian writer; CP member from 1903; *Born*: 14 Sept 1886 in Lugansk, daughter of a worker; *Career*: active in revol movement in Donbass; contributed to journal *Rabotnitsa; Publ:* verse: *Nash prazdnik* (Our Festival); *Privet* (Greetings); poem *Bogatyr'* (The Warrior Hero) (1919); non-fiction work *Pervyye shagi* (The First Steps) (1926); *Died*: 31 Oct 1960.

DAL'SKAYA (AMMAN-DAL'SKAYA), Yelizaveta Konstantinovna (1899-1962) Actress; Pop Artiste of RSFSR from 1956; *Born*: 3 Oct 1899; *Career*: 1919 stage debut at Pop House Theater, Kazan'; from 1922 toured Volga area, Kama area and Urals, first with a Russian Assoc of Proletarian Musicians ensemble, then with groups of the Ural Theater Assoc; from 1934 at Sverdlovsk Drama Theater; *Roles*: Larisa in *Bespridannitsa* (Girl Without a Dowry); Anna Karenina; Lida in Korneychuk's *Platon Krechet*; Liza Murav'yova in Chirskov's *Pobediteli* (The Victors); Varvara in Pavlenko and Radzinskiy's *Schast'ye* (Happiness); Nadezhda in Gorky's *Varvary* (The Barbarians); Lyubov' in Trenev's *Lyubov' Yarovaya*; Philomena in de Filippo's *Philomena Marturano*; Berezhkova in Ugryumov's *Kreslo No. 16* (Seat No. 16), etc; *Died*: 25 Aug 1962.

DAMSKIY, Al'bert Yakovlevich (1868-1949) Urologist; *Born*: 1868; *Career*: worked in field of urology for over 50 years; pioneer of Sov urology; 1921-49 head, Chair of Urology, Med Fac, Smolensk Univ (from 1930 Smolensk Med Inst); advocated urology as compulsory subject at all med colleges and proposed the establishment of independent chairs of urology; performed first endovesicular prostatectomy in Russia; designed a cystoscope for use in operations; wrote over 50 works and a textbook on urology; *Publ*: articles "A New Operative Cystoscope" (1913); "Transvesicular Prostatectomy on the Basis of 60 Cases Observed by the Author" (1926); *Urologiya* (Urology) (1936); *Died*: 1949.

DAN, F. I. (real name: GURVICH, Fyodor Il'ich) (1871-1947) Mensheviks leader; *Born*: 1871; *Career*: physician; 1894 joined Soc-Democratic movement; 1896 worked for executive of Petersburg "League for the Liberation of the Working Class"; 1898 exiled for three years to Vyatka Province; 1902 *Iskra* deleg at Belostok Conference; late 1903, after arrest and exile to Yenisey Province, escaped abroad and joined Mensheviks; 1905 returned to Russia; worked for ed staff, *Nachalo*; took a leading part in RSDRP (Mensheviks) activities; early 1906 with ed staff, amalgamated centr organ *Patiynyye izvestiya* Presidium member, 4th Amalgamative RSDRP Congress in Stockholm; at this Congress elected member, ed staff, Party centr organ; headed so-called *Vocalists* foreign liquidationist group; co-ed and ideological leader of their organ *Golos sotsial-demokrata;* contributed to legal liquidationist periodicals *Delo zhizni, Nasha zarya;* ed, periodicals Luch, Novaya rabochaya gazeta, etc; before WW 1 exiled to Siberia; during WW 1 officially centrist, but actually sympathized with defensism, demanding assoc with mil-ind comts; after 1917 Feb Revol head, RSDRP (Mensheviks); 1917 Presidium member, Petrograd Sov; member, ed staff, *Izvestiya SR i SD;* at 1st All-Russian Socialist-Revol Party and Soc-Democratic Party Congress delivered a report on the war; elected Presidium member, All-Russian Democratic Conference, where he defended the further coalition with Constitutional Democrats; Presidium member, All-Russian Centr Exec Comt; on its behalf opened 2nd All-Russian Congress of Soviets; after 1917 Oct Revol did not formally side with those who advocated armed struggle against Sov regime; 1919–20 worked as physician for RSFSR Pop Comrt of Health; 1920 dep; Moscow Sov; RSDRP Menshevik faction deleg to 7th and 8th Congresses of Soviets; early 1922 exiled from RSFSR as irreconcilable enemy of Sov regime; 1923 helped organize United 2nd Socialist Workers' International; one of RSDRP (Mensheviks) leaders abroad and ed of their centr organ *Sotsialisticheskiy vestnik; Publ: Dva goda skitaniy* (Two Years of Wanderings); *Died:* 1947.

DAN, Lidiya Osipovna (1878-1963) Revolutionary; Menshevik; *Born*: 21 May 1878; *Career*: 1899 arrested for revol activities; 1901 emigrated to Munich and joined her brother Yu. O. Martov (Tsederbaum); shortly afterwards sent to Moscow by ed bd of newspaper *Iskra*; early 1902 arrested and exiled to Eastern Siberia; winter of 1904-05 escaped abroad; from summer of 1905 worked for secretariat of *Iskra*; late 1905 returned to Russia; late 1907-late 1911 with her husband in Paris, then returned to Petersburg; 1914 followed husband into exile in Minusinsk and Irkutsk (Siberia); after 1917 Feb Revol lived in Petersburg, then in Moscow; 1922 together with several leaders of RSDRP (Mensheviks) banished from Russia by CC, RCP(B); 1922-33 in Berlin; 1933-40 in Paris; from 1940 in New York; for a while represented RSDRP foreign deleg at Socialist Women's International; *Died*: 28 Mar 1963 in New York.

DANELIA, Sergey Iosifovich (1888-1963) Geo lit historian; prof, Tbilisi Univ; *Born*: 15 Oct 1888 in vil Nadzhikhao, now Geo SSR; *Educ*: 1911 grad History and Philology Fac, Moscow Univ; *Publ*:

"An Outline History of 19th-Century Russian Literature" (4th ed, 1959); "The Philosophy of Griboyedov" (1940); "The World Outlook of the Author of the Poem 'The Lay of the Host of Igor'" (1938); *Died*: 21 Mar 1963 in Tbilisi.

DANIEL' (real name: MEYEROVICH, Daniil), Mark Naumovich (1900-1940) Jewish writer and playwright; *Born*: 1900 in Dvinsk; *Career*: while a young man worked in tailor's shop; joined workers' movement; *Publ*: noveletee "At Such a Time" (1924); stories and novelettes: "Towards Lenin" (1924); "The Night Watchman Rakhmiel" (1925); "On the Seventh Line" (1928); "On the Threshhold" (1928); "Julius" (1930); plays: *Zyamka Kopach* (1936); "The Inventor and the Comedian" (1937); *Pyotr Lukomskiy* (1938); "Johann Gutenberg" (1938); *Solomon Maymon* (1940), etc; his plays were staged at Jewish theaters in Moscow, Khar'kov, Belostok and at the Khar'kov Children's Theater; *Died*: Dec 1940.

DANIEL'SON (pseudonym: NIKOLAY-ON), Nikolay Frantsevich (1844-1918) Writer and translator; populist ideologist; *Born*: 1844; *Educ*: grad Petersburg Business College; *Career*: after graduation worked for Petersburg Mutual Credit Soc; 1860's-70's involved in revol youth groups; early 1870 arrested; after arrest of G.A. Lopatin, the first Russian translator of Marx's "Kapital," completed translation of Vol 1, which was published in 1872; after Lopatin was re-arrested translated Vol 2 (published in 1885) and Vol 3 (published in 1896); during this work corresponded with Marx and Engels, discussing, inter alia, the econ development of Russia; *Publ: Ocherki nashego poreformennogo obshchestvennogo khozyaystva* (Outline of Our Reformed Public Economy) (1880), etc; *Died*: 1918.

DANIELYAN, Aykanush Bagdasarovna (1893-1958) Opera singer (lyric coloratura soprano); Pop Artiste of USSR from 1939; CP member from 1941; *Born*: 15 Dec 1893 in Tiflis; *Educ*: 1920 grad class of N. A. Iretskaya, Petrograd Conservatory; *Career*: 1920-22 performed in Petrograd; 1922-32 at Tbilisi Paliashvili Opera and Ballet Theater; 1932-48 soloist, Spendiarov Opera and Ballet Theater; 1943-51 prof, Yerevan Conservatory; possessed a remarkably beautiful voice and great stage presence; dep, USSR Supr Sov of 1946 convocation; dep, Arm Supr Sov of 1938 and 1951 convocations; *Roles*: Anush in Tigranyan's *Anush*; Olimpiya in Chukhadzhyan's *Arshak II*; Antonida in Glinka's *Ivan Susanin*; Margarete Valois in Meyerbeer's "Hugenotten," etc; *Awards*: Stalin Prize (1946); *Died*: 19 Apr 1958 in Yerevan.

DANILEVSKAYA, Rozaliya Grigor'yevna (1888-1953) Russian actress; Hon Artiste of RSFSR from 1935; *Born*: 16 Sept 1888; *Career*: 1908 began acting career in Krasnoyarsk Theater; worked at theaters in Stavropol', Tula, Astrakhan', Moscow, Kiev and Kursk; 1929-41 and from 1943 at Voronezh Theater; *Roles*: Lyubov' Yarovaya in Trenev's play of the same name; Klara in *Strakh* (Fear); Glafira in Glebov's *Inga*; Safonova in *Russkiye lyudi* (Russian People); Kharitonova in Lavrenyov's *Za tekh, kto v more!* (For Those at Sea), etc; also acted in Gorky's plays - Vasilisa in *Na dne* (The Lower Depths); Melan'ya in *Deti solntsa* (Children of the Sun); Sof'ya in *Posledniye* (The Last Ones); acted also in Ostrovsky and Chekhov's plays; often acted gratis for soldiers of Red Army; *Died*: 9 May 1953.

DANILEVSKIY, Aleksandr Yakovlevich (1839-1923) Biochemist; Dr of Med from 1863; corresp member, USSR Acad of Sci; brother of V.Ya.Danilevskiy; *Born*: 10 Dec 1839 in Khar'kov; *Educ*: 1860 grad Med Fac, Khar'kov Univ; *Career*: 1863-71 prof of med chemistry, Kazan' Univ; 1871 resigned with other professors in protest against dismissal of Prof P.F.Lesgaft; 1871-85 worked mostly abroad, inter alia with R.Wirchow and E. Du Bois Reymond; 1886-92 prof of physiological chemistry, Khar'kov Univ; 1892-1906 prof, 1906-10 dir, Petersburg Mil Med Acad; founded first Russian school of biochemistry; established chairs of physiological chemistry at Kazan' and Khar'kov univ and Petersburg Mil Med Acad; did research on the chemistry of digestion, protein chemistry and the physiology of the nervous system; while still a student did research on "Natural and Artificial Pancreatic Juices with Specific Functions," a subject on which he subsequently wrote his doctor's thesis; discovered the formation of plasteins from the reaction of abomasal ferment with the products of the peptic digestion of proteins; also studied gastric autodigestion, the content of antiferments in the intestinal wall, the nature of muscle protein and the chemical composition of the haptogenous membrane of milk globules; was first to obtain amilase and trypsin from the pancreas by selective absorption with colloidal particles; proved colloidal nature of ferments; proved experimentally that the reaction of pancreatic juice with proteins is a hydrolytic reaction as a result of which the proteins are converted into peptones; 1886 demonstrated reversibility of this process by synthesizing protein from peptones by fermentation; developed method of obtaining the basic muscle protein myosin; did research on liver, kidney and brain protein; proposed globulinstromin-nuclein classification for protein components; devised first sci classification of brain proteins; 1888 devised original theory on structure of protein molecules; also studied relation of various protein components among themselves and to other substances in the cytoplasm of the living cell; 1901 detected presence of antipepsin and antitrypsin in the gastric and intestinal tissue which prevent autodigestion; 1888-1891, together with his brother, published first Russian physiology journal *Fiziologicheskiy sbornik*; chm, Russian Army Food Review Commission; *Publ*: doctor's thesis *O spetsificheski deystvuyushchikh telakh natural'nogo i iskusstvennogo sokov podzheludochnoy zhelezy* (Elements of Natural and Articifial Pancreatic Juices with Specific Functions) (1863); *Ocherk organoplasticheskikh sil organizmov* (A Study of the Organoplastic Powers of Organisms) (1886); *Osnovnoye vechestvo protoplazmy i yego vidoizmeneniya zhizn'yu* (The Basic Substance of Protoplasm and Its Modification by the Vital Process) (1894), etc; *Died*: 8 June 1923.

DANILEVSKIY, Vasiliy Yakovlevich (1852-1939) Physiologist; member, Ukr Acad of Sci from 1926; Prof Emeritus of Ukr SSR from 1926; Hon Sci Worker of Ukr SSR; *Born*: 13 Jan 1852 in Khar'kov, son of a craftsman; *Educ*: 1874 grad Med Fac, Khar'kov Univ; *Career*: while still a student worked at Chair of Physiology, doing research on the biochemistry of tetanus, etc; 1874 presented famous paper on "The Influence of the Cerebrum on Respiration and Circulation"; 1876 expanded this paper into doctor's thesis, proving that moderate or weak electr stimulation of the cerebral cortex creates impulses not in the subcortical centers but in the cells of the cortex itself, which exerts a regulatory influence on respiration and circulation; worked in the laboratories of K. Ludwig and J. d'Arsonval, where he did research on the effect of anoxemia and asphyxia on the nervous system; 1904-05 demonstrated possibility of restoring the vagal stimulus by perfusion of the coronary vessels of the heart 24 hours or more after clinical death; 1876 performed first Russian experiments on recording electr phenomena in the cerebrum of a dog; 1891 published full results of these experiments, in which he demonstrated that perception of sensation during stimulation of the receptor is objectively recorded in the form of a negative fluctuation of current in cortex of cerebral hemispheres; 1879 by adjusting the strength and frequency of excitation of peripheral ending of a dog's vagus nerve, he demonstrated cumulative effect of inhibition of cardiac activity; was a pioneer of physiological research on hypnosis in animals and humans; 1881 interpreted hypnotism as the inhibition of the "voluntary" reflexes supported by the active state of the forebrain; explained the mechanism of "nervous asthma" and dyspnea in a series of experiments with frogs; founder, Ukr Inst of Labor; helped to set up ind production of endocrine drugs; from 1927 founder and life-dir, All-Ukr Inst of Endocrinology and Organotherapy; 1880-1906 prof of Physiology, Khar'kov Veterinary Inst; 1883-1909 and 1917-26 prof, Khar'kov Univ; 1917-26 prof, Khar'kov Med Inst; 1885-1896 wrote 25 papers on hemosporidia; wrote numerous works on blood parasites in birds, notably plasmodia, which he was the first to decribe; 1888 published large monograph on comparative blood parasitology; was first to demonstrate that hemosporidia living on erythrocytes are widespread among host vertebrates; this provided proof of A. Laveran's hypothesis that parasites in human erythrocytes are the real agents of malaria; his research on blood parasites on birds yielded a model on the basis of which R. Ross proved that mosquitoes are the carriers of malaria; birds infected with plasmodia proved suitable for research on malaria and its chemotherapy; 1910, despite the opposition of the Min of Health, founded the Khar'kov Women's Med Inst, of which he was dir and also head, Chair of Physiology; wrote 217 works, including a three-vol physiology textbook; *Publ*: article "The Influence of the Cerebrum on Respiration and Circulation" (1875); doctor's thesis *Issledovaniya po fiziologii golovnogo mozga* (Research on the Physiology of the Cerebrum) (1876); *O proiskhozhdenii muskul'noy sily* (The Origin of Muscular Strength) (1876); *O summirovanii elektricheskikh razdrazheniy myshts i dvigatel'nykh nervov* (The Cumulation of Electrical

Stimuli of the Muscles and Motor Nerves) (1879); *Elektricheskiye yavleniya v golovnom mozgu* (Electrical Phenomena in the Cerebrum) (1891); *Issledovaniya nad fiziologicheskim deystviyem elektrichestva na rasstoyanii* (Research on the Physiological Effect of Electricity at a Distance) (Vol 1-2, 1900-01); *Fiziologiya cheloveka* (Human Physiology) (3 vol, 1913-15); *Ocherki po fiziologii sotsial'nykh nedugov* (Studies on the Physiology of Social Ailments) (1914); *Vrach, yego prizvaniye i obrazovaniye* (The Physician, His Vocation and Training) (1921); *Zhizn' i solntse. Fiziologicheskiye ocherki* (Life and the Sun. Physiological Studies) (1923); *Gipnotizm* (Hypnotism) (1924); *Fiziologiya truda* (The Physiology of Labor) (1927); *Uchebnik fiziologii cheloveka* (A Textbook of Human Physiology) (1929); *Died*: 25 Feb 1939.

DANILEVSKIY, Viktor Vasil'yevich (1898-1960) Sci historian; member, Ukr Acad of Sci from 1948; prof, Leningrad Polytech Inst; CP member from 1944; *Born*: 4 Sept 1898; *Career*: from 1929 organized expeditions to study ancient mines, dams and fortifications; wrote numerous works on the history of eng; *Publ: I.I.Polzunov. Trudy i zhizn' pervogo russkogo teplotekhnika* (I.I.Polzunov. The Life and Works of the First Russian Thermal Engineer) (1940); *Istoriya gidrosilovykh ustanovok Rossii do XIX veka* (The History of Water-Powered Machines in Russia Prior to the 19th Century) (1940); *Russkaya tekhnika* (Russian Engineering) (1949); *Lomonosov na Ukraine* (Lomonosov in the Ukraine) (1954); *Awards*: two Stalin Prizes (1942, 1948); *Died*: 9 Aug 1960.

DANILIN, Nikolay Mikhaylovich (1878-1945) Choirmaster; prof, Moscow Conservatory from 1923; *Born*: 3 Dec 1878 in Moscow; *Educ*: 1897 grad Moscow Synodal School for Choral Conductors; 1907 grad piano class, Moscow School of Drama and Music, Moscow Philharmonic Soc; *Career*: from 1907 asst conductor, from 1910 conductor, Synodal Choir; 1911 with Synodal Choir on successful foreign tours; from 1918 instructor at Choral Acad (former Synodal School); 1919-23 choral dir, Moscow Bolshoy Theater; 1936-37 dir, Leningrad Choir; 1937-39 dir, USSR State Choir; *Died*: 6 Feb 1945 in Moscow.

DANILOV, Sergey Sergeyevich (1901-1959) Lit and theater historian; Dr of Arts from 1947; prof from 1947; *Born*: 5 June 1901 in Petersburg; *Educ*: 1925 grad Higher Arts Courses, Inst of Art History, Leningrad; *Career*: 1925-58 (with interruptions) assoc, Theater, Music and Cinematography Research Inst; from 1945 head, Chair of Theory and History of Russian Pre-Revol and Sov Art, Ostrovskiy Stagecraft Inst, Leningrad; *Publ*: works on history of theater in Russia; *'Revizor' na stsene* ("The Government-Inspector" on the Stage) (1933); *Gogol' i teatr* (Gogol and the Theater) (1936), *Russkiy teatr v khudozhestvennoy literature* (The Russian Theater in Fiction) (1939), *Ocherki po istorii russkogo dramaticheskogo teatra* (Outline History of Russian Drama) (1948); *Russkiy dramaticheskiy teatr 19 v.* (Russian Drama in the 19th Century) (1957); *Gor'kiy na stsene* (Gorky on the Stage) (1958); essays on dramatic works of Sukhovo-Kobylin and Gorky, and on Russian actors, etc; *Died*: 31 Dec 1959 in Leningrad.

DANILOV, S. S. (1877-1939) Politician; CP member from 1904; *Born*: 1877; *Career*: 1911-17 journalist; after 1917 Oct Revol in Red Army: staff comr; from July 1921 member, Revol Mil Council, Red Army; 1929-30 at Marx-Engels Inst; expelled from Party for Trotskyist activities; arrested by State Security organs; *Died*: 1939 in imprisonment.

DANILOV, Vitaliy Ivanovich (1902-1954) Physicist; member, Ukr Acad of Sci from 1951; *Born*: 28 Mar 1902 in vil Zhyoltoye, now Lugansk Oblast, son of a teacher; *Educ*: 1926 grad Dnepropetrovsk Inst of Educ; *Career*: from 1931 head, Crystallization Laboratory, Dnepropetrovsk Physical Eng Inst; 1934-41 simultaneously prof, Dnepropetrovsk Univ; from 1946 dept head, and from 1951 dir, Laboratory of Metal Physics, Ukr Acad of Sci; the first sci in USSR to apply radiographic methods to study the structure of rare metals, alloys and electrolytes; solved a number of problems on the physics of phase transformations; wrote over 70 sci works; *Publ*: monograph *Rasseyaniye rentgenovskikh luchey v zhidkostyakh* (Dispersion of X-Rays in Liquids); *Stroyeniye i kristallizatsiya zhidkostey* (Structure and Crystallization of Liquids) (1956); *Awards*: Stalin Prize (1950); Order of the Red Banner of Labor; Order of the Red Star; *Died*: 19 Mar 1954.

DANILOV-CHALDUN, Maksim Nikolayevich (1893-1944) Chuvash writer; CP member from 1920; *Born*: 21 Dec 1893 in vil Usli, now Bashkir ASSR, son of a peasant; *Career*: miner; WW 1, Civil War and WW 2 veteran; 1922 published stories and novelettes about partisan struggle in Siberia in which he had taken part; *Publ: Na shakhte* (In the Mine); *Mogila Levendeya* (Levendey's Grave) (1922); *Dve sily* (Two Powers) (1922); *Bezvremennaya smert'* (Untimely Death) (1924); *Za lisoy* (After the Fox) (1929); *Iz kol'tsa* (Out of the Ring) (1930); *Kolkhoznyye rasskazy* (Kolkhoz Stories) (1936); *Pered 34 atakoy* (Before the 34th Attack) (1943); *Krasnoarmeyets Samsonov* (Red Army Soldier Samsonov) (1943); *Lizaveta Yegorovna* (1944), etc; *Died*: 2 Mar 1944.

DANILOVA-DOBRYAKOVA, Appollinariya Prilidianovna (1894-1967) Party official; CP member from 1916; *Born*: 12 Jan 1894; *Career*: took part in 1917 Oct Revol in Petrograd; 1917-18 instructor, Petrograd Province Zemstvo; member, Vologda Province Party Comt; 1920-22 worked for Pop Comrt of Educ and Main Polit Educ Bd; 1922-24 ed, newspaper *Rabochaya Moskva*; from 1924 teaching work; from 1955 pensioner; *Died*: 6 Nov 1967.

DANISHEVSKIY (Party pseudonym: GERMAN), Karl Yuliy Khristianovich (1884-1941) Govt and Party official; CP member from 1900; *Born*: 1884, son of Lat nobiliary family; *Career*: from 1900 active in revol movement; late 1906 represented Lat Soc-Democratic Party in CC, RSDRP; 1907 elected to CC, RSDRP at 5th RSDRP Congress; 1907-14 Party work in Petersburg, Baku, Tiflis, Warsaw, Riga and Moscow; arrested many times; Jan 1917 fled from exile and went to Moscow illegally; after 1917 Feb Revol member, Moscow RSDRP Comt and Moscow Sov; from May 1917 co-ed, Soc-Democratic newspaper *Zihna* and the Bolshevik newspaper *Okopnaya pravda*; July 1917 at 5th Congress of the Lat Soc-Democratic Party re-elected to CC; until June 1918 illegal work in Riga; Jan-May 1919 dep chm, Sov Lat Govt; during Civil War member, Revol-Mil Council of Lat Republic and Eastern Front; chm, RSFSR Revol Tribunal; at 8th RCP(B) Congress elected cand member, CC, RCP(B); from 1921 secr, Siberian Bureau, CC, RCP(B); chm, Bd, Northern Timber Trust, For Trade Bank and Timber Export Trust; 1932-37 USSR Dep Pop Comr of the Timber Ind; deleg, 5th, 8th and 10th Party Congresses; from 1919 repeatedly elected member or cand member, All-Russian and All-Union Exec Comt; arrested by State Security organs; *Publ: Nakanune sotsial'noy revolyutsii* (On the Eve of the Socialist Revolution) in 3 vol; *Professional'nyye soyuzy* (The Trade Unions); *Bor'ba za Sovetskuyu Latviyu* (The Struggle for Soviet Latvia), etc; *Died*: 1941 in imprisonment; posthumously rehabilitated.

DAN'KO (real name: DAN'KO-ALEKSEYENKO), Nataliya Yakovlevna (1891-1942) Sculptor; *Born*: 1891; *Educ*: studied at Moscow Stroganov College and Vilnius Art School; *Career*: 1909-14 specialized in decorative and monumental sculpture, and in ornamenting buildings; 1911 sculptural work at the Rome and Turin exhibitions; 1914-42 worked for the Petersburg Imperial Porcelain Factory (later the Leningrad Lomonosov Factory); from 1919 head, sculpture dept of this factory; *Works*: "Partisan on the March" (1919); "Female Worker Embroidering a Banner" (1921); "Chess" (1922); porcelain desk set picturing "Discussion of Stalin's Constitution at an Uzbek Kolkhoz" (1937); sculptural portraits of Lenin, Stalin, Gorky, Pushkin, the ballerina Pavlova, Anna Akhmatova, etc; 14 porcelain bas-reliefs on the theme "Dances and Games of the Peoples of USSR"; decorated Sverdlov Square, Moscow Metro station (1937-38); over 300 porcelain sculptures, noted for their vitality, brilliant composition and skillful utilization of the artistic possibilities of porcelain; many of her works are displayed in the Leningrad Porcelain Museum and Moscow Ceramics Museum; *Died*: 18 Mar 1942.

DAN'KO, Yelena Yakovlevna (1898-1942) Russian writer; *Born*: 1898 in Moscow; *Career*: worked at puppet theater; painter at a china factory; shortly after 1917 Oct Revol began to write plays for puppet shows; *Publ: Krasnaya shapochka* (Little Red Riding Hood) (1919); books for children, verse and novelettes: *Vaza bogdykhana* (The Chinese Emperor's Vase), *Farforovaya chashechka* (The Porcelain Cup) and "Johann Gutenberg" (1925); *Shakhmaty* (Chess) (1929); one of first sci fiction works for children *Kitayskiy sekret* (The Chinese Secret) (1929); historical novelette *Derevyannyye aktyory* (The Wooden Actors) (1931); *Avtobiografiya* (Autobiography) (1937); fairy tale *Pobezhdyonnyy Karabas* (Defeated Karabas) (1941); wrote works on decorative chinaware and on Russian lit of 18th century; *Died*: 1942 killed in Leningrad blockade.

DANOVSKAYA, Zorya Nikolayevna (1930-1957) Russian writer; *Born*: 19 Sept 1930 in Odessa; *Educ*: 1954 grad Iranian Dept,

Philological Fac, Moscow Univ; *Career*: 1957 ran club in vil Dmitriyevskoye, Moscow Oblast; *Publ*: verse: *Partbilet* (The Party Card); *Reportazh mira* (World Report); plays: *Lyubka-Lyubov'* (1956); *Vol'nyye mastera* (Free Masters) (1957); *Died*: 2 Oct 1957 killed in traffic accident near Moscow.

DANYUSHEVSKIY, Izrail' Isaakovich (1890-1950) Defectologist; specialist in socio-legal protection of children; *Born*: 29 Dec 1890; *Career*: 1923-30 methods specialist and dep head, Dept for Socio-Legal Protection of Adolescents, Pop Comrt of Educ; 1923-26 also dep head, Socio-Legal Protection Experimental Station and dep chm, RSFSR Children's Extraordinary Commission; 1930-1943 dir, Experimental Defectological Inst (1936 reorganized into Sci Practical Inst of Special Schools and Children's Homes); from 1943 dir, Centr Sci Methods Center of Children's Homes, RSFSR Min of Educ; from 1938 for many years ed, periodical *Byulleten'* of Sci Practical Inst (renamed *Uchebno' vospitatel'naya rabota v spetsial'nykh shkolakh); Died*: 19 July 1950.

DARASELI, Vanion Alekseyevich (1909-1954) Geo writer and playwright; CP member from 1940; *Born*: 25 May 1909; *Career*: 1928 began lit work; *Publ*: plays: *Kikvidze* (1941); *Gamakhare* (1948); "The Elder Brother"; "Moscow - Tbilisi," etc; *Died*: 14 Apr 1954.

DARKSHEVICH, Liveriy Osipovich (1858-1925) Neuropathologist and neurohistologist; Hon Prof from 1913; *Born*: 29 June 1858; *Educ*: 1882 grad Med Fac, Moscow Univ; *Career*: after grad worked for a number of years in France and Germany under Charcot, Vulpian, Flechsig, Meynert, Goltz, Munk, etc; 1887 defended doctor's thesis; from 1887 assoc prof of neuropathology, Moscow Univ; from 1892 extraordinary prof, Chair of Nervous Diseases, Kazan' Univ, where he established a clinic for nervous diseases and the first Russian center for treating alcoholics; together with V.M. Bekhterev founded Kazan' Soc of Neuropathologists and Psychiatrists; from 1917 until death prof of neuropathology, 1st Moscow Univ and dir, Moscow Women's Med Inst; 1917-23 co-founder and rector, Moscow Higher Med School, where he established a chair of psychology, a propaedeutic clinic and a hospital clinic for nervous diseases; co-founder, Sci Soc of Neuropathologists, 1st Moscow State Univ; did original research on anatomy and histology of centr nervous system; was first to describe the nucleus of the posterior cerebral commissure below the anterior corpora quadrigemina (Darkshevich's nucleus); while studying retrograde lesions of the peripheral nerves discovered special structures in their centr segments (Darkshevich's bodies); analysed structure of the pupillary fibers of the optic nerve; established that tabes dorsalis is a syphilitic disease of the nervous system; did research on muscular atrophy in joint diseases; was one of first sci to study epidemic encephalitis in Russia; wrote over 70 works, including first Russian manual on nervous diseases; *Publ*: doctor's thesis *O provodnike svetovogo razdrazheniya s setchatoy obolochki glaza na glazodvigatel'nyy nerv. Anatomo-fiziologicheskoye issledovaniye* (The Conductor of Photic Stimulation from the Retina to the Oculomotor Nerve. An Anatomical and Physiological Study) (1887); *Vozvrashchayushchiysya paralich glazodvigatel'nogo nerva* (Recurrent Paralysis of the Oculomotor Nerve) (1890); *Stradaniya sustavov i myshts pri cherepnomozgovykh gemiplegiyakh* (Joint and Muscle Disorders in Craniocerebral Hemiplegia) (1891); *Spinnaya sukhotka kak sifiliticheskoye stradaniye nervnoy sistemy* (Tabes Dorsalis as a Syphilitic Disease of the Nervous System) (1895); *O tak nazyvayemom retrogradnom pererozhdenii perifericheskikh nervnykh volokon* ("Retrograde Regeneration" of Peripheral Nerve Fibers) (1897); *Sluchay polinevrita cherepnykh nervov na pochve razlitogo sarkomatoza* (A Case of Polyneuritis of the Cranial Nerves During Diffused Sarcomatosis) (1899); *Kurs nervykh bolezney* (A Course in Nervous Diseases) (3 vol, 1904-17); *Travmaticheskiy nevroz* (Traumatic Neurosis) (1916); *Died*: 28 Mar 1925.

DARSKIY (real name: SHAVROV), Mikhail Yegorovich (1865-1930) Actor and stage dir; *Born*: 1865; *Educ*: studied at Petersburg Univ; *Career*: from 1882 appeared in amateur productions; 1884-85 acted for Petersburg clubs and summer theaters (Pavlovsk, Oranienbaum, etc); then acted in Vitebsk, Minsk, Zhitomir, Vilnius, etc; 1892-94 impressario in Petersburg; 1894-98 toured provinces; 1898-99 at Moscow Arts Theater; from 1905 taught stagecraft; 1902-24 actor and dir, Alexandrine Theater; *Roles*: Hamlet, Shylock; title role in Gutskov's *Uriel Akosta*; Boris Godunov in A. K. Tolstoy's *Smert' Ioanna Groznogo* (The Death of Ivan the Terrible); *Productions*: Chekhov's *Chayka* (The Seagull), etc; *Died*: 1930.

DASHICHEV, Ivan Fedorovich (1897-1963) Mil commander; Russian Army officer; Civil War veteran; maj-gen from 1941; CP member from 1929; *Born*: 1897 in vil Timonovka, Bryansk Oblast, son of a peasant; *Educ*: 1916 grad Chuguyev Mil College; *Career*: from 1918 in Red Army; in Civil War asst chief of staff, then chief of staff, 80th Brigade, 27th Omsk Infantry Div; distinguished himself by his bravery; 1921 helped suppress Kronstadt Mutiny; after Civil War regt chief of staff; head, Operations Dept, Staff of 4th Infantry Corps; chief of staff, 27th Infantry Div, 2nd Infantry Corps; commander, 35th Infantry Div; asst commander, 2nd Infantry Corps; commander, 47th Infantry Corps; 1941-45 commander, 35th and 9th Infantry Corps; commander, 44th Army; from 1945 retired; 1937 arrested by State Security organs; 1941 released and rehabilitated; *Awards*: three Orders of the Red Banner (received during Civil War); *Died*: Apr 1963.

DASHKEVICH, P.V. (1888-1942) Party and govt official; CP member from 1910; *Born*: 1888; *Career*: began Party work in Petersburg; contributed to newspapers *Zvezda* and *Pravda*; in WW 1 did revol work among soldiers during mil service; after 1917 Feb Revol helped to organize and run Mil Org, Petrograd Comt and CC, RSDRP(B); during 1917 Oct Revol member, Petrograd Mil Revol Comt; took part in storming of Winter Palace; after Oct Revol mil-polit work in Red Army, then exec and admin work for Sov govt; *Died*: 1942.

DASHKOVSKIY, Nikolay Antonovich (1892-1946) Operetta singer (tenor); Hon Artiste of RSFSR from 1941; *Born*: 1892 in Kiev; *Educ*: grad Kiev School of Music; *Career*: 1913-15 with Kiev Opera; 1915-22 in operetta; 1922-24 with operetta theater in Moscow; from 1925 at Leningrad Maly Opera Theater; also with Sverdlovsk and Khabarovsk Musical Comedy Theaters; many tours of USSR; *Roles*: Edvin and Radzhami in Kalman's *Sil'va* and *Bayadera*; Simon in Millöcker's "The Begger Student," etc; possessed fine stage presence and excellent voice; *Died*: 3 Apr 1946 in Pyatigorsk.

DASHTOYAN, Ruben Petrosovich (1879-1937) Party and govt official; CP member from 1902; *Born*: 1879 in Nor Bayazet (now Kamo), son of a postal and telegraph official; *Educ*: studied at theological school, Echmiadzin Theological Seminary and Nereisyan Seminary in Tiflis; *Career*: 1898-99 worked in Baku oil fields; 1900-07 mil service in Tiflis; after demobilition worked in Tiflis municipal laboratory; 1902 helped organize underground printing press, publishing first Arm Soc-Democratic newspaper "Proletariat"; 1907-14 worked for Party newspaper "Days" in Baku; 1914 drafted into army; at time of 1917 Feb Revol in Akhaltsikhe, where he founded a local Party org and was elected first chm, Akhaltsikhe Sov of Workers and Peasants' Dep; 1919-20 in Arm; Dec 1920 appointed chm, Kamarlin Rayon Revol Comt; 1921 chm, Nor-Bayazet Revol Comt; from 1922 chm, Karaklis Exec Comt; 1924 chm, Exec Comt, Arm Pop Comrt of Agric; then secr, Arm Centr Exec Comt and chm, Gori Exec Comt; 1930-37 secr, Arm Centr Exec Comt; 1927-34 member, Arm Centr Control Commission; 1921-35 member, Arm Centr Exec Comt; 1922-36 member, Transcaucasian Federation Centr Exec Comt; deleg at all congresses of CP Arm and at three congresses of Transcaucasian Party orgs; arrested by State Security organs; *Died*: 1937 in imprisonment.

DAUGUVETIS, Borisas Frantsevich (1885-1949) Lith theatrical figure and playwright; Pop Artiste of USSR from 1948; *Born*: 26 Mar 1885 in Lith; *Educ*: 1908 grad theater school in Petersburg; *Career*: 1910-13 actor and stage dir, Petersburg Theater of Lit and Art Soc; 1913-21 actor and stage dir at various Russian provincial theaters; from 1923 actor, stage dir and teacher, drama studio of State Theater, Kaunas (Lith); from 1940 directed this theater; from 1944 chief stage dir, Lith Drama Theater, Vilnius; dep Lith Supr Sov of 1947 convocation; *Works*: staged: "Othello" (1924); "A Winter's Tale" (1925); "The Robbers" (1928); "Don Carlos" (1931); *Vishnyovyy sad* (The Cherry Orchard) (1937); *Dokhodnoye mesto* (A Lucrative Post) (1938); Sophocles' "Oedipus at Colonna" (1939); *Meshchane* (The Philistines) (1940); Gorky's *Vragi* (The Enemies) (1946), etc; *Roles*: the baron in Pushkin's *Skupoy rytsar'* (The Miserly Knight) (1924); Claudius in "Hamlet" (1930); Autolicus in "A Winter's Tale" (1949), etc; *Publ*: plays *Novaya borozda* (The New Furrow) (1945); *Zadacha* (The Mission) (1947) about the partisan movement against the German troops; *Usad'ba Zhaldokasa* (Zhaldokas' Estate) (1948); *Awards*:

Stalin Prize (1947); *Died*: 13 July 1949 in Vilnius.

DAUGE, Pavel Georgiyevich (1869-1946) Co-founder, Lat Soc-Democratic Workers' Party; historian; publicist; Dr of Med; Hon Cultural Worker of Lat SSR; CP member from 1903; *Born*: 10 Aug 1869 in Saukas Volost, Lat, son of a teacher; *Educ*: 1897 grad Moscow Dental Surgery School; studied at Berlin Dental Surgery Inst; studied in Petersburg; *Career:* 1888–93 teacher; 1888–97 member of student Marxist circles in Dept, Petersburg and Moscow; founded Soc-Democratic circles in Lat; from 1897 dental surgeon in Moscow and active in revol work; 1905–07 member, lit lecturers' group of Moscow RSDRP Comt; contributed to Bolshevik newspaper *Svetoch;* 1905–06 attended congresses of Lat Soc-Democratic Workers' Party; 1907–12 engaged in lit and publishing work, translated into Russian and published works by F. Engels, for which he was arraigned; 1917 fought with Red Guards in Moscow; from Dec 1917 Sov Lat Pop Comr of Educ; 1918–19 Collegium member, RSFSR Pop Comrt of Health; 1928–33 prof, Moscow Odontological and Stomatological Inst; wrote many works on stomatology and public health, soc sci and history of revol movement in Lat; assoc, Inst of Philosophy and History, Communist Acad; then worked at USSR Acad of Sci; 1945–46 at Riga Inst of Party History, CC, CP(B) Lat; *Publ:* "I. Raynis - Bard of Struggle, Sun and Love" (1920); *O zubovrachebnom obrazovanii* (The Training of Dental Surgeons) (1926); *Sotsial'nyye osnovy sovetskoy stomatologii* (The Social Basis of Soviet Stomatology) (1933); *Revolyutsiya 1905–07 gg. v Latvii* (The 1905–07 Revolution in Latvia) (1949); *Rassasyvaniye korney zubov pri sklerodermii* (The Resorption of Teeth Roots in Cases of Scleroderma); *O kombinirovannom deystvii vnusheniya i mestnoy anestezii* (The Combined Effect of Suggestion and Local Anesthesia); *Karias kak sotsial'naya bolezn'* (Caries - a Social Aliment); *Osnovy sotsial'nogo zubovrachevaniya* (Principles of Social Dental Treatment), etc; *Died:* 2 Sept 1946.

DAUMAN, Àns Ernestovich (1885-1920) Lat revolutionary; CP member from 1903; *Born*: 1885 in Riga, son of a peasant; *Educ*: studied at Pskov Land Survey College and Moscow Mil Acad; *Career*: 1903 joined illegal Soc-Democrat group; 1904 member, *Atskabarga* group, Riga org, Lat Soc-Democratic Workers' Party; 1905 helped to organize workers' strike in Riga; 1907 drafted for mil service; established contact with local Party group while on duty in Warsaw; 1911-14 land-surveyor in Vilnius Province; 1914 again drafted for mil service; reached rank of battalion commander; during 1917 Feb Revol mayor of Narva, then chm, Narva Sov; early 1918 commanded partisan unit in Narva area; organized Red Guard regt of Narva workers, which formed the nucleus of the 6th Div; comr, 6th Div; 1919 member, then chm, Revol-Mil Council, Sov Lat Army; commander, 2nd Brigade, Lat Div and commandant, Dvina Fortress; commander in chief, Sov Lat Army; member, Revol Mil Council, 16th Army; member, Dvina Uyezd Comt, CP Lat; deleg, 6th Congress of CP Lat; 1920 commander, 10th Div during war with Poland; *Died*: Aug 1920 in action near Brest-Litovsk.

DAVIDENKO, Aleksandr Aleksandrovich (1899-1934) Composer specializing in mass songs; *Born*: 13 Apr 1899 in Odessa; *Educ*: 1918-19 studied at Odessa Conservatory; 1921-22 studied at Khar'kov Music Inst; 1929 grad Moscow Conservatory under P. Lier and A. Kastal'skiy; *Career*: 1919-21 in Red Army; from 1924 with amateur choirs of workers, soldiers and children's circles; 1925-29 founder-dir, "Production Collective of Student-Composers," Moscow Conservatory; 1929-32 member, Russian Assoc of Proletarian Musicians; *Works*: mass choral songs: "Budyonnyy's Cavalry Army" (1925), "At the Tenth Verst" (1927), "The Uneasy Street" (1927), "The First Cavalry Army" (1929), opera *1919 god* (1919) (1929); coauthor, opera *1905 god* (1905) (1935); romances: "Mother" and "The Letter" (1929); "Selected Choral and Mass Songs" (1938); arranged some French and Russian revol songs; *Publ: Kak ya rabotal nad pesney "Nas pobit', pobit' khoteli"* (How I Worked on the Song "They Wanted to Beat, to Beat Us Down") and *O tvorcheskoy rabote muzykal'nogo kruzhka* (The Creative Work of a Music Circle) (1931); *Awards*: Prize of USSR Pop Comrt of Educ (posthumously); *Died*: 1 May 1934 in Moscow.

DAVIDENKOV, Nikolay Nikolayevich (1879-1962) Mech eng; Dr of Physics and Mathematics; prof, Leningrad Polytech Inst from 1925; member, Ukr Acad of Sci from 1939; head, Dept of Mech Properties of Metals, Leningrad Inst of Physical Eng, USSR Acad of Sci from 1925; *Born*: 26 Mar 1879 in Riga; *Educ*: 1902 grad Petersburg Inst of Communications Eng; *Career*: 1909-18 lecturer, Petersburg Polytech Inst; 1920-21 lecturer, Don Polytech Inst; 1921-22 prof, Kiev Polytech Inst; 1923-26 prof, Moscow Inst of Trans Eng; worked on mech properties of metals; devised mech theory of cold-conditioned brittleness; established the significance of "series" experiments for determining critical brittleness temperature; devised methods of measuring and eliminating residual tension in products; *Publ: Dinamicheskiye ispytaniya metallov* (Dynamic Tests of Metals) (2nd ed, 1936); *Strunnyy metod izmereniya deformatsiy* (The Chord Method of Measuring Deformations) (1933); *Problema udara v metallovedenii* (Problem of Impact in Metallurgy) (1938); *Nekotoryye problemy mekhaniki materialov* (Some Problems of Material Mechanics) (1943); *Ustalost' metallov* (Metal Fatigue) (1949), etc; *Awards*: Stalin Prize (1943); Order of the Red Banner of Labor (1959); *Died*: 30 Sept 1962.

DAVIDENKOV, Sergey Nikolayevich (1880-1961) Neuropathologist; prof from 1919; Dr of Med from 1911; Hon Sci Worker of RSFSR from 1934; member, USSR Acad of Med Sci from 1945; hon member and bd member, Leningrad Soc of Neuropathologists and Psychiatrists; *Born*: Sept 1880; *Educ*: 1904 grad Med Fac, Moscow Univ; *Pos*: after grad nation intern, Moscow and Khar'kov zemstvo psychiatric hospitals; 1912-19 assoc prof, then prof, Chair of Nervous and Mental Diseases, Khar'kov Women's Med Inst; from 1920 prof, Chair of Nervous Diseases, Baku Univ; 1920-23 dean, then rector, Baku Univ; 1925-31 head, Dept of Nervous Diseases, Obukh Inst of Labor Hygiene and Occupational Diseases, Moscow; simultaneously lecturer in neuropathology, Postgrad Med Training Courses, Moscow Health Dept; 1932-1961 head, Chair of Nervous Diseases, Kirov Postgrad Med Training Inst, Leningrad; 1933 head, Neurosis Clinic, All-Union Inst of Experimental Med; 1934-36 dir, Pavlov's Clinic of Nervous Diseases, Leningrad; 1942-44 consultant, Leningrad mil hospitals; *Career*: in 1920's described numerous neuropathological syndromes; 1949 described consecutive viral meningitis-encephalitis; co-ed, *Bol'shaya meditsinskaya entsiklopediya* (Large Medical Encyclopedia); member, ed bd, journal *Nevropatologiya i psikhiatriya*; chief ed of a multi-vol manual on neurology; made important contribution to neuropathology and founded own school; 1948-50 subjected to ideological criticism for trying to reconcile Morgan's genetic theory with Pavlov's teachings on neuropathology; wrote over 200 works; *Publ*; doctor's thesis *K ucheniyu ob istorii ataksii Leyden-Vestfalya* (The History of Leyden-Westphal Ataxia) (1911); *Materialy k ucheniyu ob afazii. Simptomatologiya rasstroystv ekspressivnoy rechi* (Material on the Theory of Aphasia. Syndromes of Expressive Speech Disorders) (1915); *Zashchitnyye refleksy* (Defensive Reflexes) (1918); *Nasledstvennyye bolezni nervnoy sistemy* (Hereditary Diseases of the Nervous System) (1925); *Problemy polimorfizma nasledstvennykh bolezney nernoy sistemy* (Problems of the Polymorphism of Hereditary Diseases of the Nervous System) (1934); *Evolyutsionno-geneticheskiye problemy v nevropatologii* (Evolutionary Genetic Problems in Neuropathology) (1947); *Nevrozy v svete ucheniya I.P. Pavlova o vysshey nervnoy deyatel'nosti* (Neuroses in the Light of Pavlov's Theory of Higher Nervous Activity) (1948); *Klinicheskiye lektsii po nervnym boleznyam* (Clinical Lectures on Nervous Diseases)(1952-61); *Awards*: Order of Lenin (1960); Order of the Red Star; three medals; *Died*: 2 July 1961.

DAVIDOVSKIY, Konstantin Alekseyevich (1882-1939) Actor; Hon Artiste of RSFSR from 1933; *Born*: 19 Mar 1882; *Educ*: 1905 grad Khar'kov Technol Inst; took Ye. A. Lepkovskiy's private drama courses; *Career*: 1906 stage debut with Assoc of New Drama under Meyerkhol'd's direction; 1907-08 at Komissarzhevskaya Theater in Petersburg; 1908-24 acted at provincial theaters in Kherson, Odessa, Kursk, Saratov and Vilnius, etc; from 1925 actor, Theater of Moscow City Trade-Union Council in Moscow; *Roles:* Gapon in Shapovalenko's *Georgiy Gapon;* General Kondratenko in Nikulin's *Port Artur* (Port Arthur); Comr Furmanov in the stage adaptation of Furmanov's *Myatezh* (The Mutiny) (1927); Derri Mair in "The Man Who Laughs," after Victor Hugo; Li-Bertran in Shapovalenko's *Chern'* (The Rabble); Nikolay Skrobotov in *Vragi* (The Enemies); *Productions*: Nikulin's *Delo ryadovogo Shibunina* (The Case of Private Shibunin) (1936); *Vragi* (The Enemies) (1937), etc; *Publ*: play *Zoloto* (Gold) (1930); dramatization of Nekrasov's *Komu na Rusi zhit' khorosho* (Who Lives Well in Russia) (1938); also celebrated as a master of dramatic readings; *Died*: 1 Mar 1939.

DAVIDOVSKIY, Grigoriy Mitrofanovich (1866-1952) Choir conductor and composer; Hon Artiste of Ukr SSR from 1951; *Born*: 18 Jan 1866 in vil Mel'nya, near Konotop, Ukr; *Educ*: 1902 grad composition and singing class, Petersburg Conservatory; *Career*: from 1892 conducted workers' choirs; 1896-1900 directed students' choir at Petersburg Conservatory; 1908-17 founded and conducted Ukr choral group, with which he toured Russia; founded more than 35 choirs in Vinnitsa, Zhitomir, Lubny, Kerch, Poltava, Rostov-on-Don and Moscow; *Works*: vocal trilogy based on Ukr folk songs *Bandura* (1896), *Kobza* and *Kuban'*; musical poem; waltzes; arranged Russian, Ukr, Rumanian, Polish and other folk songs; *Died*: 13 Apr 1952 in Poltava.

DAVITASHVILI, Nina Shioyevna (1882-1958) Geo actress; Pop Artiste of Geo SSR from 1943; *Born*: 30 Nov 1882; *Career*: 1902 stage debut at pop theater of Avchala Auditorium in Tiflis; 1903 worked in Tiflis then Kutaisi theaters; from 1921 at Rustaveli Theater in Tiflis; *Roles*: Turpa and Patara Kakhi in Tseretelli's work of the same name; Ketevan in D. Eristavi's *Rodina* (The Homeland); Antigone in Sophocles' *Antigone* Gertrud in Schiller's "Wilhelm Tell" (1928); Ksidias in Slavin's *Interventsiya* (Intervention) (1934); Mariya Tarasovna in *Platon Krechet* (1935); Zeynab in Sumbatov-Yuzhin's *Izmena* (Betrayal) (1940); Fat'ma in Mosashvili's *Potoplennyye kamni* (Sunken Stones) (1949); Shushan in Sundukyan's *Pepo* (1951), etc; *Died*: 20 Oct 1958.

DAVKARAYEV, Nazhim (1905-1953) Karakalpak writer and lit historian; Dr of Philology; CP member from 1942; *Born*: 1905 in what is now Karakalpak ASSR; *Career*: 1935 first work published; collected, studied and published Karakalpak folklore and poetry of 18-19th centuries; worked out syntax of Karakalpak language; wrote articles on Karakalpak lit and works by Pushkin, Gorky, A. Navoi, G. Nizami, Shota Rustaveli, etc; translated into Karakalpak works by Pushkin, Nekrasov, etc; dep, Uzbek Supr Sov of 1947 convocation; *Publ*: stories: "Partisans" (1934); "In a Boarding School" (1935); *Bibikhan* (1936); musical drama based on nat epic *Alpamys* (1940); critical and research works; "Pre-Revolutionary Karakalpak Literature" (1945); "Outline History of Pre-Revolutionary Karakalpak Literature" (1959); "Karakalpak Grammar for Seven-Year and Secondary Schools" (1960), etc; *Died*: 20 July 1953 in Nukus, Karakalpak ASSR.

DAVLETSHIN Farrakh Davletshovich (1887-1956) Impromptu folk tale narrator; Pop Bard of Bash ASSR from 1944; *Born*: 24 Feb 1887 in vil Staryy Urtay, now Bash ASSR, son of a peasant; *Career*: orphan from age of eight; worked for estate-owners and as laborer at Ural plants; 1916 blinded as a result of ind accident; began to compose songs; during the Civil War satirized estate-owners and speculators; *Publ: Istoriya zakona* (The History of Law); *Muzhik popavskiy v bedu iz za porubki pomeshchich'yego lesa* (The Peasant Who Got into Trouble for Felling Trees in the Landlord's Forest); *Voyna 1914 goda* (The First World War); collections; *Baity slepogo Farrakha* (Blind Farrakh's Tales) (1928); *Stikhi i baity* (Verse and Tales) (1939); *Sovety sesena* (A Bard's Counsel) (1947), etc; *Died*: 12 Jan 1956 in vil Novo-Baishevo, Bash ASSR.

DAVLETSHIN, Gubey Kireyevich (1893-1938) Bash writer; CP member from 1917; *Born*: 29 Dec 1893 in vil Tashbulat, now Kuybyshev Province, son of a farmhand; *Career*: from 1914 in Russian Army; after 1917 Oct Revol active Party and govt official; 1917 first work published; *Publ*: stories "A Cheerless Life" and "The Guest" (1925); "The Main Profession" (1928); noveltte *Zel'skiy* (1927); stories: "The Comedy" (1928); "Alarm" (1928); "In the Clutch of the Flame" (1930), etc; arrested by State Security organs; *Died*: 11 July 1938 in imprisonment; posthumously rehabilitated.

DAVLETSHINA, Khadiya Lutfullovna (1905-1954) Bashkir writer; *Born*: Mar 1905 in vil Khasanovo, Kuybyshev Oblast, daughter of a peasant; *Career*: 1927 first work printed; *Publ*: novelette *Aybike* (1930); novel *Irgiz* (1957); *Died*: 5 Dec 1954 in Birsk.

DAVTYAN, Markar Daniyelovich (1910-1964) Arm writer and translator; *Born*: 1910 in vil Shoru, now Nakhichevan ASSR; *Publ*: 1929 first work published; collections of stories; "The Last Cry"; "Happiness," etc; novelettes "The Return"; "Under the Willow"; "When the Sun Rises"; "Karashen Summer"; "The Bright Path, " etc; novels "In Our Town"; "The Grapevine," etc; translated into Arm Azer classics Akhundov, Mamedkudizade and contemporary writers Ibragimov, Guseyn, Veliyev, Rakhman, etc; co-ed, G. Sevunets' collected works; *Died*: 30 Oct 1964.

DAVUDOVA, Marziya Yusuf-kyzy (1901-1962) Azer actress; Pop Artiste of USSR from 1949; CP member from 1942; *Born*: 8 Dec 1901 in Astrakhan'; *Career*: 1917 stage debut at Astrak an' Drama Theater; from 1920 at Baku Drama Theater (now Azer Azizbekov Drama Theater); 1943 film debut; dep, Azer Supr Sov of 1947, 1951, 1955 and 1959 convocations; *Roles*: Gul'tekin in *Aydyn* (1922); Solmaz in "Bride of Fire" (1928); Sevil' and Khayat in plays of the same name by M. Dzhabarly and M. Ibragimov; Lyubov' in Trenev's *Lyubov' Yarovaya* (1929); Lady Macbeth (1936); Shirin in S. Vurgun's "Farkhad and Shirin" (1941); Kabanikha in Ostrovskiy's *Groza* (The Thunderstorm); Gyul'zar in E. Mamed-khanly's "Dawn of the East" (1947); Vassa Zheleznova in Gorky's play of the same name (1954); Senem in "A True Friend" (1959), etc; *Awards*: Stalin Prize (1948); Badge of Hon (1959), etc; *Died*: 9 Jan 1962.

DAVYDOV (real name: LEVENSON), Aleksandr Mikhaylovich (1872-1944) Opera singer (lyric and dramatic tenor); Hon Artiste of RSFSR from 1924; *Born*: 1872 in Poltava Province; *Educ*: studied under Prof K. Everardi at the Moscow Conservatory; *Career*: 1889 began stage career at the Kiev Opera House; until 1900 sang in various opera and operetta enterprises in Tiflis, Yekaterinoslav, Khar'kov, Nizhniy Novgorod, Kazan', etc; 1900-17 soloist, Petersburg Mariinskiy Theater; from 1917 specialized exclusively in chamber singing; possessed a mellow-timbred voice and a perfect command of musical phrasing; 1924 lost his hearing, left the stage and went abroad; 1934 stage dir, Paris Opera ensemble with which Chaliapin was singing; 1935 returned to USSR; from 1936 worked at evening singing school of Kirov Opera and Ballet Theater; *Roles*: German in *Pikovaya dama* (The Queen of Spades); Siegfried, Loki and Mime in Wagner's "Ring des Nibelungen"; Kanio, Jose and Sinodal; title role in Napravnik's opera *Dubrovskiy,* etc; *Died*: 28 June 1944 in Moscow.

DAVYDOV, Boris Vladimirovich (1884-1925) Russian hydrographer and geodesist; explorer of the Arctic Ocean and the Pacific coast; *Born*: 1884; *Educ*: 1910 grad Hydrographic Dept, Naval Acad; subsequently specialized in astronomy and geodesy at Pulkovo Observatory; *Career*: 1910-13 commander, hydrographic ship *Taymyr* which took part in Vil'kitskiy's sci expedition; as astronomer of this expedition determined the coordinates of a number of points from Cape Dezhnev to the Kolyma River and worked out sailing directions for this region; from 1913 head, hydrographic expedition in the Pacific; made a nautical survey of the Okhotsk littoral and began an inventory of the Bering coast; during the Civil War arranged his collated material and prepared for publication in 1923 the book *Lotsiya poberezhiy RSFSR, Okhotskogo morya i vostochnogo berega poluostrova Kamchatki s ostrovom Karaginskim vklyuchitel'no* (Sailing Directions Along the Coast of the RSFSR, the Sea of Okhotsk and the Eastern Coast of the Kamchatka Peninsula Including Karaginskiy Island), which became a model for modern hydrographic works; after the establishment of Sov regime in the Far East headed the Far Eastern Regional Bd for Navigation Safety; 1924-25 headed expedition on the gunboat *Krasnyy Oktyabr'* to Wrangel Island, sent in connection with dispute with Canada and USA over ownership of this island and which hoisted Sov flag on island; a bay on Wrangel Island was named for him; *Publ: Materialy dlya izucheniya Severnogo Ledovitogo okeana ot mysa Dezhneva do r. Kolymy* (Material for the Study of the Arctic Ocean from Cape Dezhnev to the Kolyma River) (1912); *V tiskakh l'da. Plavaniye kanlodki 'Krasnyy Oktyabr' 'na ostrov Vrangelya* (In the Clutches of the Ice. The Voyage of the Gunboat *Krasnyy Oktyabr'* to Wrangel Island) (1925); *Died*: 30 Sept 1925.

DAVYDOV, I.A. (1866-1942) Party official; pedag; CP member from 1920; *Born*: 1866; *Career*: took part in Moscow's first Marxist circles; several times arrested and exiled for revol activities; after 1917 Oct Revol worked for educ organs and publ houses in Petrograd; 1924-33 lecturer, then Prof of polit econ, Leningrad Univ; *Publ: Chto zhe takoye ekonomicheskiy materializmm?* (What Is Economic Materialism?) (1900); *Died*: 1942.

DAVYDOV, Vladimir Nikolayevich (real name: GORELOV, Ivan Nikolayevich) (1849-1925) Russian actor; Pop Artiste of RSFSR from 1922; rep of *Shchepkin* school of acting; *Born*: 19 Jan 1849 in Novomirgorod, Ukr, son of an officer; *Educ*: studied at Moscow Univ; studied drama under I. V. Samarin; *Career*: 1867-80 acted at provincial theaters and with P. Medvedev's company; 1880-86 and 1888-1924 at Petersburg Aleksandrinskiy Theater; 1886-88 at Moscow Korsh Theater; from 1924 at Moscow Maly Theater; from 1883 teacher, Petersburg Theater College; among his students were the following prominent actors: V. Komissarzhevskaya, A. Viv'yen, V. Yureneva and K. Zubov;

noted for his subtle psychological interpretation of a role and fine tech presentation; *Roles:* Rasplyuyev in *Svad'ba Krechinskogo* (Krechinskiy's Marriage) (1875); Famusov in Griboyedov's *Gore ot uma* (Woe from Wit) (1879); Moshkin in Turgenev's *Kholostyak* (The Bachelor) (1882); Shylock in Shakespeare's "Merchant of Venice" (1897); Luka in Gorky's *Na dne* (The Lower Depths) (1903); Falstaff in Shakespeare's "Merry Wives of Windsor" (1904); Firs in Chekhov's *Vishnyovyy sad* (The Cherry-Orchard) (1905); Chebutykin in Chekhov's *Tri sestry* (Three Sisters) (1910); Bunt in Lunacharskiy's *Faust i gorod* (Faust and the City) (1920); Akim in L. Tolstoy's *Vlast' t'my* (Power of Darkness); the mayor in Gogol's *Revizor* (The Inspector-General), etc; performed over 30 roles in Ostrovskiy's plays: Khlynov in *Goryacheye serdtse* (A Warm Heart); Karakunov in *Serdtse ne kamen'* (The Heart Is Not a Stone); Obroshenov in *Shutniki* (The Jokers), etc; performed many other roles of Russian classic repertoire; *Died*: 23 June 1925 in Moscow.

DAVYDOV, Zinoviy Samoylovich (1892-1957) Russian writer; *Born*: 28 Apr 1892 in Chernigov; *Educ*: 1912-17 studied at Kiev Univ; *Career*: 1919 first work published in Chernigov; lit fame dates from 1933; Gorky described him as a "writer familiar with the history of his land. . a man with a subtle feel for history"; *Publ*: verse collection *Veter* (The Wind); novel *Beruny* (1933) based on an actual incident described in Acad P. L. Lerua's book *Priklyucheniya chetyryokh rossiyskikh matrosov, k ostrovu Ost-Shpitsbergenu bureyu prinesyonnykh* . . . (The Adventures of Four Russian Sailors Driven to East Spitzbergen by a Storm . . .), republished in 1947 under title *Russkiye robinzony* (The Russian Robinsons); novel set in early 17th century *Iz Goshchi gost'* (A Guest From Goshcha) (1940); novel about the 1854-55 Crimean War *Korabel'naya storona* (Navel District) (1957) (children's ed in 1955 under title *Korabel'naya slobodka* (Navel Settlement); historical novel for children *Razorennyy god* (A Ruined Year) (1958); *Zvyozdy na bashnyakh. Obrazy starogo Kremlya* (Stars on the Towers. Scenes of the Old Kremlin) (1963), etc; *Died*: 7 Oct 1957 in Moscow.

DAVYDOVA, Natal'ya Yakovlevna (1873-1926) Artist; *Born*: 1873; *Career*: together with team of artists (Serov, Rubel', Yakuntikova, Nevrev, Ostroukhov, Korovin, etc), worked on development of arts and crafts ind, popularizing peasant art; worked at Abramtsev School and Moscow Province Zemstvo establishments; after 1917 Oct Revol worked at Moscow Crafts Museum; *Died*: 1926.

DAYREDZHIYEV, Boris Leonidovich (1902-1955) Russian lit critic; CP member from 1919; *Born*: 30 Dec 1902 in Moscow; *Career*: member, Literary Front Group; wrote articles on Ostrovskiy, Sobolev, Yanovskiy, Vershigor, Bazhov, etc; also theater reviews; *Publ*: novel *Cherez otmeli* (Over The Shallows) (1928); articles "Na.A. Dobrolyubov, His Enemies and Heirs" (1936); "Dobrolyubov and 'What Is to Be Done? '"; study of Sholokhov *O 'Tikhom Done'* (About "Quiet Flows the Don") (1962, posthumously); *Died*: 31 July 1955 in Moscow.

DAYTS, Iosif Abramovich (1897-1954) Graphic artist; *Born*: 16 Aug 1897; *Educ*: 1921-29 studied at Khar'kov Art Inst; *Career*: 1935-47 instructor, from 1947 prof, Khar'kov Art Inst; *Works*: illustrations for: Barbusse's novel "Fire" (1937); Zabil's works (1941 and 1949); an ed of Anderson's fairy-tales (1946); Panch's novelettes; *Died*: 29 Dec 1954.

DEBORIN (IOFFE), Abram Moiseyevich (1881-1963) Philosopher and historian; member, USSR Acad of Sci from 1929; CP member from 1928; *Born*: 16 June 1881 in Kaunas; *Educ*: 1897 grad Kovno Jewish Public School; 1908 grad Philosophy Fac, Bern Univ; *Career*: 1903-07 member, Bolshevik Party; 1907-17 Menshevik and Menshevik-Internationalist; from 1920 research, ed and teaching work at 2nd Moscow State Univ, Inst of Red Prof, Communist Acad, Marx-Engels Inst, Inst of History of Sci and Eng; 1926-30 simultaneously exec ed, periodical *Pod znamenem marksizma*; helped found Militant Materialists Soc and Friends of Hegel's Dialectics Soc; 1935-45 Presidium member, USSR Acad of Sci and acad secr, Dept of History and Philosophy, USSR Acad of Sci; from 1945 senior assoc, Inst of Philosophy, USSR Acad of Sci; worked on the history of philosophy, soc-polit thought and Marxist philosophy; 1931 criticised for "taking Menshevik idealistic stands on a number of important problems"; *Publ*: *Vvedeniye v filosofiyu dialekticheskogog materializma* (Introduction to the Philosophy of Dialectical Materialism) (1915); *Lyudvig Feyerbakh. Lichnost' i mirovozzreniye* (Ludwig Feuerbach - the Man and His Outlook) (1923); *Lenin kak myslitel'* (Lenin the Thinker) (1924); *Diktatura proletariata i teorya marksizma* (Dictatorship of the Proletariat and Marxist Theory) (1927); *Ocherki po istorii materializma 17 i 18 vv.* (Outline History of 17-18th Century Materialism) (3rd ed, 1930); *Lenin i krizis noveyshey fiziki* (Lenin and the Crisis of Modern Physics) (2nd ed, 1930); *Dialektika i yestestvoznaniye* (Dialectics and Natural Science) (4th ed, 1930); *Karl Marks i sovremyonnost'* (Karl Marx and Contemporary Period) (1933); *Sotsial'no-politicheskoye ucheniye novogo i noveyshego vremeni* (Modern and Contemporary Socio-Political Theory) (Vol 1, 1958); *Materializm i dialektika v drevneindiyskoy filosofii* (Materialism and Dialectics in Ancient Indian Philosophy) (1956); *Filosofiya i politika* (Philosophy and Politics) (1961), etc; *Awards*: two Orders of the Red Banner of Labor; *Died*: 8 Mar 1963.

DEGOT', Vladimir Aleksandrovich (1889-1944) Party and govt official; CP member from 1904; *Born*: 20 Feb 1889 in vil Golubovka-Brikvanovo, Podol'sk Province, son of a worker; *Educ*: two years of night school; studied at a Party school in France; *Career*: from 1903 in revol movement; worked at Vysotskiy Factory, Odessa; 1906-07 staged several strikes at Odessa enterprises; 1908 emigrated to France, where he met Lenin; 1909 returned to Odessa and set up illegal printing press; 1910 arrested, held for two years in jail, then exiled to Yenisey Province; 1912 fled from exile to Odessa, thence abroad; 1915 together with Inessa Armand translated into French Lenin's work *Sotsializm i voyna / Otnosheniye RSDRP k voyne* (Socialism and War / The RSDRP's Attitude to War) and arranged its publication; July 1917 returned to Odessa, worked at a factory and was elected to Odessa City Sov of Worker's Dep; then chm, Printers' union; deleg at 3rd All-Russian Congress of Soviets; late 1918, on instructions from the Odessa Oblast Party Comt, set up and directed the "For Bd" which carried out propaganda work among French sailors; Feb 1919 set up an underground revol comt; from Apr 1919 again in charge of the "For Bd," now engaged in propaganda work in Europe; Aug 1919 Comintern assignments in France and Italy; Aug 1920 returned to France, was arrested and after few months' imprisonment returned via Germany to RSFSR; from 1921 chm, Ivanovo-Voznesensk Province Trade-Union Council; from 1924 head, Agitation and Propaganda Dept, and dep chm, All-Union Centr Trade-Union Council; deleg at 3rd, 4th, 5th and 6th Comintern Congresses; from 1931 Collegium member, then USSR Dep Pop Comr of Labor; later RSFSR Dep Pop Comr of Justice and RSFSR Procurator; 31 July 1938 arrested and convicted; *Publ: Pod znamenem bol'shevizma. Zapiski podpol'shchika* (Under the Banner of Bolshevism. Notes of an Underground Worker) (1933); *Died*: 3 Apr 1944 in imprisonment; posthumously rehabilitated.

DEGTYAREV, Vasiliy Alekseyevich (1879-1949) Maj-gen, Artillery Eng Corps; designer of firearms; Dr of Tech sci; CP member from 1941; *Born*: 21 Dec 1879 in Tula, son of a gunsmith; 1901 drafted into Russian Army and assigned to weapons workshop of officers' weapons school; 1905 transferred to reserve, assigned to workshop of testing range at officers' weapons school; 1914-17 foreman at Sestroretskiy Ordinance Plant; after 1917 revol for a long time haded first Sov weapons design bureau; in 1920's designed submachine-gun; then designed plane, tank and army heavy machine guns; in late 1930's designed machine-pistol and anti-tank rifle used during WW 2; dep, USSR Supr Sov of 1937 and 1946 convocations; *Publ: Moya Zhizn'* (My Life) (1949); *Awards*: four Stalin Prizes (1941, 1942, 1944 and 1949); Hero of Socialist Labor (1940); three Orders of Lenin; four other orders; medals; *Died*: 16 Jan 1949; buried in Kovrov where a monument has been erected in his memory.

DEGTYAREVA-BOKSBERG (Party pseudonym: ZENTA), Avgusta Yakovlevna (1887-1964) Lat revolutionary; CP member from 1904; *Born*: 17 Aug 1887; *Career*: 1905-07 took part in Lat revol, stored illegal lit and weapons; maintained contacts with polit prisoners; did propaganda and org work in Krasnaya Dvina distr, Riga; 1908 arrested with other members of Riga Soc-Democratic Comt and sentenced to four years at hard labor; 1913 emigrated to USA, where she worked at factories in Boston and Philadelphia; joined emigré org of Lat Soc-Democrats; after 1917 Oct Revol returned to Russia and worked for soc security service in Moscow; from 1933 pensioner; *Died*: 21 Mar 1964.

DEKANOZOV, Vladimir Georgiyevich (1898-1953) Govt official; *Born*: 1898; *Career*: 1938 dep chm, Geo Council of Pop Comr; from 1939 USSR Dep Comr of For Affairs; 1940-41 simultaneously USSR amb to Germany with rank of amb extraordinary and plen; 1939-41 cand member, 1941-50 member,

CC, CPSU(B); June 1953 relieved of his post as Geo Min of Internal Affairs; 18-23 Dec 1953, together with Beriya and others, sentenced to death for the liquidation of Party and govt personnel; *Died*: 23 Dec 1953 executed.

DEKHOTI, Abdusalom Pirmukhammadovich (1911-1962) Tadzh poet, playwright and translator; CP member from 1941; *Born*: 14 Mar 1911 in vil Bagi Maydan (Tadzh), son of an artisan; *Career*: translated into Tadzh works of Krylov, Nekrasov, Shevchenko and other Russian and for classics; ed bd member, Tadzh periodicals *Sharki Surkh, Tozhikistan,* "Pioner" and *Khorpushtak*; 1958 attended Tashkent Conference of Afro-Asian writers; Bd member, Tadzh Writers' Union; *Publ*: verse "In Honor of March 8th," "The Spring of Working People" (1929), stories "Unhappy Khamida," "The Farzand Road" and satirical stories *Djinni*, "The Last Miracle" (1930); verse collection "Songs of Labor" (1932); "The Fruits of October" (1934); play "Khosrov and Shirin" (1936); coauthor, libretto, first Tadzh opera "The Vose Mutiny" (1939); collection "Verse and Stories" (1940); song "Waiting for You" (1944); letter of Tadzh soldiers to Tadzh people in verse "For the Soviet Regime" (1944-45); "Selected Verse" (1945); play "Light in the Mountains" (1947); "Selected Verse and Prose" (1949); coauthor, one-act comedy *Tarifkhodzhayev* (1954); selected children's tales "A Gift for Kiddies" (1954); "Running Water" (1957), etc; *Awards*: two Orders of the Red Banner of Labor; two Badges of Hon; *Died*: 30 Jan 1962 in Dushanbe.

DE-LAZARI, Aleksandr Nikolayevich (1880-1942) Sov mil historian and geographer; lt-col, Russian Gen Staff; *Born*: 1880; *Educ*: grad Russian Gen Staff Acad; *Career*: from 1918 in Red Army; during Civil War chief, Operations Dept, Staff of Western Front; chief of staff, West Siberian Mil Distr; from 1921 editing mil research work; instructor at various Red Army acads; pioneer of Russian Civil War studies; 1937 arrested by State Security organs while working as instructor at USSR Mil Acad of Chemical Defense; *Died*: 1942 in imprisonment; posthumously rehabilitated.

DELONE, Nikolay Borisovich (1856-1931) Pioneer of Russian glider designer; publicized and popularized aviation theory and practice; pupil of N. Ye. Zhukovskiy; *Born*: 2 Feb 1856; *Career*: 1906-28 prof of mech, Kiev Polytech Inst; 1908-09 designed several biplane gliders which accomplished a great number of flights; simultaneously organized an aeronautic circle at the Kiev Polytech Inst, from which many prominent aviators originated; *Publ*: wrote one of the first glider-flying handbooks *Ustroystvo deshyovogo i lykogo planera i sposoby letaniya na nyom* (Building and Flying a Cheap Light Glider) (1910); *Died*: 20 Mar 1931.

DEMCHENKO, Nikolay Nesterovich (1897-1943) Party and govt official; CP member from 1916; *Born*: 1897 in Lebedin, Khar'kov Province; *Career*: after 1917 Oct Revol worked in Volhynian Oblast as: Ukr Dep Pop Comr of Workers and Peasants Inspection; dep chm, Centr Party Control Commission, CP(B) Ukr; Ukr Pop Comr of Agric; from 1932 secr, Kiev, then Khar'kov Oblast Comt, CP(B) Ukr; from 1936 USSR First Dep Pop Comr of Agric; from 1937 USSR Pop Comr of Grain and Cattle-Breeding Sovkhozes; 1924 at 8th Conference of CP(B) Ukr elected cand member, CC, CP(B) Ukr; at 10th, 11th and 12th Congresses of CP(B) Ukr elected member, CC, CP(B) Ukr; from 1928 cand member, from 1931 member, Politburo, CC, CP(B) Ukr; deleg at 13th-17th CPSU(B) Congresses; at 17th Congress elected cand member, CC, CPSU(B); was member of All-Ukr and All-Russian Centr Exec Comt; arrested by State Security organs; *Died*: 1943 in imprisonment.

DEMCHUK, Pyotr Ivanovich (1900-1943) Philosopher; corresp member, Ukr Acad of Sci from 1932; CP member from 1925; *Born*: 11 June 1900 in Gorodenka, now Ivano-Frankov Oblast; *Educ*: 1924 grad Vienna Law Inst; 1927 completed postgrad studies at Philosophy Fac, Inst of Marxism-Leninism; *Career*: 1919 joined Communist Party of Western Ukr; 1925 moved to USSR with a group of polit emigres and lived in Khar'kov; from 1927 head, Chair of Philosophy, All-Ukr Assoc of Marxist-Leninist Research Institutes; also head, Chair of Dialectic and Historical Materialism, Khar'kov Inst of Sov Construction and Law; *Publ: Raspad sovremennoy burzhuaznoy filosofii* (The Collapse of Modern Bourgeois Philosophy) (1931); *Died*: 30 Jan 1943.

DEMENT'YEV, Nikolay Ivanovich (1907-1935) Russian poet; *Born*: 1907; *Educ*: studied at Bryusov Inst of Lit and Art, and at Lit Fac, Moscow Univ; *Career*: 1925-28 member, All-Union Komsomol; until 1928 member, *Pereval* (The Pass) lit group; later joined Russian Assoc of Proletarian Writers; traveled about USSR with *Pravda* teams; worked on the construction of a chemical combine at Bobriki; learned from writers Pasternak and Aseyev; *Publ*: 1924 first verse published; works published in such journals and newspapers as *Krasnaya nov', Komsomol'skaya pravda, Molodaya gvardiya* and *Oktyabr'*, etc; verse collection *Shosse entuziastov* (The Highway of Enthusiasts) (1930); verse collections for children "Roald Amundsen" and *Samolet* (The Aircraft) (1931); collection *Ovladeniye tekhnikoy* (Mastering Technology) (1933); *Rasskazy v stikhakh* (Stories in Verse) (1934); rhymed pamphlet *Rozhdeniye atoma azota* (The Birth of the Nitrogen Atom) and poem "The City" (1931-32); stories in verse *Pastukh* (The Shepherd), *Novyy metod* (A New Method), *Tanya, Zakon* (The Law), *Mat'* (Mother); *Izbrannyye stikhotvoreniya* (Selected Verse) (1936), etc; together with E. Bagritskiy translated verse of Nazym Khikmet; *Died*: 28 Oct 1935.

DE-METTS, Georgiy Georgiyevich (1861-1947) Physicist; specialist in methods of teaching physics; *Born*: 21 May 1861 in Odessa, son of an eng; *Educ*: 1885 grad Novorossiysk Univ, Odessa; *Career*: 1891-1930 prof of physics, Kiev, Univ and Kiev Inst of Public Educ; from 1898 prof of physics, Kiev Polytech Inst; 1934-47 head, Chair of Physics, Kiev Teachers' Training Inst; *Died*: 3 Feb 1947.

DEMICHEV, Mikhail Afanas'yevich (1885-1937) Mil commander; ensign, Russian Army; div commander from 1935; CP member from 1920; *Born*: 1885; *Pos*: until WW 1 worked at a printing house; from 1918 in Red Army; 1918-20 commander of a cavalry regt, cavalry brigade and 8th Red Cossack Div; fought against the Germans, Petlyura and Denikin's forces and Polish troops; 1921-34 commander, 1st Zaporozhian Cavalry Div, Red Cossack Army; 1934-37 commander 1st Cavalry Corps; 1937 arrested by State Security organs; *Died*: 20 Sept 1937 in imprisonment; posthumously rehabilitated.

DEMIDENKO, Andrey Makarovich (1899-1961) Film sound operator; *Born*: 21 Sept 1899; *Career*: from 1934 sound operator, Kiev's Dovzhenko Feature Film Studio; *Works*: associated with films: *Divnyy sad* (The Miraculous Garden) (1935); *Natalka-Poltavka* (1936); "Tom Sawyer" (1937); *Kubantsy* (The Kuban Cossacks) (1940); *Veter s Vostoka* (Wind from the East) (1941); *Gody molodyye* (The Young Years) (1943); *Golubyye dorogi* (Blue Roads) (1948); *Shchedroye leto* (Generous Summer) (1951); *Maksimka* (1953); *Zaporozhets za Dunayem* (A Dnieper Cossack Beyond the Danube) (1953); *Komandir korablya* (The Ship Commander) (1954); *Lymerivna* (1955); *Matros Chizhik* (Seaman Chizhik) (1956); *Ivan Franko* (1956); *More zovyot* (The Sea Calls) (1956), etc; *Died*: 17 May 1961.

DEMIDENKO, Tit Trofimovich (1891-1959) Plant breeder; corresp member, Ukr Acad of Sci from 1951; CP member from 1947; *Born*: 2 Apr 1891 in vil Trushivtsy, now Cherkassy Oblast; *Educ*: 1921 grad Khar'kov Agric Inst; *Career*: for ten years worked at Moscow's Timiryazev Agric Acad; from 1944 dept head, Ukr Acad of Agric Sci; published some 70 research works and articles; *Died*: 21 July 1959.

DEMIDOV, Aleksey Alekseyevich (1883-1934) Russian writer; *Born*: 1 June 1883 in vil Bobriki, Tula Province, son of a peasant; *Career*: worked as clerk, then as bank official in Petrograd and Moscow; contributed to Tula newspapers; 1911 first work published; *Publ*: essay *Dva chasa u Tolstogo* (Two Hours with Tolstoy) (1911); stories *Na shakhte* (At the Mine) (1923); play *Geroy* (The Hero) (1927); stories *Zelyonyy luch* (The Green Ray) (1928); three-part autobiographical novel *Zhizn' Ivana* (The Life of Ivan), *Vikhr'* (The Vortex) and *Selo Yekaterininskoye* (The Village of Yekaterininskoye) (1926-29); novel *Les* (The Forest) (1933), etc; particularly successfull in portraying peasant types; *Died*: 12 Apr 1934 in Moscow.

DEMIRCHYAN, Derenik Karapetovich (1877-1956) Arm poet, writer and playwright; Hon Art Worker of Arm SSR from 1940; member, Arm Acad of Sci from 1953; *Born*: 18 Feb 1877 in Akhalkalaki (Geo), son of a craftsman; *Educ*: 1909 grad Teachers' Training Fac, Geneva Univ; *Career*: 1893 first work published; 1905-09 lived in Switzerland; 1910-22 teacher in Tiflis; from 1925 lived in Yerevan; after establishment of Sov regime in Arm set up Union of Working Writers of Arm and was its chm until 1931; member, Arm and Transcaucasian Centr Exec Comts of several convocations; *Publ*: "Collected Verse" (1899); play *Vasak* (1912); "Collected Verse" (1913); poem *Lenk-Timur*; stories: "The Violin and the Pipe"; "The Superfluous Women"; "The Smile"; "The Link"; drama "The Reprisal"; collected verse "Spring" (1919); fairy-tale drama *Brave Nazar* (1924); stories:

Sato (1929); *Rashid*: (1930); "Friends" (1931); "New and Monumental" (1932); comedy *Napoleon Korkotyan*; play *Kaputan* (1938); historical drama "My Native Land" (1939); novel *Vardanidy* (1943-46); "Selected Works" (1950); "Stories" (1954); *Chargay* (1956); unfinished novel *Mesron-Mashtots* (1956), etc; works translated into Russian, Azer, Geo and other languages; *Awards*: Order of Lenin; Order of the Red Banner of Labor; *Died*: 6 Dec 1956 in Yerevan.

DEMKOV, Mikhail Ivanovich (1859-1939) Educationist; *Born*: 24 Mar 1859; *Educ*: 1877 grad Nezhin High School; 1881 grad Kiev Univ; *Career*: from 1881 taught physics and natural sci at Chernigov Girls' High School and Glukhov Teacher's Inst; in 1890's contributed to journals *Russkaya shkola, Vestnik vospitaniya, Pedagogicheskiy sbornik, Gimnaziya,* and *Russkiy nachal'nyy uchitel'* on educ methods, didactics and history of educ; 1905-11 dir, Moscow Teachers' Inst; from Oct 1911 dir, Vladimir Province pop colleges; after 1917 Oct Revol taught educ methods and history of pedag at Priluki Teachers' Training Technicum; wrote first major textbooks on pedag for teachers' inst, teachers' seminars, etc; *Publ: Russkaya pedagogika v glavneyshikh yeyo predstavitelyakh* (Russian Pedagogics in Its Main Exponents) (1898); *Ocherki po istorii russkoy pedagogiki* (An Outline History of Russian Pedagogics) (1909); *Staryye i novyye pedagogi, ikh zhizn', mysli i trudy* (Old and New Pedagogues, their Life, Ideas and Works) (1912); *Nachatki sel'skogo khozyaystva* (The Rudiments of Agriculture) (1913); *Yestestvennaya istoriya dlya narodnoy shkoly* (Natural History of the Public School) (1914); *Dary yunosti* (The Gifts of Youth) (1915); *Ugolok detskoy zhizni* (A Corner of Children's Life) (1915); *Died*: 27 Mar 1939.

DEMUTSKIY, Daniil Porfir'yevich (1893-1954) Cameraman; Hon Art Worker of Uzbek SSR from 1944 and Ukr SSR from 1954; *Born*: 16 July 1893 in vil Okhmatov, now Cherkassy Oblast; son of composer P. D. Demutskiy; *Educ*: 1917 grad Law Fac, Kiev Univ; *Career*: a keen amateur photographer in his youth, he later became a professional photographer; from 1925 head, Photography Dept, All-Ukr Bd of Photography and Cinematography in Kiev; 1926-32 worked with film dir Dovzhenko; during WW 2 worked for Tashkent Film Studio; from 1947 again at Kiev Film Studio; *Works*: helped screen films: *Vasya-reformator* (Vasya the Reformer) (1926); *Dva dnya* (Two Days) (1927); *Kapriz Yekateriny II* (The Whim of Catherine II) (1928); *Arsenal* (The Armory) (1929); *Zemlya* (The Earth) (1930); *Ivan* (1932); *Poslednyaya ochered'* (The Last Burst) (1941); *Boyevoy kinosbornik No. 9* (Combat Film Collection No. 9) (1942); *Nasreddin v Bukhare* (Nasreddin in Bakhara) (1943); *Takhir i Zukhra* (Takhir and Zukhra) (1945); *Pokhozhdeniya Nasreddina* (Nasreddin's Adventures) (1947); *Podvig razvedchika* (The Scout's Feat) (1947); *V mirnyye dni* (In Peacetime) (1950); *Taras Shevchenko* (1951), etc; *Awards*: gold medal at 1925 Paris Int Exhibition of Applied Arts; prize at 6th Int Film Festival in Karlovy Vary, 1951; Stalin Prize (1952); *Died*: 7 May 1954.

DEMUTSKIY, Porfiriy Danilovich (1860-1927) Physician; folklorist; choral conductor and composer; *Born*: 10 Mar 1860 in vil Yanishivtsy, Kiev Province; *Educ*: grad theological seminary; 1889 grad Med Fac, Kiev Univ; *Career*: 1874 began to record folk songs; in his student years sang in N. V. Lysenko's choir; after graduating from Univ physician in vil Okhmatov; organized a chorus of local peasants, which performed Ukr songs in folklore harmonization, preserving distinctive features of peasants' manner of singing and polyphony; under his direction this choir toured many Ukr cities; from 1918 member, Ethnographic Commission, Ukr Acad of Sci; lectured on folk songs at Kiev's Lysenko Inst of Music and Drama; during his last years he worked with the *Dumka* Chorus; *Publ*: collected recordings of Ukr folk songs which for the first time recordet both the melody and the harmony: *Lira i yeyo motive* (The Lyre and Its Tunes) (1903); *Narodnyye ukrainskiye pesni na Kiyevshchine* (Ukrainian Folk Songs of the Kiev Region) (1905-07); two collections of folk songs he recorded were published in 1928; *Died*: 3 June 1927 in Kiev.

DEM'YANOV, Grigoriy Stepanovich (1885-1958) Infectionist and therapist; Dr of Med; prof from 1928; *Born*: 1885, son of a Cossack peasant; *Educ*: 1905 grad teachers' training seminary; 1913 grad Med Fac, Moscow Univ; *Career*: 1905-08 worked as a teacher; after grad from Moscow Univ worked as a country physician in Kuban'; 1920 co-founder and assoc, 1928-58 head, Chair of Infections Diseases, Kuban' Med Inst, Krasnodar; wrote some 50 works on infectious diseases and epidemiology, including several monographs; *Died*: 1958 in Krasnodar.

DEM'YANOV, Nikolay Ivanovich (1888-1961) Choral conductor; founder of amateur choirs; *Born*: 14 May 1888 in Moscow; *Career*: from 1944 taught at State Choral College, Moscow; wrote aids on choral singing and mass musical work; *Died*: 23 June 1961 in Moscow.

DEM'YANOV, Nikolay Yakovlevich (1861-1938) Organic chemist; Dr of Chemistry from 1899; member,USSR Acad of Sci from 1929; *Born*: 27 Mar 1861 in Tver' (now Kalinin); *Educ*: 1886 grad Moscow Univ; *Career*: 1887-1894 assoc, from 1894 prof, Petrine Forestry and Agric Acad, Moscow (now Timiryazev Agric Acad); 1907-17 simultaneously lecturer in chemistry, Golitsyno Higher Women's Courses; 1920 co-founder, Workers' Fac, Moscow Agric Acad; from 1935 laboratory head, Inst of Organic Chemistry, USSR Acad of Sci; 1895 defended master's thesis on "The Reaction of Nitrous Acid with Tri- Tetra- and Pentamethylenediamines", in which he described a gen method of obtaining normal saturated glycols, unsaturated alcohols and their isomeric oxides in the γ and δ series; obtained and studied tetra- and pentamethylene glycols and their oxides; 1899 defended doctor's thesis on "The Reaction of Nitric Anhydride and Hyponitrous Oxide with Ethylene Hydrocarbons", in which he demonstrated that the reaction of N_2O_5 with unsaturated hydrocarbons produces nitric ethers of glycol and the derivatives N_2O_3, N_2O_4 and N_2O_5; did research on the products obtained by reduction of these compounds and established that this reaction may be used to obtain diamines and oxyamines; 1934 summarized his findings in an article entitled "The Reaction of Nitrous Oxides N_2O_5, N_2O_4 and N_2O_3) with Unsaturated Hydrocarbons"; these findings provided the basis for the development of a new trend in organic chemistry; further developed the work of Gustavson and Markonovnikov on cyclic polymethylene hydrocarbons and their derivatives; studied the isomeric conversion of the simplest carbocyclic compounds; proved that the reaction of zinc dust and alcohol with dibromo-derivated saturated hydrocarbons (Gustavson's reaction) in which the two bromine atoms are separated by no more than one CH_2 group produces a trimethylene cycle; was thus able to obtain the first homologue of trimethylene - methyl cyclopropane; 1901 began research which led to discovery of the laws governing the isomerization of carbocyclic systems (Dem'yanov regrouping); was first to synthesize such compounds as vinyl trimethylene, methylene cyclobutane, cyclopropane, etc; also did research on agrochemistry and plant chemistry; coauthored textbook on plant chemistry and wrote textbook on organic chemistry; *Publ*: doctor's thesis *O deystvii azotnogo angidrida i azotnovatoy okisi na etilenovyye uglevodorody* (The Reaction of Nitric Anhydride and Hyponitrous Oxide with Ethylene Hydrocarbons) (1899); *Zhiry i vosk. Khimiya i analiz* (Fats and Wax. Chemistry and Analysis) (3rd ed, 1932); coauthor, *Khimiya rastitel'nykh veshchestv* (The Chemistry of Vegetable Substances) (1933); coauthor, *Efirnyye masla, ikh sostav i analiz* (Essential Oils, Their Composition and Analysis) (2nd ed, 1933); coauthor, *Obshchiye priyomy analiza rastitel'nykh veshchestv* (General Methods of Analysing Vegetable Substances) (1934); *Sbornik izbrannykh trud* (Selected Works) (1936); *Organicheskaya khimiya* (Organic Chemistry) (3rd ed, 1944); *Awards*: A.M. Butlerov Prize (1924); *Died*: 19 Mar 1938.

DEM'YANOVICH, Mikhail Pavlovich (1879-1957) Dermatologist and venerologist; Dr of Med; prof; *Born*: 1879 in vil Labinskaya, Kuban' Province, son of an office worker; *Educ*: 1904 grad Med Fac, Moscow Univ; *Career*: after grad worked for a number of years as a country physician in Yerevan Province; 1908-11 extern, Prof A.I. Pospelov's Skin and Venerological Clinic, Moscow; 1911-14 asst to Prof A.I. Lants, Skin Clinic, Moscow Higher Women's Courses (now 2nd Moscow Med Inst); 1914-18 mil service; 1917 consultant venerologist, Western Front; after 1917 Oct Revol returned to Moscow and became a member, Centr Commission for Combatting Venereal Diseases, Pop Comrt of Health; 1919-21 dir, model venerological outpatients' clinic, Moscow; 1921-57 co-founder, prof, dep dir and sci dir, State Venerological Inst (now Central Skin and Venerological Inst, USSR Min of Health); 1935-39 founder-dir, 1939-50 sci dir, State Inst of Veterinary Dermatology; read papers at numerous All-Union and int med congresses; bd member and hon member, All-Union Dermatological Soc; hon member and dep chm, Moscow Soc of Dermatologists; co-ed, journal *Sovetskaya meditsina* etc; member, various commissions, USSR Min of Health; developed method of treating scabies with solutions of hyposulphate and hydrochloric acid which became known abroad as the "Russian method"; also did research on the physiotherapy of skin diseases and cosmetic treatment; wrote over 130 works; *Publ: Chesotka* (Scabies); *Gribovyye zabolevaniya kozhi* (Fungus Diseases of the Skin); *Ekzema* (Eczema); *Tvyordyy shankr i sifilidy* (Hard Chancre and Syphilis), etc; *Awards*: Order of Lenin; Badge of Hon; medals; *Died*: 7 Aug 1957.

DEN, Vladimir Eduardovich (1867- ?) Econ and geographer; prof; *Born*: 1867; *Career*: from 1898 assoc prof, Moscow Univ; from 1902 prof of econ geography, Petersburg Polytech Inst; his works on econ geography, which may be interpreted as reviews of the various branches of econ, are notable for their wealth of facts and figures; *Publ*: *Naseleniye Rossii do pyatoy revizii* (The Population of Russia Before the Fifth Census) (2 vol, 1902); *Kamennou-gol'naya i zhelezodelatel'naya promyshlennost'* (The Coal and Iron Industry) (1907); *Sel'skoye khozyaystvo* (Agriculture) (1908); *Polozheniye Rossii v mirovom khozyaystve* (Russia's Position in the World Economy) (1922); *Novaya Yevropa* (The New Europe) (1922); *Kurs ekonomicheskoy geografii* (A Course of Economic Geography) (1924); *Died*: date and place of death unknown.

DENI (real name: DENISOV), Viktor Nikolayevich (1893-1946) Graphic artist; Hon Art Worker of RSFSR from 1932; *Born*: 24 Feb 1893 in Moscow; *Educ*: studied under N. P. Ul'yanov; *Career*: from 1913 published caricatures and cartoons in satirical and theater magazines *Bich, Satirikon, Sontse Rossii, Rampa i zhizn'*, etc; during the Civil War poster-painter in Kazan', later in Moscow; after 1917 turned to soc and polit subjects; from 1921 permanent caricaturist, newspaper *Pravda*; pioneer of Sov polit propaganda poster; exerted great influence upon Sov caricaturist school; *Works*: posters "Capital" (1919); "Constituent Assembly" (1919); "At the Grave of the Counter-Revolution" (1920); "To Moscow! Hurrah! From Moscow: Ouch!" (1941); "Kill the Fascist Savages!" (1942); "Our Day Has Come" (1943), etc; caricatures and cartoons "A Ghost Roams Europe" (1924); *K. Kautskiy's 'Marksism'* (1925); "The Face of Fascism" (1927); "Stalin's Pipe" (1930); "Two Lines" (1931); "They Stride Towards Their Death" (1937), etc; *Died*: 3 Aug 1946.

DENIKIN, Anton Ivanovich (1872-1947) Mil commander; lt gen, Russian Army; leader of White opposition during Civil War; mil author; *Born*: 4 Dec 1872 in Wloclawsk, Warsaw Province, son of border-guard major who rose trough the ranks and an impoverished Polish noblewoman; *Educ*: 1892 grad Kiev Cadet College; 1899 grad Gen Staff Acad; *Pos*: 1892-95 junior artillery officer; 1902-04 command and staff work with infantry and cavalry units; 1904-05, during Russo-Japanese War, chief of staff, 3rd Trans-Amur Brigade, Transbaykal and Ural-Transbaykal Cossack Div in Far East; 1905-14 cavalry corps staff officer, chief of staff of a reserve brigade in Saratov, commander, 17th Arkhangel'sk Infantry Regt in Zhitomir and commissions gen, Kiev Mil Distr; 1914-17 quartermastergen, 8th Army; commander, 4th Iron Rifle Brigade, 4th Iron Rifle Div, 8th Army Corps; 1917 chief of staff to Supreme Commander in Chief, and commander in chief, Western and Southwestern fronts; *Career*: 1914 from outbreak of WW 1 supervised mobilization and establishment of staffs of 3rd and 8th Armies and other units on Southwestern Front; 1914-15 his 4th Iron Rifle Brigade (subsequently expanded into the 4th Iron Rifle Div), which served as a permanent reserve for the 8th Army, displayed great tenacity in fighting in Galicia and the Carpathians; Aug 1917 supported Gen Kornilov in the latters' attempt to restore order in Petrograd but was arrested along with Kornilov by Provisional Govt and interned in Bykhov Prison; 19 Sept 1917 freed by Gen Dukhonin and made his way to the Don, where in 1918, together with Gen Alekseyev and Gen Kornilov, he formed the Volunteer Army to fight against the Soviets; Apr 1918, after death of Kornilov, took command of Volunteer Army; soon became commander in chief of anti-Sov forces in Southern Russia; summer-fall 1918, with the help of the Entente, launched a largescale offensive against the Red Army and captured the Northern Caucasus; 1919 captured the Donbas, the Ukr and centr Russia as far as the line Tsaritsyn-Voronezh-Orel; failed to understand the social motives of the Civil War and proclaimed the ideal of a "united and indivisible Russia" without offering a positive political program; permitted efforts to restore the monarchy in the rear and thus failed to gain pop support; Oct 1919 suffered defeats near Voronezh and Orel, retreated south and consolidated forces in Crimea; March 1920 after transferring remainder of his troops from Novorossiysk to Crimea, handed over command to Gen Wrangel and emigrated; *Publ: Ocherki russkoy smuty* (Studies of Russian Strife) (4vol, 1920-25); *Put' russkogo ofitsera* (The Career of a Russian Officer) (1953); *Died*: 7 Aug 1947 in USA.

DENISOV, Vasiliy Ivanovich (1880-1944) Ivory and bone carver; *Born*: 1880; *Career*: helped found the Tobol'sk bone carving assoc; numerous carvings realistically reflecting the way of life of northern peoples; frequently exhibited his carvings in Russia and abroad; some of his works are in Museum of Moscow Inst of Arts Ind; active in training young bone carvers; *Works*: "The Trading Station of the Northern Seaway Administration" (1935); "Reindeer in Harness" (1936); "The Dispensary"; "Elections in the Tundra" (1938), etc; *Awards*: gold medal at the 1937 Paris Exhibition; *Died*: 1944.

DEPP, Georgiy Filippovich (1854-1921) Thermal eng; *Born*: 29 Nov 1854; *Educ*: 1881 grad Petersburg Technol Inst; *Career*: from 1899 prof, Petersburg Technol Inst; lectured on steam boilers; founded Boiler Laboratory and supervised its research on the combustion of powdery fuel, smokeless combustion, the calculation of boiler burners, etc; pioneered production of Russia's first compression-ignition internal combustion engines; chm, 2nd (Mech) Dept, Russian Eng Soc; *Publ: Parovyye kotly* (Steam Boilers) (1902-03); *Parovyye mashiny* (Steam Machinery) (2nd ed, 1899); *Bezdymnoye sozhiganiye topliva v topkakh parovykh kotlov* (The Smokeless Combustion of Fuel in the Burners of Steam Boilers) (1895); *Died*: 17 Mar 1921.

DERATANI, Nikolay Fyodorovich (1884-1958) Philologist; historian of ancient lit; prof; Hon Sci Worker of RSFSR; CP member from 1940; *Born*: 5 Mar 1884 in Moscow; *Educ*: grad Philology Fac, Moscow Univ; *Career*: prof, Moscow State Univ and Moscow Lenin Teachers' Training Inst; wrote on the lit of ancient Rome; on Vergil, Lucretius and vulgar Latin; ed, *Khrestomatiya po antichnoy literature. T.2: Rimskaya literatura* (Anthology of Ancient Literature. Vol 2: Roman Literature) (1935); *Publ*: "Rhetoric in Ovid's Early Works" (1916), in Latin; "Quintilian's Orations" (1929), in French; *Vergiliy i Avgust. K voprosu o probleme vlasti i o patrioticheskikh ideyakh v Rime, 1 v. do n. e.* (Vergil and Augustus. The Regime and Patriotic Ideas in Rome in the 1st Century B. C.) (1946); coauthor, *Aristofan. Sbornik statey* (Aristophanes. Collection of Articles) (1956); *Died*: 13 Jan 1958 in Moscow.

DERBYSHEV, Nikolay Ivanovich (1879-1955) Party and govt official; CP member from 1896; *Born*: 22 Mar 1879 in Tomsk, son of a leatherworker; *Educ*: grad municipal college; *Career*: worked as type-setter mechanic; 1896 in Tomsk joined org of Siberian Soc-Democratic Union; member, Tomsk RSDRP Comt; from 1901 member Omsk RSDRP Comt; from 1905 member, Ural Oblast RSDRP Comt; from 1907 Party work in Petersburg; member, Vasiliy Ostrov Rayon RSDRP Comt, Petersburg; 1900, 1902, 1906 arrested and imprisoned or exiled for revol activities; after 1917 Feb Revol chm, Centr Council of Factory and Plant Comts, Petrograd; Ural Oblast Party Org deleg at 6th RSDRP(B) Congress; after 1917 Oct Revol Pop Comr of the Press; Nov 1917 ousted from Council of Pop Comr along with V. Nogin, A. Rykov, etc, for disagreeing with Party line; secr, Petrograd Trade-Union Bureau; 1920 dep chm, Northern Region Sovnarkhoz, then head, Main Admin of Polygraphic Ind; 1921-26 chm, Press Workers' Union; 1922-24 member, All-Russian Centr Exec Comt and USSR Centr Exec Comt; from 1927 admin work; then pensioner; *Died*: 13 Feb 1955.

DERIBAS, Terentiy Dmitriyevich (? -?) Govt official; comr of state security, 1st class; CP member from 1903; *Career*: 1903 exchanged school bench for revol circle organized by Bolsheviks in Kremenchug at Gebgol'd Plant and Durunchi Factory; 1904 arrested but escaped, went underground and worked in joiner's shop; again arrested for membership in RSDRP(B) and deported to Tobol'sk Province; again escaped; during Civil War in Red Army as head, div polit dept, 3rd Army; later head, Polit Dept, 5th Army; from 1920 operational work for All-Union Cheka, then for State Polit Admin and OGPU; from 1930 OGPU plen; from 1934 NKVD chief in Far Eastern Kray; elected member, USSR Centr Exec Comt of 7th convocation; from 1934 cand member, CC, RCP(B); arrested by State Security organs; *Awards*: two Orders of the Red Banner; *Died*: date and place of death unknown.

DERMAN, Abram Borisovich (1880-1952) Russian lit historian and theater expert; *Born*: 2 Nov 1880 in vil Lisichansk, Bakhmut

Uyezd, Yekaterinoslav Province; *Educ*: grad mining college; 1918 grad Law Fac, Moscow Univ; *Career*: head miner, Donets Basin coal mines; 1903 began writing fiction; from 1912 lit critic; main works on A. P. Chekhov, V. G. Korolenko and actor M. S. Shchepkin; also articles on Lev Tolstoy, Sholom-Aleichem, Gorky, Bunin, Kuprin, Shmelyov and A. N. Tolstoy, etc; ed, *Perepiska A. P. Chekhova i O. L. Knipper* (Correspondence of A. P. Chekhov and O. L. Knipper) (1934-36); edited various publ of Chekhov's and Korolenko's works; *Publ: Strannyy vopros* (A Strange Question) (1903); *Akademicheskiy intsident* (Academic Incident) (1923); *Pisateli iz naroda i V. G. Korolenko* (Writers of the People and V. G. Korolenko) (1924); *Tvorcheskiy portret Chekhova* (Creative Image of Chekhov) (1929); *Mikhail Semyonovich Shchepkin* (1937); *Anton Pavlovich Chekhov* (1939); novel *Delo ob igumene Parfenii* (The Case of Father-Superior Parfeniy) (1941); *Zhizn' V. G. Korolenko* (Life of V. G. Korolenko) (1946); *Moskva v zhizni i tvorchestve A. P. Chekhova* (Moscow in A. P. Chekhov's Life and Works) (1948); *Moskovskogo Malogo teatra artist Shchepkin* (Shchepkin, Actor of the Moscow Maly Theater) (1951); *O masterstve Chekhova* (Chekhov's Craftmanship) (1959); *Died*: 3 Aug 1952 in Moscow.

DERMANIS, Vilis (1875-1938) Revolutionary, publicist and critic; CP member from 1922; *Born*: 28 May 1875 in vil Bukashi, Lat, son of a peasant; *Educ*: 1897 grad teachers' seminary, Kuldiga; *Career*: worked as teacher and helped found the first Marxist circles in Lat; 1902-03 member, CC and Riga Comt, Baltic Lat Soc-Democratic Workers' org; 1904-07 Party posts in Riga, Saratov and Petersburg; took part in 1905-07 Revol; 1907 sentenced to hard labor; 1914 escaped to USA; 1920 returned to Lat; from 1919 contributed to Communist publ; 1920-21 represented Lat Soc-Democratic Party in Constituent Assembly and Riga City Duma; helped to organize Lat trade unions; represented his Party as deleg to Stockholm and London RSDRP Congresses; 1922 arrested for Communist activities and deported to RSFSR; 1923-38 lecturer at Moscow higher educ establishments, Communist Univ of Western Peoples and at an Ind Teachers' Training Inst; early 1920's began to work as lit critic; arrested by State Security organs; *Publ*: "An Outline of Gorky's Life and Work) (1901); "Original Latvian Drama" (1904); "Types of Intellectuals Depicted by A. Niedras" (1902); coauthor, "What Does A. Niedras Advocate? " (1905); articles "The Contemporary Proletariat and Art" (1913); "Revolution and Art" (1929), etc; *Died*: 1938 in imprisonment; posthumously rehabilitated.

DERUNOV, Konstantin Nikolayevich (1866-1929) Bibliographer and librarian; *Born*: 13 June 1866; *Educ*: studied at Petersburg Univ; expelled for involvement in populist revol movement; *Career*: 1898 began career as librarian; worked at library of Min of Finance; after 1917 Oct Revol worked at library of USSR Pop Comrt of Finance; toward end of life head librarian, Russian Assoc of Soc Sci Research Inst; his major work was a bibliography of Russian reviews in 325 Russian periodicals from 1850 to 1928 (some 300,000 titles in his unpublished card index); *Publ: Primernyy bibliotechnyy katalog. Svod luchshikh knig na russkom yazyke s 60-kh godov po 1905* (A Model Library Catalog. A List of the Best Books Published in Russian from the 1860's Through 1905) (2 vol, 1906); *Zhiznennyye zadachi bibliografii* (The Vital Tasks of Bibliography) (1913); *Tipichnyye cherty v evolyutsii russkoy 'obshchestvennoy' biblioteki* (Typical Features of the Evolution of the Russian "Public" Library) (1924); *Tipichnyye cherty v evolyutsii russkikh tsentral'nykh gosudarstvennykh knigo-khranilishch* (Typical Features of the Evolution of the Russian Central State Book Depositories) (1926); *Died*: 29 July 1929.

DERYABINA, Serafima Ivanovna (pseudonym: IVANOVA, Nina /Antonina/ Vyacheslavovna; Party pseudonym: SIMA, Yelena) (1888-1920) Revolutionary; CP member from 1904; *Born*: 1888 in Yekaterinburg; *Career*: 1907 secr, Yekaterinburg RSDRP Org; frequently arrested and exiled; did Party work in Rostov-on-Don, Moscow, Tula, Petersburg and Samara;1913 took part in "summer" conference of CC, RSDRP and Party workers; 1914 member, Exec Commission, Petrograd RSDRP Comt; after 1917 Feb Revol member, Samara Province RSDRP(B) Comt and Samara Sov; 1918 after capture of Samara by White Army arrested and sent to Siberia, whence she escaped; Mar 1919 elected member, Ural-Siberian Bureau, CC, RCP(B) at 2nd All-Russian Conference of Underground Bolshevik Org; underground Party work in Urals, was arrested and freed after the Red Army occupied Yekaterinburg; member, Org Bureau, Yekaterinburg RCP(B) Comt; 1919 elected member, All-Russian Centr Exec Comt at 7th All-Russian Congress of Soviets; *Died*: 1920 of tuberculosis.

DERYUGIN, Konstantin Mikhaylovich (1878-1938) Zoologist; Dr of Zoology from 1915; *Born*: 7 Feb 1878 in Pskov Province; *Educ*: 1900 grad Physics and Mathematics Fac, Petersburg Univ; *Career*: from 1919 prof, Leningrad Univ; studied hydrology and fauna of the Kola Bay, White Sea, Gulf of Finland, Neva Inlet and dried-up Lake Mogil'noye; directed establishment of marine research stations on the White Sea and Pacific littoral; worked out methods for comprehensive study of reservoirs and bio-geographical analysis of fauna as a basis for understanding the evolution of the sea and the genesis of its fauna; discovered internal waves in the Gulf of Finland and Neva Inlet and catalogued zones; directed compilation of a register of USSR water and a manual on USSR seas; initiated and edited publ of the series *Issledovaniya morey SSSR* (Studies of the Seas of the USSR) (25 vol); *Publ: Fauna Kol'skogo zaliva i usloviya yeyo sushchestvovaniya* (Fauna of the Kola Bay and Its Environment) (1915); *Gidrologiya i bentos Nevskoy guby* (Hydrology and Benthos of the Neva Inlet) (1923); *Barentsovo more po Kol'skomu meredianu* (The Barents Sea Along the Kola Meridian) (1924); *Novyye dannyye o perelyote ptits* (New Data on the Migration of Birds) (1924); *Gidrologiya i bentos vostochnoy chasti Finskogo zaliva* (Hydrology and Benthos of the Eastern Gulf of Finland) (1925); *Reliktovoye ozero Mogil'noye* (Residual Lake Mogil'noye) (1925); *Issledovaniya Barentsova i Belogo morey i Novoy zemli* (Studies of the Barents and White Seas and of Novaya Zemlya) (1925); coauthor, *Issledovaniye morey SSSR* (Studies of the Seas of the USSR) (No. 7-9, 1927-28); *Died*: 27 Dec 1938.

DERZHAVIN, Konstantin Nikolayevich (1903-1956) Russian lit critic and translator; theater critic; prof of Leningrad Univ; corresp member, Bulgarian Acad of Sci from 1946; *Born*: 18 Feb 1903 in Batumi, son of the famous historian N. S. Derzhavin; *Educ*: 1924 grad Leningrad Univ; *Career*: 1918-20 actor at Pop Comedy Theater; secr, Collegium, RSFSR Pop Comrt of Educ; 1921-22 stage dir, Ligova Drama Theater and New Drama Theater; repertoire manager, Acad Drama Theater; worked at State Theater, Music and Cinematography Research Inst; active at the Inst of Russian Lit and the Slavic Inst, USSR Acad of Sci; 1945-46 lectured at Sofia Univ, Bulgaria; did research on history of lit and theater of France, Spain and Slavic countries; wrote screenplay for *Iudushka Golovlev* and libretto for ballet *Gayane*; translated from Spanish novelette "La Vida de Lasarillo de Tormes" (1931; 2nd ed 1955) and F. Quevedo y Villegas' novel "Historia y Vida del Buscon" (1950); *Publ: Teatr Frantsuzskoy revolyutsii 1789-99* (The Theater of the French Revolution 1789-99) (1932); *Epokhi Aleksandrinskoy stseny* (The Epochs of the Alexandrine Stage) (1932); *Servantes i 'Don Kikhot'* (Cervantes and "Don Quixote") (1933; 2nd ed 1934); *Ye. P. Korchagina-Aleksandrovskaya* (1937); *Vol'ter* (Voltaire) (1946); *V. A. Michurina-Samoylova* (1948); *A. N. Ostrovskiy* (1950); *Bolgarskiy teatr. Ocherk istorii* (The Bulgarian Theater. An Outline of Its History) (1950); *Ivan Vazov* (1951); *Servantes. Zhizn' i tvorchestvo* (Cervantes. His Life and Work) (1958), etc; *Died*: 2 Nov 1956 in Leningrad.

DERZHAVIN, Mikhail Stepanovich (1903-1951) Actor; Pop Artiste of RSFSR from 1946; *Born*: 25 July 1903; *Educ*: 1928 grad Vakhtangov Theater Studio; *Career*: worked at a steel plant; 1928 joined Vakhtangov Theater; *Roles*: Kutuzov in Solov'yov's *Fel'dmarshal Kutuzov* (Fieldmarshal Kutuzov); Yegor Bulychyov in Gorky's *Yegor Bulychyov i drugiye* (Yegor Bulychyov and Co); Kirov in Kremlyov's *Krepost' na Volge* (The Fort on the Volga); Bos'n Shvats in *Razlom* (Break-Up); Dudykin in Pogodin's *Temp* (Tempo); Ragnau in Edmond de Rostand's"Cyrano de Bergerac"; Tikhon in *Groza* (The Storm); film roles: Vels in *Sem'ya Opengeym* (The Oppenheim Family); Zimin in *Paren' iz taygi* (The Lad from the Taiga); Pyotr in *Delo Artamonovykh* (The Artamonov Case); Gen Murav'yov in *Velikiy perelom* (The Great Change), etc; *Awards*: Stalin Prize (1946); *Died*: 30 July 1951.

DERZHAVIN, Nikolay Sevast'yanovich (1877-1953) Slavist and lit historian; Dr of History; prof; member, USSR Acad of Sci from 1931; hon member, Bel Acad of Sci and Bulgarian Acad of Sci from 1946; CP member from 1945; *Born*: 15 Dec 1877 in vil Preslav, now Zaporozh'ye Oblast; son of a teacher; *Educ*: 1896 grad high school in Simferopol'; 1896-1900 studied at Fac of History and Philology, Petersburg Univ and Nezhin Inst of History and Philology; *Career*: 1900-07 taught at high schools a in Batumi and Tiflis; 1912-17 assoc prof, from 1917 prof, Chair of Slavic Studies, Petersburg Univ; 1922-25 rector, 1925-53 head, Chair of Slavic Philology, Leningrad Univ; simultaneously dir, Inst of Occidental and Oriental Lit and Language, then State Inst of Spoken Language; 1931-34 dir, Inst of Slavic Studies, USSR Acad of Sci; 1947-53 head, Leningrad Group, Inst of Slavic Studies, USSR Acad of Sci; from 1942 chm, Anti-Fascist Comt of Sov Scholars; 1942-47 member, Pan-Slavic Comt; 1947-53 member, USSR Slavic Comt; wrote over 500 works on Slavic philology, the history of the Slavic peoples (notably the Bulgarians), gen linguistics, and Russian language and lit; 1952 accused of being influenced by N.Ya. Marr's views on Slavic ethnogenesis and forced to make public admission of "errors"; 1929 attended Congress of Philologists in Prague; 1933 attended 5th Int Congress of Historical Sci in Warsaw; *Publ: Bolgarskiye kolonii v Rossii* (Bulgarian Colonies in Russia) (2 vol, 1914-15); *Osnovnyye metodiki prepodavaniya russkogo yazyka i literatury v sredney shkole* (Basic Methods of Teaching Russian Language and Literature at Secondary Schools) (1917); *Uchebnik russkoy grammatiki. Opyt nauchno-elementarnogo kursa* (A Textbook of Russian Grammar. An Experimental Scientific Elementary Course) (1918); *T.G.Shevchenko* (1921); *Tvorchestvo T.G.Shevchenko v yego istoricheskom i ideologicheskom okruzhenii* (The Works of T.G.Shevchenko in Their Historical and Ideological Context) (1932); *A.Konstantinov* (1935); *Sbornik statey i issledovaniy v oblasti slavyanskoy filologii* (Collected Articles and Papers on Slavic Philology) (1941); *Proiskhozhdeniye russkogo naroda - Velikorusskogo, ukrainskogo i belorusskogo* (The Origin of the Russian People - The Great Russians, the Ukrainians and the Belorussians) (1944); *Plemennyye i kul'turnyye svyazi bolgarskogo i russkogo naroda* (Tribal and Cultural Links Between the Bulgarian and Russian Peoples) (1944); *Istoriya Bolgarii* (A History of Bulgaria) (4 vol, 1945-48); *Slavyane v drevnosti* (The Slavs in Antiquity) (1946); *Khristo Botev - poet-revolyutsioner* (Khristo Botev - Poet and Revolutionary) (1948); *Ivan Bazov. Zhizn' i tvorchestvo* (Ivan Bazov. Life and Works) (1948); *Awards*: Stalin Prize (1948); two Orders of Lenin; Order of Alexander (Bulgarian) (1946); *Died*: 26 Feb 1953 in Leningrad.

DERZHINSKAYA, Kseniya Georgiyevna (1889-1951) Russian opera singer (soprano); Pop Artiste of USSR from 1937; *Born*: 25 Jan 1889 in Kiev, daughter of a teacher; *Educ*: studied singing under Ye. I. Terian-Korganova in Petersburg; *Career*: 1913-14 with Sergiyevskiy Pop Center Opera Company in Moscow; 1915-48 with Bolshoy Theater; 1926 performed in Paris; from 1947 prof, Moscow Conservatory; *Roles*: Liza, Mariya and Nastas'ya in Tchaikovsky's *Pikovaya dama* (The Queen of Spades), *Mazeppa* and *Charodeyka* (The Sorceress); Yaroslavna in Borodin's *Knyaz' Igor'* (Prince Igor'); Brunhild in Wagner's "Walküre"; Margarethe in Gounod's "Faust" etc; *Awards*: Stalin Prize (1943); Order of Lenin; Order of the Red Banner of Labor; medals; *Died*: 9 June 1951 in Moscow.

DESNITSKIY (pseudonym: STROYEV), Vasiliy Alekseyevich (1878-1958) Lit critic and pedag; prof; Hon Sci Worker of RSFSR from 1957; *Born*: 11 Feb 1878 in vil Pokrov, Nizhniy Novgorod Province; *Educ*: studied at Nizhniy Novgorod Theological Seminary and at Fac of History and Philology and Law Fac, Yur'yev Univ; *Career*: 1897 joined Soc-Democratic movement in Sormovo and Nizhniy Novgorod; 1903 joined Bolshevik faction; 1903-08 attended RSDRP congresses and was elected to CC; ed, newspaper *Vperyod*; 1905-06 ed, anthology *Tekushchiy moment*; 1909 co-founder and instructor, RSDRP(B) school on Capri; withdrew from Party work; until 1917 taught in Yur'yev; from Apr 1917 member, CC, Soc-Democratic Internationalist Party; co-founder and ed, newspaper *Novaya zhizn'*; Nov 1917-Mar 1918 Soc-Democratic Internationalist Party rep in All-Russian Centr Exec Comt; 1919 abandoned politics; 1919-58 taught and did research at Herzen Teachers' Training Inst, Leningrad, Leningrad Univ, the Communist Univ and the Inst of Russian Lit, USSR Acad of Sci; prof, dept head and senior assoc, Leningrad Inst of Sci Pedag; specialized in the history and theory of lit; pioneer of research on Gorky; together with S. D. Balukhatyy organized Gorky Commission at Inst of Russian Lit, USSR Acad of Sci; ed, series *M. A. Gor'kiy. Materialy i issledovaniya* (M. A. Gorky. Material and Research); *Publ: M. Gor'kiy* (1919); *Vvedeniye v izucheniye iskusstva i literatury* (An Introduction to the Study of Art and Literature) (1926); *O predelakh spetsifikatsii v literaturnoy nauke* (The Limits of Specification in Literary Science) (1930); *'Myortvyye dushi' Gogolya kak poema dvoryanskogo vozrozhdeniya* (Gogol's "Dead Souls" as a Poem of the Rebirth of the Nobility) (1931); *Teoriya iskusstva dlya iskusstva v esteticheskoy sisteme G. V. Plekhannova* (The Theory of Art for Art's Sake in G. V. Plekhanov's Esthetic System) (1932); *V. I. Lenin i nauka o literature* (V. I. Lenin and the Science of Literature) (1933); *O zadachakh izucheniya russkoy literatury XVIII veka* (The Tasks of the Study of 18th-Century Russian Literature) (1933); *Na literaturnyye temy* (On Literary Themes) (2 vol, 1933-36); *V. I. Lenin i M. Gor'kiy* (V. I. Lenin and M. Gorky) (1934); *M. Gor'kiy nizhegorodskikh let* (Gorky's Years in Nizhniy Novgorod) (1935); *O realizme Gogolya* (Gogol's Realism) (1935); *Yeshchyo raz k voprosu ob izuchenii literatury XVIII veka* (More About the Study of 18th-Century Literature) (1935); *Marks i khudozhestvennaya literatura* (Marx and Fiction) (1936); *Zadachi izucheniya zhizni i tvorchestva Gogolya* (Tasks of the Study of Gogol's Life and Work) (1936); *M. Gor'kiy na Kapri* (Gorky on Capri) (1938); *Reforma Petra I i russkaya literatura XVIII veka* (The Reform of Peter I and 18th-Century Russian Literature) (1941); *Izbrannyye stat'i po russkoy literature XVIII-XIX vekov* (Selected Articles on 18th and 19th-Century Russian Literature) (1958); *Gor'kiy. Ocherki zhizni i tvorchestva* (Gorky. A Study of His Life and Works) (1959); *Died*: 22 Sept 1958 in Leningrad.

DESNYAK, A. (real name: RUDENKO, Aleksey Ignat'yevich (1909-1942) Ukr writer; CP member from 1939; *Born*: 17 Mar 1909 in vil Bondarovka, now Chernigov Oblast; *Educ*: 1931 grad Chernigov Inst of Public Educ; *Career*: 1928 first work printed; 1940 head, L'vov Branch, Sov Writers' Union; *Publ*: novel *Desnu pereshli batal'ony* (The Battalions Cross the Desna) (1937); novelette *Polk Timofeya Chernyaka* (Timofey Chernyak's Regiment) (1938); novel *Uday-reka* (The Uday River) (1938); *Turgayskiy sokol* (The Turgay Falcon) (1940); *Begstvo* (Escape), *Mat'* (Mother) and *Znamya* (The Banner) (1941-42); *Died*: 25 May 1942 killed in action near vil Pavlovka Vtoraya, Khar'kov Oblast.

DEVLET, Vladimir Pavlovich (1890-1958) Opera singer (baritone); singing teacher; Pop Artiste of Uzbek SSR from 1945; *Born*: 1890; *Educ*: studied singing in Kiev under Bedyayeva-Tarasevich; *Career*: 1918 opera debut in Kiev; 1920-35 at opera theaters in Odessa, Tbilisi, Sverdlobsk, Vladivostok, etc; 1936-49 soloist, Navoi Opera and Ballet Theater, Tashkent; from 1938 taught at Tashkent Conservatory; *Roles*: Yevgeniy Onegin; Mazepa; Yeletskiy; Igor; Demon; Rigoletto; German; Tonio; Escamiglio; Kachura in Chishko's *Bronenosets Potyomkin* (The Battleship Potyomkin), etc; *Died*: 1958.

DEYCH (YEVGEN'YEV), Lev Grigor'yevich (1855-1941) Politician; Populist, then Soc-Democrat; *Born*: 26 Sept 1855 in settlement Tul'chino, Kamenets-Podol'sk Province, son of a merchant; *Educ*: studied at Kiev high school; *Career*: 1874-75 began revol work as member, Populist movement; 1877 helped organize peasant revolt in Chigirin Uyezd, Kiev Province; 1879 in Petersburg joined Populist org *Zemlya i volya* (Land and Freedom); after its break-up joined *Chyornyy peredel* (Land Distribution) movement; repeatedly arrested and imprisoned; 1880 emigrated abroad; 1883 together with G. V. Plekhanov, J. B. Aksel'rod, V. I. Zasulich, etc; founded first Russian Marxist group *Osvobozhdeniye truda* (Liberation of Labor); founded printing-house in Geneva, organized printing and illegal trans of revol lit into Russia; 1884 in Germany arrested and extradited to tsarist authorities; sentenced by Odessa mil court to 13 years' penal labor and exiled to Eastern Siberia; 1901 escaped from Blagoveshchensk, fled abroad and joined *Iskra* (The Spark) group in Munich; co-opted into admin, For League of Russian Revol Soc-Democrats; helped edit and distribute *Iskras* and *Zarya*; member, For Bureauk, Org Comt for Convocation of 2nd RSDRP Congress (1903); Congress deleg from *Osvobozhdeniye truda* (Liberation of Labor) group; joined Soc-Democrats (Mensheviks); late 1905 illegally returned to Russia; 1906 in Petersburg arrested and exiled to Turukhan Kray; on the way there escaped to Petersburg and later to Terioki; 1907-11 in London; 1907 non-voting deleg, 5th RSDRP Congress in London; attended 1907 Stuttgart Int Socialist Congress; 1911-16 in USA; 1913-16 in New York ed, periodical *Svobodnoye slovo*; after 1917 Feb Revol returned to Petrograd, joined rightist Menshevik defensists; ed, Menshevik newspaper *Yedinstvo*; after 1917 Oct Revol abandoned politics; edited G. V. Plekhanov's lit legacy; edited six issues of *Gruppa osvobozhdeniya truda. Iz arkhivov G. V. Plekhanova, V. I. Zasulich i L. G. Deycha*

(Liberation of Labor Group. From the Archives of G. V. Plekhanov, V. I. Zasulich and L. G. Deych) (1923-28); from 1928 pensioner; *Publ: 16 let v Sibiri* (16 Years in Siberia) (3rd ed, 1924); *Chetyre pobega* (Four Escapes) (2nd ed, 1926); *G. V. Plekhanov. Materialy dlya biografii* (G. V. Plekhanov. Biographical Materials) (1922); memoirs and a number of articles on history of Russian liberation movement; *Died*: 4 Aug 1941.

DEYEV-KHOMYAKOVSKIY (real name: DEYEV), Grigoriy Dmitriyevich (1888-1946) Russian poet; CP member from 1918; *Born*: 6 Feb 1888 in vil Khomyakovka, Kaluga Province, son of a peasant; *Educ*: 1906 qualified as uyezd teacher; *Career*: in his youth worked as shepherd; moved to Moscow and worked as cobbler, baker and mailman; from 1909 teacher; 1907 first work printed; from 1908 assoc, then chm, Surikov Lit and Music Circle (1921 merged into All-Russian Soc of Peasant Writers); 1912 founded *Druzhba* (Friendship) Cooperative Publ House, whose members in 1915-16 published journal *Drug naroda*; 1922-27 chm, All-Russian Soc of Peasant Writers; 1928 abandoned lit work and returned to teaching; compiled four collections of revol and folk songs; *Publ*: verse collections: *Mashina bashnya* (The Tower Machine) (1911); *Zor'ka* (First Light) (1917); *Borozdy* (Furrows) (1919); *Kudel'* (Tow) (1926); play *Molodel'* (1924), etc; *Died*: 1946.

DIATROPTOV, Pyotr Nikolayevich (1860-1934) Hygienist and microbiologist; pioneer of Russian hygiene and bacteriology; Hon Sci Worker of RSFSR from 1928; *Born*: 2 Jan 1860; *Educ*: 1883 completed advanced med training; *Career*: 1884-89 health officer, Yelizavetgrad Uyezd, Kherson Province; specialized in microbiology under I.I. Mechnikov at Pasteur Inst, Paris, and under F. F. Erisman; 1889 health officer, Odessa; 1892-1907 head, first Russian bacteriological station, Odessa; during this period did major research on methods of combatting cholera and plague; launched vaccination campaign, produced diphtheria and other sera and made bacteriological checks on mains water; 1910-25 prof, Chair of Public (later Gen) Hygiene, Moscow Higher Women's Courses; (2nd Moscow State Univ); helped to organize municipal health service; bd member, Pirogov Soc; ed, journal *Obshchestvennyy vrach*; co-founder and member, Learned Med Council, USSR Pop Comrt of Health; co-founder, State Public Health Inst and Sanitation and Hygiene Inst, Pop Comrt of Health; 1918-28 co-chm, from 1928 chm, Learned Med Council, USSR Pop Comrt of Health; 1928-31 dir, State Inst of Therapy and Vaccine and Serum Control; did research on cholera, diphtheria, Siberian plague and bubonic plague; proved that cholera vibrios of different origin do not have the same pathogenic effect on animals; wrote over 50 works, including a hygiene textbook for secondary schools; co-ed, hygiene and bacteriology section, *Publ:* "BME (Large Medical Encyclopedia); *Publ: O chume* (Plague) (1897); *O neobkhodimosti postoyannogo nadzora v vodoprovodnom dele* (The Need for Constant Supervision of Water Supplies) (1899); *Obzor zabolevaniya chumoy na poberezh'ye Sredizemnogo morya i v portovykh gorodakh Yevropy v 1900-01 godakh* (A Survey of the Incidence of Plague on the Mediterranean Littoral and in the Ports of Europe in 1900-01) (1901); *O nositelyakh zarazy* (Carriers of Infection) (1910); coauthor, *Meditsinskaya mikrobilogiya* (Medical Microbiology) (1912-13); *Nachal'nyy kurs gigieny* (An Initial Hygiene Course) (1913-15); *Died*: 25 Feb 1934.

DICHENKO, Mikhail Petrovich (1863-1932) Astronomer; specialist in astrometry and theoretical astronomy; *Born*: 27 Jan 1863 in vil Budaivka, now Boyarka, Kiev Oblast; *Educ*: 1891 grad Kiev Univ; *Career*: 1891-98 astronomer, Pulkovo Observatory, where he determined the positions of 125 near-polar stars on the meridian circle; from 1898 astronomer-observer, Kiev Observatory; from 34 years' observation of stars on the meridian circle compiled a catalogue of Zodiacal stars; studied motion of the sun by re-observing stars in the zone of Argelander; *Publ: Argelanderi DLX stellarum fixarum positiones. Mouvement propre du Soleil* (1914); "A Catalogue of 640 Zodiacal Stars" (1933); *Died*: 4 Dec 1932.

DIDRIK, Karl Genrikhovich (1897-1955) Pharmacist; *Born*: 1897 in Est, son of a peasant; *Educ*: 1918 qualified as pharmacy asst at Petrograd Mil Med Acad; 1935 grad Leningrad Pharmaceutical Inst; *Career*: 1914-16 pharmacy apprentice; 1916-18 served in Tsarist Army; 1918-35 worked for Leningrad Pharmacy Bd; 1935-55 founder-head, Leningrad Pharmacy Laboratory, State Pharmacy Bd, which became a major center of drug control, pharmacy org and advanced pharmaceutical training; 1951-55 co-founder and dep chm, Leningrad Pharmaceutical Soc; contributed to information releases published by the Leningrad City Dept, RSFSR Main Pharmacy Bd; wrote a number of articles on various aspects of pharmacy; *Awards*: Order of Lenin; Leningrad Defense Medal; medal "For Valiant Labor During the Great Fatherland War"; "Distinguished Health Worker's" Badge; *Died*: 1955 in Leningrad.

DIDZHYULIS, Karolis (1894-1958) Lawyer; chm, Lith Supr Court from 1947; CP member from 1919; *Born*: 20 July 1894; *Educ*: 1923-25 studied at Communist Univ of Nat Minorities of the West, Moscow; *Career*: from 1919 Party work in Lith; arrested for polit activities; from 1940 dep chm, Presidium, Lith Supr Sov; dep, USSR Supr Sov of 1950 convocation; dep, Lith Supr Sov; member, CC, CP Lith; *Awards*: two Orders of Lenin; two Orders of the Red Banner of Labor; *Died*: 24 May 1958.

DIGMELOV, Aleksandr Davidovich (1884-1957) Cameraman; Hon Art Worker of Geo SSR; *Born*: 1884; *Career*: from 1910 film work; made short newsreels and landscape films in Tbilisi; after the establishment of Sov regime in Geo worked for Film Dept, Geo Pop Comrt of Educ; shot the first Sov historico-revol film *Arsen Dzhordzhiashvili; Works*: shot films: *Obezglavlennyy trup* (Beheaded Corpse) (1919); *Ognepoklonniki* (Fire-Worshippers); *Khristina* (1920); *Arsen Dzhordzhiashvili* (1921); *Izgnannik* (The Exile) (1922); *Krasnyye d'yavolyata* (Red Little Devils) (1923); *Razboynik Arsen* (Arsen, the Brigand) (1923); *Tri zhizni* (Three Lives) (1925); *Delo Tariela Mklavadze* (The Case of Tariel Mklavadze) (1925); *Dvunogiye* (The Bipeds) (1926); *Nakazaniye* (Punishment) (1926); *V tryasine* (In the Quagmire) (1927); *Molodost' pobezhdayet* (Youth Wins) (1928); *Kamera No. 79* (Room No. 79) (1930); *Posledniye krestonostsy* (The Last Crusaders) (1934); *Arsen* (1937); *U zastavy* (At the Frontier) (1940); *Devushka s togo berega* (Girl from the Other Shore) (1941); *Georgiy Saakadze* (1942-43); *Vesna v Sakene* (Spring in Saken) (1950); *Keto and Kote* (1953); *Lurdzha Magdany* (1956); etc: *Awards*: Stalin Prize (1946); *Died*: 1957.

DIK (real name: DICESCU), Ivan Osipovich (1893-1938) Leader of Rumanian workers' movement; CPSU (B) official; CP member from 1917; *Born*: May 1893 in Bucharest; son of a house-painter; *Educ*: grad Higher Business College; 1921-22 studied at Frunze Mil Acad; *Career*: 1909-16 member, Rumanian Soc-Democratic Workers' Party; 1910-12 co-ed, Soc-Democratic newspaper *Rominia muncitoare*; 1911-13 published atheist journal *Ratiune*; during WW 1 served as an ensign, was wounded and deserted from Royal Rumanian Army; Apr 1917 jouned RCP(B) in Petrograd; Nov 1917-Jan 1918 and May 1918-Apr 1919 worked for RSFSR Pop Comrt of For Affairs; Feb-May 1918 secr, Rumanian Mil-Revol Comt, Odessa; Apr 1919-Dec 1920 fought in Civil War; polit comr on Eastern, Turkestani and Southwestern fronts; helped to form int detachments of Red Army and to organize foreign CP cells and groups; met Lenin; Jan-Nov 1921 head, Balkan Section, Staff Registration Bd, Revol-Mil Council; 1922-37 teaching and research work in Moscow; wrote numerous works on statistics and building calculations; arrested by State Security organs; *Died*: Apr 1938 in imprisonment; posthumously rehabilitated.

DIKIY, Aleksey Denisovich (1889-1955) Actor and stage dir; prof; Pop Artiste of USSR from 1949; *Born*: 25 Feb 1889 in Yekaterinoslav (now Dnepropetrovsk), son of an artisan; *Educ*: S. V. Khalyutina's private theatrical school in Moscow; *Career*: 1910 stage debut at Moscow Arts Theater; from 1911 actor, First Studio, Moscow Acad Arts Theater (subsequently 2nd Moscow Arts Theater); 1912 ran amateur circle, Prechistenka Workers' Courses; 1914-17 with the army on Caucasian Front; later stage dir; from 1919 film actor; from 1928 stage dir, various theaters in Moscow and Leningrad; 1931 organized "Theater and Lit Workshop" studio, which subsequently became the nucleus of the Stalinabad Russian Theater; 1932-36 head, All-Union Centr Trade-Union Council Theater; then at Leningrad Bol'shoy Drama Theater; 1942-43 actor and stage dir, Vakhtangov Theater; 1944-52 at Maly Theater; from 1952 stage dir, Moscow Pushkin Theater; worked also as producer in Palestine; typical of his work was his liking for monumental, strikingly expressive forms; on the screen portrayed Russian mil leaders - Kutuzov and Nakhimov; frequently played Stalin; *Stage Roles*: Alyoshka in *Na dne* (The Lower Depths) (1911); Misha in Turgenev's *Provintsialka* (A Provincial Girl); the bailiff in *Zhivoy trup* (Living Corpse); Barend in Kheyermans' *Gibel' 'Nadezhdy'* (Loss of the "Nadezhda") (1913); Yepikhodov and L'vov in Chekhov's *Vishnyovyy sad* (The

Cherry-Orchard) and *Ivanov* (1917); Molchanov in Leskov's *Rastochitel'* (The Squanderer) (1924); Col Platov in Leskov's *Blokha* (The Flea) (1925); Mathias Klausen in Hauptmann's "Before the Sunset"; Ivan Gorlov in Korneychuk's *Front* (The Front) (1942), etc; *Film Roles*: Andrey in "Andrey Gudok" (1921); Kedenek in *Vosstaniye rybakov* (Mutiny of the Fishermen) (1934); Kutuzov in *Kutuzov* (1943); Nakhimov in"Admiral Nakhimov" (1947) and *Pirogov* (1947); the surgeon Vasiliy Vasil'yevich in *Povest' o nastoyashchem cheloveke* (Tale of a Real Man) (1948); Stalin in *Tretiy udar* (The Third Assault) (1948) and *Stalingradskaya bitva* (Battle of Stalingrad) (1949); *Productions*: operas: Triodin's *Stepan Razin* (1925); Prokofiev's *Lyubovk' tryom apel'sinam* (Love of Three Oranges) (1927); Glière's ballet *Krasnyy mak* (Red Poppy) (1929); produced plays; Leskov's *Blokha* (The Flea) (1925); A. M. Fayko's *Chelovek s portfelem* (Man with a Briefcase) (1928); V. V. Vishnevskiy's *Pervaya konnaya* (First Mounted Army) (1930); Leskov's *Ledi Makbet Mtsenskogo uyezda* (Lady Macbeth of Mtsensk) (1931); Cervantes' *Intermedia* (1931); V. Vol'f's *Matrosy iz Katarro* (Sailors from Katarro) (1932); Mikitenko's *Devushki nashey strany* (Girls of Our Country) (1933); Finn's *Vzdor* (Nonsense) (1933); Svetlov's *Glubokaya provintsiya* (In the Depths of the Provinces) (1935); Sukhovo-Kobylin's *Smert' Tarelkina* (Tarelkin's Death) (1936); *Pushkinskiy spektakl'* (Pushkin Matinee) (1936); *Meshchane* (Philistines) (1937, 1946); Kirshon's *Bol'shoy den'* (The Big Day) (1937); A. V. Sofronov's *Moskovskiy kharakter* (Moscow Character) (1948); A. Ye. Korneychuk's *Kalinovaya roshcha* (Viburnum Grove); Saltykov–Shchedrin's *Teni* (The Shadows) (1953), etc; *Publ:* numerous articles in newspapers and periodicals; book *Povest' o teatral'noy yunosti* (Tale of Theater Youth) (1957); *Awards*: Order of Lenin; Order of the Red Banner of Labor; medals; prize at the 1947 Int Film Festival in Venice; five Stalin prizes (1946, 1947, 1949 /twice/ and 1950); *Died*: 1 Oct 1955.

DIKOVSKAYA (YAKIMOVA), Anna Vasil'yevna (1856- ?) Revolutionary; member, Exec Comt, *Narodnaya volya* (People's Will) Party; *Born*: 1856; *Career*: propaganda work among peasants; 1875 arrested, arraigned but, acquitted; involved in preparations for assassination of Alexander II; Aug 1879 in Aleksandrovsk, Yekaterinoslavl' Province, with Zhelyabov; 1880 in Petersburg and Odessa with Isayev and in Petersburg with Kibal'chich helped to manufacture explosives; with Bogdanovich under the alias of Kobozevaya kept a dairy-shop on Malaya Sadovaya Street, Petersburg, from which a tunnel was dug with a view to assassinating the Tsar with a mine; 1 Mar 1881 after assassination of Alexander II went into hiding; 21 Apr 1881 arrested; received death sentence, subsequently commuted to life imprisonment at hard labor; 1883 transferred from Peter-Paul Fortress to Karu; 1897 transferred to Akatuy; 1899 deported to Chita; 1904 fled to Siberia; 1905 joined Soc-Revol Party; Aug 1905 arrested and sentenced to 8 months imprisonment; deported to Chita again; 1917 returned to Petrograd; 1935 member, Soc of Polit Prisoners; *Died:* date and place of death unknown.

DIKOVSKIY' Sergey Vladimirovich (1907-1940) Russian writer; *Born*: 14 Mar 1907 in Moscow, son of a teacher; *Career*: after grad elementary school subsequently messenger, opera chorus singer, poster sticker, railroad porter, librarian; from 1925 reporter, Novorossiysk newspaper *Krasnoye Chernomor'ye*; later wrote feuilletons for newspaper *Molodoy leninets*; 1928-29 began lit work; during his army service fought along the Chinese-Eastern Railroad; 1929 published mil sketches in corps-newspaper *Otpor*; from 1930 roving correspondent, Moscow newspaper *Pravda; Publ: Boy* (The Battle) (1929); collected stories *Zastava N* (Frontier Post N) (1932); *Ryb'ya karta* (Fishing Card) (1935); *Patrioty* (Patriots) (1937); *Yegor Tsygankov* (1938); *Priklyucheniya katera 'Smelyy'* (Adventures of the Cutter "Courageous") (1938); *Rasskazy* (Stories) (1951); *Izbrannyye proizvedeniya* (Selected Works) (1956); stories; *Nastoyashcheye* (The Present) (1958); *Patrioty* (Patriots) (1962); *Died*: 6 Jan 1940 killed in action in Finno-Russian War near Suomi-Salmi.

DILLON, Yakov Grigor'yevich (1873-1951) Roentgenologist; Hon Sci Worker of RSFSR; *Born*: 1873; *Educ*: 1895 grad Med Fac, Kiev Univ; *Career*: from 1919 asst prof, then assoc prof, 2nd Moscow State Univ; from 1934 head, Chair of Roentgenology affiliated to the Moscow Oblast Clinical Research Inst, where he organized a major center of the Moscow Oblast X-ray service; founded clinic for treatment of patients suffering from intrathoracic tumors; 1915-19 proved, contrary to established opinion, that it is necessary to flush the esophagus and stomach when the former has been damaged by caustic substances; atributed gastric ulcers to malfunctions of the centr nervous system and hyperfunction of certain parts of the stomach's muscular envelope; 1928 on the basis of research into the pathology and physiology of the diaphragm confirmed the theory that idiopathic dilation of the esophagus is caused by phrenospasm; devised theory of gastric respiration and test for viviparturition for use in forensic med; did major research on the diagnosis and treatment of lung cancer; used method of weak multipolar irradiation permitting the exposure of tumors to larger X-ray doses; hon member, Moscow Soc of Roentgenologists and Radiologists; 1942-43 founder-chm, Fergana Sci Soc; wrote over 80 works; *Publ*: articles "Persistent Unilateral Distension of the Diaphragm" (1928); "Phrenic Blockage of the Esophagus" (1938); *Pervichnyy rak lyogkogo* (Primary Lung Cancer) (1947); articles "New Achievements in the Diagnosis and Treatment of Lung Cancer" (1948); "Preliminary Gastrostomy as a Basis for Treatment for Cancer of the Esophagus" (1950); "The Early Diagnosis of Lung Cancer" (1951); *Awards*: Prof Mochutkovskiy Prize; Prize of Pop Comrt of Educ (1928); Stalin Prize (1949); *Died*: 1951.

DIMANSHTEYN, Semyon Markovich (1886-1939) Party and govt official; CP member from 1904; *Born*: 1886, son of a poor artisan; *Career*: 1904 joined RSDRP in Vilnius and sided with Bolsheviks; 1904 arrested; on release form prison transported illegal lit and worked in underground printing house of Northwestern Party Comt in Minsk; 1907 propaganda among workers in Riga; member, Riga Party Comt; 1908 arrested in Riga and sentenced to 6 months' hard labor; 1913 escaped from hard labor and emigrated; during war worked in France as metal turner and conducted propaganda among French workers; after 1917 Feb Revol worked for Riga mil org and edited newspaper *Okopnaya pravda*; after German occupation of Riga worked in Petrograd for CC, Metal Workers' Union; after 1917 Oct Revol worked for Collegium, Pop Comrt of Labor; Jan 1918 appointed comr for Jewish nat affairs; helped to found and edit first Jewish Communist newspaper *Der Emes*; 1919 CC member, and Pop Comr of Labor of Lit and Bel; 1920 worked in Turkestan as Pop Comr of Educ; 1922 chm, Main Bd of Polit Educ and head Agitation and Propaganda Dept, CC, CP (B) Ukr; member, CC and CC Org Bureau CP(B) Ukr; from 1924 dep head, Agitation and Propaganda Dept, CC, RSP(B) and head, of its Nat Section (until Feb 1930); from 1930 dep secr, Council of Nationalities, USSR Centr Exec Comt; then chm, Centr Bd, All-Union Soc for the Land Allotment of Working Jews; member, Communist Acad; dir, Inst of Nationalities, USSR Centr Exec Comt; ed, journal *Revolyutsia i natsional'nosti*; arrested by State Security organs; *Died*: 1939 in imprisonment.

DIMITROV, Georgiy Mikhaylovich (1882-1949) Bulgarian revol and Comintern official; *Born*: 18 June 1882 in vil Kovachevtsy, Radomir Distr, Bulgaria, son of a worker; *Career:* from age 15 worked as type-setter and engaged in revol activities; from 1901 secr, Printers' Trade Union, Sofia; from 1902 member, Bulgarian Workers' Soc-Democratic Party (Tesnyaki); helped to organize strikes; 1904-23 one of leaders, Bulgarian League of Revol Trade Unions; from 1909 member, CC, Tesnyaki Party (from 1919 CP Bulgaria); 1910 and 1925 deleg, 1st and 2nd Conferences of Balkan Soc-Democrats; repeatedly arrested and imprisoned for revol activities; during WW 1 protested gen mobilization and Bulgarian involvement in war; after 1917 Oct Revol actively championed Sov cause; 1921 took active part in 3rd Comintern Congress, where he met Lenin, and in 1st Profintern Congress, at which he was elected to CC; Sept 1923 one of leaders of Bulgarian workers' uprising; after suppression of uprising lived abroad as professional revol and worked for Comintern Exec Comt; 1933 arrested in Berlin on charge of having set fire to Reichstag; 21 Sept-23 Dec 1933 tried in Leipzig; 27 Feb 1934 arrived in USSR after being released on the intercession of the Sov govt, which granted him Sov citizenship; 1935-43 secr-gen, Comintern Exec Comt; 1937-45 dep, USSR Supr Sov; 1942 helped to organize Patriotic Front of Bulgaria and Bulgarian partisan movement; 1944 helped to organize armed uprising of 9 Sept which led to overthrow of Bulgarian monarchy; Nov 1945 returned to Bulgaria; from 1946 until death secr-gen, CP Bulgaria and chm, Bulgarian Council of Min; *Publ: Izbrannyye proizvedeniya* (Selected Works) (2 vol, 1957); *Awards*: Order of Lenin (1945); *Died*: 2 July 1949; buried in Dimitrov Mausoleum, Sofia.

DIMO, Nikolay Aleksandrovich (1873-1959) Soil scientist; Dr of Geology and Mineralogy; prof, Kishinyov Univ from 1945; member, All-Union Lenin Acad of Agric Sci from 1948; CP member from 1949; *Born*: 30 Nov 1873; *Educ*: 1899 grad Novo-Aleksandrovsk Inst of Agric and Forestry; *Career*: until 1908 organized and directed soil research in Saratov, Penza and Chernigov Provinces; 1908-30 did soil and botanical research in Centr Asia from the viewpoints of irrigation, reclamation, dry cropping and pasturage; co-founder, Centr Asian Univ, Tashkent; co-founder and until 1931 dir, Inst of Pedology and Botanics, Centr Asian Univ; from 1932 studied the land resources of the Transcaucasus; from 1945 head, Pedology Section, then Pedology Inst, Mold Branch, USSR Acad of Sci (later Mold Acad of Sci); head, Chair of Pedology, Kishinyov Univ; *Publ*: coauthor, *V oblasti polupustyni* (In the Semi-Desert Regions) (1907); *Pochvennyye issledovaniya v basseyne reki Amu-Darya* (Soil Research in the Amu-Darya Basin) (1913); *Opytno-proizvodstvennyye issledovaniya v kolkhozakh i sovkhozakh pravoberezh'ya Alazanskoy doliny* (Research on Experimental Agricultural Production at Kolkhozes and Sovkhozes on the Right Bank of the Alazani River Valley) (1951); *Nablyudeniya i issledovaniya po faune pochv* (Observations and Research on Soil Fauna) (1955), etc; *Awards*: Order of Lenin; two Orders of the Red Banner of Labor; *Died*: Aug 1959.

DINAMOV, Sergey Sergeyevich (1901-1939) Russian lit historian; CP member from 1919; *Born*: 16 Sept 1901 in Moscow, son of a worker; *Educ*: studied at Soc Sci Fac, 1st Moscow Univ; 1926-29 postgrad studies at Inst of Language and Lit; *Career*: textile worker and lithographer; 1919-26 in Red Army; from 1930 assoc and Collegium member, Inst of Language and Lit; dep chm, Western Lit Sub-Section, Communist Acad; 1935 head, Arts Section, Culture and Propaganda Dept, CC, CPSU(B); Secretariat member, Int Org for Aid to Revol Fighters; exec ed, this org's centr organ *Internatsional'naya literatura*; 1921 first work published; contributed to journals *Knigonosha, Pechat' i revolyutsiya, Na literaturnom postu*, etc; specialized in 20th-Century English and American lit and works of Shakespeare; wrote articles on Wells, Shaw, Rolland, Proust, Goethe, Gorky, Edgar Allan Poe, Jack London, Mark Twain, John Reed, Hemingway, etc; helped prepare several ed of Shakespeare; worked on study of English drama, publishing the chapters "King Lear" (1935), "The Language of 'Othello'" (1936) and "The Characters in 'Othello'" (1936); arrested by State Security organs; *Publ: M. Gor'kiy i Zapad* (Maxim Gorky and the West) (1932); collected articles *Zarubezhnaya literatura* (Foreign Literature) (1960, posthumously); *Died*: 20 Nov 1939 in imprisonment; posthumously rehabilitated.

DINMAGOMAYEV, Radzhab Dinmagomayevich (1905-1944) Dag writer; CP member from 1925; *Born*: 1905 in vil Urma, now Levashi Rayon, Dagh ASSR, son of a peasant; *Educ*: studied at Communist Univ of Workers of the East, Moscow; *Career*: 1916-17 boy-servant in Petrograd; 1917 returned to Dag; 1919-20 served in 1st Free Dag Revol regt; 1920-31 Komsomol and Party work; ed, oblast newspapers "Banner of Socialism" and "Bolshevik of the Mountains"; 1926 began lit work (in Avarian language); 1942 volunteered for the army; *Publ*: stories: *Mullah* (1928); "Blood for Blood" (1929); "Galina's Guests"(1935); "The Brown Snake" (1941); *Klyatva* (The Oath) (1942, in Russian); novel "Heroes in Fur-Coats" (1936); *Died*: 1944 killed in action.

DINNIK, Aleksandr Nikolayevich (1876-1950) Scientist; specialist in mechanics and the theory of elasticity; member, Ukr Acad of Sci from 1929; member, USSR Acad of Sci from 1946; Hon Sci and Tech Worker of Ukr SSR from 1943; *Born*: 21 Mar 1876 in Stavropol'; *Educ*: 1899 grad Kiev Univ; *Career*: from 1899 at Chair of Physics, Kiev Polytech Inst; from 1911 lectured at Don Polytech Inst; 1914-41 prof, Inst of Mining and Inst of Metallurgy, Dnepropetrovsk; from 1944 prof, Kiev Univ; studied theory of elasticity, stability of structural elements, especially rods and arches with permanent or varying cross-sections, stability and oscillation of sheets, laminas and membranes; application of the theory of elasticity to rock pressure in mines, strength of mine cables, etc; *Publ: Udar i szhatiye uprugikh tel* (Impact and Compression in Elastic Bodies) (1909); *Primeneniye funktsiy Besselya k zadacham teorii uprugosti* (Application of Bessel's Functions to Problems of the Theory of Elasticity) (2 vol, 1913-15); *Prodol'nyy izgib. Teoriya i prilozheniya* (Longitudinal Flexing. Theory and Applications) (1939); *Krucheniya. Teoriya i prilozheniya* (Torsion. Theory and Applications) (1938); *Ustoychivost' uprugikh sistem* (The Stability of Elastic Systems) (1950); *Izbrannyye trudy* (Selected Works) (3 vol, 1952-56); *Died*: 22 Sept 1950.

DITERIKHS, Mikhail Mikhaylovich (1871-1941) Surgeon; Hon Sci Worker of RSFSR from 1936; pupil of N.A. Vel'yaminov; *Born*: 22 Nov 1871; *Educ*: 1898 grad Mil Med Acad; *Career*: after grad worked at Vel'yaminov's Surgical Clinic, Mil Med Acad; 1901 defended doctor's thesis on lipoma arborescens of the joints; from 1912 prof of surgery, Kiev Univ; from 1934 prof of surgery, 3rd Moscow Med Inst; specialist in field surgery and the pathology of bones and joints; devised own classification of diseases of the joints; developed splint for the treatment of gunshot fractures of the thigh (Diterikh's splint); wrote over 100 works, including monographs and manuals, notably on field surgery; also wrote papers on the history of med, e.g., on Paré and Lister; his article "The Soul of the Surgeon" (1925) elicited strong reaction in the press; *Publ*: doctor's thesis *Tak nazyvayemyy drevovidnyy zhirovik sustavov* (Lipoma Aborescens of the Joints) (1901); article "Heliotherapy of 'Surgical' Tuberculosis" (1913); *Posleoperatsionnyy period* (The Postoperative Period) (1924); *Khirurgicheskoye lecheniye tuberkulyoza lyogkikh* (Surgical Treatment of Lung Tuberculosis) (1926); *Vvedeniya v kliniku zabolevaniy sustavov* (An Introduction to the Clinical Treatment of Diseases of the Joints) (1937); ed and coauthor, *Voyenno-polevaya khirurgiya* (Field Surgery) (3rd ed, 1938); *Died*: 12 Jan 1941.

DITERIKS, Mikhail Konstantinovich (1874-1937) Mil commander; gen, Russian Army; commanded White units in Siberia and Far East; *Born*: 1874; *Educ*: 1900 grad Gen Staff Acad; *Career*: fought in 1904-05 Russo-Japanese War; Aug 1914-16 various staff posts in acting army; 1916-17 commanded Russian Corps in Salonika; 1917 chief of staff, Gen Krymov's Mounted Corps; quartermaster-gen, Gen Headquarters; Nov 1917, escaped just before Gen Headquarters was captured by Sov troops; 1918 chief of staff, Czechoslovak Corps (formed from former POWs); 26-29 June 1918 commanded Czechoslovak troops which took Vladivostok; late 1918, after all Russian officers were obliged to leave Czechoslovak Corps, joined Kolchak's troops; 1919, on Kolchak's orders, made a thorough investigation of the execution of the Tsar's family in Yekaterinburg (now Sverdlovsk); 2 July 1919 appointed commander-in-chief, Kolchak's army; 10 Aug 1919 appointed Kolchak's chief of staff and Min of War, Omsk Govt; 4 Nov 1919 resigned while Kolchak's army was in full retreat; summer 1922 elected by Maritime Oblast's Zemstvo Congress "ruler of Maritime Region"; Oct 1922 emigrated as Japanese troops withdrew from Maritime Region; headed Far Eastern Dept, Russian Mil Union; *Died*: 1937 in Shanghai.

DIVAYEV, Abubakir Akhmetzhanovich (1856-1933) Bash turkologist, folklorist, ethnographer and linguist; *Born*: 19 Dec 1856; *Educ*: grad Neplyuyev Cadet Corps, Orenburg; *Career*: from 1876 worked for mil-nat admin in Tashkent; in 1920's and 1930's prof, Centr Asian Inst and Turkestani Eastern Inst; also directed Dept to Ethnography and Dept of Archeology at the Regional Museum in Tashkent; wrote numerous works on folklore, ethnography and language of Kazakhs, Uzbeks, Kirghiz and Karakalpaks; printed in *Izvestiya Obshchestva arkheologii, istorii i etnografii pri Kazanskom universitete, Zapiski Vostochnogo otdela Russkogo arkhivnogo obshchestva*, ect;*Publ: Sbornik materialov dlya statistiki Syr-Dar'inskoy oblasti* (A Collection of Materials for Statistics on the Syr-Darya Oblast) (13 vol, 1891-1907); *Batyrlar* (No. 1-7, 1922), Kirghiz-Kazakh heroic epic; collections *Podarok* (The Gift) (1924); *Podarok detyam* (Gift to Children) (1926); *Bogatyrskiye pesni* (Heroic Songs) (1939), etc; *Died*: 5 Feb 1933.

DIVIL'KOVSKIY (Party pseudonym: AVDEYEV), Anatoliy Avdeyevich (1873-1932) Party official and lit critic; CP member from 1898; *Born*: 1873, son of a physician; *Educ*: studied at Kiev Univ; *Career*: joined revol movement while still a student; 1903 member, Petersburg RSDRP (*Iskra*) Comt; 1903 arrested and 1904 exiled to Arkhangel'sk; Oct 1905 returned to Petersburg and began to organize Vyborg Rayon Sov of Workers' Dep; later fled to Viborg in Finland, where he worked for the Russian Section of local Soc-Democratic Comt; 1906 emigrated to Switzerland and joined Plekhanov's Menshevik group; 1912 broke with Mensheviks; during WW 1 supported internationalism; early 1918 joined Bolshevik group in Geneva; Nov 1918 returned to Russia, worked as an agitator and propagandist in Moscow, as asst to the business-manager, Council of Pop Comr and for newspapers *Bednota* and *Pravda*; toward end of life devoted himself entirely to lit work; *Died*: 1932.

DIZHBIT, Andrey Martynovich (1889-1966) Revolutionary; govt official; CP member from 1912; *Born*: 18 Dec 1889; *Educ*: grad Frunze Mil Acad; *Career*: 1914 arrested for revol activities and exiled to Narym Kray, whence he escaped; revol work in Samara, the Urals and Petrograd; July-Sept 1917 worked for newspaper *Tsinya* and *Okopnaya pravda*; deleg, 6th Party Congress; active in Oct Coup in Petrograd; 1917-18 comr of refugee affairs at Pop Comrt of Internal Affairs in Moscow; May 1918-Jan 1919 chief, RSFSR Police; 1919-23 in Red Army as head, Special Dept, 10th and 16th Armies; staff comr, 1st Mounted Army; 1923-26 worked abroad; until 1934 worked for various organs of Pop Comrt of For Trade; from 1935 worked for USSR Pop Comrt of Agric and for Moscow and Kiev research institutes; from 1945 at Lat Min of Agric; from 1958 pensioner; *Died*: 29 Dec 1966.

DMITRENKO, Leonid Filippovich (1875-1957) Therapist; prof; Dr of Med; *Born*: 1875; *Educ*: 1901 grad Med Fac, Kiev Univ; *Career*: 1916 defended doctor's thesis on the effect of gastric reflexes on circulation and respiration; from 1919 assoc prof, from 1920 head, Diagnostic (later Propaedeutical) Clinic; 1920-50 prof, Odessa Med Inst; his still valid research on gastric reflexes and interoceptors received int acclaim; specialized in the role of the nervous system in the pathogenesis of hypertonic diseases, arteriosclerosis and angina pectoris; described the clinical aspects and prognosis of mitral stenosis, croupous pneumonia, etc; also described the "velvety tone" of the heart in endocarditis; devised new classification for croupous pneumonia; his studies of clinical pharmacology included descriptions of the use and effects of nitroglycerine, purine diuretics, camphor, coffein, etc; also did research on the clinical aspects of epidemic jaundice and the effect of lead-poisoning on the cardiovascular system, wrote 96 works, including four monographs; *Publ: Znacheniye serdechnykh i sosudodvigatel'nykh sredstv pri krupoznom vospalenii lyogkikh* (The Significance of Heart and Vasomotor Drugs in Croupous Pneumonia) (1907); doctor's thesis *Eksperimental'nyye materialy dlya izucheniya serdechnykh i dykhatel'nykh rasstroystv zheludochno-kishechnogo proiskhozhdeniya* (Experimental Material on the Study of Heart and Respiratory Disorders of Gastrointestinal Origin) (1916); *K voprosu o vliyanii voyny na serdtse* (The Effect of War on the Heart) (1919); *Epidemicheskaya zheltukha 1917-ogo goda v tylu i na fronte* (The 1919 Jaundice Epidemic in the Rear and at the Front) (1921); *Died*: 1957.

DMITREVSKIY, Georgiy Aleksandrovich (1900-1953) Conductor; Hon Art Worker of RSFSR from 1946; *Born*: 21 Mar 1900 in Moscow; *Career*: 1944-53 artistic dir and chief conductor, Leningrad's Glinka Acad Capella; prof, Moscow Conservatory; from 1945 prof, Leningrad Conservatory; *Publ: Khorovedeniye i upravleniye khorom* (Choral Conducting and Choir Management) (1948); *Died*: 2 Dec 1953 in Leningrad.

DMITRIYEV, Adam Martynovich (1902-1036) Russian writer; CP member from 1920; *Born*: 6 Nov 1902 in Mogilev Province; *Career*: 1926 first work printed; leading member, Red Army and Navy Lit Assoc; ed, journal *Zalp; Publ*: stories: *Za khishchnikami* (After the Predators) (1926); *Kreyser 'Nippo'* (The Cruiser "Nippo") (1929); novel *Yest' – Vesti korabl'* (Aye, Aye. Man the Ship) (1931); novel "Admiral Makarov" (vol 1, 1934); *Died*: 15 Jan 1936 in Yalta.

DMITRIYEV, Aleksandr Ivanovich (1878-1959) Architect and eng; Hon Member, USSR Acad of Construction and Architecture from 1956; *Born*: 14 Oct 1878 in Pskov; *Educ*: 1900 grad Inst of Civil Eng; 1903 grad Petersburg Acad of Arts; *Career*: from 1913 member, Petersburg Acad of Arts; taught architecture; *Works*: Nakhimov College, Leningrad; Southern Railroad admin offices in Khar'kov (1908-10); wharfs in Tallinn (1913-17); Khar'kov Cooperative Center (late 1920's); Khar'kov Workers' Palace (or Railroad Workers' Club) (1928-33); Kramatorsk Theater Club (1930), etc; *Died*: 2 Dec 1959.

DMITRIYEV, Andrey Mikhaylovich (1878-1946) Plant breeder; geobotanist, meadow specialist and agronomist; Dr of Agric from 1936; prof and head, Chair of Meadow Culture, Timiryazev Agric Acad from 1922; *Born*: 30 Dec 1878 in Rybinsk, now Yaroslavl' Oblast; *Educ*: 1897 grad Rybinsk classical high school; 1901 grad natural sci div, Physics and Mathematics Fac, Petersburg Univ; 1901-07 meadow-culture inspector for Yaroslavl' Province Dept of Agric; 1907-10 worked for Yaroslavl' Province Zemstvo and chm, Yaroslavl' Regional Studies Soc; 1911-14 research assignments to Germany, Sweden, Denmark and the USA; 1912 recruited by V. R. Vil'yams as asst to organize advanced courses in meadow culture at the Petrine (later Timiryazev) Agric Acad and served as asst dir of these courses until 1922; 1916-22 lecturer, 1922-46 prof and head, Dept of Meadow Culture, Timiryazev Agric Acad; 1916-23 simultaneously prof of meadow culture, Golitsyn Higher Agric Courses; 1930-36 prof and head, Dept of Fodder Production, Moscow Zootechnical Inst; 1932-41 prof of meadow culture, Moscow's Stalin Ind Acad; V. R. Vil'yams' pupil and successor; together with V. R. Vil'yams founded State Meadow Research Inst (from 1930 All-Union Fodder Research Inst); 1922-30 served as its dir; advocated introduction of meadow and pasture crop rotation and compulsory regulation of grazing; worked out classification of meadow lands of the non-chernozem zone of the USSR and a system of measures to improve fodder production in the various zones; *Publ: O pastbishchakh romanovskoy ovtsy* (Romanov Sheep Pastures) (1901); *Luga Kholmogorskogo rayona* (Meadows of the Kholmogory Rayon) (1904); *Luga Yaroslavskoy gubernii i opyty po ikh uluchsheniyu* (Meadows of the Yaroslavl' Province and Their Experimental Improvement) (1904); *Vozdelyvaniye bolot* (Swamp Cultivation) (1905; 3rd ed, 1914); *O razrabotke zapushchennykh zemel', lugovodstve i skotovodstve* (Fallow Land Tillage, Meadow Culture and Cattle Breeding) (1906); *Kul'tura lugov v severnoy Rossii* (Meadow Culture in Northern Russia) (1908); *Luga, ikh uluchsheniye i vozdelyvaniye* (Meadow, Their Improvement and Cultivation) (1911); *Kurs lektsiy po lugovodstvu* (A Series of Lectures on Meadow Culture) (1914); *Obzor meropriyatiy po kul'ture kormovykh rasteniy 1908-13 gg.* (A Review of 1908-13 Fodder Growing Measures) (1914); *Luga, ikh zhizn', uluchsheniye i vozdelyvaniye* (Meadows, Their Ecology, Improvement and Cultivation) (1920); *Azbuka lugovodstva* (The ABC of Meadow Culture) (1923; 2nd ed, 1929); *Luga i ikh ispol'zovaniye* (Meadows and Their Utilization) (1925); coauthor, *Kormodobyvaniye. 1. Lugovoye kormodobyvaniye* (Fodder Production. 1. Fodder from Meadows) (1934); *Lugovodstvo s osnovami lugovedeniya* (Meadow Culture and the Fundamentals of Meadow Control) (1941), etc; *Awards*: Stalin Prize (1946, posthumously); *Died*: 25 July 1946 in Moscow.

DMITRIYEV, Ivan Ivanovich (1903-1954) Film sound-operator; *Born*: 8 Feb 1903; *Educ*: 1928 grad radio eng courses; *Career*: from 1930 cinema work; asst sound-operator, from 1932 sound-operator, Leningrad Film Studio; *Works*: recorded sound for films: *Groza* (The Storm) (1934); *Krest'yane* (Peasants) (1935); *Podrugi* (The Girl-Friends) (1936); *Velikiy grazhdanin* (The Great Citizen) (2 parts, 1938-39); *Nepobedimyye* (The Unconquerable) (1943); *Nashestviye* (Invasion) (1945); *Dragotsennyye zyorna* (Precious Grains) (1948); *Kortik* (1954); *Muzykal'naya istoriya* (Musical History) (1940); *Anton Ivanovich serditsya* (Anton Ivanovich Gets Angry) (1941); *Died*: 11 July 1954.

DMITRIYEV, Nikolay Izmaylovich (1886-1957) Geographer; *Born*: 9 Apr 1886 in vil Ul'yanovka,, now Sumy Oblast: *Career*: 1922-57 prof, Khar'kov Univ; founder-dir, Khar'kov Branch, USSR Geographical Soc; made a round-the-world tour, including Western Europe, America, Hawaii, Australia, New Zealand, New Guinea, Japan and China; wrote some 50 works on geomorphology (including geomorphological zones of Ukr SSR), Ukr paleogeography and the history of geography; *Died*: 8 Feb 1957.

DMITRIYEV, Nikolay Konstantinovich (1898-1954) Philologist; Dr of Philology; prof; corresp member, USSR Acad of Sci from 1943; member, RSFSR Acad of Pedag Sci; *Born*: 28 Aug 1898; *Educ*: 1920 grad History and Philology Fac, Moscow Univ; 1921 grad Middle East Fac, Moscow Inst of Oriental Studies; *Career*: from 1921 assoc, Russian Assoc of Soc Sci Research Institutes; 1949-53 head, Turkic-Mongolian Peoples' Schools Section, RSFSR Acad of Pedag Sci; specialist in Turkic languages; worked on methods of teaching Russian and native languages in national schools; wrote textbooks, teaching aids, etc for nat schools; ed, first *Russko-bashkirskiy slovar'* (Russian-Bashkir Dictionary) (1948); *Publ: Grammatika kumykskogo yazyka* (A Kumyk Grammar) (1940); *Grammatika bashkirskogo yazyka* (A Bashkir Grammar) (1948); coauthor, *Ocherki po metodike prepodavaniya russkogo i rodnogo yazykov v tatarskoy shkole* (Studies in Methods of Teaching Russian and the Native Language in Tatar Schools) (1952); coauthor, *Ocherki po metodike prepodavaniya russkogo i rodnykh yazykov v natsional'noy shkole* (Studies in Methods of Teaching Russian and Native Languages in National Schools) (1954), etc; *Died*: 23 Dec 1954.

DIMITRIYEV, Vladimir Vladimirovich (1873-1946) Power eng; Hon Sci and Tech Worker of RSFSR from 1934; *Born*: 1873; *Educ*: 1898 grad Petersburg Electr Eng Inst; *Career*: from 1909 prof, Petersburg Electr Eng Inst; 1896-1917 designed and built electr power plants in various Russian cities; suggested centralized combined heating and power plants; 1908-10 built heating and electr power plant for Petersburg's largest hospital (now Mechnikov Hospital); after 1917 Oct Revol worked for State Commission for Electrification of Russia; helped build many electr plants; 1923 provided plan for district heating of Leningrad on basis of 3rd Leningrad Hydroelectr Plant; developed theory of low-vacuum heating turbines; did research on gasification of peat and shale; *Publ: Osnovy proyektirovaniya tsentral'nykh elektricheskikh stantsiy* (Principles for the Design of Central Electric Plants) (1923); *Elektricheskiye silovyye ustanovki* (Electric Power Plants) (1928); *Osnovnyye voprosy teplofikatsii gorodov* (Basic Aspects of Municipal Heating Plants) (1933); *Died*: 1946.

DMITRIYEV, Vladimir Vladimirovich (1900-1948) Russian stage designer; Hon Art Worker of RSFSR from 1944; *Born*: 31 July 1900; *Educ*: 1918-21 studied at Petrograd Acad of Arts; *Career*: from 1917 theatrical work; in early period influenced by formalism; from 1928 at Moscow Arts Theater; from 1941 chief designer, Moscow Arts Theater; wrote a number of articles and ballet libretti; *Works*: designed sets for about 150 plays in leading USSR theaters, among them: Lev Tolstoy's *Voskreseniye* (Resurrection) (1930); *Pikovaya dama* (The Queen of Spades) (1931 and 1944); Gorky's *Yegor Bulychyov i drugiye* (Yegor Bulychyov and Co) (1932); Gorky's *Vragi* (The Enemiess) (1935); Tolstoy's *Anna Karenina* (1937); N. F. Pogodin's *Chelovek s ruzh'yom* (Man with a Gun) (1937); K. A. Trenyov's *Na beregu Nevy* (On the Bank of the Neva) (1937); Chekhov's *Tri sestry* (Three Sisters) (1940); *Kremlyovskiye kuranty* (Kremlin Chimes) (1942); A. Ye. Korneychuk's *Front* (The Front) (1942); K. M. Simonov's *Russkiye lyudi* (Russian People) (1943); Ostrovskiy's *Poslednyaya zhertva* (The Last Victim) (1944); Tchaikovsky's *Orleanskaya deva* (The Maid of Orleans) (1945); Prokofiev's *Voyna i mir* (War and Peace) (1946); A. N. Serov's *Vrazh'ya sila* (The Evil Force) (1948); Smetana's "The Bartered Bride" (1948); N. Ye. Virta's *Khleb nash nasushchnyy* (Our Daily Bread) (1948), etc; *Awards*: four Stalin Prizes (1946 [twice], 1948, 1949); *Died*: 6 May 1948.

DMITRIYEV, Timofey Pavlovich (1893-1963) Russian writer; *Born*: 1 Feb 1893 in vil Ivanovo, Vologda Province, son of a peasant; *Educ*: 1911 grad Penza teachers' seminary; *Career*: 1918 first work printed; from 1923 member, *Kuznitsa* (The Smithy) lit group; wrote mainly in 1920's; *Publ*: novelette *Razbrod* (Disorder) (1925); novel *Zelyonaya zyb'* (Green Swell) (1927); *Puti-dorozhki* (Ways and Byways) (1927); *Rasskazy* (Stories) (1927); *Krivaya tropa* (The Winding Trail) (1928); *Povesti i rasskazy* (Tales and Stories) (1928); *Died*: 27 Jan 1963.

DMITRIYEVA, Valentina Iovovna (1859-1948) Russian writer; *Born*: 1859; *Educ*: grad Tambov High School and med courses; *Career*: vil teacher, then zemstvo physician, Voronezh Zemstvo; active in People's Will circles; several times arrested; 1879 first work printed; *Publ*: stories, novelettes and novels: *Derevenskiye rasskazy* (Country Stories) (1892); *Mityukha-uchitel'* (Mityukha the Teacher) (1900); *Chervonnyy khutor* (The Red Farmstead) (1901); children's stories: *Volchyonok* (The Wolf-Cub) (1927); *Malysh i Zhuchka* (Malysh and Zhuchka) (1896), etc; *Povesti i rasskazy* (Tales and Stories) (1909); *Rasskazy* (Stories) (1913); *Povesti i rasskazy* (Tales and Stories) (1916); *Tak bylo. Put' moyey zhizni* (That's How It Was. My Career) (1930); *Died*: 1948.

DMOKHOVSKIY, Vladislav Karlovich (1877-1952) Eng; expert in foundations and groundwork; maj-gen, Eng Corps; Hon Sci and Tech Worker of RSFSR from 1940; *Born*: 18 Apr 1877; *Educ*: 1898 grad Moscow Univ; 1902 grad Petersburg Inst of Communications Eng; *Career*: 1902-12 construction work; 1912-17 instructor, higher tech educ institutions; 1917-24 rector, Moscow Inst of Civil Eng; from 1918 prof, Moscow Inst of Trans Eng, later Mil Eng Acad and other inst; conducted theoretical and experimental research in the field of pile foundations (theory of conic piles), dynamic stability of foundations, tunnels and hydraulic structures; helped plan and construct major Sov constructing projects (Dneprostroy, Moscow Subway, Magnitostroy, Moscow mulstistoreyed buildings, etc); *Publ: Staticheskiye metody raschyota tsilindricheskikh i konicheskikh svay* (Static Calculation Methods for Cylindric and Conic Piles) (1918); *Vliyaniye sil stsepleniya grunta na ustoychivost' inzhenernykh sooruzheniy* (The Effects of Soil Cohesion on the Stability of Engineering Structures) (1922); *Proyektirovaniye i raschyot zemlyanykh rabot* (Planning and Calculation of Exavation Work) (3rd ed, 1928); coauthor, *Osnovaniya i fundamenty* (Groundwork and Foundations) (1940), etc; *Died*: 26 May 1952.

DNEPROV, Mitrofan Ivanovich (1881-1966) Russian operetta singer (baritone) and stage dir; Hon Artiste of RSFSR from 1947; *Born*: 1 June 1881 in Uman'; *Educ*: 1900-06 studied on O. Bestrikh's opera courses in Petersburg; *Career*: from 1907 with various operetta companies; 1933-39 on tour in USSR; 1939-51 actor, Moscow Operetta Theater; 1946-47 stage dir in Pyatigorsk; *Roles*: Fairfax in Jones' "Geisha"; Danilo in Lehar's "The Merry Widow"; Paris in Offenbach's "Fair Helena"; the billiard-player in Dunayevskiy's *Zhenikhi* (Bridegrooms); Mr. X in Kalman's "Circus Princess"; Koretskiy in Aleksandrov's *God spustya* (One Year Later); Igonin in Milyutin's *Bespokoynoye schast'ye* (Restless Luck); Muromskiy in Kovner's *Akulina*, etc; *Works*: producted B. Aleksandrov's *Svad'ba v Malinovke* (Wedding at Malinovka); Kalman's "Silva" and "Bayadere"; *Publ: Polveka v operette* (Half a Century in Operetta) (1961); *Died*: 11 Jan 1966 in Moscow.

DNEPROV, Sergey Ivanovich (1884-1955) Russian actor; Hon Artiste of RSFSR from 1949; *Born*: 16 Oct 1884; *Educ*: 1904 grad Law Fac, Moscow Univ; 1908 grad A. I. Adashev's drama courses; *Career*: 1908-11 at Moscow Arts Theater; 1912-23 and 1925-31 at various provincial theaters; 1923-25 at Maly Theater; 1931-36 at 2nd Moscow Arts Theater; from 1936 at Moscow Sov Theater; also taught; *Roles*: Chatskiy, Neznamov, Zhadov, Ferdinand and Karl Moor; Rivares in Voinich's *Ovod* (Gadfly); Count Myshkin in Dostoyevskiy's "The Idiot"; Teryokhin in Kirshon's *Rzhavchina* (Rust); Yarovoy; Godun in *Razlom* (The Break-Up); Volgin in Afinogenov's *Chudak* (The Crank); Karandyshev; Kolychev in Ostrovskiy's *Vasilisa Melent'yeva*; Pastor in Lunacharskiy's *Medvezh'ya svad'ba* (Bear Wedding); Beregovoy in *Myatezh* (Mutiny); chairman of revol comt in Nikitin's *Apsheronskaya noch'* (The Night of Apsheron), etc; *Died*: 14 Mar 1955.

DNIPROVSKIY, I. (**pseudonym of: SHEVCHENKO, Ivan Danilovich**) (1895-1934) Ukr writer, poet and playwright; *Born*: 24 Feb 1895 in vil Kalanchak, former Kherson Province, son of a peasant; *Educ*: 1923 grad Philological Dept, Kamenets-Podol'sk Inst of Educ; *Career*: 1916 first work published; helped organize Ukr writers' soc *Gart* and Free Acad of Proletarian Lit; his works reflect the events of WW 1, the Civil War and the New Econ Policy period; wrote in Ukr language; *Publ*: poems: "The Donets Basin" (1922); "The Plough" (1924); "Good Morning, Lenin" (1924); numerous stories; plays: "Love and Smoke" (1926); "The Apple-Tree Prison" (1926); "The 'Mariya' Mine" (1931); collection "Works" (1931-33); *Died*: 1 Dec 1934 in Yalta.

DOBIASH-ROZHDESTVENSKAYA, Ol'ga Antonovna (1874-1939) Medieval historian; specialist in medieval history and ancient manuscripts; Dr of Gen History from 1918; prof from 1916; corresp member, USSR Acad of Sci from 1929; *Born*: 19 May 1874; *Career*: first woman in Russia to hold a master's degree (from 1915); from 1916 prof of medieval history, Higher Women's Courses; then prof, Leningrad Univ;1922-39 simultaneously in Manuscripts Dept, Saltykov-Shchedrin State Public Library; studied paleography, culture and religion of medieval Europe; first to introduce into univ syllabus teaching of Latin paleography and other collateral medieval subjects; studied, published, catalogued and analysed ancient Latin texts of Leningrad Public Library; *Publ*: textbook on West-European paleography *Istoriya pis'ma v sredniye veka* (History of Writing in the Middle Ages) (1923); *Tserkovnoye obshchestvo vo Frantsii v 13 v.* (Ecclesiastic Society in France in the 13th Century) (1914); *Kul't sv. Mikhaila v latinskom srednevekov'ye* (The Cult of Saint Michael in the Latin Middle Ages) (1917); *Drevneyshiye latinskiye rukopisi Publichnoy biblioteki. Rukopisi 5-7 vv.* (The Oldest Latin Manuscripts of the Public Library. Manuscripts of the 5-7th Centuries) (1929); *Masterskiye pis'ma na zare zapadnogo srednevekov'ya i ikh sokrovishcha v Leningrade* (Manuscript Masterpieces from the Dawn of the Western Middle Ages and Their Rich Collection in Leningrad) (1930); *Agrikul'tura v pamyatnikakh zapadnogo srednevekov'ya* (Agriculture in Monuments of the Western Middle Ages) (1936); *Akty Kremony*

10-13 vv. v sobraniyakh AN SSSR (Cremona Documents of the 10-13th Centuries in Collections of the USSR Academy of Sciences) (1937); *Histoire de l'atelier graphique de Corbie de 651 a 830 reflètée dans les manuscrits de Leningrad* (1934); *Died*: 30 Aug 1939.

DOBKEVICH, Anatoliy Ivanovich (1896-1942 (?)) Russian actor; Hon Artiste of RSFSR from 1937; *Born*: 19 Oct 1896; *Educ*: 1913 grad Moscow Philharmonic College; *Career*: from 1913 actor, Moscow Korsh Theater and theaters in Khar'kov, Kiev, Odessa, Kazan' and Novosibirsk; from 1931 until his death with Simferopol' Drama Theater; during WW 2 toured Red Army units with theater and concert groups; often addressed urban intelligentsia meetings, appealing for defense of the Fatherland; after occupation of the Crimea arrested by German army; *Roles*: Shadrin in *Chelovek s ruzh'yom* (Man with a Gun); Godun in *Razlom* (The Break-Up); Aleksey in *Optimisticheskaya tragediya* (Optimistic Tragedy); Gayday in *Gibel' eskadry* (The End of a Squadron); Platon in *Platon Krechet*; Boris Godunov, Neschastlivtsev, Satin, etc; *Died*: 1942 (?) in German imprisonment.

DOBROGEANU-GHEREA, Alexander (1879-1937) Rumanian revolutionary; founder-member, CP Rumania; member, CPSU(B) from 1927; *Born*: 2 July 1879, son of a Rumanian Soc-Democrat, Constantin Dobrogeanu-Gherea; *Educ*: studied eng; *Career*: 1904-20 member, Rumanian Soc-Democratic Party, from 1918 one of its left-wing leaders; 1920 member, Rumanian Soc-Democratic Party deleg to Moscow for negotiations on Comintern membership; took part in talks with Lenin; 1919 and 1920 dep, Rumanian Parliament; from 1921 one of most active members of newly-founded CP Rumania; 1922 and 1924 deleg, 2nd and 3rd Congresses, CP Rumania; 1922-24 member, Auditing Commission, CC, CP Rumania; 1924-25 member, CC, CP Rumania; frequently arrested; during imprisonment went on hunger-strike 14 times, the last of which (in 1929) lasted for 46 days and was abandoned only on orders from the CC, CP Rumania; 1925 sent to Moscow to work for Comintern Exec Comt; 1927 joined CPSU(B); 1928-31 Party work in Rumania; from 1932 until death lived in USSR; Nov 1932 member, Auditing Commission, 1st World Congress of Int Org for Aid to Revol Fighters; subjected to reprisals by State Security organs; *Died*: 4 Dec 1937 in imprisonment; posthumously rehabilitated.

DOBROKHOTOV, Aleksandr Nikolayevich (1868-1942) Metrologist; *Born*: 13 Dec 1868; *Educ*: 1894 grad Petersburg Univ; *Career*: from 1894 at the Main Chamber of Weights and Measures where he worked until his death; 1922-29 dir, Checking Inst of this Chamber; wrote works on exact weights and weighing devices; studied grain scales to determine the volumetric weight of grain, as commissioned by D. E. Mendeleyev; did much to reform the system of measures in the USSR; invented or improved various measuring devices (standard grain scales, volume meter, isochronous scales, metrological scales, etc); *Died*: 1942.

DOBROKHOTOV, Mikhail Sergeyevich (1878-1952) Neuropathologist; Dr of Med from 1913; prof from 1920; Hon Sci Worker of RSFSR; *Born*: 1878 in Kronstadt, son of a physician; *Educ*: 1904 grad Med Fac, Moscow Univ; *Career*: 1904-09 intern, Clinic for Nervous Disease, Moscow Univ; 1909-13 head, Nerve Dept, Saki Mud-Treatment Sanatorium, Crimea; from 1913 worked at various hospitals in Poltava, then as assoc prof, Chair of Nervous Diseases, Don Univ, Rostov-on-Don; from 1921 prof and head, Chair of Psychiatry and Nervous Diseases, Voronezh Univ; 1924-32 head, Chair of Nervous Diseases, Dnepropetrovsk Med Inst; 1932-34 senior assoc, Yalta Inst of Climatic Treatment, where he studied the influence of climate on the course and treatment of mental and nervous diseases; 1935-52 head, Chair of Nervous Diseases, Dag Med Inst, where he founded a clinic for nervous and mental diseases; member, Dag Med Soc; 1938-51 dep, 1947-51 dep chm, Dag Supr Sov; wrote 36 works; *Awards*: Badge of Hon; three medals; *Died*: 1952.

DOBROKHOTOV, Nikolay Nikolayevich (1889-1963) Metallurgist and thermal eng; prof from 1926; member, Ukr Acad of Sci from 1939; Hon Sci and Tech Worker of Ukr SSR from 1951; *Born*: 26 Mar 1889 in Arzamas, now Gorky Oblast; *Educ*: 1914 grad Petrograd Mining Inst; *Career*: 1914-20 at various plants; 1921-24 instructor, Petrograd Mining Inst; from 1926 prof, Ural Polytech Inst; 1935-45 prof and head, Chair of Steel Metallurgy, Dnepropetrovsk Inst of Metallurgy; simultaneously from 1940 at Inst of Ferrous Metallurgy, Ukr Acad of Sci; 1945 set up Chair of Steel Metallurgy and Construction Furnaces, Kiev Polytech Inst; 1949-52 dir, from 1952 senior assoc, Inst of Gas Utilization in Public Utilities and Ind, Ukr Acad of Sci; from 1959 member of a commission, State Sci and Tech Comt, Ukr Council of Min; studied gasification of hard fuels, theory and practice of building furnaces, technol of steel smelting and casting, application of thermodynamics in metallurgy; *Publ: Raschyot gazogeneratora i generatornogo protsessa* (Calculation of Gas Generators and the Gas Generation Process) (1922); *Sovremennaya tekhnologiya vyplavki stali v martenovskikh pechakh* (Modern Steel Smelting Technology in Open-Hearth Furnaces) (1951); *Primeneniye termodinamiki v metallurgii* (The Application of Thermodynamics in Metallurgy) (1955); *Awards*: Order of Lenin; Order of the Red Banner of Labor; medals; *Died*: 15 Oct 1963.

DOBROKHOTOVA, Aleksandra Ivanovna (1884-1958) Pediatrician and infectionist; corresp member, USSR Acad of Med Sci; Hon Sci Worker of RSFSR; *Born*: 1884 in Kineshma, daughter of a teacher; *Educ*: 1912 grad Med Fac, Moscow Higher Women's Courses; *Career*: after grad intern, Morozov Children's Hospital and asst prof under P. V. Tsiklinskaya, Chair of Microbiology; 1921-46 head, Dept of Children's Infections, Centr Inst of Mother and Child Care (now Inst of Pediatrics, USSR Acad of Med Sci); 1935-50 also head, Chair of Pediatrics, 3rd Moscow Med Inst; for 10 years chief pediatrician, USSR Min of Health; specialized in such infectious diseases as measles, whooping cough, dysentery and scarlet fever; supervised writing of over 300 sci works; contributed to planning of state-sponsored measures against measles, whooping cough and other infections, which led to a reduction in child mortality; also contributed to the solution of important theoretical, practical and organizational problems connected with the treatment of children's diseases, notably scarlet fever; studied the relation between age and the course of infection; Presidium member, Learned Councils, USSR and RSFSR Min of Health; chm, Acute Infections Section, Anti-Epidemic Comt; dep chm, Pediatric Commission, USSR Min of Health; chm, Problems Commission on Children's Infections; member, Bureau of Clinical Med, USSR Acad of Med Sci; co-ed, pediatrics section, *Bol'shaya meditsinskaya entsiklopediya* (Large Medical Encyclopedia); trained numerous pediatricians and infectionists; wrote over 150 sci and popular works on pediatrics and the clinical aspects, therapy and prevention of children's infections; *Publ: K voprosu o roli Bacilli coli v patogeneze ostrykh rasstroystv pitaniya* (The Role of Escherichia coli in the Pathogenesis of Acute Alimentary Disorders) (1926); *Kishechnaya flora i yeyo znacheniye v patologii grudnogo vozrasta* (Intestinal Flora and its Significance in Infant Pathology) (1927); *Nekotoryye itogi i perspektivy profilaktiki i lecheniya kori* (Results and Prospects for the Prevention and Treatment of Measles) (1936); *Kor' i bor'ba s ney* (Measles and the Campaign Against It) (1940); *Osobennosti techeniya skarlatiny za posledniye gody* (Peculiarities of the Course of Scarlet Fever in Latter Years) (1949); *Koklyush* (Whooping Cough) (1954); *Sostoyaniye i perspektivy nauchno-issledovatel'skoy raboty v oblasti bor'by s ostrymi detskimi infektsiyami* (The Status and Prospects of Research in the Campaign Against Acute Children's Infections) (1955); *Awards*: Order of Lenin; Order of the Red Banner of Labor; "Outstanding Health Worker" Badge; two medals; *Died*: 1958.

DOBROKLONSKIY, Mikhail Vasil'yevich (1886-1964) Art historian; corresp member, USSR Acad of Sci from 1943; prof, I. Ye. Repin Inst of Painting, Sculpture and Architecture from 1923; *Born*: 3 Nov 1886; *Career*: from 1919 assoc, Hermitage; prof, Leningrad Univ; studied and attributed West European graphic works in Sov museums; compiled Hermitage catalogues: *Risunki ital'yanskoy shkoly 15 i 16 vekov* (Italian-School Drawings of the 15th and 16th-Century) (1940); *Risunki Rubensa* (Rubens' Drawings) (1940); *Risunki flamandskoy shkoly 17-18 vekov* (Flemish-School Drawings of the 17-18th Centuries) (1955); *Novaya atributsiya risunka Paolo Gvidoni* (A New Attribution of Paolo Guidoni's Drawing) (1960); *Risunki ital'yanskoy shkoly 17-18 vekov* (Italian-School Drawings of the 17-18th Centuries) (1961); author and ed, several sections of *Istoriya iskusstva . zarubezhnykh stran* (A History of Foreign Art) (1962-63); *Died*: 16 Nov 1964.

DOBROMYLSKIY, Filipp Isaakovich (1893-1967) Otolaryngologist; prof from 1943; Dr of Med from 1938; CP member from 1943; *Born*: June 1893 in Yelizavetgrad (now Kirovograd); *Educ*: 1922 grad Crimean Med Inst; *Career*: after grad intern, Sevastopol' Inst of Physical Therapy; then intern, tuberculosis sanatorium in

Alupka; late 1923-28 intern, then asst prof, Clinical Otolaryngological Dept, Moscow Inst of Tuberculosis; 1933-36 extern, Otolaryngological Clinic, 2nd Moscow Med Inst; 1936-41 senior asst prof, Chair of Otolaryngology, 3rd Moscow Med Inst; 1941-43 consultant on otolaryngology, Gel'mgol'ts Centr Ophthalmological Inst; from 1943 head, Dept of Ear, Nose and Throat Diseases, Ulan Bator Republ Hospital; from 1945 head, Dept of Otolaryngology, Gel'mgol'ts Centr Ophthalmological Inst and consultant, various Moscow med establishments; wrote over 50 works, the most important of which are his monographs on the early diagnosis and treatment of tuberculosis of the larynx; his monograph *Pridatochnyye pazukhi nosa i ikh svyaz' s zabolevaniyami glaznitsy* (Accessory Sinuses of the Nose and Their Relation to Diseases of the Eyesocket) became a standard reference work for otolaryngologists and ophthalmologists and has been translated into English; *Died*: 11 Feb 1967 after a protracted illness.

DOBROMYSLOV, Dmitriy Konstantinovich (1901-1944) Russian actor; *Born*: 1901; *Educ*: grad Kazan' Theater studio; *Career*: worked in Cheboksary, Bryansk, Vologda, Bel'tsy and Leningrad; from 1931 actor, Simferopol' Theater; in WW 2, after the occupation of Simferopol' by the German army, joined underground group commanded by N. A. Baryshev, chief designer of Simferopol' Theater; 1944 all members of the group were arrested; *Roles*: Lizogub in Korneychuk's *Bogdan Khmel'nitskiy*; Vos'mibratov in Ostrovskiy's *Les* (The Forest); Kleshch in Gorky's *Na dne* (The Lower Depths); Napoleon in Solov'yov's *Fel'dmarshal Kutuzov* (Field-Marshal Kutuzov), etc; *Died*: 1944 executed by a German firing squad.

DOBRONITSKIY, Viktor Vasil'yevich (1910-1948) Cameraman; *Born*: 4 Apr 1910; *Educ*: 1935 grad Cameraman Dept, All-Union State Inst of Cinematography; *Career*: worked mainly on documentary films; 1939 helped film the Khalkhyn-Gol action, Sov break-through at the Mannerheim Line in 1939-40 Sov-Finnish War, etc; in WW 2 cameraman, front-line film teams; *Works*: filmed or helped to film: *Kontsert frontu* (Concert for the Front) (1942); *Orlovskaya bitva* (The Battle of Oryol) (1943); *Konferentsiya tryokh ministrov* (Conference of Three Ministers) (1943); *27 Oktyabr'* (The 27th of October) (1944); *Prokonvoirovaniye voyennoplennykh nemtsev cherez Moskvu* (Escorting German POW's Through Moscow) (1944); *Berlinskaya konferentsiya* (The Berlin Conference) (1945); *Parad pobedy* (Victory Parade) (1945); *Vozrozhdeniye Stalingrada* (Renaissance of Stalingrad) (1946); *Molodost' nashey strany* (The Youth of Our Country) (1947); *Moskva-stolitsa SSSR* (Moscow-Capital of the USSR) (1947); *Awards*: four Stalin Prizes (1943, 1946, 1947 and 1948); *Died*: 16 June 1948.

DOBRONRAVOV, Boris Georgiyevich (1896-1949) Russian actor; Pop Artiste of USSR from 1937; *Born*: 4 Apr 1896 in Moscow, son of a priest; *Educ*: studied at Mathematics Dept, Moscow Univ; *Career*: 1915 passed competitive examinations and joined Moscow Arts Theater; 1919 organized in Ufa a company to perform for army units; 1920-21 performed in North Caucasian cities; 1922-24 on tour with Moscow Arts Theater in Germany, Czechoslovakia, France and America; from 1920 film actor; *Roles*: in theater: Vas'ka Pepel in Gorky's *Na dne* (The Lower Depths) (1924); Narkis in Ostrovskiy's *Goryacheye serdtse* (A Warm Heart) (1926); Captain Myshlayevskiy in Bulgakov's *Dni Turbinykh* (Days of the Turbin Family) (1926); Tikhon in Ostrovskiy's *Groza* (The Thunderstorm) (1934); title role in Korneychuk's *Platon Krechet* (1935); Lopakhin in Chekhov's *Vishnyovyy sad* (The Cherry Orchard) (1935); Yarovoy in *Lyubov' Yarovaya* (1936); Listrat in Virta's *Zemlya* (The Earth) (1937); Tsar' Fyodor in A. K. Tolstoy's *Tsar Fyodor Ioannovich* (1940); Safonov in Simonov's *Russkiye lyudi* (Russian People) (1943); Voynitskiy in Chekhov's *Dyadya Vanya* (Uncle Vanya) (1947); in films: Stepan in *Domovoy agitator* (The House Agitator) (1920); Yegor Yefimov in *Peterburgskaya noch* (Petersburg Night) (1934); Shabanov in "Aerograd" (1935); Gromov in *Zaklyuchyonnye* (The Prisoners) (1936); Davydov in *Podnyataya tselina* (Virgin Soil Upturned) (1940); commission chairman in *Povest' o nastoyashchem cheloveke* (Tale of a Real Man) (1948), etc; *Awards*: Order of Lenin; Order of the Red Banner of Labor; *Died*: 27 Oct 1949 in Moscow on stage while playing the role of Tsar' Fyodor.

DOBROTVOR (ALEKSANDROV), Nikolay Mikhaylovich (1897-1967) Historian; Dr of History from 1957; prof; CP member from 1917; *Born*: 12 Apr 1897 in Tula, son of a bookbinder; *Educ*: 1933 grad Inst of Red Prof; *Career*: helped to establish Sov regime in Tula Province; served as volunteer on Civil War fronts; during 1920's worked for Tula Sovnarkhoz, cooperative Organs and Tula Province Inst of Party History; 1935-67 worked at Inst of Marxism-Leninism in Gorky, then head, Dept of Sov History and prof, Gorky Teachers' Training Inst; works on history of Bolshevik movement and establishment of Sov regime; *Publ*: *Bor'ba za khleb - bor'ba za sotsializm* (The Struggle for Bread Is the Struggle for Socialism) (1935); *Revolyutsionnaya rabota bol'shevikov v III gosudarstvennoy Dume* (The Bolsheviks' Revolutionary Work in the Third State Duma) (1957), etc; *Awards*: Order of the Red Banner of Labor (1956); Badge of Hon (1961); *Died*: 30 Apr 1967.

DOBROVEYN (real name: BARABEYCHIK), Isay Aleksandrovich (1894-1953) Russian pianist, conductor and composer; prof from 1917; *Born*: 15 Feb 1894 in Nizhniy Novgorod; *Career*: 1917-21 prof, Moscow Conservatory; from 1919 conductor, Bolshoy Theater; from 1923 abroad; as conductor toured many countries; from 1941 conductor, Stockholm Opera; *Works*: opera *1001 noch'* (1001 Nights) (1922); sonatas; concerto; romances; *Died*: 9 Dec 1953 in Oslo.

DOBROVOL'SKIY, Lev Mikhaylovich (1900-1963) Bibliographer, archivist and historian; *Born*: 4 Oct 1900 in Petersburg; *Career*: 1929-34 helped write bibliographical dictionary *Deyateli revolyutsionnogo dvizheniya* (Figures of the Revolutionary Movement); 1933-63 sci curator of the manuscripts of Pushkin House (Inst of Russian Lit), USSR Acad of Sci; from 1950 simultaneously ed, *Byulleteni rukopisnogo otdela Pushkinskogo doma* (No. 2-7 and 9); author of scholarly analyses of manuscripts and bibliographical works about 19th-century Russian classics and books proscribed and destroyed by Tsarist censorship; *Publ*: coauthor, *Kniga o knige* (The Book About Books) (1932); coauthor, *M.Ye. Saltykov-Shchedrin v pechati* (M.Ye. Saltykov-Shchedrin in Print) (1949); coauthor, *Bibliographiya pushkinskoy bibliografii za 1846-1950 gg.* (A Bibliography of Pushkin Bibliography 1846-1950) (1951); coauthor, *Bibliografiya proizvedeniy A. S. Pushkina i literatury o nyom, 1918-36* (A Bibliography of the Works of A. S. Pushkin and Literature About Him, 1918-36) (Part 1 1952); coauthor, *Bibliografiya literatury o N. A. Nekrasove, 1917-52* (A Bibliography of Literature About N. A. Nekrasov, 1917-1952) (1953); *Bibliografiya literatury o M. Ye. Saltykov-Shchedrine, 1848-1917* (A Bibliography of Literature About M. Ye. Saltykov-Shchedrin, 1848-1917) (1961); *Zapreshyonnaya kniga v Rossii 1825-1904. Arkhivno-bibliograficheskiye razyskaniya* (Proscribed Books in Russia 1825-1904. Archival and Bibliographical Finds) (1962); *Died*: 24 Apr 1963 in Leningrad.

DOBROVOL'SKIY, Victor Afanas'yevich (1884-1963)) Mech eng; Dr of Technol from 1936; prof from 1923; Hon Sci and Tech Worker of RSFRS from 1944; CP member from 1950; *Born*: 2 Feb 1884 in vil Trostyanets, now Sumy Oblast; *Educ*: 1908 grad Khar'kov Technol Inst; *Career*: 1908-11 at machine-building plants in Petersburg and Khar'kov; 1911-18 engaged in railroad construction; 1928-41 dep dir, 1946-56 dir, Odessa Polytech Inst; *Publ*: numerous works on machine-building and machines; textbooks and teaching aids; coauthor, textbook *Detali mashin* (Machine Parts) (4th ed, 1956-60); *Awards*: Order of Lenin; Order of the Red Banner of Labor; medals; *Died*: 22 Dec 1963.

DOBROVOL'SKIY, Vladimir Vladimirovich (1880-1956) Specialist in the theory of mechanisms; corresp member, USSR Acad of Sci from 1946; Hon Sci and Tech Worker of RSFSR from 1948; *Born*: 6 June 1880; *Career*: 1938 developed system of classifying mechanisms on the basis of their structural characteristics, which contributed to development of kinematics and kinestatics of mechanisms; 1940-45 worked out a theory of spherical mechanisms based on the use of analogy between plane and spherical mechanisms; *Publ*: major works on design of mechanisms; studied theory and calculation of cogged mechanisms, methods of calculating their efficiency factor, etc; wrote several textbooks and manuals for secondary and higher educ establishments; *Dinamika raschyotnoy tsepi* (Dynamics of a Calculated Chain) (Parts 1-2, 1930-31); coauthor, *Struktura i klassifikatsiya mekhanizmov* (The Structure and Classification of Mechanisms) (1939); *Sistema mekhanizmov* (A System of Mechanisms) (1943); *Teoriya sfericheskikh mekhanizmov* (The Theory of Spherical Mechanisms) (1947); *Teoriya mekhanizmov* (The Theory of Mechanisms) (1951); *Died*: 18 Aug 1956.

DOBRUSHIN, Iekhezkil' Moiseyevich (1883-1953) Jewish

playwright, poet and critic; prof from 1948; *Born*: 28 Nov 1883; *Career*: 1910 first work published; worked for the Moscow State Jewish Theater, writing plays and adapting works for the stage; wrote in Yiddish; taught at 2nd Moscow State Univ, etc; member, ed bd, Jewish periodical *Shtorm* (1922-24) and Jewish newspaper *Eynikayt* (1942-48); adapted for stage works by Goldfaden, Mendele-Moykher-Sforim and Sholom-Aleykhem, etc; subjected to reprisals by State Security organs; *Publ*: plays: "At the Hut" (1928); "The Trial Proceeds" (1930); "At the 62nd" (1931); "Brigadier Telepey" (1937), etc; books: *Veniamin Zuskin* (1939); "Solomon Mikhoels, the Actor" (1941); "David Bergelson" (1947); "Dramaturgy of the Classics" (1948) dealing with the work of Goldfaden, Mendele-Moykher-Sforim, Sholom-Aleykhem and Perets; *Died*: 11 Aug 1953 in imprisonment; posthumously rehabilitated.

DOBRUSKINA (married name: MIKHAYLOVA), Genriyetta Nikolayevna (1862- ?) Revolutionary; *Narodnaya volya* (People's Will) functionary; later member, Socialist-Revol Party; *Born*: 1862, daughter of a teacher; *Educ*: studied in Petersburg at Higher Courses for Women; *Career*: as student active in revol circles; after 1 Mar 1881 joined *Narodnaya volya* Party; worked for a while in Warsaw with officials of the Polish revol *Proletariat* Party; 1883 returned to Petersburg and contacted leaders of the Young *Narodnaya volya* Party Yakubovich, Sukhomlin, etc; at their suggestion went to do underground work in Rostov-on-Don, where she became an active member of the local *Narodnaya volya* movement; helped set up a secret printing shop; 1884 arrested; 1887 sentenced to death sentence commuted to eight years' hard labor; served sentence in Kara; 1900 moved to Chita; later joined Socialist-Revol Party; 1905 member of Chita comt which arranged P..V. Karpovich's escape, planned M. Maslikovaya's abduction from Chita Prison and organized the assassination of prison inspector Metus; 1907 returned to European Russia; 1917 member, Odessa Sov of Workers' Dep; *Died*: date and place of death unknown.

DOBRYNIN, Boris Fyodorovich (1885-1951) Geographer; Dr of Geography; *Born*: 26 May 1885; *Educ*: 1911 grad Physics and Mathematics Fac, Moscow Univ; *Career*: 1916-23 assoc prof, Moscow Univ; 1923-30 prof of geography, 2nd Moscow Univ; from 1931 prof, 1st Moscow Univ; member, Geographical Research Inst, Moscow Univ; ed, physical geography section, "Large Soviet Atlas of the World"; geographic field study in the Crimea, Caucasus, centr Russian plain and in the middle Volga area; studied geomorphological zones of European USSR; textbooks on geography of European USSR and Western Europe; numerous articles; *Publ: Landshaftnyye rayony i rastitel'nost' Dagestana* (Morphological Zones and Vegetation of Daghestan) (1925); *Geografiya Dagestanskoy ASSR* (Geography of the Daghestan ASSR) (1926); *Landshafty gornogo Kryma* (Landscape of the Crimean Highlands) (1928); coauthor, *Geomorfologicheskiye i pochvennyye rayony Yugo-Vostochnoy chasti Moskovskoy oblasti* (Geomorphological and Soil Zones of the Southeastern Moscow Oblast) (1931); *Fizicheskaya geografiya SSSR. Yevropeyskaya chast' i Kavkaz* (Physical Geography of the USSR. European USSR and the Caucasus) (2nd ed, 1948); *Fizicheskaya geografiya Zapadnoy Yevropy* (The Physical Geography of Western Europe) (1948); *Died*: 4 Sept 1951.

DOBRYNIN, Pyotr Georgiyevich (1894-1917) Revolutionary; participated in 1917 Oct Revol in Moscow; *Born*: 1894 in Tula Province, son of a worker; *Career*: joined RSDRP(B) while working at a Moscow telegraph and telephone equipment plant; after 1917 Feb Revol helped to muster Red Guards in Zamoskvorech'ye Rayon, Moscow; from May 1917 member, Moscow City and Zamoskvorech'ye Rayon Center of Red Guards Staffs; Oct 1917 member, Zamoskvorech'ye Rayon Mil-Revol Comt; led a Red Guards detachment in fighting against the mil cadets in the area of Prechistenka (now Kropotkin Street) and Ostozhenka (now Metrostroyevskaya Street) for possession of the Moscow Mil Distr Headquarters, was fatally wounded; *Died*: 1 Nov 1917; former Serpukhov Square in Moscow named after him.

DOBRZHINSKIY, Gavriil Valer'yanovich (1883-1946) Russian writer; *Born*: 25 Apr 1883 in Vol'sk, Saratov Oblast; *Career*: 1901 first publicistic work published; participated in 1905 Revol; lost eyesight in exile; *Publ*: historical novel *Bozh'i kogti* (The Claws of God) (1930); collected stories *Zyb' perekatnaya* (Ground Swell) (1930); novel *Vladimir Ravnoapostol'nyy* (1931); stories: *Osvobozhdeniye Kryma* (Liberation of the Crimea) (1932); *Kholop Ivashka Bolotnikov* (Ivashka Bolotnikov, the Serf) (1932); novel *Trekhgortsy* (Men from the Three Mountains) (1935); plays: *Velikiy yeretik* (The Great Heretic) (1936); *Ivan Bolotnikov* (1938); *Russkaya devushka* (Russian Girl) (1943); *Died*: 8 Mar 1946 in Moscow.

DOBUZHINSKIY, Mstislav Valerianovich (1875-1958) Painter, graphic artist and stage designer; prof from 1922; *Born*: 2 Aug 1875 in Nizhniy Novgorod; *Educ*: studied at a Munich art school; 1899-1903 studied under Khalloshi and 1905 under Mate in Petersburg; *Career*: 1903 joined *Novyy mir* (New World) Soc; from 1906 taught at various art schools in Russia; from 1907 theater work; after 1917 Oct Revol helped organize Petrograd Bolshoy Drama Theater; 1922 prof, Leningrad Acad of Arts; 1926 emigrated to Lith, henceforth lived and worked abroad; *Works*: sets for plays: *Igra o Robene i Marion* (Robin and Marion) (1907); D'Annunzio's "Francesca da Rimini" (1908); Turgenev's *Mesyats v derevne* (A Month in the Country) (1909); *Nakhlebnik* (The Parasite); *Gde tonko, tam i rvyotsya* (The Better Worn, the Sooner Torn); Turgenev's *Provintsialka* (The Provincial Girl) (1912); *Nikolay Stavrogin* (1913); *Gore ot uma* (Woe from Wit) (1914); *Selo Stepanchikovo* (Stepanchikovo Village) (1917); "Die Räuber" (1919); "King Lear" (1920); as an emigre designed sets for plays: *Boris Godunov* (1941, London); Gogol's *Sorochinskaya yarmarka* (Sorochinsk Fair) (1942, New York); Prokofiev's *Lyubov' k tryom apel'sinam* (Love of Three Oranges) (1949, New York), etc; *Died*: 1958 in New York.

DOBZHINSKIY, Konstantin Andreyevich (1889-1967) Russian actor; Pop Artiste of Geo SSR from 1954; *Born*: 25 Dec 1889; *Career*: 1906 began stage work in Nikolayev, then at various Russian towns; from 1936 at Griboyedov Russian State Drama Theater in Tbilisi; *Roles*: Frol Fedulych in Ostrovskiy's *Poslednyaya zhertva* (The Last Victim); Chugunov in Ostrovskiy's *Volki i ovtsy* (The Wolves and the Sheep); Berest in Korneychuk's *Platon Krechet*; Dzerzhinskiy in Pogodin's *Kremlevskiye kuranty* (Kremlin Chimes); Bessmenov in Gorky's *Meshchane* (Philistines); Zheleznov in Gorky's *Vassa Zheleznova*; Storozhev in Virta's *Zemlya* (The Earth), etc; *Died*: 27 Apr 1967.

DODONOVA, Anna Andreyevna (1888-1967) Revolutionary; Party official; CP member from 1911; *Born*: Dec 1888; *Educ*: grad Higher Courses for Women in Moscow; completed postgrad course; *Career*: from 1909 took part in Soc-Democratic circles of Higher Courses for Women in Moscow; arrested for revol activities; after 1917 Feb Revol secr, Moscow Sov of Workers' dep; Oct-Nov 1917 secr, Mil-Revol Comt; 1918 head, Cultural Dept, Moscow Sov; 1920-32 chm, Moscow cultural and educational org *Proletarian Culture* and member of its CC Presidium; from 1932 postgrad student; later active in research and educ work; from 1957 pensioner; *Died*: May 1967.

DOGADIN, Aleksandr Adrianovich (1869-circa 1920) Collector of Cossack folk songs; *Born*: 1869; *Educ*: grad Orenburg Cossack Cadets College; *Career*: until 1907 served in Cossack units; as an expert in folk songs, worked for a commission collecting historical materials on Astrakhan' and the Cossack Army; recorded and prepared for publ a collection of songs for male-voice choir *Byliny i pesni astrakhanskikh kazakov* (Ballads and Songs of the Astrakhan' Cossacks) (1911); this collection, the only ed of Astrakhan' Cossack's songs, contains 210, mainly historical, songs (about Stepan Razin, Suvorov, the 1812 Franco-Russian War, etc); *Publ: Rasskazy o sluzhbe kazakov Astrakhanskogo kazach'yego voyska* (Stories of Service in the Astrakhan' Cossack Army) (1908); *Died*: circa 1920.

DOGADOV, Aleksandr Ivanovich (1888-1938) Govt and trade-union official; CP member from 1905; *Born*: 1888 in Kazan' Province, son of a worker; *Educ*: grad Party school in Longjumeau near Paris; *Career*: worker; from early childhood worked as apprentice in casting shops at Libigkht Plant in Kazan'; 1905 joined RSDRP and sided with Bolsheviks; soon rose to membership of plant and rayon Party comt; from 1906 secr, Metal Workers' Union in Kazan' and Bureau member, illegal Kazan' Trade-Union Council; 1907 arrested for membership of RSDRP and exiled to Vologda Province for two years; 1909-10, after return from exile, worked in Baku and Balakhany oil fields; active in local Party org; 1911 sent to Party school in Longjumeau near Paris; after grad returned to Party work in Russia; 1912 Kazan' org deleg to Prague RSDRP Conference; then worked for Petrograd org; arrested and exiled to Vologda Province; 1914 conscripted into army; 1917 chm, brigade, then div and army comt on Southwestern Front; from 1918 chm, Tatar Trade-Union Council and member, Tatar Council of Pop Comr in Kazan'; 1921 at 4th All-Russian Trade-Union Congress elected to Presidium, All-Union Centr Trade-Union Council, of which for a number of years he was secr and in 1930 dep chm; member, Trade-Union International; until 1930 dep, USSR Supr Sovnarkhoz; member, Anglo-Sov Unity Comt; 1925 All-Union Centr Trade-Union Council rep at trade-union congress in Scarborough; along with leadership of All-Union Centr Trade-Union Council took a right-wing stand on trade-union questions; after 8th Trade Union Congress abandoned this stand; from 1931 worked for Pop Comrt of Workers and Peasants' Inspection; from 1934 with Sov Control Commission; at 10th Party Congress elected cand member, Centr Control Commission; at 13th, 14th and 15th Party Congresses elected CC member, at 16th cand member, CC, CPSU(B); at 17th Congress elected member, Sov Control Commission; 1930-33 cand member, Org Bureau, CC, CPSU(B); arrested by State Security organs; *Died*: 1938 in imprisonment.

DOGEL', Aleksandr Stanislavovich (1852-1922) Histologist; pioneer of Russian neurohistology; *Born*: 27 Jan 1852; *Educ*: 1879 grad Med Fac, Kazan' Univ; *Career*: 1878 while still a student did research on innervation of the ureter under K. A. Arnshteyn; 1881 was awarded a scholarship to prepare for professorship at Kazan' Univ; 1883 defended doctor's thesis on the structure of the retina in ganoids and was sent abroad for further specialist training; from 1885 dissector and lecturer, Chair of Histology, Kazan' Univ; 1888-95 head, Chair of Histology, Tomsk Univ, where he established a first-class histological laboratory; from 1895 until death prof, Chair of Histology, Petersburg Univ; from 1897 simultaneously prof, Petersburg Women's Med Inst; specialized in the histology of the nervous system and the sense organs; he, his pupil and his successors (V. F. Martynov, A. V. Nemilov, D. I. Deynek, etc) discovered and described almost all the forms of nerve endings in the tissues and organs of verebrates known to modern histology; obtained dato on innvervation of the skin, muscles, glands, heart and other human and animal organs; these findings are of particular importance for the physiology of interoception; his research on sensory innvervation of the heart was acclaimed by I. P. Pavlov; studied the fine structure of sensory and vegetative nerve ganglia, explained their interrelationship and detected pericellular plexi belonging to the sympathetic nerve fibers; established the presence of three types of neurons in vegetative ganglia and demonstrated the effector nature of the Dogel' Type 1 cell; this research provided a basis for the study of synapses in the vegetative nervous system; contributed to the study of evolutionary histology with his research on the philogenesis of the nervous system and sense organs; developed method of supravital staining of nerve elements with methylene blue (Dogel' method); from 1903 member and Russian rep, Int Assoc for the Study of the Nervous System; 1915 founded journal *Russkiy arkhiv anatomii, gistologii i embriologii*; wrote over 100 sci and popular works; *Publ:* doctor's thesis *Stroyeniye retiny u ganoid* (The Structure of the Retina in Ganoids) (1883); *Stroyeniye obonyatel'nogo organa u ganoid, kostistykh ryb i amfibiy* (The Structure of the Olfactory Organ in Ganoids, Teleosts and Amphibians) (1886); *Gistologicheskiye issledovaniya* (Histological Research) (1897); *Okonchaniya chuvstvitel'nykh nervov v serdtse i krovenosnykh sosudakh mlekopitayushchikh* (Sensory Nerve Endings in the Heart and Blood Vessels of Mammals) (1897); *Tekhnika okrashivaniya nervnoy sistemy metilenovoyu sin'yu* (A Technique of Staining the Nervous System With Methylene Blue) (1902); *Kontsevyye nervnyye aparaty v kozhe cheloveka* (Terminal Nerve Apparatuses in the Human Skin) (1904); "Der Bau der Spinalganglien des Menschen und der Säugetiere" (The Structure of the Spinal Ganglia in Man and Mammals) (1908); *Krov' kak osnova zhizni cheloveka i zhivotnykh* (Blood as a Basis of Human and Animal Life) (1922); *Starost' i smert'* (Old Age and Death) (1922); *Stroyeniye i zhizn' kletki* (The Structure and Life of the Cell) (1922); *Pochki i ikh znacheniye dlya zhizni nashego tela* (The Kidneys and Their Importance for Our Body's Life) (1923); *Died*: 1922.

DOGEL', Valentin Aleksandrovich (1882-1955) Zoologist; corresp member, USSR Acad of Sci from 1939; son of A. S. Dogel'; *Born*: 10 Mar 1882; *Educ*: 1902 grad Nat Sci Dept, Fac of Physics and Mathematics, Petersburg Univ; *Career*: after grad remained at univ to prepare for professorship; 1913-55 head, Chair of Invertebrate Zoology, Petersburg (Leningrad) Univ; founderhead, Laboratory of Fish Diseases, All-Union Research Inst of Fresh-Water Fishery; head, Laboratory of Protozoology, Zoological Inst, USSR Acad of Sci; did important research on morphology, taxonomy, reproduction and philogeny of certain parasitic infusorians; 1951 published maj work on gen protozoology; 1941 pioneer of ecological parasitology, the basic tenets of which he outlined in his course of gen parasitology; 1954 during studies of comparative anatomy he came to conclusion that oligomerization is one of main evolutionary paths of animals; elaborated principles of oligomerization and polymerization of animal organs in process of philogenesis; wrote over 250 works on protozoology, parasitology and comparative anatomy, including textbooks for higher educ establishments; *Publ: Catenata, organizatsiya roda Haplozoon i nekotorykh skhodnykh s nim form* (Catenata, the Organization of the Genus Haplozoon and Some Related Forms) (1910); *Materialy po istorii razvitiya Pantoda* (Material of the History of the Development of Pantoda) (1913); *Polgoda v tropikakh* (Half a Year in the Tropics) (1924); "Die Geschlechtsprozesse bei Infusorien (speziell bei den Ophryoscoleciden). Neue Tatsachen und theoretische Erwägungen" (Sexual Processes in Infusorians (Especially Ophryoscolecidae). New Facts and Hypotheses) (1925); *Sravnitel'naya anatomiya bespozvonochnykh* (Comparative Invertebrate Anatomy) (2 vol, 1938-40); *Kurs obshchey parazitologii* (A Course of General Parasitology) (2nd ed, 1947); *Zoologiya bespoznonochnyykh* (Invertebrate Zoology) (4th ed, 1947); *Obshchaya protistologiya* (General Protistology) (1951); *Oligomerizatsiya gomologichnykh organov kak odin iz glavnykh putey evolyutsii zhivotnykh* (The Oligomerization of Homologous Organs as One of the Main Paths of Animal Evolution) (1954); *Awards*: Lenin Prize (1957, posthumously); *Died*: 1 June 1955.

DOK (BLYUM), P.O. (1869-1921) Party official; *Born*: 1869; *Career*: 1904 joined Soc-Democratic movement; 1907 member, CC, Lat Soc-Democratic Party; frequently subjected to reprisals by Tsarist authorities; exiled to Siberia; 1912 fled to Irkutsk, where he did underground revol work; Riga Soc-Democratic Org deleg at 5th RSDRP Congress; after 1917 Oct Revol worked in Siberia; *Died*: 1921.

DOKTUROVSKIY, Vladimir Semyonovich (1884-1935) Botanist and geographer; swamp specialist and paleobotanist; *Born*: 18 Nov 1884 in Nikolayev; *Educ*: 1907 grad Natural Sci Div, Physico-Mathematical Fac, Moscow Univ; *Career*: 1908-12 botanist, Petersburg Botanical Garden; from 1912 at Russian Dept of Agric; from 1915 head of botanical studies, peat section, Dept of Soil Improvement, Russian Dept of Agric, later RSFSR Pop Comrt of Agric, Moscow; simultaneously 1922-30 head, Botanical Dept, Experimental Peat Inst; also lectured at Land Survey Inst (1918-23), Veterinary Inst (1919-25), Peat Dept, Acad of Mining (1927-30), Ind Acad (1932), Inst of Land Exploitation, Moscow Univ and Bel Univ; explored swamplands in Transcaucasia, Siberia, European RSFSR and Bel, etc; catalogued their precise characteristics; developed method of studying the connection between the flora, water conditions and geological structure of swamps and the chemical composition of peat; introduced method of pollen analysis and studying distribution of pollen of arboreal plants in peat, etc; examined stratigraphy of swamps, vegetation of interglacial deposits, buried peats; 1908 visited Japan, 1910 Finland, 1925 and 1929 Sweden, 1925 Norway, 1928-29 Germany, 1928 Czechoslovakia and 1928-29 Poland; took part in 4th and 5th Int Botanico-Geographical Expeditions; member, comt which founded Int Assoc of Swamp Specialists; chm, Commission for Swamp Research, Int Assoc of Soil Scientists; *Publ: Bolota, stroyeniye i razvitiye ikh* (Swamps, Their Structure and Development) (1915); *Bolota i torfyanniki, razvitiye i stroyeniye ikh* (Swamps and Peat Bogs, Their Structure and Development) (1922); *Torfyanyye bolota kak predmet izucheniya na ekskursiyakh i v shkole* (Peat Bogs as an Object of Study for Field Trips and at School) (1926); coauthor, *Slovar'-spravochnik po torfyanomu delu* (Reference Dictionary on Peat Working) (1928); "Peat Bogs, Their Origin and Development" (1930); *Torfyanyye bolota. Kurs lektsiy po bolotovedeniyu* (Peat Bogs. A Course of Lectures on Swamp Study) (1932); *Torfyanyye bolota. Proiskhozdeniye, priroda i osobennosti bolot SSSR* (Peat Bogs. Origin, Nature and Features of Swamps in the USSR) (1935); "Die Moore Osteuropas und Nordasiens" (1938); *Awards*: Gold Medal of Russian Geographical Soc (1924); *Died*: 20 Mar 1935.

DOL'D-MIKHAYLYK, Yuriy (real name: MIKHAYLYK, Yuriy Petrovich) (1903-1966) Ukr writer and playwright; CP member from 1949; *Born*: 17 Mar 1903 in vil Butenki, now Poltava Oblast; *Educ*: grad Dnepropetrovsk Inst of Educ; *Career*: until 1922 lecturer-librarian, then head, uyezd educ dept and dir, Lozovaya Children's Labor Colony; from 1922 journalist in Dnepropetrovsk, Kherson and Vinnitsa; 1925 worked for Dnepropetrovsk periodical *Zorya*; from 1929 with Khar'kov newspaper *Kommunist*; during WW 2 head, Theater Dept, Turkm Bd of Art Problems; subsequently head, Lit Dept, Shchors Theater; *Publ*: 1925 first work published; novels: "For the Soviet Regime" (1925); "Between Two Fatherlands" (1930); "The Steppe-Dwellers" (1948); "A Warrior Alone in the Field" (1957); plays: *Shchors; Kotovskiy* (1937-38); "Mother"; "Fire in the Night"; "The Earth"; "The Big River" (1942-45); "The Restless Neighbor" (1946); "The Great Law" (1948); "Borislav Tragedy" (1953); tales and essays: "The Thirsty Steppe" (1951); "Kakhovka Tales" (1952); "Portrait of a Mother" (1954); film scripts: "Far from the Fatherland"; "With the Mountain Knights" (1964); *Died*: 17 May 1966.

DOLGOPOLOV, Nifont Ivanovich (1857-1922) Health service official and revolutionary; *Born*: 1857 in Biryuch, Voronezh Province, son of an office worker; *Educ*: 1887 grad Med Fac, Khar'kov Univ; *Career*: 1879 deported to Kurgan, Tobol'sk Province, for involvement in student riots; later exiled to Tyukalinsk and Ishim for illegal med practice; after return from exile and graduation worked as surgeon in Kursk and other provincial hospitals; took part in Pirogov congresses, delivering papers on soc sci; co-founder, Commission for the Propagation of Hygiene; 1905 joined Soc-Revol Party; from Dec 1905 until death worked as a physician in Astrakhan', where he was exiled for revol activities in Nizhniy-Novgorod; 1907 elected to 2nd State Duma as rep of Populist bloc; the former Babushkin Hospital and Pesochnaya Street in Gorky are named after him; wrote a dozen sci works and numerous newspaper articles; *Died*: 1922 in Astrakhan' of typhus during an epidemic; buried at Novodevich'ye Cemetery, Moscow.

DOLGORUKOV, Pavel Dmitrievich (1866-1930) Politician; prince; major landowner; member, Constitutional Democratic Party; *Born*: 1866; *Career*: 1893-1906 uyezd Doyen of Nobility, Moscow Province; co-founder, Constitutional Democratic Party; 1905-11 chm of its CC; chm, Constitutional-Democratic faction in 2nd Duma; after 1917 Oct Revol active in plots against Sov regime; sentenced for counterrevol activity; *Died*: 1930 in imprisonment.

DOLGO–SABUROV, Boris Alekseyevich (1900-1960) Anatomist; corresp member, USSR Acad of Med Sci from 1945; prof from 1939; Dr of Med from 1935; *Born*: 11 Nov 1900 in Kostroma, son of a med orderly; *Educ*: 1925 grad Mil Med Acad; *Career*: 1922, while still a student, began med research work under V.N. Tonkov; 1927-40 lecturer, then dep head, Chair of Normal Anatomy, Mil Med Acad; 1937-40 simultaneously head, Chair of Normal Anatomy, 3rd Leningrad Med Inst; 1940-50 head, Chair of Normal Anatomy, Naval Med Acad; 1950-60 head, Chair of Normal Anatomy, Kirov Mil Med Acad; specialized in functional morphology; did research on the plasticity of veins and arteries in relation to collateral circulation; during study of the interneuronal gaps in the vagus nerve discovered pericellular apparatus and depicted the vagal trunk as a system of different conductors; in collaboration with fellow-scientists and pupils made major contribution to the study of afferent innervation of the veins; 1953 presented new data on nervovascular relations in the centr nervous system; detected synaptic structures on the sanguiferous capillaries around nerve cells; supervised writing of over 300 papers and 20 theses; trained numerous prof of anatomy; helped to organize 5th and 6th All-Union Congresses of Anatomists, Histologists and Embryologists; 1955 and 1957 attended Int Congresses of Morphologists in Paris and Atlantic City; member, ed bd, Swiss journal *Acta anatomica*; co-ed, morphology section *Bol'shaya meditsinskaya entsiklopediya* (Large Medical Encyclopedia); from 1954 ed, journal *Arkhiv anatomii, gistologii i embriologii*; from 1950 chm, Leningrad Sci Soc of Anatomists, Histologists and Embryologists; from 1958 dep chm, All-Union Sci Soc of Anatomists, Histologists and Embryologists; member, Morphological Comt, Presidium of USSR Acad of Med Sci; wrote over 100 works, including five monographs; *Publ*: "Die potentiellen Eigenschaften der Arterien der vorderen Extremität bei Tieren unter den Bedingungen des Experiments" (Potential Properties of the Arteries in the Forelegs of Animals Under Experimental Conditions) (1931); doctor's thesis *Kollateral'noye krovoobrashcheniye i potential'nyye svoystva arteriy* (Collateral Circulation and Potential Properties of the Arteries) (1935); *Anastomozy i puti okol'nogo krovoobrashcheniya u cheloveka* (Anastomoses and Collateral Circulation Paths in Man) (1956); *Nevronnaya teoriya - osnova sovremennykh predstavleniy o stroyenii i funktsii nervnoy sistemy* (The Neuron Theory - the Basis of Contemporary Concepts of the Structure and Function of the Nervous System((1956); *Innervatsiya ven* (Innervation of the Veins) (1958); *Plastichnost' krovenosnykh sosudov* (The Plasticity of the Blood Vessels) (1960); *Awards*: for orders; medals; *Died*: 24 Apr 1960.

DOLGOV, Pyotr Ivanovich (1920-1962) Test-parachutist; col from 1960; Master of Sport of USSR; CP member from 1945; *Born*: 21 Feb 1920; *Educ*: 1942 grad infantry school; *Career*: from 1940 in Sov Army; fought in WW 2; subsequently devoted all his time to improving parachutes and other aviation rescue devices; pioneered use of ejector seats; helped to devise landing technique of *Vostok* space ships; made 1,409 parachute jumps; *Awards*: Stalin Prize (1952); Hero of the Sov Union (1962, posthumously); Order of Lenin; two Orders of the Red Banner; two Orders of the Red Star; six medals; *Died*: killed 1 Nov 1962 in a parachute jump from the stratospheric balloon *Volga,* from an altitude of 25,458 meters.

DOLIDZE, Viktor Isidorovich (1890-1933) Geo composer; *Born*: 18 July 1890 in Ozurgeti (now Makharadze), son of a peasant; *Educ*: 1917 grad Kiev Business Inst; simultaneously studied violin and composition at Kiev Music College; *Career*: while a student organized a mandolin and guitar orchestra; composed first Geo comic operaa "Keto and Kote"; his compositions are based on Geo urban musical folklore; arranged over 200 Ossetian folk songs and dances; *Works*: operas: "Keto and Kote" (1918); *Leyla* (1922); *Tsisana* (1929); *Zamira* (1931, unfinished); fantasia *Iveriada* (1925); symphony *Azerbaydzhan* (1931-32); nine romances; *Awards*: gold medal at the 1910 Mandolin Competition in Tiflis; *Died*: 24 May 1933 in Tiflis.

DOLINA (real name: GORLENKO: nee: SAYUSHKINA), Mariya Ivanovna (1868-1919) Russian opera singer (contralto); *Born*: 1 Apr 1868; *Educ*: private music courses in Petersburg; *Career*: 1886-1904 at Petersburg Mariinskiy Theater; from 1904 concert work, popularizing Russian music in Russia and abroad; 1907-09 appeared in "Russian Song" and "Slavic Song" concert series, which also involoved foreign tours; *Roles*: Vanya and Ratmir in Glinka's *Ivan Susanin* and *Ruslan i Lyudmila* (Ruslan and Ludmilla); Ol'ga and Basmanov in Tchaikovsky's *Yevgeniy Onegin* and *Oprichnik*; Grunya and Izyaslav in A. N. Serov's *Vrazh'ya sila* (The Evil Force) and *Rogneda*; Siebel in Gounod's "Faust," etc; *Died*: 2 Dec 1919.

DOLINA (real name: POPIKOV), Pavel Trofimovich (1888-1955) Film dir; CP member from 1945; *Born*: 12 Nov 1888 in vil Myshelovki near Kiev; *Educ*: 1915 grad Theater College, Kiev Arts and Lit Soc; *Career*: 1918 joined company of "Young Theater"; 1919-25 actor and stage dir at various Ukr theaters; 1925-29 film dir, Odessa Film Studio; 1929-40 film dir, Kiev Feature Films Studio; 1941-43 film dir, Tech Film Studio, Kiev-Tashkent; 1947-55 dir, Kiev State Theater Museum; main subjects of films are Civil War, establishment of kolkhozes and campaign against the kulaks; *Works*: directed films: *Chertopolokh* (The Thistle) (1928); *Burya* (Storm) (1928); *V sugrobakh* (In the Snowdrifts) (1929); *Novymi putyami* (By New Paths) (1929); *Sekret rapida* (Rapid's Secret) (1930); *Chyornyye dni* (Rainy Days) (1930); *Chatuy* (1931); *Prazdnik Uniri* (Uniri Holiday) (1932), etc; *Died*: 15 Sept 1955.

DOLIVO (real name: DOLIVO-SOBOTNITSKIY), Anatoliy Leonidovich (1893-1964) Russian singer (bass); Dr of Arts; Hon Art Worker of RSFSR from 1944; *Born*: 29 Sept 1893 in Pavlograd; *Educ*: studied under Mazetti; *Career*: from 1918 chamber singer; prof, Moscow Conservatory; *Publ: Pevets i pesnya* (The Singer and the Song) (1948); *Zametki ob istokakh russkoy klassischeskoy i sovremyonnoy vokal'noy shkoly* (Notes on the Origin of the Russian Classic and Modern Vocal School) (1954); *Ispolnitel' (pevets) i khudozhestvennyye printsipy Musorgskogo* (The Performer (Singer and the Artistic Principles of Moussorgsky) (1958); *Died*: 20 Apr 1964 in Moscow.

DOLLER, Mikhail Ivanovich (1889-1952) Film dir and actor; *Born*: 1889; *Career*: 1910-23 actor and stage dir; from 1923 film work; from 1926 worked with film dir Pudovkin; *Works*: co-directed films: *Kirpichiki* (Bricklets) (1925; *Ekh, yablochko* (Hey, Little Apple) (1926); *Konets Sankt-Peterburga* (The End of St Petersburg) (1927); *Salamandra* (Salamander) (1928); *Chiny i lyudi* (Titles and People) (1929); *Prostoy sluchay* (A Simple Case) (1932); *Gorizont* (Horizon) (1933); *Vosstaniye rybakov* (Mutiny of the Fishermen) (1934); *Gibel' sensatsii* (End of a Sensation) (1935); *Minin i Pozharskiy* (Minin and Pozharskiy) (1939); *Suvorov* (1940); *Pir v Zhirmunke* (The Feast at Zhirmunka) (1941); *Roles*: the student Filonov in *Salamandra* (Salamander);

Smith in *Gorizont* (Horizon); *Awards*: Stalin Prize (1941); *Died*: 1952.

DOMASHYOVA, Mariya Petrovna (1875-1952) Russian actress; Pop Artiste of RSFSR from 1951; *Born*: 2 Jan 1875; *Educ*: 1893 grad Moscow Philharmonic College; *Career*: 1893-95 actress, Moscow Korsh Theater; 1895-99 actress, Petersburg Theater, Lit and Arts Soc; from 1899 actress, Petersburg Aleksandrinskiy Theater (now Leningrad Pushkin Theater); during WW 2 performed in front-line concerts, plays and radio broadcasts in Leningrad; *Roles*: title role in *In Snegurochka* (The Snow Maiden); Varya in Solov'yov and Ostrovskiy's *Dikarka* (The Savage); Liza in Griboyedov's *Gore ot uma* (Woe from Wit); Tanya in *Plody prosveshcheniya* (Fruits of Enlightenment); Polina in Ostrovskiy's *Dokhodnoye mesto* (A Lucrative Job); Verochka in Ostrovskiy's *Shutniki* (The Jokers); Rosie in Sudermann's "Battle of the Butterflies"; Mariya Timofeyevna in Turgenev's *Dvoryanskoye gnezdo* (A Nest of Gentlefolk); Prof Polezhayev's wife in the film *Deputat Baltiki* (Baltic Deputy), etc; *Died*: 8 May 1952.

DOMINIKOVSKIY, Fyodor Nikolayevich (1905-1949) Agrochemist; soil expert and swamp specialist; Cand of Agric from 1935; prof, Bel State Univ; *Born*: 11 Jan 1905 in vil Glubokoye, now Vitebsk Oblast; *Educ*: 1927 grad Natural Sci Div, Pedag Fac, Voronezh Univ; *Career*: 1933-43 asst prof, from 1943 prof and head, Chair of Soil Sci, Bel State Univ; in 1930's studied soils and marshland in Berezina River Basin and in Borisov Reserve; studied buried peat lignites of the Poles'ye region; simultaneously studied the effect of mineral fertilizers on the stomata and transpiration of wheat, and the effect of soil reactions and fertilizers on plants; established agrophisiological importance of trace elements in Khibinsk apatites; determined genesis of bog phosphates and their significance as a source of phosphate nourishment for plants; *Publ: Kaliyevyye udobreniya v usloviyakh BSSR* (Potassium Fertilizers in the Belorussian SSR) (1931); *Fosfornyye udobreniya i ikh deystviye na podzol'nykh pochvakh* (Phosphoric Fertilizers and Their Effect on Podzolic Soils) (1934); coauthor, *Viviant. Novyy vid mestnogo udobreniya* (Viviant. A New Type of Local Fertilizer) (1938); *Issledovaniye mikroelementov i azotosoderzhashchikh veshchestv kak udobreniy* (A Study of Trace Elements and Nitrogenous Substances as Fertilizers) (1948), etc; *Died*: 1949 in Minsk.

DOMOGATSKIY, Vladimir Nikolayevich (1876-1939) Sculptor; Hon Art Worker of RSFSR from 1937; *Born*: 20 Apr 1876 in Odessa; *Educ*: grad Law Fac, Moscow Univ; simultaneously studied sculpture under S. M. Volnukhin at Moscow School of Painting and Sculpture; *Career*: 1904 and 1912 perfected his skill and technique in Paris; first exhibition 1904; subsequently a number of exhibitions in Russia and abroad (Paris, Venice, New York); until 1912 influenced by impressionism; during revol soc and research work; *Works*: sculpted mostly in marble; numerous realistic busts and historical busts, tomb sculptures, animal carvings, etc; busts: *Vladimir Solov'yov* (1916); *Byron* (1919); "Portrait of V. A. Vatagin" (1924); "Portrait of My Son" (1926); "Portrait of V. V. Veresayev" (1929); "Head of an Old Man" (1934); bas-reliefs: "Michelangelo" and *Mickiewicz* (1918); busts: Pushkin (1926-27); L. N. Tolstoy (1928), etc; tomb sculptures for A. I. Sumbatov-Yuzhin (1928), A. V. Petrov-Sergeyev (1934), both at the Novodevich'ye Cemetery in Moscow, etc; a number of his sculptures are displayed at the Moscow Tret'yakov Gallery, the Leningrad Russian Museum and other Sov museums; the bronze bust of Pushkin is set up on a square in Shanghai; *Died*: 30 Mar 1939.

DOMRACHEV, Ivan Vladimirovich (1889-1960) Surgeon; Dr of Med from 1926; prof from 1936; Hon Sci Worker of RSFSR from 1940; CP member; *Born*: 25 Oct 1889 in vil Adzhima, now Kirov Oblast; *Educ*: 1913 grad Med Fac, Kazan' Univ; *Career*: after grad asst dissector, Chair of Normal and Pathological Anatomy, Kazan' Univ; also extern, Chair of Gen Surgery, Kazan' Univ; 1914 drafted into Russian Army and served as a regt physician; from 1915 head, Surgical Dept, Kazan' Distr Mil Hospital and intern, Hospital Surgery Clinic, Kazan' Univ, where he continued surgical studies under Prof A. V. Vishnevskiy; from 1917 chief physician and surgeon of a mobile field hospital with a Red Army div; 1921 returned to Kazan' after demobilization and completed his internship at Hospital Surgery Clinic to become an asst prof; 1926 defended doctor's thesis on secretory innervation of the prostata; from 1933 assoc prof; 1933-60 head, Surgical Dept, 3rd Kazan' Municipal Hospital; 1936-60 also prof and head, Chair of Gen Surgery, and head, Chairs of Fac and Hospital Surgery, Pediatric Fac, Kazan' Med Inst; during WW 2 surgical consultant, various evacuation hospitals, Kazan'; as a pupil and assoc of Prof A. V. Vishnevskiy, was one of first Russian surgeons to work on the development of local infiltration anaesthesia; did research on the healing properties of novocain, which he used to block the splanchnic nerves and neighboring sympathetic trunks in inflammatory processes of the abdomen and viscera; developed new technique of preparing catgut which was introduced at the Kazan' Catgut Works; devised several methods of operating for gastric and duodenal ulcers; also devised an intestinal suture for the treatment of anastomosis; in the course of his career performed some 30,000 complex operations and trained many outstanding surgeons; attended numerous surgical congresses and was dep chm, Tatar Surgical Soc and bd member, All-Russian Surgeons' Soc; wrote over 50 works; *Publ*: doctor's thesis *Sekretornaya innervatsiya predstatel'noy zhelezy* (Secretory Innervation of the Prostata) (1926); *Mestnaya infil'tratsionnaya anasteziya pri operativnom udelenii fibrom osnovaniya cherepa* (Local Infiltration Anaesthesia for the Surgical Removal of Fibromas at the Base of the Skull); *Otdalyonnyye rezul'taty posle operativnogo udaleniya raka grudnoy zhelezy pod mestnoy anesteziyey* (Long–Term Results of the Surgical Removal of Mammary Cancer Under Local Anaesthesia); *K tekhnike operativnogo vmeshatel'stva po povodu posleoperatsionnoy pepticheskoy yazvy, anastomoza zheludka i toshchey kishki* (Surgical Treatment Techniques for Postoperative Peptic Ulcer and Anastomosis of the Stomach and the Jejunum); *Awards*: Order of Lenin; two Orders of the Red Banner of Labor; medals; *Died*: 28 Apr 1960.

DON, Ts. (real name: DONDUBON, Tsydenzhap Dondupovich) (1905-1938) Buryat writer; CP member from 1925; *Born*: 31 Mar 1905 in settlement Ayaga, Bichura Ryon, son of a peasant; *Career*: Buryat-Mongolian Pop Comr of Educ; ed, newspaper *Buryat-Mongoloy Unen*; 1930 first work published; hist story "Lunar Eclipse" is the first major of Buryat fiction; collected oral folklore material; arrested by State Security organs; *Publ*: stories "Massacre" (1930); "Lunar Eclipse" (1932); "Sheep's-Cheese Poisoning" (1935); *Died*: 1938 in imprisonment; posthumously rehabilitated.

DONAURI (real name: MARDZHANISHVILI), Yelena Iosifovna (1890-1955) Geo actress; Pop Artiste of Geo SSR from 1950; *Born*: 15 Mar 1890; *Educ*: actors' courses in Tiflis and Petersburg; *Career*: 1908 began stage work with L. B. Yavorskaya's road show; 1913-14 at Petersburg Kommissarzhevskaya Theater, then in Taganrog, etc; 1918-20 at Tiflis Russian Theater; from 1920 in Geo theaters; 1920-26 at Rustaveli Theater; from 1928 at Mardzhanishvili Theater; played heroic and dramatic, later character roles; also taught; *Roles*: Khasinta in *Ovechiy istochnik* (The Sheep's Well) (1922); Katerina in Pogodin's *Poema o topore* (Poem of the Axe) (1931); Ketevana in Dadiani's *Guriya Ninoshvili* (1934); Otarov's widow in Chavchavadze's *Slomannyy most* (Broken Bridge) (1935); Tebro in Mrevlishvili's *Ochag Kharateli* (Kharateli's Hearth) (1949), etc; *Died*: 16 Oct 1955.

DONCHENKO, Oles' (Aleksandr) Vasil'yevich (1902-1954) Ukr writer and poet; *Born*: 19 Aug 1902 in Velikiye Sorochintsy, Poltava Province, son of a teacher; *Educ*: 1919 grad Lubny high school; *Career*: member, *Molodnyak* and *Proletfront* lit groups; member, All-Ukr Union of Proletarian Writers; *Publ*: 1918 first work published in Lubny Rayon newspaper; collected verse "Red Writing" (1926); "The Outskirts" (1928); novelettes and novels about industrialization of USSR: "Two Springs" (1931); "Star Fortress" (1933); "The Sea Retreats" (1934); "Prospectors" (1934); "The Martynovs" (1934); novelettes and novels for children "Native Land" (1936); "The School Above the Sea" (1937); *Lukiya* (1939); *Karafuto* (1940); "The Heart of the Golden Eagle" (1944); "The Story of the New House" (1946); "Sacred Word" (1948); "The Forester's Wife" (1945); "The Garden" (1949); "The Mine in the Steppe" (1949); novel "The Gold Medal" (1949); *Yurko Vasyuta* (1950), etc; works dealt with problems of Communist training of children and adolescents at home and at school; many works were translated into languages of other peoples of USSR; *Died*: 12 Apr 1954 in Lubny.

DONENTAYEV, Sabit (1894-1933) Kaz poet and journalist; *Born*: 1894 in aul No. 4, Aksysk Volost', former Semipalatinsk Province, son of a peasant; *Career*: worked as teacher, then miner in Ekibastuz; 1913 first work published; continued satirical tradition of Abay Kunanbayev; influenced by Saltykov-Shchedrin and Nekrasov; his pre-revol works dominated by ideas of enlightment; critic of feudalistic soc; later works deal with victory of Revol, emancipation and equality of women, collectivization, etc; one of first Kaz poets to write about Lenin; translated Russian and Tatar poets into Kaz; 1917-20, according to Sov press, deviated from official Party line; *Publ*: verse "My Dream" (1913); "The Lark"; collected verse: "Everyday Trifles" (1915); "The Unforgettable" (1924); "To the Leader" (1924), etc; also wrote essays, feuilletons and publicistic articles; *Died*: 23 May 1933.

DONETS, Mikhail Ivanovich (1883-1941) Opera singer (bass); Pop Artiste of Ukr SSR from 1930; CP member from 1940; *Born*: 23 Jan 1883 in Kiev; *Educ*: private lessons; *Career*: 1905-13 soloist at Zimin Opera Theater, Moscow; 1913-17 and from 1923 at Kiev Municipal Theater (now Shevchenko Opera and Ballet Theater); also appeared at Khar'kov Opera and Ballet Theater and as concert singer; *Roles*: Karas' in Gulak-Artemovskiy's *Zaporozhets za Dunayem* (A Dnieper Cossack Beyond the Danube); Taras in *Taras Bul'ba*; the delegate in Lysenko's *Natalka-Poltavka* (Natalya from Poltava); Dosifey in Moussorgsky's *Khovanshchina*; Mephistopheles in Gounod's "Faust"; Boris in Moussorgsky's *Boris Godunov*; the Miller in Dargomyzhskiy's *Rusalka*, etc; *Died*: 10 Sept 1941.

DONSKOY, D. D. (1881-1936) Politician; *Born*: 1881; *Career*: member, CC, Socialist-Revol Party; 1918, after Bolsheviks dispersed Constituent Assembly, represented Party CC in Council of Mil Commission; 7 Aug 1922 convicted in trial of right-wing Socialist-Revolutionaries; sentenced by Supr Tribunal to be executed by firing squad; Presidium of All-Russian Centr Exec Comt confirmed the sentence but stayed execution on condition that the Socialist-Revol Party cease its struggle against Sov regime; the Presidium of the All-Russian Centr Exec Comt ordered that Donskoy be held in strict confinement; *Died*: 1936 in prison.

DORLIAK, Kseniya Nikolayevna (1882-1945) Opera and concert singer (soprano); Hon Art Worker of RSFSR from 1944; Dr of Arts; *Born*: 11 Jan 1882 in Petersburg; *Educ*: studied under S. Gladkaya and N. Iretskaya; *Career*: from 1918 prof, Petrograd (Leningrad) Conservatory; from 1930 prof, Moscow Conservatory; *Died*: 8 Mar 1945 in Moscow.

DOROFEYEV, Zakhar Fyodorovich (1890-1952) Mordovian poet and public functionary; CP member from 1918; *Born*: 5 Apr 1890 in vil Salazgar', now Mordovian ASSR, son of a peasant; *Educ*: 1909 grad Kazan' seminary; *Career*: while still at seminary joined student revol movement; later worked as teacher; after 1917 Revol educ official and publishing work in Mordovian ASSR; *Publ*: 1905 first work published in Kazan' Russian-language newspapers; one of the founders of Mordovian lit; collected Mordvinian verse *Pesni i dumy narodnogo uchitelya* (Songs and Thoughts of a Teacher) (1912); a series of textbooks for schools; *Izbrannoye* (Selected Works) (1959); etc; *Died*: 8 July 1952 in Moscow.

DOROGOYCHENKO, Aleksey Yakovlevich (1894-1947) Mordovian writer (in Russian); CP member from 1919; *Born*: 13 Mar 1894 in vil Bol'shaya Kamenka, Samara Province; *Educ*: studied at Rovno Teachers' Seminary, then at Petersburg and Moscow Univ; *Career*: active in Civil War and establishment of Sov regime; 1917 first work printed; translated Mordovian folklore and verse into Russian; *Publ*: verse collections: *Boyevyye pesni krasnoarmeytsa* (The Battle Songs of a Red Army Soldier) (1919); *Radost' truda* (The Joy of Labor) (1920); *Inaya derevnya* (A Different Village) (1923); *Zemnyye nebesa* (Heaven on Earth) (1923); novels: *Bol'shaya Kamenka* (1927); *Zhivaya zhizn'* (Vital Life) (1930); novelettes: *Stepanovna* (1924); *Prazdnik* (The Holiday) (1934), etc; *Died*: 21 Feb 1947 in Kuybyshev.

DOROKHIN, Nikolay Ivanovich (1905-1953) Actor; Pop Artiste of RSFSR from 1948; CP member from 1958; *Born*: 18 May 1905; *Educ*: grad Lunacharskiy Theater Technicum, Moscow; *Career*: 1922 stage debut in Yelets; from 1927 at Moscow Arts Theater; 1935-37 lecturer, *Mosfilm* actors' studio; 1950-53 lecturer at All-Union State Inst for Cinematography and at studio school, Moscow Arts Theater; *Roles*: stage roles: Styopa in Korneychuk's *Platon Krechet*; Minutka in Chirskov's *Pobediteli* (The Victors); Veretennikov in Kron's *Ofitser flota* (Officer of the Fleet); Ryabinin and Grekov in Gorky's *Dostigayev i drugiye* (Dostigayev and Co) and *Vragi* (Enemies); Fedotik in Chekhov's *Tri syestry* (Three Sisters), etc; film roles: Andreyev in *Volochayevskiye dni* (Volochayev Days); Pyotr in *Poslednyaya noch'* (The Last Night), etc; *Publ: Aktyor i rezhissyor* (Actor and Director) (1937); *Po dorogam voyny...* (Along the Roads of War) (1950); *Awards*: two Stalin Prizes (1941 and 1947); *Died*: 31 Dec 1953.

DOROKHOV, Pavel Nikolayevich (1886-1942) Russian writer; *Born*: 1886 in vil Malaya Tarasovka, Samara Province, son of a peasant; *Educ*: Samara 6-grade school; *Career*: in his youth worked in various Siberia cities mainly in statistics and agric cooperative system; 1905 member, illegal Socialist-Revol org in Samara; 1917 chm, Chelyabinsk Sov of Workers and Soldiers' Dep and member, Petrograd Exec Comt of Peasants' Dep; during Civil War public and polit work in Siberia; 1920 joined CPSU(B), but left Party the same year; 1911 first work published; in 1930's member, All-Russian Soc of Peasant Writers; 1938 arrested by State Security organs; *Publ: Derevenskoye* (Rural Life) (1915-17); semi-fictitious chronicle *Kolchakovshchina* (Kolchak Era) (1923; 10 ed until 1933); story *Novaya zhizn'* (The New Life) (1924); novelette *Front uchitel'nitsy Perepyolkinoy* (The Front of Teacher Perepyolkina) (1926); *Avtobiografiya* (Autobiography) (1926); stories and novelettes *Istoriya goroda Tarabarska* (The History of the Town Tarabarsk) (1928); novel *Krepost'* (The Fortress) (1933), etc; *Died*: 8 May 1942 in imprisonment; posthumously rehabilitated.

DOROKHOV, Roman Aleksandrovich (1915-1964) Russian; Party and govt official; CP member from 1942; *Born*: 1915; *Educ*: grad Tomsk Teachers' Training Inst; *Career*: from 1934 headmaster of a primary school, dir of a short-course secondary school, inspector of a rayon educ dept; 1939-47 in the Sov Army; from 1947 exec Party and public posts; 1958-60 chm, Altay Kray Exec Comt; 1960-64 first secr, Gorno-Altay Oblast CPSU Comt; dep, RSFSR Supr Sov of 1955 convocation; dep, and member, Budget Commission, Sov of Nationalities, USSR Supr Sov of 1962 convocation; *Awards*: medal "For Valiant Labor" (1959); *Died*: 17 May 1964.

DOROSHEVICH, Aleksandr Mikhaylovich (1874-1950) Actor, Pop Artiste of RSFSR from 1946; *Born*: 1874; *Career*: 1891 stage debut; until 1901 acted with Derchak, Kropivnitskiy and Staritskiy Ukr companies; 1901-14 at Russian provincial theaters; 1914-17 acted in Petersburg at Yarovskiy and Nezlobin Theaters; from 1919 till end of life acted in Moscow for rayon theaters and Revol Satire Theater; 1923-38 with Moscow Municipal Trade-Union Council Theater; from 1938 with Centr Theater of Transport; *Roles*: Grossman in Yushkevich's *Korol* (The King); Onufriy in Andreyev's *Gaudeamus*; Count Osterhausen in Sumbatov-Yuzhin's *Dzhentl'men* (The Gentleman); Karapetyants and Lysenko in Bill'-Belotserkovskiy's *Shtil'* (Style) and *Golos nedr* (The Inner Voice); Shel'menko in Kvitka-Osnovyanenko's *Shel'menko-denshchik* (Shel'menko the Journeyman), etc; *Awards*: Hero of Labor (1932); *Died*: 1950.

DOROSHKEVICH, Aleksandr Konstantinovich (1889-1946) Lit critic and historian; prof; *Born*: 27 Sept 1889 in Bronnitsy, Moscow Province; *Educ*: 1913 grad Kiev Univ; *Career*: at univ worked under Acad V. N. Peretts; 1908 began lit work; 1917 made his mark as educationist, lecturer and lit historian; 1920-30 taught Ukr lit at higher educ institutions; 1943 head, Dept of Ukr Pre-Oct Lit, Shevchenko Inst of Lit, Ukr Acad of Sci, and head, Dept of Ukr Lit, Kiev Univ; his main studies (in Ukr language) deal with work of Shevchenko, Marko Vovchok, Kulish, Dragomanov, Karpenko-Karyy, Kotsyubinskiy, Samiylenko and other Ukr classics; *Publ*: "Ukrainian Literature" (1922); "Marko Vovchok. Biographic Data" (1928); "The Influence of Herzen on Shevchenko" (1928); "Selected Works" (1930); "Ukrainian Culture in Two Russian Capitals" (1945), etc; 1926-28 prepared and annotated 4-vol ed of Marko Vovchok's works; *Died*: 1 Apr 1946 in Kiev.

DOROZHNYY, Sergey (real name: SERADA, Sergey Mikhaylovich) (1906-1945) Bel poet; member, Bel Writers' Union from 1934; *Born*: 25 Feb 1906 in Slonim, now Grodno Oblast, son of an office worker; *Educ*: grad Minsk Teachers' Training Technicum; early 1930's grad Lit and Linguistics Dept, Pedag Fac, Bel State Univ; *Career*: from 1930 on ed bd of various Bel newspapers and journals; from 1925 member, *Maladnyak* proletarian writers assoc; from 1926 founder-member *Uzvyshsha* lit assoc; 1926 first work published; in 1930's censured for membership of *Uzvyshsha* assoc; 1937 arrested by State Security organs; *Publ*: collected poems and verse *Zvon vyasny* (Chime of Spring) (1926); *Vasil'kovaya rossyp* (The Vasilkovo Deposit) (1929); *Vybranyya vershy* (Selected Verse) (1966); *Died*: 1945 in imprisonment; posthumously rehabilitated.

DORZHIYEV, Agvan (1853-1938) Religious leader of the Buddhists in Buryat-Mongolian ASSR; former plen of Dalai Lama govt in Moscow; *Born*: 1853 in Verkholensk, Irkutsk Province; *Educ*: higher theological training in Tibet; *Career*: after his return to

Russia elected spiritual leader (Pandida Khamba Lama) of the Buddhists in Buryatia; founded the Kerminskiy and Khoymorskiy monasteries in Irkutsk Province and a monastery in Burguzinsk Rayon; besides his religious work did much to spread secular educ among the Buryats and Kalmyks; author of Buryat alphabet, named for him; helped collect Buryat folklore; published historical work *Khukhu debter,* which became very popular among the Mongols; maintained close contact with Russian pre-revol acad-orientalists and with their assistance built a Buddhist temple in Petersburg in 1913; repeatedly visited Tibet, became confidant and personal friend of the Dalai Lama; acted as intermediary between Dalai Lama and Russian Govt; after 1917 Oct Revol reformed the structure of life at Buddhist monasteries and also reorganized syllabus of theological schools at monasteries; his opponents compared these reforms with the efforts of Orthodox "Living Church" clergy to establish itself under Communist regime; accepted as Dalai Lama's plen in Moscow by Sov Govt, which at that time, according to its current Eastern policy, was interested in dipl relations with the Dalai Lama govt; in the 1930's, after establishment of Mongolian Pop Republ, the Buddhist clergy in USSR was subjected to mass annihilation; 1936 Dorzhiyer was exiled from Buryat-Mongolian ASSR; lived in Lakhta near Leningrad; 1937 arrested, exiled to Ulan-Ude (former Verkhneudinsk) and confined; *Died*: 1938 in imprisonment.

DOSMUKHAMEDOV, Khalil Dosmukhamedovich (1883-1939) Kaz physician and health service official; prof from 1927; corresp member, USSR Acad of Sci from 1924; *Born*: 1883 in Kzyl-Kuga Rayon, Gur'yev Oblast, son of a cattle-farmer; *Educ*: received primary educ at Russian-Kir school in Kzyl-Kuga; 1903 grad Ural High-School; 1908 grad Petersburg Mil Med Acad with distinction; *Career*: after grad served as mil surgeon with 2nd Turkestani Cossack Battalion, then with 2nd Ural Cossack Battalion; during mil service spent a year on advanced med training at Ural'sk City Hospital, where he helped to combat a plague epidemic; 1913 resigned from Army and became a distr physician in Temir Uyezd; from 1920 intern, Tashkent Inst of Physiotherapeutic Methods, then intern, Surgical Clinic, Med Fac, Centr Asian Univ, Tashkent; also taught anatomy and physiology and worked as a physician at Kaz Inst of Public Educ, Tashkent; soon gave up internship to devote himself to educ and org work as dep chm, then chm, Kir Sci Commission; in this capacity supervised school plannings, curricula, the standardization of sci terminology, the publ of teaching aids, etc; simulataneously Collegium member, Kaz Pop Comrt of Health and chm, Plague Elimination Commission; from 1924 member, Soc for the Study of Kaz and member, Sci Workers' Section, Educ Workers' Union; 1926-28 dep rector and assoc prof, Kaz Higher Teachers' Training Inst, where he lectured on hygiene and reflexology; also taught hygiene at Kaz Experimental Model Nine-Grade School, Tahkent; and held the post of Tashkent municipal school health officer; 1927 co-founder, Kaz State Univ, Alma-Ata, where he was also pro-rector and prof; simultaneously head, Planning and Org Dept, Kaz Pop Comrt of Health; 1932-39 dept head, Voronezh Inst of Publ Health; attended numerous congresses on med, history, ethnography, linguistics, etc; contributed to various Kaz journals and translated a number of books on natural sci from Russian into Kaz; wrote numerous tech and pop works, mainly in Kaz; *Publ*: "Anatomy and Physiology"; "Zoology"; "Nature Study"; "Hygiene for Schoolchildren," etc; *Died*: 1939 in Voronezh.

DOSSER (Party names: "Leshiy"; "Semyon Petrovich"), Zinoviy Nikolayevich (1882-1938) Party and govt official; CP member from 1917; *Born*: 1882; *Career*: 1902 began revol work; summer 1903 first arrested in Perm'; from autumn 1904 worked in Petersburg; non-voting member, Petersburg RSDRP(B) Comt; went to Moscow and was co-opted to Moscow RSDRP(B) Comt; summer 1905 arrested; Oct 18 escaped and joined triumvirate of Moscow Party Comt elected to direct uprising; in direct charge of uprising in Presnya; summer 1906 re-arrested; spring 1907, after release, regained legal status and abandoned contact with the Party; after 1917 Feb Revol worked for Oil Workers' Union; July 1917 resumed Party work in Petrograd; took part in 1917 Oct Coup; then worked for Supr Sovnarkhoz as chm, Main Oil Ind Bd; head, All-Russian Oil Syndicate; from late 1922 member, Higher Arbitration Commission, Labor and Defense Council; from July 1924 All-Russian Oil Syndicate rep in China; from 1926 Sov trade rep in Italy; 1928-37 head, Bd, RSFSR Pop Comrt of Trade; arrested by State Security organs; *Died*: 1938 in imprisonment.

DOSVITNYY, Oles' (real name: SKRIPAL', Aleksandr Fyodorovich) (1891-1934) Ukr writer; CP member from 1919; *Born*: 8 Nov 1891 in Volchansk, Khar'kov Province, son of a merchant; *Educ*: studied at Petersburg Univ; *Career*: worked at an office and a sugar refinery; 1914 drafted into Russian Army; arrested and court-marshalled for revol activities among soldiers, but managed to escape; lived in America, China and Japan; 1918 returned to Ukr; 1919-22 journalist; 1925 toured Europe; for a while was one of the ideologists of the Free Acad of Proletarian Culture; 1927 expelled from Acad for favoring use of European lit to improve standard of Ukr lit; arrested by State Security organs; *Publ*: collected novellae about China *Tyunguy* (1924); novels "The Americans" (1925); "Who" (1927); "Alay" (1927); *Gyulle* (1927); "We Were Three" (1929); "Quartzite" (1932); *Died*: 9 June 1934 in imprisonment; posthumously rehabilitated.

DOVATOR, Lev Mikhaylovich (1903-1941) Mil commander; maj-gen from 1941; outstanding cavalry leader in WW 2; CP member from 1928; *Born*: 20 Feb 1903 in vil Khotino, Beshenkovichi Rayon, Vitebsk Province, son of a peasant; *Educ*: 1929 grad Leningrad Cavalry School; 1939 grad Frunze Mil Acad; *Career*: from 1924 in Red Army; 1929-36 cavalry platoon leader, polit officer and squadron commander; 1939-41 chief of staff, Special Cavalry Regt, USSR Pop Comrt of Defence, then chief of staff of a cavalry brigade, 36th Cavalry Div; 1941 commander, Cavalry Group, Western Front; commander, 3rd Cavalry Corps, renamed in Nov 1941 as 2nd Guards Cavalry Corps; July-Sept 1941 led cavalry group in a raid against German rear echelons in the forests of Smolensk area; Oct-Nov 1941 took part in defense of Moscow on the Volokolamsk sector; 13 Dec 1941 his 2nd Guards Cavalry Corps crossed front line and struck at Germans' rear; *Awards*: Hero of Sov Union (1941, posthumously); Order of Lenin; Order of the Red Banner; *Died*: 19 Dec 1941 killed in action at vil Palashkino, near Ruza.

DOVBISHCHENKO, Viktor Semyonovich (1910-1953) Ukr film and stage dir; Hon Artiste of Ukr SSR from 1946; *Born*: 3 Nov 1910 in Khar'kov; *Educ*: 1934 grad Khar'kov Inst of Music and Drama; *Career*: 1934-41 dir, Kiev Film Studio and Khar'kov and Odessa theaters; 1941-47 art dir, Voroshilovgrad (now Lugana) Musical Drama Theater; 1947-52 art dir, Kiev Young Playgoers' Theater; from 1947 instructor, Kiev Inst of Stagecraft; wrote articles on Sov theater; *Works*: produced: B. Chirskov's *Pobediteli* (The Victors); I. Popov's *Sem'ya* (The Family); Lesya Ukrainka's *Lesnaya pesnya* (Forest Song); Gogol's *Zhenit'ba* (Marriage), etc; *Died*: 24 Sept 1953.

DOVGAL', Aleksandr Mikhaylovich (1904-1961) Graphic artist; Hon Art Worker of Ukr SSR from 1951; CP member from 1949; *Born*: 27 Jan 1904 in vil Debaltsevo; *Educ*: 1929 grad Khar'kov Inst of Arts; *Career*: author of graphic series "Building the Dnieper Hydroelectric Power Plant) (1929-32); *Socialist Khar'kov* (1935-37); "Classics of World Culture" (1939-60); "Suvorov's Men" (1945-48); poster series: "Besprinkle Freedom with the Foe's Evil Blood" (19142); illustrated works of Tychina, Marko-Vovchok, Pushkin, etc; *Died*: 12 Mar 1961.

DOVGALEVSKIY, Valerian Savel'yevich (1885-1934) Eng; govt official; dipl; CP member from 1908; *Born*: 23 Nov 1885 in Kiev Province; *Educ*: 1913 grad Toulouse Electr Eng Inst; *Career*: electr eng by profession; from 1904 in revol movement; 1905 member, Workers and Peasants' Union, South Russian RSDRP Bureau; 1906 arrested in connection with Uman' RSDRP org case; 1907 sentenced to exile for life; 1908 fled from Angara region to Krasnoyarsk and thence abroad; 1908 joined Bolsheviks; 1908-10 secr, Liège (Belgium) Bolshevik group, then member, Bolshevik group in Davos (Switzerland); 1911-14 secr, Toulouse Bolshevik org; since he lived in towns with no Russian colonies, 1915 joined left wing of French Socialist Party; moved to Paris and headed operation and tech dept of a large electr eng enterprise; July 1917 returned to Russia; drafted into Russian Army; after 1917 Oct Revol in Red Army; fought on Southern Front, in Siberia and on Petrograd Front; 1919 began work for Pop Comrt of Means of Communication; 1920 inspector of communications and comr, Kiev Okrug Eng Bd; May 1921 appointed RSFSR Pop Comr of Posts and Telegraphs; 1923 USSR Dep Pop Comr of Posts and Telegraphs; simultaneously rector, Moscow Inst of Civil Eng; 1924-25 USSR plen in Sweden; 1925-27 USSR plen in Japan; 1928-34 USSR plen in France; Oct 1929 in London signed protocol for resumption of Anglo-Sov dipl relations; 1932 signed in Paris Franco-Sov Non-Aggression Pact; attended Geneva Disarmament Conference; member, USSR Centr Exec Comt; *Died*: 14 July 1934; buried in Moscow's Red Square.

DOVGYALLO, Nikolay Dmitriyevichh (1899-1967) Anatomist; Dr of Med; prof; CP member from 1945*Born*: 1899;*Educ*: 1925 grad Odessa Med Inst; *Career*: 1925-28 postgrad student; 1928-30 asst prof, Chair of Normal Anatomy, Odessa Med Inst; 1930 established Chair of Anatomy at Stalino (Donetsk) Med Inst and restored it after the German withdrawal from the Donbas; 1941-43 head, Chair of Normal Anatomy, Kaz Med Inst; 1943-67 head, Chair of Normal Anatomy, head, Correspondence Studies Dept and dep dir, Stalino (Donetsk) Med Inst; bd member, All-Union Soc of Anatomist, Histologists and Embryologists; member, Soc for the Dissemination of Sci and Polit Knowledge; member, ed council, journal *Arkhiv anatomii, gistologii i embriologii*; wrote over 40 works; *Publ: Obshcheye ucheniye o forme sustavnykh poverkhnostey i dvizheniya v sochleneniyakh* (The General Theory of the Form of the Joint Surfaces and the Movement of Articulations); coauthor, *Prakticheskiy kurs anatomii* (A Practical Anatomy Course) (1939); *O nekotorykh voprosakh artrologii* (Some Problems of Arthrology) (1958); *Kibernetika i nekotoryye problemy morfologii* (Cybernetics and Some Problems of Morphology) (1964), etc; *Awards*: Order of the Red Banner of Labor; medal "For Labor Valor During the Great Fatherland War"; "Outstanding Health Worker" Badge; *Died*: 1967.

DOVNAR-ZAPOL'SKIY, Mitrofan Viktorovich (1867-1934) Bel; historian and soc worker; Dr of History from 1905; *Born*: 2 July 1867 in Rechitsa, Bel; *Educ*: 1894 grad History and Philology Fac, Kiev Univ; *Career*: 1898-1901 lecturer, Moscow Univ; 1901-18 prof of Russian history, Kiev Univ; simultaneously 1908-17 dir, Business Inst and 1917-18 dir, Inst of Geography and Archeology; from 1905 founder-dir, Higher Womens' Training Courses; from 1902 dir, students history and ethnography circle; 1920-25 head, Chair of History, then rector, Baku Univ; 1925-26 prof, Bel Univ and chm, History and Archeology Commission, Inst of Bel Culture, Minsk; worked on history of Bel and Russia; 1918 active member of Bel Rada; established in Kiev and wrote pamphlet "Foundations of Belorussian Statehood" for which he was later censured by Party; 1925-26 organized publication of the "Belorussian Archives," three volumes of which were published in Minsk until 1930; Feb 1926 made unsuccessful bid to publish his "History of Belorussia"; *Publ: Dokumenty Moskovskogo arkhiva Ministerstva yustitsii* (Ministry of Justice Documents from the Moscow Archives) (1897); *Akty Litovsko-Russkogo gosudarstva* (Acts of the Lithuanian–Russian State) (1899); *Pol'sko-Litovskaya uniya na seymakh do 1569 g.* (The Polish-Lithuanian Union at Sejms up to 1569) (1898); *Gosudarstvennoye khozyaystvo Velikogo knyazhestva Litovskogo pri Yagellonakh* (State Economy of the Grand Duchy of Lithuaniapality Under the Yagellon Dynasty) (1901); *Spornyye voprosy v istorii Litovsko-Russkogo seyma* (Moot Issues in the History of the Lithuanian-Russian Sejm) (1901); *Taynoye obshchestvo Dekabristov* (The Secret Society of the Decembrists) (1906) *Memuary dekabristov* (The Decembrists' Memoirs) (1906); *Idealy dekabristov* (The Decembrists' Ideals) (1907); *Issledovaniya i stat'yi* (Research and Articles) (1909); *Torgovlya i promyshlennost' Moskvy 16-17 vv'* (Trade and Industry in Moscow in the 16th and 17th Centuries) (1910) *Barkulabovskaya letopis'* (The Barkulab Chronicle) (1909); *Russkaya istoriya v ocherkakh i stat'yakh* (History of Russia in Essays and Articles) (3 vol, 1909-12); *Istoriya russkogo narodnogo khozyaystva* (History of the Russian National Economy) (1911); *Obzor istorii khozyaystvennoy zhizni Rossii* (Historical Review of Russian Economic Life) (1914);; "Foundations of Belorussian Statehood" (1919); *Narodnoye khozyaystvo Belorussii 1861-1914 gg.* (National Economy of Belorussia in 1861-1914) (1926); "Socio-Economic Structure of the Lithuanian-Belorussian State in the 16th-18th Centuries" (1927); *Died*: 30 Sept 1934 in Moscow.

DOVZHENKO, Aleksandr Petrovich (1894-1956) Film dir and writer; prof from 1955; Hon Art Worker of Ukr SSR from 1939; Pop Artiste of USSR from 1950; *Born*: 11 Sept 1894 in settlement Sosnitsy, former Chernigov Province, son of a peasant; *Educ*: 1914 grad Glukhov Teachers' Inst; studied at Kiev Business Inst, Kiev Acad of Arts and Berlin Art College; *Career*: 1914-17 teacher in Kiev and Zhitomir; 1917-21 worked for Ukr Pop Comrt of Educ; 1921-23 dipl work in Warsaw and Berlin; 1923-26 newspaper illustrator; from 1926 film work; from 1929 produced films based exclusively on his own scripts; during WW 2 mil correspondent at the front; 1940-46 worked exclusively on documentary films; 1949-51 lecturer, from 1955 prof, All-Union State Inst of Cinematography; 1958 Brussels Film Festival rated his film *Zemlya* (The Earth) among the 12 best films of all times and all peoples; *Publ:* stories: *Mat'* (Mother); *Otstupnik* (The Apostate); *Noch' pered boyem* (Night Before the Battle) (1941-45); novelette *Zacharovannaya Desna* (Enchanted Desna) (1955); plays: *Potomki zaporozhtsev* (Descendants of the Zaporozhian Cossacks); *Zhizn' v tsvetu* (Blossoming Life); film scripts[unproduced]: *Taras Bul'ba* (1941); *Ukraina v ogne* (The Ukraine in Flames) (1943); *Proshchay, Amerika* (Good-bye, America) (1949); *Otkrytiye Antarktidy* (Discovery of the Antarctic) (1952); *Poema o more* (Poem of the Sea) (1955); *Works*: produced films: *Yagodka lyubvi* (The Love Berry) (1926) ; *Sumka dipkur'yera* (The Diplomatic Bag) (1927); *Zvenigora* (1928); *Arsenal* (The Armory) (1929); *Zemlya* (The Earth) (1930); *Ivan* (1932); *Aerograd* (1935); *Shchors* (1939); *Osvobozhdeniye* (The Liberation) (1940); *Bitva za nashu Sovetskuyu Ukrainu* (The Battle for Our Soviet Ukraine) (1943); *Pobeda na Pravoberezhnoy Ukraine* (Victory in the Right-Bank Ukraine) (1945); *Rodnaya strana* (Native Country) (1946); *Michurin* (1949); *Awards*: Order of Lenin; Order of the Red Banner; other orders and medals; prizes at the 4th World Film Festival at Marianske Lazne (Czechoslovakia, 1949) and 2nd Workers' World Film Festival in Gotvaldov (Czechoslovakia, 1949); two Stalin Prizes) (1941 and 1949); Lenin Prize (1959, posthumously); *Died*: 25 Nov 1956.

DOYNIKOV, Boris Semyonovich (1879-1948) Neuropathologist; specialist in the pathomorphology of the nervous system; member, USSR Acad of Med Sci; Hon Sci worker of RSFSR; maj-gen, Army Med Corps; *Born*: 1879; *Educ*: 1902 grad Mil Med Acad; *Career*: after graduation worked for V.M. Bekhterev; 1904-05 served in Russo-Japanese War; 1906 sent to Germany, where he worked at neurological clinics and studied the normal and pathological histology of the nervous system; 1911 published major work on the normal and pathological histology of the peripheral nerves and the histology of neuritis, in which he devoted particular attention to regeneration and which received int acclaim; from 1917 until death worked at Clinic of Nervous Diseases, Mil Med Acad; 1926 founded laboratory for the study of the histology of the nervous system, Leningrad Inst of Surgical Neuropathology (now Polenov Neurosurgical Inst); 1932-48 founder-head laboratory of normal and pathological morphology of the nervous system, Inst of Experimental Med; 1936-48 after death of predecessor M. I. Astvatsaturov, head, Chair of Nervous Diseases, Mil Med Acad; during 1939-40 Sov-Finnish War established neurosurgical dept at his clinic; as a clinical neuropathologist continued the tradition of Bekhterev, Zhukovskiy and Astvatsaturov; as a neuropathologist he was an adherent of "total" research on the nervous system; studied the nervous system during infectious diseases (diphtheria, rabies, scarlet fever, typhoid) and intoxication; a number of his pupils now head chairs of nervous diseases and neuropathological laboratories; *Publ: Izbrannyye trudy po nevromorfologii i nevropatologii* (Selected Works on Neuromorphology and Neuropathology) (1955), etc; *Died*: 1948.

DOYNIKOVA, Yelena Dmitriyevna (1906-1938) Plant biochemist; *Born*: 10 Mar 1906 in Smolensk; *Educ*: grad Moscow Univ; *Career*: worked at All-Union Inst of Rubber and Guttapercha; helped to develp technol processing of rubber-bearing plant *Scorzonera Tau-Saghyz* after studying it at an experimental station in the Karatau range in 1930; worked on nucleic acid; 1936 concluded that thymonucleic acid was widespread in plants; *Publ: Nukleal'naya reaktsiya u rasteniy* (Nuclear Reaction in Plants) (1936); *O reaktsii rastitel'noy kletochnoy stenki s fuksino-sernistoy kislotoy* (Reaction of the Plant Cellular Wall to Fuchsine-Sulphuric Acid) (1937); *Sovremennoye sostoyaniye ucheniya o nukleproteidakh* (Current Data on Nucleoproteids) (1937); *Died*: 18 Sept 1938 in Moscow.

DOZITIS, Karl M. (1894-1937) Lat mil commander; brigade comr; helped establish Sov regime in Lat in 1919; Red Army polit official; CP member from 1916; *Born*: 21 Oct 1894 in vil Yaunveveri, now Lat, son of a farm laborer; *Educ*: 1928 grad Frunze Mil Acad; *Pos*: until 1908 farm laborer for German baron; 1908-16 stonemason's apprentice, then stonemason in Riga; 1916-17 private in 2nd Riga Lat Regt, Russian Army; from Jan 1918 Red Army polit official; 1918-20 mil comr, mil emissary, then again mil comr, Lat Sov Infantry Div; 1920-21 mil comr, Red Army Infantry Div; 1921 mil comr, cavalry brigade; 1922-23 mil comr, cavalry school and cavalry brigade in Taganrog; 1929-30 acting commander, Slavgorod Territorial Regt; 1930-33 worked for USSR Pop Comrt of Army and Navy Affairs; 1933-37 asst commandant (polit), College of Special Railroad Corps; *Career*: from Mar 1917 member, Exec Comt, Lat Infantry Regt; fought in Oct Revol in Valka; 1918-19 fought against German troops to defend and liberate Lat; fall 1919 helped rout Denikin's troops near Oryol; 1921 fought against Basmachi in Centr Asia; 1937 arrested by NKVD; *Awards*: Order of the Red Banner; *Died*: 1937 in imprisonment; posthumously rehabilitated.

DRABKINA (Party pseudonym: Natasha), Feodosiya Il'inichna (1883-1957) Party official; CP member from 1902; *Born*: 5 Jan 1883 in Rostov-on-Don; *Career*: from 1900 Soc-Democratic propaganda among workers; 1903 in Geneva joined Bolsheviks; 1904 returned to Russia; 1905 in Petersburg member, Bolshevik militant org; during 1905 Dec armed rebellion delivered ammunition to Moscow; 1906 secr, Narva Rayon Party Org in Petersburg, then acting secr Petersburg RSDRP Comt; contributed to Bolshevik journals *Voprosy strakhovaniya* and *Prosveshcheniye*; member, ed bd, journal *Rabotnitsa* and "Breakers" Publ House; Feb 1914 arrested and exiled to Vilnius, then to Yekaterinburg and Cherdyn' (Perm' Province); 1917, on return to Petrograd, worked for Financial Commission, Russian Bureau, and for secretariat, CC, RSDRP(B); contributed to *Pravda*; on ed staff, *Izvestiya Petrogradskogo soveta*; directed propaganda work; secr at Party conferences and 5th RSDRP(B) Congress; Oct 1917 one of secr, Petrograd Mil-Revol Comt; 1918-24 head, Non-Local Dept, Supr Sovnarkhoz; helped to organize Communist higher educ institutions; 1924-25 head, Secretariat, Inst for the Study of Party History, CC, RCP(B); 1925-38 broadcasting dir, "Radio Broadcasting"; member, Presidium and Secretariat, CC, Int Org for Aid to Revol Fighters; head, Archives of the Oct Revol (now Centr State Archives of the Oct Revol and the Building of Socialism); exec ed, Party Publishing House, etc; from 1938 pensioner; *Died*: 10 Jan 1957.

DRANISHNIKOV, Vladimir Aleksandrovich (1893-1939) Conductor, stage dir and composer; Hon Artiste of RSFSR from 1933; *Born*: 10 June 1893 in Petersburg; *Educ*: 1909 grad Court Choir School; 1916 grad piano, composition and conducting class, Petrograd Conservatory; *Career*: 1914-18 first violinist, 1918-25 conductor and 1925-36 chief conductor, Mariinskiy Theater (now Kirov Opera and Ballet Theater), Leningrad; 1936 artistic dir and chief conductor, Shevchenko Opera and Ballet Theater, Kiev; *Works*: while at Kirov Opera and Ballet Theater staged: Strauss' "Salome" (1924); Prokofiev's *Lyubov' k tryom apel'sinam* (Love of Three Oranges) (1926); Moussorgsky's *Boris Godunov* (1928); Asaf'yev's ballet *Plamya Parizha* (The Flame of Paris); *U Parizhskoy zastavy* (At the Paris Gate); *Pikovaya dama* (The Queen of Spades) (1935), etc; while at Shevchenko Opera and Ballet Theater staged: Lysenko's *Taras Bul'ba* (1937), Lyatoshinskiy's *Shchors* and *Polkovodets* (The General) (1938); Meytus, Rybal'chenko and Tits' *Perekop* (1939); also staged Deshevov's *Lyod i stal'* (Ice and Steel), Wagner's "Rheingold," Verdi's "Traviata" and Tchaikovsky's *Mazeppa*; composed: two symphonic poems, a piano scherzo, études and vocal works; *Died*: 6 Feb 1939 in Kiev.

DRAVERT, Pyotr Lyudovikovich (1879-1945) Russian poet and geologist; specialist in meteorites; *Born*: 16 Jan 1879 in Vyatka; *Educ*: 1914 grad Fac of Physics and Mathematics, Kazan' Univ; *Career*: 1905 twice exiled to Perm' Province and Yakutia for involvement in students' movement; 1918-40 asst prof, then prof of mineralogy, gology and geophysics at higher educ establishments in Omsk, 1927-45 chm, Omsk Meteorite Commission; 1939-45 member Meteorite Committee, USSR Acad of Sci; wrote verse depicting life of Yakuts, Zvenki and other Siberian peoples; his sci works included studies of meteorites and a catalog of bright bolids observed in Western Siberia; *Publ*: collected verse: *Teni i otzvuki* (Shades and Echoes) (1904); *Sibir'* (Siberia) (1923); *Stikhi o Sibiri* (Siberian Verse) (1937), etc; sci works *O nakhodke kamennogo meteorita Khmelevka, upavshego 1-ogo marta 1929-ogo goda* (The Discovery of the Khmelevka Meteorite Which Fell on 1 March 1929) (1941); *O nakhodke kamennogo meteorita Yerofeyevka* (The Discovery of the Yerofeyevka Meteorite) (1941); *O padenii kamennogo meteorita Kuznetsovo* (The Descent of the Kuznetsovo Meteorite) (1941); *Utrachennyye meteority Aziatskoy chasti SSSR* (Lost Meteorites of the Asian USSR); *Died*: 12 Dec 1945 in Omsk.

DRAY-KHMARA, Mikhail Afanas'yevich (1889-1939) Ukr poet, translator and lit historian; *Born*: 10 Oct 1889 in vil Malyye Kanevtsy, Poltava Province, son of a peasant; *Educ*: 1913 grad Kiev Univ; *Career*: assoc, Ukr Acad of Sci; prof of Ukr lit at Kiev higher educ establishments; belonged to the "neo-classic" lit group; wrote virtually nothing on soc-polit topics, preferring neutral landscapes and love themes; *Publ*: verse collection "Green Shoots" (1926); monograph *Lesya Ukrainka* (1926); lit research on Bel poet M. Bohdanovich and Polish writer K. Tetmaier; translated works of Pushkin, Bohdanovich and many for poets; *Died*: 19 Jan 1939.

DRENNOVA, Kapitolina Alekseyevna (1897-1963) Otolaryngologist; prof from 1948; Dr of Med from 1947; *Born*: 1897; *Educ*: 1923 grad 1st Petrograd Women's Med Inst; *Career*: 1923-27 intern for ear, nose, throat, and eye diseases, hospitals in Tashkent and Ashkhabad; 1927-47 extern, intern, then asst prof, Otolaryngological Clinic, Leningrad Mil Med Acad; simultaneously lecturer in pathological anatomy and biochemistry, 1st and 2nd Leningrad Med Inst; 1930-45 head, Biochemical Dept, Leningrad Research Inst for Ear, Nose and Throat Diseases; 1941-45 head, surgical and otolaryngological dept, various Leningrad hospitals; 1948-63 head, Chair of Ear, Nose and Throat Diseases, Tashkent Inst of Postgrad Med Training; chief otolaryngologist of Tashkent; chm, Uzbek Soc of Otolaryngologists; member, Learned Council, Uzbek Min of Health; member, ed council, journal *Vestnik otorinolaringologii*; wrote over 60 works on histology of reticuloendothelial system of upper respiratory tract, barrier function of nose, pharynx and larynx in animals, biochemical blood research in various ear, nose and throat diseases, influence of vitamins on these organs and war wounds; *Awards*: Badge of Hon (1961); *Died*: 23 Apr 1963.

DREY, Mikhail Ivanovich (1860- ?) Revolutionary; member, *Narodnaya volya* (People's Will) Party; *Born*: 1860 in Odessa, son of a physician; *Educ*: studied at a high school; *Career*: while still a student joined N.L. Gekker's revol group in Berdyansk; 1880 after return to Odessa, joined local *Narodnaya volya* org; was introduced to centr group by N.M. Trigoni; propaganda work among workers and soldiers and acted as go-between for centr org and workers' groups; after Trigoni's arrest worked with V.N. Figner as rep of *Narodnaya volya* Exec Comt in Odessa; 30 Sept 1881 arrested; 3 Apr 1883 sentenced by mil tribunal to 15 years at hard labor; served sentence at Kara; 1898 enforced settlement; 1900-11 in emigration; after 1917 Feb Revol worked for various publ houses; until 1928 at library of Communist Acad; 1931 member, Soc of Polit Prisoners; *Died*: date and place of death unknown.

DREYMAN, R.A. (1887-1938) Party and govt official; CP member from 1905; *Born*: 1887; *Career*: did Party work in Libava and Riga; after 1917 Feb Revol member, Exec Comt, Tomsk Sov of Soldiers' Dep; after 1917 Oct Revol served in Red Army; later Pop Comr of Means of Communication, Sov of Lat Govt; from 1920 bd member, Angara Metal Trust; Nov 1921-1926 mang, Ridder mines in Altay; 1926-29 dir, Karsakpay Copper-Smelting Combine; arrested by State Security organs; *Died*: 1938 in imprisonment.

DREYTSER' Yefim Aleksandrovich (1894-1936) Party official; CP member; *Born*: 1894; *Career*: Aug 1936 tried in connection with *Trotskiy-Zinoviev Center* on charges of organizing a terrorist center simed at assassinating Sov govt and Party leaders; sentenced to death by Mil Collegium of USSR Supr Court; *Died*: Aug 1936 executed.

DRIZHENKO, Fyodor Kirillovich (1858-1922) Russian hydrographer and geodesist; *Born*: 1858; *Educ*: 1886 grad Moscow Acad; *Career*: 1891-94 directed survey of Lake Onega; 1897-1903 supervised hydrographic expedition to Lake Baykal; made series of magnetic measurements and astronomical observations; from 1903 concentrated on seas of Russian North; 1903-05 headed hydrographic expedition to Arctic Ocean; 1905-08 headed special survey of White Sea; 1908-12 asst head, Main Hydrographic Bd; 1912 head, special Murmansk Coastal Survey; after 1917 Oct Revol served on Northern Seaway Comt, Siberian Revol Comt; directed hydrographic study of Siberian rivers and seas; cape in northern tip of Novaya Zemlya named for him; *Publ: Kratkiy otchyot o rabotakh gidrograficheskoy ekspeditsii Baykal'skogo ozera za 1898* (Short Report on the Work of the 1898 Hydrographic Expedition to Lake Baykal) (1899); *Kratkiy otchyot o rabotakh gidrograficheskoy ekspeditsii Baykal'skogo ozera za 1899* (Short Report on the Work of the 1899 Hydrographic Expedition to Lake Baykal) (1900); *Gidrograficheskoye issledovaniye Baykala* (A Hydrographic Study of Baykal) (1902); *Lotsiya i fizikogeograficheskiy ocherk ozera Baykal* (Sailing Directions and a Physical Geographic Study of Lake Baykal) (1908); *Died*: 1922.

DROBNIS, Yakov Naumovich (1890-1937) Party and govt official; CP member from 1906; *Born*: 1890; *Career*: 1906 joined RSDRP in Glukhov; 1908 in custody for 10 months before being tried for membership of RSDRP; later sentenced to five years in prison by Kiev Assizes; Jan 1915 exiled on suspicion of anti-mil agitation to Poltava, where he worked for underground RSDRP(B) org; 1918 helped to found CP(B) Ukr and was member of its CC; during Civil War sent to Ukr on underground work and to organize partisan struggle against Petlyura's army; 1919-20 fought against Denikin's army; 1920-21 supported Democratic Centralism Group; 1922 member, RSFSR Small Council of Pop Comr; 1923 served as its chm and member, Admin and Financial Commission, USSR Council of Pop Comr; 1924-27 dep chm, RSFSR Small Council of Pop Comr; 1927 expelled from Party by resolution of 15th Party Congress for siding with Trotskyite opposition; 1929 reinstated; worked in Pop Comrt of Communications; later expelled again from Party and sentenced to death in trial of the "Anti-Sov Trotskyite Center"; *Died*: 30 Jan 1937 executed.

DROBOT'KO, Viktor Grigor'yevich (1885-1966) Microbiologist and epidemiologist; Dr of Biology; Hon Sci Worker of Ukr SSR from 1966; member, Ukr Acad of Sci from 1948; prof; *Born*: 23 Nov 1885 in vil Degtyari, now Chernigov Oblast; *Educ*: 1913 grad Med Fac, Kiev Univ; *Career*: 1914-25 physician in Romny, now Poltava Oblast; 1925-31 asst prof, Kiev Bacteriological Inst; from 1931 senior assoc, then head, Dept of Med Microbiology, Zabolotnyy Inst of Microbiology and Epidemiology, Kiev (now Inst of Microbiology, Ukr Acad of Sci); from 1944 until death dir, Inst of Microbiology, Ukr Acad of Sci and head of its Dept of Pathogenic Microorganisms; obtained new vegetable antibioticum *imanin*; developed method of differential staining of microorganisms and synthetic culture media; designed original filter for working with bacteriophages; member, ed council, journal *Antibiotiki*; (1948-58) bd chm, Ukr Soc of Microbiologists, Epidemiologists and Infectionists; exec ed, *Mikrobiologicheskiy zhurnal*; wrote over 120 works;*Publ:Mikrobiologiya. Populyarni narysy* (Microbiology. A Popular Outline) (1936); *Suchasna khimioterapiya infektsiynykh khvorob* (The Modern Chemotherapy of Infectious Diseases) (1946); *Novoye gribkovoye zabolevaniye loshadey i lyudey (stakhibotriotoksikoz)* (A New Fungus Disease in Horses and Humans - Stachybotryotoxicosis) (1949); *Sovremennaya khimioterapiya infectsionnykh bolezney* (The Modern Chemotherapy of Infectious Diseases) (1949); *Imanin - novyy rastitel'nyy antiobiotik* (Imanin - A New Vegetable Antibioticum) (1954); *Antimikrobnyye veshchestva vysshikh rasteniy* (Antimicrobic Substances in Higher Plants) (1958); *Awards*: two Orders of Lenin; Order of the Red Banner of Labor; medals; *Died*: 10 Sept 1966.

DROZD, Valentin Petrovich (1906-1943) Naval officer; vice-admiral from 1941; CP member from 1930; *Born*: 1906; *Educ*: 1928 grad Frunze Naval College; 1931 grad Advanced Training Courses for Naval Officers; *Career*: from 1925 in Red Navy; 1933-35 commanded a destroyer; 1935-36 first officer on a battleship; 1936-37 mil adviser and chief of staff, Destroyer Flotilla of Spanish Republican Navy; 1937-48 commanded a naval brigade; 1938-40 commander, Northern Fleet; 1940-41 commandant of a naval college; 1941-43 commander, detachment of light vessels, then squadron commander, Baltic Fleet; *Awards*: Order of Lenin; two Orders of the Red Banner; *Died*: 29 Jan 1943 drowned near Kronstadt in a car that broke through the ice; buried in mil cemetery at Aleksandr Nevskiy Monastery, Leningrad; a vessel of the Baltic Fleet was named after him.

DROZDOV, Nikolay Fyodorovich (1862-1953) Artillery eng; col-gen; Dr of Tech Sci from 1938; Hon Sci and Tech Worker of RSFSR from 1940; *Born*: 1862 in Chernigov Province, son of a technician; *Educ*: 1886 grad Mathematical Fac, Kiev Univ; 1893 grad Mikhail Artillery Acad; *Career*: 1887-90 ensign in Russian Army; from 1896 worked for Artillery Comt, Main Artillery Bd; sent abroad to study artillery production in England, France, Germany and Austria; from 1898 instructor, Artillery Acad; 1911-14 taught course in the planning of artillery systems at Artillery Acad; from 1914 asst head, Centr Research Laboratory, War Dept; 1916-17 co-dir, Putilov Plant; from 1918 in Red Army; 1920-26 dep dir, Centr State Sci and Tech Inst, Supr Sovnarkhoz; from 1926 prof and head, Chair of Special Eng, Artillery Acad; simultaneously taught internal ballistics at Naval Acad; during late 1920's and 1930's helped to develop and test new weapon systems; 1933 compiled "Tables for Solving Internal Ballistic Problems"; 1936-40 extended his precise method of solving internal ballistic problems to progressive powders; from 1942 life-member, Artillery Comt, Main Artillery Bd; 1946-53 member and Presidium member, Acad of Artillery Sci; *Publ; Soprotivleniye artilleriyskikh orudiy i ikh ustroystvo* (The Resistance of Artillery Pieces and Their Mechanism); *Teoriya soprotivleniya avtoskreplyonnykh trub v primenenii k artilleriyskim orudiyam* (The Theory of Resistance of Autofretted Tubes Applied to Artillery Weapons) (1935); *Resheniye zadachi vnutrenney ballistiki v obobshchyonnykh peremennykh dlya zaryadov prostykh i sostavnykh* (The Solution of Internal Ballistic Problems in Generalized Variables for Simple and Compound Charges) (1952); *Awards*: two Orders of Lenin; Order of the Red Banner; Order of the Red Banner of Labor; Order of the Red Star; Order of the Fatherland War; Lenin Prize (1943); *Died*: late Dec 1953; buried in Novodevich'ye Cemetery, Moscow.

DROZDOVSKIY, Mikhail Gordeyevich (1881-1919) Col, Russian Army; maj-gen, Denikin's Volunteer Army; *Born*: 1881; *Educ*: 1908 grad Gen Staff Acad; *Career*: fought in 1904-05 Russo-Japanese War; 1914-17 staff posts in Russian Army at the front; 1917 commander, 60th Zamost'skiy Regt, then commander, 14th Infantry Div on Rumanian Front; Dec 1917 began to muster volunteer brigade in Yassy area to fight against Sov regime in Russia; Mar 1918 began forced march to link up with Denikin's Volunteer Army, routing Red Army detachments and dissolving local soviets on route; May 1918 linked up with Volunteer Army; 1918 commander, 3rd Div, Volunteer Army; 31 Oct 1918 wounded in action near Stavropol'; *Died*: 1 Jan 1919 as a result of his wounds; the 3rd Div, Volunteer Army was named after him.

DROZHZHIN, Spiridon Dmitriyevich (1848-1930) Russian poet; *Born*: 18 Dec 1848 in vil Nizovka, former Tver' Province, son of a serf; *Career*: 1860-78 subsequently cleaner, bar help, store clerk, worker, book-salesman; 1873 first work published; influenced by Pushkin, Kol'tsov, Nekrasov and Nikitin; 1896 returned to Nizovka and concentrated on his favorite pursuits--lit and agric; portrayed Russian rural way of life; a number of his works were set to music by composers Rebikov, Kyui, Bakaleynikov, etc; his songs were in the repertoires of Chaliapin, Vyal'tseva, etc; 1938 a memorial-lit museum dedicated to him was founded in settlement Zavidovo, Kalinin Oblast; *Publ: Pesni rabochikh* (Songs of the Workers) (1875); poem "A Mother's Confession" (1877); *V izbe* (In a Peasant's Hut) (1882); *V stolitse* (In the Capital) (1884); *Zimniy den'* (A Winter Day) (1892); *V zasukhu* (In the Drought) (1897); *Pesnya plovtsa* (Swimmer's Song) (1906); *Iz mraka k svetu* (From Darkness to Light) (1912); *Opyat' zima na sanochkakh* (Winter on Sledges Again) (1918); *Zapevka* (Leading the Chorus), *Na skhodke* (At the Meeting) (1920); *Avtobiografiya* (Autobiography) (1923); *Bayan* (Accordion) (1923); *Pamyati V. I. Lenina* (In Memory of Lenin) (1924); *Sveti mne, solnyshko* (Light Me, Dear Sun) (1926); his verse *Pesnya rabotnika* (Song of the Farm-Hand), *Pervaya borozda* (First Furrow), *Pesnya Mikuly Selyaninovicha* (Song of Mikula Selyaninovich), *Vesenneye tsarstvo* (Spring Kingdom), *Lyublyu ya zhguchiye morozy* (I Love the Burning Frosts); sang of labor, nature, etc; *Died*: 24 Dec 1930 in vil Nizovka, Kalinin Oblast.

DROZZHIN, Mikhail Mikhaylovich (1907-1941) Puppet-master; Hon Artiste of RSFSR from 1939; pupil of Yu. M. Yur'yev; *Born*: 1 July 1907; *Career*: 1928 debut at Leningrad Marionette Theater (now Leningrad Puppet Theater); later performed at this theater as puppet-master, designer, puppet-maker and producer; from 1936 simultaneously producer and from 1939 artistic dir, Leningrad Sovkhoz-Kolkhoz Puppet Theater; July 1941 headed 1st Front Brigade of Theater Artists; *Roles*: Gulliver in Dan'ko's *Gulliver v strane liliputov* (Gulliver in the Land of Lilliput); Zhigalin and Dymba in Chekhov's *Svad'ba* (The Wedding), etc; *Productions*: Goldoni's "Servant of Two Masters," etc; *Died*: 14 Feb 1941 killed in action near Leningrad.

DRUZYAKINA, Sof'ya Ivanovna (1880-1953) Opera singer (lyric dramatic soprano); prof, Moscow Conservatory from 1930; *Born*: 29 May 1880 in Kiev; *Educ*: grad Kiev Music College; advanced training in Milan; *Career*: 1900 opera debut in Odessa; 1901-02 in Kiev; 1903-04 in Khar'kov; 1906-07 with Maksakov in Moscow; 1907-08 at the Bolshoy Theater; performed with Chaliapin, Sobinov and Figner; 1910-11 performed in Paris and Palermo; 1910-17 soloist, Zimin Opera Theater; performed with Battistini and Galvani during their tour of Russia; 1917-24 soloist, Theater of Moscow Sov of Workers' Dep; 1920-28 instructor, State Inst of Stagecraft, Moscow; 1924 left the stage; 1930-45 prof, Moscow Conservatory; trained such prominent singers as: Kh. Nasyrova, A. Kuznetsova, K. Mal'kova, N. Rozhdestvenskaya and O. Leont'yeva; *Roles*: Masha in *Dubrovskiy*; Natasha in *Rusalka* (The Water Nymph); the Godmother in Tchaikovsky's *Charodeyka* (The

Sorceress); Marina Mnishek in *Boris Godunov*; Aida; Mimi; Margarita in "Faust"; Nedda in "Pagliacci"; Amelia in Verdi's "Masquerade," etc; *Died*: 3 Oct 1953 in Moscow.

DUBELIR, Georgiy Dmitriyevich (1874-1942) Highway eng; prof from 1916; *Born*: 1 Sept 1874; *Educ*: 1898 grad Petersburg Inst of Communications Eng; *Career*: 1898 began working as a railroad eng; from 1904 instructor, Kiev Polytech Inst; 1916-30 prof, Petrograd (Leningrad) Inst of Communications Eng; 1930-40 prof, Leningrad Highway Inst; from 1941 prof, Moscow Highway Inst; specialized in highway-planning but also worked on town-planning and streetcar and railroad systems; *Publ: Planirovka gorodov* (Town-Planning) (1910); *Gorodskiye ulitsy i mostovyye* (Urban Streets and Sidewalks) (1912); *O normakh stoka livnevykh vod* (The Run-off Rates of Rainwater) (1926); coauthor, *Ekspluatatsiya avtoguzhevykh dorog* (The Use of Motor Roads) (1934); *Osnovy proyektirovaniya avtomibil'nykh dorog* (The Principles of Planning Motorways) (2 vol, 1938-39); coauthor, *Izyskaniya avtomobil'nykh dorog* (Highway Surveying) (1939); *Died*: 10 Sept 1942.

DUBINA, Kuz'ma Kondrat'yevich (1906-1967) Historian; Dr of Historical Sci; prof; hon member, Ukr Acad of Sci; CP member from 1931; *Born*: 23 Oct 1906 in vil Podgorodnoye, Dnepropetrovsk Oblast, son of a peasant; *Educ*: 1930's grad Leningrad Inst of Journalism and Inst of Red Prof; *Career*: from 1937 taught CPSU history; 1939-41 head, Chair of Marxism-Leninism, Kiev Univ; during WW 2 worked for CC, CP Ukr; after WW 2 worked for Ukr Council of Min, then for Ukr Radio Telegraph Agency; from 1951 taught at Kiev Higher educ institutions; 1956-65 rector and assoc prof, then prof, Inst of Advanced Training for Soc Sci Teachers, Kiev Univ; 1965-67 dir, Inst of History, Ukr Acad of Sci; 1965 attended Sov-German Historians Conference, East Berlin; 1965 also attended 12th Int Congress of Historical Sci, Vienna; *Publ: Varvary XX veka* (Twentieth-Century Barbarians) (1942); *Zlodeyaniya nemtsev v Kiyeve* (The Misdeeds of the Germans in Kiev) (1945); *778 tragicheskikh dney Kiyeva* (Kiev's 778 Tragic Days) (1945); *Leninskaya teoriya sotsialisticheskoy revolyutsii i yeyo vsemirno-istoricheskoye znacheniye* (Lenin's Theory of Socialist Revolution and Its World Historical Significance) (1959); *Kommunisticheskaya partiya Ukrainy v gody Velikoy Otechestvennoy voyny* (The Communist Party of the Ukraine During the Great Fatherland War) (1961); *V gody tyazhyolykh ispytaniy* (Years of Tribulation) (1962); *Nemerknushchiy podvig* (An Undying Exploit) (1966); *Died*: 22 Sept 1967.

DUBINSKIY, David Aleksandrovich (1920-1960) Graphic artist; corresp member, USSR Acad of Arts from 1958; *Born*: 10 June 1920; *Educ*: 1946 grad Moscow Art Inst; *Works*: illustrations for Gaydar's *Chuk and Gek*, R.V.S. and *Golubaya chashka* (The Blue Goblet); Chekhov's *Dom s mezoninom* (The House with the Attic) and *Nevesta* (The Bride); Il'f and Petrov's *Tonya*; Kuprin's *Poyedinok* (The Duel); painting "The Gymnastics Lesson," etc; *Awards*: Stalin Prize (1951); *Died*: 3 May 1960.

DUBINSKIY, Sergey Aleksandrovich (1884-?) Historian and archeologist; senior assoc, Inst of History, Bel Acad of Sci; *Born*: 25 Oct 1884 in vil Naroyki, Grodno Province, son of a priest; *Educ*: 1905 grad Vilnius Theological Seminary; 1905-07 studied first at Med Fac then at History and Philology Fac, Yur'ev (Tartu) Univ; 1914 grad History and Philology Fac, Petersburg Univ; *Career*: 1914-19 history lecturer at Vilnius colleges; 1919-21 taught history, Russian language and law in Belebey, Ufa Province; simultaneously member, uyezd extraordinary commission for eliminating illiteracy; from 1921 in Minsk; 1921-24 member, Bel Centr Commission for Eliminating Illiteracy; also lecturer in Russian language and social sci at Minsk higher educ establishments; from 1924 member, Archeological Commission, Inst of Bel Culture; then researcher, Archeology Section, Bel Acad of Sci; pupil of noted archeologist A. Spitsyn; 1910-14 conducted archeological excavations in Bel'sk Uyezd, Grodno Province, from 1925 directed archeological studies and excavations in Bel SSR; with A. N. Lyavdanskiy and K. M. Polikarpovich studied paleolithic encampment near vil Berdyzh, Chechersk Rayon; excavated painted ceramic ware sites, Bantserovo township and also Germanovo and Circassian townships near Orsha; directed excavation of Zaslavl' and other burial mounds; published monograph on *Bibliyahrafiya pa arkhealogii Belarusi i sumezhnikh krain* (Bibliography on the Archeology of Belorussia and Neighboring Regions) (1932); May 1937 arrested by NKVD; *Died*: in imprisonment.

DUBKOVETSKIY, Fyodor Ivanovich (1894-1960) Ukr; administrator; CP member from 1926; *Born*: 2 May 1894 in vil Zarozhany, Khotin Uyezd, Bessarabia Province, son of a peasant; *Educ*: partial secondary educ; *Career*: from 1908 worked in agric; participant in 1919 uprising in Khotin Uyezd; 1919-22 served in Red Army; 1922 organized first agric commune in Tal'kov Rayon, which was later converted into agric artel "Achievements of the Oct Revol" and which he managed until his death; deleg, 19th, 20th and 21st CPSU Congresses and 17th, 18th, 19th and 20th CP Ukr Congresses; 1956 at 20th CPSU Congress elected member, CPSU Centr Auditing Commission; at 17th-19th CP Ukr Congresses elected member, CC, CP Ukr; dep, USSR Supr Sov of 2nd, 3rd, 4th and 5th convocations; *Publ: Trudovyye budni kolkhoza 'Zdobutok Zhovtnya'* (Workdays of the Kolkhoz "Achievements of the October Revolution") (1957); *Rozhdyonnyye oktyabryom* (October's Children) (1957); *Zdravstvuy zavtra! Na dorogakh k kommunizmu* (Hello, Tomorrow! On the Roads to Communism) (1960); *Died*: 6 Mar 1960.

DUBOV, Nikolay Ivanovich (1875-1950) Impressario, actor and stage dir; *Born*: 1875; *Educ*: studied at Petersburg Theatrical College and Raphof Courses; *Career*: from 1890 with amateur theatrical groups; actor with provincial theaters; played in Pyatigorsk, Odessa, Saratov, Smolensk and Tula; 1913-14 with Sinel'nikov Theater; from 1914 impressario at theaters in Omsk, then Irkutsk; 1920 founded and directed in Irkutsk first Siberian theatrical school; also did polit and theater cartoons; contributed theater cartoons to journal *Budil'nik*; after 1917 Oct Revol acted at theaters in Omsk, Irkutsk and Cheremkhov; specialized in character roles; wrote reminiscences of provincial theatrical life; *Roles*: Uriel' in Gutskov's *Uriel' Akosta*; Paratov in Ostrovskiy's *Bespridannitsa* (Girl Without a Dowry); Podkolesin in *Zhenit'ba* (The Marriage), etc; *Died*: 12 Dec 1950.

DUBOVIK, Leontiy Fyodorovich (1902-1952) Stage dir; drama teacher from 1925; assoc prof from 1949; Pop Artiste of Ukr SSR from 1947; CP member from 1947; *Born*: 30 Oct 1902 in Kiev; *Educ*: 1925 grad Kiev Inst of Music and Drama; *Career*: 1925-50 stage dir, *Berezil'* Theater (since 1934 Shevchenko Ukr Drama Theater), Khar'kov; *Works*: produced plays: Kulish's "97" (1930); Mikitenko's *Kadry* (Cadres) (1931); Gorky's *Vassa Zheleznova* (1936); Korneychuk's *Bankir* (The Banker) (1937); Sholom-Aleykhem's "Tevier, the Milkman" (1940); Ostrovskiy's *Groza* (The Thunderstorm) (1946); Staritskiy's *Talant* (Talent) (1941); Dmiterko's *General Vatutin* (1948); Korneychuk's *Gibel' eskadry* (The End of a Squadron) (1951); etc; *Awards*: Stalin Prize (1948); *Died*: 22 Aug 1952.

DUBOVOY, Ivan Naumovich (1896-1938) Ukr; army comr, 2nd Class from 1935; commander, Khar'kov Mil Distr; CP member from 1917; *Born*: 12 Sept 1896 in vil Chmyrivtsy, Kiev Province, son of a peasant; *Educ*: Mar 1917 grad Ensigns' School, Irkutsk; 1926 grad advanced officers training courses at Frunze Mil Acad; *Pos*: 1916 drafted into Russian Army; 1917-18 junior officer, Krasnoyarsk training depot; 1918-19 mustered Bakhmut (now Artemovsk) Red Guard detachment; mil comr, Novo-Makeyev rayon; commandant, Centr Staff, Donbass Red Guard; 1919 chief of staff, Kiev Forces Group; chief of staff, 10th Army; commander, 1st Ukr Army; from Apr 1919 commander, 3rd Border Div (renamed 44th Infantry Div); Aug 1919 asst chief, 44th (Shchors) Div; 1919-24 again chief, 44th Div; 1924-29 commander, 14th Infantry Corps; 1929-35 asst, then dep commander, Ukr Mil Distr; from 1934 simultaneously member, Mil Council, Pop Comrt of Defense; 1935-37 commander, Khar'kov Mil Distr; *Career*: in 1919 his 44th Infantry Div won renown in Ukr in liberation of Zhitomir, Chernigov and Kiev; 1930, together with Yakir, managed to quash trial of group of former officers of Russian Army who had served on staff of Ukr Milit Distr, were arrested by OGPU and unwarrantedly accused of organizing an anti-Sov plot; 1933, during Ukr famine, together with Yakir and other Party functionaries sent Stalin a letter requesting end to grain procurement in Ukr and seeking authorization to use mil supplies to aid regions worst hit by famine; 21 Aug 1937 arrested by NKVD organs; *Awards*: Order of the Red Banner; *Died*: executed 28 July 1938; 14 July 1956 rehabilitated.

DUBROVIN, Aleksandr Ivanovich (1855-1918) Politician; cofounder, monarchistic Union of the Russian People; *Born*: 1855; *Career*: physician by profession; 1905 helped found Union of the Russian People; until 1910 permanent chm of the Union's Council; 1905-17 ed, newspaper *Russkoye znamya*; accused by Sov press of instigating Jewish pogroms and terrorist acts; to him were attributed the murders of members of the 1st State Duma M. Ya.

Gertsenshteyn (1906), G. P. Iollos and A. L. Karavayev (1907); opposed Stolypin and Witte; *Died*: fall 1918 executed after Oct Coup.

DUBROVINSKIY, Yakov Fyodorovich (1882-1918) Professional revol; CP member from 1900; *Born*: 1882 in vil Pokrovsko-Lipovitsy, Oryol Province; *Educ*: studied at Oryol Tech High School and Perm' Mining College; *Career*: Party work in Perm'; 1905 worked for Moscow Soc-Democratic org; active in Decembrist uprising; member, Odessa Soc-Democratic Comt and Mil Org; from 1908 member, Krasnoyarsk RSDRP Comt; during WW 1 opponent of *defensism*; repeatedly arrested and exiled; after 1917 Feb Revol chm, Krasnoyarsk Sov and Exec Comt; member, Krasnoyarsk RSDRP(B) Comt; after 1917 Oct Revol chm, Krasnoyarsk Sov of Workers, Peasants and Cossacks' Dep; during Czechoslovak campaign voluntarily went to front with a detachment of Red Guards; arrested by Czechoslovaks and imprisoned; *Died*: 24 Oct 1918 executed.

DUBROVSKIY, Konstantin Konstantinovich (1888-1956) Astronomer; specialist in astrometry and celestial mech; *Born*: 10 Oct 1888; *Educ*: 1911 grad Petersburg Univ; *Career*: until 1933 prof, Perm' Univ; 1933-52 prof, Gorky Univ; from 1936 prof, Gorky Inst of Water Transport Eng; 1917-27 made systematic observations of planetoids and comets at Engelhardt Observatory near Kazan'; calculated the final orbit of comet 1907 (I); from 1937 chm, Gorky Dept, All-Union Astronomical and Geodetic Soc; 1939-53 ed, *Astronomicheskiy kalendar'*; proposed establishment of a latitudinal station in Gorky, which began in 1951 to study the movement of the Earth's poles; *Publ*: articles "The Application of Gibbs Formula to the Method of Varying Geocentric Distances" (1925); "The Gorky Latitudinal Station" (1951); *Died*: 15 June 1956.

DUBROVSKIY-ESHKE, Boris Vladimirovich (1897-1963) Film actor; prof, All-Union State Inst of Cinematography from 1940; Hon Art Worker of RSFSR from 1940; CP member from 1948; *Born*: 12 Apr 1897; *Educ*: 1919-23 studied at Leningrad Acad of Arts; *Career*: 1917 set designer, Opera Theater, Leningrad Pop Center; 1921 at Drama and Comedy Theater, etc; 1924 film debut; for many years leading actor for number of Sov film studios: "Lenfilm," "Mosfilm" and Centr United Film Studio, Alma Ata; from 1929 founder-instructor, Special Cinema dept for Training Film Actors; from 1938 lectured at All-Union State Inst of Cinematography; his pupils included V. Ivanov, M. Bogdanov, L. Mil'chin, P. Pashkevich, P. Dulenkov, etc; *Works*: set designer or producer in films: *Turbina No. 3* (Turbine No. 3), *Sar-Pige, Order na zhizn'* (Order For Life) and *Na dal'nem beregu* (On the Far Shore) (1927); *Goluboy ekspress* (The Blue Express) and *Myatezh* (Mutiny) (1929); *Yest', Kapitan* (Aye Aye, Captain), *Transport ognya* (Cargo of Fire) and *Zagovor myortvykh* (Conspiracy of the Dead) (1930); *Vstrechnyy* (Encounter) (1932); *Lenin v Oktyabre* (Lenin in October) (1937); *Lenin v 1918 godu* (Lenin in 1918) (1939), etc; *Publ*: coauthor, *Lenin v Oktyabre* (Lenin in October) (1938); *Died*: 7 Sept 1963.

DUDAR, Ales' (real name: DAYLIDOVICH, Aleksandr Aleksandrovich) (1904-1946) Bel poet; member, Bel Writers' Union from 1934; *Born*: 24 Dec 1904 in vil Novoselki (now Gomel' Oblast), son of a peasant; *Educ*: 1921 grad Minsk secondary school; studied at Lit and Linguistic Dept Teachers' Training Fac, Bel State Univ; *Career* :1923 helped organize *Maladnyak* lit soc of proletarian writers; 1927 helped found *Polymya* lit soc; 1921 first work published; although a poet of "revol-romantic" school, he committed "ideological errors" especially in 1927-28 during the so-called "theater controversy"; 1928 arrested and exiled until 1933 to Smolensk; 1933 returned to Minsk; 3 Nov 1936 re-arrested and sent to a concentration camp; *Publ*: collections of verse and poems: *Rebellious Belorussia* (1925); "Sunny Paths" (1925); "Purer than Gold and Steel" (1926); "The Tower" (1928); collected stories "Marseillaise" (1927); poems "Shanghai Silk" (1926); *Slutsak* (1933); "War for Peace" (1934); translated into Bel works of Pushkin, Blok's *Dvenadtsat'* (The Twelve), Goethe's "Faust" and Schiller's "Wilhelm Tell"; *Died*: 25 Feb 1946 in imprisonment; posthumously rehabilitated.

DUDAREV, Dmitriy Aleksandrovich (1890-1960) Actor, Pop Artiste of Ukr SSR from 1947; CP member from 1939; *Born*: 2 Oct 1890 in Yekaterinoslav; *Career*: 1910 professional stage debut; 1920-24 comr, dir, actor, Kremenchug Province Polit Educ Comt Theater; then worked for Ukr and Russian touring theaters; from 1927 actor, Zankovetskaya Theater; *Roles*: Voznyy in Kotlyarevskiy's *Natalka Poltavka* (Natalya from Poltava); Stadnik in A. Khizhnyak's *Na bol'shuyu zemlyu* (To the Big Country); Galushka in *Stepi Ukrainy* (Steppes of the Ukraine); Polezhayev in *Bespokoynaya starost'* (Restless Old Age); Karp in Mirnyy's *Limerivna*; Maryn in Tobilevich's *Martyn Borulya*; Shpak in Kvitka Osnov'yanenko's *Shel'menko-denshchik* (Shel'menko the Journeyman); Shmaga in *Bez viny vinovatyye* (Guilty Without Guilt); Chebutykin in Chekhov's *Tri sestry* (Three Sisters); Lenin in Korneychuk's *Pravda* (Truth) (1947), etc; *Awards*: Stalin Prize (1950); *Died*: 6 Aug 1960.

DUDINOV, Olimpiy Avramiyevich (1895-1955) Kir ophthalmologist; Dr of Med from 1940; prof from 1941; corresp member, Kir Acad of Sci from 1954; Hon Sci Worker of Kir SSR; *Born*: 1895 in Beryozovo, Tobol'sk Province; *Educ*: 1915 grad Tomsk Boys' High-School; 1920 grad Med Fac, Tomsk Univ;sI *Career* : 1920-25 worked at various hospitals in Ural'sk and specialized in ophthalmology; 1925-27 head, Therapy Section, and consulting oculist, Kzyl-Orda Health Dept, Kaz; from 1927 head, Eye Disease Dept, Regional Clinical Hospital, Alma-Ata; 1928-31 chm, Kaz Regional Assoc of Med Workers; 1931 member, Kzyl-Orda City Sov; 1933-38 head, Clinical Dept, then Experimental Dept, Kaz Ophthalmological Inst, Alma-Ata; 1934-35 exec secr, periodical *Meditsinskiy zhurnal Kazakhstana*; 1934-38 member, Alma-Ata City Sov; 1940-55 prof and head, Chair of Eye Diseases, Kir State Med Inst; also chm, Learned Council and chief ophthalmologist, Kir Min of Health; 1946-49 dep, Frunze City Sov; 1950 dep, USSR Supr Sov of 3rd convocation; bd member, All-Union Soc of Ophthalmologists; chm, Kir Soc of Ophthalmologists; dep ed, journal *Sovetskoye zdravookhraneniye Kirgizii*; devised original method of treating strabismus by shortening the weakened muscle with cartilage from the auricle and plexiglass; modified Kunt-Shimanovskiy's operation for atonic ectropion; developed a smallpox vaccine therapy for herpetic keratitis and an operation for partial enucleation in atrophy of the eyeball with shortening of the fornices; also devised methods of diagnosing cerebral hernia, pathoanatomical lesions in ocular cholesterinasis, arteriosclerotic arachnoiditis of the optic nerve, etc; also made a major contribution to the campaign against trachoma; wrote 84 works, including 19 on the campaign against trachoma in Kaz and Kir; *Publ: Eksperimental'naya tularemiya glaza* (Experimentally Induced Tularemia of the Eye) (1940), etc; *Awards*: three Orders of the Red Banner of Labor; "Outstanding Health Worker" Badge; medals; *Died*: 7 Dec 1955.

DUDNIK, Akim Minovich (1881-1934) Govt official; CP member from 1917; *Born*: 1 Oct 1881 in vil Moshni, now Cherkassy Oblast; *Career*: from 1918 govt posts in the Urals, Volga area and Moscow; 1921 Ukr Dep Pop Comr of Food Supplies; from 1922 Ukr Dep Pop Comr of Agric and simultaneously chm, Ukr Agric Bank; 1924-26 Ukr Dep Pop Comr of Workers and Peasants' Inspection and Ukr Pop Comr of Agric; 1926-33 chm, Ukr Gosplan and dep chm, Ukr Council of Pop Comr; at 13th RCP(B) Congress elected member, Centr Control Commission, CC, RCP(B); at 8th CP(B) Ukr Conference elected member, Centr Control Commission, CC, CP(B) Ukr; at 10th and 12th CP(B) Ukr Congresses elected member, CC, CP(B) Ukr; 1924-25 Presidium member, Centr Control Commission, CC, CP(B) Ukr; *Died*: 14 Mar 1934.

DUKA, Stepan Kharitonovich (1907-1960) Botanist; specialist in the selection and genetics of fruit- and berry-bearing plants; member, Ukr Acad of Agric Sci from 1959; CP member from 1939; *Born*: 10 Apr 1907 in vil Zhovte, now Dnepropetrovsk Oblast, son of a blacksmith; *Educ*: 1929 grad Uman' Agric Inst; *Career*: 1929-38 worked at Chair of Selection and Seed-Growing, Uman' Agric Inst; from 1938 assoc, from 1949 dir, Ukr Fruit Research Inst (now Ukr Horticultural Research Inst); bred new varieties of strawberry ("Early Kiev Nr 2," "Jubilee" and "Little Ukr"), sweet cherry ("Kiev Nr 2," "Nr 5," "Nr 9"), cherry ("Uman' Praecox"), apple ("Kiev Ranet"), etc; *Awards*: Stalin Prize (1952); three Orders of the Red Banner of Labor; Order of the Red Star; Order of the Great Fatherland War, 2nd Class; medals; *Died*: 23 June 1960.

DUKHONIN, Nikolay Nikolayevich (1876-1917) Mil commander; lt gen, Russian Army from 1917; leading functionary of Provisional Govt; *Born*: 1876; *Educ*: 1902 grad Gen Staff Acad; *Pos*: until WW 1 senior adjutant, Intelligence Branch, Staff of Kiev Mil Distr; 1914-17 senior adjutant, Intelligence Branch, Staff of 3rd Army; regt commander, quartermaster-gen of an army, Southwestern Front; 5 Sept 1917 appointed by Kerenskiy as chief of staff to Supr Commander; *Career*: day after 1917 Oct uprising in Petrograd telegraphed front commanders informing them that Gen Headquarters had decided to protect the army by all possible means against the influence of the "dissident elements" and fully supported the Provisional Govt; 1 Nov 1917 lost communication with commander in chief Kerenskiy and himself assumed the functions of commander in chief; refused to obey order of the Council of Pop Comr to negotiate with the German Command for a cessation of hostilities on all fronts, since he refused to recognize the Council of Pop Comr as the govt; 9 Nov 1917 outlawed by the latter body; remained at Gen Headquarters at Mogilev doing nothing to protect himself and taking no measures against the Sov regime; 19 Nov 1917 released Gen Kornilov, Gen Denikin, etc, arrested by the Provisional Govt, whose life was threatened by Red Guards sent to Mogilev by the Council of Pop Comr to rout Gen Headquarters; 20 Nov 1917 voluntarily went to meet Krylenko--Bolshevik commander in chief--on his arrival in Mogilev; *Died*: 20 Nov 1917 at Mogilev railroad station bayoneted and trampled to death by a mob of seamen and Red Guards, who pushed aside Krylenko and his guards.

DUKHOV, Nikolay Leonidovich (1904-1964) Design eng; lt gen, Army eng and tech corps; corresp member, USSR Acad of Sci from 1953; three-time Hero of Socialist Labor; CP member from 1941; *Born*: 26 Oct 1904 in vil Veprik, now Poltava Oblast; *Educ*: 1932 grad Leningrad Polytech Inst; *Career*: from 1932 eng, dep chief designer, then chief designer, Kirov Plant, Leningrad; from 1946 simultaneously chief eng, Leningrad Tank Plant No. 100; during WW 2 dep chief designer, USSR Pop Comrt of the Tank Ind; from 1948 dep sci dir and chief designer at a research inst; from 1954 chief designer and sci dir, Design Bureau of the USSR Defense Ind; along with A. A. Morozov and I. Ya. Kotin ranked as one of top Sov tank designers; 1939 helped to develop KV (Klim Voroshilov and KV-2 heavy tanks, an updated version of which, the KV-85, was produced in 1943; 1944 produced an improved version, the IS (Iosif Stalin), which was succeeded by the IS-2, IS-3 and IS-4; designed self-propelled cannon and howitzers based on the KV, ISU-122, ISU-152 and other tank chassis; *Awards*: five Stalin Prizes; Lenin Prize; four Orders of Lenin; medals; *Died*: 1 May 1964.

DUKIS, Karl Yanovich (1890-1966) Govt official; CP member from 1917; *Born*: 1890; *Career*: 1918-19 commandant, Moscow Okrug Cheka; 1919-47 worked for All-Russian Cheka and NKVD; 1948-58 econ admin work; from 1958 pensioner; *Died*: 16 Sept 1966.

DUL'CHEVSKIY, Dmitriy Antonovich (1878-1961) Eng; specialist in welding; CP member from 1953; *Born*: 29 Sept 1878; *Educ*: 1895 grad Odessa Tech College; *Career*: from 1897 worked at maintenance sheds, Roslavl' Railroad, then at electr welding workshop, Odessa Railroad maintenance sheds; 1924 designed first Sov electr welding machine; 1927 invented electr arc welder using cuprite under a layer of powdered fuels; a method of automatic electr welding was developed by other Sov sci on the basis of this system; *Publ*: *Dugovaya elektrosvarka krasnoy medi* (A Cuprite Electric Arc Welder) (1929); *Avtomat dlya metallicheskoy dugi sistemy D. A. Dul'chevskogo* (An Automatic Welder for D. A. Dul'chevskiy's Metallic Arc System) (1936); *Awards*: Stalin Prize (1951); *Died*: 4 Oct 1961.

DUMANSKIY, Anton Vladimirovich (1880-1967) Chemist; pioneer of Russian colloidal chemistry; corresp member, USSR Acad of Sci from 1933; member, Ukr Acad of Sci from 1945; Hon Sci Worker of Kaz SSR from 1942; Hon Sci Worker of Ukr SSR from 1950; CP member from 1940; *Born*: 20 June 1880 in Ivanovo-Voznesensk, now Ivanovo; *Educ*: 1903 grad Kiev Polytech Inst; *Career*: 1903-13 did research at Kiev Polytech Inst; 1913-42 founder-dir, Colloidal Chemistry Laboratory, from 1932 All-Union Colloidal Chemistry Research Inst; 1946-60 dir, Inst of Gen and Inorganic Chemistry, Ukr Acad of Sci; from 1935 founder-ed, *Kolloidnyy zhurnal*; studied solvation of colloidal particles; developed theory of bonded water; used physiochemical diagram method to study colloidal systems; 1908 devised applications for colloidal membranes; 1912 proposed use of centrifuges for measuring the size of colloidal particles; *Publ*: *Liofil'nost' dispersnykh sistem* (The Lyophylic Nature of Dispersen Systems) (1940); *Ucheniye o kolloidakh* (Colloid Theory) (3rd ed, 1948); coauthor, *Bibliograficheskiy ocherk razvitiya otechestvennoy kolloidnoy khimii* (A Bibliographic Study of the Development of Colloidal Chemistry in the USSR) (3 vol, 1949-58); *Awards*: two Orders of Lenin; Order of the Red Banner of Labor; *Died*: 14 May 1967.

DUMAVI, Nadzhib (real name: TAKHTAMYSHEV) (1888-1933) Tatar writer and pedag; *Born*: 19 May 1883 in vil Novoye Dumkino, Kazan' Province; *Educ*: studied at Kazan' medressah and at a Russian school; *Career*: 1903 first work printed; 1905-21 worked for Tatar newspapers and journals, writing articles, verse, stories and novelettes; 1906-09 taught at Kizel' mines in the Urals; after 1917 Oct Revol taught in Uzbekistan; *Publ*: verse: "The Coal-Miners" (1907); "Siberia" (1907); "The Voice" (1908); "The Prisoner" (1908); "War" (1908), etc; also wrote for children; *Died*: 5 May 1933 in Bulungur, Samarkand Oblast.

DUNAYEV, Yevlampiy Aleksandrovich (Party alias: Aleksandr) (1877-1919) Revolutionary; *Born*: 1877 in vil Lezhnevo, Vladimir Province, son of a peasant; *Career*: from 1894 worked at a weaving mill in Ivanovo-Voznesensk; 1897 joined revol movement; from 1898 attended Soc-Democratic circles run by Ivanovo-Voznesensk Workers' Union; 1899 imprisoned for 18 months in *Kresty* Jail, Petersburg; 1905 member, Ivanovo-Voznesensk City RSDRP Comt and member, Ivanovo-Voznesensk Sov of Workers' Dep; 1906 deleg from Moscow Party org at 4th RSDRP Congress; 1907 arrested and exiled to Sol'vychegodsk; 1909 returned from exile and worked in Petersburg and Moscow; Oct 1911 exiled to Nizhniy Novgorod; Feb 1914 returned to Petersburg and conducted Party work in "Bureau for Supplying Illegal Lit from Abroad"; 1916 arrested and assigned to mil unit at Shadrinsk, but fled to Nizhniy Novgorod, where he took an active part in 1917 Feb Revol; 1917 asst chm and Presidium member, Nizhniy Novgorod City Sov; Bolshevik rep in State Duma; after 1917 Oct Revol worked for Nizhniy Novgorod Province Food Comt and Sovnarkhoz; *Died*: 14 Mar 1919.

DUNAYEVSKIY, Isaak Osipovich (1900-1955) Composer; pioneer of Sov musical comedy and mass songs; Hon Art Worker of RSFSR from 1936; Pop Artiste of RSFSR from 1950; *Born*: 30 Jan 1900 in Lokhvitsa, Poltava Province; *Educ*: 1919 grad I. Akhron's violin class, Khar'kov Conservatory; studied composition under prof S. Bogatyryov; *Career*: 1919-24 orchestra violinist, first violinist; later lecturer, Pop Univ; musical dir, Khar'kov Province, Dept of Educ; 1924-26 musical dir, Hermitage Theater, then Moscow City Trade-Union Council Theater, then Korsh Theater; 1926-29 musical dir, Moscow Satyrical Theater; 1929-34 chief conductor and musical dir, Leningrad Music-Hall; 1938-48 artistic dir, Song and Dance Ensemble, Railroad Worker's Centr House of Culture in Moscow; 1937-41 chm, Org Comt, Leningrad Composers' Union; 1939-48 Presidium member, Org Comt, USSR Composers' Union; dep, RSFSR Supr Sov of 1938 convocation; first of Sov composers to include into light music elements of jazz, because of this repeatedly criticized; while his early operettas were already forgotten by the 1930's, he is better known as a creator of mass songs and composer of film-music; the first musical phrase of his song "Broad Is My Native Land" has become the call-sign of Radio Moscow; closely associated with poet Lebedev-Kumach, who wrote the texts of his songs; *Works*: ballets: *Otdykh Favna* (Recreation of a Faun); *Murzilka*; operettas: *I nashim i vashim* (To Us and to You) (1924); *Zhenikhi* (Bridegrooms) (1926); *Kar'yera prem'yera* (The Prime Minister's Career) (1928); "Ballet Suite" [Polar Passion] (1929); operetta *Million terzaniy* (A Million Torments) (1932); music for the film *Pervyy vzvod* (First Platoon) (1933); march "Jolly Fellows"; music for the film *Vesyolyye rebyata* (Jolly Fellows) (1934); "Song of Kakhovka"; music for the film *Tri tovarishcha* (Three Comrades) (1935); "Song of the Fatherland"; music for the films: *Vratar'* (The Goalkeeper); *Tsirk* (Cirkus); *Deti kapitana Granta* (Captain Grant's Children) (1936); operetta *Zolotaya dolina* (Golden Valley) (1937); "March of the Athletes"; music for the film *Kontsert Betkhovena* (Beethoven's Concerto) (1937); "Song of the Red Sailors"; operetta *Solomennaya shapka* (Straw Hat); music for the film *Volga-Volga* (1938); song "Heroes of Khasan"; "Song of the Sea" (1939); song "At the Enemy, for the Fatherland, Forward!" (1941); song "My Moscow" (1942); "Military March of the Railroad Workers" (1944); music for the film *Novyy dom* (New House) (1946); song "Inspiring Word"; music for the films: *Stadion* (Stadium), *Kubanskiye kazaki* (Kuban' Cossacks) (1949); "Song of Youth" (1951); music for the film *Krylataya zashchita* (Winged Defense) (1953); song "Moscow Lights"; music for the films: *Zapasnoy igrok* (Reserve Player), *Ispytaniye vernosti* (Test of Loyalty) (1954), etc; *Awards*: Badge of Hon; Order of the Red Star; Order of the Red Banner of Labor (1936); Stalin Prizes (1941, 1951); Prize at World Festival of Democratic Youth in Berlin; *Died*: 25 July 1955 in Moscow.

DUNDICH, Oleko (real name: CHOLICH, Milutin) (1893-1920) Mil commander; Serb; Russian Civil War veteran; prior to WW 1 member, Soc-Democratic group; *Born*: 24 Jan 1893 in vil Drenovicy (Serbia), son of a vil teacher; *Educ*: 1916 grad Odessa Ensign School; *Career*: until 1913 mechanic in Belgrade; 1913 drafted into Serbian Army; fought in WW 1; 1916 captured by Austrian Army, escaped and fled to Russia; 1916-17 in Russian Army on the Rumanian Front; during 1917 Oct Revol joined the Bolsheviks; 1917-20 commanded Serbian detachment of the Red Guard Int Brigade; battalion commander, 3rd Int Brigade; commanded squadron, Don-Stavropol' Cavalry Brigade; was liaison officer to Budennyy; asst regt commander, 1st Cavalry Army; fought at Odessa, in the Donbas and at Tsaritsyn; took part in the 1st Cavalry Army's thrust into Galicia; displayed outstanding valor; brilliant at cavalry raids in the enemy's rear; *Awards*: Order of the Red Banner; *Died*: 7 July 1920 killed in action at Rovno, where he is buried.

DURDENEVSKIY, Vsevolod Nikolayevich (1889-1963) Lawyer; specialist in int law; Hon Sci Worker of RSFSR from 1957; Dr of Law from 1946; Envoy Extraordinary and Plen, 2nd Class from 1947; *Born*: 9 Feb 1889; *Educ*: 1911 grad Law Fac, Moscow Univ; *Career* :from 1915 lecturer, Moscow Univ; from 1917 prof, Perm' Univ; from 1922 prof, Moscow Univ; 1923-39 lectured at Bel Univ, Irkutsk and Sverdlovsk Law Inst; from 1941 expert consultant, Treaty Law Dept, USSR Min of For Affairs; from 1957 member of Sov group at Permanent Court of Arbitration, the Hague, and member, Exec Comt, Sov Assoc of Int Law; from 1948 worked at Moscow Inst of Int Relations; from 1958 member, Sov—Belgian Frienship Soc; author and coauthor of works on int law; *Publ: Sovetskaya territoriya v aktakh mezhdunarodnogo prava za posledniye tridtsat' let* (Soviet Territory in International Law Documents of the Past Thirty Years) (1947); *Gosudarstvennyy stroy Shvetsii* (The State Structure of Sweden) (1947); *Agressiya i interventsiya na Dal'nem Vostoke v svete mezhdunarodnogo prava* (Aggression and Intervention in the Far East in the Light of International Law) (1952); *Neytralitet v sisteme kollektivnoy bezopasnosti* (Neutrality Within the Framework of Collective Security) (1957); *Nesovmestimost' ispol'zovaniya atomnogo oruzhiya s normami mezhdunarodnogo prava* (Incompatibility of the Use of Nuclear Weapons with the Standards of International Law) (1959); *Neytralitet i atomnoye oruzhiye* (Neutrality and Nuclear Weapons) (1960), etc; *Died*: 13 Nov 1963.

DURNOV, Modest Aleksandrovich (1868-1928) Painter (watercolorist), graphic artist and architect; *Born*: 1868; *Educ*: 1887 grad Moscow College of Painting, Sculpture and Architecture; leading exponent of Modernism in his architectural designs (often utterly distorted by the builders), paintings and graphic works; subsequently switched from allegory and symbolism to realistic portraiture, landscapes and still-lifes; master of water-color technique; maintained close ties with "Union" and "World of Art" groups; after 1917 Oct Revol specialized in art ind and town planning; worked as eng on "Greater Moscow" plan; *Works*: design for Meyerhold Theater; portraits: Bryusov; Bal'mont; his wife and son; L. V. Sobinov, etc; illustrations for Russian editions of Oscar Wilde's "Portrait of Dorian Grey," "Salome" and "The Ballad of Reading Jail"; landscape "In the Palisades" *Died*: 1928.

DUROV, Anatoliy Anatol'yevich (1887-1928) Satirical clown and animal trainer; *Born*: 1887, son of famous animal trainer and clown, A. L. Durov; *Career*: 1914 debut in Ryazan' circus; 1914 also appeared with Nikitin Circus, Moscow; for an anti-war joke exiled to Kotel'nich, Vyatka Province; 1917 resumed circus work; 1920-23, 1925 and 1927 foreign tours; performed with large, well-trained group of animals; *Died*: 19 Nov 1928 in Izhevsk as a result of an accident.

DUROV, Vladimir Leonidovich (1863-1934) Animal trainer and clown; Hon Artiste of RSFSR from 1927; brother of A. L. Durov; *Born*: 1 Apr 1863; *Educ*: grad teachers' training courses; attended Sechenov's lectures on animal physiology; *Career*: from his early youth attracted to animal training; 1883 debut at Vinkler's Circus-Menagery in Moscow; 1885 with Bezano Circus in Astrakhan'; performed as clown, strongman, singer of satiric songs, conjurer, impersonator and animal trainer; 1887 with Salamonskiy Circus in Moscow; 1912 set up and ran an experimental station in Moscow; 1919 set up a laboratory for animal psychology; performed with large groups of animals; also gave pop sci lectures; founded a school of circus art and compiled a curriculum for it; worked out a system of animal training based on study of natural instincts in animals and humane treatment of animals; presented mimes involving trained animals, best known of which was "The Railroad" (1901); *Publ: Dressirovka zhivotnykh* (The Training of Animals) (1924); *Zveri dedushki Durova* (Grandfather Durov's Animals) (1925); *Moi zveri* (My Animals) (1927), etc; *Died*: 13 Aug 1934.

DURYLIN (pseudonyms: S. SEVERNYY; S. RAYEVSKIY; N. KUTANOV; D. NIKOLAYEV), Sergey Nikolayevich (1877-1954) Lit, art and theater critic; Dr of Philology from 1943; prof from 1945; *Born*: 26 Sept 1877 in Moscow; *Educ*: 1914 grad Moscow Archeological Inst; *Career*: 1906 first work published; wrote poetry and belles-lettres; from 1904 worked for *Posrednik* Publ House; 1924-28 worked for State Acad of Arts; from 1945 assoc, Inst of History of the Arts, USSR Acad of Sci; also lectured at State Inst of Stagecraft and other higher educ establishments; *Publ*: numerous works on: history of Russian theater (M. N. Yermolova, K. S. Stanislavskiy, the Sadovskiys, A. K. Tarasova, etc); history of painting (V. I. Surikov, M. V. Nesterov, etc); research into Russian lit (M. Yu. Lermontov, A. N. Ostrovskiy, V. M. Garshin); history of Moscow theaters; *Rikhard Vagner i Rossiya* (Richard Wagner and Russia) (1913); *Grad Sofii...* (The City of Sophia) (1915); *Repin i Garshin* (Repin and Garshin) (1926); *Russkiye pisateli u Gyote v Veymare* (Russian Writers with Goethe in Weimar) (1932); *Kak rabotal Lermontov* (How Lermontov Worked) (1934); *Teatr Saltykova-Shchedrina* (The Theater of Saltykov-Shchedrin) (1939); *Geroy nashego vremeni 'M. Yu. Lermontova'* (M. Yu Lermontov's "Hero of Our Time") (1940); *Russkiye pisateli v Otechestvennoy voyne 1812 g.* (Russian Writers in the 1812 Patriotic War) (1943); *Vrubel' i Lermontov* (Vrubel' and Lermontov) (1948); *P. M. Sadovskiy. Zhizn' i tvorchestvo* (P. M. Sadovskiy. Life and Work (1950); *Pushkin na stsene* (Pushkin on Stage) (1951); *Maria Zankowecka* (1955); *Ocherki istorii russkogo sovetskogo dramaticheskogo teatra* (Outline History of the Soviet Russian Drama Theater) (1954-60), etc; *Died*: 14 Dec 1954 in Moscow.

DUSHECHKIN, Aleksandr Ivanovich (1874-1956) Agrochemist and specialist in plant physiology; Dr of Agric from 1934; prof from 1923; member, Ukr Acad of Sci from 1945; Hon Sci Worker of Ukr SSR from 1949; CP member from 1944; *Born*: 13 Aug 1874 in vil Opechenskiy Ryadok, now Novgorod Oblast; *Educ*: 1897 grad Petersburg Univ; 1897-99 studied at Zurich Polytech Inst; *Career*: 1903-12 worked at agrochemical laboratory of a network of experimental fields set up by All-Russian Soc of Sugar-Growers; 1915-30 head, Dept of Agrochemistry, Kiev Oblast Experimental Station; 1923-56 founder, prof and head, Chair of Agrochemistry, Kiev Agric Inst; 1946-53 dir, Inst of Plant Physiology and Agrochemistry, Ukr Acad of Sci (now Ukr Research Inst of Plant Physiology); specialized in plant nutrition and fertilizers; *Publ: Khod postupleniya glavneyshikh pitatel'nykh veshchestv v sakharnuyu svekly v svyazi s khodom yeyo rosta* (The Absorption Rate of the Main Nutriments in Sugar Beet in Relation to the Growth Rate) (1911); *Voprosy tekhniki vneseniya udobreniya pod sarkharnuyu sveklu i yeyo podkormki* (Techniques of Applying Fertilizers to Sugar Beet and Its Auxiliary Nutrition) (1937); *Itogi rabot laboratorii po fosfornym udobreniyam* (Work Results of the Laboratory for Phosphoric Fertilizers) (1956), etc; *Awards*: three Orders of Lenin; Order of the Red Banner of Labor; medals; *Died*: 8 Apr 1956.

DUSHENOV, Konstantin Ivanovich (1895-1940) Russian naval officer; squadron commander, 1st class from 1935; CP member from 1919; *Born*: 28 July 1895 in vil Ivanovskoye, Vologda Province, son of a peasant; *Educ*: 1928 grad Naval Acad; *Pos*: until 1915 worker at chemical supply depots in Petrograd; 1915 drafted into Russian Navy; 1916-17 petty officer, cruiser *Avrora*; from 1918 in Red Navy; 1918-20 asst chief of supply, Volga Naval Flotilla; asst commandant, Nizhniy Novgorod, and Astrakhan' ports; commandant, Saratov and Astrakhan' ports; 1921-22 commandant and comr, Sevastopol' and Baku mil docks; 1928-30 commander, training ship *Komsomolets*; chief of staff, brigade of battleships, Baltic Fleet; 1930 commandant and comr, Naval Acad; 1930-34 chief of staff, Black Sea Fleet; 1935-37 commander, Northern Naval Flotilla; 1937-38 commander, Northern Fleet; *Career*: 1917 member, ship comt on cruiser *Avrora*; helped storm the Winter Palace then headed guard detail for Winter Palace and Hermitage; in late 1920's, during controversy over how to develop Sov Navy, advocated the building of light naval vessels and naval aircraft; co-founder, Northern Fleet; dep, USSR Supr Sov of 1937 convocation; 22 May 1938 arrested by State Security organs; *Publ: K istorii voprosa o 'maloy voyne' na more* (The History of "Small—Scale"

Naval Warfare) (1928); *Awards*: four Orders of the Red Banner; Red Star; *Died*: 4 Feb 1940 in imprisonment; according to one version died in Kolyma from starvation; according to another version he was executed by firing squad; posthumously rehabilitated.

DUTOV, Aleksandr Il'ich (1864-1921) Mil commander, col, Russian Army; helped lead anti-Sov Cossack movement in Urals; *Born*: 1864, son of an Orenburg Cossack; *Educ*: grad Gen Staff Acad; *Career*: prior to 1917 Revol served with Orenburg Cossack Army; June 1917 chm, All-Russian Cossack Congress, Petrograd, which elected him chm, All-Russian League of Cossack Forces; advocated abolishing dichotomous rule of Provisional Government and Petrograd Sov; Sept 1917 elected ataman, Orenburg Cossack Army; receiving news of Bolshevik coup in Petrograd, joined with Socialist-Revolutionaries and Mensheviks to found in Orenburg the Comt for the Salvation of the Country and the Revol; in the early hours of 28 Nov 1917 arrested Bolshevik members of Orenburg Sov and Mil Revol Comt; mobilized Cossack troops and seized Troitsk, and Verkhne-Ural'sk cutting Centr Russia's rail link with Siberia and Centr Asia; then fought against Sov troops in Southern Urals; from Nov 1918 his troops, re-formed into Orenburg Separate Cossack Army, operated as part of Admiral Kolchak's forces;; Mar 1920 retreated to China with the remnants of his army; *Died*: Mar 1921 killed by a Cossack at his headquarters in Suidin.

DVIZHKOV, Pavel Pavlovich (1898-1966) Pathoanatomist; prof; Dr of Med; Hon Physician of RSFSR; *Born*: 1898 in Petersburg; *Educ*: 1923 grad Med Fac, 1st Moscow State Univ; *Career*: 1923-27 assoc, 1927-30 asst prof, Chair of Pathological Anatomy, 1st Moscow State Univ; 1923-27 assoc, 1927-41 head, Dept of Pathological Anatomy, Mechnikov Inst of Infectious Diseases, Moscow; 1939-41 head, Dept of Pathological Anatomy, 5th Sov Clinical Hospital, Moscow, and senior assoc, Obukh Inst of Occupational Diseases; 1941-46 mil anatomist in Sov Army; 1941-66 head, Dept of Pathological Anatomy, then chief physician, Med Section, 5th Sov Clinical Hospital, Moscow; 1946-56 chief pathological anatomist, RSFSR Min of Health; 1949-66 head, Laboratory of Pathological Anatomy, Inst of Labor Hygiene and Occupational Diseases, USSR Acad of Med Sci; 1958-60 dep chm, Learned Med Council, USSR Min of Health; co-ed, pathology and morphology section, *Bol'shaya meditsinskaya entsiklopediya* (Large Medcial Encyclopedia) (2nd ed); member, ed bd, journal *Arkhiv patologii*; member, ed councils, journals *Gigiyena truda professional'nyye zabolevaniya* and *Gigiyena i sanitariya*; dep ed and coauthor, multi-vol work on pathological anatomy; bd member, All-Union Soc of Pathological Anatomists; dep chm, Moscow Soc of Pathological Anatomists; dep chm, Inter-Institute Learned Council on Morphology, USSR Acad of Med Sci; member, Experts' Commission, Higher Certifying Commission, USSR Min of Higher Educ; founder, Inst of Oblast and Kray Pathological Anatomists; wrote over 100 works on various aspects of pathological anatomy, including the effect of trauma on the morphology of blood, the pathological anatomy of rabies, tuberculosis and other infectious diseases, the pathology of war wounds, hematology, comparative oncology, cardiovascular pathology, etc; *Publ: Pnevmokoniozy* (Pneumoconiosis) (1965); *Patologicheskaya anatomiya ognestrel'nykh raneniy grudnoy kletki* (The Pathological Anatomy of Gunshot Wounds of the Thorax); coauthor, various vol, *Opyt sovetskoy meditsiny v Velikoy Otechestvennoy voyne 1941-45 godov* (Soviet Medicine in the 1941-45 Great Fatherland War); *Awards*: Badge of Hon (1961); medals; govt prize for work on pathology of gunshot wounds; *Died*: 20 Sept 1960.

DVORISHCHIN, Isay Grigor'yevich (1876-1942) Opera producer; Hon Artiste of RSFSR from 1933; *Born*: 1876; *Career*: from 1889 sang in chorus of opera troupe in Voronezh; from 1904 Chaliapin's secr and dir of shows in which he appeared; 1918-19 dir, Svobodnyy Theater in Voronezh; from 1920 chorist, from 1923 producer, from 1936 producer-inspector, Kirov Opera and Ballet Theater; *Productions*: in Leningrad *Pagliacci*; *Lakmé*; *Rusalka; Yevgeniy Onegin; La Traviata* (last two during Leningrad blockade), etc; *Died*: 1942.

DVORNIKOV, Prokofiy Ignat'yevich (1905-1967) Horticulturist; specialist in vegetable cultivation; corresp member, All-Union Lenin Acad of Agric Sci; member, Mold Acad of Sci; dir, Mold Research Inst of Irrigation Farming and Vegetable Cultivation from 1956; CP member; *Born*: 1905; Educ: 1933 grad Agrobiology Fac, Khar'kov Univ; *Career*: 1925, after studying at a school of horticulture and vegetable cultivation, worked as an agronomist in Ukr; 1933-34 dir, Khar'kov Vegetable Strain-Testing Station; 1934-41 head, Vegetable Crop Dept, then sci dir and dir, Mold Experimental Station of Irrigation Fruit and Vegetable Farming, Tiraspol' (now Mold Research Inst of Irrigation Farming and Vegetable Cultivation; 1946-50 reorganized this experimental station after war-time destruction; 1950-52 Mold First Dep Min of Agric; and head, Mold Main Bd for Sci and Agric Propaganda; 1952-56 dir, Mold Research Inst of Pedology, Agrochemistry and Land Reclamation; member, CC, CP Mold; during last 15 years of life contributed to development of three new varieties of tomato, a new variety of onion, seven varieties of cucumber and three varieties of sweet corn; studied the effects of new local strains on the immunity of vegetable crops; *Publ: Orosheniye ovoshchnykh kul'tur i kartofelya* (The Irrigation of Vegetable Crops and Potatoes) (1965); *Awards*: Hero of Socialist Labor (1967); Order of the Red Banner of Labor; medal "For Valiant Labor in the Great Fatherland War"; inscribed in golden honor book of Mold SSR; *Died*: 19 June 1967.

D'YACHENKO, Dar'ya Grigor'yevna (1924-1944) Partisan leader during WW 2; Hero of the Sov Union from1958 (posthumously); Komsomol member from 1938; *Born*: 1924 in vil Kumari, Nikolayev Oblast; daughter of a peasant; *Educ*: studied at secondary school in vil Krymka, Pervomaysk Rayon; *Career:* during WW 2 co-founder and leader, *Partisan Spark* underground Komsomol org; set up contacts with partisan detachments in neighboring rayons; led Novoandreyevka underground group, did propaganda work and fought against German and Rumanian troops; Mar 1943 arrested by occupation authorities; *Died*: 2 Mar 1944 executed in Tiraspol' Prison.

DYACHENKO, Vadim Yevgen'yevich (1896-1954) Mathematician; corresp member, Ukr Acad of Sci from 1934; *Born*: 30 Dec 1896 in Nizhniy Novgorod; *Career*: from 1935 prof, Kiev Univ; did research on applied mathematics in solving problems of physics and mech; 1946 devised physicotech methods of computer mathematics; worked on design of computers; supervised construction of first electrointegrator in Kiev; founded Laboratory of Computer Mathematics at Kiev Univ; *Died*: 2 June 1954.

DYADYUKOV, Ivan Tikhonovich (1896-1955) Udmurt writer; *Born*: 10 Sept 1896, son of a peasant; *Educ*: studied at zemstvo elementary school; *Career*: during Civil War served with Chapayev Div; 1920's began to write; *Publ*: novelette *Pashka Pyodor* (1925); verse collections "Dawn", (1930); "The Road" (1933), etc; *Died*: 24 Apr 1955.

D'YAKONOV, Mikhail Mikhaylovich (1907-1954) Historian and orientalist; Dr of History from 1946; prof from 1949; Hon Sci Worker of Tadzh SSR from 1951; CP member from 1946; *Born*: 25 June 1907; *Educ*: 1930 grad Fac of Language and Civilization, Leningrad Univ; *Career*: from 1931 postgrad student, then head, Oriental Dept, Hermitage Museum, Leningrad; senior assoc, then head, Section of Centr Asian Archeology, Inst of the History of Civilization (now Inst of Archeology), USSR Acad of Sci; lecturer, Leningrad State Univ, Acad of Arts and Moscow State Univ; then head, from 1953 prof, Oriental Dept, Fac of History, Moscow State Univ;1941-44 served in Sov Army; from 1946 member, from 1953 (after death of predecessor A.Yu.Yakubovskiy) head, Tadzh Archeological Expedition; took special interest in history of ancient Bactria, where he excavated several graves and towns; helped to decipher Parthian archives discovered in Nisa, the ancient capital of Parthia; *Publ: Ocherk istorii Drevnego Irana* (An Outline History of Ancient Persia) (1961), etc; *Died*: 8 June 1954.

D'YAKOV, Mikhail Iudovich (1878-1952) Zootech; member, All-Union Lenin Acad of Agric Sci from 1948; CP member rom 1942; *Born*: 2 Oct 1878; *Educ*: 1908 grad Moscow Agric Inst; *Career*: from 1915 prof, Stebutov Inst of Agric and Forestry, Petrograd; from 1925 head, Detskoye Selo Zootech Experimental Station; did research on efficient feeding of agric animals; studied methods of researching metabolism in animals; also studied efficacy of fodder mixtures; *Publ: Osnovy ratsional'nogo kormleniya ptitsy* (The Prinicples for the Efficient Feeding of Poultry) (1915); *Fizicheskiye osnovaniya kormleniya sel'skokhozyaystvennykh zhivotnykh kombikormami* (The Physical Principles of Feeding Agricultural Animals with Combined Fodder) (1931); *Mineral'noye pitaniye sel'skokhozyaystvennykh zhivotnykh (kombinirovaniye kormovykh ratsionov v otnoshenii mineral'nogo pitaniya)* (The Mineral Feeding of Agricultural Animals[The Combination of Feed Rations in Relation to Mineral Nutrition]) (1947); *Awards*: Order of Lenin; Order of the Red Banner of Labor; medals; Stalin Prize (1942); *Died*: 5 Oct 1952.

DYBCHO, Sergey Afanas'yevich (1894-1952) Operetta singer; Hon Artiste of RSFSR from 1944; *Born*: 17 July 1894 in Odessa; *Educ*: grad Odessa Stagecraft School; *Career*: played in drama and variety theaters; from 1922 at various musical theaters in Nikolayev and other cities; from 1933 with Sverdlovsk Musical Comedy Theater; also produced operettas; *Roles*: Plyushchikhin in Shcherbachov's *Tabachnyy kapitan* (The Tobacco Captain); Saveliy and Popandopulo in Aleksandrov's *Sotyy tigr* (The Hundredth Tiger) and *Svad'ba v Malinovke* (Wedding at Malinovka); Kutaysov in Strel'nikov's *Kholopka* (The Bondswoman); Sapun-Tyufyakin in Milyutin's *Devichiy perepolokh* (Girlish Confusion); Korzhin in Kovner's *Bronzovyy byust* (The Bronze Bust); Negush in Lehar's "The Merry Widow"; Zupan in Strauss' "The Gipsy Baron," etc; *Productions*: Kalman's "Maritza" (1940), etc; *Awards*: Stalin Prize (1946); *Died*: 29 Nov 1952 in Sverdlovsk.

DYBENKO, Pavel Yefimovich (1889-1938) Mil commander; Ukr; army commander, 2nd Class from 1935; Oct Revol and Civil War veteran; CP member from 1912; *Born*: 16 Feb 1889 in vil Lyudkov, Chernigov Province, son of a peasant; *Educ*: 1922, as external student, grad Red Army Mil Acad; *Pos*: until 1912 farm laborer, then longshoreman; 1912 drafted into Russian Navy; 1917-18 Sov Pop Comr of Navy; 1918-20 commander of sailors' detachment, commander of partisan detachment, commander of 1st Trans-Dnieper Div, commander of Red Army in the Crimea, commander of 37th Infatry Div and other units; 1921-25 commander, 51st Perekop Infantry Div, then commanded an infantry corps; 1925-28 chief, Red Army Artillery Bd, chief, Red Army Supply Bd; 1928-37 commander, Centr Asian Mil Distr and Volga Mil Distr; from 1934 simutaneously member, Mil Council, USSR Pop Comrt of Defense; 1937 commander, Leningrad Mil Distr; *Career*: 1915 classified as politically unreliable and assigned to a sailors' battalion deployed as infantrymen; after 1917 Feb Revol returned of his own accord to naval base at Helsinki, where he was elected chm, Baltic Fleet Centr Bd; July 1917 took part in Bolshevik riots in Petrograd, was arrested and imprisoned; after two months released upon demand of revol sailors and again became chm, Baltic Fleet Centr Bd; chm, 2nd Congress of Baltic Sailors; during 1917 Oct Revol directed dispatch of sailors and naval vessels to Petrograd to support Bolsheviks; when Gen Krasnov launched his campaign against the Bolsheviks, entered into personal negotiations with him and escorted him to Bolshevik headquarters at Smol'nyy; late Feb 1918 led 1,000th Sailors Saved to Narva to fight German troops, but the anarchistically mindet sailors refused to fight and surrendered Narva and Yamburg; for this Dybenko was court-marshalled but acquitted and returned to Ukr where he worked in underground against Ukr nationalists and German troops; fall 1918 arrested in Sevastopol' and later exchanged by Sov Govt for captured German officers; 1919 his div broke through to Tsaritsyn (later Stalingrad, now Volgograd), held by Gen Denikin; 1921, while a student at mil acad, commanded a composite div which helped suppress Kronstadt Mutiny and crush Antonov revolt in Tambov Province; 1937 member, Special Judicial Office which tried Marshal Tukhachevskiy and other high-ranking mil leaders; dep, USSR Supr Sov of 1937 convocation; late 1937 arrested by NKVD; *Publ: Voyennaya doktrina i evolyutsiya armii* (Military Doctrine and Evolution of the Army) (1922); *Myatezhniki* (Mutineers) (1923); *Iz nedr tsarskogo flota k Velikomu Oktyabryu* (From the Depths of the Tsarist Navy Towards the Great October Revolution) (1928); *Awards*: three Orders of the Red Banner; engraved watch of the RSFSR Centr Exec Comt; *Died*: 29 July 1938 executed by firing squad; posthumously rehabilitated.

DYGAY, Nikolay Aleksandrovich (1908-1963) Govt official; CP member from 1929; *Born*: 2 Nov 1908 in vil Pokrovskiy, now Rostov Oblast; *Educ*: 1935 grad Red Army Mil Eng Acad; *Career*: 1925-26 worked on Don Okrug Komsomol Comt; 1927-29 boilermaker at Taganrog Steel Plant; 1935-36 worked on construction of Novyy Tagil Steel Combine; 1937 chm, Nizhniy Tagil City Exec Comt; 1938-39 manager, Ural Heavy Ind Construction Trust; 1940-45 head, Ural Main Construction Bd and Collegium member, USSR Pop Comrt of Construction; 1946 USSR First Dep Min, and 1947-49 USSR Min for the Construction of Mil and Naval Enterprises; 1950-52 USSR Min for the Construction of Machine-Building Enterprises; 1953-57 USSR Min of Construction; 1958 dep chm, 1958-59 first dep chm, RSFSR Council of Min; 1959-61 chm, Commission for Capital Investments, Presidium, USSR Council of Min, with the rank of USSR Min; 1961 USSR First Dep Min of Trans Construction; from Sept 1961 chm, Moscow City Sov of Workers' Dep; 1952-61 cand member, from 1961 member, CC, CPSU; dep, USSR Supr Sov of 1954, 1958 and 1962 convocations; 1955 headed Sov deleg of specialists to 26th Construction Exhibition in London; 1958 member, USSR Supr Sov deleg to India; 1960 headed USSR govt deleg to Somali; *Awards*: two Orders of Lenin; two other Orders; medals; *Died*: 6 Mar 1963.

DYKHNO, Aleksandr Mikhaylovich (1909-1957) Surgeon; Dr of Med from 1937; *Born*: 1909; *Educ*: 1931 grad Med Fac, Kazan' Univ; *Career*: from 1933 asst prof under N. I. Napalkov, Chair of Fac Surgery, Rostov Med Inst; 1937 defended doctor's thesis on fractures of the femoral neck; from 1938 head, Chair of Hospital Surgery, Khabarovsk Med Inst; from 1944 dir, Khabarovsk Med Inst; 1941-45 chief surgeon, evacuation hospitals, Khabarovsk Kray; 1951-57 head, Chair of Hospital Surgery, Krasnoyarsk Med Inst; was one of first Sov physicians to use plastics in surgery; his work on alloplasty is cited in Sov surgical textbooks; devised method of transplanting ureter to intestine, circumventing rectum; also devised modified resection of stomach for gastric ulcers; devised new and more effective methods of surgical intervention in cases of lung tuberculosis; wrote over 80 works on surgical techniques, restorative surgery, etc; *Publ*: doctor's thesis *Eksperimental'nyye dannyye k ucheniyu o perelomakh sheyki bedra* (Experimental Data on the Study of Fractures of the Femoral Neck) (1937); *Zametki po vosstanovitel'noy khirurgii* (Notes on Restorative Surgery) (2 vol, 1942-44); *K tekhnike rezektsii zheludka pri yazvennoy bolezni* (Stomach Resection Techniques for Gastric Ulcers) (1946); *Rak zheludka* (Stomach Cancer) (1955); *Neotlozhnaya khirurgicheskaya pomoshch' pri nekotorykh ostrykh zabolevaniyakh organov bryushnoy polosti* (Emergency Surgery for Certain Acute Diseases of the Viscera) (1956); *Khirurgicheskoye lecheniye opukholey i kist sredosteniya*(The Surgical Treatment of Tumors and Cysts of the Mediastinum) (1957); *Died*: 1957.

DYKHOVICHNYY, Vladimir Abramovich (1911-1963) Russian satirical writer; geological eng; *Born*: 25 Mar 1911 in Moscow; *Career*: worked as eng and actor; during WW 2 contributed to frontline press for Northern and Baltic Fleets; from 1945 regularly collaborated with M. R. Slobodskiy; *Publ*: comedy *Svadebnoye puteshestviye* (Wedding Journey) (1940); collections: *Dorozhniye znaki* (Road Signs) (1951); *Kto seyet veter* (He Who Sows the Wind) (1952); *Gde eta ulitsa, gde etot dom?* (Where Is This House, Where Is This Street?) (1953); *Pokhozhdeniye Petukhova* (Petukhov's Adventure) (1954); novelette *Stakan vody* (A Glass of Water) (1955); *Po lichnomu voprosu* (On a Personal Matter) (1957); *Bespoleznyye iskopayemyye* (Useless Minerals) (1958); *Sleduyushchiy nomer programmy* (The Next Number on the Program) (1960); *Klyaksy* (Blots) (1961); *Na zemle, v nebesakh i na more* (On the Earth, in the Sky, on the Sea) (1962), etc; his comedies, sketches, feuilletons and satirical poems mocked the petty bourgeoisie, philistinism and careerism; the sketch *Guriy L'vovich Sinichkin* (1963), written in conjunction with M. Slobodskiy, Vl. Mass and M. Chervinskiy, unmasked faults of theater world; *Died*: 24 June 1963 in Rostov-on-Don; buried in Moscow.

DYLA, Iosif Leonidovich (1880-?) Bel writer, historian and economist; senior assoc, Bel Acad of Sci from 1928; CP member from 1918; *Born*: 1880 in Slutsk, now Minsk Oblast; *Educ*: Slutsk high school; studied at Tartu Veterinarian Inst; *Career*: expelled from Tartu (Yur'yev) Veterinarian Inst for revol activities; until 1905 worked for ed bd, Minsk newspaper *Severo-Zapadnyy kray*; participated in 1905 Revol in Petersburg, then returned to Minsk, conducted RSDRP revol work among peasants in surrounding area; before and during WW 1 worked for ed bds and publ houses in Petersburg, Moscow and Kazan'; subsequently with cooperative system; at this time joined Bel nat liberation movement; helped found first Bel SSR (1 Jan 1919); as rep of Bel Communist Section, RCP(B), became member, Bel Govt, holding the post of Pop Comr of Labor; early Feb 1919 removed from this post and polit activity altogether for "nationalistic diversion"; early 1920's head, Bel Cooperative System, then Bel State Planning Commission, and Commission for Admin Div of Bel Territory; simultaneously lectured on the history of Bel revol movement at Minsk higher educ institutions; from 1924 head, Arts Dept, Inst of Bel Culture; later same post at Bel Acad of Sci (since 1936 Acad of Sci of Bel SSR); simultaneously dir, 1st Bel Drama Theater and dep head, Bel State Comt for Cinematography; under the pseudonyms Nazar Byvayevskiy and Todar Kulesh wrote a number of dramatic and prose works and critical articles; 1930 arrested and exiled from Bel for "nationalistic" activities; 1956 rehabilitated, did not return to Bel, but settled in Saratov; after rehabilitation wrote historical novelettes: " In the Name of Children"; "Prodigal Son" dealing with Simeon Polotskiy; worked on a novelette covering the life and work of Frantsishek Skorina in Italy; *Died*: date and place of death unknown.

DYOSHEVOV, Vladimir Mikhaylovich (1889-1955) Russian composer; *Born*: 30 Jan 1889 in Petersburg; *Educ*: studied at Petersburg Conservatory (piano under A. Vinkler and L. Nikolayev, counterpoint and fugue under A. Lyadov and L. Nikolayev, harmony under V. Kalafati, instrumentation under M. Shteynberg, musical form under I. Vitol'); *Career*: 1914-17 in Tsarist Army; 1917-19 secr, Musical Educ Comt in Yelizavetgrad; 1920 founder, teacher and dir, Sevastopol' Pop Conservatory and Choir; 1922 head, Ukr institutions of musical educ; 1923-33 teacher, Leningrad musical technicums; musical dir at various theaters (Red Theater, Working Youth Theater, etc); during WW 2 stayed in besieged Leningrad; *Works*: opera *Lyod i stal'* (Ice and Steel) (1930); musical comedy *Druzhnaya gorka* (The Friendly Hill) (1929); ballets *Krasnyy vikhr'* (Red Whirlwind) (1924); *Dzhebella* (1926); *Bela* (1941); *Skazka o myortvoy tsarevne i o semi bogatyryakh* (Tale of the Dead Princess and the Seven Heroes) (1949); orchestral and chamber works: "Samarkand Suite" (1931); "The Dance of the Medicine-Man" (1931); "Memorials of Military Glory of the Russian People" (1947); "Russian Fairy Tale" (1947); "Russian Overture" (1950); "Leningrad" (1954), etc; music for over 100 plays: Pushkin's *Skupoy rytsar'* (The Miserly Knight) and *Kamennyy gost'* (The Stone Guest); Chekhov's *Vishnyovyy sad* (The Cherry-Orchard); Sophocles' "Oedipus Rex"; Aeschylus' "Prometheus"; Molière's "Tartuffe"; Shakespeare's "Othello" and "King Lear", etc; music for over 20 films; romances, etc; *Awards*: medal "For the Defense of Leningrad"; other medals; *Died*: 27 Oct 1955 in Leningrad.

DYOSHIN, Aleksandr Aleksandrovich (1869-1945) Anatomist; prof; Dr of Med; *Born*: 3 Jan 1869 in Kaluga Province; *Educ*: 1893 grad Med Fac, Moscow Univ; *Career*: from 1895 asst dissector (extern), Chair of Topographic Anatomy and Operative Surgery, Moscow Univ; simultaneously intern under P. I. D'yakonov, Surgical Dept, Red Cross Hospital; 1896-97 worked in Paris and Montpelier; 1902 defended doctor's thesis on "The Anatomy of the Umbilical Region in Relation to the Development of Umbilical Hernias"; from 1903 assoc prof, Novorossiysk Univ; from 1903 prof and head, Chair of Normal Anatomy, 2nd Moscow State Univ, then 2nd Moscow Med Inst; 1917-45 ran this chair in the tradition of D. N. Zernov, editing and enlarging the latter's textbook on normal anatomy, expanding the Anatomical Museum, conducting research and engaging in pedag and soc work; studied historical anatomy; made important contributions to the study of the centr nervous system, adding to knowledge of the nerve-fibrils of the spine and the cerebrum; analysed the mechanism of the hip joint; opened new prospects for brain research with his improved method of macroscopic brain dissection; endeavored to unify med theory and practice; wrote numerous works on anatomy and related subjects; *Publ*: doctor's thesis *Anatomiya pupochnoy oblasti primenitel'no k razvitiyu pupochnykh gryzh* (The Anatomy of the Umbilical Region in Relation to the Development of Umbilical Hernias) (1902); article "An Outline of the Development of Medical Theories in Relation to the General Philosophical Ideas of the Age" (1915); *K voprosu o mnogoobrazii form chelovecheskogo zheludka* (The Multiformity of the Human Stomach) (1923); article "A Short Outline of the Theory of the Nerve-Fibrils of the Spine and Cerebrum and of the Vegetative Nervous System" (1926); *Died*: 1945.

DYSHEKOV, Magomet Pshikanovich (1902-1937) Circassian writer; founder of Circassian fiction; *Born*: 1902 in vil Zeyuko, now Karachay-Circassian Autonomous Oblast; *Publ*: verse "Komsomol Song" (1929); historical novel "The Glow" (1934); stories depicting econ and cultural changes of the 1930's; textbook *Prakticheskaya grammatika kabardino-cherkesskogo yazyka* (A Practical Grammar of the Kabardo-Circassian Language) (1932); compiled and translated many other textbooks; arrested by State Security organs; *Died*: 1937 in imprisonment; posthumously rehabilitated.

DZARAKHOKHOV, Khadzhi-Murat Uariyevich (1875-1948) Revolutionary; Civil War veteran; CP member from 1917; *Born*: 1875 in vil Zil'gi, now North Ossetian ASSR, son of peasant; *Career*: 1906 went abroad in search of work; lived in USA, Mexico and Alaska; worked as unskilled laborer, riveter and miner; joined Russian Socialist Circle in USA; 1914 returned to Russia; 1914-17 fought in WW 1 in mounted div; after 1917 Feb Revol dep chm, regt comt; Aug 1917, when Gen Kornilov's "Savage Div" was sent against Petrograd to overthrow the govt, Dzarakhokhov defected to the side of the govt with 350 horsemen of that div; fought in Oct Revol; Oct-Nov headed Red Guard detachment and helped repulse Kerensky's troops near Petrograd and capture Gen Krasnov; from 1918 in Red Army; 1918-21 commanded Caucasian Mounted Detachment on Northern Front, then commanded separate cavalry div in Budenny's 1st Cavalry Army; after Civil War returned to native vil; dep, North Ossetian ASSR Supr Sov of 1938 convocation; *Awards*: two Orders of the Red Banner; *Died*: 1948.

DZBANIVSKIY, Aleksandr Tikhonovich (1870-1938) Ukr composer; *Born*: 1870 in vil Man'kivtsy (now Cherkassy Oblast); *Educ*: studied singing under Prof Everardi in Moscow; grad corresp course, Kiev Univ; *Career*: from 1898 taught singing at Zhitomir high schools; from 1909 assoc prof, Chair of Musical Theory and History, Petersburg Inst of Music; music critic; after 1917 Oct Revol inspector, Kiev and Khar'kov opera houses; worked for Ukr Pop Comrt of Educ; assoc prof, Khar'kov Inst of Music and Drama; 1928 organized Musical Dept at Centr Sci Library, Ukr Acad of Sci; 1928-38 headed this library and collected a large stock of musical scores; *Publ*: collected works: *Shkol'noye peniye* (Singing at School); *Khorovoye peniye* (Choral Singing); *Detskiye igry i pesni* (Games and Songs for Children); *Works*: about 40 choral works, romances, arrangements of folk songs; *Died*: 28 Oct 1938.

DZERZHINSKAYA (neé MUSHKAT; Party names: BOGDANA; CHARNA), Sofiya Sigizmundovna (1882-1968) Revolutionary; veteran Bolshevik; CP member from 1905; wife of F. E. Dzerzhinkiy; *Born*: 1882 in Warsaw, daughter of a white-collar worker; *Educ*: studied in high school and later at Warsaw Conservatory; *Career*: 1905 joined Soc-Democratic Party in Poland; Party duties connected with publishing and distributing Soc-Democratic lit; later propagandist; Dec 1906 arrested for the first time and imprisoned; after release continued Party work in various Polish cities; 1908 Warsaw Comt deleg to 6th Congress of Soc-Democratic Party of Poland and Lith in Prague; then returned to Poland; Sept 1909 arrested and after three months in prison deported; while a member of Cracow Section, Soc-Democratic Party of Poland and Lith, worked for Main Party Bd; late 1910 went on Party orders to Poland, where she was again arrested and exiled to Irkutsk Province; 1912 fled from exile and escaped abroad; after 1917 Oct Revol worked for secretariat of emigre funds in Switzerland; from 1918 worked at Sov embassy in Bern; Jan 1918 returned to RSFSR and worked in Polish Comrt, Pop Comrt of Nationality Affairs; later worked for nat minorities subdept, Pop Comrt of Educ and in Sverdlov Communist Univ; from 1924 exec secr, Polish Bureau, Agitation and Propaganda Dept, CC, CPSU(B); from 1929 research and exec ed, Marx-Engels-Lenin Inst; from 1937 worked for Comintern Exec Comt; from 1946 retired; dep chm, Centr Bd, Sov-Polish Friendship Soc; *Awards*: three Orders of Lenin; Order of the Red Banner of Labor; *Died*: 27 Feb 1968.

DZERZHINSKIY, Feliks Edmundovich (1877-1926) Govt and Party official; active in Polish and Russian workers' revol movement; CP member from 1895; *Born*: 11 Sept 1877, son of petty gentry on the Dzerzhinovo Estate, Vilnius Province; *Educ*: studied at high school; *Career*: 1894 joined Soc-Democratic circle; 1895 joined left wing of Lith Soc-Democratic org in Vilnius; propaganda among artisans; 1897 revol propaganda for Lith Soc-Democratic org among Kovno workers; ed, illegal Polish-language newspaper "Kovno Worker"; 17 July 1897 arrested and imprisoned in Kovno until May 1898; 1898 exiled for three years to Nolinsk, Vyatka Province; while working at a tobacco factory there engaged in revol propaganda, for which the police soon transferred him to the remote vil of Kaygorodskoye; 28 Aug 1899 fled from exile to Vilnius and later to Warsaw, where he helped to found the combined Soc-Democratic Party of Poland and Lith; reorganized Soc-Democratic org in Warsaw after its suppression by the police and created a strong nucleus of Soc-Democratic workers; 23 Jan 1900 re-arrested, imprisoned in Warsaw Citadel and later transferred to Siedlce Prison; 1902 exiled for five years to Vilyuysk, Eastern Siberia; because of illness was kept in Verkholensk, whence he escaped in June 1902; returned to Warsaw; later went to Berlin, where in July 1903 took an active part in 4th Congress of the Soc-Democratic Party of Poland and Lith and was elected to its Main Bd; during 1905-07 Revol helped to organize revol struggle against Tsarist govt; 1905 headed May Day demonstration in Warsaw; 17 July 1905 at Warsaw Party Conference arrested for the third time and imprisoned in Warsaw Citadel; Oct 1905 released from prison under an amnesty; 1906 attended 4th (Amalgamative) RSDRP Congress in Stockholm where he first met Lenin; joined CC, RSDRP as rep of Soc-Democratic Party of Poland and Lith; Aug-Oct 1906 member, CC, RSDRP in Petersburg; in connection with State Duma election campaign went to Poland and was again arrested on 13 Dec 1906; at 5th RSDRP Congress in 1907 elected in absentia to CC, RSDRP; May 1907 released from prison on bail and returned to Warsaw; 3 Apr 1908 re-arrested; Aug 1909 permanently exiled to Siberia, whence he fled to Berlin in late Nov 1909; Jan 1910 sent by Party to Capri for treatment; Mar 1910 returned to Cracow; 1910-12 underground work for Party org of Warsaw, Czestochowa and other ind distr of Poland; 1911 in Paris attended conference of members of CC, RSDRP living abroad; 1 Sept 1912 again arrested and improsoned in Warsaw Citadel; 1914 sentenced by Warsaw Distr Court to three years hard labor; July sent to Mtsensk Uyezd Prison, then to Oryol Province and later to the Oryol Centr Penitentiary; 1916 again convicted by a Moscow court for revol work from 1910 to 1912 and sentenced to a further six years at hard labor; spent a total of 11 years in prison, at hard labor and in exile; liberated by 1917 Feb Revol from Butyrka Prison in Moscow; resumed Party work; 3-4 Apr 1917 deleg, 1st Moscow City Party Conference; 14 Apr attended meeting of Moscow RSDRP(B) Comt which discussed the formation of the Red Guard; Moscow City Party Comt deleg, 7th (Apr) RSDRP(B) Conference and 6th RSDRP(B) Congress; at congress elected member, CC, RSDRP(B); from 1917 permanent CC member; took part in Oct Revol; 29 Oct 1917 at expanded session of CC, RSDRP(B) elected to Mil-Revol Party Center to direct armed rebellion; elected by Petrograd Sov to Mil-Revol Comt; one of organizers of 1917 Oct Rebellion; 7 Nov 1917 workers and soldiers under his leadership occupied Main Post and Telegraph Office; attended 2nd All-Russian Congress of Soviets and was elected member and Presidium member, All--Russian Centr Exec Comt; 20 Dec 1917 at Lenin's suggestion appointed chm, All-Russian Cheka; retained chairmanship of All-Russian Cheka (1922 renamed OGPU) until his death, displaying incredible cruelty in his work; ruthlessly liquidated the Comt for the Salvation of the Homeland and Freedom, the Officers' Union, the Nat Center, the Tactical Center, and the Renaissance League, etc; June 1918 captured while trying to crush the revolt of left-wing Socialist-Revolutionaries in Moscow; negotiated his release and then crushed the revolt with extreme ruthlessness; after attempted assassination of Lenin in Aug 1918 directed "Red Terror"; during Brest Peace Treaty controversy opposed conclusion of a peace treaty; during Civil War, besides directing All-Russian Cheka, performed various exec commissions for the Party CC and govt; Jan 1919 went to Eastern Front with RCP(B) CC Commission; 29 May 1920, after Polish invasion of RSFSR, appointed rear commander, Southwestern Front; summer 1920 member, Polish Provisional Revol Comt in Bialystok; Apr 1920 elected cand member, Org Bureau, CC, RCP(B); 14 Apr 1921 appointed Pop Comr of Communications while continuing as chm, All-Russian Cheka and as Pop Comr of Internal Affairs; 27 Jan 1921 appointed chm, All-Russian Centr Exec Comt Commission to Improve the Welfare of Children; 2 Feb 1924 appointed chm, Supr Sovnarkhoz, while remaining OGPU chm; from 1917 member, All-Russian and then All-Union Centr Exec Comt; from June 1924 cand member, Politburo and Org Bureau, CC, CPSU(B); *Publ: Izbrannyye proizvedeniya* (Selected Works) (2 vol, 1957); *Dnevnik. Pis'ma rodnym* (Diary. Letters to Relatives) (2nd ed, 1958); *Awards*: Order of the Red Banner; *Died*: 20 July 1926 during a joint plenary session of the CPSU(B) CC and Centr Control Commission; buried in Moscow beside the Kremlin Wall on Red Square.

DZERZHINSKIY, Yan Feliksovich (1911-1960) Party official; CP member from 1939; *Born*: 23 July 1911 in Warsaw Prison, where his mother S. S. Dzerzhinskaya was confined; F. E. Dzerzhinskiy's son; *Educ*: 1936 grad higher educ establishment; *Career*: 1927 joined Komsomol; after grad from higher educ establishment worked as construction eng; 1939-43 held exec posts in Comintern Exec Comt; from 1943 worked for CC, CPSU; *Died*: 2 Oct 1960.

DZEVALTOVSKIY, Ignatiy L'vovich (1888- ?) Mil commander; junior capt, Russian Army; *Born*: 1888; *Career*: fought for Bolsheviks in 1917 Oct Revol; first commandant, Winter Palace; comr, All-Russian Chief Staff; member, Revol Mil Council, 12th Army; asst commander, Eastern Front; member, Far Eastern Bureau, CC, RCP(B); Min of War and Min of For Affairs, Far Eastern Republ; 1925 emigrated from USSR; *Died*: date and place of death unknown.

DZHABARLY, Dzhafar (1899-1934) Azer writer, playwright and translator; Hon Art Worker of Azer SSR from 1933; *Born*: 22 Mar 1899 in vil Khiza near Baku, son of a peasant; *Educ*: grad Azer Univ; *Career*: 1915 first work published; from 1927 film work; first Azer film script writer; translated into Azer works of Lev Tolstoy, Gorky, Shakespeare, Schiller, etc; 1960 his name was given to the Azer Film Studio; *Publ*: essays "Aslan and Farkhad"; "Mansur and Sitara" (1916); dramas "The True Sariyaa" (1915); *Nasreddin-Shah* (1916); "Withered Flowers" (1917); "Bride of Fire" (1928); plays *Aydyn*; *Oktay El'-ogly* (1922-23); *Sevil'* (1928); "The Year 1905" (1931); *Almas* (1931); *Yashar* (1932); "The Turning Point" (1932); poem "The Tower of the Virgins" (1923-24); libretto for R. M. Glière's opera *Shakhsenem*; film scripts *Gadzhi Kara* (1929); *Seville* (1929); *Almas* (1936) etc; *Died*: 31 Dec 1934 in Baku.

DZHAFAROV, Saftar Mamed ogly (1900-1961) Govt and Party official; *Born*: 1900; *Educ*: studied at Law Fac, Azer Univ; *Career*: 1921 volunteered for Red Army; during mil service advanced from private to polit comr; 1932-35 Azer Procurator and Pop Comr of Justice; 1935-40 govt posts; 1940-47 Azer Min of Agric; 1947-59 secr, Nov 1959-Nov 1961 chm, Presidium, Azer Supr Sov; 1960-61 member, and Politburo member, CC, CP Azer; 1961 member, CPSU Centr Auditing Commission; dep, Azer Supr Sov of 1938, 1947, 1951, 1955 and 1959 convocations; *Awards*: two Orders of Lenin; two Orders of the Red Banner; medals; *Died*: 18 Nov 1961.

DZHALIL' (real name: DZHALILOV), Musa Mustafiyevich (1906-1944) Tatar poet; Hero of Sov Union from 1956 (litle coferred posthumously); CP member from 1929; *Born*: 2 Feb 1906 in vil Mustafa, Orenburg Province, son of a peasant; *Educ*: 1931 grad Lit Fac, Moscow State Univ; *Career*: 1919 first work published; 1931-35 ed, Tatar periodicals "Young Comrades" and "Child of October"; from 1935 lit dir, Opera Studio, Moscow Conservatory; later lit dir, Kazan' Opera House (1953 named for him); 1939-41 exec secr, Tatar Writers' Union; from 1941 in Sov Army; 1942 seriously wounded, taken prisoner by the German army and interned in concentration camp, where he organized an underground group, managed escapes of POW's, etc; *Publ*: collected verse and poems; "We Go" (1925); verse "Beaten Paths" (1924-28); "On Death" (1927); "Partisan Shock-Troops" (1930); "A Letter from the Volga" (1933); "Songs of a Fisherwoman" (1933); "Decorated Millions" (1934); "Jim" (1935); "From the Hospital" (1941); "Before the Attack" (1942); cycle, written in German imprisonment "Moabite Notebook"; poems: *Dzhigan*; "The Postman" (1938); opera libretti; "The Girl with the Golden Hair" (1941); *Il'dar* (1941); book "A Letter from the Trenches" (1944); *Awards*: Lenin prize (1957; posthumously for the cycle "Moabite Notebook"); *Died*: 25 Aug 1944 executed in Berlin's Spandau Mil Prison.

DZHALILOV, Abid (1896-1963) Uzbek actor; Pop Artiste of Uzbek SSR from 1939; CP member from 1943; *Born*: Nov 1896; *Career*: 1918 began stage work; from 1919 actor, Karl Marx Theater; from 1930 actor, Khamza Theater; also acted in films; *Roles*: Vershinin in Ivanov's *Bronepoyezd 14-69* (Armored Train 14-69); Arslan in Yashin's *Dva kommunista* (Two Communists); Pulatov in Yashin's *Chest' i lyubov'* (Honor and Love); Pulat in Safarov's *Zarya Vostoka* (Dawn of the East); Koshkin in Trenev's *Lyubov' Yarovaya*; Madzhiddin in Uygun and Sultanov's *Alisher Navoi*; Mavlon in Kakhkhar's *Silken Susanna*; Graf Moor in Schiller's "Die Räuber," etc; *Awards*: Stalin Prize 1949); *Died*: Sept 1963.

DZHAMBUL DZHABAYEV (1846-1945) Kaz folk poet and bard ("akyn") *Born:* 28 Feb 1846 in Semirech'ye at the foot of Mount Dzhambul, for which he was named; son of a nomad; *Career*: from early youth sang and accompanied himself on the *dombra* (Kaz nat string instrument); narrated fairy-tales and legends; learned the art of improvisation from the bard Suyumbay; his creative work was based mainly on the bards' poetic competitions; at such competitions won against famed 19th-20th century bards - Kulmambet (1881), Sarbas, Dosmagambet and Shashubay; after the 1917 Oct Revol his songs won nation-wide fame; his work was varied in form and genre; responded to all major events of Sov polit, econ and cultural life: non-stop flights, founding of new schools, centenary of Pushkin's death, cattle-breeders' congress, etc; lauded achievements of Revol and its leaders; dedicated a number of his songs to Stalin and other members of Sov and Party leadership; during WW 2 created a number of patriotic songs which won wide popularity; his works have been translated into almost all languages of the USSR peoples and into many for languages; dep, Kaz Supr Sov from 1938; *Works*: poems: "Hero Utegen"; "Hero Suranshi"; "My Life"; "A People in Arms"; "Stalin's Great Law" (1936); "My Fatherland" (1936); tales: "The Khan and the Bard"; "Tale of the Lazy Man," etc; songs: "The Complaint"; "Fate of the Poor"; "The Will"; "Black Decree"; "Bay Kandyrbay's Dog"; "To the Bolsheviks' Congress"; "To the 10th Congress"; "Alatau"; "October Anthem"; "In the Lenin Mausoleum" (1936); "Lenin and Stalin" (1936); "Song of the Brotherhood of Peoples" (1937); "Greetings to the Caucasus" (1937); "Soviet Union" (1937); "Song of Moscow" (1937); cycle of songs about the Sov Army: "Stalin's Heroes"; "To the Red Army"; "Hero Chapay" (1937); "Eagles of Our Country" (1938), etc; WW 2 patriotic songs: "The Hour When Stalin Calls" (1941; "A Bullet for the Enemy"; "Leningraders, My Children" (1941); "Song of the Iron People's Commissar" (1941); "The Command of the Fatherland" (1942); "To the Heroes of Voronezh" (1942); "New-Year Letter to the Defenders of Stalingrad" (1942); "Vow Upon the Banner" (1943); "Death of a Son" (1943), and many others; *Awards*: Order of Lenin; other orders and medals; Stalin Prize (1941); *Died*: 22 June 1945 in Alma-Ata; bried in his native vil; a mausoleum was erected on his grave and his house converted into a lit-memorial museum; a town and an oblast in Kaz has been named for him.

DZHANAN (real name: DZHANANYAN), Mkrtich Migranovich (1892-1938) Arm actor and playwright; Hon Artiste of Arm SSR from 1932; *Born*: 1892 in Istanbul; *Educ*: grad Law Fac, Istanbul Univ; 1919 external student, stagecraft classes at Paris Conservatory; *Career*: 1911 began stage work; 1918 helped organize Arm Dramatic Soc in Istanbul; from 1922 actor, First Arm State Theater in Yerevan (now Sundukyan Theater); worked also as stage dir; 1928 helped organize Yerevan Azer Theater; author of articles on theatrical problems; *Roles*: Oksen in Paromyan's "Old Bagdasar"; Petruccio in "The Taming of the Shrew"; Iago; Macbeth; Satin in Gorky's *Na dne* (The Lower Depths); Godun in *Razlom* (Break-Up); Yarovoy in *Lyubov' Yarovaya*; Zeir in "Shakh-name" (1935); *Publ*: plays "Old Workingman" (1929); "Shakh-name" (1935); *Died*: 1938.

DZHANASHIA, Simon Nikolayevich (1900-1947) Geo historian; Dr of Historical Sci from 1938; prof from 1935; member, Geo Acad of Sci from 1941; member, USSR Acad of Sci from 1943; Hon Sci Worker of Geo SSR from 1946; CP member from 1940; *Born*: 13 July 1900; *Educ*: 1922 grad Tbilisi Univ; *Career*: 1922-30 asst prof, 1930-35 assoc prof, from 1935 prof, Tbilisi Univ; 1936-41 dir, Inst of Language, History and Material Culture, Geo Branch, USSR Acad of Sci; from 1941 vice-pres, from 1943 at same time dir, Inst of History, Geo Acad of Sci; 1940-47 headed Mtskheta Archeological Expedition; worked on history of origin and genetic ties of Geo people with peoples of Caucasus and Ancient East; studied origins of ancient Geo state and historical geography of Geo; also studied Geo, Svan, Abkhazian, Adyge and other languages; *Publ: Proiskhozhdeniye obshchestvennykh klassov i gosudarstva sredi gruzinskikh plemyon* (Origins of Social Classes and the State Among Georgian Tribes) (1932); *Tubal-Tabal, Tibaren, Iber* (1937); *Drevneysheye natsional'noye predaniye o pervonachal'nom rasselenii gruzinskikh plemyon v svete istorii Blizhnego Vostoka* (Ancient National Traditions on the Original Resettlement of Georgian Tribes in the Light of the History of the Middle East) (1940); *Gruziya na puti ranney feodalizatsii* (Georgia on the Path of Early Feudalization) (1937); *Georgiy Shervashidze. Kul'turno-istoricheskiy ocherk* (Georgiy Shervashidze. A Cultural and Historical Study) (1946); coauthor, *Istoriya Gruzii* (The History of Georgia) (vol 1, 1946); *Izbrannye trudy* (Selected Works) (3 vol, 1949-59), etc; *Awards*: two Stalin Prizes (1942 and 1947); two Orders of Lenin; Order of the Red Banner of Labor; medals; *Died*: 15 Nov 1947.

DZHANELIDZE, Yustin Yulianovich (1883-1950) Surgeon; member, USSR Acad of Med Sci from 1944; Hero of Socialist Labor from 1945; Hon Sci Worker of RSFSR from 1936; lt-gen, Naval Med Service; *Born*: 1 Aug 1883 in vil Samtredia, Kutaisi Province; *Educ*: 1903-05 studied at Med Fac, Khar'kov Univ; 1905 expelled for involvement in student riots; obtained med degree in Switzerland; 1911 returned to Russia and obtained med qualifications in Moscow; *Career*: from 1911 asst prof under A.A. Kad'yan, Chair of Hospital Surgical Clinic, Women's Med Inst; assoc and (after death of N.A. Vel'yaminov) head, then from 1921 prof, Chair of Gen Surgery, Women's Med Inst; from 1927 prof, Chair of Hospital Surgical Clinic, 1st (Pavlov) Leningrad Med Inst; took special interest in org and improvement of ambulance service; from 1939 chief surgeon, Sov Navy; during Sov-Finnish War and WW 2 worked on org of mil med service; from 1943 until death, head, Chair of Hospital Surgery, Leningrad Naval Med Acad; made major contribution to clinical surgery; 1911 did first heart operation; 1913 was first surgeon in the world to successfully suture a wound of the ascending aorta; 1927 summed up his experience of heart surgery in the monograph *Rany serdtsa i ikh khirurgicheskoye lecheniye* (Heart Wounds and Their Surgical Treatment); in subsequent years specialized in diseases of the abdominal cavity, particularly acute appendicitis and intestinal obstruction; at 24th All-Union Congress of Surgeons delivered important paper on the treatment of burns; during WW 2 changed his views on this subject and rejected open treatment methods; took a special interest in traumatology and developed original methods of treating dislocations of the hip and shoulder, fractures of the patella, habitual dislocations of the elbow, etc; did major theoretical and practical work on skin-grafting and other plastic operations, in which he reestablished the preeminence of such Russian surgeons as A.A. Abrazhanov and S.M. Yanovich-Chaynskiy; in the latter years of his life did major research on surgery of the heart, the pericardium and the major vessels; devised a successful simple palliative operation for angina pectoris; 1937-41 ed, journal *Vestnik khirurgii imeni I.I. Grekova*; 1946 chm, 25th All-Union Congress of Surgeons; chm, All-Union Sci Soc of Surgeons; member, Learned Med Council, USSR Min of Health; member, Med Bd, Sov Army; wrote over 100 works, including a number of substantial monographs; *Publ: Rany serdtsa i ikh khirurgicheskoye lecheniye* (Heart Wounds and Their Surgical Treatment) (1927); *Ozhogi i ikh lecheniye* (Burns and Their Treatment) (1941); *Svobodnaya peresadka kozhi v Rossii i v Sovetskom Soyuze* (Free Skin-Grafting in Russia and the Soviet Union) (1945); article "The Successful Treatment of Certain Acute Diseases of the Abdominal Cavity During 30 Years of the Soviet Health Service" (1948); *Bronkhial'nyye svishchi ognestrel'nogo proiskhozhdeniya* (Bronchial Fistulae Resulting From Gunshot Wounds) (1948); *Sobraniye sochineniy* (Collected Works) (5 vol, 1953); *Awards*: two Orders of Lenin; Stalin Prize (1949); Order of the Red Banner; medals; *Died*: 14 Jan 1950.

DZHANGIL'DIN, Alibey Togzhanovich (1884-1953) Govt official; CP member from 1915; *Born*: 1884 in vil Koydaul Turgay (now Kustanay) Oblast, son of a peasant; *Educ*: 1903 grad Orenburg Theological College; 1903-06 studied at Kazan' Teachers' Seminary and Moscow Theological Acad; *Career*: for participation in revol movement expelled from Moscow Theological Acad; 1910 emigrated; for over two years toured Poland, Austro-Hungary, Yugoslavia, Bulgaria, Turkey, Syria, Palestine, Egypt, Abyssinia, the Arabian Peninsula, Persia, India, Ceylon, the Malay Archipelago, Indo-China, Southern China, Formosa and Japan; paid his way by working as photographer; 1911 met Lenin in Geneva; 1913, on return to Kazakhstan, conducted revol work; summer 1913 went first to Simferopol' and worked for branch of Pulkovo Observatory, then moved to Petrograd; one of leaders of 1916 Centr Asian rebellion; 1917 polit work in Kazakhstan; Nov 1917 appointed extraordinary mil comr for Turgay Oblast by RSFSR Council of Pop Comr; chm, 1st Turgay Oblast Congress of Soviets; from May 1918 extraordinary comr for Steppe Kir (Kaz) Kray; directed mustering of Kaz Red Army units; active in establishing Sov regime in Turgay Oblast; July 1919appointed dep chm, Revol Comt for the Admin of the Kir (Kaz) Kray; from Oct 1920 dep chm, Presidium, Kaz Centr Exec Comt and Kaz Pop Comr of Soc Security; from 1938 member, from 1951 dep chm, Presidium, Kaz Supr Sov; *Awards*: Order of Lenin; Order of Red Banner; *Died*: 14 Aug 1953.

DZHANSUGUROV, Il'yas (1894-1937) Kaz poet and translator; CP member from 1924; *Born*: 1 May 1894 at aul No. 4 (now Taldy-Kurgan Rayon, Alma-Ata Oblast, Kaz SSR), son of a peasant; *Educ*: 1928 grad Moscow Communist Inst of Journalism; *Career*: one of the founders of Kaz nat poetry; 1915 first work published; in the 1920's wrote on the socialist reorganization of Kaz; wrote lit criticism; translated into Kaz works of Pushkin, Lermontov, Nekrasov, Gorky and Mayakovskiy, etc; arrested by State Security organs; *Publ*: poems: "The Steppe" (1930); "The Musician" (1935); "Kulager" (1936); novel "Comrades (1933); plays: "Turksib"; "Hatred"; "Isatay Makhambet" (1936); collection of satirical works "The Law" (1933); *Died*: 1937 in imprisonment; posthumously rehabilitated.

DZHAPARIDZE (Party pseudonym: ALYOSHA), Prokofiy Aprasionovich (1880-1918) Azer revolutionary and Party official; CP member, from 1898; *Born*: 20 Sept 1880 in vil Shardometi, Kutaisi Province; *Educ*: studied at Tiflis Teachers' Training Inst; *Career*: 1900 helped to organize May Day demonstration of Tiflis workers; Aug 1900 expelled from Teachers' Training Inst for involvement in railroad workers' strike, arrested and imprisoned for 11 months in Metekhi Castle; then exiled to Kutaisi Province; 1901-04 member, Imeritian-Mingrelian and Caucasian Union RSDRP Comts; Aug 1904 sent to Baku by Caucasian Union RSDRP Comt, where he did Party work among the oil workers; set up Party org in Balakhany region; member, Baku RSDRP Comt and co-founder of its *Gummet* group; Dec 1904 led gen strike in Baku; 1905 deleg from Baku RSDRP Org at 3rd RSDRP Congress; 1906-08 worked for Baku Bolshevik newspapers *Bakinskiy rabochiy, Prizyv, Devet-Koch, Gudok, Vol'na*, etc; 1906-09 Bd secr, Oil Workers' Union, in which capacity he attempted to negotiate a collective labor agreement; 1908-11 arrested several times and finally exiled for three years to Velikiy Ustyug; from June 1914 worked for Tis RSDRP(B) Org; May 1915 again arrested and exiled to vil Kamenka (Yenisey Provine), from which he soon fled to Tiflis; sent to Trebizond, where he did revol among soldiers under the alias of Baratov; after 1917 Feb Revol member, Baku RSDRP(B) Comt; elected member, CC at 4th RSDRP(B) Congress; Sept 1917, as strike comt chm, led gen strike of Baku workers; from Dec 1917 asst chm, from Jan 1918 chm, Exec Comt, Baku Sov; from Mar 1918 member, Revol Defense Comt; from Apr 1918 Comr of the Interior, Baku Council of Pop Comr; from June 1918 Comr of Food; 31 July 1918 arrested after the Sov defeat in Baku; *Publ: Izbrannyye stat'i, rechi i pis'ma* (Selected Articles, Speeches and Letters) (1964); *Died*: 20 Sept 1918 executed by firing squad along with 25 other Baku comr.

DZHAVAKHISHVILI, Ivan Aleksandrovich (1876-1940) Geo historian; prof; member, USSR Acad of Sci from 1939; *Born*: 11 Apr 1876 in Tiflis; *Educ*: 1899 grad Fac of Oriental Languages, Petersburg Univ; *Career*: from 1902 assoc prof, Chair of Arm-Geo Philology; 1918 co-founder, prof and dean, Philological Fac, Geo Univ (now Tbilisi State Univ); 1919-26 rector, Geo Univ; 1919-25 chm, Geo Historical and Ethnographic Soc; 1937-40 dir, Shota Rustaveli Museum and head, Mtskheta Archeological Expedition; studied the history of the Geo and neighboring peoples, Geo law, paleography, diplomacy, and the history of Geo music and drama; wrote numerous works on these subjects, mostly in Geo; *Publ*: "The State Structure of Ancient Georgia and Armenia" (1906); "Political and Social Movements in Georgia in the 19th Century" (1906); "A History of the Georgian People" (4 vol, 1908-49); "The Tasks, Sources and Methods of Ancient and Modern History" (4 vol, 1916-26); "The Ancient Georgian Historical Written Language" (1916); "Georgian Numismatics and Metrology" (1925); "Georgian Paleography" (1926); "Georgian Diplomacy" (1926); "The History of Georgian Law" (2 vol, 1928-29); "An Economic History of Georgia" (2 vol, 1930-34); "An Introduction to the History of the Georgian People" (1937); "Fundamentals of the History of Georgian Music" (1938); *Awards*: Order of the Red Banner of Labor; *Died*: 18 Nov 1940.

DZHAVAKHISHVILI (real name: ADAMISHVILI, Mikhail Savvich) (1880-1937) Geo writer; *Born*: 20 Nov 1880 in vil Tserakvi, Geo, son of a peasant; *Educ*: 1901 grad Yalta College of Horticulture and Viticulture; *Career*: worked at Allaverdy Copper Smeltery; 1903 first work printed; from 1904 ed, newspaper *Iveria*; also ed, newspaper *Glekhi*; 1906 indicted for printing articles against autocratic regime in *Glekhi*; managed to make his way abroad and from 1907 studied lit, art and polit econ at the Sorbonne; traveled throughout Italy, Switzerland, North America, Britain, Belgium, Germany and Turkey; 1909 returned to Geo with a false passport and headed group of writers which began to publish journal *Eri*; journal soon closed down and he himself brought to trial; held for twelve months in Metekhi Prison, then banished from Caucasus; after 1917 Oct Revol resumed lit work; 1917 elected member, Transcaucasian Centr Exec Comt; translated Maupassant; Sienkewicz and Chekhov into Geo; arrested by State Security organs; *Publ*: story "The Wood-Goblin" (1923); novels; *Kvachi Kvachantiradze* (1924); *Dzhakos Khiznebi* (1925); *Givi Shaduri*; novelette "The White Collar" (1936); novel "Arsen from Marabda"; novel "Woman's Fate" (1936); "Collected Works" (4 vol, 1933-34); *Died*: 1937 in imprisonment; posthumously rehabilitated.

DZHAVAKHISHVILI, Natal'ya Grigor'yevna (1882-1950) Actress; Pop Artiste of Geo SSR from 1941; *Born*: 26 Aug 1882; *Career*: 1901 began stage career with amateur shows of Avchala Auditorium's Pop Theater; 1902 joined professional company in Tiflis; worked at theaters in Kutaisi, Tbilisi and Sukhumi; from 1921 actress, Rustaveli Theater; *Roles*: Mayko in Sumbatov-Yuzhin's *Izmena* (Treason); Galchikha in Ostrovskiy's *Bez viny vinovatyye* (Guilty Without Guilt); Matryona in *Vlast' t'my* (The Power of Darkness); *Died*: 7 Sept 1950.

DZHAVID, Guseyn (real name: RASI-ZADE) (1884-1944) Azer poet and playwright; *Born*: 24 Oct 1884 in Nakhichevan, son of a Moslem priest; *Career*: lived for some time in Constantinople; disciple and student of the Turkish philosopher and poet Riza-Tevfik-bey; after his return to Azer taught and wrote; 1906 first work published in Baku periodical *Fiyuzat* under the name Rasi-Zade; in Constantinople his works were published in pan-Islamic organ *Syratul Mustakim*; in early period influenced by Persian Sufism (mysticism); at the height of the Kemal movement turned to a peculiar combination of rationalism, subjectivism, soc idealism and mysticism; arrested by State Security organs; *Publ*: dramas: "Mother" (1910); "Maral" (1912); collection of poetry "Bygone Days" (1913); tragedy "Sheikh Senan" (1914); drama "Sheyda" (1916); tragedy "Satan" (1918); poem "Azer" (1926); drama "The Prince" (1929); historical dramas in verse "Siavush" (1933); "Khayyam" (1935); dramas: "Satan's Revenge" (1936); "Tamerlane", etc; *Died*: 1944 in imprisonment; posthumously rehabilitated.

DZHIMIYEV, Georgiy Savel'yevich (1906-1944) Ossetian playwright and writer; *Born*: 18 Dec 1906 in Vladikavkaz (now Ordzhonikidze); *Career*: film work in Ashkhabad and Baku: actor, asst film dir and playwright; wrote mainly for the Ordzhonikidze Ossetian Theater; *Publ*: film script: "Two Epochs"; play "Friendship of Enemies" (1934); comedies: "Marriage" (1937); "The New Daughter-in-Law" (1940); "Days of Battle, or Hero of the Soviet Union" (1941); heroic drama "Black Fog" (1944); *Died*: 25 Sept 1944.

DZHIVELEGOV, Aleksey Karpovich (1875-1952) Russian historian; lit and art critic; Dr of Arts from 1936; prof; corresp member, Arm Acad of Sci from 1945; *Born*: 26 Mar 1875 in Rostov-on-Don; *Educ*: 1897 grad History and Philology Fac, Moscow Univ; *Career*: 1898-1939 helped direct compilation of *Entsiklopedicheskiy slovar'* (Encyclopedic Dictionary); from 1915 lectured at Nizhniy Novgorod Pop Univ and at Shanyavskiy Pop Univ; 1919-23 lecturer, from 1923 prof, 1st Moscow Univ; also lectured at Higher Lit Courses, Moscow Inst of Philosophy, Lit and History; from 1930 head, Dept of Foreign Theater, State Inst of Stagecraft; from 1939 senior assoc, Inst of World Lit; from 1945 senior assoc, Inst of History of the Arts, USSR Acad of Sci; helped publish Romance series of lit monuments for *Academia* Publ House, also multi-vol *Istoriya zarubezhnogo teatra* (History of Foreign Theater); pupil of P. G. Vinogradov; concentrated on West European culture of Renaissance era; translated into Russian plays: Machiavelli's *Mandragora,* Poggio Bracciolini's *Fezetia* and plays by Goldony; *Publ: Gorodskaya obshchina v sredniye veka* (The City Community in the Middle Ages) (1901); *Srednevekovyye goroda v zapadnoy Yevrope* (Medieval Cities in Western Europe) (1902); *Torgovlya na zapade v sredniye veka* (Trade in the West in the Middle Ages) (1904); *Istoriya sovremennoy Germanii* (The History of Modern Germany) (2 vol, 1908-10); *Krest'yanskoye dvizheniye na zapade* (The Peasant Movement in the West) (1906); *Nachalo ital'yanskogo Vozrozhdeniya* (The Beginnings of the Italian Renaissance) (1908); *Armiya Velikoy Frantsuzskoy revolyutsii i yeyo vozhdi* (The Army of the Great French Revolution and Its Leaders) (1923); *Ocherki ital'yanskogo Vozrozhdeniya* (An Outline of the Italian Reaissance) (1929); *Dante Alig'yeri. Zhizn' i tvorchestvo* (Dante Alighieri. Life and Work) (1933); *Leonardo da Vinci* (1935); *Mikel'-Andzhelo* (Michelangelo) (1938); coauthor, *Istoriya zapadnoyevropeyskogo teatra* (The History of West European Theater) (1941); *Ital'yanskaya narodnaya komediya* (Italian Popular Comedy) (1954), etc; *Died*: 14 Dec 1952 in Moscow.

DZHURA SULTAN (1910-1943) Uzbek poet; CP member from 1942; *Born*: 1910 in vil Kogoltam, Bukhara Oblast; *Career*: 1927 first work printed; in his early verse concerned with patriotism, alliance of working class and peasantry, etc; *Publ*: verse: "Bruno" (1936-37); "Song of Moscow", "Death of a Hero" and "May Song" (1938); "Karim and Kunduz" (1939); "Family, Love and Child," "Two Tales" and "Mukhammad the Machine-Gunner"

(1941); "A Letter to My Children" (1943); "The Whole World Greets Thee" (1943); also wrote children's verse; *Died*: 1943 in vil Kogoltam.

DZIDZARIYA, Kondrat Fyodorovich (1898-1943) Abkhazian impressario; *Born*: 1898; *Career*: one of the founders of Abkhazian nat theater; 1922 taught in Sukhumi; organized among his students a music and drama circle which performed Abkhazian songs on the stage; from this circle originated the following Abkhazian actors: Pachaliya, Kabakhiya, A. and R. Agrba, Chochua, Kaslandziya, etc; the circle also staged the first Abkhazian plays: Chanba's *Makhadzhiry*, Darsaliya's *Bygone Days*, Bzhaniya's *Kuchita*, etc; 1927-34 artistic dir, Abkhazian Theater; organized a "shock detachment," which toured Abkhazia propagandizing collectivization; *Died*: 1943.

DZYUBINSKIY, Vladimir Ivanovich (1860-1927) Politician; *Born*: 1860; *Career*: 1881 arrested in Kamenets-Podol'sk for revol activities and 1883 exiled for three years to Western Siberia; after serving his term of exile lived in various West Siberian towns; active in public work and contributed to many Siberian newspapers; Tobol'sk Province deleg in 3rd and 4th State Dumas, where he was a leading member of the *Trudoviki* (Laborites) faction; after 1917 Feb Revol member, Provisional Exec Comt, State Duma; member, CC, Labor Pop Socialist Party; also member, Main Org Comt, Peasant League; helped organize 1st All-Russian Congress of Peasant Deputies; member, All-Russian Exec Comt, Sov of Peasants' Deputies; after 1917 Oct Revol abandoned politics; from 1920 lived in Moscow and worked at Lefortov Mil Historical Archives and other establishments; *Died*: 1927.

E

EDEL'SHTEYN, Vitaliy Ivanovich (1881-1965) Prof; Dr of Agric; hon member, All-Union Acad of Agric Sci from 1956; CP member from 1952; *Born*: 29 Apr 1881; *Educ*: 1902 grad Petersburg Forestry Inst; *Pos*: 1902-07 at Dept of Botany, Petersburg Univ; 1907-13 lecturer, Uman Acric College; 1913-16 head, Tula Horticultural Station; 1916-23 prof, Moscow Agric Inst; from 1923 head, Dept of Vegetable Growing, and from 1946 prof, Moscow Timiryazev Agric Acad; *Career*: founded first Sov dept of vegetable growing and experimental vegetable station at Timiryazev Agric Acad; *Publ*: *Vvedeniye v sadovodstvo* (An Introduction to Horticulture) (1926); *Novoye v ogorodnichestve* (What's New in Market Gardening) (1931); *Osnovy ovoshchevodstva* (Principles of Vegetable Growing) (1934); *Rukovodstvo k prakticheskim zanyatiyam po ovoshchevodstvu* (Handbook of Practical Studies in Vegetable Growing) (1939); *Individual'nyy ogorod* (The Individual Market Garden) (1956); *Nekotoryye zakonomernosti rosta, razvitiya i formirovaniya urozhaya ovoshchnykh kul'tur, kak osnovy agrotekhniki* (Rules for the Growth, Development and Formation of Vegetable Crops as the Foundation of Agrotechnology) (1962); *Awards*: three Orders of Lenin; Badge of Hon; Hero of Socialist Labor (1961); medal for Valiant Labor (1959); Stalin Prize (1946); *Died*: 1 Aug 1965.

EDEL'SHTEYN, Yakov Samoylovich (1869–1952) Geologist and geographer; Hon Sci Worker of RSFSR from 1936; prof, Leningrad Univ from 1925; *Born*: 1869; *Educ*: 1895 grad Khar'kov Univ; *Career*: from 1897 did geological research in Far East (Sikhota-Alin', Manchuria, Northern China) and in the Pamirs; from 1908 worked for Geological Comt, then for All-Union Geological Research Inst; did geological research in Minusinsk Basin and neighboring mountains; wrote first general description of the geological features of the West Siberian Plain; specialized in geomorphology; member, USSR Geographical Soc; co-ed, anthology series *Geologiya SSSR*; *Publ*: *Severnyy i sredniy Sikhota-Alin* (Northern and Central Sikhota-Alin) (1905); *Geomorfologicheskiy ocherk Minusinskogo kraya* (A Geomorphological Study of Minusinsk Kray) (1936); *Skhema tektonicheskogo deleniya Sibiri i DVK* (The Tectonic Division of Siberia and the Far Eastern Kray) (1944); *Osnovy morfologii* (The Principles of Morphology) (1947); *Awards*: Order of Lenin; Order of the Red Banner of Labor; *Died*: 21 Jan 1952.

EFENDIYEV, Rashid-bek Ismail-ogly (1869-1942) Azer educationist, poet and writer; *Born*: 1869 in Nukha; *Educ*: 1882 grad Transcaucasian Teachers' Seminary; *Career*: 1882-93 teacher and supervisor at Kutakashkin and Kokhlukha rural schools; 1895-96 helped found and direct Moslem girls college in Tiflis and collect funds for establishment of other girls chools; 1900-17 taught Azer language and Islam theology at Transcaucasian Teachers' Seminary; from 1918 dir, Baku Teachers' Seminary; 1926-33 taught Russian at teachers' training technicum; then worked for Azer Branch, USSR Acad of Sci; *Publ*: textbook "The Kindergarten" (1898); reader "The Child's World" (1901); fiction works: "The Rose"; "The Bloody Hearth"; "The Miraculous Beard"; "The Women Problem"; *Died*: 1942.

EFENDIYEV, Sultan Medzhid (1887-1938) Party and govt official; physician; CP member from 1904; *Born*: 1887; *Educ*: 1915 grad Med Fac, Kazan' Univ; *Career*: co-founder "Gummet" soc-democratic org, Baku; 1907 exiled to Kazan', where he joined the Med Fac ot the Univ; after graduation physician at Vasil'sursk cholera quarantine center; combined med treatment of Volga region sailors with revol polit work; during 1917 Feb Revol returned to Baku, was elected member, Baku Sov and joined Baku RSDRP(B), Comt; simultaneously worked as a physician at Baku Municipal Hospital; July 1917 deleg, 6th RSDRP(B) Congress; 1917-19 exec work for CC, RCP(B) and RSFSR Pop Comrt of Nationality Affairs; 1920 fought against Gen Wrangel's army on Southern Front; 1920, after establishment of Sov rule in Azer, Comr Extraordinary, Gyandzha Province; 1921 Pop Comr of Agric; 1922-26 chm, Centr Control Comt, CP(B) Azer and head, Azer Pop Comrt of Workers and Peasants' Inspection; 1927-38 dep chm, then chm, Centr Exec Comt, Azer Sov; member CC, CP(B) Azer; member, Transcaucasian Rayon CPSU(B) Comt; Bureau member, CC, CP(B) Azer; member, Azer, Transcaucasian and USSR Centr Exec Comt; member, CPSU(B) Centr Control Commission at 13th and 14th Congresses; 1938 subjected to reprisals by State Security organs; *Died*: 1938 in imprisonment; posthumously rehabilitated.

EFFENDIYEV, Fuad Aladdin-ogly (1909-1963) Surgeon; prof; Dr of Med from 1942; corresp member, Azer Acad of Sci from 1959; Hon Sci Worker of Azer SSR; *Born*: 1909; *Educ*: 1929 grad Med Fac, Azer State Univ; *Career*: from 1929 intern, asst prof, assoc prof, then prof, Fac Surgical Clinic, Azer Med Inst; 1941-45 chief surgeon, special evacuation hospital in Baku; 1942 defended doctor's thesis; 1945-63 head, chair of Fac Surgery, Pediatric Fac and Fac of Sanitation and Hygiene, Azer Narimanov Med Inst; founder and sci dir, Azer Blood Transfusion Research Inst; chief surgeon; Azer Min of Health; 1961-63 head, Dept of Thoracic Surgery, Inst of Experimental and Clinical Med, Azer Acad of Sci; one of first Azer surgeons to perform lung and heart operations; devised various surgical and therapeutic techniques, including: a cytological test for closed hemothorax; methods of treating hemothorax and hemarthrosis; three-stage section of the thoracic wall in thoracotomy; open treatment of burns with a mixture of novocaine, furacilin and pyoctanin; discovered anticoagulative effect of calcium chloride and method of blood stabilization; proved that non-coagulation of blood in pleural cavity is caused by fibrinolysis and fibrogenolysis, not by defibrination or saturation with antithrombic substances; did considerable research on diseases of blood system; wrote over 120 works; *Publ*: *Patogenez, klinika i lecheniye krovoizliyaniy v plevral'nuyu polost' pri raneniyakh grudnoy kletki* (The Pathogenesis, Clinical Aspects and Treatment of Hemorrhage in the Pleural Cavity as a Result of Thoracic Wounds); various articles in *Opyt sovetskoy meditsiny v Velikoy Otechestvennoy voyne 1941-45 godov* (Soviet Medicine in the 1941-45 Great Fatherland War); *Awards*: Order of the Red Banner of Labor; Order of the Red Star; medals; Burdenko Prize; *Died*: 1963.

EFROS, Abram Markovich (1888-1954) Art historian and translator; *Born*: 25 Apr 1888; *Career*: 1911 began lit work; 1911-17 head, Art Criticism Dept, newspaper *Russkiye vedomosti*; contributed to journals Apollon Kul'tura i zhizn', Vestnik teatra, Iskusstvo, *Teatral'noe obozreniye, Teatr i muzyka, Novaya rampa, Rabochiy i teatr* and *Teatr*; after 1917 Oct Revol worked for Museum Dept, RSFSR Pop Comrt of Educ and Tret'yakov Gallery; 1920-26 artistic and sets mang, Moscow Arts Theater, 1940-50 taught at State Inst of Stagecraft; 1950-54 prof, Tashkent Theatrical Inst; lectured on history of Russian theater and set designing; wrote several studies on history of Russian and Western fine arts and articles on work of painters F.F. Fedorovskiy, V.V. Dmitriyev, P.V. Vil'yams, etc; translated and edited a number of works by Italian, French and Ancient writers; *Publ*: *Zhivopis' teatra* (Theatrical Painting) (1914); *Dekoratsiya Pushkinskogo spektaklya* (Sets for Pushkin's Plays) (1915); *Luidzhi Pirandello* (Luigi Pirandello)

(1926); *L.N. Bakst* (1930); *Mladshiye khudozhniki Khudozhestvennogo teatra* (Junior Artists of the Arts Theater) (1927); *Teatr i khudozhnik v gody revolyutsii* (The Theater and the Artist in the Years of Revolution) (1928); "Hofmannsthal" (1930); coauthor, *Dekoratsii teatral'nyye v Rossi* (Theater Sets in Russia) (1931); preface to album *Kamernyy teatr i yego khudozhniki* (The Chamer Theater and Its Artists) (1934); *Dva mastera teatral'noy zhivopisi (Sar'yan, Fedorovskiy)* (Two Masters of Set Designing [Sar'yan and Fedorovskiy]) (1941), etc; *Died*: 19 Nov 1954.

EFROS, Nikolay Yefimovich (pseudonyms: CHUZHOY; STARYY DRUG; PRINCE MYSHKIN; STARIK; MOSKVICH, etc) (1867-1923) Journalist, theater critic and theater historian; *Born*: 1867; *Educ*: 1889 grad Law Fac, Moscow Univ; *Career*: 1891 first work published; leading theater critic of newspaper *Russkiye vedomosti*; regular contributor to many other pre-revol periodicals (*Teatral, Novosti dnya*); from 1898 reviewed Moscow theater productions for *Yezhegodnik imperatorskikh teatrov* (Annual of Imperial Theaters) publicized work of Moscow Arts Theater and Chekhov's plays; his reviews, articles and books on Arts Theater showed his profound understanding of balancing tradition and innovation; wrote monographs on Yermolova, Shchepkin, Yuzhin, etc; co-ed, first vol of *Istoriya russkogo teatra* (History of Russian Theater); 1921-22 ed, journals *Kul'tura teatra* and *Teatral'noye obozreniye*; worked for Theater History Section, Theater Dept, Pop Comrt of Educ; chm, Theater Section, Russian Acad of Arts; translated Victor Hugo's "Angelo," Hauptmann's "The Lonely" (1899); *Publ: M. M. Yermolova* (1896); play *Delo Tarnovskiy, ili Vsemirnyy protsess* (The Tarnovskiy Case, or The World Trial) (1910); *K. S. Stanislavskiy (Opyt kharakteristiki)* (K. S. Stanislavsky. A Study) (1918); *V. I. Kachalov* (1919); *M. S. Shchepkin* (1920); *A. I. Yuzhin - 1882-1922* (1922); *A. N. Ostrovskiy* (1922); *Moskovskiy Khudozhestvennyy teatr 1898-1923* (The Moscow Arts Theater 1898-1923) (1924); *Died*: 6 Oct 1923.

EISENSTEIN, Sergey Mikhaylovich (1898-1948) Film dir; Hon Art worker of RSFSR from 1935; Dr of Arts; *Born*: 23 Jan 1898 in Riga, son of an architect; *Educ*: 1916-18 studied at Inst of Civil Eng, Petrograd; 1917 volunteer in students' pop militia unit; 1918 joined Red Army; 1921-24 designer and dir, First Workers' *Proletkul't* Theater, Moscow; here staged *Meksikanets* (The Mexican), *Na vsyakogo mudretsa dovol'no prostoty* (There's a Simpleton in Every Sage), *Moskva, slyshish'* (Moscow, Can You Hear?) and *Protivogazy* (Gas Masks); from 1924 film work; 1925 directed film *Stachka* (Strike), noted for its monumental crowd scenes, realistic episodes and sequences reflecting his absorption with formal experiments in means of cinematic expression; one great creative triumph was his direction of *Bronenosets Potyomkin* (The Battleship Potemkin) (1925); the innovatory ideas in the film laid down new cinematographic forms for rhythmical montage, strict frame composition, drama and laconicism of crowd scenes combined with clarity and accuracy of detail; the film was a milestone in the development of the cinema; together with C. V. Aleksandrov directed *Oktyabr'* (October) (1927) and *Staroye i novoye* (The Old and the New) (1929); 1929-31 lived in USA, studied film production, worked on film *Da zdravstvuyet Meksika!* (Viva Mexico!) (unfinished); from 1932 head, Dept of Direction, from 1937 prof, All-Union State Inst of Cinematography; *Works*: films: *Bezhin Lug* (Bezhin Meadow) not released because of alleged"formalist errors"; *Aleksandr Nevskiy* (1938); monumental epic *Ivan Groznyy* (Ivan the Terrible) (Part 1, 1945) recreated the atmosphere of 16th Century Rus; figures of centr heroes, Alexander Nevsky and Ivan the Terrible, were notable for elements of modernization and idealization; 1940 produced Wagner's "Die Walküre" at the USSR Bolshoy Theater; *Publ*: articles on theory and history of cinema, and cinematic technique (montage, lighting, stereoscopy); *Awards*: Order of Lenin; Badge of Hon; two Stalin Prizes (1941 and 1946); *Died*: 11 Feb 1948.

EKKERT, Ferdinand Ferdinandovich (1865-1941) Composer; French horn virtuoso; conductor; prof; Hon Art Worker of RSFSR from 1931; *Born*: 1 Mar 1865 in Prague; *Career*: 1895-1912 soloist, Bolshoy Theater Orchestra; conductor at Hermitage Theater, Int Theater and Nikitin Theater, Moscow; from 1921 conductor, Moscow Operetta Theater; directed production of his own operettas and also Dunayevskiy's *Zhenikhi* (The Suitors) and Bagrinovskiy's *Igra s dzhokerom* (Playing with the Joker), etc; prof, Moscow Conservatory; *Works*: composed operettas: *Amur i Psikheya* (Cupid and Psyche) (1902); *Vozvrashcheniye Menelaya* (The Return of Menelaus) (1903); *Korol' kormilits* (King of the Wet-Nurses) (1907); *Vesyoloye puteshestvіye* (A Merry Journey) (1910); *Atlantida* (Atlantis) (1924); *Charito* (1935); comic opera *Frina:* (1909), etc; *Died*: 17 Aug 1941 in Moscow.

EKSKUZOVICH, Ivan Vasil'yevich (1883-1942) Theater dir *Born*: 1883; *Educ*: grad Petersburg Inst of Civil Eng; *Career*: worked as architect; after 1917 Revol, directed Petrograd State Acad Theaters; 1924-28 head, State Acad Theaters in Moscow and Leningrad; wrote first Russian book on stagecraft; *Publ: Tekhnika teatral'noy stseny v proshlom i nastoyashchem* (Stagecraft Past and Present) (1930); *Died*: 1942.

ELIAVA, Georgiy Grigor'yevich (1892-1937) Microbiologist; pioneer of the Geo school of microbiology; *Born*: 1892; *Educ*: studied at Med Fac, Novorossiysk (Odessa) and Geneva Univ; 1916 grad Moscow Univ; *Career*: after graduation head, Trebizond (front-line), then Tiflis centr Laboratory, League of Cities; 1918-21 and 1925-27 worked at Pasteur Inst, Paris; from 1927 head, Chair of Hygiene, from 1929 head, Chair of Microbiology, Tbilisi Univ; one of the originators and major researchers of microbiology in Geo; 1923 co-founder, Tbilisi Bacteriological Inst; won renown for his research on bacteriophagy; directed the development of ind bacteriophage production and the use of bacteriophages in Geo med practice; co-founder and dir, All-Union Inst of Bacteriophagology, Tbilisi; supported hypothesis that bacteriophages are living viruses; along with d'Herelle established the presence of lysine in bacteriophage cultures independent of the bacteriophage corpuscles; along with E. Pozerskiy observed the specific effect of quinine compounds on bacteriophages; one of first to study the significance of bacteriophages as a factor determining bacterial mutability; obtained first bacteriophage against gas gangrene, which was used with success in Sov army; wrote numerous works on microbiology and bacteriophagology; 1937 accused of deliberatively infecting children in Signakh Rayon, Geo SSR and executed along with his wife; *Publ*: coauthor, "Sur les charactères noveaux présentés par le Bacille de Shiga, ayant résisté à l'action du bakctériophage de d'Hérelle" (1921); coauthor, "Unicité du bactériophage, sur la lysine du bactériophage" (1921); article "The Nature of d'Hérelle's Bacteriophage" (1923); coauthor "Au sujet de l'ultrafiltration du corpuscule bacteriophage" (1927); coauthor, "Dimensions du corpuscule bactériphage" (1927); *Died*: 1937 executed posthumously rehabilitated.

ELIAVA, Shal'va Zurabovich (1885-1937) Party and govt official; CP member from 1904; *Born*: 1885; *Educ*: grad Kutaisi High School; 1903 entered Law Fac, Petersburg Univ; *Career*: 1904 in Tiflis, joined RSDRP; sided with Bolsheviks and worked in Tiflis and Kutaisi Province as agitator and propagandist; twice arrested; 1906, on return to Petersburg, worked for student Party organizations and took part in student movement; 1909 exiled from Petersburg but returned in same year; 1910 exiled to Olonets Province for three years for student revol activities; 1913, after short stay in Caucasus, returned to Petersburg where he worked for a health insurance fund and contributed to *Pravda*; 1915 arrested and again exiled; spent exile in Arkhangelsk and Vologda Provinces; after 1917 Feb Revol elected chm, Vologda Sov of Workers and Soldiers' Dep; sided for a while with defensists; after 1917 Oct Revol, deleg to 2nd All-Russian Congress of Soviets; then until spring 1918 chm, Vologda Province Exec Comt and member, Vologda Province Party Comt; 1918 appointed Collegium member, RSFSR Pop Comrt of Trade and Ind; 1919-21 during Civil War served with Red Army on Eastern and Turkestani Fronts as member of army and front revol-mil councils; 1921 active in campaign against democratic govt of Geo; from 1921 Pop Comr for Mil and Naval Affairs of Geo and Transcaucasian Federation; from 1923 chm, Geo Council of Pop Comr; from 1930 chm, Council of Pop Comr of Transcaucasian Federation; from 1931 plen for meat procurement, USSR Council of Pop Comr, then USSR Dep Pop Comr of For Trade; from 1918 member, All-Russian, then USSR Centr Exec Comt, Transcausian Centr Exec Comt and Geo Centr Exec Comt; also member, CC, CP, Geo; Bureau member, Transcaucasian Kray Party Comt; elected cand member, CC, CPSU(B) at l5th and 16th CPSU(B) Congresses; arrested by State Security organs; *Died*: 1937 in imprisonment.

EMDIN, Pavel Iosifovich (1883-1959) Neuropathologist and neurosurgeon; Hon Sci Worker of RSFSR from 1941; *Born*: 1883; *Educ*: 1909 grad Med Fac, Kazan' Univ; *Career*: after graduation worked at L.O.Darkshevich's Clinic; 1914 defended doctor's thesis on lesions of the striated muscles after neurotomy; during 1917 Oct Revol helped to organize med service for Red Guards; 1920-24 head, neurology dept of a Rostov clinic; from 1924 head of a chair, Rostov Med Inst, where he founded Clinic of Nervous Diseases and Neurosurgery which became the neurological and neurosurgical center for the Northern Caucasus and the southern USSR; he and his pupils were the first Sov physicians to make extensive use of pneumoencephalography and ventriculography; devised method of cisternal puncture; was one of first Sov physicians to describe clinical aspects and histopathology of Economo's epidemic encephalitis; did considerable research on neurooncology, notably on atypical growth of neuroglias, multiform glioblastomas, neurinomas of auditory nerve, gliomas of posterior cranial fossa, and surgical and radiation therapy of brain tumors; during WW 2 developed phase theory of course of cerebral wounds and devised various surgical treatments for injuries of peripheral nerves; described sacral syndrome; devised silk mesh for use in cranio-plasty; coauthor, neurology section, *Bol'shaya meditsinskaya entsiklopediya* (Large Medical Encyclopedia) (2nd ed); member, ed council, journal *Voprosy neyrokhirurgii*;; wrote over 150 works; *Publ*: doctor's thesis *Izmeneniya v poperechno-polosatoy myshtse skeleta posle pererezki nerva* (Lesions of the Striated Muscle of the Skeleton After Neurotomy) (1914); articles "Three Ideas" (1936); "Basic Ideas in the Theory of Brain Tumors" (1937); "The Late Stage of Craniocerebral Injuries" (Third and Fourth Phases) (1944); "Solved and Unsolved Problems of Open Craniocerebral Trauma" (1905); *Died*: 1959.

ENDRUP (VIDIN'), R.Ya. (1878-1939) Party official; CP member from 1902; *Born*: 1878; *Career*: did Party work in Mitava, Libava and Riga Soc-Democratic org; 1905-07 took active part in Revol as organizer of vigilante groups in Riga; member, Riga RSDRP Federative Comt; deleg from Riga org, 5th RSDRP Congress; frequently arrested by Tsarist authorities; 1910-14 ed, Riga trade-union newspaper *Arodnieks*; after 1917 Feb Revol chm, Riga Sov of Workers and Soldiers' Dep; 1919 Lat Comr of Finance, later Comr of Food; 1922-35 co-dir, "Prometheus" Publ House, Moscow; arrested by State Security organs; *Died*: 1939 in imprisonment.

ENDZELIN, Yanis (1873-1961) Lat linguist; Baltic language specialist; *Born*: 1873; *Educ*: grad Tartu (Yur'yev) Univ; *Career*: from 1903 assoc prof in Tartu and from 1908 in Khar'kov; from 1911 prof, Khar'kov Univ; from 1920 prof, Riga Univ; from 1946 member, Lat Acad of Sci; from 1929 corresp member, USSR Acad of Sci; studied connections between Baltic and Ugro-Finnish languages; did much to establish standards for the modern Lat lit language; *Publ*: master's thesis *Latyshskiye predlogi* (Latvian Prepositions) (2 parts, 1905-06); doctor's thesis *Slavyano-baltiyskiye etyudy* (Balto-Slavic Studies) (1911); main works deal with Lat dialects and history of Lat and Baltic languages: "Latvian Grammar" (1922); "Sounds and Forms of Latvian" (1938); "Ancient Russian" (1943); "Ancient Russian Grammar" (1944); "Sounds and Forms of the Baltic Languages" (1938); "Latvian Grammar" (1951); coauthor, "Dictionary of the Latvian Language" (4 vol, 1923-32); *Died*: 1961.

ENGEL'KRON (ENGEL'-KRON) (real name: FILIPPOV), Vsevolod Mikhaylovich (1891-1961) Actor and stage dir; Hon Art Worker of RSFSR from 1946; *Born*: 9 Mar 1891; *Career*: 1920-22 at theaters in Nizhniy Novgorod; 1922-23 at Moscow "Free Drama" Theater; 1923-25, 1930-35 and 1938-51 chief dir at theaters in Voronezh and Voronezh Oblast; 1926-27 chief dir, theaters in Fergana, Derbent; 1927-28 Cheboksar; 1928-29 Morshansk; 1929-30 Arkhangelsk; 1951-53 Kuybyshev; 1953-61 Bryansk, etc; in 1930's staged numerous shows about working class; *Productions*: Kirshon's *Rel'sy gudyat* (The Rails Are Humming); Pogodin's *Temp* (Tempo) and *Moy drug* (My Friend); Golichnikov's *Master* (The Foreman) *Deti solntsa* (Children of the Sun) (1935 and 1946); Prut's *Knyaz' Mstislav Udaloy* (Prince Mstislav Udaloy) (1933); *Bez viny vinovatye* (Guilty Without Guilt) (1933); Romashov's *Boytsy* (The Warriors); Gutskov's *Uriel' Akosta and Gibel' eskadra* (The End of a Sqadron) (1934); Afinogenov's *Dalyokoye* (The Distant Past) (1935); Griboyedov's *Gore ot uma* (Woe From Wit) (1936); Globa's *Pushkin* (1937); Lavrenyov's *Razlom* (Break-Up) (1938); Lench and Voytekhov's *Pavel Grekov* (1939); Pogodin's *Kremlyovskiye kuranty* (The Kremlin Chimes) (1940); Solov'yov's *Fel'dmarshal Kutuzov* (Fieldmarshal Kutuzov) (1942); *Front* (1945); Ostrovskiy's *Na vsyakogo mudretsa dovol'no prostoty* (There's a Simpleton in Every Sage) (1945); Simonov's *Russkiy vopros* (The Russian Question) (1947); *Molodaya gvardiya* (The Young Guard) (1948); Beryozko's *Muzhestvo* (Courage) (1948); *Lyubov' Yarovaya* (1948, 1952); Korneychuk's *Platon Krechet* (1952), etc; *Pubbl: Kak my rabotayem* (How We Work) (1935); *Died*: 1 Aug 1961.

ENTIN, David Abramovich (1888-1957) Stomatologist; Hon Sci Worker of RSFSR; pioneer of Sov mil jaw and facial surgery; maj-gen, Army Med Service; *Born*: 1888; *Educ*: 1924 grad Mil Med Acad; *Career*: after graduation lecturer in odontoloy, Mil Med Acad; 1929-51 founder-head, Chair of Stomatology and Jaw and Facial Surgery, Mil Med Acad; during WW 2 chief stomatologist, USSR Armed Forces; wrote over 200 works, including several textbooks and monographs, on caries, paradontosis, sepsis of the oral cavity and the treatment of jaw and facial wounds; drew up supply tables for stomatological establishments of the Sov Army in time of peace and war; *Publ: Opty rekonstruktii litsevogo skeleta* (Reconstruction of the Facial Skeleton) (1924); coauthor, *Terapevticheskaya stomatologiya* (Therapeutic Stomatology) (1938); article "Front-Line Aid for Jaw and Facial Wounds" (1940); *Voyennaya chelyustno-litsevaya khirurgiya* (Military Jaw and Facial Surgery) (1941); *Awards*: Order of the Fatherland War, 2nd Class; Order of the Red Star; medal "For the Defense of Leningrad"; medal "For 20 Years of the Red Army"; *Died*: 1957.

EPIMAKH-SHIPILA, Bronislav Ignat'yevich (1859-1931) Bel linguist and lit historian; prof of classical languages, Petersburg Univ; senior assoc, Bel Acad of Sci from 1928; *Born*: 4 Sept 1859 at farmstead Bud'kavshchina, now Lepel' Rayon, Vitebsk Oblast; *Educ*: grad Polish secondary school in Riga; grad Classical Languages Dept, History and Philology Fac, Petersburg Univ; *Career*: from late 1880's prof, Petersburg Univ; also lecturer, Petersburg Roman-Catholic Theological Acad and teacher, Chernyayev's Gen Educ Courses; 1889-24 simultaneously dep dir, Library of Petersburg Univ; from 1925 member and ed, from 1927 dir, Commission for Compiling Dictionary of Living Bel Language, Minsk Inst of Bel Culture; from 1928 member, Humanities Dept, Bel Acad of Sci; besides teaching classical languages at Petersburg higher educ institutions, worked on Bel language and history of Bel lit; 1900 under his guidance Bel students published illegal Bel newspaper *Svaboda*, which was confiscated and proscribed; from 1902 head, Bel student org Bel Educ and Culture Circle, which illegally published Bel books and distributed them throughout Bel; from 1906, after the ban on Bel language was lifted, headed legal Bel publishing company "The Sun Will Shine in Our Window Too"; simultaneously ideological leader, Bel Sci and Lit Circle of Petersburg Univ Students, whose statutes were not ratified until 1912; edited and published works of Yanka Kupala; 1909-14 also financed Yanka Kupala's existence and his study on Chernyayev's Gen Educ Courses; among his papers was the manuscript of the "Anthology of Belorussian Literature," on which he had worked for 40 years and collected a vast amount of material on Bel lit history from ancient times to the 20th Century; after his arrest the manuscript was confiscated by GPU organs; it is presently kept at Bel State Archives of Lit and History; the "Dictionary of Belorussian Living Language," on which he worked in the last years of his life also has never been published; summer 1930 arrested for "bourgeois and nationalistic" activities and exiled from Bel; *Died*: 1931 in Leningrad; posthumously rehabilitated.

EPSHTEYN, German Veniaminovich (1888-1935) Protistologist; *Born*: 17 May 1888; *Educ*: 1912 grad Natural Science Dept, Fac of Physics and Mathematics, Moscow Univ; 1915 grad Med Fac, Moscow Univ; *Career*: from 1919 until death worked at Mechnikov Inst of Infectious Diseases; specialist in pathogenic protozoa; also studies hematology; 1922 used Rickettsia agglutination reaction for the diagnosis of typhus; *Publ*: monographs *Patogennyye prosteyshiye, spirokhety i gribki* (Pathogenic Protozoa, Spirochetes and Fungi) (1931); *Praktikum po paraziticheskim prosteyshim i spirokhetam* (A Practical Course on Parasitic Protozoa and Spirochetes) (1940); *Paraziticheskiye ameby* (Parasitic Amoebae) (1941); *Died*: 1935.

EPSHTEYN, Moisey Solomonovich (1890-?) Revolutionary; Party official; CP member from 1919; *Born*: 1890; *Career*: from 1905 took part in Jewish worker's movement, first as a member of the Soc-Democratic Party of Poland and Lith and later as a member of the Bund; before 1917 arrested many times and imprisoned; 1919 joined CP; served in Red Army as member, Revol-Mil Council 6th Army; later held Party posts: secr, Kuban'-Black Sea Oblast Comt; secr, CC, CP Turkestani; from 1923 Collegium member, RSFSR Pop Comrt of Educ; wrote various articles on promoting the Party and cultural development; arrested by State Security organs; *Died*: date and place of death unknown.

EPSHTEYN (BEN-YAKIR), Sh. (1883-1946) Party official; CP member from 1920; *Born*: 1883; *Career*: from 1903 member, Bund; worked in Warsaw and Bialystok; Bialystok Distr Bund deleg at 5th RSDRP Congress; secr, Bund Foreign Comt; 1920 joined RCP(B); later member, Centr Bureau, Jewish Section, CC, CPSU(B); lived in the USA for several years, where he was a prominent figure in the Communist movement; returned to the USSR; worked for Trade-Union International; from 1941 exec secr, USSR Jewish Anti-Fascist Comt; *Died*: 1946.

ERDENKO (real name: YARDENKO), Mikhail Gavrilovich (1885-1940) Violinist and teacher; Hon Art Worker of RSFSR from 1935; *Born*: 4 July 1885 in vil Baranovo, Kursk Province; *Educ*: 1904 grad Moscow Conservatory under I. V. Grzhimali; 1911 advanced training under Isaia in Belgium; *Career*: at age of five made concert tour of Russia; took part in 1905 revol; exiled from Moscow; from 1906 numerous concert tours of Russia, Western Europe, Japan and China; 1910-20 prof, Kiev Conservatory; 1935-40 prof, Moscow Conservatory; one of most pop Sov artists noted for the emotion, simplicity and immediacy of his rendition; *Works*: composed sonatas in ancient style for violin and piano, cadenzas for concertos by Brahms, Paganini, etc; many transcriptions and arrangements for violin; *Died*: 21 Jan 1940, Moscow.

ERDMANN, Boris Robertovich (1899–1960) Stage designer; Hon Worker of RSFSR from 1957; *Born*: 16 Feb 1899; *Career*: 1917-18 actor, Moscow Chamber Theater; 1918 began work as set designer in Merezhkovskiy's *Pavel I* (Paul I) at Smolensk Theater; introduced innovations in stage settings and costumes; worked with ballet-master K. Ya. Goleyzovskiy at Experimental Theater and with dir B. A. Mordvinov at Experimental-Heroic Theater; 1941-45 chief set designer, State Circus; 1950-60 chief set designer, Stanislavsky Drama Theater, Moscow; in early stage of career sided with constructivists; later switched from conventional decor (Labish's "Kopilka," Sophocles' "Oedipus Rex" at the Experimental–Heroic Theater) to more realistic sets conveying the local color of the period, modified by the author's original style; specialist in the planning of stage space; designed excellent sets for premiere opera, ballet and dramatic productions, circus shows and musical comedies; *Works*: sets for: Lenskiy's *Lev Gurych Sinichkin* (1924); Solovyov's *Fel'dmarshal Kutuzov* (Field Marshal Kutuzov) (1940) at Vakhtangov Theater; Olyosha's *Tri tolstyaka* (Three Fat Men) (1930); "Maria Stuart" (1957) at Moscow Arts Theater; Falla's "The Girl from the Suburbs" (1928); Krzenek's "Johnny" (1929); Offenbach's "Tales of Hoffmann" (1946); Molchanov's *Ulitsa del' Korno* (Del Corno Steet) (1960) at the Stanislavsky and Nemirovich-Danchenko Musical Theater; Dunayevskiy's *Polyarnyye strasti* (Polar Passions) (1928) at the Moscow Operetta Theater; *Vanina Vanini* after Stendhal (1955); Jurandot's "Those Were the Days" (1955) at the Maly Theater; Stein's "Astoria Hotel" (1956) at the Mayakovskiy Theater; *Chayka* (The Seagull) (1954); Bulgakov's *Dni Turbinykh* (Days of the Turbins) (1954) at Moscow's Stanislavsky Drama Theater; Prokofiev's *Zolushka* (Cinderella) (1946) at Leningrad's Kirov Opera and Ballet Theater; Vishnevskiy's *Na zapade boy* (Battle in the West) (1933) at Khar'kov's Shevchenko Theater, etc; *Died*: 28 Dec 1960.

ERENBURG, Il'ya, Grigor'yevich (1891-1967) Russian writer, publicist and translator; Jew; bd, member, USSR Writers' Union from 1934; non-Party man; *Born*: 27 Jan 1891 in Kiev; *Educ*: studied at 1st Moscow High School; *Career*: expelled from school for participating in 1905-07 revol movement; later arrested but released without trial; 1908 emigrated to Paris; 1908 began lit work; 1914-17 corresp, Russian newspapers *Birzhevyye vedomosti, Utro Rossii,* etc, on Franco-German Front; during 1917 Revol returned to Russia; 1917-21 worked for newspapers in Kiev, Khar'kov, Rostov-on-Don, Tiflis and other publications supporting anti-Communist White movement; 1921 sent by *Izvestia* as special corresp to Paris but was soon deported to Belgium; continued his assignment there, then moved to Berlin and back to Paris; visited a number of European, Asian and American countries, all the time contributing to Sov press; 1936-37 USSR mil corresp in Spain; 1937-40 in Paris, contributing to Sov centr press; 1940, with the German invasion of France, returned to USSR; 1941-45 wrote for newspapers *Pravda* and *Krasnaya zvezda*; dep, USSR Supr Sov of 1950, 1954, 1958, 1962 and 1966 convocations; member, For Affairs Commission, Sov of Nationalities of the same convocations; Presidium member and vice-pres, World Peace Council; addressed int congresses in Paris, Wroclaw, Warsaw and Helsinki; from 1955 dep chm, Sov Comt for Defense of Peace; Bd chm, Franco-Sov Friendship and Cultural Relations Soc; member, Lenin Peace Prize Commission; 1960 member, Sov Comt for Defense of Peace deleg at World Peace Council Bureau Session, Stockholm; 1954 sharply criticized for his novelette *Ottepel'* (The Thaw); 1959 attacked for articles on lit and art problems; translated works of Francois Villon and works by old Spanish and contemporary French poets; his works have run through Sov ed of about 8.8 million copies in 30 languages; from 1956 member, ed collegium, journal *V zashchitu mira*; *Publ*: verse collection *Parizh* (Paris) (Paris, 1910); *Stikhi o kanunakh* (Evening Poems) (1916); *Molitva o Rossii* (Prayer for Russia) (1918); collection *Lik voyny* (The Face of War) (1920); pamphlet novel *Neobychaynyye pokhozhdeniya Khulio Khurenito* (The Unusual Adventures of Julio Jurenito) (Berlin, 1921; 2nd ed Moscow, 1923); in Paris were published: *Trest D. E., ili istoriya gibeli Yevropy* (The D. Ye. Trust, or the History of the Downfall of Europe) (1923); *Lyubov' Zhanny Ney* (Jeanne Ney's Love) (1924); *Rvach* (The Self-Seeker) (1925); *Zhizn' i gibel' Nikolaya Kurbova* (The Life and Death of Nikolay Kurbov) (1925); *Leto 1925 goda v Parizhe* (Summer 1925 in Paris) (1927); *Fabrika snov* (The Dream Factory) (1927); *Zagovor ravnykh* (Conspiracy of Equals) (1927); *V protochnom pereulke (In Channel Lane) (1927);* Moscow publications: *Skornyak* (The Furrier) (1928); novel *Den' vtoroy* (The Second Day) (1934); *Ne perevodya dykhaniya* (In One Breath) (1935); collection *Voyna* (The War) (1941-42); novels: *Padeniye Parizha* (The Fall of Paris) (1942); *Burya* (The Storm) (1947); *Devyatyy val* (The Ninth Wave) (1951); *Sochineniya* (Works) (5 vol, 1952-54); novelette *Ottepel'* (The Thaw) (vol 1, 1954; vol 2, 1960); book on art *Frantsuzskiye tetradi* (French Notebooks) (1958); poem "Northern Spring" (1959); *Lyudi, gody, zhizn'* (People, Years, Life) (1960-65), etc; *Awards*: Stalin Prizes (1942, 1948); Int Stalin (1952) and Lenin (1960) Prizes for "strengthening peace among peoples"; two Orders of Lenin; Order of the Red Banner of Labor; Order of the Red Star; medals; *Died*: 31 Aug 1967.

ERISTAVI-KHOSHTARIYA, Anastasiya Georgievna (1868-1951) Geo writer; *Born*: 1868 in vil Ptsa near Gori; *Educ*: Gori High School; *Career*: teacher in Kartli vils; early 1890's first work published in Geo press; wrote children's stories which occupy a prominent place in Geo children's lit; *Publ*: stories: "Lazare Overdid It"; "The Earth"; "The Commission," etc; story "Around the Church"; novels: "On a Slippery Path"; "Perversities of Fate"; "The Cliff"; in Russian translation *Rasskazy* (Stories) (1957); *Died*: 1951.

ERMANS, Viktor Konstantinovich (1888-1958) Journalist and theater critic; *Born*: 1888; *Career*: 1908 began lit work; after 1917 Oct Revol lit dir, Rybinsk, then Yaroslavl' theaters; contributed theater reviews to Moscow periodicals: *Teatral'naya gazeta, Vestnik rabotnikov iskusstv, Rabis, Rabochiy i iskusstvo, Teatral'naya dekada, Dekada moskovskikh zrelishch* and *Teatral'naya Moskva;* from 1931 contributed to newspapers *Sovetskoye Iskusstvo* and *Literatura i iskusstvo;* from 1953 ed, then head, Circus and Variety Dept, and ed mang, newspaper *Sovetskaya kul'tura; Died*: 1958.

ERMLER, Fridrikh Markovich (1898-1967) Film dir and scriptwriter; member, Presidium, USSR Cinematographers Union from 1960; Pop Artiste of USSR from 1948; CP member from 1919; *Born*: 1898; *Educ*: 1923-25 studied at Inst of Cinematography, Leningrad; *Career*: 1924 film debut, first as asst dir, then as dir and scriptwriter; *Works*: films *Kat'ka - bumazhnyy ranet* (Kat'ka the Paper Apple) (1926); *Oblomok imperii* (Fragment of an Empire) (1929); *Krestyane* (Peasants) (1935); *Velikaya grazhdanskaya voyna* (The Great Civil War) (Parts 1-2, 1938-39); *Velikiy perelom* (The Great Breakthrough) (1945); *Neokonchennaya povest'* (An Unfinished Story) (1955); *Pered sudom istorii* (Before the Court of History) (1965), etc; *Awards*: four Stalin Prizes (1941, 1946 /twice/ and 1951); Order of Lenin; Order of the Red Banner of Labor; *Died*: July 1967.

ERZYA (ER'ZYA; real name: NEFEDOV), Stepan Dmitriyevich (1876-1959) Sculptor; *Born*: 28 Oct 1876; *Educ*: 1902-06 studied at Moscow College of Painting, Sculpture and Architecture; *Career*: 1918-20 worked on propaganda monument plans in Sverdlovsk; from 1921 in Transcaucasia; 1926-50 lived abroad, mainly in Argentina; specialized in wood sculpture; *Works*: monument to Lenin in Batumi; *Lev Tolstoy* (1930); "The Argentinian" (1941); "Moscow Girl" (1953), etc; *Died*: 24 Nov 1959.

ESHPAY (real name: **ISHPAYKIN**), **Yakov Andreyevich** (1890-1963) Composer; choirmaster; teacher; folklorist; Cand of Arts from 1946; Hon Art Worker of Mari ASSR from 1941; *Born*: 29 Oct 1890 in vil Koshmary, Kazan' Province; *Educ*: 1930 grad Moscow Conservatory under G. E. Konyus; 1933 completed post-grad training; *Career*: 1913-27 singing teacher, musician, choirmaster, pioneer of Mari professional music; collected and studied Mari folk songs and instrumental melodies (over 500 items); *Works*: from his material on the folklore of the Volga region composed several suites for orchestra and ensembles, piano pieces, arranged for unaccompanied choir and for voice and piano; composed songs, including children's songs; wrote music for Mari Theater productions: Shketan's *Shurko;* Chavayn's *Mulshatar* and "The Mari Company" (1934); also works in other genres; *Publ*: *Natsional'nyye muzykal'nyye instrumente mariytsev* (National Musical Instruments of the Mari) (1940); *Died*: 20 Feb 1963 in Moscow.

ESSEN, Aleksandr Magnusovich (Party pseudonyms: BUR and MYAMLIN) (1880-1930) Eng; writer; Party and govt official; CP member from 1920; *Born*: 1880, son of a nobleman; *Career*: 1899 joined student movement; from 1902 worked for Soc-Democratic org; 1903-05 member, Yekaterinoslav, Petersburg and Moscow Party Comts; 1905 non-voting deleg at 3rd Party Congress; Dec 1905 arrested in Petersburg and help in custody for eight months; until late 1906 Party work in Moscow; 1907 refrained from Party work due to illness; after 1917 Feb Revol joined internationalists; agitator for Tiflis Sov of Workers' Dep; edited internationalist newspaper in Tiflis; 1922 ed, journal *Kavkazskiy rabochiy;* 1923-25 rector, Tiflis Polytech Inst; 1925 moved to Moscow; dep chm, RSFSR Gosplan; from 1929 chm, Tech-Econ Agency, USSR Pop Comrt of Communications; *Publ: Tri internatsionala* (The Three Internationals); *Puti stroitel'stva SSSR* (Paths of Soviet Construction); *Osnovy general'nogo plana khozyaystva SSSR* (The Fundamentals of the USSR General Economic Plan), etc; *Died*: 1930.

ESSEN, Eduard Eduardovich (1879-1931) Party and govt official; CP member from 1898; *Born*: 1879 son of an aristocrat; *Educ*: studied at Acad of Arts; *Career*: at age 14 broke with familiy and went to work on railroad; 1898 after joining RSDRP conducted Party propaganda in student circles and smuggled illegal lit through Finland; Party emissary to Yekaterinoslavl'; 1903 helped to organize strike in Southern Russia; from 1903 after 2nd RSDRP Congress worked in Volga area, Yekaterinoslavl', Khar'kov, Odessa, Minsk and Petersburg; 1914-15 did Party work among soldiers on Riga Front; 1917 chm, Vasiliy Ostrov Rayon Sov, Petrograd; after 1917 Oct Revol Dep Pop Comr of State Control; 1918 captured by White Army in Crimea; after liberation of Crimea member, Revol Comt; worked as front-line agitator in 7th Army; after Civil War rector, Tolmachyov Inst; head, Polit Dept of Maritime Colleges; prof, Naval Acad; 1924 rector, Inst of Nat Econ; 1925-29 rector, Acad of Arts; from 1929 pensioner; *Died*: 1931.

ESSEN, Mariya Moiseyevna (Party pseudonyms: ZVER'; ZVEREV; ZVERUSHKA; SOKOL), Nina L'vovna (1872-1956) Party functionary; CP member from 1920; *Born*: 1872; *Career*: early 1890's joined revol movement; active in workers' circles in Yekaterinoslav, Kiev and Yekaterinburg; 1899 arrested and imprisoned for 20 months, then exiled to Yakutsk Province; 1902 escaped from exile and fled abroad; after return from abroad worked for Petersburg *Iskra* Comt; late 1903 coopted into Party CC; agitated for 3rd Party Congress; member, Bureau of Bolshevik Comts; 1904 arrested; summer 1905 exiled to Arkhangelsk Province; managed to escape en route and returned to Party work with Petersburg Comt; 1906 member, Moscow Party Comt; from 1907 discontinued Party work; after 1917 Feb Revol joined Soc-Democrat internationalists and was member, Tiflis Sov of Workers' Dep; 1921-25 head, Dept of Agitation, CC, CP Geo; member, Tiflis City Party Comt; member, Transcaucasian Kray RCP(B) Comt; 1925 moved to Moscow and worked at State Publ House; 1927-30 worked at Inst of Party History, then at Lenin Inst; from 1930 at Communist Inst of Journalism; from 1931 head of the Institute's main section; from 1938 member, USSR Writers' Union; wrote her memoirs of Lenin and a series of articles and lit reviews; *Died*: 1956.

ETINGOF, Boris Yevgen'yevich (1886-1958) Party and govt official; CP member from 1903; *Born*: 1886; *Career*: 1903, after joining Party, arrested by Tsarist authorities; served several prison terms and was repeatedly exiled; 1905 active in Revol; did underground Party work in Vilnius, Warsaw, Vyborg and Tiflis; during WW 1 did Party work on Persian and Turkish Fronts; Oct 1917 deleg, 2nd Congress of Soviets; took part in storming of the Winter Palace; member, ed bd, newspaper *Izvestia*; during Civil War helped to establish Sov rule in Northern Caucasus; did underground work for Bolsheviks in Azer and Geo; after Civil War held' exec positions in RSFSR Pop Comrt of Educ; head, Middle East Dept, RSFSR Pop Comrt of For Affairs; Sov consul-gen in Turkey; member, USSR Supr Court; *Died*: Feb 1958 after a protracted illness.

EVARNITSKIY (YAVORNITSKIY), Dmitriy Ivanovich (1855-1940) Ukr historian, archeologist and ethnographer; writer; member, Ukr Acad of Sci from 1929; *Born*: 25 Oct 1855 in vil Borisovka, now Dergachyov Rayon, Khar'kov Oblast, son of a vil deacon; *Educ*: 1881 grad History and Philology Fac, Khar'kov Univ; *Career*: 1881-86 at Khar'kov Univ; 1886-91 high-school teacher and instructor, Teachers' Training Courses in Petersburg; for revol-polit activities exiled to Tashkent; 1896-1902 assoc prof, Moscow Univ; from 1902 for 30 years dir, Archeological History Museum, later State Historical Museum in Yekaterinoslav-Dnepropetrovsk; also instructor, Dnepropetrovsk Univ; works deal with history of Dnieper Cossacks, archeology and ethnography of Southern Ukr; wrote several fiction works, among them novel *Za chuzhoy grekh* (For Another's Sins) (1907) and verse collection in Ukr language "Evening Stars" (1910); *Works*: in Russian and Ukr language: *Istoriya zaporozhskikh kazakov* (History of the Dnieper Cossacks) (3 vol, 1892-97); *Vol'nosti zaporozhskikh kazakov* (Liberties of the Dnieper Cossacks) (1898); *Zaporozh'ye v pamyatnikakh stariny i skazaniyakh naroda* (Zaporozh'ye in Old Reminiscences and Legends) (2 vol, 1887); *Istochniki dlya istorii zaporozhskikh kazakov* (Sources for the History of the Dnieper Cossacks) (2 vol, 1903); *Ukrainskiye narodnyye pesni* (Ukrainian Folk Songs) (1906); *Slovar' ukrainskogo yazyka* (Ukrainian Dictionary) (vol 1, 1920); *K istorii stepnoy Ukrainy* (History of the Ukrainian Steppes) (1929), etc; *Died*: 5 Aug 1940.

EYDEMAN, Robert Petrovich (1895-1937) Mil commander; Lat writer; CP member from 1917; *Born*: 9 May 1895 in vil Leyastsiem, Valga Uyezd, now Lat SSR, son of a teacher; *Educ*: high school; from 1914 studied at Petrograd Forestry Inst; attended Kiev Infantry College; course at Higher Mil Acad of German General Staff; *Career*: Oct 1916 sent as ensign to 16th Siberian Infantry Reserve Regt at Kansk; while still a student at Petrograd Forestry Inst joined "Union of Maximalist Socialist-Revolutionaries" and subsequently, while serving with his regt, carried out revol work among troops; after 1917 Feb Revol elected chm, Regt Comt; Apr 1917 became chm, Kansk Sov of Soldiers' Dep and dep chm, Joint Kansk Sov of Workers, Peasants and Soldiers' Dep; Oct 1917 elected dep chm, Siberian Exec Comt; Jan 1918 deleg to 3rd All-Russian Congress of Soviets, where he was elected member, All-Russian Centr Exec Comt; 1918, together with other Maximalists who favored with CPSU(B) program, admitted to CP membership; in view of his revol services and active support of the Bolsheviks, the Party CC, after 14th Congress backdated his Party record to Mar 1917; spring 1918, helped direct West Siberian Mil Staff; then commanded 1st Siberian (Partisan) Army; on Eastern Front until late 1918 as commander of 2nd Ural, then 3rd Ural Div; from Jan 1919 on Southern and Southwestern Fronts, commanding 16th Kikvidze, 41st and 46th Div and then the Right-Bank Forces Group (Kakhov Bridgehead); 1921-24 dep commander, Ukr and Crimean forces; 1924-25 commander, Siberian Mil Distr; 1925-32 commandant and comr, Frunze Mil Acad; 1932-35 member, USSR Revol Mil Council; from 1935 member, Mil Council, USSR Pop Comrt of Defense; from Mar 1932 chm, Centr Council of Soc for Promoting Defense, Aviation and Chemical Constr, with rank of army commander; from 1929 member, Section for Studying Mil Problems, Communist Acad, and head of its history sub-section; member, ed bd, milit journals; co-ed, *Istoriya grazhdanskoy voyny* (History of the Civil War) and *Sovetskaya voyennaya entsiklopediya* (Soviet Military Encyclopedia); one of foremost Sov mil writers; member, Sov Writers' Union and head of its Lat Section; works translated into Russian, Ukr, German and other languages; deleg 14th, 16th and 17th CPSU(B) Congresses and 15th and 16th CPSU(B) Conferences; often elected member, and in 1935 Presidium member, All-Russian Centr Exec Comt; 1937 arrested by NKVD; *Publ*: mil works: *Povstanchestvo i yego rol' v sovremennoy voyne* (Insurgency and Its Role in Modern Warfare) (1922); *M. V. Frunze i oborona SSSR* (M. V. Frunze and the Defense of the USSR) (1926); *Voprosy voyenno-*

nauchnoy raboty (Problems of Military Research) (1929); *Kharakter operatsiy sovremennykh armiy* (The Nature of Modern Military Operations) (1930); *K voprosu o kharaktere nachal'nogo perioda voyny* (The Initial Stage of War) (1931); *K izucheniyu istorii grazhdanskoy voyny* (Studying the History of the Civil War) (1932); lit works: collected verse: *V potoke* (In the Flood) (1910); *Po solnechnoy trope* (Along the Sun's Trail) (1912); *Zemlya i khleb blagoukhayut* (The Aroma of Land and Grain) (1924); *Neotvratimoye shestviye* (The Inexorable Campaign) (1925); stories: *Shpion* (The Spy); *Vosstaniye kamney* (The Revolt of the Stones); *Rasskaz o portnom Faytel'sone* (The Story of Feitelson the Tailor); *Vo imya dolga* (In the Name of Duty); *Poyedinok* (The Duel); etc; *Awards*: two Orders of the Red Banner; Order of the Red Star; other awards; *Died*: June 1937 sentenced to death at a secret trial for violating his mil duty and betraying his country; 12 June 1937 executed by firing squad.

EYDUK, A.V. (1886-1938) Govt official; CP member from 1903; *Born*: 1886; *Career*: 1917-19 member, Army Comt and chm, Revol Tribunal, 5th Army; plen, Pop Comrt of the Navy; head, Polit Dept, 6th Army; 1919-21 Collegium member, All-Union Cheka; special plen, Main Fuel Bd, Defense Council; dep contruction chief, then construction chief, Balkhash Combine, Lower Amur Shipyard and eastern section of Moskva-Volga Canal; Sov rep, American Aid Admin; arrested by State Security organs; *Died*: 1938 in imprisonment.

EYKHE, Genrikh Khristoforovich (1893-1968) Mil commander, officer, Russian Army; Civil War veteran historian; *Born*: 1893, son of a worker; *Career*: took part in 1917 Oct Revol; helped muster Red Guard detachments; from 1918 in Red Army; 1918-19 regt commander, brigade commander, commander of 26th Infantry Div on the Eastern Front, where his div captured Zlatoust and Chelyabinsk held by Kolchak's forces; 1919-20 commander, 5 th Army on the Eastern Front; 1920-22 commander in chief, Armed Forces of the Far Eastern Republic; 1922-37 exec work for USSR Supr Sovnarkhoz and foreign trade network; 1937 arrested by State Security organs; 1937-55 in imprisonment; 1955 rehabilitated and pensioned; *Awards*: Order of Lenin; Order of the Red Banner; *Died*: 1968.

EYKHE, Robert Indrikovich ("Andrey") (1890-1940) Party and govt official; CP member from 1905; *Born*: 31 July 1890, son of a peasant, in Kurland Province, now Lat SSR; *Career*: carpenter by trade; several times arrested by Tsarist police and exiled for revol activities; 1908 emigrated; 1911 returned to Riga and organized Bolshevik faction in Lat Soc-Democratic Party; Jan 1914 at Brussels Congress elected member, CC, Lat Soc-Democratic Party; on return to Riga arrested and 1915 exiled to Siberia for life; 1916 fled to Irkutsk; 1917 moved to Riga and became member, CC, Lat Soc-Democratic Party; after capture of Riga by German forces engaged in underground work; Jan 1918 arrested and interned in concentration camp; summer 1918 fled to RSFSR and worked for RSFSR Pop Comrt of Food; 1919 Sov Lat Pop Comr of Food; 1919-23 worked for RSFSR Pop Comrt of Food; from 1924 dep chm, then chm, Siberian Kray Exec Comt; from 1929 secr. West Siberian Kray Party Comt; 1937-38 USSR Pop Comr of Agric; at 14th Party Congress elected cand member, at 16th Congress elected member, CC, CPSU(B); Feb 1935 elected cand Politburo member, CC, CPSU(B); member, USSR Centr Exec Comt; arrested by State Security organs; *Awards*: Order of Lenin (1935); *Died*: 2 Feb 1940 in imprisonment.

EYKHENBAUM, Boris Mikhaylovich (1886-1959) Lit historian; pioneer of Russian formalism; *Born*: 22 Sept 1886 in Krasnyy, Smolensk Province, son of a physician; *Educ*: 1912 grad History and Philology Fac, Petersburg Univ; *Career*: 1907 began research career; early works studied connections between Russian and for lit; from 1918 lecturer; connected with Soc for the Study of Poetic Language; made an analysis of Russian poetic language; studied soc, philosophical and psychological factors in lit; prepared textual criticism of scholarly editions of Lermontov. Gogol, Tolstoy, Turgenev and Saltykov-Shchedrin's works; *Publ: Molodoy Tolstoy* (Young Tolstoy) (1922); *Melodika russkogo liricheskogo stikha* (The Melodics of Russian Lyric Verse) (1922); *Anna Akhmatova* (1923); *Skvoz' literaturu* (Through Literature) (1924); *Lermontov* (1924); *Literatura* (Literature) (1927); *Lev Tolstoy* (2 vol, 1928-31); *Moy vremmenik* (My Contemporary) (1929); *Tolstoy posle 'Voyny i mira'* (Tolstoy After "War and Peace") (1940); *Literaturnaya pozitsiya Lermontova* (Lermontov's Literary Stand) (1941), etc; *Died*: 24 Nov 1959.

EYKHENVAL'D, Anton Aleksandrovich (1875-1952) Composer, folklorist and conductor; Pop Artiste of Bashkir ASSR from 1945; *Born*: 13 May 1875 in Moscow; *Educ*: studied composition theory under Klenovskiy and Taneyev and instrumentation under Rimsky-Korsakov; *Career*: from 1894 opera choirmaster and symphonic conductor, artistic dir of opera theaters and impresario; 1927-28, as opera conductor, toured France; collected musical folklore; recorded some 4,000 Bashkir, Tat, Uzbek and Turkm folk songs; *Works*: operas: *Step'* (The Steppe) (1931); *Mereyen* (1940); *Ashkazar* (1944); *Solnechnyy kamen'* (The Sun-Stone) (1946); musical comedy *Tabachnyy kapitan* (The Tobacco Captain) (1942); ballets *Yolochka (Zima)* (The Little Fir Tree [Winter]) (1913); *Vsadniki* (The Horsemen) (1947); pantomime ballets *Zhar-ptitsa* (The Phoenix) and *Ivan-Tsarevich* (1925); symphonic, vocal, instrumental and chamber works; *Died*: 1952 in Leningrad.

EYSMONT, Nikolay Boleslavovich (1891-1935) Govt official; lawyer; CP member from 1907; *Born*: 1891, son of a forester; *Educ*: grad law fac; *Career*: from 1907 worked in Soc-Democratic student org; from 1912 worked for *Mezhrayontsy* Soc-Democratic group; member, Petersburg Rayon Duma, and asst mayor of Petersburg; 1917 joined RCP(B); 1919 member, Mil-Revol Council, Ural Railroad; dep plen for supply of the Red Army and Navy; Presidium member, Supr Sovnarkhoz; 1922 chm, North Caucasian Econ Council; 1923 dep chm, RSFSR Supr Sovnarkhoz; 1924 chm, North Caucasian Kray Exec Comt; from 1926 RSFSR Pop Comr of Trade and USSR Dep Pop Comr of Trade; from Dec 1930 RSFSR Pop Comr of Supply and Collegium member, USSR Pop Comrt of Supply; member, All-Uninon Centr Exec Comt; *Died*: 1935.

F

FABRITSIUS, Yan Fritsevich (1877-1929) Mil commander; Lat; Civil War veteran; CP member from 1903; *Born*: 26 June 1877 at farmstead Vankayreybey, Kurland Province, now Lat SSR, son of a farm-hand; *Educ*: 1894 grad Riga Alexandrine High School; 1924 grad Higher Acad Courses for Red Army Commanders; *Pos*: 1895-98 farm-hand; 1898-99 private, NCO, then ensign, Lith Bodyguard Regt; 1900-03 factory-worker in Riga, Vindava and Mitava; 1914-15 on Sakhalin as office worker, Aleksandrovsk Forestry Bd; 1915-18 private, NCO, company commander, battalion commander in Russian Army; from Feb 1918 in the Red Army; 1918-19 mil comr, Gdovsk Rayon, Petrograd Province; then mil comr, 3rd Brigade, 3rd Petrograd Div and mil comr, 10th Div; 1919-20 commander, composite detachment; 1st brigade, 13th Infantry Div; 3rd and 48th Brigades, 16th Infantry Div; 1921-23 commandant and comr, 43rd Combined Courses for Red Army Commanders; 1923 commander, 2nd Bel Div; 1924-27 commander, 17th Infantry Corps; 1927 demoted, than commander, 4th Infantry Corps; 1928-29 asst commander, Red Banner Separate Caucasian Army; *Career*: 1891, while still at school, participated in political riots in Vindava; from 1901, after having been arrested for illegal anti-govt propaganda, under secret police surveillance; 1903 again arrested for participating in May Day demonstration and for resisting authorities; Feb 1904, after eight months in prison, sentenced to four years at hard labor, followed by exile for life; 1915 volunteered for active duty with Russian Army on Northwestern Front; 1917 elected chm, regt commission for elections to Constituent Assembly; conducted Bolshevik propaganda work in 12th Army; 1918 member, Mil Section, Centr Exec Comt of 3rd convocation; 1918-20 Civil War service on Leningrad, Southern and Polish Fronts; 1921, as commander of 501st Rogozhsk Regt, helped crush Kronstadt Mutiny; deleg at 11-15th CPSU(B) Congresses; from 1927 member, CPSU(B) Centr Control Commission; cand, USSR Centr Exec Comt of 5th convocation; *Awards*: four Orders of the Red Banner; Arms of Honor; inscribed gold watch; *Died*: 24 Aug 1929 killed in plane crash near Sochi.

FADEYEV (real name: BULYGA), Aleksandr Aleksandrovich (1901-1956) Russian writer; public and polit figure; CP member from 1918; *Born*: 24 Dec 1901 in Kimry, Tver'Province; both his parents were med assistants; *Educ*: studied at Vladivostok Business College; 1921-22 at Moscow Mining Inst; *Career*: until 1918 lived in vil Chuguyevka, South Ussuri Kray; 1918 left school in 8th grade to undertake underground revol work; 1919-21 with partisans, then in Red Army; Apr 1920 seriously wounded near

Spassk; deleg, 10th RCP(B) Congress; Mar 1921 helped crush Kronstadt Mutiny; seriously wounded for the second time; 1923-26 Party and newspaper work in Moscow and Northern Caucasus; 1923 first work published; from 1926 active in founding Sov lit associations; helped direct Russian, then All-Union Proletarian Writers' Assoc and, after its liquidation in 1933, the USSR Writers' Union; Bd and Presidium member, USSR Writers' Union; his works deal with Oct Revol, Civil War, Stalin's five-year plans and partisan and underground activities in WW 2; 1933 together with Dovzhenko worked on a film script on Sov Far East; together with M. S. Narokov wrote stage adaptation of his novel *Razgrom* (Rout), which continues to be staged in Sov theaters; the novel *Molodaya gvardiya* (The Young Guard) has also been dramatized and staged; the novel "Young Guard" has also provided the basis for an opera, a symphony and the ballet *Lyubka*, etc; wrote articles on dramaturgy and stagecraft; at 18th and 19th CPSU(B) Congresses elected member and at 20th cand member CC, CPSU; elected dep, USSR Supr Sov of 2nd, 3rd and 4th convocations; dep, RSFSR Supr Sov of 3rd convocation; headed Sov deleg at various Int peace Congresses; 1948 in Wroclaw, 1949 in Paris, 1949 in New York, 1950 in Warsaw, etc; Bureau member, World Peace Council and Presidium member, USSR Comt for the Defense of Peace; *Publ:* novelette *Razliv* (Flood) (1923); story *Protiv techeniya* (Against the Current) (1923); novels: *Razgrom* (Rout) (1927); *Posledniy iz Udege* (The Last Man from Udege) (unfinished: Parts 1-4 in 1929-36; some chapters of Part 5 published 1941); book *Leningrad v dni blokady. Iz dnevnika* (Leningrad During the Blockade. Diary Notes) (separate ed. 1944); novels *Molodaya gvardiya* (The Young Guard) (1946); 2nd revised ed, 1951); *Chyornaya metallurgiya* (Ferrous Metallurgy) some chapters published in 1954); book *Literatura i zhizn'* (Literature and Life) (1939); *Za 30 let. Izbrannyye stat'i, rechi i pis'ma o literature i iskusstve* (Thirty Years. Selected Articles, Speeches and Letters on Literature and Art (1957); *Sobraniye sochieneniy* (Collected Works) (5 vol, 1959–61); *Awards:* Stalin Prize (1946); two Orders of Lenin; other orders; medals; *Died:* 13 May 1956 committed suicide for reasons unknown.

FADEYEV, Anatoliy Vsevolodovich (1908-1965) Historian; Dr of Historical Sci from 1954; prof from 1958; senior assoc from 1953 and from 1960 head, section for publ of multi-vol *Istoriya SSSR s drevneyshikh vremyon do nashikh dney (dooktyabr'skiy period)* (History of the USSR from Ancient Times to the Present /Pre-October Period/), Inst of History, USSR Acad of Sci; *Born*: 9 Apr 1908 in Irkutsk; *Educ*: 1929 grad Leningrad Teachers' Training Inst; *Career*: 1931-39 assoc, Abkhazian Inst of Language and History, Geo Branch, USSR Acad of Sci; 1939-41 assoc prof and head, Chair of USSR History, Odessa Univ; 1941-49 active service and training in Red Army; 1949-51 taught history at Rostov Univ; 1951-58 assoc prof, from 1958 prof, Chair of History, History Fac, Moscow State Univ; works deal with history of Caucasian pop, Tsarist colonial policy and int relations in early 19th Century; helped compile a number of school and higher educ textbooks on USSR history; headed team of writers which compiled *Istoriya Kabardino-Balkarii* (History of Kabardo-Balkaria); edited *Ocherki po istorii Abkhazii* (Outline History of Abkhazia) and *Ocherki po istorii Severnoy Osetii* (Outline History of Northern Ossetia); *Publ*: coauthor and ed, *Istoriya SSSR. S drevneyshikh vremyon do 1861 g.* (History of the USSR. From Ancient Times to 1861) (1956); *Kavkaz v sisteme mezhdunarodnykh otnosheniy* (The Caucasus in the System of International Relations) (1956); *Ocherki ekonomicheskogo razvitiya Stepnogo Podkavkaz'ya* (Outline Economic Development of Steppe Regions Adjoining the Caucasus) (1957); *Rossiya i 'Vostochnyy krizis' 20-kh godov 19-go veka* (Russia and the "Eastern Crisis" of the 1820's) (1958); *Doreformennaya Rossiya, 1800-1861 gg.* (Pre-Reform Russia, 1800-61) (1960); *Rossiya i Kavkaz v pervoy treti 19-go veka* (Russia and the Caucasus in the First 30 Years of the 19th Century) (1960); *Peredovaya russkaya intelligentsiya i tsarskiy kolonializm v doreformennyy period* (The Russian Progressive Intelligentsia and Tsarist Colonial Policy in the Pre-Reform Period) (1963); *Awards*: Badge of Hon (1955); *Died*: 4 Oct 1965.

FALALEYEV, Fyodor Yakovlevich (1899-1955) Air Force commander; Marshal of the Air Force from 1944; CP member from 1918; *Born*: 31 May 1899 in vil Polyanskaya, Udmurt ASSR, son of a peasant; *Educ*: 1928 grad Higher Infantry Tactical Courses; 1933 grad Kacha Mil Pilots' School; 1934 grad Air Force Acad; *Pos*: 1919 volunteered for Red Army; 1919-26 army polit worker; 1926-32 battalion commander, then infantry regt commander; 1934-36 pilot in the Air Force; 1936-40 commander, air force squadron, then air force brigade; dep commander, air force strategic command; 1940-41 inspector-gen and dep commander, Main Bd, Red Army Air Force; 1941-42 air force commander, Southern Front, then Southwestern Sector; 1942-46 chief of staff and dep commander, Sov Air Force; 1946-50 commandant, Air Force Acad; *Career*: fought in Civil War; in WW 2, as rep of Gen Headquarters, coordinated the activities of Army Groups' Air Force units in the Battle of Stalingrad (1942-43) and in the Crimea (1944), Belorussia (1944) and East Prussia (1945); *Awards*: Order of Lenin; three Orders of the Red Banner; three Orders of Suvorov, 1st and 2nd Class; Order of Kutuzov, 1st Class; Order of the Red Star; Badge of Hon; medals; *Died*: 12 Aug 1955 after long illness.

FAL'KIVSKIY, Dmitriy Nikanorovich (1898-1934) Ukr poet; *Born*: 3 Nov 1898 in vil Lepesy, Bel SSR; *Educ*: studied at Brest-Litovsk high school; *Career*: from his youth participated in revol work; 1920 in Red Army; 1920-23 worked for Bel Cheka; 1924 first work published in periodical *Chervonyy shlyakh*; contributed also to the periodical *Literaturnyy yarmarok*; main themes of his poetry are his native Poles'ye, its natural beauties, the peasant's love of their native land; Party critics termed him an "old fashioned singer of rural beauties," hinting that he stood "on the other shore of the epoch"; 1926-28 member, lit org "Workshop of Lit Speech"; arrested by State Security organs; *Publ*: poem "Chaban" (The Shepherd) (1925); collections: "Works" (1927); "On the Fire Site" (1928); "Poles'ye" (1931); *Died*: 17 Dec 1934 in imprisonment.

FAL'KNER, S.A. (1890-1938) Econ; prof; *Born*: 1890; *Career*: 1918-21 dep head, Econ Research Dept, Supr Sovnarkhoz; econ, Price Comt, Supr Sovnarkhoz; asst organizer, of registration and statistical work, Main Fuel Comt, Supr Sovnarkhoz and at Socialist Acad; 1921-24 member, Econ-Statistics Section, Gosplan; simultaneously Collegium member, Inst of Econ, 1st Moscow State Univ; 1925-27 head, World Econ Section, Market Council, Gosplan; arrested by State Security organs; *Died*: 1938 in imprisonment.

FARMAKOVSKIY, Boris Vladimirovich (1870-1928) Archeologist; specialist in classical and Northern Black Sea region archeology and ancient art; corresp member, Acad of Sci from 1914; member, Acad of Material Culture History from 1919 and 1921-28 its learned secr; *Born*: 12 Feb 1870 in Vyatka (now Kirov); *Educ*: 1892 grad Novorossiysk Univ, Odessa; *Career*: 1898-1901 learned secr, Russian Inst of Archeology, Constantinople; 1901-18 member, Archeology Commission; 1906-19 learned secr, Russian Archeological Soc; from 1919 prof, Leningrad Univ; for many years conducted archeological studies of Olvia; excavations of Olvia (1896, 1901-15, 1924-26) represent a model of archeological research on an ancient town; managed to determine the basic territory, the planning and defense system of Olvia, the lay-out of dwellings and public buildings, features of the city's cultural life, etc; also conducted excavations in Kiev (at Desyatinnaya Church, 1908-09), Yevpatoriya (1916-17), etc; *Publ: Atticheskaya vazovaya zhivopis' i yeyo otnosheniya k iskusstvu monumental'nomu v epokhu neposredstvenno posle greko-persidskikh voyn* (Attic Vase Painting and Its Relation to the Monumental Art of the Epoch Immediately Following the Greco-Persian Wars) (1902); *Arkhaicheskiy period v Rossii* (The Archaic Period in Russia) (1914); *Pamyatniki antichnoy kul'tury, naydennyye v Rossii* (Monuments of Antique Culture Found in Russia) (1902-15); *Khudozhestvennyy ideal demokraticheskikh Afin* (The Artistic Ideal of Democratic Athens) (1918); *Tri polikhromnyye vazy v forme statuetok, naydennyye v Fanagorii* (Three Polychrome Vases in the Form of Statuettes Found at Fanagoria) (1921), etc; *Died*: 29 July 1928.

FAT'YANOV, Aleksey Ivanovich (1919-1959) Russian poet; *Born*: 1919; *Career*: many of V. Solov'yov-Sedoy's best songs were written to Fat'yanov's lyrics: "The Nightingales," "In the Sunny Glade," "Our Town," "Where Are You, Brother Soldiers," "Where Are You, My Garden," etc; Fat'yanov's verse also set to music: by B. Mokrousov in "On Your Porch," "I'm Not Going to Brag, Dear," etc; by M. Blanter in "In the City Park"; by I. Dzerzhinskiy in his series "The Earth"; by A. Babayev, L. Bakalov, S. Kats, A. Novikov, Yu. Milyutin, V. Shorin, etc; collection of songs to Fat'yanov's lyrics published in 1960; *Died*: 1959.

FAVITSKIY, Vladimir Viktorovich (1896-1938) Mil commander; col; prof from 1935; specialist in use of armored forces; *Born*:

1896; *Career*: from 1918 in Red Army; active in Civil War; 1930-35 instructor, then head, Chair of Motorization and Mechanization of Troops, Frunze Mil Acad; 1936-38 commander and comr, 1st Separate Heavy Tank Brigade; 1938 arrested by NKVD; *Died*: 1938 in imprisonment; posthumously rehabilitated.

FAVORSKIY, Aleksey Vasil'yevich (1873-1930) Neuropathologist; Dr of Med from 1900; prof from 1918; *Born*: 1873; *Educ*: 1896 grad Med Fac, Kazan' Univ; *Career*: after grad worked at L.O. Darkshevich's Clinic of Nervous Diseases; 1900 defended doctor's thesis on "Pathological Anatomical Lesion of the Spinal Cord by Compression"; 1903-06 completed specialist training abroad under Oppenheim, Bilszowski, Vogt and Mechnikov; 1910 studied under Altzheimer; from 1907 assoc prof; read lectures on "An Anatomical and Physiological Introduction to a Course on Nervous Diseases"; 1912 worked at Pavlov's laboratory; from 1918 prof, Chair of Nervous Diseases, Kazan' Univ; 1926-30 head, Chair of Nervous Diseases, Kazan' Inst of Postgrad Med Training; studied nerve endings of bulbus olfactorius; did research on effect of botulism on lower vertebrates, establishing that these animals transmit the bacterial poison freely; also did research on pathological anatomical lesions of the nerve tissue in tabes dorsalis; was first Russian sci to read course on the pathological histology of the nervous system for physicians; wrote over 30 works; *Publ: K ucheniyu ob ostrom rtutnom polinevrite* (The Theory of Acute Mercurial Polyneuritis) (1899); doctor's thesis *Materialy k voprosu o patologoanatomicheskom izmenenii spinnogo mozga pri sdavlenii yego* (Material on Pathological Anatomical Lesion of the Spinal Cord by Compression) (1901); *Progress v uchenii ob anatomii i patologii nervnoy kletki* (Progress in the Theory of the Anatomy and Pathology of the Nerve Cell) (1902); *Deystviye botulicheskogo toksina na nizshikh pozvonochnykh v svyazi s izmeneniyami nervnoy sistemy ikh* (The Effect of Botulin Poisoning on Lower Vertebrates in Relation to Lesions of Their Nervous System) (1909), etc; *Died*: 1930.

FAVORSKIY, Aleksey Yevgrafovich (1860-1945) Organic chemist; Dr of Chemistry from 1895; prof from 1896; member, USSR Acad of Sci from 1929; Hero of Socialist Labor from 1945; *Born*: 3 Mar 1860 in vil Pavlovo, Nizhniy Novgorod Province, son of a priest; *Educ*: 1882 grad Petersburg Univ; *Career*: after grad asst, A.M.Butlerov's laboratory; 1891 defended master's thesis; 1895 defended doctor's thesis; from 1896 prof, Petersburg Univ; after 1917 Oct Revol worked at Leningrad Univ, Leningrad Inst of Chemical Eng and USSR Acad of Sci; 1921-29 corresp member, USSR Acad of Sci; 1934-38 dir, Inst of Organic Chemistry, USSR Acad of Sci; pioneer of chemistry of unsaturated organic compounds, especially acetylene chemistry; 1900-05 during research on the condensation of acetylene hydrocarbons with ketones in the presence of potassium hydroxide discovered new method of synthesizing tertiary alcohols on the basis of which he devised a method of obtaining isoprene; proposed model of alcohol fermentation and devised theory of the biosynthesis of terpenes; made major contribution to the ind production of synthetic rubber, vinyl ethers, dioxan, etc; founded influential school of organic chemistry; *Publ: Sbornik izbrannykh trudov* (Selected Works) (1940); *Awards*: Stalin Prize (1941); four Orders of Lenin; Order of the Red Banner of Labor; *Died*: 8 Aug 1945.

FAVORSKIY, Vladimir Andreyevich (1886-1964) Painter, engraver; prof from 1921; member, USSR Acad of Arts from 1962; Pop Artiste of RSFSR from 1958 and of USSR from 1963; member, Bd, USSR Painters' Union; *Born*: 1886; *Educ*: 1905-08 studied at Munich Univ, subsequently at History and Philology Fac, Moscow Univ; *Career*: 1915-17 in Russian Army; 1919-21 in Red Army; from 1921 instructor, Moscow art colleges; 1923-25 rector, Moscow Higher Tech Art Workshops; then prof, Moscow State Higher Tech Art Inst, Moscow Polytech Inst, Inst of Fine Arts and Inst of Architecture; 1958-62 corresp member, USSR Acad of Arts; specialized in wood-cuts for book illustrations; 1925 helped found "Assoc of Easel Painters"; designed facade for Sov pavilion at 1937 Paris World Fair; decorated stage portal for Moscow Sov Army Theater and did ceiling paintings for a Moscow subway station (1935); did sets for numerous plays in Sov theaters; illustrated Russian and for classics; his works were exhibited at 1958 Brussels Fair; *Works*: sculptures: "Chess" (1910); "Battle of David and Goliath" (1911); painting "Autoportrait" (1910); wood-cuts: *Dostoyevsky* (1929); *Lermontov* (1931); *Kutuzov*, (1945); engraving "Triple Portrait" (1910); illustrations for *Slovo o polku Igoreve* (The Lay of the Host of Igor (1950), *Boris Godunov* and *A.S. Pushkin* (1954); mosaic at Sov Embassy in Warsaw (1955); *Awards*: Lenin Prize (1962); medals at Brussels Fair; *Died*: Dec 1964.

FAYDYSH, Andrey Petrovich (1919-1967) Sculptor; Hon Art Worker of RSFSR; corresp member, USSR Acad of Arts from 1964; *Born*: 10 Jan 1919; *Educ*: 1948 grad Moscow Surikov Inst of Arts *Works*: "V. I. Lenin Speaking at the Finnish Terminus in April 1917"; "Lenin in 1905"; "Worker on Strike"; "Red Guardsman"; monuments to: the "Heroes of the Civil War in the Far East" (Khabarovsk), the "Bryansk Partisans" (Bryansk), *K.E. Tsiolkovskiy* (Kaluga); together with architects A. Barshch and A. Kolchin sculpted a monument commemorating the mastery of space and a monument to K. Tsiolkovskiy, both erected in Moscow; did sculptural portraits of cosmonauts A. Leonov, P. Belyayev and Acad S. Korolyov ("Alley of Heroes" in Moscow); *Awards*: Stalin Prize (1950); RSFSR State Prize (1967); *Died*: 13 Aug 1967.

FAYNSHMIDT, Isaak Il'ich (1875-1940) Therapist; specialist in tuberculosis; Hon Sci Worker of Ukr SSR; *Born*: 18 June 1875 in Orel; *Educ*: 1899 grad Med Fac, Khar'kov Univ; *Career*: after grad specialized three years in Germany and Switzerland; after return to Ukr intern, then asst prof, Khar'kov Hospital Therapy Clinic; asst prof, Khar'kov Women's Med Inst; was active in Anti-Tuberculosis League; 1917-22 founder-dir, 1st Ukr Tuberculosis Inst, Khar'kov; from 1923 head, Chair of Tuberculosis, then Chair of Fac Therapy, Khar'kov Med Inst; helped to organize first Ukr congresses of specialists on internal diseases and tuberculosis; wrote works on tubercular and non-tubercular lung diseases, cardiology and metabolism; *Publ: K voprosu o tuberkulyoze i gipertireoze* (Tuberculosis and Hyperthyroidism) (1926); co-ed, *Tuberkulyoz v gorode i na sele* (Urban and Rural Tuberculosis) (vol 1, 1927); *Rak lyogkogo i tuberkulyoz* (Lung Cancer and Tuberculosis) (1940); *Died*: 25 Apr 1940.

FAYZI, Akhmed Safiyevich (1903-1958) Tatar poet and playwright; Hon Art Worker of RSFSR from 1957; *Born*: 11 Mar 1903; *Educ*: grad Orenburg Oriental Inst; *Career*: teacher and cultural worker in Donbas, Turkm and Kazan'; 1918 began career as playwright in Ufa with the comedy "The World of Beauty"; while in Donbas founded "Teadus" (Friends of the Theater) drama ensemble, which performed at workers' settlements; translated *Boris Godunov* Shevchenko's *Katerina* and the works of Mayakovsky into Tatar; *Works*: plays "Tukay" (1939) and "Pugachev in Kazan'" (1948); libretti for operas "The Fugitive", (1939), "Dzhalil'" (1957) and "The Poet" (1947) (music by Zhiganov); libretti for Yarullin's balett "Shurale" (1945) and D. Fayzi's musical comedy "The Seagull" (1944); *Died*: 11 Aug 1958.

FAYZI, Mirkhaydar (1891-1928) Tat playwright; *Born*: 31 Oct 1891 in vil Kukshel', Orsk Uyezd, Orenburg Province, son of a peasant; *Educ*: studied at Orenburg medressah; *Career*: from 1907 worked at various libraries in Orsk; studied Russian and Tat lit; 1910 began lit work; 1912 first play published; his works demonstrate a deep knowledge of everyday life; first Tat playwright to display panorama of vil life; *Publ*: plays: "Galiyabanu" (1916-17); "Beloved" (1920); "On the Banks of the Ural" (1922); "White Cap" (1923); "A Soul Gone Astray" (1922); "Red Star" (1923), etc; verse collections: "My Poems" (1912); "Young Soul" (1913), etc; *Died*: 9 July 1928.

FAZLULLIN, Mukhametkhan Ashrafyanovich (1883-1964) Tatar philologist; prof; Hon Sci Worker of Tatar ASSR from 1940; corresp member, RSFSR Acad of Pedag Sci from 1950; CP member from 1943; *Born*: 14 Dec 1883; *Educ*: 1903 grad Moslem high school; 1908 grad Tatar Teachers' Training School, Kazan'; *Career*: 1905-07 took active part in Revol; 1908-18 teacher, Russian-Tatar College, Mamadysh; from 1918 taught at various schools in Kazan'; co-founder, Tatar educ journal "Maarif"; 1926 member, "New Alphabet" Comt for Latinization of the Tatar Script; 1939 member, Commission for Russification of the Tatar Script; 1930-64 prof, Kazan' Teachers' Training Inst; specialized in Tatar philology, history of Tatar script and methods of teaching Tatar in primary schools; *Publ: Tatarskiy yazyk v nachal'noy shkole* (The Tatar Language at Primary School) (1934); *Kniga dlya chteniya. Dlya shkol vzroslykh* (A Reading Book for Adult Schools) (1939); *Metodika tatarskogo yazyka* (Methods of Teaching Tatar) (1954); etc; *Died*: 16 Feb 1964.

FEDARAVICHYUS, Pyatras (1896-1967) Party and govt official; CP member from 1917; *Born*: 25 June 1896; *Educ*: grad Sverdlov Communist Univ; *Career*: participated in 1917 Oct Revol in Petrograd and in struggle to establish Sov regime in Lith; 1917 agitation and propaganda work among Lith soldiers in Petrograd; fought in Civil War; after completion of Univ course, teaching and Party work; from 1944 Party and govt work in Lith: secr, Vilnius and Shaulyay City Party Comt; chm, Kaunas Oblast Exec Comt; Lith First Dep Min of State Control; 1946-56 dep, Lith Supr Sov; member, CC, CP Lith; from 1958 pensioner; *Died*: 24 Mar 1967.

FEDCHENKO, Boris Alekseyevich (1872-1947) Botanist and geographer; prof; *Born*: 1872; *Educ*: 1895 grad Moscow Univ; *Career*: from 1900 worked at Petersburg Botanical Gardens (later Botanical Inst, USSR Acad of Sci; 1918-31 prof, Geographical Inst, then Leningrad Univ; 1908-17 led various botanical expeditions to Centr Russia, Urals, Far East, Caucasus, Centr Asia, Asia Minor, Western Europe and Algeria; wrote numerous works on plant geography and taxonomy; 1912-20 and 1923-24 ed, series *Flora Aziatskoy Rossii*; 1929-41 ed, series *Flora Zabaykal'ya*; 1929-41 ed, series *Flora Yugo-Vostoka Yevropeyskoy chasti SSSR; Publ: Perechen' rasteniy, dikorastushchikh v Russkom Turkestane* (A Catalog of Wild Plants in Russian Turkestan) (vol 1, 1906, vol 2-6, 1900-16); coauthor, *Flora Yevropeyskoy Rossii* (The Flora of European Russia) (3 vol, 1908-10); *Rastitel'nost' Turkestana* (The Vegetation of Turkestan) (1915); *Ocherki rastitel'nosti Turkestana* (Studies of the Vegetation of Turkestan) (1925); ed, *Sornyye rasteniya SSSR* (Weeds of the USSR) (4 vol, 1934-35); *Died*: 1947.

FED'KO, Ivan Fyodorovich (1897-1939) Ukr; mil commander; army commander, 1st class from 1938; Civil War veteran; CP member from 1917; *Born*: 24 June 1897 in vil Khmelov, Poltava Province, son of a Zaporozhian Cossack; *Educ*: 1917 grad 4th Kiev Ensign School; 1922 grad Red Army Mil Acad; *Pos*: 1913-16 joiner; 1916 drafted into Russian Army; 1916-17 private, machine-gunner, platoon commander, elected batallion commander; 1917-18 in the Red Guard; from 1918 in Red Army; 1918-20 commanded detachment, regt, then column; commander, Caucasian Armed Forces; commander, 11th Army; member, Crimean Republ Revol Mil Council and dep commander, Crimean Red Army; commander, 58th Crimean Div, then commander, 46th Infantry Div; commander, shock army group; 1922-27 commander, 18th Yaroslavl' Infantry Div; commander, 13th, then 2nd Infantry Corps; 1927-28 chief of staff, North Caucasian Mil Distr; 1928 asst commander, Leningrad Mil Distr; 1931-32 commander, Red Banner Caucasian Army; 1932-34 commander, Volga Mil Distr; 1934-37 commander, Maritime Forces Group and asst commander, Personnel Dept, Far Eastern Army; from 1934 simultaneously member, Mil Council, USSR Pop Comrt of Defense; 1937-38 commander, Kiev Mil Distr; 1938 USSR Dep Pop Comr of Defense and member, Supr Mil Council; 1938 arrested by NKVD; *Career*: participated in the Oct 1917 Revol in Feodosiya; 1921, being a student at the Mil Acad and commander of a student brigade, helped crush Kronstadt Mutiny; later, commanding a mil sector, helped crush Antonov Revolt in Tambov Province; 1924-25 fought against Basmachi; 1923 deleg, 12th CPSU(B) Congress; cand member, CC, CP Uzbek; member, Centr Exec Comt, Transcaucasian Sov Federative Socialist Republic; member, USSR Centr Exec Comt; 1937-38 member, CC, CP Ukr; dep and Presidium member, USSR Supr Sov of 1937 convocation; *Awards*: Order of Lenin; four Orders of the Red Banner; *Died*: 26 Feb 1939 died in imprisonment; posthumously rehabilitated.

FEDORENKO, Yakov Nikolayevich (1896-1947) Mil commander; Ukr; Marshal of Armored and Tank Forces from 1944; CP member from 1917; *Born*: 20 Oct 1896 in vil Krasnyy Oskol, Izyum Rayon, Khar'kov Oblast, son of a longshoreman; *Educ*: grad Khar'kov Higher Artillery School; 1934 grad Frunze Mil Acad; *Pos*: until 1915 herdsman, miner in Donets Basin, merchant seaman; 1915 drafted into Russian Navy, served as helmsman; from 1917 in Red Guard; 1918-47 in Red Army; 1918-20 company commander, Red Guard detachment; mil comr, Tiraspol' City; staff comr, 2nd Revol Army in Yekaterinoslav; commander, Armored Train N° 4; 1920-31 commander and comr, armored train group, then commander, armored train regt; 1934-37 commander, separate tank regt, Moscow Mil Distr; commander, 15th Mechanized Brigade, Kiev Mil Distr; 1937-40 commander, mechanized, armored and tank forces, Kiev Mil Distr; 1940-42 head, Mechanized, Armored and Tank Forces Bd, Red Army; 1942-47 commander, Armored, Tank and Mechanized Forces of Sov Army; *Career*: participated in Oct 1917 Revol in Odessa; fought in the Civil War; at Dec 1940 Pop Comrt of Defense conference suggested resumed production of T-34 tanks and increased production of "KV" tanks; 1942 directed formation of first four tank armies; dep, USSR Supr Sov of 1946 convocation; *Awards*: four Orders of Lenin; three Orders of the Red Banner; Order of Suvorov, 1st Class; Order of Kutuzov, 1st Class; *Died*: 26 Mar 1947.

FEDOROVSKIY, Fyodor Fyodorovich (1883-1955) Stage designer; Pop Artiste of USSR from 1951; vice-pres, USSR Acad of Arts from 1947; *Born*: 26 Dec 1883 in Chernigov; *Educ*: 1907 grad Interior Decoration Dept, Stroganov Art College, Moscow; *Career*: 1907-23 taught composition at Stroganov Art College; from 1907 also painted sets for numerous operas and musicals, his first commission being for a production of "Carmen" at the Zimin Opera Theater; 1909 at the same theater designed sets for the musical "Demon", followed in 1910 and 1914 by *Snegurochka* (The Snow Maiden) and *Zhizn' za tsarya* (A Life for the Tsar); 1912-13 designed sets for "Russian Seasons" in Paris and London and for Diaghilev in Paris; in this early period his work was characterized by its affinity to the music of the operas to which it provided a framework and by its predilection for Russian folk motifs; after 1917 Oct Revol painted posters glorifying the new regime; 1921-41 and 1947-53 mang, set-design unit, then chief designer, Bolshoy Theater, where his first major works were sets for "Carmen" (1922), "Lohengrin" (1923) and the ballet *Ispanskoye kaprichchio* (Spanish Capriccio) to music by Rimsky-Korsakov (1923); adapting motifs from folk art to the dimensional peculiarities of the stage, he subsequently designed sets for the Bolshoy Theater's productions of the operas "Boris Godunov" (1927), *Tsarskaya nevesta* (The Tsar's Bride) (1931), and *Pskovityanka* (The Girl from Pskov) (1932); a few years later the experience gained in these productions found expression in his monumental sets for *Knyaz' Igor'* (Prince Igor) (1934) and "Sadko" (1935); other major sets which he designed for the Bolshoy Theater included *Tikhiy Don* (Quiet Flows the Don) (1936), *Knyaz' Igor'* (Prince Igor) (1944), "Boris Godunov" (1947); "Sadko" (1949); *Khovanshchina* (1950); commissioned by Kirov Theater of Opera and Ballet, Leningrad, to design sets for "Ivan Susanin" (1939); his works are displayed in the State Theatrical Museum, the Bolshoy Theater Museum and the French Nat Gallery in Paris; *Awards*: Order of Lenin; two Orders of the Red Banner of Labor; medalss; *Died*: 7 Sept 1955 in Moscow.

FEDOROVSKIY, Nikolay Mikhaylovich (1886-1956) Mineralogist; corresp member, USSR Acad of Sci from 1933; CP member from 1904; *Born*: 12 Dec 1886; *Educ*: 1915 grad Moscow Univ; *Career*: 1917 member, Nizhniy Novgorod Province Exec Comt and Revol Comt; 1918-19 member, All-Russian Centr Exec Comt; 1919 head, Mining Dept, Supr Sovnarkhoz; 1919 Presidium member, Ukr Supr Sovnarkhoz; 1921-22 head, Berlin Bureau of For Sci and Tech; 1922-27 Collegium member, Dept of Sci and Tech, Supr Sovnarkhoz; 1918-23 co-founder and head, Chair of Mineralogy, Moscow Mining Acad; 1923-37 co-founder and dir, All-Union Research Inst of Mineral Raw Materials; under his direction inst was first to undertake comprehensive study of minerals, from prospecting and assaying to developing the production technol; this helped establish raw material base for numerous branches of non-metallic mining ind; from 1954 head, Applied Mineralogy and Metallurgy Section, All-Union Research Inst of Mineral Raw Materials; wrote an original classification of minerals according to their energetic indices; also compiled a mineralogy course, which ran through a number of ed; *Publ: Kurs mineralogii* (A Mineralogy Course) (5th ed, 1934); *Geneticheskaya mineralogiya* (Genetic Mineralogy) (1920); *Opredeleniye mineralov* (The Determination of Minerals) (3rd ed, 1934); *Opyt prikladnoy mineralogii* (Experience of Applied Mineralogy) (1924); *Mineraly v promyshlennosti i sel'skom khozyaystve* (Minerals in Industry and Agriculture) (2nd ed, 1927); *Nashi dostizheniya v oblasti prikladnoy mineralogii* (Our Achievements in the Field of Applied Mineralogy) (1935); *Rekonstruktsiya mineralogii kak nauki* (Reconstruction of Mineralogy as a Science) (1932); *Klassifikatsiya poleznykh iskopayemykh po energeticheskim pokazatelyam* (The Classification of Minerals According to Their Energetic Indices) (1935); *Died*: 27 Aug 1956.

FEDOSEYENKO, Pavel Fyodorovich (1898-1934) Balloonist and airship designer; *Born*: 3 Jan 1898 in Novaya Sotnya, Voronezh Province, son of a worker; *Educ*: 1932 grad Airship-Building Fac, Zhukovskiy Air Force Acad; *Career*: until 1918 modeller; from 1918 in Red Army; 1918-20 officer cadet; aerostat pilot; commander, aerostat detachment; from 1921 specialist in aeronautics; 1919-20 fought in the Civil War on Southern Front; in 1920's accomplished a number of record balloon flights; 1925 together with A. A. Fridman in a spherical balloon reached an altitude of 7,400 meters; 30 Jan 1934, as commander of the stratospheric balloon *Osoaviakhim - 1* (vol: 24,920 cubic meters) together with A. B. Vasenko and I. D. Usyskin carried out a stratopheric study flight reaching an altitude of 22,000 meters and recording important sci data; the balloon crashed and all the crew were killed; *Awards*: Order of Lenin (posthumously); Order of the Red Banner; *Died*: 30 Jan 1934 killed in above-mentioned balloon crash; the urns containing the ashes of the balloon's crew were immured in the Kremlin Wall, Moscow.

FEDOTOV, Nikolay Petrovich (1901-1966) Hygienist and med historian; prof; Dr of Med from 1950; CP member from 1920; *Born*: 1901; *Educ*: 1930 grad Med Fac, Tomsk Univ; *Career*: 1912-19 lathe operator at Ural factories; 1919-20 served in Red Army; 1930-39 postgrad student and asst prof, 1939-51 assoc prof and head, Chair of Soc Hygiene, Tomsk Med Inst; 1944-49 head, Tomsk Oblast Sanitary Inspectorate; 1951-66 head, Chair of Soc Hygiene, Health Service Org and Med History, Tomsk Med Inst; also dean, Sanitation and Hygiene Fac, Tomsk Med Inst; from 1959 bd chm, Tomsk Section, All-Union Soc of Med History; from 1960 member, Problems Commission Nr 46, USSR Acad of Med Sci; member, Experts' Commission, Higher Certifying Commission, USSR Min of Higher and Secondary Special Educ; member, ed council, journal *Sovetskoye zdravookhraneniye*; co-ed, history of med section, "BSE" (Large Soviet Encyclopedia) (2nd ed); chm, philosophy seminar at Tomsk Med Inst; organized conferences on med history for physicians in Urals and Siberia; supervised compilation of study *Zdorov'ye naseleniya v Tomskoy oblasti* (The Health of the Population in Tomsk Oblast); for two years rector, Tomsk Med Inst; frequently elected to Party Bureau, Tomsk Med Inst; attended plenary sessions of Tomsk City CPSU Comt; chm, Okrug Election Comt; wrote over 70 works on soc hygiene and med hist in Siberia; *Publ: Zdravookhraneniye za 30 let v Tomskoy Oblasti* (Thirty Years of the Health Service in Tomsk Oblast) (1947); doctor's thesis *Ocherki po istorii meditsiny Sibiri v svayazi s istoriyey yeyo kolonizatsii, 1585-1861* (The History of Medicine in Siberia in Relation to the History of Siberian Colonization, 1585-1861) (1948); coauthor, *Zdravookhraneniye v Tomskoy oblasti* (The Health Service in Tomsk Oblast) (1957); *Awards*: Order of the Red Banner of Labor; medal "For Valiant Labor in the Great Fatherland War"; *Died*: 1966.

FEDOT'YEV, Pavel Pavlovich (1864-1934) Chemical eng; corresp member, USSR Acad of Sci from 1933; *Born*: 1864 in Blagoveshchensk, now Amur Oblast; *Educ*: 1888 grad Petersburg Technol Inst; *Career*: after grad worked at chemical plants; from 1904 prof, Petersburg Polytech Inst; 1913 devised sodium carbonate process using sodium nitrate as a basic raw material; 1930 devised similar process using sodium sulphate; 1910 began research, partly with V.P. Il'inskiy, which enabled him to formulate physiochemical theory of aluminum production by the electrolysis of molten cryolite and aluminum oxide; 1929 supervised production of first Sov aluminum at *Krasnyy vyborzhets* Plant, Leningrad; 1914-15 studied production of magnesium by the electrolysis of molten carnallite; 1930 completed research program on which the ind production of magnesium in the USSR is based; 1914-15 also did research on production of sodium perborate; 1912-13 on production of barium amalgams; 1928 on production of Berthollet's salt; 1914 on production of iron; 1929 on production of zinc; 1923-28 on production of nickel and cobalt; during WW I worked on production of chlorine, soda and other chemicals; 1924 commissioned by govt to set up a silver refinery in Leningrad; *Publ: Sbornik issledovatel'skikh rabot* (Collected Research Papers) (1936); *Sovremennoye sostoyaniye khimicheskoy promyshlennosti v Rossii* (The Present State of the Chemical Insustry in Russia) (1902); *Tekhnicheskiy analiz mineral'nykh veshchestv* (The Technical Analysis of Minerals) (1922-26); *Krupnaya mineral'naya khimicheskaya promyshlennost' za posledneye desyatiletie* (The Last Decade in the Large-Scale Mineral and Chemical Industry) (1925); *Khimiko-tekhnologicheskiye ocherki* (Studies in Chemical Engineering) (1930); *Elektroliz i metallurgiya* (Electrolysis and Metallurgy) (1935); coauthor, *Nauchniye trudy po metallurgii alyuminiya* (Scientific Papers on Aluminum Metallurgy) (1950); *Died*: 20 Mar 1934.

FEFER, Isaak Solomonovich (1900-1952) Jewish poet; CP member from 1919; *Born*: 23 Sept 1900 in vil Shpola, Ukr, son of a teacher; *Career*: from 1912 worked as a typesetter; fought in Civil War; 1920 began lit career; *Publ*: poems: "Found Sparks" (1928); "Strata" (1934); verse novel "Great Frontiers" (1939); collected verse: "Posters in Bronze" (1931); "Lyrics" (1934); "The Fatherland at War" (1942); "Far-Flying Arrows" (1935); "Collected Works" (1957), etc; *Died*: 12 Aug 1952.

FEL'DMAN, Boris Mironovich (1890-1937) Mil commander; Jew; corps commander from 1935; CP member from 1919; *Born*: 1890; *Educ*: 1921 grad Red Army Mil Acad; *Pos*: until 1917 private, Russian Army; during Civil War chief of staff, Red Army brigade, then div; from 1921 chief of staff, various mil distr; 1928-31 chief of staff, Leningrad Mil Distr; 1931-37 head, Red Army Main Bd and head, Bd for Red Army Commanders; 1934-37 member, Mil Council, USSR Pop Comrt of Defense; supported efforts to motorize and mechanize Red Army; May 1937 arrested by NKVD organs; *Publ: K kharakteristike novykh tendentsiy v voyennom dele* (New Trends in Military Technique) (1931); *O budushchey voyne* (Future Warfare) (1933); *Died*: 11 June 1937 sentenced to death together with Marshal Tukhachevskiy; 12 June 1937 executed.

FEL'DMAN (PAVLOVETS), G. K. (1893-1936) Govt official; CP member from 1914; *Born*: 1893; *Career*: 1917 secr, Moscow Mikhel'son (now Vladimir Il'ich) Plant's factory comt; 1918-23 member and Presidium member, Moscow Sov; 1921 chm, Collegium of Moscow Municipality; 1923-33 worked for Sov trade mission in Berlin; manager, Centr Asian Econ Council; dep head, Cotton Supply, Main Cotton Comt; 1927 expelled from the Party; from 1933 lit work; arrested by State Security organs; *Died*: 1936 in imprisonment.

FEL'DT, Pavel Emil'yevich (1905-1960) Composer and conductor; Hon Art Worker of RSFSR from 1955; *Born*: 21 Feb 1905; *Educ*: 1930 grad Leningrad Conservatory; *Career*: 1929-34 first violinist, 1934-41 conductor, Leningrad Maly Opera Theater; from 1941 conductor, Leningrad Kirov Opera and Ballet Theater; conducted ballets: Shostakovich's *Svetlyy ruchey* (Bright Stream) (1935); Asaf'yev's *Kavkazskiy plennik* (Caucasian Prisoner) (1938) and *Ashik-Kerib* (1940); Chulaki's *Skazka o pope i rabotnike yego Balde* (Tale of the Priest and His Workman Balda) (1940); Khachaturyan's *Gayaneh* (1942, 1952); *Zolushka* (Cinderella) (1946); Yarullin's *Shurale* (1950); Solov'yov-Sedoy's *Taras Bul'ba* (1955); Khachaturyan's *Spartacus* (1956), etc; *Works*: operetta *Don Maurizio* (1946); coauthor, operetta *Prichudy revnosti* (Whims of Jealousy (1947); musical ed, Delibe's ballet *Fadetta* (1936); *Died*: 1 July 1960.

FENIGSHTEYN, Ya. G. (1888-1937) Polish and Russian revol; Party and govt official; member, Soc-Democratic Party of Poland and Lith from 1904; *Born*: 1888; *Career*: Party work in Poland and abroad; 1917 member, Petersburg RSDRP(B) Comt and its Exec Commission; simultaneously member, CC, Soc-Democratic Party of Poland and Lith; member, ed bd, Polish Bolshevik periodical *Trybuna*; 1918 Leftist Communist; from late 1918 member, CC, CP Lith and Bel, and dep chm, Lith and Bel Council of Pop Comr; 1920, during the Red Army's Warsaw offensive, with Polish Bureau, CC, and Polish Revol Comt; after the Civil War govt work; exec dir, Russian Telegraph Agency, then TASS; arrested by State Security organs; *Died*: 1937 in imprisonment.

FENSTER, Boris Aleksandrovich (1916-1960) Choreographer; Pop Artiste of RSFSR from 1957; *Born*: 30 Apr 1916; *Educ*: 1936 grad Leningrad Choreographic College; 1940 grad Ballet-Masters Dept, Leningrad Choreographic College; *Career*: from 1936 dancer, Leningrad Maly Opera Theater; from 1941 ballet-master, 1945-53 artistic dir, Leningrad Maly Opera Theater; 1956-59 chief ballet-master, Leningrad Kirov Opera and Ballet Theater; *Roles*: Harlequin in Drigo's "Harlequinade"; René in Delibe's "Fadetta"; Kolen in *Tshchetnaya predostorozhnost'* (Futile Precaution); under L. M. Lavrovskiy's guidance directed his first ballets: Gladkovskiy's "Tom Sawyer" (1939); Asaf'yev's *Ashik-Kerib* (1940); Deshevov's "Bela" (1941); *Productions*: Chulaki's *Mnimyy zhenikh* (Imaginary Bridegroom) (1946) and *Yunost'* (Youth) (1949); Morozov's *Doktor Aybolit* (1948); Korchmaryov's *Vesyolyy obmanshchik* (The Jolly Deceiver) (1951); Asaf'yev's *Baryshnya-krest'yanka* (The Peasant Miss) (1951); Bitov's *Dvenadtsat' mesyatsev* (Twelve Months) (1954); Solov'yov-Sedoy's *Taras Bul'ba* (1955); Auster's *Tiyna* (1955); Strauss' "Blue Danube" (1956); Laputin's *Maskarad* (Masquerade) (1960); *Awards*: two Stalin Prizes (1947 and 1949); *Died*: 29 Dec 1960.

FEONA, Aleksey Nikolayevich (1879-1949) Actor and operetta dir; Hon Art Worker of RSFSR from 1940; Pop Artiste of Karelian

ASSR from 1943; *Born*: 30 Mar 1879; *Educ*: 1905 grad V. N. Davydov's class, Drama School, Petersburg Aleksandrinskiy Theater; *Career*: 1905-10 at V. F. Komissarzhevskaya Theater; 1911-17 with Petersburg operetta theaters *Bouffe* and *Palas*; 1919-29 actor and dir, Leningrad Operetta Theater; 1919-27 simultaneously dir, Leningrad Maly Opera Theater; from 1928 dir, (1929-31 and 1934-36 artistic dir), Leningrad Operetta Theater; 1937-40 artistic dir, Leningrad Oblast Operetta Theater and 1942-45 Karelian ASSR Operetta Theater; *Productions:* Auber's "Fra Diabolo" (1920); "La Bohème" (1921); Rimsky-Korsakov's *Mayskaya noch'* (May Night) (1921); Kalman's "Silva" (1917); Dunayevskiy's *Zhenikhi* (The Suitors) (1927); Strel'nikov's *Kholopka* (The Bondwoman) (1929); Frimel and Stothart's "Rosemarie" (1928); Loginov and Mityushin's *Kamrad* (1932); Bogoslovskiy's *Kak yeyo zovut* (What's-Her-Name) (1935); Dunayevskiy's *Zolotaya dolina* (Golden Valley) (1938), etc; *Died*: 20 Sept 1949.

FERSMAN, Aleksandr Yevgen'yevich (1883-1945) Mineralogist and geochemist; member, USSR Acad of Sci from 1919; pupil of V. I. Vernadskiy; *Born*: 8 Nov 1883 in Petersburg, son of a soldier; *Educ*: 1901-03 studied at Novorossiysk Univ, Odessa; 1903-07 studied at Moscow Univ; *Career*: 1907-09 worked under French mineralogist and petrographer A. Lacroix in Paris and at W. Goldschmidt's crystallographic laboratory in Heidelberg, where he coauthored the almanach "Der Diamant" (1911); during this period also visited Elba, where he began research on pegmatites; from 1909 worked at Moscow Univ; from 1910 prof, Shanyavskiy Pop Univ; 1912 began reading course on geochemistry at this univ; 1911 resigned from Moscow Univ in protest against Tsarist educ policy; from 1912 senior custodian, Mineralogical Museum, Russian Acad of Sci and prof, Petersburg Higher Women's Courses; from 1912 also co-founder and ed, pop-sci journal *Priroda*; during WW 1 worked for Raw Materials Commission, Mil Tech Aid Comt, and for Commission for the Study of Natural Resources, Acad of Sci; did field research in Urals, Altay, Transbaykal, Northern Mongolia and Crimea; 1920 began large-scale survey of Khibiny tundra, leading in 1926 to the discovery of a large apatite deposit and in 1929 to the ind exploitation of the resources of the Kola Peninsula; also did research at the Tyuya-Muyunsk radium deposit in Fergana, the sulphur deposits in Karakumy, on Cheleken Island, at the emerald mines in the Urals, at the tungsten deposits in the Transbaykal, etc; also made field trips to Sweden, Norway, Denmark, Italy, Germany, Czechoslovakia, Switzerland and Belgium; 1926-29 vice-pres, from 1934 Presidium member, USSR Acad of Sci; his most important research project was the study of pegmatites, on which he spent 25 years; 1939 published his findings in the classic monograph *Pegmatity* (Pegmatites); expert on precious stones and artificial gems, on which he wrote several pop works; died important research on natural compounds of variable composition (notably magnesium silicates and zeolites) in the upper strata of the earth's crust; together with V. I. Vernadskiy pioneered research on geochemistry, which he defined as the study of the chemical elements in the earth's crust and their behavior under different thermodynamic and physiochemical conditions; 1933-39 published his major contribution to this field in the 4-vol work *Geokhimiya* (Geochemistry); studied the frequency of elements in the Earth and published several Clark tables; 1920 and 1941 contributed to regional geochemistry with his studies of European Russia and the Kola Peninsula; attributed great importance to the theoretical principles of ore prospecting based on large-scale mineralogical and geochemical survey techniques; 1940 summarized his experience in this field in the book *Geokhimicheskiye i mineralogicheskiye metody poiskov poleznykh iskopayemykh* (Mineralogical and Geochemical Methods of Ore and Mineral Prospecting); wrote excellent pop-sci works; *Publ: Dragotsennyye i tvetnyye kamni Rossii* (The Precious and Semi-Precious Stones of Russia) (2 vol, 1920-25); *Tsveta mineralov* (The Colors of Minerals) (1936); *Vospominaniya o kamne* (Recollecting Gems) (1940); *Poleznyye iskopayemyye Kol'skogo poluostrova. Sovremenoye sostoyaniye, analiz, prognoz* (The Minerals of the Kola Peninsula. Present State, Analysis and Prognosis) (1941); *Zanimatel'naya mineralogiya* (Mineralogy as a Hobby) (1950); *Zanimatel'naya geokhimiya* (Geochemistry as a Hobby) (1950); *Izbrannyye trudy* (Selected Works) (2 vol, 1952-53); *Ocherki po istorii kamnya* (Outline History of Gems) (1954); *Kristallografiya almaza* (Diamond Crystallography) (1954), etc; *Awards*: Lenin Prize (1928); Stalin Prize (1942); Wollaston Medal of London Geological Soc (1943); Order of the Red Banner of Labor; *Died*: 20 May 1945 in Sochi; buried in Novo-Devich'ye Cemetery, Moscow.

FETISOVA, Lyudmila Mikhaylovna (1925-1962) Actress; Hon Artiste of RSFSR from 1955; *Born*: 7 Oct 1925; *Educ*: grad Shchukin Theater College; *Career*: actress, Moscow Centr Theater of the Sov Army; specialized in interpretation of her coevals and contemporaries; *Roles*: Nevvi in Gow's and D'Usso's "Deep Roots"; Katya Belyayeva in Baryanov's *Na toy storone* (On the Other Side); Vera Berezina in Vinnikov's *Step' shirokaya* (The Broad Steppe); Zhen'ka Shul'zhenko in Volodin's *Fabrichnaya devchonka* (Factory Girl); Nila Snizhko in Salynskiy's *Barabanshchitsa* (Drummer-Girl); Shura Azarova in Gladkov's *Davnym davno* (Long, Long Ago); Sandra Finchly in *Zakon Likurga* (Lycurgean Law), based on Dreiser's "An American Tragedy"; Tanya Yegorova in Sobko's *Za vtorym frontom* (Behind the Second Front); Yuliya in Chepurin's *Sovest'* (Conscience); Faustina in Balzac's "Cinola's Dreams"; Ol'ga Nikolayevna in Agranovich and Listov's *Lyotchiki* (The Flyers); Lyuka Shergina in Gladkov's *Do novykh vstrech* (Till We Meet Again); Lyubka in Danovskaya's *Lyubka-Lyubov'*; Rina in Zorin's *Uvidet' vovremya* (To See in Time); Lyolya in Shteyn's *Okean* (Ocean); *Died*: 21 Apr 1962.

FEYNBERG, Samuil Yevgen'yevich (1890-1962) Composer, pianist and music teacher; Dr of Arts from 1940; prof, Moscow State Conservatory from 1922; Hon Art Worker of RSFSR from 1937; *Born*: 26 May 1890 in Odessa; *Educ*: 1911 grad Piano Class, Moscow Conservatory; *Career*: from 1912 gave piano concerts in Russia and abroad; performed 2nd vol, Bach's "Wohltemperiertes Klavier" and all Beethoven's and Skryabin's sonatas; jury member at a number of All-Union and int piano competitions; *Works*: three concertos (1931, 1944, 1947); 12 sonatas (1915-18, 1921, 1923, 1924, 1933, 1939, 1940, 1954); two suites (1926, 1936); two fantasias (1916-17, 1924); four preludes (1926); 10 romances (1922, to texts by Pushkin; 1937, seven to texts by Lermontov); three romances to poems by A. Blok; collection *25 chuvashskikh pesen* (25 Chuvash Songs) (1935); five songs of pop of the West (1932); arranged piano pieces by Bach, Vivaldi, Borodin, Tchaikovsky, etc; *Ispolnitel' i proizvedeniye* (Performer and Musical Composition) (1960); piano pieces *Detskiy al'bom* (A Children's Album) (1963); piano pieces on folklore motives (1963) *Publ*: memoirs *Uchitel' i drug* (Teacher and Friend) (1960); *Awards*: Stalin Prize (1946); Order of Lenin (1954); two Orders of the Red Banner of Labor (1937 and 1946); medals; *Died*: 23 Oct 1962 in Moscow.

FIALKOV (Naftulovich), Yakov Anatol'yevich (1895-1958) Pharmacologist; Dr of Pharmacy from 1941; prof from 1944; corresp member, Ukr Acad of Sci from 1945; *Born:* 20 Nov 1895 in Kiev, son of an office worker; *Educ:* from 1912 pharmacist's apprentice in Kiev; 1915 passed pharmacy examin at Kiev Univ; 1925 grad Kiev Polytech Inst; *Career:* until 1920 worked at various pharmacies in Kiev; from 1925 lecturer in pharmaceutical chemistry, Kiev Pharmaceutical Inst; 1929-41 also lecturer in inorganic chemistry, Kiev Polytech Inst; 1936 obtained diploma of Cand of Chemistry and wrote manual on the analysis of pharmaceutical preparations; 1937 completed postgrad studies; 1938-44 head, Dept of Inorganic Chemistry, Kiev Polytech Inst; and Dept of Gen and Inorganic Chemistry, Ukr Acad of Sci; 1939-54 head, Chair of Pharmaceutical Chemistry, Kiev Pharmaceutical Inst; from 1944 until death prof, Chair of Inorganic Chemistry, Kiev Univ; from 1945 head, Laboratory of Complex Compounds, Inst of Gen and Inorganic Chemistry, Ukr Acad of Sci; 1954-58 taught pharmaceutical chemistry at Kiev Inst of Postgrad Pharmacy Training; member, USSR State Pharmacopoeial Comt; bd member, All-Union and All-Ukr Pharmaceutic Soc; ed, *Entsiklopedicheskiy slovar aptechnogo rabotnika* (The Pharmacy Worker's Encyclopedic Dictionary); co-ed, 8th and 9th ed, *Gosudarstvennaya farmakopeya* (State Pharmacopoeia); 1927 founded first Ukr pharmacy research and control laboratory at Kiev Pharmacy Bd; 1944-54 founder and consultant, Centr Research Laboratory, Main Pharmacy Bd, Ukr Min of Health; 1944 also founded Kiev Inst of Postgrad Pharmacy Training; 1936-41 ed, practical sci section, *Ukrainskiy farmatsevticheskiy zhurnal* devised varios new methods of analyzing medicines and other pharmaceutical preparations; wrote over 220 works, mainly on such complex compounds as interhalogen compounds, aluminum halogenides, phosphoric halogenides, antimonic halogenides, compounds of iodine with organic substances, various rare and non-ferrous metals, nitrogen fertilizers, medicinal plants, etc; *Publ: Dikorastushchiye lekarstvennyye rasteniya Bashkirii* (Wild Medicinal Plants of Bashkiria) (1942); *Primeneniye lekarstvennykh rasteniy Bashkirskoy ASSR* (The Use of Medicinal Plants of the Bashkir ASSR) (1944); *Dikorastushchiyh lekarstvennyye rasteniya USSR* (The Wild Medicinal Plants of the Ukrainian SSR) (1946); *Lekarstvennyye rasteniya i ikh primeneniye. Rukovodstvo dlya aptechnykh rabotnikov* (Medicinal Plants and Their Use. A Manual for Pharmacy Workers) (1947); *Doslidzhennya v galuzi kompleksnykh spoluk galogenidiv alyuminiyu ta poligelogenidiv* (Research on Complex Compounds of Aluminum Halogenides and Polyhalogenides) (1947); *Zatrudnitel'nyye, neratsional'nyye i nesovmestimyye propisi. Farmatsevticheskiy spravochnik* (Complex, Irrational and Incompatible Prescriptions. A Pharmaceutical Reference Book) (1949); *Issledovaniya v oblasti kompleksnykh soyedineniy yoda i galogenidov yoda* (Research on Complex Compounds of Iodine and Iodine Halogenides) (1952); *Mezhgaloidnyye soyedineniya* (Interhalogen Compounds) (1958); *Rukovodstvo po analizu farmatsevticheskikh preparatov* (Manual on the Analysis of Pharmaceutical Preparations) (1935, 1938, 1946); *Awards:* two Mendeleyev Prizes (1951, 1953); *Died:* 16 Nov 1958.

FIGATNER, Yuriy Petrovich (1889-?) Party official; CP member from 1903; *Born:* 1889; *Career*: metal worker by trade; worked in Odessa, Warsaw, Moscow; repeatedly arrested; late 1906-early 1909 emigré in Belgium and France; 1909 secr, Moscow Party Comt; late 1911 sentenced to seven yearts at hard labor; 1917-22 Party, govt and trade-union work in Northern Caucasus and Transcaucasian region; member, Transcaucasian Kray Comt; secr, Caucasian Bureau, CC, RCP(B); chm, Caucasian Bureau, All-Union Centr Trade-Union Council; from 1922 chm, Siberian Bureau, All-Union Centr Trade-Union Council; member, Siberian Bureau, CC, CPSU(B); member, Siberian Revol Comt; 1924-30 Presidium member, All-Union Centr Trade-Union Council; 1925-29 chm, CC, Sov Trade Employees' Union; from 1929 Presidium member, USSR Supr Sovnarkhoz, and head, Main Inspectorate; from 14th Party Congress member, CPSU(B) Centr Control Commission; member; USSR and All-Russian Centr Exec Comt; *Died:* date and place of death unknown.

FIGNER (nee: MEY), Medeya Ivanovna (1859-1952) Italian opera singer (dramatic soprano); *Born:* 4 Apr 1859; *Educ:* studied singing under Bianca, G. Panofki, K. Zucchi; *Career:* very successfully performed in Italy, Spain, South America at first as mezzo-soprano, then as dramatic soprano; in Italy met the Russian singer N. N. Figner and became his regular partner; 1887 came to Russia; 1889 married N. N. Figner; 1887-1912 soloist, Petersburg Mariinskiy Theater; until 1923 stage work, then instructor; 1930 left Russia; possessed great acting talent and a voice of rare beauty and compass; under Tchaikovsky's guidance prepared and was the first to perform the roles of Liza in *Pikovaya dama* (The Queen of Spades) and the title role in "Iolanthe"; *Roles:* Desdemona in Verdi's "Othello"; Margarethe in "Faust"; Carmen; Brunhilde in Wagner's "Walküre"; Valentina in "The Huguenots"; Mimi; Tat'yana; Natasha in Tchaikovsky's "Oprichnik", etc; *Publ: Moi vospominaniya* (My Memoirs) (1912); *Died*: 8 July 1952 in Paris.

FIGNER (FILIPPOVA), Vera Nikolayevna (1852-1942) Populist revol; *Born:* 7 July 1852 in vil Khristoforovka Kazan' Province, daughter of a nobleman; *Educ*: 1869 grad Kazan' Inst for Daughters of the Nobility; 1872-75 studied at Med Fac, Zurich and Bern Univ; *Career*: together with Russian students B. Kaminskaya, S. Bardicha and the Lyubatovich sisters, etc, studied polit econ, history of socialistic teaching and revol movements in Europe preparing herself for revol propaganda work in Russia; 1876 joined "Separatist" circle, attached to "Northern Revolutionary-Populist Group" (from 1878 *Zemlya i volya* (Land and Liberty)), whose basic aim was to conduct revol propaganda in rural areas; 1877-79 asst physician in Samara and Saratov Province; together with her sister Yevgeniya conducted educ work among peasants; 1879 attended Voronezh congress of *Zemlya i volya*; 1879, after the schism in *Zemlya i volya* org together with S. Perovskaya, A. Zhelyabov, M. Frolenko, etc, joined Exec Comt, *Narodnaya volya* (People's Will) org, which aimed at assassinating Tsar; 1880 helped prepare the attempt on the life of Alexander II near Odessa; conducted revol propaganda in Southern Russia and in Petersburg among officers who had joined the mil org of *Narodnaya volya*; Jan 1881, together with G. P. Isayev, arranged Petersburg premises to plan the assassination of Alexander II; after the assassination (1 Mar 1881) helped plan the assassination of mil prosecutor Stel'nikov in Odessa; early 1882 moved to Khar'kov, continued revol work there; tried to restore *Narodnaya volya*, which had disintegrated after a series of failures; Feb 1883 arrested; Sept 1884 sentenced to death by Petersburg Mil Distr Court; sentence commuted to penal servitude for life; for 20 years imprisoned in Shlissel'burg Fortress; from 1904 in exile in Arkhangel'sk and Kazan' Provinces and in Nizhniy Novgorod; 1906-15 abroad; collected funds to help prisoners and convicts; attended Socialist-Revol trial of the agent-provocateur Azef; 1915 returned to Russia; after 1917 Oct Revol lit work; *Publ: Polnoye sobraniye sochineniy* (Complete Works) (7 vol, 2nd ed, 1932); *Died:* 15 June 1942.

FIGURNOV, Konstantin Mikhaylovich (1887-1961) Obstetrician and gynecologist; Dr of Med from 1923; prof from 1931; corresp member, USSR Acad of Med Sci from 1946; maj-gen, Army Med Corps; *Born*: 9 June 1887; *Educ*: 1905 grad Voronezh high school; 1912 grad Mil Med Acad; *Career:* after grad intern under Prof D. D. Popov, Chair of Obstetrics and Gynecology, Mil Med Acad; during WW 1 mil surgeon; 1918 resumed former post at Mil Med Acad; from 1919 senior physician, Red Army rifle regt; from 1920 asst chief physician, Clinical Mil Hospital and acting asst prof, Clinic of Obstetrics and Gynecology, Mil Med Acad; from 1921 asst prof, Chair of Obstetrics and Gynecology, Mil Med Acad; 1923 defended doctor's thesis on "The Anatomical Foundations for an Effective Operation to Cure Enuresis in Women"; from 1931 prof, then head until death, Chair of Obstetrics and Gynecology, Mil Med Acad; 1952-61 also sci dir, Leningrad Inst of Obstetrics and Gynecology, USSR Acad of Med Sci; devised two operations for the cure of enuresis in women resulting from childbirth trauma; did research on the duration of pregnancy; studied cyclic changes in the endometrium, perforation of the uterus in abortions, the operative treatment of cancer of the womb by the extended abdominal method, ect; took special interest in the soc aspects of gynecology, notably in his book *Trud i beremennost'* (Work and Pregnancy); chm, Problems Commission for Planning Research at Chairs of Obstetrics and Gynecology at Sov Higher Med Training Establishments, USSR Acad of Med Sci; chm, Leningrad Sci Soc of Obstetricians and Gynecologists; member, *Znaniye* (Knowledge) Soc; member, ed collegium, journal *Akusherstvo i ginekologiya*; co-ed, obstetrics and gynecology section, *Bol'shaya meditsinskaya entsiklopediya* (Large Medical Encyclopedia) (2nd ed); founder-chm, Samarkand Sci Soc of Obstetricians and Gynecologists; wrote over 70 works; *Publ:* coauthor, *Opredeleniye sroka beremennosti vo vtoroy yeyo polovine* (Determining the Duration of Pregnancy in its Second Half) (1929); coauthor, *Opredaleniye sroka beremennosti i dorodovogo otpuska* (Determining the Duration of Pregnancy and the Length of Maternity Leave) (1931); *Khirurgicheskoye lecheniye nederzhaniya mochi u zhenshchin* (The Surgical Treatment of Enuresis in Women) (1948); *Obezbolivaniye rodov* (Painless Childbirth) (1953); ed, *Voprosy neyrogumoral'noy regulyatsii fiziologicheskikh i patologicheskikh protsessov zhenskoy polovoy sfery* (The Neurohumeral Regulation of Physiological and Pathological Processes in the Sexual Life of Women) (1956); *Istoriya razvitiya akushersko-ginekologicheskoy pomoshchi v Rossii i SSSR* (The History of the Development of the Obstetric and Gynecological Service in Russia and the USSR) (1961); *Termicheskiye ozhogi kozhi u zhenshchin v techeniye menstrual'nogo tsikla i beremennosti pri nikh* (Thermic Skin Burns in Women During the Menstrual Cycle and Pregnancies in the Presence of Such Burns) (1961); *Awards*: Order of Lenin, two Orders of the Red Banner; Order of the Red Banner of Labor; four medals; *Died*: 1 Oct 1961.

FIGURNOV, Pyotr Konstantinovich (1901-1963) Econ; prof from 1938; Dr of Econ from 1962; CP member from 1917; *Born*: 29 Jan 1901; *Educ*: 1925 grad Lenin Mil Eng Acad; 1932 grad Econ Inst of Red Prof; *Career*: 1915 began work as turner at Sormovo Plant; 1917 joined Red Guards; participated in 1917 Feb and Oct Revol; 1918-22 fought in the Civil War; from 1925 teaching and research work; during WW 2 in Sov Army; after the war at: State Inst of Econ; Inst of Econ, USSR Acad of Sci; Acad of For Trade; from 1954 at Acad of Soc Sci, CC, CPSU; *Died*: 6 May 1963.

FILATOV, Nikolay Alekseyevich (1891-?) Party and govt official; CP member from 1912; *Born*: 1891 in vil Pushkino, Moscow Oblast, son of a weaver; *Educ*: 1922-23 attended Marxism courses, Communist Acad; *Career*: tailor by trade; 1911 in Moscow joined in strike at the tailor's workshop where he was working; 1912 helped found a Soc-Democratic Bolshevik circle, through which he joined the RSDRP(B); Apr 1912 took part in major tailor assistants' protest demonstration in Moscow; helped found Moscow Tailors' Union and a number of other trade unions (woodworkers', tanners', plumbers', etc); repeatedly arrested, sentenced and exiled from Moscow; Mar 1917 served with Kostroma Reserve Infantry Regt and elected member, Sov of Soldiers' Dep after 1917 Oct Revol mil comr, Kostroma Province; helped crush Yaroslavl' Mutiny and revolts in Vetluga and Varnavino Uyezds; 1919 on orders of CC, CPSU(B) sent to 14th Army, Southwestern Front, and formed a separate infantry brigade; as comr of this brigade, fought against Denikin until late 1919; 1920-21 mil comr, Chernigov Province; from 1921 govt work: chm, Chernigov, then Penza Province Exec Comt; late 1923-34 Party work: secr, Novo-Nikolayevsk Province CPSU(B) Comt; secr, Omsk Okrug CPSU(B) Comt; instructor, CC, CPSU(B); secr, Astrakhan' Okrug CPSU(B) Comt; secr, Moscow Lenin (former Zamoskvorech'ye) Rayon CPSU(B) Comt; chm Moscow City Control Commission, Workers and Peasants' Inspectorate; from Feb 1934 chm, Moscow Oblast Exec Comt; member, USSR Centr Exec Comt and RSFSR All-Russian Exec Comt of several convocations; Presidium member, All-Union Centr Exec Comt; at the 17th CPSU(B) Congress elected cand member, CC, CPSU(B); arrested by State Security organs; *Awards*: Order of Lenin; *Died*: in imprisonment; date and place of death unknown.

FILATOV, Nikolay Mikhaylovich (1862-1935) Mil commander; maj-gen, Russian Army from 1915; co-founder, sci theory of small-arms ballistics in Russia; Hero of Labor from 1928; *Born:* 11 Oct 1862; *Educ:* 1887 grad Mikhail Artillery Acad; *Career:* 1887-92 taught artillery and ballistics at Moscow Infantry School; 1892-96 worked in Infantry Officers School; 1896-1905 member, Artillery Comt; 1905-15 founder-commander, Rifle Range; 1915-17 mil school commandant; from 1892 simultaneously tested automatic infantry weapons, studied automatic weapons in various European countries, formed the first machine- and sub-machine-gun detachments in the Russian Army (in WW 1 - reserve machine-gun regts); supported early Russian inventors and designers of automatic weapons: V. G. Fyodorov, F. V. Tokarev, Ya. U. Roshchepey, V. A. Degtyaryov, I. N. Kolesnikov, etc; after 1917 Oct Revol helped train first Sov infantry commanders; Nov 1918 organized *Vystrel* Infantry School; until late 1922 commandant of this school; from late 1922 worked for Infantry Inspection; chm, Red Army Infantry Comt; *Publ: Zapiski po teorii strel'by* (Notes on Ballistics Theory) (1895); *Died:* 24 Feb 1935.

FILATOV, Vladimir Petrovich (1875-1956) Ophthamologist; Dr of Med from 1908; prof from 1911; member, Ukr Acad of Sci from 1939; member, USSR Acad of Med Sci from 1944; Hon Sci Worker of Ukr SSR from 1935; Hero of Socialist Labor from 1950; prof and head, Chair and Clinic of Eye Diseases, Odessa Med Inst; *Born:* 27 Feb 1875 in vil Mikhaylovka, Penza Province; son of a zemstvo oculist; *Educ:* 1892 grad Simbirsk high school; 1897 grad Med Fac, Moscow Univ; *Career:* after grad intern, A. A. Kryukov's Eye Disease Clinic; 1899-1903 intern, Moscow Eye Hospital, then intern and from 1906 asst prof, Eye Disease Clinic, Novorossiysk Univ, Odessa; 1908 defended doctor's thesis; 1909-11 assoc prof, from 1911 until death prof and head, Chair and Clinic of Eye Diseases, Novorossiysk Univ; founded school of ophthalmology from which numerous clinical specialists emerged; from 1931 founder-dir, first Sov glaucoma center at Eye Clinic, Odessa Med Inst; from 1936 also founder-dir, Ukr Inst of Eye Diseases, Odessa (now Filatov Experimental Research Inst of Eye Diseases and Tissue Therapy); 1941, after German invasion, evacuated to Pyatigorsk, where he worked as consultant and sci dir, Evacuation Hospital No. 2172; then moved to Tashkent, where he resurrected the Ukr Inst of Eye Diseases at the Main Evacuation Hospital; Sept 1944 returned to Odessa and resumed former posts; from 1911 chm, Odessa Ophthalmological Soc; 1936-56 dep, Odessa City Sov; from 1939 dep, Ukr Supr Sov of 1st, 2nd and 3rd convocations; founder-ed, *Oftal'mologicheskiy zhurnal*; member, ed collegium, journal *Vestnik oftal'mologii*; made major contributions to plastic surgery and ophthalmology; pioneered restorative and plastic surgery of the nose, lips, esophagus, urinary tract, skin, etc with his "progressive flap" operation and "Filatov's circular stem" operation; 1924 devised new corneal transplant method; devised method of transplanting corneas from corpses; designed numerous ophthalmological instruments; discovered "biogenic stimulators" which elicit the organism's vital reactions; 1933 devised "tissue therapy" which proved successful in the treatment of eye and other diseases (atrophy of the optic nerve, lupus, Oriental sores, etc); devised major method of treating macula corneae with secretion from the salivary gland and an operation for transferring the parotid duct to behind the lower palpebra; his method of "elastotonometry" proved to be one of the best means of early diagnosis of glaucoma; made many new contributions to clinical research on eye diseases, indluding new methods of diagnosing and treating trachoma, glaucoma, trauma, etc; performed over 1,000 corneal grafts; hon member, numerous acad and sci soc; 1955 his 80th birthday was marked by the whole Sov med profession; wrote over 430 works; *Publ:* doctor's thesis *Ucheniye o kletochnykh yadakh v oftal' mologii* (The Theory of Cell Poisons in Ophtalmology) (1908); *Plastika na kruglom steble* (Plastic Surgery with a Circular Stem) (1917); *O plastike na kruglom stranstvuyushchem steble* (Plastic Surgery with a Moving Circular Stem) (1923); *Opticheskaya peresadka rogovitsy i tkanevaya terapiya* (Corneal Transplants and Tissue Therapy) (1945); *Tkanevaya terapiya. Lecheniye biogennymi stimulyatorami* (Tissue Therapy. Treatment With Biogenic Stimulators) (1948); *Moi puti v nauke* (My Career in Science) (1955); *Operatsii na rogovoy obolochke i sklere* (Operations on the Cornea and Sclera) (1960); *Izbrannyye trudy* (Selected Works) (4 vol, 1961); *Awards:* four Orders of Lenin; Order of the Red Banner of Labor; Order of the Great Fatherland War, 1st Class; Stalin Prize (1941); Mechnikov Gold Medal of USSR Acad of Sci (1951); medals; *Died:* 30 Oct 1956 in Odessa; buried in Odessa.

FILIPCHENKO, Yuriy Aleksandrovich (1882-1930) Geneticist; prof from 1918; *Born:* 1882; *Educ:* 1906 grad Petersburg Univ; *Career:* after grad asst to Prof Shevyakov, Chair of Invertebrate Zoology, Petersburg Univ; 1916-17 wrote doctor's thesis on "The Variability and Hereditary Characteristics of the Cranium in Mammals", which served as a basis for his further research in this field; 1919 founded first Sov chair of genetics at Leningrad Univ; 1920 founded Laboratory of Genetics and Experimental Zoology, Peterhof Natural Sci (now Biological) Inst; 1924 gave up research on variablity to study quantitative genetic features; 1921 founded Eugenics Bureau (later renamed Laboratory of Genetics and now Inst of Genetics), USSR Acad of Sci, where he evaluated questionnaires on heredity filled out by scientists, artists, etc; toward end of life study the genetics of wheat; also acquired fame as a teacher and popularizer; after death his views were criticized as "errors typical of bourgeois genetics"; condemned for his defense of the theory of autogenesis and the dualist theory of heredity according to which the chromosomes determine only intraspecific racial characteristics while the basic organisatory features are determined by extranuclear elements; many of his works on eugenics contain ideas to be found in Western genetics; wrote over 100 works; *Publ:* doctor's thesis *Izmenchivost' i nasledstvennost' cherepaumlekopitayushchikh* (The Mutability and Hereditary Characteristics of the Cranium in Mammals) (1916-17); *Nasledstvennost'* (Heredity) (1917); *Evolyutsionnaya ideya v biologii* (The Idea of Evolution in Biology) (1923); *Izmenchivost' i yeyo znacheniye dlya evolyutsii* (Mutability and Its Significance for Evolution) (1924); *Obshchedostupnaya biologiya* (Biology for Everyman) (1925); *Frensis Gal'ton i Gregor Mendel'* (Francis Galton and Gregor Mendel) (1925); *Chastnaya genetika* (Specialized Genetics) (2 vol, 1927-28); "Variabilität und Variation" (Variability and Variation) (1927); *Genetika* (Genetics) (1929); *Izmenchivost' i metody yeyo izucheniya* (Mutability and Methods of Studying it) (1929); *Eksperimental'naya zoologiya* (Experimental Zoology) (1932); *Genetika myagkikh pshenits* (The Genetics of Soft Wheat) (1934); *Died:* 1930

FILIPPOV, Vladimir Aleksandrovich (1889-1965) Russian theater historian, critic and teacher; prof from 1930; Hon Art Worker of RSFSR from 1956; *Born*: 18 June 1889; *Educ*: 1912 grad Moscow Univ; *Career*: 1909 began theater and public work as actor and reader; helped found and direct first Sov children's theater; 1920-29 chm, Theater Sections, Pop Comrt of Educ, Moscow Sov and State Acad of Arts; 1921-24 head, Theater Bd, Moscow Sov; 1926-30 dir, State Pedag Theater; 1933-37 dir, Maly Theater Museum; 1934-47 head, Ostrovskiy Section, All-Russian Theater Soc; 1933-65 learned consultant, State Centr Theater Museum; wrote monographs and essays on classics of Russian and world dramaturgy and on leading Russian and Sov actors of Maly Theater; edited and annotated numerous Sov ed, among them various collections of Ostrovskiy's and Griboyedov's works; reviewed numerous theater exhibitions; 1913-65 simultaneously taught at: Moscow Philharmonic Soc College; Shchepkin Theater College; Nemirovich-Danchenko Studio; State Inst of Theater

History, etc; consultant for a number of stage productions in Moscow and country theater; *Publ: Mol'yer v Rossii 18-go veka* (Molière in 18th-Century Russia) (1915); *Besedy o teatre. Opyt vvedeniya v teatrovedeniye* (Talks on the Theater. An Introduction to Theater History) (1924); coauthor, *Moskovskiy Malyy Teatr* (The Moscow Maly Theater) (1924); *Puti samodeyatel'nogo teatra* (Development of the Amateur Theater) (1927); *Zhenit'ba' Gogolya i rezhissyorskiy kommentariy k ney* (Gogol's "Wedding" with Director's Comments) (1930); *Moskovskiy Malyy teatr i yego znacheniye* (The Moscow Maly Theater and Its Significance) (1935); *A. P. Lenskiy. Stat'yi. Pis'ma. Zapiski* (A. P. Lenskiy. Articles. Letters. Notes) (1935); *M. S. Shchepkin i yego rol' v istorii russkogo teatra* (M. S. Shchepkin and His Role in the History of the Russian Theater) (1938); *Aktyor Yuzhin* (Yuzhin, the Actor) (1941); *A. I. Yuzhin-Sumbatov. Zapisi. Stat'i. Pis'ma* (A. I. Yuzhin-Sumbatov. Notes. Articles. Letters) (1943); *A. A. Ostrovskiy* (1945), etc; *Died*: 20 May 1965.

FILIPPOVICH, Artemiy Nikitich (1901-1961) Infectionist; Dr of Med from 1950; prof; corresp member, USSR Acad of Med Sci from 1960; *Born*: 1901 in vil Yevlichi, Bel; *Educ*: 1917 grad school for med orderlies; 1926 grad Leningrad Med Inst; *Career*: 1917-21 med orderly in Yevlichi; 1926-39 country dr in Bel, then clinic intern and asst prof, Minsk Med Inst; 1939-50 head, Chair of Infectious Diseases, Izhevsk Med Inst; 1951-61 head, Chair of Infectious Diseases, Minsk Med Inst; member, ed council, journal *Zdravookhraneniye Belorussii;* described clinical aspects of recurrent typhus; studied bile-pigment metabolism and its dynamics in typhus, scarlet fever, measles, malaria, leptospirosis and serum disease; established efficacy of *osarsol* (a Sov preparation against whipworm) in the treatment of tertian malaria; described the five phases of septic sore throat and proved that the hematogenic function is rapidly restored during the period of convalescence; proved that the continuous method is better than the cyclic when treating typhus with syntomycin; detected the presence of Q-fever in Bel and described its course; used combination of antibiotics, sulphonamides and dysentery vaccine to treat chronic dysentery; was one of first group of Sov sci to detect and describe serous meningitis and its transmission by ticks in Udmurtiya; described the epidemiology and clinical aspects of brucellosis in Udmurtia, Bel SSR and Vologda Oblast, establishing that this disease is not transmitted from cattle to sheep, goats and hogs and that it is an independent nosological unit in humans; wrote over 60 works on the clinical aspects and epidemiology of infectious diseases; *Publ*: coauthor *Osobennosti klinicheskogo techeniya sypnogo tifa za posledniye gody* (Peculiarities of the Clinical Course of Typhus in Recent Years) (1955); *K voprosu o klinicheskom techenii ostrykh sezonnykh virusnykh neyroinfektsiy* (The Clinical Course of Acute Seasonal Viral Nerve Infections) (1956); *K kharakteristike klinicheskogo techeniya sporadicheskikh sluchayev vodnoy likhoradki* (The Characteristics of the Clinical Course of Sporadic Cases of Water Fever) (1957); *K voprosu kliniki Ku-likhoradki v Belorussii* (The Clinical Aspects of Q-Fever in Belorussia) (1957); *Epidemiologiya i klinika Bangovskoy infektsii (brutsellyoz) u cheloveka* (The Epidemiology and Clinical Aspects of Bangov's Infection [Brucellosis] in Humans) (1957); coauthor, *O leptospiroze tipa bataviya v BSSR* (Batavian Leptospirosis in the Belorussian SSR) (1958); *Awards*: Order of the Red Banner of Labor (1961), etc; *Died*: 1961.

FILYANSKIY, Konstantin Dmitriyevich (1903–1950) Zootechnician; CP member from 1943; *Born*: 1903; *Educ*: 1931 grad Moscow Zootech Inst; *Career*: 1931-38 senior zootechnician, *Bolshevik* Sheep-Breeding Sovkhoz, Stavropol' Kray; from 1938 chief zootechnician, Main Admin of Sheep-Breeding Sovkhozes, USSR Pop Comrt of Sovkhozes; bred new high-yield Caucasian fine-fleeced sheep; *Publ: Povysheniye produktivnosti zhivotnovodstva* (Increasing the Productivity of Animal Husbandry) (1949); *Organizatsiya i tekhnika tonkorunnogo ovtsevodstva* (The Organization and Techniques of Breeding Fine-Fleeced Sheep) (1949); *Zametki ovtsevoda. O metodakh otsenki i ispol'zovaniya baranov-proizvoditel'ey i o lineynom razvedenii v tonkorunnom ovtsevodstve* (Notes of a Sheep-Breeder. Methods of Evaluating and Using Stud-Rams and the Linear Breeding of Fine-Fleeced Sheep) (1948); *Awards*: Stalin Prize (1946); three orders; medals; *Died*: 27 Aug 1950.

FININBERG, Ezra Iosifovich (1899-1946) Jewish poet; *Born*: 1899 in Uman', Ukr; *Educ*: studied at Kiev Pop Univ; *Career*: 1920 first work printed; 1941 volunteered for the home guard; seriously wounded in battle near Moscow; translated into Yiddish Goethe's "Faust" (1937), works of Pushkin, Lermontov, Nekrasov, Mayakovskiy, Gorky, Fadeyev, Ukr classics and Sov writers; *Publ*: verse collections in Yiddish: "Breathing" (1922); "Verse" (1925); "Country and Love" (1928); "Lenin's Arrival in Moscow" (1928); "The Haystack" (1929); "At the Beginning of the Year" (1929); "The Battle Continues" (1930); "15 Years" (1933); "The Other Land" (1934); "With a Song on the Lips" (1936); poem "Osher Shvartsman" (1938); books "From the Battlefield" (1943); "In the Big Fire" (1946); "Against Death" (1944); a collection of selected works was published in 1948; *Died*: 1946.

FINN-YENOTAYEVSKIY, Aleksandr Yul'yevich (1872-1943) Econ; writer; member, Soc-Democratic Party from early 1890's; 1903-14 sided with the Bolsheviks; 1928-30 member, Russian Soc-Democratic Menshevik Party; *Born*: 1872; *Educ*: univ grad; *Career*: 1906 worked on commission to draft agrarian program of 4th (Amalgamative) RSDRP Congress; compiled one of the four drafts of agrarian program, presented to the Stockholm Congress (rejecting nationalization, demanding requisition of large estates and their partition as private property among the peasants); during WW 1 ardent defensist and chauvinist; after 1917 Oct Revol worked for Menshevik newspaper *Novaya zhizn*; assoc prof, then prof, Petrograd State Univ; wrote a number of works on econ problems; 1931 sentenced in trial of RSDRP (Mensheviks) Union Bureau counterrevol org; *Died*: 1943 in imprisonment.

FIOLETOV, Ivan Timofeyevich (Party pseudonym: "Vanechka") (1884-1918) Professional revol; Party and govt official from 1903; CP member from 1906; *Born*: 1884 in vil Tugulukov, Tambov Province, son of a peasant; *Educ*: elementary school; *Career*: at age of 11 started work as metalworker's apprentice, Nobel mech workshops in Baku; July 1903 participated in strike at Balakhan oilfields; repeatedly arrested and imprisoned; during the Dec 1904 Baku strike, member of strike comt; later worked in Groznyy and Vladikavkaz; early 1905 returned to Baku; elected bd member, Oil Workers' Union; repeatedly elected member, Baku Bolshevik Comt; 1908 exiled for three years to Sol'vychegodsk, Vologda Province, then to Yarensk; after serving his term returned to Baku, continued Party work, but because of police persecution was forced to move to Tashkent and later to Cheleken Island; 1914 returned to Baku; one of the leaders, Baku gen strike; after 1917 Feb Revol member, Exec Comt, Baku Sov; May 1917 elected chm, Baku Oil Workers' Union; Sept 1917, together with P. A. Dzhaparidze, leader, Baku workers' strike; from Apr 1918 Sovnarkhoz chm, Baku Council of Pop Comr; Aug 1918, arrested after the collapse of Sov regime in Baku; *Died*: 19 Sept 1918 executed together with 25 other Baku comr.

FIRSOV, Georgiy Petrovich (1892-1961) Educationist and philologist; Dr of Pedag; corresp member, RSFSR Acad of Pedag Sci from 1957; Hon Schoolteacher of RSFSR from 1956; *Born*: 20 Sept 1892; *Educ*: 1915 grad Fac of History and Philology, Kiev Univ; *Career*: 1916-17 taught at Poltava high school, 1917-20 taught Russian at high schools in Novocherkassk; 1923-34 at schools in Samarkand; 1930-34 at Uzbek Communist Univ; 1934-61 taught at schools in Moscow; 1939-41 taught at Moscow Municipal Postgrad Teachers' Training Inst; 1945-61 taught at Inst of Teaching Methods, RSFSR Acad of Pedag Sci; 1954-57 taught at Moscow Univ; specialized in elocution, phonetics, syntax and punctuation; his major work, *Znacheniye raboty nad intonatsiey dlya usvoyeniya sintaksisa i punktuatsii* (The Importance of Classwork on Intonation for the Learning of Syntax and Punctuation), demonstrated the role of the study of the phonetic aspects of the Russian language (notably intonation) in the learning of punctuation; studied the problem of relating the study of phonetics to the acquisition of orthoepic and orthographic skills in teaching practice, as well as the problem of relating the study of syntax to the development of elocutionary and punctuational skills; demonstrated the feasibility of teaching orthoepy as early as the 5th grade; his works are of interest to both teachers and linguists specializing in the syntactic structure of modern Russian; *Publ: Kak ya obuchayu pravil'nomu literaturnomu proiznosheniyu na urokakh fonetike* (How I Teach Correct Pronunciation in Phonetics Lessons) (1947); *Rabota nad pravil'nym proiznosheniyem i vyrazitel'nym chteniyem na urokakh grammatiki* (Classwork on Correct Pronunciation and Elocution During Grammar Lessons) (1949); *Obosoblennyye vtorostepennyye chleny predlozheniya* (Detached and Secondary Clauses and Phrases) (1955); *Izucheniye fonetiki v 5-om klasse* (The Study of Phonetics in the 5th Class) (1957); coauthor, *Sbornik statey dlya izlozheniya v 5-om po 7-oy klass* (A Collection of Articles for Analysis in the 5th-7th Classes) (1958); coauthor, *Sbornik diktantov po orfografii i punktuatsii* (A Collection of Dictations on Orthography and Punctuation) (1958); *Nablyudeniya nad zvukovoy i intonatsionnoy storonoy rechi na urokakh russkogo yazyka* (Observations on the Phonetic and Intonational Aspects of Speech During Russian Language Lessons) (1959); *Vyrazitel'noye chteniye na urokakh russkogo yazyka* (Elecution During Russian Language Lessons) (1960); *Znacheniye raboty nad intonatsiyey dlya usvoyeniya sintaksisa i punktuatsii v shkole* (The Importance of Classwork on Intonation for the Learning of Syntax and Punctuation at School) (1962); *Died*: 18 Aug 1961.

FISHER, Genrikh Matveyevich (1871-1935) Revolutionary; founder-member, Russian Soc-Democratic Workers Party; govt official; CP member from 1921; *Born*: 1871; *Career*: metalworker; from early 1890's active in Petersburg workers' circles; personal acquaintance of Lenin; directed workers' propaganda circles; 1894 arrested and interrogated in investigation of a *Narodnaya volya* (People's Will) group; for three years kept under overt police surveillance in Arkhangel'sk Province; afterwards moved to Saratov; joined Saratov "Workers' Comt," consisting of exiled workers; 1900 helped publish mimeographed newspaper *Rabochaya gazeta*; 1891 went abroad and lived for a long time in England, where participated in workers' movement; helped organize depot of arms to be sent to Russia; joined newly-founded British Communist Party; 1921 returned to RSFSR and joined CPSU(B); held various admin posts; *Publ: V Rossii i v Anglii. (Nablyudeniya i vospominaniya peterburgskogo rabochego, 1890-1921)* (In Russia and England. Observations and Memoirs of a Petersburg Worker, 1890-1921) (1922); *Died*: 1935.

FISHMAN, Yakov Moiseyevich (1887-1961) Mil commander; Jew; corps eng from 1935; maj-gen of eng troops from 1956; chemical warfare specialist; *Born*: 1887; *Career*: fought in Civil War as dep chm, Comt Against Counter-revolution, Sabotage and Pogroms (1917) and Bureau member, Comt for Revol Defense of Petrograd (1918); after Civil War head, Red Army Chemical Warfare Bd; 1934-37 simultaneously member, Mil Council, USSR Pop Comrt of Defense; 1937 arrested by NKVD organs; 1956 released from imprisonment and rehabilitated; *Publ: Khimicheskoye oruzhiye* (Chemical Weapons) (1924); *Gazovaya voyna* (Gas Warfare) (1924); *Voyenno-khimicheskoye delo v sovremyonnoy voyne* (Chemical Weapons in Modern Warfare) (1930); *Khimicheskaya oborona i zadachi Osoaviakhima* (Chemical Defense and the Aims of the Society for the Promotion of Defense, Aviation and Chemical Industry Construction) (1931); *Died*: 1961.

FITRAT (real name: RASHIDOV, Abdurauf) (1886-1938) Uzbek writer, playwright and lit historian; *Born*: 1886; *Educ*: studied at Bukhara medressah; 1911 grad Lit Fac, Istanbul Univ; *Career*: 1909 began lit work; 1921-23 Vizier of Educ, Nat Econ, etc, Bukhara Pop Republ; 1928 prof; taught Uzbek and gen lit at Uzbek higher educ institutions; arrested by State Security organs; *Publ:* plays "Dispute Between a French Scientist and a Bukhara Sage" (1911); "Blood" (1915); "Bekzhon" (1916); "Tamerlane's Tomb" (1919); "Oguzkhan" (1919); "Indian Revolutionaries"; "True Love" (1920); "Abulfaizkhan"; "Abomuslim"; "Satan's Revolt Against God"; "Arslan" (1926); works on lit (in Uzbek): "Theory of Literature" (1925); "Uzbek Classical Music and Its History" (1927); "Samples of Uzbek Classical Literature" (vol 1, 1928); "Research on Ancient Turkic Literature" (1930), etc; *Died*: 1938 in imprisonment; posthumously rehabilitated.

FLAVIAN (secular name: IVANOV, Vladimir Leonidovich) (1889-1958) Archbishop of Rostov and Kamenets, Russian Orthodox Church; *Born*: 1889; *Educ*: grad Stavropol' Theological Seminary; studied at Kazan' Theological Acad for three years; *Career*: 1913 ordained priest; archpriest, Kuban' Eparchy; was at one time an adherent of Church reform but then recanted and was admitted to Moscow Patriarchy; 1945 took monastic vows, adopted name of Flavian; appointed Bishop of Krasnodar, in which capacity he toured the vils of the eparchy; from 1949 Bishop of Oryol and Bryansk; 1950 met Chinese church deleg at Sino-Sov border on behalf of Moscow Patriarchy; from 1955 archbishop; 1956-58 Archbishop of Rostov and Kamenets; *Died*: 7 Oct 1958.

FLORIN, Viktor Anatol'yevich (1899-1960) Hydraulic eng; specialist in ground water and foundations; corresp member, USSR Acad of Sci from 1953; *Born*: 6 Dec 1899; *Educ*: 1922 grad Petrograd Inst of Communications Eng; *Career*: after grad helped to design and build hydroelectr and thermal power plants (Volkhov, Svir', etc); 1930-43 lecturer, from 1943 prof, Leningrad Polytech Inst; 1942-48 worked at All-Union Hydraulic Eng Research Inst; from 1950 worked at Inst of Mech, USSR Acad of Sci; 1936 published method of calculating girder plates of fixed and variable rigidity installed in a linearly deformable foundation; devised theory of sealing and filtering groundwater under various conditions; did research on the sinkage of hydraulic structures, the strength of foundations, the front anchorage of dam spillways, sluices, etc; during construction of Narva Hydroelectric Power Plant devised technique of installing temporary working joints in hydraulic structures to reduce internal pressure and adjust the loads on their base; during the construction of the Kuybyshev, Gorky and other hydroelectric power plants used explosion technique to study the dilution of the water-logged sandy subsoil; *Publ: Raschyoty osnovaniy gidrotekhnicheskikh sooruzheniy* (Calculating the Foundations of Hydraulic Structures) (1948); *Teoriya uplotneniya zemlyanykh mass* (The Theory of Sealing Earth Masses) (1948), etc; *Died*: 1960.

FLYORINA, Yevgeniya Aleksandrovna (1888-1952) Educationist; specialist in preschool training; Dr of Pedag; corresp member, RSFSR Acad of Pedag Sci from 1950; *Born*: 24 Dec 1888; *Educ*: 1909 grad Stroganov Art College, Moscow; 1917 grad three-year teachers' training course, "Child Work and Recreation" Soc; *Career*: 1909 began teaching career; principal of a nursery in Moscow and simultaneously teacher, Preschool Section, Tikhomirov Pedag Courses; also taught on short preschool courses in other towns; after 1917 Oct Revol began pedag research at 1st Experimetal Station for Public Educ, RSFSR Pop Comrt of Educ; from 1922 taught at higher educ establishments in Moscow; made major contribution to the study of the laws of the development of esthetic appreciation in preschool children; described the esthetic awareness, imagination and games of preschool children; devised methods of developing expressive speech in children; *Publ: Detskiy risunok* (Children's Drawings) (1924); *Kakaya igrushka nuzhna doshkol'niku* (The Proper Toys for the Preschool Child) (1933); *Zhivoye slovo v doshkol'nykh uchrezhdeniyakh* (The Living Word in Preschool Classes) (1933); *Izobrazitel'noye iskusstvo v doshkol'nykh uchrezhdeniyakh* (The Fine Arts in Preschool Classes) (1934); *Rasskazyvaniye dlya detey doshkol'nogo vozrasta* (Storytelling for Preschool Children) (1940); ed, *Zhivoye slovo doshkol'niku* (The Living Word for the Preschool Child) (1945); ed, *Doshkol'naya pedagogika* (Preschool Pedagogy) (1946); *Izobrazitel'noye tvorchestvo detey doshkol'nogo vozrasta* (Art Work by Preschool Children) (1956); *Esteticheskoye vospitaniye doshkol'nika* (The Esthetic Training of the Preschool Child) (1961), etc; *Died*: 10 Nov 1952.

FLYOROV, Vsevolod Aleksandrovich (1860-1919) Educationist; *Born*: 22 Feb 1860; *Educ*: 1885 grad Moscow Theological Acad; *Career*: 1885 after grad worked at Tula Theological College; 1887-95 subsequently taught Russian language and methods of its tuition at Novotorzhsk Teachers' Training Seminary; 1892 compiled curriculum for teaching Russian language at teachers' training seminaries; directed numerous teachers' summer courses; 1896 at Nizhniy Novgorod Exhibition lectured on methods of elementary schooling; proposed improvements in analytical synthetic vocal method of teaching reading; this technique, known under his name, is based largely on visual immediacy and helps to develop independent active thinking; 1895-98 inspector, Tver' Province pop colleges, and dir, Novinsk Teachers' Training Seminary; taught pedagogics and directed teachers' and methodologists' practical exercises; supported progressive projects of zemstvos and advanced teachers; helped to improve public educ; 1901 head, Moscow Congress of Educ Workers; 1901-06 dir, Vologda Province colleges; active in defense of teachers' rights; 1905-06 connected with illegal teachers' org, helping to distribute its appeals and proclamations; as member of Vologda City Duma subscribed to its oppositional declarations; his progressive activities were the cause of his numerous transfers; 1906 dir, Nizhniy Novgorod pop colleges; later Vilnius Okrug inspector; asst trustee, Vilnius Okrug colleges; 1908 same post in Kiev Okrug; 1909 quit working for Min of Educ; 1906 compiled and edited *Novyy russkiy bukvar' dlya obucheniya chteniyu i pis'mu* (New Russian Primer for Teaching Reading and Writing), a methodic directory for its use and other textbooks and directives for elementary schooling; his textbooks and aids have gone through dozens of ed; directed private Froebel courses; rep, Kiev Froebel Soc; on the invitation of various zemstvos, directed teachers' training courses in Ukr; from 1914 in Moscow; combined univ lectures with research and lit methodolgical work; after 1917 Oct Revol lecturer and head, methodologist lecturers group, teachers' training courses; *Publ:*

Novyy russkiy bukvar' (New Russian Primer) (1923); *Podrobnyy plan zanyatiy po obucheniyu gramote s ukazaniyem priyomov obucheniya* (Detailed Exercise Plan for Teaching Reading and Writing with a Directory of Teaching Methods) (1923); *Naglyadnyye uroki pis'ma. Posobiye dlya uchashchikhsya* (Visual Lessons in Writing. A Pupils' Primer) (3 vol, 1923); *Naglyadnost' pis'ma v osveshchenii sovremyonnoy psikhologii* (Neat Handwriting in the Light of Modern Psychology) (1923); *Died*: 26 Dec 1919.

FOKHT, Aleksandr Bogdanovich (1848-1930) Pathophysiologist; Dr of Med from 1873; prof from 1880; Hon Sci Worker of RSFSR from 1926; hon member, Union of All-Russian Therapeutic Congresses from 1922; *Born*: 28 Sept 1848 in Moscow, son of a teacher; *Educ* 1871 grad Med Fac, Moscow Univ; *Career*: after grad asst prof, Chair of Pathological Anatomy, Moscow Univ; from 1878 assoc prof, from 1880 prof, Chair of Gen Pathology, Moscow Univ; 1879-80 studied abroad, inter alia, under Cohnheim in Germany; 1891 founded Inst of Gen and Experimental Pathology; from 1909 prof, Chair of Gen Pathology, Moscow Women's Higher Courses; founded Inst of Experimental Pathology at 2nd Municipal Hospital; 1911 resigned from Moscow Univ in protest against policies of Educ Min Kasso but continued teaching and research work at Women's Higher Courses; after 1917 Oct Revol resumed teaching at Moscow Univ; 1920-23 read course in organic pathology at reinstituted Moscow Higher Med School; pioneer of modern pathological physiology as a basic discipline in experimental med; did major research on heart pathology, edema and dropsy, pericarditis, functional and anatomical lesions of the heart in coronary artery embolism, circulatory cardiac disturbances in pulmonary artery embolism, etc; specialized in the role of the nervous system in pathological processes; edited four vol of papers written at Inst of Gen and Experimental Pathology; founder, Moscow Med Soc, Moscow Therapeutic Soc, and All-Russian Endocrinological Soc; led school of pathological physiology which included such eminent pathologists as G.P. Sakharov, F.A.Andreyev. G.I.Rossolimo and D.M.Rossiyskiy; *Publ*: doctor's thesis *K ucheniyu o pereponchatoy dismenoreye* (The Theory of Membranous Dysmenorrhea) (1873); *Isskustvennoye krupoznoye vospaleniye na slizistoy obolochke zeva i dykhatel'nogo gorla i yego otnosheniye k difteritu* (Artificial Croupous Inflammation of the Mucous Menbrane of the Mouth and Trachea and its Relation to Diphtheria) (1875); *Issledovaniya o vospalenii okoloserdechnoy sumki* (Research on Pericarditis) (1899); *O funktional'nykh i anatomicheskikh narusheniyakh serdtsa pri zakrytii venechnykh arteriy* (Functional and Anatomical Disturbances of the Heart in Coronary Artery Blockage) (1901); *Lektsii obshchey patologii* (Lectures on General Pathology) (2 vol, 1910-13); *Otyok i vodyanka* (Edema and Dropsy) (1919); *Patologiya serdtsa* (Heart Pathology) (1920); *Died*: 23 Aug 1930.

FOKIN, Ignatiy Ivanovich (pseudonym: IGNAT) (1889-1919) Party official; CP member from 1906; *Born*: 19 Dec 1889 in Kiev, son of a machinist; *Career*: from 1906 draftsman, Lyudinov Plant, Bryansk Province; 1907 arrested for the first time and after serving a two-year prison term sentenced to three years' fortress detention; 1910 released; Party work in Bezhitsa; 1911 rearrested and exiled to Vologda Province; from 1913 draftsman at metallurgical plant and Party work in Petersburg; member, Petersburg RSDRP(B) Comt; organized propaganda collegium; 1916 went to Saratov, helped restore crushed Bolshevik org; shortly before 1917 Febr Revol rearrested and exiled to Siberia; Mar 1917 returned to Petrograd; agitator, Petrograd RSDRP(B) Comt, and member, agitation collegium, Vyborg Rayon Comt; Apr 1917 arrived in Bryansk; May 1917 elected secr, Bryansk RSDRP(B) org; during 1917 Oct Revol head, Bryansk Mil-Revol Comt; after 1917 Oct Revol chm, Bryansk Uyezd Sov Exec Comt; head, Extraordinary Mil Staff for Mustering Red Army Detachments; deleg, 8th RCP(B) Congress; returning from Congress, contracted typhus; *Died*: 13 Apr 1919; a Bryansk rayon, streets and a kolkhoz were named for him; a monument was erected to him in Bryansk.

FOKIN, Vitaliy Alekseyevich (1906-1964) Naval commander; admiral from 1953; member, CC, CPSU from 1961; CP member from 1927; *Born*: 17 Mar 1906; *Educ*: 1927 grad Frunze Naval College;Pos: 1922,following Komsomol levy, volunteered for Sov Navy; 1927-41 consecutively deck officer on cruiser "Avrora"; patrol boat commander; commander, destroyer *Uritskiy*; 1941-44 commander, destroyer squadron, Northern Fleet; chief of staff, Caspian Flotilla; naval detachment commander; 1944-47 squadron commander, Northern Fleet; 1947-48 chief of staff, Northern Fleet; 1948-58 dep commander, then commander, Operations Dept, Gen (later Main) Staff of the Navy; dep chief, then chief, Main Naval Staff; 1958-62 commander, Pacific Fleet; 1962-64 first dep commander, Sov Navy; *Career*: in 1930's his destroyer *Uritskiy* ranked first in mil training in Sov Navy; helped modernize Pacific Fleet; 1959 commander of a naval detachment which visited Indonesia; dep, RSFSR Supr Sov of 1959 and USSR Supr Sov of 1962 convocations; deleg at 21st (1959) and 22nd (1961) CPSU Congresses; *Awards*: Order of Lenin; four Orders of the Red Banner; Order of Nakhimov, 1st Class; Order of Ushakov, 2nd Class; Order of the Red Star; medals; *Died*: 23 Jan 1964 after a long illness; buried at Novodevich'ye Cemetery in Moscow.

FOL'BORT, Georgiy Vladimirovich (1885-1960) Physiologist; Dr of Med from 1912; prof from 1916; member, Ukr Acad of Sci from 1951; Hon Sci Worker of Ukr SSR from 1953; *Born*: 4 Feb 1885 in Petersburg; *Educ*: 1909 grad Petersburg Mil Med Acad; *Career*: while still a student began working in I.P.Pavlov's physiological laboratory; 1908 published first paper on the physiology of conditioned reflexes; 1912 defended doctor's thesis on negative conditioned reflexes; 1912-14 asst prof, 1914-26 senior lecturer and dep head, Chair of Physiology, Mil Med Acad; 1916-23 prof, Chair of Animal Physiology, Women's Higher Agric Courses; 1923-26 head, Chair of Physiology, Leningrad Univ; 1926-46 head, Chair of Normal Physiology, Khar'kov Med Inst; 1946-60 head, Chair of Normal Physiology, Kiev Med Inst and head, Dept of Higher Nervous Activity and Trophism, Bogomolets Inst of Physiology, Ukr Acad of Sci; 1927 set up laboratory for the study of the physiology of digestion at the Ukr Inst of Experimental Endocrinology; established large physiology dept at the Ukr Mechnikov Inst of Experimental Biology and Med, Khar'kov; from 1926 head, Laboratory of Conditioned Reflexes, Ukr Psychoneurological Inst, considered by Pavlov to be the first branch of his own laboratory; discovered negative conditioned reflexes resulting from the formation of temporary assoc based on inhibition of the cerebral cortex centers; did research on the working capacity of the cortex of the cerebral hemispheres, on tracking phenomena in the cortex and on conditioned stimuli formed by words and their connections; analysed bile secretion and its entry into the intestine; devised double bile fistula test; proved that the fibers of the splanchnic nerve stimulate gastric secretion; studied the function of excitosecretory substances produced by the pylorus; devised new method of obtaining secretin; made major contribution to dietetics with his research on the effects of vegetable juices and atropine on gastric secretion; also made important contributions to the study of exhaustion and recuperation with his "Fol'bort rules," which define the basic laws of these processes; knowledge of these laws made it possible to determine the functional limits of various systems in the organism; wrote over 130 works; *Publ*: doctor's thesis *Tormoznyye uslovnyye refleksy* (Inhibitory Conditioned Reflexes) (1912); *K metodike nablyudeniya nad sekretsiyey zhyolchi i na yeyo vykhodom v dvenadtsatiperstnuyu kishku* (Methods of Observing Bile Secretion and Its Entry into the Duodenum) (1917); *Ob istoshchenii slyunnykh zhelyoz pri ikh deyatel'nosti* (Functional Exhaustion of the Salivary Glands) (1924); *Fiziologicheskaya kartina protsessov istoshcheniya i vosstanovleniya organov* (A Physiological Description of the Processes of Exhaustion and Recuperation of Organs) (1941); *Adaptatsionno-troficheskoye vliyaniye simpaticheskoy nervnoy sistemi na zhelezistyye organy* (The Adaptive Trophic Influence of the Sympathetic Nervous System on the Glandular Organs) (1947); *Puti razvitiya moikh issledovaniy* (The Development of My Research Work) (1958); *Osnovnyye napravleniya nashikh rabot po vysshey nervnoy deyatel'nosti* (The Basic Trends in Our Work on Higher Nervous Activity) (1959); *Izbrannyye trudy* (Selected Works) (1962); *Awards*: Pavlov Prize; Order of Lenin; *Died*: 16 Apr 1960 in Kiev.

FOMIN, Ivan Aleksandrovich (1872-1936) Architect; *Born*: 3 Feb 1872 in Oryol, son of a postal official; *Educ*: 1890-93 studied at Fac of Mathematics, Moscow Univ; 1909 grad Petersburg Acad of Arts; *Career*: 1894 soon after joining Fac of Architecture, Petersburg Acad of Arts, expelled for involvement in student riots; 1905, after spending some time abroad and passing builders' examination, returned to Acad of Arts; 1909, after grad, was sent on a tour of Greece, Egypt, Italy, France and Germany; his best-known pre-Revol works are Polovtsev's house on Kamenny Island and Abamalek-Lazarev's house on the embankment of the Moyka River, Petersburg; took part in numerous architectural competitions; from 1915 member, Petersburg Acad of Arts; 1918-19 took part in competitions for the Workers' Palace in Narva distr, the

Leningrad Crematorium and various memorials; 1922 contributed to designs for All-Union Agric Exhibition; 1925 took part in competition for Bryansk House of Soviets; 1924 designed "Arcos" House, Moscow; 1925 designed Sverdlovsk Ind Bank; 1927-30 worked on design for Ivanovo-Voznesensk Polytech Inst; also designed a number of sanatoria; however, most of these projects were never realized; 1919-21 mang, Architectural Studio, Leningrad Sov; 1929 moved to Moscow, where he took charge of designing and building an office block on Dzerzhinskiy Street which house the Min of Internal Affairs and the KGB; from 1933 mang of a planning and architectural studio, Moscow Sov; designed buildings of USSR Pop Comrt of Communications, USSR Pop Comrt of Heavy Ind, Red Army Theater; planned reconstruction of Red Square; designed Ashkhabad Theater and Radio House; designed Sanatorium of Commission for Aid to Scientists, USSR Council of Pop Comr, Sochi; also designed Sverdlov Square and Red Gates stations, Moscow Subway; 1934-38 designed and built Ukr Govt House, Kiev; 1916-24 prof, 2nd Polytech Inst; 1918-29 and 1934-35 taught at Leningrad Acad of Arts; trained such famous Sov architects as Gegello, Trotskiy, Polyakov, Abrosimov, Minkus, Rozhin, Khryakov, Fomin junior and Levinson; wrote several works on history and theory of architecture; *Publ: Moskovskiy klassitsizm* (Muscovite Classicism) (1904); *Kratkiy kurs teorii perspektivy* (A Short Course in the Theory of Perspective), etc; *Died*: 12 June 1936 in Moscow.

FOMIN, Nikolay Petrovich (1864-1943) Composer, pianist and music teacher; *Born*: 1864 in Petersburg; *Educ*: 1891 grad Petersburg Conservatory, where he studied under N.A.Dubasov (piano), A.G.Rubinstein (conducting) and A.K.Lyadov (harmony); *Career*: prof of folk orchestration, Leningrad Conservatory; specialized in Russian instrumental folk music; with V.V.Andreyev developed variants of Russian pizzicato instruments (dombras, balalaykas, etc); developed improved psaltery with range of five octaves and devised plectrum to facilitate the playing of arpeggios and increase the volume of sound; developed orchestration principles for folk instruments; wrote orchestral arrangements of numerous Russian folk songs and adapted compositions by Russian and West European musicians for folk orchestras; made major contribution to the development of Russian folk instrumentation; *Works*: composed a number of symphonies and operas, including *Pir Baltasara* and *Skazka o spyashchey krasavitse i semi bogatyryakh* (The Tale of Sleeping Beauty and the Seven Heroes); ballets *Zhizn' i son* (Life and Dream), *Dva mira* (Two Worlds), etc; *Died*: 1943 in Leningrad.

FOMIN, Semyon Fomich (1903-1936) Chuvash writer; *Born*: 1903; *Educ*: 1920-21 studied at Chuvash Teachers' Training Courses in Kazan'; *Career*: first work published in 1920's; 1922-23 switched to prose; in his works Chuvash vil life plays an important role; translated Russian and German works into Chuvash; *Publ*: collection "Verse and Songs" (1922); novelette "Hungry Years" (1924); collection "Komsomol Stories" (1926); *Timush* (Timosha) (1929); *Shupashkar* (1929); novelette "Childhood" (1931); collection of stories "On the Way" (1933); drama *Anyukpa Vanyuk*, etc; *Died*: 1936.

FOMIN, V. V. (1884-1942) Govt official; CP member from 1910; *Born*: 1884; *Career*: Party work in Orenburg; repeatedly arrested and exiled; after 1917 Feb Revol ed, front-line newspaper *Zvezda*; 1918-20 Collegium member, All-Russian Cheka; mil comr, railroad trans; 1921-22 dept head, All-Russian Cheka; 1923 comr, Main Communications Bd; 1924 Dep Pop Comr of Means of Communication; 1925 member, Centr Control Commission; 1926-30 with Pop Comrt of Internal Trade, then Dep Pop Comr of Water Trans; 1938 manager, All-Union Bureau, All-Union Textile and Tailoring Trade Trust; arrested by State Security organs; *Died*: 1942 in imprisonment.

FORSH, Ol'ga Dmitriyevna (1873-1961) Russian writer; *Born*: 16 May 1873 at Gunig Fortress, Dag *Educ*: grad draftsmanship school in Kiev; *Career*: raised in the Caucasus, where her father commanded a div; until 1917 taught drawing at Petersburg schools; 1908 began to write; contributed to journals *Dlya vsekh, Zavety, Skify* and *Nash put'*; from 1919 worked for a while for Kiev All-Union Publ House; 1929 traveled abroad; 1934 helped prepare 1st Constituent Congress of Sov Writers' Union and was elected to its Auditing Commission; *Publ*: stories: *Byl general* (There Was a General) (1908); *Medved' Panfamil* (Panfamil the Bear) (1908); novels: *Rytsar' iz Nyurenberga* (The Knight from Nuremberg) (1908); *Sumashedshiy korabl'* (The Crazy Ship) (1931); historical novel: *Odety kamnem* (Stone-Clad) (1925); scripts for historical films: *Dvorets i krepost'* (Palace and Fortress) (1924); *Pugachev* (1937); novel *Sovremenniki* (The Contemporaries) (1926); novel *Goryachiy tsekh* (The Hot Shop) (1927); collected stories *Pod kupolom* (Under the Dome) (1929); novel *Voron* (The Raven) (1934); *Radishchev* (1939); novel *Mikhaylovskiy zamok* (Mikhail Castle) (1946), intended as first part of trilogy *Bessmertnyy gorod* (Immortal City); novel about the Decembrists *Perventsy svobody* (Pioneers of Liberty) (1953); *Vchera i segodnya* (Yesterday and Today) (1959); article "Meeting with Tolstoy" (1960); collection *Istoricheskiye romany* (Historical Novels) (1949); *Izbrannyye proizvedeniya* (Collected Works) (1953); *Awards*: Order of Lenin; other orders; *Died*: 17 July 1961.

FORTUNATOV, Aleksandr Alekseyevich (1884-1949) Historian and pedagogue; *Born*: 12 July 1884; *Educ*: 1908 grad History and Philology Dept, Moscow Univ; *Career*; 1908 taught history and lit at Prechistenskiy workers' courses; then teacher, private girls' secondary schools; 1919-25 assoc of S. T. Shatskiy at 1st Educ Experimental Station, RSFSR Pop Comrt of Educ; head, teachers' extra-scholastic work; specialized in problems of art training; 1926-39 taught history, lit and pedag at teachers' training technicums; simultaneously instructing and research work at higher educ institutions: Shanyavskiy Pop Univ; Moscow State Univ; Inst of History, Russian Assoc of Soc Sci Research Institutes; from 1939 lecturer, from 1940 head, Chair of History, and from 1947 dean, History Dept, Mosow's Potyomkin State Teachers' Training Inst; in his works on development of elementary schooling and methods of teaching history in secondary schools stressed the importance of visual-aids and utilization of artistic images in tuition; wrote a number of works on the history of labor schools, etc; *Publ*: coauthor, *Pervyy god obucheniya v nachal'noy shkole* (The First Year of Instruction in Elementary School) (2nd ed, 1914); coauthor, *Vtoroy i tretiy god obucheniya v nachal'noy shkole* (Second and Third Year of Instruction in Elementary School) (1915); *Teoriya trudovoy shkoly v yeyo istoricheskom razvitii, chast' 1. Ot Tomasa Mora do Karla Marksa* (Theory of the Labor School in Its Historical Development. Part 1. From Thomas More to Karl Marx) (1925), etc; *Died*: 19 Sept 1949.

FRANK, Semyon Lyudvigovich (1877-1950) Philosopher; *Born*: 29 Jan 1877 in Moscow, son of a physician; *Educ*: studied at Moscow and Kazan' Univ; *Career*: while a student, joined revol movement; 1899-1901 in exile and abroad (Berlin); from 1901 translated German philosophical books; 1904 attended 1st Foreign Congress of Liberation League; 1905 attended 1st Congress of Constitutional Democratic Party, Moscow; from Dec 1905, together with Struve, edited weekly *Polyarnaya zvezda*; from Mar 1906 editeed weekly *Svoboda i kul'tura*; assoc, journal *Russkaya mysl'*; 1909 contributed to anthology *Vekhi*; from 1912 assoc prof, Petersburg Univ; from 1917 at Saratov Univ; from 1921 dean, Acad of Spiritual Culture, Moscow; 1922 exiled from Sov Union; 1922-37 in Germany; 1937-45 in France; 1945-50 in England; *Publ: Predmet znaniya* (The Subject of Knowledge) (1915); *Dusha cheloveka* (The Soul of Man) (1917); *Vvedeniye v filosofiyu* (An Introduction to Philosophy); *Metodologiya obshchestvennykh nauk* (The Methodology of Social Sciences); *Krusheniye kumirov* (The Collapse of Idols) (1924); *Smysl' zhizni* (The Purpose of Life) (1925); *Dukhovnyye osnovy obschestva* (The Spiritual Principles of Society) (1930); "God Is With Us" (1946); *Svet vo t'me* (Light in Darkness) (1949); *Died:* 10 Dec 1950 in London.

FRANKO (née: KHORUZHINSKAYA), Ol'ga Fyodorovna (1864-1941) Ukr soc worker and ed; wife of Ukr writer Ivan Franko; *Born*: 1864 in vil Birki (now Sumy Oblast), daughter of a nobleman; *Career*: active in democratic women's movement in Galicia; 1894-97 together with Franko edited periodical *Zhizn' i slovo; Publ: Karpatskiye boyki i ikh semeynaya zhizn'* (Carpathian Boykis and Their Family Life) (1887); *Died*: 1941.

FRANKO, Pyotr Ivanovich (1890-1941) Ukr writer and educationist; son of Ukr writer I. Ya. Franko; *Born*: 21 June 1890; *Educ*: grad L'vov Polytech Inst; *Career*: teacher in Kolomiya; from 1927 lived in Ukr; worked as eng in Khar'kov factories; 1936 returned to Western Ukr (Poland); 1939 attended West Ukr Pop Assembly; 1940 elected dep. Ukr Supr Sov; after 1939 dept head, L'vov Inst of Trade and Econ; dir, L'vov Ivan Franko Museum; wrote memoires, articles and textbooks; film script based on Ivan Franko's novelette *Borislav smeyotsya* (Borislav Laughs); translated into Ukr Jack London's works; *Publ*: memoirs about his father *Ivan Franko vblizi* (Ivan Franko at Close Quarters) (1937); *Died*: 1941.

FREDERIKS, Vladimir Borisovich (1838-1927) High court official in the last years of Tsarist regime; Adjutant-Gen; gen of cavalry; member, State Council; *Born*: 1838; *Career*: descendant of Baltic barons; major landowner; 1897-1917 Min of Imperial Court; in this period one of most influential dignitaries; exerted great influence on the Tsar; from 1913 titular count; 2 Mar 1917, as Min of the Court, ratified abdication of Nicholas II; *Died*: 1927.

FRENKEL', Semyon Romanovich (1875-1937) Roentgenologist; prof; *Born:* 1875; *Educ*: 1898 grad Med Fac, Khar'kov Univ; *Career:* expelled from Kiev Univ for involvement in student riots; after grad worked as physician in Uman', Kiev Province; 1905 imprisoned for revol activity; after release elected to 1st State Duma; after dissolution of Duma tried on charge of distributing illegal propaganda material and sentenced to two years imprisonment; 1908-10 served sentence in Uman' fortress; 1911 went abroad and studied roentgenology under Levi-Dorn for three years; also studied under other specialists in Berlin, Hamburg, Vienna and Paris; after 1917 Oct Revol for 15 years head, Roentgenological Dept, Kremlin Hospital and head, Radiological Dept, Centr Oncological Inst; prof of roentgenology, 1st Moscow Med Inst; founder-chm and bd member, Moscow Soc of Roentgenologists; Presidium member, All-Union Assoc of Roentgenologists; chm, Russian Soc of Roentgenologists; co-ed, *Bol'shaya meditsinskaya entsiklopediya* (Large Medical Encyclopedia) (1st ed); read papers at all major Sov roentgenological conferences; also read papers at int radiological and roentgenological congresses in London, Stockholm and Zurich; wrote 47 works; *Publ:* "The Practical Application of Encephalography" (1926); coathor, *Noveyshiye metody khirurgicheskoy rentgenodiagnostiki* (The Latest Methods of Surgical X-Ray Diagnosis) (1928); coauthor, "Die Encephalographie bei psychischen und Nervenkrankheiten des Kindes- und Säuglingsalters" (The Encephalography of Mental and Nervous Diseases in Childhood and Infancy) (1933); coauthor, *Tysyacha sluchayev vnutrivennoy piyelografii* (A Thousand Cases of Intravenous Pyelography) (1935); *Died:* 1937.

FRENKEL', Yakov Il'ich (1894-1952) Physicist; corresp member, USSR Acad of Sci from 1929; *Born:* 9 Feb 1894 in Rostov-on-Don; *Educ:* 1916 grad Petrograd Univ; *Career:* from 1921 worked at Leningrad Inst of Physics and Eng; simultaneously taught at Leningrad Polytech Inst, where he headed the Chair of Theoretical Physics for 30 years; formulated first version of quantum theory of electron motion in metal; pioneered modern theory of ferromagnetism; 1931 divised theory of light absorption in dielectrics (Frenkel's excitons); did major research on the formation and role of defects in crystal lattices (atoms in interstitial spaces and vacant spaces); 1925 was first to point out the analogy between liquid and solid states; his findings were subsequently confirmed in experiments and for many years served as a basis for research on liquidity; 1945 summarized his findings on liquid state physics in the monograph *Kineticheskaya teoriya zhidkostey* (The Kinetic Theory of Liquids); made further important contributions to nuclear physics with his research on the emission of particles during evaporation; 1939, after the experimental discovery of uranium fission, formulated first quantitative theory of the phenomenon on which the practical utilization of nuclear energy is based; did major research on atmospheric electricity; also studied atmospheric physics, geomagnetism, biophysics and astrophysics; wrote first Sov courses on theoretical physics; *Publ: Elektrodinamika* (Electrodynamics) (2 vol, 1934-35); *Statisticheskaya fizika* (Statistical Physics) (1948); *Teoriya yavleniya atmosfericheskogo elektrichestva* (The Theory of the Phenomenon of Atmospheric Electricity) (1949); *Vvedeniye v teoriyu metallov* (An Introduction to Metal Theory) (3rd ed, 1958); *Printsipy teorii atomnykh yader* (The Principles of the Theory of Atomic Nuclei) (2nd ed, 1955); *Sobraniye izbrannykh trudov* (Selected Works) (2 vol, 1956-58); *Awards:* Stalin Prize (1947); Order of the Red Banner of Labor; medals; *Died:* 23 Jan 1952.

FREYBERG, Nikolay Gustavovich (1859-1927) Health service official; specialist in Sov and int med and sanitary legislation; *Born:* 1859; *Educ:* 1882 grad Mil Med Acad; *Career:* after grad regt physician in Baltic Kray; worked as a surgeon under K. K. Reyer; from 1892 sanitary official, Bd of Chief Med Inspector; 1913-16 business mang, Commission for the Review of Med and Sanitary Legislation, chaired by G. E. Reyn; after 1917 Oct Revol helped to establish RSFSR Pop Comrt of Health, becoming its business mang and a member of its Learned Med Council; 1908-17 attended all int conferences and congresses on sanitary affairs and visited Int Bureau of Soc Hygiene; after 1917 represented USSR at Warsaw and Paris Internat conferences on sanitary conventions; wrote numerous works on Russian and int med and sanitary legislation; *Publ: Mezhdunarodnyye sanitarnyye konferentsii poslednego desyatiletiya* (International Sanitary Conferences in the Last Decade) (1898); *Vrachebno-sanitarnoye zakonodatel'stvo v Rossii* (Medical and Sanitary Legislation in Russia) (1901, 1913); *Sbornik zakonov i raspoyazheniy pravitel'stva RSFSR po vrachebno-sanitarnomu delu s l-ogo sentyabrya 1919-ogo goda po l-oye yanvarya 1925-ogo goda* (A Collection of Medical and Sanitary Laws and Decrees Issued by the RSFSR Government from 1 September 1919 to 1 January 1925) (1925); *Mezhdunarodnaya sanitarnaya konferentsiya 1926-ogo goda* (The 1926 International Sanitary Conference) (1927); coauthor, *Gigiyena* (Hygiene) (7th ed, 1928); *Died*: 1927.

FREYDENBERG, Mikhail (Moisey) Filippovich (1858-1920) Inventor; *Born:* 21 Jan 1858 in Prasnyshe, Polotsk Province, son of a craftsman; *Career:* worked as a printer and then as a journalist in Odessa; 1881 built and flew an aerostat in Odessa; 1893 together with I. A. Timchenko invented the *kinetoscope* movie projector; 1893 together with S. M. Apostolov-Berdichevskiy designed his first automatic telephone switchboard (British Patent 3954, 1895); designed improved switchboards in which he included preselectors (British Patent 10155, 1895), mech selectors (British Patent 18912, 1896) and group assemblies (Russian Patent 8668, 1898); 1908 designed a machine for casting metal type; from 1902 lived in Petersburg; after 1917 Oct Revol mang, 15th Printing Hause, Petrograd; *Died:* 1 Aug 1920.

FREYMAN, Imant Georgiyevich (1890-1929) Radio eng; *Born*: 1890; *Educ*: 1913 grad Petersburg Inst of Electr Eng; *Career*: from 1916 lecturer, from 1921 prof, Petrograd Inst of Electr Eng; from 1922 taught at Leningrad Naval Acad; 1911-17 helped to build radio stations on Runo Island, in Riga and Arkhangel'sk, at Yugorskiy Shar and in Vladivostok; invented several radio devices; 1924 published *Kurs radiotekhniki* (A Corse in Radio Engineering) which remained a standard work for a number of years; *Died*: 1929.

FRICHE, Vladimir Maksimovich (1870-1929) Lit and art historian; Party and govt official; member, USSR Acad of Sci; CP member from 1917; *Born*: 16 Oct 1870 in Moscow of German parents; *Educ*: univ grad; *Career*: during 1890's worked as critic, reader and journalist; 1904-10 lecturer, Moscow Univ, then lit critic and historian; early 1910's joined Soc-Democratic movement; after 1917 Oct Revol worked for Party and govt; Comr of For Affairs; Moscow Sov; collegium member, Moscow Dept of Public Educ; agitator, Moscow RCP(B) Comt; head, Lit Dept, USSR Pop Comrt of Educ; from 1922 dir, Inst of Language and Lit, Russian Assoc of Soc Sci Research Inst; head, Lit Dept, Inst of Red Prof; head, Lit Dept, Communist Acad; dean, Lit Dept, Moscow Univ; member, State Learned Council; dir, Inst of Archeology and Art History; Presidium chm, Russian Assoc of Sci Research Inst; Presidium member, Communist Acad; chief ed, *Literaturnaya entsiklopediya* (Literary Encyclopedia); ed, journal *Literatura i marksizm*; member, ed bd, journal *Krasnyy arkhiv; Publ: Khudozhestvennaya literatura i kapitalizm* (Fiction and Capitalism) (1906); *Ocherki po istorii zapadno-yevropeyskoy literatury* (Essays on the History of West-European Literature) (1908); *Leonid Andreyev. Opyt kharakteristiki* (Leonid Andreyev. A Character Study) (1909); *Ot Chernyshevskego k 'Vekham'* (From Chernyshevskiy to the Anthology "Landmarks") (1910); *Poeziya koshmarov i uzhasa* (The Poetry of Terror and Horror) (1912); *Yevropeyskaya literatura na kanune voyny, 1900-14* (European Literature on the Eve of the War, 1900-14) (1915); *Germanskiy imperializm v literature* (German Imperialism in Literature) (1916); *Ital'yanskaya literatura XIX veka* (Nineteenth-Century Italian Literature) (1916); *Poeziya imperializma i poeziya demokratii* (The Poetry of Imperialism and the Poetry of Democracy) (1918); *Ocherki istorii mirovogo rabochego dvizheniya. 3. Rabocheye dvizheniye v Rossii* (A Study of the History of the World Workers' Movement. 3. The Workers' Movement in Russia) (1918); *Proletarskay poeziya* (Proletarian Poetry) (1918); *Noveyshaya yevropeyskaya literatura. 1. Kapitalizm i sotsializm v literature 1908-14* (Modern European Literature. 1. Capitalism and Socialism in Literature 1908-14) (1919); *Verkharn* (Emil Verhaeren) (1919); *Zolya* (Emile Zola) (1919); *Sotsializm* (Socialism) (1919); *A. I. Gertsen, 1812-70* (A. I. Herzen, 1812-70) (1920); *Pisateli raboche-krest'yanskoy Italii* (The Writers of Workers-and-Peasants' Italy) (1921); *Korifei mirovoy literatury v Sovetskoy Rossii* (The Coryphaei of World Literature in Soviet Russia) (1922); *Ocherki sotsial'noy istorii iskusstva* (Essays on the Social History of Art) (1923); *Zapadno-yevropeyskaya literatura XX veka v yeyo glavneyshikh* *proyevleniyakh* (Twentieth-Century West European Literature in Its Main Manifestations) (1926); *Vil'yam Shekspir* (William Shakespeare) (1926); *Sotsiologiya iskusstva* (The Sociology of Art) (1926); *Ocherki po istorii rabochego dvizheniya na Zapade* (A Study in the History of the Workers' Movement in the West) (1926); *Ocherk razvitiya zapadnykh literatur* (A Study of the Development of Western Literatures) (1929) *L. N. Tolstoy* (1929); *Zametki o sovremennoy literatury* (Notes on Contemporary Literature) (1928); *A. P. Chekhov. Biograficheskiy ocherk* (A. P. Chekhov. A Biographical Study) (1929); *Problemy iskusstvovedeniya* (Problems of the Study of art) (1930); *Died*: 4 Sept 1929.

FRIDBERG, V. I. (1885-1938) Govt official; CP member from 1920; *Born:* 1885; *Career:* 1904-07 sided with the Bolsheviks; after 1917 Feb Revol sided with Mensheviks; head, food sub-dept, Moscow's Arbat Rayon Duma; after 1917 Oct Revol worked for food dept, Moscow's Khamovniki Rayon Sov; 1918-23 Collegium member and head, Transport Dept, Moscow Sov; in following years publ prosecutor, Oryol Province, Pop Comrt of Justice, Rostov Kray, then East Siberian Oblast; arrested by State Security organs; *Died:* 1938 in imprisonment.

FRIDE, Nina Aleksandrovna (1859-circa 1940) Russian opera singer (mezzo-soprano, contralto); *Born:* 1859; *Educ:* studied at Petersburg Conservatory; further studies in Paris and Italy (under G. Ronconi); *Career:* 1883 began stage work at Florence Opera Theater in the role of Pierotto in Donizetti's "Linda di Chamonix"; 1884 performed in Lisbon and Madrid; 1884-91 and 1895-1907 soloist, Petersburg Mariinskiy Theater; 1891-95 gave concerts in Moscow, Odessa, Paris, Warsaw, Monte-Carlo, etc; rep of bel canto school; possessed a beautiful voice and elegant stage presence; her talent was highly rated by Tchaikovsky, Rimsky-Korsakov, Rubinstein and Gounod; *Roles:* Ol'ga, Larina, the nurse in *Yevgeniy Onegin;* Basmanov; the Princess; Ionna in Tchaikovsky's *Oprichnik, Charodeyka* (The Sorceress) and *Orleanskaya deva* (Maid of Orleans); Lyubava in *Sadko;* Fyodor in *Boris Godunov;* Delilah in Saint-Saens' "Samson and Delilah," etc; *Died*: after 1940.

FRIDOLIN, V. Yu. (pseudonyms: VAREN'KA, DASHIN) (1879-1942) Party official; CP member from 1904; *Born:* 1879; *Career*: Party work in Samara, Ufa and Petersburg; Ural RSDRP Union deleg at 3rd RSDRP Congress; 1906 member, Bolshevik mil org, Petersburg RSDRP Comt; subsequently quit polit work; 1910-17 lived in France; during WW 1 contributed to Menshevik newspaper *Nashe slovo*; from 1918 research and teaching work in Leningrad; arrested by State Security organs; *Died*: 1942 in imprisonment.

FRIDRIKHSON, L. Kh. (1889-1937) Party and govt official; CP member from 1908; *Born*: 1889; *Career*: did Party work in Lat; after 1917 Feb Revol member, Vol'mar Uyezd Zemstvo Admin; after 1917 Oct Revol member, Penza Province Party Comt and chm, Penza Province Exec Comt; 1921-24 Collegium member, Pop Comrt of Agric; 1924-29 Sov trade rep in Denmark, then in Germany; 1929-32 head Grain Trading Bd, then dep chm, Timber Export Bd; 1932-37 dep head, USSR Trade Mission in Germany; from Sept 1937 USSR Dep Min of For Trade; arrested by State Security organs; *Died*: 1937 in imprisonment.

FROLENKO, Mikhail Fyodorovich (1848-1938) Populist revol; CP member from 1936; *Born*: 1848 in Stavropol', son of a retired sergeant; *Educ*: studied at Petersburg Inst of Technol; later at Moscow's Petrine Agriculture and Forestry Acad; *Career*: took an active part in populist movement; to avoid arrest went underground; displayed exceptional courage, energy and resourcefulness; 1877 liberated from Odessa Prison the populist V. Kostyurin; 1878, obtaining the post of a Kiev prison guard, liberated the populists Ya. V. Stefanovich, L. G. Deych and I. V. Bokhanovskiy; the same year tried to liberate P. I. Voynaral'skiy; 1879 helped the populist F. N. Yurkovskiy to undermine the Kherson Treasury; 1879, after the schism in the *Zemlya i volya* (Land and Freedom) movement, joined the *Narodnaya volya* (People's Will) fraction and was a member of its exec comt; helped prepare several attempts on the life of Alexander II; 1881 arrested; 1882 sentenced to death; sentence commuted to hard labor for life; imprisoned in Peter and Paul and Shlissel'burg Fortresses until 1905; 1905 released, but until 1917 remained under police surveillance; from 1922 lived in Moscow; member, ed bd, journal *Katorga i ssylka*; *Publ: Sobraniye sochineniy* (Collected Works) (2 vol, 1930-31); *Died*: 1938.

FROLOV, Aleksandr Matveyevich (1870-1964) Civil and hydraulic eng; member, Ukr Acad of Sci from 1939; Hon Sci and Tech Worker of RSFSR from 1947; dir-gen (3rd class) of road construction; *Born*: 6 Sept 1870 in Tsarskoye Selo (from 1917 Detskoye Selo, from 1937 Pushkin), Leningrad Oblast; *Educ*: 1894 grad Petersburg Inst of Communications Eng; *Career*: from 1894 research, planning and railroad construction work; from 1909 instructor, Petersburg Inst of Communications (now Leningrad Inst of Rail Trans Eng); main works deal with railroad construction and hydrotech structures; *Publ: O perekhodakh cherez vodotoki* (Bridging Streams) (3 vol, 1912); *Mery obespechivaniya ustoychivosti zemlyanykh mass i sooruzheniy* (Means of Stabilizing Earth Masses and Structures) (2 vol, 1949-54); *Awards*: Order of Lenin; Badge of Hon; medals; *Died*: 15 July 1964.

FROLOV, Aleksandr Nikolayevich (1863-1939) Eng; specialist in operation of rail trans; *Born*: 24 Aug 1863; *Educ*: 1885 grad Moscow and Petersburg Inst of Transport Eng; *Career*: railroad work; from 1924 prof, Leningrad Inst of Rail Trans Eng; pioneered maneuver operation theory; worked on the problem of rail traffic capacity, planning and regulation of trans, designing and organization of railroad station work; *Publ*: coauthor, *Obshchiy kurs ekspluatatsii zheleznykh dorog* (General Course of Railroad Operation) (vol 1, 1926); *Obshchiye osnovy zheleznodorozhnogo khozaystva* (General Principles of Railroad Management) (1920); *Ekonomicheskaya otsenka razlichnykh sistem grafikov dvizheniya poyezdov* (Economic Estimate of Various Railroad Time-Table Systems) (1932); *Osnovnyye priyomy peresostavleniya poyezdov* (Basic Techniques of Remarshalling Trains) (1929); coauthor, *Soprotivleniye vagonov pri skatyvanii s gorki* (Car Resistance in Down-Hill Motion) (1939); *Died*: 1939.

FROLOV, Markian Petrovich (1892-1944) Composer, pianist and teacher; Hon Art Worker of RSFSR from 1944; CP member from 1938; *Born*: 6 Dec 1892; *Educ*: 1924 grad I. S. Miklashevskaya's class, Leningrad Conservatory; *Career*: from 1924 instructor; Kiev's Lysenko Inst of Music and Drama; 1928-34 at Sverdlovsk Musical Technicum; 1934-37 and 1943-44 dir, from 1939 prof, Ural Conservatory; *Works*: opera *Enkhe-Bulat bator* (1940); oratorio "The Ural Poem" (1932); orchestral music: symphonic picture "The Gray Ural" (1936), etc; piano concerto (1924); piano sonata, classical suite, etc; chorales, songs; *Died*: 30 Oct 1944.

FROLOV, Valerian Aleksandrovich (1895-1961) Mil commander; col-gen from 1943; CP member from 1919; *Born*: 7 June 1895 in Petersburg, son of an office worker; *Educ*: 1932 grad Frunze Mil Acad; *Pos*: 1915-18 private, then NCO, Moscow Guards regt; from 1918 in Red Army; 1918-21 private; company, then batallion commander; 1921-29 various commands; 1932-37 regt commander; chief of staff, 54th Infantry Div; 1937-39 mil advisor, Spanish Revol Army; 1939 commander, Infantry Corps; 1939-41 commander, 14th Army; 1941-44 commander, Karelian Front; 1945-56 commander, Arkhangel'sk (later White Sea) Mil Distr; from 1956 in retirement; *Career*: veteran of WW 1 (1915-17), Civil War (1918-20), Spanish Civil War (1937-39), Sov-Finnish War (1939-40); deleg at 18th (1939), 19th (1952) and 20th CPSU Congresses; dep, RSFSR Supr Sov of 1951 and USSR Supr Sov of 1946 and 1954 convocations; *Awards*: two George Crosses (WW 1); three Orders of Lenin; four Orders of the Red Banner; Order of Kutuzov, 1st Class; Order of Bogdan Khmel'nitskiy, 1st Class; Order of the Red Banner; medals; *Died*: 6 Jan 1961.

FROMGOL'D, Yegor Yegorovich (1881-1942) Therapist; *Born*: 1881; *Educ*: 1905 grad Med Fac, Moscow Univ; *Career*: external student, intern, then asst, Fac Therapy Clinic, Moscow Univ; 1911-20 assoc prof, from 1920 prof, Propedeutic Therapy Clinic, 1st Moscow Univ; from 1922 asst chm, Moscow Therapeutic Soc; from 1928 bd member, USSR Therapists' Soc; attended and read papers at congresses and conferences of therapists; twice sent abroad on sci assignments, working at Salkovsky and Hofmeister's chemical laboratory and touring Krauss and Wenkebach's clinics; introduced and studied urobilinogen in Russia and traced its importance in the explanation of urobilinuria; first to induce artificial urobilinuria; 1921 first to isolate bile pigment from the urine and make a chemical analysis of it; in latter years specialized in metabolism in the course of prolonged starvation; co-ed, therapy section, 1st ed of *Bol'shaya meditsinskaya entsiklopediya* (Large Medical Encyclopedia); wrote more than 30 works, including textbooks; *Publ: Issledovaniye ob urobiline* (A Study of Urobilin) (1911); *O zhyolchnom pigmente pri zheltukhe* (Bile Pigment in Jaundice) (1914); *Kartina bolezni pri otravlenii udushlivymi gazami* (The Syndrome of Suffocative Gas Poisoning) (1917); *Bolezni obmena veshchestv* (Metabolic Diseases) (1928); *Patogenez zheltukhi* (The Pathogenesis of Jaundice) (1936); *Died*: 1942.

FRONSHTEYN, Rikhard Mikhaylovich (1882-1949) Urologist; Dr of Med from 1916; prof from 1922; member, USSR Acad of Med

Sci from 1946; Hon Sci Worker of RSFSR from 1936; *Born*: 20 Feb 1882; *Educ*: grad Med Fac, Moscow Univ; *Career*: 1906-10 intern, 1911-17 asst prof, Urological Clinic, Moscow Univ; 1916 defended doctor's thesis; from 1917 assoc prof, Hospital Surgical Clinic directed by V.Martynov; from 1922 prof, Chair of Urology, Moscow Higher Med School; from 1923 prof, Chair of Urology, 1st Moscow State Univ (from 1930 1st Moscow Med Inst); from 1921 simultaneously head, Men's Gonorrhea Dept and Chair of Gonorrhea, State Venerological Inst; consultant, various med establishments; 1925-44 founder-ed, journal *Urologiya*; co-ed, surgery section, *Bol'shaya meditsinskaya entsiklopediya* (Large Medical Encyclopedia) (1st ed); member, learned Med Council, USSR Pop Comrt of Health; founder-chm Moscow and All-Russian Sci Soc of Urologists; wrote over 142 works; *Publ*: doctor's thesis *Vaktsinoterapiya i vaktsinodiagnostika gonorreynykh zabolevaniy* (The Vaccinotherapy and Vaccinodiagnosis of Gonorrheal Diseases) (1916); *Konspekt lektsiy po gonorree i rasstroystvu polovykh funktsiy u muzhchin* (A Summary of Lectures on Gonorrhea and Disorders of the Male Sexual Functions) (1922); *Gonorreya i rasstroystva polovykh funktsiy u muzhchin* (Gonorrhea and Disorders of the Male Sexual Functions) (1926); *Khronicheskiye gonorroynyye i paragonorroynyye zabolevaniya polovykh zhelyoz* (Chronic Gonorrheal and Paragonorrheal Diseases of the Gonads) (1926); *Rasstroystvo polovoy deyatel'nosti muzhchin* (Disturbances of the Male Sexual Activity) (1929); *Metodika issledovaniya i obshchaya diagnostika zabolevaniy mochevykh putey* (Methods of Studying and the General Diagnosis of Diseases of the Urinary Tract) (1931); *Zlokachestvennyye opukholi yaichek, pridatkov i semennykh kanatikov* (Malignant Tumors of the Testicles, Epididymis and the Spermatic Cords) (1934); *Zlokachestvennyye opukholi mochevogo puzyrya, semennykh puzyr'kov i predstatel'noy zhelezy* (Malignant Tumors of the Urinary Bladder, the Seminal Vescicles and the Prostate) (1934); *Zlokachestvennyye opukholi muzhskoy uretry i polovogo chlena* (Malignant Tumors of the Male Urethra and Penis) (1934); co-ed *Operativnaya urologiya* (Operative Urology) (1934); coauthor, *Uchebnik po kozhnym i venericheskim boleznyam* (Textbook of Skin and Venereal Diseases) (1936); *Urologiya* (Urology) (1938); *Izbrannyye trudy* (Selected Works) (1953); *Awards*: Order of the Red Banner of Labor; medals; *Died*: 14 Apr 1949.

FRUMINA, Anna Yefremovna (? -1959) Surgeon, traumatologist and orthopedist; Dr of Med from 1951; prof from 1951; *Born*: in Borisoglebsk, Tambov Province; *Educ*: 1911 grad Med Fac, St Vladimir Univ, Kiev; received surgical training at hospitals and clinics in Kiev; *Career*: from 1919 intern, Kiev Home for Crippled Children; after reorg of home as Kiev Children's Orthopedic Inst later Ukr Inst of Orthopedics and Traumatology head, Bone-Tuberculosis Dept; from 1930 dir, Children's and Adolescents' Orthopedic and Traumatological Clinic, Kiev Children's Orthopedic Inst; 1923-36 lecturer, 1936-37 assoc prof, 1937-41 acting head, from 1941 head, Chair of Orthopedics and Traumatology, Kiev Inst of Postgrad Med Training; during WW 2 head surgeon and traumatologist, various mil hospitals in Kaz; simultaneously, assoc prof of orthopedics and traumatology, Chair of Hospital Surgery, Kaz Med Inst; also lecturer, Kaz postgrad med training and specialization courses; 1944 resumed former posts at Kiev Inst of Postgrad Med Training and Ukr Inst of Orthopedics and Traumatology; 1951 received doctorate for thesis on "The Open Correction of Congenital Dislocation of the Hip in Children and Adolescents"; member, ed council, journal *Ortopediya, travmatologiya i protezirovaniye*; wrote over 50 works on various aspects of orthopedics, notably on the clinical aspects and treatment of bilateral coxitis, periarthritic osteal foci of infection and the advisability of early surgical intervention in such cases; developed and modified several methods of stabilizing the feet after infantile paralysis; devised improved method of open treatment of congenital dislocation of the thigh; *Awards*: orders and medals; *Died*: 9 Feb 1959.

FRUMKIN, Anatoliy Pavlovich (1897-1962) Surgeon and urologist; Dr of Med from 1939; prof from 1962; Hon Sci Worker of RSFSR; *Born*: 1897; *Educ*: 1921 grad Med Fac, 1st Moscow State Univ; *Career*: after grad intern, I.K.Spizharnyy's clinic; 1924-26 asst to Prof P.D.Solovov (with whom he worked until 1940), Chair of Hospital Surgery, 2nd Moscow State Inst; 1926-62 intern, then head, Urological Dept, S.P.Botkin Hospital; 1939 defended doctor's thesis on "Intravenal Pyeolography"; 1946-62 prof, Chair of Urology, Moscow Centr Inst of Postgrad Med Training; during WW 2 Chief Urologist, Sov Army; made important contributions to uretography, the treatment of acute suppurative infections of the kidneys, plastic surgery of the ureter and the urinary bladder with sections of the intestines, and the surgical treatment of urogenital fistulae; devised new operational techniques of resection of the cervix vesicae in cases of cancer, of superior and subcapsular pyelotomy, and of restoration of the urinary bladder in extrophy; ed, urology section, *BME* (Large Medical Encyclopedia); ed urology section *Opyt sovetskoy meditsiny v Velikoy Otechestvennoy voyne 1941-45 godov* (The Experience of Soviet Medicine During the 1941-45 Great Fatherland War); wrote over 150 works; *Publ*: coauthor, *Rentgenovskiy atlas khirurgicheskikh zabolevaniy mochepolovoy sistemy* (An X-Ray Atlas of Surgical Disorders of the Urogenital Tract) (1930); *Nephritis apostematosa* (1939); *Voyennaya travma mochepolovoy sistemy* (War Wounds of the Urogenital Tract) (1944); *Gematurgiya i yeyo klinicheskoye znacheniye* (Hematurgy and Its Clinical Significance) (1946); *Rekonstruktivno-plasticheskiye operatsii v urologii* (Restorative Plastic Operations in Urology) (1946); *Operatsii na pochkakh i mochetochnikakh* (Kidney and Ureter Surgery) (1951); *Vostanovitel'naya khirurgiya posle ognestrel'nykh raneniy i povrezhdeniy mochepolovykh organov i pryamoy kishki* (Restorative Surgery of the Urogenital Tract and Rectum After Gunshot Wounds and Injuries) (1955); *Tsistoskopicheskiy atlas* (A Cystoscopic Atlas) (1954); ed and coauthor, *Aktual'nyye voprosy urologii* (Contemporary Problems of Urology) (1962); *Died*: 1962.

FRUMKIN, Moisey Il'ich (L. GERMANOV) (1878-1939) Statistician; govt official; CP member from 1898; *Born*: 1878; *Career*: from 1894 in workers' and Soc-Democratic movement; worked in Petersburg, Moscow, Vitebsk, Minsk, Vilnius and Smolensk; member, Northwestern Oblast Comt and local comts; 1906 in Petersburg, member, Bolshevik mil org; at the time of Kronstadt and Sveaborg Mutinies arrested; May 1908 released on bail; under an alias fled to Baku and engaged in illegal Party and trade-union work; helped edit and publish polit trade-union newspaper *Gudok*; early 1908 ed, Moscow trade-union periodicals *Rabocheye delo, Vestnik truda* and *Nash put'*; Feb 1911 arrested and exiled to Kansk Uyezd; after 1917 Revol member, Krasnoyarsk Province Party Comt and Presidium member, Province Exec Comt; 1918 member, West Siberian Kray Sov in Omsk and member, Kray Party Comt; 1918-22 Collegium member, the Dep Pop Comr of Food; 1920 dep chm, Siberian Revol Comt and member, Siberian Oblast Bureau, CC; subsequently plen, Pop Comrt of Food; dep chm, Rostov Kray Sovnarkhoz and until May 1921 Bureau member, CC; 1922-24 Dep Pop Comr of For Trade; 1924 Collegium member, Pop Comrt of Finance; 1925-26 Dep Pop Comr of Trade; from late 1926 Dep Pop Comr of Finance; 1929-30 chm, State Fishing Syndicate; from 1931 head, Supply and Marketing Section, USSR Supr Sovnarkhoz; then Collegium member, USSR Pop Comrt of Food Supply; 1928-29 sided with right-wing deviationists and opposed CC, CPSU(B) policy of industrialization and collectivization; 1937 expelled from the Party for anti-Party activities; arrested by State Security organs; *Died*: 1939 in imprisonment.

FRUMKINA (pseudonym: ESTER), Mariya Yakovlevna (1880 - ?) Party official; CP member from 1920; *Born*: 1880; *Career*: from 1897 directed Minsk Jewish workers' propaganda circles; same year joined Bund; worked in Minsk, Vilnius, Odessa, etc; repeatedly arrested and exiled; member, Lit Collegium, CC, Bund; member, ed staff, centr Bund newspapers; from Apr 1917 member, CC, Bund; during WW 1 abroad; sympathized with right-wing Centrists (Kautskiy group); as CC Bureau, member, ed, newspaper "Der Wecker," member, Sov Exec Comt, and member, Minsk City Duma, until 1919, followed Bund policy and opposed Bolsheviks; from 1919 helped lead leftwing Bund faction; after the schism in the Bund joined Sov platform; head, Minsk Dept of Educ; member, Centr Exec Comt, Lith-Bel Sov Republ; at 12th Conference member, CC, "Communist Bund"; 1920 joined CPSU(B); 1921-30 member, Centr Bureau, Jewish Sections, CC, CPSU(B); head, Jewish Section, Main Polit Educ Bd for Women Workers, CC, CPSU(B); celited first Jewish eight-vol publ of Lenin's collected works; also ed, journals "Jungwald" and *Na novykh putyakh*; from 1925 rector, Communist Univ for Western Nat Minorities; *Died*: date and place of death unknown.

FRUNZE (pseudonyms: MIKHAYLOV; ARSENIY; TRIFONYCH), Mikhail Vasil'yevich (1885-1925) Party official and mil commander; former chief of staff, Red Army; head, Mil Acad; chm,

USSR Revol Mil Council; Pop Comr of the Army and Navy; member, and cand Politburo member, CC, RCP(B); CP member from 1904; *Born*: 2 Feb 1885 in Pishpek, now Frunze, son of a mil med orderly; *Educ*: 1904-05 studied at Petersburg Politech Inst; *Career*: 1904 arrested and exiled from Petersburg for participating in Nov demonstration; 1905 head, Ivanovo-Voznesensk RSDRP(B) org; 1906 deleg, 4th RSDRP Congress; Mar 1907 arrested and sentenced to four years' hard labor; during imprisonment brought to trial for armed attack on policeman and sentenced to death; sentence commuted to six years' hard labor; from 1914 in exile; late 1915 co-ed, journal *Vostochnoye obozreniye*; Apr 1916 under the pseudonym Mikhaylov began to work for the Western Front Comt of the All-Russian Zemstvo Union; after 1917 Feb Revol headed Bolshevik orgs in Bel; Sept 1917 sent to Shuya where he was elected chm, Shuya Sov of Workers, Soldiers and Peasants' Dep; Oct 1917 led workers squads in battles in Moscow; deleg, 2nd All-Russian Congress of Soviets; during spring and summer 1918 chm, Ivanovo-Voznesensk Province Exec Comt, Sov of Workers, Soldiers and Peasants' Dep; secr, Ivanovo-Voznesensk Province Party Comt; mil comr of Ivanovo-Voznesensk and chm, Ivanovo-Voznesensk Province Sovnarkhoz; July 1918 helped to crush Leftist Socialist-Revol revolt in Moscow and Yaroslavl', after which he was appointed mil comr, Yaroslavl' Mil Distr; late 1918 appointed commander, 4th Army, Eastern Front; then commander, Southern Army Group, Eastern Front; commander, Eastern and Turkestani Fronts; Sept 1920 appointed commander, Southern Front; Nov 1920 at 5th Congress of CP(B) Ukr elected member, CC, CP(B) Ukr and member, Ukr Centr Exec Comt; Dec 1920 appointed RSFSR Revol-Mil Council's plen in the Ukr, commander of Ukr and Crimea Armed Forces, and dep chm, Ukr Council of Pop Comr; Nov 1921-Jan 1922 headed special mission to Turkey and established diplomatic relations between Ukr and Turkey; Mar 1924 appointed dep chm, USSR Revol Mil Council and USSR Dep Pop Comr of Mil and Naval Affairs; from Apr 1924 simultaneously chief-of-staff, Red Army and commandant, Mil Acad (which now bears his name); Jan 1925 appointed chm, USSR Revol Mil Council and USSR Pop Comr of the Army and Navy; Feb 1925 member, USSR Labor and Defense Council; together with senior mil specialists reorganized the mil admin, transferred land forces to the territorial-police system, founded national mil units, introduced the principle of one-man command, trained commanders, etc; attended 1st All-Union Congress of Soviets where he reported on the formation of the USSR on behalf of the Ukr govt; member, All-Union Centr Exec Comt, all convocations beginning with the 3rd Congress of Soviets; from 1921 member, CC, RCP(B); from 1924 cand Politburo member, CC; his birthplace Pishpek (Kir SSR), mil training establishments, vil, rayons and streets of many towns in the USSR have been named after him; *Publ: Reorganizatsiya Krasnoy armii* (The Reorganization of the Red Army) (1921); *Yedinaya voyennaya doktrina i Krasnaya armiya* (Unified Military Doctrine and the Red Army) (1921); *Regulyarnaya armiya i militsiya* (The Regular Army and the Police) (1922); *Pamyati Perekopa i Chongara* (In Memory of Perekop and Chongar) (1922); *Dobryy chas* (In the Nick of Time) (1923); *Budem gotovy* (Let Us Be Ready) (1923); *Front i tyl v voyne budushchego* (The Front and the Rear in Future Warfare) (1924); *Yevropeyskiye tsivilizatory i Marokko* (European Civilizers and Morocco) (1925); *Kadrovaya armiya i militsiya* (The Regular Army and the Police) (1925), etc; *Awards*: two Orders of the Red Banner; Hon Revol Weapon; *Died*: 31 Oct 1925 in govt hospital from a heart attack without regaining consciousness after an ulcer operation; buried beside the Kremlin Wall in Moscow.

FRUNZE, Timur Mikhaylovich (1923-1942) Fighter-pilot; Komsomol member from 1938; *Born*: 5 Apr 1923 in Khar'kov, son of M.V. Frunze; from 1931 brought up in K.Ye. Voroshilov's family; *Educ*: 1941 grad Kacha Mil Aviation School; *Career*: from 1941 fighter-pilot in Sov Air Force; 19 Jan 1942 killed in action, defending damaged plane of his commander; *Awards*: Hero of the Sov Union (posthumously).

FUKS-MARTIN (FUCHS), Georgiy Samoylovich (1905-1957) German conductor; member, CP Germany from 1931; *Born*: 1905; *Educ*: 1925 grad Sondershausen Higher Music School; *Career*: first violinist, Sondershausen Opera House; opera conductor, theaters in Leipzig and other German and Dutch cities; 1931-33 musical dir, Hamburg "Assoc of Revol Actors"; 1933, after Hitler's accession to power, emigrated to USSR; 1937 granted Sov citizenship; from 1933 dir, Moscow Operetta Theater; *Works*: conducted operettas: Kalman's "Violet of Montmartre" (1933); Offenbach's "Madame Favar" (1935); Dunayevskiy's *Zolotaya dolina* (Golden Valley) (1938); *Vol'nyy veter* (Free Wind) (1947); Aleksandrov's *God spustya* (A Year Later) (1939); Shcherbachyov's *Tabachnyy kapitan* (Tobacco Captain) (1943); Fel'tsman's *Vozdushnyy zamok* (Castle in the Air) (1948); Milyutin's *Devichiy perepolokh* (Girlish Confusion) (1950); *Died*: 5 June 1957.

FUNTIKOV, Fyodor Adrianovich (1876-1926) Politician; member, Socialist-Revol Party from 1905; *Born*: 1876 in Saratov Province, son of a peasant; *Career*: railroad worker; after 1917 Feb Revol one of the leaders, Socialist-Revol Party in Transcaspian Oblast; summer 1918 headed anti-Sov revolt in Transcaspian Oblast, which ended with the overthrow of Sov regime in Ashkhabad and establishment of Transcaspian Provisional Govt; looking for allies in his fight against Bolshevism, he negotiated with Gen Denikin and the command of the English expeditionary corps in Meshede (Iran); official Sov sources maintain that in 1918 he pursued a policy of White terror; 24 July 1918 involved in the execution of nine Ashkhabad comr (Zhitnikov, Rozanov, Kuliyev, etc); 20 Sept 1918 involved in execution of the 26 Baku comr; 1926, after Sovietization of the Transcaspian Oblast, arrested and tried before Mil Collegium, Supr Court; *Died*: 6 May 1926 executed.

FURMANOV, Dmitriy Alekseyevich (1891-1926) Writer; CP member from July 1918; *Born*: 7 Nov 1891 in vil Sereda, former Kostroma Province (now Furmanov, Ivanov Oblast), son of a peasant; *Educ*: 1912-14 studied at Philological Fac, Moscow Univ; 1922 grad Soc Sci Fac, Moscow Univ; *Career*: at the start of WW 1 volunteered as male nurse; in summer 1917 member, then dep chm, Ivanovo Sov of Workers, Peasants and Soldiers' Dep; during 1917 Oct Revol chm, Revol staff, and from early 1918 member, Ivanovo-Voznesensk Province Exec Comt; maintained close ties with local Socialist-Revol Party group and local anarchists group; summer 1918 broke with these parties, joined CP and helped crush Yaroslavl' mutiny; late 1918 elected secr, Ivanovo-Voznesensk Province RCP(B) Comt; early 1919 comr, 25th *Chapayev* Div; then head, Polit Bd, Turkestani Front, Kuban' Army; wounded in action; 1921, after his discharge from the army, went to Moscow and began lit work; worked for State Publ House and Press Dept, CC, RCP(B); from 1923 secr, Moscow Writers' Org; first verse published 1912, first prose work 1916; *Publ*: stories and novelettes: *Krasnyy desant* (Red Landing Operation) (1922); *V semnadtsatom godu* (In 1917) (1923); *Chapayev* (1923); *Invalid* (1925); novel *Myatezh* (Mutiny) (1925); essays: *Kak ubili ottsa* (How Father Was Killed) (1925); *Tovarishch M. V. Frunze pod Ufoy* (Comrade M. V. Frunze at Ufa) (1925), etc; collected essays *Morskiye berega* (Sea Shores) (1926); critical articles: *Zavyadshiy buket* (Withered Bouquet); *O 'Zheleznom potoke' A. Serafimovicha* (A. Serafimovich's "Iron Stream"), etc; *Sobraniye sochineniy* (Collected Works) (4 vol, 1960-61); *Chapayev* and *Mutiny* were subsequently dramatized and staged in Sov theaters; these works then formed the basis for the operas *Myatezh* (Mutiny) (1938) and *Chapayev* (1941); 1934 *Chapayev* adapted for the screen; *Awards*: Order of the Red Banner of Labor; *Died*: 15 Mar 1926.

FYODOROV, G.F. (1891-1936) Party and govt official; CP member from 1907; *Born*: 1891; *Career*: Party work in Petersburg, Helsinki, Moscow, Nizhniy Tagil, etc; 1917 member, Exec Comt, Petrograd Sov; during 1917 Oct Revol member, Petrograd Mil-Revol Comt; after 1917 Revol Dep Pop Comr of Labor; 1918 chm, Nizhniy Novgorod, then Saratov Province Exec Comt; 1919-21 head, Polit Dept, 13th and 14th Armies; after Civil War exec Party, trade-union and govt work; 1927 at 15th CPSU(B) Congress expelled from Party as active member of Trotskyist opposition; 1928 reinstated in the Party by a decree of the Presidium, CPSU(B) Centr Control Commission; 1934 expelled again for anti-Party activity; arrested by State Security organs; *Died*: 1936 in imprisonment.

FYODOROV, Lev Nikolayevich (1891-1952) Physiologist; member, USSR Acad of Med Sci from 1948; CP member from 192O; *Born*: 1891; *Educ*: 1914 grad Med Fac, Tomsk Univ; *Career*: after grad army physician; from 1923 worked at I.P.Pavlov's laboratory, Inst of Experimental Med; 1927-31 dep dir, 1931-32 dir, Inst of Experimental Med; 1932-38 founder-dir, All-Union Inst of Experimental Med; founder-dir, Laboratory of Higher Nervous Activity, Inst of Neurosurgery, USSR Acad of Med Sci; head, Chair of Higher Nervous Activity, Moscow Univ; took active part in work of USSR Acad of Med Sci; did major research on the interaction of the stimulatory and inhibitory processes in experimentally-induced neuroses; also did research on convulsive states; developed method of inducing experimental reflex epilepsy; made electroencephalographic neurophysiological analyses of the cerebral cortex in hypnotic and posthypnotic states; 1948-50 chm, Learned Med Council, USSR Min of Health; *Publ*: *Deystviye bromistogo kal'tsiya pri narushenii balansa mezhdu protsessami vozbuzhdeniya i tormozheniya u vozbudimogo tipa nervnoy sistemy sobaki* (The Effect of Calcium Bromide in a Case of Imbalance of the Stimulatory and Inhibitory Processes in a Dog with a Stimulated Nervous System) (1926); *Deystviye nekotorykh farmatsevticheskikh preparatov pri eksperimental'nom nevroze u sobaki* (The Effect of Certain Pharmaceutical Preparations on Dogs With Experimentally-Induced Neuroses) (1927); *Narusheniye ravnovesiya mezhdu protsessami vozbuzhdeniya i tormozheniya u vozbudimogo tipa sobaki ot povtornykh primeneniy differentsirovki na chastotu kozhno-mekhanicheskogo razdrazhitelya i vosstanovleniye ravnovesiya bromom* (Imbalance of the Stimulatory and Inhibitory Processes Induced in a Stimulated Dog by Irregular Mechanical Stimulation of the Skin, and the Restoration of Balance With Bromide) (1928); *Died*: 1952.

FYODOROV, Mikhail Mikhaylovich (1858-?) Govt official; member, Constitutional Democratic Party; *Born*: 1858; *Career*: Min of Trade under Vitte; during Civil War chm, National Center, which played a major role in the campaigns of Denikin and Yudenich; member, National Center deleg in Volunteer Army; member, deleg sent to Yassy to confer with allied ambassadors on organizing the struggle against the Bolsheviks; member, special advisory group under Denikin; sponsored formation of army council responsible for econ org and relations with for and local govts; *Died*: date and place of death unknown.

FYODOROV, Mikhail Mikhaylovich (1867-1945) Mining eng; member Ukr Acad of Sci from 1929; Hon Sci Worker of RSFSR from 1932; *Born* 1 Sept 1867 in Yekaterinodar (now Krasnodar); *Educ*: 1895 grad Petersburg Mining Inst; *Career*: from 1895 worked at Donbas mines; from 1905 lectured at various higher educ establishments; from 1923 prof, Moscow Mining Acad (Moscow Mining Inst); from 1932 worked at Inst of Mine Mech (now Mining Inst), Ukr (Acad of Sci, which now bears his name; devised system of dynamic control to give mine elevators constant winching radius; developed harmonic lift system which guaranteed full dynamic counterpoising of mine elevators with heavy terminal cables; devised method of calculating mine turbines on the basis of hydrodynamic analogy; *Publ: Teoriya i raschyot garmonicheskogo rudnichnogo pod'yoma* (The Theory and Calculation of a Harmonic Mine Lift) (1914); *Sravneniye naiboleye rasprostranyonnykh sistem rudnichnykh ventilyatorov na osnovanii ikh kharakteristik* (A Comparison of the Commonest Mine Ventilation Systems on the Basis of Their Characteristics) (2 vol, 1911); *Naivygodneyshiye diametr i profil' nagnetatel'noy truby v rudnichnykh vodootlivnykh ustanovkakh* (The Optimum Diameter and Section of the Stand Pipe in Mine Drainage Installations) (1925); *Naivygodneyshiy dinamicheskiy rezhim v nekotorykh tipakh rudnichnykh pod'yomnykh ustanovok* (The Optimum Dynamic Specifications of Certain Types of Mine Elevator) (1926), etc; *Awards*: Order of Lenin; *Died*: 29 Mar 1945.

FYODOROV, Sergey Petrovich (1869-1936) Surgeon and urologist; Hon Sci Worker of RSFSR from 1928; *Born:* 23 Jan 1869 in Moscow, son of a physician; *Educ:* 1891 grad Med Fac, Moscow Univ; *Career:* after grad worked at A.A.Bobrov's Clinic; 1895 defended doctor's thesis on tetanus; 1903-36 head, Chair of Hospital Surgery Clinic, Mil Med Acad; in early stages of career specialized in bacteriology and immunology; 1892 obtained and used first Russian cholera antitoxin; also obtained tetanus toxin and antitoxin and proved that tetanus does not occur if both are injected simultanously; 1893 obtained anti-tetanus serum for med use; while abroad studied aseptic operation techniques under Schimmelbaum and ureter cystoscopy and cauterization techniques under Kasper; also studied new methods of endoscopy; devised a number of new operations, including pyelotomy in situ and subcapsular nephrectomy; invented new surgical instruments, including renal clamps and spatulas; became known as the father of Russian urology for his major research on surgery of the urinary and biliary tracts; wrote classic textbooks on surgery and urology; also did research on abdominal and brain surgery; developed trepaning techniques, operations on the Gasserov ganglion and the hypophysis, and a technique for removing brain tumors; made studies of spine surgery; used all newly developed methods for treating malignants tumors, including mobile x-ray equipment for irradiating the operating area during their removal; tested methods of treating neoplasms by fulguration and with high-frequency electr currents; was one of first surgeons to use intravenous narcosis (hedonal); his clinic was also one of the first in Russia to work on the problem of blood transfusion, to operate on the sympathetic nervous system and to study trophic ulcerous processes; toward end of life studied problems of surgery of the centr and peripheral nervous systems; for a number of years sci dir and dir, Leningrad State Inst of Surgical Neuropathology; co-founder, journal *Novyy khirurgicheskiy arkhiv*, which was virtually the first Sov surgery journal to appear after WW 1; 1923 co-founder, journal *Urologiya*; 1907 founder-chm, first Russian Urological Soc; developed the best traditions of Russian clinical med, combining vast practical experience with a stictly sci approach to the patient and a precise grasp of pathological processes; as a surgeon he was noted for the extreme precision of his operating technique, which derived from his excellent knowledge of anatomy and pathology; foundet a major school of surgery which brought forth scores of leading surgeons; wrote over 120 works; *Publ*: doctor's thesis *Eksperimental'no-klinicheskoye issledovaniye po voprosu o stolbnyake* (Experimental Clinical Research on Tetanus) (1895); *Atlas tsistoskopii i rektoskopii* (An Atlas of Cystoscopy and Rectoscopy) (1911); *Zhyolchnyye kamni khirurgiya zhyolchnykh putey* (Gallstones and Surgery of the Biliary Tract) (1918); *Khirurgiya pochek i mechetochnikov* (Kidney and Ureter Surgery) (6 vol, 1923-25); co-ed, *Rukovodsvto prakticheskoy khirurgii* (A Manual of Practical Surgery) (9 vol, 1929-33); *Izbrannyye trudy* (Selected Works) (vol 1, 1957); *Awards:* five orders from Tsarist govt; granted hereditary nobility and rank of Councillor of State by Tsar; Order of Lenin; *Died*: 15 Jan 1936.

FYODOROV, Vladimir Grigor'yevich (1874-1966) Weapons designer; lt-gen, Eng Corps; Dr of Tech Sci; prof; *Born:* 3 May 1874 in Petersburg, son of an office worker; *Educ:* 1895 grad Mikhaylov Artillery College; 1900 grad Mikhaylov Artillery Acad; *Career:* 1895-97 ensign, 1st Artillery Brigade; 1900-14 weapons designer, Artillery Dept, Artillery Committee; 1911 designed first Russian automatic rifle; during WW 1 arms factory controller, Main Artillery Board; 1917-18 dir of a machine-gun plant; 1918-31 head, first Sov arms planning and design bureau and dir of a tool plant; from 1931 worked for Pop Comrt of Defense, Min of Armaments and Acad of Artillery Sci; during 1930's devised method of reducing production time of Degtyaryov machine-guns; from 1953 in retirement; *Publ: Vooruzheniye russkoy armii za 19 stoletiy* (The Weapons of the Russian Army Through 19 Centuries) (1901); *Vliyaniye ognya pekhoty na deystviya artillerii* (The Effect of Infantry Fire on Artillery Operations) (1903); *Avtomaticheskoye oruzhiye* (Automatic Weapons) (1907); *Osnovaniya ustroystva avtomaticheskogo oruzhiya* (The Mechanical Principles of Automatic Weapons)(1931); *K voprosu o date poyavleniya artillerii v Rusi* (The Date of the First Appearance of Artillery in Rus) (1949), etc; *Awards:* Hero of Labor (1928); Order of Lenin; other awards; *Died:* 18 Sept 1966.

FYODOROV, Yevgraf Yevgrafovich (1880-1965) Climatologist; corresp member, USSR Acad of Sci from 1946; *Born:* 20 Nov 1880; *Educ:* 1909 grad Petersburg Univ; *Career:* 1910 assoc, Main Physical Observatory; 1911-34 assoc, Pavlovsk Observatory of Magnetism and Meteorology; 1934-55 assoc, Inst of Geography, USSR Acad of Sci; *Publ: Klimat kak sovokupnost' pogod* (Climate as an Aggregate of Weather) (1925); *Raspredeleniye dozhdlivykh pogod i ikh tipov po ravnine Yevropeyskoy chasti SSSR v letneye polugodiye* (The Distribution of Rainy Weather and its Varieties on the European Plain of the USSR in the Summer Half of the Year) (1938); *Klimat Yevropeyskoy chasti SSSR v pogodakh* (The Climate of the European USSR as Expressed in Weather) (1949); *Award:* Order of Lenin; Order of the Red Star; medals: *Died:* July 1965.

G

GABASHVILI, Gigo (real name: Georgiy Ivanovich) (1862-1936) Painter; prof; Pop Artist of Geo SSR from 1929; one of the founders of Geo realistic painting; *Born*: 9 Nov 1862 in Tiflis; *Educ*: 1886-88 studied at Petersburg Acad of Arts and 1894-97 at

Munich Acad of Arts; *Career*: created over 2,000 genre, landscape and portrait paintings; 1891 staged first exhibition; in his youth influenced by I.Ye. Repin; visited Centr Asia, Italy and Greece; 1922 helped found Tbilisi Acad of Arts; until 1930 prof of this Acad; a number of his works are on display at Geo Art Museum; *Works*: "After the Rain"; "Tea Marchant"; "Mullah"; "Ancient Eastern Weapons Shop"; "At the Melon Field"; (1891); "Three Townsmen" (1893); "Bazaar in Samarkand" (1894); "Divan-Begi Basin in Bukhara" (1895); "Daba-Khana" (1896); "Sleeping Khevsur" (1898); "Drunken Khevsur" (1899); "Temple Holiday" ("Alaverdoba") (1899); "Khevsur Patrol" (1899?); "Defense of Arkhoti" (1899-1901); "On the Rafts" (1902); "Dawn at Cemetery Church" (1904); portraits of: musician De-Roza (1902); unknown Geo prince; I. Chavchavadze (1907-08); A. Tsereteli (1908-13); Sh. Rustaveli; N.Ya. Nikoladze (1925); I.V. Stalin; *Died*: 28 Oct 1936.

GABBE, Tamara Grigor'yevna (1903-1960) Russian playwright; *Born*: 16 Mar 1903; *Educ*: 1928 grad Lit Fac, Inst of Art History; *Career*: 1929 began to write plays; wrote children's plays based on Russian folk tales and legends and Flemish fairy tales; *Works*: plays: *Zhan Besstrashnyy* (Jean the Indomitable) (1941); *Gorod masterov, ili skazka o dvukh gorbunakh* (The City of Master Craftsmen, or the Tale of the Two Hunchbacks) (1944); *Avdot'ya Ryazanochka* (1946); *Khrustal'nyy bashmachok* (The Glass Slipper) (1944); *Olovyannyye kol'tsa* (Tin Rings) (1953); *Skazka pro soldata i zmeyu* (The Tale of the Soldier and the Snake) (1958); *Gorod masterov. P'yesy, skazki* (The City of Master Craftsmen. Plays and Tales) (1958); *Died*: 2 Mar 1960.

GABIYEV, Said Ibragimovich (1882-1963) Lit historian; govt official; CP member from 1918; *Born*: 1882 in Opochek, Pskov Province, son of an office worker exiled from Dagh; *Educ*: grad Petersburg Univ; *Career*: 1904 enrolled at Petersburg Univ and conducted illegal revol work among students; from 1912 published Russian- and Lak-language newspaper *Zarya Dagestana* and *Musul'manskaya gazeta* in Petersburg; brought to trial for anti-govt articles; after 1917 Feb Revol member, Dagh Socialist Group; from May 1918 member, Dagh Oblast Mil-Revol Comt, member, Dagh Oblast Sov, chm, Terek Pop Sov and ed, newspaper *Revolyutsionnyy gorets*; organizer and comr of an int detachment in Terek area; from Feb 1919 member, Dagh Oblast RCP(B) Comt; 1920-21 chm, Dagh Revol Comt, member, North Caucasian Revol Comt, member, Revol Sov of Southeast Russian Labor Army; 1921-37 Dagh Pop Comr of Educ and Finance, Dep Pop Comr of Finance of Transcaucasian SFSR and dep head, Transcaucasian Water Management Bd; also research and lit work; pioneer of Sov Lakian lit; translated into Lakian Lermontov's verse and Krylov's fables, etc; *Publ*: monograph *Laki, ikh proshloye i byt* (The Laks, Their Past and Way of Life) (1905); collected verse *Zvuki lakskoy chungury* (Sounds of the Lakian Chungura) (1927), etc; *Died*: 1963.

GABOVICH, Mikhail Markovich (1905-1965) Russian ballet dancer; Pop Artiste of RSFSR from 1951; CP member from 1936; *Born*: 7 Dec 1905 in vil Bol'shiye Gulyanki, now Kiev Oblast; *Educ*: 1924 grad Moscow Choreographic College; *Career*: from 1924 at Moscow State Acad Bol'shoy Theater; from 1954 instructor at Moscow Choreographic College (1954-58 artistic dir of this college); author of a number of articles on ballet art; *Parts*: Siegfried and Desiré in Tchaikovsky's *Lebedinoye ozero* (Swan Lake) and *Spyashchaya krasavitsa* (Sleeping Beauty); Vatslav in Asaf'yev's *Bakhchisarayskiy fontan* (Fountain of Bakhchisaray); Andrey in Solov'yov-Sedoy's *Taras Bul'ba*; Romeo and the Prince in Prokofiev's "Romeo and Juliet" and *Zolushka* (Cinderella); Yevgeniy and Ma Li-cheng in Gliere's *Mednyy vsadnik* (The Bronze Horseman) and *Krasnyy mak* (Red Poppy), etc; *Awards*: Stalin Prizes (1946, 1950); Order of the Red Banner of Labor; Badge of Hon; medals; *Died*: 12 July 1965.

GABRIYELYAN, Gurgen Bakhshiyevich (1903-1956) Arm actor, stage dir, teacher and playwright; Pop Artiste of Arm SSR from 1950; CP member from 1946; *Born*: 3 Dec 1903; *Educ*: grad Arm Drama Studio in Tiflis; *Career*: from 1924 at Yerevan Sundukyan Theater; from 1926 film actor; taught acting and stage directing at Yerevan Inst of Stagecraft; leading Arm comedy actor; *Roles*: Kinto in *Pepo* (1935); Tatul in *Karo* (1937); Armen in *Zangezur* (1938); Gonchar in "Mountain March" (1939); Sako in "Girl from the Ararat Valley" (1950); Old Asatur in "Mystery of the Mountain Lake" (1954); Nadzharyan in "The Golden Steer" (1955); the preacher in "The Path of Thunder" (1956); Karinyan in "For Honor" (1956); *Productions*: Shakespeare's "Merry Wives of Windsor" (1939) and "Comedy of Errors" (1947); *Publ*: play *Gikor*; coauthor, play "Girl from the Ararat Valley" (1948); *Died*: 23 Mar 1956.

GABYSHEV, Ivan Yakovlevich (1887-1918) Mil commander; *Born*: 1887; *Career*: Dec 1917 chm, Centr Staff for the Org of the Red Guard in Baku; 1918 member, Mil Revol Comt, Caucasian Army; *Died*: 1918; executed by firing squad along with 25 other Baku comr.

GACHEV, Dmitriy Ivanovich (1902-1945) Bulgarian and Russian writer and musicologist; husband of musicologist and assoc prof, M.S. Bruk; *Born*: 29 Jan 1902 in Bratsigovo (Bulgaria); *Career*: 1926 came as polit emigré to USSR; author of works on Gluck, Wagner, Diderot, Stendhal, Heine and Rolland; examined the mutual relations between arts, relation of lit and music to modern philosophical thought; 1938 arrested by State Security organs; *Died*: 17 Dec 1945 in Adygolokh, Magadan Oblast; posthumously rehabilitated.

GADIYEV, Tsomak Sekayevich (Mikhail Yur'yevich) (1883-1931) Ossetian poet, writer and lit historian; CP member from 1919; *Born*: 2 Jan 1883 in vil Ganisi (now Geo SSR), son of a writer; *Educ*: grad History and Philology Fac, Derpt (now Tartu) Univ; *Career*: for participation in 1905-07 Revol sentenced to death; sentence commuted to penal servitude for life; after 1917 Feb Revol liberated; participated in 1917 Oct Revol and in the struggle to establish Sov regime in Northern Ossetia; *Publ*: verse: "The People," "Alarm," "Call to Struggle" (1907); cycle "Prison Notes" (1908-09); drama "En Route to Happiness" (1928); novelette "Ancestral Honor" (1931); articles on the work of K. Khetagurov, Ye. Britayev, S. Gadiyev, S. Bagrayev, etc; *Died*: 24 Oct 1931.

GADZHIBEKOV, Uzeir Abdul Guseyn-ogly (1885-1948) Azer composer, musicologist, teacher and playwright; founder of Azer opera; prof from 1938; Pop Artiste of USSR from 1938; member, Azer Acad of Sci from 1945; CP member from 1938; *Born*: 5 Sept 1885 in vil Agzhabedy, Shushinsk Uyezd, son of a clerk; *Educ*: 1899-1904 at Gori Teachers' Training Seminary; 1911-12 studied at College of Music and Drama, Moscow Philharmonic Soc; 1913-14 at Petersburg Conservatory; *Career*: 1905 writer and publicist in Baku; after 1917 Oct Revol head, Music Section, Azer Radio Comt; 1922 founded first Azer Music School (later converted to Conservatory); 1926 organized first Azer choir; 1931 founded orchestra of Azer nat instruments; 1936 founded Azer State Choir; from 1938 dir and prof, Azer Conservatory (1949 named for him); from 1945 dir, Research Inst of Azer Art, Azer Acad of Sci; dep USSR Supr Sov of 1st and 2nd convocations; *Works*: operas: "Leyli and Medzhnun" (1907); "Sheykh Senan" (1910); "Rustam and Zakhrab" (1910); "Shakh Abbas and Khurshid Banu" (1912); "Asli and Kerem" (1912); "Garun and Leyli" (1915); "Kyor-ogly" (1937); "Firuza" (unfinished); musical comedies: "Man and Wife" (1910); "If Not One, Then the Other" (1910); "Arshin mal alan" (1913); melody of Azer State Anthem (1945); orchestral, choral and other musical works; wrote the libretti of all his operas and musical comedies; book *Osnovy azerbaydzhanskoy narodnoy muzyki* (Origins of Azerbaydzhan Folk Music) (1945); *Awards*: Stalin Prizes (1941, 1946); Order of Lenin; Order of the Red Banner of Labor; medals; *Died*: 23 Nov 1948 in Baku.

GADZHIBEKOV, Zul'fugar Abdul Guseyn ogly (1884-1950) Composer; Hon Art Worker of Azer SSR from 1943; *Born*: 16 Sept 1884; *Educ*: taught himself music; *Works*: musical comedies "The Fifty-Year-Old Youth" (1909); "The Rich Man" (1910); "The Married Bachelor" (1911); opera "Ashik Garib" (1916); symphonic and vocal works; *Died*: 30 Sept 1950.

GADZHIYEV, Nazim Mamediya ogly (1924-1962) Party official; CP member from 1945; *Born*: 1924; *Educ*: 1950 grad Azer State Univ; *Career*: during WW 2 worked for Rayon newspaper *Nukha fekhlyasi*; then at a Nukha school; 1944-47 worked for Azer State Security organs; Dec 1947-Mar 1950 secr, Baku Comt, Azer Komsomol; 1951-52 secr for propaganda, CC, Azer Komsomol; 1952-56 first secr, CC, Azer Komsomol; member, CC, and cand member, CC Bureau, Azer Komsomol; 1956-58 head, Sci and School Dept, CC, CP Azer; June 1958-Feb 1960 worked for CC, CPSU; from Feb 1960 member, then Bureau member and secr, CC, CP Azer; dep, Azer Supr Sov of 4th and 5th convocations; *Died*: 30 July 1962.

GAFUR-GULYAM (real name: GULYAMOV, Gafur Gulyamovich) (1903-1966) Uzbek writer; Pop Writer of Uzbek SSR from 1963; member, Uzbek Acad of Sci from 1943; *Born*: 11 May 1903;

Career: 1923 first work published; translated into Uzbek the works of Mayakovskiy, Gorky, Lavrenev, etc; *Publ*: collected verse: *Dynamo* (1931); "I Come from the East" (1943); collection "Humorous Stories" (1931); poems: "Kukan, the Farmhand" (1930); "Chinese Pictures" (1932); verse: "I Am a Jew"; "You Are Not An Orphan"; "Time"; "A Feast in Our Street"; "Feast in Yangi-Yer" (1957); "Yadgar" (1961); "Lenin and the East" (1961); etc; *Awards*: Stalin Prize (1946); *Died*: 10 July 1966.

GAFURI, Mazhit (real name: GAFUROV, Gubdulmazhit Nurganiyevich) (1880-1934) Bash and Tat poet; founder of Bash and Tat lit; public figure; Pop Poet of Bash ASSR from 1923; *Born*: 20 July 1880 in vil Yelem-Karanovo, now Gafur Rayon, Bash ASSR, son of a teacher; *Educ*: studied at medressah; partly self-taught; mastered Arabic, Persian and Russian, history, geography and Tat, classical Oriental and Russian lit; *Career*: 1902 began lit work; 1905 participated in student demonstrations in Kazan'; from 1911 confined to Ufa under police surveillance; 1915 for the poem "It's Clear You Don't Exist, Allah" cursed by Moslem clergy; opposed WW 1; after 1917 Oct Revol worked in Bash, founding schools; member, Sci-Acad Center, Bash Pop Comrt of Educ; member, Waifs Commission; main themes of his work were hatred of Tsarism and the bourgeoisie, the struggle for the liberation of his people, dissemination of educ, propaganda of socialist-realism, Sov patriotism, friendship of peoples, internationalism, diligence; wrote in Bash and Tat languages; his works are included in textbooks for Bash and Tat gen educ schools, teacher's training inst and univ; *Publ*: story "A Life Spent in Poverty" (1903); poem "Siberian Railroad" (1904); verse collections "My Young Life" (1906) and "Love of One's Nation" (1907) were confiscated by the censorship; verse: "In the Days of Freedom", "Song of Joy," "Change" (1905-07); "I Went to the Bazaar" (1907); "The Rich Man and the Worker" (1908); "Beggars," "Hope!" (1909); "Truth" (1911); "I Am Where the Poor Moan," "I And My People" (1912); verse of WW 1 period: "Lament," "One Glomy Day," "Fate," "Soldier's Wife," "Who Is He? " (1915); "It's Clear You Don't Exist, Allah" (1915); "Morning of Freedom" (1917); "Down With War," "The Dragon," "Red Banner"; poem "The Worker" (1921) subsequently adapted as an opera libretto; "Thoughts of an Old Hero" (1925); play "Red Star" (1926); "National Holiday," "In the Flower-Garden" (1927); novelette "The Disgraced" (1927); "Song of the Red Soldiers" (1929); "Poisonous Dreams," "Steps of Life" (1930); autobiographical novelette "Gold Mines of a Poet" (1931); "He Did Not Die" (1933); "Symphony of Great Victories"; numerous fables, etc; *Died*: 28 Oct 1934.

GAFUROV, Abutalib Gafurovich (1882- ?) Lakian poet; Pop Poet of Dag from 1939; *Born*: 21 Nov 1882 in vil Shuni, son of a peasant; *Career*: from 11 years of age worked as itinerant tinsmith; during Civil War in Dagh musician and combatant with partisan detachment; fought against counterrevol forces of Imam Gotsinskiy; 1932 first work printed; wrote in Lakian language; the first poet to introduce rhyme in Lakian versification; *Publ*: verse "Before and Now"; "Native Mountains"; "These Things We Like"; "Lenin" (1932); collection "New World" (1934); "The Rivers Strive for the Sea"; "I Bequeath My Heart to My Friends" (1940); "March of the Heroes" (1942); "Son of the Mountains"; "Conversation with A Horse"; "The Wish" (1943); "Aul Kuli" (1952); "Khadizha" (1955); "There Is Only One Way for the Sun in the World" (1958); *Died*: date and place of death unknown.

GAKKEL', Yakov Modestovich (1874-1945) Aircraft and motor locomotive designer; Hon Sci and Tech Worker of RSFSR; *Born*: 12 May 1874; *Educ*: 1897 grad Petersburg Electr Eng Inst; *Career*: for participating in student revol activities exiled for five years to Siberia; until 1903 worked at Lena gold-fields directing construction and later operation of one of the first Russian hydroelectr power stations; after returning to Petersburg worked on design, construction and operation of Petersburg tram system; simultaneously taught electr traction course at Electr Eng Inst; from 1921 prof of this inst; from 1936 worked at Leningrad Inst of Railroad Eng; 1909 designed a biplane (YaMG) which he built at the workshops of the 1st Russian Aeronautical Assoc (Shchetinin Plant); 1910 designed and built the G-III enclosed biplane with a 35 hp air-cooled engine, known as "bimonoplane"; 1911, as a modification of previous types, built the G-IV one-stanchion biplane with a 100 hp engine; 1911 also designed the G-V first Russian amphibious hydroplane, a two-seater monoplane with two floats and a 50 hp water-cooled engine; his G-VI biplane accomplished the first Russian inter-city flight from Tsarskoye Selo to Krasnoye Selo; 1911, at the first competition of Russian planes, his G-VII biplane proved to be the only plane to conform to all the competition requirements; for his G-VIII biplane he was awarded a diploma and a gold medal at the 1912 Moscow Aeronautical Exhibition; at the 1912 Petersburg competition of mil planes he displayed the G-IX-- the World's first cross-braced monoplane--with an 80 hp water-cooled engine; 1920-21 designed a 600 hp diesel-generator locomotive; 1924 a 1,000 hp motor locomotive was built to his design; at the 1927 All-Union Locomotive Competition his designs took 1st and 4th places; 1932-36 a two-stroke 300 hp welded diesel engine was built to his design; 1934 designed a steam tractor, incorporating vacuumless steam condensation, an original welded boiler and a valve-operated steam-engine developing 600 rpm; river steamers were equipped with such steam-engines; *Died*: 12 Dec 1945.

GALAGAN, Nikolay Ivanovich (1890-1967) Govt official; CP member from 1917; *Born*: 1 Dec 1890; *Career*: started work at age 13 as a metal worker's apprentice; then worked as mechanic at factories in Poltava Province, in the Far East and in Novgorod; repeatedly arrested for revol activities; Mar-Oct 1917 member, Corps Comt of Soldiers' Dep, 39th Army Corps; Oct 1917 member, Revol Comt, Special Army; 1918-19 held prisoner by Ukr troops, then staff work on Western Front; 1920 member, North Caucasian Kray Comt; member, Batumi Oblast Party Comt; 1921-24 plen, OGPU; then worked for Pop Comrt of For Trade; 1945–47 chief eng, Saratov-Moscow gas main; from 1953 pensioner; *Died*: 15 July 1967.

GALAKTIONOV, Mikhail Romanovich (1893-1948) Sov mil commander; ensign in Russian Army; div comr from 1935; maj-gen from 1943; Red Army polit worker and mil writer; CP member from 1917; *Born*: 1893; *Educ*: before revol studied at philological fac; grad ensign school during WW 1; 1920's grad Frunze Mil Acad; *Career*: from 1918 in Red Army; worked in mil comrt in Samara, Smolensk and Omsk; 1919-21 mil comr, Operations Bd, Field Headquarters, RSFSR Revol Mil Council; from 1921 polit worker, Bd, RSFSR Revol Mil Council; also worked for other institutions of RSFSR Pop Comrt of Mil and Naval Affairs; member, Defense Group, Council of Pop Comr; during Yezhov terror expelled from CPSU(B) and dismissed from Red Army for ties with "enemies of the people"; after six months reinstated in CPSU(B); worked for newspaper *Krasnaya zvezda*; from 1943 member, ed bd, newspaper *Krasnaya zvezda*; ed, mil section, newspaper *Pravda*; Apr 1946 represented *Pravda* at int conference of journalists in the USA; *Publ: Tempy operatsiy* (The Pace of Military Operations) (1936); *Marnskoye srazheniye* (The Battle of the Marne) (1938); *Marna* (The Marne) (1939); *Died*: 5 Apr 1948 committed suicide.

GALAN, Yaroslav Aleksandrovich (pseudonyms: ROSOVICH, Volodimir; YAGA) (1902-1949) Ukr writer and publicist; member, CP West Ukr from 1924; CPSU(B) member from 1949; *Born*: 14 July 1902 in settlement Dynov near Peremyshl', son of an office worker; *Educ*: 1923-26 studied at Vienna and 1926-28 at Cracow Univ; *Career*: active in illegal revol work; worked for the periodical *Vikna* helped found *Gorno* proletarian writers' group; 1926 member, CP Poland; 1927 first work published; helped organize 1936 L'vov Anti-Fascist Congress for the Defense of Culture; subjected to reprisals, twice arrested (1934 and 1937); contributed to Polish Communist press; during WW 2 with front-line newspapers and commentator, front broadcasting stations; 1945-46 correspondent, newspaper *Rodyanska Ukraina* at Nuremberg Trial; wrote pamphlets against fascist, nationalist and clerical reaction; his works have been translated into Russian, Geo, Arm, Lat, Lith, Est and other languages; *Publ*: plays: "Don Quixote of Ettenheim" (1926-27); "The Burden," "Veronika" (1930); comedy "99 %" (1930); "The Cell" (1932); stories: "Execution," "Virgin Soil", "Unknown Petro" (1932); drama "Roll On, Maritsa" (1942); collection "Etherial Front" (1943); tragedy "Under the Golden Eagle" (1947); books covering the Nuremberg Trial "Their Faces" (1948); "In the Face of the Facts" (1949); play "love at Dawn" (1949); pamphlets: "With Cross or Dagger," "Spiders in a Jar," "People Without Fatherland," "In Satans's Service," "Father of Darkness And Accomplices," etc; *Awards:* Stalin Prize (1952, posthumously); orders and medals; *Died*: 24 Oct 1949 killed in L'vov by a Ukr nationalist.

GALANIN, Ivan Vasil'yevich (1899-1959) Mil commander; lt-gen; CP member from 1919; *Born*: 13 July 1899 in vil Pokrovtsy, Gorky Oblast; *Educ*: 1936 grad Frunze Mil Acad; *Career*: from

1919 in Red Army; fought in Civil War; during 1930's regt commander, Moscow Proletarian Div; 1938-39 commander, 57th Rifle Div, Transbaykal Mil Distr, then in Mongolia; 1939 fought at Khalkin Gol in Mongolia; 1939-41 commander, 17th Rifle Corps; 1941-45 commander, 59th Army; dep commander, 1st Guards Cavalry Corps; commander of a mobile group on Western Front; commander, 24th, 70th, 53rd and 4th Guards Armies; 1941-42 fought in battles on Volkhov River; 1942 fought in battle of Stalingrad; 1943 fought in battle of Kursk; 1944 took part in Kirovograd and Korsun'-Shevchenkovskiy operations; after WW 2 in retirement; *Awards*: two Orders of Lenin; other orders and medals; *Died*: 12 Nov 1959.

GAL'BERSHTADT, R. S. (pseudonyms: FISHER; FRANK; KONSTANTINOV; KOSTYA) (1877-1940) Party official; *Born*: 1877; *Career*: 1896 joined Plekhanov's Soc-Democratic circle in Geneva; 1898 returned to Russia; worked in Odessa, Kishinev and Yekaterinoslav; member, *Iskra* (Spark) org; at Feb 1903 Oryol Conference appointed member, Org Comt for Convening 2nd RSDRP Congress; non-voting deleg from Org Comt at 2nd RSDRP Congress; sympathized with *Iskra* minority; after the Congress active Menshevik; Novocherkassk RSDRP (Mensheviks) org deleg at 5th Congress; 1905 Menshevik member, United CC; adopted liquidationist, then defensist stand; after 1917 Feb Revol quit polit work; from 1933 pensioner; *Died*: 1940.

GALERKIN, Boris Grigor'yevich (1871-1945) Eng; specialist in elasticity theory, member USSR Acad of Sci from 1935; member, USSR Acad of Architecture; Hon Sci and Tech Worker of RSFSR from 1934; *Born*: 4 Mar 1871 in Polotsk, now Vitebsk Oblast; *Educ*: 1899 grad Petersburg Technol Inst; *Career*: 1906 sentenced to 18 months' imprisonment for revol activities; from 1909 taught from 1920 prof and head, Chair of Construction Mech, Leningrad Polytech Inst; 1928-35 corresp member, USSR Acad of Sci; specialized in construction mech and elasticity theory, particularly theory of disk and plate buckling and shell theory; devised effective methods for precise and approximate integration of elasticity theory equations; 1915 proposed a method for the approximate solution of boundary-value problems, calculus of variation and mathematical physics; 1913-15 designed a bold and original steel carcass for electr power plant in Peterburg; sonsultant on design and construction of major hydro- and thermoelectr power plants, and also for Palace of Soviets in Moscow; head, All-Union Sci Eng and Tech Soc of Civil Engineers; *Publ*: *Uprugiye tonkiye plity* (Elastic Thin Plates) (1933); *Sobraniye sochineniy* (Collected Works) (2 vol, 1952-53); *Awards*: two Orders of Lenin; Stalin Prize (1942); *Died*: 12 July 1945.

GALEYEV, Mukhamet Valeyevichh (pseudonym: M. GALI) (1893-1952) Tatar writer and lit historian; *Born*: 24 Mar 1893, son of a mullah; *Educ*: 1933 grad Kazan' Univ; *Career*: 1914 began lit work; wrote about life in Tat vil and collectivization of agric; *Publ*: stories: "While Waiting for a Guest", "At the Party" and "Village Lads" (1914-15); "Old Samigyl" (1919); "The Years of Drought" (1921); "Firemen" (1923); "At Threshing Time", "Rakhmatulla, the Tailor", "Sharafi", etc. (1929-31); monograph on playwright G. Kamal (1941); coauthor, play *Kayum Nasyri* (1944); *Died*: 16 May 1952.

GALKIN, Samuil Zalmanovich (1897-1960) Jewish poet and playwright; *Born*: 5 Dec 1897 in settlement Rogachevo, Bel, son of an office worker; *Career*: 1920 first work published; translated into Yiddish the works of Pushkin, Shakespeare, Mayakovskiy, Blok, Yesenin; *Publ*: verse collections: "Pain and Courage" (1929); "For A New Foundation" (1932); "Contact" (1935); "Verse" (1939); "Earthly Journeys" (1945); "Tree of Life" (1948); plays: "Bar-Kokhba" (1939); "Sulamif" (1940); "The Soul That Sings" ("Musician") (1941); "Ghetto Rebellion" ("For Life") (1947); etc; 1950 arrested by State Security organs; exiled; after Stalin's death rehabilitated; *Died*: 21 Sept 1960 in Moscow.

GALLER, Lev Mikhaylovich (1883-1950) Naval Commander; Russianized German; capt, Russian Navy; admiral from 1940; CP member from 1932; *Born*: 17 Nov 1883 in Petersburg, son of a nobleman and mil eng; *Educ*: 1905 grad Naval Cadet School; 1912 grad Artillery Classes; 1926 Officers Advanced Training Courses, Naval Acad; *Pos*: 1905-11 officer of the deck, cruisers *Aziya*, "General-Admiral" and battleship "Slava", Baltic Fleet; 1912-16 junior, then senior gunner, battleship *Andrey Pervozvannyy*; gunner, flagship of battleship brigade, Baltic Fleet; 1916-18 commander, destroyer "Avtroil"; senior officer, battleship "Slava"; commander, destroyer *Turkmenets-Stavropol'skiy*, Baltic Fleet; from 1918 in Red Navy; 1918-20 commander, destroyer *Mechislav*, cruiser *Bayan*, then battleship *Andrey Pervozvannyy*; 1920-21 commander, destroyer squadron; 1921-27 chief of staff, Baltic Fleet; 1927-32 commander, battleship brigade; 1932-37 commander, Baltic Fleet; 1937-38 dep commander, Red Army Naval Forces; 1938-40 chief of Main Staff, Sov Navy; 1940-46 USSR Dep Pop Comr of the Navy in charge of shipbuilding and armament; 1947-48 head, Krylov Shipbuilding and Armament Acad; *Career*: 1918 involved in transfer of Baltic Fleet units from Helsinki to Kronstadt via the frozen Gulf of Finland; 1919 directed artillery fire of battleship *Andrey Pervozvannyy* suppressing anti-Sov revolt of the forts *Krasnaya Gorka* and *Seraya Loshad'*; winter 1929-30 commanded the transfer of a naval detachment from the Baltic to the Black Sea; early 1930's supported efforts to strengthen Sov Navy by increasing the output of submarines and naval aircraft, 1939-40 directed operations of the Baltic Fleet in Sov-Finnish War; 1941-45 acting First Dep Pop Comr of the Navy; member, USSR Centr Exec Comt of 7th convocation; 1948 arrested together with Admirals N. Kuznetsov and G. Stepanov; accused of divulging mil secrets; *Awards*: three Orders of Lenin; three Orders of the Red Banner; other orders and medals; *Died*: 12 Aug 1950 in imprisonment; posthumously rehabilitated.

GALLING, Andrey Karlovich (1893-1937) Mil commander; capt, 2nd class, Russian Army; brigade commander from 1935; Civil War veteran; CP member from 1930; *Born*: 1893; *Educ*: 1925 grad Red Army Commanders' Advanced Courses; *Career*: fought in WW 1; from Mar 1918 in Red Army; 1918-21 commanded Kostroma Sov Regt, then brigade in 21st Infantry Div; from 1921 guard and defense chief, Altay Branch Line, Tomsk Railroad; commanded Gorny Altay Forces Group; commanded brigade, 62th Novorossiysk Regt; asst commander, 21st Infantry Div; Sept 1920 distinguished himself in battles against Poles near Lida; Mar-Apr 1922 helped crush anti-Sov insurrection in Gorny Altay; 1925-33 commanded 8th Infantry Div; asst head, *Vystrel* Tactical Infantry Courses; taught at Frunze Mil Acad; 1933-37 dep chm, Ukr Council, Soc for Furthering the Defense, Aviation and Chemical Ind of the USSR; 1937 arrested by NKVD; *Awards*: two Orders of the Red Banner; *Died*: 1937 in imprisonment; posthumously rehabilitated.

GAL'PERIN, Aleksandr L'vovich (1896-1960) Historian; Dr of Historical Sci from 1947; prof from 1958; *Born*: 17 June 1896; *Educ*: 1922 grad Petrograd Univ; 1924 grad Leningrad Inst of Living Oriental Languages; *Career*: 1934-40 senior assoc, Inst of World Econ and World Politics; 1942-50 senior assoc, Pacific Inst; from 1950 senior assoc, Inst of Oriental Studies, USSR Acad of Sci; 1932-34 also taught at Frunze Mil Acad; 1941-47 taught at Moscow's Lenin Teachers' Training Inst; from 1947 also taught at Moscow Univ; wrote numerous works on history of Japan and int relations in Far East; *Publ*: *Khronika sobytiy na Tikhom okeane - 1776-1930* (A Chronicle of Events in the Pacific - 1776-1930) (1935); *Anglo-yaponskiy soyuz, 1902-1921* (The Anglo-Japanese Alliance of 1902-1921) (1947); *Mezhdunarodnyye otnosheniya na Dal'nem Vostoke, 1840-1949* (International Relations in the Far East, 1840-1949) (2nd ed, 1956); coauthor, *Ocherki noveyshey istorii Yaponii* (An Outline Modern History of Japan) (1957); coauthor, *Ocherki novoy istorii Yaponii, 1640-1917* (An Outline History of Japan from 1640 to 1917) (1958); *Died*: 12 Aug 1960.

GAL'PERN, Yakov Osipovich (1876-1941) Surgeon; Hon Sci Worker of Ukr SSR from 1934; *Born*: 1 Jan 1876 in Vilnius, son of an office worker; *Educ*: grad Med Fac, Kiev Univ; *Career*: 1899 worked under Prof R. R. Vreden and S. I. Spasokukotskiy; 1907-22 head, Surgical Dept, Tver' Hospital; 1910 defended doctor's thesis on benign ailments of the stomach and duodenum and their treatment; from 1922 prof, Hospital Surgical Clinic, Yekaterinoslav (from 1926 Dnepropetrovsk) Med Inst; for many years sci dir, Inst of Blood Transfusion; 1921-41 ed, journal *Novyy khirurgicheskiy arkhiv*; wrote over 60 works on surgery; *Publ*: *Dobrokachestvennyye zabolevaniya zheludka i 12-perstnoy kishki i ikh lecheniye* (Benign Ailments of the Stomach and Duodenum and their Treatment) (1910), *O raskhozhdenii bryushnoy rany s vypadeniyem vnutrennostey* (Divergences Between the Abdominal Wound and the Egress of the Internal Organs) (1912); *K voprosu o plastike pishchevoda* (Plastic Surgery of the Oesophagus) (1913); *Pepticheskaya yazva tonkoy kishki* (Peptic Ulcer of the Small Intestines) (1921); *V zashchitu obezbolivaniya* (In Defense of Anesthesia) (1933); *Bolezni operirovannogo zheludka i bor'ba s nimi* (Diseases of the Operated Stomach and Countermeasures) (1939); *Died*: 22 Dec 1941.

GALYNIN, German Germanovich (1922-1966) Composer; *Born*: 1922 in Tula, son of a worker; *Educ*: 1950 grad composition class, Moscow Conservatory; *Career*: 1941-43 directed amateur musical groups in Sov Army; from 1951 invalid; *Works*: oratorio *Devushka i smert'* (The Maiden and Death) (1950); symphonic works: "Epic Poem" (1950); "Youth Festival Overture" (1951); piano works: four sonatas (1939, 1940, 1941 and 1946); suite (1944); five preludes (1939); choral works: "Russia" (1948) and "Don't Weep Over Corpses" (1948); music for shows; aria for violin and string orchestra (1963); string quartets and piano concertoes; *Awards*: Stalin Prize (1951); *Died*: 18 July 1966.

GAMALEYA, Nikolay Fyodorovich (1859-1949) Microbiologist and epidemiologist; pioneer of microbiology, immunology, virology and the theory of disinfection; hon member, USSR Acad of Sci from 1940; member, USSR Acad of Med Sci from 1945; Hon Sci Worker of RSFSR from 1934; CP member from 1948; *Born*: 17 Feb 1859 in Odessa; *Educ*: 1880 grad Natural Sci Dept, Fac of Physics and Mathematics, Novorossiysk Univ, Odessa; 1883 grad Petersburg Mil Med Acad; *Career*: after grad intern, Odessa State Hospital, where he worked under O. O. Mochutovskiy; did research on the bacteriology of tuberculosis and Siberian plague with I. I. Mechnikov; from Feb 1886 worked with Pasteur in Paris; improved Pasteur's method of obtaining anti-rabies vaccine and introduced the vaccine in Russia in June of that year; 1886, together with Mechnikov, established bacteriological station in Odessa, which trained numerous microbiologists and coordinated their research; together with Mechnikov studied Russian cattle plague and established that it is caused by a filtrable virus; 1887-91 did major research on rabies, tuberculosis, cholera and inflammatory processes; 1888 discovered fowl cholera vibrio (Vibrio Metschnikovi); 1892 founded bacteriological laboratory at Prof F. I. Pasternatskiy's Therapeutic Clinic, Petersburg Mil Med Acad; 1892 also defended doctor's thesis on "The Etiology of Cholera from the Viewpoint of Experimental Pathology"; 1899 founded Odessa Bacteriological and Physiological Inst, which produced med preparations and trained bacteriologists; 1898 discovered bacteriophages, which he named "bacteriolysants"; 1901-02 directed anti-epidemic measures during Odessa plague; combatted cholera in Transcaucasus, Volga Region, Odessa, Petersburg and Donbas; 1908 established that typhus can be transmitted in epidemic proportions by lice; 1910-13 founder-ed, journal *Gigiyena i sanitariya*, the first such publ in Russia; made major contribution to the development of Russian and Sov med and veterinary med; developed techniques of vaccinating humans against cholera; drew up program of sanitary and hygienic measures to combat cholera in the cities and exterminate rats during epidemics; 1910 established the importance of disinfection and the extermination of insects in combatting relapsing fever; made major contribution to knowledge of the notability (heteromorphism) of microbes; 1918 launched vaccination program in Petrograd which was subsequently made compulsory for the whole country; 1929-38 sci dir, Centr Inst of Epidemiology and Bacteriology; member, Learned Med Council, USSR and RSFSR Pop Comrt of Health; sci consultant, All-Union Inst of Experimental Med; consultant, Inst of Veterinary Med; consultant, Biochemical Inst; chm, Expertise and Certifying Commission on Microbiology, All-Union Comt for High-School Affairs; from 1938 until death prof, Chair of Microbiology, 2nd Moscow Med Inst; laboratory head, Inst of Epidemiology and Microbiology, USSR Acad of Med Sci, which now bears his name; from 1939 chm, then hon chm, All-Union Soc of Microbiologists, Epidemiologists and Infectionists; 1940 head, Laboratory for the Study of the Variability and Evolution of Microbes, USSR Acad of Sci; 1942 founded laboratory for the specific treatment of tuberculosis; *Publ: Ob opytakh po issledovaniyu chumy rogatogo skota* (Experimental Research on the Russian Cattle Plague) (1886); "Vibrio Metschnikovi (N.Sp.) et ses rapports avec le microbe de choléra asiatique" (Vibrio Metschnikovi [N.Sp.] and its Relation to the Asian Cholera Microbe) (1888); *Etiologiya kholery s tochki zreniya eksperimental'noy patologii* (The Etiology of Cholera from the Viewpoint of Experimental Pathology) (1893); *Bakteriynyye yady* (Bacterial Poisons) (1893); *Osnovy obshchey bakteriologii* (The Principles of General Bacteriology) (1899); coauthor, *Istoriya predokhranitel'nykh ot beshenstva privivok v Odesse* (The History of Anti-Rabies Vaccinations in Odessa) (1902); *Chuma v Odesse* (The Odessa Plague) (2 vol, 1903-04); *Bakteriofagi i bakteriolizіny* (Bacteriophages and Bacteriolysants) (1923); *Osnovy immunologii* (The Principles of Immunology) (1928); *Fil'truyushchiyesya virusy* (Filtrable Viruses) (1930); *Ospoprivivaniye* (Vaccination) (3rd ed, 1934); *Infektsiya i immunitet* (Infection and Immunity) (1939); *Uchebnik meditsinskoy mikrobiologii* (A Textbook of Medical Microbiology) (1943); *O metode Pastera* (Pasteur's Method) (1945); coauthor, *Paster 1822-1895* (Pasteur 1822-1895) (1946); *K voprosu ob izmenchivosti mikrobov* (The Mutability of Microbes) (1946); *Vospominaniya* (Memoirs) (vol 1, 1947); *Sobraniye sochineniy* (Collected Works) (4 vol, 1954-58); *Awards*: two Orders of Lenin; Order of the Red Banner of Labor; Stalin Prize (1943); *Died*: 29 Mar 1949.

GAMARNIK, Yan Borisovich (1894-1937) Party official and mil comr; CP member from 1916; *Born*: 2 June 1894 in Zhitomir, son of an office worker; *Educ*: studied at Law Fac, Kiev Univ; *Career*: 1914 joined student revol group in Kiev; until 1917 Oct Revol member and secr, Kiev RSDRP(B) Comt; helped to prepare Revol in Kiev; 27 Oct 1917 joined Revol Comt; spring 1918 elected by Bolshevik aktiv in Taganrog to Org Bureau for Preparation of 1st Congress of CP(B) Ukr; 1918-20 member, underground All-Ukr Center and one of leaders, Odessa, Khar'kov and Crimean Comts, CP(B) Ukr; 1919 member, Revol Mil Council, Southern Group, 12th Army, then comr, 58th Rifle Div; took part in capture of Kiev; 1920-23 chm, Odessa and Kiev Province Comts, CP(B) Ukr and chm, Kiev Province Exec Comt; 1923-28 chm, Far Eastern Kray Exec Comt and secr, Far Eastern Kray Comt; 1928 secr, CC, CP Bel; held various Army posts; from Apr 1927 member, Revol-Mil Council, Siberian Mil Distr; from Dec 1928 member, Revol-Mil Council, Bel Mil Distr; from Oct 1929 chief, Red Army Polit Bd and member, USSR Revol Mil Council; exec ed, newspaper *Krasnaya zvezda*; from June 1930 USSR Dep Pop Comr of Defense and dep chm, USSR Revol Mil Council; co-founder and member, ed council, *Sovetskaya voyennaya entsiklopediya* (Soviet Military Encyclopedia); member, main ed bd, *Istoriya grazhdanskoy voyny v SSSR* (History of the Civil War in the USSR); from 1935 army comr, 1st class; elected cand member, CC, CPSU(B) at 14th Congress and member, CC, CPSU(B) at 15th, 16th and 17th Congresses; 1934-37 member, Org Bureau, CC, CPSU(B); elected cand member, CC, CP(B)Ukr at 2nd Congress and member, CC, CP(B)Ukr at 3rd Congress and 4th Conference; member, USSR and All-Ukr Centr Exec Comt; 1937 arrested by State Security organs; committed suicide; *Awards*: Order of Lenin; Order of the Red Banner; *Died*: 31 May 1937; posthumously rehabilitated.

GAMBASHIDZE, Shalva Ksenofontovich (1899-1955) Geo actor; Pop Artiste of Geo SSR from 1939; CP member from 1940; *Born*: 1 Aug 1899 in Zestafoni (Geo), son of a priest; *Educ*: studied at Tiflis Drama Studio; *Career*: 1920 began stage work; 1921-28 at Tbilisi Rustaveli Theater; from 1928 actor, and 1937-47 head and artistic dir, Kutaisi Theater (later Tbilisi Mardzhanishvili Theater); from 1926 film actor; dep, Geo Supr Sov of 1st, 2nd and 3rd convocations; *Roles*: in theater: Estevan in "The Sheep's Spring" (1922); de Silva in Gutskov's "Uriel' Akosta" (1929); Othello (1932); Borodin in *Strakh* (Fear) (1932); Archil in Chavchavadze's *Slomannyy most* (Broken Bridge) (1935); Kutuzov in Samsoniy's "Bragration" (1944); MacPherson in *Russkiy vopros* (Russian Problem) (1947); the Mayor in *Revizor* (The Goverment Inspector) (1951); Shrewsbury in "Maria Stuart" (1955), etc; in films: the butcher in *Trubka Kommunara* (The Communard's Pipe) (1929); Andukapar in *Georgiy Saakadze* (1943); Adamur in *Vesna v Sakene* (Spring in Saken) (1951); Tumanishvili in *Pokoriteli vershin* (Summit Conquerors) (1952); Professor Irakliy in *Strekoza* (The Dragon-Fly) (1954), etc; *Works*: stage productions: Kakabadze's *Svad'ba kolkhoznika* (A Kolkhoznik's Marriage) (1938); Shakespeare's "Taming of the Shrew" (1944); *Died*: 18 May 1955.

GAMBURG, Iosif Karlovich (1887-1965) Party and govt official; CP member from 1904; *Born*: 31 Dec 1887; *Career*: took part in 1905-07 Revol; deleg at Tammerfors Conference; 1907 arrested, sentenced to six years at hard labor and exiled for life; 1915 fled from exile; took part in 1917 Oct Revol and helped establish Sov regime in Bel and in Ivanovo-Voznesensk; after Civil War exec admin posts; during WW 2 inspector, Main Quartermaster Bd, USSR Comrt of Defense; 1946-49 dep dir, *Sovetskaya entsiklopediya* Publ House; from Aug 1949 dep dir, Lenin State Library; then pensioner; *Died*: 13 Jan 1965.

GAMBURTSEV, Grigoriy Aleksandrovich (1903-1955) Geophysicist; corresp member, USSR Acad of Sci from 1946, full member from 1953; *Born*: 23 Mar 1903; *Educ*: 1926 grad Moscow Univ; *Career*: 1938-48 assoc, from 1948 dir, Geophysical Inst, USSR Acad of Sci; worked on geophysics of the Earth's crust, gravimetry and seismography; developed new seismograph equipment and devised a theory of seismograph functions; proposed a new method) for geological prospecting of minerals and a seismographical method for hapogene sounding of the Earth's crust; also phical method for hypogene sounding of the Earth's crust; also studied methods of earthquake forecasting; *Publ: O sostavlenii elektromekhanicheskikh analogiy* (Compiling Electromechanical Analogies) (1935); *Metody interpretatsii gravitatsionnykh nablyudeniy* (Methods of Interpreting Gravitation Observations) (1936); *Seysmicheskiye metody razvedki* (Seismic Sounding Methods) (2 vol, 1937-38); *O korrelyatsionnom metode prelomlyonnykh voln* (Refracted Wave Correlation Method) (1942); *Awards*: Order of Lenin; *Died*: 28 June 1955.

GAMREKELI, Irakliy Il'ich (1894-1943) Geo set designer; Hon Art Worker of Geo SSR from 1934; CP member from 1939; *Born*: 17 May 1894; *Educ*: 1922-24 studied at Tiflis Acad of Arts; *Career*: from 1922 with Tiflis Rustaveli Theater (from mid-1920's chief artist of this theater), with Tbilisi's Paliashvili Opera and Ballet Theater, and with theaters in Moscow, Leningrad, Kiev and other Sov cities; worked in Geo film studio; his sets were noted for their power, volume, picturesqueness and laconicism; *Works*: sets for plays: "Hamlet" (1925); Shanshiashvili's *Anzor* (1928); *Razlom* (The Break-up) (1928); Dadiani's *Tetnul'd* (1931); "Die Räuber" (1933); Shanshiashvili's "Arsen" (1936); "Othello" (1937); Paliashvili's "Abesalom and Eteri" (1937); Dadiani's *Iz iskry* (From the Spark) (1937) *Chelovek s ruzh'yom* (Man With a Gun) (1939); Korneychuk's *Bogdan Khmel'nitskiy* (1940); Sumbatov-Yuzhin's *Izmena* (Treason) (1940); Daraseli's *Kikvidze* (1941); Kiladze's *Lado Ketskhoveli* (1941); Balanchivadze's *Serdtse gor* (Heart of the Mountains) (1938); Gol'doni's "Poster Bride" (1942); Gokieli's *Patara Kakhi* (1943), etc; *Awards*: Badge of Hon; *Died*: 10 May 1943.

GAMSAKHURDIYA, Roman Sergeyevich (1860-1939) Geo circus dir; Hon art Worker of Geo SSR from 1933; Hero of Labor from 1933; *Born:* 14 Dec 1860; *Career:* from 1882 circus administrator; 1914 co-founded Circus and Variety Artists' Union; 1926-30 directed circuses in Odessa, Tula, Sverdlovsk and Kazan'; 1930-39 directed circus in Tbilisi; *Died*: 29 Sept 1939.

GANDER, Vladimir Aleksandrovidh (1864-1939) Specialist in teaching of the blind; prof; *Born*: 1864; *Career*: head, (inspector), school for the blind in Voronezh (1898-1910), then Khar'kov (1910-13); 1913-19 at Moscow College for the Blind; from 1918 worked for Pop Comrt of Educ on educ and training of blind children; 1920-23 head, Moscow Inst for the Blind; then member, Methods Commission for Program and Methods Problems, Pop Comrt of Educ; from 1922 head, Chair of Blind Pedag, Inst for Training Teachers of Handicapped Children, then Lenin Teachers' Training Inst; 1932-39 edited works on educ of handicapped children for Teaching and Educ Publ House; specialized in Braile lit and textbooks for the blind; *Publ: Pervonachal'noye vospitaniye i obucheniye slepykh detey* (The Elementary Training and Education of Blind Children) (1934); *Died*: 10 Jan 1939.

GANDURIN (LUKICHEV), K.D. (1884-1953) Govt official; CP member from 1905; *Born*: 1884; *Career*: Party work in Ivanovo-Voznesensk, Moscow and Petersburg; secr, Ivanovo-Voznesensk City RSDRP Comt; helped organize the first trade-unions; Bolshevik .deleg at 5th RSDRP Congress from Ivanovo-Voznesensk RSDRP org; repeatedly arrested by Tsarist authorities; shortly before 1917 Oct Revol, disagreeing with Party policy, left the Party; worked for Petrograd City Comrt of Educ; 1921 re-admitted to RCP(B); 1922-29 admin work in Moscow; from 1929 with Repertoire Comt, RSFSR Pop Comrt of Educ; dep dir, Moscow Maly Theater; 1937-39 worked for Arts Comt, USSR Council of Pop Comr; from 1939 pensioner; *Died*: 1953.

GANETSKIY (FÜRSTENBERG), Yakov Stanislavovich (Party pseudonyms: Genrikh; Kuba; Mikolay; Mashinist) (1879-1937) Polish and Russian revolutionary; Sov diplomat; CP member from 1896; *Born*: 15 Mar 1879 in Warsaw; *Educ*: studied at Berlin, Heidelberg and Zurich univ; *Career*: began revol career as member, Soc-Democratic Party of the Kingdom of Poland and Lith; 1903-09 member, Main Bd, Soc-Democratic Party of the Kingdom of Poland and Lith; 1903, 1906 and 1908 deleg, 4th, 5th and 6th Congresses of Soc-Democratic Party of the Kingdom of Poland and Lith; deleg, 2nd RSDRP Congress, where he discussed possibility of Party merger; 1905 helped lead Warsaw workers' uprising; 1906 deleg, 4th RSDRP Congress; elected in absentia member, CC, RSDRP at 5th Congress; 1903, 1906 and 1907 arrested and sentenced to terms of exile; 1913 attended Poronin Bolshevik conference; 1912-16 during schism of Soc-Democratic Party of the Kingdom of Poland and Lith, member, Kray Party Bd and one of leaders of *Rozlamowcy*, the Party faction which supported Lenin; 1912 attended Int Socialist Congress, Basle; during WW 1 sided with "Zimmerwald leftists"; 1917 member, For Bureau, CC, RSDRP(B); after Oct 1917 Revol Collegium member, USSR Pop Comrt of Finance, Comr and mang, USSR Pop Bank; from 1920 held dipl posts; 1920 Sov plen and trade rep in Lat; 1921-23 Collegium member, USSR Pop Comrt of For Affairs; 1923-30 Collegium member, USSR Comrt of For Trade and USSR Comrt of Trade; 1930-32 Presidium member, RSFSR Supr Sovnarkhov; from 1935 dir, USSR Museum of the Revol; wrote articles and pamphlets on econ and polit subjects; arrested by State Security organs; *Publ: F.Dzerzhinskiy* (1926), etc; *Died*: 26 Nov 1937 in imprisonment; posthumously rehabilitated.

GANIYEV, Nabi (1904-1952) Actor, scriptwriter and film dir; Hon Art worker of Uzbek SSR; *Born*: 1904; *Educ*: 1925 grad Higher Art and Tech Workshops; *Career*: from 1925 with Uzbek State Film Studio as actor, asst film dir, then film dir and producer; playwright and stage dir, children's plays; actor and dir, synchronizing Russian films into Uzbek ("Chapayev," etc); *Works*: Directed films: *Pod'yom* (Ascent) (1931); *Udivitel'noye delo* (Surprising Affair) (1932); *Ramazan* (1933); *Kolodets smerti* (The Well of Death) (1934); *Yegit* (1935); *Otvazhnyye druz'ya* (Brave Friends) (1941); "Takhir and Zukhra" (1945); *Pokhozhdeniya Nasreddina* (Nasreddin's Adventures) (1947); *Doch' Fergany* (Fergana's Daughter) (1948), etc; helped write scripts for films: *Pod'yom* (Ascent); film scripts for *Ramazan; Doch' Fergany (Fergana's* Daughter), etc; *Died*: 29 Oct 1952.

GANNUSHKIN, Pyotr Borisovich (1875-1933) Psychiatrist; Dr of Med from 1904; prof from 1918; *Born*: 9 Mar 1875; *Educ*: 1898 grad Med Fac, Moscow Univ; *Career*: after grad worked under S.S.Korsakov and V.P. Serbskiy; 1904 defended doctor's thesis on acute paranoia; 1904-11 assoc prof, Chair of Mental Diseases, Moscow Univ, where he read a course on "The Theory of Pathological Characters" in which he elaborated his theory of "minor psychiatry"; frequently visited Munich for postgrad work at Krepelin's clinic; 1911 resigned from Moscow Univ with other members of staff in protest against policies of Min of Educ Kasso; 1908-14 intern, Aleksey Psychiatric Hospital, Moscow (now Kashchenko Psychiatric Hospital); 1914 intern, Petrograd Naval Hospital; 1918-33 prof and head, Chair of clinical Psychiatry, Moscow Univ (later 1st Moscow Med Inst); co-founder and later chm, Russian Union of Psychiatrists and Neurologists; 1907-14 founder-ed, journal *Sovremennaya psikhiatriya*; founded maj school of psychiatry with a following throughout the USSR; wrote numerous sci works; *Publ*: doctor's thesis *Ostraya paranoya (Paranoia acuta). Klinicheskaya storona voprosa* (Clinical Aspects of Acute Paranoia) (1904); *Rezoniruyushcheye pomeshatel'stvo i rezonyorstvo* (Reasonable Insanity and Reasoning) (1905); *Psikhastenicheskiy kharakter* (The Psychasthenic Character) (1907); *Postanovka voprosa o shizofrenicheskoy konstitutsii* (The Question of a Schizophrenic Constitution) (1914); *Klinika psikhopatiy, ikh statistika, dinamika, sistematika* (The Clinical Aspects of Psychopaths, Their Statistics, Dynamicss and Taxonomy) (1933); *Died*: 1933 in Moscow.

GANSHINA, Klavdiya Aleksandrovna (1881-1952) Philologist and methodologist; Dr of Philology; prof; corresp member, RSFSR Acad of Pedag Sci from 1945; *Born*: 15 Aug 1881; *Educ*: 1901 grad Warsaw For Language Teachers' Training Courses; from 1901 high-school French teacher; from 1918 instructing and research work at higher educ institutions; 1944-52 head, Chair of For Languages, Moscow City Potyomkin Teachers' Training Inst; works deal mainly with methods of teaching French language in secondary and higher educ institutions; *Publ: Metodika prepodavaniya inostrannykh yazykov. Zadaniya 1 - 16* (Methods of Teaching Foreign Languages. Exercises 1 - 16) (1930-31); *Kak izuchit' inostrannyy yazyk* (How to Learn a Foreign Language) (1936); *Metodika prepodavaniya frantsuzskogo yazyka* (Methods of Teaching French) (1946); coauthor, *Sovremyonnyy frantsuzskiy yazyk* (Contemporary French) (1947); *Frantsuzsko-russkiy slovar'* (French-Russian Dictionary) (4th ed, 1960); *Died*: 21 Oct 1952.

GAPEYEV, Aleksandr Aleksandrovich (1881-1958) Geologist; specialist in coal deposits; Hon Sci and Tech Worker of RSFSR from 1933; CP member from 1904; *Born*: 19 Aug 1881; *Educ*: 1910 grad Petersburg Mining Inst; *Career*: before grad engaged in revol work, for which he was exiled; contributed to Party organs

Molodaya Rossiya and *Golos molodoy Rossii;* deleg, 4th RSDRP Congress; 1918 gave up Party polit work; from 1920 prof and dir, Ural Mining Inst; from 1926 prof, Moscow Mining Acad; 1930-48 prof, Moscow Mining Inst; from 1930 also prof, Moscow Geological Survey Inst; from 1944 member, Ind Mining Section, Council of Sci and Tech Expertise, USSR Gosplan; from 1954 pensioner; 1908 began geological field trips; took part in Donbas survey; 1914 did field research in Kuznetsk coal basin; established that the Karaganda coal deposits were the largest in the USSR; also studied coal deposits in Northeast Kaz, Sakhalin, the Caucasus, Urals and Centr Asia; 1924 advocated survey and opencast mining of the lower formations of the Bogoslov lignite deposit; made valuable contributions to the ind evaluation of coal deposits throughout the USSR; did important work on the classification of reserves of coal and other solid minerals; *Publ: Kuznetskiy kamennougol'nyy basseyn* (The Kuznetsk Coal Basin) (1919); *Karagandinskoye kamennougol'noye mestorozhdeniye* (The Karaganda Coal Deposit) (1922); *Geologicheskiy ocherk zapadnoy okrainy Donetskogo basseyna* (A Geological Study of the Western Fringe of the Don Basin) (1927); *K voprosu o klassifikatsii zapasov poleznykh iskopayemykh* (The Classifications of Mineral Reserves) (1938); *Fatsii osadochnykh otlozheniy i ikh rol' v obrazovanii ugol'nykh mestorozhdeniy Donetskogo basseyna* (The Facies of Sedimentary Deposits and Their Role in the Formation of the Coal Deposits of the Don Basin) (1949); *Tvyordyye goryuchiye iskopayemyye (kaustobiolity)* Solid Combustible Minerals [Caustobioliths]) (1949); *Awards*: Stalin Prize (1948); *Died*: 25 July 1958.

GAPICH, Nikolay Ivanovich (1901-1964) Mil commander; maj-gen from 1940; veteran of signal troops; CP member from 1927; *Born*: 1901, son of a peasant; *Educ*: in 1930's grad Frunze Mil Acad; 1938 grad Gen Staff Acad; *Career*: 1916-20 signalman and telegrapher; 1920-22 partisan in the Far East; from 1923 in Red Army; 1935-36 chief of communications, Bel Mil Distr; 1938-40 taught at Gen Staff Acad; July 1940-23 June 1941 head, Communications Bd, USSR Pop Comrt of Defense; from 1953 reserve officer; wrote more than 30 works on organizing mil communications and mil admin; contributed to manuals, handbooks and textbooks on mil communications; *Awards*: Order of Lenin; other orders and medals; *Died*: 16 Mar 1964.

GAPRINDASHVILI, Valerian Ivanovich (1889-1941) Geo poet, critic and translator; *Born*: 2 Jan 1889 in Kutaisi, son of a teacher; *Educ*: 1914 grad Law Fac, Moscow Univ; *Career*: 1914 first work published; ed, Geo periodical *Meotsnebe Niamorebi*; theorist of Geo symbolism; helped found "Blue Horns" symbolist group; after revol left symbolism; translated into Geo Blok's *Dvenadtsat'* (The Twelve), Potier's "Marseillaise" and "International," Schiller's "Die Räuber," and other works of Russian, French, German and English poets; translated into Russian N. Baratashvili's poetry; *Publ*: verse collection "Sunset" (1918); anthology *Poety Gruzii* (Georgian Poets) (1921); poems: "Return to Earth," "October Lines" (1925); "Paris Commune" (1925); "Lenin," "Stalin" (1941), etc; wrote articles and works on the theory of lit; *Died*: 31 Jan 1941.

GARDIN, Vladimir Rostislavovich (1877-1965) Actor, film dir and scriptwriter; Pop Artiste of USSR from 1947; *Born*: 18 Jan 1877 in Tver' (now Kalinin); *Career*: 1898 began stage work; 1904-06 at Petersburg Komissarzhevskaya Drama Theater; then actor in Petersburg, Moscow, etc; 1907 founded in Terioki "Free Theater," where he staged plays forbidden by the censorship; toured in Paris, London and other West European cities; 1908 founded Russian theater in Paris; 1912 with Moscow Korsh Theater; from 1913 film work as dir and scriptwriter and from 1915 as actor; helped create the so-called Russian Golden Film Series on themes from Russian classic lit; after 1917 Oct Revol member, Photography and Cinematography Comt, Pop Comrt of Educ; 1919-21 co-founder and head, First State Cinematography School (later State Inst of Cinematography); 1922-24 film dir, All-Ukr Photography and Cinematography Bd; 1929, after his film *Poet i tsar'* (Poet and Tsar) had been sharply criticized, stopped work as film dir; *Roles*: in theater: the President in "Kabale und Liebe"; F. P. Karamazov in *Brat'ya Karamazovy* (The Brothers Karamazov); Krogstad in Ibsen's "Dolls' House"; Shalimov in Gorky's *Dachniki* (Summer Residents); Protasov in L. Tolstoy's *Zhivoy trup* (The Living Corpse), etc; in films: Babchenko in *Vstrechnyy)* (Chance Encounter) (1932); title role in Saltykov-Shchedrin's *Iudushka Golovlyov* (1934); Count Tolstoy in *Pyotr I* (Peter I) (1939); the Boyar Kivrin in *Stepan Razin* (1939); Potanin in *Paren' iz taygi* (A Lad from the Taiga) (1941); Bakh in *Anton Ivanovich serditsya* (Anton Ivanovich Is Angry) (1941); Dilon in *Sekretnaya missiya* (Secret Mission) (1950), etc; *Works*: among the 68 films he directed are: "Anna Karenina" (1914); *Dvoryanskoye gnezdo* (Nest of Gentlefolk) (1915); *Nakanune* (On the Eve) (1915); *Serp i molot* (Hammer and Sickle) (1921); *Prizrak brodit po Yevrope* (A Ghost Stalks Through Europe) (1923); *Slesar' i kantsler* (Mechanic and Chancellor) (1924); *Krest i mauzer* (Cross and Mauser) (1925); *Poet i tsar'* (Poet and Tsar) (1927), etc; *Publ: Moi vstrechi* (My Encounters) (1946); *Vstrecha s geroyami* (A Meeting with Heroes) (1950); *Vospominaniya* (Memoirs) (1952); *Zhizn' i trud artista* (Life and Work of an Actor) (1960), etc; *Awards*: Three Orders of the Red Banner of Labor; Badge of Hon; medals; *Died*: 28 May 1965.

GAR'KAVYY, Il'ya Ivanovich (1888-1937) Mil commander; Ukr; lt, Russian army; corps commander from 1935; CP member from 1917; *Born*: 19 July 1888 in vil Muskenkovo, Yekaterinoslav Province, son of a peasant; *Educ*: grad teacher's training seminary; 1916 grad Ensign School; *Pos*: until WW 1 teacher; 1914 drafted into Russian Army; company commander, Rumanian Front; 1917 chm, Exec Comt, Tiraspol' Sov; formed and commanded Tiraspol' Red Guard unit; from 1918 in Red Army; 1919-20 chief of staff, Yakir's 45th Infantry Div; 1920-21 commander, 45th Infantry Div; then asst commander, Kiev Mil Distr; 1925-28 commander, 8th, then 14th Infantry Corps, Ukr Mil Distr; 1928-31 chief, Red Army Command Bd; 1931-35 dep commander, Leningrad Mil Distr; 1935-37 commander, Ural Mil Distr; 1934-47 member, Mil Council, USSR Pop Comrt of Defense; early 1937 arrested by NKVD organs; his friend and brother-in-law Yakir pleaded for him before Stalin, but without results; *Awards*: Order of the Red Banner; *Died*: 1 July 1937 in imprisonment; posthumously rehabilitated.

GARRI, Aleksey Nikolayevich (1903-1960) Russian writer; *Born*: 6 Jan 1903 in Paris; *Career*: fought in the Civil War as member of Kotovskiy Cavalry Brigade; 1920 first work published; 1938 arrested on basis of false denunciation; after 16 years rehabilitated; worked in Far North; wrote a number of stories about pioneers of the North; *Publ: Puteshestviye chudakov po Yevrope* (Cranks' Journey Through Europe) (1929); *Yevropa pod nogami* (Europe Under Foot) (1930); *Panika na Olimpe* (Panic on Olympus) (1934); coauthor, *Potolok mira* (The Roof of the World) (1934); *Ogon'. Epopeya Kotovskogo* (Fire. Epopee of Kotovskiy) (1934); *Struny. Rasskazy* (The Strings. Stories) (1935); *Zaychik* (Little Hare) (1951); *V glukhoy tayge* (Deep in the Taiga) (1952); *Posledniy karavan* (Last Caravan) (1955); *Bitva v tundre* (Battle in the Tundra) (1956); *Rasskazy o Kotovskom* (Stories of Kotovskiy) (1959); novel *Bez fanfar* (Without Fanfare) (1962); *Died*: 20 May 1960 in Moscow.

GARSHIN, Vladimir Georgiyevich (1887-1956) Pathoanatomist; prof from 1938; member, USSR Acad of Med Sci from 1945; *Born*: 19 Dec 1887; *Educ*: 1913 grad Med Fac, Kiev Univ; *Career*: after grad specialized at Chair of Pathological Anatomy, Kiev Univ; 1938-52 prof, Chair of Pathological Anatomy, 1st Leningrad Med Inst; 1938-50 simultaneously head, Dept of Pathological Anatomy, Inst of Experimental Med; during WW consultant, various mil hospitals in Leningrad; did important research on atypical inflammatory epithelization and metaplasia of the epithelium; discovered the role of these processes in the rejection of foreign and decayed matter; studied lesions of the epithelium of the trachea and bronchi due to foreign bodies and to A-avitaminosis; also studied delayed wound healing and the effects of x-rays on inflammatory processes (e.g. the inhibitory effect of certain dosages on phagocytosis and granulation); compiled reference material on alimentary dystrophy and tuberculosis from the files of the Leningrad Dissection Laboratory as well as valuable material on leptospirotic jaundice, gunshot osteomyelitis and the nature and function of inflammatory process; wrote 42 works; *Publ: Eksperimental'nyye issledovaniya atipicheskikh razrastaniy epiteliya kozhi* (Experimental Research Atypical Epithelization of the Skin) (1927); *O znachenii eksogennogo faktora v geneze atipicheskikh razrastaniy epiteliya* (The Significance of the Exogenous Factor in the Genesis of Atypical Epithelization) (1937); *Vospaleniye i allergiya* (Inflammation and Allergy) (1938); *O vliyanii predvaritel'nogo osveshcheniya rentgenovymi luchami na techeniye vospalitel'nogo protsessa* (The Effect of Preliminary X-Ray Irradiation on the Course of the Inflammatory Process) (1938); *Vospalitel'nyye razrastaniya epiteliya, ikh biologicheskoye znacheniye* (Epithelization and Its Biological Significance) (1939); *O geneze i patologicheskom znachenii metaplazii epiteliya pri avitaminoze* (The Genesis and Pathological Significance of Metaplasia of the Epithelium in Avitaminosis) (1946); *Patologicheskaya anatomiya alimentarnoy distrofii u vzroslykh* (The Pathological Anatomy of Alimentary Dystrophy in Adults) (1947); coauthor, *Morfologiya zazhivleniya ran* (The Morphology of Wound Healing) (1951); *Died*: 20 Apr 1956.

GARTNYY, Tishka (real name: ZHILUNOVICH, Dmitriy Fyodorovich) (1887-1937) Bel writer, politician and public figure; member, Bel Acad of Sci from 1928; member, Bel Writers' Union from 1934; CP member from 1917; *Born* 4 Nov 1887 in settlement Kopyl', now Minsk Oblast, son of a peasant; *Educ*: 1905 grad Kopyl' elementary school; *Career*: 1906-09 after futile attempts to enter Nesvizh Teachers' Training Seminary and Goretsk Agric School worked at a tannery in Kopyl'; member, Kopyl' RSDRP org; 1909-12 toured many Ukr and Bel cities in search of work; from 1913 in Petersburg; worked for some time at "Vulkan" Plant; then ran a Bel publ house and worked for Bel Refugees Comt; ed, Bel newspaper *Dzyan'nitsa*; member, Bel Socialist Party and inter-rayon RSDRP org; 1917 from various Bel Socialist Party org in Petrograd helped found Bel Soc-Democratic Workers' Party (Bolsheviks); from Feb 1918 secr, Bel Nat Comt, RSFSR Council of Pop Comr; ed, newspaper *Dzyan'nitsa*; Jan 1919 chm, Bel Provisional Govt and member, Centr Bureau, CP(B) Bel; 1919-20 with staff, 14th Army; then with Polit Dept, Western Front; 1921-30 ed, newspaper *Savetskaya Belarus'*; from 1923 ed, periodical *Polymya*; simultaneously Collegium member, Bel Pop Comrt of Educ; dir, Bel Centr Archives; head, Bel State Publ House; from 1923 member, Inst of Bel Culture; from 1928 member, Bel Acad of Sci; 1909 first work published; belonged to the so-called "proletarian writers" and observed all norms of "revol romanticism"; 1918 played an active part in the liquidation of the "Northwestern Oblast" (later "Western Cummune") and founding of Bel SSR on its basis; with the establishment of the first Bel SSR (late Dec 1918) at odds with Moscow central authorities and local Bolsheviks from the Northwest Oblast RCP(B) Comt in demanding territorial integrity for Bel and more seats for Bel in the govt and in the Centr Bureau, CP(B) Bel; early Feb 1919 expelled from Bel Govt and Centr Bureau, CP(B) Bel as "nationalist" together with other Bel; in 1920's worked on development of Bel press and publ houses; in this connection 1929-30 subjected to Party criticism for "nationalistic" activities and deprived of all his posts; continued at Bel Acad of Sci and tried to defend lit freedom but 1933 failed here also; 1936 arrested by State Security organs; *Publ*: verse collections; "Songs" (1913); "Labor and Fighting Songs" (1922); "Triumph" (1925); collected stories: "Slivers on the Waves" (1924); "Speech of Lightning" (1932); novels: "Sap of the Virgin Soil" (1929), etc; dramas: "Waves of Life" (1918); "Socialist Woman" (1924); "Two Forces" (1926); collection of lit criticism "Highlands and Lowlands" (1928); "Collected Works" (4 vol, 1929-32); "Selected Stories" (1962); *Died!* 11 Apr 1937 in Mogilev in imprisonment; posthumously rehabilitated.

GARTSMAN, Matvey Davidovich (1909-1943) Jewish poet; *Born*: 20 Dec 1909 in Berdichev, son of a painter; *Educ*: 1934 grad Lit Fac, Moscow Lenin State Teachers' Training Inst; *Career*: 1929 first work published; translated T. Shevchenko's and I. Franko's works; *Publ*: "My Second Youth" (1931); "Good Morning, My Country" (1935); "I Love You, Life" (1937); "Golden Torches" (1939); "The Song and the Sword" (1939); "Ballad of Budyonnyy," "Ukraine," "My Republic," etc, *Died:* 15 Dec 1943 killed in action.

GASANOV, Gotfrid Aliyevich (1900-1965) Dag composer and pedagogue; Hon Art Worker of Dag ASSR from 1943; *Born*: 1900 in Derbent, Dagh; *Educ*: 1926 grad piano and composition classes, Leningrad Conservatory; *Career*: founder and pedagogue, Buynak Music College (now in Makhachkala); participated in musical and ethnographic expeditions in Dag; 1935 organized Song and Dance Ensemble of Dag ASSR; musical dir, Kumyk Drama Theater; from 1948 Bd member, USSR Composers' Union; from 1955 Bd chm, Dag Composers' Union; dep, Dagh Supr Sov of 1938, 1947 and 1951 convocations; *Works*: opera *Khochbar* (1937); musical comedy "If the Heart Wishes" (1945); ballet for children *Karachach* (The Black-Haired Girl) (1945); oratorio "Dzhigits of Daghestan" (1943); "Daghestan Fantasy" for symphony orchestra (1942); *Daghestan Stalin Cantata* (1950); "Song of the Awakened East" (1959); "Piano Concerto" (1948); "Lezghin Overture" (1951); "Song Cycle of the Great Fatherland War"; instrumental works, romances and songs; music for plays of the Makhachkala Kumyk and Russian theaters; music for a number of films; collections "100 Daghestan Folk Songs" (1948) and "20 Kumyk Folk Songs" (1955); song "My Fatherland" (1963); "Rhapsody" (1963); *Awards:* Badge of Honor (1944); Order of the Red Banner of Labor (1950); two medals; two Stalin Prizes (1949 and 1951); *Died:* 1965.

GASTELLO, Nikolay Frantsevich (1907-1941) Mil pilot; Hero of the Soviet Union (26 July 1941, posthumously); capt; CP member from 1928; *Born*: 23 Apr 1907; *Educ*: grad mil aviation school; *Career*: before mil service cupola furnace worker, Moscow-Kazan' Railroad and railroad foreman in Murom; 1939 fought at Khalkhin-Gol and 1939-40 in Sov-Finnish War; 26 June 1941 his squadron bombed a German motorized column on the road from Molodechno to Radoshkovichi; an anti-aircraft grenade damaged the gas tank of his plane; sacrificing his own life, he rammed the massed enemy vehicles with his burning plane; *Died*: 26 June 1941 killed in action.

GASTEV, Aleksey Kapitonovich (pseudonym: I. DOZOROV) (1882-1941) Russian poet and researcher; CP member from 1931; *Born*: 26 Sept 1882 in Suzdal', son of a teacher; *Educ*: studied at Moscow Teacher's Training Inst and Paris Higher School of Soc Sci; *Career*: from 1900 in revol movement; for polit activities expelled from Inst; worked as mechanic; subjected to arrests and exile; several times emigrated to Paris; 1901-08 RSDRP(B) member, 1904 first work published; 1905 chm, Exec Comt, Kostroma Sov of Workers' Dep; 1906 deleg, 4th Stockholm RSDRP Congress; from 1906 trade-union official in Petersburg; 1917-18 first secr, CC, All-Russian Metalworkers' Union; 1920 founded in Moscow Centr Inst of Labor, All-Union Centr Trade Union Council; until 1938 head of this Inst; worked on methods of analysing and teaching labor processes, org of labor and reorganization of production; anticipated some ideas characteristic of the much later sci of cybernetics; 1938 arrested by NKVD; *Publ*: verse: "We Grow from Iron," "Whistles," "Rails," "Tower," "At the Tram Depot," Ivan Vavilov etc; collections: *Poeziya pervogo udara* (Poetry of the First Stroke) (1918); *Pachka orderov* (A Batch of Orders) (1921); a number of works on problems of sci org of labor: *Kak nado rabotat'* (How to Work) (1921); *Yunost', idi!* (Youth, March!) (1923); *Vosstaniye kul'tury* (Rebellion of Culture) (1923); *Novaya kul'turnaya ustanovka* (New Cultural Line) (1923); *Trudovyye ustanovki* (Labor Directions) (1924); *Ustanovka proizvodstva metodom TsIT* (Industrial Adjustment to Methods of the Central Insitute of Labor) (1927); *Normirovaniye i organizatsiya truda* (Standardization and Organization of Labor) (1929); *Died*: 1941 in imprisonment; posthumously rehabilitated.

GAUK, Aleksandr Vasil'yevich (1893-1963) Conductor and music teacher; prof from 1927; Hon Art Worker of RSFSR from 1947; Pop Artiste of RSFSR from 1954; *Born*: 3 Aug 1893 in Odessa; *Educ*: 1917 grad Petersburg Conservatory; *Career*: 1920-27 ballet conductor (later chief ballet conductor), Leningrad Acad Opera and Ballet Theater (former Mariinskiy, now S. M. Kirov Theater); 1927-34 prof, Leningrad Conservatory; among his students were Ye. Mravinskiy, A. Melik-Pashayev, etc; 1930-34 artistic dir and chief conductor, Leningrad Philharmonic; from 1934 in Moscow: conductor, Grand Symphony Orchestra, All-Union Radio and USSR State Symphony Orchestra; from 1948 prof, Moscow Conservatory; restored orchestral score of Rachmaninov's First Symphony; *Awards*: Order of the Red Banner of Labor; medals; *Died*: 30 Mar 1963 in Moscow.

GAUZNER, Grigoriy Osipovich (1907-1934) Russian writer; husband of writer Zh. V. Gauzner; *Born*: 1907; *Career*: late 1920's began lit work; sided with "constructivists"; *Publ*: essays *Nevidannaya Yaponiya* (Mysterious Japan) (1929); cycle of stories *9 let v poiskakh neobyknovennogo* (Nine Years in Search of the Unusual) (1934); *Died*: 4 Sept 1934 in Gagry.

GAUZNER, Zhanna Vladimirovna (1912-1962) Russian writer; wife of G. O. Gauzner; *Born*: 10 Sept 1912 in Odessa, daughter of poetess V. M. Inber; *Educ*: 1939 grad Moscow's Gorky Lit Inst; *Career*: 1925-32 in France; 1934 first work published; from 1945 in Leningrad; made French-Russian and Russian-French translations; *Publ*: novel *Ya uvizhu Moskvu* (I Shall See Moscow) (1952); novelettes: *Parizh - vesyolyy gorod* (Paris Is a Gray City) (1934); *Vot my i doma...* (Now We Are Home) (1947); *Mal'chik i nebo* (The Boy and the Sky) (1959); *Died*: 9 Sept 1962 in Leningrad.

GAVENIS (GAVEN), Yu. P. (DAUMAN, Ya. E.; DONNER) (1884-1937) Party and govt official; CP member from 1902;

Born: 1884; *Career:* Lat Kray Soc-Democratic Party deleg to 5th RSDRP Congress; member, CC, Lat Kray Soc-Democratic Party; arrested by Tsarist authorities; after 1917 Oct Revol member, Minusinsk RSDRP(B) Comt; late 1917 chm, Crimean Mil–Revol Comt; worked for USSR Gosplan and other govt and Party org; arrested by State Security organs; *Died:* 1937 in imprisonment.

GAVRILOV, Nikolay Andreyevich (1886-1919) Party official; RSDRP member from 1903; *Born*: 1886 in vil Dal'ne-Konstantinovo, Nizhniy- Novgorod Province, son of a peasant; *Career*: worked as teacher in Moscow Province; from 1907 exec organizer, Orekhovo-Zuyev Rayon, Moscow Okrug RSDRP Comt; 1906 and 1907 arrested; 1909 sentenced to hard labor; 1915 exiled for life to Siberia; from Mar 1917 member, Irkutsk RSDRP(B) Comt and member, Exec Comt, Irkutsk Sov; Nov 1917 helped establish Sov regime in Irkutsk; from Feb 1918 Presidium member, Centr Siberian Sov; after 1918 collapse of Sov regime in Transbaikal area conducted underground work in Blagoveshchensk and Khabarovsk; 29 May 1919 arrested by White Guards; *Died*: 1919 executed by firing squad in Makaveyev Prison.

GAVRILOVA, Aleksandra Ivanovna (1895-1940) Ballerina; *Born*: 10 May 1895; *Educ*: 1911 grad I. Chistyakov's Choreographic School, Petersburg; *Career*: from 1911 with company of Petersburg Pop Center; 1918-36 prima-ballerina, Kiev Opera and Ballet Theater; from 1918, together with Chistyakov, directed Kiev Choreographic School; *Roles*: Odette-Odille in Tchaikovsky's *Lebediynoye ozero* (Swan Lake); Kitri in "Don Quixote"; the Tsar-Maiden in *Konyok-gorbunok* (The Little Hunchback Horse); Swanilda in "Coppelia"; Tao Hoa in *Krasnyy tsvetok* (The Red Flower), etc; *Died*: 6 Apr 1940.

GAVRILYUK, Aleksandr Akimovich (1911-1941) Ukr writer; *Born*: 23 Apr 1911 in vil Zabolot'ye, now Poland, son of a peasant; *Career*: during WW 1 evacuated with his parents to Russia and lived in Petrograd, Voronezh Province and Ukr; 1919 returned to native vil; from 1929 member, CP Western Bel (abolished by orders from Moscow in 1938); then secr, distr comt of this CP and worked for underground ed staff of its CC; arrested 14 times by Polish authorities and twice interned in Berioza Kartuzska concentration camp; from 1929 lit work; wrote on revol themes with a great deal of autobiographical material; *Publ*: novelette *Berioza* (1941); collections: *Poeziya* (Poetry) (1941); *Vybrane* (Selected Verse) (1955); in Russian translation: *Izbrannoye* (Selected Works) (1952); *Pesni iz Beryozy* (Songs from Berioza) (1954); *Died*: 22 June 1941 killed in air raid on L'vov.

GAVRO, Layosh (Lyudvig) Matveyevich (1894–1937) Mil commander; Hungarian; brigade commander from 1935; Civil War veteran; Soc-Democrat from 1912; CP member from 1917; *Born*: 1894; *Educ*: 1933 grad Frunze Mil Acad; *Pos*: fought in WW 1 in Austro-Hungarian Army; 1916 captured by Russians; from 1918 in Red Army; 1918-21 commanded detachment, battalion, regt and brigade; after Civil War chief inspector of gen mil training, Ukr Mil Distr; commander, Kiev Fortified Distr; Kiev Province Mil Comr; 1924-25 worked for Comintern; 1926-30 Sov consul-gen in China; commander and comr, 50th Infantry Div; 1936-37 commanded 22nd Infantry Div, Special Red Banner Far Eastern Army; commandant, fortified distr; *Career*: during WW 1 sentenced to execution for anti-war propaganda; sentence commuted to assignment to the front; 1917-18 helped found Red Guard and int units among prisoners-of-war; 1919-20 repeatedly distinguished himself in battles against Denikin's and Petlyura's troops and on Polish Front; 1937 arrested by NKVD; *Awards*: two Orders of Red Banner; *Died:* 1937 in imprisonment; posthumously rehabilitated.

GAY (BZHISHKYAN), Gay Dmitriyevich (1887-1937) Mil commander; Arm; corps from 1935; Civil War veteran; CP member from 1903; *Born*: 6 Feb 1887 in Tiflis, son of a teacher and Soc-Democrat (Menshevik); *Educ*: 1922 grad advanced officer training courses, Gen Staff Acad; 1927 grad Frunze Mil Acad; *Pos*: 1914 drafted into Russian Army; served on the Turkish Front; for bravery promoted officer; 1918-19 detachment commander; commander, 24th "Iron" Infantry Div; commander, 1st Army, Eastern Front; 1919-20 commander, 1st Caucasian Cavalry Div; commander, 2nd Mounted Corps, Southern and Caucasian Fronts; 1920 commander, 3rd Mounted Corps, Western Front; 1922 Arm Pop Comr of Mil and Naval Affairs; 1924 commander and comr, 3rd Mounted Corps; 1927-29 junior asst, Chair of History of Wars, Frunze Mil Acad; later pedag work; 1933-37 head, Chair of Art of War, Zhukovskiy Air Force Acad; *Career*: from his youth conducted revol work; served two prison terms; 1912 exiled from Transcaucasus; 1918 his div liberated Simbirsk and Samara from White forces; 1919 his army helped liberate Buguruslan, Buzuluk, Orenburg and Ufa; 1920 his 3rd Mounted Corps broke through the front and deep into the rear of Pilsudskiy's troops at Zapadnaya Dvina, played a decisive part in the battles of Vilnius, Grodno and Osovets and reached the Vistula; Aug 1920, covering the retreat of the 4th Army to the East, he was cut off, crossed into Germany and was interned; *Awards*: three Orders of the Red Banner; *Died*: 11 Dec 1937 killed while resisting arrest by NKVD organs; posthumously rehabilitated; 1968 the Sov Postal Service issued a stamp with his portrait.

GAYDAR (real name: GOLIKOV), Arkadiy Petrovich (1904-1941) Children's writer; *Born*: 9 Feb 1904 near L'vov, son of a teacher; *Educ*: 1919 grad officer training courses in Kiev; 1921 grad Higher Infantry School; *Career*: from 1918 volunteer in the Red Army; from 1921 regt commander; 1924 demobilized from army in consequence of a wound; 1925 began lit work; on the basis of his novelette *Timur i yego komanda* (Timur and His Crew) (1940) originated the "Timurovtsy," mass children's movement, whose aim was to help the families of front soldiers; on his works were based numerous plays and films: *Shkola muzhestva* (School of Courage), *Chuk i Gek* (Chuk and Gek), *Mal'chish Kibal'chish, Sud'ba barabanshchika* (The Drummer's Fate), etc; from start of WW 2 mil correspondent, newspaper *Komsomol'skaya pravda*; late 1941 stayed behind enemy lines as machine-gunner in a partisan detachment; *Publ*: stories for children: *RVS* (Revolutionary Military Council) (1926); *Shkola* (School) (1930); *Dal'niye strany* (Far Lands) (1932); *Voyennaya tayna* (Military Secret) (1935); *Golubaya chashka* (The Blue Cup) (1936); *Chuk i Gek* (Chuk and Gek) (1939); *Timur i yego komanda* (Timur and His Crew) (1940), etc; mil essays: *Most* (The Bridge), *U perepravy* (At the River Crossing) (1941); film scripts: *Klyatva Timura* (Timur's Oath), *Komendant snezhnoy kreposti* (Commandant of the Snow Fortress); *Died*: 26 Oct 1941 killed in action; monument erected to him, at his grave on the bank of the Dnieper in Kanev.

GAYDAY, Zoya Mikhaylovna (1902-1965) Ukr opera singer (soprano); Pop Artiste of USSR from 1944; *Born:* 19 June 1902 in Tambov, daughter of a folklore specialist; *Educ:* 1927 grad Kiev Lysenko Inst of Music and Drama; *Career*: 1928-30 and 1934-55 soloist, Kiev Ukr Shevchenko Acad Opera and Ballet Theater; 1930-34 soloist, Khar'kov Lysenko State Acad Opera and Ballet Theater; from 1947 instructor, Kiev State Conservatory; toured USA, Canada, Iran, Iraq, China, Pakistan, etc; 1955 left stage; 1960 visited China with Sov deleg; *Roles*: Tat'yana in Tchaikovsky's *Yevgeniy Onegin*; Eteri in Paliashvili's "Abesalom and Eteri"; Rosina in Rossini's "Barber of Seville"; Micaela in Bizet's "Carmen"; title role in Lysenko's *Natalka-Poltavka*, etc; *Awards*: Stalin Prize (1941); First Prize, Moscow All-Union Competition of Musical Performers (1933); First Prize, All-Ukr Competition for the Performance of Sov Musical Works (1937); two Orders of the Red Banner of Labor; medals; *Died*: 21 Apr 1965 in Kiev.

GAYDEBUROV, Pavel Pavlovich (1877-1960) Russian actor and stage dir; Pop Artiste of RSFSR from 1940; *Born*: 15 Feb 1877, son of a writer, contributor to Nekrasov's periodical *Sovremennik* and ed, liberal populist newspaper *Nedelya; Educ*: 1896-99 studied at Law Fac, Petersburg Univ; *Career*: at his father's house met Miklukho-Maklay, Repin, Kyui, Borodin, Rimsky-Korsakov, Moussorgsky, Leskov, Veresayev, Nadson, Pleshcheyev, the actors Svobodin, Davydov, etc; 1899 expelled from univ for participation in student demonstrations; while still a student began stage work; 1893 together with his future wife, actress N. F. Skarskaya, founded Petersburg Public Theater (1905-28 Mobile Drama Theater); 1929-44 actor and stage dir in various cities; 1944-50 actor, Moscow Chamber Theater; 1950-54 at Simferopol' Oblast Gorky Drama Theater; 1954-56 at Moscow Vakhtangov Theater; conducted pedag work; from 1956 member, Artistic Council for the Theater, USSR Min of Culture; *Roles*: played over 500 roles, among them Oswald in Ibsen's "Ghosts"; title role in Shakespeare's "Hamlet"; Pyotr in Tolstoy's *Vlast' t'my* (Force of Darkness); the old man in Gorky's *Starik* (Old Man); Sorin in Chekhov's *Chayka* (The Sea-Gull), etc; *Works:* produced over 300 plays: all Chekhov's plays; Gogol's *Revizor* (The Government Inspector) (1934); Tolstoy's *Vlast' t'my* (Force of Darkness) (1935); Korneychuk's *Platon Krechet* (1936); *Boris Godunov* (1937); Leonov's *Nashestviye* (Invasion) (1943); Gorky's *Starik* (The Old Man) (1951), etc; *Publ: Zarozhdeniye spektaklya* (Origin of a Play) (1922); *Problema p'yesy "Starik"* (Problem of the Play "The Old Man") (1948); *Polveka s Chekhovym* (Half a

Century with Chekhov) (1948); coauthor, *Na stsene i v zhizni* (On the Stage and in Life) (1959); *Awards*: Stalin Prize (1952); *Died*: 4 Mar 1960.

GAYEVOY, Anton Ivanovich (1907-1962) Party official; CP member from 1930; *Born*: 17 Jan 1907 in vil Zalizne, now Donetsk Oblast; *Educ*: 1952 grad correspondence course, CC, CPSU Higher Party School; *Career*: 1919 started work as apprentice at Gorlovka Machine-Building Plant; 1933-40 exec trade-union, Party and govt work: chm, Gorlovka City Trade-Union Council; secr, Gorlovka City Party Comt; second secr, Donetsk Oblast Comt, CP Ukr; chm, Donetsk Oblast Exec Comt; 1940-42 and 1943-51 first secr, Lugansk Oblast Comt, CP Ukr; 1952-57 first secr, Zaporozh'ye Oblast Comt, CP Ukr; 1957-61 first secr, Dnepropetrovsk Oblast Comt, CP Ukr; from Dec 1957 Presidium member, CC, CP Ukr; from 1961 secr, CC, CP Ukr; dep, USSR Supr Sov of 2nd - 6th and Ukr Supr Sov of 3rd - 5th convocations; 1956-62 member, CC, CPSU; 1940-62 member, CC, CP Ukr; *Awards*: Order of Lenin (1957); medals; *Died*: 3 July 1962.

GAYGEROVA, Varvara Adrianovna (1903-1944) Composer; *Born*: 17 Oct 1903 in Orekhovo-Zuyevo; *Career*: pianist and concertmaster in Orekhovo-Zuyevo; 1937-40 pianist at Karabalyk Sovkhoz, Kaz; then pianist-concertmaster, State Inst of Stagecraft and Bolshoy Theater, Moscow; *Works*: three symphonies (1928, 1934 and 1937); opera "The Fortress at Kamennyy Brod" (1940); suite "Diary of a Frontline Soldier" (1943); other suites, quartets, sonatas, romances and songs; arrangements of Russian and Kalmyk folk songs; *Died*: 6 Apr 1944 in Moscow.

GAYLIT, Yan Petrovich (1894-1938) Mil commander; Lat; corps commander from 1935; CP member from 1918; *Born*: 25 May 1894 in vil Neyland, Lifland Province, son of a peasant; *Educ*: 1916 grad Chistopol' Officer Cadet School; 1931 grad Special Dept, Frunze Mil Acad; *Pos*: 1915 drafted into Russian army; from 1918 in Red Army, 1918-21 commander, 1st Lat Detachment; chief of staff, later commander, Penza Army Group; dep commander, 5th Army, Eastern Front; chief of staff, then commander, Infantry Brigade; commander, 26th Infantry Div; commander, Altay Mil Distr; 1921 commander, expeditionary corps in the Far East; 1922-30 commander, 10th Infantry Corps; dep commander, Siberian, then North Caucasian Mil Distr; 1930 dep head, Red Army Main Bd; 1931-37 commander, Siberian Mil Distr; 1934-37 member, Mil Council, USSR Pop Comrt of Defense; *Career*: 29 Aug 1918, commanding a combined detachment, repulsed an attack by Gen Kappel''s troops on Sviyazhsk, where Trotskiy's train was then stationed; although wounded, refused to leave the battlefield; 1937 arrested by NKVD; *Awards*: Order of the Red Banner; *Died*: 1938 in imprisonment; posthumously rehabilitated.

GAYSINOVICH, Samuil Yevseyevich (1901-1939) Educ official; Dr of Pedag; prof; member, State Learned Council; *Born*: 16 Feb 1901; *Educ*: 1921-25 studied at Soc-Sci Dept, Moscow State Univ; *Career*: from 1921 helped to organize factory-and-workshop schools in Moscow and Moscow Oblast; from 1926 assoc prof, Liebknecht Ind Training Inst, then at Krupskaya Acad of Communist Training; 1932-37 prof and head, Chair of Polytech Educ, Higher Communist Inst of Pedag; 1931-37 simultaneously dep dir, Research Inst of Polytech Training; first works dealt with org and teaching in factory-and-workshop schools, and with gen aspects of polytech training; arrested by State Security organs; *Publ*: *Letnyaya shkola* (The Summer School) (1926); *Politekhnizm i politekhnicheskiye navyki* (Polytechnic Training and Polytechnic Practice) (1929); *Narkompros, VSNKh i TsiT o politekhnizme* (Polytechnic Training from the Standpoint of the People's Commissariat of Education, the Supreme Sovnarkhoz and the Central Institute of Labor) (1929); *'Dinta'--Fashizm v rabochem obrazovanii* ("Dinta"--Fascism in Labor Training) (1929); *Problema industrial'nogo pedagoga* (The Problem of the Industrial Trainer) (1930); *Problema kachestva novogo rabochego* (The Problem of Quality with New Workers) (1930); *Proizvodstvo i formy proizvodstvennogo obucheniya* (Production and Forms of Production Training) (1930); *Printsipy organizatsii politekhnicheskogo obucheniya* (Organizational Principles of Polytechnic Training) (1931); *Soderzhaniye i organizatsiya trudovoy politekhnicheskoy podgotovki v FZS* (The Content and Organization of Polytechnic Labor Training in Factory-and-Workshop Schools) (1931), etc; *Died*: 14 May 1939 in imprisonment; posthumously rehabilitated.

GAZA, Ivano Ivanovich (1894-1933) Party official; CP member from 1917; *Born*: 5 Jan 1894 in Petersburg, son of a Putilov Plant fitter; *Career*: from 1909 fitter, New Mech Workshops, Putilov Plant; Feb 1916 sent to punishment barracks for organizing a strike; revol work among soldiers and sailors at Oranienbaum; helped muster Red Guard squads at Putilov Plant; from Aug 1917 dep, Petrograd Sov; took part in 1917 Oct Revol in Petrograd; from 1918 comr, Putilov Armored Train No 6; fought against Krasnov, Kornilov, Yudenich and White Polish forces; until 1925 mil comr, Red Army; from late 1925 Party work in Leningrad; 1931-33 secr, Leningrad City Party Comt; member, CPSU(B) Centr Control Commission of 16th convocation; deleg, 15th CPSU(B) Congress; an alley in Leningrad is named after him; *Died*: 5 Oct 1933; buried on Leningrad's Field of Mars.

GE, Aleksandr (real name: GOLBERG) (? -1919) Journalist; anarchist-Communist; *Born*: in Germany; *Career*: during WW 1 took internationalist stand and worked against Kropotkin and other anarchists who advocated defending Russia; after 1917 Oct Revol joined the Bolsheviks and was member, All-Russian Centr Exec Comt of 3rd and 4th convocations; summer 1918 underwent med treatment in North Caucasus and became member of North Caucasian Sov Govt; for a while held the post of dep chm, Pyatigorsk Cheka; later was plen of North Caucasian Govt in Yessentuki; *Died*: 1919 executed together with his wife Kseniya Serdyukova when Yessentuki was captured by the White Army.

GEDEONOVSKIY, Aleksandr Vasil'yevich (1859-1928) Professional revol; member, Socialist-Revol Party from 1902; *Born*: 1859 in vil Shablykino, Oryol Province, son of an archpriest; *Educ*: studied at a vil school, at Oryol Theological Seminary, and at Demidovo Lyceum; *Career*: conducted revol work among students; spring 1884 represented Yaroslavl' revol circle at a *Narodnaya Volya* (People's Will) conference in Petersburg; 1885 helped publish periodical *Narodnaya Volya*; 1888 exiled to Siberia; while en route to exile involved in Tyumen' in a fight between polit prisoners and guards, was arraigned and sentenced to six months' imprisonment; 1892 returned to Russia and, together with Natanson and Tyutchev, set up *Narodnoye pravo* (People's Right) party; 1896 again exiled to Verkholensk, East Siberia, for five years; 1902 joined Socialist-Revol Party and worked in its organizations in the Caucasus and in southern Russia; 1905 left Voronezh to attend a Party congress in Finland but was arrested at the railroad station and exiled for three years to Narym; 1906 on med grounds permitted to leave Russia, went abroad and worked for Party CC; 1909 returned to Russia; after 1917 Feb Revol was chm, Sov of Rayon Dumas; 1923 became active member, Assoc of Polit Prisoners and Deportees; *Died*: 1928.

GEDIKE, Aleksandr Fyodorovich (1877-1957) Composer, organist, pianist, instructor; prof from 1909; Pop Artiste of RSFSR from 1946; *Born*: 20 Feb 1877 in Moscow, son of a musician (organist); *Educ*: 1898 grad piano class, Moscow Conservatory with gold medal; *Career*: from 1909 prof, piano class, from 1922 organ class and from 1923 chamber music class, Moscow Conservatory; gave concerts; was the most prominent organist of the USSR; *Works*: operas: *Virineya* (1916); *U perevoza* (At the Ferry) (1933); *Zhakeriya* (1938); *Makbet* (Macbeth) (1944); three symphonies; cantatas, overtures, marches, concertoes, etc; arrangements of Russia and Kir folk songs; organ settings for a number of Russian and West European classic music pieces; *Awards*: Prize at 1900 Int Rubinstein Competition, Vienna; Stalin Prize (1948); Order of the Red Banner of Labor; medals; *Died*: 9 July 1957 in Moscow.

GEDRIS, Kazis Yuozovich (1891-1926) Lith revol; CP member from 1917; *Born*: 3 Mar 1891; *Career*: Oct 1917 organized Lith detachment to fight against Krasnov's forces; 1918 worked for Lith Section, RCP(B); later rep, Lith Provisional Revol Workers and Peasant's Govt on RSFSR Council of Pop Comr; 1919 CP Lith and Bel deleg, 1st Comintern Congress; fall 1919-summer 1920 member, illegal Vilnius Kray Bureau, CP Lith and Bel; June 1920 arrested by Polish Security Police and imprisoned; spring 1921 released (exchanged), went to Moscow; 1922-23 secr, Lith Section, CC, RCP(B) in Moscow; from Oct 1923 underground work in Kaunas; Oct 1924 arrested; July 1926 released; illegal work for Lith CC, Int Org for Aid to Revol Fighters; *Died*: 27 Dec 1926 executed after dictatorial coup.

GEDROYTS, Konstantin Kaetanovich (1872-1932) Pedologist and agrochemist; member, USSR Acad of Sci from 1929; *Born*: 6 Apr 1872; *Educ*: 1898 grad Petersburg Forestry Inst; *Career*: from 1900 worked at P.S. Kossovich's agrochemical laboratory, Russian Min of Agric; 1913-29 founder-dir, Agrochemistry Dept, Nosov Experimental Agric Station, Ukr; from 1918 prof, Petrograd

Forestry Inst; 1928-30 dir, Soil Inst, USSR Acad of Sci; from 1930 head, agrochemical laboratory, Dolgoprudnyy Experimental Station near Moscow; 1928-30 pres, Int Soc of Pedologists; from 1915 ed, *Zhurnal opytnoy agronomii*; developed theory of soil colloids and their role in the formation and fertility of soils; his findings were applied not only in pedology but also in geochemistry and agrochemistry to develop land reclamation techniques; devised several new methods of soil analysis; the All-Union Research Inst for Fertilizers, Agropedology and Agrotech is named after him; wrote over 100 papers and books and some 2,500 articles; *Publ: Osoloneniye pochv* (The Salination of Soils) (1928); *Solontsy, ikh proiskhozhdeniye, svoystva i melioratsiya* (Solonetz Soils, Their Origin, Properaties and Improvement (1928); *Ucheniye o poglotitel'noy sposobnosti pochv* (The Theory of Soil Sorption) (4th ed, 1933); *Pochvennyy pogloshchayushchiy kompleks i pochvennyye pogloshchyonnyye kationy, kak osnova genticheskoy pochvennoy klassifikatsii* (The Soil Absorption Complex and Soil-Absorbed Cations as a Basis for the Genetic Classification of Soils) (2nd ed, 1927); *Khimicheskiy analyz pochvy* (Chemical Soil Analysis) (4th ed, 1935); *Izbrannyye sochineniya* (Selected Works) (3 vol, 1955); *Awards*: Lenin Prize (1927); *Died*: 5 Oct 1932.

GEGECHKORI, Aleksandr Alekseyevich (1887-1928) Party and govt official; CP member; *Born*: 1887, son of a Mingrelian nobleman; *Career*: 1901-02 worker in Batumi, where he became acquainted with Marxist ideology; after demonstrations in Batumi went to Baku, joined the RSDRP and participated in Baku-Sabunchi workers' campaigns; 1904, after the discovery of an illegal printing press, went to Tiflis; 1905 founded terrorist battle-groups and participated in partisan activities; 1907 headed Party work in Borzhom-Akhaltsikh Rayon; 1908 arrested and exiled to Chelyabinsk Uyezd but escaped en route and fled to Chelyabinsk, where he worked with underground Bolshevik faction; to avoid arrest returned to Mingrelia, organized first Mingrelian Bolshevik circles; 1910 arrested and exiled to Don Oblast; escaped again and conducted underground work in Rostov, then in Poltava; exiled to Astrakhan' Province; after 1917 Feb Revol moved to Geo; helped found Kutaisi Bolshevik Bureau; 1918 elected chm, mil staff, West Geo Party Comt; repeatedly arrested for staging Bolshevik revolts in West Geo; summer 1918 insurrectional work in Terek Province; 1919 wounded and lost right leg; after some time went to Tiflis; arrested and exiled from Geo; 1921, after the establishment of Sov regime in Geo, continued revol work in Geo SSR; 1921-22 chm, Tiflis City Revol Comt; 1922-23 Geo Pop Comr of Internal Affairs and dep chm, Geo Council of Pop Comr; 1924-28 Geo Pop Comr of Agric and dep chm, Geo Council of Pop Comr; *Died*: 1928, committed suicide after becoming incapacitated by illness.

GEGECHKORI, Yevgeniy Petrovich (1879-1954) Lawyer; govt official; member, RSDRP (Mensheviks) from 1903; *Born*: 1879; *Educ*: 1906 grad Moscow Univ; *Career*: 1903-04 active in student movement; 1905 in Geo revol movement; 1907-12 Kutaisi Province dep in 3rd State Duma; co-leader, Duma Soc-Democratic faction; contributed to legal Soc-Democratic newspapers; during 1917 Feb Revol comr for Provisional Govt in Kutaisi Province; chm, Transcaucasian Sov of Soldiers' Dep of 1st convocation; at June 1917 Congress of Soviets elected member, All-Russian Centr Exec Comt; late 1917-18 chm, Transcaucasian Govt; from May 1918, after establishment of Geo Democratic Republ, Geo Min of For Affairs and dep chm, Geo Govt; from 1921, after the sovietization of Geo, lived in exile abroad; in emigration member, For Delegation, Geo Soc-Democratic Party; *Died*: 1954.

GEKHT, Semyon Grigor'yevich (1903-1963) Jewish writer (in Russian); *Born*: 27 Mar 1903 in Odessa; *Career*: 1922 first work published; during WW 2 mil correspondent, newspaper *Gudok*; main theme of his works was the transformed life of the Jews under Sov regime; also wrote for children; *Publ*: novelettes: *Chelovek, kotoryy zabyl svoyu zhizn'* (The Man Who Forgot His Life) (1927); *Syn sapozhnika* (The Shoemaker's Son) (1931); novelettes for children: *Yefim Kalyuzhnyy iz Smidovichey* (Yefim Kalyuzhnyy of the Smidovidiches) (1931); *Vesyoloye otrochestvo* (Gay Adolescence) (1932); *Parokhod idyot v Yaffu i obratno* (The Steamer Plies to Jaffa) (1936); novel *Pouchitel'naya istoriya* (A Cautionary Story) (1939); *Budka solov'ya* (Nightingale Box) (1957); stories *Tri plova* (Three Pilaffs) (1959); collection *V gostyakh u molodyozhi* (Guests of Youth) (1960); stories *Dolgi serdtsa* (The Heart's Debts) (1963), etc; *Died*: 10 June 1963 in Moscow.

GEKKER, Anatoliy Il'ich (1888-1937) Mil commander; corps commander from 1935; CP member from 1917; *Born*: 25 Aug 1888 in Tiflis, son of a surgeon in the Caucasian Army; *Educ*: 1909 grad Vladimir Mil College in Petersburg; 1917 grad courses at Gen Staff Acad; *Pos*: from 1907 in Russian army; veteran of WW 1; after Oct 1917 Revol elected chief of staff, 33rd Infantry Corps, later 8th Army; commander, 8th Army; from 1918 in Red Army; 1918-19 commander, Donets Workers' Army; chief of staff, Gen Command of Sov Ukr troops; comr, White Sea Mil Distr; commander, Vologda rear area, Kotlas Distr, then Astrakhan' fortified distr; 1919 commander, 13th Army; 1920 chief of staff, RSFSR Internal Security Troops; 1920-21 commander, 11th Army, then Separate Caucasian Army; 1922 asst commandant, Red Army Mil Acad; from 1922 mil attache in China; from 1929 mil and dipl work in Turkey; 1934-37 head, Dept of Foreign Relations, Red Army Gen Staff; *Career*: 1918 helped crush anti-Sov mutiny in Yaroslavl'; 1921 directed mil occupation of Geo; crushed anti-Sov revolt in Arm; 1937 arrested by NKVD; *Awards*: Order of the Red Banner; Order of the Red Banner of Azer; Order of the Red Banner of Arm; *Died*: 1 July 1937 executed; posthumously rehabilitated.

GEKKER, Naum Leont'yevich (1861-1920) Revolutionary; member, *Narodnaya Volya* (People's Will) party; *Born*: 1861 in Bakhmut, of Jewish parents; *Educ*: grad Berdyansk high school; studied at Novorossiysk Univ; *Career:* in youth joined *Chyornyy peredel* (Black Redistribution) org and was member and propagandist, South Russian Workers' Union, Odessa; 1881 arrested; 22 Nov 1882 sentenced by mil tribunal to 10 years at hard labor in Kara; took part in a prisoners' protest; then tried to commit suicide; 1892 resettled in Yakutsk Oblast, began to study life of Yakuts and contributed to newspapers; 1895 took part in Sibiryakov expedition; then worked for newspapers *Vostochnoye obozreniye,* Irkutsk, and *Odesskiye novosti,* Odessa; contributed to centr journals; *Publ: Politecheskaya katorga na Kare* (Political Convicts in Kara) (1906); "A. A. Spandoni" (1906); *Died*: 1920.

GEL'DYYEV, Alleberdy (1912-1967) Journalist; ed, journal *Turkmenistan kommunisti* from 1964; CP member from 1941; *Born*: 1912 in vil Ashkhabad, son of a peasant; *Educ*: 1953 grad Evening Branch, Turkm State Univ; *Career*: from 1931 assoc, Party newspaper *Sovet Turkmenistani*; then exec ed, newspaper *Signal*; 1939-50 head, Agric Dept, newspaper *Sovet Turkmenistani*; 1950-57 ed, Turkm youth newspaper *Yash kommunist*; 1957-64 head, Wire Agency, Turkm Council of Min; 1964 dir, *Turkmenistan* Publ House; 1964-67 ed, journal *Turkmenistan kommunisti*; 1959-62 also chm, bd, Turkm Journalists' Union and secr, USSR Journalists' Union ; 1963-66 member, Auditing Commission, CC, CP Turkm; 1963 member, Sov journalists deleg at Afro-Asian Conference in Indonesia; *Awards*: Order of the Red Banner of Labor; two Badges of Hon; medals "For Labor Valor," etc; *Died*: 12 July 1967.

GEL'FREYKH, Vladimir Georgiyevich (1885-1967) Architect; prof; *Born*: 24 Mar 1885; *Educ*: 1906-14 studied at Petersburg Acad of Arts; *Career*: while still a student began work with Acad V. A. Shchuko; from 1918 mutually designed a number of major architectural projects; this partnership continued for more than 20 years until Shchuko's death in 1939; 1922-23 they designed in Leningrad the Smol'nyy Propyleum gateway; 1924-25 three Volkhovstroy sub-stations; 1924-25 the architectural part of the Lenin Monument at Smol'nyy and 1928 of the Lenin Monument at Leningrad's Finnish Terminus; 1930 their designs were used for the construction of the monumental Lenin USSR Library in Moscow; 1932-33 took part in competition for the design of Palace of Soviets in Moscow; from 1933, together with V. A. Shchuko and B. M. Iofan, worked on design of the Palace of Soviets (on the basis of an original design by B. M. Iofan); Gel'freykh and Shchuko designs were basis for: 1931-35 Gorky Theater in Rostov-on-Don; Abkhazian Govt Building in Sukhumi; 1936-38 the Grand Stone Bridge across the Moskva River (together with M. A. Minkus); 1939 Main Pavilion, All-Union Agric Exhibition in Moscow (together with A. P. Velikanov and Yu. V. Shchuko); 1943 co-designed the ground-level entrance-hall of the Novokuznetskaya and 1944 the Elektrozavodskaya subway station; 1948 together with M. A. Minkus designed the 27-story admin building (after an original 20-story design) on Moscow's Smolensk Square; from 1919 taught at architectural institutes; from 1959 taught at Moscow Higher Ind Arts college (former Stroganov College); 1947-56 member, USSR Acad of Architecture; 1956-63 member, USSR Acad of Construction and Architecture; head, No 4 Main Workshop Moscow Design Inst; *Awards*: two Orders of the Red Banner of Labor; two Badges of Hon; medals; two Stalin Prizes (1946 and 1949); Hero of Socialist Labor (1965); *Died*: 7 Aug 1967.

GELOVANI, Mikhail Georgiyevich (1893-1956) Geo actor and film dir; Pop Artiste of USSR from 1950; *Born*: 6 Jan 1893; *Educ*: 1918-20 studied at Tbilisi Theater Studio; *Career*: 1913 began stage work; played in Baku, Tbilisi and Kutaisi theaters; 1921-22 and 1936-39 at Tbilisi Rustaveli Theater; 1942-48 at Moscow Acad Arts Theater; from 1924 also film actor; from 1927 film dir, Arm Film Studio; first Geo actor to play the role of Stalin; *Roles*: on the stage: Kotsio in Dadiani's "Things of Yesterday"; Tariel Mklavadze in Ninoshvili's *Tariel Mklavadze*; Stalin in Dadiani's "From the Spark..." (1937) and *Chelovek s ruzh'yom* (Man With A Gun) (1939), etc; in films: Bakhva Pulava in *Tri zhizni* (Three Lives) (1925); Avalov in *Devyatyy val* (The Ninth Wave) (1926) Rostom in *Posledniy maskarad* (Last Masquerade) (1934), etc; Stalin in the films: *Velikoye zarevo* (The Great Glow) (1938), *Chelovek s ruzh'yom* (Man With a Gun) (1938), *Vyborgskaya storona* (The Vyborg Side) (1939), *Lenin v 1918 godu* (Lenin in 1918) (1939); *Valeriy Chkalov* (1941), *Oborona Tsaritsyna* (Defense of Tsaritsyn) (1942), *Klyatva (The Oath) (1946), Padeniye Berlina* (The Fall of Berlin) (1950); *Works*: directed films: *Zloy dukh* (The Evil Spirit) (1927); *Molodost' pobezhdayet* (Youth Wins) (1929); *Delo doblesti* (A Matter of Valor) (1931); *Nastoyashchiy kavkazets* (A True Caucasian) (1934), etc; *Awards*: Stalin Prizes (1941, 1942, 1947, 1956); *Died*: 21 Dec 1956.

GEL'SHTEYN, Eliazar Markovich (1897-1955) Therapist and clinicist; Hon Sci Worker of RSFSR; *Born*: 1897; *Educ*: 1919 grad Med Fac, Moscow Univ; *Career*: after grad served in Red Army; 1920-30 intern and asst, therapeutic clinics, 2nd Moscow Med Inst; 1931-52 head, Fac Therapy Clinic, above inst; during WW 2 chief therapist, Leningrad Front; did research on rheumatism, hypertonia and myocardic infarct, alimentary dystrophy and experimental chemotherapy; wrote chapter on mil field therapy for encyclopedic dictionary of mil med; bd member, All-Union and dep chm, Moscow Therapeutic Soc; wrote more than 60 works; *Publ: Uchebnik vnutrennikh bolezney* (A Textbook of Internal Diseases) (1935); *Klinicheskoye znacheniye rentgenokimografii serdtsa* (The Clinical Importance of Cardiac Roentgenokymography) (1937); coauthor, *Uchebnik chastnoy patologii i terapii vnutrennikh bolezney* (A Textbook on the Special Pathology and Therapy of Internal Diseases) (1947); *Infarkt miokarda* (Myocardic Infarct) (1948); coauthor, *Chastnaya patologiya i terapiya vnutrennikh bolezney* (The Special Pathology and Therapy of Internal Diseases) (1950); coauthor, *Opyt sovetskoy meditsiny v Velikoy Otechestvennoy voyne 1941-1945 godov* (The Experience of Soviet Medicine in the 1941-45 Great Fatherland War) (1951); *Died*: 1955.

GEL'TSER, Yekaterina Vasil'yevna (1876-1962) Ballet dancer; Pop Artiste of RSFSR from 1925; *Born*: 14 Nov 1876 in Moscow, daughter of a ballet dancer; *Educ*: 1894 grad Moscow Theater College; *Career*: 1894-96 and 1898-1934 at Moscow Bol'shoy Theater; 1896-98 at Petersburg Mariinskiy Theater; 1910 on tour abroad (Brussels, Berlin, Paris, London, USA) propagandizing Russian ballet art; also taught ballet; from 1934 tours of USSR; *Roles*: Odetta in Tchaikovsky's *Lebedinoye ozero* (Swan Lake); Aurora in Tchaikovsky's *Spyashchaya krasavitsa* (Sleeping Beaty); Esmeralda in Puni's "Esmeralda"; Medora in Puni and Adan's "The Corsair"; the Fisherwoman in Grieg's "Fast is Love"; Tao Hoa in Glier's *Krasnyy mak* (Red Poppy); Raymonda in Glazunov's *Raymonda; Awards*: Stalin Prize (1943); Order of Lenin; Order of the Red Banner of Labor; medals; *Died*: 12 Dec 1962.

GENDEL'MAN, Mikhail Yakovlevich (YAKOBI) (1881-?) Politician; lawyer; member, Socialist-Revol Party from 1902; *Born*: 1881; *Career*: 1917 at 3rd and 4th Socialist-Revol Party Congresses elected member, Party CC; July 1917 member, comt of inquiry that investigated alleged dealings of some members of the Bolshevik faction with the Germans; member, Constituent Assembly; 1922 received suspended death sentence in trial of CC, Socialist-Revol Party on charges of organizing armed overthrow of Sov regime; *Died*: date and place of death unknown.

GENERALOV, Fyodor Stepanovich (1899-1962) Russian; promoted kolkhoz system; CP member from 1940; *Born*: 1899, son of a peasant; *Educ*: partial secondary educ; *Career*: from 1919 in Red Army; then agric work; from 1931 kolkhoz worker; 1932-37 dep chm, 1937-42 chm, *Krasnyy Oktyabr'* (Red October) kolkhoz, Lukhovitsk Rayon, Moscow Oblast; from 1942 chm, Lenin kolkhoz, same rayon; dep, USSR Supr Sov of 3rd, 4th, 5th and 6th convocations; *Awards*: Hero of Socialist Labor (1949 and 1957); *Died*: 3 May 1962.

GENTER, German Genrikhovich (1881-1937) Obstetrician and gynecologist; *Born*: 1881; *Educ*: 1904 grad Mil Med Acad; *Career*: 1913 defended doctor's thesis on premature partition of placenta; from 1925 prof, Clinic, 2nd Leningrad Med Inst; studied prophylaxis of female gonorrhea and org of rural midwifery service; devised a method of surgical sterilization; described parametritis symptom (dull percussive tone over anterior upper spine of the ilium) and other diagnostic techniques; wrote 57 works, including monographs and guides; *Publ: Prezhdevremennoye otdeleniye detskogo mesta* (Premature Partition of the Placenta) (1913); *Akusherskiy seminariy* (An Obstetrics Seminary) (3 vol, 1931-33); *Uchebnik akusherstva* (An Obstetrics Textbook) (1937); *Died*: 1937.

GEORGIYEVSKIY, Adol'f Georgiyevich (1886-1945) Actor; Hon Artiste of RSFSR from 1931; CP member from 1940; *Born*: 18 Jan 1886; *Educ*: grad Law Fac, Moscow Univ; *Career*: from 1904 at theaters in Nizhniy Novgorod, Rostov-on-Don and Sverdlovsk; *Roles*: Repetilov in Griboyedov's *Gore ot uma* (Woe from Wit); Krutitskiy in Ostrovskiy's *Na vsyakogo mudretsa dovol'no prostoty* (There's a Simpleton in Every Sage); Yusov in Ostrovskiy's *Dokhodnoye mesto* (A Lucrative Post); Arkashka Schastlivtsev in Ostrovskiy's *Les* (The Forest); Lyubim Tortsov in Ostrovskiy's *Bednost' ne porok* (Poverty Is No Vice); Kutuzov in Solov'yov's *Fel'dmarshal Kutuzov* (Fieldmarshal Kutuzov); Galushka in Korneychuk's *V stepyakh Ukrainy* (In the Steppes of the Ukraine), etc; *Died*: 1945.

GERASIMCHUK, Lidiya Pavlovna (1922-1958) Ballet dancer; Hon Artiste of Ukr SSR from 1952; *Born*: 5 Apr 1922 in Kiev, daughter of a worker; *Educ*: 1937 grad Choreographic School; *Career*: 1937-41 and from 1944 soloist, Kiev Opera and Ballet Theater; 1941-44 soloist, Leningrad Opera and Ballet Theater; *Roles*: Marusya in A. Svechnikov's *Marusya Boguslavka*; Mariula in K. Dan'kevich's *Lileya*; Raymonda in Glazunov's *Raymonda*, etc; *Died*: 5 Dec 1958.

GERASIMENKO, Konstantin Mikhaylovich (1907-1942) Ukr poet and playwright; *Born*: 11 May 1907 in vil Prikhod'ki, Poltava Oblast, son of a teacher; *Educ*: grad Piryatinsk Teachers' Training College; *Career*: teacher in Donets Basin; 1932 first work published; from 1935 lit work in Kiev; in WW 2 mil corresp on North Caucasian Front; wrote mainly in Ukr; *Publ*: verse collections: "Growth" (1933); "September" (1935); "Remembrance" (1938); "The Road" (1939); "Portrait" (1941); *Na Yuzhnom fronte* (On the Southern Front) (1942, in Russian); plays: "On the High Road" (1939); "Legend" (1941), etc; libretto for M. Verikovskiy's opera "The Hired Woman," etc; poem "Oath for the Leader" (1942); *Died*: Sept 1942 killed in action.

GERASIMENKO, Mikhail Petrovich (1902-1961) Agric econ; Dr of Econ from 1961; CP member from 1944; *Born*: 21 Nov 1902 in vil Lebedin', Kiev Province, son of a peasant; *Educ*: 1926 grad Kiev Inst of Nat Econ; *Career*: until 1941 lecturer in polit econ, Kiev Univ; simultaneously senior assoc, Sugar Ind Research Inst; 1946-52 lecturer, L'vov Trade and Econ Inst; 1952-61 head, Econ Dept, L'vov Inst of Soc Sci, Ukr Acad of Sci; wrote works on history and econ of Western Ukr; *Publ: Bor'ba trudyashchikhsya Zapadnoy Ukrainy za vossoyedineniye s Sovetskoy Ukrainoy* (The Struggle of the Workers of the Western Ukraine for Unification with the Soviet Ukraine) (1955); *Agrarnyye otnosheniya v Galitsii v period krizisa krepostnogo khozyaystva* (Agrarian Relations in Galicia During the Crisis of the Feudal Economy) (1959); *Died*: 26 Nov 1961.

GERASIMENKO, Vasiliy Filippovich (1900-1961) Mil commander; lt-gen from 1940; CP member from 1920; *Born*: 11 Apr 1900 in vil Velikiye Burimtsy, Cherkassy Oblast, son of a peasant; *Educ*: 1927 grad infantry school; 1931 grad Frunze Mil Acad; *Career*: from 1918 in Red Army; fought in Civil War; 1938-41 dep commander, Kiev Special Mil Distr; commander, Volga Mil Distr; 1940-41 member, CC, CP Ukr; 1941-42 commander, Volga and Stalingrad mil distr; 1942 fought in battle of Stalingrad; 1942-43 commander, 28th Army; 1943 took part in mopping-up operations near Melitopol'; 1945-53 dep commander, Baltic Mil Distr; from 1953 in retirement; *Awards*: three Orders of Lenin; other orders and medals; *Died*: 13 Feb 1961.

GERASIMOV, Aleksandr Mikhaylovich (1881-1963) Painter; Pop Artist of the USSR from 1943; member, USSR Acad of Arts from 1947; CP member from 1950; *Born*: 12 Aug 1881 in Kozlov (now Michurinsk); *Educ*: 1903-15 studied portraiture and architecture at Moscow College of Painting, Sculpture and Architecture; *Career*: 1915-18 in the Army; 1925 joined Painters' Assoc of Revol Russia; 1947-57 pres, USSR Acad of Arts; chm, Org Comt, USSR Painters' Union; dep, RSFSR Supr Sov of 2nd, 3rd and 4th convocations; specialized in portrait, historical, genre, landscape and still-life painting, set designing and illustrations; a number of his works are displayed in the Tret'yakov Gallery and other Sov museums; *Works*: portraits: "V. I. Lenin on the Tribune" (1929-30); "I. V. Stalin at the 16th CPSU(B) Congress" (1933); "I. V. Stalin and K. Ye.Voroshilov in the Kremlin" (1938); O. V. Lepeshinskaya (1939); I. I. Fisanovich (1942); group portrait of the four senior Sov painters (1944); I. V. Stalin (1945-47); V. M. Molotov (1948), etc; group compositions: "October Anthem" (1942); "Teheran Big-Three Conference" (1945); "I. V. Stalin at A. A. Zhdanov's Grave" (1948), etc; paintings: "Troyka in Winter" (1914); "Burgeoning Steppe" (1924); "After the Rain" (1935); series "Mother Rye" (1946), etc; illustrated: "Taras Bul'ba" (1947); "Yevgeniy Onegin" (1949), etc; designed numerous stage sets; *Publ: V. I. Surikov - vydayushchiysya predstavitel' russkoy kul'tury* (V. I. Surikov, A Prominent Representative of Russian Culture) (1948); *Sovetskoye izobrazitel'noye iskusstvo i zadachi AKh SSSR* (Soviet Fine Arts and the Tasks of the USSR Academy of Arts) (1949); *Zadachi AKh SSSR v dele khudozhestvennogo obrazovaniya* (The Tasks of the USSR Academy of Arts in the Sphere of Artistic Education) (1949); *Za sovetskiy patriotizm v iskusstve* soviet Patriotism in Art) (1949); *Awards*: four Stalin Prizes (1941, 1943, 1946 and 1949); Grand Prix at Paris Int Exhibition (1937); Order of the Red Banner of Labor; medals; *Died*: 23 July 1963.

GERASIMOV, Aleksandr Pavlovich (1869-1942) Geologist; Hon Sci Worker of RSFSR; *Born*: 11 Sept 1869; *Educ*: 1893 grad Petersburg Mining Inst; *Career*: assoc, Geological Comt, USSR Acad of Sci; senior geophysicist, Inst of Physics and Mathematics, USSR Acad of Sci; did field work in Caucasus, Siberia, the Kola Peninsula, the Maritime Region and other regions of the USSR; made geological surveys of the Transbaykal and Kir steppe; made systematic study of the geology of the Caucasus and supervised the compilation of a gen geological map of this region; was one of first geologists to correlate the development of tectonic folding to manifestations of vulcanism in the Caucasus; did many years of research on the Mineral'nyye Vody region and igneous rocks of the Caucasus; *Publ: Geologicheskiye issledovaniya v Lenskom gornom okruge v 1903-em godu* (Geological Research in the Lena Mountain District in 1903) (1907); *Geologicheskiye issledovaniya v Tsentral'nom Zabaykal'ye* (Geological Research in the Central Transbaykal) (1910); *Tektonika, vulkanicheskiye tsikly i metallogeniya Severnogo Kavkaza* (The Tectonics, Volcanic Cycles and Metallogeny of the Northern Caucasus) (1933); *Geologicheskoye stroyeniye Mineralovodskogo rayona* (The Geological Structure of the Mineral'nyye Vody Region) (2 vol, 1935-37); *Stratigrafiya dokembriyskikh obrazovaniy Kavkaza* (The Stratigraphy of the Precambrian Formations of the Caucasus) (1939); *Died*: 10 Nov 1942.

GERASIMOV, Mikhail Prokof'yevich (1889-1939) Russian poet; CP member from 1905; *Born*: 12 Oct 1889 near Buguruslan, Samara Province, son of a railroad worker; *Educ*: studied at Samara Railroad Tech College; *Career*: 1906-07 subjected to reprisals and arrested for revol activities; from 1907 emigré in Belgium and France; 1913 first work published; member, Paris workers' circle together with A. Lunacharskiy, F. Kalinin, A. Gastev, P. Bessal'ko, etc; 1914 volunteered for French Army; 1915 exiled to Russia for anti-mil propaganda; from 1917 exec Party and govt work: chm, Samara Province Exec Comt; mil comr, Samara Province; chm, Samara Sov of Soldiers' Dep; dep chm, Samara Revol Comt; 1918 chm, Samara Proletarian Culture Comt; fought in Civil War; 1920-23 co-founder and member, *Kuznitsa* lit group in Moscow; member, first bd of All-Russian Assoc of Proletarian Writers and Bd member, All-Russian Writers' Union; with the introduction of the New Econ Policy experienced an ideological and creative crisis and 1921 left the Party; 1937 arrested by NKVD; *Publ*: collected verse: *Veshniye zovy* (Vernal Calls) (1917); *Zavod vesenniy* (Spring at the Factory) (1919); *Zheleznyye tsvety* (Iron Flowers) (1919); *Elektrifikatsiya* (Electrification) (1922); *Zemnoye siyaniye* (Terrestrial Radiance) (1927); *Dobroye utro* (Good Morning) (1928); *K sorevnovaniyu'* (For Competition) (1930); *Liricheskiy vecher* (Lyrical Evening) (1927), etc; poems: *Mona Liza* (1918); *Chyornaya pena* (Black Foam) (1921); *Prostyye stroki* (Simple Lines) (1920); *Elektropoema* (Electro-Poem) (1923), etc; collected stories *Tsvety pod ognyom* (Flowers Under Fire) (1919); *Prazdnik zhizni'* (Holiday of Life) (1925); *Died*: 1939 in imprisonment; posthumously rehabilitated.

GERASIMOV, Sergey Vasil'yevich (1885-1964) Painter and graphic artist; member, USSR Acad of Arts from 1947; Pop Artist of USSR from 1958; *Born*: 27 Sept 1885 in Mozhaysk; *Educ*: 1901-07 studied at Moscow Stroganov Arts College; 1912 grad Moscow College of Painting, Sculpture and Architecture; *Career*: 1940-51 chm, Moscow Painters' Union; from 1947 presidium member, USSR Acad of Arts; 1958-63 first secr, Bd, USSR Painters' Union; dep, RSFSR Supr Sov of 1963 convocation; from 1960 member, Lenin Prizes Comt for Lit and Arts, USSR Council of Min; from 1964 Bd chm, USSR Painters' Union; illustrated Russian lit classics; also taught; specialized in landscape, historical and genre painting; a number of his works are displayed in Moscow's Tret'yakov Gallery and other Sov museums; *Works*: "Male Portrait" (1912); "Portrait of G. Ye. Malasov" (1913); paintings: "Old Woman with a Mortar" (1920-21); "Village Soviet" (1924-25); "Communists' Arrival at a Village" (1927); "October 1917," "Partisan Oath" (1932-33); "Kolkhoz Watchman" (1933); "Kolkhoz Holiday" (1937); "Winter" (1939); "Partisan's Mother" (1943); "The Pugachev Rebellion" (1945); "April" (1950); "Spring Rain" (1954); "For the Soviet Regime" (1957); "Mozhaysk Landscapes" (1957); series "Russian Land," etc; *Awards*: Lenin Prize (1966, posthumously); several Orders of the Red Banner of Labor; medals; *Died*: 20 Apr 1964.

GERBIL'SKIY, Nikolay L'vovich (1900-1967) Biologist; pioneer of ichthyology and evolutionary morphology; Dr of Biological Sci from 1947; prof from 1952; maj, Med Corps from 1945; CP member from 1945; *Born*: 10 Dec 1900 in Yekaterinoslav (now Dnepropetrovsk), son of a physician; *Educ:* 1919 grad Yekaterinoslav Boys' High School; 1920-25 studied at Biological Fac, Dnepropetrovsk Inst of Public Educ; 1928 grad Biological Fac, 1st Moscow Univ; *Career*: from 1921, while still a student, worked as asst, Chair of Invertebrate Zoology, Dnepropetrovsk Inst of Public Educ; 1922-24 with Azov-Black Sea Ichthyological Expedition; from 1924, while completing studies, dissector and asst, Chair of Biology, Dnepropetrovsk Med Inst; 1928 for a while asst, Chair of Histology, Moscow Univ; 1928-32 taught biology at a school and at Workers' Fac, Leningrad Univ; 1932-67 lecturer, asst prof, then prof of biology, Leningrad Univ; 1941-45 in Sov Army; head of laboratory, evacuation hospital; 1945-48 head, Chair of Developmental Dynamics of Organisms, Leningrad Univ; also dir, Laboratory of Fish-Breeding Principles, Main Fishery Bd; also section head, Biological Inst, Leningrad Univ; 1952-67 head, Chair of Ichthyology and Hydrobiology, Leningrad Univ; studied morphology, physiology, endocrinology, ecology, axonomy and evolution of fish and founded new biological trend - ecological histophysiology; on the basis of this made valuable proposals for increasing Sov fish stocks; wrote over 100 works, including textbooks and teaching aids; *Awards*: Order of the Red Banner of Labor (1939); Order of the Red Star (1944); Badge of Hon (1951); "Outstanding Fishery Worker" Badge (1950); scrolls of hon; various prizes; *Died*: 1967.

GEREYEV, Yusup (1903-1941) Kumyk writer; CP member; *Born*: 20 Dec 1903 in a Russian family; early orphaned, was brought up by a Kumyk peasant; *Career*: from 1927 exec Party and govt work; pioneered satire in Dagh prose; *Publ*: collection of anti-religious stories "A Panacea for All Ills" (1927); stories: "Mullah Nasreddin's Companion" (1927); *Abaz; Basmilla; Azhay's Plans; Marzhanat's Troubles; Ustaz*; novelette "Spring From the North" (1934); collected stories and novelettes "Misfortune" (1935); "Stories" (1955); collection "Spring from the North" (1959); *Died*: 27 Nov 1941 killed in an accident.

GERMAN, Aleksandr Petrovich (1874-1953) Mining eng; Gen Mine Dir, 2nd Class; member, USSR Acad of Sci from 1939; *Born*: 1 Feb 1874; *Educ*: 1897 grad Fac of Physics and Mathematics, Petersburg Univ; 1903 grad Petersburg Mining Inst; *Career*: from 1907 lecturer, from 1914 prof, Petersburg (Leningrad) Mining Inst; did research on the theoretical principles of mining mech and wrote studies of mine elevators, pumps, ventilators and pneumatic equipment, and also on machinery for the heat treatment of metals; *Publ: Opredeleniye osnovykh razmerov parovykh turbin*

(Determining the Basic Dimensions of Steam Turbines) (1912); *O sovmestnoy rabote rudnichnykh ventilyatorov* (The Tandem Operation of Mine Ventilators) (1922); *Turbomashiny* (Turbines) (1925); *Teoriya i raschyot turbovozdukhoduvnykh mashin* (The Theory and Calculation of Turbo-Blowers) (1928); *Primenenye szhatogo vozdukha v gornom dele* (The Mining Applications of Compressed Air) (1933); *Gornaya mekhanika* (Mining Mechanics) (2 vol, 1934-35); *Rudnichnyye pod'yomnyye ustanovski* (Mine Elevators) (1947); *Vliyaniye teploobmena mezhdu stenkami tsilindra i vozdukhom na rabotu porshnevykh kompressorov* (The Effect of the Heat Exchange Between the Cylinder Walls and the Air on the Operation of Piston Compressors) (1947), etc; *Awards*: Order of Lenin; three other orders; *Died*: 30 Nov 1953.

GERMAN, I. E. (1884-1942) Professional revol; RSDRP member from 1904; *Born*: 1884; *Career*: member, Riga City RSDRP(B) Comt; acitve in 1905 Revol; frequently subjected to reprisals by tsarist authorities; 1909 emigrated to Berlin; helped organize Bolshevik groups of Lat Soc-Democratic Party abroad; strove for amalgamation of the party with RSDRP(B); 1914 deleg at 4th Congress of Lat Soc-Democratic Party in Brussels, where was elected member, CC, member of Party's For Comt and member, ed bd, newspaper *Zihna*; after 1917 Feb Revol member, ed bd, newspapers *Sotsial-demokrat* and *Svobodnyy strelok*; after 1917 Oct Revol Party and govt work; chm, Tambov RCP(B) Comt and member, Tambov Province Exec Comt; from 1920 financial work in various Sov organizations; deleg at 8th RCP(B) Congress; later worked in lit and journalism; *Died*: 1942.

GERMAN, Valentin Aleksandrovich (1904-1957) Veterinary surgeon; prof from 1942; Hon Sci Worker of Ukr SSR from 1951; CP member from 1940; *Born*: 20 June 1904 in Poltava; *Educ*: 1926 grad Khar'kov Veterinary Inst; *Career*: from 1942 prof and head, Chair of Surgery, Alma-Ata Zooveterinary Inst; from 1944 prof, from 1948 head, Chair of Surgery, Khar'kov Veterinary Inst; wrote some 50 works on animal blood transfusion; *Publ*: *Perelivaniye krovi u loshadey i drugikh domashnikh zhivotnykh* (Blood Transfusion in Horses and Other Domestic Animals) (1948); *Perelivaniye krovi i drugiye vidy gemoterapii u zhivotnykh* (Blood Transfusion and Other Forms of Animal Hemotherapy) (1954), etc; *Died*: 30 Aug 1957.

GERMAN, Yuriy Pavlovich (1910-1967) Russian writer; CP member from 1958; *Born*: 4 Apr 1910 in Riga, son of an office worker; *Career:* 1926 first work published; from 1965 Bd member, RSFSR Writers' Union; works deal with "socialist morals," re-education of people and historical themes; *Publ:* novels: *Rafael'iz parikmakherskoy* (Raphael from the Barber's Shop) (1931); *Nashi znakomyye* (Our Acquaintances) (1934-36); *Bednyy Genrikh* (Poor Genrikh) (1934); *Rossiya molodaya* (Young Russia) (1952); *Odin god* (One Year) (1960); *Dorogoy moy chelovek* (My Dear Man) (1961); novelettes: *Aleksey Zhmakin* (1937-38); *Studyonoye more* (Gold Sea) (1943); stories: *Medsestra Nadya Grechukha* (Nurse Nadya Grechukha) (1942); plays: *Syn naroda* (Son of the People) (1939); *Za tyuremnoy stenoy* (Behind the Prison Wall) (1956); film scripts: *Semero smelykh* (The Courageous Seven) (1936), coauthor); *Doktor Kalyuzhnyy* (1939); *Doktor Pirogov* (1947); *Delo Rumyantseva* (The Rumyantsev Case) (1956); *Vechnyy ogon'* (Eternal Fire) (1962, coauthor); *Ver'te mne, druz'ya* (Believe Me, Friends) (1965); TV film *Slushay* (Listen!) (1964); trilogy about Dr Ustimenko: *Delo, kotoromu ty sluzhish'* (The Cause You Serve), *Dorogoy moy chelovek* (My Dear Man), *Ya otvechayu za vyso* (I Take Full Responsibility) (1965); *Awards:* Stalin Prize (1948); *Died:* 16 Jan 1967.

GERMANO (real name: GERMAN), Aleksandr Vyacheslavovich (1893-1955) Writer; *Born*: 7 June 1893 in vil Startsevo-Lepyoshkino, Oryol Province; *Career*: wrote in Russian and Romany; 1915 first work published; 1926 moved from Oryol to Moscow and became interested in the Gipsies; collected Gipsy folklore, songs and fairy-tales; his plays were staged at the Gipsy theater *Romen*; *Publ*: in Russian: *Cherv' gryzyot* (The Gnawing Worm) (1915); play *V nekoyem uchrezhdenii* (In a Certain Institution) (1921); *Bibliografiya o tsyganakh. Ukazatel' knig i statey s 1780 po 1930* (Gipsy Bibliography. Index of Books and Articles from 1780 to 1930) (1930); essay *Tsygane* (Gipsies) (1931); *Stikhi i pesni* (Poems and Songs) (1937); *Povesti i rasskazy* (Novelettes and Stories) (1960); in Romany: "His Name Was Wolf and Other Stories" (1933); "Be On Your Guard" (1934); "Red Fires" (1934); "Ganka Chamba and Other Stories" (1935); "Poems" (1935); plays: "Life on Wheels," "Between the Fires"; *Died*: 22 May 1955 in Moscow.

GERMANOVICH, Markian Yakovlevich (1895-1937) Mil commander; ensign, Russian army; corps commander from 1935; CP member from 1918; *Born*: 1895; *Pos*: from 1918 in Red Army; 1918-21 consecutively comr; brigade commander; chief of staff, Minsk Rayon; brigade commander, 46th Infantry Div; commander, 52nd, 15th and 23rd Infantry Div; 1921-37 commander, 5th Infantry Corps; asst commander, Bel, Centr Asian and Moscow Mil Distr; commandant, Red Army Acad of Motorization and Mechanization; dep commander, Leningrad Mil Distr; 1934-37 member, Mil Council, USSR Pop Comrt of Defense; 1937 arrested by NKVD; *Died*: 1937 in imprisonment; posthumously rehabilitated.

GERMOGEN (secular name: KOZHIN, Vasiliy Vasil'yevich) (1880-1954) Exarch of the Moscow Patriarchy in America; Master of Divinity from 1917; Dr of Divinity from 1949; *Born*: 1880 in vil Kumylzhinskaya, now Volgograd Oblast, son of a psalm-reader; Educ: grad Don Theological Seminary; 1916 grad Kazan' Theological Seminary; *Career:* 1907 entered priesthood; 1916 ordained monk with name of Germogen; 1917 attended All-Russian Council of the Russian Orthodox Church and ordained Bishop of Kazan' and Sviyaga; from Nov 1947 prof, Chair of Occidental Religions and rector, Moscow Theological Acad; simultaneously rector, Moscow Theological Seminary; 1948 speaker and chm, Commission for the Sci Evaluation of Reports, Moscow conference of bishops and rep of 11 autocephalous Orthodox churches; 1948 also delivered policy statement on theol training and the attitude of the Moscow Patriarchy to ecumenism; 1949 ordained Bishop of Krasnodar and Kuban'; 1950 member, Russian Orthodox Church deleg to Palestine; 1951 deleg, 3rd All-Union Peace Conference, Moscow; 1953 accompanied deleg from Antiochian Orthodox Church on tour of USSR; 1954 ordained metropolitan and appointed Exarch of Moscow Patriarchy of North and South America (Aleutia and North America); *Publ: Popytka Vatikana podchinit' svoyemu vliyaniyu pravoslavnyye tserkvi yuzhnykh slavyan na Balkanakh* (The Vatican's Attempt to Subject the Orthodox Churches of the Southern Slavs in the Balkans to Its Influence); *Missiya druzhby* (A Mission of Friendship); *K yubileyu Khalkidonskogo sobora* (The Anniversary of the Council of Chalcedon); *Starokatolicheskoye dvizheniye* (The Old Catholic Movement), etc; *Awards*: right to wear cross on cowl; *Died*: 3 Aug 1954; buried in Krasnodar.

GERNET, Mikhail Nikolayevich (1874-1953) Lawyer and criminologist; law historian; Dr of Law from 1936; prof from 1911; Hon Sci Worker of RSFSR from 1928; *Born*: 12 July 1874 in Ardatov, former Simbirsk Province, son of a polit exile; *Educ*: 1897 grad Law Fac, Moscow Univ; *Career*: from 1902 assoc prof and lecturer, criminal law course, Moscow Univ; 1911 left Moscow Univ in protest against reactionary policy of Min of Educ; from 1911 prof, Chair of Criminal Law, Petersburg Inst of Psychoneuropathology; from 1919 prof, Moscow Univ; 1919-30 simultaneously head, Dept of Moral Statistics; USSR Centr Statistical Bd; from late 1930's, although now blind, engaged in research on history of Tsarist jails; *Publ: Obshchestvennyye prichiny prestupnosti* (Social Reasons of Criminality) (1905); *Detoubiystvo* (Infanticide) (1911); *Smertnaya kazn'* (Capital Punishment) (1913); *Prestupleniye i bor'ba v svyazi s evolyutsiyey obshchestva* (Crime and Prevention in Connection with the Evolution of the Society) (1916); *Prestupnost' i samoubiystvo vo vremya voyny i posle neyo* (Criminality and Suicide During and After War) (1927); *Prestupnost' za granitsey i v SSSR* (Criminality Abroad and in the USSR) (1931); *Istoriya tsarskoy tyur'my* (History of Tsarist Jails) (5 vol, 1941-56); *Awards*: Stalin Prize (1947); Order of the Red Banner of Labor (1944); *Died*: 16 Jan 1953.

GERSEVANOV, Nikolay Mikhaylovich (1879-1950) Eng; ground-soil specialist; corresp member, USSR Acad of Sci from 1939; Hon Sci and Tech Worker of RSFSR from 1936; *Born*: 28 Feb 1879; *Educ*: 1901 grad Petersburg Inst of Communications Eng; *Career*: from 1923 prof, Moscow Inst of Communications Eng; from 1931 head, Chair of Hydrotech Structures, Mil Transport Acad and sci dir, All-Union Inst of Foundations and Substructures; 1914 devised method of calculating wide-span pier structures which was extensively used for building wharves in Sov ports; 1917 developed still-valid formula for determining the failure rate of piles; specialized in the mech of ground soil as a material for foundations in civil eng; was one of first eng to apply new mathematical methods to eng calculations; 1906-08 pioneered nomography in Russia; 1923 experimented with the application of algebraic logic to eng calculations; *Publ: Osnovaniya nomograficheskogo ischisleniya s prilozheniyem ikh k inzhernernomu delu* (The Principles of Nomographic Calculus and Their Engineering Applications) (2 vol, 1906-08); *Ob opredelenii soprotivleniya svay po ikh otkazu* (Determining the Failure Rate of Piles) (1917); *Raschyoty fundamentov gidrotekhnicheskikh sooruzheniy na osnovanii uchyota deformatsiy postroyennykh* sooruzheniy (Calculations for the Foundations of Hydrotechnical Structures Based on Calculation of the Deformation of Finished Structures) (1923); *Osnovy dinamiki gruntovoy massy* (The Principles of Ground Soil Mass Dynamics) (3rd ed, 1937); *Opyt razvitiya dinamiki gruntovoy massy* (The Experimental Development of Ground Soil Mass Dynamics) (1940);*Teoriya dvizheniya smesi vozdukha i vody v primenenii k erliftam* (The Theory of the Motion of an Air-Water Mixture as Applied to Air Lifts) (1941); coauthor, *Teoreticheskiye osnovy mekhaniki gruntov i ikh prakticheskiye primeneniya* (The Theoretical Principles of Ground-Soil Mechanics and Their Practical Applications) (1948); *Sobraniye sochineniy* (Collected Works) (2 vol, 1948); *Awards:* two Orders of the Red Banner of Labor; Stalin Prize (1948); *Died:* 20 Jan 1950.

GERSHENZON, Mikhail Osipovich (1869-1925) Lit and social historian; Jew; *Born*: 13 July 1869 in Kishinyov; *Educ*: 1887-89 studied at Berlin Polytechnicum; 1894 grad Philology and History Fac, Moscow Univ; *Career*: helped edit journals *Nauchnoye slovo, Kriticheskoye obozreniye, Russkaya mysl'* and *Vestnik Yevropy*; wrote for the Constitutional-Democratic Party's organ *Vekhi*; after 1917 worked with Pop Comrt of Educ and Centr Records Office; taught at Bryusov Higher Inst of Lit and Arts; full member, Russian Assoc of Soc Sci Research Institutes; chm, Lit Section, State Acad of Arts; helped found and subsequently head All-Russian Writers' Union; followed ideas of philosophic idealism; his works, based on very thorough research, deal with Russian writers, social theorists, Moscow intellectual life of early 19th Century and religious and philosophical problems; these latter works are imbued with idealism and religiosity contrary to positivism and materialism; did extensive translations from German, French and Italian; published valuable archive materials; *Publ: Sotsial'no-politicheskiye vzglyady Gertsena* (Herzen's Social and Political Views) (1906); *P. Ya. Chaadayev. Zhizn' i myshleniye* (P. Ya. Chaadayev' Life and Thought) (1908); *Istoriya molodoy Rossii* (History of Young Russia) (1908); *Istoricheskiye zapiski o russkom obshchestve* (Historical Notes on Russian Society) (1910); *Zhizn' V. S. Pecherina* (V. S. Pecherin's Life) (1910); *Obrazy proshlogo* (Images of the Past) (1912); *Griboyedovskaya Moskva* (Griboyedov's Moscow) (1914); *Dekabrist Krivtsov i yego brat'ya* (Decembrist Krivtsov and His Brethren) (1914); *Russkiye propilei. Materialy* (Russian Propyleas. Documents) (6 vol, 1915-19); *Videniye poeta* (The Poet's Vision) (1918); *Troystvennyy obraz sovershenstva* (The Triple Image of Perfection) (1918); *Mudrost' Pushkina* (Pushkin's Wisdom) (1919); *Mechta i mysl' I. S. Turgeneva* (I. S. Turgenev's Dream and Thought) (1919); coauthor, *Perepiska iz dvukh uglov* (Correspondence from Two Angles) (1921); *Klyuch very* (Key to Faith) (1922); *Gol'fstrem* (Gulf Stream) (1922); *Sud'by yevreyskogo naroda* (The Fortunes of the Jewish People) (1922); *Novyye propilei* (New Propyleas) (1923); *Stat'i o Pushkine* (Articles on Pushkin) (1926); *Pis'ma k bratu* (Letters to My Brother) (1927); *Died*: 19 Feb 1925 in Moscow.

GERSHUN, Andrey Aleksandrovich (1903-1952) Lighting specialist; physicist; prof; *Born*: 22 Oct 1903, son of a Russian physicist; *Educ*: grad Petrograd Univ; *Career*: from 1920 at State Optical Inst; applied to photometric calculations field force theory and vector analysis methods which made it possible to produce a number of generalized formulas and perform calculations for non-homogeneous and diffuse media; did much work on practical lighting technique, particularly development of theoretical methods and substantiation of light masking; also worked on underwater lighting, economics of natural lighting and development of specialpurpose illuminants; *Publ: Svetovoye pole* (The Light Field) (1936); *Osnovnyye predstavleniya teorii svetovogo polya* (Fundamentals of Light Field Theory) (1936); *Printsypy i priyomy svetovoy maskirovki* (Principles and Methods of Light Masking) (1943); *Raschyot yackosti proshektornogo snopa* (Calculating the Brightness of a Projector Beam) (1944); *K teorii svetovogo polya v rasseivayushchey srede* (Theory of the Light Field in a Diffuse Medium) (1945); *Teletsentricheskiy metod izmereniya sily sveta* (The Telecentric Method of Measuring Luminous Intensity) (1946); *Awards*: Stalin Prize (1942); *Died*: 6 Dec 1952.

GERSON, V.L. (1891-1941) Govt official; CP member from 1917; *Born*: 1891; *Career*: Aug 1918-1937 worked for All-Russian Cheka and NKVD organs; from 1937 worked for Centr Council, *Dynamo* Sports Soc; arrested by State Security organs; *Died*: 1941 in imprisonment.

GERTSEN, Pyotr Aleksandrovich (1871-1947) Surgeon; pioneer of Sov oncology; Dr of Med from 1897; prof from 1917; Hon Sci Worker of RSFSR from 1934; corresp member, USSR Acad of Sci from 1939; *Born*: 8 May 1871 in Florence, son of physiologist Prof A.A.Herzen; *Educ*: 1896 grad Med Fac, Lausanne Univ; 1898 grad Med Fac, Moscow Univ summa cum laude; *Career*: studied surgery under Roux; 1897 defended doctor's thesis in Lausanne on "Causes of Death After Bilateral Vagotomy" and, in accordance with the wishes of his grandfather A.I. Herzen, moved to Moscow; for 22 years worked at Staro-Yekaterinskaya Hospital; served in Russo-Japanese War; 1909 defended doctor's thesis on nephrolysine in Moscow; from 1910 assoc prof, Fac Surgery Clinic, Moscow Univ; from 1917 prof, Chair of Operative Surgery and Topographical Anatomy, 2nd Moscow State Univ; during WW 1 and Civil War, consultant and head surgeon, various hospitals; from 1921 head, Chair of Gen Surgery, 1st Moscow State Univ; from 1934 until death head, Chair of Hospital Surgery, 1st Moscow Med. Inst; 1921-47 also dir, Inst for the Treatment of Tumors (now P.A. Gertsen Centr Oncological Inst); chm, Moscow Surgical Soc; from 1923 chm, Surgical Expertise Commission, State Learned Council; member, Int Surgical Soc; trained large school of oncologists; wrote over 90 works; *Publ: O nefrolizinakh* (Nephrolysines) (1910); *Khirurgicheskoye lecheniye travmaticheskikh anevrizm (po nablyudeniyam Russko-Yaponskoy voyny i posleduyushchikh let)* (The Surgical Treatment of Traumatic Aneurisms [on the Basis of Observations Made During the Russo-Japanese War and Subsequent Years]) (1911); *O nekotorykh novykh sposobakh obezzarazhivaniya ruk i operatsionnogo polya* (Some New Methods of Disinfecting the Hands and the Operating Area) (1911); *O krovotecheniyakh* (Bleeding) (1940); *O granitsakh operativnogo lecheniya rakovykh opukholey v svyazi s ikh patologicheskimi svoystvami* (The Limits of the Operative Treatment of Carcinomas in Relation to Their Pathological Properties) (1934); *Vvedeniye v kliniku khirurgicheskikh form raka* (An Introduction to the Clinical Aspects of Surgical Forms of Cancer) (1930); *O rake yazyka* (Cancer of the Tongue) (1928); *Izbrannyye trudy* (Selected Works) (1956); *Died*: 2 Jan 1947 in Moscow.

GESSEN, Iosif Vladimirovich (1866-1943) Publicist; helped found and lead Constitutional-Democratic Party; member of its CC; *Born*: 1866; *Career*: together with P. N. Milyukov edited Party newspapers *Narodnaya Svoboda* (Dec 1905) and *Rech'* (until 1918); Petersburg dep to 2nd State Duma; after 1917 Oct Revol opposed Sov regime; during Civil War actively supported Gen Yudenich; then emigrated; from 1921 edited and published newspaper *Rul'* in Berlin; *Died*: 1943.

GESSEN, S. M. (1898-1938) Party official; CP member from 1916; *Born*: 1898; *Career*: deleg, Petrograd City RSDRP(B) Conference and 7th (April) All-Russian RSDRP(B) Conference; after 1917 Oct Revol exec Party work in Petrograd, Samara, Yekaterinburg and Minsk; 1926 joined "New Opposition"; 1927 at 15th CPSU(B) Congress expelled from the Party as active member of Trotskyist opposition; 1928 re-admitted to the Party; 1934 re-expelled for anti-Party and anti-Sov activities; later imprisoned; *Died*: 1938 in imprisonment.

GESSEN, Yuliy Isidorovich (1871-1939) Historian and writer; *Born*: 8 Mar 1871; *Career*: until 1917 worked mainly on Jewish history and the contemporary situation of the Jews in Russia; member and secr, Comt for the Equity of Jews; helped found *Yevreyskaya entsiklopediya* (Jewish Encyclopaedia); after 1917 concerned himself chiefly with history of the working class in Russia; from 1921 in Leningrad edited periodicals *Arkhiv istorii truda v Rossii* and *Russkoye proshloye*; 1925 ed, *Khrestomatiya po istorii rabochego klassa v Rossii* (Reader on the History of the Working Class in Russia); 1930-35 ed, *Vestnik AN SSSR*; also exec secr and co-ed, 1st vol, collection *Metallurgicheskiye zavody na territorii SSSR s 17-go v. po 1917 g.* (Metallurgical Plants on Present Soviet Territory from the 17th Century to 1917) (1937); during the last years of life ed, Records Dept, Leningrad Oblast NKVD Bd; *Publ: Istoriya yevreyskogo naroda v Rossii* (History of the Jewish People in Russia) (2 vol, 1906); *Istoriya gornorabochikh SSSR do 60-ykh godov* (History of Russian Miners until the 1860's) (2 vol,

1926-29); *Died*: 22 Aug 1939.

GETMAN, David Grigor'yevich (1884-1946) Stage dir and playwright; *Born*: 1884; *Career*: 1903-13 asst stage dir, then stage dir at theaters in Nizhniy Novgorod, Khar'kov, Kiev, Kazan', etc; helped sponsor movement for establishment of theaters of miniatures in Russia and produced reviews at these theaters; during WW 1 directed Mamon and Petrine Theaters of Miniatures, Moscow; 1917-19 directed Free Theater, Voronezh Province Educ Dept; 1926-29 leading stage dir, Moscow Satire Theater; stage dir, Leningrad Satire Theater; also staged music hall shows; 1924-29 stage dir, Moscow Operetta Theater; 1941 founded *Yastrebok* frontline theater; *Works*: helped write plays: *Moskva s tochki zreniya* (Moscow from One Point of View) (1924); *Sem' let bez vzaimnosti* (Seven Years Without Mutuality) (1925); *Oy, ne khody, Grytsyu, na zagovor imperatritsy* (Oh, Grytsya, Don't Be Taken in by the Empress' Plot!) (1925); *Died*: 1946.

GETSOV, S.A. (1883-1937) Govt official; *Born*: 1883; *Career*: 1918 Presidium member, South-Russian Sovnarkhoz; 1918-23 dep chm, Main Coal Comt; 1919 head, Main Coal Bd in Khar'kov; from 1920 head, Moscow Coal Bd; then various admin posts in coal ind; arrested by State Security organs; *Died*: 1937 in imprisonment.

GET'YE, F.A. (1863-1938) Internist; personal physician to Lenin from 1919; *Born*: 1863; *Career*: dir, various Moscow hospitals; chief physician, Basmanov Hospital; founder and chief physician, Botkin (formerly Soldatenkov) Hospital; member, Kremlin Therapeutic and Sanitary Bd; arrested by State Security organs; *Died*: 1938 in imprisonment.

GEVELING, Nikolay Vladimirovich (1897-1946) Metallurgist; inventor; Hon Sci and Tech Worker of RSFSR from 1940; maj-gen of Air Force Eng Corps; *Born*: 19 June 1897; *Educ*: 1924 grad Moscow Higher Tech College; *Career*: from 1933 prof, Zhukovskiy Air Force Acad; specialized in airframe metallurgy; collated data in this field and submitted physico-chemical explanations for a number of metallurgical problems, particularly in the heat treatment of special steels; studied rapid steel-tempering processes, the effect of the rate of cooling on the structure of special steels, internal cohesion in liquid alloys, etc; 1931 introduced a method for surface tempering of alloys by means of contact electr heating and until 1936 elaborated and theoretically explored this method; *Publ: K voprosu issledovaniya bystroprotekayushchikh teplovykh izmeneniy v metallicheskikh splavakh termicheskim metodom* (Research into Rapid Thermal Changes in Metallic Alloys by Thermic Methods) (1920); *O prirode evtektiki* (The Nature of Eutectics) (1934); *Issledovaniye svarnoy tochki* (Research on the Welding Point) (1935); *Poverkhnostnaya elektrotermoobrabotka* (Surface Electro-Thermic Treatment) (1936); *Metallovedeniye* (The Study of Metals) (Part 1, 2nd ed, 1938); *Awards*: Order of Lenin; four other orders; medals; *Died*: 20 May 1946.

GEY, Konstantin Veniaminovich (1896-1940) Party and govt official; CP member from 1916; *Born*: 1896, son of an office worker; *Educ*: studied at Khar'kov Univ; *Career*: took part in student polit circles; after 1917 Revol worked in Pskov: secr, Dept of Labor; chm, Pskov Province Exec Comt; secr, Pskov Province Party Comt; 1920-21 Presidium chm, Saratov Railroad Workers Union Comt; during the trade-union controversy sympathized with Trotskyist platform; from 1922 exec Party work: secr, Pskov Province Party Comt; head, Org Dept, Northwestern Bureau, CC; Secr, Sverdlovsk Province Party Comt; secr, Perm' Okrug Party Comt; head, Org Dept, Ural Oblast Party Comt; head, Org and Distribution Dept, CC; from 1926 second secr, Ural Oblast Party Comt; secr, CC, CP Bel; secr, Moscow CPSU(B) Comt; from 1934 govt work in Uzbekistan and Gorky Oblast; after 14th Congress member, CC, CPSU(B); at 13th, 15th and 16th Congresses cand member, CC, CPSU(B); arrested by State Security organs; *Died*: 1940 in imprisonment.

GEYMANOVICH, Aleksandr Iosifovich (1882-1958) Neurologist; Hon Prof of Ukr SSR from 1927; *Born*: 4 Aug 1882; *Educ*: 1908 grad Med Fac, Moscow Univ; *Career*: 1904 expelled from Khar'kov Univ for revol activities and exiled; 1905 took active part in Revol; early 1906 arrested; after grad worked at clinic for nervous diseases; during WW 1 founded Neurological Center in Khar'kov; from 1920 founder-dir, Ukr Psychoneurological Inst, Khar'kov; from 1932 vice-pres, Ukr Psychoneurological Acad; 1937-53 dir, Clinic for Nervous Diseases and head, Neurohistological Laboratory, Ukr Psychoneurological Inst; from 1953 consultant, Centr Psychoneurological Hospital, Neurosurgical Hospital, USSR Min of Communications, and Clinic, Khar'kov Balneological Hospital; during WW 2 consultant, various field hospitals; 1919 together with Raymist (Odessa) was first to describe epidemic encephalitis in Ukr; 1920 devised new clinicial and morphological concept of typhus; 1936 devised classification of tumors of the nervous system; obtained new data on blast injuries; trained over 200 sci, including 14 prof and dr of med; wrote over 300 works, half of them on neurosurgery, the remainder on infections of the nervous system, the theory of tonus and motility, etc; *Publ*: coauthor, *Infektsiya i nervnaya sistema* (Infection and the Nervous System) (1927); ed and coauthor, *Opukholi tsentral'noy nervnoy sistemy* (Tumors of the Central Nervous System) (1936); coauthor, *Problemy motoriki v nevrologii i psikhiatrii* (Problems of Motility in Neurology and Psychiatry) (1937); coauthor, *Sanitarnaya sluzhba v dni Otechestvennoy voyny* (The Medical Corps During the Fatherland War) (1943); coauthor, *Travmaticheskiye porazheniya tsentral'noy i perifericheskoy nervnoy sistemy* (Traumatic Lesions of the Central and Peripheral Nervous System) (1946); coauthor, *Voprosy profilakticheskogo i predupreditel'nogo lecheniya nervnykh i psikhicheskikh zabolevaniy* (The Prophylactic and Preventive Treatment of Nervous and Mental Diseases) (1956-57); *Died*: 18 Apr 1958.

GEYMANOVICH, Zakhar Iosifovich (1884-1948) Neurosurgeon; *Born*: 1884 in Khar'kov; *Educ*: 1909 grad Med Fac, Khar'kov Univ; *Career*: from 1909 specialized in surgery particularly neurosurgery; intern and asst prof, Khar'kov surgical hospitals; 1922 founded Laboratory of Experimental Neurosurgery at Ukr Psychoneurological Research Inst, Khar'kov; from 1931 for many years directed Neurosurgical Clinic, founded on the basis of this laboratory; studied topographical anatomy of centr nervous system, neurooncology, surgical treatment of neuralgia, methods of treating hyperkinesis, plastic surgery, etc; *Awards*: Order of the Red Star; medals; *Died*: 3 Nov 1948.

GEYROT, Aleksandr Aleksandrovich (1882-1947) Actor; Hon Artiste of RSFSR from 1933; *Born*: 20 Mar 1882; *Career*: 1911-12 at Ancient Theater, Petersburg; 1913-23 and 1935-47 with Moscow Arts Theater; 1924-35 actor, 2nd Moscow Arts Theater; displayed great originality, irony and wit in his acting; *Roles*: Prince Volkovskiy in *Unizhyonnyye i oskorblyonnyye* (The Oppressed and the Insulted), after Dostoyevsky; Mozart in Pushkin's *Motsart i Sal'yeri* (Mozart and Salieri); Fabrizzio in Goldoni's "The Innkeeper's Wife"; Prince Dulebov in *Talanty i poklonniki* (Talents and Admirers); Repetilov in Griboyedov's *Gore ot uma* (Woe from Wit); Cléant in Molière's "Tartuffe"; Baron in Gorky's *Na dne* (The Lower Depths), etc; *Died*: 8 Feb 1947.

GIATSINTOV (real name: BULOCHNIKOV), Aleksandr Mikhaylovich (1896-1957) Actor and stage dir; Hon Art Worker of RSFSR from 1956; *Born*: 28 July 1896; *Career*: 1921 stage debut at Red Army Theater; after demobilization from Red Army became professional actor; actor, stage dir and artistic dir at theaters in Kamyshin, Cheboksary, Murom, Tyumen', Michurinsk, Torzhok, etc; from 1942 chief stage dir, dir and actor of theater he founded in Kimry, Kalinin Oblast; *Productions*: Gorky's *Yegor Bulychyov i drugiye* (Yegor Bulychyov and Co) (1945); Gorky's *Platon Krechet* (1946); Gorky's *Na dne* (The Lower Depths) (1947); Gogol's *Revizor* (The Government Inspector) (1952); Ostrovskiy's *Groza* (The Storm) (1954); Rozov's *V dobryy chas* (In the Nick of Time) (1955), etc; *Roles*: Polezhayev in Rakhmanov's *Bespokoynaya starost'* (Restless Old Age); Stepanov in Alyoshin's *Direktor* (The Director); Jan Grubek in Simonov's *Pod kashtanami Pragi* (Under the Chestnut Tress of Prague); Losev in Shteyn's *Zakon chesti* (The Law of Honor); Major Peterson in Galan's *Pod zolotym orlom* (Under the Golden Eagle); Gorlokhvatskiy in Krapiva's *Kto smeyotsya poslednim* (Who Laughs Last), etc; *Died*: 15 June 1957.

GIBER, Grigoriy Vladimirovich (1893-1951) Cameraman; *Born*: 1893; *Career*: 1913 began film work; after 1917 Oct Revol filmed documentary films on various fronts of the Civil War; took part in propaganda-train tours; from 1920's in feature filmwork; during WW 2 filmed mil newsreels; of historical value are his films of Lenin at 3rd Comintern Congress, 10th Party Congress, etc; his films were used in the motion-picture *Vladimir Il'ich Lenin* (1948); *Works*: feature films: *Bog mesti* (God of Vengeance) (1918); *Timbute - groza Parizha* (Timbute, Terror of Paris) (1919); *Besprizornyye* (The Waifs) (1923); *Nemyye svideteli* (Dumb Witnesses) (1925); *V tylu u belykh* (In the Rear of the Whites) (1925); *Kashtanka* (1926); *Iuda* (1930); *Vlastelin mira* (Master of the World) (1932), etc; documentary films: *Sibiryaki* *frontu* (Siberians to the Front) (1942); *Parad pobedy* (Victory Parade) (1945); *Pervoye maya* (First of May) (1947); *Sovetskaya Latviya* (Soviet Latvia) (1947); *Den' Vozdushnogo flota SSSR* (USSR Air Force Day) (1949); *Zhivotnovody Podmoskov'ya* (Cattlebreeders of the Moscow Region) (1949); *Moskva golosuyet* (Elections in Moscow) (1950), etc; *Publ: Kak my rabotali v Krymu* (Our Work in the Crimea) (1926); *Stranitsa iz vospominaniy operatora* (A Page from the Memoirs of a Cameraman) (1927); *Awards*: Stalin Prize (1949); *Died*: 20 Mar 1951.

GIKALO, Nikolay Fyodorovich (1897-1939) Party and govt official; first secr, CC, CP(B) Bel from 1932; CP member from 1917; *Born*: 8 Mar 1897 in Odessa; *Educ*: 1915 grad Tiflis mil med oderlies school; *Career*: 1918 chm, Groznyy Sov; commander, Red Army units in Groznyy; leader, partisan detachment; during the campaign against Denikin's troops in Northern Caucasus group commander, insurgent forces in Tersk Oblast; from 1919 member, Caucasian Kray RCP(B) Comt; commander and mil comr, Terek Oblast mil forces and dep chm, Terek Oblast Exec Comt; 1922-24 secr, Gorsk Oblast RCP(B) Comt; 1924-26 head, Dept of Agitation and Propaganda and member, Northeastern Bureau, CC, RCP(B); 1926-32 secr, North-Caucasian Kray CPSU(B) Comt; first secr, CC, CP(B) Uzbek and CC, CP(B) Azer; then worked for CC, CPSU(B); 1932-37 first secr, CC, CP(B) Bel; from 1934 cand member, CC, CPSU(B); 1937 arrested by NKVD; *Died*: 1939 in imprisonment; posthumously rehabilitated.

GIKOV, Rafail Borisovich (1905-1946) Film dir; CP member from 1942; *Born*: 2 Sept 1905; *Educ*: 1929 grad Cameraman Fac, State Inst of Cinematography; 1930 grad Fine Arts Dept, Moscow Univ; *Career*: 1929-32 film reporter, All-Union Newsreel Studio; from 1933 directed documentary films; 1932-41 assoc prof, Chair of Camera Technique, All-Union State Inst of Cinematography; *Works*: films: *Moskva - stolitsa mira*, (Moscow, Capital of the World) (1933); *Vozdushnyy parad* (The Air Parade) (1934); *A. V. Lunacharskiy* (1934); *Moskva - Volga* (Moscow-Volga) (1937); *Odinnadtsat' stolits* (Eleven Capitals) (1939); *Na zashchitu rodnoy Moskvy* (The Defense of Our Native Moscow) (1941); *Orlovskaya bitva* (The Battle of Oryol) (1943); *Bitva za Pribaltiku* (The Battle of the Baltic) (1944); *Podpisaniye deklaratsii o porazhenii Germanii* (The Signing of the Declaration on the Defeat of Germany) (1945), etc; *Died*: 17 July 1946.

GILYAROV, Aleksey Nikitich (1856-1938) Philosopher; member, Ukr Acad of Sci from 1922; *Born*: 1856; *Career*: taught philosophy, at first as assoc prof, Moscow Univ and from 1888 as prof, Kiev Univ; wrote works on philosophy from idealistic standpoint and works on organic chemistry and Western lit; *Publ: Platonizm, kak osnovaniye sovremeonnogo mirovozzreniya* (Platonism as the Basis of a Modern Weltanschauung) (1887); *Znacheniye filosofii* (The Significance of Philosophy) (1888); *Grecheskiye sofisty* (The Greek Sophists) (1888); *Istochniki o sofistakh. Platon kak istoricheskiy svidetel'* (Sources on the Sophists. Plato as an Eyewitness of History) (1891); *Obzor trudov po grecheskoy filosofii* (A Review of Works on Greek Philosophy) (1896); *Obzor filosofskoy literatury za posledniye gody* (A Review of Philosophic Literature in Recent Years) (1898); *Chto takoye filosofiya i chto ona mozhet i chego ne mozhet dat'* (What Philosophy Is and What It Can and Cannot Furnish) (1899); *Noveyshiye popytki filosofskogo sinteza na nauchnoy pochve* (Latest Attempts at a Scientific Philosophic Synthesis) (1901); *Chto nuzhno chitat', chtoby zanimat'sya filosofiyey* (What to Read in Studying Philosophy) (1901); *Filosofiya v yeyo sushchestve, istorii i znachenii* (Philosophy--Its Essence, History and Significance) (2 vol, 1916-19); *Skhema istorii filosofii v osveshchenii istoricheskogo materializma* (A Schematic History of Philosophy as Viewed by Historical Materialism) (1926); *Predsmertnyye mysli 19-go v. vo Frantsii* (Final Reflections Before Death in 19-th-Century France) (1926), etc; *Died:* 1938.

GILYAROVSKIY, Vasiliy Alekseyevich (1875-1959) Psychiatrist; Dr of Med from 1909; prof from 1917; member, USSR Acad of Med Sci from 1944; Hon Sci Worker of RSFSR from 1936; CP member from 1940; *Born*: 26 Dec 1875 in Buzulik, now Kúybyshev Oblast, son of an office worker; *Educ*: 1899 grad Med Fac, Moscow Univ; *Career*: after grad intern, Prof V. K. Rot's Clinic for Nervous Diseases, Moscow Univ; 1904-05 psychiatrist, neuropathologist and dissector, Khar'kov Province Mental Hospital; senior intern and dissector, Centr Mental Patients' Admission Building, Moscow; 1909 defended doctor's thesis and began to read lectures on the pathological anatomy of psychoses at Moscow Postgrad Med Training Courses; from 1910 asst prof, Preobrazhenskiy Psychiatric Hospital, Moscow; from 1916 acting head, Chair of Psychiatry, Moscow Women's Higher Courses; 1917-32 head, Chair of Psychiatry, 2nd Moscow State Univ; 1932-52 head, Chair of Psychiatry, 2nd Moscow Med Inst (now Pirogov Med Inst); 1945-52 founder-dir, 1952-59 sci dir, Inst of Psychiatry, USSR Acad of Med Sci, which later came under the control of the USSR Min of Health; trained numerous psychiatrists and pioneered Sov child psychiatry; 1950-52 criticized for "underestimating" the importance of Pavlov's theory; chm, All-Union Sci Soc of Neuropathologists and Psychiatrists; co-ed, psychiatry section, *Bol'shaya Meditsinskaya Entsiklopediya* (Large Medical Encyclopedia) (2nd ed); member, ed collegium, *Zhurnal nevropatologii i psikhiatrii imeni S. S. Korsakova; Publ*: doctor's thesis *K voprosu o patologicheskoy anatomii i patogeneze parentsefalii* (The Pathological Anatomy and Pathogenesis of Parencephalia) (1909); *Vvedeniye v anatomicheskoye izucheniye psikhozov* (An Introduction to the Anatomical Study of Psychoses) (1925); *Staryye i novyye problemy psikhiatrii* (Old and New Problems of Psychiatry) (1946); *Ucheniye o gallyutsionatsiyakh* (The Theory of Hallucinations) (1949); coauthor, *Elektroson* (Elecrically-Induced Sleep) (1954); *Psikhiatriya* (Psychiatry) (4 ed, 1918-56); *Awards*: two Orders of Lenin; Order of the Red Banner of Labor; *Died*: 10 Mar 1959 in Moscow.

GILYAROVSKIY, Vladimir Alekseyevich (pseudonym: GILYAY) (1853-1935) Writer; *Born*: 8 Dec 1853 in Vologda Province, son of an office worker; *Educ*: studied at Vologda high-school; *Career*: 1871 left home to undertake populist work on the Volga; until 1881 worked as barge hauler, longshoreman, fireman, worker, circus and stage actor, etc; volunteer in 1877-78 Russo-Turkish War; 1873 first work published; prior to 1917 engaged in journalism; his works deal with the life of barge haulers, raftsmen, workers and poor townsfolk; 1887 his first book *Trushchobnyye lyudi* (Slum-Dwellers) was burnt by the censorship; translated Shevchenko's works; *Publ: Trushchobnyye lyudi* (Slum-Dwellers) (1887); verse collection *Zabytaya tetrad'* (Forgotten Notebook) (1896); stories: *Moskovskiye nishchiye* (Beggars of Moscow) (1896); *Byli* (True Stories) (1909); *Shutki* (Jokes) (1912); poems: *Peterburg* (Petersburg) (1922); *Zaporozhtsy* (Dnieper Cossacks) (1926); *Sten'ka Razin* (1926); research works: *Na rodine Gogolya* (Gogol's Homeland) (1902); *Ot angliyskogo kluba k Muzeyu revolyutsii* (From the English Club to the Museum of Revolution) (1926); memoirs: *Moskva i moskvichi* (Moscow and the Muscovites) (1926); *Moi skitaniya* (My Wanderings) (1928); *Lyudi teatra* (Theater People) (1941); *Na zhiznennoy doroge* (Journey Through Life) (1959); *Moskva gazetnaya* (Moscow of the Press) (1960), etc; *Died*: 1 Oct 1935 in Moscow.

GINDIN (real name: GINZBURG), Ya. I. (1892-1938) Govt official, CP member from 1917; *Born*: 1892; *Career*: after 1917 Oct Revol admin and Party work; 1918-21 dept head, Pop Comrt of Labor and head, Dept of Labor, at Special Army Supply Agency; member, Small Council of Pop Comr; from 1922 with Supr Sovnarkhoz, Pop Comrt of Supply and Pop Comrt of Workers and Peasants' Inspection; arrested by State Security organs; *Died*: 1938 in imprisonment.

GINETSINSKIY, Aleksandr Grigor'yevich (1895-1962) Physiologist; Dr of Med; prof from 1932; corresp member, USSR Acad of Med Sci; *Born*: 1895; *Career*: 1920-36 asst prof, Acad L. A. Orbeli's Physiological Laboratories; 1932-51 head, Chair of Physiology, Leningrad Pediatric Inst; 1936-50 dep dir, Physiological Inst, USSR Acad of Sci; 1951-55 head, Chair of Physiology, Novosibirsk Med Inst; 1955-62 head, Laboratory for the Evolution of Secretory Processes and dep dir, Sechenov Inst of Evolutionary Physiology, USSR Acad of Sci; co-ed, physiology section, *Bol'shaya Meditsinskaya Entsiklopediya* (Large Medical Encyclopedia) (2nd ed); member, ed council, *Fiziologicheskiy zhurnal SSSR imeni I. M. Sechenova*; did research on the adaptive trophism of the sympathetic nervous system; described the influence of the nervous system on the activity of the skeletal muscles (Orbeli-Ginetsinskiy phenomenon); analysed the ontogenetic characteristics of the oxygen-binding properties of hemoglobin and adaptation to hypoxidosis in antenatal and early postnatal ontogenesis; 1950, after dissolution of Orbeli's physiology school, was forced to move to Novosibirsk; 1955 returned to Leningrad and was rehabilitated along with Orbeli; wrote over 80 works; *Publ: Vliyaniye simpaticheskoy nervnoy sistemy na funktsii poperechno-polosatoy myshtsy* (The Influence of the Sympathetic Nervous System on the Functions of the Striated

Muscle) (1923); *Transport kisloroda v embrional'nom periode* (Oxygen Transmission in the Embryonic Stage) (1936); coauthor, *Prakticheskiy kurs fiziologii* (A Practical Physiology Course) (1938); *Kholinergicheskaya struktura myshechnogo volokna* (The Cholinergic Structure of the Muscle Fiber) (1947); *Osnovy fiziologii cheloveka i zhivotnykh* (The Principles of Human and Animal Physiology) (1947); *Funktsiya pochek v rannem post-natal'nom periode* (The Function of the Kidneys in the Early Postnatal Period) (1952); coauthor, *Kurs normal'noy fiziologii* (A Course in Normal Physiology) (1956), etc; *Died*: 20 Oct 1962 in Leningrad.

GINTSBURG, Il'ya Yakovlevich (1859-1939) Sculptor; member, Acad of Arts from 1911; *Born*: 1859 in Grodno; *Educ*: 1886 grad Petersburg Arts Acad; *Career*: student and personal friend of M. M. Antokol'skiy and V. V. Stasov; rep, late itinerant school; did sculptural portraits and monuments of Russian writers, scientists, musicians and artists; during his last years lit work; *Works*: sculptural portraits of L. N. Tolstoy, Turgenev, D. I. Mendeleyev, Rimsky-Korsakov, V. I. Surikov, I. I. Shishkin, I. N. Kramskoy, I. Ye. Repin, etc; genre-statuettes "Boy About to Bathe" (1886); "Young Musician" (1890); "The First Fairy-Tale" (1892), etc; portrait statuettes "V. V. Stasov" (1889); "V. V. Vereshchagin at Work" (1892), etc; tombstone of V. V. Stasov; monuments to Gogol' in Sorochintsy (1911), G. V. Plekhanov in Leningrad (1921-25), D. I. Mendeleyev in Leningrad (1929), I. K. Ayvazovskiy in Feodosiya (1930), M. M. Kotsyubinskiy in Chernigov (1939), etc; *Publ: Iz moyey zhizni* (From My Life) (1908); *Iz proshlogo* (From the Past) (1924); art criticism; *Died*: 3 Jan 1939.

GINZBURG (KOL'TSOV), B. A. (1863-1920) *Born*: 1863; *Career*: mid-1890's member, Petersburg *Narodnaya volya* (People's Will) org; late 1890's joined Soc-Democratic Party; from 1893 abroad; member, 1895-98 secr, League of Russian Soc-Democrats Abroad; worked for the League's organ *Rabotnik*; 1900 left the League after its schism; contributed to newspapers *Iskra* and *Zarya; Iskra* consultative deleg at 2nd RSDRP Congress; after 2nd Congress active Menshevik; 1905 returned to Russia and conducted Party work; contributed to almost all Menshevik organs; during WW 1 defensist; contributed to defensist newspapers and periodicals; after 1917 Feb Revol Comr of Labor, Petrograd Sov of Workers and Soldiers' Dep; opposed 1917 Oct Revol; RSDRP (Menshevik) cand, Constituent Assembly; 1918-19 worked for Petrograd cooperative system; *Died*: 1920.

GINZBURG, Grigoriy Romanovich (1904-1961) Pianist; prof from 1935; Hon Art Worker of RSFSR from 1946; *Born*: 16 May 1904 in Nizhniy Novgorod; *Educ*: 1924 grad Moscow Conservatory; *Career*: from 1924 concert work in USSR and abroad; from 1928 instructor and from 1935 prof, Moscow Conservatory; continued traditions of Prof A. B. Gol'denveyzer; among his students were G. Aksel'rod, S. Dorenskiy and A. Skavronskiy; *Publ: Zametki o masterstve* (Notes on Technique) (1963); *Awards*: fourth prize at 1st Int Pianists Competition in Warsaw (1927); Stalin Prize (1949); various orders and medals; *Died*: 5 Dec 1961 in Moscow.

GINZBURG, Moisey Yakovlevich (1892-1946) Architect; prof; member, USSR Acad of Architecture; *Born*: 1892; *Educ*: 1914 grad Milan acad; 1917 grad Architecture Dept, Riga Polytechnicum; *Career*: prof, Moscow Higher Tech College and Higher Arts and Tech Workshops; ed, periodical *Sovremeonnaya arkhitektura;* 1925 helped found Modern Architects Soc; in early period influenced by "Düsseldorf School" and 1920-22 sided with the constructivists; a number of his articles were published in for press; *Works*: State Insurance Building in Moscow (1926-27); Kaz Govt Building in Alma-Ata (1928-29); apartment house in Sverdlovsk (1929), etc; *Publ: Ritm v arkhitekture* (Rhythm in Architecture) (1922); *Stil' i epokha* (Style and Epoch) (1924), etc; *Died*: 1946.

GINZBURG, Vera Genrikhovna (1892-1967) Econ; CP member from 1917; *Born*: Aug 1892; *Educ*: 1923-24 studied at Moscow Univ; *Career*: 1917-23 trade-union and Party work with Smolensk Province Exec Comt; member, Smolensk Province Party Comt; cand member, Western Oblast CPSU(B) Comt; member, Smolensk Province Exec Comt and member, Western Oblast Exec Comt; deleg at 8th RCP(B) Congress; from 1924 planning eng and econ at various enterprises; from 1954 pensioner; *Died*: Sept 1967.

GIPPIUS, Zinaida Nikolayevna (real name: MEREZHKOVSKAYA; pseudonym: Anton KRAYNIY) (1869-1945) Poetess, fiction writer, playwright and lit critic; wife of writer D. S. Merezhkovskiy; *Born*: 20 Nov 1869 in Belev; *Career*: 1888 first work published; one of the founders and rep of symbolism; active in mystico-idealistic trend of 1890-1900's; helped found Petersburg Religious-Philosophic Soc; 1902-04 ed staff member, periodical *Novyy put'*; in her early works themes of sensual love and non-resistance to evil alternated with religious humility, fear of death and decay; opposed 1917 Revol; from 1920 abroad; in verse and articles sharply attacked Sov regime; published anti-Sov newspaper in Warsaw; *Publ*: novels: *Chortova kukla* (Devil's Puppet) (1911); *Roman-tsarevich* (Tsarevich Roman) (1913); plays: coauthor, *Makov tsvet* (Poppy Blossom) (1908); *Zelyonoye kol'tso* (The Green Ring) (1916); collected stories: *Novyye lyudi* (New People) (1896); *Zerkala* (Mirrors) (1898); *Rasskazy* (Stories) (1902); *Alyy mech* (Red Sword) (1906); *Chyornoye po belomu* (In Black and White) (1908); *Lunnyye murav'i* (Lunar Ants) (1912); *Nebesnyye slova* (Heavenly Words) (1921); collected verse: *Posledniye stikhi* (Latest Verse) (1914-18); *Stikhi* (Verse) (1922); *Siyaniya* (Radiances) (1938); memoirs *Zhivyye litsa* (Living Faces) (1925); collection of critical articles *Literaturnyy dnevnik* (Literary Diary) (1908), etc; *Died*: 9 Sept 1945 in Paris.

GIRA, Lyudas Konstantinovich (1886-1946) Lith writer and poet; politician; Pop Poet of Lith SSR; member, Lith Acad of Sci from 1945; *Born*: 27 Aug 1886 in Vilnius; *Educ*: studied at pharmacy school and theol seminary; *Career*: 1921-26 journal and newspaper ed and dir, Kaunas State Theater; dep, Pop Sejm of Lith; 1940 member, deleg to 7th session of USSR Supreme Sov which petitioned for inclusion of Lith in USSR; during WW 2 served with Lith detachment of Sov Army; *Publ*: verse collections "Peep-Peep—Pipe" (1909); "The Green Meadow" (1911); "On the Roads of My Homeland" (1912); "Sparks" (1921); tragedy "Vengeance" (1910); two plays; other verse collections "Grünwald's Lithuania" (1942); "Force and Decisiveness" (1942); "On Distant Roads" (1945); in Russian *Slovo bor'by* (Battle-cry) (1943); collected essays "Critical Works" (1928); translated Pushkin, Shevchenko, etc into Lith; *Died*: 1 July 1946 in Vilnius.

GIRGOLAV, Semyon Semyonovich (1881-1957) Surgeon and traumatologist; Dr of Med from 1907; prof from 1919; member, USSR Acad of Med Sci from 1944; Hon Sci Worker of RSFSR from 1935; lt-gen, Army Med Corps; *Born*: 1881 in Tiflis; *Educ*: 1904 grad Petersburg Mil Med Acad; *Career*: worked at Kronstadt Hospital and as ship's surgeon on the cruiser *Rossiya*; 1908 worked at clinic, Chair of Gen Surgery, Petersburg Mil Med Acad; 1909 sent to Germany to study under Prof Hertwig, Prof Friedberg, etc; 1912-19 assoc prof, from 1919 prof and head, Chair of Gen Surgery, Petersburg (Petrograd) Mil Med Acad; from 1919 simultaneously prof, Petrograd State Inst of Med Knowledge; 1932-57 dep sci dir, Leningrad Inst of Traumatology and Orthopedics; 1937-54 head, Chair of Hospital Surgery, Kirov Mil Med Acad, Leningrad; 1941-45 Dep Chief Surgeon of Sov Army; from 1954 consulting prof, Leningrad Mil Med Acad; leading member, Pirogov Surgical Soc, Leningrad; member, then dep chm, Learned Med Council, USSR Min of Health; ed and author, various sections, *Opyt sovetskoy meditsiny v Velikoy Otechestvennoy voyne 1941-45* (Soviet Medicine During the 1941-45 Great Fatherland War); ed and co-ed, various med journals; dep, Leningrad City and Rayon sov; established new four-degree classification of frostbite and devised new fast-treatment method which is widely used in the USSR; wrote over 120 works, including 75 original research papers; *Publ:* doctor's thesis, *Eksperimental'nyye dannyye k voprosu o primenenii izolirovannogo sal'nika v bryushnoy khirurgii* (Experimental Data on the Use of the Isolated Omentum in Abdominal Surgery) (1907); coauthor, *Obshchaya khirurgiya* (General Surgery) (1935); *Otmorozheniye* (Frostbite) (1940); *Kratkiy kurs travmatologii* (A Short Course on Traumatology) (1940); coauthor, *Chastnaya khirurgaya* (Regional Surgery) (1941); coauthor, *Uchebnik chastnoy khirurgii* (A Textbook of Regional Surgery) (2 vol, 1944-47); *Ognestrel'naya rana* (The Gunshot Wound) (1956), etc; *Awards*: two Orders of Lenin; Stalin Prize (1943); three Orders of the Red Banner; Order of the Red Banner of Labor; Red Star; Moscow Defense Medal; Red Army 20th Anniversary Medal; *Died*: 1957 in Leningrad.

GITTIS, Vladimir Mikhaylovich (1881-1938) Mil commander; col, Russian army; corps commander from 1935; CP member from 1925; *Born*: 24 Juni 1881 in Petersburg, son of middle-class parents; *Educ*: 1902 grad Infantry Cadet School; *Pos*: until 1917 regt commander, Russian Army; from 1918 in Red Army; 1918-19 commander, 6th, then 8th Army; 1919 commander, Southern, 1919-20 Western, 1920-21 Caucasian Front; 1921-30 commander, Leningrad Mil Distr; dep commander, Red Army Supply Dept; 1930-37 head, Dept of External Orders, Pop Comrt of Defense and plen, Pop Comrt of Defense at Pop Comrt of For Trade; *Career*: fall 1919 commanded counter-offensive of 7th and 15th Armies near Petrograd, which led to the defeat of Gen Yudenich's troops; 1937 arrested by NKVD; *Died*: 22 Aug 1938 in imprisonment; posthumously rehabilitated.

GIZZAT, Tazi (real name: GIZZATOV, Tadzhi Kalimovich) (1895-1955) Tat playwright and actor; Hon Art Worker of RSFSR from 1940; CP member from 1942; *Born*: 15 Sept 1895 in vil Varzi-Umga, now Krasnoborodsk Rayon, Tat ASSR, son of a peasant; *Career*: 1920-48 actor, various Tat theaters; 1922 began lit work; *Publ*: plays "Silver Coin" (1923); "The Taymasovs" (1941); "Sacred Mission" (1944); "True Love" (1947); "Victim of Egoism" (1950-54); dramas "The Employer" (1928); "Bishbulyak" (1932); "Sparks" (1935); trilogy "Streams" (1937); "The Flame" (1940); comedies: "Glorious Epoch" (1936); "Bold Girls" (1939), etc; *Died*: 7 Mar 1955 in Kazan'.

GLADKIY, Dmitriy Spiridonovich (1911-1959) Party and trade-union official; CP member from 1940; *Born*: 1911 in vil Martonosha, Novo-Mirgorod Rayon, Kirovograd Oblast, son of a peasant; *Educ*: from 1935 studied at Khar'kov Workers Fac and Tiraspol Communist Higher Educ Establishment; 1938-39 at mil school; grad Higher Party School, CC, CPSU; *Career*: 1933-35 in Red Army; after graduating Communist Higher Educ Establishment worked as dept head, Mold Oblast Komsomol Comt; from 1939 commands in Sov army; from 1946 exec Party work; instructor, Kirov Rayon Party Comt; after graduating Higher Party School first secr, Kalarash Rayon Party Comt; dept head, CC, CP Mold; from 1951 secr, from Oct 1952 first secr, and from 1954 second secr, CC, CP Mold; from Mar 1959 chm, Mold Republ Trade-Union Council; elected dep, USSR Supr Sov of 4th convocation; dep, Mold Supr Sov; elected member, CC, CP Mold; *Awards*: Order of Lenin; Order of the Fatherland War, 2nd Class; medals; *Died*: 27 Oct 1959 in Kishinev.

GLADKOBORODOVA, Anna Ivanovna (1893-1943) Narrator; *Born*: 20 Nov 1893 in vil Konetsgor'ye, Pinezh Rayon, Arkhangel'sk Oblast; *Career*: her father and grandfather were narrators and ballad singers; from 14 years of age itinerant tailor; knew many old folksongs, proverbs, wedding and funeral lamentations, spiritual verse, fairy-tales; from 1936 composed tales on Sov themes; *Works*: narrations: *Priyezd papanintsev* (Return of Papanin's Crew); *Velichal'nyye pesni poyot nash narod* (Songs of Honor Sing Our People); *Pro vybory prezhniye i sovetskiye* (Former and Soviet Elections); *Slovo Stalina nerushimoye* (Stalin's Inviolable Word); *Beyte voroga, moi sokoly* (Kill the Enemies, My Eagles); *Istrepal Gitler smaznye sapogi* (Worn Out Are Hitler's Blackened Boots); story *Kak tyoshcha k zyatyu v gosti khodila* (Mother-in-law Visiting Her Son-in-law); *Publ: Skazy i pesni* (Tales and Songs) (1947); *Died*: 20 May 1943.

GLADKOV, Fyodor Vasil'yevich (1883-1958) Novelist and short-story writer; CP member from 1920; *Born*: 21 June 1883 in vil Chernavka, Saratov Province, son of an old-believer peasant; *Educ:* 1901 grad Yekaterinodar Municipal College as primary school teacher; 1906 grad Tiflis Teachers' Training Inst; *Career*: worked as trainee store salesman, trainee pharmacist and typesetter; from 1902 taught in Transbaykal; 1905 went to Tiflis to obtain teacher's diploma and joined local Soc-Democratic org; 1906 went to Yeysk on Party work and became full member of RSDRP; was arrested and exiled to Verkholensk Uyezd for three years, after which he settled in Novorossiysk; 1914-17 taught at a preparatory school in vil Pavloskaya, Kuban'; from 1918 did undercover work for Bolsheviks and volunteered for service in Red Army; from 1920 ed, Novorossiysk newspaper *Krasnoye Chernomor'ye*; 1921 transferred to Moscow; 1923 joined *Kuznitsa* (Smithy) lit group; from 1932 member, ed bd, jounal *Novyy mir*; during WW 2 Ural correspondent for *Pravda* and *Izvestia* based in Sverdlovsk; 1945-48 dir, Gorky Lit Inst; 1900 first work published; from 1902 corresponded with Gorky; wrote lit portraits of numerous writers and public figures; wrote articles on lit and language; *Publ*: short story *K svetu* (Toward the Light) (1900); novella *Izgoi* (The Outsiders) (1922); short story *Yedinorodnyy syn* (The Only Son); short story *Ognennyy kon'* (Fiery Steed) (1923); plays *Burelom* (Windfall Wood) (1921) and *Vataga* (The Gang) (1923); novel *Tsement* (Cement) (1925); short story *Krov'yu serdtsa* (With the Heart's Blood) (1928); collected short stories *Malen'kaya trilogiya* (Little Trilogy) (1932); *Novaya zemlya* (New Land) (1930); *P'yanoye solntse* (The Drunken Sun) (1932); novel *Energiya* (Energy) (revised ed 1939 and 1947); novellae *Beryozovaya roshcha* (The Birch Grove) (1941); *Klyatva* (The Oath) (1944); autobiographical trilogy *Povest'o detstve* (A Tale of Childhood) (1949), *Vol'nitsa* (Freemen) (1950) and *Likhaya godina* (Hard Times) (1954); 4-part autobiographical novella *Myatezhnaya yunost'* (Rebellious Youth) (unfinished); *Sobranniye sochineniy* (Collected Works) (3 vol, 1926; 3 vol 1929-30; 5 vol 1950-51; 8 vol, 1958-59); *Myatezhnaya yunost', Ocherki, Stat'i, Vospominaniya* (Rebellious Youth, Essays. Articles. Memoirs) (1961); collected articles *O literature* (On Literature) (1955); *Awards*: two Stalin Prizes (1950, 1951); *Died*: 20 Dec 1958 in Moscow.

GLAGOLEV, Nil Aleksandrovich (1888-1945) Mathematician; specialist in geometry; *Born*: 3 Dec 1888; *Career*: 1916-31 lecturer, from 1931 prof, Moscow Univ; directed first research seminar on nomography; also directed All-Union Nomographic Bureau; wrote first theoretical course on nomography in Russian; studied wurf calculus; wrote studies of geometrical axioms; *Publ: Elementarnaya geometriya* (Elementary Geometry) (2 vol, 1944-45); *Died*: 2 July 1945.

GLAGOLEV, Vasiliy Pavlovich (1883-1938) Mil commander; brigade commander from 1935; *Born*: 23 May 1883 in Petersburg, son of a nobleman; *Educ*: 1909 grad Gen Staff Acad; *Career*: during WW 1 rose to rank of col; from Apr 1918 served in Red Army; commander, 1st Kursk Infantry Div, then commander, reserve army; chief of staff, Ukr Front; commander, 6th Army, Northern Front; commander, 16th Army, Western Front; from Sept 1919 commanded 11th, then 12th Cavalry Div in battles against Gen Denikin's Army; summer 1920 commanded 10th Army on search-and-destroy missions in Tver' Oblast; after Civil War held following posts in succession: dep chief of staff, Amur Kray; chief of staff, 5th Army; special duties, Red Army Weapons Dept; asst to chm, USSR Revol Mil Council; special duties, Red Army centr organs; 1937 arrested by NKVD; *Died*: 14 Mar 1938 in imprisonment; posthumously rehabilitated.

GLAGOLEVA-ARKAD'YEVA, Aleksandra Andreyevna (1894-1945) Physicist; prof; *Born:* 28 Feb 1884; *Educ:* 1910 grad Fac of Physics and Mathematics, Moscow Higher Women's Courses; *Career*: from 1910 asst prof, Chair of Physics, Moscow Higher Women's Courses; 1914-18 worked in x-ray dept of a mil hospital in Moscow; from 1918 taught at Moscow Univ; from 1930 prof, 2nd Moscow Med Inst; 1939 gave up teaching for health reasons; 1916 invented roentgen stereometer for locating bullets and shrapnel in the human body; 1923 used emitter of own design to obtain ultra-short waves in the range of several centimeters to 82 microns; did extensive research on these wavelengths with equipment which she designed herself; *Publ: Sobraniye trudov* (Collected Works) (1948); *Died*: 30 Oct 1945.

GLAVCHE, Yegor Stepanovich (1871-1919) Venereologist; *Born*: 21 Jan 1871 in Kishinev; *Educ*: 1895 grad Med Fac, Moscow Univ; from 1895 specialized at Prof A.I. Pospelov's Clinic of Skin and Venereal Diseases, Moscow Univ; 1897-1900 intern at this clinic; fall 1900-1902 outpatients physician, 1902-17 intern and head, Male Outpatients Dept, Odessa City Hospital; also conducted extensive private practice and worked on microbiology and serology at N.F. Gamaleya's laboratory; 1902 passed initial doctorate examinations in Moscow; completed first part of thesis *Limfaticheskiye zhelezy i sifilis* (The Lymph Glands and Syphilis); 1903 further med studies at Prof Jadasson's clinic in Berne; from 1911 gave public lectures on venereal diseases and prostitution, recruiting other physicians for this work; arranged printing of thesis lectures for public distribution; 1912 popularized prophylactic method of treating persons who had had sexual or non-sexual contact with syphilis sufferers; 18 June 1917 opened Russia's first polyclinic of skin, venereal and urogenital diseases which accepted patients on Sundays in order to afford treatment to workers and other persons bound by their jobs; recruited external students of staff and arranged short sources to train civilian and mil physicians in dermatovenerology; established serological and pathoanatomical laboratories at the polyclinic at his own expense; 1922 polyclinic reorganized into Dermato-Venerological Inst and named after him; reported and lectured to Moscow Venerological and Dermatological Soc; member and for many years secr, Odessa Dermatological Soc; presented papers at conferences of dermatologists and venerologists; 1902 read paper at 3rd All-Russian Congress of Odontologists; for many years lectured on syphidology at Odessa Dental School; wrote several dozen works on eczema, new anti-syphilis drugs, serodiagnosis of syphilis, effects of war on development of prostitution and spread of venereal diseases, prophylaxis of venereal disease, etc; *Publ: Vassermanovskaya reaktsiya i sifilis v Odesskom gorodskom priyute dlya maloletnikh detey po statisticheskim dannym 1911-1912 godov* (The Wassermann Reaction and Syphilis at the Odessa Municipal Orphanage from Statistics Covering 1911 and 1912) (1913); *Limfaticheskiye zhelezy i sifilis* (The Lymph Glands and Syphilis) (1916), dental textbook *Kratkaya skhema ucheniya o sifilise* (A Brief Outline of Syphilis Theory); *Venericheskiye bolezni i voyna* (Venereal Disease and War); *Sifilis v izyashchnoy literature* (Syphilis in Fiction); *Died*: 17 Aug 1919 in Odessa.

GLAZENAP, Pyotr Vladimirovich (1882-1951) Lt-gen, White Army; *Born*: 2 Mar 1882 in Gzhatsk, Smolensk Province, son of a hereditary Russian Army officer; *Educ*: 1903 grad Nikolay Cavalry College, Petersburg; 1913 grad Petersburg Cavalry Officers' School; *Career*: 1903-11 officer, 37th Dragoon Regt and Guards Cavalry Reserve Regt; 1913-14 officer, Petersburg Cavalry Officers' School; 1914-17 active war service in command of a partisan unit operating behind German lines; from Dec 1917 served with Gen Alekseyev's Volunteer Army; 1918-19 commanded a group, a squadron, a cavalry regt and a brigade; 1918 mil governor, Stavropol' Province after withdrawal of Sov troops; 1919-20 commander, Petrograd group of forces and force commander, Northwestern Army; 1919 also mil governor, Petrograd area after withdrawal of Sov troops; 1920 mustered Russian units for Pilsudski's Army in Poland; from 1920 in emigration, 1948-51 chm, League of the Banner of St Andrew, an anti-Communist emigre organization in West Germany; *Died*: 27 May 1951 in Munich of brain hemorrhage; buried in Munich.

GLAZENAP, Sergey Pavlovich (1848-1937) Astronomer; specialist in double and variable stars and practical astronomy; corresp member from 1927 and hon member from 1929, USSR Acad of Sci; Hon Sci Worker of RSFSR; Hero of Labor; *Born*: 25 Sept 1848 in Tver' Province; *Career*: 1870-78 astronomer at Pulkovo Observatory; 1871-82 studied motion of Jupiter's moons; 1874 attended expedition to Eastern Siberia to observe Venus pass across the disk of the Sun; 1881 astronomical observatory at Petersburg Univ, built to his design, was put into operation; 1889-1924 prof, Petersburg (Petrograd) Univ; 1882-97 at Petersburg, Domkin (near Luga), Gurzufa and Abastuman' made over 5,000 observations of double stars; results of these observations published in 5 vol; advanced a new and now widley used analytical method for computing the orbits of double stars; 1890 helped found Russian Astronomical Soc and for a number of years was its chm; 1901 directed wort on determination of astronomical points in Siberia; designed "sun ring," the simplest instrument for determining time and latitude; wrote popular books on astronomy for gen public; also textbooks on mathematics and cosmography; compiled widely-used mathematical tables; also specialist in theory and practice of gardening and bee-keeping; for 24 years ed, periodical *Vestnik Russkogo obshchestva pchelovodov; Publ: Sravneniye nablyudeniy zatmeniy sputnikov Yupitera s tablitsami zatmeniy i mezhdu soboy* (Comparison of the Eclipse of Jupiter's Moons with Eclipse Tables and Among Themselves) (1874); *Refraktsionnyy uklon* (Refractive Deviation) (1881); *Komety i padayushchiye zvyozdy* (Comets and Falling Stars) (1881); *O nablyudenii peremennykh zvyozd* (Observation of Variable Stars) (1892); *Astronomicheskiye opredeleniya geograficheskikh mest rayonov pozemel'no-ustroitel'nykh rabot v chetyryokh Sibirskikh guberniyakh* (Astronomical Determination of Geographical Locations of Land-Organization Work in Four Siberian Provinces) (1909); *Matematicheskiye i astronomicheskiye tablitsy* (Mathematical and Astronomical Tables) (1932); *Katalog astronomicheskikh punktov, lezhashchikh v predelakh Yakutskoy ASSR* (Catalogue of Astronomical Points Within the Yakutian ASSR) (1934); *Shestiznachnyye tablitsy logarifmov summ i raznostey po Gaussu* (Six-Digit Gauss Logarithmic Tables of Sums and Differences) (1935); pop sci books: *Komety* (Comets) (1910); *Druz'yam i lyubitelyam astronomii* (For Fans and Amateurs of Astronomy) (3rd ed, 1936); *Died*: 12 Apr 1937.

GLAZUNOV, Aleksandr Konstantinovich (1865-1936) Composer, conductor and music teacher; Dr of Music; prof; Pop Artiste of RSFSR from 1922; *Born*: 10 Aug 1865 in Petersburg; *Educ*: studied under N.A. Rimsky-Korsakov; *Career*: member, Belyayev Circle; from 1899 prof, 1905-28 dir, Petersburg (Leningrad) Conservatory; 1907 awarded doctorates by Oxford and Cambridge Univ; from 1922 lived in France, where he went for med treatment; *Works*: eight symphonies (1881, 1886, 1890, 1893, 1895, 1896, 1902, 1906); unfinished symphony (1909); symphonic arrangements: *Sten'ka Razin* (1885); "The Forest" (1887); "The Sea" (1889); "The Kremlin" (1890); "Spring" (1891); various overtures, including "Solemn Overture" (1900); various suites, including "From the Middle Ages" (1902); two piano concertos (1911, 1917); violin concerto (1904); ballad-concerto for cello (1931); arrangement of "The Volga Boatmen" for choir and orchestra (1905); together with Rimsky-Korsakov, finished Borodin's opera *Knyaz' Igor'* (Prince Igor); seven quartets; over 20 romances; music for the ballets - "Raymonda" (1897); *Vremena goda* (The Seasons) (1899); *Baryshnya-sluzhanka* (The Noble Maidservant) or *Ispytaniye Damisa* (Damis' Trial) (1898); Lermonotov's *Maskarad* (Masquerade) (1917), etc; *Died*: 21 Mar 1936 in Paris.

GLAZUNOV, Mikhail Fyodorovich (1896-1967) Pathoanatomist and oncologist; prof; Dr of Med from 1935; member, USSR Acad of Med Sci from 1960; *Born*: 1896 in Tsarskoye Selo (now Pushikn); *Educ*: 1919 grad Petrograd Mil Med Acad; 1923 completed postgrad course at above inst; *Career*: 1919-21 mil surgeon, Red Army; 1924-25 junior lecturer, 1926-41 senior lecturer, Chair of Pathological Anatomy, Leningrad Mil Med Acad; 1929-41 head, Pathological Dept, Inst of Oncology; 1941-42 pathoanatomist of a front, 1942-45 chief pathoanatomist, Sov Army; 1945-50 head, Chair of Pathological Anatomy, Leningrad State Inst of Advanced Med Training; 1945-63 senior assoc and head, Pathomorphological Laboratory, Inst of Oncology, USSR Acad of Med Sci; 1963-67 consultant, above inst and dir, Int Center for Tumors of the Ovaries, World Health Org; dep chm, Presidium, All-Union Soc of Pathoanatomists; member, ed collegium, journal *Voprosy onkologii*; member, ed council, journal *Arkhiv patologii*; co-ed, "Pathology and Morphology" section, 2nd ed of *Bol'shaya meditsinskaya entsiklopediya* (Large Medical Encyclopedia); co-ed, *Opyt sovetskoy meditsiny v Velikoy Otechestvennoy voyne 1941-45 gg* (Soviet Medical Experience in the 1941-45 Great Fatherland War); studied nature of malaria pigmentation, morphology and histogenesis of tumors, etc; wrote some 80 works; *Publ:* doctor's thesis *O vliyanii vitamina C na rost kostey v eksperimente* (The Experimental Effects of Vitamin C on Bone Development) (1935); *Ukazaniya po patologoanatomicheskoy sluzhbe* (Pathoanatomical Service Instructions); *Zlokachestvennyye opukholi* (Malignant Tumors) (1947); *Opukholi yaichnikov* (Tumors of the Ovaries) (1954), etc; *Awards*: Order of Lenin; Order of the Red Banner; Order of the Red Star; Badge of Hon; medals; *Died*: 1967.

GLEBOV (real name: GLEBOV-KOTEL'NIKOV), Anatoliy Glebovich (1899-1964) Russian writer; CP member from 1919; *Born*: 9 Dec 1899 in Poltava; *Educ*: high-school grad; also studied Japanese at a univ; *Career*: from 1917 ed, newspaper *Svobodnaya shkola*; 1918 served as a med orderly with a Red Guard unit; 1919 ed, Tula newspaper *Proletarskoye stroitel'stvo;* 1920-24 held dipl post in Turkey; 1924-27 head, Rural Corresp Dept, *Krest'yanskaya gazeta;* 1924 worked with various amateur acting groups which performed his plays; subsequently became full-time writer; *Publ:* plays: *Nashi dni* (Our Times) *or V dalyokiye dni* (In Distant Days) (1919); *Kanun* (The Eve) or *Prestupleniye starosty Dembovskogo* (Headman Dembovskiy's Crime) (1924); *Zagmuk* (1925); *Vlast'* (Power) 1927); *Rost* (Growth) (1927); *Inga* (1929); *Nachistotu* (Frankly) or *Pravda* (The Truth) (1940), etc; prose works: *Liniya druzhby. Rasskazy o Turtsii* (The Friedship Line. Tales of Turkey) (1960); *Pravdokha. Zapyataya. Rasskazy* (The Just Man. The Comma. Short Stories) (1962), etc; *Died:* 6 Feb 1964 in Moscow.

GLEBOV (real name: SOROKIN), Gleb Pavlovich (1899-1967) Actor; Pop Artiste of USSR from 1948; *Born*: 11 May 1899; *Career*: 1921 began stage work at Ukr provincial theaters; from 1926 at 1st Bel Drama Theater (now Minsk Kupala Theater); also film actor; *Roles*: Pavel Nemira in Chornyy's *Otechestvo* (Fatherland); Khalimon and Tulyaga in Krapiva's *Partizany* (Partisans) and *Kto smeyotsya poslednim* (He Who Laughs Last); Garpagon in Moliere's "The Miser"; Kroplya in Movzon's *Konstantin Zaslonov*, etc; *Awards*: Stalin Prizes (1941 and 1948); *Died*: 3 Mar 1967.

GLIER, Reyngol'd Moritsevich (1875-1956) Composer and conductor; Dr of Arts; Pop Artiste of USSR from 1938, Azer SSR from 1934, RSFSR from 1935, Uzbek SSR from 1937; *Born*: 11 Jan 1875 in Kiev; *Educ*: 1894 grad Kiev Music College; 1900 grad

Moscow Conservatory; *Career*: from 1908 conductor; 1913-20 prof, from 1914 dir, Kiev Conservatory; 1920-41 dir, Moscow Conservatory; a milestone in Sov ballet history was his *Krasnyy mak* (Red Poppy), written on a modern revol theme; his nat operas played an important part in development of Azer and Uzbek music; 1938-48 chm, Org Comt, USSR Writers' Union; among his students were: B. Aleksandrov, A. Davidenko, N. Ivanov-Radkevich, G. Litinskiy, B. Revutskiy, M. Frolov, etc; *Works*: five operas including *Shakhsenem* (1925; new ed, 1934); coauthor, *Leyli i Medzhnun* (Leyli and Medzhnun) (1940); coauthor, *Gyul'sara* (1949); six ballets, including: *Krasnyy mak* (Red Poppy) (1927) renamed *Krasnyy tsvetok* (Red Flower) in 1957; *Komedianty* (The Comedians) (1930, new ed 1955 renamed *Doch' Kastilii* [Daughter of Castille]); *Mednyy vsadnik* (The Bronze Horseman) (1949); musical drama *Gyul'sara* (1936); three symphonies (1900, 1907, 1911 [Il'ya Muromets]); poem for symphony orchestra *Sirens* (1908); symphonic pictures *Dnieper Cossacks* (1921) and *Commandment* (1929); five overtures; five concertos for harp (1938), voice (1942), cello (1946), French horn (1951), violin (concert allegro, 1955, completed and instrumented by B. Lyatoshinskiy); works for brass band; three string sextets; four string quartets (1st, 1899; 4th, 1946); pieces for piano and other instruments; choral works; about 130 romances, etc; *Awards:* three Orders of Lenin; Order of the Red Banner of Labor; Badge of Hon; medals; Stalin Prizes (1946, 1948, 1950); Glinka Prizes (1902, 1909, 1914); *Died:* 23 June 1956 in Moscow.

GLINKA, Konstantin, Dmitriyevich (1867-1927) Pedologist; prof from 1895; member, USSR Acad of Sci from 1927; *Born*: 5 July 1867 in Smolensk Province; *Educ:* 1889 grad Petersburg Univ as a mineralogist; *Career*: after grad lecturer, Petersburg Univ; from 1895 prof, Chair of Mineralogy and Geology, from 1901 prof, Chair of Pedology, Novo-Aleksandriiskiy Agric Inst; from 1913 founder-dir and lecturer in pedology, Voronezh Agric Inst; from 1922 rector and prof, Leningrad Agric Inst; from 1927 dir, Soil Inst, USSR Acad of Sci; devised method of performing mineralogical research on fine soil fractions; did major research on erosion and founded influential school of Russian soil mineralogy; 1889 made first pedological studies of gray forest soils; 1894 made soil survey of Poltava Province under the supervision of G. Dokuchayev; 1899-1906 studied the soils of Pskov Provine; 1902-03 surveyed Smolensk Province; 1903 studied the soils of Novgorod Province; 1908-14 organized and led pedological and geographical expeditions to Siberia and Centr Asia which resulted in the discovery of vast agric land resources; contributed to compilation of first soil map of Asian USSR; took a special interst in the study of soil zones and the genesis and classification of soils; pioneered paleopedology in the USSR; *Publ: Pochvoobrazovaniye, kharakteristika pochvennykh tipov i geografiya pochv (Vvedeniye v izucheniye pochvovedeniyaa)* (Soil Formation, the Characteristics of Soil Types and Soil Geography[An Introduction to the Study of Pedology]) (1923); *Pochvy Rossii i prilegayushchikh stran* (The Soils of Russia and the Neighboring Countries) (1923); *Solontsy i solonchaki Aziatskoy chasti SSSR (Sibir' i Turkestan)* (The Solonetz and Solonchak Soils of the Asian USSR [Siberia and Turkestan]) (1926); *Skhematicheskaya pochvennaya karta zemnogo shara* (A Schematic Soil Map of the World) (1908); *Dispersnyye sistemy v pochve* (Dispersion Systems in the Soil) (1924); *Ocherki pochv Yakutii* (An Outline of the Soils of Yakutia) (1927); *K voprosu o klassifikatsii turkestanskikh pochv* (The Classification of the Soils of Turkestan) (1909); *Pochvy* (Soils) (2nd ed, 1929); *Russkoye pochvovedeniye (Kratkiy istoricheskiy ocherk)* (Russian Pedology [A Brief Historical Study]) (1924); *Zadachi istoricheskogo pochvovedeniya* (The Tasks of Historical Pedology) (1904); *Kratkaya svodka dannykh o pochvakh Dal'nego Vostoka* (A Resume of Data on the Soils of the Far East) (1910); *Pochvovedeniye* (Pedology) (6th ed, 1935); *Died*: 2 Nov 1927 in Leningrad; buried at Shuvalov Cemetery, Leningrad.

GLIVENKO, Ivan Ivanovich (1868-1931) Lit historian; prof; *Born*: 24 Apr 1868 in Lebedin, Khar'kov Province; *Career*: from 1906 assoc prof, then prof, various univ; from 1921 prof, Moscow Univ; 1921-23 dir, Main Bd of Sci, Museum and Artistic Establishments; specialized in Western lit; *Publ: Rukovodstvo k izucheniyu ital'yanskogo yazyka* (A Guide to the Study of Italian) (1899); *Vittorio Al'f'yeri. Zhizn' i proizvedeniya* (Vittorio Alfieri. His Life and Works) (vol 1, 1912); *Chteniya po istorii vseobshchey literatury* (Readings on the History of Universal Literature) (1914); *Etyudy po teorii poezii* (Studies in the Theory of Poetry) (vol 1, 1920); *Poeticheskoye izobrazheniye i real'naya deystvitel'nost'* (Poetic Imagery and Reality) (1929); *Ital'ynsko-russkiy slovar'* (An Italian-Russian Dictionary) (1930), etc; *Died*: 22 Dec 1931 in Moscow.

GLOBA, Andrey Pavlovich (1888-1964) Russian writer; *Born*: 26 Nov 1888 in Romny, Poltava Province; *Career*: 1915 first work printed; specialized in translating into Russian folklore of peoples of USSR and other countries; his translations are free renditions rather than exact reproductions of the original; many of his works have been included in the repertoire of Sov theaters; *Publ: Dramaticheskiye stseny* (Dramatic Scenes) (1916); poem *Watt Tyler* (1922); tragedy *Famar'* (1923); drama *Venchaniye Kh'yuga* (Hugo's Wedding) (1924); verse collection *Korabli izdaleka* (Ships from Afar) (1922); tragedy *Pushkin* (1936); dramas: *Prolitaya chasha* (The Spilled Cup) (1952), after the Chinese classic Vash Shi-fu; *Russkaya doroga* (The Russian Road) (1959); *Komedianty* (The Comedians) (1960), etc; *Poemy* (Poems) (1922); *Zapadnyy sbornik pesen* (Collection of Western Songs) (1936); *Pesni narodov SSSR* (Songs of the Peoples of the USSR) (1947); *Dramy i komedii* (Dramas and Comedies) (1960); *Died*: 9 Feb 1964 in Moscow.

GLOVATSKIY, Gavriil Vladimirovich (1866-1939) Actor and stage dir; Hon Artiste of RSFSR from 1934; *Born*: 25 Mar 1866; *Educ*: 1890-92 studied at drama school; *Career*: 1887 began stage work in Moscow on the stage of the Small Hall, Nobles' Assembly; actor, Abramova Theater; 1896 began directing work; worked for Soc for Pop Entertainment (staged plays at Moscow plants and workers' suburbs), for large actors' assoc and enterprises (with M.M. Boroday, Ye. Belyayev, K.N. Nezlobin); 1905-15 stage dir, Lit-Artistic Assoc Theater (so-called Suvorin Theater) in Petersburg; after 1917 Oct Revol organized in Odessa first Sov theaters (*Krasnyy moryak, Moroborona*); 1930 founded and directed theater in Yakutia; subsequently worked in the Far East in Blagoveshchensk, Petropavlovsk-on-Kamchatka and Vladivostok; from 1907 instructor at Stagecraft College, Lit-Artistic Soc and N.N. Arbatov Drama School; *Roles*: Lyubim Tortsov; Shylock; Richard III; Garpagon; etc; *Productions:* Kolyshko's *Del'tsy* (Businessmen); Zhukovskaya's *Deti* (Children) and *Osobnyak* (Private Residence) (1907, 1908, 1910); *Bez viny vinovatyye* (Guilty Without Guilt) (1906); Belyayev's *Tsarevna-lyagushka* (The Frog Princess) (1913); Trenyov's *Pugachyovshchina* (The Pugachev Mutiny) (1926); *Platon Krechet* (1935); Zarkhi's *Ulitsa radosti* (Street of Joy) (1937), etc; *Died:* 17 Oct 1939.

GLUKHACHENKOV, Ivan Kuz'mich (1886-1966) Govt official; CP member from 1907; *Born*: 15 May 1886; *Career*: from 1904 in revol movement; helped organize strikes at Kolpino Izhorskiy Plant; arrested; served time at Baku jail; 1914 drafted into the army; participated in 1917 Oct Revol; Collegium member, Cheka; 1918-19 chm, Petrograd City Rayon Dept of Pop Court; 1919-38 in the Navy; 1938-43 worked for Navy Museum; from 1957 pensioner; *Died*: 25 July 1966.

GLUSHCHENKO, Aleksandra Petrovna (1887-1967) Party official; CP member from 1914; *Born*: 1887; *Career*: 1907 began work as tutor; for revol activities placed under police surveillance; after 1917 came to Petrograd, worked for the soc insurance system at the Neva Shipyard; 1918-30 and from 1932 journalistic, govt, trade-union and work in Vologda and Vologda Oblast; 1931 Party work in Vol'sk; from 1945 pensioner; *Died*: July 1967.

GLUSHKOV, Pyotr Arkad'yevich (1880-1937) Stomatologist; Dr of Med; prof from 1920; *Born*: 1880 in vil Melekess, Samara Province, son of a zemstvo physician; *Educ*: 1904 grad Med Fac, Kazan' Univ with distinction; *Career*: from 1904 asst to Prof V. N. Tonkov, Chair of Anatomy, Kazan' Univ; 1905 served in Russo-Japanese War; 1908 began specialist training in stomatology under Dr Dombrovskiy; 1911 attended Zverzhkhovskiy's course on conservative dentistry and Dr Nemenov's course on roentgenology in Petersburg; from 1912 lectured on conservative dentistry at 2nd Kazan' School of Dentistry; after 1917 Oct Revol founder-head, Odontological Dept, Med Fac, Kazan' Univ, where he lectured on stomatology; from 1920 member, Learned Council, Med Fac and founder-head, Chair of Stomatology, Kazan' Univ; Nov 1923 attended 1st All-Russian Odontological Congress; 1924 offered professorship in odontology at 2nd Moscow Univ but Kazan' Univ refused to release him; from 1928 founder-dir, Special Stomatological Clinic, Kazan' Univ; 1930, after the conversion of the Odontological Dept at Kazan' Univ into an independent stomatological inst, moved to Leningrad, where he worked under Acad A. D. Speranskiy at the Inst of Experimental Med; trained such prominent stomatologists as Ye. A. Domrachev, K. A. Korchatin, I. M. Oksman and Z. A. Shishkin; wrote over 20 works; *Publ: Iz kliniki zaderzhki prorezyvaniya zubov v detskom vozraste* (The Clinical Aspects of Delayed Childhood Dentition); *Metod plasticheskoy rezektsii nizhney chelyusti* (A Method of Plastic Resection of the Lower Jaw); *O kostnoy plastike nizhney chelyusti po metodu P. I. D'yakonova* (Osteoplasty of the Lower Jaw by P. I. D'yakonov's Method); *K patogenezu i terapii al'veolyarnoy piorrei* (The Pathogenesis and Treatment of Alveolar Pyorrhea); *Died*: 5 Mar 1937.

GLUSHKOV, Viktor Grigor'yevich (1883-1939) Hydrologist; prof; *Born*: 1883; *Career*: from 1918, head, "White Coal" Dept, Commission for the Study of Natural Resources, USSR Acad of Sci; from May 1918 dir, Bureau for the Electrification of Russia, then dir, Bureau for the Electrification of the Northern Region; from 1922 dir, State Hydrological Inst, Leningrad; specialized in hydrology and hydrometry; designed pumps and other hydrotech equipment; 1910 founded Turkestani Hydrometric Unit; 1912 organized similar unit in European Russia; 1915 set up "White Coal" Dept, Commission for the Study of Natural Resources; 1918 organized Electrification Planning Bureau; 1919 founded State Hydrological Inst; 1924 and 1928 organized All-Union Hydrological Congresses; arrested by State Security organs; *Died*: 1939 in imprisonment.

GLYASSER, M. I. (1890-1951) Party and govt official; CP member from 1917; *Born*: 1890; *Career*: 1918-24 with Secretariat, RSFSR Council of Pop Comr; subsequently at Lenin Inst; then at Marx-Engels-Lenin Inst, CC, CPSU(B); *Died*: 1951.

GNESIN, Mikhail Fabianovich (1883-1957) Composer and musical writer; Dr of Arts; Hon Art Worker of RSFSR from 1927; *Born*: 2 Feb 1883 in Rostov-on-Don; *Educ:* 1909 grad Petersburg Conservatory; *Career:* taught at music colleges in Yekaterinodar, Rostov-on-Don and Moscow; 1925-35 prof, Moscow and 1935-44 Leningrad Conservatories; 1944-51 prof, Moscow Gnesin Musical Teachers' Training Inst; Bd member, USSR Writers' Union; among his students were: B. Klyuzner, A. Leman, G. Mushel', N. Narimanidze, V. Salmanov, A. Stepanyan, A. Khachaturyan, T. Khrennikov, etc; his *Symphonic Monument* was one of the first Sov symphonic works on revol subjects; wrote a number of musical works on nat themes; *Works*: opera *Yunost' Avraama* (Abraham's Youth) (1923); works for choir and orchestra (1905-17); "Symphonic Monument" (1925); "To the Red Army" (1943); for voice and orchestra *Vrubel'* (symphonic dithyrambs to lyrics by Bryusov) (1911); symphonic works; ensembles, including piano sectet *Adygeya* (1933); for string quartet: variations on a Jewish folk theme (1914) and on Azer folk songs (1930); sonata-fantasia for piano quartet (1945); piano trio "In Memory of Our Perished Children" (1943) and other instrumental works; choral works; song cycle for voice and piano "Story of the Red-Haired Motel'" (1926-29); about 50 romances; music for plays, including Gogol's *Revizor* (The Government Inspector) (1926); recordings and arrangements of folk songs, etc; lit works: *Nachal'nyy kurs prakticheskoy kompozitsii* (Elementary Course in Practical Composition) (1941; revised and supplemented ed, 1962); *O russkom simfonizme* (Russian Symphonic Music) (1948, 1949, 1950); *Mysli i vospominaniya o N. A. Rimskom-Korsakove* (Thoughts and Reminiscences About N. A. Rimsky-Korsakov) (1956); *Awards*: Stalin Prize (1946); Order of the Red Banner of Labor; medals; *Died*: 5 May 1957 in Moscow.

GNESINA, Yelena Fabianovna (1874-1967) Pianist and piano teacher; prof from 1943; Hon Art Worker of RSFSR from 1935; *Born*: 30 May 1874 in Rostov-on-Don; her sisters Yevgeniya, Mariya and Ol'ga and her brother M. Gnesin were also musicians; *Educ*: 1893 grad Moscow Conservatory; *Career*: 1895 together with sister Yevgeniya founded and directed a music college; 1944-53 founder-dir, Gnesiny Musical Training Inst, Moscow; *Works*: manuals on piano teaching; *Fortepiannaya azbuka* (The ABC of Piano-Playing); *Malen'kiye etyudy dlya nachinayushchikh* (Short Etudes for Beginners); *Vospominaniya* (Memoirs) (1964), etc; *Died*: 4 June 1967.

GNEZDILOV, Vladimir Georgiyevich (1898-1958) Parasitologist; Dr of Med from 1945; *Born*: 1898; *Educ*: 1926 grad Leningrad Mil Med Acad; *Career*: from 1956 head, Chair of Gen Biology and Parasitology, Leningrad Mil Med Acad; specialized in med helminthology, protozoology and gen biology; did major research on the propagation of helminthiasis; determined the potential hosts of broad tapeworm and pork tapeworm; also made important study of protozoal intestinal infestations; conducted mass examinations in various regions of USSR, North Korea and Kwantung Leased Territory to determine the incidence of protozoal intestinal infections; determined the laws governing the relationship between Entamoeba histolylica and the host organism; made major contribution to the study of the morphology and cultivation of intenstinal protozoa; together with Ye.N. Pavlovskiy achieved medically-important breakthrough in the study of parasitocenoses in the host organism; did research on the cultivation of Balantidium coli and Trichomonas hominis; analysed the intraspecific and interspecific relations among animals artificially infested with pleurocercoids of the broad tapeworm; also devised experiments to determine factors of the evolutionary formation of host organisms and parasites; wrote over 55 works; *Publ:* doctor's thesis, *Dizenteriynyye amyoby i drugiye kishechnyye prosteyshiye cheloveka v svyazi s voprosom ob adaptivnykh modifikatsiyakh* (Entamoebae Histolylicae and Other Human Intestinal Protozoa in Relation to Adaptive Modifications) (1944); *Vnutrividovyye i mezhvidovyye otnosheniya sredi komponentov parazitotsenoza kishechnika khozyaina* (Intraspecific and Interspecific Relations Among the Components of Parasitocenosis of the Host Intestine) (1953); *Died*: 1958.

GOBI (SHNITNIKOVA), L. Kh. (Irina) (1878-1944) Govt official; CP member from 1923; *Born*: 1878; *Career*: from 1901 active in Soc-Democratic movement; distributed illegal revol lit; 1902-04 tech secr, Petersburg Comt; 1903 CC liaison agent for Petersburg Province; 1905 maintained a weapons cache at her Petersburg apartment; subsequently quit Party work; 1923-27 worked for Grain Export Comt; 1928-33 with Comt for the Application of Chemistry in Nat Econ; *Died*: 1944.

GODIN, Yuriy Nikolayevich (1912-1962) Geologist; Dr of Geology and Mineralogy; prof from 1959; Presidium member, Turkm Acad of Sci from 1959; dir, Inst of Geology, Turkm Acad of Sci from 1959; member, ed bd, journal *Izvestiya Akademii nauk Turkmenskoy SSR*; CP member from 1951; *Born*: 23 May 1912; *Educ*: 1930 grad Courses for Field Geophysicists; 1939 grad Leningrad Mining Inst as external student; *Career*: specialized in geophysical survey methods and regional geology; 1930 embarked on first field trip; 1939-43 in charge of geophysical survey teams; 1943-54 dir, Turkm Geophysical Service; 1954-59 head, Regional Studies Section, All-Union Research Inst of Geophysical Survey Methods; made numerous survey and research expeditions in USSR; compiled new tectonic zone maps of Turkestan and the western regions of Centr Asia; supervised large-scale seismic and geophysical regional studies of Centr Asia and the Volga-Ural oil-bearing region; wrote over 50 works; *Publ: Rol' razvedochnoy geofiziki i otkrytiya novykh neftyanykh i gazovykh mestorozhdeniy v Turkmenistane* (The Role of Geophysical Prospecting Techniques and the Discovery of New Oil and Gas Deposits in Turkestan) (1960); *Seysmicheskiye issledovaniya zemnoy kory v rayone Ferganskoy mezhgornoy vpadiny* (Seismic Studies of the Earth's Crust in the Fergana Depression) (1960); *Seismicheskiye issledovaniya zemnoy kory v Bukharskom rayone Uzbekskoy SSR* (Seismic Studies of the Earth's Crust in the Bukhara Region of the Uzbek SSR) (1960); *Awards:* 2 Badges of Hon; three medals; Stalin Prize (1950); Lenin Prize (1962, posthumously); *Died*: 1 Jan 1962.

GODINER, Shmuel Davidovich (1892-1941) Jewish writer; *Born*: 1892 in Minsk Province; *Career*: 1913-20 in the army; WW 1 veteran; fought in Civil War in Ukr; *Publ*: 1921 first work published; novelettes "The Dolls," "Nudity" and "Ivan-Town" (1922-24); "Man with a Rifle" (1928); collection "Other People" (1940); in Russian translation *Povesti i rasskazy* (Novelettes and Stories) (1961); *Died*: 1941 killed in action during defense of Moscow.

GOFFE, Vladimir Ivanovich (1907-1961) Mil commander; lt-gen of artillery; CP member from 1938; *Born*: 1907; *Educ*: 1927 grad Mil Artillery School; *Career*: from 1924 in Red Army; from 1927 commanded various artillery units; artillery commander of a mil distr; after WW 2 in USSR Min of Defense; Aug 1945 artillery commander in campaign against Japanese Kwangtung Army; *Awards*: two Orders of Lenin; three Orders of the Red Banner; two Orders of Kutuzov, 2nd Class; Order of the Red Star; Badge of Hon; medals; *Died*: 17 May 1961 along with Army Gen V. Ya. Kolpakchi and others in an airplane crash during tactical exercises; buried in Moscow's Novodevich'ye Cemetery.

GOFMAN, Modest Lyudvigovich (1887-1959) Russian lit historian; *Born:* 29 June 1887 in Petersburg; *Educ:* grad mil school and

History and Philology Fac, Petersburg Univ; *Career*: 1907 published first verse collection *Kol'tso. Tikhiye pesni skorbi* (The Ring. Gentle Songs of Grief); closely connected with the symbolists; in the collection *Gimny i ody* (Hymns and Odes) (1910) tried to introduce into Russian poetry complex antique meter; 1909 published *Kniga o russkikh poetakh poslednego desyatiletiya* (Book on Russian Poets of the Last Decade) and article on Pushkin's work *Kapitanskaya dochka* (The Captain's Daughter); 1914-15 edited Ye.A. Baratynskiy's complete works; from 1920 assoc, Pushkin House, Acad of Sci; 1922 published textological works *Propushchennyye stroki "Yevgeniya Onegina"* (Omitted Lines in "Yevgeniy Onegin") and *Pushkin. Pervaya glava nauki o Pushkine* (Pushkin. First Chapter of Studies on Pushkin); in this book he declared the main problem to be the determination of Pushkin's original ("canonical") texts; however, in his own works he replaced a critical study of Pushkin's texts with the mechanical reproduction of the last authorized ed, as is evident from his studies *Domik v Kolomne* (The House in Kolomna) and *Posmertnyye stikhotvoreniya Pushkina, 1833-1836* (Pushkin's Posthumous Poems, 1833-36) (1922); 1923 went on a research mission to Paris, but did not return to Russia; in France taught a Russian lit course at the Sorbonne; edited Pushkin's works and books dealing with Pushkin; *Publ: Poeziya Baratynskogo* (The Poetry of Baratynskiy) (1915); *Pushkin. Psikhologiya tvorchestva (vtoraya glava nauki o Pushkine)* (Pushkin. The Psychology of Creative Work [Second Chapter of Studies on Pushkin]) (1928); "Pouchkine"(1931); coauthor, "Histoire de la litérature russe depuis les origines jusqu'a nos jours" (1934); "Pouchkine et la Russie" (1947); coauthor, "Le drame de Pouchkine" (1948); *Died*: 6 Mar 1959 in Paris.

GOFUNG, Yefim Mikhaylovich (1876-1944) Stomatologist; Hon Prof of Ukr SSR; Hon Sci Worker of Ukr SSR from 1941; *Born*: 1876 in Konstantinograd (now Krasnograd), Khar'kov Province, son of a teacher; *Educ*: 1899 grad Warsaw Dental School; 1924 grad Khar'kov Med Inst; *Career*: 1899-1903 gave free dental treatment at Red Cross outpatients' clinic in Poltava; from 1904 lecturer, Yekaterinoslav Dental School; 1906-21 clinic head, 1st Khar'kov Dental School; after 1917 Oct Revol helped to organize higher stomatological training in Ukr; 1921-29 founder-dean, Odontological Fac, Khar'kov State Med Inst, which became the prototype of modern Sov stomatological institutes; devised still valid classification of pulpites; 1910-35 chm, Khar'kov Dentists' Soc; 1911 secr, Org Comt, 6th All-Russian Congress of Odontologists; edited transactions of this congress; 1913 co-chm, Moscow Congress of Dental Soc Delegates; helped to organize and attended All-Union and Ukr stomatological conferences and congresses; wrote numerous textbooks and papers on stomatology, including an original study of the active mesenchyme of the pulpa; *Publ: Klinika bolezney zubov i polosti rta* (The Clinical Treatment of Diseases of the Teeth and Oral Cavity) (1930); *Osnovy proteznogo zubovrachevaniya* (The Principles of Dental Prosthetics) (1935); coauthor, *Klinika bolezney zubov i polosti rta* (The Clinical Treatment of Diseases of the Teeth and Oral Cavity) (1936); coauthor, *Stomatologiya* (Stomatology) (1937); coauthor, *Terapevticheskaya stomatologiya* (Therapeutic Stomatology) (1938); *Uchebnik bolezney zubov i polosti rta* (A Textbook on Diseases of the Teeth and Oral Cavity) (1945) *Uchebnik terapevticheskoy stomatologii* (A Textbook on Therapeutic Stomatology) (1946); *Died*: 29 Sept 1944.

GOGOBERIDZE, Levan Davidovich (1896-1937) Party official; CP member from 1916; *Born*: 1896; *Educ*: 1930-34 studied in Moscow; *Career*: after 1917 Feb Revol dep chm, Dzhivizlik (near Trapezund) Sov of Workers and Soldiers' Dep; assoc, Bolshevik newspaper *Kavkazskiy rabochiy*; from Feb 1918 Party and govt posts in Baku; after collapse of Sov regime in Baku engaged in exec underground activities; Nov 1918 attended a conference of Transcaucasian Bolshevik organizations in Tiflis, was arrested and deported to Baku; from Dec 1918 Bureau member, Baku Party Comt, then member, Caucasian Kray Party Comt; May 1919 helped organize Baku workers' strike; summer 1919 seriously wounded; late 1920 Presidium member, Nizhniy Novgorod Province RCP(B) Comt; 1921-30 exec posts in Geo; chm, Tiflis Revol Comt; secr, Tiflis RCP(B) Comt; 1923 dep chm, Geo Council of Pop Comr; 1926-30 secr, CC, CP Geo; 1930-34 worked and studied in Moscow; from May 1934 secr, Yeysk Rayon CPSU(B) Comt; from Jan 1935 secr, *Rostsel'mash* Plant Party Comt; deleg at 15th and 16th CPSU(B) Congresses; arrested by State Security organs; *Died*: 1937 in imprisonment; posthumously rehabilitated.

GOLANT, Raisa Yakovlevna (1885-1953) Psychiatrist; Hon Sci Worker of RSFSR from 1940; *Born*: 1885; *Career*: initially spezialized in experimental physiology and clinical neuropathology; 1913 defended doctor's thesis on immotility of vertebra; from 1928 head, Chair of Psychiatry, 2nd Leningrad Med Inst; specialized in exogenous psychoses of syphilitic, vascular or traumatic origin; described new symptoms and syndromes, including syndromes of hallucinatory lingual speech movements, violent states, sense of weightlessness, rare gnostic and mnestic dystrophy, phases of encephalitis, etc; popularized new methods of studying and treating mental patients; for many years bd member, Leningrad and All-Union Soc of Neuropathologists and Psychiatrists; helped organize congresses and conferences and served on ed bd of several periodicals and publ; sci dir, Bekhteryov Psychoneurological Inst; wrote 125 works; *Publ:* doctor's thesis *O nepodvizhnosti pozvonochnika* (The Immotility of the Vertebra) (1913); *O rasstroystve pamyati* (Memory Disturbances) (1935); *Died*: 1953.

GOL'DBERG, B. I. (1884-1946) Govt official; CP member from 1902; *Born*: 1884; *Career*: revol work in Yekaterinoslav, Chita, Krasnoyarsk and Ufa; after 1917 Feb Revol chm, Tomsk Garrison Sov; 1917-25 in Red Army; 1919-21 commander, RSFSR and Volga Mil Distr Reserve Army; 1921-22 dep chm, Main Comt of State Installations, All-Russian Sovnarkhoz; 1922-23 dep head, Main Bd, RSFSR Air Force; 1923-24 RSFSR Revol-Mil Council rep with Pop Comrt of For Trade; from 1925 exec admin work; *Died*: 1946.

GOL'DBERG, Isaak Grigor'yevich (1884-1939) Russian writer; *Born*: 8 Nov 1884 in Irkutsk, son of an exiled blacksmith; *Career*: at age 19 arrested for belonging to a high-school circle which published the manuscript periodical *Bratstvo*; from 1904 until the establishment of Sov regime in Siberia member, Socialist-Revol Party; 1907-12 in exile; 1903 first work printed; his works deal with the life of Northern peoples, Civil War in Siberia, and the country's industrialization and collectivization; arrested by NKVD; *Publ: Tungusskiye rasskazy* (Tunguz Stories) (1914); stories: *Chelovek s ruzh'yom* (The Man With a Gun) (1921); *Grob podpolkovnika Nedochyotova* (The Tomb of Lieutenant-Colonel Nedochyotov) (1924); *Bab'ya pechal'* (Woman's Grief) (1925); collected stories *Put' ne otmechennyy na karte* (Unmapped Road) (1927); novelette *Sladkaya polyn'* (Sweet Absinth) (1928); *Tsvety na snegu* (Flowers on the Snow) (1930); novel *Poema o farforovoy chashke* (Poem of the China Cup) (1930); *Kak Yukhartsa poshyol po novym tropam* (How Yukhartsa Came to Walk New Paths) (1932); novelettes *Glavnyy shtrek* (Main Drift) (1932); *Tayga v ogne* (Burning Taiga) (1932); *Troye i syn* (Three and the Son) (1933); novel *Zhizn' nachinayetsya segodnya* (Life Begins Today) (1934); *Povesti i rasskazy* (Novelettes and Stories) (1934); *Povesti* (Novelettes) (1934); *Povesti i rasskazy* (Novelettes and Stories) (1958); poem *Pesnya o Fed'ke - krasnom boytse* (Song of the Red Warrior Fed'ka) (1963); *Died*: 2 Dec 1939 in imprisonment; posthumously rehabilitated.

GOL'DBERG, Nikolay Maksimovich (1891-1962) Historian; *Born*: 1891 in Moscow; *Educ*: studied at Lausanne and Heidelberg Univ and at Petrine Agric Acad; *Career*: during Civil War worked for Pop Comrt of For Affairs and For Relations Dept, Turkestani Commission, All-Russian Centr Exec Comt; from late 1920 assoc, Turkestani Dept, Comintern Exec Comt; 1926-27 TASS corresp in Turkey; from 1928 worked for Comintern; from 1938 assoc, various sci establishments, USSR Acad of Sci, including Inst of the Peoples of Asia; wrote over 40 works on India; *Publ*: coauthor and exec ed, *Novaya istoriya Indii* (The New History of India), etc; *Died*: 1962.

GOL'DENBERG (pseudonym: LYUSHKOVSKIY), Iosif Petrovich (1873-1922) Politician; CP member from 1920; *Born*: 1873; *Educ*: higher educ in Paris; *Career*: from 1892 in Soc-Democratic movement; from 1903 Bolshevik; returned to Russia and engaged in trade-union and Party work; worked in Saratov, then Petersburg; 1905-07 helped edit Bolshevik publications; 1905 attended 5th (London) RSDRP Congress; 1905-10 member, CC, RSDRP; 1910-14 in exile; 1914 switched from Bolsheviks to Mensheviks and supported Plekhanov; 1917-19 sided with *Novaya zhizn'* (New Life) group; opposed Lenin; summer 1917 went abroad with deleg of Menshevik All-Russian Centr Exec Comt and remained there after 1917 Oct Revol; 1920 reconciled with Bolsheviks and admitted to RCP(B); 1921 returned to USSR; *Died*: 1 Jan 1922 of a heart attack.

GOL'DENVEYZER, Aleksandr Borisovich (1875-1961) Pianist, teacher and composer; Pop Artiste of USSR from 1946; Dr of Arts from 1940; *Born:* 10 Mar 1875 in Kishinev; *Educ:* 1895 grad Piano Class under A. I. Ziloti and P. A. Pabst and 1897 Composition Class, Moscow Conservatory under S. I. Tanev, A. S. Arenskiy and M. M. Ippolitov-Ivanov; *Career*: 1895 began concert work; from 1896 teacher; 1904-06 prof, Piano Class, College of Music and Dramatic Art, Moscow Philharmonic Soc; from 1906 prof, 1922-24 and 1939-42 dir, Moscow Conservatory; among his students were G. R. Ginzburg, D. B. Kabalevskiy, V. V. Nechayev, T. P. Nikolayev, S. Ye. Feynberg and R. V. Tamarkina; *Works*: three operas: *Pir vo vremya chumy* (Feast During the Plague) (after Pushkin); *Pevtsy* (The Singers) and *Veshniye vody* (Spring Freshets) (after Turgenev); cantata "October Light"; chamber music, piano pieces, romances, two symphonic suites on themes of Russian folksongs, etc; edited piano works of Beethoven, Schumann, etc; wrote memoirs *Vblizi Tolstogo. Zapisi za pyatnadtsat' let* (Near Tolstoy. Records of Fifteen Years) (2 vol, 1922-24); *Awards*: Stalin Prize (1947); two Orders of Lenin; two Orders of the Red Banner of Labor; medals; *Died*: 26 Sept 1961 in Moscow.

GOL'DMAN, L. I. (Akim) (1877-1939) Govt official; *Born*: 1877; *Career*: from 1893 in revol movement; 1899 arrested, managed to escape, worked in Odessa; from 1900 abroad; joined *Iskra* (Spark) org; early 1901 met Lenin in Munich and discussed with him plans for founding an *Iskra* printing house in Russia; May 1901 founded in Kishinev illegal printing house, where *Iskra* and other Soc-Democratic publ were printed; Mar 1902 arrested and exiled to Siberia; 1905 fled to Geneva, where he joined Soc-Democrats (Mensheviks); after 1917 Oct Revol returned to Russia; admin, ed and publ work; arrested by State Security organs; *Died*: 1939 in imprisonment.

GOL'DSHTEYN, Dmitriy Yefimovich (1899-1967) Roentgenologist; Dr of Med; prof; Hon Sci Worker of Tatar ASSR from 1959; CP member from 1925; *Born*: 1899; *Educ*: 1924 grad med fac; *Career*: from 1929 asst prof, assoc prof, then full prof, Chair of Roentgenology and Radiology, Kazan' Inst of Postgrad Med Training; member, ed council, journal *Vestnik rentgenologii*; dep chm, Tatar Soc of Roentgenologists and Radiologists; Presidium member, Tatar Branch, *Znaniye* (Knowledge) Soc; bd member, All-Russian Soc of Roentgenologists and Radiologists; did research on various aspects of roentgenology and devised method of fistulography; wrote over 60 works on experimental and clinical studies of bone pathology, diseases of the digestive tract, contrast x-ray techniques, the biological effect of x-rays, the lymphatic system, etc; *Publ*: coauthor, *Voprosy kliniko-rentgenologicheskoy diagnostiki zakrytykh perelomov trubchatykh kostey* (The Clinical X–Ray Diagnosis of Closed Fractures of the Tubular Bones) (1960), etc; *Awards*: Order of the Red Banner of Labor; "Outstanding Health Worker" Badge; Hon Scroll of Presidium of Tatar Supr Sov; *Died*: 1967.

GOLENKIN, Fyodor Il'ich (1871-1936) Mil eng; *Born*: 1871; *Educ*: studied at 3rd Moscow Cadet School, Nikolayev Eng College and Nikolayev Eng Acad; *Career*: 1901-17 instructor, Nikolayev Eng Acad; specialized in field and permanent fortifications (especially armored installations); was first Sov commandant, Mil Eng Acad; during the Civil War helped fortify Petrograd and the Kronstadt fortress; simultaneously taught fortification theory at Mil Eng Acad; *Publ: Vliyaniye noveyshikh sredstv porazheniya na polevuyu fortifikatsiyu u nas i zagranitsey* (Effect of Modern Fire Weapons on Field Fortifications in Russia and Abroad) (1903); *Zametki po polevoy fortifikatsii* (Notes on Field Fortification) (2nd ed, 1907); *Bronevyye ustanovki. Sovremennoye ikh razvitye, ustroystvo i primeneniye v sukhoputnykh krepostyakh* (Armored Installations. Present Development, Structure and Use in Land Fortresses) (1910); coauthor, *Dolgovremennaya fortifikatsiya. Kurs Nikolayevskogo inzhenernogo uchilishcha* (Permanent Fortification. A Course for the Nikolayev Engineering College) (1912); coauthor, *Sovremennoye sostoyaniye dolgovremennoy i vremennoy fortifikatsii. Kurs Nikolayevskoy inzhenernoy akademii* (Present State of Permanent and Temporary Fortification. A Course for the Nikolayev Engineering Academy) (1913); *Podgotovka gosudarstva k oborone v inzhenerno-tekhnicheskom otnoshenii. Kurs srednego klassa Voyenno-inzhenernoy akademii* (Engineering and Technical Preparation of State Defenses. A Middle Class Course for the Military Engineering Academy) (1920); *Died*: 1936.

GOLIKOV, Aleksandr Grigor'yevich (1896-1937) Mil commander; lt, Russian Army; brigade commander from 1935; Civil War veteran; *Born*: 1896; *Educ*: early 1920's grad Red Army Mil Acad; *Career*: fought in WW 1; from June 1918 in Red Army; 1918-21 chief of artillery, 23rd Infantry Div; commanded 23rd and 7th Infantry Div; commanded shock troops, 12th Army; commander, 15th Cavalry Div; 1920 distinguished himself in Warsaw campaign and subsequent rear-guard battles; after Civil War cavalry inspector, Western Mil Distr; commander 7th Cavalry Div; directed Red Army Commanders' Advanced Cavalry Courses; head, Cavalry Dept, Frunze Mil Acad; Red Army asst inspector of cavalry; 1937 arrested by NKVD; *Awards*: two Orders of the Red Banner; *Died*: 1937 in imprisonment; posthumously rehabilitated.

GOLIKOV, Ivan Ivanovich (1887-1937) Painter of Palekhian miniatures; Hon Art Worker of RSFSR from 1933; *Born*: 6 Jan 1887; *Career*: his work was dominated by themes and images of the old and new vil life, folk-songs, tales and everyday subjects; based on the ancient Stroganov style he developed his own technique, noted for its expressive line, dynamics, brilliant and pure colors, subtle patterns and decorativeness; painted on various materials: canvas, wood, glass, china, parchment, metal, etc; helped create and develop the art of Palekhian miniature painting on papier-mache; *Works*: illustrations for the 1934 ed of *Slovo o polku Igoreve* (Lay of the Host of Igor) (1932-33); "The Ploughman" (1923); "Agricultural Work" (1925); "The Execution of Stenka Razin" (1926); "Song" (1926); "Ten Years Since the October Revolution" (1927); "The Reaper" (1927); "Third International" (1927); "Boar Hunt" (1928); "Demons" (1928); "Boris Godunov" (1932); "Romeo and Juliet" (1932); "Tale of Tsar Saltan" (1933); "Partisans" (1935-37), etc; *Died*: 31 Mar 1937.

GOLITSYN, Nikolay Dimitriyevich (1850-1925) Govt official; prince; last chm, Council of Min, Tsarist Govt (1916-17); *Born*: 1850; *Career*: from 1871 official, Min of Internal Affairs; 1885-1903 governor of Arkhangel'sk, Kaluga, then Tver'; from 1903 senator; from 1915 right-wing member, Council of State; simultaneously appointed chm, Commission for Aid to Russian Prisoners of War; 27 Dec 1916 appointed chm, Council of Min; after 1917 Feb Revol took no further part in polit life; *Died*: 1925.

GOLLERBACH, Erikh Fyodorovich (1895-1942) Lit and art historian; *Born*: 23 Mar 1895; *Publ*: 1915 first work published; books *V. V. Rozanov. Zhizn' i tvorchestvo* (V. V. Rozanov's Life and Work) (1922); *Aleksey N. Tolstoy* (1927); anthology *Tsarskoye selo v poezii* (Tsarskoye Selo in Poetry) (1922); *Obraz Akhmatovoy* (Akhmatova's Image) (1925); *Gorod muz* (City of Muses) (1927); *A. S. Pushkin v portretakh i illyustratsiyakh* (A. S. Pushkin in Portraits and Illustrations) (1937); *N. A. Nekrasov v portretakh i illyustratsiyakh* (N. A. Nekrasov in Portraits and Illustrations) (1938); coauthor, *M. Ye. Saltykov-Shchedrin v portretakh i illyustratsiyakh* (M. Ye. Saltykov-Shchedrin in Portraits and Illustrations) (1939); coauthor, *M. Yu. Lermontov v portretakh i illyustratsiyakh* (M. Yu. Lermontov in Portraits and Illustrations) (1941); books about painters: *Risunki M. Dobuzhinskogo* (The Drawings of M. Dobuzhinskiy) (1923), *Risunki i gravyury V. D. Zamiraylo* (The Drawings and Engravings of V. D. Zamiraylo) (1925), *Siluety Ye. I. Narbuta* (Ye. I. Narbut's Silhouettes) (1926), *Grafika M. A. Kirnarskogo* (The Drawings of M. A. Kirnarskiy) (1928), *Akvareli M. A. Voloshina* (The Water Colors of M. A. Voloshin) (1927); *Died*: 1942 killed during the blockade of Leningrad.

GOLODED, Nikolay Matveyevich (1894-1937) Bel; Party and govt official; chm, Bel Council of Pop Comr from 1927; CP member from 1918; *Born*: 1894 in vil Staroy Kryvets, now Gomel' Oblast, son of a peasant; *Educ*: from 1922 studied at Workers' Fac, Goretsk Inst of Agric; *Career*: from 1910 eng and electrician at Krivoy Rog Basin mines; from 1917 in the army; revol work among Southwestern Front units and later in 1917 Oct Revol; from 1918 Party and govt work in Novozybkov Uyezd; 1919 directed suppression of Starokopytov mutiny in Gomel'; 1921-22 chm, Exec Comt, Gorki Uyezd Sov; from 1922 studied and bd member, Goretsk Inst of Agric; 1924 member, Provisional Bel Bureau, CC, RCP(B) in Gomel'; subsequently member, CC, CP(B) Bel; 1925-27 second secr, CC, CP(B) Bel; from 1927 chm, Bel Council of Pop Comr; member, Bel Centr Exec Comt; Bureau and Secretariat member, CC, CP(B) Bel; cand member, CC, CPSU(B); arrested by State Security organs; *Awards*: Order of Lenin (1935); *Died*: 1937 in imprisonment; posthumously rehabilitated.

GOLODNYY, Mikhail (real name: EPSHTEYN, Mikhail Semyonovich) (1903-1949) Russian poet; CP member from 1939; *Born*: 24 Dec 1903 in Bakhtum (now Artyomovsk) of Jewish parents;

Educ: from 1923 studied at Moscow Workers' Fac, at Bryusov Higher Inst of Lit and Arts and later at 1st Moscow Univ; *Career*: at age 12 began work at a comb factory; 1920 first verse published in Yekaterinoslav journal *Yunyy proletariy*; from 1923, simultaneously with his studies, headed lit section, journal *Molodaya gvardiya*; 1919-28 Komsomol member; belonged to *Molodaya gvardiya* (Young Guards) lit assoc; specialized on events of Civil War; translated works of Polish, Ukr and Bel poets; *Works*: verse collections *Svai* (Piles) (1922); *Zemnoye* (Earthly Things) (1924); *Novyye stikhotvoreniya* (New Poems) (1928); *Stikhi i pesni* (Poems and Songs) (1930); in 1930's wrote ballads and songs, some of which were put to music: "Shchors Song," "Partisan Zheleznyak," "The Revolutionary Tribunal Judge," "Execution of a Communist in Berlin," "Wolves," etc; these works were published in collections: *Stikhi o grazhdanskoy voyne* (Verse on the Civil War) (1932); *Slovo pristrastnykh* (Word of the Biassed) (1934), etc; in 1942 he published *Pesni i ballady Otechestvennoy voyny* (Songs and Ballads of the Fatherland War) and *Stikhi ob Ukraine* (Poems of the Ukraine); *Matrosskaya legenda* (Seamen's Legend) (1944), etc; *Izbrannoye* (Selected Works) (1956); *Stikhotvoreniya Ballady. Pesni.* (Poems. Ballads. Songs.) (1959); *Died:* 20 Jan 1949 in Moscow.

GOLOSHCHYOKIN, Filipp Isayevich (pseudonym: Filipp FRAM) (1876-1941) Party and govt official; CP member from 1903; *Born*: 1876 in Nevel', Vitebsk Province, son of a contractor; *Career*: Party work in Petersburg, Kronstadt, Sestroretsk, Moscow and other towns; 1906 elected member, Petersburg RSDRP Comt; after dissolution of 1st State Duma arrested and sentenced to two years' imprisonment; released after one year but re-arrested on 1 May 1907; upon release worked as exec organizer and member, Petersburg RSDRP Exec Comt; 1909 attended *Proletariya* expanded ed bd meeting in Paris; upon return to Russia worked for Moscow RSDRP Comt; 1909 arrested and exiled to Narym Kray; 1910 fled from exile and conducted Party work in Moscow; at 6th (Prague) Conference elected member, CC, RSDRP; again worked in Moscow, was re-arrested and exiled to Tobol'sk Province; 1913 escaped from exile and worked in Petrograd, then in the Urals, where was re-arrested and exiled to Turukhan Kray, where he remained until 1917 Feb Revol; deleg at 7th (April) RSDRP(B) Conference and 6th RSDRP(B) Congress; after 1917 Oct Revol secr, Perm' and Yekaterinburg Province Party Comt; secr, Ural Oblast Party Comt and member, Siberian Bureau, CC, RSDRP(B); during Civil War mil comr, Ural Oblast; chief, Polit Dept, 3rd Army; member, Revol-Mil Council, Turkestani Army; at 7th RCP(B) Congress sided with mil opposition; 1922-25 chm, Samara Province Exec Comt and secr, Samara Province RCP(B) Comt; from Oct 1924 secr, Kray Comt, CP Kaz; at 12-14th Party Congresses elected cand member and at 15th and 16th Party Congresses elected member, CC, CPSU(B); from 1933 chief arbitrator, USSR Council of Pop Comr; arrested by State Security organs; *Publ: Partiynoye stroitel'stvo v Kazakhstane. Sbornik rechey i statey 1925-30* (Building the Party Apparatus in Kazakhstan. Collected Speeches and Articles, 1925-30) (1930); *Kazakhstan na putyakh sotsialisticheskogo pereustroystva. Sbornik statey i rechey* (Kazakhstan on the Path of Socialist Reconstruction. Collected Articles and Speeches) (1931); *Died*: 1941 in imprisonment; posthumously rehabilitated.

GOLOSOV, Il'ya Aleksandrovich (1883-1945) Architect; *Born*: 1883; *Educ*: 1906 grad Weaving and Metalworking Dept, Stroganov College; 1912 grad Architecture Dept, Moscow College of Painting, Sculpture and Architecture; *Career*: from 1918 helped with Moscow city planning; 1925 helped found Soc of Modern Architecture; over 60 of his designs received prizes in various competitions; most important among the numerous buildings constructed from his designs are: the Communal Workers' Club-House (1927-29); the apartment house on Pokrovskiy Boulevard (1936); a residential block in the housing area of the Stalin Automobile Plant (1937); Higher Trade-Union School Builing (1938); admin building on Pirogov Street (1939); several apartment houses at the Molotov Automobile Plant in Gorky; 1918-45 simultaneously taught architecture; from 1920 prof, Moscow Higher Art and Tech Workshops; *Publ: Moy tvorcheskiy put'* (My Career) (1933); *Died*: 1945.

GOLOSOV, Panteleymon Aleksandrovich (1882-1944) Architect; *Born*: 1882; *Educ*: 1905 grad Stroganov College as artist in metal; 1911 grad Architecture Dept, Moscow College of Painting, Sculpture and Architecture; *Career*: 1914 designed apartment house in Italian Renaissance style in Moscow's Ulanskiy Lane, and grandstand of Moscow Race course; from 1918 helped compile Moscow reconstruction plans with Moscow Planning Workshops, Moscow City Sov; together with I. Zholtovskiy designed cattle-breeding complex at 1923 All-Russian Agric Exhibition; 1929-35 designed the newspaper *Pravda* building and 1931-34 the Fertilizer Research Inst building on Sadovo-Kudrinskaya Street in Moscow; 1934 compiled gen city plan of Chirchik; compiled plans for reconstruction and development of various Moscow rayons (Frunze and Dorogomilov Embankments, part of Boulevard Ring); 1941 designed apartment-block on Dorogomilov Embankment, etc; 1918-44 teaching work; prof at a number of specialized higher educ institutions (Chair of Architectural Planning); *Publ*: coauthor, *Nashi pervyye raboty* (Our First Works) (1934); *Died*: 1944.

GOLOVACH, Platon Romanovich (1903-1937) Bel writer; member, Bel Writers' Union from 1934; CP member from 1922; *Born*: 18 Apr 1903 in vil Pobokovichi, now Bobruysk Rayon, Mogilev Oblast, son of a smallholder; *Educ*: 1926 grad Bel Communist Univ; *Career*: 1920-22 Komsomol work in Borisov; from 1922 at Minsk Party School; after grad instructor, Borisov Komsomol Comt; 1926-29 head, Org Dept, then first secr, CC, Bel Komsomol and ed, newspaper *Chyrvonaya z'mena*; helped run *Maladnyak* (Youth) lit assoc; from late 1928 head, Bel Assoc of Proletarian Writers; for some time ed, periodicals *Maladnyak* and *Polymya*; from 1934 exec secr, Bel Writers' Union; elected to exec organs, CC, CP(B) Bel and to Bel Centr Exec Comt; 1925 first work published; works deal with Bolshevik Revol and progress of soc reorganization; in the last years of his life worked on the novel "Road into the World" dealing with the "generation of the builders of socialism" and also collected material on 1863-64 Bel uprising; arrested by State Security organs; *Publ*: collected stories: "The Little Things of Life" (1927); "Lust for Life" (1930); "Stories" (1934); novelettes: "Scare in the Fields" (1930); "Guilty" (1930); "Bearers of Hate" (1936); "They Shall Not Pass" (1937); novel "Through the Years" (1935); "Collected Works" (3 vol, 1958); *Died*: 29 Oct 1937 in imprisonment; posthumously rehabilitated.

GOLOVANOV, Nikolay Semyonovich (1891-1953) Conductor, composer and pianist; Pop Artiste of USSR from 1948; *Born*: 21 Jan 1891 in Moscow; *Educ*: 1900-09 studied at Moscow Synodal College, from which he graduated as a choirmaster; 1909-14 studied composition under M.M. Ippolitov-Ivanov and S.N. Vasilenko at Moscow Conservatory; *Career*: conducted Synodal Choir and Choir of Russian Choral Soc; from 1915 choirmaster, 1918-28 and 1930-36 conductor, Bolshoy Theater; 1919 cofounder, Bolshoy Theater Opera Studio (later Stanislavsky Opera Theater); 1922-23 made concert tour of Western Europe as accompanist to his wife A.V. Nezhdanova; 1925-29 prof of opera and orchestration, Moscow Conservatory; 1926-28 opposed attempts to change the repertoire of the Bolshoy Theater to encompass themes on "socialist construction" but finally yielded to criticism and contributed to the development of Sov music, becoming one of the country's foremost conductors; from 1937 chief conductor, Bolshoy Symphony Orchestra, All-Union Radio Comt; from 1948 chief conductor, Bolshoy Theater; displayed particular brilliance in his treatment of works with a marked national epic character, notably those of Borodin, Rimsky-Korsakov and Moussorgsky; *Works*: over 200 romances; operas *Printsessa Yurata* (Princess Yurata) (1954) and *Bogatyrskiy kurgan* (The Hero's Tomb) basend on a theme by Ibsen; also composed symphonies and symphonic poems, and arranged folk-songs; *Awards*: Order of Lenin; Order of the Red Banner of Labor; four Stalin Prizes (1946, 1949, 1950 and 1951); medals; *Died*: 28 Aug 1953 in Moscow.

GOLOVATYY, Ferapont Petrovich (1890-1951) Kolkhoznik; co-initiator, movement to collect funds for Sov Army during WW 2; Hero of Socialist Labor from 1947; CP member from 1944; *Born*: 5 June 1890; *Career*: began work in Kiev, then moved to Krasnodar, where he worked on the railroad and at a brewery; during WW 1 in Russian Army; during Civil War served with Red Army; kolkhoznik, 1946-51 chm, *Stakhanovets* Kolkhoz, Saratov Oblast; dep, USSR Supr Sov of 1946 and 1950 convocations; member, Council for Kolkhoz Affairs, USSR Council of Min; Dec 1942 and May 1944 allegedly contributed 100,000 rubles (a total of 200,000 rubles) to Sov Army fund for the construction of warplanes; simultaneously urged all kolkhozniks in USSR to donate their savings for war needs; for this he was twice thanked in person by Stalin; however an ordinary kolkhoznik is in no position to save 200,000 rubles from his "earnings," and possession of such a sum would entail immediate criminal proceedings for embezzlement, speculation, etc; this indicates that his "donations" were fictitious and dreamed up by Sov authorities in order ot boost the "public movement for the collection of funds for the Sov Army and Navy"; *Died*: 25 July 1951.

GOLOVCHINER, Viktor Yakovlevich (1905-1961) Stage dir and playwright; Pop Artiste of Bel SSR from 1944; Pop Artiste of Lith SSR from 1959; CP member from 1944; *Born*: 28 June 1905; *Educ*: 1921 enrolled at, 1926 grad Bel Opera and Ballet Studio, Moscow; *Career*: 1926 stage debut at State Jewish Theater, Minsk; until 1928 actor, then stage dir; until 1949 performed in Bel; 1926-30, 1932-38 and 1942-46 at State Jewish Theater, Minsk; 1939-42 at Kupala Theater and at a workers' theater; also performed at State Russian Theater of Bel SSR; 1949-51 chief stage dir, Irkutsk Theater; 1951-53 at Mukimi Theater, Tashkent; 1953-54 at Gorky Russian Drama Theater, Tashkent; from 1955 chief stage dir, Russian Theater in Vilnius; from 1938 simultaneously taught at Bel Theater School, Tashkent Theater Inst and Vilnius Conservatory; *Works*: staged: Bezymenskiy's *Vystrel* (The Shot) (1930); Ben Johnson's *Volpone* (1934); Gorky's *Fal'shivaya moneta* (False Coin) (1937); Goldfaden's *Koldun'ya* (The Witch) (1941); in Vilnius staged Korneychuk's *Kryl'ya* (Wings) and *Varvary* (The Barbarians) (1955); Smirnov's *Krepost' nad Bugom* (Fortress on the Bug) (1956); Tsao-Yuy's *Typhoon* (1958); dramatization of Nikolayeva's novel *Bitva v puti* (Battle En Route) (1960); *Publ*: drama *Velikodushiye* (Generosity); play *Urok zhizni* (Life's Lesson) (1935, 1942); *Awards*: State Prize of Lith SSR (1960); *Died*: 15 July 1961.

GOLOVENCHENKO, F. M. (1899-1963) Lit historian; CP member from 1920; *Born*: 16 Feb 1899 in vil Letnitskoye, Stavropol' Province; *Educ*: 1932 grad Inst of Red Prof; *Career*: 1924 first work printed; lectured on 19th-Century Russian lit at higher educ establishments; specialized in realism, populism and Party commitment of lit and work of Russian revol democrats; *Publ*: *Slovo o polku Igoreve* (The Lay of the Host of Igor) (1955-63); *Velikiy russkiy revolyutsioner-demokrat N.G. Chernyshevskiy* (The Great Russian Revolutionary Democrat N.G. Chernyshevsiy) (1953); *Realizm Gogolya* (Gogol's Realism) (1953); *Istoriya russkoy literatury XIX veka* (The History of 19th-Century Russian Literature) (2 vol, 2nd ed, 1963-64); *Vvedeniye v literaturovedeniye* (An Introduction to Literary History) (1963); *Died*: 10 May 1963 in Moscow.

GOLOVIN, Nikolay Mikhaylovich (1889-1954) Educationist; corresp member, RSFSR Acad of Pedag Sci from 1944; Hon Schoolteacher of RSFSR from 1943; *Born*: 8 Aug 1889; *Educ*: 1907, as external student, passed elementary schoolteachers' examinations; *Career*: from 1908 taught at vil elementary school in Yaroslavl' Province; 1914-51 at Chebakovo school, Tutayevo Rayon, Yaroslavl' Oblast; then at Chebakovo Teachers' Training College; specialized in methods of teaching Russian, regional studies, etc; *Publ*: coauthor, *Krayevedeniye v shkole* (Regional Studies at School) (1935); coauthor, *Russkiy yazyk v nachal'noy shkole* (Russian at the Elementary School) (2nd ed, 1939); coauthor, *Razvitiye pis'mennoy rechi* (The Development of Written Speech) (1940); *Bukvar'* (An ABC Primer) (8th ed, 1944); *Zapiski uchitelya* (A Teacher's Notes) (1949); *Krayevedeniye v nachal'noy sel'skoy shkole* (Regional Studies in the Elementary Village School) (1949); *Krayevedeniye v nachal'noy shkole* (Regional Studies in the Elementary School) (1950); *Awards*: Order of Lenin; *Died*: 20 Nov 1954.

GOLOVIN, Sergey Selivanovich (1866-1931) Ophthalmologist; *Born*: 14 July 1866 in Bolkhov, Oryol Province; *Educ*: 1889 grad Med Fac, Moscow Univ; *Career*: from 1889 worked at Eye Clinic, Med Fac, Moscow Univ; 1895 defended doctor's thesis; 1903-11 founder and prof, Odessa Eye Clinic; 1911-18 chief physician, Moscow Eye Hospital; 1918-31 prof, Chair of Ophthalmology, Moscow Univ; devised simple and bone orbitotomy, orbito-sinus operation, ossioplastic opening of the frontal sinuses, fixation of a displaced tear gland, plastic surgery of the conjunctival sac, etc; invented retrobulbar diaphanoscopy and method of localizing foreign bodies in the eye; designed an ophthalmoscope without a centr opening; proposed theory of genesis of cataracts and development of sympatitis; wrote some 100 works; *Publ*: *Oftal'motonometricheskiye issledovaniya* (Ophthalmotonometric Studies) (1895); *Operativnoye lecheniye pul'siruyushchego pucheglaziya* (The Operative Treatment of Pulsating Exophthalmus) (1900); *Neuectomia opticociliaris pri absolyutnoy glaukome* (Neuectomia opticociliaris with Absolute Glaucoma) (1900); *Opukhol' zritel'nogo nerva i ikh operativnoye lecheniye* (Tumors of the Optic Nerve and Their Surgical Treatment) (1904); *O slepote v Rossii* (Blindness in Russia) (1910); *Vospalitel'nyye intradural'nyye opukholi zritel'nogo nerva i ikh operativnoye lecheniye* (Inflammatory Intradural Tumors of the Optic Nerve and Their Surgical Treatment) (1914); *Klinicheskaya oftal'mologiya* (Clinical Ophthalmology) (1923); *Issledovaniya nad subvital'nymi protsessami v izolirovannom glazu* (Research on Subvital Processes in the Isolated Eye) (1927); *Died*: 28 Apr 1931.

GOLOVKO, Arseniy Grigor'yevich (1906-1962) Naval commander; admiral; CP member from 1927; *Born*: 23 June 1906 in Prokhladnyy, now Kabardo-Balkar ASSR, son of an office worker; *Educ*: 1928 grad Frunze Naval College, Leningrad; 1931 grad special command staff courses; 1938 grad Voroshilov Naval Acad, Leningrad; *Career*: from 1925 in Sov Navy; 1928-33 commander of a torpedo boat, then commander of a torpedo-boat squadron, Pacific Fleet; 1933-36 chief of staff and commander of a torpedo-boat flotilla, Pacific Fleet; 1938-40 commander of a destroyer squadron and chief of staff, Northern Fleet; then commander, Caspian and later, Amur Flotilla; 1940-46 commander, Northern Fleet, in which capacity he provided escorts for British and American convoys delivering vital war matériel to USSR; 1946-47 dep chief, 1947-50 chief of Main Staff, Sov Navy; 1950-52 Chief of Naval Gen Staff and First Dep Min of the Navy; 1952-56 commander, 4th Fleet in the Baltic; 1956 commander, Baltic Fleet; 1956-62 First Dep Commander in Chief, Sov Navy; 1960 criticized for his memoirs *Vmeste s Flotom* (With the Navy); dep, USSR Supr Sov of 1946, 1950, and 1954 convocations; dep, RSFSR Supr Sov of 1959 convocation; voting deleg, 20th, 21st and 22nd CPSU congresses; *Awards*: four Orders of Lenin; three Orders of the Red Banner; Suvorov Order; Ushakov Order; other orders and medals; *Died*: 17 May 1962.

GOL'ST, Leopol'd Leopol'dovich (1888-1939) Roentgenologist; *Born*: 1888; *Educ*: 1911 grad Med Fac, Freiburg Univ; 1911 also passed state examinations in Kazan'; *Career*: 1913 specialized in roentgenology under Rieder in Munich; 1919-24 head, X-Ray Dept, 1st Communist Hospital; from 1932 head, Chair of Roentgenology, Moscow's Centr Inst of Postgrad Med Training; specialized in x-ray diagnosis of cardiovascular diseases, pneumoconiosis, vocational diseases, roentgenological picture of spondylites after typhus and x-ray therapy of bronchial asthma, wound surfaces, pneumonia, etc; coauthor and ed, monograph on pneumoconiosis, a summary of the x-ray diagnosis of heart and lung diseases, a manual of x-ray technique and a textbook on x-ray diagnosis; co-founder, Moscow Soc of Roentgenologists and Radiologists; organized All-Russian congresses and conferences on roentgenology; wrote some 50 works; *Publ*: coauthor, *Osnovy rentgenodiagnostiki zabolevaniy serdtsa i lyogkikh* (The Principles of the X-Ray Diagnosis of Heart and Lung Diseases) (1939); coauthor, *Rukovodstvo po rentgenodiagnostike* (A Manual on X-Ray Diagnosis) (1940); *Died*: 1939.

GOL'TS, Georgiy Pavlovich (1893-1946) Architect and teacher; member, USSR Acad of Architecture; *Born*: 6 Mar 1893; *Educ*: studied at Moscow School of Painting, Sculpture and Architecture; 1922 grad Higher Art Workshops, Moscow; *Career*: for several years collaborated with I.V. Zholtovskiy and A.V. Shchusev; 1924-25 studied architecture in Italy; 1927 helped design factory building at Ivanteyevka and State Bank building in Ivanovo; 1930-36 helped design *Vsekokhudozhnik* art supplies factory in Moscow; directed architectural planning workshop engaged in replanning Moscow; redesigned numerous Moscow districts, embankments and apartment houses; 1937 designed Ustinskiy Bridge over Moscow River; 1940 designed lock on River Yauza; designed apartment house on Bol'shaya Kaluzhskaya Street, Moscow; in 1940's did designs for redevelopment of Smolensk, Vladimir and other cities; 1934-46 dir of postgrad studies, USSR Acad of Architecture; from 1924 also designed theater sets and costumes, including sets for Sophocles' "Electra" at the Vakhtangov Theater (1946); *Awards*: Badge of Hon; medals; Stalin Prize (1941); *Died*: 27 May 1946.

GOL'TSEV, Viktor Viktorovich (1901-1955) Russian lit critic; CP member from 1940; *Born*: 28 July 1901 in Moscow; *Educ*: until 1923 studied at Bryusov Higher Lit and Art Inst; *Career*: 1923 first work printed; 1949-55 chief ed, almanach (then journal) *Druzhba narodov*; wrote on work of Blok, Tikhonov, Pavlenko and lit of peoples of the USSR, particularly Geo lit; edited and prefaced some 80 books on non-Russian Sov writers;

Publ: G. Leonidze. Kritiko-biograficheskiy ocherk (G. Leonidze. A Critical and Biographical Study) (1955); *Literaturno-kriticheskiye stat'i* (Literary Criticism Articles) (1957); *Stat'i i ocherki* (Articles and Essays) (1958); *Died*: 9 May 1955 in Moscow.

GOL'TSMAN, Abram Zinov'yevich (1894-1933) Govt official; CP member from 1917; *Born*: 1894, son of a loader; *Educ*: completed secondary tech educ; *Career*: worker; 1910 joined revol movement; 1911 sentenced to one year's fortress detention for his connection with Odessa RSDRP org; 1913 exiled to Narym; fled from exile; early 1917 re-arrested; after 1917 Revol trade-union and admin posts; 1917-20 member, CC, Metal Workers' Union; 1920-21 Presidium member, All-Union Centr Trade-Union Council and head of its Tariff Dept; during trade-union debate sided with Trotsky; from 1922 head, Main Electr Eng Ind Bd, Supr Sovnarkhoz; group head, Centr Control Commission, Workers and Peasants' Inspection; assoc chm, Main Civil Aviation Bd; at 14th Party Congress elected member, CC, RCP(B); specialized in org of labor and production; *Publ: Regulirovaniye i naturalizatsiya zarabotnoy platy* (Wage Regulation and Payment in Kind) (1918); *Organizatsiya truda v SSSR* (Labor Organization in the USSR) (1925); *Reorganizatsiya cheloveka* (The Reorganization of Man) (1925); *Rezhim ekonomii i stroitel'stvo sotsializma* (The Policy of Economy in Building Socialism) (1926); *Died*: 1933.

GOLUBENKO, Nikolay Vasil'yevich (1898-1937) Mil commander; Party official; CP member from 1914; *Born*: 1898 in Ukr; *Career*: until 1917 metalworker in Kiev; from 1918 in Red Army; 1918 member, Revol Mil Council, 3rd Ukr Army; chm, underground Odessa Insurgent Comt; 1919-20 comr, 45th Infantry Div; 1920-21 polit work in Ukr and Crimean armed forces; fought against Petlyura, French interventionists, Denikin's forces and Pilsudski's troops; from 1921 Party and govt work; 1923-24 sympathized with Trotskyist opposition; 1936 arrested by NKVD; *Awards*: Order of the Red Banner; *Died*: 1937 in imprisonment; posthumously rehabilitated.

GOLUBEV, Aleksandr Vasil'yevich (1899-1968) Mil commander and historian; col; CP member from 1917; *Born*: 10 Nov 1899 in Novoloki, now Ivanovo Oblast; son of a worker who took an active part in the 1905 Revol; *Educ*: 1928 grad Frunze Mil Acad; *Career*: until 1917 worked at a cotton mill in Novoloki; from Sept 1917 in Red Guard; early 1918 instructor, Ivanovo-Voznesensk Province Sovnarkhoz and ed of an uyezd newspaper published in Kineshma; from May 1918 in Red Army; 1918-21 instructor, Polit Dept, Troop Mustering Bd, Eastern Front; comr of an artillery battery; brigade comr, 1st Caucasian Cavalry Div; 1921-25 brigade comr, 2nd Cavalry Div; head, Polit Dept, 9th Don Rifle Div and 3rd Independent Cavalry Brigade, 11th Cavalry Div; 1928-29 commanded a rifle battalion and a combined mechanized group in Moscow Mil Distr; 1929-36 adjunct, senior instructor, then head, Fac of Mil History, Frunze Mil Acad; 1936-42 senior instructor, then head, Chair of Operations, Gen Staff Acad; 1942-43 worked for Gen Staff evaluating experience of war with Germany and revision of Field Regulations in the light of this experience; from 1954 in reserve, then retired; wrote books and articles on mil history, notably on the Russian and Spanish Civil Wars and on the war with Germany; 1943-63 writing career interrupted, probably because of imprisonment; *Publ: Vrangelevskiye desanty na Kubani. Avgust-sentyabr' 1920 goda* (Wrangel's Kuban' Landing Operations. August-September 1920) (1921); *Grazhdanskaya voyna 1918-20 godov* (The 1918-20 Civil War) (1932); *Voprosy frontovoy i armeyskoy operatsii* (Problems of Front and Army-Scale Operations) (1940); *M. V. Frunze o kharaktere budushchey voyny* (M. V. Frunze on the Future Nature of Warfare) (1931); *Died*: 26 Apr 1968.

GOLUBEV, Ivan Mikhaylovich (1875-1938) Govt official; CP member from 1900; *Born*: 1875; *Career*: from the age of 14 worked at a leather factory in Torzhok; 1896 worked at Maxwell Factory, Petersburg; early 1900 joined RSDRP; 1901, while working at a foundry, joined with a group of workers who went to help strikers at the Obukhov Arsenal; June 1901 arrested and exiled to Tver' Province; May 1903 organized a three-week strike of textile workers in Vyshniy-Volochok; arrested together with other members of strike comt; 22 Feb 1904 took part in a demonstration in Tver' and was again arrested; after seven months' imprisonment resettled in Baku where joined Baku Rayon Party Comt; active in Nov 1904 Baku strike; founded militant org, but Jan 1905 arrested, together with 14 soldiers; acquitted and moved to Moscow; worked as Party organizer in Rogozhsk Rayon and took part in 1905 uprising; from spring 1909 member, Moscow RSDRP Comt and member of its Exec Commission; 13 Dec 1909 arrested while attending a session of Moscow RSDRP Comt and exiled to Vologda Province; 1914 returned to Moscow, helped to rebuild Moscow RSDRP org, set up agency for illegal newspaper *Pravda*; during 1917 Feb Revol elected member, Moscow Sov and member, Exec Comt of 1st convocation; during 1917 Oct Revol comr, Bauman (then Basmannyy) Rayon Mil-Revol Comt; then chm, Bauman Rayon Sov; from Aug 1918 plen of Pop Comrt of Food for grain procurement in Oryol Province; Feb 1919-21 Collegium member, RSFSR Pop Comrt of Agric; also chm, All-Russian Workers' Comt for the Promotion of Agric, RSFSR Pop Comrt of Agric; later worked for: All-Union Centr Trade-Union Council; Main Electr Eng Ind Bd; Pop Comrt of Workers and Peasants' Inspection; 1924-30 member, RSFSR Supr Court; arrested by State Security organs; *Died*: 1938 in imprisonment.

GOLUBEV, Viktor Maksimovich (1916-1945) Fighter-pilot; maj, Sov Air Force; CP member from 1942; *Born*: 17 Jan 1916 in Petrograd; *Career*: 1941-45 commanded flight, then squadron; navigator, Air Force regt on Sov-German fronts; *Awards*: twice Hero of Sov Union (1942 and 1943); Order of Lenin; other orders and medals; *Died*: 17 May 1945.

GOLUBEV, Vladimir Vasil'yevich (1884-1954) Mathematician; specialist in mech; corresp member, USSR Acad of Sci from 1934; Hon Sci and Tech Worker of RSFSR from 1943; *Born*: 3 Dec 1884; *Educ*: 1908 grad Moscow Univ; *Career*: from 1917 prof, Saratov Univ; from 1930 sen eng, Centr Aerodynamics Inst and prof, Moscow Univ; from 1932 head, Chair of Higher Mathematics, Zhukovskiy Air Force Eng Acad; spezialized in aeromech and the theory of the function of a complex variable; further developed S. A. Chaplygin's work on aerodynamics; devised method of calculating airfoils of finite span, the theory of wings of minor elongation and the theory of the laminar boundary layer; did major research on the theory of mechanized wings, fully explaining the functions of fore and aft flaps and devising methods of calculating the lift of mechanized wings; devised theory of flapping wings; in pure mathematics worked on the development of the theory of analytical functions and the analytical theory of differential equations; also wrote books on the history of Russian sci; *Publ: Odnoznachnyye analiticheskiye funktsii s sovershennym mnozhestvom osobykh tochek* (Univalent Analytical Functions with an Absolute Set of Singular Points) (1916); *Lektsii po analiticheskoy teorii differentsial'nykh uravneniy* (Lectures on the Analytical Theory of Differential Equations) (2nd ed, 1950); *Lektsii po teorii kryla* (Lectures on Airfoil Theory) (1949); *Awards*: four orders and medals; *Died*: 4 Dec 1954.

GOLUBEVA-YASNEVA, Mariya Petrovna (1861-1936) Govt official; CP member from 1901; *Born*: 1861; *Career*: worked as vil teacher and engaged in populist propaganda; in 1880's member, populist revol group; 1891 exiled to Samara, where she met Lenin; in Saratov distributed newspaper *Iskra*; 1903-Nov 04 secr, Saratov RSDRP Comt; from late 1904 in Petersburg; member, org comt to convene 3rd Party Congress; Oct 1905 her flat was used for Petersburg Party Comt meetings; early 1906 it was used as secret address by Lenin; 1907 organized illegal Bolshevik printing house in Petersburg; after 1917 Oct Revol worked for Centr Council of Factory Comts, for Pop Comrt of Justice and for Petrograd Cheka; 1920-28 with CC, CPSU(B); from 1928 pensioner; *Died*: 10 May 1936.

GOLUBINSKIY (real name: TROSTYANSKIY), Dmitriy Mikhaylovich (1880-1958) Actor; Pop Artiste of Ukr SSR from 1947; *Born*: 29 Nov 1880 in vil Golubinskaya, Don Oblast; *Career*: 1905 stage debut with Astrakhan' theater; acted at theaters in Yelizavetgrad, Rostov, Samara and Leningrad; 1928-31 at Dnepropetrovsk theater; 1931-33 at Kiev theater; 1933-54 with Sov Army Theater in Kiev, Odessa and L'vov; also did film work; *Roles*: Lopakhin in Chekhov's *Vishnyovyy sad* (The Cherry Orchard); Bessemenov in Gorky's *Meshchane* (The Philistines); Gloster in Shakespeare's "King Lear"; Peshek in Buryakovskiy's *Praga ostayotsya moyey* (Prague Remains Mine); Kostyukovich in Movzon's *Konstantin Zaslonov; Awards*: Stalin Prize (1952); *Died*: 29 Jan 1958.

GOLUBKINA, Anna Semyonovna (1864-1927) Sculptress; *Born*: 28 Jan 1864 in Ryazan' Province; *Educ*: 1889-90 studied at private art school in Moscow; 1891-93 studied at Moscow College of Painting, Sculpture and Architecture; 1894 studied at Petersburg

Acad of Arts; *Career*: in 1890's made two study trips to Paris; 1902 visited Paris again and studied under Rodin; after return to Russia sentenced to one year imprisonment for revol activities; 1913-16 taught at Prechistenskiy Workers' Courses, Moscow; 1916 gave up monumental sculpture for health reasons and specialized in busts, relief landscapes and fable themes; also taught at Free Art Studios and Higher Art Studios; 1914 and 1944 had exhibitions in Moscow; her best works are in the Tret'yakov Gallery in Moscow and the Russian Museum in Leningrad; *Works*: "The Toiler" (1900); "Walking Man" (1903); bust of Marx (1905); " Old Izergil'" (1904); "Sanchetta" (1905); bust of A. N. Tolstoy (1911); bust of V. G. Chertkov (1926), etc; *Publ: Nes-kol'ko slov o remesle skul'ptora* (A Few Words about the Sculptor's Craft) (1923); *Died*: 7 Sept 1927.

GOLUBKOV, Aleksandr Pavlovich (1880-1945) Health service official; CP member from 1903; *Born*: 13 June 1880 in Moscow, son of a bookkeeper; *Educ*: 1903 grad Med Fac, Moscow Univ; *Career*: 1900 joined revol Marxist org; 1901 arrested for involvement in student revol movement; 1903 joined RSDRP Bolshevik faction; after grad physician, Smolensk Province Rural Hospital; at same time assoc, from 1904 head, local tech bureau, Russian Section, CC, RSDRP; Dec 1904-spring 1905 in prison; after release subject to travel restrictions; from 1905 member, Moscow RSDRP Comt; co-founder and ed, Bolshevik newspaper *Vperyod*; 1906 arrested again; 1907 went abroad but returned to Russia six months later, where be became acting secr, Petersburg "Group of Five" commissioned by the CC, RSDRP to conduct revol work in Russia; Dec 1908 attended All-Russian RSDRP Conference in Paris; 1909 arrested again; 2 Oct 1910 exiled to Minusinsk, Eastern Siberia, where he opened a med practice and printed and distributed Bolshevik propaganda; after 1917 Feb Revol returned to Moscow; as member, All-Russian Rural League helped to organize health service; deleg, 1st Congress of Soviets, Petrograd; from Oct 1917 member, Moskvorech'ye Revol Comt; after Oct Revol for a while Comr of Health, Moscow Province; member, Council of Doctors' Collegia; campaigned against the Pirogov Memorial Soc of Russian Physicians on the pages of the journal *Izvestiya sovetskoy meditsiny*; from July 1918 Collegium member, RSFSR Comrt of Health; dep chm, Russian Red Cross Soc; 1930-36 co-ed, *Bol'shaya metitsinskaya entsiklopediya* (Large Medical Encyclopedia) (1st ed); bd chm, State Med Publ House; *Publ:* memoirs *Na dva fronta* (To Two Fronts) (1933); *Died:* 1945.

GOLUBKOVA, Marem'yana Romanovna (1893-1959) Russian narrator; member, USSR Writers' Union from 1943; CP member from 1943; *Born*: 1 Mar 1893 in vil Golubkovo, Nizhnepechersk Rayon, Arkhangel'sk Province, daughter of a peasant; *Career*: from childhood worked on farm, later kolkhoz work; cherished traditions of folklore: from her narrations were recorded over 400 songs, numerous lamentations, proverbs and riddles; her outstanding talent for improvisation found its expression in lamentations; her tales of past and present life deal with peasants and fishermen of Pechora Region; to the events of WW 2 responded with songs: "A Curse on Hitler"; "Let Drop a Mother's Words"; "He Gave His Life Without Regret"; *Publ*: together with the writer and folklorist N. P. Leont'yev wrote the books: *Dva veka v pol veka* (Two Lives in Half a Century) (1946); *Olen'i kraya* (Reindeer Country) (1947); *Mat' -Pechora* (Mother Pechora) (1950); novel *Marishka* (1960); *Died*: 8 Sept 1959 in Moscow.

GOLUBOK, Vladislav Iosifovich (1882-1937) Bel writer and playwright; Pop Artiste of Bel SSR from 1930; *Born*: 15 May 1882 near Baranovichi, son of a railroad worker; *Educ*: grad Minsk city college; *Career*: until 1919 railroad worker; simultaneously active in Bel Drama and Comedy Soc, founded in Minsk; 1919-25 with Western Railroad Bd and Bel Pop Comrt of Educ; 1920 founded drama soc; 1926-32 head, Bel Mobile Theater; 1932-37 manager, 3rd Bel Drama Theater in Gomel'; during his theater career worked as manager, playwright, set designer, actor and stage dir; 1908 first work printed in newspaper *Nasha niva*; 1937 arrested by State Security organs; *Publ*: collected stories "Stories" (1913); over 40 plays: "The Scribe's Name-Day," "Trial," "Last Encounter," "Madonna of Pinsk," "The Frivolous," "Raftsmen," "Ganka," "Innocent Girl," "Lechery," "Landowner Surynta," "A Visitor from the Penitentiary," "Grugany," etc; *Awards:* Scroll of Hon of Bel Centr Exec Comt; private car and assignments to Moscow and Leningrad (1935); *Died*: 1937 in imprisonment; posthumously rehabilitated.

GOLUBOV, Sergey Nikolayevich (1894-1962) Russian writer; *Born*: 20 June 1894 in Saratov, son of an office worker; *Educ*: grad Law Fac, Moscow Univ; *Career*: during Civil War served as commander with Red Army on Eastern Front, in Caucasus and Kuban'; 1933 first work printed; wrote on Russian mil historical themes; also wrote several biographies of V. I. Bazhenov (1937), I. I. Polzunov (1937), A. A. Bestuzhev-Marlinskiy (1938) and the Bulgarian revolutionary-poet Khristo Botev; (1958); *Publ:* novels: *Soldatskaya slava* (Soldier's Glory) (1939); *Iz iskry - plamya* (From the Spark a Flame) (1940); "Bagration" (1943); *Sotvoreniye veka* (The Making of an Age) (1947); *Kogda kreposti ne sdayutsya* (When Forts Refuse to Yield) (1953); *Izbrannyye proizvedeniya* (Selected Works) (2 vol, 1958); *Died*: 8 Feb 1962 in Moscow.

GOLUBOVICH, Vsevolod Aleksandrovich (1885-?) Ukr revolutionary; member, CC, Ukr Socialist-Revol Party; *Born:* 1885; *Career:* worked as a civil eng; 1903 began polit career by joining the "Revol Ukr Party"; 1912 joined Kiev group, Ukr Socialist-Revol Party; from Mar 1917 chm, Odessa Comt, Ukr Socialist-Revol Party; Ukr socialist-revol dep from Kherson Province, All-Russian Constituent Assembly; July 1917, after agreement between the Provisional Govt and the Ukr Centr Rada, Secr-Gen of Communications, then Secr-Gen of Trade and Ind, Gen Secretariat (govt) of the Autonomous Ukr; 1918 head, Ukr Centr Rada deleg, Brest-Litovsk peace talks; Dec 1917-May 1918 chm, Centr Rada Council of Min, which replaced the Gen Secretariat; 1918 ed, anti-Bolshevik newspapers *Trudova respublika, Trudova hromada*, etc; 1920, as chm, CC, Ukr Socialist-Revol Party, signed draft constitution of Ukr Pop Republ; Aug 1920 arrested in Kamenets-Podol'sk by Special Dept, 14th Army; 1921 tried with other Ukr Socialist-Revolutionaries and sentenced to five years in a concentration camp; late 1921 amnestied by the All-Ukr Centr Exec Comt; after release worked as civil eng for Ukr Sovnarkhoz; *Died*: date and place of death unknown.

GOLUBTSOV, Ivan Aleksandrovich (1887–1966) Historian; Dr of Historical Sci from 1963; senior assoc, Inst of History, USSR Acad of Sci from 1945; member, USSR Geographical Soc from 1950; *Born*: 1887, son of archeologist Prof A. P. Golubtsov; *Educ*: 1910 grad Moscow Univ; *Career*: 1910-30 lectured at Moscow Higher Women Courses, Moscow Univ and Archives Courses; simultaneously and later worked for Main Records Office, Min of For Affairs, Red Army Centr Archives and Moscow Records Office of Nat Econ, Culture and Way of Life, etc; 1930-59 compiled geographical handbooks, historical charts and atlases which became widely known; specialist in source research, historical geography and cartography, archeography and archives mang; compiled *Akty sotsial'no-ekonomicheskoy istorii Severo-Vostochnoy Rusi* (Records of Social and Economic History of Northeastern Russia) (3 vol, 1952-64); studied and annotated historical documents included in this collection; *Died*: 4 Nov 1966.

GOLUBYATNIKOV, Dmitriy Vasil'yevich (1866-1933) Geologist; oil deposits specialist; *Born*: 7 Nov 1866; *Educ*: grad Petersburg Mining Inst; *Career*: while still a high-school student joined *Narodnaya volya* (People's Will) Party, formed student group and conducted propaganda among workers and poor Don Cossacks; 1883 arrested; 1886 joined Aleksandr Ul'yanov's student terrorist group; 1887 exiled; 1900 entered Petersburg Mining Inst; after grad worked for Geological Comt; 1922-25 prof, Moscow Mining Acad; from 1903 made surveys of Baku oil deposits; devised method of compiling structural maps of oil deposits; 1909 after years of prospecting, established that the Bibi-Eybat oil deposit extends under the sea-bed; 1908 detected vast oil reserves at the Surakhan deposit, which was formerly thought to contain only gas; proved the presence of oil at the Puta and Kara-Chukhur deposits and pioneered their ind exploitation; wrote a monograph proving the existence of a large oil deposit on Svyatoy Ostrov (Artyom Island); also discovered an oil deposit to the east of Surakhanov; correctly predicted that the Mardakyany region was petroliferous; advocated study of the hydrogeology of oil deposits; proposed the use of electr methods of studying wells (carottage) and organized their large-scale application; *Publ: Surakhanskaya gazonosnaya i neftenosnaya ploshchad'* (The Surakhan Gas and Oil-Bearing Area) (1908); *Svyatoy ostrov* (Artyom Island) (1908), etc; *Died*: 2 Jan 1933.

GOLUNSKIY, Sergey Aleksandrovich (1895-1962) Diplomat; Dr of Law; prof, Moscow Univ from 1954; corresp member, USSR Acad of Sci; Amb Extraordinary and Plen, 1st Class from 1948; CP member from 1941; *Born*: 4 July 1895 in Moscow; *Educ*: 1917 grad Law Fac, Moscow Univ; 1917-19 postgrad studies, Moscow Univ; *Career*: 1923-39 worked for Public Porsecutor's office;

1939-43 section head, Inst of Law, USSR Acad of Sci; simultaneously head of a chair, Mil Law Acad; 1943-45 consulting expert, Treaty Law Dept, USSR Pop Comrt of For Affairs; 1945-51 head, Treaty Law Dept and collegium member, USSR Min of For Affairs; 1946-53 prof, Chair of Law, Acad of Soc Sci CC, CPSU; 1954-58 dir, All-Union Criminology Research Inst; from 1958 section head, Inst of State and Law, USSR Acad of Sci; simultaneously chief ed, journal *Sovetskoye gosudarstvo i pravo*; 1952-53 member, UN Int Court of Justice; attended numerous int conferences and congresses; 1943 advisor, Moscow Four-Power Conference attended by US, USSR, UK and China; 1944 advisor, Sov deleg Dumbarton Oaks Conference at which the US, USSR and UK agreed on proposals for the foundation of the UN; 1945 attended UN Conference on Int Organization, San Francisco; 1945 also attended Yalta and Potsdam Conferences; 1946-48 chief Sov prosecutor, Tokyo war crimes trials; 1954 advisor, Berlin Conference of for min of US, USSR, UK and France; 1956-58 member, from 1958 vice-pres, Sov Assoc for Cooperation with the UN; *Publ: Uchebnik po sudoustroystvu* (A Textbook on the Judicial System (1939); *Kriminalistika* (Criminology) (1939); *Sudoustroystvo SSSR* (The Soviet Judicial System) (1946); *Novyye osnovy ugolovnogo sudoproizvodstva SSSR i soyuznykh respublik* (New Principles of Criminal Legal Procedure in the USSR and Union Republics) (1958); *Politicheskaya organizatsiya obshchestva v period razvyornutogo stroitel'stva kommunizma* (The Political Organization of Society in the Period of the Extended Building of Communism), etc; *Died*: 29 Nov 1962.

GOLUZIN, Gennadiy Mikhaylovich (1906-1952) Mathematician; Dr of Physics and Mathematics from 1936; prof from 1938; *Born*: 24 Jan 1906 in Torzhok; *Educ*: 1929 grad Leningrad Univ; *Career*: 1929-52 worked at Leningrad Univ on theory of analytical functions; developed theory of single-sheet functions; *Publ: Vnutrenniye zadachi odnolistnykh funktsiy* (Internal Tasks of Single-Sheet Functions) (1939); *Otsenki dlya analiticheskikh funktsiy s ogranichennym srednim modulem* (Criteria for Evaluating Analytical Functions with Limited Mean Modulus) (1946); *O teoremakh iskazheniya i koeffitsientnykh odnolistnykh funktsiy* (Distortion Theorems and Coefficient Single-Sheet Functions) (1946); *Metod variatsiy v konformnom otobrazhenii* (The Variation Method in Conformal Mapping) (1946-47); *Nekotoryye voprosy teorii odnolistnykh funktsiy* (Some Aspects of the Theory of Single-Sheet Functions) (1949), etc; *Awards*: Stalin Prize (1948); *Died*: 17 Jan 1952.

GOLYAKOV, Ivan Terent'yevich (1888-1961) Lawyer; prof from 1940; dep dir, All-Union Inst of Law 1956-59; CP member from 1918; *Born*: 1888 in vil Peshkovo, Moscow Province; *Educ*: 1925 grad Law Fac, Rostov Univ; *Career*: 1910-17 soldier in Russian army; 1917-19 member, regt and army comts; later secr, member and chm, volost comt; 1919-20 in Red Army; instructor, Polit Dept, 9th Army on Southeastern Front; polit comr, infantry regt, 23rd Div; chm, Revol-Mil Tribunal, 14th Infantry Div; 1920-33 with Red Army mil tribunals; 1933-36 member, Mil Collegium, USSR Supr Court; 1936-38 holding the rank of divisional mil lawyer, court reserve member, Mil Collegium, USSR Supr Court at show trial of "Trotsky and Zinov'yevite terrorist center"; 1938-49 chm, USSR Supr Court; headed show trial of the "joint Trotsky and Zinov'yevite terrorist center" (L. Kamenev, I. Smirnov, G. Yevdokimov, etc); 1938-58 prof, Law Fac, Moscow State Univ; Moscow Inst of Law and other higher educ institutions; 1938-56 dir, All-Union Inst of Law and chm, Experts' Commission on Law, Higher Certifying Commission and member, plenum of this commission; 1936-38 assisted in Red Army purge; 1941-45 headed work of mil tribunals and rear area mil courts in the compaign against mil and labor deserters; 1947-58 member, ed bd, periodicals *Sovetskoye gosudarstvo i pravo* and *Sotsialisticheskaya zakonnost'*; dep, and chm, Draft Bills Commission, RSFSR Supr Sov of 1938 convocation; dep, USSR Supr Sov of 1946 convocation and member, Ed Commission for Amendments and Additions to USSR Constitution; also helped to codify various branches of Sov legislation, including drafting new Criminal Code of RSFSR; wrote numerous articles on criminal law, judicial system, state law, org of higher legal training, etc; *Publ: Sud i zakonnost'v khudozhestvennoy literature* (The Court and Legality in Fiction) (1958), etc; *Awards*: two Orders of Lenin; Order of the Red Banner; Order of the Red Banner of Labor; *Died*: 1961.

GOMARTELI, Ivan Gedevanovich (1875-1938) Physician; member, RSDRP (Mensheviks) from 1889; *Born*: 1975; *Educ*: 1889 grad Med Fac, Moscow Univ; *Career*: 1906 elected Kutaisi Province deleg, 1st State Duma; after the dissolution of the Duma, senteced to three months' imprisonment for signing Vyborg Proclamation; after serving the term took no active part in Soc-Democratic movement; 1913 left Menshevik org because of differences on the nationalities problem: defended territorial autonomy of Geo; after 1917 Oct Revol worked for Geo Democratic Govt; 1919 cand member, Tiflis City Duma; from 1921, after Sovietization of Geo, left Mensheviks and cooperated with Sov regime; worked as physician and writer (publicist, fiction writer, playwright); arrested by State Security organs; *Died*: 1938 in imprisonment.

GONCHAR, Ivan Tarasovich (1888-1944) Ukr ceramic artist; *Born*: 1888 in vil Krishentsi, now Vinnitsa Oblast, son of a potter; *Career*: from 1905 master ceramic artist; his best works include satirical and humorous ceramic sculptures and other ceramic products depicting, folk fable and fairy-tale scenes; also made ceramic toys; *Works*: "One with Smallfry, Seven with Spoons) (1910); "Animal Musicians" (1935); "How the Mice Belled the Cat) (1936); "Budyonny's Men"; Kolkhoz Dancers"; "Kolkhoz Orchestra," etc; *Died*: 1944.

GONCHAROV, Vasiliy Leonidovich (1896-1955) Mathematician; Dr of Physics and Mathematics; prof; corresp member, RSFSR Acad of Pedag Sci from 1944; *Born*: 24 Nov 1896; *Educ*: 1919 grad Physics and Mathematics Fac, Khar'kov Univ; *Career*: from 1921 taught higher mathematics at Khar'kov Geodesic Technicum (1922 expanded into inst); 1944-55 head, Mathematical Methods Section, Inst of Teaching Methods, RSFSR Acad of Pedag Sci; specialized in mathematical analysis, especially interpolation theory; *Publ: Teoriya interpolirovaniya i priblizheniya funktsiy* (The Theory of Functional Interpolation and Approximation) (1934); *Voprosy metodiki matematiki* (Problems of Mathematical Methods) (1946); *Arifmeticheskiye uprazhneniya i funktsional'naya propedevtika v srednikh klassakh shkoly* (Arithmetical Exercises and Functional Propedeutics in the Middle Grades of School) (1947); *Vychislitel'nyye i graficheskiye uprazhneniya s funktsional'nym soderzhaniyem v starshikh klassakh shkoly* (Calculus and Graphic Exercises Using Functions in the Senior Grades of School) (1948); *Metodicheskiye ukazaniya dlya prepodavateley k materialu po algebre. 6 klass* (A Teachers' Methods Aid for Algebra Material. 6th Grade) (1949); *Algebra* (2 vol, 1949-50); *Nachal'naya algebra* (Beginning Algebra) (2nd ed, 1960); *Died*: 31 Oct 1955.

GOPNER, D. Yu. (1884-1925) Govt official; CP member from 1921; RSDRP member from 1900; *Born*: 1884; *Career*: 1913-17 abroad; during 1917 Oct Revol fought for establishment of Sov regime in Yekaterinoslav; from 1920 exec work in Turkm Republ: member, Turkm Bureau; with Pop Comrt of For Affairs; Dep Pop Comr of Justice; *Died*: 1925.

GOPNER, Serafima Il'inichna (1880-1966) Historian; Party and int Communist movement official; Dr of Historical Sci from 1934; prof; CP member from 1903; *Born*: 7 Apr 1880 in Kherson, daughter of a merchant; *Career*: from 1901 in revol movement; 1901 joined RSDRP, 1903 joined Bolsheviks; agitation and propaganda work in Odessa, Kiev, Nikolayev and Yekaterinoslav; 1905 arrested for the first time; during 1905-07 Revol member, Yekaterinoslav RSDRP Comt; 1910 emigrated to France; member, Paris Bolshevik group; early 1916 returned to Russia; stayed in Irkutsk, moved from there to Yekaterinoslav; illegal work at Bryansk metallurgical plant; early 1917 arrested and imprisoned; Mar 1917 released; after 1917 Feb Revol member, Yekaterinoslav RSDRP(B) Comt and Yekaterinoslav Sov; deleg, 7th (April) RSDRP(B) Conference; participated in 1917 Oct Revol and the Civil War in Ukr; 1918 in Oryol with For Bureau, CC, CP(B) Ukr as secr, CC, CP(B) Ukr; 1919 Ukr Dep Pop Comr of Educ; 1920 directed polit educ courses for 12th Army; 1920-25 head, Agitation and Propaganda Dept, Yekaterinoslav, Donetsk, then Khar'kov Province Party Comts; from 1927 ed, newspaper *Vseukrainskiy proletariy;* 1918-22 member, All-Russian Centr Exec Comt; 1922-29 member, USSR Centr Exec Comt; 1927-38 member, CC, CP(B) Ukr; deleg , 1st - 7th Comintern Congresses; 1928-43 cand member, Comintern Exec Comt; 1929-39 head, Agitation and Propaganda Dept, Comintern Exec Comt; 1938-45 dep chief ed, periodical *Istoricheskiy zhurnal* ; from 1945 member, Learned Council, Inst of Marxism-Leninism, CC, CPSU; also teaching and research work; wrote memoirs and works on Party history; during the last years of life pensioner; *Publ: Pod znamenem mirovoy proletarskoy revolyutsii* (Under the Banner of the World Proletarian Revolution) (1929); *V.I. Lenin v*

Parizhe (V.I. Lenin in Paris) (1956), etc; *Awards*: three Orders of Lenin; *Died*: 26 Mar 1966.

GORASH, Vladimir Antonovich (1878-1942) Urologist; prof from 1932; Dr of Med from 1918; *Born*: 1878; *Educ*: 1903 grad Mil Med Acad; *Career*: worked in S.A. Fyodorov's clinic, Mil Med Acad; 1918 defended doctor's thesis; from 1932 head, Chair of Urology, 2nd Leningrad Med Inst; from 1934 head, Chair of Urology, 3rd Leningrad Med Inst; 1920 devised a conservative method of nephropexy which ensures almost normal anatomic and physiological conditions for a displaced kidney; developed technique of partial nephrectomy for kidney stones; contributed to study of painful perinephritis and described its characteristic symptom - a sense of pain with depression of the 12th rib; wrote some 100 works; *Publ: Ognestrel'nyye raneniya pochki* (Gunshot Wounds of the Kidney) (1918); *Novyy metod fiksatsii smeshchyonnoy pochki (fastsioplikatsiya)* (A New Method of Fixing a Displaced Kidney [Fascioplication]) (1925); *Plotnyye opukholi pochek* (Compact Tumors of the Kidneys) (1930); *Nefrity i ikh khirurgicheskiye lecheniye* (Nephritis and Its Surgical Treatment) (1931); *Chastichnaya nefrektomiya, ili rezektsiya pochki kak odin iz metodov operativnogo lecheniya nekotorykh form kamennoy bolezni* (Partial Nephrectomy, or Resection of the Kidney as One of the Methods for the Surgical Treatment of Some Forms of Calculous Disease) (1933); *Povrezhdeniya i raneniya pochek* (Injuries and Wounds of the Kidneys) (1940); *Died*: 1942.

GORBACHOV, Georgiy Yefimovich (1897-1942) Lit historian and critic; CP member from 1919; *Born*: 26 Sept 1897 in Petersburg; *Educ*: 1922 grad Petrograd Univ, *Career*: 1917 worked with a group of Menshevik Internationalists; participated in the 3-5 July 1917 Bolshevik revolt; arrested by Provisional Govt organs and imprisoned for two months; 1919-21 polit work in Red Army; from 1923 assoc prof, Leningrad State Univ; teaching history of Russian lit; worked at Research Inst of Comparative History of Languages and Lit of Western and Eastern Peoples; 1925-26 ed, journal *Zvezda*; until 1925 dissociated himself from lit debate and organized proletarian lit movement; early 1925 adopted the basic principles of the "On Guard" lit group; after the schism in this group joined its minority, faction and subscribed to all its printed and verbal statements; from early 1925 member, Leningrad Proletarian Writers' Assoc; Presidium member and chm, *Stroyka* (Construction) proletarian writers' group; in his works he assessed the lit movement of the late 1920's and early 1930's; his works gave rise to sharp polemic and criticism in the press, aroused great public interst and sustained several ed; arrested by State Security organs; *Works*: books *Ocherki sovremennoy russkoy literatury* (Outline of Contemporary Russian Literature) (1924); *Kapitalizm i russkaya literatura* (Capitalism and Russian Literature) (1925); *Dva goda literaturnoy revolyutsii* (Two Years of Literary Revolution) (1926); *Sovremennaya russkaya literatura* (Contemporary Russian Literature) (1928); *Protiv literaturnoy bezgramotnosti* (Against Ignorance in Literature) (1928); *Nazad k Shulyatikovu i Aykhenval'du* (Back to Shulyatikov and Aykhenval'd) (1930); articles: *Otkrytoye pis'mo redaktoru 'Zvedzdy'* (Open Letter to the Editor of "Zvezda") (1925); *K yubileyu odnoy revolyutsii* (On the Anniversary of a Revolution) (1926); *Literaturnoye 'zatish'ye' i yego prichiny* (The Literary "Lull" and Its Reasons) (1928); *Bytiye i soznaniye v ponimanii Pereverzeva* (Existence and Consciousness in Pereverzev's Interpretation) (1929), etc; *Died*: 10 Oct 1942 in imprisonment; posthumously rehabilitated.

GORBACHOV, Yemel'yan Grigor'yevich (1892-1965) Party and govt official; CP member from 1910; *Born*: 31 July 1892; *Career*: 1910 began revol career in Kiev; frequently arrested; three times exiled; deleg at 7th (April) Party Conference; 1917-18 chm, Kiev Metal Workers' Union; then Bd chm, Moscow Metal Works (now "Serp i Molot" Plant); 1920-22 chm, Kiev and Odessa Metal Workers' Union; chm, Kiev Council of Workers' Cooperatives; 1923-26 Ukr Dep Comr, then Comr of Labor; 1926-30 chm, Ukr Metal Workers' Union; 1931-44 exec admin posts; from 1945 exec trade-union work; at 9th, 10th and 11th Congresses, CP Ukr, elected member, CC, CP Ukr; member, All-Ukr and USSR Centr Exec Comt; *Died*: 21 Oct 1965.

GORBACHYOV, Boris Sergeyevich (1892-1937) Mil commander and comr; Civil War veteran; corps commander from 1935; CP member from 1917; *Born*: 1892; *Educ*: 1927 grad Frunze Mil Acad; *Career*: from 1918 served in Red Army; during Civil War mil comr, Igumen' Uyezd; commander, special cavalry regt; commander, special cavalry brigade, 8th Army; commander, 3rd Cavalry Brigade, 4th Petrograd Div, Budyonnyy's 1st Cavalry Army; 1927-29 commander, 2nd Brigade, 11th Cavalry Div; commander, 12 Cavalry Div; 1929-37 commandant and comr, All-Union Centr Exec Comt Joint Mil School; commander and comr, Training Establishments Corps; asst, then dep commander, Moscow Mil Distr; commander, Transbaykal and Ural Mil distr; member, USSR Centr Exec Comt of seven convocations; 1937 arrested by NKVD; 1938 at Bukharin-Rykov trial incriminated in "generals' plot"; *Awards*: three Orders of the Red Banner; *Died*: 1937 in imprisonment; posthumously rehabilitated.

GORBATOV, Boris Leontiyevich (1908-1954) Russian writer and journalist; CP member from 1930; *Born*: 15 July 1908 at Pyotr Mar'yev Mine, Donbas; *Career*: apprentice planing-machine operator, Kramatorsk Plant; from 1922 workers' corresp, various newspapers; 1924 joined Komsomol and became dep ed, newspaper *Molodoy shakhtyor*, the organ of Donetsk Province Komsomol Comt; 1924 also helped to organize the *Zaboy* Assoc of Proletarian Writers; 1925 attended 1st Congress of Proletarian Writers; from 1926 bd member, All-Union Assoc of Proletarian Writers; 1930-31 served in Sov Army and edited regt newspaper; from 1931 roving corresp for *Pravda*; 1935 member, Arctic expedition to Dixon Island; 1936 accompanied V.S. Molokov, Hero of the Sov Union, on his flight from Krasnoyarsk to Moscow via Kolyma, the Sea of Okhotsk, the Bering Straits, Wrangel Island, Dixon Island and Arkhangel'sk; 1939 covered the Finno-Sov War; 1941-45 corresp, newspaper *Vo slavu Rodiny*; also wrote short stories, novels and plays; dep, RSFSR Supr Sov; *Publ*: short story *Sytyye i golodnyye* (The Fed and the Hungry) (1922); novella *Yacheyka* (The Cell) (1928); novel *Nash gorod* (Our Town) (1930); essay collections *Komintern* (1932); *Mastera* (The Masters) (1933); *Gornyy pokhod* (Mountain Tour) (1932); novella *Moyo pokoleniye* (My Generation) (1933); non-fiction *Obyknovennaya Arktika* (The Ordinary Arctic) (1940); *Pis'ma k tovarishchu* (Letters to a Comrade) (1942); novella *Aleksey Kulikov, boyets* (Aleksey Kulikov, Warrior) (1942); short stories *Rasskazy o soldatskoy dushe* (Tales of Esprit de Corps) (1943); play *Yunost' otsov* (Our Fathers' Youth) (1943); novella *Nepokoryonnye* (The Undefeated) (1943); essay collection *V Yaponii i na Filippinakh* (In Japan and the Philippines) (1946-47); novel *Donbass* (1st vol, 1950); coauthor, film scripts *Nepokoryonnyye* (The Undefeated) (1945); *Eto bylo v Donbasse* (It Happened in the Donbas) (1945); *Donetskiye shakhtyory* (The Donets Miners) (1950); *Sobraniye sochineniy* (Collected Works) (5 vol, 1955-56); his play *Odna noch'* (One Night) was filmed in 1957; *Awards:* Badge of Hon; two Stalin Prizes (1946 and 1952); *Died*: 20 Jan 1954 in Moscow.

GORBOV, Aleksandr Ivanovich (1859-1939) Chemist; prof from 1918; *Born*: 1859; *Educ*: 1883 grad Petersburg Univ; *Career*: from 1894 head, chemistry laboratory, from 1918 prof, Mil Eng Acad; from 1882 active member, Russian Physiochemical Soc; from 1927 ed, *Zhurnal prikladnoy khimii*; member, Commission for the Study of Natural Resources, USSR Acad of Sci; 1885, together with A.E. Kessler designed original equipment for fractional distillation at reduced pressure; did research on the properties of concrete; devised methods of obtaining hydrogen under field conditions by the reaction of a caustic soda solution with aluminum or silicon and the reaction of water with calcium hydride; 1904-05 the first of these methods was used during the Russo-Japanese War; designed smoke-pots for mil use; 1907-10, together with V.F. Mitkevich, built first Russian installation for obtaining nitric acid from air by the arc method; *Publ*: textbook *Khimicheskiye elementy i ikh prosteyshiye soyedineniya. Chast' 1 - Metalloidy* (Chemical Elements and Their Simplest Compounds. Part 1 - Metalloidy) (1908); *Died:* 1939.

GORBUNOV, Boris Nikolayevich (1901-1944) Eng; specialist in construction mech; corresp member, Ukr Acad of Sci from 1939; *Born*: 22 Jan 1901 in Kiev; *Educ*: 1925 grad Kiev Polytech Inst; *Career*: from 1926 worked for Ukr Acad of Sci and taught at higher tech educ establishments; wrote over 90 works; *Publ*: coauthor, *Stal'nyye mosty* (Steel Bridges) (2 vol, 1935-36), etc; *Died*: 28 July 1944.

GORBUNOV, Nikolay Petrovich (1892-1944) Lenin's personal secr; Party and govt official; chemical eng; member and life-secr, USSR Acad of Sci from 1935; *Born*: 1892, son of an eng; *Educ*: 1917 grad Chemistry Dept, Petersburg Technol Inst; *Career*: 1917 joined *Mezhrayontsy*, then the RSDRP Bolshevik faction; from mid-1917 head, Information Bureau, All-Russian Centr Exec Comt; from Nov 1917 secr, Council of Pop Comr and Lenin's personal secr; from Aug 1918 head, Sci and Tech Dept, Supr Sovnarkhoz; fall 1919 member, Revol-Mil Council, 13th and 14th Armies; from Dec 1920 business mang, RSFSR Council of Pop Comr; Dec 1922-32 business mang, USSR Council of Pop Comr and Labor and Defense Council; 1923-29 simultaneously rector, Moscow Higher Tech College; 1928-32 chm, Sci Commission, Comt for Chemization; 1931-33 dep dir, L. Ya. Karpov Chemical Inst; 1931-34 member, USSR Gosplan; 1928 leader, Sov-German Pamir expedition; 1929 co-founder and dep pres, All-Union Lenin Acad of Agric Sci; 1932 leader, USSR Acad of Sci joint expedition to study natural resources of Tadzh; arrested by State Security organs; *Publ: Kak rabotal Vladimir Il'ich. Sbornik statey i vospominaniy* (How Vladimir Il'yich [Lenin] Worked. A Collection of Articles and Reminiscences) (1933); *Awards*: Order of the Red Banner; *Died*: 1944 in imprisonment.

GORBUNOV, P. P. (1885-1937) Govt official; CP member from 1918; *Born*: 1885; *Career*: 1917-18 member, Omsk Sov of Cossacks' Dep; Omsk Mil Comr; member, Omsk Exec Comt; 1918-20 comr, div staff, 3rd Army; dep head, Polit Bd; member, Yekaterinoslav Revol Comt and member, Revol-Mil Council, 1st Cavalry Army; Feb 1921-Feb 1922 mang, Pop Comrt of For Affairs; subsequently Party, admin and econ work: with Pop Comrt of Finance, Party CC, State Bank, etc; arrested by State Security organs; *Died*: 1937 in imprisonment.

GORBUNOV-POSADOV (real name: GORBUNOV), Ivan Ivanovich (1864-1940) Publisher and educationist; *Born*: 16 Apr 1864 in Kolpino distr, Petersburg, son of an eng; *Educ*: grad business college; *Career*: from 1884 promoted ideas of L. N. Tolstoy; 1885-97 assoc, from 1897 life-dir, Tolstoy's *Posrednik* Publ House, which published mainly fiction and home-study books for the gen publ; compiled numerous anthologies of short stories, verse, parables, etc; published children's journal *Mayak*, journal *Svobodnoye vospitaniye*, etc, in which he preached educ through work; was subjected to reprisals by tsarist authorities for his Tolstoian views; Oct 1917-25 resumed directorship of *Posrednik* Publ House; continued work in pedag and children's lit; *Publ: Biblioteka dlya detey i yunoshestva* (Children's and Youth Library); *Kalendar' dlya vsekh* (Everyman's Calender); *Bor'ba s pyanstvom* (The Fight Against Drink); *Azbuka-kartinka* (A Picture-Alphabet) (1889); *Osvobozhdeniye cheloveka. Poema o dvadtsatom veke* (The Liberation of Man. A Poem of the Twentieth Century) (vol 1, 1918); *Pesni bratstva i svobody i nabroski v proze* (Songs of Fraternity and Freedom and Prose Sketches) (vol 1, 1928); *Died*: 12 Feb 1940 in Moscow.

GORCHAKOV, Nikolay Mikhaylovich (1898-1958) Stage dir and theater critic; Dr of Arts; Hon Art Worker of RSFSR from 1943; *Born*: 1898; *Educ*: grad 3rd Studio, Maly Arts Theater (directed by Vakhtangov); *Career*: from 1922 actor and producer, 3rd Studio Maly Arts Theater; 1924 joined Maly Acad Arts Theater; 1925 helped Stanislavsky to stage *Gore ot uma* (Woe from Wit); 1928 helped V. I. Nemirovich-Danchenko to stage Katayev's *Kvadratura kruga* (Squaring the Circle); his other co-productions at this theater included Virta's *Zemlya* (Earth) (1937), Sheridan's "School for Scandal" (1940), Marshak's *Devnadtsat' mesyatsev* (Twelve Months) (1948), Kron's *Ofitser flota* (An Officer of the Fleet) (1946) and Hellmann's "Autumnal Garden" (1956); his own productions included Bulgakov's *Mol'yer* (Molière) (1936) and *Bespokoynaya starost'* (Restless Old Age) (1956); 1933-41 and 1943-48 also artistic dir, Moscow Satire Theater, where he co-produced Shkvarkin's *Chuzhoy rebyonok* (Another's Child) (1933) and *Fakir na chas* (Fakir for an Hour) (1946); 1941-43 worked at Moscow Drama Theater, where he staged *Russkiye lyudi* (Russian People), *Front* (The Front Line), etc; also worked as a theater critic and taught production techniques; from 1939 prof and head, Chair of Production, State Inst of Stagecraft; *Publ: Besedy o rezhissure* (Talks on Stage Production) (1941); *V. I. Kachalov - Chatskiy* (1906-38); coauthor, *Rabota rezhissyora nad sovetskoy p'yesoy* (The Producer's Work on the Soviet Play) (1950); *Rezhissyorskiye uroki K. S. Stanislavskogo* (K. S. Stanislavsky's Lessons in Production) (1950); *Rezhissyorskiye uroki Vakhtangova* (Vakhtangov's Lessons in Production) (1957); *Spektakl' khudozhestvennoy samodeyatel'nosti* (The Amateur Show) (1954); *Kak postavit' spektakl'* (How to Produce a Show) (1955); *Rabota rezhissyora nad spektaklem* (The Work of the Show Producer) (1956); "Show Production and the Work of the Play Producer" (1956, in Latvian); "The Actor's Training and Craft" (1957, Latvian); *V. G. Sakhnovskiy* (1947); *V. V. Luzhskiy* (1946(; *V. G. Sakhnovskiy. Zhizn'i tvorchestvo* (V. G. Sakhnovskiy. His Life and Work) (1948); *M. M. Tarkhanov* (1950); *Nikolay Petrovich Batalov* (1952); *Vladimir I. Nemirovich-Danchenko v rabote nad p'yesoy K. Treneva 'Lyubov' Yarovaya'* (Vladimir I. Nemirovich-Danchenko During Work on K. Trenev's Play *Lyubov' Yarovaya*) (1958); *Fizicheskiye deystviya v protsesse repetitsii* (Physical Movement at Rehearsals) (1951); *Rezhissyory dvukh teatrov. Zametki o rezhissure dramaticheskikh teatrov Latvii* (Producers at Two Theaters.) Notes on Production Techniques at Drama Theaters in Latvia) (1956), etc; *Awards*: two Stalin Prizes (1946 and 1952); *Died*: 28 Aug 1958.

GORCHILIN, Andrey Ivanovich (Party pseudonym: GRENADYOR) (1886-1956) Party official; CP member from 1904; *Born*: 1886; *Career*: metalworker at workshops of Moscow-Kazan' Railroad; member, Moscow Railroad Rayon RSDRP Comt; 1905 co-opted member, Moscow RSDRP Comt; active in 1905 Dec armed uprising in Moscow (head, Moscow-Kazan' Railroad workers' battle squad); 1906-12 illegal Party work in Kiev, Moscow, Petersburg and Simbirsk; 1912-17 abroad; participated in 1917 Oct Revol as member, Moscow Lefortovo Rayon Red Guards detachment; during Civil War served with special units combatring counter-revol; subsequently Party and admin work; *Publ: 1905 g. na Kazanke. Vospominaniya podpol'shchika* (1905 on the Kazan' Railroad. Memoirs of an Underground Man) (2nd ed, 1934); *Bor'ba za Nikolayevskiy vokzal* (The Battle for the Nikolayev Terminus) (1955); *Rasskaz Il'ichu* (A Story for Il'ich) (1960); *Died*: 22 July 1956.

GORDLEVSKIY, Vladimir Aleksandrovich (1876-1956) Orientalist and Turcologist; prof; member, USSR Acad of Sci from 1946; *Born*: 7 Oct 1876 in Sveaborg, son of a mil official; *Educ*: 1899 grad Moscow Lazarev Inst of Oriental Languages; 1904 grad History and Philology Dept, Moscow Univ; *Career*: 1907-18 taught Turkish language and lit at Lazarev Inst; 1918 prof, Near East Inst; 1920-48 prof, Moscow Inst of Oriental Studies; 1948-56 head, Near and Middle East Languages and Lit Section, Inst of Oriental Studies, USSR Acad of Sci; 1929-46 cand member, USSR Acad of Sci; specialist in Turkish language and lit, Turkish ethnography, history and folklore, which he collected and studied during his numerous visits to Turkey; *Publ: Ocherki po novoy osmanskoy literature* (Studies on New Osman Literature) (1912); *Obraztsy osmanskogo narodnogo tvorchestva* (Samples of Osman Folklore) (1916); *Grammatika turetskogo yazyka* (Grammar of the Turkish Language) (1928); *Turetskaya khrestomatiya so slovaryom* (Turkish Reader and Dictionary) (1931); ed, *Turetsko-russkiy slovar'* (Turko-Russian Dictionary) (1931); *Khodzha Nasreddin* (1936); *Vnutrenneye sostoyaniye Turtsii vo vtoroy polovine 16-go v.* (Internal Situation of Turkey in the Late 16th Century) (1940); *Gosudarstvo Sel'dzhukidov Maloy Azii* (The Seljukian State in Asia Minor) (1941); *Ekspluatatsiya nedr zemli v Turtsii* (Exploitation of Mineral Wealth in Turkey) (1945); *Izbrannyye sochineniya* (Selected Works) (3 vol, 1960-62); *Died*: 10 Sept 1956.

GORDON, Konstantin Vasil'yevich (1910-1962) Film sound operator; Hon Art Worker of Lat SSR from 1947; CP member from 1948; *Born*: 1910; *Educ*: 1936 grad Leningrad Inst of Cinema Eng; *Career*: 1935-52 sound operator, Leningrad, Alma Ata, Riga and Moscow Film Studios; from 1952 sound operator, Moscow Film Studio; *Works*: did sound for films: *Chelovek s ruzh'yom* (The Man with a Gun) (1938); *Maskarad* (Masquerade) (1941); *Vo imya Rodiny* (In the Name of the Country) (1943); *Pesnya Abaya* (The Song of Abay) (1946); *Serdtse b'yotsya vnov'* (The Heart Beats Anew) (1956); "Pygmalion" (1958); *Trizhdy voskresshiy* (Thrice Resurrected) (1960), etc; *Died*: 1962.

GORDOV, Vasiliy Nikolayevich (1896-1951) Mil commander; col-gen; CP member from 1918; *Born*: 12 Dec 1896 in vil Matveyevtsy, now Tatar ASSR; *Educ*: 1921 grad *Vystrel* Advanced Infantry Tactical Courses; 1932 grad Frunze Mil Acad; *Career*: from 1918 in Red Army; fought in Civil War; after Civil War held various commands; 1939 chief of staff, 7th Army; 1941-45 chief of staff, Volga Mil Distr; 1941-42 chief of staff, then commander, 21st Army; 1942 commander, 64th Army; 22 July-9 Aug 1942 commander, Stalingrad Front; Aug-Sept 1942 dep commander, Stalingrad Front; 1942-43 commander, 33rd Army; June 1943 sent a letter to Stalin and Zhukov suggesting the abolition of the army mil soviets as useless institutions and the conversion of army polit departments into corresp staff departments; 1945-46 commander, Volga Mil Distr; 1945 took part in Berlin operations; 1946 compulsorily retired because of his negative attitude to the army polit organs; arrested by State Security organs; *Awards*: two Orders of Lenin; other orders and medals; *Died*: 12 Dec 1951 in imprisonment; posthumously rehabilitated.

GORDYAGIN, Andrey Yakovlevich (1865-1932) Geobotanist, ecologist and pedologist; prof from 1901; corresp member, USSR Acad of Sci; *Born*: 29 Oct 1865 in Perm'; *Educ*: 1888 grad Kazan' Univ; *Career*: 1891-1901 assoc prof, from 1901 prof, Kazan' Univ; made extensive geobotanical and floristic surveys of the eastern part of the European USSR and Western Kaz; 1900-01 published a major work entitled *Materialy dlya poznaniya pochv i rastitel'nosti Zapadnoy Sibiri* (Material on the Identification of the Soils and Vegetation of Western Sibera), in which he described the gen geography of the region, examined the sequence of formation of its present forest and steppe vegetation and analysed the origin of the Siberian chernozem and solonchak soils; during the WW 1 shortage of cotton-wool proposed use of peat-moos (Sphagnum) as a substitute; *Publ: K biologii Helianthus annuus L.* (The Biology of Helianthus annuus L.) (1891); *Nablyudeniya nad izmenchivost'yu Anemone patens L.* (Observations on the Mutability of Anemone patens L.) (1920), etc; *Awards*: Hero of Labor; *Died*: 15 Jan 1932 in Kazan'.

GORELOV, Gavriil Nikitich (1880-1966) Painter; Hon Art Worker of RSFSR from 1947; member, USSR Acad of Arts from 1953; *Born*: 4 Apr 1880; *Educ*: 1903-11 studied at Petersburg Acad of Arts under I. Ye. Repin and F. A. Rubo; *Career*: early works deal with themes from Russian history and are noted for their skill in depicting historical scenes, situations, costumes and utensils ("Mockery of Heretics," 1908, etc); from 1912 member, Mobile Art Exhibitions Assoc; from 1924 member, Assoc of Painters of Revol Russia; under the Sov regime turned to themes from revol-liberation movement, events of the Civil War, WW 2 and scenes of Sov everyday life; *Works*: "With the Poor on the Volga" (1924); "Revolution in the Village" (1924); "At the Leader's Coffin in the Hall of Columns" (1925); "Pugachev Judging a Land-Owner" (1925); "Budyonnyy's Cavalry Corps at Voronezh" (1928); group portrait of Gorky Automobile Plant executives (1935); "Red Soldiers at the Tret'yakov Gallery" (1938); helped design diorama sketch "Battle at Chongar Bridge" for the panorama "The Perekop Assault" (1937-38); "Return of Hero of the Soviet Union, Lieutenant P. A. Brin'ko from a Flight Mission" (1942); "The Bolotnikov Mutiny" (1944); "Minin's First Appeal to the People" (1945); "Minin Greets the People After the Victory" (1947); "Dog-Knights" (1947); portraits of the steelfounder A. S. Subbotin and the foreman I. V. Grachyov; "Eminent Steelfounder M. G. Gusarov with His Brigade at the 'Hammer and Sickle' Plant" (1948-49); *Awards*: Stalin Prize (1950); *Died*: 16 Aug 1966.

GORETSKIY, Maksim Ivanovich (1893-1939) Bel writer and lit historian; senior assoc, Bel Acad of Sci from 1928; *Born*: 18 Feb 1893 in vil Malaya Bogot'kovka, now Mstislavl' Rayon, Mogilyov Oblast, son of a peasant; *Educ*: 1913 grad Gory-Goretsk (now Gorki) Agronomical College; 1918 studied at Smolensk Inst of Archeology; *Career*: from 1914 student, Petersburg Pavel Mil College; later on active service in army; 1917, after being wounded in action, discharged; 1918 in Smolensk worked for Smolensk Sov newspaper *Izvestiya* and newspaper *Zvezda*, organ of Northwestern Oblast RCP(B) Comt; 1919-22 in Vilnius first on govt work with newspaper *Zvezda*, then teacher, Vilnius Bel High-School; worked for ed staff, newspaper *Belaruskiya vedamas'tsi*; 1922 for his connections with Bel SSR arrested by Polish authorities and exiled to Lith; from 1923 in Minsk, worked for Inst of Bel Culture; from late 1928 with Bel Acad of Sci; simultaneously history teacher, Bel State Univ; 1926-28 taught Bel language and lit at Bel Acad of Agric in Gorki (Bel SSR); 1912 first work printed; writer and lit historian of great talent; 1930 together with his brother, the economist G. I. Goretskiy, a member of the Bel Acad of Sci, arrested and sentenced to five years' hard labor for "nationalist" activities; served sentence in Vyatka (now Kirov); 1935 released and permitted to live in Kirov (former Pesochnya), Kaluga Oblast; taught Russian lit at high school; 1937 re-arrested by NKVD and sent to a concentration camp in Komi ASSR; *Publ*: collected stories "Winter Crop" (1914); "Dawns" (1926); "What Is His Guilt?" (1926); "Quiet Songs" (1926); novelettes: "Two Souls" (1919); "Melancholy" (1928); "Quiet Stream" (1930); collected dramatic works: "The Jesting Scribe" (1928); essays: "Imperialistic War" (1926); novel "Vilnius Communards" (1965, posthumous ed); scholarly works: "Belorussian-Russian Dictionary" (1919); "History of Belorussian Literature" (1920); "Reader of Belorussian Literature" (1922 and 1924); coauthor, "Folksongs with Melodies" (1928); *Died*: 20 Mar 1939 in imprisonment; posthumously rehabilitated.

GOREV, Aleksandr Aleksandrovich (1884-1953) Electr eng; *Born*: 16 May 1884; *Educ*: 1907 grad Petersburg Polytech Inst; *Career*: 1902-07 took active part in student revol movement; after grad lecturer, from 1919 prof, Petersburg Polytech Inst; 1920 helped to draft State Plan for the Electrification of Russia and to plan several power plants; for several years chm, Electr Planning Comt, Main Admin of the Electrotech Ind; also member, USSR Gosplan; 1924 head, Sov deleg to World Power Conference, London; from 1933 consultant, Centr Volga Construction Trust; then consultant, State Hydropower Planning Bd; Specialized in high-tension and power transmission technol; supervised construction of 300,000-kilowatt generator for testing high-voltage equipment; devised reliability criteria for the combined operation of any number of power generators under any given conditions; during last years of life supervised research on the linear compensation, reliability, internal overloading and lightning protection of transformer substations; *Publ: K voprosu ob izolyatsii liniy vysokogo napryazheniya* (The Insulation of High-Tension Lines) (1922); *Vysokovol'tnyye linii peredachi elektricheskoy energii* (High-Voltage Power Transmission Lines) (1927); *Vvedeniye v teoriyu ustoychivosti parallel'noy raboty elektricheskikh stantsiy* (An Introduction to the Theory of the Reliability of Power Stations Operating in Parallel) (Vol 1, 1935); coauthor, *Impul'snyye kharakteristiki bol'shikh iskrovykh promezhutkov* (The Pulse Characteristics of Large Spark Gaps) (1948); *Perekhodnyye protsessy sinkhronnoy mashiny* (The Transitional Processes of a Synchronous Machine) (1950); *Awards*: Stalin Prize (1948); *Died*: 15 Apr 1953.

GOREV, (pseudonym: GOL'DMAN), Boris Isaakovich (1874-?) Mil instructor; *Born*: 1874; *Educ*: studied at high school, then at Petersburg Univ; *Career*: from 1893 in revol movement; after the first arrests of its members, joined League for the Liberation of the Working Class; from late 1896 one of its leaders; 1902 *Iskra* (The Spark) agent; member, Org Commission for Convening 2nd RSDRP Congress; on his way to the Congress arrested and imprisoned for two years; 1905 worked in Vilnius and later in Petersburg as member, Petersburg RSDRP(B) Comt; from 1907 Soc-Democrat (Menshevik); at London Party Congress elected cand member, CC; 1908 emigrated; worked with RSDRP (Mensheviks) foreign org; 1912 attended RSDRP Aug Conference; after 1917 Feb Revol ed, RSDRP (Mensheviks) centr organ *Rabochaya gazeta*; member, CC, RSDRP (Mensheviks) and member, All-Russian Centr Exec Comt of 1st convocation; 1920 officially left RSDRP (Mensheviks) Party and engaged in teaching work; his research, teaching and lit work dealt mainly with historical materialism and its adaptation to the problem of war, and with the history of socialism in Western Countries and in Russia; wrote a number of books and articles on these themes; *Publ: Ocherki istoricheskogo materializma* (Outline of Historical Materialism) (1925); collection of articles *Na ideologicheskom fronte* (On the Ideological Front) (1923); *Istoriya sotsializma na Zapade* (History of Socialism in the West) (3rd ed, 1925); *Populyarnaya istoriya sotsializma na Zapade i v Rossii* (Popular History of Socialism in the West and in Russia) (1926; *Materializm - filosofiya proletariata* (Materialism, the Philosophy of the Proletariat) (5th ed, 1924); *Anarkhizm v Rossii* (Anarchism in Russia) (1930); biographies of: Blanka (2nd ed, 1923), Bakunin, Plekhanov and Mikhaylovskiy (1925), etc; *Died*: date and place of death unknown.

GORINEVSKAYA, Valentina Valentinovna (1882-1953) Surgeon; Dr of Med from 1935; prof from 1919; Hon Sci Worker of RSFSR from 1943; *Born*: 1882, daughter of a physician and physical culture enthusiast; *Educ*: 1908 grad Petersburg Women's Med Inst; *Career*: after grad worked under A. A. Kad'yan and G. I. Turner at Surgical Clinic, Peter and Paul Hospital; 1914 first woman to be appointed senior surgeon at a hospital in the rear of the Western Front; from 1919 prof, Chair of Gen Surgery, Samara Univ; later head, Surgical Dept, Obukh Inst, Moscow, then head, Traumatological Dept, Inst of Therapy and Prosthetics; from 1931 head, Chair of Field Surgery, Centr Inst of Postgrad Med Training; simultaneously head, Traumatological Clinic, Sklifosovskiy Inst; 1939 worked in field hospitals during fighting against Japanese at Khalkin-Gol; also served in war against Finland; during WW 2 senior inspector, Main Mil Med Bd, Sov Army; specialized in occupational and mil traumatism; advocated the functional trend in the treatment of traumas; was one of first Sov surgeons to introduce the primary surgical treatment of wounds resulting from ind and other accidents; as a pioneer of traumatology as separate branch of surgery, made a major contribution to the org of treatment for minor injuries; wrote some 90 works; *Publ*: coauthor and ed, *Osnovy travmatologii* (The Principles of Traumatology) (1936); coauthor, *Pervaya khirurgicheskaya pomoshch' pri travmakh voyennogo i mirnogo vremeni* (Surgical First Aid for Traumas in Wartime and Peace) (1942); *Sovremennyye metody lecheniya ran* (Modern Methods of Wound Treatment) (1942); *Kompleksnoye lecheniye v gospitalyakh dlya legkoranenykh* (Comprehensive Treatment in Hospitals for the Lightly Wounded) (1944); ed, *Lecheniye legkoranenykh* (The Treatment of the Lightly Wounded) (1946); *Awards*: numerous orders and medals; *Died*: 1953.

GORINEVSKIY, Valentin Vladislavovich (1857-1937) Hygienist, pediatrist and gymnastics specialist; Dr of Med; *Born*: 5 Oct 1857; *Educ*: grad Med Fac, Heidelberg Univ; 1887 grad Petersburg Mil Med Acad; *Career*: 1887 defended doctor's thesis and thereafter worked for 30 years in Petersburg as a pediatrist and factory and school physician; simultaneously lectured on school hygiene and physical training at various higher educ establishments; a follower of P. F. Lesgaft's theories, he pioneered physical training in schools and campaigned for a school med program; 1912 established one of first Russian school biometric laboratories at Tenishevskiy College, Petersburg; founder-head, Chair of Research Methods on Physical Development, Lesgaft's Higher Courses; after 1917 Oct Revol helped to organize research on and training of med specialists in physical training; first dean, Med Fac, Samara Univ, where he lectured on hygiene, biology and physiology; 1921 founded research dept at Main Mil Physical Training School, Moscow; 1923 founded first Sov Chair of Med and Pedag Control of Physical Training and a number of laboratories at Moscow Inst of Physical Training; until 1934 lectured on physical training and school and labor hygiene at 2nd Moscow State Univ; trained hundreds of med physical training specialists at Min of Health courses, Centr Inst of Postgrad Med Training, Inst of Balneology, Child and Adolescent Welfare Dept, etc; was one of first Sov sci to develop new physical therapy methods; wrote over 60 works; *Publ: O zakalivanii kak sredstve vospitaniya* (Toughening-Up as Means of Education) (1900); *Fizicheskoye obrazovaniye* (Physical Education) (1913); *Kul'tura tela* (Bodybuilding) (1927); *Gigiyena fizicheskikh uprazhneniy i sporta* (The Hygiene of Physical Exercises and Sport) (1930); coauthor, *Rukovodstvo po fizicheskoy kul'ture i vrachebnomu kontrolyu* (A Manual on Physical Education and Medical Supervision) (1935); *Fizicheskaya kul'tura i zdorov'ye* (Physical Education and Health) (1945); *Izbrannyye proizvedeniya* (Selected Works) (1951); *Died*: 13 Feb 1937 in Moscow.

GORIN-GALKIN, Vladimir Filippovich (pseudonyms: N. GRABOVSKIY; SIROTININ) (1863-1925) Govt official; *Born*: 1863 in Mogilev; *Career*: in 1880's worked for *Narodnaya volya* (People's Will) circles in Sevastopol', Khar'kov, Odessa and Mogilev; 1888 arraigned for above activities and exiled for eight years to Eastern Siberia; while in exile joined RSDRP; from 1902 member, Saratov RSDRP Comt; 1903 represented Saratov Party org at 2nd RSDRP Congress and sided with Lenin; then worked for Bolshevik organizations abroad; maintained contact with Karl Liebknecht and Rosa Luxemburg; after 1917 Feb Revol returned to Russia; from Aug 1917 worked for Petrograd RSDRP(B) Comt; as member, Petrograd Mil-Revol Comt helped prepare 1917 Oct Revol; helped set up Pop Comrt of For Affairs; from 1918 exec mil-polit work in Red Army; after the end of Civil War research and educ work in Moscow; *Publ: Doloy materializm! 'Kritika empiriokriticheskoy kritiki'* (Down with Materialism! "A Critique of Empiriocriticism") (1910); *Died*: 1925.

GORKY, Maksim (real name: PESHKOV, Aleksey Maksimovich) (1868-1936) Writer; *Born*: 28 Mar 1868 in Nizhniy Novgorod, son of a carpenter; *Educ*: self-taught; *Career*: from age 11 worked as errand boy in a store, as dish-washer on a steamer and as asst in a bakery, etc; 1884 tried to enroll at Kazan' Univ; in Kazan' joined Populist "self-educ circle" and began propaganda among workers and peasants; became acquainted with Marxist lit; 1887 shot himself through the lung in a suicide attempt; 1889 arrested for links with revolutionaries and kept under police surveillance; 1888-89 and 1891-92 toured Russia, reaching Tiflis, where he worked at the railroad workshops and engaged in revol propaganda among workers; 1892 first work printed; 1898 his two-vol *Ocherki i rasskazy* (Essays and Stories) attracted wide attention; late 1890's closely linked with Marxist circles in Nizhniy Novgorod and Sormovo; sided with Lenin's *Iskra* group; 1901 wrote proclamation urging campaign against Tsarism; Apr 1901 published "Song of the Stormy Petrel" heralding coming revol; 1901 arrested for complicity in establishing an underground printing press and exiled to Arzamas; 1902 elected hon member, Russian Acad of Sci, but his election was quashed on orders from Nicholas II; prior to 1905 Revol directed progressive democratic "Knowledge" Publ House, which published a series of socio-polit pamphlets; evening of 8 Jan 1905, together with other public figures, met Tsarist ministers to plead for withdrawal of troops from Petersburg streets in a bid to avert bloodshed; after bloody events of 9 Jan wrote revol proclamation, leading to his internment in Peter and Paul Fortress; released after massive public protests; Oct 1905 helped found first legal Bolshevik paper *Novaya zhizn'*; 27 Nov 1905 met for first time Lenin, with whom for many years he was close friends; early 1906 went to America and wrote essays, pamphlets and appeals in support of Russian revol; fall 1906 settled on Capri, where he lived for seven years; May 1907 non-voting deleg at 5th (London) RSDRP Congress; 1909-10 sided with *Vperyod* (Forward) group; his interest in *bogostroitel'stvo* / the idea of establishing a new, "socialist" religion/ dates from this time; 1913 returned to Russia; 1912-14 contributed to Bolshevik newspapers *Zvezda* and *Pravda* and journal *Prosveshcheniye*; during WW 1 adopted internationalist stand; 1915 founded anti-war journal *Letopis'*; 1915-17 directed *Parus* (Sail) Publ House, which published a series of pamphlets entitled "Europe Prior to and During the War"; at time of 1917 Feb Revol published newspaper *Novaya zhizn'*; 1917-18, disagreeing with Bolshevik policy, printed his "Untimely Thoughts" in above newspaper; his attitude to Oct Revol drew sharp criticism from Lenin; 1918-20 nevertheless contributed to establishment of Sov cultural organs; founded "World Lit" Publ House; helped found 1st Workers and Peasants' Univ; worked for Commission to Improve Welfare of Scientists; 1921 went abroad to recover from tuberculosis; from 1924 lived at Sorrento, Italy; July-Aug 1928 and 1929 toured USSR; 1929 at 5th All-Union Congress of Soviets elected member, USSR Centr Exec Comt; 1931 returned for good to USSR; directed many periodicals: *Nashi dostizheniya, SSSR na stroyke, Literaturnaya uchyoba, Za rubezhom, Kolkhoznik*, etc; 1934 elected chm, bd, Sov Writers' Union; 1930's sponsored and organized work on publ *Istoriya grazhdanskoy voyny v SSSR* (The History of the Civil War in the USSR) and series *Istoriya fabrik i zavodov*; edited lit history and biographical series *Istoriya molodogo cheloveka 19 veka* (The History of a Young Man of the 19th Century), *Istoricheskiye romany* (Historic Novels) and *Zhizn' zamechatel'nykh lyudey* (The Lives of Remarkable People), etc; *Publ:* stories: *Makar Chudra* (1892); *Goremyka Pavel* (Pavel the Woebegone) (1894); *Chelkash* (1895); *Pesnya o Sokole* (Song of the Falcon) (1895); *Starukha Izergil'* (Izergil', the Old Woman) (1895); *Byvshiye lyudi* (Bygone People) (1897); *Suprugi Orlovy* (Mr and Mrs Orlov) (1897); *Mal'va* (The Hollyhock) (1897); novels: *Foma Gordeyev* (1899); *Troye* (The Three) (1900-01); *Pesnya o Burevestnike* (The Song of the Stormy Petrel) (1901); plays: *Meshchane* (The Philistines) (1902); *Na dne* (The Lower Depths) (1902); *Dachniki* (The Summer Villa Residents) (1904); *Deti solntsa* (Children of the Sun) (1905); *Varvary* (The Barbarians) (1906); novel *Mat'* (Mother) (1906); novelette *Ispoved'* (The Confession) (1908); play *Posledniye* (The Last Ones) (1908); novelettes: *Zhizn' nenuzhnogo cheloveka* (The Life of a Useless Man) (1907-08); *Gorodok Okurov* (Fume City) (1909); *Zhizn' Matveya Kaussnyakina* (The Life of Matvey Kaussnyakin) (1910-11); play *Chudaki* (The Cranks) (1910); *Skazki ob Italii* (Tales of Italy) (1911-13); collected stories and essays *Po Rusi* (Round and About Rus) (1912-16); trilogy: *Detstvo* (Childhood) (1912-13), *V lyudyakh* (Out in the World) (1914) and *Moi universitety* (My Universities) (1923); novel *Delo Artamonovykh* (The Artamonov Case) (1925); series of essays *Po Sovetskomu Soyuzu* (Around the Soviet Union) (1929); plays: *Yegor Bulychyov i drugiye* (Yegor Bulychyov and Co) (1932); *Dostigayev i drugiye* (Dostigayev and Co) (1933); novel *Zhizn' Klima Samgina* (The Life of Klim Samgin) (1925-36, unfinished); *Sobraniye sochineniy* (Collected Works) (30 vol, 1949-55); *Died*: 16 June 1936; buried on Moscow's Red Square; his name has been conferred on: former Nizhniy Novgorod (now Gorky); Moscow Acad Arts Theater; Leningrad Bolshoy Drama Theater; Inst of World Lit, USSR Acad of Sci; five univ; Lit Inst, USSR Writers' Union; hundreds of cultural facilities, plants, sovkhozes and kolkhozes.

GORNFEL'D, Arkadiy Georgiyevich (1867-1941) Russian lit historian; *Born*: 30 Aug 1867 in Simferopol'; *Educ*: grad Law Fac, Khar'kov Univ; studied poetry under A. A. Potebni, founder of the psychological school in Russian linguistics, then in Berlin under Lazarus and Geiger; *Career*: from early 1890's collaborated with journals *Russkoye bogatstvo, Zhurnal dlya vsekh* and *Voskhod*; contributed to collections *Voprosy teorii i psikhologii tvorchestva* (Problems of Creative Theory and Psychology); typical of his theoretical works are his interest in the author's style and the effort to fathom his psychology and poetic thought; wrote articles on the theory of lit in encyclopedic works: Brockhaus and Ephron's *Entsiklopedicheskiy slovar'* (Encyclopedic Dictionary); *Yevreyskaya entsiklopediya* (Jewish Encyclopedia); 1st ed, *Bol'shaya Sovetskaya Entsiklopediya* (Large Soviet Encyclopedia); *Publ: Muki slova* (The Torments of Speech) (1906); *Knigi i lyudi* (Books and People) (1908); *Na Zapade* (In the West) (1910); *O russkikh pisatelyakh. Tom 1 - Minuvshiy vek* (Of Russian Writers. Vol 1 - The Last Century) (1912); *Puti tvorchestva* (Creative Paths) (1922); *Novyye slovechki i staryye slova* (New Slogans and Old Words) (1922); *Boyevyye otkliki na mirnyye temy* (Militant Response to Peaceful Themes) (1924); *Romany i romanisty* (Novels and Novelists) (1930); *Died*: 25 Mar 1941 in Leningrad.

GORODETSKIY, Aleksey Afanas'yevich (1897-1967) Roentgenologist and radiologist; Dr of Med from 1940; prof; corresp member, Ukr Acad of Sci from 1957; *Born*: 1897 in vil Novo-Kostichi, now Kuybyshev Oblast; *Educ*: 1924 grad Med Fac, Saratov Univ; *Career*: 1919-20 med orderly in Red Army; 1920-22 male nurse; 1924-34 worked as a physician in the vil and towns of Ural Oblast; 1926 began research on radio therapy and roentgenology; 1935-41 lecturer in roentgenology, Bashkir Med Inst, Ufa; during WW 2 head, roentgenological dept, various mil hospitals; 1944-49 dep sci dir, Kiev Roentgenological, Radiological and Oncological Inst; 1944-67 head, Chair of Roentgenology and Radiology, Kiev Inst of Postgrad Med Training; 1945-50 chief roentgenologist, Ukr Min of Health; from 1945 also chm, Radiological Commission, Ukr Min of Health and bd chm, Kiev Soc of Roentgenologists and Radiologists; 1953-67 head, Roentgenological and Radiological Dept, Kiev Inst of Experimental Biology and Pathology and head, Biophysics Laboratory, A. A. Bogomolets Inst of Physiology, Ukr Acad of Sci; from 1956 bd chm, Ukr Soc of Roentgenologists and Radiologists; member, ed council, journal *Vestnik rentgenologii i radiologii*; devised several new therapeutic techniques, including x-ray therapy of gunshot wounds, massive single-dose irradiation and complex treatment for breast cancer; complex treatment for radiation damage and radioactive phosphorus treatment for tumors; wrote over 60 works; *Awards*: Order of Lenin, etc; *Died*: 1967.

GORODOVIKOV, Oka Ivanovich (1879-1960) Kalmyk mil commander; col-gen from 1941; Civil War veteran; brilliant cavalry tactician; CP member from 1919; *Born*: 12 Sept 1879 in vil Mokraya El'muta, now Rostov Oblast, son of a Kalmyk peasant; *Educ*: 1923 grad Higher Acad Courses; 1932 grad special fac, Frunze Mil Acad; *Career*: 1903 drafted for mil service with 9th Don Cossack Regt; from 1904 junior warrant officer; 1905 helped to put down revol movement in Poland; 1908-14 farm worker; 1914-16 served on Southwestern Front; 1916-17 part of a Cossack detachment guarding a factory and mines near vil Sulin, Don Oblast; late 1917 joined Red Guard detachment; from 1918 in Red Army; commander, cavalry squadron, Budyonnyy's Cavalry Regt; brigade commander, then commander, 6th Cavalry Div, Budyonnyy's 1st Cavalry Army; commander, 2nd Cavalry Army; commander, 6th Cavalry Div, which broke through the Chongar fortifications during the storming of Perekop; 1921-29 commander of a cavalry div; inspector of cavalry, North Caucasian Mil Distr; then commander and comr, 1st Cavalry Corps; 1932-38 dep commander, Centr Asian Mil Distr; 1938-45 inspector of cavalry, Red Army; 1941-45 supervised formation of cavalry units; Headquarters rep overseeing cavalry raids behind enemy lines; coordinated cavalry operations during battle of Stalingrad; 1945-47 Dep Commander of Cavalry, Sov Army; from 1947 in retirement; 1937 dep, USSR Supr Sov; *Publ: Vospominaniya* (Reminiscences) (1957); *Awards*: Hero of the Sov Union (1958); three Orders of Lenin; six Orders of the Red Banner; other orders and medals; *Died*: 26 Feb 1960.

GORODTSOV, Vasiliy Alekseyevich (1860-1945) Archeologist; Dr of Archeology; prof, Moscow Univ from 1918; Hon Sci Worker of RSFSR from 1943; CP member from 1938; *Born*: 11 Mar 1860; *Career*: 1903-29 worked at State Historical Museum; from 1907 until death taught archeology; prior to 1917 Revol worked at Shanyavskiy Univ, Archeological Inst, Inst of History, Philosophy and Lit and Moscow Univ; 1888 studied neolithic settlements on the Oka River; also did research on ethnography and historical geography in relation to archeology; took a special interest in the Paleolithic and Bronze ages and ancient Slavic civilizations; 1928 discovered and studied Timonov Paleolithic settlement; made major contribution to knowledge of the Bronze Age in the forest and steppe regions of the USSR and devised a still-valid classification of civilizations; studied relics of the early Iron Age at Bel'skoye and Yelizavetinskiy and medieval relics at Staraya Ryazan' and Madzhary; wrote over 200 works; *Publ: Pervobytnaya arkheologiya* (The Archeology of Primitive Man) (1908); *Bytovaya arkheologiya* (The Archeology of Civilized Man) (1910); *Kul'tury bronzovoy epokhi v Sredney Rossii* (Bronze-Age Civilizations in Russia) (1915); *Arkheologiya. Tom 1, Kamennyy period* (Archeology. Volume 1, The Stone Age) (1923); *Starsheye Kashirskoye gorodishche* (The Oldest Kashir City Site) (1933); *Timonovskaya paleoliticheskaya stoyanka* (The Timonov Paleolithic Settlement) (1935); *Yelizavetinskoye gorodishche i soprovozhdayushiye yego mogil'niki po raskopkam 1935-ogo goda* (The Yelizavetinskiy City Site and the Neighboring Tombs After the Excavations of (1935) (1936), etc; *Awards*: Order of Lenin (1944); *Died*: 3 Feb 1945.

GORSHKOV, Iosif Stepanovich (1896-1965) Agronomist; specialist in fruit-growing; Dr of Agric; corresp member, USSR Acad of Agric Sci; popularizer of Michurin's theories; CP member; *Born*: 1896; *Educ*: 1917 grad horticulture college; *Career*: from 1919 gardener in Kozlov (later Michurinsk); from 1920 asst selectionist to I. V. Michurin; from 1935 dir, Michurin Centr Genetic Laboratory, Michurinsk; also directed work of many other laboratories of the Michurin Combine; wrote works on selection and genetics of berry fruits and melons; produced many new fruit and berry varieties; dep, RSFSR Supr Sov of three convocations; for many years member, Tambov Oblast CPSU Comt and Michurinsk City CPSU Comt; deleg at 19th and 20th CPSU Congresses; *Publ: Kratkiy obzor sortov Michurina* (A Brief Review of Michurin's Varieties) (1925); *Selektsiya--moguchee sredstvo bor'by za vysokiy urozhay* (Selection, an Important Means of Achieving High Yields) (1934); *Velikiy uchyonyy-plodovod* (The Great Fruit-Growing Researcher) (1935); *Ispol'zovaniye dostizheniy I. V. Michurina v praktike selektsionnykh rabot* (The Use of Michurin's Achievements in Practical Selection Work) (1937); *Metody Michurina v selektsionnoy rabote* (Michurin's Methods in Selection Work) (1940); *Prodvizheniye vinogradstva v novyye rayony* (Expansion of Viticulture into New Areas) (1947); coauthor, *I. V. Michurin* (1960); *Michurinskiye printsipy i metody selektsii--osnova sovetskogo rasteniyevodstva* (Michurin's Principles and Selection Methods as the Basis of Soviet Plant-Growing) (1961); *Awards*: three Orders of Lenin; two Orders of the Red Banner of Labor; *Died*: 21 Oct 1965.

GORSHKOV, Ivan Ivanovich (1885-1966) Party official; CP member from 1904; *Born*: 24 June 1885; *Career*: 1905 secr, Yegor'yevsk Sub-Rayon Party Comt, Ryazan' Province; member, Moscow Okrug RSDRP Comt; 1905 staged Yegor'yevsk textile workers' gen strike; repeatedly arrested; 1911 exiled to Siberia; May 1917 returned to Yegor'yevsk; exec Party and trade-union work; during 1917 Oct Revol member, Yegor'yevsk Party Comt and secr, Yegor'yevsk Textile Workers' Union; organized Red Guards detachments; from 1919 member, Ryazan' Province Exec Comt and chm, Ryazan' Province Party Comt; 1921 chm, Ufa Revol Tribunal; secr, Yegor'yevsk then Dmitriyev Uyezd Party Comt; 1928-29 Presidium member and dep secr of Party Collegium, Moscow RCP(B) Control Commission; 1933-39 admin work in Moscow; from 1939 pensioner; deleg, 8th - 14th Party Congresses; at 15th Party Congress elected member, CPSU(B) Centr Control Commission; *Died*: 6 Mar 1966.

GORSKIY, Aleksandr Alekseyevich (1871-1924) Ballet dancer, ballet-master and teacher; Hon Artiste of RSFSR; *Born*: 18 Aug 1871; *Educ*: 1889 grad Petersburg Theater College; *Career*: from 1889 ballet dancer at Petersburg Mariinskiy Theater; performed classical, character and grotesque parts: the Prince in *Spyashchaya krasavitsa* (Sleeping Beauty); the Satyr in "Tannhaeuser"; Chinese dance in *Shchelkunchik* (Nut-Cracker), etc; 1896 appointed instructor at Moscow Bolshoy Theater; from 1904 taught at Moscow Choreographic College; influenced creative development of many eminent ballet-masters; arranged new original versions of ballets: "Don Quixote" (1900); *Lebedinoye ozero* (Swan Lake); Puni's *Konyok-Gorbunok* (Hunch-Backed Horse) (1901); Koreshchenko's *Volshebnoye zerkalo* (Magic Mirror) (1905); *Raymonda* (1908); Adam's "The Corsair" (1912); his main new ballets are: *Doch' Guduly* (Gudula's Daughter) to Simon's score (1902); Arends' *Salambo* (1910); *Lyubov' bystra* (Love Is Fleet) to music by Grieg (1913); *Evnika i Petroniy* (Eunice and Petronius) to music by Chopin (1915), etc; worked on the ballet *Sten'ka Razin* (after Glazunov) (1918); devised new choreographic arrangements of several classical ballets, including "The Nut-Cracker" (1919) and "Swan Lake," etc; *Died*: 20 Oct 1924.

GORVITS, Aleksandr Borisovich (Party pseudonym: SASHA) (1897-1918) Party official; CP member from 1915; *Born*: 1897; *Career*: during WW 1 underground Party work; from Apr 1917 member, Kiev City RSDRP(B) Comt, then member, Exec Comt, Kiev Sov; from Dec 1917 member, CC, Ukr Soc-Democratic Party; at 1st All-Ukr Congress of Soviets elected member, Centr Exec Comt; Jan 1918 Sov plen for organizing in Kiev uprising against Ukr Govt--the Centr Rada; *Died*: 1918 killed in the course of the above uprising.

GORYACHKIN, Vasiliy Prokhorovich (1868-1935) Specialist in agric machine-building; hon member, USSR Acad of Sci from 1932; Hon Sci and Tech Worker of RSFSR from 1935; member, All-Union Acad of Agric from 1935; *Born*: 29 Jan 1868 in Moscow; *Educ*: 1890 grad Fac of Physics and Mathematics, Moscow Univ; 1894 grad Moscow Tech College; *Career*: from 1896 lecturer, Moscow Agric Inst (renamed the Petrine Acad of Agric, then the Moscow K. A. Timiryazev Acad of Agric); from 1899 asst prof, from 1913 prof of this Acad; from 1913 founder-head, machine-testing station, which became an experimental base of his sci work; 1919-22 rector, Petrine Acad of Agric, from 1929 dir, All-Union Inst of Agric Mech; also sci dir, All-Union Inst of Mechanization and Electrification of Agric; together with V. R. Vil'yams helped found Moscow Inst of Mechanization and Electrification of Agric; until his death headed the Chair of Agric Machinery at this inst; postulated theoretical principles for the calculation and construction of agric machinery and implements; much of his research, such as the mass and speed theory of agric machinery and implements, the principle of similarity and homogeneity, and the impact theory applied to the work of agric machines is of gen significance for the theory of machines; pioneered and developed the sci of agric mech and established methods of theoretical and experimental research; designed a number of testing devices and instruments (micromanometer, profile meter, traction and rotatory dynamometers, etc); his works served as basis for further research work in agric mechanization; from 1935 founder-ed, publishing house *Teoriya, konstruktsiya i proizvodstvo sel'skokhozyaystvennykh mashin* (Theory, Design and Production of Agricultural Machinery); *Publ: Sobraniye sochineniy* (Collected Works) (7 vol, 1937-49); *Died*: 25 Sept 1935.

GORYUNOV (real name: BENDEL'), Anatoliy Iosifovich (1902-1951) Actor; Pop Artiste of RSFSR from 1946; *Born*: 17 Dec 1902; *Educ*: 1924 grad Theater School at 3rd Studio, Moscow Acad Arts Theater; *Career*: after the early death of his father was greatly influenced by his mother's brothers, the actors I. M. Moskvin and M. M. Tarkhanov; 1920 joined Vakhtangov's Studio (1926 reorganized into Vakhtangov Theater); *Roles*: the Sage in Gozzi's "Princess Turandot" (1922); the Young Soldier in Seyfullina and Pravdukhin's *Virineya* (1925); Puzyr' in Lavrenyov's *Razlom* (Break-Up) (1927); Globa in *Russkiye lyudi* (Russian People) (1942); one of his most significant roles was the jocular French soldier Celestin in Slavin's *Interventsiya* (Intervention) (1933); vividly and acutely performed negative roles: Ivan Babichev in Olesha's *Zagovor chuvstv* (Conspiracy of the Senses) (1929); Baron Nusengen after Balzac's "Human Comedy" (1934); Tonkikh in Afinogenov's *Dalyokoye* (Things Far Away) (1935); Tkachenko in Katayev's *Shyol soldat s fronta* (A Soldier Returned from the Front) (1938); other roles: Benedict in "Much Ado About Nothing" (1936); the seaman Dymov in Pogodin's *Chelovek s ruzh'yom* (Man with a Gun) (1937); the Mayor in *Revizor* (The Government-Inspector) (1939); Sancho Panza in Bulgakov's "Don Quixote" after Cervantes (1941); Globa in *Russkiye lyudi* (Russian People) (1942); the Colonel in Herve's "M'lle Nitouche (1944); Kosta Varra in Virta's *Zagovor obrechyonnykh* (Conspiracy of the Doomed) (1950); also worked as stage dir: co-staged Priestley's "Dangerous Turn" (1940); production and lit manager and dep artistic manager, Vakhtangov Theater; from 1927 teacher, Vakhtangov Theater College; from 1931 taught at State Inst of Stagecraft; from 1932 also film actor; roles: the Party committee secretary in *Partiynyy bilet* (Party Card); Karasik in *Vratar'* (The Goalkeeper), etc; *Awards*: Stalin Prize (1950); Order of the Red Banner of Labor; medals; *Died*: 10 July 1951.

GOTLIB, Yakov Grigor'yevich (1888-1951) Urologist; Dr of Med from 1935; *Born*: 1888; *Career*: 1914-18 country physician and mil surgeon; 1918-21 assoc, Chair of Urology, Kiev Inst of Post-grad Med Training; 1921-23 asst prof, Chair of Urology, Moscow Higher Med School; 1923-31 asst to Prof R. M. Fronshteyn, then assoc prof, Chair of Urology, 1st Moscow Med Inst; from 1931 founder-dir, Urological Clinic, Moscow Oblast Clinical Inst, on the basis of which he later established a chair of urology; also founded Chair of Urology, Centr Inst of Postgrad Med Training; 1944-50 head, Chair of Urology, Med Inst, RSFSR Min of Health; specialized in X-ray diagnosis, the diagnosis of anomalies of the kidneys and ureter, the treatment of nephrolithiasis and the early diagnosis of tumors of the urogenital tract; was first Sov sci to propose prophylactic examinations of workers in the aniline industry for early diagnosis of cancer of the urinary bladder; from 1950 hon member, Moscow Soc of Urologists; wrote over 100 works; *Publ: O fiziologii i patologii mochetochnika* (The Physiology and Pathology of the Ureter) (1926); *O pnevmorene* (Pneumokidney) (1926); *O boleye ranney diagnostike novoobrazovaniy pochki* (The Earlier Diagnosis of Neoplasms of the Kidney) (1927); "Nieren- und Harnleiteranomalien (Klinik und Diagnostik)" (Anomalies of the Kidneys and Ureter [Clinical Aspects and Diagnosis]) (1929); "Zur Kliniktherapie der Nieren- und Harnleitersteine" (The Clinical Treatment of Kidney and Ureter Stones) (1929); *Pochechnaya gematuriya iz malogo ochaga* (Renal Hematuria from a Minor Focus) (1931); *Osnovnyye voprosy prakticheskoy urologii* (Basic Aspects of Practical Urology) (1939); *Died*: 1951 in Moscow.

GOTS, Abram Rafailovich (1882-1940) Politician; CC member, Socialist-Revol Party; *Born*: 1882 of Jewish parents; *Career*: from 1906 active in militant org, Socialist-Revol Party; 1907 sentenced to eight years at hard labor; after 1917 Feb Revol led Socialist-Revol faction in Petrograd Sov; 1917 asst chm, All-Russian Centr Exec Comt of 1st convocation; during 1917 Oct Revol member, Comt for Saving the Fatherland and the Revol; 28-29 Oct 1917 helped stage officer cadet mutiny in Petrograd; 1920 arrested for complicity in acts of terrorism against leaders of Sov regime; 1922 sentenced to death in trial of right-wing Socialist-Revolutionaries; sentence commuted to five years' imprisonment; later amnestied and worked for Simbirsk Province Planning Comt; arrested by State Security organs; *Died*: 1940 in imprisonment.

GOTSINSKIY, Nazhmutdin (1859-1925) Dagh revol; *Born*: 1859; *Educ*: Arabic educ; *Career*: served as bodyguard to Dagh Mil Governor; then chief of police, Kopsubulinsk Precinct; after 1917 Feb Revol member, Dagh Oblast Sov; as mufti served in Mountainous Region Govt; 1917 at a congress of Dagh and Chechen tribes elected 4th Imam of Northern Caucasus; Mar 1918 his troops overthrew Sov regime in Port Petrovsk; 1918 fought against Red Army in Dagh; 1920-21 helped stage anti-Sov revolt in Dagh highlands; after revolt was crushed he fled to the mountains; 1925 discovered by accident and arrested; committed for trial in Rostov-on-Don and sentenced to death; *Died*: 1925 executed.

GOT'YE, Yuriy Vladimirovich (1873-1943) Historian and archeologist; prof; member, USSR Acad of Sci from 1939; *Born*: 18 June 1873; *Educ*: 1895 grad History and Philology Fac, Moscow Univ; *Career*: 1903-15 assoc prof, 1915-41 with some intervals, prof, Moscow Univ; simultaneously taught at Moscow Higher Women's Courses (1902-18), Land-Surveying Inst (1907-17), Shanyavskiy Univ (1913-18), Inst of Eastern Pop (1928-30) and Moscow Inst of Philosophy, Lit and History (1934-41); 1898-1930 learned secr, later dep dir, now All-Union V. I. Lenin Library; 1909-24 simultaneously chief librarian, Rumyantsev Museum; from 1922 corresp member, USSR Acad of Sci; specialist in econ and soc polit history of 17-18th-century Russia; from 1900 conducted archeological excavations and was one of the first to demand that a synthesis of historical and archeological materials should be adopted in research on ancient Slav history; extracted from Swedish archives and published *Pamyatniki oborony Smolenska 1609-1611 gg.* (Monuments on the Defense of Smolensk 1609-1611) (1912) and translated from English *Angliyskiye* *puteshestvenniki v Moskovskom gosudarstve 16-go v.* (English Travellers in 16th-Century Muscovy) (1937); as a follower of V. O. Klyuchevskiy's school, adhered to the "Norman" theory of Kiev Rus' origin; in late 1920's and early 1930's persecuted for this as a "bourgeois" historian, but subsequently, after the censure of M. N. Pokrovskiy's historical teachings, held an eminent place in Sov historiography; *Publ: Zamoskovnyy kray v 17-m v.* (The Trans-Moscow Region in the 17th Century) (1906); *Istoriya oblastnogo upravleniya v Rossii ot Petra I do Yekateriny II* (The History of Regional Administration in Russia from Peter I to Catherine II) (2 vol, 1913-41); *Ocherki istorii zemlevladeniya v Rossii* (Outline History of Land—Ownership in Russia) (1915); *Ocherki po istorii material'noy kul'tury Vostochnoy Yevropy do osnovaniya pervogo Russkogo gosudarstva* (Outline History of Material Culture in Eastern Europe Prior to the Establishment of the First Russian State) (1925); *Zheleznyy vek v Vostochnoy Yevrope* (The Iron Age in Eastern Europe) (1930); *Died*: 17 Dec 1943.

GOVOROV, Leonid Aleksandrovich (1897-1955) Mil commander; Marshal of the Sov Union from 1944; outstanding strategist; member, Acad of Artillery Sci from 1946; cand member, CC, CPSU from 1952; CP member from 1942; *Born*: 21 Feb 1897 in vil Butyrki, Vyatka Province, son of an office worker of peasant descent; *Educ*: 1917 grad Constantine Artillery College, Petrograd; 1933 grad Frunze Mil Acad; 1938 attended Gen Staff Acad; *Career*: 1916 drafted into Russian Army while studying at Petrograd Polytech Inst; 1917 officer, Tomsk garrison; 1918 drafted into Gen Kolchak's Army but deserted in Oct 1919; Jan 1920 joined Red Army; during 1920's tried repeatedly to join CP but was refused for having fought with Gen Kolchak; 1920-21 commander, artillery battalion, 51st Rifle Div; 1921-29 commander artillery regt, then commander of artillery, 51st Rifle Div; 1929-36 commander of artillery, 14th and 15th Rifle Corps and a number of fortified areas in the southern USSR; 1938 transferred from Gen Staff Acad without explanation; 1938-39 taught tactics at Dzerzhinskiy Artillery Acad; 1939-40 chief of artillery staff, 7th Army, Sov-Finnish Front; during Finno-Sov War advocated the direct laying of heavy artillery against pill-boxes, a tactic which won the approval of Gen Timoshenko; 1940-41 dep inspector-gen of artillery, Main Artillery Bd; 1941 commandant, Dzerzhinskiy Artillery Acad; spring 1941 proscribed by NKVD for having fought with Gen Kolchak but spared by Kalinin's personal intervention; from 22 July 1941 commander of artillery, Western Sector, Reserve Front; from 17 Oct 1941 commander, 5th Army, Western Front, which played an important part in the counter-offensive near Moscow in Dec of that year; Apr 1942-45 commander, Leningrad Front; 1943 supervised break-through of Leningrad Blockade; 1944 in charge of liberation of Leningrad Oblast; 1945 in charge of mopping-up operations in Baltic; 1945-46 commander, Leningrad Mil Distr; 1946-47 Chief Inspector Sov Army; 1947-55 commander in chief, Anti-Aircraft Defense and USSR Dep Min of Defense; dep, USSR Supr Sov of 1946, 1950 and 1954 convocations; *Awards*: Order of the Red Star (1920); five Orders of Lenin; Order of Victory; other orders and medals; *Died*: 19 Mar 1955.

GOYDA, Yuriy Andreyevich (1919-1955) Ukr poet; CP member from 1945; *Born*: 15 Mar 1919 in vil Znyatsevo, Transcarpathia; *Educ*: studied at Debrecen Univ, Hungary; *Career*: 1939 first work published; after 1945 reunification of Transcarpathia with Ukr worked on ed staff of newspaper *Zakarpatskaya pravda,* Uzhgorod; headed Transcarpathian Branch, Ukr Writers' Union; *Publ*: collections "My Landsmen" (1948); "Verkhovinsk Poem" (1949); "Verkhovinsk Kray" (1950); "The Sun over Tissa" (1950); "The Sun over the Carpathians" (1951); "Lyrics" (1954); "Hungarian Melodies" (1955); also wrote for children; in Russian translation: *Rozhdeniye skazki. Stikhi i poemy* (The Birth of a Tale. Verse and Poems) (1955); *Izbrannoye. Stikhi i poemy* (Selected Verse and Poems) (1960); *Died*: 2 June 1955.

GOYKHBARG, Aleksandr Grigor'yevich (1883-1962) Lawyer; 1904-17 member, RSDRP (Mensheviks); 1919-24 RCP(B) member; *Born*: 1883; *Career*: co-ed, newspaper *Novaya zhizn'*; prior to Revol wrote, commentaries on contemporary novellae dealing with civil law; 1918 joined Bolsheviks; worked for Pop Comrt of Justice; 1919 on Eastern Front; 1920 member, Siberian Revol Comt and Siberian Oblast Comr of Justice; 1920 prosecutor at Omsk trial of Siberian Govt ministers; Oct 1920-24 Collegium member, Pop Comrt of Justice and simultaneously member and chm, Small Council of Pop Comr; 1921-24 helped draft Sov legislation for initial period of New Econ Policy and directed compilation of RSFSR Civil Code; in following years legal adviser, Pop Comrt of For Trade; despite his dogmatic views and assistance with Sov legislative policy, he was officially criticized for errors in assessing various legal trends and tendencies; *Publ: Khozyaystvennoye pravo RSFSR* (Economic Law of the RSFSR) (Vol 1, 1923); *Sravnitel'noye semeynoye pravo* (Comparative Family Law) (2nd ed, 1927); *Ocherki khozyaystvennogo prava* (An Outline of Economic Law) (1927); *Kurs grazhdanskogo protsessa* (Civil Lawsuit Course) (1928); *Died*: 1962.

GOZHANSKIY (SANYKH), S. N. (1867-1943) Govt official; CP member from 1919; *Born*: 1867; *Career*: from 1897 member, Bund; left-wing Bund leader; member, CC, Bund; worked in Lith and Bel cities; after 1917 Oct Revol member, Moscow Rayon Admin in Petrograd; 1918-19 secr, Tula Province Dept of Labor; from 1922 teacher; from 1939 pensioner; *Died*: 1943.

GRABAR', Igor' Emmanuilovich (1871-1960) Painter and art historian; Pop Artist of USSR; member, USSR Acad of Arts from 1947; *Born*: 25 Mar 1871 in Budapest; *Educ*: 1894-96 studied at Petersburg Acad of Arts under Repin, etc; 1896-1901 lived abroad and studied in Munich; *Career*: 1880 moved to Russia; from 1901 taught art; joined "World of Art" soc; early 1900's painted sensitive landscapes "September Snow" (1903), "February Blue" (1904), etc; some of his works show traces of impressionism; also worked as architect; 1909-14 designed *Zakhar'ino* Sanatorium near Moscow; 1909-16 supervised publ of capital work *Istoriya russkogo iskusstva* (History of Russian Art); 1913-25 directed Tret'yakov Gallery, where he re-arranged the exhibits (1914-15) and published a catalogue (1917); after 1917 Oct Revol headed Dept of Museums and Protection of Art Monuments and Antiquities, Centr State Restoration Workshops; from 1944 dir, Inst of Art History, USSR Acad of Sci; from 1920 prof, Moscow Univ; from 1928 Hon Art Worker of RSFSR; from 1945 Pop Artist of RSFSR; *Works*: paintings: "A Sunny Winter Day" (1941); portraits of N. D. Zelinskiy (1932); "Svetlana" (1933); S. A. Chaplygina (1935), etc; "V. I. Lenin on the Direct Line" (1933); "Peasant Messengers Received by Lenin in 1920" (1938); *Publ:* works on Rublyov (1926) and Repin (1937); study of 18th-century Russian architecture; coauthor and ed, *Istoriya russkogo iskusstva* (History of Russian Art) (5 vol, 1953-60); monographs: *Fyodor Yakovlevich Alekseyev* (1907); coauthor, *Isaak Il'ich Levitan* (1913); *Valentin Alekseyevich Serov.* (1914); *Awards*: two Orders of Lenin; two Orders of the Red Banner of Labor; Stalin Prize (1941); *Died:* 16 May 1960.

GRABAR', Vladimir Emmanuilovich (1865-1956) Lawyer and historian; member, Ukr Acad of Sci from 1926; Dr of Law from 1918; prof of int law; *Born*: 22 Jan 1865 in Vienna; *Educ*: 1888 grad Moscow Univ; *Career*: from 1893 assoc prof, from 1901 prof, Derpt Univ; from 1918 prof, Voronezh, 1922-24 Moscow Univ; 1922-29 consultant, USSR Pop Comrt of For Trade; 1922-23 expert, Sov deleg at Lausanne Conference; 1890-1947 published over 130 works in Russian, Ukr, French, German and English on problems of int law history and dipl law, rights of war, air law, the Status of the Black Sea Straits and for trade monopolies; wrote treatises on ambassadorial law; revised List's textbook on int law (six Russian ed, 1902-26); 1926 helped compile USSR Consular Code; *Publ: Rimskoye pravo v istorii mezhdunarodno-pravovykh ucheniy* (Roman Right in the History of International Law Teachings) (1901); *Materialy k istorii literatury mezhdunarodnogo prava v Rossii (1647-1917)* (Materials on the History of International Law Literature in Russia [1647-1917]) (1958), etc; *Died*: 26 Nov 1956.

GRACHEVA, Yekaterina Konstantinovna (1866-1934) Educ specialist; defectologist; *Born*: 1866; *Career*: devoted 40 years to the care of children with serious physical and psychological defects (among her pupils were even blind deaf-mutes); 1894 founded in Petersburg one of the first Russian asylums for the mentally retarded and epileptics; her success in training very backward pupils was so great that in 1898 the asylum founded the first Russian school for mentally deficient children; 1900 founded a Russian welfare org to help the mentally deficient; 1900 founded courses for training nurses to work with mentally deficient and epileptic children; in early 20th century sponsored and directed the establishment of mental asylums in Moscow, Vyatka, Kursk, etc; visited France, Germany and Sweden to study experience with mentally deficient children; campaigned for compulsory elementary educ of all retarded children and their training in a useful trade; worked to improve conditions at special institutions for retarded children; 1918-20 gave course of lectures in Petrograd to train staff for institutions for defective children; wrote first Russian books on training and educ of retarded children; ***Publ***: main work *Vospitaniye i obucheniye gluboko otstalogo rebyonka* (The Upbringing and Training of Retarded Children) (1932); *Died*: 1934.

GRAFTIO, Genrikh Osipovich (1869-1949) Power eng; prof; member, USSR Acad of Sci from 1932; pioneer of Sov hydroelectr eng; *Born*: 26 Dec 1869 in Dvinsk, son of a railroad eng; *Educ*: 1892 grad Fac of Physics and Mathematics, Novorossiysk Univ, Odessa; 1896 grad Petersburg Inst of Communications Eng; *Career*: 1896-1900 studied hydroelectr plants and electr railroads in Western Europe and USA; 1900-17 designed and supervised construction of railroads in southern and eastern Russia; helped to plan and build Petersburg street-car system; 1905 designed power plant on Malaya Imatra River; 1910-11 planned power plant on Volkhov River; 1917-18 head, Electr Eng Section, Railroad Bd, RSFSR Min of Means of Communication; 1918-20 asst chief eng, 1921-27 chief eng and construction mang, Volkhov Hydroelectr Plant; simultaneously worked for State Commission for the Electrification of Russia; 1928-38 chief eng and construction mang, Lower Svir Hydroelectr Plant, which now bears his name; 1938-45 chief inspector for the construction of hydroelectr power plants, USSR Pop Comrt (Min) of Power Stations; during WW 2 simultaneously in charge of the construction of hydroelectr plants in Uzbek and Arm; 1907-21 lecturer, from 1921 prof and 1945-49 head, Chair of Power Stations, Petersburg (Leningrad) Electr Eng Inst; member, USSR Centr Exec Comt; *Publ*: co-author, *Elektrifikatsiya i transport* (Electrification and Transport) (1921); *Volkhovstroy* (The Construction of the Volkhov Hydro-electrical Plant) (1928); *Awards*: Order of Lenin; Order of the Red Banner of Labor; medals; *Died*: 30 Apr 1949.

GRAN, Moisey Markovich (1867-1940) Hygienist; health service official; *Born*: 27 Apr 1867; *Educ*: 1892 grad Med Fac, Kazan' Univ; *Career*: after grad worked in rural hygiene service, Samara Province; mang, Sanitary Bureau, Samara Province Zemstvo; 1893-97 published several works on the campaign against cholera, malaria, syphilis and malnutrition in Samara Province; chm, Soc Comt for Aid to the Starving; 1908 left rural service and moved tc Petersburg; 1910-14 ed, journal *Vestnik narodnykh universitetov*; 1912 co-founder, Jewish Health Soc; from 1915 head, Refugee Dept and Statistics Dept, Oblast League of Cities; delivered papers on soc hygiene and public health at numerous congresses of the Pirogov Soc of Physicians; also worked for Public Health Soc; founder, Petersburg Chemical and Bacteriological Sanitary Inst; after 1917 Oct Revol head, Sanitary Statistics Dept, "Northern Commune" Pop Comrt of Health; 1920-24 chm, Commission for the Study of the Sanitary Consequences of War, RSFSR Pop Comrt of Health; 1921 chm, Commission for Aid to the Hungry of the Volga Distr; from 1925 asst to Prof N. A. Semashko, Chair of Soc Hygiene, 1st Moscow State Univ; from 1926 ed, journal *Voprosy biologii i patologii yevreyev*; from 1928 prof, Chair of Soc Hygiene, Kazan' Univ; while in Kazan' did research on sanitary conditions in Tatary; 1933 returned to Moscow and continued research on the sanitary consequences of the Civil War at the Hygiene Inst, 1st Moscow Med Inst; apart from rural med, alcoholism, syphilis, malaria and malnutrition also studied occupational hygiene among educ and bakery workers; wrote over 60 works; *Publ: Iz materialov po sifilisu Samarskoy gubernii* (Statistics on Syphilis in Samara Province) (1897); *Kholera i bor'ba s ney* (Cholera and Anti-Cholera Measures) (1919); coauthor, *Profvrednost' i profpatologiya pedagogov* (The Incidence of Disease Among Teachers and Their Occupational Pathology) (1928), etc; *Died*: 1940.

GRANOVSKIY (AZARKH), Aleksey Mikhaylovich (1890-1937) Jewish stage dir; Hon Artiste of RSFSR from 1926; *Born*: 1890; *Educ*: 1910-11 studied at Petersburg School of Stagecraft; 1911-13 at Munich Theater Acad; simultaneously practical work at Munich Arts Theater under Reinhardt, etc; 1914-17 abroad, studying stagecraft; *Career*: 1914 began work as stage dir at Riga New Theater with Verhaeren's "Philip II"; this was followed in 1918 by the staging of "Macbeth" and Sophocles' "King Oedipus" at the Petrograd State Circus; operas "Faust" and "Sadko" at Petrograd Bolshoy Theater; 1921 at Moscow Circus staged Meyakovskiy's *Misterii buf* (Mystery Bouffe); 1919 in Petrograd founded Jewish Theater Studio, which in 1920 was transferred to Moscow and reorganized into State Jewish Chamber Theater; until 1929 artistic manager of this theater; directed plays: *Vecher Sholom Aleykhema* (Sholom Aleykhem's Party) (1921); *Koldun'ya* (Sorceress) after Goldfaden (1922); "200,000" after Sholom Aleykhem (1923); Dobrushin and Oyslender's *Tri yevreyskikh izyuminki* (Three Jewish Raisins) (1924); Perets' *Noch' na starom rynke* (Night at the Old Market) (1925); *Puteshestviye Veniamina III* (Benjamin III's Journey) after Mendele Moykher-Sforim (1927); *Chelovek vozdukha* (Air Man) after Sholom Aleykhem (1928); his shows depicted the old Jewish settlement with its typical way of life and inhabitants; he accepted the comical and sad traits of the settlement's life, applying the technique of grotesque irony; taught a number of famous actors at this theater, including M. S. Mikhoels and V. L. Zuskin; directed film *Yevreyskoye schast'ye* (Jewish Luck) (1925); 1928 decided not to return to USSR from a tour abroad; worked in for film ind; *Died*: 14 Mar 1937.

GRASHCHENKOV, Nikolay Ivanovich (1901-1965) Neurologist and neurophysiologist; prof; Dr of Med from 1935; corresp member, USSR Acad of Sci from 1939; member, Bel Acad of Sci from 1947; member, USSR Acad of Med Sci from 1944; CP member from 1918; *Born*: 26 Mar 1901 in vil Zabor, now Smolensk Oblast; *Educ*: 1926 grad Med Fac, Moscow Univ; 1932 grad Inst of Red Prof in philosophy and natural sci; *Career*: 1926-33 worked at Med Fac, Moscow Univ (from 1930 1st Moscow Med Inst) and at All-Union Gorky Inst of Experimental Med; 1935-37 studied the physiology of the sensory organs and the electrophysiology of the nervous system at Cambridge, New York, New Haven, Boston and Montreal univ laboratories; 1937-39 First Dep, then acting USSR Pop Comr of Health; 1939-44 dir, All-Union Inst of Experimental Med; 1941-45 consultant on neuropathology and neurosurgery to Army Med Corps; 1944-48 dir, Inst of Neurology, USSR Acad of Med Sci; 1947-51 president, Bel Acad of Sci; 1951-58 head, Chair of Nervous Diseases, Centr Inst of Post-grad Med Training, Moscow and head, Clinical Neurophysiological Laboratory, USSR Acad of Med Sci; 1958-65 head, Chair of Nervous Diseases, 1st Moscow Med Inst and head, Laboratory for the Study of Nervous and Humoral Regulation, USSR Acad of Sci; 1951-58 chm, Learned Med Council and member, Higher Certifying Commission, USSR Min of Health; dep chief ed, *Bol'shaya meditsinskaya entsiklopediya* (Large Medical Encyclopedia) (2nd ed); member, ed council, journals *Voprosy neyrokhirurgii, Zhurnal nevropatologii i psikhiatrii imeni S. S. Korsakova,* etc; vice-pres, European Regional Comt, World Health Org; 1955 attended Int Congress of Neuropathologists, London; 1957 attended 10th session, Gen Assembly, World Health Org; 1959 accompanied the dir-gen of the World Health Org, Dr Marcolino Gomes Candau, on a tour of Uzbek SSR; 1950 helped to break-up L. A. Orbeli's school of physiology; wrote over 160 works; *Publ*: doctor's thesis *Eksperimental'noye izucheniye patogeneza epilepsii* (Experimental Research on the Pathogenesis of Epilepsy) (1935); coauthor, *Uchebnik nervnykh bolezney* (A Textbook on Nervous Diseases) (1939); *Raspoznavaniye i lecheniye raneniy perifericheskikh nervov* (The Detection and Treatment of Injuries to the Peripheral Nerves) (1942); *Anaerobnaya infektsiya mozga* (Anaerobic Infection of the Brain) (1944); *Ognestrel'nyye raneniya pozvonochnika i spinnogo mozga* (Gunshot Wounds of the Spine and Spinal Cord) (1946); *Cherepnomozgovyye raneniya i metody ikh lecheniya* (Craniocerebral Wounds and Methods of Treating Them) (1947); *Komarinyy (yaponskiy) entsefalit* (Mosquito [Japanese] Encephalitis) (1947); *Mezhnevronnyye apparaty svyazi-sinapsy i ikh rol' v fiziologii i patologii* (Interneuronal Synapse Links and Their Role in Physiology and Pathology) (1948); *Ocherki virusnykh porazheniy tsentral'noy nervnoy sistemy* (Studies of Viral Affections of the Central Nervous System) (1951); coauthor and ed, *Rukovodstvo po nevrologii* (Neurology Manual) (1957); *Awards*: Order of Lenin; *Died*: 8 Oct 1965 in Moscow.

GRASIS, K.Ya. (1894-1937) Party official; member, Lat Soc-Democratic Party from 1909; 1913-17 Menshevik; CP member from May 1917; *Born*: 1894; *Career*: Mar-Oct 1917 chm, Cheboksary Sov of Workers and Soldiers' Dep; 1917-19 chm, Kazan' Revol Headquarters; chm, Cheka and head, Special Dept, Caspian-Caucasian Front; subsequently head, Information Bureau, RSFSR State Publ House; 1927, by decree of CPSU(B) Centr Control Comission, expelled from the Party for taking advantage of his positions for personal gain; arrested by State Security organs; *Died*: 1937 in Imprisonment.

GRATSIANSKIY, Nikolay Pavlovich (1886-1945) Medievalist; Dr of Historical Sci; prof; *Born*: Oct 1886; *Educ*: 1910 grad History and

Philology Fac, Kazan' Univ; *Career*: 1914-21 assoc prof, then prof, Kazan' Univ; from 1922 prof, 2nd Moscow Univ; 1934-36 and 1941-45 prof, Moscow State Univ; also head, Chair of Medieval History, Moscow's Lenin Teachers' Training Inst; 1921-45 (with brief intervals) also worked for Inst of History, Russian Assoc of Soc Sci Research Institutes and for Inst of History, USSR Acad of Sci; specialized in socio-econ history of early and classic Middle Ages; studied agrarian history of late Roman Empire and early Middle Ages, history of Ancient Germans, Western Slavs, etc; *Publ: Parizhskiye remeslennyye tsekhi v XIII-XIV stoletiyakh* (Parisian Craft Workshops in the 13th-14th Centuries) (1911); *Krest'yanskiye i rabochiye dvizheniya v sredniye veka* (Peasant and Workers' Movements in the Middle Ages) (1924); *Zapadnaya Yevropa v sredniye veka. Istochniki sotsial'no-ekonomicheskoy istorii* (Western Europe in the Middle Ages. Sources of Socio-Economic History) (1925); *Burgundskaya derevnya v X-XII stoletiyakh* (The Burgundian Village in the 10th-12th Centuries) (1919-35); *Iz sotsial'no-ekonomicheskoy istorii zapadno-yevropeyskogo srednevekov'ya* (The Socio-Economic History of the West European MiddleAges) (1960); *Died*: 4 Nov 1945.

GRAUERMAN, Grigoriy L'vovich (1861-1921 Obstetrician and gynecologist; *Born*: 1861; *Educ*: 1885 grad Natural Sci Fac, Petersburg Univ; 1889 grad Med Fac, Moscow Univ; *Career*: 1889-94 asst, from 1894 taught obstetrics and women's diseases at Med Orderlies and Midwifes School, Staro-Yekaterininskaya Hospital; from 1898 head, Maternity Ward, which he expanded from 13 to 60 beds; 1907-21 founder-dir, Moscow's Lepekhin City Maternity Clinic; 1910-21 founder-dir, Timister Postnatal Diseases Hospital, the first of its kind in Russia (now Moscow Oblast Obstetrics and Gynecology Research Inst); founded at these establishments gynecological outpatients departments, infant consultation clinics, milk kitchens and diagnosis rooms; from 1918 worked for Moscow City Health Dept; helped organize Sov mother and child care system; a Moscow maternity home is named for him; *Publ: K voprosu ob organizatsii akusherskoy pomoshchi v Moskve* (The Organization of Obstetrical Care in Moscow) (1901); *K statistike poslerodovykh zabolevaniy i smertnosti pri nikh v Moskve za vremya s 1897 po 1903 god v svyazi s voprosom ob uchrezhdenii spetsial'nogo otdeleniya dlya zabolevshikh poslerodovymi formami* (Statistics on Postnatal Diseases and Their Mortality Rate in Moscow from 1897 to 1903 in Connection with the Establishment of a Special Department for Patients Suffering from Puerperal (Diseases) (1905); *Chto takoye okhrana materinstva i kak yeyo sleduyet osushchestvit'* (Maternity Care and How to Organize It) (1919); *Died:* 1921 in Moscow.

GRAVE, Dmitriy Aleksandrovich (1863-1939) Mathematician; Dr of Mathematics from 1896; prof; member, Ukr Acad of Sci from 1919; hon member, USSR Acad of Sci from 1929; *Born*: 6 Sept 1896 in Kirillov, now Vologda Oblast; *Educ*: 1885 grad Petersburg Univ; *Career*: 1889-97 taught at Petersburg Univ, Inst of Communications Eng and Higher Women Courses; 1897-99 prof, Khar'kov Univ; from 1899 prof, Kiev Univ, Inst of Nat Econ and other higher educ institutions; 1934-39 dir, Inst of Mathematics, Ukr Acad of Sci; specialist in integration of differential equations, mathematical theory of geographical mapping, algebra and numbers theory; created Kiev algebra and numbers theory school; *Publ: Ob integratsii chastnykh differentsial'nykh urovneniy pervogo poryadka* (The Integration of Particular Differential Equations of the First Order) (1889); *Ob osnovnykh zadachakh matematicheskoy teorii postroyeniya geograficheskikh kart* (Main Problems of the Mathematical Theory of Geographical Mapping) (1896); *Teoriya konechnykh grupp* (Theory of Finite Groups) (1908); *Kurs algebraicheskogo analiza* (Course of Algebraic Analysis) (1910); *Kratkiy kurs matematicheskogo analiza* (Short Course of Mathematical Analysis) (1924); *Teoreticheskaya mekhanika na osnove tekhniki* (Theoretical Mechanics on the Basis of Technology) (1932); *Awards:* Order of the Red Banner of Labor; *Died:* 19 Dec 1939.

GRAVE, Ivan Platonovich (1874-1960) Maj-gen of eng; Dr of Tech Sci; prof; member, Acad of Artillery Sci from 1947; expert on internal ballistics; *Born*: 1874; *Educ*: 1900 grad Mikhail Artillery Acad; *Career*: 1900-04 taught at Konstantin and Mikhail Artillery Colleges; 1904-17 taught at Mikhail Artillery Acad; from 1918 head, Training Dept and prof, Red Army Artillery Acad; *Publ: Kurs teoreticheskoy vnutrenney ballistiki* (A Course of Theoretical Internal Ballistics) (1933-38); *Ballistika poluzamknutogo prostranstva* (The Ballistics of Semi-Closed Space) (1940); *Awards*: Stalin Prize, 1st Class (1942); two Orders of Lenin; two Orders of the Red Banner; Order of the Fatherland War; medals; *Died*: Mar 1960; buried in Moscow's Novodevich'ye Cemetery.

GRDINA, Yuriy Vyacheslavovich (1901-1967) Metallurgist; Dr of Tech Sci; prof from 1943; Hon Sci and Tech Worker from 1961; CP member from 1943; *Born*: 6 July 1901; *Educ*: 1945 grad Tomsk Technol Inst; *Career*: 1925-27 assoc, Tomsk Inst of Applied Physics; 1927-32 at Tomsk Univ; from 1928 simultaneously assoc, from 1958 head, Chair of Physics, Siberian Metal Inst, Tomsk; specialized in rail production technol; *Awards*: USSR State Prize (1967); *Died*: 13 Nov 1967.

GREBENSHCHIKOV, Il'ya Vasil'yevich (1887-1953) Chemist; prof; member from 1932 and Presidium member from 1947, USSR Acad of Sci; *Born*: 24 June 1887 in Petersburg; *Educ*: 1910 grad Petersburg Univ; *Career*: 1912-14 worked at Russian Mint; from 1912 taught at Petersburg Electrotech Inst; 1922-32 prof of chemistry and theoretical electrochemistry, Leningrad Electrotech Inst; helped found Leningrad State Optical Inst; founder and head, chemical laboratory of this inst; 1933 founded laboratory of silicate chemistry, which in 1948 was reorganized into Leningrad Inst of Silicate Chemistry; chemical laboratory head and dir of this inst; 1909-12, studied the effects of high pressure (up to 3,000 atmospheres) on cristallization temperatures of some organic compounds and was the first to study the effects of pressure (up to 4,000 atmospheres) on the structure and temperature of eutectics in double systems; during his research work on adiabatic compression and expansion of a number of liquids discovered anomalies, which he explained as allotropic conversion in liquids; 1915 together with N. N. Kachalov laid the groundwork of Russian optical glass production; his studies on interaction of molten glass with gases and the conditions for the formation of homogeneous glass were of great value for sci theory of optical glass production; 1931 obtained new porous glasses with adsorption properties; devised a surface treatment of optical parts, the so-called clarification of optics (covering glass with a thin translucent film, which reduces light reflection); devised new chemical theory for polishing glass and metals and worked out new polishing pastes, from 1944 directed research on physical and chemical properties and the synthesis of new transparent plastics to be used in optics; dep, USSR Supr Sov of 3rd convocation; *Publ*: coauthor, *O khimicheskoy stoykosti stekla* (Chemical Stability of Glass) (1931); *Khimicheskiye reaktsii na poverkhnosti silikatov i ikh znacheniye dlya tekhniki* (Chemical Reactions on the Surface of Silicates and Their Technical Significance) (1937); coauthor, *Prosvetleniye optiki. Umen'sheniye otrazheniya sveta poverkhnost'yu stekla* (Clarification of Optics. Reduction of Glass Surface Reflection) (1946); coauthor and ed, *Fiziko-khimicheskiye svoystva troynoy sistemy okis' natriya-okis' svintsa-kremnezyom* (Physical and Chemical Properties of the Triple Sodium Oxide-Lead Oxide-Silica System) (1949), etc; *Awards*: two Orders of Lenin; other orders; two Stalin Prizes (1942 and 1952); *Died*: 8 Feb 1953.

GREBNER, Georgiy Eduardovich (1892-1954) Scriptwriter; *Born*: 13 Apr 1892; *Educ*: 1911 grad Navigators' College; *Career*: 1918-22 mil correspondent at Civil War fronts; from 1922 film work; worked for *Mezhrabpom-Rus'* film studio; scripted feature and cartoon films; his works vary greatly in themes and genres; specialized in screen adaptation of lit works and Russian historical events; *Works*: wrote scripts for films: *Chetyre i pyat'* (Four and Five) (1924); *Doroga k schast'yu* (Road to Happiness) (1925); *Kirpichiki* (Bricklets) (1925); coauthor, *Medvezh'ya svad'ba* (Bears' Wedding) (1926) and *Salamandra* (Salamander) (1928); adaptations of lit works: Lavrenyov's *Razlom* (The Break-Up) (1929); Zegers' *Vosstaniye rybakov* (Revolt of the Fishermen) (1934); Jules Verne's "The Young Captain" (1946); Dubov's *Ogni na reke* (Lights on the River) (1954), etc; scripts on historical themes: coauthor, *Suvorov* (1941); Zolotovskiy's *Gibel' 'Orla'* (The Loss of the "Eagle") (1941); *Kreyser 'Varyag'* (The Cruiser "Varyag") (1947); feature films: *Posledniy vystrel* (The Last Shot) (1926); *Sluchay na mel'nitse* (The Incident at the Mill) (1926); *Chuzhaya* (The Stranger) (1927); coauthor, Lazhechnikov's *Ledyanoy dom* (The Ice House) (1928); *Sopernitsy* (The Rivals) (1929); A. Tolstoy's *Khromoy barin* (The Lame Landowner) (1929); *Zavtra noch'* (Tomorrow Night) (1930); *Gibel' sensatsii* (End of a Sensation) (1935); Gogol's *Kak possorilis' Ivan Ivanovich s Ivan Nikiforovichem* (How Ivan Ivanovich Quarreled with Ivan Nikiforovich) (1941); *Prokuror* (The Prosecutor) (1941); *Doch' moryaka* (The Sailor's Daughter) (1942);

Kuprin's *Belyy pudel'* (The White Poodle) (1956); cartoon films: *Lisa i drozd* (The Fox and the Blackbird) (1946); *U strakha glaza veliki* (Fear Takes Molehills for Mountains) (1947); *Volshebnyy kover* (The Magic Carpet) (1948); Aksakov's *Alen'kiy tsvetochek* (The Little Red Flower) (1952); Kelyan-Gruy's *Orekhovyy prutik* (The Nut-Tree Twig) (1955); coauthor, Andersen's "The Snow Queen" (1957); pop sci films: *Sputnik malogo cheloveka* (The Little Man's Companion); *Kurs-nord* (Course North); *Nepreryvnyy potok* (Continuous Stream); *Zhidkoye solntse* (Liquid Sun); *Tungusskiy meteorit* (The Tungus Meteorite); "Roald Amundsen"; *Awards*: Stalin Prize (1947); Order of the Red Banner of Labor; *Died*: 24 June 1954.

GRECHISHCHEV, Ksenofont Mikhaylovich (1873-1957) Hygienist; *Born*: 1873; *Educ*: 1894-99 studied at Tomsk Univ but was expelled for involvement in student riots; 1899-1900 completed med training at Berlin Univ; *Career*: from 1901 health official in Siberia; 1902 organized public health facilities in Tomsk; after 1917 Oct Revol helped to organize health service in Siberia and combatted infectious diseases and other consequences of the Civil War; head, Sanitary Section, Irkutsk Province Health Dept; head, Sanitary Epidemiological Section, Siberian Health Dept; while working as an epidemiologist in Omsk co-founded Omsk Med Inst; 1921-40 founder-head, Chair of Communal Hygiene, Tomsk Med Inst; supervised training of over 200 health officials and hygienist; founder and life-chm, Tomsk Branch and bd member, All-Union Soc of Hygienists; from 1926 dep, Omsk City Sov; wrote over 150 works; *Publ: Opyt massovogo krysoistrebleniya v gorode Tomske* (Experience in the Mass Extermination of Rats in Tomsk) (1913); *Materialy dlya kharakteristiki sanitarnogo sostoyaniya pereselencheskikh posyolkov Sibirskogo kraya* (Material on the Sanitary Conditions of Resettlement Villages in the Siberian Kray) (1928); ed, *Sanitarnoye sostoyaniye, usloviya truda i byta, fizicheskoye razvitiye i zabolevayemost' promyshlennykh rabochikh Sibiri* (The Sanitary, Working and Living Conditions, the Physical Development and Sick-Rate Among Industrial Workers in Siberia) (1929); *Ubornyye i ikh ustroystvo v nekanalizovannykh vladeniyakh* (Toilets and Their Installation on Properties Without Sewers) (1934); *Gigiyena na polevykh rabotakh* (Hygiene During Field Work); *Died*: 1957.

GREKOV, Boris Dmitriyevich (1882-1953) Historian; Dr of Historical Sci; prof; member, USSR Acad of Sci from 1935; member, USSR Acad of Architecture from 1939; member, Polish and Bulgarian Acad of Sci and hon member, Bel Acad of Sci from 1947; Hon Dr of Philosophy, Prague Univ from 1947; *Born*: 22 Apr 1882 in Mirgorod, now Poltava Oblast; *Educ*: 1901-05 studied at Warsaw Univ; 1907 grad Moscow Univ; *Career*: from 1910 teacher at higher educ institutions in Petersburg, Perm', Simferopol' and Moscow; 1920's-early 1930's prof, Leningrad Univ and member, Permanent Historical and Archeological Commission, USSR Acad of Sci; 1937-53 dir, Inst of History, USSR Acad of Sci and prof, Moscow Univ; simultaneously 1944-46 dir, Inst of Material Culture (now Inst of Archeology), USSR Acad of Sci; 1947-51 dir, Inst of Slavic Languages and Lit, USSR Acad Sci; 1946-53 acad secr, Dept of History and Philosophy, USSR Acad of Sci; from 1946 also head, Chair of USSR History, Acad of Soc Sci, CC, CPSU; very active in the campaign against M. N. Pokrovskiy's historical school and against the "nationalistic" teaching of the Ukr historian M. S. Grushevskiy; after the collapse of these schools, headed so-called "anti-Norman" school of Sov historiography; in this connection rejected the formal juridical treatment of feudalism, criticized thesis of slavo-holding and mercantile nature of the Eastern Slav's development, introducing conception of developed agriculture and feudalism; also advanced the theory of transition of Eastern Slavs from communal structure to feudalism, by-passing the slave-holding stage; founded and directed acad publ *Ocherki istorii SSSR* (Outline History of the USSR) and helped publish document collections, including *Krepostnaya manufaktura v Rossii* (Feudal Industry in Russia) (4 vol, 1930-34) and *Pravda Russkaya* (Russian Truth) (2 vol, 1940-47); dep, RSFSR Supr Sov of 2nd convocation and USSR Supr Sov of 3rd convocation; 1941-45 Presidium member, Slavic Comt; 1949-50 member, Permanent Comt, World Peace Congress; from 1951 dep chm, USSR Peace Comt; *Publ: Novgorodskiy dom sv. Sofii* (Novgorod House of St. Sophia) (Part 1, 1914); *Opyt obsledovaniya khozyaystvennykh anket 18-go v.* (A Study of 18th-Century Economic Forms) (1929); *Ocherki po istorii feodalizma v Rossii* (Outline History of Feudalism in Russia) (1934); *Feodal'nyye otnosheniya v Kiyevskom gosudarstve* (Feudal Relations in the State of Kiev) (1936); *Bor'ba Rusi za sozdaniye svoyego gosudarstva* (Russia's Struggle to Establish Its Own State) (1942); *Kul'tura Kiyevskoy Rusi* (The Culture of Kiev Rus) (1944); *Krest'yane na Rusi s drevneyshikh vremyon do 17-go v.* (Peasants in Rus from Ancient Times to the 17th Century) (1946); *Vinodol'skiy statut ob obshchestvennom i politicheskom stroye Vinodola* (The Vinodol Statute on the Social and Political Structure in Vinodol) (1948); coauthor, *Zolotaya orda i yeyo padeniye* (The Golden Horde and Its Downfall) (1950); *Politsa. Opyt izucheniya obshchestvennykh otnosheniy v Politse 15-17 vv.* (Politsa. A Study of Social Relations in 15-17th-Century Politsa) (1951); coauthor and exec ed, *Istoriya kul'tury drevney Rusi* (History of the Culture of Ancient Rus) (2 vol, 1951); *Kiyevskaya Rus'* (Kiev Rus) (6th ed, 1953); coauthor, *Ocherki istorii SSSR. Period feodalizma 9-15 vv.* (Outline History of the USSR. The Period of 9-15th-Century Feudalism) (2 vol, 1953); *Kratkiy ocherk istorii russkogo krest'yanstva* (A Brief Outline History of the Russian Peasantry) (1958); *Izbrannyye trudy* (Selected Works) (2 vol, 1957-60); *Awards*: three Stalin Prizes (1943, 1947, 1952); *Died*: 9 Sept 1953.

GREKOV, Ivan Ivanovich (1867-1934) Surgeon; Dr of Med from 1901; Hon Sci Worker of RSFSR from 1932; *Born*: 17 Mar 1867; *Educ*: 1894 grad Med Fac, Yur'yev (Tartu) Univ; *Career*: from grad until death worked at Obukhov Hospital, Petersburg (Leningrad), where he was one of A. A. Troyanov's most brilliant pupils and became chief physician; 1901 defended doctor's thesis on the surgical treatment of cranial defects, for which he recommended the use of calcined bone; 1913 performed almost total resection of pancreas for cancer; from 1915 until death also prof, Fac Surgery Clinic, then Hospital Surgery Clinic, State Inst of Med Knowledge; did important research on penetrating wounds of the thorax, for which he advocated predominantly conservative treatment; 1922 was first Russian surgeon to succeed in forming an artificial oesophagus by the Roux-Herzen method; 1928 performed open heart surgery (ventriculotomia cordis explorativa) for the removal of a bullet and predicted the possibility of open surgery for heart diseases; made major contribution to abdominal surgery; devised two operations on the sigmoid colon (Grekov I and Grekov II) which won universal recognition; detected the functional relationship between Bauhin's valve and the pylorus; used Pavlov's theory to explain the pathogenesis of certain diseases (stomach ulcers, appendicitis, etc); maintained close contacts with Pavlov; 1928 established special laboratory and clinic at Obukhov Hospital to study digestive disorders; from 1932 founder-dir, Med Inst, Obukhov Hospital; wrote still-valid papers on intestinal blockage, peritonitis and ulcers of the stomach and duodenum; from 1911 dep chm, after WW 2 chm, Pirogov Surgical Soc; from 1922 ed, journal *Vestnik khirurgii i pogranichnykh oblastey* (formerly *Khirurgicheskiy arkhiv Vel'yaminova* and now *Vestnik khirurgii imeni I. I. Grekova*); 1924 chm, 16th All-Union Congress of Surgeons; *Publ*: doctor's thesis *Materialy k voprosu o kostnykh defektakh cherepa i ikh lechenii* (Material on Cranial Bone Defects and Their Treatment) (1901); *Materialy k voprosu o lechenii razlichnykh gnoynykh peritonitov* (Material on the Treatment of Various Suppurative Forms of Peritonitis) (1914); *Svyaz' yazvy zheludka i dvenadtsatiperstnoy kishki s appenditsitom* (The Relationship of Ulcers of the Stomach and Duodenum to Appendicitis) (1923); *K lecheniyu zavorotov sigmovidnoy kishki* (The Treatment of Obstructions of the Sigmoid Colon) (1924); *Bauginospazmy i bauginoplastika. L voprosu o tak nazyvayemom khronicheskom appenditsite* (Bauhin's Spasms and Bauhin's Plastic Operation. "Chronic Appendicitis") (1927); *Oshibki v khirurgii bryushnoy polosti* (Errors in Surgery of the Abdominal Cavity) (1927); *Ileus* (1928); *Iz oblasti oshibok i opasnostey v khirurgii krovenosnykh sosudov* (Errors and Dangers of Surgery of the Blood Vessels) (1933); *Izbrannyye trudy* (Selected Works) (1952); *Died*: 11 Feb 1934.

GEKOV, Konstantin Dmitriyevich (1879-1927) Operetta singer and producer; *Born*: 27 Oct 1879; *Career*: stage debut in Novocherkassk; worked for Blyumental'-Tamarin Theater, Moscow; worked at operetta theaters in Kiev, Odessa, Khar'kov and Rostov; then with S.N. Novikov's Operetta Theater, Petersburg; from 1910 producer, Ye. V. Potopchina's Operetta Theater, Moscow; 1918-22 at operetta theaters in Khar'kov, Baku and Tbilisi; 1922-27 at Moscow Operetta Theater; translated into Russian the score of many Viennese operettas; *Died*: 28 June 1927.

GREKOV, Mitrofan Borisovich (until 1911: MARTYSHCHENKO,

Mitrofan Pavlovich) (1882-1934) Painter; specialist in battle scenes; *Born*: 3 June 1882 at farmstead Sharpayevka, Don Army Oblast; *Educ*: 1899-1903 studied at Odessa Arts College; 1911 grad Petersburg Acad of Arts; *Career*: 1911 after graduating acad, entitled "free artist" for his picture "Oxen at the Plough"; 1913 painted pictures on subjects from the history of the Grenadier, Cuirassier and Pavel regts; in WW 1 served in the ranks and made many sketches; volunteered for Red Army; fought in Civil War and in his sketches and paintings depicted operations of the 1st Cavalry Army; 1923 joined Assoc of Revol Russian Painters and organized its Novocherkassk branch; *Works*: paintings "Kornilov's Men" (1919); "Transport of Shells at Novocherkassk" (1920); "Volodarskiy Regiment Entering Novocherkassk" (1921), etc; "Machine-Gun Cart" (1925; 2nd version 1933); "Joining Budyonny's Detachment" (1923); "The Battle of Yegorlykskaya" (1927; 2nd version 1930), etc; "Red Banner in the Sal'sk Steppe" (1923); "Mopping Up General Krzhyzhanovskiy's Army"; "At a Cossack Farm" (1924); "Zhlobin's Men at Novocherkassk" (1925); "Budyonnyy's Detachment in 1918," "Retreat of Denikin's Army" (1926); "Retreat of Denikin's Army from Novocherkassk," "Battle for Rostov at Bol'shiye Saly," "General Pavlov's Frozen Cossacks," "Cavalry Attack" (1927); "I. V. Stalin and K. Ye. Voroshilov in the Trenches on the Tsaritsyn Front," "Next Day at Platovskaya Village," "To the Kuban," "Trumpeters of the 1st Horse Army" (1934), etc; 1929 painted diorama "Capture of Rostov"; 1935 a posthumous exhibition was held in Moscow; his works are displayed at Moscow galleries: State Tret'yakov Gallery, Centr Sov Army Museum, Museum of USSR Revol, and at galleries of other cities; 1935 the Stalin Special Cavalry Brigade founded a soldiers' amateur art workshop named for him; this subsequently developed into the Grekov Mil Painters' Studio, under the Sov Army's Main Polit Bd; *Awards*: gold watch with inscription: "To M. B. Grekov, Master-Painter of Battle Scenes, From the 1st Horse Army"; *Died*: 27 Nov 1934.

GRENDAL', Vladimir Davidovich (1884-1940) Mil commander, col, Russian Army; col-gen of artillery from 1940; *Born*: 22 Mar 1884 in Sveaborg; *Educ*: 1902 grad Pskov Cadet School; 1905 grad Mikhaylov Artillery College; 1911 grad Mikhaylov Artillery Acad; *Pos*: from Dec 1917 in Red Army; 1917-20 senior artillery experimentalist, Main Artillery Range; artillery inspector, Southern and Southwestern Fronts; 1921-25 artillery commander, Kiev, then Petrograd Mil Distr; commandant, Artillery Acad; Red Army dep artillery inspector; 1925-32 Red Army artillery inspector; 1932-35 Red Army dep artillery inspector; worked for Main Artillery Bd; 1935-38 senior instructor, Chair of Artillery, Frunze Mil Acad; dept head, Artillery Acad; 1938-40 dep head, Main Artillery Bd and chm, Comt for Design and Production of New Artillery Pieces; in 1939-40 Sov-Finnisch War field artillery inspector; army group commander; commander, 13th Army; *Publ*: *Ogon' artillerii* (Artillery Fire) (1926); *Polevaya sluzhba artilleriyskogo kommandovaniya i shtabov* (Field Service of Artillery Headquarters and Staffs) (1927); *Rol' artillerii v obshchevoyskovom boyu* (Artillery in Combined Military Action) (1937); *Artilleriya v pozitsionnoy voyne* (Artillery in Stabilized Warfare) (1938); *Razvitiye artilleriyskoy tekhniki* (Development of Artillery Engineering) (1938); *Artilleriya vo vstrechnom, nastupatel'nom i oboronitel'nom boyu strelkovogo korpusa i divizii* (Artillery in Encounter, Offensive and Defensive Action of the Infantry Corps and Division) (1938); *Artilleriya v osnovnykh vidakh boya* (Artillery in the Basic Forms of Battle) (1940); *Awards*: Order of Lenin; Order of the Red Banner; *Died*: Nov 1940 of lung cancer.

GRIBKOV, Mikhail Petrovich (1909-1964) Party official; CP member from 1939; *Born*: 2 Sept 1909; *Educ*: 1934 grad Omsk Agric Inst; 1952 grad Higher Party School, CC, CPSU; *Career*: 1934-40 zootech, senior zootech, then dep dir of various sovkhozes in Omsk Oblast; 1941-45 in Sov Army; from 1945 Party and govt work; 1947-49 secr, Omsk City CPSU(B) Comt; 1949-56 worked for CC, CPSU; 1956-58 chm, Kuybyshev Oblast Exec Comt; 1958-60 with RSFSR Council of Min; from 1960 second secr, CC, CP Lat; dep, USSR Supr Sov of 5th and 6th convocations; from 1961 member, Centr Auditing Commission, CC, CPSU; *Awards*: Order of Lenin (1957); medal "For Valiant Labor" (1959); *Died*: 14 Jan 1964.

GRIBKOV, Vladimir Vasil'yevich (1902-1960) Actor; Hon Artiste of RSFSR from 1948; *Born*: 15 May 1902; *Educ*: studied at Moscow Acad Arts Theater school; *Career*: 1924-38 and 1944-60 with Moscow Acad Arts Theater; 1938-44 film actor only; also gave recitations and performed in variety; did sound for cartoon films; *Roles*: in theater: Abram in Katayev's *Kvadratura kruga* (Squaring the Circle) (1928); the Trumpeter in *Yegor Bulychyov i drugiye* (Yegor Bulychyov and Co) (1934); Pickwick in "The Pickwick Papers" after Dickens (1934); Dorimedont in *Pozdnyaya lyubov* (Late Love) (1944); Kostylyov in *Na dne* (Lower Depths) (1955); Smerdyakov in *Brat'ya Karamazovy* (The Brothers Karamazov) (1960), etc; film roles: Mikhaylov in *Poslednyaya noch'* (The Last Night) (1937); the peasant Nikita Gur'yanov in *V poiskakh radosti* (In Search of Joy) (1940), etc; also played in varous comedy series: the manager Obolenskiy in *Aktrisa* (The Actress) (1943); the house-manager in *Bliznetsy* (Twins) (1945); the orthopedic appliances specialist Zuyev in *Povest' o nastoyashchem cheloveke* (The Tale of a Real Man) (1948), etc; *Awards*: Stalin Prize (1952); *Died*: 22 Oct 1960.

GRIBOV, Sergey Yefimovich (1895-1938) Bel mil commander; staff capt, Russian Army; corps commander, Red Army from 1935; Civil War veteran; CP member from 1926; *Born*: 5 July 1895 in Roslavl', Smolensk Province, son of a railroad worker; *Educ*: 1915 grad Kiev Ensigns' School; 1924 grad Higher Acad Courses; *Career*: 1915-17 platoon, company and battalion commander; from 1918 in Red Army; during Civil War adjutant, 65th Rifle Regt; then commander, 72nd Rifle Regt, 8th Rifle Div; commander 23rd Rifle Brigade, 8th Rifle Div; 1923 adjutant, 2nd Tula Div; 1924-28 served in Main Admin, Red Army; 1928-34 commander and comr, 5th Rifle Corps; 1934-37 dep commander, 1937 commander, North Caucasian Mil Distr; 1934-37 member, Mil Council, USSR Pop Comrt of Defense; 1937 arrested by NKVD; *Awards*: three Orders of the Red Banner; imperial orders for service in WW 1; *Died*: 1938 in imprisonment; posthumously rehabilitated.

GRIDASOV, Nikita Sergeyevich (1891-1967) Govt official; CP member from 1912; *Born*: 1891; *Educ*: 1921-23 studied at Gen Staff Acad; *Career*: at 13 years of age farm-hand, then ind worker in Kursk Province; participated in 1917 Oct Revol in Petrograd; comr, then chief of staff, 1st Infantry Div, Murmansk Front; head, Intelligence Dept, 2nd Infantry Div, Petrograd Front; Mar 1921 helped crush Kronstadt Mutiny; 1923-24 in Red Army; later admin and econ work; from 1953 pensioner; *Died*: 5 Jan 1967.

GRIGORENKO, Grits'ko (real name: SUDOVSHCHIKOVA-KOSACH, Aleksandra Yevgen'yevna) (1867-1924) Ukr writer; *Born*: 1867 in vil Makar'yevo, Kostroma Province; *Career*: wrote short stories about rural life at the turn of the century; *Publ*: short-story collections *Nashi lyudi na sele* (Our Villagers) (1898); *Pereselentsy* (The Settlers); *Niyak ne vmre* (He Just Won't Die); *Vona 'hramotna'* (She's "Educated"); *Lyudyam* (For People); children's short stories *Detki* (The Kids) (1918); play *Bat'ko* (The Father); essays *Pochuttya i nastroi* (Moods and Feelings); *Narysy* (Sketches); *Smerdy* (The Serfs); *Son syl'nishyy* (Deepest Sleep); *Krasa* (Beauty); *Sochineniya* (Works) (2 vol, 1930), *Izbrannyye sochineniya* (Selected Works) (1959); *Died*: 27 Apr 1924.

GRIGOROVICH, Dmitriy Pavlovich (1883-1938) Plane designer; *Born*: 6 Feb 1883 in Kiev; *Educ*: 1909 grad Kiev Polytech Inst; *Career*: designed about 80 planes, many of which saw serial production and were used by the Sov Air Force; 1912 designed his first hydroplane, the M-1, and in 1914 the M-5 hydroplane of the same type with 100 hp engine; the plane was used by the Russian Army for reconnaissance and training; 1915 designed the 150-hp M-9, the first-hydroplane to be fitted with 37-mm cannon; 1916 for the first time in hydroplane history an M-9 performed a Nesterov loop; 1916-17 the M-5, M-9 and M-15 designs were passed on to allied naval authorities, and the M-9 was then produced in various for countries; 1916 designed the M-11, the world's first armored hydroplane; 1916-17 designed a twin-engined torpedo-plane and also several M-9 versions; his best Sov designs were the I-2 and I-2b fighters, the M-24 hydroplane and the ROM-2 naval reconnaissance plane with two 500 hp engines and a speed of 220 km/h; 1930 designed the I-5 fighter, noted for its great maneuverability; 1931-32 designed the Z, the first cannon-armed fighter plane, etc; *Died*: 26 July 1938.

GRIGOROVICH, Ivan Konstantinovich (1835-1930) Russian naval commander; admiral from 1911; *Born*: 26 Jan 1835; *Career*: 1904-05 commanded battleship *Tsesarevich* during Russo-Japanese War; from Mar 1904 port commander, Port Arthur; 1905 chief of staff, Black Sea Fleet and ports; 1906 commander, Liepaja Port; 1908 commander in chief, Kronstadt Port; from 1909 dep, 1911-Feb 1917 Navy Minister; supervised various shipbuilding programs: 1911 and 1914 for the Black Sea Fleet,

1912 for the Baltic Fleet; 1916 proposed for premiership by progressive bourgeois circles but rejected by Tsaritsa because of his liberal views; after 1917 Oct Revol worked for the Naval Historical Commission, for which he wrote his memoirs; 1923 permitted to emigrate to France; *Died*: 3 Mar 1930.

GRIGORIY (secular name: CHUKOV, Nikolay Kirillovich) (1870-1955) Metropolitan of Leningrad and Novgorod; permanent member, Most Holy Synod, Russian Orthodox Church; chm, Educ Comt, Holy Synod, Russian Orthodox Church; Hon Dr of Divinity from 1949; *Born*: 1870 in Olonets Province; *Educ*: 1889 grad theological seminary; 1895 grad Philological Dept, Petersburg Theological Acad; *Career*: 1889-91 supervisor and custodian, Petrozavodsk Theological College; from 1895 taught theology; from 1897 priest and eparchic inspektor of church parish schools; 1907 elevated to archpriest; in the course of his rural work established some 300 libraries, organized "Sunday readings" for adults and campaigned against "pan-Finnish and Lutheran influences"; from 1911 rector, Petrozavodsk Theological Seminary; 1914 as chm, Petrozavodsk Dept, League of Cities, supervised the establishment of field hospitals and organiszed aid for soldiers' families; 1918 named dean, Petrograd Univ Church, then dean, Kazan' Cathedral and rector, Kazan' Divinity Inst; 1922 arrested and sentenced to death in connection with the case of Metropolitan Veniamin of Petrograd, who was charged with opposing the confiscation of Church property; after receiving a pardon adopted a conciliatory attitude to the Sov regime and soon advanced to high Church office; during this period organized Higher Divinity Courses in Leningrad; 1926 defended master's thesis on "The Messianic Concepts of the Judeans According to the Targum of Jonathan Ben-Uriel"; 1939 became a widower; 1942 entered monkhood and assumed the name Grigoriy, after which he was appointed Bishop of Saratov and Stalingrad; after appointment of Patriarch served as business mang, Moscow Patriarchy; 1944 transferred to See of Pskov and Porokhovsk and also appointed temporary business mang, Leningrad, Novgorod and Olonets Eparchies; simultaneously elected to Holy Synod; 1945 founded divinity courses in Leningrad, which were expanded into a theological seminary in 1946, when the Theological Acad was re-opened; 1948 organized correspondence-course sections at both the seminary and the Acad; 1945 appointed Metropolitan of Leningrad and Novgorod with autority over the Baltic parishes; simultaneously permanent member, Holy Synod and chm of its Educ Comt; also undertook several diplomatic missions; 1945 broke the autonomy of the Orthodox Churches of Lat and Est; helped to heal the split between the "old-style" and "new-style" factions on Valaam island and in the Orthodox parishes of Finland, uniting them with the Moscow Patriarchy; 1946 accompanied Patriarch Aleksiy on trips to Bulgaria and Rumania; attended the funeral of Metropolitan Yevlogiy in Paris; visited the heads of the Eastern Orthodox churches; visited USA; *Awards*: right to bear cross during divine service; right to wear double amulet with personal message from the Patriarch (1950); three foreign orders and medals; *Died*: 5 Nov 1955; buried in Leningrad.

GRIGORYAN, Grant Aramovich (1919-1962) Arm composer; Hon Art Worker of RSFSR from 1958; Hon Art Worker of Yakut ASSR from 1957; *Born*: 10 Apr 1919 in Sukhumi; *Educ*: 1952 grad Moscow Conservatory; *Career*: 1949 began composing; did much research on Yakut folk music; made wide use of Yakut melodies, modernizing them in the light of modern operatic technique; from 1953 instructor, Yakutsk Musical Arts College; *Works*: opera "Lookut and Nyurgusun" (1959); first Yakut nat operetta "Flower of the North" (1962); oratorio "Northern Spring" (1955); symphony (1955); concerto on Yakut themes; arranged Yakut folk songs, etc; *Died*: 27 Jan 1962 in Yakutsk.

GRIGOR'YEV, N.A. (1878-1919) Mil commander; staff captain, Russian Army; div commander, Red Army; *Born*: 1878; *Career*: during WW 1 on active service; 1918 supported Ukr Centr Rada govt; spring 1919 transferred allegiance to Soviets; 18 Feb 1919 appointed commander, 1st Trans-Dnieper Ukr Sov Brigade, subsequently reformed as the 6th Sov Ukr Div; Mar-Apr 1919 fought with this div in the battles for Nikolayev, Kherson and Odessa; early May 1919 moved with his div near Yelizavetgrad; 7-9 May 1919 disobeyed order to transfer div to Rumanian Front to support Hungarian Sov Republ and raised a rebellion behind the Red Army lines with his army of 20,000 men, 50 pieces of artillery and 10 armored trains; this army, which was manned by Ukr peasants and staffed by leftist Ukr Socialist-Revolutionaries, fought under the slogans "Power to the Soviets of the Ukr People Without the Communists" and "The Ukraine for the Ukrainians"; the rebels seized large areas of territory between the Dnieper and Southern Bug, including the towns of Cherkassy, Uman', Kremenchug, Yekaterinoslav, Yelizavetgrad, Kherson and Nikolayev; in many towns the garrisons joined Grigor'yev without a fight; the rebel army refused, however, to enlist manual and office workers and was supported by the peasantry, which was dissatisfied by the food and land policies of the Sov regime; Grigor'yev supported the leftist Ukr Socialist-Revolutionaries (activists) and the Soc-Democratic activists; late May 1919 the rebellion was put down by Red Army units under the command of K. Ye. Voroshilov, P. Ye. Dybenko, A. I. Yegorov, M. K. Levandovskiy, A. Ya. Parkhomenko, etc; Grigor'yev escaped to the headquarters of Ataman Makhno, who killed him; *Died*: 27 July 1919.

GRIGOR'YEV, Pavel Semyonovich (1879-1940) Dermatologist and venereologist; prof from 1919; Hon Sci Worker of RSFSR from 1935; *Born*: 28 Aug 1879; *Educ*: 1903 grad Petersburg Mil Med Acad; *Career*: 1903-07 mil surgeon in Russo-Japanese War; 1915-17 asst to Prof A.C. Bogomolets, Chair of Gen Pathology and Microbiology, Saratov Univ; from 1919 prof, Chair of Skin and Venereal Diseases, Saratov Univ; from 1936 prof, Chair of Skin and Venereal Diseases, 1st Moscow Med Inst; did research on experimentally-induced syphilis and studied the biological properties and variability of Spirocheta pallida; 1933 together with M.M. Rapoport devised simplified method for the serodiagnosis of syphilis (Grigor'yev-Rapoport reaction); 1934 devised new method of cultivating Spirocheta pallida; made major contribution to dermatology with his studies of Kaposi's sarcoma (multiple idiopathic hemorrhagic sarcoma), skin leukemia, etc; devised original classification of leukemic skin affections and used x-rays to treat actinomycosis; founder, Saratov Dermatolgical Soc and Saratov Kray Dermatological Inst; chm, Moscow Skin and Venerological Soc; exec ed, journal *Vestnik venerologii i dermatologii*; wrote over 70 works; *Publ: K voprosu o mnozhestvennoy idiopaticheskoy gemorragicheskoy sarkome kozhi Kapozi* (Kaposi's Multiple Idiopathic Hemorrhagic Skin Sarcoma) (1915); *K voprosu o leykemii kozhi* (Skin Leukemia) (1917); coauthor, *K voprosu o spetsificheskikh aortitakh pri eksperimental'nom sifilise krolikov* (Specific Forms of Aortitis in Rabbits Experimentally Infected With Syphilis) (1928); *Vrozhdyonnyy sifilis, peredannyy krol'chikhoy, zarazhyonnoy cherez perednyuyu kameru glaza* (Congenital Syphilis Transmitted by a Doe Rabbit Infected Via the Anterior Chamber of the Eye) (1928); *Rukovodstvo po venericheskim boleznyam* (A Manual on Venereal Diseases) (1930); *O patogennosti chistykh kul'tur blednoy spirokhety* (The Pathogenicity of Pure Cultures of Spirocheta Pallida) (1938); *Uchebnik venericheskikh i kozhnykh bolezney* (A Textbook of Venereal and Skin Diseases) (1938); *Kratkiy kurs venericheskikh i kozhnykh bolezney* (A Short Course on Venereal and Skin Diseases) (3rd ed, 1946); *Died*: 1940.

GRIGOR'YEV, Sergey Grigor'yevich (1874-1931) Geographer and bio-geographer; *Born*: 24 Oct 1874 in Moscow; *Educ*: 1897 grad Natural Sci Dept, Physics and Mathematics Fac, Moscow Univ; *Career*: from 1897 teacher, secondary school; from 1906 simultaneously teacher at: Tikhomirov's Teachers' Training Courses; Inst of Commerce; Higher Women Courses; from 1909 assoc prof, Moscow Univ; 1911 left Moscow Univ in protest against the policy of the Min of Educ Kasso; 1917 returned to Univ; from 1919 prof, 1st Moscow Univ and assoc, Inst of Geography of this univ; from 1901 conducted expeditions in the Pamirs, Southern Urals, Caucasus, Ukr, Kola Penisula and in the Crimea; 1913-14 headed expedition, equipped by Russian Geographic Soc, to explore Kanin Peninsula; 1929 commissioned by Inst of Geodesy and Cartography to direct geographic work in the Urals; also travelled through Scandinavia, Western Europe, Egypt and Syria; member, Northern Commission, USSR Centr Exec Comt; State Comt for Nature Conservation; member, Natural History Section, Soc for Exploring the Urals, Siberia and the Far East, etc; together with A. A. Kruber, A. S. Barkov and S. V. Chefranov wrote a number of geographic readers and textbooks for secondary schools; *Publ: Krysha mira (Pamir)* (Roof of the World [The Pamirs]) (1905); *Vokrug yuzhnogo polyusa* (Around the South Pole) (2nd ed, 1915); *Shestaya chast' sveta (Antarktida)* (The Sixth Continent [The Antarctic]) (1925); *Poluostrov Kanin* (Kanin Peninsula) (1929), etc; *Died*: 29 Aug 1931 in Moscow.

GRIGOR'YEV (real name: GRIGOR'YEV-PATRASHKIN), Sergey

Timofeyevich (1875-1953) Russian writer; *Born*: 14 Oct 1875 in Syzran', son of a railroad worker; *Career*: 1899 first work printed; travelled extensively through Russia; contributed to provincial and metropolitan journals and newspapers; 1923 began writing for children; wrote historical novels and children's novelettes; *Publ*: story *Krasnyy baken* (Red Buoy) (1923); novelettes and novels *S meshkom za smert'yu* (Tracking Death with a Bag) (1924); *Tayna Ani Gay* (The Mystery of Ana Gay) (1925); *Mal'chiy bunt* (Boys' Mutiny) (1925); *Amba-polosatyy* (The Striped Amba) (1927); *Berko-kantonist* (Berko, the Cantonist) (1927); *Aleksandr Suvorov* (1939); *Malakhov kurgan* (Malakh's Burial Mound) (1941); *Pobeda morya* (Victory of the Sea) (1945); *Krugosvetka* (Round-the-World Voyage) (1946); *Sobraniye sochineniy* (Collected Works) (Vol 1-4 and 8, 1927); *Istoricheskiye rasskazy* (Historical Stories) (1955); *Sobraniye sochineniy* (Collected Works) (Vol 1-4, 1959-61; *Awards*: Order of the Red Banner of Labor; *Died*: 20 Mar 1953 in Moscow.

GRIN, Aleksandr (real name: GRINEVSKIY, Aleksandr Stepanovich) (1880-1932) Russian writer; *Born*: 23 Aug 1880 in Slobodskoy, Vyatka Province, son of a Polish office-worker who participated in 1863 mutiny and at the age of 16 was exiled to Siberia; *Educ*: 1896 grad Vyatka junior college; *Career*: 1896 went to Odessa; tramped through Russia, worked as seaman, fisherman, gold-prospector in the Urals, soldier; in the army joined Soc-Democratic Party; deserted from the army; conducted revol work among seamen and soldiers in Sevastopol'; jailed several times; three times exiled; from 1912 in Petersburg; 1924 moved to Feodosiya; 1930 to Staryy Krym; his first story, a propaganda pamphlet signed A. S. G., *Zasluga ryadovogo Panteleyeva* (Private Panteleyev's Service) (1906) was confiscated and burned by the Secret Polit Police Dept; the second story *V Italiyu* (To Italy) (1906) was signed A. M-v; the next - *Apel'siny* (Oranges) (1908) was for the first time signed A. S. Grin (an abbreviation of the author's name); at that time the author was an escaped convict and as such was wanted by the Secret Polit Police Dept; by the time of 1917 Oct Revol he was an acknowledged writer with numerous novelettes to his credit; his stories, novels and novelettes are imbued with romantic attitude; excellent at landscape descriptions and a fine psychologist; by the force of his imagination he lent life to non-existant countries and cities, strange events and characters; his rare gift of romantic phantasy distinguished him from most Sov writers; did not belong to any lit groupings; his novelette *Alyye parusa* (Red Sails) was the basis for a ballet and film of the same name (1961); many of his works have been translated into for languages; *Publ: Sobraniye sochineniy* (Collected Works) (3 vol, 1913); *Polnoye sobraniye sochineniy* (Complete Collected Works) (15 vol, 1927-29); *Blistayushchiy mir* (Sparkling World) (1924); *Doroga nikuda* (Road to Nowhere) (1930); *Fantasticheskiye novelly* (Phantastic Novellae) (1934); autobiographical novelette *Zolotaya tsep'* (Golden Chain) (1939); *Izbrannoye* (Selected Works) (1956); *Izbrannoye* (Selected Works) (2 vol, 1962), etc; *Died*: 8 July 1932 in Staryy Krym.

GRINBERG, Aleksandr Abramovich (1898-1966) Inorganic chemist; member, USSR Acad of Sci from 1958; prof, Leningrad Inst of Technol from 1936; *Born*: 2 May 1898 in Petersburg; *Educ*: 1924 grad Leningrad State Univ; *Career*: 1943-58 corresp member, USSR Acad of Sci; specialist in the chemistry of complex compounds; studied acid base and reduction and oxidation properties of complex compounds, the balance of their aqueous solutions, and the use of marked atoms in complex compounds; *Publ: Vvedeniye v khimiyu kompleksnykh soyedineniy* (Introduction to the Chemistry of Complex Compounds) (1951); *K voprosu ob obmene broma v monopiridintribromoplatoate kaliya* (The Problem of Bromine Exchange in Potassium Monopyridinetribromineplatoate) (1961); *K voprosu o novykh solyakh uranshchavelevoy kisloty* (New Salts of Oxalic Uranium Acid) (1962); *O konstantakh nestoykosti platinovykh kompleksov* (The Instability Constants of Platinum Complexes) (1962); *Ob izotopnom obmene khlora v soli Tseyze* (Isotopic Exchange of Chlorine in Zeise Salt) (1962); *K voprosu o sushchestvovanii soley ammiakatov chetyryokhvalentnoy platiny* (Existence of Ammoniate Salts of Tetravalent Platinum) (1962); *Awards*: Stalin Prize (1946); *Died*: 16 July 1966.

GRINBERG, Grigoriy Izrayliyevich (1886-1966) Otolaryngologist; Dr of Med from 1943; *Born*: 26 July 1886 in vil Kartuz-Beryoza, now Grodno Oblast; *Educ*: 1911 grad Med Fac, Yur'yev (Tartu) Univ; *Career*: after grad worked at Obukhov Hospital, Petersburg and qualified as an otolaryngologist at the Inst of Postgrad Med Training; 1914-22 on mil service; 1923-31 assoc, Prof V. I. Voyachek's Ear, Nose and Throat Clinic, Leningrad Mil Med Acad; 1931-34 assoc, Leningrad Practical Sci Inst of Ear, Nose and Throat Diseases and Speech Defects; 1934-40 asst prof, Chair of Otolaryngology, 3rd Leningrad Med Inst; 1937 defended cand thesis; 1940-43 asst prof, 1943-52 assoc prof and dep head of a chair, Naval Med Inst; 1943 defended doctor's thesis on "Electroacoumetry in Clinical Practice"; 1952-66 head, Acoustics Laboratory, Leningrad Research Inst of Ear, Nose and Throat Diseases and Speech Defects; as a specialist in deafmutism also acquired fame outside the USSR; was one of first Sov sci to advocate and apply audiometric methods to the study of the auditory fac; trained numerous specialists in deafmutism, a discipline in which he propagated the physiological theories of his teacher V. A. Voyachek; devised widely-used table for locating defects of the sound analyzer at various levels; active member, Leningrad Sci Soc of Otolaryngologists; wrote over 50 works; *Publ*: coauthor, standard work *Osnovy fiziologii i prakticheskiye metody issledovaniya slukhovogo, vestibulyarnogo i obonyatel'nogo analizatorov* (The Physiological Principles and Practical Methods of Studying the Auditory, Vestibular and Olfactory Analyzers); *Died*: 29 Sept 1966 in Leningrad.

GRINBERG, Mark Iosifovich (1896-1957) Eng; specialist in turbine construction; prof from 1935; Dr of Tech Sci from 1947; *Born*: 22 Feb 1896; *Educ*: 1922 grad Leningrad Polytech Inst; *Career*: from 1923 worked at a Leningrad metal plant, from 1944 as chief designer of gas and steam turbines; simultaneously from 1929 research and teaching work at Leningrad tech insts; helped design the 200,000-kw PVK-200-130 steam turbine; *Awards*: two Stalin Prizes (1946 and 1948); Lenin Prize (1963, posthumously); *Died*: 25 Feb 1957.

GRINBERG, Z.G. (1889-1949) Govt official; 1906-14 Bund member; 1917-22 RCP(B) member; *Born*: 1889; *Career*: after 1917 Oct Revol comr, newspaper *Novaya Rus'*; member, State Comt for Public Educ; Dep Pop Comr of Educ, Union of Northern Region Communes; from Feb 1920 Collegium member, RSFSR Pop Comrt of Educ; later bd member, Historical Museum and dep dir, Armory; 1927-45 teaching and research work, 2nd Moscow Univ and Gorky Inst of World Lit, USSR Acad of Sci; *Died*: 1949.

GRINCHENKO, Mariya Nikolayevna (lit pseudonyms: M. ZAGIRNYA; M. CHAYCHENKO; M. DOLENKO, etc) (1863-1928) Ukr writer; wife of the Ukr writer B. Grinchenko; *Born*: 1863 in Bogodukhov, Khar'kov Province; *Career*: teacher by profession; 1891 first lit work published; translated into Ukr works of Turgenev, Mamin-Sibiryak, Lev Tolstoy, Ibsen, Mark Twain, etc; wrote pop studies of P. Sagaydachnyy and Abraham Lincoln, also memoirs of I. Nechuy-Levitskiy and V. Samoylenko; helped prepare for publ acad *Slovar' ukrainskogo yazyka* (Dictionary of the Ukrainian Language), compiled by B. Grinchenko and published 1927-29 under the editorship of A. Yu. Krymskiy; *Publ*: verse "Dawn" (1891); collected stories "Below the Earth" (1897); "The Shepherd and the Girl" (1905); novelette *V shakhtakh* (In the Mines) (in Russian, 1911), etc; *Died*: 15 July 1928.

GRINEVETSKIY, Vasiliy Ignat'yevich (1871-1919) Thermal eng; *Born*: 1871; *Educ*: 1896 grad Moscow Higher Tech College; *Career*: from 1900 prof, Chair of Applied Mech and Machine-Building, from 1914 dir, from 1917 rector, Moscow Higher Tech College; began work supervising designing of machine and crane parts; subsequently concentrated on problems of thermal eng; introducted into heat eng a thorough study of actual working processes within steam engines and internal combustion engines; 1905 developed a complete heat calculation diagram for steam boiler units, based on correct understanding of heat transmission processes; 1906 presented econ theory of steam engine operation; reorganized steam economy in textile factories, installing very efficient combined thermal power units; 1906 designed a two-stroke double-expansion internal combustion engine for motor locomotives, which was built in 1909 and gave good test results; 1907 devised heat calculation diagram for internal combustion engines, which continues to be the basis of planning and analyzing the working processes of these engines; correctly appraised the significance of motor locomotives for railroads and planned the technology of motor locomotive production; opposed to Sov regime; in his book *Poslevoyennyye perspektivy russkoy promyshlennosty* (Post-War Prospects of Russian Industry) tried to prove that the restoration and development of Russian ind could not be achieved without the return to capitalism and for capital investment; *Publ: Graficheskiy raschyot parovogo kotla* (Calculation Diagram of a Steam Boiler) (1905); *Ekonomika rabochego protsessa parovoy mashiny* (Economics of Steam Engine Operation) (1906); *Rabochiy protsess parovoy mashiny. Atlas chertezhey* (Operation of the Steam Engine. An Atlas of Blueprints) (1906); *Teplovoy raschyot rabochego protsessa dvigateley vnutrennego sgoraniya* (Heat Calculation of the Working Process of an Internal Combustion Engine) (1907); *Problema teplovoza i yego znacheniye dlya Rossii* (Motor Locomotives and Their Significance for Russia) (1923); *Poslevoyennyye perspektivy russkoy promyshlennosti* (Post-War Prospects of Russian Industry) (1919); *Parovyye mashiny. Teoriya rabochego protsessa* (Steam Engines. Theory of Operation) (2nd ed, 1926); *Died*: 27 Mar 1919 in Yekaterinodar.

GRIN'KO, Grigoriy Fyodorovich (1890-1938) Govt official; CP member from 1919; *Born*: 30 Nov 1890 in vil Shtepivka, now Sumy Oblast, son of an official; *Educ*: grad secondary school; studied at Moscow Univ; *Career*: from 1906 in revol movement as member, Socialist-Revol Party; 1913 for participation in student strike expelled from univ and drafted as private into the army; during the 1914-17 war at the front; promoted officer; after 1917 Oct Revol member and CC member, Ukr *Borot'bisty* (Fighters) Party; 1919 joined Bolsheviks; 1919-26 worked for Ukr Bolshevik Govt; member, All-Ukr Mil-Revol Comt; Pop Comr of Educ; Gosplan chm; chm, Exec Comt, Kiev Province Sov of Workers and Peasants' Dep; 1925; 26 dep chm, Ukr Council of Pop Comr; Dec 1926-29 dep chm, USSR Gosplan; from 1929 USSR Dep Pop Comr of Agric; 1930-37 USSR Pop Comr of Finance; member, USSR Centr Exec Comt of all convocations; 1924-26 elected member, CC, CP(B) Ukr; 1934, at 17th CPSU(B) Congress, elected cand member, CC; elected member, USSR Centr Exec Comt of all convocations; 1938 tried with the "Rightist Trotskyite Bloc" on charges of alleged membership of this bloc, counter-revol activity and efforts to undermine the financial might of the USSR; *Died*: 15 Mar 1938 executed.

GRINSHTEYN, Aleksandr Mikhaylovich (1881-1959) Neuropathologist; Dr of Med from 1910; prof from 1921; member, USSR Acad of Med Sci from 1945; consulting prof, 4th Main Bd, USSR Min of Health; Hon Sci Worker of RSFSR from 1945; *Born*: 10 Aug 1881 in Tula, son of a physician; *Educ*: 1904 grad Med Fac, Moscow Univ; *Career*: after grad intern, Clinic for Nervous Diseases, Moscow Univ; from 1906 asst prof, Clinic of Nervous Diseases, Moscow Higher Women's Med Courses; 1921-24 prof and head, Chair of Nervous Diseases, Voronezh Med Inst; 1924-40 prof and head, Chair of Nervous Diseases, 1st and 2nd Khar'kov Med Inst; 1940-55 head, Chair of Nervous Diseases, 2nd Moscow Med Inst; until death consultant, Kremlin Therapy and Sanitary Bd, now 4th Main Bd, USSR Min of Health; late 1952 arrested on charges of spying for the USA and deliberately giving CPSU and Red Army leaders wrong med treatment; after Stalin's death freed and fully rehabilitated; for a number of years Bureau member, Clinical Dept and member, Coordinating Comt, Presidium, USSR Acad of Med Sci; *Publ*: doctor's thesis *Materialy k ucheniyu o provodyashchikh putyakh corporis striati* (Material on the Theory of the Conduction Paths of the Corpus Striatus) (1910); *Kozhno-vistseral'naya semiotika organicheskikh zabolevaniy nervnoy sistemy* (The Dermovisceral Semiotics of Organic Diseases of the Nervous System) (1928); *Lokalizatsiya troficheskikh funktsiy v nervnoy sisteme* (Localizing Trophisms in the Nervous System) (1936); *Puti i tsentry nervnoy sistemi* (Paths and Centers of the Nervous System) (1946); coauthor, *Lecheniye sosudistykh zabolevaniy putyom operatsiy na pogranichnom stvole* (The Treatment of Vascular Diseases by Operating on the Truncus Sympathicus) (1950); *Problema dinamicheskoy lokalizatsii funktsiy v eksperimente i klinike* (The Dynamic Location of Functions in Experimental and Clinical Practice) (1956), etc; *Awards:* Order of the Red Banner of Labor; medals; *Died*: 10 Mar 1959 in Moscow.

GRISHASHVILI (real name: MAMULAYSHVILI), Iosif Grigor'yevich (1889-1965) Geo poet; member, Geo Acad of Sci from 1946; Pop Poet of Geo SSR from 1959; Hon Art Worker of Arm SSR; Bd member, Geo Writers' Union; Presidium member, Bd, Geo Theater Soc; Member, Geo Comt for the Defense of Peace; Bd member, Geo Coc for the Dissemination of Polit and Sci Knowledge; *Born*: 24 Apr 1889 in Tiflis, son of an artisan; *Career*: in his youth began to write plays and poems; from 1908 for several years prompter in Geo theaters; 1916, 1920 and 1923 published own lit-artistic journal *Leyla*; simultaneously active member, ed bd, Geo Writers' Union periodical *Khomli* and lit newspapers *Lomisi* and *Kartuli sitkva*; 1959 member, ed bd, multi-vol *Tolkovyy slovar' gruzinskogo yazyka* (Dictionary of the Georgian Language); contributed to periodicals *Dila, Pioneri* and *Norchi Lenineli*; Bd member, House of Art Workers; member, learned councils of: Rustaveli Theater Inst, Geo Book Chamber, Marx Public Library; member, Geo Orthography Comt; member, Artistic Councils, Mardzhanishvili Theater and Geo Philharmonic; translated into Geo works of Arm (Ovanes, Tumanyan, Shirvanzede, etc) and Azer lit (Mirza-Fatali Akhundov, Fizuli), also Russian classical and contemporary poets; *Publ*: lit essays: "The Origins of Georgian Romanticism"; "Correlations Between Georgian Literature and the Literature of Brother Peoples"; "Pre-Revolutionary Georgian Theater"; "Forgotten and Lost Names"; "History of Tbilisi" (5 vol, 1952); "Lermontov and Georgian Literature"; "Ostrovskiy and the Georgian Theater"; collected verse "A Bunch of Roses" (1906); "Phantasy" (1907); "Dream Kiss" (1911); "Fare-well to Old Tbilisi" (1925); "A Letter to the Leader from My Electoral District" (1937); "To Dzhambul" (1938); "On David's Mountain" (1938); "Grigor Orbeliani on Komsomol Avenue" (1938); "Fatherland and Victory" (1941); "To Mothers and Sisters" (1941); "To the Heroes of Stalingrad" (1943); "In Pushkin's City" (1944); poems: "Light" (1947); "There Goes the Georgian Automobile"; "New Kutaisi"; "Georgian Citruses in the Ukraine"; "You Were Born in April" (1960); "Singer of the Homeland" (1960), etc; *Awards*: Order of the Red Banner of Labor (1944); Stalin Prize (1950); *Died*: 3 Aug 1965.

GRISHIN-ALMAZOV (real name: GRISHIN), Aleksey Nikolayevich (1880-1919) Mil commander; lt-col of artillery, Russian Army; maj-gen, Whitist Siberian Army; *Born*: 1880; *Career*: from Jan 1918 mustered anti-Sov officers squads in towns of Western Siberia and became chief of staff of these units; June 1918, together with Capt Gayda, a brigade commander with the Czech Corps, overthrew Sov regime in Novo-Nikolayevsk; followed up by overthrowing Sov regime from Chelyabinsk to Baykal and became commander of Siberian Army and acting Mil Min of Siberian Provisional Govt; by Aug 1918 completed formation of three-corps Siberian Army; fall 1918 removed from his posts on charges of "Bonapartism"; Oct 1918 joined Gen Denikin and was appointed last Commandant of Odessa; Mar 1919 removed from this post and expelled from Odessa in connection with the French command's policy of dismissing Denikin's local authorities in the French occupation zone; May 1919 tried to cross Sov front on steamer on the Caspian Sea, intending to return to Siberia; 5 May 1919 the steamer was detained by Sov warship; *Died:* 5 May 1919 committed suicide to avoid falling into Sov hands.

GRISHKO, Grigoriy Yeliseyevich (1906-1959) Party official; maj-gen; CP member from 1930; *Born*: 25 Jan 1906 in vil Velikaya Fyodorovka, Nikolayev Oblast; *Educ:* 1923-28 studied at a cooperative school; 1928-36 at Odessa Agric Inst; *Career*: 1937-39 head, Nikolayev Oblast Land Dept; 1939-41 chm, Volhynian Oblast Exec Comt; during WW 2 member, mil council of an army; 1946-48 chm, Ternopol' Oblast Exec Comt; 1949-51 first secr, Kherson Oblast Comt, CP Ukr; 1951-52 secr, CC, CP Ukr; 1952-57 first secr, Kiev Oblast Comt, CP Ukr; 1957-59 inspector, CC, CP Ukr; 1952-56 member, CPSU Centr Auditing Commission; 1956-61 cand member, CC, CPSU; at 16th, 17th, 18th and 19th CP Ukr Congresses elected member, CC, CP Ukr; 1952 cand Bureau member, CC, CP Ukr; 1953-57 cand Presidium member, CC, CP Ukr; dep, USSR Supr Sov of 3rd and 4th convocations; dep, Ukr Supr Sov of 2nd convocation; *Awards*: four Orders of Lenin; three Orders of the Red Banner of Labor; *Died*: 9 Feb 1959.

GRITSEVETS, Sergey Ivanovich (1909-1939) Air Force maj; Fighter-pilot; first twofold Hero of Sov Union; CP member from 1931; *Born*: 6 July 1909 in vil Borovtsy, Minsk Province, son of a peasant; *Educ*: 1932 grad Orenburg Mil Pilots School; *Career*: 1927-39 worked at Zlatoust machine plant; from 1929 in Sov Air Force; 1936-39 fighter-pilot with Spanish Republ Air Force; 1939 commanded Air Force regt during fighting at Khalkin Gol; shot down some 40 enemy planes; rescued his commanding officer from a forced landing in enemyheld territory in Manchuria; *Awards*: twice Hero of Sov Union (23 Feb and 29 Aug 1939); Order of Lenin; Order of Mongolian Pop Republ; *Died*: 16 Sept 1939 killed in the execution of his duty.

GROMADIN, Mikhail Stepanovich (1899-1962) Mil commander;

col-gen; CP member from 1925; *Born*: 8 Nov 1899; *Educ*: 1933 grad Frunze Mil Acad; *Career*: from 1918 in Sov Army; fought in Civil War; on eve of WW 2 dep commander, Anti-Aircraft Defense Forces, Moscow Mil Distr; June-Nov 1941 commander, Moscow Anti-Aircraft Defense Zone; 9 Nov 1941-June 1943 Dep Pop Comr of Defense and commander, USSR Anti-Aircraft Defense Forces; 1943-45 commander, Anti-Aircraft Defense Forces, Western, Northern and Centr Fronts; 1946-48 again commander, USSR Anti-Aircraft Defense Forces; after 1948 exec posts in USSR Min of Defense; from 1954 in retirement; dep, USSR Supr Sov of 2nd convocation; *Awards*: two Orders of Lenin; two Orders of the Red Banner; Order of Suvorov, 1st Class; two Orders of Kutuzov, 1st Class; other orders and medals; *Died*: 4 June 1962.

GROMAN (pseudonym: GORN), Vladimir Gustavovich (1873-?) Statistician and econ; Hon Sci Worker of RSFSR from 1927; *Born*: 1873 of a German father and Russian mother; *Educ*: studied at Moscow Univ; *Career*: 1898 exiled to Vyatka for polit activities; 1902-05 in Siberian exile; 1905 took active part in Revol as member, RSDRP (Mensheviks); 1909 sent to penza, where he worked as mang, statistics bureau; from outbreak of 1917 Feb Revol chm, Food Commission, Petrograd Sov of Workers and Soldiers' Dep; after 1917 Oct Revol continued to serve the Sov regime but retained Menshevik allegiance; 1918 chm, Northern Food Bd; 1919-20 worked for Main Fuel Comt and "Commission for Investigating the Effects of War and Intervention on the Nat Econ"; from 1921 contributed regular econ reviews to the journal *Ekonomicheskaya zhizn'*; 1927 member, Sov deleg, Geneva Conference; 1928 chm, Econ Council and chm, Internal Econ Section, USSR Gosplan; Presidium member, USSR Gosplan and collegium member, USSR Centr Statistical Bd; at beginning of period of reconstruction opposed ind and collectivization policies; 1929 removed from office; 1930 arrested with other econ; *Publ*: ed, *Statistika. Materialy po statistike Vyatskoy gubernii, tom XII. Obshchaya svodka po gubernii, chast' 2* (Statistics. Statistical Material on Vyatka Province, Vol 12. A General Survey of the Province, Part 2) (1900); ed, *Itogi otsenochno-statisticheskogo issledovaniya Penzenskoy gubernii, 1909-13 gody* (The Results of a Statistical Estimation Study of Penza Province, 1909-13) (1923); *Voprosy prodovol'stviya i organizatsii narodnogo khozyaystva* (Food Problems and the Organization of the National Economy) (1915); *Agrarnyy vopros. Krest'yanskiye dvizheniya za poltora veka* (The Agrarian Question. Peasant Movements During One and a Half Centuries) (1909) *Soderzhaniye russkoy revolyutsii* (The Content of the Russian Revolution) (1906); *Krest'yanskiye dvizheniya do 1905-ogo goda* (Peasant Movements Until 1905) (1909), etc. *Died*: in imprisonment; date and place of death unknown.

GROMOVA, Ul'yana Matveyevna (1924-1943) Member of underground Komsomol org during WW 2; *Born*: 3 Jan 1924 in vil Pervomayevka, Krasnodon Rayon, Lugansk Oblast, daughter of a worker; *Career*: Sept 1942 helped to organize in German-occupied Pervomayevka an underground Komsomol group which was a part of *Molodaya Gvardiya* underground Komsomol org in Krasnodon; as staff member of *Molodaya Gvardiya,* distrubuted leaflets, collected medicine for wounded Sov soldiers, helped the arrested underground agents to escape; arrested by German mil authorities, barbarically tortured and thrown into a coal mine; *Awards*: Hero of the Sov Union (1943); *Died*: 15 Jan 1943.

GROSSGEYM, Aleksandr Al'fonsovich (1888-1948) Botanist and geographer; Dr of Biological Sci from 1935; prof from 1929; member, USSR Acad of Sci from 1946; member, Azer Acad of Sci from 1945; *Born*: 6 Mar 1888 in vil Likhovka, former Yekaterinoslavl' Province; *Educ*: 1907-11 studied at Khar'kov Univ; 1912 grad Natural Sci Dept, Physics and Mathematics Fac, Moscow Univ; *Career*: 1917-30 with Tiflis Polytech Inst; from 1929 prof, 1934-46 prof and head, Chair of Plant Morphology and Taxonomy, Azer Univ; from 1930 simultaneously head, Chair of Botany, Azer Teachers' Training Inst; 1914-26 botanist and florist, Tiflis Botanical Garden; 1927-30 botanist for study of Azer pastures, Pop Comrt of Agric; 1931-32 section head, Azer Research Inst in Baku; 1932-36 head, Botany Section, Azer Dept, Transcaucasian Branch, USSR Acad of Sci; 1936-45 dir, Inst of Botany, Azer Branch, USSR Acad of Sci; 1947-48 head, Caucasian Flora Section, Inst of Botany, USSR Acad of Sci and prof, Leningrad Univ; explored various Caucasian and Transcaucasian regions; accomplished expeditions to Centr Asia and Northern Iran; research dealt with taxonomy and geography of Caucasian flowering plants; described a great number of new flora species and advanced a new phylogenetic taxonomy of flowering plants; a plant genus and many plant species were named for him; hon member, All-Union Botanical Soc; member, Moscow Soc of Nature Researchers and member, All-Union Geographic Soc; wrote over 250 research works; *Publ*: coauthor, *Opredelitel' rasteniy okrestnostey Tiflisa* (A Guide to Plants in the Tiflis Area) (1920); *Tipy rastitel'nosti severnoy chasti nagornogo Dagestana* (Vegetation Types in the Northern Daghestan Highlands) (1925); *Flora Talysha* (The Flora of Talysh) (1926); *Flora Kavkaza* (Caucasian Flora) (4 vol, 1928-34); *Flora Azerbaydzhana* (Azerbaydzhani Flora) (3 vol, 1934-36); *Analiz flory Kavkaza* (Analysis of Caucasian Flora) (1936); coauthor, *Lekarstvennyye rasteniya Azerbaydzhana* (Pharmaceutical Plants of Azerbaydzhan) (1942); *Rastitel'nyye resursy Kavkaza* (Caucasian Vegetation Resources) (1946); *Rastitel'nyy pokrov Kavkaza* The Vegetation of the Caucasus) (1948); *Opredelitel' rasteniy Kavkaza* (A Guide to Caucasian Plants) (1949); *Awards*: Gold Medal of Russian Geographic Soc; USSR Acad of Sci V.L. Komarov Prize (1946); Stalin Prize (1948); *Died*: 4 Dec 1948 in Leningrad.

GROSSMAN, Leonid Petrovich (1888-1965) Russian writer, lit historian and critic; Dr of Philology from 1940; *Born*: 24 Jan 1888; *Educ*: 1911 grad Law Fac, Odessa Univ; *Career*: 1914 began lit work; from 1911 teacher; from 1945 prof; *Publ*: *Teatr Turgeneva* (Turgenev's Theater) (1924); *Pushkin v teatral'nykh kreslakh. Kartiny russkoy stseny 1817-1820 godov* (Pushkin in Theater Seats. Scenes of the Russian Stage 1817-1820) (1926); *Prestupleniye Sukhovo-Kobylina* (Sukhovo-Kobylin's Crime) (2nd ed, 1928); *Teatr Sukhovo-Kobylina* (Sukhovo-Kobylin's Theater) (1940); *Lermontov i kul'tura Vostoka* (Lermontov and the Culture of the East) (1941); *N.S. Leskov* (1945); *Lermontov i Rembrandt* (Lermontov and Rembrandt) (1946); *Tvorcheskiy put' L.M. Leonidova* (L.M. Leonidov's Career) (1946); *Stil' Leonidova* (Leonidov's Style) (1947); *Yubileynaya postanovka "Gore ot uma"* (Anniversary Production of "Woe from Wit") (1947); *Dramaturgicheskiye zamysly Turgeneva* (Turgenev's Dramaturgical Conceptions) (1955); *Problematika "Gamleta"* (Problems of "Hamlet") (1955); *Pushkin* (3rd ed, 1960); *Dostoyevskiy* (1963); biographical novels and novelettes; *Zapiski D'Arshiaka* (D'Archiac's Memoirs) (1930); *Ruletenburg* (1932); *Barkhatnyy diktator* (The Velvet Dictator) (1933), etc; *Died*: 15 Dec 1965.

GROSSMAN, Vasiliy Semyonovich (1905-1964) Russian writer; Bd member, USSR Writers' Union from 1954; *Born*: 12 Dec 1905 in Berdichev; *Educ*: 1929 grad Moscow Univ; *Career*: 1930-41 eng in the Donbas; 1941-45 reporter for newspaper *Krasnaya zvezda; Publ*: novel "Glückauf" (1934); collected stories: *Schast'ye* (Happiness) (1936); *Chetyre dnya* (Four Days) (1936); novel *Stepan Kol'chugin* (1937-40); collected stories *Gody voyny* (The War Years) (1945); novelette *Narod bessmerten* (The Public Is Immortal) (1942); novel *Za pravoye delo* (For the Right Cause) (1952); its sequel *Zhizn' i sud'ba* (Life and Destiny) (1960); helped translate Arm work by Rachiya Kochar "Children of the Big House" (1962); story *Los'* (The Elk) (1963), etc; play *Yesli verit' pifagoreytsam* (To Credit the Pythagorians) (1946) was sharply criticized by Sov press; *Awards*: Order of the Red Banner of Labor (1956); *Died*: 4 Sept 1964 in Moscow.

GROZIN, Boris Dmitriyevich (1898-1962) Specialist in metals; corresp member, Ukr Acad of Sci from 1939; head, Dept of Metals and Contact Capacity, Inst of Construction Mech, Ukr Acad of Sci from 1944; CP member from 1924; *Born*: 15 Oct 1898 in Kiev; *Educ*: 1930 grad Kiev Polytech Inst; *Career*: 1930-35 head, Dept of Thermal Surface Treatment of Metals, Research Inst of Construction Mech, Ukr Acad of Sci; works deal with mech properties of tempered steel; developed complex method for studying "active" metal spheres; one of the first in USSR to apply radioactive isotopes to investigate fatigue in machine components; *Publ*: coauthor, *Povysheniye ekspluatatsionnoy nadyozhnosti detaley mashin* (Increasing the Operation Reliability of Machine Components) (1960); exec ed, *Povysheniye iznosostoykosti i sroka sluzhby mashin* (Increasing Fatigue Resistance and Prolonging the Working Life of Machines) (1960); *Strukturnyye izmeneniya v stali pri vozdeystvii potoka szhatykh gazov vysokoy temperatury* (Structural Changes in Steel in a Stream of Compressed High-Temperature Gases) (1962); *Died*: 28 Oct 1962.

GRUM(M)-GRZHIMAYLO, Grigoriy Yefimovich (1860-1936) Explorer and geographer; explored Centr Asia; member, Russian Geographical Soc; *Born*: 17 Feb 1860 in Petersburg; *Educ*: 1884 grad Fac of Physics and Mathematics, Petersburg Univ; *Career*: 1884-87 explored the Bukhara, Altay, Pamir, Kashgar and Tyan'-Shan' mountains; 1889-90 led major expedition of Russian Geographical Soc to explore the Eastern Tyan'-Shan', Dzungaria, Bey-Shan', Nanshan and Gobi; during this expedition established that the Bey-Shan' range links the Tyan'-Shan' and Nanshan systems; in Tyan'-Shan' discovered the Turfan (Lukchun) depression, one of the world's deepest; compiled extensive zoological and botanical collections; 1903 explored Western Mongolia and Tuva; 1908 the Far East; 1911 Turkmenia; 1912 the Transcaucasus; 1914 Siberia and Tuva; 1921-30 lecturer, Leningrad Univ, Geographical Inst and Inst of Living Oriental Languages, where he read a course on the study of Asian countries; wrote over 200 works on his travels, including numerous monographs containing detailed information on the geography, geology, anthropology, ethnography, botany, zoology and history of the areas explored; *Publ: Ocherk Pripamirskikh stran* (A Study of the Pamir Lands) (1886); *Pamir i yego lepidopterologicheskaya fauna* (The Pamirs and Their Lepidoptera) (1890); *Opisaniye Amurskoy oblasti* (A Description of the Amur Region) (1894); *Opisaniye puteshestviya v Zapadnyy Kitay* (Account of a Journey to Western China) (3 vol, 1896-1907); *Istoricheskoye proshloye Bey-Shanya v svyazi s istoriyey Sredney Azii* (The Historical Past of Bey-Shan' in Relation to the History of Central Asia) (1898); *Zapadnaya Mongoliya i Uryankhayskiy kray* (Western Mongolia and Uriankhai) (3 vol, 1914-30); *Awards*: Przewalski Prize (1891); Tchihatchef Prize of the French Acad (1893); *Died*: 3 Mar 1936.

GRUM-GRZHIMAYLO (GRUMM-GRZHIMAYLO), Vladimir Yefimovich (1864-1928) Metallurgist; corresp member, USSR Acad of Sci from 1927; *Born*: 24 Feb 1864 in Petersburg; *Educ*: 1885 grad Petersburg Mining Inst; *Career*: from 1885 worked at Ural metallurgical plants; from 1907 junior asst, 1911-18 prof, Chair of Steel Metallurgy, Petersburg Polytech Inst; 1918-24 prof, Ural Mining Inst; 1924 founded in Moscow Bureau of Metallurgical and Heat Eng, USSR Supr Sovnarkhoz; worked with this Bureau planning metallurgical and other factory furnaces; 1889 wrote article describing Bessemer method introduced by K. P. Polenov at Nizhne-Saldinsk Plant in the 1870's; this method, later known as the "Russian Bessemer Method," differed from previous methods by enabling steel to be produced from cast-iron with a low silicon and manganese content; 1908 was the first to apply the laws of physical chemistry (law of balanced state of a system, depending on temperature changes and the law of mass activity) to explain the processes in an Bessemer converter and in the steel bath of an open-hearth furnace; 1910 introduced calculation theory for flame furnaces applying hydraulic laws to the motion of flue gases; the motion of a flame in air he compared to the motion of a light liquid in heavy liquid; together with I. G. Yes'man furnished a means of calculating the "height of the gas fountain" and the "gaseous flux" in furnaces; his hydraulic calculation method for flame furnaces was the first attempt to devise a gen sci method of furnace calculation; at one time this method was widely used in Russia and abroad and stimulated the further development of metallurgical furnace construction theory; by studying the properties of refractory materials, especially dinas bricks, developed "theory of dinas regeneration" which is still the basis of dinas production technol; his work *Prokatka i kalibrovka* (Rolling and Gaging) was the first attempt to explain gaging methods which had been a trade secret; directed design of various heating furnaces: for heating ingots before rolling; forging furnaces for thermal treatment of metals; drying, annealing and open-hearth furnaces; his work *Plamennyye pechi* (Flame Furnaces) (1925) summarized his methods of designing ind furnaces and introduced a number of original designs for various furnaces; *Publ: Plamennyye pechi* (Flame Furnaces) (5 vol, 1925); *Proizvodstvo stali* (Steel Production) (1925); *Prokatka i kalibrovka* (Rolling and Gaging) (1933); *Sobraniye trudov* (Collected Works) (1949); *Died:* 30 Oct 1928.

GRUNT, Yan Yanovich (1892-1950) Party official; CP member from 1907; *Born*: 12 Apr 1892 in Valmiyer, Lifland Province; *Career*: Party work in Valmiyer, Riga, Moscow; over 10 years in exile; helped found Lat Soc-Democratic org, the so-called Tver' RSDRP(B) Group; from Apr 1917 chm, Kolomna Uyezd RSDRP(B) Comt; helped establish Sov regime in Kolomna; 1919-50 worked for various newspapers (*Pravda, Tikhookeanskaya zvezda*, etc); *Publ: Gody bor'by* (Years of Struggle) (1933); *Stranitsy proshlogo* (Pages of the Past) (1923); *V tyur'me i na katorge* (In Prison and in Exile) (1923); *Oktyabr' v Kolomne* (October in Kolomna) (1922); *Kandal'nyy zvon. Stikhi* (The Clink of Fetters. Poems) (1918); *Died*: 8 Dec 1950.

GRUODIS, Yuozas Matveyevich (1884-1948) Composer and conductor; Hon Art Worker of Lith SSR; *Born*: 20 Dec 1884 in vil Rokenay, Lith, son of a musical instrument maker; *Educ*: 1914-16 studied under Ippolitov-Ivanov at Moscow Conservatory; 1924 grad Leipzig Conservatory; *Career*: 1924-27 opera conductor, 1927-37 dir, Kaunas Musical College; from 1933 prof and dir, Kaunas Conservatory; wrote symphonic and choral works and many songs; *Works*: ballet *"Yurate and Kastitis"* (1932); symphonic suite; poems; variations; string quartet; sonatas; choral works; songs; folk song arrangements; *Awards*: Order of the Red Banner of Labor; *Died*: 16 Apr 1948 in Kaunas.

GRUSHEVSKIY, Mikhail Sergeyevich (1866-1934) Ukr historian and one of the leaders of the Ukr nat-liberation movement; member, Ukr Acad of Sci from 1924; member, USSR Acad of Sci from 1929; *Born:* 17 Sept 1866 in Kholm, son of a teacher; *Educ*: 1890 grad History and Philology Dept, Kiev Univ; *Career*: 1894-1914 prof and head, Chair of World History, L'vov Univ; lectured on history of Ukr; from 1897 simultaneously chm, Ukr Shevchenko Sci Assoc and ed of its organ *Zapiski*; 1898 set up periodical *Literaturno-naukovyy vistnyk*; during 1905 Revol lived in Kiev, directing the Shevchenko Assoc; at the outbreak of WW 1 settled in Kiev, was arrested and exiled to Simbirsk; after 1917 Feb Revol returned to Kiev and took active part in establishing independent Ukr; 1917-18 chm, Ukr Centr Rada; early 1919, when Ukr was occupied by Bolsheviks, emigrated to Austria, set up Ukr Sociological Inst in Vienna and directed its activities; 1924 broke with Ukr emigre circles and returned to Kiev; head, History of Ukr Section, History Dept, Ukr Acad of Sci; edited regional studies journal *Ukraina*; from 1930 lived in Moscow; 1933 accused of setting up the "counter-revolutionary" Ukr Nat Center and of participating in the activities of Ukr Socialist-Revol Party; while a follower of V. B. Antonovich compiled the first work on the history of Ukr from ancient times to the mid-17th Century and founded a Ukr historical school classified by Sov historiography as "nationalistic school"; interpreted the history of Kiev Rus as the history of Ukr people, the continuation of which he saw in the Duchy of Galicia and Volhynia and to some extent in the Grand Duchy of Lith and the Cossack Ukr; similarly denied the theory of the existence of an "All-Russian" language and nationality during the Kiev Rus epoch; according to his theory, right from the ancient period of Slavic colonization the Eastern Slavic group consisted of three principal nat groups: Ukr, Russian and Bel; each developing independently from the others; did extensive research on the history of Ukr lit, rejecting the "All-Russian" theory and connecting Ukr lit traditions with those of Kiev Rus; *Publ: Barskoye starostvo* (The Barin Eldership System) (1894); "A History of Ukrainian Rus" (10 vol, 1898-1936); *Ocherk istorii ukrainskogo narody* (Outline History of the Ukrainian People) (1904); "An Illustrated History of the Ukraine" (1911) *Ukrainskiy narod v yego proshlom i nastoyashchem* (The Ukrainian People in the Past and in the Present) (1914); "History of Ukrainian Literature" (5 vol, 1923-27); "Sources for the History of Ukrainian Rus" (22 vol, 1895-1924); *Died*: 25 Nov 1934 in Kislovodsk.

GRUZDEV, Il'ya Aleksandrovich (1892-1960) Lit critic and historian; *Born*: 1 Aug 1892 in Petersburg; *Educ*: 1918 grad Philological Fac, Petrograd Univ; *Career*: from 1914 published notices, critical articles, feuilletons; early 1920's belonged to lit group *Serapionovy brat'ya* (Serapion Brethren); famed mainly as Gorky's biographer and for his research on Gorky's works; his works on Gorky include archives and memoir materials connected with the writer's biography; also annotated and edited Gorky's works (Collected Works, Vol 1 - 23, 1928-30); his work was facilitated by his long acquaintance and correspondence with Gorky; *Publ: Gor'kiy i yego vremya* (Gorky and His Age) (1938); *Gor'kiy. Biografiya* (Gorky. A Biography) (1946); *Molodyye gody Maksima Gor'kogo. Po yego rasskazam* (Maxim Gorky's Youth as Related by Gorky) (1954); *Gor'kiy* (1958); *Moi vstrechi i perepiska s M. Gor'kim* (My Meetings and Correspondence with Gorky) (1961); *Gor'kiy i yego vremya* (Gorky and His Age) (Vol 1, 1868-1896), etc; *Died*: 11 Dec 1960 in Leningrad.

GRUZDEV, Viktorin Sergeyevich (1866-1938) Obstetrician and gynecologist; Dr of Med from 1894; prof from 1900; Hon Sci Worker of RSFSR from 1934; *Born*: 6 Feb 1866; *Educ*: 1891 grad Petersburg Mil Med Acad; *Career*: after grad, intern, Obstetrical and Gynecological Clinic, Petersburg Mil-Med Acad; 1894 defended doctor's thesis on ovarian sarcomas, after which he was sent abroad for further specialist training; from 1897 assoc prof, Obstetrical and Gynecological Clinic, Petersburg Mil Med Acad; 1900-31 prof and head, from 1931 consultant, Chair of Obstetrics and Women's Diseases, Kazan' Univ, which he turned into a major research center; did important research on the physiology of the female sexual organs and their innervation; used x-ray therapy to treat malignant neoplasms of the womb; together with his pupils, made studies of ovarian and cervical sarcomas and primary and metastatic cancer of the female sexual organs; also studied fistulas of the urogenital tract, for which he devised a classification and treatment; did research on miscarriages; ed, *Kazanskiy meditsinskiy zhurnal*; 1912 attended 6th Int Congress of Obstetricians and Gynecologists, Berlin; 1926, 1928 and 1934 co-organizer and hon chm, 7th, 8th and 9th All-Union Congresses of Obstetricians and Gynecologists; 1923 organizer and chm, 1st Sci Congress of Volga Physicians; trained many outstanding Sov obstetricians and gynecologists; wrote over 100 works, including one of best Russian manuals on obstetrics and gynecology; also wrote studies of the history of these disciplines and translated five manuals into Russian; *Publ:* doctor's thesis *Sarkomy yaichnikov* (Ovarian Sarcomas) (1894); *Kurs akusherstva i zhenskikh bolezney* (A Course of Obstetrics and Women's Diseases) (2 vol, 1919-22); *Ginekologiya* (Gynecology) (1922); *Died*: 1938.

GRUZINOV, Ivan Vasil'yevich (1893-1942) Russian poet; *Born*: 20 Nov 1893 in vil Shebarshino, Smolensk Province, son of a peasant; *Career*: 1912 first work published; until 1924 theoretician of *Imaginists* group; 1924 left the group together with S. A. Yesenin; works dealt primarily with rural life; *Publ: Bubny boli* (Diamonds of Pain) (1915); collected verse *Izbyanaya Rus'* (Peasant-Hut Russia) (1925); *Imazhinizma osnovnoye* (The Keynotes of Imaginism) (1921); *Zapadnya slov* (The Snare of Words); *Rody* (Childbirth) (1926); *Malinovaya shal'* (The Crimson Shawl) (1926); *S. Yesenin razgovarivayet o literature i iskusstve* (S. Yesenin Talks of Literature and Art) (1927); *Mayakovskiy i literaturnaya Moskva* (Mayakovskiy and Literary Moscow) (1939-40); *Died*: 1942 in Moscow.

GRUZINSKIY, Aleksandr Sergeyevich (1881-1954) Ukr philologist and paleographer; prof; *Born*: 22 Dec 1881 in Nezhin; *Educ*: 1909 grad Kiev Univ; *Career*: taught at higher educ institutions in Nezhin, Khar'kov, Leningrad, Mogilyov and Kiev; works deal with language, illustration and ornamentation of ancient Ukr writings; examined also the works of G. Skovoroda and F. Prokopovich; *Publ: Peresopnitskoye yevangeliye kak pamyatnik iskusstva epokhi Vozrozhdeniya v Yuzhnoy Rossii v 16-m veke* (The Peresopnitsk Gospel, a Renaissance Monument of 16th-Century Southern Russia) (1911); *Iz istorii perevoda yevangeliya v Yuzhnoy Rossii v 16-m veke, Letkovskoye yevangeliye* (The History of Gospel Translation in 16th-Century Southern Russia. The Letkov Gospel) (1911); *Paleograficheskiye i kriticheskiye zametki o Peresopnitskom yevangelii* (Paleographic and Critical Notes on the Peresopnitsk Gospel) (1912); "Critical Notes on the Work of Skovoroda" (1927); *Died*: 11 Jan 1954.

GRUZINSKIY, Aleksey Yevgen'yevich (1858-1930) Lit historian; *Born*: 3 May 1858 in Moscow; *Educ*: 1883 grad Philological Fac, Moscow Univ; *Career*: taught at secondary school, Moscow Higher Women's Courses, Shanyavskiy Univ and Moscow Univ; helped found Moscow Commission for Home Reading; from 1896 member, 1909-21 chm, Friends of Russian Linguistics Soc; until 1930 custodian of Tolstoy's manuscripts at All-Union Lenin Public Library; 1886 first work published; began research on ethnography and folklore (articles published in *Etnograficheskoye obozreniye* and *Russkiye vedomosti*); ed, A. N. Afanas'yev's *Russkiye narodnyye skazki* (Russian Folk Tales) (1897 and 1913-14) and *Pesni, sobrannyye P.N. Rybnikovym* (Songs Collected by P.N. Rybnikov) (3 vol, 1909-10); made efforts to popularize Russian and West European lit (pop essays on Fonvizin, Belinskiy, Dante, Shakespeare, Lermontov, Turgenev, etc); gave much attention to teaching of lit; read a course of lectures on teaching of methods Russian language and lit; 1907 compiled together with A. D. Alferov a reader on 18th-Century Russian lit; helped publish *Istoriya russkoy literatury 19-go veka* (History of 19th-Century Russian Literature) (5 vol, 1908-10) and works in Library of History and Literature and Library of European Classics series; also known as translator of "Arabian Nights" (1922-23) and Nizami (1922) and R. Tagora's (1918) works; one of the first to analyze Turgenev and L. N. Tolstoy's texts; helped prepare anniversary ed of L. N. Tolstoy's collected works; *Istoriko-literaturnyye raboty V. Ya. Stoyunina* (V. Ya. Stoyunin's Works on the History of Literature) (1889); *K istorii 'Zapisok okhotnika' Turgeneva* (The History of Turgenev's "A Huntsman's Notes") (1903); *M. I. Glinka* (1904); *Literaturnyye ocherki* (Literary Studies) (1908); *P. N. Rybnikov. Biograficheskiy ocherk* (P. N . Rybnikov. A Biographical Outline) (1909); *Metodika russkogo yazyka i literatury. Kurs lektsiy, chitannyy na Moskovskikh Vysshikh zhenskikh kursakh* (Methods of Teaching Russian Language and Literature. Course of Lectures Held at Moscow Higher Women's Courses) (1917); *I.S. Turgenev* (1918); *Yasnaya Polyana* (1922); *K novym tekstam iz romana 'Voyna i mir' L. N. Tolstogo* (New Texts from L. N. Tolstoy's Novel "War and Peace") (1925), etc; *Died*: 22 Jan 1930 in Moscow.

GRUZMAN, Shulim Ayzikovich (? -1919) Jewish revol; helped establish Sov regime in Ukr; CP member from 1912; *Career*: 1917 chm, Gorlovka-Shcherbinovka RSDRP(B) Comt; deleg, 1st All-Russian Congress of Soviets; member, Centr Exec Comt of 1st convocation; founder-member, Donbass Mil Revol Comt and Centr Staff; 1918 deleg, 1st (July) and 2nd (Oct) Congress of the CP(B) Ukr, which were held in Moscow; from Oct 1918 member, Exec Bureau, CC, CP(B) Ukr, which operated in the German-occupied Ukr; *Died*: 1919 in battle with Petlyura forces.

GRYAZNOV, Ivan Kensarionovich (1897-1938) Mil commander; officer, Russian Army; corps commander from 1935; Civil War veteran; CP member from 1922; *Born*: 11 Jan 1897 in Perm' Province, son of chm of a credit company; *Educ*: Kazan' Business College; 1917 grad Chistopol' Ensign School; 1923 grad Higher Acad Courses; *Pos*: 1916 drafted into Russian Army; 1917 company commander; asst commander, army training group; from June 1918 in Red Army; 1918-20 draft inspector for Krasnoufimsk Front; commander of a forces group; regt, then brigade commander, Eastern Front; 1920-22 commander, 30th Infantry Div; 1922-30 commander, 7th, 18th, 11th, 8th then 6th Infantry Corps; 1930-31 asst commander, Centr Asian Mil Distr; 1931-33 dep head, Red Army Bd of Motorization and Mechanization; 1933-35 commander, Transbaykal Army Group; 1935-37 commander, Transbaykal Mil Distr; 1937 commander, Centr Asian Mil Distr; 1934-37 member, Mil Council, USSR Pop Comrt of Defense; *Career*: 1918, as regt commander, helped suppress anti-Sov peasant revolt in Krasnoufimsk Uyezd; 1920 his troops seized Irkutsk and participated in the Perekop assault; 1930-31 fought against Basmachi movement; 1937 arrested by NKVD organs; *Awards*: two Orders of the Red Banner; silver sabre; engraved Mauser automatic; *Died*: 29 July 1938 in imprisonment (or 21 Aug 1940 according to other sources); posthumously rehabilitated.

GUBAYDULLIN, Gaziz Salikhovich (pseudonym: GAZIZ, G.) (1887-1938) Tat historian and writer; *Born*: 27 June 1887 in Kazan', son of a merchant; *Educ*: 1914 grad Historical and Philological Fac, Kazan' Univ; *Career*: 1919-25 taught Tat history at various higher educ institutions in Kazan'; from 1925 prof and head, Chair of the History of Turkic Peoples, Baku (Azer) Univ; also dean, Oriental Fac of this Univ and lecturer on Oriental history at Samarkand Univ; works deal with history of Tat and Turkic peoples and history of Turkic-Tat lit; 1907 began lit career, writing humorous stories about everyday life; arrested by State Security organs; *Publ*: coauthor, *Materialy po istorii tatarskoy literatury drevnego perioda* (Materials on the History of Ancient Tatar Literature) (3 vol, 1920's); *Istoriya tatar* (History of the Tatars) (1922); *Nauchno-pedagogicheskiye trudy K. Nasyri* (K. Nasyri's Academic and Pedagogic Works) (1922); coauthor, *Istoriya tatarskoy literatury* (History of Tatar Literature) (2nd ed, 1925; *Razvitiye istoricheskoy literatury u tyurko-tatarskikh narodov* (Development of the Historical Literature of the Turkic-Tatar Peoples) (1926); *Pugachyovshchina i tatary* (The Pugachov Mutiny and the Tatars); *K voprosu o proiskhozhdenii tatarskogo naroda* (The Origin of the Tatar People), etc; *Died*: 16 Sept 1938 in imprisonment; posthumously rehabilitated.

GUBARYOV, Aleksandr Petrovich (1855-1931) Gynecological surgeon and obstetrician; Dr of Med from 1887; Hon Prof; *Born*: 11 Mar 1855 in Moscow; *Educ*: 1882 grad Med Fac, Moscow Univ; *Career*: did postgrad work at Moscow Univ; from 1893 dissector, Chair of Operative Surgey and Topographical Anatomy, Moscow Univ, under N.V. Vorontsovskiy and A.A. Bobrov; then assoc, Chair of Normal Anatomy, Moscow Univ, under D. N. Zernov; simultaneously specialized in gynecology at V. F. Snegiryov's clinic; 1887 defended doctor's thesis on the surgical anatomy of the abdominal cavity and internal impaction of the intestines; 1893-97 head, Chair of Obstetrics and Gynecology, Yur'yev (Tartu) Univ; 1897-1901 assoc, 1901-22 dir, Gynecological Clinic, Moscow Univ; 1910 published classic manual on operative gynecology and the principles of abdominal surgery; devised several gynecological and urological operations, including a radical operation for cancer of the womb, an extraperitoneal approach to pelvic abscesses, a method of suturing the ureter and an operation without preliminary tying-off of the blood vessels; developed a number of gynecological instruments, including a cervical expander, a diagnostic trocar, an infusion cannula and a special curet; did research on the clinical anatomy of the female pelvis, classified the pelvic cellular tissue and lymphatic system and studied the propagation of infections and malignant diseases; 1897 read paper on his radical operation for cancer of the womb, which anticipated the method of the Viennese gynecologist E. Wertheim, at 12th Int Congress of Physicians; founded a school of gynecology in the tradition of V. F. Snegiryov; even in retirement he took an active interest in the prevention of women's diseases in keeping with the prophylactic trend in Sov med; chm, Moscow Obstetrical and Gynecological Soc; co-founder and ed, journal *Ginekologiya i akusherstvo*; co-ed, *Bol'shaya meditsinskaya entsiklopediya* (Large Medical Encyclopedia) (1st ed); wrote 135 works, including 19 monographs and manuals on obstetrics and gynecology, notably on the anatomy of the female pelvic organs; *Publ*: doctor's thesis *Khirurgicheskaya anatomiya bryushnoy polosti i operatisya pri vnutrennem ushchemlenii kishok* (The Surgical Anatomy of the Abdominal Cavity and an Operation for Internal Impaction of the Intestines) (1887); *O sovremennom znachenii ginekologii i o metodakh yeyo klinicheskogo prepodavaniya* (The Present-Day Significance of Gynecology and Methods of Teaching It in Clinics) (1893); *Korennaya operatsiya pri rake matki* (A Radical Operation for Cancer of the Womb) (1897); *Akusherskoye issledovaniye naruzhnoye i vnutrenee* (External and Internal Obstetrical Examination) (1898); *Operativnaya ginekologiya i osnovy abdominal'noy khirurgii* (Operative Gynecology and the Principles of Abdominal Surgery) (1910) *Meditsinskaya ginecologiya* (Medical Gynecology) (1917); *Meditsinskoye akusherstvo ili akusherstvo prakticheskogo vracha* (Medical Obstetrics or Obstetrics for the General Practitioner) (1923); *Vospaleniye bryushiny i osnovaniya dlya yego lecheniya. Klinicheskiy ocherk* (Peritonitis and the Basis for its Treatment. A Clinical Study) (1926); *Klinicheskaya anatomiya tazovykh organov zhenshchiny* (The Clinical Anatomy of the Female Pelvic Organs) (1926); coauthor, *Rukovodstvo prakticheskoy khirurgii* (A Manual of Practical Surgery) (1931); *Awards*: Bush Prize; Snegiryov Prize; Hon Dr of Dublin Univ; *Died*: 24 Oct 1931.

GUBEL'MAN, Moisey Izrailevich (1884-?) Party official; CP member from 1902; *Born*: 1884; *Career*: 1902 joined RSDRP; frequently arrested and imprisoned for public and revol activities; 1910 sentenced to eight years at hard labor; after 1917 Oct Revol secr, Exec Comt, Vladivostok Sov; member, Far-Eastern Oblast RSDRP(B) Comt and Pop Comr of Food Supply and Agric in first Sov Far-Eastern Kray Govt in Khabarovsk; active in overthrowing Provisional Govt in Far East; active in partisan movement; Mar 1918 helped suppress White Guards revolt in Blagoveshchensk; from 1924 worked for Moscow Party org; member, Zamoskvorech'ye Rayon and Moscow City CPSU(B) Comt; from 1928 Presidium member, Moscow Party Control Commission; from 1924 edited journals *Soyuz potrebiteley, Smychka* and *Informatsionnyy byulleten' Tsentrosoyuza; Died:* date and place of death unknown.

GUBER, Boris Andreyevich (1903-1937) Writer; *Born*: 9 July 1903 in vil Kamenka, Kiev Province, son of an agronomist; *Career*: 1920 volunteered for Red Army and fought in Civil War; 1920 first verse published; from 1925 member, *Pereval* lit group; arrested by State Security organs; *Publ*: articles and reviews on A. Malyshkin *Padeniye Daira* (The Downfall of Dair) (1926), and Gorky *On i my. O romane Gor'kogo 'Zhizn' Klima Samgina'* (He and We. Gorky's Novel "Klim Samgin's Life") (1936), etc; collected stories *Sharashkina kontora* (A Phony Office) (1926); book *Izvestnaya Shurka Shapkina* (The Well-Known Shurka Shapkina) (1927); novelettes: *Bab'ye leto* (Indian Summer) (1934); "April" (1937), etc; stories and essays: *Nespyashchiye* (The Watchful) (1931); coauthor, *Eshelon opazdyvayet* (The Echelon Is Late) (1932); stories *Sapogi* (Boots) (1927); *Karagach* (1927); *Prostaya prichina* (A Simple Reason) (1928); *Passazhir* (The Passenger) (1928); *Died*: 1937 in inprisonment; posthumously rehabilitated.

GUBER, Pyotr Konstantinovich (1886-1941) Writer and lit historian; *Born*: 26 Sept 1886 in Poltava; *Career*: 1912 first work published; translated and annotated Erazm Rotterdamskiy's book *Pokhval'noye slovo gluposti* (A Word in Praise of Stupidity) (1931); critico-biographical sketch "Anatole France" (1922); biographical essay "Jack London" (1927); preface to V. A. Sollogub's memoirs (1931), etc; arrested by State Security organs; *Publ*: books *Iov Dulder; Don Zhuanskiy spisok Pushkina* (Pushkin's Don Juan List) (1923); *Khozhdeniye na vostok venitseyskogo gost'ya Marko Polo, prozvannogo millionshchikom* (Oriental Travels of Marco Polo, a Guest from Venice Dubbed a Millionaire) (1929); novels *Kruzheniya serdtsa. Semeynaya drama Gertsena* (Heart Vertigo. Herzen's Family Drama) (1928); *Mesyats tumanov* (The Month of Fogs) (1929); "1830" (1930); *Died*: 13 Apr 1941 in imprisonment; posthumously rehabilitated.

GUBER-GRITS, David Solomonovich (1893-1967) Neuropathologist; Cand of Med from 1936; *Born*: 1893; *Educ*: 1914 began med studies at Edinburgh Univ; 1920 grad Med Fac, Yur'yev (Tartu) Univ, which was evacuated to Voronezh during WW 1; *Career*: 1919-22 mil surgeon in Red Army; 1921-28 intern, then asst prof, Clinic for Nervous Diseases, Khar'kov Med Inst; from 1928 worked for railroad med service in Khar'kov; 1931 read course on ind and occupational psychoneurology at Ukr Inst of Postgrad Med Training; 1938-39 head, Chair of Nervous Diseases, Stalingrad Med Inst; 1941-43 worked for med service, Turkestan-Siberian Railroad and various hospitals; specialized in the org of psychoneurological outpatients facilities, occupational diseases and the semiotics of nervous diseases; did major research on syphilis of the nervous system and diseases of the peripheral nervous system, a subject on which he wrote a standard monograph; member, Psychoneurological Section, Learned Med Council, Ukr Pop Comrt of Health; member, Learned Council, Centr Ukr Psychoneurological Inst; Bureau member, Psychoneurological Section, Khar'kov Med Inst; member, Learned Council and Bureau for Psychoneurological Conferences, Centr Hospital, Min of Means of Communication; wrote 39 papers, two monographs and over 20 popular works; *Awards*: Order of Lenin; "Hon Railroad Worker" badge; two medals; *Died*: 20 May 1967.

GUBERGRITS, Maks Moiseyevich (1886-1951) Therapist; Dr of Med from 1917; member, Ukr Acad of Sci from 1948; Hon Sci Worker of Ukr SSR from 1935; *Born*: 19 Jan 1886 in Romny, now Sumy Oblast, son of a physician; *Educ*: 1911 grad Med Fac, Kiev Univ; *Career*: after grad assoc, V. P. Obraztsov's Clinic, Kiev Univ; 1917, while working at Pavlov's Laboratory, defended doctor's thesis on an improved method of differentiating external stimuli; from 1920 head, Chair of Diagnosis and Regional Pathology, then Chair of the Propaldeutics of Internal Diseases, Kiev Med Inst; did major research on the physiology and pathology of blood circulation and neurohumoral regulation; studied the third normal sound of the heart and the phenomenon of cardiac murmur; made widely-acclaimed studies of the clinical physiology and pathology of the digestive system, notably of the pancreas, intestines, stomach and liver; studied the clinical aspects of chronic appendicitis and described several new symptoms; also did research on pain, describing several biochemical changes in the blood and some internal organs in its presence; a pupil of V. P. Obraztsov, he himself trained a large number of internists, including 12 prof; co-ed, therapy section, *Bol'shya meditsinskaya entsiklopediya* (Large Medical Encyclopedia); *Publ*: doctor's thesis *Boley vygodnyy sposob differentsirovaniya vneshnikh razdrazheniy* (A More Advantageous Method of Differentiating External Stimuli) (1917); *Klinicheskaya diagnostika* (Clinical Diagnosis) (1939); *Izbrannyye trudy* (Selected Works) (1958), etc; *Died*: 6 May 1951.

GUBKIN, Ivan Mikhaylovich (1871-1939) Geologist and petroleum specialist; prof; member, USSR Acad of Sci from 1939; CP member from 1921; *Born*: 21 Sept 1871 in vil Pozdnyakovo, Murom Uyezd, Vladimir Province, son of a peasant; *Educ*: 1890 grad Kirzhach Teachers' Seminary; 1898 grad Petersburg Teachers' Inst; 1910 grad Petersburg Mining Inst; *Career*: from 1910 assoc, Geological Comt; from 1918 with Main Petroleum Comt and held exec posts in centr Sov organs directing oil ind and geological services; 1919-24 simultaneously chm, Main Shale Comt, then dir, Shale Ind Bd; 1920-25 chm and sci dir, Special Commission for the Study of the Kursk Magnetic Anomaly, then chm, Council for Oil Ind; 1930-36 chm, Council for the Study of Sov Production Resources; from 1920 prof, 1922-30 rector, Moscow Mining

Acad; from 1930 rector, Moscow Oil Inst; 1924-34 founder-dir, Oil Research Inst; from 1934 dir, Inst of Combustible Minerals, USSR Acad of Sci; from 1936 simultaneously vice pres, USSR Acad of Sci and from 1937 chm of its Azer branch; from 1920 founder-ed, journal *Neftyanoye i slantsevoye khozyaystvo* (from 1925 *Neftyanoye khozyaystvo);* 1908 began research work, studying mineral deposits on northern shore of Lake Ladoga and in Maykop oil-bearing area (North Caucasus); 1912-13 in works on geology and oil content of Maykop area suggested a new method of mapping subterranean relief of oil-bearing strata; was the first to establish special configuration of oil deposits later known as "shoestring deposits"; geological explorations conducted after 1917 solved a number of major problems; proposed hypothesis covering rules of distribution and origin of mud volcanoes and the connection between them and oil deposits; 1921 recommended a detailed survey of the Volga-Ural area as a promising new oilfield; later directed surveying work there; 1932 produced a detailed plan for and then directed oil prospecting in the West Siberian plain, the Kuznetsk Basin, the Minusinsk Depression, the Baikal area and the Yakut ASSR; in his classic work *Ucheniye o nefti* (The Science of Oil) (1932) he summed up the results of his research on the origin of oil and the conditions for the formation of oil deposits; while directing USSR geological service headed several commissions on the study and exploitation of USSR natural resources; instrumental in the development of the raw materials base of the Ural-Kuznetsk Combine, Karaganda and Great Altay, and in the ind development of Siberia, the Far East, Geo, Turkm, Maritime Kray, Arctic areas, etc; from 1932, as chm of the Commission for Studying the Quarternary period, organized and directed work along these lines; co-founder, Int Assoc for the Study of Quarternary Deposits in Europe; 1932 organized its 2nd Conference in Leningrad, over which he presided; member, Sov Section of above Assoc; 1933 led Sov deleg at 16th Session, Int Geological Congress, Washington; 1937 elected pres, 17th Int Geological Congress, Moscow; 1936 attended Brussels Int Peace Congress; Inst of Geology of Azer Acad of Sci and Moscow Oil Inst were named after him; *Publ: Problemy Akchagyla v svete novykh dannykh* (The Akchagyl Problem in the Light of New Data) (1931); *Ucheniye o nefti* (The Science of Oil) (1932); *Bashkirskaya neft', yeyo znacheniye i perspektivy razvitiya* (Bashkir Oil, its Importance and Prospects for its Development) (1932); *Mirovyye neftyanyye mestorozhdenya* (The World's Oil Deposits) (1934); *Volzhskaya neftenosnaya oblast'* (The Volga Oil-Bearing Area) (1940); *Izbrannyye proizvedeniya po geologii Azerbaydzhana* (Selected Works on the Geology of Azerbaidzhan) (1949); *Izbrannyye sochineniya* (Selected Works) (2vol, 1950-53); *Died*: 21 Apr 1939 in Moscow.

GUCHKOV, Aleksandr Ivanovich (1862-1936) Moscow property owner and industrialist; founder and leader, Octobrist Party; *Born*: 1862; *Career*: from 1905 played an active role in politics after he appealed to the tsar to make peace and convene the Zemstvo Council; 1905 took a right-wing stand at zemstvo and city congresses and spoke out against parliamentarianism; 10 Nov 1905, together with other minority leaders of the zemstvo and city congresses (Count P. A. Geyden and D. N. Shipov), proclaimed foundation of the "League of Oct 17" (Octobrist Party); 1905 approved the introduction of field courts martial; May 1907 elected trade and ind rep to the State Council; Oct 1907 resigned from State Council; elected to 3rd State Duma; Mar 1910 elected Duma chm; Mar 1911 resigned chairmanship in protest against Stolypin's law on the Zemstvo in the Western provinces; Nov 1911 elected chm, Octobrist Faction; 1915-17 chm, Centr Mil Ind Comt; elected member, State Council; member, Special Defense Council; active in "Progressive Bloc"; 2 Mar 1917, together with other members of the State Council, persuaded Nicholas II to abdicate in favor of his brother Mikhail; 15 Mar-15 May 1917 Min of War and the Navy in the first cabinet of the Provisional Govt; resigned min portfolio and founded Soc for the Rebirth of Russia; Aug 1917 helped arrange Gen Kornilov's march on Petrograd; arrested at the front; liberated by the Provisional Govt; member, Democratic Conference and Pre-Parliament; helped found Volunteer Army; 1918 emigrated to Berlin; made speeches abroad against the Sov regime; *Publ: Rechi po voprosam gosudarstvennoy oborony i ob obshchey politike 1908-17 gg* (Speeches on State Defense and General Policy, 1908-17) (1917); *Died*: 1936 in Paris.

GUDKOV, Viktor Panteleymonovich (1899-1942) Karelian poet; composer and folklorist; Hon Art Worker of Karelian-Finnish SSR from 1940; *Born*: 16 Sept 1899 in Voronezh, son of a notary; *Career*: from 1918 lived in Petrovodsk; after mastering Finnish, used folk runes and legends in his poetry; made instrumental and choral arrangements of folk songs; perfected the kantele, a string folk instrument; founded the first kantele orchestra (now the "Kantele" State Song and Dance Ensemble of Karelian ASSR); 1937 elected dep, Karelian-Finnish Supr Sov of 1st convocation; *Publ*: verse collection "From the North" (1929); cycle of poems "The Choice" (1939); poem "Girl at the Sea" (1941); libretto for the opera "Three Brothers" (1941); play in verse "Sampo" (1940) based on "Kalevala" themes; *Died*: 17 Jan 1942.

GUDTSOV, Nikolay Timofeyevich (1885-1957) Metallurgist; Dr of Tech Sci from 1934; prof; member, USSR Acad of Sci from 1939; Hon Sci Worker of RSFSR; *Born*: 13 Nov 1885; *Educ*: 1910 grad Petersburg Polytech Inst; *Career*: from 1910 worked at A. A. Baykov's Laboratory, Petersburg Polytech Inst; 1913-28 head, Metallographic Laboratory, Putilov Plant, Petersburg; 1928-33 worked at Leningrad Inst of Metals; simultaneously lectured at Leningrad Polytech Inst; from 1930 prof at above Inst; from 1939 exec assoc, Inst of Metallurgy, USSR Acad of Sci; from 1943 simultaneously prof and head, Chair of Thermal Treatment, Moscow Steel Inst; helped design thermal-treatment shops at various machine-building plants; did research on phenomena occuring in metals during their crystallization, processing and use; developed a theory of the genesis of tetragonal iron lattices, a theory of deformation in crystal bodies and a theory of physical changes in steel during cooling; developed a method of applying X-ray analysis to the study of tempered steel; suggested a new hypothesis on ferrocarbon alloys; *Publ*: basic textbooks for metallurgical students *Spetsial'naya stal', yeyo svoystva, obrabotka i primeneniye* (Special Steel. Its Properties, Processing and Use) (1920-28) and *Metallografiya i termicheskaya obrabotka stali* (The Metallography and Thermal Treatment of Steel) (1924-32); *Stal, yeyo priroda i svoystva* (Steel, Its Nature and Properties) (1927); *Teoriya obrazovaniya flokenov* (The Theory of Floccule Formation) (1941); *Ucheniye o prochnosti i plasticheskoy deformatsii* (The Theory of Strenght and Plastic Deformation) (1948), etc; *Awards*: Order of Lenin; Order of the Red Star; medals; Stalin Prize; *Died*: 29 Jan 1957.

GUDZIY, Nikolay Kallinikovich (1887-1965) Lit historian; prof from 1922; member, Ukr Acad of Sci from 1945; *Born*: 3 May 1887 in Mogilyov-Podol'skiy; *Educ*: 1911 grad Kiev Univ; *Career*: from 1915 assoc prof, Kiev Univ; from 1922 prof, Moscow Univ; simultaneously 1938-47 head, Dept of Ancient Russian Lit, Inst of World Lit, USSR Acad of Sci; 1945-52 head, Dept of Russian Lit and 1952-61 head, Dept of Ancient Ukr Lit, Inst of Lit, Ukr Acad of Sci; also chm, Commission for the Study of History of Philology, Dept of Lit and Language, USSR Acad of Sci; worked on the history of Russian and Ukr lit and textology and history of philological sci; spent many years studying L. N. Tolstoy's works and prepared for publ a 10-volume ed of his works; *Publ*: univ course *Istoriya drevney russkoy literatury* (History of Ancient Russian Literature) (1938); *Khrestomatiya po drevney russkoy literature* (Anthology of Ancient Russian Literature) (1935); *Kak rabotal L. Tolstoy* (How L. Tolstoy Worked) (1936); *Frantsuzskaya burzhuaznaya revolyutsiya i russkaya literatura* (The French Bourgeois Revolution and Russian Literature) (1944); *Lev Tolstoy. Kritiko-biograficheskiy ocherk* (Lev Tolstoy. Critical and Biographical Outline) (1949); *Pushkin. Kritiko-biograficheskiy ocherk* (Pushkin. Critical and Biographical Outline) (1949); *N. S. Tikhonravov* (1956); *I. Franko i russkaya kul'tura* (I. Franko and Russian Culture) (1957); *Literatura Kiyevskoy Rusi i drevneyshiye inoslavyanskiye literatury* (The Literature of Kiev Rus and the Ancient Literature of Other Slavic Peoples) (1958); *Khrestomatiya po drevney russkoy literature XI-XVII vv.* (Anthology of Ancient Russian Literature of the 11th-17th Centuries) (7th ed, 1962); *Istoriya drevney russkoy literatury* (History of Ancient Russian Literature) (7th ed, 1966); *Died*: 29 Oct 1965.

GUKASYAN, Gukas Oganesovich (1899-1920) Party official; CP member from 1917; *Born*: 1899 in vil Kalara, Erivan Province, son of a peasant; *Career*: founded workers and peasants' youth org in Arm; Sept 1919 at first illegal Transcaucasian conference of Communist youth leagues in Baku elected member, Transcaucasian Center, Communist Youth League; early 1920 at illegal conference of Arm Bolshevik org elected member, Arm Exec Bolshevik Center (Arm Comt); assigned by the Center to head Kars Bolshevik org; May 1920, during the revolt against Arm

Democratic Govt, chm, Kars Mil-Revol Comt; *Died*: 1920 killed during the suppression of this revolt; a rayon in Arm SSR was named for him and a monument to him erected in Yerevan.

GUKOVSKIY, Grigoriy Aleksandrovich (1902-1950) Lit historian, specialist in 18th-and early 19th-Century Russian poetry; *Born*: 1 May 1902; *Educ*: 1923 grad Soc Sci Fac, Petrograd Univ; *Career*: prof, Leningrad and Saratov Univ; headed Group for Study of 18th-Century Lit at Pushkin House in Leningrad (Inst of Russian Lit, USSR Acad of Sci); one of the first Sov lit historians to study Russian lit of 18th and early 19th Centuries; wrote a number of works on Pushkin and Gogol' notable for their thorough lit and historical analysis; expressed very clearly his conception of Russian realism; investigated the inner laws of lit development, where each successive school solves the contradictions of the previous period; although all his works were based on profound knowledge of 18th-Century social life, in the 1930's he was subjected to Party criticism for applying formalistic methods in lit research and in 1949 was arrested by State Security organs; *Publ: Russkaya poeziya 18-go v.* (Russian Poetry in the 18th Century) (1936); *Ocherki po istorii russkoy literatury i obshchestvennoy mysli 18-go veka* (Outline History of 18th-Century Russian Literature and Social Theory) (1938); *Russkaya literatura 18-go veka* (Russian Literature in the 18th Century) (1939); *Sumarokov i yego literaturno-obshchestvennoye okruzheniye* (Sumarokov and His Literary and Social Environment) (1941); *Karamzin* (1941); *Fonvizin, Radishchev i dr.* (Fonvizin, Radishchev and Co) (1947); *Pushkin i russkiye romantiki* (Pushkin and the Russian Romanticists) (1946); *Pushkin i problemy realisticheskogo stilya* (Pushkin and the Problems of Realistic Style) (1957); *Realizm Gogolya* (Gogol's Realism) (1959); *Died*: 2 Apr 1950 in imprisonment; posthumously rehabilitated.

GUKOVSKIY, Isidor Emmanuilovich (1871-1921) Party and govt official; CP member from 1898; *Born*: 1871; *Career*: from 1898 in revol movement as member, Petersburg Revol Workers' Group; 1898 arrested for his connections with Bielostok printing house and for inciting Izhorsk ind workers to strike; imprisoned in a fortress and then exiled for five years to Yeniseysk Province; after his return from exile in 1904 stayed in Baku and worked for local Soc-Democratic org under the alias of Fyodor IZMAYLOVICH; 1906 secr, ed bd, newspaper *Novaya zhizn'*; after being questioned by the police in connection with the newspaper, went abroad; 1907 returned and worked in Moscow; re-arrested again and brought to trial; after 1917 Feb Revol treasurer, CC, RSDRP(B); after 1917 Oct Revol appointed Dep Pop Comr, then Pop Comr of Finance; 1919 Collegium member, Pop Comrt of State Control; 1919-20 RSFSR plen in Est; *Died*: 1921.

GULAKYAN, Armen Karapetovich (1899-1960) Stage dir; Pop Artiste of Arm SSR from 1940; CP member from 1941; *Born*: 1 Nov 1899 in Tiflis; *Educ*: 1921-25 studied at Arm Drama Studio in Moscow and at State Inst of Stagecraft; *Career*: 1918 began stage work as actor, Tbilisi Zubalov Pop House; from 1925 stage dir, Tbilisi Arm Drama Theater; from 1927 stage dir, 1930-38 and 1944-53 chief stage dir, Yerevan Sundukyan Theater; 1938-46 and from 1958 chief stage dir, Yerevan Spendiarov Opera and Ballet Theater; his work helped to establish Sov dramaturgy on Arm stage, to improve stagecraft and to expand Arm theater; from 1947 taught at Yerevan Inst of Arts and Theater (prof, Chair of Acting and Directing); dep, USSR Supr Sov of 2nd and 3rd convocations; *Works*: directed plays: Sundukyan's "Khatabala" (1927) and "Pepo" (1929); Vagarshyan's "Encircled" (1930); "Marriage of Figaro" (1933); Tigranyan's *Anush* (1935); *Platon Krechet* (1935); *Groza* (Thunderstorm) (1935); Sundukyan's "Broken Hearth" (1938); "Othello" (1940); *Ivan Susanin* (1942); "The Huguenots" (1943); Chukhadzhyan's *Arshak II* (1946); *Maskarad* (Masquerade) (1949); Boryan's "On the Heights" (1947); Ter-Grigoryan and Karagezyan's "These Our Stars" (1950); *Zhivoy trup* (Living Corpse) (1951); Tigranyan's *David bek* (1952); *Kremlyovskiye kuranty* (The Kremlin Chime) (1956); Stepanyan's *Lusabatsin* (1960), etc; wrote plays: *Na zare* (At Dawn) (1937); *Velikaya druzhba* (Great Friendship) (1939); *Klad* (Hidden Treasure) (1940); *Dni, lyudi nezabyvayemyye* (Unforgettable Days and People) (1957); *Awards*: two Stalin Prizes (1946 and 1950); Order of Lenin; Order of the Red Banner of Labor; medals; *Died*: 22 Sept 1960.

GULEVICH, Vladimir Sergeyevich (1867-1933) Biochemist; prof; member, USSR Acad of Sci from 1929 and member, German Leopold Acad of Natural Sci in Halle from 1928; *Born*: 18 Nov 1867 in Ryazan'; *Educ*: 1890 grad Med Fac, Moscow Univ; *Career*: from 1896 assoc prof, Med Fac, Moscow Univ; from 1899 prof, Khar'kov Univ; 1901-33 prof and from 1907 head, Chair of Med Chemistry and head, Chemical Laboratory, Moscow Univ; 1908-29 simultaneously prof and head, Chair of Biological Chemistry, Moscow Higher Women's Courses (later 2nd Moscow Med Inst); 1910-33 prof and head, Chair of Organic Chemistry, Moscow Business Inst (later Plekhanov Inst of Nat Econ); from 1933 head, Biochemistry Section, All-Union Inst of Experimental Med and head, Leningrad Laboratory of Physiology and Biochemistry of Animals, USSR Acad of Sci; chm, Assoc of Sci Research Inst, Physics and Mathematics Fac, 1st Moscow State Univ; his doctor's thesis *O kholine i neyrone* (Choline and Neuron) (1896) proved the absence of neurons in the brain and thus disproved Liebreich's theory, which attributed a number of mental diseases to poisoning of the body by the accumulation of poisonous neurons in the brain; studied organic nitrous animal extracts and the chemistry of proteins and amino acids; together with his assoc discovered and analyzed five new amino acids: carnosin, anserin, carnitin, methylguanidin and creaton; these studies were the basis for comparative biochemistry and helped to solve some nutrition and endocrinology problems; discovered new methods of synthesizing amino acids and thus obtained a number of new, hitherto unknown amino acids and various derivatives of already known amino acids; *Publ: O kholine i neyrone* (Choline and Neuron) (1896); *Analiz mochi* (Urinoscopy) (1901); *Kurs biologicheskoy khimii* (Course of Biological Chemistry) (reprinted 1947); *Izbrannyye trudy* (Selected Works) (1954); *Died*: 6 Nov 1933.

GULIA, Dmitriy Iosifovich (1874-1960) Abkhazian writer, linguist, historian and ethnographer; CP member from 1955; *Born*: 21 Feb 1874 in vil Uarcha, now Abkhazian ASSR, son of a peasant; *Educ*: studied at teachers' seminary in Gori; *Career*: teacher; 1924-26 taught Abkhazian language at Tbilisi State Univ; 1892 helped compile Abkhazian alphabet; 1919-20 ed, first Abkhazian newspaper *Apsny*; 1921 founded and headed first Abkhazian theater company; wrote poems, lyric verse, ballads and fables, a novel, stories and a play; wrote studies on history of oral folk art, language and ethnography; compiled terminological dictionary on lit and linguistics, as well as textbooks and readers; translated into Abkhazian verse of Pushkin, Shevchenko, Chavchadze, Tsereteli and Shota Rustaveli's "The Man in the Tiger Skin"; dep, USSR Supr Sov of 4th and 5th convocations; *Publ:* "Collected Verse" (1912); poem "Love Letter" (1913); "Selected Works" (1934); verse cycle "My City" (1952); novella "Under an Alien Sky" (1919); novel *Kamachich* (1940); play *Ghosts* (1946); "A History of Abkhazia" (vol 1, 1925); "The Abkhazians' Love of Hunting and Hunting Language"; "The Goat Cult"; "A Collection of Abkhazian Proverbs, Conundrums, Tongue-Twisters, Homographs, Folk Weather Signs, Charms and Curses" (1939); "Literature and Linguistic Terminology" (1930); *Awards*: Order of Lenin; *Died*: 7 Apr 1960 in vil Agudzera, Abkhazia; buried in center of Sukhumi; Abkhazian Inst of Language, Lit and History, various streets, schools and other Abkhazian establishments are named for him.

GULOMALIYEV, Gulomkhaydar (1904-1961) Musician, ballet-master, composer; Pop Artiste of USSR from 1957; CP member from 1943; *Born*: 1904; *Career*: helped organize amateur artistic activities in the Pamirs; 1943 founded Children's Song and Dance Ensemble; 1956 founded Pamir Ethnographic Song and Dance Ensemble; *Died*: 19 Apr 1961.

GULYAM (real name: GULYAMOV), Gafur Gafurovich (1903-1966) Uzbek poet; member, Uzbek Acad of Sci from 1943; secr, Bd, Uzbek Writers' Union and Bd member, USSR Writers' Union; CP member from 1946; *Born*: 10 Mar 1903 in Tashkent; *Educ*: elementary educ at old Moslem school; *Career*: orphaned at an early age; worked as bootblack, newsboy, gardener, teacher, then on newspapers and journals; 1923 first work printed; translated into Uzbek works of Pushkin, Mayakovskiy, Rustaveli, Shevchenko, etc; 1956-60 member, CC, CP Uzbek; dep, Uzbek Supr Sov of 1955, 1959 and 1963 convocations; *Publ*: letters in verse: "Letter from the Happy Uzbek People to the Leader of Peoples, the Great Stalin, at the 18th CPSU(B) Congress" (1939); "Letter from the Builders of the Great Fergana Canal to I. V. Stalin" (1939); "Letter from the Uzbek People to the Soldiers of the Great Fatherland War" (1942); "To Comrade Stalin" (1949); novelette "Yadgar" (1938); collected verse and poems: "I Come from the East" (1943); "The Fortune of My Homeland" (1951); "The Time Hymn" (1959); "Selected Works" (1963); "Colloquy of Hearts" (1964), etc; *Awards*: Stalin Prize (1946); 1st Republ Prize (1959); *Died*: 10 July 1966.

GUMILYOV, Nikolay Stepanovich (1886-1921) Russian poet; *Born*: 15 Apr 1886 in Kronstadt, son of a ship's dr; *Educ*: 1906 grad high-school; 1906-08 attended lectures at Sorbonne; from 1910 studied at Fac of History and Philology, Petersburg Univ; *Career*: 1902 first work published; 1910 married the poetess A. A. Gorenko (Anna Akhmatova); established Acmeist "Poets' Workshop" and became the leader of the Acmeist movement; made several trips abroad, visiting Italy and Africa; 1914-17 on active service with Russian Army, then with Russian Expeditionary Corps in Paris; early 1918 returned to Russia; member, ed bd "World Lit" Publ House; apart from poetry also wrote fiction and lit criticism; translated the Babylonian epic "Gilgamesh," French folk songs and works by Gautier, Villon, Wilde and Coleridge into Russian; 1921 arrested in Petrograd for alleged involvement in an anti-Sov plot; *Publ: Put' konkvistadorov. Stikhi* (The Road of the Conquistadores. Poems) (1905); *Romanticheskiye tsvety. Stikhi* (Romantic Flowers. Poems) (1908); *Zhemchuga* (The Pearl) (1910); *Chuzhoye nebo* (Another Sky) (1912); *Kolchan* (The Quiver) (1916); *Kostyor* (The Camp-Fire) (1918); *Mik. Afrikanskaya poema* (Mik. An African Poem) (1918); *Farforovyy pavil'on. Kitayskiye stikhi* (The Porcelain Pavilion. Chinese Poems) (1918); *Ditya Allakha. Arabskaya skazka* (The Children of Allah. An Arab Legend) (1921); *Shatyor* (The Marquee) (1921); short stories *Ten' ot pal'my* (Palm-Shade) (1922); lit criticism *Pis'ma o russkoy poezii* (Letters on Russian Poetry) (1923); *Died*: 24 Aug 1921 executed by firing squad in Petrograd.

GURARIY, Mikhail Samar'yevich (1909-1965) Eng; dep head, Main Bd for the Construction of State Highways from 1953; member, Tech Council, USSR Min of Trans Construction; member, Sci Council, USSR Research Inst of Roads and Highways from 1953; *Born*: 1909; *Career*: 1931-48 with road-building organizations; chief eng and head, Kir Road Trans Bd, then head, Moscow-Brest, Moscow-Gorky-Kazan' and Moscow-Minsk Highways Bd; 1948-51 head, Moscow-Khar'kov-Simferopol' and Kiev-Khar'kov-Rostov Highway Construction Bd; 1951-53 dep head, Kuybyshev Hydroelectric Power Plant Construction Bd; *Awards*: Order of the Red Banner of Labor; Order of the Red Star; Badge of Hon; Stalin Prize; *Died*: June 1965.

GUREVICH, Emmanuil L'vovich (lit pseudonyms: Ye. SMIRNOV; V. DANEVICH; K. PETROV) (1866-?) Publicist; *Born*: 1866; *Career*: 1884 arrested for involvement in self-educ circles; late 1885 exiled to Ufa Province; 1889 moved to Zurich, but deported in same year; until 1890 member, *Narodnaya volya* (People's Will) group; from 1901 member, RSDRP; first lit work printed in French Socialist press; from 1897 contributed to Russian legal and illegal press; 1901, together with Yu. Steklov and D. B. Ryazanov, founded Soc-Democratic *Bor'ba* (Struggle) group; after schism in RSDRP joined Mensheviks; 1905 member, ed staff, Menshevik organ *Nachalo*; 1910 sided with the liquidationists; member, Soc-Democratic faction of State Duma; in this connection 1911 arrested and after six months' imprisonment exiled from Petersburg; during WW 1 defensist; 1917 ed, rightist cooperators' newspaper *Vlast' Naroda;* worked for Inst of Marx and Engels; helped edit Russian editions of works of Marx, Engels, Lafarge, Kautskiy, etc; *Died*: date and place of death unknown.

GUREVICH, Lyubov' Yakovlevna (1866-1940) Russian writer, theater historian and critic; *Born*: 1 Nov 1866 in Petersburg, daughter of a teacher; *Educ*: 1888 grad Philological Dept; Besstuzhev Higher Women's Courses; *Career*: while still a student began writing stories and translating; 1891-98 ed and publisher, journal *Severnyy vestnik*; persuaded such eminent writers as L. N. Tolstoy, Chekhov, Leskov and Gorky to contribute to the journal; contributed to journals *Mir bozhiy, Zhizn', Obrazovaniye*, etc; 1912 published the collection *Literatura i estetika* (Literature and Aesthetics), which included articles on Gogol', Pushkin, L. Tolstoy, Chekhov, Leskov and Al'bov and articles on aesthetics with valuable observations on the nature of artistic creative work; from early 1900's concentrated on history, theater history and theater criticism; with the opening of the Moscow Arts Theater, became its ardent advocate and friend of K. S. Stanislavskiy; first to edit Stanislavskiy's theoretical works, including the book *Moya zhizn' v iskusstve* (My Life in Art); after 1917 Oct Revol active in Sov theater studies; translated Spinoza's letters, M. K. Bashkirtseva's *Dnevnik*, Baudelaire's "Verse in Prose", works of Guy de Maupassant, Anatole France and Schnitzler; edited L. Tolstoy's letters for the anniversary ed of his works; *Publ: Sedok i drugiye rasskazy* (The Horseman and Other Stories) (1904); *Tvorchestvo aktyora* (The Actor's Work) (1927); *K. S. Stanislavskiy* (1929); *Istoriya russkogo teatral'nogo byta* (History of Russian Theatrical Life) (Vol 1, 1939); *K. S. Stanislavskiy* in the collection *Mastera MKhAT* (Masters of the Moscow Academic Arts Theater) (1939), etc; *Died*: 17 Oct 1940 in Moscow.

GUREVICH, Mikhail Osipovich (1878-1953) Psychiatrist; Dr of Med from 1908; member, USSR Acad of Med Sci; *Born*: 1878; *Educ*: 1902 grad Med Fac, Moscow Univ; *Career*: after grad intern, Psychiatric Clinic, Moscow Univ; then intern, Petersburg Mil-Med Acad; 1908 defended doctor's thesis on nerve fibrils and their lesions under certain pathological conditions; later worked at psychiatric hospitals in Tver' and Saratov; 1918-25 asst to Prof P. B. Gannushkin, from 1937 dir, Psychiatric Clinic, Moscow Univ; in the course of his career was also associated with the Brain Inst, the All-Union Inst of Experimental Med, the Centr Inst of Psychiatry, the Serbskiy Inst of Forensic Psychiatry, the Moscow Oblast Psychiatric Clinic, etc; wrote some 115 works; *Publ*: doctor's thesis *O nevrofibrillyakh i ikh izmeneniyakh pri nekotorykh patologicheskikh usloviyakh* (Nerve Fibrils and Their Lesions under Certain Pathological Conditions) (1908); *Psikhopatologiya detskogo rosta* (Child Psychopathology) (1927); coauthor, *Uchebnik psikhiatrii* (A Psychiatry Textbook) (1928); *Nervnyye i psikhicheskiye rasstroystva pri zakrytykh travmakh cherepa* (Nervous and Mental Disorders from Closed Traumas of the Cranium) (1948); *Psikhiatriya* (Psychiatry) (1949); *Died*: 1953.

GUREVICH, Nikolay Il'ich (1871-1960) Surgeon; *Born*: 1871 in Kiev; *Educ*: 1894 grad Med Fac, Kiev Univ; *Career*: 1894-1902 external student, Obukhov Women's Hospital, Petersburg; also for two years dissector, Chair of Normal Anatomy; 1898 defended doctor's thesis; 1902-08 head, Surgical Dept, Petrozavodsk Province Zemstvo Hospital; 1903 founded Olonets Province Physicians' Soc; from 1918 chief surgeon, Moscow's Beryozkin Hospital; 1931-35 head, Surgical Dept, Moscow's Blagushchinskaya Hospital; from 1935 prof, Hospital Surgical Clinic, 3rd Moscow Med Inst; 1942-52 consultant and sci dir at Moscow hospitals; from 1952 chief surgeon, Moscow's Bauman Hospital; advocated early surgery for acute appendicitis; proposed intraabdominal resection of intestine in case of constricted hernia; did research on patency of large intestine's descending section when separated from mesentery; wrote more than 50 works on abdominal surgery and urology; *Publ: K voprosu o lechenii prostykh perelomov massazhem* (Treating Simple Fractures with Massage) (1898); *O zhiznesposobnosti niskhodyashchey obodochnoy kishki pri otdelenii yeya ot bryzheyki* (The Patency of the Descending Colon when Separated from the Mesentery) (1900); *Ostryye khirurgicheskiye zabolevaniya bryushnoy polosti* (Acute Surgical Diseases of the Abdominal Cavity) (1949); *Died:* 25 Oct 1960 in Moscow.

GURIY (real name: YEGOROV, Vyacheslav Mikhaylovich) (1891-1965) Metropolitan of Simferopol' and the Crimea and vicar of the Dnepropetrovsk Eparchy from 1961; Cand of Theology from 1916; *Born:* 1891; *Educ:* 1916 grad Petrograd Theological Acad; *Career:* 1915 took monastic orders under name of Guriy and ordained priest-deacon, then priest-monk; 1917 treasurer, Aleksandr Nevskiy Monastery (Petrograd); 1922 ordained archimandrite; from 1925 father superior, Monastery's Anchorite Section and head, Theological Pastoral College; from 1928 father superior, Kiev Monastery Church in Leningrad; 1929 arrested and imprisoned in a forced labor camp; subsequently exiled to Northern Kray; 1944 appointed dean, Samarkand Pokrov Cathedral and acting secr, Eparchial Council, Tashkent Eparchy; 1945 helped restore Troitsa-Sergiev Monastery in Zagorsk; 1945-46 father superior of this monastery; 1946 Bishop of Tashkent and Centr Asia; 1952 consecrated Archbishop; 1953 Archbishop of Saratov; 1954 Archbishop of Chernigov and Nezhin; 1955 Archbishop of Dnepropetrovsk and Zaporozh'ye; 1959 consecrated Metropolitan of Minsk and Bel; 1960 Metropolitan of Leningrad and Ladoga and permanent member, Holy Synod, Moscow Patriarchate; organized clergy congresses in Kir and Uzbek SSR; 1954 assisted in return to Chernigov of the relics of St Feodosiy, which until then had been displayed at Leningrad Anti-Religious Museum; *Awards*: right to wear two breast-crosses (1946); Moscow Patriarchate Order of St Vladimir, 1st Class (1963); *Died*: 12 July 1965.

GURKO-KRYAZHIN (real name: GURKO), Vladimir Aleksandrovich (1887-1931) Historian; *Born*: 9 May 1887; *Educ*: 1912 grad Historical and Philological Fac, Moscow Univ; *Career*: 1920 head, Information Dept, RSFSR Mil and Dipl Mission in Turkey and

Iran; 1921 head, Oriental Dept, Caucasian Branch, Russian Telegraphic Agency; 1924-31 lecturer; from 1928 prof, Leningrad Univ; 1922-28 Presidium member, Learned Assoc of Orientology and dep ed, journal *Novyy Vostok*; works deal with history of int relations, history of Near and Middle East, ethnography and archeology of Caucasian peoples; *Publ: Natsional'no-osvoboditel'noye dvizheniye na Blizhnem Vostoke* (The National-Liberation Movement in the Near East) (1932); *Blizhniy Vostok i derzhavy* (The Near East and the Great Powers) (1925); *Istoricheskiye sud'by Afganistana* (The Historical Fortunes of Afghanistan) (1923); *Kratkaya istoriya Persii* (Short History of Persia) (1925); *Arabskiy Vostok i imperializm* (The Arabic East and Imperialism) (1926); *Khevsury* (The Khevsurs) (1928); *Died*: 17 Oct 1931.

GURLO, Ales' (full name: Aleksandr Kondrat'yevich) (1892-1938) Bel poet; *Born*: 31 Jan 1892 in Kopyl', now Minsk Oblast; *Educ*: 1908 grad elementary school; *Career*: from 1909 worked as farmhand; later at Petersburgg "Vulkan" Plant; from 1909 RSDRP member; from 1913 served with the Baltic Fleet; 1917 joined Bolsheviks and participated in the storming of the Winter Palace in Petrograd during the Bolshevik Revol; during the Civil War served with the Red Volga Flotilla; from 1921 on ed staff, Minsk newspaper *Sovetskaya Belarus'*; in the 1930's worked for Inst of Linguistics, Bel Acad of Sci; 1909 first work published in Bel newspaper *Nasha niva; Publ*: collected verse: "Periwinkle" (1924); "Meetings" (1925); "Constellations" (1926); "Starry Sky" (1927); "Boundaries" (1929); "Selected Works" (1950); "Verse" (1953); *Died*: 4 Feb 1938 in Minsk.

GURSHTEYN, Aron Sheftelevich (1895-1941) Lit critic; *Born*: 2 Oct 1895 in Krolevets, Chernigov Province; *Educ*: studied at Petrograd Univ; *Career*: at age 16 printed first work; 1920 volunteered for Red Army; lectured on lit at Kiev and Odessa Teachers' Training Inst; wrote many works on Jewish lit and theater in Yiddish and Russian; wrote articles on work of D. Bergel'son and A. Fininberg, verse of S. Galkin, acting of S. Mikhel's and V. Zuskin, A. Gol'dfaden and book "Sholom-Aleykhem" (1939); also wrote on lit theory; *Publ: Voprosy marksistskogo literaturovedeniya* (Problems of Marxist Literary Studies) (1931); *Problemy sotsialisticheskogo realizma* (Problems of Socialist Realism) (1941); *Died*: 1941 killed in action at the front.

GURVICH, Aleksandr Gavrilovich (1874-1954) Biologist and histologist; prof from 1906; Dr of Med from 1908; *Born*: 1874; *Educ*: 1897 grad Med Fac, Munich Univ; *Career*: until 1905 worked at Strasbourg and Berne Univ; 1906-18 prof of histology, Petersburg (Petrograd) Higher Women's Courses; 1918-24 prof of histology, Crimean Univ, Simferopol'; 1924-29 prof of histology, 1st Moscow Univ; 1930-45 head, Dept of Experimental Biology, All-Union Inst of Experimental Med; 1945-48 dir, Inst of Experimental Biology, USSR Acad of Med Sci; specialized in embryology, histophysiology, biophysics and theoretical biology; developed important hypotheses on the restorative processes (regulation) of the ovum after centrifuging and on standardization and determination as important modes of embryonic development; did major research on the causes of cell division and its mechanisms; 1923 discovered weak ultraviolet radiation as a by-product of exothermic (mainly ferment) reactions, which play an important role in the vital activity of organisms; the discovery of mitogenetic radiation led him to research in the new field of "mitogenetics," the study of molecular phenomena in biological processes; devised "physiological theory of protoplasm," which views protoplasm as a structured process and sees an extreme dynamic quality in all phenomena of life; expanded these concepts into a "biological field" theory which attributes all basic vital phenomena to a complex interrelationship between the elements of an organism and the organism as a whole; considered the source of the "biological field" to be the chromatine synthesizing process; in late 1920's and early 1930's his ideas were criticized as being "reactionary and mystical," and he was considered to be an extreme proponent of "vitalism"; *Publ*: "Morphologie und Biologie der Zelle" (The Morphology and Biology of the Cell) (1904); doctor's thesis *O yavleniyakh regulyatsii v protoplazme* (Regulation Phenomena in Protoplasm) (1908); *Lektsii po obshchey gistologii dlya yestestvennikov* (Lectures on General Histology for Natural Scientists) (1923); "Die histologischen Grundlagen der Biologie" (The Histological Principles of Biology) (1930); coauthor, *Mitogeneticheskoye izlucheniye* (Mitogenetic Radiation) (1934); *Teoriya biologicheskogo polya* (The Theory of the Biological Field) (1944); coauthor, *Mitogeneticheskoye izlucheniye, fiziko-khimicheskiye osnovy i prilozheniya v biologii i meditsine* (Mitogenetic Radiation, Its Physiochemical Principles and Applications in Biology and Medicine) (1945); coauthor, *Vvedeniye v ucheniye o mitogeneze* (An Introduction to the Theory of Mitogenesis) (1948); *Awards*: Stalin Prize; *Died*: 1954.

GURVICH, Lev Gavrilovich (1871-1926) Specialist in oil chemistry; *Born*: 1871; *Educ*: 1892 grad Kiev Univ; *Career*: from 1899 worked in sugar ind; 1904-09 chemist, Centr Oil Laboratory, Baku Nobel Plants; from 1909 head, oil laboratory in Petersburg; 1920 founder and head, Centr Chemical Laboratory, Azer Oil Trust in Baku; from 1920 prof, Azer Univ and Azer Polytech Inst; from 1924 head, Oil Laboratory, Moscow Inst of Heat Eng; collated and analysed vast experimental material on oil chemistry and physical chemistry obtained in Russia and abroad; 1911-12 studying the phenomenon of adsorbtion, advanced hypothesis on physic-chemical attraction, intermediate between chemical bonding and molecular attraction; on the basis of these ideas explained the formation of floridine (bleaching earth) and metal suspension in liquids and the formation of colloidal solutions and also adsorbtion and desorbtion processes; his works on adsorbtion helped develop methods of oil refining; his book *Nauchnyye osnovy pererabotki nefti* (Scientific Principles of Oil Refining) (1913) is among the classic works on oil refining and is still largely valid; his research on adsorbtion and catalysis led him to a hypothesis on heterogeneous catalysis (1916); 1908, while studying the steam refining of oil, found the explanation for this process; his research on surface tension of an oil product/aqueous solution face/ helped ascertain the reason for the formation and destruction of emulsions, especially during the refining of oil products in alkaline solutions; *Publ: Osnovnyye yavleniya, zakony i teorii neorganicheskoy khimii* (Basic Phenomena, Laws and Theories of Inorganic Chemistry) (1926); *Nauchnyye osnovy pererabotki nefti* (Scientific Principles of Oil Refining) (3rd ed, 1940); *Died*: 30 May 1926.

GURVICH, Yevgeniya Adol'fovna (1861-?) Translator; *Born*: 1861; *Career*: 1879 arrested in Petersburg and for her connections with the *Narodnaya volya* (People's Will) group exiled to Minsk; in 1890's worked in Soc-Democratic circles; joined Bund; during the "legal Marxism" period on her own initiative translated (together with L. M. Zaks) the Vol 1 of Marx's "Kapital," which was to be published illegally; eventually it was published legally by O. N. Popova under the editorship of P. B. Struve; July 1898 arrested; 1900 exiled to eastern Siberia; fled abroad; 1906 returned to Russia and continued to work for RSDRP (Mensheviks) until 1917 Feb Revol; 1917 member, Exec Comt, Minsk Sov of Worker's Dep; from 1922 assoc, Inst of Marx and Engels, Moscow; *Died*: date and place of death unknown.

GUSAKOV, Grigoriy Vasil'yevich (1893-1967) Physician and publ health official; CP member from Mar 1917; *Born*: 1893; *Career*: took part in Oct Revol and Civil War; at time of 1917 Oct Revol physician, 30th Reserve Infantry Regt; then physician, 1st Communist Regt, 10th Army on Southern Front; from 1920 public health work; from 1951 pensioner; *Died*: 24 July 1967.

GUSEV, Dmitriy Nikolayevich (1894-1958) Mil commander; col-gen from 1944; CP member from 1932; *Born*: 26 Oct 1894 in Karsun, now Ul'yanovsk Oblast, son of an office worker; *Educ*: 1917 grad Orenburg Ensigns' School; 1926 grad *Vystrel* Higher Command Staff Courses; 1950 grad Higher Educ Courses, Gen Staff Acad; *Career*: 1916 drafted into Tsarist Army; from 1919 in Red Army; fought in Civil War as company commander and dep regt commander; from 1938 instructor, Frunze Mil Acad; 1941 chief of staff, Baltic Mil Distr, chief of staff, 48th Army and staff chief of operations, Leningrad Front; Nov 1941-Apr 1944 chief of staff, Leningrad Front; from Apr 1944 until end of war commander, 21st Army; took part in Vyborg, Weichsel-Oder, Lower Silesian, Upper Silesian and Prague operations; 1946-55 commander, Leningrad, East Siberian and Transbaykal Mil Distr; 1955 transferred to reserve for health reasons; dep, USSR Supr Sov of 1946 convocation; 1952 deleg, 19th CPSU Congress; *Awards*: Hero of the Soviet Union (1944); four Orders of Lenin; three Orders of the Red Banner; Order of Suvorov, 1st Class; Order of Kutuzov, 1st Class; Order of the Red Star; medals; *Died*: 25 Aug 1958 after a long illness.

GUSEV, Nikolay Ivanovich (1897-1962) Mil commander; col-gen; CP member from 1919; *Born*: 27 Nov 1897, son of a worker; *Educ*: 1941 grad Gen Staff Acad; *Career*: from 1918 in Red Army; fought in Civil War; 1941 comr, Gen Staff; 1941-45 commander of a cavalry div, 13th Cavalry Corps and commander, 4th, 47th and 48th Armies; 1941 led cavalry sortie behind enemy lines; 1943 took part in battle of Leningrad; 1944 took part in Bel operations; 1945 fought in East Prussian campaign; after WW 2 commander of an army and a mil distr, then held exec posts on Gen Staff; toward end of life head, Main Bd, USSR Min of Defense; *Awards:* two Orders of Lenin; four Orders of the Red Banner; other orders and medals; *Died*: 6 May 1962 in the course of duty.

GUSEV, Sergey Ivanovich (real name: DRABKIN, Yakov Davidovich) (1874-1933) Party and govt official; CP member from 1896; *Born*: 1 Jan 1874 in Sapozhok, Ryazan' Province; *Educ*: grad Rostov high-school; 1896 entered Petersburg Technol Inst; *Career*: 1896 began revol activity as member, League for the Liberation of the Working Class; 1897 arrested and exiled to Orenburg; from 1899 did Party work in Rostov; member, Don RSDRP Comt; 1902 one of leaders of Rostov strike; Mar 1903 co-organizer, Rostov demonstration; 1903 deleg, 2nd RSDRP Congress; commissioned by Lenin to report on work of congress in southern Russia; Dec 1904-May 1905 secr, Petersburg RSDRP Comt and member, Bureau of Bolshevik Comts; then secr, Odessa RSDRP Comt; from 1906 member, Moscow RSDRP Comt and Party organizer, Zheleznodorozhnyy Rayon; 1906 deleg, 4th (Amalgamative) RSDRP Congress; 1909 did Party work in Petersburg; frequently subjected to reprisals by Tsarist authorities; Oct 1917 secr, Petrograd Mil-Revol Comt; 1918-20 in succession member, Revol-Mil Council, 5th and 2nd Armies; member, Revol-Mil Council, Eastern, Southeastern and Southern Fronts; commander, Moscow Defense Sector; member, RSFSR Revol-Mil Council; from spring 1921 chm, RSFSR Polit Bd; 1921-22 cand member, CC, RCP(B); from 1923 member, then secr, Centr Control Commission, RCP(B); Collegium member, Pop Comrt of Workers' and Peasants' Inspection; 1925-26 head, Press Dept, CC, CPSU(B); 1928 cand member, Comintern Exec Comt; 1929-33 Presidium member, Comintern Exec Comt; *Publ: Reorganizatsiya Krasnoy armii* (The Reorganization of the Red Army) (1921); *Uroki grazhdanskoy voyny* (The Lessons of the Civil War) (1921); *Nashi raznoglasiya v voyennom dele* (Our Differences on Military Affairs) (1925); *Grazhdanskaya voyna i Krasnaya armiya* (The Civil War and the Red Army) (1958); *Died*: 10 June 1933.

GUSEV, Viktor Mikhaylovich (1909-1944) Russian poet and playwright; *Born*: 30 Jan 1909 in Moscow; *Educ*: 1925-26 studied at Moscow Theatrical College and Higher Lit Courses; 1930-31 studied at Fac of Lit and Art, Moscow Univ; *Career*: 1927 began writing poetry and verse plays; wrote cabaret sketches for "Blue Blouse" ensemble; 1928 first play published; *Publ*: comedy review *Tri volneniya odnogo dnya* (Three Upsets in One Day) (1928); prose plays *Zakrytiye Ameriki* (The Closing of America) (1933); verse comedy *Slava* (Glory) (1935); verse play *Druzhba* (Friendship) (1938); verse play *Syn Rybakova* (Rybakov's Son) (begun 1939, finished by V.V. Vinnikov); lyrical comedy *Vesna v Moskve* (Spring in Moscow) (1941); verse play *(Moskvichka* (The Girl from Moscow) (1943); verse play *Synov'ya tryokh rek* (The Sons of Three Rivers) (1944); film scripts: *Svinarka i pastukh* (The Swine-Maiden and the Shepherd); *Pesnya o Moskve* (Song of Moscow); *V shest' chasov vechera posle voyny* (At Six in the Evening After the War); lyrics for the films *Aerograd* (Aeropolis) (1935); *Udarom na udar* (Blow for Blow) (1936); *Dal'nem Vostoke* (In the Far East) (1937); *Traktoristy* (The Tractor-Drivers) (1939); *Doch' moryaka* (The Sailor's Daughter) (1942); *Aleksandr Parkhomenko* (1939); songs: "The Wide, Wide Field," "Song of Moscow," "Beyond the Kama River," etc; *Awards:* two Stalin Prizes (1942 and 1946); *Died*: 24 Jan 1944 in Moscow.

GUSEV, Vladimir Nikolayevich (1904-1956) Electrochemical eng; CP member from 1956; *Born*: 26 July 1904; *Educ*: 1930 grad Leningrad Polytech Inst; *Career*: 1930-36 worked at *Bolshevik* Plant, Leningrad; from 1936 at a research inst; conducted research on new technol for electr machining of metals; devised methods of electrochemical boring (1928), electrochemical finishing of metal surfaces (1930), methods of obtaining complex-profile holes with the help of anode diffusion (1933) and the formation of complex profiles by electrochemical means (1951); 1938 introduced new method of protecting machine parts against wear; *Publ: Sovremennoye sostoyaniye sposoba anodno-mekhanicheskoy obrabotki metallov* (The Modern Anode-Mechanical Processing of Metals) (1951); *Anodno-mekhanicheskaya obrabotka metallov* (Anode-Mechanical Metal Processing) (1952), etc; *Awards*: three Stalin Prizes (1942, 1948 and 1949); *Died*: 19 Nov 1956.

GUSEYN, Dzhavid (real name: GUSEYN Rasi-zade) (1882-1944) Azer poet and playwright; *Born*: 24 Oct 1882 in Nakhichevan', son of an ecclesiastic; *Educ*: elementary ecclesiastical school; 1909 grad Lit Fac, Istanbul Univ; *Career*: 1906 began lit work; wrote 18 plays, a number of which have been staged in Sov theaters; arrested by State Security organs; *Publ*: verse "Bygone Days" (1910); "Spring Dew" (1914); plays: "Mother" (1910); "Siberian Stag" (1912); "Sheyda" (1916); "Satan" (1918); "Shakhla" (1935); poem "Azer" (1926-37); drama "The Prince" (1929); historical drama "Siavush" (1930); "Khayam" (1935); play "Satan's Revenge" (1936); "Selected Works" (1957), etc; *Died*: 1944 in imprisonment; posthumously rehabilitated.

GUSEYN Mekhti (real name: GUSEYNOV, Mekhti Ali ogly) (1909-1965) Azer writer, playwright and critic; first secr, Bd, Azer Writers' Union from 1957; secr, USSR Writer's Union from 1959; member, CC, CP Azer from 1961; CP member from 1941; *Born*: 1909 in vil Shikhly, now Kaz SSR; *Educ*: 1930 grad Azer State Univ; 1938 grad All-Union State Inst of Cinematography; *Career*: from 1930 exec secr, Proletarian Writers' Assoc; then exec secr, Org Comt, Azer Writers' Union; from 1934 head, Fiction Dept, Azer State Publ House; dir, Baku Film Studio; 1963 visited Turkey, Bulgaria and Austria; dep, USSR Supr Sov of 1962 convocation; *Publ*: novels "High Water" (1936); "Tarlan" (1947); "Apsheron" (1947); collected stories "Flaming Sword" (1943); "As One Family" (1948); "Commissar" (1949); novelettes "Dawn" (1950); "Hard Autumn" (1961); dramas "Glory" (1938); "Nizami" (1940); *Dzhavanshir* (1942); coauthor, "Expectation" (1944), etc; *Awards*: Stalin Prize (1949); *Died*: 10 Mar 1965.

GUSEYNOV, Geydar Nadzhaf-ogly (1908-1950) Azer philosopher and publicist; member, Azer Acad of Sci from 1945; CP member from 1938; *Born*: 3 Apr 1908 in Erevan; *Educ*: grad Azer Univ; *Career*: pres, Azer Branch, USSR Acad of Sci; subsequently 1945-50 vice-pres, Azer Acad of Sci; 1945-50 simultaneously dir, Inst of Party History, CC, CP Azer; also head, Chair of Philosophy, Azer Univ; worked on soc and philosophical thought in Azer; translated Marxist lit into Azer and edited four-vol *Russko-azerbaydzhanskiy slovar'* (Russian-Azerbaydzhan Dictionary) (1940-46); 1950 accused of polit blunders; *Publ: Filosofskiye vzglyady M. F. Akhundova* (Akhundov's Philosophical Views) (1942); *Stat'i po istorii razvitiya filosofskoy i obshchestvennoy mysli v Azerbaydzhane* (Articles on the History of the Development of Social and Philosophical Thought in Azerbaydzhan) (1948); *Iz istorii obshchestvennoy i filosofskoy mysli v Azerbaydzhane v XIX v.* (From the History of Social and Philosophical Thought in Azerbaydzhan in the 19th Century) (1949); *Died*: 15 Aug 1950 committed suicide in Baku.

GUSEYNOV, Mirza Davud Bagir ogly (1894-1938) Govt official; CP member from Nov 1918; *Born*: 1894 in Baku; *Educ*: studied at Moscow Business Inst; *Career*: early 1919 joined "Gummet" Azer Soc-Democratic org and became a member of its comt; then member, Caucasian Kray RCP(B) Comt; from Feb 1920 member, CC, CP Azer; as member, Mil-Revol Staff, helped prepare armed uprising against Azer democratic govt; 1920-21 after establishment of Sov regime in Azer, Azer Pop Comr of Finance; chm, Higher Econ Council, Azer Council of Pop Comr; then Azer Pop Comr of For Affairs; 1922 RSFSR Dep Pop Comr of Nationalities; 1923-29 dep chm, Council of Pop Comr, Pop Comr of For Affairs, then Pop Comr of Finance, Transcaucasian SFSR; 1930-33 first secr, CC, CP Tadzh; deleg at 14th and 16th CPSU(B) Congresses; towards the end of his life worked for RSFSR Pop Comrt of Educ in Moscow; arrested by State Security organs; *Died*: 1938 in imprisonment; posthumously rehabilitated.

GUTOROV, Ivan Vasil'yevich (1906-1967) Bel lit historian and writer; Dr of Philology from 1947; prof, Bel Univ, Minsk from 1951; corresp member, Bel Acad of Sci from 1953; *Born*: 1906 in vil Volkovtsy, now Mogilyov Oblast; *Educ:* 1928 grad Bel Univ, Minsk; *Career*: after grad taught Bel and Russian languages at Mogilyov Teacher's Training Inst and other educ establishment in Mogilyov; 1932 began lit research; during WW 2 fought in Sov Army and partisan detachments; 1939-47 Cand of Philology; 1943-47 studied for doctorate at Inst of World Lit, USSR Acad of Sci; 1947-51 worked for CC, CP Bel; *Publ*: "The Struggle and Work of the People's Avengers" (1949); "The Poetic Skill of V. Mayakovskiy" (1950); "The Aesthetic Principles of Soviet Literature" (1950); "The Philosophical and Aesthetic Views of A.S. Pushkin" (1957); memoirs "The Elusive Youth" (1965), etc; *Awards*: Order of Lenin; Order of the Red Banner; Order of the

Red Banner of Labor; medals; *Died*: 1967.

GUTTARI, Tobias Osipovich (pseudonym: Lea KHELO) (1907-1953) Poet; *Born*: 29 Jan 1907 in vil Muya (now Mga Rayon, Leningrad Oblast), son of a Finnish peasant; *Educ*: grad Gatchiny Teachers' Training Technicum; *Career*: worked as teacher; wrote in Finnish; 1927 first work printed; his verse is emotional, fresh and expressive, close to folk song style; many of his poems have been included in Karelian school readers; translated into Finnish Chernyshevskiy's *Chto delat'?* (What Should We Do?), and works of Chekhov, Gorky, Fadeyev, Novikov-Priboy, Sholokhov, etc; *Publ*: verse collection "Young Thoughts" (1930); "I'm Stepping Over" (1931); "Red Army - the True Guard" (1933); "Poems" (1936); "Spring Song" (1940); "My Country" (1947); children's books "Paper Grows in the Karelian Woods"; "How a Book Is Born" (1932-33); essays "Conquerors of the River" (1933); in Russian translation *Moya strana* (My Country) (1950); *Izbrannyye stikhotvoreniya* (Selected Poems) (1950); *Died*: 14 Dec 1953.

GUTYAR, Nikolay Mikhaylovich (1866-1930) Lit historian; *Born*: 15 Mar 1866 in Gorbatovo, Nizhniy Novgorod Province; *Educ*: grad Moscow Univ; *Career*: teacher in Orenburg, Tarus and Yalta; after 1917 assoc prof, Krasnodar Teachers' Training Inst; 1892 first work published; his main work, "I.S. Turgenev" (1907), composed from a number of his articles, was the first serious research on Turgenev's biography; it includes thorough collection of memoirs and letters; compiled the first chronological annals of Turgenev's life; *Publ: I.S. Turgenev* (1907); *I.S. Turgenev i V.G. Belinskiy* (I.S. Turgenev and V.G. Belinskiy) (1900); *I.S. Tugenev i semeystvo Viardo-Garsia* (I.S. Turgenev and the Viardo-Garcia Family) (1908); *K biografii Turgeneva* (Biographical Materials on Turgenev) (1908); *I.S. Turgenev i yego ne-literaturnyye druz'ya* (I.S. Turgenev and His Non-Literary Friends) (1909); *Khronologicheskaya kanva dlya biografii I.S. Turgeneva* (Chronological Outline of I.S. Turgenev's Biography) (1910); *Poyezdki I.S. Turgeneva v Angliyu* (I.S. Turgenev's Visits to England) (1929); *Died*: 1930 in Krasnodar.

GVETADZE, Razhden Matveyevich (1897-1952) Geo writer; *Born*: 10 Aug 1897 in vil Tsikhia, Kutaisi Rayon; *Career*: 1915 began lit work; member, Geo "Blue Horns" symbolist group; after establishment of Sov regime in Geo one of the first to abandon symbolism; translated into Geo the Indian epic "Ramayana" (1943), Arm epic "David Sasunskiy," works of Russian and Ukr writers; *Publ*: stories: "Teo" (1930); "The Camp-Fire" (1932); "The Nights of Lashaur" (1934); "Belorussian Novellae" (1935); "Life Begins Anew" (1949); cycle "True Novellae" (1943); verse; *Died*: 1 Dec 1952.

GVOZDEV, Aleksandr Nikolayevich (1892-1959) Philologist; Dr of Philological Sci; prof; corresp member, RSFSR Acad of Pedag Sci from 1945; *Born*: 15 Mar 1892; *Educ*: 1918 grad History and Philology Dept, Moscow State Univ; *Career*: 1918 began teaching Russian language and lit, Penza Teachers' Seminary; from 1920 research and teaching work at higher educ institutions; 1944-59 prof, Kuybyshev Teachers' Training Inst; worked on dialectology of contemporary Russian, orthography, stylistic grammar, etc; gave much attention to methods of teaching Russian in schools; *Publ: Voprosnik dlya sostavleniya dialektologicheskogo atlasa russkogo yazyka* (Questionnaire for Compiling a Dialectological Atlas for the Russian Language) (1939); *Usvoyeniye rebyonkom zvukovoy storony russkogo yazyka* (Mastering the Phonetic Aspects of Russian by Children) (1948); *Formirovaniye u rebyonka grammaticheskogo stroya russkogo yazyka* (Teaching Children Russian Grammar) (2 vol, 1949); *O fonologichekikh sredstvakh russkogo yazyka* (The Phonological Resources of Russian) (1949); *Voprosy russkoy orfografii i metodika yeyo prepodavaniya* (Problems of Russian Orthography/ and Methods of Teaching It) (1950); *Sbornik uprazhneniy po sovremennomu russkomu yazyku* (Collection of Exercises in Modern Russian) (3rd ed, 1953); *Osnovy russkoy orfografii* (Principles of Russian Orthography) (4th ed, 1954); *Ocherki po stilistike russkogo yazyka* (Outline Stylistics of the Russian Language) 2nd ed, 1955); *K. S. Stanislavskiy o foneticheskikh sredstvakh yazyka* (K. S. Stanislavskiy on the Phonetic Resources of Language) (1957); *Ob osnovakh russkogo pravopisaniya. V zashchitu morfologicheskogo printsipa russkoy orfografii* (Principles of Russian Spelling. In Defense of Morphological Principle in Russian Orthography) (1960); *Voprosy izucheniya detskoy rechi* (The Study of Children's Speech) (1961); *Sovremennyy russkiy literaturnyy yazyk* (Modern Literary Russian) (2 vol, 2nd ed, 1961); *Died:* 19 Dec 1959.

GVOZDEV, Aleksey Aleksandrovich (1887-1939) Russian theater and lit historian, critic and instructor; *Born*: 9 Mar 1887; *Educ*: studied at Leipzig and Munich Univ; 1913 grad Philological Fac, Petersburg Univ; *Career*: 1917-20 taught history of West European lit at Tomsk Univ and 1920-39 at Leningrad Herzen Teachers' Training Inst; from 1920 founder-chm, Theater History and Theory Dept, Petrograd State Inst of History of Arts (now Leningrad State Theater, Music and Cinematography Research Inst); introduced a new discipline into the curriculum of higher educ institutions: - history of West European theater; *Publ*: over 200 works dealing with the history of Sov and West European theater, critical articles and theater notices; *Iz istorii teatra i dramy* (From the History of Theater and Drama) (1923); *O smene teatral'nykh sistem* (The Change of Theater Systems) (1926); *Teatr im. V. Meyerkhol'da 1920-1926* (V. Meyerhol'd Theater 1920-1926) (1927); *Khudozhnik v teatre* (The Theater Artist) (1931); *Teatr v epokhe feodalizma* (The Theater in the Feudalist Epoch) (1931); *Istoriya zapadnoyevropeyskoy literatury. Sredniye veka i Vozrozhdeniye* (History of West European Literature. Middle Ages and Renaissance) (1935); *Zapadnoyevropeyskiy teatr na rubezhe 19-go i 20-go stoletiy* (West European Theater at the Turn of the 19th Century) (1939), etc; *Died*: 10 Apr 1939.

GYULLING (GYLLING), Edvard Otto Vil'gel'm (1881-1944) Finnish revol and Sov govt official; member, Finnish Soc-Democratic Party from 1905; CP member from 1920; *Born*: 30 Nov 1881; *Career*: 1908-18 dep, Finnish Sejm; 1910-18 assoc prof, Helsinki Univ; 1905 joined Soc-Democratic Party of Finland (SDPF) and sided with its left (Marxist) wing; 1913-17 member, Exec Comt, SDPF; 1917-18 chm, SDPF; during the 1918 Workers' Revol in Finland member, Revol Govt; chief of main staff, Red Guards; late 1918, after the collapse of revol, emigrated to Sweden where he worked with For Bureau, CC, CP Finland; 1920 emigrated to USSR and received Sov citizenship; helped found Karelian Labor Commune (from 1923 Karelian ASSR); 1920-23 chm, Karelian Oblast Exec Comt; 1923-35 chm, Karelian Sovnarkhoz; 1935-37 with Int Econ Inst in Moscow; member, USSR Centr Exec Comt of all convocations; 1937 arrested by State Security organs; *Died*: 19 Aug 1944 in imprisonment; posthumously rehabilitated.

GYUNTER, Nikolay Maksimovich (1871-1941) Mathematician; corresp member, USSR Acad of Sci from 1924; prof, Leningrad Univ; Hon Sci Worker of RSFSR; *Born:* 17 Dec 1871; *Career:* initial works dealt with gen theory of differential equations in common and special derivatives; did extensive research on mathematical physics; proved the existence and uniqueness of a solution to the equation for the hydrodynamics of an ideal liquid in the presence of an external potential force; 1934 first to give a strict and systematic exposé of the current state of the potential theory; widely used the ideas and methods of the theory of the function of a real variable and functional analysis in solving problems of mathematical physics; coauthor of a standard book on problems of higher mathematics; *Publ: O prilozhenii teorii algebraicheskikh form k integrirovaniyu lineynykh differentsial'nykh uravneniy* (Application of the Theory of Algebraic Forms to the Integration of Linear Differential Equations) (1903); *K teorii kharakteristik sistem uravneniy v chastnykh proizvodnykh* (The Theory of the Characteristics of Equation Systems in Partial Derivatives) (1913); *Ob osnovnoy zadache gidrodinamiki* (The Basic Problem of Hydrodynamics) (1927); *O dvizhenii zhidkosti zaklyuchyonnoy v dannom peremeshchayushchemsya sosude* (The Motion of a Liquid Confined in a Shifting Vessel) (1926-28); coauthor *Sbornik zadach po vysshey matematike* (A Collection of Higher Mathematical Problems) (1949-51); *Died*: 4 May 1941.

GZHEL'SHCHAK (GRZELSZCZAK), Frantsishek Yanovich (Party pseudonyms: MEKHANIK; Martsin GZHEGOZHEVSKIY [GRZEGORZEWSKI]) (1881-1937) Polish and Russian revolutionary; member, Soc-Democratic Party of Poland and Lith from 1904; *Born*: 1 Jan 1881 in Warsaw, son of a worker; *Career*: participated in 1905 Revol in Warsaw; Warsaw deleg, 5th (London) RSDRP Congress; repeatedly arrested by Tsarist authorities; 1914 drafted into the army; member, soldiers' revol movement; 1917 elected member, Bolshevik faction, 2nd Army Comt; Sept 1917 attended All-Russian Democratic Conference in Petrograd; elected member, Preparliament; together with Bolshevik faction left Preparliament; at 2nd Congress of Soviets elected member, All-Russian Centr Exec Comt; early 1918 went to Poland; member, Warsaw Comt, Soc-Democratie Party of Poland and Lith; helped organize Sov of Workers' Dep; worked illegally, repeatedly subjected to arrests; Dec 1918 at 1st

(Amalgamative) Congress of Soc-Democratic Party of Poland and Lith and Polish Socialist Party· elected member, CC, Communist Workers' Party of Poland (from 1925 CP Poland); attended all Congresses and Conferences of CP Poland; May 1925 arrested; 1928 with other polit prisoners exchanged by USSR Govt; in USSR worked for Comintern, Profintern, Int Revol Fighters Assistance Org; 1924 at 5th Comintern Congress elected member, Comintern Exec Comt; 1937 arrested by State Security organs; *Died*: 25 Dec 1937 in imprisonment; posthumously rehabilitated.

GZOVSKAYA, Ol'ga Vladimirovna (1889-1962) Russian actress; *Born*: 10 Oct 1889; *Career*: 1906-10 and 1917-19 at Moscow Maly Theater; 1917-19 at Moscow Acad Arts Theater; gave stage recitations to music; 1920-32 abroad; 1943-56 at Leningrad Pushkin Acad Theater; also film actress; taught stagecraft; *Roles*: Beatrice in Shakespeare's "Much Ado About Nothing"; Ophelia in Shakespeare's "Hamlet"; Cleopatra in Shaw's "Caesar and Cleopatra"; Mirandolina in Goldoni's "The Innkeeper's Wife"; Sof'ya in Griboyedov's *Gore ot uma* (Woe from Wit); Marina Mnishek in Ostrovskiy's *Dmitriy Samozvanets i Vasiliy Shuyskiy* (Dmitriy the Impostor and Vasiliy Shuyskiy); Lidiya in Ostrovskiy's *Beshenyye den'gi* (Mad Money), etc; *Died*: 2 July 1962.

I

IBRAGIMOV, Akhmedzhan (1899-1957) Party and govt official; CP member from 1921; *Born*: 1899; *Educ*: grad Centr Asian Communist Univ; *Career*: 1917 volunteered for Red Guard in Turtkul' and fought in campaign for the establishment of Sov rule in Turtkul' and Khorezm; 1920-22 commander, Tashauz Oblast partisan detachment; then chm, Tashauz Oblast Revol Comt and Cheka; 1925-29 did govt work in Khorezm Oblast; from 1930 first secr, Shavat Rayon CPSU(B) Comt; from 1931 studied at Centr Asian Communist Univ; after grad secr, Party bureau at this univ; from 1935 first secr, Shafrikan Rayon CPSU(B) Comt, Bukhara Oblast; from 1937 first secr, Khorezm Oblast Comt, CP Uzbek; 1941-46 dir, "Five Years of the Uzbek SSR" Sovkhoz; first secr, Uychi Rayon Comt, CP Uzbek, Namagan Oblast; from 1950 directed various sovkhozes, Tashkent Oblast; dep, USSR Supr Sov of 1st and 2nd convocations; *Awards*: Order of Lenin; three Orders of the Red Banner; three Orders of the Red Banner of Labor; two Orders of the Red Star; medals; *Died*: 29 Sept 1957.

IBRAGIMOV, Galimdzhan (1887-1938) Tatar writer; CP member from 1917; *Born*: 12 Mar 1887 in vil Sultan-Muratovo, now Bash ASSR, son of a mullah; *Educ*: studied at Orenburg medressah, then at *Galiya* Medressah in Ufa; *Career*: 1906 arrested for revol activities; 1912-13 propaganda work among Moslem students in Kiev; from 1914 taught Tatar language and lit at *Galiya* Medressah; at time of 1917 Feb Revol edited Leftist Socialist-Revol newspaper *Irek* in Ufa; Jan 1918 dep, Constituent Assembly, walked out together with Bolshevik faction; 1918 as Leftist Socialist-Revol elected member, All-Russian Centr Exec Comt at 3rd All-Russian Congress of Soviets; dep chm, Moslem Comrt, Pop Comrt of Nationalities; chm, commission to translate and publish Lenin's works in Tatar; ed, Tatar journal "Our Path" and "Enlightenment"; 1925-27 chm, Acad Center, Tatar Pop Comrt of Educ; 1926 chm, Tatar delegation at 1st Turkological Congress in Baku, where he headed the Arabist group and bitterly opposed introduction of the new Turkic alphabet; 1927 issued statement recanting his errors on this matter and urged Tatars to support latinized Tatar orthography; outlined his views on Tatar nat culture in article "Along What Lines Will Tatar Culture Develop? "; these views were at odds with the Party line and were denounced by the Tatar Party org; taught on mil courses, at Tatar Oblast Sov-Party School and at Tatar Communist Univ, lecturing on history of lit, history of CPSU(B) and history of revol movement among Tatars; officially joined CP in 1920 but in view of his revol services the Party CC backdated his membership from 15 Apr 1917; 1917 first work printed; in 1930's arrested by State Security organs; *Publ*: stories and novelettes: "Expulsion from the Zakishakird Medressah" (1907); "The Fate of a Tatar Woman" (1910); "Pages from the Life of Young People" (1911); "At Sea" (1911); "The Old Farmhand" (1912); "The Mullah is a Thief" (1912); "Children of Nature" (1914); novels: "Young Hearts" (1912); "Our Times" (1920); "The Tale of the Red Flowers" (1922); "Almachuvar" (1922); "Daughter of the Steppes" (1924); "Deep Roots" (1928); works on Tatar philology and linguistics: "A Tatar Grammar" (1911); "Principles of Tatar Orthography" (1924); "The Theory of Literature" (1916); "Methods of Teaching Our Native Language" (1918), etc; historical works: "The Great October Revolution and Dictatorship of the Proletariat" (1922); "From the History of the Tatar Student Movement" (1922); articles on the life and work of Kayum Nasyra, Mullanur Vakhitov, etc; "1905 Revolutionary Movements Among the Tatars" (1925); *Died*: 21 Jan 1938 in imprisonment; posthumously rehabilitated.

IBRAGIMOV, Khabibula Kalimullovich (1894-1959) Bash playwright and composer; Hon Art Worker of Bash ASSR; *Born*: 29 Dec 1894 in Orenburg; *Educ*: grad Leningrad Inst of Music; *Career*: wrote numerous plays and musical works, mainly songs and marches; *Works*: musical comedies "Little Boots" (1921); "Son-in-Law" (1945); plays: "Fellow from the City," etc; composed pop songs to lyrics by Bash and Tat poets and also to lyrics of his own ("Girl-Harvester," "Akushey," "Mastyura, the Kolkhoz Woman," "My Present," etc) and marches ("Salavat's March," "Komsomol March," "Kolkhoz March," "March of the Shockworkers," etc); *Died:* 7 Mar 1959.

IBRAGIMOVV, Usman Ibragimovich (1915-1962) Lawyer; CP member from 1942; *Born*: 1915; *Career*: 1926 began work at age of 11; 1937 began legal career-pop judge, member of an okrug court, dep chm and chm, Surkhan Darya Oblast Court; from 1952 chm, Uzbek Supr Court; member, USSR Supr Court; 1961-62 cand member, CC, CP Uzbek; 1956-61 member, Auditing Commission, CC, CP Uzbek; dep, Uzbek Supr Sov of 1959 convocation; *Awards*: two Badges of Hon; *Died*: 6 July 1962 killed in the performance of his duties.

IBRAGIMOV, Yu. I. (1895-1961) Govt official; *Born*: 1895; *Career*: during 1917 Oct Revol fought on Northern Front; 1918 member, Turkestani Centr Exec Comt and Turkestani Mil-Polit Staff; 1919 member, Moslem Mil Collegium, RSFSR Pop Comrt of Mil and Naval Affairs; 1920 member, Revol-Mil Council, Turkestani Front; 1921 Collegium member, Turkestani NKVD; then admin work: *Died*: 1961.

IDAYATZADE, Ismail Guseyn-ogly (1901-1951) Azer actor, stage dir and theater dir; Pop Artiste of Azer SSR from 1938; *Born*: 19 Aug 1901; *Career*: 1917 began acting career while still a student, performing with several professional Azer ensembles; from 1920 actor, Azer State Theater (now Azizbekov Theater); from 1934 also worked as a producer; from 1938 chief producer, from 1941 also dir, Akhundov Opera and Ballet Theater; dep, Azer Supr Sov; *Roles*: Abdulalibek in Dzharbaly's *Sevil'* (1928); Shvandya in *Lyubov' Yarovaya* (1929); Sharif in Dzhabarly's *Almas* (1931); Salamov in Dzhabarly's "In the Year 1905" (1931); Célestin in Slavin's *Interventsiya* (Intervention) (1932); Sheikh Nasrulla in Mamedkulizade's "The Corpses" (1933); Shmaga in *Bez viny vinovatyye* (Guilty Without Guilt) (1935); Hadji Kar in Akhundov's "The Miser's Adventure" (1937), etc; *Productions*: shows: Dzhavid's *Siyavush* (1934) and Dzhanan's "Shah-name" (1935); Gadzhibekov's opera *Kyor-ogly* (1937) and musical *Arshin mal alan* (1938); Badalbeyli's "Tower of Virgins" (1940); Tigranyan's *Anush* (1941); Niyazi's *Khosrov and Shirin* (1942); Karayev and Gadzhiyev's *Veten* (1945); Bizet's "Carmen" (1946); Badalbeyli's *Nizami* (1948); *Died*: 11 Nov 1951.

IDEL'SON, Naum Il'ich (1885-1951) Astronomer and sci historian; *Born*: 14 Mar 1885; *Career*: prof, Leningrad Univ and senior assoc, Pulkovo Observatory; 1941-43 ed, *Astronomicheskiy yezhegodnik SSSR* (Astronomical Yearbook of the USSR), for which he wrote two papers on reduction values and basic constants in astronomy; did research on the motion of Encke and Méchain-Toutle's comets; wrote monographs on the theory of potential, the least squares method and the history of the calendar, as well as biographies of Copernicus, Galileo, Newton, Lagrange, Clairaut and Lobachevskiy; *Publ: Istoriya kalendarya* (The History of the Calendar) (1925); *Teoriya potentsiala s prilozheniyami k teorii figury Zemli i geofizike* (The Theory of Potential with Applications to the Theory of the Shape of the Earth and Geophysics) (1936); *Sposob naimen'shikh kvadratov i teoriya matematicheskoy obrabotki nablyudeniy* (The Least Squares Method and the Theory of the Mathematical Processing of Observations) (1947); *Died*: 14 July 1951.

IGNATIYENKO, Varfolomey Andrianovich (1892-1943) Ukr bibliographer; *Born:* 25 Aug 1892 in vil Ozeryany, now Chernigov Oblast, son of a peasant; *Educ*: 1919 grad Kiev Business Inst;

Career: 1923-31 head, Bibliographic Section, Ukr Bibliographical Research Inst; teacher; wrote numerous works on book history and Ukr press; *Publ: Bibliografiya ukrainskoy pressy. 1816-1916* (Bibliography of the Ukrainian Press. 1816-1916) (1930); *Died*: 7 Dec 1943.

IGNATOV, Geniy Petrovich (1925-1942) Kuban' partisan in WW 2; Komsomol member; *Born*: 12 Mar 1925, son of an eng and writer; *Educ*: studied in 9th Grade at School Nr 8 in Krasnodar; *Career*: Aug 1942, as German troops advanced into the Caucasus, together with his father, mother and elder brother joined partisan detachment; his father, P. K. Ignatov (partisan alias: *Batya*) described the operations of this detachment in his book *Zapiski partizana* (A Partisan's Notes) (1949); *Awards*: Hero of the Sov Union (1943, posthumously); *Died*: 10 Oct 1942 killed in action.

IGNATOV, K. M. (1872-1939) Eng; *Born*: 1872; *Career*: from 1907 lecturer, 1918-24 prof, Moscow Higher Tech College; 1921 appointed rector of this College by Main Bd of Vocational Training, RSFSR Pop Comrt of Educ; helped plan and construct Moscow water-supply system; consultant to Supr Sovnarkhoz, Pop Comrt of Labor and other org; wrote works on water-supply, sewerage, fire-proof construction methods, etc; *Died*: 1939.

IGNATOV, Nikolay Fyodorovich (1914-1967) Party and govt official; USSR Dep Min of Machine-Building for the Light and Food Ind and Domestic Appliances from 1966; CP member from 1939; *Born*: 1914; *Educ*: 1934 grad Moscow Streetcar Technicum; 1948 grad Higher Party School, CC, CPSU; *Career*: 1934-42 naval pilot; 1942-49 Party and govt work in Moscow; 1949-54 first secr, Bauman Rayon CPSU Comt, Moscow; 1954-56 secr, from 1956 second secr, Moscow Oblast CPSU Comt; 1956-59 chm, Exec Comt, Moscow Oblast Sov of Workers' Dep; 1960-62 first secr, Oryol Oblast CPSU Comt; 1963-64 first secr (for agric), Oryol Oblast Comt; 1964-65 first secr, Oryol Oblast CPSU Comt; 1956-66 member, CC, CPSU; dep, USSR Supr Sov of 1954, 1958 and 1962 convocations; dep, RSFSR Supr Sov of 1955 convocation; *Awards*: Order of Lenin; *Died*: Apr 1967.

IGNATOV, Nikolay Grigor'yevich (1901-1966) Party and govt official; CP member from 1924; *Born*: 16 May 1901 in vil Tishenskaya, Khoper Okrug, now Volgograd Oblast; *Educ*: 1934 grad Marxism-Leninism Courses, CC, CPSU(B); *Career*: 1917-32 in Red Army and OGPU; from 1934 Party work; 1934-37 secr, Party Comt, Leningrad *Gosznak* Plant; first secr, Lenin Rayon Party Comt, Leningrad; 1937-40 second, then first secr, Kuybyshev Oblast CPSU(B) Comt; 1941-48 second, then first secr, Oryol Oblast CPSU(B) Comt; 1949-52 first secr, Krasnodar Kray CPSU(B) Comt; 1952-53 USSR Min of Procurement; 1952-53 and 1957-60 secr, CC, CPSU; 1953 second secr, Leningrad Oblast CPSU Comt and first secr, Voronezh, then Gorky Oblast CPSU Comt; 1952-53 cand Presidium member, CC, CPSU; 1956-57 and 1962-66 member, Bureau for RSFSR, CC, CPSU; 1957-61 Presidium member, CC, CPSU; 1959 Presidium chm, RSFSR Supr Sov; 1960-62 dep chm, USSR Council of Min; 1962-62 simultaneously chm, State Comt for Procurement, USSR Council of Min; 1962 chm, USSR Comt for Agric; from 1962 Presidium chm, RSFSR Supr Sov; from 1963 Presidium dep chm, USSR Supr Sov; from 1952 member, CC, CPSU; dep, USSR Supr Sov of 1st-7th convocations; *Awards*: Hero of Socialist Labor (1961); *Died*: 14 Nov 1966.

IGNATOV, Nikolay Konstantinovich (1870-1951) Hygienist; Dr of Med from 1898; member, USSR Acad of Med Sci; Hon Sci Worker of RSFSR; *Born*: 1870; *Educ*: 1893 grad Med Fac, Moscow Univ; *Career*: while still a student began research work under Prof F. F. Erisman, Chair of Hygiene, Moscow Univ; 1898 defended doctor's thesis on copper salts in vegetable preserves; 1899-1906 performed extensive research on the water of the Moskva River for the Moscow Water Supply Hygiene Research and Planning Commission; determined the suitability of new, untested filter systems for purifying river water; from 1912 head, Chair of Hygiene, Moscow Women's Med Inst; from 1917 head, Chair of Experimental Hygiene, Higher Med School; from 1924 head, Chair of Experimental Hygiene, 2nd Moscow State Univ; 1930-51 head, Chair of Hygiene, Moscow Med Inst; wrote over 140 works; *Publ*: doctor's thesis *K voprosu o podkrashivanii solyami medi rastil'nykh konservov* (The Use of Copper Salts for Coloring Vegetable Preserves) (1898); *Amerikanskiye mekhanicheskiye fil'try s sanitarnoy tochki zreniya* (American Mechanical Filters from the Sanitary Viewpoint) (1905); *Angliyskiye pesochnyye fil'try* (English Sand Filters) (1908); *Pitaniye detey vsekh vozrastov v svyazi s primeneniyem surrogatov i zamenoyu odnikh produktov drugimi* (The Feeding of Children of All Ages in Connection with the Use of Surrogates and the Use of Substitute Products) (1922); *Metody sanitarno-gigiyenicheskikh issledovaniy* (Sanitation and Hygiene Research Methods) (1938); *Died*: 1951.

IGNATOV, Sergey Sergeyevich (1887-1959) Lit historian and critic; prof from 1939; *Born:* 1 July 1887; *Educ:* 1913 grad Romano-Germanic Dept, Fac of History and Philology, Moscow Univ; *Career:* began lit career after grad; 1921-25 lit dir, Moscow Chamber Theater; wrote articles on this theater's actors and productions; 1921 began teaching course on history of West European lit and theater; taught at various theaters (including Mayakovskiy Theater) and at Inst of Philosophy, History and Lit; from 1934 taught at State Inst of Stagecraft; specialized in the history of West European, notably Spanish and Slavic theater, and was one of first Sov scholars to do research on East bloc theater; wrote numerous press articles; *Publ: Istoriya zapadnoyevropeyskogo teatra novogo vremeni* (The History of the West European Theater in Modern Times) (1940); *Ispanskiy teatr XVI-XVII vekov* (16th-17th Century Spanish Theater) (1939); *Zarozhdeniye slavyanskogo teatra na Balkanakh* (The Birth of the Slavic Theater in the Balkans) (1957); *Nachalo russkogo teatra i teatr Petrovskoy epokhi* (The Beginnings of the Russian Theater and the Theater of the Petrine Age) (1918); *Pol'skiy teatr* (The Polish Theater) (1957); *Lope de Vega i yego teatr* (Lope de Vega and His Theater) (1935); *Vklad slavyan v teatral'nuyu kul'turu Yevropy* (The Slavic Contribution to the European Theater) (1947); *Printsipy postroyeniya istorii teatra zapadnykh i yuzhnykh slavyan* (The Structural Principles of the History of the Theater of the Western and Southern Slavs) (1948); *Visente Zhil', Lope de Vega i drugiye* (Vicente Gil, Lope de Vega and Others); translations: Hofmann's "Don Juan," "Kavalier Glück" (1918) and "Prinzessin Blandina" (1925); Lope de Rueda's "Olivas" (1919); Goldoni's "Pamela" (1936); Sol'skiy's *Vospominaniya* (Reminiscences) (1961); *Died:* 7 Mar 1959.

IGNATOV, Ye. Nr. (1890-1938) Politician and trade-union official; CP member from 1912; *Born:* 1890; *Educ:* grad Marxism courses at Communist Acad; studied at Inst of Red Prof *Career:* worker; prior to 1917 Oct Revol active in trade-union movement; 1913 helped found Bolshevik newspaper "Nash put'" in Moscow; 1914 arrested for staging a May Day strike; from 1917 Feb Revol until mid-1921 member, Exec Comt, Moscow Sov and several times elected to its Presidium; during 1917 Oct Revol member, Mil-Revol Comt in Moscow; member, All-Russian Centr Exec Comt of several convocations; 1918 called for revision of Sov Constitution; Dec 1918, together with Rakovskiy, Ioffe, Bukharin, Radek and Markhlevskiy, represented All-Russian Centr Exec Comt at 1st All-German Congress of Soviets; active trade-unionist; Presidium member, Public Nutrition League and Presidium member, All-Union Centr Trade-Union Council; 1921 chm of Russian deleg sent to Poland to negotiate repatriation of prisoners-of-war; 1920-21 during the trade union controversy helped Pead anarcho-syndicalist "Ignatov" group which sided with "workers' opposition"; withdrew from opposition after 10th RCP(B) Congress; subsequently held various exec Party and govt posts; worked for Vitebsk Province RCP(B) Comt; chm, Vitebsk Province Exec Comt; from 1929 dir, Higher Sov Construction Courses, All-Union Centr Exec Comt; arrested by State Security organs; *Publ: Moskovskiy sovet rabochikh deputatov v 1917 g.* (The Moscow Soviet of Workers' Deputies in 1917); *Rayonnyye sovety* (The Rayon Soviets); *Died:* 1938 in imprisonment.

IGNATOV, Yevgeniy Petrovich (1915-1941) Design eng; Kuban' partisan in WW 2; CP member from 1941; *Born:* 2 Sept 1915, son of an eng and writer; *Career:* Aug 1942, as German troops advanced into the Caucasus, together with his father, mother and younger brother joined partisan detachment; devised techniques of partisan mining and sabotage against the German troops; his father, P. K. Ignatov (partisan alias: "Batya") described the operations of the partisan detachment in his book *Zapiski partizana* (A Partisan's Notes) (1949); *Awards:* Hero of the Sov Union (1943, posthumously); *Died:* 10 Oct 1942 killed in action.

IGNATOVICH, Nikolay Kliment'yevich (1899–1950) Hydrogeologist; *Born:* 1899; *Educ:* 1925 grad Moscow Mining Acad; *Career:* helped survey subterranean water resources in the Caucasus, the Urals, Kaz and the Far East; wrote a number of works on regional hydrogeology; extrapolating from extensive hydrogeological data on the Russian Plateau, was the first to state the main principles for zonal location of subterranean water resources; *Publ: Psekupskiye mineral'nyye istochniki* (Psekupsk Mineral Springs) (1932); *O zakonomernostyakh raspredelentya i formirovaniya podzemnykh vod* (Principles for the Distribution and Appearance of Subterranean Waters) (1944); *K voprosu o gidrogeologicheskikh usloviyakh formirovaniya i sokhraneniya neftyanykh zalezhey* (Hydrogeological Conditions for the Formation and Preservation of Oil Deposits) (1945); *Zonal'nost', formirovaniye i deyatel'nost' podzemnykh vod v svyazi s razvitiyem geostruktury* (Zones of Distribution, Formation and Activity of Subterranian Waters in Connection with the Development of the Geological Structure) (1950); *Awards:* F. P. Savarenskiy Prize (1949); *Died:* 1950.

IGNATOVSKIY, Afanasiy Sergeyevich (1858-1935) Forensic med specialist; *Born:* 1858; *Educ:* 1884 grad Med Fac, Kiev, Univ; *Career:* from 1884 intern, Fac Surgical Clinic, Kiev Univ; 1892 defended doctor's thesis on skull fractures; 1894 studied under Virchow and Hofmann in Germany; returned to Russia and lectured on forensic med at Kiev Univ; from 1895 prof of forensic med, Yur'yev Univ; after 1917 Oct Revol prof of forensic med, Voronezh Univ and Voronezh Med Inst; studied causes of death in the case of hanging; described heart and skeletal muscle changes after phosphorus poisoning; explained hemorrhaging of stomach's mucous lining in people who freeze to death; traced mechanism of formation of hemochromogen crystals 1910-12 published some of most original Russian lectures on forensic med; *Publ; K voprosu o perelomakh cherepa* (Skull Fractures) (1892); *Proiskhozhdeniye i sostav sudebnoy meditsiny* (The Origin and Content of Forensic Medicine) (1895); *Znacheniye krovoizliyaniy v zheludke dlya sudebnomeditsinskoy diagnostiki* (The Signifiance of Stomach Hemorrhages for Forensic Medical Diagnosis) (1903); *Sudebnaya meditsina* (Forensic Medicine) (1910-12); *Died:* 1935.

IGNATOVSKIY, Vsevolod Makar'yevich (1881-1931) Bel historian; prof, Bel State Univ from 1921; member and pres, Bel Acad of Sci from 1928; CP member from 1920; *Born:* 1881 in former Grodno Province, son of a teacher; *Educ:* until 1905 and in 1906 studied at Historical and Philological Fac, Petersburg Univ; 1911 grad Historical and Philological Fac, Derpt (Tartu) Univ; *Career:* member, Socialist-Revol Party; 1906 expelled from Petersburg Univ for revol activities and exiled to Olonets Province; 1911-14 secondary-school teacher in Vilnius; from 1914 history teacher, Minsk Teachers' Training Inst; late July 1920 on behalf of Bel Communist org signed Constitutional Act to establish second Bel SSR; member, Bel Mil-Revol Comt; late 1920 - early 1926 Bel Pop Comr of Agric, then Bel Pop Comr of Educ; 1925-28 simultaneously Presidium chm, Inst of Bel Culture; from late 1928 member and pres, Bel Acad of Sci; member, CC and CC Bureau, CP(B) Bel and member, Bel Centr Exec Comt; worked on Bel history and history of Bel lit; helped found Bel higher educ institutions, the Inst of Bel Culture and Bel Acad of Sci; 1929-31, during the reprisals against Bel "Nat-Democrats" was charged with belonging to the counter-revol Bel Liberation League; *Publ:* "Brief Outline of the National and Cultural Revival of Belorussia" (1921); "Brief Outline of Belorussian History" (5th ed, 1925); "History of Belorussia in the 19th and Early 20th Century" (1925); "Notes on the Origin of the Belorussian Movement" (1926), etc; *Died:* 20 Feb 1931 committed suicide.

IGNAT'YEV, Aleksandr Mikhaylovich (1879-1936) Inventor; CP member from 1903; *Born:* 13 Dec 1879; *Educ:* from 1901 studied at Petersburg Univ; *Career:* 1905 took part in Revol as member, mil eng group, CC, RSDRP; 1908 worked abroad for CC, RSDRP; 1909 returned to Russia; 1911 resumed studies at Petersburg Univ; 1914 drafted into Russian Army, where he designed a new anti-aircraft gun-sight; after 1917 Oct Revol in Red Army; inspector of Petrograd anti-aircraft defenses; 1920-25 Sov trade rep in Finland; 1925-29 worked at Sov trade mission in Berlin; 1926 designed self-sharpening cutting tool (Sov patent 14451 for 1926); this invention was also patented in the USA, Britain, France, Germany, Italy and Belgium; after return to USSR worked at A. M. Ignat'yev State Research Laboratory, Moscow; in the course of research on the production of multilayered tools devised a method of electr welding under pressure which made it possible to weld together any quantity of individual strips or disks of different thickness in any sequence; designed welding press and continuous welding machine for this process; made numerous other inventions; *Died:* 27 Mar 1936.

IGNAT'YEV, Aleksey Alekseyevich (1877-1954) Russian mil diplomat and writer; *Born:* 14 Mar 1877 in Petersburg, son of a count and commander of a cavalry guards regt; *Educ:* grad Page Corps and Gen Staff Acad: *Career:* during 1904-05 Russo-Japanese War served as adjutant to commander in chief, Gen Kropotkin; 1906-17 mil-diplomatic posts in Denmark, Sweden, Norway and France; during WW 1 liaison rep of Russian Army Headquarters at French Army Headquarters; after 1917 Oct Revol, while serving as mil attache in France, sided with Sov regime and helped to secure for it money deposited by tsarist govt in French banks; 1924, upon establishment of first Sov embassy in France, turned over to it documents and considerable amount of money; granted Sov citizenship and worked in Sov trade mission; 1937 returned to Moscow; 1937-47 worked in Red Army mil schools and in the Mil Publ House; 1943 promoted lt-gen; 1947 retired and concentrated on lit work; *Publ: Pyat'desyat let v stroyu* (Fifty Years in Military Service) (2 vol, 1939-40) describing life of Russian soc and court, the Russo-Japanese War and why it was lost, life in Russia, Scandinavian countries and France prior to and after WW 1; *Died:* 20 Nov 1954 in Moscow.

IGNAT'YEV (pseudonym: ARGUS), Nikon Vasil'yevich (1895-1941) Mari writer; CP member from 1918; *Born:* 31 Mar 1895 in vil Chalomkino, now Mountain-Mari Rayon, Mari ASSR, son of a peasant; *Career:* worked as a farm-hand and Volga boatman; served in Russian Army; 1919 began to write verse, prose and plays in Mari; under pseudonym Argus also wrote satirical press articles; translated Pushkin, Gorky, etc into Mari; *Publ:* novels: "The Steel Wind" (1930-31); "Savik" (1934); "The Fatherland" (1935); novellae: "The Girl from the Komsomol" (1933); "Old Things Fade Away" (1935); *Died:* 4 Mar 1941.

IGNAT'YEV, Varnava Yefimovich (1867-1927) Hygienist; specialist in school hygiene; *Born:* 1867; *Educ:* 1882 grad Med Fac, Moscow Univ; *Career:* after grad physician, Moscow Orphanage; from 1886 asst prof, then assoc prof, Chair of Hygiene, Moscow Univ; 1903 defended doctor's thesis on diffuse lithting of classrooms; 1911 resigned from Moscow Univ in protest against policies of Educ Min Kasso; 1918-23 founder-dir, Moscow Inst of Physical Training and Sport; in his latter years consultant on school hygiene and physical training, USSR Pop Comrt of Health and USSR Pop Comrt of Educ; head, Chair of School Hygiene, Moscow Teachers' Training Inst; studied sanitary conditions and physical training in elementary and forest schools and children's colonies; *Publ: Trebovaniya shkol'noy gigiyeny pri postroyke shkol'nykh zdaniy i klassnykh pomeshcheniy dlya narodnykh shkol* (School Hygiene Requirements in the Construction of School Buildings and Class Accommodation for Public Schools) (1902); *Shkoly v lesu, ikh organizatsiya i sovremennoye sostoyaniye* (Schools Sited in Forests, Their Organization and Modern State) (1913); *Osnovy fizicheskoy kul'tury* (The Principles of Physical Training) (1925); *Okhrana zdorov'ya uchashchikhsya fabrichno-zavodskikh shkol* (Health Care for Students at Factory and Plant Schools) (1925); *Issledovaniye fizicheskogo razvitiya cheloveka doshkol'nogo, shkol'nogo i prizyvnogo vozrastov* (A Study of the Physical Development of Persons in the Preschool, School and Military Draft Age Categories) (1927); *Biologiya trudyashchegosya cheloveka* (The Biology of the Working Man) (1927); *Died:* 1927.

IGNAT'YEV, Vladimir Ivanovich (1887-?) Politician; lawyer; *Born:* 1887; *Career:* 1905 member, Socialist-Revol Party; 1906 sided with Party's maximalist wing; 1917 member, CC, Labor Group, then member, CC, Pop Socialist Party and chm of its Petrograd City Comt; late 1917 and 1918 engaged in underground work against Sov regime in Petrograd and Vologda; member, anti-Sov Renaissance League; 1918 comr, Arkhangelsk Province; until Aug 1919 member, Northern Oblast Govt; 1920 founded All-Siberian Peasants' Union, which directed anti-Sov revolts in Siberia; 1920 arrested; 1922 defendant in trial of CC, Right-Wing Socialist-Revol Party; sentenced to death but amnestied after publicly recognizing Sov regime; subsequently worked for Sov organs; later arrested by State Security organs; *Publ: Nekotoryye fakty i itogi 4 let grazhdanskoy voyny. Chast' I, oktyabr' 1917 - avgust 1919* (Some Facts and Consequences of Four Years of Civil War. Part 1. October 1917 - August 1919); *Died:* date and place of death unknown.

IGUMNOV, Konstantin Nikolayevich (1873-1948) Pianist and music teacher; Dr of Arts; Pop Artiste of USSR from 1946; *Born:* 1 May 1873 in Lebedyan', Tambov Province: *Educ:* began music studies under N.S.Zverev; 1894 grad Moscow Conservatory, where he studied under A.I.Ziloti, P.A.Pabst and S.I. Taneyev; *Career:* 1895 received hon mention at Int Rubinstein Competition; 1899-1948 prof, 1924-29 rector, Moscow Conservatory; from 1932 bd member, USSR Composers' Union; made concert tours in Russia and abroad; included many forgotten works of Russian composers in his concert repertoire, including pieces by Tchaikovsky and A.G.Rubinstein; premiered Glazunov's "1st Concerto," Rachmanioff's "1st Sonata", Skryabin's "Fantasia Sonata Nr 2" and A.K.Lyadov's "Variations on a Theme by Glinka"; as a teacher continued the traditions of the Russian realist school of music; trained several generations of musicians; his pupils included L.N.Oborin, A.N.Aleksandrov, V.I.Argamakov, Ya.V.Fliyer and M.I.Grinberg: *Publ:* ed, various editions of piano works by Rachmaninoff, Skryabin, Lyadov, Glazunov and Rubinstein; *Awards:* Stalin Prize (1946); Order of Lenin; Order of the Red Banner of Labor; medals; *Died:* 24 Mar 1948.

IKOV, V. K. (pseudonyms: MIROV; V. GORODETSKIY) (1882-?) Menshevik: *Born:* 1882; *Career:* voting deleg from Yekaterinoslav RSDRP org at 4th Amalgamative RSDRP Congress; adopted liquidationist stand; 1931 sentenced to imprisonment for his Menshevik views; *Died:* date and place of death unknown.

IKRAMOV, Akmal' (1898-1938) Uzbek Party and govt official; co-founder, CP Uzbek; CP member from 1918; *Born:* 1898 in Tashkent, son of a peasant; *Educ:* grad Sverdlov Communist Univ, Moscow; *Career:* Party work in Fergana, Tashkent and Namangan; dep chm, Namangan Revol Comt; secr, Fergana and Syr-Darya Oblast RCP(B) Comt; 1921-22 head, Org Dept and secr, CC, CP Turkm; after grad from Communist Univ became secr, Tashkent Oblast Comt, CP Uzbek; from Mar 1925 secr, CC, CP Uzbek; from 1929 first secr, CC, CP Uzbek and secr, Centr Asian Bureau, CC, CPSU(B); deleg at 12-17th CPSU(B) Congresses; at 14th, 15th and 16th Party Congresses elected cand member and at 17th Party Congress member, CC, CPSU(B); member, USSR Centr Exec Comt and cand Presidium member of this body; 1937 arrested by State Security organs; sentenced to death for connections with "anti-Sov right-wing-Trotskyite bloc"; *Died:* 15 Mar 1938 executed; posthumously rehabilitated.

IL'CHENKO, Pyotr Yakovlevich (1893-1958) Surgeon; Dr of Med from 1938; prof from 1939; *Born:* 1893 in Krasnograd, Khar'kov Province, son of a worker; *Educ:* 1926 grad Med Fac, Kazan' Univ; *Career:* 1926-29 head of a distr hospital and surgical intern in Sverdlovsk and Ivanovo Oblasts; 1930-35 postgrad student and asst to Prof P. A. Gertsen, Moscow Oncological Inst; 1935 defended cand thesis and advanced to assoc prof; in same year sent by RSFSR Pop Comr of Health to take over the Chair of Operative Surgery, Far Eastern Med Inst; during Finno-Soviet War served as mil surgeon, surgery chief and dep dir of a mil hospital; from 1939 prof and head, Chair of Hospital Surgery, Voronezh Med Inst; from 1941 head, Chair of Fac Surgery, Dag Med Inst; during WW 2 chief surgeon, various front-line hospitals; 1944 seriously wounded and shell-shocked; 1946-Aug 1954 head, Chair of Gen Surgery, Stanislav Med Inst; 1954-58 head, Chair of Operative Surgery and Topographical Anatomy, Dnepropetrovsk Med Inst; devised several new surgical techniques, including: a plastic method of amputation at the thigh to provide a durable stump surface; a method of osteoplastic amputation at the knee; a method of plastic closure of extensive hernial defects of the abdominal wall; an osteotomy to prevent the displacement of bone-splinters, etc; designed a new ski-stretcher for carrying wounded; improved techniques for the immobilization of a fractured leg during transport; also designed improved shoulder and forearm splints; in his latter years designed equipment for the immobilization of an injured spine and pelvis and a fractured thigh during transport of casualties in mines; the first-aid sections at all Krivoy Rog mines were supplied with this equipment; wrote 52 works on the diagnosis, clinical aspects and treatment of malignant tumors, and on surgical anatomy, field surgery, plastic surgery, etc; *Publ: Anatomicheskiye puti rasprostraneniya ostrykh gnoynykh protsessov v myagkikh tkanyakh stopy* (The Anatomical Propagation Paths of Acute Suppurative Processes in the Soft Tissues of the Foot) (1938), etc; *Awards:* five orders and medals; *Died:* 1958 in Dnepropetrovsk.

IL'F, Il'ya (real name: FAYNZIL'BERG, Il'ya Arnol'dovich) (1897-1937) Russian satirical writer; *Born:* 15 Oct 1897 in Odessa, son of a bank clerk; *Educ:* 1913 grad tech school; *Career:* worked for drafting bureau, telephone switchboard, aircraft plant, as statistician, for Southern Bureau, Russian Wire Agency and then for newspaper *Moryak*; ed, humorous journal *Sindetikon*; 1923 moved to Moscow and began writing fiction; re-wrote stories and reports of worker-correspondents for newspaper *Gudok*; contributed essays, feuilletons and film reviews to periodicals *Zheleznodorozhnik, 30 dney, Smekhach, Sovetskiy ekran* and *Vechernyaya Moskva*; 1926 began his long collaboration with Ye. Petrov; 1935 toured USA together with Petrov; *Publ:* essay *Luchshaya v mire strana* (The Best Country in the World) (1924); series of essays *Moskva-Aziya* (Moscow-Asia) (1925); coauthor, novel *Dvenadtsat' stul'yev* (The Twelve Chairs) (1928); coauthor, novelette *Svetlaya lichnost'* (A Radiant Personality) (1928); coauthor, series of satirical novellae *1001 den', ili Novaya Shakherezada* (1001 Days, or the New Sheherezade) (1929); coauthor, novel *Zolotoy telyonok* (The Golden Calf) (1931); coauthor, collection of humorous stories *Kak sozdavalsya Robinzon* (How Robinson Was Created) (1933); coauthor, book of essays *Odnoetazhnaya Amerika* (One-Story America) (1936); coauthor, comedy *Bogataya nevesta* (The Rich Bride) (1936); coauthor, play *Nervnyye lyudi* (Nervous People) (1937); coauthor, collected stories *Tonya* (1937); *Zapisnyye knizhki* (Notebooks) (1939, posthumously); *Died:* 13 Apr 1937.

IL'ICHYOV, Aleksandr Semyonovich (1898-1952) Mining eng; corresp member, USSR Acad of Sci from 1939; Hon Sci and Tech Worker of RSFSR from 1943; CP member from 1941; *Born:* 12 Apr 1898; *Educ:* 1925 grad Moscow Mining Acad; *Career:* 1925-29 at State Inst for Designing Coalmining Equipment; from 1929 lectured at Moscow Mining Acad; from 1930 prof, Moscow Mining Inst; main works deal with the theory of lifting gear and pneumatic installations; 1926 first to recommend the construction of bicylindrical conical drums based on equalization of the torque moment; 1934 laid down principles for standardizing mine lifting gear and suggested unique criteria for counterbalancing mine lifting gear with variable winding radius; studied the operation of piston and rotary compressors; *Publ: Rudnichnyye podyomnyye mashiny* (Mine Hoisting Gear) (2nd, ed, 1933); *Rudnichnyye pnevmaticheskiye ustanovki* (Pneumatic Mine Equipment) (3rd ed, 1949); *K voprosu ob osnovakh standartizatsii rudnichnykh podyomnykh mashin s tsilindricheskimi barabanami* (Principles for Standardizing Mine Hoisting Gear with Cylindrical Drums) (1934); *Kriteriy uravnoveshennosti podyomnykh ustanovok s peremennym radiusom naviki* (Counterbalancing Criterium for Hoisting Gear with a Variable Winding Radius) (1951); *Sobraniye trudov* (Collected Works) (4th ed, vol 1, 1953); *Awards*: Order of Lenin; three other orders; medals; *Died*: 29 Feb 1952.

IL'IN, Aleksey Alekseyevich (1858-1942) Historian; specialist in Russian numismatics; corresp member, USSR Acad of Sci from 1928; *Born*: 26 Sept 1858; *Career*: in the 1920's head, Dept of Numismatics, Hermitage and head, Section of Numismatics and Glyptics, State Acad of History of Material Culture; wrote a number of papers on money circulation in ancient Russia; *Publ: Topografiya kladov serebryanykh i zolotykh slitkov* (Topography of Silver and Gold Bar Troves) (1921); *Topografiya kladov drevnikh russkikh monet 10 - 11-go vv. i monet udel'nogo perioda* (Topography of Troves of 10th-11th Century Ancient Russian Coins and Coins of the Independent Principalities Period) (1925); *Klassifikatsiya russkikh udel'nykh monet* (Classification of Russian Coins of the Independent Principalities Period) (1940); *Died*: 1942.

IL'IN, F. N. (1876—1944) Revolutionary; govt official; CP member from 1897; *Born*: 1876; *Career*: helped stage 1905 armed uprising in Rostov; 1907 returned from exile and emigrated to France and Switzerland, where he remained until 1917 on active Party work; after 1917 Oct Revol returned to Russia and held exec posts in Moscow Sov, Revol Tribunal, Moscow Province Court, Supr Court and RSFSR Gosplan, etc; from 1930 pensioner; *Died*: 1944.

IL'IN, Fyodor Nikolayevich (1872-1959) Obstetrician and gynecologist; Dr of Med from 1907; prof; Hon Sci Worker of Azer SSR; *Born*: 1872; *Educ*: 1898 grad Petersburg Mil Med Acad; *Career*: after grad mil surgeon in Warsaw, where he specialized in obstetrics and gyneocology under Prof N. Jastrebow; 1905 retired from Army and worked for a year at Prof Bumm's clinic in Germany; 1907-20 worked at Prof D. O. Ott's Midwifery and Gynecological Inst, Petersburg (Petrograd); 1907 defended doctor's thesis on pubic section; from 1915 assoc prof, 1920-59 head, Chair of Obstetrics and Gynecology, Med Fac, Azer State Univ (now Azer Narimov State Med Inst), Baku; delivered papers at obstetrical, gynecological and oncological congresses; chm, Obstetricians and Gynecologists Section, Azer Med Soc; head, Maternity Dept, Inst of Mother and Child Care; wrote over 100 works on various obstetrical and gynecological subjects, inter alia on: aeroembolism; decapsulation of the kidneys in eclampsia; the treatment of malignant neoplasma of the womb with radium and x-rays; amenorrhea in wartime and in malnutrition; osteomalacia; physical therapy methods; napththalene therapy; the treatment of uterine fibroma; trained numerous specialists, including three prof and several cand of med; *Awards*: Order of Lenin; two Orders of the Red Banner of Labor; *Died*: 1959.

IL'IN, Lev Aleksandrovich (1880-1942) Architect; corresp member, USSR Acad of Architecture; *Born*: 1880; *Educ*: 1909 grad Petersburg Inst of Civil Eng; *Career*: 1906-16 designed and constructed in Petersburg the Peter I (now I. I. Mechnikov) Hospital, four bridges and a number of other buildings and apartment houses; most notable for its architecture was the house on Pharmaceutical Island; prior to Oct Revol sided with a group of progressive architects, following the traditions of classical Russian and world art; after 1917 Oct Revol distinguished as city planner; from 1925 for 15 years chief architect of Leningrad; devised and directed new gen city plan of Leningrad; 1930-36 directed compilation of Baku gen plan; designed and constructed Baku Nagornyy Park with monumental buildings and Kirov monument; published a number of works on problems of city planning; *Publ: Moy tvorcheskiy put'* (My Career) (1938); *Died*: 1942.

IL'IN, Lev Fyodorovich (1871-1938) Pharmacologist; Dr of Med; specialist in organic pharmaceutics and forensic chemistry; *Born*: 24 May 1871 in Petersburg; *Educ*: grad Mil Med Acad; *Career*: prof, Mil Med Acad; member, State Acad of the History of Material Culture; head, Leningrad Oblast Forensic Med Laboratory; wrote works on pharmacy, pharmacological botany and forensic chemistry; *Publ*: doctor's thesis *K voprosu ob izuchenii deystvuyushchikh nachal kornevishcha zmeyevika - Polygonum Bistorta L.* (A Study of the Active Components of Polygonum Bistorta L. Root) (1905); *Died*: 1938.

IL'IN M. (real name: MARSHAK, Il'ya Yakovlevich) (1896-1953) Russian writer; *Born:* 10 Jan 1896 in Bakhmut (Artyomovsk), brother of S. Ya. Marshak; *Educ*: 1925 grad Leningrad Technol Inst; *Career*: worked as technol eng at Neva Stearin Works; 1924 began writing for children; contributed to children's journal *Novyy Robinzon*, for which he wrote the chemistry section; most of his books are popular accounts of developments in sci and eng; *Publ:* book *Solntse na stole* (The Sun on the Table) and *Kotoryy chas?* (What's the Time) (1927); short story *Chyornym po belomu* (In Black and White) (1928); book *Sto tyisych pochemu* (A Hundred Thousand Why's) (1929); essays *Kak avtomobil' uchilsya khodit'* (How the Automobile Learned to Drive) (1930); *Rasskaz o velikom plane* (The Story of the Great Plan) (1930); *Gory i lyudi* (Mountains and People) (1935); *Rasskazy o veshchakh* (Stories About Things) (1936); coauthor, *Kak chelovek stal velikanom* (How Man Became a Giant) (2 vol, 1946); *Preobrazovaniye planety* (Reshaping the Planet) (1951), etc; *Died*: 15 Nov 1953 in Moscow.

IL'IN, Nikifor Il'ich (1884-?) Party and govt official; CP member from 1910; *Born*: 1884, son of a peasant; *Career*: worked as a fitter; 1906 joined revol movement in Petersburg; 1908 arrested; from 1912 active in workers' insurance movement; 1913 rearrested; 1914 member, Workers' Insurance Council; 1917-18 member, factory comt, Erikson Plant and member, Petrograd Sov; 1917 member, Petrograd City Duma; 1918-19 Collegium member, Pop Comrt of Labor; 1919-20 worked for Supr Sovnarkhoz; 1920-23 worked for USSR Pop Comrt of Communications; from 1925 RSFSR Pop Comr of Workers and Peasants' Inspection and Collegium member, USSR Pop Comrt of Workers and Peasants' Inspection; Presidium member and member, Budget Commission, All-Russian Centr Exec Comt; member, USSR Centr Exec Comt; elected Presidium member; Central Control Commission at 12th CPSU(B) Congress and rep of this commission in Politburo, CC, CPSU(B); after 17th CPSU(B) Congress member, Sov Control Commission, USSR Council of Pop Comr; arrested by State Security organs; *Died*: date and place of death unknown.

IL'IN , Sergey Ivanovich (1891-1948) Geologist; Dr of Geology and Mineralogy from 1947; prof from 1947; *Born*: 10 Jan 1891; *Educ:* 1925 grad Leningrad Mining Inst; *Career:* worked for geological and geological survey institutions; 1941-44 dir, Geological Inst and dep dir (for sci), Tadzh Branch, USSR Acad of Sci; 1937-43 also head, Chair of Geology, Stalinabad State Teachers' Training Inst; from 1944 at All-Union Petroleum Research Inst, Leningrad; *Awards*: Lenin Prize (1960, posthumously): *Died*: 28 Feb 1948.

IL'IN, Vsevolod Sergeyevich (1888-1930) Hydrogeologist; *Born:* 1888; *Educ*: 1910 grad Moscow Univ; *Career*: helped found first Sov hydrogeological research establishments; devised theory of zonal distribution of ground waters; contributed expertise for first major hydraulic eng projects; *Publ: Karty gruntovykh vod Yevropeyskoy chasti SSSR [masshtab 60 verst v dyuyme] i Tsentral'noy Promyshlennoy Oblasti [masshtab odna milliionnaya]* Charts of Ground Water in the European USSR [Scale: 60 versts to the inch] and in the Central Industrial Region [Scale: one to one million]) (1925); *Gruntovyye vody Tsentral'noy Promyshlennoy Oblasti* (Ground Waters in the Central Industrial Region) (1925); *Gidrogeologiya* (Hydrogeology); *Died*: 1930.

IL'IN, Yakov Naumovich (1905-1932) Russian writer; CP member from 1924; *Born*: 23 Oct 1905 in Kiev; *Career*: 1922 began work at *Krasnaya Presnya* Publ House, Moscow; twice elected member, CC, Komsomol; worked for newspaper *Komsomol'skaya pravda* as dep dir and member of its ed bd; from 1929 worked for newspaper *Pravda*; in response to Gorky's appeal to record the history of Sov factories, directed the compilation of a collective work *Lyudi Stalingradskogo traktornogo* (People of the Stalingrad Tractor Plant) (1933); *Publ*: novels: *Shestoye chuvstvo* (The Sixth Sense) (1933); *Bol'shoy konveyer* (The Big Conveyor) (1934); *Died*: 20 Dec 1932 in Moscow.

IL'IN-ZHENEVSKIY, Aleksandr Fyodorovich (1894-1941) Party and govt official; publicist; CP member from 1912; *Born*: 1894 in Petersburg; *Career*: contributed to illegal publications; 1913-14 lived abroad; 1914 assoc, newspaper *Pravda* and journal *Voprosy strakhovaniya*; 1914-17 ensign in Russian Army; 1917 active Party work among Baltic Fleet seamen; edited Bolshevik newspapers *Volna, Golos Pravdy* and *Soldatskaya pravda*; member, Petrograd Sov of Workers and Soldiers' Dep; during 1917 Oct uprising Petrograd Mil-Revol Comt appointed him comr, Guards Reserve Grenadier Regt; then given seamen's detachment and sent to Moscow to help Bolsheviks; upon return to Petrograd became secr in Pop Comrt of Mil Affairs, then comr, Main Mil Judicial Bd; 1918-20 head, Mil Bd, Petrograd Mil Distr; comr, Main Bd for Gen Mil Training; 1922-23 in Press Dept, CC, RCP(B); from 1923 edited various newspapers and journals and headed Leningrad Oblast Party History Comt; from Aug 1930 counsellor, USSR Embassy in France, then in Czechoslovakia; from 1932 dep dir, Leningrad Inst of Party History; arrested by State Security organs; *Publ: Odin dens Leninym* (A Day with Lenin) (1956); *Bol'sheviki u vlasti. Vospominaniya o 1918 g.* (The Bolsheviks in Power. Recollections of 1918) (1929); *Oktyabr'skaya revolyutsiya* (The October Revolution) (1957); *Died*: 1941 in imprisonment; posthumously rehabilitated.

IL'INA, Yelena (real name: PREYS, Liya Yakovlevna) (1901-1964) Russian writer; S. Ya. Marhak's sister; *Born*: 29 June 1901 in Ostrogozhsk, Voronezh Province; *Educ*: 1926 grad Leningrad Inst of Art History; *Career*: 1925 first work printed; wrote novelettes, stories, poems and verse tales for children; *Publ*: collections: *Dva detdoma* (Two Children's Homes) (1928); "Tip-top" (1954), etc; novelettes: *Chetvyortaya vysota* (The Fourth Height) (1945); *Eto moya shkola* (This Is My School) (1955); *Neutomimyy putnik* (The Indefatigable Traveller) dealing with Marx's childhood and youth (1964), etc; *Died*: 2 Nov 1964 in Moscow.

IL'INSKIY, Aleksandr Konstantinovich (1903-1966) Actor, Vitebsk Kolas Drama Theater from 1945; Pop Artiste of USSR from 1953; CP member from 1945; *Born*: 1903; *Educ*: 1926 grad Moscow Bel Theater Studio; *Career*: 1920 began stage work; played mainly comedy roles; 1926-40 actor, 1940-45 artistic manager, Vitebsk Kolas Theater; dep, Bel Supr Sov of 1955 and 1959 convocations; *Roles*: Khlestakov in Gogol's *Revizor* (The Government Inspector); Schastlivtsev in Ostrovskiy's *Les* (Forest); Rasplyuyev in Sukhovo-Kobylin's *Svad'ba Krechinskogo* (Krechinskiy's Wedding); Shvandya in Trenyov's *Lyubov' Yarovaya;* Talash in Kolas' *V pushchakh Poles'ya* (In the Volga Thickets); Nesterka in Vol'skiy's *Nesterka*; Sganarelle in Moliere's "Le Médecin Malgré Lui"; Korzh in Polesskiy's *Pesnya nashikh serdets* (Song of Our Hearts); Pytlyovannyy in Krapiva's *Poyut zhavoronki* (The Larks Are Singing); Mochek-Mochul'skiy in Danilov's *Lyavonikha*; etc; *Awards*: Order of Lenin; two Orders of the Red Banner of Labor; Badge of Hon; Stalin Prize (1946); *Died*: Mar 1966.

IL'INSKIY, Aleksandr Vasil' yevich (1896-1956) Russian operetta dir and singer; Pop Artiste of RSFSR from 1955; *Born*: 1896; *Career*: 1918 began stage work in Rostov-on-Don; until 1922 with Rostov Miniature Theater; 1922-27 with mobile musical comedy theaters; 1927-35 with Khar'kov, Rostov-on-Don, Minsk and Vitebsk theaters; from 1935 with Volgograd Musical Comedy Theater; *Roles*: Count Kutaisov in Strel'nikov's *Kholopka* (The Bondwoman); Suvorov in Fel'tsman's *Doch' fel'dmarshala* (The Field-Marshal's Daughter); Plyushchikhin in Shcherbachyov's *Tabachnyy kapitan* (Tobacco Captain); Master-Sgt Mal'tsev in Blanter's *Na beregu Amura* (On the Banks of the Amur); Popandopulo in Aleksandrov's *Svad'ba v Malinovke* (Wedding in Malinovka); Chashkin in Bogoslovskiy's *Odinnadtsat' neizvestnykh* (Eleven Unknowns); Louis Philippe in Calman's "Bayadère"; Frosch in Strauss' "Fledermaus," etc; staged Enke's opera *Lyubov' Yarovaya*, Zaslavskiy's operetta *Solov'inyy sad* (Garden of Nightingales), etc; *Died*: 21 Aug 1956.

IL'INSKIY, Mikhail Aleksandrovich (1856-1941) Organic chemist and chemical eng; specialist in synthetic dyes; Dr of Chemistry from 1934; hon member, USSR Acad of Sci from 1935; Hon Sci and Tech Worker of RSFSR from 1934; *Born*: 13 Nov 1856 in Petersburg; *Educ*: 1875 entered Petersburg Technol Inst but was soon expelled for involvement in student riots; 1882 grad Berlin Higher Tech School; *Career*: after grad asst to K. Liebermann, Berlin Higher Tech School; 1885, together with G. Knorre, pioneered the use of organic reagents in analytical chemistry by suggesting 1-nitroso-2-naphthol as a reagent for cobalt and trivalent iron; also hypothesized that nitrosonaphthols have a hydrogen bond; 1887 and 1888 read papers to the German Chemistry Soc and the Russian Physics and Chemistry Soc on his theory of "atomicity" (Valence), proposing a number of now-accepted hypotheses, including the divisibility of valences, the existence of free radicals, hydrogen bonds and ion solvation; from 1889 dep production mang, then production mang, Rabeneck Alizarin Works at Shchelkovo, near Moscow; 1891 established that, in the presence of mercury, the sulfonation of anthraquinone is accompanied by the formation of alpha-sulfoacids and disulfoacids instead of the normal beta-sulfoacids; added sodium chloride to eliminate the harmful catalytic reaction of mercury in the sulfonation process; proposed the use of lime for the conversion of anthraquinone sulfoacids into oxy compounds; 1891 also devised method of obtaining primary blue from alizarin-sapphirol-type acidic anthraquinone dyes; from 1899 worked for R. Wedekind and Company, Uerdingen, Germany; 1911 developed new absorption dying method; 1914, at outbreak of WW 1, refused to adopt German citizenship and was sent to Muenster, Westphalia, under police escort; late 1916 escaped to Russia via Holland; 1916-20 member, Tech Council, Russian Dye and Paint Bd (later Main Bd of the Aniline Ind); 1918-24 assoc prof, Moscow Univ; from 1925 in charge of the development of alizarin dye technol for the Aniline Trust and Inst of Organic Semi-Products and Dyes; 1928-32 did research on the oxidation conversion of anthracene into anthraquinone; 1936, together with A. N. Nikolayeva and A. I. Perel'man, obtained alizarin directly from anthraquinone by oxidation synthesis, bypassing the sulfonation and alkalization stages; *Publ: Nekotoryye obobshcheniya teorii atomnosti* (Some Generalizations on the Theory of Atomicity) (1897); *Died*: 18 Nov 1941.

ILLARIONOV, Ivan Ivanovich (pseudonym: Ivan MUCHI) (1895-1946) Chuvash writer; *Born*: 29 Nov 1895 in vil Chural'kasy, Kosmodem'yansk, Uyezd, Kazan' Province; son of a peasant; *Career*: took part in Civil War; from 1922 contributed stories and topical satirical articles to oblast newspapers *Chuvashskiy kray* and *Kanash*; translated Russian classics into Chuvash; helped initiate first Chuvash satirical journal *Kapkan; Publ*: collected stories and novelettes: "Red Laughter" (1931); "En Route to Collectivization" (1931); "Tales for Laughter, not for Pleasure" (1936); "Humorous Stories" (1940); stories: "Taneta," "The Seeker Did Not Find"; "Blessed Ubanka"; "On the Threshing Floor," etc; *Died:* 28 Apr 1946 in Cheboksaey.

IL'MER, Karl Petrovich (1891-1919) Revolutionary; CP member from 1908; *Born*: 1891; *Career*: worker; 1905 member, workers militant squad; conducted Party work in Riga and Baku; 1914 exiled to Narym Kray; 1916 fled from exile to Petrograd and worked for local Bolshevik mil org; after 1917 Feb Revol assoc, Lat workers' newspaper *Bor'ba*; after 1917 Oct Revol Comr for Food, Aleksandr Nevsky Rayon, Petrograd; 1918 sent to Siberia to procure food supplies for Petrograd; Comr for Food in Akmolinsk Oblast; June 1918, after collapse of Sov regime in Omsk, sent to do underground work in Tomsk; headed the underground Tomsk RSDRP Comt, helped to organize underground RCP(B) Center in Siberia and prepared overthrow of Siberian govt under Admiral Kolchak; together with other members of underground Tomsk RCP(B) Comt arrested by Kolchak mil authorities; *Died*: 1919 executed by firing squad.

ILOVAYSKIY, Aleksandr Semyonovich (1873-1954) Eng; specialist in building mech and hydrotech; prof from 1920; Hon Sci and Tech Worker of Ukr SSR from 1949; CP member from 1938; *Born*: 12 Mar 1873 in vil Serskoye, Tambov Province, son of a priest; *Educ*: grad Petersburg Inst of Communications Eng; *Career*: while still a student joined revol movement; 1899-1920 worked for water transport system, Kiev Road Distr; from 1907 lecturer, higher tech educ establishments in Yekaterinoslav (now Dnepropetrovsk), Khar'kov, etc; wrote works on construction mech and hydrotech; *Died*: 22 Sept 1954.

ILOVAYSKIY, Davyd Ivanovich (1878-1935) Paleontologist; prof; *Born*: 1878; *Educ*: 1900 grad Moscow Univ; *Career*: from 1919 prof, Moscow Mining Acad (later Moscow Oil Inst); studied ammonites and stratigraphy of Jurassic and Lower Cretaceous deposits of Moscow area, Arctic Ural region and Gen Syrt; studied features of boreal fauna in Jurassic deposits and outlined methods of studying ammonites; *Publ: Verkhneyurskiye ammonity Lyapinskogo kraya* (The Upper Jurassic Ammonites of Lyapin Kray) (2 vol, 1917); *Rukovodstvo po paleozoologii bespozvonochnykh* (A Guide to the Paleozoology of Invertebrates) (2 vol, 1934); coauthor, *Verkhneyurskiye ammonity basseynov rek Urala i Ileka* (Upper Jurassic Ammonites of the Ural and Ilek River Basins) (1941); *Died*: 1925.

ILOVAYSKIY, Serafim Dmitriyevich (1904-1944) Russian actor; Hon Artiste of RSFSR from 1942; CP member from 1939; *Born*: 12 Aug 1904; *Career*: 1925 began stage work; from 1929 played in Omsk and Irkutsk theaters; from 1932 actor, Novosibirsk *Krasnyy fakel* (Red Torch) Theater; from 1939 artistic manager and stage dir, same theater; *Roles*: Ivan the Terrible in A. K. Tolstoy's *Smert' Ioanna Groznogo* (Death of Ivan the Terrible); Karenin in *Anna Karenina*; Firs in *Vishnyovyy sad* (The Cherry Orchard); Zhuv in Slavin's *Interventsiya* (Intervention); Vlas in Afinogenov's *Dalyokoye* (Things Far Away); title-role in Leonov's *Skutarevskiy*; Zabelin in *Kremlyovskiye kuranty* (Kremlin Chimes); Hamlet, etc; *Died*: 8 Feb 1944.

ILOVAYSKIY, Sergey Aleksandrovich (1891-1924) Protozoologist and parasitologist; *Born*: 1891; *Educ*: 1915 grad Natural Sci Dept, Moscow Univ; *Career*: 1915-18 asst prof, Moscow Univ; 1918-21 asst prof, Chair of Invertebrate Zoology, Saratov Univ; 1921-24 assoc, Parasitological Dept, Saratov *Microbe* Inst; did research on parasitic amoebozoa, infusoria, trypanosomes and plague-transmitting ectoparasites; collected and published material on amoebozoic liver abscesses in man; did research on amoebozoic hepatitis in amphibians which proved valuable for the comparative pathology of amoebiasis; 1921-24 made valuable studies of trypanosomosis in camels and horses in southeastern RSFSR; also studied infusorial cysts; initiated research on rodent ectoparasites as transmitters of plague to humans and animals; wrote several works; *Died*: 1924.

IL'YENKOV, Vasiliy Pavlovich (1897-1967) Russian writer; CP member from 1918; *Born*: 24 Mar 1897; *Educ*: studied at Yur'yev Univ; *Career*: from 1918 Party work; 1927 first stories published; *Publ*: novels: *Vedushchaya os'* (Driving Axle) (1931); *Solnechnyy gorod* (A Sunny Town) (1935); *Bol'shaya doroga* (The Great Road) (1949); collected stories *Lichnost'* (Personality) (1938); *Rodnoy dom* (My Native Home) (1942); *Na tot bereg* (To the Far Shore) (1945); *Bogatstvo* (Wealth) (1947); *Morskoye serdtse* (The Heart of the Sea) (1964); play *Ploshchad' tsvetov* (An Area of Flowers) (1944), etc; *Awards*: Stalin Prize (1950); *Died*: 15 Jan 1967.

IMAMALIYEV, Salar Agrafiyevich (1898-1959) Epidemiologist, microbiologist and health service official; Dr of Med from 1957; CP member; *Born*: 1898 in Petrovsk, (now Makhachkala); *Educ*: 1924 grad Med Fac, 1st Moscow Univ; *Career*: after grad distr physician and Party worker in vil Akhty, Dag SSR, then Dag Pop Comr of Health; 1931-34 dir, Baku Centr Municipal Polyclinic; from 1934 dir, Azer Research Inst of Microbiology and Epidemiology, which became a center for the production of bacterial preparations; founder-dir, Dag Anti-Plague Station, Baku; 1941 obtained culture of tularemia bacteria from rodents; during WW 2 head, Epidemiology Service, 46th Army, which he accompanied through Rumania, Hungary, Yugoslavia, Austria and Czechoslovakia; 1942 defended cand thesis on fungus diseases; after war worked at Chair of Epidemiology, Azer State Med Inst and Inst of Postgrad Med Training; founded special section at Med Inst for the publ of med lit in Azerbaydzhani; toward end of life head, Dept of Dangerous Infectious Diseases, Azer Republ Sanitary-Epidemiological Station; 1957 defended doctor's thesis on endemic typhus in Baku; wrote over 60 works; *Publ: Opyt sanitarnogo i protivoepidemicheskogo obespecheniya chastey deystvuyushchey Armii v Velikoy Otechestvennoy voyne* (Experience in Providing Units of the Active Army with Sanitary and Anti-Epidemic Protection During the Great Fatherland War) (1948); *Epidemicheskiy (krysinyy) sypnoyy tif v gorode Baku* (Epidemic [Rat-Borne] Typhus in Baku) (1957), etc; *Awards*: Order of the Red Star; Order of the Fatherland War, 2nd class; medals "For the Capture of Berlin," "For the Capture of Vienna", "For the Capture of Belgrade," "For the Capture of Budapest" and "For Victory Over Germany"; med lit prize (1948); *Died*: 7 Jan 1959 in Baku.

IMANZHANOV, Mukan (1916-1958) Kaz writer; CP member from 1945; *Born*: Dec 1916 in Atbasarskiy Uyezd, Akmolinsk Province (now Ulutau Rayon, Karaganda Oblast); *Career*: late 1930's first work published; wrote plays which were staged at Kaz theaters; *Publ*: collected stories "Youth" (1948); "A Girl I Knew" (1952); novelette "The First Months" (1950); novel "The Green Horizon" (Part 1, 1958); plays "Youth" (1948); "My Love" (1952); "Smoldering Brands" (1958); *Died*: 18 Mar 1958 in Alma Ata.

IMASHEV, Temir-Bulat Gubaydulovich (1908-1946) Bash actor and stage dir; Hon Art Worker of Bash ASSR from 1942; Hon Artiste of RSFSR from 1944; CP member from 1940; *Born*: 1908; *Educ*: 1930 grad Theater Dept, Ufa Technicum of Arts; *Career*: from 1929 actor, later stage dir, Bash Drama Theater in Ufa; 1937-40 artistic manager of this theater, 1940-43 chief dir, Bash Opera and Ballet Theater, which he helped found; 1944 founded Kolkhoz and Sovkhoz Theater in Ugiliy Rayon; taught at Bash Theater Technicum; *Roles*: Salavat Yulayev in Bikbay's *Salavat*; Yula in Miftakhov's *Sakmar*; Karl Moor; Yarovoy; Zhadov; Neznamov; Platon Krechet; *Works*: staged plays: *Bez viny vinovatyye* (Guilty Without Guilt) (1933); *Lyubov' Yarovaya* (1937); Miftakhov's *Druzhba i lyubov'* (Friendship and Love) (1939); operas: Chemberdzhi's "Swallow" (1941); Spadavekia and Zaimov's *Akbuzat* (1942); *Died*: 7 Apr 1946.

IMEDASHVILI, Aleksandr Solomonovich (1882-1942) Geo actor; Pop Artiste of Geo SSR from 1932; *Born*: 2 Mar 1882; *Career*: from 1900 with Tiflis Geo Theater; 1902-03 with Kutaisi Theater; 1903-09 with Tiflis Theater; 1917-20 manager, Kutaisi Theater; 1921-24, after establishment of Sov regime in Geo, with Rustaveli Theater; 1928-31 with Kutaisi Theater under K. Mardzhanishvili; 1939-42 with Mardzhanishvili Theater; toured all major Geo towns; from 1925 also film actor; *Roles*: Otiya in Guniy's "Brother and Sister"; Shadiman in Shanshiashvili's "Kings Without Crowns"; Gigua in Gedevanishvili's "Victim"; Leonidze in Eristavi's "Fatherland"; Vanyushin in Naydyonov's *Deti Vanyushina* (Vanyushin's Children); Protosov in Lev Tolstoy's *Zhivoy trup* (The Living Corpse); Bersenev in *Razlom* (Break-Up); Karl Moor; title roles in Shakespeare's Othello, Macbeth, King Lear; Oedipus in Sophocles' "Oedipus Rex," etc; *Died:* 26 Sept 1942.

IMEDASHVILI, Iosif Zakhar'yevich (1876-1952) Geo journalist and theater man; *Born*: 4 Apr 1876; *Career*: 1893 helped found Tiflis Pop Theater and was first stage dir of this theater; 1910 founder and ed, journal *Teatri da tskhovreba*; in his articles supported the development of Geo nat theater; translated plays; *Died*: 5 May 1952.

IMINAGAYEV, Aziz (1885-1944) Darginian (Dag) poet; *Born:* 1885 in vil Aymau-makhi, now Dag ASSR, son of a peasant; *Career*: 1910 began writing verse; pioneered satirical genre in Darginian lit; many of his poems are propagandistic in nature and directed against old customs; fought in WW 2; *Publ*: verse "The Worker's Life" (1911); "The Mullah's Labor" (1935); "October" (1938); "What the Mullah Did to Musa"; "Down with the Dagger"; "My Difficulties"; "Down with the Swine," etc; *Died*: 1944.

INAR, Gyustav (INARD, Gustave) (1847-1932) French revolutionary; member, 1871 Paris Commune; capt, Nat Guard, 17th Arondissement; *Born*: 1847; *Career*: after suppression of the Commune lived in emigration; subsequently returned to France; engaged in lit work; from 1925 in USSR; in spite of his advanced age active in Sov soc and polit affairs; *Died*: 1932.

INGAL, Vladimir Iosifovich (1901-1966) Sculptor; Hon Art Worker from 1957; corresp member, USSR Acad of Arts from 1958; CP member from 1945; *Born*: 29 Mar 1901; *Educ*: 1930 grad Leningrad Acad of Arts; *Career*: from 1929 worked in partnership with sculptor V. Ya. Bogolyubov; together they produced: statue of G. K. Ordzhonikidze (1937); monuments of Lenin in Riga (1947-50), Rimsky-Korsakov in Leningrad (unveiled 1952), etc; designed Lenin monument in Sverdlovsk (1957), a number of busts, etc; prof, Leningrad Mukhina Higher Art and Ind College; *Awards*: Stalin Prize (1941); *Died*: 29 Mar 1966.

INGULOV, Sergey Borisovich (1893-?) Journalist; Party official; CP member from 1918; *Born*: 1893; *Career*: worked as typesetter; 1919 directed underground Bolshevik org in Nikolayev; then member, underground Odessa Oblast Party Comt; 1920 secr, Odessa Province Party Comt; 1921 head, Agitation and Propaganda Dept, CC, CP(B) Ukr in Khar'kov; 1923-30 worked for CC, CPSU(B) as head, Press Bureau, Agitation and Propaganda Dept and then dep head, Agitation and Propaganda Dept; from 1935 head, Main Lit and Publ Bd; co-ed, *Malaya sovetskaya entsiklopediya* (Small Soviet Encyclopedia); wrote several books on press work, also polit pamphlets and pop textbooks on Leninism; *Died*: date and place of death unknown.

INNOKENTIY (secular name: SOKAL', Ivan Ivanovich) (1883-1965) Bishop of Smolensk and Dorogobug from 1959; *Born*: 1883; *Educ*: Warsaw Theological College; Kholmy Theological Seminary; 1910 grad Kiev Theological Acad; *Career*: 1910-12 asst inspector, Kursk Theological Seminary; subsequently inspector, parallel classes at Kursk Theological Seminary in Ryl'sk; ordained priest; 1919 with Russian Ecclesiastical Mission in Palestine; 1921-31 inspector, Yugoslav theological seminaries; 1931-50 vicar, Belgrade Trinity Church; 1945-50 in charge of Moscow Patriarchate parishes in Yugoslavia; 1950 deported to USSR by order of Yugoslav Govt; 1950-53 rector, Saratov, 1953-56 Minsk, 1956-57 Odessa Theological Seminaries; 1957 appointed vicar, Smolensk Cathedral and secr to the incumbent bishop; 1959 took monastic vows; consecrated archimandrite and bishop; 1948 attended Moscow Conference of leaders and rep of autocephalous orthodox churches; *Awards*: Moscow Patriarchate Order of St Vladimir, 2nd Class (1963); *Died*: 14 May 1965.

IOANN (real name: IVANOV, Ivan Spiridonovich) (1912-1966) Bishop of Kirov and Sloboda from 1962; Cand of Theology from 1954; *Born:* 1912 in Pskov; *Educ:* 1954 grad Leningrad Theological Acad; *Career:* 1925-35 psalm-reader in various Pskov churches and sub-deacon to Pskov bishops; 1938-41 secular work; 1941 ordained deacon, then priest, Pskov Cathedral; 1943 vicar in Pskov; 1944 vicar, Kretingen (Lit SSR) orthodox church; 1945-48 dean, Pskov Cathedral; 1948 vicar, various Leningrad churches; 1958 took monastic vows; until 1962 rural dean of an okrug, Leningrad Eparchy; during WW 2 in partisan movement against German forces; *Died*: 1966.

IOANN-BAPTIST (real name: TSEPLYAK) (1857-1926) Administrator and vicar-gen, Mogilyov Archbishopric and titular Archbishop of Archis, Roman Catholic Church; *Born*: 1857 in vil Dubrowno, Poland; *Educ:* 1873 entered Kielce Roman Catholic Theological Seminary; grad Petersburg Roman Catholic Theological Acad; *Career:* ordained priest while still a student; after grad remained at Petersburg Roman Catholic Theological Acad as an instructor for 26 years; simultaneously catechist at various teaching establishments; from 1908 suffragan Bishop of Mogilyov; administered Lat Parishes of Mogilyov Archbishopric; commissioned by Metropolitan of Mogilyov to tour Catholic settlements in Siberia; 1919 appointed administrator and vicar-gen of Mogilyov Archbishopric; made titular Archbishop of Archis by Pope Benedict XV for services to Church; 1920 arrested and jailed in Petrograd Prison; 1922 arrested again for refusing to hand over Church treasures; 1923 summoned to Moscow and arrested again; 21-25 Mar 1923 faced show trial with other priests, in the course of which he and the prelate Budkevich were sentenced to death by firing squad; the death sentence was commuted to 10 years imprisonment, and in 1924 he was expelled from the USSR over the Lat border; *Died*: 13 Feb 1926 of pneumonia; buried in Vilnius Roman Catholic Cathedral.

IOANNISYAN, Ioannes Mkrtichevich (1864-1929) Arm poet; *Born*: 26 Apr 1864 in vil Vagarshapat, son of a peasant; *Educ*: from 1877 studied at Lazarev Inst of Oriental Languages, Moscow; 1888 grad History and Philology Fac, Moscow Univ; *Career*: 1888 returned to Arm; 1888-1912 taught Russian language and general lit at Echmiadzin Theological Acad; 1912 moved to Baku; 1918 during the Baku Commune, directed Baku City Educ Dept; from 1922 worked for Legislative Commission, Arm Council of Pop Comr, and for inst compiling dictionaries and developing terminology; helped establish Sov regime in Arm; translated: Homer, Pushkin, Nekrasov, Yakubovich, Mickiewicz, Goethe, Schiller, Heine and other poets; *Publ*: collections "Verse" (1887, 1908 and 1912); verse: "Village Shrine"; "Grain," "Farewell, Sun and Spring"; *Ashug; Araz;* "Alagyaz Paled, Fell Silent"; "A New Spring"; "All Ahead, All Above!"; "The Mother"; "There Are Moments"; "I Believe I Am Immortal," etc; Ballads and legends: *Tsar Artavazd* and "The Birth of Vaagno," etc; *Died*: 29 Sept 1929 in Yerevan.

IOASAF (real name: ZHURMANOV, Aleksandr Yefremovich) (1877-1962) Archbishop of Tambov and Michurinsk from 1946; *Born*: 1877; *Educ*: 1915 grad Petrograd Business Inst; *Career*: 1915 entered monkhood and adopted name of Ioasaf; ordained priest-monk; 1922 appointed archimandrite, Aleksandr Nevskiy Monastery, Petrograd; 1944-46 Bishop of Simferopol' and Tavricheskoye; *Awards*: right to wear cross on cowl (1960); *Died*: 18 Mar 1962.

IOFF, Il'a Grigor'yevich (1897-1953) Parasitologist; *Born:* 1897; *Educ:* 1922 grad Med Fac, Saratov Univ; *Career:* 1928-34 founder-head, Parasitological Dept, Rostov Mcrobiological Inst; from 1934 founder-head, Parasitoligical Dept, Stavropol' Anti-Plague Station (1952 reorganized into Caucasian and Transcaucasian Anti-Plague Research Inst); first to establish role of non-synanthropic rodent fleas in the epizootology and epidemiology of plague; founded study of flea ecology and used this data in the epizootology and prophylaxis of plague; 1949 proposed a system for typing foci of plague enzooty throughout the world; together with V. Ye. Tiflov, O. I. Skalon and M. A. Mikulin, established fundamental classification keys to fleas in the various parts of the USSR; made a unique collection of fleas inhabiting the USSR; helped organize campaign to eliminate plague foci in the north-western Caspian area; 1928-44 devised new methods of surveying areas in relations to plague by collecting and studying rodent corpses and by the mass analysis of fleas; 1928-34 directed a laboratory for the study and prevention of malaria in the Northern Caucasus; 1922 perfected malarial blood analysis methods; wrote over 140 works on plague, malaria, tularemia and pathogenic protozoa; *Publ: O geograficheskom rasprostranenii suslikovykh blokh v svyazi s istoriyey rasseleniya suslikov* (The Geographic Distribution of Gopher Fleas in Connection with the Historical Distribution of Gophers) (1936); *Posobiye dlya opredeleniya blokh (Aphaniptera) Yugo-Vostoka yevropeyskoy chasti SSSR* (An Aid to the Classification of Fleas [Aphaniptera] in the Southeastern European USSR) (1938); *Voprosy ekologii blokh v svyazi s ikh epidemiologicheskim znacheniyem* (The Ecology of Fleas in Connection with Their Epidemiological Significance) (1941); *Opredelitel' blokh v svyazi s ikh epidemiologicheskim znacheniyem* (A Classification key to Fleas in Connection with Their Epidemiological Significance) (1941); *Opredelitel' blokh Vostochnoy Sibiri, Dal'nego Vostoka i prilezhashchikh rayonov* (A Classification Key to the Fleas of Eastern Siberia, the Far East and Neighboring Areas) (1954); *Blokhi Turkmenii* (The Fleas of Turkmenia) (1956), etc; *Awards*: Stalin Prize; *Died*: 1953.

IOFFE, Abram Fyodorovich (1880-1960) Physicist; member, USSR Acad of Sci from 1920; CP member from 1942; *Born*: 29 Oct 1880; *Educ*: 1902 grad Petersburg Technol Inst; 1905 grad Munich Univ, where he worked under Roentgen; *Career*: 1906-13 assoc, from 1913 prof, Petersburg Polytech Inst; 1913 entitled Master of Physics; 1915 entitled Dr of Physics for his research on the elastic and electric properties of quartz; 1918-20 corresp member, USSR Acad of Sci; from 1918 founder-head, Physical Eng Dept, State Roentgenological and Radiological Inst, Petrograd; then until 1951 dir, Physical Eng Inst, USSR Acad of Sci, founded from this dept; from 1932 dir, Physico-Agronomical Inst; from 1951 head, Laboratory of Semiconductors, USSR Acad of Sci (elevated to Inst of Semiconductors in 1954); 1909-13 did research on quantum theory; 1910 experimentally proved that cathode rays exert a magnetic field; specialized in mech properties of semiconductors; studied mechanism of solid-state rectifiers and developed theory of plasticity and brittleness; devised methods for calibrating semiconductors, which led him to divide them into electronic and hole-type semiconductors; 1937 postulated new theory rectification; established major school of Sov physicists; hon member, American Acad of Sciences and Arts from 1928; corresp member, Goettingen Acad of Sci from 1924; corresp member, Berlin Acad of Sci from 1928; Hon Dr of California (1928), Paris (1944) and Bucharest (1945) Univ, etc; wrote several textbooks; *Publ: Elementarnyy fotoelektricheskiy effekt. Magnitnoye pole katodnykh luchey* (An Elementary Photoelectric Effect. The Magnetic Field of Cathode Rays) (1913); *Lektsii po molekulyarnoy fizike* (Lectures on Molecular Physics) (2nd ed, 1923); *Fizika kristallov* (The Physics of Crystals) (1929); *Poluprovodniki v fizike i tekhnike* (Semiconductors in Physics and Technology) (1940); *Moya zhizn' i rabota. Avtobiograficheskiy ocherk* (My Life and Work. An Autobiographical Sketch) (1933); *Osnovnyye predstavleniya o sovremennoy fizike* (The Basic Concepts of Modern Physics) (1949); *Poluprovodniki v sovremennoy fizike* (Semiconductors in Modern Physics) (1954); *Poluprovodniki i ikh primeneniye* (Semiconductors and Their Applications) (1956); *Poluprovodnikovyye termoelementy* (Semiconductor Thermocouples) (1956), etc; *Awards:* two Orders of Lenin; Hero of Socialist Labor (1955); Stalin Prize (1942); Lenin Prize (1961, posthumously); *Died*: 14 Oct 1960.

IOFFE, Adol'f Abramovich (pseudonym: Victor KRYMSKIY) (1883-1927) Govt official; CP member from 1903; *Born:* 1883 in Simferopol'; *Educ*: 1903 completed high-school; studied at Med Fac, Berlin Univ and Law Fac, Zurich Univ; *Career*: 1899 connected with and did commissions for Soc-Democrat org; 1902 joined RSDRP and worked for Propagandists and Agitators Bd, Simferopol' RSDRP Org; 1903 went to Berlin and enrolled at Med Fac; 1904 Party CC sent him to Baku to smuggle illegal propaganda lit; failed in this Baku commission and in subsequent work in Moscow; left for Berlin, but soon returned to Russia; Party work in Crimea: Simferopol', Sebastopol, Yalta and Yevpatoriya; reprisals by Tsarist authorities impelled him to return to Berlin; 1906, after Stockholm RSDRP Congress, joined For Bureau, CC, RSDRP; spring 1907 deported from Germany as an "undesirable alien"; returned to Crimea and co-opted to Crimean Oblast RSDRP Comt; after this org was crushed, moved to Moscow and to Baltic; again emigrated to Zurich, where he worked for Swiss Socialist Party and for local groups supporting RSDRP; 1908 joined Trotsky's "Vienna Club" group and helped edit Viennese *Pravda*; 1910 toured Russian orgs on behalf of *Pravda*; helped found anti-Bolshevik "Aug Bloc"; 1910 signed appeal for a conference of all anti-Bolshevik orgs and was a member of the org commission to convene such a conference; 1912 Party work for *Pravda* in Russia; 1912 arrested by Tsarist authorities and exiled for 4 years to Tobol'sk Province, followed by settlement for life in Siberia; after 1917 Feb Revol went to Petrograd and became a member, Petrograd Sov of Workers and Soldiers' Dep; then returned to Crimea; deleg, Congress of United Soc–Democrats (Mensheviks), but walked out of the congress and wrote pamphlet "The Collapse of Menshevism"; 1917 at 6th RSDRP Congress admitted to RSDRP(B) along with the *mezhrayontsy* (org of revol internationalists) and elected member, CC, RSDRP(B); member, Petrograd City Duma and member, first All-Russian Centr Exec Comt; Bolshevik deleg for Pskov in Constituent Assembly; Bolshevik Presidium member, Petrograd Sov of Workers and Peasants' Dep; active in 1917 Oct Revol as member, Petrograd Mil Revol Comt; after Oct Revol went to Dvinsk Front; 1918 chm, Sov deleg at armistice and peace talks with Germany, Austro-Hungary, Bulgaria and Turkey; 1918 "Leftist Communist"; opposed signing of Brest-Litovsk Peace Treaty; Presidium member, Petrograd Sov; member, Council of Northern Commune; member, CC, RSDRP(B); Pop Comr of For Affairs, then Pop Comr of Soc Security; 1918 at 7th RCP(B) Congress elected cand member, CC, RCP(B); Apr-Nov 1918 RSFSR plen in Germany; then Party work in Ukr; after Petlyura captured Kiev, he retreated with the army to Chernigov as a member, Ukr Defense Council; member, Petrograd Civil Defense Council during Yudenich's march on Petrograd; 1919-21 headed Workers and Peasants' Inspection in Petrograd; member, Sov deleg at peace talks with Est, Lith, Lat and Poland; signed peace treaty with Est; 1922 member, Sov deleg at Genua Conference; 1922 appointed Sov plen in China; simultaneously conducted negotiations with Japan; sustained nervous breakdown and sent to Vienna for cure; 1924 member, Sov deleg to UK and remained in London as Sov dep plen in UK; then Sov plen in Austria; from March 1925 Presidium member, RSFSR Gosplan and dep chm, Main Concessions Comt; from 1925 sided with Trotskyists; *Died*: 17 Nov 1927 committed suicide.

IOGANSON (JOHANSSON), Oskar Erlandovich (1892-1939) Finno-Karelian writer; CP member from 1920; *Born*: 11 June 1892 in Helsinki, son of a worker; *Educ*: grad Finnish public school; *Career*: 1918 fought in Red Guard during Finnish workers' revol; arrested after revol was put down and fled two years later to USSR; worked as a teacher in Murmansk Oblast, then as ed, Karelian newspaper *Kollektivisti*; arrested by State Security organs; *Publ*: novels "Red Partisans" (1931) and "Iron Vortex" (1935); collected stories "In the Forests and Mountains" (1935); *Died*: 1939 in imprisonment; posthumously rehabilitated.

IONOV (KOYGEN), F. M. (1870-1923) Soc-Democratic politician; Bund leader; CP member from 1917; *Born*: 1870; *Career*: from 1893 in Soc-Democratic movement; member, CC, Bund; deleg, 4th (Amalgamative) RSDRP Congress; deleg from Polish Rayon, Bund at 5th RSDRP Congress; 1908 sided with Mensheviks; later favored conciliatory attitude toward the liquidationists; during WW 1 belonged to Bund's Internationalist Wing which held a near-Center position; after 1917 Oct Revol joined RCP(B); worked for Sov Mission in Berlin and in Votyak Oblast Party Comt; *Died*: 1923.

IONOV, Nikolay Ivanovich (1894-1965) Party official; CP member from 1913; *Born*: 19 Dec 1894; *Career*: frequently arrested for revol activities; member, Petersburg 1st City Rayon RSDRP Comt; member, Petersburg City RSDRP Comt and member of its Exec Commission; member, steering group of Bolshevik faction in 4th State Duma; contributed to newspaper *Pravda*; 1917 chm, Novgorod City RSDRP Comt; deleg at 7th (Apr) All-Russian RSDRP(B) Conference; after 1917 Oct Revol held exec trade-union posts and worked for USSR Pop Comrt of Means of Communication; during WW 2 Party work; until 1951 assoc, Centr Lenin Museum; then pensioner; *Died*: 9 June 1965.

IONOV, Vsevolod Mikhaylovich (1851-1922) Ethnographer, folklorist and linguist; specialist on Yakutia; journalist and teacher; *Born*: 1851; *Educ*: 1873-74 studied at Petersburg Technol Inst; *Career*: 1876 arrested for involvement in Populist movement and sentenced to five years at hard labor, after which he was exiled to Yakutsk Oblast; during exile collected valuable material on the life, folklore, language and pre-Christian religions of the Yakuts; member, Sibiryakov and Nel'kan-Ayanka expeditions to Yakutia; devised Yakut alphabet; engaged in teaching and journalism; helped to compile E.K. Pakarskiy's *Slovar' yakutskogo yazyka* (Yakutian Dictionary); 1910 returned to Petersburg, where he continued evaluation of his ethnographic material, which is now kept at the Leningrad Inst of Oriental Studies, USSR Acad of Sci; *Publ: K voprosu o skotovodstve u yakutov Yakutskogo okruga* (Cattle-Farming Among the Yakuts of Yakutsk Okrug) (1896); *Poyezdka k mayskim tungusam* (A Trip to the Mayskiy Tungus) (1904); *Oryol v vozzreniyakh yakutov* (The Eagle in the View of the Yakuts) (1913); *Obzor literatury po verovaniyam yakutov* (A Survey of Literature on Yakut Religious Beliefs) (1914); *Dukh - khozyain lesa u yakutov* (The Yakuts' Spirit-Lord of the Forest) (1916); *K voprosu ob izuchenii dokhristianskikh verovaniy u yakutov* (The Study of Pre-Christian Yakut Religious Beliefs) (1918); *Died*: 1922.

IORDAN, Artur Pavlovich (1886-1945) Dermatologist; *Born*: 1886; *Educ*: grad Med Fac, Yur'yev Univ; *Career*: 1892 defended doctor's thesis on effects of derivatives of guanidine; specialist training in Berlin and Viennese clinics and at Moscow's Myasnitskaya Hospital; until 1910 worked at 1st and 2nd Moscow Hospitals; also intern, Myasnitskaya Hospital; 1911-25 asst prof, 1925-32 prof, Chair of Skin and Venereal Diseases, Higher Women's Courses (now 2nd Moscow Med Inst); demonstrated role of dystrophy of neuro-endocrine system and internal organs in pathogenesis and course of skin diseases; 1917 gave account of Norwegian itch; 1924 described purulent psoriasis; 1928 described nodular skin disease of the joints; 1930 described nodular chondrodermatitis of the aural helix; attended many Pirogov Congresses, int dermatological congresses and All-Union congresses of venereologists; hon member, Moscow, Saratov, Gorky and Kuban' Dermatological Soc; corresp member, Danish, Czechoslovakian and Berlin Dermatological Soc; wrote 142 works; *Publ*: "Über die Wirkungsweise zweier Derivate des Güanidins" (The Active Mechanism of Two Derivatives of Guanidine) (1892); *O sluchaye norvezhskoy chesotki* (A Case of Norwegian Itch) (1917); *Atipichnyy gnoynyy cheshuychatyy lishay* (Atypical Purulent Scaly Herpes) (1924); *Ekzema* (Eczema) (1928); *Klinika bolezney kozhi* (The Clinical Treatment of Skin Diseases) (1931); *Bolezni kozhi u detey i podrostkov* (Skin Diseases in Children and Adolescents) (1936); *Died*: 1945.

IORDANSKIY, Nikolay Ivanovich (pen name: NEGOREV) (1876-1928) Journalist; govt official; CP member from 1921; *Born*: 16 Dec 1876 in Novokhopersk, now Voronezh Oblast; *Educ*: studied at univ; *Career*: late 1890's participated in student movement in Petersburg; populist, then from 1889 Soc-Democrat; frequently arrested, then exiled; after 2nd RSDRP Congress sided with Mensheviks and became a leading Menshevik journalist, contributing to Menshevik *Iskra* and editing the legal *Sovremennyy mir*; 1905 elected to Exec Comt, Petersburg Sov of Workers' Dep; 1906 attended Stockholm RSDRP Congress and was elected cand member, CC and appointed to ed bd of centr organ; 1910 represented Mensheviks in *Zvezda* org but soon resigned; 1909-17 ed, journal *Sovremennyy mir*; during WW I took defensist stand; 1917 member, Plekhanov's "Unity" group; after 1917 Feb Revol appointed Provisional Govt comr for armies on Southwestern Front; after 1917 Oct Revol for a while abandoned politics but then pledged his support for Sov regime; 1921 ed, Sov newspaper *Put* in Finland; from Nov 1921 Collegium member, Pop Comrt of Educ; 1922 worked for Pop Comrt of For Affairs and for State Publ House; 1923-24 Sov plen in Italy; from 1924 in Moscow, engaged in lit work; *Publ: Zemskiy liberalizm* (Zemstvo Liberalism) (1906); *Konstitutsionnoye dvizheniye 60-kh godov'* (The Constitutional Movement of the Sixties) (1906); *Lev Tolstoy i sovremennoye obshchestvo* (Lev Tolstoy and Contemporary Society) (1910); *Pokoleniye 'lishnikh lyudey'* (The Generation of "Superfluous Men") (1923); *Yevropa nashikh dney* (Europe in Our Time) (1926), etc; *Died*: Dec 1928.

IORDANSKIY, Nikolay Nikolayevich (1863-1941) Pedag; prof; Dr of Pedag; *Born*: 30 Apr 1863; *Career*: 1887 began teaching career; taught Russian language at secondary schools in Nizhniy Novgorod; worked for Nizhniy Novgorod Soc of Elementary Educ; co-founder and teacher, Nizhniy Novgorod Women's Sunday School; 1905 co-founder, first Russian public library for children, Nizhniy Novgorod; also helped to introduce meal service at primary schools and to establish "day shelters" for poor urban schoolchildren; 1911 exiled to Baltic Kray on polit grounds; inspector of public colleges, Riga Educ Distr; 1911 deleg, All-Zemstvo Congress; 1913 deleg, Khar'kov Congress on School Statistics; 1913-14 co-organizer and deleg, All-Russian Teachers' Congress; 1914-17 worked in public educ system, Moscow Zemstvo; from Sept 1917 Dep Min of Educ; 1918-19 head, Culture Dept, Council of All-Russian Cooperative Congresses; 1921-22 Collegium member, RSFSR Pop Comrt of Educ and chm, Main Bd of Soc Educ; 1922-32 prof of pedag, 2nd Moscow State Univ; in 1930's worked at pedag research establishments in Moscow and studied problems of school mang; did research on gen educ, the org of primary schools and teachers' training; *Publ: Voprosy narodnogo obrazovaniya sredi staroobryadtsev* (Problems of Public Education Among Old-Believers) (1909); *Rukovodstvo shkoloy* (School Management) (1918); *Kul'turno-prosvetitel'naya deyatel'nost' kooperativnykh soyuzov* (The Cultural and Educational Activities of the Cooperative Unions) (1919); *Detskiy dom-kommuna* (The Children's Commune-Home) (1919); *Osnovy i praktika sotsial'nogo vospitaniya* (The Principles and Practice of Social Education) (1925); *Massovaya trudovaya shkola i progammy GUSa* (The Mass Labor School and the Progams of the State Learned Council) (1925); *Shkolovedeniye* (School Mangement) (1929); *Died*: 9 Jan 1941.

IOSAFAT (secular name: Iosif KOTSILOVSKIY) (1876-1947) Dr of Divinity and Philosophy; former Bishop of Peremyshl' and Sambor (Greek Catholic Church); *Born*: 1876 in vil Pakoshivka, Galicia; *Educ*: studied at univ; grad mil college; studied divinity in Rome; *Career*: served in Austro-Hungarian Army as senior lt; 1907 took holy orders and appointed prof at theological training establishments in Stanislawow; 1913 took monastic vows under name Iosafat and sent to St. Onufrius Monastery, L'vov; 1914 emigrated to Moravia and organized theological seminary for Galician emigres; consecrated bishop and 1916 assigned to See of Peremyshl'; during WW 2 arrested by State Security organs and imprisoned at Tarnow; 1945 transferred to L'vov Prison and 1947 to Kiev; *Died*: 1947 in imprisonment.

IOSIF (real name: OREKHOV, Iosif Stefanovich) (1871-1961) Metropolitan of Voronezh and Lipetsk from 1959; *Born*: 1871; *Educ*: grad Kiev Theological Acad as Cand of Theology; *Career*: 1894 ordained priest; subsequently ordained senior priest; took monastic vows; 1945 consecrated Bishop of Voronezh and Ostrogozhsk; 1950 consecrated archbishop; from 1954 Archbishop of Voronezh and Lipetsk; 1959 consecrated metropolitan; *Awards*: right to wear cross on cowl (1954); *Died*: 14 Jan 1961.

IOSIFOV, Gordey Maksimovich (1870-1933) Anatomist; CP member from 1931; *Born*: 15 Jan 1870; *Educ*: 1894 grad Med Fac, Khar'kov Univ; *Career*: 1899 defended doctor's thesis; from 1906 prof, Chair of Anatomy, Tomsk Univ; from 1923 prof, Chair of Anatomy, Voronezh Univ; specialized in human lymph system; outlined types and variants of lymph system; studied role of passive and active mechanisms in convection of lymph; *Publ*: doctor's thesis *K voprosu o nervakh gl. thymus u cheloveka* (Nerves of the Human Thymus Gland) (1899); *Limfaticheskaya sistema cheloveka s opisaniyem adenoidov i organov dvizheniya limfy* (The Human Lymph System, with an Account of the Adenoids and Lymph Propulsion Organs) (1914); *Died*: 24 Mar 1933.

IOST, Vladimir Ivanovich (1886-1959) Surgeon; Dr of Med from 1927; prof from 1931; CP member from 1930; *Born*: 1886; *Educ*: 1919 grad Med Fac, Saratov Univ; *Career*: after grad worked for a brief period as intern, Hospital Surgery Clinic, Saratov Univ under Prof S. I. Spasokukotskiy but was soon drafted into the Red Army; served as a mil surgeon in V. I. Chapayev's div; 1920 returned to Hospital Surgery Clinic, Saratov Univ as asst prof, then assoc prof; from 1931 head, Chair of Hospital Surgery Clinic, Gorky Med Inst; co-founder, Gorky Blood Transfusion Center; from 1939 head, Chair of Hospital Surgery Clinic, Khar'kov Med Inst; during WW 2 held several important posts in Sov Army; 1944 campaigned for wide-scale use of penicillin, sanazine and other antibiotics in surgical practice; after war head, Chairs of Fac and Hospital Surgery, Sanitary-Hygiene and Pediatric Fac, Khar'kov Med Inst; dep, Gorky and Khar'kov City Sov; member, various soc, sci and Party org; sponsored some 25 doctor's theses; 1958 retired on pension for health reasons; wrote over 60 works on surgery, blood transfusion, stomach ulcers, microtraumas, chronic suppurative processes, lung cancer, ind safety, etc; *Died*: 3 May 1959 in Khar'kov.

IPAT'YEV, Vladimir Nikolayevich (1867-1952) Organic chemist; prof from 1900; member, Russian (USSR) Acad of Sci from 1916; *Born*: 21 Feb 1867; *Educ*: 1892 grad Mikhaylov Artillery Acad, Petersburg; *Career*: 1892-1900 asst head, Chemical Laboratory, from 1900 prof, Mikhaylov Artillery Acad; also worked for Acad of Sci and State High-Pressure Chemical Research Inst; 1921-22 Presidium member and head, Dept of the Chemical Ind, Supreme Sovnarkhoz; 1927 sent abroad on official business and never returned to USSR; from 1930 worked for Universal Oil Products Company, Chicago; prof, Northwestern Univ, Chicago; did first research on the reaction of tertiary alcohols and bromine; devised new methods of synthesizing hydrocarbons; 1900 began research on catalytic reactions at high pressures and temperatures, especially the reactions of hydrogenation, dehydration (over aluminum oxide), olefine polymerization, destructive hydrogenation and alkylation; developed polymerization process for the production of high-octane gasoline; devised several new catalysts for the extraction of fuels and dies; was one of first sci to try to determine the chemical affinity of catalysts, especially mixed catalysts; pointed out the role of promoters in the process of catalysis; made major contribution to ind catalysis; 1936 expelled from USSR Acad of Sci for refusal to return to USSR; *Publ*: coauthor, *Glinozyom kak katalizator v organizheskoy khimii* (Alumina as a Catalyst in Organic Chemistry) (1927); *Kataliticheskiye reaktsii pri vysokikh temperaturakh i davleniyakh, 1900-03* (Catalytic Reactions at High Temperatures and Pressures, 1900-03) (1936); *Died*: 1952.

IPPOLITOV-IVANOV (real name: IVANOV), Mikhail Mikhaylovich (1859-1935) Composer and conductor; Pop Artiste of RSFSR from 1922; prof from 1893; *Born*: 19 Nov 1859 in Gatchina; *Educ*: 1872-75 attended music classes arranged by Choir of Petersburg's Isaac Cathedral; 1882 grad Petersburg Conservatory; *Career*: 1882-93 lived in Tiflis and headed a musical college and Tiflis Dept, Russian Musical Soc; from 1893 prof, 1906-22 dir, Moscow Conservatory; 1895-1901 conductor, Russian Choral Soc; 1899-1906 conductor, Mamontov and Zimin Opera Theaters, Moscow; from 1925 conductor, Bolshoy Theater; married singer V. Zarudnaya; *Works*: operas: *Ruf'* (1887); *Aera* (1890); *Asya* (1900); *Izmena* (Treason) (1910); *Ole iz Nordlanta* (Ole of Nordlant) (1916); *Zhenit'ba* (Marriage) - 2nd, 3rd and 4th acts of Moussorgsky's unfinished opera, performed 1931; *Poslednyaya barrikada* (The Last Barricade) (1933); cantatas and orchestral works: "Hymn to Labor" (1934); symphony (1907); suites: "Caucasian Sketches" (1894); "Iberia" (1895); "Turkic Fragments" (ca 1930); "Musical Pictures of Uzbekistan" (1934); "Catalonian Suite" (1934); "Hop Slopes. A Spring Overture" (1881); tone poem *Mtsyri* (1924); "Jubilee March" (1931); instrumental and vocal works; romances, etc; *Awards*: Order of the Red Banner of Labor; *Died*: 28 Jan 1935 in Moscow.

IRCHAN, Miroslav (real name: Andrey Dmitriyevich BABYUK) (1897-1937) Ukr writer; CP member from 1920; *Born*: 14 July 1897 in vil Pyadiki, now Ivano-Franko Oblast, son of a poor peasant; *Educ*: 1914 grad L'vov Teachers' Seminary; *Career*: during WW 1 drafted into Austrian Army; early 1920 defected to Red Army; began lit career in Western Ukr; from 1922 lived in Prague, studying at univ, while active in Czechoslovak workers' orgs; Oct 1923, upon invitation from Farm Workers' Soc, emigrated to Canada and engaged in publ, lit work and journalism: journals *Rabotnitsa* and *Mir molodyozhi*; secr, trans-oceanic branch of "Gart" soc; leading exec in Ukr Farm Workers' Center assoc; June 1929 returned to Sov Ukr; from 1930 headed "Western Ukr" writers' assoc in Khar'kov; ed, journal *Zakhidna Ukraina*; his dramatic and prose works won recognition as early as the 1920's, were translated into English, German, French, Czech, Bel and Yiddish and were staged successfully at many theaters; subjected to reprisals by State Security organs; *Publ*: non-fiction work "The Laughter of Nirvana" (1918); collected novellae: "Films of the Revolution" (1923); "The Tragedy of the First of May" (1923); "In the Tall Weeds" (1925); plays: "The Twelve" (1923); "Underground Galicia" (1926); "The Family of Brush-sellers" (1927); "Radium" (1928); novelette "Carpathian Night" (1927); stagecraft textbook "The Stage"; *Died*: 1937 in imprisonment; posthumously rehabilitated.

ISAAKYAN, Avetik Saakovich (1875-1957) Arm poet; member, Arm Acad of Sci from 1943; *Born*: 30 Oct 1875 in vil Kazarapat, near Aleksandropol' (now Leninakan); *Educ*: 1889-92 studied at Echmiadzin Theological Seminary; 1893-95 studied at Leipzig Univ; *Career*: 1892 first work published; 1893 moved to Germany and attended Leipzig Univ, studying lit, history and philosophy; toured Italy and Greece; 1895 interrupted studies due to family circumstances and returned home; a year later arrested for anti-tsarist activities; after release from prison published first collection of verse; most of his works were either entirely banned or drastically cut by the tsarist censorship; 1911 emigrated and lived in Constantinople, Geneva, Berlin and Paris; 1930-36 favored Sov regime; 1926 returned to Sov Arm; 1936 returned permanently to Paris; member, Sov Peace Comt; 1946-57 chm, Arm Writers' Union; dep, Arm Supr Sov of 2nd and 4th convocations; *Publ*: collected verse "Songs and Wounds" (1897); poem *Abul Ala Maari* (1909-11); in emigration wrote Oriental legends and poems in prose: *Litit*, *Li Tai-bo*, etc; lyrical verse and unfinished novel "The Lips of Karo"; historical ballad "Our Forefathers" (1917); epic poem *Sasma Mger* (1919); collected verse; stories "The Patience Pipe" (1928); legend in prose *Lilit*, etc; verse cycle "Our Historians and Our Gusans" (1939); "To My Country" (1940); "Armenian Architecture" (1942), etc; verse: "Battle Cry" (1941); "My Heart is on the Mountain Tops" (1941); "To the Eternal Memory of S. G. Zakiyan" (1942); "The Great Victory Day" (1945), etc; *Awards*: two Orders of Lenin; Stalin Prize (1946); *Died*: 17 Oct 1957.

ISACHENKO, Boris Lavrent'yevich (1871-1948) Microbiologist; Dr of Botany from 1917; Dr of Biology from 1934; member, Ukr Acad of Sci from 1945; member, USSR Acad of Sci from 1946; Hon Sci Worker of RSFSR from 1936; *Born*: 14 June 1871 in Petersburg; *Educ*: 1895 grad Nat Sci Dept, Fac of Physics and Mathematics, Petersburg Univ; *Career*: 1895 studied the botanical gardens of Vienna, Triest, Heidelberg, Amsterdam and Berlin; studied North Sea algae on Helgoland Island; 1895-1900 asst prof, 1900-18 assoc prof; 1918-29 head, Chair of Microbiology, Petersburg (Leningrad) Univ; 1902-35 prof, Leningrad Agric Inst; 1917-30 dir, Main Botanical Garden (now Botanical Inst), USSR Acad of Sci; 1930-37 head, Laboratory of Gen Microbiology, All-Union Inst of Experimental Med; from 1937 dir, Inst of Microbiology, USSR Acad of Sci; 1896 visited Germany; 1898 - France and Holland; 1900 - France; 1902 - Austria, France, Germany, Hungary and Switzerland; 1904 - Belgium and Germany; 1906 and 1910 - Germany; 1912 - France; 1922 - Czechoslovakia, England, France, Germany and Holland; 1924 - England; 1926 Spain, Canada and USA; 1928 - Germany, France and Italy; did research on the propagation of microorganisms in nature and their role in geological processes; also studied individual groups of microorganisms; his research on marine microbiology received wide acclaim; 1914 made first study of the microflora of the Arctic Ocean as part of a project which was subsequently extended to the Sea of Japan, the Baltic Sea, the Kara Sea, the Sea of Marmora, the Black Sea, the Caspian Sea and the Sea of Azov; 1927 did research on salt-water lakes and medicinal muds; established the role of Actinomyces in imparting an earthy odor to water; described new microorganism (Bact Issatschenkoi) which causes epizooty in mice and was subsequently used for rodent extermination; studied the role of microorganisms in the formation of calcium; 1900 read one of first Russian courses on microbiology at Petersburg Univ and Agric Inst; wrote 234 works, including some 50 on seed-growing and a number of monographs and textbook chapters on microbiology; *Publ: Izbrannyye trudy* (Selected Works) (3 vol, 1951-57), etc; *Awards*: Order of Lenin; Order of the Red Banner of Labor; Hon Dr of Charles Univ, Prague (1948); *Died*: 17 Nov 1948 in Moscow.

ISAIYA (real name: KOVALYOV, Vladimir Dmitriyevich) (1882-1961) Bishop of Uglich from 1954; vicar of Yaroslavl' Eparchy from 1957; *Born*: 1882 in Uglich, now Yaroslavl' Oblast; *Educ*: 1903 grad Rybinsk River Transport School; *Career*: until 1946 worked in river transport system; 1946 entered monkhood with name of Isaiya and ordained priest-monk; priest, Yaroslavl' Cathedral; member, Yaroslavl' Eparchic Council; 1949 father-superior, from 1951 archimandrite and acting custodian and treasurer, Archpriest's Residence; 1952 dean, Yaroslavl' Cathedral; 1954 ordained bishop; vicar, Yaroslavl' Eparchy; *Died*: 1961.

ISAKOV, Ivan Stepanovich (1894-1967) Naval commander; fleet admiral from 1944; novelist; prof, Chair of Strategy and Operations; corresp member, USSR Acad of Sci; CP member from 1939; *Born*: 10 Aug 1894 in vil Adzhikent, Arm, son of an office worker; *Educ*: 1917 grad Naval College; 1928 grad Higher Acad Courses, Naval Acad; *Career*: 1914 volunteered for Russian Navy while still a student; during WW 1 master chief petty officer, destroyer *Izyaslav*; from 1918 in Sov Navy; during Civil War took part in Arctic campaign of Baltic Fleet; commander, destroyer escort *Kobchik* at Kronstadt; commander, destroyer "Karl Marx," Volga-Caspian Flotilla; commander of a minesweeper and destroyer, Baltic Fleet 1923-27 commander of a destroyer, Black Sea Fleet, then operational duties with Fleet and Coastal Defense staffs; 1931-33 instructor, Voroshilov Naval Acad; 1933-35 chief of staff, Baltic Fleet; dep, USSR Supr Sov of 1937 convocation; 1937-38 commander, Baltic Fleet; 1938-46 USSR First Dep Pop Comr of the Navy; until 1939 simultaneously dir, Voroshilov Naval Acad; 1940-41 chief of Main Staff, Sov Naval Forces; 1941-43 also member, Mil Council, Leningrad, North Caucasian and Transcaucasian Fronts; 1946-47 dep commander in chief and chief of Main Staff, Sov Naval Forces; 1947-50 dep chief of staff, Sov Naval Forces in charge of evaluating experience of WW 2; 1949-54 exec ed, *Morskoy atlas* (Marine Atlas); 1950-54 in retirement and member, ed collegium, *Atlas mira* (World Atlas); 1954-55 USSR Dep Min of the Navy; from 1956 worked for USSR Min of Defense; 1956-64 member, Lenin Prize Comt for Sci and Technol; *Publ: Desantnaya operatsiya* (Landing Operations) (1934); *Operatsiya yapontsev protiv Tsindao* (The Japanese Tsingtao Operation) (1936); *Kharakter sovremennoy voyny i operatsii na more* (The Nature of Modern Warfare and Naval Operations) (1940); *Primorskiye kreposti* (Coastal Fortifications) (1945-46), etc; *Awards*: Hero of the Sov Union (1965); Stalin Prize (1951); five Orders of Lenin; three Orders of the Red Banner of Labor; two Orders of Ushakov, 1st Class; other orders and medals; *Died*: 11 Oct 1967 in Moscow after a long illness; buried in Novodevich'ye Cemetery.

ISAMETDINOV, Mamadzhan Isametdinovich (1912-1957) Uzbek govt and Party official; CP member from 1940; *Born*: 1912 in Andizhan; *Educ*: 1924-31 studied at secondary school; 1937 grad All-Union Bank Workers' Courses; *Career*: from 1931 worked at Andizhan branch, State Bank; from 1937 mang, Pap Branch, State Bank; 1941 chm, Andizhan Oblast Bd, State Bank; 1943 first secr, Altyn-Kul' Rayon Comt, CP Uzbek; 1945 secr, Andizhan Oblast Comt, CP Uzbek; from 1946 Uzbek Min of Finance; elected member, CC, CP Uzbek at 10th-13th Congresses; dep, Uzbek Supr Sov of 1951 and 1955 convocations; *Awards*: two Orders of the Red Banner of Labor; two Badges of Hon; medals; *Died*: 12 Sept 1957.

ISAYEV, Dmitriy Yefremovich (1905-1930) Chuvash writer and lit critic; *Born*: 1905; *Educ*: studied for a while at Communist Univ of the Workers of the East; *Career*: took part in Komsomol work; was exec ed, Chuvash youth newspaper *Molodoy krest'yanin* and other periodicals; one of the first Chuvash Marxist lit critics; *Publ*: stories: "The Girl Student at a Workers Faculty" (1927); "The Detachment" (1928); "A Village Aflame" (1928); novelette "Lizuk the Weaver" (1929); collected stories "The New Generation" (1930); collection of lit criticism "For Proletarian Literature" (1931); *Died*: 1930.

ISAYEV, Uraz Dzhayzakovich (1899-?) Govt official; CP member from 1921; *Born*: 1899 of Kir parents; *Career*: chm, Kaz Council of Pop Comr; cand Presidium member, USSR Centr Exec Comt; at 16th and 17th CPSU(B) Congresses elected cand member, CC, CPSU(B); 1937 arrested by State Security organs; *Died*: date and place of death unknown.

ISETSKIY (real name: TER-IOANESYANTS), Leon Nikolayevich (1890-1946) Opera singer (bass); Pop Artiste of Geo SSR from 1943; Hon Artiste of Arm SSR from 1933; *Born*: 20 Sept 1890; *Educ*: 1914 grad Brussels Univ; same year, after moving to Tiflis, studied singing under A. A. and V. I. Zelyonyy; further training in Milan; *Career*: from 1916 soloist, Tiflis Opera House; from 1937 soloist, Paliashvili Theater; 1923 helped organize Aleksandropol' (now Leninakan) Opera Theater, where he performed in Arm language; at Paliashvili Theater performed following roles in Russian and Geo: Tsangala in Paliashvili's "Daisi," Tsar Georgiy in M. Balanchivadze's "Daredzhan the Perfidious"; Nadir-Shah in Spendiarov's "Almast"; Ogsen in Stepanyan's *Lusabatsin*; Konchak; the miller, Don Basilio, Mephisto; Tsuniga in "Carmen," etc; helped found Spendiarov Opera and Ballet Theater; *Died*: 10 May 1946.

ISHANOV, Kemal (1911-1948) Turkm writer; Hon Poet of Turkm SSR from 1939; *Born*: 1911; *Career*: from 1933 worked on ed staff of various newspapers; 1933 first stories, essays and articles on Red Army published; from 1937 chm, bd, Turkm Writers' Union; *Publ*: play "The Red Army Man" (1940); collected verse; "Red Star" (1939); "Letters from the Front" (1947); children's novelette "The Young Patriot" (1947); *Died*: 1948.

ISHEMGULOV, Bulat Zakirovich (1900-1938) Bash writer; CP member from 1920; *Born*: 29 Mar 1900 in vil Chebenli, now Ziyanchura Rayon, Bash ASSR; *Educ*: studied at medressah in Ufa; *Career*: fought in Civil War; exec Party and Komsomol work in Bash; 1917 first work published; wrote verse, stories, essays, satirical sketches, feuilletons and songs; arrested by State Security organs; *Publ*: collections "Komsomol Songs" (1925); "Godless Laughter" (1930); stories "Mullah Sabir's Letter from the Grave" (1924); "A Prayer by Agreement" (1926); "The Atheists' Decree" (1927), etc; poems "Tractor Driver Aykhylu" (1933); "Roads" (1933); "Zianchura" (1934); in Russian translation *Izbrannoye* (Selected Works) (1957); *Died*: 1938 in imprisonment; posthumously rehabilitated.

ISKENDEROV, Mamed Salmanovich (1908-1965) Party official; Dr of History from 1964; *Born*: 30 Dec 1908 in vil Urud, Zangezur Uyezd, son of a peasant; *Educ*: 1933 grad Transcaucasian Communist Univ; 1947-50 studied at Acad of Soc Sci, CC, CPSU; *Career*: from 1933 worked for Transcaucasian Kray CPSU(B) Comt and simultaneously taught at Transcaucasian Higher Communist Agric School; from 1936 exec Party work in Azer and Arm; from 1937 instructor, CC, CP(B) Arm; then dep ed, newspaper *Kyzyl Shafak*; first secr, Vedinskiy Rayon Party Comt; from May 1938 secr, Yerevan City Party Comt; during WW 2 secr, CC, CP(B) Arm; from 1950 dep dir, then dir, Azer Branch, Inst of Marxism-Leninism, CC, CPSU; also dir, Inst of History; Azer Acad of Sci; 1952-56 head, Propaganda and Agitation Dept, CC, CP Azer; from 1956 dir, Azer Branch, Inst of Marxism-Leninism, CC, CPSU; member, CC, CP Azer and CC, CP Arm; dep, Arm, Azer and USSR Supr Sov; *Publ*: over 50 works; *Iz istorii bor'by kommunisticheskoy partii Azerbaydzhana za pobedu Sovetskoy vlasti* (history of the Azerbaidzhan Communist Party's Struggle for the Victory of the Soviet Regime); *Ocherki istorii Kommunisticheskoy partii Azerbaydzhana* (Outline History of Azerbaidzhan Communist Party); *S. M. Kirov v Azerbaydzhane* (S. M. Kirov in Azerbaidzhan), etc; *Awards*: Order of the Fatherland War, 1st Class; Order of the Red Banner; Badge of Hon; medals; *Died*: May 1965 in Baku.

ISMAILOV, Abib Akper-ogly (1906-1967) Stage and film dir; Hon Art Worker of Azer SSR from 1960; CP member from 1930; *Born*: 1906; *Educ*: 1931 grad Production and Acting Fac, Centr Stagecraft Technicum; 1954 completed postgrad studies on theatrical history; *Career*: 1931-43 artistic dir, chief producer and theater dir in Baku, Kirovabad and Makhachkala; 1938-41 also taught acting at Baku Conservatory; 1940-41 dir, Akhundov Theatrical College; from 1943 film dir, Baku Film Studios; 1949-50 probationary dir, *Mosfilm* Studios; 1943-48 worked mainly on documentary films; from 1946 also worked as dubbing dir; *Works*: documentary films: *Ordenli Azerbaydzhan*, "25th Anniversary of the Nakhichevan ASSR", *Dzhafar Dzhabarly* and "25th Anniversary of the Dagestani ASSR," (1943-48) (wrote scripts for last two); dubbed: *Raduga* (The Rainbow), *Chevlovek Number 217* (Man Number 217) and *Bez viny vinovatyye* (Guilty Without Guilt); tech documentary "The Use of Advanced Methods in Cotton Farming" (1956, own script); feature films: "The Step-Mother" (1959, own script) and "The Great Support" (1963); *Awards*: 3rd Prize, 2nd All-Union Film Festival (1959); *Died*: Jan 1967.

ISMAILOV, Khadzhi (1913-1948) Turkm writer; *Born*: 1913 in vil Bagir, near Ashkhabad; *Career*: 1929 first work published; worked as an ed; specialist in Turkm folklore; collated and published material on lit monuments; translated into Turkm works of Russian lit and Victor Hugo's "1893," etc; *Publ*: poem "Two Strangers United" (1930); story "The Reading Room" (1937); novelettes: "The Rivals" (1944); "A Son of Two Fathers" (1946); "The Teacher's Daughter" (1947); in Russian translation *Povesti voyennykh let* (Tales of Wartime) (1950); *Died*: 6 Oct 1948.

ISMAILOV, Yesmagambet Samuratovich (1911-1966) Philologist and lit historian; Dr of Philology from 1957; prof; corresp member, Kaz Acad of Sci from 1958; member, USSR Writers' Union; *Born*: 1911 in Enbekshil'der Rayon, Kokchetav Oblast; *Educ*: grad Philological Fac, Kaz Teachers' Training Inst; *Career*: 1943-57 cand of Philology; from 1957 head, Folklore Dept, Inst of Language and Lit, Kaz Acad of Sci; 1957-66 directed publ in Russian and Kaz of *Ocherk istorii kazakhskoy sovetskoy literatury* (An Outline History of Soviet Kazakh Literature); *Publ*: coauthor, *Istoriya kazakhskoy literatury* (A History of Kazakh Literature) (1948); *Akyny* (Folk Bards) (1957); *Istoriya Kazakhskoy SSR* (The History of the Kazakh SSR) (vol 1, 1957); *Antologiya kazakhskoy poezii* (An Anthology of Kazakh Poetry) (1958); *Tema revolyutsii v kazakhskoy literature* (The Theme of the Revolution in Kazakh Literature) (1960); *Awards*: Badge of Hon; medals; *Died*: 29 Aug 1966.

ISTOMIN, Konstantin Konstantinovich (1874-1942); Lit historian; *Born*: 12 Apr 1874 in Khar'kov; *Career*: taught lit at Petrograd schools; 1904-06 published studies of Ancient Russian lit; from 1913 wrote articles on Russian prose fiction of 1840's and 1850's and style and composition of Turgenev and Dostoyevsky's early works; *Publ*: *K voprosu o redaktsiyakh Tolkovoy Palei* (Editions of the Critical Old Testament Edition) (1905); *'Staraya manera' Turgeneva* (Turgenev's "Old Manner") (1913); *Roman 'Rudin.' Iz istorii turgenevskogo stilya* (The Novel "Rudin." The History of Turgenev's Style) (1923); *Iz zhizni i tvorchestva Dostoyevskogo v molodosti* (The Life and Work of the Young Dostoyevsky) (1924); *Parodiynaya komediya M.I. Veryovkina 'Imyaninniki'* (M. I. Veryovkin's Parody-Comedy "Name-Day Celebrants") (1934); *Died*: 1942 in Leningrad.

ISTRIN, Vasiliy Mikhaylovich (1865-1937) Lit historian; member, Russian Acad of Sci from 1907; *Born*: 10 Feb 1865 in vil Pekhra, Moscow Uyezd; *Educ*: grad Moscow Univ; studied under Prof N. S. Tikhonravov; *Career*: 1891-97 assoc prof, Moscow Univ; 1897-1907 prof, Novorossiysk (Odessa) Univ; 1902-07 corresp member, Russian Acad of Sci; did comparative research on religious works in Russian and other Slavonic literatures and their relationship to the Byzantine originals; published material from the archives of the Turgenev brothers and biographies of V. A. Zhukovskiy and Gogol; did research on the works of Pushkin; helped run Dictionary Commission, Russian Acad of Sci; *Publ*: *Aleksandriya russkikh khronografov* (The Alexandria of the Russian Chroniclers) (1893); *Skazaniye ob Indiyskom tsarstve* (The Legend of the Indian Empire) (1893); *Otkroveniye Mefodiya Patarskogo i apokrificheskiye videniya Daniila v vizantiyskoy i Slavyano-russkoy literaturakh* (The Revelation of Methodius of Patara and the Apocryphal Visions of Daniel in Byzantine and Russian Slavonic Literature) (1897); *Zamechaniya o sostave Tolkovoy Palei* (Notes on the Compilation of the Critical Old Testament Edition) (1897-98); *Khronika Ioanna Malaly* (The Chronicle of John Malalas) (1903-13); *Khronika Georgiya Armatola* (The Chronicle of George Hamartolos) (3 vol, 1920-30); *Issledovaniya v oblasti drevne-russkoy literatury* (Studies on Ancient Russian Literature); *Ocherki po istorii drevne-russkoy literatury domoskovskogo perioda. 11-13 vekov* (Studies on Ancient Russian Literature of the Pre-Muscovite Period. 11th-13th Centuries) (1922), etc; *Died*: 19 Apr 1937 in Leningrad.

ISTRINA, Yevgeniya Samsonovna (1883-1957) Linguist; prof; corresp member, USSR Acad of Sci from 1943; *Born*: 1883; *Career*: specialist in lit Russian language, grammar, style and historical syntax; did research on Russian lexicography, orthography and methods of teaching Russian; prepared publ of A.A. Shakhmatov's *Sintaksis russkogo yazyka* (Russian Syntax); *Publ*: *Sintaksicheskiye yavleniya Sinodal'nogo spiska pervoy Novgorodskoy letopisi* (Syntactic Aspects of the Synodal Register of the 1st Novgorod Chronicle) (1923); *Normy russkogo literaturnogo yazyka i kul'tura rechi* (Norms of Literary Russian and Linguistic Standards) (1948); coauthor, *Grammatika russkogo yazyka* (Russian Grammar) (1952); *Zametki po dvuyazychnym slovaryam* (Notes on Bilingual Dictionaries) (1944); *Died*: 1957.

ISUV, I.A. (pseudonyms: M. Mikhail) (1878-1920) Menshevik Party official; *Born*: 1879; *Career*: 1903 member, Yekaterinoslav RSDRP Comt; after 2nd RSDRP Congress worked in Moscow and Petersburg; elected in absentia member, CC at 4th RSDRP Congress; during period of new revol upsurge became a supporter of liquidationism and contributed to the journal *Nasha zarya* and other liquidationist publ; during WW 1 was a soc chauvinist; 1917 member, Moscow Menshevik Comt; member, Moscow Sov Exec Comt and All-Russian Centr Exec Comt of 1st convocation; after 1917 Oct Revol worked at Labor Museum; *Died*: 1920.

ITKIS, Mark Borisovich (1921-1967) Mold historian; Cand of Historical Sci; *Born*: 31 Dec 1921 in Kishinev; *Educ*: completed grad and postgrad studies at Historical Fac, Mold Teachers' Training Inst; *Career*: from 1936 in underground Bessarabian Komsomol Org; 1938 arrested and sentenced to six months' imprisonment; after grad taught; from 1956 senior assoc, Inst of History, Mold Acad of Sci; specialized in history of Mold peasant movement in 1917-18 and history of revol movements; *Publ*: coauthor, *Istoriya Moldavskoy SSR* (The History of the Moldavian SSR) (vol 11, 1968); *Died*: 30 July 1967.

ITSENKO, Nikolay Mikhaylovich (1889-1954) Neuropathologist; Dr of Med from 1923; prof; *Born*: 1889; *Educ*: until 1913 studied at Petersburg Mil Med Acad but was expelled for revol activities; 1918 obtained med diploma; *Career*: 1923 defended doctor's thesis on epidemic encephalitis; from 1929 head, Chair of Physiotherapy, Rostov Med Inst; from 1933 head, Chair of Nervous Diseases, Ivanovsk Med Inst; from 1939 prof, Voronezh Med Inst; specialized in nerve infections, diseases of the vegetative nervous system and brain tumors; described interhypophysical disease (Itsenko-Cushing disease) and a new form of subcortical epilepsy (Vorsaba-Itsenko epilepsy); wrote over 100 works, including six monographs; *Publ*: doctor's thesis *Klinika i patologicheskaya anatomiya khronicheskogo epidemicheskogo entsefalita* (The Clinical Aspects and Pathological Anatomy of Chronic Epidemic Encephalitis) (1924); *Kleshchevoy (vesenneletniy) entsefalit* (Tick [Spring-Summer] Encephalitis) (1945); *Problema nachal'nykh form i faznosti v razvitii mozgovogo arterioskleroza* (The Initial Forms and Phases in the Development of Cerebral Arteriosclerosis) (1947); coauthor, *Klinika metastaticheskikh opukholey golovnogo mozga* (The Clinical Aspects of Metastatic Brain Tumors) (1949); *Died*: 1954.

IVAKHNENKO, Grigoriy Sergeyevich (1902-1956) Surgeon and hematologist; prof from 1945; *Born*: 1902; *Educ*: 1927 grad Med Fac, Don Univ, Rostov-on-Don; *Career*: after several years' work as a gen practitioner in the country specialized in surgery at Rostov Med Inst, where he was trained by Prof N. N. Napalkov; simultaneously assoc, from 1938 dir, Rostov Blood Transfusion Inst; after the inst was transformed into the Rostov Oblast Blood Transfusion Center remained as its dir and, subsequently, sci dir; during WW 2 chief surgeon, various mil hospitals; from 1945 head, Chair of Surgery, from 1950 also rector, Rostov Med Inst; member, ed council, journal *Problemy gematologii i perelivaniya krovi*; member, various sci soc; wrote some 50 works on surgery, traumatology and blood transfusion; *Awards*: Order of the Red Star; Badge of Hon; medals; *Died*: 1956 in Rostov-on-Don.

IVANNIKOV, Georgiy Ivanovich (1908-1959) Party and govt official; CP member from 1929; *Born*: 1908 in Tashkent; *Educ*: 1949 grad Higher Party School, CC, CPSU; *Career*: 1923 joined Komsomol; 1924 chm, Chimkent City Pioneer Bureau; then exec Komsomol work in Tashkent and Ashkhabad; from 1934 Party and govt work; Party organizer, CC, CP Turkm; section head, CC, CP Turkm; secr, rayon Party comt in Ashkhabad; first dep chm, Turkm Council of Min; first secr, Ashkhabad Oblast Comt, CP Turkm; from 1949 counsellor, Nov 1951-Nov 1953 USSR amb to Mongolian Pop Republ; from Nov 1953 head, Dept of Adm Trade and Finance Organs, CC, CP Turkm; held the rank of amb extraordinary and plen; dep, Turkm and USSR Supr Sov, member, CC, CP Turkm; *Awards*: two Orders of the Red Banner of Labor; two Badges of Hon; medals; *Died*: June 1959.

IVANOV, Aleksandr Aleksandrovich (1867-1939) Astronomer; specialist in celestial mech and practical astronomy; prof, Petersburg (Leningrad) Univ (1908-29); corresp member, USSR Acad of Sci from 1925; Hon Sci Worker of RSFSR from 1935; *Born*: 1867; *Career*: 1890-1901 astronomer, 1919-30 dir, Pulkovo Observatory; 1901-11 inspector, Main Bd of Weights and Measures; 1932-38 dep dir, All-Union Research Inst of Metrology; research concerned latitude changes of Pulkovo Observatory; developed theory of the Earth's shape and the distribution of gravity upon its surface; research work on celestial mechanics dealt with the motion of small planets and comets; taught a number of univ courses on the main branches of astronomy; 1906-10 and 1913 chm, Russian Astronomers' Soc; *Publ: Vrashchatel'noye dvizheniye zemli. O peremeshchenii polyusov osi vrashcheniya po poverkhnosti zemnogo sferoida* (Rotation of the Earth. The Shift of the Rotationary Axis Poles on the Surface of the Terrestrial Spheroid) (1895); *Teoriya pretsessii* (Wobbling Theory) (1899); *Kurs sfericheskoy astronomii* (Course of Spherical Astronomy) (1923); *Osnovnoy kurs teoreticheskoy astronomii* (Basic Course of Theoretical Astronomy) (1923); *Prakticheskaya astronomiya* (Practical Astronomy) (1923); *Kometa Galileya* (Galileo's Comet), etc; *Died*: 1939.

IVANOV, Aleksandr Fyodorovich (1867-1935) Otolaryngologist; Dr of Med from 1900; prof from 1914; pioneer of otolaryngology as an independent discipline in Russia; Hon Sci Worker of RSFSR from 1934; *Born*: 24 Dec 1867; *Educ*: 1890 grad Fac of Physics and Mathematics, Moscow Univ; 1893 grad Med Fac, Moscow Univ; *Career*: after grad worked as surgeon at hospital in vil Tikhoretskaya; 1900 defended doctor's thesis on the treatment of malaria with methylene blue; became interested in otolaryngology and worked under S. F. Shteyn at Bazanova Hospital, Moscow; from 1914 prof, Chair of Otolaryngology, Med Fac, Moscow Univ (later 1st Moscow Med Inst); 1921 founded Laryngological Dept, Moscow Prosthetics Inst, where he developed methods of restoring the lumen of the laryns and trachea in cases of chronic stenosis caused, mainly, by perichondritis; devised new operation on the bulb of the jugular vein in thrombosis; developed modified operations for persistent stenosis of the larynx and trachea and operations on the frontal and maxillary sinuses; improved various intranasal surgical techniques; described maxillary sinusitis as a separate disease entity; studied suppurative otitis media and improved techniques for treating this disease; devised a new laryngostomy; 1905 did research on osteophony; 1911 studied the sensitivity of the larynx; trained numerous otolaryngologists, includung such prominent specialists as L. D. Rabotnikov, K. A. Orleanskiy, A. G. Likhachyov, M. I. Vol'fkovich, N. N. Usol'tsev and A. M. Gel'fon; established otolaryngological sections at Pirogov congresses; 1908 co-organizer, 1st Russian Congress of Otolaryngologists; chm, Moscow Sci Otolaryngological Soc; co-ed, *Bol'shaya Meditsinskaya Entsiklopediya* (Large Medical Encyclopedia) (1st ed); wrote 72 works; *Publ: Vskrytiye lukovitsy yaremnoy veny pri piyemiyakh ushnogo proiskhozhdeniya* (The Opening of the Bulb of the Jugular Vein in Pyemia of Aural Origin) (1905); *O lobnoreshyotchatoy trepanatsii* (Ethmofrontal Trepanning) (1911); *Vnutrinosovaya khirurgiya pridatochnykh polostey nosa* (Intranasal Surgery of the Nasal Accessory Sinuses) (1914); *O lechenii stenozov gortani* (Treating Stenosis of the Larynx) (1925); *O khronicheskom vospalenii chelyustnoy pazukhi* (Chronic Maxillary Sinusitis) (1925); coauthor, *Kratkoye rukovodstvo po boleznyam nosa, gorla i ukha* (A Short Manual of Ear, Nose and Troat Diseases) (1933); *Died*: 1935 in Moscow.

IVANOV, Aleksandr Vasil'yevich (1899-1959) Artist and film-cartoonist; CP member from 1955; *Born*: 5 June 1899; *Educ*: grad Tambov Teachers' Training Inst and Tambov Art Studios; *Career*: worked as cartoonist for newspapers *Gudok, Rabochaya Moskva,* etc; from 1923 specialized in cartoon films; one of first Sov cartoon-film artists; 1924 did animation sequences for film *K nadzemnym pobedam* (Victories on Land); 1926 founded animation studio at *Sovkino* Film Studios, where he produced propaganda films; also drew political posters and cartoons, notably "Political Toys" (1925), "Second Industrialization Loan" (1928) and "The Chinese-Eastern Railroad" (1929); *Productions: Vor* (The Thief) (1935, co-production); *Lisa-stroitel'* (Builder-Fox) (1936); *Lyubimets publiki* (The Popular Favorite) (1937); *Volshebnaya fleyta* (The Magic Flute) (1938); *Okhotnik Fyodor* (Theodore the Hunter) (1939); *Ne toptat' fashistskomu sapogu nashey Rodiny* (Don't Let Fascist Boots Trample Our Fatherland) (1941, co-production); *Lisa i drozd* (The Fox and the Trush) (1947); *Kvartet* (Quartet) (1948); *Chempion* (The Champion) (1948); *Zay i Chik* (Rab and Bit) (1952); *Krashenyy lis* (The Painted Fox) (1953); *V lesnoy chashche* (In the Depths of the Forest) (1954); *Trubka i medved'* (The Pipe and the Bear) (1955); *Podpis' nerazborchiva* (The Illegible Signature) (1955); *Lesnaya istoriya* (The Forest Story) (1956); *Chudesnitsa* (The Sorceress) (1957), etc; *Awards*: diploma at British Festival of For Films (1957); 1st prize, Moscow All-Union Film Festival (1958); *Died*: 13 Mar 1959.

IVANOV, Aleksey Andreyevich (pseudonym: KYUNDE) (1898-1934) Yakut writer; *Born*: 16 Jan 1898 in vil Suntarskiy now Yakut ASSR, son of a peasant; *Educ*: 1917 grad teachers' seminary, Irkutsk; *Career*: 1923 first work published; wrote several plays staged by Yakut Theater; also wrote lit criticism; *Publ*: verse collection "Scarlet Haze" (1926); verse: "A New Faith" (1926); "The Force of Reason" (1926); "Coming Time" (1926); "The First Snow"; "Summer Time"; "Morning," etc; stories: "Marba"; "The Doromon Family"; "The Card Players"; "Stories" (1927); plays: "In the Tayga Backwoods" (1927); "Lelya" (1928); "Lights of the Commune"; "Those Years"; *Died*: 20 Oct 1934 in Yakutsk.

IVANOV, Aleksey Nikolayevich (1869-1958) Geologist and stratigrapher; *Born*: 21 Feb 1869; *Career*: from age 17 worked in coal mines; 1896 passed examinations to qualify as foreman of underground mining work; 1917-25 lecturer, Perm' Univ; from 1925 lecturer, Sverdlovsk Mining Inst; for many years worked for Geological Comt and Ural Geological Bd; then head, Stratigraphy and Paleontology Laboratory, Geological and Mining Inst, Ural Branch, USSR Acad of Sci; studied stratigraphy of western slopes of Northern and Centr Urals; compiled geological maps and stratigraphic tables of various areas; his work led to the discovery of several coal deposits in the Kizel Basin; *Died*: 22 June 1958.

IVANOV, Andrey Vasil'yevich (1888-1927) Party official; CP member from 1906; *Born*: 1888 in vil Kukshevo, Kostroma Province, son of a peasant; *Career*: fitter at railroad depot, Aleksandrovo Station, Vladimir Province; 1905 took active part in revol; 1916 drafted into Russian army and posted to Arsenal Plant, Kiev; after 1917 Feb Revol member and leader of Bolshevik faction, 1st Kiev Sov of Workers' Dep; simultaneously member, Kiev City RSDRP(B) Comt; Kiev deleg at 6th RSDRP(B) Congress; during 1917 Oct Revol chm, Kiev Mil Revol Comt; helped to prepare and conduct 1st All-Ukr Congress of Soviets, which proclaimed Sov rule in the Ukr; member, Ukr Centr Exec Comt; Jan 1918 one of leaders of uprising against Ukr Centr Rada; RSDRP(B) CC plen responsible for supplying partisans with arms and propaganda material; member, Ukr Centr Mil Revol Comt; 1918 also elected Presidium member, Ukr Centr Exec Comt at 2nd All-Ukr Congress of Soviets; from 1919 chm, Kiev Exec Comt; from 1920 chm, Khar'kov Province Exec Comt; from 1921 simultaneously secr, Ukr Centr Exec Comt; from late 1922 chm, Odessa Province Exec Comt; from 1925 member, USSR Centr Exec Comt; subsequently Presidium member, dep chm, Budget Commission and secr, Sov of the Union, USSR Centr Exec Comt; from 1924 cand member, CC, RCP(B); from Mar 1920 member, from 1922 Politburo member, CC, CP(B) Ukr; *Died*: 1927; buried in Kiev.

IVANOV, Arkadiy Aleksandrovich (1902-1956) Geologist; corresp member, USSR Acad of Sci from 1953; CP member from 1942; *Born*: 19 Nov 1902; *Educ*: 1926 grad Tomsk Technol College; *Career*: from 1926 worked in the Urals; from 1944 dir, Sverdlovsk Inst of Mining and Geology, Ural Branch, USSR Acad of Sci; main works deal with mineralogy, geochemistry and petrography of gold, platinum and rare metal deposits; advanced theory of vein structures' origin; discovered new type of fundamental niobium and osmious iridium deposits; *Publ: Lokalizatsiya zolotogo i svyazannogo s nim redkometal'nogo orudneniya na Srednem i Severnom Urale v svyazi s geologicheskimi strukturami* (Localization of Combined Gold and Rare-Metal Ore in the Central and Northern Urals in Connection with Geological Structures) (1941); *Mestorozhdeniya osmistogo iridiya* (Osmious Iridium Deposits) (1944); *Geologiya korennykh mestorozhdeniy zolota na Urale* (Geology of Fundamental Gold Deposits in the Urals) (1948); coauthor, *O magmaticheskikh rudnykh mestorozhdeniyakh* (Magmatic Ore Deposits) (1955); *Died*: 20 July 1956.

IVANOV, Boris Ivanovich (1887-1965) Party and trade-union official; CP member from 1906; *Born*: 6 Aug 1887; *Career*: 1905-07 took active part in Revol; one of first workers' corresp of *Pravda*; frequently arrested and exiled for distributing illegal lit and other revol activities; spring 1917 member, Petrograd Sov of Workers and Soldiers' Dep; after 1917 Oct Revol held trade-union posts; founder-member, CC, Food-Ind Workers' Union; member, All-Russian Centr Exec Comt; dep, Moscow and Leningrad Sov; from 1952 pensioner; wrote books on revol subjects; *Publ: Po stupenyam bor'by. Zapiski starogo bol'shevika* (In the Footsteps of Struggle. Notes of an Old Bolshevik) (1934); *Zapiski proshlogo. Povest' iz vospominaniy detstva i yunoshestva rabochego sotsialista* (Notes of the Past. A Story from the Childood and Youth of a Socialist Worker) (1919), etc; *Awards*: Hero of Socialist Labor (1962); *Died*: 31 May 1965.

IVANOV, Dmitriy Dmitriyevich (1871-1930) Art historian; specialist in decorative art and art ind; *Born*: 1871; *Career*: from 1918 with Museum Dept, Pop Comrt of Educ; from 1922 dir of Kremlin museums; re-catalogued exhibits of Kremlin Weaponry Dept; assoc, State Acad of Material Culture and State Acad of Arts; taught at higher educ establishments and on special courses; *Publ: Ob'yasnitel'nyy putevoditel' po khudoz-hestvennym sobraniyam Peterburga* (An Explanatory Guide to Petersburg's Art Collections) (1904); *Iskusstvo mebeli* (The Art of Furniture) (1924); *Iskusstvo farfora* (The Art of Porcelain) (1924); *Iskusstvo keramiki* (The Art of Ceramics) (1925); *Germanskoye iskusstvo epokhi Vozrozhdeniya v byte drevney Rusi* (German Renaissance Art in the Everyday Life of Ancient Rus) (1925); *Died*: 1930.

IVANOV, Georgiy Fyodorovich (1893-1956) Anatomist; Dr of Med; prof from 1930; CP member; *Born:* 1893 in vil Gory, Mogilyov Province, Bel, son of a peasant; *Educ*: 1922 grad Petrograd Mil Med Acad; *Career*: 1922-25 asst to Prof V. N. Tonkov, Chair of Anatomy, Petrograd (Leningrad) Mil Med Acad; 1925-39 lecturer, then assoc prof, Leningrad Mil Med Acad; 1930-56 head, Chair of Normal Anatomy, 1st Moscow Med Inst, where he enlarged the Anatomical Museum; as a rep of the school of functional anatomy did research in conjunction with pathophysiologists and clinicians; made new contributions to knowledge on collateral blood circulation, the lymphatic system, the circulation of cerebrospinal fluid, the motor apparatus and innvervation of the cardiovascular system; trained several outstanding anatomists; member, Higher Certifying Commission and Experts' Commission, USSR Min of Higher Educ; chm, Methods Commission for Theoretical Chairs, 1st Moscow Med Inst; co-founder and chm, Moscow Branch, and dep chm, All-Union Soc of Anatomists, Histologists and Embryologists; 1952-54 coordinating ed, journal *Arkhiv anatomii, gistologii i embriologii*; wrote over 90 works for Sov, German and French journals and several monographs; *Publ: Khromaffinovaya i interrenal'naya sistemy* (The Chromaffine and Interrenal Systems) (1930); *Nervy i organy chuvstva serdechnososudistoy sistemy* (The Sensory Nerves and Organs of the Cardiovascular System) (1945); textbook *Osnovy normal'noy anatomii cheloveka* (The Principles of Normal Human Anatomy) (2 vol, 1949); *Nervy serdechnososudistoy sistemy* (The Nerves of the Cardiovascular System) (1956); *Died*: 1956 in Moscow.

IVANOV, Il'ya Ivanovich (1870-1932) Biologist and veterinarian; *Born*: 1 Aug 1870 in Shchigry, now Kursk Oblast, son of a civil servant; *Educ*: 1896 grad Khar'kov Univ; *Career*: after grad worked at Inst of Experimental Med; did research on the role of the accessory sexual glands in the fertilization of mammals and devised artificial insemination method; 1901 founder-dir, Experimental Station for the Artificial Insemination of Horses, vil Dolgom, Oryol Province; in the following period established several other artificial insemination centers; 1908, with the aid of I. P. Pavlov, founded a physiological dept at the Petersburg Veterinary Admin Laboratory (later Laboratory for the Biology of Reproduction, Inst of Experimental Veterinary Med); 1928-31 carried out large-scale artificial insemination programs at the "Sheep-Breeder" and "Cattle-Breeder" Sovkhozes; from 1931 head, Chair of the Physiology of Reproduction, Alma-Ata Zoological and Veterinary Inst and head, Alma-Ata Artificial Insemination Laboratory; also worked on the interspecific hybridization of animals; 1910 bred several hybrids of wild and domestic animals at his zootech station in Askaniya-Nova; 1926-27 led USSR Acad of Sci expedition to West Africa to experiment with the interspecific hybridization of anthropoid apes; trained numerous zootechnicians and veterinarians; *Publ: Iskusstvennoye oplodotvoreniye u mlekopitayushchikh* (The Artificial Fertilization of Mammals) (1906); *Iskusstvennoye oplodotvoreniye domashnikh zhivotnykh* (The Artificial Fertilization of Domestic Animals) (1910); "De la fécondation artificielle des mammifères et des oiseaux" (The Artificial Fertilization of Mammals and Birds) (1924); *Iskusstvennoye osemeneniye domashnikh zhivotnykh* (The Artificial Insemination of Domestic Animals) (1930); *Died*: 20 Mar 1932.

IVANOV, Il'ya Ivanovich (1899-1967) Ordinance designer; lt-gen, Eng and Tech Corps; member, Acad of Ordinance from 1946; CP member from 1946; *Born*: 1899 in Petersburg; *Educ*: 1921 grad Petrograd Tech Artillery Courses; 1928 grad Artillery Acad; *Career*: during Civil War commanded artillery units; 1932-37 prof, Dzerzhinskiy Artillery Acad; after 1937 design work; *Publ: Osnovy raschyota i proyektirovaniya lafetov* (Principles of Gun-Carriage Calculation and Design) (1933); *Awards*: four Orders of Lenin; other orders and medals; two Stalin Prizes (1943 and 1946); Hero of Socialist Labor (1940); *Died*: May 1967.

IVANOV, Ivan Alekseyevich (1906-1948) Diplomat; envoy extraordinary and plen, 2nd class; *Born*: 1906; *Career*: from 1939 in dipl service; 1939-47 USSR plen, then envoy to Mongolian Pop Republ; 1948 USSR amb in Afghanistan; *Died*: 1948.

IVANOV, Ivan Ivanovich (1909-1941) Russian fighter pilot; senior lt; *Born*: 1909 in vil Chizhovo, Moscow Province; *Educ*: 1934 grad Odessa Mil Pilots' School; *Career*: from 1931 in Red Army; 1941 commander, flight of fighter aircraft; 22 June 1941 in an air battle over Western Ukr performed the first ramming of an enemy aircraft in the history of WW 2 and died in so doing; *Awards*: Hero of the Sov Union (posthumously); *Died*: 1941 killed in action.

IVANOV, Ivan Ivanovich (1862-1939) Mathematician; Dr of Mathematics from 1901; corresp member, USSR Acad of Sci from 1924; prof, Leningrad Polytech Inst; Hon Sci Worker of RSFSR from 1933; *Born*: 11 Aug 1862; *Career*: established that Ye. I. Zolotaryov and R. Dedekind's formally different theories of algebraic numbers were in fact equivalent; 1901 defended doctor's thesis, in which he obtained several results on the distribution of prime numbers; *Died*: 17 Dec 1939.

IVANOV, Ivan Ivanovich (1862-1929) Lit historian and critic; *Born*: 4 Oct 1862; *Educ*: 1886 grad Fac of History and Philology, Moscow Univ; *Career*: in 1890's contributed to *Severnyy vestnik, Russkaya mysl'* and *Mir bozhiy*; 1913-17 prof, Moscow Univ; adherent of cultural-historical school; wrote numerous works on gen history and history of Western European lit; *Publ: Politicheskaya rol' frantsuzskogo teatra v svyazi s filosofiyey 18-go veka* (The Political Role of the French Theater in Connection with the Philosophy of the 18th Century) (1895); *Shekspir* (Shakespeare) (1896); *Pisemskiy* (1898); *Iz zapadnoy kul'tury. Stat'i po voprosam literatury, filosofii, politiki* (Western Culture. Articles on Literature, Philosophy and Politics) (1899-1900); *Istoriya russkoy kritiki* (A History of Russian Criticism) (2 vol, 1900); *Sen-Simon i sensimonizm* (Saint-Simon and Saint-Simonism) (1901); *Rytsar' slova i zhizni. Servantes i yego 'Don-Kikhot'* (A Knight of Word and Life. Cervantes and His "Don Quixote") (1911); *V. Shekspir. Biograficheskiy ocherk* (W. Shakespeare. A Biographical Sketch) (1904); *F. Shiller. Biograficheskiy ocherk* (F. Schiller. A Biographical Sketch) (1905); *Uchitel' vzroslykh i drug detey. Bicher-Stou* (Teacher of Adults and Friend of Children. Beecher-Stowe) (1907); *I. S. Turgenev* (1914); *Died*: 1929 in Moscow.

IVANOV, Leonid Aleksandrovich (1871-?) Botanist; prof from 1904; corresp member, USSR Acad of Sci from 1922; *Born*: 1871; *Educ*: 1895 grad Moscow Univ; *Career*: 1904-41 prof, Chair of Botany (later Chair of Plant Anatomy and Physiology), Timber Inst (now Kirov Forestry Acad); 1938-47 head, Photosynthesis Laboratory, Inst of Plant Physiology, USSR Acad of Sci; from 1944 simultaneously head, Laboratory of the Physiology and Ecology of Wood Varieties, Inst of Timber, USSR Acad of Sci; did research on the effects of light and moisture on trees; devised original method of studying photosynthesis; designed a phytoactinometer to study photosynthesis and a phytoatmometer to measure evaporation rates, etc; established theoretical priciples of tapping conifers; wrote numerous works on wood anatomy, the taxonomy of lower plants, fermentation, respiration and phosphorus conversion in plants; *Publ: Biologicheskiye osnovy ispol'zovaniya khvoynykh SSSR v terpentinovom proizvodstve* (The Biological Principles of the Exploitation of the Conifers of the USSR for Turpentine Production) (1934); *Fiziologiya rasteniy* (Plant Physiology) (1936); *Obshchiy kurs sistematiki rasteniy* (A

General Course on Plant Taxonomy) (1937); *Anatomiya rasteniy* (Plant Anatomy) (1939); *Svet i vlaga v zhizni nashikh drevesnykh porod* (Light and Moisture in the Life of Our Trees) (1946); *Awards*: two Orders of the Red Banner of Labor; *Died*: date and place of death unknown.

IVANOV, Leonid Gordeyevich (1898-1936) Circus artist and animal trainer; *Born*: 1898; *Career*: from age of seven worked with a team of acrobats under the leadership of his father; performed in the "Icarus Games" number; from 1925 worked with performing animals (horses, camel, dogs, monkeys, parrots, etc); included in his program Russian folk elements, wearing Russian folk dress (shirt, breeches, high boots); his technique with animals was unconstrained, natural and often funny; introduced comic episodes (races with dogs dressed as jockeys; a waltzing camel, etc; *Died*: 1936.

IVANOV, Lev Nikolayevich (1903-1957) Historian; specialist in int econ relations; member, USSR Acad of Sci from 1943; CP member from 1944; *Born*: 28 July 1903; *Educ*: 1923 grad Fac of Soc Sci, Moscow State Univ; *Career*: 1924 began teaching and research work; 1925-47 worked at Inst of World Econ and World Politics, Communist Acad (from 1936 USSR Acad of Sci); 1930-38 worked at Higher Diplomatic School, USSR Min of For Affairs; 1939-43 corresp member, USSR Acad of Sci; 1940-41 worked at Lenin Mil–Polit Acad; from 1943 worked at Inst of Int Relations; 1946 adviser to Sov deleg, Paris Peace Conference; from 1948 head, Section of British Empire Countries, Inst of Econ, USSR Acad of Sci; *Publ: Mirovaya politika posle Versalya* (World Politics After Versailles) (1927); *Anglo-frantsuzskoye sopernichestvo 1919-27 godov* (Anglo-French Rivalry, 1919-27) (1928); *Liga natsiy* (The League of Nations) (1929); *Anglo-amerikanskoye morskoye sopernichestvo* (Anglo-American Maritime Rivalry) (1933); *Morskoye sopernichestvo imperialisticheskikh derzhav* (The Maritime Rivalry of the Imperialist Powers) (1936); *Ocherki mezhdunarodnykh otnosheniy v period vtoroy mirovoy voyny 1939-45 godov* (Studies of International Relations During World War 2, 1939-45) (1958); *Died*: 6 Mar 1957.

IVANOV, Mikhail Fyodorovich (1871-1935) Veterinary surgeon; specialist in animal-husbandry; prof from 1906; member, All-Union Lenin Acad of Agric Sci from 1935; Hon Sci Worker of RSFSR from 1929; *Born*: 2 Oct 1871; *Educ*: 1897 grad Khar'kov Veterinary Inst; *Career*: after grad worked as veterinary surgeon in Oryol Province; 1898 sent abroad to study West European animal-breeding methods; studied at Agric Dept, Zurich Univ; from 1900 taught animal-husbandry and hygiene at Khar'kov Veterinary Inst; 1903 defended master's thesis on changes in nitrogenous substances in moldy fodder; from 1906 prof, Khar'kov Veterinary Inst; 1914-35 prof, Moscow Agric Inst (now Timiryazev Agric Acad); 1925 established experimental breeding station at Aksaniya-Nova, where he did research on stock-breeding; 1935 member, USSR Centr Exec Comt; apart from stock-breeding, did major research on animal selection and acclimatization; devised methods of breeding new stock and improving old, taking feeding, maintenance, constitution and productivity as his main criteria; bred fine-fleeced Askanian sheep with a high wool and meat yield, white Ukr steppe hog, etc; the All-Union Animal Hybridization and Acclimatization Inst at Askaniya-Nova now bears his name; wrote numerous works, including manuals on sheep-, hog- and poultry-breeding; *Publ: Izbrannyye sochineniya* (Selected Works) (3 vol, 1949-50), etc; *Died*: 1935.

IVANOV, N. I. (1883-1937) Govt official; CP member from 1905; *Born*: 1883; *Career*: worker; took part in 1905-07 Revol in Lugansk and Sevastopol'; in 1917 chm, rayon Party comt in Petrograd; after 1917 Oct Revol dep chm, then chm, Petrograd Metal Workers' Union and Presidium member, All-Russian Centr Trade-Union Council; mid-1918 Comr of Labor, Northern Oblast League of Communes; subsequently head, Labor Dept, Petrograd Province Sov; other exec trade-union, admin and govt work; arrested by State Security organs; *Died*: 1937 in imprisonment.

IVANOV, Nikolay Nikolayevich (1884-1940) Physiologist and biochemist; Dr of Biology; prof from 1918; *Born*: 25 Oct 1884 in Gatchina, Petersburg Province; *Educ*: 1909 grad Petersburg Univ; *Career*: from 1909 asst prof, Chair of Plant Physiology, Petersburg Univ; 1914-25 simultaneously lecturer, Froebel Teachers' Training Course, Inst of Preschool Training; 1918-22 prof, Agronomical Inst; from 1922 assoc, Inst of Applied Botany and New Cultures; 1926-30 prof, Technol Inst; also head, Biochemistry Laboratory (Dept), All-Union Inst of Phytoculture; from 1929 prof, Chair of Microbiology, Leningrad Univ; 1936-48 co-founder and ed, multi-vol work *Biokhimiya kul'turnykh rasteniy* (Crop Biochemistry); compiled large body of information on various plants, especially on protein content; devised original biochemical plant selection methods which led to the cultivation of new crops (alkaloid-free lupin and sweet clover with a low coumarin content); also did research on the biochemisty of microorganisms, notably on the ureal metabolism of fungi and bacteria; also sought new vegetable sources of vitamins; *Publ*: coauthor, *O mochevine u bakteriy* (Bacterial Urea) (1927); *Obrazovaniye i prevrashcheniye mocheviny v gribakh* (The Formation and Conversion of Urea in Fungi) (1928); *Metody fiziologii i biokhimii rasteniy* (Methods of Plant Physiology and Biochemistry) (1946); *Problema belka v rasteniyevodstve* (The Problem of Protein in Phytoculture) (1947), etc; *Died*: 3 Dec 1940 in Leningrad.

IVANOV, Nikolay Pavlovich (1905-1967) Electr eng; Cand of Tech Sci from 1962; *Born*: 25 Dec 1905; *Educ*: 1926 grad Kagan-Shabshay State Inst of Electr Machine-Building; *Career*: 1927-41 worked at "Elektrosila" Plant; 1941-49 worked at "Uralelektro-apparat" Plant, Sverdlovsk; 1949-50 worked for USSR Pop Comrt of the Electr Ind; from 1950 chief designer, "Elektrosila" Plant; helped to design generators for Bratsk Hydroelectr Plant; *Awards*: two Stalin Prizes (1946 and 1949); USSR State Prize (1967); *Died*: 1 Jan 1967.

IVANOV, Stoyan Mineyevich (1890-1959) Party and trade-union official; member, Bulgarian Soc-Democratic Workers' Party from 1907; CP member from 1916; *Born*: 21 Aug 1890 in Bulgaria, son of a peasant; *Career*: 1915 Bulgarian Youth League deleg at Int Conference of Progressive Youth, Berne; 1916 joined Geneva RSDRP(B) org; active in setting up Comt of Supporters of 3rd international; co-founder and ed, revol newspaper *Novyy internatsional,* Geneva; held exec positions in Comintern Exec Comt; during and after WW 2 research and teaching work; senior assoc, Inst of World Economics and Int Relations, USSR Acad of Sci; wrote numerous works on int Communist and Workers' movement; *Awards*: Order of Lenin; medal "For Valiant Labor in the 1941-45 Great Fatherland War"; *Died*: 4 May 1959.

IVANOV, Sergey Nikolayevich (1892-1967) Party official; CP member from 1918; *Born*: 1892 in Tula; *Career*: worked at Zindal Plant in Tula; during Civil War commander, then polit worker with Red Army on Southeastern Front; subsequently chm, Comt of Mil Organizations, RCP(B); chm, Tula City and Tula Oblast Mil Draft Bd; from 1921 exec secr, Tula City and Centr Rayon Party Comts; head, Dept of Agitation and Propaganda, Tula Province Party Comt; from mid-1920's exec ed, newspaper *Kommunar* and ed, journal *Avangard,* organ of Tula Oblast CPSU(B) Comt; from 1929 in Moscow on trade-union work; then dep ed, newspaper *Rabochaya Moskva*; exec ed, newspaper *Vechernyaya Moskva*; during this period member, Moscow City CPSU(B) Comt and member of its Control Commission; from 1943 ed, Polit Publ House; pensioner; *Awards*: Order of the Red Banner of Labor; Badge of Hon; medals; *Died*: 1967.

IVANOV, S. V. (1880-1955) Party and govt official; CP member from 1904; *Born*: 1880; *Career*: Party work in Kronstadt, Arkhangelsk and Libava; subjected to reprisals by tsarist authorities; after 1917 Feb Revol member, Smolensk Uyezd Sov of Peasants' Dep; after 1917 Oct Revol Party and govt work; member, Smolensk Province Party Comt and Smolensk Province Exec Comt; member, Bel Pop Comr of Internal Affairs; member CC, CP Bel; dep chm, Lith and Bel Centr Exec Comt; member, All-Russian and USSR Centr Exec Comt; Smolensk Province RCP(B) Comt rep at 8th All-Russian Party Conference; 1938-54 exec work in coal ind; from 1954 pensioner; *Died*: 1955.

IVANOV, Vadim Nikolayevich (1892-1962) Internist; Dr of Med; prof from 1933; member, Ukr Acad of Sci from 1957; Hon Sci Worker of USSR from 1946; *Born*: 30 Apr 1892 in Mariupol'; *Educ*: 1916 grad Med Fac, Kiev Univ; *Career*: 1918-34 intern, asst prof, then assoc prof, Kiev Med Inst; 1928 devised technique for examining gastric secretions using stimulants of various strength; 1933-41 head, Chair of Fac Therapy, Kiev Med Inst; 1944-50 head, Chair of Therapy, Kiev Med Inst; 1946-53 corresp member, USSR Acad of Med Sci; 1951-57 head, Chair of Hospital Therapy Clinic, Kiev Med Inst; 1953-62 head, Bogomolets Dept of Clinical Physiology, Ukr Acad of Sci; 1958-62 head, Chair of Fac Therapy Clinic, Bogomolets Med Inst, Kiev; bd member, All-Union Oncologists' Soc; dep chm, Ukr Therapists' Soc; hon member, All-Union Therapists' Soc; member, ed collegium, *Fiziologichnyy zhurnal*; member, ed council, journals *Klinicheskaya meditsina,*

Terapevticheskiy arkhiv, Vrachebnoye delo, etc; coauthor, internal diseases section, *Bol'shaya meditsinskaya entsiklopediya* (Large Medical Encyclopedia) (2nd ed); did research on the motor activity of the stomach, gastric secretion, the duodenal fasting contents, normal and pathological digestion, etc; also studied stomach ulcers, achylia, cancer of the diverticulum and stomach, lung cancer and gen lesions in patients suffering from cancer of the internal organs; wrote over 80 works; *Publ: O dvizheniyakh toshchego zheludka u zdorovykh ludey* (Movements of the Jejunum in the Healthy) (1926); *O zabrasyvanii soderzhimogo dvenadtsatiperstnoy kishki v toshchiy zheludok vne pishchevareniya* (The Non-Digestive Injection of the Contents of the Duodenum into the Jejunum) (1926); *Klinichni formy kartsinomy shlunku* (Clinical Forms of Stomach Cancer) (1932); *Pro kyslotnist' shiunkovogo vmistu u sekretsiyu pri vyraztsi shlunka ta dvanadtsatipaloi kyshky* (Gastric Acidity and Secretion in Distension of the Stomach and Duodenum) (1935); *Divertikuly zheludka* (The Gastric Diverticula) (1947); *Diagnostika raka lyogkikh* (The Diagnosis of Lung Cancer) (1949); *Diagnosticheskoye i klinicheskoye znacheniye tomofluorografii lyogkikh* (The Diagnostic and Clinical Importance of Tomofluorography of the Lungs) (1950); *Dostizheniya vnutrenney meditsiny v Ukrainskoy SSR za 40 let* (The Achievements of Internal Medicine in the Ukrainian SSR in the Last 40 Years) (1957), etc; *Awards*: Order of Lenin; Stalin Prize (1951); Order of the Red Banner of Labor (1961); other orders and medals; *Died*: 15 Jan 1962 in Kiev.

IVANOV, Vasiliy Vasil'yevich (1896-1957) Surgeon and health service official; Hon Physician of Ukr SSR from 1940; CP member from 1938; *Born*: 1896 in vil Baltazarovka, Kherson Province; *Educ*: 1916 grad Kakhovka High-School; 1922 grad Med Fac, Novorossiysk Univ, Odessa; *Career*: after grad worked as distr physician, based in vil Stroganovka; from 1927 head, Surgical Dept and dir, Chaplino Rayon Hospital; from 1929 head, Kirovograd Oblast Health Dept and acting chief physician and surgeon, 2nd Kirovograd Hospital; from 1938 head, Kirovograd Oblast Health Dept; during WW 2 chief surgeon, various field evacuation hospitals, Southern and Volkhov Fronts; 1945-57 head, Kiev Oblast Health Dept; wrote several articles on surgery and health service org; *Awards*: two Orders of Lenin; Order of the Red Banner of Labor; three medals; *Died*: 1957 in Kiev.

IVANOV, Vladimir Ivanovich (1893-1938) Party and govt official; CP member from 1915; *Born*: 1893, son of a peasant; *Career*: 1917-18 Party and govt work in Bauman Rayon, Moscow; 1919-20 in Red Army on the Southern Front; 1920-21 secr, Yaroslavl' Province RCP(B) Comt; 1921-24 head, Org Dept, Moscow City RCP(B) Comt and chm, Moscow Party Control Commission; 1924-27 secr, CC, CP Uzbek; 1927-31 secr, North Caucasian Kray CPSU(B) Comt; from 1931 first secr, Northern Kray CPSU(B) Comt; from 1937 USSR Pop Comr of Timber Ind; at 13th Party Congress elected member, CPSU(B) Centr Control Commission; at 15th and 16th Party Congresses elected cand member and at 17th Party Congress member, CC, CPSU(B); subjected to reprisals by State Security organs; sentenced to death in the trial of the "Rightist-Trotskyite Bloc"; *Died*: 15 Mar 1938 executed by firing squad.

IVANOV, Vladimir Vladimirovich (1873-1931) Dermatologist and venereologist; Dr of Med from 1900; prof from 1913; *Born*: 1873; *Educ*: 1897 grad Petersburg Mil Med Acad; *Career*: after grad intern, Therapeutic Clinic, Petersburg Mil Med Acad; from 1899 worked at T. P. Pavlov's Clinic for Skin and Venereal Diseases; 1900 defended doctor's thesis on the histological structure of skin syphilids; 1900-02 worked abroad under I. I. Mechnikov and A. M. Bezredka at Pasteur Inst and Gallopo, Brock, Darier and Fournier's clinics in Paris and at Neisser, Unna and Jadassohn's clinics in Germany; from 1904 assoc prof, Petersburg Mil Med Acad; 1913-17 head, Chair of Skin and Venereal Diseases, Petrograd Psychoneurological Inst; 1917-25 head, Chair of Skin and Venereal Diseases, Moscow Univ; from 1925 head, Dermatological Dept, Obukh Inst of Occupational Diseases; 1916 initiated production of salvarsan preparations in Russia; founded school of dermatological occupational pathology; made important contributions to the study of the chemotherapy of syphilis, papular-necrotic tuberculosis of the skin, multiple sarcomatosis of the skin, epidermitis in the region of wounds and experimental leprosy; 1917 chm, All-Russian League Against Venereal Diseases; 1923 chm, 1st All-Russian Congress on Venereal Diseases; 1919-28 chm, Moscow Venerological and Dermatological Soc; hon member, Moscow, Kiev, Odessa and Don dermatological soc; corresp member, Berlin Dermatological Soc; 1904 attended 5th Int Dermatological Congress; 1923 Sov deleg, 3rd Int Congress on Leprosy; 1913-14 ed, journal *Dermatologiya*; 1924-31 founder-ed, journal *Russkiy vestnik dermatologii; Publ*: doctor's thesis *K ucheniyu o gistologicheskom stroyenii sifilidov kozhi kondilomatoznogo i gummoznogo periodov* (The Theory of the Histology of Skin Syphilids in the Condylomatous and Gummatous Periods) (1900); *K voprosu o mnozhestvennom sarkomatoze kozhi* (Multiple Skin Sarcomatosis) (1900); *K voprosu o sud'be palochek prokazy v organizme zhivotnykh (morskikh sviney)* (The Fate of Leprosy Rods in the Organism of Animals [Guinea Pigs]) (1903); *K etiologii papulo-nekroticheskogo tuberkulyoza (folliclis)* (The Etiology of Papular-Necrotic Tuberculosis [Folliclis]) (1910); *O boleznyakh kozhi v voyennoye vremya* (Skin Diseases in Wartime) (1916); *Zapiski po kozhnym i venericheskim boleznyam* (Notes of Skin and Venereal Diseases) (1923); *Died*: 1931.

IVANOV, Vsevolod Vyacheslavovich (1895-1963) Writer and playwright; Bd member, USSR Writers' Union from 1959; *Born*: 24 Feb 1895 in vil Lebyazh'ye, Semipalatinsk Province; *Educ*: studied at Pavlodar Agric School; *Career*: before 1917 Oct Revol worked as sales-clerk, sailor, type-setter, circus juggler, wrestler, sorter at an emerald mine and ditch-digger; 1915 first work published; 1917-18 simultaneously a member of the Soc-Revolutionary Party and the RSDRP; 1918-20 instructor in Red Army; 1920-41 secr, Petrograd (Leningrad) Lit Studio; regular contributor to journals *Krasnaya nov'* and *Novyy mir*; also worked for "Circle" and "Nucleus" Publ Houses before becoming full-time writer; from 1922 member, Serapion Brethren Lit Soc; during 1920's criticized for "political blindness" and classified a "fellow-traveler"; 1941-45 worked for Sov Information Bureau in Kuybyshev, on film location in Tashkent and as a war corresp; 1945 visited Berlin and attended Nuremberg war-crimes trial as special corresp for *Izvestia*; 1958 attended Constituent Congress, RSFSR Writers' Union; 1959 deleg, 3rd USSR Writers' Congress; dep chief ed, journal *Voprosy yazykoznaniya*; member, Leningrad Oblast CPSU Comt; *Publ*: short story *Priishim'ye* (The Ishim River Region) (1915); collection of short stories *Rogul'ki* (Odds and Ends) (1919); novella *Partizany* (The Partisans) (1921); novella *Bronepoyezd No. 14-19* (Armored Train Number 14-19) (1922); novel *Tsvetnyye vetra* (Colored Winds) (1922); *Sopki. Partizanskiye povesti* (The Hills. Partisan Tales) (1923); novella *Golubyye peski* (Blue Sands) (1923); novella *Khabu* (1925); novella *Vozvrashcheniye Buddy* (Buddha's Return) (1925); anthology *Taynoye taynykh* (The Mystery of Mysteries) (1927); *Sobrannyye sochineniya* (Collected Works) (5 vol, 1928-29); play *Bronepoyezd No. 14-19* (Armored Train Number 14-19) (1927); *Povesti brigadira M. N. Sinitsin* (The Tales of Brigadier M. N. Sinitsin) (1930); novel *Pokhozhdeniye fakira* (The Fakir's Adventure) (1934-35); novel *Parkhomenko* (1938-39); film script *Aleksandr Parkhomenko*; novel *Prospekt Il'icha* (Il'ich Avenue); *V boyakh za Oryol* (The Battle of Oryol); play *Kantsler* (The Chancellor); short stories *Pod Berlinom, u Gal'skikh vorot* (By Berlin, at Hallesches Tor) (1941-45); sketches *Leto 1948-ogo goda* (Summer 1948); play *Lomonosov* (1953); *Izbrannyye proizvedeniya* (Selected Works) (2 vol, 1954); novel *My idyom v Indiyu* (We're Walking to India) (1956); autobiographical novella *Istoriya moikh knig* (The Story of My Books) (1958); *Sobrannyye sochineniya* (Collected Works) (vol 1, 1958), etc; *Awards*: Order of the Red Banner of Labor; *Died*: 15 Aug 1963 in Moscow.

IVANOV, Vyacheslav Ivanovich (1866-1949) Russian poet, playwright, historian and art theoretician; Dr of Classical Philosophy from 1923; *Born*: 28 Feb 1866; *Educ*: studied at History and Philology Fac, Moscow Univ, then studied history, philology and philosophy in Berlin: *Career*: specialized in Dionysian cult and origins of tragedy; from 1891 for a number of years toured many European countries, visited Palestine and Alexandria and returned occasionally to Russia, but primarily domiciled in Italy; 1903 first poetry printed; 1905 settled in Petersburg and became one of the leaders of symbolism; active in Petersburg Religious Philosophy Soc and in *Ory* Publ House; contributed to journal *Zolotoye runo,* almanach *Severnyye tsvety* and journals *Vesy, Apollon, Novyy put',* etc; taught on Higher Women's Courses; after 1917 Oct Revol worked for History of Theater Dept, Pop Comrt of Educ, Moscow; from 1921 in Baku where he was a prof and for a while rector, Baku Univ and Azer Dep Pop Comr of Educ; Ivanov's symbolist ideas affected Proletkul't theoreticians; shied away from official commissions on

Sov themes and emigrated from USSR; from 1924 lived in Italy and translated Dante; *Publ: Kormchiye zvyozdy* (Pilot Stars) (1903); *Prozrachnost'* (Translucence) (1904); *Tantal* (Tantalus) (1905); *Serdtse goryashcheye* (Cor Ardens) (2 vol, 1911-12); *Nezhnaya tayna* (Tender Secret) (1912); poem *Mladenchestvo* (Infancy) (1918); tragedy *Prometey* (Prometheus) (1919), etc; non-fiction: *Ellinskaya religiya stradayushchego Boga* (The Hellenic Religion of the Suffering God) (1904); *Religiya Dionisa* (The Religion of Dionysus) (1905); *Po zveyodam* (By the Stars) (1909); *Borozdy i mezhi* (Furrows and Boundaries) (1916); *Rodnoye i vselenskoye* (The Particular and the Universal) (1917); *Dionisiystvo i pradionisiystvo* (Dionysianism and Pra-Dionysianism) (1923), etc; translations: Pindar's "Ipiphean Ode" (1899), "Alcheus and Sappho" (1914), etc; *Died*: 16 July 1949.

IVANOV-BARKOV, Yevgeniy Alekseyevich (1892-1965) Film dir and scriptwriter; Hon Art Worker of Turkm SSR; *Born*: 4 Mar 1892; *Educ*: 1911-15 studied at Stroganov Arts College; *Career*: from 1915 set designer with private film studios and State Skobelev Comt film enterprises; after 1917 Oct Revol helped organize Sov film ind; 1918-24 dir, then production manager, State Film Studio; 1919 took part in first experimental production of State Film Studio School - screening excerpts from Jack London's novel "The Iron Heel"; 1924 set designer, films *Iz iskry plamya* (Fire from the Spark) and *Krasnyy tyl* (Red Home Front); from 1925 worked as film dir; his first film was *Moroka* (Fuss), produced in conjunction with Yu. Tarich; in late 1920's produced films: *Mabul* (1927, after Sholom-Aleykhem's novelette "Bloody Stream"); *Yad* (Poison) (1927); *Geroi domny* (Heroes of the Blast-Furnace) (1929); *Iuda* (Judas) (1930); from 1938 with Ashkhabad Film Studio (now Turkm Film Studio); from 1945 artistic dir of this studio; helped develop Turkm film ind and produced films: *Dursun* (1940) and *Prokuror* (Public Prosecutor) (1941); 1948 directed lyric comedy *Dalyokaya nevesta* (Distant Bride); 1956 at Odessa Film Studio produced comedy *Sharf lyubinoy* (Scarf of the Beloved) 1958 at Turkm Film Studio helped direct adventure film *Osoboye porucheniye* (Special Mission); *Awards*: two Stalin Prizes (1941), 1949); *Died*: 20 May 1965.

IVANOV-BORETSKIY, Mikhail Vladimirovich (1874-1936) Musicologist, teacher and composer; *Born*: 26 June 1874 in Moscow; *Educ*: 1896 grad Law Fac, Moscow Univ; 1894-1896 studied composition under N. S. Klenovskiy in Moscow and 1898-1900 under Rimsky-Korsakov in Petersburg; 1901-05 studied music history in Italy; *Career*: 1905 returned to Russia and became active in various music socs and educ organizations, including Comic Opera Circle, which staged his opera *Adol'fina* in 1908; 1913 composed opera *Koldun'ya* (The Sorceress), after Chirikov, which was banned by the censors and not produced until 1918; from 1922 prof, Moscow Conservatory; edited *Materialy i dokumenty po istorii muzyki* (Material and Documents on the History of Music) (2 vol, 1934); ed, *Muzykal'no-istoricheskaya khrestomatiya* (An Anthology of Musical History) (3 vol, 1929); ed, collection *Muzykal'noye nasledstvo* (Musical Heritage) (1935), containing material on the history of Russian and for opera; *Works*: operas: *Adol'fina* (1908); *Koldun'ya* (The Sorceress) (1913, staged 1918); symphonic suite (1893); various instrumental works, choral pieces, romances, etc; *Publ: Zabytyy muzykant. E. T. A. Gofman* (E. T. A. Hoffmann, a Forgotten Musician) (1908); *Stranichka proshlogo. Dve opery epokhi Velikoy frantsuzskoy revolyutsii* (A Page from the Past. Two Operas from the Period of the Great French Revolution) (1924); "Gioacchino Rossini" (1930); *Ot opery k oratorii. G. F. Gendel'* (From Opera to Oratorio. G. F. Handel) (1935); *Tablitsy po obshchey istorii muzyki* (Tables on the General History of Music) (1924); *Pervobytnoye muzykal'noye iskusstvo* (Original Musical Art) (1925); *Muzykal'no-istoricheskaya khrestomatiya* (An Anthology of Musical History) (1929), etc; *Died*: 1 Apr 1936 in Moscow.

IVANOV-NEZNAMOV, Vladimir Ivanovich (1902-1958) Clinician and therapist; Dr of Med from 1955; assoc prof; Kremlin physician; *Born*: 1902 in Moscow; *Educ*: 1926 grad Med Fac, Tomsk Univ; *Career*: after grad intern, then asst prof, Therapeutic Clinic, Tomsk Univ; 1931-42 therapist, various Moscow hospitals, then asst prof and assoc prof, Therapeutic Clinic, 1st Moscow Med Inst; during WW 2 mil surgeon in Sov Army, where he held several high posts; 1952-58 worked for 4th Main Bd, USSR Min of Health as head, Therapeutic Dept, 1st Kremlin Hospital and consultant, 1st Polyclinic; wrote 22 works on internal med; *Awards*: Order of the Great Fatherland War, 1st and 2nd Class; Order of the Red Star; medals; *Died*: 1958 in Moscow.

IVANOV-RADKEVICH, Nikolay Pavlovich (1904-1962) Composer; Cand of Arts from 1939; prof from 1930; Hon Art Worker of RSFSR from 1957; *Born*: 1904 in Krasnoyarsk; *Educ*: 1928 grad Moscow Conservatory; *Career*: from 1930 prof of instrumentation, Moscow Conservatory; 1948-57 bd member, USSR Composers' Union; from 1952 head, Chair of Instrumentation, Mil Conductors' Inst, Sov Army; *Works*: arrangement of the Sov national anthem for brass band (1943); symphonic works: 5 symphonies (1928, 1932, 1937, 1944, 1962); 12 suites; "Russian Overture" (1938); "Heroic Poem" (1942); "Rhapsody on Ukrainian Folk Themes"; works for brass band: "Grand Overture" (1948); "Suite on Russian Folk Themes" (1950); "Victory-Day Poem" (1958); "Second Russian Rhapsody" (1963); 28 marches; also wrote music for 17 films; *Awards*: Stalin Prize (1943); *Died*: 4 Feb 1962 in Moscow.

IVANOV-RAZUMNIK (real name: IVANOV, Razumnik Vasil'yevich) (1878-1946) Russian lit historian and sociologist; *Born*: 24 Dec 1878 in Tiflis, son of a nobleman; *Educ*: grad Mathematics Fac, Petersburg Univ; *Career*: 1902 exiled from Petersburg for participating in student demonstration; 1904 published first article *N. K. Mikhaylovskiy* in *Russkaya mysl'*; then contributed to journals *Russkoye bogatstvo* and *Zavety* and to newspaper *Russkiye vedomosti*, etc; in works on the history of Russian social thought and in books about Belinskiy and Herzen presented the history of 19th-century Russian lit as the history of the Russian intelligentsia, a "classless" group struggling against the petty bourgeoisie; regarded the history of Russian social thought as the history of heroic personalities; after 1917 Oct Revol joined Leftist Socialist-Revolutionaries; 1918 co-ed, anthologies "Skify"; 1941 found himself in German-occupied territory (Pushkin); subsequently lived in Germany; *Publ: Istoriya russkoy obshchestvennoy mysli* (A History of Russian Social Thought) (1907); *O smysle zhizni. F. Sologub, L. Andreyev, Lev Shestov* (The Meaning of Life. F. Sologub, L. Andreyev and Lev Shestov) (1908); *Literatura i obshchestvennost'* (Literature and the Public) (1911); *Lev Tolstoy* (1912); *A. I. Herzen 1870-1920* (1920); *Vladimir Mayakovskiy. Misteriya ili Buff* (Vladimir Mayakovskiy. Mystery or Buffo) (1922); *Kniga o Belinskom* (A Book on Belinskiy) (1923); *M. Ye. Saltykov-Shchedrin. Zhizn' i tvorchestvo* (M. Ye. Saltykov-Shchedrin's Life and Work) (1930); *Tyur'my i ssylki* (Prisons and Exile) (1953); *Died*: 9 June 1946 in Germany.

IVANOVSKIY, Boris Aleksandrovich (1890-1941) Physician; specialist in physical educ; *Born*: 1890; *Educ*: 1914 grad Med Fac, Kazan' Univ; *Career*: from 1924 worked under Prof V. V. Gorinevskiy at Moscow Inst of Physical Educ; 1931 founded Chair of Physical Educ, Centr Inst of Postgrad Med Training; 1935-39 head, Med Control Dept for Physical Educ, Inst of Physiotherapy; did research on the scientific principles of physical educ, physical therapy and med control; introduced rational organizational forms and methods of med control and therapeutical exercises; wrote some 100 works; *Publ: Boks kak fizicheskoye upryazhneniye* (Boxing as Physical Exercise) (1926); *Zadachi i metody vrachebno-pedagogicheskogo kontrolya v shkolakh 1 i 2 stupeni* (Tasks and Methods of Medical and Pedagogical Control in 1st-and 2nd-Grade Schools) (1927); *Zdorov'ye i fizicheskoye razvitiye studenchestva i zadachi yego fizicheskogo vospitaniya* (The Health and Physical Development of Students and the Objectives of Their Physical Education) (1928); *Vrachebnyy kontrol' nad fizicheskoy kul'turoy* (Medical Control of Physical Education) (1935); *Died*: 1941.

IVANOVSKIY, Dmitriy Iosifovich (1864-1920) Botanist and microbiologist; pioneer of virus theory; prof from 1901; Dr of Botany from 1903; *Born*: 28 Oct 1864 in Petersburg; *Educ*: 1888 grad Natural History Dept, Fac of Physics and Mathematics, Petersburg Univ, where he studied under A. N. Beketov, A. S. Famintsyn and Kh. Ya. Gobi; *Career*: after grad stayed on at univ to prepare for professorship; 1895 defended master's thesis on spirit fermentation; as assoc prof read a course on the physiology of lower organisms and, a year later, on plant physiology and anatomy; from 1901 extraordinary prof, Warsaw Univ; 1903 defended doctor's thesis on tobacco mosaic at Warsaw Univ and became ordinary prof; 1887, together with V. V. Polovtsev, studied tobacco mosaic in Southern Russia; established that the two forms of tobacco mosaic are two different diseases and that one form (wildfire) is caused by a fungus; was unable to establish the cause of the other; 1890-92 and 1898-1902 did further research on tobacco mosaic and developed counter-measures; 1892 discovered filtrable viruses; noticed that the sap of diseased leaves strained through a fine filter retains its infectious properties, while the filtrate contains no microbes detectable under the microscope and does not grow in normal nutrients; established that disinfectants deprive the filtrate of its infectious capacity; by making a comparative study of the diffusion of the filtered sap of diseased plants in agar and the organic matter in suspension by determining the infectious properties of fractions of the filtrate, he came to the conclusion that the disease agent has a corpuscular structure; suggested that the agent of tobacco mosaic is a minute organism; described crystalloid deposits which he detected in the cells of diseased plants; *Ivanovskiy's crystal* turned out to be accumulations of the tobacco mosaic virus; also did research on spirit fermentation; established a similarity between the absorption spectra of chlorophyll in colloidal solutions and the living leaf; also did research on soil microbiology; was an advocate of Darwinism; wrote some 50 works; *Publ: Iz deyatel'nosti mikroorganizmov v pochve* (Microorganic Activity in the Soil) (1891); *O dvukh boleznyakh tabaka* (Two Tobacco Diseases) (1892); *Issledovaniya nad spirtovym brozheniyem* (Research into Spirit Fermentation) (1894); *Eksperimental'nyy metod v voprosakh evolyutsii* (The Experimental Method in Questions of Evolution) (1908); *Fiziologiya rasteniy* (Plant Physiology) (1924); *Izbrannyye proizvedeniya* (Selected Works) (1953), etc; *Died*: 20 June 1920 in Rostov-on-Don.

IVANOVSKIY (IVANOV), Nikolay Pavlovich (1893-1961) Ballet-dancer; *Born*: 3 Aug 1893; *Educ*: 1911 grad Petersburg Ballet College; *Career*: from 1911 with corps-de-ballet, Mariinskiy Theater; 1912-15 with the Diaghilev Ballet; from 1915 again with Mariinskiy Theater; 1930-31 with Tbilisi Opera Theater; performed character parts: Anthony in Arenskiy's *Yegipetskiye nochi* (Egyptian Nights); Eusebio in "Carnival"; the toreador in "Don Quixote," etc; from 1925 taught classical ballroom dancing at Leningrad Choreographic College; 1940-52 and 1954 artistic manager of this college; while teaching ballroom dancing, he took a keen interest in ancient dances and founded a new discipline - the historical dance - which was included in the curriculum of Sov and for choreographic colleges; *Publ: Bal'nyy tanets 16-19 vv.* (Ballroom Dances of the 16th-19th Centuries) (1948); *Died*: 28 Dec 1961.

IVANOVSKIY, Pavel Maksimilianovich (1885-1953) Hygienist; specialist in school hygiene; *Born*: 22 Mar 1885; *Educ*: 1911 grad Natural Sci Dept, Fac of Physics and Mathematics, Moscow Univ; 1918 grad Med Fac, Moscow Univ; *Career*: 1912 began teaching chemistry and physics at secondary schools in Moscow; 1915-18 mil surgeon; 1918 resumed school work as a teacher and physician; 1926-35 asst prof, 1935-47 assoc prof, 1947-53 head, Chair of School Hygiene, Med Fac, Moscow State Univ; simultaneously dean, Fac of Sanitation and Hygiene, 1st Moscow Med Inst; believed that the allround development of children requires a rational combination of mental and physical work; studied the hygienic principles of physical education, which he considered to be an integral part of school life; developed experimental method for school hygiene; together with Prof A. V. Mol'kov, compiled first school hygiene programs and wrote teaching aids for physicians and teachers; chm, School Hygiene Section, Moscow Sci Soc of Hygienists; *Publ*: coauthor, *Fizicheskoye vospitaniye v shkole pervoy stupeni* (Physical Education in First-Grade School) (1927); coauthor, *Planirovka detskikh uchrezhdeniy v svyazi s rekonstruktsiyey goroda* (The Planning of Children's Institutions in Connection with Urban Reconstruction) (1933); *Sanitarnyy rezhim detskikh uchrezhdeniy* (Sanitary Conditions in Children's Institutions) (1934); *Programmy proyektirovaniya zdaniy obshcheobrazovatel'noy sredney shkoly Moskvy* (Planning Programs for the Buildings of Secondary General Education Schools in Moscow) (1953); *Died*: 2 Mar 1953.

IVANTER, Ben'yamin Abramovich (1904-1942) Russian writer; CP member from 1931; *Born*: 28 June 1904 in Vilnius; *Educ*: 1921 studied at Meyerhold's Training Studio for Stage Dir; *Career*: 1920 joined Komsomol and volunteered for Red Army; 1921 first work published; 1923-25 wrote agitation plays for the *Komsomol'skiy teatr* series; from 1925 contributor, 1933-38 ed, journal *Pioner*; from Aug 1941 worked for div newspaper *Vraga - na shtyk; Publ*: plays: *Rozhdestvo popa Sergeya* (Priest Sergey's Christmas) (1923); *Zemlya zazhglas'* (The Earth Inflamed) (1924); *Ten' Karla Libknekhta* (Karl Liebknecht's Shade) (1925); coauthor, *Mamay* (1930), etc; novelettes: *Vesyoloye zveno* (A Cheerful Team) (1930); *Vystrel* (The Shot) (1938); books: *Vit'ya* (1939); *Moya znakomaya* (My Friend) (1941); *Mal'chishka* (The Urchin) (1941); *Chetyre tovarishcha* (Four Comrades) (1956). *Vystrel* (The Shot) (1956); *Died*: 5 July 1942 killed in action.

IVASHCHENKO, Aleksandr Fyodorovich (1908-1961) Lit historian; CP member from 1930; *Born*: 21 Apr 1908 in Aleksandrovsk-Grushevskiy (now Shakhty), Rostov Oblast; *Career*: taught at Moscow Univ, Moscow Inst of Philosophy, Lit and Art, etc; did research on critical realism in French lit, the results of which appeared in his studies of Stendhal, Honoré de Balzac and Gustave Flaubert; also wrote studies of socialist realism and contemporary realism in foreign lit; edited modern editions of Balzac and Flaubert; *Publ: Belinskiy o frantsuzskom sotsial'no-utopicheskom romane* (Belinskiy on the French Social-Utopian Novel) (1949); *Gyustav Flober* (Gustave Flaubert) (1958); *K voprosu o kriticheskom realizme i realizme sotsialisticheskom* Critical Realism and Socialist Realism) (1959); coauthor, *Istoriya frantsuzskoy literatury* (A History of French Literature); *Zametki o sovremennom realizme* (Notes on Contemporary Realism) (1961), etc; *Died*: 9 Dec 1961.

IVASHCHENTSOV, Gleb Aleksandrovich (1883-1933) Infectionist; prof from 1927; *Born*: 11 Mar 1883 in Petersburg, son of a lawyer; *Educ*: 1907 grad Petersburg Mil Med Acad; *Career*: excluded from competitive examination for continuation of studies at Mil Med Acad because of involvement in student revol movement; for 15 years worked at Obukh Hospital; 1913-14 sent abroad for postgrad med training; 1920-21 head, Therapy Section, Petrograd Province Health Dept; 1922-33 chief physician, Botkin Municipal Infection Hospital, which became a model med establishment under his direction; from 1927 prof, Chair of Infectious Diseases, 1st Leningrad Med Inst; did important research on the etiology of complications in relapsing fever; 1922 together with M. A. Rappoport, isolated microbe now known as Bacterium paratyphi N and described a complication in relapsing fever known as N-paratyphobacillosis; helped to organize Leningrad health service; co-founder, Leningrad Sci Therapeutic Soc; wrote over 30 works; *Publ: Ob opsonicheskom pokazatele pri kholere* (The Opsonic Index in Cholera) (1909); *K voprosu o pervichnoy sibirskoy yazve kishok* (Primary Siberian Intestinal Plague) (1910); coauthor, *O svoyeobraznoy N-paratifobatsillyoznoy epidemii sredi bol'nykh vozvratnym tifom* (An Unusual Epidemic of N-Paratyphobacillosis Among Relapsing Fever Patients) (1922); *Paratifoznyye zabolevaniya* (Paratyphoid Diseases) (1929); *Bryushnoy tif i bor'ba s nim* (Typhoid and Countermeasures) (1933); coauthor, *Kliniko-laboratornyye paralleli pri tifozno-paratifoznykh zabolevaniyakh* (Clinical and Laboratory Parallels in Typhoid and Paratyphoid Diseases) (1934); coauthor, *Kurs ostrykh infektsionnykh bolezney* (A Course on Acute Infectious Diseases) (1925); *Died*: 9 Dec 1933.

IVCHENKO, Mikhail Yevdokimovich (1890-1939) Ukr writer; *Born*: 1890 in Priluki, now Poltava Oblast, son of a peasant; *Educ*: tech high school; *Career*: worked as a statistician; until Oct 1917 Ukr Progressivist; member, Constitutional Democratic Party; 1917-18 member, Socialist-Revol Party; 1930, in the trial of the Union for the Liberation of the Ukr, accused of systematic agitation and propaganda of bourgeois nationalistic ideas in his works and sentenced to imprisonment (suspended); later arrested by State Security organs; main theme of Ivchenko's stories was the "power of the earth"; his typical heroes were strong peasants holding on to their farms; extolled patriarchal village as the symbol and guarantee of the nat independence of the Ukr; *Publ*: novel *Rabochiye sily* (Manpower) (1929); *Died*: 1939 in imprisonment.

IVING, Viktor Petrovich (other pseudonyms: SERPUKHOVSKOY; TSOKI; real name: IVANOV) (1888-1952) Theater critic; Cand of Arts from 1944; *Born*: 19 Nov 1888; *Educ*: 1916 grad Law Fac, Moscow Univ; *Career*: 1917-26 ballet dancer, Theater of Revol Satire, etc; 1923 began writing ballet reviews for the newspapers *Pravda, Izvestia, Sovetskoye iskusstvo*, etc and the journals *Teatr i muzyka, Zrelishcha, Rampa, Zhizn' iskusstva*, etc; also wrote a number of monographs; 1940-41 and 1946-52 taught at State Inst of Stagecraft; 1943-47 taught at Moscow Choreographic College; *Publ: A. I. Abramova* (1928); *Viktorina Kriger* (1928); *Put' teatra* (The Way of the Theater) (1936); *Tantsy Buryat-Mongolii* (The Dances of Buryat-Mongolia) (1941); *O russkoy shkole klassicheskogo tantsa* (The Russian School of Classical Dance) (1947); coauthor, *Ye. V. Gel'tser* (1948); *O russkoy plyaske* (Russian Dance) (1953); *Soderzhaniye postanovochnoy raboty po* *tantsu so shkol'nikami* (The Contents of Choreographic Arrangements for Schoolchildren) (1956); *Died*: 8 Sept 1952.

IVNIK, Ivan Nikolayevich (1914-1942) Chuvash poet and translator; *Born*: 10 June 1914 in vil Syaval, Kazan' province, son of a peasant; *Career*: 1929 first verse published; translated the works of Russian and Ukr writers into Chuvash, including Pushkin's *Bakhchisarayskiy fontan* (The Fountain of Bakhchisaray) and *Kamennyy gost'* (The Stone Guest), Lermontov's *Mtsyri* (The Solitary Monks), Shevschenko's *Son* (Sleep) and poems by Mayakovskiy, M. V. Isakovskiy, etc; also put Chuvash folk tales into verse; *Publ*: poems: *Pavlik Morozov* (1934); *Kirka Ilene* (1935); versification of fairy tale "The Road to Happiness" (1938); verse collections: "Spring" (1937); "New Verse" (1937); "Lyrics" (1939); "A Book of Verse" (1940); children's verse: "Warm Wind" (1939); "Our Happiness" (1939), etc; *Died*: 28 May 1942 in Cheboksary.

IYERUSALIMSKIY, Nikolay Dmitriyevich (1901-1967) Microbiologist; Dr of Biology from 1946; member, USSR Acad of Sci from 1966; CP member; *Born*: 4 Jan 1901; *Educ*: 1931 grad Biology Fac, Moscow State Univ; *Career*: 1930-35 laboratory asst, then assoc, Moscow Chemical and Pharmaceutical Research Inst; 1935-50 senior assoc, 1950-62 dep dir, Inst of Microbiology, USSR Acad of Sci; 1935-38 also dep section head of a yeast research laboratory; from 1954 prof of microbiology, Moscow Univ; 1958 attended International Symposium on the Continuous Cultivation of Microorganisms, Prague, and the Int Microbiology Congress, Stockholm; 1960 attended an int symposium in Rome; 1960-66 corresp member, USSR Acad of Sci; 1961-66 dep dir, 1966-67 dir, Inst of the Biochemistry and Physiology of Microorganisms, USSR Acad of Sci; 1963 dep acad secr, Dept of Biological Sci, USSR Acad of Sci; specialized in the development of microorganisms in various nutrients; *Publ: Stroyeniye bakteriy* (The Structure of Bacteria) (1940); *Mikrobiologiya tsellyulozy* (The Microbiology of Cellulose) (1953); *O zakonomernosti rosta i razvitiya mikroorganizmov* (The Laws of the Growth and Development of Microorganisms) (1959); coauthor, *Otnosheniya Bacillus megaterium k usloviyam sredy v protsesse prokhozhdeniya zhiznennogo tsikla* (The Relation of Bacillus megaterium to Environmental Conditions in the Course of the Life Cycle) (1960); *O pervom Mezhdunarodnom simpoziume po brozheniyu i fermentatsii v Italii* (The First International Fermentation Symposium in Italy) (1961); *Metod protochnogo kul'tivirovaniya organizmov i vozmozhnosti yego primeneniya* (A Method of Continuous Cultivation of Organisms and its Potential Applications) (1962); coauthor, *Izmeneniye nekotorykh fiziologicheskikh potrebnostey drozhzhey v rezul'tate adaptatsii k streptomitsinu* (The Change in Some Physiological Requirements of Yeast as a Result of Adaptation to Streptomycin) (1963); *Died*: 16 May 1967.

IYEZUITOV, Nikolay Mikhaylovich (1899-1941) Film historian and critic; *Born*: Nov 1899; *Educ*: 1924 grad History of Art Section, Soc Sci Fac, Moscow Univ; *Career*: began teaching at Moscow Conservatory, lecturing on historical materialism and sociology of arts; 1932 in charge of film criticism section and postgrad course at Acad of Arts, Leningrad; from 1936 head, Chair of Cinema History, All-Union State Inst of Cinematography; 1941 joined Moscow civil defense corps; *Publ: Kino v prepodavanii istorii* (The Cinema in the Teaching of History) (1929); *Kino kak istochnik istorii zavodov* (The Cinema as a Source for Factory History); *Nekotoryye problemy metodologii uchebnogo fil'ma* (Some Methodological Aspects of the Educational Film) (1931); *Dramaturgiya 'Bol'shevika'* (The "Bolshevik" Dramaturgy) (1933); *Problemy zanimatel'nosti* (Problems of Entertainment) (1934); essay *Kinematografiya* (Cinematography) (1936); *Na putyakh k realizmu* (The Paths to Realism); *'Groza' V. Petrova* (V. Petrov's "Thunderstorm") (1934); preface to book by V. Pudovkin *Aktyor v fil'me* (The Film Actor) (1934); *Puti khudozhestvennogo fil'ma* (Feature Film Trends) (1934); *Pudovkin* (1937); *Aktyory MKHAT v kino* (Moscow Academic Arts Theater Actors in Film Work) (1938); *Aktyor V. Gardin* (The Actor V. Gardin) (1940); coauthor, *Istoriya sovetskogo kino* (History of the Soviet Cinema) (1958); *Died*: 1941 killed in action.

IZGARYSHEV, Nikolay Alekseyevich (1884-1956) Electrochemist; corresp member, USSR Acad of Sci from 1939; *Born*: 16 Nov 1884; *Educ*: 1908 grad Moscow Univ; *Career*: 1908-12 with Chair of Chemistry, Moscow Univ; from 1912 taught at Moscow Business Inst (now Inst of Nat Econ); from 1917 prof of this Inst; taught also at other higher educ institutions, including Moscow Inst of Chemical Technol; 1915-25 advanced new theory of galvanic elements; 1921 introduced new theory of overtension in the separation of oxygen and hydrogen; 1921-29 his research work led to the discovery of "Izgaryshev's effect," which consists in altering the polarization by introducing into the solution "foreign" electrolytes which do not participate directly in the electrode reactions; "Izgaryshev's effect" can either reduce or increase polarization, with a capacity of several hundred millivolts; together with his students discovered, explored and developed production technol for method of metal-plating steel products in metal salt vapors; a number of early works deal with corrosion of metals and anti-corrosion treatment; founded a large school of electrochemists, instrumental in developing the electrochemistry of non-ferrous metals, galvanic technol and other branches of electrochemical ind; *Publ: Issledovaniya v oblasti elektrodnykh protsessov* (Research on Electrode Processes) (1914); *Sovremennaya teoriya rastvorov* (Modern Solution Theory) (1924); *Elektrokhimiya i yeyo tekhnicheskoye primeneniye* (Electrochemistry and Its Technical Application) (2nd ed, 1930); *Elektrokhimiya tsvetnykh i blagorodnykh metallov* (Electrochemistry of Non-Ferrous and Precious Metals) (1933); coauthor, *Kurs teoreticheskoy elektrokhimii* (Course of Theoretical Electrochemistry) (1951); *Awards*: Stalin Prize (1949); *Died*: 24 Mar 1956.

IZHAKEVICH, Ivan Isidorovich (1864-1962) Painter and illustrator; Pop Artist of Ukr SSR from 1951; *Born*: 18 Jan 1864; *Educ*: 1884-88 studied at Petersburg Acad of Arts as an external student; *Career*: 1888-1917 became widely known for his drawings on Ukr historical and folk subjects which appeared in the journal *Niva*; 1907 moved to Kiev, where he began working as a painter; *Works*: historical canvases "Landlord Exchanging a Serf for Dogs" (1935), etc; illustrations to L. Ukrainka's "Forest Song" (1937); I. Ya. Franko's "Tales of Borislav" (1937); T. G. Shevchenko's "Bard" (1939); I. L. Le's "The Ukraine" (1940); G. F. Kvitka-Osnov'yanenko's "Pan Chalawski" (1941); I. P. Kotlyarevskiy's *Eneida* (The Aeneid), *Natalka Poltavka* and "The Soldier-Sorcerer" (1948-49); *Awards*: Order of the Red Banner of Labor; Badge of Hon; *Died*: 19 Jan 1962.

IZMAILOV, Nikolay Arkad'yevich (1907-1961) Physicochemist; prof from 1948; corresp member, Ukr Acad of Sci from 1957; head, Chair of Physical Chemistry, Khar'kov Univ from 1944; Hon Sci Worker of Ukr SSR; CP member from 1948; *Born*: 1907 in Sukhumi; *Educ*: 1926 grad Khar'kov Technicum of Econ and Finance; 1931 completed postgrad course at Khar'kov Univ; *Career*: main research work concerns electrochemistry of solutions, thermodynamics of non-aqueous solutions, theory of absorption from solutions and its practical application in technol; *Publ*: monograph *Elektrokhimiya rastvorov* (Electrochemistry of Solutions) (1959); *Podschyot khimicheskikh energiy sol'vatatsii i gidratatsii s perenosom i bez perenosa* (Calculation of Chemical Energies of Solutation and Hydration With and Without Transfer) (1960); coauthor, *Vzaimodeystviye aminov s butilovym spirtom, atsetonom i uksusnoy kislotoy* (Interaction of Amines with Butyl Alcohol, Acetone and Acetic Acid) (1960); coauthor, *Konstanty dissotsiatsii osnovaniy v bezvodnoy uksusnoy kislote* (Dissociation Constants of Bases in Anhydrous Acetic Acid) (1961); *Awards*: USSR Acad of Sci Mendeleyev Prize; *Died*: 2 Oct 1961.

IZOTOV, Nikita Alekseyevich (1902–1951) Miner; one of the founders of the Stakhanov movement in the Donbas; CP member from 1936; *Born:* 9 Feb 1902 in vil Malaya Dragunka, Oryol Province, son of a peasant; *Educ*: 1935-37 studied at Ind Acad, Moscow; *Career*: from 1914 worked in the Donbas as apprentice at a briquette plant; from 1922 coal-faceman, *Kochegarka* No 1 Mine, Gorlovka; 1932 became highly proficient in coal mining, achieved high productivity and initiated movement to pass on advanced mining techniques to young and inexperienced miners; 1933 set up a practical training school for improving the skills of young miners; such "Izotov schools" became a feature of the coal and other ind; 11 Sept 1935, at an early stage in the Stakhanov movement, mined 240 tons of coal in six hours, overfulfilling the shift quota 30-fold; Nov 1935 attended 1st All-Union Conference of Stakhanovite Workers in the Kremlin; from late 1937 various exec posts in the coal ind; from 1935 member, USSR Centr Exec Comt; 1937 elected dep, USSR Supr Sov of 1st convocation; 1939 at 18th CPSU(B) Congress elected member, CPSU(B) Centr Auditing Commission; *Publ: Moya zhizn'. Moya rabota* (My Life and Work) (1933); *Awards*: Order of Lenin; Order of the Red

Banner of Labor: medals; *Died*: 4 Jan 1951.

IZVEKOV, Nikolay Pavlovich (1886-1942) Theater historian; specialist in stage equipment and properties; *Born*: 14 Nov 1886; *Career*: 1923 founded and headed first Sov Theater Laboratory at State Inst of Arts History (now Leningrad State Inst of Theater, Music and Cinematography); this laboratory studied and proposed a number of tech innovations for the theater (relief projection, color filters, sound montage, etc); *Publ: Klassifikatsiya teatral'nykh protsessov* (The Classification of Theatrical Processes) (1926); *Stsena. 1 - Arkhitektura stseny* (The Stage. 1 - Stage Architecture) (1935); *Stsena. 2 - Svet na stsene* (The Stage. 2 - Stage Lighting) (1940); *Tekhnika stseny* (Stage Equipment) (1940); *Died*: 19 Jan 1942.

K

KABAK, Nistor Petrovich (1913-1941) Mold poet; *Born*: 23 Nov 1913 in vil Staraya Kul'naya, Odessa Oblast, son of a shepherd; *Career*: in 1930's wrote on Komsomol themes connected with first Five-Year Plans; arrested by State Security organs; *Publ*: verse collections: "First Furrow" (1932); "Fiery Tongues" (1934); "Poems" (1935); "With All My Heart" (1935); in Russian wrote: *Pesnya poley. Stikhi* (Song of the Fields. Poems) (1959); *Died*: 10 July 1941 in imprisonment; posthumously rehabilitated.

KABAKCHIYEV, Khristo Stefanov (1878-1940) Bulgarian revolutionary; official, Bulgarian and int workers' movements; journalist; CPSU member from 1928; *Born*: 14 Jan 1878 in Galati, Rumania, son of a teacher; *Educ*: studied at high-school in Varna; 1897-1902 studied in Geneva; *Career*: 1894 took part in Varna high-school riots; 1896 organized student socialist groups in Gabrovo; 1897 joined Bulgarian Workers' Soc-Democratic Party; 1905-19 member, CC, Bulgarian Workers' Soc-Democratic Party (Close Socialists); 1919-28 member, CC, Bulgarian CP; 1910-23 ed, Party organ *Rabotnicheski vestnik*; deleg, Stuttgart (1907), Copenhagen (1910) and Basel (1912) Congresses of 2nd Internationale; 1914-23 dep, Bulgarian National Assembly; 1920 met Lenin; deleg, 1921, 1922, 1924 and 1928 Comintern Congresses; 1924 elected member, Centr Control Commission, 5th Comintern Congress; 1923 secr, CC, Bulgarian CP; 1923, 1925-26 served prison terms; 1926 emigrated to Vienna after release; 1927 emigrated to USSR ; 1928 joined CPSU(B); assoc, Marx-Engels-Lenin Inst and Inst of History, USSR Acad of Sci; specialized in the history of the Bulgarian CP, Bulgarian history and the history of the Balkans in gen; *Publ: D. Blagoyev i bolgarskiye tesnyaki* (D. Blagoyev and the Bulgarian "Close Socialists") (1935); *Lenin i bolgarskiye tesnyaki* (Lenin and the Bulgarian "Close Socialists") (1934); *Partiya tesnykh sotsialistov, revolyutsiya v Rossii i tsimmerval'dskoye dvizheniye* (The "Close Socialist" Party, the Revolution in Russia and the Zimmerwald Movement) (1957), etc; *Died*: 6 Oct 1940.

KABAKOV, Ivan Dmitriyevich (1891-?) Party official, member, CC, CPSU(B); CP member from 1914; *Born*: 1891; *Career*: worked as a fitter at the Sormovo Plant; until 1916 member, Sormovo Bolshevik Comt; from Mar 1917 Bolshevik dep, Nizhniy Novgorod and Sormovo Sov of Workers' Dep; 1918 chm, Sormovo RSDRP(B) Comt; 1919 chm, Nizhniy Novogorod RCP(B) Comt; 1920-21 chm, Voronezh City Sov; 1922-24 secr, Yaroslavl' Province RCP(B) Comt; 1924 instructor, CC, CPSU(B); 1924-28 secr, Tula Province CPSU(B); Comt; 1928-29 chm, Ural Oblast Exec Comt; from 1929 secr, Ural Oblast CPSU(B) Comt; from 1934 secr, Sverdlovsk Oblast CPSU(B) Comt; elected cand member, CC, CPSU(B) at 13th Congress and member, CC at 14-17th Congresses; arrested by State Security organs; *Died*: date and place of death unknown.

KABLUKOV, Ivan Alekseyevich (1857-1942) Physiochemist; Dr of Chemistry from 1891; prof from 1899; Hon member, USSR Acad of Sci from 1932; Hon Sci Worker of RSFSR from 1929; pioneer of Russian physiochemistry; *Born*: 2 Sept 1857, son of a rural dentist; *Educ*: 1880 grad Moscow Univ with gold medal; *Career*: from 1880 lecturer, Moscow Univ; 1881 sent to Petersburg Univ to do research under A. M. Butlerov on a new method of obtaining formaldehyde; from 1885 assoc prof, Moscow Univ; 1887 defended master's thesis; in same year demonstrated that the formation heat of isomeric organic molecules is not identical; 1889 worked with Arrhenius in Leipzig; from 1899 prof of Chemistry, Moscow Agric Inst (now Timiryazev Agric Acad); 1903-10 prof, from 1910 emeritus prof, Moscow Univ; 1905 used thermal analysis to study mutual salt solutions and established that complete exchange between silver nitrate and silver chloride and between potassium bromide and potassium iodide is accompanied by separation; 1915-33 also head, V. P. Luginin Thermal Laboratory, Moscow Univ; 1928-32 corresp member, USSR Acad of Sci; 1933-41 head, Chair of Chemistry, Moscow Ind Acad; consultant, Moscow Inst of Fertilizers and Insecto-Fungicides and Inst of Applied Mineralogy; pioneered the electrochemistry of anhydrous solutions; introduced the concept of hydration (ion solvation) which provided a basis for the unification of D. I. Mendeleyev's chemical and Van't Hoff and Arrhenius' physical theory of solutions; also studied the history of chemistry; *Publ: Glitseriny, ili tryokhatomnyye spirty i ikh proizvodnyye* (Glycerines or Trivalent Alcohols and Their Derivatives) (1887); *Ob elektroprovodnosti khloristogo vodoroda i sernoy kisloty v razlichnykh rastvoritelyakh* (The Electrical Conductivity of Hydrogen Chloride and Sulfuric Acid in Various Solvents) (1890); *Sovremennyye teorii rastvorov (Vant-Goffa i Arreniusa) v svyazi s ucheniyem o khimicheskom ravnovesii* (Modern Theories of Solution [Van't Hoff and Arrhenius'] in Relation to the Theory of Chemical Equilibrium) (1891); *Osnovnyye nachala neorganicheskoy khimii* (The Basic Principles of Inorganic Chemistry) (1900); *Osnovnyye nachala fizicheskoy khimii* (The Basic Principles of Physical Chemistry) (1900); coauthor, *Krymskiye solyanyye ozera* (The Salt Lakes of the Crimea) (1915); *Pravilo faz v primenenii k nasyshchennym rastvoram soley* (The Phase Rule Applied to Saturated Salt Solutions) (1934); *Termokhimiya* (Thermochemistry) (1934); *O mede, voske pchelinom kleye i ikh podmesyakh* (Honey, Wax, Bees-Gum and Their Admixtures) 1941; coauthor, *Fizicheskaya i kolloidnaya khimiya* (Physical and Colloid Chemistry) (1949); *Awards*: Order of Lenin; Order of the Red Banner of Labor; *Died*: 5 May 1942.

KABLUKOV, Nikolay Alekseyevich (1849-1919) Russian econ and statistician; *Born*: 1849; *Career*: prof, Moscow Univ from 1903; 1885-1907 headed statistical section, Moscow Provincial Zemstvo; 1877-79 supervised compilation of *Sborniki statisticheskikh svedeniy po Moskovskoy gubernii* (Collections of Statistical Information on Moscow Province); contributed to many newspapers and journals; 1917 participated in work of Main Land Comt, Provisional Govt; after 1917 Oct Revol worked for Centr Statistical Bd; taught and wrote research works; in various of his works, especially *Razvitiye kapitalizma v Rossii* (The Development of Capitalism in Russia), Lenin sharply criticized Kablukov's views; *Publ: Vopros o rabochikh v sel'skom khozyaystve* (Workers in Agriculture) (1884); *Lektsii po ekonomii sel'skogo khozyaystva* (Lectures on the Economics of Agriculture) (1897); *Ob usloviyakh razvitiya krest'yanskogo khozyaystva v Rossii* (Conditions of the Development of Peasant Agriculture in Russia) (1899); *Statistika* (Statistics) (1904); *Politicheskaya ekonomika* (Political Economy) (1918), etc; *Died*: 1919.

KACHALOV, Nikolay Nikolayevich (1883-1961) Glass technologist; Dr of Tech Sci from 1935; prof from 1930; corresp member, USSR Acad of Sci from 1933; Hon Sci and Tech Worker of RSFSR from 1935; *Born*: 1883 in Dresden, Germany; *Educ*: 1911 grad Ore Dept, Petersburg Mining Inst; *Career*: 1911-23 laboratory asst, technician, then tech dir, Petrograd Phosphorus Works; 1916-18 construction chief, Petrograd Glass Works; 1918-20 member, Sci Collegium, 1920-29 dep dir, from 1929 chm, Sci Collegium, State Ceramic Research Inst, Leningrad; 1923-30 simultaneously tech dir, Leningrad Optical Glass Works; from 1930 prof and head, Chair of Glass Technol, 1937-39 dep sci and studies dir, Leningrad Sov Technol Inst; 1932-46 dep dir and laboratory head, from 1937 also consultant, State Optical Inst, Leningrad; 1948-51 dep dir, from 1951 head, Laboratory of Cold Silicate Processing, Inst of Silicate Chemistry, USSR Acad of Sci; from 1951 also bd member, Leningrad Dept, All-Union Soc for the Dissemination of Polit and Sci Knowledge; *Publ: Osnovy protsessov shlifovki i polirovki stekla* (The Principles of Glass Grinding and Polishing) (1946); *Osnovy proizvodstva opticheskogo stekla* (The Principles of Optical Glass Production) (1960), etc; *Awards*: Stalin Prize (1947); Order of Lenin; two Orders of the Red Banner of Labor; Order of the Red Star; medals; *Died*: 19 June 1961.

KACHALOV (real name: SHVERUBOVICH), Vasiliy Ivanovich (1875-1948) Russian actor; Pop Artiste of the USSR from 1936; *Born*: 11 Feb 1875 in Vilnius, son of a priest; *Educ*: studied at Petersburg Univ; *Career*: while at high school played Khlestakov,

Podkolyosin in *Zhenit'ba* (The Marriage), Neschastlivtsev, etc; 1893 began to study law at Petersburg Univ and took part in student drama circle; 1996-97 worked at Suvorin Theater (Theater of the Lit and Art Soc, Petersburg); summer 1897 accompanied V. P. Dalmatov on tour and performed major roles, such as Boris Godunov in A. K. Tolstoy's *Smert' Ioanna Groznogo* (The Death of Ivan the Terrible); 1897-1900 performed in Kazan' and Saratov with Assoc of Actors roles of: Mitya in *Bednost' ne porok* (Poverty Is No Vice); Dudukin in *Bez viny vinovatyye* (Guilty Without Guilt); Prince Shakhovskoy in A. K. Tolstoy's *Tsar' Fyodor Ivanovich*; Ivan the Terrible in Ostrovskiy and Gedeonov's *Vasilisa Melent'yeva* and in A. K. Tolstoy's *Smert' Ioanna Groznogo* (The Death of Ivan the Terrible); Horatio in "Hamlet"; Cassius in "Julius Caesar"; the President in "Kabale und Liebe," etc; spring 1900 moved to Moscow Arts Theater and soon became one of its leading actors; his work under Stanislavskiy and Nemirovich-Danchenko caused him to revise much of his acting experience and exchange his high-flown declamatory style for a restrained, profound and noble simplicity; 1900-48 performed 55 roles at Moscow Arts Theater; his first performance at this theater in 1900 in the role of Tsar Berendey in *Snegurochka* (The Snow Maiden) was a tremendous success; possessed tremendous stage presence, an unusually colorful voice and great plasticity of movement; 1902 played the tramp Baron in *Na dne* (The Lower Depths), one of his most celebrated roles which he continued to perform for 45 years; 1903-04 Bolshevik N. E. Bauman hid in his apartment (the police had Kachalov listed as a suspect person); during the years preceding the 1905 Revol and later took part in student charity concerts; 1906, during a Moscow Arts Theater foreign tour, read Gorky's *Pesnya o Burevestnike* (Song of the Storm Petrel) in Berlin; *Roles*: Pimen in *Boris Godunov* (1907); Glumov in *Na vsyakogo mudretsa dovol'no prostoty* (There's a Simpleton in Every Sage) (1910); Karenin in *Zhivoy trup* (The Living Corpse) (1911); Gorskiy in Turgenev's *Gde tonko, tam i rvyotsya* (The Chain Is No Stronger Than Its Weakest Link) (1912); Chatskiy (1906 and 1914); Don Juan in Pushkin's *Kamennyy gost'* (The Stone Guest) (1915); Brand in Ibsen's "Brand" (1906); Ivan Karamazov in *Brat'ya Karamazovy* (The Brothers Karamazov) after Dostoyevsky (1910); Hamlet (1911); Nikolay Stavrogin in the play of the same name (1913), after Dostoyevsky's novel *Besy* (The Devils); Fyodor Krasnokutskiy in Merezhkovskiy's *Budet radost'* (There Will Be Joy) (1916); after 1917 Revol appeared in concerts reading works of Gorky and Shakespeare, monologues from Byron's "Manfred" and Blok's *Dvenadtsat'* (The Twelve) and *Skify* (The Scythians); July 1919, during a Khar'kov tour by part of the Moscow Arts Theater troupe, cut off from Sov Russia by White Army; 1919-22 headed the Moscow Arts Theater's "Kachalov Group" and appeared with it in Bulgaria, Yugoslavia, Czechoslovakia, Germany, Austria and Scandinavia; 1922 returned to Moscow; 1922-24 took part in Moscow Arts Theater tours of Europe and America; appeared abroad in three new roles: Tsar Fyodor in A. K. Tolstoy's *Tsar' Fyodor Ivanovich*, Gayev in *Vishnyovyy sad* (The Cherry Orchard), Stockman in Ibsen's "Doctor Stockman"; 1926 played Nicholas I in Kugel"s *Nikolay I i dekabristy* (Nicholas I and the Decembrists); 1927 played partisan leader Vershinin in *Bronepoyezd 14-69* (Armored Train 14-69); 1930 his performance of the Author in *Voskreseniye* (Resurrection) after L. N. Tolstoy was one of the highlights of his career; also did radio work with an unusually large repertoire which included, besides excerpts from Russian and foreign classics, the prose of Gogol, Tolstoy, Chekhov and Gorky and the poetry of Pushkin, Lermontov, Blok, Mayakovsky, Yesenin, Bagritskiy and others; at concerts he characterized: Egmont in Goethe's "Egmont"; Richard III; Brutus and Anthony in Shakespeare's "Julius Caesar"; Famusov; performed Don Quixote in the radio adaptation of Cervantes' novel, etc; created special genre of dramatic performance, so-called"arrangements" in which he took several roles: scenes from Act 4 of *Na dne* (The Lower Depths); Act 2 of "Hamlet", Act 1 of *Na vsyakogo mudretsa dovol'no prostoty* (There's a Simpleton in Every Sage), etc; played the Governor in the film *Belyy oryol* (The White Eagle); read the introduction in the film *Putyovka v zhizn'* (A Start in Life); *Awards*: Stalin Prize (1943); Order of Lenin; Order of the Red Banner of Labor; medals; *Died*: 30 Sept 1948 in Moscow; Bolshoy Drama Theater in Kazan' named after him.

KADATSKIY (pseudonym: KODATSKIY), Ivan Fyodorovich (1893-1939) Party and govt official; CP member from 1914; *Born*: 1893, son of a worker; *Career*: lathe-operator; did Party work in Petrograd; after 1917 Feb Revol member for Vyborg Distr, Petrograd RSDRP(B) Comt and member, Petrograd Sov; deleg, 6th RSDRP(B) Congress; after 1917 Oct Revol did exec work in Party and econ admin; chm, Leningrad Oblast Exec Comt; elected cand member, CC, at 14th and 15th, and member, CC, at 16th and 17th CPSU(B) Congresses; arrested by State Security organs; *Died*: 1939 in imprisonment.

KADOMTSEV, Erazm Samuilovich (pseudonyms: Pyotr, Pavel) (1884-1965) Revolutionary; CP member from 1901; *Born*: 8 Mar 1884 in Birsk; *Career*: 1896 joined revol movement; 1904-05 did propaganda work among soldiers in Far East; 1905-07 member, Combat Center, CC, RSDRP during Revol; late 1905 in charge of armed workers' detachments in Ufa; 1906 in the Urals, then in Petersburg; deleg Tammerfors Conference of Armed Combat Organizations, RSDRP; 1908 arrested and exiled to Tobol'sk Province; 1909 escaped and emigrated to France; during 1917 Oct Revol helped to organize armed workers' detachments in the Urals for the campaign against Dutov; 1922 commanded OGPU troops; one of the founders of the Sov film ind; before WW 2 worked for Min of Agric; from 1941 pensioner; *Died*: 6 Mar 1965.

KADYRI, Abdulla (pseudonym: DZHULKUNBAY) (1894-1939) Uzbek writer; *Born*: Apr 1894 in Tashkent, son of a gardener; *Educ*: 1915-17 studied at a medressah; mastered Arabic and Persian; *Career*: one of the pioneers of Uzbek prose; 1915 first work published; in his early period influenced by Djadidism; after 1917 Oct Revol contributed to satirical journal *Mushtum*; helped compile Russian-Uzbek Dictionary; translated into Uzbek Gogol's *Zhenit'ba* (The Wedding) and Chekhov's *Vishnyovyy sad* (Cherry Orchard), etc; *Publ*: play "The Unfortunate Bridegroom" (1915); story "The Libertine" (1915); satirical stories "What Wicked Tashpulat Is Saying"; "From Kalvak Makhsum's Notebook"; novels "Bygone Days" (1923-24); "The Scorpion from the Altar" (1929); novelettes "I Shall Fight Against the Sun"; "Abid-Ketmen"' (1935); *Died*: 26 Aug 1939.

KADYRLI (ISRAFILBEKOV), Movsum Nadzhmeddin-ogly (1892-1941) Physician; pioneer of Azer health service; CP member from 1911; *Born*: 1892 in Azer; *Educ*: 1917 grad Med Fac, Kiev Univ; *Career*: after grad returned to Baku, where he did revol work; member Baku RSDRP Comt; 1920, after establishment of Sov rule in Azer, head, Polit Bd, Azer Pop Comrt of the Navy, then Azer Pop Comr of Soc Security; 1922-34 Azer Pop Comr of Health; directed the establishment of med facilities in the towns and villages of the Azer SSR; paid particular attention to the hospital building program, especially in rural areas; 1934 supervised campaign against malaria, which was then widespread in the Azer SSR; from 1934 prof of the history of med, Azer Med Inst; 1920-35 member, CC, CP(B) Azer; member, Azer and Transbaykal Centr Exec Comt; wrote numerous works on health service org, epidemiology and the history of med; *Publ*: coauthor, *Vvedeniye k materialam po izucheniyu Isti-Su* (An Introduction to Study Material on Isti-Su) (1930); *Problema bor'by s malariyey v Azerbaydzhanskoy SSR* (The Campaign Against Malaria in the Azerbaydzhani SSR) (1937); *Died*: 1941.

KAGAN, Avrom Yakovlevich (1901-1965) Jewish writer; *Born*: 9 Jan 1901 in Berdichev, son of an office worker; *Career*: 1922 first work printed; member, Jewish Section, All-Ukr Proletarian Writers' Union; ed secr, Jewish monthly *Prolit*; translated into Yiddish works of Gorky, Korolenko, Gaydar, P. Panch, I. Mikitenko, etc; *Publ*: verse collection *Notches* (1923); collection *Tripol'ye* (1925); novelette "Alcove People" (1928); stories "Brokhe from the Children's Home" (1925); "On a Spring Night"; "Milk"; collection of stories "Fragments" (1930); play "Energy" (1932); novels "Engineers" (1932); "Arn Liberman" (1935); novelette "On the Gnilopyatka River" (1937); novel *Sholom-Aleykhem* (1961), etc; *Died*: 17 Dec 1965 in Kiev.

KAGAN, Naum Iosifovich (1918-1963) Eng; specialist in pipe manufacturing; CP member from 1954; *Born*: 10 Sept 1918; *Educ*: 1941 grad Dnepropetrovsk Metallurgical Inst; *Career*: July-Sept 1941 worked at Southern Pipe Metallurgical Plant, Nikopol', then at First Ural New Pipe Plant; from Aug 1943 designer, technologist and asst shop mang at a pipe-rolling plant in Chelyabinsk; helped to develop standard furnace unit for continuous high-speed pipe-welding; *Awards:* Lenin Prize (1963); *Died*: 22 May 1963.

KAGAN, Veniamin Fyodorovich (1869-1953) Mathematician; Dr of Mathematics; Hon Sci Worker of RSFSR from 1929; *Born*: 1869; *Educ*: 1892 grad Kiev Univ; *Career*: from 1897 assoc prof,

Novorossiysk Univ; before 1917 Oct Revol co-founder, Odessa Women's Courses; ed, journal *Vestnik opytnoy fiziki i elementarnoy matematiki*; co-founder and assoc, *Mathesis* Sci Publ House; 1922-30 held seminars on tensor calculus at Mathematical Research Inst, Moscow Univ; from 1923 prof, Moscow Unic; from 1890 onwards popularized N.I. Lobachevskiy's mathematical teachings; in his book "The Principles of Geometry" he expounded the axiomatics of Euclidian space and analyzed their consistency and independence; in his studies of tensor calculus and its applications to geometry he developed the theory of subprojective spaces representing a broad generalization of Lobachevskiy's space; founded the Sov school of differential geometric tensor calculus; *Publ: Ocherk geometricheskoy sistemy Lobachevskogo* (A Study of Lobachevskiy's System of Geometry) (1900); *Osnovaniya geometrii* (The Principles of Geometry) (2 vol, 1905-07); *Osnovy teorii poverkhnostey v tenzornom izlozhenii* (The Principles of the Theory of Surfaces in Tensor Presentation) (2 vol, 1947-48); *Lobachevskiy* (1948); *Osnovaniya geometrii* (The Principles of Geometry) (Part 1, 1949); *Awards*: Order of the Red Banner of Labor; Stalin Prize (1943); *Died*: 1953.

KAGANOVICH, Mikhail Moiseyevich (1889- ?) Govt official; CP member from 1905; *Born*: 1889; *Career*: metalworker by profession; often arrested for revol activities; 1917 chm, Mil Revol Comt in Arzamas; then chm, Surazh Sov of Workers and Peasants' Dep; from 1920 plen, Arzamas Province Exec Comt; food comr in Arzamas; from 1921 secr, Vyksa Uyezd CPSU(B) Comt; 1923-27 chm, Nizhniy Novgorod Province Sovnarkhoz; at 15th and 16th CPSU(B) Congresses elected member, CPSU(B) Centr Control Comission; group leader and Collegium member, USSR Pop Comrt of Workers and Peasants' Inspection; from 1930 Presidium member, CPSU(B) Centr Control Commission; from 1931 head, Main Machine Building Bd, and dep chm, USSR Supr Sovnarkhoz; from 1932 USSR Dep Pop Comr of Heavy Ind; 1935 appointed head, Main Bd of the Aircraft Ind; from 17th Congress (1934) member, CC, CPSU(B) and cand member, Org Bureau, CC, CPSU(B); member, All-Russian and USSR Centr Exec Comt; arrested by State Security organs; *Awards*: Order of Lenin (1936); *Died*: date and place of death unknown.

KAKHIANI, Mikhail Ivanovich (1896- ?) Party official; CP member from 1917; *Born*: 1896; *Career*: after 1917 Oct Revol held exec party posts; 1922-30 secr, CC, CP(B) Geo; from 1931 secr, Centr Asian Bureau, CC, CPSU(B); elected cand member, CC at 16th CPSU(B) Congress; member, Party Control Commission at 17th CPSU(B) Congress; arrested by State Security organs; *Died*: date and place of death unknown.

KAKTYN', Artur Martynovich (1893-1937) Party and govt official; CP member from 1916; *Born*: 1893; *Career*: 1914 began revol work among Petrograd student circles; during 1917 Feb Revol member, Lat Rayon RSDRP(B) Comt, Petrograd; ed, Lat Party organ, "Prol. Cina"; deleg from Lat Rayon to 6th RSDRP(B) Congress; instructor, Centr Council of Factory and Plant Comts; 1918 plenum member, Supr Sovnarkhoz; from 1919 member, Fergana Oblast Revol Comt; chm Centr Sovnarkhoz of Turkestan; member, Turkestan Kray CP(B) Comt; from 1920 Presidium member, then chm, Ukr Sovnarkhoz; 1922-25 dep exec ed, "Ekonomicheskiy zhurnal"; member, Centr Control Commission of 12th and 13th convocations; 1925 Collegium member, Pop Comrt of Domestic Trade; 1926 collegium member, Pop Comrt of Trade and exec ed, journal "Torgovyye izvestiya"; 1926-29 asst business mang, USSR Sovnarkhoz and secr, Labor and Defense Council; 1930 dep bd chm, State Bank; 1931 exec ed, newspaper "Za pishchevuyu industriyu"; bd member USSR Pop Comrt of Supply; 1931-34 Collegium member, USSR Pop Comrt of Workers and Peasants' Inspection; and head, Cotton Irrigation Group; from 1934 dep chm, Tadzh Sovnarkhoz; arrested by State Security organs; *Died*: 1937 in imprisonment.

KAKURIN, Nikolay Yevgen'yevich (1883-1936) Mil commander and historian; col, Gen Staff, Russian Army; *Born*: 4 Sept 1883 in Orel, son of a nobleman; *Educ*: grad Mikhail Artillery College; 1910 grad Nikolay Mil Acad; *Career*: 1914-18 senior staff officer, 10th Army Corps; chief of staff, 71st Infantry Div, 3rd Transbaykal Cossack Brigade; commander, 7th Caucasian Rifle Regt on active duty; from Dec 1918 volunteer, Galician Army, West Ukr Pop Republ, which fought simultaneously against Poland and the RSFSR; from early 1920 in Red Army; 1920 div chief of staff, then commander, 10th Rifle Div; commander, 3rd Army; dep to commander (Tukhachevsky), Western Front; 1921 chief of staff, army group assigned to put down Antonov rebellion; 1922 troop commander, Bukhara-Fergana Distr, where he fought against the Basmachi, 1921-22 senior tactics instructor, Red Army Mil Acad; from 1923 head, Dept (then Section) for the History of the Civil War, Red Army Staff; wrote numerous books and articles on the history of the Civil War and over 300 works on operations, tactics and strategy; in his works on the war against Poland he expressed the opinion that the Sov setbacks at Warsaw in 1920 were the result of commander Tukhachevskiy's miscalculations and the failure of the command on the Southwestern Front (A. I. Yegorov and Stalin) to transfer three armies to the Western Front; June 1930 arrested by OGPU; 19 Feb 1932 sentenced to 10 years imprisonment; *Publ: Kak srazhalas' revolyutsiya* (How the Revolution Was Fought) (2 vol, 1925-26), etc; *Awards*: Order of the Red Banner; Order of Bukhara; Red Star, 1st Class; *Died*: 29 July 1936 in imprisonment; 5 Jan 1957 posthumously rehabilitated.

KALANDARISHVILI, Grigoriy Matveyevich (1904-1965) Philosopher; Dr of Philosophy from 1962; CP member from 1957; *Born*: 1904; *Educ*: 1931 grad Tbilisi Univ; 1935 completed post-grad studies at Moscow Inst of Philosophy, Lit and History; *Career*: 1940-60 lectured on philosophy and did research on dialectical logic; from 1960 head, Dept of Logic, Inst of Philosophy, Geo Acad of Sci; *Publ: Ocherki po istorii logiki v Gruzii* (Studies on the History of Logic in Georgia) (1952); *O sootnoshenii dialekticheskoy logiki i logiki formal'noy* (The Relationship of Dialectical Logic and Formal Logic) (1959); coauthor, *V. I. Lenin o 'Nauke Logiki' Gegelya* (Lenin on Hegel's "Science of Logic") (1959); *Dialekticheskaya logika ob otrazhenii v myshlenii ob'yektivnykh protivorechiy* (Dialectical Logic on Reflection in the Ratiocination of Objective Contradictions) (1961); *Died*: 1965.

KALANDARISHVILI (pseudonyms: NESTOR; DEDUSHKA), Nestor Aleksandrovich (1867-1922) Revolutionary; partisan leader in Eastern Siberia during Civil War; CP member from 1917; *Born*: 1876 in Geo; *Educ*: studied at Tiflis Teachers' Training Seminary; *Career*: 1903 joined Socialist-Revol Party while studying in Tiflis; 1905 took part in Geo peasant uprising; frequently imprisoned and exiled; 1917 joined "Anarchist-Communist" Party and helped to establish Sov rule in Irkutsk; spring 1918 organized a partisan detachment on orders from the Irkutsk RCP(B) Comt; summer 1919 fought in the rear of Gen Kolchak's army; spring 1920 fought against Japanese in Transbaykal; Jan 1921 joined RCP(B) with membership backdated to 1917; from spring 1921 in charge of Korean revol detachments in Far East; from Dec 1921 commander of armed forces, Yakutsk Province; *Died*: 6 Mar 1922 killed while suppressing a peasant revolt.

KALANTAR, Levon Aleksandrovich (1891-1959) Arm stage dir and actor; prof from 1944; Pop Artiste of Arm SSR from 1954; CP member from 1942; *Born*: 16 Jan 1891; *Educ*: 1916 grad Oriental Fac, Petersburg Univ; studied under stage dir of Alexandrine Theater and under stage dir A. Sanin and I. Shmidt; *Career*: 1916 began stage work in Tiflis as actor and stage dir; 1921 founded Arm Shaumyan Theater in Tbilisi; helped found Yerevan Sundukyan Theater and until 1928 chief stage dir of this theater; 1928-30 chief stage dir, Baku Arm Theater; 1931 founded in Yerevan Gorky Workers' Theater and until 1935 chief stage dir of this theater; 1937-43 and 1957-59 chief stage dir, Yerevan Russian Theater; also taught stagecraft; from 1944 prof, Yerevan Arts and Theater Inst; wrote reviews and articles on theater; translated into Arm Gogol's *Revizor* (The Government Inspector), *Zhenit'ba* (The Wedding), etc; *Works*: staged plays: "Die Räuber" (1922); Hauptmann's "Sunken Bell" (1922); "Taming of the Shrew" (1923); Lunacharskiy's *Yad* (Poison) (1926); Paronyan's *Dyadya Bagdasar* (Uncle Bagdasar) (1927); "Lyubov' Yarovaya" (1927); *Na dne* (Lower Depths) (1929); *Revizor* (The Government Inspector) (1930); *Myatezh* (Mutiny) (1930); *Svad'ba Krechinskogo* (Krechinskiy's Wedding) (1933); *Les* (Forest) (1934); "Merchant of Venice" (1937); Rakhmanov's "Professor Polezhayevv" (1957); Shirvanzade's "Evil Spirit" (1959), etc; *Died*: 29 Oct 1959.

KALASHNIKOV, Aleksey Georgiyevich (1893-1962) Physicist, pedag and educ official; Dr of Physics and Mathematics; prof; member, RSFSR Acad of Pedag Sci from 1947; CP member from 1942; *Born*: 28 Feb 1893; *Educ*: 1917 grad Fac of Physics and Mathematics, Moscow Univ; *Career*: from 1917 taught physics and mathematics at high-schools in Moscow; 1919 began pedag research; head, Moscow Dept of Professional Training; head,

Teachers' Training Dept, Main Professional Training Bd; head, Ed Section, State Publishing House; from 1941 in charge of research work at Inst of Theoretical Physics; USSR Acad of Sci; 1945-46 RSFSR Dep Pop Comr of Educ; 1946-48 RSFSR Pop Comr of Educ; from 1948 worked at Inst of Geophysics, USSR Acad of Sci; from 1953 senior assoc, Inst of Teaching Methods, RSFSR Acad of Pedag Sci; dep, USSR Supr Sov of 2nd convocation; specialized in pedag theory and methods of teaching physics in secondary schools and polytechnicums; wrote numerous works on the pedag process, the public educ and workers' polytechnic systems, the practical training of students, etc; 1927-29 ed, "Pedagogicheskaya entsiklopediya" (3 vol); did research on the design and utilization of visual aids for physics teaching and trade training; also did considerable work on theoretical physics and geophysics; *Publ: Opyt postroyeniya industrial'no-trudovoy shkoly blizhayshego budyshchego* (Experience in Building Industrial Trade Schools for the Immediate Future) (1922); *Industrial'no-trudovaya shkola* (The Industrial Trade School) (1924); ed, *Sovetskaya proizvodstvenno-trudovaya shkola* (The Soviet Trade Apprenticeship School) (2 vol, 1928); *Ocherki marksistkoy pedagogiki* (Studies on Marxist Pedagogics) (Vol 1, 1929); *O podgotovke uchashchikhsya semiletnikh i srednikh shkol k prakticheskoy deyatel'nosti* (Training the Pupils of Seven-Year and Secondary Schools for Practical Work) (1949); ed, *Voprosy politekhnicheskogo obucheniya v shkole* (Polytechnic Training at School) (1953); *Died*: 2 Jan 1962.

KALASHNIKOV, Vasiliy Dmitriyevich (1904-1958) Govt official; CP member from 1926; *Born*: 1904 in vil Balanda, Saratov Province; *Career*: from 1926 held exec Komsomol, Party and govt posts; from 1940 worked in grain procurement system; rep for Irkutsk and Kuybyshev oblasts, USSR Pop Comrt of Procurement; 1944 rep for Ukr, USSR Min of Procurement; from 1954 rep, RSFSR Min of Procurement; from July 1956 RSFSR First Dep Min of Grain Products; dep, Ukr Supr Sov; dep RSFSR Supr Sov of 1956 convocation; *Awards*: Order of Lenin; Order of the Fatherland War, 1st Class; Order of the Red Banner of Labor; medals; *Died*: 23 Aug 1958.

KALASHNIKOV, Viktor Petrovich (1893-1959) Pharmacologist; maj-gen, Med Corps; Dr of Med from 1938; prof from 1939; *Born*: 1893 in Bugul'ma, Samara Province; *Educ*: 1917 grad Petrograd Mil Med Acad; *Career*: after grad served as mil surgeon in Russian Army and Red Army; returned to Petrograd (Leningrad) for two years of postgrad studies at Mil Med Acad; 1926-35 senior lecturer, Chair of Pharmagnostics and Pharmacy, Leningrad Mil Med Acad; 1935 defended cand thesis; 1935-39 assoc prof, from 1939 prof, Chair of Pharmacology and Pharmacy; Leningrad Mil Med Acad; from 1943 until death head, Chair of Pharmacy and Medicinal Botany, Leningrad Mil Med Acad; apart from problems relating to mil pharmacy also did research on raw materials, techniques of obtaining drugs from medicinal plants, the rationalization of pharmacopoeial stocking, etc; 1945 established nursery at Chair of Pharmacology and Pharmacy containing over 170 varieties of medicinal plants; Bureau member, Pharmacopoeia Comt, USSR Min of Health; member, Learned Med Council, Main Mil Med Bd, USSR Armed Forces; member, Learned Council, Leningrad Chemical Pharmaceutical Research Inst; co-ed, pharmacology section, *Bol'shaya meditsinskaya entsiklopediya* (Large Medical Encyclopedia) (2nd ed); *Publ: Ob efirnom masle kavkazskoy valeriany* (The Ethereal Oil of the Caucasian Valerian) (1919); *K voprosu o sile deystviya landysha i o kharakteristike yego preparatov* (The Efficacy of Lily of the Valley and the Characteristics of Its Derivatives) (1924); *O zhirnom masle semyan fistashek* (The Fatty Oil of Pistachio Seeds) (1927); *Kak sobirat lekarstvennyye rasteniya* (How to Gather Medicinal Plants) (1929); *Ob emil'giruyushchikh i obvolakivayushchikh svoystvakh vishnyovogo kleya* (The Emulsifying and Encapsulating Properties of Cherry Gum) (1934); coauthor, *Rezul'taty ispytaniya tryokh obraztsov otechestvennogo revenya* (The Results of Tests with Three Varieties of Rhubarb in the USSR) (1937); doctor's thesis *Soderzhaniye i kharakteristika deystvuyushchikh nachal kul'tiviruyemykh i otechesvtvennykh dikorastushchikh vidov lobelii* (The Contents and Characteristics of the Effective Agents of Cultivated and Wild-Growing Species of Asthma Weed in the USSR) (1937); *Farmako-khimicheskiye i farmakologicheskiye issledovaniya nekotorykh otkharkivayushchikh sredstv* (Pharmochemical and Pharmocological Investigations of Certain Expectorants) (1937); *Biologicheskiye ispytanya lobelina, vydelennogo iz odutloy lobelii, kul'tivirovannoy pod Leningradom* (Biological Tests of Lobeline Extracted from Indian Tobacco Grown Near Leningrad) (1939); *O soderzhanii alkaloidov v kul'tiviruyemykh i dikorastushchikh vidov lobelii* (The Alkaloid Content of Cultivated and Wild-Growing Species of Asthma Weed) (1939); *O lekarstvennoy flore Sredney Azii* (The Medicinal Flora of Central Asia) (1942); coauthor, *Opyt kul'tury odutloy lobelii v subtropicheskikh usloviyakh Sredney Azii* (Experience in Cultivating Indian Tobacco in the Subtropical Conditions of Central Asia) (1942); *Khimiya i lekarstvovedeniye* (Chemistry and Pharmacology) (1944); *Botanika i lekarstvovedeniye* (Botany and Pharmacology) (1945); *Zoologiya i lekarstvovedeniye* (Zoology and Pharmacology) (1946); *Predvaritel'nyye dannyye o sostavnykh nachalakh yasentsa turkestanskogo* (Preliminary Data on the Composite Elements of Turkestani Dittany) (1946); *Opyt dvukhletnikh nablyudeniy na uchastke lekarstvennykh rasteniy kafedry farmatsii* (The Results of Two Years of Observations at the Medicial Plants Section of the Chair of Pharmacy) (1947); *Rukovodstvo po retsepture* (A Prescription Manual) (1954); *Lekarstvennyye rasteniya severo-zapadnoy chasti RSFSR* (The Medicial Plants of the Northwestern RSFSR) (1957); *Died*: 1959.

KALEDIN, Aleksey Maksimovich (1861-1918) Don Cossack; cavalry gen, Russian Army; one of leaders of anti-Sov campaign on the Don in 1917 Oct Revol; *Born*: 1861; *Career*: 1914-17 commanded cavalry div, army corps, then 8th Army on Southwestern Front; May 1917 removed from command of 8th Army by Brusilov for opposing new democratic trends in army; 30 June 1917 elected ataman of Don Army and head, Don Army Govt; Nov 1917 refused to recognize Sov regime and proclaimed autonomy of Don Oblast; when the Sov regime attempted to subdue the Don area by force, he joined Gen Alekseyev's Volunteer Army; late Dec 1917 became member, of triumvirate (Alekseyev, Kaledin and Kornilov) which directed the anti-Sov campaign in southern Russia; 11 Feb 1918 resigned as ataman of the Don Army, convinced of the futility of further resistance after the Volunteer Army's withdrawal from the Don; *Died*: 11 Feb 1918 committed suicide.

KALININ, Fyodor Ivanovich (1882-1920) Russian lit critic; CP member from 1903; *Born*: 14 Feb 1882 in vil Shilkovo, Vladimir Province, son of a weaver; *Career*: started work at age 15 (joiner, typesetter, weaver); 1905 led armed rebellion in Aleksandrov; 1909-11 attended Party schools on Capri and in Bologna; member, CC, "Proletkul't" cultural and educ org; wrote lit criticism; 1918-20 contributed to journals "Proletarskaya kul'tura," "Gorn" and "Gryadushcheye"; *Publ:* article "The Worker Type in Literature" Oct Revol Collegium member, RSFSR Pop Comrt of Educ; member, CC, *Proletkul't* cultural and educ org; wrote lit criticism; 1918-20 contributed to journals *Proletarskaya kul'tura, Gorn* and *Gryadushcheye; Publ*: article "The Worker Type in Literature" (1912); coauthor, anthology *Problemy proletarskoy kul'tury* (Problems of Proletarian Culture) (1919); *Died*: 5 Feb 1920 of typhus in Moscow.

KALININ, Konstantin Alekseyevich (1889-1940) Aircraft designer; CP member from 1923; *Born*: 29 Dec 1889 in Valuyki, Voronezh Province, son of a soldier; *Educ*: 1925 grad Kiev Polytech Inst; *Career*: 1925 designed K-1 passenger plane; from 1926 head, Design Bureau, Ukr Air Fleet; 1926-27 designed K-2 and K-3 aircraft; 1928-29 designed K-4 and K-5 passenger planes, which replaced foreign-built airliners in USSR; 1930-33 designed several aircraft, including the K-7 airliner for 120 passengers and 12 crew; 1937 designed K-12 tailless bomber; 1938 designed K-13 special-purpose bomber with rear gun-turret; *Died*: 21 Apr 1940.

KALININ, Mikhail Ivanovich (1875-1946) Party and govt official; Presidium chm, USSR Supr Sov; CP member from 1898; *Born*: 19 Nov 1875 in vil Verkhnyaya Troitsa, Tver' Province (now Kalinin Oblast); *Educ*: 1889 grad vil school; *Career*: from 1893 apprentice lathe operator, "Old Arsenal" Plant, Petersburg; from 1896 lathe operator, Putilov Plant, where he joined the revol movement; organized Marxist group which became part of the Petersburg League for the Liberation of the Working Class; July 1899 arrested for involvement with League; Apr 1900, after ten months in jail, exiled to Tiflis, where he worked as a lathe operator at the Main Railroad Sheds and joined the center group of the Tiflis RSDRP Org; Aug 1900 helped to organize strikes, arrested and imprisoned in Metekhi Castle; Mar 1901 exiled to Revel, where he found lathe work first at the "Volta" Plant, then in the railroad sheds; 1902 organized a Marxist group and an underground printing shop; worked as an agent and corresp for the newspaper

"Iskra"; Jan 1903 arrested and imprisoned in "Kresty" jail, Petersburg; July 1903 exiled to Revel again; early 1904 arrested and exiled to Povenets, Olonets Province; 1905 moved illegally to Petersburg on orders from the Bolshevik Center; Oct 1905 pardoned and, after establishing legal residence, headed the Bolshevik org at Putilov Plant; member, Narva Distr RSDRP Comt; 1906 took work at a pipe plant and was elected to Petersburg RSDRP Comt; 1906 deleg, 4th RSDRP Congress; 1908-10 worked in Moscow as a fitter at Lubyanka Power Plant and Mius streetcar substation; Sept 1910 arrested; Nov 1910 exiled to home village; 1911-12 worked as a gage-maker at an artillery plant in Petersburg; member, Petersburg RSDRP Comt and head, Vyborg Distr RSDRP Org; elected cand member, CC and member, Russian Bureau, CC at 6th RSDRP Congress in Prague; co-founder, newspaper *Pravda*; collaborated with Bolshevik faction in 4th State Duma; summer 1912 led strike at artillery plant; 1913-15 worked at "Ayvaz" Plant and continued Party Work; during WW 1 sided with internationalists; Jan 1916 arrested for involvement with Petersburg RSDRP Comt; after a year in jail sentenced to exile in Eastern Siberia but went into hiding and did underground Party work in Petrograd; early 1917 took active part in Feb Revol; member, first legal Petrograd RSDRP(B) Comt and its rep in the Bureau, CC, RSDRP(B); member, ed bd, "Pravda"; Spet 1917 elected member, Petrograd City Duma, and chm, Lesnovsk Distr Council; after 1917 Oct Revol again elected to Petrograd City Duma, which elected him Mayor of Petrograd; 1918 Petrograd Comr of Municipal Econ; Mar 1919 elected member, CC, at 8th RCP(B) Congress; 30 Mar 1919 elected chm, All-Russian Centr Exec Comt; from 1919 also cand member, Politburo, CC, RCP(B); 1918-20, during Civil War, conducted agitation and propaganda campaigns among workers, peasants and soldiers; made 12 tours of centr Russia, Ukr, Northern Caucasus, Siberia and most fronts with the "Oct Revol" agitation train; Dec 1922, after formation of USSR, elected chm, USSR Centr Exec Comt; 1925 elected Politburo member, CC, after 14th CPSU(B) Congress; Jan 1938-Mar 1946 Presidium chm, USSR Supr Sov; Mar-June 1946 Presidium member, USSR Supr Sov; *Publ: Izbrannyye proizvedeniya* (Selected Works) (3 vol, 1960-62); *Awards*: two Orders of Lenin; two Orders of the Red Banner; Hero of Socialist Labor (1944); *Died*: 3 June 1946; buried on Red Square, Moscow.

KALININ, Semyon Ivanovich (1887-1963) Govt official; CP member from 1904; *Born*: Apr 1887; *Career*: began working in Revel at age 13; worked at factories in Petersburg and Baku; 1905 took part in 9 Jan demonstration; 1917 joined Red Guard; fought in Caucasus during Civil War; from 1921 admin work; 1938-44 dir, "Red Instrument-Maker" Plant, Leningrad; from 1945 dir, "Komsomol" Plant; from 1947 worked for USSR Min of Machine-Building and Instrument-Manufacturing; *Died*: May 1963.

KALININA, Ol'ga Pavlovna (1907-1959) Russian opera singer (lyric-coloratura soprano); Hon Art Worker of RSFSR from 1950; *Born*: 23 July 1907; *Educ*: 1938 grad Sverdlovsk Musical College; *Career*: 1938-39 with Sverdlovsk Opera and Ballet Theater; 1939-40 at Alma-Ata Opera and Ballet Theater (now Abay Theater); 1940-41 at Gorky Opera and Ballet Theater; 1941-42 at Perm' Opera and Ballet Theater; from 1942 with Saratov Opera and Ballet Theater; also gave concerts; *Roles*: Queen Shemakhan in Rimskiy-Korsakov's *Zolotoy petushok* (Golden Cockerel); the Snow-Maiden; Lyudmila; Antonida in "Ivan Susanin"; Gilda; Violetta; Rosina; Lakme; Juliet in Gounod's "Romeo and Juliet"; Cerline in Ober's "Fra Diabolo", etc; performed also in comic operas and operettas: Keto in Dolidze's "Keto and Kote"; Rosalinde in Strauss' "Fledermaus"; Laura in Millöcker's "Bettelstudent", etc; *Awards*: Stalin Prize (1947); *Died*: 28 June 1959.

KALININA, Yekaterina Ivanovna (1882-1960) Revolutionary; govt and Party official; wife of M. I. Kalinin; CP member from Mar 1917; *Born*: 2 July 1882; *Career*: in youth worked as a weaver in Revel (Tallinn) and Petersburg; 1905 joined revol movement and elected member, Petersburg Sov of Workers' Dep; Feb 1917 took active part in Revol; during Civil War helped to organize children's facilities and toured the fronts with the "Oct Revol" agitation and instruction train of the All-Russian Centr Exec Comt; after Civil War held various posts in govt and ind; member, RSFSR Supr Court; from 1946 pensioner; *Died*: 22 Dec 1960.

KALINOVICH, Mikhail Yakovlevich (1888-1949) Linguist; member, Ukr Acad of Sci from 1939; *Born*: 13 Oct 1888 in Zhakhnivtsy, now Vinnitsa Oblast; *Educ*: 1912 grad Kiev Univ; *Career*: from 1916 taught at Kiev Univ and other higher educ establishments in Kiev; from 1924 also worked at Ukr Acad of Sci; 1930-39 dept head, from 1939 dir, Inst of Linguistics and head, Soc Sci Dept, Ukr Acad of Sci; did research on Ukr and gen linguistics, lexicography and lit history; translated works of Joseph Conrad and H. G. Wells into Ukr; *Publ: Ponyatiye otdel'nogo slova* (The Concept of the Discrete Word) (1935); *Nauka protiv religii v voprosakh proiskhozhdeniya yazyka* (Science Versus Religion in Questions of the Origin of Language) (1938); *Vvedeniye v yazykoznaniye* (An Introduction to Linguistics) (1940); *Proiskhozhdeniye yazyka* (The Origin of Language) (1946); coauthor and exec ed, *Russko-ukrainskiy slovar'* (A Russian-Ukrainian Dictionary) (1948), etc; *Died*: 16 Jan 1949.

KALINOVSKIY, Konstantin Bronislavovich (1897-1931) Mil commander of Polish origin; tank specialist; CP member from 1920; *Born*: 1897 in Smolensk, son of a nobleman; *Educ*: attended 2nd Moscow High-School; 1919 grad Higher Mil Automobile and Armor School; 1925 grad Red Army Mil Acad; *Career*: July 1917 quit 8th grade at 2nd Moscow High-School and volunteered for Russian Army; served as a gunner with a heavy artillery field battalion; June 1918 volunteered for Red Army; served with a special artillery battalion on Northern Front; from 1919 artillery officer in the "Raskol'nikov" armored train, Western Front; 1921 commander, armored train No 35, Caucasian Front; 1921-22 inspector, Armor Parts Bd, Separate Red-Banner Caucasian Army; 1925-29 inspector, Red Army armored forces; 1929-31 dep commander, Red Army Mechanization Bd; a mechanized corps was named after him; after his death he became an unperson and his name was expunged from all encyclopedias and mil textbooks published from 1937 to 1956; *Publ: Tanki* (Tanks) (1925); *Ispol'zovaniye tankov v vzaimodeystvii s pekhotoy* (The Use of Tanks in Conjunction with Infantry) (1927); *Vzaimodeystviye pekhoty s tankami* (Joint Infantry and Tank Operations) (1928); *Tanki v gruppe DD* (Tanks Operating in a Long-Range Group) (1931); *Died*: 12 July 1931 in a plane crash near Moscow.

KALITIN, Nikolay Nikolayevich (1884-1949) Geophysicist and actinometrist; Dr of Physics and Mathematics; prof; *Born*: 29 Mar 1884 in vil Sirkovitsy, Yamburg Uyezd, Petersburg Province; *Educ*: 1911 grad Physics and Mathematics Fac, Petersburg Univ; *Career*: worked for Main Geophysical Observatory where he supervised the actinometric dept, which was reorganized in 1930 into the Inst of Actinometry and Atmospheric Optics; 1925 founded and headed Permanent Actinometrical Commission of the Main Geophysical Observatory, which played an important role in org the network of Sov actinometrical stations; 1925-40 edited *Byulleten' postoyannoy aktinometricheskoy komissii glavnoy geofizicheskoy observatorii*; planned Palace of the Sun, built 1931 and specially equipped for actinometry and atmospheric optics; invented and built more than 30 original actinometrical instruments; *Publ: Aktinometriya* (Actinometry) (1938); *Razvitiye aktinometricheskikh rabot v SSSR za posledniye 30 let* (The Development of Actinometry in the USSR in the Past 30 Years) (1947); *Luchi solntsa* (The Rays of the Sun) (1947); *Died*: 21 Aug 1949.

KALITSKIY, Kazimir Petrovich (1873-1941) Geologist and oil ind worker; *Born*: 4 Mar 1873 in Petersburg; *Educ*: 1899 grad Mining Inst in Petersburg; *Career*: from 1901 worked for Geological Comt (1941 reorganized as Oil and Geological Survey Research Inst); led numerous geological expeditions in oil districts of USSR (Centr Asia, the Caucasus, etc); compiled still valid geological maps and accounts of oil deposits; invented method of drafting structural maps for correct surveying and operation of oil deposits; compiled one of first textbooks on the geology of oil from a course of lectures which he read in 1920-22 at the Petrograd Mining Inst; investigated stratigraphy and tectonics of various regions, also the origin of oil and formation of oil deposits; developed hypothesis that oil originated from marine plants; *Publ*: coauthor, "Cheleken" (1911); *Podzemnoye kartirovaniye* (Subterranean Cartography) (1933); *Geologiya nefti* (The Geology of Oil) (1921); *Nauchnyye osnovy poiskov nefti* (Scientific Principles of Oil Prospecting) (1944), etc; *Died*: 28 Dec 1941 in Leningrad.

KALIZHNYUK, Semyon Konstantinovich (1900-1964) Hydraulic eng; CP member from 1921; *Born*: 2 Feb 1900; *Educ*: grad Tashkent Inst of Irrigation and Agric Mechanization Eng; *Career*: 1912-19 hired hand and shoemaker; 1920-27 served in Sov Army; 1927-35 worked for Centr Asian Water Bd; 1935-37 mang,

Excavator Trust, USSR Pop Comrt of Agric; 1939-40 dep construction chief, Katta-Kurgan water reservoir; 1941-42 in Sov Army; 1942-43 construction chief, Northern Tashkent Canal; 1943-50 construction chief, various hydropower plants; 1950-53 construction chief, Main Turkm Canal; 1953-54 mang, Centr Asian Hydropower Plant Construction Trust; 1954-60 mang, Turkm Hydropower Plant Construction Trust; from 1960 pensioner; 1961-62 construction chief, Nurek Hydropower Plant; dep, Turkm Supr Sov of 3rd and 4th convocations; member, CC, CP Uzbek; cand member, CC, CP Turkm; member, CC, CP Tadzh; *Awards*: Lenin Prize (1965); *Died*: 29 Oct 1964.

KALMANOVICH, Moisey Iosifovich (1888-1937) Party and govt official; CP member from 1917; *Born*: 1888; *Career*: office worker; after 1917 Oct Revol worked mainly in food admin; 1917-20 member, Western Oblast RSDRP(B) Comt; member Smolensk Province RCP(B) Comt; dep chm, Bel Centr Exec Comt; member, CC, CP Bel; member, Bel Labor and Defense Council; Bel Pop Comr of Food; chm, Special Food Commission, Western Front; 1920 Ukr Dep Pop Comr of Food; 1921-24 chm, Siberian Food Comt; RSFSR Pop Comr of Food; chm, Grain Produce Bd; 1924-37 admin work; 1927 elected member, Centr Control Commission at 15th CPSU(B) Congress; from 1928 chm, Grain Trust Bd; from Dec 1929 also USSR Dep Pop Comr of Agric; from 1930 chm, USSR State Bank; also USSR Dep Pop Comr of Finance; 1934-37 USSR Pop Comr of Grain and Food Sovkhozes; elected cand member, CC at 16th and 17th CPSU(B) Congresses; arrested by State Security organs; *Died*: 1937 in imprisonment.

KALMYKOV, Betal Edykovich (1893-1940) Kabardo-Balkar Party and govt official; CP member from Mar 1918; *Born*: 24 Oct 1893 in Kuba, now Kabardo-Balkar ASSR; *Educ*: attended two-grade school; *Career*: from age 14 worked as a farmhand; 1913 helped lead a peasant uprising against rich horse-breeders; 1915-16 set up illegal *Karakhalk* (Poverty) revol-democratic peasants' org; arrested by Tsarist authorities and Provisional Govt; 1917 helped to prepare and carry out Oct Revol in Northern Caucasus; 1918 deleg to all five Terek Oblast nationalities congresses; chm, 1918 Nal'chik Okrug Congress, after its proclamation as Kabardia and Balkaria by the Sov govt in Mar; extraordinary comr and Nationalities Comr, Terek Oblast; during Civil War organized and led North Caucasian partisan detachments; Red Army regt and div commander; 1921-24 in charge of operations against rebels in Kabardia and Balkaria; 1920-29 chm, Kabardo-Balkar Oblast Exec Comt; 1929-38 first secr, Kabardo-Balkar Oblast CPSU(B) Comt; member, RSFSR Supr Centr Exec Comt and USSR Centr Exec Comt of all convocations; deleg 11-17th CPSU(B) Congresses; arrested by State Security organs; *Publ: Stat'i i rechi* (Articles and Speeches) (1961); *Awards*: Order of the Red Banner (1926); Order of Lenin (1931); *Died*: 27 Feb 1940 in imprisonment; posthumously rehabilitated.

KALMYKOV, Mikhail Vasil'yevich (1888-1937) Mil commander; corps commander from 1935; Civil War veteran; CP member from 1917; *Born*: 4 Dec 1888 in Vyshniy Volochek Uyezd, Tver' Province, son of a glass-blower; *Educ*: 1924 grad Red Army Mil Acad; *Career*: until 1910 glass-blower (Bohemian) at various Russian glassworks; 1910-17 private and noncom, various Russian Army eng units; fought in WW 1; 1918 commander of a Red Guard unit, then commander and mil comr of all Red Guard Units, Krasnousol'skiy Sov Republ in rear of White Army; commander, Bogoyavlensk Red Guard Detachment; from Sept 1918 in Red Army; 1918 also took part in Blucher's march behind the White Army lines in the Southern Ural to join up with Red Army; 1918-20 commander, 269th Rifle Regt, 86th Brigade, 30th Rifle Div on Eastern and Southern Fronts; 1920 also took part in storming of Perekop; 1920-21 commander, 42nd Rifle Div in Ukr; 1924-27 commander, 2nd Turkestani Rifle Div in Centr Asia, where he fought against the Basmachi and became member, Uzbek Centr Exec Comt and cand member, CC, CP Uzbek; 1927-30 commander, 1st Rifle Corps; head, Red Army Command (Personnel) Bd; 1930-32 corps commander and dep commander, Special Red Banner Far Eastern Army; 1932-37 commander, Special Far Eastern (Kolkhoz) Corps, which was created at his suggestion to combine mil service with agric work at special kolkhozes; 1937 arrested by NKVD; *Awards*: Order of Lenin; two Orders of the Red Banner; *Died*: 27 Dec 1937 in imprisonment; posthumously rehabilitated.

KALMYKOVA, Aleksandra Mikhaylovna (1849-1926) Revolutionary; *Born*: 26 Dec 1849 in Yekaterinoslav; *Educ*: grad high school; *Career*: in 1880's helped found and ran Sunday schools in Khar'kov and Petersburg; worked for *Narodnaya Volya* (People's Will) movement; connected with Liberation of Labor group and later with Petersburg League for Liberation of the Working Class; member, ed bd, Legal Marxist journals "Novoye slovo" and "Nachalo"; 1890-1902 in charge of pop lit book depot which served as a secret address for Soc-Democrats; helped finance publ of Lenin's "Iskra" and "Zarya"; 1902 deported from Russia; gave Bolsheviks financial aid; after 1917 Oct Revol worked for Leningrad Dept of Educ and Ushinskiy Teachers' Training Inst in Leningrad; wrote about children's lit; *Publ: Zhizn' prezhde i teper'* (Life Then and Now); *Sily prirody i trud cheloveka* (The Forces of Nature and the Labor of Man); *Died*: 1 Apr 1926.

KALNIN, (Party pseudonym: UGIS), Oskar Yur'yevich (1895-1920) Lat revolutionary; mil comr; *Born*: 1895 in vil Ogre, Liflyand Province, Lat; son of a peasant; *Educ*: attended mil ensigns' school; *Career*: worker in Riga and Daugavpils; 1915 evacuated to Moscow, from where he was exiled a year later for revol activities; took refuge in Baku, where he worked for the Baku RSDRP(B) Org; went abroad; Aug 1917 returned to Moscow; during Oct Revol led a Red Guard detachment during the storming of the Kremlin; Presidium member, Rogozhsko-Simonov Distr Sov and mil comr and police chief of this distr; Feb 1918 sent to Eastern Front; member, Revol-Mil Sov, 1st Army; from spring 1919 performed special duties for Revol-Mil Council in Lat (later 15th) Army; comr, 11th Rifle Div during battle of Pskov; 1920 comr, 143rd Brigade, 16th Army; *Died*: 21 Nov 1920 in action.

KALNIN', T. P. (KALNIN, Werner) (1871-1938) Lat Party official; CP member from 1903; *Born*: 1871; *Career*: 1900 began working for underground Soc-Democratic groups; smuggled illegal literature from abroad and did Party work in Riga; from 1904 in charge of underground printing-shop of CC, Lat Soc-Democratic Workers' Party, where the newspaper "Zihna" was printed; member, Riga Comt, Lat Soc-Democratic Workers' Party; 1905-07 took active part in Revol in Lat; deleg, 5th RSDRP Congress, London; deleg, several congresses of Lat Soc-Democratic Workers' Party and Soc-Democratic Party of Lat Kray; 1908 sentenced to four years at hard labor after discovery of underground press; after serving sentence exiled to Siberia; after 1917 Oct Revol worked for Irkutsk cooperative system; from 1920 worked for Foreign Bureau, CC, CP Lat; later transferred to other Party and govt work; *Died*: 1938.

KALNYN', Al'fred Yanovich (1879-1951) Lat composer, organist, teacher and musical and public figure; prof from 1947; Pop Artiste of Lat SSR from 1945; *Born*: 23 Aug 1879 in settlement Tsesis; *Educ*: 1901 grad Composition Class (under A. K. Lyadov and N. F. Solov'yov) and Organ Class (under L. F. Gomilius), Petersburg Conservatory; *Career*: in 1900's began composing work; worked as organist, piano accompanist and conductor in Riga, Pyarnu, Liepaya and Tartu; 1923-26 dir, Lat Nat Opera House; 1927-33 in USA; from 1933 in Riga; 1944-47 rector, from 1947 prof, Lat Conservatory in Riga; pioneer of Lat opera; did a great deal to encourage Lat vocal and piano music; a number of his works were written under the direct influence of Ya. Raynis' poetry; *Works:* operas "Banyuta" (1919); *Ostrovityane* (The Islanders) or *Probuzhdeniye rodiny* (Awakening of the Fatherland) (1924); ballet "Staburag" (1943); symphonic poem *U Staburaga* (At Staburag); cantatas "To Music," "The Sea," "Day of Wrath," "Labor and Song," etc; suite "Song of the Fatherland," "Overture" (1950); "Ten Latvian Folk Songs" for symphony orchestra (1951); over 300 romances; choral works; works for organ; music for plays: Van Lerberg's "Pan"; "Daugava"; Raynis' *Korol' mukh* (King of Flies), etc; arranged Lat folk songs, etc; *Awards*: Prize of Lat SSR (1958); *Died*: 23 Dec 1951 in Riga.

KALNYN', Fridrikh K. (1887-1938) Mil commander; Lat junior-capt in Russian Army; Civil War veteran; *Born*: 1887; *Career*: from 1918 in Red Army; 1918-19 commander, 8th Lat Sov Regt, Lat Brigade; from 20 Oct 1919 head, Lat Infantry Div; Lat Infantry Div which he headed was one of the most disciplined and battleworthy Red Army formations and played a decisive role in repelling Denikin's offensive near Oryol (Oct 1919) and an important role in battles against Makhno and Grigor'yev (Jan 1920) and in the operation to seize the bridgehead near Kakhovka (summer 1920); from 1921 various command posts; then taught at Frunze Mil Acad; 1937 arrested by NKVD; *Awards*: Order of the Red Banner; *Died*: 1938 in imprisonment; posthumously rehabilitated.

KALYUGA, Lukash (real name: VASHYNA, Konstantin Petrovich)

(1909-1937) Bel writer; *Born*: 27 Sept 1909 in vil Skvortsy, now Dzerzhinsk Rayon, Minsk Oblast; *Educ*: studied at Bel Polytech School in Minsk; *Career*: 1927 first work published; from 1929 belonged to *Uzvyshsha* lit assoc; his novellas and novelettes, including novelettes "Neither Guest Nor Host" and "The Zablotskiys' Misfortune," were carried in the journals "Uzvyshsha" and "Polymya"; 1931 expelled from Bel Polytech School; later worked for Sovnarkhoz research inst, then on radio comt in Minsk; Jan 1933 arrested, tried and exiled for five years to Irbit in Western Siberia; 1935 interned in concentration camp; *Died*: 2 Oct 1937 in inprisonment; posthumously rehabilitated.

KAMAL (real name: KAMALETDINOV), Galiaskar Galiaskarovich (1879-1933) Tat playwright, publicist and public figure; Hero of Labor from 1923; Pop Playwright of Tat from 1926; *Born*: 6 Jan 1879 in Kazan', son of an artisan; *Educ*: 1900 grad Kazan' medressah; subsequently furthered his own educ and mastered several languages; *Career*: 1900 wrote first play; 1901 published illegal newspaper "Terakkyy" and founded Tat lit publishing house "Megarif"; 1906 worked for newspaper "Azad"; after suppression of this newspaper founded newspaper "Azad khalyk"; printed articles of Tat revol Kh. Yamashev, G. Kulakhmetov, etc; disseminated revol ideas, fought against nationalists; in Sept 1906 he was arrested and the newspaper suppressed; 1907-17 worked for newspaper "Yulduz"; 1908-09 together with G. Tukay edited satirical journal "Yashen"; 1910-17 ed, journal "Yalt-Ult"; after 1917 Oct Revol contributed to Bolshevik newspapers "Esh" ans "Kyzyl bayrak"; worked for Red Army theaterclubs; helped found "Sayyar" theater group; opposed Pan-Turkism and demanded purification of Tat language from Turkish and Arabic words; helped establish Tat lit language; translated into Tat Gogol's *Revizor* (The Government Inspector), Ostrovskiy's *Groza* (Thunderstorm), Gorky's *Na dne* (Lower Depths), etc; reviewed the work of Tat writers G. Tukay, G. Kulakhmetdinov, M. Gafuri, etc; the Kazan' Acad Theater was named for him; *Publ*: plays: "The Unfortunate Youth" (1898; 2nd version, 1907); "Three Luckless Men" (1900); "Poor Child"; comedies: "First Play" (1908); "Because of the Gift" (1908); "The Mistress" (1911); "Mystery of Our City" (1911); "Bankruptcy" (1912); plays: "Dear Khafiza" (1921); "Three Lives" (1933); "Blind Masters" (1935), etc; *Died*: 8 June 1933 in Kazan'.

KAMAL, Sharif (real name: BAYGIL'DIYEV, Sharif Kamalovich) (1884-1942) Tat writer and public figure; Hon Art Worker of Tat SSR from 1940; CP member from 1919; *Born*: 28 Mar 1884 in vil Pishlya, Penza Province (now Kuznetsk Rayon, Mordovian ASSR), son of a mullah; *Educ*: studied at medressah; *Career*: 1900 began work on construction of Moscow-Kursk Railroad; 1901-03 in Istanbul; 1903-05 worked in Donets Coalfields, then for Caspian fisheries; 1905 in Petersburg taught at Tat elementary school and simultaneously proof-reader, newspaper "Nur"; 1905-10 taught at vil school and engaged in agric work; 1906 first work printed; 1910-20 in Orenburg contributed to Tat newspapers "Vakt" and "Eshchelyar Dunyasy"; in 1910's became closely ayquainted with representatives of revol Tat lit G. Tukay and G. Kamal; 1923-25 contributed to Orenburg newspapers "Yul" and "Saban"; 1934 translated into Tat Sholokhov's *Podnyataya tselina* (Virgin Soil Upturned); from 1935 worked for Kazan' newspapers, House of Tat Culture, Tat Main Lit Bd and Tat Proletarian Writers' Assoc, etc; during WW 2 wrote a number of patriotic articles; many of his works have been translated into Russian; in his early period was strongly influenced by Gorky; *Publ*: verse collection "Voice" (1906); novellae: "In Search of Happiness," "In a Strange Land," "The Tramp" (1909–12); novelettes: "The Crow's Nest" (1910); "Sea Gulls" (1915); feuilletons and stories "Withered Flower" (1909); "The Eagle," "The Deputy" (1910); "At the Time of the Plague," "Boredom" (1912); satirical comedy "Khadzhi Efendi Gets Married" (1915); novels: "At Dawn" (1927); "When Beauty Is Born" (1938); "With Firm Steps" (1940); plays: "Fire" (1928); "The Crow's Nest" (1930); "Mountains" (1932); "Beyond the Mist" (1934); "When Beauty Is Born" (1938) after his novel of the same title, etc; *Awards*: Order of Lenin; *Died*: 22 Dec 1942 in Kazan'; a museum named for him was opened in Kazan'.

KAMENEV (real name: ROZENFEL'D), Lev Borisovich (1883-1936) Party official; CP member from 1901; *Born*: 1883, son of eng; *Educ*: studied at Moscow Univ; *Career*: joined Marxist circle in Tiflis while still at high-school; 1901 joined RSDRP while studying at Moscow Univ; 13 Mar 1902 arrested for taking part in a demonstration; after release expelled from univ, banished from Moscow and placed under police surveillance; fall 1902 went to Paris; after schism in RSDRP sided with Bolsheviks; returned to Russia and worked in Tiflis, Moscow and Petersburg; deleg, London Party Congress; then worked in Russia as Party CC agent; 1905-07 agitator and propagandist in Petersburg; contributed to legal and illegal Party publ; 1908 arrested, then emigrated; member, ed bd, newspaper "Proletariy"; contributed to newspaper "Sotsial-demokrat"; 1910 sponsored attempt at reconciliation with Trotskiy; upon instructions from Party CC joined ed staff, newspaper "Pravda" in Vienna but resigned shortly afterwards; early 1914 sent to Russia to direct publ of "Pravda" and work of Bolshevik Duma faction; 4 Nov 1914 arrested at meeting between this faction and Party workers at Ozerki, near Petersburg; 1915 tried with Bolshevik faction of State Duma and exiled to Siberia; after 1917 Feb Revol returned to Petrograd and joined "Pravda"; Apr 1917-1927 member, CC, CPSU(B); Politbureau member, CC, CPSU(B); 1917 frequently opposed Lenin's policies: after 1917 July demonstration arrested; fall 1917 opposed planned Bolshevik coup; after 1917 Oct Revol advocated coalition govt of all socialist parties and resigned from CC, RSDRP(B); at 2nd Congress of Soviets elected chm, All-Russian Centr Exec Comt but replaced a few days later by Sverdlov; member, Sov deleg at Brest peace talks; 1918-26 chm, Moscow Sov; from 1922 dep chm, Council of Pop Comr; from 1924 chm, Labor and Defense Council; first dir, Lenin Inst; 1926 USSR Pop Comr of Trade; 1927 Sov plen in Italy; 1923-24 sided with Zinov'yev against Trotskiy; 1925 joined leftist opposition; 1926 sided with Trotskiy; 1926-28 one of most active leaders, Trotskite opposition; Dec 1927 expelled from CPSU(B) at the decision of 15th Party Congress; 1928 re-admitted to Party after recanting his errors; from 1928 head, Bd, Supr Sovnarkhoz; from 1929 chm, Main Concessions Comt; elected member, All-Russian and USSR Centr Exec Comt; 1932 again expelled from Party; 1933 re-admitted; 1934 expelled from Party for third time; Jan 1935 sentenced to five years imprisonment; July 1935 retried and sentenced to 10 years' imprisonment; Aug 1936 sentenced to death in trial of "Trotskyite-Zinov'yev Center"; *Publ: Dve Partii* (The Two Parties); *Mezhdu dvumya revolyutsiyami* (Between Two Revolutions); *Bor'ba za mir* (The Struggle for Peace), etc; edited collected ed of Lenin's works and *Leninskiye sborniki* (Lenin Collections): *Died*: 15 Aug 1936 executed.

KAMENEV, Sergey Sergeyevich (1881-1936) Mil commander; col, Russian Army Gen Staff; army commander, 1st class from 1935; CP member from 1930; *Born*: 4 Apr 1881 in Kiev, son of mil eng; *Educ*: 1900 grad Alexandrine Mil College; 1907 grad Gen Staff Acad; *Pos*: from 1898 in Russian Army; 1900-04 officer, 165th Lutsk Infantry Regt; 1907-14 staff work in Vilnius Mil Distr; 1914-17 junior, then senior postgrad mil student, then head, Staff Operations Dept, 1st Army; 1917 commander, 30th Poltava Infantry Regt; chief of staff, 15th Army Corps; 1917-18 chief of staff, 3rd Army; from Apr 1918 in Red Army; 1918 commander, Nevel' Rayon, Western Flank; Sept 1918 - July 1919 commander, Eastern Front; 8 July 1919 - Apr 1924 commander in chief, RSFSR Armed Forces; Apr 1924 - Nov 1925 inspector, Red Army; from Jan 1925 also chief of staff, Red Army; Nov 1925 - Aug 1926 chief inspector, Red Army; Aug 1926 - May 1927 head, Main Bd, Red Army; also directed instruction in tactics at Frunze Mil Acad; 20 May 1927-1934 USSR Dep Pop Comr of Mil and Naval Affairs and chm, USSR Revol Mil Council; July 1934 - 25 Aug 1936 head, Red Army Antiaircraft Defense Bd; from Nov 1934 also member, Mil Council, USSR Pop Comrt of Defense; *Career*: spring 1919 devised plan for routing Admiral Kolchak's forces; late 1919 devised and carried out plan for routing Gen Denikin's forces; summer 1920, during Western Front's offensive against Warsaw, displayed indecisiveness in commanding Southwestern Front, resulting in delay in transferring 1st Mounted Army, 12th Army and 14th Army to reinforce Tukhachevskiy's forces; member, All-Russian and USSR Centr Exec Comt of all convocations; *Publ: Ocherednyye voyennyye zadachi* (Routine Military Tasks) (1922); coauthor, *Osnovnyye voprosy sovremennoy taktiki* (Basic Problems of Modern Tactics) (1925); *Podgotovka pekhoty v inostrannykh armiyakh* (Infantry Training in Foreign Armies) (1927); coauthor, *Voyennaya podgotovka naseleniya* (Public Military Training) (1926); *Awards*: Order of the Red Banner; Golden Arms with badge of Order of Red Banner (Sabre); Hon Firearm with Order of Red Banner; Order of Red Banner of Khorezm SSR; Order of Red Crescent of Bukhara Sov Republ; *Died*: 25 Aug 1936 of heart disease; ashes immured in

Kremlin Wall; 1937 his remains were removed from Kremlin Wall and his name expunged from Sov records; after 20th CPSU Congress rehabilitated.

KAMENSKIY, Anatoliy Pavlovich (1876-1941) Russian writer; *Born*: 29 Nov 1876 in Astrakhan'; *Career*: from 1920 in emigration; early 1930's returned to Russia; 1903 published first collection of stories *Stepnyye golosa* (Voices of the Steppe); cult of "natural" and "strong" personality, frank eroticism and praise of free love are characteristic of his work; arrested by State Security organs; *Publ: Rasskazy* (Stories) (1908-10); *Legkomyslennyye rasskazy* (Frivolous Stories) (1910); novel *Lyudi* (People) (1910); *Zverinets. Novyye rasskazy* (The Menagerie. New Stories) (1913); *Knyazhna Dudu. Novyye rasskazy* (Princess Dudu. New Stories) (1914); *Moy garem. Rasskazy o lyubvi* (My Harem. Love Stories) (1923); comedy *Chizhukhinskiye alimenty* (Chizhukhin's Alimony) (1927); *Belaya noch'. Rasskazy* (A White Night. Stories) (1928); *Petersburgskiy chelovek. Povesti i rasskazy 1905-15* (The Petersburg Man. Novelettes and Stories 1905-15) (1936); *Died*: 1 Dec 1941 in imprisonment; posthumously rehabilitated.

KAMENSKIY, A. Z. (1885-1938) Party and govt official; CP member from 1917; *Born*: 1885; *Career*: deleg from Lugana RSDRP(B) Org at 6th Party Congress; after 1917 Oct Revol held Party, govt and trade-union posts; 1920-21 RSFSR Dep Pop Comr of Nationalities; 1921-22 secr, Don Oblast RCP(B) Comt; during trade-union controversy joined the "democratic centralists" in opposition to the Party; rejected Lenin's draft resolution "On Party Unity" at the 10th RCP(B) Congress; 1922-23 Collegium member, Pop Comrt of Agric; 1925-26 sided with Trotskyite opposition; 1927-33 dir, Ind Acad; 1933-36 Collegium member, Pop Comrt of Light Ind; from 1936 worked for RSFSR Pop Comrt of Finance; arrested by State Security organs; *Died*: 1938 in imprisonment.

KAMMARI, Mikhail Davidovich (1898-1965) Philosopher; Dr of Philosophy; prof; senior assoc, Inst of Philosophy, USSR Acad of Sci; corresp member, USSR Acad of Sci from 1953; CP member from 1919; *Born*: 1 Mar 1898; *Educ*: 1931 grad Inst of Red Prof; *Career*: 1936-40 worked at Marx-Engels-Lenin-Stalin Inst, CC, CPSU(B) (now Inst of Marxism-Leninism, CC, CPSU); 1940-50 member, Radio Development and Broadcasting Comt; 1951-54 chief ed, journal *Kommunist*; 1954-59 chief ed, journal *Voprosy filosofii*; 1959-63 member, ed council, from 1953 Bureau member, Dept of Economical, Philosophical and Legal Sci (now Dept of Philosophy and Law), USSR Acad of Sci; *Publ: O novom vydayushchemsya vklade I. V. Stalina v marksistko-leninskuyu filosofiyu* (A Brilliant New Contribution to Marxist-Leninist Philosophy by I. V. Stalin) (1952); *Torzhestvo ideologii druzhby narodov* (The Triumph of the Ideology of Peoples' Friendship) (1954) *O roli narodnykh mass v revolyutsii 1905-ogo goda* (The Role of the Popular Masses in the 1905 Revolution) (1955); *Revionistskiy mif ob 'osvobozhdenii' nauki ot ideologii* (The Revisionist Myth of the "Liberation" of Science from Ideology) (1958); *V. I. Lenin o yedinstve dialekticheskogo i istoricheskogo materializma* (V. I. Lenin of the Unity of Dialectical and Historical Materialism) (1959); coauthor, *Nekotoryye voprosy razvitiya i dal'neyshego sblizheniya sovetskikh natsiy v period razvernutogo stroitel'stva kommunizma* (Questions of the Development and Further Rapprochement of the Soviet Peoples in the Period of the All-Round Communist Construction) (1962); *Awards*: Order of Lenin; medals; *Died*: Sept 1965.

KAMINSKIY, Grigoriy Naumovich (1895-1939) Party and govt official; CP member from 1913; *Born*: 1 Nov 1895 in Yekaterinoslav (now Dnepropetrovsk), son of a worker; *Educ*: from 1915 studied at Med Fac, Moscow Univ; *Career*: conducted propaganda among workers and students; after 1917 Feb Revol member, Moscow Oblast RSDRP(B) Bureau; transferred to Tula; from Mar 1917 secr, Tula RSDRP Joint Comt, then Tula RSDRP(B) Comt; deleg, 6th RSDRP(B) Congress; after 1917 Oct Revol chm, Tula RSDRP(B) Org; member, command staff of a fortified region and member, Revol-Mil Council, 2nd Army; 1920 sent to Baku as secr, CC, CP Azer and chm, Baku Sov; 1922-29 chm, Land and Forestry Workers' Union and All-Union Council of Kolkhozes; 1929 head, Agitation Dept, CC, CPSU(B); 1930-31 secr, Moscow CPSU(B) Comt; 1932-34 chm, Moscow Oblast Exec Comt; 1934-36 RSFSR Pop Comr of Health; 1936-37 USSR Pop Comr of Health; member, All-Russian and USSR Centr Exec Comt; elected cand member, CC, CPSU(B) at 14th-17th congresses; arrested by State Security organs; *Died*: 9 Feb 1939 in imprisonment; posthumously rehabilitated.

KAMKOV (KATS), B. D. (1885-1938) Party official; *Born*: 1885; *Career*: member, Socialist-Revol Party; co-organizer and leader, leftist Socialist Revolutionaries; 1918 opposed the conclusion of the Peace of Brest-Litovsk; co-organized assassination of German ambassador Mirbach and Moscow uprising; sentenced for anti-Sov activity by Mil Tribunal; later worked as a statistician in Voronezh; arrested by State Security organs; *Died*: 1938 in imprisonment.

KAMO, (real name: TER-PETROSYAN, Simon Arshakovich) (1882-1922) Revolutionary; Civil War veteran; CP member from 1901; *Born*: 27 May 1882 in Gori, Geo; *Educ*: 1920-21 studied at Mil Acad; *Career*: 1901 began revol activities; distributed illegal lit in Tiflis, Baku, Batumi, Kutaisi, Gori and other cities; organized underground printing presses; Nov 1903 arrested; Sept 1904 escaped from prison; 1905 Party work organizing and training armed workers squads and collecting weapons; during Dec 1905 uprising in Tiflis led detachment of armed workers; wounded five times in battles with Cossacks; imprisoned in Metekh Castle and tortured but managed to deceive police and escape; Mar 1906 went to Petersburg, where he first met Lenin; on Lenin's orders went abroad to buy weapons and smuggle them into Russia; 1905-06 organized various robberies to collect funds for the Party; 1907 arranged theft of 250.000 rubles of treasury funds on Erivan Square in Tiflis; the money was taken to Petersburg and turned over to the Party; 1905-17 smuggled arms and munitions from Petersburg to Tiflis; Nov 1907 betrayed by an agent-provocateur and arrested in Berlin by German police; simulated insanity to escape trial and extradition to Russia; late 1909 turned over to Tsarist authorities, taken to Tiflis, imprisoned in Metekh Castle and court-martialed; 15 Aug 1911 escaped from prison hospital and fled to Paris; on Lenin's orders arranged transport of Party lit to Russia; 1912 returned to Russia, arrested and sentenced to death; under 1913 amnesty (in connection with 300th anniversary of Romanovs) sentence commuted to 20 years' hard labor, to be served in the Kharkov Penitentiary; 6 Mar 1917 released; Dec 1917 sent by S. G. Shaumyan to Petersburg with a letter for Lenin; 8 Jan 1918 brought Lenin's letters to Tiflis and resolution of RSFSR Council of Pop Comr appointing Shaumyan provisional comr extraordinary of the Caucasus; 1919 arrived in Astrakhan' by boat from Baku with G. K. Ordzhonikidze; spring 1919 commissioned by Lenin to organize a partisan detachment for operations behind enemy lines; 1919 formed partisan detachment which operated near Kursk and Oryol and later behind the lines of Denikin's forces on the Southern Front; brought arms and money for North Caucasian underground Party org and partisans by way of Astrakhan' in a fishing boat; 15 Jan 1920 arrested in Tiflis by Menshevik govt; 18 months later released and given 24 hours to leave Geo; moved to Baku and helped to prepare Bolshevik uprising; May 1920, after liberation of Baku by the Red Army, moved to Moscow; studied at mil acad; 1921 worked for RSFSR Min of For Trade; from early 1922 worked for Geo Pop Comrt of Finance; *Died*: 14 July 1922 killed in traffic accident.

KANATCHIKOV, Semyon Ivanovich (1879-1940) Party official; CP member from 1898; *Born*: 1879, son of a peasant; *Educ*: elementary school; *Career*: from the age of 15 worked at plants in Moscow, Petersburg, etc; modeller by trade; 1898 joined the League for the Liberation of the Working Class; from 1905 professional revolutionary; repeatedly in prison and exile; member, Moscow and Petersburg Party Comt; deleg, Stockholm Congress; 1917 member, Novaya Nikolayevka Party Comt; then chm, Mil Revol Staff in Tomsk; 1919 Collegium member, Pop Comrt of Domestic Affairs; then member, Small Sovnarkhoz; 1920-21 Party work in the Urals and Tatary; 1921-24 dean, Leningrad Communist Univ; from 1924 press official; head, Press Dept, CC, CPSU(B); member, Commission for CP History; edited various newspapers and journals; 1923 spoke out vehemently against Trotsky in a pamphlet entitled *Istoriya odnogo uklona* (The History of a Deviation); 1926 temporarily sided with "Leningrad opposition"; from 1928 worked for "Krasnaya nov' "; chm, ed council, "Federation" Publishing House; ed, "Literaturnaya gazeta"; member, All-Russian Soc of Peasant Writers; chief ed, State Fiction Publishing House; ed, "Sov Writer" Publishing House; arrested by State Security organs; *Publ: Istoriya odnogo uklona* (The History of a Deviation) (1923); *Kak rozhdalas' Oktyabr'skaya revolyutsiya* (How the October Revolution Was Born), etc; *Died*: 1940 in imprisonment.

KANCHAVELI, Zakhariy Alekseyevich (1890-1932) Botanist; prof from 1928; *Born*: 16 Dec 1890 in Signakhi Uyezd, Tiflis Province; *Educ*: 1910 grad Geo High-School, Tiflis; 1915 grad Biology and Agronomy Section, Natural Sci Dept, Khar'kov Univ; *Career*: while still a student commissioned by Tiflis Botanical Garden to tour Kakhetiya and Tushetiya to study local flora; 1915, after grad, did botanical research for tanning industry in Black Sea Province and Sukhumi Okrug; 1916 worked for Batumi Botanical Garden; 1917 asst prof, Chair of Botany, Tiflis Polytech Inst; from 1918 asst prof, Chair of Botany, Tiflis Univ; 1921 secr, Pedag Fac, Tbilisi Univ; from 1921 in charge of botany course at pedag, agronomy and med fac, Tbilisi Univ; from 1922 head, Chair of Botany, Tbilisi Univ; from 1923 also head, Floristics Dept, Botanical Inst, Geo Acad of Sci; from 1928 until death dir, Tbilisi Botanical Garden; made numerous botanical field trips: 1920 and 1922 to Tushetiya; 1924-25 to Samgori Steppe; 1926-27 to Shiraki-El'dari Steppe; 1928-29 to Tsivgombari Range; 1929-30 to Inner Kakhetiya; *Publ*: *Opredelitel' paporotnikoobraznykh i tsvetkovykh rasteniy* (A Classification Key of Pteridophyta and Spermatophyta) (1919); *Tetrad' dlya opredeleniya rasteniy* (A Plant Classification Notebook) (1920); *Botanika. 1. Obshchaya chast'* (Botany. 1. General Section) (1927); *Botanika. 2. Sistematika rasteniy* (Botany. 2. Plant Taxonomy) (1927); *Novyy vid roda Campanula iz Kakhetii i novyye dannyye o rasprostranenii nekotorykh rasteniy na Kavkaze* (A New Species of the Genus Campanula from Kakhetiya and New Data on the Distribution of Certain Plants in the Caucasus) (1930); *Tetrad' dlya opredeleniya tsvetkovykh rasteniy* (A Notebook for the Classification of Spermatophyta) (1934); *Died*: 24 Jan 1932 in Tbilisi.

KANIN, Aleksandr Ignat'yevich (1877-1953) Actor and stage dir; Hon Art Worker of RSFSR from 1926; CP member from 1950; *Born*: 6 Dec 1877 in Saratov; *Educ*: 1904 grad Moscow Arts Theater School (class of V. I. Nemirovich-Danchenko); *Career*: from 1904 actor and stage dir, Meyerhold Ensemble in Tiflis; 1905-06 actor; Studio on Povarskaya (run by Stanislavskiy and Meyerhold); 1908-17 with various theaters in Voronezh, Rostov-on-Don, Taganrog, Samara, Kazan', Orenburg, Irkutsk, Odessa, Astrakhan'; from 1917 in Saratov; 1920 organized a youth troupe at Saratov's Karl Marx Theater; artistic dir with theaters in Ashkhabad (1927-29), Penza (1929-30), Samara (1930-31), Voronezh (1931-34), Kursk (1934-41), Engel's (1941-43), Kurgan (1943-46), Ulan-Ude (1946-47), Velikiye Luki (1947-48); from 1948 chief stage dir, Ryazan' theater; produced almost all of Gorky's plays; founded and taught at theater studios in Saratov, Kiev, Samara, Penza, Voronezh and Kursk; the Kursk Studio was named for him; *Works*: staged plays: *Meshchane* (Philistines) (1907 and 1951); *Vassa Zheleznova* (1910 and 1935); *Lyubov' Yarovaya* (1926); *Yegor Bulychov i drugiye* (Yegor Bulychov and Co) (1933 and 1946); *Razlom* (Break-Up) (1937); *Chelovek s ruzh'yom* (Man with a Gun) (1938); *Poslednyaya zhertva* (The Last Victim) (1948), etc; *Roles*: Bessemenov in *Meshchane* (Philistines); Firs in *Vishnyovyy sad* (Cherry Orchard); the Old Cook in *Plody prosveshcheniya* (Fruits of Enlightenment); Ferapont in *Tri sestry* (Three Sisters); Osip in *Revizor* (The Government Inspector); Lup Kleshnin in *Tsar' Fyodor Ioannovich*, etc; *Awards*: Stalin Prize (1951); *Died*: 3 Nov 1953.

KANNABIKH, Yuriy Vladimirovich (1872-1939) Psychiatrist and psychotherapist; specialist in the history of psychiatry; Dr of Med from 1914; prof from 1920; Hon Sci Worker of RSFSR from 1937; *Born*: 5 Oct 1872; *Educ*: 1896 grad Dept of Natural History, 1899 grad Med Fac, Moscow Univ; *Career*: while still a student worked at Krepelin's Clinic; after grad worked as an intern at a propaedeutic clinic to obtain the knowledge of internal diseases that he deemed necessary for a psychiatrist; 1905-09 worked at Moscow Centr Admission Unit for Mental Patients directed by A. N. Bernshteyn; delivered lectures on the history of psychiatry at postgrad med training courses for psychiatrists; worked at Kryukovo Sanatorium for Nervous Diseases and Alekseyevskiy Psychiatric Hospital, where he became a follower of S. S. Korsekov and a specialist in "minor psychiatry"; 1914 defended doctor's thesis on cyclothymia, a still valid classical study of this subject; from 1918 assoc prof, Moscow Univ; from 1920 prof, Chair of Psychiatry, Turkestani Univ, Tashkent; 1921 returned to Moscow to read course on med psychology, Higher Med School, then course on psychotherapy at P. B. Gannushkin's Clinic; 1925 read course on "minor psychiatry" and psychotherapy, at Postgrad Med Training Courses, Pop Comrt of Health; from 1929 head, Dept of the History of Psychiatry, Inst of Neuropsychiatric Prophylaxis, Pop Comrt of Health (now Centr Inst of Psychiatry, RSFSR Min of Health); from 1936 head, Chair of Psychiatry, 3rd Moscow Med Inst; approached psychotherapy from the Pavlovian viewpoint; collected psychographic data on Guy de Maupassant, Dostoyevskiy and Hegel; *Publ*: doctor's thesis *Tsiklotimiya (cyclothymia), yeyo simptomatologiya i techeniya* (Cyclothymia, Its Symptoms and Course) (1914); *Istoriya psikhiatrii* (The History of Psychiatry) (1929); *Psikhoterapiya* (Psychotherapy); *Mesto gipnoza v sovetskoy sisteme psikhoterapii i gipnoza* (The Place of Hypnosis in the Soviet System of Psychotherapy and Hypnosis), etc; *Died*: 1939.

KAPANTSYAN, Grigoriy Ayvazovich (1887-1957) Arm linguist and historian; prof from 1925; member, Arm Acad of Sci from 1943; *Born*: 29 Dec 1887; *Educ*: 1913 grad Petersburg Univ; *Career*: from 1925 prof, Yerevan State Univ, where he taught ancient Arm (Grabar), comparative historical grammar of Arm and Urart, and gen linguistics; 1943-48 acad secr, Dept of Social Sci, Arm Acad of Sci; specialized in the history of Urartu and ancient Armenia and studied the languages of Asia Minor (Hittite, Urart, Hurrian, Palaic, etc); *Publ*: "Chetto-Armeniaca. A Comparative Linguistic Study Explaining Some 200 Common Words and Forms" (1931-33); "Elements Common to Urart and Hittite" (1936); "The Historical Linguistic Significance of Toponymy in Ancient Armenia" (1940); "Hittite Gods and the Armenians" (1940); "Hajasa - the Cradle of the Armenians. The Ethnogenesis of the Armenians and their Early History" (1947); "The Origin of the Armenian Language" (1946); *Suffiksy i suffigirovannyye slova v toponomike drevney Maloy Azii* (Suffixes and Suffixed Words in the Toponymy of Ancient Asia Minor) (1948); "Stone Columns in the Mountains of Armenia" (1952); "Historical and Linguistic Papers. The Early History of the Armenians of Ancient Asia Minor" (1956); *Died*: 5 May 1957.

KAPELYUSHNIKOV, Matvey Alkunovich (1886-1959) Petroleum eng; corresp member, USSR Acad of Sci from 1939; Hon Sci and Tech Worker of RSFSR from 1947; *Born*: 13 Sept 1886; *Educ*: 1914 grad Tomsk Technol Inst; *Career*: 1914-37 worked at Baku Research Inst; 1937-48 laboratory head, Oil Inst, USSR Acad of Sci; 1958-59 laboratory head, Inst of Geology and Mineral Deposits, USSR Acad of Sci; 1922 designed a turbo-drill for a new oil-drilling technique, which he developed; 1924-31, together with V. G. Shukhov designed and constructed first Soviet cracking plant; 1952 established the presence of oil in solution in gas under high pressure; *Publ*: *O mekhanizatsii i avtomatizatsii burovykh rabot* (The Mechanization and Automation of Drilling Operations) (1945); *Fizicheskoye sostoyaniye nefti, gaza i vody v usloviyakh neftyanogo plasta* (The Physical State of Oil, Gas and Water in an Oil Bed) (1952); *K voprosu o migratsii i akkumulyatsii rasseyannoy nefti v osadochnykh gornykh porodakh* (The Migration and Accumulation of Dispersed Oil in Sedimentary Rocks) (1954), etc; *Awards*: Order of Lenin; four other orders and medals; *Died*: 5 July 1959.

KAPIYEV, Effendi Mansurovich (1909-1944) Dag writer of Lak descent; *Born*: 13 Mar 1909 in vil Kukhum, now Lak Rayon, Dag ASSR, son of a tinsmith and engraver; *Educ*: 1928 grad secondary school; 1928-31 studied at Leningrad Machine-Building Inst; *Career*: wrote in Russian; taught Russian language at Aksay vil school; 1931-35 exec secr, Dag Writers' Org; ed, Dag State Publ House; contributed to Kumyk newspaper "Yeldash," then to newspaper "Melodoy leninets" in Pyatigorsk; during WW 2 front-line corresp for newspaper "Dagestanskaya pravda"; also worked for newspaper "Vperyod za Rodinu," which was published on the North Caucasian Front; influenced by Russian classical lit and Dag folklore; translated verse of Suleyman Stal'skiy and Caucasian folk ballads into Russian; *Publ*: sketches *Dagestanskaya tetrad'* (Dagestani Notebook) (1934-40); authologies *Pesni gortsev* (Songs of the Mountaineers) (1939) and *Rez'ba po kamnyu* (Stone-Carving) (1940); novella cycle "Poet" (1940); *Frontovoy dnevnik* (Front-Line Journal) (1941-44); *Died*: 27 Jan 1944 in Pyatigorsk.

KAPLANSKIY, Samuil Yakovlevich (1897-1965) Biochemist; Dr of Med from 1936; prof from 1938; CP member from 1937; *Born*: 1897; *Educ*: 1921 grad Med Fac, Moscow Univ; *Career*: did biochemical research at Acad V. S. Gulevich's laboratory; 1921-25 asst dissector, 1925-29 asst prof and head, Biochemical Laboratory, Chair of Gen Pathology, Moscow Univ; worked simultaneously as biochemist for Inst of Skin Tuberculosis; 1929-31 assoc prof, Moscow Univ, where he taught course on mineral metabolism; 1931-35 head, Biochemical Dept, Biological

Research Inst, Communist Acad, Moscow; 1935-36 dep head, Dept of Metabolism, All-Union Inst of Experimental Med; 1939-51 head, Chair of Biochemistry, 2nd Moscow Med Inst; 1939-65 dep sci dir, All-Union Inst of Experimental Med; 1944-65 head, Dept of Physiochemistry, Inst of Biological and Med Chemistry, USSR Acad of Med Sci; co-ed, chemistry section and author of several entries, *Bol'shaya meditsinskaya entsikopediya* (Large Medical Encyclopedia) (2nd ed); member, ed collegium, journal "Byulleten' eksperimental'noy biologii i meditsiny," etc; wrote numerous works on biochemical extracts, amino acid synthesis, skin chemistry, metabolism, etc; *Publ: Biokhimiya kozhi* (The Biochemistry of the Skin) (1931); *Kislotnoshchelochnoye ravnovesiye v organizme i znacheniye yego narusheniy v patologii* (The Body's Acid-Alkaline Balance and the Pathological Significance of Its Disturbances) (1932); *Mineral'nyy obmen* (Mineral Metabolism) (1938); *Kislotnoshchelochnoye ravnovesiye v organizme i yego regulyatsiya* (The Body's Acid-Alkaline Balance and Its Regulation) (1940); *O narusheniyakh obmena aminokislot pri belkovoy nedostatochnosti i ikh ustranenii* (Disturbances of the Amino Acid Metabolism in Protein Insufficiency and Their Elimination) (1957); *Died*: 1965.

KAPLUN, Sergey Il'ich (1897-1943) Hygienist and health service official; CP member from 1917; *Born*: 9 May 1897; *Educ*: 1917 grad Moscow Univ; *Career*: 1914 joined student revol movement and Soc-Democratic org; 1918-27 worked for RSFSR and USSR Pop Comrt of Labor; 1925, together with V. A. Levitskiy, founded State Inst of Labor Welfare which specialized in the sci study of labor hygiene, ind sanitation and accident-prevention; 1927-32 dir of this inst; 1924 founded first Sov chair of hygiene at 2nd Moscow Med Inst; from 1926 until death founder-head, Chair of Labor Hygiene, 1st Moscow Med Inst; supervised compilation of labor welfare sections of Labor Code, which served as a basis for legislation on ind sanitation and accident-compensation; supervised the establishment of sanitary, tech and legal inspectorates within the framework of the Pop Comrt of Labor to control working conditions, labor welfare and ind safety regulations; for many years dep chm, Soc of Materialist Physicians, Communist Acad; from 1923 founder and exec ed, journal "Gigivena truda"; co-ed, *Tekhnicheskaya entsiklopediya* (Technical Encyclopedia) and *Bol'shaya meditsinskaya entsiklopediya* (Large Medical Encyclopedia) (1st ed); read papers on ind hygiene at numerous Sov and for congresses; Sov rep at various int org for labor hygiene and occupational diseases; wrote over 200 works, including first manual on labor hygiene for Sov med colleges; edited various translations of for works on soc hygiene and labor hygiene and pathology (Grotian, Koelsch, Levy, etc); compiled bibliographic index on labor welfare; *Publ: Sanitarnaya statistika truda* (Sanitary Labor Statistics) (1924); *Osnovy obshchey gigiyeny truda* (The Principles of General Labor Hygiene) (2 vol, 1925-26); *Teoriya i praktika okhrany truda* (The Theory and Practice of Labor Welfare) (2 vol, 1926-27); *Obshchaya gigyena truda* (General Labor Hygiene) (1940); *Died*: 1943 killed in action.

KAPP, Artur Iosifovich (1878-1952) Est composer; Hon Art Worker of Est SSR from 1945; one of first professional Est composers; *Born*: 28 Feb 1878 in Suure Jaani, Liflyand Province; *Educ*: 1898 grad organ class, 1900 composition class, Petersburg Conservatory, where he studied under N. A. Rimsky-Korsakov and A. K. Lyadov; *Career*: 1904-20 instructor, then dir, Astrakhan' Music College; 1020-24 conductor, "Estonia" Theater; 1920-25 instructor, 1925-40 prof, Tallinn Conservatory; *Works*: symphonies (1924, 1945, 1947), "Youth Symphony" (1949); "Peace Symphony" with soloist and choir accompaniment (1951); three cantatas "To the Sun"; four symphonic poems "Don Carlos"; oratorio "Job"; orchestral suites based on Est folk themes; solo instrumental concertos; chamber and choral music; *Awards*: Stalin Prize (1950); *Died*: 14 Jan 1952.

KAPPEL', Vladimir Oskarovich (? - 1920) Mil commander; col, Russian Army Gen Staff; gen under Admiral Kolchak; helped lead Whitist Forces in Volga, Urals and Siberia; *Career*: fought in WW 1; spring 1918 formed anti-Communist force in Samara; summer 1918, at head of this force, successively liberated Singiley, Simbirsk and Kazan' from Sov troops; then commanded 1st Volga Corps; Nov-Dec 1919 commanded 3rd Army; Dec 1919 appointed by Kolchak as commander in chief, Eastern Front; after rout of Kolchak's forces in Western Siberia directed their retreat from Omsk to Irkutsk; in the course of this action he broke through the ice, caught a severe chill and sustained frost-bitten legs; *Died*: 26 Jan 1920 of gangrene and croupous pneumonia; buried in Chita; Kolchak's forces were long termed *Kappelites* in his honor.

KAPUSTIN, Nikolay Yakovlevich (1878- ?) Mil commander; gen, Russian Army; *Born*: 1878; *Career*: during WW 1 at Russian Supr Commander in Chief's Headquarters; from 1918 training work with Red Army; lectured at Frunze Mil Acad; *Publ: Operativnoye iskusstvo v pozitsionnoy voyne* (The Art of Operations in Positional Warfare) (1927); *Died*: date and place of death unknown.

KARAKHAN, Lev Mikhaylovich (1889-1937) Govt official; lawyer and diplomat; CP member from 1904; *Born*: 1889 in Kutaisi Province; *Educ*: 1910-15 studied at Law Fac, Petersburg Univ; *Career*: from 1912 member, trade-union movement; from 1913 member, Org of Revol Internationalists (Mezhrayontsy); fall 1915 arrested and exiled to Tomsk; 1917 Presidium member and secr, Petrograd Sov and member, Petrograd Mil-Revol Comt; during 1917 Oct Revol, at which time he held the rank of ensign, elected chm, Corps Comt, 6th Army Corps; from Nov 1917 in Diplomatic Service; 1918-20 Collegium member, RSFSR Pop Comrt of For Affairs and RSFSR Dep Pop Comr of For Affairs; 1918 secr and member, Sov deleg at Brest-Litovsk; 1921 Sov plen in Warsaw; 1922 again RSFSR Dep Pop Comr of For Affairs; 1923-26 Sov plen in China; from 1927 USSR Dep Pop Comr of For Affairs; from 1930 USSR Second Dep Pop Comr of For Affairs and rep of this min at RSFSR Council of Pop Comr; from June 1934 Sov plen in Turkey; deleg, 16th and 17th CPSU(B) Congresses; member, USSR Centr Exec Comt; 16 Dec 1937 sentenced to death by the Mil Collegium, USSR Supr Court, on charges of terrorism and espionage; *Died*: Dec 1937 executed by firing squad.

KARAVAYEV, Pyotr Nikolayevich (1884-1952) Party official; CP member from 1903; *Born*: 1884 in Kologriva, Kostroma Province; *Educ*: from 1904 studied at Law Fac, Moscow Univ; *Career*: from early age participated in revol struggle; 1903 joined Party; organizer and member, Party comts in Kostroma, Ivanovo-Voznesensk, Moscow and Siberia; repeatedly arrested; until 1917 in exile; after 1917 Feb Revol member, Irkutsk Party Comt; during the Kolchak era worked underground in the Amur area; 1920 ed, "Amurskaya pravda"; member, Amur Party Comt; 1921-22 on orders of Party CC worked in America as member, govt deleg of the Far Eastern Republ; on his return from America appointed newspaper ed; elected member, Chita Control Commission; from 1924 member, Party Collegium, Centr Control Commission; 1928-34 secr, then chm, Party Collegium, Moscow Oblast Control Commission; member, Centr Control Commission of the 12th, 14th, 15th and 16th convocations; at 17th CPSU(B) Congress elected member, Party Control Commission; deleg, 18th CPSU(B) Congress; from Apr 1939 asst head, Centr Party Archives, Inst of Marxism-Leninism, CPSU CC; *Publ: Vtoraya konferentsiya RSDRP (Pervaya Vserossiyskaya)* (The 2nd [1st All-Russian] RSDRP Conference) (1950); *Tret'ya konferentsiya RSDRP (Vtoraya Vserossiyskaya)* (The 3rd [2nd All-Russian] RSDRP Conference) (1951); *V dooktyabr'skiye gody* (The Years Prior to the October Revolution) (1953), etc; *Died*: 10 June 1952.

KARAYEV, Dzhuma Durdy (1910-1960) Party and govt official; first secr, CC, CP Turkm from 1958; CP member from 1939; *Born*: 10 Jan 1910; *Educ*: 1917-26 attended boarding-school; 1933 grad Bayram-Ali Agric Technicum; 1950-52 studied at Higher Party School, CC, CPSU; *Career*: from 1932 dir, Bayram-Ali Boarding-School; 1935-37 dep dir and teacher, Bayram-Ali Educ Combine; from 1937 kolkhoz agronomist; from 1938 dir of a machine and tractor station; from 1940 member, Auditing Commission, CC, CP(B) Turkm; 1941-42 first secr, Takhta-Bazar Rayon Comt, CP(B) Turkm; 1942-43 Turkm Dep Pop Comr of State Control); 1943-47 first secr, Kerki Oblast Comt, CP(B) Turkm; 1947-50 Turkm Min of Agric; from 1950 member, CC, CP Turkm; 1952-58 first secr, Tashauz Oblast Comt, CP Turkm; from Jan 1958 chm, Turkm Council of Min; from 1958 also Bureau member, CC, CP Turkm; dep, USSR Supr Sov of 1950, 1954 and 1958 convocations; dep, Turkm Supr Sov of 1947, 1951 and 1959 convocations; *Awards*: four Orders of Lenin; two Orders of the Red Banner of Labor; Badge of Hon; medals; *Died*: 4 May 1960.

KARBYSHEV, Dmitriy Mikhaylovich (1880-1945) Mil commander; lt-col, Russian Army; lt-gen, Sov Army from 1940; prof; Dr of Mil Sci; specialist in mil fortifications; CP member from 1940; *Born*: 14 Oct 1880 in Omsk, son of a mil official; *Educ*: 1900 grad Nikolay Eng College; 1911 grad Nikolay Eng Acad; *Career*: 1898 joined Russian Army; 1904-05 eng on active service in Far East; took part in defense of Port Arthur; 1911-14 in charge of construction of forts at Brest Fortress and commander of one of these forts; 1914-17 div, then corps eng on Southwestern Front; from 1917 detachment eng, Red Guard in Mogilev-Podol'skiy; from 1918 in Red Army; Mar-Aug 1918 junior, then senior eng, RSFSR Eng Defense Collegium; from Aug 1918 mil eng on Eastern and Southern fronts; 1920 in charge of eng operations at Kakhov bridgehead; 1922 chief eng, Ukr Mil Distr; 1923 chm, Eng Comt, Red Army Main Mil Eng Bd; from 1923 instructor at mil academies; head, Chair of Eng, Frunze Mil Acad; dep head, Chair of Eng, Gen Staff Acad; at outbreak of WW 2 suffered shell-shock while inspecting fortification works on Western border and captured; refused to cooperate with Germans and was interned in various prison camps; died at Mauthausen camp, where a memorial was erected in his memory; a Sov Army research inst bears his name and his story is told in S. N. Golubev's novel *Kogda kreposti ne sdayutsya* (When Fortresses Do not Yield) (1953); *Publ: Vliyaniye usloviy bor'by na formy i printsipy fortifikatsii* (The Influence of Battle Conditions on the Forms and Principles of Fortification) (1921); *Inzhenernaya podgotovka Kakhovskogo platsdarma* (The Engineering Organization of the Kakhov Bridgehead) (1922); *Inzhenernaya podgotovka granits SSSR* (Engineering Organization on the Borders of the USSR) (1924); *Inzhenernaya razvedka* (Engineering Intelligence) (1928); *Sluzhba zagrazhdeniy i yeyo boyevoye ispol'zovaniye* (Obstacle-Building and Its Use in Battle) (1930); *Oborona Port-Artura 1904* (The 1904 Defense of Port Arthur) (1933); *Kratkiy spravochnik po voyenno-inzhenernomu delu* (A Short Reference Manual on Military Engineering) (1936); *Uroki Verdena* (The Lessons of Verdun) (1938); *Inzhenernoye obespecheniye oboronitel'noy operatsii* (Engineer Support in Defensive Operations) (1938); *Inzhenernoye obespecheniye nastupatel'noy operatsii* (Engineer Support in Offensive Operations) (1939); *Inzhenernoye obespecheniye boyevykh deystviy strelkovykh soyedineniy* (Engineer Support of Military Operations with Infantry Forces) (1939-40); *Awards*: Hero of the Sov Union (1946); Order of Lenin; Order of the Red Banner; *Died*: 18 Feb 1945.

KARDOVSKIY, Dmitriy Nikolayevich (1866-1943) Artist; Hon Art Worker of RSFSR from 1929; prof from 1907; member, Acad of Arts from 1915; *Born*: 5 Sept 1866 in vil Osurovo, Vladimir Province; *Educ*: 1892-1902 studied at Petersburg Acad of Arts under P. P. Chistyakov and I. Ye. Repin; 1896-1900 at Azhbe's studio in Munich; *Career*: prominent realist, master draftsman and expert on everyday life and art of 19th-century Russia; did illustrations for plays of Griboyedov, Gogol, Tolstoy and Chekhov; taught at Acad of Arts; 1920-29 designed theater sets, mainly for the Malyy Theater; designed sets for: *Les* (The Forest) (1921); *Revizor* (The Government Inspector) (1922, 1949); *Bednost' ne porok* (Poverty Is No Vice) (1924, 1953); Turgenev's *Nakhlebnik* (The Parasite) and *Zavtrak u predvoditelya* (Breakfast at the Marshal's) (1924); *Svoi lyudi - sochtyomsya* (Birds of a Feather Flock Together) (1929); A. N. Tolstoy's *Lyubov' - kniga zolotaya* (Love Is a Golden Book) (1923); helped design sets for Kugel's *Nikolay I i dekabristy* (Nicholas I and the Decembrists) (1926); *Died*: 10 Feb 1943.

KARELIN, Vladimir Aleksandrovich (1891-1938) Politician and govt official; founder-member, Leftist Socialist-Revolutionary Party; *Born*: 1891; *Career*: from Dec 1917 member, RSFSR Council of Pop Comr; Pop Comr of State Property; Collegium member, Pop Comrt of Justice; member, All-Russian Centr Exec Comt; member, Sov deleg at Brest-Litovsk; Mar 1918 ousted from RSFSR Council of Pop Comr after protesting Peace of Brest-Litovsk; July 1918 helped to organize uprising against Sov rule and emigrated after it was suppressed; Nov 1918 sentenced in absentia to three years' imprisonment by Sov court; in his latter years retired from politics; *Died*: 1938.

KARELINA-RAICH (real name: POPOVKINA), Raisa Andreyevna (1880-1957) Actress; Hon Art Worker of RSFSR from 1947; *Born*: 1880; *Educ*: studied at Blyumenfel'd Theatrical School, Kiev, under N. P. Roshchin-Insarov and Ye. Ya. Nedelin: *Career*: 1897, while still a student, joined ensemble at N. N. Solovtsov Theater, Kiev; 1900-25 performed in Novocherkassk, Kishinev, Kazan', Khar'kov, Kiev, etc; 1904-06 and 1925-33 acted at Korsh Theater, Moscow; from 1933 at Moscow Trade-Union Council Theater; 1948 retired from stage; *Roles*: Tanya in *Plody prosveshcheniya* (The Fruits of Enlightenment); Glafira in *Volki i ovtsy* (The Wolves and the Sheep); Liza in *Gore ot uma* (Woe from Wit); Catherine in Sardou's "Madame Saint-Jean"; title roles in "Larisa", "Anna Karenina", "Nora", etc; *Died*: 28 Sept 1957.

KAREYEV, Nikolay Ivanovich (1850-1931) Historian, sociologist and journalist; prof from 1879; hon member, USSR Acad of Sci from 1929; *Born*: 6 Dec 1850 in Moscow; *Educ*: 1873 grad Moscow Univ; *Career*: 1879-84 prof, Warsaw Univ; 1886-99 and from 1906 prof, Petersburg Univ; 1906 joined Constitutional Democratic Party; member, 1st State Duma; 1910-29 corresp member, Russian (USSR) Acad of Sci; achieved int fame for studies of agrarian history of France; *Publ: Krest'yane i krest'yanskiy vopros vo Frantsii v posledney chetverti XVIII veka* (The Peasants and the Peasant Question in France in the Last Quarter of the 18th Century) (1879); *Ocherk istorii frantsuzskikh krest'yan s drevneyshikh vremyon do 1789-ogo goda* (A Study of the History of the French Peasantry from Ancient Times to 1789) (1881); *Osnovnyye voprosy filosofii istorii* (Fundamental Questions of the Philosophy of History) (3 vol, 1883-90); *Pol'skiye reformy XVIII veka* (The 18th-Century Polish Reforms) (1890); *Istoriya Zapadnoy Yevropy v novoye vremya* (The Modern History of West Europe) (7 vol, 1892-1917); *Istoriki Frantsuzskoy revolyutsii* (The Historians of the French Revolution) (3 vol, 1924-25), etc; *Died*: 18 Feb 1931.

KARI-YAKUBOV, Mukhitdin (1896-1957) Uzbek opera singer (baritone) and theater dir; Pop Artiste of Uzbek SSR from 1936; *Born*: 1896 in Fergana, son of a worker; *Career*: until 1917 sang in mosques; 1918 joined "Moslem Youth Drama Ensemble"; 1918-21 performed at front-line theaters during Civil War; 1925 sang Uzbek folk songs at World's Exhibition in Paris and Berlin; performed as a dramatic actor with the "Polit Ensemble"; 1926 formed an "ethnographic" concert ensemble which became the nucleus of the Uzbek Musical Theater; 1926-34 dir, 1928-32 also artistic dir of this theater; from 1936 artistic dir, Uzbek Philharmonic Orchestra and soloist, Uzbek Theater of Opera and Ballet; *Roles*: Khosrov in Uspenskiy and Mushel"s "Farkhad and Shirin"; the Governor in Ashrafi and Vasilenko's "Snowstorm"; Naufal' in Glier and Sadykov's "Leyli and Medzhnun"; title role in Kozlovskiy's *Uglubek*; title role in Brusilovskiy's *Yer-Targyn; Died*: 1957.

KARIBZHANOV, Fazyl (1912-1960) Kaz Party and govt official; CP member from 1940; *Born*: 1912; *Educ*: 1933 grad Workers' Fac, Omsk; 1938 grad Siberian Agric Inst; *Career*: agronomist; from 1941 Party work; 1946-51 second secr, Karaganda Oblast Comt, CP Kaz; 1951 chm, Exec Comt, Karaganda Oblast Sov of Workers' Dep; 1951-53 head, Agric Dept, CC, CP Kaz; from Apr 1953 Kaz Min of Agric; 1954-58 secr, 1958-60 second secr, CC, CP Kaz; from Jan 1960 Presidium chm, Kaz Supr Sov; dep, USSR Supr Sov of 4th and 5th convocations; dep Kaz Supr Sov of 3rd-5th convocations; *Died*: Aug 1960.

KARIMI, Fatykh (real name: KARIMOV, Fatykh Gil'manovich) (1871-1946) Tatar writer and journalist; *Born*: 1871; *Career*: 1900 first work published; 1906-17 founder-ed, Tatar newspaper "Vakt"; the voice of progressive Tatar intellectuals, which set a nationalist tone; after 1917 Feb Revol resigned and founded new newspaper "Yanga Vakt," which pleaded for an independent Tatar state; after 1917 Oct Revol sided with the Soviets; during Sov period worked for the newspaper "Yul" and as Centr Asian corresp for the newspaper "Kzyl Tatarstan"; also worked for the Centr Publ House of the Peoples of the USSR; 1937 arrested by State Security organs; *Publ*: short stories "Dzhiangir Makhzum"; "Zikhangir Makhmud" (1900); "Shakird and the Student" (1903); "The Wedding of Salikh-babay", etc; *Died*: 1946 in imprisonment; posthumously rehabilitated.

KARINSKIY, Nikolay Mikhaylovich (1873-1935) Linguist and paleographer; specialist in Russian dialectology; corresp member, USSR Acad of Sci from 1921; *Born*: 3 Apr 1873; *Career*: from 1931 chm, Dialectology Commission, Inst of Language and Thought, USSR Acad of Sci; did research on the history of Russian and ancient Bulgarian, Russian dialectology and the paleography of the Russian and other Slavic peoples; *Publ: Khrestomatiya po drevne-tserkovnoslavyanskomu i russkomu yazykam. Chast' 1 - Drevneyshiye pamyatniki* (An Old Church Slavonic and Russian Reader. Part 1 - The Earliest Relics) (1904); *Obraztsy glagolitsy* (Specimens of the Glagolitic Alphabet) (1908); *Yazyk Pskova i yego oblasti v XV veke* (The Language of Pskov and Its Environs in the 15th Century) (1909); *Ocherki iz istorii pskovskoy pis'mennosti i yazyka. Vypusk 1 - Issledovaniye yazyka Pskovskogo Shestodneva 1374-ogo goda* (Studies in the History of the Written and Spoken Language of Pskov. Part 1 - A

Study of the Language of the 1374 Pskov Manuscript on the Six Days of Creation) (1916); *Ocherki iz istorii pskovskoy pis'mennosti i yazyka. Vypusk 2 - Musin-Pushkinskaya rukopis' Slova o polku Igoreve kak pamyatnik pskovskoy pis'mennosti XV-XVI vekov* (Studies in the History of the Written and Spoken Language of Pskov. Part 2 - The Musin-Pushkin Manuscript of the Lay of the Host of Igor as a Monument of the 15th-16th Century Language of Pskov) (1917);*Obraztsy pis'ma drevneyshego perioda istorii russkoy knigi* (Specimens of Lettering from the Earliest Period of the History of the Russian Book) (1925); *Ocherki yazyka russkikh krest'yan. Govor derevni Vanilovo* (Studies in Russian Peasant Speech. The Dialect of the Village Vanilovo) (1936), etc; *Died*: 14 Dec 1935.

KARIYEV, Abdulla (real name: KHAYRULLIN, Minnibay) (1886-1920) Tatar actor and producer; pioneer of Tatar national theater; *Born*: 20 May 1886; *Career*: 1907 began acting with "Sayyar" Tatar Drama Ensemble; 1918-19 actor-producer, Orsk Tatar Ensemble; specialized in character studies of rich Centr Asian landowners; was an adherent of critical realism in acting; trained such outstanding actors as G. Bolgarskaya, N. Arapova, N. Tadzharova, F. Il'skaya, G. Mangushev, Z. Sultanov and K. Tingurina; *Roles*: Khamza, Khafiz and Sirazetdin Tuktagayev in G. Kamal's comedies "First Introduction", "Our Town's Secrets" and "Bankrupt", which he also produced; Yunus Khadzhi in Sh. Kamal's "Khadzhi Effendi Gets Married" (1915); Badri in Fayzi's *Galiyabanu* (1918); classical roles: Podkolesin (1909); Dikoy in *Groza* (The Thunderstorm) (1913); Besemenov in *Meshchane* (The Philistines) (1917); the President in "Kabale und Liebe" 1909); Lopakhin in *Vishnyovyy sad* (The Cherry Orchard) (1918); *Productions*: "Kabale und Liebe" (1909); *Dokhodnoye mesto* (A Lucrative Post) (1915); Kulakhmetov's "Young Life" (1918), etc; *Died*: 28 Jan 1920.

KARNAUKHOV' Mikhail Mikhaylovich (1892-1955) Metallurgist; prof from 1927; member, USSR Acad of Sci from 1953; *Born*: 14 Mar 1892 in Orenburg; *Educ*: 1914 grad Petrograd Polytech Inst; *Career*: after grad worked at metallurgical plants in Alapayevsk, Taganrog, etc; 1920-27 lecturer, from 1927 prof, Petrograd Polytech Inst; 1939-53 corresp member, USSR Acad of Sci; from 1953 head, Leningrad Laboratory, Inst of Metallurgy, USSR Acad of Sci; helped to plan new metallurgical plants; specialized in the physiochemical principles of steel alloying processes, particularly the acid open-hearth process; *Publ: Metallurgiya stali* (Steel Metallurgy) (3 vol, 1933-34); *Awards*: Stalin Prize (1943); *Died*: 22 Dec 1955.

KARNAUKHOVA, Irina Valer'yanovna (1901-1959) Writer; folklorist; reciter of folk tales; *Born*: 20 Nov 1901 in Kiev; *Career*: 1926-32 took part in northern folklore expeditions (Zaonezh'ye, Pinega, Mezen', Pechora and Pomor'ye); arranged various anthologies of folk poetry for children; wrote novelettes and plays for children; many of her works translated into other languages; *Publ*: novelettes *Khruzhevo na machte* (Lace on the Mast); *Oy-kho. Povest' o samoyedskom mal'chike* (Oy-kho. The Story of a Samoyed Boy) (1931); plays *Starinka starodavnyaya pro moguchego russkogo bogatyrya Il'yu Muromtsa* (An Ancient Tale of the Mighty Russian Hero Il'ya Muromets) (1938); coauthor, *Alen'kiy tsvetochek* (The Little Scarlet Flower) (1946); *Zolotyye ruki* (Golden Hands) (1948); *Kolokola-lebedi* (The Swan Bells) (1948); *Skazki i predaniya Severnogo kraya* (Tales and Legends of the North) (1934); *Skazki babushki Ariny* (Grandmother Arina's Fairy Tales) (2nd ed, 1939); *Skazki* (Fairy Tales) (1940); *Raduga-duga* (The Rainbow Arc) (1946); *Zhar-ptitsa* (The Fire Bird) (1947); *Nenaglyadnaya krasota* (The Darling Beauty) (1949); *Russkiye bogatyri. Byliny* (Russian Mythical Heroes. Epics) (1949); *Povest' o druzhnykh* (A Story of Friends) (1954); *Banderol'* (The Wrapper) (1957); novelette *Nashi sobstvennyye* (Our Own People) (1958); *Died*: 13 Apr 1959 in Leningrad.

KARPINSKIY, Aleksandr Petrovich (1847-1936) Geologist; member, Imperial Acad of Sci in Petersburg from 1886; first elected pres, Russian Acad of Sci (from 1925 USSR Acad of Sci) 1917-36; *Born*: 7 Jan 1847 at Bogoslovskiy Plant, Verkhotur'ye Uyezd in the Urals (now Karpinsk, Sverdlovsk Oblast), son of mining eng; *Educ*: 1866 grad Mining Inst, Petersburg; 1869 defended cand thesis; *Career*: from 1869 junior sci asst, Dept of Geology and Geognosy, 1877-96 prof of geology, Mining Inst, Petersburg; 1882 helped found, 1885-1903 directed, Geological Comt, Acad of Sci; 1899-1936 pres, Mineralogical Soc of Russia and then of USSR; for many years headed Geological Section, Leningrad Soc of Naturalists; May 1916 - May 1917 acting vice-pres, Russian Acad of Sci; attended many int geological congresses; 1897 chm, Org Comt and pres, 7th session, Int Geological Congress in Petersburg; model research on tectonics and paleography of the European USSR; extensive research on geological surveying, stratigraphy, paleontology, tectonics, mineralogy and petrography of ferrous and non-ferrous deposits; compiled summary geological maps of the Urals and the European USSR; originally specialized in petrography; from 1880 concentrated on geology and paleontology; from 1910 worked on fossils; his works on tectonics and paleogeography are especially well known; first to propose now accepted theory on structure of the Russian Platform; *Publ*: about 300 monographs and articles; cand thesis *Ob avgitovykh porodakh derevni Muldakayevoy i gory Kachkanar na Urale* (Augitic Rocks of Muldakayevaya Village and Mount Kachkanar in the Urals) (1869); *Zamechaniya ob osadochnykh obrazovaniyakh Yevropeyskoy Rossii* (Notes on Sedimentary Formations of European Russia) (1880); *Zamechaniya o kharaktere dislokatsiy porod v yuzhnoy polovine Yevropeyskoy Rosii* (Notes on the Rock Distribution of the Southern Part of European Russia) (1883); *Ocherk fiziko-geograficheskikh usloviy Yevropeyskoy Rossii v minuvshiye geologicheskiye periody* (A Study of the Physical and Geographical Conditions of European Russia in Past Geological Periods) (1887); *Obshchiy kharakter kolebaniy zemnoy kory v predelakh Yevropeyskoy Rossii* (The General Character of Movements of the Earth's Crust Within European Russia) (1894); *K tektonike Yevropeyskoy Rossii* (The Tectonics of European Russia) (1919); *Ob ammoneyakh artinskogo yarusa i o nekotorykh skhodnykh s nimi kamennougol'nykh formakh* (Ammonites of the Artinsky Layer and Some Similar Coal Forms) (1889); *Ob ostatkakh yedestid i o novom ikh rode* (Edestidae Remnants and a New Genus of Edestidae) (1899); *O trokhiliskakh* (Trochilisci) (1906), etc; *Died*: 15 July 1936 in Moscow; ashes immured in Kremlin Wall.

KARPINSKIY, Vyacheslav Alekseyevich (1880-1965) Journalist; Party official; Dr of Econ; CP member from 1898; *Born*: 16 Jan 1880 in Penza, son of an intellectual; *Educ*: studied at Khar'kov Univ; *Career*: at age 17 began organizing Soc-Democratic groups in Penza; expelled from Khar'kov Univ for revol activities and exiled to Penza; travelled secretly to Rostov, where he continued his polit work; on return to Khar'kov co-founded local "League for the Liberation of the Working Class"; 1900 arrested; 1922 exiled to Vologda Province; fall 1903-fall 1904 in hiding; 1904 emigrated; met Lenin in Geneva and worked for the newspapers "Vperyod" and "Proletariy"; after 1917 Oct Revol ed, newspaper "Bednota"; head, Dept of Agitation and Instruction, All-Russian Centr Exec Comt; during Civil War made polit agitation cruises on SS "Krasnaya zvezda" and published the newspaper "Krasnaya zvezda"; member, All-Russian Centr Exec Comt if 1st-7th convocations; 1918-27 member, Main Ed Bd, newspaper "Pravda"; also edited other newspapers and journals; received over 100 letters from Lenin; 1936-37 worked for CC, CPSU(B); from 1937 engaged in research and propaganda; from 1959 Bd member, USSR Journalists' Union; wrote numerous pop-sci works as well as articles on Lenin and Communism; *Publ: Besedy o Leninizme* (Talks on Leninism) (1933); *Besedy o kommunizme* (Talks on Communism) (1958); *V. I. Lenin - vozhd', tovarishch, chelovek* (V. I. Lenin - the Leader, the Comrade, the Man) (1960), etc; *Awards*: two Orders of Lenin; Hero of Socialist Labor (1962); *Died*: 20 Mar 1965.

KARPOV, Aleksandr Terent'yevich (1917-1944) War hero; fighter-pilot; capt; CP member from 1942; *Born*: 17 Oct 1917 in vil Filenevo, Kaluga Oblast, son of a peasant; *Educ*: 1940 grad mil pilots' school; *Career*: from 1939 in Sov Air Force; 1941-44 flight and squadron commander, Leningrad and 1st Ukr Front; *Awards*: twice Hero of the Sov Union; Order of Lenin; other orders; *Died*: 20 Oct 1944 in aerial combat.

KARPOV (Party pseudonym: VLADIMIR), Lev Yakovlevich (1879-1921) Party and govt official; chemist; CP member from 1897; *Born*: 18 Feb 1879 in Kiev, son of a store clerk; *Educ*: 1910 grad Moscow Higher Tech College; *Career*: 1897 joined revol movement; 1898 helped to organize Moscow League for the Liberation of the Working Class; from 1900 worked in Voronezh and maintained contacts with Northern Workers' League; head, RSDRP CC Eastern Bureau, Samara; from late 1903 head, RSDRP CC, Southern Bureau, Kiev; July 1904 coopted to CC, RSDRP; from 1905 worked in Moscow; helped to organize distribution of newspaper "Vperyod"; Aug 1906-May 1907 secr, RSDRP Credentials Commission; frequently arrested; 1911-15 worked in Russian rosin and terpentine ind as a chemical eng; 1915-17 dir, Bondyuzhskiy Chemical Plant and Bolshevik group leader; from Feb 1918 Presidium member and head, Chemical Dept, Supr Sovnarkhoz; co-founder, Centr Chemical Laboratory (now the Karpov Physiochemical Research Inst); *Died*: 6 Jan 1921; buried on Red Square, Moscow.

KARPOV, Mikhail Yakovlevich (1898-1937) Writer; CP member from 1918; *Born*: 16 Nov 1898 in vil Timoshevka, Ufa Province; *Educ*: studied at univ and Communist Univ; *Career*: 1922 first work published; arrested by State Security organs; *Publ*: short story collection *Aprel'skiye preli* (April Moulds) (1925); novella "Karbush" (1926); novels: *Pyataya lyubov'* (Fifth Love) (1927); *Nepokornyy* (Unruly) (1930); "Aznayevo" (1934), etc; *Died:* 1937 in imprisonment; posthumously rehabilitated.

KARSKIY, Yevfimiy Fyodorovich (1861-1931) Linguist; pioneer of Bel linguistics and philology; prof from 1894; member, Russian (USSR) Acad of Sci from 1916; *Born*: 20 Dec 1861 in vil Lashi, now Grodno Oblast; *Educ*: 1885 grad Nezhin Historical and Philological Inst; *Career*: from 1894 prof, Warsaw Univ; 1901-16 corresp member, Russian Acad of Sci; from 1905 ed, journal "Russkiy filologicheskiy vestnik"; from 1920 ed, journal "Izvestiya otdeleniya russkogo yazyka i slovesnosti Akademii nauk"; specialized in the history of the Bel and Russian languages, Bel dialectology and Bel folklore; *Publ: Obzor zvukov i form belorusskoy rechi* (A Survey of Belorussian Sounds and Speech Forms) (1885); *K istorii zvukov i form belorusskoy rechi* (The History of Belorussian Sounds and Speech Forms) (1893); *O yazyke tak nazyvayemykh litovskikh letopisey* (The Language of the So-Called Lithuanian Chronicles) (1894); *Zapadnorusskiye perevody psaltyri v XV-XVII vekakh* (West Russian Psaltery Translations in the 15th-17th Century) (1896); *Materialy dlya izucheniya belorusskikh govorov* (Material for the Study of Belorussian Dialects) (6 vol, 1897-1910); *Listki Undol'skogo, otryvok kirillovskogo yevangeliya XI veka* (The Undol'skiy Papers. A Fragment of the 11th-Century Cyrillic Gospel) (1904); *Belorusy* (The Belorussians) (3 vol, 1903-22); *Russkaya dialektologiya* (Russian Dialectology) (1924); *Lavrent'yevskaya letopis'* (The Lavrent'yev Chronicle) (1926-28); *Slavyanskaya kirillovskaya paleografiya* (Slavonic Cyrillic Paleography) (1928); *Russkaya Pravda po drevnemu spisku* ("Russkaya Pravda," the Ancient Roll) (1930); *Trudy po belorusskomu i drugim slavyanskim yazykam* (Papers on Belorussian and Other Slavonic Languages) (1962); *Died*: 29 Apr 1931.

KARTASHOV, Nikolay Ivanovich (1867-1943) Locomotive designer; prof from 1903; Hon Sci and Tech Worker of RSFSR; *Born*: 17 Oct 1868; *Educ*: 1891 grad Khar'kov Technol Inst; *Career*: after grad worked for Russian railroad service; from 1893 worked on Ussuri Railroad; from 1903 prof, Tomsk Electromech Inst for Railroad Eng; specialized in the theory and design of steam locomotives; 1936 propagated Stakhanov movement in railroad service; *Publ: Parovoznyye paroraspredelitel'nyye sistemy. Zolotniki i kulissy* (Steam Distributing Systems for Locomotives. Slide Valves and Rocker Dies) (1914); *Parovozostroyeriye 2 - Kulissnyy mekhanizm Geysingera* (Steam Locomotive Construction 2 - Heisinger's Rocker Die Mechanism) (1929); *Kurs parovozov* (A Course on Steam Locomotives) (6 vol, 1929-33); *Proyektirovaniye parovozov. Raschyot glavnykh razmerov i sostavleniye eskiznogo proyekta* (Steam Locomotive Design. The Calculation of the Major Dimensions and the Preparation of Rough Blueprints) (2nd ed, 1936); *Awards*: Stalin Prize (1941); Order of Lenin; Badge of Hon; *Died*: 1943.

KARTVELISHVILI (Party pseudonym: LAVRENT'YEV), Lavrentiy Iosifovich (1891-1938) Party and govt official; CP member from 1910; *Born*: 1891 in Samtredia, Geo, son of a peasant; *Educ*: 1910 grad Kutaisi High-School; 1911-14 studied at Kiev Business Inst; *Career*: 1905 joined revol movement; 1915-16 did revol work in Saratov; 1917-18 chm, Kiev City Distr RSDRP(B) Comt; from May 1918 member Provisional All-Ukr Comt, Workers' CP; from July 1918 member, CC, CP(B) Ukr; continued Party work in Ukr during German occupation; late 1918-Aug 1919 member, Odessa Oblast and City Comt, CP(B) Ukr; member, Odessa Revol Comt; 1919 member, Revol-Mil Council, Southern Group, 12th Army; 1920 head, Org Dept, Odessa Oblast Comt, CP(B) Ukr and ed, newspaper "Kommunist"; 1921-23 secr, Kiev Province Comt, CP(B) Ukr; 1923-28 secr, CC, CP(B) Geo; 1929-31 head, Polit Bd, Ukr Mil Distr; later 2nd secr, Transcaucasian Kray CPSU(B) Comt; then chm, Geo Council of Pop Comr; 1931 again secr, Transcaucasian Kray CPSU(B) Comt, then secr, West Siberian Kray CPSU(B) Comt; 1933-36 secr, Far Eastern Kray CPSU(B) Comt, and member, Mil Council, Special Far Eastern Army; Jan-July 1937 secr, Crimean Oblast CPSU(B) Comt; deleg, 10th-17th CPSU(B) Congresses; cand member, CC at 16th CPSU(B) Congress; member, CC at 17th CPSU(B) Congress; arrested by State Security organs; *Died*: 1938 in imprisonment; posthumously rehabilitated.

KARUZIN, Pyotr Ivanovich (1864-1939) Anatomist; Dr of Med from 1894; prof from 1900; Hon Sci Worker of RSFSR from 1936; *Born*: 1864; *Educ*: 1888 grad Med Fac, Moscow Univ; *Career*: from 1889 asst dissector, Chair of Normal Anatomy, Moscow Univ; 1894 defended doctor's thesis on nerve fibers of the spinal cord; 1894-1923 lectured on anatomy at Moscow College of Painting, Sculpture and Architecture; 1900-30 prof, Chair of Normal Anatomy, Moscow Univ; also lectured at Higher State Tech Art Studios, State Inst of Stagecraft and Inst of Physical Educ; organized chairs of normal anatomy in Tbilisi, Astrakhan, Smolensk and Minsk, which he visited on a lecture tour; 1924 helped to embalm Lenin's corpse; 1928 supervised planning and construction of new building for Anatomical Inst, 1st Moscow Med Inst on Mokhovaya Street; was one of first Russians to study the conduction paths of the centr nervous system; divided the white matter of the spinal cord into two major groups depending on the period of myelination: 1. early development group (the sensory fibers and, in part, the motor fibers); 2. late development group (the corticospinal tract and the fibers of the Lissauer zone); distinguished different fiber systems in embryos and fetuses on the basis of development; member, various planning and educ reform commissions; member, Sci Methods Commission on Physical Educ, USSR Supr Sov; edited several anatomy manuals; *Publ*: doctor's thesis *O sistemakh volokon spinnogo mozga, vydelyayemykh na osnovanii istorii ikh razvitiya* (The Fiber Systems of the Spinal Cord Divided on the Basis of the History of Their Development) (1894); *Zametki o sovremennom prepodavanii anatomii v nemetskikh universitetakh* (Notes on Modern Methods of Teaching Anatomy at German Universities) (1900); *Zapiski po plasticheskoy anatomii chelovecheskogo tela* (Notes on the Plastic Anatomy of the Human Body) (1901); *Rukovodstvo po plasticheskoy anatomii* (A Guide to Plastic Anatomy) (1921); *O razmerakh, roste i proportsiyakh chelovecheskogo tela* (The Dimensions, Growth and Proportions of the Human Body) (1921); *Slovar' anatomicheskikh terminov* (A Dictionary of Anatomical Terms) (1928); *Died*: 25 Sept 1939.

KASATKIN, Nikolay Alekseyevich (1859-1930) Painter; member, Russian Acad of Painting from 1898; member, Petersburg Acad of Arts from 1903; Pop Artiste of RSFSR from 1923; *Born*: 13 Dec 1859 in Moscow; *Educ*: 1873-83 studied at Moscow College of Painting, Sculpture and Architecture; *Career*: carried on tradition of Russian realism; from 1891 active member, Soc of Itinerant Art Exhibitions; 1907-17 taught at Moscow School of Painting, Sculpture and Architecture and at Sytin Art School; 1922 exhibited several cycles of paintings at 47th Itinerant Art Exhibition; in same year joined Assoc of Artists of Revol Russia; 1924 visited England; helped to organize several art museums; several of his paintings are on display in the Tret'yakov Gallery and the Moscow Museums; *Works*: "The Rivals" (1890); "Orphaned" (1891); "The Joke" (1892); "It's a Hard Life" (1892); "The Stormy Petrel" (1892); "Slander" (1893); "The Girl at the Fence" (1893); "Streetcar Arrival" (1894); "The Poor Digging Coal at a Worked-Out Mine" (1894); "The Mine-Girl" (1894); "Change of Shift at a Coal-Pit" (1895); "The Coal-Hauler" (1895); "In the Corridor of a Circuit Court" (1897); "Visiting Hour at a Women's Jail" (1898); "January 9"; "After the Search"; "The Spy's Last Walk" (1905); "Women Workers Storm the Factory" (1906); "The Serf Performer in Disgrace" (1912); series of paintings on Sormovo Plant (1919); "English Miners Leaving the Pit" (1927); "The Great Strike in England" (unfinished); "The Rural Correspondent" (1927); portraits of Young Pioneers and Komsomol members; "Writing the School Newspaper" (1927); *Died*: 30 Dec 1930.

KASHAKASHVILI, Valerian Sardionovich (pseudonyms: KASHELI;TORELI) (1899-1954) Geo opera singer (baritone); prof from 1945; Hon Art Worker of Geo SSR from 1943; *Born*: 20 May 1899; *Educ*: 1923 grad Prof A. Dzhakeli's class, Tbilisi Conservatory; 1925 further training in Milan under the "La Scala" soloist, Prof M. Sammarco; *Career*: 1923-25 at Tbilisi Opera and Ballet Theater; 1925 performed in Milan, Rome, Pisa and other Italian cities; from 1928 soloist, Paliashvili Opera and Ballet Theater; at first sang baritone parts, from 1933 dramatic tenor; from 1928 instructor; from 1945 prof, Tbilisi Conservatory; *Roles:* Kiazo in Paliashvili's "Daisi"; Valentin in "Faust"; Tonio, Canio in "Bajazzo"; Amonasro and Radames in "Aida"; Scarina and Cavaradossi in "Tosca"; Manrico in "The Troubadour"; Othello and Iago in Verdi's "Othello"; Rigoletto, etc; *Died*: 19 Aug 1954.

KASHCHENKO, Vsevolod Petrovich (1870-1943) Child defectologist; prof; pioneer of advanced training in defectology; *Born*: 21 Mar 1870; *Educ*: 1891-94 studied at Med Fac, Moscow Univ; expelled for involvement in student revol circles and exiled from Moscow; 1897 grad Med Fac, Kiev Univ; *Career*: 1908, deprived of right to hold publ office for polit "unreliability," opened a private sanatorium-school for abnormal children; 1918, on the basis of this school, founded a "Child-Study Home" (later Med Pedag Experimental Station), the sections of which subsequently developed into the Experimental Defectological Inst, the Practical and Sci Inst of Special Schools and, in 1943, the Inst of Defectology; 1918 and 1919 organized training courses for defectologists in Moscow; 1920-24 rector and prof, Moscow Pedag Inst of Child Defectiveness; in latter years specialized in logopedics and worked at the Kremlin Polyclinic and the polyclinic of the 2nd Moscow Med Inst; in his treatment of defective children made extensive use of natural physiotherapy (sun, air, water), special diets, occupational therapy, gymnastics and rest; his training and educ programs were based on the use of methods encouraging a maximum of activity and independence; stressed the necessity of developing the qualities, vitality and cognitive powers of defective children rather than inculcating quantitative knowledge; made considerable use of visual aids, manual work and games for instruction purposes; emphasized the individual approach to the educ and training of abnormal children on the basis of thorough preliminary analysis of the capabilities of each child; interpreted the purpose of such educ as consisting in instilling in the defective child a relationship to self and environment which elicits the desire to acquire normal behavior patterns; in late 1930's his writings were criticized for containing idealistie trends; was censured for belief that defects are hereditary or "congenital"; *Publ*: ed, *Defektivnyye deti i shkola* (Defective Children and School) (1912); coauthor, *Vospitaniye-obucheniye trudnykh detey* (The Training and Instruction of Difficult Children) (1913); ed, *Putyom tvorchestva* (By Creative Means) (1922); *Died*: 30 Nov 1943.

KASHIRIN, Ivan Dmitriyevich (1890-1937) Mil commander; CP member from 1919; *Born*: 1890; *Career*: Cossack staff capt; from 1918 in Red Army; during Civil War commander, Upper Ural Detachment; commander, Independent Cavalry Brigade; after Civil War worked for All-Russian Cheka; arrested by State Security organs; *Died*: 1937 in imprisonment.

KASHIRIN, Nikolay Dmitriyevich (1888-1938) Mil commander; army commander, 2nd class from 1935; Civil War veteran; CP member from 1918; *Born*: 4 Feb 1888 in vil Verkhneural'sk, Orenburg Province, son of a Cossack teacher who later became the vil ataman; *Educ*: 1909 grad Orenburg Junkers' College; *Career*: 1912 discharged from 5th Orenburg Cossack Regt for agitation against the govt; during WW 1 reached rank of staff capt; 1916 wounded and returned home; Mar 1917 fought for Soviets with a Cossack unit; 1918 formed Cossack detachment at Verkhneural'sk to oppose troops of Ataman Dudov; from 16 July 1918 commander in chief, after being wounded dep commander, Southern Ural Composite Partisan Detachment operating behind the lines of the White Army in the Southern Urals; from Sept 1918, after induction into Red Army, dep commander, then commander, 4th Ural (later 30th Rifle) Div; 1919 commandant, Orenburg Fortified Region; commander, 49th Fortress Div, Turkestani Front; 1920 chm, Orenburg-Turgay Province Exec Comt; commander, 3rd Cavalry Corps, Southern Front; commander, Aleksandrov Group of Forces in campaign against Ataman Makhno; 1923-25 commander, 14th Rifle Corps; special duties for Red Army Gen Staff; commander, 1st Red Cossack Cavalry Corps; 1925-31 dep commander, various mil distr; 1931-37 commander, North Caucasian Mil Distr; from 1934 member, USSR Mil Council; June 1937 member, Special Tribunal of RSFSR Supr Court in trial of Marshal Tukhachevskiy and others, who were sentenced to death by firing squad; July-Aug 1937 head, Main Mil Training Bd; late 1937 arrested by State Security organs; *Awards*: six orders for WW 1 services; *Died*: 14 June 1938 in imprisonment; posthumously rehabilitated.

KASHKAROV, Daniil Nikolayevich (1878-1941) Zoologist; specialist in vertebrate ecology; prof; Dr of Biology from 1934; prof; CP member from 1941; *Born*: 30 Mar 1878 in Ryazan'; *Educ*: 1903 grad Natural Sci Dept, 1908 Med Fac, Moscow Univ; *Career:* from 1908 worked in Tübingen, Graz, Vienna and Bergen; from 1914 lecturer, Moscow Univ; 1916 defended master's thesis on zoology and comparative anatomy; 1919-33 head, Chair of Vertebrate Zoology, Centr Asian Univ, Tashkent; 1934-41 head, Chair of Vertebrate Zoology, Leningrad Univ; made numerous field trips to study vertebrate animals of Centr Asia; favored the ecological approach to the study of animals; 1934-39 ed, periodical "Voprosy ekologii biotsenologii"; *Publ: Kurs biologii pozvonochnykh* (A Course of Vertebrate Biology) (1929); coauthor, *Kholodnaya pustynya Tsentral'nogo Tyan'-Shanya* (The Cold Desert of the Central Tyan'-Shan') (1937); *Ekologiya domashnikh zhivotnykh* (The Ecology of Domestic Animals) (1937); coauthor, *Kurs zoologii pozvonochnykh zhivotnykh* (A Course of Vertebrate Animal Zoology) (1940); *Osnovy ekologii zhivotnykh* (The Principles of Animal Ecology) (1945); *Died*: 26 Dec 1941.

KASHKIN, Ivan Aleksandrovich (1899-1963) Russian translator and critic; *Born*: 24 June 1899 in Moscow; *Educ*: 1924 grad 2nd Moscow Univ; *Career*: taught at Moscow higher educ establishments; trained many Sov translators working from English; laid down principles for reproducing in Russian the style and individual traits of 20th-century poets and prose writers; these principles were implemented in Kashkin's translations of Conrad, Stevenson, Hardy, Hemingway, Caldwell, etc; wrote about English and American writers Chaucer, Frost, Caldwell, Sandburg, Faulkner, etc; wrote works on theory of translating; wrote first Sov studies of Hemingway; 1959 edited two-vol ed of Hemingway's works; *Publ*: co-translator of Chaucer's "Canterbury Tales" (1946); *Perechityvaya Khemingueya* (Rereading Hemingway) (1956); *Kheminguey na puti k masterstvu* (Hemingway on the Path to Craftmanship) (1957); *O samom glavnom. Proza E. Khemingueya* (The Main Aspects of Hemingway's Prose) (1960); *Tekushchiye dela. Zametki o stile perevodcheskoy raboty* (Current Affairs. Notes on Translation Style) (1959); anthology of American poets *Slyshu, poet Amerika* (I Hear You, Poet America) (1960); *Ispaniya v rasskazakh Khemingueya* (Spain in Hemingway's Stories) (1964); "Hemingway" (1966); "Ernest Hemingway" (1966), etc; *Died*: 26 Feb 1963 in Moscow.

KASTAL'SKIY, Aleksandr Dmitriyevich (1856-1926) Composer; specialist in musical folklore and choral music; teacher; prof from 1923; *Born*: 28 Nov 1856 in Moscow; *Educ*: 1882 grad Composition Class, Moscow Conservatory (student of Tchaikovsky, N. A. Gubert and S. I. Taneyev); *Career*: while still a student directed railroad workers' chorus; from 1887 teacher and choral precentor, Moscow Synodal College; from 1910 dir of this college; 1918-23 dir, Pop Choral Acad, founded according to his plan from the former college; from 1923 prof, Moscow Conservatory; taught many Russian composers and choral specialists, including D. S. Vasil'yev-Buglay, A. A. Davidenko, etc; prior to Revol wrote mainly sacred music; one of the first to compose Sov revol songs and choral songs to lyrics by Sov poets; played an important part in the development of Russian choral music; of great value are his papers on folklore; *Works*: opera "Klara Milich" (1907); "Agricultural Symphony" (1923); "V. I. Lenin (At His Tomb)" (1924); choral works: "1905" (1925); Russia; Ekh, Troika; "Song of Razin's Companions"; arranged the anthem "The Internationale"; eight piano pieces "Trough Georgia," etc; *Publ: Osobennosti narodno-russkoy muzykal'noy sistemy* (Characteristics of the Russian Folk Music System) (1923); *Osnovy narodnogo mnogogolosiya* (The Basis of Folk Polyphony) posthumous ed, 1948); *Died*: 17 Dec 1926 in Moscow.

KASTORSKIY, Sergey Vasil'yevich (1898-1962) Russian lit historian; *Born*: 1 Oct 1898 in vil Sigontino, Kostroma Province; *Educ*: 1927 grad Leningrad Herzen Teachers' Training Inst; *Career*: prof, Leningrad Teachers' Training Inst; senior assoc, Inst of Russian Lit, USSR Acad of Sci; 1928 first work published; specialized on life and work of Gorky; contributed to 10-vol *Istoriya russkoy literatury* (The History of Russian Literature) compiled by USSR Acad of Sci; contributed to Inst of Russian Lit serial publications *M. Gor'kiy. Materialy i issledovaniya* (M. Gorky. Material and Research), *Voprosy sovetskoy literatury*

(Soviet Literature), etc; *Publ: M. Gor'kiy i poety 'Znaniya'* (Gorky and the "Znaniye" Poets); articles and lit studies: "Gorky and Bunin" (1936); "A Hero of Our Time" (1941); "Gorky and the Realist Writers of the Late 19th and Early 20th Centuries" (1948); novelette *Leto* (Summer) (1951); "Gorky's Poems" (1951); "Gorky's Novelette 'Mother,' Its Social, Political and Literary Significance" (1954); "The Traditions of Gorky in the Modern Essay" (1956); "Herzen and Gorky" (1962); "Gorky's Novelette 'The Artamonov Affair'" (1961); "L. Tolstoy and Gorky" (1961); *Gor'kiy - khudozhnik* (Gorky the Artist) (1963); *Dramaturgiya M. Gor'kogo. Nablyudeniya nad ideyno-khudozhestvennoy spetsifikoy* (Gorky's Plays. Observations on Their Ideological and Artistic Character) (1963), etc; *Died*: 26 June 1962 in Leningrad.

KASTORSKIY, Vladimir Ivanovich (1871-1948) Russian opera singer (bass); Hon Art Worker of RSFSR from 1939; *Born*: 14 Mar 1871 in vil Bol'shiye Soli, Kostroma Province; *Career*: 1894 began stage career in opera troupe which toured Russia; from 1898 soloist, Mariinskiy Theater (later Kirov Opera and Ballet Theater); his performance of Sobakin in the premiere of *Tsarskaya nevesta* (Bride of the Tsar) was praised by Rimsky-Korsakov; 1907-08 performed in "Russian Seasons Abroad" concerts; 1907 organized vocal quartet which performed in Russia and abroad; prof, Leningrad Conservatory; *Roles*: the Marriage-Broker; the Miller in *Rusalka* (The Water Nymph); Ruslan; Dosifey in "Khovanshchina"; Pimen in "Boris Godunov"; Gudal in "Demon"; Gremin in "Yevgeniy Onegin"; Tomskiy in "Pikovaya dama" (The Queen of Spades); Wotan in Wagner's "Ring der Nibelungen," etc; *Died:* 2 July 1948 in Leningrad.

KASUMOV, Mir Bashir Fattakh ogly (1879-1949) Party and govt official; CP member from 1905; *Born*: 1879 in vil Dashbuly, Tabriz Vilayet; son of a peasant; *Career*: 1905-07 took active part in Revol; frequently arrested for polit activities; 1918-20 Baku proletariat leader; 1920 elected member CC at 1st Congress, CP(B) Azer; from 29 Apr 1920 member, Baku Revol Comt; 1920-21 head, Baku Workers and Peasants' Inspectorate; 1921-25 and 1931-35 dep chm, Azer Centr Exec Comt; 1935-37 Azer Pop Comr of Soc Security; dep, USSR Supr Sov of 1st and 2nd convocations; also dep chm, Presidium, USSR Supr Sov; 1938-49 Presidium chm, Azer Supr Sov; *Awards*: two Orders of Lenin; other orders and medals; *Died*: 1949.

KAS'YAN (TER-KASPARYAN), S. I. (1876-1938) Arm Party and govt official; CP member from 1905; *Born*: 1876; *Career*: did revol work in Transcaucasus; ed, illegal Bolshevik newspaper "Benvori Dzayn"; frequently arrested and exiled; after 1917 Oct Revol resumed work in Transcaucasus; 1920 first chm, Arm Revol Comt; 1923-27 rector, Transcaucasian Communist Univ; 1927-31 chm, Transcaucasian and Arm Centr Exec Comt; member, USSR Centr Exec Comt; arrested by State Security organs; *Died*: 1938 in imprisonment.

KAS'YANOV, Aleksandr Mikhaylovich (1906-1961) Architect; corresp member, Ukr Acad of Building and Architecture from 1958; CP member from 1940; *Born*: 23 Feb 1906 in Khar'kov, son of a teacher; *Educ*: 1930 grad Khar'kov Art Inst; *Career*: 1930-50 taught at Khar'kov Building Inst and other educ establishments; 1943-50 chief architect of Khar'kov; 1950-61 dir, Urban Building Research Inst, Ukr Acad of Architecture; helped to compile gen building plans for Khar'kov, L'vov, Chernigov, Lugansk, Kamenets-Podol'sk and other Ukr towns; also worked on individual projects, including the design for the centr square in Novaya Kakhovka; *Publ: Sovetskoye gorodskoye stroitel'stvo na Ukraine* (Soviet Urban Building in the Ukraine) (1955); *Gorod budushchego* (The City of the Future) (1957), etc; *Died*: 23 Sept 1961.

KAS'YANOV, Vladimir Pavlovich (pseudonym: Villi NAD) (1883-1960) Film dir, scriptwriter and actor; *Born*: 12 July 1883; *Career*: 1905 actor in P. Orlenev's provincial troupe; 1912 wrote his first film script; subsequently worked mainly as film dir; after 1917 Oct Revol helped develop Sov cinematography; films of this period deal with Civil War and Revol; film actor; 1938-57 with Main Film Hire Bd; *Works*: directed about 30 films: *Moroz po kozhe* (Goosepimples) (1912); *Nakhlebnik* (The Parasite) (1913); *Zavet materi* (A Mother's Legacy) (1913); *Rannyaya mogila* (Early Grave) (1913); *Devushka iz podvala* (The Girl from the Basement) (1914); *Drama v kabare futuristov Nr 13* (Drama in the Futurists' Cabaret Nr 13) (1914); *Kak malo prozhito, kak mnogo perezhito* (Life Is So Short, Experience So Great) (1914); *Guttaperchevyy mal'chik* (The India-Rubber Boy) (1915); *Son'ka – zolotaya ruchka* (Son'ka with the Golden Hand) (1915); *Rokovaya zhenshchina* (Fatal Woman) (1916); *Gde pravda?* (Where Is the Truth?) (1917); *Zhizn' pobezhdyonnaya smert'yu* (Life Conquered by Death) (1917); *Podpol'ye* (Underground) (1918); *Za krasnoye znamya* (For the Red Banner) (1919); *Pod vlast'yu adata* (Under the Power of the Moslem Law) (1926); "Leon Couturier" (1927); *Sed'moy sputnik* (The Seventh Companion) (1928); *Te, kotoryye prozreli* (Those Who See Clearly) (1931); wrote scripts for a number of his own films: *Moroz po kozhe, Rannyaya mogila, Kak malo prozhito, kak mnogo perezhito* and *Guttaperchevyy mal'chik*, etc; *Died*: 24 Nov 1960.

KATANYAN, Ruben Pavlovich (1881-1966) Party and govt official; CP member from 1903; *Born*: 1881, son of a teacher; *Educ*: studied at Moscow Univ; *Career*: 1901 joined revol movement; frequently arrested by Tsarist authorities; 1903-04 worked in student soc-democratic org in Moscow, for which he was arrested; 1905 worked in Soc-Democratic org on Orenburg Railroad; 1906-08 did undercover work in Moscow and Tbilisi; 1908-09 co-ed, Bolshevik journal "Bor'ba," Tiflis; 1909-13 conducted lit-propaganda work for Tiflis RSDRP(B) Org; 1917 member, Moscow Centr Trade-Union Bureau; Mar-Sept 1917 member, Internationalist Group; during 1917 Oct Revol worked for "Izvestiya Voyenno-revolyutsionnogo komiteta"; 1919 served on front with 11th Army as ed, newspaper "Krasnyy voin," then head, Polit Dept, Army Polit Bd; 1920-21 head, Agitation and Propaganda Dept, CC, RCP(B); from 1923 asst to RSFSR State Prosecutor; senior asst to Supr Court Prosecutor; 1933-37 senior asst, USSR State Prosecutor; prosecutor in a number of polit trials; 1938 arrested by State Security organs; 1955 rehabilitated and pensioned; *Died:* 6 June 1966.

KATAYEV, Ivan Ivanovich (1902-1939) Russian writer; CP member from 1919; *Born*: 27 May 1902 in Moscow, son of a prof; *Educ*: studied at Econ Fac, Moscow Univ; *Career*: 1919 volunteered for the Red Army; 1921 first work published; originally wrote verse but later changed to prose; 1923-25 member, All-Russian Assoc of Proletarian Writers; 1926-32 helped run "Pereval" lit assoc; 1934 elected bd member, USSR Writers' Union; 1937 arrested by State Security organs; *Publ*: novelette *Serdtse* (The Heart) (1928); collected stories: *Dvizheniye* (Movement) (1932); *Chelovek na gore* (The Man on the Mountain) (1934); novelettes *Moloko* (Milk) (1930); *Vstrecha* (The Encounter) (1934); *Na krayu sveta* (On the Edge of the World) (1933); *Ledyanaya Ellada* (Icy Hellas) (1933); *Otechestvo* (The Fatherland) (1934); story *Pod chistymi zvyozdami* (Under Pure Stars) (written 1937, first published 1956); *Died*: 2 May 1939 in imprisonment; posthumously rehabilitated.

KATENINA, Lidiya Mikhaylovna (1878-1965) Party and govt official; CP member from 1904; *Born*: 1878; *Career*: 1901 arrested for involvement in student riots; from 1903 worked for Petersburg RSDRP org; 1904 member, Bureau of Bolshevik Committees; worked as cipher-clerk and corresponded with other Soc-Democratic groups; 1905-10 tech secr, Petersburg's Moscow and City Rayon RSDRP Comt; 1911-13 worked for Kostroma health service, then in Moscow, Tyumen', Simferopol' and Ufa; helped to consolidate Sov rule in Kineshma; 1936-50 contributed to history of Civil War published in journal "Istorik-marksist"; worked for Historical Records Inst, Lit Archive and Main Records Bd; from 1956 pensioner; *Died*: 4 June 1965.

KATIN-YARTSEV, Viktor Nikolayevich (1875-1928) Otolaryngologist; revolutionary; explorer; *Born*: 10 Jan 1875 in Samara Province, son of an office worker who was expelled from Petersburg Med Surgical Acad for revol activities; *Educ*: 1892 grad Saratov boys' high-school; 1904 grad Petersburg Mil-Med Acad; *Career*: from 1892 worked together with G. V. Plekhanov in Saratov revol circles; after entering Mil-Med Acad continued revol work in Petersburg with K. M. Takhtaryov, V. P. Invashin, M. Ya. Sitnikov, N. E. Bauman, etc; 1895 joined Marxist movement and was coopted to CC, League for the Liberation of the Working Class, most of whose members (including Lenin) were arrested; 1896 and 1897 took part in Petersburg workers' strikes; Mar 1897 arrested for involvement in student demonstration after the suicide of student M. F. Vetrovaya in Peter-Paul Fortress; 1899 exiled to Eastern Siberia for five years after spending nine months in prison and 13 months under investigative custody; spent exile in Yakutsk, where he taught, did med work and wrote for journal "Vostochnoye obozreniye"; 1902 joined E. Toll's polar expedition to the Novosibirsk islands and Sannikov Land; in the course of the expedition covered 3,000 kilometers on horse and sledge, traveling along the Lena and Aldan, through the Upper Kolyma and Verkhoyansk regions, along the River Yana and the Arctic littoral; visited many Arctic islands with the MS *Zarya*; 1904 obtained med qualifications at Mil-Med Acad after return from exile; drafted into army and sent to Japanese front as junior surgeon, 88th Petrine Infantry Regt; after Russo-Japanese War opened med practice in Petersburg and worked as a physician at Okhtinskiy Gunpowder Works, where he resumed revol activities; from 1908 specialized in otolaryngology; 1913 studied otolaryngology in London and attended Int Med Congress; 1914 drafted into army and appointed intern, Ear Dept, Nikolay Mil Hospital, Petersburg; at this time joined Lit Soc, to which Gorky also belonged; 1917 treated Lenin in Petrograd; 1918 med adviser, then head, Bureau of Med Expertise, Petrograd Province Health Dept; head, Petrograd Bureau, Soc Insurance Comt; in latter years of life senior assoc, Leningrad Inst of Mother and Child Care; also worked at Otophonetic Inst and Inst of Occupational Diseases, where he lectured on otolaryngology; wrote numerous works on soc insurance, otolaryngology, exploration, reminiscences of the Revol and lit works; published articles in med journals and in such journals as *Voprosy strakhovaniya, Katorga i ssylka, Mir Bozhiy* and *Byloye*; also wrote a book on the Petersburg strike of 1896 entitled *Istoricheskaya stachka* (A Historic Strike) (1926); *Died*: 1 Nov 1928 in Leningrad of lung tuberculosis; buried in Volkovyy Cemetery near his friend G. V. Plekhanov.

KATS, Yakov Yur'yevich (1869-1933) Health service official; prof; *Born*: 1 Jan 1869 in Bessarabia Province; *Educ*: 1890 grad Natural Sci Dept, Fac of Physics and Mathematics, 1893 grad Med Fac, Moscow Univ; *Career*: for 25 years worked in zemstvo sanitary and health service; from 1894 distr physician, Tula Province; from 1908 health officer, Dmitrov Uyezd, Moscow Province; from 1917 Bd member, Pirogov Soc and chm, All-Russian League of Physicians' Professional Assoc; 1917 transferred to Moscow Sanitary Bureau, where he did research and statistical work; from 1918 prof of child hygiene, Pedological Courses, RSFSR Pop Comrt of Health; 1919-20 dep head, from 1920 head, Sanitary Epidemic Section, Moscow Health Dept, where he adopted and developed the "Moscow dispensary system"; from 1920 also prof, Moscow Pedological Inst and Pedag Fac, 2nd Moscow State Univ; Bureau member, Physicians' Section, All-Russian Med and Sanitary Workers' Union; from 1925 member, Moscow Sov of Workers and Peasants' Dep of several convocations; from 1925 ed, anthology *Trud i zdorov'ye rabochikh* (Workers' Labor and Health); *Publ: Moskva, yeyo sanitarnoye i epidemiologicheskoye sostoyaniye* (Moscow and its Sanitary and Epidemiological Conditions) (1924); *Sistema i metody dispanserizatsii* (The Dispensary System and its Methods) (1925); *Dispansernaya sistema obsluzhivaniya v svete dvukhletnego opyta goroda Moskvy i Moskovskoy gubernii* (The Dispensary Service in the Light of Two Years of Experience in Moscow and Moscow Province) (1926); *Sanitarnaya organizatsiya Moskovskoy gubernii* (The Sanitary Organization of Moscow Province) (1928); *Yedinyy dispanser* (The Common Dispenser) (1930); *Died*: 1933.

KATTS, Azariy Yakovlevich (1883-1952) Stomatologist; Dr of Med from 1935; *Born*: 1883; *Educ*: 1924 grad Leningrad Mil Med Acad; *Career*: from 1929 assoc, Chair of Normal Anatomy, Leningrad Mil Med Acad; 1935 defended doctor's thesis on the structure of the lower jaw; from 1936 founder-head, Chair of Orthopedic Stomatology, Leningrad Stomatological Inst; specialized in the functional anatomy of the jaws, biological methods of orthodontic treatment, the functional diagnosis of occlusal anomalies, the mechanism of dentition, and methods of treating neoplasms of the jaw; made major contribution to the development of the functional trend in Sov orthopedic stomatology; designed several stomatological corrective devices, including special jacket-crowns, a bite-plate and sprung braces; wrote over 60 works; 1940 together with N. A. Astakhov and Ye. M. Gofung, wrote first Sov textbook on orthopedic stomatology; *Publ*: coauthor, *Sovremennyye problemy stomatologii* (Contemporary Problems of Stomatology) (1935); *Lecheniye sformirovavshikhsya anomaliy prikusa* (The Treatment of Acquired Malocclusions) (1936); coauthor, *Ortopedicheskaya stomatologiya* (Orthopedic Stomatology) (1940); *Znacheniye perestroyki kostnoy tkani i rosta al'veolyarnykh otrostkov v mekhanizme prorezyvaniya zubov* (The Significance of Bone Tissue Changes and the Growth of the Alveolar Appendices in the Dentition Mechanism) (1940); *Funktsional'nyye metody lecheniya ognestrel'nykh raneniy chelustey* (Functional Methods of Treating Gunshot Wounds of the Jaws) (1944); *Died*: 1952.

KATUL'SKAYA, Yelena Kliment'yevna (1888-1966) Opera singer (coloratura soprano); teacher; prof from 1950; Hon Art Worker of RSFSR from 1958; Pop Artiste of USSR from 1965; *Born*: 2 June 1888 in Odessa; *Educ*: 1909 grad Petersburg Conservatory (Prof N. A. Iretskaya's class); *Career*: 1909-13 soloist, Mariinskiy Theater in Petersburg; 1913-45 at Moscow Bol'shoy Theater; also performed as chamber singer; 1945-52 consultant, Bol'shoy Theater; from 1948 teacher, from 1950 prof, Moscow Conservatory; among her students were A. Maslennikov, T. Milashkina, L. Gritsenko, etc; wrote articles on vocal technique; compiled and edited collections of vocal music; *Roles*: the Snow Maiden, Marfa, Volkhova, the Swan Princess in Rimskiy-Korsakov's *Snegurochka* (The Snow Maiden), *Tsarskaya nevesta* (The Bride of the Tsar), *Sadko, Skazka o tsare Saltane* (The Tale of Tsar Saltan); Lyudmila and Antonida in Glinka's *Ruslan i Lyudmila* (Ruslan and Lyudmila) and *Ivan Susanin*; Gilda and Violetta in Verdi's "Rigoletto" and "La Traviata"; Juliet in Gounod's "Romeo and Juliet"; title role in Delibe's "Lakme"; Rosina in Rossini's "Barber of Seville," etc; *Awards*: Stalin Prize (1950); two orders; medals; *Died*: 19 Nov 1966.

KAUCHUKOVSKIY, Grigoriy Danilovich (1898-1942) Party official; CP member from 1917; *Born*: 1898; *Career*: 1918 secr, Simbirsk City Comt; member, Simbirsk Province Party Comt; then various Party and govt posts; helped crush Murav'yov rebellion; *Died*: 1942.

KAVAL', Vasil' (KOVALEV, Vasiliy Petrovich) (1907-1937) Bel writer; member, Bel Writers' Union from 1934; *Born*: 17 Aug 1907 in vil Sova, now Mogilyov Oblast, son of a poor peasant; *Educ*: studied at Mogilyov Teachers' Training Technicum; attended gen educ courses in Gorky; then studied at Dept of Lit and Linguistics, Teachers' Training Fac, Bel State Univ; *Career*: from 1925 member, *Maladnyak* lit assoc; 1925 first work published; 1937 arrested by State Security organs; *Publ*: collected stories "How Spring Was Called" (1927); "On the Strips" (1928); "The Spring" (1929); "Selected Works" (1959); novelle *Il'ka* (1928); "The Examination" (1932); "Night at Sea" (1934); "Hatred" (1935); novelettes "The Day Blazes" (1932); "San'ka the Signalman" (1936); *Died*: 29 Oct 1937 in imprisonment; posthumously rehabilitated.

KAVERIN, Fyodor Nikolayevich (1897-1957) Stage dir; teacher; prof from 1949; Hon Art Worker of RSFSR from 1948; *Born*: 13 Feb 1897 in Moscow; *Educ*: 1922 grad Maly Theater School (studied under N. A. Smirnova and V. N. Pashennaya); *Career*: during his high-school and student years performed in amateur plays, studied at Polenov Pop House and wrote one-act plays; from 1922 stage dir, Maly Theater; worked as stage dir, and from 1925 head, Theater Studio, Maly Theater (from 1932 New Theater, 1936-43 Moscow Drama Theater); stage dir at Music Hall, Moscow State Jewish Theater and Moscow Drama Theater; from 1925 instructor at Maly Theater Studio, State Inst of Stagecraft Theater College of State Jewish Theater and Moscow Conservatory; prof from 1949; wrote articles and booklets on amateur stage directing and producing plays on a small stage, etc; *Works*: staged plays: Ostrovskiy's *Komik 17-go stoletiya* (Comic of the 17th Century) (1922); Kayzer's *Kinoroman* (Cinema Novel) (1926); *Pokhozhdeniya Bal'zaminova* (Bal'zaminov's Adventures) after Ostrovskiy (1926); Shkvarkin's *Vrednyy element* (Harmful Element) (1927); Shakespeare's "All's Well That Ends Well" (1928); Dobrushin's *Sud idyot* (The Trial Proceeds) (1929); *Bez viny vonovatyye* (Guilty Without Guilt) (1930); Dem'yan Bednyy's *Kak 14-ya diviziya v ray shla* (How the 14th Division Marched to Paradise) (1932); Gutskov's *Uriel' Akosta* (1934); Kron's *Trus* (Coward) (1936); Leonov's *Obyknovennyy chelovek* (The Common Man) (1945); Markish's *Vosstaniye v getto* (Ghetto Revolt) (1946), etc; *Publ: Rol' samoobrazovaniya v tvorchestve aktyora* (The Importance of Self-Training in an Actor's Work) (1934); *Rabota nad spektaklem* (Producing a Play) (1938); *Rabota rezhissyora samodeyatel'nogo teatra* (The Work of an Amateur Stage Director) (1945); *Oformleniye spektaklya na maloy stsene* (Staging a Play on a Small Stage) (1951); *Died*: 20 Oct 1957 in Moscow.

KAVRAYSKIY, Vladimir Vladimirovich (1884-1954) Geodesist, cartographer and astronomer; rear-admiral; prof; *Born*: 22 Apr 1884; *Career*: prof, Leningrad Univ; developed position lines method to determine the position of a ship at sea and esimate the accuracy of the fix; helped to introduce the rectangular coordinates system in Sov geodesy; developed method of determining time and position simultaneously by stellar elevation; designed several optical instruments, including an inclinometer and a direction-finder for use by the Sov Navy; wrote a number of papers and manuals on mathematical cartography; *Publ: Graficheskoye resheniye astronomicheskikh zadach* (The Graphic Solution of Astronomical Problems) (1913); *Issledovaniya po matematicheskoy kartografii* (Research on Mathematical Cartography) (1934); *Awards*: Stalin Prize (1952); *Died*: 26 Feb 1954.

KAVSADZE, Vladimir (Lado) Longinovich (1887-1953) Geo operetta and opera singer (lyric tenor); Pop Artiste of Geo SSR from 1943; *Born*: 7 Jan 1887; *Educ*: studied singing under E. Brodzhi in Tiflis; *Career*: 1908 began stage career in Moscow; until 1917 with various operetta theaters in Moscow, Orenburg, Petersburg, Smolensk and other Russian cities; helped found Tashkent Opera and Ballet Theater; 1921 helped found Geo Theater of Musical Comedy; from 1921 soloist, Paliashvili Opera and Ballet Theater; very successful in comic roles; acted in films; *Roles*: Gippert in Evert's "Frinash"; Katan in Jones' "Geisha"; Gennadiy in Valentinov's *Noch' lyubvi* (Night of Love); Paris in Offenbach's "Helen the Fair"; Orpheus in Offenbach's "Orpheus in Hell"; Baron in Strauss' "Zigeunerbaron"; Abesalom in Paliashvili's "Abesalom and Eteri"; title role in Arakishvili's *Shota Rustaveli*; Kote and Sako in Dolidze's "Keto and Kote"; Lenskiy; Alfred; Almaviva, etc; *Died*: 30 Nov 1953.

KAYDANOVA, Ol'ga Vladimirovna (1867 - ?) Pedag; educ official; *Born*: 1867; *Educ*: 1885 grad high-school; 1896-97 attended courses on experimental pedag and natural sci at Sorbonne; *Career*: spent childhood and youth in Tiflis; 1885, after grad from high-school, founded a Sunday school for a hundred pupils with the aid of a youth group; 1888 founded the "Cheap Library" with which Gorky and Kalinin were associated; studied pedag and taught 8th grade at a women's high-school; 1904 taught at workers' courses in Prechistenka Distr, Moscow and at Vyazemskaya's private high-school; 1904 arrested for revol activity and exiled to Podol'sk, where she continued teaching; 1906-09 worked at P. Maksimovich's Women-Teachers' Seminary, Tver'; exiled from Tver' and lived in Tarus, Kaluga Province, until 1917; after 1917 Oct Revol resumed educ and cultural work; 1918 worked in Kursk; 1921-22 taught in Tomsk; 1923-24 cared for homeless children in Moscow; from 1920 also worked for Main Polit Educ Bd; regular contributor to pedag journals *Svobodnoye vospitaniye, Obrazovaniye, Vestnik vospitaniya, Vestnik prosveshcheniya,* and *Na putyakh k novoy shkole*; also contributed to the anthology *Obshcheye delo* and to the "Free Training and Educ Library"; in 1930's emigrated to Canada, where she wrote her 3-vol book "Studies in the History of Public Education in Russia"; *Publ: Otchyot o deyatel'nosti Tiflisskoy Deshyovoy Biblioteki za 10 let sushchestvovaniya, 1888-1898* (A Report on the Work of the Tiflis Cheap Library During the Ten Years of Its Existence, 1888-1898) (1902); *Shkola. Istoricheskiy ocherk* (The School. A Historical Study) (1902); *Assotsiatsiya po izucheniyu dorevolyutsionnoy pedagogiki v svyazi s sovremennost'yu* (The Association for the Study of Pre-Revolutionary Pedagogics in Relation to Present Needs) (1926); *Besprizornyye deti. Praktika raboty opytnoy stantsii* (Homeless Children. The Practical Work of an Experimental Station) (1926); coauthor, *Krasnyy pakhar'. Derevenskiy bukvar' dlya vzroslykh* (The Red Plowman. A Rural ABC for Adults) (1930); *Podrostok. Bukvar' dlya sel'skikh shkol podrostkov* (The Adolescent. An ABC for Rural Adolescent Schools) (1930); *Nash bukvar'. Dlya gorodskikh shkol podrostkov* (Our ABC-Book. For Urban Adolescent Chools) (1930); *Ocherki po istorii narodnogo obrazovaniya v Rossii* (Studies in the History of Public Education in Russia) (Vol 1, 1938); *Died*: date and place of death unknown.

KAZAKEVICH, Emmanuil Genrikhovich (1913-1962) Jewish and Russian writer; Bd member, USSR Writers' Union from 1959; CP member from 1944; *Born*: 24 Feb 1913 in Kremenchug, son of a teacher and journalist; *Educ*: 1930 grad Khar'kov Machine-Building Technicum; *Career*: began work in Birobidzhan as construction superintendent, kolkhoz chm, then theater dir; contributed to newspapers; in WW 2 commanded reconnaissance unit; began lit work in mid-1930's in Yiddish; translated into Yiddish works of Pushkin, Lermontov and Mayakovskiy; from 1947 wrote in Russian; 1948 criticized for "distorting Sov reality"; 1956 chief ed, lit collections *Literaturnaya Moskva* (Literary Moscow); *Publ*: collection "Big World" (1939); novelettes *Zvezda* (Star), *Dvoye v stepi* (Two in the Steppes) (1948); novel *Vesna na Odere* (Spring on the Oder) (1949); novelette *Serdtse druga* (Heart of a Friend) (1953); novel *Dvoye na ploshchadi* (Two on the Square) (1956); story *Pri svete dnya* (By Daylight) (1961); novelette *Sinyaya tetrad'* (Blue Notebook) (1961); *Sobraniye sochineniy* (Collected Works) (2 vol, 1963); *Awards*: two Stalin Prizes (1948, 1950); *Died*: 22 Sept 1962 in Moscow.

KAZAKOV, Aristarkh Andreyevich (1878-1963) Turkestani revolutionary; Party and govt official; *Born*: 1878; *Career*: worker; during Civil War chm, Turkestani Centr Exec Comt of Soviets and chm, Turkestani Revol-Mil Council after Civil War secr, Samara Province, RCP(B) Comt; member, All-Russian Centr Exec Comt of two convocations; for 20 years held exec posts in Party and govt; worked for Polit Dept, Donbas Railroad and for Construction Bd, Turkestan-Siberian Railroad; 1937 arrested by State Security organs; 1956 rehabilitated and given a state pension; *Publ*: memoirs in anthology *Oktyabr'skaya sotsialisticheskaya revolyutsiya i grazhdanskaya voyna v Turkestane* (The October Socialist Revolution and the Civil War in Turkestan) (1957); *Za Sovetskiy Turkestan* (For Soviet Turkestan) (1963); *Died*: 1963.

KAZANLI, Dmitriy Nikolayevich (1904-1959) Geologist and geophysicist; Cand of Geology and Mineralogy from 1949; *Born*: 22 Oct 1904; *Educ*: 1930 grad Leningrad Univ; *Career*: 1932-41 head, Geodetic Service; Main Construction Bd of the Far North; 1941-46 worked in Centr Asian gold fields; 1946-59 dept head, Inst of Geophysical Sci, Kaz Acad of Sci; specialized in the physics of the earth's crust, the relationship between tectonic and seismic activity, metallogeny, magnetism and gravity; *Awards*: Lenin Prize; *Died*: 12 Nov 1959.

KAZANSKIY, Gilyaz (1891-1938) Tat actor and stage dir; *Born*: 1891; *Career*: from 1912 with professional Tat ensemble *Nur*, founded by S. Gizzatullina-Volzhskaya in Ufa; during Civil War with army ensembles; 1922 organized in Ufa Tat ensemble *Urnek*; 1924 helped found Bash State Theater; 1931 at Kazan' Kamal Theater; 1935 helped found Menzelin Kolkhoz-Sovkhoz Theater; until 1938 with this theater; *Roles*: Zagid in Fayzi's "The Wretch"; Khalil in *Galiyabanu*; Zakir in *Neschastnyy yunosha* (The Unfortunate Youth); Ferdinand; Akhmetzhan in *Rasputstvo* (Dissipation), etc; *Died*: 1938.

KAZANSKIY, Yevgeniy Sergeyevich (1896-1937) Mil commander; junior-capt in Russian Army; div commander from 1935; Civil War veteran; CP member from 1917; *Born*: 21 Jan 1896 in vil Naryshkino, Oryol Province, son of a vil priest; *Educ*: 1912 grad Oryol Theological Seminary; 1913 grad first course at Kiev Polytech School; 1914 grad Pavel Mil College; 1924 grad Red Army High Command Mil Acad Courses; *Pos*: from 1913 in Russian Army; 1914-18 platoon, then company commander; commanded regt machine-gun unit; from 1918 in Red Army; 1918 machine-gunner; commanded squad, then armored car; 1919-20 commanded rebel detachments in the Black Sea littoral behind the White lines; commander, Black Sea Sov "Green" (partisan) Army; 1920-25 asst head, 6th Petrograd Infantry Courses; commandant and comr, Petrograd Sklyanskiy Infantry School; 1926-31 commander, 2nd, then 1st Turkestani Div in Centr Asia, Stepin 2nd Caucasian Infantry Div, then 13th Dagestan Infantry Div in the Caucasus; 1932-36 chief of staff for mil training establishments, Main Red Army Bd; head, Red Army Mil Training Establishments Bd; 1934-36 simultaneously member, Mil Council, USSR Pop Comrt of Defense; 1936-37 commander, 5th Infantry Corps; *Career*: after 1917 Feb Revol carried out Bolshevik work on soldiers' comt in Batumi; Aug 1918 conducted underground Bolshevik work in Baku against local democratic authorities until he was tracked down and had to flee to Geo; 1919 arrested by Menshevik govt organs and imprisoned; liberated under Menshevik Geo pledge to Sov Russia not to persecute Bolsheviks; Mar 1921 during suppression of Kronstadt Mutiny headed Northern Combat Sector, Sov Punitive Force; 1926-28 fought against Basmachi in Centr Asia; 1937 arrested by NKVD; *Awards*: two Orders of the Red Banner; Hon Revol Arms; Order of the Turkm Red Banner of Labor; *Died*: 26 Sept 1937 in imprisonment; posthumously rehabilitated.

KAZANTSEV, Florentiy Pimenovich (1877-1940) Designer; railroad eng; *Born*: 1877; *Career*: designed brakes for passenger and freight trains; 1909 developed and tested double air brake for passenger trains at Chelkar Station on the Orenburg Railroad; from 1921 worked in Moscow; 1923 tested his double air brake on a passenger train on the Oct Railroad; the brake was subsequently installed in oil-fired trains on the Baku-Batumi line; 1925 designed single-acting rigid brake (type AP); 1927 designed semi-rigid brake (type K); these types were used in Sov freight trains until the introduction of I. K. Matrosov's improved designs; 1930-32 worked on the development of electr control systems for air-brakes; 1926 helped to design engine crane for Sov freight trains at Moscow Brake Factory; *Awards*: Order of the Red Banner of Labor; *Died*: 1940.

KAZ'MIN, Nikolay Dimitriyevich (1904-1963) Dir, Centr Lenin Museum; CP member from 1928; *Born*: 1904; *Educ*: 1938 grad Acad of Communist Training; *Career*: began work at age 14; from 1938 teaching and educ admin work; secr, Ivanovo Oblast CPSU(B) Comt; dep dir, Higher Party School, CC, CPSU(B); dir, Lenin Courses; from 1943 head, Agitation Dept, Main Bd of USSR Armed Forces; 1948-61 exec Party work: 1949-55 secr, Leningrad Oblast CPSU Comt; head, Dept of Schools, CC, CPSU; head, Dept of Sci, Schools and Culture for RSFSR, CC, CPSU; at 20th CPSU Congress elected member, Centr Auditing Commission; dep, RSFSR Supr Sov of 4th and 5th convocations; *Awards*: Order of the Fatherland War; Order of the Red Star; medals; *Died*: 29 Oct 1963.

KAZ'MIN, Pyotr Mikhaylovich (1892-1964) Folklorist; Pop Artiste of USSR from 1961; *Born*: 17 Oct 1892 in vil Tret'yaki, Voronezh Province; *Career*: from 1927 artistic dir, Pyatnitskiy Russian State Choir; *Publ*: *Stranitsy iz zhizni M. Ye. Pyatnitskogo* (Pages from the Life of M.Ye.Pyatnitskiy) (1961); *Awards*: Stalin Prize (1952); *Died*: 30 June 1964 in Moscow.

KECHEK'YAN, Stepan Fyodorovich (1890-1967) Lawyer and state law historian; Dr of Law; prof from 1918; head, Dept of History of State and Law, Moscow Univ from 1942; member, ed bd, journal *Vestnik Moskovskogo universiteta - Law* series; *Born*: 1890 in Nakhichevan'-on-Don; *Educ*: 1911 grad Law Fac, Moscow Univ; *Career*: from 1911 at Moscow Univ; from 1915 assoc prof; 1918 elected prof, Saratov Univ and later Don, Azer and other univ; from 1934 at various higher educ establishments and research inst in Moscow: Moscow Law Inst; All-Union Law Acad; Moscow Inst of Legal Relations; All-Union Inst of Juridical Sci; Law Inst, USSR Acad of Sci; Acad of Soc Sci, CPSU CC, etc; member, ed bd, journal *Sovetskoye gosudarstvo i pravo*; wrote more than 120 research works, monographs and textbooks; *Publ*: *Vseobshchaya istoriya gosudarstva i prava. Chast' I. Drevniy Vostok i Drevnyaya Gretsiya* (A General History of State and Law. Part I. The Ancient Orient and Ancient Greece) (1944); *Ucheniye Aristotelya o gosudarstve i prave* (Aristotle's Teachings of State and Law) (1947); *Pravootnosheniya v sotsialisticheskom obshchestve* (Legal Relations in Socialist Society) (1959); coauthor, textbooks *Teoriya gosudarstva i prava* (Theory of State and Law) (1949 and 1955); *Istoriya gosudarstva i prava* (History of State and Law) (1949); *Istoriya politicheskikh ucheniy* (History of Political Doctrines) (1955); *Died*: June 1967.

KEDROV, Mikhail Sergeyevich (1878-1941) Party and govt official; CP member from 1901; *Born*: 1878 in Moscow, son of a notary; *Educ*: studied at Moscow Univ and Yaroslavl' Lyceum; 1897 entered Moscow Univ; *Career*: 1899 expelled from univ for revol activities; joined RSDRP while a student at Yaroslavl' Lyceum; worked in Nizhniy Novgorod, Yaroslavl' and Simferopol' Soc-Democratic org; 1904 helped to dig a tunnel under Taganka Prison in Moscow to liberate N. E. Bauman; early 1905 helped supply arms to Moscow detachments of armed workers; Oct 1905 in Kostroma; member, Kostroma Bolshevik Comt; helped to organize detachments of armed workers; after defeat of Dec armed rebellion worked in Tver' and Petersburg Bolshevik org; RSDRP CC agent for dissemination of Party lit; 1908 while dir of *Zerno* Publ House published collection of Lenin's articles entitled *Za 12 let* (For Twelve Years); 1908-11 imprisoned for publishing illegal lit; 1912 emigrated to Switzerland; 1916 returned to Russia on Lenin's orders; from 1916 dr on the Caucasian Front; Mar-Apr 1917 chm, Sherif-Khanes Sov; from May 1917 in Petrograd; member, Mil Org, CC, RSDRP(B) and All-Russian Bureau of Bolshevik Mil Org; ed, newspaper *Soldatskaya pravda*; helped found newspapers *Rabochiy i soldat* and *Soldat*; from Nov 1917 Collegium member, Pop Comrt of Mil Affairs; Comr for Demobilization of the Old Army; from Aug 1918 commander, Northeastern Sector, Western Barrier; from Sept 1918 member, Revol-Mil Comt, 6th Army, Northern Front; from Mar 1919 chm, Special Dept, All-Russian Cheka; Collegium member, NKVD; RCP(B) CC plen for Southern and Western Fronts; participated in defense of Petrograd; 1921-23 Labor and Defense Council plen for the Southern Caspian fishing ind; member, Baku Sov; 1924-25 with Supr Sovnarkhoz and Pop Comrt of Health; 1926-27 asst prosecutor, Dept of the Mil Prosecutor's Office, USSR Supr Court; 1931-34 Presidium member, RSFSR Gosplan; dir, Mil Health Inst; elected member, All-Union Centr Exec Comt; late 1938 retired because of poor health; streets in Moscow, Arkhangel'sk and Vologda named after him; Apr 1939 arrested by State Security organs; *Publ*: *Iz krasnoy tetradi ob Il'iche* (From A Red Notebook About Il'ich) (1956-57); *Za Sovetskiy Sever. Lichnyye vospominaniya i materialy o pervykh etapakh grazhdanskoy voyny 1918 g.* (For th Soviet North. Memoirs and Material on the First Stages of the Civil War in 1918) (1927); *Bez bol'shevistskogo rukovodstva* (Without Bolshevik Leadership) (1930); *Pod igom angliyskikh gromil* (Under the Yoke of the British Thugs) (1927); *Awards*: Order of the Red Banner; Badge of Hon Chekist; *Died*: Nov 1941 in imprisonment; 1953 posthumously rehabilitated after arrest and execution of Beriya.

KEDROVSKIY, Vasiliy Ivanovich (1865-1937) Bacteriologist and pathological anatomist; Dr of Med from 1896; prof from 1915; *Born*: 30 Dec 1865; *Educ*: 1891 grad Med Fac, Moscow Univ; *Career*: after grad assoc, Chair of Pathological Anatomy, Moscow Univ; 1896 defended doctor's thesis on the life of anerobic microbes in oxygen; from 1898 assoc prof of bacteriology, from 1902 dissector and asst prof of pathological histology; 1910-23 dir, G. N. Gabrichevskiy Bacteriological Inst, Moscow Univ; 1915-18 prof, Chair of Pathological Anatomy, Moscow Univ; from 1925 head, Morphological Dept, Inst of Experimental Endocrinology; from 1926 head, Leprosy Dept, Tropical Inst; specialized in leprosy and tuberculosis; 1910 cultivated the pathogenic agent of leprosy in vitro and proved the possibility of injecting it into animals; 1912 proposed hypothesis on the mutability of microorganisms and established that the considerable differences in bacteria in the same colony are determined by the properties of the microorganisms and environmental conditions; from 1926 member, Int Assoc of Leprologists; wrote over 30 works on pathological anatomy and microbiology; *Publ*: doctor's thesis *Usloviya kislorodnoy zhizni anaerobnykh bakteriy* (The Life Conditions of Anerobic Bacteria in Oxygen) (1896); *Ob isskustvennykh razvodkakh vozbuditeli prokazy* (Artificial Leprosy Cultures) (1900); *Eksperimental'nyye issledovaniya po voprosu o privivayemosti prokazy zhivotnym* (Experimental Research on the Feasibility of Injecting Leprosy into Animals) (1911); *Prokaza i yeyo vozbuditel'* (Leprosy and its Pathogenic Agent) (1918); *Epidemiologiya prokazy v svete noveyshikh izyskaniy* (The Epidemiology of Leprosy in the Light of the Latest Scientific Investigations) (1935); *Died*: Dec 1937.

KEDROV-ZIKHMAN, Oskar Pavlovich (1885-1964) Agrochemist; Dr of Agric and Chemistry; member, All-Union Lenin Acad of Agric Sci from 1935; member, Bel Acad of Sci from 1939; Hon Sci Worker of Bel SSR from 1940; CP member from 1919; *Born*: 1885; *Educ*: 1913 grad Kiev Univ; *Career*: 1913-20 worked as agronomist and chemist at laboratories and experimental stations in Kiev Oblast; 1921-31 prof, Bel Agric Acad; from 1931 dir, Soil Liming Laboratory, All-Union Inst of Fertilizers, Agrotechnics and Agropedology; 1931-41 also prof, Timiryazev Agric Inst, Moscow; 1941-46 acad secr, Dept of Natural and Acric Sci, Bel Acad of Sci; member, Learned Council, USSR Min of Agric; attended 3rd Int Congress of Pedologists, Oxford; 1955 attended Int Atomic Energy Conference, Geneva; member, USSR Comt for the Development of the Chemical Ind; member, Mendeleyev All-Union Chemical Soc; chm, Agrochemistry and Pedology Section, House of Scientists, USSR Acad of Sci; member, ed bd, journal *Pochvovedeniye*; wrote some 300 works; *Publ*: *Vliyaniye izvestkovaniya na mobilizatsiyu pitatel'nykh veshchestv* (The Effect of Liming on the Mobilization of Nutrients) (1936); *Udobreniye kak faktor uluchsheniya semennoy produktsii sel'skokhozyaystvennykh rasteniy* (Fertilizer as a Factor in Improving the Seed Production of Agricultural Plants) (1948); *Izvestkovaniye pochv v BSSR* (Soil Liming in the Belorussian SSR) (1951); *Died*: Feb 1964.

KEKCHEYEV, Krikor Khachaturovich (1893-1948) Physiologist; Dr of Med; prof; corresp member, RSFSR Acad of Pedag Sci from 1947; CP member from 1944; *Born*: 2 Apr 1893; *Educ*: 1919 grad Med Fac, Moscow Univ; *Career*: while still a student began to work under Prof V. Henri at the Labor Inst, Moscow Sci Inst Soc; after grad worked at Psychoneurological Inst and Labor Inst, All-Union Centr Trade-Union Council, where he specialized in the psychophysiology of labor; 1933 founded Laboratory of Labor Physiology, All-Union Inst of Experimental Med, Moscow; from 1941 until death founder-head, Laboratory of Psychophysiology, Inst of Psychology, RSFSR Acad of Pedag Sci; lecturer, Chair of Physiology, Moscow Univ; from 1938 head, Chair of Physiology, Moscow Stomatological Inst; did research on the physiology and psychophysiology of labor and the psychophysiology of the human sense organs; studied the dependence of visual functions on indirect (inadequate) stimuli, proving the possibility of forming conditioned sensory reflexes and establishing the influence of certain imperceptible stimuli, the inversion of the effect of some stimuli in relation to their intensity and the possibility of improving twilight vision; obtained interesting data on proprioception in relation to working processes; devised "series method" of studying proprioception; described the role of interoception in the visual process and did comparative research on the muscular sensitivity of the sighted and the blind; analysed the physiological mechanisms of controlled movement; *Publ: Fiziologiya truda* (The Physiology of Labor) (1931); *Psikhofiziologiya maskirovki i razvedki* (The Psychophysiology of Camouflage and Reconnaissance) (1942); *Interoretseptsiya i proprioretseptsiya i ikh znacheniye dlya kliniki* (Interoception and Proprioception and Their Significance for Clinical Practice) (1946); *Nochnoye zreniye* (Night Vision) (1946); *Died*: 3 Sept 1948.

KEKILOV, Shali (1906-1943) Turkm poet; *Born*: 1906 in vil Keshi near Ashkhabad; son of a peasant; *Career*: 1927 first work published; 1932-36 exec secr, Turkm Writers Union; contributed to newspaper *Sovet Turkmenistany* and journal *Sovet edebiyaty; Publ*: "The Girls' Request" (1928); "Garden of Freedom" (1928); "For the Girls" (1932); "The Kolkhoz Path Is the Path of Socialism" (1931); "At the Kyzyl-Arvat Repair Plant" (1932), etc; poems "Uncle Ivan" (1942); "In the Karelian Forest" (1943); in Russian translation *Slava. Izbrannyye stikhi* (Glory. Selected Verse) (1952); *Died*: 8 Oct 1943 killed in action during WW 2.

KELDYSH, Vsevolod Mikhaylovich (1878-1965) Architect; specialist in ferro-concrete structures; prof from 1918; maj-gen, Eng Corps; member, USSR Acad of Building and Architecture from 1956; Hon Sci and Tech Worker of RSFSR from 1944; CP member from 1945; father of Mstislav Vsevolodovich Keldysh (pres, USSR Acad of Sci); *Born*: 13 June 1878; *Educ*: 1902 grad Riga Polytech Inst; *Career*: after grad worked on various railroad construction projects; from 1918 prof, various building inst; from 1932 prof, Moscow Mil Eng Acad; worked as designer and advisor on many maj Sov construction projects; supervised development of standards for ferro-concrete; pioneered the limiting state calculation of structures; *Publ: Raschyot i proyektirovaniye elementov zhelezobetonnykh konstruktsiy po razrushayushchim usiliyam* (The Calculation and Design of the Elements of Ferro-Concrete Structures on the Basis of Breaking Strength) (1940); *Fiziko-mekhanicheskiye svoystva betona i zhelezobetona* (The Physical and Mechanical Properties of Concrete and Ferro-Concrete) (1952), etc; *Died*: 19 Nov 1965.

KEL'IN, Fyodor Viktorovich (1893-1965) Russian lit historian; specialist in Spanish lit; translator of poetry; *Born*: 22 Apr 1893 in Moscow; *Educ*: 1917 grad History and Philology Fac, Moscow Univ; *Career*: 1923 first work published; 1937 attended 2nd Int Congress of Writers in Defense of Culture, in Barcelona, Madrid and Valencia; received hon doctorate of Madrid Univ from Republ govt; during and after WW 2 edited journal *Sovetskaya literatura* in Spanish with Spanish writer S. M. Arconada; wrote many works on classical and contemporary Spanish and Latin American lit; translated poems of Spanish and Latin American poets and plays of Lope de Vega, Calderon, Ruiz de Alarcon y Mendoza, Machado y Ruiz, Garcia Lorca, Alberti, Aconada, etc; compiled first Sov Spanish-Russian dictionaries; vice-pres, Sov Assoc of Friendship and Cultural Cooperation with Latin America; *Publ*: introductory articles to *Servantes M. Nazidatel'nyye novelly* (M. Cervantes. Didactic Novellas) (1935); *Tirso-de-Molina i yego vremya* (Tirso de Molina and His Time) (1935); *Puti razvitiya sovremennoy ispanskoy literatury* (Trends in the Development of Contemporary Spanish Literature) (1940); *Ispaniya. Literatura* (Spain. Literature) (1947); *Progressivnaya literatura Latinskoy Ameriki* (Progressive Literature of Latin America) (1952); prefaces to *Amadu Zh. Podpol'ye svobody* (J. Amadu. Freedom Underground) (1954); *Gravina A. Granitsy, otkrytyye vetru* (A. Gravina. Borders Open to the Wind) (1954); introductory article to *Garsia Lorka F. Teatr* (Garcia Lorca. The Theater) (1957); preface to *Dario R. Stikhi* (R. Dario. Verse) (1958); introductory article to *Servantes M. Sobrannyye sochineniya v 5 tomakh, t. I* (M. Cervantes. Collected Works in Five Volumes, Volume I) (1961); *Died*: 29 Sept 1965 in Moscow.

KELL', Nikolay Georgiyevich (1883-1965) Geodesist and photogrammetrist; prof from 1923; corresp member, USSR Acad of Sci from 1946; *Born*: 1883; *Educ*: 1915 grad Petrograd Mining Inst; *Career*: 1908-10 topographer, Kamchatka expedition of Russian Geographic Soc; 1917-22 worked for Ural Mining Inst, Sverdlovsk (1919-20 as rector); from 1922 member, Russian Geographic Soc; from 1923 prof, Leningrad Mining Inst; from 1947 dir, Laboratory of Aerial Survey Methods, USSR Acad of Sci; specialized in the development of aerial photogrammetric methods for the compilation of geographic and geodetic maps; *Publ: Graficheskiy metod v deystviyakh s pogreshnostyami i polozheniyami (raspredeleniyami)* (The Graphic Method Applied to Movements with Margins of Error and Positions [Distribution]) (1948); *Vysshaya geodeziya i geodezicheskiye raboty* (Advanced Geodesy and Geodetic Operations) (2 vol, 1932-33); *Fotografiya i fotogrammetriya* (Photography and Photogrammetry) (1937); *Karta vulkanov Kamchatki* (A Volcano Map of Kamchatka) (1928); *Awards*: Order of Lenin; three other orders; medals; *Died*: Dec 1965.

KELLER, Boris Aleksandrovich (1874-1945) Botanist and ecologist; prof from 1913; member, USSR Acad of Sci from 1931; member, All-Union Lenin Acad of Agric Sci from 1935; Hon Sci Worker of RSFSR from 1929; Hon Sci Worker of Turkm SSR from 1944; CP member from 1930; *Born*: 28 Aug 1874 in Petersburg; *Educ*: 1892-95 studied at Med Fac, then Fac of Physics and Mathematics, Moscow Univ but was expelled for revol activity and exiled from Moscow; 1902 grad Fac of Physics and Mathematics, Kazan' Univ; *Career*: 1902-10 asst prof, from 1910 assoc prof, Kazan' Univ; 1913-31 prof of botany, Voronezh Agric Inst; 1919-31 also prof of botany, Med Fac and Fac of Physics and Mathematics, Voronezh Univ; 1931-37 dir, Botanical Inst, USSR Acad of Sci, Leningrad; for a time also dir, Soil Inst, USSR Acad of Sci; 1937-45 dir, Moscow Botanical Garden, USSR Acad of Sci; 1941-45 also chm, Turkmen Branch, USSR Acad of Sci, Ashkhabad; 1908-36 made numerous botanical field trips and expeditions, inter alia to the Volga basin, the Gornyy Altay, the steppes of Kazakhstan, Sweden and Norway; devised new methods for research on the interrelationship of plants and their environment (ecological series method); introduced "semi-desert" concept; developed principles of differentiating steppe and semi-steppe vegetation; studied evolution from the viewpoint of ecology and physiology, giving special consideration to the universal role of vegetation, the question of the individual plant and hereditary changes of plants under the influence of their environment; wrote over 300 works and gave his name to several plant varieties; *Publ: Botaniko-geograficheskiye issledovaniya v Zaysanskom uyezde Semipalatinskoy oblasti* (Botanical and Geographical Research in Zaysan Uyezd, Semipalatinsk Oblast) (2 vol, 1911-12); *Po dolinam i goram Altaya. Botaniko-geograficheskiye issledovaniya* (Through the Valleys and Mountains of the Altay. Botanical and Geographical Research) (1914); *Rastitel'nost' Voronezhskoy gubernii* (The Vegetation of Voronezh Province) (1921); *Sorno-polevaya rastitel'nost' na ravninakh Yevropeyskoy chasti SSSR* (Weeds of the Plains of the European USSR) (1929); *V stepnoy dubrave* (In the Oak Groves of the Steppe) (1930); *Botanika s osnovami fiziologii* (Botany and the Principles of Physiology) (1932); *Genetika. Kratkiy ocherk* (Genetics. A Short Study) (1933); *Botanika. Glavnyye faktory i zakonomernosti* (Botany. The Main Factors and Laws) (1935); *Osnovy evolyutsii rasteniy* (The Principles of Plant Evolution) (1948); *Izbrannyye sochineniya* (Selected Works) (1951); *Awards*: two Orders of the Red Banner of Labor; *Died*: 29 Oct 1945.

KERTSELLI, Sergey Vasil'yevich (1869-1935) Expert on reindeer breeding; explorer; *Born*: 1869 in Bendin, Poland; *Educ*: 1896 grad Khar'kov Veterinary Inst; *Career*: 1897-1907 veterinarian in the Caucasus; from 1908 in the Far North, specializing as a reindeer breeder; 1910 founded in Pechora Russia's first reindeer breeding research station, which he directed until 1912; studied reindeer breeding and fur trading in the Bol'shezemel'skaya Tundra (1908-09), the Kolguyev and Vaygach islands (1911), the Kamchatka Peninsula (1916-18); Eastern Sayan (1927), Anadyr' Kray (1929-30), Karagasiya and Taymyr (1931); 1933 worked in the Northern Pechora region; 1934-35 on Kola Peninsula; believed in "cottage-scale reindeer breeding," i.e., breeding reindeers in semi-permanent settlements; experimented in reindeer breeding and studied pastures; helped found the Inst of Reindeer Breeding in Leningrad; *Publ: Po Bol'shezemel'skoy tundre s kochevnikami* (Through the Bol'shezemel'skaya Tundra with Nomads) (1911), etc; *Died*: 5 Mar 1935.

KEUL'KUT, Viktor Grigor'yevich (1929-1963) Chukot (Luoravetlan) poet; *Born*: 15 Jan 1929 in settlement Tumanskaya, Anadyr' Rayon, Chukotka, son of a hunter and reindeer breeder; *Educ*: attended school for training of kolkhoz specialists in Anadyr'; *Career*: worked as a livestock expert; from 1954 worked for newspaper *Sovetken Chukotka,* later for Magadan publ house; 1954 first work published; in his verses depicted work and daily life of reindeer breeders and hunters and landscape of Chukotka; wrote lyric love poetry, satires, journalistic verse and verse about and for children; *Publ*: in Russian translation *Moya Chukotka* (My Chukotka) (1958); *Pust' stoit moroz* (Let There Be Frost) (1958); *Died*: 9 June 1963.

KEZMA, Taufik Gavrilovich (1882-1958) Ukr philologist and Arabist; *Born*: 7 Feb 1882 in Damascus, of Arab parents; *Educ*: 1906 grad Kiev Theological Acad; *Career*: taught Arabic at higher educ establishments; 1939-48 lecturer, from 1948 prof at univ; until 1941 assoc, Ukr Acad of Sci; wrote various works on Oriental studies; *Works*: "A Popular Account of the Elementary Principles of Arabic Grammar" (1928); translated into Ukr from Arabic: "The Arab Historian Abu-Khodzhi Rudraverskiy's 11th-Century Study of Rus's Conversion to Christianity" (1927); also translated M. Nuajme's stories "The Notables" (1958) and M. Tejmur's "What the Eyes See" (1957); *Died*: 9 Apr 1958.

KHADYKA, Vladimir Martynovich (1905-1940) Bel poet; member, Bel Writers' Union from 1934; *Born*: 3 Jan 1905 in vil Tsitva, now Minsk Oblast; *Educ*: 1923 grad Gen Educ Courses, Minsk; 1928 grad Cherven' Teachers' Training Technicum; *Career*: 1923-25 served in Sov Army; 1925-28 secr, Dudichi Vil Sov; 1926 first work published; from 1929 ed secr, journal *Polymya*; member, *Maladnyak* Lit Assoc and Bel Assoc of Proletarian Writers; 1929 criticized by Party for lack of "class vigilance"; late 1936 arrested by State Security organs; *Publ*: verse collection *Sunitsy* (Strawberries) (1926); *Vybranyya vershy* (Selected Verse) (1932); *Radasny budzen'* (Happy Days) (1935); *Vybranyya vershy* (Selected Verse) (1957); *Died*: 1 July 1940; killed by rock-fall in labor-camp quarry; posthumously rehabilitated.

KHAKHAN'YAN, Grigoriy Davidovich (1895-1939) Mil commander; Civil War hero; CP member from 1917; *Born*: 28 Dec 1895 in vil Ruisi, Gori Uyezd, Geo; son of an Arm vil teacher; *Educ*: 1915-16 studied at Fac of History and Philology, Moscow Univ; 1917 grad Moscow Ensigns' School; 1924 grad Higher Acad Courses; *Career*: 1916 joined Russian Army; 1917 ensign in reserve regt in Kamyshlov, Perm' Province and Gorodok, Vitebsk Province; court-martialed for conducting Bolshevik propaganda among troops; took active part in Oct Revol in Petrograd; 1917-18 asst chm, Mil Revol Comt, 5th Army, Western Front; secr, Pskov Province Cheka; chief, Operations Dept, Mil Revol Comt, Velikiye Luki Rayon; mil comr, Novorzhev Rayon; 1918-19 fought on Eastern Front during Civil War; 1918 mil comr, Pskov Div; dep chief, Staff Operations Dept, 5th Army; commanded defense of Sviyazhsk on Eastern Front; 1919 chief, Staff Operations Dept, 5th Army; 1919-23 commanded a rifle brig; 1920 fought against Poland; 1921 helped to put down Kronstadt Mutiny and anti-Sov uprising in Volga area; 1923 commander, 27th Omsk Div; 1924-27 head, Tactics Fac, Air Force Acad; dir and comr, *Vystrel* Higher Infantry Tactics School; 1927-29 commander and comr, 19th Maritime Rifle Corps, Khabarovsk; 1930-34 member, Revol Mil Council and head, Polit Bd, Ukr Mil Distr; 1934 deleg, 17th CPSU(B) Congress; 1934-36 chief of mil group, Sov Control Commission; 1937 member, Mil Council and head, Polit Bd, Special Red Banner Far Eastern Army; fall 1937 recalled from Far East to Moscow and suspended from duties; 1 Feb 1938 arrested by NKVD; *Publ: Osnovy voyennoy psikhologii* (The Principles of Military Psychology) (1929); *Awards*: three Orders of the Red Banner; Revol Arms of Honor; *Died*: 22 Feb 1939 in imprisonment; posthumously rehabilitated.

KHALATOV, Artemiy Bagratovich (1896-1938) Party and govt official; CP member from 1917; *Born*: 26 Apr 1896 in Baku; *Educ*: from 1912 studied at Moscow Business Inst; *Career*: after 1917 Feb Revol worked for food agencies; chm, Moscow City Food Comt; Oct 1917 member, Zamoskvorech'ye Rayon Mil Revol Comt; after 1917 Oct Revol Collegium Member, RSFSR Pop Comrt of Food; head, Red Army Main Food Supply Bd; then chm, Workers' Supply Commission, RSFSR Pop Comrt of Food; from 1921 chm, Centr Commission to Improve Scientists' Living Conditions; 1922-27 Collegium member, Pop Comrt of Means of Communication; 1923-29 simultaneously chm, Public Nutrition Assoc; 1927-32 Collegium member, USSR Pop Comrt of Educ; chm, bd, State Publ House; 1927-29 rector, Plekhanov Inst of Nat Econ; from 1932 again Collegium member, USSR Pop Comrt of Means of Communication; then chm, All-Union Inventors' Soc; member, All-Russian and USSR Centr Exec Comt; wrote various pop pamphlets; arrested by State Security organs; *Died*: 27 Oct 1938 in imprisonment.

KHALATOV, Semyon Sergeyevich (1884-1951) Pathophysiologist; Dr of Med from 1917; Hon Sci Worker of RSFSR; CP member from 1921; *Born*: 1884; *Educ*: 1908 grad Natural Sci Fac, Petersburg Univ; 1912 grad Petersburg Mil Med Acad; *Career*: from 1912 assoc, Petersburg Mil Med Acad; 1917 defended doctor's thesis on cholesterol diathesis; specialized in metabolism, endocrinology and gerontology; 1911-12 contributed to knowledge of the pathology of lipoid metabolism with his research on the reaction of the liver to various edible fats; 1912-13 established the role of cholesterol in a number of pathological processes during research on the origin and properties of liquid crystals in animals - a pioneer project in the study of the pathology of cholesterol metabolism; demonstrated the role of brain damage in the origin of lipoidemia; 1922-29 head, Chair of Gen Pathology, 1st Leningrad Med Inst; 1929-47 head, Chair of Pathological Physiology, 1st Moscow Med Inst; 1947-50 head of an experimental laboratory, Centr Oncological Inst; 1950-51 head, Pathophysiological Laboratory, Centr Skin and Venerological Inst; also did extensive research on the hormonal properties of the fetal membrane; wrote 70 works, including eight monographs and three textbooks on pathological physiology; helped to reorganize chairs of gen pathology into chairs of pathophysiology; *Publ: Ob otnoshenii pecheni k razlichnym sortam pishchevykh zhirov* (The Reaction of the Liver to Various Kinds of Edible Fat) (1913); *O zhidkikh kristallakh v zhivotnom organizme, ob usloviyakh ikh vozniknoveniya i ikh svoystvakh* (Liquid Crystals in the Organism of Animals, the Conditions of Their Genesis and Their Properties) (1913); doctor's thesis *K voprosu o kholesterinovom diateze* (Cholesterol Diathesis) (1917); "Die anisotrope Verfettung im Lichte der Pathologie des Stoffwechsels" (Anisotropic Fatty Degeneration in the Light of the Pathology of Metabolism) (1922); *Ucheniye o diateze* (The Theory of Diathesis) (1930); *Fiziologicheskaya endokrinnaya sistema i endokrinopatiya v svete novoy teorii prirody i proiskhozhdeniya gormonal'nykh nachal* (The Physiological Endocrinal System and Endocrinopathy in the Light of the New Theory of the Nature and Origin of the Hormonal Primordia) (1944); *Kholesterinovaya bolezn'* (Cholesterol Disease) (1946); *Died*: 1951.

KHALEPSKIY, Innokentiy Andreyevich (1893-1938) USSR Pop Comr of Communications from Apr 1937; army commander, 2nd class from 1935; specialist in mil communications, mechanization and motorization; CP member from 1918; *Born*: 1893 in Minusinsk, son of a tailor; *Career*: 1918 joined Red Army; in same year fought against the White Army and Czech Legion in Urals with a Party volunteer unit; commander and Extraord Comr of Communications, 3rd Army; RSFSR Extraordinary Comr of Mil Post and Telegraph Offices; Nov 1918-Aug 1919 Ukr Pop Comr of Posts and Telegraphs; 1919-20 chief of communications, Southern and Caucasian Fronts; June 1920-24 Red Army Chief of Communications and Collegium member, USSR Pop Comrt of Posts and Telegraphs; 1924-29 head, Red Army Mil-Tech Bd; 1929-36 head, Red Army Bd of Motorization and Mechanization; 1932-34 also member, USSR Revol Mil Council; 1934-37 member, Mil Council, USSR Pop Comrt of Defense; 1936-37 also Red Army Chief of Armaments; Mar-Apr 1937 USSR First Dep Pop Comr of Means of Communication; 5 Apr-Aug 1937 USSR Pop Comr of Means of Communication; Aug 1937 arrested by NKVD; *Awards*: Order of Lenin; Order of the Red Banner; *Died*: 1938 in imprisonment; posthumously rehabilitated.

KHALYUTINA, Sof'ya Vasil'yevna (1875-1960) Actress; teacher; Pop Artiste of the RSFSR from 1948; *Born*: 22 Jan 1875; *Educ*: studied under Nemirovich-Danchenko at the College of Music and Drama, Moscow Philharmonic Soc; *Career*: from 1898 actress, Moscow Arts Theater; noted for clear and precise portrayal of character, imbued with subtle psychological touches; 1909-14 in charge of drama courses (Khalyutina School); taught drama at various studios and schools; 1921 founded Blok Theater, which lasted one season; *Roles*; Eylif in Ibsen's "Doctor Stockmann"; Anyutka in *Vlast' t'my* (The Power of Darkness); Olaf in Ibsen's "The Pillars of Society"; Dunyasha and Sharlotta in *Vishnyovyy sad* (The Cherry Orchard); Til-til in Maeterlinck's "The Blue Bird"; Sonka in L. Andreyev's *Anathema*; Ose in Ibsens's "Peer Gynt"; Amaliya in *Strakh* (Fear); Mrs. Wardle in "Pickwick Papers"; Gornostayeva in *Lyubov' Yarovaya*; the Dowager Countess in *Gore ot uma* (Woe From Wit), etc; *Died*: 10 Mar 1960.

KHAMZA, Khakim zade (pseudonym: NIYAZI) (1888-1929) Uzbek writer and composer; Pop Poet of Uzbek SSR from 1926; CP member from 1920; *Born*: 6 Mar 1926 in Kokand, son of a healer; *Educ*: studied at medressah, then continued his educ through his own studies; studied composition theory at Samarkand Music Inst; *Career*: began to write verse and songs at age 16; 1911-15 ran a free school for poor children, taught at this school, wrote primary-school aids and tried to incorporate oral folk work into the curriculum; the authorities claimed his school was harmful and barred him from teaching; his textbooks remained in manuscript; 1915 founded in Kokand a semi-professional drama company which staged his plays and the plays of Azer writers; 1918 founded itinerant theater company and, together with this company, joined the Red Army; wrote a number of plays for this theater; studied and arranged folk music, composed his own melodies and collected folk songs throughout Uzbekistan, performing them on nat folk instruments; *Works*: drama "Poisoned Life" (1916); collected verse: "Red Flower," "White Flower" and "Pink Flower" (1915-17); plays: "The Bey and the Farmhand" (1917); "Firuza Khanum"; "The Use of Science"; "The Misdeeds of Normukhamed Domulla"; "Ferghana Tragedies"; "The Tragedy of the Conscripts"; "The Slanderers' Punishment"; "The Case of the Den-Keeper's Wife, or Parandzha's Secrets" (1926); "The Last Days of World Capitalism" (1927), etc; songs: "We Are the Workers"; "Long Live the Soviets!"; " Do Not Surrender Freedom"; "Awake, Workers!"; *Died*: 18 Mar 1929 killed in vil Shakhimardan (now Khamzaabad); the Uzbek State Acad Theater, schools and kolkhozes have been named after him.

KHANDZHYAN, Agasi Gevondovich (1901-1936) Arm Party official; CP member from 1917; *Born*: 1901 in Aane, Western Arm, son of a teacher; *Educ*: studied in Yerevan and Echmiadzin; grad Communist Univ in Moscow; *Career*: helped found workers and peasants' youth orgs in Arm; from May 1919 co-ed, underground Komsomol newspaper *Spartak*; Aug 1919 arrested; after his release from jail active in preparing 1st Conference of Arm Communist Organizations; held illegally in Yerevan in Jan 1920; 1920 after defeat of May Rebellion in Arm, appointed secr, underground Yerevan Party Comt; Oct 1920 arrested and sentenced to ten years in prison; Dec 1920-Feb 1921, after establishment of Sov regime in Arm, appointed secr, Yerevan Party Comt; Feb-Apr 1921 on the Sevan Front; 1921 sent to study at Sverdlov Communist Univ, Moscow; after grad Party work in Leningrad; head, Agitation and Propaganda Dept, Vyborg Rayon Comt, then head, Org Dept, Moscow-Narva Rayon Comt, Leningrad; 1928 sent back to Arm by CC, CPSU(B); 1928-30 second secr, May 1930-36 first secr, CC, CP Arm; *Died*: 1936.

KHANIK, Lev Osipovich (1902-1934) Office worker; CP member; *Born*: 1902; *Career*: arrested in connection with 1 Dec 1934 Leningrad murder of secr of CC and Leningrad Oblast CPSU(B) Comt S. M. Kirov and charged with belonging to underground anti-Sov group of former Zinov'yev followers; 29 Dec 1934 sentenced to death with co-defendants by Assizes of Supr Court Mil Collegium; *Died*: 29 Dec 1934 executed.

KHANSON (KHANSEN), Bernkhard (Benno) Bernkhardovich (1891-1952) Opera singer (bass); Hon Artiste of the Est SSR from 1946; *Born*: 20 Mar 1891; *Educ*: 1914-17 studied singing at Petersburg Conservatory under M. M. Chuprynnikov; 1925 advanced training in Italy; *Career*: 1908-12 at *Estoniya* Operetta and Drama Theater in Tallin; 1912-18 member of the chorus, Mariinskiy Theater in Petersburg; 1918-27 and 1929-52 opera soloist, *Estoniya* Theater; possessed a beautiful voice with a velvety timbre of great range; in his youth he also sang some baritone parts; possessed natural musical talent and artistic ability; *Roles*: Onegin and Gremin in *Yevgeniy Onegin*; Boris Godunov, Pimen and Varlaam in *Boris Godunov*; Konchak in *Knyaz' Igor'* (Prince Igor); Germon in "La Traviata"; Falstaff in Nicolai's "The Merry Wives of Windsor"; Simone Boccanegra in Verdi's opera of the same name; Don Basilio in "The Barber of Seville"; Vakho in Aav's *Vikertsy* (The Men of Viker); Ako in Vedro's *Kaupo*; Timoshka in Lemba's *El'ga*; Mekhis in Kapp's *Ogni mshcheniya* (The Fires of Revenge); the Pastor and the Tavernkeeper in Ernesaks' *Plyukhayarv* and *Bereg bur'* (Shore of Storms), etc; *Died*: 26 Apr 1952.

KHANZHONKOV, Aleksandr Alekseyevich (1877-1945) Film producer and distributor; pioneer of Russian film ind; *Born*: 8 Aug 1877; *Career*: Russian Army officer; 1906, after retirement from army, founded film distribution office in Moscow from which he sold for films and equipment; 1907 founded film studio which survived until 1920 and produced some 400 films; apart from feature films also supervised the production of documentary, pop sci and cartoon films of a high quality for the time; 1920-23 lived abroad; 1923 returned to USSR, where he worked for the *Rusfil'm* and *Proletkino* studios; *Publ: Pervyye gody russkoy kinematografii. Vospominaniya* (The First Years of Russian Cinematography. Reminiscences) (1937); *Died*: 26 Sept 1945.

KHARAZYAN, Amo (Amazasp) Gevondovich (1880-1957) Actor and stage producer; Pop Artiste of the Arm SSR from 1933; *Born*: 20 Apr 1880; *Educ*: 1896-98 studied at the College of the Moscow Philharmonic Soc under Nemirovich-Danchenko; *Career*: 1898 began stage career in Tiflis; staged plays in working distr of Tiflis and for workers of the Baku oilfields; 1908 founded "New Drama" troupe; from 1915 head, Arm Drama Troupe, Zubalov House of the People; 1920 founded one of the first modern theaters in Karaklis and a touring theater in Yerevan which performed in Arm and other Transcaucasian republics; 1928 State Touring Theater founded from this troupe (named after Kharazyan in 1933); from 1950 worked in Echmiadzin (theater closed in 1952); from 1955 Artashat Theater named after Kharazyan; *Roles*: Uriel' in Gutskov's *Uriel' Akosta*; King Oedipus in Sophocles' "Oedipus Rex"; Othello; Corrado in Giacometti's "The Criminal's Family"; the Knight in *Traktirshchitsa* (The Tavernkeeper); Bersenev in *Razlom* (Break-Up); Elizbarov in Shirvanzade's "Because of Honor"; Rayevskiy in *Rozhdyonnyye burey* (Spawn of the Storm), after Ostrovsky, etc; *Works*: staged: *Yarost'* (Fury) (1930), after Yanovskiy; *Stantsionnyy smotritel'* (The Station Master) (1937), after Pushkin; *Volki i ovtsy* (The Wolves and the Sheep) (1940); *Iz-za khleba* (Because of Bread) (1936), after Proshyan, etc; *Publ*: translated plays and scripts: Pushkin's "The Station Master"; Proshyan's "Because of Bread"; Ostrovsky's "Spawn of the Storm"; *Died*: 6 Aug 1957.

KHARECHKO, T. I. (1893-1937) Party official; CP member from 1914; *Born*: 1893; *Career*: revol work in Petrograd, Donbas and Moscow; after 1917 Feb Revol chm, Bakhmut (now Artemovsk) Uyezd Party Comt and Bakhmut Uyezd Sov of Peasants' Dep; after 1917 Oct Revol chm, Donets Basin Mil Revol Comt; chm, Centr Staff, Donbas Red Guards; during German occupation of Ukr illegal Party work in Khar'kov; member, Donetsk-Krivoy Rog Party Comt; head, Org Dept, CC, CP(B) Ukr; secr, Donetsk Province Party Comt; then taught in Leningrad; 1927 expelled from Party by 15th Congress for membership of anti-Party Sapronov group; 1936 arrested by State Security organs and sentenced for alleged Trotskyist activities; *Died*: 1937 in imprisonment.

KHARIK, Izi (Issak Davydovich) (1898-1937) Jewish poet; corresp member, Bel Acad of Sci; CP member; *Born*: 1898 in vil Zembin, Minsk Oblast, son of a shoemaker; *Educ*: 1921-23 studied at Bryusov Lit Inst, Moscow; 1924-27 studied at Philology Fac, Bel Univ; *Career*: 1920 first work published; wrote poems about the fate of the Jewish population during the Oct Revol and Civil War and the changes in the rural patriarchal system; was strongly influenced by Jewish and Bel folklore; member, Bd Centr Exec Comt; arrested by State Security organs; *Publ*: verse collections: "Rain" (1922) and "On the Land" (1926); poems: "The Marshes of Minsk" (1924); "Bread" (1925); "Body and Soul" (1927); "Non-Stop" (1932); "From Pole to Pole" (1934); "Bearing Another's Burden" (1936); *Died*: 1937 in imprisonment.

KHARITONOV, M. M. (1887-1948) Party official; CP member from 1905; *Born*: 1887; *Career*: from 1912 lived in Switzerland; member, then secr, Zurich Section of Bolsheviks; 1915 deleg, Conference of For Bolshevik Sections in Bern; Apr 1917 returned to Russia; secr, Petrograd 2nd City Comt; member, Petrograd RSDRP(B) Comt; after 1917 Oct Revol Party, admin and mil work in Petrograd and Kiev; 1920-21 supported Trotsky in trade-union controversy; 1922-25 secr, Ural Bureau, CC, RCP(B); secr, Perm' and Saratov Province Party Comt; at 14th CPSU(B) Congress sided with "new opposition," then joined Trotskiy-Zinov'evite bloc; 1927 expelled for this from the Party at the 15th Congress; 1928, after reinstatement in Party, worked for Centr Control Commission, Pop Comrt of Workers and Peasants' Inspection, then for Pop Comrt of For Trade; 1935 again expelled from the Party for anti-Party activities; arrested by State Security organs; *Died*: 1948 in imprisonment.

KHARKEVICH, Aleksandr Aleksandrovich (1904-1965) Electronics and radio eng; member, USSR Acad of Sci from 1964; *Born*: 3 Feb 1904; *Educ*: 1930 grad Leningrad Electrotech Inst; *Career*: 1929-32 worked at Centr Electrotech Radio Laboratory; 1932-38 assoc, Mil Electrotech Acad; 1938-41 worked at Leningrad Inst of Communications Eng; 1941-44 at Physical Eng Inst, USSR Acad of Sci; 1944-48 assoc, L'vov Polytech Inst; 1948-52 worked at Inst of Physics, Ukr Acad of Sci; 1952-62 at Moscow Electrotech Communications Inst; 1960-64 corresp member, from 1964 member, USSR Acad of Sci; from 1962 dir, Inst of Information Transmission Problems, USSR Acad of Sci; specialized in the theory, calculation and design of electroacoustical equipment and the theory of information transmission; *Died*: 30 Mar 1965.

KHARMANDAR'YAN, Gurgen Ivanovich (1893-1938) Roentgenologist; pioneer of Sov x-ray and oncological services; *Born*: 1893; *Educ*: 1910-13 studied at Petersburg Mil Med Acad; expelled for revol activities and exiled from Petersburg; 1913-14 studied at Yur'yev Univ; 1917 grad Med Fac, Khar'kov Univ; 1932 grad Khar'kov Electrotech Inst; *Career*: 1914 drafted into army as mil surgeon; after grad specialized in roentgenology under Prof S. P. Grigor'yev in Khar'kov; from 1923 dir, Khar'kov Roentgenological and Radiological Inst; simultaneously, head, Dept of Transport Med, then head, Main State Sanitary Inspectorate, Ukr Pop Comrt of Health; Ukr Dep Pop Comr of Health; 1928 head, Chair of Roentgenology, Khar'kov Med Inst; pioneered network of oncological dispensaries in Ukr; founder, journal *Voprosy onkologii*; 1931 organized All-Union Congress of Oncologists, Khar'kov; provided x-ray facilities in rural areas, inter alia at the Donbas mines; attended several int congresses on roentgenology; did research on the limits of x-ray identification of lesions in the skeleton; made x-ray study of the peristaltic and evacuatory function of the stomach during hypnosis to prove how it is influenced by emotions; 1937 Chief State Sanitary Inspector, USSR Pop Comrt of Health; 1937 arrested by NKVD; *Publ: K voprosu ob organizatsii rentgenologicheskoy pomoshchi naseleniyu i podgotovke spetsialistov-rentgenologov* (The Organization of the Roentgenological Service and the Training of X-Ray Specialists) (1927); *K voprosu o rentgenometricheskoy diagnostike khronicheskikh kolitov* (The Roentgenometric Diagnosis of Chronic Colitis) (1927); *Kholetsistografiya i yeyo klinicheskaya tsennost'* (Cholecystography and Its Clinical Value) (1927); coauthor, *Klinicheskaya tsennost' rentgenovskogo issledovaniya pri vnutrigrudnykh opukholyakh* (The Clinical Value of X–Ray Examination of Intrathoracic Tumors) (1936); *Died*: 1938 in imprisonment.

KHARUZINA, Vera Nikolayevna (1866-1931) Ethnographer; sister of eminent ethnographers Aleksey, Mikhail and Nikolay Kharuzin; *Born*: 29 Nov 1866; *Educ*: studied in Berlin and Paris; *Career*: from 1907 lecturer, Moscow Higher Women's Courses and Archeological Inst; then taught at Moscow Univ; acoompanied her brother Nikolay on his expeditions to the Olenek and Arkhangel'sk Provinces, the Altay, Barabin Steppe, the Baltic area, Crimea and the Caucasus; *Publ*: travel notes *Na severe* (In the North) (1890); *Skazki russkikh inorodtsev* (Fairy-Tales of the Non-Slavic Russians) (1898); *Etnografiya* (Ethnography) (4 vol, 1901-05); *Materialy dlya bibliografii etnograficheskoy literatury* (Material for a Bibliography of Ethnographic Literature) (1904); *Vvedeniye v etnografiyu. Opisaniye i klassifikatsiya narodov zemnogo shara* (An Introduction to Ethnography. An Account and Classification of the World's Peoples) (1941) (3rd, ed, 1941); *Died*: 17 May 1931.

KHASHCHEVATSKIY, Moisey Izrail'yevich (1897-1943) Jewish poet; *Born*: 1897 in vil Buki, Cherkassy Province; *Career*: worked as librarian; 1918 first work printed; starting as Symbolist, progressed to depicting Sov reality from a proletarian stand; translated some works of Lermontov's; fought in WW 2; *Publ*: verse collections: "Thirst" (1922); "Implacable Reality" (1924); "Hand in Hand" (1935); "Homeland" (1940); "Today and Tomorrow" (1943); poem "Lenin" (1934); play "Dreams" (1933); *Died*: 1943 killed in action.

KHASSIS, Abram Isaakovich (1894-1927) Diplomat; CP member from 1916; *Born*: 1894; *Educ*: 1924 grad Oriental Dept, Mil Acad; *Career*: after 1917 Oct Revol served with Red Army as commander and polit comr; from Oct 1924 worked for Far Eastern Dept, USSR Pop Comrt of For Affairs; Feb 1925 appointed secr, USSR Consulate-Gen in Shanghai; then secr, USSR Consulate-Gen in Hankow; from Dec 1926 USSR vice-consul in Canton; *Died*: Dec 1927 killed in Canton.

KHATAYEVICH, Mendel' Markovich (1893-1939) Party official; CP member from 1913; *Born*: 22 Mar 1893 in Gomel; *Career*: dental tech by trade; 1913 member, Poles'ye RSDRP(B) Comt; several times arrested; 1914 arrested while printing polit proclamations, sentenced and deported to Angara Kray; after 1917 Feb Revol worked for Gomel RSDRP(B) Org; 1918 chm, Samara City Party Comt; helped crush counter-revol uprising; as the Czech Legion advanced on Samara, went underground but was soon arrested and tortured (right hand paralysed); released from prison by Red Army; 1919 worked for Samara Province RCP(B) Comt; then served on Polish Front; 1921 secr Gomel' Province Party Comt; 1923 secr, Odessa Province Party Comt; 1924-25 worked for org and distribution organs of CC, CPSU(B); 1925 elected secr, Tatar Oblast Party Comt; 1928-32 secr, Centr Volga Kray Party Comt; 1933 elected secr, Dnepropetrovsk Oblast Party Comt; also secr and Politburo member, CC, CP(B) Ukr; member, USSR Centr Exec Comt; deleg at 8th-17th Party Congresses; at 14th CPSU(B) Congress elected member, Centr Auditing Commission; at 15th Party Congress elected cand member, CC, CPSU(B); at 16th and 17th Congresses elected member, CC, CPSU(B); at 12th and 13th Ukr Party Congresses elected member, CC, CP Ukr; 1937 arrested by State Security organs; *Awards*: Order of Lenin (1935); *Died*: 1939 in imprisonment; posthumously rehabilitated.

KHATENEVER, Leonid Moiseyevich (1896-1948) Microbiologist; Dr of Med from 1935; *Born*: 1896; *Educ*: 1925 grad Med Fac, 1st Moscow Univ; *Career*: from 1928 did research on the diagnosis, treatment, epidemiology, immunology and prophylaxis of tularemia; established first Sov tularemia laboratory; developed and introduced allergic intradermal diagnostic test; helped to develop vaccinotherapy for tularemia; devised rational system of anti-tularemic measures; wrote over 50 works, including seven monographs; *Publ: Tulyaremiya i yeyo profilaktika* (Tularemia and Its Prevention) (1942); *Allergicheskaya diagnostika, spetsificheskaya profilaktika i vaktsinoterapiya tulyaremii* (The Allergy Diagnosis, Specific Prophylaxis and Vaccinotherapy of Tularemia) (1943); coauthor and ed, *Tulyaremiynaya infektsiya* (Tularemic Infection) (1943); *Died*: 1948.

KHAYRI, Gaynan Badretdinovich (1903-1938) Bash writer; *Born*: 1903 in vil Iske-Kulevo, now Nurimanov Rayon, Bash ASSR, son of a peasant; *Educ*: studied at Bash Teachers' Training Inst; *Career*: worked for polit educ institutions and Bash newspapers; in 1920's first work published; subjected to reprisals by State Security organs; *Publ*: novelettes: "The Cooperators," "The Wife," etc; *Died*: 1938 in imprisonment.

KHESSIN, Aleksandr Borisovich (1869-1955) Conductor; teacher; Hon Art Worker of the RSFSR from 1929; *Born*: 19 Oct 1869 in Petersburg; *Educ*: 1899 grad Petersburg Conservatory in N. F. Solov'yov's composition class; 1899-1900 studied conducting under A. Nikis in Leipzig; 1900 studied under F. Motl in Karlsruhe; *Career*: 1904-05 dir, Moscow Philharmonic College; from 1910 artistic dir and chief conductor, Sheremetev Music and History Soc; 1915-17 opera conductor, House of the People in Petrograd; 1918-19 conducted at various Mariinskiy Theater productions in Petrograd; 1922 helped found Moscow Philharmonic; from 1935 artistic dir and chief conductor, Opera Studio, Moscow Conservatory; 1943-53 directed, Sov Opera Ensemble, All-Russian Theatrical Soc in Moscow, where he supervised the production of more than 20 new Sov operas, including: Prokofiev's *Voyna i mir* (War and Peace) (1944); Koval's *Sevastopol'tsy* (The People of Sebastopol) (1948); Kas'yanov's *Foma Gordeyev* (1946), etc; staged various operas neglected by the Moscow theaters, such as: Taneyev's *Oresteya* (1945); Gershwin's "Porgy and Bess" (1945); Moniuszko's "The Enchanted Castle" (1946); Smetana's "Dalibor" (1944), etc; from 1924 taught at State Inst of Stagecraft; *Publ: Iz moikh vospominaniy* (From My Memoirs) (1959); *Died*: 3 Apr 1955 in Moscow.

KHIDOYATOV, Abrar (1900-1958) Uzbek actor; Pop Artiste of

USSR from 1945; CP member; *Born*: 1900 in Tashkent; *Educ*: 1924-27 studied at Uzbek Studios, Moscow; 1927 grad Theatrical Studios, Uzbek House of Educ, Moscow; *Career*: from 1918 performed with M. Uygur's Theatrical Group (from 1919 Karl Marx Ensemble); from 1927 actor, Uzbek Centr State Ensemble (from 1929 Khamza Theater); *Roles*: Arslan in Yashen's *Dva kommunista* (Two Communists) and *Razgrom* (Defeat); Gafur in Khamza's "The Bey and the Farmhand"; Zer Sibane in Glebov's *Zagmuk*; Brodskiy in Slavin's *Interventsiya* (Intervention); Gay in Pogodin's *Moy drug* (My Friend); Kokumbay in *Myatezh* (Mutiny), after Furmanov; Gratanov in Fayko's *Chelovek s portfelem* (The Man with the Briefcase); Aman in Ismailov's *Vrediteli khlopka* (The Cotton Pests); Aripov in Safarov and Said's "History Spake"; Toigbek in Fatkhullin's "Unmasked"; *Awards*: Stalin Prize (1949); *Died*: 3 Oct 1958 in Tashkent.

KHIKHLOVSKIY, Vladimir Vasil'yevich (1921-1961) Mil commander; col; official, USSR Min of Defense; CP member from 1943; *Born*: 1921, son of a peasant; *Educ*: 1941 grad Mil Artillery College; after WW 2 grad Frunze Mil Acad; *Career*: from 1939 in Red Army; 1941-45 commanded artillery units in the field; after grad from mil acad, worked for USSR Min of Defense; *Awards*: Order of Aleksandr Nevskiy; Order of the Fatherland War, 1st Class; Order of the Fatherland War, 2nd Class; two Orders of the Red Banner; medals; *Died*: 17 May 1961 killed with Gen of the Army V. Ya. Kolpakchi and others in a plane crash during tactical exercises; buried in Moscow's Novodevich'ye Cemetery.

KHIKMET NAZYM (full name: NAZYM KHIKMET RAN) (1902-1963) Turkish poet and soc figure; member, Turkish CP from 1924; Bureau member, World Peace Council; *Born*: 1902 in Salonika, of artistocratic parents; *Educ*: studied at naval college; then studied at Communist Univ of Workers of the East; *Career*: expelled from naval college for revol activities on board training ship; 1917 first work printed; active in 1918-22 Turkish nat-liberation movement; 1921-28 lived in USSR; from 1928 helped publish progressive journal *Resimli ay*; arrested for Communist activities and spent 17 years in Turkish prisons; 1937 sentenced to 28 years' imprisonment; 1950 released; 1951 moved to USSR; introduced free verse to Turkish poetry; *Publ*: verse collection "835 Lines" (1929); collections of verse and poems: "La Gioconda and Hsi Ya-wu" (1929); "The Coming Z" (1930); "Why Benerdji Wanted to Commit Suicide" (1932); "The Night Telegram" (1932); "Letters to Taranta-Bab" (1935); "The Poem of Sheikh Bedreddin Simavi, Son of the Kadi of Simavne" (1936); plays: "The Skull" (1932); "The Deceased's House" (1932); "The Forgotten Man" (1935); articles "German Fascism and Racism" (1936) and "Soviet Democracy on the Basis of the New Constitution" (1936); plays: Iosif the Handsome" (1948); "A Legend of Love" (1948; Russian translation 1952); "Stories of Turkey" (1952); "First Day of the Holiday" (1953); "The Crank" (1954); comedy "Was There an Ivan Ivanovich? " (1956), etc; *Awards*: Int Peace Prize (1950); *Died*: 3 June 1963.

KHINCHIN, Aleksandr Yakovlevich (1894-1959) Mathematician; prof; Dr of Mathematics; corresp member, USSR Acad of Sci from 1939; member, RSFSR Acad of Pedag Sci from 1944; *Born*: 19 July 1894; *Educ*: 1916 grad Physics and Mathematics Fac, Moscow Univ; *Career*: 1919 began to teach; taught successively at Ivanovo-Voznesensk Polytech Inst, then at Moscow Karl Liebknecht Teachers' Training Inst; from 1927 prof, Moscow Univ; from 1939 did research at Mathematics Inst, USSR Acad of Sci; dealt with functions of real variables, introducing concept of asymptotic derivative, generalizing the Dangeois integral and studying the structure of measurable integrals; applied metric functions theory methods to numbers and probability theory; in numbers theory did research on the theory of diophantic approximations; discovered new aspects of the metric theory of constant fractions; together with Acad A. I. Kolmogorov, founded Sov probability theory school; also studied limiting theorems, discovered the law of the repeating logarithm, defined the random stationary process and laid the basis for the theory of tsuch processes; made wide use of probability theory as a mathematical tool of statistical physics; *Publ*: textbooks: *Osnovnyye ponyatiya matematiki i matematicheskiye opredeleniya v sredney shkole* (Basic Mathematical Concepts and Mathematical Calculations in the Secondary School) (1940); *O formalizme v shkol'nom prepodavanii matematiki* (Formalism in School Mathematics Teaching) (1944); *Tsennyye drobi* (Value Fractions) (1935); *Velikaya teorema Ferma* (Ferme's Great Theorem) (1932); *Tri zhemchuzhiny teorii chisel* (Three Pearls of the Theory of Numbers) (1947), etc; *Sluchay i kak nauka s nim spravlyayetsya* (Chance and How Science Copes with It) (1934); *Predel'nyye zakony dlya summ nezavisimykh sluchaynykh velichin* (Limitation Laws for Sums of Independent Random Values) (1938); *Matematicheskiye osnovaniya statisticheskoy mekhaniki* (The Mathematical Principles of Statistical Mechanics) (1943); *Vosem' lektsiy po matematicheskomu analizu* (Eight Lectures on Mathematical Analysis) (1948); *Awards*: Order of Lenin; three other orders; medals; Stalin Prize (1941); *Died* 18 Nov 1959.

KHINCHUK (pseudonyms: FYODOROV; MIRON), Lev Mikhaylovich (1869-1944) Govt official;CP member from 1920;*Born*: 1869; *Career*: 1890-91 founded Soc-Democratic circles in Tula; 1893 arrested in Tula and spent two and a half years in prison, followed by six years' exile to Yakutsk Oblast; after serving term in exile worked in Simferopol' and joined *Iskra* org; after collapse of Crimean Soc-Democratic org moved to Tula, then to Moscow; 1901 founded Moscow RSDRP Comt together with Vaynshteyn and Teodorovich; corresponded with *Iskra*; May 1902 re-arrested, spent 18 months in prison, then exiled to Yenisey Province; 1903 fled from exile and escaped abroad; after 2nd RSDRP congress joined Mensheviks; early 1905, after return to Russia, founded Menshevik group in Petersburg; May 1905 at All-Russian Conference of Mensheviks elected to Menshevik Center; 1906 at Stockholm (Joint) RSDRP Congress elected Menshevik member, CC, RSDRP; 1905 member, Exec Comt, Petersburg Sov of Workers' Dep; Dec 1905 arrested for this but escaped from custody, evaded trial and went underground, calling himself Miron; active in trade-union and cooperative movement in Moscow; sympathized with "liquidationists"; Feb-Sept 1917 chm, Moscow Sov; walked out of 2nd Congress of Soviets along with right-wing Mensheviks; 1917-19 member, CC, RSDRP (Mensheviks); 1920 joined CPSU(B); from late 1919 member, Collegium, Pop Comrt of Food; from 1921 chm, Centr Union of Consumer Org; Nov 1926-June 1927 Sov trade rep and chm, USSR trade deleg in Britain; 1927 attended Int Econ Conference in Geneva; from 1927 USSR Dep Pop Comr of Trade; 1930-34 Sov plen in Germany; from Aug 1934 RSFSR Pop Comr of Domestic Trade; member, USSR Centr Exec Comt; 1937arrested by State Security organs; *Died*: 1944 in imprisonment.

KHITAROV, Rafail Moiseyevich (1901- ?) Party official; CP member from 1919; *Born*: 1901; *Career*: from 1919 exec Komsomol work; 1927-28 secr, Exec Comt, Communist Youth International; from 1928 Presidium member, Comintern Exec Comt; *Died*: date and place of death unknown.

KHLOPIN, Grigoriy Vital'yevich (1863-1929) Hygienist; Dr of Med and prof from 1896; Hon Sci Worker of RSFSR from 1927; *Born*: 28 Jan 1863 in vil Dobryanka, Perm' Province; *Educ*: 1886 grad Natural Sci Dept, Fac of Physics and Mathematics, Petersburg Univ; 1893 grad Med Fac, Moscow Univ; *Career*: after grad Petersburg Univ worked at I. M. Sechenov's physiological laboratory; twice arrested for involvement with D. N. Blagoyev's Soc-Democratic group and sent under police escort to Cherdyn', Perm' Province; later transferred to Perm', where he worked first as asst, then dir, Zemstvo Health Laboratory; 1890 entered Med Fac, Moscow Univ and worked simultaneously at Prof F. F. Erisman's Hygiene Inst; after grad stayed on at Moscow Univ to prepare for professorship; from 1896 prof of hygiene, Yur'yev (Tartu) Univ; 1903 head, Chair of Hygiene, Novorossiysk Univ, Odessa; 1904-06 head, Chair of Hygiene, Petersburg Women's Med Inst; 1906-18 head, Chair of Hygiene, Petersburg Inst of Postgrad Med Training; 1918-29 head, Chair of Hygiene, Petrograd (Leningrad) Mil Med Acad; ranked with F. F. Erisman and A. P. Dobroslavin as one of the foremost pioneers of Russian hygiene; did research on water hygiene, including the effect of petroleum products on river fish and the quality of the water of the Volga; studied the composition and properties of coal-tar paints and their effect on the human body; conducted experiments on labor hygiene and occupational diseases in the chemical and ore-mining ind; helped to develop principles of sanitary-chemical protection; wrote over 140 works, including 25 on hygiene research methods; *Publ: K metodike opredeleniya rastvorennogo v vode kisloroda* (Methods of Determining the Dissolved Oxygen-Content of Water) (1896); *Kamennougol'nyye kraski* (Coal-Tar Paints) (1903); *Materialy po ozdorovleniyu Rossii* (Material on the Improvement of Health Standards in Russia) (1911); *Khimicheskiye metody issledovaniya pit'yevykh i stochnykh vod* (Chemical Methods of Examining Drinking and Waste Water) (1913); *Khimicheskaya promyshlennost' i narodnoye zdorov'ye* (The Chemical Industry and Public Health) (1920-24); *Trudovoy rezhim i professional'nyye vrednosti* (Working Conditions and Occupational Diseases); *Osnovy gigiyeny* (The Principles of Hygiene) (1921-22); *Issledovaniya v oblasti fiziologii i gigiyeny umstvennogo truda* (Research on the Physiology and Hygiene of Mental Work) (1922); *Voyenno-sanitarnyye osnovy protivogazovogo dela* (The Military Sanitary Principles of Gas Defense) (1926); *Metody sanitarnykh issledovaniy* (Sanitary Research Methods) (1928-29); *Died*: 30 July 1929 in Leningrad.

KHLOPIN, Nikolay Grigor'yevich (1897-1961) Histologist; maj-gen, Med Corps; member, USSR Acad of Med Sci from 1945; *Born*: 28 July 1897, son of G. Khlopin, prof of hygiene, Petersburg Mil Med Acad; *Educ*: 1921 grad Leningrad Mil Med Acad; 1922 grad Natural Sci Dept, Fac of Physics and Mathematics, Leningrad Univ; *Career*: 1921-36 lecturer, 1936-55 head, Chair of Histology and Embryology, Mil Med Acad, where he specialized in histology under Prof A. A. Maksimov; 1928-38 founder-head, Cytology Laboratory, Leningrad Oncological Inst, 1932 founded Chair of Histology, I. I. Mechnikov Training Hospital; 1932-41 founder-head, Laboratory of Experimental Histology and Tissue Cultures, 1945-54 founder-head, Histology Dept, Inst of Experimental Med; 1955-61 head, Laboratory of Experimental Morphology, Oncological Inst, USSR Acad of Med Sci; pioneered study of evolutionary histology in USSR; made extensive use of tissue culture method to study specifically histological problems of tissue differentiation, determination and classification; established that intra vitam stains accumulate in granules formed under the influence of the staining media; did research on the epithelial and muscular tissues, neuroglia and vasal endothelium; performed experimental histological analyses of tumor tissues on the basis of which he hypothesized the specificity of the properties of vertebrate tissues; devised classification of tissues in vertebrates; postulated theory of divergent tissue evolution which parallels Darwin's theory of the divergent evolution of whole organisms; *Publ*: "Experimentelle Untersuchungen über die sekretorischen Prozesse im Zytoplasma" (Experimental Investigations of the Secretory Processes in Cytoplasm) (1927); *Kul'tura tkaney* (Tissue Cultures) (1940); *Obshchebiologicheskiye i eksperimental'nyye osnovy gistologii* (The General Biological and Experimental Principles of Histology) (1946); *Gistogenez opukholevykh tkaney v svete eksperimental'nogo gistologicheskogo analiza* (The Histogenesis of Tumor Tissues in the Light of Experimental Histological Analysis) (1947); *Spetsifichnost' endoteliya, regenerativnyye vozmozhnosti i vzaimootnosheniya tkaney susudistoy stenki* (The Specificity of the Endothelium, the Regenerative Potential and Interrelationship of the Tissues of the Vasal Wall) (1958); *Razvitiye mnogokletochnoy i tkanevoy organizatsii zhivotnykh* (The Development of Multicellular and Tissue Organization in Animals) (1959); *Awards*: Order of Lenin; Stalin Prize (1947); other orders and medals; *Died*: 1961.

KHLOPIN, Vitaliy Grigor'yevich (1890-1950) Chemist; member, USSR Acad of Sci from 1939; Hon Sci and Tech Worker of RSFSR from 1940; *Born*: 26 Jan 1890 in Perm'; *Educ*: 1911 grad Göttingen Univ; 1912 grad Petersburg Univ; *Career*: 1912-15 did postgrad work at Petersburg Univ; 1915-21 assoc, Radiological Laboratory, Russian (USSR) Acad of Sci; until 1917 specialized in the inorganic and analytical chemistry of metals in the platinum group; 1918-21 supervised the construction of the first Russian radium plant, where he obtained radium preparations and organized research on the chemistry and geochemistry of radioactive elements; 1922-39 assoc, from 1939 dir, Radium Inst, USSR Acad of Sci; from 1924 also lecturer, Leningrad Univ, where he read a course on radioactivity and the chemistry of radioactive elements; 1933-39 corresp member, USSR Acad of Sci; formulated the law of the distribution of microcomponents between solid and liquid states; devised method of determining the composition of unstable chemical compounds by studying their co-crystallization conditions; made a major contribution to geochemistry with his study of the migration of radioactive elements in the Earth's crust and his radioactive dating of the Earth's geological age; also developed a number of methods of gas, volumetric, weight and calorimetric analysis; *Awards*: Order of Lenin; two Stalin Prizes (1943 and 1946); Medals; *Died*: 10 July 1950.

KHLOPLYANKIN, Ivan Ivanovich (1890-?) Govt official; CP member from 1917; *Born*: 1890, son of a peasant; *Career*: from 1911 in trade-union movement; from 1914 chm, bd, trade employees union; 1916 arrested; after 1917 Oct Revol worked for cooperative and supply organs; 1922-23 chm, Kursk Province Exec Comt; 1923 RSFSR Dep Pop Comr of Internal Affairs; 1924-26 mang, Labor and Defense Council; 1926-29 Collegium member, Pop Comrt of Trade; 1929-30 dep chm, Moscow Sov; from 1931 chm, bd, Moscow Oblast Trade-Union Council; *Died*: date and place of death unknown.

KHLOPLYANKIN, Mikhail Ivanovich (1892-?) Gov official; CP member from 1917; *Born*: 1892, son of a peasant; *Career*: before 1917 Oct Revol office worker; 1918-19 bd member, Pop Comrt of Labor; 1919-21 fought on Eastern and Southern fronts in Civil War; 1921-23 again worked for Pop Comrt of Labor; 1923-24 bd member, State Bank; 1924-25 bd member, Pop Comrt of For Trade; 1925-26 Sov trade rep in London; 1927 chm, Grain Export Bd; 1928-30 chm, Lower Volga Kray Exec Comt; from 1930 USSR Dep Pop Comr of Supply; member, USSR Centr Exec Comt; elected cand member, CC, CPSU(B) at 16th Party Congress; *Died*: date and place of death unknown.

KHMEL'NITSKIY, Boris Moiseyevich (1885-1959) Phthisiatrist and health official; Dr of Med from 1927; prof from 1931; *Born*: 1885 in Yekaterinoslav; *Educ*: 1910 grad Med Fac, Khar'kov Univ; *Career*: 1910-14 intern, Khar'kov Hospital Therapy Clinic; during WW 1 served at mil hospitals; after 1917 Oct Revol chm, Khar'kov Province Tuberculosis Council; head, Tuberculosis Section, Khar'kov Province Health Dept, then head, Tuberculosis Dept, Ukr Pop Comrt of Health; cofounder, and for 20 years head, Adults' Tuberculosis Clinic, 1940-52 dir, Ukr Inst of Tuberculosis; 1931-59 head, Chair of Tuberculosis, Khar'kov Med Inst; bd member, Khar'kov Med Soc, Ukr Soc of Phthisiatrists and All-Union Soc of Therapists; attended numerous All-Union, republ and oblast conferences of therapists and phthisiatrists; wrote some 90 works; *Publ: Smeshannaya infektsiya pri lyogochnom tuberkulyoze* (Mixed Infection in Pulmonary Tuberculosis) (1927); *Ranniye formy otkrytogo lyogochnogo tuberkulyoza u vzroslykh* (Early Forms of Open Pulmonary Tuberculosis in Adults) (1932), etc; *Awards*: Order of the Red Star; A. Ya. Shternberg Prize (1932); medals; *Died*: 1959 in Khar'kov.

KHMELYOV, Nikolay Pavlovich (1901-1945) Russian actor and producer; Pop Artiste of USSR from 1937; CP member from 1941; *Born*: 10 Aug 1901 in Sormovo, son of a factory foreman; *Educ*: 1919 began to study acting at 2nd Studio, Moscow Arts Theater; *Career*: from 1924 actor, Moscow Acad Arts Theater; was strongly influenced by Stanislavsky and Nemirovich-Danchenko; from 1932 founder-dir, Moscow Theater-Studio; 1937-45 artistic dir, Yermolova Theater, Moscow, with which his Theater-Studio merged; 1943-45 artistic dir, Moscow Acad Arts Theater; also taught acting and performed in films; *Roles*: King Tmu-Tarakansk in *Skazka ob Ivanushke* (The Tale of Little Ivan); Yelevferiy in Sologub's *Uzor iz roz* (Pattern of Roses); Petrushka in Griboyedov's *Gore ot uma* (Woe From Wit); Ushakov and Biron in Smolin's *Yelizaveta Petrovna*; Prince Vasiliy Shuyskiy in A. K. Tolstoy's *Tsar' Fyodor Ivanovich*; Zabelin in *Kremlyovskiye kuranty* (Kremlin Chimes); Dubelt in Bulgakov's *Posledniye dni* (Last Days); Ivan the Terrible in A. N. Tolstoy's *Trudnyye gody* (Hard Years); *Productions*: Ostrovskiy's *Ne bylo ni grosha, da vdrug altyn* (From Rags to Riches) (1934); Shakespeare's "As You Like It" (1940); *Front* (The Front-Line) (1942); *Russkiye lyudi* (Russian People) (1943); *Poslednyaya zhertva* (The Last Victim) (1944); *Deti solntsa* (Children of the Sun) (1944); *Awards*: three Stalin Prizes (1941, 1942 and 1946); Order of the Red Banner of Labor; *Died*: 1 Nov 1945 during dress rehearsal of "Ivan the Terrible".

KHOBTA, Yelena Semyonovna (1882-1960) Agric innovator; CP member from 1940; *Born*: 27 May 1882 in vil Tayshino, nov Kiev Oblast, daughter of a peasant; *Career*: from 1930's kolkhoz worker; from 1936 field-team leader, Ivan Franko (now "Lenin's Spark") Sovkhoz, Kiev Oblast; 1947 led team which harvested 75.7 centners [metric] of corn per hectare; 1950 harvested 145 centners of corn and 565 centners of potatoes per hectare; 1952 harvested 102.75 centners of corn and 517.2 centners of potatoes per hectare; deleg, 17th, 18th and 19th Congresses, CP Ukr; dep, Ukr Supr Sov of 3rd and 4th convocations; *Awards*: two Orders of Lenin; *Died*: 23 Apr 1960.

KHODOROVSKIY, Iosif Isayevich (1885-1940) Party and govt official; CP member from 1903; *Born*: 1885; *Career*: 1905 arrested for smuggling illegal lit and sentenced to eight months in prison; from Nov 1905 member, then secr, Nikolayev RSDRP(B) Comt; Jan 1906 arrested and exiled to Vologda Province whence he escaped to Nikolayev; re-arrested and exiled to Olonets Province, whence he also escaped; 1907 worked in Moscow as Party organizer in Lefortov Rayon, then exec rayon organizer; member, Moscow City Bolshevik Comt; 1910 tried by Moscow City Court for membership in the Party; from 1912 contributed to Bolshevik journal *Prosveshcheniye*; 1917 member, Moscow Group, Soc-Democratic amalgamationists; during 1917 Oct rebellion fought in Moscow's Sushchevsko-Mar'inskiy Rayon; chm, Sushchevsko-Mar'inskiy Rayon Sov of Workers, Peasants and Soldiers' Dep; early 1918 head, Polit Dept, and member, Revol Mil Comt, Southern Front; 1919 Moscow Comr of Labor; chm, Kazan' Province Exec Comt; 1920 chm, Tula Province Exec Comt; then secr, Siberian Bureau, CC, CPSU(B); 1922-28 Dep Pop Comr of Educ; 1928-32 Sov plen in Italy, then Turkey; 1932-34 dep chm, Comt of Higher Tech Educ, USSR Centr Exec Comt; 1934-38 head, Therapy and Sanitation Bd, USSR Council of Pop Comr; 1938 arrested by State Security organs; *Died*: 1940 in imprisonment.

KHODUKIN, Nikolay Ivanovich (1896-1957) Parasitologist and epidemiologist; corresp member, USSR Acad of Med Sci from 1945; corresp member, Uzbek Acad of Sci from 1947; Hon Sci Worker of Uzbek SSR from 1940; *Born*: 1896; *Educ*: 1919 grad Med Fac, Kazan' Univ; 1921 completed postgrad studies at Moscow Tropical Inst (now Inst of Malaria, Med Parasitology and Tropical Med); *Career*: during Civil War served as physician in Red Army; after postgrad training established malaria station in Mary, Centr Asia; 1924 head, Mirzachulinsk Malaria Station, then head, Tashkent Malaria Station; from 1925 head, Parasitological Dept, Tashkent Inst of Epidemiology and Microbiology; taught course of gen and special parasitology at Centr Asian Univ; did major research on canine leishmaniosis; also studied virus infections (encephalitis, Pappatacci's fever, etc) and rickettsial diseases (Q-fever); established that encephalitis in Dzhalavgara was of alimentary origin and helped to wipe out the disease in this area; wrote 147 works on malaria, leishmaniosis and the regional diseases of Centr Asia, especially Uzbek SSR; *Publ: Osnovnyye problemy epidemiologii 'kala-azar' v svyazi s epidemiologiyey sobach'yevo leyshmanioza v Sredney Azii* (The Basic Problems of the Epidemiology of "Kala-Azar" in Connection with the Epidemiology of Canine Leishmaniosis in Central Asia) (1929); coauthor, *Ocherki po istorii parazitologii* (Outline History of Parasitology) (1953); *Izbrannyye trudy* (Selected Works) (1959), etc; *Died*: 1957.

KHODZHA-EYNATOV, Leon Aleksandrovich (1904-1954) Arm composer; Hon Art Worker of Arm SSR from 1945; *Born*: 23 Mar 1904 in Tiflis; *Educ*: 1926-28 studied under A. A. Spendiarov in Yerevan; 1931 grad P.B. Ryazanov's composition class, Centr Musical Technicum, Leningrad; *Career*: 1931-36 conductor and musical dir in Leningrad drama theaters; *Works*: operas: *Shlyuz* (The Lock) (1931); *Myatezh* (Mutiny) (1938), after Furmanov; *Semya* (The Family) (1940); *Namus* (Honor) (1945), etc; coauthor, operetta *Moya lyubimaya* (My Beloved) (1938); arranged and orchestrate Chukhadzhyan's opera *Arshak II* (1945) and Tigranyan's opera *David-bek* (1950); composed pieces for variety orchestra, a string quartet, romances, music for plays, symphonies, suites, overtures, dances, etc; *Died*: 7 Oct 1954 in Leningrad.

KHODZHAYEV, Fayzula Abaydullayevich (1896-1938) Govt official; CP member from 1920; *Born*: 1896; *Career*: one of leading Communist figures of Centr Asia; from 1913 active in "nat revol movement", spearheaded by the Young Bukhara Party; 1917 joined CC, Young Bukhara Party; 1917 helped stage demonstration against the Emir of Bukhara; 1918 appointed chm, Bukhara Revol Comt; participated in armed campaign against the Emir, for which he was sentenced in absentia to death; after the failure of the campaign fled to Moscow; arrested in Orenburg and spent four months in prison; late 1919 went to Tashkent; chm, Turkestani Bureau, Young Bukhara Party; then ed, newspaper *Uchkun*; 1920 fought in Sept armed uprising and with Red Army during the campaign to capture Bukhara; 1920-24 chm, Bukhara Sov of Pop Comr; member, CC, CP Bukhara; member, Revol Mil Comt; during the establishment of the Sov regime in Centr Asia helped crush the Basmachi revolt; Oct 1924-June 1937 chm, Uzbek Council of Pop Comr; member, CC, CP Uzbek; 1922-36 member, Centr Asian Bureau, CC, CPSU(B); 1925-June 1937 chm, USSR Centr Exec Comt; 1937 arrested for membership in a "bourgeois nationalist org"; accused of having founded in 1920 the *Milli Ittihad* illegal counter-revol org aimed at divorcing Centr Asia from the USSR; sentenced to death in "Anti-Sov Rightist Trotskyite Center" trial; *Awards*: Order of the Red Banner; *Died*: 18 Mar 1938 executed by firing squad.

KHOKHLOV, Aleksandr Yevgen'yevich (1892-1966) Actor; Pop Artiste of RSFSR from 1946; *Born*: 4 Mar 1892; *Career*: 1910 stage debut at Smolensk theater; 1910-19 worked at theaters in Vinnitsa, Tambov, Irkutsk, Tashkent, Yaroslavl' and Nizhniy Novgorod; from 1919 at State Model Theater, 1st Theater of the RSFSR and Comedy Theater, Moscow; 1931-64 with Centr Theater of the Sov Army; *Roles*: Chatskiy, Molchalin, Zagoretskiy, Repetilov and Skalozub in Griboyedov's *Gore ot uma* (Woe from Wit); Erekle, Dato and Soleyman in Sumbatov-Yuzhin's *Izmena* (Treason); Glukhovtsev and von Franken in Andreyev's *Dni nashey zhizni* (The Days of Our Life); Kutuzov in Gladkov's *Davnym-davno* (Long, Long Ago) and in Trenyov's *Polkovodets Kutuzov* (General Kutuzov); Potyomkin in Bakhterev and Razumovskiy's *Suvorov* and in Shteyn's *Flag admirala* (The Admiral's Flag); the Comr in Ovchina-Ovcharenko's *Voyenkom* (The Military Commissar); Derzhavin in Prut's *Mstislav Udaloy*; Lenchitskiy in Romashov's *Boytsy* (Warriors); Gaydar in *Front*; the Commander in Chepurin's *Stalingradtsy* (The Stalingraders); Lynyayev in *Volki i ovtsy* (The Wolves and the Sheep); Mamayev in Ostrovskiy's *Na vsyakogo mudretsa dovol'no prostoty* (There's a Simpleton in Every Sage); Krutitskiy in Ostrovskiy's *Ne bylo ni grosha, da vdrug altyn* (From Rags to Riches); Muromskiy in Sukhovo-Kobylin's *Delo* (The Case); *Died*: 1966.

KHOKHLOV, Konstantin Pavlovich (1885-1956) Actor and producer; Pop Artiste of USSR from 1944; *Born*: 1 Nov 1885; *Educ*: 1908 grad Moscow Theatrical College, where he studied under A. P. Lenskiy; *Career*: 1908-20 actor, Moscow Arts Theater; from 1921 actor, then chief producer, Bolshoy Drama Theater, Petrograd (Leningrad); from 1922 also taught acting; 1925-30 producer, Leningrad (now Pushkin) Acad Drama Theater; 1931-38 producer, Maly Theater, Moscow; 1938-54 artistic dir and chief producer, Lesya Ukrainka Russian Theater, Kiev; from 1954 chief producer, Bolshoy Theater, Leningrad; taught acting at Shchepkin Theatrical College, Moscow, Lesya Ukrainka Theatrical Studio and Karpenko-Karyy Ukr Theatrical Inst, Kiev; from 1946 prof, Ostrovskiy Theatrical Inst, Leningrad; *Roles*: at Moscow Arts Theater: Karenin in *Zhivoy trup* (The Living Corpse); Horatio in "Hamlet"; Yeletskiy in Turgenev's *Nakhlebnik* (The Parasite); at Bolshoy Drama Theater, Leningrad: Salluste de Bazin in Hugo's "Ruy Blas"; the Consul in Bryusov's *Zemlya* (Earth); Mark Antony in Shakespeare's "Julius Caesar"; *Productions*: at Bolshoy Drama Theater, Leningrad: "Julius Caesar" (1922); Kaiser's "Gas" (1922); Benelli's "La Cena delle beffe" (The Jester's Supper) (1923); Fayko's "Teacher Bubus" (1925); Leonov's *Polovchanskiye sady* (The Polovtsian Gardens) (1954); Hauptmann's "Vor Sonnenaufgang" (Before Dawn) (1955); at Leningrad Acad Drama Theater: Sophocles' "Oedipus Rex" (1924); Lunacharskiy's *Yad* (Poison) (1925); *Pugachyovshchina* (The Pugachev Rebellion) (1926); Lunacharskiy and Shtukken's *Barkhat i lokhmot'ya* (Velvet and Rags) (1927); *Dokhodnoye mesto* (A Lucrative Post) (1928); *Gore ot uma* (Woe from Wit) (1928); at Malyy Theater, Moscow: *Plody prosveshcheniya* (The Fruits of Enlightenment) (1932); *Vragi* (The Enemies) (1933); Romashov's *Boytsy* (The Warriors) (1934); *Volki i ovtsy* (The Wolves and the Sheep) (1935); Trenyov's *Na beregu Nevy* (On the Banks of the Neva) (1937); at Lesya Ukrainka Theater, Kiev: Lesya Ukrainka's *Kamennyy vlastelin* (The Stone Sovereign) (1939, 1946); Paustovskiy's *Prostyye serdtsa* (Simple Hearts) (1939); *Zykovy* (The Zykovs) (1940); Solov'yov's *Fel'dmarshal Kutuzov* (Fieldmarshal Kutuzov) (1940); Shaw's "Pygmalion" (1945); Shteyn's *Zakon chesti* (The Law of Honor) (1948); Alyoshin's *Direktor* (The Director) (1950); Turgenev's *Mesyats na derevne* (A Month in the Country) (1954); *Awards*: Order of Lenin; three other orders; medals; *Died*: 1 Jan 1956.

KHOKHOL, Yelena Nilolayevna (1897-1965) Pediatrician; Dr of Med from 1945; prof from 1946; corresp member, USSR Acad of Med Sci from 1953; Hon Sci Worker of Ukr SSR from 1958; cand member, CC, CP Ukr from 1954; CP member from 1953; *Born*: 3 June 1897 in Ustilug, now Volhynian Oblast; *Educ*: 1921 grad Kiev Med Inst; *Career*: 1921-25 worked as physician in Uman'; 1925-27 pediatrician at various hospitals and clinics, Kiev; 1927-41 asst prof, then assoc prof, Chair of Pediatrics, Kiev Inst of Postgrad Med Training; 1941-42 worked at various mil hospitals and for evacuated Ukr Pop Comrt of Health; 1943-45 head, Bd of Therapeutic and Prophylactic Service, USSR Min of Health; 1945-46 assoc prof, from 1946 head, Chair of Children's Diseases, Bogomolets Med Inst, Kiev; dep, Ukr Supr Sov of 3rd and 4th convocations; member, Ukr deleg, 7th and 8th sessions of UN Gen Assembly; attended various int conferences on pediatrics; bd chm, Ukr Soc of Pediatricians; bd member, All-Union Soc of Pediatricians; member, ed council, journal *Pediatriya*; developed various methods of baby-feeding, inter alia with ionitic milk; established experimentally that disturbances of the peripheral circulation and lesions of the connective tissue occur in intestinal toxicosis; established laboratory for testing new baby-foods; supervised research program on baby-feeding at USSR Acad of Med Sci; studied immunological reaction of babies during first months of life; wrote some 80 works; *Publ: Materialy k voprosy o narusheniyakh kapillyarnogo krovoobrashcheniya pri toksicheskoy dispepsii u detey* (Material on Disturbances of Capillary Circulation in Children Suffering from Toxic Dyspepsia) (1945); *Pytannya diahnostyky, kliniky likuvannya ditey khvorykh na tuberkul'oznyy meninhit* (The Diagnosis and Clinical Treatment of Children Suffering from Tubercular Meningitis) (1959); *Gipoproteinemiya i gipogammaglobulinemiya u detey pervykh mesyatsev zhizni* (Hypopproteinemia and Hypogammaglobulinemia in Babies During the First Months of Life) (1957); *Awards*: Order of Lenin; etc; *Died*: 1965 in Kiev.

KHOKHRYAKOV, Semyon Vasil'yevich (1915-1945) Mil commander; maj; CP member from 1935; *Born*: 1915 in vil Koyelga, Chelyabinsk Uyezd, Orenburg Province; *Educ*: 1941 grad Mil Infantry College; 1943 grad Higher Officers' Tank School; *Career*: from 1937 in Red Army; 1941-42 commanded platoon, then company; 1943-45 commanded tank battalion on 1st Ukr Front; 1944 fought at Pereyaslavl-Khmel'nitskiy; 1945 fought at Czestochowa, Poland; *Awards*: twice Hero of the Soviet Union (1944 and 1945); Order of Lenin; other orders and medals; *Died*: 17 Apr 1945 killed in action.

KHOL'TSOV, Boris Nikolayevich (1861-1940) Urologist; Dr of Med from 1892; prof; Hon Sci Worker of RSFSR from 1936; *Born*: 1861; *Educ*: 1884 grad Natural Sci Fac, Odessa Univ; 1887 grad Petersburg Mil Med Acad; *Career*: specialized in surgery under A. A. Troyanov; specialized in urology under Kasper; 1901-10 head, Surgical Dept, from 1910 head, Urological Dept, Obukhov Hospital, where he established the first urological in-patient ward in Petersburg; 1915 chief surgeon of a large mil hospital; from 1916 prof, Chair of Urology, Psychoneurological Inst (now 2nd Leningrad Med Inst); from 1926 prof of urology, Leningrad State Inst of Postgrad Med Training; head, Urological Dept, "Victims of the Revolution" Memorial Hospital, Leningrad; devised two- and three-phase methods of removing enlarged prostates; also devised operative techniques for the treatment of fistulas and stricture of the urethra, constriction of the cervix vesicae and tumors of the urinary bladder; trained numerous specialists, many of whom now head chairs of urology; hon member and chm, Leningrad Urologists' Soc; member, Leningrad City Sov; wrote over 100 works, including many monographs and textbooks: *Publ*: doctor's thesis, *Ob ostanovke krovotecheniya pri raneniyakh bolshikh ven i o perevyazke obshchey bedrennoy veny v chastnosti* (Hemostasis in Injury of the Major Veins and the Ligation of the Vena Femoralis in Particular) (1892); *Povrezhdeniya i zabolevaniya predstatel'noy zhelezy* (Injuries and Diseases of the Prostate Gland) (1909); *Diagnostika bolezney mochepolovykh organov* (The Diagnosis of Diseases of the Urogenital Tract) (1911); *Gonoreya i yeyo oslozhneniya* (Gonorrhea and its Complications) (1926); *Rukovodstvo po urologii* (A Urology Manual) (1924); *Chastnaya urologiya* (Special Urology) (1927); *Died*: 1940.

KHOL'ZUNOV, Viktor Stepanovich (1905-1939) Air Force commander; div commander; CP member from 1927; *Born*: 1905 in Tsaritsyn, now Volgograd, son of a worker; *Educ*: 1925 grad Leningrad Mil Theory Air Force School; 1928 grad Borisoglebsk Mil Pilots School; 1933 grad Advanced Commanders Training Courses; 1936 grad Higher Flight Tactics School; *Career*: 1918 served with his father in Red Army in defense of Tsaritsyn; from 1923 in Sov Air Force; 1936-37 pilot, flight commander, then squadron commander with bomber units of Spanish Republ Air Force; 1937-39 commanded Air Force operations group; dep, USSR Supr Sov of 1937 convocation; *Awards*: Hero of Sov Union (1937); Order of Lenin; Order of the Red Banner; *Died*: 1939 killed on mission; monument erected to him in Volgograd.

KHOLODNYY, Nikolay Grigor'yevich (1882-1953) Botanist; prof from 1919; member, Ukr Acad of Sci from 1929; Hon Sci Worker of Ukr SSR from 1945; *Born*: 22 June 1882 in Tambov, son of a teacher; *Educ*: 1906 grad Kiev Univ; *Career*: 1906-19 lecturer, from 1919 prof, Kiev Univ; 1920-49 also worked at Inst of Botany, Ukr Acad of Sci; did research on plant physiology, anatomy and ecology, microbiology and pedology; postulated phytohormonal theory of tropism to explain the growth movements of plants; studied the morphology and physiology of iron bacteria; also studied the vegetative reproduction of the houseleek Sempervivum soboliferum, the pollination of sage, the escape of caryopsides from Gramineae during long periods of rain, etc; spent latter years studying soil gases and their biological significance; speculated on the origin of life on Earth; *Publ: O vliyanii metallicheskikh ionov na protsessy razdrazhimosti u rasteniy* (The Influence of Metallic Ions on Plant Stimulation Processes) (1918); *Fitogormony* (Phytohormones) (1939); *Darvinizm i evolyutsionnaya fiziologiya* (Darwinism and Evolutionary Physiology) (1943); *Zhelezobakterii* (Iron Bacteria) (1953); *Gazy pochvy i ikh biologicheskoye znacheniye* (Soil Gases and Their Biological Importance) (1953); *Izbrannyye trudy* (Selected Works) (3 vol, 1956-57); *Died*: 4 May 1953.

KHOMENKO, Vitya (Viktor Kirillovich) (1926-1942) WW 2 partisan; member, Young Pioneer Org; *Born*: 12 Nov 1926 in Kremenchug; *Career*: 1941-42 did liaison and reconnaissance work for partisan movement near Nikolayev; 1942, together with Sh. Kober, crossed through enemy lines to deliver information to partisan headquarters in Moscow; Nov 1942 captured by German troops; *Died*: 5 Dec 1942; executed by German firing squad.

KHOROSHKO, Vasiliy Konstantinovich (1881-1949) Neuropathologist; Dr of Med from 1912; member, USSR Acad of Med Sci from 1945; Hon Sci Worker of RSFSR; *Born*: 7 Apr 1881; *Educ*: 1904 grad Med Fac, Moscow Univ; *Career*: after grad clinical intern, Novo-Yekaterina Hospital; 1911, together with other sci, resigned from Moscow Univ in protest against policies of Educ Min L. Kasso; 1912-23 taught at Moscow Higher Women's Courses; 1915-20 also worked at Traumatological Inst; 1916 resumed duties at Moscow Univ as assoc prof; from 1929 head, Neurological Clinic, Inst of Physical Therapy and Orthopedics; from 1929 also sci dir, Experimental Therapy Research Laboratory and head, Chair of Nervous Diseases, 4th, then 3rd, Moscow Med Inst; Presidium member, Soc of Neuropathologists and Psychiatrists; member, Learned Med Council, RSFSR Pop Comrt of Health; ed and member, ed collegia of several journals; co-ed, neuropsychiatric section, *Bol'shaya meditsinskaya entsiklopediya* (Large Medical Encyclopedia); member, All-Union Assoc of Sci and Tech Workers for the Promotion of Socialist Construction; 1906 hypothesized the subcortical origin of compulsive actions and muscle-tone disorders; 1912 expounded his biological therapy methods in doctor's thesis; in same year located the center of active attention and initiative in the frontal lobes and described a number of injury syndromes; did original research on diseases of the vegetative nervous system, the diagnosis of nervous diseases and the theory of neuroses; made extensive studies of neurotraumatism and neurosurgery; was first specialist in Moscow to use lumbar puncture for diagnosis and treatment; devised original method of pneumoencephalography; also did considerable research on the physical therapy of nervous diseases; wrote 208 works; *Publ: Klinicheskaya forma professora Kozhevnikova epilepsia partialis continua* (The Clinical Form of Professor Kozhevnikov's Epilepsia Partialis Continua) (1907); *Klinicheskiye nablyudeniya v svyazi s punctio lumbalis* (Clinical Observations Concerning Lumbar Puncture) (1908); *Ob otnoshenii lobnykh doley mozga k psikhologii i psikhopatologii* (The Pertinence of the Frontal Lobes to Psychology and Psychopathology) (1912); doctor's thesis *Reaktsiya zhivotnogo organizma na vvedeniye nervnoy tkani* (The Reaction of the Animal Organism to the Introduction of Nerve Tissue) (1912); *Bolezni vegetativnoy nervnoy sistemy* (Diseases of the Vegetative Nervous System) (1929); ed and coauthor, *Lyumboishialgiya* (Lumbar Sciatica) (1938); *Ucheniye o nevrozakh* (The Theory of Neuroses) (1943), etc; *Died*: 26 June 1949.

KHORUZHAYA, Vera Zakharovna (1903-1942) Revolutionary in Bel and Poland; CP member from 1921; *Born*: 1903; *Educ*: grad Party school; 1919 grad labor school in Mozyr'; *Career*: taught at rural school in Poles'ye; 1920, after establishment of Sov regime, joined the Komsomol; fought against counter-revol forces; Komsomol work; ed, newspaper *Malady araty*; from 1924 underground work in Western Bel; helped found Bel Komsomol; secr, CC, West Bel Komsomol; member, CC, Polish Komsomol and CC,

CP Western Bel; 1924-32 imprisoned in Poland; from 1932 in USSR; Party work; at outset of WW 2 joined Bel partisan detachment and sent behind enemy lines; underground Party work in occupied Vitebsk; arrested by German occupation authorities; *Publ*: *Pis'ma na vol'yu* (Letters to Freedom) (1931); *Awards*: Hero of the Soviet Union (1960, posthumously); *Died*: 1942 in imprisonment in Vitebsk.

KHOTEYEVA, Mavra Maksimovna (1865-1938) Karelian storyteller; specialist in epic folk songs (runes), fairy tales and laments; *Born*: 1865 in vil Ukhta, now Kalevala Rayon, Karelian ASSR, daughter of a peasant; *Career*: during 1930's became well-known as a composer of runes of Sov themes, including *Toyvo Antikaynen*, "The Soviet Constitution", etc; 1935 performed in Kalevala's 100th anniversary celebrations; 1937 related runes at Karelian Art Festival in Leningrad; some of Khoteyeva's works published in the anthology *Karel'skiye epicheskiye pesni* (Karelian Epic Songs) (1950) and in other collections; *Died*: 1938.

KHOTIMSKIY, Valentin Ivanovich (1892-1939) Party official, statistician; CP member from 1918; *Born*: 1892 in Glukhov, Chernigov Province, son of a teacher; *Educ*: studied at Petersburg Polytech Inst; *Career*: 1913 expelled from Petersburg Polytech Inst for revol activities; 1914 reinstated at request of teaching staff; 1917 took active part in Feb Revol; member of a revol comt in Urals and oblast comr of agric; 1918 switched allegiance from Leftist Socialist-Revol Party to RSDRP(B); fought with partisan units during Civil War and did Party work in Urals, Ukr, Siberia and Far East; 1921-22 head, Propaganda Section, CC, RCP(B); helped to develop Party educ policy; after Civil War engaged in research, publishing and teaching work; 1933 head, Polit Dept, Far Eastern Kray Machine and Tractor Station; subjected to reprisals by State Security organs; *Publ: Vyravnivaniye statisticheskikh ryadov po metody naimen'shikh kvadratov (sposob Chebyshyova)* (The Adjustment of Statistical Series by the Method of Least Squares [Chebyshyov's Method]) (1925); *Ob odnoy formule parabolicheskogo interpolirovaniya* (A Parabolic Interpolation Formula) (1925); *Ob ekstremal'nykh znacheniyakh sredney arifmeticheskoy* (The Extreme Values of the Arithmetical Mean) (1928); *Ob ekstremal'nykh znacheniyakh kvadraticheskogo ukloneniya* (The Extreme Values of Second-Order Deviation) (1928); coauthor and ed, *Teoriya matematicheskoy statistiki* (The Theory of Mathematical Statistics) (1930); *Obshchaya teoriya statistiki* (The General Theory of Statistics) (1931); ed, textbook *Statistika* (Statistics) (1932); *Died*: 1939 in imprisonment.

KHOTKEVICH, Gnat Martynovich (pen and stage name: GALAYDA, Gnat) (1877-1938) Ukr writer, playwright, translator, stage dir and composer; *Born*: 31 Dec 1877 in Khar'kov; *Educ*: 1900 grad Khar'kov Technol Inst; *Career*: worked as railroad eng; 1895 founded peasant theater in vil Dergachi, Khar'kov Province; 1903 founded and directed first Ukr workers' theater in Khar'kov; from 1896 gave concerts as bandura virtuoso; active in 1905-07 Revol, then emigrated to Galicia; 1910 founded Hutsul Theater; 1912 returned to Ukr; after 1917 Oct Revol worked as instructor; 1927 founded bandura group in Poltava; from 1934 taught bandura class at Khar'kov Musical Drama Inst; translated into Ukr plays of Shakespeare, Molière, Schiller; Victor Hugo, etc; *Publ*: plays on revol themes (banned from the stage): "A Troubled Time," "The Railroad Workers" and "They" (1906); "The 1905 Village" (1929); "Hutsul Year"; "Difficult Times"; "Dovbush"; dramas: "The Sea," "Fortune" and "The Emigrees" (1910); "I Love a Woman" (1913), etc; historical plays: *Rogned'* and *Slovo o polku Igoreve* (The Lay of the Host of Igor); tetralogy *Bogdan Khmel'nitskiy* (*Subotov, Kiev, Berestechko* and *Pereyaslav*); "The Popular and Medieval Theater in Galicia" (1925); "The Theater in 1848" (1932); "Musical Instruments of the Ukrainian People" (1930), etc; *Died*: 8 Oct 1938.

KHOVANSKIY (real name: ULUPOV), Aleksandr Pankrat'yevich (1890-1962) Actor; Pop Artiste of the RSFSR from 1954; *Born*: 31 Mar 1890; *Career*: 1908 began stage career at Arkhangel'sk Theater; then performed in Vilnius, Vladivostok, Voronezh, Petrograd Acad Drama Theater (1919-24) and Saratov; from 1933 at Centr Theater of the Red Army (now Centr Theater of the Sov Army); 1944-46 simultaneously performed at the Moscow Arts Theater; *Roles*: Lenchitskiy in Romashov's *Boytsy* (The Fighters); Fyodor Talanov in *Nashestviye* (Invasion); Kobz in *Gibel' eskadry* (The End of a Squadron); Skundrel in Lavrenyov's *Golos Ameriki* (The Voice of America); Nelson in Steyn's *Flag admirala* (The Admiral's Flag); Glumov in *Na vsyakogo mudretsa dovol'no prostoty* (There's a Simpleton in Every Sage); Berkutov in *Volki i ovtsy* (Wolves and Sheep); Tarelkin in Sukhovo-Kobylin's *Delo* (The Affair); Prokhor in *Vassa Zheleznova*; Erskin in Kh'yellann's *On skazal net* (He Said No); Gardner in Shaw's "Mrs Warren's Profession"; Semyon Rak in Romashov's *Vozdushnyy pirog* (Meringue); also played Chatskiy, Neznamov, Khlestakov, Ferdinand, Baron, Shvandi, Karandyshev, and Zhadov, etc; *Awards*: Stalin Prize (1951); *Died*: 12 Dec 1962.

KHRIPIN, Vasiliy Vladimirovich (1893-1937) Mil commander and aviation pioneer; corps commander from 1935; CP member from 1919; *Born*: 1893; *Career*: 1916 ensign, Russian Army Air Corps; 1917 commander-elect, 5th Air Regt; 1918 joined Red Army; 1918-21 commander, army air force; dep commander of Air Force on Southeastern and Caucasian fronts; 1921-37 Inspector of Sov Air Force; chief of staff, Sov Air Force; 1934-37 member, Mil Council, USSR Pop Comrt of Defense; 1937 commander, Special Air Army; 1937 arrested by NKVD; *Publ: Voprosy strategii i taktiki Krasnogo vozdushnogo flota* (The Strategy and Tactics of the Red Air Force) (1925); coauthor, *Vozdushnaya voyna* (Aerial Warfare) (1934); *O gospodstve v vozdukhe* (Aerial Supremacy) (1936); *Died*: 1937 in imprisonment; posthumously rehabilitated.

KHRISANFOV, Nikolay Yefremovich (1884-1950) Balneologist; Dr of Med; prof; *Born*: 1884; *Educ*: 1909 grad Med Fac, Moscow Univ; *Career*: worked as surgeon during WW 1 and Civil War; from 1921 in charge of health resort hygiene and construction for Main Health Resort Bd, RSFSR Pop Comrt of Health; 1930-40 head, Sanitary, Health Resort and Workers' Recreation Planning Group, Health Service Section, USSR Gosplan; incorporated planning results into health service section of 2nd and 3rd five-year plans; 1932 took part in 1st All-Union Conference of USSR Gosplan; 1933 member, various govt commissions in charge of planning Geo health resorts; 1935 member, commission for reconstruction of Sochi-Matsesta health resort; member, commissions for reconstruction of Caucasian Mineral'nyye Vody and Southern Crimean health resorts; during WW 2 head, Dept of Evacuation Hospitals, USSR Main Health Resort Bd; from 1945 until death worked at Centr Inst of Balneology; member, Various Sov and for sci soc; wrote over 100 works; *Publ*: coauthor, *Lechebnyye sredstva kurortov mestnogo znacheniya* (The Curative Resources of Regional Health Resorts) (1930); *Lechebnyye mestnosti Tadzhikistan* (Potential Health Resorts of Tadzhikistan) (1933); *Lechebnyye sredstva kurortov SSSR* (The Curative Resources of the Health Resorts of the USSR) (1951); *Died*: 1950.

KHRULEV, Andrey Vasil'yevich (1892-1962) Mil commander; corps comr from 1935; army gen from 1943; logistics expert; CP member from 1918; *Born*: 30 Sept 1892 in vil Bol'shaya Aleksandrovka, Petersburg Province, son of a blacksmith; *Educ*: 1925 grad Red Army Higher Mil and Polit Acad Courses; *Pos*: 1915-17 metalworker at the Okhtinskiy Plant in Petrograd; 1917 Red Guard; took part in the storming of the Winter Palace and in battles against Gen Krasnov's troops near Petrograd; from 1918 in Red Army; 1918-19 commandant, Revol Guard of Porokhovskiy Rayon, Petrograd; worked for div polit dept, then mil comr of a regt; 1919-22 head, Polit Dept, 11th Cavalry Div, Budennyy's 1st Mounted Army; 1922-24 regt mil comr, 4th Cavalry Div; 1925-30 mil comr, 10th Cavalry Div; dep head, Polit Bd, Moscow Mil Distr; 1930-37 head; Centr Finance and Planning Bd, USSR Pop Comrt of Defense; 1934-37 simultaneously member, Mil Council, USSR Pop Comrt of Defense; 1938-39 head, Kiev Distr Mil Eng Bd; 1940-41 chief of supply, then chief quartermaster of the Red Army; 1941-45 USSR Dep Pop Comr of Defense and head, Main Logistics Bd; from 1943 chief of logistics, Red Army; 1942-43 simultaneously fulfilled duties of USSR Pop Comr of Means of Communication, although Kaganovich officially held this office; 1945-51 USSR Dep Pop Comr of Defense, USSR Min of the Armed Forces, then USSR War Min (for logistics); 1945-50 simultaneously member, Main Mil Council; 1951-57 USSR Dep Min of Construction Materials Ind; USSR Min of Road Transport and Highways; then USSR Min of Construction; *Career*: 1941 drafted Red Army logistic regulations based on pre-revol *Polozheniye o polevom upravlenii voysk v voyennoye vremya* (Regulations for the Wartime Command of Troops in the Field) and laid the foundation for centralized logistics of the Sov Armed Forces; 1937, during purge of Red Army commanders, he was relieved of his exec duties in the Red Army centr organs; late 1940's his wife was arrested by the MVD, although Stalin continued to receive Khrulev himself; 1951 relieved of duties at the War Min; *Awards*: two Orders of Lenin; four Orders of the Red Banner; two Orders of Suvorov, 1st Class; other orders and medals; *Died*: 9 June 1962 after a long illness; buried in Moscow's Novodevich'ye Cemetery.

KHRUNICHEV, Mikhail Vasil'yevich (1901-1961) Govt official; member, CC, CPSU from 1952; lt-gen of eng; CP member from 1921; *Born*: 1901 in Donbass, now Voroshilovgrad Oblast; *Educ*: 1930-32 studied at the Voroshilovgrad branch of the Ukr Ind Acad, then at the All-Union Inst of Econ Managers; *Career*: from the age of 13 errand-boy, postman, then factory worker; 1920-24 in Red Army; 1924-29 on the police force; 1930-32 admin work at the Artem Plant in Voroshilovgrad; 1932-37 dep dir, then dir, mil plant; 1937-38 head, Main Bd, USSR Pop Comrt of the Defense Ind; 1938-39 USSR Dep Pop Comr of the Defense Ind; 1939-42 USSR Dep Pop Comr of the Aircraft Ind; 1942-46 USSR First Dep Pop Comr of Munitions; 1946-53 USSR Pop Comr, then USSR Min of the Aircraft Ind; 1953-55 USSR First Dep Min of Medium Machine-Building; 1955-56 dep chm, USSR Council of Min; 1956-57 dep chm, USSR State Econ Commission; 1957-61 dep chm, USSR Gosplan with rank of USSR Min; from Apr 1961 dep chm, USSR Council of Min and chm, State Comt for the Coordination of Research, USSR Council of Min; dep, USSR Supr Sov of the 1946 and 1958 convocations; *Awards*: Hero of Socialist Labor; two Stalin Prizes; seven Orders of Lenin; Order of the Red Banner of Labor; Order of Suvorov, 2nd Class; five medals; *Died*: 2 June 1961 in Moscow.

KHRUSHCHEVA-YELAGINA, Agaf'ya Aleksandrovna (1886-1967) Revolutionary; CP member from 1905; *Born*: 16 Apr 1886; *Career*: 1905 fought in armed workers squad, then member, Zlatoust City Party Comt; 1909 and 1911 arrested; 1913 exiled; Apr 1917 returned to Zlatoust; 1919-21 worked for mother and child care org; 1923-29 worked in Ufa, helping orphans, then in revol museum; 1929-31 head, Revol Museum in Smolensk; 1932 retired; *Died*: 11 Nov 1967.

KHRUSHCHOV, Grigoriy Konstantinovich (1897-1962) Histologist; Dr of Biology; prof from 1933; corresp member, USSR Acad of Sci from 1953; Hon Sci Worker of RSFSR from 1947; CP member from 1940; *Born*: 3 Mar 1897; *Educ*: 1919 grad Natural Sci Dept, Fac of Physics and Mathematics, Moscow Univ; *Career*: 1919-30 asst prof, Chair of Histology, Moscow Univ; 1933-45 prof of histology, Moscow Zooveterinary Inst; 1939-49 dir, Moscow Inst of Cytology, Histology and Embryology; 1945-62 head, Chair of Histology, 2nd Moscow Med Inst; 1949-62 dir, N. A. Severtsev Inst of Animal Morphology, USSR Acad of Sci; for many years ed, journal *Uspekhi sovremennoy biologii*; co-ed, pathology and morphology section, *Bol'shaya meditsinskaya entsiklopediya* (Large Medical Encyclopedia) (2nd ed); member, ed council, journal *Arkhiv anatomii, gistologii i embriologii* member, ed collegium, journal *Izvestiya Akademii nauk SSSR, Seriya biologicheskaya*; Bureau member, Dept of Biological Sci, USSR Acad of Sci; did research on comparative and experimental histology, cytology and hematology; developed I. I. Mechnikov's theory of the evolution of the body's defensive mechanisms against infection and tissue damage and studied the stimulatory role of leucocytes in regenerative processes; *Publ: Fizicheskiye svoystva zhivoy kletki i metody ikh issledovaniya* (The Physical Properties of the Living Cell and Methods of Studying Them) (1930); *Rol' leykotsitov krovi v vosstanovitel'nykh protsessakh v tkanyakh* (The Role of Leucocytes in Tissue Regeneration Processes) (1945); *Leykotsitarnyye sistemy mlekopitayushchikh i ikh evolyutsiya* (The Leucocytic Systems of Mammals and Their Evolution) (1951), etc; *Awards*: Order of Lenin; Order of the Red Banner of Labor; medals; *Died*: 22 Dec 1962.

KHRUSHCHOV, Vasiliy Mikhaylovich (1882-1941) Electr eng; prof from 1920; member, Ukr Acad of Sci from 1939; CP member from 1940; *Born*: 12 June 1882 in Petersburg, son of an office worker; *Educ*: grad Tomsk Technol Inst; *Career*: 1914-20 instructor, from 1920 prof, Tomsk Technol Inst; from 1923 prof, Khar'kov Technol Inst; from 1930 prof, Khar'kov Electr Eng Inst; from 1939 co-founder and dir, Inst of Power Eng (later Inst of Electr Eng), Ukr Acad of Sci; specialized in the transmission and distribution of electr power; during latter years developed a high-tension arc rectifier and a heavy-duty mech rectifier; wrote 78 works; *Publ: Elektricheskiye seti i linii* (Electric Grids and Transmission Lines) (2 vol, 1932-35); *Died*: 19 Dec 1941.

KHRYUKIN, Timofey Timofeyevich (1910-1953) Mil commander; col-gen, Sov Air Force from 1944; CP member from 1929; *Born*: 31 June 1910 in Yeysk, now Krasnodar Kray, son of a stone mason; *Educ*: 1933 grad Lugansk (Voroshilovgrad) Pilots' School; 1941 grad Advanced Command Staff Courses, Gen Staff Acad; *Career*: 1932 drafted into Sov Air Force via Party muster; 1933-40 pilot; commanded bomber wing, squadron and brigade; 1936-37 flew bomber for Republicans in Spanish Civil War; 1938, as bomber pilot in China, personally sank a Japanese aircraft carrier; 1941-42 commander Sov Air Force units on Karelian and Southeastern Fronts; 1942 commanded air force of Southeastern and Stalingrad Fronts; took part in Battle of Stalingrad; 1942-44 commander, 8th Air Army on Southern and 4th Ukr Fronts; took part in liberation of Crimea; 1944-45 commander, 1st Air Army, 3rd Bel Front; 1945 took part in East Prussian operations; after WW 2 held various commands in Sov Air Force; 1950-53 dep commander in chief, Soviet Air Force; *Awards*: twice Hero of the Sov Union (1938, 1945); Order of Lenin; Order of the Red Banner; Order of Suvorov, 1st Class; Order of Kutuzov, 1st Class; other orders and medals; *Died*: 19 July 1953.

KHUDAYBERDIN, Shagit Akhmetovich (1896-1924) Party and govt official; *Born*: 1896 in vil Psyanchino (now Khudayberdino), Bash ASSR, son of a peasant; *Educ*: attended parish school; 1915 grad med orderlies courses; *Career*: during childhood worked for landowner; 1914 expelled from parish school for participating in pupils' revol movement; early 1915, after finishing courses for med orderlies, he was sent to the front; wounded and returned to Ufa; 1917 headed revol movement among Bash and Tatars in Ufa Province; member, Ufa Province Provisional Revol Comt and Revol Tribunal; joined CP and conducted agitation and propaganda; organized detachments to fight counter-revol forces; Collegium member, Centr Moslem Comrt in Moscow; then assigned to 5th Army on the Eastern Front for work among Bash and Tatars; late 1919 returned to Bash; chm, Bash Centr Exec Comt; secr, Bash Minor Oblast Comt; chm, Bash Council of Pop Comr; 1921, while a deleg to the 10th CPSU(B) Congress, helped crush the Kronstadt Mutiny, in the course of which he was wounded and shell-shocked; member, USSR and All-Russian Centr Exec Comt; *Awards*: Order of the Red Banner; *Died*: 21 Dec 1924 in Moscow.

KHUDYAKOV, Nikolay Nikolayevich (1866-1927) Microbiologist; prof from 1896; *Born*: 1866; *Educ*: studied at Berlin and Leipzig Univ; *Career*: from 1896 prof, Moscow Agric Inst (now Timiryazev Agric Acad); 1896 proved the possibility of cultivating anaerobes in the presence of oxygen and hypothesized that bacterial anaerobiosis is a form of adaptation to environmental conditions; 1909-17 also prof, Moscow Business Inst (now Plekhanov Inst of Nat Econ); in course of research on soil microbiology discovered the phenomenon of the absorbtion of bacteria by soil particles; *Publ: K ucheniyu ob anaerobioze* (The Theory of Anaerobiosis) (1896); textbook *Sel'skokhozyaystvennaya mikrobiologiya* (Agricultural Microbiology) (1926), etc; *Died*: 1927.

KHUDYAKOV, Pyotr Kondrat'yevich (1858-1935) Physicist; specialist in applied mech; prof from 1890; Hon Sci and Tech Worker of RSFSR from 1933; *Born*: 4 Mar 1858; *Educ*: 1877 grad Moscow Tech College; *Career*: 1877-90 lecturer, 1890-1904 prof, from 1904 emeritus prof, Moscow Tech College; specialized in the resistance of materials and machine parts; developed course on this subject which served as a basis for training several generations of eng; also did research on steam engines and boilers; made major contribution to Russian pump-manufacture with his pump manuals and catalogs; *Publ: Atlas porshnevykh nasosov, ispolnennykh russkimi i zagranichnymi mekhanicheskimi zavodami* (An Illustrated Catalog of Piston Pumps Manufactured by Russian and Foreign Engineering Plants) (2 vol, 1890); *Postroyeniye nasosov* (Pump Manufacture) (1899); *Put' k Tsusime* (The Road to Tsushima) (1907); coauthor, *Detali mashin* (Machine Parts) (2 vol, 1907-11); *Soprotivleniye materialov* (Material Resistance) (2 vol, 1930), etc; *Awards*: Order of the Red Banner of Labor; Hero of Labor (1928); *Died*: 17 Sept 1935.

KHURSHID (real name: SHARAFUTDINOV), Shamsudtdin (1892-1960) Uzbek poet, playwright, producer and translator; pioneer of Uzbek musical theater; Hon Art Worker of Uzbek SSR from 1941; *Born*: May 1892; *Career*: 1912 began writing verse and lit criticism; 1915 began stage career with *Turan* amateur ensemble in Tashkent, with which he played several well-delineated character and comedy roles in plays by Azer, Tatar and Uzbek dramatists; 1924-29 producer, Uzbek *Tilak* theater ensemble; translated plays by Azer, Russian and other authors into Uzbek (U. Tadzhibekov, Mamedkulizade, Schiller, Bill'-

Belotserkovskiy, etc); helped to establish and develop native Uzbek theater; *Publ*: plays: "The Illiterate Bai" (1918); "The New and the Old" (1918); "The Little Soldier" (1919); tragedy "Siyavush's Sentence" (1920); drama "The Blacksmith's Son" (1920); historical drama "Turkestan" (1920); musical comedies "The Best Girl" (1924) and "Laughter and Tears" (1926); first Uzbek nat musicals "Farkhad and Shirin" and "Leyli and Medzhnun" (1923-24) after Navoi; libretti for the operas "Leyli and Medzhnun" (1940) and "Farkhad and Shirin" (1957); "Selected Works" (1967); *Died*: 13 Sept 1960.

KHVESIN, T. S. (1895-1941) Govt official; CP member from 1911; *Born*: 1895; *Career*: 1917 member, Exec Comt, Saratov Sov of Workers' Dep; during Civil War commander, 4th Army on Eastern Front; commander, 8th Army on Southern Front; then commander of an expeditionary force sent to crush a revolt on the Don; exec Party and govt posts; gen rep, RSFSR State Export and Import Trading Office in Berlin; chm, USSR Gosplan; dep chm, Moscow Sov of Workers' Dep; bureau member, Saratov Kray Party Comt; RSFSR Dep Pop Comr of Communal Econ; arrested by State Security organs; *Died*: 1941 in imprisonment.

KHVOL'SON, Orest Danilovich (1852-1934) Physicist; corresp member from 1895, hon member from 1920, Russian (USSR) Acad of Sci; *Born*: 4 Dec 1852 in Petersburg, son of the Russian Orientologist and Semitologist D. A. Khvol'son; *Educ*: 1873 grad Petersburg Univ; *Career*: from 1876 lecturer, from 1891 prof, Petersburg Univ; also taught at Higher Women's Courses, Electr Eng Inst, Teachers' Training Inst, Leningrad Communist Univ, etc; 1886-89 studied internal diffusion of light; 1892-96 studied diffusion of solar energy; designed actinometer and pyrheliometer which were for a long while standard equipment at Russian meteorological stations; from 1896 concentrated mainly on his *Kurs fiziki* (Physics Course), used for years in Russian high schools; this work went through several ed and was translated into German, French and Spanish; gave public lectures and published many pop sci books and pamphlets; *Publ: Kurs fiziki* (Physics Course) (6 vol, 1892-1928); *Fizika i yeyo znacheniye dlya chelovechestva* (Physics and Its Importance for Mankind) (1923); *Awards*: Hero of Labor (1926); Order of the Red Banner of Labor (1926); *Died*: 11 May 1934.

KHVYLYOVYY, Mykola (pen name: Nikolay Fitilyova) (1893-1933) Ukr writer and publicist; CP member; *Born*: 13 Dec 1893 in Trotsyanets, now Sumy Oblast; *Career*: fought in Civil War in Ukr; 1922 began writing poetry, then switched to prose; co-founder, *Gart* proletarian writers' assoc; 1925 founded new writers' assoc - Free Acad of Proletarian Writers and published its journal *VAPLITE*; preached orientation on West European lines as a counter-balance to Moscow; 1927 criticized by CC, CP(B) Ukr for nationalistic ideas, whereupon he stopped advocating pro-Western orientation; 1927 Free Acad of Proletarian Writers abolished; joined All-Ukr League of Proletarian Writers; his views were taken up by the "Lit Fair" (1928-30) and "Polit Front" (1931) writers' assoc; *Publ: V elektricheskiy vek* (Into the Electrical Age) (1921); collections of novellae: *Siniye etyudy* (Blue Studies) (1922); *Mysli protiv techeniya* (Thoughts Against the Current) (1925-27); novel *Val'dshnepy* (Woodcocks) (vol 1, 1927); *Sotsiologicheskiy ekvivalent tryokh kriticheskikh vzglyadov* (The Sociological Equivalent of Three Critical Views) (1927); *Tvory* (Works) (3 vol, 1927-30); *Vybrani tvory* (Selected Works) (vol 1, 1932), etc; *Died*: 13 May 1933 comitted suicide after incessant Party criticism.

KIACHELI, Leo (real name: SHENGELAYA, Leon Mikhaylovich) (1884-1963) Geo writer; *Born*: 19 Feb 1884 in vil Obudzhi, Geo, son of a nobleman; *Educ*: 1904 grad Kutaisi High-School; and entered Law Fac, Khar'kov Univ; 1907 studied in Moscow; studied at Geneva Univ; *Career*: 1905 joined revol movement; 1906 arrested; 1907 escaped from Kutaisi Prison and lived illegally in Moscow; 1912-17 lived abroad; after 1917 Feb Revol returned to Geo; *Publ*: story "The Past in the Present" (1909); novels: "Tariel Golua" (1917); "Blood" (1927); "Gvali Bigva" (1938); "The Man of the Hills" (1948); novellas: "Princess Mayya" (1927); "Almasgir Kibulan" (1928); "Khaki Adzba" (1933), etc; also did translations and wrote children's works; his works have been translated into many for languagues; *Awards*: Stalin Prize (1941); *Died*: 19 Dec 1963 in Tbilisi.

KIDIN, Aleksandr Nikolayevich (1909-1959) Party official; CP member from 1930; *Born*: 17 Mar 1909 in Kaluga, son of a railroad worker; *Educ*: 1936 grad Higher Law Courses; *Career*: 1927 started working on the railroad as laborer, metal worker, then locomotive driver; 1936 worked for prosecutor's office, then first secr, Vereya Rayon CPSU(B) Comt, Moscow Oblast; during WW 2 secr, Klin City CPSU(B) Comt; fought with partisans; 1942 dep chm, Moscow Oblast Exec Comt; from 1945 chm, Exec Comt, Smolensk Oblast Sov of Workers' Dep; 1951-55 first secr, Vladimir Oblast CPSU Comt; from 1955 exec work for CPSU CC; from 1959 first secr, Udmurt Oblast CPSU Comt; at 14th Party Congress elected CC member; at 20th Congress elected member, Centr Auditing Commission; dep, USSR Supr Sov of 4th and 5th convocations; *Awards*: two Orders of the Red Banner of Labor; Badge of Honor; medals; *Died*: 6 June 1959; buried in Novodevich'ye Cemetery, Moscow.

KIKODZE, Gerontiy Dimitriyevich (1886-1960) Geo writer; critic; lit historian; translator; *Born*: 16 Sept 1886 in vil Bakhvi; *Educ*: grad Philosophy Fac, Univ of Leipzig and Bern; *Career*: 1905 published first articles in Geo journal *Mozgauri*; 1905 and 1910 arrested for left-wing polit speeches; 1921-22 Geo Dep Pop Comr of Agric; lectured on the history of West European lit; 1928 joined *Arifioni* lit group; wrote lit criticism, reviews, art criticism and studies on esthetics; translated into Geo classic works of Marxism-Leninism and Balzac, Stendhal, Mérimée, Daudet, France, etc; *Publ*: "Articles on Art" (1936); "A History of Georgian Literature" (1947); "Memoirs, Speeches, Letters" (1956); "Studies and Portraits" (1958); in Russian translation *Gruzinskiye klassiki* (Georgian Classics) (1942); *Irakliy Vtoroy* (Irakli the Second) (2nd ed, 1948); *Died*: 1 Aug 1960 in Tbilisi.

KIKVIDZE, Vasiliy Isidorovich (1895-1919) Mil commander; Civil War veteran; *Born*: 28 Feb 1895 in Kutaisi, Geo, son of a civil servant; *Educ*: grad Kutaisi High-School; *Career*: joined revol movement while still a student; during WW 1 volunteered for cavalry service; arrested three times for revol activity; 1917 chm, Soldiers' Comt, 6th Cavalry Div and co-chm, Mil–Revol Comt, Southwestern Front; Dec 1917 led Rovno Red Guard detachment in battle against German troops and troops of Ukr Nat Govt; May 1918 his unit was turned into a rifle div (subsequently the 16th); from June 1918 commanded this unit near Tsaritsyn, where he displayed military prowess and great courage; 10 Jan 1919 received fatal wounds; after death his name was given to the 16th Rifle Div; 1936 the vil Preobrazhenskaya was named after him; 1959 monuments were erected to him in Kutaisi and Tbilisi; *Died*: 12 Jan 1919.

KILADZE, Grigoriy Varfolomeyevich (1902-1962) Composer; prof, Tbilisi Conservatory from 1941; Hon Art Worker of Geo SSR; conductor, Opera Studio, Tbilisi Conservatory from 1953; CP member from 1940; *Born*: 25 Oct 1902 in Batumi; *Educ*: 1924-27 studied at Baku Conservatory; 1927-29 at Leningrad Conservatory; 1931 grad Composition Class, Tbilisi Conservatory; *Career*: 1929-52 conductor, 1941-45 dir, Tbilisi Opera and Ballet Theater; 1929-52 conductor, 1952-53 chief conductor, Tbilisi Philharmonic; 1929-52 conductor, Tbilisi Radio; 1931-41 taught special instrumentation; 1938-41 and 1945-52 dir, Tbilisi Conservatory; 1937-38 chm, Bd, Geo Composers' Union; *Works*: operas *Bakhtrioni* (1936) and *Lado Ketskhoveli* (1941); ballet "Light" (1947); symphonic works: two symphonies (1944 and 1955); two suites (1925 and 1928); tone poem "Lile", the name of a folk hymn to the sun (1925); poem "The Hermit" (1937); "Festival Overture" (1957); music for films: "The Last Masquerade" (1934); "Arsenic" (1937); "The Winged Painter" (1937); "Friendship" (1941); "Dzhurday's Shield" (1944); *Awards*: two Orders of the Red Banner of Labor (1946 and 1952); Badge of Hon (1937); medals; Stalin Prizes (1941 and 1948); *Died*: 3 Apr 1962 in Tbilisi.

KIMONKO, Dzhansi Batovich (1905-1949) Udegey writer; founder of Udegey lit; CP member from 1946; *Born*: Dec 1905 in vil Gvasyugi, Khabarovsk Kray; *Educ*: 1934-36 studied at Inst of the Peoples of the North, Leningrad; 1937 grad Centr Sov Construction Courses; *Career*: spent childhood in extreme poverty, wandering with his parents through the Ussuri taiga and along the Sukpay River and living from the hunt; during the Civil War helped partisans in the Far East; founded the first Udegey kolkhoz and was the first Udegey to receive an educ; after grad chm, Gvasyugi Vil Sov; encouraged to write by Yu. A. Shestakova; *Publ*: novelettes "Glow Above the Forest" (1948) and "The Red Flag" (1950), published jointly under the title "Where the Sukpay Flows" (1950); *Died*: 17 June 1949 in hunting accident in Khabarovsk Kray.

KIN (real name: SUROVIKIN), Viktor Pavlovich (1903-1937) Russian writer; CP member from 1920; *Born*: 1903 in

Borisoglebsk, son of a railroad worker; *Educ*: grad Inst of Red Prof; *Career*: 1918 one of first Komsomol members; organized youth activities in his home town; during Civil War polit work on Polish Front; 1922 did underground Party work in Far East; 1923 began writing career in Sverdlovsk, then moved to Moscow; wrote satirical articles and lit reviews for *Pravda* and *Komsomolskaya pravda*; joined "Lit Front" group; 1931-36 TASS corresp in Italy and France; 1937 ed, "Journal de Moscou"; 1937 arrested by NKVD; his novel "On the Other Side" has been adapted for the stage and screen under such titles as *Nasha molodost'* (Our Youth) (in mid-1930's by S. Kartashyov) and *Kogda gorit serdtse* (When the Heart Is Aflame) (1957 by V. Gol'dfel'd); it has also been translated into several languages; *Publ*: novel *Po tu storonu* (On the Other Side) (1928); collection of essays and satirical articles *Pytka elektrichestvom* (Torture by Electricity) (1931); article *Gamletizm i nigilizm v tvorchestve Turgeneva* (Hamletism and Nihilism in the Works of Turgenev) (1929); *Izbrannoye* (Selected Works) (1965); *Died*: 1937 in imprisonment; posthumously rehabilitated.

KINGISEPP, Sergey Viktorovich (1909-1941) Govt official; CP member from 1929; *Born*: 1909 in Arensburg (now Kingisepp), Est; *Educ*: 1927 grad secondary school in Leningrad; *Career*: from 1923 lived in polit emigres hostel in Moscow; 1925 sent to school in Leningrad by Int Org for Aid to Revol Fighters; 1924 joined Komsomol; secr, school Komsomol cell; 1927 worked for int firefighting unit in Tambov; 1929 enrolled in campaign to eliminate the kulaks; from June 1930 worked for State Security organs: 1930-31 in Tambov; 1931-34 in Voronezh; 1934-36 in Kursk; 1936-37 in Kalinin; 1937-40 in Moscow; 1940-41 worked for Est Pop Comrt of State Security in Tallin; member, then secr, Party Comt of Kalinin NKVD Bd; member, Part Comt, Tambov, Voronezh and Kursk NKVD Bds; elected cand member, CC, CP Est; 1940 directed investigation and arranged arrest of Sergey Viktorovich Nymmik-Linkkhorst, who allegedly betrayed his father, V. E. Kingisepp to the Est authorities in 1922; 1941 commanded battalion in defense of Tallin during WW 1; *Died*: 29 Aug 1941 killed on S. S. *Yarvamaa* on Baltic during German air raid.

KIPSHIDZE, Nikolay Andreyevich (1888-1954) Internist; prof; member, Geo Acad of Sci from 1946; Hon Sci Worker of Geo SSR from 1941; *Born*: 18 Dec 1888; *Educ*: 1914 grad Mil Med Acad; *Career*: from 1931 prof, Tbilisi Med Inst; 1949-54 prof, Tbilisi Inst of Postgrad Med Training; specialized in helminthism and enterozoa; described Coccidia, Lamblia and Balantidia; wrote first description of Taenia flavopunctata and Strongyloides stercoralis et intestinalis; isolated Trichomonas elongata in apes and obtained a pure culture; 1936, together with Desh'yen, developed highly effective nutrient for cultivating protozoa; studied long-term sequelae of operations for stomach and duodenal ulcers; made extensive use of conservative treatment for amoebic abscesses of the liver; also studied the clinical aspects and diagnosis of subdiaphragmal gas abscesses; did research on the clinical aspects of brucellosis; studied the Geo health resorts of Borzhomi, Bakhmaro, Kodzhori, etc; dep. USSR Supr Sov of 2nd and 3rd convocations; wrote 70 works on internal med and helminthology; *Publ*: "Internal Diseases" (1946); "Bormozhi and Its Gorge" (1952); *Awards*: Order of Lenin; two other orders; medals; *Died*: 6 June 1954.

KIREYEV, Grigoriy Petrovich (1890-1938) Mil commander; flag officer, 1st class from 1935; Sov naval officer; CP member from 1918; *Born*: 21 Jan 1890 in vil Lyudinovo, Kaluga Province, son of a foundry worker; *Educ*: 1927 grad Red Army High Command Advanced Courses, Naval Acad; 1933 grad Special Course, Naval Acad; *Pos*: 1908-11 worked at Lyudinovo Plant; 1911 conscripted into Russian Navy and assigned to 1st Baltric Fleet; during WW 1 ship's mechanic; 1919-22 chm, Bryansk City Sov, then chm, Sevsk Uyezd Exec Comt; second secr, Bryansk Province RCP(B) Comt; 1922 via Party muster joined Red Navy; 1923-26 member, Revol Mil Council, Black Sea Navy; 1928-30 member, Revol Mil Council, Baltic Navy; 1933-34 commander and comr, Caspian Fleet; 1934-37 dep commander, Pacific Fleet; from Aug 1937 commander, Pacific Fleet; *Career*: after 1917 Feb Revol chm, Sailors' Section, Helsinki Sov; comr of a revol sailors squad which guarded naval property in Finland; 1929-30 helped work battleship *Parizhskaya kommuna* and cruiser *Profintern* from Kronstadt to Sevastopol'; Nov 1937 proposed as dep to the USSR Supr Sov, but his name was not entered on the lists of dep cand; Nov 1937 dismissed from command of the Pacific Fleet and expelled from the CPSU(B); Jan 1938 arrested by NKVD; *Awards*: Order of the Red Star; *Died*: 1938 in imprisonment;posthumously rehabilitated.

KIREYEV, Mikhail Petrovich (1873-1943) Infectionist; Dr of Med from 1905; prof from 1918; Hon Sci Worker of RSFSR from 1940; *Born*: 1873 in Moscow, son of an employee of Moscow Discount Bank; *Educ*: 1899 grad Med Fac, Moscow Univ; *Career*: after grad intern, Sokolniki (now Red Sov) Hospital, Moscow; 1907-10 assoc prof, Moscow Univ; from 1910 until death, head, Dept of Infectious Diseases, Soldatyonkov (now Botkin) Hospital, Moscow; 1914-18 also chief physician, Khodynskaya Hospital of Infectious Diseases; 1918-36 prof, Chair of Infectious Diseases, 1st Moscow Univ (now 1st Moscow Med Inst); 1932-43 prof, Centr Inst of Postgrad Med Training; described diagnostic symptoms of typhus; was one of first Sov sci to use Weil-Felix reaction to diagnose this disease; used blood-drop test to diagnose recurrent fever; developed specific therapy for diphtheria and scarlet fever; devised isolation and treatment measures for nosocomial diseases at infection hospitals; during Civil War combatted epidemics and worked on various med commissions; member, Learned Med Council, RSFSR and USSR Pop Comrt of Health; member, ed collegia, various med journals; co-ed, *Bol'shaya meditsinskaya entsiklopediya* (Large Medical Encyclopedia); from 1931 dep, Moscow City Sov of several convocations; from 1938 dep, RSFSR Supr Sov; from 1939 dep chm, All-Union Soc of Microbiologists, Epidemiologists and Infectionists; wrote over 70 works; *Publ: K voprosu o diagnosticheskom i prognosticheskom znachenii sypi pri sypnom tife* (The Diagnostic and Prognostic Significance of the Exanthema in Typhus) (1905); doctor's thesis *Nablyudeniya nad izmeneniyami krovi pri sypnom tife* (Observations on Blood Lesions in Typhus) (1905); coauthor, *Znacheniye reaktsii Veyl'-Feliksa pri raspoznavanii sypnogo tifa* (The Importance of the Weil-Felix Reaction in Diagnosing Typhus) (1922); co-ed, *Rukovodstvo po ostrym infektsionnym boleznyam* (A Manual on Acute Infectious Diseases) (1931); *Ratsional'noye stroitel'stvo infektsionnykh otdeleniy - osnovnoye meropriyatiye v dele bor'by s vnutribol'nichnymi zarazheniyami* (The Efficient Construction of Infection Departments - A Basic Measure in Combatting Hospital Infections) (1934); *Died:* 7 Aug 1943 in Moscow in the performance of his duties.

KIRICHENKO, Il'ya Nikitich (1889-1955) Ukr linguist and lexicographer; corresp member, Ukr Acad of Sci from 1951; *Born*: 19 July 1889 in vil Ryabukhi; now Chernigov Oblast, son of a peasant; *Educ*: 1914 grad Nezhin Teachers' Training Inst; *Career*: secondary and high-school teacher; from 1931 assoc, Inst of Linguistics and lecturer, Kiev Univ; from 1946 head, Dictionary Dept, Inst of Linguistics; from 1952 also head, Chair of Classical Philology, Kiev Univ; wrote some 40 works; *Publ: Slovar' meditsinskoy terminologii* (A Dictionary of Medical Terminology) (1936); *Printsipy postroyeniya ukrainsko-russkogo slovarya* (The Principles of Compiling a Ukrainian-Russian Dictionary) (1948); *Orfograficheskiy slovar'* (An Orthographic Dictionary) (1948); *Russko-ukrainskiy slovar'* (A Russian-Ukrainian Dictionary) (1948); coauthor and ed, *Ukrainsko-russkiy slovar'* (A Ukrainian-Russian Dictionary) (6 vol, 1953-63); *Ukrainskaya leksikografiya sovetskogo perioda* (Ukrainian Lexicography During the Soviet Period) (1954); *Died*: 13 July 1955.

KIRILLOV, Pyotr Semyonovich (1910-1955) Mordvinian writer and playwright; CP member from 1942; *Born*: 10 July 1910 in vil Malyy Tolkay, now Kuybyshev Oblast; *Educ*: 1929 grad Mordvinian Teachers' Training School; 1934 grad Moscow Inst of Editing and Publishing; 1938 grad Script Dept, Inst of Cinematography in Moscow; *Career*: 1926 began professional lit career; also wrote film scripts; many of his works have been incorporated in the repertoire of Sov theaters; *Publ*: collected verse: *Bez mezhi* (Boundless) (1932); *Po trudnoy doroge* (A Hard Road) (1933); *Po dorogam voyny* (Along the Roads of War) (1945); poem "Morning on the Sura" (1935); novelettes: *V Spasskom monastyre* (At Spasskiy Monastery) (1935); *Pervyy urok* (The First Lesson) (1940); plays: *Litova* (1939); *Uchitel'nitsa* (The Mistress) (1955); *Dva brata* (Two Brothers) (1941); *Nasha slava* (Our Glory) (1947); *Svet nad dal'nim uglom* (Light Over a Far Corner) (1951), etc; *Died*: 24 Nov 1955 in Moscow; buried in Saransk.

KIRILLOV, Vladimir Timofeyevich (1890-1943) Russian poet; *Born*: 14 Oct 1890 in vil Kharino, Smolensk Province, son of a peasant; *Educ*: primary schooling; *Career*: seaman with Black Sea Merchant Fleet; visited Turkey, Greece and Egypt; for part in seamen's revol activities in 1905-06 Revol exiled for three years to Ust'-Sysol'skaya, where he joined Soc-Democratic circle; 1911 went to America; 1912 returned to Russia; 1914 drafted into Tsarist Army and sent to front; took part in 1917 Feb and Oct Revol; 1913 first work published; 1917-18 with Petrograd, from 1919 with Tambov Proletarian Culture Orgs; visited front with agitation teams; from 1920 in Moscow; member, "Smithy" lit group but subsequently expelled and joined All-Russian Writers' Union; 1918 published collection *Stikhotvoreniye* (Verse) covering revol events; Dec 1917 wrote poem in response to Lunacharsky's resignation from the govt in protest against the destruction of Russian cultural monuments; the poem contained lines which later became one of the Proletarian Culture Org's slogans: "For the sake of our Tomorrow, we shall burn Raphael, destroy the museums and trample the flowers of art"; 1923 broke with above org, while his verse departed increasingly from the principles of proletarian poetry; during the New Econ Police period his work renounced the basic themes of his preceding period; from 1929 published very little; 1937 arrested by State Security organs; *Publ*: collection *Stikhotvoreniya* (Verse) (1918); *Zori gryadushchego* (Dawns of the Future) (1919); *Parusa* (Sails) (1921); *Zheleznyy messiya* (The Iron Messiah) (1921); *Otplytiye* (Sailing) (1923); *Stikhotvoreniya* (Verse) (vol. 1, 1924); *Rabochiye shagi* (Workers' Steps) (1924); *More* (The Sea) (1925); *Krov' i sneg* (Blood and Snow) (1925); coauthor, stories *Prazdnik zhizni* (Festival of Life) (1925); *O detstve, more i krasnom znameni* (Life, the Sea and the Red Banner) (1926); *Golubaya strana* (The Blue Country) (2 vol, 1927); *Vecherniye ritmy* (Evening Rhythms) (1928); *Vesenniy svet. Stikhotvoreniya* (Spring Light. Poems) (2nd ed, 1928); coauthor, *Liricheskiy vecher* (Lyrical Evening) (1927); *Stikhotvoreniya* (Verse) (1958); *Died*: 18 Dec 1943 in imprisonment; posthumously rehabilitated.

KIRKHENSHTEYN (KIRCHENSTEIN), Avgust Martynovich (1872-1963) Lat Govt official, microbiologist and veterinary surgeon; Dr of Agronomy from 1923; Dr of Biology from 1945; prof from 1923; member and vice-pres, Lat Acad of Sci from 1946; Presidium chm, Lat Supr Sov from 1940; CP member from 1941; *Born*: 1872 on Waltenberg Estate, Mazsalaca, Valmera Uyezd; *Educ*: 1902 grad Tartu Veterinary Inst; 1907-08 studied at Zurich Univ; *Career*: 1902-04 veterinary surgeon in Valmera and Limbazi; 1905 forced to emigrate because of revol activities; 1911-14 assoc, Davos Inst of Tuberculosis, Switzerland; 1914-16 veterinary surgeon in Serbian Army; 1916 assoc, Inst of Hygiene, Geneva Univ; 1917 bacteriologist, Lugano Chemical and Bacteriological Laboratory; returned to Lat in same year and resumed revol work; 1917-19 head, Valka Veterinary Dept; 1919 head, Riga Veterinary Dept and assoc prof, Fac of Agric, Riga Univ, where he established a microbiological laboratory; 1920-23 assoc prof of bacteriology, various fac, Riga Univ; 1921-37 regularly attended Baltic Veterinary Congresses in Kaunas; 1922 established microbiological laboratory at Pasteur Inst, Paris; also organized production of serum against swine-erysipelas in Lat; 1923 attended Pasteur memorial celebrations in Paris; in same year founded serological unit at Riga Univ and Anti-Tuberculosis Soc; 1925 organized production of tuberculosis vaccine; in same year dep, Riga City Duma; 1926 attended Int Congress on Dairy Farming, Paris; 1927 - Int Conference on Tuberculosis, Oslo; 1929 - Conference of Int Writers' Union, Vienna; 1930 - 1st Int Congress of Microbiologists, Paris, and another Int Conference on Tuberculosis, Oslo; 1935 - Baltic Veterinary Congress, Tallinn; 1936 - Conference of Dir of Baltic Serological Stations, Tartu; 1937 - Conference of Int Writers' Union, Paris; 1938 - 13th Int Congress on Veterinary Med, Zurich; 1939 - Conference of Int Writers' Union, Prague; 1940 pres and prime-minister of Lat; 1940-52 Presidium chm, Lat Supr Sov; from 1940 dep and member, Sov of Nationalities, 1941-54 dep chm, USSR Supr Sov; dep and Presidium member, Lat Supr Sov of 1959 convocation; wrote some 800 works; *Publ: Vvedeniye v molochnoye khozyaystvo* (An Introduction to Dairy Farming) (1905); "Die Bedingungen der Phagozytose von Tuberkelbazillen" (The Conditions for the Phagocytosis of Tubercle Bacilli) (1913); "Beobachtungen über die Entwicklung und Zahl der Tuberkelbazillen im Sputum in Abhängigkeit vom klinischen Verlauf" (Observations on the Development and Number of Tubercle Bacilli in the Sputum in Relation to the Clinical Course) (1914); "Structure intérieure et et mode de développement des bactéries" (The Internal Structure and Development of Bacteria) (1922); *Problemy mikrobiologii i immunologii* (Problems of Microbiology and Immunology) (1954); *Vitaminy i immunitet* (Vitamins and Immunity) (1955); *Znacheniye normal'noy mikroflory dlya organizma* (The Importance of Normal Microflora for the Organism) (1955); *K voprosu o znachenii polnotsennogo pitaniya v protsessakh infektsii i immuniteta* (The Importance of Proper Nutrition in the Processes of Infection and Immunity) (1956); *Rol' vitaminov v profilaktike infektsionnykh bolezney* (The Role of Vitamins in the Prevention of Infectious Diseases) (1957), etc; *Awards*: five Orders of Lenin; two Orders of the Red Banner of Labor; Order of the Fatherland War, 1st Class; two medals; Hon Scroll of the Lat Supr Sov; Gamaleya Prize; Small Gold Medal for services to agric (1955); Hero of Socialist Labor (1957); *Died*: 3 Nov 1963.

KIRKIZH, Kupriyan Osipovich (1886-1932) Party and govt official; CP member from 1910; *Born*: 29 Sept 1886 in vil Smolyanka, Vitebsk Province, son of a peasant; *Career*: 1910 Party work in Riga; organized workers' strikes; at beginning of war secr of sick fund at Khar'kov Plant of Gen Electr Company; from 1917 chm, plant comt; member, Khar'kov City Sov; member, Khar'kov Province Party Comt; during Civil War helped form 2nd Proletarian Regt; polit comr of separate Donets Brigade; comr, right wing of Yekaterinoslav Sector; 1922 secr, Khar'kov Province Party Comt; 1923 member, CC, CP(B) Ukr; 1925 head, Org Dept, CC, CP(B) Ukr; 1926-27 Ukr Pop Comr of Workers and Peasants' Inspection; 1925-27 Politburo, member, CC, CP(B) Ukr; at 13th Party Congress elected cand member, CC, CPSU(B); at 14th and 15th member, CC, CPSU(B); 1927-29 secr, CC, CP(B) Uzbek; then dep secr, USSR Centr Exec Comt; 1929-31 chm, CC, Union of Sov Trade Employees; 1930 member, CPSU(B) Centr Control Commission of 16th convocation; 1931 chm, CC, Union of Machine-Building Workers; member, All-Ukr and USSR Centr Exec Comt of several convocations; *Awards*: Order of the Red Banner; *Died*: 24 May 1932 killed in an automobile accident; his ashes are immured in the Kremlin Wall in Moscow.

KIROV (KOSTRIKOV), Sergey Mironovich (1886-1934) Party and govt official; CP member from 1904; *Born*: 27 Mar 1886 in Urzhum, Vyatka Province; *Educ*: 1897-1901 studied at Urzhum City College; 1904 grad Kazan' Mech Eng College; *Career*: orphaned at an early age, he and his two sisters were cared for by their grandmother; put into an Orphanage at age 7; 1904 moved to Tomsk; from July 1905 member, Tomsk RSDRP Comt; managed an underground printing press and did revol work among railroad workers; 1905-06 arrested several times by police; 1907 sentenced to 16 months of fortress arrest; June 1908 moved to Irkutsk after release and rebuilt local RSDRP org, which had been broken up by police; May 1909 moved to Vladikavkaz to avoid arrest and took over local Bolshevik org; after 1917 Feb Revol member, Vladikavkaz Sov; Oct 1917 deleg, 2nd All-Russian Congress of Soviets; took active part in Oct Revol in Petrograd; after return to Vladikavkaz worked to establish local Sov rule; persuaded Pop Congress of Tver' Oblast (Feb-Mar 1918, Pyatigorsk) to recognize authority of RSFSR Council of Pop Comr; from Feb 1919 chm, Provisional Mil-Revol Comt, Astrakhan Kray; from 7 May 1919 member, Revol Mil Council, 11th Army; from 7 July 1919 member; Revol Mil Council, Southern Forces Group, Red Army; helped to defend Astrakhan against Gen Denikin's army and establish Sov rule in Northern Caucasus; from 29 May 1920 RSFSR plen with Geo Democratic Govt; 1-12 Oct 1920 headed Sov deleg at concluding session of peace talks with Poland; 1921 elected cand member, CC, at 10th RCP(B) Congress; Apr 1921 chm, Constituent Congress of Gorskaya ASSR; July 1921 elected secr, CC, CP Azer; co-founder, Transcaucasian SFSR; 1923 elected member, CC, at 12th RCP(B) Congress; 1926 elected first secr, Leningrad Province CPSU(B) Comt and North Caucasian Bureau, CC, CPSU(B); cand Politburo member, CC, CPSU(B); campaigned against various anti-Party groups (Trotskyites, Bukharinites, Zinov'yevites, etc); from 1934 Politburo member, CC,CPSU(B); from 1934 member, Org Bureau and secr, CC, CPSU(B); Presidium member, USSR Centr Exec Comt; 1 Dec 1934 murdered by Chekist Nikolayev at Smol'nyy in Leningrad — an act which served as pretext for mass reprisals throughout the USSR; *Publ: Izbrannyye stat'i i rechi. 1912-34* (Selected Articles and Speeches. 1912-34) (1957); *Awards:* Order of the Red Banner (1928); Order of Lenin; *Died:* 1 Dec 1934; buried on Moscow's Red Square.

KIRPICHNIKOV, V. D. (1881-1940) Technol eng; *Born*: 1881;

Career: from 1907 worked at 1st Moscow Electr Plant; from 1918 member, Electr Eng Council, Main Comt of State Installations, Supr Sovnarkhoz; helped direct Bureau for Planning State Peat-Fired Distr Electr Plants; helped plan Shatura and other electr plants of the Moscow Ind Distr; 1920-24 dep exec dir, Hydropeat Trust, Supr Sovnarkhoz; helped invent hydraulic method of extracting peat and wrote various works on peat extraction; *Died*: 1940.

KIRPICHYOV, Mikhail Viktorovich (1879-1955) Thermal eng; member, USSR Acad of Sci from 1939; *Born*: 23 Aug 1879, son of mech eng V. L. Kirpichyov; *Educ*: 1907 grad Petersburg Technol Inst; *Career*: 1907-19 assoc, 1919-34 prof, Petersburg (Leningrad) Polytech Inst; 1929-39 corresp member, USSR Acad of Sci; from 1933 worked for Power Eng Inst, USSR Acad of Sci; 1937-49 also prof, Moscow Power Eng Inst; also worked for Inst of Physical Eng, USSR Acad of Sci, Centr Boiler and Turbine Inst, etc; did research on improving the efficiency of steam boilers and the accuracy of thermal calculations; studied the combustion of coal dust and the use of high-pressure steam in power plants; studied the physical properties of the operation of thermal equipment; devised model-operation theory (Kirpichyov-Gukhman theorem), whose third similarity theorem is widely used in hydraulics, thermal eng, power eng, chemistry, etc; *Publ: O teploperedache v kotlakh* (Heat Transfer in Boilers) (1924); coauthor, *Modelirovaniye teplovykh ustroystv* (The Modelling of Thermal Equipment) (1936); coauthor, *Teploperedacha* (Heat Transfer) (1940); *Teoriya podobiya kak osnova eksperimenta* (The Theory of Similarity as a Basis of Experimentation) (1945), etc; *Awards*: Stalin Prize (1941); *Died*: 10 Jan 1955.

KIRPICHYOV, Nil L'vovich (1850-1927) Mil eng; lt-gen, Russian Army; chm of first mil aeronautic eng comt in Russia; *Born*: 1850; *Career*: until 1917 prof, Nikolay Mil Eng Acad; 1918-20 chm, Eng Comt, Main Mil Eng Bd, Sov Army; chm, Kuybyshev Mil Eng Acad; well-known for his works on theoretical and building mechanics; invented a calculation method and deduced a formula for the resistance of fortified installations under artillery fire; helped to plan and build bridges across the Neva in Petersburg (Okhtenskiy, Troitskiy, Dvortsovy) and across the Syr-Dar'ya; planned hydrotech installations such as the ship basin on the Amur, the Ladoga water main, etc; worked out standards for the capacity of various types of bridges; *Publ: Osnovy teoreticheskoy mekhaniki* (The Principles of Theoretical Mechanics) (Parts 1-3, 1903-04); Parts 2-3 entitled *Teoreticheskya mekhanika* (Theoretical Mechanics); *Stroitel'naya mekhanika* (Construction Mechanics) (1898); *Died*: 1927.

KIRPONOS' Mikhail Petrovich (1892-1941) Ukr; med orderly in Russian Army; colonel-gen from 1941; cand member, CC, CPSU(B) in 1941; CP member from 1918; *Born*: 9 Jan 1892 in vil Vertiyevka, Chernigov Province, son of a peasant; *Educ*: 1916 grad med orderlies school; 1927 grad Frunze Mil Acad; *Career*: 1915 drafted into Russian Army; fought in WW 1 on Rumanian Front; after 1917 Feb Revol chm, regt comt; member, div comt; Feb 1918 demobilized; fought with partisans against Germans and Petlyura' forces; from 1918 in Red Army; 1918-20 asst commander, 1st Ukr Div and one of its regt commanders; asst commandant, Div School of Red Commanders, 44th Div; after Civil War held various commands; 1927-34 chief of staff, 41st Perekop Infantry Div; 1934-39 commandant, Kazan' Infantry College; 1939-40 commander, 70th Infantry Div on the Northwestern Front (Soviet-Finnish War); his div distinguished itself in the operation to capture Vyborg by crossing the thin ice of the Straits of Finland behind the Finnish lines in Vyborg; June 1940-Jan 1941 commander, Leningrad Mil Distr; Feb-June 1941 commander, Kiev Special Mil Distr; from 22 June 1941 commander, Southwestern Front; 14 Sept 1941 his troops, and 20 Sept 1941 his headquarters were encircled near Kiev; *Awards*: Hero of the Sov Union (1940); Order of Lenin; *Died*: 20 Sept 1941, while breaking out of the encirclement, fatally wounded by mortar fire; buried where he fell; later reinterred in Kiev.

KIRSANOV, Aleksandr Trofimovich (1880-1941) Agrochemist, pedologist and plant breeder; Dr of Agric; prof from 1909; *Born*: 15 Aug 1880 in Saratov Province; *Educ*: 1908 grad Berlin Agric Inst; *Career*: 1909-17 prof, Kamennyy Ostrov Agric Courses; 1918-22 prof and dean, Agronomical Fac, Ivanovo-Voznesensk Polytech Inst; 1927-31 prof, then rector, Leningrad Agric Inst; 1931-41 head, Agrochemical Laboratory, Soil Inst, USSR Acad of Sci; specialized in bog cultivation, fertilizers, plant growth factors and soil fertility; devised methods of determining how much phosphate and potassium fertilizer various soils require; made long-term studies of the bogs of Bel; co-founder Minsk Bog Research Station; *Publ: K voprosam opytnogo izucheniya bolot Poles'ya v tselyakh kul'tury* (The Experimental Study of the Poles'ye Bogs with a View to Cultivation) (1914); *Kul'tura bolot* (Bog Cultivation) (1918); *Sravnitel'noye agronomicheskoye pochvovedeniye* (Comparative Agronomical Pedology) (1927); coauthor, *Slovar'-spravochnik po torfyanomu delu* (A Reference Dictionary on Turf and Peat) (1928); *Teoriya Mitcherlikha, yeyo analiz i prakticheskoye primeneniye* (Mitscherlich's Theory, Its Analysis and Practical Application) (1929); *Kislovaniye obyknovennogo chernozyoma* (The Acidulation of Common Chernozem) (1932); *Mineral'nyye udobreniya v Zapadnoy Sibiri* (Mineral Fertilizers in Western Siberia) (1932); *Usvoyayemost' rasteniyem legkopodvizhnykh form pitatel'nykh veshchestv iz razlichnykh gorizontov pochvy* (The Capacity of Plants to Absorb Mobile Forms of Nutrients from Various Soil Layers) (1935); *Died*: 30 Oct 1941 in Tashkent.

KIRSANOV, P. N. (1897-1937) Govt official; CP member from 1905; *Born*: 1897; *Career*: Party work in Petersburg and Moscow; after 1917 Feb Revol chm, Railroad Comt, Northern Railroad Bd; 1918-19 member, Collegium, Pop Comrt of Means of Communication; 1919-22 dir, Finance Bd, Pop Comrt of Means of Communication; from 1922 dep chm, Moscow-Kiev Railroad Bd; admin and econ posts with Pop Comrt of Communications; arrested by State Security organs; *Died*: 1937 in imprisonment.

KIRSANOV, Stepan Pavlovich (1908-1966) Diplomat; amb extraordinary and plen; *Born*: 1908; *Career*: from 1937 in diplomatic service; 1943-44 counsellor, Sov mission in Bulgaria; 1944-45 dep head, then head, Polit Dept, Allied Control Commission in Rumania; 1945-48 polit advisor to chm, Allied Control Commission in Bulgaria; 1948-49 dep head, Dept of Balkan Countries (Albania, Bulgaria, Greece, Hungary, Rumania and Yugoslavia), USSR Min of For Affairs and polit adviser, Sov Balkan Command; 1949-50 head, 4th European Dept, USSR Min of For Affairs; 1953-59 Sov amb to Holland; 1959-66 dep head, Dept of Scandinavian Countries, USSR Min of For Affairs; *Awards*: Badge of Hon (1955); *Died*: Oct 1966.

KIRSANOVA, Klavdiya Ivanovna (1888-1947) Party official; CP member from 1904; *Born*: 1888; *Career*: Party work in Perm'; arrested for revol activities; 1908 deported for life to Irkutsk Province, whence she escaped; worked for Party org of Tula, Khar'kov and Saratov; 1909 rearrested and spent four years at hard labor in Perm' prison; 1913-17 exiled to Yakutsk Oblast; during Civil War fought with machine-gun detachment, 14th Volhynian Regt, Ural Composite Div; after Civil War dir, Party educ establishments; rector, Sverdlovsk Univ; dir, Sverdlovsk Uyezd Party Officials' Courses, CC, CPSU(B) and Lenin School; from 1941 rector, Propaganda and Agitation Bd, CC, CPSU(B); member, Anti-Fascist Comt of Sov Women; attended int women's congresses in Paris; *Awards*: Order of Lenin; Order of the Red Star; medals; *Died*: 10 Oct 1947.

KIRSHON, Vladimir Mikhaylovich (1902-1938) Playwright; CP member from 1920; *Born*: 19 Aug 1902 in Nal'chik, son of a Menshevik lawyer who gave up politics after 1905-07 Revol; *Educ*: completed six grades of high-school; 1923 grad Sverdlov Communist Univ, Moscow; *Career*: 1918 joined Komsomol and served on Caucasian Front; 1922 first work published; 1923-25 dir of studies, Rostov-on-Don Sov Party School, then dep head, Rostov-on-Don Agitation and Propaganda Dept; organized Rostov and North Caucasian Assoc of Proletarian Writers; from 1925 secr, All-Russian Assoc of Proletarian Writers, Moscow; 1926-28 member, ed bd, journal *Molodaya gvardiya*; 1928-32 member, ed bd, journal *Na literarnom postu*; 1930-34 exec ed, journal *Rost*; in early 1930's secr, Russian Assoc of Proletarian Writers and chm of its Film Section; leading member, All-Union League of Assoc of Proletarian Writers; during 1930's visited Germany; his plays have been translated into many for languages; 1937 arrested by NKVD; *Publ*: film script *Bor'ba za ul'timatum* (The Struggle of the Ultimatum) (1923); coauthor, play *Konstantin Terekhin (Rzhavchina)* (Konstantin Terekhin [Rust]) (1927); plays *Rel'sy gudyat* (The Rails Are Humming) (1928); *Gorod vetrov* (City of the Winds) (1929); *Khleb* (Bread) (1930); *Sud* (The Trial) (1933); *Chudesnyy splav* (Miraculous Alloy) (1934); *Bol'shoy den'* (The Great Day) (1937); *Stat'i i rechi o dramaturgii, teatre i kino* (Articles and Speeches on Dramaturgy, the Theater and Cinema) (1962); *Died*: 28 July 1938 in imprisonment; posthumously rehabilitated.

KISEL', Aleksandr Andreyevich (1859-1938) Pediatrician; Dr of Med; prof; Hon Sci Worker of RSFSR from 1933; *Born*: 31 Aug 1859 in Kiev; *Educ*: 1883 grad Med Fac, Kiev Univ; *Career*: after grad worked at S. P. Botkin's clinic in Moscow; 1890-1938 assoc, Ol'ga Children's Hospital, Moscow; 1892-1911 assoc prof, Moscow Univ; resigned in protest against policies of Educ Min Kasso; from 1910 lecturer, then prof and dir, Children's Clinic, Higher Women's Courses (now 2nd Moscow Med Inst); 1927-38 dir, Inst of Child Welfare, Moscow; specialized in preventive med; campaigned for the improvement of living conditions, hygiene and nutrition for children; developed child balneology and founded several children's sanatoria and health resorts; campaigned for inoculation of new-born babies with BCG antitubercular vaccine; did original research on rheumatism, malaria, scarlet fever, dysentery, infectious hepatitis, tuberculosis, etc; organized several pediatric conferences; co-ed, *Bol'shaya meditsinskaya entsiklopediya* (Large Medical Encyclopedia) (1st ed); wrote over 600 works; *Publ*: *K voprosu o patologoanatomicheskikh izmeneniyakh v kostyakh rastushchikh zhivotnykh pod vliyaniyem minimal'nykh doz fosfora* (Pathological Anatomical Lesions in the Bones of Growing Animals under the Influence of Minimal Doses of Phosphorus) (1887); *Trudy zasluzhennogo deyatelya nauki professora A. A. Kiselya* (The Works of Professor A. A. Kisel', Honored Scientific Worker) (1940-44), etc; *Died*: 2 Mar 1938 in Moscow.

KISELEV, Aleksandr Ivanovich (1903-1967) Ukr writer and lit critic; Dr of Philosophy; senior assoc, Inst of Lit, Ukr Acad of Sci from 1939; *Born*: 29 Mar 1903 in vil Satanovka, now Khmel'nitskiy Oblast; *Educ*: 1936 grad Kiev Univ; *Career*: until 1925 teacher; from 1926 corresp for various newspapers; during WW 2 in Sov Army at the front; *Publ*: wrote studies of P. Grabovskiy, I. Kotlyarevskiy, T. Shevchenko, etc; coauthor, Vol 1 of *Istoriya ukrainskoy literatury* (A History of Ukrainian Literature); "Ivan Franko's Life and Work" (1959); "The Life and Work of Pavel Grakobskiy" (1959), etc; *Died*: 24 Feb 1967.

KISELEV, Aleksey Semyonovich (1879-1938) Party and govt official; CP member from 1898; *Born*: 1879 in vil Avdot'ino, near Ivanovo-Voznesensk, son of a worker; *Career*: from age of 14 metal-worker in a factory; Party work in Ivanovo-Voznesensk, Moscow, Khar'kov, Baku and Odessa; repeatedly arrested and exiled; 1914 sent on Party business to Austria, where he met Lenin; coopted member, CC, RSDRP(B); summer 1914 arrested and exiled to Yeniseysk, but son escaped and lived illegally in Yeniseysk, Krasnoyarsk and Verkhne-Udinsk; after 1917 Feb Revol returned to Ivanovo-Voznesensk; elected chm, City Sov and member, Ivanovo-Voznesensk RSDRP(B) Comt; at 6th RSDRP(B) Congress elected cand member, CC; at 1st All-Russian Congress of Soviets elected member, All-Russian Centr Exec Comt; after 1917 Oct Revol chm, Centr Union of Textile Ind; Presidium member, Supr Sovnarkhoz; later member, Commission for Turkestani Affairs, Supr Sovnarkhoz; 1918 head, Orenburg Defense Group against Kolchak and Dutov's troops; 1920 chm, Miners' Union; during trade-union controversy sided with "workers' opposition"; 1921-23 chm, Small Sovnarkhoz; after 2nd All-Union Congress of Soviets member, USSR Centr Exec Comt; 1923 at 12th RCP(B) Congress elected member, RCP(B) Centr Control Commission; Presidium member, RCP(B) Centr Control Commission; RSFSR Pop Comr of Workers and Peasants' Inspection; USSR Dep Pop Comr of Workers and Peasants' Inspection; at 10th, 11th, 14th, 15th and 16th Party Congresses elected cand member, CC; at 17th Congress elected member, Auditing Commission; from 1924 secr, All-Russian Centr Exec Comt; Presidium member, All-Russian Centr Exec Comt; arrested by State Security organs; *Died*: 1938 in imprisonment; posthumously rehabilitated.

KISELEV, Andrey Petrovich (1852-1940) Mathematician, *Born*: 12 Dec 1852; *Educ*: 1875 grad Fac of Physics and Mathematics, Petersburg Univ; *Career*: 1875-91 taught mathematics, mech and tech drawing at Voronezh High School; 1892-1901 taught mathematics and physics at Voronezh Cadet Corps; 1901 retired from teaching to write textbooks; in 1920's resumed teaching and continued textbook writing; 1937-38 his revised textbooks on elementary arithmetic, algebra and geometry, which had already run into dozens of editions, were adopted as standard textbooks for Sov secondary schools, where they have been in use until recent times; *Publ: Sistematicheskiy kurs arifmetiki dlya srednikh uchebnykh zavedeniy* (A Systematic Arithmetic Course for Secondary Educational Establishments) (1884); *Elementarnaya algebra* (Elementary Algebra) (1888); *Elementarnaya geometriya* (Elementary Geometry) (1892); *Dopolnitelnyye stat'i algebry* (Algebraic Appendices) (1906); *O tekh voprosakh elementarnoy geometrii, kotoryye reshayutsya obyknovenno pomoshch'yu predelov* (Problems of Geometry Commonly Solved by Limitation) (1916); *Kratkaya algebra* (A Short Algebra) (1917); *Nachala differentsial'nogo i integral'nogo ischisleniy* (The Principles of Differential and Integral Calculus) (1917); *Kratkaya arifmetika dlya gorodskikh i uyezdnykh uchilish* (A Short Arithmetic Primer for Urban and Uyezd Colleges) (1918); *Graficheskoye izobrazheniye nekotorykh funktsiy, rassmatryvayemykh v elementarnoy algebre* (The Graphic Representation of Some Functions Treated in Elementary Algebra) (1923); *Irratsional'nyye chisla, rassmatryvayemyye kak beskonechnyye desyatichnyye, neperiodicheskiye drobi* (Irrational Numbers Treated as Recurring Non-Periodic Decimal Fractions) (1923); *Elementy algebry i analiza* (The Elements of Algebra and Analysis) (1930-31); *Arifmetika* (Arithmetic) (1955); *Geometriya* (Geometry) (1962); *Algebra* (1964); *Awards*: Order of the Red Banner of Labor (1933); *Died*: 8 Nov 1940.

KISELEV, Ivan Andreyevich (1902-1958) Mil theoretician; maj-gen; *Born*: 1902; *Educ*: grad Mil Acad of Armored and Mechanized Troops; *Career*: served with Sov Army Gen Staff; *Publ*: article "Motorized and Mechanized Units" (1930); *Protivotankovaya oborona marsha* (Anti-Tank Defense of the March Echelon) (1934); *Died*: 1958.

KISELEV, Sergey Vladimirovich (1905-1962) Archeologist and historian; Dr of History from 1946; prof from 1939; corresp member, USSR Acad of Sci from 1953; CP member from 1949; *Born*: 17 July 1905 in Mytishchy, near Moscow; *Educ*: 1926 grad Dept of History and Archeology, Moscow Univ; 1930 completed postgrad studies at Research Inst of Archeology and Art Studies; *Career*: from 1927 did archeological research in Southern Siberia, Kazakhstan and Transbaykal; 1929-38 senior assoc, State Historical Museum, Moscow, and later member of its Learned Council; from 1930 simultaneously senior assoc, State Acad of the History of Civilization (now Inst of Archeology, USSR Acad of Sci); from 1939 prof, Chair of Archeology, Moscow Univ; 1945-51 dep dir, Inst of Archeology, USSR Acad of Sci; 1947-62 head, Neolithic and Bronze Age Section, Inst of Archeology, USSR Acad of Sci; from 1949 exec ed, journal *Vestnik drevney istorii*; 1953-54 dep acad secr, Dept of Historical Sci, USSR Acad of Sci; specialized in the ancient and medieval history and archeology of Southern Siberia and Centr Asia; 1948-49 led joint excavations of USSR Acad of Sci and Mongolian Sci Comt at Karakorum, Khar-Balgas and other Mongolian towns; later led other archeological expeditions to Tuva ASSR, Chita Oblast and Mongolia; *Publ: Drevnyaya istoriya Yuzhnoy Sibiri* (The Ancient History of Southern Siberia) (1949); ed, *Materialy i issledovaniya po arkheologii Sibiri* (Material and Studies of the Archeology of Siberia) (1952); coauthor and ed, *Drevnemongol'skiye goroda* (Ancient Mongolian Cities) (1957); *Drevniye goroda Zabaykal'ya* (Ancient Cities of the Transbaykal) (1958); *Iz istorii kitayskoy cherepitsy* (The History of Chinese Tile) (1959); *Neolit i bronzovyy vek Kitaya* (The Neolithic and Bronze Ages in China) (1960); *Awards*: Order of Lenin; Badge of Hon; Stalin Prize (1950); *Died*: 8 Nov 1962 after a long illness.

KISELEV, Yevgeniy Dmitriyevich (1908-1963) Diplomat; CP member from 1938; *Born*: 1908 in Solikamsk in the Urals, son of a teacher; *Educ*: 1930 grad Moscow's Plekhanov Inst of Nat Econ; *Career*: eng-econ in Ural mining ind; from 1937 dipl work; 1940-41 USSR consul, then consul-gen in Königsberg; 1941-42 in Sov Army; 1943-45 USSR consul-gen in New York; 1945-48 polit adviser (with the rank of envoy), USSR High Commissioner with Allied Commission in Austria; 1948-49 head, Dept of Balkan Countries, USSR Min of For Affairs; 1949-54 USSR ambassador to Hungary; 1954 head, Protocol Dept, Min of For Affairs; 1955-58 USSR amb to Egypt; from Aug 1956 simultaneously envoy to Yemen; 1958-59 USSR amb to United Arab Republic and envoy to Yemen; 1959-62 head, Middle Eastern Dept, USSR Min of For Affairs; 1962-63 Dep UN Secr-Gen; held rank of amb extraordinary and plen; *Awards*: Order of the Red Banner of Labor; Order of the Fatherland War, 2nd Class; medals; *Died*: 17 Apr 1963 in New York.

KISHKIN, N. M. (1864-1930) Politician; leader, Constitutional-Democratic Party; *Born*: 1864; *Career*: dr by profession; Min of State Charity in the last Russian Provisional Govt; on the eve of the 1917 Oct Revol appointed Mayor of Petrograd; 1919 active in the Tactical Center, an anti-Sov org in Moscow; Aug 1920 given a five-year suspended prison sentence in absentia by the Supr Revol Tribunal of the All-Union Centr Exec Comt for his connections with the Tactical Center; 1921 member, All-Russian Comt for Famine Relief; during last years of his life worked at the Pop Comrt of Health; *Died*: 1930.

KISTYAKOVSKIY, Vladimir Aleksandrovich (1865-1952) Physicochemist and electrochemist; Dr of Chemistry from 1910; prof from 1903; member, Ukr Acad of Sci from 1919; member, USSR Acad of Sci from 1929; *Born*: 12 Oct 1865 in Kiev, son of a prof; *Educ*: 1889 grad Petersburg Univ as Cand of Natural Sci; *Career*: 1889-90 worked at Prof W. F. Ostwald's laboratory; 1890 formulated hypothesis of double salts and complex ions and applied Kohlrausch's law to them; 1894 made experimental and mathematical analyses of reversible chemical reactions; 1900 discovered new photocatalysts; 1903-34 prof, Petersburg (Leningrad) Polytech Inst; 1904 did research on associated liquids and formulated rule of capillary attraction; 1907 worked on method of determining electron potential; 1907-10 devised new theory of the passivity and accretion process of metals; 1914 devised evaporation heat formula; 1916-35 developed film theory of metal corrosion; 1922 made mathematical analysis of chemical equilibrium and reformulated the third principle of thermodynamics; 1925-29 corresp member, USSR Acad of Sci; 1930-34 founder-head, Laboratory of Colloid and Electrochemistry, USSR Acad of Sci; 1934-39 dir, Inst of Colloid and Electrochemistry (now Inst of Physical Chemistry), USSR Acad of Sci; wrote over 100 works, including 20 on metal corrosion; *Publ: Razbor vozrazheniy na teoriyu elektroliticheskoy dissotsiatsii* (A Review of Objections to the Theory of Electrolytic Dissociation) (1902); *Elektrokhimiya* (Electrochemistry) (1912-16); *Ob odnoy zakonomernosti dlya kapillyarnogo pod'yoma* (A Law of Capillary Attraction) (1913); *Kolloido-elektrokhimiya* (Colloid and Electrochemistry) (1938); *Prikladnaya fizicheskaya khimiya* (Applied Physiochemistry) (1926), etc; *Awards*: two Orders of Lenin; medals; *Died*: 19 Oct 1952.

KIZEVETTER, Aleksandr Aleksandrovich (1866-1933) Russian historian and politician; Dr of Historical Sci from 1909; *Born*: 10 May 1866; *Educ*: 1888 grad Moscow Univ; *Career*: 1903-11 assoc prof, Moscow Univ; then taught on Moscow Advanced Courses for Women; believed in constitutional monarchy; 1904 joined League for the Liberation of the Working Class; from 1906 member, CC, Constitutional-Democratic Party; member, 2nd State Duma; contributed to Constitutional-Democratic journals *Russkaya mysl'* and *Russkiye vedomosti*; 1922 deported from the USSR for counter-revol activities; 1922-33 prof of Russian history, Prague Univ; adhered to S. M. Solovyov and V. O. Klyuchevskiy's school of history; worked on Russian history of the 18th and early 19th centuries; wrote various studies on the history of Russia in the 1860's and on social history; *Publ: Posadskaya obshchina Rossii v 18 st.* (The Russian Artisan and Mercantile Community in the 18th Century) (1903); *Gorodovoye polozheniye Yekateriny II 1785 g.* (Catherine II's 1785 Urban Charter) (1909); *Istoricheskiye ocherki* (Historical Studies) (1912); *Istoricheskiye otkliki* (Historical Comments) (1916); *Istoricheskiye siluety. Lyudi i sobytiya* (Historical Silhouettes. People and Events) (1931), etc; *Died*: 1933 in Prague.

KIZHNER, Nikolay Matveyevich (1867-1935) Organic chemist; Dr of Chemistry from 1900; prof from 1901; hon member, USSR Acad of Sci from 1934; *Born*: 2 Dec 1867 in Moscow; *Educ*: 1890 grad Moscow Univ; *Career*: while still a student did work on hexahydrobenzene, providing the mathematical basis for the solution of a fundamental question in the chemistry of alicyclic compounds - the isomerization of cycles; 1895, on the basis of extensive research on typical alicyclic amines, wrote first detailed description of this group and deduced that the chemical properties of alicyclic amines are close to those of amines of the fatty series; 1900 devised method of obtaining substituted hydrazines; detected the intermediate formation of fatty diazo compound during the reaction of free hydroxyl amine and dibromo-amines; from 1901 prof, Tomsk Technol Inst; 1913 resigned in disagreement with educ policy; 1911 discovered catalytic hydrazine decomposition reaction (Kizhner's reaction), which was widely used in hydrocarbon synthesis; 1914-17 taught at Shanyavskiy Pop Univ, Moscow; from 1918 sci dir, Aniline Trust Research Inst, Moscow; contributed to development of Sov paint and dye ind with his subsequent work on organic dyes; 1929-34 corresp member, USSR Acad of Sci; *Publ*: master's thesis *Aminy i gidraziny polimetilenogo ryada, metody obrazovaniya ikh i prevrashcheniya* (Amines and Hydrazines of the Polymethylene Series, Methods of Formation and Conversion) (1895); doctor's thesis *O deystvii okisi serebra i gidroksilamina na bromaminy. O stroyenii geksagidrobenzola* (The Effect of Silver Oxide and Hydroxy Amine Oxide on Bromo-Amines. The Structure of Hexahydrobenzene) (1900); *Issledovaniya v oblasti organicheskoy khimii* (Research in Organic Chemistry) (1937); *Awards*: two Butlerov Prizes (1893, 1914); *Died*: 28 Nov 1935.

KLASSON, Robert Eduardovich (1868-1926) Electr eng; *Born*: 12 Feb 1868 in Kiev, son of a physician; *Educ*: 1891 grad Petersburg Technol Inst; *Career*: 1891 helped M. O. Dlivo-Dobrovol'skiy in experiments on the long-range transmission of electr current with a three-phase generator; 1891-93 worked in Germany; 1895-96 installed one of first Russian earthed three-phase plants at Okhtenskiy Gunpowder Works; designed and supervised construction of power stations in Moscow and Petersburg; 1900-06 worked on the electrification of the Baku oil fields; 1912-14 supervised construction of first Russian peat-fired distr power plant at Bogorodsk (now Noginsk, Moscow Oblast), which is still in operation and now bears his name; 1914 devised hydraulic peat extraction method and techniques of peat dehydration; also established a pilot plant for the manufacture of peat briquets in Bogorodsk; *Publ: Elektricheskaya peredacha sily tryokhfaznymi tokami na Okhtenskikh zavodakh bliz Svyatogo-Peterburga* (The Transmission of Electrical Power with Three-Phase Currents at the Okhtenskiy Gunpowder Works near Saint Petersburg) (1897); *Gidrotorf* (Hydropeat) (1923); *Gidrotorf v svyazi s rayonnymi elektricheskimi stantsiyami* (Hydropeat in Relation to District Power Plants) (1923); *Died*: 11 Feb 1926.

KLEMBOVSKIY, Vladislav Napoleonovich (1860-1921) Mil commander; gen of infantry, Russian Army from 1915; *Born*: 28 June 1860; *Educ*: 1879 grad Alexandrine Mil College; 1885 grad Nikolay Mil Acad; *Career*: 1904-05 regt commander and corps chief of staff in Russo-Japanese War; 1914-17 commander, 9th Infantry Div; commanded 16th Army Corps; chief of staff, Southwestern Front; asst chief of staff to supr commander in chief and commander in chief of Northern Front; 1918 sided with Sov regime; worked for Commission to Examine and Utilize the Experience of the 1914-18 War; 1920 member, Special Conference at Command Headquarters of RSFSR Armed Forces; *Publ: Partizanskiye deystviya* (Partisan Operations) (1894); *Taynyye razvedki* (Secret Reconnaissance) (2nd ed, 1911); Vol 5 of *Strategicheskiy ocherk voyny 1914-18* (A Strategic Outline of the 1914-18 War) (1920); *Died*: 19 July 1921 executed on charges of treason.

KLIMENKO, Ivan Yevdokimovich (1891-1938) Party and govt official; CP member from 1912; *Born*: 1891 in vil Rivchaki, now Chernigov Oblast, son of a peasant; *Career*: worked for Bolshevik orgs; underground work in Kiev, Rostov, Poltava and Khar'kov; subjected to reprisals by Tsarist authorities; imprisoned for two years then exiled for three years to Narym Kray; 1916 fled to Irkutsk, then to Novonikolayevsk (now Novosibirsk), where he continued revol activities; after 1917 Feb Revol dep chm, Novonikolayevsk Sov of Workers and Peasants' Dep; May 1917 went to Kiev and elected member, Centr Council of Factory and Plant Comts; Jan 1918 fought in Kiev armed uprising; underground work in Kiev; late 1918 moved to Odessa to direct underground Odessa Mil Revol Comt; 1919-20 chm, Odessa Province Exec Comt and Odessa Province Revol Comt; dep chm, Kiev Revol Comt; mil comr, 45th Div; then chm, Yekaterinoslav Province Exec Comt; Bureau member, Odessa, Kiev and Yekaterinoslav Province Comts, CP(B) Ukr; 1922-24 Ukr Pop Comr of Agric; Jan 1925-Oct 1927 secr, CC, CP(B) Ukr; 1927-30 chm, Tractor Center; RSFSR and USSR Dep Pop Comr of Agric; chm, Siberian Kray Exec Comt; Nov 1930 removed from post as chm, Siberian Kray Exec Comt by order of the CC, CPSU(B); 1930-33 head, Centr Asian and Ryazan'-Ural Railroads and Collegium member, Pop Comrt of Means of Communication; from 1934 head, Grain Bd, USSR Pop Comrt of Agric; deleg at 1st-3rd 9th and 10th Congresses of CP(B) Ukr and 6th-7th Conferences of CP(B) Ukr; at 8th Conference and 9th and 10th Congresses of CP(B) Ukr elected member, CC; May 1924-Oct 1927 Org Bureau and Politbureau member, CC, CP(B) Ukr; deleg at 11th and 13th RCP(B) Congresses and 14th-16th CPSU(B) Congresses; at 14th-16th Congresses elected member, CC, CPSU(B); several times elected member, All-Ukr and USSR Centr Exec Comt; arrested by State Security organs; *Died*: 1938 in imprisonment.

KLIMKOVICH, Mikhail Nikolayevich (1899-1954) Bel poet, playwright and lit critic; member, Bel Writers' Union; CP member from 1920; *Born*: 20 Nov 1899 in vil Selitriniki, now Minsk Oblast, son of a poor peasant; *Educ*: grad Borisov City College; 1917 qualified as teacher after course of external studies; *Career*: 1921-22 in Red Army; afterwards taught for a short time; later worked in Party organs and in Bel Writers' Union; 1926 first work published; 1944 wrote the words for the state anthem of the Bel SSR; *Publ*: historical dramas *Katerina Zhernosek* (1938), *Georgiy Skorina* (1946), *Kastus' Kalinovskiy* (1947) and *Vsya vlast' Sovetam* (All Power to the Soviets) (1947); collected stories "The Forest Lake" (1946); lit study "The Vitalizing Influence of Russian Literature on Belorussian Literature" (1955); "Georgiy Skorina. A Dramatic Poem" (1958); "Collected Works" (1959); "Literary Criticism" (1962); *Died*: 5 Nov 1954 in Minsk.

KLIMOV, Aleksey Filippovich (1878-1940) Veterinary anatomist; Dr of Veterinary Med from 1912; prof from 1916; Hon Sci Worker of RSFSR from 1940; *Born*: 16 Feb 1878; *Educ*: 1909 grad Kazan' Veterinary Inst; *Career*: from 1916 prof of histology and embryology, Novocherkassk Veterinary Inst; from 1921 prof of anatomy, Moscow Veterinary Inst; from 1939 prof, Moscow Mil Veterinary Acad; did research on the structure of animal organs (the outer ear, the skin, etc); *Publ*: doctor's thesis *K ucheniyu o naruzhnom ukhe sobaki* (The Study of the Outer Ear of Dogs) (1912); *Anatomiya domashnikh zhivotnykh* (The Anatomy of Domestic Animals) (3 vol, 1937-38); *Anatomiya i fiziologiya sel'skokhozyaystvennykh zhivotnykh* (The Anatomy and Physiology of Agricultural Animals) (5th ed, 1946); *Awards*: Stalin Prize; *Died*: 11 June 1940.

KLIMOV, Mikhail Georgiyevich (1881-1937) Choirmaster; *Born*: 21 Oct 1881 in vil Zavidovo, Moscow Province, son of a peasant; *Educ*: grad Moscow Synodal College; 1908 grad Petersburg Conservatory, where he studied composition under Rimsky-Korsakov and conducting under N. N. Cherepnin; *Career*: from 1902 asst conductor, from 1913 until death chief conductor, 1919-31 dir, Court Choir (Leningrad State Acad Choir); 1908-37 also prof, Petersburg (Leningrad) Conservatory; *Publ: Uchebnik sol'fedzhio* (Solfeggio Textbook), etc; *Died*: 20 Feb 1937 in Leningrad.

KLIMOV, Mikhail Mikhaylovich (1880-1942) Actor; Pop Artiste of USSR from 1937; *Born*: 20 Nov 1880 in Petersburg; *Career*: 1897-1900 worked in office of Putilov Plant; simultaneously performed in amateur plays; 1900 began stage career with Petersburg clubs and summer theaters; 1902-04 played in provinces (Dvinsk and Odessa); 1905-09 in Moscow at Korsh Theater; 1909-42 (except 1918-19 and 1925-27 when he played at Korsh Theater) performed at Moscow Maly Theater; excellent comedy actor of realist school; *Roles*: stage roles: Zemlyanik in Gogol's *Revizor* (The Government Inspector) (1922, 1938); Telyatev and Gorodulin in Ostrovsky's *Beshenyye den'gi* (Mad Money) and *Na vsyakogo mudretsa dovol'no prostoty* (There's a Simpleton in Every Sage) (1935); Famusov in Griboyedov's *Gore ot uma* (Woe from Wit) (1938); Tolokonnikov in Uspenskiy's *Rasteryayeva ulitsa* (Rasteryayev Street) (1929); Yelisatov and Shmetsger in *Trenyov's Lyubov' Yarovaya* (1926) and *Na beregu Nevy* (On the Banks of the Neva) (1937); Petrygin in Leonov's *Skutarevskiy* (1934); film roles: the banker Ornano in *Protsess o tryokh millionakh* (The Trial Over Three Million) (1926); the Head Waiter in *Chelovek iz restorana* (The Man from the Restaurant) (1927); Volkov in *Khromoy barin* (The Lame Gentleman) (1929); the Vicar in *Prazdnik svyatogo Iorgena* (The Feast of Saint Iorgen) (1930); Knurov in *Bespridannitsa* (The Girl Without a Dowry) (1937); Squire Trelawny in "Treasure Island" (1938), etc; *Died*: 9 July 1942 in Tbilisi.

KLIMOV, Vladimir Yakovlevich (1892-1962) Aviation engine designer; member, USSR Acad of Sci from 1953; lt-gen, Aviation Eng Corps; *Born*: 23 July 1892 in Moscow; *Educ*: 1917 grad Moscow Higher Tech College; *Career*: 1926-28 head, Dept of Aviation Engines, Zhukovskiy Air Force Acad; head, Dept of Light Internal-Combustion Engines, Aviation Engine Research Inst; 1930-31 head, Tech Control Dept, and dir, Frunze Engine Plant; 1931-34 head, Dept of Gasoline Engines, Baranov Centr Inst of Aviation Machine-Building; member of Russia's first aeronautical circle founded by Zhukovskiy at the Moscow Higher Tech College; 1923 helped establish Russia's first Laboratory of Automobile and Tractor Engines which was developed into the Sci Automobile and Tractor Inst; 1924 headed a commission to Germany to buy and receive German aviation engines; 1928 headed a commission to France to receive airplane motors which had been bought there for the USSR Air Force; 1943-53 corresp member, USSR Acad of Sci; read course on devices and theory of balancing airplane motors at Moscow Higher Tech College, Moscow Aviation Inst, etc; invented the VK series of liquid-cooled, reciprocating airplane engines; 1948 invented VK-5A jet motor (VK I modification) which was used for the MiG-15, MiG-15b and MiG-17; 1955 designed the VK-3b motor which was built into the Tu-104 in 1956; dep, USSR Supr Sov of 1946 convocation; dep, RSFSR Supr Sov of 1955 convocation; *Awards*: twice Hero of Socialist Labor; four Stalin Prizes (1941, 1943, 1946, 1949); five Orders of Lenin; four other orders; medals; *Died*: 9 Sept 1962.

KLODNITSKIY, Nikolay Nikolayevich (1868-1939) Epidemiologist and microbiologist; Dr of Med from 1902; prof from 1920; *Born*: 21 Nov 1868 in vil Krasnoye, Vilnius Province, son of a priest; *Educ*: 1886 grad Mariampol' High-School, Suvalki Province; 1894 grad Petersburg Mil Med Acad with distinction; *Career*: while still a student helped to combat typhus epidemic in Saratov Province; 1894-99 served in Russian Army as junior physician; 1899 worked at I. I. Pavlov's laboratory; 1899-1904 head, bacteriological laboratory and infection barrack, Chinese-Eastern Railroad; 1902 combatted outbreak of plague among railroad construction workers in Manchuria; 1903-05 and 1906 worked under I. I. Mechnikov in Paris and P. Ehrlich in Frankfurt-on-Main; 1905 helped to combat plague in Transbaykal; 1906-14 head, Astrakhan' Anti-Plague Laboratory; 1907 devised new method of hemoculture; 1909 did research on experimental infection of guinea-pigs with typhus; 1911 isolated plague culture from camel; established the presence of primary bacteriemia in bubonic plague; 1915-17 commander, 43rd Sanitation and Hygiene Detachment, Galician Front, then consultant, Centr Mil Hospital, Helsinki; 1917 supervised campaign against typhus in Petrograd; from 1920 prof, Chair of Infectious Diseases, Mil Med Acad; 1920-24 founder-dir, Infection Clinic, Tashkent Med Inst; 1924-25 head, Biological Dept, then Diagnosis Dept, Baku Bacteriological Inst; from 1925 prof, Chair of Microbiology, Irkutsk Univ and dir, Irkutsk Bacteriological Inst, where he founded an anti-plague unit in 1929; from 1932 prof of epidemiology, Moscow Med Inst; 1934 devised new method of cultivating agar jelly; also did research on the microbiology and epidemiology of relapsing fever, paratyphus, malaria, scarlet fever, tuberculosis, etc; *Publ: Ob endemicheskom kharaktere astrakhanskoy chumy* (The Endemic Nature of the Astrakhan' Plague) (1910); *K voprosu o vozniknovenii i rasprostranenii lyogochnoy chumy* (The Origin and Propagation of Pneumonic Plague) (1911); *K voprosu o vospriimchivosti verblyudov k bubonnoy chume* (The Susceptibility of Camels to Bubonic Plague) (1912); *Voprosy epidemiologii astrakhanskoy chumy* (The Epidemiology of the Astrakhan' Plague) (1926); *Voprosy epidemiologii zabaykal'skoy chumy* (The Epidemiology of the Transbaykal Plague) (1927), etc; *Died*: 31 Aug 1939 in Moscow of cerebral hemorrhage.

KLUBOV, Aleksandr Fyodorovich (1918-1944) Fighter pilot; WW 2 hero; capt; CP member; *Born*: 18 Jan 1918 in vil Yerunovo, Vologda Province, son of a peasant; *Educ*: 1940 grad mil pilots' school; *Career*: 1941-44 wing and squadron commander on North Caucasian and 4th Ukr fronts; shot down 39 German planes in aerial combat; suffered burns as a result of enemy fire; sentenced to a year's imprisonment (to be served after war) for using a weapon in a brawl; *Awards*: twice Hero of the Soviet Union; Order of Lenin; two Orders of the Red Banner; Order of the Fatherland War; Order of Aleksandr Nevskiy; *Died*: 1 Nov 1944 killed in abortive landing after a training flight; buried in L'vov.

KLUMOV, Yevgeniy Vladimirovich (1878-1944) Surgeon and gynecologist; prof from 1939; *Born*: 1878 in Moscow; *Educ*: 1902 grad Med Fac, Moscow Univ; *Career*: 1902-04 worked at various med establishments in Moscow; 1905 served in Russo-Japanese War as junior intern at a mil hospital; 1904-14 dir, Sutkov Rural Distr Hospital, Minsk Province, where he specialized in gen and gynecological surgery; 1911 delivered paper on distr hospital org at 2nd Congress of Physicians of Minsk Province; 1914-20 mil surgeon in Russia, then Red Army; from 1921 head, Surgical Dept and chief physician, 2nd Sov City Hospital, Minsk; 1935-39 assoc prof, from 1939 prof and dir, Gynecological Clinic, Minsk Med Inst; remained in Minsk during German occupation and collaborated with local partisans and underground Communist org; 1943 arrested by German police; the 3rd Clinical Hospital and a street in Minsk are named after him; *Awards*: Order of Lenin; Gold Star; Hero of the Sov Union (1965); *Died*:

June 1944 executed by German firing squad.

KLYASHTORNYY, Todar Todaravich (1903-1938) Bel poet; member, Bel Writers' Union from 1934; *Born*: 11 Mar 1903 in vil Porech'ye, now Vitebsk Oblast, son of a peasant; *Educ*: grad Workers' Fac in Orsha and Dept of Lit and Linguistics, Teachers' Training Fac, Bel State Univ; *Career*: on ed staff, journals *Maladnyak, Uzvyshsha,* and *Polymya* and newspapers *Savetskaya Belarus', Zvyazda* and *Chyrvonaya zmena*; 1925-27 member, *Maladnyak* lit assoc; 1928-31 member, *Uzvyshsha* lit assoc; 1924 first work published; 1929 subjected to Party criticism for belonging to *Uzvyshsha* lit assoc; 1936 arrested by NKVD; *Publ*: collected poems and verse "Maple Snow Storms" (1927); "Light and Shade" (1928); "The Sails" (1929); "The Fields Have Spoken" (1930); "May Over the World" (1934); "Through a Storm to a Storm" (1934); "Bloom, Order-Bearer" (1935); "We Work Like a United Family" (1935); "The Blooming of a Young Spring" (1935); "The Golden Binding" (1960); *Died*: 1938 in imprisonment; posthumously rehabilitated.

KLYCHKOV (real name: LESHENKOV), Sergey Antonovich (1889-1940) Russian writer; *Born*: 13 July 1889 in vil Dubrovki, Tver' Province, son of a shoemaker; *Career*: fought in WW 1; 1908 first work published; from first collections of poems — *Pesni* (Songs) (1911) and *Potayonnyy sad* (The Hidden Garden) (1913) — onwards belonged to so-called "new peasant" school (N. Klyuyov, S. Yesenin, etc); developed themes from Russian songs and fairy-tales, re-interpreted them in the spirit of symbolism and appeared as a romanticist; in 1920's turned to prose with the novels *Sakharnyy nemets* (The Sugar-Coated German) (1925); *Chertukhinskiy balakir'* (The Chertukhin Pitcher) (1926), etc; the rejection of modern reality and machine civilization, a fondness for olden times and the patriarchal system and preoccupation with motifs of doom and pessimism are clearly expressed in Klychkov's works; in prose adhered to the narrative style and was a master at rich colloquial speech; in 1930's did translations and lit versions of folk epics of the peoples of the USSR (Vogul and Kir epics, Shota Rustaveli, etc); 1937 arrested by State Security organs; *Publ: Domashniye pesni* (Home-Made Songs) (1923); *Gost' chudesnyy* (The Miraculous Guest) (1923); *Seryy barin* (The Gray Gentleman) (1926); *Talisman* (The Talisman) (1927); *Knyaz' mira* (The Prince of Peace) (1928); *V gostyakh u zhuravley* (A Visit with the Cranes) (1930); *Saraspan. Stikhotvoreniya. Obrabotki fol'klora i perevody* (Saraspan. Poems. Folklore Arrangements and Translations) (1936); *Madur Vaza - pobeditel'* (Madur Vaza the Conqueror) (1936), a free rendition of M. Plotnikov's poem 'Yangal - Maa'; *Died*: 21 Jan 1940 in imprisonment; posthumously rehabilitated.

KLYKOV, Nikolay Prokop'yevich (1861-1944) Artist; specialist in Mstyora miniatures; *Born*: 21 Mar 1861; *Career*: painted everyday scenes on papier-maché boxes, plates, etc; also took subjects from Russian folk songs and lit works; "Near the Town of Slavyansk" (1933-35); "Red Army Men in the Camps"; "Dubrovskiy" (1935); "The Kolkhoz Harvest"; "The Lumber Camp" (1936); "Russian Heroes" (1944), etc; excelled at typical Russian landscapes; *Died*: 9 Jan 1944.

KLYSHKO, N. K. (1880-1937) Govt official; CP member from 1904; *Born*: 1880; *Career*: from 1898 in the revol movement; often arrested and exiled; 1907 went to Britain; after Oct Revol returned to Russia and held govt, dipl and admin posts; dep head, State Publ House; RSFSR plen in Estonia; secr, Sov trade deleg in London; from 1923 head, Export Dept, Pop Comrt of For Trade; June 1924-June 1926 Sov trade rep in China; then worked for Supr Sovnarkhoz; 1937 head, Planning Dept, State Rubber Ind Trust; arrested by State Security organs; *Died*: 1937 in imprisonment.

KLYUCHNIKOV, Yu. V. (1886-1938) Lawyer; specialist in int law; *Born*: 1886; *Career*: prof, Moscow Univ; member, Constitutional Democratic Party; 1918 took part in Yaroslavl' uprising of Leftist Socialist-Revolutionaries; consultant and co-min, "Ufa Directorate", then Min of For Affairs, Kolchak's "Omsk Govt"; from 1919 in emigration; member, Paris Comt, Constitutional Democratic Party; 1921-22 contributed to emigre symposium *Smena vekh* and newspaper *Nakanune*; 1922 invited to advise Sov deleg at Genua Conference on questions of int law; 1923 returned to USSR, where he resumed teaching and research; arrested by State Security organs; *Died*: 1938 in imprisonment.

KLYUSS, Ivan Aleksandrovich (1899-1948) Mil surgeon; Dr of Med from 1946; lt-gen, Med Corps; specialist in org of mil med service; CP member from 1918; *Born*: 1899; *Educ*: 1927 grad Leningrad Mil Med Acad; *Career*: 1918 volunteered for Army after outbreak of Civil War; after grad postgrad student, then asst prof and assoc prof under V. A. Oppel"s at Mil Med Acad; from 1939 head, Chair of Field Surgery, Kuybyshev Mil Med Acad; served in Finno-Sov War as med corps commander; during WW 2 head, Med Bd, Karelian and 3rd Ukr Fronts; after war headed a chair at a med college; wrote 22 works on the org of the army med service and field surgery; *Publ*: ed, *Ocherki khirurgii voyny* (Studies of Field Surgery), etc; *Died*: 1948.

KLYUYEV, Leonid Lavrovich (1880-1943) Mil commander and instructor; officer, Russian Army Gen Staff; lt-gen, Sov Army from 1940; prof; CP member from 1919; *Born*: 4 Aug 1880 in Kazan', son of a craftsman; *Educ*: 1904 grad Kazan' Infantry College; grad Gen Staff Acad; *Career*: fought in Russo-Japanese War; 1914-17 commanded company, then senior adjutant, corps staff; after 1917 Oct Revol elected commander, 5th Army Corps; from 1918 in Red Army; 1918-19 head, Operations Bd, Staff of Southern Front; 1919 chief of staff, 10th Army; 26 May-28 Dec 1919 commander, 10th Army; June 1920-Feb 1921 chief of staff, Budyenny's 1st Cavalry Army; 1921-24 commandant, infantry school, then asst commandant, *Vystrel* Infantry Tactics Courses; 1924-30 worked for USSR Pop Comrt of Mil and Naval Affairs; from 1930 taught at higher educ establishments and Mil Chemical Acad; *Died*: 29 Jan 1943.

KLYUYEV, Nikolay Alekseyevich (1887-1937) Poet; *Born*: 1887 in Olonets Province, son of a peasant; *Educ*: educated by parents; *Career*: tramped through Russia and joined religious sect; his early works were written in the style of schismatic chants, religious verse and apocryphal writing; he then developed into a symbolist and led the "neo-rustic" movement in poetry (S. Yesenin, S. Klychkov, P. Oreshin); 1917-18 supported by "Scythian" group; adhered to ancient Russian values and opposed urbanism and Western cultural influences; held utopian views of future of Russian ("No communes without stove-couches") but welcomed certain aspects of the Revol; championed conservative Russian beliefs and institutions; was criticized for opposing course of history and interpreting the Revol from a patriarchal and religious viewpoint; influenced the early work of Yesenin and other "rustic" poets; arrested by State Security organs; early 1930's exiled to Siberia; *Publ*: verse collections: *Sosen perezvon* (The Ringing of the Pines) (1912); *Bratskiye pesni* (Fraternal Songs) (1912); *Pesnoslov* (Book of Songs) (1919); *Mednyy kit* (The Bronze Whale) (1919); *L'vinyy khleb* (Lion's Bread) (1922); *Chetvyortyy Rim* (The Fourth Rome) (1922); *Lenin* (1924); *Izba na pole* (The Hut in the Field) (1928); *Died*: 1937 in imprisonment while working on Siberian Railroad.

KLYUYEVA, Vera Nikolayevna (1894-1964) Russian philologist, translator and poetess; *Born*: 17 Mar 1894 in Mariupol, daughter of a teacher; *Educ*: grad Philology Fac, Kazan' Univ; *Career*: asst prof, Moscow Teachers' Training Inst of For Languages and Acad of Soc Sci; 1944-50 head, Russian Language Dept, Mongol Univ (Ulan Bator); member and lecturer, Org Comt, Int Seminar of Russian Language Teachers; *Publ*: collected verse *Akvareli* (Water Colors) (1920); translated poems of: Verhaeren in *Perevody* (Translations) (1921); Zakhida Iffat in *Zvezda Vostoka* (Star of the East) (1922); Heine in *Sobrannyye sochineniya* (Collected Works) (vol 2, 1957); published various Mongolian tales and articles on folklore: *Pevtsy, poety i pisateli Mongol'skoy Narodnoy Respubliki* (Bards, Poets and Writers of the Mongolian People's Republic) (1952); *Narodnoye tvorchestvo Mongolii* (The Folk Art of Mongolia) (1958); *Batarchinskiye skazy* (Batarchin Tales) (1959); *Serebryanoye derevo i desyat' tysyach let schast'ya* (The Silver Tree and Ten Thousand Years of Happiness) (1961); articles on language and style: *O yazyke romana M. Yu. Lermontova 'Geroy nashego vremeni'* (The Language of Lermontov's Novel "A Hero of Our Time"); *O stilisticheskom analize* (Analyzing Style) (1960); *Kratkiy slovar' sinonimov russkogo yazyka* (A Short Dictionary of Russian Synonyms) (1956); articles on lexicology in *Kratkaya literaturnaya entsiklopediya* (Short Literary Encyclopedia); workbook to *Vvedeniye v yazykoznaniye* (Introduction to Linguistics) (1962); helped write textbooks of Russian for foreigners: "Le russe vivant" (1962-64), etc; *Died*: 13 Feb 1964 in Moscow.

KNIGA, Vasiliy Ivanovich (1882-1961) Mil commander; major-gen from 1940; Civil War veteran; CP member from 1919; *Born*: 1882 in Stavropol' Province, son of a peasant; *Educ*: 1931-32 studied in special group (deserving, but semi-illiterate mil leaders) at Frunze Mil Acad; *Career*: from the age of nine farm laborer for landowner; 1905-08 private in Russian Army stationed at Kutaisi; 1914-17 private, sergeant and sergeant-major on Caucasian Front; 1917-18 mil comr and chm, Mil Revol Comt, Stavropol' Province; from 1918 in Red Army; 1918-19 commander, 4th Sov Stavropol' Cavalry Regt; 1919-21 brigade commander with 6th Cavalry Div, Budennyy's 1st Mounted Army; from 1921 various commands; during WW 2 commander, 6th Reserve Cavalry Brigade; from 1945 retired; *Awards*: Order of Lenin; four Orders of the Red Banner; medals; *Died*: 20 May 1961 in Stavropol'.

KNIPOVICH, Nikolay Mikhaylovich (1862-1939) Zoologist and ichthyologist; hon member, USSR Acad of Sci from 1935; Hon Sci and Tech Worker of RSFSR from 1935; dean of Sov school of ichthyology; *Born*: 6 Apr 1862 in Suomenlinna /Sveaborg/, son of a physician; *Educ*: 1886 grad Fac of Physics and Mathematics, Petersburg Univ; *Career*: 1887 imprisoned for involvement with D. N. Blagoyev's Soc-Democratic group and kept under police surveillance for five years after release; 1892 defended masters thesis on Ascothoracida; 1893 assoc prof, Petersburg Univ; fired for polit unreliability; 1894-1921 sci custodian, junior and senior zoologist, Zoological Museum (now Zoological Inst), Petersburg Acad of Sci; from 1898 vice-pres, Int Marine Research Council; 1911-30 prof, Chair of Zoology and Gen Biology, Women's (1st Leningrad) Med Inst; 1921 commissioned by Lenin to take part in talks with Finland; 1927-35 corresp member, USSR Acad of Sci; helped to organize Sov fishing ind; organized and led numerous oceanological expeditions: 1898-1901 in the Sea of Murmansk, for which the world's first oceanographic vessel, the *Andrey Pervozvannyy*, was built; 1886, 1904, 1912-13 and 1914-15 in the Caspian Sea; 1902 in the Baltic Sea; 1922-27 in the Sea of Azov and the Black Sea; 1931-32 led the All-Caspian Expedition; organized and took active part in numerous sci commissions and conferences; helped found various marine research inst; apart from sci works wrote numerous pop-sci books; *Publ*: master's thesis *Materialy k poznaniyu gruppy Ascothoracida* (Material on the Recognition of Ascothoracida) (1892); *Nauchno-promyslovyye issledovaniya u Murmanskogo Berega* (Research on the Fishery Potential of the Coastal Waters of the Sea of Murmansk) (1897); *Osnovy gidrologii Yevropeyskogo Ledovitogo okeana* (The Principles of the Hydrology of the European Part of the Arctic Ocean) (1906); *Gidrologicheskiye issledovaniya v Kaspiyskom more 1914-15 goda* (Hydrological Research in the Caspian Sea, 1914-15) (1921); *Kaspiyskoye more i yego promysly* (The Caspian Sea and Its Fishing Grounds); *Ocherk prirody i promyslov russkikh morey* (The Nature and Fishing Grounds of the Russian Seas) (1923); *Opredelitel' ryb Chyornogo i Azovskogo morey* (A Classification Key to the Fish of the Black Sea and the Sea of Azov) (1923); *Kurs obshchey zoologii* (A General Zoology Course) (1924); *Opredelitel' ryb morey Barentsova, Belogo i Karskogo* (A Classification Key to the Fish of the Barents Sea, the White Sea and the Kara Sea) (1926); *Opredelitel'nyye tablitsy morskikh i prokhodnykh ryb Yevropeyskogo Ledovitogo okeana i morey Belogo i Karskogo* (Classification Tables of the Indigenous and Transient Fish of the European Part of the Arctic Ocean and the White and Kara Seas) (1926); *Gidrologicheskiye issledovaniya v Azovskom more* (Hydrological Research in the Sea of Azov) (1932); *Gidrologicheskiye issledovaniya v Chyornom more* (Hydrological Research in the Black Sea) (1932); *Gidrologiya morey i solonovatykh vod v primenenii k promyslovomu delu* (Marine and Salt-Water Hydrology Applied to Fishery) (1938); *Died*: 23 Feb 1939 in Leningrad.

KNIPPER-CHEKHOVA, Ol'ga Leonardovna (1868-1959) Actress; Pop Artiste of USSR from 1937; wife of Anton Chekhov from 1901; *Born*: 21 Sept 1868 in Glazov, daughter of an eng; *Educ*: 1898 grad College of Music and Drama, Moscow Philharmonic Soc; *Career*: 1898 invited by her teacher V. I. Nemirovich-Danchenko to join newly-created Moscow Arts Theater, where she immediately became a star performer; *Roles*: Princess Irina in A. K. Tolstoy's *Tsar Fyodor Ioannovich* (1898); Arkadina, Yelena Andreyevna, Anna Petrovna, Masha and Ranevskaya in Chekhov's *Chayka* (The Seagull) (1898), *Dyadya Vanya* (Uncle Vanya) (1899), *Ivanov* (1904), *Tri sestry* (Three Sisters) (1901) and *Vishnyovyy sad* (The Cherry Orchard) (1904); Yelena Krivtsova, Nastya, Melaniya and Polina Bardina in Gorky's *Meshchane* (The Philistines) (1902), *Na dne* (The Lower Depths) (1902), *Deti solntsa* (Children of the Sun) (1905) and *Vragi* (The Enemies) (1935); Nataliya Petrovna in Turgenev's *Mesyats v derevne* (A Month in the Country) (1909); *Anna Andreyevna* in Gogol's *Revizor* (The Government Inspector) (1908); Belina in Molière's "Le Malade Imaginaire" (1913); Khlyostovaya in Griboyedov's *Gore ot uma* (Woe From Wit) (1925); Nadezhda L'vovna in V. V. Ivanov's *Bronepoyezd 14-69* (Armored Train 14-69) (1927); Mar'ya Aleksandrovna in *Dyadyushkin son* (Uncle's Dream) (1929) after Dostoevsky; Countess Charskaya in *Voskreseniye* (Resurrection) (1930) after L. N. Tolstoy; Madame Pernelle in Molière's "Tartuffe" (1939), etc; *Publ*: coauthor, *O Stanislavskom. Sbornik vospominaniy* (Stanislavskiy. An Anthology of Reminiscences) (1948); *Awards*: Order of Lenin; two Orders of the Red Banner of Labor; Stalin Prize (1943); medals; *Died*: 22 Mar 1959 in Moscow.

KNORIN, Vil'gel'm Georgiyevich (1890-1939) Lat Party official; Party historian; Dr of History from 1935; CP member from 1910; *Born*: Aug 1890, son of a poor Lat peasant; *Educ*: 1910 grad Valmiyer Teachers' Training College; *Career*: from 1910 Party propaganda work in Lat; from 1914 in army on Western Front, where he helped to found Bolshevik orgs; from May 1917 member, Minsk RSDRP(B) Comt; secr, then dep chm, Minsk Sov; from Nov 1917 member, Northwestern Oblast RSDRP(B) Comt; member, Mil Revol Comt, Northwestern Oblast (Bel) and Front; at the same time ed, newspaper *Zvezda*; 1918 in Smolensk as secr, Northwestern Oblast CPSU(B) Comt; then comr, Northwestern Mil Distr; also ed, newspaper *Zapadnaya kommuna*; 1919-20 member, Centr Bureau, CP(B) Bel; secr, Centr Bureau, CP(B) Lat and Bel; then one of the three members, Bel Mil-Revol Comt; 1920-22 first secr, CC, CP(B) Bel; 1922-26 head, Dept of Information, CC, CPSU(B); then head, Dept of Agitation and Propaganda, CC, CPSU(B); 1927-28 first secr, CC, CP(B) Bel; 1928-31 chm, Exec Comt, Comintern; 1931-35 member, Polit Secretariat, then head, Centr European Secretariat, Comintern; then chief ed, journal *Kommunisticheskiy Internatsional*; from 1932 simultaneously dir, Inst of Party History of the Red Professorate and member, ed bd, newspaper *Pravda*; 1935-37 dep head, Dept of Agitation and Propaganda, CC, CPSU(B); member, ed bd, journal *Bol'shevik*; wrote about the history of the CP(B) Bel, the CPSU(B) and the Comintern; 1937 arrested by State Security organs; *Publ: Revolyutsiya i kontrrevolyutsiya v Belorussii* (Revolution and Counterrevolution in Belorussia) (1920); *Pyat' let. Kratkiy konspekt k istorii KP(b) Belorussii* (Five Years. A Short Summary of the History of the Communist Party [Bolsheviks] of Belorussia) (1922); *1917 god v Belorussii i na Zapadnom fronte* (1917 in Belorussia and on the Western Front) (1925); *V period mezhdu nemetskoy i pol'skoy okkupatsiyami* (The Period Between the German and Polisch Occupations)(1927); *Zametki k istorii diktatury proletariata v Belorussii* (Notes on the History of the Dictatorship of the Proletariat in Belorussia) (1934); ed, *Kratkaya istorya VKP(b)* (A Short History of the All-Union Communist Party [Bolsheviks]) (1934); coauthor, *Istoriya VKP(b). Populyarnyy ocherk* (A History of the All-Union Communist Party [Bolsheviks]. A Popular Study) (1935), etc; *Awards*: Order of the Red Banner (1928); *Died*: 1939 in imprisonment; posthumously rehabilitated.

KNUSHEVITSKIY, Svyatoslav Nikolayevich (1908-1963) Cellist; prof, Moscow Conservatory from 1950; Hon Art Worker of RSFSR from 1956; *Born*: 6 Jan 1908; *Educ*: 1936 grad cello class, Moscow Conservatory; *Career*: 1929-43 orchestral soloist; 1931-36 with quartet of USSR State Acad Bolshoy Theater; 1940-50 lecturer, Moscow Conservatory; from 1941 performed with sonata ensemble; gave concerts in Czechoslovakia, Finland, Sweden, Belgium, Hungary, Austria, France, Britain, Iran, etc; *Awards*: First Prize at All-Union Competition of Performing Musicians (1933); Stalin Prize (1950); *Died*: 19 Feb 1963.

KNYAZEV, Vasiliy Vasil'yevich (1887-1937) Russian poet; *Born*: 18 Jan 1887 in Tyumen', son of a merchant; *Career*: 1905 first work published in satirical leaflets and journals; wrote revol songs and ballads, but was mainly a satirist and author of fables, parodies, fairy tales and topical folk ballads; his verse appeared in *Zvezda* and *Pravda*; wrote satire exposing the evils of the time: collection *Satiricheskiye pesni* (Satirical Songs) (1910) and *Dvunogiye bez per'yev* (Two-Legged Without Feathers) (1914); collected proverbs and topical folk ballads, book *Zhizn' molodoy derevni. Chastushki-korotushki S.-Peterburgskoy gubernii* (The Life of Young Villagers. Folk Ballads of Saint Petersburg Province) (1913); used folklore genres in his verse, i.e. facetious sayings, intoned verse, and songs as in the cycle *Podpitershchina* (Around and About Saint Petersburg) (1915); after 1917 Oct Revol contributed to *Krasnaya zvezda*; such verse as "Alarum of the Red Bell Ringer," "Songs of the Red Poet," "Feuilletons of Sofronov's Grandson from Velikiye Luki," "Talks with Grandfather Nefed," etc, appeared almost daily in *Krasnaya zvezda*; during the defense of Petrograd Knyazev joined the Red Guards, went with a mobile propaganda unit to the front and worked for *Boyevaya pravda*; verse from the collections *Krasnoye Yevangeliye* (The Red Gospel) (1918), *Krasnyye zvony i pesni* (Red Chimes and Songs) (1918), *Pesni Krasnogo zvonarya* (Songs of the Red Bell Ringer) (1919) and *O chyom pel kolokol* (What the Bell Sang) (1920) were set to music ("Song of the Commune": "Never, Never, Never! Never Will Communards Be Slaves..." [1919], etc) and translated into for languages; 1924 published anthology *Kaplya krovi Il'icha* (A Drop of Il'ich's Blood); in 1920's and 1930's contributed to periodicals, published collections of new topical folk ballads and worked on *Poslovichnaya entiklopediya* (An Encyclopedia of Proverbs), part of which he published in the anthologies *Rus'* (1924) and *Kniga poslovits* (A Book of Proverbs) (1930); 1934, under pseudonym Ivan Sedykh, published novel *Dedy* (Grandfathers) about the life of Siberian merchants; arrested by State Security organs; *Publ: Kniga izbrannykh stikhotvoreniy* (A Book of Selected Poems) (1930); *Poslednyaya kniga stikhov 1918-30* (The Last Book of Verse, 1918-30) (1933); *Za chetvert' veka 1905-30* (A Quarter Century, 1905-30) (1935); *Izbrannoye* (Selected Works) (1959); *Died*: 10 Nov 1937 in Kolyma, in imprisonment; posthumously rehabilitated.

KOBER, Shura (Aleksandr Pavlovich) (1926-1942) Partisan; *Born*: 5 Nov 1926 in Nikolayev, son of a worker; *Educ*: 1941 grad secondary school; *Career*: after German occupation of Nikolayev helped distribute Sov Information Bureau communiques among population; then joined Nikolayev underground org and worked as messenger and scout; spring 1942 crossed front lines with message for partisan headquarters in Moscow; after returning to Nikolayev continued working for underground until it was discovered and its members arrested by German occupation authorities; *Died*: 5 Dec 1942 executed in Nikolayev along with other resistance workers; monument erected to him in Nikolayev by Ukr Pioneers.

KOBETSKIY, Mikhail Veniaminovich (1881-1937) Party and govt official; diplomat; CP member from 1903; *Born*: 1881; *Career*: worked for RSDRP org in Petersburg, Baku, Kursk and Yekaterinoslav; frequently arrested and imprisoned by Tsarist police; 1908 emigrated to Denmark and organized dispatch of Bolshevik newspaper *Proletariy* and RSDRP centr organ *Sotsial-Demokrat* to Russia; forwarded correspondence for Lenin from Russia; 1917 returned to Russia; 1917-18 worked at machine-gun works in Kovrov; from 1919 worked for Comintern; 1920-21 secr, 1921-23 dep head, Comintern Exec Comt; 1924 Sov plen in Est; 1924-33 Sov plen in Denmark; 1933 USSR Pop Comrt of For Affairs plen with Transcaucasian SFSR Council of Pop Comr; arrested by State Security organs; *Died*: 1937 in imprisonment.

KOBEYEV, Spandiyar (1878-1956) Kaz writer and teacher; CP member from 1940; *Born*: 13 Oct 1878 in Turgay Oblast, now Kustanay Oblast, Kaz SSR; *Educ*: grad Russo-Kaz school and teachers' training courses in Kustanay; *Career*: 1901 began teaching; popularized Russian lit in Kaz with public recitations of Pushkin, Gogol and Chekhov; Hon Teacher of Kaz SSR; dep, Kaz Supr Sov; *Publ*: translation of Krylov's fables "A Model Translation" (1910); reader "An Exemplary Boy" (1912); novel "The Ransom" (1913); memoirs "Dreams Come True" (1951); *Awards*: two Orders of Lenin; *Died*: 2 Dec 1956.

KOBOZEV, Pyotr Alekseyevich (1878-1941) Govt official; CP member from 1898; *Born*: 1878; *Educ*: 1904 grad Riga Polit Inst; *Career*: took part in student polit movement; 1898 arrested for revol activities and exiled to Riga; until 1914 worked in Riga as an eng; active in Riga Bolshevik Org; member, Riga RSDRP Comt; 1905-07 worked for Bolshevik newspaper *Golos soldata*; 1914 exiled to Orenburg; helped found Orenburg Bolshevik Comt; 1915 worked on construction of Murmansk Railroad; May 1917 summoned by Party to Petrograd and elected member, Petrograd City Council; Nov 1917-Feb 1918 directed operations against Ataman Dutov's army as special comr for Orenburg-Turgay Oblast; 1918 special comr for Western Siberia and Centr Asia; RSFSR Pop Comr of Means of Communications; chm, Revol Mil Council of Eastern Front; 1919 member, Turkestani Commission, All-Union Centr Exec Comt and RSFSR Council of Pop Comr; 1919-20 Collegium member, Pop Comrt of Peasants and Workers' Inspection; fought in Civil War on the Southern Front; 1922-23 chm, Far Eastern Republ Council of Min; from 1923 rector, prof and dept head, Moscow Survey Inst (later Moscow Inst of Geodesy, Aerial Photography and Cartography Eng); *Died*: 1941.

KOBYAKOV, Vasiliy Andreyevich (1906-1937) Khakass writer; *Born*: 1906 in vil Fyrkal, Minusinsk Province, son of a shepherd; *Career*: in 1920's worked in provincial theater; promoted publ of books in Khakass language in Novosibirsk and Abakan; pioneer of Khakass lit; guided by song traditions, he wrote many popular poems; novelette *Aydo* (1934), stories and essays are first works of Khakass narrative prose; translated and popularized Russian lit; also wrote textbooks; arrested by State Security organs; *Died*: 1937 in imprisonment; posthumously rehabilitated.

KOBYLYANSKAYA, Ol'ga Yulianovna (1863-1942) Ukr writer; member, USSR Writers' Union from 1940; *Born*: 27 Nov 1863 in Gura Gumora, Kimpolung Uyezd, Southern Bukovina; *Educ*: completed German-language grade school; *Career*: in 1880's began to write (at first in German); 1890's first work published; *Publ: Chelovek* (The Human Being) (1894); *On in Ona* (He and She) (1895); *Tsarevna* (1896); *Pokornost'* (Obedience) (1898); *Chto ya lyubil* (What I Loved) (1896); *Impromtu phantasie* (1894); "Valse mélancolique" (1894); novelettes *Cherez mostki* (Across Little Bridges) (1911); *V poiskakh situatsiy* (In Search of Situations) (1913); stories *U svyatogo Ivana* (With Saint John) (1896); *Nekul'turnaya* (The Uncultured Woman) (1896); *Sel'skiy bank* (The Rural Bank) (1895); *Na polyakh* (In the Fields) (1898); novel *Zemlya* (The Land) (1902); poetic novelette *V voskresen'ye utrom zel'ye kopala...* (On Sunday Morning She Dug for a Potion) (1909) based on the Ukr folk song "Oh, Don't Go to the Party, Gritsya"; stories: *Iuda* (Judas) (1915); *Navstrechu sud'be* (To Meet Fate) (1915); *Pis'mo osuzhdyonnogo soldata k svoyey zhene* (A Condemned Soldier's Letter to His Wife); *Soshyol s uma* (Gone Mad) (1923), etc; novelette *Volchikha* (The She-Wolf) (1923); *Sochineniya* (Works) (9 vol, 1927-29); *Sochineniya* (Works) (3 vol, 1956); *Sochineniya* (Works) (5 vol, 1962-63); *Izbrannoye* (Selected Works) (1953); *Died*: 21 Mar 1942 in Chernovtsy; 1944 Kobylyanskaya Memorial Museum opened in Chernovtsy.

KOCHAR (real name: GABRIYELYAN, Rachiya Kocharovich), Rachiya (1910-1965) Arm writer; member, Arm Writers' Union; CP member from 1939; *Born*: 2 Feb 1910 in vil Kumplipuchi, Alashker Rayon, Western Arm; *Career*: 1931 first work published; 1954 at 17th Congress of CP Arm elected member, CC, CP Arm; *Publ*: novelette *Vagan Vardyan* (1939); humorous novel *Ogsen Vaspur's Journey* (1937); novel "Children of a Large House" (1952); collected stories: "The Birth of Heroes" (1942); "On the Eve" (1943); "A Sacred Oath" (1946); lit criticism "Literature and Life" (1949), etc; in Russian translation: *Frontovyye ocherki* (Essays from the Front) (1944); *Rasskazy* (Stories) (1950); film script *Severnaya raduga* (The Northern Rainbow) (1959), etc; *Died*: 3 May 1965 in Yerevan.

KOCHERGA, Ivan Antonovich (1881-1952) Ukr playwright; Hon Art Worker of Ukr SSR from 1950; *Born*: 6 Oct 1881 in vil Nosovka near Nezhin, son of railroad official; *Educ*: 1903 grad Law Fac, Kiev Univ; *Career*: began lit career as journalist; from 1903 worked in offices in Chernigov and Zhitomir; from 1917 worked for Workers and Peasants' Inspection in Zhitomir; then worked for local newspaper; active in Ukr Union of Sov Writers and Comt on Art Affairs; 1941 ed, journal *Teatr*; 1941-45 ed, newspaper *Literatura i iskusstvo*; *Publ: Pesnya v bokale* (Song in a Goblet) (1910); *Devushka s myshkoy* (The Girl with the Mouse); *Polchasa lyubvi* (A Half-Hour of Love); *Feya gor'kogo mindalya* (The Bitter Almond Fairy) (1926); *Almaznyy zhyornov* (The Diamond Millstone) (1927); *Svad'ba Svichki* (Svichka's Wedding) (1931); *Marko v adu* (Marko in Hell) (1928); *O chyom poyot rozh'?* (What Sings the Rye?); *Natura i kul'tura* (Nature and Culture) (1928-1931); *Chasovshchik i kuritsa* (The Watchmaker and the Hen); *Mastera vremeni* (Masters of Time) (1933); *Poydyosh' - ne vernyosh'sya* (If You Go, You Won't Return) (1936); *Imya* (The Name) (1937); *Chornyy val's* (The Black Waltz) (1937); *Vybor* (The Selection) (1938); *Ekzamen po anatomii* (The Anatomy Examination) (1940); *Chasha* (The Cup) (1942); *Nochnaya trevoga* (Night Alarm) (1943); *Kitayskiy flakon* (The Chinese Flacon) (1944); *Yaroslav Mudryy* (Yaroslav the Wise) (1946); *Istina* (The Truth) (1947); *Prorok* (The Prophet) (1948), etc; *Awards*: Stalin Prize (1947); two Orders of Red Banner of Labor; *Died*: 29 Dec 1952 in Kiev.

KOCHERIN, Dmitriy Illarionovich (1889-1928) Hydrologist; *Born*: 1889; *Educ*: 1915 grad Petrograd Polytech Inst; *Career*: from 1923 worked for Main Electr Eng Ind Bd, USSR Supr

Sovnarkhoz; from 1928 at Moscow's Timiryazev Agric Acad; 1927 compiled first maps of European USSR showing mean annual flow, surface evaporation from river basins and mean annual flow factors; devised modular coefficients for calculating the flow of rivers and devised a method for calculating the fluctuation in mean annual passage of water; collated and processed data on 178 snow- and torrent-conditioned maximum river flows and worked out their qualitative and quantitative characteristics; *Died*: 1928.

KOCHETOV, Nikolay Razumnikovich (1864-1925) Musicologist, composer and conductor; *Born*: 8 July 1864 in Oranienbaum, son of A. D. Aleksandrova-Kochetova, a prof at Moscow Conservatory; *Educ*: 1889 grad Law Fac, Moscow Univ; studied music under G. A. Larosh; *Career*: 1886 began writing music reviews for newspapers *Moskovskiye vedomosti* and *Moskovskiy listok,* the journal *Artist,* etc; also conducted opera and symphony orchestras; after advent of Sov rule worked for Music Dept, RSFSR Pop Comrt of Educ; 1921 co-founder, State Inst of Musicology; taught at Moscow Conservatory, etc; *Works*: "Arab Suite" (1888); two symphonies (1894, 1911); opera *Strashnaya mest'* (Terrible Vengeance) (1901); choral pieces "May 1 March" (1919) and "Hammer and Sickle" (1922); piano concerto (1922); romances, etc; *Publ: Ocherk istorii muzyki* (An Outline History of Music) (1909); *Vokal'naya tekhnika i yeyo znacheniye* (Vocal Technique and Its Importance) (1930), etc; *Died*: 3 Jan 1925.

KOCHIN, Nikolay Yevgrafovich (1901-1944) Mathematician; specialist in mech; member, USSR Acad of Sci from 1939; *Born*: 19 May 1901; *Educ*: 1923 grad Petrograd Univ; *Career*: 1919 drafted into Red Army while still a student; fought against Yudenich and Kronstadt rebels; 1924-34 taught at Leningrad Univ; 1923 demonstrated that a compressible liquid can be moved by conservative forces and form vortices without an external energy source; 1924 solved equations for the movement of compressible liquids on the rotating Earth; 1924-25 did research on shockwaves from explosions in compressible liquids; 1931 determined the conditions of the formation of a cyclone wave from air masses at the interface; 1933-34 dir, Inst of Theoretical Meteorology; 1935 devised method of determining the pole of the velocities and pressures of air masses attracted by the rotating Earth, taking into account viscosity and non-uniform atmospheric temperature; 1936 on the basis of this method developed model of zonal atmospheric circulation; 1937 devised general method of solving plane problem of a submerged hydrofoil and formula for the resistance of a ship's body; 1938-44 taught at Moscow Univ; 1939-44 also head, Mech Dept, Inst of Mech, USSR Acad of Sci; 1941-44 provided first strict solutions for a wing of finite span; also did research on pure mathematics and theoretical mech; wrote numerous works, including textbooks on hydromech and vector calculus; co-authored a monograph on dynamic meteorology and edited the posthumous memoirs of A. M. Lyapunov and I. A. Lappo-Danilevskiy; *Publ: Ob odnom sluchaye adiabaticheskogo dvizheniya* (A Case of Adiabatic Motion) (1923);-*Opredeleniye tochnogo vida voln konechnoy amplitudy na poverkhnosti razdela dvukh zhidkostey konechnoy glubiny* (Determining the Exact Form of a Wave of Finite Amplitude at the Interface of Two Liquids of Finite Depth) (1928); *Ob ustoychivosti poverkhnosti razryva Margulesa* (The Stability of Margules' Surface of Separation) (1931); *Ob uskorenii liniy razryva i poverkhnostey razryva v atmosfere* (The Acceleration of Lines and Surfaces of Separation in the Atmosphere) (1932); *K teorii voln Koshi-Puasson* (Cauchy and Poisson's Wave Theory) (1935); *O volnovom soprotivlenii i pod'yomnoy sile pogruzhennykh v zhidkosti tel* (The Wave Resistance and Buoyancy of Submerged Bodies) (1937); *Teorii voln, vynuzhdayemykh kolebaniyami tela pod svobodnoy poverkhnost'yu tyazhyoloy neszhimayemoy zhidkosti* (The Theory of Waves Induced by the Oscillations of a Body Under the Free Surface of a Heavy Incompressible Liquid) (1940); *Died*: 31 Dec 1944.

KOCHUBEY, Anton Danilovich (1911-1966) Govt official; Dep chm, Ukr Council of Min; chm, Ukr Gosplan from 1963; member, CC, CP Ukr from 1965; CP member from 1942; *Born*: 1911 in vil Komendantovka, now Poltava Oblast; *Educ*: 1933 grad Kiev Finance and Econ Inst; *Career*: 1936-38 worked for Ukr Pop Comrt of Finance; 1938-40 in Sov Army; 1940-41 exec work for Ukr Council of Pop Comr; 1941-45 in Sov Army; 1945-54 exec work for Ukr Council of Min; 1954-57 dep chm, Ukr Gosplan; 1957-61 inspector, CC, CP Ukr; then dept head, Ukr Gosplan; 1961-63 first dep chm, Ukr Gosplan; 1960-61 headed Ukr deleg to UN European Econ Commission in Geneva; 1961-65 cand member, CC, CP Ukr; dep, Ukr Supr Sov of 1963 convocation; *Died*: 14 Dec 1966.

KOCHUBEY, Ivan Antonovich (1893-1919) Kuban' Cossack; Civil War veteran; *Born*: 25 July 1893 at Roshchinskiy farmstead, Kuban' Oblast, son of a Cossack; *Career*: during WW 1 active service on the Caucasian Front; early 1918 founded Red Guard mounted squad which he led in numerous battles against White troops in the Northern Caucasus, then commanded 3rd Kuban' Cavalry Brigade, 11th Army; brave and resolute commander with excellent command of partisan tactics; Feb 1919 the 11th Army was disbanded because of demoralization by order of the Revol Mil Comt of the Caspian-Caucasian Front; the 3rd Kuban' Cavalry Brigade was hereby also subject to disbandment, but Kochubey refused to carry out the order for which he was relieved of his command and his brigade disarmed; tried to get to Prikum'ye to found a partisan detachment but was captured by the Whites and refused to side with them; *Died*: 4 Apr 1919 hanged in Svyatoy Krest (now Prikumsk, Stavropol' Kray).

KOCHUROV, Yuriy Vladimirovich (1907-1952) Composer and music teacher; *Born*: 24 June 1907 in Saratov; *Educ*: 1931 grad Leningrad Conservatory; *Career*: from 1947 instructor, Leningrad Conservatory; *Works*: cantata for the 15th anniversary of the 1917 Oct Revol (1932); prelude "In Memory of Pushkin" (1937); "Heroic Aria" for voice and orchestra (1942); "Song of Leningrad" for soloist, choir and orchestra (1943); aria "The Fortress City" (1943); symphony "Macbeth" (1948); completed Tchaikovsky's opera *Voyevod* (The General) (1949) and Glinka's "Etudes" for voice and piano (1950); "Petrarch's Sonnets" for voice and organ (1951); sonata for cello and piano; some 40 romances: "The Dedication," "The Joy of Life," "Spring," "After the Rain," "Love," "The Source," etc; 34 songs and folksong arrangements; stage music for *Zapadnya* (The Trap) (1934), after Zola; *Gore ot uma* (Woe from Wit) (1941); Brushteyn's "Tristan and Isolda" (1947); "Boris Godunov" (1949); music for the films: *Padshiy angel* (The Fallen Angel) (1933); *Sokrovishcha pogibshego korablya* (The Treasure of the Sunken Ship) (1935); *Yunost' poeta* (The Poet as a Young Man) (1937); *Vragi* (The Foes) (1938); "Professor Mamlok" (1938); "Aleksander Popov" (1949), etc; *Awards*: Stalin Prize (1952); *Died*: 22 May 1952 in Leningrad.

KODZHOYAN, Akop Karapetovich (Gerasimovich) (1883-1959) Graphic artist and painter; Pop Artist of Arm SSR from 1935; *Born*: 1 Dec 1883, son of a master engraver and chaser; *Educ*: 1900-07 studied art in Moscow and Munich; *Career*: although a versatile artist, he displayed special talent for book-illustration and graphic art; 1918-20 painted polit posters and worked as a cartoonist and sketcher; 1922-55 also taught art; *Works*: portrait *David Sasunskiy* (1922); illustrations for the legnd *Azaran Blbul* (1925); designs for Gorky's *Skazki i legendy* (Fairy-Tales and Legends) (1933); *Sayat Nova* (1945); "Armenian Tales" (1954); illustrations for S. Zoryan's fairy-tales (1957); *Awards*: two Orders of the Red Banner of Labor (one in 1956); *Died*: 24 Apr 1959.

KOGAN, Boris Borisovich (BERKOVICH, Borukh) (1896-1967) Internist; Dr of Med from 1939; prof from 1939; Hon Sci Worker of RSFSR from 1960; CP member from 1917; *Born*: 1896 in Zhitomir, son of a med orderly; *Educ*: 1923 grad Med Fac, 1st Moscow Univ; *Career*: 1917-19 did Party work in Ukr; chm, Zhitomir RSDRP(B) Comt; deleg All-Russian RCP(B) Conference and 9th RCP(B) Congress; 1923-31 intern and asst prof, Moscow Inst of Soc and Occupational Diseases; 1931-39 consultant, intern, asst prof, then assoc prof, Chair of Hospital Therapy Clinic, 1st Moscow Med Inst; 1939-67 dept head, Chair of Hospital Therapy Clinic, 1st Moscow Med Inst at Moscow Clinical Hospital Nr 67; bd member, All-Russian and Moscow Sci Therapists' Soc; Presidium member, All-Russian Cardiological Soc; member, Learned Med Council, RSFSR Min of Health; 1930-40 co-founder and dep chm, All-Union Therapists' Soc; dep ed, journal *Terapevticheskiy arkhiv*; co-ed, internal diseases section, *Bol'shaya meditsinskaya entsiklopediya* (Large Medical Encyclopedia) (2nd ed) and *Malaya meditsinskaya entsiklopediya* (Small Medical Encyclopedia); delivered papers at 13th-15th All-Union and 1st-2nd All-Russian Therapists' Congresses; 1960 also delivered paper at Int Congress on Diseases of the Thoracic Organs, Vienna; devised original classification of allergies and chronic pulmonary heart; 1944 hypothesized the existence of hypertony of the pulmonary circulatory system as an independent nosological unit; 1954 described the intra vitam diagnosis and clinical aspects of subacute pulmonary heart and devised rational therapy; 1958 introduced "euphylline test" to clinical practice; did major research on the histological substratum in bronchial asthma before and after an attack; wrote over 140 works on the history of med, soc hygiene, occupational diseases, internal diseases, etc; *Publ*: *Byt rabochey molodyozhi* (The Way of Life of Young Workers) (1929); *Uchebnik professional'nykh bolezney* (A Textbook on Occupational Diseases); *Uchebnik terapii vnutrennikh bolezney* (A Textbook on the Treatment of Internal Diseases); *Gemodinamika pri lyogochnom serdtse* (The Hemodynamics of Pulmonary Heart) (1949); *Bronkhial'naya astma* (Bronchial Asthma) (1950); *Klinika infarkta miokarda, oslozhnennogo anevrizmoy serdtsa* (The Clinical Aspects of Myocardial Infarct Complicated by Cardiac Aneurysm) (1958); coauthor, *Klinicheskaya fiziologiya khronicheskogo lyogochnogo serdtsa* (The Clinical Physiology of Chronic Pulmonary Heart); *Awards*: Order of the Red Banner of Labor (1965); other orders and medals; *Died*: 14 Nov 1967 suddenly in the performance of his duties.

KOGAN, Pyotr Semyonovich (1872-1932) Jewish lit critic and historian; specialist in West European and Russian lit; *Born*: 20 May 1872 in Lida, now Bel SSSR, son of a physician; *Educ*: grad Moscow Univ; *Career*: from 1900, after passing master's examination at Petersburg Univ, retained as assoc prof, Chair of Germanic and Romance Philology; also lectured at Higher Women's Courses; after 1917 Oct Revol worked for Pop Comrt of Educ; prof, Moscow Univ; from 1921 pres, State Acad of Arts; *Publ*: *Ocherki po istorii zapadnoyevropeyskoy literatury* (An Outline History of West European Literature) (3 vol, 1903-10); *Ocherki po istorii drevnikh literatur* (An Outline History of Ancient Literatures) (vol 1, 1907); *Ocherki po istorii noveyshey russkoy literatury* (An Outline History of Modern Russian Literature) (3 vol, 1908-12); *Istorya russkoy literatury s drevneyshikh vremyon do nashikh dney* (The History of Russian Literature from Ancient Times to the Present) (1928); *Lev Tolstoy i marksistskaya kritika* (Lev Tolstoy and Marxist Criticism) (1928); *Ocherki po istorii zapadno-yevropeyskogo teatra* (An Outline History of West European Theater) (1934), etc; *Died*: 2 May 1932.

KOGAN, Ye. S. (1886-1938) Party and govt official; CP member from 1907; *Born*: 1886; *Career*: did Party work in Uman', Odessa, Yekaterinoslav, Kiev, Khar'kov and Samara; after 1917 Feb Revol member, Samara RSDRP(B) Comt, then secr, Samara Province RSDRP(B) Comt; member, Exec Comt, Samara Sov of Workers and Soldiers' Dep; deleg, 6th RSDRP(B) Congress; after 1917 Oct Revol held a variety of Party and govt posts; 1934 elected to Auditing Commission at 17th CPSU(B) Congress; arrested by State Security organs; *Died*: 1938 in imprisonment.

KOGAN-YASNYY, Viktor Moiseyevich (1889-1958) Therapist; Dr of Med from 1924; prof from 1930; Hon Sci Worker of RSFSR from 1941; *Born*: 16 July 1889 in Poltava; *Educ*: 1913 grad Med Fac, Khar'kov Univ; *Career*: 1919 founded Organotherapy Inst (later Ukr Inst of Endocrinology); 1924 defended doctor's thesis on the preparation, physiological effects and applications of insulin; from 1930 founder-dir first Sov Endocrinological Inst; from 1930 also prof, Chair of Gen Therapy, then head, Chair of Fac and Hospital Therapy, Khar'kov Med Inst; 1931 founded Ukr Nutrition Inst; obtained first Sov insulin samples at V. Ya. Danilevskiy's laboratory; specialized in endocrine diseases, especially diabetes and Basedow's disease, metabolic disturbances in certain diseases, hypertony, ulcers, pneumonia, etc; proposed the use of insulin-glucose for treating pneumonia; wrote 175 works on internal med and endocrinology and edited numerous textbooks and symposia; co-founder and exec ed, journal *Vrachebnove delo*; co-ed, internal diseases section, *Bol'shaya meditsinskaya entsiklopediya* (Large Medical Encyclopedia); *Publ*: doctor's thesis *Nekotoryye dannyye ob insuline: yego podgotovleniye i primeneniye* (Data on Insulin: Its Preparation and Application) (1923); coauthor, *Osnovy terapii ta likuval'noy profilaktyky* (The Principles of Therapy and Medical Prophylaxis) (3 vol, 1934); *Siflis endokrinnykh zhelez* (Syphilis of the Endocrine Glands) (1939); *Diabet* (The Diabetic) (1945); *Sovremennyye predstavleniya o lechenii razlichnykh form gipertonii* (Modern Concepts of the Treatment of Different Forms of Hypertony) (1949); *Nasha kontseptsiya ob etiologii i patogeneze gipertonicheskoy bolezni v svete Pavlovskogo ucheniya* (Our Conception of the Etiology and Pathogenesis of Hypertony in the Light of Pavlovian Theory) (1950); *Nekotoryye kliniko-eksperimental'nyye dannyye o kortiko-vistseral'nykh faktorakh pri gipertonii i yazvennoy bolezni* (Clinical and Experimental Data on the Cortico-Visceral Factors in Hypertony and Ulcers) (1952); *Sakharnaya bolezn'* (Sugar Diabetes) (1957); *Died*: 20 July 1958 in Khar'kov.

KOKOVIKHIN, Mikhail Nikolayevich (1883-1965) Party official; CP member from 1903; *Born*: 23 Jan 1883, son of a peasant; *Career*: 1904 member, Soc-Democratic mil org, Brest-Litovsk Fortress; 1907-09 helped lead Min'yar Soc-Democratic org; arrested several times by Tsarist authorities; 1910 exiled to Astrakhan' Province; 1913 returned to Min'yar and headed Soc-Democratic org; from 1914 revol work among soldiers in Ufa, then in Grodno; dep chm, Revol Comt, Southwestern Front; deleg to Constituent Assembly; 1918 chm, Min'yar, then Sim Okrug Exec Comt; 1919-20 Party and govt posts in Vyatka and Ufa Provinces; from 1923 worked for Centr Control Commission, Workers and Peasants' Inspection; elected member, CPSU(B) Centr Control Commission; worked for CC, CPSU(B); member, USSR and All-Russian Centr Exec Comt; RSFSR Dep Pop Comr of Soc Security; finally pensioner; deleg, 12th-17th Party Congresses; *Died*: 13 Sept 1965.

KOKOVTSOV, Pavel Konstantinovich (1861-1942) Russian orientalist and semitist; prof, Petersburg (Leningrad) Univ from 1900; member, Russian (USSR) Acad of Sci from 1906; *Born*: 1 July 1861 in Pavlovsk, now Leningrad Oblast; *Educ*: 1884 grad Fac of Oriental Languages, Petersburg Univ; *Career*: from 1884 assoc prof, from 1900 prof, Petersburg (Leningrad) Univ; from 1903 junior asst, from 1906 member extraordinary, from 1912 member, Russian (USSR) Acad of Sci; prominent Semitist with a knowledge of all Semitic languages, including Assyro-Babylonian cuneiform and the monuments of Ethiopian lit; discovered scores of new Oriental sources; researched and published a major text of Semitic epigraphy, a trade treaty of the city state Palmira, the Aramaic inscriptions of Nibar from the 9th Century B.C. and 10th-Century monuments of Hebrew-Khazar relations; for several decades sorted and catalogued the Hebraic and Arabic manuscripts of the State Public Library in Petrograd (Leningrad); from 1919 head, Dept of Hebraic Books; *Publ*: *K istorii srednevekovoy yevreyskoy filologii i yevreysko-arabskoy literatury* (A History of Medieval Hebraic Philology and Hebraic and Arabic Literature) (2 vol, 1893-1916); *Novyy yevreyskiy dokument o khazarakh i khazaro-russko-vizantiyskikh otnosheniyakh v X veke* (A New Hebraic Document About the Khazars and Khazar-Russian-Byzantine Relations in the 10th Century) (1913); *Novyye materialy dlya kharakteristiki Iyekhudy Khayyudzha, Samuila Nagida i nekotorykh drugikh predstaviteley yevreyskoy filologicheskoy nauki v X-XII vv* (New Material on Judah Hayyuj, Samuel ha-Nagid and Various Other Hebrew Philologists of the 10th and 11th Centuries) (1916); *Yevreysko-khazarskaya perepiska v X veke* (Hebrew-Khazar Correspondence in the 10th Century) (1932); *Died*: 1 Jan 1942 in Leningrad.

KOLAS, Yakub (real name: MITSKEVICH, Konstantin Mikhaylovich) (1882-1956) Bel poet and writer; member and vice-pres, Bel Acad of Sci from 1928; Pop Poet of the Bel SSR from 1926; member, Bel Writers' Union from 1934; CP member from 1943; *Born*: 3 Nov 1882 in vil Akinchitsy in Bel, son of a landless peasant forester; *Educ*: 1902 grad Nesvizh Teachers' Training Seminary; *Career*: 1902-06 taugth at rural schools in Pinsk and Igumen Distr; 1906-08 brought to trial and forbidden to teach for organizing the League of Bel Teachers in the vil Mikolayevshchina; 1908-11 in Minsk Prison; 1911-15 taught at parish school in Pinsk; 1915-18 served in army at Aleksandr Mil College, on Rumanian Front, then in Oboyan' in Kursk Province; 1918-21 after discharge taught, then instructor for Oboyan' Dept of Educ; 1921 returned to Bel SSR, where he worked for the Terminology Commission, Bel Pop Comrt of Educ, at the Inst of Bel Culture, then at the Bel Acad of Sci; taught at Minsk Teachers' Training Inst and Bel State Univ; 1941-44 lived in Tashkent; from 1944 member, CC, CP Bel; Bd member, USSR and Bel Writers' Unions; dep, Bel and USSR Supr Sov; for a number of years head, Bel Comt for the Defense of Peace; 1906 first work published; his works are strong on local color and deal mainly with soc problems; in 1920's criticized Sov nationality policy toward Bel and attacked Party interference in lit, although he mostly supported the new Sov regime; 1927 joined *Polymya* lit assoc, which was loyal to the Sov regime; *Publ*: poems "The New Land" (1923); "Simon Music" (1925); "The Trial in the Forest" (1943); "Repayment" (1944); "The Fisherman's Hut" (1947); collected poems: "Songs of Sorrow" (1910); "A Man Is Missing" (1913); "The Farm Hand" (1913); "The Echo" (1922); "Our Days" (1937); "Under Stalin's Sun" (1940); "We Shall Avenge" (1942); "The Voice of the Earth" (1943); collected stories: "Stories" (1912); "The Thick Log" (1913); "Neman's Gift" (1913); "Native Phenomena" (1914); "Fairy Tales of Life" (1921); the novelettes "In the Backwoods" (1923), "In the Depth of Polessie" (1927) and "At the Crossroads" (1954) were combined into the trilogy "At the Crossroads" (1955); novelettes: "The Renegade" (1932); "Quagmire" (1934); children's books: "Mikhasyov's Adventures" (1935); "Sovos' the Mischief-Maker" (1936); "The Mustachioed Crab" (1938); "Among the Acient Oaks" (1941); "Sunrise" (1948); "The Morning of Life" (1950); collections: "Collected Works" (Vol 1, 1928); "Collected Works" (7 vol, 1952); "Collected Works" (12 vol, 1961-64); *Awards*: four Orders of Lenin; Order of the Red Banner; Order of the Red Banner of Labor; two Stalin Prizes (1945 and 1949); *Died*: 13 Aug 1956 in Minsk after a long illness.

KOLBAS'YEV, Sergey Adamovich (1898-1942) Russian writer; *Born*: 17 Mar 1898 in Petersburg, son of a civil servant; *Educ*: grad Naval Cadet Corps; *Career*: during Civil War commanded a torpedo-boat div; worked as interpreter at Sov embassy in Kabul and Sov trade mission in Helsinki; member, Lit Assoc of Red Army and Navy; arrested by State Security organs; *Publ*: poem *Otkrytoye more* (The Open Sea) (1922); short stories *Povorot vse vdrug* (About Face) (1930); short stories *Pravila sovmestnogo plavaniya* (Sailing in Convoy) (1935); children's books *Salazhonok* (1931); *Khoroshiy komanduyushchiy* (The Good Commander) (1932); *Kren* (List) (1935); pop sci works *Radio - nam* (Radio for Us) (1929); *Radioknizhka* (The Little Radio Book) (1931); *Died*: 30 Oct 1942 in imprisonment; posthumously rehabilitated.

KOLBAS'YEV, Yevgeniy Viktorovich (1862-1920) Marine inventor; capt, 1st class; *Born*: 15 June 1862; *Career*: from 1891 instructor, Kronstadt Divers' School; during 1880's designed ship telephone systems, shipdiver intercom sets and underwater lamps; 1893 opened a workshop in Kronstadt for the manufacture of diving equipment and ship's telephones; also designed a floating mine and several submarines; *Died*: 1920.

KOLCHAK, Aleksandr Vasil'yevich (1873-1920) Admiral, Russian Navy; politician; leader of anti-Bolshevik movement in Siberia during Civil War; *Born*: 1873 in Petersburg, son of a maj-gen; *Educ*: 1894 grad Naval Corps; *Career*: from 1891 in Russian Navy; 1894-99 officer on various warships in Baltic and Pacific Fleets; took part in several extended voyages; 1900-02 hydrologist and magnetologist, Baron Tol's polar expedition organized by Acad of Sci; 1903-04 headed expedition to the New Siberian Islands in search of Baron Tol's expedition; 1904 officer, cruiser *Askol'd*; commander, destroyer *Serdityy*; fought in Russo-Japanese War; laid minefields on approaches to Port Arthur, leading to destruction of the Japanese cruiser "Takosado"; 1904-05 in Japanese captivity; 1905-06 worked for Acad of Sci and for Geographic Soc; 1906 founded at Naval Acad a Naval Circle which worked on modernization of the Navy; Apr 1906 recommendations of this circle led to establishment of Naval Gen Staff; 1906-07 naval expert in mil commissions, State Duma; 1906-08 head, Baltic Theater of Operations, Naval Gen Staff; 1908 helped plan exploration of Northern Sea Route from Pacific to Atlantic; 1908-09 directed construction of icebreakers *Taymyr* and *Vaygach* which were to take part in this expedition; 1909-10 commanded icebreaker *Vaygach* in expedition; 1910-12 again head, Baltic Theater of Operations, Naval Gen Staff; 1912-13 commander, destroyer *Ussuriyets*; 1913-15 flag-officer for operations, Baltic Fleet Staff; with the start of WW 1 directed laying of minefields in the Gulf of Finland and later in German waters; 1915-16 commander, Destroyer Div, Baltic Fleet; from 28 June 1916 commander, Black Sea Fleet; commanded a number of operations which secured Black Sea waters from attacks of fast German cruisers "Goeben" and "Breslau" and paralyzed activities of German submarines; Mar 1917, after the abdication of Nicholas II, swore allegiance to Provisional Govt; June 1917, in protest against Sebastopol Sov's order to disarm the officers of the Fleet, relinquished command of Black Sea Fleet; Aug 1917, on invitation of the American Navy Dept, left for USA with consent of the Provisional Govt to work as adviser on minefields and scheduled Dardanelles operations; Nov 1917 left USA for Russia, learning of the Oct Revol en route; volunteered to continue fighting against Germany with the English Army; sent to Mesopotamian Front but en route ordered to the Far East; from Apr 1918 in Harbin consolidated anti-Sov mil formations in Transbaykal Region; July 1918 went to Tokyo to improve liaison with Japanese Command; Oct 1918 arrived in Omsk as a civilian; 4 Nov 1918 accepted the post of Min of War and Navy, Directory coalition govt; 18 Nov 1918, as a result of a coup staged by the Directory's Council of Min and Cossack officers, became Supr Ruler and commander in chief of Russian anti-Bolshevik forces; himself a democrat, tolerated development of pre-revol bureaucratism in govt organs and abuse of power by individual officials and officers in the rear; as a result of these abuses his troops, after several major victories in Mar-Apr 1919, which took them to the Volga, were left without supplies and late 1919 were incapable of further action; 14 Nov 1919 Omsk was ceded; 27 Dec 1919 Kolchak was arrested by officers of the Czechoslovak Corps in Nizhneudinsk; 4 Jan 1920 relinquished supr power and command; 5 Jan 1920 entered train of Entente reps who guaranteed his safe conduct to the Far East; 15 Jan 1920 at Innokent'yevskaya railroad station turned over to opposition Polit Center, which had seized power in Irkutsk; scheduled for trial by Polit Center's Investigation Commission; 25 Jan 1920 fell into hands of Irkutsk Sov of Workers and Soldiers' Dep, which had in turn seized power; *Died*: 7 Feb 1920 executed by orders of Irkutsk Mil Revol Comt.

KOLCHITSKIY, Nikolay Feodorovich (1890-1961) Protopresbyter, Russian Orthodox Church; administrator, Moscow Patriarchy from 1941; dean, Patriarchal Cathedral of the Epiphany, Moscow; chm, Training Comt, Holy Synod; *Born*: 1890; *Educ*: 1910 grad theological seminary; 1914 grad Moscow Theological Acad as Cand of Theology; *Career*: 1914 took holy orders; until 1923 served in Khar'kov, then transferred to Moscow as dean, Church (now Patriarchal Cathedral) of the Epiphany; 1945 accompanied Patriarch on trip to Egypt and Palestine; 1948-49 - on tour of USSR; 1954 sent to England, Germany, Belgium, etc; 1953 member, Russian Orthodox Church deleg at funeral ceremonies for Stalin; stood in honor guard at Stalin's tomb; took part in Moscow dialogue between US National Council of Churches of Christ, the Russian Orthodox Church and other Christian churches in the USSR; 1949, 1950 and 1952 deleg All-Union Peace Conference; *Awards*: medal; *Died*: 11 Jan 1961.

KOLEGAYEV, Andrey Lukich (1887-1937) Politician; member, Socialist-Revol Party from 1906; CP member from 1918; *Born*: 1887; *Career*: 1917 helped found Leftist Socialist-Revol Party; Dec 1917 appointed Pop Comr of Agric by RSFSR Council of Pop Comr; Mar 1918, because of Leftist Socialist-Revol Party's objections to the signing of the Treaty of Brest-Litovsk, resigned from the govt; 1918 broke with the party after the suppression of the Leftist Socialist-Revol revolt; Nov 1918 joined RCP(B); during Civil War supply chief and member, Revol Mil Council, Southern Front; 1920 Collegium member, RSFSR Pop Comrt of Communications, then chm, Main Transport Commission, Labor and Defense Council; from 1921 admin work; arrested by State Security organs; *Died*: 1937 in imprisonment; posthumously rehabilitated.

KOLENKOVSKIY, Aleksandr Konstantinovich (1880-1942) Mil commander and historian; lt-col, Gen Staff, Russian Army; lt-gen, Sov Army from 1940; Dr of Mil Sci; prof; CP member from 1940; *Born*: 23 Aug 1880 in Nikolayev, son of an officer; *Educ*: 1900 grad Odessa Infantry Cadet College; 1912 grad Nikolay Gen Staff Acad; *Pos*: from 1897 in Russian Army; fought in 1904-05 Russo-Japanese War and in WW 1; from 1918 in Red Army; 1918-19 chief of staff, Eastern Front; 1919-20 commander, Volga Mil Distr; 1920-21 Sov mil attache in Lithuania; 1921-24 head, Operations Bd, Red Army Staff; from 1924 taught and did research at Frunze Mil Acad, where he headed the Dept of Mil History; *Publ: O nastupatel'noy operatsii armii, vkhodyashchey v sostav fronta* (The Offensive Operations of an Army Assigned to a Front) (1929); *Zimnyaya operatsiya v Vostochnoy Prussii v 1915 g* (The 1915 Winter Campaign in East Prussia) (1930); *Dardanell'skaya operatsiya* (The Dardanelles Operation) (1930); *Manevrennyy period pervoy mirovoy imperialisticheskoy voyny* (The Maneuvering Period of the Imperialist First World War) (1940); *Died*: 23 May 1942.

KOLESNIK, Ivan Danilovich (1900-1953) Agronomist; plant breeder; member, All-Union Lenin Acad of Agric Sci from 1948; CP member from 1942; *Born*: 1900; *Educ*: 1930 grad Poltava Agric Inst; *Career*: 1931-35 worked at Kiev Research Inst of Fruit and Berry Farming; from 1938 worked for All-Union Lenin Acad of Agric Sci; from 1947 head, Mass Production Experimental Laboratory of this acad; developed methods of increasing the Yield of millet and bred fast-growing poplar; *Publ: Letniye posadki kartofelya v tsentral'noy zone SSSR* (The Summer Planting of Potatoes in the Central Region of the USSR) (1941); *Agrotekhnika prosa* (The Agrotechnics of Millet) (1947); *Awards*: Stalin Prize (1943); Order of the Red Banner of Labor; medals; *Died*: 1953.

KOLESNIKOV, Aleksey Konstantinovich (1895-1967) Govt official; CP member from 1917; *Born*: 1895; *Educ*: 1931-33 studied at Ind Acad in Moscow; *Career*: 1910 began work; 1917-19 exec secr, Orel Province Party Comt; 1919-22 in Red Army; worked for Special Dept, All-Russian Cheka on he Southwestern Front; 1922-30 dept head, All-Russian Cheka and OGPU; 1930-31 manager, USSR Supr Sovnarkhoz in Moscow; 1933-41 worked for NKVD in Moscow City and Oblast; 1941-46 dep head, Main Bd, Far Eastern Railroad Construction Trust in Magadan; 1946-47 admin work in Moscow; 1947-50 retired; 1950-52 admin work in Kazakhstan; from 1952 pensioner; *Died*: Nov 1967.

KOLESNIKOV, Nikolay Nikolayevich (1899-1959) Actor; Pop Artiste of RSFSR from 1951; CP member from 1938; *Born*: 1899; *Educ*: 1923 grad State Higher Stagecraft Studios; *Career*: from 1927 acted at theaters in Orenburg, Arkhangelsk and Omsk; from 1949 actor, Kuybyshev Theater; *Roles*: Godun and Levinson in Fadeyev's *Razlom* (Break-Up) and *Razgrom* (Rout); Zhukhray, Talanov Senior and Svekolkin in Leonov's *Kak zakalyalas' stal'* (How the Steel Was Tempered), *Nashestviye* (Invasion) and *Obyknovennyy chelovek* (The Common Man); Lenin in Pogodin's *Chelovek s ruzh'yom* (The Man with a Gun), *Kremlyovskiye kuranty* (Kremlin Chimes) and *Tret'ya pateticheskaya* (The Third Pathètique); Glagolin in Pogodin's *Sotvoreniye mira* (The Creation of the World); Lenin in Kapler and Zlatogorova's *Lenin v 1918-om godu* (Lenin in 1918); Antip Zykov, Vasnetsov and Chesnok in Korneychuk's *Zykovy* (The Zykovs), *Paren' iz nashego goroda* (A Lad from Our Town) and *V stepyakh Ukrainy* (In the Steppes of the Ukraine), etc; *Died*: 1959.

KOLESNIKOV, Vladimir Prokof'yevich (1902-1948) Paleontologist; Dr of Geological and Mineralogical Sci from 1935; *Born*: 1902; *Educ*: studied at Don Polytech Inst, Novocherkassk; *Career*: from 1925 worked for Geological Comt and for Geological Museum, USSR Acad of Sci; later worked for Geological Inst, USSR Acad of Sci; specialized in the fauna and stratigraphy of the Neogene in the southern USSR; did major research on the mollusks of the Sarma, Akchagyl and Apsheronperiods; studied the laws governing the development of mollusks in relation to their physical and geographical environment, analyzed the characteristics of closed basins and devised syngenetic diagrams to illustrate the process of fauna change; also studied the origin of Caspian mollusks, described the stratigraphy of the Neogene deposits in the Ponto-Caspian region and observed the parallel development of sedimentation in isolated basins; *Publ: Sarmatskiye mollyuski* (The Mollusks of Sarma) (1935); *Neogen SSSR* (The Neogene in the USSR) (1940); *Akchagyl'skiye i apsheronskiye mollyuski* (The Mollusks of the Akchagyl and Apsheron Periods) (1950); *Died*: 1948.

KOLESNIKOVA (DROBINSKAYA), Nadezhda Nikolayevna (1882-1964) Party official; CP member from 1904; *Born*: 12 Sept 1882 in Moscow, daughter of a white-collar worker; *Educ*: studied at Moscow Teachers' Training Courses; *Career*: worked as teacher; Dec 1905 participated in armed uprising in Moscow; 1907-16 worked in Moscow and Baku; member, Baku RSDRP Comt; after 1917 Feb Revol secr, Moscow Okrug RSDRP(B) Org; from Apr 1918 Pop Comr of Educ, Baku Council of Pop Comr; at the same time her husband Ya. D. Zevin, who was later shot along with 25 other Baku comr, was Comr of Labor of the Baku Council of Pop Comr; early Aug 1918 evacuated with her children to Astrakhan' and worked for the Province Exec Comt; from late 1918 chm, Astrakhan' Province RCP(B) Comt; 1919 worked for Pop Comrt of Educ in Moscow; 1920-21 admin work for Azer Pop Comrt of Educ; 1920 worked for Pop Comrt of Educ in Baku; elected member, CC, Azer CP(B); from 1923 head, Propaganda and Agitation Dept, Moscow Province CPSU(B) Comt, then Yaroslavl' Province Party Comt; 1929-32 rector, Acad of Communist Educ; 1933-57 research work at Inst of Marxism-Leninism, CC, CPSU and the Lenin Museum; from 1957 retired; *Publ: Massoviki-podpol'shchiki. Vospominaniya o bakinskikh rabochikh* (Underground Leaders. Memoirs of Baku Workers) (1935); *Ivan Fioletov* (1948); *Yakov Zevin* (1948); *Iz istorii bor'by za Sovetskuyu vlast' v Baku. Avgust 1917-iyul' 1918. Vospominaniya* (History of the Struggle for the Soviet Regime in Baku. August 1917-June 1918. Memoirs) (1958); *Awards*: two Orders of Lenin; *Died*: 18 Mar 1964.

KOLESSA, Filaret Mikhaylovich (1871-1947) Music historian, folklorist and ethnographer; Dr of Music (Vienna); member, Ukr Acad of Sci from 1929; *Born*: 17 July 1871 in vil Khodovichi, now L'vov Oblast; *Educ*: grad Philological Fac, L'vov Univ; completed postgrad studies in Vienna; *Career*: 1898-1930 worked as high-school teacher; from 1939 prof, L'vov Univ; dir, L'vov Branch, Inst of Art Studies, Folklore and Ethnography, Ukr Acad of Sci; dir, L'vov Ethnographical Museum; wrote numerous studies of Ukr and Slavic folklore and compiled several anthologies of Ukr folk Songs; wrote choral arrangements of poems by T. G. Shevchenko; maintained contacts with the foremost rep of Ukr lit and folklore and with Ukr, Russian and for specialists in this field; wrote valuable studies of N. V. Lysenko, I. Ya. Franko and Lesya Ukrainka; attended int congresses of folklorists and music historians; *Publ: Rytmika ukrains'kykh narodnykh pisen'* (The Rhythmics of Ukrainian Folk Songs) (1906-07); *Melodii ukrains'kykh narodnykh dum* (The Melodies of Ukrainian Folk Ballads) (2 vol, 1910-13); *Varianty melodiy ukrains'kykh narodnykh dum, ikh kharakterystyka i gruppovaniye* (Melody Variants of Ukrainian Folk Ballads, Their Characteristics and Classification) (1913); *Pro genezu ukrains'kykh narodnykh dum* (The Origins of Ukrainian Folk Ballads) (1922); *Ukrainska narodna pisnya na perelomi XVII-XVIII vekov* (The Ukrainian Folk Song in the Late 17th and Early 18th Century) (1928); *Ob ukrainskom fol'klore* (Ukrainian Folklore) (1940); *Fol'klor Vitchizyanoi viyny* (The Folklore of the Fatherland War) (1945); *Narodno-pisenni melodii ukrains'koho Zakarpattya* (Folk Song Melodies of Ukrainian Transcarpathia) (1946), etc; *Awards*: Order of the Red Banner of Labor; *Died*: 3 Mar 1947.

KOLLONTAY, Aleksandra Mikhaylovna (1872-1952) Govt and Party official; CP member from 1915; *Born*: 31 Mar 1872 in Petersburg, daughter of Gen Domontovich; *Educ*: from 1898 studied soci sci and econ at Zurich Univ; *Career*: in 1890's joined revol movement; 1903-06 affiliated to no party but worked for Bolsheviks; 1906 joined Mensheviks and attended Int Conference of Women Workers at Mannheim; member, Int Bureau of Women Socialists; 1907 member, RSDRP deleg at Int Socialist Congress in Stuttgart; late 1908 emigrated to escape police persecution; worked for Socialist Parties of Germany, Britain, France and Scandinavian countries as agitator and publicist; 1909-10 worked for Viennese *Pravda* and for centr organ of Soc-Democratic Party; lectured at "Forward" second Party school in Bologna; 1910 attended Copenhagen Congress; 1912 attended Basel Congress; contributed to *Pravda*; 1913 worked in Britain; permanent corresp for Int Bureau of Women Party Workers; 1914, at start of WW 1, worked in Switzerland and took revol-internationalist stand, leading to her expulsion from Switzerland in Dec 1914; worked for Paris publ *Golos* and *Nashe slovo*, internationalist organs; 1915-17 in Denmark and Norway in close contact with Lenin; sided with Bolsheviks, conducted anti-war agitation and Bolshevik propagenda among leftist-internationalist Soc-Democrats of Sweden, Norway, Denmark and America; contributed to journal "Kommunist"; 1915 commissioned by Lenin to write pamphlet "Who Needs the War" for Russian soldiers and prisoners-of-war; 1915 -16 twice visited America at invitation of German faction of American Soc-Democratic Party to press "Zimmerwald leftist policy" among Soc-Democrats; Mar 1917 returned to Russia and became member of Exec Comt, Petrograd Sov of Dep on behalf of the Bolshevik Mil Org, for which she agitated among the seamen of the Baltic Fleet and among Petrograd soldiers; member, ed bd, Bolshevik journal *Rabotnitsa*; 1917 attended RSDRP(B) Apr Conference; June 1917 attended Conference of Zimmerwald Leftists in Stockholm; Aug 1917 arrested by Provisional Govt together with other Bolshevik leaders but was soon released; Aug 1917 at 6th RSDRP(B) Congress elected member, CC and head, Bureau for Work Among Women; Oct 1917 attended 2nd Congress of Soviets and elected to Congress Presidium; Pop Comr of State Poor Relief in first Council of Pop Comr, but resigned as Leftist Communist in connection with the Brest Peace Treaty controversy; 1918 staged 1st Congress of Women Workers and Peasants; 1919 sent to Ukr and worked at the front, in the Donbass, Khar'kov and Crimea; then appointed Pop Comr of Propaganda and Agitation in the Crimean Republ, then in Ukr; 1920 head, Women's Dept, CC RCP(B); member, All-Russian

Centr Exec Comt; 1921-22 secr, Int Women's Secretariat of Comintern; Nov 1920 and Mar 1921, during the trade-union controversy, one of the leaders of the "workers' opposition", but broke with this group after the 11th Party Congress; deleg, 7th, 8th and 10th RCP(B) Congresses; from 1922 on dipl work; fall 1922 counsellor, Sov mission in Norway; May 1923-26 Sov plen in Norway; 1926 Sov plen and trade rep in Mexico; 1927 again Sov plen in Norway; 1930-45 USSR envoy, then amb in Sweden; 1935-38 member, Sov deleg at League of Nations, Geneva; 1945-52 counsellor, USSR Min of For Affairs, with the rank of amb extraordinary and plen; as Sov plen in Norway negotiated de jure recognition of Sov govt; 15 Feb 1924 signed act establishing dipl relations between USSR and Norway; spring 1926 signed trade agreement with Norway stipulating position and extraterritorial status of Sov trade mission; during WW 2, as Sov amb in Sweden, negotiated armistice with Finland; also negotiated and signed various trade agreements with Norway, Sweden and Finland; wrote numerous works on women's movement, also articles and pamphlets on sexual problems; wrote lit works under the name of Domontovich; *Publ: Polozheniye rabochego klassa v Finlyandii* (The Position of the Working Class in Finland) (1903); *Klassovaya bor'ba* (Class Struggle) (1906); *Sotsial'nyye osnovy zhenskogo voprosa* (The Social Principles of the Women's Movement) (1908); *Po rabochey Yevrope* (Working Europe) (1912); *Novaya moral' i rabochiy klass* (The New Morality and the Working Class) (1918); *Rabochaya oppozitsiya* (The Workers' Opposition) (1921); *Komu nuzhna voyna* (Who Needs the War) (1916); *Lyubov' pchyol trudovykh* (The Love of Worker Bees) (1923); *Bol'shaya lyubov'. Povest'* (Great Love. A Novelette) (1927); stories *Syostry* (Sisters) (1927); novelette *Vasilisa Malygina* (1927); *Doroga krylatomu Erosu* (The Road to Winged Eros) (1927); *Iz vospominaniy* (Memoirs) (1945); *Molodomu pokoleniya. Vospominaniya* (To the Younger Generation. Memoirs) (1946), etc; *Awards*: Order of Lenin; two Orders of the Red Banner of Labor; Norwegian Grand Cross of the Order of St. Olaf, 1st Class; supr Mexican Order of Augil Aztec; *Died*: 9. Mar 1952 in Moscow.

KOLOKOLOV, Vasiliy Grigor'yevich (1875-1948) Pharmacist; Master of Pharmaceutics from 1906; prof from 1941; helped to organize Sov pharmaceutical ind; *Born*: Dec 1875; *Educ*: 1893 grad Nursing School, Golitsyn Hospital; 1895 obtained asst pharmacist's diploma at Moscow Univ; 1900 grad Pharmaceutical Dept, Moscow Univ; 1902 passed master's examination at Moscow Univ but did not defend thesis until 1906; *Career*: 1893-94 male nurse in Kursk zemstvo; 1895-1918 asst pharmacist, pharmacist, then pharmacy mang, Golitsyn Hospital, Moscow; spring 1908-late 1920 also head, Control and Analysis Laboratory, R. Keller and Company; after 1917 Oct Revol helped to organize galenical production and pharmaceutical service in Moscow; head, Org Section, Pharmaceutical Dept, USSR Pop Comrt of Health; dep chm, Moscow Pharmacy Bd; established first laboratory in Moscow for control of pharmacy-produced drugs, where he supervised the development of 20 state-approved standards for complex drugs; organized production of various galenic and clinical drugs, including cincophen, novocain, anesthesin and phenobarbital; supervised cultivation of rhubarb, belladonna, asthma weed and other medicinal plants at *Bittsa* Sovkhoz; helped to compile 7th and 8th ed of State Pharmacopeia; from 1934 head, Chair of Medicinal Forms and Galenic Drug Technol, Moscow Pharmaceutical Inst; made major contribution to the development of this budding branch of pharmaceutics; edited first textbooks on the technol of medicinal forms written by S. F. Shubin; member, Pharmacological Comt, Learned Med Council, USSR Pop Comrt of Health; member, Commission for Testing and Introducing New Drugs, USSR Pop Comrt of Health; member, Pharmacopeia Commission, USSR Pop Comrt of Health; member, Pharmacy Manual Commission; member, ed collegium, journal *Farmatsiya*; member, Learned Council, Centr Pharmaceutical Research Inst; member, Commission on Plant Resources, USSR Pop Comrt of Health; wrote over 100 works, including numerous entries in 7th and 8th ed of State Pharmacopeia; *Awards*: Order of Red Star; "Outstanding Health Worker" badge; *Died*: Aug 1948.

KOLOSOV, Aleksandr Aleksandrovich (1862-1937) Histologist; *Born*: 2 Aug 1862; *Educ*: 1886 grad Med Fac, Khar'kov Univ; *Career*: after grad remained at Univ to work in Histology Dept; from 1889 asst prof, Dept of Histology, Embryology and Comparative Anatomy, Moscow Univ; 1892 defended doctor's thesis on the structure of pleuroperitoneal and vascular epithelia (endothelia); from 1895 prof, Histology Dept, Warsaw Univ; from 1915 in Rostov-on-Don; from 1930 prof, Rostov Med Inst; did research on structure of epithelia and muscle tissue; to determine minute cellular structures proposed original method using osmium impregnation; analysed the structure of smooth muscular tissue, integumentary and glandular epithelia and described the so-called juice canals in them; established nature of the secretory canals in the lining of the stomach glands; designed an excellent laboratory paraffin bath; *Publ*: large number of works on histology in Russian and German; thesis *O stroyenii plevroperitoneal'nogo i sosudistogo epiteliya (endotelia)* (The Structure of Pleuroperitoneal and Cellular Epithelia - Endothelia) (1892); *O stroyenii poperechnopolosatykh myshechnykh volokon u pozvonochnykh i chlenistonogikh* (The Structure of Transversostriated Muscle Fibers in Vertebrates and Anthropoda) (1910); *O vzaimootnosheniyakh kletok i o sokovykh kanal'tsakh v pokrovnykh i zhelezistykh epiteliyakh i v gladkoy myshechnoy tkani* (The Relationship of Cells and Juice Canals in Integumentary and Glandular Epithelia and in Smooth Muscle Tissue) (1925); *Died*: 26 Mar 1937.

KOLOSOV, Aleksey Ivanovich (1897-1956) Russian writer and journalist; *Born*: 23 Dec 1897 in Ardatov, Simbir' Province, son of an agronomist; *Educ*: studied at Law Fac, Yaroslavl' Univ; *Career*: 1917 first work published; 1917 dep, Syzran' Uyezd Sov and newspaper ed in Syzran'; head, Syzran' Uyezd Public Educ Dept; 1919-22 war corresp attached to polit bd, Turkestani Front; helped to put down uprising in Vernyy (Alma-Ata); ed secr, journal *Put' MOPRa* and roving corresp for *Izvestia*; 1928-56 *Pravda* special corresp; *Publ: Idut legiony. Rasskazy* (The Marching Legions. Short Stories) (1927); *Byloye i nastoyashcheye* (Past and Present) (1950); *Liniya zhizni* (Lifeline) (1958); *Svetlyye vody* (Bright Waters) (1958); *Sluchay u shlagbauma* (Border Incident) (1958); *Devochka iz Poles'ya* (The Girl from Poles'ye) (1959), etc; *Awards*: Order of the Fatherland War, 1st Class; *Died*: 18 Dec 1956 in Moscow.

KOLOSOV, Mikhail Alekseyevich (1878-1958) Obstetrician and gynecologist; Dr of Med from 1910; prof from 1920; *Born*: 1878; *Educ*: 1903 grad Med Fac, Moscow Univ; *Career*: 1903-09 intern, Obstetrical Clinic, Moscow Univ, then zemstvo physician; 1910 defended doctor's thesis on placental adhesion; 1920-23 prof, Chair of Obstetrics, Moscow Univ; after 1917 Oct Revol worked for Pop Comrt of Health and made major contribution to the org of the midwifery service; also active in mother and child care; wrote a number of exemplary pop-sci brochures on obstetrics and 46 sci works, including five monographs; *Publ*: doctor's thesis *K voprosu o prirashchenii posleda* (Placental Adhesion) (1909); *Zhizn' cheloveka do rozhdeniya* (Human Life Before Birth) (1913); *Rozhdeniye cheloveka* (Human Birth) (1914); *Sushchnost' zhenshchiny* (The Essence of Woman) (1927); *Operativnoye akusherstvo* (Operative Obstetrics) (1929); *Died*: 1958.

KOLOTILOV, Nikolay Nikolayevich (1885-1937) Party and govt official; CP member from 1903; *Born*: 1885; *Educ*: grade school; *Career*: metal worker by trade; Party work in Ivanovo-Voznesensk, Bryansk, etc; subjected to reprisals by Tsarist authorities; spent more than six years in prison, then four years in exile; after 1917 Feb Revol secr, Ivanovo-Voznesensk City, then Province Party Comt; 1920-21 chm, Gomel' Revol Comt, then chm, Exec Comt, Gomel' Sov; 1921-22 dep chm, Ivanovo-Voznesensk Province Exec Comt; 1922-25 secr, Don Oblast Comt, then North Caucasian Kray Party Comt; 1925-32 secr, Ivanovo-Voznesensk Province (later Ivanovo Oblast) CPSU(B) Comt; at 12th Congress elected cand member, and at 13th-16th Congresses member, CC, CPSU(B); arrested by State Security organs; *Died*: 1937 in imprisonment.

KOLOTILOVA, Antonina Yakovlevna (1890-1962) Musician; Pop Artiste of RSFSR from 1960; *Born*: 23 Mar 1890; *Career*: from 1924 soloist, Northern Dvina Radio Comt; 1926 founded amateur Russian folk choir, later reorganized into Russian Northern Folk Song Choir; wrote more than 100 ballads and songs; *Publ*: collection *Severnyye russkiye narodnyye pesni* (Northern Russian Folk Songs) (1936); *Awards*: Stalin Prize (1949); *Died*: 6 July 1962.

KOLPAKCHI, Vladimir Yakovlevich (1899-1961) Army gen from 1961; CP member from 1918; *Born*: 7 Sept 1899; *Educ*: 1928 grad Frunze Mil Acad; *Career*: 1916 drafted into Russian Army; from Sept 1917 in Petrograd Red Guard; participated in Oct

Revol; 1918-20 commanded a company, then a battalion; chief of staff of a detachment; after Civil War various commands; 1928-36 battalion and regt commander; chief of staff, then commander of a div; 1936-39 mil adviser in Spain during Civil War; 1941 chief of staff, Khar'kov Mil Distr; chief of staff, then commander, 18th Army; 1941-42 chief of staff, Bryansk Front; 1942-44 commanded operational groups on Kalinin Front; commander, 62nd Army deployed in Stalingrad sector; commanded 63rd Army on the Bryansk and Bel Fronts; 1944 chief of staff, 2nd Bel Front; 1944-45 commander, 69th Army on 1st Bel Front; after WW 2 dep commander of a mil distr; commander, Northern Mil Distr; 1956-61 head, Main Ground Forces Combat Training Bd; 1961 dep commander in chief of Ground Forces; head, Main Ground Forces Combat Training Bd; 1941-42 fought at Moscow; 1942 at Stalingrad; 1943 at Kursk; 1944 in Bel operation; 1945 in Berlin operation; dep, Karelian-Finnish Supr Sov of 1955 convocation; *Awards*: Hero of the Soviet Union (1945); three Orders of Lenin; three Orders of the Red Banner; three Orders of Suvorov, 1st Class; two Orders of Kutuzov, 1st Class; Order of the Red Star; medals; *Died*: 17 May 1961 killed in plane crash during tactical exercises.

KOL'TSOV, (real name: FRIDLYAND) Mikhail Yefimovich (1898-1942) Russian writer and journalist; corresp member, USSR Acad of Sci from 1938; CP member from 1918; *Born*: 12 June 1898 in Kiev, son of a craftsman; *Educ*: 1915 enrolled at Petrograd Psychoneurological Inst; *Career*: during 1917 Feb Revol active with soldiers and sailors at the Tauride Palace and served with workers' militia in the arrest of tsarist ministers; 1918-21 fought in Civil War on Southern, Southwestern and Polish Fronts; from 1920 worked in Moscow for Press Dept, Pop Comrt of For Affairs and for Russian Wire Agency; 1921 helped crush Kronstadt Mutiny; 9 July 1920 first sketch entitled *Makhno* appeared in *Pravda*; from 1922 contributed feuilletons almost daily to *Pravda*; from 1923 member, ed bd, *Pravda*; from 1923 founder-ed, journal *Ogonyok*; 1928-30 ed, journal *Chudak*; 1934-38 ed, journal *Krokodil*; with Gorky, co-edited journal *Za rubezhom*; as head, Journal-Newspaper Assoc, directed publ of *Zhizn' zamechatel'nykh lyudey* (The Lives of Notable Persons), *Biblioteka romanov* (Library of Novels), *Istoriya molodogo cheloveka 19-go veka* (The History of a Young Man of the 19th Century) and the book *Den' mira* (Day of Peace) (1937); 1935, as head of For Commission, Sov Writers' Union, attended Int Writers' Congress in Paris; 1937 head, Sov deleg at writers' congress in Spain; co-founder and secr, Int Writers' Assoc; 1938 elected dep, RSFSR Supr Sov; toured Sov Union and made many foreign trips; 1927 visited Budapest under an alias; to went Germany, gained admission to Sonnenburg Prison and visited Max Helz there; 1932 contrived to interview and photograph Gen Shatilov; 1931 and 1936 visited Spain; covered Spanish Civil War for *Pravda*; specialized in feuilletons, particularly denunciatory ones such as: "The Voronezh Pinkertons" (1927) about bureaucratism; "Acrobats, Incidentally" (1930) about architectural monstrosities; "A Very Bad Lapse" (1930) about public facilities and services; "On the Question of Obtuseness" (1931) about red-tape and official bungling; "Night-Blindness" (1930) about excessive form-filling, etc; outstanding was his series of novellas under the gen title *Ivan Vadimovich, chelovek na urovne* (Ivan Vadimovich, Man at the Top) (1933), in which he depicted the typical philistine and time-server with a Party card in his pocket; among his best feuilletons lauding new aspects of life are: "145 Lines of Lyrics" (1924) about the Soviet hard ruble; "Birth of a Firstling" (1925) about the Shatura Power Plant; "White Paper" (1926) about the construction of the Balakhna Paper Combine, etc; also wrote numerous sketches, to gain experience for which he worked as a school-teacher ("Seven Days in a Class" (1935)), drove a taxi in Moscow ("Three Days in a Taxi" (1934)) and served in a registry office ("In the Registry Office" (1936)), etc; wrote various sketches about Lenin: "The Last Trip" (1924); "Wife. Sister..." (1924); "January Days" (1925), etc; wrote sketches about the 1917 Revol: "October" (1919); "The February March" and "Dust and Sun" (1921); "Distant Tracks" (1925), etc; 1938 arrested by State Security organs; *Publ: Ispanskaya vesna* (Spanish Spring) (1933); *Ispanskiy dnevnik* (Spanish Diary) (1958); *Fel'yetony i ocherki* (Feuilletons and Sketches) (1961); *Pisatel' v gazete. Vystupleniya, stat'i, zametki* (A Newspaper Writer. Items, Articles and Notes) (1961); *Khochu letat'* (I Want to Fly); *29 gorodov* (29 Cities); *Sotvoreniye mira* (The Creation of the World) (1928), etc; his works have been translated into many for languages; *Awards*: Order of Lenin; Order of the Red Star; Order of the Red Banner; *Died*: 4 Apr 1942 in imprisonment; posthumously rehabilitated.

KOLTYPIN, Aleksandr Alekseyevich (1883-1942) Clinical pediatrician; Hon Sci Worker of RSFSR; *Born*: 1883; *Educ*: 1908 grad Med Fac, Moscow Univ; *Career*: 1908-12 zemstvo physician; from 1912 worked at A. A. Kisel''s Clinic; from 1927 head, Chair of Infantile Diseases, 2nd Moscow State Univ; 1932-38 head, Chair of Pediatric Fac, 2nd Moscow Med Inst; 1938-42 sci dir, Centr Pediatric Inst, RSFSR Pop Comrt of Health; after detailed study of the clinical and pathogenic aspects of scarlet fever, diphtheria, dysentery, measles, influenza, cerebrospinal meningitis, etc, devised unified classification of infectious diseases; analyzed the forms and course of both acute and chronic infections (rheumatism and tuberculosis) and established how they damage the nervous system; devised phase theory of the infection process and tripartite classification of pathogenesis - toxic, allergic and by secondary microbic infestation - on the basis of which developed and used a complex system of differentiated treatment; introduced the concept of the "infectious heart" in clinical practice; did research on serum disease; contributed to the theory of infectious allergy by establishing its clinical syndrome; wrote over 100 works on infectious pathology; *Publ: Ob issledovanii vegetativnoy nervnoy sistemy u detey pri ostrykh infektsiyakh (skarlatina i kor')* (Research on the Vegetative Nervous System of Children Suffering from Acute Infections [Scarlet Fever and Measles]) (1924); *K voprosu o klassifikatsii klinicheskikh form skarlatina u detey* (The Classification of Clinical Forms of Scarlet Fever in Children) (1925); *Ostryye infektsionnyye bolezni* (Acute Infectious Diseases) (1928); *Klinicheskiye osobennosti grippa v detskom vozraste* (Clinical Peculiarities of Influenza in Childhood) (1935); *Uchebnik detskikh bolezney* (A Textbook of Children's Diseases) (1939); *Metodika klinicheskogo issledovaniya infektsionnogo bol'nogo i semiotika infektsionnogo protsessa u detey* (Methods of the Clinical Examination of Infected Patients and the Semiotics of the Infection Process in Children) (1941); *Osnovnyye cherty dinamiki infektsionnogo protsessa* (The Basic Features of the Dynamics of the Infection Process) (1943); *Patogeneticheskiye osnovy klinicheskoy klassifikatsii ostrykh infektsionnykh bolezney u detey* (The Pathogenic Principles of the Clinical Classification of Infectious Diseases in Children) (1948); coauthor, *Detskiye bolezni* (Children's Diseases) (1957); *Died*: 1942 in Moscow.

KOLYADA (alias: BATYA), Nikifor Zakharovich (1891-1954) Ukr; partisan leader during 1918-20 Civil War and WW 2; CP member from 1920; *Born*: 9 Feb 1891 in Khar'kov Province, son of a poor peasant; *Educ*: 1925-30 studied at Eastern Fac, Far Eastern Univ; *Career*: fought in WW 1; 1917 chm, regt comt; 1918-19 commanded partisan detachment in Podol'sk Province; 1920 mil commander, 57th Infantry Div on Polish Front; 1922 dep commander, partisan detachments in the Far East, then member, Mil Council of Maritime Partisan Detachments; after liberation of the Far East head, Maritime Workers and Peasants' Police; 1932-41 worked for USSR Pop Comrt of Forests, USSR Pop Comrt of State Procurement and USSR Pop Comrt of the Navy; June 1941 sent by CC, CPSU(B) to Smolensk Oblast to organize partisans behind enemy lines; commanded *Batya* group of partisan detachments; during WW 2 arrested by Sov counter-intelligence; until 1954 in imprisonment, then released and rehabilitated; *Awards*: Order of Lenin (1942); *Died*: 1 Mar 1954.

KOMAR, Anatoliy Nikolayevich (1909-1959)Civil eng; member, Ukr Acad of Construction and Architecture from 1956; member, USSR Acad of Construction and Architecture from 1957; pres, Ukr Acad of Construction and Architecture from 1956 to 1959; CP member from 1940; *Born*: 25 Dec 1909 in Kiev, son of a worker; *Educ*: 1934 grad Dnieper Civil Eng Inst in Zaporzh'ye; *Career*: assisted with numerous major construction projects, such as the blast furnaces for the *Zaporozhstal'* Steel Plant, metallurgical enterprises in the Urals, etc; directed construction of hydraulic eng projects, roads, houses and public buildings; did research on the org and mechanization of construction; dep, Ukr Supr Sov of 5th convocation; *Awards*: two Orders of Lenin; other orders and medals; *Died*: 26 Oct 1959.

KOMAROV, Nikolay Pavlovich (1886-1937) Party and govt official; CP member from 1909; *Born*: 1886, son of a peasant; *Career*: metalworker by trade; Party work in Petersburg; arrested by Tsarist authorities; 1917 member, Vyborg Rayon and Petrograd City Party Comt; during Civil War comr of a battalion on the

Eastern Front, head of a special dept, then chm, Petrograd Province Cheka; from 1921 secr, Petrograd Province Exec Comt; from 1925 secr, Northwestern Bureau, CC, CPSU(B); chm, Leningrad Sov and Leningrad Province Exec Comt; chm, Bd, All-Union Construction Trust; member, Presidium, USSR Supr Sovnarkhoz; from 1931 RSFSR Pop Comr of Communal Utilities; at the 11th and 17th Party Congresses, elected cand member, at the 10th, 12th, 14th, 15th and 16th Congresses elected member, CC, CPSU(B); arrested by State Security organs; *Died*: 1937 in imprisonment.

KOMAROV, Pyotr Stepanovich (1911-1949) Poet; CP member from 1943; *Born*: 25 July 1911 in vil Boyevo, Novgorod Province, son of a worker who moved to the Far East with his family in 1918; *Career*: 1926 first work published; 1929-39 worked for newspapers *Nabat molodyozhi, Tikhookeanskaya zvezda*, etc; from 1939 secr and member, ed bd, journal *Na rubezhe* Khabarovsk; 1943-46 exec secr, Khabarovsk section, USSR Writers' Union; wrote verse about the conquest of the taiga, building, collectivization and the life of border-guards, geologists and hunters in the Sov Far East; *Publ*: collected verse *U beregov Amura* (On the Banks of the Amur) (1940); unfinished verse-novel *Vladimir Atlasov* (1944-45); verse cycles *Man'chzhurskaya tetrad'* (Manchurian Notebook), *Novyy peregon* (New Stage), *Zelyonyy poyas* (Green Belt), etc; *Awards*: Stalin Prize (1950); *Died*: 30 Sept 1949 in Khabarovsk.

KOMAROV, Sergey Petrovich (1891-1957) Film actor and dir; Hon Artiste of RSFSR from 1935; *Born*: 1891; *Career*: taught at All-Union State Inst of Cinematography; *Roles*: the Commissar in *Derevnya na perelome* (A Village at the Turning-Point) (1921); the ration squad officer in *Serp i molot* (Hammer and Sickle) (1921); the one-eyed man in *Neobychaynyye priklyucheniya mistera Vesta v strane bol'shevikov* (The Remarkable Adventures of Mr West in the Land of the Bolsheviks) (1924); the Adventurer in "Miss Mend" (1926); Hans in *Po zakonu* (By Due Process) (1926); the Jesuit Brzezinski in *Salamandra* (The Salamander) (1928); Bul'di senior in *Dva-Bul'di-dva* (Two-Bul'di-Two) (1930); Greshin in *Okraina* (The Outskirts) (1933); Burakov in *Lyudi doliny Sumbar* (The People of the Sumbar Valley) (1938); Prince Trubetskoy in *Minin i Pozharskiy* (Minin and Pozharskiy) (1939); Terentiy in *Sibiryaki* (The Siberians) (1940); the Chaplain in *Prints i nishchiy* (The Prince and the Pauper) (1943); the Minister in *Sinegoriya* (Blue Mountains) (1946); the Doctor in *Molodaya gvardiya* (The Young Guard) (1948); Ivanov in *Nakhlebnik* (The Parasite) (1953); the prof of oceanography in *Tayna dvukh okeanov* (The Secret of Two Oceans) (1957), etc; *Productions: Potseluy Meri Pikford* (Mary Pickford's Kiss) (1927); *Kukla s millionami* (The Millionaire Doll) (1928); *Died*: 1957.

KOMAROV, Vladimir Leont'yevich (1869-1945) Botanist and geographer; Dr of Botany from 1911; prof from 1918; pres, USSR Acad of Sci from 1936; *Born*: 13 Oct 1869 in Petersburg; *Educ*: 1894 grad Fac of Physics and Mathematics, Petersburg Univ; from 1894 worked at Main Botanical Garden (Botanical Inst, USSR Acad of Sci); 1902-18 assoc prof, 1918-37 prof and head, Chair of Botany, Petersburg (Leningrad) Univ; also taught at other higher educ establishments; 1914-20 corresp member, 1920-30 member, 1930-36 vice-pres, Russian (USSR) Acad of Sci; 1931-45 dir, Plant Taxonomy and Geography Dept, Botanical Inst, USSR Acad of Sci; 1944-45 also dir, Inst of the History of Nature Studies, USSR Acad of Sci; specialized in taxonomy, floristics and plant geography; made several field trips: 1892-93 to Centr Asia; 1896-97 to Manchuria and Korea; 1913, 1930, 1932 and 1935 to Far East; 1934, 1936 and 1937 to France; proved the necessity of considering both latitudinal and meridional characteristics in biogeographical zoning; attached prime importance to the environment in the development of species and considered a given species to be a definite stage in the process of evolution; from 1934 supervised the compilation and publ of the encyclopedic work *Flora SSSR* (The Flora of the USSR); 1930-45 chm, All-Union Botanical Soc; 1936 dep, USSR Supr Sov; wrote some 300 works and gave his name to several plant genera and species, as well as to the Botanical Inst, USSR Acad of Sci; *Publ: Flora Man'dzhurii* (The Flora of Manchuria) (3 vol, 1901-07); *Flora poluostrova Kamchatki* (The Flora of the Kamchatka Peninsula) (3 vol, 1927-30); *Tipy rasteniy* (Plant Types) (1939); *Ucheniye o vide u rasteniy* (The Theory of Species Applied to Plants) (1940); *Prakticheskiy kurs anatomii rasteniy* (A Practical Course in Plant Anatomy) (1941); *Proiskhozhdeniye rasteniy* (The Origin of Plants) (1943); *Vvedeniye v botaniku* (An Introduction to Botany) (1949); *Izbrannyye sochineniya* (Selected Works) (12 vol, 1945-58), etc; *Awards*: N. M. Przheval'skiy Medal (1897); K. M. Ber Prize (1909); three Orders of Lenin; two Stalin Prizes (1941, 1942); Hero of Socialist Labor; *Died*: 5 Dec 1945 in Moscow.

KOMAROV, Vladimir Mikhaylovich (1927-1967) Russian cosmonaut; col, Eng Corps; Pilot-Cosmonaut of USSR from 1964; mil pilot, 3rd class; Hon Master of Sport of USSR from 1964; CP member from 1952; *Born*: 16 March 1927 in Moscow, son of a janitor; *Educ*: 1945 grad Special Air Force School in Moscow; 1949 grad Bataysk Mil Pilots College; 1959 grad Zhukovsky Air Force Eng Acad; postgrad studies at above acad; *Career*: 1945 joined Sov Air Force; 1949-54 fighter pilot with air force units of North Caucasian Mil Distr; 1959-60 worked for air force research inst; 1960-67 served with cosmonauts team; 12-13 Oct 1964, as commander of first threeman spaceship *Voskhod*, made first group 24-hour flight together with K. P. Feoktistov and B. B. Yegorov, whereby *Voskhod* completed 16 orbits of the Earth and covered over 700.000 kilometers; 23-24 Apr 1967 performed fatal test space flight of *Soyuz-1* spaceship; *Awards*: twice Hero of the Sov Union (1964 and 1967, posthumously); Order of Lenin; Order of the Red Star; medals; *Died*: 24 Apr 1967 killed during landing after space flight; buried by the Kremlin Wall on Moscow's Red Square.

KOMAROVICH, Vasiliy Leonidovich (1894-1942) Russian lit historian; *Born*: 13 Jan 1894 in vil Voskresensk, Makar'yev Uyezd, Nizhniy Novgorod Province; *Educ*: 1917 grad Petrograd Univ; *Career*: 1924-28 taught at Leningrad Univ and Inst of Art History; 1916 first work published; wrote many studies on Dostoevsky, Pushkin, poets of the period, and the Petrashevskiy poets; edited and compiled anthology *Poety-petrashevtsy* (The Petrashevskiy Poets) (1940); did research on ancient Russian lit, especially the history of Russian manuscripts and local legends; wrote various chapters on ancient Russian lit in *Istoriya russkoy literatury* (A History of Russian Literature) (1941-46); translated and annotated Stendhal's works; *Publ: Neizvestnyaya stat'ya F. M. Dostoyevskogo "Peterburgskiye snovideniya v stikhakh i proze"* (F. M. Dostoyevsky's Unknown Article "Petersburg Dreams in Verse and Prose") (1916); *Dostoyevskiy i shestidesyatniki* (Dostoevsky and the Men of the 1860's) (1917); *Nenapisannaya poema Dostoyevskogo* (An Unwritten Poem of Dostoevsky's) (1922); *Mirovaya garmoniya Dostoyevskogo* (Dostoevsky's "World Harmony") (1924); *Roman Dostoyevskogo "Podrostok" kak khudozhestvennoye yedinstvo* (Dostoevsky's Novel "The Juvenile" as an Integral Artistic Work) (1924); *Dostoyevskiy. Sovremennyye problemy istoriko-literaturnogo izucheniya* (Dostoevsky. Modern Problems of Historical and Literary Studies) (1925); *Kitezhskaya legenda. Opyt izucheniya mestnykh legend* (The Kitezh Legend. A Study of Local Legends) (1936); *Vtoraya kavkazskaya poema Pushkina* (Pushkin's Second Caucasian Poem) (1941), etc; *Died*: 17 Feb 1942 killed during the German blockade of Leningrad.

KOMENDANTOV, Leonid Yefimovich (1883-1939) Otolaryngologist; Dr of Med from 1916; prof; *Born*: 1883; *Educ*: 1907 grad Petersburg Mil Med Acad; *Career*: after grad worked at mil hospitals and studied pathological anatomy; specialized in otolarynogology at Saratov Ear, Nose and Throat Clinic; 1916 defended doctor's thesis on the pathological anatomy of the temporal bone in rachitis and its relation to the pathology of the ear; 1921, as head, Chair of Ear, Nose and Throat Diseases, Perm' Univ, founded an otolaryngological clinic; from 1923 head, Chair of Otolaryngology, North Caucasian Univ, Rostov-on-Don, where he also founded a special clinic; from 1930 until death head, Chair of Ear, Nose and Throat Diseases, 1st Leningrad Med Inst; contributed several new hypotheses to the theory of hearing and balance; did major research on the normal anatomy of various sections of the temporal bone, otosclerosis, hearing fatigue, ototopy and lesions of the temporal bone in congenital syphilis; pioneered study of health resort treatment for ear, nose and throat diseases; 1925 founded Otolaryngological Soc, North Caucasian Univ; wrote over 90 works; *Publ*: doctor's thesis *Patologoanatomicheskiye osobennosti visochnoy kosti pri rakhite i ikh znacheniye v patologii ukha* (Pathological Anatomical Features of the Temporal Bone in Rachitis and Their Significance in the Pathology of the Ear) (1916); *O primenenii matsestinskoy (serovodorodnoy) vody dlya terapii verkhnikh dykhatel'nykh putey i slukhogo organa* (The Use of Matsesta [Hydrogen Sulphide] Water for the Therapy of the Upper Respiratory Tract and the Auditory Apparatus) (1928); *O slukhovoy funtsii* (The Auditory Function) (1936); *Protsessy summatsii i tormozheniya v slukhovoy funktsii* (The Summation and Retardation Processes in the Auditory Function) (1938); *Boleźni ukha, nosa i gorla* (Ear, Nose and Throat Diseases) (1939); *Died*: 1939.

KOMISSAROV, Nikolay Valerianovich (1880-1957) Russian actor; Pop Artiste of Ukr SSR from 1946; *Born*: 17 Jan 1890 in Petersburg; *Educ*: grad Petersburg Business College; *Career*: after grad worked for Kiev branch of Gosbank; simultaneously acted with P. P. Struyskiy's company; 1930 began professional acting career; worked at theaters in Kiev, Staryy Oskol, Kremenchug and other Ukr cities; 1925-27 at Leningrad Comedy Theater, then at theaters in Far East, Yaroslavl', etc; 1934-45 at Odessa Theater; from 1939 also film work; 1946-57 with Maly Theater, Moscow; *Roles*: Famusov (1946); Vyshnevskiy in *Dokhodnoye mesto* (A Lucrative Post) (1948); Ioakim Pino in Virta's *Zagovor obrechyonnykh* (Conspiracy of the Doomed) (1949); Trabskiy in Pogodin's *Minuvshiye gody* (Bygone Years) (1948); Prince Abrezkov in L. Tolstoy's *Zhivoy trup* (The Living Corpse) (1951), etc; film roles in: *Karmelyuk; Kavaler Zolotoy Zvezdy* (Knight of the Gold Star); *Ubiystvo na ulitse Dante* (Murder on Dante Street); *Shchors; Tainstvennyy ostrov* (Mystery Island); *Stalingradskaya bitva* (The Battle of Stalingrad), etc; *Awards*: Stalin Prizes (1951 and 1952); *Died*: 30 Sept 1957.

KOMLEV, Vasiliy Terent'yevich (1882-1967) Party official; CP member from 1905; *Born*: 10 Mar 1882; *Educ*: 1922 grad mil polit school; 1924-27 at Inst of Polit Educ; *Career*: fought in 1905 Revol in Moscow; typesetter in illegal Party printing shop; 1909 arrested; 1911 sentenced to seven years hard labor; 1917-19 worked for newspapers *Sotsialdemokrat* and *Pravda*; fought in Civil War; from 1922 instructor, polit dept of a div in Turkestan; 1928-32 admin work for *Pravda* Publ House; 1932-34 secr, Party Collegium, Krasnogorsk CPSU(B) Auditing Commission; until 1944 admin work in Krasnogorsk Rayon; from 1944 pensioner; *Died*: 20 Sept 1967.

KOMYAKHOV, Vasiliy Grigor'yevich (1911-1966) Ukr Party and govt official; Presidium member, CC, CP Ukr from 1962; member, CC, CP Ukr from 1952; CP member from 1941; *Born*: 31 Mar 1911 in Slavyansk, now Donetsk Oblast; *Educ*: 1936 grad Odessa Agric Inst; *Career*: 1936-38 served in Red Army; 1938-41 and 1945-49 bd chm, head of an oblast land dept, then chm of an oblast agric bd; 1941-45 polit officer and comr in Sov Army; 1949-53, chm, Exec Comt, Kirovograd Oblast Sov of Workers' Dep; 1953-55 first secr, Sumy Oblast Comt, CP Ukr; 1955-60 first secr, Crimean Oblast Comt, CP Ukr; 1960-62 first secr, Poltava Oblast Comt, CP Ukr; 1962-64 chm, Agric Bureau, CC, CP, Ukr; 1956-66 cand member, CC, CPSU; 1966 elected member, CC, at 23rd CPSU Congress; dep, USSR Supr Sov of 1954, 1958, 1962 and 1966 convocations; dep, Ukr Supr Sov of 1947, 1951 and 1963 convocations; *Awards*: two Orders of Lenin; other orders and medals; *Died*: 16 Oct 1966.

KON, Feliks Yakovlevich (1864-1941) Polish and Russian revolutionary; Party and govt official; CP member from 1918; *Born*: 30 May 1864 in Warsaw, son of an intellectual; *Educ*: studied at Warsaw Univ; *Career*: joined revol movement while still a student; 1892 joined Polish "Proletariat" Party; 1884 sentenced by mil tribunal to ten years and eight months at hard labor for revol activities; released after serving six years of sentence at Kara, Eastern Siberia; 1891-1904 exiled to Yakutia; 1904 returned to Warsaw; from 1906 member, CC, Polish Socialist Party (Leftists); from 1907 in emigration; during WW 1 sided with internationalists; May 1917 went to Russia; 1919 member, Kiev Province Party Comt, and secr, CC, CP(B) Ukr; summer 1920, together with F. E. Dzerzhinskiy and Yu. Yu. Markhlevskiy, member, Provisional Revol Comt of Poland; 1922-23 secr, Comintern Exec Comt; 1924-35 member, Int Control Commission, Comintern Exec Comt; 1925-28 ed, newspaper *Krasnaya zvezda*; then ed, newspaper *Rabochaya gazeta*; 1930-31 head, Art Section, RSFSR Pop Comrt of Educ; 1931-33 chm, All-Union Radio Broadcasting Comt; from 1933 head, Music Dept, RSFSR Pop Comrt of Educ; from 1934 member, USSR Writers' Union; 1937-41 ed, journal *Nasha strana*; member, All-Ukr Centr Exec Comt and Presidium member, USSR Centr Exec Comt; *Publ: Pod znamenem revolyutsii. Vospominaniya* (Under the Banner of Revolution. Reminiscences) (1926); *Istoriya revolyutsionnogo dvizheniya v Rossii* (The History of the Revolutionary Movement in Russia) (1929); *1905* (1930); *F. E. Dzerzhinskiy* (1939); *Za 50 let* (The Past Fifty Years) (4 vol, 1936); *Died*: 28 July 1941.

KONASHKOV, Fyodor Andreyevich (1860-1941) Illiterate storyteller; member, USSR Writers' Union; *Born*: 1860 in vil Semyonovo, Olonets Province, now Karelian ASSR, son of a peasant; *Career*: worked as a farmer and fisherman; learned Russian epics from grandfather and uncle; at turn of century the epics were written down by O. M. Dobrolyubov but the manuscripts were subsequently destroyed; 1928 the members of an expedition following the trail of Rybnikov and Gil'ferding (V. M. Sokolov, S. P. Borodin, E. G. Borodina-Morozova, Yu. A. Smarin, V. I. Chicherov and V. I. Yakovleva) recorded 19 epic texts; other epics (22 themes), fairy-tales, folk-poems and religious verses were written down by folklorists from Petrozavodsk, Leningrad and Moscow; *Publ*: epics *Il'ya Muromets i goli kabatskie* (Ilya Muromets and the Poor Inn-Keepers); *Dobrynya i Zmey* (Dobrynya and the Dragon); *Mikhaylo Potyk; Samoye dorogoye* (The Dearest) (1939); *Skazka o Yorshe* (The Tale of Yorsh); *Died*: 1941.

KONCHALOVSKIY, Maksim Petrovich (1875-1942) Internist; Dr of Med from 1911; prof from 1918; Hon Sci Worker of RSFSR from 1934; *Born*: 13 Oct 1875 in Odessa; *Educ*: 1899 grad Med Fac, Moscow Univ; *Career*: 1899-1912 intern, then asst prof, from 1912 assoc prof, Fac Therapy Clinic, Moscow Univ, where he worked under Prof V. D. Shervinskiy and Prof L. Ye. Golubinin; from 1918 prof, Hospital Therapy Clinic, Women's Higher Courses (now 2nd Moscow Med Inst); 1919-23 co-chm, from 1923 chm, Moscow Therapists' Soc; from 1923 also founder-ed, journal *Terapevticheskiy arkhiv*; 1927-29 dean, Med Fac, 2nd Moscow Univ; from 1928 sci dir, Inst of Hematology and Blood Transfusion and chm, All-Union Rheumatism Comt; from 1929 also dir, Fac Therapy Clinic, 1st Moscow Med Inst; from 1931 chm, All—Union Therapists' Soc; from 1933 dir, Therapeutic-Clinic, All-Union Inst of Experimental Med; from 1936 vice-pres, Int Rheumatism League; trained numerous internists, including prof A. A. Bagdasarov, B. Ye. Votchal, M. S. Dul'tsin, S. A. Gilyarevskiy, A. G. Gukasyan, Ye, A. Kost, S. A. Pospelov, K. I. Shirokova, V. N. Smotrov and Ye. M. Tareyev; did major research on the pathology of the digestive tract, rheumatism and hematology; also studied cholelithiasis, the pathology of the liver, spleen, stomach, etc; favored the Pavlovian clinical physiological approach to med; viewed disease as a failure of the body's ability to adapt to its environment; attributed great importance to disturbances of the cerebral cortex in the pathogenesis of internal diseases; bases his clinical cerebral cortex in the pathogenesis of internal diseases; based his clinical (syndromes); hypothesized that rheumatism is a hyperergic reaction of the sensitized organism in which the actual infection is short-lived; founder, Congress of Russian Therapists; member, Methods Commission, Main Bd of Professional Training, RSFSR Pop Comrt of Educ; member, Learned Med Council, RSFSR Pop Comrt of Health; chm and hon member, Sci Health Resort Soc; pres, 4th Int Rheumatism Congress; member, Int Balneological Soc; co-ed, *Bol'shaya meditsinskaya entsiklopediya* (Large Medical Encyclopedia) and series *Biblioteka prakticheskogo vracha* (The Practical Physician's Library); wrote over 150 works; *Publ: Zheludochnaya akhiliya* (Achylia gastrica) (1911); coauthor, *Sakharnaya bolezn', yeyo diagnoz i lecheniye* (Diabetes, Its Diagnosis and Treatment) (1928); *Klinika lyogochnogo raka* (The Clinical Treatment of Lung Cancer) (1930); *Klinicheskiye lektsii* (Clinical Lectures) (1935-37); *Uchebnik vnutrennikh bolezney* (A Textbook on Internal Diseases) (1946), etc; *Died*: 29 Nov 1942 in Moscow.

KONCHALOVSKIY, Pyotr Petrovich (1876-1956) Painter and set designer; Pop Artist of RSFSR from 1946; member, USSR Acad of Arts from 1947; *Born*: 21 Feb 1876 in Slavyansk, now Donetsk Oblast; *Educ*: 1897-1898 studied in Paris; 1899-1907 at Petersburg Acad of Arts; *Career*: close friend of Russian painters V. I. Surikov and V. A. Serov; co-founder, "Jack of Diamonds" artists' assoc; 1918-21 and 1926-29 taught painting; *Works*: canvases: "The Bull Fight" (1910); "Portrait of Siena" (1912); "Portrait of My Daughter" (1925); "From the Fair" (1926); "Lilac" (1933); "Dead Game" (1937); "Wood-Grouse" (1940); "The First Snow" (1940); "Birch Tops" (1941); "Noon" (1947); "Return from Mowing" (1948); "Eglantine" (1951), etc; portraits of stage dir and actors: "V. E. Meyerhold"; "S. S. Prokofiev"; "N. S. Golovanov", etc; designed sets for: Bryuni's *Uragan* (The Hurricane) at Mamontov's Private Opera Theater in Moscow (1904); Anton Rubinshteyn's *Kupets Kalashnikov* (The Merchant Kalashnikov) (1912) and Mozart's "Don Juan" (1913) at the Zimin Opera Theater; Offenbach's "Perikola" at the Nemirovich-

Danchenko Musical Studio (1922); *Khozyayka gostinitsy* (The Mistress of the Inn) at the Moscow Arts Theater (1933); Wolf-Ferrari's "Four Despots" at the Bolshoy Theater (1933), etc; *Awards*: Order of the Red Banner of Labor (1946); medals; Stalin Prize (1943); *Died*: 2 Feb 1956.

KONDAKOV, Nikolay Alekseyevich (1883-1967) Party and govt official; CP member from 1905; *Born*: 22 Oct 1883; *Career*: 1905 joined revol movement; 1917 sent to Kaluga Province to do Party work among peasants; 1918-26 exec Party and govt work in Kaluga; 1926-35 worked for USSR Pop Comrt of Sovkhozes; 1935-36 dir, Zheleznovodsk and Shafranovo health resort admin and Bira Rest Home, Bashkir ASSR; after 1936 held a variety of minor govt posts; from 1955 pensioner; *Died*: 29 Jan 1967.

KONDAKOV, Vadim Aleksandrovich (1886-1959) Pedag, geographer and local historian; prof; corresp member, RSFSR Acad of Pedag Sci from 1945; *Born*: 8 Apr 1886; *Educ*: 1911 grad Natural Sci Dept, Fac of Physics and Mathematics, Kazan' Univ; *Career*: from 1911 taught at girls' and boys' high-schools, business colleges and Teachers' Training Inst in Ufa; 1916 commissioned by Ufa Province Zemstvo to organize first Tatar-Bashkir teachers' training seminary in Russia; after 1917 Oct Revol helped to organize new schools in Urals, Western Siberia and Altay (Yekaterinburg, Tomsk, Biysk and Perm'); lectured and taught on teachers' training courses, inspected schools and helped to develop local teaching programs; 1920 began teaching at higher educ establishments; 1923-24 ed, pedag journal *Na tret'yem fronte*, Perm'; 1923-30 worked at Perm' Univ, then at Sverdlovsk Univ and Steel Inst; 1925-27 ed, pedag journal *Ural'skiy uchitel'*, Sverdlovsk; 1932-47 head, Chair of Physical Geography, Perm' Teachers' Training Inst; from 1947 worked at Kazan' Teachers' Training Inst; did research on methods of teaching geography and natural sci and on the local history and physical geography of the Urals; supervised compilation of first Sov teaching map of Urals; *Publ: K voprosu o ponyatii interesa i samodeyatel'nosti sredi uchashchikhsya* (The Concept of Pupil Interest and Independent Work) (1912); *Letnyaya shkola* (The Summer School) (1923); *Krayevedeniye i shkola* (Local History and the School) (1925); *Krayevedcheskiy printsip v prepodavanii geografii* (The Local History Principle in Geography Teaching) (1950), etc; *Died*: 25 May 1959.

KONDRATENKO, Stepan Fyodorovich (1906-1942) Party and govt official; CP member from 1929; *Born*: 29 Aug 1906 in vil Sherstyukovka, Poltava Province, son of a peasant; *Career*: Komsomol and govt work in Poltava Oblast; from 1939 secr, Poltava Oblast Comt, CP Ukr, with responsibility for agitation and propaganda; from Sept 1941 first secr, underground Poltava Oblast Comt, CP Ukr; staff commander of an oblast partisan unit; *Awards*: Order of Lenin (posthumous); *Died*: 17 Jan 1942 killed in action near vil Veprik, Poltava Oblast.

KONDRAT'YEV, Aleksandr Aleksandrovich (1886-1962) Mil commander; senior lt, Russian Navy; helped found Sov Navy; *Born*: 25 Feb 1886 in Kronstadt, son of a port employee; *Educ*: 1910 grad Naval School; *Career*: 1908-14 cadet, midshipman, then warrant officer on various ships of the Black Sea and Baltic Fleets; 1914-17 inspector, then company commander on the battleship "Aleksandr II"; after 1917 Feb Revol elected commander of the same battleship, which was renamed "The Dawn of Freedom"; July 1917 led a column of Baltic sailors in armed Bolshevik demonstration and sustained concussion; Oct 1917, by order of the Kronstadt Sov, took his ship into battle station to shield an insurgent Petrograd against possible attack by troops of the Provisional Govt; late 1917-late 1919 served on Baltic Fleet Personnel Bd, selecting detachments of sailors to be sent to the Civil War fronts; then fought personally against Yudenich's troops; 1920-21 chief of staff, Sea and River Forces on the Southwestern Front, then in charge of defense of Caucasian littoral of the Black and Azov Seas; 1921-22 chief of staff, Black Sea Fleet; 1922-23 worked for centr naval organs in Moscow; Nov 1923 discharged; subsequently worked for merchant marine and for Bd of Special Submarine Assignments; fought in WW 2; *Died*: 14 Dec 1962 in Leningrad.

KONDRAT'YEV, Nikolay Dmitriyevich (1892- ?) Economist; prof; *Born*: 1892; *Career*: 1917-19 member, Socialist Revol Party; pupil of economist and historian Tugan-Baranovskiy, a one-time assoc of Petlyura's Ukr govt; 1920-28 dir, Market Inst; prof, Timiryazev Agric Acad; assoc, USSR Pop Comrt of Finance and Pop Comrt of Agric; wrote reports for USSR Gosplan and lectured at Communist Acad; compiled first five-year agric plan for RSFSR; 1924 visited British Exhibition; 1925 sent to US for econ talks; developed econ theses and concepts contradicting Party line; defended private farming and proposed a redistribution of nat income in favor of the peasantry; opposed the state's monopoly on for trade and market manipulation; pleaded for slower industrialization on the grounds that econ health depends on the harmonious interplay of ind and agric; gained considerable support among fellow-economists and students and gave added impetus to "rightist deviation" within the Party, especially with his concept of "restorative prices", which was adopted by the Trotskyites; late 1930 arrested by OGPU on charges of "facilitating counter-revol activities", econ misplanning and spreading false information about USSR; was also accused of involvement with the Working Peasants' Party (an affiliate of the Ind Party) during collectivization; after his arrest his econ theories were condemned by the Agrarian Inst at the Communist Acad and by the Int Agrarian Inst; *Publ: Agrarnyy vopros* (The Agrarian Question); *Mirovoye khozyaystvo i yego konyunktury vo vremya i posle voyny* (The World Economy and Its Situation Before and After the War); *Sotsializatsiya zemli* (Socialization of the Land) (1918); *Proizvodstvo i sbyt maslichnykh semyan v svyazi s interesami krest'yanskogo khozyaystva* (The Production and Marketing of Oil-Producing Seeds in Relation to the Interests of the Peasant Economy) (1919); *Mikhail Ivanovich Tugan-Baranovskiy* (1923); *Perspektivnyy plan razvitiya sel'skogo khozyaystva 1923-28 godov* (The 1923-28 Long-Term Agricultural Development Plan); *Sovremennoye sostoyaniye narodnogo khozyaystva v svete vzaimootnosheniya industrii i sel'skogo khozyaystva* (The Present State of the National Economy in the Light of the Interrelationship of Industry and Agriculture) (1925); *Zadachi v oblasti sel'skogo khozyaystva v svyazi s obshchim razvitiyem narodnogo khozyaystva i yego industrializatsii* (The Tasks of Agriculture in Relation to the General Development of the National Economy and Its Industrialization) (1927); *Bol'shiye tsikly kon'yunktury* (The Great Economic Cycles) (1928); *Died*: date and place of death unknown.

KONDRATYUK, Yuriy Vasil'yevich (1900-1942) Inventor and rocketry pioneer; *Born*: 7 Sept 1900 in Lutsk, son of a teacher; *Educ*: 1918 grad Paul and Galagan College, Kiev; *Career*: studied the problems of space-flight; designed interplanetary rockets and suggested the feasibility of a manned lunar orbital station; worked at Ukr Ind Power Eng Research Inst; before WW 2 helped to design wind-operated electr power plant in Crimea; *Publ: Zavoyevaniye mezhplanetnykh prostorov* (The Conquest of Interplanetary Space) (1929); *Died*: 1942.

KONDYREV, Leonid Alekseyevich (1897-1961) Actor and producer; Pop Artiste of North Ossetian ASSR from 1953; Hon Artiste of RSFSR from 1957; *Born*: 17 June 1897; *Educ*: studied on V. P. Martynov's acting courses; *Career*: 1916 began stage career at Izhevsk Theater; 1923-29 and 1933-34 acted at theaters in Taganrog, Kazan', Stalingrad, etc; 1939-48 actor-producer, North Caucasian Mil Distr Theater, Rostov-on-Don; from 1948 actor-producer, Russian Theater of North Ossetian ASSR, Ordzhonikidze; *Roles*: Khlynov in *Goryacheye serdtse* (Warm Heart); Mamayev in *Na vsyakogo mudretsa dovol'no prostoty* (There's a Simpleton in Every Sage); Rasplyuyev in *Svad'ba Krechinskogo* (Krechinskiy's Wedding); Akim in *Vlast' t'my* (The Powers of Darkness); title role in Gorky's *Starik* (The Old Man); title role in Bakhterev and Razumovskiy's *Polkovodets Suvorov* (General Suvorov); the Sapper in Smirnov's *Lyudi, kotorykh ya videl* (People I Have Seen); *Productions: Vassa Zheleznova* (1951); *Vlast' t'my* (The Powers of Darkness) (1954); *Svoi lyudi - sochtyomsya* (Blood Is Thicker Than Water) (1954); Zola's *Rabourdin's Heirs* (1954), etc; *Died*: 23 Nov 1961.

KONI, Anatoliy Fyodorovich (1844-1927) Lawyer and publ figure; hon member, Russian (USSR) Acad of Sci from 1900; *Born*: 28 Jan 1844 in Petersburg, son of the writer and theater critic F.A. Koni; *Educ*: 1865 grad Law Fac, Moscow Univ; *Career*: from 1867 worked for judiciary; from 1871 prosecutor, from 1877 chm, Petersburg Okrug Court; 1878 presided over trial which acquitted V.I. Zasulich of shooting Petersburg's mayor F.F. Trepov; 1881-85 chm, Civil Dept, Petersburg Judicial Bd; from 1885 senior prosecutor, Criminal Appeals Dept, Senate; 1906 turned down proferred Min of Justice post; as a liberal, hoped to eliminate soc ills through reforms and spread of educ; defended idea of publ trial and trial by jury; from 1907 head, State Council; 1918-22 prof of criminal jurisprudence, Petrograd Univ; specialist in Russian lit and theater; wrote articles, reviews and read lectures and papers on the theater; a friend of Nekrasov, Goncharov, Tolstoy, Dostoyevskiy, Turgenev, etc; suggested to L. Tolstoy the subjects for his novel *Voskreseniye* (Resurrection) and his play *Zhivoy trup* (The Living Corpse) from cases in his legal practice; on his 75th anniversary elected hon member, Alexandrine Theater; 1919 founded Turgenev Soc; donated his lit archives to Pushkin Center, Leningrad; *Publ: Sudebnyye rechi* (Court Pleas) (1888); *Izbrannyye proizvedeniya* (Selected Works) (2 vol, 2nd ed 1959); *Na zhiznennom puti* (In Life's Career) (5 vol, 1912-29); *Died*: 17 Sept 1927.

KONONENKO, Pyotr Petrovich (1900-1965) Civil eng; Ukr Dep Min of Construction from 1956; Hon Builder of Ukr SSR from 1960; *Born*: 1900; *Educ*: 1924 grad Odessa Polytech Inst; *Career*: 1921-41 worked on various building projects, including metallurgical and coking plants; 1941-47 dep chief eng, Magnitogorsk Building Trust; 1947-48 dep chief eng, Zaporozh'ye Building Trust; 1948-55 chief eng, Dzerzhinsk Building Trust; 1955-56 dep dir, Main Dnieper Building Trust; *Awards*: Lenin Prize (1959); *Died*: Sept 1965.

KONOPLYOVA, L. V. (1891-1940) Politician; member, Socialist-Revolutionary Party; *Born*: 1891; *Career*: Bureau member, Mil Commission, CC, Socialist-Revolutionary Party and member, Centr Fighting Unit for Terrorism; helped to organize fighting units to combat Sov rule; 1922 sentenced to death by firing squad at trial of rightist Socialist-Revolutionaries but amnestied by All-Russian Centr Exec Comt; later arrested by State Security organs; *Died*: 1940 in imprisonment.

KONOVALOV, Dmitriy Petrovich (1856-1929) Chemist; Dr of Chemistry from 1885; prof from 1886; member, USSR Acad of Sci from 1923; *Born*: 22 Mar 1856; *Educ*: 1878 grad Petersburg Mining Inst; 1880 grad Petersburg Univ; *Career*: 1880-82 worked at A. M. Butlerov's laboratory and did research on the vapor tension of solutions under Prof Kundt at Strasbourg Univ; 1882-86 asst prof, 1886-91 prof, 1891-1907 head, Chair of Inorganic Chemistry, Petersburg Univ; also prof, Petersburg Inst of Communication Eng; 1884 defended master's thesis on the vapor tension of solutions, in which he formulated Konovalov's laws and, by a development of Mendeleyev's theory, proved that there is no clear-cut division between compounds and solutions and that the latter are just a special state of the former; 1885, in his doctor's thesis on the role of catalytic elements in dissociation phenomena, introduced the concept of the active surface, which played an important part in the development of the theory of heterogeneous catalysis; 1900-04 prof, from 1904 dir, Petersburg Mining Inst; 1907 dir, Russian Mining Dept; 1908-15 Russian Dep Min of Trade and Ind; 1916 resumed acad career as prof, Petrograd Technol Inst; 1918-19 prof, 1919-22 dir, Petrograd Mining Inst; also prof, Dnepropetrovsk Research Inst of Chemistry and Power Eng; after WW 1 helped to restore and develop Ukr chemical ind; from 1922 pres, Main Chamber of Weights and Measures; in research on thermal chemistry made a study of the relationship between the combustion heat of organic compounds and their structure; also did research on various aspects of chemical eng; from 1922, chm, Chemistry Branch, from 1923 pres, Russian Physiochemical Soc; hon member, various for soc; *Publ*: master's thesis *Ob uprugosti para rastvorov* (The Vapor Tension of Solutions) (1884); doctor's thesis *Rol' kontaktnykh deystviy v yavleniyakh dissotsiatsii* (The Role of Catalytic Factors in Dissociation Phenomena) (1885); *Materialy i protsessy khimicheskoy tekhnologii* (The Materials and Processes of Chemical Technology) (2 vol, 1924-25), etc; *Died*: 6 Jan 1929.

KONOVALOV, Nikolay Vasil'yevich (1900-1966) Neuropatholigist; prof from 1939; Dr of Med from 1937; member, USSR Acad of Med Sci from 1950; CP member from 1943; *Born*: 1900; *Educ*: 1924 grad Med Fac, 1st Moscow State Univ; *Career*: specialized under Prof L. O. Darkshevich, G. I. Rossolimo and Ye. K. Seppa at Dept of Neuropathology, Moscow Univ; 1934-36 head, Dept of Nervous Diseases, 3rd Moscow Med Inst; 1935-47 sci dir, Neurological Dept, Semashko Hospital, USSR Min of Communications; 1948-66 dir, Inst of Neurology, USSR Acad of Med Sci; 1950-58 vice-pres, USSR Acad of Med Sci; directed research on neurology for the entire USSR; specialized in degenerative disorders of the nervous system; studied connection between liver disorders and the pathology of the nervous system; described torula meningitis caused by torula histolytica; described clinical, pathomorphological and pathogenic features of hepatolenticular degeneration, termed the Westfall-Wilson-Konovalov disease in the USSR; co-ed, neurology section of *Bol'shaya meditsinskaya entsiklopediya* (Large Medical Encyclopedia) (2nd ed); member, ed bd, *Zhurnal nevropatologii i psikhiatrii imeni S. S. Korsakova*; chm, Expert Commission on Neuropathology and Psychiatry; chm, Higher Certifying Commission, USSR Min of Higher Education; chm Problem Commission for Basic Nervous and Mental Diseases, USSR Acad of Med Sci; wrote more than 60 works; *Publ*: doctor's thesis *Patofiziologiya i patologiya mozzhechka* (The Pathophysiology and Pathology of the Cerebellum) (1939); *Gepatolentikulyarnaya degeneratsiya* (Hepatolenticular Degeneration) (1948); *Gepato-tserebral'naya distrofiya* (Hepatocerebral Dystropy) (1960), etc; *Awards*: Lenin Prize (1961); other awards; *Died*: Apr 1966.

KONSTANTINOV, Pyotr Nikiforovich (1877-1959) Plant selectionist; member, All-Union Lenin Acad of Agric Sci from 1935; *Born*: 10 June 1877; *Career*: 1929-35 prof, Kuybyshev Agric Inst; from 1938 prof, Timiryazev Agric Acad, Moscow; bred (occasionally in teamwork) new strains of wheat, barley, millet, peas, chick-pea, flax, fodder plants and Euagropyrum for specific agroclimatic zones; *Publ: Lyutserna i yeyo kul'tura na yugo-vostoke Yevropeyskoy chasti SSSR* (Lucerne and Its Cultivation in the Southeast of the European USSR) (1932); *Zhitnyak* (Euagropyrum) (1936); *Metodika polevykh opytov (s elementami teorii oshibok)* (Field Experiment Methods [With Elements of Error Theory]) (1939); *Osnovy sel'skokhozyaystvennogo opytnogo dela (v polevodstve)* (The Principles of Agricultural Field Experimentation) (1952); *Awards*: two Orders of Lenin; Stalin Prize (1943); other orders; *Died*: Oct 1959.

KONSTANTINOVICH, A.S. (1866-1939) Party official; CP member from 1913; *Born*: 1866; siter-in-law of I.F. Armand; *Career*: 1905 joined revol movement; 1908 arrested and exiled to Vologda Province; 1911 emigrated; after 1917 Oct Revol worked for Moscow RSDRP(B) Comt and Comintern Exec Comt; *Died*: 1939.

KONSTANTINOV, Nikolay Aleksandrovich (1894-1958) Educ historian; Dr of Pedag; prof; member, RSFSR Acad of Pedag Sci from 1945; Hon Sci Worker of Uzbek SSR from 1943; *Born*: 7 June 1894 in Telšiai, Lith; *Educ*: 1918 grad Fac of History and Philosophy, Moscow Univ; 1918 studied at Shelaputin Higher Teachers' Training Inst; 1920 completed postgrad studies at Red Army Mil Teachers' Training Course; *Career*: 1920-24 worked for Main Bd of Mil Educ Establishments; from 1924 worked for Krupskaya Communist Training Acad, Inst of Non-Russian Schools, Inst of Schools, etc; 1945-57 head, Chair of Pedag, Moscow Univ; 1946-49 also dir, Inst of the Theory and History of Pedag, RSFSR Acad of Pedag Sci; from 1949 prof, Potyomkin Teachers' Training Inst, Moscow; 1952-57 head, Dept of the History of Pedag, Inst of the Theory and History of Pedag, RSFSR Acad of Pedag Sci; *Publ*: Ocherki po istorii sredney shkoly v Rossii (Studies in the History of the Secondary School in Russia) (1947); *Ocherki po istorii sovetskoy shkoly RSFSR za 30 let* (The 30-Year History of Soviet Schools in the RSFSR) (1948); *Shkol'naya politika v kolonial'nykh stranakh v XIX-XX vekakh* (School Policy in Colonial Countries During the 19th and 20th Century) (1948); *Ocherki po istorii nachal'nogo obrazovaniya v Rossii* (Studies in the History of Primary Education in Russia) (1949); *Ocherki po istorii sredney shkoly* (Studies in the History of the Secondary School) (1956); textbook *Istoriya pedagogiki* (The History of Pedagogics) (1958); *Awards:* Order of Lenin; Order of the Red Banner of Labor; Badge of Hon; *Died*: 18 Apr 1958.

KONSTANTINOV, Vasiliy Dmitriyevich (1899-1952) Inventor; designed cinematographic equipment; CP member from 1947; *Born*: 1899; *Career*: from 1929 cameraman with Soyuzkinokhronika in Moscow; 1932, while working at Moscow studios of Soyuzkinokhronika, helped invent *Khronikon* motion picture sound camera which was widely used for newsreels; 1937 invented *Konvas* cine-camera and tripod; 1940 invented "Konvas Sound Camera" for simultaneous photography and sound recording on the same film; 1948 invented popular portable "Konvas Automatic" cine-camera for newsreel photography; 1950 invented original gate mechanism and telescopic viewfinder, which he incorporated in a new model of the universal "Konvaskhronikon-3 Rodina" cine-camera; *Died*: 29 June 1952.

KONYUS, Georgiy Eduardovich (1862-1933) Musicologist, composer and music teacher; *Born*: 13 Oct 1862 in Moscow; *Educ*: 1889 grad Moscow Conservatory, where he studied under Tchaikovsky, S. I. Taneyev and A. S. Arenskiy; *Career*: 1891-99 taught at Moscow Conservatory; 1901-05 taught at Music and

Drama College, Moscow Philharmonic Soc; from 1912 prof, Saratov Conservatory; from 1920 prof, Moscow Conservatory; taught music theory to the composers A. N. Skryabin, A. F. Gedike, S. N. Vasilenko, R. M. Glier and A. B. Gol'denveyzer; developed theory of metrotectonism, according to which all music has a common abstract principle of composition; *Works*: romances and piano pieces; suite for orchestra and choir *Iz detskoy zhizni* (From Childhood); symphonic poem *Les shumit* (The Rustling Forest) to words by V. G. Korolenko (1890); ballet "Daita" (1896); symphonic arrangement of French revol song "Carmagnole", etc; *Publ: Sbornik zadach, upryazhneniy i voprosov (1,001) dlya prakticheskogo izucheniya elementarnoy teorii muzyki* (A Thousand and one Tasks, Exercises and Questions for the Practical Study of Elementary Music Theory) (1892); *Zadachnik po instrumentovke* (A Task Book on Instrumentation) (3 vol, 1906-09); *Kritika traditsionnoy teorii v oblasti muzykal'nykh form* (A Critique of the Traditional Theory of Musical Forms) (1932); *Nauchnoye obosnovaniye muzykal'ogo sintaksisa* (The Scientific Foundation of Musical Syntax) (1935); *Died*: 28 Aug 1933 in Moscow.

KOPEL'MAN, Solomon Lazarevich (1889-1966) Roentgenologist; assoc prof; *Born*: 1889, son of an office worker; *Educ*: 1925 grad Med Fac, 2nd Moscow Univ; *Career*: 1925-28 postgrad student, Moscow Roentgenological Inst, then intern and asst prof, Chair of Roentgenology, 2nd Moscow Med Inst; 1928-41 roentgenological consultant, Centr Inst of Hematology and Blood Transfusion; 1932-34 asst prof, 1934-66 assoc prof, Chair of Roentgenology, Centr Inst of Postgrad Med Training; 1932-41 senior assoc, 1941-46 head, X-Ray Diagnosis Dept, State Roentgenological and Radiological Research Inst, RSFSR Min of Health; 1941-45 roentgenological consultant at various evacuation hospitals in Moscow; member, then hon member, All-Union, All-Russian and Moscow Soc of Roentgenologists and Radiologists; member, ed council, journal *Vestnik rentgenologii i radiologii*; did research on diseases of the gastro-intestinal and biliary tracts; devised new method of examining the upper section of the stomach; described the x-ray semiotics of cancer of the cardiac region of the stomach, salverform cancer, etc; wrote over 70 works; including several monographs and textbook articles; *Died*: 1966 in Moscow.

KOPENKIN, Ivan Iosifovich (1917-1942) Commander of partisan detachment during WW 2; *Born*: 1917 in vil Novobokovo, now Ryazan' Oblast, son of a peasant; *Educ*: high school; *Career*: early in WW 2 Kopenkin founded Budennyy Partisan Detachment on instructions from the Zaporozhian Oblast Comt CP Ukr; Oct-Dec 1941 commanded partisan detachment in Khar'kov and Poltava Oblasts; May 1942 operated with his detachment behind the German lines in Lugansk and Khar'kov Oblasts; *Awards*: Hero of the Sov Union; *Died*: June 1942 in battle with German troops near Novaya Vodolaga, Khar'kov Oblast.

KOPP, Issidor Filippovich (1898-1963) Ophthalmologist; Dr of Med; prof; *Born*: 1898; *Educ*: 1923 grad Odessa State Med Inst; *Career*: from 1923 specialized in ocular diseases at the Clinic of the Odessa Med Inst; 1924-25 at Grishman Ukr Inst of Ocular Diseases, Khar'kov; 1925-41 head, Dept of Ocular Diseases, Zaporozh'ye City Hospital; 1941-44 in Sov Army; 1944-63 head, Dept of Ocular Diseases, Stalin (now Donets) Med Inst; compiled research works on various fields of ophthalmology, especially corneal transplants, eye injuries and glaucoma; his work on eye injuries enabled him to assess various new methods of surgical treatment of eye wounds; 1960 attended congress of European Ophthalmological Soc in Athens; wrote more than 80 works; *Publ*: co-ed, manuals: *Voprosy glaznoy travmy* (Eye Injuries) (1956); *Rukovodstvo po glaznym boleznyam* (Manual of Ocular Diseases) (1960); *Osnovy terapii zabolevaniy glaz* (The Principles of Ocular Therapy) (1963), etc; *Awards*: Order of the Red Banner of Labor; Order of the Red Star; medals "For the Defense of Stalingrad" and "Victory over Germany"; Public Health Badge; *Died*: 1963.

KOPP, Viktor Leont'yevich (1880-1930) Diplomat; CP member from 1917; *Born*: 1880; *Career*: 1898 joined Soc-Democratic movement; 1903-05 organized smuggling of illegal lit across the German border; 1904 favored reconcilation with the Mensheviks, then joined them; fall 1905 returned to Russia; 1909 arrested and deported abroad where he contributed for a while to Trotsky's Viennese *Pravda*; 1913 returned to Russia, then conscripted; 1914 sent to the front; 1915-18 prisoner-of-war in Germany; 1919-30 worked for USSR Pop Comrt of For Affairs, 1919-21 plen, RSFSR Pop Comrt of For Affairs and RSFSR Pop Comrt of For Trade, then RSFSR rep in Germany; 1921 RSFSR rep for prisoner-of-war affairs in Germany; 1923 RSFSR plen at talks with Poland; 1924-25 Collegium member, USSR Pop Comrt of For Affairs and the latter's plen with the RSFSR Council of Pop Comr; 1925-27 USSR plen in Japan; 1927-30 USSR plen in Sweden; *Died*: 1930.

KOPTELOV, Mikhail Yefremovich (1904-1952) Diplomat; envoy extraordinary and plen, 2nd class; *Born*: 1904; *Career*: from 1936 in diplomatic service; 1938-40 administrator, Sov Consulate-Gen in Danzig; 1941 Sov consul-gen in Vienna; 1941-42 Sov consul-gen in Pehlevi, Iran; 1945-48 dep polit adviser, Sov Section, Allied Control Commission in Austria; 1948-51 Soviet political representative attached to Austrian government; 1951-52 deputy head, 3rd European Department, USSR Ministry of Foreign Affairs; 1952 dep head, Consular Bd, USSR Min of For Affairs; *Died:* 1952.

KOPYLENKO, Aleksandr Ivanovich (1900-1958) Ukr writer; CP member from 1950; *Born*: 1 Aug 1900 in Konstantinograd, Poltava Province (now Krasnograd, Khar'kov Oblast), son of a railroad worker; *Educ*: 1920 grad teachers' seminary; 1920-25 studied at Biology Fac, Khar'kov Inst of Public Educ; *Career*: 1921 first work published; wrote for various newspapers and journals; began lit career in *Plug* (Plough) Union of Peasant Writers; member, *Gart* (Type-Metal) and *Vaplit* (All-Union Assoc of Proletarian Lit) unions; *Publ:* story collections: *Kara-Krucha* (1923); "In the Name of the Ukrainian People" (1924); "A Boisterous Booze-Up" (1925); "Tough Stuff" (1928); "The Brothers" (1944); "Indomitable Life" (1945); novels: "A City is Born" (1932); "Very Well" (1936); "The Kids in the Tenth Grade" (1938); "The Lieutenants" (1947); "The Big Land" (1957); children's books: "The Boy from Petrograd" (1947); "How They Are" (1948), etc; *Died*: 1 Dec 1958 in Kiev.

KOPYLOV, N. V. (1889-1940) Party and govt official; CP member from 1912; *Born*: 1889; *Career*: participant in 1905-07 Revol in Tula; Party work in Petrograd and Yekaterinoslav; subjected to reprisals by Tsarist authorities; after 1917 Oct Revol chm, Tula Province Party Comt; 1922-24 member, ed bd, newspaper *Bednota*; 1921-22 sided with "workers' opposition"; signed 22-signatory declaration to Comintern; after 11th Party Congress left the "workers' opposition"; from 1924 admin work; Supr Sovnarkhoz plen in France; head, Road and Machine Building Trust; head, All-Union Assoc of Power Eng, USSR Pop Comrt of Heavy Ind; arrested by State Security organs; *Died*: 1940 in imprisonment.

KORCHAGINA-ALEKSANDROVSKAYA (née KORCHAGINA; added husband's name as ALEKSANDROVSKAYA), Yekaterina Pavlovna (1874-1951) Russian actress; Pop Artiste of the USSR from 1936; dep, USSR Supr Sov of 1st convocation; *Born*: 23 Dec 1874 in Kostroma; daughter of provincial actors whose stage name was Ol'gin; *Career*: from early childhood acted on the stage; 1887 under the stage name of Ol'gin began independant career as actress (signed her first contract in Perm'); until 1890 worked in various Russian cities (Arkhangel'sk, Mogilyov, Yelets, Tula, Tambov, etc); 1890-95 played in Ivanovo-Voznesensk; 1896-1903 in Pskov; married provincial actor V. V. Aleksandrovskiy; from 1895 performed under the name of Korchagina-Aleksandrovskaya; 1915 made debut at Aleksandrinskiy Theater (now Leningrad Pushkin Theater) and was given permanent engagement; performed many of her best roles there; 1937 elected dep, USSR Supr Sov; *Roles*: about 400 on the provincial stage; Lipochka in *Svoi lyudi - sochtyomsya* (Birds of a Feather Flock Together); Varvara in *Groza* (The Storm); Mar'ya Antonovna in *Revizor* (The Government Inspector); Liza in *Gore ot uma* (Woe From Wit); Yelena in *Meshchane* (The Philistines); Nastya in *Na dne* (The Lower Depths); played in vaudeville and melodramas; 1904-07 worked at Komissarzhevskaya Theater in Petersburg; Domna Pantelevna in *Talanty i poklonniki* (Talents and Admirers) (1904); Kaurova in Turgenev's *Zavtrak u predvoditelya* (Lunch with the Marshal) (1905); later played exclusively elderly women; at Krasov Theater in Petersburg played Ulita in *Les* (The Forest) (1907) and Poshlyopkina in *Revizor* (The Government Inspector) (1907) which later became her best roles; 1908-15 engagement at Theater of the Lit and Arts Soc (Petersburg); specialized in "comic old women", Galchikha in *Bez viny vinovaty* (Guilty Without Guilt) (1908); Matryona in *Vlast' t'my* (The Powers of Darkness) (1908); Emma Shtark in Lunacharskiy's *Kantsler i slesar'* (The Chancellor and the Locksmith) (1923); Ivan Kalyayev's mother in Kalugin and Berenshtam's *Ivan Kalyayev*

(1926); Pugachyov's mother in Trenyov's *Pugachyovshchina* (The Pugachyov Revolt) (1926); the nurse Khristina Arkhipovna in *Platon Krechet* (1935); Kozlikha in Seyfullina and Pravdukhin's *Virineya* (1926); Dobzhina in Afinogenov's *Chudak* (The Crank) (1930); Karaulova in Shkvarkin's *Chuzhoy rebyonok* (Another's Child) (1934); Demid'yevna in *Nashestviye* (Invasion) (1943); from 1943 performed in films; Ulita in *Iudushka Golovlyov*; Feklyusha in *Groza* (The Storm), etc; *Publ: Moy put'* (My Career) (1934); 2nd ed entitled *Stranitsy moyey zhizni* (Pages of My Life) (1939); *Awards*: two Orders of Lenin; Order of the Red Banner of Labor; Stalin Prize (1943); *Died*: 15 Jan 1951 in Leningrad.

KORCHAK-CHEPURKOVSKIY, Avksentiy Vasil'yevich (1857-1947) Epidemiologist and hygienist; Dr of Med from 1898; prof; member, Ukr Acad of Sci; *Born*: 28 Feb 1857 in Konstantinograd, now Krasnograd, Khar'kov Oblast; *Educ*: 1883 grad Med Fac, Khar'kov Univ; *Career*: 1883-99 worked as rural hygienist in Ukr and Bessarabia; 1898 defended doctor's thesis on the epidemiology of diphtheria; 1899-1904 health officer, 1904-07 head, Health Dept, Kiev Town Council; 1907 dismissed for polit reasons; 1903-18 assoc prof, Chair of Hygiene, Kiev Univ; during this period did research on the relationship between wars and epidemics, the role of the state in the health service and various problems of epidemiology and hygiene; after 1917 Oct Revol dean, Med Fac and head, Chair of Hygiene, Kiev Univ; 1927-34 member, All-Ukr Centr Exec Comt; 1928-33 secr, Ukr Acad of Sci; during Sov period did research on health statistics, the working conditions of miners and the classification and nomenclature of diseases, compiling first nomenclature in Ukr; also studied the history of med; *Publ: Epidemicheskiye voprosy v sisteme issledovaniy sanitarnogo sostoyaniya naseleniya* (The Question of Epidemics in Research on Public Health) (1896); doctor's thesis *Materialy dlya izucheniya epidemiy difterii (epidemiologii) v Rossii* (Material for the Study of Diphteria Epidemics [Epidemiology] in Russia) (1898); *Voyny i epidemii* (Wars and Epidemics) (1904); *Nomenklatura khvorob* (A Nomenclature of Diseases) (1927); *Died*: 27 Nov 1947 in Kiev.

KORCHMARYOV, Klimentiy Arkad'yevich (1899-1958) Composer; Hon Art Worker of Turkm SSR from 1944; *Born*: 3 July 1899 in Verkhnedneprovsk; *Educ*: 1919 grad Odessa Conservatory; *Career*: one of first composers of Sov revol music; 1939-47 worked in Turkm, where he wrote first Turkm nat ballets, including "The Gay Deceiver" (1940); *Works*: operas *Ivan-soldat* (Soldier John) (1927) and *Ditya radosti* (Child of Joy) (1953); ballets *Krepostnaya balerina* (Ballerina Serf) (1927); *Alen'kiy tsvetochek* (The Little Crimson Flower) (1949); two operettas; three vocal symphonies, including *Gollandiya* (Holland) (1950); symphonic and instrumental pieces and folk-song arrangements; music for the films: *Troye s odnoy ulitsy* (Three from the Same Street) (1936); *Poyedinok* (The Duel) (1945); *Dalyokaya nevesta* (The Distant Bride) (1948); *Ten' u pirsa* (The Shadow by the Pier) (1955), etc; *Awards*: Stalin Prize (1951); *Died*: 7 Apr 1958 in Moscow.

KOREPANOV-KEDRA, Dmitriy Ivanovich (1892-1949) Udmurt writer; CP member from 1923; *Born*: 28 Sept 1892 in vil Igra, son of a peasant; *Educ*: studied at Kazan' Teachers' Training Seminary; *Career*: expelled in last year at Seminary for his free-thinking ideas; fought with Siberian partisans during Civil War; 1923-26 ed, Udmurt newspaper *Gudyri*; helped establish Udmurt orthography and lit language; arrested by State Security organs; *Publ*: tragedy *Eshterek* (1915); novelette *Vuzhgurt* (1926), reissued as *Vuzhgurt Shudders* in 1958; novel "The Heavy Yoke" (1929), etc; *Died*: 12 Nov 1949 in imprisonment; posthumously rehabilitated.

KORF, Rafail Grigor'yevich (1893-1942) Actor and producer; Hon Artiste of RSFSR from 1934; *Born*: 13 Mar 1893; Educ; studied at Vocal Dept, Odessa Conservatory; *Career*: 1913 began stage career in Odessa; 1922 actor, Theater of the Revol; from 1924 actor and producer, Moscow Satire Theater, where he specialized in comic character studies; also played light comedy in partnership with Ya. M. Rudin; 1942 accompanied concert troupe to the front and was killed in encirclement; *Roles*: Naryvaytis and Nabaldashnikov in Ardov and Nikulin's *Skloka* (The Squabble) and *114-aya stat'ya* (Article 114); Ugryum-Burcheyev in *Gorod Glupov* (Foolstown) after Saltykov-Shchedrin; Chechkov in Sumbatov-Yuzhin's *Dzhentel'men* (The Gentleman); the Prime Minister in A. N. Tolstoy's *Chyortov most* (The Devil's Bridge); Grifelev in Shkvarkin's *Prostaya devushka* (A Simple Girl); Tulyaga in Krapiva's *Kto smeyotsya poslednim* (He Who Laughs Last); *Productions*: Krapiva's "He Who Laughs Last" (1939); Finn's *Sashka* (1940); *Died*: 1942.

KORGANOV, Grigoriy Nikonovich (1886-1918) Revolutionary; comr of Baku Commune; *Born*: 1886 in Tiflis, son of a mil official; *Educ*: 1914 grad Moscow Univ; *Career*: 1905 expelled from 8th grade of high school for taking part in a student demonstration and strike; moved to Baku, where he graduated from high school after external studies; enrolled at Fac of History and Philology, Moscow Univ; continued Party work in Moscow in underground Bolshevik circles and headed assoc of Caucasian students; 1911-12 served with artillery in Russian Army; 1914 re-drafted into the army and sent to the Caucasian Front; as an officer carried out revol propaganda in the army; after 1917 Feb Revol active in revol army orgs; May 1917 headed Bolshevik faction at 1st Congress of Caucasian Army (Tiflis); 10-23 Dec 1917 elected chm, 2nd Congress of Caucasian Army, held in Tiflis; the Congress adopted Bolshevik resolutions and founded a new Distr Army Council headed by Korganov; 12 Dec 1917 the Council elected Korganov head of its exec organ - the Mil Revol Comt of the Caucasian Army; Jan 1918 Korganov moved from Tiflis to Baku, where he helped muster regular Red Army units to fight the Transcaucasian anti-Sov coalition; Mar 1918 appointed member, Comt for the Revol Defense of Baku; from Apr 1918 Pop Comr of Naval Affairs, Baku Council of Pop Comr; led revol troops during German-Turkish assault of Baku; Aug 1918 arrested after collapse of Sov regime in Baku; *Died*: 20 Sept 1918 shot with 25 other Baku comr.

KORGUYEV, Matvey Mikhaylovich (1883-1943) Russian story-teller; member, USSR Writers' Union; *Born*: 1883 in vil Keret', now Loukhi Rayon, Karelian ASSR, son of a poor peasant; *Career*: orphaned at an early age; began work at the age of nine; member of a fishing kolkhoz; in 1930's more than 100 of Korguyev's fairy tales were written down by A. N. Nechayev (78 of them were published in 1939); could also relate various epics and Karelian runes which he had learned from his mother; his repertoire included magic tales notable for their sustained epic style and abundant details of everyday life; gave narrations in Moscow, Leningrad and Petrozavodsk; *Publ* fairy tales *Andrey Strelets* (Andrey the Archer); *Shkip* (The Urchin); *Yelena Prekrasnaya* (Helen the Beautiful); *Pro Chapaya* (About Chapay); *Died*: 1943.

KORIN, Pavel Dmitriyevich (1892-1967) Painter; member, USSR Acad of Arts from 1958; Pop Artist of RSFSR from 1958; Pop Artist of USSR from 1962; *Born*: 7 July 1892 in vil Palekh, now Ivanovo Oblast, son of a peasant icon-painter; *Educ*: 1916 grad Moscow College of Painting, Sculpture and Architecture; *Career*: from 1957 bd member, USSR Artists' Union; 1963 exhibited paintings in Moscow; from 1965 member, All-Russian Soc for the Preservation of Historical and Cultural Monuments; 1965 visited US, France and Italy and exhibited paintings in New York; *Works*: portraits: M. Gorky (1932); M. Nesterov (1939); A. Tolstoy (1940); V. Kachalov (1940); N. Gamaleya (1941); G. Zhukov (1945); P. Rybalko (1947); S. Konenkov (1947); M. Sar'yan (1956); the cartoonists M. V. Kupryanov, P. N. Krylov and N. A. Sokolov (1958); various WW 2 generals; landscapes: "My Fatherland" (1928-47); "Smolensk" (1953); triptych *Aleksandr Nevskiy* (1942-47); mosaics and glass paintings for the Moscow subway stations Komsomol'skaya kol'tsevaya (1951) and Novoslobodskaya; mosaic for an auditorium at Moscow Univ (1952); portrait suites of the folk painter R. Simonov, the artist M. Mar'yan, the Italian painter R. Guttuzo and the cartoonists Kupryanov, Krylov and Sokolov (1963), etc; *Awards*: Stalin Prize (1953); Lenin Prize (1963); Order of Lenin (1967); *Died*: Nov 1967.

KORK, Avgust Ivanovich (1887-1937) Est mil commander; lt-col, Gen Staff, Russian Army; army commander, 2nd class, Sov Army from 1935; CP member from 1927; *Born*: 22 July 1887 in vil Ardlakyulya, Liflyand Province, son of a peasant; *Educ*: 1908 grad Chuguyev Infantry Cadet College; 1914 grad Nikolay Mil Acad; *Pos*: from 1905 in Russian Army; 1908-11 officer, 98th Infantry Yur'yev Regt; 1914 worked on staff, Vilnius Mil Distr; 1914-17 senior officer-at-large, 20th Army Corps Staff; senior adjutant, 3rd Siberian Army Corps and 8th Infantry Div Staffs; asst senior adjutant, Operations and Intelligence Branches, 10th Army Staff; Air Force field officer, Western Front Staff; acting chief, Operations Dept, Western Front Staff; awarded five battle-field orders; 14 June 1918 joined Red Army; 1918 junior clerk, then branch head, Operations Dept, All-Russian Gen Staff; head,

Operations and Intelligence Dept, 9th Army Staff; 1918-19 consultant for Est Labor Commune, RSFSR Pop Comrt of Mil Affairs; chief of staff, Est Army; asst commander, 7th Army; June 1919-Oct 1920 commander, 15th Army at Petrograd and on Western Front; Oct 1920-May 1921 commander, 6th Army, Southern Front; 1921-22 commander, Khar'kov Mil Distr; 1922 asst commander, Ukr and Crimean Armed Forces; 1922-23 commander, Turkestani Front; 1923 asst head, Main Bd, Red Air Force, 1923-25 asst commander, then commander, Western Mil Distr; 1925 commander, Caucasian Red Banner Army; 1925-27 commander, Western Mil Distr; 1927-28 commander, Leningrad Mil Distr; 1928-29 mil attaché in Germany; 1929 chief of supply, Red Army; 1929-35 commander, Moscow Mil Distr; 1935-37 head, Frunze Mil Acad; from 1934 member, Mil Council, Pop Comrt of Defense; *Career*: fall 1919 his 15th Army played an important role in repelling Yuredich's attack on Petrograd; May 1920 fought in counterattack on the Polish Front; Nov 1920 his 6th Army forded the Sivash, attacked Gen Wrangel's troops from the rear and opened the way to the Crimea for the Red Army; May 1937 arrested by NKVD; 11 June 1937 sentenced to be shot along with Marshal Tukhachevskiy and others; *Awards*: two Orders of the Red Banner; Golden Weapon; *Died*: 12 June 1937 executed; posthumously rehabilitated.

KORNEYEV, Il'ya Il'ich (1887-1957) Party and govt official; CP member from 1912; *Born*: 1887; *Educ*: 1934 grad Moscow Ind Acad; *Career*: started work at the age of 12 at Putilov Plant (Petrograd) first as an apprentice, then as a lathe operator; 1914-15 elected Bd member, then chm, Putilov Plant Sick Fund; 1915 arrested and deported from Petrograd to the Urals, where he worked at the Lys'venskiy Plant; 1916 returned to Petrograd, where he worked for the "Promet" Plant; 1917 moved to Taganrog, where he helped plan armed rebellion; member, Mil Revol Comt, Russo-Baltic Plant; after Bolshevik seizure of power elected dep, Taganrog City Sov; 1920-23 Ukr Pop Comr of Soc Security; 1923-24 exec secr, Taganrog Okrug Party Comt; 1925-26 Ukr Dep Pop Comr of Workers and Peasants' Inspection and chm, Ukr Centr Control Commission; 1927-31 chm, Stalingrad Province Sovnarkhoz and construction chief, Stalingrad Shipyard; 1935-53 exec work in the aircraft ind; from 1953 pensioner; *Died*: Sept 1957.

KORNILOV, Boris Petrovich (1907-1938) Russian poet; *Born*: 16 July 1907 in vil Pokrovskoye, Nizhniy Novgorod Province; *Career*: 1923 first verse published; late 1920's active in lit soc of journal *Smena* in Leningrad; member, Leningrad Branch, Russian Assoc of Proletarian Writers; arrested by State Security organs; *Publ: Kniga stikhov* (Book of Verse) (1933); poems "Salt" (1931); "The Theses of a Novel" (1933); "Criminal Investigation Agent" (1933); "The Beginning of the Earth" (1936); "Samson" (1936);; "Tripol'ye" (1933); "My Africa" (1935); songs "Song of a Man I Met"; "The Komsomol Red Fleet," etc; propaganda play *Vosh'* (The Louse); chilren's verse *Kak ot myoda u medvedya zuby nachali bolet'* (How the Bear's Teeth Ached from Honey), etc; *Stikhotvoreniya i poemy* (Verse and Poems) (1960); *Died*: 21 Nov 1938 in imprisonment; posthumously rehabilitated.

KORNILOV, Konstantin Nikolayevich (1879-1957) Psychologist; Dr of Pedag Sci; prof from 1921; member, RSFSR Acad of Pedag Sci from 1944; *Born*: 21 Mar 1879 in Tyumen'; *Educ*: 1898 grad Omsk Teachers' Seminary; 1910 grad Moscow Univ; *Career*: 1898-1905 worked as schoolteacher in Siberia; 1910-16 assoc, from 1916 assoc prof, Psychological Inst, Moscow Univ; from 1918 propagandist; from 1920 member, State Learned Council, RSFSR Pop Comrt of Educ; 1921 founded Pedag Fac, Moscow Univ, which was expanded into the State Lenin Teachers' Training Inst; became dean and head, Chair of Psychology at this inst; 1923-30 and 1938-41 dir, Psychological Research Inst; 1923-57 dep, Moscow Sov; 1923 and 1924 read papers at 1st and 2nd All-Russian Psychoneurological Congresses, Moscow, on the necessity of reorganizing psychology on the basis of dialectical materialism; criticized G. I. Chelpanov's school of psychology; 1931 criticized for adhering to mechanistic concepts, for striking a compromise between subjectivism and objectivism and for committing ideological errors; 1944-50 vice-pres, RSFSR Acad of Pedag Sci; 1945-56 ed, journal *Sem'ya i shkola*; 1955-57 member, ed collegium, journal *Voprosy psikhologii*; wrote over 100 works on psychology and pedag, notably on will-power training; *Publ: Sovremennaya psikhologiya i marksizm* (Modern Psychology and Marxism) (2nd ed, 1925); *Ocherk psikhologii rebyonka doshkol'nogo vozrasta* (A Study of the Psychology of the Pre-School Child) (3rd ed, 1927); *Ucheniye o reaktsiyakh cheloveka (Reaktologiya)* (The Theory of Human Reactions [Reactology]) (3rd ed, 1927); *Uchebnik psikhologii* (A Psychology Textbook) (5th ed, 1931); *Psikhologiya. Uchebnik dlya pedagogicheskikh uchilishch* (Psychology. A Textbook for Teachers' Training Colleges) (1946); *Awards*: Order of Lenin; *Died*: 10 July 1957.

KORNILOV, Lavr Georgiyevich (1870-1918) Mil commander; infantry gen, Russian Army; co-founder, Volunteer Army; *Born*: 31 Aug 1870 in Ust'-Kamenogorsk, son of a retired officer of Siberian Cossack Army; *Educ*: 1889 grad Siberian Cadet Corps; 1892 grad Mikhail Artillery College; 1898 grad Gen Staff Acad; *Career*: 1892-95 served in Turkestan; 1898-1904 reconnaissance officer, Staff of Turkestani Mil Distr, surveilling Afghan border, Eastern Turkestan, India and eastern provinces of Persia; 1904-05 chief of staff, 1st Infantry Brigade with army in the field in the Far East; after Russo-Japanese War officer with Main Bd of Gen Staff; 1907-11 mil agent in China; 1914-15 commanded brigade, then 48th Infantry Div against Austrians; Apr 1915 wounded and captured; July 1916 escaped from imprisonment; 1915-17 commander, 25th Army Corps; Mar-Apr 1917 commanded Petrograd Mil Distr; May-July 1917 commanded 8th Army on Southwestern Front; 31 July-9 Sept 1917 supr commander in chief; early Sept 1917, with the consent of Kerenskiy's close aides, such as Savenkov, began to concentrate near Petrograd troops of Gen Krymov's 3rd Mounted Corps with the aim of crushing the Bolshevik orgs in Petrograd, eliminating the dichotomous rule of the Provisional Govt and the Petrograd Sov, and establishing a mil dictatorship or an authoritarian govt; 9 Sept 1917, because of this, Kerenskiy dismissed him as supr commander in chief and 15 Sept 1917 ordered his arrest; 2 Dec 1917, after Oct Coup, escaped with his supporters from Bykhov Prison, made his way to the Don and helped muster the Volunteer Army to fight Sov regime; 12 Apr 1918 mortally wounded by shrapnel in the storming of Yekaterionodar; *Died*: 12 Apr 1918 of his wounds, without regaining consciousness; 15 Apr 1918 buried at German colony Gnachbau; after Sov troops seized the colony his remains were exhumed and destroyed.

KORNOUKHOV, Nikolay Vasil'yevich (1903-1958) Civil eng; prof; member, USSR Acad of Sci from 1951; assoc, Inst of Construction Mechanics, USSR Acad of Sci from 1935; prof, Kiev Civil Eng Inst from 1948; Hon Sci and Tech Worker of USSR from 1954; CP member from 1941; *Born*: 23 Oct 1903 in Nezhin, now Chernigov Oblast, son of a teacher; *Educ*: 1928 grad Kiev Politech Inst; *Career*: 1928-31 designed bridges; 1931-48 lecturer, Kiev Civil Eng Inst; 1940-44 dir, Inst of Construction Mechanics, USSR Acad of Sci; 1939-41 corresp member, USSR Acad of Sci; devised various exact and approximate methods of calculating stability and of making combined calculations of the strength and stability of structures; worked on theory of the stability of structures within and beyond the limits of elasticity; *Publ: Prochnost' i ustoychivost' sterzhnevykh sistem i interpolyatsionno-integratsionny metod resheniya diferentsial'nykh uraveneniy prochnosti i ustoychivosti neprozmaticheskikh sterzhney* (The Strength and Stability of Pivotal Systems and the Interpolation-Integration Method of Solving Differential Equations of the Strength and Stability of Non-Prismatic Pivots) (1949); *Opredeleniye chastot sobstvennykh kolebaniy svobodnykh ramnykh sistem po metodu osnovnykh neizvestnykh* (Determining the Self-Oscillation Frequencies of Free Frame Systems by the Basic Unknown Quantities Method) (1951); *Osobyy sluchay poteri ustoychivosti, konechnyye deformatsii i ustoychivost' prosteyshey formy* (A Special Case of Stability Loss, Final Deformations and Stability of the Simplest Form) (1952); *Raschyot slozhnykh ram po metodu peremeshcheniy s uchyotom sdviga i shiriny sterzhney* (Calculating Complex Frames by the Travel Method with Allowance for Shift Deformations and Breadth of Pivots) (1959), etc; *Awards*: Stalin Prize (1950); *Died*: 2 June 1958.

KORNYANU, Leonid Yefimovich (1909-1957) Mold poet and playwright; CP member from 1945; *Born*: 1 Jan 1909 in vil Koshnitsi, now Mold SSR; *Educ*: grad Tiraspol' Teachers' Training Inst; postgrad studies at Inst of Philosophy, Lit and History; *Career*: 1928 first work published; wrote mainly on Mold and Sov themes; translated the works of the Ukr writers I. Franko and P. Tychine; *Publ*: play "In the Valleys of Moldavia" (1944); coauthor, musical comedy "Marika's Happiness" (1951); drama "Iljana's Carpet" (1953); play "Beyond the Blue Danube" (1955); variety show

"The Bitterness of Love" (1957); historical drama "The Source of Friendship," etc; *Died*: 26 Nov 1957.

KORNYUSHIN, Fyodor Danilovich (1893-1940) Party, govt and trade-union official; CP member from 1917; *Born:* 1 Mar 1893 in vil Danilovka, now Kaluga Oblast; *Career*: helped establish Sov regime in Odessa; during Civil War underground Party work; member, Odessa Province CP(B) Ukr Comt; member, Odessa Revol Comt; 1921-23 chm, Odessa Province Trade-Union Council; dep chm, Western Bureau, All-Union Centr Trade-Union Council; 1924-25 secr, Odessa Province Comt, CP(B) Ukr; head, Org and Instruction Dept, CC, CP(B) Ukr; from late 1925 secr, CC, CP(B) Ukr; Nov 1926-Mar 1928 secr, Kiev Okrug Comt, CP(B) Ukr; in 1930's worked for Pop Comrt of Supply and carried out other Party and govt work; deleg, 12th and 13th RCP(B) Congresses and 14th, 15th and 17th CPSU(B) Congresses; deleg, 7th and 8th CP(B) Ukr Conferences and 9th and 10th CP(B) Ukr Congresses; at 7th CP(B) Ukr Conference elected cand member, CC; at 8th Conference and 9th and 10th CP(B) Ukr Congresses elected member, CC, CP(B) Ukr CC; 1926-28 cand Politburo member, CC, CP(B) Ukr; repeatedly elected Presidium member, All-Ukr Centr Exec Comt and member, USSR Centr Exec Comt; arrested by State Security organs; *Died*: 1 Jan 1940 in imprisonment.

KOROBCHANSKIY, Ivan Yevstaf'yevich (1895–1956) Fuel technologist; prof from 1945; corresp member, Ukr Acad of Sci from 1951; CP member from 1945; *Born*: 16 Jan 1895 in vil Kekino, now Sumy Oblast; *Educ*: 1917 grad Khar'kov Technol Inst; *Career*: from 1917 worked at various ind plants; 1924-30 tech dir at various by-product coke plants in Donbas; from 1933 also taught fuel technol; 1935-56 head of a chair, Donetsk Ind Inst; did research on coking, concentration and the underground gasification of coal; *Died*: 1 Apr 1956.

KOROBEYNIKOVA, Yuliya Ivanovna (1883-1950) Plant selectionist; Cand of Agric; *Born:* 17 June 1883 in Blagoveshchensk-on-Amur; *Educ:* 1917 grad Stebut Women's Higher Agric Courses, Petrograd; *Career*: 1911-12 took part in exploration of Amur Oblast; 1919-24 worked at Khar'kov Experimental Agric Station; 1924-26 head, Agric Dept, Amur Land Bd; 1927-30 head, Geobotanical Research Dept, Primor'ye settlement; 1930-32 asst prof, Selection Dept, Ukr Inst of Grain Farming; 1933-50 assoc, Khar'kov Selection Station; established that there is no connection between the planting depth of the bushing node of winter wheat and its winter-resistance; *Publ: Sorta ozimoy pshenitsy selektsii Khar'kovskoy opytnoy stantsii* (A Winter Wheat Strain Bred at Khar'kov Experimental Station) (1937); *Glubina zaleganiya uzla kushcheniya i yeyo svyazi s zimostoykost'yu u raznykh sortov ozimoy pshenitsy* (The Planting Depth of the Bushing Node and Its Relation to the Winter-Resistance of Various Strains of Winter Wheat) (1947); *Died*: 1 Apr 1950.

KOROBKO, Vasya (Vasiliy Ivanovich) (1927-1944) WW 2 partisan; *Born*: 31 Mar 1927 in vil Pogorel'tsy, Semyonov Rayon, Chernigov Oblast, son of peasant; *Educ*: secondary educ; *Career*: during German occupation of vil Pogorel'tsy joined partisan detachment; messenger and scout; took part in raids; *Awards*: Order of Lenin; two Orders of the Red Banner; *Died:* 1 Apr 1944 killed on mission; Pioneer Detachment of Pogorel'tsy Secondary School named after him.

KOROBKOV, Vitya (Viktor Mikhaylovich) (1929-1944) WW 2 partisan; Pioneer; *Born*: 4 Mar 1929 in Feodosiya, son of worker; *Educ*: secondary educ; *Career*: during WW 2 lived in Feodosiya; helped local underground partisan groups collect reconnaissance information on German troop positions; helped print and disseminate leaflets; then scout for headquarters, 3rd Brigade, Eastern Command of Crimean Partisans; after returning to Feodosiya arrested by German mil authorities; *Died*: 9 Mar 1944 executed in Starokrymskaya Prison; school which he attended and street in Feodosiya named after him; monument erected to him by Ukr Pioneers.

KOROBOV, Anatoliy Vasil'yevich (1907-1967) Govt official; econ; CP member from 1942; *Born*: 26 Dec 1907; *Educ*: 1931 grad Kirov Teachers' Training Inst; completed post-grad training at Moscow Inst of Planning; *Career*: began working as vil schoolteacher; from 1936 assoc prof, Moscow Planning Inst; 1938-51 assoc, 1951-53 dep chm, USSR Gosplan; 1953-58 business mang, USSR Council of Min; 1958-60 USSR Dep Min of Finance; 1961-62 dep chm, State Learned Econ Council, USSR Council of Min; from June 1963 dep chm, USSR Gosplan; wrote several works on Sov econ; *Died*: 3 Oct 1967.

KOROBOV, Ivan Grigor'yevich (1882-1952) Metallurgist; CP member from 1941; *Born*: 26 Jan 1882 in vil Kanomichna, now Kursk Oblast; *Career*: from 1897 employed at metallurgical plants as worker and foreman; 1918-52 senior foreman, Makeyevka Metallurgical Plant; proposed many improvements in blast-furnace production techniques; dep, USSR Supr Sov of 2nd and 3rd convocations; dep, Ukr Supr Sov of 1st convocation; deleg, 16th and 17th Congresses of CP Ukr; *Awards:* three Orders of Lenin; other orders and medals; *Died*: 28 Jan 1952.

KOROBOV, Pavel Ivanovich (1902-1965) Metallurgical eng; member, USSR State Expert-Commission; exec ed, journal *Stal'*; CP member from 1934; *Born*: 1902 in Makeyevka, now Donetsk Oblast; *Educ*: 1928 grad Moscow Acad of Mines; *Career*: from 1916 in blast furnace shop, Makeyevka Metallurgical Plant as unskilled worker, metal worker's apprentice, transporter and gas fitter; from 1926 researcher, shift eng and dep asst head, blast furnace shop; from 1928 asst head, then head, blast furnace shop, Yenakiyevo Plant; 1936-39 head of blast furnace shop, chief eng, then dir, Magnitogorsk Combine; 1939-54 USSR First Dep Pop Comr of Ferrous Metallurgy; 1955 first dep chm, State Comt of New Technol, USSR Council of Min; dep, USSR Supr Sov of 1937 convocation; *Awards*: Hero of Socialist Labor (1943); six Orders of Lenin; Order of the Red Banner of Labor; medals; *Died*: Aug 1965.

KOROL'CHUK, Aleksandr Ivanovich (1883-1925) Actor and stage dir; *Born*: 12 Oct 1883 in Volhynia; *Career*: 1909 began acting; 1917 dir, All-Ukr Professional Stagecraft Assoc; 1920 worked in Romny and Poltava; from 1921 at Kiev Pop Theater; co-founder, Zan'kovetskaya Ukr Drama Theater; *Productions*: Lesya Ukrainka's "In the Virgin Forest"; Franko's "Stolen Happiness"; Gogol's *Revizor* (The Government Inspector); Ibsen's "Ghosts"; also performed in these plays; *Died*: 3 Mar 1925.

KOROLENKO, Vladimir Galaktionovich (1853-1921) Russian writer, publicist and soc figure; *Born*: 27 July 1853 in Zhitomir, son of a distr judge; *Educ*: from 1871 studied at Petersburg Technol Inst; from 1874 at Petrine Agric Acad; 1877-1878 at Mining Inst; *Career*: 1876 expelled from Petrine Agric Acad for taking part in student riots; late 1870's close contacts with revol Populist circles in Petersburg; 1879 arrested and spent some six years in prison and exile (Vyatka Province and Perm'; 1881 exiled to Yakutia); 1885-95 lived in Nizhniy Novgorod, where he continued his writing and engaged in soc-polit work; contributed to provincial press, *Russkaya mysl', Russkiye vedomosti, Severnyy vestnik*, etc; 1896 moved to Petersburg and helped publish Populist journal *Russkoye bogatstvo*; described pop life from humanistic and democratic standpoint; helped mitigate horrors of 1891-92 famine; 1900 elected hon member, Russian Acad of Sci; 1902, together with Chekhov, renounced hon membership in protest against rejection of Gorky's candidature; from 1900 lived in Poltava; as peasant democrat, attacked autocratic excesses, anti-semitism, mil field courts and death penalty; 1887-1895 active member, Nizhniy Novgorod Province Archives Commission; this work inspired in him an interest in Russian history and led him to write several works of historical fiction; 1890's began collecting material for historical novel on Pugachev rebellion - *Nabeglyy tsar* (The Marauding Tsar), but the novel was never completed; 1906 worked on biography of Populist revolutionary I. N. Myshkin, with whom he was personally acquainted; his interest in history is most clearly expressed in his *Istoriya moyego sovremennika* (The History of My Contemporary) (1922), reflecting many soc aspects of pre-reform Russia; wrote articles and reminiscences of many soc and lit figures, including N. G. Chernyshevskiy, L. N. Tolstoy, N. K. Mikhaylovskiy, G. I. Uspenskiy; wrote some 700 articles, reports, essays and notes; *Publ*: stories: *Epizody iz zhizni iskatelya* (Episodes from the Life of a Seeker) (1879); *Chudnaya* (A Strange Woman) (1880); *Yashka* (1880); *Ubivets* (The Assassin) (1882); *Son Makara* (Makar's Dream) (1883); *Sokolinets* (The Falconer) (1885); *Fyodor Bespriyutnyy* (1885); *V durnom obshchestve* (In Bad Company) (1885); *Slepoy muzykant* (The Blind Musician) (1886); *Les shumit* (The Sound of the Forest) (1886); *Cherkes* (The Circassian) (1888); *Reka igrayet* (The Babbling River) (1891); *Bez yazyka* (Without a Tongue) (1895); *Marusina zimka* (Mariya's Homestead) (1899); *U kazakov* (With the Cossacks) (1901); *Ne strashnoye* (Dreadless) (1903); *V Krymu* (In the Crimea) (1907); *Nad limanom* (Above the Estuary) (1909); *Plennyye* (The Captives) (1917); *Pis'ma* (Letters) (1888–1921); essays*: Pis'ma iz Poltavy* (Letters from Poltava) (1919); *Zemli, Zemli!* (Lands, Lands!) (1922); *Pis'ma k A. V. Lunacharskomu*

(Letters to A. V. Lunacharskiy) (1922), etc; *Sobraniye sochineniy* (Collected Works) (18 vol, 1953-56); *Died*: 25 Dec 1921 in Poltava.

KOROLYOV, Sergey Ivanovich (1894–1946) Plant-breeder and selectionist; Dr of Agric Sci; prof from 1940; *Born*: 26 Mar 1894 in Kostroma; *Educ*: 1918 grad Natural Sci Dept, Physics and Mathematics Fac, Moscow Univ; 1922 grad experimental agric course at Timiryazev Agric Acad; *Career*: 1921-22 took part in Northern Soil-Study Expedition in Arkhangel'sk, Vologda and Kostroma Provinces; 1923 sci assoc, Experimental Field, Chair of Gen Agric, Timiryazev Agric Acad; 1924-34 specialist, State Strain-Testing System, in charge of testing and zoning strains of oats, barley and rice; wrote numerous guides for testing basic varieties of oats and barley; made field trips to Centr Asia, Caucasus and Siberia to organize new test strips and collect local seed material for various agric plants; 1929-33 on expedition to study agric areas of Kazakhstan, especially along Turkestani-Siberian Railroad; drafted plan for siting agric crops in Kazakhstan's main zones; 1936-46 prof and head, Chair of Field Crop Selection and Seed-Growing, Gorky Agric Inst; studied ways of increasing sunflower-seed production in Gorky Oblast; dean, Agronomic Fac, Gorky Agric Inst; *Publ*: coauthor, *Opredelitel' i opisaniye sortov ovsa RSFSR. Rukovodstvo k aprobatsii selektsii sortov vazhneyshikh polevykh kul'tur RSFSR* (A Key and Account of Oat Varieties in the RSFSR. A Guide to the Approbation and Selection of the RSFSR's Main Field Crop Varieties) (1928); *Glavneyshiye dostizheniya v oblasti selektsii i semenovodstva polevykh kul'tur v SSSR* (Major Achievements in the Selection and Development of Field Crops in the USSR) (1929); *Sravnitel'naya urozhaynost' ovsa, yachmenya i yarovoy pshenitsy v razlichnykh rayonakh SSSR* (The Comparative Yield of Oats, Barley and Spring Wheat in the Various Areas of the USSR) (1930); *Skhema rayonov nailuchshikh sortov ovsa chernozemnoy polosy RSFSR* (A Diagram of the Best Oat Variety Areas in the Black-Earth Zone of the RSFSR) (1930); *Golozernyye yachmeni i problema ikh ispol'zovaniya v SSSR* (Naked Barleys and the Problem of Their Use in the USSR) (1931); *O novykh problemakh ispol'zovaniya vysokoproteinnykh yachmeney iz yuzhnykh rayonov SSSR* (New Problems in the Use of High-Protein Barleys from the Southern USSR) (1932); *Osobennosti metodiki provedeniya opytov po sortoispytaniyu v usloviyakh krupnogo mekhanizirovannogo khozyaystva* (Methods of Conducting Experiments for Variety-Testing on Large Mechanized Farms) (1932); *Yuzhnaya zona. Yachmen' na yuge SSSR* (The Southern Zone. Barley in the Southern USSR) (1932); *Oveyos v Leningradskoy oblasti* (Oats in the Leningrad Oblast) (1933); *Sravnitel'naya urozhaynost' yarovoy pshenitsy, yachmenya, ovsa i kukuruzy* (The Comparative Yield of Spring Wheat, Barley, Oats and Corn) (1933); *Yachmen' v Leningradskoy oblasti* (Barley in the Leningrad Oblast) (1933); *Proso* (Millet) (1942), etc; *Died*: 26 Mar 1946 in Gorky.

KOROLYOV, Sergey Pavlovich (1906-1966) Mech eng; spaceship designer; member, USSR Acad of Sci from 1958; laboratory head, Inst of Mech Eng, USSR Acad of Sci; CP member from 1952; *Born*: 30 Dec 1906 in Zhitomir, son of a teacher; *Educ*: 1930 grad Moscow Higher Tech College and pilots school; *Career*: from 1927 worked in aviation ind while pursuing high-school studies; 1933 helped form Jet Propulsion Study Group; designed space rocket systems used to launch the world's first artificial satellites; directed design of manned spaceships used for first manned space flight and first space walk; 1953-58 corresp member, USSR Acad of Sci; *Awards*: twice Hero of Socialist Labor; Lenin Prize; *Died*: 14 Jan 1966.

KOROLYOV-BATYSHEV (YULIY), I. G. (1885–1958) Party official; RSDRP member from 1905; *Born*: 1885; *Career*: summer 1909 sent by Moscow Party org (Rogozhskiy Rayon) to school on Capri where he joined group of Leninists; at Lenin's invitation attended a course of lectures in Paris which were organized by the Bolshevik Center for those who had been expelled from the Capri school; 1910, after return to Moscow, arrested and exiled to Yekaterinoslav; 1913 exiled to Olonets Province; later transferred to Radom; 1916 released; after 1917 Oct Revol trade-union, Party and govt work in Gorky, Ukr and Moscow; *Died*: 1958.

KOROSTELEV, Aleksandr Alekseyevich (1887-1937) Party and govt official; CP member from 1905; *Born*: 1887 in Samara; *Educ*: attended three-grade parish school; *Career*: metalworker and lathe operator; 1903 joined workers' movement; member, Samara RSDRP Comt and bd member, Samara Metalworkers' Union; 1907 arrested; 1908 arrested and exiled to Ust'sysol'sk; 1910-21 worked in Orenburg; after 1917 Feb Revol chm, Orenburg Sov; arrested twice by Ataman Dutov's troops but escaped from prison with group of Bolsheviks; took active part in Civil War; 1918 chm, Orenburg Province Exec Comt; from 1920 comr, Tashkent Railroad; from 1921 Collegium member, Pop Comrt of Workers and Peasants' Inspection and chm of its Commission for Cooperation with Econ Organs; Presidium member, All-Union Trade-Union Council; 1921 supported Ignatov during trade-union controversy; 1922-29 chm, CC, Educ Workers' Trade Union; from 1928 head, Org Dept and Presidium member, All-Union Trade-Union Council; from 1929 chm, Metal Trust; at 11th, 12th and 15th CPSU(B) Congresses elected member, Centr Control Commission; arrested by State Security organs; *Died*: 1937 in imprisonment.

KOROSTELEV, Georgiy Alekseyevich (1885-1932) Party official; CP member from 1905; *Born*: 1885 in Samara; *Educ*: elementary parish school; *Career*: coppersmith by trade; prof revol; repeatedly imprisoned in Tsarist jails for revol activities; 1917-18 member, Orenburg Province Food Comt; 1918-19 on Aktyubinsk Front; 1919-22 chm, Orenburg Province Sovnarkhoz; comr, Tashkent Railroad; 1922-25 secr, Kir Oblast CPSU(B) Comt; later head, Dept of Agric Inspection, Pop Comrt of Workers and Peasants' Inspection; chm, Moscow Control Commission, CPSU(B); from 1925 member, Party Collegium, CPSU(B) Centr Control Commission; Collegium member, Pop Comrt of Workers and Peasants' Inspection; at 13th Party Congress elected cand member, CC, CPSU(B); elected member, CPSU(B) Centr Control Commission at 11th, 14th, 15th and 16th Party Congresses; *Died*: 1932.

KOROTEYEV, Konstantin Appolonovich (1901-1953) Mil commander; col-gen; CP member from 1938; *Born*: 25 Feb 1901 in vil Shcheglovtsy, Khar'kov Province, son of a worker; *Educ*: 1947 grad Higher Acad Courses, Gen Staff Acad; *Career*: 1918 joined Red Army; fought in Civil War, after which he held a succession of commands; 1941-42 commander of a rifle div; 11th Guards Rifle Corps; 1942-43, as commander, 9th Army, took part in defense of Caucasus and counter-offensive; 1943 commander, 18th, 9th and 37th armies; 1943-44 took part in Kirovograd operation; 1943-45 commander, 52nd Army; 1944 took part in Korsun'-Shevchenkovskiy and Uman'-Botoshansk operations; 1945 took part in Oder-Vistula operation; 1947-53 commander, Transbaykal and North Caucasian Mil Distr; dep, USSR Supr Sov of 1950 convocation; *Awards*: Hero of the Sov Union; three Orders of Lenin; other orders and medals; *Died*: 4 Jan 1953 of heart disease.

KOROTKOV, Aleksey Andreyevich (1910-1967) Organic chemist; corresp member, USSR Acad of Sci from 1958; assoc, All-Union Research Inst of Synthetic Rubber from 1945 and Inst of High-Molecular Compounds, USSR Acad of Sci from 1953; CP member from 1942; *Born*: 1910; *Educ*: 1931 grad Leningrad Inst of Chemical Technol; *Career*: 1931-45 at synthetic rubber factories; worked on processing by-products of synthetic rubber; *Publ*: coauthor, *Opredeleniye stroyeniya kauchukov metodom infrakrasnoy spektroskopii* (Determining the Structure of Rubber with Infrared Spectroscopy) (1950); coauthor, *Vliyaniye mikrostruktury poliizoprena na yego svoystva* (The Effect of the Microstructure of Polyisoprene on Its Properties) (1956); coauthor, *K voprosu o prirode deystviya kompleksnykh katalizatorov* (The Action of Complex Catalysts) (1957); *Kataliticheskaya sopolimerizatsiya stirola i divinila* (The Catalytic Copolymerization of Styrene and Divinyl) (1960); coauthor, *Polimerizatsiya pentena-I v prisutstvii izoprena na kompleksnom katalizatore* (The Polymerization of Pentene-I with an Isoprene Complex Catalyst) (1964); coauthor, *Vyvod uravneniy kinetiki reaktsii nestatsionarnoy polimerizatsii* (Deducing the Kinetic Equations of the Reaction of Non-Stationary Polymerization) (1966); *Died*: Feb 1967.

KOROTKOV, Ivan Ivanovich (1885-1949) Party official; CP member from 1905; *Born*: 1885; *Career*: painter by trade; fought in 1905-07 Revol; Party work in Ivanovo-Voznesensk; fought in Oct Revol; 1918-20 chm, Teykovo Uyezd Party Comt; chm, Shuya Uyezd Exec Comt; head, Org and Instruction Dept, then secr, Ivanovo-Voznesensk Province Party Comt; 1923-39 worked for CC, CPSU(B) and for CPSU(B) Centr Control Commission; 1923-24 head, Org Dept, CC, CPSU(B); Presidium and Party Collegium member, CPSU(B), Centr Control Commission; 1939-44 dir, State Pushkin Museum of Fine Art; at 11th and 12th

Party Congresses elected member, CC, CPSU(B); at 13th and 17th Congresses elected member, CPSU(B) Centr Control Commission and Party Control Commission; *Died*: 1949.

KOROVIN, Mikhail Kalinikovich (1883-1956) Geologist; Hon Sci and Technol Worker of RSFSR from 1944; CP member from 1947; *Born*: 19 Nov 1883; *Educ*: 1914 grad Tomsk Technol Inst; *Career*: 1914-48 asst prof, prof and head, Dept of Historical Geology, Tomsk Technol Inst; 1928-30 worked for Siberian Geological Comt and later for various geological trusts and bd; 1943-44 member of a commission of the USSR Acad of Sci to found the West Siberian Branch of the USSR Acad of Sci; helped to found geological service in Western Siberia; explored Irkutsk, Kan, Chulym-Yenisey and Tunguska coal-fields and established their ind significance; also worked in Kuznets and Minusin Basins; shed new light on the geological structure of Irkutsk and Tomsk Oblasts and Usolka salt deposits; plotted the tectonic structure of Western Siberia against its oil deposits; *Publ*: textbook *Istoricheskaya geologiya* (Historical Geology) (1941); *Awards*: Lenin Prize (1964, posthumously) for helping to establish the oil and gas potential of the West Siberian lowland; *Died*: 19 Feb 1956.

KOROVIN, Yevgeniy Aleksandrovich (1892-1964) Historian; specialist in the history of int law and int relations; prof from 1923; Dr of Juridical Sci from 1938; corresp member, USSR Acad of Sci from 1946; Hon Sci Worker of RSFSR from 1946; Hon Sci Worker of Uzbek SSR from 1951; *Born*: 12 Oct 1892; *Educ*: 1915 grad Moscow Univ; *Career*: from 1915 did research and taught at Moscow Univ, Moscow Inst of Oriental Studies and Higher Dipl School of USSR Min of For Affairs, etc; included in Sov deleg at many int conferences; 1929 expert at Paris Conference of Aviation Law; 1945 adviser, USSR deleg to UN Preparatory Commission (London); 1945-46 consultant expert at London and Paris sessions of Council of For Min; 1956-61 Sov rep on various UNESCO commissions; from 1957 member, Permanent Chamber, Court of Arbitrations; from 1959 chm, Commission on Legal Problems of Interplanetary Space, USSR Acad of Sci; wrote 13 books, 16 pamphlets and more than 200 articles published in 12 world languages, including the first Sov textbooks on int law; *Publ: Mezhdunarodnoye pravo perekhodnogo vremeni* (International Law of the Transitional Period) (1924); *Sovremennoye mezhdunarodnoye publichnoye pravo* (Modern International Public Law) (1926); coauthor, *Razoruzheniye* (Disarmament) (1930); *Katolitsizm kak faktor sovremennoy mirovoy politiki* (Catholicism as a Factor of Modern World Politics) (1931); *Istoriya mezhdunarodnogo prava* (The History of International Law) (1946); *Osnovnyye problemy sovremennykh mezhdunarodnykh otnosheniy* (The Main Problems of Modern International Relations) (1959), etc; *Awards*: Order of Lenin; Order of the Red Banner of Labor; medals; *Died*: 1964.

KOROYEV, Kazbeg Aleksandrovich (1908-1964) Ossetian poet; CP member from 1928; *Born*: 18 Sept 1908 in vil Yerman, son of a peasant; *Career*: 1930 first work pbulished; translated Raspe's "The Adventures of Baron Münchhausen" from Russian into Ossetian; 1937 arrested by State Security organs; 1957 rehabilitated; *Publ*: collected verse "The Steel Law" (1932); book of children's verse "The New Voice" (1934); *Died*: 9 Mar 1964 in Leningrad.

KORSHIKOV, Aleksandr Arkad'yevich (1889-1942) Botanist; Dr of Biology; prof; *Born*: 9 Nov 1889 in Sumy; *Educ*: 1915 grad Khar'kov Univ; *Career*: after grad stayed on at univ to train for professorship; after 1917 Oct Revol prof, Khar'kov Inst of Public Educ; from 1926 prof, Khar'kov Univ; from 1930 also dir, Botanical Research Inst, Khar'kov Univ; during WW 2 fought with Ukr partisans; did research on the morphology, taxonomy and evolution of fresh-water algae, particularly colored flagellates; discovered oogamy and the existence of contractile vacuoles in Protococcales order; made special study of Vovocales order; studied the algoflora of the Ukr, Gorky Kray, the Kola Peninsula, etc; *Publ: Materialy k flore vodorasley Gor'kovskogo kraya* (Material on the Algoflora of Gorky Kray) (1938); *Materialy k flore vodorasley Kol'skogo poluostrova* (Material on the Algoflora of the Kola Peninsula) (1941), etc; *Died*: 1942 executed by Germans in Ukr.

KORSHUN, Stepan Vasil'yevich (1868-1931) Microbiologist and immunologist; Dr of Med from 1903; prof from 1910; *Born*: 6 Sept 1868 in Glukhov, Chernigov Province; *Educ*: 1893 grad Med Fac, Khar'kov Univ; *Career*: after grad specialized in bacteriology under V. K. Vysokovich; 1901-02 sent abroad for further study, inter alia under Prof P. Ehrlich; 1903 returned to Russia to defend doctor's thesis on the biochemical link between toxins and enzymes, in which he demonstrated that rennin, like toxins, has an antigenic property and precipitates the formation of antirennin; devised method of freeing horse's serum from the substances inhibiting its neutralizing action on rennin; also demonstrated the existance of a modification of rennin analogous to toxoids; from 1908 dir, Khar'kov Bacteriological Inst; from 1910 extraordinary prof, Chair of Hygiene, Khar'kov Univ; during WW 1 helped to develop method of obtaining tetanus serum, which had previously been imported; 1923-30 dir, Mechnikov Inst, Moscow; proposed use of neutral mixture of diphtheria toxin and antitoxin, as well as a combined scarlet-fever vaccine consisting of dead hemolytic scarlatinal streptococci and scarlatinal toxin; 1924 introduced vaccine for intestinal infections made from dead formalin cultures; wrote some 80 works; *Publ: O biokhimicheskoy svyazi mezhdu toksinami i enzimami* (The Biochemical Link Between Toxins and Enzymes) (1903); *Ob antagonizme mezhdu normal'nymi i immunnymi bakteriologicheskimi syvorotkami* (Antagonism Between Normal and Immune Bacteriological Sera) (1906); *K voprosu o vaktsinatsii protiv kholery* (Vaccination Against Cholera) (1922); *Immunizatsiya smes'yu difteriynogo toksina s antitoksinom v bor'be s difteriyey* (Immunization with a Mixture of Diphtheria Toxin and Antitoxin in the Campaign Against Diphtheria) (1924); *Etiologiya i profilaktika skarlatiny* (The Etiology and Prevention of Scarlet Fever) (1924); *Opyt aktivnoy immunizatsii protiv skarlatiny* (Experience in Active Immunization Against Scarlet Fever) (1926); *Opyt odnovremennoy immunizatsii protiv difterii i skarlatiny* (Experience in Simultaneous Immunization Against Diphtheria and Scarlet Fever) (1930); *Died*: 1931 in Khar'kov.

KORSUN, Nikolay Georgiyevich (1876-1958) Mil commander; maj-gen, Gen Staff, Russian Army; lt-gen, Sov Army from 1940; Dr of Mil Sci; prof; mil historian; *Born*: 1876; *Educ*: 1905 grad Nikolay Mil Acad; *Career*: participated in WW 1; after Oct Revol sided with Soviets; 1917-18 with Gen Staff, Sov Army; 1918-21 on army staff, Eastern Front and on Field Staff, RSFSR Revol Mil Sov; from Oct 1918 lectured at Gen Staff Acad; 1922-54 senior instructor, dept head, and head of mil history disciplines at the Red Army Mil Acad (later Frunze Mil Acad); 1942 helped plan operations for defense of the Caucasus; from 1954 retired; *Publ: Sarakamyshskaya operatsiya* (The Sarykamysh Operation) (1935); *Erzerumskaya operatsiya na Kavkazskom fronte v 1915-1916 godakh* (The 1915-16 Erzerum Operation on the Caucasian Front) (1938); *Italo-abissinskaya voyna 1935-1936 godov* (The 1935-36 Italo-Abyssinian War) (1939); *Balkanskiy front mirovoy voyny 1914-1918 godov* (The Balkan Front of the 1914-18 World War) (1939); *Alashkertskaya i Khamadanskaya operatsii na Kavkazskom fronte mirovoy voyny v 1915 godu* (The 1915 Alashkert and Khamadan Operations on the Caucasian Front of the World War) (1940); *Awards*: two Orders of Lenin; two Orders of the Red Banner; two Orders of the Red Star; medals; *Died*: Nov 1958 after a long illness.

KORYAK, Vladimir Dmitriyevich (1889-1939) Ukr lit historian and critic; CP member from 1920; *Born*: 14 Jan 1889 in Slavyansk; *Career*: 1909-15 wrote about lit in Ukr Soc-Democratic press; active in illegal Ukr Soc-Democratic organizations; 1911-14 maintained Ukr Soc-Democratic positions of that period in his critical and journalistic work; 1915 arrested and exiled for revol activities to Turgay Oblast, where he remained until 1917 Feb Revol; after 1917 Oct Revol wrote about various problems of Marxist-Leninist lit history; 1919-25 worked for Ukr Pop Comrt of Educ and Ukr State Publ House; from 1925 lectured on Ukr lit at Khar'kov Inst of Educ, Artyom Communist Univ, etc while continuing lit work; active in organizing proletarian writers; helped found *Gart* lit assoc; after dissolution of *Gart* helped found new proletarian lit soc; founder and member, All-Ukr Union of Proletarian Writers; participated in discussions on lit criticism; some of his works were berated by Sov critics for "vulgar sociologism"; 1937 arrested by State Security organs; *Publ*: book "To the Gates" (1913); "Taras Shevchenko" (1920); "Six and Six" (1923); "M. Kotsyubinskiy, Poet of the Ukrainian Intelligentsia" (1923); "On the Literary Front. Ukrainian Literature Before October 1917" (1924); "The Organization of October Literature. Newspaper and Magazine Articles 1919-24" (1925); "The Shevchenko Campaign" (1925); "An Outline History of Ukrainian Literature" (2 vol, 1925-29); "Khvyl'ovyy's Sociological Equivalent. An Ignorant Person's Letter" (1927), etc; worked on "Istoriya ukrainskoy literatury" (A History of Ukrainian

Literature); *Died*: 12 Apr 1939 in imprisonment; posthumously rehabilitated.

KORZHENEVSKIY, Nikolay Leopol'dovich (1879-1958) Geographer; Dr of Geography from 1937; prof from 1922; corresp member, Uzbek Acad of Sci from 1947; Hon Sci Worker of Uzbek SSR from 1939; *Born*: 6 Feb 1879 in vil Zaverzh'ye, Vetebsk Province; *Educ*: 1901 grad Kiev Mil College; 1906 grad Mil Quarter Acad; *Career*: 1903 made first expedition to Pamirs; 1904 reached unexplored territory in middle reaches of Muksu River; 1905 explored Alay mountain range and valley; from 1922 prof and head, Chair of Physical Geography, Centr Asian Univ; 1922 led expedition to Muyun-Kun desert; 1926 led expedition of USSR Acad of Sci, which discovered Acad of Sci Range in 1928; subsequently explored the foothills of the Tyan'Shan'; determined the exact location of the Kir range; described Lake Karakul' and compiled a catalog of the Centr Asian glaciers; studied the rivers of Centr Asia; gave his name to a glacier in the Trans-Alay range and the Trans-Ili Alatau; *Publ: Muksu i yeyo ledniki* (The Muksu and its Glaciers) (1927); *Katalog lednikov Sredney Azii* (A Catalog of Central Asian Glaciers) (1930); *Alayskaya dolina* (The Alay Valley) (1930); *Ozero Kara-Kul'. Fiziko-geograficheskiy ocherk* (Lake Karakul'. A Physical Geographical Study) (1936); *Fiziko-geograficheskiy ocherk Sredney Azii* (The Physical Geography of Central Asia) (1941), etc; *Awards*: two Orders of the Red Banner of Labor; *Died*: 31 Oct 1958.

KORZINOV, G. N. (1886-1926) Party and govt official; CP member from 1904; *Born*: 1886; *Career*: 1905-07 took active part in Revol; did Party work in Petersburg, Riga, Helsinki and Moscow; subjected to reprisals by Tsarist authorities; 1917 took part in Oct Revol in Moscow; after Oct Revol held various Party, govt and admin posts; member, Exec Comt, Moscow Sov; member, Moscow RCP(B) Comt; 1921-26 dir, "Proletarian Labor" Plant; 1921-22 sided with "workers' opposition"; sided with Ignatov in trade-union controversy; *Died*: 1926.

KOSAREV, Aleksandr Vasil'yevich (1903-1939) Party and Komsomol official; CP member from 1919; *Born*: 27 Feb 1903 in Moscow, son of a worker; *Educ*: parochial school; 1920 grad polit courses; *Career*: at the age of 11 went to work at zinc and tin plant; early 1918 joined Komsomol; fought in Civil War; at the age of 15 went to the front as a volunteer; fought in defense of Petrograd against Gen Yudenich's troops; after returning from Civil War did Komsomol work in Leningrad; from 1921 secr, Bauman Rayon Komsomol Comt, Moscow; from late 1924 secr, Penza Province Komsomol Comt; early 1926 sent to Leningrad and elected secr, Moscow-Narva Rayon Komsomol Comt; later elected secr, Moscow Komsomol Comt; 1927 secr, CC, All-Union Komsomol; Mar 1929 elected secr-gen, CC, All-Union Komsomol; at 15th CPSU(B) Congress elected member, CPSU(B) Centr Control Commission; at 16th Party Congress elected cand member, CC, CPSU(B); at 17th Party Congress elected member, CC, CPSU(B); member, Org Bureau, CC, CPSU(B); member, USSR Centr Exec Comt; when mass reprisals began (after Kirov's murder) against govt, Party and Komsomol officials, Kosarev rejected claims that there were enemies of the people among the Party leaders; he protested against it and did his best to shield people from accusations; 19-22 Nov 1938 All-Union Komsomol CC held a plenum, attended by Stalin, Molotov and Malenkov, at which Kosarev and other Komsomol leaders were accused of hostile activities and relieved of their posts; Kosarev was then arrested by State Security organs; *Awards*: Order of Lenin (1933); *Died*: 23 Feb 1939 in imprisonment; posthumously rehabilitated.

KOSAREV, Vladimir Mikhaylovich (1881-1945) Party official; CP member from 1898; *Born*: 1881; *Career*: late 90s began revol activities in Moscow; member, Lefortov Rayon RSDRP Comt; 1907 arrested and exiled to Nizhniy Novgorod; summer 1909 sent by Moscows' Lefortov Rayon Party org to school on Capri; after his return to Russia arrested and exiled to Narym Kray; 1916 conscripted; worked for underground soldiers' org in Tomsk; after 1917 Oct Revol exec Party and govt work; chm, Tomsk Province Exec Comt; member, Siberian Revol Comt and Siberian Bureau, CC, RCP(B); chm, Novonikolayevsk Province Exec Comt; member, Moscow Party Comt; member, Centr Control Commission; *Died*: 1945.

KOSENKO, Viktor Stepanovich (1896-1938) Composer; *Born*: 23 Nov 1896 in Petersburg; *Educ*: 1918 grad Petrograd Conservatory; *Career*: from 1918 taught music in Zhitomir; 1929 moved to Kiev; prof, Music and Drama Inst and Conservatory; piano soloist at concerts and in ensembles; reproduced Ukr folk music in his varied, lyrical compositions; used many Sov themes; Zhitomir Music College named after him; *Works*: "Heroic Overtures" (1932); "Symphonic Poems on Moldavian Folk Themes" (1937); 35 romances and 37 songs to lyrics by Ukr and Russian poets, including: "Ballad of Stalin"; "As I Come from Work at the Plant"; "On the Square"; "In Memory of the Paris Communards"; "A Message to Siberia"; piano compositions: three sonatas; etudes; preludes; tone poems; 24 children's pieces; stage and film music; compiled first Ukr collection of Sov folk songs *Pooktyabr'skiye pesni* (October Songs) (1936); *Awards*: Order of the Red Banner of Labor; *Died*: 3 Oct 1938 in Kiev.

KOSHEVOY, Oleg Vasil'yevich (1926-1943) Komsomol activist; led underground youth org *Molodaya gvardiya* during WW 2; Komsomol member from 1940; *Born*: 8 June 1926 in Priluki, Chernigov Oblast; *Educ*: studied at secondary school in Krasnodon; *Career*: July 1942, after seizure of Krasnodon by German troops, helped found underground Komsomol org *Molodaya gvardiya*; elected its secr and comr, *Molodaya gvardiya* headquarters; *Molodaya gvardiya* had more than 100 members; Oct 1942 it switched from distributing leaflets to partisan activities and open attacks on German troops; 26 Jan 1943 Koshevoy was arrested by German troops; mines, sovkhozes, ships, schools and pioneer detachments in the USSR and abroad have been named after him; *Awards*: Hero of the Sov Union (posthumously 1943); *Died*: 1943 in Roven'ki Prison; 20 Mar 1943 buried in Roven'ki, Voroshilovgrad Oblast, after the city was liberated by the Sov Army.

KOSHLYAKOV, Nikolay Sergeyevich (1891-1958) Mathematician; prof; corresp member, USSR Acad of Sci from 1933; *Born*: 23 June 1891; *Educ*: 1914 grad Petersburg Univ; *Career*: 1925-42 prof, Leningrad Univ; 1926-42 prof and head, Chair of Mathematics, Leningrad Electrotech Inst; specialized in the theory of higher transcendental functions and differential equations in mathematical physics; *Publ*: "Application of the Theory of Sum-Formulae to the Investigation of a Class of All-Valued Analytical Functions in the Theory of Numbers" (1928); "On an Extension of Some Formulae of Ramanujan" (1936); *Osnovnyye differentsial'nyye uravneniya matematicheskoy fiziki* (The Basic Differential Equations of Mathematical Physics) (1936); coauthor, *Vvedeniye v teoriyu malykh kolebaniy, imeyushchikh primeneniye v akustike* (An Introduction to the Theory of Small Oscillations Applicable to Acoustics) (1937); *Issledovaniye odnogo klassa differentsial'nykh uravneniy s dvoyako-periodicheskimi koeffitsientami* (An Investigation of a Class of Differential Equations with Double Periodic Coefficients) (1952); *Died*: 23 Sept 1958.

KOSHOVA, Anna Denisovna (1871-1948) Kolkhoz innovator and shock-worker; *Born*: 2 Oct 1871 in vil Malopolovetskoye, now Kiev Oblast, daughter of a peasant; *Career*: joined one of first kolkhozes; 1935 directed kolkhoz field-team which harvested 537 centners of sugar beet per hectare; active in champion beet-growers' campaign among Ukr beet raisers; 1957 "Red Giant" kolkhoz in vil Velikopolovetskoye, in which she worked as field-team leader for some 17 years, was named after her; 1955 monument was erected to her at All-Union Agric Exhibition; *Awards*: two orders; medals; *Died*: 9 Mar 1948.

KOSHTOYANTS, Khachatur Sedrakovich (1900-1961) Physiologist; Dr of Med; prof from 1935; corresp member, USSR Acad of Sci from 1939; member, Arm Acad of Sci from 1943; CP member from 1927; *Born*: 26 Sept 1900 in Aleksandropol' (now Leninakan), Arm; *Educ:* 1926 grad Med Fac, 2nd Moscow Univ; completed postgrad studies at Timiryazev Biological Research Inst, Moscow; *Career*: 1915-21 pharmacy worker in Pyatigorsk, Northern Caucasus; 1920-21 laboratory asst, Pyatigorsk Balneological Inst and lecturer, Pyatigorsk Pop Univ; 1923-30 head, Workers' Fac, Karl Liebknecht Ind Teachers' Training Inst, Moscow; 1928-29 asst prof, Chair of Physiology, Moscow Univ; 1929-37 head, Biology Dept and member, Timiryazev Agric Inst, Moscow, where he established a laboratory of comparative physiology in 1930; from 1930 bd member, Moscow and All-Union Soc of Physiologists, Biochemists and Pharmacologists; 1930-31 sent to Holland to study Dutch laboratories of comparative physiology; 1933-36 head, Dept of Evolutionary Physiology; 1937-43 dep dir, Severtsev Inst of Animal Morphology; 1939-47 acad secr, USSR Acd of Sci; 1943-61 head, Chair of Animal Physiology, Biology Fac, Moscow Univ; 1943-46 acad secr, Dept of Biological Sci, Arm Acad of Sci; 1946-53 dir, Inst of the History of Natural Sci, USSR Acad of Sci; chief ed, physiology section, *Bol'shaya meditsinskaya entsiklopediya* (Large Medical Encyclopedia) (2nd ed); 1951-52 dep chief ed, journal *Vestnik Akademii nauk SSSR*; wrote over 300 works; *Publ: Fiziologiya i teoriya razvitiya* (Physiology and the Theory of Evolution) (1932); *O sostoyanii funktsiy vegetativnykh i animal'nykh organov v svete ikh evolyutsii* (The State of the Functions of Vegetative and Animal Organs in the Light of Their Evolution) (1937); *Osnovy sravnitel'noy fiziologii* (The Principles of Comparative Physiology) (1940); *Ocherki po istorii fiziologii v Rossii* (Outline History of Physiology in Russia) (1946); *Belkovyye tela, obmen veshchestv i nervnaya regulyatsiya* (Proteic Bodies, Metabolism and Nerve Regulation) (1951), etc; *Awards*: Stalin Prize (1946); Lomonosov Prize (1952); order of Lenin; two Orders of the Red Banner of Labor; Badge of Hon, etc; *Died*: 2 Apr 1961.

KOSICH, Dmitriy Iosifovich (1886-1937) Mil commander; corps quartermaster from 1935; CP member from 1918; *Born*: 1886; *Career:* during Civil War commanded regt, then mil comr, 5th Army Staff on Eastern Front; after Civil War commander and comr, 9th Infantry Div; chief of supply, North Caucasian Mil Distr; inspector of Red Army formations; asst commander, Moscow Mil Distr; head, Red Army Baggage Train Supply Bd; 1937 arrested by NKVD; *Died*: 1937 in imprisonment; posthumously rehabilitated.

KOSIOR, Iosif Vikent'yevich (1893-1937) Govt official; CP member from 1908; *Born*: 1893 in vil Vengerov, Sedlets Province, son of a Polish laborer; *Career*: from 1907 worked at Yur'yevskiy Plant in the Donets Basin; active in Donbass Bolshevik underground orgs; repeatedly imprisoned by Tsarist authorities; 1909-17 exiled in Yenisey Province; 1917 escaped from exile and worked illegally in Moscow; Oct 1917 chm, Mil Revol Comt, Zamoskvorech'ye Rayon; after 1917 Oct Revol chm, Zamoskvorech'ye Rayon Sov; from 1918 during Civil War commands in Red Army, regt comr; member, Revol Mil Comt of an army; army commander on South and North Caucasian Fronts; from 1923 head, Groznyy Oil and Gas Trust; 1926 chm, Bd, Southern Steel Ind Trust, Khar'kov; 1927-32 dep chm, USSR Supr Sovnarkhoz; chm, Bd, All-Union Metal Plants Construction Trust; chm, Bd, Eastern Steel Ind Trust; from 1932 USSR Dep Pop Comr of Heavy Ind; head, Main Coal Ind Bd; from 1933 USSR Pop Comrt of Heavy Ind rep in the Far Eastern Kray; 1925 at 14th Party Congress elected cand member, CC, CPSU(B); at 15th, 16th and 17th Party Congresses elected member, CC, CPSU(B); member, USSR Centr Exec Comt; arrested by State Security organs; *Awards*: Order of the Red Banner; Order of the Red Banner of Labor; *Died*: 1937 in imprisonment.

KOSIOR, Stanislav Vikent'yevich (1889-1939) Party and govt official; CP member from 1907; *Born*: 18 Nov 1889 in Vengerov, Sedlets Province, son of a Polish laborer; *Educ*: primary school; *Career*: worked at Sulin Steel Works; from 1905 worked at Donets-Yur'yevskiy Steel Works; 1907 member, RSDRP Party Comt, Donets-Yur'yevskiy Steel Works; 1907-11 repeatedly arrested for revol work; 1912-14 illegal Party work in Khar'kov, Poltava and Kiev; 1915 Party work in Moscow, then arrested and exiled to Irkutsk Province for three years; after 1917 Feb Revol member, Narva-Peterhof RSDRP(B) Comt, and member, Exec Commission, Petrograd RSDRP(B) Comt; deleg, 7th (Apr) RSDRP(B) Conference and 6th RSDRP(B) Congress; fought in 1917 Oct rebellion in Petrograd; comr, Petrograd Mil Revol Comt; 1918 directed underground Party work in German-occupied Ukr; Oct 1918 elected secr, underground Right-Bank Comt, CP(B) Ukr; member of oblast Party comt appointed to plan armed rebellion; during Brest–Litovsk peace talks sided with "Leftist" Communists; 1919 head, Rear Bureau, CC, CP(B) Ukr; directed underground work behind the lines of Denikin's forces; 1920 secr, CC, CP(B) Ukr; 1921-22 arranged food supplies; late 1922 with CC, CP(B) Ukr; from Nov 1922 secr, Siberian Bureau, CC, CPSU(B); Dec 1925-July 1928 secr, CC, CPSU(B); July 1928-Jan 1938 secr-gen, CC, CP(B) Ukr; Jan 1938 at first session of USSR Supr Sov elected dep chm, USSR Council of Pop Comr, and chm, Sov Control Commission; deleg at 12th-17th Party Congresses; at 12th CPSU(B) Congress elected cand member, CC; at 13th-17th Party Congresses elected member, CC, CPSU(B); 1927-30 cand Politburo member, from 1930 Politburo member, CC, CPSU(B); deleg at 6th and 7th Comintern Congresses; Presidium member, USSR Centr Exec Comt; at 1st, 3rd, 11th, 12th and 13th Congresses of CP Ukr elected member, CC, CP Ukr; 1919-20 and July 1928-Jan 1938 Politburo member, CC, CP Ukr; arrested by State Security organs; *Awards*: Order of Lenin (1935); *Died*: 26 Feb 1939 in imprisonment; posthumously rehabilitated.

KOSIOR, V. V. (1891-1938) Govt official; CP member from 1907; *Born*: 1891; *Career*: Party work in Donbass, Khar'kov and Kiev; after 1917 Feb Revol instructor, Moscow Union of Metal Workers; after 1917 Oct Revol mil, trade-union and admin work; 1920-21 during trade-union controversy sided with Trotsky; thereafter active member of Trotskyite opposition; deleg, 9th and 11th RCP(B) Congresses; 1929 expelled from Party for alleged anti-Party activities; arrested by State Security organs; *Died*: 1938 in imprisonment.

KOSMINSKIY, Yevgeniy Alekseyevich (1886-1959) Medievalist; Dr of History from 1936; prof from 1919; member, RSFSR Acad of Pedag Sci from 1945; member, USSR Acad of Sci from 1946; Hon Sci Worker of RSFSR from 1947; *Born*: 2 Nov 1886 in Warsaw; *Educ*: 1910 grad Fac of History and Philology, Moscow Univ; *Career*: 1915-19 lecturer, from 1919 prof, Moscow Univ; from 1921 member, Inst of History, Russian Assoc of Soc Sci Research Inst; from 1926 also taught at Inst of Red Prof, Inst of Philosophy, Lit and History and Acad of Soc Sci, CC, CPSU; from 1929 assoc, Inst of History, Communist Acad; 1934-49 head, Chair of Medieval History, Moscow Univ; 1936-52 head, Medieval History Section, 1952-59 senior assoc, Inst of History, USSR Acad of Sci; 1939-46 corresp member, USSR Acad of Sci; from 1942 exec ed, periodical *Sredniye veka*; 1944-48 assoc, Inst of Teaching Methods, RSFSR Acad of Pedag Sci; from 1952 exec ed, English-language ed, journal *Novosti* (News); specialized in Medieval history of Western Europe, especially England; concentrated on Medieval agrarian and social problems; also did research on Medieval historiography, the history of the 17th-Century English revol and Byzantine history; 1949 criticized by Party for "cosmopolitan errors" and "econ materialism"; accused of belittling Sov Medievalism and the importance of Russia and Slavdom in European history and dismissed from Chair of Medieval History, Moscow Univ; 1950 performed self-criticism and revised his textbooks on Medieval history; 1952 dismissed from Medieval History Section, Inst of History, USSR Acad of Sci; *Publ: Angliyskaya derevnya v XIII veke* (The English Village in the 13th Century) (1935); *Istoriya diplomatii* (The History of Diplomacy) (Vol 1, 1941); *Issledovaniya po agrarnoy istorii Anglii XIII veka* (Research on the Agrarian History of 13th-Century England) (1947); coauthor and ed, textbook *Istoriya srednikh vekov* (Medieval History) (1952); *Angliyskaya burzhuaznaya revolyutsiya XVII veka* (The 17th-Century English Bourgeois Revolution) (2 vol, 1954); *Istoriografiya srednikh vekov. V - seredina XIX veka* (Medieval Historiography. From the 5th to the Middle of the 19th Century) (1963); *Problemy angliyskogo feodalizma v istoriografii srednikh vekov* (The Problem of English Feudalism in Medieval Historiography) (1963), etc; *Awards*: Stalin Prize (1942); Order of Lenin; two Orders of the Red Banner of Labor; *Died*: 24 July 1959.

KOSMODEM'YANSKAYA (alias: TANYA), Zoya Anatol'yevna (1923-1941) WW 2 partisan; Komsomol member from 1938; *Born*: 13 Sept 1923 in Osinovyye Gai, Tambov Oblast, daughter of an office worker; *Educ*: 10th grade at Secondary School Nr 201 in Moscow; *Career*: Oct 1941 volunteered for partisan unit; crossed the front into enemy-occupied territory at the vil of Obukhovo near Naro-Fominsk with a group of Komsomol partisans; late Nov 1941 captured by German troops in the vil of Petrishchevo, Vereya Rayon, Moscow Oblast while on a mission to destroy a German mil supply dump; Kosmodem'yanskaya did not reveal her real name, but called herself Tanya; subject of various works by Sov writers, sculptors and artists; also inspired motion picture *Zoya*; her former school and many pioneer orgs named after her; monument to her erected on the Minsk Highway near vil Petrishchevo; *Awards*: Hero of the Sov Union (1942, posthumously); *Died*: 29 Nov 1941 hanged in vil Petrishchevo; buried in Moscow's Novodevich'ye Cemetery.

KOSMODEM'YANSKIY, Nikolay Pavlovich (1891-1953) Mil commander and instructor; maj-gen, Quartermaster Corps; *Born*: 1891; *Career*: during Civil War chief of staff of an army and mil distr air force; then commands with Sov Air Force; also taught at Air Force Acad; *Died*: 1953.

KOSONOGOV, Iosif Iosifovich (1866-1922) Physicist; prof from 1903; member, Ukr Acad of Sci from 1922; *Born*: 1866 in Kamensk-Shakhtinskiy, now Rostov Oblast; *Educ*: 1889 grad Kiev Univ; *Career*: 1889-1903 asst prof, from 1903 prof, Kiev Univ; specialized in electr and optical phenomena; 1902 discovered optical resonance in visible spectrum and attributed the color gradation of structurally heterogeneous bodies to this phenomenon; was first to use ultramicroscope to study electrolysis; *Publ: K voprosu o dielektrikakh* (Dielectrics) (1901), etc; *Died*: 22 Mar 1922.

KOST, Nikolay Andreyevich (1883-1943) Hygienist; pioneer of Sov health service; Cand of Med; CP member from 1904; *Born*: 1883, son of a merchant; *Educ*: 1910 grad Med Fac, Moscow Univ; *Career*: from 1904 member, Tech Group, Moscow RSDRP Comt; 1905 took active part in Revol in Moscow; in same year imprisoned in Taganka Jail, after which he resumed revol work although under police surveillance; after grad worked as zemstvo health officer in Kostroma, Nizhniy Novgorod and Vladimir Provinces; in course of duties did research on living and working conditions of peasants, smallpox, intestinal infections, children's diseases, tuberculosis and syphilis rates, water supplies, etc; 1914 drafted into Russian Army; during 1917 Oct Revol member, Mil-Revol Comt and dept chm, Sov of Soldiers' Dep, Southwestern Front; dep chm, Kamenetsk-Podol'sk Sov of Workers' Dep; chm, Zhitomir RSDRP(B) Comt; chm, Zhitomir Sov of Workers' Dep; Dec 1917 member, 1st Ukr Centr Exec Comt; fought against Gen Kornilov; 1918 Collegium member, Main Mil Health Bd, Council of Physicians' Collegia; 1919-20 acting Ukr Pop Comr of Health; 1920-24 RSFSR Pop Comrt of Health's chief plen for Kuban' and Black Sea health resorts; 1926-33 exec secr, USSR Red Cross and Red Crescent Soc; 1927-28 asst prof, Chair of Soc Hygiene, 2nd Moscow Univ; from 1928 head, sanitary unit, Donbas water prospecting and planning group; head, Water Hygiene and Sanitary Hydraulic Eng Dept, All-Union Inst of Communal Hygiene, USSR Pop Comrt of Health; also worked for Main State Sanitary Inspectorate, RSFSR Pop Comrt of Health; 1941-43 worked for All-Union State Sanitary Inspectorate, USSR Pop Comrt of Health; *Publ: K voprosu o novom techenii v zemskoy sanitarii* (The New Trend in the Zemstvo Sanitary Service) (1913); *Statisticheskiye dannyye o rasprostranenii "ispanskoy" bolezni v Respublike* (Statistical Data on the Incidence of "Spanish" Influenza in the RSFSR) (1919); *Meropriyatiya v oblasti vodosnabzheniya i kanalizatsii* (Water-Supply and Sewage Measures) (1933); *O proyektirovanii zon sanitarnoy okrany vodoprovodov* (Planning Sanitary Protection Zones for Water Mains) (1941), etc; *Died*: 1943.

KOSTEL'NIK, Gavriil (1886-1948) Greek Catholic priest; prof, L'vov Theological Acad; *Born*: 1886 in vil Russky Kerestur, Yugoslavia; *Career*: 1926-30 taught at theological acad; relieved of teaching duties and placed under supervision of eparchial bd for publishing various articles on theological questions; 1945-46 vehemently criticized papacy and church unity; 1945 headed group of Greek Catholic clergymen who prepared 1946 convocation of L'vov Synod, which proclaimed liquidation of 1596 Brest Union and merger of Galician Church with Russian Orthodox Church; *Publ*: *Spor pro Epiklezu mezhdu Vostokom i Zapadom* (The East-West-Epiclesis Dispute); *Novoye vremya nashey tserkvi* (The New Epoch of Our Church), etc; *Died*: 1948 murdered by unknown assailants.

KOSTENKO, Fyodor Yakovlevich (1896-1942) Ukr mil commander; lt-gen from 1940; CP member from 1941; *Born*: 6 Dec 1896 in vil Bol'shaya Martynovka, Rostov Oblast, son of a peasant; *Educ*: completed two grades of vil school; 1941 completed Red Army Advanced Commanders Courses; *Career*: 1915 drafted into Russian Army and rose to rank of senior noncommissioned officer; 1917 took part in Feb Revol in Petrograd and Oct Revol in Novgorod; from 1918 in Red Army; fought in Civil War; four times wounded; 1921–39 commanded cavalry squadron, then commandant of regt school and commander of cavalry regt, div, then corps; 1939 commanded army cavalry group, Ukr Front; 1939 took part in West Ukr Campaign; 1941 commander, 26th Army, and dep commander, Southwestern Front; 1941, with part of the 26th Army, broke out of encirclement in Kiev area; 9 Dec 1941 his Southwestern Front operations group liberated Yelets; 1941-42 commander, Southwestern Front; Apr-May 1942 dep commander, Southwestern Front; May 1942 commanded troops which made a vain attempt to break out of encirclement near Khar'kov; *Awards*: Order of Lenin; Order of the Red Banner; *Died*: 26 May 1942 in action.

KOSTIKOV, Andrey Grigor'yevich (1899-1950) Artificer; corresp member, USSR Acad of Sci from 1943; maj-gen, Eng Corps; Hero of Socialist Labor from 1941; CP member from 1922; *Born*: 1899; *Educ*: 1934 grad Zhukovskiy Air Force Eng Acad; *Career*: designed many new types of weapons; *Awards*: Stalin Prize (1942); Order of Lenin; three other orders; medals; *Died*: 1950.

KOSTINSKIY, Sergey Konstantinovich (1867-1936) Astronomer; specialist in photographic astrometry; corresp member, USSR Acad of Sci from 1915; *Born*: 12 Aug 1867; *Educ*: 1890 grad Moscow Univ; *Career*: 1896-1936 photographed the satellites of the outer planets and, using a normal astrograph, acquired photographs of a large numer of celestial bodies on the basis of which he studied the proper motion of stars and determined the parallaxes of some 200; 1902-36 senior astronomer, Pulkovo Observatory; did research on astronomical latitudes; developed universally recognized method of plotting the motion of the poles; pioneered astrophotography and photographic astrometry; devised method of measuring the position of stars from photographic plates and deduced reduction formulae for these measurements; 1906 detected double image on photographic plates indicating the presence of close binaries (Kostinskiy's phenomenon); *Publ: Ob izmenenii astronomicheskikh shirot* (Change of Astronomical Latitudes) (1893); "Untersuchungen auf dem Gebiete der Sternparallaxen mit Hilfe der Photographie" (The Photographic Investigation of Star Parallaxes) (1905); *Died*: 21 Aug 1936.

KOSTROMSKOY (real name: CHALEYEV), Nikolay Feodosiyevich) (1874-1938) Actor; Pop Artiste of RSFSR from 1937; *Born*: 5 July 1874; *Career*: did amateur acting; 1902 began professional stage career; actor, Meyerkhol'd and Kasheverov ensembles, Kherson; also acted in Tiflis, Sebastopol, Nikolayev, Kostroma, Baku, Astrakhan and Nizhniy Novgorod; from 1917 actor, Korsh Theater, Moscow; from 1918 actor, Maly Theater, Moscow; noted for his clear and skillful delineation of character; from 1919 also taught acting; 1919-25 teacher, Maly Theater Studios; taught at Komissarzhevskiy and Yermolovaya Studios; from 1932 teacher, Shchepkin Theatrical College; also worked as a producer; *Roles*: Mitrofanushka and Starodum in Fonvizin's *Nedorosl'* (The Ignoramus); Osip, Zemlyanika and the Governor in *Revizor* (The Government Inspector); Molchalin, Skalozub and Famusov in *Gore ot uma* (Woe from Wit); Gayev, Firs and Lopakhin in *Vishnyovyy sad* (The Cherry Orchard); Shabel'skiy in *Ivanov*; Mamayev in *Na vsyakogo mudretsa dovol'no prostoty* (There's a Simpleton in Every Sage); Kuchumov in *Beshenyye den'gi* (Easy Money); Gornostayev in *Lyubov' Yarovaya*; Lynyayev in *Volki i ovtsy* (The Wolves and the Sheep); Vos'mibratov in *Les* (The Forest); *Died*: 3 Nov 1938.

KOSTROV, Taras (real name: Aleksandr MARTYNOVSKIY) (1901-1930) Critic and publicist; *Born:* 1901 in a Russian prison, to Soc-Democratic revol parents; *Career*: 1919 helped found underground Bolshevik org in Odessa; set up underground printing press, directed rebel detachment and helped lead Odessa Party org; after end of Civil War secr, Lugansk Okrug Comt, CP(B) Ukr; directed Kiev newspaper *Proletarskaya pravda* and contributed to Khar'kov *Kommunist;* in 1920's chief ed, newspaper *Komsomol'skaya pravda*; sided with Shatskin-Lominadze-Sten leftist Communist group; late 1928 dismissed from editorship of *Komsomol'skaya pravda*; 1929 edited journal *Molodaya gvardiya;* later founded journal *Za rubezhom*; *Died*: Sept 1930.

KOSTYAKOV, Aleksey Nikolayevich (1887-1957) Agronomist; specialist in soil improvement; prof from 1919; corresp member, USSR Acad of Sci from 1933; member, All-Union Lenin Acad of Agric Sci from 1935; Hon Sci and Tech Worker of RSFSR from 1936; *Born*: 28 Mar 1887; *Educ*: 1912 grad Moscow Agric Inst; *Career*: from 1919 prof, Timiryazev Agric Acad, Moscow; from 1930 prof, Moscow Inst of Water Management; pioneered experimental research on soil improvement techniques in USSR and developed their theoretical basis; devised and introduced several irrigation techniques involving the use of temporary irrigation ditches; *Publ: Melioratsiya v bor'be s neurozhayami* (Soil Improvement in the Campaign Against Harvest Failures) (1924); *Perspektivy melioratsii v SSSR. Yevropeyskaya chast'* (The Prospects of Soil Improvement in the European USSR) (1925); *Predupreditel'nyye meropriyatiya protiv zabolachivaniya i zasoleniya zemel' pri oroshenii* (The Prevention of Swamping and Salting in Irrigation) (1945); *Osnovy melioratsii* (The Principles of Soil Improvement) (1951); *Awards*: Order of Lenin; two Stalin Prizes (1951, 1952); other orders and medals; *Died*: 30 Aug 1957.

KOSTYAYEV, Fyodor Vasil'yevich (1878-1925) Mil commander; maj-gen, Russian Army Gen Staff; prof; *Born*: 8 Feb 1878 in Mitava (Yelgava), son of a retired capt; *Educ*: 1899 grad Nikolay

Eng College; 1905 grad Gen Staff Acad; *Career*: 1914-17 various staff and command posts in Russian Army, leading to command of 132nd Infantry Div; from Mar 1918 in Red Army; 1918 chief of staff, Pskov Area; commander, Petrograd Div; mustering inspector and mil commander, Petrograd Area; chief of staff, Northern Front; from Sept 1918 chief, Field Staff of RSFSR Commander in Chief; June 1919 dismissed from this post and arrested along with Commander in Chief I. I. Vatsetis in connection with failures on the Southern Front; from Sept 1919 prof, Red Army Mil Acad; 1921-23 member and mil rep, Russian-Ukr-Bel Commission for Establishing the State Border with Poland; 1924-25 chm, Sov Commission for Establishing the State Border with Finland; consultant for the establishment of borders with Rumania, Iran and other states; wrote numerous works on mil geography, history of the Civil War and gen staff service; *Died*: 27 Dept 1925.

KOSTYCHEV, Sergey Pavlovich (1877-1931) Phytophysiologist; biochemist and microbiologist; member, USSR Acad of Sci from 1923; *Born*: 8 May 1877 in Petersburg, son of Prof P. A. Kostychev, the soil scientist; *Educ*: 1900 grad Petersburg Univ; *Career*: 1907-14 assoc prof, from 1914 prof of plant anatomy and physiology, Petersburg Univ; 1922-23 corresp member, USSR Acad of Sci; from 1923 dir, State Inst of Experimental Agronomy (from 1930 Inst of Agric Microbiology, All-Union Lenin Acad of Agric Sci); studied chemism of respiration and fermentation, nitrogen metabolism of yeasts and mold funghi, air nutrition of higher plants, etc; wrote phytophysiology course, translated into German and English, and monograph on plant respiration; *Publ: Fiziologiya rasteniy* (The Physiology of Plants) (vol 1, 3rd ed, 1937); coauthor, *Khimicheskiye issledovaniya nad svyazyvaniyem molekulyarnogo azota mikrobom Azotobacterium agile* (Chemical Study of Molecular Nitrogen Binding by Azotobacterium agile) (vol 1, 1926); *Fiziologokhimicheskiye issledovaniya nad dykhaniyem rasteniy* (Physiochemical Studies of Plant Respiration) (1911); *K voprosu ob okislenii spirta vysshimi rasteniyami* (The Oxydation of Alcohol by Higher Plants) (1916), etc; *Died*: 21 Aug 1931 in Alushta, Crimea.

KOSTLYOV, Valentin Ivanovich (1884–1950) Russian writer; CP member from 1944; *Born*: 1884 in Moscow, son of a railroad official; *Career*: 1903 first story, *Melkiy sluchay* (A Minor Incident), published in journal *Razvlecheniye*; in various works described suburban life; story *V gospitale* (In Hospital) (1911) reflects 1905 revol; greatly influenced by his correspondence and contacts with Gorky and his acquaintance with Veresayev, Tolstoy, Teleshov and Serafimovich; in 1930's wrote historical novels; *Publ*: novels *Khvoynyy shtorm* (The Coniferous Storm) (1935), revised ed entitled *Schastlivaya vstrecha* (A Happy Encounter) (1947); *Pitirim* (1936); *Zhretsy* (The Priests) (1937); *Kuz'ma Minin* (1939); historical drama *Kuz'ma Minin* (1942); trilogy depicting Ivan IV's role in founding a centralized Russian state *Ivan Groznyy* (Ivan the Terrible), including: *Moskva v pokhode* (Moscow on the March) (1943), *More* (The Sea) (1946) and *Nevskaya tverdynya* (The Neva Fortress) (1947); *Awards:* Stalin Prize (1948); *Died:* 29 Aug 1950 in Moscow.

KOSYNKA (real name: STRELETS), Grigoriy Mikhaylovich (1899-1934) Ukr writer; *Born*: 17 Nov 1899 in vil Shcherabanivka, now Kiev Oblast, son of a peasant; *Educ*: uncompleted higher educ; *Career*: as a youth worked as hired laborer at sugar refinery; 1913 moved to Kiev, worked in offices and attended high-school; attended college but did not graduate; in WW 1 served at front; 1919 first work published; 1925 returned to Kiev and worked as secr, cooperative journal; member, *Lanka* and *Mars* lit orgs; wrote mainly about Ukr country life; 1934 arrested by State Security organs; 15 Dec 1934 sentenced to death by Assizes of Mil Collegium, USSR Supr Court; *Publ:* "Beyond the Gate" (1924); "Mother" (1925); "Politics" (1926); "The Plot" (1930); "Heart" (1933); "Harmony" (1933), etc; *Died*: 17 Dec 1934 executed by firing squad in Kiev.

KOTEL'NIKOV, Aleksandr Petrovich (1865-1944) Mathematician; specialist in geometry and mech; Hon Sci Worker of RSFSR from 1934; *Born*: 20 Oct 1865; *Career*: prof, higher educ establishments in Kiev, Kazan' and Moscow; did research on the applications of the theory of quaternions and complex numbers to geometry and mech; developed principles of mech and vector calculus in non-Euclidean space; *Awards*: Stalin Prize (1943); *Died*: 6 Mar 1944.

KOTEL'NIKOV, Gleb Yevgen'yevich (1872-1944) Parachute designer; *Born*: 30 Jan 1872 in Petersburg; *Educ*: 1894 grad Kiev Mil College; *Career*: after a brief mil career retired from army; worked as a civil servant, then as an actor; 1911 designed satchel parachute RK-1, which passed tests in 1912 but was rejected by mil authorities; 1914 the RK-1 was accepted for *Il'ya Muromets* bombers; 1921-24 improved design of parachute, developing marks RK-2 and RK-3, and designed supply parachutes; *Publ: Istoriya odnogo izobreteniya. Russkiy parashyut* (The Story of an Invention. The Russian Parachute) (1939); *Awards*: cash prize of Supr Sovnarkhoz (1921); "Designer" Badge of USSR Soc for the Promotion of Aviation, Defense and Chemical Ind (1936); *Died*: 22 Nov 1944.

KOTIK, Valentin Aleksandrovich (1930-1944) WW 2 partisan in Ukr; *Born*: 11 Feb 1930 in vil Khmelivtsy, Khmel'nitskiy Oblast; *Educ:* 1941 grad secondary school; *Career:* from 1941 lived and studied in Shepetovka; after occupation of Shepetovka by German troops joined underground org and carried out its assignments; then joined partisan detachment and took part in assaults; *Awards*: Order of the Fatherland War; Partisan of Fatherland War Medal; Hero of Sov Union (1958, posthumously); *Died*: 17 Feb 1944 in battle near Izyaslav, Khmel'nitskiy Oblast; Shepetovka school which he attended, pioneer club and pioneer units named after him and monument erected to him in Shepetovka.

KOTLUBAY, Kseniya Ivanovna (1890-1931) Actress, producer and teacher; Hon Artiste of RSFSR; *Born*: 1890; *Career*: close assoc of Ye. B. Vakhtangov; 1913 co-founder, Vakhtangov Student Drama Studio; taught Stanislavskiy's method; from 1922 producer, Moscow Acad Arts Theater and Nemirovich-Danchenko Musical Theater; *Roles:* Hortense and Virginia in Materlinck's "Le Miracle de Saint-Antoine" (The Miracle of Saint Anthony); Kseniya in Zaytsev's *Usad'ba Laninykh* (The Lanin Estate); helped produce: Bizet's "Carmen" (1924); Rachmaninoff's "Aleko" (1926); Knipper's *Severnyy veter* (North Wind); *Died:* 29 Mar 1931.

KOTOLYNOV, Ivan Ivanovich (1905-1934) Student; CP member; *Born*: 1905; *Career*: expelled from Party for belonging to Zinov'yev Group but reinstated after declaring complete solidarity with the policies of the Party and Sov regime; after secr of the CPSU(B) CC Kirov was assassinated on 1 Dec 1934, Kotolynov was arrested along with 14 others; 25 Dec 1934 tried in Leningrad by assizes of the Mil Collegium, USSR Supr Court as the leader of the illegal terrorist "Leningrad Center," allegedly founded in Leningrad by former members of the Zinov'yev Group; 29 Dec 1934 sentenced to death; *Died*: 1934 executed by firing squad.

KOTOV, Anatoliy Konstantinovich (1909-1956) Russian lit historian; CP member from 1940; *Born*: 5 Feb 1909 in Petersburg, son of a peasant; *Educ*: 1931 grad Lit Fac, 2nd Moscow Univ; 1936 completed postgrad course at Moscow's Lenin Teachers' Training Inst; *Career*: 1931 first work printed; studied life and work of Korolenko, Chekhov and Podyachev; 1948-56 dir, Fiction Publ House; *Publ: Kak zakalyalas' stal'* (How the Steel Was Tempered) (1933); *V. G. Korolenko, ocherk zhizni i literaturnoy deyatel'nosti* (V. G. Korolenko, a Study of His Life and Literary Work) (1957); *Stat'i o russkikh pisatelyakh* (Articles on Russian Writers) (1962); *Died*: 28 Nov 1956 in Moscow.

KOTOV, Pyotr Ivanovich (1889-1953) Artist; Hon Art Worker of RSFSR from 1946; member, USSR Acad of Art from 1949; *Born*: 8 July 1889 in vil Vladimirskaya, Astrakhan' Province, son of an icon-painter; *Educ*: 1903-09 studied at Kazan' Art School; 1909-16 studied at Petersburg Acad of Arts; *Career*: during 1920's painted historical and revol subjects; 1923 joined Assoc of Artists of Revol Russia; during 1930's painted subjects based on the first five-year plans; during 1940's specialized in portrait-painting; *Works*: "The Battle of Chongar"; "The Battle of Gorbat Bridge, 1905"; "The Storming of Perekop" (1929); "The Stoker"; "Portrait of a Bukhara Revolutionary"; "Blast Furnace Number 1" (1931); "Red Sormovo" (1937); portraits of the sculptor I. D. Shadr (1936), Acad N. N. Burdenko (1943), Gen I. Kh. Bagramyan (1946), Acad N. D. Zelinskiy (1947), Stakhanovite Ye. K. Mikheyeva (1948), etc; *Awards*: Stalin Prize (1948); *Died*: 1953.

KOTOVSKIY, Grigoriy Ivanovich (1881-1925) Mold anarchist revol; Sov mil commander; Civil War veteran; Leftist Socialist-Revol from 1917; CP member from 1920; *Born*: 12 June 1881 in vil Gancheshty, Bessarabia, son of a mechanic; *Educ*: 1900 grad Agric College; *Career*: 1900-02 agronomist and steward for a landowner; Dec 1902 arrested and imprisoned in Kishenev Prison for forging a letter of recommendation; 1903-05 laborer on an estate, forester, day laborer and brewery worker; Feb 1905 conscripted into Russian Army and assigned to 19th Kostroma Infantry Regt in Zhitomir; May 1905 deserted; late 1905 during peasant uprisings in Russia founded small partisan detachment in his native parts and began campaign of terror against local landowners, burning estates and distributing the valuables among the poor; Nov 1907 after repeated arrests and escapes sentenced to 12 years' hard labor; Feb 1913 escaped from construction gang building Amur Railroad; early 1915 returned to Bessarabia and resumed terrorist activities against the rich and local admin; June 1916 captured, tried and sentenced to hanging, which the commander of the Southwestern Front commuted to indefinite hard labor; May 1917, after Feb Revol, released on parole and sent to the army on the Rumanian Front; from 1918 in Red Army; 1919-20 commanded cavalry brigade and fought against White troops in the Ukr and near Petrograd; fought in the Sov-Polish War; 1920-21 commander, 17th Cavalry Div, then separate cavalry brigade; helped liquidate Makhno's troops and crush Antonov rebellion in Tambov Province and the anti-Sov insurrection in the Ukr; 1921-22 commander, 9th Cavalry Div; 1922-25 commander, 2nd Cavalry Corps in the Ukr; member, USSR Centr Exec Comt and All-Ukr Centr Exec Comt; *Awards*: three Orders of the Red Banner; Gold Cap with the Order of the Red Banner; *Died*: 6 Aug 1925 murdered by former colleague; the real motive for the murder was never revealed (according to the official Stalinist version, he was murdered by Trotskyite agents of a for intelligence service); buried in Birzul (now Kotovsk).

KOTS, Arkadiy (Aaron) Yakovlevich (pen names: A. DANIN; A. BRONIN; A. SHATOV) (1872-1943) Russian poet and translator; CP member from 1903; *Born*: 13 May 1872 in Odessa, son of a minor official; *Educ*: grad Gorlovka Mining College; grad Paris Mining Inst; *Career*: after grad Gorlovka Mining College worked as head miner; 1897-1902 in Paris, studying at mining inst; became acquainted with RSDRP officials in emigration; 1902 returned to Russia; 1903 joined RSDRP and conducted agitation and propaganda in Mariupol' and Odessa; 1907-14 abandoned party work; 1914-20 sided with Mensheviks; 1920 joined Bolsheviks; 1902 translated and published text of "The Internationale," which became the Sov nat anthem after Oct Revol and from 1943 (with the adoption of a new nat anthem) became the anthem of the CPSU; *Publ*: translated Lafargue pamphlet "The Worship of Gold" (1905) and Mirabeau's play "The Bad Shepherds" (1905), etc; verse: *Gornaya ballada* (Mountain Ballad) (1938); *Skazaniye o Stakhanove* (The Tale of Stakhanov) (1940); *Tebe, Ural* (To Thee, Urals!), *Parizh* (Paris), *Tulonskiy vzryv* (The Toulon Explosion), *Mayskaya pesn'* (May Song), *9 yanvarya* (9 January) and *Pesni proletariyev* (Songs of the Proletariat) (1907); *Kak myshi kota khoronili* (How the Mice Buried the Cat) (1921); *Died*: 13 May 1943 in Sverdlovsk.

KOTSKO, Vasiliy Fyodorovich (1873-1942) Party official; one of the founders and leaders of the Communist movement in the Western Ukr; CP member from 1918; *Born*: Apr 1873 in vil Mlinki Shkol'nyye, now L'vov Oblast; *Educ*: studied at Drogobych High School; *Career*: from 1888 revol agitation among Drogobych Uyezd peasants; from 1913 participated in strikes of Drogobych and Borislav oil workers; 1915 went to Russia; 1915-18 worked as a joiner in Kremenchug; helped establish Sov regime in Poltava Province; later returned to Drogobych; Nov 1918 founded Communist Socialists' Group; helped found Sov of Workers' Dep at salt works in Stebnka and Drogobych; 1919 helped organize Drogobych rebellion; 1918-21 member, uyezd and okrug comts and member, CC, East Galician CP; deleg, 3rd Comintern Congress; persecuted and arrested by Polish authorities; 1939, after establishment of Sov regime in Western Ukr, helped to set up Sov admin apparatus; during WW 2 underground work; arrested by German authorities along with 39 others including his daughter Olga (a Party official); *Died*: 26 Jan 1942 shot near Drogobych in Bronnitskiy Forest.

KOTSOYEV, Arsen Borisovich (1872-1944) Ossetian writer; *Born*: 15 Jan 1872 in vil Gizel', now North Ossetian ASSR, son of a peasant; *Educ*: grad Ardon Theological College; *Career*: 1897-1906 teacher; dismissed from his job for teaching atheist ideas; from 1895 published his work in Russian newspapers in Vladikavkaz; 1909-10 ed, Tiflis sociolit illustrated journal *Afsir*; 1912 proof-reader, newspaper *Pravda*, which published his stories "They Dreamed," "Comrade," etc; 1927-29 ed, lit journal *Fidiuag*; translated Pushkin's verse into Ossetian; *Publ*: stories: "The Hunters"; "Friends"; "At Dawn"; "It's Sometimes Like That"; "The Ram and the Goat"; "Twenty-Four Days"; "A Nameless Story," etc; novelette *Dzhanaspi* (1940); play *Paskha Gigo;* also wrote satirical works such as "The Monster," etc; *Awards*: All-Union Competition Prize (1940); *Died*: 4 Feb 1944 in Ordzhonikidze.

KOTSYUBA, Gordey Maksimovich (1892-1939) Ukr writer; *Born*: 15 Jan 1892 in vil Kostev, Khar'kov Province; *Educ*: 1917 grad Law Fac, Petrograd Univ; *Career*: 1919 first work published; collaborated with writer V. Blakitnyy (Yellan); sided with Ukr proletarian writers group; co-founder, *Gart* lit assoc; together with nucleus of this org, joined *Vaplite* lit assoc and remained a member until its disbandment; 1937 arrested by State Security organs; *Publ*: story "Two Worlds" (1919); collected stories: "On the Boundary" (1924); "Workdays and Holidays" (1927); "The Conspiracy of Masks" (1929); "Bronze People" (1930); "Sagas of the Dnieper" (1931); novel "New Shores" (2 vol, 1932-36); novel "Fruitfulness" (1934); novel "Before the Storm" (1937); *Died*: 22 Mar 1939 in imprisonment; posthumously rehabilitated.

KOTSYUBINSKIY, Yuriy Mikhaylovich (1895-1937) Govt official; CP member from 1913; *Born*: 9 Dec 1895, son of the Ukr writer M. M. Kotsyubinskiy; *Educ*: studied at Chernigov High School; from 1922 studied at Socialist Acad of Soc Sci; *Career*: 1913 joined Chernigov RSDRP Comt; from 1916 in Russian Army; revol and propaganda work among soldiers; during 1917 Oct Revol member, Petrograd Mil Revol Comt; took part in the storming of the Winter Palace; Dec 1917 at 1st All-Ukr Congress Soviets elected member, Pop Secretariat, Ukr Workers and Peasants' Republic and appointed Dep Pop Secr of Mil Affairs; Jan 1918 appointed commander in chief of Ukr Republic's armed forces; 1918 at 1st Congress of CP(B) Ukr elected member, CC, CP(B) Ukr; 1919 chm, Chernigov Province Comt, CP(B) Ukr; 1920 member, Poltava Province Comt, CP(B) Ukr; member, Poltava Province Exec Comt; 1921-22 Ukr dipl rep in Austria; 1927-30 councilor, USSR plen mission in Poland; Ukr Dep Pop Comr of Agric; dep chm, Ukr Council of Pop Comr; at the same time chm, Ukr Gosplan; member, Org Bureau, CC, CP(B) Ukr; repeatedly elected member, CC, CP(B) Ukr; arrested by State Security organs; *Died*: 1937 in imprisonment.

KOTYAGIN, Aleksandr Fyodorovich (1882-1943) Artist; master and co-founder of Mstyora miniature painting; *Career*: painted a number of original, excellent compositions on papier-mâché boxes and other articles on Sov themes, historical motifs and subjects from lit works; *Works*: "The Eroica of the Soviet Union" (1935); "The Prosperous Life of the Kolkhozniks" (1937); "By the Bay" (1936); "Igor Speaking Before the Campaign Against the Polovtsians" (1940), etc; *Died*: 18 Sept 1943.

KOVAL'-SAMBORSKIY, Ivan Ivanovich (1893-1962) Actor; Hon Artiste of Kir SSR from 1944; *Born*: 16 Sept 1893; *Career*: 1922–23 worked at Meyerkhol'd Theater in Moscow; first major screen role was as the worker Andrey in *Yego prizyv* (His Summons) (1925); *Roles*: Arthur Storn in "Miss Mend" (1926); Govorukha-Otrok in *Sorok pervyy* (The 41st) (1927); Sokolin in *Chelovek iz restorana* (The Man from the Restaurant) (1927); Il'ya Snegiryov in *Devushka s korobkoy* (The Girl with the Basket) (1927); Yakov in *Zemlya v plenu* (Land in Bondage) (1928); Belyaev in *Lyotchiki* (The Fliers) (1935); Mark, a typesetter, in *Troye s odnoy ulitsy* (Three from the Same Street) (1936); eng Viskovskiy in *Ushchel'ye Alamasov* (Alamasov Canyon) (1937); Val'ter in *Bolotnyye soldaty* (Swamp Soldiers) (1938); the Elder in *Prolog* (The Prologue) (1956); circus dir in *Guttaperchevyy mal'chik* (The India-Rubber Boy) (1957); Selivanov in "Poet" (1957); Bogomolov in *Shtorm* (The Storm) (1958); Shcherbina in *Smena nachinayetsya v shest'* (The Shift Begins at Six) (1959); the Forester in *Zelyonyy pastukh* (The Green Shepherd) (1961), etc; *Died*: 1962.

KOVALENKO, Boris L'vovich (1903-1938) Lit historian and critic; CP member from 1927; *Born*: 25 Nov 1903 in vil Khatunichi, now Chernigov Oblast; *Career*: member, Ukr Union of Proletarian Writers, *Molodnyak* and other Ukr lit assoc; active member, All-Union League of Proletarian Writers' Assoc; 1931-35 worked in Moscow; fell into disfavor for sharing the proscribed views of the leadership of the Russian Assoc of Proletarian Writers on the methods of socialist realism; arrested by State Security organs; *Publ: V bor'be za proletarskuyu literaturu* (The Struggle for Proletarian Literature) (1928); *Proletarskiye pisateli* (Proletarian Writers) (1931); *Ukrainskaya literatura. Posobiye dlya sredney shkoly* (Ukrainian Literature. A Textbook for Secondary Schools) (1935); *Literaturno-kriticheskiye stat'i* (Articles on Literary Criticism) (1962); *Died*: 24 Aug 1938 in imprisonment;

posthumously rehabilitated.

KOVALENKOV, Valentin Ivanovich (1884-1960) Communications eng; maj-gen, Eng Corps; corresp member, USSR Acad of Sci from 1939; Hon Sci and Tech Worker of RSFSR from 1935; CP member from 1945; *Born*: 1884 in vil Mezhnik, now Novgorod Oblast; *Educ*: 1909 grad Petersburg Electrotech Inst; 1911 completed postgrad studies at Fac of Physics and Mathematics, Petersburg Univ; *Career*: 1940-48 worked at Inst of Automation and Telemech; 1948-56 dir, Line Communications Development Laboratory, USSR Acad of Sci; specialized in line transmission theory, the analysis of transient processes in communications lines and research on magnetic circuits; *Publ*: thesis *Ustanavlivayushchiyesya protsessy i rasprostraneniye preryvistogo toka po telegrafnym provodam* (Stabilizing Processes and the Propagation of Intermittent Current in Telegraph Wires) (1914); *Telefonirovaniye na bol'shiye rasstoyaniya* (Long-Distance Telephony) (1924); *Teoriya peredachi po liniyam elektrosvyazi* (Electrical Line Transmission Theory) (1937-38); *Osnovy teorii magnitnykh tsepey i primeneniya yeyo k analizu releynykh skhem* (The Principles of Magnetic Circuit Theory and Its Application to the Analysis of Relay Diagrams) (1940); *Ustanavlivayushchiyesya elektromagnitnyye protsessy vdol' provodnykh liniy* (Stabilizing Electromagnetic Processes Along Transmission Lines) (1945), etc; *Awards:* A. S. Popov Prize; Stalin Prize (1941); two Orders of Lenin; Order of the Red Banner of Labor; Order of the Red Star; four medals; *Died:* 14 July 1960.

KOVAL'SKAYA (née: SOLNTSEVA), Yelizaveta Nikolayevna (1851-1943) Revol populist; *Born*: 17 July 1851 in Khar'kov; *Career*: in 1870's revol work in Khar'kov and Petersburg; closely associated with "Land and Freedom" (Zemlya i Volya) movement; 1879, after its schism, joined "Black Reallotment" (Chyornyy Peredel) faction; 1880, together with N. P. Shchedrin, founded the "Southern Russian Workers' League" in Kiev, for which she was sentenced (1881) to an indefinite term at hard labor; 1882 sent to Kara; 1903–17 in emigration, where she joined the Socialist-Revol Party (Maximalists); late 1917 returned to Russia; from 1918 worked for Petrograd Archives of Revol History; from 1923 member, ed bd, journal *Katorga i ssylka*; member, Soc of Polit Convicts; *Publ: Yuzhnorusskiy rabochiy soyuz 1880-1881* (The 1880-1881 Southern Russian Workers' League) (1926); *Moi vstrechi s S. L. Perovskoy* (My Encounters with S. L. Perovskaya) (1931); *Died*: 1943.

KOVALYOV, Sergey Ivanovich (1886–1960) Historian; prof from 1949; Dr of History from 1938; *Born*: 25 Sept 1886; *Educ*: 1922 grad Fac of History and Philology, Leningrad Univ; *Career*: 1919-38 taught at Lenin Mil Polit Acad in Leningrad; 1924-34 taught at Leningrad State Univ and Herzen Teachers' Training Inst; 1930-37 head, Dept of Ancient History, State Acad of the History of Material Culture; 1934-56 head, Dept of Greek and Roman History, Leningrad State Univ; 1938-50 senior assoc, Leningrad Branch, Inst of History, USSR Acad of Sci; 1956-60 dir, Museum of the History of Religion and Atheism; did research on the polit, soc and econ history of ancient Greece and Rome; did research on the origins of Christianity and the Marxist conception of ancient soc; *Publ*: textbooks *Istoriya antichnogo obshchestva* (A History of Ancient Society) (1936); *Istoriya Rima* (A History of Rome) (1948), etc; *Kurs vseobshchey istorii* (A Course of General History) (1923-25); *Aleksandr Makedonskiy* (Alexander the Great) (1937); coauthor, *Ocherki istorii Drevnego Rima* (An Outline History of Ancient Rome) (1956); *Osnovnyye voprosy proiskhozhdeniya khristianstva* (The Origin of Christianity) (1964); *Died*: 12 Nov 1960.

KOVALYOVA, Ol'ga Vasil'yevna (1881-1962) Singer (contralto); collector and performer of Russian folk songs; Pop Artiste of the RSFSR from 1947; *Born*: 4 Aug 1881 in vil Lyubovka, Saratov Province, daughter of a peasant; *Educ*: 1903-06 studied music in Samara; 1907-09 took opera courses in Petersburg; *Career*: 1909-11 toured various Russian cities with private opera troupe; sang Vanya in *Ivan Susanin*, Olga in *Yevgeniy Onegin*, etc; from 1913 performed Russian folk songs; in 1920's repeatedly performed with USSR folk groups abroad; performed in Sweden, Norway, Finland, France and Germany; from 1924 sang in radio concerts; at first performed mainly folk songs which she had learned as a child in Saratov Province (from time to time songs which had been written by other collectors); later Kovalyova greatly extended her repertoire; excelled at wedding songs and old lyrical songs for women; *Died*: 2 Jan 1962.

KOVPAK, Sidor Artyom'yevich (1887–1967) Ukr govt official and mil commander; maj-gen; member, CC, CP Ukr; CP member from 1919; *Born*: 2 June 1887 in vil Kotel'va, now Poltava Oblast, son of a poor peasant; *Career*: 1909-12 private in Russian Army; 1912-18 worked at tram depot; 1918-19 commanded partisan unit in Ukr; 1919 in Sov Army on Eastern Front; 1921-26 uyezd, then okrug mil comr; 1926 demobilized; from 1937 head, Dept of Roads, Putivl' Rayon Exec Comt; 1939-41 chm, Putivl' City Exec Comt; during WW 2 commanded partisan units behind the German lines in Ukr and Bel; 1943 led partisan raid deep into Galicia; 1944 wounded and evacuated; 1947-67 dep chm, Presidium, Ukr Supr Sov; dep, USSR Supr Sov of 1946, 1950, 1954, 1958, 1962 and 1966 convocations; deleg, 11th, 12th and 13th CPSU Congresses; from 1956 dep chm, Sov War Veterans Comt; *Publ: Ot Putivlya do Karpat* (From Putivl' to the Carpathians) (1946); *Awards*: twice Hero of the Sov Union (1942 and 1944); four Orders of Lenin; Order of the Red Banner; Order of Suvorov, 1st Class; medals; *Died*: 11 Dec 1967.

KOVTUN, Ivan Dmitriyevich (pen names: Yuriy VUKHNAL'; Ivan UKHNAL) (1906-1937) Ukr writer; *Born*: 5 Oct 1906 in vil Chernobayevka, now Khar'kov Oblast; *Career*: wrote short stories, novelettes and novels; arrested by State Security organs; *Publ*: collections of satyrical and humourous pieces: "For Malice" (1927); "The Life and Work of Fed'ka Gusko"; "The Convinced Ukrainian" (1929); novels: "The Hawks" (1928); "The Asiatic Aerolith" (1931); *Died*: 15 July 1937 in imprisonment.

KOVTYUKH, Yepifan Iovich (1890-1938) Mil commander; captain, 2nd class, Russian Army; corps commander, Sov Army from 1935; Civil War veteran; CP member from 1918; *Born*: 21 May 1890 in vil Baturino, Kherson Province, son of a poor peasant; *Educ*: 1916 grad ensign school; 1922 grad Red Army Mil Acad; 1927 grad advanced officer-training courses; *Pos*: from 1911 in Russian Army; 1914-18 served on Caucasian Front; from 1918 in Red Army; 1918 commander, revol company; dep commander, Red Army detachment in Kuban'; commander, Taman Army; 1919-20 commander, 3rd Taman Infantry Div and 50th Infantry Div; 1920 commander, composite corps, 11th Army; 1922-36 commanded rifle div, then rifle corps; 1936-38 army inspector and dep commander, Bel Mil Distr; *Career*: Aug-Sept 1918 during retreat of Taman Army from Kuban' along the Black Sea through Novorossiysk on the Tuapse and thence across the mountains to Armavir brilliantly commanded advance-guard 1st Column against all odds; these events are described in A. S. Serafimov's novel *Zheleznyy potok* (The Iron Stream), in which he figured as the hero under the name of Kozhukh; fall 1920 headed landing operation in the rear of White Gen Ulagay in Kuban'; 1921, while a cadet at the Mil Acad, helped crush Kronstadt Mutiny; 1938 arrested by NKVD; *Publ: Zheleznyy potok* (The Iron Current) (mil version, 1935); *Awards*: three Orders of the Red Banner; *Died*: 28 July 1938 executed; posthumously rehabilitated.

KOVYLKIN, S. T. (1887-1943) Govt official; CP member from 1905; *Born*: 1887; *Career*: 1908-17 in exile; after 1917 Feb Revol chm, plant comt, railroad shops in Saratov; then member, Exec Comt, Saratov Sov of Workers, Peasants and Soldiers' Dep; from 1919 transport work; Collegium member, Pop Comrt of Communications; head, Transport Dept, All-Russian Cheka; 1921 head, Southwestern Railroad with plen authority for measures against crimes affecting railroads and water transport; 1922-23 Pop Comrt of Communications plen for Simbirsk Okrug; 1922 chm, Volga State River Shipping Trust; 1931 head, Ural Railroad Construction Trust; arrested by State Security organs; *Died*: 1943 in imprisonment.

KOZAK, Semyon Antonovich (1902-1953) Ukr; lt-gen; CP member from 1923; *Born*: 10 May 1902 in vil Iskorost' (later incorporated into city of Korosten'), Zhitomir Oblast, son of a peasant; *Educ*: 1938 grad Frunze Mil Acad; *Career*: from 1924 in Red Army; 1941–43 dep chief of staff of an army; 1943–45 commander, 73rd Guards Infantry Div; 1943 fought at Kursk; 1944 fought in liberation of Yugoslavia; *Awards*: twice Hero of the Soviet Union (1943 and 1945); two Orders of Lenin; other orders and medals; *Died*: 24 Dec 1953.

KOZAKOV, Mikhail Emmanuilovich (1897-1954) Writer; *Born*: 23 Aug 1897 in vil Romodan; *Educ*: 1916-17 studied at Kiev Univ; 1922 grad Law Fac, Petrograd Univ; *Career*: joined revol movement while still a student; 1922 embarked on lit career; *Publ*: short stories *Popugayevo schast'ye* (Parrot Happiness) (1924); novelette *Meshchanin Adameyko* (Adameyko the Philistine) (1927); *Poltora Khama* (A Boor and a Half) (1927); short stories *Chelovek, padayushchiy nits* (The Toppling Man)

(1929); plays *Chekisty* (The Chekists) (1939) and *Neistovyy Vissarion* (Violent Vissarion) (1948); novel *Devyat' tochek* (Nine Points) (4 vol, 1929-37), later published in full under the title *Krusheniye imperii* (The Fall of an Empire) (1956); novel *Zhiteli etogo goroda* (The People of This Town) (1955); novelette *Petrogradskiye dni* (Petrograd Days) (1957); *Died*: 16 Dec 1954 in Moscow.

KOZHANOV, Ivan Kuz'mich (1897-1938) Naval commander; warrant officer, Russian Navy; flag officer, 2nd class, from 1935; CP member from 1917; *Born*: 24 May 1897 in vil Voznesenskaya, Kuban' Oblast; *Educ*: 1917 grad naval cadet classes in Petrograd; 1927 grad Naval Acad; *Career*: from 1916 in Russian Navy; from 1918 in Sov Navy; 1918-20 fought in Civil War on Volga and in Ukr; commanded seamen's detachment on the Volga, then landing units, naval expeditionary corps on the Caspian Sea, naval expeditionary div in the Azov area and in the Kuban'; 1921 helped crush Kronstadt Mutiny; 9 Mar-6 May 1921 head, Baltic Naval Forces; 1921-22 member, Revol Mil Council, Black Sea and Azov Sea Naval Forces; 1922-23 head, Far Eastern Naval Forces; from 1927 naval attaché in Japan; senior vice-commander, then commander, destroyer *Uritskiy*; chief of staff, Baltic Naval Forces; 27 June 1931-1 Jan 1935 chief, Black Sea and Azov Sea Naval Forces; 11 Jan 1935-Oct 1937 commander, Black Sea Fleet; from 22 Nov 1934 simultaneously member, Mil Council, USSR Pop Comrt of Defense; Oct 1937 arrested by NKVD; *Awards*: Order of the Red Banner; *Died*: 22 Aug 1938 in imprisonment; posthumously rehabilitated.

KOZHEVNIKOV, S. N. (1896-1938) Party official; CP member from 1917; *Born*: 1896; *Career*: 1918 extraordinary comr, Donets Basin; then commands and polit work in Red Army; from 1935 head, Polit Admin, Khar'kov Mil Distr; arrested by State Security organs; *Died*: 1938 in imprisonment.

KOZHEVNIKOV, Savva Yelizarovich (1903-1962) Writer; CP member from 1924; *Born*: 14 Sept 1903 in vil Krivinskaya, now Altay Kray, son of a peasant; *Educ*: 1928 grad Communist Univ; *Career*: for many years worked for okrug and kray newspapers; during WW 2 war corresp; 1946-53 chief ed, journal *Sibirskiye ogni*; wrote lit criticism and studies of lit history; 1953-55 lived in China; *Publ*: essays *Yedinstvennyy pravil'nyy put'* (The Only Right Way) (1933); *Vyshe 56-y paralleli. Ocherki* (Above the 56th Parallel. Essays) (1948); *Literaturnyye ocherki* (Literary Essays) (1949); *O chyom shumyat sosny* (What the Pine Trees Say) (1950); *Nikolay Ivanovich Naumov. Ocherk o zhizni i tvorchestve* (Nikolay Ivanovich Naumov. A Study of His Life and Work) (1952); *Yuy-gun peredvigayet gory* (Yu-Kung Moves Mountains) (1956); *Radi etogo stoit zhit'* (This Makes Life Worthwhile) (1958); *Belaya tayga* (The White Taiga) (1958); *Zemlya Sibirskaya. Rasskazy* (The Land of Siberia. Short Stories) (1958); *Moya Sibir'* (My Siberia) (1962); *Po zakonam krasoty. Ocherki i rasskazy* (By the Laws of Beauty. Essays and Short Stories) (1963); *Gor'kiy i Sibir'* (Gorky and Siberia); *Bytopisatel' staroy Sibiri. N. Naumov* (A Portrayer of the Manners and Morals of Old Siberia. N. Naumov); *Chelovek strashnoy sud'by. I. Tachalov* (A Man of Terrible Fate. I. Tachalov), etc; *Died*: 23 Oct 1962 in Yalta; buried in Novosibirsk.

KOZHEVNIKOVA (GURVICH), V. V. (1873-1940) Politician; *Born*: 1873; *Career*: 1894-95 worked for Petersburg League for the Liberation of the Working Class; 1901 subpoenaed in the "Workers' Banner' and "Socialists" cases; later went abroad and worked as a tech secr for *Iskra*; fall 1902 sent to Moscow by *Iskra* org to restore the Moscow RSDRP Comt; Dec 1902 arrested and exiled to Eastern Siberia for six years; 1904 fled abroad and worked for Menshevik org; 1915 left Mensheviks; 1925-39 head, tech library, Boiler Turbine Trust; *Died*: 1940.

KOZHIN, Mikhail Vladimirovich (1886-1966) Party and govt official; CP member from 1917; *Born*: 18 Apr 1886; *Educ*: grad Stroganov Ind Art College; *Career*: took part in 1905 Revol; distributed leaflets and the newspaper *Iskra*; active in 1917 Revol; during Civil War asst comr, Gen Staff of the Navy; head, Polit Dept and comr, Staff of North Sea Naval Forces; deleg, 10th Party Congress and 8th Congress of Soviets; from 1923 worked for Supr Sovnarkhoz; then dep chm, Standardization Comt, USSR Centr Exec Comt; wrote works on standardization; *Died*: 26 Mar 1966.

KOZHUKHOVA, Mariya Alekseyevna (1897-1959) Ballet dancer and teacher; Hon Art Worker of RSFSR from 1937; *Born*: 22 Feb 1897; *Educ*: 1915 grad Petrograd Theatrical College; *Career*: 1915-33 dancer, Maria Theater; from 1919 also ballet teacher, Petrograd Choreographic College and 1st Choreographic Technicum; 1933 retired from stage and moved to Moscow, where she became one of the best ballet instructors at Moscow Choreographic College; co-founder, 6-year training course for talented children; from 1949 taught advanced ballet training at the Bolshoy, Stanislavskiy and Nemirovich-Danchenko theaters; *Roles:* Aurora and Lisa in *Tshchetnaya predostorozhnost* (Vain Precaution); the Tsar-Maiden in Puny's *Konyok gorbunok* (The Little Hump-Backed Horse); friend of Fleur de Lys in "Esmeralda," etc; *Died*: 13 Nov 1959.

KOZLANYUK, Pyotr Stepanovich (1904-1965) Ukr writer; Bd member, USSR Writers' Union from 1954 and Ukr Writers' Union from 1959; member, ed bd, journal *Zhovten'*; CP member from 1943; *Born*: 1904 in vil Pererovo, now Ivano-Frankov Oblast; *Career*: 1927-30 contributed to newspaper *Sel'rob*; 1930-32 ed, newspaper *Sila*; 1930-39 on several occasions imprisoned in Poland for revol activities; from 1939 worked for newspaper *Vil'na Ukraina*; during WW 2 corresp for front newspapers and contributed to Radio Dnipro; 1945-51 ed, journal *Radyans'kyy L'viv*; from 1944 for several years headed L'vov Branch of Ukr Writers' Union; 1952-54 chm, exec comt, L'vov Oblast Sov of Workers' Dep; helped found Ukr writers' org *Horno* and journal *Vikna;* at 13th and 14th CP Ukr Congresses elected cand member, CC, CP Ukr; dep, USSR Supr Sov of 1950, 1954 and 1958 convocations; author of numerous articles, pamphlets, humorous stories and feuilletons; works translated into many Sov languages and into Polish, Czech, Rumanian, German, Chinese, etc; 1926 first work published; *Publ*: collected stories "In the Village" (1928); "Peasant Prosperity" (1928); collected feuilletons "A Smile from Behind Bars" (1930); collected stories "From Bygone Days" (1941); collected feuilletons "A Parade of Corpses" (1943); trilogy "Yurko Kruk" (1946-56); "The Storks Have Come" (1953); humorous stories "My Acquaintances" (1962); *Awards*: two Orders of Lenin (1954 and 1960); other orders and medals; *Died*: Mar 1965.

KOZLOV, Frol Romanovich (1908-1965) Russian govt and Party official; metallurgical eng; CP member from 1926; *Born*: 18 Aug 1908 in vil Loshchinino, Ryazan' Oblast; *Educ*: 1928-31 studied at Communist higher educ establishment, then at Workers' Fac, Leningrad Mining Inst; 1936 grad Leningrad Polytech Inst; *Career*: 1923-26 worker; then asst shop foreman at Red Textile Worker Plant in Kasimov; 1926-28 secr, Komsomol Comt at this factory; then head, Econ Dept, Kasimov Uyezd Komsomol Comt; 1936-39 eng and head of the blooming mill at a metallurgical plant in Izhevsk; 1939-40 Party CC organizer and secr of the Party Comt at this plant; 1940-41 secr, Izhevsk City CPSU(B) Comt; 1941-44 coordinated arms production and deliveries to front; 1944-47 worked for CC, CPSU(B); 1947-49 second secr, Kuybyshev Oblast CPSU(B) Comt; 1949 worked for CC, CPSU(B); then Party organizer for CC, CPSU at the Kirov Plant in Leningrad; 1949-52 secr, 1952-53 second secr, 1953-57 first secr, Leningrad Oblast CPSU Comt; 1956-57 and 1958 member, Bureau for the RSFSR, CC, CPSU; from 1952 member, CC, CPSU; Feb-June 1957 cand member, June 1957-64 member, Presidium, CC, CPSU; from 1962 member, Presidium, USSR Supr Sov; 1957-58 chm, RSFSR Council of Min; 1958-60 first dep chm, USSR Council of Min; 1960-64 secr, CC, CPSU; dep, USSR Supr Sov of 1950, 1954, 1958 and 1962 convocations; dep, RSFSR Supr Sov of 1955 and 1959 convocations; *Awards*: Hero of Socialist Labor (1961); three Orders of Lenin; two Orders of the Red Banner of Labor; Order of the Fatherland War, 2nd Class; Order of the Red Star; medals; *Died*: 30 Jan 1965.

KOZLOV, Ivan Andreyevich (1888-1957) Party official; writer; CP member from 1905; *Born*: 24 June 1888 in vil Sandyri, Moscow Province, son of a peasant; *Educ*: 1923-25 studied at Higher Lit Inst; *Career*: 1905-07 took active part in Revol; sentenced to four years' imprisonment and life exile in Siberia for revol activities; fled from exile to Switzerland; after 1917 Feb Revol returned to Russia; during Civil War did underground Party work in Sevastopol' and Khar'kov; 1920 first lit work published; 1925 resumed Party work after lit studies; during WW 2 did Party work among partisans in Crimea; secr, Simferopol' CPSU(B) Comt; *Publ*: plays: *Podpol'ye* (The Underground) (1920); *Stena* (The Wall) (1924); *Konets Kabayevshchiny* (Kabayev's End) (1929); *V volch'yey pasti* (In the Wolf's Maw) (1934); novelettes: *Vstryaska* (Shake-Up) (1926); *V Krymskom podpol'ye* (In the Crimean Underground) (1947); *V gorode russkoy slavy* (In the City of Russian Glory) (1950); memoirs *Zhizn' v bor'be* (A Life in

Struggle) (Part 1, 1955); *Awards*: Stalin Prize (1948); *Died*: 26 Mar 1957.

KOZLOV, Pyotr Kuz'mich (1863-1935) Explorer of Centr Asia; member, Ukr Acad of Sci from 1928; hon member, Dutch Geographical Soc from 1896, Russian Geographical Soc from 1910 and Hungarian Geographical Soc from 1911; *Born*: 15 Oct 1863 in Dukhovshchina, now Smolensk Oblast; *Educ*: 1887 grad mil college; *Career*: 1883-85, 1888-90 and 1893-95 member, N. M. Przheval'skiy, M. V. Pevtsov and V. I. Roborovskiy's Centr Asian expeditions; 1899-1901 led Mongolia-Tibet expedition, which traveled from Kyakhta to Eastern Tibet and back via the Mongolian Altay, Centr Gobi and Tsaidam; during this expedition collected valuable material on the orography, geology, climate, flora and fauna of Tibet and on the East Tibetan tribes; 1907-09 led Mongolia-Szechuan expedition, which discovered the remains of the ancient city of Hara-Hoto in the Gobi Desert; excavation led to the discovery of numerous relics, including some 2.000 books written in Hsihsia, the language of the Tangut tribe, Chinese and other languages; also collected other valuable material on the peoples of Mongolia and Tibet during this expedition; 1923-26 made last expedition to Mongolia and Tibet, during which an Eastern Hun burial mound dating from the beginning of the first millenium A. D. was discovered in the Hengt'ei mountains; this expedition also found the ruins of the ancient Chinese town of Shungwui-Cheng and continued excavations at Hara-Hoto; Kozlov's name has been given to a genus and several varieties of plants; *Publ: Mongoliya i Kam. Trudy ekspeditsii 1899-1901 godov* (Mongolia and Kham. The Transactions of the Expedition of 1899-1901) (4 vol, 1905-08); *Mongoliya i Kam. Tryokhletnee puteshestvie po Mongolii i Tibetu, 1899-1901* (Mongolia and Kham. A Three-Year Journey Through Mongolia and Tibet, 1899-1901) (1913); *Mongoliya i Amdo i myortvyy gorod Khara-Khoto. Ekspeditsiya v Nagornoy Azii 1907-09 godov* (Mongolia, Amdo and the Dead City of Hara-Hoto. The 1907-09 Expedition to Mountainous Asia) (1923); *V aziatskikh prostorakh. Kniga o zhizni i puteshestviyakh N. M. Przheval'skogo* (In the Expanse of Asia. A Book About the Life and Travels of N. M. Przheval'skiy) (1947); *Puteshestviye v Mongoliyu, 1923-26. Dnevniki* (Journey to Mongolia, 1923-26. Journals) (1949); *Awards*: Przheval'skiy Silver Medal (1891); Constantine Medal of Russian Geographical Soc (1902); Grand Gold Medal of Italian Geographical Soc (1911); medal of British Geographical Soc (1911); Tchihatchef Prize of Paris Acad (1913); *Died*: 26 Sept 1935.

KOZLOV, Vasiliy Ivanovich (1903-1967) Bel Party and govt official; chm, Presidium, Bel Supr Sov and dep chm, USSR Supr Sov from 1948; maj-gen; member, Presidium, Sov War Veterans' Comt from 1956; member and Bureau (Presidium) member, CC, CP Bel from 1956; member, CC, CPSU from 1966; CP member from 1927; *Born*: 18 Sept 1903 in vil Zagrad'ye, now Gomel' Oblast; *Educ*: 1929-33 grad Lenin Communist Univ in Minsk; *Career*: 1919-25 metal worker at Zhlobin railroad depot; 1925-27 in Red Army; 1927-29 switchman at Zhlobin Station; 1929 instructor, Zhlobin Rayon Exec Comt; 1934-37 dir, Starobin Machine and Tractor Station; 1937-40 first secr, Starobin and Cherven' Rayon Comt, CP Bel; 1940-41 dep chm, Bel Council of Pop Comr; Apr-July 1941 second secr, from July 1941 first secr, Minsk Oblast (Underground) CP Comt; 1944-48 first secr, Minsk Oblast and City Party Comt; 1947-48 chm, Bel Supr Sov; 1956-66 cand member, CC, CPSU; 1941-43 plen, CC, CP Bel for development of partisan movement; commanded partisan detachments in Minsk, Bobruysk and Polotsk Oblasts; dep, USSR Supr Sov of 1946, 1950, 1954, 1958, 1962 and 1966 convocations; dep, Bel Supr Sov of 1938, 1947, 1951, 1955, 1959 and 1963 convocations; member, Constitution Commission; *Awards*: three Orders of Lenin; Order of the Red Banner; two Orders of the Fatherland War, 1st Class; Hero of the Sov Union; medals; *Died*: 2 Dec 1967.

KOZLOVSKIY, Mechislav Yul'yevich (1876–1927) Party and govt official; took part in Polish, Lith and Russian revol movements; CP member from 1900; *Born*: 1 Dec 1876 in Vilnius, son of a teacher; *Educ*: 1894 entered Moscow Univ but was arrested a year later and imprisoned for participation in student riots; *Career*: 1896-99 member, League of Lith Workers and ed of its newspaper *Przeglad Robotniczy*; 1899-1901 member, Main Bd, Soc-Democratic Party of Poland and Lith; 1900-05 member, Vilnius Comt, Soc-Democratic Party of Poland and Lith; 1905 took active part in Revol and was arrested that fall; 1906-08 in emigration 1907 attended 5th RSDRP Congress; from 1909 lived in Petersburg, where he contributed to the Polish weekly *Nowa Trybuna* and held a post in the Metalworkers' Trade Union; after 1917 Feb Revol member, Exec Comt, Petrograd Sov and Centr Exec Comt of 1st convocation; chm, Vyborg Rayon Duma; July 1917, along with Lenin and Ya. S. Ganetskiy, accused of being a German spy, arrested and released early in Oct; after 1917 Oct Revol chm, Petrograd Investigation Commission and Collegium member, Pop Comrt of Justice; Mar 1918-Nov 1920 chm, RSFSR Small Council of Pop Comr; Jan-Apr 1919 did govt work in Lith; Lith-Bel Pop Comr of Justice; deleg, 8th RCP(B) Congress; 1922-23 Sov consul-gen in Vienna and dep plen rep in Austria; from 1923 main legal consultant, Pop Comrt of Means of Communication; *Died*: 3 Mar 1927.

KOZLOVSKIY, Nikolay Feofanovich (1887-1939) Cameraman; *Born*: 1887; *Career*: worked as photographer and taught himself movie-camera technique; 1908, together with A. Drankov, filmed first Russian feature *Ponizovaya vol'nitsa* (*Sten'ka Razin i knyazhna*) (The River Pirate [Stenka Razin and the Princess]); by 1917 filmed some 60 movies; after Oct Revol filmed over 20 features for various Sov studios; also did newsreel and cartoon work; 1921 and 1922 filmed 3rd and 4th Comintern Congresses; worked with dir I. Perestiani, Panteleyev, G. Roshal', A. Dovchenko, etc; 1932 played eng Lazarev in film *Vstrechnyy* (The First Comer); *Works*: historical films *Bogdan Khmel'nitskiy* (1910) and *Pokoreniye Kavkaza* (The Conquest of the Caucasus) (1913); psychological dramas *Prestupnaya strast'* (Crime of Passion) (1913) and *Podlets* (The Rogue) (1915); classics *Obryv* (The Precipice) (1913) and *Brat'ya Karamazovy* (The Brothers Karamazov) (1915); *Krest'yanskaya svad'ba* (The Peasant Wedding) (1910); comedy *Chudotvorets* (The Miracle-Worker) (1922); *Za vlast' Sovetov* (For Soviet Power) (1923); *Komediantka* (The Comedienne) (1923); *Serdtsa dollary* (The Dollar's Hearts) (1924); *Palachi* (The Executioners) (1925); *Gospoda Skotininy* (Mssrs Skotinin) (1927); *Yego prevoskhoditel'stvo* (His Excellenxy) (1928); *Sumka dipkur'yera* (The Courier's Bag) (1928), etc; *Died:* 1939.

KOZLOVSKIY, Sergey Vasil'yevich (1885-1962) Stage designer; Hon Art Worker of RSFSR from 1940; Pop Artist of RSFSR from 1944; CP member from 1940; *Born*: 3 Apr 1885; *Educ*: 1900-03 studied at Shvaykovich's Art Workshop; also attended Odessa Art College; *Career*: 1903-13 actor and set designer in Ukr theater; from 1913 in film work; designed sets for many pre-revol Russian films, in many of which he also took part as dir and actor; these include: *Mnogo li cheloveku zemli nuzhno* (Does A Man Need Much Land?) (1915); *Privalovskiye milliony* (The Privalov Millions) (1916); *Molchite, proklyatyye struny* (Be Still, Cursed Strings) (1917), etc; worked on over 100 Sov films; 1923-30 set designer, Russian Int Workers' Aid Film Studio; designed or helped design sets for: *Polikushka* (1919); *Aelita* (1924); *Mat'* (Mother) (1926); *Sorok pervyy* (The Forty-First) (1927); *Konets Sankt-Peterburga* (The End of St Petersburg) (1927); *Don Diyego i Pelageya* (Don Diego and Pelagea) (1928); *Potomol Chingiskhana* (Descendant of Genghis Khan) (1929); *Prazdnik Svyatogo Iorgena* (The Feast of Saint Jorgen) (1930); also directed or co-directed a number of films, for many of which he designed the sets and wrote the scripts; *Ditya Gostsirka* (A Child of the State Circus) (1925); *Doroga k schast'yu* (The Road to Happiness) (1925); *Sluchay na mel'nitse* (The Incident at the Mill) (1926); designed sets for sound films: *Dezertir* (The Deserter) (1933); *Okraina* (The Outskirts) (1933); *Marionetki* (The Puppets) (1934); *Posledniy tabor* (The Last Camp) (1936); *Ostrov sokrovishch* (Treasure Island) (1938); *Lermontov* (1943); *Eto bylo v Donbasse* (It Happened in the Donbass) (1945); *Pyatnadtsatiletniy kapitan* (The Fifteen-Year-Old Captain) (1946); *More studyonoye* (The Chill Sea) (1955), etc; also devised many measures for increasing efficiency in film work, introduced at film studios throughout the USSR; helped devise the pre-fabricated, standardized fundus system of building sets from basic, standard units, thus saving time and money; from 1924 taught at All-Union State Inst of Cinematography; *Publ:* coauthor, *Khudozhnik-arkhitektor v kino* (The Cinema Set Designer) (1930); *Awards*: Order of the Red Banner of Labor; *Died*: 22 Nov 1962.

KOZ'MIN, Boris Pavlovich (1883-1958) Historian and lit critic; Dr of History; prof; *Born*: 27 Dec 1883 in Moscow; *Educ*: 1910 grad Law Fac, Moscow Univ; *Career*: 1920-30's senior assoc, Inst of Lit, Russian Assoc of Soc Sci Research Inst; simultaneously chief ed, Publ House of the Soc of Ex-Polit Prisoners and journal *Katorga i ssylka*; from 1939 senior assoc, Inst of World Lit, USSR

Acad of Sci; 1944-46 dep dir, 1946-54 dir, State Lit Museum; 1946-58 also senior assoc, Inst of History, USSR Acad of Sci; contributed to journals *Krasnyy arkhiv, Pechat' i revolyutsiya, Literatura i marksizm* and *Novyy mir* and to the almanac *Literaturnoye nasledstvo*; did research on soc movements in Russia during the late 19th Century; wrote studies of A. I. Herzen, N. G. Chernyshevskiy, N. A. Dobrolyubov, D. I. Pisarev, P. L. Lavrov, P. N. Tkachyov and N. K. Mikhaylovskiy; edited and annotated the works of Herzen, Chernyshevskiy, Dobrolyubov, M. L. Mikhaylov, G. S. Uspenskiy, etc; also wrote commentaries to memoirs of V. N. Zasulich, N. A. Morozov, P. D. Boborykin, Ye. N. Vodovozovaya, etc; *Publ:P. N. Tkachyov i revolyutsionnoye dvizheniye 1860-ykh godov* (P. N. Tkachyov and the Revolutionary Movement of the 1860's) (1922); *Revolyutsionnoye podpol'ye v epokhu 'belogo terrora'* (The Revolutionary Underground During the "White Terror") (1929); *Kazanskiy zagovor 1863-yego goda* (The Kazan' Plot of 1863) (1929); *Ot 'devyatnadtsatogo fevralya' k 'pervomu marta'. Ocherki po istorii narodnichestva* (From "February 19" to "March 1." Studies in the History of Populism) (1933); *Russkaya sektsiya Pervogo Internatsionala* (The Russian Section of the First International) (1957); *Iz istorii revolyutsionnoy mysli v Rossii* (The History of Revolutionary Thought in Russia) (1961), etc; *Awards*: Prize of the Presidium of the USSR Acad of Sci (1957); *Died*: 5 July 1958 in Moscow.

KOZO-POLYANSKIY, Boris Mikhaylovich (1890-1957) Botanist; prof from 1920; corresp member, USSR Acad of Sci from 1932; *Born*: 19 Jan 1890; *Educ*: grad Moscow Univ; *Career*: from 1920 prof, Voronezh Univ; 1921-28 did research on the evolutionary system of flowering plants; 1922-51 did parallel research on vegetation as a whole; from 1937 dir, Voronezh Botanical Garden; developed evolutionary taxonomy of Umbelliferae and devised new carpoanatomical classification method; discovered area abounding in vegetational relicts (Kozo-Polyansky Center) in Kursk Oblast; studied the history of vegetational cover and compiled botanical maps of Centr Chernozyom Oblast; did reseacrh on various commercial plants at Voronezh Botanical Garden; also studied the history of Russian and Sov botany; *Publ: O filogenii rodov Umbelliferae Kavkaza* (The Philogeny of Umbelliferae in the Caucasus) (1914); *Zontichnyye* (Umbelliferae) (2 vol, 1915-20); *Vvedeniye v filogeneticheskuyu sistematiku vysshikh rasteniy* (An Introduction to the Philogenetic Taxonomy of the Higher Plants) (1922); *Predki tsvetkovykh rasteniy* (The Forebears of the Flowering Plants) (1928); *V strane zhivykh iskopayemykh* (In the Land of Living Fossils) (1931); *Osnovnoy biogeneticheskiy zakon s botanicheskoy tochki zreniya* (The Basic Biogenetic Law From the Viewpoint of Botany) (1937); *Znacheniye razlichnykh metodov v sistematike rasteniy* (The Importance of Different Methods in Plant Taxonomy) (1950); *Awards*: two Orders of the Red Banner of Labor; *Died*: 21 Apr 1957.

KOZOLUPOV, Semyon Matveyevich (1884-1961) Cellist and music teacher; Dr of Arts; Pop Artiste of RSFSR from 1946; *Born*: 10 Apr 1884 in vil Krasnokholmskaya, Orenburg Province; *Educ*: 1907 grad Petersburg Conservatory; *Career*: 1908-12 and 1924-31 soloist, Bolshoy Theater, Moscow; 1912–16 prof, Saratov Conservatory; 1916–21 prof, Kiev Conservatory; from 1922 prof, Moscow Conservatory; performed as a soloist and with S. I. Taneyev, K. N. Igumnov, A. B. Gol'denveyzer's and other ensembles; was a leading proponent of the Sov school of cello-playing; trained such outstanding cellists as S. Z. Aslamazyan, S. N. Knushevitskiy, G. S. Kozolupov, F. P. Luzanov, M. L. Rostropovich and A. K. Vlasov; wrote numerous cello arrangements; *Publ*: coauthor, *Shkoly dlya violincheli* (A Cello School) (1947); *Awards*: 1st Prize, Moscow Cellists' Competition (1911); Order of the Red Banner of Labor; medals; *Died*: 18 Apr 1961 in Moscow.

KRACHKOVSKIY, Ignatiy Yulianovich (1883-1951) Arabist and Orientalist; prof from 1918; member, USSR Acad of Sci from 1921; member, Arab Acad of Sci, Damascus, from 1923; *Born*: 16 Mar 1883 in Vilnius; *Educ*: 1905 grad Fac of Oriental Languages, Petersburg Univ; *Career*: specialized in Arabic languages and ancient, modern and contemporary Arabic lit; 1908-10 sent to Syria and Egypt to study living Arabic languages and modern lit; 1918-51 prof, Leningrad Univ; also worked at Inst of Oriental Studies, USSR Acad of Sci; pioneered systematic study of modern and contemporary Arabic lit; conceived plan of publishing complete catalog of Arabic-language sources on the history of the peoples of Eastern Europe, the Caucasus and Centr Asia; member, Polish Acad of Sci; hon member, Iranian Acad of Sci; member, British Royal Asian Soc; 1934 published in *Sogdiyskiy sbornik* document on the history of Arab conquests in Centr Asia found during excavations on Mount Mug, Tadzh SSR; *Publ: Istoricheskiy roman v sovremennoy arabskoy literature* (The Historical Novel in Modern Arabic Literature) (1911); *Abu-l Faradzh al-Vava Damaskiy* (Abu 'l-Faraj el-Wawa of Damascus) (1914); *Nad arabskimi rukopisyami* (Arabic Manuscripts) (2nd ed, 1946); *Ocherki po istorii russkoy arabistiki* (Outline History of Russian Arabic Studies) (1950); *Izbrannyye sochineniya* (Selected Works) (6 vol, 1955-60); *Awards*: two Orders of Lenin; Stalin Prize (1951); *Died*: 24 Jan 1951.

KRAINSKIY, Nikolay Vasil'yevich (1869-1951) Psychiatrist; Dr of Med from 1896; prof from 1928; *Born*: 1869; *Educ*: 1893 grad Med Fac, Khar'kov Univ; *Career*: from 1894 worked at P. I. Kovalevskiy's Psychiatric Clinic, Khar'kov Univ; 1896 defended doctor's thesis on the pathology of epilepsy; 1918 assoc prof, Chair of Neuropathology and Psychiatry, Kiev Univ; 1919 evacuated with White Army to Novorossiysk, from where he made his way to Greek island of Lemnos; from Lemnos moved to Yugoslavia; 1921-28 assoc prof, Chair of Psychiatry, Zagreb Univ; from 1928 prof, Chair of Psychiatry and Experimental Psychology, Belgrade Univ; 1946 returned to USSR and worked for the rest of his life at the Ukr Psychoneurological Research Inst; also head, Kiev Biophysical Laboratory; opposed plans to decentralize the psychiatric service on the grounds that this would lead to duplication and a lowering of med standards; devised toxic theory of epilepsy and established that the toxic agent in epileptics is ammonium carbamate, a hypothesis which was later confirmed by I. F. Sluchevskiy; also did important research on hysteria; wrote over 200 works; *Publ: Issledovaniye vremeni psikhofizicheskoy reaktsii na taktil'nyye i bolevyye razdrazheniya u zdorovykh i nervno- i dushevno-bol'nykh lyudey* (A Study of the Reaction Time to Tactile and Pain Stimuli in Healthy Persons and Nervous and Mental Patients) (1893); *Issledovaniye obmena veshchestv u epileptikov* (A Study of the Metabolism of Epileptics) (1895); *Porcha, klikushi i besnovatyye kak yavleniya russkoy narodnoy zhizni* (Bewitchment, Hysteria and Insomnia as Phenomena of Russian Folk Ways) (1900); *Po voprosu ob organizatsii prizreniya dushevno-bol'nykh* (Organizing the Care of the Mentally Ill) (1903); *Energetika nervnogo protsessa* (The Energetics of the Nervous Process) (1914); *Awards*: Prize of Brussels Acad of Sci (1901); Prize of New York Soc for the Study of Epilepsy (1902); Mochutkovskiy Prize (1914); *Died*: 1951.

KRAINSKIY, Sergey Vasil'yevich (1876-1936) Botanist and horticulturist; prof from 1919; *Born*: 5 May 1876 in vil Shebekino, Kursk Province; *Educ*: 1907 grad Natural Sci Dept, Fac of Physics and Mathematics, Kiev Univ; *Career*: 1904-09 secr, Kiev Dept, Russian Pomological Soc; 1907-17 taught pomology, vegetable-gardening and phytopathology at Kiev Higher Agric Courses; from 1912 member, Kiev Soc of Natural Scientists; from 1913 ed, journal *Sadovod i ogorodnik*; from 1919 prof of pomology and vegetable-gardening, Voronezh Agric Inst; from 1920 prof, Taurian (Crimean) Univ; prof, Simferopol' Agric Inst; prof, founder and rector, Crimean Inst of Special Crops; from 1925 prof, Kuban' Agric Inst; from 1926 chm, Kuban' Pomological Commission, Okrug Land Bd and dir, Research Inst of Special Crops, Kuban' Agric Inst; from 1929 chm, Black Sea Okrug Pomological Commission, Novorossiysk; from 1931 prof, Chair of Horticulture and Pomology, Azer Agric Inst; co-ed, section on vegetable-gardening, *Polnaya entsiklopediya russkogo sel'skogo khozyaystva* (The Complete Encyclopedia of Russian Agriculture); *Publ: Posadka ogorodnykh rasteniy* (The Planting of Garden Vegetables) (1902); *V voprosu o sevooborote v ogorode* (Crop Rotation in the Vegetable Garden) (1904); *Razmnozheniye ogorodnykh rasteniy* (The Reproduction of Garden Vegetables) (1908); *Dokhodnaya kul'tura sparzhi* (Growing Asparagus for Profit) (1908); *Dokhodnyy yagodnyy sad. Prakticheskoye rukovodstvo k posadke i ukhodu za yagodnymi kustarnikami* (The Profitable Berry Orchard. A Practical Guide to the Planting and Care of Berry Bushes) (1908); *Neobkhodimost' vvedeniya vysshevo sadovogo obrazovaniya v Rossii* (The Necessity of Introducing Advanced Horticultural Training in Russia) (1913); *Glavneyshiye vrediteli plodovogo sada i bor'ba s nimi* (The Major Fruit Orchard Pests and How to Combat Them) (1915); *Kul'tura tsvetnoy kapusty na semena* (Growing Cauliflower for Seed) (1925); *Kul'tura yagodnykh rasteniy* (The Cultivation of Berry Plants) (1926); *Plodovyye rayony i luchshiye sorta dlya*

Chernomorskogo okruga (Fruit Zones and the Best Varieties of the Black Sea Okrug) (1930), etc; *Died*: 12 Feb 1936 in Baku.

KRAMARENKO, Leonid Petrovich (1881-1960) Eng; specialist in agric machine-building; corresp member, Ukr Acad of Sci from 1939; *Born*: 15 Dec 1881 in Balta, now Odessa Oblast, son of an office-worker; *Educ*: 1907 grad Kiev Univ; 1913 grad Kiev Polytech Inst; *Career*: 1915-29 lecturer, then head, Chair of Agric Machinery, Kiev Polytech Inst; 1929-38 lecturer, from 1938 prof, Khar'kov Mech and Machine-Building Inst; 1945-60 worked for Khar'kov Research Inst for Stock-Raising in the Forest-Steppe and Polessie Regions of the Ukr SSR; *Publ: Sel'skokhozyaystvennyye mashiny i orudiya* (Agricultural Machinery and Implements) (1935); *Sel'skokhozyaystvennyye mashiny. Teoriya, konstruktsiya i raschyot* (Agricultural Machinery. Theory, Design and Calculation) (2 vol, 1937-41); *Died*: 15 May 1960.

KRAMER, Vasiliy Vasil'yevich (1876-1935) Neuropathologist; prof from 1920; Hon Sci Worker of RSFSR; attendant physician to Lenin during last years of Lenin's life; *Born*: 1876; *Educ*: 1900 grad Med Fac, Moscow Univ; *Career*: after grad worked at clinics for nervous diseases under Prof V. K. Rot and Prof L. S. Minor; from 1929 head, Neurological Section and co-founder and sci dir, Moscow Neurosurgical Clinic (later Inst of Neurosurgery); did research on the localization of functions; described cerebellar thread syndrome, quadrigeminal lid syndrome, and ape's foot syndrome; studied the semiotics of the fundus of the third cerebral ventricle, the diagnosis of extramedullary tumors of the spinal cord and tumors of the postcranial fossa; also did research on the visual perception of light, color and shape and on stereoscopic vision; studied the localization of vestibular vertigo, the pathogenesis of myasthenia and epilepsy, dextrality and sinistrality, etc; wrote 42 works; *Publ: Ucheniye o lokalizatsiyakh* (The Theory of Localization) (1931); *K ucheniye ob opticheskom vospriyatii formy* (The Theory of the Optical Perception of Shape) (1934), etc; *Died*: 1935.

KRAMOL'NIKOV (PRIGORNYY), Grigoriy Inokent'yevich (1880-1962) Party official and researcher; CP member from 1919; *Born*: 1880; *Career*: from 1898 in Soc-Democratic movement; began Party work for Siberian RSDRP Union; worked in Omsk, Tomsk, Samara, Moscow, Petersburg, Kazan', etc; after 2nd RSDRP Congress sided with Bolsheviks; frequently arrested by Sov authorities; deleg, 3rd and 5th RSDRP Congresses; 1907-09 sided with Mensheviks; 1909 abandoned Party work; 1919 joined RCP(B) and engaged in research and teaching work at Moscow higher educ establishments; instructor, Inst of Red Prof; from 1924 at Inst of Marx and Engels (then Inst of Marx-Engels-Lenin); from 1943 pensioner; *Died*: 1962.

KRAMOV, Aleksandr Grigor'yevich (1885-1951) Actor, stage dir and impressario; Pop Artiste of USSR from 1944; *Born*: 23 Dec 1885 in Kiev; *Educ*: 1908 grad Law Fac, Kiev Univ; 1903-05 also at a stagecraft studio; *Career*: 1905-09 at N. N. Solovtsov's Theater, Kiev; then actor and stage dir, theaters in Kherson and Samara; 1913-15 at Nezlobin Theater, Petersburg; 1917-33 in Moscow; 1919-20 actor, Moscow Show Theater; then actor, Theater of the Revol; 1924-33 at Moscow City Trade-Union Council Theater; from 1933 actor, stage dir, then artistic dir and chief stage dir, Khar'kov's Pushkin Russian Drama Theater; prof, Khar'kov Theatrical Inst; dep, Ukr Supr Sov of 1st convocation; dep, USSR Supr Sov of 2nd convocation; *Roles*: Protasov in Lev Tolstoy's *Zhivoy trup* (The Living Corpse); Chebutykin in Chekhov's *Tri sestry* (The Three Sisters); Perchikhin in Gorky's *Meshchane* (The Philistines); Chapayev in *Chapayev*, after Furmanov; Polezhayev in Rakhmanov's *Bespokoynaya starost'* (Restless Old Age); Kostya in Pogodin's *Aristokraty* (The Aristocrats); Lenin in Pogodin's *Chelovek s ruzh'yom* (The Man with a Gun); *Productions*: staged plays by Ostrovskiy, Lev Tolstoy, Chekhov, Gorky, Pogodin, Afinogenov, Korneychuk, etc; *Awards*: Order of the Red Banner of Labor; medal; *Died*: 17 May 1951.

KRAPIVYANSKIY, Nikolay Grigor'yevich (1889-1948) Ukr mil commander and Cheka agent; lt-col, Russian Army; CP member from 1917; *Born*: 5 Dec 1889 in vil Volod'kova-Devitsa, Chernigov Province, son of a peasant; *Educ*: 1913 grad Chuguyev Mil College; *Career*: 1908 drafted into Russian Army as private; promoted to junior nco; 1913-14 junior officer, infantry regt; 1914-17 commanded company, then battalion in Russian Army on Southwestern Front; 1917-18 elected commander, 12th Army Corps; from 1918 in Red Army; Aug 1918 directed revolt against Austro-German troops in parts of Chernigov and Kiev Provinces; 1918-21 chief of staff, 2nd Sov Ukr Army; organized revolts against Austro-German troops in Ukr; commander, 1st Ukr Insurgent Sov Div; inspector of troops for Sov Ukr; chm, Nezhin Uyezd Comt, CP Ukr; chm, Extraordinary Mil Staff to Combat Anti-Sov Revolts in Chernigov Province; commander, Nezhin Mil Distr, 60th Infantry Div; rear commander, 12th Army and commander, 47th Div; 1919-23 ruthlessly suppressed anti-Sov revolts in the Ukr; 1921-23 head, Dept for Suppressing Anti-Sov Revolts, Ukr Cheka; acting commander, Ukr and Crimean Cheka Forces; 1923-24 inspector of training, Red Army Staff; from 1924 admin work at River Emba oilfields; Collegium member, USSR Pop Comrt of Sovkhozes; 1933-36 engaged in secret work, preparing partisan movement for the event of war; 1936-38 inspector, USSR NKVD; senior NKVD official at the Volga Construction Project in Rybinsk; 31 May 1938 arrested by NKVD; until 1940 in solitary confinement; then in concentration camp, working on construction of Kotlas-Vorkuta Railroad; 1944 released and worked as forester, then watchman at a food warehouse in Tula Oblast; Apr 1948 hospitalized in Moscow; Sept 1948, though paralysed, exiled to Nezhin by admin order; *Awards*: Order of the Red Banner; *Died*: 22 Oct 1948; 1956 rehabilitated and reinstated in CPSU; a monument to him was erected in Nezhin and a street in Nezhin also named after him.

KRASEV, Mikhail Ivanovich (1898-1954) Composer; *Born*: 16 Mar 1898 in Moscow; *Educ*: took music lessons from composers A. T. Grechaninov, I. A. Dobroveyn, etc; *Career*: wrote mainly music for children; *Works*: operas: *Skazka o myortvoy tsarevne i semi bogatyryakh* (The Tale of the Dead Princess and the Seven Heroes) (1924); *Duma pro Opanasa* (The Ballad of Opanas) (1937); *Toptygin i lisa* (Toptygin and the Fox) (1943); *Masha i medved'* (Masha and the Bear) (1946); *Nesmeyana-tsarevna* (The Princess Who Could Not Laugh) (1947); *Mukha-tsokotukha* (The Clicker Fly) from K. Chukovskiy's fairy tale; *Terem-teremok* (The Little Tower Chamber) (1948); *Morozko* (1949); operettas: *Parizhskiy volchok* (The Little Parisian Wolf) (1928); *Pavlin v voron'ikh per'yakh* (The Peacock in Raven's Feathers) (1930); *Pevets iz zavkoma* (The Singer from the Factory Committee) (1931); *U morya* (At the Seashore) (1934); cantata *Moscow* (1947) for three-part children's choir, soloists and symphony orchestra; cantata "Glory to October" (1947) for four-part choir; various works for folk instruments; arrangements of folk songs for voice and piano (1948, 1949), etc; *Awards*: Stalin Prize (1950); *Died*: 24 Jan 1954 in Moscow.

KRASHENINNIKOV, Fyodor Nikolayevich (1869-1938) Botanist; Dr of Botany from 1901; prof; specialist in plant physiology and anatomy; *Born*: 24 Dec 1869 in Voronezh; *Educ*: 1893 grad Moscow Univ; *Career*: 1893-1938 asst prof, assoc prof, then prof, Moscow Univ; did research on photosynthesis; proved experimentally that plants absorb the energy of sunlight in the process of photosynthesis; determined the combustion heat of the products of photosynthesis; *Publ*: doctor's thesis *Nakopleniye solnechnoy energii v rastenii* (The Accumulation of Solar Energy in Plants) (1901); *Lektsii po anatomii rasteniy* (Lectures on Plant Anatomy) (1937), etc; *Died*: 14 Dec 1938 in Moscow.

KRASHENINNIKOV, Nikolay Aleksandrovich (1878-1941) Writer; *Born:* 26 Nov 1878 in vil Petrovskoye, Orenburg Province; great-great-grandson of explorer S. P. Krasheninnikov; *Educ*: grad Law Fac, Moscow Univ; 1899 first work published; contributed to journals *Russkiye vedomosti, Russkaya mysl', Russkoye bogatstvo,* etc; *Publ:* stories and sketches *Ugasayushchaya Bashkiriya* (Dying Bashkiria) (1907); play *O malen'koy Tase* (Little Tasa) (1908); play *Plach Rakhili* (Rachel's Lament) (1910); novel *Baryshni* (The Young Ladies) (1911); novelette *Skazka lyubvi* (A Tale of Love) (1912); novel *Devstvennost'* (Virginity) (1913); novel *Amelya* (Amelia) (1915); *Sobrannyye sochineniya* (Collected Works) (8 vol, 1911-16; vol 9, 1926); *Pod solntsem Bashkirii* (Under the Sun of Bashkiria) (1936); *K zemle obetovannoy. Rasskazy* (To the Promised Land. Short Stories) (1963); dramatizations: Turgenev's *Veshniye vody* (Spring Freshets) (1913); Gorky's *Mat'* (Mother) (1928); Fadeyev's *Razgrom* (Rout) (1934); Sholokhov's *Podnyataya tselina* (Virgin Soil Upturned) (1934); Pushkin's *Kapitanskaya doch'* (The Captain's Daughter) (1937); L. N. Tolstoy's *Voyna i mir* (War and Peace) (1938), etc; *Died*: 11 Oct 1941 in Ufa.

KRASIKOV (Party pseudonyms: IGNAT; PAVLOVICH), Pyotr Anan'yevich (1870-1939) Govt and Party official; lawyer; CP member from 1892; *Born*: 4 Oct 1870 in Krasnoyarsk, son of a lawyer; *Educ*: 1891 entered Physics and Mathematics Fac, then Law Fac, Petersburg Univ; *Career*: 1892 began revol activities in

Petersburg; 1892 went to Switzerland where he established contact with "Liberation of Labor" group; 1893 expelled from univ for revol activities; 1894 imprisoned in Peter and Paul Fortress, then exiled to Krasnoyarsk; 1896 became acquainted with Lenin in exile; 1900, returning to Pskov from exile, worked for the Pskov group as an agent of Lenin's *Iskra*; 1902 member, Org Comt, 2nd Party Congress at which he was a deleg from the Kiev Soc-Democratic Comt; member, Congress Presidium; vice-chm, 2nd Party Congress; 1904 attended conference of 22 leading Bolsheviks in Geneva; Bolshevik deleg, Amsterdam Congress of Second International; 1905 member, Petersburg Party Comt; member, Exec Comt, Petersburg Sov; from 1908 worked as asst barrister in Leningrad; active as defense counsel in polit and labor cases; 1917 member, Exec Comt, Petrograd Sov; chm, Investigating Commission for the Struggle Against Counter-revolution; Collegium member, Pop Comrt of Justice; 1919-24 ed, journals *Revolyutsiya i tserkov'* and *Voinstvuyushchiy ateist*; from 1924 procurator, USSR Supr Court; 1933-38 dep chm, USSR Supr Court; elected member, All-Russian Centr Exec Comt and USSR Centr Exec Comt; 1936 member, Commission to Draft the Constitution of the USSR; deleg, 2nd, 3rd, 6th, 8th, 14th, 15th, 16th and 17th Party Congresses; Sept 1938 relieved of his duties; *Died*: 20 Aug 1939 in Zheleznovodsk; buried in local cemetery.

KRASIN (Party pseudonyms: ZIMIN; NIKITIN; VINTER), Leonid Borisovich (1870-1926) Govt official; CP member from 1890; *Born*: 15 July 1870 in Kungur, son of a minor official; *Educ*: grad tech high school in Tyumen'; 1887-91 studied at Petersburg Technol Inst; 1900 grad Khar'kov Technol Inst; *Career*: 1887 entered Petersburg Technol Inst; became acquainted with Marxist lit in student circles; joined M. I. Brusnev's Soc-Democratic Group; propagated Marxism in Petersburg weavers' circles along Obvodnyy Canal; 1891 expelled from the inst and exiled to Nizhniy Novgorod for helping organize an anti-govt student-worker demonstration at the funeral of the writer N. V. Shchelgunov; 1892 re-arrested in connection with the closure of M. I. Brusnev's circle and imprisoned in Taganka Prison; 1895 exiled to Irkutsk for three years; 1897 returned from exile and entered Khar'kov Technol Inst; 1900-04 asst dir on construction of large electric power plant in Baku; at the same time active in underground work; helped turn electric power plant into underground base of the Baku *Iskra* Soc-Democratic org; fugitive *Iskra* members were hired at the plant, documents and illegal lit stored and passports forged, etc; 1903 helped re-establish the centr Party printing office, founded by Lado Ketskhoveli, which served Lenin's *Iskra*; used social, private and business contacts to arrange the tech side of transporting illegal lit and to canvas money for the Bolshevik underground; after the schism at the 2nd RSDRP Congress (1903), joined the Bolsheviks; late 1903 coopted member, CC, RSDRP(B); after 2nd Congress, while Lenin was campaigning against the Mensheviks, Krasin took a reconciliatory stand toward the Mensheviks; with his consent Mensheviks were coopted to the Party CC; later Krasin broke his ties with the Mensheviks; 1905 at 3rd RSDRP(B) Congress Krasin delivered the CC report in which he condemned his reconciliatory errors; at 3rd Party Congress elected member, CC; active in preparing 1905-07 rebellion; displayed talent as organizer and conspirator in forming battle squads, in stealing and transporting mil equipment and in outfitting Party printing offices; after 17 Oct 1905 helped found legal Bolshevik newspaper *Novaya zhizn'*; Party CC rep in Petersburg Sov of Workers' Dep; 1906 at 4th (Amalgamative) Party Congress led the campaign against the Mensheviks according to Lenin's directions; re-elected member, CC; at 5th London Congress elected cand member, CC; member, Bolshevik Center; 1908 arrested in Finland; went abroad after his release; 1908 for a while sided with Bogdanov's *Vperyod* group; then abandoned polit activities and worked as an eng; with start of 1917 Oct Revol immediately sided with Bolsheviks; 1918 chm, Special Commission to Supply the Red Army; Presidium member, Supr Sovnarkhoz, and Pop Comr of Means of Communication; 1918 participated in Brest-Litovsk talks; helped draft Aug Supplementary Agreement with Germany, which was signed in Berlin; Mar 1921 signed Anglo-Sov treaty; Sov plen in Britain; attended Genua and Hague conferences; appointed Pop Comr of For Trade; at 12th Party Congress made various "right-wing opportunistic" proposals regarding for and domestic policies; objected to Lenin's proposed reorganization of Centr Control Commission; late 1924, while remaining a Pop Comr, appointed Sov plen in Paris; 1926 again Sov plen in Britain; at 13th and 14th Party Congresses elected member, CC, CPSU(B); *Publ*: *Dela davno minuvshikh dney. Vospominaniya* (The Affairs of Bygone Days. Memoirs) (3rd ed, 1934); *Died*: 24 Feb 1926 in London.

KRASITSKIY, Fotiy Stepanovich (1873-1944) Painter and graphic artist; *Born*: 24 Aug 1873 in vil Zelyonaya Dubrova, now Chernigov Oblast; *Educ*: 1888-1892 studied at Kiev Art School; 1894 grad Odessa Art College; 1901 grad Petersburg Acad of Arts; *Career*: from 1903 lived and worked in Kiev; 1927-37 taught at Kiev Art Inst; *Works*: "At the Well" (1900); "A Guest from Zaporozh'ye" (1901); "To the Festival" (1902); landscapes: "Khatki Farmstead on the River Psel" (1898); "The Road to Kazatskoye Village" (1899); "Kirillovka Village" (1904); "T. G. Shevchenko" (1906-10); "I. Franko" (1907-14), etc; *Died*: 2 June 1944.

KRASNOBAYEV, Timofey Petrovich (1865-1952) Surgeon; pioneer of child surgery; Hon Dr of Med from 1935; member, USSR Acad of Med Sci from 1945; Hon Sci Worker of RSFSR; *Born*: 5 Mar 1865; *Educ*: 1888 grad Med Fac, Moscow Univ; *Career*: after grad worked at Vladimir and Olga children's hospitals, Moscow; from 1903 senior physician, Surgical Dept, Morozov Children's Hospital (1st Moscow Children's Clinical Hospital); 1894 introduced primary blind suture of trachea in tracheotomy; used chalk dressing for treating burns; devised technique of crushing bladder stones which can be used with minimum risk even on infants; 1922 performed first Sov operation for congenital pylorostenosis on a baby; designed support for plaster-cast work and traction blocks which are still in use; viewed bone tuberculosis as a disease of the whole organism and suggested it be treated by strengthening the constitution and increasing its resistance, especially by spa treatment; considered removal of bone a last resort; *Publ*: coauthor, *Rezul'taty lecheniya ostrykh empiyem* (The Results of Treatment of Acute Empyema) (1925); *Kostno-sustavnoy tuberkulyoz u detey* (Tuberculosis of the Bones and Joints in Children) (1950); *Lecheniye penitsilinom ostrogo infektsionnogo gematogennogo osteomiyelita u detey* (The Penicillin Treatment of Acute Infectious Hematogenous Osteomyelitis in Children) (1951); *Awards*: Stalin Prize; two Orders of Lenin; Filatov Prize; Order of the Red Banner of Labor; *Died*: 11 Oct 1952 in Moscow; a monument to him stands outside the 1st Children's Clinical Hospital, Moscow.

KRASNOSEL'SKAYA, Tat'yana Abramovna (1884-1950) Plant physiologist; Dr of Biology; prof from 1935; *Born*: 1 Jan 1884 in Petersburg; *Educ*: 1904 grad Fac of Physics and Mathematics, Bestuzhev Higher Women's Courses; 1910 passed State Examination as external student, 1912 obtained master's degree, Petersburg Univ; *Career*: 1905-07 asst prof, Chair of Botany, Petersburg Univ; 1907-09 asst prof, Chair of Botany, Petersburg Agric Courses; 1909-14 asst prof, Chair of Botany, Petersburg Higher Women's Courses; 1914-19 lecturer, Tiflis Higher Women's Courses and Transcaucasian Univ and assoc, Tiflis Botanical Garden; 1919-21 lecturer, Chair of Plant Physiology and Anatomy, Krasnodar Agric Inst; 1921-25 and 1932-35 lecturer, Leningrad Inst of Textile Crops, Leningrad Timber Inst, etc; 1925-35 researcher, Laboratory of Plant Physiology, All-Union Phytological Research Inst; 1935-37 prof and head, Chair of Plant Physiology and Microbiology, Saratov Agric Inst; from 1938 until death prof and head, Chair of Botany, Lenin Teachers' Training Inst, Moscow; did research on plant respiration and fermentation, water econ and drought resistance, photosynthesis, growth and development, the influence of trace elements and the history of plant physiology; translated works on plant physiology by Hans Molisch, J. Lilian and Clarke into Russian; edited several biological and agric dictionaries; *Publ: Dykhaniye i brozheniye plesnevykh gribov na tvyordom substrate* (The Respiration and Fermentation of Mold Fungi on a Hard Substratum) (1904); *Sutochnyye kolebaniya soderzhaniya vody v list'yakh* (Diurnal Fluctuations in the Water Content of Leaves) (1917); *Nablyudeniya nad elastichnost'yu kletochnoy obolochki* (Observations on the Elasticity of the Cellular Membrane) (1925); *Novyye dannyye po fiziologii prorastaniya semyan* (New Data on the Physiology of Seed Germination) (1929); *Opyt vyyasneniya vnutrenney prichiny zaderzhki vykolashivaniya u ozimykh* (An Attempt to Explain the Intrinsic Reason for the Delayed Earing of Winter Crops) (1931); *Opyt fiziologicheskogo analiza zakhvata pri pomoshchi iskusstvennogo sukhoveya* (An Experiment in the Physiological Analysis of Entrapment with the Aid of an Artificial Dry Wind) (1931); *Vliyaniye gormonov zhivotnogo proiskhozh-*

deniya na nastupleniye vykolashivaniya i na nakopleniye sukhoy massy u ovsa (The Effect of Animal Hormones on the Inception of Earing and the Accumulation of Dry Bulk in Oats) (1933); coauthor, *Anglo-russkiy sel'skokhozyaystvennyy slovar'* (An English-Russian Agricultural Dictionary) (1944); *K voprosu o probuzhdenii pochek drevesnykh rasteniy ot zimnego pokoya* (Dehibernation of Ligneous Plant Buds) (1945); *M. S. Tsvet. Kratkaya biografiya* (M. S. Tsvet. A Short Biography) (1946); *Rol' M. S. Tsveta v sozdanii khromatograficheskogo adsorbtsionnogo analiza* (The Role of M. S. Tsvet in the Development of Chromatographic Absorption Analysis) (1946); *Letnyaya praktika po fiziologii rasteniy* (Practical Summer Studies of Plant Physiology) (1948), etc; *Died:* 17 Feb 1950 in Moscow.

KRASNOSHCHYOKOV, A. M. (1880-1937) Govt official; CP member from 1917; *Born*: 1880; *Career*: 1920-21 member, Far Eastern Bureau, CC, RCP(B); Min of For Affairs and chm, Govt of Far Eastern Republ; from early 1922 Dep Pop Comr of Finance; from 1922 Presidium member, Supr Sovnarkhoz; 1923 chm, Bd, USSR Ind Bank; from 1929 at USSR Pop Comrt of Agric; arrested by State Security organs; *Died*: 1937 in imprisonment.

KRASNOV, Pyotr Nikolayevich (1869-1947) Don Cossack; lt-gen, Russian Army; mil leader of anti-Sov movement in Don area; *Born*: 10 Nov 1869; *Educ*: grad Paul Mil College; grad Officers Cavalry School; *Career*: 1914-17 commanded Cossack brigade, Cossack div, then 3rd Mounted Corps in Russian Army at the front; during 1917 Oct Revol appointed by Kerenskiy to command troops sent from the front to Petrograd to crush the Bolshevik coup; his troops were halted by Red Guards at Pulkovo; after the Cossacks refused to meddle in "purely Russian affairs," he was captured and then released on his cognizance that he would stop opposing the revol; went to the Don area; May 1918 elected Ataman of the Don Army; concluded pact with German occupation forces; helped found Federation of Cossack Regions and turn it into an independent state; opposed Denikin, who was allied with the Entente countries; Jan 1919, with the end of German occupation, recognized Denikin's rule; 19 Feb 1919, lacking Denikin's support, declined to stand for re-election as Ataman of the Don Army; emigrated to Germany and engaged in lit work; 1941-45 helped form Cossack units from Soviet prisoners-of-war, used in operations against Sov troops; advocated formation of a separate Cossack State under German protection; 1945 captured by Allied troops and turned over to Sov authorities; *Died*: 17 Jan 1947 hanged by order of the Mil Collegium, USSR Supr Court.

KRASNUSHKIN, Yevgeniy Konstantinovich (1885-1951) Psychiatrist; Hon Sci Worker of RSFSR; *Born*: 16 Apr 1885 in Moscow; *Educ*: 1910 grad Med Fac, Moscow Univ; *Career*: after grad worked on free-lance basis at Prof G. I. Rossolimo's Clinic; 1912-14 worked for psychiatrist A. N. Bernshteyn at Moscow Centr Admission Clinic for Mental Patients; 1920-30 head, Chair of Forensic Psychiatry, Soc Sci Fac, 1st Moscow Univ; also head, Section for the Study of the Criminal Personality; from 1921 co-founder and chm, Experts Commission, Serbskiy Inst of Forensic Psychiatry; specialized in the clinical and pathological aspects of psychosis, neurosis and psychopathy; 1929 devised classification of psychogeny; sought a physiological explanation for neurotic states and the transition from the "functional" to the "organic" disorder; made major contribution to the understanding of the pathogenesis, treatment and prevention of neurosis; from 1931 psychiatric consultant, Moscow Oblast Clinical Research Inst, where he founded the Psychiatric Clinic of the 4th Moscow Med Inst and lectured on psychiatry; 1938 criticized the static interpretation of psychopathy and hypothesized that it is a dynamic and variable process influenced by external factors; was one of first Sov psychiatrists to use active therapy for psychoses; from 1943 until death dir, Moscow Oblast Neuropsychiatric Clinic; 1945-46 provided forensic expertise at Nuremberg Trials; wrote 86 works; *Publ: Sovremennaya terapiya progressivnogo paralicha* (The Modern Therapy of Progressive Paralysis) (1925); *O psikhogeniyakh* (Psychogeny) (1929); *O nervno-psikhicheskikh rasstroystvakh pri arterioskleroze i gipertonii* (Neuropsychic Disorders in Arteriosclerosis and Hypertony) (1937); *Problema dinamiki i izmenchivosti psikhologii* (The Dynamics and Mutability of Psychology) (1949); *V voprosu o roli kardiovazal'nogo faktora v psikhiatricheskoy klinike* (The Role of the Cardiovascular Factor in Psychiatric Clinical Practice) (1946); *Psikhogenii voyennogo vremeni* (Psychogeny in War Time) (1948); *Died*: 3 Mar 1951 in Moscow.

KRASOVSKIY, Feodosiy Nikolayevich (1878-1948) Geodesist; prof from 1917; corresp member, USSR Acad of Sci from 1939; Hon Sci and Tech Worker of RSFSR from 1943; *Born*: 26 Sept 1878 in Galich, now Kostroma Oblast; *Educ*: 1900 grad Moscow Survey Inst; *Career*: 1907-17 instructor, from 1917 prof, 1919-21 rector, Moscow Survey Inst, on the basis of which he established the Moscow Inst of Geodetic, Aerial Survey and Cartographic Eng; 1928 co-founder, Moscow Research Inst of Geodesy and Cartography (now Centr Inst of Geodesy, Aerial Survey and Cartography); 1928 developed schem for the introduction of a union-wide geodetic reference grid system and demonstrated the necessity of expanding it into an astronomical-geodetic grid system; devised one of the best methods of coordinating the astronomical-geodetic grid and elaborated the principles of processing triangulation figures; the triangulation, gravimetric and astronomical data which he coordinated made it possible to determine the shape of the Earth on new sci principles (Krasovskiy's ellipsoid); found new approaches to the sci problems of geodesy and gravimetry on the basis of geophysical and geological principles; trained a large number of geodesists; *Publ: Rukovodstvo po vysshey geodezii* (A Manual of Advanced Geodesy) (2 vol, 1926-32); *Izbrannyye sochineniya* (Selected Works) (4 vol, 1953-56); *Awards*: Order of Lenin; Order of the Red Banner of Labor; two Stalin Prizes (1943, 1952); medals; *Died*: 1 Oct 1948.

KRASOVSKIY, Ivan Fyodorovich (1870-1938) Actor; Hon Artiste of RSFSR from 1937; *Born*: 17 Jan 1870; *Educ*: 1896 grad Moscow Univ; *Career*: while still a student acted at clubs, including Pushkino Summer Theater, and played in vaudeville; joined Stanislavskiy's Art and Lit Soc; from 1898 (under pseudonym Krovskiy) with Moscow Arts Theater; 1899 transferred to Maly Theater; *Roles*: Shuyskiy in A. K. Tolstoy's *Tsar' Fyodor Ioannovich*; Tesman in Ibsen's "Hedda Gabler"; the Priest in Hauptmann's "The Sunken Bell"; Molchalin in Griboyedov's *Gore ot uma* (Woe from Wit); Lynyayev and Velikatov in *Volki i ovtsy* (The Wolves and the Sheep) and *Talanty i poklonniki* (Talents and Admirers); Chichikov in *Myortvyye dushi* (Dead Souls), after Gogol; the Captain in Smolin's *Ivan Kozyr' i Tat'yana Russkikh* (Ivan Kozyr' and Tat'yana of the Russians); Georgiy Bogorodskiy in Trenyov's *Zhena* (The Wife), etc; *Died*: 1938.

KRASUSKIY, Konstantin Adamovich (1867-1937) Chemist; prof; corresp member, Ukr Acad of Sci from 1926; corresp member, USSR Acad of Sci from 1933; Hon Sci Worker of Azer SSR from 1936; *Born*: 14 Sept 1867 in Zaraysk Uyezd, Ryazan' Province; *Educ*: 1891 grad Petersburg Univ; *Career*: from 1916 prof, Khar'kov Univ; from 1930 prof, Azer Polytech (Ind) Inst; did research on the reactions of the formation of aliphatic alpha-oxides and their numerous conversions; also studied the synthesis reactions of amino alcohols by the interaction of ammonia and amines with aliphatic alpha-oxides; explained the mechanism of these reactions and determined the interaction of alpha-oxides with hydrogen chloride; *Publ: Issledovaniye izomernykh prevrashcheniy, sovershayushchikhsya pri uchastii organicheskikh okisey* (A Study of Isomeric Conversions Involving Organic Oxides) (1902); *Issledovaniye reaktsiy ammiaka i aminov s organicheskimi okisyami* (A Study of the Reactions of Ammonia and Amines with Organic Oxides) (1911); *Died*: 7 Apr 1937.

KRASYUK, Anatoliy Aleksandrovich (1886-1933) Pedologist, geographer and explorer of North European USSR, Yakutia, Kamchatka and Sakhalin; *Born*: 21 Feb 1886 in Rostov, Yaroslavl' Province; *Educ*: 1911 grad Moscow Univ; *Career*: spent over 20 years studying the soils and landscapes of remote regions of USSR; 1919-23 founder-head, Chair of Pedology, Ivanovo-Voznesensk Polytech Inst; compiled numerous soil maps; 1931-33 supervised study of soils of kolkhozes and sovkhozes in Leningrad Oblast; 1933 head, Chair of Arable Farming, All-Union Stalin Communist Agric Inst; *Publ: Ukazaniye k proizvodstvu polevykh pochvennykh issledovaniy* (Instructions for Soil Research in the Field) (1917); *Pochvennyye issledovaniya Severnogo kraya* (Soil Research in the Northern Kray) (1922); *Pochvy i grunty po linii Podol'skoy zheleznoy dorogi* (The Soils and Ground Soils Along the Podol'sk Railroad) (1922); *Opisaniye pochv i gruntov vdol' Vologodsko-Arkhangel'skoy linii Severnykh zheleznykh dorog na protyazhenii 240 verst ot stantsii Bandysh do goroda Vologdy* (A Description of the Soils and Ground Along a 240-Verst Stretch of the Vologda-Arkhangel'sk Line of the Northern Railroad from Bandysh Station to Vologda) (1923); *Kratkiy ocherk pochv Kostromskoy oblasti* (A Short Study of the Soils of Kostroma

Oblast) (1924); *Pochvy Severo-vostochnoy oblasti i ikh izucheniye. 1921-1924 gg.* (The Soils of the Northeastern Oblast and Their Study. 1921-1924) (1925); *Yestyestvenno-istoricheskoye opisaniye Ivanovo-Voznesenskoy gubernii* (A Natural Historical Account of Ivanovo-Voznesensk Province) (1927); *Pochvy i ikh issledovaniye v prirode* (Soils and Their Study under Natural Conditions) (1931), etc; *Died*: 18 Nov 1933 in Leningrad.

KRAVCHENKO, Aleksandr Diomidovich (1881-1923) Ukr; partisan leader in Siberia during Civil War; CP member from 1920; *Born*: 1881 in Voronezh Province, son of a peasant; *Educ*: grad Saratov Agric School; *Career*: 1902 sentenced to two years imprisonment for revol activity; 1907-14 agronomist; vil Shushenskoye, Siberia; 1914-17 served in Achinsk with Russian Army; 1918 organized partisan detachment in Achinsk to fight against Gen Kolchak's army; Apr 1919 took command of partisan army formed in Yenisey Province, which rose to a strength of 18,000 men and joined the Red Army in Jan 1920 after a series of victories in Tuva region; 1920-22 worked for RSFSR Pop Comrt of Agric; 1922-23 head, Pyatigorsk Province Land Dept; *Died*: 21 Nov 1923 in Rostov-on-Don of tuberculosis.

KRAVCHENKO, Aleksey Il'ich (1889-1940) Artist; *Born*: 11 Feb 1889 in vil Pokrovskoye (now town of Engel's, Saratov Oblast); *Educ*: 1911 grad Moscow College of Painting, Sculpture and Architecture; *Career*: worked as painter; member, Assoc of Itinerant Art Exhibitions; after 1917 Oct Revol founded poster workshop; then specialized in graphic art; did brilliant woodcuts, linocuts and etchings; displayed keen imagination, romantic fervor and dynamism in his woodcuts and drawings to illustrate the works of L. M. Leonov (1923), Charles Dickens (1925), Gogol (1923 and 1931), Anatole France (1929), Gorky (1932), Goethe (1932), Byron (1932 and 1937), Pushkin (1934, 1937, 1939-40), Stefan Zweig (1936) and Victor Hugo (1940), etc; 1935-40 prof, Moscow Art Inst; *Works*: landscapes: "The Moscow Kremlin" (1924); *Dneprostroy* (1931); *Azovstal'* (1938); paintings to illustrate his trips to India, Italy, Paris, etc; series "The Life of a Woman" (1928); "The Paris Commune" (1924 and 1926); engravings "The Barricades on the Presna" (1925); "Stradivarius in His Workshop" (1926); series of drawings in memory of Lenin; *Died*: 31 May 1940.

KRAVCHENKO, Andrey Grigor'yevich (1899-1963) Ukr mil commander; col-gen, armored troops from 1944; CP member from 1925; *Born*: 30 Nov 1899; *Educ*: 1923 grad Poltava Infantry School; 1928 grad Frunze Mil Acad; *Career*: from 1918 in Red Army; fought in Civil War; 1923-41 various commands and staff posts; 1941 took part in Moscow counter-offensive; 1941-42 chief of staff, mechanized corps; commander, 31st Tank Brigade; commander of armored and tank forces, 61st Army; 1942 took part in encirclement of 6th German Army at Stalingrad; 1942-44 commanded 2nd, 4th, then 5th Guards Tank Corps; 1943 took part in liberation of Kiev; 1944 took part in Korsun'-Shevchenkovo and Yassy-Kishinev operations; 1944-45 commander, 6th Tank Army; 1945 helped rout Kwantung Army in Manchuria; after WW 2 commanded armored and mechanized forces of various mil distr; dep, USSR Supr Sov of 1946 convocation; from 1955 retired; *Awards*: twice Hero of the Sov Union (1944 and 1945); two Orders of Lenin; four Orders of the Red Banner; two Orders of Suvorov, 1st Class; Order of Bogdan Khmel'nitskiy, 1st Class; Order of Suvorov, 1st Class; Order of Kutuzov, 1st Class; medals; *Died*: 18 Oct 1963.

KRAVCHENKO, Grigoriy Panteleyevich (1912-1943) Ukr fighter-pilot; lt-gen of the Air Force from 1940; CP member from 1931; *Born*: 10 Oct 1912 in vil Golubivka, Dnepropetrovsk Oblast, son of a peasant; *Educ*: 1932 grad Kachin Flying School; 1941 grad Advanced Commanders Courses at Gen Staff Acad; *Career*: 1930-31 worked for Zverinopol' Rayon Komsomol Comt, Urals; 1931 admitted to Air Force on Komsomol draft; 1932-36 flying instructor, Kachin Flying School; commanded flight, then squadron in fighter unit; from 1936 test-pilot; 1938-39 with Republ Spanish Air Force; 1939-40 commanded air regt in Transbaikal and took part in fighting at Khalkhin Gol; commanded special air force brigade on Soviet-Finnish Front; air force commander, Baltic Mil Distr; 1941-43 commanded air force group, then air force commander, 3rd Army on Bryansk Front; commander, air force div; *Awards*: twice Hero of the Sov Union (1939); Order of Lenin; two Orders of the Red Banner; Badge of Hon; Order of the Mongolion Pop Republ; *Died*: 23 Feb 1943 in an air battle.

KRAVCHENKO, Vsevolod Ignat'yevich (1915-1961) Bel writer; member, Bel Writers' Union; CP member from 1949; *Born*: 14 Oct 1915 in vil Kaplichi, now Gomel' Oblast, son of a teacher; *Educ*: 1933 grad Workers' Fac, Minsk Univ; *Career*: 1933 first work published; 1935-41 worked for oblast newspaper *Bal'shavik Palessya*; during WW 2 worked for newspaper *Savetskaya Belarus'* in Moscow; 1945-61 worked for several lit journals in Minsk, then as chief ed, children's journal *Byarozka*; wrote mainly short stories, novellae and novelettes; *Publ:* collections of stories and novellae: *Na krutym pavarotse* (Sharp Bend) (1937); *Kalgasnyya navely* (Kolkhoz Novellas) (1940); *Zyamlya gudze* (The Earth Groans) (1945); *Dzve syabrouki* (Two Friends) (1948); *U imya Radzimy* (In the Name of the Fatherland) (1948); *Padarunak* (The Gift) (1950); *Zhyta krasuye* (The Flourishing Rye) (1951); *Vyasna na Palessi* (Spring in Poles'ye) (1952); *Krygakhod* (The Ice-Breaker) (1957); *Zorka Venera* (The Planet Venus) (1960); stories *Rygor Shybay* (1947) and *Rygor Takuyeu* (1957); *Died*: 27 Aug 1961 committed suicide by jumping from window of hotel in Caen, France, after refusing to return to USSR with tourist group.

KRAVCHUK, Mikhail Filippovich (1892-1942) Mathematician; Dr of Physics and Mathematics from 1924; prof from 1922; member, Ukr Acad of Sci from 1929; *Born*: 21 Nov 1892 in vil Chernovitsy, now Volhynian Oblast; *Educ*: 1914 grad Kiev Univ; *Career*: from 1921 lecturer, Kiev Polytech Inst; from 1922 prof, Kiev Univ; wrote papers on higher mathematics, mathematical statistics and the history of mathematics; *Died*: 9 Mar 1942.

KRAVETS, Torichan Pavlovich (1876-1955) Physicist; specialist in optics; prof from 1913; corresp member, USSR Acad of Sci from 1943; *Born*: 22 Mar 1876 in vil Volkovo, now Tula Oblast; *Educ*: 1898 grad Moscow Univ, where he also did postgrad studies; *Career*: 1898-1914 taught at Moscow Eng College and other higher educ establishments; from 1913 prof, Khar'kov Univ; from 1921 prof, Moscow Means of Communication Inst; from 1923 prof, Irkutsk Univ; from 1926 worked at State Optical Inst; from 1938 prof, Leningrad Univ; did research on light absorption in colored media on the basis of electron theory; 1923-26 studied fluctuations in the level of the water basins of the USSR; 1926, while in charge of photographic laboratory at State Optical Inst, supervised research on the nature of the latent photographic image; also studied the history of physics; *Publ: Absorbtsiya sveta v rastvorakh okrashennykh veshchestv* (Light Absorption in Colored Solutions) (1912); coauthor, *Predvaritel'naya zametka o prilivakh Baykala* (A Preliminary Note on the Tides of Lake Baykal) (1926); *Sovetskiye issledovaniya v oblasti fotografii* (Soviet Photographic Research) (1939), etc; *Awards*: Order of Lenin; Stalin Prize (1946); Order of the Red Banner of Labor; *Died*: 21 May 1955.

KRAVKOV, Nikolay Pavlovich (1865-1924) Pharmacologist; Dr of Med from 1894; prof from 1899; corresp member, Russian Acad of Sci from 1920; *Born*: 8 Mar 1865 in Ryazan'; *Educ*: 1888 grad Natural Sci Dept, Fac of Physics and Mathematics, Petersburg Univ; 1892 grad Petersburg Mil Med Acad; *Career*: after grad from Mil Med Acad studied hydrocarbon metabolism at V. V. Pashutin's Laboratory; 1894 defended doctor's thesis on experimentally induced amyloid in animals; obtained first experimental liver amyloid and described the biochemical features of this process; 1898-99 assoc prof, Chair of Gen Pathology, 1899-1924 prof and head, Chair of Pharmacology, Mil Med Acad; 1924 head, Dept of Pharmacology, Inst of Experimental Med; believed that pharmacology should be treated as a branch of biology; did research on the effect of toxic agents in relationship to dosage, the combined effect of such agents, how they are affected by temperature changes and how the body tissues adapt to them; devised hypothesis of the phased action of drugs and demonstrated the existence of three stages of tissue reaction to them - the "entry," "absorption" and "exit" stages; also devised new methods of studying isolated organs which are still in gen use; 1904 perfused isolated organs with Ringer and Locke's solution to study vascular pharmacology; also used this method to study the endocrine glands and the reaction of their secretion to toxic agents; pioneered comparative and evolutionary pharmacology and the pharmacology of pathological processes; used isolated human fingers, hearts, kidneys and spleens to investigate the functional capacity of the blood vessels, established that the reaction of human coronary vessels to adrenalin changes with age; also did major research on the relationship between the effect of drugs and their chemical structure with special reference to narcotics and soporifics of the fatty series; pioneered the use of hedonal and other non-volatile soporifics as gen anesthetics; *Publ*: doctor's thesis *Ob amiloide, eksperimental'no vyzyvayemom u zhivotnykh* (Experimentally Induced Amyloid in Animals) (1894); *Osnovy farmakologii* (The Principles of Pharmacology) (1904); *O vnutrivenno-gedonalovom narkoze* (Intravenous Narcosis with Hedonal) (1910); *O razlichnykh fazakh deystviya yadov na izolirovannoye serdtse* (Different Phases in the Action of Toxic Agents on an Isolated Heart) (1911); *O deystvii yadov v razlichnyye periody prebyvaniya ikh v tkanyakh* (The Effect of Toxic Agents at Various Stages of Their Presence in the Tissues) (1915); *O samostoyatel'nykh sokrashcheniyakh sosudov* (Independent Constractions of the Vessels) (1916); "Über die funktionellen Eigenschaften der Blutgefässe isolierter Organe von Tieren und Menschen" (The Functional Properties of the Blood Vessels of Isolated Animal and Human Organs) (1922); "Über die Grenzen der Empfindlichkeit des lebenden Protoplasmas" (The Sensitivity Limits of Living Protoplasm) (1923); *Awards*: Lenin Prize (1926); *Died*: 24 Apr 1924 in Leningrad.

KRAVKOV, Sergey Pavlovich (1873-1938) Soil scientist and agronomist; *Born*: 21 June 1873 in Ryazan'; *Educ*: grad Ryazan' high school and Natural Sci Dept, Physics and Mathematics Fac, Petersburg Univ; *Career*: after grad stayed on at Chair of Agronomy, Petersburg Univ; 1898 made geobotanical study of Derkul Steppe, Khar'kov Province; 1901-02 directed experimental farm at Novo-Aleksandriya Inst of Agric and Forestry; from 1904 assoc prof, Petersburg Univ; 1908 defended master's thesis; 1912 defended Dr of Agronomy thesis; from 1912 prof, Chair of Agronomy, Petersburg Univ; then until his death head, Chair of Agronomy, Leningrad Univ; also taught on Stebutov Women's Agric Courses; from 1901 also taught farming at Kamennyy Ostrov Agric Inst (of which he was a co-founder in 1908); after 1917 Oct Revol until 1932 head, Chair of Gen Farming, Leningrad Agric Inst; from 1932 also head, Chair of Gen Farming, Higher Communist Agric School; 1921-25 head, Dept of Applied Pedology, Northwestern Oblast Agric Experimental Station; from 1934 Hon Sci Worker of RSFSR; *Publ: Kurs obshchego zemledeliya. 1. Agronomicheskoye pochvovedeniye* (A Course in General Farming. 1. Agronomical Pedology) (1925); *Uchebnik pochvovedeniya* (A Pedology Textbook) (1930); *Pochvovedeniye* (Pedology) (1934), etc; *Died*: 12 Aug 1938 in Leningrad.

KRAVKOV, Sergey Vasil'yevich (1893-1951) Physiologist; prof; corresp member, USSR Acad of Sci and USSR Acad of Med Sci from 1946; Hon Sci Worker of RSFSR; *Born*: 31 May 1893; *Educ*: 1915 grad Philosophy Dept, Moscow Univ; *Career*: after grad stayed on at univ to study for professorship and did research at Moscow Inst of Psychology; from 1919 asst to Prof P. P. Lazarev, Dept of Sense Organs, Inst of Biophysics, RSFSR Pop Comrt of Health; from 1932 head, Laboratory of the Psychophysiology of Sensation, Moscow Inst of Psychology; 1936-51 founder-head, Laboratory of Physiological Optics, Helmholtz Inst of Eye Diseases; shortly before death established a laboratory for the psychophysiology of the sense organs at Inst of Philosophy, USSR Acad of Sci; read lectures on the physiology of the sense organs at Moscow Univ, etc; did important research on the functions of vision in the human organism as a whole, the relationship of the visual organ to other sense organs and the influence of the centr nervous system on the visual functions; discovered that the photosensitive apparatus can react in the shortwave range to some incidental stimuli in a manner diametrically opposed to apparatus receiving long-wave radiation; on the basis of experimental data on the opposite effect of potassium and calcium ions and adrenaline on green and red vision (short- and long-wave radiation), attributed great importance to the role of ionic processes and vegetative influences in this phenomenon; bd member, USSR Soc of Physiologists; co-founder, Commission on Physiological Optics, USSR Acad of Sci, which published 12 collections of articles on this subject; wrote over 100 works; *Publ: Ocherk psikhologii* (An Outline of Psychology) (1925); *Ocherk obshchey psikhofiziologii organov chuvstv* (An Outline of the General Psychophysiology of the Sense Organs) (1946); *Vzaimodeystviye organov chuvstv* (The Interaction of the Sense Organs) (1948); *Glaz i yego rabota* (The Eye and Its Function) (1950); *Tsvetovoye zreniye* (Color Vision) (1951), etc; *Died*: 16 Mar 1951.

KRAVTSOV, Ivan Kondrat'yevich (1896-1964) Mil commander; lt-gen; CP member from 1925; *Born*: 1896 in Orel Province, son of a worker; *Educ*: grad Frunze Mil Acad and Gen Staff Acad; *Career*: 1918 joined Red Army; fought in Civil War, after which he held a variety of command and staff posts; 1941-45 commander of a rifle div, chief of staff of a rifle corps, 8th Guards Army, then commander, 64th (29th) Guards Rifle Corps; 1944 took part in Danube offensive and liberation of Yugoslavia; 1945 took part in fighting at Lake Balaton; *Awards*: Hero of the Sov Union (1944); two Orders of Lenin; three Orders of the Red Banner; Order of Kutuzov, 2nd Class; Order of Bogdan Khmel'nitskiy, 2nd Class; Partisan's Star, 1st Class (Yugoslavia); other orders and medals; *Died*: 19 Oct 1964 in plane crash while flying to Belgrade for celebration of Yugoslav liberation anniversary.

KRAVTSOV, Pyotr Vasil'yevich (1871-1942) Agronomist; specialist in med plants and ind crops; *Born*: 1871 in Sumy, Khar'kov Province; *Educ*: 1890 grad Khar'kov Agric College; then studied for a while at Petrine (now Timiryazev) Agric Acad; *Career*: agronomist in Khar'kov Province, Black Sea Caucasian littoral, Krasnodar Kray, etc; from 1921 head, Seed-Growing Sub-Dept, Kuban' Cooperatives Union; then dep head, Agric Dept, Kuban' Okrug Land Admin; from 1926 agronomist, Kuban' Agric Credit Union; 1927-30 specialist on med plants and tech cultures for Kuban' Special Crops Assoc; 1931-33 head, Krasnodar Nursery, All-Russian Med and Tech Raw Material Assoc; 1935-41 head, Azov-Black Sea Station, All-Union Inst of Med and Aromatic Plants; pioneered cultivation of hoary basil and Dalmatian chrysanthemum; *Publ: Ogorodnichstvo i ogorodnoye semenovodstvo v melkikh trudovykh khozyaystvakh* (Olericulture and Seed-Growing on Small Labor Farms) (1923); *Kormovyye rasteniya* (Fodder Plants) (1924); *Sakharnaya svyokla* (Sugar Beet) (1924); *Polozheniye ogorodnichestva i ogorodnogo semenovodstvo na Kubani* (The Situation of Olericulture and Seed-Growing in the Kuban') (1925); coauthor, *Novyye lekarstvenno-tekhnicheskiye kul'tury dlya Severnogo Kavkaza* (New Medicinal and Technical Crops for the Northern Caucasus) (1928); *Kleshchevina i vozdelyvaniye yeyo v usloviyakh kuban'skogo okruga* (The Castor-Bean and Its Cultivation in the Conditions of the Kuban' District) (1929); *Kamfornyy bazilik i dalmatskaya romashka i ikh kul'tura v Azovo-Chernomorskom kraye* (Hoary Basil and Dalmatian Chrysanthemum and Their Cultivation in the Azov-Black Sea Region) (1937); *Kamfornyy bazilik i dalmatskaya romashka* (Hoary Basil and Dalmatian Chrysanthemum) (1940); *K voprosu povysheniya urozhaynosti dalmatskoy romashki* (Increasing the Yield of Dalmatian Chrysanthemum) (1941); *Died*: 3 Dec 1942.

KRAYSKIY (real name: KUZ'MIN), Aleksey Petrovich (1891-1941) Russian poet; *Born*: 17 Feb 1891 in Novgorod; *Career*: errand boy and shop asst in Petersburg; 1916 first verse published; after 1917 Oct Revol contributed to publications of Petrograd Proletkul't org; from 1926 sided with creative minority movement of Russian Assoc of Proletarian Writers; fought in WW 2; *Publ*: verse collection *Ulybki solntsa* (The Smiles of the Sun) (1919); *U goroda-razboynika* (At the Brigand City) (1922); *Povest' o soldatskikh kostyakh, pokhoronennykh v Turtsii* (The Tale of the Soldiers' Bones Buried in Turkey) (1927); *Na panel'nykh kvadratakh* (On the Panel Squares) (1930); *Lirika. Izbrannyye stikhotvoreniya. 1916-1937* (Lyrics. Selected Verse. 1916-1937) (1939); *Chto nado znat' nachinayushchemu pisatelyu* (What the Budding Writer Needs to Know) (2nd ed, 1928); *Died*: 11 Dec 1941 killed at the front while serving with a Civil Defense unit.

KRECHETOVICH, Lev Mel'khisidekovich (1878-1956) Botanist; specialist in methods of teaching botany; Dr of Biological Sci; prof; corresp member, RSFSR Acad of Pedag Sci from 1944; *Born*: 23 Nov 1878; *Educ*: 1900 grad Natural Sci Dept, Physics and Mathematics Fac, Moscow Univ; *Career*: 1901 began to teach at non-classical high school in Moscow; from 1903 at higher educ establishments in Moscow; 1942-48 head, Dept of Natural Sci and Geographical Disciplines, Inst of Teaching Methods, RSFSR Acad of Pedag Sci; worked on morphology and taxonomy of plants and methods of teaching botany in secondary schools and higher educ establishments; compiled botany textbooks for zootech and veterinary colleges; translated sci and methodological works and textbooks on botany from English, German, Danish, etc; *Publ: Yadovityye rasteniya, ikh pol'za i vred* (Poisonous Plants, Their Uses and Dangers) (1931); *Yadovityye rasteniya SSSR* (The Poisonous Plants of the USSR) (1940); *Voprosy evolyutsii rastitel'nogo mira* (The Evolution of the Vegetable Kingdom) (1952); *Died*: 17 Dec 1956.

KREPTYUKOV, Daniil Aleksandrovich (1888-1957) Writer; CP member; *Born*: 23 Dec 1888 in Skvira, Kiev Province, son of a peasant; *Educ*: studied at a land-survey college; *Career*: joined underground Populist org in Ukr; arrested by Tsarist police and exiled to Arkhangel'sk Province; 1914 first poem published; after 1917 Oct Revol appointed Murmansk Province Comr of Educ and member, Murmansk Oblast Comt; 1921 expelled from CP; 1925 first short story published; from 1928 member, Soc of Peasant Writers; *Publ*: verse *Lesnyye muzy* (The Forest Muses) (1914); story *Mikisha* (1925); novelettes and stories *Podzhigateli* (The Incendiaries) (1926); novelette *Mamzer* (1928); novel *Vremena* (Times) (1928); novel *Pukh-pero* (Feather Down) (1929); sketches *Pionery v stepi* (Pioneers in the Steppe) (1930) and *Stepnyye vskhody* (The Burgeoning Steppe) (1931); stories *Step' zovyot* (The Call of the Steppe) (1931), etc; *Died*: 22 Oct 1957 in Moscow.

KRESTINSKIY, Nikolay Nikolayevich (1883–1938) Party and govt official; diplomat; USSR First Dep Pop Comr of For Affairs; CP member from 1903; *Born*: 13 Oct 1883 in Mogilev; *Educ*: grad Law Fac, Petersburg Univ; *Career*: from 1901 in revol movement; from 1907 contributed to Bolshevik press; many times arrested and exiled for revol activities; after 1917 Feb Revol dep chm, Yekaterinburg and chm, Ural Oblast RSDRP(B) Comt; elected to Constituent Assembly; after 1917 Oct Revol Northern Commune Comr of Justice; Aug 1918-late 1922 RSFSR Pop Comr of Finance; 1919-21 also secr, CC, RCP(B); 1922-30 Sov polit rep in Germany; 1930-37 USSR First Dep Pop Comr of For Affairs; member, CC, RCP(B); 1917-21 member, USSR Centr Exec Comt; 1922 attended Hague Conference; sided with Leftist Communists during Brest Peace Talks controversy; 1921 sided with Trotsky in trade-union debate; later dissociated himself from Trotsky's stand; 1917-21 member, CC, RCP(B); member, All-Russian and USSR Centr Exec Comt; Mar 1938 sentenced to death in trial of "anti-Sov Rightist-Trotskyite Bloc"; *Died*: 15 Mar 1938 executed.

KRESTOVNIKOV Aleksey Nikolayevich (1885-1955) Physiologist; corresp member, USSR Acad of Med Sci; Hon Sci Worker of RSFSR; *Born*: 1885; *Educ*: 1912 grad Natural Sci Fac, Moscow Univ; 1923 grad 1st Leningrad Med Inst; *Career*: from 1923 senior assoc, I. P. Pavlov's Laboratory, then asst to L. A. Orbeli, Physiological Dept, and from 1927 prof and head, Chair of Physiology, P. F. Lesgaft Sci Inst; specialized in the physiology of physical exercise and sport; demonstrated experimentally that physical exercise affects all systems of the internal organs, increases the strength and motility of nervous processes, enhances the stimulus level and lability of the respiratory apparatus and improves the functions of the visual, motor and vestibular analyzers; contributed to the discovery of the basic laws governing the formation of motor habits and the development of motor characteristics; demonstrated that the improvement of working capacity by physical exercise is a complex integral process resulting from the improvement of the regulatory mechanisms; also did considerable research on sport training and the effect of individual exercises; worte over 200 works; *Publ: O vliyanii udaleniya chasti mozzhechka na nekotoryye svoystva poperechnopolosatoy muskulatury* (The Effect of the Removal of Part of the Cerebellum on Certain Properties of the Cross-Striated Muscles) (1928); *Magnusovskiy propriotseptivnyy refleks na diafragmu u cheloveka* (Magnus' Proprioceptive Reflex on the Human Diaphragm) (1938); *Fiziologiya cheloveka* (Human Physiology) (1938); *Fiziologiya sporta* (The Physiology of Sport) (1939); *Fiziologicheskiye osnovy sportivnoy trenirovki* (The Physiological Principles of Sport Training) (1944); *Ocherki po fiziologii fizicheskikh uprazhneniy* (Studies in the Physiology of Physical Exercises) (1951); *Ucheniye o vysshey nervnoy deyatel'nosti kak yestestvennonauchnaya osnova teorii fizicheskogo vospitaniya* (The Theory of Higher Nervous Activity as the Natural Scientific Basis of the Theory of Physical Education) (1953); *Died*: 1955.

KREYN, Aleksandr Abramovich (1883-1951) Composer; Hon Art Worker of RSFSR from 1934; *Born*: 20 Oct 1883 in Nizhniy Novgorod; *Educ*: 1908 grad Moscow Conservatory; *Career*: 1912-17 taught at Moscow Pop Conservatory; his work was strongly influenced by Arabic, Jewish and Spanish music; *Works*: two symphonies (1925, 1945); "Threnody for Lenin" (1926); opera *Zagmuk* (1930); symphonic eulogy "The USSR - Shock Brigade of the World Proletariat" (1932); ballets *Laurensiya* (1937) and *Tat'yana* (1943), revised as *Doch' naroda* (Daughter of the People) (1947); "Song of the Falcon" for soloist, choir and symphony orchestra (1949); symphonic suites, tone poems, music for the theater and films, etc; *Died*: 21 Apr 1951 in vil Staraya Ruza, Moscow Oblast.

KREYSBERG, Isaak Mironovich (1898-1919) Revolutionary; CP member; *Born*: 7 Mar 1898 in Kiev; *Career*: started work at age 13; 1912 active in revol movement in Minsk and Dvinsk; from 1913 Bolshevik propagandist in Kiev; from 1914 underground Party work in Russian Army; after 1917 Feb Revol member, Kiev Exec Comt; secr, Kiev City RSDRP Comt; shortly before 1917 Oct Revol joined Kiev City Revol Comt; helped lead Jan 1918 armed rebellion in Kiev; at Taganrog Party Conference elected member, Org Bureau to Prepare 1st Congress of CP(B) Ukr; at 1st and 2nd Congresses of CP(B) Ukr elected member, CC, CP(B) Ukr; 1918-19 helped found Bolshevik underground in Odessa and prepare armed rebellion against Directorate in Khar'kov and Yekaterinoslav; *Died*: Jan 1919 executed by Petlyura troops in Poltava.

KREYTNER, Georgiy Gustavovich (1903–1958) Composer; CP member from 1946; *Born*: 30 Dec 1903 in Libava (Liepaja); *Educ*: 1928 grad V. Abramov's piano class, Moscow's Skryabin Musical Technicum; studied composition independently, with advice from Kabalevskiy, Myaskovskiy and Shebalin; 1930 grad Dipl and Econ Fac, Inst of Oriental Studies; *Career*: 1922-25 taught polit econ and polit affairs in Penza; 1930-33 worked for Pop Comrt of For Trade and in various Mideast countries; 1933-38 taught mil geography and aerography at Zhukovskiy Air Force Acad; taught history of econ of Mideast countries and gen history at Inst of Oriental Studies; 1939-40 artistic dir, Moscow Philharmonic; 1940-41 dep head, Main Musical Establishments Bd, Arts Comt, USSR Council of Min; 1941-44 in Sov Army; 1949-52 ed, Music Publ House; Cand of Mil Sci from 1938; *Works*: operas: *Gibel' Pushkina* (The Death of Pushkin) (1936-37); *Vozvrashcheniye Don-Zhuana* (The Return of Don Juan) (1941); *Vadim (V groznyy god)* (Vadim [An Ominous Year]) (1951-52); *Tanya* (1953-54); *V litovskom zamke* (In a Lithuanian Castle) (1942); operettas: *Vesennyaya noch'* (A Spring Night) (1944); *Rokovaya pyatnitsa* (A Fateful Friday) (1945); *Duen'ya* (The Duenna) (1954); *Yad blagodarnosti* (The Poison of Gratitude) (1955); *Samozvanets ponevole* (The Unwitting Pretender) (1955); cantatas: "Life and Struggle" (1939); "We Shall Conquer" (1941); suite for soloist, choir and orchestra "Russian People" (1942); symphonic suite on Sov folk themes (1947); five symphonic pieces from music for "The Duenna" (1943); tone picture "The Steppe" (1952); piano works: "Small Suite" (1939-40); two pieces (1936); ten variations on a dance theme (1947); "Concert Fantasy" (1949); monologue for baritone and orchestra "The Sword" (1947); monologue for bass and orchestra "Lenin" (1948); for small symphony orchestra: "Suite on Lithuanian, Latvian and Estonian Themes" (1946); "Russian Suite" (1952); for brass orchestra: "Rhapsody on Rumanian Folk Themes" (1950); for variety orchestra: "Suite on Czech and Slovak Folk Themes" (1950); 30 other pieces (1946-55); string and piano "Sextet" (1945); "Quintet" (1941-45); "Quartet" (1944); "Trio" in memory of Zoya Kosmodem'yanskaya (1942); nine piano pieces on Sov folk themes (1944); waltz (1940); "Dramatic Poem" for violin and piano (1943-46); six pieces for woodwinds and piano (1946); four songs for choir and piano (1936); six romances to words by Lermontov (1937); two songs to works by Shevchenko; (1938); two albums to words by Blok (1940 and 1946); "Songs of the Great Fatherland War, 1941-42" (1942-46); variety songs to words by Russian, English and French poets; (1944), etc; music for the production of Sheridan's "The Duenna" (1943); music for cartoon films *Pesenka radosti* (The Song of Joy) (1944); *Severnaya skazka* (A Northern Tale) (1955); *Died*: 14 July 1958 in Moscow.

KRICHEVSKIY, Aleksandr Moiseyevich (1896-1956) Dermatologist and venerologist; prof from 1930; *Born*: 1896; *Educ*: 1919 grad Med Fac, Kiev Univ; *Career*: from 1919 intern, Centr Skin and Venerological Polyclinic, Kiev; 1924-37 head, Dermatological Dept, 1937-56 dir, Ukr Skin and Venerological Inst; 1926, together with Z. I. Sinel'nikov, obtained rat cancer strain by grafting malignant melanomas from humans; from 1930 head of a chair, Khar'kov Inst of Postgrad Med Training; helped to organize and supervise campaign against venereal and skin diseases in Ukr; devised etiological and pathogenic classification of dermatosis; did research on the role of sensitization and viruses in the pathogenesis and etiology of various skin diseases; 1939 achieved immunoprophylaxis of Brown-Pearce cancer in rabbits; introduced bipolar electrocoagulation treatment for skin cancer and devised complex treatment for occupational pyodermia; also developed original penicillin immunotherapy; was one of first Sov sci to describe and obtain a culture of the agent of Reuter's disease (an infection involving polyarthritis, urethritis and conjunctivitis); also introduced radioactive phosphorus treatment for dermatosis; wrote over 120 works; *Publ: Novyy shtam sarkomy shchuriv, oderzhanyy vid pryshchepleniya melanosarkomy lyudyny* (A New Strain of Rat Cancer Obtained by Grafting Human Melanomas) (1927); *Rol' sensibilizatsii v patogeneze bolezney kozhi* (The Role of Sensitization in the Pathogenesis of Skin Diseases) (1932); *Preliminarna etiolchichna i patchenetichna klasifikatsiya dermatoziv* (A Preliminary Etiological and Pathogenic Classification of Dermatosis) (1935); *Metodika bor'by s piodermiyami na proizvodstve* (Methods of Combatting Pyodermia in Industry) (1937); coauthor, *Metod lecheniya bol'nykh piodermiyami vnutrikozhnymi vpryskivaniyami smesi malykh doz penitsillina i stafilovaktsiny* (A Method of Treating Pyodermia Patients with Low-Dosage Hypodermic Injections of a Mixture of Penicillin and Staphylovaccine) (1954); coauthor, *Materialy k etiologii, klinike i terapii tak nazyvayemogo uretro-okulo-sinoval'nogo sindroma* (Material on the Etiology, Clinical Aspects and Treatment of the "Urethral-Ocular-Synovial Syndrome") (1954); *Died*: 1956.

KRICHEVSKIY, Fyodor Grigor'yevich (1879-1947) Artist and art teacher; prof; Hon Art Worker of Ukr SSR from 1940; *Born*: 10 May 1879 in Lebedin, now Sumy Oblast; *Educ*: 1896-1901 studied at Moscow College of Painting, Sculpture and Architecture; 1907-10 studied at Petersburg Acad of Arts; *Career*: 1913 began teaching art; 1922-32 and 1934-41 taught at Kiev Art Inst; 1932-33 at Khar'kov Art Inst; *Works*: "The Bride" (1910); portrait of G. Pavlutskiy (1922-23); "Self-Portrait"; "Life" (1925-27); "The Match-Makers" (1928); "The Mother" (1929); "Dovbush" (1931); "Victors over Wrangel" (1934-35); "The Merry Milkmaids" (1937); cycle of pictures based on Taras Shevchenko's poem "Katerina," etc; *Died*: 30 July 1947.

KRICHEVSKIY, Vasiliy Grigor'yevich (1872-1952) Architect, painter and graphic artist; Hon Art Worker of Ukr SSR from 1940; prof; *Born*: 31 Dec 1872 in vil Vorozhba, now Sumy Oblast; *Educ*: attended lectures at Khar'kov Univ; *Career*: 1913-15 artistic dir, weaving workshop; 1922-41 taught at Kiev Art Inst; *Works*: designed building and decoration of: former Poltava Zemstvo (1905-09); Shevchenko Museum in Kanev (1936–38); landscapes: "Kvitka-Osnov'yanenko Dam" (1899); "On the Dnieper" (1900); "Romny in the Poltava Region" (1917); "Sorochintsy Fair" (1938); various book illustrations; sets for films: "T. Shevchenko" (1925); "Taras Tryasilo" (1926); "Zvenigora" (1927); *Died:* 15 Nov 1952.

KRINITSKIY, Aleksandr Ivanovich (1894-1938) Party official; CP member from 1915; *Born*: 1894 in Tver'; *Educ*: studied at Moscow Univ; *Career*: fall 1915 arrested and exiled to Irkutsk Province; after 1917 Feb Revol member, Tver' City Bolshevik Comt; 1918 chm, Tver' Province Party Comt; member, Tver' Province Exec Comt; 1919 Party work in Vladimir; 1919-20 secr, Saratov Province Comt; 1920-21 head, Org Dept, Moscow RCP(B) Comt; 1921 secr, Rogozhsko-Simonovskiy Rayon RCP(B) Comt in Moscow; 1922 secr, Omsk Province Party Comt; 1923 member, Siberian Bureau, CC, RCP(B); 1923-24 secr, Donetsk Province Comt, CP(B) Ukr; 1924-27 secr, CC, CP Bel; from 1927 head, Agitation and Propaganda Dept, CC, CPSU(B); simultaneously member, ed bd, journal *Bol'shevik*; 1933-34 head, Polit Bd, USSR Pop Comrt of Agric; from 1934 first secr, Saratov Kray CPSU(B) Comt; deleg, 9th-17th Party Congresses; at 13th, 14th, 15th and 16th Congresses elected cand member, CC, CPSU(B); at 17th Congress elected member, CC, CPSU(B); from 1934 cand member, Org Bureau, CC, CPSU(B); 1937 arrested by NKVD along with his wife Yu. F. Alekseyeva; *Died*: 1938 in imprisonment; posthumously rehabilitated.

KRINITSKIY, Mark (real name: SAMYGIN, Mikhail Vladimirovich) (1874-1952) Russian writer; *Born*: 16 Mar 1874 in Moscow; *Educ*: 1896 grad History Fac, Moscow Univ; *Career*: taught lit in Ryazan' Province; *Publ*: collected stories: *V tumane* (In the Fog) (1895); *Tsvety repeynika* (Burdock Flowers) (1899); *Chayushchiye dvizheniya vody* (Water Diviners) (1903); *Dusha zhenshchiny* (A Woman's Soul) (1915); stories: *Na puti k vyzdorovleniyu* (On the Road to Recovery) (1895); *Smert' Rozy Val'ter* (The Death of Roza Val'ter) (1899); *Angel strakha* (The Angel of Fear) (1902); *Poshlost'* (Banality) (1905); *Yefim* (1905); *Lozh'* (The Lie) (1906); *Muzh* (The Husband) (1907); *Lyubov'* (Love) (1910); *Verochka* (1913); novelettes *Molodyye gody Doletskogo* (Doletskiy's Young Years) (1911); *Svetozar Oktyabryov* (1925); novels *Vami kaznyonnyy* (Executed by You) (1914); *Maskarad chuvstv* (Masquerade of Feelings) (1915); *Zhenshchina v lilovom* (The Woman in Purple) (1916); *Devushka s Ladogi* (The Girl from Ladoga) (1927); *Moy brat Kain* (My Brother Cain) (1928); drama *U vas v domakh* (In Your Homes) (1916); plays: *Raby* (The Slaves) (1922); *Prodnalog* (Tax in Kind) (1924); *Sovetskaya kvartira* (The Soviet Apartment) (1924), etc; *Died*: 19 Feb 1952 in Gorky.

KRIPYAKEVICH, Ivan Petrovich (1886-1967) Ukr historian; prof, member, Ukr Acad of Sci from 1958; Hon Sci Worker of Ukr SSR from 1961; *Born*: 25 May 1886 in L'vov; *Educ*: 1908 grad Dept of History and Philology; L'vov Univ; *Career*: specialized in 16–17th Century Ukr history; from 1911 member, Shevchenko Sci Soc, L'vov; until 1939 taught history at private Ukr high-schools in Galicia; 1939-41 and from 1945 prof and head, Chair of Ukr History, L'vov Univ; head, L'vov Dept, Inst of History, Ukr Acad of Sci; 1951-53 head, Dept of Ukr History, 1953-62 dir, Inst of Soc Sci, Ukr Acad of Sci, L'vov; from 1962 pensioner; *Publ: Studii o gosudarstve B. Khmel'nitskogo* (Studies of Bogdan Khmel'nitskiy's State) (1925-31); *Otnosheniya Zapadnoy Ukrainy s Rossiyey do serediny XVII veka* (The Western Ukraine's Relations with Russia until the Middle of the 17th Century) (1953); *Bogdan Khmel'nitskiy* (1954); *Uchebnik istorii Ukrainy* (A Textbook on Ukrainian History) (1954); *Istochniki po istorii Galitsii perioda feodalizma* (Sources on the History of Galicia During the Feudal Period) (1962); *Died*: 22 Apr 1967 in L'vov.

KRISHTAFOVICH, Nikolay Iosifovich (1866-1941) Geologist and hydrologist; Dr of Geology and Mineralogy from 1919; prof from 1920; *Born*: 23 Oct 1866 in Smolensk Province; *Educ*: secondary educ at mil school; 1888-92 attended lectures on natural sci at Fac of Physics and Mathematics, Moscow Univ; *Career*: 1890 discovered and described interglacial deposits with fossil flora at Troitskoye, near Moscow; also described fossil Larix sibirica from Poland; from 1893 librarian, Novaya Aleksandriya Inst of Agric and Forestry; 1895 while in Novo-Aleksandriya founded the journal *Yezhegodnik po geologii i mineralogii v Rossii*, which ran to 154 issues by 1918, and collected a library of 67.000 books; made special study of Quaternary deposits in Russia; 1915-20 assoc prof, 1920-30 prof, Khar'kov Agric Inst; 1925-32 also head, Geology Section, Univ Research Inst; after retirement on pension continued to work as geologist and hydrologist for various govt agencies; wrote 214 works, of which some 100 were published; *Publ*: "Anzeichen einer interglaziären Epoche in Zentralrussland" (Indications of an Interglacial Period in Central Russia) (1890); "Note préliminaire sur les couches interglaciales de Troïtzkoïe, gouvernement de Moscou" (A Preliminary Note on the Interglacial Deposits of Troitskoye, Moscow Province) (1890); *O poslelednikovom vozraste ozernykh otlozheniy sela Troitskogo* (The Postglacial Age of the Lake Deposits of Troitskoye Village) (1892); *Nekotoryye novyye dannyye k voprosu o vozraste troitskogo ozernogo otlozheniya Moskovskoy gubernii* (Some New Data on the Age of the Troitskoye Lake Deposit in Moscow Province) (1893); *O poslednem lednikovom periode v Yevrope i Severnoy Amerike* (The Last Ice Age in Europe and North America) (1910); *Sibirskaya listvennitsa (Larix sibirica) v posletretichnykh otlozheniyakh Pol'shi* (Larix Sibirica in Polish Post-Tertiary Deposits) (1910); *Doistoricheskiy les* (The Prehistoric Forest) (1911), etc; *Awards*: Hon Doctorate of Erlangen Univ, Germany (1899); *Died*: 4 Jan 1941 in Khar'kov.

KRISHTOFOVICH, Afrikan Nikolayevich (1885-1953) Paleobotanist; member, Ukr Acad of Sci from 1945; corresp member, USSR Acad of Sci from 1953; *Born*: 8 Nov 1885 in vil Krishtopovka, Yekaterinoslav Province; *Educ*: 1908 grad Novorossiysk Univ, Odessa; *Career*: from 1908 assoc, Novorossiysk Univ; from 1914 member, Russian Geological Comt; from 1924 assoc, Main Botanical Garden, Leningrad (now V. L. Komarov Botanical Inst, USSR Acad of Sci); studied the paleobotany of the Tertiary, Mesozoic and Paleozoic deposits of the USSR, Northern China, Korea and Japan; also did major research on the geology and stratigraphy of carboniferous Tertiary and Mesozoic deposits in Northeast Asia; established the zonal distribution of vegetation in past geological epochs and refuted the theory that the earth had a uniform climate in the Carboniferous; also studied plant evolution; *Publ: Katalog rasteniy iskopayemoy flory SSSR* (A Catalog of Plants from the Fossil Flora of the USSR) (1941);

textbook *Paleobotanika* (Paleobotany) (1941); *Awards*: Order of Lenin; Order of the Red Banner of Labor; Stalin Prize (1946); medals; *Died*: 8 Nov 1953.

KRISTI, M. P. (1875-1956) Govt official; CP member from 1898; *Born*: 1875; *Career*: from 1893 in revol movement; 1905-06 active in Revol; after 1917 Feb Revol worked in Kerch', then Petrograd; 1918-26 Pop Comrt of Educ plen in Petrograd; from 1926 dep head, Main Bd of Sci, Museum and Artistic Research Establishments; 1928-37 dir, State Tret'yakov Gallery; 1938-48 artistic dir, Moscow Assoc of Artists; *Died* 1956.

KRITSMAN, Lev Natanovich (1890-1938) Economist; CP member from 1905; *Born*: 1890; *Career*: lived abroad; early 1918 returned to Russia and held various senior posts with Supr Sovnarkhoz; 1920-21 headed Commission for the Use of Material Resources, Supr Sovnarkhoz (then Labor and Defense Council); from 1921 Presidium member, Gosplan; 1923 member, ed staff, newspaper *Pravda*; from 1927 Collegium member, from 1928 dep mang, USSR Centr Statistical Bd; from 1923 Presidium member, Communist Acad and head of its Econ Section and Agrarian Inst; ed, *Ekonomicheskaya entsiklopediya* (Economic Encyclopedia); edited journals *Problemy ekonomiki* and *Na agrarnom fronte*; member, ed bd, *BSE* (Large Soviet Encyclopedia); from 1932 research work; wrote on econ of USSR, agrarian problem and econ theory; arrested by State Security organs; *Publ: Geroicheskiy period velikoy russkoy revolyutsii* (The Heroic Period of the Great Russian Revolution); *Klassovoye rassloyeniye v sovetskoy derevne* (Class Stratification in the Soviet Village); *Proletarskaya revolyutsiya v derevne* (The Proletarian Revolution in the Village); *Ob usloviyakh ravnovesiya kapitalisticheskogo khozyaystva* (Conditions for the Stability of Capitalist Economy); *O nakoplenii kapitala i 'tret'ikh litsakh'* (Capital Accumulation and "Third Parties"); *Died*: 1938 in imprisonment.

KRIVCHENKO, Georgiy Alekseyevich (1883-1960) Economist, statistician and geographer; prof from 1932; *Born*: 15 Apr 1883 in vil Kibintsi, now Poltava Oblast; *Educ*: studied at Petersburg Polytech Inst; 1910 grad Munich Univ; *Career*: 1905 expelled from Petersburg Polytech Inst for revol activities and exiled to Velikiy Ustyug; later permitted to emigrate; after return to Russia worked for statistical offices in Penza and Saratov; after 1917 Oct Revol worked mainly for sci and higher educ establishments in Kiev; 1919-20 assoc, Inst of Demography, Ukr Acad of Sci; 1922-31 and 1956-60 prof, Kiev Inst of Nat Econ; 1932-33 head, Econ Group, Kuybyshev Hydropower Complex Planning Office; 1943-52 prof, Kiev Univ and assoc, Kiev Inst of Geography; also worked for Ukr statistical offices and various econ planning bodies; wrote a number of monographs and economic reviews of Ukr SSR, etc; compiled various statistical handbooks; *Died*: 11 Apr 1960.

KRIVONOSOV, Vladimir Mikhaylovich (1904-1941) Composer and teacher; Hon Art Worker of Chuvash ASSR from 1935; *Born*: 6 Oct 1904 in Moscow; *Educ*: 1930 grad Moscow Conservatory; *Career*: did research on Chuvash folk songs; arranged folk songs; composed music for the theater; fought in WW 2; *Works*: musical comedy *Radost'* (Joy) (1935); cantata "October"; overture and suite for orchestra "Dance Tune"; music for Osipov's *Aydar*, Ayzman's "After the Ball," etc; co-composer of ancient Russian folk comedy *Tsar' Maksimilian* (1938); *Died*: 4 Oct 1941 in action near Smolensk.

KRIVOPOLENOVA, Mariya Dmitriyevna (1843-1924) Russian storyteller and singer; *Born*: 31 Mar 1843 in vil Ust'-Yezhuga on the Pinega, daughter of a peasant; *Career:* 1900 A. D. Grigor'yev made first records of Krivopolenova's stories and published them in 1904; 1915 the Moscow actress O. E. Ozarovskaya became acquainted with her and took her to Moscow, then to Petrograd; 1916 Krivopolenova travelled throughout the country accompanied by Ozarovskaya, reciting folk poems and fairy-tales; knowing many songs, she was the source of the unique epic *Vavilo i skomorokhi* (Vavilo and the Buffoons); performed epics *Il'ya Murovich i Kalin-tsar'* (Il'ya Murovich and Tsar Kalin) and *Ivan Groznyy i yego syn* (Ivan the Terrible and His Son); 1921 received pension for her contribution to Russian culture; sat for several artists and sculptors; her repertoire was published in A. D. Grigor'yev's *Arkhangel'skiye byliny i istoricheskiye pesni* (Arkhangel'sk Epics and Historical Songs) (2 vol, 1904), in O. E. Ozarovskaya's *Babushkiny stariny* (Grandmother's Days) (2nd ed, 1922) and in the monograph *Byliny, skomoroshiny, skazki* (Epics, Folk Poems and Fairy Tales) (1950); *Died*: 2 Feb 1924 in vil Veyegory on the Pinega River.

KRIVORUCHKO, Nikolay Nikolayevich (1887-1939) Mil commander; Ukr; corps commander from 1935; Civil War veteran; outstanding cavalry commander; CP member from 1919; *Born*: 6 Dec 1887 in vil Bereznyaki, Cherkassy Province, son of a peasant; *Educ*: 1932-33 studied with "special group" (promising but poorly educated mil commanders) at Frunze Mil Acad; *Career*: fought in WW 1; Oct 1917 joined Red Guards with a detachment which he had founded; from 1918 in Red Army; during Civil War commander, cavalry regt, Kotovskiy Cavalry Brigade; 1921-25 commander, cavalry brigade, then div; 1925-37 commander, 2nd Cavalry Corps; 1937 dep commander of cavalry, Kiev, then Bel Mil Distr; member, Ukr Centr Exec Comt; 1937 arrested by NKVD; *Awards*: Order of Lenin; two Orders of the Red Banner; *Died*: 7 July 1939 in imprisonment; posthumously rehabilitated.

KRIVOSHEIN, Aleksandr Vasil'yevich (1858-1923) Govt official; *Born*; 1858; *Career*: 1896-1902 asst head, 1902-05 acting head, Resettlement Bd, Min of the Interior; then closely associated with Stolypin in the implementation of his agrarian reforms; 1905-06 asst gen mang, 1908-15 gen mang for land allotment and agric (1906-18 Asst Min of Finance, and mang, Nobility and Peasantry Land Banks); from 1907 member, State Council; took extreme rightist stand; after 1917 Oct Revol helped lead counterrevol "Rightist Center"; 1920 headed Russian Govt in Crimea; emigrated to France after evacuation of Gen Wrangel's forces; *Died*: 1923.

KRIVOSHEYEVA, Yefimiya Petrovna (1876-1936) Mordovian narrator; *Born*: 14 June 1867 in vil Tarasovka, Saratov Province; *Career*: 1922 made first written records of her improvisations; 1936 attracted wide attention when *Pravda* published her *Plach o S.M. Kirove* (Lament for S.M. Kirov); a collection of her laments and poems was published posthumously; outstanding among these was "The World-Land Is Born Again," written in 1934 and known in Dem'yan Bednyy and A. Dorogoychenko's translation as *Zaveshchaniye* (The Testament); *Publ*: in Russian translation: *Golos materi. Skazy* (A Mother's Voice. Tales) (1940); *Died*: 24 July 1936.

KRIVOV, Timofey Stepanovich (1886-1966) Party official; CP member from 1905; *Born*: 5 Mar 1886, son of a peasant; *Career*: worked as fitter; from 1903 active in revol movement; 1905 helped organize strikes and battle squads, leading to his arrest; spent seven years in prison and 18 months in emigration; 1910 worked abroad as Party organizer and propagandist; returned to Russia; 1911 interned in Peter and Paul Fortress and sentenced to indefinite term at hard labor; 1917 and 1918 helped form mil orgs in the Urals; 1919 polit work in 5th Army; 1920 secr, Ural Bureau, CC, RSDRP(B); 1922 senior instructor, Org Dept, Party CC; then worked for Pop Comrt of Workers and Peasants' Inspection; managed Financial Inspectorate, USSR Pop Comrt of Workers and Peasants' Inspection; then Collegium member of Comrt, and from 1928 USSR Dep Pop Comr of Workers and Peasants' Inspection; from 1934 govt and trade-union work; from 1940 pensioner, but continued agitation and propaganda work; cand member, CC, CPSU(B); member, Centr Control Commission of 10th-16th convocations; Presidium member, Centr Control Commission of 12th-16th convocations; *Awards*: Hero of Socialist Labor (1966); *Died*: 16 Aug 1966.

KROGIUS, Avgust Adol'fovich (1871-1933) Psychologist; *Born*: 18 Mar 1871; *Educ*: 1898 grad Med Fac, Yur'yev (Tartu) Univ; *Career*: 1898-1900 worked at Clinic of Nervous and Mental Diseases, Yur'yev Univ; 1900-05 taught psychology at Yur'yev Univ; 1905-07 taught at Petersburg Psychoneurological Inst; 1907-18 at Petersburg Teachers' Training Acad; 1912-18 at Petersburg Univ; 1919-31 at Saratov Univ; 1929-32 at German Teachers' Training Inst, Pokrovsk; 1932-33 at Herzen Teachers' Training Inst, Leningrad; specialized in the psychology of the blind; helped to reorganize schools for the blind after Revol; demonstrated that it is possible to overcome the blind person's reduced perception and restricted spatial awareness by systematic training of attention, memory, speech and thought; wrote over 50 works; *Publ: Iz dushevnogo mira slepykh* (The Spiritual World of the Blind) (1909); *Psikhologiya slepykh i yeyo znacheniye dlya obshchey psikhologii i pedagogiki* (The Psychology of the Blind and Its Significance for General Psychology and Pedagogics) (1926), etc; *Died*: 1 July 1933.

KROKHMAL' (pseudonyms: VTOROV, ZAGORSKIY), V. N. (1873-1933) Party official; Menshevik; *Born*: 1873; *Career*: from mid-1890's in Soc-Democratic movement; Party work in Kiev and Ufa; 1902 went abroad, where joined Foreign League of Russian

Revol Soc-Democracy; deleg, 2nd, 4th and 5th RSDRP Congresses; after 2nd Congress sided with Mensheviks; late 1904 cand member, CC, RSDRP (Mensheviks); after 1917 Feb Revol ed, *Rabochaya gazeta*; after 1917 Oct Revol head, Petrograd Branch, Centr Union of Consumer Cooperatives; legal consultant in various Leningrad institutions; *Died*: 1933.

KROL', Mikhail Borisovich (1879-1939) Neuropathologist; Dr of Med from 1918; corresp member, USSR Acad of Sci; member, Bel Acad of Sci; Hon Sci Worker of RSFSR; *Born*: 1879; *Educ*: 1901 grad Med Fac, Moscow Univ; *Career*: from 1904 worked at various clinics in West Europe; 1906-24 worked at L. S. Minor's Clinic, Higher Women's Courses (now 2nd Moscow Med Inst); 1918 defended doctor's thesis on apraxia; 1921 organized Med Fac; Bel Univ, Minsk; from same year head, Chair of Nervous Diseases, Bel Univ; from 1932 head, Chair of Nervous Diseases, 2nd Moscow Med Inst; from 1933 until death dir, Clinic of Nervous Diseases, All-Union Inst of Experimental Med; treated gnosis, praxis and speech as interconditioning parts of a single process; studied synergic and tonic reflexes; did research on chronaxie, repercussion, etc; also studied viral nervous infections (leprosy, rabies, typhus, epidemic encephalitis); 1937-38 did research on then new Taiga encephalitis; analyzed adaptive role of nervous system; wrote over 120 works; his handbook *Nevrologicheskiye sindromy* (Neurological Syndromes) has become a standard work for specialists in the USSR and abroad; *Publ*: "Klinische Studien über Synergiereflexe der unteren Extremitäten 'Réflexes de Défense'" (Clinical Studies of Synergic Reflexes of the Lower Extremities "Réflexes de Défense") (1914); "Magnus de Kleynsche Tonusreflexe bei Nervenkrankheiten" (Magnus de Kleyn's Tonic Reflexes in Nervous Diseases) (1925); *Tonicheskiye refleksy pri giperkinezakh* (Tonic Reflexes in Hyperkinesis) (1927); *Nevropatologicheskiye sindromy* (Neuropathological Syndromes) (1933); *Khronaksimetriya v nervnoy klinike* (Chronaximetry in the Clinical Treatment of Nervous Diseases) (1934); "Flecktyphus des Zentralnervensystems" (Typhus of the Central Nervous System) (1935), etc; *Died*: 1939.

KRONTOVSKIY, Aleksey Antoninovich (1885-1933) Bacteriologist and pathologist; Dr of Med from 1917; *Born*: 12 Mar 1885 in Penza; *Educ*: 1911 grad Med Fac, Kiev Univ; *Career*: after grad worked under Prof V. K. Lindeman at Chair of Gen Pathology, Kiev Univ; 1917-21 assoc prof, from 1923 prof, Chair of Bacteriology, Kiev Univ; 1923-24 head, Chair of Gen Pathology, Kiev Univ; 1924 retired to devote himself to full-time research at Dept of Experimental Med, Kiev Bacteriological Inst and Cancer Dept and Dept of Experimental Biology which he organized at Kiev Roentgen Inst; from 1925 co-founder and ed, journal "Archiv für experimentelle Zellforschung, besonders Gewebezüchtung," Jena; member, Int Soc of Cytologists and various Sov sci soc; did research on the comparative and experimental pathology of tumors, the pathology of heredity, the physiology of regeneration and the effect of x-rays and bacterial toxins on tissue growth; devised improved method of studying tissue cultures outside the organism; apart from studying the morphological development of tissue cultures developed several exact physiochemical and microchemical observation techniques; these made possible to study cultures of tissues which are not subject to volumetric growth (the gray matter in adult animals, etc) and led to the discovery of several features of the vital activity of the cells; helped to establish that any normal tissue deprived of the body's regulating influence begins to display metabolic features typical of malignant tumors; wrote some 80 works, including five monographs; *Publ: Materialy k sravnitel'noy i eksperimental'noy patologii opukholey* (Material on the Comparative and Experimental Pathology of Tumors) (1916); *Metod tkanevykh kul'tur* (A Tissue Culture Method) (1917); *Sovremennoye ucheniye o sypnom tife* (The Modern Theory of Typhus) (1920); *Nasledstvennost' i konstitutsiya* (Heredity and Constitution) (1925); *Novyy metod izucheniya vnutrenney sekretsii posredstvom eksplantatsii* (A New Method of Studying Internal Secretion by Explantation) (1927); *Metod izolirovaniya opukholey v organizme i vne organizma* (A Method of Isolating Tumors Inside and Outside the Organism) (1928); *Died*: 15 Aug 1933 in Kiev.

KROPACHYOVA, Mariya Vyacheslavovna (1909–1967) Educationist; Hon Schoolteacher of RSFSR; corresp member, RSFSR Acad of Pedag Sci; *Born:* 1909; *Career:* specialized in methods of teaching Russian and Sov history in secondary schools; *Publ: Uchitel' i komsomol'skaya organizatsiya shkoly* (The Teacher and the School Komsomol Organization) (1950); *Moi druz'ya komsomol'tsy* (My Komsomol Friends) (1951); *Vospitatel'naya rabota komsomol'skoy organizatsii shkoly* (The School Komsomol Organization's Training Work) (1953); *Lingvisticheskiye vzglyady frantsuzskikh prosvetiteley 18-go veka* (The Linguistic Views of the French 18th-Century Educationists) (1959); *Awards*: Ushinskiy Medal; *Died*: 21 June 1967.

KROPOTKIN (KRAPOTKIN), Prince Pyotr Alekseyevich (1842-1921) Revolutionary, anarchist and geographer; 1862 grad Page Corps; *Born*: 27 Nov 1842 in Moscow; *Career*: officer, Amur Cossack Army; toured Amur Oblast and Northern Manchuria; commissioned by Russian Geographical Soc, of which he was a member, to accompany Olekminsk-Vitim expedition; did geographical research in Amur Basin and Eastern Siberia and published results in journal *Zapiski Russkogo geograficheskogo obshchestva*; 1872 joined revol movement; sided with Bakunin faction in 1st Int; played leading role in N. V. Chaykovskiy's Populist org and did propaganda work among Petersburg workers; 1873 and 1874 outlined anarchist program in the pamphlets "Should We Consider the Ideal of the Bourgeois System? " and "A Revolutionary Propaganda Program", which displayed the influence of P. Proudhon and M. A. Bakunin; 1874 arrested; 1876 escaped to England; 1877 moved to Geneva, where he published the journal "Le Révolte," which became the organ of European anarchism; 1881 expelled from Switzerland; 1883 sentenced by French court to five years' imprisonment for preaching anarchy and belonging to Int Workers' Assoc; 1886 settled in London after amnesty and did lit and research work; soon became acknowledged theoretician of European anarchism and influenced the formation of anarchist groups in Russia; 1903 assoc, anarchist journal *Khleb i volya*, which was published in Geneva; 1905-07 played active role in Russian revol; 1914-18 supported Russian "defensist" ideas; 1917 returned to Russia and preached the idea of a "class peace, and war until victory"; 1917 attended Congress of State convoked by Provisional Govt; after Oct Revol opposed "dictatorship of the proletariat"; May 1919 met with Lenin; 1920, at request of British workers' deleg, appealed to int proletariat to unite against for intervention in Russia; came to terms with the Revol; spent last years in Dmitrov; a mountain ridge, a town in Krasnodar Kray, a vil in Irkutsk Oblast and a street and square (*Kropotinskiye vorota*) in Moscow bear his name; *Publ: Obshchiy ocherk orografii Vostochnoy Sibiri* (A General Study of the Orography of Eastern Siberia) (1875); *Materialy dlya orografii Vostochnoy Sibiri* (Material on the Orography of Eastern Siberia) (1875); *Issledovaniya o lednikovom periode* (Research on the Ice Age) (1876); *Anarkhiya, yeyo filosofiya, yeyo ideal* (Anarchy, Its Philosophy and Its Ideal); *Anarkhiya i yeyo mesto v sotsialisticheskoy revolyutsii* (Anarchy and Its Place in the Socialist Revolution) (1906); *Sobrannyye sochineniya* (Collected Works) (Vol 1, 4, 5 and 7, 1906-07); *Rechi buntovshchika* (The Speeches of a Rebel) (1921); *Sovremennaya nauka i anarkhiszm* (Modern Science and Anarchism) (1921); *Etika* (Ethics) (1922); *Vzaimnaya pomoshch' sredi zhivotnykh i lyudey, kak dvigatel' progressa* (Mutual Aid Among Animals and Humans as a Motive Force of Progress) (1922); *Velikaya frantsuzskaya revolyutsiya. 1789-93* (The Great French Revolution. 1789-93) (1922); *Dnevnik* (Journal) (1923); *Zapiski revolyutsionera* (Notes of a Revolutionary) (1933); *Perepiska Petra i Aleksandra Kropotkinykh* (The Correspondence Between Pyotr and Aleksandr Kropotkin) (2 vol, 1932-33); *Died*: 8 Feb 1921 of pneumonia in Dmitrov; buried in Novodevich'ye Cemetery, Moscow.

KROSHNER, Mikhail Yefimovich (1900-1942) Composer; *Born*: 1900 in Kiev; *Educ*: 1918-21 studied at Kiev Conservatory; 1923-26 at Skryabin Music Technicum, Moscow; 1931-33 studied composition under V. Zolotaryov at Sverdlovsk Music Technicum; 1937 grad Zolotaryov's class at Minsk Conservatory; *Career*: for many years worked as pianist; Hon Artiste of Bel SSR from 1940; *Works*: ballet *Solovey* (The Nightingale), after Z. Byadulya's novelette (1937-39); cantata "The Drowned Man," to words by Pushkin; symphonic dances; quartet; "Piano Variations on a Belorussian Theme"; romances to words by Pushkin, Yanka Kupala, Yakub Kolas, etc; arrangements of Bel and Jewish folk songs; *Awards*: Order of the Red Banner of Labor; *Died*: 1942 in Minsk during WW 2.

KRUCHININ (real name: KHLEBNIKOV), Nikolay Nikolayevich (1885-1962) Russian ethnographer; guitarist; Hon Artiste of

RSFSR from 1947; *Born*: 29 Oct 1885 in Moscow; *Career*: collected Gypsy folklore; 1925-29 head, Old Gypsy Songs Ethnographic Ensemble, which developed from the Studio he founded in 1920; *Publ: Starinnyye russkiye pesni, sokhranyonnyye muzykal'noy traditsiyey tsygan* (Ancient Russian Songs Preserved by the Gypsies' Musical Tradition) (1929); *Died*: 1 Jan 1962 in Moscow.

KRUG, Karl Adol'fovich (1873-1952) Electr eng; corresp member, USSR Acad of Sci from 1933; Hon Sci and Tech Worker of RSFSR from 1937; *Born*: 6 July 1873; *Educ*: 1898 grad Moscow Higher Tech College; 1903 grad Moscow Univ; *Career*: from 1905 taught at Moscow Higher Tech College, where he established an electr eng dept and, after the 1917 Oct Revol, an electr eng fac; 1920 helped to develop plans for the electrification of Russia; co-founder and assoc, All-Union Electr Eng Inst and Moscow Power Eng Inst; 1921-30 dir, All-Union Electr Eng Inst; specialized in electr eng theory and techniques of converting direct into alternating current; did research on electromagnetic processes in controlled mercury rectifiers; *Publ: Elektromagnitnyye protsessy v ustanovkakh s upravlyaemymi rtutnymi vypryamitelyami* (Electromagnetic Processes in Installations with Controlled Mercury Rectifiers) (1935); *Osnovy elektrotekhniki* (The Principles of Electrical Engineering) (2 vol, 1946); *Perekhodnyye protsessy v lineynykh elektricheskikh tsepyakh* (Transient Processes in Linear Electrical Circuits) (1948); *Died*: 24 Apr 1952.

KRUMIN, Garal'd Ivanovich (1894-1943) Economist; writer; CP member from 1909; *Born*: 1894, son of a white-collar worker; *Educ*: completed higher educ; *Career*: from 1908 (while still at school) in the revol movement; 1917 member, ed bd, Lat communist organ *Sotsial-Demokrat*; 1918 ed, Supr Sovnarkhoz journal *Narodnoye khozyaystvo*; 1919-29 chief ed, newspaper *Ekonomicheskaya zhizn'*; from 1928 member, ed bd, *Pravda*; 1931 chief ed, newspaper *Izvestiya*; 1935 dep ed, *Bol'shaya sovetskaya entsiklopediya* (Large Soviet Encyclopedia) and ed, journal *Problemy ekonomiki*; at 16th CPSU(B) Congress elected member, CPSU(B) Centr Control Commission; arrested by State Security organs; *Died*: 1943 in imprisonment.

KRUMIN', Yan Martynovich (Party name: PILAT) (1894-1938) Lat revol; CP member from 1912; *Born*: 13 Sept 1894 in Lat, son of a peasant; *Educ*: 1932 grad Inst of Red Prof; *Career*: 1915 coopted member, CC, Lat Kray Soc-Democratic Party; then elected to CC at 5th-7th Congresses of CP Lat; 1917 dep chm, Exec Comt, Lat Council of Workers, Soldiers and Landless Peasants; edited its organ *Ziniotays*; from Feb 1918 organized underground Party work in German-occupied Vidzeme (former Liflyand Province); 1919 similar work in Kurland; 1919 member, CC, CP Lat and member, Sov Lat Govt; taught at Communist Univ; from 1932 head, Lat Section, Comintern Exec Comt; arrested by State Security organs; *Died*: 1938 in imprisonment; posthumously rehabilitated.

KRUPENINA, Mariya Vasil'yevna (1882-1950) Educationist; prof; CP member; *Born*: 7 Nov 1882; *Educ*: completed Higher Women's Courses; *Career*: after grad taught at secondary schools and extracurricular establishments in Moscow; helped found and run Inst of School Work Methods; 1921 member, Sci Pedag Section, State Learned Council, RSFSR Pop Comrt of Educ; teaching and research work at Krupskaya Acad of Communist Training and at Moscow Oblast and Tomsk Teachers' Training Inst; specialized in gen pedag, curricula and teaching methods; arrested by State Security organs; *Publ*: coauthor and ed, *Ot shkoly uchyoby k shkole obshchestvenno-poleznogo truda* (From the School of Study to the School of Socially Useful Labor) (1927); *Detskoye kommunisticheskoye dvizheniye, yego sushchnost' i zadachi* (The Children's Communist Movement, Its Essence and Tasks) (1928); *Kommunisticheskoye detskoye dvizheniye i shkola* (The Communist Children's Movement and the School) (1928); coauthor, *V bor'be za marksistskuyu pedagogiku* (The Campaign for Marxist Pedagogics) (1929); coauthor and ed, *Pedagogika sredy i metody yeyo izucheniya* (The Pedagogics of Environment and Methods of Studying It) (1930); *Died*: 18 Dec 1950 in imprisonment; posthumously rehabilitated.

KRUPSKAYA (UL'YANOVA), Nadezhda Konstantinovna (Party pseudonyms: SABLINA; LENINA, N. K.; ARTAMONOVA; ONEGINA; "RYBA"; "MINOGA"; RYBKINA; SHARKO; KATYA; FREY; GALLILEY) (1869-1939) Wife of Lenin; Govt and Party official; theoretician of Marxist pedag; CP member from 1898; *Born*: 26 Feb 1869 in Petersburg; *Educ*: after completing high school studied for a year on Higher Women's Courses; *Career*: from 1890 active in Marxist student circles in Petersburg; 1891-96 taught gratis at evening and Sunday workers' school on Nevskaya Zastava and engaged in revol propaganda among workers; 1894 met Lenin; 1895 helped Lenin found and run Petersburg League for the Liberation of the Working Class; helped prepare 1st RSDRP Congress; Aug 1896 arrested; 1898 exiled for three years to Ufa; allowed to change her place of exile and accompany Lenin (arrested in Dec 1895) to exile in vil Shushenskoye, Siberia, where they were married; spent last year of her exile in Ufa; 1901, after term of exile expired, emigrated and settled in Munich, where she became secr, ed staff, newspaper *Iskra*; co-founder of Bolshevik Party; helped prepare 2nd RSDRP Congress, at which she was a non-voting deleg; from Dec 1904 secr, newspaper *Vperyod*; helped arrange 3rd Party Congress; Nov 1905 returned to Russia with Lenin; lived in Petersburg, and from late 1906 in Kuokkala; secr, CC, Party; managed liaison with Party comts; helped prepare and attended 4th Party Congress; late 1907 moved with Lenin to Geneva; secr, newspaper *Proletariy*; 1911 helped found and taught at Party School at Longjumeau, near Paris; 1912 helped prepare 6th (Prague) RSDRP Congress; then moved to Cracow, where she helped Lenin to maintain liaison with Party orgs in Russia, with newspaper *Pravda* and with Bolshevik Faction of 4th State Duma; late 1913-early 1914 helped found journal *Rabotnitsa*; 1915 deleg for Russian Bureau, CC, RSDRP at Int Women's Anti-War Conference in Bern; secr, Party organ *Sotsial-demokrat*; 3 Apr 1917 returned to Russia with Lenin; helped prepare and attended 7th (Apr) RSDRP(B) Conference; 13 May 1917 published article "A Page from the History of the Russian Social-Democratic Party" in the newspaper *Soldatskaya pravda*; the article was, in effect, the first biography of Lenin; organized socialist youth leagues; drafted public educ demands for new Party program; did considerable agitation and propaganda work among the masses, particularly in the Vyborg Distr as member, Vyborg Rayon Party Comt; June 1917 elected member, Vyborg Rayon Duma; helped prepare and attended 6th Party Congress; carried out assignments for Lenin, forced into hiding after July 1917 riots; kept him abreast of polit developments, involving two trips to see him in Finland; during preparations for 1917 Oct Revol acted as his agent, conveying his letters with secret instructions to CC, RSDRP(B), Petrograd Party Comt and Mil Revol Comt; after 1917 Oct Revol served as govt comr for extracurricular work; Collegium member, RSFSR Pop Comrt of Educ; together with Lunacharskiy and Pokrovskiy, drafted first Sov decrees on public educ; organized polit training work; 1918 elected member, Socialist Acad; 1919 cruised the Volga with SS "Red Star" agitation steamer; from Nov 1920 chm, Main Polit Educ Comt, RSFSR Pop Comrt of Educ; from 1921 chm, Sci Methods Section, State Learned Council, RSFSR Pop Comrt of Educ; founded and helped run a number of benevolent societies, such as "Down with Illiteracy," "Children's Friend," etc; chm, Soc of Marxist Educationists; 1931 elected hon member, USSR Acad of Sci; from 1936 Dr of Pedag Sci; member, ed staff, journals: *Na putyakh k novoy shkole*; *O nashikh detyakh; Pomoshch' samoobrazovaniyu; Krasnyy bibliotekar; Shkola vzroslykh; Kommunisticheskoye prosveshcheniye; Izbachital'nya;* 1930 sponsored foundation of newspaper *Krest'yanskaya gazeta dlya nachinayushchikh chitat'*; wrote numerous works on educ and Communist training; attended all Komsomol Congresses (apart from 3rd); attended all Party Congresses (apart from 1st and 5th); from 1924 member, Centr Control Commission; from 1927 member, CC, CPSU(B); member, All-Russian and USSR Centr Exec Comt of all convocations; dep and Presidium member, USSR Supr Sov of 1st convocation; deleg at 2nd, 4th, 6th and 7th Comintern Congresses; at 4th Comintern Congress co-reporter on "Work with Youth"; transmitted to CC, RCP(B) transcript of Lenin's last instructions and advice, including his "Letter to the Congress"; 1924 began to write her *Vospominaniya o Lenine* (Recollections of Lenin); campaigned for retention of Lenin's ideas, principles and traditions in the Party; her latter years were embittered by developments in the USSR; she witnessed the falsification of many aspects of Party history and reprisals against her Party comrades; Dec 1925, at 14th CPSU(B) Congress, sided with Zinov'yevist opposition group, but dissociated herself from it in the fall of 1926; 1934 *Pravda* reviewed her "Recollections of Lenin", accusing her of errors in covering Party history and depicting Lenin; she was also accused of "deviations" on fundamental issues of educ and training; *Publ: Zhenshchina-rabotnitsa* (The Woman Worker) (1899); *Narodnoye obrazovaniye i demokratiya* (Public Education and Democracy) (1915); *Osnovy politprosvetraboty* (The Principles of Political Education Work) (1927); *Vospominaniya o Lenine* (Recollections of Lenin) (1957); *Pedagogicheskiye sochineniya* (Pedagogic Works) (11 vol, 1957), etc; *Awards*: Order of Lenin; Order of the Red Banner of Labor; *Died*: 27 Feb 1939 in Moscow.

KRUSHEL'NITSKAYA, Solomeya Amvros'yevna (1873-1952) Ukr opera singer (lyric-coloratura soprano); Hon Art Worker of Ukr SSR from 1951; *Born*: 23 Nov 1873 in vil Bilyavintsy, Ternopol' Province; *Educ*: 1893 grad Prof. V. Vysotskiy's piano class, L'vov Conservatory; *Career*: 1893 opera debut in L'vov; went to Milan for further voice training under Prof Crespi; sang at opera theaters in Italy, France, South America, Canada, etc; also appeared in L'vov, Cracow, Odessa, Petersburg and other cities; had a voice of enormous power and range (two and a half octaves) and great stage presence and acting ability; very popular as chamber singer, particularly with Ukr folk songs and works of Lysenko and other Ukr composers; 1939-46 instructor, from 1946 prof, L'vov Conservatory; *Roles*: Tat'yana and Liza; Aida; Carmen; Madame Butterfly; Leonora in Donizetti's "The Favorite"; title role in Ponchielli's "La Gioconda"; *Died*: 16 Nov 1952 in L'vov.

KRUSHEL'NITSKIY, Anton Vladislavovich (1878-1941) Ukr writer; *Born*: 4 Aug 1878 in vil Lan'tsut, Western Galicia, son of minor official; *Educ*: grad Philosophy Fac, L'vov Univ; *Career*: joined group of writers headed by I. Ya. Franko; 1898 first work published; taught in Galicia; 1917-20 influenced by Ukr bourgeois nationalists; Min of Educ of Ukr Pop Republ; 1919 emigrated to Austria; helped found movement to reunite Western Ukr with Sov Ukr; wrote novels and novelettes about events in Ukr between 1918 and 1920; 1929-32 ed, L'vov journal *Novi shlyakhy*; 1933 ed, journal *Kritika*; subjected to reprisals for defending socialist system in Ukr; 1932-33 in Polish prison; 1934 moved to Sov Ukr; exposed ideology of bourgeois nationalism in journalistic articles and fervently propagated Sov system; arrested by State Security organs; *Publ*: novelettes "Felling the Forest" (2 vol, 1919); "Daily Bread" (1920); collected stories "The Proletarians" (1899); comedy "The Eagles" (1906); *Died*: 13 Nov 1941 in imprisonment; posthumously rehabilitated.

KRUSHEL'NITSKIY, Ivan Antonovich (1905-1934) Ukr poet and playwright; *Born*: 12 Nov 1905 in Kolomyya, now Ivano-Frankovsk Oblast, Ukr; *Educ*: 1927 grad Prague Univ; *Career*: from 1929 worked for Ukr journal; active in campaign for annexation of Western Ukr to Sov Ukr; from 1932 assoc, Inst of History of Material Culture, Ukr Acad of Sci, Khar'kov; arrested by State Security organs; *Publ*: verse collections: *Vesnyana pisnya* (Spring Song) (1924); *Yuzhnyy spokiy* (Southern Peace) (1929); *Radoshchi zhyttya* (Joy of Life) (1930); *Buri i vikna* (Storms and Windows) (1930); *Zalizna korova* (The Iron Cow) (1930); play *Na skelyakh* (On the Cliffs) (1932); *Died*: 17 Dec 1934 in imprisonment in Khar'kov; posthumously rehabilitated.

KRUSHEL'NITSKIY, Mar'yan Mikhaylovich (1897-1963) Ukr actor, stage dir and impressario; prof from 1947; Pop Artiste of USSR from 1944; CP member from 1943; *Born*: 18 Apr 1897 in vil Pilyavo, now Ternovka Rayon, Ukr; son of a peasant; *Educ*: studied at Philosophy Fac, L'vov Univ; 1924 grad Philosophy Fac, Prague Univ; *Career*: 1915-17 acted with Ukr Ternopol' Theatrical Evenings co; 1918 co-founder, New L'vov Theater; 1920 Franko Theater founded in Vinnitsa from this co and from a group of actors from Young Theater; 1921-23 worked for Russian Conversation Soc's Ukr Theater, L'vov; 1924 moved to USSR; 1924-33 actor, Berezil' Theater; 1933-52 actor and artistic dir, Shevchenko Theater, Khar'kov; from 1952 actor and stage dir, 1954-61 chief stage dir, Franko Theater; one of first actors to portray Lenin in Ukr; from 1926 also film work; from 1932 taught stagecraft; 1946-52 taught at Khar'kov Theater Inst; from 1952 at Kiev Inst of Stagecraft; dep, Ukr Supr Sov of 3rd-4th convocations; *Productions:* Afinogenov's *Portret* (The Portrait) (1934); Kropivnitskiy's *Day serdtsu volyu, zavedyot v nevolyu* (Give the Heart Its Will and It Leads You into Thraldom) (1934); Ostrovskiy's *Groza* (The Storm) (1938); Korneychuk's: *Pravda* (Truth) (1937); *Bogdan Khmel'nitskiy* (1939); "Front" (1942); "Makar Dubrava" (1948); *Kalinovaya roshcha* (Viburnum Grove) (1950); "Eugene Grandet", after Balzac (1940); *Molodaya gvardiya* (The Young Guard), after Fadeyev (1945); Kocherga's *Yaroslav Mudryy* (Yaroslav the Wise) (1947); Virta's *Zagovor obrechyonnykh* (Conspiracy of the Doomed) (1949); Dmiterko's *Naveki vmeste* (Forever Together) (1948); Karpenko-Karyy's *Martyn Borulya* (1951); Gorky's *Yegor Bulychyov i drugiye* (Yegor Bulychyov and Co) (1952); Shteyn's *Personal'noye delo* (A Personal Affair) (1956); Dan'kevich's opera *Bogdan Khmel'nitskiy* (1953); *Roles*: the Abbé Honoré in Merimee's "Jacqueries" (1925); Maloshtan in Mikitenko's *Diktatura* (Dictatorship) (1936); Sergeant Bednya in Irchan's *Platsdarm* (Bridgehead) (1934); Martyn in Karpenko-Karyy's *Martyn Borulya* (1934); Ivan Nepokrytyy in Kropivnitskiy's "Give the Heart It's Will and It Leads You into Thraldom (1935); Bukhta, Bublik, Deacon Gavrilo and Galushka in *Gibel' eskadry* (End of the Squadron) (1933), *Platon Krechet* (1934), *Bogdan Khmel'nitskiy* (1939) and *V stepyakh Ukrainy* (In the Steppes of the Ukraine) (1940); Schastlivtsev and Murzavetskiy in *Les* (The Forest) (1939) and *Volki i ovtsy* (The Wolves and the Sheep) (1939); Tev'ye in Sholom Aleykhem's *Tev'ye-molochnik* (Tev'ye the Milkman) (1940); Bulychyov in *Yegor Bulychyov and Co* (1947); Shvandya in *Lyubov' Yarovaya*: (1937); Vatutin in Dmiterko's "General Vatutin" (1948); Poludin in Shteyn's "A Personal Affair" (1956); Gulya in Sukhodol'skiy's "Arsenal" (1957); *Awards*: Order of Lenin (1960); Stalin Prizes (1947 and 1948); *Died*: 5 Apr 1963.

KRUSSER, Aleksandr Semyonovich (1893-1919) Mil commander; CP member from 1913; *Born*: 1 Sept 1893 in vil Skulyany, Bessarabian Province, son of a nobleman; *Educ*: 1912-16 studied at Petersburg Power Eng Inst, then at Petrograd Univ; *Career*: worked for Petersburg RSDRP Comt; 1916 drafted into Russian Army and trained at ensigns' school; from Mar 1918 member, Revol Comt and comr for artillery inspection, 8th Army; from Apr 1918 commanded 4th Army, then asst commander, 5th Donetsk Army; from Nov 1918 head, Mil Control Dept, 10th Army; 1919 for a while secr, Collegium, Ukr Pop Comrt of Internal Affairs; member Ukr Centr Exec Comt; *Died:* 1919.

KRYLENKO, Nikolay Vasil'yevich (Party name: COMRADE ABRAM) (1885-1938) Govt and Party official; CP member from 1904; *Born*: 14 May 1885 in vil Bekhteyevka, Smolensk Province, son of an exiled official; *Educ*: grad History and Philology Fac and Law Fac, Petersburg Univ; *Career*: 1904-05 played leading part in student revol movement; 1905-06 Party agitation and propaganda in Petersburg and surrounding area and in Moscow for Petersburg and Moscow RSDRP Comts; June 1906 emigrated; returned to Russia; as member, Mil Org, Petersburg RSDRP Comt, carried out active propaganda among troops of Petersburg garrison; 1907 re-arrested and exiled to Lyublin; from 1911 contributed to *Zvezda* then to *Pravda*; on instructions from Lenin organized smuggling of Party lit and arranged travel of underground Bolshevik agents to and from Russia; summer 1912 went to Petersburg for Lenin to help prepare elections for 4th State Duma; Aug 1913, after completing mil service, sent to Petersburg by CC, RSDRP(B) to work for newspaper *Pravda* and Duma's Bolshevik faction; denounced by agent-provocateur Malinovskiy, arrested and Mar 1914 exiled to Khar'kov; helped prepare Southern Russian Party Conference; to avoid further arrest emigrated to Austria, then moved to Switzerland; attended Bern Conference of For RSDRP Sections; summer 1915 sent by Party CC on underground work to Moscow; Nov 1915 re-arrested; Apr 1916 drafted into Russian Army and sent to the front; after 1917 Feb Revol elected chm, regt, then div comt, 11th Army; as rep of CC, RSDRP(B) attended Southwestern Front Congress at Kremenets; Apr 1917 elected chm, Army Comt, 11th Army; May 1917 deleg of Frontline Army Congress in Petrograd; deleg, 1st All-Russian Congress of Soviets; as Bolshevik cand elected to Presidium of Congress and elected member, first All-Russian Centr Exec Comt; active propaganda among workers and soldiers; contributed to newspaper *Soldatskaya pravda*; June 1917 helped prepare All-Russian Conference of Frontline and Rear RSDRP(B) Organizations and presented report on "War, Peace and Offensive"; elected member, Centr Bureau of All-Russian Mil Org, CC, RSDRP(B); June-Aug 1917 arrested by Provisional Govt; Oct 1917 helped organize Congress of Northern Oblast Soviets; played active role in 1917 Oct Revol; member, Petrograd Mil Revol Comt; member, first Council of Pop Comr, as member, Comt for Mil and Naval Affairs; 9 Nov 1917 appointed Supr Commander in Chief and Pop Comr for Mil Affairs; from Mar 1918 worked for Soc Justice organs and helped estabiseh Sov legal and Public prosecution system; 1918–31 State Prosecutor for major political cases, including: Tactical Center; Rightist Socialist-Revolutionaries; Shakhty Case; Ind Party; trial of Soc-Democrats

(Mensheviks), etc; 1922-31 RSFSR Asst Prosecutor, then Prosecutor; from 1931 RSFSR Pop Comr of Justice; from 1936 USSR Pop Comr of Justice; at 15th and 16th Party Congresses elected member, Centr Control Commission; member, All-Russian Centr Exec Comt of many convocations; 1935 elected Presidium member, All-Russian Centr Exec Comt; from 1934 Dr of State and Legal Sci; member, Commissions to Draft the Constitution of the RSFSR and USSR and Commission to Draft Legal Codes; helped prepare publ *Istoriya grazhdanskoy voyny* (History of the Civil War); co-founder *BSE* (Large Soviet Encyclopedia); taught at higher educ establishments, including Inst of Red Prof; head, Chair of Criminal Law, Moscow Inst of Sov Law; 1928–34 helped lead six USSR Acad of Sci expeditions to the Pamirs; for a number of years head, All-Union Soc of Proletarian Tourism; directed Sov chess org; 1925-36 organized int chess tournaments; wrote many works on theory and practice of Sov state system and law; arrested by State Security organs; *Publ: Sud i pravo v SSSR* (Court and Law in the USSR) (3 vol, 1927-30); *Chto takoye revolyutsionnaya zakonnost'* (What Revolutionary Legality Is) (1927); *Lenin o sude i ugolovnoy politike* (Lenin on the Courts and Criminal Policy) (1934); *Sovetskoye pravosudiye. Sud i prokuratura v SSSR* (Soviet Jurisprudence. The Courts and Prosecutor's Office in the USSR) (1936), etc; *Awards*: Order of Lenin; Order of the Red Banner; *Died*: 1938 in imprisonment posthumously rehabilitated.

KRYLOV, Aleksey Nikolayevich (1863-1945) Mathematician; specialist in mech and naval architecture; member, Russian (USSR) Acad of Sci from 1916; *Born*: 15 Aug 1863 in vil Visyaga, Simbirsk Province, son of an artillery officer; *Educ:* 1884 grad Naval College; 1890 completed postgrad studies at Petersburg Naval Acad; *Career*: 1884 joined Compass Dept, Main Hydrographic Bd, where he began research on compass deviation under I. P. Kolong; subsequently specialized in ship theory; 1888 entered Shipbuilding Dept, Petersburg Naval Acad after a year's practical training at a shipyard; from 1890 assoc, from 1892 lecturer in mathematics and ship theory, Petersburg Naval Acad, where he worked for almost 50 years; also taught at Petersburg Polytech Inst and other higher educ establishments; from 1900 head, Model Testing Basin, where, inter alia, he experimented on the capsizability of a model of the battleship *Petropavlovsk*; also designed changes in the armor-plating of battleships to improve their buoyancy and stability; devised techniques of determining the effect of roll on the accuracy of ships' guns; 1908-10, as Chief Inspector of Shipbuilding and chm, Naval Tech Comt, co-designed first *Sebastopol* class ships; introduced several innovations in ship design; 1910-17, after resignation from Naval Tech Comt, worked as consultant, Metal Works, Obukhov Plant, Putilov Plant, etc; from 1916 dir, Main Physical Observatory and head, Main Naval Meteorological Bd; from 1917 dir, Physics Laboratory (later Inst), Russian Acad of Sci; from 1919 dir, Naval Acad; 1921 sent abroad by Russian Acad of Sci as member, Commission for the Restoration of Sci Relations; while abroad also supervised the construction of ships ordered for the Sov Navy; 1927 returned to USSR and resumed teaching post at Naval Acad and directorship of Inst of Physics, USSR Acad of Sci; *Publ: O priblizhyonnykh vychisleniyakh* (Approximative Calculations) (1907); *Vibratsiya sudov* (Ship Vibration) (1908); *O nekotorykh differentsial'nykh uravneniyakh matematicheskoy fiziki, imeyushchikh prilozheniye v tekhnicheskikh voprosakh* (Some Differential Equations from Mathematical Physics with Engineering Applications) (1913); Russian translation of Isaac Newton's *Philosophiae Naturalis Principia Mathematica* (Mathematical Principles of Natural Philosophy) (1915); *O raschyote balok, lezhashchikh na uprugom osnovanii* (The Calculation of Beams Resting on an Elastic Base) (1930); Russian translation of Leonhard Euler's *Theoria motuus lunae* (A Theory of the Motion of the Moon) (1934); *Sobraniye trudov* (Collected Works) (12 vol, 1936-56); *Vozmushcheniya pokazaniy kompasa, proiskhodyashchiye ot kachki korablya na volnenii* (False Compass Readings Due to Ship's Roll on Choppy Seas); *O teorii girokompasa Anshyuttsa* (The Theory of Anschütz's Gyrocompass); *Osnovaniya teorii deviatsii kompasa* (Principles of the Compass Deviation Theory) (1938-40); *Moi vospominaniya* (My Memoirs); also wrote studies of the life and works of Newton, Euler, Gauss, Lagrange, P. L. Chebyshev, etc; *Awards*: Stalin Prize (1941); Hero of Socialist Labor (1943); three Orders of Lenin; *Died*: 26 Oct 1945.

KRYLOV, Nikolay Mitrofanovich (1879-1955) Mathematician; prof from 1912; member, Ukr Acad of Sci from 1922; member, USSR Acad of Sci from 1929; Hon Sci Worker of Ukr SSR from 1939; *Born*: 29 Nov 1879 in Petersburg; *Educ*: 1904 grad Petersburg Mining Inst; *Career*: from 1912 prof, Petersburg Mining Inst; from 1917 prof, Crimean Univ, Simferopol'; from 1922 head, Chair of Mathematical Physics, Ukr Acad of Sci; 1928-29 corresp member, USSR Acad of Sci; did research on the theory of interpolation, on the approximative integration of differential equations in mathematical physics and on non-linear mechanics; *Publ*: "Sur quelques idées de P. Tchebycheff qui peuvent être rattachées à la solution approchée des problèmes du calcul des variations" (Some of P. Chebyshev's Ideas Applicable to the Approximate Solution of Differential Calculus Problems) (1929); *Osnovni problemy matematychnoy fizyky i tekhniky* (The Basic Problems of Mathematical Physics and Engineering) (1932); *Vvedeniye v nelineynuyu mekhaniku* (An Introduction to Non-Linear Mechanics) (1937); coauthor, *Zbirnik prats' z neliniynoi mekhaniky* (A Collection of Papers on Non-Linear Mechanics) (1937); *Awards*: Order of Lenin; two Orders of the Red Banner of Labor; medals; *Died*: 11 May 1955.

KRYLOV, Sergey Borisovich (1888-1958) Lawyer; specialist in int law; Dr of Law; prof; Hon Sci Worker of RSFSR; CP member from 1946; *Born*: 1 Jan 1888; *Educ*: 1910 grad Law Fac, Petersburg Univ; *Career*: after graduation embarked on legal career; prof of state and int law, Leningrad Law Inst and Higher Diplomatic School, USSR Min of For Affairs; 1942-46 and 1952-58 consultant, USSR Min of For Affairs; from 1943 head, Chair of Int Law, Inst of Int Relations; 1944 member, Sov deleg, Dumbarton Oaks Conference; 1945 member, Sov deleg, UN Conference on Int Org, San Francisco; in same year attended Washington session of Comt of Jurists; attended first session of UN Gen Assembly; 1953-56 member, UN Int Law Commission; 1956 attended 47th Conference, Int Law Association, Dubrovnik; vice-pres, Sov Int Law Association; wrote over 160 works on int law; *Publ*: textbook *Mezhdunarodnoye chastnoye pravo* (International Private Law) (1930); coauthor, *Kurs vozdushnogo prava* (A Course in Aviation Law) (1933); coauthor, textbook *Mezhdunarodnoye publichnoye pravo* (International Public Law) (1946), etc; *Died*: 24 Nov 1958.

KRYLOV, S.N. (1892-1938) Govt official; CP member from 1909; *Born*: 1892; *Career*: Party work in Smolensk and Moscow; after 1917 Feb Revol chm, regt, div, then corps soldiers' comt; after 1917 Oct Revol commandant and commander, Vitebsk Garrison; chm Vitebsk Province RCP(B) Comt; deleg at 8th RCP(B) Congress; 1918 sided with Leftist Communists in opposing Brest Peace Treaty; then govt and Party work; member, Commission for Dealing with the Harvest Failure, Council of Pop Comr; Collegium member, Pop Comrt of Trade; chm, Middle Volga Kray CPSU(B) Comt; 1937 expelled from Party for alleged anti-Party activities; arrested by State Security organs; *Died*: 1938 in imprisonment.

KRYMOV, Aleksey Petrovich (1872-1954) Surgeon; Dr of Med from 1906; prof from 1912; member, USSR Acad of Med Sci from 1945; Hon Sci Worker of Ukr SSR from 1940; *Born*: 1872 in Moscow, son of a well-known artist; *Educ*: 1898 grad Med Fac, Moscow Univ; *Career*: while still a student won a gold medal for a paper on nephrolithiasis; after grad worked for a year as intern at Prof A. A. Bobrov's Clinic; 1899 joined Russian Army and worked as a surgeon at Smolensk Mil Hospital; also worked under Prof S. I. Spasokukotskiy at Smolensk Zemstvo Hospital; for ten years head, Surgical Dept, Moscow City Hospital for the Poor run by the Med Fac, Moscow Univ; 1905 served in Russo-Japanese War; 1906 defended doctor's thesis on peritoneal-inguinal apophysis; 1911 assoc prof, Prof P. I. D'yakonov's Hospital Surgical Clinic, where he lectured on field and clinical surgery; simultaneously head, Surgical Dept, Moscow Mil Hospital; also consultant, Alexandrine (now Semashko) Hospital; from 1912 prof, Chair of Hospital Surgery, Saint Vladimir Univ, Kiev; during WW 1 hospital consultant, Southwestern Front; after establishment of Sov rule in Ukr banned from teaching for anti-Sov statements and temporary allegiance to White Army; found work at several hospitals in Kiev; 1929 rehabilitated and appointed head, Chair of Fac Surgery, Kiev Med Inst; from 1936 bd chm, Ukr Republ and Kiev Surgeons' Soc, then chm, All-Union Surgical Soc and Presidium member, Learned Med Council, Ukr Min of Health; during WW 2 evacuated to Chelyabinsk, where he worked as a consultant and surgeon at various mil hospitals; after WW 2 until death head, Fac Surgical Clinic, Kiev Med Inst; devised original operating techniques for the fixation of floating livers and kidneys, corrosion of the fistula in arteriovenous aneurism, amputation of the legs and half of the pelvis, etc; described new symptom of acute appendicitis; trained numerous outstanding surgeons; wrote 135 works; *Publ*: doctor's thesis *O bryushinno-pakhovom otrostke* (Peritoneal-Inguinal Apophysis) (1906); *Ucheniye o gryzhakh* (Celology) (1911); *Voyenno-polevaya khirurgiya* (Field Surgery) (1935); *Izbrannyye lektsii po voyenno-polevoy khirurgii* (Selected Lectures on Field Surgery) (1937); coauthor, *Chastnaya khirurgiya* (Special Surgery) (1940); *Ognestrel'naya anevrizma* (Gunshot Aneurism) (1943); *Spetsial'na khirurgiya* (Special Surgery) (2nd ed, 1948); *Bryushnyye gryzhy* (Abdominal Hernia) (1950); *Awards*: Bush Prize (1911); Order of Lenin; S. P. Fyodorov Prize (1940); Order of the Red Banner of Labor; Order of the Red Star; medal "For Valiant Labor During the Great Fatherland War"; *Died*: 1954 in Kiev.

KRYMOV, Nikolay Petrovich (1884-1958) Landscape painter; corresp member, USSR Acad of Arts from 1949; Hon Art Worker of RSFSR from 1942; Pop Artist of RSFSR from 1956; *Born*: 2 May 1884; *Educ*: 1904-11 studied at Moscow College of Painting, Sculpture and Architecture; *Career*: member *Golubaya roza* (Blue Rose) art group; member, Russian Painters' Union; taught at various art schools; his works are marked by a plethora of detail, precision of execution and tonal harmony; they are on exhibition at the Tret'yakov Gallery and many other Sov art galleries; from 1910 also worked as stage artist; *Works*: landscapes: "Snow-Covered Roofs" (1906); "A Hot Day" (1911); "Bathing Woman" (1916); "Reedy Pond" (1917); "Garden Nook" (1921); "A Gray Day" (1924-25); "The Riverlet" (1926); "Provincial Winter" (1933); "A Summer Day" (1939); "In Tarus" (1948); "Morning" (1953), etc; stage sets for: *Ne bylo ni grosha, da vdrug altyn* (From Rags to Riches) (1910, 1926); *Goryacheye serdtse* (Warm Heart) (1926); Ostrovskiy's *Bespridannitsa* (Girl Without a Dowry) (1932), etc; *Awards*: Order of the Red Banner of Labor; *Died*: 6 May 1958.

KRYMSKIY, Agafangel Yefimovich (1871-1942) Ukr historian, philologist and orientalist; prof from 1898; member, Ukr Acad of Sci from 1918; Hon Sci Worker of Ukr SSR from 1940; *Born*: 15 Jan 1871 in Vladimir-Volynsk (Wlodzimierz), son of a teacher; *Educ*: 1892 grad Lazarev Inst of Oriental Languages, Moscow; 1896 grad Fac of History and Philology, Moscow Univ; *Career:* 1896-98 did research in Syria and Lebanon; 1898-1918 prof, Lazarev Inst of Oriental Languages; 1918-28 member, from 1928 life-secr, Ukr Acad of Sci; wrote major works on the history and lit of the Arab countries, Iran, Turkey, Abyssinia, as well as historical studies of the Ukr, Azer and Tadzh; also wrote philological studies, translations, novels, short stories and verse; *Publ: Povesti i rasskazy* (Stories and Novelettes) (1895); *Ivan Franko* (1897); verse collection *Pal'move gillya* (Palm-Branches) (3 vol, 1901, 1908, 1922); *Istoriya Persii, yeyo literatury i dervishskoy filosofii* (The History of Persia, Its Literature and Dervish Philosophy) (3 vol, 1903, 1910, 1917); *Istoriya musul'manstva* (The History of Islam) (3 vol, 1903-04); novel *Andrey Lagovskiy* (1905); *Istoriya Sasanidov i zavoyevaniye Irana arabami* (The History of the Sassanids and the Arab Conquest of Iran) (1905); *Drevnekiyevskiy govor* (The Ancient Kievan Dialect) (1906); *Ukrainskaya grammatika* (Ukrainian Grammar) (2 vol, 1907-08); *Istoriya Turtsii i yeyo literatury* (The History of Turkey and Its Literature) (2 vol, 1910–16); *Istoriya arabov i arabskoy literatury* (The History of the Arabs and Arabic Literature) (3 vol, 1911-13); *Istoriya Persii ta ii Pys'menstva* (The History of Persia and Its Written Language) (1923); *Khafiz ta yoho pisni* (Hafiz and His Songs) (1924); *Per'skyy teatr* (Persian Theater) (1925); *Do istorii vyshchoi osvity u arabiv* (The History of Arabic Higher Education) (1928); *Tyurky, ikh movy ta literatury* (The Turks, Their Languages and Literatures) (1930); *Studii z Krymu* (Studies of the Crimea) (1930); translations from Arabic of works by 'Antara and ul-Ma'arri; translations from Persian of part of *Shah-name* (Book of Kings) and works by Omar Khayyam, Sa'di, Hafiz and Jami; translations from Turkish of works by Mihri-hatun and Halid Ziya, etc; *Awards*: Order of the Red Banner of Labor; *Died*: 25 Jan 1942 in Kokchetav.

KRYUKOV, Aleksandr Nikolayevich (1878-1952) Therapist; pioneer of Sov hematology; Dr of Med from 1909; prof from 1918; member, USSR Acad of Med Sci from 1948; Hon Sci Worker of Uzbek SSR; *Born*: 31 Aug 1878; *Educ*: 1901 grad Med Fac, Moscow Univ; *Career*: after grad worked at various hospitals in Moscow; 1909 defended doctor's thesis on the origin and interrelationship of leucocytes and leucocytosis; from 1917 co-founder and dir, Fac Therapy Clinic, Centr Asian Univ; from 1918 prof, Moscow Univ; 1923 wrote first Sov description of smallpox and proved the existence of brucellosis in the USSR, which he identified along with V. A. Smirnov from hemocultures; 1927-30 head, Clinic of Tropical Diseases, Centr Asian Univ; from 1930 dir, Emergency Therapy Clinic, Sklifosovskiy Inst, Moscow, and prof, Chair of Therapy, Centr Inst of Postgrad Med Training; during WW 2 chief therapist, various evacuation hospitals, RSFSR Pop Comrt of Health; did research on hematology, emergency therapy and tropical pathology; developed "sub-unitarian" theory of hematogenesis according to which all the blood cells derive from a lymphoid-reticular tissue cell which has turned into a hemocytoblast (Kryukov and Pappenheim's lymphoidocyte) from which all blood elements develop by differentiation; this theory has been confirmed with blood cell cultures, from embryological observations and by the morphogenesis of blood elements in pathological blood states (mainly leucosis); wrote over 80 works; *Publ*: doctor's thesis *O proiskhozhdenii i vzaimootnosheniyakh leykotsitov i o leykotsitoze* (The Origin and Interrelationship of Leucocytes and Leucocytosis) (1909); *Morphologiya krovi* (The Morphology of Blood) (3 vol, 1920); *Atlas krovi* (A Blood Atlas) (1946); *Klinicheskaya simptomatologiya ostrykh vnutrennikh zabolevaniy* (The Clinical Symptomatology of Acute Internal Diseases), etc; *Died*: 19 Dec 1952.

KRYUKOVA, Marfa Semyonovna (1876-1954) Russian narrator; *Born*: 17 July 1876 in vil Nizhnyaya Zimnyaya Zolotitsa, Arkhangel'sk Province; *Career*: talented narrator of traditional heroic folk epics; also composed original tales and legends; performed as narrator from age 15, learning the epics and legends from her mother and grandfathers, etc; first written record of her stories made in 1900's by A. V. Markov (seven folk epics and two religious poems); 1934 V. P. Chuzhimov and 1937-38 A. M. Astakhova, E. G. Borodina-Morozova and R. S. Lipets recorded her entire repertoire of over 150 folk epics and epic-style arrangements; Kryukova then began to compose original epics and stories, including "The Tale of Lenin," "How the Whites Tried to Take the North," "Broad and Great Is Our Kolkhoz Land," "The Tale of the Pole," "Stony Moscow All A-Wailing," etc; from 1939 member, Writers' Union; *Publ: Byliny* (Folk Epics) (2 vol, 1939-41); *Noviny* (New Epics) (1939); *Skazki* (Tales) (1941); *Na Zimnem berege, u morya Belogo* (On the Winter Shore by the White Sea) (1950); *O bogatyryakh staroprezhnikh i nyneshnikh* (Folk Heroes, Ancient and Modern) (1946); *Awards*: Order of Lenin; Order of the Red Banner of Labor; *Died*: 7 Jan 1954.

KRYZHANOVSKIY, Vladimir Petrovich (1901-1937) Mil commander; specialist in theory of tank operations; *Born*: 1901; *Educ*: 1926 grad Frunze Mil Acad; 1930 grad Advanced Commanders Courses; *Career*: 1918 joined Red Army; during Civil War infantry instructor; 1930-37 held admin posts with Red Army Mechanization and Motorization Bd; 1937 arrested by NKVD; *Publ: Samostoyatel'nyye mekhanizirovanniye soedineniya na otkrytom flange armii v nastupatel'noy operatsii* (Independent Mechanized Units on the Open Flank of an Army During an Offensive Operation) (1932); *Preodoleniye zagrazhdeniy motomekhanizirovannymi chastyami* (Obstacle Surmounting for Motorized and Mechanized Units) (1932); *Problemy samostoyatel'nykh motorizovannykh strelkovykh soyedineniy* (The Problems of Independent Motorized Rifle Units) (1934); *Died*: 1937 in imprisonment.

KRZHEVSKIY, Boris Apollonovich (1887–1954) Lit historian; translator; *Born*: 25 Sept 1887 in Kiev *Educ*: grad Petersburg Univ; 1914-16 completed educ in Spain; *Career*: taught Romance philology at Leningrad higher educ establishments; one of the greatest experts on European Renaissance lit; studied French lit (Rabelais, Saint-Evremond, classicist theater, etc) and ties between Russian and Spanish lit; translated Cervantes' "Novelas Ejemplares," Prévost d'Exiles' Histoire du Chevalier Des Grieux et Manon Lescaut," etc; *Publ:* articles *Servantes i yego novelly* (Cervantes and His Novellae) (1916); *Don Kikhot na fone ispanskoy literatury XVI–XVII stoletiy* (Don Quixote Against the Background of Spanish Literature of the 16th and 17th Centuries) (1929); "Cervantes" (1936); works on the Spanish theater "Tirso de Molina" (1923); *Tvorchestvo Lope de Vegi* (Lope de Vega's Works) (1940), etc; *Died*: 15 July 1954 in Leningrad.

KRZHIZHANOVSKAYA-NEVZOROVA (LANIKHA), Zinaida Pavlovna (1870-1948) Party and govt official; CP member from 1898; *Born*: Aug 1870 in Nizhniy Novgorod, daughter of a teacher; *Educ*: 1894 grad Higher Women's Courses in Petersburg; *Career:* from 1890's active revol; worked for Petersburg League for the Liberation of the Working Class; June 1896 arrested for involvement in the League; exiled along with G. M. Krzhizhanovskiy to vil Tesinskoye, Minusinsk Okrug, Yenisey Province, then to Minusinsk; 1899 among 16 other Soc-Democrats who signed Lenin's "Protest of the Russian Social-Democrats" against the "Economists' Creed"; after 2nd RSDRP Congress sided with Bolsheviks and active in *Iskra* org; 1902 secr, Centr Bureau, Russian org of the newspaper *Iskra*; in charge of secretariat, CC, RSDRP(B) in Kiev; 1904 arrested in this connection; 1905 worked for Bolshevik periodicals; from Feb 1917 in Moscow Oblast Sov; after 1917 Oct Revol dep head, Extra-Scholastic Dept, Pop Comrt of Educ; from 1924 member, Methods Section, State Learned Council; then dean, Acad of Communist Educ; from 1927 incapacitated by illness; *Publ: Nabroski vospominaniy o 'Soyuze bor'by za osvobozhdeniye rabochego klassa'* (Rough Memoirs of the League to Liberate the Working Class) (1926); *Died*: 24 Apr 1948.

KRZHIZHANOVSKIY, Gleb Maksimilianovich (1872-1959) Revolutionary; power eng; member, USSR Acad of Sci from 1929; CP member from 1893; *Born*: 24 Jan 1872 in Samara, son of a lawyer; *Educ*: 1889-94 studied at Petersburg Technol Inst; *Career*: 1891 joined Marxist movement; helped Lenin to organize Petersburg League for the Liberation of the Working Class; Dec 1895 arrested and imprisoned; while in jail wrote the song "Vicious Whirlwinds Blow Above Us"; 1897 sentenced to three years' exile in vil Tesinskoye, Minusinsk Okrug; 1899 signed the exiled Lenin's "Protest of the Russian Soc-Democrats," which was directed against the Economists' "Credo"; 1901 returned to Samara, where he managed the local "Iskra" center; member, Org Comt for the convocation of the 2nd RSDRP Congress, at which he was elected to CC in absentia; campaigned against the Mensheviks; June 1904 quit CC because of disagreement with majority's conciliatory attitude toward Mensheviks; 1905 helped to prepare 3rd RSDRP Congress; 1905-07 took active part in Revol; Oct 1905 chm, Strike Comt, Southwestern Railroad; early 1906 worked in Petersburg for Bolshevik newspaper *Volna*, journal *Mysl'*, etc; 1910 moved to Moscow, where he worked as mang-eng, Cable Electr Network and for Moscow RSDRP(B) Org; 1912 mang, "Electrosupply" Power Station; during 1917 Feb Revol member, Bolshevik faction, Moscow Sov; 1920 commissioned by Lenin to write a study of "The Basic Tasks of the Eletrification of Russia"; 1920 also appointed chm, State Comt for the Electrification of Russia; 1921-30 chm, USSR Gosplan; helped to draft first Sov five-year plan; 1929-39 vice-pres, USSR Acad of Sci; late 1930-32 chm, Main Power Eng Bd, USSR Pop Comrt of Heavy Ind; 1932-36 chm, Comt for Higher Tech Educ, USSR Centr Exec Comt, then RSFSR Dep Comr of Educ; 1930 founder-dir, Power Eng Inst, USSR Acad of Sci; elected member, CC at 13th-17th Party Congresses; member, All-Russian and USSR Centr Exec Comt; dep, USSR Supr Sov of 1st convocation; *Publ: Sochineniya* (Works) (3 vol, 1933-36); *O Vladimire Il'iche* (Vladimir Il'ich) (1956); *Izbrannoye* (Selected Works) (1957), etc; *Awards*: five Orders of Lenin; two Orders of the Red Banner of Labor; Hero of Socialist Labor (1957); *Died*: 31 Mar 1959.

KRZHIZHANOVSKIY, Sigizmund Dominikovich (1887-1950) Russian writer; *Born*: 11 Feb 1887 in Kiev; *Educ*: grad Law Fac, Kiev Univ; *Career*: 1910 first work printed; wrote studies of Shakespeare, Shaw, Chekhov and Ostrovskiy, also wrote original philosophical novellae and essays; translated Shaw, Mickiewicz Tuvim, Zheromskiy, etc; wrote several plays, opera librettos and stage adaptations, including *Tot tretiy* (The Third One), *Suvorov, Kola Bryun'yon* and *Chelovek, kotoryy byl chetvergom* (The Man Who Was Thursday); wrote scripts for films: *Prazdnik svyatogo Yorgena* (The Feast of St Jorgen) (1930); *Novyy Gulliver* (The New Gulliver) (1935); *Publ: Poetika zaglaviy* (The Poesy of Titles) (1931); *Karabel'naya slobodka* (The Shipyard District) (1943); *Pop i poruchik* (The Priest and the Lieutenant) (1939); *Dramaturgicheskiye priyomy Bernarda Shou* (The Dramatic Techniques of Bernard Shaw) (1934); *Shagi Fal'stafa* (The Steps of Falstaff) (1934); *Komediynyy syuzhet Shekspira* (Shakespeare's Comedy Subjects) (1935); *B. Shou, yego obrazy, mysli i obraz mysley* (Bernard Shaw, His Characters, Ideas and Way of Thinking) (1935); *Poetika Shekspirovskikh khronik* (The Poesy of Shakespeare's Chronicles) (1936); *Russkaya istoricheskaya p'yesa* (The Russian Historical Play) (1937); *Chekhonte i Chekhov* (Chekhonte and Chekhov) (1940); *Zabytyy Shekspir* (Forgotten Shakespeare) (1939); *Ay, Chyornoye more* (Oh, Black Sea!) (1939); *Dve shelkovinki* (Two Silk Threads) (1941); *Died*: 28 Dec 1950 in Moscow.

KUBYAK, Nikolay Afanas'yevich (1881-1942) Party and govt official; CP member from 1898; *Born*: 1881 in Meshchevsk, son of a worker; *Career*: began revol activities as a worker at a Bryansk plant; from 1902 member, Bryansk RSDRP Comt; took part in 1905-07 Revol; 1907 Bryansk RSDRP Comt deleg at 5th RSDRP Congress; after the congress arrested; 1908-12 in prison, then three years in exile; 1917 active in Oct Revol; Sestroretsk Plant dep in Petrograd Sov; chm, Sestroretsk Zemstvo Admin; chm, Sestroretsk Rayon RSDRP(B) Comt; 1918-19 and 1920 chm, Petrograd Province RCP(B) Comt and dep chm, Petrograd Province Exec Comt; chm, CC, Land and Forestry Workers' Union; deleg at 5th All-Russian Congress of Soviets; during Civil War member, Revol Mil Council, Petrograd Front; 1920 for a while sided with Workers' Opposition, but then dissociated himself from it; 1921-22 instructor, CC, RCP(B); 1922-26 secr, Far Eastern Bureau, CC, CPSU(B); 1927 secr, CC, CPSU(B); from 1928 RSFSR Pop Comr of Agric; chm, Power Eng Center, USSR Pop Comrt of Heavy Ind; from 1931 chm, Ivanovo Oblast Exec Comt; 1934-37 chm, All-Russian Council for Communal Management, USSR Centr Exec Comt; at 12th-16th Party Congresses elected member, CC, CPSU(B); member, All-Russian Centr Exec Comt; 1937 arrested by State Security organs; *Died*: 13 Aug 1942 in imprisonment; posthumously rehabilitated.

KUCHAIDZE, Grigoriy Leont'yevich (1886-1943) Govt official; Geo Pop Comr of Health from 1921; CP member from Oct 1902; *Born*: 1886; *Educ*: 1916 grad Med Fac, Moscow Univ; *Career*: took active part in Geo revol movement as RSDRP(B) member; organized workers' groups in Kutaisi, worked for an underground printing press and wrote articles for Bolshevik newspaper *Iskra*; arrested several times for distributing Party lit against WW 1; 1916 drafted into army and posted to reserve mil hospital in Orel; during 1917 Oct Revol member, Orel Province Mil-Revol Comt, then head, Orel Province Health Dept and chm, Refugee Evacuation Comt; 1920, after establishment of Sov rule in Northern Caucasus, dir, Caucasian Spa Bd; supervised restoration of war-damaged health resorts; in same year began organizing Azer Pop Comrt of Health as plen, RSFSR Pop Comrt of Health; 1921-34 Geo Pop Comr of Health; from 1924 also health plen, Transcaucasian Railroad; from 1929 chm, Malaria Commission, Council of Pop Comr, Transcaucasian SFSR; represented Azer, Arm and Geo Pop Comrt of Health at Council of Pop Comr, Transcaucasian SFSR; member, Tiflis City Sov; member, Geo Centr Exec Comt; member, Centr Exec Comt, Transcaucasian SFSR; member, Control Commission, CP Geo; 1935–38 dir, Centr Serum and Vaccine Control Inst, Moscow; from 1938 dir, Centr Inst of Balneology, Moscow; from Feb 1943 until death dep dir, Gorky All-Union Inst of Experimental Med; wrote several works on the Sov health service; *Publ: Zdravookhraneniye na sotsialisticheskoy stroyke* (The Health Service in Socialist Construction) (1932); *Died*: 1943.

KUCHERENKO, Pavel Aleksandrovich (1882-1936) Pathoanatomist; prof; *Born*: 15 Oct 1882 in Rostov-on-Don, son of an office worker; *Educ*: 1908 grad Petersburg Mil Med Acad; *Career*: 1910 began specializing in pathological anatomy under prof V. K. Vysokovich; from 1921 until death prof and head, Chair of Pathological Anatomy, Kiev Med Inst; also head, Sci Dept, Kiev Med Inst; prof, Kiev Inst of Postgrad Med Training; did research on diabetic lesions of the kidneys, endemic goiter, lymphogranulematosis, oncology (notably on the state of the endocrine glands in persons suffering from malignant neoplasms), physical chemistry, etc; 1927 co-founder, Dept of Pathological Anatomy, Ukr Acad of Sci; *Publ: Patolohichna anatomiya* (Pathological Anatomy) (1936), etc; *Died*: 28 May 1936.

KUCHERENKO, Vladimir Alekseyevich (1909-1963) Govt and Party official; member, CC, CPSU from 1956; CP member from 1942; *Born*: 1909 in vil Lozovaya, now Khar'kov Oblast; *Educ*: 1933 grad Khar'kov Construction Inst; *Career*: 1925-29 worked at Lozovaya Railroad Station; 1933-36 worked on construction of Kupyansk Sugar Refinery and at locomotive-building plant in Ulan-Ude; 1936-39 chief eng at construction of plants in the Donbass; 1939-50 directed construction and ind trusts in Khar'kov, Sterlitamak and Dnepropetrovsk; 1950 Collegium member, then USSR Dep Min for the Construction of Medium Machine-Building Enterprises; 1953 at USSR Min of Medium Machine-Building; 1954 dep chm, Moscow City Exec Comt and head of its Main Housing and Civil Construction Bd; 1955 dep chm, USSR Council of Min; 1956 dep chm, State Econ

Commission; 1955-61 chm, State Comt for Construction, USSR Council of Min; 1961-63 pres, USSR Acad of Construction and Architecture; from Aug 1963 USSR Min and dep chm, State Comt for Construction, USSR Council of Min; 1956-63 member, USSR Acad of Construction and Architecture; dep, RSFSR Supr Sov of 1955, and USSR Supr Sov of 1958 and 1962 convocations; *Awards*: Order of Lenin; Order of the Red Banner of Labor; Order of the Red Star; medals; Stalin Prize (1951); *Died*: 26 Nov 1963.

KUCHINSKIY, Dmitriy Aleksandrovich (1898–1938) Mil commander, div commander from 1935; CP member from 1918; *Born:* 1898; *Educ*: 1917 grad Ensigns' School; in 1920's grad Red Army Mil Acad; *Career*: 1918 joined Red Army; 1918-21 held various staff posts on Civil War fronts; after Civil War continued staff work and commanded a rifle corps; 1935-36 chief of staff, Kiev Mil Distr; 1934-37 member, Mil Council, USSR Pop Comrt of Defense; 1936-37 commander, Gen Staff Acad; 1937 arrested by NKVD; *Died*: 1938 in imprisonment; posthumously rehabilitated.

KUCHIYAK, Pavel Vasil'yevich (1897-1943) Altai-Oirot poet, storyteller and folklorist; playwright; actor and dir; *Born*: 17 Mar 1897 in vil Kuyum in Oirotia, now Gorno-Altay Oblast, son of a shaman; raised by his grandfather, who had adopted Christianity; *Educ*: attended a parochial school for two years; 1929 grad Communist Univ of Eastern Workers in Moscow; *Career*: after establishment of Sov regime in the Altay became secr, rural welfare comt; taught in Sov Party school; directed itinerant red yurt; 1938-43 head, Lit Section, Gorno-Altai Theater; 1928 first work published; recorded epics and translated them into Russian; knew Russian lit well and translated it into his native language; acted in plays; performed in concerts as storyteller and musician; *Publ*: poem in Altai *Arbachi* (1933); story *Zheleznyy kon'* (The Iron Steed) (1933); poem of a legend *Zazhglas' zolotaya zarya* (The Golden Dawn Was Lit) (1934); novelette *Aza Yalan* (1940); unfinished novel *Adyyok* (1943), etc; plays *Bor'ba* (The Struggle) (1932); *Petlya* (The Noose) (1934); *Yama* (The Pit) (1936); *Neozhidannaya vstrecha* (An Unexpected Encounter) (1936); *Vragi v kapkane* (Enemies in a Trap) (1937); *Cheynesh* (1940); *Tri sestry* (Three Sisters) (1941); collections *Zolotaya zarya* (The Golden Dawn) (1948); *V gorakh Altaya* (In the Altai Mountains) (1957); *Died*: 2 July 1943.

KUCHUGURA-KUCHERENKO, Ivan Yovich (1878-1943) Ukr kobza-player; Pop Artiste of Ukr SSR; *Born*: 1878 in vil Murafi, now Khar'kov Oblast; *Career*: 1908-10 taught kobza-playing at M. Lysenko's Music School, Kiev; his repertoire included such kobza ballads as "Aleksey Popovich," "The Slaves' Lament," "Khmel'nitskiy and Barabash" and "Khmel'nitskiy's Death"; wrote several songs, including "Upon a Precipice So High"; *Died*: 1943.

KUDRYASHOV, Vladimir Sidorovich (1909-1942) Party official; WW 2 partisan; CP member from 1932; *Born*: 21 Oct 1909 in Kiev, son of a worker; *Career*: 1935-41 shop foreman, Kiev Locomotive and Railroad-Car Repair Plant; Sept 1941 Party work in Kiev; helped found sabotage groups, underground printing offices, etc; from spring 1942 commanded partisan detachment; arrested by German authorities; *Awards*: Hero of the Sov Union; *Died*: 15 July 1942 executed.

KUFTIN, Boris Alekseyevich (1892–1953) Archeologist and ethnographer; Dr of History; member, Geo Acad of Sci from 1946; *Born*: 21 Jan 1892; *Career*: from 1919 lecturer, Moscow Univ; 1933-53 learned consultant, Geo State Museum; did research on the ethnography, ethnogenesis and archeology of the peoples of Siberia and the Crimea; from 1933 studied archeological relics of Geo; discovered traces of previously unknown Geo and Caucasian Bronze Age culture which existed in the region of Trialeti in the 2nd Century BC; also studied the Kur-Araka Aeneolithic civilization; *Publ: Arkheologicheskiye raskopki v Trialeti, 1936-40-ogo goda* (Archeological Excavations at Trialeti, 1936-40) (1941); *Materialy k arkheologii Kolkhidy* (Material on the Archeology of Colchis) (2 vol, 1949-50); *Awards:* Stalin Prize (1942); *Died:* 2 Aug 1953.

KUK, Aleksandr Ivanovich (1886-1937) Mil commander; capt, Russian Army; Sov mil commander; CP member from 1927; *Born*: 1886; *Pos*: from 1918 in Red Army; helped crush Kronstadt mutiny; 1918-21 head, Operations Dept, Estland and 15th Armies; commander, 16th Army, then chief of staff, Southern Group of Seventh Army; after Civil War at Red Army headquarters; chief of staff, Western Mil Distr; asst commander, Leningrad Mil Distr; commandant, Karelian Fortified Area; Sov mil attaché to Japan; 1937 arrested by NKVD; *Died*: 1937 in imprisonment; posthumously rehabilitated.

KUKLEV, Ivan Abramovich (1889-1967) Govt official; CP member from 1905; *Born*: 25 Oct 1889; *Career*: from 1904 active in revol movement; during 1907 Revol organized workers' battle squads at a factory in vil Kokhma; 1907 arrested; 1908 sentenced to 20 years' hard labor; released after 1917 Feb Revol; from 1918 in Red Army on Southern Front and at Perekop; from 1921 dept head, 2nd Infantry Div of All-Russian Cheka in Ukr; from 1922 mil and Party work; from 1928 mil prosecutor; from 1953 pensioner; *Died*: 26 Oct 1967.

KUKLIN, Georgiy Osipovich (1903-1939) Russian writer; *Born*: 25 May 1903 in vil Ignat'yevo, Irkutsk Province; *Educ*: 1925 grad Leningrad Univ; 1926 first work printed; member, *Pereval* (The Pass) lit group; took part in trips by writers' brigades to Karelia, the Kuzbass, Chuvashia, etc; arrested by State Security organs; *Publ*: novelette *Kratkosrochniki* (The Short-Termers) (1929); novels: *Na gore* (On the Mountain) (1932); *Uchitelya* (The Teachers) (1935); children's stories *Derevenskiye rebyata* (Village Lads) (1926); stories *Nepredvidennyye zapisi* (Unforeseen Records) (1931); novelettes *Shkola* (The School) (1931); *Died:* 9 Nov 1939 in imprisonment in Krasnoyarsk; posthumously rehabilitated.

KUKLINSKIY, Sergey Ivanovich (1900-1967) Artist; *Born*: 1900; *Educ*: grad Moscow's Stroganov Art College; *Career*: 1918 volunteered for Red Army; Nov 1920 took part in the storming of Perekop as a member of the signals unit of the 52th Infantry Div; 1921-22 participated in All-Russian competition to design the Order of the Red Banner of Labor; 20 Mar 1922 the drawing of the order which Kuklinskiy submitted was approved by the Competition Commission of the All-Russian Centr Exec Comt; Kuklinskiy, as the designer, was asked to supervise the casting of the first models; this model of the order was used until 1933; *Died*: 18 Jan 1967.

KUKUSHKIN, Stepan Mikhaylovich (1903-1964) Party official; specialist in Party history; prof; CP member from 1930; *Born*: 1903, son of a peasant; *Educ*: 1923 grad Biysk Teachers' Training Technicum; 1929 grad 2nd Moscow Univ; *Career*: until 1938 school-teacher; from 1938 head, Propaganda and Agitation Dept, Proletarian Rayon CPSU(B) Comt, Moscow; then head, Propaganda and Agitation Dept, Moscow City CPSU(B) Comt; from 1944 dir and lecturer in Party history, Higher Party School, CC, CPSU(B); 1958-64 dep sci dir, Moscow Oblast and Moscow City CPSU Comt; wrote a number of books and pamphlets on Party history; *Died*: 12 Mar 1964 after a long illness.

KULAKOVSKIY, Aleksey Yeliseyevich (1877-1926) Yakut poet; founder of written Yakut lit; *Born*: 16 Mar 1877 in vil Baturus, Yakutia, son of a herder; *Educ*: 1897 grad Yakut Non-Classical College; *Publ*: "Are the Russians Entitled to Be Proud of Their Name? " (1897); "The Chief Merits of Pushkin's Poetry" (1897); song "The Cursing of Bayanay" (1900); poems "Portraits of Yakut Women" (1904); "The Song of a 100-Year-Old Woman" (1906); "The Miserly Rich Man" (1907); "The Gifts of the River" (1909); "The Shaman's Dream" (1910); "Cursed Before Birth" (1913); "The Onset of Summer" (1924); verse: "The Song of the Drunken Bourgeois" (1915); "A City Girl" (1916); "Vodka" (1916); "The Aeroplane" (1924); "The Army of a Snow-and-Ice Country" (1925); "An Old Man's Tale" (1924); "Collected Verse" (2 vol, 1924-25); "Material for Studying the Beliefs of the Yakuts" (1923); "Yakut Proverbs and Sayings" (1925); "The Manchars" (1945); "Articles and Material on the Yakut Language" (1946); *Died*: 6 June 1926 in Moscow.

KULAYEV, Sozyryko (Siko) Aleksandrovich (1900-1938) Ossetian writer; CP member from 1919; *Born*: Jan 1900 in vil Zgubir, son of a peasant; *Educ*: 1928 grad Timiryazev Agric Acad; *Career*: fought in the Civil War in Southern Ossetia and the Northern Caucasus; twice arrested for revol activities; during last years of his life South Ossetian Pop Comr of Educ; arrested by State Security organs; *Publ*: stories: "A Shepherd's Thoughts"; "A Highlander's Lament"; "The Second Wife"; "Thirteen"; "In a Museum"; "The Marauder"; "The Man with One Hand"; "The Iron Giant"; "Oshuak the Jew"; "The Mussa School"; "The New Road"; "Comrade Mal'tsev" (1933); novel "Osman the Tatar"; drama "A Good Start" (1930); poem "The Song of Totradze," etc; major works translated into Russian and Geo; *Died*: 1938 in imprisonment.

KULEMIN, Vasiliy Lavrent'yevich (1921-1962) Russian poet; CP member from 1942; *Born*: 9 Apr 1921 in vil Ovcharovka, now Tula oblast; *Educ*: 1951 grad Moscow Univ; *Career*: 1940 first work printed; *Publ*: verse collections: *Ot serdtsa k serdtsu* (From Heart to Heart) (1956); *Russkiye vechera* (Russian Evenings) (1957); *Ozhidaniye* (Expectation) (1959); *Oblaka* (Clouds) (1961); *Ya - malakhit* (I Am Malachite) (1961); *Vechnyy ogon'* (Eternal Fire) (1962); *Otets* (The Father) (1962); poems: *Respublika - Yunost'* (The Republic Is Youth) (1960); *Magnitogorskaya ballada* (Magnitogorsk Ballad) (1960); *Vremya polyota* (Flight Time) (1960); *Pravo na nezhnost'* (The Right to Tenderness) (1963); *Tol'ko o lyubvi k tebe* (Only for Love of Thee) (1963); *Izbrannaya lirika* (Selected Lyrics) (1964); *Died*: 2 Dec 1962.

KULESHOV, Pavel Nikolayevich (1854-1936) Zootechnician; corresp member, USSR Acad of Sci from 1928; *Born*: 27 Aug 1854; *Educ*: 1875 grad Khar'kov Veterinary Inst; 1879 grad Petrine Agric and Forestry Acad; *Career*: 1889-94 prof, Petrine Agric and Forestry Acad; from 1921 prof, Moscow Zootech Inst; summarized experience of Russian sheep breeders; developed new strain of short-fleeced sheep termed the New Caucasian Merino; wrote textbooks and guides on various aspects of animal-breeding; *Publ: Teoreticheskiye raboty po plemyennomu zhivotnovodstvu* (Theoretical Works on Pedigree Animal-Breeding) (1947); coauthor, *Konevodstvo* (Horse-Breeding) (1933); *Svinovodstvo* (Pig-Breeding) (10th ed, 1930); *Krupnyy rogatyy skot* (Cattle) (7th ed, 1925); *Metody plemyennogo razvedeniya domashnikh zhivotnykh* (Methods of the Pedigree Breeding of Domestic Animals) (2nd ed, 1932); *Vybor po ekster'yeru loshadey, skota, ovets i sviney* (Selecting Horses, Cattle, Sheep and Hogs on Their Outward Points) (1937); *Rabochaya loshad'* (The Work-Horse) (3rd ed, 1926); *Grubosherstnoye ovtsevodstvo* (Coarse-Fleece Sheep-Raising) (3rd ed, 1925); *Myasosherstnoye ovtsevodstvo* (Meat and Fleece Sheep-Raising) (1933); *Died*: 5 Oct 1936.

KULIK, Ivan Yulianovich (pseudonyms: R. ROLINATO; Vasil' ROLENKO) (1897-1941) Ukr writer and critic; Party and govt official; CP member from 1914; *Born*: 26 Jan 1897, son of a teacher; *Educ*: studied at Odessa Art College; *Career*: 1914 emigrated to USA, where he was employed as an unskilled worker and took part in activities of RSDRP; 1917 returned to Ukr, where he took part in Oct Revol and fought in Civil War; from 1917 member, Main Comt, Ukr Soc-Democratic Party; member, Kiev Mil-Revol Comt; helped to establish Sov rule in Kremenchug and Uman'; 1918 first work published; from 1919 Collegium member, Pop Comrt of For Affairs; 1919-20 did underground Party work in West Ukr; 1923 joined *Gart* Proletarian Writers' Org; 1924-26 Sov consul in Canada; from 1927 member, All-Ukr Union of Proletarian Writers'; ed, journal *Chervonyy shlyakh*; from 1934 chm, Ukr Writers' Union; from 1937 member, CC, CP Ukr; member, All-Ukr Centr Exec Comt; subjected to reprisals by State Security organs; *Publ*: verse collections: *Moi kolomiyki* (My West-Ukrainian Dances) (1921); *Vyzdorovleniye* (Regeneration) (1923); *V okruzhenii* (Encircled) (1927); poem *Chyornaya epopeya* (Black Epic) (1919); verse collection *Vozmuzhaniye* (Maturation) (1935); helped compile and translate *Antologiya amerikanskoy poezii* (An Anthology of American Poetry) (1928); translated verse by A. Akopyan, E. Bagritskiy, N. Baratashvili, N. Tikhonov, B. Yasenskiy, etc; *Died*: 14 Oct 1941 in imprisonment; posthumously rehabilitated.

KULIK, Leonid Alekseyevich (1883-1942) Mineralogist; specialist on meteorites; pioneer of Sov meteorite studies; cand CP member from 1941; *Born*: 31 Aug 1883 in Tartu, son of a physician; *Educ*: 1924 grad Leningrad Univ; *Career*: studied circumstances involved in the fall of many meteorites; greatly expanded USSR Acad of Sci meteorite collection; 1921-22 directed meteorite expedition to check the USSR Acad of Sci's reports on fallen meteorites in the USSR; 1927-30 and 1938-39 headed expedition to study the fall of the Tungus meteorite; at start of WW 2 joined Civil Defense unit; wounded and taken prisoner by Germans; *Publ: Dannyye po tungusskomu meteoritu k 1939 godu* (Data on the Tungus Meteorite up to 1939); *Kamennyy meteorit "Zhigaylovka"* (The "Zhigaylovka" Stone Meteorite) (1935); *Died*: 1942 in German captivity.

KULIKOVSKIY, Grigoriy Grigor'yevich (1890-1955) Otolaryngologist; Dr of Med from 1935; prof; maj-gen, Med Corps; *Born*: 1890; *Educ*: 1916 grad Med Fac, Moscow Univ; *Career*: after grad joined Army Med Corps; 1922-24 detached to Otolaryngological Clinic, Leningrad Mil Med Acad for specialist training; from 1924 head, Otolaryngological Dept, 1st Moscow Communist Hospital (now Burdenko Main Mil Hospital); 1935 defended doctor's thesis on osteophony, which contained new concepts in the physiology of hearing; 1941 prof, Chair of Ear, Nose and Throat Diseases, Leningrad Mil Med Acad; from 1942 Chief Otolaryngologist, Sov Army; did major research on aviation med; made original studies of vestibular training for pilots, pilot selection and paratroop training; developed new techniques for the treatment of ear, nose and throat wounds and shell-shock; designed several ear-protectors (a helmet-liner, a pilot's head-band, etc) and otolaryngological instruments (a needle for puncturing the maxillary sinus, a needle for suturing the palatine arch and a simplified diaphanoscope for examining the frontal sinus); *Publ*: doctor's thesis *K voprosu o mekhaniszme kostnoy provodimosti* (The Mechanism of Bone Conduction) (1935); *Vestibulyarnaya trenirovka lyotchika* (Vestibular Training for Pilots) (1939); *Otorinolaringologiya dlya voyskovogo vracha* (Otolaryngology for the Military Surgeon) (1940); *Istoricheskiy obzor razvitiya otolaringoligicheskoy pomoshchi ranenym, bol'nym i kontuzhenym* (A Historical Review of the Otolaryngological Treatment of Wounded, Sick and Shell-Shocked Servicemen) (1951); *Obshchaya kharakteristika raneniy nosa, gorla i ukha i kontuzionnykh porazheniy* (A General Description of Ear, Nose and Throat Wounds and Shell-Shock Injuries); *Died*: 1955.

KULISH, Mykola (Nikolay Gur'yevich) (1892-1937) Ukr writer; CP member from 1919; *Born*: 6 Dec 1892 in vil Chaplinka, Kherson Province, son of a peasant; *Educ*: completed high-school correspondence course; *Career*: 1915-17 fought in WW 1; active in 1917 Oct Revol and Civil War; member, Olyoshka (now Tsuryupinsk) Revol Comt; from 1923 inspector of soc training, Odessa; from 1925 inspector of soc training in Khar'kov; from 1925 concentrated exclusively on lit work; 1924-25 member, *Gart* lit assoc; 1925, together with Khvylyovyy and others, left *Gart* and joined *Vaplite* lit assoc; contributed to almanach *Literaturnyy yarmarok*; active in *Korelis* playwrights' soc; worked for *Berezil'* Theater; 1928, together with Khvylyovyy and co, founded new org "Proletfront," which joined the Federation of Proletarian Writers; accused of nationalist deviation and distorting Sov reality by Party critics; 1934 arrested by Sov Security organs; *Publ*: plays: "97" (1924); "Commune in the Steppe" (1925); "Sonata Pathetique" (1931); "Maklena Grasa" (1932); "Farewell, Village!" (1933); comedies: "How Guska Died" (1932); "Mina Mazaylo" (1929); tragedies: "The Folk Malachi" (1927); *Died*: 1937 in imprisonment; posthumously rehabilitated.

KULISHENKO, Grigoriy Yakimovich (1903-1939) Fighter-pilot; *Born*: 1903 in vil Cherepyn', Cherkassy Oblast, son of a peasant; *Educ*: 1934 grad air force college; *Career*: prior to joining Red Army, worked at sugar refinery; June 1939 volunteered for service in China, where he commanded a squadron of Sov pilots; shot down six Japanese planes; *Died*: 14 Oct 1939 killed in air battle; buried at Wanxian.

KULISHER, Anna Semyonovna (1888-1961) Russian translator; *Born*: 1 May 1888 in Petersburg, son of an office worker; *Educ*: grad History Fac, Brussels Univ and Leningrad Inst of New Languages; *Career*: 1928 began lit translating work; translated into Russian: A. Segers' "A Prized Head" (1935); Thomas Mann's stories and articles (1938 and 1960); Stefan Zweig's "Magellan's Exploit" (1947); Alphonse Daudet's stories (1948); Stendhal's "Life of Napoleon" (1950); Balzac's novelettes (1951); Victor Hugo's "The History of a Crime" (1954); Forster's "Paris Sketches" (1956); de Musset's novellae (1957); also translated Sov Russian works into German; edited German ed of Gorky's collected works (5 vol, 1934-37); *Died*: 10 Jan 1961 in Leningrad.

KULIYEV, Mustafa Zakariya ogly (1893-1938) Azer politician, publicist, critic and theater historian; CP member from 1918; *Born*: 1893 in Nukha, son of a merchant; *Educ*: studied at Kiev Univ; *Career*: while a student joined revol movement; 1918 joined RCP(B); member, Moslem Section, Kiev RCP(B) Comt; 1922-28 Azer Pop Comr of Educ; 1923–26 ed, journal "Enlightenment and Culture"; wrote works intended to bring modern history of Azer in line with Marxist tenets; arrested by State Security organs; *Publ*: "October and Turkic Literature" (1930); "Modern Turkic Literature" (1926); "Proletarian Literature" (1928); "Form and Content in Literature" (1930); "The Work of M. F. Akhundov" (1928); *Died*: 1938 in imprisonment.

KUL'KOV, Mikhail Maksimovich (1891-1939) Party official; CP member from 1915; *Born*: 9 May 1891 in vil Konstantinovo, Moscow Province, son of a worker; *Educ*: 1903 grad zemstvo school; from 1926 took Marxism-Leninism courses in Moscow; *Career*: 1903 started work at age 12; from 1905 active in revol movement; several times arrested; Apr 1917 helped found

Bryansk RSDRP org; 1918 dep chm, Bryansk Province Cheka and head, Internal Management Dept, Bryansk Province Exec Comt; 1919 elected chm, Bryansk Province RCP(B) Comt; 1920 chm, Bezhitsa Sov; from late 1920 member, Zamoskvorech'ye Rayon Party Comt; 1924-25 worked for Centr Control Commission, Workers and Peasants' Inspection; after completing Marxism-Leninism courses appointed CPSU(B) Centr Control Commission's dep plen with Centr Asian Bureau, CC, CPSU(B); member, Turkm Centr Control Commission; 1929-30 first secr, Kir Oblast CPSU(B) Comt; member, Centr Asian Bureau, CC, CPSU(B); 1931-35 secr, Zamoskvorech'ye, then Proletarskiy Rayon Moscow Party Comt; 1935-37 secr, Moscow City CPSU(B) Comt; from Feb 1937 plen, Azov-Black Sea Kray Party Control Commission; at 13th Congress elected member, CPSU(B) Centr Control Commission; at 18th Congress elected cand member, CC, CPSU(B); 1937 dep, USSR Supr Sov of 1st convocation; Oct 1938 arrested by State Security organs; 1965 a street in Bryansk was named after him; *Died*: 1939 in imprisonment; posthumously rehabilitated.

KULYABKO, Aleksey Aleksandrovich (1866-1930) Physiologist; emeritus prof, Tomsk Univ; *Born*: 27 Mar 1866 in Omsk; *Educ*: 1888 grad Natural Sci Dept, Fac of Physics and Mathematics, Petersburg Univ; 1893 grad Med Fac, Tomsk Univ; also grad Berlin and Leipzig Univ; *Career*: worked at I. M. Sechenov and F. V. Ovsyannikov's physiological laboratories; specialized in reanimation; Aug 1902 reactivated the heart of an infant 20 hours after death from pneumonia; 1903-24 head, Chair of Normal Physiology, Med Fac, Tomsk Univ; also taught physiology at Siberian Higher Women's Courses, Tomsk; conducted numerous experiments on the reanimation of warm-blooded animals; succeeded in reactivating the isolated and frozen hearts of animals as much as seven days after death; together with the physiologist Kodis froze a rabbit's heart solid and elicited contractions of the cardiac muscle after gradual thawing; also experimented successfully with restoration of the vital functions of the cerebrum of ganoids and Osteichthyes, whose isolated heads he reanimated by perfusion with Locke's solution; also studied the pathogenesis of petroleum product poisoning and devised means of prevention; attended various int congresses and was a member of numerous sci soc; his research was continued by F. A. Andreyev, I. A. Birillo, S. S. Bryukhonenko, etc; *Publ: K voprosu o zhyolchnykh kapillyarakh* (The Bile Ducts) (1897); *Opyty ozhivleniya serdtsa* (Experiments in Cardiac Reactivation) (1902); *Dal'neyshiye opyty ozhivleniya serdtsa* (More Experiments in Cardiac Reactivation); *Otets russkoy fiziologii. Pamyati professora I. M. Sechenova* (The Father of Russian Physiology. In Memory of Professor I. M. Sechenov) (1916); *Opyty ozhivleniya serdtsa i golovy i ikh znacheniye* (Experiment of Cardiac and Cerebral Reactivation and Their Significance) (1928); *Died:* 6 Aug 1930.

KULYABKO, P. I. (Party names: INSAROVA; MYSH') (1874-1959) Party official; CP member from 1898; *Born*: 1874; *Career*: 1893 began revol activities in Samara, where she met Lenin, Sklyarenko, Lalayanets and other members of a Marxist circle; helped establish Yekaterinoslav League for the Liberation of the Working Class; 1900 exiled to Eastern Siberia; summer 1902 emigrated to Geneva; member, For League of Russian Revol Soc-Democrats; after 2nd RSDRP Congress sided with Bolsheviks; helped prepare 3rd Party Congress; after 1917 Oct Revol Party work; during WW 2 polit work in Leningrad; *Died*: 1959.

KUN, Bela (1886-1939) Hungarian revol; CP member from 1916; *Born*: 20 Feb 1886 in vil Lele, son of a country clerk; *Career*: from the age of 16 active in workers' movement; 1902 joined Hungarian Soc-Democratic Party; propaganda work among students in Budapest, where he helped found Marxist student org; 1905 instigated strikes which resulted in clashes with the police, for which he was repeatedly arrested; 1914 during WW 1 conscripted into the army; 1916 in Russia as a prisoner of war; 1916 in prisoner-of-war camp in Tomsk joined local RSDRP(B) org; conducted Soc-Democratic propaganda among prisoners of war; after 1917 Feb Revol worked for Tomsk Province RSDRP(B) Comt, then for Bolshevik journal *Sibirskiy rabochiy* and weekly *Znamya revolyutsii*; after 1917 Oct Revol went to Petrograd where he became acquainted with Lenin; co-ed, Hungarian newspaper "Nemzetközi Szocialista," then newspaper "Szocialis forradalom," which was distributed among prisoners of war; Mar 1918 founded Hungarian Group of RCP(B); chm, Centr Federation of For RCP(B) Groups, which was founded in May 1918; led int Red Army squads; fought in the defense of Petrograd and at Narva; helped crush Socialist-Revol revolt in Moscow; helped spread propaganda among German and Austro-Hungarian troops in the Ukr; Nov 1918 returned to Hungary illegally and helped other Hungarian Communists found the Hungarian Communist Party; Feb 1919 arrested with a group of other Communists; imprisoned until 21 Mar 1919, when the Hungarian Sov Republic was proclaimed; from the first days of the Sov regime in Hungary Pop Comr of For Affairs, then Pop Comr of Mil Affairs; after the defeat of the Hungarian Sov Republic, emigrated to Austria where he was interned; 1920 went to Sov Russia and fought against the White Guards in the Crimea; member, Revol Mil Council, Southern Front; chm, Crimean Revol Comt; 1921 in Germany; helped stage Mar proletariat demonstrations; 1921-23 exec Party work in the Urals; Presidium member, All-Union Centr Exec Comt; Sept 1923 appointed CPSU(B) CC plen with the CC, Russian Komsomol; active in Comintern; from 1921 member, Comintern Exec Comt; at the same time head, Hungarian Communist Party; 1928 arrested in Vienna but soon released; returned to the USSR and continued polit activities; Presidium member, Comintern Exec Comt; wrote works on the history ot the int workers' movement; 1937 arrested by State Security organs; *Publ: Uroki proletarskoy revolyutsii v Vengrii* (Lessons of the Proletarian Revolution in Hungary) (1960); *Awards*: Order of the Red Banner (1927); *Died*: 30 Nov 1939 in imprisonment; posthumously rehabilitated.

KUNIKOV, Tsezar' L'vovich (1909-1943) Major; WW 2 hero; *Born*: 1909 in Baku, son of an eng; *Educ*: 1935 grad tech inst; *Pos*: 1935-41 eng; 1941-43 comr, then commander of a river gunboat unit on the Don River and in the Sea of Azov, then commander of an amphibious marine unit; *Career*: in the early hours of 4 Feb 1943 in the course of a poorly planned amphibious operation near Novorossiysk his marine unit of 870 men landed successfully near the vil of Stanichka, captured a small beachhead and held it for three days until reinforcements arrived; fall 1943 this beachhead played a decisive role in the liberation of Novorossiysk; *Awards*: Hero of the Sov Union (posthumously); Order of Aleksandr Nevskiy; *Died*: 12 Feb 1943 killed in action on the Stanichka beachhead; a monument to him has been erected in Novorossiysk.

KUPALA, Yanka (real name: LUTSEVICH, Ivan Dominikovich) (1882-1942) Bel poet; Pop Poet of the Bel SSR from 1925; member, Bel Acad of Sci from 1928; member, USSR Acad of Sci from 1929; member, Bel Writers' Union from 1934; *Born*: 7 July 1882 in vil Vyazynka, formerly Minsk Province, son of a landless peasant; *Educ*: 1898 grad Beloruchi Pop College; 1909-13 studied on Chernyayev Educ Courses in Petersburg; *Career*: from 1902, after his father's death, worked as itinerant teacher, investigator's clerk in Radoshkovichi, then brewery laborer; 1908-09 worked for the Bel newspaper *Nasha niva* and for the *Znaniye* Library in Vilnius; from 1909 under the patronage of Prof B. I. Epimakh-Shipila in Petersburg; 1914-15 ed, newspaper *Nasha niva* in Vilnius; 1915 evacuated to Russia, where he attended the Shanyavskiy Free Univ in Moscow; 1916-18 with road-building gang of the home guard in Minsk, Polotsk and Smolensk; from 1919 in Minsk; active in Bel lit life; worked at the Inst of Bel Culture, then at the Bel Acad of Sci; 1905 first work published; pioneer of modern Bel fiction; wrote mainly about Bel soc, historical and modern nat and polit subjects; welcomed and supported socialist changes, although he repeatedly spoke out against "proletarization" of peoples and forcible collectivization; 1927 joined *Polymya* lit assoc, which was loyal to the Sov regime; late 1920's subjected to Party criticism and even arrest; from 1933 turned to purely Sov subjects and wrote various odes in honor of kolkhozes, Stalin, Voroshilov, Sov Constitution, elections, etc; from 1941 in Moscow, then settled in vil Pechishchi near Kazan'; Presidium member, Pan-Slavic Comt; involved in anti-German propaganda; *Publ*: poems: "In Winter" (1906); "The Burial Mound," "The Psaltery Player," "Excerpt From a Poem" (1910); "Bandarouna," "Yana and I," "The Lion's Grave" (1913); "The Abandoned Violin," "Christmas Eve," "The Night of Kupala," "The Sorcerer," "Parents' Day" (1908-13); "Nameless" (1924); "Above the Oressa River" (1933); "Taras' Fate" (1939); dramatic poems: "An Age-Old Song" (1910); "Dream on a Burial Mound" (1910); "Lodgings" (1912); plays: "Paulinka" (1912); "The Spongers" (1913); "The Ravaged Nest" (1913); "The Local People" (1922); collected verse: "The Fife" (1908); "The Psaltery Player"; "The Paths of Life" (1913); "The Inheritance" (1922); "Nameless" (1925); "The Fable Song" (1930); "Falling Blossoms" (1930); "Song to Construction"

(1936); "To Decorated Belorussia" (1937); "To the Young Eagles" (1940); "From the Heart" (1940); "My Land" (1958); "Verse and Poems" (1958); "Collected Works" (6 vol, 1925-32); "Selected Works" (1952); "Poems and Plays"; "Collected Works" (6 vol, 1961-63); many of Kupala's works which were banned in the USSR were published in Munich in 1955 in the anthology *Spadchyna* (Heritage); *Awards*: Order of Lenin (1939); Stalin Prize, 1st Class (1941), for collection of odes in honor of Stalin entitled "From the Heart"; *Died*: 28 June 1942 committed suicide by throwing himself out of a window of the Hotel Moskva in Moscow.

KUPALOV, Pyotr Stepanovich (1888-1964) Physiologist; Dr of Med; prof; member, USSR Acad of Med Sci from 1946; Hon Sci Worker of RSFSR from 1943; *Born*: 13 Oct 1888 in vil Lipinishki, Vitebsk Province, now Lat SSR; *Educ*: 1915 grad Petrograd Mil Med Acad; *Career*: specialized in physiology under Acad I. P. Pavlov; 1925-36 sci asst to Pavlov, Physiological Dept, Pavlov All-Union Inst of Experimental Med (now Inst of Experimental Med, USSR Acad of Sci); 1926, under Pavlov's supervision, conducted research on the functions of the cerebral hemispheres which provided the basis for the theory of the dynamic stereotype; 1928–30 did research at Prof Hill's Physiological Laboratory, London; 1931–52 head, Chair of Normal Physiology, 1st Leningrad Med Inst and head, Physiological Laboratory, State Roentgenological Inst; from 1936 member, British Royal Soc of Physiologists; 1936-64 head, Physiological Dept and sci dir, Pavlov All-Union Inst of Experimental Med; 1949 published Pavlov's *Lektsii po fiziologii* (Lectures on Physiology); 1949-64 did research on the analytic and synthetic activity of the cerebral cortex in animals under natural behavioral conditions; designed special chamber to study the situational reflexes of dogs in various spatial conditions; from 1950 chm, Leningrad Soc of Physiologists, Biochemists and Pharmacologists; 1959-64 chm, Centr Council, Pavlov All-Union Physiological Soc; organizer and exec secr, 1st All-Union Congress of Physiologists; delivered papers at 13th, 15th, 19th and 20th Int Congresses of Physiologists and at 1st Int Neurological Congress, Brussels; devised improved methods and apparatus for studying conditioned reflexes, including sound-proof chambers and equipment for recording higher nervous processes; also studied the functional structure of cortical excitation and contributed to the further development of Pavlov's theory of neuroses; attributed great significance in the development of neuroses to inertness and inadequate regeneration of the cortical cells, pathological irradiation of the process of inhibition, disturbance of the guard mechanism, explosivity and new pathogenic factors; added considerably to knowledge of the tonic reflexes of the spinal cord; also did research on the effect of ionizing radiation on the central nervous system in animals; member, ed bd, journals *Byulleten' eksperimental'noy biologii i meditsiny* and *Fiziologicheskiy zhurnal SSSR imeni I. M. Sechenova*; chief ed, *Zhurnal vysshey nervnoy deyatel'nosti imeni I. P. Pavlova*; co-ed, physiology section, *Bol'shaya meditsinskaya entsiklopediya* (Large Medical Encyclopedia) (2nd ed); wrote some 150 works; *Publ: O vliyanii sistemy ritmicheskikh uslovnykh refleksov na obrazovaniye i sushchestvovaniye novogo uslovnogo refleksa* (The Effect of a System of Rhythmic Conditioned Reflexes on the Formation and Existence of a New Conditioned Reflex) (1933); *Fiziologicheskoye izucheniye vysshikh proyavleniy zhiznennoy deyatel'nosti zhivotnykh* (The Physiological Study of Higher Aspects of Vital Activity in Animals) (1946); *Ob eksperimental'nykh nevrozakh u zhivotnykh* (Experimentally Induced Neuroses in Animals) (1952); *Nekotoryye problemy fiziologii vysshey nervnoy deyatel'nosti* (Some Problems of the Physiology of Higher Nervous Acitity) (1956), etc; *Awards*: Order of Lenin; Pavlov Gold Medal, etc; *Died*: 17 Mar 1964 in Leningrad.

KUPER, Emil' Al'bertovich (1887-1960) Conductor; *Born*: 13 Dec 1877; *Educ*: 1891 grad violin and composition classes, Odessa Music College; *Career*: until 1898 performed as violinist; taught himself conducting; 1899 toured various Russian cities with Chaliapin and Sobinov as opera conductor; worked in Rostov, Kiev and Petersburg; 1907-09 in Moscow, first at Solodovnikov Theater, then at Zimin Opera Theater, where he conducted opera "Boris Godunov," premiere of opera *Zolotoy petushok* (The Golden Cockerel) and first Russian production of Wagners "Die Meistersaenger von Nuernberg"; 1909-14 took part in Diaghilev's Paris and London tours - "Russian Seasons Abroad"; 1911 conducted first performance of "Khovanshchina" in Paris; 1913 conducted first performance of *Pskovityanka* (The Woman of Pskov) in London; 1910-19 conductor, Bolshoy Theater; 1919-20 conductor, Petrograd Acad Opera and Ballet Theater; from 1918 prof, Moscow Conservatory; from 1921 artistic dir, Moscow Philharmonic; 1924 emigrated from USSR; *Publ: Kratkiy obzor moyey muzykal'noy deyatel'nosti* (A Brief Review of My Musical Career) (1923); *Died*: 16 Nov 1960.

KUPREYANOV, Nikolay Nikolayevich (1894-1933) Graphic artist; prof; *Born*: 16 July 1894; *Educ*: grad Petersburg Univ; studied art at Petrov-Vodkin and Kardovskiy's studios and xylographic techniques at Ostroumova-Lebedeva's studio; *Career*: 1916 made first woodcuts; 1917 held first exhibition; 1921-26 prof, Higher Art Technique Studios; 1926-30 prof, Higher Art Technique Inst; also prof, Polygraphic Inst; his works are exhibited in the Tret'yakov Gallery and the Pushkin Museum of Fine Arts in Moscow, the Lit Museum, the Red Army Museum and the State Russian Museum in Leningrad and in the British Museum and South Kensington Museum in London; *Works*: engravings "Ironing Woman" (1921); "The Cruiser Aurora" (1923); ink drawings "The Herds" (1926-29); "Evenings in Selishche" (1926-29); "The Railroads" (1926-27); lithograph series "The Baltic Fleet"; illustrations for Gorky's *Mat'* (Mother) and *Delo Artamonovykh* (The Artamonov Affair) (1930); for Fadeyev's *Razgrom* (Rout) (1932); for Nekrasov's *Dedushka Mazay* (Grandfather Mazay) (1933); *Awards*: Gold Medal of Int Exhibition, Paris (1925); *Died*: 1933 drowned while swimming.

KUPRIN, Aleksandr Ivanovich (1870-1938) Russian writer; *Born*: 7 Sept 1870 in Narovchat, now Penza Oblast, son of an official; *Educ*: 1890 grad Alexandrine Cadets College; *Career*: 1877-80, after death of his father, raised in Razumovskiy Boarding School, Moscow; 1880-90 at mil training establishments; 1890-94 served with Russian Army in Podol'sk Province; 1894 abandoned mil service and tried a variety of professions; from 1901 lived mainly in Petersburg; from 1903 worked for "Knowledge" Publ House, founded by Gorky; 1919 left Russia with his family and lived mainly in Paris; wrote anti-Sov articles and pamphlets for Russian emigre press, then abandoned politics; spring 1937, seriously ill, returned to USSR; began writing back in Cadet College; wrote many stories, essays, novelettes and several novels; specialized in essay form; exponent of critical realism in Russian lit; *Publ*: novel *Poyedinok* (The Duel) (1905); *Sobraniye sochineniy* (Collected Works) (12 vol, 1909-16); *Sobraniye sochineniy* (Collected Works) (12 vol, 1921-25), in Berlin; novel *Yunkera* (The Cadets) (1928); novel *Zhaneta* (Jeannette) (1932-33); *Sobraniye sochineniy* (Collected Works) (6 vol, 1957-58); *Sobraniye sochineniy* (Collected Works) (9 vol, 1964); *Died*: 25 Aug 1938 in Leningrad.

KUPRIYANOV, Pyotr Andreyevich (1893-1963) Surgeon; Dr of Med; prof from 1930; lt-gen, Med Corps; member, USSR Acad of Med Sci from 1944; Hon Sci Worker of RSFSR from 1942; *Born*: 7 Feb 1893; *Educ*: 1915 grad Petrograd Mil Med Acad; *Career*: 1915-17 mil surgeon in Russian Army and surgical intern, S. P. Fyodorov and V. A. Oppel's clinics, Petrograd Mil Med Acad; 1918-24 lecturer, asst prof, then assoc prof, 1924-38 senior intern and head, Surgical Dept, Leningrad Mil Hospital; 1926-29 assoc prof, 1930-49 prof and head, Chair of Operative Surgery and Topographical Anatomy, 1st Leningrad Med Inst; 1938-40 chief surgeon, Leningrad Mil Distr; served in Finno-Sov War; 1940-49 head, Chair of Fac Surgery, 1st Leningrad Med Inst; 1941-45 front-line surgeon; 1944-63 dir, 2nd Fac Surgical Clinic and Surgical Clinic, Fac of Postgrad Med Training, Leningrad Mil Med Acad; 1944-50 vice-pres, USSR Acad of Med Sci; ed, section on thoracic wounds, multivol *Opyt sovetskoy meditsiny v Velikoy Otechestvennoy Voyne* (Soviet Medicine in the Great Fatherland War); chm and hon member, All-Union Soc of Surgeons; hon member, Pirogov Surgical Soc, Leningrad; member, ed bd, and co-ed, surgery section, *Bol'shaya meditsinskaya entsiklopediya* (Large Medical Encyclopedia) (2nd ed); member, ed bd, journal *Vestnik khirurgii imeni N. N. Grekova;* member, ed council, journal *Khirurgiya*; 1955 attended 16th Int Surgical Congress, Copenhagen, and visited surgical clinics in Norway and Sweden; 1957 attended 3rd Int Surgical Congress, Turin; from 1959 chm, Commission for Competitive Surgical Prizes, USSR Acad of Med Sci; from 1961 hon member, Soc of Polish Surgeons; pioneered Sov lung and thoracic surgery; was one of first Sov surgeons to treat congenital and acquired heart diseases; introduced hypothermy in Sov clinical practice and performed open-heart operations; trained many top surgeons, including Professors M. S.

Grigor'yev, I. S. Kolesnikov, A. P. Kolesov, V. I. Kolesov, S. L. Libov and P. K. Romanov; the clinic of the Leningrad Mil Med Acad at which he worked now bears his name; wrote over 100 works; *Publ: Kratkiy kurs voyenno-polevoy khirurgii* (A Short Course on Field Surgery) (1942); *Atlas ognestrel'nykh raneniy* (An Atlas of Gunshot Wounds) (1946-55); *Sovremennyye problemy grudnoy khirurgii* (Current Problems of Thoracic Surgery) (1954); *Gnoynyye zabolevaniya plevry i lyogkikh* (Suppurative Diseases of the Pleura and the Lungs) (1955); *Posleoperatsionnoye vedeniye bol'nykh, osnovannoye na Pavlovskoy fiziologii* (The Postoperative Care of Patients Based on Pavlovian Physiology) (1956); *Problema iskusstvennoy gipotermii v khirurgii serdtsa* (The Problem of Artificial Hypothermy in Heart Surgery) (1956); *Yavlyayetsya li vyalo protekayushchiy revmokardit protivopokazaniyem k mitral'noy komissurotomii?* (Is Sluggish Rheumocarditis a Contraindication to Mitral Commissurotomy?) (1957); *Nekotoryye voprosy grudnoy khirurgii* (Some Problems of Thoracic Surgery) (1959); *Zaprosy sovremennoy anesteziologii k farmakologii i farmatsevticheskoy khimii* (Modern Anaesthesiology's Demands on Pharmacology and Pharmaceutical Chemistry) (1960); *Awards*: two Orders of Lenin; Lenin Prize (1961); five other orders and medals; *Died*: 13 Mar 1963 in Leningrad.

KURAKO, Mikhail Konstantinovich (1872-1920) Metallurgist; blast-furnace specialist; CP member; *Born*: 23 Sept 1872 in Kozelya, now Mogilev Oblast; *Educ*: self-educated; *Career*: from 1890 worked as roller, gas fitter and furnace chief at various metallurgical plants in south of Russia; taught himself physics, chemistry, laboratory techniques, several for languages, history and philosophy; also took an interest in soc and econ problems; after acquiring a thorough knowledge of blast-furnace techniques was made mang of the blast-furnace plant at Kramatorsk Metallurgical Works; 1905 exiled to Vologda Province for involvement in revol and spent two years there, after which he was kept under permanent police surveillance; 1908 returned to Donbas; at outbreak of 1917 Oct Revol joined sov of workers and peasants' dep at Yuzov Plant, Donbas; later that year began planning and construction of Kuznetsk Metallurgical Plant; made a number of improvements to existing blast-furnaces; 1903 designed first Russian inclined elevator with automatic distribution of furnace charge; developed original design for a blast-furnace hearth which is now in common use in USSR; introduced improved blast box and four types of standardized section-shaped refractory bricks for furnace repair work; trained numerous blast-furnace eng; *Died*: 2 Feb 1920.

KURASHOV, Sergey Vladimirovich (1910-1965) Health service official; USSR Min of Health from 1959; Cand of Med; assoc prof; corresp member, USSR Acad of Med Sci from May 1965; CP member from 1938; *Born*: 1 Oct 1910; *Educ*: 1931 grad Med Fac, Kazan' Univ; *Career*: 1929-31 med orderly; 1931-41 intern, asst prof, then assoc prof, Psychiatric Clinic, Kazan' Med Inst, where he defended his cand thesis; simultaneously held admin posts in Tatar Pop Comrt of Health; 1935-36 chief physician, Kazan' Clinical Hospital; 1936-41 chief physician, Kazan' Psychiatric Hospital; 1941-42 dir, Kazan' Med Inst; 1942-46 RSFSR Dep Pop Comr of Health; 1946-51 Collegium member and head, Main Health Resort and Sanatorium Bd, USSR Min of Health; 1950-53 dep dir, Centr Inst of Postgrad Med Training, Moscow; 1953-55 head, Main Bd of Training Establishments, USSR Min of Health and USSR Dep Min of Health; 1954-61 chief ed, journal *Zdorov'ye*; 1955-65 head, Chair of Health Service Org, 1st Moscow Med Inst; 1959-65 USSR Min of Health; 1961-65 cand member, CC, CPSU; dep, RSFSR Supr Sov of 1955 and 1959 convocations; dep, USSR Supr Sov of 1958 and 1962 convocations; 1954 led Sov med deleg to England; 1957 attended Int Congress on Soc Med, Vienna; 1959 attended 4th Congress of Ministers of Health of the Socialist Countries, Sofia; 1960 led Sov med deleg to Cambodia, Norway and Sweden; lectured at Carolinian Hospital, Stockholm; 1960 also led deleg to 13th World Health Assembly, Geneva; 1961 led deleg to 14th World Health Assembly, Delhi and attended Congress of Ministers of Health of the Socialist Countries, Budapest; 1962 chm, 15th World Health Assembly, Geneva; ed, section on health service org, *Bol'shaya meditsinskaya entsiklopediya* (Large Medical Encyclopedia) (2nd ed); member, ed council, *Zhurnal nevropatologii i psikhiatrii imeni S. S. Korsakova*; the Kazan' Med Inst now bears his name; *Publ: Kurortnyye bogatstva nashey Rodiny* (Our Country's Health Resorts) (1950); *Sorok let zdravookhraneniya Rossiyskoy Federatsii* (Forty Years of the RSFSR Health Service) (1957); *Sovetskoye zdravookhraneniye v shestoy pyatiletke* (The Soviet Health Service in the Sixth Five-Year Plan) (1957); coauthor and ed, *Kurorty SSSR* (The Health Resorts of the USSR) (2nd ed, 1961); *Bol'nichnaya pomoshch' na sovremennom etape* (The Modern Hospital Service) (1963); *Awards*: Hon Scroll of World Peace Council (1959); Order of Lenin (1960); *Died*: 27 Aug 1965 of cancer in Moscow.

KURAYEV, V.V. (1892-1938) Party and govt official; CP member from 1914; *Born*: 1892; *Career*: Party work in Petrograd and Penza, also among troops during WW 1; after 1917 Feb Revol helped found Penza Sov of Soldiers' Workers and Peasants' Dep; deleg, 1st All-Russian Congress of Soviets; member, Centr Exec Comt; after 1917 Oct Revol chm, Exec Comt, Penza Province Sov; secr, Penza Province Party Comt; 1918 took part in operations against Czechoslovak Legion; then mil polit work in Red Army; from Mar 1920 Collegium member, Pop Comrt of Agric; Presidium member, Supr Sovnarkhoz; then exec work for USSR Gosplan; arrested by State Security organs; *Died*: 1938 in imprisonment.

KURBANGALIYEV, Mukhitdin Khafizovich (1873-1941) Tatar linguist and methodologist; prof; Hon Sci Worker of Tatar ASSR; *Born*: 26 Oct 1873; *Educ*: 1895 grad Kazan' Teachers' Training School; *Career*: 1895 began to teach at rural Russo-Tatar zemstvo school, then taught Russian and Tatar in Malmyzh (now Kirov Oblast); from 1903 worked in Kazan', first as teacher then for various newspapers; helped found schools and shelters for orphans; after 1917 Oct Revol taught Tatar and Russian at primary and secondary schools, at schools for adults, teachers' training courses, and at Kazan' Teachers' Training Inst; also head, Chair of Tatar Language, Kazan' Univ; from 1940 assoc, Tatar Inst of Language, Lit and History; member, Tatar Centr Exec Comt; founder-head, Tatar United Labor Schools Bd; dep chm, Sci Center, Tatar Pop Comrt of Educ; wrote numerous works on Tatar grammar, lexicography and teaching methods; 1918 helped publish first full grammar of Tatar language; 1938 published Tatar syntax textbook for secondary schools, which ran through 20 editions; compiled Russo-Tatar and Tatar-Russian dictionaries; worked on Tatar sci terminology, Tat lit standards, principles of Tatar orthography based on Cyrillic; *Died*: 3 June 1941.

KURBANOV, Shikhali Kurbanovich (1925-1967) Party official; secr and Bureau member, CC, CP Azer from 1966; *Born*: 1925 in Baku; *Educ*: studied at Azer Teachers' Training Inst; *Career*: from 1942 in Sov Army; taught at Azer Teachers' Training Inst; 1953-61 secr, rayon Party comt, then head, Propaganda Dept, Baku City Comt and head, Propaganda Dept, CC, CP Azer; from 1961 worked for Inst of Lit and Language, Azer Acad of Sci; *Died*: 24 May 1967.

KURBAS, Aleksandr (Les') Stepanovich (1887-1942) Ukr actor and producer; Pop Artiste of the Ukr SSR from 1925; *Born*: 12 Sept 1887 in Staryy Skalat, now Ternopol' Oblast, son of an actor whose stage name was Yanovich; *Educ*: 1909 grad Fac of History and Philology, Vienna Univ; *Career*: 1909 began acting career at Khotkevich Gutsul Theater; 1910 worked at L'vov Theater of the "Russian Conversation" Assoc; 1915 with "Ternopol' Theatrical Evenings" company; 1916 at Sadovskiy Theater in Kiev; 1916 founded theater studio which developed into the "Young Theater" (1918-19); at this theater Kurbas produced Sophocles' "Oedipus Rex," Grillparzer's "Weh' dem, der lügt," Olesya's "Etudes," etc; acted at theaters in Belaya Tserkov' and Uman'; 1922 helped found "Berezil'" Theater (from 1934 Khar'kov Shevchenko Theater), which he directed until 1933; early plays were remarkable mainly for experimental stage effects; criticized for "Berezil'"Theater productions which specialized in intricate contradictions and because he opposed not only the stereotypes and clichés of the pre-revol Ukr theater but also its best realistic traditions; Kurbas sought reflection of current events in so-called "scenic compositions" and in unique dramatization as in *Haydamaki* (The Haydamaks), *Ivan Gus* after Shevchenko, "Macbeth" after Shakespeare, "Gas" after Kaiser, "Jimmy Higgins" after Sinclair, etc; completely revised all these plays; at the same time the critics recognized him as a talented producer whose plays were notable for their originality although the search for melodramatic effects and the stream of the producer's imagination often became an end in themselves and obscured the message of the play; paid much attention to casting; assembled such brilliant Ukr actors around him in the "Berezil'" Theater as: A. Buchma, N. Uzhviy, I. Mar'yanenko, V. Vasil'ko, Mr.

Krushel'nitskiy, A. Serdyuk, D. Antonovich, V. Chistyakova, V. Tyagno, L. Gakkebush, S. Fedortseva, L. Dubovik, V. Sklyarenko, etc; scripted and produced films: "Vendetta," *Makdonal'd* (MacDonald), *Arsenal'tsy* (The Arsenal Guards) and *Shvedskaya spichka* (The Swedish Match); late 1933 dismissed as director of "Berezil'" Theater and accused of nationalism; 1937 arrested by State Security organs; *Roles*: Gnat in Karpenko-Karyy's *Bestalannaya* (The Luckless Woman); Gurman in Franko's *Ukradennoye schast'ye* (Stolen Happiness); Astrov in *Dyadya Vanya* (Uncle Vanya); Khlestakov; Oedipus in Sophocles' "Oedipus Rex"; *Died*: 15 Oct 1942 in imprisonment; posthumously rehabilitated.

KURCHATOV, Igor' Vasil'yevich (1903-1960) Physicist; member, USSR Acad of Sci from 1943; threefold Hero of Socialist Labor; CP member from 1948; *Born*: 12 Jan 1903 in vil Simskiy Zavod, Ufa Province (now Sim, Chelyabinsk Oblast), son of a surveyor; *Educ*: 1923 grad Physics and Mathematics Fac, Crimean Univ, Simferopol'; *Career*: from 1924 at Magnetometeorological Observatory at Pavlovsk, near Leningrad; from 1925 at Physics Eng Inst, USSR Acad of Sci and other Acad establishments; 1927-29 also taught at Leningrad Polytech Inst; 1935-41 taught at Leningrad Teachers' Training Inst; Presidium member, USSR Acad of Sci; after WW 2 dir, Inst of Atomic Energy, USSR Acad of Sci; studied electr properties of Seignette salt crystals and laid basis for study of Seignette electr; from 1933 studied nuclear physics and helped establish high-voltage proton accelerator at Physics Eng Inst, USSR Acad of Sci; also directed installation of cyclotron at Radium Inst; 1935 discovered important property of nuclear isomerism in artificially radioactive elements; then studied fission of heavy nuclei in field of neutron physics; 1940 supervised research which led to discovery of autonomous fission of uranium-238 atoms; during WW 2 worked for defense ind; then studied uses of atomic energy; helped develop first Sov atomic bomb; instrumental in establishing Sov atomic eng ind; did research on controlled thermonuclear reactions and studied econ applications of atomic energy; designed and built 10-Bev proton accelerator; also designed 50-Bev accelerator; wrote some 90 works; 1955 member, Sov deleg at Int Conference on Peaceful Uses of Atomic Energy in Geneva; 1956 accompanied Khrushchev and Bulganin in their tour of Britain; dep, USSR Supr Sov of 1950, 1954 and 1958 convocations; *Publ: Segnetoelektriki* (Seignette Electrics) (1933); *Rasshechepleniye atomnogo yadra* (Splitting the Atomic Nucleus) (1935); *O vozmozhnosti sozdaniya termoyadernykh reaktsiy v gazovom razryade* (The Possibility of Triggering Thermonuclear Reactions in a Gas Discharge) (1956), etc; *Awards*: five Orders of Lenin; two Orders of the Red Banner of Labor; four Stalin Prizes; Lenin Prize; *Died*: 7 Feb 1960; buried by Kremlin Wall on Moscow's Red Square; Inst of Atomic Energy, USSR Acad of Sci and Beloyarsk Atomic Electr Plant named for him.

KURKIN, Pyotr Ivanovich (1858-1934) Health service official; specialist in health statistics; Hon Sci Worker of RSFSR from 1928; *Born*: 1858; *Educ*: 1882 grad Natural Sci Dept, Fac of Physics and Mathematics, Petersburg Univ; 1886 grad Med Fac, Moscow Univ; *Career*: worked as distr physician in Mozhaysk and Serpukhov Uyezds, Moscow Province; from 1886 health officer, Serpukhov Uyezd; from late 1895-1925 head, Med Statistics Dept (later Health Statistics Bureau), Moscow Province Zemstvo Health Bureau; bd member and treasurer, Pirogov Soc; ed, journal *Obshchestvennyy vrach*; 1911 helped to organize Dresden Hygiene Exhibition; 1913 helped to organize All-Russian Hygiene Exhibition; after 1917 Oct Revol helped to establish Sov health statistics service; 1919 chm, Joint Health Statistics Commission, RSFSR Pop Comrt of Health and Centr Statistical Bd; member, Registration Commission which compiled "General Rules and Forms of Medical Statistical Registration" - the basis for the compilation of health statistics in the USSR; head, Moscow Oblast Health Statistics Dept; head, Health Statistics Dept, F. F. Erisman Inst; founder-chm, Permanent Statistics Commission for the Unification of Health Statistics Methods in Rural Provinces; contributed to compilation of "Pirogov's Nomenclature of Diseases," which was in use from 1899 to 1924; wrote over 140 works; the Chair of Health Statistics, 1st Moscow Med Inst, bears his name; *Publ: Detskaya smertnost' v Moskovskoy gubernii i yeyo uyezdakh v 1883-97-om godakh* (Child Mortality in Moscow Province and Its Uyezds in 1883-97) (1902); *Statistika dvizheniya naseleniya v Moskovskoy gubernii v 1883-97-om godakh* (Statistics on Population Movement in Moscow Province in 1882–97) (1902); *Statistika boleznennosti naseleniya v Moskovskoy gubernii za period 1883-1902* (Statistics on Sickness Among the Population of Moscow Province in the Period 1883-1902) (4 vol, 1907-12); *Sanitarno-statisticheskiye tablitsy* (Health Statistics Tables) (1910); *Zemskaya sanitarnaya statistika* (Rural Health Statistics) (1912); *Statistika fizicheskogo razvitiya rabochego naseleniya* (Statistics on the Physical Development of the Working Population) (1925); *Smertnost' grudnykh detey* (Infant Mortality) (1925); coauthor, *Zabolevayemost' naseleniya Moskovskoy gubernii i goroda Moskvy za 1926-oy god* (The Sick Rate of the Population of Moscow Province and the City of Moscow for 1926) (1929); *Statistika boleznennosti naseleniya v SSSR* (Statistics on Sicknes Among the Population of the USSR) (1929); *Rozhdayemost' i smertnost' v kapitalisticheskikh gosudarstvakh Yevropy* (Birth and Death Rates in the Capitalist States of Europe) (1938), etc; *Died*: 1934 in Moscow.

KURLOV, Mikhail Georgiyevich (1859-1932) Balneologist and internist; Dr of Med from 1886; prof from 1890; *Born*: 1859; *Educ*: 1884 grad Petersburg Mil Med Acad; *Career*: after grad intern, V. A. Manassein's Clinic, Petersburg Mil Med Acad; 1886 defended doctor's thesis on the assimilation and metabolism of nitrogenous substances in Debov's diet for consumptives; 1890-1929 head, Chair of Therapy, Tomsk Univ; in course of research on hematology observed lesions of monocytes and lymphocytes in blood after splenectomy and discovered "Kurlov's corpuscules" in the monocytes of guinea-pigs; did major research on balneology; devised classification for mineral waters and proposed a widely-used formula for representing them, consisting of a fraction with the anions in the numerator and the cations in the denominator; wrote over 100 works; *Publ*: coauthor, *Materialy k rasprostraneniyu tuberkulyoza v Tomske* (Material on the Incidence of Tuberculosis in Tomsk) (1913); *Opyt klassifikatsii sibirskikh tselebnykh mineral'nykh vod* (A Practical Classification of the Curative Mineral Waters of Siberia) (1921); *Klinicheskiye lektsii po vnutrennim boleznyam* (Clinical Lectures on Internal Diseases) (1927); *Perkussiya i auskul'tatsiya serdtsa i yego izmereniye* (Percussion and Auscultation of the Heart and Its Mensuration) (1928); *Bibliograficheskiy spravochnik po sibirskoy balneologii* (A Bibliographic Guide to Siberian Balneology)(1929); *Died*: 1932

KURLYANDSKAYA, Ettel' Borisovna (1903-1966) Hygienist; Dr of Biology from 1940; prof from 1955; *Born*: 1903; *Educ*: 1927 grad Natural Sci Fac, Khar'kov Univ; *Career*: 1927-43 senior asst, assoc, then senior assoc, Inst of Labor and Occupational Diseases Hygiene, USSR Acad of Med Sci; 1943-66 founder-head, Pathophysiological Laboratory, above inst; also member, Radiological Commissions, USSR Acad of Sci and USSR Acad of Med Sci; member, ed bd, journal *Gigiyena truda i professional'nyye zabolevaniya*; edited four collections of works of his Pathophysiological Laboratory on toxicology of radioactive substances and biological effects of high-energy protons; did research on ind toxicology, radiobiology and radiotoxicology; wrote over 50 works; *Publ: K mekhanizmu deystviya luchistoy energii na organizm* (The Mechanism of the Physiological Effects of Radiant Energy); coauthor and co-ed, *Materialy po toksikologii novykh radioaktivnykh veshchestv (toriy-232, uran-238)* (Material on the Toxicology of New Radioactive Substances [Thorium-232 and Uranium-238]) (1964 and 1965); *Awards:* Order of the Red Banner of Labor; Badge of Hon; medals; *Died*: May 1966.

KURNAKOV, Nikolay Semyonovich (1860-1941) Chemist; pioneer of physiochemical analysis; Dr of Chemistry from 1893; prof from 1893; member, Russian (USSR) Acad of Sci from 1913; Hon Sci Worker of RSFSR from 1940; *Born*: 6 Dec 1860 in Nolinsk, Vyatka (Kirov) Province, son of an officer; *Educ*: 1877 grad Nizhniy Novgorod Mil High-School; 1882 grad Petersburg Mining Inst; *Career*: 1885-93 adjunct prof, 1893-99 prof of inorganic chemistry, from 1899 prof of analytic chemistry, Chair of Metallurgy, Halurgy and Assaying, Petersburg Mining Inst; 1893 defended doctor's thesis on complex metallic bases, with which he pioneered systematic Russian research on the structure and properties of complex compounds; synthesized and studied several new platinum compounds and discovered the Kurnakov reaction by which the structure of the derivatives of bivalent platinum can be determined; 1898 began research on metallic alloys; 1899-1908 prof of physical chemistry, Petersburg Electrotech Inst; 1900 compiled basic composition charts showing the fusibility of binary systems; 1902-30 prof of gen chemistry, Petersburg (Leningrad) Polytech Inst; 1903 designed self-recording pyrometer which greatly improved thermal analysis methods; 1906, together with S. F. Zhemchuzhnyy, developed basic composition charts on the electr conductivity of binary systems (the Kurnakov-Zhemchuzhnyy rules); demonstrated that tech alloys with a high electr resistance consist of solid solutions; 1908-09, again with Zhemchuzhnyy, developed composition charts on solidity; 1908-13 devised new method of determining emission pressure; 1914, in course of research on tempered and quenched copper-and-gold alloys, observed the formation of specific chemical compounds of solid solutions; gave impetus to the study of the physical and mech properties of metallic systems in relation to composition and temperature; 1915, together with V. I. Vernadskiy and A. Ye. Fersman, organized Commission for the Study of Russia's Natural Productive Forces, Russian Acad of Sci; from 1918 founder-dir, Inst of Physiochemical Analysis, Russian Acad of Sci; 1919 founded journal *Izvestiya Instituta fiziko-khimicheskogo analiza*; 1919-27 dir, State Inst of Applied Chemistry; from 1920 dir, Chemical Laboratory (later Gen Chemistry Laboratory), Russian Acad of Sci; 1920 and 1924 organized Congresses of Russian Physiochemical Soc (now All-Union Mendeleyev Chemical Soc) and Russian Metallurgical Soc, of which he was an active member; from 1922 dir, Inst for the Study of Platinum and Other Precious Metals, Russian Acad of Sci; 1928 organized conference on salts, 1929 on solid metallic solutions, 1933 on physiochemical analysis; 1930-34 chm, Chemical Assoc, USSR Acad of Sci; from 1934 dir, Inst of Gen and Inorganic Chemistry, USSR Acad of Sci, which was named after him in 1944; 1936 founded journal *Izvestiya Sektora fiziko-khimicheskogo analiza*; contributed to the development of Sov chemical engineering and trained numerous chemists and metallurgists; *Publ*: doctor's thesis *O slozhnykh metallicheskikh osnovaniyakh* (Complex Metallic Bases) (1893); *Sobraniye izbrannykh rabot* (Selected Works) (2 vol, 1939-39); *Vvedeniye v fiziko-khimicheskiy analiz* (An Introduction to Physicochemical Analysis) (4th ed, 1940), etc; *Awards*: Lenin Prize (1928); Stalin Prize (1941); Order of the Red Banner of Labor; *Died*: 19 Mar 1941.

KURSKIY (Party alias: DIK), Dmitriy Ivanovich (1874-1932) Lawyer; govt official; CP member from 1904; *Born*: 26 Oct 1874 in Kiev, son of an eng; *Educ*: 1900 grad Law Fac, Moscow Univ; *Career*: participated in revol movement from the age of 19; 1895 arrested; 1905 fought in Dec armed uprising in Moscow; from 1906 member, Moscow Oblast Party Bureau; simultaneously worked as legal consultant for illegal workers' trade union; defense counsel in polit trials and labor cases; 1908 co-ed, illegal Bolshevik newspaper *Rabocheye znamya* and Moscow Okrug Party Comt organ *Krasnoye znamya*; Sept 1909 arrested for involvement in the Moscow Oblast Bureau and imprisoned; 1912 active in election campaign for the State Duma; 1914 sent to the front as a reserve ensign; elected chm, Sov of Soldiers' Dep of the Rumanian Front and deleg to 1st Congress of Soviets; Oct 1917 member, Odessa Revol Comt; 1918 returned to Moscow and founded first pop courts on govt instructions; 1918-28 Pop Comr of Justice; first Sov prosecutor-gen; supervised compilation of the civil and criminal codes; implemented regulations on the judicial system, the prosecutor's office, etc; 1919 during Civil War appointed comr, Main and Field Headquarters and member, Revol Mil Council; from 8th Party Congress member, 1924-27 chm, Auditing Commission, CC, CPSU(B); 1927 at 15th Congress elected member, CPSU(B) Centr Control Commission; 1928-32 USSR plen in Italy; from 1921 Presidium member, All-Russian Centr Exec Comt; from 1923 Presidium member, USSR Centr Exec Comt; *Publ: Izbrannyye stat'i i rechi* (Selected Articles and Speeches) (2nd ed, 1958); *Died*: 20 Dec 1932.

KUSHITASHVILI, Vasiliy Pavlovich (1894-1962) Geo stage dir; Pop Artiste of Geo SSR from 1958; *Born*: 7 May 1894; *Educ*: 1913 entered Moscow Univ; 1914-16 simultaneously trained at Komissarzhevskaya Theater Studio; *Career*: 1918-19 staged his first plays in Tbilisi; 1919-33 lived abroad; stage dir at various Paris theaters and theaters in USA; 1933 returned to Geo; from 1934 at Mardzhanishvili Theater; 1948 directed theater in Zugdidi; 1950-52 directed theaters in Gori; 1952-54 directed theaters in Kutaisi, and 1961-62 in Sukhumi; 1933-58 taught stagecraft at Geo Theatrical Inst and theatrical studios; *Productions*: "Marriage of Figaro" (1937); Victor Hugo's "Ruy Blas" (1941); "Masquerade" (1946); Simonov's *Russkiy vopros* (The Russian Question) (1947); Schiller's "Maria Stuart" (1955); Mrevlishvili's "Landslide" (1956); Shakespeare's "Richard III" (1957); *Died*: 20 Jan 1962.

KUSHNER, B. A. (1888-1937) Journalist and writer; CP member from 1917; *Born*: 1888; *Career*: 1920-21, in addition to writing, worked as dep dept head for Electr Trust, Supr Sovnarkhoz; then exec posts with Pop Comrt of Domestic and For Trade; arrested by State Security organs; *Died*: 1937 in imprisonment.

KUSHNERIK, Fyodor Danilovich (1875-1941) Ukr folk bard (kobzar); *Born*: 19 Sept 1875 in vil Bol'shaya Bogachka, Poltava Province; went blind at age six; *Career*: learned to play the violin as a youth; at age 35 began to study under the celebrated kobzar M. Kravchenko, whose repertoire and techniques he inherited; performed ballads, historical, satirical and genre songs, accompanying himself on the bandura; some of his songs and ballads brought him to the attention of the police; after 1917 Oct Revol active in cultural and polit life; composed a number of songs (words and music) on kolkhoz themes; also composed two ballads about Lenin: *Bat',o Lenin* (Father Lenin) and "Pro Lenina and Stalina"; from 1939 member, Ukr Writers' Union; *Died*: 23 Feb 1941.

KUSHNIROV, Aron Davidovich (1890-1949) Jewish poet; CP member from 1942; *Born*: 7 Jan 1890 in vil Boyarki, Kiev Province, son of an office worker; *Career*: fought in WW 1 and awarded George Cross; after 1917 Oct Revol volunteered for Red Army; first work printed in Russian; 1920 first verse in Russian "Again the Day of Danger Comes" printed; founded Jewish Section, Moscow Assoc of Proletarian Writers; at outset of WW 2 volunteered for front-line service; extricated a large group of soldiers from encirclement; after the war edited newspaper "Einigkeit"; then ed, almanach "Heimland"; translated into Yiddish: *Slovo o polku Igoreve* (The Lay of Igor's Host); Gorky's poem "The Maiden and Death"; Pushkin and Lermontov's verse; plays of Shakespeare and Lope de Vega, etc; *Publ*: first collection of poetry "Walls" (1921); lyrical poem "In Memoriam" (1922); story "Children of One People" (1928); verse cycles: "The Train," "The Call," "Loyalty," "Walls" and "East and West" (1940); "Father-Commander" (1948), etc; verse drama "Hirsh Lekkert" (1929); *Died*: 7 Sept 1949.

KUSKOVA, Yekaterina Dmitriyevna (1869-1958) Politician, soc worker and publicist; *Born*: 1869; *Career*: in mid 1890's joined group of League for the Liberation of Labor while abroad; soon came under the influence of Eduard Bernstein's version of Marxist theory; wrote "Credo," which laid bare the essence of "economism" and elicited strong protests from Russian revol Marxists; shortly before 1905 Revol joined Liberation League; 1906, together with S. N. Prokopovich, published journal *Bez Zaglaviya*; contributed to newspaper of leftist Constitutional Democrats *Tovarishch*; after 1917 Oct Revol opposed Sov rule; 1921 member, All-Russian Famine Relief Comt; 1922 expelled from USSR; in exile campaigned against Sov regime; *Died*: 1958.

KUSTODIYEV, Boris Mikhaylovich (1878-1927) Painter, graphic artist, set designer and sculptor; member, Russian Acad of Painting from 1909; *Born*: 7 Mar 1878 in Astrakhan'; *Educ*: 1896-1903 studied under I. Ye. Repin at Petersburg Acad of Arts; *Career*: member, League of Russian Artists; during 1905-07 Revol painted a number of political caricatures; 1907-08 set designer, Mariinskiy Theater; 1911 joined "World of Art" group; before 1917 Oct Revol specialized in Russian provincial scenes; after Revol painted numerous portraits of Lenin; illustrated works by Pushkin, Nekrasov, Leskov, Marshak, etc; *Works*: "Country Fair" (1906, 1908); "The Tea-Party" (1913); "Shrove Tuesday" (1916); "The Bolshevik" (1920); "Demonstration on Uritskiy Square" (1921); "Night Festival on the Neva" (1923); busts of Lenin, etc; *Died*: 26 May 1927 after a long illness.

KUTEPOV, Aleksandr Pavlovich (1882- ?) Mil commander; col, Russian Army; infantry gen, White Army from 1920; organized and led anti-Bolshevik struggle; *Born*: 16 Sept 1882 in Cherepovets, Novgorod Province, son of a forester of noble descent; *Educ*: 1904 grad Petersburg Mil College; *Career*: from 1902 in Russian Army; 1904-05 junior officer with reconnaissance unit of 85th Vyborg Infantry Regt serving in Far East; 1905-14 asst training officer, machine-gun squad commander, reconnaissance commander, company commander, then training officer, Preobrazhenskiy Household Regt; 1914-17 company, then battalion commander with Preobrazhenskiy Household Regt on Southwestern Front; Feb 1917, while on leave in Petrograd, on orders from commandant of Petrograd garrison headed punitive squad in attempt to crush the Revol; from 24 Dec 1917 served with Gen Alekseyev's Volunteer Army; 1918-19 commandant, Taganrog Garrison; company commander, 1st Officers Regt; asst commander, 1st Officers Regt; commander, Kornilov Regt; provisional commander, 1st Div, Volunteer Army; then Black Sea Mil Governor; from May 1919 commander, 1st Army Corps, then commander, Separate Corps of Volunteer Army; commander, 1st Army; during Civil War his troops were noted for their discipline and staunchness; ruthlessly stopped any pillaging, plundering and anti-Semitism; Nov 1920 evacuated from Russia with the remnants of the White Army; in mid-1920's, living abroad, founded and headed "Kutepov Org," a reconnaissance and terrorist org which operated clandestinely in the USSR until the late-1920's; from 1928, after the death of Gen Wrangel, headed the White emigre mil org Russian Gen Soldiers' League; 26 Jan 1930 kidnapped in Paris by OGPU agents and smuggled to USSR; *Died*: further fate unknown.

KUTLER, Nikolay Nikolayevich (1859-1924) Russian politician; *Born*: 1859; *Career*: 1899-1904 dept dir, Russian Min of Finance; 1904-05 Russian Asst Min of Interior and Finance; 1905-06 gen mang for land utilization and farming; forced to resign from this post after drafting liberal proposals for expropriation and redistribution of large estates; from 1906 leading member, Constitutional Democratic Party; helped to draft its agrarian program; dep, 2nd and 3rd State Dumas; closely linked with banking and ind circles; 1917 headed Council of Congresses of Ind and Trade Reps, etc; member of various Provisional Govt commissions; after 1917 Oct Revol worked for State Bank; from 1922 bd member, USSR State Bank; *Died*: 1924.

KUTUY, Adel' (real name: KUTUYEV, Adel'sha Nurmukhamedovich) (1903-1945) Tatar writer and journalist; CP member from 1943; *Born*: 28 Nov 1903 in vil Tatarskiye Kynady, now Saratov Oblast, son of a peasant craftsman; *Educ*: studied at Samara Univ; 1929 grad Kazan' Teachers' Training Inst; *Career*: from 1922 lived in Kazan'; 1923 first work published; 1929-40 worked as a teacher; member, A. S. Neverov's lit circle, co-founder *Sulf* (Left Front) Tatar lit group and "Sulfa Front" theatrical studio; also co-founder, "Bomba" drama ensemble, which staged agitation plays; translated Mayakovskiy's *Levyy marsh* (Left March) into Tatar; his novelette "Unposted Letters" was adapted for the stage by G. Minskiy and turned into an opera by Dzh. Fayzi (performed in 1960-61); *Publ*: verse collection "The Passing Days" (1925); plays: "The Sister-in Law"; "The Little Gray Dove"; "Kazan'"; "Director Dzhamilev"; "Song of Joy"; "The Answer"; stories "Sultan's Day" and "What Shall We Do? "; novelette "Unposted Letters" (1936); war writings: "With Giant Strides"; "Duma"; "Take That, Germany!"; "Tremble, Berlin!"; "One of Many"; "The Artist," etc; children's fantasy "The Adventures of Rustam" (1945); "We Are the People of Stalingrad" (1947); *Died*: 16 June 1945 in a Polish mil hospital.

KUTUZOV, A. V. (1892-1942) Journalist; CP member from 1917; *Born*: 1892; *Career*: 1917 worked for army Bolshevik newspaper in Sveaborg; 1918 with Penza Province Press Commission; edited newspapers *Penzenskaya bednota, Penzenskaya kommuna*, etc; mil corresp, *Pravda* and Russian Telegraphic Agency on Eastern Front; taught Penza machine-gun courses; from 1922 worked in Moscow for TASS, newspaper *Vechernyaya Moskva* and other organs; *Died*: 1942.

KUTUZOV, Ivan Ivanovich (1885-1943) Govt official; CP member from 1917; *Born*: 1885, son of peasant; *Career*: textile-worker by trade; from 1906 in revol movement; 1908 founded textile-workers' union; then arrested; after 1917 Feb Revol chm, Moscow Oblast Textile-Workers' Union; 1919-21 Presidium member, All-Russian Centr Exec Comt; 1920 member, CC, RCP(B); 1920-21 sided with "workers' opposition"; 1924 member, Sov deleg in negotiations with Britain; Presidium member, USSR Centr Exec Comt of 1st-4th convocations; 1929 member, All-Russian Centr Exec Comt; then chm, Commission for Furthering State Credit and Savings, All-Russian Centr Exec Comt; arrested by State Security organs; *Died*: 1943 in imprisonment.

KUTYAKOV, Ivan Semyonovich (1897-1942) Mil commander; corps commander from 1935; Civil War veteran; CP member from 1917; *Born*: 6 Jan 1897 in vil Krasnaya Rechka, Samara Province, son of a peasant; *Educ*: 1923 grad Red Army Mil Acad; 1931 grad Red Army Advanced Officer Training Courses; *Career*: 1916 conscripted into Russian Army; 1916-18 junior warrant officer; elected commander and comr, 20th Turkestani Infantry Regt; 1918 chm, volost revol comt; commander, Red Guards detachment; 1918-19 commander, 73rd Brigade in 25th Chapayev Infantry Div; 1919-20 commander, 25th Infantry Div; 1923-36 commander, infantry div, then various infantry corps; 1936-37 dep commander, Volga Mil Distr; 1937 arrested by NKVD; *Awards*: three Orders of the Red Banner; *Died*: 23 Sept 1942 in imprisonment; posthumously rehabilitated.

KUUSINEN, Otto Vil'gel'movich (1881-1964) Finn; govt and Party official; historian; member, USSR Acad of Sci from 1958; secr and Presidium member, CC, CPSU from 1957; member, CC, CPSU from 1941; CP member from 1904; *Born*: 1881 in Finland; *Educ*: 1905 grad History and Philology Fac, Helsingfors Univ; *Career*: led left wing of Finnish Soc-Democratic Party; 1906-08 ed, "Socialist journal"; 1907-16 ed, newspaper "Työmies"; 1908-17 Sejm dep and leader, Soc-Democrat faction of parliament; 1912 attended Basel Congress of 2nd International; 1917-18 helped lead Bolshevik revol in Finland; educ plen in "Finnish Revol Govt"; 1918 founded Finnish CP; member, CC, Finnish CP until 1944; deleg at 1st, 3rd, 4th, 5th, 6th and 7th Comintern Congresses; at 3rd Comintern Congress elected member, Comintern Exec Comt; 1921-39 secr, Comintern Exec Comt; 1939 headed "Pop Govt of Democratic Republ of Finland," proclaimed in Terijoki; 1940-56 chm, Presidium, Karelian-Finnish Supr Sov; simultaneously until 1958 dep chm, Presidium, USSR Supr Sov; late 1952-Mar 1953 Presidium member, CC, CPSU; 1958-62 chm, USSR Parliamentary Group; dep, USSR Supr Sov of 1940—1962 convocations; dep, RSFSR Supr Sov of 1959 and 1963 convocations; chm, For Affairs Commission, Sov of Nationalities, USSR Supr Sov of 1962 convocation; wrote several works on the history of the int Communist movement; *Publ: Revolyutsiya v Finlyandii* (Revolution in Finland); *Osvoboditel'noye dvizheniye v kolonial'nykh i polukolonial'nykh stranakh* (The Liberation Movement in the Colonial and Semi-Colonial Countries); *Lenin i organizatsionnyy vopros na 3 kongresse Kominterna* (Lenin and the Organizational Problem at the 3rd Comintern Congress) (1934); *Pretvoreniye v zhizn' idey Lenina* (The Implementation of Lenin's Ideas) (1960); textbook *Osnovy marksizma-leninizma* (The Principles of Marxism-Leninism) (2nd ed, 1962), etc; *Awards*: three Orders of Lenin; Hero of Socialist Labor (1961); *Died*: 17 May 1964 in Moscow.

KUVSHINNIKOV, Pyotr Afanas'yevich (1889-1954) Physician; specialist in health statistics; prof; member, USSR Acad of Med Sci from 1945; *Born*: 16 Mar 1889; *Educ*: 1914 grad Moscow Univ; *Career*: from 1918 head, Statistics Dept, RSFSR Min of Health; 1935-41 prof, 1st Moscow Med Inst, where he taught a course on health statistics; simultaneousely head, Bureau of Sci Health Statistics Methods, 1st Moscow Med Inst, then head of a similar bureau at USSR Min of Health; from 1946 until death head, Health Statistics Dept, Semenko Inst of Health Service Org and Med History; long-time assoc of P. I. Kurkin; during early years of Sov rule helped to set up statistics offices at local health service org and to develop med registration and accounting systems; did major research on epidemic and tuberculosis statistics; also supervised the compilation of demographic, sick-rate and physical development statistics; *Publ: Sotsial'nyye bolezni v Moskovskoy gubernii* (Social Diseases in Moscow Province) (1926); *Zabolevayemost' moskovskikh promyshlennykh rabochikh v 1925-27-om godakh* (The Sick-Rate Among Moscow Industrial Workers in 1925-27) (1929); *Statisticheskiy metod v klinicheskikh issledovaniyakh* (The Statistical Method in Clinical Research) (1955), etc; *Died*: 25 Jan 1954 in Moscow.

KUYBYSHEV, Nikolay Vladimirovich (1893-1938) Mil commander; Civil War veteran; capt, Russian Army; corps commander from 1936; brother of Politburo member V. V. Kuybyshev; CP member from 1918; *Born*: 13 Dec 1893 in Kokchetav, now Kaz SSR, son of an officer; *Educ*: 1914 grad Alexandrine Mil College; 1922 grad Higher Acad Courses; *Career*: 1914-17 commanded company, then battalion in Russian Army at the front; 1917-18 elected regt commander; from 1918 in Red Army; 1918 member, Higher Mil Inspectorate; 1919-20 mil comr, 3rd Infantry Div, then brigade commander in 9th Infantry Div; 1919-21 active in Civil War on Southern Front and in Transcaucasia; 1920-21 commanded 9th Infantry Div; 1921 commanded infantry corps; 1922-23 commandant and comr, Kronstadt Fortress; 1923-25 commandant, *Vystrel* Higher Infantry School; 1925 asst commander, Turkestani Front; summer 1925 replaced Blyukher as chief adviser in Chiang Kai-shek's forces; intrigued against Chiang Kai-shek, siding with his main rival Wang Tsyn-wei; spring 1926 returned to USSR; 1926 commanded infantry corps; 1927-28 head, Red Army Command Bd; asst commander, Moscow Mil Distr; 1929 commander, Siberian Mil Distr; 1930 head, Red Army Main Bd;

1931-34 head, Naval Inspectorate, USSR Pop Comrt of Workers and Peasants' Inspection; 1934-35 member, Party Control Commission, CC, CPSU(B) and head of its Naval Group; 1934-38 member, Party Control Commission, CC, CPSU(B); 1935-37 Bureau member, above commission; 1937-38 commander, Transcaucasian Mil Distr; dep, USSR Supr Sov of 1937 convocation; 1938 arrested by NKVD; *Awards*: three Orders of the Red Banner; Order of Azer SSR; *Died*: 1 Aug 1938 in imprisonment; posthumously rehabilitated.

KUYBYSHEV, Valerian Vladimirovich (1888-1935) Govt and Party official; CP member from 1904; *Born*: 6 June 1888 in Omsk, son of an officer; *Educ*: 1905 grad Cadet Corps; 1905-06 studied at Mil Med Acad; 1909-10 at Law Fac, Tomsk Univ; *Career*: at the age of 16, while studying in Omsk Cadet Corps, joined the Bolsheviks and the Omsk RSDRP Org; from 1905 active in Petersburg Bolshevik org while a student at Mil Med Acad; spring 1906 expelled from the acad; went to Omsk to hide from the police; elected member, Omsk RSDRP Comt; 1906-16 revol work in Omsk, Kainsk (now Kuybyshev, Novosibirsk Oblast), Tomsk, Petropavlovsk, Barabinsk, Petersburg (from Dec 1914 member, Petersburg RSDRP Comt), Vologda and Khar'kov; arrested Nov 1906, July 1908, Apr 1909, Feb 1910, Nov 1910, June 1912, June 1915 and Sept 1916; tried three times; exiled to Kainsk, Narym Kray, Tutury in Verkholensk Uyezd of Irkutsk Province and Turukhansk Kray; Mar 1917 returned to Samara from exile; then head, Samara RSDRP(B) Org; 1917 deleg, 7th (Apr) RSDRP(B) Conference; helped organize armed rebellion to establish the Sov regime in Samara; chm, Samara Revol Comt; during Civil War polit leader in Red Army; from July 1918 polit comr and member, 1st Army Revol Mil Comt; from Sept 1918 polit comr and member, 4th Army Revol Mil Comt on the Eastern Front; from Apr 1919 member, Revol Mil Comt, Southern Group on the Eastern Front; M. V. Frunze's adviser in campaign against Kolchak; from July 1919 directed defense of Astrakhan' along with S. M. Kirov; appointed member, 2nd Army Revol Mil Comt; from Aug 1919 member, Revol Mil Comt, Turkestani Front; helped establish Sov regime in Centr Asia; Oct 1919 appointed dep chm, Commission for Turkestani Affairs, All-Union Centr Exec Comt and RSFSR Council of Pop Comr; Sept 1920 RSFSR plen with Bukhara govt; after Civil War admin work; Dec 1920 elected Presidium member, All-Union Centr Trade-Union Council and head of its Econ Dept; 1921 at 10th RCP(B) Congress elected cand member, CC, RCP(B); from May 1921 Presidium member, Supr Sovnarkhoz; head, Main Bd of the Electrical Ind; head, State Commission for the Electrification of Russia; 1922 at 11th RCP(B) Congress elected member, CC; Apr 1922 elected secr, CC, RCP(B); 1923 at 12th RCP(B) Congress elected member, Centr Control Commission; chm, Centr Control Commission, Workers and Peasants' Inspection; from 1926 chm, Supr Sovnarkhoz; 19 Dec 1927 elected Politburo member, Party CC; from Nov 1930 chm, USSR Gosplan; simultaneously dep chm, USSR Council of Pop Comr and Labor and Defense Council; from Feb 1934 chm, Sov Control Commission; from May 1934 First Pop Chm, USSR Council of Pop Comr and Labor and Defense Council; helped draft 1st and 2nd five-year plans; the city of Samara was named after him; *Publ: Stat'i i rechi* (Articles and Speeches) (Vol 5 [1930-35], 1937); *Stat'i i rechi* (Articles and Speeches) (1935); *Izbrannyye stat'i i rechi* (Selected Articles and Speeches) (1931, 1934, 1944); *Died*: 25 Jan 1935 of sclerosis of the heart; at the trial of the "right-wing Trotskyite bloc" in Mar 1938 it was claimed that the bloc had him murdered by means of "injurious med treatment"; his brother N. V. Kuybyshev, a mil commander, died in imprisonment on 1 Aug 1938 shortly after his arrest by State Security organs.

KUZ'MICH, Vladimir Savvich (1904-1943) Ukr writer; CP member from 1924; *Born*: 27 June 1904 in Bakhmach, Chernigov Oblast, son of a laborer; *Educ*: 1929 grad Khar'kov Inst of Econ; 1932 grad Ukr Inst of Red Prof; *Career*: member, All-Ukr Union of Proletarian Writers and Ukr lit org *Molodnyak*; 1925 first work published; during WW 2 arrested by State Security organs; *Publ*: collected stories *Nagan* (The Nagant Revolver) (1927); stories and novelettes "The Italian Women from Magento" (1927); "Hao-Jen" (1928); "The Cherry Orchards" (1936); novels: "The Wings" (1930); "The Turbines" (1932); children's novelette "The Ocean" (1939); collected stories "A Hundred Loaves" (1940); war stories "A Pilot's Wife" and "Into the Storm" (1941); *Died*: 4 Oct 1943 in imprisonment in Alma-Ata; posthumously rehabilitated.

KUZ'MIN, Georgiy Pavlovich (? -1943) Russian mil commander; capt; fighter pilot; *Born*: in Zaozyornyy, Krasnoyarsk Kray; *Educ*: grad Mil Aviation College; *Pos*: 1941-43 pilot, squadron commander, then dep commander, Air Force fighter guards regt; *Career*: Nov 1941 lost both feet; learned to fly a fighter plane with artificial limbs; flew about 300 missions; shot down 21 enemy aircraft; *Awards*: Hero of the Sov Union (1943); Order of Lenin; Order of the Red Banner; *Died*: 18 Aug 1943 in an air battle.

KUZ'MIN, N. N. (1883-1939) Mil commander; Party official; CP member from 1903; *Born*: 1883; *Career*: Party work in North; 1917-18 comr, Southwestern Front; from Aug 1918 with Soviet forces in the North; comr, 6th Army; then member, Revol Mil Councils of 3rd and 6th Armies; mil comr, Baltic Fleet; commander, 12th Army; asst commander, Baltic Fleet; 1925-34 member, Revol Mil Council and head, Polit Bd, Turkestani Front; head, Red Army's Main Mil Training Establishments Bd; member, Revol Mil Council and head, Polit Bd, Siberian Mil Distr; then dipl, admin and Party work; arrested by State Security organs; *Died*: 1939 in imprisonment.

KUZ'MIN-KARAVAYEV, V. D. (1859-1927) Mil lawyer; gen; leader, Right Wing of Constitutional-Democratic Party; *Born*: 1959; *Career*: Tver' Province dep, 1st and 2nd State Duma; helped crush 1905-07 Revol; during WW 1 leading zemstvo official and member, Mil Ind Comt; after 1917 Oct Revol actively opposed Sov regime; during Civil War member, Yudenich's Polit Consultative Bd; from 1920 lived in emigration; *Died*: 1927.

KUZMINSKAYA, Tat'yana Andreyevna (1846-1925) Russian writer; *Born*: 10 Nov 1846, daughter of the physician A. Ye. Bers; a close friend and sister-in-law of Lev Tolstoy; *Career:* spent much of her youth with the Tolstoys; 1919 moved to Yasnaya Polyana, where she lived until her death; according to Tolstoy, she (and her sister Sof'ya Andreyevna) served as the prototype for Natasha Rostova in his novel *Voyna i mir* (War and Peace); early 1880's began to write at the prompting of Tolstoy, who read and corrected the manuscript of her stories; *Publ*: stories *Bab'ya dolya* (A Woman's Fate) and *Beshenyy volk* (Mad Wolf) (1886); reminiscences of Tolstoy and his family (from 1908); *Moya zhizn' doma i v Yasnoy Polyane* (My Life at Home and at Yasnaya Polyana) (4th ed, 1964); *Died*: 8 Jan 1925 in Yasnaya Polyana.

KUZNETSOV, Aleksey Aleksandrovich (1905-1949) Party and govt official; CP member from 1925; *Born*: 20 Feb 1905 in Borovichi, son of a worker; *Career*: from 1922 worked at Borovichi sawmill; 1923 joined Komsomol; 1924 elected secr, volost Komsomol comt; 1924-32 exec Komsomol work in Novgorod Province and Leningrad Oblast; from 1932 instructor, Leningrad City CPSU(B) Comt; from 1936 second secr, Smol'nyy Rayon Party Comt, Leningrad; then secr, Dzerzhinskiy Rayon Party Comt, Leningrad; 1937-38 second secr, Leningrad Oblast Party Comt; 1938-45 second secr, Leningrad City Party Comt; 1939-46 member, Mil Council, Baltic Fleet; 1939 at 18th Party Congress elected member, CC, CPSU(B); during WW 2 helped organize defense of Leningrad; member, Mil Council, Leningrad Front; 1942 entitled maj-gen and 1943 lt-gen; 1945-46 first secr, Leningrad Oblast and City CPSU(B) Comt; 1946-Feb 1949 secr, CC, CPSU(B); 1946 member, Org Bureau, CC, CPSU(B); dep, USSR Supr Sov; dep, RSFSR Supr Sov; arrested by State Security organs; tried and sentenced in "Leningrad Case"; *Awards*: two Orders of Lenin; Order of the Red Banner; Order of Kutuzov, 1st and 2nd Class; Order of the Fatherland War, 1st Class; medals; *Died*: 1949 in imprisonment; posthumously rehabilitated.

KUZNETSOV, Fyodor Isidorovich (1898-1961) Mil commander; col-gen from 1941; CP member from 1938; *Born*: 29 Sept 1898 in vil Balbechino, Mogilev Province, son of a peasant; *Educ*: 1916 grad Russian Army Ensigns' School; 1926 grad Frunze Mil Acad; *Career*: 1916 joined Russian Army; 1916-18 platoon commander, reconnaissance officer and staff operations officer, 5th Infantry Div, Western Front; 1918 secr, Balbechino Rayon Sov and commander of local Red Guard unit; from 1918 in Red Army; 1918-21 battalion and regt commander on various fronts of Civil War, notably in operations against anti-Sov rebels in Bel; 1926-30 again regt commander; 1930-32 commander, Training Dept, Moscow Red Banner Infantry School; 1932-35 commander, Moscow Red Banner Infantry School; 1935-38 head, Chair of Tactics, Frunze Mil Acad; commander, 20th Tadzh Mountain Cavalry Div; 1938-40 dep commander, Western Special Mil Distr; 1940-41 commander, Baltic Special Mil Distr; 1941 commander, Northwestern Front, 21st Army, Central Front, Special 51st Army in Crimea, 61st Army near Moscow; 1941-42 dep commander, Western Front; 1942-43 commandant, Gen Staff Acad; 1943-44 dep commander, Volkhov Front; from 1943 commander, Ural Mil Distr; from 1947 in reserve; *Publ: Motorizatsiya i mekhanizatsiya i sluzhba zagrazhdeniya* (Motorization, Mechanization and Obstacle Construction) (1930); *Boyevaya mashina segodnyashnego dnya i problema unifikatsii* (The Modern Military Machine and the Problem of Unification) (1931); *Awards*: two Orders of Lenin; three Orders of the Red Banner; Order of Suvorov, 2nd Class; Order of the Red Star; medals; *Died*: Mar 1961 in Moscow; buried in Novodevich'ye Cemetery, Moscow.

KUZNETSOV, Nikolay Adrianovich (1904-1924) Poet; *Born*: 1904, son of a worker; *Career*: worked at a plant; at age 15 joined Komsomol and contributed to Komsomol press; from 1922 member, "Workers' Spring" and "October" lit groups; 1924 transferred to *Pereval* (The Pass) group along with M. Golodnyy, Artyom Vesyolyy, etc; together with Bezymenskiy, Doronin, Svetlov, etc founded proletarian lyric school; *Publ*: verse: "I Shall Cover the White Sheets with Bits of My Heart in the Form of Lines"; "The Radio Tower"; "The Captured Bandit"; collection *Stikhi* (Verse) (1925); *Rabocheye serdtse* (The Worker's Heart) (1925); *Died*: 20 Sept 1924 committed suicide.

KUZNETSOV, Nikolay Ivanovich (Party name: GRACHOV, N. I.) (1911-1944) Engineer; WW 2 partisan; CP member from 1942; *Born*: 1911 in vil Zyryanka, Sverdlovsk Oblast, son of a peasant; *Career*: eng at "Uralmash" Plant in Sverdlovsk, then at automobile plant in Moscow; Aug 1942 joined D. N. Medvedev's partisan unit which operated in the German-occupied Poles'ye area of the Ukr; posing as German Senior-Lt Paul Siebert, collected and passed on to partisans valuable reconnaissance and intelligence data in Rovno; performed various acts of sabotage and killed or kidnapped several German generals and occupation officials; his exploits are covered in D. N. Medvedev's books *Eto bylo pod Rovno* (It Happened at Rovno) and *Sil'nyye dukhom* (The Strong at Heart) and in the film *Podvig razvedchika* (An Intelligence Agent's Feat); *Awards*: Hero of the Sov Union (1944, posthumously); *Died*: 9 Mar 1944 killed in a battle in vil Boratin, L'vov Oblast; buried in L'vov.

KUZNETSOV, Nikolay Ivanovich (1864-1932) Geobotanist; Dr of Botany; prof from 1895; corresp member, Russian (USSR) Acad of Sci from 1904; *Born*: 17 Dec 1864 in Petersburg; *Educ*: 1888 grad Petersburg Univ; *Career*: from 1888 worked for Min of State Property; from 1891 junior assoc, Petersburg Botanical Garden; 1894 lectured on botany at Petersburg Teachers' Training Courses for Women; from 1895 prof, Yur'yev (Tartu) Univ; 1915-18 dir, Nikitskiy Botanical Garden, Crimea; 1918-21 prof, Taurian Univ, Simferopol'; from 1921 prof, Leningrad Univ; 1922-32 head, Geobotanical Dept, Main Botanical Garden, USSR Acad of Sci; did research on the flora of the Caucasus and its history and on the botanical zoning and mapping of the Caucasus and the European USSR; founder-ed, journal *Trudy botanicheskogo sada Yur'yevskogo universiteta* (later *Vestnik russkoy botaniki*); *Publ: Elementy Sredizemnomorskoy oblasti v Zapadnom Kavkaze* (Mediterranean Features of the Western Caucasus) (1891); *Printsipy deleniya Kavkaza na botaniko-geograficheskiye rayony* (The Principles of the Geobotanical Zoning of the Caucasus) (1909); *Vvedeniye v sistematiku tsvetkovykh rasteniy* (An Instroduction to the Taxonomy of Flowering Plants) (1914); *Osnovy botaniki* (The Principles of Botany) (1914-19); *Botaniko-geograficheskiy atlas zemnogo shara* (A Geobotanical Atlas of the World) (1923); *Botaniko-geograficheskaya karta Yevropeyskoy chasti SSSR* (A Geobotanical Map of the European USSR) (1924); *Zhizn' i stroyeniye rasteniy* (The Life and Structure of Plants) (1924); *Politopnoye proiskhozhdeniye rasteniy* (The Polytopian Origin of Plants) (1924); *Geobotanicheskiye karty Yevropeyskoy chasti SSSR* (Geobotanical Maps of the European USSR) (1928); *Died*: 22 May 1932 in Leningrad.

KUZNETSOV, Stepan Leonidovich (1879-1932) Russian actor; Pop Artiste of RSFSR from 1929; *Born*: 14 Jan 1879 in Kishinev; *Educ*: completed parish school; *Career*: salesclerk in book stores; 1897 amateur acting debut; 1901 became professional actor with Tomskiy Company in Orel; 1902-06 served in Russian Army and engaged in revol work among the troops; 1907-08 at Solovtsov Theater, Kiev; 1908 joined Moscow Arts Theater; from 1910 at theaters in Kiev, Odessa, Khar'kov, etc; 1923-25 actor, Moscow City Trade-Union Council Theater; from 1925 at Malyy Theater; *Roles*: Gayev, Yepikhodov and Firs in Chekhov's *Vishnyovyy sad* (The Cherry Orchard); Vaflya and Astrov in Chekhov's *Dyadya Vanya* (Uncle Vanya); Luka, Baron and Alyoshka in Gorky's *Na dne* (The Lower Depths); almost all the roles in Gogol's *Revizor* (The Government Inspector); Blokhin in Andreyev's *Dni nashey zhizni* (The Days of Our Life); Fredrikson' in Hamsun's "In the Clutches of Life"; the Tsar in A. K. Tolstoy's *Tsar' Fyodor Ioannovich*; Ferdyshchenko in *Idiot* (The Idiot), after Dostoyevsky; Doolittle in Shaw's "Pygmalion"; Lemm in *Dvoryanskoye gnezdo* (A Nest of Gentlefolk), after Turgenev; Razlyulyayev in *Bednost' ne porok* (Poverty Is No Vice); Sganarelle in Molière's "Don Juan"; Vikent'yev in *Obryv* (The Precipice), after Goncharov; Krutitskiy in Ostrovskiy's *Ne bylo ni grosha, da vdrug altyn* (From Rags to Riches); Dubrovin and Buketov in Romashov's *Ognennyy most* (Bridge of Fire) and *Smena geroyev* (New Generation of Heroes), etc; *Died*: 18 Apr 1932 in Moscow.

KUZNETSOV, Vasiliy Ivanovich (1894-1964) Mil commander; ensign, Russian Army; col-gen, Sov Army from 1943; CP member from 1928; *Born*: 1894; *Career*: fought in WW 1; from 1918 in Red Army; during Civil War commanded regt; after Civil War commander, 2nd Turkestani Div in Centr Asia, where he fought against Basmachi movement; 1937-41 commander, infantry corps; then commander, 3rd Army; 1939 fought in West Bel campaign; 1941-42 commander, 21st and 1st Shock Armies; then 63rd and 1st Guards Armies; fought in defense of Kiev, in Moscow counter-offensive and in battle of Stalingrad; 1942-43 dep commander, Southwestern Front; 1943-45 commander, 1st Guards Army, then 5th and 3rd Shock Armies; fought in liberation of Donbass, Warsaw, East Pomeranian operation and storming of Berlin; after WW 2 served with Sov occupation forces in East Germany; chm, Centr Comt, Voluntary Org for the Promotion of the Sov Army, Air Force and Navy; 1952-57 commander, Volga Mil Distr; 1957-60 research work; 1960 retired on med grounds; dep, USSR Supr Sov of 1946 and 1954 convocations; 1956 deleg at 20th CPSU Congress; *Awards*: Hero of the Sov Union; two Orders of Lenin; five Orders of the Red Banner; two Orders of Suvorov, 1st Class; medals; *Died*: June 1964.

KUZNETSOV, Vasiliy Vasil'yevich (1866-1938) Meteorologist; pioneer of aerological research in Russia; *Born*: 2 Apr 1866; *Career*: from 1896 made photogrammetric measurements of cloud height, speed and direction in Petersburg; made free balloon ascents and used first sounding-balloons; 1902 established special kits dept (from 1912 Aerological Observatory) at Pavlovsk Magnetism and Meteorology Observatory, where he flew over 2.000 kites and released over 300 sounding-balloons by 1919; 1905 organized aerological research in Kuchino and, for the first time, used a searchlight for the optical sounding of the atmosphere up to a height of 15 kilometers; 1907 organized aerological research in Nizhneye Olchedayevo, then in Irkutsk, Yekaterinburg, Omsk and Tashkent; also did aerological research at sea; 1917 compiled first Russian cloud atlas; designed several meteorological instruments (including a thermograph) and the following aerological instruments: an aerological theodolite, a cylindrical kite (1899), a kite-borne meteorograph (1899), a meteorograph for sounding-balloons (1902), a nephoscope (1905) and a wind-gust recorder (1905-06); also made hydrological instruments, including a dynamograph to study the strength of wave impact on the shore, and a hydrostatic tide-gage; *Publ: Opytnyye issledovaniya nad soprotivleniyem vozdukha na konechnyye poverkhnosti* (Experimental Research on Air Resistance on Terminal Surfaces) (1899); *Ob opredelenii skorosti i napravleniya dvizheniya oblakov* (Determining the Speed and Direction of Cloud Movement) (1899); *Atlas oblakov* (A Cloud Atlas) (2nd ed, 1926); *Died*: 6 Mar 1938.

KUZNETSOV, Vladimir Dmitriyevich (1887-1963) Physicist; prof from 1920; member, USSR Acad of Sci and Presidium member, Siberian Branch from 1958; Hon Sci Worker of RSFSR from 1934; CP member from 1945; *Born*: 12 May 1887 in Mias, now Chelyabinsk Oblast; *Educ*: 1910 grad Petersburg Univ; *Career*: from 1911 taught at various higher educ establishments in Tomsk; 1917-20 asst prof, from 1920 prof, Tomsk Univ; from 1929 dir, Siberian Physics and Eng Inst; specialized in solid-state physics and technol; *Publ: Fizika tvyordogo tele* (Solid-State Physics) (1937-49); *Kristally i kristallizatsiya* (Crystals and Crystallization) (1953); *Poverkhnostnaya energiya tvyordykh tel* (The Surface Energy of Solids) (1954); *Narosty pri rezanii i trenii* (Excrescences in Cutting and Friction Processes) (1956); *Awards*: Order of Lenin; Stalin Prize (1942); Hero of Socialist Labor (1957); medal; *Died*: 13 Oct 1963.

KUZNETSOV, Yevgeniy Mikhaylovich (1900-1958) Theater historian and critic; Hon Art Worker of RSFSR from 1939; *Born*: 30 Jan 1900; *Career*: specialist in variety, circus and mass shows; 1919 began to work on theater criticism, writing theater reviews from Petrograd for newspaper *Krasnaya gazeta*; from 1928 head, Leningrad Circus Museum; 1938-57 artistic dir, Leningrad and Moscow Circuses and artistic dir, USSR Circuses Bd; Leningrad Circus used his scripts for the pantomimes *Lyudi morskogo dna* (Seabed People) (1935), *Shamil'* (1936) and *Tayga v ogne* (The Taiga on Fire) (1938); 1957-58 founder-ed, journal *Sovetskiy tsirk*; wrote first books on history of Sov and European circus; *Publ*: coauthor, *Arena'. Teatral'nyy al'manakh* (The Arena. A Theatrical Almanach) (1924); *Tsirk* (The Circus) (1931); *Sovetskiy tsirk* (The Soviet Circus) (1938); *Arena i lyudi sovetskogo tsirka* (The Arena and People of the Soviet Circus) (1947); *I. F. Borbunov* (1947); *Iz proshlogo russkoy estrady* (From the Russian Variety Stage's Past) (1958); *Posledniy posluzhnoy spisok F. I. Shalyapina* (F. I. Chaliapin's Last Service Record) (1958); *Komissar teatrov* (Theater Commissar) (1961); *Died*: 27 Mar 1958.

KVARATSKHELIYA, Tarasiy Karamanovich (1889-1951) Agronomist; specialist in subtropical agric; Dr of Agric from 1926; prof from 1928; member, Geo Acad of Sci from 1941; member, All-Union Lenin Acad of Agric Sci from 1948; Hon Sci Worker of Geo SSR from 1936; CP member from 1943; *Born*: 25 Feb 1889 in vil Nikifu, Kutaisi Province; *Educ*: 1914 grad Petrograd Higher Agric Courses; 1925 grad Tiflis Univ; *Career*: 1926-30 dir, Sukhumi Agric Experimental Station; 1930-37 dir, All-Union Inst of Tea Farming; from 1937 prof, Chair of Subtropical Fructiculture, Geo Agric Inst; collected material on the root systems of fruit trees and tea shrubs; developed the principles of differentiated tea cultivation; did considerable work on the development of tea and fruit farming in Geo SSR; *Publ: Materialy k biologii kornevoy sistemy plodovykh derev'yev* (Material on the Biology of the Root System of Fruit Trees) (1927); *Sel'skokhozyaystvennyye rayony Abkhazii. Opyt sel'skokhozyaystvennogo rayonirovaniya na ekologicheskikh osnovakh* (The Agricultural Regions of Abkhaziya. An Experiment in Agricultural Zoning on Ecological Principles) (1930); *Chaynyy kust i soputstvuyushchiye yego kul'tury* (The Tea Shrub and Concomitant Plants) (1934); *Chayevodstvo* (Tea Growing) (1950); *Died*: 23 Aug 1951.

KVIRING, Emmanuil Ionovich (1888-1939) Party and govt official; Dr of Econ Sci; CP member from 1912; *Born*: 14 Sept 1888; *Career*: from 1906 worked in Saratov pharmacy; 1913 secr, Bolshevik faction, 4th State Duma; arrested and exiled for revol activities; Oct 1917 secr, Yekaterinoslav RSDRP(B) Comt; chm, Ukr Supr Sovnarkhoz; dep dir, Polit Bd, 12th Army; 1920-22 secr, Donets Province Party Comt; 1918-25 member, CC, CP(B) Ukr; 1923-25 first secr, CC, CP(B) Ukr; 1925-27 dep chm, USSR Supr Sovnarkhoz; 1927-30 dep chm, USSR Gosplan; 1931 USSR Dep Pop Comr of Communications; 1932-34 dep chm, Comt of Commodity Stocks, Labor and Defense Council; 1932-36 dir, Econ Inst, Communist Acad; from 1934 dep chm, USSR Gosplan; at 12th-16th CPSU(B) Congresses elected member, CC, CPSU(B); member, USSR Centr Exec Comt of various convocations; wrote several books on building socialism; 1937 arrested by State Security organs; *Publ: Ocherki razvitiya promyshlennosti SSSR 1917-27* (Outline Development of Soviet Industry 1917-27) (1929); *Zadachi postroyeniya sotsializma v SSSR* (The Task of Building Socialism in the USSR) (1931), etc; *Died*: 1939 in imprisonment; 1956 posthumously rehabilitated.

KVITKA, Kliment Vasil'yevich (1880-1953) Folklorist and music historian; husband of Ukr writer Lesya Ukrainka; *Born*: 4 Feb 1880 in Kiev; *Educ*: 1902 grad Kiev Univ; *Career*: from 1920 prof at music and drama inst in Kiev; from 1933 prof, Moscow Conservatory; 1937-53 founder-dir, Studio for the Study of the Music of the Peoples of the USSR; studied and collected folk music of Slavs, Greeks, Moldavians, Geo, Arm, etc; reconstructed historical geography of folk music; many of Kvitka's notations of Ukr folk songs were adopted by choirs and radio broadcasts; made valuable studies of harmony and rhythm of folk songs, folk musical instruments and their technique; collected over 6.000 folk songs; *Publ:* "Folk Melodies. Sung by Lesya Ukrainka" (2 vol, 1917–18); "Ukrainian Folk Melodies" (1922); "Ukrainian Songs About a Girl Who Travelled with a Pimp" (1926); "Ukrainian Songs About a Child Seducer" (1927); "Le système anémitonique pentatonique chez les peuples slaves. Comptes rendus du 2-me congrès des géographes et ethnographes slaves" (1930); *Died*: 19 Sept 1953 in Moscow.

KVITKO, Leyb Moiseyevich (1895-1952) Jewish poet; CP member from 1941; *Born*: 11 Nov 1895 in vil Goloskovo, near Podol'sk, son of a poor peasant; *Career*: orphaned at an early age, he worked as a shoemaker, hide peddler and painter; toured length and breadth of the Ukr; 1917 first work published; 1921-25 lived in Germany; 1926 returned to USSR and worked for a Jewish journal in Khar'kov; 1934 deleg, 1st All-Union Writers' Congress; from 1936 lived in Moscow; during WW 2 worked for Sov Information Bureau and Jewish Anti-Fascist Comt; 1949 arrested by State Security organs; wrote mainly children's verse, which was translated into Russian by S. Marshak, S. Mikhalkov, M. Svetlov, Ye. Blaganina, etc; *Publ*: poem "The Red Storm" (1918); children's verse "Little Songs" (1919); verse collection "Steps"; novella "Lyam and Pete" (1930); novel "Young Years"; poems "A Letter to Voroshilov," "The Little Horse," "The Pussy-Cat," "The Raylet," "Hallo," "The Bagpipes," etc; children's verse "Toward the Sun" (1948); "Verse" (1948); verse collection "Soul Song" (1956); "Visiting" (1962), etc; *Died*: 12 Sept 1952 in imprisonment; posthumously rehabilitated.

KVYATEK (KWIATEK), Kazimir Frantsevich (1888-1937) Mil commander; Pole; div commander from 1935; CP member from 1917; *Born*: 21 Nov 1888 in Warsaw, son of a worker; *Educ*: 1918 grad Kremlin Red Commanders' Courses; *Career*: 1904-06 worked at an enameling plant in Warsaw; 1904-06 also member, Polish Socialist Party; 1905 took active part in revol; May 1906 involved in attempted assassination of governor-gen of Warsaw and sentenced to 20 years at hard labor; served 11 years, six of them in chains; 1917 freed during Feb Revol; from July 1917 in Red Guard; took part in Oct Revol in Ukr and fought against Germans; from 1918 in Red Army; 1918-20 commanded a platoon, company and battalion before being appointed dep commander, 1st Bogun Regt; 1920-22 commander, 130th Bogun Brigade; 1922–37 asst commander, 44th Kiev Rifle Div; commander, 99th Rifle Div, 17th Rifle Corps; dep commander, Khar'kov Mil Distr; Nov 1937 arrested by State Security organs; *Awards*: Order of the Red Banner; Scroll of the All-Ukr Centr Exec Comt; *Died*: 1937 in imprisonment; 8 Sept 1956 rehabilitated.

KYARNER (KÄRNER), Yaan (1891-1958) Est writer; Hon Writer of Est SSR from 1946; *Born*: 27 May 1891 in Kirepm, Est, son of a peasant; *Educ*: 1911-14 studied at Shanyavskiy Pop Univ in Moscow; *Career*: 1906 first work published; in 1920's combined lyrical description of nature with soc themes and account of workers' life in his poetry; in 1930's wrote anti-fascist poetry; wrote plays, memoirs, works on history of culture; 1940 welcomed Sov annexation of Est; translated into Est: Pushkin, Griboyedov, Lermontov, Schiller, Heine, Mayakovskiy, Antokol'skiy, etc; *Publ:* collected verse "Shades of the Stars" (1913); "Song of Time" (1921); "The Month of Reaping" (1925); "Man at the Cross-Roads" (1932); "The Stirring Word" (1936); "Order of the Motherland" (1943); "Hatred, Only Hatred" (1944); novels: "Byanka and Ruf'" (1923); "A Woman from the Poor World" (1930); collected articles "Foliage in the Wind" (1924-37), etc; *Died*: 3 Apr 1958 in Tartu.

KYASPERT, Iokhannes Yur'yevich (1886-1938) Party and govt official; CP member from 1912; *Born*: 8 May 1886 in Narva, son of a worker; *Career*: office worker in Narva; helped publish newspaper *Kiir*, then conducted Party work in Revel; Apr 1916 arrested and exiled to Kustanay Uyezd, where he was released after 1917 Feb Revol; member, Tallin RSDRP(B) Comt; directed publ of Bolshevik newspapers in Est; member, Exec Comt, Estland Kray Sov and press comr for Estland Kray; helped muster Red Guard units; from Feb 1918 in Petrograd and Moscow; worked for newspaper *Pravda* and Pop Comrt of Nationalities; from Nov 1918 member, Govt and Pop Comrt of Interior of Estland Labor Commune; from 1919 worked for Red Army Staff and All-Russian Cheka; from 1925 exec secr, Commission to Collect and Study Material on the History of the Communist Party, CC, CP Est; edited journal *Proletarne revolutsioon Eestis*; from 1927 Party work in Leningrad; from 1930 secr, Bureau, Est Section, Comintern; arrested by State Security organs; *Died*: 1938 in imprisonment; posthumously rehabilitated.

KYUNER, Nikolay Vasil'yevich (1877-1955) Orientalist; specialist in the history, geography and ethnography of Eastern Asia; *Born*: 25 Sept 1877 in Tiflis; *Educ*: 1900 grad Oriental Fac, Petersburg Univ; *Career*: from 1902 prof, Oriental Inst (from 1920 Far Eastern Univ), Vladivostok; 1909 defended master's thesis on Tibet; from 1925 prof, Leningrad Univ; 1925-28 also taught at

Leningrad Oriental Inst; from 1932 senior assoc, then head, East and Southeast Asian Section, Inst of Ethnography, USSR Acad of Sci; wrote over 300 works on the history, ethnography, geography and culture of China, Japan and Korea; also translated classic and modern writings on source-research and compiled bibliographies; *Publ: Geografiya Kitaya* (A Geography of China) (1903-04); master's thesis *Opisaniye Tibeta* (A Description of Tibet) (4 vol, 1907-08); *Statistiko-geograficheskiy i ekonomicheskiy ocherk Korei* (A Statistical Geographical and Economic Study of Korea) (1912); *Lektsii po istorii razvitiya glavneyshikh osnov kitayskoy material'noy i dukhovnoy kul'tury* (Lectures on the History of the Development of the Main Principles of Chinese Civilization and Culture) (1921); *Geografiya Yaponii (Fizicheskaya i politicheskaya)* (The Physical and Political Geography of Japan) (1927); *Ocherki noveyshey politicheskoy istorii Kitaya* (Studies in Modern Chinese Political History), etc; *Died* 5 Apr 1955.

L

LADINSKIY, Antonin Petrovich (1896-1961) Writer; *Born:* 31 Jan 1896 in vil Obshcheye Pole, now Pskov Oblast; *Career:* from 1921 lived in Paris; in 1930's published several vol of poetry; 1946 acquired Sov citizenship; 1955 returned to USSR; translated works by P. Bourget and Voltaire into Russian; *Publ:* biographical sketch *Posledniye gody I. A. Bunina* (I. A. Bunin's Last Years) (1955); historical novels: *Kogda pal Khersones...* (When Chersonesus Fell...) (1959); *V dni Karakally* (in the Age of Caracalla) (1961); *Anna Yaroslavna - koroleva Frantsii* (Anna Yaroslavna - Queen of France) (1961); *Died:* 4 June 1961 in Moscow.

LADYGINA-KOTS, Nadezhda Nikolayevna (1889-1963) Psychologist; Dr of Biology; Hon Sci Worker of RSFSR from 1960; *Born:* 19 May 1889 in Penza; *Educ:* 1916 grad Moscow Higher Women's Courses; *Career:* specialized in comparative psychology; 1913 established a psychological laboratory at Darwin Museum, where she did most of her research; from 1945 senior assoc, Inst of Philosophy, USSR Acad of Sci; did research on higher forms of adaptive activity in primates; devised "specimen sampling" method to study the cognitive abilities of chimpanzees; used "problem cage" method to study habit formation in the lower apes; made a comparative analysis of the behavior of chimpanzees and infants which revealed a qualitative mental difference (while the primate's elementary thinking is based solely on the use of space-time relations, human thinking reveals cause-and-effect relationships); compiled and analyzed much data on the use of tools by chimpanzees and on the constructive and imitative activities of primates and pre-school children; *Publ: Issledovaniye poznovatel'nykh sposobnostey shimpanze* (A Study of the Cognitive Abilities of Chimpanzees) (1923); *Prisposobitel'nyye motornyye navyki makaka v usloviyakh eksperimenta* (The Adaptive Motor Habits of a Macaco Under Experimental Conditions) (1928); *(Ditya shimpanze i ditya cheloveka v ikh instinktakh, emotsiyakh, igrakh, privychkakh i vyrazitel'nykh dvizheniyakh* (Chimpanzee and Human Children in Their Instincts, Emotions, Games, Habits and Expressive Movements) (1935); *Razvitiye psikhiki v protsesse evolyutsii organizmov* (Mental Development in the Evolution of Organisms) (1958); *Konstruktivnyye i orudiynaya deyatel'nost' vysshykh obez'yan (shimpanze)* (Consturctive and Tool Activity in the Higher Apes "Chimpanzees") (1959); *Awards:* Order of Lenin (1955); *Died:* 3 Sept 1963.

LADYZHNIKOV, Ivan Pavlovich (1874-1945) Publisher; revolutionary; *Born:* 25 Jan 1874 in vil Peskovskoye, Perm' Province; *Career:* late 1890's and early 1900's active in revol movement; close friend and assistant of Gorky in his publishing work; 1905, on orders from the CC of the RSDRP, founded together with Gorky the "Demos" Publ House in Geneva, which was transferred to Berlin the same year and named the "Bühnen- und Buchverlag russischer Autoren J. Ladyschnikow"; this org published Marxist lit and the works of Gorky and writers of the "Znaniye" group; 1913 it was closed down; 1914-17 Ladyzhnikov worked with Gorky in the "Sail" Publ House and on the journal "Letopis' "; 1918-21 member, ed bd, "World Lit" Publ House; 1921-30 co-dir, "Book" and "Int Book" Limited Companies; 1937-43 sci consultant, Gorky Archives; *Publ:* coauthor, *Opisaniye rukopisey M. Gor'kogo* (A Description of Maxim Gorky's Manuscripts) (vol 1, 1948); *Died:* 20 Oct 1945 in Moscow.

LAKERBAY, Mikhail Aleksandrovich (1901-1965) Abkhazian writer; *Born:* 19 Jan 1901 in vil Merkheuli, now Gul'ripshi Rayon, Abkhazian ASSR; *Educ:* studied law in Tbilisi; *Career:* 1919 first work published; wrote plays, libretti, film-scripts, etc; *Publ:* film script "Flower of the Sun" (1934); musical comedy "Khadzharati" (1938) to a score by V. Kurtidi; comedies "Scion of the Gech" (1940) and "In Sadyby Ravine" (1941); opera "Mzia" (1951) to a score by A. Balanchivadze; drama "Danakay" (1956); "Abkhazian Novellas" (1957); film script "Flourishing Abkhazia" (1959); book "Alamys" (1961); operetta "Happiness" (1961) to a score by A. Balanchivadze; "Outline History of the Abkhazian Theater" (1962); *Died:* 15 Nov 1965.

LAKHUTI, Abol'gasem Akhmedzade (1887-1957) Iranian poet; one of the founders of Sov Tadzh poetry; CP member from 1924; *Born:* 31 Dec 1887 in Kermanshah, Western Iran; *Career:* active in 1905-11 Revol in Iran; 1916 published revol-democratic Kermanshah newspaper "Bisotup"; 1917 emigrated to Turkey following British occupation of Iran; published in Istanbul Persian- and French-language newspaper "Pars"; 1922 headed 2nd Tabriz Revolt (the "Lakhuti-Khan Revolt") and, after this was suppressed, emigrated to USSR; 1923-25 worked for Centr Publ House of Peoples of the USSR, Moscow; secr, city Party comt; Thadzh Dep Pop Comr of Educ; exec secr, USSR Writers' Union; 1907 first verse published wrote on Persian, Tadzh and int themes; in his latter years published three books of selected verse, mainly from his wartime period, worked on an autobiographical book and translated Russian and world classics; translated: Pushkin's poetry; Griboyedov's *Gore ot uma* (Woe from Wit); Mayakovskiy's *Razgovor s tovarishchem Leninym* (A Conversation with Comrade Lenin); Shakespeare's tragedies; Lope de Vega's "The Sheep's Spring", etc; many of his works have been translated into Russian and the other Sov languages; 1948 his poem "Pearl of Happiness" (1947) was proclaimed "alien to socialist realism", and from mid-1949 his works were seldem published; toward end of WW 2 wrote text for nat anthem of Tadzhik SSR; 1941 his poem *Kuznets Kova* (Kova the Smith) served as the libretto for A. Balasanyan's opera of the same name; *Publ:* ballad *Lenin zhiv* (Lenin Lives) (1924); poems: *Kreml'* (The Kremlin) (1923); *Korrespondentsiya* (The Report) (1932); *Gora i zerkalo* (Mountain and Mirror) (1933); *Klassu-sozidatelyu* (To the Founder-Class) (1933); *Puteshestviye v Yevropu* (A Journey to Europe) (1934); *Rodina radosti* (Homeland of Joy) (1935); *Korona i znamya* (Crown and Banner) (1935); *Kuznets Kova* (Kova the Smith) (1939); "Mardestan" (1941); *Pobeda Tani* (Tanya's Victory) (1942); *Sputniki* (Companions) (1943); *Perl schast'ya* (The Pearl of Happiness) (1947), etc; *Awards:* Order of Lenin; Order of the Red Banner of Labor; Dushanbe Drama Theater is named for him; *Died:* 16 Mar 1957 in Moscow.

LALAYAN, Yervan Aleksandrovich (1864-1931) Arm ethnographer, archeologist and folklorist; *Born:* 13 Mar 1864 in Alexandropol', now Leninakan; *Educ:* 1894 grad Fac of Soc Sci, Geneva Univ; *Career:* 1896-1916 published Arm ethnographic journal "Azgagrakan andes"; 1906-17 co-founder and active member, Arm Ethnographical Soc; 1909 co-founder, Tbilisi Ethnographical and Archeological Museum, which was transferred to Yerevan in 1921; dir, Arm State Historical Museum; collected valuable material on Arm ethnography and folklore; *Publ:* "The Perfume of Dzhavakhka" (2 vol, 1892); "Pearls of Armenian Folklore" (3 vol, 1914-16); "Tomb Excavations in Soviet Armenia" (1931), etc; *Died:* 24 Feb 1931 in Yerevan.

LAMM, Pavel Aleksandrovich (1882-1951) Musicologist; Dr of Arts from 1943; *Born:* 27 July 1882 in Moscow; *Educ:* 1900-01 studied at Law Fac, Bonn, then Cologne Univ; 1912 grad piano courses, Moscow Conservatory; *Career:* from 1912 art dir, Russian Musical Publ House (later State Musical Publ House); 1912 began research in archives of musical manuscripts; catalogued works of leading Russian composers; edited and arranged Russian musical classics; from the papers left by various composers he restored original score of Moussorgsky's "Boris Godunov" and "Khovanshchina" and Dargomyzhskiy's *Rusalka* (The Water-Nymph); edited Moussorgsky's opers *Sorochinskaya yarmarka* (Sorochintsy Fair) and Borodin's "Prince Igor"; arranged over 150 symphonic works for two pianoes; 1918-39 lecturer; from 1939 prof, Moscow Conservatory; Awards: Order of the Red Banner of Labor; medal; *Died:* 5 May 1951 in vil Nikolina Gora, near Moscow.

LAMPERT, Feliks Moiseyevich (1893-1958) Surgeon and oncologist; Dr of Med from 1938; prof from 1940; pupil of P. A. Gertsen; *Born:* 1893; *Educ:* 1912 grad Warsaw Boys' High-School; 1920 grad Med Fac, Rostov-on Don-Univ; *Career:* during Civil War served as mil surgeon with Budyonnyy's Cavalry Army; from 1921 intern, P. A. Gertsen's Propaedeutical Surgical Clinic, Moscow Univ; 1924-25 worked at Surgical Dept, N. V. Sklifosovskiy First Aid Inst; 1026-30 asst prof, Propaedeutic Clinic, First Moscow Univ and Tumor Therapy Inst; 1930-33 surgeon, Volokolamsk Hospital, Moscow Oblast; 1930-32 dep, Volokolamsk City Sov; 1930 in charge of a distr cancer center during the org of Moscow municipal and oblast cancer service; 1934-41 surgeon, Blagushinsk Hospital; 1938 defended doctor's thesis on surgery of the vegetative nervous system and the surgical treatment of hypertonia; during 1930's also studied endarteritis obliterans; 1939-45 dep, Stalin Rayon Sov, Moscow; from 1940 prof, Chair of Gen Surgery, 3rd Moscow Med Inst then head, Chair of Hospital Surgery, Perm, Med Inst; 1941-42 chief hospital surgeon, Perm' Oblast; 1942-45 dir, Surgical Clinic, Moscow Oncological Inst; 1945 founded a 150-bed oncological dept at the "Medsantrud" Hospital, Moscow, which became a major center for the study and combined treatment of malignant tumors; pioneered the hormone treatment of mammary cancer in the USSR; also developed methods for the combined treatment of cancer of the thyroid gland, cervix, bones, urinary bladder, etc; 1953-58 sci dir, Moscow Municipal Oncological Hospital; member, various sci soc; delivered papers at numerous conferences and at bd sessions of the All-Union, Moscow and Leningrad Oncological Soc; from 1952 bd member, All-Union and Moscow Oncological Soc, wrote over 60 works, *Died:* 1 Aug 1958 in Moscow.

LANDA, M. M. (1890-1939) Party and govt officail; CP member from 1918; *Born:* 1890; *Career:* 1907-16 member, RSDRP (Mensheviks); 1916-18 member, Soc-Democratic Internationalist Party; revol work in Kiev, Tula and Moscow; 1917 member, Moscow Sov; after 1917 Oct Revol polit work in Red Army; dep head, Polit Bd, Red Army; head, Polit Bd, Bel, then Siberian Mil Distr; asst prosecutor, USSR Supr Court and mil prosecutor; exec ed, newspaper "Krasnaya zvezda" and journal "Znamya"; arrested by State Security organs; *Died:* 1939 in imprisonment.

LANDER, K. I. (1884-1937) Govt official; CP member from 1905; *Born:* 1884; *Career:* Party work in Lat, Moscow, Petersburg, Samara, etc; fought in 1905-07 revol in Moscow; 1917 member Minsk and Northwestern Oblast RSDRP(B) Comt; after establishment of Sov regime in Bel appointed chm, Western Oblast Council of Pop Comr; from May 1918 RSFSR Pop Comr of State Control; after Civil War took up writing; arrested by State Security organs; *Died:* 1937 in imprisonment.

LANDSBERG, Grigoriy Samuilovich (1890-1957) Physicist; member, USSR Acad of Sci from 1946; *Born:* 22 Jan 1890 in Vologda; *Educ:* 1913 grad Moscow Univ; *Career:* 1913-15, and 1947-51 at Moscow Univ; from 1934 at Physics Inst, USSR Acad of Sci; 1932-46 corresp member, USSR Acad of Sci; specialized in optical physics, particularly spectral analysis and the molecular diffusion of light; 1926 detected and studied molecular diffusion in crastals; 1928 together with L. I. Mandel'shtam discovered phenomenon of combination diffusion of light; 1931 the two discovered and studied the selective diffusion of light; used optical methods to study inter-and intra-molecular reactions in crystals, liquids and gases laid the groundwork for the spectral analysis of metals and devised special equipment for such analysis; 1949 developed methods for the molecular spectral analysis of complet organic mixtures, including motor fuel; chm, Spectroscopy Commission, USSR Acad of Sci; *Publ:* coauthor, *"Novoye yavleniye pri rasseyanii sveta"* (A New Phenomenon in the Diffusion of Light) (1928); *"Mezhdumolekulyarnyye sily i kombinatsionnoye rasseyaniye sveta"* (Inter-Molecular Forces and the Combination Diffusion of Light) (1938); coauthor, *"Vliyaniye temperatury na spektr rasseyaniya Kristallov, soderzhashchikh OH-gruppy"* (The Effect of Temperature on the Diffusion Spectrum of Crystals Containig OH-Groups) (1952); "Optika" (1952); *Awards:* two Orders of Lenin; medals; Stalin Prize (1941); *Died:* 2 Feb 1957.

LANG, Georgiy Fyodorovich (1875-1948) Internist; Dr of Med from 1901; member, USSR Acad of Med Sci from 1944; Hon Sci Worker of RSFSR; *Born:* 28 July 1875 in Petersburg; *Educ:* 1899 grad Petersburg Mil Med Acad; *Career:* 1901 defended doctor's thesis on the osmotic stability of blood corpuscles in stomach ulcers; 1901-19 intern, then dept head, Petropavlovsk (now F. F. Erisman) Hospital; 1905-19 also lecturer, Petersburg (Petrograd) Mil Med Acad; 1919-22 dir, Therapeutic Clinic, Leningrad Inst of Postgrad Med Training; from 1922 dir, Fac Therapeutic Clinic, 1st Leningrad Med Inst; did major research on cardiology and hypertonia; 1922 concluded that hypertonia is an independent nosological entity unrelated to primary kidney damage; laid the foundations of the modern concept of hypertonia as a disease related to disturbances of the system of cortical and subcortical nervous regulation; also did research on the pathology of the myocardium; undertook first Sov clinical-anatomical study of Hiss's (atrioventricular) tract; established that electrocardiograms can indicate certain biochemical disturbances in the cardiac muscle and devised the term "myocardic dystrophy" to describe diseases of the cardiac muscle caused by reversible exogenous and endogenous disturbances of biochemical and physiochemical processes in the heart; developed a classification system for circulatory diseases bases on etiological, pathoanatomical, pathophysiological (functional) and clinical-symptomatological principles; initiated functional trend in hematology; did research on hemolytic anemia and devised new classification of liver diseases; co-founder, journal "Terapevticheskiy arkhiv"; ed, journal "Klinicheskaya meditsina"; wrote one of best studies of pulmonary pathology - *"K voprosu o tromboarteriite lyogkikh"* (Thromboarteriities of the Lungs); wrote four-vol textbook on interior diseases that served as a standart work for many years; 1922 organized 1st Sov Congress of Therapeutists; directed All-Union therapeutic congresses; lifechm, All-Union Therapeutic Soc; trained such eminent therapeutists as A. Myasnikov, I. Teplov, D. Grotel' and B. Il'inskiy, etc; *Publ:* doctor's thesis *"O diagnosticheskom znachenii povysheniya stoykosti krasnykh krovyanykh telets i drugikh izmeneniy krovi pri rake zheludka"* (The Diagnostic Importance of Increased Stability of the Red Blood Corpuscles and Other Blood Lesions in Cancer of the Stomach) (1901); coauthor *"Chastnaya patologiya i terapiya vnutrennikh bolezney"* (Special Pathology and Therapy of Internal Diseases) (4 vol, 1927-31); *"Voprosy patologii krovoobrashcheniya i kliniki serdechno-sosudistykh bolezney"* (The Pathology of Blood Circulation and Clinical Aspects of Cardiovascular Diseases) (1936); *"Bolezni sistemy krovoobrashcheniya. Uchebnik vnutrennikh bolezney"* (Diseases of the Circulatory System. A Textbook of Internal Diseases) (Vol 1, 1938); *"Gipertonicheskaya bolezn'..* (Hypertonia) (1950), etc; *Awards:* Stalin Prize (1950); Order of Lenin; other orders; medals; *Died:* 24 July 1948 in Leningrad

LANN (real name: LOZMAN), Yevgeniy L'vovich (1896-1958) Russian writer and translator; *Born:* 13 May 1896 in Khar'kov; *Career:* specialized in British and American lit; edited, commented on and made numerous translations of Dickens, Smollett, Hardy, Conrad, Crane, Lawson, Aldington, Anderson, Belloc, Dos Passos, etc; made various translations with A. V. Krivtsova; *Publ:* novels based on British history *"Gvardiya Mak Kumgala"* (The MacCumgal Guard) (1938); *"Staraya Angliya"* (Old England) (1943); lit criticism "Joseph Konrad" (1924); *"Pisatel'skaya sud'ba Maksimiliana Voloshina"* (The Writing Career of Maksimilian Voloshin) (1926); *"Literaturnaya mistifikatsiya"* (Literary Mystification) (1930); "Dikkens" (Dickens) (1946); *Died:* 3 Oct 1958 in Moscow.

LANSERE, Yevgeniy Yevgen'yevich (1875-1946) Painter and graphic artist; member, Acad of Painting from 1912; Hon Art Worker of Geo SSR from 1933; Pop Artist of RSFSR from 1945; *Born:* 4 Sept 1875 in Pavlovsk, Petersburg Province; *Educ:* studied drawing in Petersburg and Paris; *Career:* from 1898 member, "World of Art" assoc; displayed markedly realistic bent in his work; early 1900's painted historical subjects and did illustrations for books and periodicals; 1917-34 lived in Caucasus and painted typical genre pictures; also worked as set deigner; 1920-34 dean and prof, Acad of Arts, Tbilisi; then prof fo painting, All-Union Acad of Architecture; *Works:* "The Empress Yelizaveta Petravna at Tsarskoye Selo" (1905); "Ships of Peter I's Time" (1911); Illustrations for Lev Tolstos's novelette "Khadzhi-Murat" (1912-16); paintings "Zangezur" (1926) and "Svanetiya" (1929); triptych "The Red Partisans of Daghestan" (1931); murals in Tbilisi Station's Agitation Center; 1921); murals in Kazan' Station Restaurant (1934); decorated ceiling of Moskva Hotel in Moscow (1937); Illustrations for Lev Tolstoy's "Kazaki" (Cossacks) (1937); designed sets and costumes for Griboydov's *Gore ot uma"* (Woe From Wit) at Moscow's Maly Theater (1938); guache series "Trophies of Russian Army" (1942); murals in vestibule of Kazan' Station "Victory" and "Peace" (1945-46); *Awards:* Stalin Prize (1943); two Orders of the Red Banner of Labor (1943 and 1945); medals; *Died:* 13 Spt 1946.

LAPCHINSKIY, Aleksandr Nikolayevich (1882-1938) Mil commender; brigade commander from 1935; specialist in air force theory; *Born:* 1882; *Career:* from 1918 in Red Army; during Civil War chief of an army air force; chief of staff, Sov Russian Air Force; after Civil War teaching and research work at Frunze Mil Acad and Air Force Acad; *Publ: "Taktika aviatsii".* (Air Force Tactics) (1926); *"Krasnyy Vozdushnyy flot 1918-1928"* (The Red Air Force. 1918-1928) (1928); *"Tekhnika i taktika vozdushnogo flota"* (Air Force Equipment and Tactics) (1930); *"Vozdushnyye sily v boyu i operatsii"* (The Air Force in Combat and in Operations) (1932); *"Vozdushnyy boy"* (Aerial Combat) (1934); *"Bombardirovochnaya aviatsiya"* (The Bomber Air Force) (1937); *"Vozdushnaya razvedka"* (Aerial Reconnaissance) (1938); *"Vozdushnaya armiya"* (The Air Army) (1939); *Died:* 1938.

LAPIN (real name: LAPIN'), Al'bert Yanovich (1899-1937) Mil commander; Lat; corps commander from 1935; CP member from 1917; *Born:* 27 May 1899 in Riga, son of a worker; *Educ;* 1925 grad Red Army Mil Acad; *Career:* 1917 loader at "Provodnik" Plant in Moscow; took part in 1917 Feb Revol; secr, Lefortov Rayon Working Youth League; took Part in 1917 Oct Revol in Moscow; from 1918 in Red Army; 1918-21 comr of intelligence service, 5th Army Staff; commander, 232nd Infantry Regt, 26th Infantry Div; head, 30th Infantry Div; commander, 80th Brigade, 27th Infantry Div; 1921-22 commander, Amur Army; dep commander in chief, Pop Revol Army of Far Eastern Republ; commander, Amur and Trans-Baikal Mil Distr; 1925-27 mil adviser, Kaifin Group, then chief of staff, Kalgan Group, China (under the alias of Seyfullin); 1929-30 chief of staff, Blyukher's Special Red Banner Far Eastern Army; 1929 directed Sov mil operations to restore order along Chinese-Eastern Railroad; 1930-37 commander, 19th Maritime Corps; chief of a bd, Red Army Staff; chief, Red Army Mil Training Bd; air force commander, Bel Mil Distr and Special Red Banner Far Eastern Army; 1937 arrested by NKWD; *Awards:* four Order of the Red Banner; *Died:* 1937 in imprisonment; posthumously rehabilitated.

LAPIN, Boris Matveyevich (1905-1941) Writer; *Born:* 30 May 1905 in Moscow; *Career:* mid-1920's accompanied geobotanical expedition to Centr Asia; worked at a fur factory in Chukotka and as a trainee navigator on ocean-going vessels; during this period began writing for newspapers; 1939, together with fellow war-correspondent Z. Khatsrevin, covered the battle of Khalkyn Gol; also accompanied Khatsrevin on reporting assignments during WW 2, writing "Letters from the Front" for the newspaper "Krasnaya zvezda"; *Publ:* verse collections *"Molniyanin"* (The Lightning Man) (1922) and *"1922-aya kniga stikhov"* (Tale of the Pamirs) (1929); *"Tikhookeanskiy dnevnik"* (Pacific Journal) (1929); coauthor, *Amerika granichit s nami"* (America's on Our Borders) (1932); *"Podvig"* (The Exploit) (1933); *"1869-yy god"* (1869) (1935); coauthor, *"Dal'nevostochnyye rasskazy"* (Stories of the Far East); coauthor, *"Puteshestviye"* (The Jouney) (1937); coauthor, film-script *"Yego zovut Sukhe-Bator"* (His Name Is Sukhe-Bator) (1938); *Died:* Sept 1941 killed in actions near Kiev together with Z. Khatsrevin.

LAPINSKIY, P. L. (pseudonyms: Ya. LEVINSON; MIKHAL'SKIY) (1879-1937) Polish Communist, economist and journalist; CP member from 1919; *Born:* 1879; *Career:* 1920-28 member, RSFSR (USSR) mission in Germany; arrested by State Security organs; *Died:* 1937 in imprisonment.

LAPIROV-SKOBLO, M. Ya. (1888-1947) Electr eng; *Born:* 1888; *Career:* from 1918 mang and Collegium member, Sci and Tech Dept, Supr Sovnarkhoz; worked for State Commission for Electrification of Russia; 1918-21 chm, bd administering electr tube plants; 1922 performed missions abroad for Supr Sovnarkhoz and Pop Comrt of For Trade; 1923-29 directed electr eng and radio eng institutes of Supr Sovnarkhoz and Pop Comrt of Posts and Telegraphs; co-founder, All-Union Electr Eng Inst; 1932-37 dir, Centr Research Inst of Communications; from 1924 prof and Dr of Tech Sci; *Died:* 1947

LAPITSKIY (pseudonym: MIKHAYLOV), Iosif Mikhaylovich (1876-1944) Opera producer; Hon Artiste of RSFSR from 1936; *Born:* 28 Jan 1876 in Minsk; *Career:* 1897-1900 actor and stage dir, Sablina-Dol'skaya's Theater Company; 1900-01 with E. Possart's Company in Munich; 1903-06 stage dir, Solodovnikov Opera Theater in Moscow; under the pseudonym Mikhaylov published in theatrical section journal "Birzhevyye vedomosti" a number of articles advocating opera theater reforms; his ideas were supported by Stanislavsky; 1906-08 stage dir, Bolshoy Theater; 1908-11 at various theater in Perm', Samara, Irkutsk; 1912-19 founder-dir, Petersburg Musical Drama Theater; 1919 with Malaya State Opera; 1920-22 with Moscow Musical Drama Theater; 1921, 1924-25 and 1928 dir and stage dir, Bolshoy Theater; 1923-24 managed opera company drawn from Leningrad's opera theaters; helped establish musical theaters in Ukr; 1926 helped found Kiev State Opera and 1941 Donetsk Opera and Ballet Theater; Productions; staged operas: *"Yevgeniy Onegin"* (Eugene Onegin) (1912); "Carmen" (1913); *"Pikovaya dama"* (The Queen of Spades) (1914); *"Snegurochka"* (The Snow-Maiden) (1914); "Aida" (1915); Wagner's "Parzival" (1916); Rimsky-Korsakov's *"Skazaniye o nevidimom grade Kitezhe i deve Fevronii"* (The Tale of the Invisible City of Kitezh and the Maiden Fevroniya) (1908); "Rigoletto" (1925); "Khovanshchina" (1928); Wagner's "Die Meistersinger von Nürnberg" (1929); *"Tikhiy Don"* (Quiet Flows the Don) (1936); "Lyatoshinskiy's "Shchors" (1938); Richard Strauß' "Salome" (1924); Offenbach's "Hoffmanns Erzählungen" (1924); d'Albers' "The Valley" (1920); Kalmann's "Czardasfürstin" (1921); Strel'nikov's *"Chyornyy amulet"* (The Black Amulet) (1928); *"Podnyataya tselina"* (Virgin Soie Upturned) (1938), etc; *Died:* 5 Nov 1944 in Moscow.

LAPPO-DANILEVSKIY, Ivan Aleksandrovich (1895-1931) Mathematician; corresp member, USSR Acad of Sci from 1931; *Born:* 28 Oct 1895; *Educ:* 1925 grad Leningrad Univ; *Career;* worked at various higher educ establishments in Leningrad; 1930 recaived Rockefeller grant for study abroad; developed theory of Functions from matrices and obtained fundamental results from application to the theory of linear differential equations; *Publ: "Novaya teoriya sistem lineynykh differentsial'nykh uranvneniy s ratsional'nymi koeffitsientami"* (A New Theory of Linear Differential Equation Systems with Rational Coefficients) (1929); *"Teoriya funktsiy ot matrits i sistemy lineynykh differentsil'nykh uravneniy"* (The Theory of Functions from Matrices and Linear Differential Equation Systems) (1934); "Mémoires sur la théorie des systèmes des équations différentielles linéaires" (Notes on the Theory of Linear Différential Equation Systems) (1934); *Died:* 15 Mar 1931 in Giessen, Germany, of heart disease.

LARICHEV, Pavel Afanas'yevich (1892-1963) Pedagogue; specialist in methods of teaching mathematics; corresp member, RSFSR Acad of Pedag Sci from 1950; Hon Schoolteacher of RSFSR from 1947; *Born:* 16 Feb 1892; *Educ:* 1911 grad teachers' seminar; 1923 grad Vologda Teachers' Training Inst; 1925 grad Moscow Higher Sci Pedag Courses; *Career:* 1911 began teaching at a vil school; from 1923 taught mathematics at secondary schools; lectured and held seminars on teaching methods; from 1944 consultant on mathematics, School Bd, RSFSR Pop Comrt (Min) of Educ; wrote articles on methods of teaching mathematics in secondary schools and compiled algebra task books for the 6th-7th and 8th-9th grades; *Died:* 12 Mar 1963.

LARIN, Boris Aleksandrovich (1893-1964) Linguist; Dr of Philology from 1948; prof; member, Lith Acad of Sci and corresp member, Ukr Acad of Sci from 1945; Hon Sci Worker of RSFSR; *Born:* 17 Jan 1893 in Poltava; *Educ:* grad Kiev Univ; studied Sanskrit, Persian and the Slavic, Romance and Baltic languages at Petersburg Univ; *Career:* prof, Leningrad Univ; did research on the Russian language and its history, including dialectology, lexicology, phraseology, stylistics and grammar; also did research on Indian philology; 1934-49 supervised the compilation of material for a dictionary of ancient Russian; also collected material for a bibliography of the Russian language from 1860 through 1940; *Publ: "Iz oblasti vediyskoy poezii"* (From the Realm of Vedic Poetry) (1924); *"Materialy po litovskoy dialektologii"* (Material on Lithuanian Dialectology) (1926); *"Zaodnoyevropeyskiye elementy russkogo vorovskogo argo"* (West European Elements in Russian Thieves' Cant) (1931); coauthor, *"Tolkovyy slovar' russkogo literaturnogo yazka"* (An Explanatory Dictionary of Literary Russian) (4 vol, 1934-40); *"Dialektizm v yazyke sovetskikh pisateley"* (Dialectism in the Language of Soviet Writers) (1935); *"Parizhskiy *slovar' russkogo yazyka 1586-ogo goda"* (The 1586 Paris Dictionary of Russian) (1936); *"Russkaya gramatika Ludol'fa 1696-ogo goda"* (Ludolph's Russian Grammar, 1696) (1937); ed, *"Russko-Litovskiy slovar'"* (A Russian-Lithuanian Dictionary) (1941); *"Tri inostrannyye istochniki po istorii russkogo yazyka XVI-XVII vekov"* (Three Foreign Sources on the History of the Russian Language in the 16th and 17th Centuries) (1948); *"Parizhskiy slovar' moskovitov 1586-ogo goda"* (The 1586 Paris Moscovite Dictionary) (1948); *"Iz istorii slov: 1. Lyutyy zver'; 2. Sem'ya; 3. Kavardak"* (From the History of Words: 1. The Wild Beast; 2. The Family; 3. The Muddle) (1951); *"Ocherki po frazeologii"* (Studies in Phraseology) (1956); *"Ob izuchenii i perevodakh drevneindiyskoy poetiki"* (The Study and Translation of Ancient Indian Poetics) (1957); *"Kratkiy istoricheskiy obzor litovskoy leksikografii"* (Ashort Historical Review of Lithuanian Lexicography) (1957); *"Istoricheskaya dialektologiya russkogo yazyka i yeyo sovremennoye znacheniye"* (The Historical Dialectology of Russian and Its Present-Day Importance) (1958); *"Russkiye povesti XV-XVI vekov"* (Russian Narratives of the 15th and 16th Century) (1958); *"Russko-angliyskiy slovar' iz Zapisnoy knigi Richarda Dzhemsa 1618-ogo goda"* (The Russian-English Dictionary from Richard James' Notebook for 1618) (1960), etc; *Died:* 26 Mar 1964.

LARIN, Yu. (real name: ALEKSANDROVICH, Lur'ye Mikhail) (1882-1932) Econ and writer; CP member from 1917; *Born:* 4 July 1882 in Simferopol'; *Career:* from 1900 active in revol movement in Odessa; 1901-02 headed Simferopol' Soc-Democratic org; helped found Crimean RSDRP League; 1902 exiled to Yakutsk Province; 1904 fled from exile and went to Geneva, where he sided with the Mensheviks; 1905 returned to Petersburg and helped found first Russian trade unions; 1905-13 underground Party work in Petersburg, Crimea, Ukr and Caucasus; 1912 took liquidationist stand; sided with anti-Bolshevik "Aug Bloc"; 1913 arrested in Tiflis; 1914 exiled from Russia; during WW 1 took internationalist stand; after 1917 Feb Revol returned to Russia and headed internationalist Menshevik group, publishing journal "International"; member, Exec Comt, Petrograd Sov; after 1917 Oct Revol worked for committees and commissions handling finance, nationalization of trade, establishment of sovkhozes, allotment of land to Jewish workers, etc; co-founder, Gosplan; 1918 head, Comt of Econ Policy, Supr Sovnarkhoz; 1920-21 dep chm, High Council for Haulage and Transport, Gosplan; from May 1921 member, from Nov 1921 Presidium member, Gosplan; 1921 chm, Soc for the Struggle Against Alcoholism; Feodosiya RSDRP Comt deleg at 4th (Amalgamative) RSDRP Congress; Poltava City RSDRP Comt deleg at 5th RSDRP Congress; Kostroma Province RCP(B) Comt deleg at 8th RCP(B) Congress; *Publ: "Itogi NEPa"* (The Results of the New Economic Policy); *"Voprosy krest'yanskogo khozyaystva"* (Problems of the Peasant Economy); *"Uroki krizisov"* (The Lessons of Crises); *"Novaya torgovaya politika"* (The New Trade Policy); *"Sovetskaya derevnya"* (The Soviet Village), etc; *Died:* 14 Jan 1932; buried on Moscow's Red Square.

LASHAS, Vladas Laurinovich (1892-1966) Physiologist; prof from 1926; member, Lith Acad of Sci from 1946; corresp member, USSR Acad of Med Sci from 1948; Hon Sci Worker of Lith SSR from 1945; *Born:* 1892; *Educ:* 1918 grad Med Fac Tartu Univ; *Career:* 1922-25 asst prof, then assoc prof, and 1926-50 prof, Chair of Physiology Med Fac, Kaunas Univ; 1946-62 acad secr, Dept of Natural Sci, Lith Acad of Sci 1950-66 head, Chair of Physiology, Kaunas Med Inst; co-founder, Med Fac, Kaunas Univ and several chairs and laboratories; did research on anaphylaxis and anaphylactic shock and on problems of nutrition; devised method of determining the resorption of native proteins from the intestine; made detailed study of various desensitizers and their afficacy; defined the concept of anaphylactic incubation and did research on the reflector phase of anaphylactic shock; also studied the antigen-antibody reaction phase; co-ed, physiology section, *"Bol'shaya meditsinskaya entsiklopediya"* (Large Medical Encyclopedia) (2nd ed); *Publ: "Anafilaksiya"* (Anaphylaxis) (1926); *"Osnovy nauki o pitanii"* (The Principles of Alimentology) (1945); *"Vitaminy"* (Vitamins); *"Endokrinnyye zhelezy"* (The Endocrine Glands) (1946); *"Fiziologiya myshts i nervnoy sistemy"* (The Physiology of the Muscles and the Nervous System) (1950); *"Prakticheskiye zanyatiya po fiziologii"* (Practical Studies in Physiology) (1954); *"Fiziologiya analizatorov"* (The Physiology of the Analyzers) (1954); *"Krov' i krovoobrashcheniye"* (Blood and Its Circulation) (1958); *"Sensibiliziruyushchiye svoystva nekotorykh produktov streptokokkovogo proiskhozhdeniya"* (The Sensitizing Properties of Some Drugs of Streptococcic Origin) (1950); *Died:* Jan 1966.

LASHEVICH, Mikhail Mikhaylovich (1884-1928) Party and govt official; CP member from 1901; *Born:* 1884; *Career:* from 1901 in revol movement; member, Bolshevik committees in Odessa, Nikolayev, Yekaterinburg, Petersburg, etc; after 1917 Feb Revol secr, then chm, Bolshevik faction, Petrograd Sov; during 1917 Oct Revol member, Petrograd Mil Revol Comt; fought in Oct Revol; during Civil War member, Revol Mil Council, 3rd, Southern, 7th and 15th Armies; after Civil War chm, Siberian Revol Comt; 1925-26 joined Leningrad opposition, but soon abandoned it and recanted his error; from 1926 dep chm, bd, Chinese-Eastern Railroad; at 7th, 12th and 13th Party Congresses elected member, CC, CPSU(B); at 14th Congress elected cand member, CC, CPSU(B); Jan 1926 expelled from cand membership of CC; 1927 at 15th CPSU(B) Congress expelled from Party for belonging to Trotskyist opposition; later reinstated; *Died:* 1928.

LATSIS, Martyn Ivanovich (SUDRABS, Yan Fridrikhovich) (1888-1938) Party and govt officail; CP member from 1905; *Born:* 16 Dec 1888 in Lat, son of peasant; *Educ:* attended Shanyavskiy Univ in Moscow; *Career:* teacher by profession; 1906-11 taught in Lat; 1911-13 surveyor in Northern Caucasus; 1914 in Moscow; 1915 arretsed; 1916 exiled to Irkutsk Province; fall 1916 fled from exile to Petrograd, where he did underground Party work; fought in 1905-07 Revol in Riga and in 1917 Oct Revol in Petrograd; deleg, 7th (Apr) Party Conference and 6th RSDRP(B) Congress; member, Petrograd Mil Revol Comt; after 1917 Oct Revol Collegium member, Pop Comrt of Internal Affairs; from May 1918 Collegium member, All-Russian Cheka; July-Nov 1918 chm, Cheka and Mil Tribunal, 5th Army on Eastern Front; 1919-21 chm, All-Ukr Cheka, then again worked for All-Russian Cheka; deleg, 8th and 10th RCP(B) Congresses; from 1921 exec admin and Party work; chm Main Salt Ind Bd; dep head, Main Mining Ind Bd; Collegium member, RSFSR Pop Comrt of Agric; from 1928 senior instructor, CC CPSU(B); then dep head, Rural Dept, CC, CPSU(B); from 1932 dir, Plekhanov Econ Inst; 1937 arrested by State Security organs; *Publ: "Chrezvychaynyye komissii po bor'be s kontrrevolyutsiyey"* (The Special Commissions to Combat Counterrevolution) (1921); *"Nasha doroga. Povest' iz zhizni revolyutsionera"* (Our Road. A Tale of a Revolutionary's Life) (1923); *"Agrarnoye perenaseleniye i perspektivy bor'by s nim"* (Agrarian Overpopulation and Prospects of Combatting It) (1929); *"V posledney skhvatke s tsarizmom. Vospominaniya o rabote moskovskikh* bol'she*vikov v gody imperialisticheskoy voyny"* (The Last Skirmish with Tsarism. Memoirs of Moscow Bolsheviks' Work During the Imperialistic War) (1935); *Died:* 1938 in imprisonment; posthumously rehabilitated.

LATSIS, Vilis Tenisovich (1904-1966) Lat writer; Pop Writer of Lat SSR from 1947; bd member, USSR and Lat Writer's Unions; member, CC, CP Lat from 1940; CP member from 1928; *Born:* 12 May 1904 in vil Rinuzhi, near Riga, son of a dock worker; *Eudc:* 1917 completed Ust-Dvinsk parish school; 1917-18 studied at Barnaul Teachers' Seminary; *Career:* 1917 evacuated to Barnaul in the Altay; 1921 secr, vil sov in the Altay; returned to Lat; from fall 1921 laborer, then stoker on ocean-going merchant ships; 1925-26 in Lat Army; 1928-33 underground Party work; Bd member, Dock Workers' Union; 1933-35 librarian at an urban public library; 1935-38 engaged in lit work; 1938-40 underground Party work in Riga; 1940 Min of Internal Affairs in the new Sov Lat govt; 1941-44 helped direct partisan movement in Lat; 1940-59 chm, Lat Council of Pop Comr, then Council of Min; 1952-61 cand member, CC, CPSU; 1954 member, Sov deleg at "European peace and security" conference in Moscow; 1955 member, Sov deleg at East-Bloc conference in Warsaw and at World Peace Assembly in Helsinki; 1956 led USSR Supr Sov deleg to Belgium; 1956 member, Sov deleg in Finland; dep, Lat Supr Sov of 1947, 1951, 1955, 1959, and 1963 convocations; dep, USSR Supr Sov of 1946, 1950, 1954 and 1958 convocations; dep chm, Sov of Nationalities, USSR Supr Sov of 1950 convocations; chm, Sov of Nationalities, USSR Supr Sov of 1954 convocation, 1921 first work published; *Publ:* novels: "The Stone Path"; "The Call of the Ancestors";

"People in Masks"; "The Fisherman's Son"; novelettes: "The Guilty"; "A Journey to Zakata"; "Land and Sea"; trilogy: "The Five-Story City", "On the Seven Seas" and "Wingless Birds" (1930-41); plays: "The Fiancee" (1943); "Victory" (1945); novelette "Smiths of the Future" (1942-44); novels; "The Storm" (1945-48) "To a New Shore" (1951); "Settlement by the Sea" (1954); "After the Storm" (1962(; *Awards:* four Orders of Lenin; Order of the Fatherland War, 1st Class; medals: two Stalin Prizes (1948 and 1952); *Died:* 6 Feb 1966 in Riga.

LATSIS, Yan Yanovich (1897-1937) Mil commander; Lat; corps commander from 1935; CP member from 1917; *Born:* 8 Feb 1897 on Lyudy Estate, Liflyand Province, son of farm-laborer; *Career:* 1916 drafted into Russian Army; private, then nco in 4th Lat Vidzeme Infantry Regt; after 1917 Feb Revol secr, regt comt of Bolshevik faction, then chm, soldiers' regt comt; after 1917 Oct Revol commanded 4th Lat Vidzeme Infantry Regt; Mar-May 1918 used regt to guard Kremlin; simultaneously commandant, Kremlin; 1918-20 commanded Inza Revol Div on Eastern Front and Don; 1920-21 commanded Lat Infatry Div; acting commander, 14th Army; asst rear commander, 12th and 13th Armies; rear commander, 6th Army on Southern Front; 1924-26 commandant, Kiev Joint Mil School; 1926-32 commanded infantry corps; 1932-37 commander, Red Army railroad troops; *Awards:* Order of Lenin; Order of the Red Banner; *Died:* 10 Mar 1937

LATYSHEV, Nikolay Ivanovich (1886-1951) Parasitologist; corresp member, USSR Acad of Med Sci; *Born:* 1886; *Educ:* 1912 grad Med Fac, Moscow Univ; *Career:* for over 20 years worked in various mil med org, mainly in Centr Asia; 1923 published a monograph on malaria which became a standard work for gen practitioners engaged in the campaign against this disease; 1937-51 worked in Parasitology Dept, All-Union Inst of Experimental Med; did research on tick-borne relapsing fever, Pappatacci's fever and skin leishmaniosis; by means of self-infection established that tick-bite relapsing fever of the Centr Asian type is transmitted by the tick Ornithodorus papillipes; discovered a new from of this disease associated with the gerbil Rhombomys opimus and carried by Spirochaeta latyshevi; spent eight years studying skin leishmaniosis along the Murgab river and proved that this disease is zoonotic and is transmitted to human beings by the great gerbil (Rhombomys opimus) and certain other rodents; also studied leishmaniosis along the Karakum Canal and worked out suitable countermeasures; *Publ: "Malyariya i bor'ba s ney"* (Malaria and How to Combat It) (1923); *"K epidemiologii kozhnogo leyshmanioza"* (The Epidemiology of Skin Leishmaniosis) (1941); *"Opyt likvidatsii endemicheskogo ochaga kozhnogo leyshmanioza v Turkmenii"* (The Practical Destruction of an Endemic Focus of Skin Leishmaniosis in Turkmania) (1941); *"Epidemiologiya kozhnogo leyshmanioza v usloviyakh peschanoy pustyni"* (The Epidemiology of Skin Leishmaniosis in Sand-Desert Conditions) (1941); *"Ucheniye o khozhnom leyshmanioze"* (The Theory of Skin Leishmaniosis) (1947); *"Bolezn' Borovskogo (kozhnyy leyshmanioz, pendinskaya yazva, ashkhabadskaya yazva)"* (Borovskiy's Disease (Skin Leishmaniosis, Oriental Sores and Ashkhabad Sores) (1953); *Awards:* Mechnikov Prize (1949); *Died:* 1951.

LAVOCHKIN, Semyon Alekseyevich Aircraft designer; Chief Aircraft Designer from 1935; maj-gen, Eng and Tech Corps; corresp member, USSR Acad of Sci from 1958; CP member from 1953; *Born:* 29 Aug 1900 in Smolensk, son of a teacher; *Career:* from 1927 aircraft eng in aviation ind; supervised design of "LAGG-3", "LA-5", "LA-7" and "LA-9" fighters and a number of other planes used during WW 2; after WW 2 designed first Sov plane to reach speed of sound; dep, USSR Supr Sov of 3rd-5th convocations; dep, RSFSR Supr Sov; *Award:* twice Hero of Socialist Labor; four Stalin Prizes (1941, 1943, 1946 and 1948); three Orders of Lenin; Order of Suvorov, 1st and 2nd Class; Order of the Red Banner; medals; *Died:* 9 June 1960 in Moscow.

LAVRENT'YEV, Boris Innokent'yevich (1892-1944) Histologist; founder of histophysical and experimental school of neurohistology; prof from 1927; corresp member, USSR Acad of Sci from 1939; Hon Sci Worker of RSFSR form 1940; *Born;* 13 Aug 1892 in Kazan'; *Educ:* 1914 grad Med Fac, Kazan' Univ; *Career:* while still a student began specializing in histology under D. A. Timofeyev and A. N. Mislavskiy; 1914-20 mil surgeon in Tsarist and Red Armies; 1920-26 dissector, Chair of Histology, Kazan' Univ; 1927-29 prof, Moscow Veterinary Zootech Inst; 1929-30 prof, 1st Moscow Univ; 1930-33 prof, 1st Moscow Med Inst; 1934-44 prof, 2nd Moscow Med Inst; 1927-29 head, Morphological Dept, Obukh Inst; 1932-44 head, Morphological Dept, 1937-43 dep dir, All-Union Inst of Experimental Med; did research on the peripheral nervous system; made first extensive use of the experimental morphological method involving neurotomy; studied nerve degeneration and regeneration by the silver impregnation method; did research on the interconnection of the vegetative nerves and their relation to the innervate tissues and organs; contributed to an important in vivo study of synapses; introduced new concepts in the theory of neurohistology and contributed to the theory of the neuronic structure of nervous tissue; *Publ: "Gistofiziologiya innervatsionnykh mekhanizmov (sinapsov)"* (The Histophysiology of Innervervational Mechanisms Synapses) (1936); *"Nekotoryye voprosy teorii stroyeniya nervnoy tkyni"* (Some Problems of the Theory of the Structure of Nerve Tissue) (1938); *"Chuvstvitel'naya innervatsiya vnutrennikh organov"* (Sensory Innervation of the Internal Organs) (1943); coauthor, *"Morfologiya avtonomnoy nervnoy sistemy"* (The morphology of the Autonomous Nervous System) (2nd dc, 1946); coauthor *"Morfologiya chuvstvitel'noy innervatsii vnutrennikh organov"* (The Morphology of the Sensory Innervation of the Internal Organs) (1947); *Awards:* Stalin Prize (1941); *Died:* 9 Apr 1944 in Moscow of angina pectoris.

LAVRENYOV, Boris Andreyevich (1891-1959) Russian writer; *Born:* 17 July 1891 in Kherson, son of a teacher; *Educ:* grad Law Fac, Moscow Univ; *Career:* 1915 drafted into Russian Army; 1921 began lit career; *Publ:* collections of short stories: *"Veter"* (The Wind) (1924); *"Sorok pervyy"* (The Forty-First) (1926); Plays: *"Razlom"* (Break-Up) (1928); *"Pesn' o chernomortsakh"* (The Song of the Black Sea Sailers) (1944); *"Za tehk, kto v more"* (For Those at Sea) (1945); *"Golos Ameriki"* (The Voice of America) (1949); *Awards:* two Stalin Prizes (1946 and 1950); *Died:* 7 Jan 1959.

LAVROVSKIY (real name: IVANOV), Leonid Mikhaylovich (1905-1967) Choreographer; prof from 1952; Pop Artiste of RSFSR from 1959 and USSR from 1965; CP member from 1944; *Born:* 1905; *Educ:* 1922 grad Petrograd Choreographic College; *Career:* 1922-36 with ballet ansemble, Leningrad State Acad Opera and Ballet Theater (now Kirov Opera and Ballet Theater); 1936-38 artistic dir, ballet ensemble, Maly Opera Theater; 1938-44 at Leningrad's Kirov Theater; from 1944 chief choreographer, Moscow Bolshoy Theater; artistic dir, Moscow Choreograohic College; from 1950 teacher; 1959 toured USA and Canada with ballet ensemble, Bolshoy Theater; *Works:* staged ballets Glier's *"Krasnyy mak"* (Red Poppy) (1949,1957); *"Skaz o kamennom tsvetke"* (Tale of the Stone Flower) (1954); Prokofiev's "Romeo and Juliet" (1940, 1946), etc; *Awards:* three Stalin Prizes (1946, 1947 and 1950); Order of Lenin (1967); two other orders; medals; *Died:* Nov 1967.

LAZARENKO, Fyodor Mikhaylovich (1888-1953) Histologist; prof; corresp member, USSR Acad of Med Sci from 1947; *Born:* 1888; *Educ:* 1918 grad Natural Sci Dept, Fac of Physics and Mathematics, Petrograd Univ; *Career:* from 1930 head, Chair of Histology, Orenburg Agric Inst; from 1944 also head, Chair of Histology, Orenburg Med Inst; did research on the relationship between muscles and tendons and wrote detailed description of the structure of the sarcolemma; observed the part played by the epithelium in the regenerative process; devised new methods of studying the epithelial organs and of cultivating tissues in an aseptic focus of inflammation within the body (heteroplastic method); made studies of almost all epithelial organs in the course of research on the specific properties and interrelationship of various tissues and on the role of neurohumoral regulation in localized tissue processes; provided a dynamic description of the tissue elements of the internal medium and explained the origin of non-cellular formations in the connective tissue; devised modification of Bel'shovskiy's argentation method; also did research on experimentaly induced malignant tumors of viral origin; wrote some 40 works; *Publ: "K voprosu o perekhode myshts v sukhozhiliya i o stroyenii sarkolemmy"* (The Transition of Muscles into Tendons and the Structure of the Sarcolemma) (1922); *"Opyt kul'tivirovyniya in vitro nekotorykh sarkom v geterologicheskoy plazme"* (An Experiment in the in Vitro Cultivation of Certain Sarcomas in Heterological Plasma) (1929); *"Opyt primeneniya novogo metoda k eksperimental'nomu izucheniyu tkaney i yego pred-*

varitel'nyye rezul'taty" (The Trial of a New Method for the Experimental Study of Tissues and Its Preliminary Results) (1934); *"Opyty kul'tivirovaniya tkaney i organov v organizme"* (Experiments in the in Vivo Cultivation of Tissues and Organs) (1939), etc; *Died:* 1953.

LAZARENKO, Vitaliy Vital'yevich (1912-1948) Circus artist; clown-satirist; *Born:* 15 April 1912; *Career:* began his circus debut at the age of six under the direction of his father V. Ye. Lazarenko; 1928, after completing school, became a professional circus artist; worked as acrobat, xylophonist, juggler, balancer and trick-cyclist, combining elements of all these into a single number; until 1939 performed together with his father and, after his father's death, continued his tradition of satirical publicism in circus performances; talented acrobat and tumbler; *Died:* 14 Mar 1948.

LAZARENKO, Vitaliy Yefimovich (1890-1939) Circus artist; clown-satirist; Hon Artiste of RSFSR from 1933; *Born:* 26 Apr 1890, son of a miner; *Educ:* 1898-1906 trained at a circus; *Career:* 1898 joined M. I. Kozlikov's circus; mastered various circus acts, including acrobatic leaps over obstacles; 1906, after completing his training, entered the Pervil' Circus, and met A. L. Durov, who persuaded him to specialize in clowning; 1914 made his debut with the Nikitin Circus in Moscow; set a record by performing the salto mortale over three elephants; as clown created the image of the tramp-philosopher; during the Civil War headed a circus company that performed at the front; from 1919 performed with state circuses, where he became acquainted with such satirical writer as Mayakovsky, Aduyev and Apro, who helped enlarge his repertoirs; performed Mayakovskiy's *"Azbuku"* (Alphabet) and the act *"Chempionat vsemirnoy klassovoy bor'by"* (The World Class Struggle Championship), written specially for him in 1920 by Mayakovsky; 1919, in collaboration with the artist D. R. Erdman, developed a new type of clown combining liveliness, | buffoonery and realistic features (the traits of the rypical young Soviet man); spattering his performance with various acrobatics, Lazarenko usually ended with a splendid salto mortale over obstacles; performed in a typical two-color costume, almost without make-up; among his best acts were: "Arkashka the Failure", "Little Bricks" "Court-Room Touches", "Katya the Dancer", etc; performed with circuses at the newly-developing cities of Chelyabinsk, Magnitogorsk and Kemerovo, etc; during festival demonstrations he would appear on huge stilts with a megaphone, yelling jokes and greetings; also performed in film; *Publ: "Pyatna grima"* (Grease-Paint Spots) *(1922); "Tsirk i kloun"* (Circus and Clown) (1926); *"Po afishe Vitaliy Lazarenko – kloun-prygun"* (According to the Program - Vitaliy Lazarenko, Clown and Tumbler) (1938); *Awards:* Order of the Red Banner of Labor: *Died:* 18 May 1939.

LAZAREV, Pyotr Petrovich (1878-1942) Biophysicist and geophysicist; Dr of Physics from 1911; prof from 1912; member, Russian (USSR) Acad of Sci from 1917; *Born:* 13 Apr 1878 in Moscow; *Educ:* 1901 grad Med Fac, Moscow Univ; 1903 grad Mathematical Dept, Fac of Physics and Mathematics, Moscow Univ as an external student; *Career:* 1903 asst prof, Bazanova Clinic of Ear, Nose and Throat Diseases; 1904-07 asst prof, from 1907 assoc prof, P. N. Lebedev's Laboratory, Moscow Univ; 1910 wrote classic master's thesis on thermal conductivity of rarified gasas; 1911 defended doctor's thesis the fading of paints and pigments in the visible spectrum; in same year resigned from Moscow Univ with other scholars in protest against policies of Educ Min Kasso; from 1912 prof, Moscow Higher Tech College; 1918 commissioned by Lenin to organize research on iron deposits near Kursk (Kursk Magnetic Anomaly), the results of which made an important contribution to theoretical geophysics and, subsequently, to the Sov econ; 1919-31 founder-dir, Inst of Physics and Biophysics, RSFSR Pop Comrt of Health; from 1924 also dir, Roentgen Inst from 1931 head, Dept of Biophysics All-Union Inst of Experimental Med; 1938-42 dir, Biophysical Laboratory, USSR Acad of Sci; organized the production of new x-ray equipment in the USSR; trained such outstanding biophysicists as N. T. Fyodorov, S. V. Kravkov, A. V. Lebedinskiy, P. A. Rebinder, E. V. Shpol'skiy, V. V. Shuleykin and S. I. Vavilov; from 1940 vice-pres, Moscow Soc of Natural Sci; wrote over 500 works; *Publ:* docotr's thesis *"Vytsvetaniye Krasok i pigmentov v vidnom svete. Opyt izucheniya osnovnykh zakonov khimicheskogo deystviya sveta"* (The Fading of Paints and Pigments in Visible Light. A Study of the Basic Laws of the Chemical Action of Light) (1911); *"Ionnaya teoriya vozbuhdeniya"* (The Ion Theory of Excitation) (1923); *"Osnovy fiziki zemli"* (The Principles of Geophysics) (1939); *"Sovremennyye problemy biofiziki"* (Modern Problems of Biophysics) (1945); *"Ocherki istorii russkoy nauki"* (Studies in the History of Russian Science) (1950); *"Sochineniya"* Works)) (3 vol, 1950-57); *Died:* 23 Apr 1942 in Moscow.

LAZIMIR, Pavel Yevgen'yevich (1891-1920) Revolutionary; CP member from 1918; *Born:* 21 Jan 1891, son of professional soldier; *Educ:* grad mil med orderlies school; *Career:* 1917 member, Leftist Socialist-Revol Party; med asst at hospital of Uhlan Regt and Qaurtermaster Depots in Petrograd; disseminated revol propaganda among soldiers; after 1917 Feb Revol member, Petrograd Sov; member, Exec Comt, Petrograd Sov; chm, Soldiers' Section, Petrograd Sov; shortly before 1917 Oct Revol joined Bolsheviks; first chm, Petrograd Revol Mil Comt; 27 Oct 1917 Collegium member, Pop Comrt of Mil Affairs; 9-24 Oct 1918 member, Revol Mil Council, Southern Front; then in charge of supplying Sov troops in Ukr and organizing health service in distr liberated from Gen Denikin's troops; *Died:* 20 May 1920 of typhus; buried in Kremenchug.

LAZO, Sergey Georgiyevich (1894-1920) Mil commander; ensign in Russian Army; veteran of Civil War in Siberia and Far East; CP member from 1918; *Born:* 7 Mar 1894 in vil Pyatry, now Lazo, Kishinev Province; *Educ:* studied at Petersburg Technol Inst and at Physics and Mathematics Fac, Moscow Univ; 1916 grad Aleksey Mil Acad; *Career:* June 1916 drafted into army; from Dec 1916 commanded company in 15th Siberian Reserve Regt in Krasnoyarsk; Mar 1917 placed his company at disposal of Krasnoyarsk Sov; elected chm, Soldiers' Section, Krasnoyarsk Sov; Dec 1917 led Red Guard detachment to crush anti-Sov rebellion in Irkutsk; from Feb 1918 led mil operations against Ataman Semyonov's Withe troops in Transbaykal; from fall 1918 member, underground Far Eastern Oblast RCP(B) Comt; from spring 1919 commanded Sov partisan detachments in Maritime region; from Dec 1919 head, Revol Mil Staff to Prepare Rebellion in Maritime Region; from Jan 1920 until establishment of Sov regime in Vladivostok member, Revol Mil Council and Far Eastern Bureau, CC, RCP(B); Apr 1920, after Japanese seized Vladivostok, arrested together with other members of Revol Mil Council and turned over to White Army; *Died:* late May 1920 burned alive along with other prisoners in locomotive firebox at Murav'yovo-Amurskaya Station, now Lazo station.

LAZURKIN, M. S. (1883-1937) Party Official; CP member from 1903; *Bron:* 1883; *Career:* 1903 joined RSDRP; Party work in Odessa, Moscow and Petersburg; after 1917 Feb Revol propagandist, Petrograd's 1st City Rayon Party Comt; secr, Bolshevik Faction, City Duma; 1917 Petrograd deleg at 7th (Apr) RSDRP(B) Conference; during preparation and implementation of 1917 Oct Revol active Kamenev supporter; 1918, after dissolution of Constituent Assembly, left the Party; 1920 confessed his "errors"; and was readmitted to the Party; admin works; taught in Moscow and Leningrad; arrested by State Security organs; *Died:* 1937 in imprisonment.

LEBED', Dmitriy Zakharovich (1893-1937) Govt official; CP member from 1909; *Born:* 11 Jan 1893 in vil Nikolayevka, now Dnepropetrovsk Oblast; *Career:* metalworker by trade; worked at various plants and simultaneously carried on revol activities; 1908 joined a circle of the Socialist-Revol Party; 1912-17 several times arrested; after 1917 Feb Revol chm, Yekaterinoslav Railroad Workers RSDRP(B) Comt; Oct 1917 directed seizure of power in Yekaterinoslav area; 1918 Party and govt work in the Ukr; 1919-20 head, Polit Dept, Yekaterinoslav Rainroad; ed, Yekaterinoslav "Zvezda"; from late 1920 secr, CC, CP(B) Ukr; from 1024 chm, Ukr Centr Control Commission and Ukr Pop Comr of Workers and Peasants' Inspection; from 1926 USSR Dep Pop Comr of Workers and Peasants' Inspection and Presidium member, USSR Centr Control Commission; from 1930 dep chm, RSFSR Council of Pop Comr; at 11th and 12th Party Congresses elected cand member, CC, at 13th, 16th and 17th Congresses elected member, CC, and at 14th and 15th Congresses elected member, CPSU(B) Centr Control Commission; arrested by State Security organs; *Died:* 30 Oct 1937 in imprisonment.

LEBEDEV, Aleksandr Nikolayevich (1881-1938) Biochemist; prof from 1914; *Born:* 1881; *Educ:* 1901 grad Moscow Univ; 1904 grad Petrovsko-Razumovskiy Agric Acad; *Career:* 1905 went to Germany, where he worked first at Prof Bredic's physiochemical laboratory in Heidelberg, then at E. Buchner's laboratory in Berlin; 1909 developed spirit fermentation model in which the major role is played by the trioses glycerine aldehyde and dioxyacetone; much later the phosphoric esters of these substances were recognized as essential intermediate products of the anaerobic decomposition of hydrocarbons; 1911 worked at Pasteur Inst and G. Bertrand's laboratory in Paris; in same year devised method of obtaining zymase ferment from dry yeast which superceded Buchner's method; also observed that yeast juice becomes inactive in the process of dialysis but that it can be reactivated by the admixture of a small quantity of boiled juice; obtained osazones of the intermediate products of fermentation, which he identified at hexosephosphoric esters; 1912-14 assoc prof, from 1914, after defending master's thesis, prof, Don Polytech Inst; from 1921 prof, Chair of Agrochemistry, Moscow Univ; from 1930 also head, Biochemical Laboratory, Centr Food Research Inst; 1935 established a biochemical laboratory at All-Union Inst of Experimental Med; wrote over 80 works: *Publ:* "Über die Hexosephosphorsäureester" (The Esters of Hexosephosphoric Acid) (1910); "Extraction de la zymaze par simple macération" (The Extraction of Zymase by Straight Maceration) (1911); "Über den Mechanismus der alkoholischen Gärung" (The Mechanism of Alcohol Fermentation) (1912); *"Khimicheskiye issledovaniya nad vnekletochnym spirtovym brozheniyem"* (Chemical Research on Extracellular Alcohol Fermentation) (1913); *"Sovremennoye sostoyaniye voprosa o khimizme spirtovogo brozheniya"* (The Present State of Data on Alcohol Fermentation) (1915); *Died:* 3 June 1938.

LEBEDEV, Aleksey Borisovich (1883-1941) Electr eng; specialist in electr traction; sorresp member, USSR Acad of Sci from 1939: *Born:* 29 Dec 1883; *Educ:* 1909 grad Petersburg Polytech Inst; *Career:* from 1909 worked at Petersburg Polytech Inst; 1924-41 prof, Leningrad Polytech Inst simultaneously 1930-36 prof, Moscow Power Eng Inst; 1932-41 prof, Leningrad Inst of Railroad Eng; 1914 advocated 3,000-5,000 volt. d,c, system for electrification of railroads, adopted in USSR in 1931; 1939 developed new electr traction systems at USSR Acad of Sci; did research on methods of planning electr railroads, electr calculation of contact grid and calculation of the heating of an electr traction motor for given working d conditions; *Publ: "Elektricheskiy raschyot rabochey seti elektricheskikh zheleznykh dorog"* (Electrical Calculation of an Electric Railroad's Working Grid) (1926); *"Raschyoty elementov elektricheskikh zheleznykh dorog"* (Calculating the Elements of Electric Railroads) (1930); *"Osnovy elektricheskoy tyagi"* (The Principles of Electric Traction) (1937); *"K voprosu o metodike vybora sistemy elektricheskoy tyagi"* (Methods of Selecting an Electric Traction System); *Died:* 5 July 1941.

LEBEDEV, Mikhail Nikolayevich (1877-1951) Komi writer; *Born:* 22 Oct 1877 in vil Mezhador, Vologda Province, the son of a Russian volost clerk; *Educ:* from 1886 studied at Ust'-Sysol'sk 2nd Classical College; *Career:* worked as clerk; after 1917 Oct Revol secr, comt of rural poor, then secr, pop court; 1900 first work printed; translated into Komi works of Pushkin, Lermontov, Krylov, Mayakovskyi, Isakovskiy, Rollend, etc: *Publ:* Russian-language stories: "Ivan Goloy" (1900); "Foma Lyokmorotv" (1914); novelettes:: *"V volostnom omute"* (In the Volost Whirlpool); verse *"Volya"* (Freedom) and *"Moya zemlya"* (My Land) (1919); *"Prazdnik trudovogo cheloveka"* (A Workingman's Holiday) (1919), etc; Komi-language works: A verse play "The Sorcerer" (1920); play "A Good Maid" (1921); operettas "The Beautiful Girl" (1919); "Nastya" (1929); poems "Life Under the Tsar" (1927); "Two Fists" (1929); "If You Don't Work, You Don't Eat" (1931); "How Grisha Van' Was Born and Raised" (1937); cycle of stories "Under God and the Tsar"; verse "Aggressor, Get Out of Korea!" (1950); "Down With War" (1951); *Died:* 5 Mar 1951.

LEBEDEV, Nikolay Yevgen'yevich (1898-1951) Microbiologist; CP member from 1919; *Born:* 20 Feb 1898; *Educ:* 1927 grad Leningrad Inst of Med Knowledge; *Career:* from 1929 worked at various research inst in Moscow and Leningrad; from 1949 dep dir, Inst of Epidemiology and Microbiology, USSR Acad of Med Sci; devised several new methods of cultivating microorganisms for med and agric drug production; *Awards:* two Stalin Orizes (1951 and 1952); *Died:* 1951.

LEBEDEV, Pavel Pavlovich (1872-1933) Mil commander; maj-gen, Russian Army; chief of staff, Red Army; *Born:* 21 Apr 1872, son of a nobleman; *Educ:* 1900 grad Gen Staff Acad; *Career:* during WW 1 chief of Staff, 3rd Army; 1918 joined Red Army; May 1918-Mar 1919 head, Draft Bd, All-Russian Gen Headquarters; Apr-Juny 1919 chief of staff, Eastern Front; July 1919-Feb 1921 chief, RSFSR Field Headquarters; Feb 1921-Apr 1924 chief of staff, Red Army; 1919-24 also member, Revol Mil Council; 1922-24 commandant, Red Army Mil Acad; 1924-25 plen for major assignments, USSR Revol Mil Council; 1925-28 chief of staff and asst commander, Ukr Mil Distr; 1924-27 also chief dir of all mil acad, responsible for mil admin; 1927 contracted serious illness; 1928 relieved as chief of staff but continued to act as asst commander, Ukr Mil Distr; *Awards:* Order of the Red Banner; Order of the Red Banner of Labor; *Died:* 2 July 1933 in the performance of his duty; Kiev Artillery school named after him.

LEBEDEV, Pyotr Ivanovich (1885-1948) Geologist and petrographer; corresp member, USSR Acad of Sci from 1939; *Born:* 23 Aug 1885 in Piryatin, now Poltava Oblast; *Educ:* 1909 grad Petersburg Polytech Inst; 1912 grad Petersburg Univ; *Career:* from 1915 prof at various high educ establishments; from 1920 prof, Rostov Univ, then Leningrad Politech Inst, Leningrad Mining Inst etc; from 1926 assoc, USSR Acad of Sci; did research on classificatory, theoretical and experimental petrography, mineralogy, geochemistry; carried out field studies in Kareliy, Caucasus, Transcaucasus, Ukr, Kuznetsk Alatau, Altay and Far East; wrote monograph on the Alagez volcano, tracing its development and classifying its mineralogical structure; *Publ:* coauthor, *"Petrografiya Ukrainy"* (The Petrography of the Ukraine) (1934); *Awards:* Order of Lenin; Order of the Red Banner of Labor; medals; *Died:* 3 Apr 1948.

LEBEDEV, Sergey Vasil'yevich (1874-1934) Chemist; pioneer of ind rubber synthesis in USSR; prof from 1916; member, USSR Acad of Sci from 1932; *Born:* 25 July 1874 in Lublin: *Educ:* 1900 grad Petersburg Univ; *Career:* 1900-02 worked for Rail Steel Research Commission, Petersburg Inst of Means of Communication; from 1902 worked at Petersburg (Leningrad Univ, where he founded a laboratory for the chemical processing of oil and coal in 1925; 1908-13 did research on the polymerization of hydrocarbons in the divinyl and propadiene series; 1909-10 published papers on the polymerization of isoprene and diisopropenyl; 1910 optained first rubberoid product from divinyl (butadiene); 1913 defended master's thesis on biethylene hydrocarbons, which provided the sci basis of ind rubber synthesis; 1912-15 also worked on the production of toluene by oil pyrolysis, developing a method used at a benzene and toluene plant built in Baku after WW 1; 1914 began research on the polymerization of hydrocarbons of acetylene and ethylene which provided the basis for modern ind methods of obtaining butyl rubber and polyisobutylene; from 1916 prof, Petrograd (Leningrad) Mil Med Acad; 1921-23, together with assoc, did research on the properties of sodium divinyl rubber, for which he found active fillers; 1926-28, in govt-sponsored competition to find best method of ind rubber synthesis, supervised research which led to prize-winning method of obtaining sodium divinyl rubber based on the polymerization of divinyl alcohol with metallic sodium; 1928-30 founder-dir, Synthetic Rubber Laboratory; trained numerous rubber chemists; several sci establishments now bear his name: *Awards:* Order of Lenin; *Died:* 2 May 1934.

LEBEDEV, Vladimir Nikolayevich (1882-1951) Biologist and specialist in microphotographic filming techniques; prof; *Born:* 1882 *Educ:* grad Natural Sci Dept, Fac of Physics and Mathematics, Moscow Univ; *Career:* from 1908 worked on Moscow Higher Women's Courses; 1912, on the basis of experience gained with amateur film group at Moscow Univ, filmed the life-cycle of infusoria at the studio of Khanzhonkov and Co, Ltd; from 1920 worked at Inst of Experimental Biology and from 1949 at Inst of Animal Morphology, USSR Acad of Sci; spcialized in the structure of protozoa; together with the best Sov sci film-makers (B. Dolin, N. Grachyov, M. Iiskunov, P. Kosov, A. Kudryavtsev, A. Sveshnikov, S. Zguridi) made over 40 films of microscopic processes, including *"Kul'tura tkaney"* (Tissue Culture), *"Opyty po fiziologii serdtsa"* (Experiments in Cardiac Physiology) and *"Fagotsity"* (Phagocytes); *Publ:* "Einige Beobachtungen über Trypanosoma rotatorium" (Some Observation on Trypanosoma rotatorium) (1910); "Ein neuer Parasit im Blute des Iltis, Microsoma mustelae" (A New Parasite in the Blood of the Polecat, Microsoma mustelae) (1911), etc; *Awards:* Badge of Hon; Stalin

Prize (1941); *Died:* 1951.

LEBEDEV, Vladimir Vasil'yevich (1891-1967) Artist; corresp member, USSR Acad of Arts from 1967; Pop Artist of RSFSR; *Born:* 27 May 1891; *Career:* 1910-14 worked at Rubo and Bernshteyn's workshops; contributed drawings to journal "Satirikon"; worked with poet S. Marshak on illustrated books for childran; artistic ed, Leningrad Publ House and Children's Publ House; his works are displayed at Moscow's Tret'yakov Gallery and Leningrad's State Russian Museum, etc; *Works:* series of genre drawings: "Panel of the Revolution" (1922); "New Economic Policy /NEP/" (1925-27); "Guarding the October Revolution" and other posters for the Russian News Agency (1920-22); illustrations for children's books: Kipling's "The Little Elephant" (1921); Marshak's "Tsirk" (Circus) (1924), etc: Cubist series "The Washerwomen" (1921-24); illustrations for Marshak's *"Skazki"* (Tales) (1934); illustrations for *"Okhota"* (The Hunt) (1924); *"Glupyy myshyonok"* (The Silly Mouse) (1925); Marshak's *"Mister Tvister"* (Mister Twister) (1933); Marshak's *"Sbornik"* (Collection) (1935-36); sketches of ballerinas and models (1935-37); *Died:* 21 Nov 1967.

LEBEDEV, Vsevolod Vladimirovich (1901-1938) Russian writer; *Born:* 21 Nov 1901 in vil Radda on the Amur; *Educ:* 1927 grad Archeological Fac, Leningrad Univ; *Career:* 1921 first work published; 1930-37 lived in Far North, the Urals and on the Amur; *Publ: "K severnym narodam"* (To Northern Peoples) and *"Polyarnoye solntse"* (Polar Sun) (1930-31); *"Okhotniki na Imane"* (Hunters on the Iman) (1932); *"Tovarishchi"* (Comrades) (1935); coauthor, play *"Otrady"* (Detachments) (1936); novel in chronicle form about Ural miners *"Zavody"* (Plants) (1937); *Died:* 16 Feb 1938 in Moscow.

LEBEDEV-KUMACH (real name: LEBEDEV), Vasily Ivanovich (1898-1949) Russian poet; CP member from 1940; *Born:* 8 Aug 1898 in Moscow, son of a cobbler; *Educ:* studied at History and Philology Fac, Moscow Univ; *Career:* began writing verse at age 13; 1916 first work printed; 1919-21 worked for Press Bureau, Revol Mil Council and for Mil Dept, Russian Telegraphic Agency Agitation Div, writing stories, articles, feuilletons, ditties for frontline newspapers and slogans for agitation trains; also studied at History and Philology Fac, Moscow Univ; from 1922 contributed to "Rabochaya gazeta", "Krest'yanskaya gazeta", "Gudok" and journal "Krasnoarmeyets"; later worked for journal "Krokodil", to which he contributed for 12 years; wrote many lit parodies, satirical tales, feuilletons and mass songs; from 1929 wrote revues for "Blue Blouse" Theater and for workers' amateur theatrical groups; during WW 2 served in Sov Navy; dep, RSFSR Supr Sov of 1st and 2nd convocations; *Publ:* collections: *"Chayniki v blyudtse"* (Teapots in a Saucer) (1925); *"So svekh volostey"* (From All Volosts) (1926); *"Pechal'nyye Ulybki"* (Sad Smiles) (1927), etc; theater revues: *"Za godom god"* (Year by Year); *"Kiryushina pobeda"* (Kiryushin's Victory) (1926); *"Zhena zavmaga"* (The Store Managers' Wife) (1940), etc; songs for comedy films: *"Vesyolyye rebyata"* (The Merry Lads) (1934); *"Tsirk"* (The Circus) (1936); *"Deti kapitana Granta"* (The Children of Captain Grant) (1936); *"Volga-Volga"* (1937); texts for mass songs: "The Sacred War" (1941); collection *"Spoyom, tovarishchi, spoyom!"* (Sing, Comrades, Sing!) (1941); *Komsomol'tsy-moryaki"* (Komsomol Sailors) (1943), etc; children's verse *Petina lavka"* (Petya's Store) (1927); *"Pro umnykh zveryushek"* (Clever Little Animals) (1939); *"Pod krasnoy zvezdoy"* (Under the Red Star) (1941); collections: *"Lirika, Satirika. Fel'yeton"* (Lyric Verse, Satire and Feuilletons) (1939); *"Stikhi i pesni"* (Verse and Songs) (1951); *"Pesni i stikhotvoreniya"* (Songs and Poetry) (1960); *Awards:* Stalin Prize (1941); Order of the Red Banner of Labor; Order of the Red Star; Badge of Hon; *Died:* 20 Feb 1949 in Moscow.

LEBEDEV-POLYANSKIY(real name: LEBEDEV), Pavel Ivanovich (1882-1948) Lit historian and critic; Dr of History; prof; member, USSR Acad of Sci from 1946; CP member from 1902; *Born:* 2 Jan 1882 in Melenki, Vladimir Province; *Educ:* grad Vladimir Theological Seminary; studied at Med Fac, Derpt (Tartu) Univ; *Career:* 1908-17 polit emigre in Geneva and member, *"Vperyod"* (Forward) group; 1917-19 Collegium member, RSFSR Pop Comrt of Educ and Govt comr of its Lit Publ Dept; 1918 chief ed, journal "Narodnoye prosveshcheniye"; 1918-20 chm, All-Russian Proletkul't Council; 1918-21 chief ed, journal "Proletarskaya kul'tura"; 1921-30 dir, Main Lit and Publ Bd; 1922 chief ed, journal "Tvorchestvo"; 1928-30 chief ed, journal "Literatura i marksizm"; 1929-31 chief ed, journal "Russkiy yazyk v sovetskoy shkole"; 1934-48 exec ed, symposia "Literaturnoye nasledstvo"; from 1937 dir, Inst of Lit, USSR Acad of Sci; also taught at Moscow Univ and Communist Acad and worked for Russian Assoc of Soc Sci Research Institutes; chief ed, *"Literaturnaya entsiklopediya"* (Literary Encyclopedia) and member, Main Ed Bd, "BSE" (Large Soviet Encyclopedia); specialized in 19th- and 20th-Century Russian lit; criticized the methods of Sakulin, Keltuyala, Pypin, Veselovskiy and even Plekhanov in lit history and proclaimed Lenin a lit historian; *Publ: "O proletarskoy kul'ture"* (Proletarian Culture) (1921); *"Lenin i lieratura"* (Lenin and Literature) (1924); *"Na literaturnom fronte"* (On the Literary Front) (1924); *"N. A. Nekrasov. Kritiko-biograficheskiy ocherk"* (N. A. Nekrasov. A Critical and Biographical Study) (1925); *"Voprosy sovremennoy Kritiki"* (Problems of Modern Criticism) (1927); *"N. A. Dobrolyubov. Mirovozzreniye i literaturno-kriticheskaya deyatel'nost'"* (N. A. Dobrolyubov. His Weltanschauung and Career as a Writer and Critic) (1933); *"Tri velikikh russkikh demokrata"* (Three Great Russian Democrats) (1938); *"V. G. Belinskiy. Literaturno-kriticheskaya deyatel'nost'"* (V. G. Belinskiy. His Career as a Writer and Critic) (1945); *"Lomonosov i russkaya literatura"* (Lomonosov and Russian Literature) (1947), etc; *Awards:* Order of Lenin; *Died:* 4 Apr 1948 in Moscow.

LEBEDEVA, Sarra Dmitriyevna (1892-1967) Sculptor; Hon Art Worker of RSFSR from 1945; *Born:* 23 Dec 1892; *Educ:* 1910-14 studied drawing under M. D. Bernshteyn and sculpture under L. V. Shervud at an art studio; *Career:* from 1958 corresp member, USSR Acad of Arts; specialized in busts of contemporaries; sculpted many small figures in plaster, bronze and ceramics; *Works:* series of portraits of revol figures: "L. B. Krasin" (1924); "F. E. Dzerzhinskiy" (1925); "A. D. Tsyurupa" (1927), etc; portraits of: the aviator "V. P. Chkalov" (1937); sculptor "V. I. Mikhina" (1939); actress "O. L. Knipper-Chekhova" (1940); poet "A. T. Tvardovskiy" (1949-50); architect "A. V. Shchusev" (1947); sculptor "G. I. Kepinov" (1956), etc; statues: "Girl with a Butterfly" (1936); "The Miner" (1937); monuments to; "A. S. Pushkin" (1937); "F. D. Dzerzhinskiy" (1940); "A. P. Chekhov" (1945); *Died:* 6 Mar 1967.

LEBEDEVSKIY, Boris Nikolayevich (1897-1965) Otolaryngologist, Dr of Med; prof; Hon Sci Worker of RSFSR from 1945; *Born:* 1897 in Kamyshin, Saratov Province; *Educ:* 1919 grad Med Fac Saratov Univ; *Career:* 1918 joined Red Army; 1919-35 worked in Red Army hospitals in the Volga Mil Distr; asst prof, Saratov Ear, Nose and Throat Clinic; asst Prof, Kazan' Med Inst; 1935-65 head, Chair of Ear, Nose and Throat Diseases, Perm' Med Inst; 1941-45 dir of a special ear, nose and throat hospital and head of an evacuation hospital dept; founder-chm, Perm' Soc of Otolaryngologists; dep, Perm' Oblast Sov; member, ed council, journal "Vestnik utorinolaringologii"; wrote some 90 works, notable on suppurative sinusitis, direct examination of the respiratory tract and oesophagus and the clinical treatment of gunshot wounds of the nasal accessory sinus; *Awards:* Order of Lenin; Order of the Red Star; medals; *Died:* 1 June 1965.

LEBEDINSKIY, Andrey Vladimirovich (1902-1965) Physiologist; prof; Dr of Med maj-gen, Med Corps; member, USSR Acad of Med Sci from 1960; Hon Sci Worker of RSFSR; pioneer of Sov radiobiology and space biomed; *Born:* 12 May 1902; *Educ:* 1924 grad Leningrad Mil Med Acad; *Career:* after grad worked at I. P. Pavlov and L. A. Orbeli's laboratories, then for a number of years headed Physiological Section, Psychophysiological Laboratory, Leningrad Inst of Civil Aviation Eng; also head, Physiological Laboratory, Leningrad Ophthalmological Inst; head, Physiological Section, Leningrad Brain Inst; head, Theoretical Section, Leningrad Neurosurgical Research Inst; from 1953 head, Chair of Physiology, Naval Med Acad; after it was merged with Kirov Mil Med Acad worked at latter; specialized in physiology of sense organs, particularly vision; discovered reciprocal relation between the rods and cones of the retina and determined the importance of this phenomenon in the eye's adaptation to darkness; discovered phosphene phenomenon caused by the action of electr current on the retina and studied electroretinography with glaucoma and the role of the symphathetic nervous system in the function of the accomodatory muscle; determined the trifacial nerve fiber's vasodilatory affect on the vessels of the ciliary body; in a study of neurogenic dystrophy theory demonstrated importance of disturbances of the afferential innervation; one of first to study effects of ultra-sound on the body and the somatic effects of ionizing radiation on the body; ed, radiobiology section, 2nd ed of "BME"(Large Medical Encyclopedia); member, Leningrad and Moscow Sci Ophthalmological Soc; attended numerous ophthalmological congesses and sessions; from 1955 Sov permanent rep, UN Sci Comt; wrote over 300 works; *Publ: "Problemy pronitsayemosti"* (Problems of Penetration) (1938); *"O vliyanii ioniziruyushchego izlucheniya na organizm zhivotnogo"* (The Physiological Effects of Ionizing Radiation on Animals) (1955); coauthor, *"Kurs normal'noy fiziologii"* (A Normal Physiology Course) (1956); *Awards:* many orders and medals; *Died:* 3 Jan 1965 in Leningrad.

LEBEDINSKIY, Vladimir Konstantinovich (1868-1937) Physicist; *Born:* 20 July 1868; *Educ:* 1891 grad Petersburg Univ; *Career:* from 1895 at Petersburg Electr REng Inst; from 1906 at Petersburg Polytech Inst; from 1913 at Riga Politech Inst; from 1925 prof 1st Leningrad Med Inst; from 1930 prof, Leningrad Inst of Railroad Eng; 1919-25 co-founder and assoc, Nizhniy Novgorod Radio Laboratory; from 1932 head, Chair of Physics, Mil Med Acad; 1906-10 ed, "Zhurnal Russkogo fiziko-khimicheskogo obshchestva. Fizicheskiy otdel"; 1918-28 founder and ed, journal "Telegrafiya i telefoniya bez provodov"; 1901-05 studied properties of electr sparks; 1906-16 studied theory of high-frequency transformers; 1937 studied progressive magnetization phenomena; *Publ: "Elektromagnitnyye volny i osnovaniya besprovolochnogo telegrafa"* (Electromagnetic Waves and the Principles of Wireless Telegraphy) (1906); *"Elektrichestvo i magnetizm"* (Electricity and Magnetism) (1909); *"Teoriya electrichestva"* (The Theory of Electricity) (1911); *"Printsip otnositel'nosti v sovremennoy fizike"* (The Relativity Principle in Modern Physics) (1914), *Died:* 11 July 1937.

LEBEDINSKIY, Vyacheslav Vasil'yevich (1888-1956) Chemist; specialist in complex compounds; corresp member, USSR Acad of Sci from 1946; Hon Sci and Tech Worker of RSFSR from 1947; *Born:* 14 Sept 1888; *Educ:* studied under L. N. Chugayev; *Career:* 1920-35 prof, Leningrad Univ; 1939-52 prof, Moscow Inst of Precision Chemical Eng; also taught at other higher educ establishments; obtained new complex compounds of platinum, rhodium, iridium, rhenium, indium etc; did major research on the chemistry of rhodium; synthesized all possible series of ammonium compounds of rhodium; developed the stereochemistry of rhodium compounds; devised ind methods of obtaining rhodium from natural raw material; *Awards:* Order of the Red Banner of Labor; Stalin Prize (1946); *Died:* 12 Dec 1956.

LEBEREKHT (LEBERECHT), Gans Fridrikhovich (1910-1960) Est writer; CP member from 1945; *Born:* 1 Dec 1910 in Petersburg, son of a worker; *Educ:* 1935-37 studied at Leningrad Evening Lit Inst; *Career:* spent his childhood in Est; from 1918 lived and studied in Leningrad; 1928 welder, then electr fitter, "Elektrosila" Plant; during WW 2 served with Est Corps in Sov Army; 1930 first work published; wrote in Russian; *Publ:* novelettes: *"Vechnyy koler"* (Everlasting Color) (1936); *"Svte v Koordi"* (Light at Koordi) (1948); coauthor, play *"Utro nashikh let"* (The Morning of Our Years) (1953); novels: *"Kapitany"* (Captains) (1954); *"Soldaty idut domoy"* (The Soldiers Go Home) (1956); novelette *"V odnom dome"* (In the Same House) (1957); novel *"Dvortsy Vassarov"* (Vassar Palaces) (1960); *Awards:* Stalin Prize (1949); *Died:* 10 Nov 1960 in Tallin.

LEDER, V. L. (1882-1938) Politician; active in Polish workers' movement; member, Soc-Democratic Party of Poland and Lith from 1900; *Born:* 1882; *Career:* 1905-11 member, Main Bd, Soc-Democratic Party of Poland and Lith; 1910-11 secr, Main Bd, Soc-Democratic Party of Poland and Lith; represented Soc-Democratic Party of Poland and Lith on ed staff of RSDRP centr organ "Sotsial-Demokrat"; member, For Org Commission and Tech Commission; supported the conciliationist Stand against the Bolsheviks; 1919-20 avtive in Communist Workers' Party of Poland; from 1921 exec, Comitern and Trade-Union Int; arrested by State Security organs; *Died:* 1938 in imprisonment.

LEIN'SH, Paulis Yanovich (1883-1959) Lat livestock breeder; member, Lat Acad of Sci and Corresp member, USSR Acad of Sci from 1946; Hon Sci Worker of Lat SSR from 1945; *Born:* 26 Feb 1883; *Educ:* 1907 grad Riga Polytech Inst; *Career:* from 1907 instructor, then dir, Experimental Training Farm, Jelgava Agric College; 1919-32 assoc prof, Chair of Animal Husbandry, Riga Univ; 1932-51 prof, Riga Univ and Agric Acad; 1946-51 pres, Lat Acad of Sci; dep, USSR Supr Sov of 2nd and 3rd convocations; did research on livestock fodder and local breeds of cattle; wrote a comparative study of the econ characteristics of cattle bred in Lat; helped to develop the basic fodders now used in animal husbandry in Lat; *Awards:* Order of Lenin; other orders and medals; *Died:* 27 Mar 1959.

LEKHIN, Ivan Vasil'yevich (1895-1964) Revolutionary; Oct Revol and Civil War veteran; CP member from 1917; *Born:* 21 Nov 1895; *Career:* member, Samara Province Exec Comt and Province Food Comt; chm, Special Mil Commission, Chapayev 25th Infantry Div, Eastern Front; head, Mil Food Supply Bd, Fergana Army, Turkestani Front; dep head, Mil Food Supply Bd, Volga Mil Distr; later admin work for govt agencies and Party organs; 1939-58 dir, For and Nat Dictionaries Publ House; pensioner; *Died:* 10 Apr 1964.

LELEVICH, G. (real name: Labori Gilelevich KALMANSON) (1901-1945) Russian critic and poet; CP member from 1917; *Bron:* 30 Sept 1901 in Mogilev, son of the poet G. M. Kalmanson (pen name: Perekati-pole) *Career:* Party work during the revol and Civil War; 1917 began lit career; as a critic, co-ed of the journal "Na postu" and a leading light of the All-Russian Assoc of proletarian Writers, actively involved in lit trends and factions of 1920's and early 1930's; campaigned for new, proletarian art and for Party direction of lit; in this light wrote articles about K. Ryleyev, N. Ogarev, V. Kurochkin and Sov writers-Yesenin, D. Furmanov, A. Fadeyev, S. Stal'skiy; Party critics accused Lelevich of idiological errors, such as a sectarian approach to the work of "proletarian" writers, narrow-minded class judgements, etc; arrested by State Security organs; *Publ:* collected verse: "Nabat" (1921); *"V Smol'nom"* (At Smol'nyy) (1925); poem "Famine" (1921); etc; *"Strekopytovshchina. Stranichka iz istorii kontrrevolyutsionnykh vystupleniy v gody grazhdanskoy voyny"* ("Strekopytovism." A Page from the History of Counter-Revolutionary Utterances During the Civil War) (1923); *"Stikhi raznykh let"* (Poems of Various Years) (1924); *"Na literaturnom postu. Stat'i, zametki"* (On Litersry Watch. Articles and Notes) (1924); *"Tvorcheskiye puti proletarskoy literatury"* (Creative Paths of Proletarian Literature) (1925); "Dem'yan Bednyy" (1925); *"O printsipakh Marksistskoy literaturnoy kritiki"* (The Principles of Marxist Literary Criticism) (1925); *"Marksistskoye literaturovedeniye i biografiya khudozhnika"* (Marxist Literary Studies and the Biography of the Artist) (1926); *"V. Ya. Bryusov. Ocherk zhizni i tvorchstva'* (V. Ya. Bryusov, His Life and Work) (1926); "Sergey Yesenin' (1926); *"Klinok i kniga. Pamyati Dmitriya Furmanova"* (Blade and Book. In Memory of Dmitriy Furmanov) (1926); *"Voinstvuyushchiy idealizm na fronte literaturovedeniya"* (Militant Idealism on the Literary Studies Front) (1927); *"Literaturno-kriticheskaya metodologiya N. P. Tkacheva"* (N. P. Tkachev's Methods of Literary Criticism) (1928); *"Poeziya revolyutsionnykh raznochintsev 60-80-ykh godov 19-go veka"* (The Poetry of the "Raznochintsy" Revolutionary Intellectuals of the 1860's - 1880's) (1931); "Poeziya N. P. Ogareva" (The Poetry of N. P. Ogarev) (1934); *Died:* 8 Oct 1945 in imprisonment; posthumously rehabilitated.

LEMANIS (pen names: Zars; Skultens), Indrikis Krish'yanovich (1904-1960) Lat writer; CP member from 1940; *Born:* 21 Feb 1904 in vil Kerklini, Kuldig Uyezd, son of a farmhand; *Career:* participated in Lat undergrounded revol movement; repeatedly arrested; 1922 first work printed; during WW 2 polit officer, Lat Infantry Div; ed, frontline newspaper "Za Sovetskuyu Latviyu"; 1945-60 chm, Lat Radio and Television Comt; *Publ;* story "Mother" (1943); collected stories "Modest Heroes" (1945); novelette "The Roads of Life" (1948-53); novels "Calloused Hands" (1938); "At Dawn" (1955); *Awards:* Order of the Red Banner of Labor; Order of the Red Star; *Died:* 13 Feb in Riga.

LEMBERSKIY, Boris Abramovich (1894-1967) Otolaryngologist; Cand of Med from 1941; specialist in mil otolaryngology; *Born:* 1894 in Cherkassy, Kiev Province; *Educ:* 1918 grad Med Fac, Geneva Univ; *Career:* served 30 yaers as a surgeon in the Sov Army; during Civil War chief otolaryngologist, 3rd Bel Front 1927 began research on auditory "islets" in deaf-mutes and methods of restoring hearing; 1928-30 intern, Ear, Nose and Throat Clinic, Leningrad Mil Med Acad; 1939-42 asst prof, Chair of Otolaryngology, Kuybyshev Mil Med Acad; 1941-45 studied deafness and psychic trauma induced by shell-shock; simultaneously exec ed, journal "Meditsina na Zapadnom fronte";

1945-67 assoc prof, Chair of Ear, Nose and Throat Diseases, Krasnoyarsk Med Inst; from 1945 also dep chm, Krasnoyarsk Soc of Otolaryngologists; wrote 45 works on the physiology of the ear, nose and throat, the clinical aspects and prevention of ear, nose and throat diseases, mil otolaryngology, field surgery and the history of med; *Publ: "Materialy k izucheniyu sostoyaniya lor-organov u glukhonemykh"* (Material on the Study of the State of the Otolaryngological Organs in Deaf-Mutes) (1941); *Awards:* Order of Lenin; Order of the Red Banner; Order of the Fatherland War; Order of the Red Star; medals; *Died:* 14 Nov 1967.

LEMKE, Mikhail Konstantinovich (1872-1923) Lit historian and journalist; specialist in history of the revol movement; CP member from 1923; *Born:* 12 Nov 1872 in Dem'yansk, Novgorod Province, son of a nobleman; *Educ:* 1893 grad Konstantonovka Mil College; *Career:* 1894 first work published; contributed to the journals "Byloye", "Russkoye bogatstvo", "Russkaya mysl'" and *"Mir bozhiy";* 1898-91 ed, newspaper "Orlovskiy vestnik"; 1901-02 ed, newspaper "Pridneprovskiy kray"; 1906 ed, journal "Kniga"; 1915-16 mil censor at gen headquarters of Supr Command; 1917-18 in charge of team processing State papers in Petrograd; 1920-21 member, ed bd, journal "Kniga i revolyutsiya"; from Sept 1922 dep chm, from Jan 1923 chm, Petrograd Press Trust; did research on the history of the soc movement in the 1850's and 1860's on the basis of formerly inaccessible material in the archives of the 3rd Dept /Tsarist Secret Police/, the Govt Senate and the Main Press Bd; wrote numerous works on the history of lit, journalism and censorship; prepared first complete edition of Herzen's works (22 vol) for publ; also published complete 4-vol ed of N. A. Dobrolyubov's works; *Publ: "Dumy zhurnalista"* (The Thought of a Journalist) (1903) *"Ocherki po istorii russkoy tsenzury i zhurnalistiki"* (Studies in the History of Russian Censorship and Journalism) (1904); *"Epokha tsenzurnykh reform, 1859-65"* (The Period of the 1859-65 Censorship Reforms) (1904); "N. M. Yadrintsev" (1904); *"Politicheskiye protsessy v Rossi 1860-ykh godov"* (Political Trials in Russia in the 1860's (1907); *"Nikolayevskiye zhandarmy i literatura 1826-55 godov"* Nicholas' Gendarmes and literaturs 1826-55) (1908); *"Ocherki osvoboditel'nogo dvizheniya shestidesyatykh godov po neizdannym dokumentam"* (Studies of the Liberation Movement of the 1860's Based on Unpublished Documents) (1908); *"M. M. Stasyulevich i yego sovremenniki v ikh perepiske"* (M. M. Stasyulevich and His Contemporaries in Their Correspondence) (5 vol, 1911-13); *"250 dney v tsarskoy Stavke"* (250 Days at the Tsarist General Headquarters) (1920), etc; *Died:* 18 Aug 1923 in Petrograd.

LENGNIK, Fridrikh Vil'gel'movich (Party names: ZARIN; KURPKOL) (1873-1936) Party and govt official; CP member from 1893; *Born:* 12 Jan 1873 in Grobinya, Kurlyand Province, son of a teacher; *Educ:* from 1891 studied at Petersburg Technol Inst; *Career:* 1896 arrested in connection with Petersburg League for the Liberation of the Working Class; 1898 exiled to vil Tesinskoye, Yeniseysk Province; one of 17 signatories to Lenin's "Russian Social-Democrats' Protest Against the Economists' 'Cred'"; returned from exile and did revol work in Samara and Kiev; "Iskra" agent; member, Org Comt to Convene 2nd RSDRP Congress; at 2nd RSDRP Congress elected in absentia member, CC; member, Party Council, CC, RSDRP; 1904 returned to Russian and did Party work in Moscow; went into hiding to avoid trial in the case of the Northern Bureau, CC, RSDRP, then fled abroad; 1905 returned to Russia and 1905-17 engaged in Party work in Revel, Yekaterinoslav, Moscow, Samara and Petersburg; after 1917 Oct Revol Collegium member, RSFSR Pop Comrt of Educ; worked for State Commision for the Electrification of Russia; Collegium member, Supr Sovnarkhoz; from 1921 Collegium member, Pop Comrt of For Trade; from 1923 Collegium member, Pop Comrt for Workers and Peasants' Inspection; from 1928 chm, Comt for Standardization, Labor and Defense Council; from 1929 Collegium member; Inst of Philosophy, Communist Acad; 1931-32 dir, Inst of Tech, Communist Acad; from 1932 dep chm; All-Union Soc of Old Bolsheviks; assessor, USSR Supr Court; at 12th-15th Congresses elected member, CPSU(B) Centr Control Commission; from 1926 Presidium and Party Collegium member, SPSU(B) Centr Control Commission; *Died:* 29 Nov 1936.

LENIN (real name: UL'YANOV; other pseudonyms: K. LENIN; V. IL'IN; KARPOV, etc), Vladimir Il'ich (1870-1924) Revolutionary; Bolshevik theoratician; founder and leader, Communist Party (Bolsheviks) and Comintern; organizer of 1917 Oct Revol in Russian; founder of Sov Union; *Born:*22 Apr 1870 in Simbirsk; son of IT. N. Ul'yanov, Simbirsk Province college inspector who received patent of nobility; brother of Aleksandr Ul'yanov, member of People's Will Party, executed 1887 for attempted assassination of Alexander III; *Educ:* 1887 grad Simbirsk high school; 1891 passed external examinations for Law Fac, Petersburg Univ; *Career:* 1887 arrested for attending illegal student gathering, expelled from Kazan' Univ and deported from Kazan' by police; seetled on his mother's estate in vil Kokushkino, Kazan' Province, but was barred from attending univ; from 1889 lived with his family in Samara; from 1891 asst to public notary; active in secret People's Will circles; Aug 1893 moved to Petersburg and established contacts with technol students' Marxist circle and with Marxist workers; began revol work in Petersburg workers' circles and publiched articles attacking opponents of Marxism; Apr 1895 went abroad and established contacts with Plekhanov's Liberation of Labor group; after receiving instructions, returned to Petersburg, then visited Vilnius, where he met the Soc-Democrat L. Martov, exiled there and working for the Bund; fall 1895 sponsored foundation in Petersburg of League for the Liberation of the Working Class; shortly afterwards arrested and imprisoned together with other leaders of this org; Feb 1897 exiled for three years to Siberia, to vil Shushenskoye, Minusinsk Okrug; meanwhile, 1898 illegal Soc-Democratic party RSDRP emerged in Russia, with wich Lenin allied himself; July 1900-Nov 1905 in Zurich, Munich, London and Geneva; in Geneva, together with Plekhanov, Martov, Zasulich, Aksel'rod and Potresov, published newspaper "Iskra"; Nov 1905-Aug 1906 lived in Petersburg, directing CC of RSDSRP's Bolshevik faction and directing publ of newspapers "Vperyod", "Proletariy" and "Novaya zhizn"; played no particular part in 1905-07 Revol; summer 1906 moved to Finland; Dec 1907 went abroad and until Apr 1917 lived in Paris, Cracow and Switzerland; campaigned actively against Mensheviks, Bolshevik "opportunists", West European socialists and supporters of Kautsky; with the latter he differed regarding the attitude to war and the "conversion of imperialistic wars into civil wars"; the polemic culminated in his speeches at the 1915 Zimmerwald and 1916 Kienthal Socialist Conferences; contemplated breaking with 2nd International and forming his own 3rd Communist International; developed theory of "imperialism as the last, decaying stage of capitalism" and the possibility of the victory of "socialist revolution" amd the building of socialism first in one country - Russia-which, though econ backward, represented the weakest link in the gen system of capitalism as regards "socialist" transformation of Russia, he excluded any cooperation with Soc-Democrats and Socialist-Revolutionaries, preferring to rely for support on the factionalized "petty bourgeois element" to the point of forming a provisional govt with it; 16 Apr 1917, with the assistance of the German authorities, returned to Petersburg and in his "April Theses" publicly announced a program for a Bolshevik coup d'etat; put an end to cooperation of some Bolsheviks with Mensheviks and Socialist-Revolutionaries, which had developed since 1917 Feb Revol; led Bolsheviks to adopt an opposition stand and undermine Provisional Govt and the Soviets; late June and early July 1917 Bolsheviks made an abortive bid to seize power; to evade arrest and trial Lenin went into hiding and was smuggled to Finland; since the Soviets had refused to support the Bolsheviks in their attempted coup, Lenin struck the former slogan "All Power to the Soviets" form his program and concentrated entirely on preparing an armed uprising and seizing power by conspiratorial means; when a majority of the RSDRP(B) CC objected to this, Lenin threatened to break away from them and appeal to the Baltic Fleet sailors for help; however, agreed to postpone armed uprising until opening of 2nd Congress of Soviets; situation in Russian at this time was extremly critical: demands for an end to the war came from the soldiery, demoralized by mil routs and setbacks, by Bolshevik defeatist propaganda, by the provisional Government's vacillating war-or-peace policy and by the org of the armed forces and mil discipline; the non-Russian peoples demanded a solution of the nationality problem; however, the provisional Govt postponed action on all these problems until the convening of the Constituent Assembly, elections to which were delayed; Lenin made use of all this, demagogically promising to end the war, give the peasants land, grant the non-Russian peoples selfdetermination up to and including secession from Russia, turn factories and plants over to the workers and grant the gen public the full range of polit and civil rights; in addition to this, in connection with Gen Kornilov's bid to establish an authoritarian regime in Petrograd, the Provisional Govt freed arrested Bolshevik leaders and allowed the Bolsheviks to muster their own armed formations; as a result, the Bolsheviks, under Lenin's leadership, carried off the Oct Revolt and coup d'etat very easily; Lenin headed the new Sov govt as chm, Council of Pop Comr; the Constituent Assembly; convened in Jan 1918, refused to recognize the new regime since the Bolsheviks constituted a minority in the Assembly; the Assembly was therefore dispersed by force; non-Bolshevik polit parties were banned and their leaders arrested; the non-Bolshevik press, or any freedom of speech, was also banned; the Cheka terror began; the Bolsheviks claimed to solve the agrarian problem by establishing communes on lands confiscated from the large landowners; earlier promises of self-determination for the non-Russian peoples remained a fiction; in this setting there began the protracted Civil War; 30 Aug 1918 Lenin was shot and wounded by a woman, the Socialist-Revolutionary F. Kaplan; the anti-Bolshevik forces were decimated, divided and feuded among themselves; the Whitist movement, supported by the Entente, was headed by generals who alienated from their cause the more progressive elements, the non-Russian peoples and the gen mass of workers and peasants by their unmitigated militarism; on the other hand, the policies of the German occupation forces, and then the Polish forces in Bel and the Ukr prompted much of the population in these areas to swing behind the Bolsheviks; the Bolsheviks were aided by their demagogic promises of freedom and a rosy future, by fomenting the poorer peasants' hatred of the more well-to-do and utilizing this hatred for their own polit ends; Lenin and his followers finally emerged the victors from the Civil War, but the country was increasingly discontented with "war communism", and the raging Cheka terror; in 1921 the Kronstadt sailors' garrison revolted with the slogan "The Soviets Without the Bolsheviks!"; the situation cempelled Lenin to abandon "war communism" and adopt his famous "new economic policy" - NEP, for short; he also prepared the first mass purge of his own party - the RCP(B), on the pretext of countering the "Workers' Opposition", the "Democratic Centralists" and other opposition groups within the Party; his aim was to weed out all opposition, establish iron discipline and bring Party rank-and-file fully under the control of the CC; Mar 1919 Lenin founded the 3rd Communist International (Comintern) and drew up rules for admission to the Comintern, its program and its tactics; its prime task was not to combat capitalism but to counter the socialist parties in the European countries; furthermore, the Comintern was to support Sov Russia and defend its polit and econ interests in the int forum; Lenin left a huge literary legacy; his main achievement in the theory and practice of so-called "scientific Communism" was to found "a new type of party", without which it is allegedly impossible to proceed from capitalism to socialism; in Marxist theory he is considered the "loyalest" disciple of Marx and the founder of a new body of teaching - Marxism -Leninism - which, to use the CPSU CC definition, "creatively developed Marxism" and raised it to new heights; May 1922 Lenin became seriously ill with cerebral vascular sclerosis; Mar 1923 suffered a second stroke, as a result of which he lost the power of speech and was even more paralysed throughout the right side of his body; *Died:* 21 Jan 1924 at Gorki, near Moscow; his embalmed body is displayed in the specially built Mausoleum on Moscow's Red Square; innumerable towns, factories, plants, institutions and organizations are named for him.

LENTSMAN, Yan Davydovich (Party pseudonyms: KENTSIS; MISIN'BARD; KRUMS; TSERPS; GRIKE; GRIKIS; BORIS) (1881-1939) Lat Party and govt official; CP member fom 1899; *Born:* 16 Nov 1881 in Kurland Province, son of a farmhand; *Career:* 1897 joined revol movement; 1903 exiled to Arkhangel'sk Province; Oct 1904 fled to Lepaya; member, Lepaya Comt, Lat Soc-Democratic Workers' Party; from 1905 member, CC, Lat Kray Soc-Democratic Party; 1907 deleg, 5th RSDRP Congress; from early 1908 member, CC, RSDRP on behalf of CC, Lat Kray Soc-Democratic party; late 1908-11 member, Baku RSDRP Comt; from 1911 member, Riga Comt and CC, Lat Kray Soc-Democratic Party; from 1917 also member, Riga Sov of Workers' Dep; member, All-Russian Centr Comt of 1st convocation; during German occupation of Lat did underground work in Riga; from Dec 1918 dep chm, Sov Govt of Lat and Lat Comr of Internal Affairs; 1919-21 member, Revol Mil Council, 15th Army; also worked for RSFSR Revol Mil Council; 1921-24 dir, Petrograd (Leningrad) merchant port and member, Petrograd Province RCP)B) Comt; 1925-31 bd chm, Sov Merchant Fleet; 1931-37 worked in Lat Section of Comintern; arrested by NKVD; *Died:* 1939 in imprisonment; posthumously rehabilitated.

LEONIDOV (real name: VOL'FENZON), Leonid Mironovich (1873-1941) Actor, producer and teacher; Dr of Arts; prof from 1939; Pop Artiste of USSR from 1936; *Born:* 3 June 1873 in Odessa; *Educ:* 1894-96 studied at Moscow Theatrical College; *Career:* began acting as an amateur in productions of the Fine Arts Soc at Odessa Municipal Auditorium; 1896-1901 acted at Solovtsov Theater in Kiev and Odessa; from 1903 actor, Moscow Arts Theater; 1918 made first film appearance; from 1935 instructor and dean, Acting Fac, 1939-41 artistic dir, State Inst of Stagecraft; wrote numerous articles on acting theory; Roles: Ensign Charusskiy in Sumbatov's *"Staryy zakal"* (The Old Stock); Treplyov and Murzavetskiy in *"Volky i ovtsy"* (The Wolves and the Sheep); Molchainin and Morskoy in Nemirovich-Danchenko's *"Tsena zhizni"* (The Price of Live); Leartes in "Hamlet"; Ganya Ivolgin and Prince Myshkin in "The Idiot", after Dostoyevsky; Khlestakov and Lyapkin-Tyapkin in Gogol's *"Revizor"* (The Government Inspector); Konstantin in Nadyonov's *"Deti Vanyushina"* (Vanyushin's Children); Glumov and Gorodulin in *Na vsyakogo mudretsa dovol'no prostoty"* (There's a Simpleton in Every Sage); Ivan and Dmitriy Kramazov in *"Brat'ya Karamazovy"* (The Brothers Karamazov), after Dostoyevskiy; Vas'ka Pepl in Gorky's *"Na dne"* (The Lower Depths) (1903); Lopakhin and Borkin in Chekhov's *"Vishnyovyy sad"* (The Cherry Orchard) and "Ivanov" (1904); Vagin in *"Deti solntsa"* (Children of the Sun) (1905); Solyonyy in Chekhov's *"Tri sestry"* (The Three Sisters) (1906); Skalozub in Griboyedov's *"Gore ot uma"* (Woe from Wit) (1906); the Man and Dr Kerzhentsev in Andreyev's *"Zhizn' cheloveka"* (The Life of a Man) (1907) and *"Mysl'"* (Thought) (1914); Tropachyov in Turgenev's *"Nakhlebnik"* (The Parasite) (1912); Ivan Pazukhin in Saltykov-Shchedrin's *"Smert' Pazukhina"* (Pazukhin's Death) (1914); title role in Byron's "Cain" (1920) Pugachyov in Trenyov's *"Pugachyovshchina"* (The Pugachyov Rebellion); (1925); Borodin in *"Strakh"* (Fear) (1931); Plyushkin in Gogol's *"Myortvyye dushi"* (Dead Souls) (1932); title role in "Yegor Bulychov" (1934); *Film Roles:* Peter I in *"Tsarevich Aleksey"* (Prince Alexis) (1919); Ivan the Terrible in *"Kryl'ya kholopa"* (The Serf's Wings) (1926); Prof Kochubey in *"V gorod vkhodit' nel'zya"* (You Can't Go into Town) (1929); title role in "Gobsek" (1937), etc; *Productions:* Virta's *"Zemlya"* (Earth) (1937); *"Dostigayev i drugiye"* (Dostigayev and Co) (1938), etc; *Awards:* Order of Lenin; Order of the Red Banner of Labor; *Died:* 6 Aug 1941 in Moscow.

LEONIDOV, Oleg Leonidovich (1893-1051) Scriptwriter; *Born:* 1893; *Educ:* studied at Law Fac, Moscow Univ; *Career:* 1926 began working for film ind; assoc, Lit Dept, "Mezhrabpom-Rus" (then "Mezhrabpomfil'm") Studios, for which he wrote most of his script; *Films:* coauthor, *"Ne vsyo kotu maslenitsa"* (All Good Things Come to an End) (1927); *"Moskvy v Oktyabre"* (Moscow During the October Revolution) (1927); coauthor, *"Chelovek iz restorana"* (The Man from the Restaurant) (1927); coauthor, *"Kukla s millionami"* (The Doll with the Millions) (1928); *"Chelovek rodilsya"* (A Man Was Born) (1928); coauthor, *"Don Diyego i Pelageya"* (Don Diego and Pelagea) (1928); coauthor, *"Belyy oryol"* (The White Eagle) (1928); coauthor, *"Ledyanoy dom"* (House of Ice) (1928); coauthor, *"Chiny i lyudi"* (Officials and People) (1929); coauthor, "Sasha" (1930); coauthor, *"Te, kotoryye prozreli"* (Those Who Saw the Light) (1931); coauthor, *"Poslednyaya obida"* (The Last Insult) (1931); coauthor, "Prosperity" (1933); coauthor, *"Stepnyye pesni"* (Songs of the Steppe) (1934); *"Deti kapitana Granta"* (Captain Grant's Children) (1936); coauthor, *"Gobsek"* (Gobseck) (1937); coauthor, *"Ostrov sokrovishch"* (Treasure Island) (1938); coauthor, *"Po shchuch'yemu velen'yu"* (By a Wave of the Wand) (1938); cartoons: *"Serdtse khrabretsa"* (The Heart of the Bold) (1951); *"Tayozhnaya skazka'* (Tale of the Taiga) (1951); *"Snegurochka"* (The Snow-Maiden) (1952); *Died:* 17 Sept 1951.

LEONOV, Fyodor Grigor'yevich (1892-?) Party official; CP member from 1914; *Born:* 1892; *Educ:* 1924-25 studied at Communist Acad and Inst of Red Prof; *Career:* locksmith by trade; until 1918 Party and trade-union work at various factories; 1918 helped organize committees of the poor and draft troops for Red Army; then summoned to Petrograd and elected member and senior organizer, Vyborg Rayon Exec Comt; fought against Yudenich; head, Polit Dept, Karelian Mil Sector; then head, Polit Dept; 55th Infantry Div; transferred to Baltic Fleet and appointed dep head of its Polit Bd; helped crush Kronstadt Mutiny; 1921-22 senior instructor, CC, RCP(B); 1922-24 head, Org Dept, CC, Komsomol; 1926-27 dept head, newspaper "Pravda"; late 1927 elected secr, Don Okrug Party Comt; 1928 secr, Krasnopresnenskiy Rayon Party Comt, Moscow; then secr, Moscow City CPSU(B) Comt; from 1930 secr, East Siberian Kray Party Comt; at 15th Party Congress elected and member, at 16th Party Congress elected member, CC, CPSU(B); *Died:* date and place of death unknown.

LEONTOVICH, Aleksandr Vasil'yevich (1869-1943) Neurophysiologist and histologist; Dr of Med from 1900; prof from 1913; member, Ukr Acad of Sci from 1929; Hon Sci Worker of Ukr SSR from 1939; *Born:* 1 Nov 1869 in Kiev, son of a physician; *Educ:* 1893 grad Med Fac, Kiev Univ; *Career:* while still a student worked at V. V. Podvysotskiy's Laboratory; from 1898 lecturer, Agric Dept, Kiev Polytech Inst; 1900 defended doctor's thesis on skin innervation in humans; 1913-39 prof of physiology, Moscow Agric Inst (now Timiryazev Agric Acad); 1934-36 head Electrophysiological Laboratory, All-Union Inst of Experimental Med; 1936-43 founder-assoc, Physiological Laboratory, Inst of Physiology, Ukr Acad of Sci; did research on the physiological degeneration and regeneration of nerve tissue elements in the course of the body's lifetime; described cell-containing peripheral nerve plexi in human skin and animal tissues; depicted synapses as "organoid bodies"; devised method of staining peripheral nerve structures with methylene blue; hypothesized the presence of fluctuating current in neurons; wrote first Russian guides to the application of biometrics to biology, medicine and the physiology of domestic animals; *Publ: "Novyye dannyye ob innervatsii kozhi cheloveka"* (New Data on Skin Innervation in Humans) (1900); *"Plexus nervosus autonomicus periphericus"* (The Autonomous Peripheral Nerve Plexus) (1926); *"K voprosu o sushchestvovanii 'osnovnogo nervnogo spleteniya' serdtsa"* (The Existence of a "Basic Nerve Plexus" of the Heart) (1927); "La microstructure du systéme nerveux et de ses 'neurons' comme la base des théories de conductibilité et d'excitation dans le système nerveux" (The Microstructure of the Nervous System and Its "Neurons" as a Basis for Theories on Conductivity and Excitation in the Nervous System) (1928); "Über die Ganglienzellen der Blutgefäße" (The Ganglion Cells of the Blood Vessels) (1930); *"Pro postiynu fiziolohichnu reheneratsiyu nervovoi systemy dorosloho organizmu"* (The Constant Physiological Regeneration of the Adult Body's Nervous System) (1937); *"Sovremennaya metodika prizhiznennogo okrashivaniya nervov metilenovoy sin'koy i drugimi krasitelyami"* (Modern Methods of Staining Nerves Intra Vitam with Methylene Blue and Other Dyes) (1939), etc; *Died:* 15 Dec 1943.

LEONTOVICH, Nilolay Dmitriyevich (1877-1921); Composer; exponent of Ukr choral music; *Born:* 13 Dec 1877 in vil Monastyryok, Podol'sk Province; *Educ:* 1899 grad Kamenets-Podol'sk Theological Seminary; from 1910 studied composition under B. L Yavorskiy; *Career:* abandoned intention of theological career and spent his life teaching choral singing in Ukr (Chukovo, Tul'chin, etc); recorded and arranged folk songs; 1904 passed Church choir precentor's examination in Petersburg; 1905 active in revol movement in Yekaterinoslav Province; 1916 first musical work (arrangement of folk song "A Generous Man") performed in Kiev; 1919 began to teach at lysenko Musical Drama Inst; Kiev; also worked for Ukr Pop Comrt of Educ; composed some 200 classical arrangements of folk songs; *Works: songs:* A Generous Man"; "Bearing a Cossack"; "Oh, from Beyond the Stone Mountain"; "A Mother Had a Daughter"; "Outside the Town the Ducks are Swimming"; arranged revol songs;"Internationale"; "Marseillaise"; "Warsaw Woman"; "We Are the Smiths"; etc; also arranged Russian folk songs; original choral works; "The Ice-Breaker"; "Legend"; "Summer Tones"; "My Song" and incomplete fairy-tale opera *"Na rusalchyn velykden"* (The Water-Nymph Festival); *Died:* 23 Jan 1921 killed in vil Markovka, Vinnitsa Oblast.

LEONT'YEV, Yakov Leont'yevich (1890-1948) Theater impresario; *Born:* 6 Jan 1890 *Educ:* 1907 studied at M. I. Morskaya's drama school in Odessa; 1913 grad Kiev Business Inst; *Career:* from 1908 actor and admin, Kishinev and Kiev theaters; after 1917 Oct Revol helped found new theaters and companies in provinces; 1922-26 dir, Russian and Tatar Theaters, Simferopol'; 1926-32 dir, Studio of Maly Theater; 1933-34 asst dir, Moscow Acad Arts Theater; from 1934 dep dir, Bolshoy Theater and dir of its branch; *Died:* 14 Jan 1948.

LEPESHINSKAYA, Ol'ga Borisovna (1871-1963) Biologist and histologist; Dr of Biology from 1935; prof from 1939; member, USSR Acad of Med Sci from 1950; CP member from 1898; *Born:* 18 Aug 1871; *Educ:* 1897 grad Rozhdestvenskiy Med Orderlies' Courses, Petersburg; 1902 studied at Med Fac, Lausanne Univ; 1906 studied at private med course for women in Moscow; 1915 grad Med Fac, Moscow Univ; *Career:* 1894 joined Marxist circle; 1897-1900 exiled with husband, the revolutionary P. N. Lepeshinskiy, to Siberia, where she worked as a nurse in the vil Kuragino, Yeniseysk Province; 1899 attended conference of Marxist-in-exile at which Lenin presented his anti-Economist program; 1903 accompanied her exiled husband to Minusinsk and organized his subsequent flight; 1903-06 lived in Geneva and worked with local Bolshevik emigres; 1906 returned to Russia, living first in Orsha, then in Moscow, where she continued her revol activities; after obtaining med license became asst prof, Chair of Therapy, Moscow Univ but was soon fired on polit grounds; after this worked as a distr physician at a railroad station near Moscow; also worked in Crimea; 1919-20 asst prof, Chair of Histology, Tashkent Univ; 1920-26 asst prof, Chair of Histology, 1st Moscow Univ; 1926-36 head, Histological Laboratory, Biological Inst, Timiryazev Communist Acad (now All-Union Inst of Experimental Med); 1936-49 Head, Cytological Laboratory, All-Union Inst of Experimental Med; 1949-57 head, Dept for the Development of Living Matter, Inst of Experimental Biology, USSR Acad of Med Sci; dep, USSR Supr Sov of 1950 convocation; from 1957 head, Cytological Laboratory, Inst of Experimental Biology; member, ed collegiom, journal "Uspekhi sovremennoy biologii"; member, ed council, journal "Arkhiv anatomii, gistologii i embriologii"; did research on the histology of bone tissue and on non-cellular living matter and its role in the organism; a research project on living matter which she began in 1950 failed to yield results and was strongly criticized by other sci; wrote over 150 works; *Publ: "Proiskhozhdeniye kletok iz zhivogo veshchestva i rol' zhivogo veshchestva v organizme"* (The Emergence of Cells from Living Matter and the Role of Living Matter in the Organism) (1950); *"Obolochki zhivotnykh kletok i ikh biologicheskoye znacheniye"* (The Membranes of Animal Cells and Their Biological Importance) (1952); *"Novaya kltochnaya teoriya i yeyo fakticheskoye obosnovyniye"* (A New Cell Theory and Its Factual Proof) (1955), etc; *Award:* Order of Lenin; Stalin Prize (1950); Order of the Red Banner of Labor; medals; *Died:* 2 Oct 1963.

LEPESHINSKIY, Panteleymon Nikolayevich (1868-1944) Party official; prof; Dr of Historical Sci; CP member from 1898; *Born:* 12 Mar 1868 in vil Studenets, Mogilev Province, son of a priest; *Educ:* 1886-1890 studied at Petersburg Univ; *Career:* 1890 expelled from univ for participation in student polit movement, arrested and banished from Petersburg; 1895 re-arrested; 1897 exiled to Siberia; 1898 met Lenin in exile; one of 17 signatories to Lenin's "Russian Social-Democraties' protests Against the Economists' 'Creed"; 1900 completed term of exile and on Lenin's instructions settled in Pskov, organizing and distributing newspaper "Iskra"; 1902 member, Org Comt to Convene 2nd RSDRP Congress; arrested and exiled to Siberia; 1903 fled to Switzerland; 1905 helped prepare 3rd RSDRP Congress; 1905-07 revol work in Yekaterinoslav and Petersburg; 1907-09 taught mathematics at secondary school in Orsh; 1909 again arrested; then worked for Statistics Bureau, Moscow Province Admin; during WW 1 took defeatist stand; sctive in 1917 Feb Revol; after 1917 Oct Revol headed Dept of School Reform, Pop Comrt of Educ; also Collegium member, Pop Comrt of Educ; coauthor, *"Polozheniya o yedinoy trudovoy shkole"* (Statute of the Common Labor School); 1918 helped found first experimental model commune school in vil Litvinovichi, Mogilev Province, which served as the basis for Moscow's Lepeshinskiy Experimental Model Commune School; 1919-20 Turkastani Republ Dep Pop Comr of Educ; 1921 returned to Moscow and helped found Commision to Study and Collate Material on the History of the Oct Revol and the Communist Party: co-founder, Int Org for Aid to Revol Fighters; 1925-27 chm, CC, Int Org for Aid to Revol Fighters; 1927-30 dir, Historical Museum; 1931-34 dir, Research Inst, Pop Comrt of For Trade; 1935-36 dir, Museum of the Revol; from 1936 pensioner; deleg at 14th-17th Party Congresses and 15th- 17th Party Conferences; *Publ: "Doklad o printsipakh yedinoy trudovoy shkoly"* (A Report on the Principles fo the Common Labor School) (1918); *"Shkol'nyy vopros v obstanovke sotsialisticheskoy revolyutsii'* (The School Problem in the Light of the Socialist Revolution) (1920); *"Parizhskaya kommuna i MOPR"* (The Paris Commune and the International Organization for Aid to Ravolutionary Fighters) (1927); *"Na povorote"* (At the Turning Point) (1925); also wrote memoirs of Lenin; *Awards:* Order of the Red Banner of Labor; *Died:* 29 Sept 1944.

LEPLEVSKIY, G. M. (1889-1939) Govt official, CP member from 1917; *Born:* 1889; *Career:* 1921-23 member, then chm, Small Council of Pop Comr; then exec official, USSR Council of Pop Comr; 1934-39 USSR Dep Prosecutor; arrested by State Security organs; *Died:* 1939 in imprisonment.

LEPORSKIY, Nikolay Ivanovich (1877-1952) Internist; Dr of Med from 1911; prof from 1917; member, USSR Acad of Med Sci from 1944; Hon Sci Worker of RSFSR from 1944; *Born:* 29 Jan 1877; *Educ:* 1903 grad Yur'yev (Tartu) Univ; *Career:* 1906-17 asst prof, Hospital Therapy Clinic, Yur'yev Univ; 1909-11 worked at physiological laboratories of the Russian Acad of Sci and at Pavlov's Inst of Experimental Med; 1911 defended doctor's thesis on conditioned inhibition; from 1911 assoc prof; 1912-17 lectured on the pathology and therapy of internal diseases at Yur'yev Univ; simultaneously taught fac and hospital therapy at Yur'yev Higher Med Courses; from 1917 head, Hospital Therapy Clinic, Tomsk Med Inst; from 1923 head, Hospital Thearpy Clinic, Voronezh Med Inst; from 1942 until death head, Hospital Therapy Clinic, Leningrad Naval Med Acad; strongly influenced by Pavlovianism; used Pavlov's methods in research on the pathology of blood circulation, digestion and higher nervous acticity; devised generally accepted methods of examining the functional state of the stomach; solved various problems of the clinical physiology of the Stomach, liver and pancreas;contributed to dietology with a study on the importance of vegetables for digestion; introduced optical adequatometry technique to deternine the excitability of the higher nervous centers; did research on inhibitory processes on the basis of the functional state of the digestive organs during noctural sleep; bd member, All-Union Soc of Therapists; member, various learned councils and commissions; co-ed, various med journals and *"Bol'shaya meditsinskaya entsiklopediya"* (Large Medical Encyclopedia) (1st ed); wrote over 60 works, including 5 monographs; *Publ: "Materialy k fiziologii Uslovnogo tormozheniya"* (Material on the Physiology of Conditioned Inhibition) (1911); *Sluchay dlitel'noy ostanovki serdtsa, vyzvannoy povrezhdeniyem yego igloyu* (A Case of Prolonged Cardiac Arrest Caused by Injury with a Needle) (1913); *Ovoshchi i deyatel'nost' pepsinovykh zhelez* (Vegetables and the Activity of the Peptic Glands) (1922); *Ovoshchi i ikh fiziologicheskoye znacheniye v pishchevarenii* (Vegetables and Their Physiological Importance in Digestion) (1934); *Nekotoryye voprosy klinicheskoy fiziologii podzheludochnoy zhelezy* (Some Problems of the Clinical Physiology of the Pancreas) (1950); *Bolezni podzheludochnoy zhelezy* (Diseases of the Pancreas) (1951), etc; *Awards:* Order of Lenin; Stalin Prize (1952); Order of the Red Banner of Labor; medals; *Died:* 15 June 1952 in Leningrad.

LEPSE, Ivan Ivanovich (1889-1929) Trade-union official; CP member from 1904; *Born:* 2 July 1889 in Riga, son of a worker; *Career:* foundry worker; 1905-07 head, Party org at a plant in Riga; drafted into Tsarist Army; wounded and demobilized; from 1915 worked in Riga and Petrograd; 1917 chm, Petrograd Rayon Bolshevik Comt; helped found Metal Workers' Union; from Apr 1917 member, Centr Bd, Metal Workers' Union; 1918 secr, Petrograd Comt, Metal Workers' Union; from Jan 1919 polit work in Red Army; fought in defense of Petrograd; 1920 comr, 10th and 11th Div and member, Revol Mil Council, 7th Army; 1921 helped crush Kronstadt Mutiny; 1921-29 chm, CC, All-Union Metal Workers' Union; deleg, 11th-15th Party Congresses; at 11th and 12th Congresses elected cand member, Party CC; at 13th-15th Congresses elected member, CC, CPSU(B); member, All-Russian and USSR Centr Exec Comt; member, Exec Bureau, Trade-Union Int; attended many int congresses and trade-union conferences; *Died:* 6 Oct 1929; buried on Red square in Moscow.

LESHCHENKO (Pseudonym: SHATOV), Dmitriy Il'ich (1876-1937) Revolutionary; CP member from 1900; *Born:* 1876 in Nikolayevo, son of a worker; *Educ:* grad Physics and Mathematics Fac, Petersburg Univ; *Career:* fought in 1905-07 Revol; 1906 secr, Bolshevik newspapers *Volna* and *Ekho*, 1906 Lenin lived in Levshchenko's apartment: spring 1906 Leshchenko was elected secr, Petrograd RSDRP Comt; 1907 deleg, 5th RSDRP Congress; 1910-11 worked for newspaper *Zvezda* and *Pravda;* 1917 secr, nwespaper *Izvestiya Petrogradskogo Soveta* (until the Bolsheviks withdrew from the ed staff); then in Vyborg Rayon Duma; July 1917 travelled to vil Razliv where he photographed Lenin; after 1917 Oct Revol secr, Pop Comrt of Educ; 1918-21 head, All-Russian Cinema Comt; from 1924 taught; arrested by State Security organs; *Died:* 1937 in imprisonment.

LEVANDOVSKIY, Mikhail Karlovich (1890-1937) Mil commander; junior capt, Russian Army; army commander, 2nd grade from 1935; Maximalist Socialist-Revolutionary from 1918 to 1920; CP member from 1920; *Born:* 13 May 1890 in Tiflis, son of a med orderly; *Educ:* 1912 grad Vladimir Mil College: *Career:* fought in WW 1; from 1918 in Red Army; 1918 mil comr, Terek Sov Republ; commander, Vladikavkaz-Groznyy Forces Group; 3 Jan-13 Feb 1919 commander, 11th Army; 1919-20 commanded Special, 7th Cavalry and 33rd Kuban Rifle Div, then Terek Forces Group; 29 Apr-12 July 1920 commanded 11th Army on Turkestani Front; 19 July-5 Oct 1920 and 21 Nov 1920-30 Mar 1921 commanded 9th Army; 20 Mar-18 Apr 1921 commanded 10th Terek-Daghestani Army; 22 Apr-27 May 1921 commanded 9th Army; July-Sept 1921 mil comr, Tabov Province; 1921-24 asst, then dep commander, Tambov Mil Distr; 30 Apr 1924-2 Dec 1925 commander, Turkestani Front; 1925-28 commander, Separate Caucasian Army; 1928-29 USSR Pop Comr of Mil and Naval Affairs plen with Council of Pop Comr of Transcaucasian SFSR; head, Main Bd, Red Army; 1929-37 commander, Siberian, then Transcaucasian Mil Distr; 1937 commander, Maritime Forces Group of Special Red Banner Far Eastern Army; 1934-37 also member, Mil Council, USSR Pop Comrt of Defense; 1934 deleg at 17th CPSU(B) Congress; 1937 arrested by NKWD; *Awards:* Order of Lenin; other orders and medals; *Died:* 29 Dec 1937 died in imprisonment; posthumously rehabilitated.

LEVANDOVSKIY, Vyacheslav Vyacheslavovich (1897-1962) Stage and film dir; artist; *Born:* 1897; *Educ:* 1918 studied at Kiev Theatrical Acad; 1920-22 studied at Ukr Acad of Arts; *Career:* 1920 started work as set-designer at Kiev theaters; worked for various publ houses as artist, specializing in illustrating children's books; from 1925 set-designer at Kiev Film studios, All-Ukr Film Bd; made animated cartoons using flat puppets and appliqués; made puppets and mountings for photographing them; 1926 transferred to Odessa Film Studios, All-Ukr Film Bd, where he made his first film and first Ukr animed cartoon *"Skazka o solomennom bychke"* (The Tale of the Straw Bull-Calf) (1927); 1927 returned to Kiev and used the same process to film another folk tale *"Skazka o belke-khozyayushke i myshke-zlodeyke"* (The Tale of the Kind Squirrel Hostess and the Villainous Mouse) (1928); 1932 returned to Odessa Film Studios where he started work on his first animated sound cartoon *"Tuk-Tuk i yego Priyatel' Zhuk'* (Rat-Tat and His Friend Beetle), which was finished in 1935, 1933 artist for Mosfil'm Studios; dir, script writer, scene-painter and puppeteer, maker of puppets and various devices for photographing them; 1942-45 artist and designer at Acad of Architecture in Moscow; 1945 returned to Mosfil'm Studios; worked as modeler and designer; *Works:* produced films: first three-dimensional animated cartoon *"Lisa i vinograd"* (The Fox and the Grapes) (1937) from Krylov's fable; *"Zaveshchaniye"* (The Will) (1937) from Bracciolini's novella; *"Lisa i volk"* (The Fox and the Wolf) (1937) from folk tale; *"Serebryany dozhd"* (The Silver Rain) (1938) about adventures of toys on New Year's Eve; *"Zolotoy klyuchik"* (The Little Golden Key) (1939); co-dir, *"V kukol'noy strane"* (In Doll Land) (1941); helped make *"Nebesnoye sozdaniye"* (The Creation of the Heavens) (1956); *Died:* 1962.

LEVANEVSKIY, Sigizmund Aleksandrovich (1902-?) Pilot; Hero of the Sov Union; CP member from 1934; *Born:* 1902 in Petersburg, son of a worker; *Educ: 1923-25* studied at Sebastopol School of Naval Pilots; *Career:* from 1916 laborer; 1917 joined Red Guard; 1918 worked for food squad in Vyatka Province; 1919 volunteered for Red Army and served on Eastern Front; 1919-23 company, then battalion commander, asst chief of staff of a brig, asst commander, Stavropol' Territorial Regt; 1925-29 instructor at mil school; 1929-31 senior instructor, then commandant, Nikolayev School of Soc for Promotion of the Sov Defense, Aviation and Chemical Ind; from 1931 dir of studies, Poltava School of this Soc; 1933 joined Main North Sea Passage Bd; flew to Nome, Alaska, to deliver the American pilot Mattern, who had crashed in the Anadyr distr; Feb 1934 flew to USA to organice Alaskan rescue operation for members of icebreaker "Chelyuskin" expedition; hence flew in very bad conditions via Fairbanks, Nome, Wellen to Vancarem; at 7th Congress of Soviets elected member, USSR Centr Exec Comt, Sept 1936 flew 19,000 km from Los Angeles to Moscow; after returning from America continued to work for polar aviation; early 1937 prepared for non-stop Moscow-US flight over North Pole; 12 Aug 1937 captained 4-engine N-209 plane which set of from Moscow for America; the flight encountered exceptionally bad weather; over the Barents Sea the plane ran into continuous cloud, which forced it to fly at an altitude of over 6,000 meters; approaching the North Pole strong winds cut the plane's ground speed to just over 160 km/hr; 13 Aug 1937 the plane passed over the North Pole and headed for Alaska; this marked the start of the most difficult navigational stage of the flight - 2,187 km from the North Pole to the Alaskan coast; around 2 a.m. Levanevskiy radioed that one of his engines was out of action as a result of a faulty oil lead; after this steady radio contact with the plane was lost; the few scraps of radio messages subsequently received indicate that Levanevskiy continued for a while on three engines; then the situation worsened and the plane was forced to descend into the cloud, resulting in icing-up of the plane's surfaces and an attempted forced landing on the ice; rescue efforts were immediately made by both Sov and American polar pilots, but no trace of Levanevskiy or the plane was found; *Awards:* Hero of the Sov Union (1934); Order of the Red Star (1933); Order of the Red Banner of Labor (1936); *Died:* 1937 following a plane crash in the Arctic.

LEVCHENKO, Mitrofan Vasil'yevich (1890-1955) Historian; specialist in Byzantine period; Dr of History from 1941; prof from 1938; CP Member from 1925; *Born:* 5 Dec 1890 in Sudzha, now Kursk Oblast; *Educ:* 1915 grad Bezborodko Inst of History and Philology, Nezhin; 1930-33 postgrad studies at Leningrad Inst of History; Philosophy and Linguistics; *Career:* from 1918 taught and did govt work in Sudzha; from 1933 senior assoc, State Acad of the History of Civilization; from 1938 senior assoc, Inst of History, USSR Acad of Sci, where he was in charge of the Byzantine group; 1940-44 head, Leningrad Dept, Inst of History, USSR Acad of Sci; 1944-50 founder-head, Chair of Byzantine Studies, Leningrad Univ; studied soc and econ history of early Byzantium and relations between Byzantium and Kievan Rus; *Publ: "Istoriya Vizantii. Kratkiy kurs"* (The History of Byzantium. A Short Course) (1940); coauthor, *"Sbornik deokumentov po sotsial'no-ekonomicheskoy istorii Vizantii"* (A Collection of Documents on the Social and Economic History of Byzantium) (1951); *"Agafiy. O Tsarstvovanii Yustiniana"* (Agathium. The Reign of Justinian) (1953); *"Ocherki po sitorii russko-vizantiyskikh otnosheniy"* (Studies in the History of Russo-Byzantine Relations) (1956); *Died:* 22 Jan 1955

LEVICHEV, Vasiliy Nikolayevich (1891-1937) Mil commander; junior capt, Russian Army; corps commander from 1935; CP member from 1919; *Born:* 22 Dec 1891 in vil Pochinok, Vologda Province, son of a peasant; *Educ:* grad teachers' seminary; 1915 grad Peterhof Ensigns' School; 1923 grad Mil Acad Course for Senior Commanders; *Career:* 1917 elected commander, 16th Special Regt, Russian Army; from Apr 1919 in Red Army; 1919-20 mil comr, Vologda Province; 1920-22 asst mil comr, Kiev Okrug and commander, Kiev Battle Sector and Mil Area; 1924-27 asst chief, dep chief, then chief, Red Army Main Bd, simultaneously taught on mil polit courses; 1928-29 corps commander; 1930 dep chief of staff of Red Army and head, Red Army Main Bd; exec ed, journal "Voyennyy vestnik"; 1931-33 dep chief of staff of Red Army; 1933-34 Sov mil attache in Germany; 1934-37 again dep chief of staff of Red Army and dep chief of Gen Staff; 1934-37 also member, Mil Council, USSR Pop Comrt of Defense; 1937 arrested by NKVD; *Died:* 26 Nov 1937 in imprisonment; posthumously rehabilitated.

LEVIN, Boris Mikhaylovich (1899-1940) Russian writer; *Born:* 5 Jan 1899 in vil Zagorodino, Vitebsk Province; *Educ:* 1930 grad Moscow Univ; *Career:* 1918-22 in Red Army; from 1923 worked for satirical journals and newspapers; wrote humorous stories; 1939 fought in Sov Army in Western Bel campaign; 1939-40 fought in Sov-Finnish War; *Publ:* novelette *"Zhili dva tovarishcha"* (The Were Once Two Comrades) (1931); novel *"Yunosha"* (The Youth) (1933); *plays: "Rodina"* (Native Land) (1936); *"Pod yasnym nebom'* (Under a Clear Sky) (1938); coauthor, film script *"Yakov Sverdlov"* (1940); essay *"Yevgeniy Konstantinovich Fyodorov"* (1938); novelette *"Na Vrangelya!"* (Get Wrangel!) (1939); *Died:* 6 Jan 1940 in battle near Suomussalmi during Sov-Finnish War.

LEVIN, Lev Grigor'yevich (1870-1938) Internist; *Born:* 1870; *Career:* 1896-97 postgrad student, in Berlin and Paris; 1897 returned to Russia; 1907-19 factory physician; 1919-20 intern, Health Resort Selection Hospital, RSFSR Pop Comrt of Health; 1920-38 intern, then head, Therapy Dept, Kremlin Hospital; 13 Mar 1938 sentenced to death for allegedly deliberately giving Sov leaders and the writer Maxim Gorky and his son M. A. Peshkov incorrect med treatment; *Died:* 1938 executed by firing squad in Moscow.

LEVIN, R. Ya. (1898-1937) Govt official; CP member from 1915; *Born:* 1898; *Career:* Party work in Moscow; after 1917 Feb Revol member, Tsaritsyn City Party Comt and chm, Tsaritsyn Exec Comt; after 1917 Oct Revol Party and govt work; chm, Tsaritsyn Province Party Comt; chm Tsaritsyn Exec Comt; member, Yaroslavl' Province RCP(B) Comt; Collegium member, RSFSR Pop Comrt of Finance; 1929-30 chm, RSFSR Gosplan; 1937 chm, Bd, Ind Bank; member, All-Russian and USSR Centr Exec Comt; 1919 Tsaritsyn Province RCP(B) Comt delg at 8th RCP(B) Congress; arrested by State Security organs; *Died:* 1937 in imprisonment.

LEVIN, Vladimir Solomonovich (1897-1934) Office worker; CP member; *Born:* 1897; *Career:* Expelled from Party for belonging to Zinov'yev group; Dec 1934 arrested for alleged membership of Leningrad underground terrorist center which is claimed to have murdered CC, CPSU(B) secr Kirov on 1 Dec 1934 in Leningrad; 29 Dec 1934 sentenced to death by Mil Collegium, USSR Supr Court; *Died:* 29 Dec 1934 executed.

LEVINA, Revekka Saulovna (1899-1964) Economist; Dr of Econ from 1937; corresp member, USSR Acad of Sci from 1939; CP member from 1918; *Born:* 1899; *Career:* specialized in agric econ, agrarian relations and agrarian crises; member, ed bd, journals; *"Mirovoye khozyaystvo i mirovaya politika"; "Na agrarnom fronte"; "Sotsialisticheskaya rekonstruktsiya sel'skogo khozyaystva!";* wrote more then 50 works; *Publ: "Novyye materialy k rabote V. I. Lenina"* (New Material on Lenin's Work); *"Novyye dannyye o zakonakh razvitiya kapitalizma v zemledelii"* (New Data on the Laws of Capitalist Development in Agriculture); *"Kapitalizm i zemledeliye v Soyedinyonnykh Shtatakh Ameriki"* (Capitalism and Agriculture in the United States of America) (1937); *Awards:* Order of the Red Banner of Labor; *Died:* Dec 1964.

LEVINSON-LESSING, Frants Yul'yevich (1861-1939) Geologist and petrographer; member, USSR Acad of Sci from 1925; *Born:* 9 Mar 1861 in Petersburg, son of a dr; *Educ;* 1883 grad Physics and Mathematics Fac, Petersburg Univ; postgrad course at above Univ; *Career:* 1888 began to lecture at Petersburg Univ; 1892-1902 prof, Yur'yev (now Tartu) Univ; 1902-30 prof, Petersburg (Leningrad) Polytech Inst; founded first Russian laboratory of experimental petrography at polytech Inst; 1902-20 prof, Higher Woman's Courses, Petersburg; from 1921 head, Chair of Petrography, Leningrad Univ; 1918-25 founder and dept head, Commission for the Study of Natural Production Resources, USSR Acad of Sci; 1925-29 first dir, Soil Inst, USSR Acad of Sci; 1930-38 founder-dir, Petrographic Inst, USSR Acad of Sci; founder-dir, first Vulcanological station in Kamshatka; 1934-39 chm, Commission for the Comprehensive Study of the Caspian; chm, Azer and Arm Branches of USSR Acad of Sci; 1920-23 active part in hydrogeological studies for the "Svir'stroy" construction project; head, Transcaucasian expedition of USSR Acad of Sci; member and hon member of many Sov and for learned soc; Geological Soc, London; Société Belge de Géologie, etc; specialized in theoretical petrography and petrogenesis; 1898 proposed first efficient chemical taxonomy of rocks; studied differentiation of magma, genesis and classification of ore deposits, etc; also published works on physics and chemistry; 1934 Petrographic Inst of USSR Acad of Sci named after him, as its founder; *Publ: "Variolity Yalguby Olonetskoy gubernii"* (The Varioliths of Yalguba, Olonets Province) (1884); *Olonetskaya diabazovaya formatsiya* (The Olonets Diabasic Formation) (1888); *"Issledovaniya po teoreticheskoy petrografii v svyazi s izucheniyem izverzhennykh porod Tsentral'nogo Kavkaza"* (Research on Theoretical Petrography in Connection with the Study of the Eruptive Rocks of the Central Caucasus (1898); *"Vulkany i lavy Tsentral'nogo Kavkaza"* (The Volcanoes and Lavae of the Central Caucasus) (1913); *"Uspekhi* *petrografii v Rossii"* (Progress in Russian Petrography) (1923); *"Vvedeniye v istoriyu petrografii"* (An Introduction to the History of Petrography) (1936); "Petrografiya" (1940); *Died:* 25 Oct 1939.

LEVIT, Vladimir Semyonovich (1883-1961) Surgeon; Dr of Med from 1914; prof from 1922; maj-gen, Med Corps; Hon Sci Worker of RSFSR from 1936; *Born:* 1883; *Educ:* 1906 grad Med Fac, Koenigsberg Univ; in same year obtained license at Khar'kov Univ; *Career:* 1906-14 zemstvo physician, Ardatov Uyezd, Simbirsk Province; 1914-18 head, Surgical Dept, Simbirsk Province Zemstvo Hospital; 1919-20 assoc prof, Fac Surgical Clinic, Tomsk Univ; 1922-26 prof and head, Fac Surgical Clinic, 1924-26 dean, Med Fac, Irkutsk Univ; 1926-53 head, Chair of Hospital Surgical Clinic, 1928-29 asst dean, 2nd Moscow Med Inst; 1928 performed first Sov resection of the cardiac part of the stomach for cancer; 1932-39 dep, Frunze Rayon Sov, Moscow; 1935-46 chm, Moscow and Moscow Oblast Surgical Soc; 1939-42 dep, Lenin Rayon Sov, Moscow; from 1942 dep chief surgeon of Sov Army and chief surgeon, Burdenko Main Mil Hospital; 1945-61 head, Chair of clinical and Field Surgery, Mil Fac, Centr Inst of Postgrad Med Training, Moscow; member, Learned Council, USSR Min of Health; read papers at int surgical conferences in cairo and Copenhagen; from 1955 hon member, All-Union Surgical Soc and member, Int Surgical Soc; ed, surgery section, *"Bol'shaya meditsinskaya entsiklopediya"* (Large Medical Encyclopedia) (1st ed) and co-ed, 2nd ed; co-ed; *"Entsiklopedicheskiy slovar' voyennoy meditsiny"* (Encyclopedic Dictionary of Military Medicine); member, ed bd, journal *"Khirurgiya";* performed first Sov operation for bilateral hydatid tapeworm of the liver and devised origianal methods for the treatment of gunshot wounds of the extremities and thorax; wrote over 100 works; *Publ: "K khirurgii kardial'noy chasti zheludka'* (Surgery of the Cardiac Section of the Stomach) (1932); "Materials on the investigation of the Stomach Function After Resection" (1939); *"Ognestrel'nyye raneniya krupnykh sustavov"* (Gunshot Wounds of the Large Joints) (1944); coauthor, *"Uchebnik chastnoy khirurgii"* (A Textbook on Special Surgery) 2 vol, 1944); *"Chastota i klassifikatsiya ognestrel'nykh raneniy sustavov"* (The Incidence and Classification of Gunshot Wounds of the Joints) (1953); *"Diagnostika khirurgicheskikh zabolevaniy"* (The Diagnosis of Surgical Diseases) (1959), etc; *Awards:* Order of the Red Banner; Order of the Red Banner of Labor; Order of the Fatherland War, 2nd Class; medals; *Died:* 1969 in Mosoow.

LEVITSKIY, Oleg Dmitriyevich (1909-61) Geologist; corresp member, USSR Acad of Sci from 1953; *Born:* 19 Mar 1909; *Educ:* 1930 grad Leningrad Mining Inst; *Career:* from 1938 at Inst of Geological Sci, USSR Acad of Sci; geological surveys in Eastern USSR; from 1956 at Inst of Geology, Minerla Deposits, Petrography, Mineralogy and Geochemistry, USSR Acad of Sci; studied tungsten deposits of Eastern Transbaikal; surveyed tin deposits, etc; also studied granitoids of Eastern Transbaikal and mineral deposits of Far East and Northeastern USSR; *Publ: 'Vol'framovyye mestorozhdeniya Vostochnogo Zabaykal'ya'* (The Tungsten Deposits of Eastern Transbaikal) (1939); *"Mestorozhdeniya kassiteritovo-kvartsevykh formatsiy"* (Cassiterite-Quartz Deposits) (1947); *"K voprosu o znachenii kolloidnykh rastvorov pri rudootlozhenii"* (The Significance of Colloidal Solutions in Ore Emplacement) (1953); *Awards:* Stalin Prize (1946); *Died:* 24 Jan 1961.

LEVITSKIY-TSEDERBAUM, V. O. (pen-name: LEONOV) (1883-?) Writer; Menshevik; *Born:* 1883; *Career:* worked for the Dvinsk Bund org; 1904 emigrated; 1905, after Menshevik conference in Geneva, returned to Russia; propaganda work in Petersburg; Petersburg Menshevik deleg at 4th (Amalgamative) RSDRP Congress; took liquidationist stand and worked for liqiudationist organs *"Golos sotsial-demokrata"* and *"Vozrozhdeniye";* member, ed staff, liquidationist jouranl *"Nasha zarya";* during WW 1 took extreme right-wing defensist stand; worked for defensist journal *"Delo";* after 1917 Feb Revol worked for Menshevik newspaper *"Vperyod";* hostile toward 1917 Oct Revol and fought against Sov regime; 1919 tried in case of the counterrevolutionary "tractical center" and sentenced to detention in a concentration camp until the end of the Civil War; subsequently engaged in lit work; *Died:* date and place of death unknown.

LEYBENZON, Leonid Samuilovich (1879-1951) Specialist in mech, oil technol and geophysics; member, USSR Acad of Sci from 1943; *Born:* 26 June 1879 in Khar'kov; *Educ:* 1901 grad Moscow Univ; 1906 grad Moscow Higher Tech College; *Career:* 1904 began sci work under the supervision of N. Ye. Zhukovskiy; 1908-11 taught at Moscow Univ; resigned with other staff members in protest against policies of Educ Min Kasso and went to work for Bari Company, where he designed reservoirs and oil pipelines under the supervision of V. G. Shukov; 1915 defended master's thesis on the theory of free-span roofing; 1919-21 prof, Tiflis Polytech Inst; 1921 prof, Baku Polytech Inst; 1922 returned to Moscow Univ; where he worked until his death; devised variational methods of solving elasticity problems which made it possible to reach approximate solutions and simplify boundary conditions; also did research on viscous liquids and devised a new boundary-layer equation; studied the theory of oil-extraction by deep pumping and the subterranean hydraulics of oil, water and gas; on the basis of his research on the motion strata of oil and gas in pipes developed new methods of pipeline calculation; during his considerable research on geophysics also applied the theory of elasticity to the structure of the Earth and evaluated the effect of the Earth's heterogeneity on the absolute value of the solidity of the Earth; wrote numerous works, including textbooks on theoretical mech, material resistance, hydraulics and oil mech; *Publ: "Gidravlika"* (Hydraulics) (1931); *"Priblizhyonnaya dinamicheskaya teoriya glubokogo nasosa"* (An Approximate Dynamic Theory of a Deep Pump) (1932); *"Podzemnaya gidravlika vody, nefti i gaza"* (The Subterrenean Hydraulics of Water, Oil and Gas) (1934); *"Neftopromyslovaya mekhanika"* (Industrial Oil Mechanics) (1939); *"Variatsionnyye metody resheniya zadach teorii uprugosti"* (Variational Methods of Solving Problems in the Theory of Elasticity) (1943); *"Dvizheniye prirodnykh zhidkostey i gaza v poristoy srede"* (The Motion of Natural Liquids and Gas in a Porous Medium) (1947); *"Sobraniye trudov"* (Collected Works) (4 vol, 1951-55); *Awards:* two Lenin Prizes; Stalin Prize (1943); Order of the Red Banner of Labor; medals; *Died:* 15 Mar 1951 in Moscow.

LEYTEYZEN, Gavriil Davidovich (pseudonyms: G. LINDOV; VALERIN; VYAZEMSKIY) (1874-1919) Revolutionary; physician; journalist; CP member from 1918; *Born:* 9 Nov 1874 in Oryol, son of a craftsman; *Career:* physician by profession; 1891-92 helped found Soc-Democratic circles in Yekaterinoslav; late 1920's emigrated and joined Liberation of Labor Group; from 1902 Iskra rep in Paris; 1903, after 2nd RSDRP Congress, sided with Bolsheviks; contributed to newspapers "Vperyod" and "Proletary" 1907 at 5th RSDRP Congress presented report for Bolsheviks on "the workers' congress", and elected member, CC, RSDRP; late 1907 arrested and imprisoned, then lived in Tula, practicing med and continuing Party work; after 1917 Feb Revol sided for a while with the internationalists; joined "New Life" group; after 1917 Oct Revol Collegium member, Pop Comrt of Labor; from Aug 1918 comr, Revol Mil Council, 4th Army on Eastern Front; wrote a number of historical and political studies and works on preventive med and soc security; *Publ: Profilaktika i sotsial'noye strakhovaniye* (Preventive Medicine and Social Security) (1918); *Died:* 20 Jan 1919 at the front.

LEZHAVA, Andrey Matveyevich (1870-1937) Party and govt official; CP member from 1904; *Born:* 19 Feb 1870 in Signakhi, Tiflis Province, son of peasant; *Educ:* grad Tiflis Teachers' Training Inst; *Career:* taught; late 1880's joined populist movement; 1893 arrested for helping found underground printing press in Smolensk; spent more than two years in Peter and Paul Fortress and five years in exile in Yakutsk, where he became a Marxist; revol activities in Tiflis, Voronezh, Nizhniy Novgorod, Saratov and Moscow; after 1917 Oct Revol admin and govt work; 1919-20 chm, Centr Union of Consumer Soc; 1921 RSFSR Dep Pop Comr of For Trade; 1922-24 USSR Pop Comr of Domestic Trade; 1924-20 dep chm, RSFSR Council of Pop Comr; simultaneusly chm, RSFSR Gosplan; then chm, All-Union Bd of Fisheries and Fishing Ind; 1930-37 head, USSR Main Bd of Subtropic Corps; deleg at 13th-17th Party Congresses; at 15th Congress elected member, CPSU(B) Centr Control Commission; member, All-Russian and USSR Centr Exec Comt of various convocations; 1937 arrested by State Security organs; *Died:* 8 Oct 1937 in imprisonment; posthumously rehabilitated.

LEZHNEV, A. (real name: GORELIK, Abram Zelikovich /Zakharovich/) (1893-1938); Russian lit critic and historian; *Born:* 1893 in vil Parichi, Bobruysk Uyezd; *Educ:* 1922 grad Yekaterinoslav (Dnepropetrovsk) Med Inst; *Career:* member and theoretician, pereval (The Pass-lit assoc; arrested by State security organs; *Publ: voprosy literatury i kritiki* (Literature and Criticism) (1926); *sovremenniki. Literaturno-kriticheskiye ocherki* (Contemporaries. Literary Critical Exxays) (1927); col loected articles *Literaturnyye budni* (Literary Workdays) (1929); *coauthor,* Literarury revolyutsionnogo desyatiletiya, 1917-1927 (The Literature of the Revolutionary Decade of 1917-27 (1929); *Razgovor v serdtsakh* (A Cordial Conversation) (1930); *Derevyannyy kluch'* (The Wooden Key) (1932); *Yedinstvo protivopolozhnostey* (The Unity of Opposided) (1934); *Dva poeta. Geyne, Tyurchev* (Two Poets. Heine and Tyutchev) (1934); *Ob iskusstve* (About Art) (1936); *Proza Pushkina* (Pushkin's Prose) (1937); *Died:* 29 Nov 1938 in imprisonment; posthumously rehabilitated.

LEZHNEV, I. (real name: AL'TSHULER, Isay Grigor'yevich) (1891-1955) Lit critic and journalist; CP member from 1933; *Born:* 6 Mar 1891 in Nikolayev; *Educ:* 1914 grad Fac of Philosophy, Zurich Univ; *Career:* 1906-09 member, RSDRP(B); 1909 gave up politics and wokred for newspapers in Nikolayev, Tsaritsyn and Petrograd; after 1917 Oct Revol worked for newspaper Russkaya volya and Petrograd News Agency; during Civil War worked for Red Army press and headed Information Dept, newspaper *Izvestiya TsIK;* 1922-26 ed, journal *Novaya Rossiya;* exiled abroud after closure of journal; 1930 returned to Russia; 1933 readmitted to Party on the basis of his book *Zapiski sovremenniky* (Notes of a Contemporary); in which he expounded his revised views on the Sov regime; 1935-39 head, Lit and Art Dept, newspaper *Pravda;* wrote studies of Chekhov, Chernyshevskiy, Gorky, Herzen, Pushkin, Sholokhov and A. N. Tolstoy, etc; *Publ: Zapiski sovremennika* (Notes of a Contemporary) (1934); *Vozhd' revolutsionnoy demokratii N. G. Chernyshevskiy* (N. G. Chernyshevskiy, a Leader of Revolutionary Democracy) (1939); critical biographical study Mikhail Sholokhov (1941); monograph Mikhail Sholokhov (1948); biography Put' Sholokhova (Sholokhov's Way) (1958); *Died:* 9 Oct 1955 in Moscow.

LIANOZOV, Stepn Georgiyevich (1872-1951) Oilman; *Born:* 1872; *Career:* dir; mang or bd member of over 20 oil companies and other industrial companies; co-founder, "Oil"- Russian Gen Oil Corporation, founded in 1912 by the Russian-Asian Bank, International Bank and other banks; after 1917 Oct Revol actively opposed Sov regime; head, "Northwestern Govt", founded in 1919 in Est by Gen Yudenich; then lived in emigration; 1920 in Paris helped found "Trade Finacial and Ind Comt"; from 1940, after German occupation of Paris, took an anti-Nazi stand; *Died:* 1951.

LIBEDINSKIY, Yuriy Nikolayevich (1898-1959) Russian writer; CP member from 1920; *Born:* 10 Dec 1898 in Odessa, son of a physician; *Educ:* grad Chelyabisnk High School; *Career:* spent his childhood at Myasskiy Zavod in the Urals; fought in Civil War; polit work in Siberia, Urals ans Moscow; 1922 first work printed; member, *Octyabr'* (October) lit assoc; leading contributor to journal *Na postu;* 1923-25 exec work with All-Russian Assoc of Proletarian Writers; 1925-32 exec work for Russian Assoc of Proletarian Writers; member, ed bd, journal *Na literaturnom postu;* corresp, newspaper *Pravda;* during WW 2 worked for frontline newspaper *Krasnyy voin;* corresp, newspaper *Krasnaya zvezda;* after WW 2 studied folk epics and history of Caucasus; translated and published Ossetion Nart legends, and Ossetian and Azer stories; *Publ:* novolettes: *Nedelya* (The Week) (1922); *Zavtra* (Tomorrow) (1923); *Komissary* (The Commissars) (1925); *Nakanune* (On the Eve) (1928); *Rozhdeniye geroya* (The Birth of a Hero) (1930); play *Vysoty* (Hights) (1929); novel *Rozhdeniye geroya* (The Birth of a Hero) (1930); essays: *Petya Gordyushenko; Rasskazy tovarishchey* (Comrades' Tales) (1933), etc; novel *Batash and Batay* (1939); essays and stories *Khozyayka* (The Housewife) (1943); *Zhivoy Stalingrad* (Living Stalingrad) *Gvardeytsy* (The Guardsmen) (1942); *Pushka Yugova* (1944); trilogy: *Gory i lyudi* (Mountains and People) (1947); *Zarevo* (Dawn) (1952); *Utro Sovetov* (The Morning of the Soviets) (1957); children's works; *Vospitaniye dushi* (Soul Training) (1962); coauthor, novelette *Syn partii* (A Son of the Party) (1960); memoirs *Sovremenniki* (Contemporaries) (1958); *Izbrannyye proizvedeniya* (Selcted Works) (2 vol, 1958); *Died:* 24 Nov 1959 in Moscow.

LIBER (GOL'DMAN), Mikhail Isaakovich (1880-1937) Bund and Menshevik leader; *Born:* 1880 in Vilnius, son of an office worker; *Career:* 1898 began polit career; from 1902 member, Bund CC; 1903 head, Bund deleg at 2nd RSDRP Congress; after Congress joined Mensheviks; 1907 at 5th RSDRP Congress elected to CC, RSDRP from the Bund; 1907-10 Menshevik-liquidationist; 1912 active in Aug anti-Party Bloc; during WW 1 sided with Soc-Chauvinists; after 1917 Feb Revol member, Exec Comt, Petrograd Sov of Worker and Soldiers' Dep and Presidium member, Centr Exec Comt of 1st convocation; hostile toward 1917 Oct Revol; abandoned polit activities; various admin posts; 1937 arrested by NKWD; *Died:* 1937 in imprisonment.

LIBERMAN, L. A. (1879-1938) Party official; CP member from 1921; *Born:* 1879; *Career:* 1902-04 member, RSDRP; 1905-20 member, Socialist-Revol Party; 1917-20 secr, Yekaterinoslov City Comt, Socialist-Revol Party; 1920 head, Publ Dept, Railroad Workers' Union and Main Professional Training Bd; 1921 head Centr Press Agency of All-Russian Centr Exec Comt; 1922-26 worked for State Film Studio, Pop Comrt of Educ and Higher State Art Studios; 1926-37 press instructor, CC, CPSU(B); Donbass correspondent, newspaper *Pravda;* head, Culture and Educ Section, Far Eastern Railroad Polit Dept; arrested by State Security organs; *Died:* 1938 in imprisonment.

LIBERT, Yakov Grigor'yevich (1874-1946) Jewish actor and stage dir; Hon Artiste of RSFSR; *Born:* 1874; *Career:* 1884-85 acted with A.Gol'dfaden's troupe; from 1893 with various troups touring Russia; appeared mainly in works of Jewish classic repertoire; after 1917 Oct Revol worked in Ukr; from 1926 in Kiev Jewish Theater; *Roles:* Zalman and Trakhtenberg in Gordin's *"Mirra Efros"* and *"Orphan Khasya";* Zalkind in Pinskiy's "The Mother"; Sholshovich in Sh. Ash's "God of Vengeance"; Satin in *Na dne* (The Lower Depths); Krogstad in The Dolls' House; Zayvl Ovadis in Markish's "The Ovadis Family" *Died:* 1946.

LIFSHITS, Boris Solomonovich (1896-1949) Mil corresp; CP member from 1917; *Born:* 1896; *Educ:* in 1920's grad Inst of Red Prof; *Career:* during Civil War helped muster and became first comr of 24th Samara-Ul'yanovsk Infantry Div; after Civil War dipl work and posts with Pop Comrt of For Trade; during WW 2 mil corresp; *Died:* 1949.

LIKHACHOV, Mikhail Pavlovich (1901-1945) Komi-Permian writer; *Born:* 2 Nov 1901 in vil Egve, now Komi-Permian Okrug; *Educ:* 1919 grad teachers' training seminary; 1930 studied at Moscow Editing and Publishing Inst; *Career:* worked as a teacher; compiled textbook *Vperyod* (Forward) (1925); and a Komi-Permian reader; *Publ:* colected stories "The Pioneer" (1929); "Red Flag" (1930); poem "Girl Without a Dowry" (1930); verse collection "Golden Days" (1934); novelette "Mirosh, the Worldly Son" (1936), etc; *Died:* 25 Apr 1945.

LIKHACHYOV, Aleksey Alekseyevich (1866-1942) Pharmacologist and toxicologist; Dr of med from 1893; prof from 1899; Hon Sci Worker of RSFSR from 1933; *Born:* 15 Jan 1866; *Educ:* 1890 grad Petersburg Mil Med Acad; *Career:* after grad spcialized under V. V. Pashutin at Chair of Gen Pathology, Petersburg Mil Med Acad; 1893 defended doctor's thesis on human heat generation in a state of relative rest in which, by the use of direct calorimetry on healthy individuals and feverish patients, he established that the generation and emission of heat and gas metabolism undergo various changes related to the waking and sleeping states and independently of the ingestion food; did research abroad under Prof Bauman in Freiburg and Prof Ziegler in Baden; 1899-1942 head, Chair of Pharmacology, 1906-29 head, Training Dept, Petersburg Women's Med Inst (1st Leningrad Med Inst); 1900-29 also read courses on gen and physical therapy at this inst; together with A. Studenskiy, established the heat fixation laws of rigor mortis; thgether with P. Avrorov, did research on enhanced gas and heat metabolism under the influence of alcohol; helped to develop equipment for measuring oxygen consumption in research on the gas metabolism of animals; during WW 1 organized special laboratories for the study of chemical weapons; 1921-30 founder-head, Chair of Aviation Hygiene, Leningrad Inst of Communication Eng; 1923 resumed study of chemical weapons; 1926, together with M. P. Nikolayev, made comparative study of the efficacy of testicular preparations; 1933-42 head, Chair of Pharmacology, Leningrad Pharamceutical Inst; established a laboratory for biological drug evaluation at Leningrad Chemical and Pharmaceutical Research Inst; founder-chm, Leningrad Soc of Physilogists, Pharmacologists and Biochemists; co-ed, Pharmacology section, *Bol'shaya meditsinskaya entsiklopediya* (Large Medical Encyclopedia) (1st ed); *Publ:* doctor's thesis *Teploproizvodstvo zdorovogo cheloveka pri otnositel'nom pokoye* (The Generation of Heat in Healthy Individuals in a State of Relative Rest) (1893); coauthor, *Issledovaniye gazovogo i teplovogo* *obmena pri likhoradke* (A Study of Gas and Heat Metabolism During Fever) (1902); coauthor, *O vliyanii alkogolya na teplovoy i gazovyy obmen u cheloveka* (The Effect of Alcohol on Heat and Gas Metabolism in Humans) (1906); *Deystviye na organizm boyevykh otravlyayushchikh veshchestv i lechebnyye meropriyatiya pri porazhenii imi* (The Effect of Chemical Weapons on the Body and Therapeutic Measures) (1931), etc; *Died:* Jan 1942.

LIKHACHYOV, Ivan Alekseyevich (1896-1956) Govt official; CP member from 1917; *Born:* 15 June 1896 in Tula Oblast, son of a peasant; *Educ:* studied at Acad of Mines and Inst of Electromechanics; *Career:* from the age of 12 worked at Putilov plant in Petersburg; during WW 1 sailor in Baltic Fleet; 1917-21 Red Guard; Red Army commander; then worked for All-Russian Cheka; 1921-26 trade-union work; 1926-39 dir, Moscow Automobile Plant; 1939 USSR Pop Comr of Machine-Building; 1939 at 18th CPSU(B) Congress elected member, CC; 1941 at 18th Party Conference expelled from CC for neglect of duty; 1940-50 again dir, Moscow Automobile Plant; 1950-53 dir, machine-building plant; from 1953 USSR then RSFSR Min of Motor Transport and Highways; dep, USSR Supr Sov of 1st-5th convocations; 1956 at 20th CPSU Congress elected cand member, CC, CPSU; *Awards:* Stalin Prize (1948); five Orders of Lenin; Order of the Fatherland War; Order of the Red Banner of Labor; medals; *Died:* 24 June 1956 in Moscow, buried on Red Square; June1956 Moscow Automobile Plant named after him.

LIKHACHYOV, V. M. (1882-1924) Govt official; CP member from 1902; *Born:* 1882; *Career:* Party work in Perm', Ufa, Samara, Kazan', etc; 1912-16 lived in America; after 1917 Feb Revol secr, Moscow RSDRP(B) Comt; after 1917 Oct Revol head, Admin Dept, then head, Dept of Municipal Utilities, Moscow Sov; 1921-22 chm, Moscow Sovnarkhoz; 1923-24 head, Agitation and Propaganda Dept, Moscow RCP(B) Comt; *Died:* 1924.

LIKHAREV, Boris Mikhaylovich (1906-1962) Russian Poet; CP member from 1942; *Born:* 27 Nov 1906 in Pargolova, near Petersburg; *Educ:* studied at Bryusov Higher Lit and Art Inst, Moscow and at Leningrad Univ; *Career:* raised in children's home; 1929 first work published; 1939-40 fought in Finno-Sov War; during WW 2 worked for Leningrad Front newspaper *"Na strazhe Rodiny"*, then joined writers' group, Leningrad Front Polit Bd; 1942 joined 2nd Partisan Brig behind German lines in Leningrad Oblast; *Publ:* verse collection *Sol'* (Salt) (1930); Poem *"Moisey Uritskiy"* (1938); *Stikhi o Leningrade* (Poems on Leningrad) (1938); verse collection *Yarost'* (Fury) (1943) and *Pokhod k fiordam* (Approach to the Fjords) (1947); poem "A Friend's Deed" (1951); collections *Doroga druzhby* (Friendship Road) (1954); *V strane druzey* (In the Land of Friends) (1958); *Solntse vsyo vyshe* (Ever-Rising Sun) (1959), etc; *Died:* 2 Mar 1962 in Leningrad.

LILINA, (real name: PEREVOSHCHIKOVA; married name: Alek-SEYEVA), Mariya Petrovna (1866-1943) Actress; Pop Artiste of RSFSR from 1933; co-founder, Moscow Arts Theater; *Born:* 3 July 1866 in Moscow, daughter of a notary-public; *Educ:* studied at Yekaterinin inst; *Career:* orphaned at an early age and lived at Yekatarinin inst; took part in amateur theatricals; acted in productions of Soc of Art and Lit; 1889 married K. S. Stanislavskiy (Alekseyev) and later assisted him in founding of Moscow Arts Theater; directed and taught at Stanislavskiy Studio; from 1923 Hon Artiste of RSFSR; *Roles:* Masha in Chekhov's *Chayka* (The Seagull) (1898); Sonya in Chekhov's *Dyadya Vanya* (Uncle Vanya) (1900-01); Natasha in Chekhov's *Tri sestry* (Three Sisters) (1901); Anya in Chekhov's *Vishnovyy sad* (The Cherry Orchard) (1904); Liza Bensh in Hauptmann's "Michael Kramer" (1901); Mariya Timofeyevna Lebyadkina in "Nikolay Stavrogin" (1913), after Dostoyevsky's novel *Besy* (Devils); Liza in Griboyedov's *Gore ot uma* (Woe from Wit); Toinette in Moliere's "Le Malade Imaginaire" Elina in Gamsun's *U tsarskikh vrat* (At the Imperial Gate) (1909); Anna Dmitriyevna in Tolstoy's *Zhivoy trup* (The Living Corpse) (1911); Dar'ya Ivanovna in Turgenev's *Provintsialka* (The Provincial Woman) (1912); Karpukhina in *Dyadyushkin son* (Uncle's Dream) (1931-32) after Dostoyevsky; Vronskaya in *"Anna Karenina"* (1937); *Awards:* Order of Lenin; Order of the Red Banner of Labor (1937); *Died:* 24 Aug 1943 in Moscow.

LIN'KOV, Grigoriy Matveyevich (1899-1961) WW 2 hero; writer; CP member from 1918; *Born:* 12 Jan 1899; *Career:* 1918-46 served in Sov Army; during WW 2 led partisan detachments in Bel and Western Ukr; *Publ:* *V tylu vraga* (Behind Enemy Lines) (1948); *Awards:* Hero of the Sov Union (1942); *Died:* 17 Dec 1961.

LIPATOV, Timofey Ivanovich (1888-1959) Revolutionary; CP member from 1917; *Born:* 3 Aug 1888, son of a peasant; *Career:* 1910-18 sailor on cruiser 'Aurora"; Sept-Dec 1917 member, "Aurora"; ship's comt; from 1918, after discharge, worked in ind and water transport; 1951 drafted into navy and appointed asst commander, cruiser "Aurora"; helped found museum on ship; Awards: Hero of Socialist Labor (1957); *Died:* 1 May 1959

LIPIN, Vyacheslav Nikolayevich (1858-1930) Metallurgist; corresp member, USSR Acad of Sci from 1928; *Born:* 18 Dec 1858; *Educ:* 1881 grad Petersburg Mining Inst; *Career:* worked at various plants in Urals and Petersburg; 1885,1897 and 1902 made studies of the effect of alloy components which made it possible to develop high-grade Russian Steels; organized the production of special types of steel, notably the production of tungsten steel at Putilov Plant in 1896; *Publ: Metallurgiya chuguna, zheleza i stali* (The Metallurgy of Cast Iron, Iron and Steel) (1904-11); *Died:* 19 Dec 1930.

LISHEV, Vsevolod Vsevolodovich (1877-1960) Sculptor; Pop Artiste of USSR from 1957; Pop Artiste of RSFSR from 1953; member, USSR Acad of Arts from 1949; *Born:* 7 Oct 1877 in Petersburg; *Educ:* 1906-13 studied at Petersburg Acad of Arts; *Works:* sculpture "Our Anestors" (1913); monument to Peter I (1912-14); monumental busts of P. P. Semyonov of Tyan-Shan' and M. P. Moussorgsky (1916) in Petrograd; monumental busts of Karl Marx (1918) in Novaya Ladoga and N. A. Nekrasov (1922) in Petrograd; group sculptures: "I. V. Stalin and K. Ye. Voroshilov" (1933); "October" (1935); monumental bust of S. I. Spasokukotskiy (1945-46) in Moscow; Leningrad monument to M. G. Chernishevskiy (1947); series of compositions "On the Streets of Leningrad During the Blockade" (1942-43); bronze group "Mother" (1945-46); statues for monuments to Griboyedov, K. D. Ushinskiy, I. P. Pavlov and D. I. Mendeleyev; *Awards:* Order of Lenin; Stalin Prize (1942) *Died:* 15 Aug 1960.

LISINOVA (LISINYAN), Lyusik (1897-1917) Revolutionary; helped found young workers' leagues; took part in 1917 Oct Revol in Moscow; *Born:* 1897; *Educ:* studied at Moscow Business Inst; *Career:* 1916 started working for Bolshevik Party; while a student at Moscow Business Inst ran Party circles at Mikhel'son and Brokar Plants and at Danilovskiy Textile Mill; helped print and distribute Party proclamations; co-founder, Young Workers' League in Zamoskvorech'ye Rayon; during 1917 Oct Revol in Moscow received despatches, bandaged the wounded and delivered messages; killed while fighting with Red Guards squad from Zamoskvorech'ye Rayon on Ostozhenko Street (now Metrostroyevskaya Street) in attempt to capture the headquarters of the Moscow Mil Distr; Serpukhov Street renamed Lyusinovskaya Street in her memory; *Died;* 14 Nov 1917; buried on Red Square.

LISITSYN, N. V. (1891-1939) Govt official; CP member from 1910; *Born:* 1891; *Career:* Party work in Tver', Kostroma, Vologda and Voronezh; arrested by Tsarist authorities; after 1917 Feb Revol chm, Ostrog Sov of workers, Soldiers and Peasants' Dep; after 1917 Oct Revol govt and Party work; member, Presidium, Moscow Oblast Exec Comt; head, information Dept, CC, RCP(B); 1919 Moscow RCP(B) Comt deleg at 8th RCP(B) Congress; 1920-21 supported "democratic centralism" group; from 1930 RSFSR Dep Pop Comr of Agric; from 1934 chm, Land Commission, RSFSR Pop Comrt of Agric; arrested by State Security organs; *Died:* 1939 in imprisonment.

LISKONOZHENKO, Nikolay Gavrilovich (1919-1941) Fighter-pilot; lt; Komsomol member from 1935; *Born:* 1919 in vil Novodanilovtsy, Zaporozhian Oblast; *Educ:* 1938 grad flying college; *Career:* Prior to joining Red Army, worked at Melitopol' Locomotive Dapot; fought in 1939-40 Sov-Finnish War; during WW 2 flew missions in defence of Leningrad; 2 Nov 1941 flew with Sov fighter wing which engaged 12 German planes in an air battle; after using up all his ammunition, downed two enemy planes by ramming action, himself sustaining fatal wounds; *Awards:* Hero of the Sov Union (posthumously); *Died:* 2 Nov 1941 killed in action; buried in vil Krasnenka, near Malaya Vishera.

LISKUN, Yefim Fedotovich (1873-1958) Livestock breeder; pioneer of zootech in USSR; member, All-Union Lenin Acad of Agric Sci from 1934; Hon Sci and Tech Worker of RSFSR from 1934; *Born:* 26 Oct 1873 in vil Ataki, now Chernovtsy Oblast, son of a peasant; *Educ:* grad Kherson Agric College; 1900 grad Moscow Agric Inst; *Career:* 1900-06 dir, Tomsk Agric School; then lecturer, agric colleges in Saratov Province and Kazan' 1906-18 prof; Stebut Women's Agric Courses, Petersburg (Petrograd); 1918-23 prof, Petrograd Forestry Inst; from 1923 prof, Timiryazev Agric Acad, Moscow; bred improved strains of Russian livestock; on the basis of large-scale experiments with Red-Steppe, Kir and Astrakhan' cattle proved that breed quality depends on maintenance and feeding conditions; 1936 demonstrated the feasibility of doubling and trebling milk yield with an extensive study of milking techniques at kolchozes in Moscow Oblast; developed gen guidelines for livestock breeding which ensured stock improvement; contributed large collection of animal skulls and skeletons to State Museum of Animal Husbandry, Moscow, which now bears his name; wrote over 300 works, including several textbooks on animal husbandry; *Publ: Krasnyy nemetskiy skot* (German Red Cattle) (1911); *Russkiye otrod'ya krupnorogatogo skota* (Indigenous Russian Horned Stock) (1928); *Osnovy zhivotnovodstva* (The Principles of Animal Husbandry) (1943); *Ekster'yer sel'skokhozyaystvennykh zhivotnykh* (Livestock Points) (1949); *Otechestvennyye porody krupnogo rogatogo skota* (Indigenous Breeds of Cattle in the USSR) (1949); *Krupnyy rogatyy skot* (Cattle) (1951), etc; *Awards:* Grand Gold Medal of Moscow Agric Inst (1912); Grand Medal, All-Union Agric Exhibition; two Orders of the Red Banner of Labor; four Orders of Lenin; Badge of Hon; Stalin Prize (1943); medal "For Valiant Labor During the Great Fatherland War"; 800th Aniversary of Moscow" medal; *Died:* 19 Apr 1958.

LISOVSKAYA, Sofiya Nikolayevna (1876-1951) Surgeon and urologist; Dr of Med from 1911; prof; Hon Sci Worker of RSFSR from 1935; *Born:* 1876; *Educ:* 1902 grad Petersburg Women's Med Inst; *Career:* 1904-17 worked under A. Kad'yan at Hospital Surgical Clinic, Petersburg Women's Med Inst; 1911 defended doctor's thesis on transplantation of the thyroid gland; from 1917 head, Hospital Surgical Clinic, Petrograd Women's Med Inst (now 1st Leningrad Med Inst); 1919-37 also head, Chair of Operative Surgery and Topographical Anatomy, 2nd Leningrad Med Inst; 1933-51 head, Chair of Urology, 1st Leningrad Med Inst; devised modification of Debre-Paraff reaction for the diagnosis of gonorrhea involving the location and isolation to the gonococcic antigen in the patient's urine and discharge; devised and introduced treatment for enuresis consisting of training the "guard point" in the cerebral cortex by Pavlovian techniques; wrote 86 works; *Publ:* doctor's thesis *K ucheniyu o peresadke shchitovidnoy zhelezy* (The Theory of the Transplantation of the Thyroid Gland) (1911); *K voprosu 0 syvorotochnoy anafilaksii* (Serum Anaphylaxis) (1911); *O glukozurii pri khirurgicheskikh zabolevaniyakh bryushnoy polosti* (Glucosuria in Surgical Diseases of the Abdominal Cavity) (1922); *Tripper i sposoby bor'by s nim* (Gonorrhea and How to Combat It) (1929), etc; *Died:* 1951.

LISOVYY, Pyotr Andreyevich (pen name: SVASHCHENKO) (1892-1943) Ukr writer and journalist; CP member from 1919; *Born:* 12 June 1892 in vil Dergachi, now Khar'kov Oblast; *Educ:* grad Uman Agric College; *Career:* fought in Civil War; 1924 first work printed; *Publ:* "To the Revolution" (1927); "From the Road" (1930); novels: "Mykola Yorosh" (1927); "Yuriy Dibrova's Notes" (1930); novelettes: "Beyond the Zbruch" (1932); "The Red Rocket" (1932); etc; *Died:* 17 Jan 1943.

LITOVTSEVA, (nee: LEVESTAMM; married name: KACHALOVA), Nina Nikolayevna (1878-1956) Actress and stage dir; Pop Artiste of RSFSR from 1948; *Born:* 12 Jan 1878; *Educ:* grad Nemirovich-Danchenko's class, Drama Dept, Moscow Philharmonic College; *Career:* after grad worked with M. M. Boroday's company in Kazan', Saratov and Astrkhan'; from 1901 with Moscow Arts Theater; 1908-16 absent from stage because of ill health; taught at theatrical schools; 1916-19 instructor and stage dir, 2nd Studio, Moscow Arts Theater; from 1922 actress and stage dir, Moscow Acad Arts Theater; *Roles:* Roxana in Edmond de Rostand's "Cyrano de Bergerac"; Susanna in "Marriage of Figaro"; Vera Pavlovna in Chirkov's "Ivan Mironich" (1905); Fima in *Deti solntsa* (Children of the Sun) (1905); Irina in Chekhov's *Tri sestry* (Three Sisters); Natasha and Anna in Gorky's *Na dne* (The Lower Depths); Varya in Chekhov's *Vishnyovyy sad* (Cherry Orchard); Sarra in "Ivanov"; Nataliya Dmitriyevna in *Gore ot uma* (Woe from Wit); Finochka's Mother in Gippius' *Zelyonoye kol'tso* (Green Ring); *Productions:* Andreyev's *Mladost'* (Youth) (1919); Kugel's *Nikolay I i dekabristy* (Nicholas I and the Decembrists) (1926); Kartashev's *Nasha molodost'* (Our Youth) (1930); *Bronepoyezd 14-69* (Armored Train 14-69) (1927); *Talanty i poklonniki* (Talants and Admirers) (1933); *Tri sestry* (Three Sisters) (1940); *Dyadya Vanya* (Oncle Vanya) (1947); *Plody prosveshcheniya* (The Fruits of enlightenment) (1951); *Publ: Iz proshlogo Moskovskogo khudozhestvennogo teatra* (From the Past of the Moscow Arts Theater) (1945); *Died:* 8 Apr 1956.

LITVAKOV, Moisey Il'ich (1880-1939), Jewish lit critic; CP member from 1921; *Born:* 1880 in Cherkassy, Ukr; *Career:* 1902 co-founder, Jewish Sionist-Socialist Party; from 1908 contributed to newspaper *"Kievskaya mysl"*; Feb 1917-Aug 1920 member, CC, United Jewish Socialist Workers' Party; 1920 member, Communist Bund; 1921 ed, centr Jewish Communist newspaper "Der Emmes" in Moscow; 1924-28 chief ed, "School and Book" Publ House; lectured at Jewish Dept, Moscow Teachers' Training Inst member, Inst of Jewish Culture, Ukr Acad of Sci; member, Comt for Allotment of Land to Jewish Workers; member, All-Union Soc for Allotment of Land to Jewish Workers; member, Centr Bureau of Jewish Sections, CC, CPSU(B); 1903 began to write lit criticism; 1937 arrested by State Security organs; *Publ: V buryu* (Into the Storm) (2 Vol, 1918-26); collections; *Pyat' let Gosudarstvennogo yevreyskogo kamennogo teatra* (Five Years of the State Jewish Chamber Theater) (1924); *Na dvukh frontakh* (On Two Fronts) (1932); wrote lit studies of D. Bergel'son, Nister, O. Shvartsman, D. Gofshteyn, L. Kvitko, I. Markish, A. Kushnirov, S. Galkin, etc; *Died:* 1939 in imprisonment; posthumously rehabilitated.

LITVINENKO-VOL'GEMUT, Mariya Ivanovna (1895-1966); Opera singer (dramatic lyric soprano); Pop Artiste of USSR from 1936; CP member from 1944; *Born:* 6 Feb 1895 in Kiev; *Educ:* 1912 grad Kiev Music College; *Career:* 1912-14 singer, Ukr Pop Theater, Kiev; 1914-16 singer, Petrograd Musical Drama Theater; 1920-23 singer, Ukr Pop Theater, Vinnitsa; 1923-35 soloist, Khar'kov Opera Theater; 1935-51 soloist, Shevchenko Opera and Ballet Theater, Kiev; from 1946 prof, Kiev Conservatory; also sang lieder; *Roles:* various roles in: S. S. Gulak-Artemovskiy's "Odarka" and *Zaporozhets za Dunayem* (A Dnieper Cossack Beyond the Danube); N. V. Lysenko's "Natalka-Poltavka" and "Taras Bul'ba" M. I. Berikovskiy's *Naymychka* (The Hired Girl); Borodin's *Knyaz' Igor'* (Prince Igor); Tchaikovskiy's *Pikovaya dama* (Queen of Spades), "Mazepa" and "Cherevichky" (The Slippers); A. S. Dargomyzhskiy's *Rusalka* (The Water-Nymph); Verdi's "Aida"; Meyerbeer's "The Huguenots"; Wagner's "Lohengrin", "Die Walküre" and "Tannhäuser"; *Awards:* Order of Lenin; three Orders of the Red Banner of Labor; Stalin Prize (1946); medals; *Died:* 4 Apr 1966.

LITVINOV, Maksim Maksimovich (Party pseudonyms: PAPASHA; KUZNETSOV; MAKSIMOVICH; LUVIN'YE; FELIKS; NITS) (1876-1951) Diplomat; CP member from 1898; *Born:* 17 July 1876 in Belostok, son of an office worker; *Educ:* grad tech high school; *Career:* after mil service became propagandist; 1898 began propaganda among workers; 1900 joined Kiev RSDRP Comt; arrested; Aug 1902 helped arrange escape of 11 *"Iskra"* members from Kiev Prison; emigrated to Switzerland; *"Iskra"* agent; headed one of its underground transportation centers; after 2nd RSDRP Congress Bolshevik; member, Riga RSDRP(B) Comt and member, Bureau of Bolshevik Comts; in charge of smuggling freight, arms and agents across north-western border; deleg at 3rd Party Congress; Oct 1905 helped found Bolshevik newspaper *"Novaya zhin"*; 1907 secr, London RSDRP group; secr, RSDRP deleg at Stuttgart Congress of 2nd International; Bolshevik rep Int Socialist Bureau; Feb 1915, on orders from CC, RSDRP, condemned WW 1 at London Conference of Socialists of Entente Countries; 1918 appointed RSFSR dipl rep to Britain; arrested there as hostage and exchanged for Bruce Lockhart, who had been arrested in Russia; Collegium member, Pop Comrt of For Affairs; from 1921 Dep Pop Comr of For Affairs; simultaneusly Collegium member, RSFSR Pop Comrt of Workers and Peasants' Inspection and dep chm, Main Concessions Comt; fall 1920 appointed Sov plen and trade rep in Est; 1922 dep head, Sov deleg at Genoa Conference; headed deleg at Hague Conference; 1923 chm, Moscow Int Disarmament Conference; negotiated with Britain for repeal of blockade of Sov Russia; signed various trade agreements with European countries; 1927-30 headed Sov deleg in Preparatory Commission for Geneva Disarmament Conference; 1930-39 USSR Pop Comr of For Affairs; 1932 headed Sov deleg at League of Nations Disarmament Conference; 1933 headed Sov deleg at World Econ Conference in London; 1934-38 represented USSR at League of Nations; at 17th and 18th Party Congresses elected member, CC, CPSU(B); member, USSR Centr Exec Comt; dep, USSR Supr Sov of 1st and 2nd convocations; May 1939, during Stalin purges, relieved as USSR Pop Comr of For Affairs; Feb 1941 at 18th Party Conference expelled from CC, CPSU(B) for failing in his duty as member of CC, CPSU(B); 1941-46, soon after outbreak of WW 2, reappointed USSR Pop Comr of For Affairs; 1941-43 simultaneously USSR amb to USA; from Oct 1942 also USSR envoy to Cuba; Oct 1943 attended Moscow Conference of For Min of USSR, USA and Britain; *Publ: V bor'be za mir* (In the Struggle for Peace) (1938); *V neshnyaya politika SSSR. Rechi i zayavleniya 1927-37* (The Foreign Policy of the USSR. 1927-37 Speeches and Statements) (2nd ed, 1937); *Protiv agressii* (Against Aggression) (1938); *Za vseobshcheye razoruzheniye* (In Favor of General Disarmament) (1928); *Awards:* Order of Lenin (1936); Order of the Red Banner of Labor; medals; *Died:* 31 Dec 1951

LIVSHITS, Benedikt Konstantinovich (1887-1939) Poet; *Born:* 5 Jan 1887 in Odessa; *Educ:* grad Law Fac, Kiev Univ; *Career:* 1910 first work published; his first book of verse displayed the influence of the French symbolists; 1912 joined Russian futurist group; translated the works of French poets, showing a particular penchant for Stephåne Mallarmé, Laforgue and Paul Valéry; also translated T. Tabize, I. Yashvili and G. Leonidze into Russian; his works were published in the anthologies *Poshchyochina obshchestvennomy vkusu* (A Slap at Public Taste), *Sadok sudey* (The Arbiters' Warren), etc; arrested by State Security organs; *Publ:* verse collections *Volch'ye solntse* (Vulpine Sun) (1914); *Iz topi blat* (Cant from the Swamp) (1922); *Patmos* (1926); *Krotonskiy polden'* (Noon in Crotona) (1928); translations from French *Ot romantikov do syurrealistov* (From the Romantics to the Surrealists) (1934); *Died:* 15 May 1939 in imprisonment; posthumously rehabilitated.

LIZAREV, F. S. (1882-1937) Party official; CP member from 1904; *Born:* 1882; *Career:* during 1917 Oct Revol member, Revol Comt, Butyr' Rayon; member, Moscow Council of Rayon Dumas; 1918-20 member, Moscow Province RCP(B) Bureau and Province Exec Comt; Moscow Province Food Comr; from 1920 Party and govt work in Don Oblast and Stavropol' Kray; member, Stavropol' City RCP(B) Comt; chm, Revol Comt and Don Province Exec Comt; secr, Don Province RCP(B) Comt; from 1922 exec railroad transport work; 1930 and 1933-36 dean, Moscow Inst of Rail Transport Eng; member, All-Russian and USSR Centr Exec Comt of three convocations; 1928 cand member, CC, CP(B) Ukr, arrested by State Security organs; *Died:* 1937 in imprisonment.

LOBACHYOV, I. S. (1879-1933) Govt official; CP member from 1917; *Born:* 1879; *Career:* fought in 1917 Oct Revol; from 1918 worked for food supply system in Moscow and the Ukr; from 1920 Collegium member, RSFSR Pop Comrt of Food; Ukr Pop Comr of Food; 1923 USSR Dep Pop Comr of Food; from 1924 RSFSR Pop Comr of Domestic Trade; from 1925 chm, Bd, All-Union Grain Trust; 1933 dep chm for state procurement, USSR Council of Pop Comr; member, USSR Centr Exec Comt; *Died:* 1933

LOBANOV, M. I. (STANISLAV) (1887-1937) Party official; RSDRP member from 1904; *Born:* 1887; *Career:* 1909 sent to Party school on Island of Capri; sided with Bogdanov; signed recall-ultimatum program of *Vperyod* group; after 1917 Oct Revol joined Bolsheviks; subsequently one of the leaders of the "workers' opposition"; worked for Ukr Pop Comrt of Heavy Ind; arrested by State Security organs; *Died:* 1937 in imprisonment.

LOBODA, Andrey Mitrofanovich (1871-1931) Ukr folklorist and lit historian; member, Ukr Acad of Sci from 1922; corresp member, USSR Acad of Sci from 1924; *Born:* 26 June 1871 in vil Sventsyany, Vilnius Province; *Educ:* 1894 grad Kiev Univ; *Career:* from 1898 assoc prof, from 1900 prof, Kiev Univ, specializing in history of Russian language, Russian and Ukr lit and folk art; 1923-25 vice-pres, Ukr Acad of Sci; head, Ethnographical Commision, Ukr Acad of Sci; member, various Russian and Ukr sci soc; *Publ:* "The Russian Bogatyr Epic. A Critical and Bibliographical Review of Works on the Russian Bogatyr Epic" (1896); "Russian Match-Making Legends" (1902); "Folk Elements in Russian Musical Drama a Hundred Years Ago" (1889); The 'Stefanotokos' School Drama According to the Newly-Found 1741-43 Manuscipt' (1901); "At Pushkin's Cradle" (1899); "Pushkin in Kamenka" (1899); also wrote works about Shevchenko, M. Maksomovich and P. Kulish as ethnographers; valuable studies of Ukr folklore and ethnography; his study "Shakespearism in Russian Literature" remained in his manuscript *Died:* 1 Jan 1931 in Kiev

LOBOV, Semyon Semyonovich (1888-1939) Govt Official: CP member from 1913; *Born:* 1888, son of a peasant; *Career:* metalworker by trade; 1910 worked on Amur Railroad, then in Ufa; from 1914 worked in Petersburg; at time of 1917 Feb Revol worked at Rosenkrantz Plant in Petrograd; member, Petrograd Party Comt and member, Petrograd Sov; after 1917 Oct Revol worked for Sovnarkhoz; 1918-21 worked for Cheka in Petrograd, Samara, Bashkiria and in Caucasus; then various posts in Petrograd: worked for Oil Syndicate, coal trust, member, Bd, October Railroad; from 1924 chm, Northwestern Ind Bureau; member, Main Concessions Comt; Presidium member, Supr Sovnarkhoz; from 1926 chm, RSFSR Supr Sovnarkhoz, then dep chm, USSR Supr Sovnarkhoz; from 1930 USSR Dep Pop Comr of Supply, then USSR Pop Comr of Forestry Ind; member, USSR Centr Exec Comt; at 12th Party Congress elected cand member, at 13th-17th Party Congress elected member, CC, CPSU(B); 1927-34 member, Org Bureau, CC, CPSU(B); arrested by State Security organs; *Died:* 1939 in imprisonment.

LOBOVA, V. N. (Vera) (1888-1924) Professional revolutionary; CP member from 1905; *Born:* 1888; *Career:* 1906-08 member, Ural Oblast Party Comt; 1911 member, Moscow RSDRP Comt; early 1913 secr; Russian Bureau, CC, RSDRP; secr, Bolshevik Faction, 4th State Duma; after 1917 Oct Revol Presidium member, Kiev Province Exec Comt; member Ukr Centr Exec Comt; 1922-23 worked for Agitation and Propaganda Dept, Party CC; *Died:* 1924.

LOGINOV, Fyodor Georgiyevich, (1900-1958) Hydraulic eng; govt official, CP member from 1925; *Born:* 19 Feb 1900; *Educ:* 1932 grad Leningrad Polytech Inst; *Career:* began working at age 11; during 1917 Oct Revol joined Red Guard; 1923-28 did admin and trade-union work; 1932-41 helped to build a number of hydropower plants; from 1942 USSR Dep Pop Comrt of Power Plants; 1944-46 in charge of restoration of Dnieper Hydropower Plant; from 1905 in charge of construction of Stalingrad Hydropower Plant; 1954-57 USSR Min of Power Plant Construction; from 1957 USSR First Dep Min of Power Plants; dep, RSFSR Supr Sov; *Died:* 2 Aug 1958.

LOGINOV, Saveliy Prokhorovich (1913-1960) First secr, Arkhangel'sk Oblast Party Comt from 1955; cand member, CC, CPSU from 1956; CP member from 1939; *Born:* 1913 in vil Tochna, now Mogilev Oblast, son of a peasant; *Educ:* 1932 grad Teachers' Training Technicum; 1951 grad Higher Party School; *Career:* from 1932 taught; dir, secondary school; then head, rayon educ dept; from 1938 chm, Kansk Rayon Exec Comt, Krasnoyarsk Oblast; from 1942 first secr, Kansk Rayon Party Comt; then dep dept head, Krasnoyarsk Kray Party Comt; 1943-46 worked for CC, CPSU; from 1951 secon secr, Arkhangel'sk Oblast CPSU Comt; dep, USSR Supr Sov of 5th convocation; dep, RSFSR Supr Sov of 3rd and 4th convocations; *Awards:* Order of Lenin; Order of the Fatherland War, 2nd Class; medals; *Died:* 26 Oct 1960.

LOKERMAN (pseudonyms: BAZILENKOV; TSAREV), A. S. (1880-1937) Party official; *Born:* 1880; *Career:* 1898 joined Soc-Democratic movement; worked in Rostov-on-Don; member, Don RSDRP Comt; Don Comt deleg at 2nd RSDRP Congress; after 2nd RSDRP Congress active Menshevik; worked in Southern Russian; after 1917 Feb Revol dep chm; Rostov-on-Don Sov of Workers and Soldiers' Dep; represented Menshviks in Centr Exec Comt; after 1917 Oct Revol fought against Sov regime; 1917-20 member, Don RSDRP (Mensheviks) Comt; convicted for counter-revolutionary Menshevik activities; arrested by State Security organs; *Died:* 1937 in imprisonment.

LOKTIONOV, Aleksandr Dmitriyevich (1893-1941) Mil commander; ensign, Russian Army; lt-gen, Sov Army from 1940; CP member from 1921; *Born:* 11 Aug 1893 in vil Verkhniy Lyubazh, now Kursk Oblast; *Career:* from 1918 in Red Army; 1918-21 commanded regt, then brigade; 1920 fought in Crimea; 1923-30 asst commander, then commander, 2nd Infantry Regt; 1930-33 commander, 4th Infantry Corps; 1933-37 asst commander, Bel, then Khar'kov Mil Distr; 1937 commander, Centr Asian Mil Distr; 1937-39 chief, Sov Air Force; 1940 commander, Baltic Special Mil Distr; June 1941 arrested by NKVD; *Died:* 28 Oct 1941 in imprisonment; posthumously rehabilitated.

LOMAKIN, Yakov Mironovich (1904-1958) Diplomat with the

rank of envoy extraordinary and plen, 2nd class; *Born:* 1904; *Career:* from 1941 dipl work; 1942-44 USSR co-gen in San Francisco; 1944-45 dep head, Press Dept, USSR Pop Comrt of For Affairs; 1946-48 USSR consul-gen in New York; 1949 dep head, Press Dept, USSR Min of For Affairs; 1953-56 counsellor, USSR embassy in Peking; 1956-58 counsellor, Dept of Int Econ Org, USSR Min of For Affairs; *Died:* 1958.

LOMOV (real Name: OPPOKOV), Georiy Ippolitovich (Party pseudonyms: Afanasiy, Zhorzh; pen name: A. LOMOV) (1888-1938) Party and govt official; CP member from 1903; *Born:* 28 Jan 1888 in Saratov, son of a priest; *Educ:* 1913 grad Law Fac, Petersburg Univ; *Career:* 1905 member, Saratov RSDRP Comt; head, workers squad in Saratov; 1906, while a student at Petersburg Univ, Party organizer for Railroad Rayon; 1907 member, Ivanovo-Voznesensk RSDRP Comt, then Moscow Okrug RSDRP Comt; 1909 member and secr, Petersburg Party Comt; 1910-13 exiled to Arkhangel'sk Province; took part in polar expeditions; after exile and graduation from Petersburg Univ conducted Party work in Moscow; helped found Metalworkers' Union; 1914 exiled to Saratov; 1916 exiled to Eastern Siberia; after 1917 Feb Revol, member Moscow Oblast RSDRP(B) Bureau and Moscow RSDRP(B) Comt; dep chm, Moscow Sov of Workers' Dep; deleg, 6th RSDRP(B) Congress at which he was elected cand member, CC; helped direct 1917 Oct Revol in Moscow; member, Moscow Mil Revol Comt; Pop Comr of Justice in first Council of Pop Comr; 1918, in Brest-Litovsk peace treaty debate, sided with "Lefstist Communists"; 1918-21 Presidium member and dep chm, Supr Sovnarkhoz and chm, Main Forestry Comt; 1921-23 member, Siberian Bureau, CC, RCP(B); member, Siberian Revol Comt; chm, Siberian Ind Bureau, Supr Sovnarkhoz; member, Ural Bureau, CC, RCP(B); chm, Ural Econ Council; from late 1923 chm, All-Russian Oil Syndicate; Presidium member, USSR Supr Sovnarkhoz; member, Moscow RCP(B) Comt, and Moscow Sov of Workers' Dep; fall 1926 appointed chm, Bd, Donets Basin State Coal Ind Trust; member, and Politburo member, CC, CP(B) Ukr; from 1929 chm, State Trust for Planning and Equipping Oil and Gas Ind Enterprises; Presidium member, USSR Supr Sovnarkhoz; 1931-33 dep chm, USSR Gosplan; member, Centr Exec Comt of all convocations; deleg 6th-12th and 14th-17th Party Congresses; at 6th, 7th and 14th Congresses elected cand member, Party CC; at 15th and 16th Congresses elected member, CC; at 17th Congress elected member, Sov Control Commission; 1934-37 Bureau member, Sov Control Commission ; wrote articles and pamphlets on econ and polit themes; arrested by State Security organs; *Died:* 30 Dec 1938 in imprisonment; posthumously rehabilitated.

LONGINOV, Vitaliy Vital'yevich (1886-1937) Chemist; *Born:* 31 Jan 1886; *Educ:* 1912 grad Moscow Univ; *Career:* 1912-32 taught and worked at Moscow Univ; 1920-37 co-founder and dir, Inst of Pure Chemical Reagents; did research on the reduction of sodium esters in alcohol; devised methods of synthesizing ethylene and diene hydrocarbons, alcohols, esters, terpenes and heterocyclic compounds; helped to organize and develop the ind production of pure reagents in USSR; did research on the theory and practical methods of obtaining chemically pure substances; from 1936 member, Int Standards Bureau; published numerous in the journal"Trudy Instituta chistykh khimicheskikh reaktivov"; *Died:* 7 Nov 1937.

LONGVA, Roman Vaytsekhovich (1899-1937) Sov mil commander; Pole; corps commander from 1935; *Born:* 1899; *Career:* during Civil War commanded infantry div; after Civil War chief of admin, Red Army Staff; 1926-27 Sov mil attaché in Peking; 1927-35 member, Red Army Staff, then Red Army Gen Staff; 1935-37 head, Communications Bd, USSR Pop Comrt of Defense; 1936 helped plan Chkalov's non-stop flight from Moscow to Petropavlovsk-in-Kamchatka;1937 arrested by NKWD; *Awards:* Order of the Red Banner; Order of the Red Star; *Died:* 1937 in imprisonment; posthumously rehabilitated.

LOPUKHIN, Aleksey Aleksandrovich (1864-1927) Govt official; *Born:* 1864; *Career:* 1902-05 police dept dir; 1906 uncovered printing of pogrom proclamations in police dept; 1908 informed Burtsev of the agent-provocateur Azef's services to the secret police; 1909 sentenced to five years at hard labor, subsequently commuted to exile; 1911 pardoned and reinstated; from 1913 vice-dir, Petersburg Commercial Bank in Moscow; *Publ: "Otryvki iz vospominaniy"* (Excerpts from My Memoirs) (1923); *Died:* 1927.

LORDKIPANIDZE, G. S. (pseudonyms: Grisha, Grisha KUTAISSKIY, SPIRIDONOV)(1881-1937) Geo writer; member, RSDRP (Mensheviks) from 1904; *Born:* 1881; *Career:* 1900 joinedRSDRP worked for Menshevik newspaper; Kutaisi RSDRP (Mensheviks) Comt deleg at 5th RSDRP Congress; 1918-21 member, Geo govt; arretsed by State Security organs; *Died:* 1937 in imprisonment.

LORDKIPANIDZE, Nikolay Merabovich (1880-1944) Geo Writer; *Born:* 17 Sept 1880, in vil Chuneshi, son of a commune mediator; *Educ:* until 1900 studied at Khar'kov Univ; expelled for involvement in student demonstrations; 1902 attended Leoben Mining Acad, Austria; *Career;* worked as teacher and lecturer; 1902 first work published; *Publ:* novelettes: "For the Sake of the Hearth" (1914); "Ruined Nests" (1916); "Hard Times" (1914-19); "The Terrible Ruler" (1912); "Knights" (1912); "Tie-Plate" (1926); "The Indomitable" (1938-44); "The Prisoner's Return", etc; pamphlet "Georgia for Sale"; stories; "The Woman in the Shawl" (1925); "The Feudals" (1924); "The Bishop at the Hunt" (1926); *Died:* 25 May 1944.

LORENTS, I. L. (1890-1941) Diplomat; CP member from 1919; *Born:* 1890; *Career:* 1918 secr, RSFSR plen mission in Berlin; 1919 worked for secretariat, 1st Comintern Congress; 1919-20 on Western Front; asst comr, then comr of artillery, 15th Army; senior dipl work; Sov plen in Lith, Finland, Lat and Austria; arrested by State Security organs; *Died:* 1941 in imprisonment.

LOSEV (pseudonyms: VALER'YANOV; SEMYONOV) V. N. (1878-1948) Party official; CP member from 1902; *Born:* 1878; *Career:* Party work in Voronezh, Moscow and the Urals; repeatedly subjected to reprisals by Tsarist authorities; Dec 1905 fought in Moscow uprising; 1905 Ural RSDRP Comt deleg at 3rd RSDRP Congress; 1908 worked in Southern Russia; from 1913 in Moscow; after 1917 Feb Revol chm, Nizhniy Novgorod Sov of Workers' Dep; 1918-19 food supply work in Moscow; 1919 worked for Polit Dept; 13th Army on Southern Front; from 1920 worked for newspapers and publ houses; from 1930 retired; *Died:* 1948.

LOSKUTOV, Mikhail Petrovich (1960-1940) Russian writer; *Born:* 24 Sept 1906 in Kursk; *Career:* from 1930 worked for Centr Asian Radio-Newspaper, Tashkent; toured Centr Asia; spoke Uzbek and Turkman; summer 1933, as a correspondent of the journals "Nashi dostizheniya" and "Vechernyaya krasnaya gazeta", took part in the Karakum Motor Raaley; arrested by State Security organs; *Publ:* collected essays and feuilletons: *Konets meshchanskogo pereulka* (The End of the Bourgeois Alley) (1928); *Zolotaya pustota* (Golden Void) (1929, coauthor); *Otvoyovannoye u vodki* (Won Away from Vodka) (1929); series of short stories and essays *Trinadtsatyy karavan. Zapiski o pustyne Karakum* (The Thirteenth Caravan. Notes on the Karakum Desert) (1933); *Rasskazy o dorogakh* (Stories of Roads) (1935); works published posthumously: *Belyy slon. Ocherki i rasskazy* (The White Elephant. Sketches and Stories) (1958); *Sledy na peske. Izbrannyye proizvedeniya* (Traces in the Sand. Selected Works) (1959); *Zhazhda. Rasskazy* (Thirst. Stories) (1961); *Died:* 1940 in imprisonment; posthumously rehabilitated.

LOSSKIY, Vladimir Apollonovich (1874-1946) Opera singer (bass) and producer; Hon Artiste of RSFSR from 1925; *Born:* 30 June 1874 in Kiev; *Educ:* took singing lessons from K. Everardi in Petersburg; 1899 grad Kiev Univ; *Career:* 1899 joined Moscow Private Opera House; 1901-05 singer, Kiev Private Opera House; 1905-06 again at Moscow Private Opera House; from 1906 soloist, 1920-28 chief producer, Bolshoy Theater; also produced operas in Sverdlovsk, Tbilisi, Leningrad, etc; 1920-26 appeared in shows at Musical Studio, Moscow Acad Arts Theater; 1934-36 and 1943-46 again producer, Bolshoy Theater; also taught singing at Moscow, Kiev and Odessa conservatories; *Roles:* Don Bartholo in "The Barber of Seville"; the Englishman in Auber's "Gra Diavolo"; Skoromokh in *Skazka o tsare Saltalne* (The Tale of Emperor Saltan); the Scribe in *Mayskaya noch'* (A May Night); Duda in "Sadko"; Skula in *Knyaz' Igor'* (Prince Igor); *Productions:* at Bolshoy Theater; *Kavkazskiy plennik* (The Caucasian Prisoner) (1909); *Snegurochka* (The Snow-Maiden) (1911); "Iolanthe" (1917); "Aida" (1922); "Lohengrin" (1923); "Boris Godunov" (1927); "Sadko" (1935); *Knyaz' Igor'* (Prince Igor) (1944); *Rusalka* (1944); at Leningrad Opera and Ballet Theater: *Skazka o tsare Saltane* (The Tale of Emperor Saltan) (1937); "Lohengrin" (1941); ar Sverdlovsk Theater of Opera and Ballet: "Boris Godunov" (1928-29); *Ruslan i Lyudmila* (Ruslan and Ludmilla) (1929-30); "Lohengrin" (1934); at Tbilisi Opera and Ballet Theater: "Prince Igor" (1930); at Odessa Theater of Opera and Ballet: "The

Huguenots"; "Aida" (1919-20); "The Barber of Seville" (1937-38); "Ivan Susanin"; Chishko's *Bronenosets Potyomkin* (The Battleship Potyomkin) (1930-40); *Died:* 6 July 1946 in Moscow.

LOYTER, Efraim Borisovich (1889-1963) Jewish stage dir and stagecraft teacher; Hon Artiste of Uzbek SSR from 1943; *Born:* 3 Dec 1889; *Career:* 1910 began to write theater reviews; after 1917 Oct Revol co-dir and producer, "Kulturliga" Studio (Kiev-Moscow, 1919-24), from which was founded in 1925 the State Jewish Theater of the Ukr SSR; 1925-28 chief producer of this theater; 1929-35 taught in studio of Moscow Jewish Theater; 1933-35 taught at State Inst of Stagecraft; 1935-41 and 1945-49 art dir, Odessa Jewish Theater; *Works:* staged plays: *Purimshpil;* Daniel' and Loyter's "In the Fire"; Glbos's "Zagmuk"; Gol'dfaden's "Kunelemelekh"; Lope de Vega's "Sheep's Spring" (1935); Gorky's *Mat'* (Mother) (1938); Sholom Aleykhem's "Wandering Stars" (1940); Del's *Yakov Sverdlov* (1941), etc; Lunacharskiy's *Podzhigateli* (The Instigators) (1924); Shapovlenko's 1881 god (The Year 1881) (1924); *Publ: Masterstvo sovetskogo aktyora* (The Technique of the Soviet Actor) (1933); *Slova na stsene i estrade* (Speech Delivery on the Theater and Variety Stage) (1954); *Died:* 10 Dec 1963.

LOZHECHKIN, Mikhail Pavlovich (1905-1957) Prospecting geologist; Cand of Geology and Mineralogy from 1940; CP member from 1927; *Born:* 1905, son of a foundry worker; *Educ:* 1930 grad Moscow Mining Acad; *Career:* 1916 began working at age 11, 1919 joined Komsomol; 1922-26 worked as a fitter at Samara Pipe Works and attended evening courses at workers' fac; 1930-40 surveyed gold, copper, mica and magnesite deposits in the Urals and Baykal arey; during WW 2 supervised surveys of new deposits of rare metals prior to ind exploitation; 1944-48 did admin work for USSR Council of Min; 1949-54 Collegium member, USSR Min of Geology and chm, All-Union Commision for Mineral Resources; from 1954 chm State Commision for Mineral Resources, USSR Council of Min; *Awards:* Order of the Red Banner of Labor; Badge of Hon; medals; *Died:* 5 Sept 1957.

LOZINSKIY, Mikhail Leonidovich (1886-1955) Russian poet and translater; *Born:* 20 July 1886 in Petersburg; *Educ:* grad philological Fac, Petersburg Univ; *Career:* from 1912 poet and lit critic; worked for "World Lit" Publ House; translated from English, Spanish, Italian, German, French and Iranian; translated Shakespeare, Cervantes, Moliere, Corneille, Kipling, Firdousi, etc; *Publ:* collected verse *Gornyy klyuch* (Mountains Spring) (1916); translated into Russian Fletcher's "The Spanish Priest" (1935); Sheridan's "The Duenna"; Lope de Vega's "The Widow of Valencia" (1939); Alarcon's "Dubious Truth" (1941); Dante's "Divine Comedy" (1939-45), etc; *Awards:* Stalin Prize (1946); *Died:* 1 Feb 1955 in Leningrad.

LOZOVSKIY, A. (real name: DRIDZO, Solomon Abramovich (1878-1952) Party and govt official: CP member from 1901; *Born:* 16 Mar 1878 in vil Danilovka, Yekaterinoslav Province, son of a teacher; *Career:* worked as salesclerk and blacksmith; 1903 after 2nd RSDRP Congress joined Bolsheviks; Party work in Petersburg, Kazan' and Khar'kov; took part in 1905-07 Revol in Kazan'; 1905 deleg at 1st RSDRP Conference in Tammerfors; June 1906 arrested and after teo years' imprisonment sentenced to exile in Irkusk Province; 1908, en route to exile, fled abroad; 1909-17 lived in Geneva and Paris; member, French Socialist Party; active in French trade-union movement; sided with Bolshevik-reconciliationists; during WW 1 took internationalist stand; June 1917 returned to Russia; July 1917 at 3rd All-Russian Trade-Union Conference elected secr, All-Russian Centr Trade-Union Council; Dec 1917 expelled from RSDRP(B) forcriticizingParty policy; 1918-19 headed group of Soc-Democrat internationalists; Dec 1919 re-admitted to RCP(B) together with this group; 1918-21 exec secr, Textile Workers, Then Railroad Workers Unions; chm, Moscow Trade-Union Council; during trade-union controversy supported Lenin's stand; 1921-37 secr-gen, Trade-Union International (Profintern); 1937-39 dir, State Lit Publ House; 1939-46 USSR Dep Min of For Affairs; 1941-48 also dep head, then head, Sov- Information Bureau; at 15th-17th Party Congresses elected cand member, and at 18th Congress elected member, CC, CPSU(B); attended 2nd-7th Comintern Congresses and elected member, Comintern Exec Comt; from 1939 lectured on historical sci; 1940-49 head, Chair of History of Int Relations and USSR For Policy, Higher Party School, CC, CPSU; Presidium member, Communist Acad; prof, Moscow Univ; member, All-Russian and USSR Centr Comt; dep, USSR Supr Sov of 1st and 2nd convocation; arrested by State Security organs; Publ: *Rabochiy kontrol'* (Workers' Control) (1918); *Professional'nyye soyuzy v Sovetskoy Rossii* (Trade Unions in Soviet Russia) (1920); *Anarkhosindikalizm* (Anarchic Syndicalism and Communism) (1924); *Osnovnyye momenty v razvitii mezhdunarodnogo profdvizheniya* (Main Stages in the Development of the International Trade-Union Movement) (1924); *Lenin i professional'noye dvizheniye* (Lenin and the Trade-Union Movement) (1925); *Za yedinyy front i yedinstvo profdvizheniya* (For a United Front and Unity of the Trade-Union Movement) (1935); *Died:* 12 Aug 1952 in imprisonment; posthumously rehabilitated.

LUBOTSKIY, David Naumovich (1899-1966) Anatomist and surgeon; specialist in anatomical terminology; assoc prof; *Born:* 1899, son of a physician; *Educ:* 1927 grad Leningrad Mil Med Acad; *Career:* 1919-22 served in Red Army as chief of a radio station; 1924-27 took an active part in the work of the sci circle at Prof V. N. Shevkunenko's Chair of Topographical Anatomy; Leningrad Mil Med Acad; 1927-30 junior lecturer, 1930-37 lecturer, Chair of Topographical Anatomy and Operative Surgery, Leningrad Mil Med Acad; 1939-40 asst to prof P. A. Kupriyanov, Chair of Topographical Anatomy, 1st Leningrad Med Inst; 1941-48 asst prof, then assoc prof, Chair of Topographical Anatomy, 2nd Moscow Med Inst; 1942-43 also head of a surgical dept at a Moscow evacuation hospital; from 1949 did private research as a pensioner; in the course of 32 years spent editing works on topographical anatomy and opertive surgery acquired a reputation as an authority on anatomical terminology; did major research on the surgical anatomy of the lumbosacral region of the peripheral nervous system which was used on the compilation of the *Atlas perifericheskoy nervnoy i venoznoy sistemy* (Atlas of the Peripheral Nervous and Venous System) (ed Prof V. N. Shevchenko); studied the anatomical works of N. I. Pirogov, whom he considered the founder of topographical anatomy, and translated his doctor's thesis from Latin into Russian; also translated Pirogov's experimental study on the Achilles tendon from German into Russian; 1959 edited and annotated the *Annaly Derptskoy kliniki* (Annals of the Dorpat Clinic), which constitute vol 2 of Pirogov's "Collected Works"; wrote over 50 works; *Publ: Osnovy topograficheskoy anatomii. Rukovodstvo* (The Principle of Topographical Anatomy. A Manual) (1953); coauthor, *Kurs operativnoy khirurgii s topograficheskoy anatomiyey* (A Course in Operative Surgery and Topographical Anatomy) (2nd ed, 1963); *Died:* 1966.

LUDRI, Ivan Martynovich (1895-1938) Naval commander; Est; Flag-Officer, 1st Class from 1935; *Born:* 1895; *Educ:* 1927 grad Naval Acad; *Career:* from 1919 commandant, Kronstadt Fortress; comr, Onega Naval Flotilla; 1920-21 member, Revol Mil Council, Black and Azov Sea Naval Forces; 1921-23 head, Caspian Naval Forces; 1927-32 commander, Black Sea coastal defense; chief of staff, Black and Azov Sea Naval Forces; 1932-37 dep head, Red Army Naval Forces; 1937 arrested by NKVD; *Publ: Krasnyy flot v sostave Vooruzhyonnykh sil Respubliki* (The Red Fleet as a Part of the RSFSR Armed Forces) (1927); *O taktike malogo flota* (The Tactics of a Small Fleet) (1928); *Awards:* Order of Red Star; *Died:* 1938 in imprisonment; posthumously rehabilitated.

LUGANOVSKIY (pseudonyms: ROBERTOV; YAKOV; PORTUGEYS), E. V. (1885-1940) Govt official; CP member from 1902; *Born:* 1885; *Career:* Party work in Kiev, Odessa, Yekaterinoslav, etc; repeatedly arrested by Tsarist authorities; 1903-04 lived abroad; Nizhniy Tagil RSDRP Comt deleg at 5th RSDRP Congress; Dec 1917-May 1918 member, Sov Ukr govt; from Oct 1918 plen, RSFSR Pop Comrt of Food; 1919-21 worked for Labor and Defense Council and Supr Sovnarkhoz; then various admin posts; 1927-38 chm, bd, Centr Bank of Communal Econ and Housing; arrested by State Security organs; *Died:* 1940 in imprisonment.

LUGOVSKOY, Vladimir Aleksandrovich (1901-1957) Russian poet; *Born:* 1 Juli 1901 in Moscow, son of a teacher; *Educ:* 1921 grad Mil Teachers' Training Inst; *Career:* 1918-24 served in Red Army; 1925 first work published in journal "Novyy mir"; tourned Sov Centr Asia and visited Turkey, Greece and Italy with ships of the Black Sea Fleet; traveled through Centr Europe and made several trips to Azer; apart from poetry wrote articles on lit and translated nat poets of various Sov republ; *Publ:* poetry collections: *Muskul* (Muscle) (1929); *Stradaniya* *moikh druzey* (The Sufferings of My Friends) (1930); epic poem *Bol'shevikam pustyni i vesny* (Deserts and Springs for the Bolsheviks) (3 parts, 1931, 1933 and 1948); verse collections; *Yevropa* (Europe) (1932); *Zhizn'* (Life) (1933); *Kaspiyskoye more* (The Caspian Sea) (1936); *Novyye stikhi* (New Poems) (1941); *Solntsevorot* (Solstice) (1956); *Sinyaya vesna* (Blue Spring) (1958); *Seredina veka* (Medcentury) (1958); articles *Razdum'ye o poezii* (Reflections on Poetry) (1960); *Izbrannyye proizvedeniya* (Selected Works) (2 vol, 1956); opera libretto *Oktyabr'* (October); *Died:* 5 June 1957 in Yalta.

LUGOVTSOV, Maksim Vlasovich (1885-1956) Metallurgist; member, Ukr Acad of Sci from 1939; Hon Sci and Tech worker of Ukr SSR from 1945; *Born:* 11 May 1885 in Yuzovka, now Donetsk, son of a worker; *Educ:* 1916 grad Yekaterinoslav Mining Inst; *Career:* worked at various factories and plants; after 1917 Oct Revol eng at steel plants, metalluriical trusts and groups; directed research teams and research insts; member, Sci and Tech Councils of USSR and Ukr SSR; from 1939 dir, Inst of Ferrous Metallurgy, Ukr Acad of Sci; developed statistical theory of blast-furnace processes and methods of improving cast iron quality; *Awards:* two Orders of Lenin; other orders; medals; *Died:* 7 June 1956.

LUKA (secular name: VOYNO-YASENETSKIY, Valentin Feliksovich) (1877-1961) Archibishop of Simferopol and the Crimea; Doctor of Med; prof of surgery; *Born:* 1877; *Educ:* studied painting at Kiev Art School; 1903 grad Med Fac, Kiev Univ; *Career:* head, Chair of Surgery, Kiev Univ; 1915 dir, Pereyaslavl'-Zalesskiy Mil Hospital; 1917 chief surgeon of a Tashkent hospital; 1919 became a widower and took monastic orders with the name Luka; 1920 prof, Tashkent Univ; 1921 elevated to priest and 1923 to Bishop of Tashkent and Turkestan; 1923 exiled to Yeniseysk for criticizing Bolshevik regime, then exiled to Turkhansk, where he practised med; with start of WW 2 chief surgeon, Krasnoyarsk evacuation hospitals; fall 1942 elevated to archibishop and given the Krasnoyarsk Eparchy with special dispensation to continue surgical practice; famed throughout USSR for his brilliant operation technique; 1944 appointed Bishop of Tambov and Michurinsk; 1954 elected hon member, Moscow Theological Acad; *Publ: Ocherki gnoynoy khirurgii i rezektsii pri infil'trirovannykh ognestrel'nykh raneniyakh sustavov* (Studies in Suppurative Surgery and Resection with Infiltrated Gunshot Wounds of the Joints); *Awards:* Stalin Prize, 1st Class for above work; *Died:* 11 June 1961.

LUKASHEV, Artemiy Maksimovich (1870-1942) Fruit-grower and breeder; *Born:* 1870 in Mglina, now Bryansk Oblast, son of a cobbler; *Educ:* 1897 grad Glukhov Teachers' Training Inst; *Career:* from 1901 worked as teacher in Khabarovsk; 1903 took up horticulture as hobby; bred five strains of pear (Tyoma, Polya, Olya, Lida and Vnuchka) which have become standard in Khabarovsk Kray, Maritime Kray, Siberia and the Urals; also bred several semi-wild strains of apple (Shkrab, Ded, etc); from 1934 dir of a fruit and berry nursery in Khabarovsk which now bears his name; contributed to the journals "Ussuriyskoye sadovodstvo i ogorodnichestvo" and "Plodoovoshchnoye khozyaystvo" *Publ: Plodovyy sad na Dal'nem Vostoke* (The Fruit Orchard in the Far East) (1932); *Moy Opyt* (My Experience) (1936); *Awards:* cash prize of RSFSR Pop Comrt of Farming (1936); Silver Medal at All-Union Agric Exhibition 1939); *Died:* 1942

LUKASHKIN, Nikolay Ivanovich (1898-1957) Civil eng; member, USSR Acad of Construction and Architecture from 1956; CP member from 1949; *Born:* 6 Aug 1898; *Educ:* 1930 grad Khar'kov Polytech Inst; *Career:* 1917-39 at various construction projects in Donbass, including Stalino Steel Plant; from 1939 chief eng of bds of USSR Pop Comrt of Construction; 1950-53 USSR Dep Min for Construction of Heavy Ind Enterprises; 1954-57 USSR Dep Min for Construction of Metallurgical and Chemical Ind Enterprises; from 1957 head, State Construction Comt, USSR Council of Min; devised new methods for high-speed construction and assembly of blast furnaces; developed and introduced new asbestos-cement structures; *Publ: Opyt stroitel'stva domennoy pechi Chusovskogo zavoda* (Experience in the Construction of the Chusovaya Plant's Blast Furnace) (1947); *Opyt vosstanovleniya pervoy ocheredi zavoda 'Zaporozhstal'* (Experience in the Restoration of the First Section of the' "Zaporozhstal' " Steel Plant) (1938); *Stroitel'stvo domennykh tsekhov* (The Construction of Blast-Furnace Shops) (1950); *Awards:* two Stalin Prizes (1946 and 1949); *Died:* 21 Dec 1957.

LUKHA, Artur Kheynrikhovich (1892-1953) Geologist; member, Est Acad of Sci from 1946; *Born:* 9 July 1892; *Career:* 1922-51 lecturer, 1945-51 prof, Tartu Univ; from 1947 dir, Geological Inst, Est Acad of Sci; studied stratigraphy of Silurian rocks and minerals (phosphorites and fuel shales, etc, in Est SSR; *Died:* 29 Dec 1953.

LUKIN, Avgust Mel'kisovich (1893-1966) Govt official; CP member from 1913; *Born:* 1893; *Educ:* grad For Trade Acad; *Career:* in revol movement; until 1919 propaganda work in Pavlovskiy Posad, where he helped establish Sov regime; fought in Civil War then various admin posts in timber ind; 1933 sent to work in Bel SSR; fought in WW 2; then govt work in Lat; from 1960 retired; twice elected member, CC, CP(B) Bel; *Died:* 19 Sept 1966.

LUKIN, Nikolay Mikhaylovich (pseudonym: N. ANTONOV) (1885-1940) Historian; prof; member, USSR Acad of Sci from 1929; CP member from 1904; *Born:* 20 July 1885, son of a primary school teacher; *Educ:* 1909 grad Fac of History and Philology, Moscow Univ; *Career:* from 1915 assoc prof, Moscow Univ; helped to run Moscow Bolshevik newspaper "Nash put' "; after 1917 Feb Revol member, ed collegium, Bolshevik newspaper "Sotsial-demokrat"; Oct 1918 resumed post at Moscow Univ; from 1921 dean, Fac of Soc Sci, Moscow Univ; also prof, Inst of Red Prof, Gen Staff Acad and Socialist Acad; 1925 co-founder, Soc of Marxist Historians and journal "Istorik-marksist", of which he was exec ed from 1935; 1928 attended Int Congress of Historians, Oslo; 1930 attended session of Int Comt on Historical Sci in Cambridge; 1932-36 dir, Inst of History, Communist Acad; 1932 and 1934 attended sossions of Int Comt on Historical Sci in the Hague and Paris; 1933 attended Int Congress of Historians, Warsaw; 1936-38 dir Inst of History, USSR Acad of Sci; specialized in modern European history with special reference to France (the French Revolution and Paris Commune of 1871) and Germany; wrote first Sov textbook on modern history for higher educ establishment; 1938 arrested by State Security organs; *Publ: Bor'ba za kolonii* (The Struggle for Colonies) (1914); *Maksimilian Robesp'yer* (Maximilian Robespierre) (1919); *Parizhskaya Kommuna 1871-goda* (The Paris Commune of 1871) (1922); *Noveyshaya istoriya Zapadnoy Yevropy* (The Recent History of Western Europe) (1923); *Ocherki po noveyshey istorii Germanii* (Studies in the Recent History of Germany)(1925); *Revolyutsionnoye pravitel'stvo i sel'skokhozyaystvennyye rabochiye* (The Revolutionary Government and the Agricultural Workers) (1930); *Parizhskaya Kommuna 1871-goda* (The Paris Commune of 1871) (Vol 1, 1932); *Izbrannyye trudy* (Selected Works) (3 vol, 1960-63); *Died:* 19 July 1940 in imprisonment; posthumously rehabilitated.

LUKOMSKIY, Aleksandr Sergeyevich (1868-1939) Mil commander and politician; gen, Russian Army; helped lead White forces; *Born:* 10 July 1868; *Educ:* 1897 grad Gen Staff Acad; *Career:* 1897-1909 staff officer, Kiev Mil Distr; 1909-14 head, Draft Dept; Main Bd of Gen Staff; 1913-15 head of chancelry, Min of War; 1915-16 Asst Min of War (for supply of troops); 1916 commanded 32nd Infantry Div in breaching Austrian forces; chief of staff, 10th Army; Oct 1916-Apr 1917 Quartermaster-Gen, Headquarters of supr commander in chief; 1917 commanded 1st Army Corps; June-Aug 1917 chief of staff to supr commander in chief; supported Gen Kornilov's bid to liquidate Bolshevik organizations in Petrograd and end dichotomous rule of Provisional Govt and Petrograd Sov; 14 Sept 1917 arrested by Provisional Govt; 2 Dec 1917 fled with Kornilov from Bykhov Prison and made his way to Novocherkassk on the Don, where he helped form White Volunteer Army; 1918-19 chief of staff, Volunteer Army; chief, Mil Bd; asst commander in chief, Armed Forces of Southern Russia (Denikin); July 1919-Jan 1920 chm, Special Consultative Bd, which acted as govt in areas liberated from Sov troops; Mar 1920 moved to Constantinople and represented Gen Wrangel in Entente Allied Comt; after end of Civil War lived abroad; *Publ: Vospominaniya* (Memoirs) (2 vol, 1922); *Died:* 25 Jan 1939 in Paris.

LUKOMSKIY, Il'ya Genrikhovich (1893-1958) Stomatologist; prof; Hon Sci Worker of RSFSR; *Born:* 1893; *Educ:* 1922 grad Med Fac, Moscow Univ; *Career:* after grad asst to Prof P. A. Gertsen, Chair of Propaedeutic Surgery, Moscow Univ; 1926-52 head, Chair of Stomatology, 1st Moscow Med Inst; did research on odontogenic tumors, tuberculosis of the oral cavity, oral sepsis, diseases of the mucous membrane of the oral cavity, the salivary glands and war injuries of the face and jaw; made special study of dental caries, for which he devised a preventive fluoridation treatment; devised classification of pericementites which found a wide application in Sov stomatology; 1926-58 regularly attended Sov stomatological conferences; *Publ: Odontogennyye opukholi* (Odontegenic Tumors) (1927); *Tuberkulyoz rta* (Oral Tuberculosis) (1931); *Kariyes zuba* (Dental Caries) (1948);*Bolezni zubov i slizistoy polosti rta* (Diseases of the Teeth and the Mucous Membrane of the Oral Cavity) (1959), etc; *Died:* 1958.

LUKS, Karl Yanovich (pseudonyms: MEMOR; Viktor LONDO; VOLGIN) (1888-1932) Civil War veteran; CP member from 1904; *Born:* 1888 in Lat; son of a peasant; *Career:* 1906-07 fought in revol in Liepaja and Saldus; from 1911 served six years at hard labor, then exiled to Siberia; 1919 during Civil War member, Chita Revol Comt; chief of staff, partisan detachment; 1920 member, Revol Mil Council; commander, Eastern Transbaykal and Amur partisan fronts; member, Far Eastern Republ Council of Min; after Civil rector, Inst of Northern Peoples; member, Northern Comt, All-Russian Centr Exec Comt Presidium; *Died:* 1932 killed during sci expedition.

LUK'YANOV, Sergey Vladimirovich (1910-1965) Actor; Pop Artiste of RSFSR from 1952; *Born:* 27 Oct 1910; *Career:* from 1929 actor, Donbass Theater; then worked at theaters in Ukr and RSFSR; 1924-55 and from 1963 actor, Vakhtangov Theater; 1956-63 actor, Moscow Arts Theater; *Roles:* stage roles: Kudryash in Ostrovski's *Groza* (The Storm); Lopakhin in Chekhov's *Vishnyovyy sad* (The Cherry Orchard), etc, film roles: Afanas'yev in *Delo Rumyantseva* (The Rumyantsev Case) (1956); Gordey Voron in *Kubanskiye Kazaki* (Kuban' Cossacks) (1950); Matvey in *Bolshaya sem'ya* (The Big Family) (1954), after Kochetov's novel *Sem'ya Zhurbinykh* (The Zhurbin Family); Vasiliy Bortnikov in *Vozvrashcheniye Vasiliya Bortnikova* (The Return of Vasily Bortnikov) (1953), after Nikolayeva's novel *Zhatva* (Reaping) Yegor Bulychyov in *Yegor Bulychyov i drugiye* (Yegor Bulychyov and Co) (1953); Nikanor in *Vikhri vrazhdebnyye* (Hostile Whirlwinds) (1956); Pugachev in *Kapitanskaya dochka* (The Captain's Daughter) (1958); Shkuro in *Oleko Dundich* (1958), etc; *Awards:* Stalin Prize (1951); *Died:* 1 Mar 1965.

LUNACHARSKAYA, A. A. (1883-1959) Soc worker; *Born:* 1883; *Career:* A. V. Lunacharskiy's wife; with him in emigration; 1917 returned to Russia; worked on circus boards; ed, journal "Tsirk"; in 1920's directed children's camps in Moscow; *Died:* 1959.

LUNACHARSKIY, Anatoliy Vasil'yevich (1875-1933) Govt and Party official; writer; member, USSR Acad of Sci from 1930; RSFSR Pop Comr of Educ from 1917; CP member from 1917; *Born:* 23 Nov 1875 in Poltava, son of an official; *Educ:* studied at Zurich Univ; *Career:* 1892, while studying at 1st Kiev High School, joined Soc-Democratic circle; 1893 moved to Switzerland and maintained close contacts with Liberation of Labor Group and with Plekhanov personally; studied natural sci and philosophy in R. Avenarius' circle; 1897 returned to Russia and later became member, Moscow RSDRP Comt; arrested and exiled to Kaluga; 1901-03 in exile in Vologda and Pot'ma; 1903, after 2nd RSDRP Congress, sided with Bolsheviks; 1904 moved to Geneva and joined ed staff of Bolshevik newspapers "Vperyod", then "Proletary"; 1905 attended 3rd RSDRP Congress, delivering paper on armed uprising in Russia; 1905 returned to Petersburg, where he engaged in agitation work and helped to edit legal Bolshevik news- "Novaya zhizn' "; from 1906 again in emigration, - in France, Switzerland and Italy; 1906 attended 4th RSDRP Congress; from 1907 attended Stuttgart and Copenhagen Int Socialist Congresses; drifted away from Bolsheviks and sided with "Vperyod" group, which criticized philosophical and theoretical principles of Marxism and Bolshevism; under the influence of Mach and Avenarius' philosophy sympathized with "bogostroitel'stvo", i. e., movement to establish a "socialist" religion; 1912 returned to Bolsheviks; from 1913 worked for Bolshevike nespaper "Pravda"; May 1917 returned to Russia and sided with "Mezhrayontsy" at 6th RSDRP(B) Congress admitted to RSDRP(B) along with "Mezhrayontsy" group; Oct 1917-29 RSFSR Pop Comr of Educ; during Civil War also plen, Revol Mil Council; 1929-33 chm, Learned Council, USSR Centr Exec Comt; from 1933 plen in Spain; from 1927 also sent abroud an various dipl missions; co-founder and member, Sverdlov Communist Acad; deleg at 8th, 10th, 11th, 13th, 15th and 16th Party Congresses; played key part in reorganizing higher and secondary educ in USSR and in sovetizing intelligentsia; wrote many works on philosophy, religion, lit, theater, esthetics, etc; *Publ: Osnovy pozitivnoy estetiki* (The Principles of Positive Esthetics) (1904); *Religiya i sotsializm* (Religion and Socialism) (2 vol, 1908); *Ob intelligentsii* (The Intelligentsia) (1923); *Istoriya zapadnoyevropeiskoy literatury v yeyo vazhneyshikh momentakh* (A History of the Main Aspects of West European Literature) (1924); *Teatr i revolyutsiya* (Theater and Revolution) (1924); *Osnovy prosvetitel'noy politiki sovetskoy vlasti* (The Principles of the Soviet Regime's Enlightenment Policy) (1924); *Prosveshcheniye i revolyutsiya* (Enlightenment and Revolution) (1924); *Problemy narodnogo obrazovaniya* (Problems of Public Education) (1925); *Ocherki marksistskoy teorii iskusstv* (Studies in the Marxist Theory of Arts) (1926); *Iskusstvo i molodyozh* (Art and Youth) (1929); *Klassiki russkoy literatury* (The Classics of Russian Literature) (1937); *Stat'i o teatre idramaturgii* (Articles on the Theater and Drama) (1938); *Stat'i o literature* (Articles on Literature) (1957); *Rasskazy o Lenine* (Stories of Lenin) (1959); *Stat'i o sovetskoy literature* (Articles on Soviet Literature) (1958); *O teatre i dramaturgii* (Theater and Drama) (2 vol, 1958); *Sobraniye sochineniy* (Collected Works) (6 vol, 1963-65); *Died:* 26 Dec 1933 in Menton, Southern France; buried by the Kremlin Wall on Moscow's Red Square.

LUNDBERG, Yevgeniy Germanovich (1887-1965) Russian writer and lit critic; *Born:* 12 Sept 1887 in Taurogen, Kovno Province; *Educ:* grad Paris Higher School of Soc Sci; studied at Geneva and Jena Univ; *Career:* 1901 first work printed; 1920-24 lived in Berlin; founded Skify (Scythians) Leftist Populist publ house; also founded Berlin Branch, State Publ House and Berlin Branch, State Tech Publ House; wrote critical studies of Bel, Kaz and Geo lit, articles on the works of Vazha Pshavela, Lordkipanidze, Tsereteli, etc; *Publ: Rasskazy* (Stories) (1909); stories *Moi skitan'ya* (My Wanderings) (1909); *Merezhkovskiy i yego novoye khristianstvo* (Merezhkovskiy and His New Christianity) (1914); *Ot vechnogo k perekhodyashchemu* (From the Eternal to the Ephemeral) (1923); *Lenin i legenda* (Lenin and Legend) (1924); *Zapiski pisatelya* (A writer's Notes) (1930); coauthor, *Zodchiy Andrey Nikiforovich Voronikhin. Materialy k biografii* (The Architect Andrey Nikiforovich Voronikhin. Biographic Material) (1937); critical articles; *O gruzinskoy literature 19-go veka* (Georgian 19th-Century Literature) (1939); *Abay - uchitel' zhizni* (Abay, the Teacher of Life) (1945); *Golos zemli* (Voice of the Earth) (1946); coauthor, *Vazha Pshevela; 1861-1915 gg. Zhizn' poeta* (Vazha Pshavela. 1861-1915. Life of a Poet) (1948), etc; *Died;* 30 Nov 1965 in Moscow.

LUNIN, Nikolay Ivanovich (1853-1937) Pediatrician; pioneer of vitaminology; Dr of Med from 1880; *Born:* 1 Feb 1853 in Dorpat (now Tartu, Est SSR), son of a merchant; *Educ:* 1878 grad Med Fac, Dorpat Univ; *Career:* 1880 defended doctor's thesis on the role of inorganic salts in animal fodder; from 1882 worked as pediatrician in Petersburg (Leningrad); provided first experimental proof that more than protein, fat, sugar, salts and water is needed to maintain life and demonstrated that, apart from casein, fat, lactose and salts, milk contains other vital substances (named "vitamins" by K. Funk in 1912); wrote over 40 works on pediatrics and dietetics; *Publ:* doctor's thesis "Über die Bedeutung der anorganischen Salze für die Ernährung des Tieres" (The Importance of Inorganic Salts for Animal Nutrition) (1880); *Died:* 18 Mar 1937 in Leningrad.

LUNTS, Lev Natanovich (1901-1924) Russian writer and journalist; *Born:* 2 May 1901 in Petersburg; *Educ:* 1918 grad Philology Fac, Petersburg Univ; *Career:* from 1918 did postgrad research on West European lit at Petersburg Univ; 1922 first work published; member, "Serapion Brethren" lit group; *Publ: Pochemu my 'Serapionovy brat'ya'* (Why We Are the "Serapion Brethren") (1922); *V pustyne* (In the Desert) (1922); *O publitsistike i ideologii* (Interpretative Journalism and Ideology) (1922); *Na Zapad!* (Westward!) (1923); *Vne zakona. Tragediya* (Outside the Law. A Tragedy) (1923); *Bertran de Born Tragediya* (Bertrand de Borne. A Tragedy) (1923); novella *Rodina* (Homeland) (1923); play *Obez'yany idut* (The Apes Are Coming) (1923); play *Gorod Pravdy* (The City of Truth) (1924); *Died:* 8 May 1924 in Hamburg of encephalitis.

LUPPOL, Ivan Kapitonovich (1896-1943) Russian lit historian and philosopher; member, USSR Acad of Sci from 1939; CP member from 1920; *Born:* 13 Jan 1896 in Rostov-on-Don, son of a white-collar worker; *Educ:* 1919 grad Law Fac, Moscow Univ; 1932 grad Inst of Red Prof; *Career:* from 1933 corresp member, USSR Acad of Sci; 1935-40 dir, Gorky Inst of World Lit; wrote about enlightenment in France and Russia, history of Russian and for lit and historical and methodological questions; edited works of Diderot and Béranger (1934-35), Radishchev and Heine (1938-39) and *Gor'kovskiye chteniya* (Readings from Gorky) (1940); 1935 attended 1st Int Writers' Congress in Defense of Culture, Paris; arrested by State Security organs; *Publ:* "Denis Diderot" (1924); *Tvorcheskiy put' M. Gor'kogo* (Gorky's Career) (1932); *Istoriko-filosofskiye etyudy* (Historical and Philosophical Studies) (1935); *Literaturnyye etyudy* (Literary Studies) (1940), etc; *Died:* 26 May 1943 in imprisonment.

LUR'YE, Aleksandr Yudimovich (1897-1958) Obstetrician; prof; corresp member, Ukr Acad of Sci from 1939; Hon Sci Worker of Ukr SSR from 1958; CP member from 1932; *Born:* 27 Oct 1897 in Klimovichi, Mogilev Province, son of a pharmacist; *Educ:* 1921 grad Med Fac, Moscow Univ; *Career:* 1924-32 asst prof and senior lecturer, Moscow Centr Inst of Mother and Child Care; from 1930 sci dir, Ural Inst of Mother and Child Care; 1932-38 also head, Chair of Obstetrics and Gynecology, Sverdlovsk Med Inst; from 1938 head, Chair of Obstetrics and Gynecology, Kiev Med Inst; from 1949 also Chief Obstetrician and Gynecologist, Ukr Min of Health; wrote original study of maternity consultation techniques and did research on contraceptives; campaigned for widespread use of painless childbirth techniques and compiled statistics on the mortality of mothers during childbirth; trained midwives in the psychological preparation of expectant mother; devoted considerable energy to anti-cancer campaigns, introduced mass prophylatic examinations for women and devised chordotomy for advanced cancer of the womb; deleg, 8th All-Union Congress of Soviets; member, Ed Commission for Final Draft of the Sov Constitution; wrote 110 works; *Publ: Metody raboty konsul'tatsii dlya zhenshchin* (Methods of Holding Consultations for Women) (1930); ed, *Obezbolivaniye rodov* (Painless Childbirth) (1935); *Khirurgicheskaya terapiya septicheskikh poslerodovykh zabolevaniy* (The Surgical Treatment of Septic Postnatal Diseases) (1940); *Akusherkiye oshibki i materinskaya smertnost* (Obstetrical Errors and Maternal Mortality) (1947); *Profilaktika, klinika i terapiya raka matki* (The Prophylaxis, Clinical Aspects and Treatment of Cancer of the Womb) (1947); *Awards:* Stalin Prize (1941); Order of Lenin; medals; *Died:* 21 May 1958 in kiev.

LUR'YE, G. I. (pseudonym; GIRSH) (1878-1938) Govt official; CP member from 1921; *Born:* 1878; *Career:* from 1897 in revol movement; worked in Vitebsk, Mogilyov, Belostok, Minsk, Kiev and Warsaw; Warsaw Bund Org deleg at 5th RSDRP Congress; after 1917 Oct Revol worked for Odessa cooperative system; later quit Party; from 1923 worked for Centr Union of Consumer Org, Moscow and for RSFSR Pop Comrt of Educ; from 1930 retired; arrested by State Security organs; *Died:* 1938 in imprisonment.

LUR'YE, Miron Samoylovich (1894-1967) Otolaryngologist; Dr of Med from 1947; prof from 1951; *Born:* 1894 in Vologda; *Educ:* 1915-17 studied at Petrograd Psychoneurological Inst; 1920 grad Odessa Med Acad; *Career:* 1920-25 health officer in Vologda and otolaryngologist at various local hospitals; 1925 spent four months in Leningrad studying otolaryngology under Prof L. T. Levin; from same year extern, then intern, Prof L. I. Sverzhevskiy's Ear, Nose and Throat Clinic, 2nd Moscow Univ; later head, Otolaryngological Dept, Moscow City Hospital Nr 1; 1938 defended cand thesis; from 1943 asst to Prof Sverzhevskiy; from 1947 in charge of fac course on otogenic sepsis; 1951-56 head, Chair of Ear, Nose and Throat Diseases, Samarkand Med Inst and chm, Samarkand Soc of Otolaryngologists; from 1956 pensioner, but continued to serve as consultant to various med establishments in Moscow; did research on colloidal chemistry of tonsils and devised accelerated colloidal catalysis reaction for the diagnosis of chronic tonsilitis and operative indications; while working in Moscow hospitals during WW 2 studied the local application of sulfonamides for wound treatment; also studied the otolaryngological use of ovoprotein as a gen stimulant; did research on the influence of various war factors on the incidence of suppurative ear diseases among the civilian population and noted a widespread atypical susceptibility to suppurative otitis media, mastoiditis and intracranial complications; 1947-48 introduced use of casts to study the atypical healing of surgical wounds; also made a study of hypertonia in otolaryngology; wrote numerous works, including two monographs; *Publ:* coauthor, *Angina grushevidnogo sinusa* (Angina of the Pyriform Sinus) (1938), etc; *Awards:* medals "For the Defense of Moscow" and "For Outstanding Labor During the Great Fatherland War"; "Commemorative Medal for 800th Anniversary of Moscow"; *Died:* 23 Dec 1967 in Moscow.

LUR'YE, Noyakh Gershelevich (1886-1960) Jewish writer; *Born:* 24 Dec 1886 in vil Blashna, Bel, son of a tar sprayer; *Career:* worked as stevedore, builder and teacher; tramped Lith, Poland and Ukr in search of work; 1905-18 member, Bund; fought in WW 1; 1920 volunteered for Red Army; fought in campaign against Warsaw; 1911 first work published; wrote novels and plays; translator; promoted foundation of Jewish schools in Ukr SSR; member, Jewish Section, All-Ukr Union of Proletarian Writers; *Publ:* novelettes *Zavl-nogi* (Zavl-Legs); *Lesnaya tishina* (Forest Silence) (1957); collected stories and novellas *Mosty goryat* (The Bridges Are Burning) (1929); *Died:* 18 May 1960 in Moscow.

LUR'YE, Solomon Yakovlevich (1891-1964) Hellenic historian; philologist; Dr of History and Philology from 1943; prof; *Born:* 8 Jan 1891 in Mogilev; *Educ:* 1913 grad Classics Dept, Hostory and Philology Fac, Petersburg Univ; *Career:* specialized in history, lit and sci of Ancient Greece; from 1913 junior asst, Petersburg Univ; 1918-21 prof, Samara Univ; 1921-50 lecturer and researcher at a number of higher educ and research establishments in Leningrad; prof, Leningrad Univ; 1950-53 prof, Odessa Univ; 1953-64 prof, L'vov Univ; wrote a number of works on ancient Greek history, lit linguistics, epigraphy, folklore and philosophy; *Publ: Beotiyskiy soyuz* (The Beotian League) (1914); *Istoriya antichnoy obshchestvennoy mysli* (The History of Ancient Social Thought) (1929); *Teoriya beskonechno malykh u drevnikh atomistov* (The Ancient Atomists' Theory of Infinitesimals) (1935); *Demokrit* (Democritus) (1937); *Istoriya Gretsii* (The History of Greece) (Vol 1, 1940); *Arkhimed* (Archimedes) (1945); *Ocherki po istorii antichnoy nauki. Gretsiya epokhi rastsveta* (An Outline History of Ancient Science. Greece in the Golden Age) (1947); *Gerodot* (Herodotus) (1947); *Yazyk i kul'tura mikenskoy Gretsii* (The Language and Culture of Mycenian Greece) (1957); *Latynskiy yazyk kak drevneyshiy etap frantsuzskogo yazyka* (Latin as the Most Ancient Stage of French) (1959); *Neugomonnyy* (The Indefatigable) (1962); *Died:* 30 Oct 1964 in L'vov.

LUTOVINOV, Yuriy Khrisanfovich (1887-1924) Trade-union official; CP member from 1904; *Born:* 1887; *Career:* metalworker by trade; worked in Lugansk, Aleksandrovsk and Petersburg; from 1912 active in trade-union movement; Party work in various Russian cities; repeatedly subjected to reprisals by Tsarist authorities; after 1917 Oct Revol fought in Civil War on the Don and in the Ukr; member, underground CC, CP(B) Ukr; 1920 chm, Lugansk Province Exec Comt; later trade-union and govt work; from 1920 member, CC, Metalworkers' Union; Presidium member, All-Union Centr Exec Comt; Presidium member, All-Union Centr Trade-Union Council; 1920-21, during trade-union controversy, one of the leaders of the "workers' opposition"; 1921 relieved of trade-union exec work and appointed RSFSR dep trade rep in Germany; *Died:* 1924 committed suicide.

LUTSKIY, Aleksey Nikolayevich (1883-1920) Civil War Veteran; CP member from 1918 (from 1917, according to other sources); *Born:* 10 Feb 1883 in Kozlov, now Michurinsk, son of notary-public; *Educ:* 1904 grad Tiflis Mil Acad; *Career:* from 1904 in Russian Army; after 1917 Feb Revol elected to Irkutsk Sov of Mil Dep; from Aug 1917 head of counter-intelligence in right of way of Chinese-Eastern Railroad; cooperated with Bolsheviks; from Nov 1917 member, Harbin Sov; Dec 1917 appointed Sov comr for right of way Chinese-Eastern Railroad; Jan-Sept 1918 arrested after collapse of Sov regime in Siberia and Far East; Feb 1920 member, Mil Council, Provisional Govt of Maritime Oblast, Vladivostok; 5 Apr 1920 arrested along with other council members; *Died:* late May 1920 burned alive by occupation forces along with other prisoners in locomotive firebox at Murav'yovo-Amurskaya Station, now Lazo Station.

LUZIN, Nikolay Nikolayevich (1883-1950) Mathematician; member, USSR Acad of Sci from 1929; *Born:* 9 Dec 1883 in Tomsk; *Educ:* 1908 grad Moscow Univ; *Career:* from 1917 prof, Moscow Univ; 1919-21 prof, Ivanovo-Voznesensk Polytech Inst; also worked for institutes of USSR Acad of Sci: 1929-36 and 1941-50 Mathematics Inst; 1936-1950 Inst of Automation and Telemech; 1944-1950 Inst of Seismology; pioneered research in developed of metric and descriptive theory of real variable functions; also studied functions of complex variables, differential equations and differential geometry; founded Moscow mathematical school; *Publ: Sobraniye sochineniy* (Collected Works) (2 vol, 1953-58); *Integral i trigonometricheskiy ryad* (The Intregral and the Trigonometric Series) (1915); *Lektsii ob analiticheskikh mnozhestvakh i ikh primeneniyakh* (Lectures on Analytical Multiples and Their Applications) (1930), etc; *Awards:* Order of the Red Banner of Labor; *Died:* 28 Feb 1950.

L'VOV, Nikolay Nikolayevich (1867-1944) Politician; landowner; *Born:* 1867; *Career:* dep, 1st, 3rd and 4th State Dumas; 1893-1900 Saratov Marshal of Nobility; from 1899 chm, Saratov Province Zemstvo Bd; helped found League of Liberation; attended 1904 and 1905 Zemstvo Congresses; 6 June 1905 member, deputation to Tsar; 1906 member, CC, Constitutional-Democratic Party; quit Party over differences of opinion concerning agrarian problems, etc; helped found Peaceful Renewal Party; at 3rd Duma one of leaders of Progressist groups; dep chm, 4th Duma; 1917 one of leaders of Landowners' Union; after 1917 Oct Revol journalist in territory occupied by Gen Denikin; wrote anti-Sov articles; *Died:* 1944 in emigration.

L'VOV, Sergey Dmitriyevich (1879-1959) Plant physiologist and biochemist; prof from 1931; corresp member, USSR Acad of Sci from 1946; CP member from 1946; *Born:* 2 Oct 1879; *Educ:* 1911 grad Petersburg Univ; *Career:* 1911-15 asst prof, Petersburg Forestry Inst; 1915-23 asst prof, 1923-31 assoc prof, 1931-59 prof and head, Chair of Plant Physiology, Petrograd (Leningrad) Univ; did research on the metabolism of higher plants; demonstrated the role of proteins (along with hydrocarbons) in the formation of ethereal oils in aromatic plants; also studied drought-resistance, the physiological role of sucrose and the functional role of vitamin C in plant metabolism did research on the chemical aspects of the respiratory process in plants; *Publ: Osnovnyye napravleniya v istoricheskom razvitii ucheniya o dykhanii rasteniy* (Basic Trends in the Historical Development of the Theory of Plant Respiration) (1950), etc; *Awards:* Order of Lenin; medals; *Died:* 6 Jan 1959.

L'VOV, Vladimir Nikolayevich (1872-?) Politician; landowner; *Born:* 1872; *Career:* chm, Center Faction at 3rd and 4th Dumas; after 1917 Feb Revol Synod senior prosecutor for Provisional Govt; accomplice to Kornilov revolt; commissioned by Gen Headquarters to negotiate with Kerenskiy; after 1917 Oct Revol emigrated; Nov 1921 joined *Smena vekh* (Changing Landmakrs) movement; gave speech in Paris entitled *Sovetskaya vlast' v bor'be za russkuyu gosudarstvennost'* (The Soviet Regime in the Struggle for a Russian State System), published as a separate pamphlet in Berlin in 1922; 1922 returned to USSR and worked for centr econ institutions; *Died:* date and place of death unknown.

L'VOV-ROGACHEVSKIY, V. (real name: ROGACHEVSKIY, Vasiliy L'vovich) (1874-1930) Lit historian and critic; *Born:* 9 Jan 1874 in Khar'kov; *Educ:* 1900 grad Petersburg Univ; *Career:* 1895 first work published; from 1898 member, League for the Lieberation of the Working Class; after 2nd RSDRP Congress sided with Mensheviks; after 1905 Revol took liquidationist stand; 1899 began to write lit criticism; in 1900's worked for publ *Russkoye bogastvo, Obrazovaniye, Sovremennyy mir* (head, poetry dept), and *Sovremennik*, etc; from 1917 abandoned politics and concentrated on lit criticism and teaching; *Publ:* coauthor, *Russkaya literatura XX veka* (Twentieth-Century Russian Literature) (Vol 1 covering 1890-1910, 1914); *Bor'ba za zhizn'* (Life's Struggle) (1907); *Poet-prorok. Pamyati A. A. Bloka* (The Prophetic Poet. In Memory of A. A. Blok) (1921); *Russko-yevreyskaya literatura* (Russian Jewish Literature) (1222); *Leonid Andreyev. Kriticheskiy ocherk* (Leonid Andreyev. A Critical Study) (1922); *A. P. Chekhov v vospominaniyakh sovremennikov i yego pis'makh* (A. P. Chekhov in the Recollections of His Contemporaries and in his Letters) (1923); coauthor, *Rabochekrest'yanskiye pisateli. Bibliograficheskiy ukazatel'* (Worker and Peasant Writers; A Bibliographic Index) (1926); *I. S. Turgenev. Zhizn' i tvotchestvo* (The Life and Work of I. S. Turgenev) (1926); *Ocherki proletarskoy kul'tury* (Studies in Proletarian Culture) (1927); *Noveyshaya russkaya literatura* (Modern Russian Literature) (1927); *Ot usad'by k izbe. Lev Tolstoy. 1828-1928* (From Estate to Hut. Lev Tolstoy. 1828-1928) (1928); *Died:* 30 Sept 1930 in Moscow.

LYADOV (real name: MANDEL'SHTAM), Martyn Nikolayevich (Party pseudonyms: RUSALKA; MARTIN; GRIGORIY; SEMYONOVICH; SARATOVETS; LIDIN) (1872-1947) Historian; CP member from 1893; *Born:* 1872 in Moscow, son of a merchant; *Educ:* 1889 grad trade school; *Career:* worked in chemical plants; 1891 began revol work in Moscow Populist circles; 1893 helped found Moscow "Workers' Union"; 1895 staged May Day demonstration near Moscow and was arrested; 1897 exiled for five years to Verkhoyansk; 1902 completed term of exile and was sent under police surveillance to Saratov, where he joined the Saratov RSDRP Comt; 1903 emigrated; deleg, 2nd RSDRP Congress; sided with *"Iskra"* Bolsheviks; after Congress agent CC For Dept; campaigned against Mensheviks in Russia and abroad; Aug 1904 attended Geneve Bolshevik conference; member, Bureau of Bolshevik Comts; Bolshevik deleg at Amsterdam Congress of 2nd International; helped compile Bolshevik report to this congress; active in 1905-07 Revol; member, Moscow RSDRP Comt; deleg at Tammerfors Party Conference; deleg at 3rd-5th RSDRP Congresses; 1908 again emigrated; 1909 joined "Vperyod" group and lectured at "Vperyod" Party courses on Capri and in Bologna; 1911 broke with "Vperyod" group; from 1911 worked in Baku; 1917 asst chm, Baku Sov; ed, newspaper *"Izvestiya Bakinskogo Soveta"*; took Menshevik stand; 1920 moved to Moscow and was readmitted to CPSU(B); worked for Supr Sovnarkhoz, then chm, Main Sci, Museum and Art Establishments Bd; 1923-29 rector, Sverdlov Communist Univ; member, Sci Councils, Inst of Lenin and Commission for Studying and Collating Material on History of Oct Revol and Communist Party; cand member, All-Russian and USSR Centr Exec Comt; deleg at 12th-16th Party Congresses; from 1930 retired; in his latter years worked for Lit Dept, Soc of Old Bolsheviks; *Publ: Istoriya Rossiyskoy sotsial-demokraticheskoy rabochey partii* (History of the Russian Social-Democrtic Party) (3 vol, 1906); part 2, though published was confiscated by police; part 3 was confiscated by police in manuscript from; *25 let Rossiyskoy Kommunisticheskoy partii bol'shevikov* (Twenty-Five Years of the Russian Communist Party (Bolsheviks) (1923); *Kak nachala skladyvat'sya Rossiyskaya Kommunisticheskaya Partiya* (The Formation of the Russian Communist Party) (1924); memoirs of 2nd RSDRP Congress *Iz zhizni partii v 1903-07 gg.* (The Life of the Party in 1903-07) (1926); *Died:* 6 Jan 1947.

LYAKHIN, Nikolay Yefimovich (1880-1959) Govt official; revolutionary; CP member from 1902; *Born:* 10 May 1880; *Career:* fought in 1905-07 Revol and 1917 Feb and Oct Revol; 1917 deleg at All-Russian RSDRP Conference and at 7th, 8th and 9th Party Congresses; 1920 worked for All-Russian Cheka; member, Dzerzhinskiy' Special Collegium; 1921-37 various admin posts; from 1937 retired; *Died:* 7 Mar 1959.

LYAKHOV, Vladimir Platonovich (1869-1919) Mil commander; col, Russian Army; maj-gen, Denikin's Volunteer Army; helped lead resistance ot Sov regime in Northern Caucasus; *Born:* 1869; *Career:* 1906 led Cossack brigade and helped crush nat-liberation movement in Northern Persia; during WW 1 governor-gen of occupied zone along Turkish littoral of Black Sea; 1918-19 commander, 3rd Army Corps, Volunteer Army; fought Sov troops in Northern Caucasus; Feb 1919 appointed by Denikin commander in chief and commander, Terek-Daghestani Kray; Mar 1919 forced to resign after crimes and atrocities committed by the commander of his personal bodyguard were brought to light; settled near Batum; *Died:* 1919 killed by unknown assassin(s).

LYAPUNOV, Boris Mikhaylovich (1862-1943) Linguist; specialist in Slav languages; prof from 1899; member, USSR Acad of Sci from 1923; member, Polish Acad of Sci from 1930; corresp member, Bulgarian Acad of Sci from 1932; corresp member, Czech Acad of Sci from 1934; *Born:* 6 Aug 1862 in vil Bolobonova, now Gork Oblast; *Educ:* 1885 grad Fac of History and Philology, Petersburg Univ; *Career:* 1897-99 lecturer, Khar'kov Univ; 1899-1923 prof, Novorossiysk Univ, Odessa; from 1924 worked for Inst of Language and Thought and USSR Acad of Sci in Leningrad; did research on the history of the Russian language and its dialects, Old Slavonic, comparative Slavic grammar and Slavic etymology; *Publ: Issledovaniye o yazyke sinodal'nogo spiska 1-oy Novgorodskoy letopisi* (A Study of the Language of the Synodal Roll of the 1st Novgorod Chronicle) (1899); *Formy skopleniya v staroslavyanskom yazyke* (Cumulative Forms in Old Slavonic) (1905); *Iz nablyudeniy nad yazykom drevnerusskikh i staroslavyanskikh pamyat-*

nikov (Observations on the Language of Ancient Russian and Old Slavonic Documents) (1908); *Kurs lektsiy po sravnitel'noy fonetike slavyanskikh yazykov* (A Lecture Course on the Comparative Phonetics of the Slavic Languages) (1913-14); *Yedinstvo russkogo yazyka i yego narechiy* (The Unity of Russian and Its Dialcts) 1919, etc; *Died:* 22 Feb 1943.

LYASHCHENKO, Pyotr Ivanovich (1876-1955) Economist; specialist in agrarian problems and history of Sov econ; corresp member, USSR Acad of Sci from 1943; member, Ukr Acad of Sci from 1945; Hon Sci Worker of RSFSR from 1943; *Born:* 22 Oct 1876 in Saratov; *Educ:* 1899 grad Natural Sci Dept, Physics and Mathematics Fac, Petersburg Univ; 1900 grad Econ Dept, Law Fac, Petersburg Univ; *Career:* 1900 after grad retained at Chair of Agronomy, Petersburg Univ to train for prof; from 1903 assoc prof, Chair of Agric, Petersburg Univ; 1913-17 prof, Chair of Polit Econ and Statistics, Tomsk Univ; after 1917 Oct Revol continued research and teaching work; prof, Don Univ; rector, Inst of Nat Econ, Rostov-on-Don; from 1945 senior assoc, Inst of Econ, USSR Acad of Sci; wrote 120 works on agrarian problems, history of Econ and grain problems, etc; *Publ: Khlebnaya torgovlya na vnutrennikh rynkakh Yevropeyskoy Rossii* (Grain Trading on the Domestic Markets of European Russia) (1912); *Istoriya russkogo narodnogo khozyaystva* (The History of the Russian National Economy) (1927); *Istoriya narodnogo khozyaystva SSSR* (The History of the USSR National Economy) (1939), etc; *Awards:* Stalin Prize (1949); Order of the Red Banner of Labor; Badge of Hon; *Died:* 24 July 1955.

LYASHKO (real name: LYASHCHENKO), Nikolay Nikolayevich (1884-1953) Russian writer; CP member from 1928; *Born:* 19 Nov 1884 in Lebedin, Khar'kov Province, son of a soldier; *Educ:* completed parish school; *Career:* 1895 moved to Khar'kov and worked as errand boy at a coffee-house and apprentice at a confectioner's; then metal turner at plants in Khar'kov, Nikolayev, Sebastopol and Rostov-on-Don; 1901-02 active in underground workers' circles; 1903 arrested and exiled to Olonets Province for Soc-Democratic activities; 1908-11 in exile in Vologda Province; 1914 sentenced to 12 months' fortress arrest for publishing journal *"Ogni";* 1902 first work published; 1920 leading member, *Kuznitsa* (The Smithy) lit assoc; *Publ:* stories and novelettes: *V nochnuyu* (On the Night Shift) and *V mestakh otdalyonnykh* (In Remote Parts) (1904-05); *Starik s knigoy* (The Old Man and the Book) (1911); *Pyataya kamera* (Cell No 5) (1913); *Orlyonok* (The Eaglet) (1914); *Rasskaz v kandalakh* (A Tale in Fetters) (1920); *V razlom* (For Scrap) (1924); *Domennaya pech'* (The Blast Furnace) (1925); *S otaroyu* (With the Flock) (1926); *Stena desyatykh* (The Wall of Tens) (1927); *Kamen' u morya* (Stone by the Sea) (1939); *Russkiye nochi* (Russian Nights') (1943); *Nikola iz Lebedina* (Nikola from Lebedin) (1951), etc; *Sobraniye sochineniy* (Collected Works) (1926-28); *Died:* 26 Aug 1953 in Moscow

LYAVDANSKIY, Aleksandr Nikolayevich (1893-1942) Bel archeologist and historian; *Born:* 11 Sept 1893 in vil Yur'yevo, now Minsk Oblast, son of a peasant; *Educ:* 1922 grad Smolensk Branch, Moscow Archeological Inst; also grad Historical Dept, Smolensk Univ; *Career:* asst prof, Archeological Section, then assoc prof, Smolensk Univ and assoc, Smolensk State Museum; from 1927 worked for Inst of Bel Culture, then Bel Acad of Sci, Minsk; simultaneously lecturer, Bel Univ and head, Archeological Dept, Bel State Museum; during 1920's supervised systematic research on archeological relics in Bel ranging from the Paleolithic to the early Middle Ages, including the ancient cities of Polotsk, Zaslavl', Vitebsk, and Orsha and settlements near Smolensk; also supervised the compilation of an archeological map of Bel; hypothesized that the settlements of Centr Bel belonged to the ancient Baltic tribes; from 1931 sci secr, then head, Archeological Section Inst of History, Bel Acad of Sci 1934 began research for an outline history of per-class soc in Bel; 1937 arrested by NKVD and sentenced to a long term in a concentration camp; *Publ: Raskopki i arkheolegichnyya raz'vedki u Baryseuskim pavetse* (Excavations and Archeological Research in Bosisovo Uyezd) (1925); *S'lyady neolitychnay staynaki i paz'neyshykh kul'tur kalya m. Novaga-Bykhava* (Traces of a Neolithic Settlement and Later Civilizations near Novyy Bykhov) (1926); *Belaruskiya garadzishchy* (Ancient Belorussian Town Sites) (1926); *Arkheilogicheskiye pamyatniki Smolenskoy gubernii* (The Archeological Relics of Smolensk Province) (1927); *Nekotoryye dannyye o kamennom veke i kul'tury bronzovoy epokhi Smolenskoy gubernii* (Data on the Stone-age and Bronze-age Civilization in Smolensk Province) (1927); *Archeolegichnyya dos'ledy u Smalenskay guberni za 1918-28 gadov* (Archeological Research in Smolesnk Province in 1918-28 (1928); *Arkheolegichnyya dos'ledy 1926-28 gadov u BSSR i Smalenshchyne* (Aercheological Research in the Bel SSR and the Region of Smolensk in 1926-28) (1930); coauthor, *Arkheolegichnyya dos'ledy u BSSR u 1933-34 gadov* (Archeological Research in the Bel SSR in 1933-34) (1936); *Died:* 1942 in imprisonment; 1958 rehabilitated.

LYSENKO, Nikolay Konstantinovich (1865-1941) Anatomist; Dr of Med from 1896; prof from 1902; *Born:* 4 Aug 1865 in Moscow; *Educ:* 1893 grad Moscow Univ; *Career:* after grad trained for professorship at Moscow Univ; 1896 defended doctor's thesis on cerebral hernia and its treatment; from 1896 assoc prof, Chair of Topographical Anatomy, Moscow Univ; from 1902 prof, Chair of Topographical Anatomy, Med Fac, Novorossiysk Univ, Odessa; 1917 took over Chair of Narmal Anatomy; from 1923 head, Chair of Morphology and Physiology, Novorossiysk Univ; also lectured on plastic anatomy at Odessa Inst of Fine Arts; devised new methods of disarticulating the shoulder and exsecting the third ramus of the trigeminal nerve; also devised a non-liquid method of conserving anatomical specimens with their natural volume; wrote 49 works; *Publ:* doctor's thesis *Mozgovyye gryzhi (cephalocale) i ikh lecheniye* (Cerebral Hernia /Cephalocele/ and Its Treatment) (1896); *Topografiya i operativnaya khirurgiya cherepnoy polosti* (The Topography and Operative Surgery of the Cranial Cavity (1898); coauthor, *Lektsii po topograficheskoy anatomii i operativnoy khirurgii* (Lectures on Topographical Anatomy and Operative Surgery) (1908); *Obshchaya anatomiya organov dvizheniya* (The General Anatomy of the Motor Organs) (1923); *Plasticheskaya anatomiya* (Plastic Anatomy) (1925); coauthor, *Anatomo-fiziologicheskiye osnovy fizicheskoy kul'tury chelovecheskogo tela* (The Anatomical and Physiological Principles of the Physical Training of the Human Body) (1927); coauthor, *Normal'naya anatomiya cheloveka* (Normal Human Anatomy) (1943); coauthor, *Uchebnik normal'noy anatomii cheloveka* (A Textbook on Normal Human Anatomy) (1958); etc; *Died:* 1941.

LYTKIN, Fyodor Matveyevich (POLOT-BEK, Ferik Fet'ko) (1897-1918) Russian poet; revolutionary; CP member from 1917; *Born:* 2 Aug 1897 in Tulun, Irkutsk Province, son of exiled Yezid Kurd; *Educ:* studied at Irkutsk High-School and Tomsk Univ; *Career:* at Irkutsk High-School founded illegal pupils' circle led by exiled Soc-Democrats; printed and disseminated revol proclamations among pupils; 1915 first collected verse published in Irkutsk; expelled from high school for polit unreliability; 1917, while a student at Tomsk Univ, edited Bolshevik journal "Sibirskiy rabochiy"; Dec 1917 after establishment of Sov regime in Tomsk, Press Comr, Tomsk Sov; member, Tomsk Exec Comt; Feb 1918 at 2nd All-Siberian Congress of Soviets in Irkutsk elected dep chm, Centr Exec Comt of Siberian Soviets; member, Transbaykal Red Army Staff; ed, front newspaper "Krasnoarmeyets"; July 1918, after fall of Sov regime in Irkutsk, moved with other members of Centr Exec Comt of Siberian Soviets to Transbaykal and then to Amur Oblast; Sept 1918 took refuge in taiga; *Died:* Nov 1918 in action; buried in Olekminsk.

LYUBARSKIY, N. M. (1887-1938) Diplomat; CP member from 1906; *Born:* 1887; *Career:* from 1908 lived abroad; 1917 returned to Russia; deleg at 2nd All-Russian Congress of Soviets; until 1918 ed, Vladivostok Sov organ "Krasnoye znamya"; 1918-23 various dipl posts; Collegium member, Sov Propaganda Dept, Pop Comrt of For Affairs; then various ed posts; arrested by State Security organs; *Died:* 1938 in imprisonment.

LYUBAVSKIY, Matvey Kuz'mich (1860-1936) Historian; Dr of History from 1900; prof from 1901; member, USSR Acad of Sci from 1929; *Born:* 13 Aug 1860 in vil Mozhari, now Ryazan' Oblast, son of a sexton; *Educ:* 1882 grad Fac of History and Philology, Moscow Univ; *Career:* from 1901 prof, 1911-17 rector, Moscow Univ; simultaneously lecturer, Moscow Higher Women's Courses; from 1913 chm, Moscow Historical Soc of Russian Antiquities; 1917-29 corresp member, Russian Acad of Sci; as a pupil of V. O. Klyuchevskiy was classified by Sov authorities as a historian of the "bourgeios legal school"; specialzed in the history of the Grand Principality of Lith (Medieval Bel and Lith); also studied the history of Muscovite Russia and historiography; 1931-36 worked at Bashkir

Research Inst of Nat Culture, Ufa; wrote many still-valid works; *Publ: Oblastnoye deleniye i mestnoye upravleniye Litovsko-Russkogo gosudarstva ko vremeni izdaniya pervogo Litovskogo statuta* (The Regional Zoning and Local Government of the Lithuanian-Russian State at the Time of the Proclamation of the First Statute of Lithuania) (1892); *Litovsko-Russkiy seym* (The Lituanian-Russian Sejm) (1900); *Istoricheskaya geografiya Rossiya v svyazi s kolonizatsiyey* (The Historical Geography of Russia in Relation to Colonization) (1909);*Ocherk istorii Litovsko—Russkogo gosudarstva do Lyublinskoy unii vklyuchitel'no* (An Outline History of the Lithuanian-Russian State Up to and Including the Union of Lublin) (1910); *XVIII vek i Lomonosov* (Lomonosov and the 18th Century) (1912); *S. M. Solov'yov i V. O. Klyuchevskiy* (S. M. Solov'yov and V. O. Klyuchevskiy) (1913); *Lektsii po drevney russkoy istorii do kontsa XVI veka* (Lectures on Ancient Russian History Until the End of the 16th Century) (1915); *Obrazovaniye osnovnoy gosudarstvennoy territorii velikorusskoy narodnosti* (The Formation of the Basic State-Controlled Territory of the Great-Russian People) (vol 1, 1929); *Died:* 22 Nov 1936 in Ufa.

LYUBCHENKO, Arkadiy Afanas'yevich (1899-1945) Ukr writer; *Born:* 1899; *Career: 1923* first work printed; 1923-25 member, "Gart" lit assoc; from 1925 member, All-Ukr Assoc of Proletarian Lit; from 1930 member, Proletarian Lit Front assoc; then member, All-Ukr Assoc of Proletarian Writers; 1941-42 worked for Khar'kov newspaper "Novaya Ukraina"; *Publ;* novelettes: "The Stormy Path" (1925); "She" (1929); "Vetep" (1930); "The Enemy" (1930); play "The Burning Land" (1932); etc; *Died:* 1945 in Germany.

LYUBCHENKO, Panas Petrovich (1897-1937) Party and govt official; CP member from 1920; *Born:* 14 Jan 1897 in Kiev Province; *Educ:* from 1913 studied at Kiev med orderlies school; *Career:* after 1917 Feb Revol elected member, Kiev Sov of Workers' Dep; 1918 joined Ukr Socialist-Revol Party (Borot'bisty) and worked for its centr organs; 1919 Ukr Dep Pop Comr of Food; 1920, together with other Borot'bisty, joined CP(B) Ukr; 1920-21 secr, Kiev Province Comt, CP(B) Ukr; dep head, Polit Dept, 2nd Mounted Army; chm, Chernigov Province Exec Comt; 1922-26 chm, Donetsk Province Exec Comt; chm, Bd, All-Ukr Assoc of Agric Cooperatives; chm, Kiev Province Exec Comt; chm, Kiev Okrug Exec Comt; 1927-34 secr, CC, CP(B) Ukr; 1933 also first dep chm, Ukr Council of Pop Comr; 1933-37 chm, Ukr Council of Pop Comr; deleg at 15th-17th CPSU(B) Congresses; at 17th Congress elected cand member, CC, CPSU(B); deleg at 4th, 5th and 8th Conferences and 9th-13th Congresses of CP(B) Ukr; at 9th Congress of CP(B) Ukr elected cand member, at 10th-13th Congresses elected member, CC, CP(B) Ukr; 1929-34 cand Politburo member, 1934-37 Politburo member, CC, CP(B) Ukr; elected member All-Ukr and USSR Centr Exec Comt; *Awards:* Order of Lenin; *Died:* 29 Aug 1937 committed suicide during Stalin's mass purges.

LYUBIMENKO, Vladimir Nikolayevich (1873-1937) Botanist and plant physiologist; prof; corresp member, USSR Acad of Sci from 1922; member, Ukr Acad of Sci from 1929; *Born:* 16 Jan 1873 in vil Veydelovka, Voronezh Province, son of an office worker; *Edcu:* 1898 grad Petersburg Forestry Inst; *Career:* 1908-14 worked at Nikita Botanical Garden; from 1914 worked at Petersburg Botanical Garden (later Botanical Inst, USSR Acad of Sci); prof, Leningrad Univ, Leningrad Mil Med Acad and other higher educ establishments; set up laboratories of plant physiology in Kiev and Khar'kov; did research on the formation of chlorophyll in plants, the process of photosynthesis and the formation of dry matter; detected the existence of a chemical bond between proteins and chlorophyll in the living plastid and studied the relationship between yellow and green leaf pigment; interpreted chlorophyll formation as the oxidation of colorless leucophyll into "chlorophyllogen" and subsequent conversion in the presence of light into chlorophyll; in the course of research on photosynthesis concluded that this process begins at a higher light intensity in light-demanding plants than in shadephiles; established that the intensity of photosynthesis and the accumultation of matter do not always correspond; noted that photosynthesis predominated in red light and matter accumulation in blue and violet light; wrote over 200 works; *Publ: Soderzhaniye khlorofilla v khlorofil'nom zerne i energiya fotosinteza* (The Chlorophyll Content of Chlorophyll Grain and the Energy ofPhotosynthesis) (1910); *O prevrashcheniyakh pigmentov plastid v zhivoy tkani rasteniya* (The Conversion of Plastid Pigments in the Living Tissue of a Plant) (1916); *Kurs obshchey botaniki* (A Course in General Botany) (1923); *Biologiya rasteniy* (Plant Biology) (1924); *Materiya i rasteniya* (Matter and Plants) (1924); *Fotosintez i khimosintez v rastitel'nom mire* (Photosynthesis and Chemosynthesis in the Vegetable Kingdom) (1935); *Keruvannya roslinoyu* (Plant Control) (1936); *Died:* 14 Sept 1937.

LYUBIMOV, Isidor Yevstigneyevich (1882-1939) Party and govt official; CP member from 1902; *Born:* 1882, son of a peasant; *Career:* teacher by profession; 1902-06 Party work in Yaroslavl', Kineshma, Vichuga and Kostroma; deleg at 5th (London) RSDRP Congress; 1907-10 member, Moscow RSDRP Comt; after 1917 Feb Revol chm, Minsk Sov of Workers' Dep; helped organize 1st Congress of Western Front Soldiers' Dep; after 1917 Oct Revol chm, Exec Comt, Ivanovo-Voznesensk Council; 1919-20 member, Revol Mil Council special plen for supply of Turkestani Front; 1921 Presidium member, Ukr Sovnarkhoz; 1922-24 chm, Main Cotton Comt and member, Centr Asian Bureau, CC, RCP(B); 1924-26 dep chm, Moscow Sov; Presidium member, All-Russian Sovnarkhoz; from 1926 chm, Bd, Centr Union of Consumer Soc; from 1930 USSR Dep Pop Comr of For Trade; USSR trade rep in Germany; from 1932 USSR Pop Comr of Light Ind; at 14th Party Congress elected cand member, and at 15th, 16th and 17th Congresses elected member, CC, CPSU(B); arrested by State Security organs; *Died:* 1939 in imprisonment; posthumously rehabilitated.

LYUBOMIROV, Pavel Grigor'yevich (1885-1935) Historian; prof from 1920; *Born:* 22 Aug 1885; *Educ:* 1910 grad Petersburg Univ; *Career:* from 1915 assoc prof, Petrograd Univ; 1920-30 prof and head, Chair of Russian History, Saratov Univ; 1931-35 prof and assoc, State Historical Museum, Moscow Inst of Philosophy, Lit and History and Historical Records Inst; specialized in the econ history of 17th and 18th-century Russia; also studied the history of the Schism and the Old-Believers; *Publ: Ocherk istorii Nizhegorodskogo opolcheniya 1611-13 godov* (An Outline History of the Nizhniy Novgorod Guard Force, 1611-13) (1917); *Ocherki po istorii russkoy promyshlennosti XVII, XVIII i nachala XIX vekov* (Studies in the History of Russian Industry in the 17th, 18th and Early 19th Centuries) (1947), etc; *Died:* 7 Dec 1935.

LYUBOVICH, Artemiy Moiseyevich (1880-1939) Party and govt official; CP member from 1907; *Born:* 1880 in Zhitomir; *Career:* worked as telegrapher; 1914 conscripted into army and assigned to Kronstadt signals company; from 1917 member, Kronstadt RSDRP(B) Comt; deleg, 7th (Apr) All-Russian RSDRP(B) Conference and 6th RSDRP(B) Congress; chm, first amalgamated Kronstadt Sov; deleg, 1st All-Russian Congress of Soviets; Oct 1917 comr, Keksgol'm Regt which occupied Centr Telegraph Office in Petrograd; after 1917 Oct Revol ed, "Izvestiya Kronshtadtskogo soveta"; 1918-19 chm, CC, Postal and Telegraph Workers' Union; chief of communications in army; 1920-37 USSR Dep Pop Comr of Posts and Telegraphs; USSR Dep Pop Comr of Communications; then chm, Bel Gosplan; dep chm, Bel Council of Pop Comr; deleg, 15th CPSU(B) Congress and 17th CPSU(B) Conference; arrested by State Security organs; *Died:* 10 Apr 1939 in imprisonment.

M

MADDISON, Ottomar Aleksandrovich (1879-1958) Est construction eng; bridge specialist; prof from 1936; member, Est Acad of Sci from 1946; Hon Sci Worker of Est SSR from 1945; *Born:* 31 Mar 1879 in Tallinn, son of a craftsman; *Educ:* 1906 grad Petersburg Inst of Communications Eng; *Career:* 1909-17 worked for Eng Council, Russian Min of Means of Communication; 1912-14, together with N. A. Belelyubinskiy, designed and built railroad bridges across the Volga near Kazan' and Simbirsk; 1914, across the Dnieper on the Kiev-Kursk Railroad; 1916-17 across the Irtysh near Pavlodar; 1908-21 lectured at Petersburg (Petrograd) Inst of Communications Eng; 1921-36 lecturer, Tallinn Higher Technicum and founder-head, Building Materials Testing Laboratory; 1936-50 prof, dean and head of a chair, Tallin Polytech Inst; 1946-50 acad secr, Dept of Tech, Physical and Mathematical Sci, Est Acad of Sci; also dir, Inst of Building and Building Materials, Est Acad of Sci; from 1950 pensioner; developed local Est building material made from the ash of combustible shale-kuckersite; wrote numerous sci works; *Died:* 30 Dec 1958.

MAGINSKAS, Aleksas (1907-1942) Lith writer; CP member from 1929; *Born:* 16 Dec 1907 in vil Kurishkyay, Moletay Rayon, Lith; *Career:* worked as cobbler, construction worker and stevedore; 1926-29 member, underground Lith Komsomol; 1931-36 in prison in Lith; began to write in prison; published in Communist journal "Priyekalas"; early 1940 re arrested and interned in concentration camp; released after Sov annexation of Lith; 1940-41 dep ed, newspaper "Tiesa"; ed, journal "Ipagalba"; wrote verse, short stories, essays and articles; *Publ:* story "A Letter from the USSR"; "Selected Works" (1950), etc; *Died:* 25 Jan 1942 in Kraganda.

MAGOMAYEV, Muslim Magometovich (1885-1937) Azer composer and conductor; Hon Art Worker of Azer SSR from 1935; *Born:* 18 Sept 1885 in Groznyy; *Educ:* 1904 grad Gore Teachers' Seminary; *Career:* from 1905 teacher in Lenkoran'; 1911 helped found Azer Nat Musik Theater in Baku; from 1911 violinist from 1912 first conductor, above theater; after 1917 Oct Revol directed nat drama, then opera theaters; also opera conductor; 1906 began to compose music, writing music for stage shows; first Azer composer to write music for films; *Works:* opera "Shakh Ismail" (1919); Opera "Nergiz" (1935); music for shows; Dzhabarly's "In 1905" and Mamedkulizade's "The Dead Men", etc; *Died:* 28 Dec 1937; Baku Philharmonic named after him.

MAKARENKO, Anton Semyonovich (1888-1939) Experimental pedag and writer; *Born:* 13 Mar 1888 in Belopol'ye, Khar'kov Province, son of a worker; *Educ:* 1905 grad Kremenchug City College and affiliated teachers' training course; 1917 grad Poltava Teachers' Inst; *Career:* 1905-11 teacher, Kryukov Railroad School, Kremenchug; 1911-14 teacher, Dolinskaya Station Railroad School; 1916-17 militiaman; 1917-19 dir, Kryukov Railroad School; 1919-20 dir, Poltava City College; from 1920 founder-dir of a labor colony for juvenile delinquents near Poltava; 1926 moved colony to Khar'kov, where he undertook an experiment in mass self-reeducation; from 1927 also dir, OGPU Children's Commune near Khar'kov; late 1928 forced to give up post at work colony after dispute with Ukr Pop Comrt of Educ and devoted himself to work at OGPU Children's Commune, which combined secondary educ with work in ind enterprises; 1935-37 worked at NKVD-sponsored children's institutions in Kiev; 1937 moved to Moscow, where he continued teaching work and writing; *Publ: Marsh tridtsatogo goda* (The Mrach of 1930) (1932); *Pedagogicheskaya poema* (A Pedagogic Poem) (3 vol, 1933-35); *Kniga dlya roditeley* (A Book for Parents) (1937); *Flagi na bashnyakh* (Beflagged Towers) (1938); *Awards:* Order of the Red Banner of Labor; *Died:* 1 Apr 1939.

MAKARENKO, Nikolay Yemel'yanovich (1877-1936) Archeologist, ethnographer and art historian; prof from 1933; *Born:* 1877 in vil Moskalevka, now Sumy Oblast; *Educ:* 1902 grad Stiglits Ind Art College and Petersburg Archeological Inst; *Career:* 1902-19 custodian, Medieval and Weaponry Dept, Hermitage Museum and assoc, Petersburg Imperial Archeological Commission; 1920-25 dir, Kiev Museum of Occidental and Oriental Art; 1920-29 assoc, Dept of History and Philology, Ukr Acad of Sci and member, All-Ukr Archeological Comt; from 1933 assoc, Kiev Inst of Civilization and Kiev Art Inst; specialized in the history of Ukr civilization; 1934 arrested for writing letters to the CC, CP Ukr the Govt Commission for the Reconstruction of Kiev and Stalin personally to protest against the decision to demolish the Cathedral of SS Michael and Dmitriy, Kiev; exiled to Kazan', then to Siberia; *Publ: Khudozhestvennyye sokrovishcha Ermitazha* (The Art Treasures of the Hermitage) (1916); *Muzey iskusstv Ukrainskoy Akademii nauk* (The Art Museum of the Ukrainian Academy of Sciences) (1924); *Ornamentatsiya ukrainskoy knigi XVI-XVIII vekov* (Ukrainian Book Illustration in the 16th-18th Centuries) (1926); *Borzenskiye emali i staryye emali Ukrainy* (Borzna and Ancient Ukrainian Enamel-Work) (1928); *Skul'ptura i rez'ba Kiyevskoy Rusi domongol'shikh vremyon* (The Sculpture and Carving of Kievan Rus in Pre-Mongolian Times) (1930); *Mariupol'skiy mogil'nik* (The Mariupol' Burial Ground) (1933); *Died:* 1936 in imprisonment.

MAKARIY (secular name: DAYEV, Sergey) (1890-1960) Archbishop of Mozhaysk, Russian Orthodox Church; *Born:* 1890; *Educ:* 1912 grad Bethanium Theological Seminary, Moscow; *Career:* 1912 ordained priest; 1944 elevated to archpriest and appointed dean, Church of Christ's Robe, Moscow; in same year ordained monk with name of Makariy and appointed Bishop of Mozhaysk; 1951 appointed Archbishop of Mozhaysk; head, Admin Bd and Pensions Comt, Moscow Patriarchy; close aide of Patriarch Sergey and Patriarch Aleksey; *Awards:* right to wear cross on cowl; govt medal; Antiochan Order of the Holy Apostles Peter and Paul; *Died:* 13 Jan 1960.

MAKARIY (secular Name: OSIYUK, Mikhail Fyodorovich) (1884-1961) Metropolitan of Warsaw and All Poland, Polish Autocephalous Orthodox Church; *Born:* 1884; *Educ:* 1911 grad Kiev Theological Acad; *Career:* from 1917 librarian, Ukr Acad of Sci; 1945 ordained monk with rank of archpreist and name of Makariy and appointed Bishop of L'vov and Ternopol'; 1946 ordained archbishop; 1946-49 worked on merger of Uniates with Moscow Patriarchate; 1949-51 also vicar of Uzhgorod and Mukachevo Eparchy; 1949 deleg of Russian Orthodox Church to All-Union Peace Defense Conference;organized Volhynian Theological Seminary, Lutsk; 1952 took part in Zagorsk Peace Conference attended by reps of all churches and religous bodies; 1957-59 prof ordinarius, Chair of Patrology, Warsaw Orthodox Theological Seminary; *Awards:* right to wear cross on cowl (1949); *Died:* 1961.

MAKAROV, Ivan Ivanovich (1900-1940) Russian writer; *Born:* 30 Oct 1900 in vil Saltyki, Ryazan' Province, son of peasant; *Career:* 1920 first work published; portrayed peasant life and kolkhoz reforms; various works devoted to gen "socialist" reforms and "class" struggle, changes in life of urban population and even fate of "Withe emigration"; works noted for poignant narrative and profound psychological analysis; criticized by Party for portraying individualism and passiveness of peasantry; after 1936 arrested by NKVD; *Publ:* novels *Stal'nyye ryobra* (Steel Ribs) (1929); *Golubyye polya* (The Blue Fields) (1936); novelettes *Kazachiy khutor* (A Cossack Farm) (1933); *Reyd Chyornogo zhuka* (Black Beetle's Raid) (1932), etc; *Died:* 1940 in imprisonment; posthumously rehabilitated.

MAKAROV, Sergey Ivanovich (1887-1967) Revolutionary; CP member from 1905; *Born:* 1887; *Career:* from 1903 worked at "Parostroy" Locomotive Plant in Moscow for more then 30 years; 1905 active in revol movement in Moscow; member, armed workers squad; asst Party organizer, Zamoskvorech'ye Rayon; arrested and exiled for revol activities; 1917 member, plant comt; member, rayon duma; 1917 fought in Oct Revol in Moscow; 1918 member, then chm, "Parostroy" Plant Comt; then various admin posts; from 1944 retired; *Died:* 1 July 1967.

MAKHARADZE, Filipp Iyeseyevich (1868-1941) Govt official, historian, lit critic and journalist; CP member from 1891; *Born:* 21 Mar 1868 in vil Shemokmedi, Geo; *Educ:* studied at Tiflis Theological Seminary and Warsaw Veterinary Inst; *Career:* 1891 joined revol movement; did Party work in Tiflis, Astrakhan and Baku; from 1903 member, Caucasian Joint RSDRP Comt; 1905-07 took acitve part in revol; several times arrested and exiled; 1915, together with S. G. Shaumyan, led various Party org in Transcaucasus; member, RSDRP Caucasian Bureau; after 1917 Feb Revol co-founder Tiflis Sov of Workers' Dep; Apr 1917 deleg, 7th RSDRP(B) Conference; member, Caucasian Kray RSDRP(B) Comt; 1919-20 did underground Party work in Geo; from Feb 1921 chm, Geo Revol Comt; then chm, Geo Centr Exec Comt; also chm, Transcaucasian SFSR Gosplan, chm, Geo Council of Pop Comr and chm, Transcaucasian SFSR Centr Exec Comt; from 1938 Presidium chm, Geo Supr Sov; dep Presidium chm, USSR Supr Sov; deleg at 12th, 13th, 15th, 16th, 17th and 18th Party Congresses; wrote several works on history of revol movement and Bolshevikh org in Geo; dir, Inst of Marxism-Leninism, Geo Centr Exec Comt; the town Ozurgeti now bears his name; *Publ:* "Collected Works" (8 vol, 1924-31); "Georgia in the 19th Century" (1932); coauthor, "An Outline History of the Workers' and Peasants, movement in Georgia" (1932), etc; *Awards:* Order of Lenin; *Died:* 10 Dec 1941.

MAKHARADZE, G. F. (1881-1937) Govt official; *Born:* 1881; in 2nd State Duma; member, Soc-Democratic faction; member, RSDRP (Mensheviks); 1907 convicted and exiled to Siberia in trial of Soc-Democratic faction, 2nd State Duma; after 1917 Feb Revol worked for Exec Comt, Tiflis Sov of Worker's Dep; 1920 Geo govt plen in RSFSR; after establishment of of Sov regime in Geo admin work; from 1936 retired; arrested by State Security organs; *Died:* 1937 in imprisonment.

MAKHAYSKIY, Yan Vatslav Konstantinovich (pseudonyms: VOL'-SKIY, A.; MAKHAYEV) (1867-1926) Politician; founder and theorist of the "Makhayevshchina" anarchist theory, which originated in the 1900's; *Born:* 1867 in Pinchov, Kielce Province; *Career:* while a student active in Polish revol movement; early 1890's arrested while attempting to smuggle from Switzerland illegal proclamations for Lodz workers; after five years' imprisonment exiled to Vilyuysk, Yakutsk Oblast; here in 1898 wrote *Evolyutsiya sotsialdemokratii* (The Evolution of Social-Democracy), the first part of his major work *Umstvennyy rebochiy* (The Intellectual Worker), and read it to his fellow exiles; next year wrote part 2 - *Nauchnyy sotsializm* (Scientific Socialism); both parts were hectographed in Vilyuysk; "The Intellectual Worker" immediately brought him a small group of followers; 1900 arrested on his return journey to European Russia but released on payment of a surety; May 1903 re-arrested and confined in Alexandrine Centr Jail; escaped and went abroad; 1904 in Geneva published 3rd part of "The Intellectual Worker"; 1905 all three parts were published in Geneva; after 1905 Revol returned to Russia; wrote under pen-name "A. Vol'skiy"; 1906 the first two parts of "The Intellectual Worker" were legally published in Russia; 1908-17 in emigration; after 1917 Oct Revol admin work; until Feb 1926 worked for Supr Sovnarkhoz as tech ed, journal "Narodnoye khozyaystvo" (later renamed "Sotsialisticheskoye khozyaystvo"; *Publ:* books *Umstvennyy rabochiy* (The Intellectual Worker); pamphlets: *Burzhuaznaya revolyutsiya i rabocheye delo* (The Bourgeois Revolution and the Workers' Cause) (first published abroad; 1906 reprinted in Russia); *Bankrotstvo sotsializma v 19 stoletii* (The Bankruptcy of Socialism in the 19th Century); *Died:* Feb 1926.

MAKHLIN, L. D. (pseudonyms: "Misha the Typesetter"; ORLOV; SOKOLOVSKIY) (1880-1925) Trade-union official; CP member from 1920; *Born:* 1880; *Career:* from 1900 active in Soc-Democratic movement; while abroad joined "Iskry" org; 1902 "Iskra" agent in Russia; 1903 propaganda work in Yekaterinoslav; member, Yekaterinoslav RSDRP Comt; Yekaterinoslav RSDRP Comt deleg at 2nd Party Congress, where he sided with majority "Iskra" faction; after Congress joined RSDRP (Mensheviks); worked in Vilnus, Dvinsk and Petersburg; after 1905-07 Revol emigrated; 1919 returned to Russia; various trade-union and admin posts in Leningrad; *Died:* 1925.

MAKHNO, Nestor Ivanovich (1889-1934) Ukr anarchist leader and mil commander; leader of peasant anarchist movement in Southern Ukr during Civil War; *Born:* 1889 in vil Gulyay-Pole, Yekaterinoslav Province, son of a peasant; *Career:* worked as herder and farm laborer; 1905 joined underground anarchist circle in Gulyay-Pole; 1907 arrested and sentenced to hard labor for complicity in robbery of Beryansk Treasury involving the killing of a police guard; after 1917 Feb Revol released; fall 1917 returned to Gulyay-Pole and became chm of Gulyay-Pole Land Comt and Sov; early 1918, with German occupation of Ukr, retreated with Red Guard units to Sov Russia; summer 1918, after gaining the support of Lenin and Trotsky, returned to Ukr, founded a mounted peasant insurgent unit and began to fight the Germans, Hetman Skoropadskiy's admin and the major landowners; his mounted detachment expanded to include infantry, transported on light horse-drawn carts ("tachanki") fitted with machine-guns; with the sympathy and support of the local peasantry his unit easily evaded pursuit and would attack small German units; capturing their weapons; it also stopped and derailed trains and confiscated the property of the rich, distributing it among the poor peasantry; at the same time, elements of drunkenness, anti-Semitism, licentiousness and unruliness began to appear in the unit; after Petlyura's troops drove out the Germans, Makho's forces began to fight Petlyura too; after establishment of Sov regime in Southern Ukr Makhno, preaching anarch, "free communes" and "free labor councils", turned against the Sov regime, wiping out Coummunist cells, Cheka organs, food detachments and police units in the vil and small town he captured; his rank and file were attached to the slogan "Kill the Bolsheviks, the Commissars and the Jews!"; spring 1919, when Gen Denikin began his advance on the Donbass and the Ukr, formally submitted to Sov command and, as brigade comr, fought against Whitist troops; June 1919, upon capturing Aleksandrovsk, convened a Congress of Soviets of Peasants, Workers and Insurgents' Deputies, which elected the Revol Mil Council of his forces; Sov authorities banned the Congress, which opposed their policy of centralization; therupon moved with his troops into the Red Army's rear and attacked Sov units, Towns and villages; officially outlawed; withdrew to Yelizavetgrad-Voznesensk area and demoralized Whitist forces' rear; Sept 1919 defeated Denikin's cavalry in Uman' area and captured Berdyansk and Mariupol'; Nov 1919 reoccupied and plundered Yekaterinoslav; after Red Army routed Denikin's troops, again turned against Sov regime; Oct 1920, during Gen Wrangel's offensive, Sov regime made a pact with him, and his troops were moved to the Crimean Front; after routing Wrangel's forces the Red Army concentrated on crushing Makhno's rebel forces; this compaign lasted almost a year; Aug 1921 Makhno, heading one of his detachments, broke through to Rumania, where he was interned; then lived in Poland and Paris, contributing to anarchist publ; *Publ:* memoirs *Pod udarami kontrrevolyutsii* (Under the Blows of the Counterrevolution) (Paris, 1936); *Died:* 1934 of tuberculosis.

MAKOVSKIY, Vladimir Matveyevich (1870-1941) Eng; piping specialist; CP member from 1940; *Born:* 27 July 1870 in Yeysk now Krasnodar Kray; *Educ:* 1894 grad Khar'kov Technol Inst; *Career:* 1896-99 worked at Main Steam Locomotive Sheds, Khar'kov 1899 exiled to Groznyy; 1904-30 instructior, Khar'kov Mech and Machine-Building Inst, where he established a Chair of Pipe Construction in 1932; 1933 founded first Sov gas-turbine laboratory, where a 1,000-horsepower stationary gas-turbine was designed and built in 1940; *Publ: Opyt issledovaniya turbin vnutrennego sgoraniya s postoyannym davleniyem sgoreniya* (The Results of Research on Internal Combustion Turbines with Constant Combustion Pressure) (1925); *Died:* 3 June 1941.

MAKSIMOV, Aleksandr Nikolayevich (1872-1941) Ethnographer; prof from 1919; *Born:* 1 Aug 1872; *Career:* 1894 exiled to Arkhangel'sk Province for involvement in revol movement; began study of ethnography in exile; 1919-30 prof, Moscow Univ; 1919-35 bibliographer, Lenin State Library; specialized in the history of families and family groups; also studied the history of agric; adopted a highly critical approach to ethnography, avoiding broad generalizations and rejecting evolutionistic theories of family structure, group marriage, etc; compiled exhaustive bibliography on ethnography; *Publ: Chto sdelano po istorii sem'i* (What Has Been Done in the History of the Family) (1901); *Gruppovoy brak* (Group Marriage) (1908); *Teoriya rodovogo byta* (The Theory of Family Structure and Life) (1913); *Nakanune zemledeliya* (The Antecedents of Arable Farming) (1929); *Materinskoye pravo v Avstralii* (Maternal Law in Australia) (1930), etc; *Died:* 24 Apr 1941.

MAKSIMOV, K. G. (1894-1939) Govt official; CP member from 1914; *Born:* 1894; *Career:* Party work in Samara and Moscow; after 1917 Feb Revol appointed Presidium member, Moscow Sov; one of the leaders of the Bolshevik faction, Moscow Sov; 1917 member, Moscow RSDRP(B) Comt; 1917 took part in Oct Revol in Moscow; 1918-20 chm, Food Dept, Moscow Sov; then member, Revol Mil Council and extraordinary plen for supplying the armies of the Eastern Front; 1920-22 dep chm, Ural Ind Bureau, Supr Sovnarkhoz; Labor and Defense Council plen for restoration of ind in the Urals; then dep mang, Donbass coal ind; subsequently chm, Ukr Sovnarkhoz; Presidium member, USSR Sovnarkhoz; USSR Dep Pop Comr of Trade; Presidium member, All-Russian, All-Ukr and USSR Centr Exec Comts; arrested by State Security organs; *Died:* 1939 in Imprisonment.

MAKSIMOV, Nikolay Aleksandrovich (1880-1952) Plant physiologist; prof; member, USSR Acad of Sci from 1946; *Born:* 21 Mar 1880 in Moscow; *Educ:* 1902 grad Physics and Mathematics Fac, Petersburg Univ; *Career:* from 1917 prof, Tiflis Polytech Inst; then prof, Kuban' Polytech Inst; from 1921 prof, Patrograd (Leningrad) Univ; from 1935 prof, Saratov Univ; from 1943 prof, Moscow's Timiryazev Agric Acad; from 1936 senior assoc, 1946-52 dir, Inst of Plant Physiology, USSR Acad of Sci; helped found sci of ecological plant physiology; argued that death of a plant from frost occurs gradually, as ice crystals accumulate in the plant, and that the main cause of tissue death is their dehydration and mechanical damage; this theory refuted the German scientist Metz's hypothesis that plants die when the temperature drops to "a specific minimum", accompanied by the sudden death of the plant; devised a new theory to axplain drought-resistance in plants, based largely on the plant's ability to endure temporary severe dehydration of the tissues without, or with a minimum, reduction in yield; detected a number of biochemical and physiochemical changes in the properties of plant protoplasm in the case of withering; studied light-quotia, photosynthesis, respiration, development and growth of plants under differing conditions; also wrote on the history of phytophysiology; *Publ: Izbrannyye raboty po zasukhoustoychivosti i zimostoykosti rasteniy* (Selected Works on the Drought-Resistance and Winter Hardiness of Plants) (2 vol, 1952); *Kratkiy kurs fiziologii rasteniy* (A Short Course on Plant Physiology) (9th ed, 1958); *Died:* 9 May 1952.

MAKSIMOV, Stepan Maksimovich (1892-1951) Chuvash composer and music teacher; Hon Art Worker of Chuvash ASSR from 1932; CP member from 1919; *Born:* 31 Oct 1892; *Educ:* 1935 grad Prof A. N. Aleksandrov's composition class, Moscow Conservatory; *Career:* collected and arranged Chuvash musical folklore; from 1911 taught music; his pupils included F. M. Lukin, A. G. Orlov-Shuz'm, G. Ya. Khibryu, etc; collected over 2,000 Chuvash folk songs and for melodies, some of which he published in collections; *Works;* music for plays *Alan'kiy tsvetochek* (The Crimson Flower) (1948), after S. Aksakov; Gusev's *Slava* (Glory), etc; many works in other musical genres; *Died:* 26 Aug 1951.

MAKSIMOVICH, Nikolay Ivanovich (1855-1928) Hydraulic eng; prof; *Born:* 7 Mar 1855 in Kiev, son of a prof; *Educ:* 1878 grad Petersburg Inst of Means of Communication; *Career:* 1896 designed Kiev harbor; from 1900 prof, Kiev Polytech Inst; from 1918 member, Permanent Tech Council, State Construction Comt, Moscow; from 1919 head, Hydrological Section, Ukr Acad of Sci; did research on the development of the Great Dnieper, the hydrology and dydrogeography of Kiev Oblast and the electrification of the Kiev area; *Died:* 1926 in Kiev.

MAKSIMOVICH, Sergey Olimpiyevich (1876-1942) Inventor; specialist in color photography and cinematography equipment; *Born:* 17 July 1876 in Petersburg; *Educ:* 1901 grad Darmstadt (Germany) Higher Tech College; *Career:* 1901-16 worked for dispatch office; State Mint, Petersburg; 1917-30 prof, Higher Inst of Photography (later Photography and Cinematography Technicum); from 1930 with Research Inst of Geodesy, Aerial Photography and Cartography; 1909 perfected optical system of polarization densitometer; contributed to the development of trichromatic subtractive-additive films; 1909 patented his invention of trichromatic cinematography (German patent Nr 229007, 22 Dec 1909) and was the first to make a trichromatic film; 22 Dec 1912 registered a new method of producing color films (Russian license Nr 2446); 1920 pioneered use of double-sided color film and a resolving prism eliminating parallaxes; his research on sensitometry played an important role in the development of photogrphy; also invented galvanoplastic and electrotech methods and processes; *Died:* 1942 killed during the blockade of Leningrad.

MAKSIMOVSKIY, Vladimir Nikolayevich (1887-1941) Party and govt official; CP member from 1903; *Born:* 1887, son of railroad tech; *Career:* 1903-06 worked as Party propagandist and organizer in Kolomna; 1905 savagely beaten by Cossacks; 1906-07 in Geneva Party group; 1907-09 member, Moscow Okrug Party Comt; 1910 helped establish Tula Party org; 1912-13 again in Kolomna; fall 1913 ed, Bolshevik newspaper "Nash put' "; 1914 exiled to Khar'kov and placed under police surveillance; thence deported to Samara, where he was arrested and exiled to Irkutsk Province; 1917-18 secr, Moscow Oblast Exec Comt and Moscow Oblast Party Comt; 1918-19 Collegium member, NKVD; 1919-20 head, Registration and Distribution Dept, Party CC, then head, Registration and Distribution Dept, Main Polit Bd, Pop Comrt of Means of Communication; 1919-20 chm, Ryazan' Province Food Conference; 1921 dep chm, Main Polit Educ Comt, Pop Comrt of Educ; 1922 Dep Pop Comr of Educ; then worked for All-Russian Centr Exec Comt Publ House; from 1925 dean, Econ Fac, Timiryazev Agric Acad; Presidium member, Communist Acad; taught at various higher educ establishments; during Brest-Litovsk Peace Treaty controversy sided with Leftist Communist; 1920-21 active member, "Democratic Centralism" group; 1923 joined "New Opposition"; 1925 broke with opposition after 14th Party Congress; arrested by State Security organs; *Died:* 1941 in imprisonment.

MAKSUD, Makhmud Gisamutdinovich (1900-1962) Tat writer; CP member from 1919; *Born:* 15 Jan 1900 in vil Kibyakhuza, now Tat ASSR, son of a mullah; *Educ:* until 1919 studied at a seminary; grad Communist Univ of Workers of the East and Tat Dept, Moscow Univ; *Career:* during Civil War fought at front; from 1921 worked in Moscow for Tat newspaper "Young Worker"; 1918 first work printed; wrote poetry, essays, lit criticism, lit studies and did translations; during WW 2 worked for front newspaper "Sovetskiy voin" after the war wrote several books of essays; wrote studies on work of G. Tukay, G. Ibragimov, etc; translated into Tat; works of Pushkin; Turgenev's novel "Rudin"; Lev Tolstoy's *Voyna i mir* (War and Peace); Gorky's *Mat'* (Mother); Nekrasov's poems; Feuchtwanger's novel "The Oppenheim Family"; Nizami's poem "Leyli and Medzhnun"; the "Communist Manifesto"; Plekhanov's articles about art, etc; *Publ:* "Collected Works" (1952); *Died:* 10 Feb 1962 in Moscow.

MAKSUTOV, Dmitriy Dmitriyevich (1896-1964) Optician; prof from 1944; corresp member, USSR Acad of Sci from 1946; *Born:* 23 Apr 1896; *Educ:* 1913 grad Odessa Cadet Corps; 1914 grad Mil Eng College; *Career:* until 1930 worked at Pulkovo Observatory and Inst of Physics, USSR Acad of Sci; 1930-44 dir, Laboratory of Astronomical Optics, State Optical Inst, Leningrad; from 1944 prof, State Optical Inst; from 1952 assoc, Main Astronomical Observatory, USSR Acad of Sci, Pulkovo; as a specialist in astronomical optics did research on techniques for the manufacture of and testing heavy precision optical equipment and the theory and practice of preparing aspherical surfaces; *Publ: Anaberratsionnyye otrazhayushchiye poverkhnosti i sistemy i novyye sposoby ikh ispytaniya* (Anaberrational Reflecting Surfaces and Systems and New Methods of Testing Them) (1932); *Tenevyye metody issledovaniya opticheskhi sistem* (The Shadow Method of Examining Optical Systems) (1934); *Astronomicheskaya optika* (Astronomical Optics) (1946); *Izgotovleniye i islledovaniye astronomicheskoy optiki* (The Manufacture and Testing of Astronomical Optical Systems) (1948), etc; *Awards:* two Orders of Lenin; Badge of Hon; two Stalin Prizes (1941 and 1946); *Died:* 12 Aug 1964.

MAKUSHENKO (MAKUKHA-MAKUSHENKO), Ivan Semyonovich (1867-1959) Ukr painter and teacher; *Born:* 1867 in vil Lysyantsy, now Cherkassy Oblast; *Educ:* 1892-97 studied under Repin at Petersburg Acad of Arts; *Career:* 1905-19 taught at Kiev Art School; from 1934 taught at Kiev Art Inst; depicted peasants life, views and scenes of his native vil Lysyantsy; his pictures are displayed at the Kiev and L'vov Ukr Art Museums; *Works:* "Holiday in the Ukraine" (1900); "Before the Holiday" (1904); "Grandmother's Tales"; "Peasant Woman and Child" (1936); "Lirnyk" (1938);,etc: *Died:* 6 July 1955.

MALAKHOVSKIY, Bronislav Sigizmundovich (1869-1934) End and steam locomotive designer; *Born:* 1869; *Educ:* 1895 grad Petersburg Technol Inst; *Career:* worked at Sormovo Plant; 1911 designed one of best pre-Revol Russian steam locomotives for passenger trains - the 1-3-1, series C; 1914 designed the freight locomotive 0-4-0, series Vc, after 1917 Oct Revol worked in admin of various steam-locomotive plants and for Supr Sovnarkhoz, etc; *Died:* 20 Feb 1934.

MALAKHOVSKIY, Vladimir Filippovich (1894-1940) Revolutionary; helped found Red Guard in Petrograd; Cand of Historical Sci; CP member from 1911; *Born:* 1894 in Petersburg, son of a worker; *Educ:* 1930 grad History Dept, Inst of Red Prof; *Career:* from 1909 worked at Neva Shipyards and other plants in Petersburg; 1920 joined Soc-Democratic circle; 1912 founder-member, Petersburg RSDRP Comt; 1913 arrested for revol work and banished from Petersburg; 1913-14 illegal revol work in Riga and Revel (now Tallin); 1914 rearrested and banished from Estland Province; barred from 59 cities of the Russian Empire; from 1915 in Russian Army; after 1917 Feb Revol conducted Bolshevik propaganda among soldiers in the field; member, company, regt, div and corps comt; summer 1917 arrested for the third time and discharged from the army as a polit incorrigible; from Sept 1917 instructor, then Presidium member, and secr, Red Guards Staff, Vyborg Rayon of Petrograd; 25 Oct 1917 led Red Guard squads of his rayon during Bolshevik coup; from Jan 1918 helped found Red Army in Petrograd; 1918-21 head, Polit Dept, 8th Army; head, Org and Instruction Dept, Southern Front; dep mil comr, 9th Infantry Div; after Civil War trade-union and Party work; from 1930 taught and did research at Marxism courses of USSR Centr Exec Comt; at Communist Acad, Sverdlovsk Univ, Advanced Taining Inst for Teachers and Exec Personal and at Inst of History, USSR Acad of Sci; *Publ: Iz istorii Krasnoy gvardii* (A History of the Red Guards); various articles on the history of the CPSU(B) and the populist movement; *Died:* Dec 1940; buried in Moscow's Novodevich'ye Cemetery.

MALANDIN, German Kapitonovich (1894-1961) Mil commander; officer, Russian Army; army gen, Sov Army from 1948; prof; member, Sov Armed Forces Gen Staff; CP member from 1940;

Born: 15 Dec 1894 in Nolinsk, Vyatka Province, son of an office worker; *Educ:* 1915 grad Mil Cadet College; 1929 grad Frunze Mil Acad; 1937 grad Gen Stafff Acad; *Career:* from 1915 in Russian Army; commanded company in WW 1 on Southwestern and Rumanian Fronts; from Sept 1918 in Red Army; during Civil War did mil org work in rear, commanded regt and helped crush anti-Sov revolts; after Civil War chief of staff of a brigade, then div; chief of staff, Kolkhoz Corps, Separate Red Banner Far Eastern Army; 1939 dep chief of staff, Ukr Front; took part in Galician campaign; 1940-41 chief, Operations Bd, Gen Staff; 1941 chief of staff, Western Front; 1941-42 chief, Operations Bd, Staff of Western Front; 1942-43 taught at Gen Staff Acad; 1943-45 chief of Staff, 13th Army; after WW 2 chief of staff, Centr Forces Group; chief of Gen Staff and dep commander in chief of Land Forces; dep chief on Gen Staff; 1958-61 commandant, Gen Staff Acad; dep, RSFSR Supr Sov of 1955 and 1959 convocations; deleg at 22nd CPSU Congress; *Awards:* three Orders of Lenin; three Orders of the Red Banner; two Orders of Suvorov, 1st Class; Order of Kutuzov, 1st Class; Order of Suvorov, 2nd Class; Order of the Red Star; medals; *Died:* 27 Oct 1961 buried in Moscow's Novodevich'ye Cemetery.

MALEN'KIY (real name; POPOV), Aleksey Georgiyevich (1904-1947) Russian writer; *Born:* 8 Sept 1904 in Barnaul; *Career;* co-founder and ed, Novosibirsk Komsomol newspaper "Put' molodyozhi"; 1921 first work published; toured USSR, studying Siberia and Urals; wrote essays and stories about the life of miners and factory workers before the Revol; helped write histories of factories and plants; 1937 arrested by NKVD; *Publ:* essays *Tyazhyoloye dykhaniye* (Labored Breathing) (1928); *Novyy materik. Pis'ma s Vishery* (A New Continent. Letters from Vishera) (1933); unfinished novelette *Sosedi* (Neighbors) (1936); *Izbrannoye* (Selected Works) (1963); novel *Pokoriteli tundry* (Tamers of the Tundra) (1962); about socialist reforms in Siberia in 1940's (written in concentration camp); *Died:* 16 Aug 1947 in imprisonment; posthumously rehabilitated.

MALENKOV, Yemel'yan Mikhaylovich (1890-1918) Revolutionary; veteran of Oct Revol and Civil War; CP member from 1912; *Born:* 4 Aug 1890; *Career:* metalworker by trade; worked in Moscow; from 1905 in revol movement; 1915 sentenced to four years at hard labor for antiwar agitation; 1917 founded Red Guards in Moscow's Sokol'niki Rayon; member, Moscow Centr Red Guards Staff; dep, Moscow Sov of Workers' Dep; during 1917 Oct Revol commanded Red Guard squad; after revol chm,Sokol'niki Rayon Sov; 1918 fought on Western Front; then various commands and polit work with units on Eastern Front; street and railroad station in Moscow names after him; *Died:* 5 Oct 1918 in action.

MALETSKIY, A. M. (RUBINSHTEYN, A.) (1879-1937) Professional revolutionary; *Born:* 1879; *Career:* late 1890's joined revol movement; 1904 worked in Lodz, then Warsaw; deleg at 5th RSDRP Congress from Lodz org, Soc-Democratic Party of the Kingdom of Poland and Lith; 1906 elected member, Main Bd, Soc-Democratic Party of Kingdom of Poland and Lith; 1907 attended Stuttgart Congress of 2nd International; 1909 resigned from Main Bd, due to differences of opinion with the leadership of the Polish-Lithuanian Soc-Democratic Party; 1912, after split among Polish Soc-Democrats, became one of leaders of "rozlam" opposition group, which took a stand close to that of the Bolsheviks; edited its organ "Rabochaya gazeta"; 1912 attended Basel Congress of 2nd International; 1914 attended Brussels RSDRP(B) Conference; 1921 went to Russia; 1921-22 head, Information Bureau, Pop Comrt of For Affairs; 1922-25 secr, ed bd, journal "Komintern"; 1926-35 taught at higher educ establishments; then learned consultant, Dept of Philosophy, Lenin State Library; arrested by State Security Organs; *Died:* 1937 in imprisonment.

MALEVICH, Kazimir Severinovich (1878-1935) Artist; pioneer of Suprematism school; *Born:* 11 Feb 1878 in Kiev; *Educ:* 1895-96 studied at Kiev School of Painting; 1904-05 studied at Moscow College of Painting, Sculpture and Architecture; *Career:* 1898 first work exhibited at Moscow Artists' Assoc; began as Impressionist ("Spring", "The Red Hue"); 1911-12 changed to Cubist Futurism ("The Grinder"); from 1913 employed abstract art from which he called "Suprematism" - a combination of painted geometrical surfaces portrayed in motion; then designed architecture models which he called "architectons"; his Suprematism left some traces in applied arts, especially the design of ceramics and textiles; in his latter years also turned to socialist realism ("The Pioneer Camp", "The Socialist City"); *Publ:* pamphlets *Ot Sezanna do suprematizma* (From Cézanne to Suprematism); *o novykh sistemakh v iskusstve* (New Systems in Art); *Died:* 15 May 1935.

MALININ, Mikhail Sergeyevich (1899-1960) Mil commander; army gen; dep chief of Gen Staff; CP member from 1931; *Born:* 28 Dec 1899 in Kostroma Province, son of a peasant; *Educ:* 1920 grad Moscow Infantry School; 1931 grad Frunze Mil Acad; *Career:* 1912-19 apprentice, then worker, Petrograd plants; carpenter, then joiner in Kostroma province; 1919 drafted into Red Army; 1931-38 staff duties; 1938-39 lecturing work; 1939-40 chief, Operations Dept, Army staff on Sov-Finnish Front; 1940-41 chief of staff, mechanized corps; 1941-45 chief of staff, Rokossovskiy' Forces Group, 16th Army, then Bryansk, Don, Centr, Bel and 1st Bel Fronts; took part in defense of Moscow and 1941-42 winter counter-offensive; 1942 helped with encirclement and liquidation of Paulus' army at Stalingrad; 1943 fought in battle of Kursk; 1944 campaigned in Bel; 1945 took part in Berlin campaign; 1945-48 chief of staff, Soviet Occupation Forces Group in Germany; from 1948 with centr organs of Min of Armed Forces; chief, Main Staff of Land Forces; 1956 helped crush Hungarian Revolution; 1952-60 first dep chief of Gen Staff; 1952-56 cand member, CC, CPSU; 1956-60 member, CPSU Centr Auditing Commission; dep, USSR Supr Sov of 1950 and 1954 convocations; dep, RSFSR Supr Sov of 1959 convocation; *Awards:* Hero of the Sov Union (1945); four Orders of Lenin; three Orders of the Red Banner; three Orders of Suvorov; three Orders of Kutuzov; medals; *Died:* 24 Jan 1960. buried in Moscow's Novodevich'ye Cemetery.

MALINOVSKIY, P. P. (1869-1943) Govt official; CP member from 1904; *Born:* 1869; *Career:* after 1917 Oct Revol chm, Commission for the Protection of Art and Ancient Monuments, Moscow Sov of Workers' Dep; civil comr of the Kremlin; from Mar 1918 acting RSFSR Pop Comr of Republ Property; from 1921 worked for Gosplan; then worked for construction org; *Died:* 1943.

MALINOVSKIY, Rodion Yakovlevich (1898-1967) Mil commander; Ukr; Marshal of the Sov Union from 1944; USSR Min of Defense; CP member from 1926; *Born:* 23 Nov 1898 in Odessa, son of a hospital cook; *Educ:* 1930 grad Frunze Mil Acad; *Career:* prior to 1914 worked as farm laborer for landowner and as errand boy in haberdashery; 1914 secretly joined mil echelon and went to front; 1914-17 machine-gunner with 256th Yelizavetgrad Regt, then 2nd Regt of Russian Expeditionary Corps in France; twice wounded and awarded George Cross; 1917, after the corps was disbanded, worked as laborer in Belfort area, then served with For Legion of 1st Moroccan Div, winning a French mil award; 1919 traveled from Marseilles to Vladivostok, made his way Wast and joined Red Army; from 1919 machine-gun instructor, 240th Tver' Regt, 27th Infantry Div on Eastern Front; fought at Omsk, Novonikolayevsk and Mariinsk; from 1920 commanded machine-gun platoon, then commanded machine-gun section of 246th Infantry Regt; after Civil War asst commander, then commander of a battalion; 1930-37 chief of staff, 67th Cavalry Regt; served of Staffs of North Caucasian and Bel Mil Distr; chief of staff, Timoshenko's 3rd Cavalry Corps; Jan 1937-May 1938, under pseudonym Malino, mil adviser in Republ Spain; 1938-41 senior instructor, Chair of Staff Duties, Frunze Mil Acad;Mar-Aug 1941 commander, 48th Infantry Corps, Odessa Mil Distr on Southern Front; then chief of staff and commander, 6th Army; 24-Dec 1941-28 Aug 1942 commander, Southern Front; July-Aug 1942 one of two dep commanders (under Budyonnyy) North Caucasian Front; also commander, Don Operational Forces Group; Aug-Oct 1942 commander, 66th Army Oct-Nov 1942 dep commander (under Golikov), Votonezh Front; 29 Dec 1942-Jan 1943 commander, 2nd Guards Army; Dec 1942 his 2nd Guards Army played an important role in beating off the offensive of Mannstein's Forces Group which attempted to extricate Paulus' 6th Army, encircled at Stalingrad; 2 Feb-Mar 1943 commander Southern Front; Mar-20 Oct 1943 commander, Southwestern Front; 20 Oct 1943-15 May 1944 commander, 3rd Ukr Front; 1943-44 helped liberate Donbass and Western Ukr; 15 May 1944-July 1945 commander, 2nd Ukr Front; 1944-45 took part in Yassy-Kishinev operation and in liberation of Rumania, Hungary, Austria and Czechoslovakia; July-Sept 1945 commander, Trans-Baikal Front; Aug 1945 launched main offensive against Kwantung Army in Manchuria; 1946-53 commander in chief, Far Eastern Troops; 1953-56 commander, Far Eastern Mil Distr; Mar 1956-Oct 1957 commander in chief of

Land Forces and USSR First Dept Min of Defense; Oct 1957-31 Mar 1967 USSR Min of Defense; from 1959 directed modernization of Sov Armed Forces; their armament with missiles and corresponding reorganization; dep, USSR Supr Sov of 1946, 1950, 1954, 1958, 1962 and 1966 convocations; deleg at 20th-23rd Party Congresses; 1952-56 cand member, 1956-67 member, CC, CPSU; *Awards:* twice Hero of the Sov Union (1945 and 1958); Order of Victory; five Orders of Lenin; three Orders of the Red Banner; two Orders of Suvorov, 1st Class; Order of Kutuzov, 1st Class; medals; *Died:* 31 Mar 1967; his ashes are immured in the Kremlin Wall; the Mil Acad of Armed and Tank Troops is named after him.

MALINOVSKIY, Roman Vatslavovich (1876-1918) Tsarist Secret Police agent in revol movement; *Born:* 18 Mar 1876; *Career:* metalworker; 1906-10 worked in Petersburg, then in Moscow; member, workers' comt; secr, Bd, Metalworkers' Union; from 1907 voluntarily worked as police informer; 1910 recruited as secret agent by Tsarist Secret Police; 1912 at Prague RSDRP Conference elected CC member; 1912, with help of Secret Police, elected Moscow Province Workers' Curia dep to 4th State Duma; from 1913 chm, Bolshevik Duma faction; 1914, at insistance of the Police Department which feared exposure of Malinovski's undercover activities in Duma, resigned from Duma and emigrated; expelled from Party for desertion (Malinovskiy's connection with Tsarist Secret Police was discovered in June 1917); during WW 1 prisoner-of-war in Germany; 1918 went to RSFSR and surrendered to Sov authorities; tried and sentenced to death by All-Russian Centr Exec Comt Supr Tribunal; *Died:* 5 Nov 1918 excuted.

MALKIN, B. F. (1891-1938) Govt official; CP member from 1918; *Born:* 1891; *Career:* from 1908 member, Socialist-Revol Party; helped found Leftist Socialist-Revol Party (Internationalists); member, CC, Leftist Socialist-Revol Party; after 1917 Oct Revol Presidium member, All-Russian Centr Exec Comt of 5th and 6th convocation; dir, Petrograd News Agency; helped edit newspaper "Isvestiya"; 1919-21 managed Centr Agency for Distribution of Press, All-Russian Centr Exec Comt; 1919 attended 8th All-Russian RCP(B) Conference; from 1921 dir, Ural State Publ House; 1926-30chm, bd, "Mezhrabpomfil'm" Film Studios; 1930-38 dir, State Fine Arts Publ House and Art Publ House; arrested by State Security organs; *Died:* 1938 in imprisonment.

MAL'KOV, Pavel Dmitriyevich (1887-1965) Govt official; CP member from 1904; *Born:* 17 Nov 1887; *Career:* revol work among conscripts in Russian Army; distributed revol leaflets; 1907 arrested and exiled; 1910 drafted into Baltic Fleet; worked for Bolshevik underground org; 1917 member, Helsingfors Party Comt; member, Baltic Fleet Centr Party Comt; commanded sailors squad in storming of Winter Palace; from 29 Oct 1917 Smol'ny commandant; from Mar 1918 Moscow Kremlin commandant; from 1920 served in Civil War with 15th Army; then various govt and admin posts; member, All-Russian Centr Exec Comt of three convocations; from 1934 retired; *Publ;* memoirs *Zapiski komendanta Moskovkogo Kremlya* (Notes of a Moscow Kremlin Caommandant); *Pod znamenem Sovetov*(Under the Banner of the Soviets), etc; *Died:* 22 Nov 1965.

MALOV, Sergey Yefimovich (1880-1957) Turkologist; corresp member, USSR Acad of Sci from 1939; *Born:* 4 Jan 1880; *Educ:* grad Kazan' Univ; *Career:* did research on ancient and modern Turkic languages, folklore, ethnography and history of Turkic peoples; 1909-11 and 1913-15 did research on language and life of Uigurs in Western and Centr China, in Sinkiang and Kansu Provinces, and on language of Yellow Uigurs; assembled much material on modern Uigur dialects; discovered unique Old Uigur manuscript "The Sutra of Golden Luster"; deciphered, translated and published Old Turkic lit monuments; *Publ: Sutra zolotogo bleska (Suvarnaprabhâsa)* (The Suvarnaprabhâsa, or the Sutra of Golder Luster) (10 vol, 1913-17); *Pamyatniki drevnotyurkskoy pis'mennosti* (Monuments of Old Turkic Literature) (1951); *Yeniseyskaya pis'mennost' Tyurkov* (The Yenisey Literature of the Turks) (1952); *Uygurskiy yazyk. Khamiyskoye narechiye* (The Uigur Language. The Khami Dialect) (1954); *Lobnorskiy yazyk* (The Lobnor Language) (1956); *Yazyk zhyoltykh uygurov. Slovar' i grammatika* (The Language of the Yellow Uigurs. Dictionary and Grammar) (1957); *Awards:* Order of Lenin; *Died:* 6 Sept 1957.

MAL'SAGOV, Zaurbek Kurazovich (1894-1935) Ingush writer; CP member from 1925; *Born:* 3 June 1894 in Temir-Khan-Shura, now Dag ASSR, son of a mil serviceman; *Educ:* 1930 grad Leningrad Univ; *Career:* from 1923 founder-ed, first Ingush language newspaper "Serdalo"; drafted Ingush alphabet and wrote textbook on Ingush language; 1920 first work published; *Publ:* plays "Vengeance" (1927) and "The Kidnapped Bride" (1933); *Died:* 14 May 1935.

MAL'TSEV, Anatoliy Ivanovich (1909-1967) Mathematician; prof from 1944; Dr of Physics and Mathematics from 1941; member USSR Acad of Sci from 1958; Hon Sci Worker of RSFSR from 1956; *Born:* 1909, son of a worker; *Educ:* 1931 grad Moscow Univ; *Career:* 1932-38 asst prof, 1938-42 assoc prof, Ivanovo Teachers' Training Inst; 1942-59 assoc, Mathematics Inst, USSR Acad of Sci; 1959-67 assoc, Novosibirsk Inst, and prof, Inst of Mathematics, Siberian Branch, USSR Acad of Sci; 1953-58 corresp member, USSR Acad of Sci; dep USSR Supr Sov of 1954 and 1958 convocations; wrote over 50 works on mathematical logic, theory of continous groups and theory of algebraic systems; *Publ:* "Untersuchungen aus dem Gebiete der mathematischen Logik" (1936); "On the Immersion of an Algebraic Ring into a Field" (1937); *O vklyuchenii assotiativnykh sistem v gruppy* (The Inclusion of Associative Systems in Groups) (1939); *Ob odnom obshchem metode polucheniya lokal'nykh teorem teorii grupp* (A General Method of Deriving Local Group Theory Theorems) (1941); *O poluprostykh podgruppakh grupp Li* (Semi-Simple Sub-Groups of the Lie Group) (1944); "On the Theory of the Lie Group in the Large" (1945); *Ob odnom klasse odnorodnykh prostranstv* (A Class of Uniform Simple Spaces) (1949); *K obshchey teorii algebraicheskikh sistem* (The General Theory of Algebraic Systems) (1954); *Osnovy lineynoy algebry* (The Principles of Linear Algebra) (1956); *O klassakh modeley s operatsiyey porozhdeniya* (Classes of Breeding Models) (1957); *Iterativnyye algebry i mnogoobraziya Posta* (Post's Iterative Algebra and Manifolds) (1966), etc; *Awards:* Stalin Prize (1946); Lenin Prize (1964); Order of Lenin; *Died:* 7 July 1967.

MALYAROV, Dmitriy Yevgen'yevich (1903-1942) Eng; specialist in electrovacuum instruments; *Born:* 3 July 1903; *Career:* from 1921 worked at Nizniy Novgorod Radio Laboratories; from 1929 at Centr Radio Laboratories; from 1935 worked for Leningrad research inst; 1936-37, under the dir of Bonch-Bruyevich, helped design first heavy-duty multi-resonant centimeter-band magnetron; developed a number of electrovacuum instruments; a point-modulated flourescent lamp; a vacuum contact; a helium gasotron, etc; *Publ: Yavleniya avto-toka v katodnykh lampakh* (Auto-Current Phenomena in Cathode Tubes) (1925); *Polucheniye moshchnykh kolebaniy magnetronom v santimetrovom diapazone voln* (Generating Powerful Oscillations by a Magnetron in the Centimeter Wave-Band) (1940); *Died:* 16 Feb 1942.

MALYGIN, Ivan Vasil'yevich (1888-1918) Professional revolutionary; one of 26 Baku Comr; CP member from 1905; *Born:* 1888 in vil Markovo, Vladimir Province, son of a carpenter; *Career:* founded underground Party printing press; July 1907 arrested and held in Baku jail; after release worked for underground Dag Bolshevik org; June 1911 arrested and exiled from Caucasian Kray for five years; 1912 lived in vil Petrovskoye, Stavropol' Province; after 1917 Feb Revol helped found and direct Pyatigorsk Bolshevik org and Sov of Workers and Soldiers' Dep; from summer 1917 exec member, Groznyy RSDRP(B) Comt; 1917 attended two Caucasian Army Congresses in Tiflis; Dec 1917 elected member, Mil Revol Comt of Caucasian Army; Jan 1918, after Mil Revol Comt moved from Tiflis to Baku, appointed secr, Mil Revol Comt; from Apr 1918 Collegium member, Pop Comrt of Naval Affairs, Baku Council of Pop Comr; early Apr 1918 represented Baku Council at 2nd Congress of Terek Peoples, Pyatigorsk; Aug 1918, after collapse of Sov regime in Baku, arrested along with other leading Baku Bolsheviks and taken to Krasnovodsk; *Died:* 1918 executed along with 25 other Baku comr.

MALYSHEV, Ivan Stepanovich (1902-1966) Economist and statistician; Dr of Econ; CP member from 1919; *Born:* 1902 in vil Klobuchki, now Ryazan' Oblast; *Educ:* 1930 grad Plekhanov Econ Inst; 1937 completed postgrad studies at Econ Research Inst, USSR Gosplan; *Career:* 1919 volunteered for Red Army; after mil service Party secr at various ind enterprises in Moscow; from 1937 worked for Centr Statistical Bd, USSR Gosplan; 1940-53 and 1958-66 first dep chm, USSR Centr Statistical Bd; 1953-58 dep mang, USSR Council of Min; *Publ: Natsional'nyy dokhod SSSR* (The National Income of the USSR) (1953); *Balans narodnogo khozyaystva SSSR* (The Economic Balance of the USSR) (1955); *Obshchestvennyy uchyot truda i tsena pri sotsialzme* (The Social Calcualtion of Labor and Price Under Socialism) (1960); *Ekonomicheskaya nauka i khozyaystvennaya praktika* (Economic Theory and Pratice) (1964), etc: *Awards:* Order of Lenin; Order of the Red Banner of Labor; Order of the Red Star; *Died:* 29 Nov 1966.

MALYSHEV, Sergey Vasil'yevich (1877-1938) Govt official CP member, from 1902; *Born:* 1877 son of a baker; *Career:* 1891-96 worked as tradesman; 1896 began work at obukhov Plant in Petersburg; joined Marxist workers' circle; 1903 moved to Odessa and joined "Iskra" group; 1913 returned to Petersburg and became secr, "Pravda"; 1914 arrested and exiled to Siberia; Apr 1917 moved to Borovichi and became chm, Borovichi Sov; June 1917 beaten almost to death by an enraged mob for his Bolshevik activities; Oct 1917-1918 worked for Pop Comrt of Labor; 1918-20 plen, Pop Comrt of Food; 1918 organized expedtion along Volga and Kama to barter ind goods for grain with the Volga peasantry; 1920-21 member, Revol Mil Council, Turkestani Front; 1921-22 plen, Labor and Defense Council 1922 chm, Irbit, then Nizhiniy Novgorod Market Comt; chm, All-Union Bd of Trade; then worked for Centr Council of Consumer Cooperatives; *Died:* 1938.

MALYSHEV, Vyacheslav Aleksandrovich (1902-1957) Govt official; col-gen, Sov Army; CP member from 1926; *Born:* 16 Feb 1902 in Ust'-Sysol'sk, Vologda Province (now Syktyvkar, Komi ASSR), son of a teacher; *Educ:* 1934 grad Moscow Mech and Machine-Building Inst; *Career:* 1920-24 worked as a fitter in Velikiye Luki railroad shops and studied at a railroad technicum; 1924-30 fitter, Podmoskovnaya Depot, Moscow-Bel Railroad, asst railroad eng, then railroad eng; 1934-39 successively diesel locomotive designer, senior designer, dep chief designer, mang of diesel workshop, chief eng and dir, V. V. Kuybyshev Locomotive Plant, Kolomna; from Feb 1939 USSR Pop Comr of Heavy Machine-Building; 1941-52 successively USSR Pop Comr of the Tank Ind; Min of Transport Machine-Building; chm, State Comt for the Application of Advenced Technol in the Nat Econ, USSR Council of Min; and Min of Shipbuilding Ind; from 1940 dep chm, USSR Council of Pop Comr, then dep chm, USSR Council of Min and USSR Min of Heavy and Transport Machine-Building; 1953-55 USSR Min of Medium Machine-Building; from Dec 1953 also dep chm, USSR Council of Min; from Feb 1955 simultaneously chm, State Comt on New Technol, USSR Council of Min; 1939 and 1952 elected member, CC, at 18th and 19th Party Congresses; dep USSR Supr Sov; *Awards:* Hero of Socialist Labor; Stalin Prize; four Orders of Lenin; Order of Suvorov, 1st Class; Order of Kutuzov, 1st Class; medals; *Died:* 20 Feb 1957; buried on Red Square, Moscow.

MALYUTIN, Sergey Vasil'yevich (1859-1937) Painter and graphic artist; member, Petersburg Acad of Art from 1913; *Born:* 22 Sept 1859 in Moscow; *Educ:* 1886 grad Moscow College of Painting, Sculpture and Architecture; *Career:* from 1891 exhibited with Assoc of Itinerant Art Exhibitions; from 1915 member, above assoc; co-founder, Assoc of Artists of Revol Russia; 1934 gave an exhibition of his work in Moscow; also taught art; designed sets and costumes for shows; did book illustrations and portraits; *Works:* paintings "The Girl Friends" (1889); "By Stages" (1890); "Peasant and Boy" (1893); sets for operas; Sadko (1894); *Ruslan i Lyudmila* (Ruslan and Ludmila) (1902); painting "Country Fair" (1907); portraits; "M. V. Nesterov" (1913); "K. F. Yuona" (1914); portraits of the writers Veresayev, Bryusov, Furmanov, etc; paintings: "Hay-Making at the Kolkhoz" (1933); "The Artel Dinner" (1934); "Partisan" (1936); *Died:* 6 Dec 1937.

MAMALADZE, Georgiy Petrovich (1892-1937) Health official and health resort specialist; CP member; *Born:* 1892 in vil Khevi, Geo; *Educ:* 1919 grad Med Fac, Kiev Univ; *Career:* while a student engaged in revol activities; during WW 1 junior physician in Russian Army; 1919 directed a rayon hospital in Kiev Province; early 1920's organized rest homes and sanatoria in Sochi-Anap area of Black Sea littoral; from 1925 head, Geo Health Resort Bd; co-founder, Geo Inst of Health Resort Treatment; then Geo Dep Pop Comr of Health; head, Geo Red Cross Soc; exec ed, journal "Sabchota meditsina"; from 1934 Geo Pop Comr of Health; helped found; Geo Inst of Postgrad Med Training; psychoneurological outpatients' clinic; Batumi Coffein Plant, etc; chm, Transcaucasian Malaria Comt; 1937 arrested by State Security organs; *Died:* 1937 in imprisonment; posthumously rehabilitated.

MAMBETALIYEV, Moldakun (1906-1964) Party and govt official; CP member from 1930; *Born:* 1906; *Career:* for five years secr, distr Komsomol comt, then distr exec comt; inspector, Naryn Rayon Exec Comt; then exec Party and govt posts; from 1937 USSR Pop Comrt of Procurement's plen for Kir SSR; from 1946 chm, Issyk-Kul Oblast Exec Comt; 1949-61 dep chm, Kir Council of Min; 1961-62 chm, State Control Commission, Kir Council of Min; from 1962 dep chm, Party and State Control Comt; CC, CP Kir and Kir Council of Min; *Awards:* two Orders of the Red Banner of Labor; Order of the Red Star; medal "For Labor Valor" (1964); *Died:* Oct 1964.

MAMEDALIYEV, Yusif Geydarovich (1905-1961) Organic chemist; Dr of Chemistry from 1948; prof from 1934; member, Azer Acad of Sci from 1945; corresp member, USSR Acad of Sci from 1958; Hon Sci Worker of Azer SSR; CP member from 1943; *Born:* 31 Dec 1905 in Ordubad, Azer; *Educ:* 1926 grad Azer Teachers' Training Inst; 1932 grad Chemistry Fac, Moscow Univ; *Career:* 1926-29 secondary-school teacher; 1932-33 worked at Azer Agric Inst; 1933-46 worked at Azer Oil Inst; from 1934 also prof, Azer Univ; 1945-46 dir, Oil Inst, Azer Acad of Sci; 1947 chm, Tech Council, USSR Min of the Oil Ind; 1947-50 and 1958-61 pres, Azer Acad of Sci; 1950-54 acad secr, Dept of Physical and Tech Sci, Azer Acad of Sci; 1954-58 rector, Azer Univ; from 1956 member, CC, CP Azer; specialized in petroleum and gas chemistry; during WW 2 helped to build first Sov installation for the ind production of high-grade synthetic fuel components; also helped to introduce the ind synthesis of isopropyl benzene; *Publ:* coauthor; *Sovremennoye sostoyaniye khimii i tekhnologii aviatsionnykh topliv* (The Present State of the Chemistry and Technology of Aviation Fuels) (1943); *Reaktsiya alkilirovaniya v proizvodstve aviatsionnykh topliv* (The Alkalinization Reaction in the Production of Aviation Fuels) (1945); *Alkilirovaniye tsikloparafinov* (The Alkalinization of Cycloparaffins) (1955), etc; *Awards:* Stalin Prize (1948); *Died:* 15 Dec 1961.

MAMEDKULIZADE, Dzhalil (pseudonym: Molla NASREDDIN) (1866-1932) Azer writer, playwright, satirist and publicist; *Born;* 22 Feb 1866 in Nakhichevan'; *Educ:* 1887 grad Gori Teachers' Training Seminary; *Career:* 1888-98 taught in rural schools; from 1903 in Tiflis on ed staff of Azer newspaper "Russian East"; 1906-31 founded and (with brief intervals) published satirical journal "Molla Nasreddin" in Tiflis; 1920, after fall of independent Azer Republic, emigrated to Iran; 1921 returned to Sov Azer at invitation of Sov govt; continued his work to introduce new Latinized alphabet to replace Arabic alphabet; edited first Azer newspaper in new orthography "New Path"; late 19th Century first work published; headed democratic trend in Azer lit, carring on realist traditions of Akhundov; attacked religious fanaticism, gen backwardness and ignorance in his works and in satirical journal "Molla Nasreddin"; Passionately defended ideas of soc justice and equality of women; introduced new hero into Azer lit, peasant who is fanatically religious, but kind and chivalrous; his works are popular in all Moslem countries; *Publ:* novelettes "The Loss of an Ass"; "Events in Danabash Settlement" (1894); "The Letter-Box" (1903); comedy "The Dead Men" (1909); plays "My Mother's Book" (1919); "Kemancha" (1920); "The School in Danabash Village" (1921); "A Crazy Mob" (1927); "Selected Works" (1936); "Selected Writings" (1940); "Selected Works" (1959); "Selected Works" (2 vol, 1966); *Died:* 4 Jan 1932 in Baku.

MAMED'YAROV, Mamed (1875-1933) Govt official; CP member from 1902; *Born:* 1875 in vil Mashtagi, Baku Uysezd, son of a stonemason; *Career:* from 1890 driller at Baku oilfield; from late 1890's active in first Soc-Democratic circles in Baku; 1903 helped stage May Day demonstration in Baku; July 1903 helped organize Baku gen strike; 1904 revol propaganda among Azer workers; Dec 1904, during Baku gen strike, member, Strike Comt; Oct 1905 helped instigate and organize polit demonstration in Baku; helped found Baku Sov of Workers' Dep, Oct 1907 became member, Baku RSDRP(B) Comt, frequently arrested by Tsarist authorities; 1913 and 1914 helped organize polit strikes in Baku; after 1917 Revol elected Presidium member, Baku Sov; 1918 dep province comr, Baku Council of Pop Comr; Aug 1918, after collapse of Sov regime in Baku, arrested and imprisoned; ascaped from prison and continued underground party work; Apr 1920, after re-establishment of Sov regime in Baku, performed exec govt work; 1921 deleg at

10th RCP(B) Congress; 1922-27 Azer Pop Comr of Soc Security; 1922-29 directed tech propaganda in Azer oil ind; from 1929 chm, Azer Red Crescent Soc, from 1921 repeatedly elected Presidium member, Azer Centr Exec Comt; *Died:* 1933.

MAMIN, Yakov Vasil'yevich (1873-1955) Inventor; specialist in internal combustion engines; one of first Russian tractor designers; *Born:* 27 Nov 1873; *Career:* from 1885 worked at F. A. Blinov's workshops in Balakov; 1893-95 built self-propelled cart fitted with internal combustion engine - the prototype of the modern tractor; 1899-1908 designed engine with pump-operated fuel vaporization and compression ignition; from 1913 at Balakov Plant he began to produce tractors fitted with the first 25-45 hp compression-ignition engines; from 1937 assoc, Chelyabinsk Inst for Mechanization and Electrification of Agric; where he designed various engines and instruments, *Died:* 6 Aug 1955.

MAMONTOV, Konstantin Konstantinovich (1869-1920) Whitist mil commander; col, Russian Army; cavalry commander; *Born:* 1896; *Career:* after Oct Revol made his way to the Don; 1918 helped Gen Krasnov muster his Whitist forces; 1918-19 commanded Cossack corps; Aug-Sept 1919 led his corps in a raid in the Red Army's rear, in the course of which he took Tambov, Kozlov (Michurinsk), Yelets and Gryazi - now known as the Mamontov Raid; his campaign caused panic in Moscow but, burdened by its spoils of war, his corps could no develop its success, lost its maneuvrability and after some unsuccessful battles in Oct-Nov 1919 in the Voronezh area crossed the front-line and withdrew to the Don; *Died:* 1920.

MAMONTOV, Yakov Andreyevich (1888-1940) Ukr writer, playwright and theater critic; *Born:* 22 Oct 1888 in vil Strelichnyy, now Sumy Oblast, son of a peasant; *Educ:* 1914 grad Moscow Business Inst; *Career:* from 1920 various research and teaching posts at Khar'kov higher educ and research institutions; 1907 first work published; passed from symbolism to modernism and realism, with traces of socialist realism; attacked Ukr "bourgeois nationalism"; wrote about socialist reforms in vil and formations of new Sov intelligentsia; adapted for stage works of Shevchenko, Kotsyubinskiy and Franko; wrote theoretical and critical studies of drama and theater; *Publ:* comedies and Plays: "The Pink Spider Web" (1926); "Republic on Wheels" (1927); "Princess Victoriy" (1928); "His Private Property" (1929); "His Own Boss" (1936); collected verse "Garlands Over the Water" (1924); essays "At the Theatrical Crossroads" (1925); "Dramatic Works" (1927); "I. Tobilevich's Dramatic Works" (1931); "Writings" (1932); *Died:* 31 Jan 1940 in Khar'kov.

MAMONTOV, Yefin Mefod'yevich (1885-1922) Partisan leader in the Altay; *Born:* 1885; in Altay Province, son of a peasant;*Career:* 1910-18 in Russian Army; fought in WW 1; 1917 member, soldiers' comts; deleg, 1st All-Russian Congress of Soviets; 1918 returned from front and helped found Soviets in Altay villages; early 1919 founded partisan unit which launched raids against Admiral Kolchak's army; Sept-Oct 1919 elected commander, partisan army in Western Siberia; Nov-Dec 1919 partisans cooperated with Red Army to liberate Slavgorod, Kamen', Pavlodar, Semipalatinsk and Barnaul; after rout of Kolchak's forces Mamontov fought against Wrangel's troops at head of volunteer Siberian brigade of ex-partisans; subsequently returned to Altay; *Died:* 25 Feb 1922 killed in vil Vlashikha, near Barnaul.

MANANDYAN, Yakov Amazaspovich (1873-1952) Arm historian; prof from 1926; member, USSR Acad of Sci from 1939; member, Arm Acad of Sci from 1943; Hon Sci Worker of Arm SSR from 1935; *Born:* 22 Nov 1873 in Akhaltsikhe, Geo; *Educ:* 1897 grad Philosophy Dept, Jena Univ; 1898 grad Oriental Fac, Petersburg Univ as an external student; 1909 grad Law Fac, Yur'yev (Tartu) Univ; *Career:* from 1926 prof of ancient Arm history; wrote numerous works on the soc and econ history of anvient Arm, philology, metrology and historical geography; *Publ: O torgovle i gorodakh Armenii v svyazi s mirovoy torgovley drevnykh vremyon* (Armenian Trade and Towns in Relation to World Trade in Ancient Times) (1930); *Feodalizm v drevney Armenii* (Feudalism in Ancient Armenia) (1934); *Tigran II i Rim* (Tigranus II and Rome) (1941); *Kriticheskiy obzor istorii armyanskogo naroda* (A Critical Survey of the History of the Armanian People) (3 vol, 1945-52); *Died:* 4 Feb 1952.

MANDEL'SHTAM (Party name: ODISSEY), Aleksandr Vladimirovich (1878-1929) Party official; CP member from 1902; *Born:* 1878; *Career:* until 1904 helped smuggle Party lit, then agitator and propagandist; from 1905 member, Kiev, Odessa, Petersburg and Ivanovo-Voznesensk Party Comt; during 1905 Revol member, Moscow Okrug Party Comt; helped plan Dec 1905 uprising; then worked in Kiev; from Oct 1906 in Moscow; 1907 attended London Party Congress; 1906-10 member, Moscow Party Comt; 1911 exiled for three year to Narym; 1914-17 in Russian Army; after 1917 Feb Revol member, Minsk Exec Comt; during 1917 Oct Revol member, Basmannyy Rayon Revol Comt, Moscow; 1917-19 staff comr, Moscow Mil Distr; then served with 3rd and 7th Armies; head, Agitation Dept, Main Polit Bd, Pop Comrt of Means of Communication; 1920-21 ed, newspaper "Gudok"; 1921-22 secr, Khamovniki Rayon Party Comt,Moscow; 1925-27 ed, journal "Molodaya gvardiya"; from 1927 worked for Pop Comrt of Educ; *Died:* 1929.

MANDEL'SHTAM, Leonid Isaakovich (1879-1944) Physicist; prof; member, USSR Acad of Sci from 1929; *Born:* 4 May 1879 in Odessa; *Educ:* 1879-98 studied at Novorossiysk Univ, whence he was expelled for participating in student riots; studied at Strasburg Univ; *Career:* from 1918 prof, Odessa Polytech Inst; from 1925 prof, Moscow Univ; specialized in optics, theory of oscillation and radio physics; studied phenomenon of light scattering; 1907, in his work *Ob opticheski odnorodnykh i mutnykh sredakh* (Optically Uniform and Opaque Media), disproved the English physicist John Rale's theory of the molecular scattering of light and established that a medium must be non-uniform in order to scatter light; then proved that the molecular scattering of monochromatic light must be accompained by a change in its wavelength; 1928, in collaboration with G. S. Landsberg (independently of the Indian physicist Raman), his study of the spectral composition of scattered light led to the discovery of the combination scattering of light; his study of oscillation theory led to a new trend, the so-called non-linear oscillation theory, covering the excitation of auto-oscillation and various oscillation conversions, which was widely used in various fields of eng, radio eng, automation, etc; together with N. D. Papaleksi, discovered and studied a number of new phenomena connected with non-linear oscillation (e. g., autoparametric and combination excitation); devised the parametric generator for stimulatin electr oscillation; 1937 he and Papleksi used their own radiointerference methods to revolve a number of problems connected with the dissemination of radio waves over the Earth's surface; proposed the idea that distances could be precisely measured by using radio wave techniques and together with Papaleksi invented radiointerference range-finders which were widely used in geodesy and hydrography; also did research on statistical and quantum physics and the theory of relativity; did considerable teaching work; 1945 the USSR Acad of Sci established two Mandel'shtam prizes for the best works in radio physics; *Publ: Polnoye sobraniye trudov* (Complete Collected Works) (5 vol, 1947-55); *Awards:* Mendeleyev Prize (1936); Stalin Prize (1942); *Died:* 7 Nov 1944.

MANDEL'SHTAM, Nikolay Nikolayevich (1879-1929) Party official; CP member 1902-17 and from 1919; *Born:* 1879; *Career:* started work at age 14; 1902 joined RSDRP; member, Voronezh RSDRP Comt; 1902-08 professional Party work; after RSDRP schism joined Bolsheviks; worked in Vilnius; member, Northwestern, then Riga and Yekaterinoslav RSDRP(B) Comt; 1905-07 member, Moscow RSDRP(B) Comt and exec organizer, Moscow's Railroad Rayon; worked as propagandist; 1908 unskilled factory worker; 1910-13 in emigration; 1913-17 electrician; arrested four times; spent 18 month in prison and two years in exile; escaped twice; after 1917 Feb Revol member, Exec Comt and head, Labor Dept, Nikolayev Sov, Dec 1917 sided with internationalists; 1917-20 worked for Metalworkers' Union; late 1919 returned to Bolshevik fold; 1920 dep chm, Main Bd of Electr Eng Ind; 1921 secr, Turkastani Bureau, CC, RCP(B) and secr, Turkm Commission, All-Russian Centr Exec Comt; from 1924 head, Org Dept, Moscow's Bauman Rayon Party Comt; then dep head, Org Dept, Moscow Party Comt; 1926-28 head, Agitation and Propaganda Dept, Moscow Party Comt; *Died:* 1929.

MANDEL'SHTAM, Osip Emil'yevich (1891-1938) Russian poet; *Born:* 15 Jan 1891 in Warsaw, son of a merchant; *Educ:* 1907 grad Tenishev College, Petersburg; studied ancient French language and lit at Petersburg Univ; *Career:* 1909 joined circle of poets who contributed to journal "Appolon"; 1910 first work published; 1912 joined Acmeist movement, of which he became one of the foremost proponents; 1916 began introducing lyrical elements into his poetry; 1918-21 worked in various cultural and educ establishments and spent some time in the Crimea and Geo; 1922 moved to Moscow; took and independent stand in the conflicts of local lit groups; 1934 arrested by NKVD but later released; 1938 arrested again; *Publ:* Collected verse *Kamen'* (The Stone) 3rd ed, (1923); "Tristia" (1922); *O prirode slova* (The Nature of Words) (1922); *Vtoraya kniga* (The Second Book) (1923); children's verse "Primus" (1925); *O poezii* (On Poetry) (1928); *Stikhotvoreniya* (Verse) (1928); *Razgovor o Dante* (Talking of Dante) (1933); *Died:* 27 Dec 1938 in imprisonment.

MANDEL'SHTAM, Roza Semyonovna (1875-1953) Russian bibliographer; *Born:* 29 Nov 1875 in Rostov-on-Don; *Educ:* grad Saratov Inst of Educ; *Career:* from 1922 assoc, State Acad of Arts; 1925-33, together with B. P. Koz'min, published series of manuals *Revolyutsionnoye dvizheniye v Rossii XVII-XX vekov* (The Revolutionary Movement in Russia in the 17th-20th Centuries); 1926, together with V. L. L'vov-Rogachevskiy, published bibliographical guide *Rabochekrest'yanskiye pisateli* (Worker and Peasant Writers); 1933, together with L. S. Mandel'shtam, compiled bibliography *Proletariat, fabriki i zavody tsarskoy Rossii i SSSR v Khudozhestvennoy literature* (The Proletariat, Factories and Plants of Tsarist Russian and the USSR in Fiction); also compiled bibliography of Radishchev and Lunacharskiy; 1953, together with L. S. Mandel'shtam, published *Materialy dlya bibliografii opublikovannykh pisem Ogaryova* (Material for the Bibliography of Ogaryov's Published Letters) and *Neuchtyonnyye publikatsii pisem Gertsena* (Unconsidered Publications of Herzen's Letters); coauthored *Bibliografiya pisem k Gertsenu i Ogaryovu, opublikovannykh do 1955 goda* (A Bibliography of Letters to Herzen and Ogaryov, Published Prior to 1955), published posthumously in 1955; among his unpublished works was his annotated manuscript *Bibliografiya russkoy memuarnoy i espistolyarnoy literatury 1887-1917* (A Bibliography of Russian Memoir and Epistolic Literature 1887-1917); *Publ: Bibliografiya Radishcheva* (Bibliography of Radishchev) (1926); *Knigi A. V. Lunacharskogo. Bibliograficheskiy ukazatel'* (The Books of A. V. Lunacharskiy. A Bibliographic Guide) (1926); *Khudozhestvennaya literatura v otsenke russkoy marksistskoy kritiki* (Fiction as Assessed by Marxist Critics) (1928); *Died:* 7 June 1953 in Moscow.

MANDEL'SHTAM, Sergey Osipovich (1896-1934) Office worker; CP member, *Born:* 1896; *Career:* expelled from CP for siding with Zinov'yevist opposition; reinstated after publicly expressing complete solidarity with policy of Party and Sov regime; Dec 1934 arrested and tried for complicity in assassination of Poliburo member and secr, CC, CPSU(B) S. M. Kirov on 1 Dec 1934 in Leningrad; 29 Dec 1934 sentenced to death with co-defendants by Assizes of USSR Supr Court's Mil Collegium; *Died:* 29 Dec 1934 executed in Leningrad.

MANIZER, Matvey Genrikhovich (1891-1966) Sculptor; Pop Artist of USSR from 1958; Pop Artist of RSFSR; Hon Art Worker of Ukr and Bel SSR; member, and from 1947 vice-pres, USSR Acad of Arts; CP member from 1941; *Born:* 17 Mar 1891 in Petersburg, son of an artist; *Educ:* 1914 grad Mathematics Fac, Petersburg Univ; 1916 grad Petersburg Acad of Arts; *Works:* monumental bust of Karl Marx for Kaluga (1921); sculptural portraits of the composer Glazunov (1919), the singer I. V. Yershov (1920), etc; Leningrad monument to V. Volodarskiy (1923-25); Monument to the Victimes of 9 January 1905 (1929-30), unveiled 1931 in Obukhov, near Leningrad; monuments to V. I. Chapayev in Kuybyshev (1932) and Shevchenko in Khar'kov (1935); embodied Lenin in various sculptures: in design for monument at Leningrad's Finland Station (1924); in two statues (1925-26); repeated in the monuments for Pushkin, Kirovograd, Kuybyshev and Khabarovsk; in monuments in Petrozavodsk and Minsk (1933) and Ul'yanovsk (1940); in a bust (1946); in the design of a monument for Moscow (1950), etc; similarly, did many statues of Stalin, including statues in busts in 1937, 1938, 1946, 1949 and 1950; monumental decorative series of sculpture for subway stations: twenty figures at Revolution Square Station (1936-39), in collaboration with a team of his pupils; and sculptures at Izmailovskaya Station (1944); statue of Zoya Kosmodem'yanskaya (1942); monumental statue in Tambov (1947) and Leningrad (1951); monumental portrait busts of Heroes of the Sov Union P. M. Kamozin (1950), A. I. Pokryshkin (1949); portrait busts of Russian scientists Mendeleyev, Pavlov, Michurin and Zhukovkiy, for Moscow Univ Building (1952); Pavlov monument in Ryazan' (1949); monuments to Gen Kharitonov in Shcherbakov (1949) and I. V. Michurin in Michurinsk (1950); co-sculpted multi-figure composition "The Struggle for Peace" (1950); *Publ: Skul'ptor o svoyey rabote* (A Sculptor on His Work) (2 vol, 1940-52); *Awards:* three Stalin Prize (1941, 1943 and 1950); Order of the Red Star; medals; *Died:* 20 Dec 1966.

MAN'KOVSKIY, Boris Nikitich (1883-1962) Neuropathologist; Dr of Med; prof; member, USSR Acad of Med Sci from 1944; Hon Sci Worker of Ukr SSR from 1942; *Born:* 23 Mar 1883 in Kozelets, now Chernigov Oblast; *Educ:* 1910 grad Kiev Univ; *Career:* 1904 expelled from univ for involvement in student riots; 1910-22 intern, asst prof, then assoc prof, Chair of Nervous Diseases, Kiev Univ; 1922-41 head, Chair of Nervous Diseases, Kiev Inst of Postgrad Med Training; 1922-62 also head, Chair of Nervous diseases, Kiev Med Inst; 1931-50 founder and sci dir, Kiev Psychneurological Research Inst and associated Blastomatosis Clinic; simultaneously dir, Clinic of Nervous Diseases, Kiev Oct Municipal Hospital; also dep chm, Ukr and Kiev Soc of Neuropathologists and Psychiatrists; did research on the clinical aspects and pathomorphology of diseases of the spinal cord, metastatic cancer of the centr nervous system, secondary neuroinfections from measles, typhoid, epiphyseal tumors, etc; described nasal liquor in brain tumors; foundermang, journal "Sovremennaya psikhonevrologiya"; member, ed council, journals "Nevropatologiya i psikhiatriya imeni S. S. Korsakova" and "Klinicheskaya meditsina"; co-ed, journal "Vrachebnoye delo"; co-ed, *Bol'shaya meditsinskaya entsiklopediya* (Large Medical Encyclopedia) (2nd ed); chm, Learned Med Council, Ukr Min of Health, dep, Kiev City Sov; wrote some 150 works; *Publ: Mnozhynnyy dyseminovanyy skleroz* (Encephalomyelitis diseminata scleroticans periaxilis) (1941); *Patogenez nevroinfektsionnykh zabolevaniy i reaktivnost' organizma* (The Pathogenesis of Nerve Infections and the Body's Reactivity) (1950), etc; *Awards:* two Orders of Lenin; Order of the Red Banner of Labor; Badge of Honor; *Died:* 24 Nov 1962.

MANTSEV, Vasiliy Nikolayevich (1888-1939) Govt official; CP member from 1906; *Born:* 1888; *Educ:* from 1905 studied at Moscow Univ; 1911-12 studied at Party school at Longjumeau, near Paris; studied at Grenoble Univ; *Career:* 1905 joined revol movement; 1905 helped organize strikes and Moscow uprising; from 1906 secr, Moscow Oblast Party Bureau; subjected to reprisals by Tsarist authorities; 1911 exiled to vil Nikol'skoye, Vladimir Province, whence he fled to France; Bureau member, Paris "Rabochaya gazeta" circle; also secr, Paris Section of For Party Organizations; 1913 returned to Russia and engaged in underground work; Feb 1917 in Rostov-Yaroslavsk with 206th Infantry Reserve Regt; helped prepare 1917 Oct Revol in Rostov-Yaroslavsk; secr, Moscow Oblast Party Bureau; from 1918 Party and govt work in Moscow; summer 1919 chm, Moscow Cheka; late 1919 head, Centr Bd of Ukr Cheka and Special Depts; simultaneously Collegium member, All-Russian Cheka; head, Special Dept, Southeastern and Southern (Crimean) Fronts, and chief of rear areas; from 1923 worked for Workers and Peasants' Inspection in Moscow, then for Supr Sovnarkhoz; from 1927 USSR Dep Pop Comr of Finance; from 1936 dep chm, RSFSR Supr Court; arrested by State Security organs; *Died:* 1939 in imprisonment.

MANUIL'SKIY, Dmitriy Zakharovich (Party names: MEFODIY; IONYCH; FOMA; Ivan BEZRABOTNYY) (1883-1959) Party and govt official; CP member from 1903; *Born:* 3 Oct 1883 in vil Svyatets, Volhynian Province, son of a district clerk or peasant origin; *Educ:* studied at Petersburg Univ; 1911 grad Law Fac; Sorbonne Univ; *Career:* 1905 member, Bd of Agitators, Petersburg RSDRP Comt; 1906 helped organize Kronstadt Mutiny, then Sveaborg Mutiny; arrested for this and sentenced to five years' exile in Yakutsk but escaped from Volodga Prison and fled to Kiev; joined Kiev RSDRP Comt and worked for Party Mil Org; Fall 1907 emigrated to France; joined "Vperyod" group; 1912-13 underground work in Petersburg and Moscow, then returned to France; May 1917 returned to Russia and joined "Mezhrayontsy" org; deleg at 6th RSDRP(B) Congress; joined RSDRP(B) together with other "Mezhrayontsy"; during 1917 Oct Revol comr of Krasnoye Selo during fighting with Krasnov's troops; from Dec 1917 Collegium member, Pop Comrt of Food; Apr 1918 sent by RSFSR govt to Ukr to negotiate with hetman govt; Jan 1919 headed Sov Red Cross mission in France; 1920 member, Sov deleg at peace talks with Poland in Riga; 1918 sent by CC, RCP(B) to Ukr and appointed member, All-Ukr Revol Comt and Ukr Pop Comr of Agric; July-Aug 1920 attended 2nd Comintern Congress; Dec 1921 elected first secr, CC, CP(B) Ukr; 1920-23 and 1949-52 Politburo member, CC, CP(B) Ukr; 1922 worked for Comintern; from July 1924 Presidium member, Comintern Exec Comt; 1928-43 secr Comintern Exec Comt; headed CPSU(B) deleg in this org; at 17th (1934) and 18th (1939) CPSU(B) Congresses presented report of CPSU(B) delegations' activity in Comintern Exec Comt; 1942-44 worked for CC, CPSU(B) and Red Army Main Polit Bd; from July 1944 dep chm, Ukr Council of Pop Comr and Ukr Pop Comr of For Affairs; 1946-53 dep chm, Ukr Council of Min; 1945 headed Ukr deleg at San Francisco Conference; 1946 headed Ukr Deleg at Paris Peace Conference; attended first four sessions of UN Gen Assembly; 1948 Ukr permanent rep in UN Security Council; held rank of amb extraordinary and plen; 1923-39 member, CC, CPSU(B); member, Comintern Exec Comt from 1921; member, USSR Centr Exec Comt; dep USSR Supr Sov; wrote numerous articles and studies of workers and Communist movement; wrote memoirs of his meetings with Lenin; Dr of Historical Sci; prof; from 1944 member, Ukr Acad of Sci; 1953 contracted serious illnes and retired on pension; *Publ: Itogi V Vsemirnogo kongressa Kominterna* (The Results of the 5th World Comintern Congress) (1924); *Ekonomicherkiy krizis i revolyusionnyy podyom* (The Economic Crisis and the Revolutionary Upsurge) (1930); *God posle VI kongressa* (A Year After the 6th Congress) (1929); *Itogi sotsialisticheskogo stroitel'stva v SSSR* (The Results of the Building of Socialism in the USSR) (1935); *Itogi VII Kongressa Kommunisticheskogo Internatsionala* (The Results of the 7th Communist International Congress) (1935); *Awards:* three Orders of Lenin; Order of the Red Star; medals; *Died:* 22 Feb 1959 in Kiev.

MARDZHANISHVILI (real name: MARDZHANOV), Konstantin (Kote) Aleksandrovich (1872-1933) Stage dir; Pop Artiste of Geo from 1931; *Born:* 9 June 1872 in vil Kvareli, Geo; *Career:* from 1893 actor, Kutaisi Theater; from 1894 in Tiflis; 1896-97 again in Kutaisi; from 1897 worked for Russian Theaters in Kerch', Vyatka, Tambov, Baku, Tashkent, etc; 1905-07 engaged in revol work; close friend of Gorky's 1904-05 stage dir, Nezlobin Theater, Riga; 1906-07 organized and directed Khar'kov Actors Assoc for defence of actors' rights; 1907-08 with Duvan-Tortsov's company in Kiev; gave series of lecturer shows young people; 1908-09 with Bagrov's company in Odessa; expelled from Odessa for allowing the performance of the "Marseillaise" in his production of *Gibel' 'Nadezhdy'* (The End of the "Nadezhda"); 1909 chief stage dir, Nezlobin Theater, Moscow; together with A. I. Yuzhin, founded Geo Drama Studio; 1910-13 at Moscow Arts Theater; 1913 founded Free Theater in Moscow; 1914-15, after closure of Free Theater, directed a theater in Rostov-on-Don; 1916-17 dir, Bouffe Theater, Petrograd; after 1917 Oct Revol helped establish Sov theater; 1919 in Kiev; from 1920 in Petrograd; produced massive theater shows lauding the revol; directed Free Comedy Theater and Comic Opera Theater; 1922 returned to Geo and directed Rustaveli Theater; 1928 founded in Kutaisi 2nd Geo State Theater (transferred to Tbilisi in 1930); in his latter years worked at Moscow theaters; 1931 at Korsh Theater; 1933 at Maly Theater and Moscow Operetta Theater; 1916-28 film work; *Productions: Dyadya Vanya* (Uncle Vanya) (1901); *Na dne* (The Lower Depths); *Deti solntsa* (Children of the Son); *Dachniki* (The Summer Residents) (1905); *Gibel' 'Nadezhdy'* (The End of the "Nadezhda") (1909); *Brat'ya Karamazovy* (The Brothers Karamazov) after Dostoyevsky (1910); Hamsun's "In Life's Clutches" (1911); Ibsen's "Per Gynt" (1912); Offenbach's Die schöne Helena" (1913); Mozarts "Entführung aus dem Serail"; Donizetti's "Don Pasquale"; Eristavi's "Partition" (1923); Arakishvili's "The Tale of Shota Rustaveli" (1923); "The Merry Wives of Windsor"(1924); "Lohengrin" (1924); Leoncavallo's "I Pagliacci" (1924); "Hamlet" (1925); Arakishvili's "Life Is a Joy" (1927); Suppe's "Bocaccio" (1927); Dadiani's "Right to the Heart" (1928); "Uriel' Akosta" (1929); "The Roar of the Rails" (1929); Kirshon's *Khleb* (Bread) (1931); Kutateli's "Midnight Past" (1929); Kulish's *Komuna v stepi* (The Commune in the Steppe) (1930); *Skaz ob Arsene* (The Rale of Arsene) (1931); Olesha's *Tri tolstyaka* (Three Fat Men) (1931); Pogodin's *Poema o topore* (The Poem of the Axe) (1931); Mikitenko's "Shine, Stars!" (1931); Ibsen's "The Master-Builder" (1931); Rossini's "William Tell" (1931); *strakh* (Fear) (1932); "Othello" (1932); "Don Carlos" (1933); Strauss' "Die Fledermaus" (1933), etc; *Publ: Tvorcheskoye nasalediye. Vospominqniya, stat'i i doklady* (Creative Legacy. Memoirs, Articles and Reports) (1958); *Memuary i stat'i* (Memoirs and Articles) (1947); *Died:* 17 Apr 1933 in Moscow.

MARGULYAN, Arnol'd Evad'yevich (1879-1950) Conductor and music teacher; Pop Artiste of Ukr SSR from 1932 and RSFSR from 1944; CP member from 1945; *Born:* 1 Apr 1879 in Kiev; *Career:* from 1896 violinist with Odessa Opera Orchestra; 1902-12 conductor, theaters in Petersburg, Kiev, Khar'kov, Odessa, Tiflis, Riga, Siberia and Far East 1912-18 conductor, Petrograd Musical Drama Theater; 1937-50 artistic dir and chief conductor, Sverdlovsk Opera and Ballet Theater; from 1942 prof, Sverdlovsk Conservatory; staged a number of plays, among them "Othello"; *Awards:* Stalin Prize (1946); *Died:* 15 July 1950 in Sverdlovsk.

MARIYENGOF, Anatoliy Borisovich (1897-1962) Russian poet and playwright; *Born:* 24 June 1897 in Nizhniy Novgorod; *Career:* 1918 first work printed; sided with Imaginists; friend of the poet Sergey Yesenin; *Publ:* verse *Vitrina serdtsa* (Window of the Heart) (1918); collected articles *Buyan-Ostrov. Imazhinizm* (Buyan Island. Imaginism) (1920); collected poems *Tuchelet* (Cloudfly) (1921); Historical tragedy *Zagovor durakov* (Conspiracy of Fools) (1922); collected verse and Poems *Novyy Mariyengof* (The New Marienhof) (1926); memoirs *Roman bez vran'ya* (Novel Without Lies) (1927); comedy *Shut Balakirev* (Balakirev the Fool) (1940); coauthor, play *Zolotoy obruch* (The Golden Ring); plays: *Sud zhizni* (The Court of Life) (1948); *Rozhdeniye poeta* (The Birth of a Poet) (1951), etc; *Died:* 24 June 1962 in Leningrad.

MARKARYAN, Martin Gerasimovich (1893-1963) Hygienist; Dr of Med; prof; *Born:* 1893; *Educ:* 1916 grad Natural Sci Dept, Fac of Physics and Mathematics, Petrograd Univ; 1925 grad Leningrad Mil Med Acad; *Career:* 1917-18 taught chemical warfare defense techniques to mil instructors in Petrograd; 1919-20 taught hygiene in secondary schools; 1926-29 postgrad student, then asst prof, Chair of Gen and Mil Hygiene, Leningrad Mil Med Acad 1930-35 asst prof, Chair of Hygiene, 1st Leningrad Med Inst, assoc, Leningrad Inst of Child and Adolescent Care and lecturer, Leningrad Mil Med College; 1935-55 asst prof, then assoc prof, Kuybyshev Mil Med Acad, then assoc prof, Leningrad Mil Med Acad; 1955-63 head, Chair of Hygiene, Leningrad Pediatric Med Inst; member, Learned Council, Inst of Radiation Hygiene; bd member, Leningrad Branch, All-Russian Inst of Hygienists and Health Officers; helped to build first Sov desalination plant for underground salt water in Centr Asia; wrote some 70 works on water-supply hygiene, food hygiene, clothing hygiene and the physical training of children and adolescents, including two hygiene textbooks for pediatric faculties; *Awards:* Order of Lenin; two Orders of the Red Banner; Order of the Red Star; three medals; *Died:* 17 May 1963.

MARKELOV, Grigoriy Ivanovich (1880-1952) Neuropathologist; prof; member, Ukr Acad of Sci from 1939; Hon Sci Worker of Ukr SSR from 1948; *Born:* 7 Feb 1880 in Perm', son of an office worker; *Educ:* 1906 grad Med Fac, Novorossiysk Univ, Odessa; *Career:* from 1906 intern, asst prof, then assoc prof, Chair of Nervous Diseases, Novorossiysk Univ; from 1927 head, Chair of Neuropathology, Odessa Med Inst; from 1930 also dir, Odessa Psychneurological Research Inst; did research on the physiology and pathology of the vegetative nervous system; devised a new classification for deseases of the vegetative nervous system and several new examination methods; also studied hypotonia and hypertonia, lesions of the brain's vascular system, the effect of environmental influences on the course of Physiological processes, lesions of the vegetative nervous system during malaria, etc; wrote numerous works; *Publ: Vegetativna nervova systema* (The Vegetative Nervous System) (1934-40); *Zabolevaniya vegetativnoy sistemy* (Ailments of the Vegetative Nervous System) (1948); *Died:* 8 Apr 1952.

MARKHLEVSKIY (MARCHLEWSKI) (pseudonym: KARSKIY), Yulian Yuzefovich (1866–1925) Polish revol; active in Russian and German workers' movement; *Born:* 17 May 1866 in Wloclawek, son of petty nobility; *Career:* 1880's began revol work as member of first Polish workers' revol party – "Proletariat"; helped found and lead Soc-Democratic Party of the Kingdom of Poland and Lithuania; from 1896 lived in Germany and helped Lenin found newspaper "Iskra"; Dec 1905 returned to Poland and took part in 1905–07 Revol; attended 5th (London) RSDRP Congress; elected cand member, CC, RSDRP; deleg at Zurich and Stuttgart Congresses of 2nd International; from 1909 worked mainly for German Soc-Democratic Party and was one of its left-wing leaders; helped found "Spartacus League"; frequently arrested for revol activities; May 1918 went to Russia; July 1918 until death member, All-Russian Centr Exec Comt; 1919 member, CC, German Communist Party; 1919 helped found Communist International and drafted theoretical principles of its agrarian program; 1920 headed Provisional Polish Revol Comt, founded on Polish territory liberated during the Sov-Polish War; 1923 founder and CC member, Int Org for Aid to Revol Fighters; 1918–22 fulfilled various important dipl commissions for Sov govt; took part in Sov negotiations with Poland, Lith, Finland, Japan and China; wrote works on econ, Polish history and int polit; *Publ: Sochineniya* (Works) (1931); *Died:* 22 Mar 1925 in Italy, buried in Germany in same cemetery as Rosa Luxemburg and Karl Liebknecht.

MARKIN, Nikolay Grigor'yevich (1893–1918) Sailor; Civil War Veteran; CP member from 1916; *Born:* 21 May 1893 in vil Russkiy Syromyas, Penza Province, son of a peasant; *Career:* electr fitter by trade; 1910 arrested for revol activities and imprisoned for eight months; 1914 drafted into Russian Navy and served with Baltic Fleet; 13 Mar 1917 led company of sailors from their barracks into the streets of Kronstadt to agitate for revol and aboliton of the monarchy; after 1917 Feb Revol conducted active Bolshevik propaganda among sailors; member, Petrograd Sov; deleg, 1st All-Russian Congress of Soviets; member, All-Russian Centr Exec Comt of 1st convocation; during 1917 Oct Revol commanded a squad of soldiers and sailors; from Nov 1917 secr to Trotsky; organized publ of *Sbornik sekretnykh dokumentov iz arkhivov byvshego Ministerstva inostrannykh del* (Collection of Secret Documents from the Archives of the Former Ministry of Foreign Affairs); from June 1918 comr for special assignments, Pop Comrt of the Navy; 21 June 1918 sent to NizhniyNovgorod as comr to muster the Volga Naval Flotilla; from Aug 1918 asst commander of this flotilla; Sept 1918 commanded sailors squad in the capture of Kazan'; *Died:* 1 Oct 1918 killed on the armed steamer "Vanya-Kommunist", shelled and set ablaze by White forces on the River Kama.

MARKISH, Perets Davidovich (1895–1952) Jewish writer; CP member from 1942; *Born:* 25 Nov 1895 in vil Polonnoye, Volhynian Province; *Educ:* studied at Shanyavskiy Pop Univ; then studied independently; *Career:* began work at age eight; 1917 first work published; from 1921 lived abroad, residing in Warsaw, Berlin, Paris and London; 1926 returned to USSR; his expressive and philosophic style combined lyrical, epic, realistic and romantic elements; arrested by State Security organs; *Publ:* verse – "Threshholds" (1919); "At a Loose End" (1919); "The Prank"; "Just So" (1921); "Night Theft" (1922); "The Heap" (1922); "Radio" (1922); "The Brothers" (1929); "Do Not Lose Heart" (1931); "The Thistle" (1935); "Dawn on the Dnieper"; "War" (1941–48); novels – "From Age to Age" (2 vol, 1929-41); "One for One" (1934); plays: "Earth" (1930); "The Ovadis Family" (1937); "The Chetto Uprising" (1946); *Died:* 12 Aug 1952 in imprisonment; posthumously rehabilitated.

MARKOV, A. T. (1877–1935) Party and govt official; CP member from 1917; *Born:* 1877; *Career:* after 1917 Oct Revol govt, Party and trade-union work; chm, Orekhovo-Zuyevo Uyezd Exec Comt; secr, Serpukhov Uyezd Party Comt; 1922–30 worked for Textile Workers' Union; Presidium member, All-Union Centr Trade-Union Council; member, bd, State Cotton Trust; worked for Moscow Sovnarkhoz; Moscow deleg at 11th RCP(B) Congress; *Died:* 1935.

MARKOV, Nikita Afanas'yevich (pen name: N. AMARU) (1903–1939) Mold writer; *Born:* 5 Sept 1903 in vil Korzhovo, now Mold SSR; *Career:* 1924 first work published; wrote essays, reports, lit criticism, etc; arrested by State Security organs; *Publ:* collected stories: "Panagika" (1929); "Toward a New Life" (1929); "For Soviet Rule" (1931); novelettes "The Struggle" (1933); novels: "The Party Is Calling" (1935); "The Treasure" (1936); *Died:* 4 Sept 1939 in imprisonment; posthumously rehabilitated.

MARKOV, S. D. (1880–1922) Govt official; CP member from 1901; *Born:* 1880; *Career:* 1903–04 member, Petrograd RSDRP(B) Comt; then worked in Nikolayev, Kherson and Simbirsk; from late 1918 member, Collegium, Pop Comrt of Means of Communication; from 1919 RSFSR Dep Pop Comr of Means of Communication; 1920 dir, Vladikavkaz Railroad; member, Revol Mil Council, Caucasian Front; *Died:* 1922.

MARKOV, Vladimir Nikolayevich (1884–1945) Educationist; prof; corresp member, RSFSR Acad of Pedag Sci from 1944; CP member from 1924; *Born:* 27 July 1884; *Educ:* 1904 grad Moscow Teachers' Training Inst; 1908–12 studied at Moscow Business Inst; *Career:* 1904 teacher, Likhvin City College, Tula Oblast; from 1922 high-school teacher; 1924–31 directed educ research center and worked for higher educ establishments in Saratov; 1934–41 head, Chair of Pedagogics, Moscow City Teachers' Training Inst; 1943–45 head, Chair of Pedagogics, Moscow State Univ; from 1944 dir, Inst of Teaching Methods, RSFSR Acad of Pedag Sci; specialized in gen problems of educ theory, particularly didactics and study of the Sov schoolchild; *Publ: Nauchno-obrazovatel'nyye muzei v provintsii, kak shkola prikladnykh znaniy* (Provincial Scientific Education Museums as Schools of Applied Knowledge) (1920); *Pioner v shkole* (The Pioneer in the School) (1929); *Teoriya pedagogiki pervykh dney revolyutsii* (Pedagogic Theory in the First Days of the Revolution) (1930); *Pedagogicheskaya kharakteristika sovetskogo shkol'nika* (The Pedagogic Characteristics of the Soviet Schoolchild) (1935); *Died:* 13 Dec 1945.

MARKOVICH, Vukashin (1874–1943) Revolutionary; *Born:* 12 Aug 1874 in Montenegro, son of a peasant; *Educ:* grad med schools in Kiev and Khar'kov; *Career:* from 1892 in Russia; during 1912–13 Balkan War in Serbian Army Red Cross units; 1914 mil surgeon in Russian Army on Southwestern Front; from 1903 active in Russian Soc-Democratic movement; repeatedly arrested by Tsarist authorities for revol activities; after 1917 Feb Revol elected to Petrograd Sov of Workers and Soldiers' Dep; 1917 met Lenin in Petrograd and went to the front as Bolshevik agitator on his orders; from 1918 fought in Civil War; worked among for prisoners-of-war with his wife Zh. Lyaburb; May 1918 co-founder and head, first Yugoslav Communist Group in RCP(B); chief ed of its press organ; helped found Comintern; from spring 1921 in Montenegro, where he helped lead peasant revolt; Apr 1925, after year in prison in Cetinje, escaped to Austria; summer 1926 returned to USSR; in 1930's worked for USSR Acad of Sci in Moscow; 1938 arrested by State Security organs; *Died:* 1943 in imprisonment; posthumously rehabilitated.

MARR, Nikolay Yakovlevich (1864–1934) Philologist; Orientologist; archeologist and ethnographer; member, Russian (USSR) Acad of Sci from 1909; CP member from 1930; *Born:* 25 Dec 1864 in Kutaisi, son of an agronomist (Scottish father, Georgian mother); *Educ:* 1888 grad Fac of Oriental Languages, Petersburg Univ; *Career:* from 1900 prof, Petersburg Univ; 1919–34 pres, Acad of the History of Material Culture; simultaneously dir, Japhetidological Inst, USSR Acad of Sci; specialized in Arm and Geo philology and Kartvelian languages of the Caucasus, as well as the history, archeology and ethnography of the Caucasian peoples; excavated the ancient capital of Arm – Ani – and the Urart monuments near Lake Van; also excavated Garni and Varnak; in philology concentrated on the most ancient period in the history of Geo and Arm lit; founded the series: *Teksty i razyskaniya po Armyano-gruzinskoy filologii* (Text and Research on Armenian-Georgian Philology) (13 vol, 1900–13); published earliest specimens of Arm and Geo lit with Russian translations and extensive commentaries; founded the Japhetic theory in linguistics in an attempt to prove the Caucasian languages kinship with Semitic group; around 1924, as a result of further work on his "Japhetic theory", proposed a new version of this theory termed the "new language theory"; this theory was based on the unity of the glottogonic process in the development of all the world's languages and their stage development; on the basis of this he considered that all the languages of the world derived from the so-called four elements (sal, ber, yon, rosh) and rejected the theory that there existed language groups which derived from different original material; in consequence, this theory, which took no account of the modern findings of comparative linguistics and philology, proved to be an utterly arbitrary doctrine and was completely refuted by the available specific data; yet it was imposed on Sov linguistics as a Marxist, and hence the only acceptable, theory; criticism or deviation from it was regarded as deviation from Marxism in linguistics; its basic tenets were also applied to the history of material culture (archeology and ethnography) and even to lit; in the latter case, ethnic differences were confused with class differences, and it was also maintained that the succession of archeological cultures in a given territory always reflects the stages of the local (autochthonous) development, and not the migration of peoples, etc; 1950, upon the initiative of Stalin himself, who had just published his work "Marksizm i voprosy yazykoznaniya" (Marxism and Problems of Linguistics), Marr's "new theory of language" was denounced and rejected as anti-Marxist and "anti-scientific"; Marr thus suffered the fate of other scientists, degenerating from "Marxist authority" to an "anti-Marxist"; he was rehabilitated in the early 1960's, but his "Japhetic theory" was not revived; *Publ: Grammatika drevnearmyanskogo yazyka* (An Ancient Armenian Grammar) (1903); *Osnovnyye tablitsy k grammatike drevnegruzinskogo yazyka s predvaritel'nym soobshcheniyem o rodstve gruzinskogo yazyka s semiticheskimi* (Basic Tables on the Grammar of Ancient Georgian with a Preliminary Concordance on Georgian's Kinship with the Semitic Languages) (1908); *Grammatika chanskogo (lazskogo) yazyka s khrestomatiyey i slovaryom* (A Grammar of the Chan (Laz) Language with a Reader and Lexicon) (1910); *Grammatika drevneliteraturnogo gruzinskogo yazyka* (A Grammar of the Ancient Georgian Literary Language) (1925); *Izbrannyye raboty* (Selected Works) (5 vol, 1933–1937); *Awards:* Order of Lenin; *Died:* 20 Dec 1934.

MARSHAK, Nikolay Yakovlevich (1902–1962) Stage dir; actor; founder of children's theaters; Pop Artiste of Geo SSR from 1955; CP member from 144; *Born:* 1902; *Career:* active in amateur dramatics; 1921 founded, 1921–24 actor and stage dir, 1st Geo Komsomol Proletarian Theater, Tbilisi; 1927 founded in Tbilisi first Transcaucasian Russian Young Playgoers' Theater; 1935 founded Russian Puppet Theater at this theater; for over 30 years directed Russian Young Playgoers' Theater, Tbilisi; 1961 chief stage dir, Kalinin Young Playgoers' Theater; 1962 chief stage dir, Tula Young Playgoers' Theater; *Productions:* "Don Quixote", after Cervantes (1933); "The Adventures of Tom Sawyer", after Mark Twain (1936); Brunshteyn's *Goluboye i rozovoye* (The Blue and the Pink) (1937); "The Robbers" (1938); Schwartz's "The Snow-Queen" (1939 and 1960); "Kabale und Liebe" (1944); *Molodaya gvardiya* (The Young Guard), after Fadeyev (1951); Trenyov's *Gimnazisty* (The High-School Students) (1953); Rozov's *V dobryy chas* (In Good Time) (1955); Stojenescu and Sava's "Zero for Conduct" (1959); "Romeo and Juliet" (1949);

MARSHAK, Samuil Yakovlevich (1887–1964) Russian poet, children's writer and translator; *Born:* 22 Oct 1887 in Voronezh; *Educ:* 1913–14 studied at London Univ; *Career:* 1904–06 lived with Gorky in Yalta; 1907 first work published; from 1908 worked for journal "Satirikon"; 1912–14 lived in England, studying English language and lit; on eve of WW 1 returned to Russia; 1915–17 worked for journals "Severnyye zapiski" and "Russkaya mysl'"; from 1920 head, Children's Homes and Colonies Section, Krasnodar Oblast Educ Dept; 1920 repertoire dir, Young Playgoers' Theater, Petrograd; from 1924 directed Children's Dept, Assoc of State Publ Houses; 1923–38 lit consultant and mang, children's journal "Novyy Robinzon"; 1924–25 dir, above journal; during WW 2 continued to write for children, composed texts for polit posters and cartoons and worked as journalist, critic, lit theorist and translator; from 1959 bd member, USSR Writers' Union; translated works of Shakespeare, Burns, Byron, Heine, Petöfi, etc; several of his works have been set to music; *Publ:* children's books: *Detka v kletke* (The Child in the Cage) (1923); *Pozhar* (The Fire) (1923); *Glupyy mishonok* (The Silly Bear Cub) (1923); *Bagazh* (Luggage) (1926); *Pochta* (The Mails) (1927); *Vot kakoy rasseyannyy* (Such an Absent-Minded Person) (1930); *Voyna s Dneprom* (War with the Dnieper) (1931); "Mister Twister," (1933); *Pochta voyennaya* (The Military Mails) (1944); *Ledyanoy ostrov* (Ice Island) (1947); *Lesnaya kniga* (The Forest Book) (1950); *Vesyoloye puteshestviye ot A do Ya* (A Merry Journey from A to Z) (1952); novelette *V nachale zhizni* (At the Start of Life) (1960); verse *Chudo* (The Miracle) and *Bessmertiye* (Immortality) (1960); children's books: *Redkiy sluchay* (A Rare Case) and *Moy kon'* (My Horse) (1963); fairy-tale plays *Koshkin dom* (Kitten House) (1941); *Dvenadtsat' mesyatsev* (The Twelvemonth) (1947); *Gorya boyatsya – schast'ya ne vidat'* (Shun Grief and Miss Happiness) (1954), etc; various lit critical articles; *Awards:* two Orders of Lenin; Order of the Red Banner of Labor; Order of the Fatherland War, 1st Class; four Stalin Prizes (1942, 1946, 1949 and 1951); Lenin Prize (1963); *Died:* 4 July 1964 in Moscow.

MARSHEV, M. L. (1881–1958) Trade-Union and govt official; CP member from 1918; *Born:* 1881; *Career:* from 1897 in revol movement; from Nov 1917 Presidium member, Moscow City Trade-Union Council; from 1920 chm, Presidium, Construction Workers' Union; 1926–31 senior asst prosecutor, Moscow Oblast; 1932–34 secr, Moscow Oblast Meat and Dairy Ind Union; from 1937 prosecutor, Moscow Okrug Railroad; from 1947 retired; *Died:* 1958.

MARTENS, Lyudvig Karlovich (1875–1948) Revolutionary; diplomat; Dr of Tech Sci; CP member from 1893; *Born:* 1 Jan 1875 in Bakhmut (now Artemovsk), son of a russified German factory-owner; *Educ:* until 1896 studied at Petersburg Technol Inst; *Career:* 1895 joined Lenin's League for the Liberation of the Working Class; 1896 arrested for publishing and distributing illegal lit and for organizing strikes; imprisoned for three years in Kresty Jail, then deported to Germany; 1906 moved to England; 1916 moved to USA continued revol work abroad; Jan 1919 appointed RSFSR rep in USA; US govt rejected all his efforts to establish dipl and trade relations between RSFSR and USA and ordered him deported from USA; returned to Moscow; from 1921 exec admin and teaching work in Moscow; from 1921 Presidium member, Supr Sovnarkhoz and chm, Main Metal Trust; 1926–27 chm, Comt for Inventions; 1926–29 prof and rector, Moscow Mech Inst; 1926–36 dir, research inst; from 1929 learned secr, USSR Acad of Sci; 1927–41 chief ed, *Tekhnicheskaya entsiklopediya* (Technical Encyclopedia); 1930 designed high-speed, single-valve high-compression engine; wrote numerous sci works; *Died:* 19 Oct 1948.

MARTIKYAN, Sergey Nikolayevich (1874–1957) Party and govt official; CP member from 1904; *Born:* 1874 in Tiflis; *Career:* metalworker by trade; from 1901 in revol movement; 1905–07 helped found underground Bolshevik printing presses in Baku; 1917 member Baku RSDRP Comt; co-founder and comr, Baku detachment of armed Bolshevik workers; Sept 1918–Mar 1919, after collapse of Baku Commune, Party work in Astrakhan'; from June 1919 underground work in Arm; member, Arm Party Comt; May 1920 arrested by Dashnaks; Nov 1920, after establishment of Sov regime in Arm, exec Party and admin work; repeatedly elected member and Bureau member, CC, CP(B) Arm; member, CPSU(B) Centr Control Commission; 1933–36 chm, Arm Centr Exec Comt; member, USSR Centr Exec Comt and Centr Exec Comt of Transcaucasian SFSR; deleg at 12th, 14th and 16th CPSU(B) Congresses; *Died:* 13 May 1957.

MARTOV, L. (real name: TSEDERBAUM, Yuliy Osipovich) (1873–1923) Politician; *Born:* 1873; *Educ:* studied at Petersburg Univ; *Career:* 1892 first arrested in Petersburg for membership of a circle engaged in revol work among student youth and for distributing illegal lit; after his release from prison worked for illegal "Red Cross" group and for Petersburg Liberation of Labor Group; 1893 exiled to Vilnius, where he was active in Jewish workers' movement; 1895 returned to Petersburg and joined Lenin's group of "Old Revolutionaries"; 1896 arrested and 1897 exiled for three years to Turukhansk; after his exile helped prepare and edit "Iskra"; at 2nd RSDRP Congress headed minority faction; Oct 1905–07 lived in Russia and led RSDRP (Menshevik) faction; attended London Party Congress; remained abroad and helped edit Menshevik paper "Golos sotsial-demokratov"; took moderate liquidationist stand; adopted centrist stand as regards the war; attended Zimmerwald and Kienthal Party Conferences; after 1917 Feb Revol returned to Russia and sided with Menshevik internationalists; opposed 1917 Oct Revol; 1920 member, Moscow Sov; until 1920 lived in RSFSR and led RSDRP Mensheviks; 1921 exiled from RSFSR and edited RSDRP journal "Sotsialisticheskiy vestnik"; *Publ: Krasnoye znamya v Rossii* (The Red Banner in Russia); *Proletarskaya bor'ba v Rossii* (The Proletarian Struggle in Russia); *Razvitiye krupnoy promyshlennosti i rabocheye dvizheniye v Rossii* (The Development of Heavy Industry and the Workers' Movement in Russia); *Istoriya RSDRP* (The History of the RSDRP); *Zapiski sotsial-demokrata* (Notes of a Social-Democrat), etc; *Died:* 1923.

MARTSINOVSKIY, Yevgeniy Ivanovich (1874–1934) Epidemiologist and parasitologist; Dr of Med from 1909; prof; Hon Sci Worker of RSFSR from 1934; *Born:* 19 Mar 1874; *Educ:* 1899 grad Med Fac, Moscow Univ; *Career:* 1899–1924 worked at Infection Barracks, Pavlov Hospital; 1909 defended doctor's thesis on the etiology of Oriental sores; described new acid-resistant bacillus from the tonsillar crypt; 1910–11 assoc prof, Moscow Univ, where he lectured on the role of pathogenic protozoa in animal and human pathology; 1911 resigned from Moscow Univ with other prof in protest against the policies of Educ Min Kasso; did major research on malaria; appointed chm, Malaria Commission, Pirogov Soc and organized numerous expeditions to study and combat this disease in the Caucasus and on the Black Sea littoral; 1912 founded Caucasian Malaria Comt to combat the disease in the areas of worst infection; after outbreak of WW 1 organized a special detachment to combat typhus, smallpox and cholera in the Caucasus; 1920–34 founder-dir, Tropical Inst (now Martsinovskiy Inst of Malaria, Parasitology and Helminthology); 1924–30 founder-head, Chair of Infectious Diseases, Moscow

Univ; from 1932 chm, Learned Council, RSFSR Pop Comrt of Health; member, Moscow City Sov of several convocations; ed, journals "Tropicheskaya meditsina", "Gigiyena i epidemiologiya", etc; member, various Sov and for sci soc; Sov deleg, Int Malaria Commission, League of Nations; made studies of leishmaniosis, spirochetosis, malaria, arthropodous vectors of diseases affecting man and animals, pyroplasmosis, fungus diseases, typhus, typhoid, tropical diseases, etc; wrote over 200 works; *Publ: Etiologiya "vostochnoy yazvy" (Bouton d'Orient) i kratkiye svedeniya ob etoy bolezni* (The Etiology of "Oriental Sores" [Bouton d'Orient] and Brief Data on This Disease) (1904); *Likvidatsiya malyarii vo vtorom pyatiletii* (The Elimination of Malaria During the Second Five-Year Plan) (1932); *Na fronte zdravookhraneniya* (On the Health Front) (1932); *Mysli o rabote* (Thoughts About Work) (1933); *Nashi dostizheniya* (Our Achievements) (1933); *Meditsinskaya parazitologiya i parazitarnyye bolezni* (Medical Prasitology and Parasitic Diseases) (2 vol, 1935), etc; *Died:* 25 July 1934.

MARTYNOV (PIKER), Aleksandr Samoylovich (1865–1935) Party official; CP member from 1919; *Born:* 24 Dec 1865 in Pinsk; *Career:* member, "People's Will" circles; from 1884 member, "People's Will" Party; 1886 exiled for 10 years to Siberia; in 1890's sided with Soc-Democrats; from 1899 member, Yekaterinoslav RSDRP Comt; 1900 arrested again, then emigrated; worked for ed bd, "economist" journal "Rabocheye delo" and polemicized with Lenin's newspaper "Iskra"; 1903 attacked "Iskra" group at 2nd RSDRP Congress; after Congress sided with Mensheviks; deleg at 4th and 5th RSDRP Congress; at 5th Congress elected member, CC, RSDRP; during WW 1 adopted centrist, then Menshevik-internationalist stand; opposed 1917 Oct Revol; 1918 member, left wing of CC, RSDRP(Mensheviks); subsequently drifted away from Mensheviks; 1918–22 teacher in Ukr; 1923 agitated for liquidation of Geo Soc-Democratic Party; 1923 at 12th RCP(B) Congress admitted to RCP(B); worked for Inst of Marx and Engels; from 1924 member, ed bd, journal "Kommunisticheskiy internatsional"; *Publ:* pamphlets: *Dve diktatury* (Two Dictatorships); *Moi ukrainskiye vpechatleniya i razmyshleniya* (My Ukrainian Impressions and Reflections); *Velikarya proverka* (The Great Check); *Died:* 5 June 1935.

MARTYNOV, Aleksey Vasil'yevich (1868–1934) Surgeon; Dr of Med from 1897; prof from 1904; Hon Sci Worker of RSFSR from 1904; *Born:* 24 June 1868 in vil Yerofeyevskaya Sloboda, Ryazan' Province, son of a physician; *Educ:* 1891 grad Med Fac, Moscow Univ; *Career:* 1891–95 intern, Prof A. A. Bobrov's Clinic, Moscow; from 1895 supernumerary asst to Prof I. N. Novatskiy, consultant, Prison Hospital and lecturer in dentistry; 1897 defended doctor's thesis on surgery of the pancreas; from 1898 assoc prof, Moscow Univ, where he read a course on fac surgery; 1900 sent to clinics in Germany, France and Switzerland for further specialist training; 1904 appointed prof, Propaedeutic Surgical Clinic, Khar'kov Univ; 1905–10 dir, Surgical Clinic, 1907–10 also dir, Urological Clinic, Novo-Yekaterinskaya Hospital, Moscow; 1908 sent to Prof Albarran's Urological Clinic in Paris; from 1910 until death prof and dir, Hospital Surgical Clinic, Med Fac, Moscow Univ; 1912–14 founder-ed, *Yezhegodnik russkoy meditsinskoy pechati* (Russian Medical Press Yearbook); during WW 1 consultant, various mil hospitals; before 1917 Oct Revol member, Constitutional Democratic Party; after Revol, to which he refused allegiance, consultant, various establishments of Kremlin Therapeutic and Sanitary Bd; did research on lesions of the blood after surgical intervention, the pathology of the thyroid gland, Basedow's disease, the surgical treatment of inguinal hernia and horseshoe kidney, etc; devised original methods of resection of the thyroid gland and operations for inguinal and postoperative hernia, myoceles, etc; 1928 performed operation for cholecystitis on Prof I. P. Pavlov; founder-member and chm, Soc of Russian Surgeons, Moscow; chm, 17th Congress of Russian Surgeons; hon member, Pirogov Surgical Soc in Leningrad, Saratov, Ryazan', etc; co-ed, "Bol'shaya meditsinskaya entsiklopediya" (Large Medical Encyclopedia) (1st ed); co-ed, multivol *Rukovodstvo po prakticheskoy khirurgii* (A Practical Surgery Manual); co-ed, journals "Klinicheskaya meditsina", "Russkaya klinika", "Sovetskaya khirurgiya", "Vestnik endokrinologii", "Vestnik khirurgii i pogranichnykh oblastey", etc; trained such outstanding surgeons as M. S. Astrov, V. R. Braytsev, R. M. Fronshteyn, V. R. Khesin, P. G. Melikhov, Ye. K. Molodaya, V. I. Pavlov-Sil'vanskiy, A. D. Prokin, S. M. Rubashov, I. G. Rufanov, V. N. Savvin, Ye. S. Shakhbazyan, P. P. Sitkovskiy, S. D. Ternovskiy and A. M. Zabludovskiy; wrote some 70 works; *Publ:* doctor's thesis *Khirurgiya podzheludochnoy zhelezy* (Surgery of the Pancreas) (1898); *Izmeneniya krovi v posleoperatsionnom periode* (Lesions of the Blood in the Post-operative Period) (1924); *Dostizheniya i zadachi khirurgii tsentral'noy nervnoy sistemy* (The Achievements and Tasks of Surgery of the Central Nervous System) (1925); *O khirurgicheskom lechenii pri bolezni Bazedova* (The Surgical Treatment of Basedow's Disease) (1926); *Khirurgiya zhyolchnogo puzyrya i zhyolchnykh putey* (Surgery of the Gall Bladder and Biliary Tract) (1929); *Bolezni bryushiny* (Diseases of the Peritoneum) (1931); *Povrezhdeniya i bolezni shchitovidnoy zhelezy* (Injuries and Diseases of the Thyroid Gland) (1933); *Died:* 24 Jan 1934 in Moscow.

MARTYNOV, Andrey Vasil'yevich (1879–1938) Entomologist and paleozoologist; *Born:* 1879; *Educ:* 1902 grad Moscow Univ; *Career:* from 1902 at Moscow Univ; from 1908 assoc prof, Chair of Zoology, Warsaw Univ; 1920–30 assoc, Zoological Museum, 1930–35 assoc, Zoological Inst, from 1935 assoc, Paleontological Inst, USSR Acad of Sci; co-founder, paleoentomology; from his paleoentomological studies and research on the morphology of insect wings he developed a gen taxonomy of insects, dividing them into ancient-winged and new-winged varieties; made the first review of Yura and Perm' insect fauna in the USSR; collated material on deposits of fossile insects and their historical development in connection with the Earth's geological past; also worked on the taxonomy, morphology, ecology and zoogeography of caddis flies and amphipods; *Publ: Ocherki geologicheskoy istorii i filogenii otryadov nasekomykh (Pterigota)* (Studies in the Geological History and Philogeny of Orders of Insects /Pterigota/) (vol 1, 1938); *O dvukh tipakh kryl'yev nasekomykh i ikh evolyutsii* (Two Types of Insect Wings and Their Evolution) (1924); *Ekologicheskiye predposylki dlya zoogeografii presnovodnykh bentonicheskikh zhivotnykh* (The Ecological Premises for the Zoogeography of Fresh-Water Bentonic Animals) (1929); *Died:* 29 Jan 1938.

MAR'YANENKO (real name: PETLISHENKO), Ivan Aleksandrovich (1878–1962) Actor; prof from 1946; Pop Artiste of USSR from 1944; *Born:* 9 June 1878 in vil Mar'yanovka, now Kirovograd Oblast, son of a peasant; *Educ:* 1895 completed college; studied stagecraft under his uncle, M. L. Kropivnitskiy; *Career:* 1896–1906 with Kropivnitskiy and Suslov's drama companies; 1906–18 at Sadovskiy Theater, Kiev; 1918–23 at Shevchenko and Zan'kovetskaya Theaters, Kiev; 1923–58 at Kahr'kov's Shevchenko Drama Theater; from 1917 also taught stagecraft; from 1946 prof, Khar'kov Inst of Stagecraft; from 1915 founder-dir, Assoc of Ukr Artists; 1917 co-founder, Ukr Nat Theater; played over 300 roles and staged many plays at Ukr theaters; *Roles:* Omel'ko in Karpenko-Karyy's "Martyn Borulya"; Gonta in *Gaydemaki* (The Haydemaks), after Shevchenko; Don Juan in Lesya Ukrainka's *Kamennyy vlastelin* (The Stone Sovereign); Yaroslav in Kocherga's *Yaroslasv Mudryy* (Yaroslav the Wise); Bogdan in Korneychuk's "Bogdan Khmel'nitskiy"; Prokhor in Gorky's "Vassa Zheleznova"; Dikiy in Ostrovskiy's *Groza* (The Storm); Khlestakov in Gogol's *Revizor* (The Government Inspector); Mikola in Kotlyarevskiy's "Natalka Poltavka", etc; *Awards:* Order of Lenin; Order of the Red Banner of Labor; Stalin Prize (1947); *Died:* 4 Nov 1962.

MARZEYEV, Aleksandr Nikitich (1883–1956) Hygienist and health service official; Dr of Med from 1930; prof from 1925; member, USSR Acad of Med Sci from 1944; Hon Sci Worker of Ukr SSR from 1935; *Born:* 6 Apr 1883 in Nizhniy Novgorod (now Gorky), son of a peasant; *Educ:* 1911 grad Med Fac, Moscow Univ; *Career:* 1911–14 zemstvo health officer, Yekaterinoslav Province; 1914 drafted into Russian Army; supervised campaign against scurvy on various fronts; 1917–18 chm, Comt of Soldiers' Dep, 39th Army Corps Staff; from 1918 health officer, Mariupol' City Health Dept; 1922–35 head, Khar'kov Sanitary Epidemiological Dept, Ukr Pop Comrt of Health; 1925–30 founder-head, Chair of Communal Hygiene, from 1930 prof, Chair of Gen and Communal Hygiene, Ukr Inst of Postgrad Med Training; from 1930 also head, Sanitation and Hygiene Dept, Ukr Health Inst; 1931–56 founder-dir, Ukr Centr Inst of Communal Hygiene, Khar'kov (from 1944 Kiev); from 1933 also founder-head, Chair of Communal Hygiene, Khar'kov Med Inst; 1944–56 head, Chair of Communal Hygiene, Kiev Med Inst; 1944–46 head, Chair of Communal Hygiene, Kiev Inst of Postgrad Med Training; established All-Ukr Sanitary Council, Ukr Centr Sanitary-Tech Council and various sci commissions; life-chm, Ukr Soc of Hygienists; dep chm, bd, All-Union Soc of Hygienists; member, Learned Council, Ukr Min of Health; co-ed, journal "Gigiyena i sanitariya"; established numerous publ healt centers in Ukr and helped to draft Ukr health legislation; organized first Sov admin courses for health officers; supervised hygiene campaign in Donbas; ensured hygienic conditions during the construction of the Kakhovka Hydropower Plant, the North Donets-Donbas Canal, etc; campaigned against air pollution in the ind centers of the Ukr; wrote over 130 works; *Publ: Zhilishche i sanitarnyy byt sel'skogo naseleniya Ukrainy* (The Living Conditions and Sanitary Practices of the Rural Population of the Ukraine) (1927); *Donbass i yego sanitarnoye ozdorovleniye i izucheniye* (The Study and Improvement of the Donbas from the Sanitary Point of View) (1935); *Planirovka i rekonstruktsiya kolkhoznogo sela* (The Planning and Reconstruction of the Kolkhoz Village) (1941); *Razrusheniye gorodov i sel'skikh mest Ukrainy i gigiyenicheskiye osnovy ikh vosstanovleniya* (The Destruction of Cities and Villages in the Ukraine and the Hygienic Principles of Their Reconstruction) (1946); *Voprosy kommunal'noy i shkolnoy gigiyeny* (Communal and School Hygiene) (1956); textbook *Kommunal'naya gigiyena* (2nd et, 1958), etc; *Awards:* two Order of Lenin; Badge of Hon; medals; *Died:* 1 Feb 1956 in Kiev.

MASHKIN, Nikolay Aleksandrovich (1900–1950) Historian; Dr of History and prof from 1942; *Born:* 9 Feb 1900 in vil Sokolki, Samara Province, son of a teacher; *Educ:* 1922 grad Fac of Soc Sci, Moscow Univ; 1929 completed postgrad studies at Inst of History, Russian Assoc of Soc Sci Research Institutes; *Career:* 1922–36 lecturer, Communist Univ of the Workers of the East; 1927–31 also lecturer, Sverdlov communist Univ; 1934–42 lecturer, from 1942 prof, from 1943 head, Chair of the History of the Ancient World, History Fac, Moscow Univ; 1938–48 senior assoc, from 1948 head, Ancient History Section, Inst of History, USSR Acad of Sci; specialized in the history of the Roman Republ and Empire; also did research on historiography; *Publ:* textbook *Istoriya Drevnego Rima* (The History of Ancient Rome) (1947); *Printsipat Avgusta. Proiskhozhdeniye i sotsial'naya sushchnost* (The Pricipate of Augustus. Its Origin and Social Nature) (1949), etc; *Awards:* Badge of Hon (1945); Stalin Prize (1950); *Died:* 15 Sept 1950.

MASLOV, A.M. (Pseudonyms: Aleksandr; Aleksandr Kr.; KRASNOYARSKIY) (1879–1954) Revolutionary; CP member from 1904; *Born:* 1879; *Career:* Party work in Tomsk, Irkutsk, Nizhneudinsk, Barnaul and Krasnoyarsk; 1906 chm, Krasnoyarsk RSDRP Comt; secr, Siberian Union Comt; Krasnoyarsk deleg, 5th RSDRP Congress; after 1917 Feb Revol worked in Motovilikha; member, Motovilikha RSDRP(B) Comt; from 1919 worked in Urals; 1923–36 various exec posts in Ukr; 1936–38 dir, inst of chemical technol von Moscow; from 1939 worked for USSR Pop Comrt of Chemical Ind; from 1951 retired; *Died:* 1954.

MASLOV, I. N. (1891–1938) Govt official; Cp member from 1917; *Born:* 1891; *Career:* 1918–37 Asst Pop Comr of Posts, Telegraph and Press; head, Communications Dept, Moscow Oblast Exec Comt; secr, Moscow City Rayon Party Comt; head, cotton trust; then head, Cotton Trust, Pop Comrt of Light Ind; 1920–21 during trade-union controversy supported Ye. Ignatov; sympathized with views of "workers' opposition" group; arrested by State Security organs; *Died:* 1938 in imprisonment.

MASLOV, Mikhail Stepanovich (1885–1961) Pediatrician; Dr of Med from 1913; prof from 1921; majgen, Med Corps; member, USSR Acad of Med SCi from 1945; member, Polish Acad of Sci from 1939; Hon Sci Worker of RSFSR from 1935; *Born:* 1885 in Narva; *Educ:* 1910 grad Petersburg Mil Med Acad; *Career:* 1913–14 visited pediatric clinics in Berlin, Vienna, Munich and Zurich; 1910–14 trainee, Inst of Experimental Med; 1914–18 mil surgeon at front and head of an evacuation hospital; 1918–20 asst prof, 1920–21 assoc prof, 1921–61 prof and head, Chair of Children's Diseases, Leningrad Mil Med Acad; 1921–23 prof, Chair of Child Pathology, 1923–29 sci dir for brain research, Youth Dept, Leningrad Inst of Mother and Child Welfare; 1925–30 head, Chair of Physiology, Hygiene and Infant Dietetics, 1930–31 head, Chair of Clinical Pediatrics, 1938–61 head, Chair of Fac Pediatrics, Leningrad Pediatric Med Inst; chm, Leningrad Soc of Pediatricians; bd member, All-Union and All-Russian Soc of Pediatricians; attended numerous All-Russian, All-Union and for pediatric congresses: 1947 in New York, 1952 in Vienna, 1957 in Copenhagen, 1959 in Montreal; member, Exec Comt, Int Soc of Pediatricians; hon member, various med soc, including the French Pediatric Soc and the Czechoslovak Med Soc; dep ed, Journal "Pediatriya"; ed, journal "Voprosy okhrany materinstva i detstva" and periodical "Vrachebnaya gazeta"; co-ed, pediatrics section, "Bol'shaya meditsinskaya entsiklopediya" (Large Medical Encycloedia) (1st and 2nd ed); dep, Leningrad City Sov of 1946 convocation; invented instruments and equipment for the diagnosis and treatment of children's diseases; organized several pediatric museums and exhibitions; trained over 40 prof and assoc prof; wrote over 180 works; *Publ: O biologicheskom znachenii fosfora dlya rastushchego organizma* (The Biological Importance of Phosphorus for the Growing Organism) (1913); *Ucheniye o konstitutsiyakh i anomaliyakh konstitutsii v detskom vozraste* (The Theory of Constitution and Constitutional Anomalies in Childhood) (1926); *Osnovy ucheniya o rebyonke i ob osobennostyakh yego zabolevaniy* (The Principles of Pedology and the Features of Children's Diseases) (1927); *Detskiye bolezni* (Children's Diseases) (1933); *Rukovodstvo po pediatrii* (A Pediatric Manual) (1938); *Uchebnik detskikh bolezney* (A Textbook on Children's Diseases) (1939); *Diagnoz i prognoz detskikh zabolevaniy* (The Diagnosis and Prognosis of Children's Diseases) (1948); *Bolezni pecheni i zhyolchnykh putey u detey* (Diseases of the Liver and Biliary Tract in Children) (1951); *Patogenez i lecheniye toksicheskoy dispepsii* (The Pathogenesis and Treatment of Toxic Dyspepsia) (1955); *Lektsii po fakul'tetskoy pediatrii* (Lectures on Faculty Pediatrics) (1957); *Sepsis i septicheskiye sostoyaniya u detey* (Sepsis and Septic Conditions in Children) (1959), etc; *Awards:* five orders and several medals; *Died:* 1961 in Leningrad.

MASLOV, Pyotr Nikolayevich (1898–1965) Surgeon; Dr of Med from 1946; prof; *Born:* 1898; *Educ:* 1925 grad Med Fac, Kazan' Univ; *Career:* 1918–19 mil surgeon in Red Army; 1925–30 intern, then asst prof, Surgical Clinic, Kazan' Univ; 1930–35 asst prof, Surgical Clinic, 2nd Moscow Med Inst; 1935–48 assoc prof, Surgical Clinic, Centr Inst of Postgrad Med Training, Moscow; 1948–49 head, Chair of Hospital Surgery, Vitebsk Med Inst; 1949–54 head, Chair of Gen Surgery, Minsk Med Inst; from 1955 head, Chair of Fac Surgery, Minsk Med Inst; from 1950 chm, Bel Soc of Surgeons; from 1957 member, ed bd, journal "Zdravookhraneniye Belorussii"; did research on the treatment of inflammatory processes, muscle tone disturbances of the internal organs, stomach and thoracic surgery, etc; wrote over 40 works; *Publ:* monograph *Ostraya kishechnaya neprokhodimost* (Acute Intestinal Blockage), etc; *Awards:* Order of Lenin (1961), etc; *Died:* 27 Aug 1965.

MASLOV, Pyotr Pavlovich (pen name: Iks; Dzhon) (1867–1946) Econ; Menshevik; member, USSR Acad of Sci from 1929; *Born:* 27 July 1867 in Orenburg Province, son of a Cossack; *Educ:* studied at Khar'kov Veterinary Inst; *Career:* while a student, engaged in extensive correspondence with members of N.Ye. Fedoseyev's Marxist circle; 1889 arrested for his connections with this circle and imprisoned for three years; from 1890's active in Soc-Democratic movement; 1896–97 ed, newspaper "Samarskiy vestnik"; contributed to progressive Petersburg journals; after 2nd RSDRP Congress sided with Mensheviks; 1906 at 4th RSDRP Congress advocated Menshevik program for municipalization of the land; wrote major studies of agrarian problem, revising several Marxist tenets; roundly criticized by Lenin; during WW 1 took liquidationist stand; after 1917 Oct Revol abandoned polit work; worked for Gosplan and Russian Assoc of Soc Sci Research Institutes; taught and did research at various higher educ establishments in Omsk, Irkutsk, Chita and Moscow; in his latter years studied Soc Agric econ, especially machine-and-tractor stations and sovkhozes; *Publ: Agrarnyy vopros v Rossii* (The Agrarian Problem in Russia) (2 vol, 1903–08); *Kritika agrarnykh programm i proyekt programmy* (A Critique of Agrarian Programs and a Draft Program) (1905); *Teoriya razvitiya narodnogo khozyaystva* (The Theory of Development of the National Economy); *Kapitalizm* (Capitalism); *Mirovaya sotsial'naya problema* (The World Social Problem); *Nauka o narodnom khozyaystve* (The Theory of the National Economy); *Istoriya khozyaystvennogo byta Zapadnoy Yevropy* (The History of West European Economic Practice); *Osnovy kooperatsii* (Principles of the Cooperative System); *Vliyaniye yestestvennykh i sotsial'nykh usloviy na proizvoditel'nost' truda* (The Effect of Natural and Social Conditions on Labor Productivity); *Died:* 4 June 1946.

MASLOV, Sergey Ivanovich (1880–1957) Lit historian and teacher; corresp member, Ukr Acad of Sci from 1939; *Born:* 29 Nov 1880 in Ichnay, now Chernigov Oblast; *Educ:* 1898–1900 studied at Kiev Polytech Inst; 1907 grad History and Philology Fac, Kiev Univ; *Career:* from 1900 studied at Natural Sci Fac, Kiev Univ; expelled and drafted into Russian Army for participating in student polit movement; from 1914–35 assoc prof, from 1935 prof, Kiev Univ; catalogued stocks of manuscripts and wrote on history of press in Ukr, paleography, folklore and history of language; did research on old Slavic lit, works, books published in Russia before 18th Century and lit work of various Ukr writers; *Publ: Pechataniye na Ukraine v XVI–XVIII vv* (Printing in the Ukraine in the 16th and 18th Centuries) (1924); *Ukrainskaya pechatnaya kniga XVI–XVIII vv* (The Ukrainian Printed Book of the 16th–18th Centuries) (1925); *Kul'turno-natsional'noye vozrozhdeniye na Ukraine v kontse XVI i pervoy polovine XVII stoletiya* (The Cultural and National Renaissance in the Ukraine in the Late 16th and Early 17th Century) (1943); ed, *Slovo o polku Igoreve v ukrainskikh khudozhestvennykh perevodakh i izlozheniyakh XIX–XX stoletiy* (The "Lay of the Host of Igor" in 19th– and 20th-Century Ukrainian Translations and Interpretations) (1953), etc; *Died:* 11 Jan 1957.

MASLOVSKAYA, Sof'ya Dmitriyevna (1883–1953) Opera producer; Hon Artiste of RSFSR from 1931; *Born;* 21 June 1885 in Petersburg; *Educ:* 1912 grad Drama Dept, Petersburg Theatrical College; 1912–14 studied singing at Petersburg Conservatory; *Career:* 1912–19 stage dir, Musical Drama Theater; 1914–26 lecturer, 1926–29 prof, Leningrad Conservatory; 1923 helped found Opera Studio at Leningrad Conservatory; from 1929 worked in Moscow and Sverdlovsk; 1935–38 stage dir, 1938–41 chief stage dir, Khar'kov Opera and Ballet Theater; 1939–41 founder-dir, Opera Studio, Khar'kov Conservatory; 1943–49 again prof, Opera Studio, Leningrad Conservatory; *Productions:* co-produced Auber's "Fenella" (1918); co-produced Rimsky-Korsakov's *Kashchey besmertnyy* (Kashchey the Immortal) (1919); *Pikovaja dama* (The Queen of Spades) (1937); *Knyaz' Igor* (Prince Igor) (1939); "La Traviata" (1937); Chishko's *Bronenosets Potyomkin* (The Battleship Potyomkin) (1938); Khrennikov's *V buryu* (In the Storm) (1939); *Yevgeniy Onegin* (Eugene Onegin) (1934); *Tsarskaya nevesta* (The Bride of the Tsar) (1936), etc; *Died:* 19 May 1953.

MASSALITINOVA, Varvara Osipovna (1878–1945) Actress; Pop Artiste of RSFSR from 1933; *Born:* 29 July 1878; *Educ:* 1901 grad A.P. Lenskiy's courses at Moscow Theatrical College; *Career:* acted with amateur circle in Tomsk, specializing in elderly roles; 1901–19 at Maly Theater in Moscow; 1919–21 at State Show Theater; 1922–45 again at Maly Theater; *Roles:* stage soles; Korobochka in Gogol's *Myortvyye dushi* (Dead Souls) (1902); noncom's widow in Gogol's *Revizor* (The Government Inspector) (1903); Merchutkina in Chekhov's *Yubiley* (The Anniversary) (1904); the Mad Mistress in Ostrovsky's *Groza* (The Storm) (1911); Prostakova in Fonvizin's *Nedorosl'* (The Minor) (1923); Khlyostova in Griboyedov's *Gore ot uma* (Woe From Wit) (1938); film roles: Kabanikha in Ostrovsky's "Groza"; Vasiliy Buslay's mother in "Aleksandr Nevskiy"; Grandmother Akulina Ivanovna in *Detstvo Gor'kogo* (Gorky's Childhood) and *V lyudyakh* (Out in the World); *Awards:* Stalin Prize (1941); two orders; *Died:* 20 Oct 1945.

MATIYASEVICH, Mikhail Stepanovich (1878–1941) Sov mil commander during Civil War; col, Russian Army; *Born:* 24 May 1878 in Smolensk, son of an infantry officer; *Educ:* grad Yaroslavl' Mil School; grad Odessa Mil Infantry School; 1929 grad Red Army Advanced Courses for Higher Command Staff; *Career:* 1904 officer, 220th Yepifan' Regt; fought in Russo-Japanese War; wounded five times and shell-shocked; 1914–18 commanded company, battalion then regt on Western and Northern Fronts; wounded four times; from Apr 1918 in Red Army; 1918 asst mil head, then mil head, Vitebsk Detachment on Western Front; commanded brigade, then 1st Smolensk Div; commanded right wing of 5th Army on Eastern Front; 1918–19 commanded 26th Div, 5th Army; July-Sept 1919 commander, 7th Army near Petrograd; Sept 1919–Jan 1920 commander, 3rd Army on Eastern Front; Feb 1920–Aug 1921 commander, 5th Army; from Sept 1920 simultaneously commander, Eastern Siberian Mil Distr; 1921–22 commandant, Higher Mil School in Kazan'; 1922–24 commandant, Kamenev Higher Joint Mil School in Kiev; 1924 pensioned on med grounds; taught at Kiev higher educ establishments; worked for Soc for Furthering the USSR Defense, Aviation and Chemical Ind; *Died:* 5 Aug 1941 in Kiev.

MATROSOV, Aleksandr Matveyevich (1924–1943) WW 2 hero; Komsomol member from 1942; *Born:* 1924 in Dnepropetrovsk; *Career:* orhpaned at an early age; raised at the Ivanov Orphanage, Ul'yanovsk Oblast, and at a children's labor colony in Ufa; Oct 1942 drafted into Red Army and sent to infantry college; Nov 1942 assigned to 254th Guards Infantry Regt and sent to Kalinin Front; *Died:* 23 Feb 1943 killed bodily blocking the gunports of a German pill-box in fighting for the vil Chernushka, Pskov Oblast; 19 June 1943 posthumously entitled a Hero of the Sov Union; the 254th Guards Regt is named after him; his name is inscribed in perpetuity in the rolls of the regiment's 1st company; monument to him erected in Ufa.

MATSIYEVSKAYA (married name: MORINETS), Lidiya Vladimirovna (1889–1955) Ukr actress; Pop Artiste of Ukr SSR from 1947; CP member from 1945; *Born:* 20 Dec 1889 in vil Kashperovka, now Kiev Oblast, to the Krapivnitsky family of actors; *Educ:* 1909 grad History Fac, Higher Women's Courses, Odessa; *Career:* until 1916 worked as teacher and took part in amateur dramatics; 1908–18 acted with Ukr Company of Public Sobriety Soc; 1921–24 acted with Agitation Group of Odessa Polit Educ Dept, which covered the villages of Odessa Oblast; from 1925 actress, Ukr State Drama Theater (now Oct Revol Theater), Odessa; showed particular talent for comedy and character roles; preferred psychological dramas and topical comedies; 1934–52 taught dramatic delivery and narration at Odessa Theatrical College; *Roles:* Limerikha in Staritskiy's "After Two Hares"; Dulska in Zapolska's "The Morality of Mrs Dulska"; Dun'ka in "Lyubov' Yarovaya"; Bochkaryova in "Platon Krechet"; Ganna in Karpenko-Karyy's *Bestalannaya* (The Ill-Fated Woman); Fetiniya in Ostrovskiy's *Ne bylo ni grosha, da vdrug altyn* (From Rags to Riches); Khivrya in Staritskiy's *Sorochinskaya Yarmarka* (Sorochintsy Fair), after Gogol; Nataliya Kovshik and Goritsvet in Korneychuk's *Kalinovaya roshcha* (Viburnum Grove) and *Kryl'ya* (Wings); *Died:* 24 Dec 1955.

MATUSEVICH, Nikolay Nikolayevich (1879–1950) Hydrographer and geodesist; prof from 1931; vice-admiral, Sov Navy; Hon Sci and Tech Worker of RSFSR from 1944; *Born:* 10 Apr 1879; *Educ:* 1904 grad Petersburg Naval Acad; 1909 grad Petersburg Univ; *Career:* 1911–31 in charge of hydrographic surveys in north of Russia; surveyed the shores of the White, Barents and Kara seas; from 1931 prof, Leningrad Naval Acad; 1947–50 vice-pres, All-Union Geographical Soc; a bay and a river on Oct Revol Island now bear his name; *Publ: Osnovy morekhodnoy astronomii* (The Principles of Nautical Astronomy) (1956); *Died:* 27 May 1950.

MAURER, Zhan Adamovich (1890–1960) Party official; CP member from 1907; *Born:* 9 Feb 1890 in Lat; *Educ:* 1936 grad Inst of Red Prof; *Career:* started work at age 12 as shepherd; then unskilled laborer; active in revol movement; repeatedly arrested by Tsarist authorities; during WW 1 helped found Bolshevik mil org in army; fought in 1917 Oct Revol and Civil War; dep, Soskovo Sov; 1924–29 Party investigator, Party Collegium, Centr Control Commission; then worked for Centr Control Commission, Workers and Peasants' Inspection; from 1936 taught; 1938–60 prof, Chair of CPSU History, Moscow Univ; *Died:* 20 Sept 1960.

MAVRINSKIY, Ivan Leont'yevich (1885–1966) Govt official; CP member from 1903; *Born:* 14 Jan 1885; *Career:* from 1900 worked in Ufa Railroad Shops, where he engaged in illegal revol activities; during 1905–07 Revol founded and led armed workers squads in the Urals and on the Volga; several times arrested; 1907 sentenced to eight years at hard labor; Feb 1917 returned to Samara from exile; elected member, Samara City RSDRP(B) Comt, Samara Sov of Workers and Soldiers' Dep and bd member, Samara Metalworkers' Union; during Civil War commanded partisan unit; underground work in Siberia; from 1919 admin work in Barnaul and Samara; from 1925 worked for Pop Comrt of For Trade in Moscow; from 1947 in Min of the Fishing Ind; from 1954 retired; *Died:* 17 Feb 1966.

MAY–MAYEVSKIY, Vladimir Zenonovich (1867–1920) Whitist mil commander; maj-gen, Russian Army; *Born:* 1867; *Educ:* grad Gen Staff Acad; *Career:* from 1888 in Russian Army; during WW 1 commanded brigade, then 35th and 4th Infantry Div and, finally, 1st Guards Corps; 1918, with development of Civil War in Southern Russia, commanded 12,000-strong forces group in Gen Denikin's army; from Dec 1918 commanded 3rd Infantry Div, transferred to Donbass after withdrawal of German troops; after receiving reinforcements, cleared Donbass of Soviet troops and 1919 launched offensive in north; May 1919 his group was renamed Volunteer Army of Southern Russian Armed Forces; June 1919 his troops occupied Khar'kov, whereupon Denikin appointed him commander in chief of the six provinces he had occupied; Oct 1919 his troops were defeated at Kursk and Voronezh and were forced to retreat southwards; his staff was infiltrated by Sov agents and disrupted by drunkenness; because of this, in Dec 1919 Denikin dismissed him as commander of

Volunteer Army; *Died:* 1920.

MAYAKOVSKIY, Vladimir Vladimirovich (1893–1930) Russian poet; pioneer of rhythmic verse; *Born:* 19 July 1893 in vil Bagadi, Geo, the son of a nobleman; *Educ:* studied at, but did not complete, high schools in Kutaisi and Moscow; from 1911 studied at Moscow College of Painting, Sculpture and Architecture, from which he was expelled in 1912; *Career:* 1908 sided with RSDRP(B) and did propaganda work for Party; arrested and imprisoned in Moscow's Butyrka Jail, but released as a juvenile; 1910 broke with RSDRP(B); 1912 began to publish his verse in Futurist collections; 1912, together with Khlebnikov, David Burlyuk and A. Kruchyonykh, Founded Cubo-Futurist group and signed manifesto *Poshchyochina obshchestvennomu vkusu* (A Slap in the Face for Public Taste); with start of WW 1 adopted an anti-militarist stand; 1915–17 served his mil service as a draftsman at Petrograd Automobile School; welcomed 1917 Feb Revol but was soon disillusioned with it; after 1917 Oct Revol and start of Civil War began to collaborate with Bolsheviks in so-called "Satyrical Windows of the Russian Telegraphic Agency"; from 1922 ed, journals "Lef" and "Novyy lef"; led writers grouped around these journals; lauded initial achievements of Sov regime but sharply criticized Sov bureaucracy and philistinism of Sov soc; during his lifetime was frequently attacked by Party critics; visited France, Spain, America and other Western countries and on the basis of his travels produced works critical of capitalist world; 1930 joined Russian Assoc of Proletarian Writers; 1935, after his death, Stalin declared; "Mayakovsky was and remains the best and most talented poet of our socialist epoch"; *Publ:* verse: *Voyna obyavlena* (War is Declared) and *Mama i ubityy nemtsami vecher* (Mama and the Evening Killed by the Germans) (1914); *Nash marsh* (Our March) (1917); *Oda revolyutsii* (Ode to the Revolution) (1918); *Levyy marsh* (Left March) (1918); *Vladimir Il'ich* (1920); *Neobychaynoye priklyucheniye, byvsheye s Vladimirom Mayakovskim letom na dache* (The Unusual Adventure that Befell Vladimir Mayakovskiy in Summer at His Dacha) (1920); *Poslednyaya stranichka grazhdanskoy voyny* (The Last Page of the Civil War) (1921); *Yubileynoye* (Jubilee) (1924); *Proch' ruki ot Kitaya!* (Hands Off China!) (1924); *Khristofor Kolumb* (Christopher Columbus) (1925); "Black and White" (1925); "Broadway" (1925) *Sergeyu Yeseninu* (To Sergey Yesenin) (1926); *Tovarishchu Nette, parokhodu i cheloveku* (To Comrade Nette, Steamship and Man) (1926); *Stolp* (The Pillar) (1928); *Na Zapade vsyo spokoyno* (All Quiet in the West) (1929); *Stikhi o sovetskom pasporte* (Verse on a Soviet Passport) (1929); poems: *Oblako v shtanakh* (Cloud in Trousers) (1914–15); "150,000,000" (1920); *Vladimir Il'ich Lenin* (1924); *Khorosho!* (Good!) (1927); plays: *Misteriya Buff* (Mystery-Buffo) (1918); *Klop* (The Bedbug) (1928); *Banya* (The Bathhouse) (1929), etc; *Died:* 14 Apr 1930 committed suicide in Moscow; Mayakovskiy Library-Museum founded in Moscow in 1937; 1958 monument erected to him in Moscow.

MAYLIN, Beimbet Zharmagambetovich (1894–1939) Kaz poet, playwright and writer; CP member from 1925; *Born:* 15 Nov 1894 in vil Aktyube, Now Kustanay Oblast; *Educ:* 1915 grad Ufa medressah; *Career:* 1912 began to write; 1913–17 worked for newspaper "Kazak"; 1916–19 teacher in Orenburg; 1932 exec polit ed for Kaz Publ House; member, Org Burau, Kaz Assoc of Proletarian Writers; arrested by State Security organs; *Publ:* novelette "The Shchuga Memorial" (1915); verse collection "Beimbet's Verse" (1923); novelette "Raushan the Communist" (1929); play "Front" (1933); novel "Azamat Azamatych" (1934); verse collection "Myrkymbay" (1935); plays "The Amangelds" (1935); "Our Djigits" (1935); "Zhalbyr" (1936), etc; libretto for musical drama "Zhalbyr" (1936); *Died:* 10 Nov 1939 in inprisonment; posthumously rehabilitated.

MAYOROV, Mikhail Moiseyevich (1890–1940) Party and govt official; CP member from 1906; *Born:* 1890 in vil Skorodnoye, Minsk Oblast, son of a craftsman; *Career:* Party work in Kiev, Yekaterinoslav, Saratov and Moscow; spent three years in prison, ten years in exile; 1917 head, Kiev RSDRP(B) Org and Bolshevik faction, Kiev Sov of Workers and Soldiers' Dep; deleg at 7th (Apr) RSDRP(B) Conference; at 2nd All-Russian Congress of Soviets elected member, All-Russian Centr Exec Comt; 1918 chm, All-Ukr Revol Comt; underground and partisan work in Ukr; 1919–20 in Red Army; 1922–23 and 1931–32 secr, Odessa Province Party Comt; 1924–27 secr, Tomsk Province Party Comt;1923–24chm, Astrakhan' Province Exec Comt; 1924–25 chm, Tomsk Province Exec Comt; 1927–30 dep chm, Centr Control Commission, CP(B) Ukr; 1930–31 Ukr Pop Comr of Supply; 1933–37 secr, Centr Asian Bureau, CC, CPSU(B); from 1937 dep chm, USSR Centr Council of Consumer Cooperatives; deleg at 10th, 11th, 14th–17th Party Congresses and 12th–14th and 16th Party Conferences; at 15th and 16th Party Congresses elected member, CPSU(B) Centr Control Commission; deleg at 1st–3rd and 11th Congresses and 5th–7th Conferences of CP(B) Ukr; at 3rd Congress elected cand member, CC and at 5th Conference elected member, CC, CP(B) Ukr; 1932–33 cand Politbureau member, CC, CP(B) Ukr; 1938 arrested by State Security organs; *Died:* 1940 in imprisonment; posthumously rehabilitated.

MAYSURYAN, Nikolay Aleksandrovich (1896–1967) Plant breeder; Dr of Agric; prof; member, Lenin All-Union Acad of Agric Sci from 1959; corresp member, Arm Acad of Sci from 1945; CP member from 1953; *Born:* 1896; *Educ:* 1922 grad Tiflis Polytech Inst; *Career:* from 1922 asst prof, Chair of Private Farming, Tiflis Polytech Inst; 1928–33 asst prof, assoc prof, then prof, Chair of Crop Farming, Timiryazev Agric Acad, Moscow; 1932–41 prof, All-Union Acad of Socialist Farming; from 1941 again prof, Timiryazev Agric Acad; from 1959 dean, 1st Fac, Moscow Oblast Kolkhoz Univ; did research on the biology, taxonomy and agrotech of field crops; bred several strains of quick-ripening alkaloid and non-alkaloid lupine, quick-ripening soya, quick-ripening barley for the Northern regions, etc; *Publ:* coauthor, *Opredelitel' semyan i plodov sornykh rasteniy* (A Classification Key to the Seeds and Fruit of Weeds) (1930); *Rukovodstvo po morfologii i systematike polevykh kul'tur* (A Guide to the Morphology and Taxonomy of Field Crops) (1932); *Biologicheskiye osnovy sortirovaniya semyan po udel'nomu vesu* (The Biological Principles of Seed Grading by Specific Weight) (1947); *Rasteniyevodstvo* (Crop Farming) (3rd ed, 1954); ed, *Agrotekhnika polevykh kul'tur* (The Agrotechnics of Field Crops) (1960); ed, *Rasteniyevodstvo. Uchebnik dlya vysshykh shkol* (Crop Farming. A College Textbook) (1960); *Awards:* two Orders of Lenin; Order of the Red Banner of Labor; four medals; *Died:* Nov 1967.

MAYSURYAN (real name: PUGINYAN), Ol'ga Mikhaylovna (1871–1931) Arm actress; Hon Artiste of Geo SSR from 1930; *Born:* 19 Mar 1871; *Career:* 1895 began acting at Russian theater in Tbilisi; 1900 began acting in Arm; performed in the major cities of the Transbaykal and Northern Caucasus; 1912 made guest appearances in Moscow and Petersburg; specialized in dramatic heroic roles; her acting was marked by strong character identification, verve, individuality and a powerful stage presence; also read verse and prose in Arm and Russian; *Roles:* Ophelia, Desdemona, Lady Macbeth and Kruchinina; Katerina in *Groza* (The Thunderstorm); Magda in Sudermann's "Heimat," Zeynab in Yuzhin-Sumbatov's *Izmena* (Treason); Trilby; Louisa in "Kabale und Liebe"; Marguerite Gautier in "La Dame au Camelia"; Mira Efros and Esfir in Gordon's *Za okeanom* (Beyond the Ocean); Yevgine, Susan and Margarit in Shirvanzade's "Yevgine," "Namus" and "For Honor's Sake"; Natas'ya Filippovna in "Idiot," after Dostoyevsky; *Died:* 3 Aug 1931.

MAZAY, Makar Nikitovich (1910–1941) Steel founder; CP member from 1938; *Born:* 1910 in vil Ol'ginskaya, now Ksasnodar Kray; *Educ:* grad Ind Acad; *Career:* 1930–32 asst founder, from 1932 founder, Zhdanov Metallurgical Plant; 1936 originated movement for high-speed steel founding; Oct 1936 took 15 tons of steel from every square meter of hearth for six hours and 40 minutes; cut the smelting time by one-third and doubled the steel output by using high-speed methods; 1936 deleg at 8th Extraordinary Congress of Soviets; during WW 2 arrested as Communist by German mil authorities; *Publ:* *Kak dobit'sya vysokoy s'yomki stali* (How to Achieve High Steel Output) (1937); *Zapiski stalevara* (A Steel Founder's Notes) (1940); *Awards:* Order of the Red Banner of Labor; *Died:* 1941 in imprisonment in Zhdanov.

MAZAYEV, Aleksandr Vasil'yevich (1904–1962) Govt and Party official; CP member from 1925; *Born:* 1904 in Zaraysk Rayon, Moscow Oblast; *Career:* started work at age 11; 1925–35 various Komsomol, govt and Party admin posts in Moscow Oblast; from 1935 secr, Gissar Rayon Party Comt, Tadzh SSR; 1938–60 first dep chm, Tadzh Council of Pop Comr, then Council of Min; from 1960 first dep chm, Tadzh Gosplan; elected member and Bureau member, CC, CP Tadzh; dep, Tadzh Supr Sov; dep, USSR Supr Sov of 4th convocation; *Awards:* Order of Lenin; three Orders of the Red Banner of Labor; Order of the Fatherland War, 1st Class; medals; *Died:* 14 Dec 1962.

MAZHELIS, Petras (1894–1966) Bishop and Apostolic Administrator of Tel'shai Eparchy, Roman Catholic Church of Lith from

1959; *Born:* 1894; *Educ:* 1923 grad Kovno (Kaunas) Theological Seminary; 1928 grad Philosophical Fac, Kovno Univ; *Career:* 1923 consecrated priest of Tel'shai parish; also taught Divinity at Polish school; 1928–40 instructor, Tel'shai Theological Seminary; until 1940 ed, religious journal "Zhemanchiu Prietelius"; from 1941 officiated at Tel'shai Catheadral; 1952 attended Peace Conference with reps from all Churches and religious assoc, convened in Zagorsk by the Moscow Patriarchy; 1955 consecrated bishop; until 1959 capitulary vicar, Tel'shai Eparchy; *Died:* 1966.

MAZING, Yevgeniy Karlovich (1880–1944) Eng; specialist in internal combustion engines; Hon Sci and Tech Worker of RSFSR from 1941; *Born:* 17 Apr 1880; *Educ:* 1906 grad Moscow Higher Tech College; *Career:* from 1906 at Laboratory of Internal Combustion Engines, Moscow Higher Tech College; from 1920 prof and dept head, above college; developed and refined ideas of his teacher V. I. Grinevetskiy on methods of thermal calculation of engines; studied gas generation and its use in engines; designed original pneumatic power transmission for diesel locomotives; his works on complete and partial combustion of solid and liquid fuels were widely used in the design of internal combustion engines; trained many research workers and eng; *Publ: Teplovoy raschyot rabochego protsessa dvigateley vnutrennego sgoraniya* (Heat Calculations or the Working Process of Internal Combustion Engines) (1935); *O pnevmaticheskoy peredache energii v teplovozakh* (Pneumatic Power Transmission in Diesel Locomotives) (1923); *Died:* 24 Mar 1944.

MAZNIN, Dmitriy Mikhaylovich (pseudonyms: Arseniy GRANIN; GRANIN) (1902–1938) Russian poet and critic; CP member from 1920; *Born:* 26 Oct 1902 in Petersburg; *Career:* 1918 first work printed; member, writers' orgs in Northern Caucasus; member, Russian Assoc of Proletarian Writers, contributed to journals "Na podyome" and "Krasnaya nov'"; 1920 deleg at 3rd Komsomol Congress; arrested by State Security organs; *Publ:* verse collection *V dymu pozharov* (In the Smoke of the Fires) (1921); articles: "The Idea of 'Quiet Flows the Don'" (1931); "Aleksandr Malyshkin" (1932); collected articles *Na vysshuyu stupen'* (To the Highest Degree) (1932); *O geroyakh nashego vremeni* (The Heroes of Our Time) (1933); *Cherty geroya 2-y pyatiletki* (Traits of the Hero of the 2nd Five-Year Plan) (1933), etc; *Died:* 1938 in imprisonment; posthumously rehabilitated.

MDIVANI, P. G. (Party name: BUDU) (1877–1937) Party and govt official; CP member from 1903; *Born:* 1877; *Career:* revol propaganda in Kutaisi, Batumi, Tiflis, Baku and other Transcaucasian cities; frequently arrested by Tsarist authorities; late 1918–Mar 1920 member, Revol Mil Council, 11th Army and chief, Polit Dept, 10th Army; 1920–21 member, Caucasian Bureau, CC, RCP(B); 1921 RSFSR dipl rep in Turkey; June 1921 chm, Geo Revol Comt; 1922 member, Sov deleg at Genoa Conference; 1922 Presidium member, CC, CP Geo; as regards the formation of the Transcaucasian Federation and the USSR he insisted that Geo should retain its nat individuality and that Geo should join the USSR directly, and not via the Transcaucasian Federation; Geo Party org regarded this stand by Mdivani and his supporters as nationalistic deviation; 1923 sided with Leftist Opposition; 1924 USSR trade rep in France; 1931–36 chm, Supr Sovnarkhoz, Geo Pop Comr of Light Ind and first dep chm, Geo Council of Pop Comr; member, USSR and Geo Centr Exec Comt; 1928 expelled from Party for allegiance to Trotskyite opposition; 1931 reinstated in Party; 1936 again expelled; 9 July 1937 sentenced to death by Geo Supr Court; *Died:* 10 July 1937 executed by firing squad; 1953 posthumously rehabilitated.

MECHIYEV, Kyazim Bekkiyevich (1859–1945) Balkar poet; founder of Balkar lit; *Born:* 1859 in vil Shiki, now Kabardo-Balkar ASSR, son of a cattle-farmer; *Educ:* attended theological school; studied Pharsee, Arabic, Turkish and the Oriental poets; *Career:* 1890 began writing; made two trips to Middle East; 1909–10 visited Istanbul, Baghdad, Damascus and Mecca; during pre-Revol period wrote poems about unrequited love, soc inequality, folk wisdom and the people's struggle for justice and freedom; during Sov period eulogized Sov rule, the Civil War heroes and Lenin and Stalin; 1943 in the course of mass reprisals against the Balkar people for "collaborating with the Germans", exiled to Kazakhstan; *Publ:* poems: 'I Would Fain Row O'er the River Unto Thee"; "For Whom is Thy Dwelling Warm" (1890); "The Lament" (1898); "The Maiden's Lament" (1900); "The Truth"; "Toil"; "An Honest Word" (1901); "I Make Verse and Forge Iron" (1905); "Testament for a Son" (1906); "The Wounded Aurochs" (1907); "The Song of Soltan-Khamid" (1918); "Take Up Your Weapons" (1919); "I've Seen the Bolshevik Way Is Honest" (1919); "To My Son, Mukhamad" (1919–20); verse collection "Verse and Poems" (1962); *Died:* 25 Mar 1945 in exile near Taldy-Kurgan, Kaz SSR; posthumously rehabilitated.

MEDOVIKOV, Pyotr Sergeyevich (1873–1944) Pediatrician; specialist in tuberculosis; founder of Sov children's health resort treatment; prof from 1919; Dr of Med from 1902; Hon Sci Worker of RSFSR; *Born:* 1873; *Educ:* 1897 grad Petersburg Mil Med Acad; *Career:* from 1897 specialized in pediatrics; from 1913 assoc prof, Petersburg Mil Med Acad; from 1919 prof, Chair of Children's Diseases, Khar'kov Univ; from 1920 head, Chair of Pediatrics, State Inst of Advanced Med Training, Leningrad; founded children's consultation section and various other children's establishments at Petersburg (Petrograd) Mil Med Acad; 1919–24 helped found first children's senatoria at Pushkin, Petrodvorets, Siverskaya, Tolmachevo and Sestroretsk in Leningrad area; 1937 drafted basic regulations for children's sanatoria, later approved by USSR Pop Comrt of Health; argued that sanatorium and resort care for children should be both therapeutic and prophylactic and therefore saw that sanatoria provided good physical training facilities; 1925 sponsored and organized 5th All-Union Sci and Practical Congress on Resort Treatment; 1935 organized similar conferences in Yalta, Yevpatoriya and at State Inst of Resort Treatment; 1936 promoted the construction of a model children's health resort at Yevpatoriya; 1936 work was started on reconstruction of the entire Yevpatoriya area to turn it into a children's health resort; 1935–40 studied infantile diseases, tuberculosis and rachitis in children and pathology of older children; 1937 laid down indications and contraindications for health resort treatment of children; member, ed bd, journals "Pediatriya", "Voprosy tuberkulyoza", "Okhrana materinstva i mladenchestva", etc; co-ed, "Bol'shaya meditsinskaya entsiklopediya" (Large Medical Encyclopedia); wrote some 70 works; *Publ: Fiziologiya, patologiya i terapiya pishchevareniya u detey grudnogo vozrasta* (The Physiology, Pathology and Therapy of Digestion in Unweaned Infants) (1921); *Klassifikatsiya rasstroystv pishchevareniya i pitaniya v grudnom vozraste* (Classification of Digestive and Nutritional Disorders in Infants) (1923); *Tuberkulyoz v detskom vozraste* (Child Tuberculosis) (1926); *Rakhit i yego lecheniye* (Rachitis and Its Treatment) (1927); *Biologicheskiye osnovy profilaktiki u detey i tekhnika yeyo provedeniya* (The Biological Principles of Child Prophylaxis and the Technique of Its Use) (1929); *Osnovy kurortologii* (The Principles of Health Resort Treatment) (1936); *Died:* 1944 during blockade of Leningrad.

MEDVEDEV, Aleksey Vasil'yevich (1884–1940) Party and govt official; CP member from 1904; *Born:* 22 Mar 1884, son of a worker; *Educ:* studied at parish school; *Career:* metalworker by trade; worked at various plants in Moscow, Lugansk, etc; member, Socialist-Revol Party; revol work in Moscow, Petersburg, Riga and Khar'kov; frequently arrested; after 1917 Feb Revol member, Petrograd RSDRP(B) Comt; member, Petrograd Sov of Workers and Soldiers' Dep; 1918–21 exec Party work in Syzran, Kozel'sk, Belaya Tserkov' and in Red Army; 1922 chm, Khar'kov Province Trade-Union Council; from 1923 chm, Centr Control Commission of Ukr Workers and Peasants' Inspectorate; 1924 second secr, CC, CP(B) Ukr; 1927–30 secr, CC, CP(B) Ukr; in 1930's secr, USSR Centr Exec Comt; member, USSR Supr Court; deleg at 11th–17th Party Congresses; at 13th–15th CPSU(B) Congresses elected member, CC; at 16th Congress elected member, CPSU(B) Centr Control Commission; deleg at 4th, 5th 6th and 8th Conferences and 9th and 10th Congresses of CP(B) Ukr; at 6th Conference elected cand member, and at 7th Conference member, Centr Control Commission, CP(B) Ukr; at 8th Conference and 9th and 10th Congresses elected member, CC, CP(B) Ukr; 1924–25 Politbureau member, CC, CP(B) Ukr; 1926 cand Politbureau member, 1927–30 again Politbureau member, CC, CP(B) Ukr; member, All-Ukr and USSR Centr Exec Comts; arrested by State Security organs; *Died:* 23 July 1940 in imprisonment.

MEDVEDEV, Grigoriy Sergeyevich (1904–1938) Udmurt writer; *Born:* 17 Mar 1904 in vil Malyye Lyzi, now Tatar ASSR; *Career:* 1926 first work published; after writing numerous sketches and short stories embarked on his major work – a novel trilogy; described the collectivization and "socialist" transformation of the Udmurt countryside; arrested by State Security organs; *Publ:* collections of stories "The Telegraph Poles Hum" (1930) and "Storm of Flax" (1932); trilogy "The Lozin Boundary" (1932), "On the Slopes of Kyykar" (1934) and "The Great Day" (1936, publ 1959); *Died:* 1938 in imprisonment; posthumously rehabilitated.

MEDVEDEV, Mikhail Yevgen'yevich (1898–1937) Mil commander; *Born:* 1898; *Career:* from 1918 in Red Army; during Civil War chief of staff of a brigade, commanded Gomel Serfs Brigade, then commanded 1st Kazan' Infantry Div; after Civil War chief of staff, Red Army Air Force; corps chief of staff; admin chief, Red Army Staff; 1937 arrested by NKVD; *Died:* 1937 in imprisonment.

MEDVEDEV, Pavel Nikolayevich (1892–1938) Lit critic and historian; *Born:* 4 Jan 1892 in Petersburg; *Educ:* 1914 grad Law Fac, Petrograd Univ; *Career:* 1911 first work published; in 1920's and 1930's taught at higher educ establishments in Leningrad; wrote one of first courses of Sov Russian lit; also wrote studies of Aleksandr Blok, the Russian "Formalist school" and the psychology of creative writing; criticized for "sociologism" and affinities to "neo-Kantianism"; arrested by State Security organs; *Publ:* "Dem'yan Bednyy" (1925); *Dramy i poemy A. Bloka. Iz istorii ikh sozdaniya* (The Dramas and Poems of A. Blok. The Story of Their Creation) (1928); *Formal'nyy metod v literaturovedenii* (The Formal Method in Literary History) (1928); *V laboratorii pisatelya* (In the Writer's Laboratory) (1933); *Metodicheskaya razrabotka po kursu istorii russkoy literatury epokhi imperializma i proletarskoy revolyutsii* (A Methodical Draft for a Course on the History of Russian Literature in the Age of Imperialism and the Proletarian Revolution) (1933); *Formalizm i formalisty* (Formalism and the Formalists) (1934); *Died:* 1938 in imprisonment; posthumously rehabilitated.

MEDVEDEV, S. P. (1885–1937) Trade-union official; CP member from 1900; *Born:* 1885; *Career:* revol work in Petersburg and Sevastopol'; several times arrested by Tsarist authorities; after 1917 Oct Revol polit work in Red Army; from July 1918 on Eastern Front; Sept 1918–Jan 1919 member, Revol Mil Council, 1st Army; 1920 chm, CC, Metalworkers' Union; worked for All-Russian and USSR Centr Exec Comt; then various admin posts; one of leaders of "workers' opposition" group; active in "new opposition"; 1924 wrote anti-Party letter "K bakinskim rabochim" (To the Workers of Baku), for which he was expelled from the Party; 1926 publicly recanted his former views and was reinstated in Party; elected member, All-Russian Centr Exec Comt; deleg, 11th RCP(B) Congress; during 1933 Party purge again expelled from CPSU(B) as a "double-dealer and renegade"; arrested by State Security organs; *Died:* 1937 in imprisonment.

MEDYNSKIY, Yevgeniy Nikolayevich (1885–1957) Educationist; Dr of Pedag from 1935; prof from 1926; member, RSFSR Acad of Pedag Sci from 1944; *Born:* 11 Mar 1885 in Yalta; *Educ:* 1903–05 studied at Khar'kov Technol Inst; 1914 grad Law Fac, Petersburg Univ; *Career:* 1905 expelled from Khar'kov Technol Inst for involvement in Revol; from 1909 head, Zemstvo Public Educ Dept, Tsarskoye Selo Uyezd; 1912–15 lectured on extrascholastic educ at Petersburg (Petrograd) Pedag Acad; 1915–17 taught school admin at Petersburg Higher Froebel Courses and lectured at Shanyavskiy Univ, Moscow; 1917–22 taught at higher educ establishments in Nizhniy Novgorod (Gorky) and Yekaterinburg (Sverdlovsk); 1922–26 lecturer, 1926–37 prof, 2nd Moscow Univ; 1930–37 also lecturer, Higher Communist Educ Inst; 1938–48 prof, Lenin Teachers' Training Inst, Moscow; 1944–48 head, Pedag Dept, Inst of the Theory and History of Pedag, RSFSR Acad of Pedag Sci and dir, K. D. Ushinskiy State Library of Public Educ; 1947–52 Presidium member, RSFSR Acad of Pedag Sci; wrote first Sov textbook on the history of educ, which was criticized and revised several times in the 1930's and 1940's; *Publ: Vneshkol'noye obrazovaniye, yego znacheniye, organizatsiya i tekhnika* (The Importance, Organization and Techniques of Extrascholastic Education) (1913); *Metody vneshkol'noy prosvetitel'noy raboty* (Methods of Extrascholastic Education Work) (1915); *Entsiklopediya vneshkol'nogo obrazovaniya* (An Encyclopedia of Extrascholastic Education) (3 vol, 1923–25); *Istoriya pedagogiki v svyazi s ekonomicheskim razvitiyem obshchestva* (The History of Pedagogics in Relation to the Economic Development of Society) (3 vol, 1925–29); *Klassovaya bor'ba i vospitaniye* (The Class Struggle and Education) (1931); *Narodnoye obrazovaniye v SSSR* (Public Education in the USSR) (2nd ed, 1947); *Istoriya pedagogiki* (The History of Pedagogics) (1947); coauthor, *Ocherki istorii sovetskoy shkoly RSFSR za 30 let* (An Outline History of Soviet Schools in the RSFSR in the Last 30 Years) (1948); *Bratskiye shkoly Ukrainy i Belorussii v XVI-XVII vekakh i ikh rol' v vossoyedinenii Ukrainy s Rossiyey* (The Sister-Schools of the Ukraine and Belorussia in the 16th and 17th Centuries and Their Role in the Reunification of the Ukraine with Russia) (1954); *Prosveshcheniye v SSSR* (Education in the USSR) (1955); *Awards:* Order of Lenin; Order of the Red Banner of Labor; Ushinskiy Medal; *Died:* 6 Mar 1957.

MEKHLIS, Lev Zakharovich (1889–1953) Mil commander; Party and govt official; col-gen; CP member from Mar 1918; *Born:* 13 Jan 1889 in Odessa, son of Jewish office-worker; *Educ:* 1930 grad Inst of Red Prof; *Career:* 1911 drafted into Russian Army; 1914–17 served with artillery units; from 1918 in Red Army; 1918–20 brigade comr, 46th Rifle Div, Right-Bank Shock Group, Southern Front; wounded in fighting at Kakhovka; 1921–22 exec work for Pop Comrt of Workers and Peasants' Inspection; 1922–27 worked for Stalin's secretariat; played active part in campaign against Trotsky and Zinoviev opposition; from May 1930 chief ed, newspaper "Pravda"; 1937 also head, Press and Publication Dept, CC, CPSU(B); 30 Dec 1937–Sept 1940 USSR Dep Pop Comr of Defense and head, Main Polit Bd, Red Army; helped carry out purge of Red Army ranks; Stalin's rep with operational troops in battles at Lake Khasan (1938), Khalkhin Gol (1939) and in 1939–40 Soviet-Finnish War; often disorganized and disrupted operations by his interference in command decisions; Sept 1940–June 1941 USSR Pop Comr of State Control; strongly advocated concentrating mobilized reserves in direct vicinity of Western borders, which later resulted in the German capture of most of them; with the start of the Sov-German War again USSR Dep Pop Comr of Defense and head, Red Army Main Bd; Supr Commander in Chief's Headquarters rep on various fronts; his inspection tours often led to reprisals against mil commanders; late 1941 devised idea of "freezing the Germans out," involving the destruction and firing of all villages and forests near Moscow in the German troops path; May 1942, as Supr Headquarters rep on the Crimean Front, seriously disrupted the work of the front's command, thus contributing to the defeat of the Sov forces at Krch'; this debacle led to his demotion from army comr, 1st class, to corps comr and his dismissal from the posts of USSR Dep Comr of Defense and head, Red Army Main Bd; 1942–45 member, Mil Council, Volkhov, Bryansk, Western, Baltic, 2nd Baltic, 2nd Bel and 4th Ukr fronts; 1945–27 Oct 1950 again Pop Comr (Min) of State Control; relieved of this post for health reasons; 1934–39 cand member, 1939–53 member, CC, CPSU(B); 1938–52 member, Org Bureau, CC, CPSU(B); dep, USSR Supr Sov of 1937 and 1946 convocations; dep, RSFSR Supr Sov of 1938 convocation; *Awards:* four Orders of Lenin; two Orders of the Red Banner; Order of Suvorov, 1st Class; Order of Kutuzov, 1st Class; Order of the Red Star; medals; *Died:* 13 Feb 1953; buried on Moscow's Red Square.

MEKHONOSHIN, Konstantin Aleksandrovich (1889–1938) Revolutionary; veteran of Oct Revol and Civil War; CP member from 1913; *Born:* 30 Oct 1889 in what is now Aleksandrovsk, son of a teacher; *Educ:* 1914 grad Physics and Mathematics Fac, Petersburg Univ; *Career:* from 1906 active in revol movement; 1912, still a student, twice arrested and exiled from Petersburg; 1914–15 with Caspian Ichthyological Marine Expedition; 1915–17 life-guard with Grenadier Regt in Petrograd; after 1917 Feb Revol member, Petrograd RSDRP(B) Comt and member of its Mil Commission; member, All-Russian Bureau of Front and Rear Mil Organizations, CC, RSDRP(B); member, Petrograd Sov; July 1917 arrested for Bolshevik armed demonstration against Provisional Govt and imprisoned until Oct; during preparations for Oct Coup member, Petrograd Mil Revol Comt; member, All-Russian Centr Exec Comt of 1917 convocation; from 3 Dec 1917 Asst Pop Comr for Mil Affairs; Dec 1917–Sept 1918 Collegium member, Pop Comrt of Mil Affairs; from 6 Jan 1918 member, Extraordinary Mil Staff to Defend Sov Regime Against Counterrevolution; from 3 Feb 1918 member, Bd for Mustering and Organizing the Red Army; from 21 Feb 1918 member, Extraordinary Staff of Petrograd Mil Distr; member, Comt for Revol Defense of Petrograd; from 18 Mar 1918 member, Higher Mil Council; 13 June–13 July 1918 member, Revol Mil Council to Coordinate Operations against the Mutiny of the Czechoslovak Corps; 13 July–19 Aug 1918 member, Revol Mil Council, Eastern Front; 2 Sept 1918–4 July 1919 member, RSFSR Revol Mil Council; 3 Oct 1918–26 Jan 1919 chm, Revol Mil Council of Southern Front; 9 Feb–13 Mar 1919 chm, Revol Mil Council of Caspian–Caucasian Front; 20 Mar–10 June 1919 chm, Revol Mil Council of 11th Separate Army; 15 June–13 July 1919 member, Revol Mil Council of Southern Front; July–Dec 1919 head, Polit Dept of Internal Defense; 31 Dec 1919–27 May 1920 member, Revol Mil Council of 11th Army on Southeastern Front; 20 June–31 Dec 1920 chm, Revol Mil Council of 3rd Army on Western Front; 1921 Collegium member, Main Fisheries Trust; 1921–26 dep chief, then chief of Gen Mil Training; chm, Higher Council for Physical Training and Sport; chm, Red Sports International; 1926–27 Sov mil attache in Poland; 1928 dep chm, Defense Section, USSR Gosplan; Presidium member, Centr Council, Soc for the Promotion of the USSR Aviation, Chemical and Defense Ind; 1929–31 Presidium member, USSR Gosplan and chm of its Defense Section; 1931–34 Collegium member, USSR Pop Comrt of Posts and Telegraphs and USSRPop Comrt of Communications; from 1934 dir, All-Union Research Inst of Oceanography and Marine Econ; Nov 1937 arrested by NKVD; *Died:* 7 May 1938 in imprisonment; posthumously rehabilitated.

MELENEVSKIY, M. I. (pseudonyms: BASOK, SAMOYLOVICH) (1879–1938) Politician; *Born:* 1879; *Career:* 1905 worked for Ukr Soc-Democratic org "Spilka" (Union); member, Spilka CC; Kiev Okrug Party Org and Spilka voting deleg at 14th (Amalgamative) RSDRP Congress; 1908 emigrated after suppression of Spilka; 1912 secr, re-founded Spilka For Comt; Aug 1912 attended Liquidationist Conference in Vienna; during WW 1 active in Union for the Liberation of the Ukr; after 1917 Oct Revol various admin posts; arrested by State Security organs; *Died:* 1938 in imprisonment.

MEL'GUNOV, Sergey Petrovich (1879–1956) Historian and publicist; leading member, Pop Socialist Party; *Born:* 25 Dec 1879; *Educ:* 1904 grad Moscow Univ; *Career:* 1900–10 worked for newspaper "Russkiye vedomosti"; 1913–23 co-ed, journal "Golos minuvshego"; helped edit collective historical works; *Velikaya reforma* (The Great Reform) (1911); *Otechestvennaya voyna i russkoye obshchestvo* (The Fatherland War and Russian Society) (1912) and *Masonstvo v vego proshlom i nastoyashchem* (Masonism Past and Present) (1912); opposed to 1917 Oct Revol; 1920 sentenced to death in trial of "Tactical Center", fabricated by the Cheka; sentence commuted to 10 years' imprisonment; 1921 released upon intercession of anarchist Krapotkin; 1922 rearrested; 1923 allowed to leave USSR on condition that he would never return; lived in Berlin and from 1924 in Paris; published journals "Golos minuvshego na chuzhoy storone", "Bor'ba za Rossiyu" and "Rossiyskiy demokrat"; *Publ: Iz istorii studencheskikh obshchestv v russkikh universitetakh* (The History of Student Societies in Russian Universities) (1904); *Tserkov' i gosudarstvo v Rossii* (Church and State in Russia) (2 vol, 1907–09); *Studencheskiye organizatsii 80-90-ikh godov v Moskovskom universitete* (Student Organizations of the 1880's and 1890's at Moscow University) (1908); *Tserkov' v novoy Rossii* (The Church in the New Russia) (1917); *Religiozno-obshchestvennyye dvizheniya XVII-XVIII vekov v Rossii* (Seventeenth-and Eighteenth-Century Religious and Social Movements in Russia) (1922); *Dela i lyudi Aleksandrovskogo vremeni* (Events and People of the Alexandrine Period) (1923); *Krasnyy terror v Rossii* (The Red Terror in Russia) (1924); *Tragediya admirala Kolchaka. Iz istorii grazhdanskoy voyny na Volge* (The Tragedy of Admiral Kolchak. The History of the Civil War on the Volga) (3 vol, 1930–31); *Na putyakh k dvortsovomu perevorotu* (The Approaches to a Palace Coup) (1931); *Zolotoy nemetskiy klyuch k bol'shevistskoy revolyutsii* (The Golden German Key to the Bolshevik Revolution) (1940); *Kak bol'sheviki zakhvatili vlast'. Oktyabr'skiy perevorot 1917 goda* (How the Bolsheviks Seized Power. The 1917 October Coup) (1953); *Legenda o separatnom mire* (The Legend of the Separate Peace) (1957); *Martovskiye dni 1917 goda* (The Events of March 1917) (1961), etc; *Died:* 29 May 1956 in Paris.

MELIK-PASHAYEV, Aleksandr Shamil'yevich (1905–1964) Conductor; Pop Artiste of USSR from 1951; *Born:* 23 Oct 1905 in Tiflis; *Educ:* studied at Tbilisi Conservatory; 1930 grad Leningrad Conservatory, where he studied under Prof A. V. Gauk; *Career:* from 1921 pianist-concertmaster, from 1922 conductor, Tbilisi Opera Theater, where he conducted Borodin's *Knyaz' Igor'* (Prince Igor) and Pototskiy's *Proryv* (The Breach) (1930–31); 1931 made debut at Bolshoy Theater with "Aida"; 1931–53 conductor, 1953–62 chief conductor, Bolshoy Theater; *Works:* conducted operas: "Othello" (1932); "The Huguenots" (1934); "Sadko" (1935); Chishko's *Bronenosets Potyomkin* (The Battleship Potyomkin) (1938); *Cherevichki* (The Slippers) (1941); "Wilhelm Tell" (1942); "Carmen" (1945); "La Traviata" (1953); Shaporin's *Dekabristy* (The Decembrists) (1953); Beethoven's "Fidelio" (1955); Kabalevskiy's "Nikita Vershinin" (1955); *Voyna i mir* (War and Peace) (1959); Dzerzhinskiy's *Sud'ba cheloveka* (A Man's Fate) (1961); Verdi's "Falstaff" (1962), etc; *Awards:* Order of the Red Banner of Labor; Badge of Hon; two Stalin Prizes (1942 and 1943); *Died:* 18 June 1964.

MELIKOV, Firuz Ali ogly (1902–1965) Zootech; Doctor of Agric Sci; member, All-Union Lenin Acad of Agric Sci from 1948; member, Azer Acad of Sci from 1949; Hon Sci Worker of Azer SSR from 1941; CP member from 1945; *Born:* 1902 in Sal'yany; *Educ:* 1928 grad Azer Polytech Inst; *Career:* 1926–39 lecturer, from 1939 prof, dean and dep dir, Azer Agric Inst; also dep dir, Veterinary Research Inst, dir of an experimental stock-raising station and Azer First Dep Min of Agric; 1958–60 pres, Azer Acad of Agric Sci; in latter years prof, Chair of Genetics and Darwinism, Azer State Inst; also worked on sheep-breeding and bred the Azer highland Merino, a high-yield strain of sheep; *Publ: Merinosovodstvo v Azerbaydzhane i materialy po skreshchivaniyu ikh s mestnymi ovtsami* (Merino-Breeding in Azerbaydzhan and Data on Their Cross-Breeding with Local Strains of Sheep) (1936); *Molochnoye ovtsevodstvo v Azerbaydzhane* (Sheep-Breeding for Milk in Azerbaydzhan) (1940); coauthor, *K vyvedeniyu polutonkorunnoy zhirnokhvostnoy porody ovets v Azerbaydzhane* (The Development of a Semi-Fine Fleeced Fat-Tailed Breed of Sheep in Azerbaydzhan) (1952); coauthor, *Omolochnoy produktivnosti polutonkorunnykh zhirnokhvostnykh ovets (Novaya porodnaya gruppa) v sovkhoze "Bol'shevik"* (The Milk Productivity of Semi-Fine Fleeced Fat-Tailored Sheep (the New Breed) on the Bolshevik Sovkhoz) (1952); *Azerbaydzhanskiy gornyy merinos* (The Azerbaydzhan Highland Merino) (1946); coauthor, *Vyrashchivaniye i ispol'zovaniye vysoko-produktivnykh baranov porody Azerbaydzhanskiy gornyy merinos* (Raising and Utilizing High-Yield Rams of the Azerbaydzhan Highland Merino Breed) (1954); *Uluchsheniye plemennogo kachestva sovetskogo merinosa v sovkhoze im. "28 aprelya"* (Improving the Stud Quality of the Soviet Merino on the "28 April" Sovkhoz) (1960); *Sel'skokhozyaystvennaya nauka v Azerbaydzhane za 40 let* (Forty Years of Agricultural Science in Azerbaydzhan) (1960); *Izolirovannyy rubets u buyvolov* (The Isolated Rumen in Oxen) (1962); *Awards:* Order of Lenin; two Orders of the Red Banner of Labor; Stalin Prize (1947); *Died:* 12 Nov 1965.

MELIKOV, Vladimir Arsen'yevich (1898–1942) Mil historian and instructor; maj-gen from 1940; Dr of Mil Sci; prof; CP member from 1919; *Born:* 1898; *Educ:* 1923 grad Red Army Mil Acad; *Career:* fought in Civil War; from 1923 instructor, then head, Chair of Mil History, Red Army Mil Acad (from 1925 Frunze Acad); from 1936 prof, Gen Staff Acad; *Publ: Marna, Visla, Smirna* (The Marne, Vistula and Smyrna) (1928); *Problema strategicheskogo razvyortyvaniya po opytu mirovoy i grazhdanskoy voyn* (The Problem of Strategic Deployment from the Experience of the World War and the Civil War) (1935); *Geroicheskaya oborona Tsaritsyna* (The Heroic Defense of Tsaritsyn) (1938); *Died:* 1942.

MELKHISEDEK (real name: PAYEVSKIY, Mikhail) (187? –1931) Metropolitan of Minsk and Bel, Autocephalous Orthodox Church of Bel; *Born:* 187? in Grodno Province; *Educ:* grad Kazan' Theological Acad; *Career:* after grad taught lit at various theological schools; until 1910 archimandrite and father-superior, Belynichi Monastery, Mogilev Province; 1910 transferred to Crimea for health reasons and appointed Bishop of Taurida; 1918 Bishop of Ladoga; 1919 appointed Bishop of Slutsk and administrator (from 1920 Bishop) of Minsk and Turov Eparchy; 1922 organized congress of eparchal clergy which proclaimed the Autocephalous Orthodox Church of Bel and elected him Metropolitan of Minsk and Bel; in same year ordained three Bel bishops with the assistance of several bishops from USSR with Patriarchal authority; 1923 tried by Sov court in Minsk for "concealing Church valuables" and given a suspended sentence; after accession of Metropolitan Sergiy (Stragorodskiy) Spent nine months in Butyrka Prison; after release continued to campaign for preservation of Autocephalous Orthodox Church of Bel; 1927 summoned to Moscow, deprived of metrolitanship and exiled to Krasnoyarsk; 1931 returned to Moscow, appointed archbishop and persuaded by Sergiy to attend summer session of Holy Synod; *Died:* 1931 in a Moscow church.

MELKHISEDEK (real name: Mikhail PKHALADZE) (1876–1960) Catholicos of All Geo, Geo Autocephalous Orthodox Church; Archbishop of Mtskheta and Tbilisi; *Born:* 1876 in Kakhetia, son of a psalm-reader; *Educ:* 1896 grad Tiflis Theological Seminary; 1900 grad Kazan' Theological Acad as Cand of Divinity; *Career:* until 1915 taught at theological establishments; 1915 consecrated priest; 1925 took monastic orders with the name Melkhisedek;

1925 elevated to archimandrite and soon afterwards to Bishop of Alaverda; 1927 appointed Bishop of Tskhum-Bedia (Geo SSR); 1928 resigned this see; 1935 elevated to metropolitan; 1943 appointed Metropolitan of Urbnis (Geo SSR); 1952 at 9th Synod of All-Geo Church in Tbilisi, elected Catholicos of All Geo; also Archbishop of Mtskheta and Tbilisi; *Died:* 10 Jan 1960.

MELKIKH, Sergey Mikheyevich (1877–1952) Internist; prof from 1922; *Born:* 1877 in Moscow, son of an office worker; *Educ:* 1895 grad boys' high-school in Moscow; 1900 grad Med Fac, Moscow Univ with distinction; *Career:* 1900–10 intern, Prof A. A. Ostroumov's Therapeutic Clinic, Moscow Univ; 1910–14 asst prof, Therapeutic Clinic, Moscow Higher Women's Courses; during WW 1 physician at an evacuation hospital; from Feb 1918 senior asst prof, Fac Therapy Clinic, 2nd Moscow Univ; from 26 Apr 1922 head, Chair of Fac Therapy, Bel Univ; from 1923 also dean, Med Fac, Bel Univ; 1937–41 head, Sci and Personnel Training Dept, Bel Pop Comrt of Health; founder-chm, Bel Soc of Therapists; co-ed, journal "Belaruskaya medychnaya dumka"; 1941 volunteered for Sov Army and headed therapy dept at various mil hospitals; May 1943 detached for work with Bel Acad of Sci; from Aug 1943 head, Chair of Hospital Therapy, Minsk Med Inst during and after evacuation to Yaroslavl; *Publ: diagnostika khronicheskogo pankreatita* (The Diagnosis of Chronic Pancreatitis) (1902); *Klinicheskoye znacheniye krioskopii mochi* (The Clinical Importance of Cryoscopy of the Urine) (1903); *Trudnosti differentsial'noy diagnostiki mezhdu pankreatitom i rakom podzheludochnoy zhelezy* (The Difficulties of the Differential Diagnosis of Pancreatitis and Cancer of the Pancreas) (1914), etc; *Died:* 1952 in Minsk.

MEL'NICHANSKIY, Grigoriy Natanovich (1886–1937) Trade-union official; CP member from 1902; *Born:* 1886; *Career:* metalworker by trade; carried out Party work in southern Russia, Nizhniy Novgorod and Siberia; 1905 took part in revol in Odessa and was involved in mutiny on the battleship "Potyomkin"; member, Odessa Sov of Workers' Dep; 1910 emigrated and worked for American Socialist Party; after 1917 Feb Revol returned to Russia and did Party and trade-union work in Petrograd, Donbass and Moscow; active in Oct Revol; Oct 1917 member, Moscow Mil Revol Comt; after Oct Revol trade-union and admin work; Nov 1917–18 secr, 1918–24 chm, Moscow Province Trade-Union Council; from 1926 Presidium member, All-Union Centr Trade-Union Council; chm, CC, Textile Workers' Union; 1918–20 member, Workers and Peasants' Defense Council on behalf of All-Union Centr Trade-Union Council; Presidium member, Gosplan; Collegium member, Pop Comrt of Workers and Peasants' Inspection; chm, Inventions Comt; at 18th Trade-Union Congress sided with Tomskiy, but broke with him after congress; at 1927 15th Party Congress elected cand member, CC, CPSU(B); cand Presidium member, USSR Centr Exec Comt; arrested by State Security organs; *Died:* 1937 in imprisonment.

MEL'NICHUK, Yuriy Stepanovich (1921–1963) Ukr writer, journalist and lit historian; cand of Philology; bd member, Ukr Writers' Union; CP member from 1942; *Born:* 7 May 1921 in vil Malaya Kamenka, Ukr; *Educ:* 1948 grad Higher Party School, CC, CP Ukr; 1950 grad Lvov Univ; *Career:* 1938 expelled from Kolomiya High-School for distributing Communist lit; 1939 first work published; from 1940 Komsomol work and contributed to Kolomiya newspaper "Krasnyy flag"; during WW 2 in the Red Army; from 1948 chief ed, "Soviet Writer" Publ House; from 1951 chief ed, journal "Zhovten'"; dep, USSR Supr Sov of 1962 convocation; *Publ:* collections: "Servants of the Yellow Devil" (1957); "Spawn of Judas" (1958); "The Wall Street Organ-Grinder" (1958); "The Face of God's Host" (1960); "Popes Are Born in the Smokestack" (1960); "The Flame of the Vampires" (1963); "The Wrenched Forth Heart" (1966), etc; lit-critical studies of the Ukr writers Galan, Gavrilyuk, etc, "A Word About Writers" (1958); *Awards:* Order of the Red Banner of Labor; (1961); other orders; medals; *Died:* 11 Aug 1963 in Lvov.

MEL'NIKAYTE, Mariya Yuozovna (1923–1943) WW 2 partisan in Lith; Komsomol member from 1940; *Born:* 12 Apr 1923 in Zarasay, Lith, daughter of a worker; *Career:* secr, Zarasay Uyezd Comt, Lith Komsomol; June 1942 joined 16th Lith Infantry Div, Red Army; 23 May 1943 sent behind enemy lines with partisan group; helped found Kestutis Partisan Detachment and took part in its operations; 8 July 1943 wounded and captured by German troops along with partisan group; *Awards:* Hero of Sov Union (1944, posthumously); *Died:* 13 July 1943 executed in vil Dukshtas; opera entitled "Marite" and film devoted to her; monuments erected to her in Zarasay and Druskininkay.

MEL'NIKOV, Aleksandr Vasil'yevich (1889–1958) Surgeon and oncologist; Dr of Med from 1920; prof from 1923; maj-gen, Med Corps; member, USSR Acad of Med Sci from 1948; Hon Sci Worker of RSFSR from 1942; *Born:* 12 July 1889 in Mezen', Arkhangel'sk Province; *Educ:* 1909 grad Arkhangel'sk Classical High School; 1914 grad Petersburg Mil Med Acad with Distinction; *Career:* while still a student began specializing in surgery under Prof N. A. Vel'yaminov; vice-pres, Student Surgical Soc; in last year of studies also intern, Surgical Dept, Semyonov Hospital; during WW 1 senior surgeon with an artillery brigade and head of surgical dept at various hospitals; from 1918 dissector, then senior lecturer, V. N. Shevkunenko's Chair of Operative Surgery, Petrograd Mil Med Inst; from same year member, Pirogov Surgical Soc, in which he subsequently held the posts of secr, dep chm and chm; 1920 defended doctor's thesis on the sinus eostodiaphragmaticus; 1920–22 asst to Prof S. P. Fyodorov, Surgical Clinic, Petrograd Inst of Postgrad Med Training; 1922 assoc prof, Chair of Operative Surgery, Petrograd Mil Med Acad; 1923–29 prof, Chair of Operative Surgery, 1929–32 head, Chair of Surgical Pathology and Therapy, 1932–39 head, Chair of Hospital Surgery, 1939 head, Chair of Fac Surgery, Khar'kov Med Inst; 1923–41 also head, Oncological Clinic, Ukr Centr Roentgenological; Radiological and Oncological Inst, Khar'kov; 1925–35 head, Chair of Operative Surgery, Khar'kov Stomatological Inst; 1928 founded first Sov oncological outpatients' clinic in Khar'kov; 1940 head, Chair of Oncology, Khar'kov Inst of Postgrad Med Training; Nov 1940–42 head, Chair of Hospital Surgery, from 1942 head, Chair of Fac Surgery, Leningrad Naval Med Acad; 1956–58 head, 2nd Chair of Fac Surgery, Leningrad Mil Med Acad; from 1953 hon member, Pirogov Med Sci and bd member, All-Union Soc of Surgeons; member, various other med soc, commissions, etc; ed or co-ed, journals "Vestnik khirurgii i pogranichnykh oblastey", "Voprosy onkologii", "Vrachebnoye delo", "Eksperimental'naya meditsina" and "Vestnik khirurgii imeni I. I. Grekova"; organized and read papers at numerous All-Union and republ oncological congresses; trained numerous surgeons and sponsored 53 doctor's theses; developed surgical techniques for treating gunshot stomach wounds, intestinal fistula, etc, and devised a nerve-trunk blocking technique; developed theory of the pre-cancerous state and described the metastases in the collectors of the lymphatic nodes at various stages of cancer of the stomach; wrote over 120 works; *Publ: Rezektsiya grudnogo otdela pishchevoda* (Resection of the Thoracic Section of the Oesophagus) (1922); *Klinika gazovoy infektsii ognestrel'nykh ran* (The Clinical Aspects of Gas Infection of Gunshot Wounds) (1945); *Klinika i profilaktika svishchey zheludka i kishechnika u ranenykh v bryushnuyu polost'* (The Clinical Aspects and Prevention of Gastrointestinal Fistulas in Patients Suffering from Abdominal Wounds) (1947); *Okolobryushnyye flegmony u ranenykh v zhivot* (Periabdominal Phlegmata in Patients Suffering from Stomach Wounds) (1955); coauthor, *Opyt sovetskoy meditsiny v Velikoy Otechestvennoy voyne, 1941–45* (The Experience of Soviet Medicine in the 1941–45 Great Fatherland War), etc; *Awards:* Bush Prize (1914); Burdenko Prize (1945); various orders and medals; *Died:* 18 June 1958.

MEL'NIKOV, Pyotr Ivanovich (1870–1940) Opera producer; *Born:* 1870, son of the opera singer I. A. Mel'nikov; *Career:* 1896–1905 producer, Moscow Private Russian Opera House; 1906–09, 1913–14 and 1919–21 produced operas at Bolshoy Theater; 1909–13, 1914–19 and 1921–22 producer, Mariinskiy Theater; 1922 emigrated to Lat; 1922–32 producer, Riga Opera Theater; 1932–40 worked as a producer in Milan; *Works:* produced operas: at Bolshoy Theater: "Demon" (1906); "Ruslan and Ludmilla" (1907); "Eugene Onegin" (1908); Goldmark's "A Winter's Tale" (1909); "Boris Godunov" (1920); at Mariinskiy Theater: *Knyaz' Igor'* (Prince Igor) (1909); *Skazaniye o nevidimom grade Kitezhe i deve Fevroniya* (The Legend of the Invisible City of Kitezh and the Maiden Fevronii) (1910, 1918); "Khovanshchina" (1911); *Mayskaya noch'* (May Night) (1910); Kazanli's "Miranda" and Taneyev's *Metel'* (The Blizzard) (1916); at Riga Opera Theater: Medyn's *Zhritsa* (The Priestess) (1927), etc; *Died:* 28 Dec 1940.

MEL'NIKOV-RAZVEDENKOV, Nikolay Fedotovich (1866–1937) Pathoanatomist; Dr of Med from 1895; prof from 1902; member, Ukr Acad of Sci from 1927; *Born:* 24 Dec 1866 in vil Ust'-Medveditskaya (now Serafimovich, Volgograd Oblast), son of a nobleman; *Educ:* 1889 grad Med Fac, Moscow Univ; *Career:* after grad did postgrad work at Moscow Univ; 1890–1902 asst prof, Chair of Pathological Anatomy, Moscow Univ; 1892 founded a pathoanatomical club which subsequently became the Moscow Pathoanatomists' Soc; from 1896 assoc prof of pathological anatomy; 1898 did research on Siberian plague; 1898–1900 underwent further specialist training in Freiburg (Bade); 1902–20 prof of pathological anatomy, Khar'kov Univ; 1902 did research on alveolar hydatid tapeworm in animals and humans; from 1906 co-founder and ed, journal "Khar'kovskiy meditsinksiy zhurnal"; from 1918 co-founder and ed, journal "Vrachebnoye delo"; 1920–25 head, Chair of Pathological Anatomy and Forensic Med, Kuban' Univ, Krasnodar, of which he was a founding member; 1921–25 rector, Kuban' Med Inst; co-founder and chm, Kuban' Soc of Physical Med; co-founder, journals "Kubanskiy nauchno-meditsinskiy izvestnik" and "Kubanskiy voyenno-meditsinskiy zhurnal"; 1925–30 founder-dir, Ukr Inst of Experimental Med, Khar'kov; from 1925 Presidium member, Ukr Main Sci Bd and chm, Pathology Commission, Ukr Acad of Sci; from 1926 founder and life-chm, Ukr Pathologists' Soc (with branches in Khar'kov, Kiev, Odessa and Dnepropetrovsk); Presidium member, Learned Council, Ukr Pop Comrt of Health; 1929 did research on nodular periarteritis; from 1930 head, Pathomorphological Dept, Ukr Inst of Experimental Med; 1936 studied the pathomorphology of nodular processes; co-ed, "Bol'shaya meditsinskaya entsiklopediya" (Large Medical Encyclopedia); devised conservation method used by V. P. Vorob'yov to embalm Lenin's corpse; *Publ: Novyy sposob prigotovleniya anatomicheskikh preparatov* (A New Method of Preparing Anatomical Specimens) (1896); *Issledovaniye al'veolyarnogo (mul'tilokulyarnogo) ekhinokokka u cheloveka i u zhivotnykh* (A Study of Alveolar [Multiple] Hydatid Tapeworm in Humans and Animals) (1902); *Posobiye k prakticheskomu kursu patologicheskoy gistologii* (An Aid to the Practical Course of Pathological Histology) (1916); *Aktinomikoz tsentral'noy nervnoy sistemy* (Actinomycosis of the Central Nervous System) (1930); *Patogistologiya oteka* (The Pathological Histology of Edema) (1934); *Patomorfologiya allergicheskikh protsessov* (The Pathomorphology of Allergic Processes) (1938); *Died:* 20 Dec 1937 in Khar'kov.

MENDELEYEV, Vasiliy Dmitriyevich (1886–1922) Russian inventor and designer; son of D. I. Mendeleyev; *Born:* 1886; *Educ:* 1903–06 studied at Kronstadt Naval Eng College; *Career:* 1908–16 at Baltic, Neva and other shipyards in Petersburg; 1919–22 at "Kubanol'" Shipyard in Krasnodar; 1911 proposed plans for an armored tracked mil machine (tank); 1911–15 worked on blueprints for tank; one of his blueprints provided for a tank armed with a 120-mm naval gun and a machine-gun; the tank would have a maximum speed of 24 km/hr, carry a crew of eight and weigh 170 tons; also designed submarines and minelayers; *Died:* 1922.

MENZHINSKAYA, Lyudmila Rudol'fovna (1876–1933) Educationist; CP member from 1904; sister of V. R. Menzhinskiy, chm of USSR OGPU; *Born:* 1876, daughter of a history professor; *Educ:* grad Mariinskaya Girls High-School and three-year teachers' training course; *Career:* from 1896 teacher, No. 1 Narva School; then until 1917 teacher, No. 5 Petrograd City Girls College; simultaneously taught evening and Sunday courses at Smolensk (Kornilov) School in Petrograd; from 1905 worked for Mil Section, CC, RSDRP, storing and delivering weapons and explosives; then secr, Petersburg RSDRP Comt; helped organize Soc-Democratic Teachers Congress; 1912–14 contributed to newspaper "Pravda"; 1914 member, Russian Section, ed bd of journal "Rabotnitsa"; 1914 arrested; after release active Marxist propaganda among teachers; lectured to Marxist workers' circles and at schools; after 1917 Feb Revol worked for secretariat, CC, RSDRP(B); July–Aug 1917 member, secretariat, 6th RSDRP(B) Congress; from fall 1917 member, Petrograd 1st City Rayon RSDRP(B) Comt and member, Petrograd RSDRP(B) Comt; Jan 1918 appointed govt comr, Pop Comrt of Educ; 1919 acting Dep Pop Comr of Educ; 1921 appointed dep head, Women Workers Dept, CC, RSDRP(B); then chm, All-Russian Extraordinary Commission to Eliminate Illiteracy; Aug 1922–Mar 1924 Collegium member, Ukr Pop Comrt of Educ; then worked in Moscow; 1926–27 incapacitated by ill health; 1927–28 prorector, Acad of Communist Training; from 1928 worked for Agitation and Propaganda Dept, CC, RSDRP(B); then dep head, Moscow Publ Educ Dept; from 1931 dep dir and dir of studies, Moscow Oblast Ind Teachers' Training Combine; *Died:* 12 Nov 1933; buried in Moscow's Novodevich'ye Cemetery.

MENZHINSKAYA, Vera Rudol'fovna (1872–1944) Educationist; Party and govt official; CP member from 1905; *Born:* 1872, daughter of a history prof; *Educ:* grad Maria Girls' High-School, 3-Year Teachers' Training Courses and Courses in Experimental Pedag; *Career:* from 1894 taught at a municipal school in Petersburg, then at an evening and Sunday workers' school at Moscow Gates; 1905–07 worked as an aide to N. K. Krupskaya, with whom she organized secret meetings of RSDRP(B) members, the supply of propaganda material and passports and the transmission of Party instructions; 1912–14 contributed to "Pravda"; 1915 member, Agitation and Propaganda Commission, CC, RSDRP(B); after 1917 Feb Revol worked for Secretariat, CC, RSDRP(B); 1917–29 held exec positions in RSFSR Pop Comrt of Educ; head, Unified School Dept, Theater Dept and Travelling Exhibition Section, Main Polit·Educ Comt; 1929–44 founder-dir, Centr Foreign Language Corresp Courses; *Awards:* Order of the Red Banner of Labor; *Died:* 21 Oct 1944; buried at Novodevich'ye Cemetery, Moscow.

MENZHINSKIY, Vyacheslav Rudol'fovich (1874–1934) Party and govt official; CP member from 1902; chm, USSR OGPU; *Born:* 1 Oct 1874 in Petersburg, son of a teacher; *Educ:* 1898 grad Law Fac, Petersburg Univ; *Career:* from 1895 active in revol movement; member, Yaroslavl' Party Comt and head of its Agitation and Propaganda Dept; 1903 after 2nd RSDRP Congress sided with Bolsheviks; worked in Yaroslavl' for legal newspaper "Severnyy kray"; active in 1905–07 Revol; co-ed, Bolshevik newspaper "Kazarma"; 1906 arrested in Petersburg and imprisoned; 1907 escaped and fled abroad; lived in Belgium, Switzerland and France; late 1910–spring 1911 sided with "Vperyod" faction and lectured at "Vperyod" Party school; worked for foreign orgs of Party; worked for ed bd, newspaper "Proletariy"; summer 1917 returned to Russia; helped prepare and carry out 1917 Oct Revol; Bureau member, Mil Org and ed, Bolshevik newspaper "Soldat"; after 1917 Oct Revol Pop Comr of Finance; directed nationalization of banks; 1918 RSFSR consul-gen in Berlin; 1919 Ukr Pop Comr of State Control; from 1919 exec work with All-Russian Cheka; dep chm, Cheka and head, Special Dept, Cheka; from 1922 Collegium member, State Polit Bd; from 1923 first dep chm, OGPU; from 1926, after Dzerzhinskiy's death, chm, OGPU; uncovered such alleged anti-Sov orgs and plots as: the "Shakhtinskiy Affair," the "Industrial Party," "Peasant Labor Party," the "Union RSDRP (Mensheviks) Bureau," etc; member, USSR Centr Exec Comt of 4th and 5th convocations; 1927 and 1930 at 15th and 16th Party Congresses elected member, CC, CPSU(B); *Died:* 10 May 1934; allegedly assassinated by "Righist-Trotskyite Bloc"; buried on Moscow's Red Square.

MERANVIL', L. A. (1885–1938) Govt official; CP member from 1917; *Born:* 1885; *Career:* 1904–17 member, RSDRP (Mensheviks); 1921–22 business manager, Pop Comrt of Workers and Peasants' Inspection; member, Minor Council of Pop Comr; arrested by State Security organs; *Died:* 1938 in imprisonment.

MEREZHKOVSKIY, Dmitriy Sergeyevich (1866–1941) Russian writer, philosopher and lit historian; *Born:* 14 Aug 1866 in Petersburg, son of a minor court official; *Educ:* grad History and Philology Dept, Petersburg Univ; *Career:* in early 1880's began to publish verse; 1920 emigrated; opposed to Sov regime; leader of older Symbolists; influential in religious revival among Russian intellectuals in early 1900's; *Publ:* collection *Stikhotvoreniya* (Verse) (1888); *O prichinakh upadka i o novykh techeniyakh sovremennoy russkoy literatury* (New Trends and the Reasons for the Decline in Modern Russian Literature) (1893); trilogy: *Khristos i Antikhrist* (Christ and Antichrist) (Part 1–3, 1896–1901–1905); *L. Tolstoy i Dostoyevskiy. Zhizn' i tvorchestvo* (L. Tolstoy and Dostoyevsky. Life and Work), (Part 1–2, 1901–02); *O tak nazyvayemykh religioznykh iskaniyakh v Rossii. Yevangeliye ot dekadansa* (The So-Called Religious Questing in Russia. The Gospel of Decadence) (1909); *Gryadushchiy kham* (The Future Boor) (1906); *Gogol' i chort* (Gogol and the Devil) (1906); historical plays: *Pavel I* (Paul I) (1908); "Tsarevich Aleksey" (1920); novels "Aleksandr I" and *14 dekabrya* (14 December) (1918); *Litsa svyatykh ot Iisusa k nam: Pavel, Avgustin, Frantsisk Assizskiy, Zhanna d'Ark* (The Persons of the Saints from Jesus to Us: Paul, Augustine, Francis of Assisi, Joan of Arc) (1936–38); "Dante" (2 vol, 1939), etc; *Died:* 9 Dec 1941 in Paris.

MERKULOV, Fyodor Aleksandrovich (1900–1956) USSR First Dep Min of Ferrous Metallurgy; CP member from 1919; *Born:* 1900, son of a miner; *Educ:* 1937 grad Ind Acad, Moscow; *Career:* from 1912 lamp primer, coal hauler and repairman at Donbass mines; distributed leaflets for underground Bolshevik agents; 1918 with partisan unit operating against White Army and Petlyura's forces;

1919 worked for Bolshevik Party; May 1919 volunteered for Red Army and fought in Ukr during Civil War; 1923 demobilized from Red Army and assigned Party work; 1923–31 (with intervals) Party and trade-union work; from 1931 worked on construction of Magnitogorsk Steel Combine, for three years as deputy chief (for personnel) of the Magnitostroy Construction Trust and head, Ore Mining Bd; 1937–39 head, Main Pipe Ind Bd, then head, Main Metallurgical Ind Bd; from Jan 1939 Pop Comr of Ferrous Metallurgy; 1939 at 18th Party Congress elected member, CC, CPSU(B); Feb 1941 expelled from CC for deficient work; 1940–56 USSR Dep Pop Comr, then Min of Ferrous Metallurgy; during WW 2 organized metal and ammunition production at Ural metallurgical plans; *Awards:* two Orders of Lenin; two Orders of the Red Banner of Labor; medals; *Died:* 9 Oct 1956.

MERKUROV, Sergey Dmitriyevich (1881–1952) Sculptor; Hon Art Worker of Arm SSR from 1940 and RSFSR from 1942; Pop Artiste of USSR from 1943; Hon member, USSR Acad of Arts from 1947; CP member from 1945; *Born:* 8 Nov 1881 in Aleksandropol', now Leninakan Arm; *Educ:* until 1902 studied sculpture at A. Meyer's workshop in Zurich; 1905 grad Munich Acad of Arts; 1906–09 further studies in Florence and Paris; *Career:* from 1910 worked in Moscow; after 1917 Oct Revol active in Art Workers' Union; member, Assoc of Artists of Revol Russia; founded Sculpture Factory, Assoc of State Publ Houses; helped conduct "monumental propaganda" campaign; member, Stalin Prizes Comt; dep, Moscow Sov; *Works:* "Salome", "Fifth Symphony" and "Death and the Maiden", sculpted abroad prior to 1910; composition "Thought" and statues of Lev Tolstoy and Dostoyevsky (1911–12); busts of Lev Tolstoy, G. and I. Myasoyedov and Prof P. Minakov, etc, prior to 1917; post-revol works: numerous monuments and statues of Lenin and Stalin, Party and govt officials and cultural figures, including: monument to Sverdlov (1922); monument to Timiryazev (1923); Lenin monument in Tver (1926); bust of Stalin (1930); statue of Lenin in Meeting Hall of Bel Supr Sov (1939); Stalin monument for Yerevan Victory Museum (1950), etc; composition "The Twenty-Six Baku Commissars" (1926); monuments to: Lomonosov (1943); A. N. Tolstoy (1945); Pushkin; Gogol; Kutuzov; Tsiolkovskiy, etc; did death masks of Lev Tolstoy, Lenin, Dzerzhinskiy, Sverdlov, Gorky, etc; *Awards:* Order of Lenin (1939); two Orders of the Red Banner of Labor (1947 and 1951); two Stalin Prizes (1941 and 1951); *Died:* 8 June 1952.

MERSHIN, Paval Mikhaylovich (1898–1942) Inventor; specialist in color film equipment; *Born:* 1898; *Career:* from 1927 cameraman, Moscow Film Studio; from 1935 directed research on color filming equipment; devised chrome gelatine method of preparing color films; 1938 invented hydrotype method of manufacturing color films and worked on technol for this; 1938 invented method of producing chrome matrices and a machine for the hydrotype manufacture of color films; 1936–41 this technique was used for cartoon and puppet films; *Died:* 1942.

MERTSALOV, Nikolay Ivanovich (1866–1948) Eng; specialist in mech and thermodynamics; Hon Sci and Tech Worker of RSFSR from 1944; *Born:* 1866; *Educ:* 1888 grad Moscow Univ; 1894 grad Moscow Higher Tech College; *Career:* 1895–1912 lectured at Moscow Univ; 1897–99 junior prof, 1899–1930 prof, Moscow Higher Tech College; from 1920 prof, Eng Fac, Moscow's Timiryazev Agric Acad, developed in 1930 into the Moscow Inst for the Mechanization and Electrification of Agric; wrote major works on the kinematics and dynamics of mechanism; 1914, in his course *Dinamika mekhanizmov* (The Dynamics of Mechanisms), he outlined methods for the dynamic study of mechanisms; 1916, in *Kinematika mekhanizmov* (The Kinematics of Mechanisms), he outlined the principles of kinematic geometry and their application to the study of mechanisms; these books had a great influence on the development of mech theory in Russia; on the basis of these methods he devised a new and more precise solution to the calculation of flywheels; pioneered the theory of spatial mechanisms; 1921 began a course on spatial mechanisms; wrote works on the design of spatial geared transmissions for expanding and non-expanding surfaces; 1946, in his work *Zadacha o dvizhenii tvyordogo tela, imeyushchego nepodvizhnuyu tochku* (The Problem of the Motion of a Solid Body with an Immobile Point), continued the research of S. V. Kovalevskaya and S. A. Chaplygin and resolved several special cases of the gyroscope problem; studied the hydrodynamics of lubrication theory and examined the three-dimensional solution of lubrication problems; contributed to thermodynamic theory; using the techniques of mathematical analysis, established the link between experimental results and theoretically derived thermodynamic equations; *Publ: Prostranstvennaya semizvennaya sharnirnaya tsep'* (A Spatial Seven-Bar Linkage Chain) (1936); *Postroyeniye posledovatel'nykh polozheniy zven'yev prostranstvennogo semizvennogo sharnirnogo mekhanizma* (Resolving the Consecutive Positions for the Links of a Spatial Seven-Bar Linkage Mechanism) (1940); *Izbrannyye trudy* (Selected Works) (3 vol, 1950–52); *Teoriya prostranstvennykh mekhanizmov* (The Theory of Spatial Mechanisms) (1951); *Died:* 13 Nov 1948.

MESHCHANINOV, Aleksandr Ivanovich (1878–1966) Surgeon and health service official; Dr of Med and prof from 1935; *Born:* 1878 in Putivl', Khar'kov Province, son of an office worker; *Educ:* 1904 grad Med Fac, Kiev Univ; *Career:* 1904–06 practical med in vil Smela, Kiev Province, then served in a field hospital in Manchuria during the Russo-Japanese War; 1906–09 intern, Surgical Dept, Yelizavetgrad City Zemstvo Hospital, where he specialized under the surgeon O. A. Yutsevich; 1909 opened private surgical practice in vil Petrovo, Kherson Province, then worked as a surgeon at Aleksandriya Uyezd Hospital; from 1912 surgeon and chief physician, Sumy Uyezd Zemstvo Hospital; during WW 1 dir of a large Red Cross surgical hospital in Sumy and chm, Refugee Comt; 1919–53 chief physician and head, Surgical Dept, Kholodnogorskiy Hospital, Khar'kov; 1935–66 head, Chair of Surgery, Ukr Inst of Postgrad Med Training; member, Permanent Rural Health Comt and secr, Learned Council, Ukr Pop Comrt of Health; during WW 2 continued med work in Khar'kov during German occupation; attended numerous Russian and first ten Ukr Surgical Congresses; hon member, Ukr Surgical Soc; also active member, Kharkov Med Soc and Khar'kov Surgical Soc; member, Khar'kov Oblast Bureau, Med and Sanitary Workers' Trade Union; dep, Khar'kov Distr and City Sov; wrote over 90 works; *Awards:* Order of the Red Banner of Labor; medal "For Valiant Labor During the Great Fatherland War"; medal "For Victory Over Germany"; *Died:* 1966 in Khar'kov.

MESHCHANINOV, Ivan Ivanovich (1883–1967) Linguist and archeologist; Dr of Philology from 1927; prof, Leningrad Univ from 1937; member, USSR Acad of Sci from 1932; Hero of Socialist Labor from 1945; *Born:* 24 Nov 1883 in Petersburg; *Educ:* 1907 grad Law Fac, Petersburg Univ; 1909 grad Petersburg Archeological Inst; *Career:* 1910–23 lecturer and head of archives, Petrograd Archeological Inst; 1919-32 assoc, Japhetic Inst, Leningrad; 1920–31 at State Acad for the History of Material Culture; 1926–33 directed archeological Study of ancient Van-Urart in the Caucasus; 1933–37 dir, Inst of Anthropology and Ethnography, USSR Acad of Sci; 1935–50 dir, Inst of Language and Thought, USSR Acad of Sci; from 1939 acad secr, Dept of Lit and Language, and Presidium member, USSR Acad of Sci; from 1950 senior assoc, Inst of Linguistics, USSR Acad of Sci; 1960–63 Burau member, Dept of Lit and Language, USSR Acad of Sci; 1937–62 prof, Leningrad Univ; specialist in ancient Oriental languages, especially Urart; adhered to Acad Marr's language theory, which involved him in criticism in the 1950's; *Publ: Elamskiye drevnosti* (Elam Antiquities) (1918); *Khaldovedeniye* (Chaldean Studies) (1927); *Vvedeniye v yafetidologiyu* (An Introduction to Japhetidology) (1929); *Verkhniy paleolit* (The Upper Paleolithic) (1931); *Problema klassifikatsii yazykov* (The Classification of Languages) (1934); *Yazyk vanskoy klinopisi* (The Language of the Van Cuneiform) (2 vol, 1932–35); *Novoye ucheniye o yazyke. Stadial'naya tipologiya* (The New Language Theory. Stage Typology) (1936); *Obshcheye yazykoznaniye* (General Linguistics) (1940); *Chleny predlozheniya i chasti rechi* (Parsing and Parts of Speech) (1945); *Glagol* (The Verb) (1948); *Grammaticheskiy stroy urartskogo yazyka* (The Grammatical Structure of Urart) (2 vol, 1958–62); *Struktura predlozheniya* (Sentence Structure) (1963); *Awards:* Order of Lenin; Order of the Red Banner of Labor; (1963); "Hammer and Sickle" Gold Star; two Stalin Prizes (1942 and 1945); *Died:* 16 Jan 1967.

MESHCHERSKAYA (real name: PASHCHENKO), Anna Yefimovna (1876–1951) Ukr actress; Pop Artiste of Ukr SSR from 1946; CP member from 1941; *Born:* 1 Apr 1876 in Kiev, daughter of a laborer; *Career:* from 1895 actress in Cherkassy, Kiev, Khar'kov, Yekaterinoslav, Odessa, etc; 1919–21 performed at front-line theaters, after Civil War at Ukr drama theaters; 1927–30 and 1934–51 at Odessa theater; *Roles:* Varvara and Mariya Tarasovna in Korneychuk's "Bogdan Khmel'nitskiy" and "Platon Krechet"; Vassa Zheleznova in Gorky's "Vassa Zheleznova"; Lukash's Mother in Lesya Ukrainka's *Lesnaya pesnya* (Forest Song); Mrs

Alving in Ibsen's "Ghosts," etc; *Died:* 1 Apr 1951.

MESHCHERSKIY, German Ivanovich (1874–1936) Dermatologist and venerologist; Dr of Med from 1904; prof; Hon Sci Worker of RSFSR from 1936; *Born:* 14 Nov 1874; *Educ:* 1898 grad Med Fac, Moscow Univ; *Career:* 1898–1904 worked at Skin and Venerological Clinic, Moscow Univ; 1904 defended doctor's thesis, a now classical work on progressive idiopathic atrophy of the skin and its relation to scleroderma in which he proved that both diseases are variants of the same dermatosis; 1908–20 assoc prof, 1920–25 head, Chair of Skin and Venereal Diseases, 2nd Moscow Univ; 1917–19 member, Anti-Venereal Commission; from 1923 member, all Sov dermatological and venerological soc; 1925–36 head, Chair of Skin and Venereal Diseases, 1st Moscow Univ (now 1st Moscow Med Inst); did research on gonorrheal sores, the treatment of syphilis, early renal syphilis, syphilitic reinfection and superinfection, congenital syphilis, inguinal lymphogranulomatosis, etc; devised a classification of leucoderms and herpies; developed a number of treatments for skin diseases; co-founder, State Venerological Inst; from 1926 chm, Congenital Syphilis Commission; member, org bureau of three All-Union Venerological Congresses; from 1930 chm, Moscow Dermatological and Venerological Soc; member, ed bd, journal "Russkiy vestnik dermatologii," "Moskovskiy meditsinskiy zhurnal," "Tsentral'nyy meditsinskiy zhurnal" and "Russkaya klinika"; co-ed, *Bolshaya meditsinskay entsiklopediya* (Large Medical Encyclopedia) (1st ed); supervised the translation of for med manuals into Russian; wrote over 150 works, some of which were published abroad; *Publ:* doctor's thesis *K ucheniyu ob idiopaticheskoy progressivnoy astrofii kozhi i ob otnoshenii yeyo k sklerodermii* (The Theory of Progressive Idiopathic Atrophy of the Skin and Its Relation to Scleroderma) (1904); *O pereloynykh yazvakh* (Gonorrheal Sores) (1911); *Osnovnyye svedeniya o kozhnykh i venericheskikh bolesnyakh* (Basic Information on Skin and Venereal Diseases) (1917); *Lecheniye sifilisa* (The Treatment of Syphilis) (1922); *Uchebnik po kozhnym i venericheskim boleznyam* (A Textbook on Skin and Venereal Diseases) (1936), etc; *Died:* 17 Aug 1936.

MESHCHERYAKOV, Nikolay Leonidovich (1865–1942) Eng; writer, corresp member, USSR Acad of Sci from 1939; CP member from 1901; *Born:* 25 Feb 1865 in Zaraysk, son of an agronomist; *Educ:* 1885–86 studied at Petersburg Technol Inst; grad Technol Fac, Liege Univ; *Career:* in 1880's began revol work as member, People's Will Party; 1886 arrested and exiled to Ryazan' Province; 1893 emigrated to Belgium; 1901 joined For League of Russian Soc-Democrats; chm, Belgien org of "Iskra"; 1902 went to Moscow as "Iskra" rep and joined Moscow RSDRP Comt; 27 Nov 1902 arrested and imprisoned; 1904 exiled to Yakutsk Province; 1906 member, Moscow Okrug Party Comt and Moscow Oblast Party Bureau; Oct 1906 re-arrested; 1909 exiled for life to Yeniseysk Uyezd; 1913 moved to Krasnoyarsk and worked as eng; 1917 member, Krasnoyarsk RSDRP(B) Comt and ed newspaper "Krasnoyarskiy rabochiy"; then returned to Moscow and became chm, Moscow Province Sov; at time of 1917 Oct Revol ed, "Izvestiya Moskovskogo voyennorevolyutionnogo komiteta"; after 1917 Oct Revol worked for "Izvestiya Mossoveta"; 1918–22 member, ed bd, newspaper "Pravda"; member, Bd, Centr Assoc of Consumer Soc; mang, 1921–24 chief ed, State Publ House; worked for Comintern, Krestintern and Int Agrarian Inst; from 1924 dep chief ed, "BSE" (Large Soviet Encyclopedia); 1927–38 chief ed, "MSE" (Small Soviet Encyclopedia); ed, journal "Nauka i zhizn'"; member of ed team publishing complete works of Shchedrin, Nekrasov, Chernyshevskiy, Gleb Uspenskiy, Gogol and Ostrovskiy, deleg at 13th–15th CPSU(B) Congress; *Publ: Semidesyatniki* (The Men of the "Seventies") (1935); *Died:* 3 Apr 1942.

MESHKOV, Vasiliy Vasil'yevich (1893–1963) Painter; member, from 1905; *Born:* 1885; *Career:* Party work in Petersburg and abroad; 1917 returned to Russia; fought in 1917 Oct Revol; 1918 Collegium member, RSFSR Pop Comrt of Agric; Ukr Pop Comr of Agric; then various Party and govt posts in Novgorod, Tambov and Simbirsk; 1922–28 Collegium member, Pop Comrt of Educ; dep chm, Main Polit Educ Comt, RSFSR Pop Comrt of Educ; then dep head, Agric Dept, CC, CPSU(B); 1925 at 14th CP Congress elected member, Centr Control Commission; 1930–36 worked for USSR Min of For Affairs; then various admin posts; *Died:* 1946.

MESHCHERYAKOVA, A.I. (1866–1948) Govt official; CP member from 1917; *Born:* 1866; *Career:* from 1890's active in revol movement; 1901, while in emigration in Belgium, helped smuggle "Iskra"; after 1917 Febr Revol member, Nikolayevka Rayon RSDRP(B) Comt, Krasnoyarsk; Bolshevik member, Krasnoyarsk City Duma; after 1917 Oct Revol worked for Pop Comrt of Educ; worked for Library Dept, Main Polit and Educ Comt, RSFSR Pop Comrt of Educ; then head, Library of Centr Kremlin Club; *Died:* 1948.

MESHKOV, Vasiliy Nikitich (1868–1946) Russian painter and art teacher; Pop Artiste of RSFSR from 1943; *Born:* 6 Jan 1868 in Yelets; *Educ:* studied at theological seminary; 1882–89 studied at Moscow College of Painting, Sculpture and Architecture; *Career:* for a while worked at an ikon workshop; 1891–1916 ran his own art school; sided with Itinerant Painters movement; 1922 joined Assoc of Artists of Revol Russia; *Works:* genre paintings: "Dentistry" (1891); "Evening Serenade" (1893); "The Blinded Artist" (1898); landscape "Cooling" (1898); Portraits: "Lev Tolstoy" (1910); "S.M. Budyonnyy" (1927); "V.R. Menzhinskiy" (1927); "M.I. Kalinin" (1929); "Karl Marx" and "Friedrich Engels" (1930's), etc; *Awards:* Order of the Red Banner of Labor; medals; *Died:* 26 Nov 1946.

MESHKOV, Vasiliy Vasilyevich (1893–1963) Painter; member, USSR Acad of Arts from 1958; Hon Art Worker of RSFSR from 1944; Pop Artiste of RSFSR from 1963; *Born:* 4 Apr 1893 in Moscow, son of the paintner V.N. Meshkov; *Educ:* 1917 grad Moscow College of Painting, Sculpture and Architecture; *Career:* 1911 joined "Peredvizhniki" (Itinerant Painters) group; 1913 visited France, Italy and Germany; during WW 1 worked as war artist; 1919–20 dir, State Art Studios, Ryazan, and chief set-designer, Ryazan-City Theater; from 1922 member, Assoc of Artists of Revol Russia; in mid-1920's chief set-designer, Novosibirsk Theater; before and during WW 2 painted numerous battle scenes; after WW 2 specialized in landscapes; 1953–58 corresp member, USSR Acad of Arts; *Works:* "Old Uglich" (1911); "Pskov" (1916); "Under the Flag of Freedom" (1918); "Toil" (1923); "At the 'Hamer and Sickle' Plant" (1923); "The Smoke-Screen" (1933); "The Oil-Strike" (1934); "Red Army Maneuvers" (1937); "The Black Sea in the Fall" (1945); "Villas on the Oka" (1948); "On the Enemy's Trail"; "Kryukovo After the Battle"; "A Tale of the Urals" (1945); "The Kama" (1950); "Fall in Karelia" (1951); Ural landscarpe series; *Awards:* Stalin Prize (1951); *Died:* 6 Aug 1963.

MESSING, Stanislav Adamovich (1890–1946) Govt official; CP member from 1908; *Born:* 1890, son of a musician; *Educ:* studied in high school; *Career:* Party work in Warsaw and in army; twice arrested; after 1917 Oct Revol secr, Sokol'niki Rayon Exec Comt; then exec work for All-Russian Cheka, State Polit Admin and Pop Comrt of For Trade; from 1920 Collegium member, All-Russian Cheka; second dep chm, OGPU; at 16th Congress elected member, CPSU(B) Centr Control Commission; *Died:* 1946.

MESTNIKOV, Vasiliy Vasil'yevich (1908–1958) Yakut producer and actor; Pop Artiste of USSR from 1958; CP member from 1943; *Born:* 14 Jan 1908; *Educ:* 1925 grad Yakut Teachers Training Technicum; 1931–34 studied at Lunacharskiy State Inst of Stagecraft; *Career:* did amateur acting in youth; from 1925 actor, Yakut Theater (Oyunskiy Yakut Music and Drama Theater); from 1934 producer; 1935–38 and 1942–43 art dir and chief producer, Oyunskiy Theater; made major constribution to the development of the Yakut theater, especially in conjunction with the playwright D Sivtsev and the composers M. Zhirkov and G. Litinskiy, who wrote the first Yakut musical drama "N'yurgun Bootur" in 1940 and reworked it into an opera in 1945; taught acting and translated a number of plays into Yakut; his productions were notable for their lucidity, directness, expressiveness and picturesque treatment of crowd scenes; *Productions:* Sevost'yanov's "Partisan Morozov"; Mordvinov's *Da zdravstvuyet chelovek* (Long Live Man) and *Ot kolonii k kommune* (From Colony to Commune); Sofronov's *Tina zhizni* (The Mire of Life); Korneychuk's "Makar Dubrava" (1951); *Talanty i poklonniki* (Talents and Admirers) (1952); Mukhtarov's *Sem'ya Allana* (Allan's Family) (1953); Galan's *Pod zolotym orlom* (Beneath the Golden Eagle) (1954); Tyrin's *Otets i syn* (Father and Son) (1956); Sivtsev's *Kuznets Kyukyur* (Kyukyur the Blacksmith) (1957); *Died:* 18 Oct 1958.

MESYATSEV, Ivan Illarionovich (1885–1940) Zoologist and oceanologist; CP member from 1929; *Born:* 2 July 1885; *Educ:* 1912 grad Moscow Univ; *Career:* 1921 co-founder, until 1933 dir, Floating Marine Research Inst (now All-Union Inst of Marine Fishery and Oceanography); 1922 directed construction of first Sov expeditionary vessel "Persey"; headed several maj expeditions to the Northern Seas of the USSR; from a study of the biology of swarm fish, particulatly the reasons for their concentration, established the necessity for the development of a large Sov trawling fleet; his methods were used in developing fish search techniques; *Publ: Stroyeniye kosyakov stadnykh ryb* (The Formation of Swarm Fish Shoals) (1937); coauthor, *Ob organizatsii poiskovykh rabot po treske v Dal'nevostochnykh moryakh* (Organizing the Search for Cod in the Far Eastern Seas) (1933); *Died:* 1940.

MESYATSEV, P.A. (1889–1938) Govt official; CP member from 1906; *Born:* 1889; *Career:* 1921–24 Collegium member, then plen, RSFSR Pop Comrt of Agric; then worked for cooperative system, agric bank and USSR Gosplan; joined "Trotskyist opposition"; arrested by State Security organs; *Died:* 1938 in imprisonment.

METALLIKOV, Mikhail Solomonovich (1896–1939) Sov public health official; CP member from 1917; *Born:* 1896; *Educ:* 1927 grad Med Fac, Moscow Univ; *Career:* after 1917 Oct Revol directed underground Bolshevik org against Petlyura admin in Ukr; then comr, Sanitary Bd, 14th Army; organized mil hospitals; 1921, at Lenin's suggestion, appointed polit comr, then head, Kremlin Sanitation Bd; member, Govt Commission which supervised med treatment of Lenin; 1927, after grad, worked in Surgical and Urological Depts, Botkin Hospital; together with A.P. Frumkin, discovered and popularized preparation for intravenous and retrograde pyelography, named "sergozin"; arranged for and supervised production of this preparation,; organized construction of many hospitals; sanatoria and rest homes; 1935–37 USSR dep chief sanitary inspector, USSR Council of Pop Comr; in this capacity greatly improved Sov sanitary and public health system; wrote many works on surgery, urology and public health org; *Publ: Vydelitel'naya (vnutrivennaya) piyelografiya* (Secretory/ Intravenous/ Pyelography) (1934); *Died:* 1939.

METALLOV, Vasiliy Mikhaylovich (1862–1926) Musical historian and theoretician; musical paleographer; *Born:* 1862; *Educ:* grad Moscow Theological Acad; *Career:* from 1901 prof, Chair of the History of Ancient Russian Music, Moscow Conservatory; prof, Moscow Archeological Inst; after 1917 Oct Revol member, State Acad of Arts; specialist in ancient Russian standard or hook notation; expounded this system in *Azbukva kryukovogo peniya* (The ABC of Hook Singing) (1899) and outlined its history in the paleographic atlas *Russkaya simiografiya* (Russian Simiography) (1912); *Publ: Ocherk istorii pravoslavnogo tserkovnogo peniya v* Rossii" (Outline History of Orthodox Church Singing in Russia) (1893); *Strogiy stil' garmonii* (Strict Harmony Style) (1897); *Bogosluzhebnoye peniye russkoy tserkvi v period domongol'skiy* (Russian Church Liturgical Singing in the Pre-Mongolian Period) (2 vol, 1906); *Died:* 1926.

METELEV, A.D. (1893–1937) Govt official; CP member from 1912; *Born:* 1893; *Career:* June-early Aug 1918 member, Arkhangel'sk Province Exec Comt; polit worker, 6th Army; member, Penza Provinze Exec Comt; then various exec posts; 1921 manager, All-Russian Centr Exec Comt; 1933 USSR Centr Exec Comt plen for Azov and Black Sea Kray; arrested by state Security organs; *Died:* 1937 in imprisonment.

METNER, Nikolay Karlovich (1879–1951) Composer and pianist; *Born:* 24 Dec 1879 in Moscow; *Educ:* 1900 grad Moscow Conservatory, studying piano under V. Safonov and composition under S. Taneyev; *Career:* gave concerts in Russia and Germany; 1909-10 and 1915–21 prof of piano, Moscow Conservatory; 1921 emigrated; from 1936 in England; *Works:* three piano concertoes (1918, 1927 and 1943); 14 sonates, including the "Fairy-Tale Sonata", the "Ballad Sonata" and "Triad Sonata"; "Fairy Tales"; "Forgotten Themes"; "Dithyrambs"; piano quintet; three nocturnes; two canzonets with dances; numerous romances, etc; *Publ: Muza i moda* (The Muse and Fashion) (1935); *Died:* 13 Nov 1951 in London.

METSANURK, Mait (real name: HUBEL, Eduard) (1879–1957) Est writer and playwright; member, Est Writers' Union; *Born:* 19 Nov 1879 in Yur'yev (Tartu) Uyezd, son of a peasant; *Educ:* grad Tartu City College; *Career:* 1904 first work published; 1910–16 wrote theater reviews for the newspaper "Tallinn News"; also worked as a reporter; wrote humanitarian-idealistic works criticizing soc conditions and the clergy; *Publ:* novels: *Vahesaare Villem* (William of Vahesaare) (1909); *Orjad* (The Slaves) (1912); *Punane tuul* (The Red Wind) (1928); *Ümera joel* (On the River Ümera) (1934); *Kutsutudja seatud* (The Called and the Chosen) (1937); *Tuli tuha all* (The Smouldering Fire) (1939); *Savine pööripäey* (The Summer Solstice) (1957); plays: "The Life of the Meek" (1923); "The General's Son" (1925); "The Peasant's Son" (1929); "Weed Roots" (1933), etc; *Died:* 21 Aug 1957 in Tallinn.

MEYERHOLD, Vsvevolod Emil'yevich (1874–1940) Stage dir and impressario; Pop Artiste of RSFSR from 1923; CP member from 1918; *Born:* 9 Feb 1874 in Penza; *Educ:* 1895–96 studied at Law Fac, Moscow Univ; 1896 joined Nemirovich-Danchenko's drama class, Music and Drama College at Moscow Philharmonic Soc; *Career:* 1898–1902, after grad from college, actor with Moscow Arts Theater; 1902–05 worked in Kherson, Tiflis and Nikolayev; 1906–07 chief stage dir, Komissarzhevskaya Drama Theater, Petersburg; 1908 worked at Aleksandrinskiy Theater and staged shows at Mariinskiy Theater; 1913–17 taught and did experimental work at his Studio on Barodinskaya; 1914–16, under pseudonym Dr Dapertutto, published journal "Lyubov' k tryom apel'sinam"; after 1917 Oct Revol proclaimed slogan "Theatrical October" and tried to adapt stagecraft to revol conditions; contributed to establishment of Sov theater; head, Theater Dept, Pop Comrt of Educ; 1918–19 dep head, Petrograd Branch, 1920–21 head, Theater Dept, Pop Comrt of Educ; from 1920 directed 1st RSFSR Theater (later the Meyerhold Theater); from 1923 also staged shows at Theater of the Revol; Party critics accused his work of containing "thoroughly bourgeois and formalistic attitudes, alien to Soviet art"; 1938 this theater was closed down; from 1938 stage dir, from 1939 chief stage dir, Stanislavskiy Opera Theater, Moscow; also did film work and taught drama; greatly influenced production technique in USSR and abroad; 1939 arrested by State Security organs; *Productions:* Verharen's "Dawns" (1920); Mayavovskiy's "Mystery-Buffo" (1921); Ostrovskiy's *Dokhodnoye mesto* (A Lucrative Post) (1923); Fayko's *Ozero Lyul'* (Lake Lyul) (1923); Erdman's "The Mandate" (1925); Mayakovskiy's *Klop* (The Bedbug) (1929) and *Banya* (The Bathhouse) (1930); Bezymenskiy's *Vystrel* (The Shot) (1929); Vyshnevskiy's *Posledniy reshitel'nyy* (The Crucial Last One) (1931); German's *Vstupleniye* (Introduction) (1933); classic plays: Sukhovo-Kobylin's *Smert' Tarelkina* (Tarelkin's Death) (1922); Ostrovskiy's *Les* (The Forest) (1924); Gogol's *Revizor* (The Government Inspector) (1926); Griboyedov's *Gore ot uma* (Woe from Wit) (1928); Tchaikovsky's *Pikovaya dama* (The Queen of Spades) (1935), etc; *Publ: O teatre* (The Theater) (1913); *Rekonstruktsiya teatra* (Reconstruction of the Theater) (1930); *Died:* 2 Feb 1940 in imprisonment in Moscow; posthumously rehabilitated.

MEYERZON, Zh. I. (1894–1939) Party official; CP member from 1919; *Born:* 1894; *Career:* 1917–18 Bund member; 1919–20 Party work in Bel and Ryazan'; 1920–23 secr, Tula Province RCP(B) Comt; Tula RCP(B) Comt deleg at 11th Party Congress; from 1923 exec work in CC, RCP(B); 1932–34 secr, Transcaucasian Kray Party Comt; at 17th CPSU(B) Congress elected member, Party Control Commission, CC, CPSU(B); from 1934 head, Trans and Communications Group, Party Control Commission, CC, CPSU(B); arrested by State Security organs; *Died:* 1939 in imprisonment.

MEYSNER, V. I. (1879–1938) Specialist in fish-breeding; *Born:* 1879; from 1910 worked for Min of Agric; after 1917 Oct Revol asst head, Fishing and Research Dept, Agric Comt; from July 1920 dep head, then head, Main Bd of Fish Ind; from 1923 fishery consultant, USSR Gosplan; from 1934 dir, Inst of Fishing Ind; arrested by State Security organs; *Died:* 1938 in imprisonment.

MEZHENINOV, Sergey Aleksandrovich (1890–1937) Mil commander; capt, Russian Army; corps commander from 1935; member, Sov Army Gen Staff; CP member from 1931; *Born:* 19 Jan 1890 in Kashira, son of a nobleman; *Educ:* 1910 grad Kazan' Mil College; 1914 grad Nikolay Mil Acad; 1916 grad Kiev Pilot-Observers' School; *Career:* 1914–18 officer on active duty in Russian Army; 1918 conscripted into Red Army; Sept 1918–Feb 1919 chief of staff, 4th Army on Eastern Front; Mar–Aug 1919 commanded 3rd Army on Eastern Front; Sept 1919–June 1920 commanded 12th Army on Western Front; Oct–Dec 1920 commanded 15th Army on Western Front; 1921 asst commander, then commander, Oryol Mil Distr; Mar 1925–31 asst chief, then dep chief, Red Army Air Force; 1932–33 chief of staff, Red Army Air Force; 1933–37 dep chief, Red Army Staff, then Gen Staff, 1934–37 simultaneously member, Mil Council, Pop Comrt of Defense; 1937 dept head, Red Army Gen Staff; 1937 arrested by NKVD; *Publ: Voprosy primeneniya i organizatsii aviatsii* (The Employment and Organization of an Air Force) (1924); *Osnovnyye voprosy primeneniya VVS* (Basic Aspects of Employing an Air Force) (1926); *Vozdushnyye sily v voyne i operatsii* (The Air Force in

War and Operation) (1927); *Died:* 28 Sept 1937 in imprisonment; posthumously rehabilitated.

MEZHLAUK, Ivan Ivanovich (1891–1938) Party and govt official; CP member from 1918; *Born:* 30 Sept 1891 in Khar'kov, son of a schoolteacher; *Educ:* grad Khar'kov Univ; *Career:* 1917 took part in Oct Revol; 1918 Comr of Justice and chm, Khar'kov Revol Tribunal; then Mil Comr of Kazan' Province and member, Kazan Province RCP(B) Comt; 1919–20 Chief Quartermaster, Red Army and member, Revol Mil Council, 4th and 7th Armies; 1921–23 dir, Petrov Metallurgical Plant, Yenakiyevo, and bd chm, Southern Steel Trust; 1923–24 chm, Turkestani Cotton Comt and Centr Asian Econ Council; 1924–25 secr, CC, CP(B) Turkm; 1928–29 secr, Tambov Okrug CPSU(B) Comt; 1931–36 secr, Labor and Defense Council and dep business mang, USSR Council of Pop Comr; 1936–37 chm, All-Union Comt for Higher Educ Establishments, USSR Council of Pop Comr; member, All-Russian and USSR Centr Exec Comt; Presidium member, Turkestani Centr Exec Comt; arrested by State Security organs; *Died:* 26 Apr 1938 in imprisonment; posthumously rehabilitated.

MEZHLAUK, Valeriy Ivanovich (1893–1938) Party and govt official; CP member from 1917; *Born:* 7 Feb 1893 in Khar'kov, son of a teacher; *Educ:* grad History and Philology Fac and Law Fac, Khar'kov Univ; *Career:* 1907 joined revol movement; member, Khar'kov RSDRP(B) Comt and Khar'kov Sov; helped organize Red Guards in Ukr; 1918 Pop Comr of Finance of Donetsk-Krivoy Rog Republ; member, Donetsk Oblast Comt, CP(B) Ukr; member, Donetsk Mil Headquarters; 1918–20 mil comr for Kazan' Province; member, Revol Mil Councils of 5th, 10th, 14th and 2nd Armies; member, Revol Mil Council of Southern Front; Ukr Pop Comr of Mil Affairs; member, Revol Mil Council of Tula Fortified Area; 1920–24 exec railroad work; comr, Moscow-Baltic, Moscow-Kursk and Northern Railroads; dep chief of means of communication; Collegium member, Pop Comrt of Means of Communication; 1924–26 Presidium member, USSR Supr Sovnarkhoz and dep chm, Main Metal Ind Bd; 1926–31 head, Main Metal Ind Bd and dep chm, USSR Supr Sovnarkhoz; 1931–34 first dep chm, USSR Gosplan; 1934–37 dep chm, USSR Council of Pop Comr and chm, USSR Gosplan; also dep chm, USSR Labor and Defense Council; from Feb 1937 USSR Pop Comr of Heavy Ind; from Oct 1937 dep chm, USSR Council of Pop Comr and chm, USSR Gosplan; 1937 member, Econ Council, USSR Council of Pop Comr; 1919 elected member, All-Ukr Centr Exec Comt; 1927–29 member, All-Russian Centr Exec Comt; 1927–37 member USSR Centr Exec Comt; Nov 1937 cand in elections to USSR Supr Sov; 1927 from cand member, from 1934 member, CC, CPSU(B); wrote pamphlets and articles on industrialization of Sov econ; exec ed, newspaper "Za industrializatsiyu"; lectured on "The Plan and Planning" at the High School for Party Organizers, CC, CPSU(B); 1933 presented paper at World Econ Conference, London; 2 Dec 1937 arrested by State Security organs; *Publ: Nationalizatsiya promyshlennosti i oborona SSSR* (Industrial Nationalization and Defense of the USSR) (1927); *XV let stroitel'stva sotsialisticheskoy ekonomiki* (Fifteen Years in the Construction of a Socialist Economy) (1933); *O planovoy rabote i merakh yeyo uluchsheniya* (Planning and Measures for Improving It) (1938), written in prison shortly before his death; *Awards:* Order of Lenin (1936); Order of the Red Banner (1928); *Died:* 29 July 1938 in imprisonment; posthumously rehabilitated.

MGELADZE (pseudonym: VARDIN), I. V. (1890–1943) Party official; CP member from 1907; *Born:* 1890; *Career:* after 1917 Feb Revol member, Saratov Province RSDRP(B) Comt and Saratov Exec Comt; ed, Saratov newspaper "Sotsial-demokrat"; after 1917 Oct Revol Party work; member, Saratov Province Party Comt; head, Polit Dept, 1st Mounted Army; then head, Press Section, CC, RCP(B); during Brest-Litovsk peace treaty debate sided with "Leftist Communists"; Saratov Party Org deleg at 8th All-Russian Party Conference; newspaper "Kommunar" deleg at 8th RCP(B) Congress; 1925 active in "new opposition"; then member, Trotsky-Zinov'yev Bloc; 1927 at 15th CPSU(B) Congress expelled from Party for active participation in Trotskyist opposition; 1930 reinstated; 1935 again expelled from Party and imprisoned for "anti-Party and anti-Sov activities"; *Died:* 1943 in imprisonment.

MICHURIN, Ivan Vladimirovich (1855–1935) Horticulturist and selectionist; Dr of Biology from 1935; Hon member, USSR Acad of Sci from 1935; member, Lenin All-Union Acad of Agric Sci from 1935; Hon Sci and Tech Worker of RSFSR from 1934; *Born:* 27 Oct 1855 in vil Dolgoye, Ryazan' Province, son of an impoverished nobleman; *Educ:* studied at Ryazan' High School; 1869 grad Pronsk Uyezd College; *Career:* obtained first knowledge of horticulture from father, who was a keen amateur gardener; 1872–1875 clerical worker at Kozlov Railroad station; 1875–77 senior clerk, Ryazhsk Station; from 1877 signalmaster, Kozlov-Lebedyan' Railroad Line; studied practical and theoretical horticulture in his leisure hours; by 1888 had over 600 species of fruit and berry plants; in same year opened a 32-acre commercial nursery; 1889 became full-time professional horticulturist; corresponded with leading horticulturists of Russia, France, Germany and Belgium; 1913 declined US offer to buy his collection of fruit and berry shrubs and trees; from 1918 continued to manage nursery after it became State property; 1928 the nursery was turned into a genetic selection station and named after him (subsequently renamed I. V. Michurin Centr Genetic Laboratory); did research on acclimation, hybridization and mass selection; bred about 300 new fruit and berry strains; highly revered by Sov sci, which ranks him with Lamarck, Darwin, Timiryazev, Sechenov and Pavlov and fetes him as discoverer of sci plant growth control; Fruit and Vegetable Inst and Pomological Research Inst now bear his name; town of Kozlov was renamed Michurinsk in his honor; *Publ: Vyvedeniye novykh kul'turnykh sortov plodovykh derev'yev i kustarnikov iz semyan* (The Breeding of New Commercial Strains of Fruit Trees from Seed) (1911); *Po povodu neprimenimosti zakonov Mendelya v dele gibridizatsii* (The Inapplicability of Mendel's Laws to the Problem of Hybridization) (1915); *Semena, ikh zhizn' i sokhraneniye do poseva* (Seeds, Their Life and Storage Before Sowing) (1915); *Itogi poluvekovykh rabot po vydeleniyu novykh sortov plodovykh i yagodnykh rasteniy* (The Results of Half-a-Century of Work on the Breeding of New Fruit and Berry Strains) (1929–32); *Awards:* Order of the Red Banner of Labor (1925); Order of Lenin (1931); *Died:* 7 June 1935 in Michurinsk.

MICHURINA-SAMOYLOVA, Vera Arkad'yevna (1866–1948) Actress; Pop Artiste of USSR from 1939; *Born:* 17 May 1866, daughter of actress Vera Samoylova II; *Educ:* studied acting under aunt, actress Nadezhda Samoylova; *Career:* 1886 successful debut at Aleksandrinskiy Theater (now Pushkin Drama Theater) as Vera in prologue to Mey's "Pskovityanka" (The Woman of Pskov); from this date performed uninterruptedly at that theater; after 1917 Oct Revol active in developing Sov theater; taught stagecraft at School of Russian Drama; 1941–44 remained in Leningrad during blockade, doing soc work and performing in "Teatr u mikrofona" (Theater at the Microphone), plays, concerts, etc; *Roles:* pre-revol roles: Sof'ya in Griboyedov's *Gore ot uma* (Woe From Wit); Luise and Lady Milford in Schiller's "Kabale und Liebe"; Countess Orsino in Lessing's "Emilia Galotti"; Sidoni in Daudet and Belot's "Fromont Jeune et Risler Ainé"; Reneva in Ostrovsky's *Svetit, da ne greyet* (It Lights But Does Not Warm), etc; post-revol roles: Mrs. Chivley in Oscar Wilde's "An Ideal Husband"; Kseniya Mikhaylovna and Lenchitskaya in Romashov's *Ognennyy most* (Bridge of Fire) and *Boytsy* (The Fighters); Polina Bardina in Maksim Gorky's *Vragi* (The Enemies), etc; *Publ: Polveka na stsene Aleksandrinskogo teatra* (A Half-Century on the Stage of the Aleksandrinskiy Theater) (1935); *Shest'desyat let v iskusstve* (Sixty Years in Art) (1946); *Awards:* Stalin Prize (1943); Order of Lenin; Order of the Red Banner of Labor; *Died:* 2 Nov 1948.

MIKAY (real name: GERASIMOV, Mikhail Stepanovich) (1885–1944) First Mari poet and fabulist; *Born:* 1885 in vil Ilnet', now Tatar ASSR, son of a poor peasant; *Career:* 1904 began writing in Mari; 1917 first work published; worked as a school-teacher all his life; *Publ:* poems "The Prisoner" (1905) and "Morning Sun" (1910); verse and fable collections "Sparks" (1920) and "Poems and Fables" (1948); coauthor, "Mari Literature" (1949) and "Mari Poetry" (1952); *Died:* 7 Apr 1944.

MIKENAS, Yuozas Iokubovich (1901–1964) Lith sculptor; prof; corresp member, USSR Acad of Arts from 1954; bd member, USSR Artists' Union; Hon Art Worker of Lith SSR from 1945; Pop Artist of USSR from 1961; CP member from 1952; *Born:* 25 Feb 1901 in vil Skardupis, now Lith SSR; *Educ:* 1925 grad Kaunas Art School; 1931 grad Paris Higher Art School; *Career:* specialized in monumental, decorative and portrait sculpture; from 1954 head of a chair, Lith State Art Inst; dep, Lith Supr Sov of 1955 convocation; *Work:* "Victory" group in Kaliningrad (1946); statue of the post Yu.Yanonis; bust and statue of the writer P. Tsvirk in Vilnius (1959); bust of the writer A. Ventslav; "Student Youth" group in Vilnius (1952); "Peace" composition (1960), etc; *Awards:* Stalin Prize (1947); Order of Lenin (1954); *Died:* 23 Oct 1964.

MIKHALEVSKIY, Faddey Il'ich (1876–1952) Economist; prof; corresp member, USSR Acad of Sci from 1946; CP member from 1919; *Born:* May 1876 in vil Lyakhovichi, now Minsk Oblast; *Career:* 1921–27 taught and did research at Sverdlov Univ; 1928–34 worked for USSR State Bank; 1934–37 prof, Moscow Inst of Credit and Econ; 1940–52 senior assoc, Inst of Econ, USSR Acad of Sci; 1941–50 also specialist, USSR State Bank; *Publ: Zoloto kak denezhnyy tovar* (Gold as a Monetary Commodity) (1937); *Zoloto v period mirovykh voyn* (Gold During the World Wars) (1945); *Ocherki istorii deneg i denezhnogo obrashcheniya.* (An Outline History of Money and Monetary Circulation) (1948); *Zoloto v sisteme kapitalizma posle vtoroy mirovoy voyny* (Gold in the Capitalist System After World War 2) (1952); *Awards:* Order of the Red Banner of Labor; medals; *Died:* 17 Nov 1952 in Moscow.

MIKHAYLOV, Adrian Fyodorovich (1853–1929) Revolutionary; Populist; member, "Land and Liberty" Group; *Born:* 5 Aug 1853; *Career:* 1878 took part in plot to liberate P. I. Voynaral'skiy, held on charges of assassinating Chief of Police Mezentsov; Oct 1878 arrested in Petersburg; 1880 sentenced to death; sentence commuted to 20 years' hard labor, which he served in Kara; 1907 returned to European Russia; spent his last years working for a cooperative in Rostov-on-Don; *Publ:* memoirs *Semidesyatniki* (The Men of the Seventies) and *4 avgusta 1878–4 avgusta 1918* (4 August 1878–4 August 1918); *Died:* 8 July 1929.

MIKHAYLOV (pseudonyms: YELINSON; POLITIKUS), Lev Mikhaylovich (1872–1928) Journalist; CP member from 1903; *Born:* 24 Nov 1872 in Yekaterinodar, son of an office worker; *Career:* 1890's began revol activities; from 1896 Soc-Democrat; after 2nd RSDRP Congress sided with Bolsheviks; took part in revol in Moscow; 1905 member, lit lectures group, Moscow RSDRP(B) Comt; contributed to newspapers "Bor'ba" and "Svetoch" then lived in Petersburg; helped found newspapers "Zvezda" and "Pravda"; 1917 chm, first legal Petrograd RSDRP(B) Comt; chm, Vyborg Rayon Admin; after Oct Revol Presidium member, Petrograd Province Exec Comt; 1922 Sov plen in Norway; 1923–24 Sov plen in Turkestan; member, Centr Asian Bureau, CC, RCP(B); from 1924 exec secr, All-Union Soc of Old Bolsheviks, CC, RCP(B); also worked for Gosplan; deleg at 6th, 8th, 14th and 15th Party Congresses; *Died:* 5 Mar 1928.

MIKHAYLOV, Mikhail Mikhaylovich (1892–1961) Electr eng; specialist in insulation tech; Dr of Tech Sci from 1936; prof from 1934; *Born:* 1892 in Tiflis; *Educ:* 1922 grad Electr Eng Fac, Leningrad Polytech Inst; *Career:* specialist in dielectrics and insulation products; from 1922 lecturer, 1930–34 assoc prof, Chair of Electr Insulation Materials Technol, Leningrad Polytech Inst; 1922–26 simultaneously assoc, State Ceramics Inst; from 1926 worked at State Physical Eng Laboratory, then at Leningrad Electrophysical Inst; from 1934 prof, from 1935 head, Chair of Electr Insulation and Cable Eng, Leningrad Polytech Inst; member, Dielectrics Commission, USSR Acad of Sci; *Publ: Setevyye i kabel'nyye izmereniya* (Grid and Cable Metering) (1933); *Elektrotekhnicheskiye materialy* (Electrotechnical Materials) (1933); coauthor, *Ispytaniye elektroizoliruyushchikh materialov* (Testing Electrical Insulation Materials) (1936); *Vlagopronitsayemost' organicheskikh dielektrikov* (The Moisture-Permeability of Organic Dielectrics) (1960); *Awards:* Order of Lenin; Order of the Red Banner of Labor; medals; *Died:* 1961.

MIKHAYLOV, Vasiliy Mikhaylovich (1894–1937) Party and govt official; CP member from 1915; *Born:* 1894, son of a worker; *Career:* worked as binder; Party work in Moscow; 1916 arrested; after 1917 Feb Revol member, Moscow Sov of Workers' Dep; 1917–1918 member, Moscow Sov and bd member, Moscow Printers' Union; active in 1917 Oct Revol in Moscow; then member, Moscow Party Comt; chm, Moscow City Rayon Cheka; 1918–20 fought in Civil War; 1921–22 secr, CC, RCP(B); from 1922 Party and trade-union work in Moscow; 1922–24 secr, Moscow Party Comt and secr, Zamoskvorech'ye Rayon RCP(B) Comt; 1924–29 chm, Moscow City Trade-Union Council; late 1928–early 1929 favored reconciliation with "rightist opposition"; from 1929 dir, construction of Dnieper Hydropower Plant; at 10th, 12th, 13th, 14th and 15th Party Congresses elected member, at 11th, 16th and 17th Congresses elected cand member, CC, CPSU(B); 1925–29 cand member, Org Bureau, CC, CPSU(B); arrested by State Security organs; *Died:* 1937 in imprisonment.

MIKHAYLOVA, Yekaterina Nikolayevna (1897–1952) Lit historian; CP member from 1920; *Born:* 1897 in vil Levokumskaya, Stavropol' Province; *Educ:* 1932 grad Inst of Red Prof; *Career:* 1930 first work published; 1930–37 taught Russian lit at Moscow higher educ establishments; 1937–41 learned secr, ed bd, "Literaturnaya entsiklopediya" (Literary Encyclopedia); 1941–52 head, Sov Russian Lit Section, Gorky Inst of World Lit; *Publ: Tvorcheskiy put' Lermontova* (Lermontov's Career) (1939); coauthor, *Zhizn' i tvorchestvo M. Yu. Lermontova* (The Life and Work of M. Yu. Lermontov) (1941); *Proza Lermontova* (Lermontov's Prose) (1957); *Died:* 31 Jan 1952 in Moscow.

MIKHAYLOVSKIY, Boris Vasil'yevich (1899–1965) Lit historian and art historian; *Born:* 3 Dec 1899 in Moscow; *Educ:* 1925 grad Bryusov Lit and Art Inst; 1929 completed postgrad course at State Acad of Arts; *Career:* 1930 first work published; 1942–43 research and admin work at Gorky Inst of World Lit; from 1943 prof, Moscow Univ; *Publ: Russkaya literatura XX veka. S devyanostykh godov XIX veka do 1917 goda* (Russian 20th-Century Literature. From the 1890's to 1917) (1939); coauthor, *Ocherki istorii drevnerusskoy monumental'noy zhivopisi* (Outline History of Ancient Russian Monumental Painting) (1941); *Dramaturgiya M. Gor'kogo epokhi pervoy russkoy revolyutsii* (Gorky's Plays from the Period of the First Russian Revolution) (2nd ed, 1955); *Tvorchestvo M. Gor'kogo i mirovaya literatura* (Gorky's Work and World Literature) (1965); coauthor, *O literaturno-khudozhestsvennykh techeniyakh XX veka* (Literary and Artistic Trends of the 20th Century) (1966); wrote articles about Chekhov, Lev Tolstoy, Bryusov and Serafimovich; *Died:* 23 Feb 1965 in Moscow.

MIKHAYLOVSKIY, Sergey Vasil'yevich (1896–1965) Otolaryngologist; Dr of Med and prof from 1932; Hon Sci Worker of Bashkir ASSR from 1945; *Born:* 1896; *Educ:* 1922 grad Kiev Med Inst; *Career:* 1922–32 intern, asst prof, then assoc prof, Kiev Ear, Nose and Throat Clinic; 1932–34 head, Chair of Otolaryngology, Perm' Med Inst; 1935–38 head, Chair of Otolaryngology, Crimean Med Inst, Simferopol'; 1939–46 head, Chair of Otolaryngology, Bashkir Med Inst, Ufa; during WW 2 also worked at Ufa evacuation hospitals; 1946–65 head, Chair of Otolaryngology, L'vov Med Inst; founder-chm, L'vov Branch, All-Union Soc of Otolaryngologists; from 1956 until death member, ed council, journal "Vestnik otorinolaringologii"; supervised anti-sclerosis campaign in L'vov Oblast and other parts of Western Ukr; *Publ: Skleroma dykhatel'nykh putey* (Scleroma of the Respiratory Tract) (1959), etc; *Awards:* "Outstanding Health Worker" Badge; scrolls of hon and medals; *Died:* 22 Sept 1965.

MIKHEL'S, V. A. (1892–1940) Journalist; CP member from 1918; *Born:* 1892; *Career:* fought in WW 1; after 1917 Oct Revol served in Red Army as polit worker, then corresp, Russian Telegraphic (News) Agency; Feb 1921–25 head, Information Dept, newspaper "Izvestia"; various journalistic, admin and dipl posts; *Died:* 1940.

MIKHEL'SON, Vladimir Aleksandrovich (1860–1927) Physicist; Dr of Physics and prof from 1894; *Born:* 30 June 1860 in Tul'chin, now Vinnitsa Oblast; *Educ:* 1883 grad Moscow Univ; *Career:* 1884–87 secr, Physics Section, Soc of Amateur Naturalists; from 1887 assoc prof, Moscow Univ; 1890 established the basic law governing the relationship between the composition of a burning gas mixture and the motion of the combustion front and laid the foundations of the theory of explosive combustion; 1894–1927 prof of physics and meteorology, Petrov-Razumovskiy (now Timiryazev) Agric Acad; 1899 calculated the Doppler effect of light passing through a medium with a varying refraction index; dir of an observatory, USSR Acad of Sci; in latter years did research on actinometry and meteorology; *Publ: O normal'noy skorosti vosplameneniya gremuchikh gazovykh smesey* (The Normal Ignition Rate of Detonating Gas Mixtures) (1890); *K voprosu o pravil'nom primenenii printsipa Doplera* (The Correct Application of Doppler's Principle) (1899); *Sobraniye sochineniy* (Collected Works) (1930), etc; *Died:* 27 Feb 1927.

MIKHIN, Nikolay Andrianovich (1872–1946) Veterinary microbiologist; *Born:* 16 July 1872; *Educ:* 1896 grad Yur'yev (Tartu) Veterinary Inst; *Career:* from 1896 head, Diagnostic Dept, Veterinary Laboratory, Russian Min of Int Affairs; from 1919 prof, Moscow Veterinary (now Zoological and Veterinary) Inst; 1935 discovered the agent of leptospirosis in livestock; developed methods of manufacturing vaccines for various livestock diseases (a formalin vaccine for paratyphus in calves, an antibacillary serum and complex antisera); also devised a method of hyperimmunizing horses to speed up the manufacture of sera against Siberian plague; *Publ: Kurs chastnoy mikrobiologii dlya veterinarnykh vrachey i studentov* (A Special Microbiology Course for Veterinary Surgeons and Students) (1926), etc; *Awards:* Order of the Red Banner of

Labor; medals; *Died:* 1946.

MIKHOELS, (real name: VOVSI), Solomon Mikhaylovich (1890–1948) Actor and stage dir; Pop Artiste of USSR from 1939; *Born:* 16 Mar 1890 in Dvinsk; *Educ:* studied at Kiev Business Inst and Law Fac, Petrograd Univ; *Career:* 1919 joined Petrograd Jewish Theater School and Studio; 1921 saw foundation of State Jewish Chamber Theater, later renamed Moscow State Jewish Theater; 1929 Mikhoels appointed art dir, above theater; appeared in many films; also taught stagecraft; from 1931 taught at Jewish Theater Technicum; chm, Jewish Anti-Fascist Comt; *Works:* roles: Shimile Soroker in "200 Thousand"; Tevier in "Tevier the Milkman" after Sholom Aleykhem: Veniamin in Mendele-Moykher-Sforim's "The Journey of Veniamin III"; Lear in Shakespeare's "King Lear"; productions: outstanding production of "Freylekhs" based on folklore themes; *Awards:* Order of Lenin; Stalin Prize (1946); *Died:* 1948; according to Stalin's daughter, Svetlana Alliluyeva, Mikhoels was deliberately killed by the State Security organs; on Stalin's orders, his death was officially attributed to an automobile accident; 1953 Sov Security Organs posthumously accused Mikhoels of espionage and terrorism in connection with the infamous "doctors' plot"; 1955 officially rehabilitated.

MIKITENKO, Ivan Kondrat'yevich (1897–1937) Ukr writer, playwright and publicist; secr, bd, Ukr Writers' Union; bd member, USSR Writers' Union from 1934; CP member from 1925; *Born:* 6 Sept 1897 in vil Rovnoye, now Kirovograd Oblast; *Educ:* 1914 grad Kherson Mil Med Orderlies College; 1922–26 studied at Odessa Med Inst; 1927 grad Khar'kov Med Inst; *Career:* from 1914 served at the front; from 1918 med orderly in Kherson Province; also active in cultural and educ work; 1927–32 helped lead All-Ukr Union of Proletarian Writers; 1932–34 member, Org Bureau, Ukr and USSR Writers' Union; member, Int Bureau for the Struggle Against Fascism; 1935 and 1937 attended World Anti-Fascist Congresses in Defense of Peace; from 1931 also member, Ukr Centr Exec Comt; 1924 first work published; in the 1930's his plays were staged throughout the Ukr, and also in Moscow and Leningrad; concentrated on building of socialism in the villages, mines and Komsomol construction projects; also dealt with training of "new" Sov intelligentsia, establishment of Sov regime in the Ukr and struggle against Ukr "bourgeois nationalism"; arrested by State Security organs; *Publ:* plays: "I Come" (1926); "Dictatorship" (1929); "Cadres" (1930); "A Matter of Honor" (1931); "Our Country's Girls" (1932); "Flute Solo" (1933–36); "Days of Youth" (1936); "When the Sun Rose" (1937); collected stories "On Sunny Slopes" (1926); novelette "The Urkagany" (1928); novel "Morning" (1933); "Selected Works" (2 vol, 1957); "Collected Works" (6 vol, 1964–65); "Plays" (1959); "On the Literary Front 1927–1937. Articles, Studies, Speeches" (1962); *Died:* 4 Oct 1937 in imprisonment.

MIKOLAYTIS-PUTINAS (MYKOLAITIS-PUTINAS), Vintsas Yuozovich (1893–1967) Lith writer and lit historian; member, Lith Acad of Sci from 1941; Pop Writer of Lith SSR from 1963; *Born:* 13 Jan 1893 in vil Pilotishkyay, now Lith SSR, son of a peasant; *Educ:* studied at Petrograd Theological Acad; studied at Munich Univ; grad at Swiss Univ; *Career:* 1911 first work published; from 1923 prof of lit, Kaunas Univ; 1940–50 prof of lit, Vilnius Univ; translated Pushkin, Lermontov and Mickiewicz into Lith; *Publ:* novels: "Alley in Shade" (1933); "Rebels" (1957); collected verse: "Between Two Dawns" (1927); "I Welcome the Earth" (1950); "Poetry" (1956); "The Hour of Being" (1963); "The Window" (1966); *Died:* 7 June 1967.

MIKULICH, Boris Mikhaylovich (1912–1954) Bel writer; *Born:* 19 Aug 1912 in Bobruysk, son of a med orderly; *Educ:* grad secondary school; *Career:* late 1920's–early 1930's worked for Bobruysk newspaper "Kamunist"; from 1931 worked for various Bel lit journals; wrote on such subjects as the Komsomol, "socialist" transformation of Bel and "peoples' friendship"; in late 1930's arrested by NKVD; *Publ:* story collections: *Udar* (The Blow) (1931); *Chornaya Virnya* (Black Virnya) (1931); *Nasha solntsa* (Our Sun) (1932); *Yakhant* (The Ruby) (1935); novelettes: *Uskraina* (The Boundary) (1932); *Duzhasts'* (Power) (1934); *Druzhba* (Friendship) (1936); *Vybranaye* (Selected Works) (1959); *Povesti* (Novelettes) (1960); *Died:* 17 June 1954 in imprisonment; posthumously rehabilitated.

MILEV, Dumitru (1887–1944) Mold writer; *Born:* 2 Jan 1887 in vil Baurchi-Moldoven', Bessarabia; *Career:* 1918–24 did underground Party work in Bessarabia; in 1930's chm, Mold Branch, Ukr Writers' Union and ed, Mold journal "October"; in late 1930's arrested by NKVD; *Publ:* novelettes: "At Dawn" (1928); "Sixty-Two and a Half" (1931), etc; "Works" (1958); *Died:* 13 Oct 1944 in imprisonment; posthumously rehabilitated.

MILLER, Boris Vsevolodovich (1877–1956) Orientalist; specialist in Iranian languages and lit; Dr of Philology; prof; *Born:* 12 Nov 1877; *Educ:* at turn of century grad Law Fac, Moscow Univ and Lazarev Inst of Oriental Languages; *Career:* from 1922 taught at various Oriental inst; 1943–53 founder-head, Chair of Iranian Philology, Moscow Univ; did research on the Western group of living Iranian languages (Persian, Talish, Tat and Kurdish); wrote standard works on Talish and Tat; *Publ: Taty, ikh rasseleniye i govory* (The Tats, Their Distribution and Dialects) (1929); *Talyshskiye teksty* (Talish Texts) (1930); *O nekotorykh problemakh kurdskoy fonetiki* (Some Problems of Kurdish Phonetics) (1950); *Persidsko-russkiy slovar'* (A Persian-Russian Dictionary) (1953); *Awards:* Order of the Red Banner of Labor; medal "For Valiant Labor During the Great Fatherland War"; *Died:* 6 Aug 1956 after a long illness.

MILLER, Yevgeniy (Lyudvig) Karlovich (1867–?) Mil commander; russified German; lt-gen, Russian Army; commander, White Forces in Northern Russia; *Born:* 1867; *Educ:* grad cavalry college and Gen Staff Acad; *Career:* from 1886 in Russian Army; 1914–17 chief of staff, 5th Army; commander 26th Army Corps; Jan 1919 appointed governor-gen, Northern Oblast by anti-Sov govt of Northern Oblast; then Min of War, above govt; from July 1919, with evacuation of British Expeditionary Corps from Arkhangel'sk, commanded Whites' Northern Front and refused to evacuate his forces; began assault on Vologda and won a series of victories on the River Onega and along the Northern Railroad; Feb 1920, under pressure from Sov troops, shipped out of Arkhangel'sk with the remnants of his force; settled in Paris; from 1920's dep head, Russian Gen Soldiers' League; after OGPU kidnapped Gen Kutepov, head of the League, in Jan 1930, Miller became head of the League; 22 Nov 1937 kidnapped, like Kutepov, by NKVD agents in Paris; further fate unknown; *Died:* date and place of death unknown.

MIL'NER, Mikhail Arnol'dovich (1886–1953) Jewish composer, choirmaster and singing-teacher; *Born:* 29 Dec 1886 in vil Rakitno, Kiev Province; *Career:* 1924–25 music dir, Moscow Jewish Theater; 1929–31 music dir, Khar'kov Jewish Theater; 1931–41 art dir, Leningrad Jewish Vocal Ensemble; *Works:* operas: "Die Himmel brennen" (The Skies Are Burning) (1923); *Novyy put'* (The New Way) (1933); *Flaviy* (Flavius); symphony (1937); tone poem "The Partisans" (1944); piano concerto (1946); sonatas, piano pieces and vocal arrangements; vocal suite *Mat' i ditya* (Mother and Child); romances and theater music; *Died:* 25 Oct 1953 in Leningrad.

MILOSLAVSKIY, Valerian Vladimirovich (1880–1961) Hygienist; Dr of Med from 1934; prof from 1935; Hon Sci Worker of RSFSR from 1947; *Born:* 1880 in vil Zubtsov, now Kalinin Oblast; *Educ:* 1907 grad Med Fac, Tomsk Univ; *Career:* after grad physician, Nizhneudinsk Railroad Junction, then distr health officer, Don Oblast; specialized in hygiene under Prof V. G. Khlopin at Petersburg Inst of Experimental Med; from 1910 laboratory technician, Chair of Hygiene, Kazan' Univ; 1910–26 also dir, Smallpox Vaccination Inst; 1920 defended cand thesis on pollution of Kazanka River; from 1923 head, Chair of Hygiene, Kazan' Univ (from 1930 Kazan' Med Inst); from 1924 assoc, Inst of Labor Welfare, All-Union Centr Trade-Union Council; 1927–54 consultant, Sanitary and Antiepidemic Service, Tatar ASSR; 1928–32 took part in expeditions to study endemic goiter in Mari, Ural, Transbaykal and Gornaya Shoriya regions; did research on methods of determining the nitric and nitrous acid content of sewage, studied river pollution; also supervised a study of the mineral content of food products in the Tatar and Mari ASSR which confirmed that iodine deficiency is the basic etiological factor of endemic goiter; wrote over 50 works: *Publ: Kurs obshchey gigiyeny* (A General Hygiene Course); *Uchebnik gigiyeny pitaniya* (A Textbook on Food Hygiene); *K metodike opredeleniya azotistoy kisloty v stochnoy vode* (Methods of Determining the Nitrous Acid Content of Sewage) (1911); *K voprosy o vesovom metode opredeleniya azotnoy kisloty v stochnoy vode* (The Weight Method of Determining the Nitric Acid Content of Sewage) (1912); *Issledovaniye reki Kazanki* (A Study of the Kazanka River) (1923), etc; *Awards:* Order of Lenin; two Orders of the Red Banner of Labor; medals; *Died:* May 1961.

MILYUKOV, Pavel Nikolayevich (1859–1943) Politician; leader, Constitutional-Democratic Party (Cadets); historian and journalist; *Born:* 15 Jan 1859 in Moscow, son of a prof of architecture;

Educ: 1882 grad Moscow Univ; *Career:* 1886–1895 assoc prof, Chair of Russian History, Moscow Univ; 1892 received master's degree; in 1890's and early 1900's frequently criticized tsarist policy; 1895 dismissed from Moscow Univ for his links with the liberal wing of the student movement; for next ten years lived mainly abroad; lectured at Sofia and Chicago Univ; contributed to journal "Osvobozhdeniye"; spring 1905 returned to Russia and devoted himself entirely to polit work; active for Liberation League; co-founder, League of Leagues; deleg and Bureau member at zemstvo and urban congresses; co-founder, from 1907 chm, CC, Constitutional-Democratic Party; edited its organ "Rech'"; headed Cadet faction in State Duma of all convocations; dep, 3rd and 4th Dumas; during WW 1 supported tsarist policy (demanded the annexation of Galicia, Constantinople and the Dardanelles – hence his nickname "Dardanelles Milyukov" – and continuation of the war until "its victorious end"); highly critical of the government's inability to bring the war to a successful conclusion; prominent member, "Progressive Bloc"; after 1917 Feb Revol advocated retention of monarchy and negotiated transfer of imperial power to Grand Duke Mikhail, maintaining that otherwise "the chaos of anarchy will reign"; Feb–May 1917 Min of For Affairs in Provisional Govt; then leading role in numerous org, conferences and congresses; in newspaper "Rech'" campaigned against Lenin and the Bolsheviks; after 1917 Oct Revol fled to Southern Russia and allied himself with White Army; 1920 emigrated to London; from 1921 in Paris; in emigration headed Left Wing, Cadet Party, which in 1920 was reformed into the Democratic Group, and in 1924 into the Republ Democratic Assoc; edited newspaper "Posledniye novosti" advocating "new tactics" against Sov regime involving degeneration of dictatorship of the proletariat and its subservsion from within (slogan – "The Soviets Without the Bolsheviks"); with start of WW 2 sided with those Russian emigres who refused to collaborate with the Nazis; in an article written shortly before his death he paid tribute to the successes of the Sov state and the Red Army; *Publ: Gosudarstvennoye khozyaystvo Rossii v pervoy chetverti XVIII stoletiya i reforma Petra Velikogo* (The State Administration of Russia in the First Quarter of the 18th Century and Peter the Great's Reform) (1892); *Spornyye voprosy finansovoy istorii Moskovskogo gosudarstva* (Moot Aspects of Muscovy's Financial History) (1892); *Razlozheniye slavyanofil'stva* (Demoralization of Slavophilism) (1893); *Ocherki po istorii russkoy kul'tury* (Outline History of Russian Culture) (3 vol, 1869–1903); *Glavnyye techeniya russkoy istoricheskoy mysli* (Main Trends in Russian Historical Thought) (1897); *Iz istorii russkoy intelligentsii* (The History of the Russian Intelligentsia) (1902); collected articles *God bor'by* (A Year of Struggle) (1907); *Istoriya vtoroy russkoy revolyutsii* (The History of the Second Russian Revolution) (3 vol, 1919–24); *Natsional'nyy vopros* (The Nationality Problem) (1925); *Rossiya na perelome* (Russia at the Turning-Point) (2 vol, 1927); *Died:* 31 Mar 1943 in Paris.

MILYUTIN, Nikolay Aleksandrovich (1889–1942) Govt official; CP member from 1908; *Born:* 8 Dec 1889 son of a peasant-fisherman; *Educ:* primary school; *Career:* worked at various plants in Petersburg; 1908 founded Marxist circle in youth org; from 1910 in trade-union movement; 1913 elected Bd member, Trade and Ind Workers' Union; 1914 secr, Sick Fund, Putivl' Plant; 1915 organized RSDRP(B) Rayon Comt at "Skorokhod" Plant; 1916 drafted into Tsarist Army and founded two mil Party cells; Feb 1917 arrested but escaped and continued Party work in Petersburg's Lesnoy Rayon; after 1917 Feb Revol served in workers' insurance agency; member, Petrograd Sov; July 1917 sentenced to death by regt tribunal for his part in July demonstration, but was released by soldiers of his company; during the Kornilov affair commanded Red Guards of Moscow-Narva Rayon and directed defense of main sector on approaches to Petrograd; won over first units of so-called "Savage Div" to Bolshevik cause; Oct 1917 member, Org Comt, Moscow-Narva Rayon and commanded Red Guards; from Dec 1917 chm, Petrograd City Hospital Fund; member, Exec Bureau, Petrograd Province Trade-Union Council; member, Exec Comt, Petrograd Sov; Dep Comr of Labor, League of Northern Oblast Communes; from 1918 Collegium member, Pop Comrt of Labor; 1920–21 All-Russian Centr Exec Comt and Labor and Defense Council plen for Oryol and Voronezh Provinces; Ukr Dep Pop Comr of Food; 1922–24 RSFSR Dep Pop Comr of Soc Security; 1924–29 RSFSR Pop Comr of Finance; from 1929 chm, RSFSR Small Council of Pop Comr; 1930–34 RSFSR Dep Pop Comr of Educ; 1935–37 head, RSFSR Main Cinema Expansion Bd; *Died:* 1942.

MILYUTIN, Vladimir Pavlovich (1884–1938) Party and govt official; econ and writer; CP member from 1910; *Born:* 1884; *Career:* 1903 joined Soc-Democratic movement; after 2nd RSDRP Congress sided with Mensheviks; carried out Party work in Kursk, Moscow, Oryol, Petersburg and Tula; eight times arrested for revol activities and spent five years in prison, two in exile; after 1917 Feb Revol member, Saratov RSDRP(B) Comt; chm, Saratov Sov; Apr 1917 at 7th All-Russian RSDRP(B) Conference and 6th RSDRP(B) Congress elected member, CC, RSDRP(B); Pop Comr of Agric in first Sov govt; Nov 1917 advocated coalition govt with Mensheviks and Socialist-Revolutionaries and differed with RSDRP(B) CC policy; resigned from Party CC and Council of Pop Comr; later recanted his error; 1918–21 dep chm, Supr Sovnarkhoz; at 9th and 10th Party Congresses elected cand member, CC, RCPT(B); at 13th–16th Party Congresses elected member, CPSU(B) Centr Control Commission; 1922 dep chm, Econ Council of Nortwestern Oblast; from 1924 Collegium member, Pop Comrt of Workers and Peasants' Inspection; from 1928 mang, USSR Centr Statistical Bd; dep chm, USSR Gosplan; member, Labor and Defense Council; member, USSR Centr Exec Comt; dep chm, Communist Acad; member, main ed bd, "BSE" (Large Soviet Encyclopedia); member, ed bd of various journals; wrote many works on econ; arrested by State Security organs; *Publ: Agrarnaya politika v SSSR* (Agrarian Policy in the USSR) (1926); *Istoriya ekonomicheskogo razvitiya SSSR* (The Economic Development of the USSR) (1928); *Novyy period mirovoy ekonomiki* (A New Period in World Economics); *Sotsializm i sel'skoye khozyaystvo* (Socialism and Agriculture); *Narodnoye khozyaystvo Sovetskoy Rossii* (The National Economy of Soviet Russia); *Kapitalisticheskaya ratsionalizatsiya i ratsionalizatsiya sotsialisticheskaya* (Capitalist and Socialist Efficiency); *Died:* 1938 in imprisonment; posthumously rehabilitated.

MINAYEV, Kuz'ma Afanas'yevich (1895–1950) Ukr opera singer (baritone); Pop Artiste of Ukr SSR from 1946; CP member from 1946; *Born:* 14 Nov 1895 in vil Novaya Slobodka, now Kaluga Oblast; *Educ:* 1920–24 studied at Moscow Conservatory; 1927 grad Bolshoy Theater Studio; *Career:* 1927–37 performed at opera theaters in Khar'kov, Odessa and Baku; 1937–50 soloist, Kiev Acad Theater of Opera and Ballet; *Roles:* Astap and Miron in Lysenko's "Taras Bul'ba" and "Natalka-Poltavka"; Sultan in Gulak-Artemovskiy's *Zaporozhets' za Dunayem* (A Dnieper Cossack Beyond the Danube); Protenko in Meytus' *Molodaya gvardiya* (The Young Guard); Nagul'nov in Dzerzhinskiy's *Podnyataya tselyna* (Virgin Soil Upturned); title roles in Borodin's *Knyaz' Igor'* (Prince Igor) and Verdi's "Rigoletto", etc; *Died:* 26 Jan 1950.

MININ, Sergey Konstantinovich (1882–1962) Party and govt official; CP member from 1905; *Born:* 29 June 1882 in vil Dubovka, Tsaritsyn Uyezd, Saratov Province, son of a priest; *Career:* 1903 joined revol movement; frequently arrested by Tsarist authorities; after 1917 Feb Revol chm, Tsaritsyn RSDRP(B) Comt and Tsaritsyn Sov of Workers' and Soldiers' Dep; late 1917 in charge of "defense staff" responsible for crushing opposition in Don area; from July 1918 member, Revol–Mil Councils, North Caucasian Mil Distr and 10th Army; from Oct 1918 Collegium member, NKVD; from June 1919 again with 10th Army; in same year sided with "mil opposition" at 8th RCP(B) Congress; May 1920–May 1921 member, Revol Mil Council, 1st Cavalry Army; after Civil War dep polit commander, Ukr and Crimea; member, CC, CP(B) Ukr and Ukr Council of Pop Comr; chief ed, newspaper "Kommunist"; from 1923 rector, Leningrad Communist and State Univs; member, Northwestern Bureau, CC, CPSU(B); deleg at 6th, 8th, 9th, 10th, 11th, 13th, 14th and 15th Party Congresses; 1925 joined "new opposition"; 1927 retired for health reasons; *Died:* 8 Jan 1962.

MINKEVICH, Nikolay Anatol'yevich (1883–1942) Metallurgist; Hon Sci and Tech Worker of RSFSR from 1934; *Born:* 16 Feb 1883; *Educ:* 1907 grad Petersburg Polytech Inst; *Career:* 1908–14 worked at Obukhov Plant; from 1920 prof, Moscow Mining Acad; from 1930 prof, Moscow Steel Inst, where he founded the Chair of Metallurgy and Heat Treatment of Steel; helped introduce many new technol processes in the Sov machine-building ind; studied steel strength, distortion in steel and special steels, etc; made first use of pyrolysis gas for cementation; directed studies on the exploitation of naturally alloyed ores in the Orsk-Khalil deposits; helped design heat treatment shops for first Sov automobile and tractor plants; *Publ: Stal', stal'nyye i chugunnyye* *polufabrikaty* (Steel, and Steel and Iron Semi-Products) (1930); *Svoystva, teplovaya obrabotka i naznacheniye stali i chuguna* (The Properties, Heat Treatment and Application of Steel and Cast Iron) (2 vol, 2nd ed, 1934); *Kurs termicheskoy obrabotki stali i chuguna* (A Course in the Heat Treatment of Steel and Iron) (1935); *Novyye malolegirovannyye bystrorezhushchiye stali* (New Low-Alloy East-Cutting Steels) (1940); *Awards:* Stalin Prize (1941); *Died:* 13 Oct 1942.

MINKIN, Aleksandr Yeremeyevich (1887–1955) Party and govt official; CP member from 1903; *Born:* 1887; *Career:* Party work in Warsaw and Urals; repeatedly arrested by Tsarist authorities; 1910 emigrated to North America; joined Russian Dept, American Soc-Democratic Party; after 1917 Feb Revol returned to Russia; member, Petrograd RSDRP(B) Comt and chm, rayon RSDRP(B) comt; after 1917 Oct Revol various exec Party, govt and dipl posts; chm, Penza Province Party Comt and Penza Province Exec Comt; comr, Perm' Plant, State Bd for Issue of Banknotes; chm, Perm' Province Party Comt and Perm' Province Exec Comt; secr, Arkhangel'sk Province Party Comt; Collegium member, Pop Comrt of Trade; 1934–35 USSR plen in Uruguay; dep chm, RSFSR Supr Court; Arkhangel'sk RCP(B) Comt deleg at 11th RCP(B) Congress; *Died:* 1955.

MINKOV, I. I. (1894–1935) Party official; *Born:* 1894; *Career:* 1910 emigrated to Winnipeg, Canada; 1911 joined group of Russian Soc-Democrats; 1915 member, then secr, Russian Dept of Philadelphia Comt, American Soc-Democratic Party; returned to Russia; from 1917 various Party and govt posts; member, Moscow Okrug RSDRP(B) Comt; Presidium member, Moscow Province Exec Comt; secr, then head, Org Dept, Moscow RCP(B) Comt; secr, Samara Province RCP(B) Comt; Presidium member, Samara Province Exec Comt; deleg, 8th and 9th RCP(B) Congresses; 1923–27 cand member, then member, CPSU(B) Centr Control Commission; from 1928 retired; *Died:* 1935.

MIN'KOV, M. I. (1895–1938) Party official; *Born:* 1895; *Career:* 1911 emigrated to Milwaukee, USA; 1912 joined group of Russian Soc-Democrats; secr, Russian Dept, American Soc-Democratic Party; after 1917 Feb Revol Party work in Yekaterinoslav; worked for Bolshevik newspaper "Zvezda"; after 1917 Oct Revol head, Org Dept, Zamoskvorech'ye Rayon Party Comt in Moscow; secr, Vyatka Province RCP(B) Comt; member, CC, Int Org for Aid to Revol Fighters; 9th Army Party Org deleg at 8th RCP(B) Congress; during 14th CPSU(B) Congress joined Trotsky-Zinov'yev Bloc; 1927, at 15th CPSU(B) Congress, expelled from Party for belonging to "anti-Party Sapronov group" and "Trotskyst opposition"; 1931 reinstated; 1935 again expelled from Party and charged with anti-Party and anti-Sov activities; *Died:* 1938 in imprisonment.

MINOR, Lazar' Solomonovich (1855–1942) Neuropathologist and clinician; co-founder, Moscow school of neuropathology; Dr of Med from 1884; prof from 1910; Hon Sci Worker of RSFSR from 1927; *Born:* 29 Dec 1855; *Educ:* 1879 grad Med Fac, Moscow Univ; *Career:* after grad worked at Kozhevnikov, Charcot, Westfal and Mendel's clinics; 1882 defended doctor's thesis on the corpus striatum; from 1884 assoc prof, Moscow Univ; from 1910 founder-dir and prof, Nerve Clinic, Higher Women's Courses (now 2nd Moscow Med Inst); consultant, various Moscow hospitals; edited numerous specialist publications in Russian and German, including the 3-vol "Handbuch der pathologischen Anatomie des Nervensystems" (Manual on the Pathological Anatomy of the Nervous System) (1903); hon member, various Sov sci soc; hon member, Paris Anatomical, Psychiatrical and Neurological Soc, German Neurological Soc, Est Neurological Soc, Philadelphia Neurological Soc, etc; 1931 hon deleg, 1st World Neurological Congress; specialized in clinical histological research and the histology of the nervous system; described numerous clinical forms and symptoms (Minor's centr hematomyelia, Minor's epiconus, Minor's iscias phenomenon); devised theory of polypathia; also did research on alcoholism, epilepsy and occupational nervous diseases; wrote over 160 works; *Publ: Tsentral'naya gematomiyeliya* (Central Hematomyelia) (1890); *Chisla i nablyudeniya iz oblasti alkogolizma* (Statistics and Observations on Alcoholism) (1910); *Hallux valgus hemiplegicorum. Materialy k ucheniyu o kombinozakh i diatezakh* (Hallux valgus hemiplegicorum. Material on the Theory of Combinosis and Diathesis) (1911); *Elektricheskoye soprotivleniye kozhi pri voyenno-travmaticheskikh povrezhdeniyakh nervi sympathici* (The Electrical Resistance of the Skin in War Traumas of the Sympathetic Nerve) (1915); *Lecheniye nervnykh bolezney* (The Treatment of Nervous Diseases) (1935), etc; *Died:* 1942.

MINORSKIY, Vladimir Fyodorovich (1877–1966) Orientalist; prof; *Born:* 5 Feb 1877; *Educ:* grad Law Fac, Moscow Univ and Lazarev Inst of Oriental Languages; *Career:* for many years lived in England; Hon Dr of Sci, Brussels Univ; member, British and French Acad of Sci; hon member, Paris Asian Soc; 1960 attended 25th Int Congress of Orientalists, Moscow; maintained connections with Sov Orientalists and bequeathed his extensive library to the Inst of Oriental Studies, USSR Acad of Sci; translated and published numerous source material on the lit and history of the Mideast countries; *Publ: Turkmenika* (Turkmen Studies); *Kaukazika* (Caucasian Studies); *Mongolika* (Mongolian Studies); *Istoriya Shirvana i Derbenda X-XI vekov* (The History of Shirvan and Derbend in the 10th and 11th Centuries) (1963); *Died:* 25 Mar 1966 in London; reinterred 19 June 1970 in Moscow's Novodevich'ye Cemetary.

MIRCHINK, Georgiy Fyodorovich (1889–1942) Geologist; prof from 1918; member, Bel Acad of Sci from 1941; *Born:* 13 Apr 1889; *Career:* from 1918 prof, Moscow Univ; did research on the geological conditions at paleolithic settlements; 1923 compiled map of Quaternary deposits in European USSR; 1936 read paper at 3rd Int Quaternary Conference, Vienna; applied complex method to research on Quaternary period; *Publ:* master's thesis, *Posletertichnyye otlozheniya Chernigovskoy gubernii i ikh otnosheniya k analogichnym obrazovaniyam ostal'noy Rossii* (Post-Tertiary Deposits in Chernigov Province and Their Relation to Similar Formations in the Rest of Russia) (1918); *Sootnosheniye chetvertichnykh otlozheniy Russkoy ravniny i Kavkaza* (The Relationship Between the Quaternary Deposits of the Russian Plain and the Caucasus) (1929); textbook *Geologiya chetvertichnykh otlozheniy* (The Geology of Quaternary Deposits) (1934), etc; *Died:* 10 Apr 1942.

MIR-KASIMOV, Mir Asadulla Mir Alesker ogly (1883–1958) Surgeon; prof from 1931; member, Azer Acad of Sci from 1945; Hon Sci Worker of Azer SSR from 1935; *Born:* 29 Nov 1883; *Educ:* 1913 grad Novorossiysk Univ, Odessa; *Career:* from 1913 intern, Odessa Municipal Hospital; 1918–23 worked at Mikhaylov Hospital, Baku; 1931–58 prof of surgery, Azer Med Inst, Baku; 1945–47 pres, Azer Acad of Sci; dep, USSR Supr Sov of 1st–3rd convocations; did research on the etiology and clinical aspects of bladder stones, the treatment of wounds and diffuse suppurative peritonitis; *Publ: Materialy k izucheniyu mochekamennoy bolezni v Azerbaydzhane* (Material on the Study of Bladder Stones in Azerbaydzhan) (1928); *O spontannom raspadenii kamney v organizme* (The Spontaneous Disintegration of Stones in the Body) (1930); *O rake mochevogo puzyrya* (Cancer of the Urinary Bladder) (1936); *Dinamicheskiye momenty v rasstroystve mocheispuskaniya pri tak nazyvayemoy gipertrofii predstatel'noy zhelezy* (Dynamic Factors of Micturitional Disturbance in Hypertrophy of the Prostate Gland) (1938); *O bespovyazochnom lechenii chistykh operatsionnykh ran* (The Healing of Clean Surgical Wounds Without Dressings) (1942); *Awards:* Order of Lenin; medals; *Died:* 19 July 1958.

MIROLYUBOV, Viktor Sergeyevich (1860–1939) Ed and publisher; *Born:* 3 Feb 1860 in Moscow; *Educ:* studied at Moscow Univ; *Career:* exiled to Samara for polit activity; from 1898 ed, pop sci and lit magazine "Zhurnal dlya vsekh", which was closed in 1906 for publishing articles about the revol movement; 1910 asked by Gorky to edit anthologies for the "Znaniye" (Knowledge) Publ House; 1912–13 head, Lit Dept, journal "Zavety"; 1914–17 published the magazine "Yezhemesyachnyy zhurnal literatury, nauki i obshchestvennoy zhizni"; 1917 contributed to Socialist-Revol newspaper "Volya norada"; after 1917 Oct Revol worked for the Centr Cooperative Publ House and edited the journal "Artel'noye delo"; *Died:* 26 Oct 1939 in Leningrad.

MIRONOV, Filipp Kuz'mich (1872–1921) Mil commander; lt-col, Russian Army; Civil War veteran; CP member from 1920; *Born:* 14 Oct 1872 in vil Bol'shoy, on the Don, son of a Cossack; *Educ:* 1898 grad Novocherkassk Cossack Cadet College; *Career:* 1904–05 fought in Russo-Japanese War; arrested for his part in 1905–07 Revol events in the Don area and after release dishonorably discharged from army; 1914, with the start of WW 1, volunteered for Russian Army and was sent to the front; won four mil orders and gained rapid promotion; 1917 sided with Maximalist Socialist-Revolutionaries; elected commander, 32nd Don Cossack Regt; Dec 1917 led his regt from the Rumanian Front to Ust'-Medveditsa Okrug, where he was instrumental in establishing Sov regime; 1918 Ust'-Medveditsa Okrug Comt; his terrorist policies helped spark the anti-Sov Don revolt; 1918–19 commanded regt, brigade, then 23rd Infantry Div; commanded a group of forces of the 9th Army in battles against White Gen Krasnov; Feb 1919 transferred to Western Front after vigorously protesting against the Don RCP(B) Bureau's policy of "de-Cossackization"; asst commander and 15 May–9 June 1919 commander, Bel-Lith Army; June 1919 commanded expeditionary corps on Southern Front; from July 1919 led special Cossack Corps on Southern Front; Aug 1919, alarmed at continuing Sov reprisals against the Cossacks, led his troops against Sov forces, urging them to fight to "overthrow the Communist Party and save the gains of the revol"; routed by Budyonny's Cavalry, arrested and sentenced to death by mil tribunal; at Lenin's instigation, the RCP(B) CC Politburo ordered his release, and the All-Russian Centr Exec Comt quashed the sentence; after this worked as head, Land Dept, Don Exec Comt; 6 Sept–6 Dec 1920 commanded 2nd Cavalry Army against Gen Wrangel's forces; subsequently inspector of Red Army Cavalry; Feb 1921 arrested by Cheka; *Awards:* Order of the Red Banner; Golden Arms; *Died:* 2 Apr 1921 executed; posthumously rehabilitated.

MIRONOV, Ivan Fyodorovich (1882–1964) Govt official; CP member from 1905; *Born:* 1882; *Career:* active in revol movement in Petrograd; revol work at Rechkin, Putilov and "Vulkan" Plants; exiled to Arkhangel'sk Province but fled from exile; until 1917 lived illegally in Petersburg; fought in Civil War; worked for Special Dept, Southern Front; 1921 Collegium member, Ukr Pop Comrt of Workers and Peasants' Inspection; 1925 member, Ukr Supr Court; oblast prosecutor in Zhitomir, Odessa and Khar'kov; from 1945 asst prosecutor of Lat SSR; from 1953 retired; *Died:* 29 June 1964.

MIRONOV, Nikolay Romanovich (1913–1964) Mil commander; govt and Party official; maj-gen; CP member from 1940; *Born:* 27 Dec 1913 in Dneprodzerzhinsk; *Educ:* 1946 grad Dnepropetrovsk Univ; *Career:* 1933–37 with Dnepropetrovsk Oblast Trade-Union Council and Dnepropetrovsk Oblast Comt for Physical Training and Sport; 1937–41 student; 1941–45 polit work in Sov Army; 1945–47 with Dnepropetrovsk Oblast Comt, CP Ukr; 1947–49 first secr, Dnepropetrovsk's Oct Rayon Comt, CP Ukr; 1949–51 secr, Kirovograd Oblast Comt, CP Ukr; from 1951 with Centr State Security organs; 1956–59 head, KGB Bd for Leningrad Oblast; 1959–64 head, Admin Organs Dept, CC, CPSU; 1961–64 member, CPSU Centr Auditing Commission; dep, RSFSR Supr Sov of 1959 convocation; dep, USSR Supr Sov of 1962 convocation; deleg at 19th and 22nd CPSU Congresses; *Awards:* Order of Lenin; Order of the Red Banner of Labor; Order of the Red Star; Order of the Fatherland War, 2nd Class; Badge of Hon; medals; *Died:* 19 Oct 1964 killed in plane crash en route to Belgrade.

MIRONOV, Stepan Il'ich (1888–1959) Oil geologist; member, USSR Acad of Sci from 1946; *Born:* 10 Aug 1888; *Educ:* 1914 grad Petersburg Mining Inst; *Career:* 1913–29 worked for Geological Comt in Leningrad; surveyed oil deposits on Emba and Sakhalin; 1929–31 dir, 1932–38 dep dir, 1938–46 consultant, Leningrad Inst of Oil Geology; 1946–47 dept head, Oil Inst, USSR Acad of Sci; 1947–49 dir, Sakhalin Research Base, USSR Acad of Sci; 1949–50 Presidium chm, Sakhalin Branch, USSR Acad of Sci; 1950–58 laboratory head, Oil Inst, USSR Acad of Sci; 1958–59 laboratory head, Inst of Geology and Combustible Minerals; did research on oil survey methods and the mapping of deposits with the help of wells; *Publ: Ural'skiy neftenosnyy rayon* (The Ural Petroliferous Region) (1915); *Novo-Bogatinskoye mestorozhdeniye nefti* (The Novobogatinskoye Oil Deposit) (1927); *Problema proiskhozhdeniya nefti i puti yeyo razresheniya* (The Problem of the Origin of Oil and Ways of Solving It) (1952), etc; *Awards:* Order of the Red Banner of Labor; medals; *Died:* 20 Mar 1959.

MIROSHNIKOV, I. I. (1894–1939) Govt official; CP member from 1917; *Born:* 1894; *Career:* fought in Civil War; 1921–37 dep manager, then manager, Council of Pop Comr and Labor and Defense Council; from 1937 USSR Dep Pop Comr of Finance; at 18th CPSU(B) Congress elected member, Sov Control Commission; arrested by State Security organs; *Died:* 1939 in imprisonment.

MIROTVORTSEV, Sergey Romanovich (1878–1949) Surgeon; prof from 1914; member, USSR Acad of Med Sci from 1945; Hon Sci Worker of RSFSR from 1935; CP member from 1944; *Born:* 28 May 1878; *Educ:* 1903 grad Med Fac, Khar'kov Univ, where he won two gold medals for study projects; *Career:* from 1903 intern, asst prof, then assoc prof, Petersburg Mil Med Acad, where he specialized under Prof A. A. Troyanov, S. P. Fyodorov and V. A. Oppel'; 1904 wounded while serving as a mil surgeon in besieged Port Arthur and interned by Japanese; from 1914 head, Chair of Gen Surgery, Saratov Univ; during WW 1 served on Caucasian and Western Fronts; from 1920 until death head, Chair of Fac Surgery, Saratov Univ; 1922–28 also rector, Saratov Univ; 1941–45 mil surgeon in Sov Army; did research on renal syphilis, sarcomas of the tubular bones, ligation of the carotid artery, collateral blood circulation, etc; introduced new method of transferring the ureter to the rectum; during WW 1 compiled statistics on 180,000 gun-shot wounds; chm, Saratov Surgical Soc; chm, Lower Volga Kray Physicians' Assoc; co-ed, "Zhurnal sovremennoy khirurgii"; trained numerous talented surgeons; wrote some 150 works; *Publ: Eksperimental'nyye dannyye k voprosu o peresadke mochetochnikov v kishechnik* (Experimental Data on the Transfer of the Ureters to the Intestines) (1909); *K ucheniyu o kollateral'nom krovoobrashchenii* (The Theory of Collateral Blood Circulation) (1912); *Sarkomy trubchatykh kostey* (Sarcomas of the Tubular Bones) (1914); *K patologii i klinike sarkom kishechnika* (The Pathological and Clinical Aspects of Intestinal Sarcomas) (1923); *O sifilise pochki* (Renal Syphilis) (1927); *Zlokachestvennyye novoobrazovaniya cherepnoy kryshki* (Malignant Neoplasms of the Calvaria) (1930); coauthor, *Materialy k voyenno-polevoy khirurgii* (Material on Field Surgery) (1940); *Stranitsy zhizni* (The Pages of Life) (1956), etc; *Awards:* two orders; medals; *Died:* 5 May 1949.

MIROVICH (real name: DUNAYEV), Yevstigney Afinogenovich (1878–1952) Bel playwright, actor and producer; prof; Pop Artiste of Bel SSR from 1940; *Born:* 11 July 1878 in Petersburg, son of a railroad worker; *Educ:* grad Volkov Theatrical Courses in Petersburg; *Career:* actor and producer, various Petersburg theaters: 1900–03 Admiralty Theater; 1903–10 Yekaterina Theater; 1910–12 Kronstadt Theater; 1912–13 Trinity Theater; 1914–17 Foundry Theater; 1906 began writing plays; 1919 moved to Bel; 1921–31 art dir, 1st Bel (now Kupala) Drama Theater; 1932–37 mang and art dir, Bel Kolkhoz-Sovkhoz Theater; 1937–40 art dir, Young Playgoers' Theater; 1941–45 producer, Kupala Drama Theater; from 1945 art dir, prof and head, Chair of Acting, Bel Theater Inst; wrote in Russian and Bel; on subjects ranging from Bel history to Sov reality; *Publ:* plays: *Opekuny* (The Trustees); *Teatr kuptsa Yepishkina* (The Merchant Yepishkin's Theater); *Grafinya El'vira* (Countess Elvira); *Vova prisposobilsya* (Vova Toes the Line); "Masheka" (1922); "Kastus' Kalinovski" (1923); *Kaval'-vayavoda* (The Blacksmith General) (1924); *Kar'yera Bryzgalina* (Bryzgalin's Career); *Peramoha* (Victory) (1926); *Zapayuts' veratsyony* (The Spindles Hum) (1928); collected works *P'yesy* (Plays) (1957); *Works:* produced: Charot's *Na kupalle* (At the Kupala Festival) (1921); *Myatezh* (The Uprising) (1927), after Furmanov; Romanovich's *Most* (The Bridge) (1929); Kurdin's *Mezhdubur'ye* (Storm Interval) (1929); Kobets's "Guta" (1930); *Kak zakalyadas' stal'* (How the Steel Was Tempered) (1937); Vokov's *Chudesnaya dudka* (The Magic Pipes) (1939); *Dokhodnoye mesto* (A Lucrative Post) (1941), etc; *Died:* 15 Feb 1952 in Minsk.

MIRSKIY, Dmitriy Petrovich (1890–1939) Lit historian and critic; *Born:* 27 Aug 1890 in vil Giyovka, Khar'kov Province, son of the liberal tsarist min, Prince Svyatopolk-Mirskiy; *Educ:* grad Philological Fac, Petersburg Univ; *Career:* 1911 published collection of verse, written in his youth; after 1917 Oct Revol in emigration; 1922–32 lived in England and lectured on Russian lit at London Univ and the Royal College; lit critic for journals, "Criterion" and "Échange"; 1926–28 contributed to almanach "Versty", Brussels; wrote Engl-language works "A History of Russian Literature" (1927) and "Contemporary Russian Literature" (1926); published several anthologies of Russian poetry; 1930 joined Communist Party of Britain; 1932 returned to USSR and engaged in lit work; published articles on the theory and history of Russian and Western lit; 1934 published soc essay "The Intelligentsia" based on his impressions of England; helped popularize English literature with the articles "Contemporary English Literature" (1933) about T. S. Eliot and "Ulysses" (1935); wrote preface to editions of works by Smollett, Shelley, Huxley, etc; compiled first Russian-language "Antologiya novoy angliyskoy poezii" (An Anthology of New English Poetry) (1937); wrote articles on Sov poets N. Zabolotskiy, E. Bagritskiy and P. Vasil'yev; also worked on biography of Pushkin, part of which was published in 1937; 1937 arrested by NKVD; *Publ: Russkaya lirika. Malen'kaya antologiya ot Lomonosova do Pasternaka* (Russian Lyric Poetry. A Short Anthology from Lomonosov to Pasternak) (Paris, 1924); "Pushkin" (London, 1926); "Lenin" (London, 1931); "Russia. A Social History" (London, 1931); coauthor, "Bagritskiy" (1936); *Died:* 1939 in imprisonment; posthumously rehabilitated.

MIRZA-AVAKYAN, Urutyun Grigor'yevich (1879–1937) Surgeon; prof from 1935; *Born:* 1879 in Baku; *Educ:* 1902 grad Baku high school; 1908 grad Med Fac, Kiev Univ; *Career:* 1908–21 intern, Kiev surgical clinics, then head, surgical dept of various hospitals; 1915–18 chief physician, Kiev's No 1 Hospital, League of Cities; late 1921 moved to Arm to become head, Surgical Dept, Yerevan Mil Hospital; from 1922 head, Surgical Dept, Yerevan 2nd Hospital; until 1937 chief physician, above hospital; specialized in brain and spinal operations; 1927 successfully removed bullet from thick cardiac muscle; from 1924 founder-head, Chair of Operative Surgery and Topographical Anatomy, Med Fac, Yerevan Univ; 1929 founded another surgical dept at Yerevan Univ; 1929 sent to Paris to study experience of French surgical clinics; 1933–36 head, Chair of Hospital Surgery, Med Fac, Yerevan Univ; 1936 abandoned teaching on health grounds and headed Surgical Dept, Yerevan Red Cross Hospital; *Died:* 1937.

MIRZOYAN, Levon Isayevich (1897–1938) Party official; CP member from 1917; *Born:* Nov 1897 in vil Ashan, Shusha Uyezd, Azer; *Career:* 1912, while at school, joined Soc-Democratic movement; 1917–20 trade-union work; secr, Binagada Branch of Boilermakers and Riveters Union (then Metalworkers Union); member, Bolshevik mil squad; dep, Baku Sov of Workers and Soldiers' Dep; July 1917 after collapse of Sov regime in Baku, carried out underground Party work; resumed trade-union work after establishment of Sov regime in Azer; Aug 1920 elected chm, Azer Trade-Union Council; 1921 head, Baku Comt, CP Azer; then worked for CC, CP Azer; from late 1925 secr, CC, CP Azer; from Oct 1929 secr, Perm' Okrug Party Comt; then second secr, Ural Oblast CPSU(B) Comt; 1933 elected first secr, Kaz Kray Party Comt; June 1937, with formation of CP Kaz, first secr, CC, CP(B) Kaz; at 15th and 16th Party Congresses elected cand member, at 17th Congress member, CC, CPSU(B); member, USSR Centr Exec Comt of several convocations; 1938 arrested by State Security organs; *Awards:* Order of Lenin (1935); *Died:* May 1938 in imprisonment; his fate was shared by his wife Yuliya Teodorovna Tevosyan, a CP member from 1918, who was dir, Inst of Marxism-Leninism, CC, CP Kaz; Jan 1956 Mirzoyan and Tevosyan were posthumously rehabilitated.

MISHULIN, Aleksandr Vasil'yevich (1901–1948) Historian; specialist in ancient history; Dr of History from 1943; CP member from 1927; *Born:* 1901; *Educ:* completed higher educ; 1932 completed postgrad course at Inst of History, Russian Assoc of Soc Sci Research Institutes; *Career:* 1938–40 and 1943 head, Ancient History Section, Inst of History, USSR Acad of Sci; 1944–46 work for CC, CPSU(B); 1946–48 rector, Acad of Soc Sci, CC, CPSU(B); prof and head, Chair of Ancient History, Moscow State Univ; 1938–48 ed, journal "Vestnik drevney istorii"; specialized in soc and econ history of Ancient Rome and the slave revolts; *Publ: Spartak* (Spartacus) (2nd ed, 1950); *Antichnaya Ispaniya do ustanovleniya rimskoy provintsial'noy sistemy v 197 godu do nashey ery* (Ancient Spain Prior to the Establishment of the Roman Provincial System in 197 B.C.) (1952); *Awards:* Order of the Red Banner of Labor; medals; *Died:* 19 Sept 1948.

MISLAVSKIY, Aleksandr Andreyevich (1827–1918) Surgeon; Dr of Med from 1894; *Born:* 1827, son of a Kostroma landowner; *Educ:* 1851 grad Med Fac, Kazan' Univ; *Career:* as a student specialized in obstetrics; from 1851 physician, Turinsk Mine, Urals, where he gained considerable surgical experience; later transferred to Bogoslovskiy Plant, Urals; from 1859 chief physician, Verkh-Isetsk plants; 1852 one of first Russian surgeons to perform a successful strumectomy; in the course of his career performed some 10,000 major operations and 4,000 cataract operations, treating over 300,000 patients and making over one million doctor's calls; 1867 underwent advanced ophthalmological and surgical training in Germany and France; 1879 performed first laparotomy for removal of ovarian cysts; 1901 the fiftieth anniversary of the start of his med career was celebrated throughout the Urals with the establishment of scholarships in his name and work on a Mislavskiy Eye Clinic covering the Ural mines; corresp member of Belgian, Italian, French, British, American and Austrian sci socs; wrote numerous works; presented papers at surgical and ophthalmological congresses; *Died:* 1918.

MISLAVSKIY, Aleksandr Nikolayevich (1880–1958) Histologist; Dr of Med from 1909; prof from 1918; Hon Sci Worker of RSFSR; *Born:* 1880, son of the physiologist N. A. Mislavskiy; *Educ:* 1904 grad Med Fac, Kazan Univ; *Career:* from 1904 asst dissector, Chair of Histology, Kazan' Univ; 1909 defended doctor's thesis on the microscopic structure of the merocrine glands in the skin of mammals; 1911–12 worked under Prof M. Heidenhain in Germany; 1913–18 assoc prof, from 1918 prof of histology, Med Fac, Kazan Univ; from 1921 head, Chair of Histology, Kazan Univ and Kazan' Histological Laboratory; did major research on glandular tissue; studied the cellular structure of the renal eipithelium and the role of the chondriosomes of the pancreas in secretion; supervised research at Kazan' Histological Laboratory on the morphology of the sympathetic nervous system (innervation of the digestive tract, gall-bladder, etc); trained such outstanding histologists as N. G. Kolosov, Yu. M. Lazovskiy, B. I. Lavrent'yev and G. A. Polikarpov; *Publ:* doctor's thesis *Materialy k gistologii slozhnykh trubchatykh (merokrinovykh) zhelez kozhi mlekopitayushchikh* (Material on the Histology of the Complex Tubular [Merocrine] Glands in the Skin of Mammals) (1909); *K morfologii zhelezistoy kletki* (The Morphology of the Glandular Cell) (1913), etc; *Died:* 1958.

MISLAVSKIY, Nikolay Aleksandrovich (1854–1928) Physiologist; Dr of Med from 1885; prof from 1891; corresp member, USSR Acad of Sci from 1927; Hon Sci Worker of RSFSR from 1926; *Born:* 29 Apr 1854, son of well-known Ural surgeon A. A. Mislavskiy; *Educ:* 1876 grad Med Fac, Kazan' Univ; *Career:* from 1876 until death worked at Kazan' Univ; asst prof, dissector, from 1886 assoc prof, from 1891 prof and head, Kazan' Physiological Laboratory; did research on the body's nervous regulation; 1885 defended doctor's thesis on the mammalian respiratory center, which he located in the medulla oblongata; together with V. M. Bekhterev established how the cortex of the cerebral hemispheres influences the activity of a number of internal organs (the heart, stomach, intestines, urinary bladder, etc) and described the areas of the cortex containing centers controlling movement and secretory nervous reactions; also studied the reflex regulation of blood circulation; established that blood pressure depends on the interaction of the antagonistic vasodilator and vasoconstrictor centers (an extension of the principle of reciprocal innervation of blood pressure regulation); together with V. Borman devised original method of obtaining prostatic fluid and of studying the mechanism of salivation; made first use of new preparation which made it possible to study the contraction of the smooth muscles and their reaction to various chemicals; together with D. Polumordvinov arrived at the disputed conclusion that inhibitory processes develop in the innervated organ itself and not via the nerve fibers; demonstrated the adaptivity of the nerve centers to peripheral lesions by cross-suturing nerve fibers; 1898 member, Int Commission for the Control of Graphic Research Methods; from 1900 member, "Association de l'Institut Marey"; from 1910 corresp member, French Biological Soc; hon member, Kazan' Soc of Physicians, Soc of Natural Scientists, Soc of Neurologists and Psychiatrists and Ural Med Soc; wrote over 50 works; *Publ:* doctor's thesis *O dykhatel'nom tsentre* (The Respiratory Center) (1885); *Izbrannyye proizvedeniya* (Selected Works) (1952), etc; *Died:* 28 Dec 1928.

MITKEVICH, Vladimir Fyodorovich (1872–1951) Bel electr eng; member, USSR Acad of Sci from 1929; Hon Sci and Tech Worker of RSFSR from 1938; *Born:* 3 Aug 1872 in Minsk; *Educ:* 1895 grad Petersburg Univ; *Career:* 1902–38 taught at Petersburg (Leningrad) Polytech Inst; 1903–05 did research on the nature of electr arcs; together with A. I. Gorbov devised method of oxidizing nitrogen with air; 1906–12 lecturer, Petersburg Higher Women's Courses; 1910 proposed use of split wiring for high-tension power lines; during 1920's worked for Special Tech Bureau of Mil Inventions; together with eng V. I. Bekauri developed "BEMI" remote-controlled detonator, which was adopted by Red Army in 1929; 1939–44 head, Dept of Theoretical Electr Eng, Krzhizhanovskiy Power Eng Inst, USSR Acad of Sci; helped draft plan for the electrification of Russia; 1940–42 head, Electr Communications Section, Dept of Tech Sci, USSR Acad of Sci, devised new concept of electromagnetic field; *Publ: O vol'tovoy duge* (The Electric Arc) (1905); *Kurs peremennykh tokov* (A Course on Alternating Current) (1907); *Magnetizm i elektrichestvo* (Magnetism and Electricity) (1912); *O prirode elektricheskogo toka* (The Nature of Electric Current) (1921); *Fizicheskiye osnovy elektrotekhniki* (The Physical Principles of Electrical Engineering) (3rd ed, 1933); *Magnitnyy potok i preobrazovaniya* (Magnetic Flux and Its Conversions) (1946); *Izbrannyye trudy* (Selected Works) (1956); *Awards:* Lenin Prize (1928); Stalin Prize (1943); Order of

Lenin; two other orders; *Died:* 1 Apr 1951.

MITROFAN (secular name: GUTKOVSKIY) (1897–1959) Bishop of Kuybyshev and Syzran'; *Born:* 1897 in Volhynia, son of Orthodox priest; *Educ:* 1919 grad Volhynian Orthodox Theological Seminary; 1931 grad Orthodox Theological Fac, Warsaw Univ; *Career:* 1930, while still a student, took monastic vows with name Mitrofan; after grad from univ served monastic apprenticeship at Pochayevo Monastery; simultaneously steward of Zabludov Orthodox Monastery; later steward and treasurer, Pochayevo Lavra; 1934 appointed deputy Father Superior, then Father Superior, Yablochintsy Monastery, also directing psalm-reader and deacons' courses at the monastery; at end of WW 2 in Poland; 1945 returned to USSR and assigned by Moscow Patriarchate to Bel SSR as rector of pastoral theological courses at Zhirovichi Monastery; simultaneously elevated to archimandrite; 1947 these courses were reorganized into a theological seminary, of which Mitrofan was appointed first rector; simultaneously deputy Father Superior, Zhirovichi Monastery; 1953 consecrated bishop and made Bishop of Bobruysk and vicar of Minsk Eparchy; late 1955 exchanged with Bishop of Oryol; 1956 appointed Bishop of Kuybyshev and Syzran'; *Died:* 12 Sept 1959.

MITROFANOV, A. Kh. (ROMANYCH) (1879–1942) Party official; CP member from 1903; *Born:* 1879; *Career:* Party work in Urals, Moscow and Samara; 1917 member, Samara City RSDRP(B) Comt; then member, Samara Province RSDRP(B) Comt; member, Samara Sov; edited newspaper "Privolzhskaya pravda"; 1918–19 edited newspaper "Golos trudovogo krest'yanstva" and journal "Krasnyy pakhar'"; then various admin posts; 1925–30 worked for CC, CPSU(B); from 1930 dir, Moscow Zootech Inst; then senior assoc, Inst of Marxism-Leninism, CC, CPSU(B); deleg at 5th RSDRP Congress and 8th RCP(B) Congress; *Died:* 1942.

MITSKEVICH, Sergey Ivanovich (1869–1944) Physician and health service official; revolutionary; CP member from 1893; *Born:* 18 Aug 1869 in Yaransk, Vyatka Province, son of an officer; *Educ:* 1893 grad Med Fac, Moscow Univ; *Career:* joined revol movement while still a student; 1893, together with A. N. Vinokurov, founded first Moscow Marxist group, which formed the nucleus of the subsequent "Workers' League" from which the Moscow RSDRP(B) Org emerged; 1894–96 in solitary confinement at Taganka Prison, Moscow; 1896 sentenced to five years exile in Eastern Siberia; 1898 lived in Olekminsk, Yakutia; 1899–1903 distr physician in Sredne-Kolymsk, where he organized a hospital and a leprosy station; and did research on neuroses among the local population; 1903 worked for a private psychiatric hospital in Moscow and joined the Pirogov Soc of Russian Physicians; also maintained contacts with Bolshevik underground org; 1904 exiled for polit activities to Tver' where he worked as a physician at Tver' Manufacturing Plant and did Party work; 1905 returned to the private psychiatric hospital in Moscow; Dec 1905 took active part in Revol; 1906 exiled to Nizhniy Novgorod, where he worked at the Province Psychiatric Hospital; 1914 moved to Saratov, where he worked as a school health officer; during 1917 Feb Revol elected cand member, Centr Physicians' and Health Officers' Council at Extraordinary Congress, Pirogov Soc; after 1917 Oct Revol member, Med Collegium, RSFSR Pop Comrt of Internal Affairs; from same year member, Council of Physicians' Collegia; 1918 dep head, Moscow Dept of Publ Educ; from 1919 worked on several Civil War fronts; after demobilization worked for various educ authorities in Moscow; 1922–24 Collegium member, Inst of Party History, CC, RCP(B); lecturer, Sverdlov Communist Univ and Moscow Univ; 1922 founder, from 1924 dir, USSR Museum of the Revol, a post which he gave up for health reasons in 1934; continued research work in retirement; *Publ: Menerik i emiryachen'ye – formy isterii v Kolymskom kraye* ("Menerik" and "Emiryachen'ye" – Forms of Hysteria in Kolyma Kray) (1929); *Na grani dvukh epokh – ot narodnichestva do marksizma* (On the Verge of Two Epochs – Populism and Marxism) (1937); *Revolyutsionnaya Moskva, 1888–1905* (Revolutionary Moscow 1888–1905) (1940); *Zapiski vracha-obshchestvennika, 1888–1918* (Notes of a Public Health Official, 1888–1918) (1941), etc; *Died:* 12 Sept 1944.

MITSKEVICH, V. S. (1900–1948) Party official; CP member from 1917; *Born:* 1900; *Career:* fall 1918–May 1919 worked as Lenin's librarian; May 1919 volunteered for Red Army; after Civil War polit work in Red Army and various exec posts in ind; *Died:* 1948.

MITSKYAVICHYUS-KAPSUKAS, Vintsas Simanovich (MITSKEVICH-KAPSUKAS, Vikentiy Semyonovich) (1880–1935) Party official; helped found and lead CP Lith; *Born:* 26 Mar 1880 in Lith, son of a peasant; *Educ:* studied at Mariyampole high-school; 1902–04 studied polit econ and philosophy at Bern Univ; *Career:* 1903 joined Lith Soc-Democratic Party; active in 1905–07 Revol; 1907 arrested; 1909 sentenced to eight years' hard labor; 1913 exiled to Siberia, whence he fled; 1914 lived in Cracow, where he made contact with Lenin; then lived in UK and USA; edited Lith-Soc-Democratic emigre newspapers "Rankpelnis", "Socialdemokratas" and "Kova" and journal "Naujoji gadyne", propagating Bolshevik WW 1 policy and advocating rapprochement between Lith Soc-Democrats and Bolsheviks; June 1917 returned to Petrograd and joined RSDRP(B); edited first Lith Bolshevik paper "Tiesa"; deleg at 6th RSDRP(B) Congress and 2nd All-Russian Congress of Soviets; 21 Dec 1917 appointed Comr for Lith Affairs in Sov govt; as member, Centr Bureau of Lith Section, CC, RCP(B), helped found CP Lith; 1918–35 member, CC, CP Lith; 1918–19 chm, Council of Pop Comr of Lith-Bel SSR; 1920–21, after collapse of Sov regime in Lith, did underground work in Vilnius; from late 1921 in Moscow; 1924–28 cand member, from 1928 member, Comintern Exec Comt; head, Polish-Baltic Laender Secretariat, Comintern Exec Comt; co-founder Int Org for Aid to Revol Fighters; member, CC, Int Org for Aid to Revol Fighters of 1st convocation; 1898 first work published; wrote 47 books and pamphlets on Lith Marxist history, philosophy, proletarian lit, etc; wrote studies of 1918–19 revol in Lith and history of Lith Soc-Democratic movement; *Publ: Fashistskiy perevorot v Litve* (The Fascist Coup in Lithuania) (1927); *V tsarskikh tyur'makh* (In Tsarist Prisons) (1929); *Litva* (Lithuania) (1931); *Died:* 17 Feb 1935.

MITYUSHIN, Nikolay Trofimovich (1877–1950) Railroad eng; Hon Sci and Tech Worker of RSFSR from 1947; *Born:* 17 Jan 1877; *Educ:* 1902 grad Petersburg Inst of Communications Eng; *Career:* 1902–13 worked on railroads; 1913–19 lecturer, from 1919 prof, Moscow Communications Inst; did research on track strength and the stability of trains in motion; wrote several textbooks; *Publ: Dinamicheskiye napryazheniya v rel'sakh zheleznodorozhnogo puti v krivykh* (Dynamic Tensions in the Rails of a Railroad Track in Curves) (1917); *Zheleznodorozhnyy put', skovannyy morozom* (The Frozen Railroad Track) (1924); *Raschyot verkhnego stroyeniya puti v svyazi s ustoychivost'yu dvizheniya poezdov* (Calculation of Track Superstructure in Relation to the Running Stability of Trains) (1926), etc; *Awards:* two orders and medals; *Died:* 13 Jan 1950.

MIZYUN, Grigoriy Mikhaylovich (1903–1963) Ukr playwright; *Born:* 7 Apr 1903 in vil Krivushi, now Poltava Oblast; *Educ:* 1937 grad Khar'kov Inst of Red Prof; *Career:* 1923 first work published; his plays, which were staged at Ukr and Bel theaters, deal inter alia with the collectivization of agric and the role played by youth in this process; *Publ:* plays: "The Tragedy of Tripoli" (1923); "Force on Force" (1927); "By New Paths" (1929); "Reconstruction" (1930); "The Province" (1931); "Zigzags" (1933); "The Ice-Breaker" (1934); "Liberated Conscience" (1945); coauthor, "Luk'yan Kobylitsa" (1955); "The Rattling Keys" (1962); *Died:* 15 Dec 1963.

MODEL', Moisey Iosifovich (1889–1965) Party and govt official; publisher; CP member from 1905; *Born:* 14 May 1889; *Career:* joined revol movement in Petersburg; 1906 managed an illegal Bolshevik printing press; tried for involvement in Petersburg mil org; 1910 secr, Minsk RSDRP(B) group; 1910–17 lived in USA; member, Russian Section, American Socialist Party; member, US Soc for Aid to Polit Exiles and Prisoners in Russia; after return to Petrograd member, Vasiliy Ostrov Rayon Sov of Workers' and Soldiers' Dep; during 1917 Oct Revol member, Investigative Commission, Petrograd Mil Revol Comt; 1918–19 ed, newspaper "Izvestia", publ by Revol Mil Council of Southern Front; 1921–22 mang, Head Office, newspaper "Izvestia", All-Russian Centr Exec Comt; from 1922 publ work; from 1956 pensioner; *Died:* 17 Oct 1965.

MODOROV, Fyodor Aleksandrovich (1890–1967) Painter; corresp member, USSR Acad of Arts from 1958; Hon Art Worker of Bel SSR from 1944; Hon Art Worker of RSFSR from 1950; CP member from 1946; *Born:* 28 Feb 1890 in vil Mstyora, Vladimir Province; *Educ:* studied at Mstyora Ikon Studio; from 1910 studied at Kazan' Art College; 1918 grad Petrograd Acad of Arts; *Career:* 1918–19 chm, Mstyora Sov of Workers', Peasants' and Soldiers' Dep; from 1923 member, Assoc of Artists of Revol Russia; during 1930's chief consultant, Art Affairs Comt, Bel Council of Min and lecturer, Minsk Postgrad Art Training Courses; member, Org Comt, Sov Artists' Union; from 1948 dir, V. I.

Surikov Art Inst, Moscow; *Works:* "A Thoughtful Expression" (1918); "May 1 Among the Germans" (1926); "Oil Rigs at Baku" (1928); "Komsomol Tank-Driver Brigade" (1931); "A Popular Assembly in Western Belorussia" (1940); "The Battle of Kalinin" and "The German Retreat on the Kholm Flank" (1942); "Messengers with Lenin" (1948); over 50 portraits of WW 2 partisans and group portraits of Heroes of the Sov Union; *Awards:* Order of the Red Banner of Labor; medals; *Died:* 4 Mar 1967.

MODZALEVSKIY, Boris L'vovich (1874–1928) Lit historian; specialist in Pushkin texts; corresp member, USSR Acad of Sci from 1918; *Born:* 2 May 1874 in Tiflis; *Educ:* 1898 grad Law Fac, Petersburg Univ; *Career:* from 1898 worked for Records Office, State Council; from 1899 worked for various organs of Acad of Sci; 1919–28 senior Custodian, Pushkin Center (now the Inst of Russian Lit, USSR Acad of Sci); 1896 first work published helped found Pushkin Center: 1900–18 coauthor, "Russkiy biograficheskiy slovar'" (Russian Biographical Dictionary); 1903–28 virtual ed, "Pushkin i yego sovremenniki (Pushkin and His Contemporaries); traced, annotated and published many valuable lit and historical documents: works and letters of Pushkin; documents on the Decembrists; letters of Goncharov, Turgenev, Nekrasov, Ostrovskiy, Dostoyevsky, Lev Tolstoy, Korolenko, Chekhov, etc; *Publ: Biblioteka A. S. Pushkina. Bibliograficheskoye opisaniye* (The Library of A. S. Pushkin. A Bibliographic Account) (1910); *Arkhiv Rayevskikh* (The Rayevskiy Papers) (1908–15); *Pushkin pod taynym nadzorom* (Pushkin Under Secret Surveillance) (1925); *Roman dekabrista Kakhovskogo* (The Decembrist Kakhovskiy's Novel) (1926), etc; *Died:* 3 Apr 1928 in Leningrad.

MODZALEVSKIY, Lev Borisovich (1902–1948) Lit historian and bibliographer; Dr of Philology from 1947; *Born:* 9 Aug 1902 in Petersburg, son of B. L. Modzalevskiy, the lit historian and specialist on Pushkin; *Educ:* 1925 grad Philological Fac, Leningrad Univ; *Career:* 1919 worked for book depositories and archives in Leningrad; from 1933 assoc, Pushkin Commission, USSR Acad of Sci; analysed and annotated manuscripts of Pushkin and Lomonosov; wrote commentaries on Pushkin's 1831–33 letters in *Pushkin. Polnoye sobraniye sochineniy* (Pushkin. Complete Works) (Vol 3, 1935); commented on Lomonosov's letters; edited and annotated many of the letters to Pushkin in the acad ed of his works; *Publ:* coauthor, *Rukopisi Pushkina, khranyashchiyesya v Pushkinskom dome. Nauchnoye opisaniye* (Pushkin Manuscripts at the Pushkin Center. A Scientific Account) (1937); *Rukopisi Lomonosova v AN SSSR. Nauchnoye opisaniye* (Lomonosov Manuscripts at the USSR Academy of Sciences. A Scientific Account) (1937); doctor's thesis *Lomonosov i yego literaturnyye otnosheniya v Akademii nauk (1751–1763)* (Lomonosov and His Literary Relations in the Academy of Sciences /1751–1763/) (1947); *Died:* 26 June 1948 near Leningrad.

MOGILEVSKIY, Solomon Grigor'yevich (1885–1925) Govt official; CP member from 1903; *Born:* 1885; *Educ:* completed legal training; *Career:* from 1902 took part in high-school and workers' circles; 1904 arrested and, after release from prison, emigrated; in Geneva sided with Bolsheviks; 1906 returned to Russia and did propaganda work among Yekaterinoslav railroad workers; moved to Petrograd and worked as Party organizer and propagandist until 1908; 1916 drafted into Russian Army; after 1917 Feb Revol member, Minsk Party Comt and Minsk Sov; Apr 1917 attended RSDRP Congress; after 1917 Oct Revol worked in Ivanovo-Voznesensk; from spring 1918 dep dept head, Pop Comrt of Justice and member, Prosecution Collegium, RSFSR Supr Tribunal; summer 1918 appointed member, Special Commission of All-Russian Centr Exec Comt in Saratov; directed Saratov Cheka; helped root out conspiracy in 3rd Army; from early 1919 worked for Ukr Pop Comrt of Justice; dep chm, Revol Tribunal of 12th Army; from Dec 1919 dir of investigations, Moscow Cheka and head, For Dept, All-Russian Cheka; helped crush alleged counter-revol plots and organizations, such as the "Nat Center", etc; from 1922 chm, Transcaucasian Cheka; *Died:* 22 Mar 1925 killed in plane crash.

MOGIL'NITSKIY, Boris Nestorovich (1882–1955) Pathoanatomist; prof from 1920; corresp member, USSR Acad of Med Sci; Hon Sci Worker of RSFSR; *Born:* 1882; *Educ:* 1908 grad Med Fac, Moscow Univ; *Career:* 1908–11 asst prof, Chair of Nervous Diseases, Moscow Univ; 1911 resigned in protest against policies of Educ Min Kasso; from 1913 asst prof, Chair of Pathological Anatomy, then Chair of Gen Pathology (Pathological Physiology), Moscow Univ; 1918–20 assoc prof, from 1920 head, Chair of Pathological Anatomy, Med Fac, Gorky Univ; 1928–55 head, Dept of Experimental Pathology, Centr Roentgenological and Radiological Research Inst; 1933–55 also head, Chair of Pathological Anatomy, Pediatric Fac, 2nd Moscow Med Inst; did research on the pathological anatomy of the vegetative nervous system; together with N. N. Burdenko, made a study of the pathogenesis of ulcers; also did research on capillary permeability in various diseases, the effect of radiation on the body and aspects of endocrinology; wrote some 200 works; *Publ: K voprosu o deystvii na bar'yernyye sistemy ne spetsificheskikh razdrazhateley* (The Effect of Non-Specific Stimulants on the Barrier Systems) (1935); *Vvedeniye v patologicheskuyu anatomiyu i patologiyu vegetativnoy nervnoy sistemy* (An Introduction to Pathological Anatomy and the Pathology of the Vegetative Nervous System) (1941); ed, *Voprosy pronitsayemosti krovenosnykh kapillyarov v patologii* (The Permeability of the Blood Capillaries in Pathology) (2 vol, 1949–55); *Died:* 1955.

MOGILYANSKIY, M. (1873–?) Ukr publicist and critic; *Born:* 1873; *Career:* prior to 1917 Oct Revol worked for Constitutional Democratic organ "Rech'" which in 1913 published his article sharply criticizing the slogan "Independent Ukraine", put forward by the All-Ukr Student Congress; another article entitled "Patterns of Lies", published in 1913 in "Rech'" comes out openly in defense of tsarism; after 1917 Oct Revol sided with Ukr nationalists; together with a group of neo-classicists, campaigned against proletarian lit; 1926 journal "Chervonnyy shlyakh" erroneously published his story *Ubyvstvo* (Murder), which attacked the "Sov Socialist Ukr"; this story, criticized by the Party press, lambasts the bourgeois intelligentsia for striving to cooperate with the proletariat; 1931 in Ukr Acad advocated idea of collaboration of Marxism and bourgeoi sci; *Died:* date and place of death unknown.

MOISEYENKO (Party pseudonyms: MOSEYONOK, ANISIMOV), Pyotr Anisimovich (1852–1923) Revolutionary; CP member from 1905; *Born:* 1852 in Smolensk Province, son of a peasant; *Career:* 1865, at age 13, began working at a Moscow factory; 1871–74 worked as a weaver in Orekhovo-Zuyevo; 1874–75 did similar work in Petersburg, where he joined the workers' movement; joined the revol movement after meeting Plekhanov, Khalturin and other Populists and revol workers; 1876 took part in Kazan' demonstration; active member, Northern League of Russian Workers; 1878 exiled to Smolensk Province, 1880 to Yeniseysk Province for helping to organize a strike at the New Cotton Mill; 1883 returned from exile and found work at the Morozov Textile Mill in Orekhovo-Zuyevo, where he helped to organize the "Morozov strike" in 1885; 1885–89 exiled to Arkhangel'sk Province for this offense; 1893 joined Rostov-on-Don Soc-Democratic Org; 1894 helped organize a big strike in Rostov, for which he was exiled to Vologda Province; 1898 returned from exile and resumed revol work in Donbas; 1905–07 took active part in Revol; 1909–10 worked in Baku; from 1912 in Gorlovka; wrote articles for "Pravda"; 1914–18 did Party work in Baku and Northern Caucasus, then in the Red Army; fought in Civil War; 1920–21 public educ instructor in Mineral'nyye Vody; 1922 worked in Khar'kov for the Commission for Collating and Studying Material on the History of the CP and the Sov State; *Publ: Vospominaniya, 1873–1923* (Memoirs, 1873–1923) (1924); *Died:* 30 Nov 1923 in Moscow; buried beside the Morozov Strike memorial in Orekhovo-Zuyevo.

MOISEYEV, Nikolay Dmitriyevich (1902–1955) Astronomer; CP member from 1943; *Born:* 3 Dec 1902; *Educ:* 1924 grad Moscow Univ; *Career:* 1929–47 instructor, Zhukovskiy Air Force Acad; from 1935 prof, Moscow Univ; 1939–43 dir, Shternberg State Astronomy Inst; specialized in celestial mech and stability of motion theory; in his latter years developed theory of mean and interpolation-mean problems of celestial mech; *Publ: O nekotorykh osnovnykh voprosakh teorii proiskhozhdeniya komet, meteorov i kosmicheskoy pyli. Kosmogonicheskiye etyudy* (Some Basic Aspects of the Theory of the Origin of Comets, Meteors and Cosmic Dust. Cosmogonic Studies) (1930); *Onekotorykhobshchikh metodakh kachestvennogo izucheniya form dvizheniya v problemakh nebesnoy dinamiki* (Som General Methods for the Qualitative Determination of Motion Forms in Problems of Celestial Dynamics) (1936); *O nekotorykh voprosakh teorii ustoychivosti* (Some Aspects of the Theory of Stability) (1939); *O nekotorykh metodakh teorii tekhnicheskoy ustoychivosti* (Some Methods of the Theory of Technical Stablitiy) (1945); *Ob Interpolyatsionno-osrednyonnykh variantakh ogranichennoy zdachi tryokh tochek* Interpolation-Mean Variants of the Limited Three-Points Problem) (1950), etc; *Died:* 6 Dec 1955.

MOISEYEV, S. I. (1879–1951) Party and govt official; CP member from 1902; *Born:* 1879; *Career:* revol work in Nizhniy Novgorod, Moscow and Petersburg; repeatedly subjected to reprisals by Tsarist authorities; 1905 fled from exile to Switzerland; six months later returned, went underground and worked for Party CC; 1912–17 in France; after 1917 Oct Revol worked for Comintern; from 1930 worked for USSR Pop Comrt of Domestic Trade; *Died:* 1951.

MOKROUSOV (pseudonym: SAVIN), Aleksey Vasil'yevich (1887–1959) Revolutionary; partisan leader in Crimea during Civil War and WW 2; CP member from 1928; *Born:* 21 June 1887 in Ponyri, Kursk Province, son of a peasant; *Career:* farm-hand, miner and metalworker; 1905 served with armed workers' squad; from 1908 sailor in Baltic Fleet, then arrested; 1912 fled abroad and worked as laborer in Sweden, Denmark, Britain and Argentina; also worked for trade unions; 1917 returned to Russia and fought in Oct Revol in Petrograd; after 1917 Oct Revol headed sailors' squad in fighting in Crimea, Ukr and on Don; summer 1918 commanded 4th Column on Don-Kuban' Front; then headed Bd to Muster Red Army in Crimea; commanded Southern Battle Section; 1919 commanded brigade, then 58th Div; from July 1920 commanded Crimean Rebel Army behind Gen Wrangel's lines; after Civil War founded one of first agric communes in Crimea; 1924–36 various exec govt posts; 1937 fought in Spanish Civil War; during WW 2 partisan leader in Crimea, then commanded Red Army regt; *Died:* 28 Oct 1959.

MOKUL'SKIY, Stefan Stefanovich (1896–1960) Lit historian and theater critic; Dr of Philology and prof from 1937; CP member from 1940; *Born:* 7 Aug 1896 in Tiflis; *Educ:* 1918 grad Philology Fac, Kiev Univ; *Career:* from 1918 taught and wrote theater reviews in Kiev; 1923–42 taught courses on for lit at Leningrad Univ and Herzen Teachers' Training Inst; also lectured on for theater history at Leningrad Theatrical Inst and Higher Art History Courses, Inst of the History of the Arts; 1943–52 prof, 1952–57 head, Chair of For Theater, State Inst of Theater and Art History; 1943–48 also dir of this inst; prof, Studio School, Moscow Acad Arts Theater and Acad of Soc Sci, CC, CPSU; simultaneously head, Theater Theory and History Section, Inst of the History of the Arts, USSR Acad of Sci; specialized in the history of Italian and French lit and art during the Renaissance and the Age of Enlightement and the history of West European theater as a whole; 1931 and 1933 translated T. Guardati's "Novellino" and Goldoni's "Memoirs" into Russian; his work was noted for its profound erudition and clarity of exposition; *Publ: Ital'yanskaya literatura* (Italian Literature) (1931); *Mol'yer. Problemy tvorchestva* (Molière. Problems of Creativity) (1935); *Mol'yer* (Molière) (1936); *Bomarshe i yego teatr* (Beaumarchais and His Theater) (1936); *Istoriya zapadnoyevropeyskogo teatra* (The History of West European Theater) (2 vol, 1936–39); *Rasin* (Racine) (1939); coauthor, *Istoriya frantsuzskoy literatury* (The History of French Literature) (Vol 1, 1946); coauthor, *Istoriya zapadnoyevropeyskoy literatury* (The History of West European Literature) (1947); *Komedii* (Comedies) (1953); exec ed, *Istoriya zapadnoyevropeyskogo teatra* (The History of West European Theater) (3 vol, 1956–63); *O teatre. Sbornik* (The Theater. An Anthology) (1963), etc; *Died:* 25 Jan 1960 in Moscow.

MOLCHANOV, Vasiliy Ivanovich (1868–1959) Pediatrician and infectionist; Dr of Med from 1909; prof; member, USSR Acad of Med Sci from 1945; Hon Sci Worker of RSFSR from 1935; *Born:* 31 Dec 1868 in vil Iroshnikovo, Vladimir Province; *Educ:* 1894 grad Med Fac, Moscow Univ; *Career:* 1896–1903 intern, 1904–23 head, Infection Ward, N. F. Filatov's Children's Clinic, Moscow Univ; befor 1917 Oct Revol made several trips abroad and worked at clinics in Austria, Germany and France; 1923–50 head, 1950–59 consultant, Chair of Children's Diseases, 1st Moscow Univ (1st Moscow Med Inst); did research on the effect of scarlet fever and other acute infections of the vegetative nervous system; established the genetic link between scarlet fever, rheumatism and endocarditis; described endocrine diseases in children; devised endocrinopathic classification which found recognition both in the USSR and abroad; from 1936 chm, Comt for the Study of Infantile Rheumatism; delivered proof of the infection-allergy theory of the origin of rheumatism and made an extensive study of early forms; ed, journal "Pediatriya"; co-ed, "Tsentral'nyy meditsinskiy zhurnal"; co-ed, "Bol'shaya meditsinskaya entsiklopediya" (Large Medical Encyclopedia) (1st and 2nd ed); member, various med soc; trained numerous pediatricians; wrote over 100 works; *Publ:* doctor's thesis *Nadpochechniki i ikh izmeneniya pri difterii* (The Suprarenal Glands and Their Lesions During Diphtheria) (1909); *Vago-N sympathicotonia pro skarlatine u detey* (Vago-N Sympathicotonia in Infantile Scarlet Fever) (1916); *Klinika i patogenez belogo dermografizma pri skarlatine* (The Clinical Aspects of Pathogenesis of White Dermographism During Scarlet Fever) (1925); *Rasstroystva rosta i razvitiya u detey* (Disturbances of Growth and Development in Children) (1927); *Difteriya* (Diphtheria) (1929); "Hirsutismus" (1929); *Skarlatina i porok serdtsa* (Scarlet Fever and Heart Defects) (1932); "Pubertas praecox" (1933); *Propedevtika detskikh bolezney* (The Propaedeutics of Children's Diseases) (1936); *Skarlatina* (Scarlet Fever) (1943); *Difteriya* (Diphtheria) (1947); *Awards:* Order of Lenin; Order of the Red Banner of Labor; medals; *Died:* 1959 in Moscow.

MOL'KOV, Al'fred Vladislavovich (1870–1947) Hygienist and health official; prof; Hon Sci Worker of RSFSR from 1934; CP member from 1919; *Born:* 9 Nov 1970; *Educ:* 1896 grad Med Fac, Moscow Univ; *Career:* 1896–1903 zemstvo health officer, Moscow Province; 1903–17 health officer, Vereya, Zvenigorod and Moscow Uyezds; bd member, Pirogov Soc and co-ed, journal "Obshchestvennyy vrach"; 1900–19 chm, Pirogov Commission for the Dissemination of Hygiene Knowledge, during which period he made a major contribution to sanitary educ by publishing pop lit, visual aids, etc; 1911 helped to organize Russian pavilion at Inst Hygiene Exhibition, Dresden; 1913 helped to organize the All-Russian Hygiene Exhibition, Petersburg; 1919–31 founder-dir, Museum of Soc Hygiene (from 1923 Inst of Soc Hygiene), RSFSR Pop Comrt of Health; 1922 helped found the Chair of Soc Hygiene, 1st Moscow Univ, to which he was appointed asst prof; co-founder, Bureau of Prophylactic Depts; helped to reform med educ with the introduction of active teaching methods; 1924–47 founder-head, Chair of School Hygiene, Med Fac, 2nd Moscow Univ; contributed to first studies on the dynamics of physical development in childhood and adolescence; 1930 again helped to organize Sov pavilion at Int Hygiene Exhibition, Dresden; 1934 founded Chair of School Hygiene, Centr Inst of Postgrad Med Training; from 1944 head, Chair of Educ Hygiene, Moscow Univ; also organized courses on school hygiene at various teachers' training inst; co-ed, "Bol'shaya meditsinskaya entsiklopediya" (Large Medical Encyclopedia) (1st ed); co-ed, journals "Gigiyena i epidemiologiya" and "Sotsial'naya gigiyena"; wrote some 150 works; *Publ: Zhilishche, yego znacheniye i ustroystvo* (Housing, Its Importance and Organization) (1909); *Pishcha i pitaniye* (Food and Nutrition) (1923); *Osnovy profilaktiki v meditsine* (The Principles of Prophylaxis in Medicine) (1927); *Sotsial'naya gigiyena* (Social Hygiene) (2 vol, 1927–30); *Gigiyena vospitaniya* (Education Hygiene) (1930); ed, *Praktikum-spravochnik po shkol'noy gigiyeny* (A Practical Reference Manual on School Hygiene) (1939); coauthor, *Uchebnik shkol'noy gigiyeny* (A Textbook on School Hygiene) (5th ed, 1949); *Awards:* Order of the Red Banner of Labor; *Died:* 1947 in Moscow.

MOLOKHOV, Aleksey Nikolayevich (1897–1966) Psychiatrist; Dr of Med; prof; *Born:* 1897; *Educ:* 1924 grad Med Fac, 1st Moscow Univ; *Career:* 1924–45 asst prof, then assoc prof, Psychiatric Clinic and senior assoc, V. P. Serbskiy Inst of Forensic Psychiatry; consultant, Frunze Rayon Neuropsychiatric Out-Patiens' Center, Moscow; from 1945 until death head, Chair of Psychiatry, Kishinev Med Inst and sci dir, Mold Republ Psychiatric Hospital; did research on schizophrenia, infectious psychoses, alcoholism, psychopathy, phobia, hysteria, paranoid reactions and mental disturbances caused by malaria, tularemia, tubercular meningitis, epidemic hepatitis, etc; developed a definition of paranoid reactions which gained gen acceptance in Sov psychiatry; devised differentiated methods of insulin therapy for various forms of schizophrenia; attended numerous All-Union and republ congresses of neuropathologists and psychiatrists; chm, Mold Soc of Neuropathologists and Psychiatrists; lecturer, Soc for the Dissemination of Sci and Polit Knowledge; co-ed, psychiatry section, "Bolshaya meditsinskaya entsiklopediya" (Large Medical Encyclopedia) (2nd ed); member, ed council, "Zhurnal nevropatologii i psikhiatrii imeni S. S. Korsakova"; *Publ: Formy shizofrenii i ikh lecheniye* (Forms of Schizophrenia and Their Treatment), etc; *Died:* 1966.

MOOR (real name: ORLOV), Dmitriy Stakhiyevich (1883–1946) Graphic artist and teacher; Hon Art Worker of RSFSR from 1932; CP member from 1940; *Born:* 3 Nov 1883 in Novocherkassk; *Educ:* studied at Moscow Univ; *Career:* 1906 began drawing polit cartoons for the journal "Budil'nik", etc; after 1917 Oct Revol emerged as one of the leading Sov polit poster artists; contributed cartoons to the "Okna ROSTA" (Russian Telegraph Agency Windows) and journal "Krasnoarmeyets"; in 1920's and 1930's drew cartoons for "Pravda" and "Izvestia" and the journals "Krokodil", "Bezbozhnik u stanka", etc; 1941–45 resumed work as a poster artist, specializing in anti-Fascist and anti-German subjects; also did book-illustration; *Works:* poster series "Have You Volunteered? ", "Wrangel's Still Alive, Give Him No Quarter" and "A Red Gift for the White Gentleman" (1918–20); poster for Volga famine relief campaign "Help" (1921); illustrations for: Heine's "Dispute" (1928); stories by Saltykov-Shchedrin (1934); Henri Barbusse's "Le Feu" (Fire); a new ed of *Slovo o polku Igoreve* (The Lay of the Host of Igor) (1944), etc; *Died:* 24 Oct 1946.

MORAVOV, Aleksandr Viktorovich (1878–1951) Painter; member, USSR Acad of Arts from 1949; Hon Art Worker of RSFSR from 1946; *Born:* 1878; *Educ:* 1897–1901 studied at Moscow College of Painting, Sculpture and Architecture; *Career:* from 1904 member, Peredvizhniki (Mobile Art Exhibitors) Soc, at whose exhibitions he displayed his paintings on rural themes; 1923–28 member, Assoc of Artists of Revol Russia; 1928–32 member, Assoc of Artists of the Revol; 1932–39 member, RSFSR Artists' Union; from 1939 member, USSR Artists' Union; *Works:* "The Decembrists in Chita" (1911); "A Meeting of the Poor Relief Committee" (1920); triptych depicting Lenin's arrival in Petrograd in 1917 (1933); "Stalin Speaking at the 'Dynamo' Plant in 1924" (1937), etc; *Died:* 1951.

MORDVINKIN, V. Yu. (1889–1946) Politician; CP member from 1917; *Born:* 1889; *Career:* until 1917 Oct Revol bookkeeper; member, ed bd, Irkutsk newspaper "Novaya Sibir'"; Nov 1917 – Oct 1918 exec secr, newspaper "Izvestiya VTsIK"; 1918–19 ed chief, Supr Mil Inspectorate; then edited Kiev newspaper "Krasnaya armiya"; 1919–21 asst head, Agitation and Propaganda Dept, State Publ House; simultaneously headed Press Bureau, Special Dept, All-Russian Cheka; 1922–31 worked for Main Bd of Lit and Publ Houses; then worked for Fine Arts Publ House; 1923–24 member, "Trotskyist opposition"; arrested by State Security organs; *Died:* 1946 in imprisonment.

MORDVINOV, Arkadiy Grigor'yevich (1896–1964) Architect; member, USSR Acad of Building and Architecture; CP member from 1919; *Born:* 27 Jan 1896; *Educ:* grad Moscow College of Painting, Sculpture and Architecture; in 1920's grad Architecture Fac, Moscow Higher Tech College; 1930 completed postgrad studies at Moscow Inst of Architecture and Building; *Career:* fought with Red Army during Civil War; in 1920's chm, All-Russian Soc of Proletarian Architects; bd member, Sov Architects' Union; 1939–49 vice-pres, 1949–55 pres, USSR Acad of Building and Architecture; 1943–47 chm, Architectural Affairs Comt, USSR Council of Min; chm, Architecture Section, Stalin Prize Comt; dep, RSFSR Supr Sov of 1938, 1947 and 1951 convocations; introduced "continous" construction method in house-building, which received special mention at 18th CPSU(B) Congress in 1939; 1955 critized in decree of 4 Nov "On the Elimination of Excesses in Planning and Construction"; his works include the design for the "Ukraina" Hotel and plans for the reconstruction of Moscow and other Sov cities after WW 2; *Awards:* two Stalin Prizes (1941 and 1949); *Died:* 24 July 1964.

MORDVINOV, Nikolay Dmitriyevich (1901–1966) Actor; Pop Artiste of USSR from 1949; *Born:* 15 Feb 1901 in vil Yadrin', now Chuvash ASSR; *Career:* 1925–36 performed at Zavadskiy Studio; 1936–40 at Rostov's Gorky Theater; from 1940 at Moscow Sov Theater; during latter years performed in variety, on television and radio; member, Arts Council, Moscow Sov Theater; 1953 toured Bulgaria with Moscow Sov Theater; *Roles:* 1927–36 roles: Sobolevskiy in Lavrenev's *Prostaya veshch'* (A Simple Thing); Richard in Shaw's "The Devil's Disciple"; Murzavetskiy in Ostrovskiy's *Volki i ovtsy* (Wolves and Sheep); Vagram in Pervomayskiy's *Vagramova noch'* (Vagram's Night); at Rostov Theater: Yarovoy in Trenyov's "Lybov' Yarovaya"; Petruccio in Shakespeare's "The Taming of the Shrew"; from 1940: Ognyov in Korneychuk's *Front* (The Front); Kurepin in Surov's *Rassvet nad Moskvoy* (Dawn Over Moscow); Cavalier di Rippafrat in Goldoni's "La Locandiera"; Othello in Shakespeare's "Othello"; Arbenin in *Maskarad* (The Masquerade); also roles in films: "The Masquerade"; "Bogdan Khmel'nitskiy", "Kotovskiy", etc; *Awards:* Order of the Red Banner of Labor; three Stalin Prizes (1942, 1949 and 1951); Lenin Prize (1965); *Died:* 26 Jan 1966.

MORGUNENKO, Vladimir Stepanovich (1905–1943) Partisan; teacher; CP member from 1940; *Born:* Aug 1905; *Career:* 1927–37 teacher, from 1937 school principal, vil Krimtsi, Nikolayev Oblast; during WW 2 commissioned by underground Party org to set up a Komsomol group known as the "Partisan Spark" to conduct diversionary operations against German troops; Feb 1943 arrested by Germans; *Awards:* Hero of the Sov Union (1958, posthumously); *Died:* 28 Feb 1943, executed by firing squad.

MOROKHOVETS, Yevgeniy Andreyevich (1880–1941) Historian; prof from 1920; CP member from 1905; *Born:* 23 Apr 1880; *Educ:* 1904 grad Moscow Univ; *Career:* from 1905 worked for RSDRP and taught in Ivanovo-Voznesensk and Rostov-Yaroslavskiy; from 1920 prof, Chair of Russian History, Moscow Univ and learned secr, Inst of History, Russian Assoc of Soc Sci Research Institutes and lecturer, Sverdlov Communist Univ; 1935–41 senior assoc, Inst of History, USSR Acad of Sci; specialized in the history of peasant movements in 19th–20th-Century Russia; *Publ: Krest'yanskoye dvizheniye i sotsial-demokratiya v epohku pervoy russkoy revolyutsii* (The Peasant Movement and Social-Democracy at the Time of the First Russian Revolution) (1926); *Agrarnyye programmy rossiyskikh politicheskikh partiy v 1917-om godu* (The Agrarian Programs of the Russian Political Parties in 1917) (1929); *Istoriya Rossii v period promyshlennogo kapitalizma* (The History of Russia in the Period of Industrial Capitalism) (2 vol, 1929); *Krest'yanskoye dvizheniye 1827–69. Sbornik dokumentov* (The 1827–69 Peasant Movement. A Collection of Documents) (2 vol, 1931); *Krest'yanskaya reforma 1861-ogo goda* (The Peasant Reform of 1861) (1937); *Krest'yanskoye dvizheniye v 1861-om godu posle otmena krepostnogo prava* (The Peasant Movement in 1861 After the Abolition of Feudal Law) (2 vol, 1949); *Died:* 3 Oct 1941.

MOROZ, G. S. (1893–1940) Party and govt official; CP member from 1917; *Born:* 1893; *Career:* worked for Cheka and OGPU State Security organs; 1925–28 secr, Moscow Control Commission, CPSU(B); then Collegium member, Pop Comrt of Trade; chm, CC, Trade Workers' Union; deleg for Moscow City Party Comt at 9th RCP(B) Congress; at 11th Party Congress elected member, CPSU(B) Centr Control Commission; arrested by State Security organs; *Died:* 1940 in imprisonment.

MOROZKIN, Nikolay Ivanovich (1893–1966) Infectionist; Dr of Med and prof from 1940; corresp member, USSR Acad of Med Sci from 1957; *Born:* 1893; *Educ:* 1916 grad Med Fac, Moscow Univ; *Career:* 1916–23 mil surgeon, Russian and Red Armies; 1923–39 lecturer in infectious diseases, Smolensk Med Inst, then assoc, Sanitary Epidemiological Laboratory, All-Union State Sanitary Inspectorate, Moscow; 1939–51 head, Chair of Infectious Diseases, Gorky Med Inst; 1952–65 head, Clinic of Acute Respiratory Infections and dep sci dir, Inst of Infectious Diseases, USSR Acad of Med Sci, Kiev; 1959 attented 2nd Int Congress on Infection Pathology, Milan; 1962 read paper at 3rd Int Congress on Infection Pathology, Bucharest; did research on various aspects of the pathology of infectious diseases with special reference to viral infections; also studied the effect of antibiotics on the body in the course of infections; wrote over 130 works; *Publ:* doctor's thesis *Klinika sypnogo tifa* (The Clinical Aspects of Typhus) (1940); *Pyatnadtsatiletniy opyt primeneniya gemoterapii v infektsionnoy klinike* (Fifteen Years of Experience in the Clinical Use of Hemotherapy for Infectious Diseases) (1952); *Gripp* (Influenza) (1958), etc; *Died:* Jan 1966.

MOROZOV, Anatoliy Petrovich (? –1961) Mil commander; maj-gen; CP member from 1938; *Born:* son of a worker; *Educ:* grad two mil acad; *Career:* from 1930 in Red Army; fought in WW 2; from 1945 admin posts on staffs of various mil distr; *Awards:* Order of Lenin; Order of the Red Banner; Order of the Red Star; medals; *Died:* 17 May 1961 in plane crash in line of duty.

MOROZOV, Dmitriy Georgiyevich (1888–1963) Party and govt official; CP member from 1905; *Born:* 18 Oct 1888; *Career:* textile worker by trade; revol work in Ivanovo-Voznesensk; 1913 arrested and exiled to Olenets Province; drafted in Tsarist Army; at time of 1917 Feb Revol served on Rumanian Front; member, div comt of soldiers' dep, 6th Army; 1919–22 worked for Cheka in Ivanov and Samara; 1923–28 exec Party and govt work in Ivanovo-Voznesensk Province; 1930–32 secr, Yaroslavl Okrug Party Comt; deleg at 13th–17th Party Congresses; at 14th and 15th Congresses elected member, CPSU(B) Centr Control Commission; 1932–37 worked for Party control organs; from 1937 pensioner; *Died:* June 1963.

MOROZOV, Mikhail Akimovich (1879–1964) Virologist; prof; member, USSR Acad of Med Sci from 1945; Hon Sci Worker of

RSFSR from 1943; *Born:* 1879; *Educ:* 1904 grad Med Fac, Moscow Univ; *Career:* 1904–14 head, Voronezh Zemstvo Smallpox Vaccine Station; 1914 founded Voronezh Pasteur Station; 1914–18 mil surgeon; 1918–23 head, Voronezh Pasteur Station; 1923–30 dir, Centr State Smallpox Inst; 1930–64 head, Smallpox Dept, Gamaleya Inst of Epidemiology and Microbiology, USSR Acad of Med Sci; member, ed collegium, journal "Voprosy virologii"; co-ed, microbiology section, "Bol'shaya meditsinskay entsiklopediya" (Large Medical Encyclopedia) (2nd end); 1943 devised technique for obtaining a stable combined dry smallpox vaccine; improved methods of rapid laboratory diagnosis of smallpox; did research on the etiology and pathogenesis of influenza, scarlet fever, measles, polyomyelitis, porphyria, etc; 1944 devised technique for staining microbes with tannin-chrysoidin; 1954 detected virus-like bodies in the spinal fluid of schizophrenics; 1955 advanced his hypothesis on the viral nature of schizophrenia; devised method of staining elementary viral bodies by argentation; made in-depth study of the virus of natural smallpox; identified Lipschütz's elementary bodies in cows, sheep, goats and humans and established that the disease caused by paravaccine is an independent nosological unit in the nature of a benign zoonotic viral disease; in Sov med terminology the elementary bodies formed by the viruses of these diseases are now known as Paschen-Morozov and Lipschütz-Morozov bodies; also made major contribution to knowledge concerning the mutability of viruses; considered cancer to be of viral etiology; wrote over 150 works; *Publ: Novoye o etiologii paravaktsiny* (New Facts on the Etiology of Paravaccine) (1940); "Die Färbung der Paschen'schen Körperchen durch Versilberung" (1946); *Ospa* (Smallpox) (1948); coauthor, *Atlas morfologii virusov* (An Atlas of Virus Morphology) (1951); coauthor, *Spetsificheskaya agglyutinatsiya i lizis virusov* (The Specific Agglutination and Lysis of Viruses) (1953); *K metodike virusoskopii po Morozovu* (The Morozov Method of Viroscopy) (1956), etc; *Awards:* Prize of All-Russian Hygiene Exhibition (1913); Stalin Prize (1952); *Died:* 1964 in Moscow.

MOROZOV (pseudonyms: GUDASH; M. VLADIMIROVICH; MRUZ; MURATOV), Mikhail Vladimirovich (1868–1938) Revolutionary; Russian writer and lit critic; CP member from 1901; *Born:* 20 Mar 1868 in Balta, Kamenets-Podol'sk Province; *Educ:* grad Odessa Tech High School; until 1890 studied at Petersburg Forestry Inst; expelled for taking part in student riots; *Career:* from 1887 active in revol movement; helped found Marxist circles in Odessa and Petersburg; 1891 first work published; 1892 arrested and exiled; 1901 helped found Saratov Soc-Democratic Comt, which sided with newspaper "Iskra"; 1903–04 underground revol work in Baku; 1904–07 one of leaders of revol movement in Turkestan; Bolshevik; ed, newspapers "Samarkand" and "Russkiy Turkestan"; 1907 banished from Tashkent; 1908 worked underground in Petersburg; repeatedly arrested and exiled; then on ed staff of "Literaturnyy raspad"; from 1910 in emigration; member, Lenin's Bolshevik Section in Paris; 1912–13 ed, émigré "Parizhskiy vestnik"; after 1917 Feb Revol returned to Russia; fought in 1917 Oct Revol; after 1917 Oct Revol admin work in fuel and peat ind; 1930–32 vice-pres, Acad of Arts; from 1936 dir, All-Russian Cooperative Assoc "Artist" Publ House; late 1930's arrested by NKVD; *Publ: Ocherki noveyshey literatury* (An Outline of Modern Literature) (1911); collected verse *Peresvety* (Talks) (1924); *Obraz Lenina v izobrazitel'nom iskusstve* (Lenin's Image in the Fine Arts) (1934); *Died:* 13 May 1938 in imprisonment in Moscow; posthumously rehabilitated.

MOROZOV, Nikolay Aleksandrovich (1854–1946); Revolutionary (Populist); scientist; historian; hon member, USSR Acad of Sci from 1932; *Born:* 25 June 1854 on Borok Estate, Yaroslavl' Province, son of a land-owner and a peasant girl; *Educ:* 1869–74 studied at Moscow Classical High School; *Career:* 1874 joined Moscow Populist circle; engaged in Populist "to the people" work in Yaroslavl', Kursk, Voronezh and Kostroma Provinces; late 1874 went to Geneva and contributed to newspaper "Rabotnik" and "Vperyod"; joined 1st International; spring 1875 returned to Russia, was arrested and 1877–78 tried; 1878 joined "Land and Liberty" group; co-ed, newspaper "Zemlya i volya; after schism in this org, became member, Exec Comt, People's Will org; helped edit newspaper "Narodnaya volya"; 1880 went abroad and met Marx in London; Jan 1881 arrested trying to cross Russian border illegally; sentenced to an indefinite term at hard labor; until Oct 1905 imprisoned at Shlissel'burg Fortress, where he spent the time studying chemistry, physics, astronomy, mathematics and history; after his release from the Fortress, published a number of sci works written during his imprisonment; taught chemistry and astronomy at Lesgaft Higher Courses and at Psychoneurological Inst; 1911 sentenced to a year's imprisonment (served in Dvinsk Fortress) for antireligious trends in his collected verse "Zvezdnyye pesni" (Star Songs), published in 1910; 1917 sided for a while with the Constitutional-Democratic Party and took part in the Moscow State Consultative Org; 1918 appointed dir, Lesgaft Biological Laboratory, which was soon developed into the Lesgaft Research Inst; wrote a number of books on the history of religion and Christianity: *Otkroveniye v groze i bure* (Revelation in Storm and Tempest) (1907); *Proroki* (The Prophets) (1914) and *Khristos* (Christ) (7 vol, 1924–32), which revised many gen historical dogmas and views connected with history of Christianity; his theses were rejected by Sov historians; *Publ: Periodicheskiye sistemy stroyeniya veshchestva* (Periodic Systems of the Structure of Matter) (1907); *D. I. Mendeleyev i znacheniye yego sistemy dlya khimii budushchego* (D. I. Mendeleyev and the Importance of his System for the Chemistry of the Future) (1907); *Nachala vektorial'noy algebry v ikh genezise iz chistoy matematiki* (The Principles of Vector Algebra in Their Genesis from Pure Mathematics) (1909); *Funktisya* (Function) (1912); *Printsip otnositel'nosti i absolyutnoya* (The Principle of Relativity and the Absolute) (1920), etc; memoirs *Povesti moye zhizni* (Tales of My Life) (4 vol, 1916–18). *Awards:* Order of Lenin; Order of the Red Banner of Labor; *Died:* 30 July 1946.

MOROZOV, Pavlik (Pavel Trofimovich) (1918–32) Fanatical supporter of agric collectivization; member, Young Pioneers Org; *Born:* 2 Dec 1918 in vil Gerasimovka, Sverdlovsk Oblast, son of a poor peasant; *Educ:* studied at vil school, where he led a Pionier group; *Career:* opposed richer peasants' attempts to keep private land; 1930 informed on his father, chm of a vil sov, for selling forged deeds and served as witness at subsequent trial; also informed on rich peasants who refused to meet compulsory grain delivery schedules and encouraged villagers to hide their harvest; proposed that a kolkhoz be established at vil Gerasimovka; 1932 killed together with younger brother by a group of rich peasants; the murderers were captured and executed; the kolkhoz at Gerasimovka, other kolkhozes, pioneer lodges, libraries and the Palace of Culture in Krasnaya Presna, Moscow, now bear his name; there are monuments to him in Moscow and Gerasimovka; *Died:* 3 Sept 1932.

MORSKOY (real name: MALYSHEV), Dmitriy Ivanovich (1897–1956) Mordovian poet; *Born:* 1 Nov 1897 in vil Sapozhkino, Orenburg Province, son of a peasant; *Educ:* 1923–25 studied at Bryusov Higher Lit and Art Inst; *Career:* farmhand on an estate; fought in WW 1; 1921 first work published; from 1926 member, "Nikitinskiye subbotniki" lit assoc; fought in WW 2; *Publ:* story "Poor Volodya" (1923); collected verse "Mute Blizzard" (1927) and "Rosy Morn" (1936); poems "Ul'yana Sosnovskaya" (1929) about the fate of Mordovian women prior to the Revol, and "Nuvyazi" (1930) about the Mordovians' part in the Pugachev Rebellion; *Died:* 20 Feb 1956 in vil Koltubanka, Orenburg Oblast.

MORZON, Vladimir Osipovich (1881–1954) Surgeon; public health official; Hon Physician and Hon Sci Worker of Bel SSR; CP member from 1938; *Born:* 1881 in vil Sennitsa, Minsk Uyezd, son of a volost clerk; *Educ:* grad theological college and 1904 Theological Seminary, Minsk; 1911 grad Med Fac, Yur'yev Univ; *Career:* 1904 entered Law Fac, Yur'yev Univ; 1905 involved in student revol activities, resulting in a one-year suspension of his studies; 1906 allowed to resume studies at Med Fac, Yur'yev Univ; from 1911 head of a distr zemstvo hospital, then moved to Minsk Province Hospital to study surgery; 1912 performed 293 operations, including two hernias and four amputations; 1913 transferred to Bobruysk Uyezd Hospital; 1914 sent for postgrad med training to Petrograd, where he studied surgery, gynecology and urology at I. I. Grekov, N. N. Petrov, S. P. Fyodorov and D. O. Ott's clinics; returned from Petrograd and worked for a while at the Staro-Dorozhskaya and Parich Distr Hospitals; at start of WW 1 surgeon, Bobruysk Red Cross Hospital, then surgeon, med field team in Western Front; after 1917 Oct Revol head, Bobruysk City Hospital; from 1934 head, Chair of Operative Surgery, Vitebsk Med Inst; from 1935 prof and head, Fac Surgery Clinic, Vitebsk Med Inst; during WW 2 surgeon at mil hospitals; from 1943 consultant, then head, Dept of Med Training Establishments, Bel Min of Health; 1948 head, Chair of Surgery, 1949–54 dir, Minsk Inst of Postgrad Med Training; did research on operative treatment for ailments of the visceral organs (liver and gall-bladder, gastric ulcers, appendicitis, etc) and gynecological and urological diseases; pioneered technique of two-stage transplantation of the ureters to the rectum; contributed still valid research works to journal "Belorusskaya meditsinskaya mysl'"; 1929 co-organizer, dep chm, and rapporteur, 1st Bel Congress of Surgeons and Gynecologists; 1947 chm, first postwar Bel Surgeons' Congress; chm, Bel Sci Soc of Surgeons; dep and Presidium member, Bel Supr Sov; *Publ: Klinicheskiye nablyudeniya nad ushchemlyonnymi gryzhami* (Clinical Observations of Constricted Hernias) (1921); *Dvukhmomentnyy sposob peresadki mochetochnikov v pryamuyu kishku* (A Two-Stage Method of Transplanting the Ureters to the Rectum); *Organizatsiya khirurgicheskoy pomoshchi v BSSR* (The Organization of Surgical Care in the Belorussian SSR) (1929); *Awards:* two Orders of Lenin (1943 and 1953); two Orders of the Red Banner of Labor (1932 and 1949); two medals; *Died:* 6 Sept 1954 in Minsk.

MOSASHVILI, Ilo Onisimovich (1896–1954) Geo poet and playwright; *Born:* 7 Jan 1896 in vil Chargali, now Dusheti Rayon; *Educ:* studied at Tiflis Seminary; 1914 entered Petrograd Psychoneurological Inst; transferred to Law Fac, Khar'kov Univ; *Career:* 1916 first verse published; late 1920's wrote lyric poetry on Geo civic themes; after WW 2 playwright; wrote in spirit of socialist realism; dep, Geo Supr Sov of 1938, 1947 and 1951 convocations; *Publ:* plays "The Station Master" (1947); "Sunken Stones" (1949); "His Star" (1950); "Path to the Future" (1953); various books of verse and poems for children; *Awards:* Order of Lenin; Stalin Prize (1951); *Died:* 4 Aug 1954 in Tbilisi.

MOSIN, Aleksandr Grigor'yevich (1871–1929) Opera singer (tenor); Hon Artiste of Ukr SSR from 1928; *Born:* 16 Oct 1871; *Educ:* 1897 grad Prof Ye. A. Lavroskaya's singing class; Moscow Conservatory; *Career:* began stage career in N. V. Unkovskiy's opera company; sang in Tiflis and Rostov in opera company of Petrograd House of the People; 1908–10 performed at Bol'shoy Theater in Moscow; promoted opera in the Ukr; performed in Odessa, Khar'kov, etc; 1926–29 performed at Kiev Opera Theater; *Roles:* German, Yuriy in Tchaikovsky's *Charodeyka* (The Sorceress); Sobinin in "Ivan Susanin"; Lykov in *Tsarskaya nevesta* (Bride of the Tsar); Levko; Berendey; Rual'd in Serov's "Rogneda"; Bastryukov in Arenskiy's *Son na Volge* (Dream on the Volga); Khlopusha in Pashchenko's *Orlinyy bunt* (Revolt of the Eagles); Mikola in Lysenko's *Rozhdestvenskaya noch'* (Christmas Eve); Ramses; Canio; the Caliph in Puccini's "Turandot", etc; *Died:* 9 Sept 1929.

MOSKOVIN, Ivan Mikhaylovich (1890–1939) Party official; CP member from 1911; *Born:* 1890, son of an office worker; *Career:* active in student polit movement; after 1917 Feb Revol Party organizer, Petrograd Railroad Rayon; 1918–23 various posts in Petrograd; head, Accounting and Distribution Dept, Petrograd Polit Railroads Bd; dept head, Petrograd Province Exec Comt; head, Org Dept, Petrograd Province Party Comt; from 1923 dep secr and head, Org Dept, Northwestern Bureau CC, CPSU(B); then head, Org and Distribution Dept, CC, CPSU(B); from 1927 cand Secretariat member, and member, Org Bureau, CC, CPSU(B); from Nov 1930 Presidium member, USSR Supr Sovnarkhoz; head, Personnel Dept, USSR Supr Sovnarkhoz; at 12th, 13th and 14th Party Congresses elected cand member, at 15th and 16th Congresses elected member, CC, CPSU(B); at 17th CPSU(B) Congress elected member, Sov Control Commission, USSR Council of Pop Comr; arrested by State Security organs; *Died:* 1939 in imprisonment.

MOSKVIN, Ivan Mikhaylovich (1874–1946) Russian actor; Hon Artiste of RSFSR from 1923; Pop Artiste of RSFSR from 1926; Pop Artiste of USSR from 1936; *Born:* 18 June 1874 in Moscow, son of a master watch-maker; *Educ:* 1896 completed drama class at Musical Drama College, Moscow Philharmonic Soc; studied under Nemirovich-Danchenko; *Career:* prior to 1893 errand boy in a store, then weighman and order clerk at a foundry; took part in amateur dramatics; 1896–97 actor, Z. A. Malinovskiy's company in Yaroslavl'; 1897–98 actor, Korsh Theater, Moscow; from 1898 until death actor, Moscow Arts Theater; also film parts; co-produced shows: "The Bluebird"; *Revizor* (The Government Inspector); *Mesyats v derevne* (A Month in the Country); *Smert' Pazukhina* (The Death of Pazukhin); *Tri tolstyaka* (Three Fat Man), etc; from 1943 dir, Moscow Arts Acad Theater; chm, Comt for Awarding Stalin Prizes (for art and lit); dep, USSR Supr Sov of 1937 convocation; *Roles:* in theater: Tsar Fyodor in A. K. Tolstoy's "Tsar' Fyodor Ioannovich" (1898); Tesman in Ibsen's "Hedda Gabler" (1899); Arnold in Hauptmann's "Mikael Kramer" (1901); Luka in Gorky's *Na dne* (The Lower Depths) (1902); Oswald in Ibsen's "Ghosts" (1905); Zagoretskiy in Griboyedov's *Gore ot uma* (Woe from Wit) (1906); Golutvin in Ostrovskiy's *Na vsyakogo mudretsa dovol'no prostoty* (There's a Simpleton in Every Sage) (1910); Fyodor Protasov in L. N. Tolstoy's *Zhivoy trup* (The Living Corpse) (1911); Prokofiy Pazukhin in Saltykov-Shchedrin's "The Death of Pazukhin" (1914); Foma Opiskin in *Selo Stepanchikovo* (Stepanchikovo Village) (1917), after Dostoyevskiy; Pugachev in Trenyov's *Pugachyovshchina* (The Pugachev Rebellion) (1925); Chervakov in L. M. Leonov's "Untilovsk" (1928); Prof Gornostayev in Trenyov's "Lyubov' Yarovaya" (1936); Gen Gorlov in Korneychuk's "Front" (1942); Vice-Admiral Belobrov in Kron's *Ofitser flota* (Naval Officer) (1945), etc; film roles: Polikushka in "Polikushka" (1919); Samson Vyrin in *Kollezhskiy registrator* (The Collegium Recorder) (1925), after Pushkin's novelette *Stantsionnyy smotritel'* (The Station Master); Chervyakov in *Chiny i lyudi* (Ranks and Persons) (1929), etc; *Awards:* two Stalin Prizes (1943 and 1946); two Orders of Lenin; Order of the Red Banner of Labor; *Died:* 16 Feb 1946 in Moscow.

MOSOLOV, Vasiliy Petrovich (1888–1951) Agrotech; member from 1935 and vice-pres from 1939; All-Union Lenin Acad of Agric; CP member from 1932; *Born:* 25 Aug 1888, son of a Mari peasant; *Career:* 1924–38 head, Gen Agric Dept, Kazan' Agric Inst; from 1938 worked for All-Union Lenin Acad of Agric; wrote about treatment of podsol soil, use of fertilizers, wintering of winter crops, foddergrass cultivation and crop rotation in centr USSR, etc; *Publ: Agrotekhnika* (Agrotechnics) (1952); *Mnogoletniye travy* (Perennial Grasses) (1950); *Awards:* two Stalin Prizes (1943 and 1951); *Died:* 10 Feb 1951.

MOSTOVENKO, Pavel Nikolayevich (1881–1939) Party and govt official; CP member from 1901; *Born:* 10 May 1881, son of a forester; *Educ:* grad Petersburg Polytech Inst; *Career:* joined League for the Liberation of the Working Class in Petersburg; member, Nizhniy Novgorod, Severnyy, Tver' and Moscow RSDRP Comt; several times arrested; 1905 exec Party organizer for Blagushe-Lefortov Rayon in Moscow; attented Tammerfors Party Conference; 1907 deleg at 5th Party Congress; 1917 member Petrograd Sov; deleg at 6th RSDRP(B) Congress; Petrograd Exec Comt plen on Rumanian Front; elected Bolshevik dep, Constituent Assembly; during 1917 Oct Revol member, Moscow Mil Revol Comt; helped lead 1917 Oct Revol in Moscow; late 1917 chm, Moscow Sov of Soldiers' Dep; Presidium member, Moscow City Sov of Workers' Dep; 1918 underground work in Ukr; 1919 secr, Ufa Province RCP(B) Comt; helped found Bashkir Republ; 1921–22 RSFSR plen in Lith and Czechoslovakia; from 1923 various exec admin posts; from 1929 rector, Moscow Higher Tech College; then All-Russian Supr Sovnarkhoz plen in Berlin; 1934–37 dir, Higher Acad Courses, Pop Comrt of Heavy Ind; arrested by State Security organs; *Died:* 18 Apr 1939 in imprisonment; posthumously rehabilitated.

MOSTRAS, Konstantin Georgiyevich (1886–1965) Violin teacher; Hon Art Worker of RSFSR from 1937; Dr of Art History; prof, Moscow Conservatory; *Born:* 16 Apr 1886 in vil Arzhenka, Tambovsk Province; wrote violin works and manuals; *Publ: Intonatsiya na skripke* (Intonation on the Violin (1948); *Ritmicheskaya distsiplina skripacha* (The Violinist's Rhythmic Discipline) (1951); *Dinamika v skripichnom iskusstve* (Dynamics in Violin Art) (1956); Sistema domashnikh zanyatiy skripacha *(The Violonist's System of Home Exercises) (1956); Metodicheskiye kommentarii k "24 kaprisam" dlya skripki solo N. Paganini* (Methodic Commentaries on the "24 Capriccios" for the Paganini Violin Solo) (1959); *Died:* 6 Sept 1965 in Moscow.

MOVCHAN, Vasiliy Arkhipovich (1903–1964) Ukr ichthyologist and specialist in fish-breeding; corresp member, Ukr Acad of Sci from 1951; corresp member, All-Union Lenin Acad of Agric Sci from 1955; CP member from 1927; *Born:* 14 Jan 1903 in vil Nemorozhi, now Cherkassy Oblast, son of a peasant; *Career:* 1930–41 dir, Fish Pond Farming Research Inst, Kiev; from 1945 prof, Kiev Univ; *Awards:* Stalin Prize (1949); *Died:* 2 July 1964.

MOVCHIN, Nikolay Nikolayevich (1896–1938) Mil commander; *Born:* 1896; *Educ:* grad Frunze Mil Acad; *Career:* 1918–22 fought in Civil War; in 1920's with Red Army Staff; *Publ: Komplektovaniye Krasnoy Armii* (Recruitment for the Red Army) (1926); *Posledovatel'nyye operatsii po opytu Marny i Visly* (Consistent Operations Based on the Experience of the Marne and Vistula) (1928); *Died:* 1938.

MOYROVA, Varvara Akimovna (1890–1951) Party official; CP member from 1917; *Born:* 10 Dec 1890 in Simferopol'; *Career:*

secr, Odessa newspaper "Golos proletariata"; at 2nd Congress of Rumanian-Black Sea Front elected member, Exec Comt; from 1918 Party work in Moscow; helped organize 1st All-Russian and 1st All-Ukr Congresses of Women Workers and Peasants; 1921–23 Ukr Pop Comr of Soc Security, 1923–26 worked for Centr Dept of Women Workers, CC, CPSU(B); then dir, All-Union Public Nutrition Assoc; at 4th Comintern Congress elected cand member, Comintern Presidium; for number of years managed Int Secretariat for Work Among Women; 1935–37 headed All-Russian Red Cross and Red Crescent Soc; *Award:* Order of Lenin; *Died:* 31 July 1951.

MOZURYUNAS, Vladas (1922–1964) Lith poet; member, USSR Writers' Union from 1947; CP member from 1947; *Born:* 1 Feb 1922 in Kaunas, son of a worker; *Educ:* 1956 grad Higher Lit Courses, Gorky Lit Inst; 1958 grad Higher Party School, CC, CPSU; *Career:* 1938 joined illegal Lith Komsomol; 1939 first work published; 1940 collaborated with Sov authorities after occupation of Lith; in same year began working for the newspaper "Komjaunimo Tiesa" and journal "Pionerjus"; 1942 ed, front-line newspaper "Uz Tabylu Lietuva"; 1945–48 ed, newspaper "Komjaunimo Tiesa"; 1948–54 ed, journal "Svyturys"; 1958–64 ed, lit journal "Pergale"; bd member, Lith Writers' Union; *Publ:* verse collections *Žemes sauja* (The Hollow) (1947); *Sauletekis* (Sunrise) (1950); *Vilniaus etudai* (Vilnius Etudes) (2 vol, 1958–63); film script "Steps in the Night", etc; *Died:* 9 June 1964 in Vilnius.

MRACHKOVSKIY, Sergey Vital'yevich (1888–1936) Govt official; CP member from 1905; *Born:* 1888; *Career:* several times arrested by Tsarist authorities; 1917 touring agitator for Ural Oblast RSDRP(B) Comt; after 1917 Oct Revol various polit posts and commands in Red Army; from 1925 admin work; from 1923 active Trotskyist; 1927 expelled from Party and later jailed; after release in 1929 and reinstatement in Party in 1936 again expelled from Party for alleged anti-Party and anti-Sov activities; Aug 1936 sentenced to death in trial of "Trotsky-Zinov'yevite terrorist center"; *Died:* 24 Aug 1936 executed.

MROCHKOVSKIY, Stefan Iosifovich (1885–1967) Govt official; CP member from 1905; *Born:* 1885; *Career:* lawyer by profession; 1917 member, Yelisavetgrad Sov and Mil Comt; 1919 captured and interned Gen Denikin's forces; escaped; 1921–25 chm of a comt, Supr Sovnarkhoz; 1925–27 chm, bd, Berstol' and Metakhim joint-stock companies; 1927–43 admin work for USSR Pop Comrt of Defense; from 1953 retired; *Died:* 22 Feb 1967.

MSTISLAVSKIY (real name: MASLOVSKIY), Sergey Dmitriyevich (1876–1943) Russian writer and playwright; *Born:* 23 Aug 1876 in Moscow; *Educ:* 1901 grad Natural Sci Dept, Petersburg Univ; *Career:* as a student took part in expeditions to Centr Asia; 1905 began revol work with Socialist-Revol Party; 1920 interned in Peter and Paul Fortress; fought for Bolsheviks in Oct 1917 Revol and Civil War; member, CC, Leftist Socialist-Revol Party; Presidium member, 2nd All-Russian Congress of Soviets; 1922–26 ed for Trade-Union International; then asst chief ed, "Bol'shaya sovetskaya entsiklopdiya" (Large Soviet Encyclopedia); head, Prose Workshop, Gorky Lit Inst; *Publ:* essays: *Na okraine* (On the Outskirts); *Kishlak skomorokhov* (The Village of Mountebanks); *V Samarkande* (In Samarkand); *Kuril'shchiki opiuma* (The Opium Smokers); "Kop-Kara" (1900); "Gal'cha" (1901); *Letopis' voyennoy pechati* (Chronicle of the Military Press) (1911); novels: *Krysha mira* (The Roof of the World) (1925); *Gibel' tsarizma* (The End of Tsarism) (1927); *Soyuz tyazhyoloy kavalerii* (The Heavy Cavalry League) (1928); *Bez sebya* (Without Oneself) (1930); *Grach, ptitsa vesennyaya* (The Rock, a Spring Bird) (1936); *Nakanune. 1917 god* (On the Eve. 1917) (1937); novelette *Chyornyy Magoma* (Black Magoma) (1932); plays: *Na krovi* (Blooded) (1928); *Burevestniki* (The Stormy Petrels) (1930); *Sud'ba gor* (The Fate of the Mountains); also wrote film scripts; *Died:* 22 Apr 1943 in Irkutsk.

MUDARRIS (MUDARRISOV), Sharaf Khasiyatullovich (1919–1963) Tatar poet; *Born:* 1 Nov 1919 in vil Nizhnyaya Karakitya, now Tatar ASSR, son of a peasant; *Educ:* 1939–41 studied at Kazan' Teachers' Training Inst; 1956 completed corresp course at Gorky Lit Inst; *Career:* fought in WW 2; translated Shakespeare's sonnets, verse of Byron, Shelley, Heine, Pushkin, Nekrasov, Shevchenko, etc into Tatar; *Publ:* collected verse in Tatar and Russian: *Rost* (Growth) (1937); *Frontoviki-tatary* (Tatar Front-Line Soldiers) (1944); *Put' pesni* (Path of a Song) (1947); *Solntse vskhodit* (The Sun Rises) (1951); *Moy rovesnik* (My Coeval) (1956), etc; *Died:* 2 May 1963.

MUKHADZE, Grigoriy Mikhaylovich (1879–1948) Surgeon; Dr of Med from 1912; prof from 1919; member, USSR Acad of Med Sci and Geo Acad of Sci from 1944; Hon Sci Worker of Geo SSR from 1946; *Born:* 1879; *Educ:* 1908 grad Med Fac, Tomsk Univ; *Career:* after grad intern, Minusinsk and Krasnoyarsk hospitals; from 1911 head, Surgical Dept, Chiatura Trades Hospital; 1912 completed doctor's thesis on the effect of reduced circulation on blood pressure at V.A. Oppel's clinic; from 1918 dir, Traumatological Inst; co-founder, Tbilisi Univ; 1919–21 head, Chair of Gen Surgery, 1921–48 head, Chair of Hospital Surgery, Tbilisi Univ; 1932 established blood transfusion unit which in 1935 became the Inst of Hematology and Blood Transfusion, Geo Min of Health; 1944–48 founder-dir, Inst of Experimental Surgery and Hematology, Geo Acad of Sci; pioneered modern surgical techniques in Geo SSR and trained many leading Geo surgeons; wrote 87 works, including ten monographs on surgery and blood transfusion; a hospital and street in Chiatura, the Tbilisis Surgical Soc and the Tbilisi Inst of Hematology and Blood Transfusion bear his name; *Publ:* doctor's thesis *K voprosu o vliyanii umen'shennogo krovoobrashcheniya na obshchee krovyanoye davleniye* (The Effect of Reduced Blood Circulation on General Blood Pressure) (1912); *K voprosu o kardiografii pri svezhykh ranakh serdtsa* (Cardiography in the Case of Fresh Heart Wounds) (1929); *Klinicheskiye nablyudeniya nad avertinovym narkozom* (Clinical Observations on Avertin Narcosis) (1929); *K voprosu o peresadke mochetochnikov v kishechnik* (The Transplantation of the Ureters to the Intestines) (1937); *Spravochnik po perelivaniyu krovi* (Reference Manual on Blood Transfusion) (1941), etc; *Died:* 1948 in Tbilisi.

MUKHIN, Fyodor Nikanorovich (1878–1919) Revolutionary; CP member from 1904; *Born:* 1878 in vil Zavodo-Ukovskoye, Tobol'sk Province, son of a peasant; *Career:* machinist at Ul'miya Station, Chinese-Eastern Railroad; fought in 1905–07 Revol; Feb 1918 elected chm, Amur Oblast Sov and Blagoveshchensk City Sov; then head, Amur Council of Pop Comr; late 1918 helped organize partisan movement in Amur area; 1919 helped plan armed rebellion against American and Japanese expeditionary troops and White forces; Mar 1919 captured by White forces; *Died:* 9 Mar 1919 executed.

MUKHIN, Nikolay Semyonovich (1890–1943) Mari poet; *Born:* 7 Dec 1890 in vil Olykyal, Mari ASSR, son of a teacher; *Educ:* 1909 grad teaching course; 1932 grad Mari Teachers' Training Inst; *Career:* orphaned at an early age and worked as a farmhand and shepherd; 1906 began to write verse; from 1909 worked as a teacher; wrote poems about nature and the 1917 Oct Revol; translated verse by N.A. Nekrasov, I.S. Nikitin and A.V. Kol'tsov into Mari; in late 1930's arrested by NKVD; *Publ:* poem "Change of Life" (1918); collection "Verse" (1928); play "Still Waters Run Deep" (1926); verse collection "The Fruits of Freedom" (1936), etc; *Died:* 1943 in imprisonment; posthumously rehabilitated.

MUKHINA (MUKHINA-ZAMKOVA), Vera Ignat'yevna (1889–1953) Sculptress; member, USSR Acad of Arts from 1947; Pop Artiste of USSR from 1943; *Born:* 1 July 1889 in Riga; *Educ:* 1909–11 studied at K. Yuon and I. Dudin's Art School and Sinitsyna's Sculpture Studio, Moscow; 1912–14 studied under A. Bourdelle in Paris; *Career:* 1914 studied classical sculpture and architecture in Italy; before 1917 Oct Revol her work displayed strong West-European influences; after Revol began working on monumental sculpture depicting revol themes; from 1930 considered a major proponent of socialist realism in sculpture; member, ed collegium, journal "Iskusstvo"; also taught sculpture; *Works:* marble group "Children's Dance" (1915); two-meter statue "The Peasant Girl" (1927); 24-meter steel group "The Worker and the Kolkhoz Girl" (1930); monumental statue of Gorky (1938–39, unveiled in Gorky in 1952); busts and relief portraits of Col. I. Khizhnyak, B. Yusupov and other Sov mil leaders (1941–45); cork-elm portrait of Acad A. Krylov (1944–45); statue for Tchaikovsky memorial (1945–49); headstones for the graves of L. Sobinov and L. Peshkov; coauthor, six-figure group "We Demand Peace" (1950); coauthor, Gorky memorial, Moscow (1951); coauthor, two monumental ornamental statues for Moscow Univ (1952); *Awards:* four Stalin Prizes (1941, 1943, 1946 and 1951); Order of the Red Banner of Labor; Badge of Hon; medals; *Died:* 6 Oct 1953 in Moscow.

MUKHTAROV, Khasan Bagautdinovich (1901–1963) Bash writer; *Born:* 10 Nov 1901 in vil Kamyshly, Bash ASSR, son of merchant; *Career:* left home at age 11; worked as apprentice, typesetter, proofreader and ed; fought in Civil War; 1930 first work published; depicted revol movement in Bash; translated Gorky, Chekhov, Lermontov, Fadeyev, Polevoy, etc into Bash; *Publ:*

collected essays on workers' life "The First Shock Workers" (1931); historical stories: "Long Live the Commune" (1934); "The Clash of Generations" (1936); books for children "The Lost Drawings" (1940); "In the Forest" (1944); novelette "Before the Storm" (1935); *Died:* 13 Oct 1963 in Ufa.

MUKLEVICH, Romual'd Adamovich (1890–1938) Mil commander; Pole; veteran of 1917 Oct Revol; CP member from 1906; *Born:* 7 Dec 1890 in vil Suprasl', Grodno Province, son of textile worker; *Career:* 1907–09 textile worker and secr, Belostok Comt, Soc-Democratic Party of Poland and Lith; 1911 secr, Lodz Comt, Soc-Democratic Party of Poland and Lith; 1907 imprisoned for organizing strikes in Belostok; 1912 drafted into Russian Army and sent to front; 1915–17 noncom at motor mechanics' school in Kronstadt; fought in 1917 Feb Revol; member, Petrograd Sov of Workers and Soldiers' Deputies; worked for Mil Org, CC, RSDRP; during 1917 Oct Revol helped storm Winter Palace and disarm Vladimir Acad cadets; Feb 1918 joined partisan detachment and fought against German troops; 1918–21 border comr for demarcation line established by Germans; chief of staff, Sventsyany forces group troops; mil comr of Minsk Province; comr, 16th Army and Western Front staffs; 1921–22 member, Revol Mil Comt, Western Front; 1922–25 comr, Red Army Mil Acad; 1925–26 dep chief, Red Army Air Force; simultaneously chm, ed bd, journal "Vestnik Vozdushnogo flota"; 1925 helped pioneer Moscow-Peking air route; from Aug 1926 chief, Sov Navy; member, USSR Revol Mil Council; devised and implemented program to reestablish Sov fleet; helped devise and implement first Red Army Naval Forces Field Manual and Navy Regulations; 1931–34 inspector, Sov Navy; member, USSR Revol Mil Council; chm, Commission to Determine the Feasibility of a Pacific Fleet; 1934–36 head, Main Shipbuilding Ind Bd; 1936–37 USSR Dep Pop Comr of Defense Ind; deleg at 3rd Comintern Congress (1921) and at 15th (1927) and 17th (1934) CPSU(B) Congresses; member, USSR and All-Russian Centr Exec Comt of various convocations; 1937 arrested by NKVD; *Awards:* Order of the Red Banner; *Died:* 9 Feb 1938 in imprisonment; posthumously rehabilitated.

MUL'TANOVSKIY, Boris Pompeyevich (1876–1938) Meteorologist; member, All-Union Lenin Acad of Agric Sci from 1935; *Born:* 11 Apr 1876; *Educ:* 1899 grad Petersburg Univ; *Career:* from 1900 worked at Main Physical (from 1924 Geophysical) Observatory; developed principles of long-term weather forecasting (the principle of atmospheric influence centers, the principle of dividing synoptic processes into natural synoptic periods and seasons, etc); analyzed the development characteristics of synoptic processes over long periods of time and large areas with the use of "aggregate maps"; supervised various Sov research projects on long-term weather forecasting, especially for agric; *Publ: Vliyaniye tsentrov deystviya atmosfery na pogodu Yevropeyskoy Rossii v tyoploye vremya goda* (The Effect of Atmospheric Influence Centers on the Weather in European Russia During the Warm Period of the Year) (1915); *Osnovnyye polozheniya sinopticheskogo metoda dolgosrochnykh prognozov pogody* (The Basic Principles of the Synoptic Method of Long-Term Weather Forecasting) (1933), etc; *Died:* 4 Mar 1938.

MURADOV, Ata (1914–1965) Party and govt official; CP member; *Born:* 1914 in vil Kordzhou Geok-Tepe Rayon, son of a pesant; *Educ:* grad trade technicum; 1950 grad Higher Party School, CC, CPSU; *Career:* from 1926 raised in a boarding school; worked for consumers cooperative system; 1944–47 Turk Dep Min of Trade; 1950–52 chm, Ashkhabad City Sov; from 1952 first secr, Ashkhabad Oblast Comt, CP Turkm; then dep dept head, CC, CP Turkm; Turkm Min of Procurement; Turkm Min of Agricultural Produce Production and Procurement; in his latter years head, Dept of Light and Food Ind, CC, CP Turkm; dep, USSR Supr Sov of 4th and 5th convocations; dep, Turkm Supr Sov; member and Bureau member, CC, CP Turkm; *Awards:* Order of Lenin; Badge of Hon; medals; *Died:* Sept 1965.

MURADOV, Shirin (usta Shirin) (1880–1957) Uzbek architect (Bukhara school), ornamental artist and brilliant sculptor in "ganch" (a baked mixture of gypsum and clay); hon member, Uzbek Acad of Sci and Hon Art Worker of Uzbek SSR from 1943; *Born:* 18 Aug 1880; *Career:* during 1910's built and decorated houses in Bukhara and Sitorai-Makhi-Khosa Palace near Bukhara; during Sov period worked on the restoration and ornamentation of buildings in Tashkent; 1939 designed Uzbek and Turkm pavillions at All-Union Agric Exhibition, Moscow; 1947 designed and executed decorations for the Bukhara Hall of the Navoi Opera and Ballet Theater, Tashkent; *Awards:* Stalin Prize (1947); *Died:* 12 Feb 1957.

MURADYAN, Bagrat Georgiyevich (1887–1959) Arm actor; comedian; Hon Artiste of Arm SSR from 1931; *Born:* 3 July 1887; *Career:* 1908 began stage career in Tiflis with A. Kharazyan's company; 1912–17 performed at Arm Drama Soc Theater, Tiflis; 1917–20 in Arm Cultural Sov troupe in Baku; 1924–32 performed at Sundukyan Thater; 1933–39 at Arm Theater in Baku; from 1940 at Arm Young Plaggoers' Theahter, Yerevan; popular in classical roles; *Died:* 21 June 1959.

MURALOV, Aleksandr Ivanovich (Party alias: Matvey) (1886–1938) Party and govt official; CP member from 1905; *Born:* 1886 near Taganrog, son of a farmer; *Career:* agric chemist by profession; fought in 1905–07 Revol; Party work in Serpukhov, Moscow, Petersburg and Podol'sk; arrested and imprisoned; after 1917 Feb Revol member, Serpukhov Sov; Oct 1917–19 chm, Aleksin Uyezd RCP(B) Comt and Aleksin Uyezd Exec Comt, Tula Province; then Bureau member, Tula Province RCP(B) Comt and Tula Province Mil Comt; commandant, Tula Fortified Area; 1920 chm, Moscow Sovnarkhoz; late 1920–23 chm, Donetsk Sovnarkhoz; Bureau member, Don RCP(B) Comt; 1923–28 chm, Nizhniy Novgorod Province Exec Comt; Bureau member, Nizhniy Novgorod Province RCP(B) Comt; from Mar 1928 RSFSR Dep Pop Comr of Agric; from 1929 RSFSR Pop Comr of Agric; Mar 1933–Sept 1936 USSR Dep Pop Comr of Agric; 1935–37 pres, All-Union Lenin Acad of Agric Sci; deleg at 9th and 11th–17th CPSU(B) Congresses; member, All-Russian and USSR Centr Exec Comt; arrested by State Security organs; *Died:* 1938 in imprisonment; posthumously rehabilitated.

MURALOV, Nikolay Ivanovich (1877–1937) Mil commander; revolutionary; administrator; CP member from 1903; *Born:* 1877; *Career:* until 1917 Oct Revol Party work in Podol'sk, Moscow and Tula; Oct 1917 member, Moscow Mil Revol Comt; member, Moscow Revol Staff; helped organize and lead Bolshevik coup in Moscow; 1917–18 commander, Moscow Mil Distr; 21 Feb–14 Aug 1919 member, Revol Mil Comt, 3rd Army; 19 Aug–28 Nov 1919 member, Revol Mil Council, Eastern Front; 8 Sept 1919–23 July 1920 member, Revol Mil Council, 12th Army; 1920–21 Collegium member, Pop Comrt of Agric; 1921–24 commander, Moscow Mil Distr; from 1924 commander, North Caucasian Mil Distr; then various exec posts; 1923–27 member, "Trotskyist Opposition"; 1927 expelled from CP for membership, Trotskyist Opposition; 1929 exiled to Western Siberia and assigned admin work; 23–30 Jan 1937 tried with "anti-Sov Trotskyist center" in Moscow; 30 Jan 1937 sentenced to death; *Died:* 1 Feb 1937 executed by firing squad.

MURANOV, Matvey Konstantinovich (1873–1959) Party official; CP member from 1904; *Born:* 29 Sept 1873 in vil Rybtsy, Poltava Province; *Career:* metalworker by trade; 1907 helped run Railroad Rayon Party Comt in Khar'kov; 1912 member, Khar'kov Bolshevik Comt; Khar'kov workers' dep at 4th State Duma; simultaneously revol work in Petrograd, Khar'kov, Ivanovo-Voznesensk, Vyatka, etc; worked for "Pravda"; Nov 1914 arrested along with other Bolshevik deputies of State Duma for revol activities against the war and the Tsarist govt; 1915 exiled to Turukhan Kray; after 1917 Feb Revol worked for newspaper "Pravda"; 1917–23 instructor, CC, RCP(B); 1922–34 member, CPSU(B) Centr Control Commission; from 1923 Collegium member, USSR Supr Court; 1934–37 worked for Private Amnesty Commission, All-Russian Centr Exec Comt; deleg at 10th, 13th, 15th, 16th and 17th Party Congresses; at 6th and 8th Party Congresses elected member, Party CC; at 9th Congress elected cand member, CC, RCP(B); from 1939 retired; *Died:* 9 Dec 1959.

MURASHEV, Georgiy Vasil'yevich (1892–1953) Psychologist and defectologist; *Born:* 1892; *Educ:* grad Moscow Univ; *Career:* specialized in child psychiatry at Defectology Research Inst, RSFSR Acad of Pedag Sci; worked on corrective treatment of oligophrenic children; proposed methods for group training of children in special schools; devised means of teaching retarded children geography (inculcating geographical concepts and spatial conceptions, developing powers of observation, training children to apply their acquired knowledge to the solution of problems and to understand cause-and-effect relationships, etc); wrote works of interest to defectologists, pedagogues and specialists in mass educ methods; particularly intersting in this respect is his collection of geography problems, many of which are suitable for both special and gen educ schools; *Publ:* coauthor, *Isklyuchitel'nyye deti. Deti nervnyye, trudnyye i slabo odaryonnyye. Ikh izucheniye i* *vospitaniye* (Exceptional Children. Neurotic, Problem and Untalented Children. Their Study and Training) (1929); *Sbornik zadach po geografii dlya klassnoy i kruzhkovoy raboty vo II i III klassakh* (A Collection of Geography Problems for Class and Group Study in the 2nd and 3rd Grades) (1947); *Printsip vospityvayushchego obucheniya i soderzhaniye geografii kak uchebnogo predmeta vospomogatel'noy shkoly* (The Educational Training Principle and Content of Geopgrahy as a Discipline of the Auxiliary School) (1949); *Sbornik zadach i uprazhneniy po geografii dlya nachal'noy shkoly. Posobiye dlya uchiteley* (A Collection of Problems and Exercises in Geography for Primary Schools. A Teacher's Aid) (1952); *Died:* 1953.

MURASHKA, Rygor (Grigoriy) Danilovich (1902–1944) Bel writer; CP member from 1920; *Born:* 16 Feb 1902 in vil Bezverkhovichi, now Minsk Oblast, son of a poor peasant; *Educ:* studied at Nesvizh Teachers' Training Seminary; *Career:* 1919–20 did underground Party work and fought with partisans; 1920–28 served in Red Army, after which he became a rural newspaper corresp; active member, Bel Assoc of Proletarian Writers; 1941–43 lived in Minsk during the German occupation, then joined partisans; wrote on such subjects as the 1905 Revol in Bel, the Civil War and the "internal emigration" in Bel lit during the 1920's; *Publ:* story collection *Strel nachny u lese* (A Shot in the Woods at Night) (1926); novelette *U ikhnym dome* (In Their House) (1929); novel *Syn* (The Son) (1929); story collections *Prygranichny manastyr* (The Frontier Monastery) (1930); *Zvanki* (The Bells) (1931); "Ruziki" (1932); novel *Salaui svyatoha Palikara* (The Nightingales of Saint Polycarp) (1940); *Died:* spring 1944 killed in action.

MURATOV, Mikhail Vasil'yevich (1892–1957) Writer, historian and ethnographer; *Born:* 25 Dec 1892 in vil Goryachinskoye, Transbaykal Oblast, son of a physician father and a polit prisoner mother; *Educ:* 1917 grad Fac of History and Philology, Moscow Univ; *Career:* while still a student began research on the history of pop religious movements in Russia; 1920–31 taught the history of Russian sects and publishing at higher educ establishment in Irkutsk and Moscow; *Publ: Knizhnoye delo v Rossii v XIX i XX vekakh* (Publishing in Russia During the 19th and 20th Centuries) (1931); *L. N. Tolstoy i V. G. Chertkov po ikh perepiske* (L. N. Tolstoy and V. G. Chertkov in Their Correspondence) (1934); *Dva puteshestviya kapitana Bering* (Two of Captain Bering's Journeys) (1937); *Pervyye razvedchiki velikogo puti* (The First Explorers of the Great Route) (1943); *Yunost' Lomonosova* (Lomonosov's Youth) (1944); "Lomonosov" (1945); *Zamorskiy gost'* (A Guest from Overseas) (1947); *K dalyokim beregam* (To Distant Shores) (1947); *Zhizn' Radishcheva* (Radishchev's Life) (1949); *Kapitan Golovnin* (Captain Golovnin) (1949); "Yemelyan Pugachyov" (1953); "Denis Ivanovich Fonvizin" (1953); *Navstrechu opasnostyam* (Into Danger) (1956); "A. S. Griboyedov" (1965), etc; *Died:* 20 July 1957 in Moscow.

MURAV'YOV, Mikhail Artem'yevich (1880–1918) Mil commander; member, Leftist Socialist-Revol Party from 1917; *Born:* 1880; *Career:* lt-col, Russian Army; 1917 mustered shock battalions for active army; after 1917 Oct Revol transferred allegiance to Sov regime and, as commander, Petrograd Mil Distr, helped to defend Petrograd from Kerensky and Krasnov's troops; early 1918 commanded troops fighting against Ukr Centr Rada, after which he took over command of the Southern armies and repelled the Rumanian advance on Odessa; 13 June 1918 placed in command of forces fighting the Czechoslovak Corps; played prominent role in 1918 Leftist Socialist-Revol uprising in Moscow; 10 July 1918 arrived on board a captured steamer in Simbirsk, where he raised a revolt, despatched telegrams declaring a resumption of the war with Germany and ordered the commanders of Red Army and Czechoslovak units to march on Moscow; *Died:* 11 July 1918 killed in ambush by Simbirsk Communists, led by Province Comt chm I. M. Vareykis.

MUROMTSEV, Sergey Nikolayevich (1898–1960) Microbiologist and immunologist; member, All-Union Lenin Acad of Agric Sci from 1948; CP member from 1940; *Born:* 25 May 1898; *Educ:* 1923 grad Med Fac Moscow Univ; *Career:* after grad worked at various med research inst in Moscow; did research on anaerobic infections in livestock; 1926 devised simple brain-smear method of detecting animal rabies under the microscope; 1929 introduced a vaccine and therapeutic serum for black quarter in cattle; 1931 helped to organize and supervise a system of state control of veterinary drugs in the USSR; 1934–43 developed new methods of staining Negri bodies and obtaining semi-liquid vaccines for Sov veterinary med; also did research on gen questions of microbic mutability, immunity and the phagoprophylaxis and treatment of infectious diseases in humans and animals; from 1956 until death dir, N. F. Gamaleya Inst of Epidemiology and Microbiology, USSR Acad of Med Sci; wrote some 100 works; *Publ: Poluzhidkiye vaktsiny. Izgotovleniye i primeneniye v veterinarii* (Semi-Liquid Vaccines. Their Preparation and Use in Veterinary Medicine) (1944); *Problemy sovremennoy mikrobiologii v svete michurinskogo ucheniya* (Problems of Modern Microbiology in the Light of Michurin's Theory) (1950); *Izmenchivost' mikroorganizmov i problemy immuniteta* (The Mutability of Microorganisms and Problems of Immunity) (1946), etc; *Awards:* Stalin Prize (1946); *Died:* 1960.

MURYSEV, Aleksandr Sergeyevich (1915–1962) Party official; first secr, Kuybyshev Oblast CPSU Comt from 1959; Presidium member, RSFSR Supr Sov from 1959; member, CC, CPSU from 1961; CP member from 1942; *Born:* 1915 in Gomel', now Bel SSR, son of a white-collar worker; *Educ:* 1941 grad Kuybyshev Ind Inst; *Career:* 1930 started work as railroad fitter; from 1930 Komsomol member; from 1941 eng; dep shop foreman; Komsomol CC organizer at machine-building plant; from 1945 head, Dept of Working Youth, Kuybyshev Oblast Komsomol Comt; from 1949 second, then first secr, rayon Party comt; first secr, Chapayev City CPSU Comt, Kuybyshev Oblast; 1953–58 Party organizer at Kuybyshev Hydropower Plant construction project; from 1958 second secr, Kuybyshev Oblast CPSU Comt; then chm, Kuybyshev Oblast Exec Comt; dep, USSR Supr Sov of 1959 convocation; dep, USSR Supr Sov of 1962 convocation; *Awards:* Hero of Socialist Labor (1958); Order of the Red Banner of Labor; medal "For Labor Valor" (1959); *Died:* 1962.

MURZIDI, Konstantin Gavrilovich (1914–1963) Russian writer; *Born:* 3 June 1914 in vil Anapa, now Krasnodar Kray; *Career:* 1929 first work published; fought in WW 2; 1932–55 lived in Urals; *Publ:* collected verse *Otchizna* (Native Land) (1938); *Gornyy shchit* (The Mountain Shield) (1945); *Ural'skoye solntse* (Ural Sun) (1946); *Ulitsa pushkarey* (Street of the Gunners) (1947); *Izbrannyye stikhi* (Selected Verse) (1947); *Druzhba* (Friendship) (1952), etc; novels and novelettes *U Orlinoy gory* (At Eagle Mountain) (1947); *U nas na Urale* (Here in the Urals) (1950); *Noch' v tayge* (Night in the Taiga) (1951); essays *Severodvinskiye zarisovki* (Northern Dvina Sketches) (1964), etc; collected children's verse *Vodolaz* (The Diver) (1941); *Nashi novyye igry* (Our New Games) (1947); *Dobryy velikan* (The Good Giant) (1954), etc; *Died:* 11 Mar 1963 in Moscow.

MUSA DZHALIL' (1906–1944) Tatar poet; CP member from 1929; *Born:* 1906 in vil Mustafa, Orenburg Province; *Career:* 1919 first work published in Orenburg newspaper "Krasnaya zvezda"; 1939–41 exec secr, Tatar Sov Writers' Union; from 1941 in Sov Army; seriously wounded and taken prisoner by Germans; interned in concentration camp, then executed in Moabit Prison, Berlin; *Publ:* verse: "Traveled Paths"; "At the Plant"; "Man of Oryol"; "The Shock-Worker Partisan"; "On the Spring Path"; "The Mailman"; "Before the Attack"; "The Helmet"; "In Camp"; "My Songs"; "Do Not Believe"; libretto to opera "Altyn chech", etc; *Awards:* Stalin Prize (1948); *Died:* 1944 executed in Berlin prison.

MUSABEKOV, Gazanfar Makhmud-ogly (1888–1938) Azer Party and govt official; physician; CP member from 1918; *Born:* 26 July 1888 in vil Pirebedil', Baku Province, son of a peasant; *Educ:* 1917 grad Med Fac, Kiev Univ; *Career:* joined revol movement while still a student; 1912 helped to organize an illegal congress of Moslem students; 1917 returned to Azer after grad and worked as a physician in Kuba; chm, Kuba Sov; from Dec 1917 dep chm, Baku Province Food Comt; after collapse of Sov regime moved to Astrakhan'; 1918 elected chm, Moslem Section, Astrakhan RCP(B) Comt; simultaneously chief physician at a mil hospital; 1920 travelled to Baku with A. I. Mikoyan, where he became Azer Pop Comr of Food; 1922–28 chm, Azer Council of Pop Comr; 1929–31 chm, Azer Centr Exec Comt; 1931–36 chm, Council of Pop Comr, Transcaucasian SFSR; from 1936 co-chm, USSR Centr Exec Comt; member, Comintern Exec Comt; member and Presidium member, USSR Centr Exec Comt; Presidium member, CC, CP Azer; Presidium member, Transcaucasian Kray CPSU(B) Comt; elected cand member, CC, CPSU(B) at 14th, 15th and 16th Party Congresses; made major contribution to the development of the Azer and Transcaucasian health services; co-founder, Baku Inst of Microbiology and Epidemiology, Baku Inst of Mother and Child Welfare and Baku Malaria Inst; 1937 arrested by NKVD and sentenced to death by firing squad; *Publ: Dva puti* (Two Paths)

(1930), etc; *Died:* 1938 in imprisonment; posthumously rehabilitated.

MUSIN, Alikhan Chuzhebayevich (1908–1963) Mining eng; Dr of Eng from 1957; prof from 1959; corresp member, Kaz Acad of Sci from 1958; Hon Sci Worker of Kaz SSR from 1961; CP member from 1940; *Born:* 1908; *Educ:* 1937 grad Moscow Inst of Non-Ferrous Metals and Gold; *Career:* 1949 defended cand thesis; from 1949 dir, Inst of Mining, Kaz Acad of Sci; specialized in the working of ore deposits, especially in hilly regions; introduced forced block-crushing system at Leninogorsk Polymetal Combine; *Publ: Voprosy razvitiya promyshlennosti Kazakhstana* (Problems of Industrial Development in Kazakhstan) (1960); *K metodike primeneniya ob'yomnogo opticheskogo modelirovaniya dlya izucheniya napryazhyonnosti massiva* (The Use of Volumetric Optical Modeling Methods for the Study of Stress in a Massive) (1963), etc; *Awards:* Lenin Prize (1961); *Died:* 1963.

MUSULMANKULOV, Moldobasan (1881–1961) Kir bard; narrator of Kir epic "Manas"; Pop Artiste of Kir SSR; *Born:* 1881 in Tyan'-Shan'; *Career:* during youth wandered from vil to vil singing folksongs to the accompaniment of a komuz; his recorded repertoire included two parts of the epic "Manas" ("Manas" and "Semetey"), the epics "Kurmanbek", "Kozhozhash", "Dzhanysh-Bayysh" and "Zhanyl-Myrza", and the legends "Osmon baatyr" and "Gulbara menen Asasan"; *Died:* 17 June 1961.

MUTALIYEV, Khadzhi-Bekir Shovkhalovich (1910–1964) Ingush poet; pioneer of Sov Ingush poetry; *Born:* 20 June 1910 in vil Ekazhevo, son of a highlander; *Educ:* studied at Moscow Inst of Journalism; *Career:* late 1920's first work published; wrote verse and plays in line with current Sov policy of liquidating private property in vil, eliminating old ways and traditions and combatting religion; *Publ:* plays "Cultural Soldiers"; "An Eye for an Eye, a Tooth for a Tooth"; stories "Mother and Daughter" and "The Bolsheviks Are Coming"; poems "New Guests"; "A Grim Day"; "Kunta's Revenge"; collected verse "On the Road" (1964); *Died:* 11 Sept 1964 in Grozny.

MUZYCHENKO, Aleksandr Fyodorovich (1878–1940) Ukr philologist and pedag; Dr of Pedag and prof from 1922; *Born:* 6 Sept 1878 in vil Kishlav, Crimea, son of a teacher; *Educ:* 1899 grad Novorossiysk Univ, Odessa; *Career:* 1900–08 taught at a high school in Odessa; 1908–09 studied abroad for doctorate; 1909–11 assoc prof, Nezhin Inst of History and Philology; 1911–14 inspector, Kiev 4th and 5th High Schools; 1913–14 also dir, Russian Pedag Museum, Kiev; 1914–19 principal, Naumenko High School, Kiev; 1919–21 principal, Pyatigorsk High School; 1922–25 head, Kiev Model Labor School; 1922–40 prof of pedag, Kiev Univ and Teachers' Training Inst; from 1928 member, Sci Pedag Comt, Ukr Pop Comrt of Educ; specialized in teaching methods, first as a Herbartian, then as an advocate of the "comprehensive system"; *Publ: Nekotoryye osobennosti govora krymskikh bolgar* (Some Features of the Dialect of the Crimean Bulgars) (1907); *Sovremennyye pedagogicheskiye techeniya v Zapadnoy Yevrope i Amerike* (Modern Teaching Trends in West Europe and America) (1912); *Chto takoye pedagogika i chemu ona uchit?* (What Is Pedagogics and What Does it Study?) (1912); *Chteniye i kul'tura slova v sovremennoy shkole* (Reading and Elocution in Modern Schools) (1930), etc; *Died:* 5 Aug 1940 in Kiev.

MYANNIK, Eduard (1906–1966) Est writer; Hon Writer of Est SSR; CP member from 1942; *Born:* 12 Jan 1906 in Tartu, son of a worker; *Career:* worked as digger, miner and builder; from 1921 wrote for newspapers; 1925 published first fictional work for children; wrote novels, short stories and entertaining satirical articles; 1940–41 collaborated with Sov authorities after occupation of Est; fought in WW 2; after war began writing in socialist-realist style; *Publ:* novel "The Grey House" (1930); story collections "The Trial of Hearts" (1946) and "The Fifteen Steps" (1947); novelettes: "The Fight Goes On" (1950); "Twenty Years Ago" (1953); "Behind Barbed Wire" (1954); "A Love Story" (1954), etc; *Died:* 30 Jan 1966 in Tallinn.

MYASKOV, K. G. (1881–1958) Govt official; CP member from 1912; *Born:* 1881; *Career:* after 1917 Oct Revol Comr of Food in Samara; then various exec posts; chm, Russian Agric Bank; Presidium member, All-Union Acad of Agric Sci; member, USSR Gosplan; worked for CC, CPSU; *Died:* 1958.

MYASKOVSKIY, Nikolay Yakovlevich (1881–1950) Composer; music teacher; Pop Artiste of USSR from 1946; Dr of Arts; *Born:* 8 Apr 1881 in Novo-Georgiyevsk Fortress, near Warsaw; *Educ:* 1902 grad mil eng college; 1911 grad Lyadov's composition class, Petersburg Conservatory; *Career:* from 1911 worked as music critic; 1914–18 eng officer, Russian Army; 1918–21 served with Naval Gen Staff, Petrograd; 1921–50 prof, Moscow Conservatory; helped train composers: D. B. Kabalevskiy, V. I. Muradeli, A. I. Khachaturyan, V. Ya. Shebalin, etc; *Works:* peom "Alastor" (1913); mass songs "The Wings of the Soviets" (1931) and "The Lenin Song" (1932); violin concerto (1938); poem-cantata "Kirov Is With Us" (1942); cello concerto (1945); 27 symphonies; 13 string quartets; simfoniettas, sonatas, romances, songs, etc; *Awards:* Order of Lenin; five Stalin Prizes (1941, 1946 (two), 1950 and 1951); *Died:* 8 Aug 1950 in Moscow.

MYASNIKOV (MYASNIKYAN), Aleksandr Fyodorovich (Party and lit pseudonyms: Al. MARTUNI; Alyosha; Bolshevik) (1886–1925) Arm Party and govt official; writer; CP member from 1906; *Born:* 9 Feb 1886 in Rostov-on-Don; *Educ:* studied at Arm seminary and high-school classes at Lazarev Inst of Oriental Languages, Moscow; 1911 grad Law Fac, Moscow Univ; *Career:* fall 1906 arrested, but escaped and fled to Baku, where he conducted revol work; 1912–14 asst to notary-public in Moscow; also wrote and worked as freelance journalist; from 1914 in Tsarist Army; revol propaganda among troops; from early Feb 1917 member, Front Comt, Western Front and head of its Bolshevik faction; together with Frunze founded and edited Bolshevik newspapers "Zvezda" in Minsk; deleg at 6th RSDRP(B) Congress, reporting on situation on Western Front; helped organize 1917 Oct Revol in Minsk; Sept 1917 at 1st Northwestern Oblast Bolshevik Conference elected chm, Northwestern Oblast RSDRP(B) Comt; Oct 1917 elected chm, Bolshevik Mil Revol Comt, Western Oblast; Nov 1917 at Western Front Congress of Soldiers and Officers' Dep elected commander, Western Front; for a while acting Supr Commander in Chief; spring 1918 appointed commander, Volga Front; early 1919 elected chm, Bel Centr Exec Comt; then chm, Centr Bureau, CP Bel; 1919–21 mil organizer, Moscow Party Comt; then secr Moscow Party Comt; summer 1920 head, Polit Bd and head, Main Polit Bd, Western Front; 1921 chm, Arm Council of Min and Arm Pop Comr for Mil Affairs; from 1922 chm, Transcaucasian SFSR Union Council; then first secr, Transcaucasian Kray RCP(B) Comt; at 12th and 13th Party Congresses elected cand member, CC, RCP(B); also ed, newspaper "Zarya Vostoka"; member, USSR Revol Mil Council; Presidium member, USSR Centr Exec Comt; *Publ:* "Good Deeds and Do-Gooders" (1912); "Awakening" (1914); "M. Nalbandyan" (1919); "Armenian Political Parties Abroad" (1925); "The Nationality Problem" (1919); "For the Party" (1921); "Methods of Literary Criticism" (1922), etc; *Died:* 22 Mar 1925 in a plane crash; buried in Tbilisi.

MYASNIKOV, Aleksandr Leonidovich (1899–1965) Internist; Dr of Med; prof from 1932; member, USSR Acad of Med Sci from 1948; corresp member, Rumanian Acad of Sci; *Born:* 18 Sept 1899 in Krasnyy Kholm, Tver' Province; *Educ:* 1922 grad Med Fac, Moscow Univ; *Career:* 1922–25 clinical intern, 1925–32 asst prof, Chair of Fac Therapy, Petrograd (Leningrad) Univ; 1932–38 prof, Chair of Internal Diseases, Novosibirsk Med Inst and Novosibirsk Inst of Postgrad Med Training; from 1938 head, Chair of Fac Therapy, 3rd Leningrad Med Inst and prof, Naval Fac, 1st Leningrad Med Inst; 1940–48 head, Chair of Fac Therapy, Leningrad Naval Med Acad; 1942–46 also chief therapist, Sov Navy; 1946–47 corresp member, USSR Acad of Med Sci; 1948–65 head, A. A. Ostroumov Chair of Fac Therapy, 1st Moscow Med Inst and dir, Inst of Therapy, USSR Acad of Sci, which now bears his name; also chm, Learned Council, Presidium member and acad secr, Clinical Med Section, USSR Acad of Med Sci; 1953 attendant physician to Stalin; for many years chm, Competition Awards Commission, USSR Acad of Sci; exec ed, journal "Voprosy patologii serdechnososudistoy sistemy"; co-ed, internal diseases section, "Bol'shaya meditsinskaya entsiklopediya" (Large Medical Encyclopedia) (2nd ed); attended various int therapists' congresses – 1954 in Stockholm, 1956 in Madrid, 1958 in Philadelphia and Brussels, and 1959 in London; from 1956 chm, All-Russian Soc of Therapists; 1960 read paper at All-Russian Therapists' Conference, Moscow; from 1961 member, J. E. Purkyně Med Soc, Czechoslovakia; 1962 attended 4th Int Congress of Cardiologists, Mexico; 1963 attended 6th Int Congress of Nutrition, England; also attended five congresses of East Bloc health min in Moscow, 3rd European Congress of Cardiologists in Rome and an int symposium on coronary heart diseases; comt member, Int Soc of Internal Med; member, various for cardiological soc; did research on the pathology of the liver, hypertonia and arteriosclerosis; devised new theory of epithelial and mesenchymal hepatitis; developed new methods of diagnosing and a progressive classification of arteriosclerosis; together with Prof G. F. Lang, developed neurogenic theory of hypertonia; wrote over 140 works; *Publ: Bolezni pecheni i zhyolchnykh putey* (Diseases of the Liver and Bilary Tract) (1934); *Vistseral'naya malyariya* (Visceral Malaria) (1936); *Bolezni pecheni* (Liver Diseases) (2nd ed, 1940); *Propedevtika vnutrennikh bolezney* (The Propaedeutics of Internal Diseases) (1944); *Klinika brutselloza* (The Clinical Aspects of Brucellosis) (1944); *Klinika alimentarnoy distrofii* (The Clinical Aspects of Alimentary Dystrophy) (1945); *Epidemicheskiye gepatity* (Epidemic Forms of Hepatitis) (1946); *Gipertonicheskaya bolezn'* (Hypertonia) (1954), etc; *Awards:* Order of Lenin; Order of the Red Star; Order of the Red Banner of Labor; Hon scroll of World Peace Council (1959); int "Golden Stethoscope" prize for contributions to cardiology (1965); medals; *Died:* 19 Nov 1965 in Moscow.

MYASNIKOV, G. I. (1889–1946) Party official; CP member from 1906; *Born:* 1889; *Career:* 1921 Party work in Perm' Province and then in Petrograd; 1921–22 active in "workers' opposition"; Feb 1922 expelled from Party for "anti-Party activities and systematic breach of Party discipline"; after 11th RCP(B) Congress helped direct "workers' opposition"; then emigrated; *Died:* 1946.

MYASNIKOV, Nikolay Petrovich (1900–1934) Party official; *Born:* 1900; *Career:* twice expelled from CP for siding with Zinov'yevite opposition but reinstated after publicly recanting his errors and expressing solidarity with Party and govt policy; Dec 1934 arrested and tried for alleged complicity in assassination of Kirov on 1 Dec 1934; 29 Dec 1934 sentenced to death, along with other defendants, by Assizes of Mil Collegium, USSR Supr Court; *Died:* 29 Dec 1934 executed by firing squad in Leningrad.

MYRNYY, Panas (real name: RUDCHENKO, Afanasiy Yakovlevich) (1849–1920) Ukr writer; *Born:* 1 May 1849 in Mirgorod, Ukr; *Educ:* 1862 grad Gadyach Uyezd College; *Career:* worked for Tsarist Civil Service – 1863–64 in Gadyach, 1865–67 in Priluki, 1867–71 in Mirgorod; from 1871 accountant, Poltava Province Treasury, after which he held various posts with Treasury Bd; 1872 first work published; after 1817 Oct Revol worked for Poltava Province Finance Dept; 1918–19 supported Ukr independence; his Weltanschauung and lit views were influenced by Shevchenko; translated Pushkin, Lermontov, Ostrovskiy, Shakespeare and Longfellow into Ukr; wrote new translation of "The Lay of the Host of Igor"; a number of his unpublished manuscripts are in the custody of Ukr museums; several schools, libraries, etc, now bear his name, and a monument to him was erected in Poltava in 1951; *Publ:* short stories – *Lykhyy poputav* (The Erring Demon) (1872); *P'yanitsa* (The Drunkard) (1874); *Lovv* (Capture) (1883); "Morozenko" (1885); *Sered stepiv* (In the Steppe) (1903); *K suchasnoi muze* (To a Modern Muse) (1905); *Durnytsya* (A Trifle) (1906); novelettes: "Lykhi lyudy" (The Wicked) (1877); novels – *Khiba revut voly, yak yasla povni?* (Do the Fed Complain?) (1880); coauthor, *Poviya* (The Streetgirl) (vol 1–2, 1883–84; vol 1–4, 1928); *Lykho davne i s'ohochasne* (Woes Past and Present) (1897); plays – *Peremudryv* (Over-Sly) (1885); *Zhuba* (Doom) (1896); *V chernitsyakh* (Among the Nuns) (1884); *Spokusa* (Temptation) (1901); "Lymarivna" (1883); *Died:* 1920.

MYSH, Vladimir Mikhaylovich (1873–1947) Surgeon; Dr of Med from 1898; prof from 1901; member, USSR Acad of Med Sci from 1945; Hon Sci Worker of RSFSR from 1934; CP member from 1940; *Born:* 16 Jan 1873; *Educ:* grad Petersburg Mil Med Acad; *Career:* specialized under Prof N. A. Vel'yaminov at Petersburg Mil Med Acad; from 1901 prof, Chair of Gen Surgery, 1909–31 dir, Fac Surgical Clinic, Tomsk Univ; 1912 performed first radical operation for alveolar echinococcosis of the liver in Russia; 1927 founded Surgical Clinic, Tomsk State Inst of Postgrad Med Training; 1935 co-founder, from 1936 dir, Fac Surgical Clinic, Novosibirsk Med Inst; did research on asepsis and antisepsis; also studied surgical techniques for the treatment of certain cortical varieties of epilepsy and athetosis; devised measures for preventing complications after gastroenterostomy; trained numerous surgeons; the Surgical Clinic he directed now bears his name; wrote 130 works; *Publ:* doctor's thesis *Herniae vaginales inguinales v detskom vozraste* (Herniae vaginales inguinales in Childhood) (1898); *Osnovy khirurgicheskoy patologii i terapii* (The Principles of Surgical Pathology and Therapy) (1907); *K voprosu o khirurgicheskom lechenii ekhinokokka* (Surgical Treatment for Hydatid Tapeworm) (1927); *Ocherki khirurgicheskoy diagnostiki – pozvonochnik, taz, konechnosti* (Studies in Surgical Diagnostics – the Spinal Column, the Pelvis and the Extremities) (1934); *Ocherki khirurgicheskoy diagnostiki – opukholi zhivota* (Studies in Surgical Diagnostics – Abdominal Tumors) (1944); *Ocherki khirurgicheskoy diagnostiki – opukholi zhivota, pal'tsevoye issledovaniye cherez pryamuyu kishku* (Studies in Surgical Diagnostics – Abdominal Tumors and Rectal Touch) (1948); *Awards:* two Orders of Lenin; Order of the Red Banner of Labor; medals; *Died:* 31 Dec 1947.

MYUZNIB, Ali-Abbas Mutallibzade (1883–1938) Azer writer and journalist; *Born:* 1883 in Baku; *Career:* taught himself Persian language and lit; ed, satirical journals "Babai-Emir", "Shekhabi-Sagib", etc; published book of anecdotes "Sheikh Bakhlul" and the poems of Sabir; 1911 translated and published portion of "A Thousand and One Nights" in Azer; arrested by NKVD; *Publ:* stories "The Flame of the Spirit" and "Laugh or Cry – The Choice Is Yours" (1913); lyrical poems "Siberian Letters" and "The Splinter" (1913), etc; *Died:* 1938 in imprisonment; posthumously rehabilitated.

N

NABOKOV, Vladimir Dmitriyevich (1869–1922) Politician; co-founder, Constitutional-Democratic Party; asst chm, Party CC and ed-publisher of its organ "Vestnik partii narodnoy svobody"; *Born:* 1869; *Educ:* grad Law Fac, Petersburg Univ; *Career:* taught criminal law at College of Jurisprudence; ed, law periodicals "Pravo" and "Vestnik prava"; contributed to journal "Osvobozhdeniye"; attended 1904 and 1905 Zemstvo Congresses; dep, 1st State Duma; after 1917 Feb Revol business-mang, Provisional Govt; opposed Sov regime; 1919 Min of Justice, Crimean Kray Govt; in emigration sided with Right Wing, Constitutional-Democratic Party; together with I.V. Gessen edited Berlin newspaper "Rul'"; *Publ:* memoirs *Vremennoye pravitel'stvo* (The Provisional Government) (1924, posthumously); *Died:* 28 Mar 1922 assassinated.

NADTOCHIY, Mikhail Fomich (1907–1963) Ukr govt official; CP member from 1931; *Born:* 1907, son of a peasant; *Educ:* grad Odessa Land-Reclamation Eng Inst; *Career:* 1919–21 farm-hand; from 1921 worked on sovkhoz and did Komsomol work; after grad worked on various construction projects as foreman, tech dir, then mang of a trust; 1941–47 exec Party work; from 1947 USSR Dep Min of Construction Materials Ind, USSR Dep Min of Heavy Ind Enterprise Construction, then USSR Dep Min of Construction; from 1958 RSFSR Min of Construction; dep, RSFSR Supr Sov of 1959 convocation; dep, USSR Supr Sov of 1962 convocation; *Died:* 20 Mar 1963.

NADZHMI (real name: NEZHMETDINOV), Kavi Gibyatovich (1901–1957) Tatar writer and public figure; CP member from 1919; *Born:* 15 Dec 1901 in vil Krasnyy Ostrov, now Gorky Oblast; *Educ:* 1922 grad Moscow Higher Mil Teachers' Training School; *Career:* 1919 volunteered for Red Army; 1919 first work published; comr and exec ed, Red Army Tatar-language newspaper "The Red Army Man"; after Civil War ed, journal "Sovetskaya literatura" and first chm, Tatar Writers' Union; dep, RSFSR Supr Sov of 1947 and 1951 convocations; *Publ:* novelettes and stories: "The Very Last" (1925); "The Lottery" (1926); "Coastal Beacons" (1929); "The Bright Path" (1930); "The First Spring" (1930); poems: "Khayat Apa" (1941); "Farida" (1944); novel "Spring Winds" (1948), etc; *Awards:* Stalin Prize (1951); *Died:* 24 Mar 1957.

NAGISHKIN, Dmitriy Dmitriyevich (1909–1961) Russian writer; CP member from 1947; *Born:* 13 Oct 1909 in Chita; *Educ:* 1928 grad electr eng trade school; *Career:* worked for newspapers in Khabarovsk, Blagoveshchensk and Chita as illustrator and journalist; *Publ:* fairy-tale *Kak orla pobedili* (How the Eagle Was Defeated) (1938); adventure novelette *Tikhaya bukhta* (The Still Bay) (1939); book *Mal'chik Chokcho* (The Boy Chokcho) (1945); *Amurskiye skazki* (Amur Tales) (1946); novel *Serdtse Bonivura* (Bonivur's Heart) (1947); book *Khrabryy Azmun* (Brave Azmun) (1949); *Skazka i zhizn'. Pis'ma o skazke* (Tales and Real Life. Letters About Tales) (1957); children's novelette *Gorod Zolotogo Petushka* (The City of the Golden Cockerel) (1959); novel *Sozvezdiye Strel'tsa* (Constellation of Sagittarius) (1962); *Died:* 11 Mar 1961 in Riga.

NAKASHIDZE, Nina Iosifovna (1872–1963)Geo children's writer; *Born:* 1 Jan 1872 in Kutaisi Province; *Educ:* 1892 grad Tbilisi

Gynecological Inst; *Career:* 1898 met Lev Tolstoy in Moscow; from 1904 contributed to children's journal "Nakaduli"; 1910–28 ed, journal "Nakaduli"; head, Children's Lit Section, Geo Writers' Union; *Publ:* story "The Breadwinner" (1902); play "Who's to Blame? " (1908); stories "What the Boy Toma Was Like," "Arishka," "The Adventures of Deviko and Temiko," etc; published her memoirs of Lev Tolstory (1954); translated into Geo Tolstoy's *Detstvo* (Childhood) and *Otrochestvo* (Adolescence); also translated Hans Andersen's fairy-tales; *Died:* 2 July 1963 in Tbilisi.

NAKHIMSON, Semyon Mikhaylovich (Party names: Pavel SALIN; MIKHAL'CHI) (1885–1918) Revolutionary; Dr of Philosophy and Econ; *Born:* 1885; *Career:* 1902–07 Bund member; then member, Soc-Democratic Party of the Kingdom of Poland and Lith and member, RSDRP; 1905 one of the leaders, Mil Council, Libava Mil Revol Org Bund; sentenced to death in absentia for preparing 1905 Aug mutiny of Libava garrison; 1907 Kovno Mil Revol Bund Org deleg at 5th (London) RSDRP Congress; 1907–11 in emigration; received his doctor's degree in Bern; worked for Bolshevik newspapers "Zvezda" and "Pravda"; 1915 in Russian Army; head, health detachment, League of Cities; 1917 court-martialed for revol propaganda; after 1917 Feb Revol member, Petrograd RSDRP(B) Comt; chm, Petrograd's 1st City Rayon Sov; member, Mil Section, Petrograd Sov; July 1917 dispatched to Riga; ed, newspaper "Okopnyy nabat"; comr, Lat riflemen; Oct 1917 member, Mil Revol Comt, sector of 12th Army; member, All-Russian Centr Exec Comt; 14 Nov 1917 elected chm, 12th Army Exec Comt of Soldiers' Dep and comr, 12th Army; 1918 mil comr, Yaroslavl' Mil District; from 2 July 1918 chm, Yaroslavl' Province Exec Comt; *Died:* 6 July 1918 killed during Yaroslavl' Revolt; buried on Leningrad's Field of Mars.

NALYOTOV, Mikhail Petrovich (1869–1938) Inventor; *Born:* 1869; *Career:* 1906 designed world's first underwater minelayer; 1912 "Krab" minelayer built to this design; designed for it a special mine which could be anchored at a given depth; designed several other inventions; during his latter years worked at Kirov Plant, Leningrad; *Died:* 1938.

NAMYOTKIN, Sergey Semyonovich (1876–1950) Organic chemist; prof from 1912; member, USSR Acad of Sci from 1939; Hon Sci and Tech Worker of RSFSR from 1947; *Born:* 3 July 1876 in Kazan'; *Educ:* 1902 grad Moscow Univ; *Career:* 1902–11 lecturer, Moscow Univ; 1911 resigned with other fac members in protest against policies of Educ Min Kasso; from 1912 prof, Moscow Higher Women's Courses; 1918–30 prof, 1919–24 rector, 2nd Moscow Univ; 1930–38 prof, Moscow Inst of Fine Chemical Technol; 1934–39 senior assoc, 1939–48 dir, Inst of Combustible Minerals, USSR Acad of Sci; from 1938 also prof, Moscow Univ; 1948–50 dir, Oil Inst, USSR Acad of Sci; did research on the theoretical chemistry of hydrocarbons and on theoretical and practical problems of oil chemistry; studied the processes of oil desulphurization, catalytic cracking of oil fractions, oxygen conversion of paraffin into alcohols and aldehydes, detergent production, motor oil and fuel additives, etc; discovered second-order camphene rearrangement which now bears his name; also did research on perfumes and chemical fertilizers; *Publ: Khimiya nefti* (Oil Chemistry) (2 vol, 1932–35); *Izbrannyye trudy* (Selected Works) (1949); *Sobraniye trudov* (Collected Works) (3 vol, 1954–55); *Awards:* two Stalin Prizes (1943 and 1949); Order of Lenin, etc; *Died:* 5 Aug 1950.

NAMSARAYEV, Khotsa Namsarayevich (1889–1959) Buryat poet, playwright and prose writer; founder of Buryat lit; CP member from 1925; *Born:* 27 Apr 1889 in vil Kizhinga, now Buryat ASSR; *Career:* in his youth worked as carpenter and joiner; 1917 taught at Verkhne-Kizhinga school; 1918–19 helped crush anti-Sov revolt in Kizhinga; 1919 began lit work; until 1928 taught at schools in Khori and Kizhinga; dep, USSR Supr Sov of 1946, 1950, 1954 and 1958 convocations; *Publ:* play "Darkness" (1919); "A Dark Life" (1921); verse "Dark Times Have Passed" (1924); stories "Death of the Orphans" (1929); "The Master and the Farmhand" (1930); novelettes: "Tserempil" (1935); "Once One Night" (1938); "Ray of Victory" (1942); "The Golden Arrow" (1944); "The Key of Happiness" (1947); novel "At Dawn" (1950), etc; *Awards:* Order of Lenin; other orders; medals; *Died:* 28 July 1959 in Ulan-Ude.

NANEYSHVILI, Viktor Ivanovich (1878–?) Party and govt official; CP member from 1903; *Born:* 1878; *Career:* Party work in Tiflis, Moscow, Voronezh, Yekaterinoslav, Lugansk and Baku; special corresp, Bolshevik newspaper "Pravda"; Mar 1917 elected member, Baku Sov of Workers' Dep; member, Bolshevik faction of this Sov; then worked in Daghestan; Sept 1918 chm, Astrakhan' Province Exec Comt, then secr, Astrakhan' Province RCP(B) Comt; July 1919 returned to Baku and engaged in underground Party work in Transcaucasia; coopted member, Caucasian Kray RCP(B) Comt; after establishment of Sov regime in Azer elected secr, Politburo and Org Bureau, CC, CP(B) Azer; Sept 1920 assigned to Party work in centr Russia along with a number of other Azer Party officials; secr, Tula City Party Comt; then worked in Dag, Rostov and Perm'; 1924 appointed secr, Kaz Kray CPSU(B) Comt; from 1931 until his death directed Trade Acad (later Acad of Food Ind); *Died:* date and place of death unknown.

NAPALKOV, Nikolay Invanovich (1868–1938) Surgeon; Dr of Med from 1900; prof from 1913; *Born:* 20 Nov 1868 in Moscow; *Educ:* 1893 grad Med Fac, Moscow Univ; *Career:* 1893–95 zemstvo physician in Voronezh and Vladimir Provinces; 1895–1903 asst to Prof P.I. D'yakonov, Chair of Topographical Anatomy and Operative Surgery, Moscow Univ; 1900 defended doctor's thesis on sutures of the heart and blood channels; 1900–13 assoc prof, Moscow Univ; 1909–14 ed, journal "Khirurgiya"; 1913–15 prof of surgery, Warsaw (after evacuation – Rostov) Univ; 1915–38 lived and worked in Rostov-on-Don, where he established his own surgical school; 1927 chm, 19th All-Union Surgeons' Congress; did research on the preservation of the functions of the blood channels after injury and on hemostasis; in latter years did research on preventive and final hemostasis in wounds of the liver and portal vein; also studied the pathology of the intestines at the pelvic floor and diseases of the intestinal valve; organized and chaired several sci soc and congresses, including the 19th Congress of Russian Surgeons; hon chm, Don Surgical Soc; wrote over 180 works; *Publ:* doctors's thesis *Shov serdtsa i krovenosnykh stvolov* (Sutures of the Heart and Blood Channels) (1900); *khirurgiya serdtsa i okoloserdechnoy sumki* (Surgery of the Heart and Pericardium) (1902); *Operativnoye lecheniye khronicheskikh plevral'nykh nagnoyeniy* (The Operative Treatment of Chronic Pleural Suppurations) (1905); coauthor, *Lektsii topograficheskoy anatomii i operativnoy khirurgii* (Lectures on Topographical Anatomy and Operative Surgery) (1908–09); coauthor, *Lecheniye ran* (The Treatment of Wounds) (1913); *K klinike mnozhestvennogo ekhinokokka* (The Clinical Aspects of Multiple Hydatid Tapeworm) (1932), etc; *Awards:* Prof Novitskiy Prize (1900); *Died:* 6 Jan 1938.

NAR-DOS (real name: OVANISYAN), Mikael Zakar'yevich (1867–1933) Arm writer; Pop Writer of Arm and Geo from 1927; Hon Writer of RSFSR from 1931; *Born:* 1 Mar 1867 in Tiflis; *Career:* from 1884 proof-reader, then secr, ed staff, newspaper "Nor dar"; 1886 first work printed; *Publ:* comedy "Honey and Flies" (1886); novelette "Anna Saroyan" (1888); novelette "He and I" (1889); series of novellas "Our District" (1894); novelette "The Slain Dove" (1898); novelette "One of the Hard Days" (1904); novel "Struggle" (1911); novel "Death" (1912); drama "The Man with Crutches" (1921); novelette "The Last of the Mohicans" (1930); unfinished novel "The New Man" (1935), etc; *Died:* 13 July 1933 in Tbilisi.

NARBUT, Vladimir Ivanovich (1888–1944) Russian poet; *Born:* 14 Apr 1888 at vil Narbutovka, Chernigov Province, son of a petty landowner; *Educ:* studied at History and Philology Fac, Petersburg Univ; *Career:* 1909 first verse printed; from 1910 contributed to Petersburg journals "Gaudeamus," "Giperborey," "Apollon", "Sovremenny mir," etc; 1912 joined "Poets' Shop" lit group, together with M.A. Zenkevich representing its left wing; his verse collection "Alleluia" (1912) was confiscated by the Tsarist censorship; after 1917 Oct Revol worked for Sov press; 1918–19 ed, newspaper "Izvestia" and journal "Sirena" in Voronezh; 1920–22 dir, Southern Bureau, Russian News Agency, Odessa; then dir, Ukr Radio and News Agency in Khar'kov; 1922 moved to Moscow; founder and dir, "Zemlya i fabrika" Publ House; ed, various journals; 1933–34, after a long period of silence, published in journals "Novyy mir" and "Krasnaya nov'" verse belonging to so-called "sci poetry" movement; arrested by State Security organs; *Publ:* verse collections: *Stikhi* (Verse) (1910); *Vereteno* (The Spindle) (1919); *Krasnoarmeyskiye stikhi* (Red Army Poetry) (1920); *Plot* (Flesh) (1920); *V ogennykh stolbakh* (In Pillars of Fire) (1920); *Stikhi o voyne* (War Verse) (1920); *Sovetskaya zemlya* (The Soviet Land) (1921); "Aleksandra Pavlovna" (1922); *Spiral* (Spiral); *Died:* 15 Nov 1944 in imprisonment; posthumously rehabilitated.

NARDOV (real name: KNIPPER), Vladimir Leonardovich (1876–1942) Opera producer and singer (tenor); teacher; brother of O. L. Knipper-Chekhova; Hon Artiste of RSFSR from 1933; CP member from 1941; *Born:* 22 June 1876 in Moscow; *Educ:* 1902 grad Law Fac, Moscow Univ; simultaneously studied singing under his mother, a prof at Moscow Philharmonic College; perfected his singing in Berlin and Dresden; *Career:* performed in various German towns; 1914 at Zimin Opera Theater; from 1918 opera producer; 1920–36 at Bolshoy Theater; from 1936 teaching work; from 1940 prof, Moscow Conservatory; *Roles:* Almaviva; Jose; Ottavio in "Don Juan"; Walter in "Tannhäuser"; the Singer in Richard Strauss' "Der Rosenkavalier," etc; directed operas: Auber's "Fra Diavolo" (1923); Rimsky-Korsakov's *Motsart i Sal'yeri* (Mozart and Salieri) (1926); Rimsky-Korsakov's *Skazaniye o nevidimom grade Kitezhe i deve Fevronii* (The Tale of the Invisible Town of Kitezh and the Maiden Fevroniya) (1935), etc; *Died:* 12 Nov 1942 in Moscow.

NAROKOV (real name: YAKUBOV), Mikhail Semyonovich (1879–1958) Actor and stage dir; Pop Artiste of RSFSR from 1937; *Born:* 14 Feb 1879; *Career:* 1896 appeared with P. A. Sokolov-Zhamson's company in Melitopol'; 1897–98 at Dyukovaya Theater, Khar'kov; 1899–1900 at Solovtsov Theater, Kiev; 1901–02 at Yavorskaya's New Theater; 1906–07 actor, Meyerkhol'd's New Drama Company; 1903–04 at Pop Center Theater, Nizhniy Novgorod; 1909–10 actor, Komissarzhevskaya Theater; 1916–18 at Sukhodol'skaya Theater, Moscow; 1918 at Korsh Theater; 1920–40 actor, Maly Theater, Moscow; *Roles:* Danton in Byukhner's *Smert' Dantona* (The Death of Danton) (1918); Cromwell in Lunacharskiy's "Oliver Cromwell"; Verrino in Schiller's "The Fiesco Conspiracy"; Peter in Shapovalenko's *Smert' Petra I* (The Death of Peter I); Krasnov in Ostrovskiy's *Grekh da beda na kogo ne zhivyot* (Bad Luck and Calamity Are Everyone's Lot) (1926); Petrygin in Leonov's "Skutarevskiy"; Chernykh in Gusev's *Slava* (Fame); de Silva in Gutskov's "Uriel' Akosta"; Dr Talonov in *Nashestviye* (Invasion), etc; also produced: *Rasteryayeva ulitsa* (Rasteryayeva Street) (1929); *Razgrom* (Rout) (1932); Mikitenko's *Solo na fleyte* (Flute Solo) (1935), etc; *Publ:* memoirs of the theater *Biografiya moyego pokoleniya* (A Biography of My Generation) (1956); *Died:* 25 June 1958.

NARIMANOV, Nariman Kerbelay Nadzhaf-ogly (1871–1925) Govt official; Azer writer; teacher and physician; CP member from 1905; *Born:* 14 Apr 1971 in Tiflis; *Educ:* 1890 grad Transcaucasian Teachers' Seminary, Gori; 1908 grad Med Fac, Novorssiysk Univ, Odessa; *Career:* from 1890 taught in vil Kizil-Adzhili, Tiflis Province; 1891 moved to Baku and taught Azer language at A. I. Pobedonostsev's private preparatory school and at Alexander III Boys' High-School; 1894 opened first genuinely public library and reading-room; 1902 enrolled in Med Fac, Novorossiysk Univ, Odessa; as a student took an active part in revol movement; 1905 returned to Baku and worked for Bolshevik "Gummet" org; contributed to newspapers "Irshad" and "Khayat," publishing articles on sociological and educ themes; sought by the Tsarist police, Feb 1909 moved from Baku to Tiflis; 1 Mar 1909 arrested and jailed in Metekhi Prison; Oct 1909 exiled to Astrakhan'; contributed to newspapers "Astrakhanskiy kray," "Burkhani-Taraggi" and "Idel"; lectured on educ reform; active in Astrakhan' Pop Univ and "Shurayi-Islam" Astrakhan' Moslem Soc; 1913 returned to Baku; 1917 chm, Soc-Democratic "Gummet" group of Baku Bolshevik org; 1919 head, Near East Dept, RSFSR Pop Comrt of For Affairs, Moscow; then RSFSR Dep Pop Comr for Nationality Affairs; 1920 chm, Azer Revol Comt; 1921 chm, Azer Council of Pop Comr; from 1922 chm, Transcaucasian Union Council; co-chm, USSR Centr Exec Comt; member, Caucasian Bureau, CC, RCP(B); member, Transcaucasian Kray RCP(B) Comt; Presidium member, CC, CP Azer; at 12th RCP(B) Congress elected cand member, CC, RCP(B); *Publ:* plays: "Ignorance" (1894); "Nadir shakh" (1899); novel "Bakhdur and Sona" (1896–1900); novelette "The Feast" (1913); "Short Tatar-Azerbaydzhani Grammar" (1899); "Teach Yourself Russian" (1899), etc; *Died:* 19 Mar 1925; buried on Moscow's Red Square.

NASEDKIN, Vasiliy Fyodorovich (1895–1940) Russian poet; CP member from 1914; *Born:* 13 Jan 1895 in vil Verovka, Ufa Province, now Bash ASSR, son of a peasant; *Educ:* 1914–15 attended lectures at Shanyavskiy Pop Univ; in 1920's studied at Bryusov Higher Lit Inst; *Career* fought in WW 1 and in Civil War; from 1922 professional writer; member, "Pereval" (The Pass) lit group; close friend of the poets S. A. Yesenin and V. Ya. Bryusov; in his earlier period strongly influenced by Yesenin; wrote several stories and memoirs about Yesenin; arrested by State Security organs; *Publ: Na vernom puti* (On the Right Track) (1927); story "Seid Rafik" (1927); memoirs *Posledniy god Yesenina* (Yesenin's Last Year) (1927); verse collections: *Tyoplyy govor* (Warm Talk) (1927); *Veter s polya* (Wind from the Field) (1931); *Stikhi. 1922–1932* (Verse. 1922–1932) (1933), etc; *Died:* 1940 in imprisonment, posthumously rehabilitated.

NASIMOVICH, Aleksandr Fyodorovich (1880–1947) Russian writer; *Born:* 25 Dec 1880 in Nizhniy Novgorod, now Gorky; *Educ:* 1903 grad Moscow Teachers' Training Inst; *Career:* 1905 first work printed; *Publ:* verse collection *Siluety* (Silhouettes) (1909); collected stories *Vecherniy put'* (Evening Journey) (1915); *Burelom* (Windfall) (1923); *Topor* (The Axe) (1927); *Grekh* (Sin) (1928); *Okolo smerti* (Near Death) (1928); essay *Buntovshchiki* (The Mutineers) (1930); novel "Talka" (1930); play *Torgovyy dom "Grynza i synov'ya"* ("Grynza and Sons" Warehouse) (1925); plays for school theaters *Obshcheye lukoshko* (The Common Basket) (1927); *Sochiniteli* (The Storytellers) (1928); *Zheleznaya doroga* (The Railroad) (1929); stories for children: *Kon'-ogon* (The Fiery Horse) (1922); *Groznyye dni* (Terrible Days) (1927); *Priklyucheniya malen'kogo Peti* (Little Petya's Adventures) (1928); "Finogenych" (1929); *Vulkanusova sila* (Vulkan's Strength) (1930); *Noch' pod MYuD* (The Eve of International Youth Day) (1931), etc; *Died:* 7 Jan 1947 in Moscow.

NASONOV, Arseniy Nikolayevich (1898–1965) Historian; Dr of History from 1944; *Born:* 27 Aug 1898 in Yevpatoriya, son of the zoologist Acad N.V. Nasonov; *Educ:* 1922 grad Fac of History and Philology, Petersburg Univ; *Career:* from 1924 worked at Numismatics Dept, Hermitage Museum; from 1935 assoc, Inst of History and Archeography, then Inst of History, USSR Acad of Sci; 1941–42 dir, Inst of History, Turkm Branch, USSR Acad of Sci; 1942–45 served in Red Army; from 1945 senior assoc, Inst of History, USSR Acad of Sci; specialized in the history of Kievan Rus, the Muscovite State in the 13th and 14th Centuries, historical geography, source research and archeography; did major research on Russian chronicles; co-ed, anthology "Problemy istochnikovedeniya"; *Publ: Mongoly i Rus'. Istoriya tatarskoy politiki na Rusi* (The Mongols and Rus. The History of Tatar Policies in Rus) (1940); *Tatarskoye igo na Rusi v osveshchenii M.N. Pokrovskogo* (Tatar Rule in Rus as Described by M.N. Pokrovskiy) (1940); ed, *Pskovskiye letopisi* (The Pskov Chronicles) (2 vol, 1942–55); *Novgorodskaya pervaya leopis' starshego i mladshego izvodov* (The First Novgorod Chronicle, Old and New Recensions) (1950); *"Russkaya zemlya" i obrazovaniye territorii Drevnerusskogo gosudarstva* ("The Russian Lands") and the Formation of the Territory of the Ancient Russian State) (1951); coauthor, *Ocherki istorii SSSR. Period feodalizma* (Studies in the History of the USSR. The Feudal Period) (1953–55); Nachal'nyye etapy kiyev-*skogo letopisaniya v svyazi s razvitiyem Drevnerusskogo gosudarstva* (The Beginnings of Chronicle-Keeping in Kiev in Relation to the Development of the Ancient Russian State) (1959); *Died:* 23 Apr 1965.

NASONOV, Dmitriy Nikolayevich (1896–1957) Histologist and cytophysiologist; prof from 1935; corresp member, USSR Acad of Sci from 1943; member, USSR Acad of Med Sci from 1945; *Born:* 10 Sept 1896 in Warsaw, son of the zoologist, Acad N.V. Nasonov; *Educ:* 1919 grad Natural Sci Dept, Fac of Physics and Mathematics, Petrograd Univ; *Career:* 1919–35 lecturer, from 1935 prof, Leningrad Univ; 1933–50 also senior assoc, All-Union Inst of Experimental Med, Leningrad; 1955–57 founder-dir, Inst of Cytology, USSR Acad of Sci; co-ed, biology section, "Bol'shaya meditsinskaya entsiklopediya" (Large Medical Encyclopedia) (2nd ed); member, ed council, journal "Arkhiv anatomii, gistologii i embriologii"; did research on laws governing the reaction of living tissues to environmental influences; explained the role of Golgi's body in cellular secretory processes; established a homologue between Golgi's body in the cells of metazoans and the contractile vacuole of protozoans; devised cell-damage theory, according to which the paranecrotic reaction of protoplasm to injurious agents results from denaturational lesions of the cell proteins; expanded this theory to explain cell excitation; also devised new phase theory of bio-electr currents and formulated the "law of self-regulation of divaricate excitation"; *Publ:* coauthor, *Reaktsiya zhivogo veshchestva na vneshniye vozdeystviya* (The Reaction of Living Matter to External Influences) (1940); *Protiv tak nazyvayemogo zakona "vsyo ili nichego" v fiziologii* (Against the So-Called "All or Nothing" Law in Physiology) (1952); *Mestnaya reaktsiya protoplazmy i rasprostranyayushcheyesya vozbuzhdeniye* (The Local

Reaction of Protoplasm and Divaricate Excitation) (1959); *Awards:* Order of the Red Banner of Labor; Stalin Prize (1943); medals; *Died:* 12 Dec 1957.

NASONOV, Nikolay Viktorovich (1855–1939) Zoologist; member, Russian (USSR) Acad of Sci from 1906; *Born:* 1 Mar 1855 in Moscow; *Educ:* 1879 grad Moscow Univ; *Career:* 1884 worked at Prof Kovalevskiy's Laboratory, Odessa; 1889–96 prof, Warsaw Univ; 1907–21 dir, Zoological Museum, Acad of Sci, Petersburg; 1921–31 dir, Laboratory of Experimental Zoology, USSR Acad of Sci; 1924–30 also dir, Sebastopol Biological Station; studied morphology, taxonomy, fauna, zoogeography, ekology and embryology of invertebrates (insects, lower crustaceans, turbellaria, etc.) and some vertebrates such as wild sheep, African ostrich, etc; studied organ regeneration in animals; 1916 sponsored foundation of Russian Acad of Sci Commission to Study Lake Baykal and Organize Baykal Biological Station (now the Baykal Limnological Station); 1911 began work on his major study *Fauna Rossii i sopredel'nykh stran* (The Fauna of Russia and Contiguous Countries) and then "Fauna SSSR" (Fauna of the USSR), 25 vol of which appeared under his editorship; published over 170 research works; *Publ: Materialy po yestestvennoy istorii murav'yov (sem'ya Formicariae) preimushchestvenno v Rossii* (Material on the Natural History of Ants (Family: Formicariae) Primarily in Russia) (1889); *K istorii razvitiya afrikanskogo strausa (Struthio camelus Z.)* (The Historical Development of the African Ostrich /Struthio camelus Z./) (3 vol, 1894–96); *Kurs entomologii. Chast' 1. Naruzhnyye pokrovy nasekomykh* (Entomology Course. Part 1. The External Casing of Insects) (1901); *Geografiya rasprostraneniya baranov starogo sveta* (The Geographical Distribution of Sheep in the Old World) (1923); "Zur Morphologie der Turbellaria rhabdocoelida des Japanischen Meeres" (1932); *Dobavochnyye obrazovaniya, razvivayushchiyesya pri vlozhenii khryashcha pod kozhu vzroslykh khvostatykh amfibiy* (Additional Formations Developing from the Subcutaneous Injection of Cartillage Into Adult Caudate Amphibia) (1941); *Died:* 10 Feb 1939.

NASTYUKOV, Aleksandr Mikhaylovich (1868–1941) Chemist; prof from 1908; *Born:* 11 Oct 1868; *Educ:* 1890 grad Moscow Univ; *Career:* 1903 discovered formolite reaction (the condensation of formaldehyde with aromatic hydrocarbons in the presence of concentrated sulfuric acid), which he used in petroleum research and to obtain new plastics; 1908–30 prof, Moscow Univ; 1914–19 developed methods of obtaining black and khaki sulfur dyes; from 1933 assoc, Moscow Inst of Chemical Technol; *Publ:* coauthor, *Primery tekhnicheskogo analiza* (Examples of Technical Analysis) (1910); coauthor, *Primery tekhnicheskikh preparatov* (Technical Samples) (1911); coauthor, *Tekhnicheskaya khimiya* (Industrial Chemistry) (1924); *Vvedeniye v kurs tekhnicheskoy khimii plasticheskikh mass* (An Introduction to a Course of Industrial Plastics Chemistry) (1934), etc; *Died:* 16 Feb 1941.

NASYRI, Gamir (1916–1959) Tatar playwright; CP member from 1944; *Born:* 3 Jan 1916; *Educ:* 1937 grad theatrical technicum; *Career:* 1932 first work printed; fought in WW 2; *Works:* comedies "Travel Permit"; "Director Tarkhanov"; plays: "Kushnarat" (1952); "Precious Minutes" (1953); "Native Village" (1956); "On the Banks of the Volga"; vaudeville "The Green Hat" (1957), etc; *Died:* 27 Dec 1959.

NASYRI, Imay (real name: NASYROV, Imametdin Nizametdinovich) (1898–1942) Bash writer; CP member from 1919; *Born:* 1898 in vil Nizhniye Susyly, now Bash ASSR; *Career:* worked for police; also worked as journalist; 1921 first work printed; deleg at 10th Party Congress; 1937 arrested by State Security organs; *Publ:* novelette "Buried Alive" (1926); collected stories "Swallows" and "Flowers, But the Wrong Ones" (1927); novelettes: "In the Compartment" (1929); "Sibay" (1930); novel "Kudey" (1936); novelette "The Conquered Slough" (1937), etc; *Died:* 1942 in imprisonment; posthumously rehabilitated.

NASYRLI, Yakub (1899–1958) Turkm poet; CP member from 1925; *Born:* 8 Nov 1899 in Baku, son of an artisan; *Educ:* studied at Lit Fac, Moscow Univ; *Career:* 1909 his family moved to Chardzhou; worked as apprentice in a shop, as boot-black and as confectioner's laborer; 1918 volunteer on Transcaspian Front; later contributed to Ashkhabad newspapers and journals; 1925 first work printed; translated into Turkm Russian classic poetry, works of Mayakovsky, S.Ya. Marshak, K.M. Simonov, Nizami, Navoi, Dzhambul, S. Vurgun, etc; *Publ:* verse "Book of Lenin" (1925); "The Eternal Beacon" (1925); collection "Poetry" (1941); collection "Kill the Enemy" (1943); poems "The Lieutenant's Son" (1941); "Courage" (1942); stories "Polina"; "Joy" (1949); collections: "To a Russian Comrade"; "The Oath"; "At the Silk-Mill"; "The Glass-Cutter"; play "Honor"; children's stories: "Dangatar"; "The Conquered Dragon," etc; *Died:* 11 Nov 1958 in Alupka (Crimea).

NATADZE, Georgiy Mikhaylovich (1892–1965) Hygienist; Dr of Med; prof from 1938; corresp member, USSR Acad of Med Sci; Hon Sci Worker of Geo SSR; *Born:* 1892; *Educ:* 1921 grad Med Fac, Kiev Univ; *Career:* 1922–38 health officer, Transcaucasian Railroad; assoc, various hygiene establishments; asst prof, then assoc prof, Chair of Gen Hygiene, Tbilisi Med Inst; 1938–65 prof and head of this chair; 1958–65 founder-head, Food Research Laboratory, Geo Min of Health; founded Centr Sanitation and Hygiene Laboratory, Transcaucasian Railroad; co-founder and dep dir, Tbilisi Food Inst; wrote some 120 works; *Publ:* textbook *Osnovy gigiyeny* (The Principles of Hygiene) (1951) (translated into Korean), etc; *Died:* 7 Feb 1965 in Tbilisi.

NATALI, Vladimir Frankovich (1890–1965) Zoologist; specialist in methods of teaching biology; Dr of Biology; member, RSFSR Acad of Pedag Sci from 1947; *Born:* 10 Sept 1890; *Educ:* 1912 grad Natural Sci Dept, Fac of Physics and Mathematics, Khar'kov Univ; *Career:* 1913 secondary-school teacher in Khar'kov; 1913–19 worked at Moscow Experimental Biology Laboratory and taught at various high-schools; 1919–Nov 1930 founder-dir, Moscow Biology Teachers' Training Station, where he also established an experimental laboratory for research on zoology and genetics; from 1919 also taught at various higher educ establishments, including Kalinin Teachers' Training Inst; 1921–48 lecturer, Pedag Fac (now Lenin State Teachers' Training Inst), 2nd Moscow Univ; also taught at Moscow Oblast Teachers' Training Inst; in the course of research on zoology and genetics studied the secondary sexual characteristics of animals and fish and the effect of external influences (especially x-rays) on fertility; wrote numerous works, including textbooks on biology teaching methods; *Publ: Biologiya. Rabochaya kniga dlya shkoly 2-oy stupeni* (Biology. A Work-Book for 2nd-Grade Schools) (1927); *Zoologiya. Dlya pedtekhnikumov* (Zoology for Teachers' Training Technicums) (1928); *Obshchaya biologiya* (General Biology) (1930); *Genetika. Nauchnyye osnovy selektsii i evolyutsionnoye ucheniye* (Genetics. The Scientific Principles of Selection and the Theory of Evolution) (1931); *Genetika. Uchebnik dlya vysshykh pedagogicheskikh uchebykh zavedeniy* (Genetics. A Textbook of Higher Teachers' Training Establishments) (1934); *Vliyaniye luchey Rentgena na plodovitost' i izmenchivost' Lebister reticulatus* (The Effect of X-Rays on the Fertility and Mutability of Lebister Reticulatus) (1940); *Razvitiye i differentsirovka gonad u karpovykh ryb v svyazi s problemoy prevrashcheniya polov* (The Development and Differentiation of the Gonads in Cyprinids in Relation to the Sex-Change Problem) (1947); *Zhivotnyye v ugolke zhivoy prirody* (Animals in School Nature-Study Clubs) (1955); *Zoologiya bezpozvonochnykh. Uchebnik dlya fakul'tetov yestestvoznaniya pedagogicheskikh institutov* (Invertebrate Zoology. A Textbook for Natural Science Faculties at Teachers' Training Institutes) (1963); *Zoologiya. Posobiye dlya uchashchikhsya 6-ogo klassa vecherney (smennoy) obshcheobrazovatel'noy shkoly* [Zoology. A 6th-Grade Studies Aid for Evening (Shift) General-Education Schools] (1965); *Died:* 6 Nov 1965.

NATISHVILI, Aleksandr Nikolayevich (1878–1959) Anatomist and Geo health service official; pioneer of functional morphology in Geo; Dr of Med from 1916; prof from 1918; member, Geo Acad of Sci from 1944; Hon Sci Worker of Geo SSR from 1940; CP member from 1945; *Born:* 1878 in Tiflis; *Educ:* 1905 grad Med Fac, Khar'kov Univ; *Career:* 1905–07 zemstvo physician in Khar'kov Province; 1907–14 asst dissector, from 1914 senior asst prof, Chair of Normal Anatomy, Khar'kov Women's Med Inst; Aug 1918–59 prof and founder-head, Med Fac (from 1930 Med Inst), Tbilisi Univ; 1920–30 founder-head, Chairs of Histology and Embryology, Med Fac, Tbilisi Univ; 1921–32 founder-head, Chair of Plastic Anatomy, Tbilisi Acad of Arts; 1932–46 founder-head, Chair of the Anatomy of Domestic Animals, Geo Zootech and Veterinary Inst; 1935–38 founder-head, Chair of Dynamic Anatomy, Fac of Physical Culture, Geo Zootech and Veterinary Inst; 1946–59 founder-dir, Inst of Experimental Morphology, Geo Acad of Sci; 1919 and 1928–29 dean, Med Fac, Tbilisi Univ; 1930–31 dep dir, Tbilisi Med Inst; 1926, 1928, 1940 and 1948 chm, Geo State Examinations Commission; 1934–35 chm, Med Educ Bd, Geo Pop Comrt of Health; 1944-45 dep dir, Tbilisi Inst of Postgrad Med Training; 1925–33 learned secr, 1933–59 member, Learned Med Council, Geo Pop Comrt of Health; 1918–19 chm, Geo Soc of Naturalist Physicians; chm, 3rd All-Geo Physicians' Congress; chm, Org Comt, 4th All-Geo Physicians' Congress; member, ed collegia, journals "Tanamedrove meditsina", "Sabchota meditsina" and "Arkhiv anatomii, gistologii i embriologii"; dep, Tbilisi City Sov; from 1925 member, Geo Centr Red Cross Comt; 1944–52 Bureau chm, Sci Workers' Section, Geo Med and Sanitary Workers' Union; Presidium member, Geo Soc for the Dissemination of Polit and Sci Knowledge; wrote over 70 works; *Publ: Kurs anatomii cheloveka dlya srednikh meditsinskikh shkol* (A Human Anatomy Course for Secondary Medical Schools) (1915); *Rukovodstvo k sektsii mozga* (A Guide to Brain Dissecting) (1916); in Geo: "Human Anatomy" (7 ed); "The Anatomy of the Human Jaws"; coauthor, "Plastic Anatomy"; "A Brain Dissection Aid" (5 ed); "The Anatomy of Domestic Animals" (3 ed); "An Anatomy and Physiology Textbook for Military Nurses," etc; *Awards:* two Orders of Lenin; Order of the Red Banner of Labor; Badge of Hon; medal "For Valiant Labor During the Great Fatherland War"; *Died:* 1959 in Tbilisi.

NATSARENUS, S.P. (1883–1938) Govt official; CP member from 1904; *Born:* 1883; *Career:* 1918 extraordinary mil comr, Murmansk-White Sea Region; then extraordinary mil comr, Petrograd Mil District; member, Revol Mil Councils, 7th, 14th and 15th Armies; July 1919 appointed mil comr, Khar'kov Mil District; 1921 RSFSR plen in Turkey; later exec govt and econ work; arrested by State Security organs; *Died:* 1938 in imprisonment.

NAUMOV, I.K. (1895–1938) Party and govt official; CP member from 1913; *Born:* 1895; *Career:* Party work in Petrograd; after 1917 Feb Revol member, Vyborg Rayon Comt and Petrograd RSDRP(B) Comt; after 1917 Oct Revol mil-polit, govt and Party work; deleg, 7th (April) All-Russian Conference and deleg, 6th RSDRP(B) Congress; 1927 for participation in "Trotskyist opposition" expelled from the Party; 1928 readmitted to the Party; 1935 for alleged anti-Party activities again expelled and arrested by State Security organs: *Died:* 1938 in imprisonment.

NAUMOV, Nikolay Aleksandrovich (1888–1959) Botanist; specialist in mycology and phytopathology; prof from 1926; corresp member, USSR Acad of Sci from 1946; *Born:* 18 Mar 1888; *Educ:* 1910 grad Petersburg Univ; *Career:* from 1910 assoc, Bureau of Mycology and Phytopathology, Main Bd of Land Exploitation and Arable Farming (now All-Union Plant Protection Inst); from 1926 prof, Leningrad Univ; from 1939 head, Fungus Taxonomy Laboratory, All-Union Plant Protection Inst; described over 200 new species of fungus, of which some 20 belonged to new genera; *Publ: Obshchiy kurs fitopatologii* (A General Course of Phytopathology) (1926); *Metody mikroskopicheskikh issledovaniy v fitopatologii* (Microscope Examination Methods in Phytopathology) (1932); *Bolezni sadovykh i ovoshchnykh rasteniy s osnovami obshchey fitopatologii* (Diseases of Orchard and Vegetable Plants and the Principles of General Phytopathology) (1937); *Metody mikologicheskikh i fitopatologicheskikh issledovaniy* (Mycological and Phytopathological Research Methods) (1937); *Rzhavchina khlebykh zlakov v SSSR* (Black Rust of Grain in the USSR) (1939); *Osnovy botanicheskoy mikrotekhniki* (The Principles of Microscope Techniques in Botany) (1954); *Opredelitel' nizshikh rasteniy* (A Classification Key of the Lower Plants) (1956), etc; *Awards:* Badge of Hon; medals; *Died:* 6 July 1959.

NAVASHIN, Sergey Gavrilovich (1857–1930) Biologist; specialist in plant cytology and embryology; prof from 1894; member, Russian (USSR) Acad of Sci from 1918; member, Ukr Acad of Sci from 1924; hon member, Swedish Acad of Sci, Uppsala, from 1917; Hon Sci Worker of RSFSR from 1929; *Born:* 14 Dec 1857 in vil Tsarevshchina, now Saratov Oblast, son of a physician; *Educ:* studied at Petersburg Med Surgical Acad; 1881 grad Moscow Univ; *Career:* from 1887 lecturer, Petersburg Univ; 1894–1915 prof, Kiev Univ; 1918–23 prof, Tbilisi Univ; 1923–29 dir, Timiryazev Biological Inst, Moscow; did research on the morphology and taxonomy of mosses and parasitic fungi; began embryological research on the fertilization process in angiosperms after detecting chalazogamy in monochlamydeous plants while studying the development of collar-rot in birch ovaries; 1898 discovered double fertilization in angiosperms; also did cytological research on the structure of cell nuclei and chromosomes; *Publ: Izbrannye trudy* (Selected Works) (vol 1, 1951), etc; *Died:* 1930.

NAYDYONOVA, Yelizaveta Ivanovna (1876–1951) Actress; Hon Artiste of RSFSR from 1937; *Born:* 1876; *Educ:* 1907 grad drama courses, Maly Theater; *Career:* from 1896 took part in amateur dramatics; 1902 acted for Hunters' Club under the pseudonym Tomskaya; 1907 made her debut with the Maly Theater; 1934–36 actress, Zakmetcha Branch of Maly Theater; 1942 appeared with front-line drama theater of Sov Navy and acted for All-Russian Theatrical Soc; *Roles:* in Ostrovskiy's plays: Negina in *Talanty i poklonniki* (Talents and Admirers); Katerina in *Groza* (The Thunderstorm); Annushka in *Na boykom meste* (A Lively Post); Poliksena in *Pravda khorosho, a schast'ye luchshe* (Truth Is Good, But Happiness Is Better); Mar'ya Andreyevna in *Bednaya nevesta* (The Poor Bride), etc; Mar'ya Antonovna and Anna Andreyevna in Gogol's *Revizor* (The Government Inspector); Dunya and Liza in Gnedich's *Kholopy* (Bondmen); Natal'ya Dmitriyevna in Griboyedov's *Gore ot uma* (Woe from Wit); Kseniya Bulychova in "Yegor Bulychov," etc; *Died:* 1951.

NAYMUSHIN, Georgiy Fyodorovich (1914–1965) Party and govt official; maj-gen; CP member from 1940; *Born:* 1914; *Educ:* grad Higher Party School, CC, CPSU; *Career:* 1935–40 secondary school teacher; 1940–46 in Sov Army; 1946–50 instructor and section head, oblast CPSU(B) comt; 1950-60 worked for CC, CPSU and State Security Comt, USSR Council of Min; 1960–63 chm, State Security Comt, Uzbek Council of Min; 1963–65 head, Krasnodar Kray State Security Bd; 1960–62 member and Bureau member, CC, CP Uzbek; 1962–63 cand Presidium member, CC, CP Uzebek; 1961–63 dep, Uzbek Supr Sov of 1959 convocation; dep, USSR Supr Sov of 1962 convocation; *Died:* Nov 1965.

NAZARBEKYAN, Arpenik Zakharovna (1893–1966) Party official; CP member from 1917; *Born:* 1893; *Career:* from 1910 in revol movement; 1917 Party work in Petrograd; 1919 worked for Polit Dept, 14th Army; then secr, Groznyy Okrug RCP(B) Comt; 1921–22 Party work in Arm; then exec work in Moscow; 1922 elected member, Arm Centr Exec Comt; from 1955 pensioner; *Died:* 18 Mar 1966.

NAZARETYAN, Amayak Markovich (1889–1938) Party official; CP member from 1905; *Born:* 1889 in Akhalkalaki; *Educ:* grad Law Fac, Petersburg Univ; *Career:* 1909 arrested for carrying out Party propaganda and placed under police surveillance; 1911 emigrated to Switzerland and continued Party work; 1913 returned to Russia and carried out Party work until Revol; after 1917 Oct Revol worked in Northern Caucasus and Transcaucasia; 1917–18 member, Caucasian Bureau, CC, RSDRP(B); also member, Transcaucasian Kray Party Comt; 1918 Terek Sov Republ Pop Comr of Labor and Soc Security; 1919–20 secr, underground Transcaucasian comt; Feb 1920 directed 1st Congress of CP Azer; late Feb 1920 elected secr, CC, CP Geo; 1922–23 worked in Moscow for CC, RCP(B) and for newspaper "Pravda"; from 1924 again in Tiflis; secr, Transcaucasian Kray RCP(B) Comt, then until 1930 head, Transcaucasian Kray Control Commission; from 1931 in Moscow with Centr Control Commission of Workers and Peasants' Inspection; then Bureau member, Sov Control Commission, USSR Council of Pop Comr; deleg at 2nd Comintern Congress and at 11th and 15th CPSU(B) Congresses; frequently elected member, USSR, Transcaucasian and Geo Centr Exec Comt; arrested by State Security organs; *Died:* 1938 in imprisonoment.

NAZAROV, Ivan Nikolayevich (1906–1957) Organic chemist; prof from 1947; member, USSR Acad of Sci from 1953; CP member from 1934 assoc, Inst of Organic Chemistry, USSR Acad of Sci; Oblast; *Educ:* 1931 grad Timiryazev Agric Acad, Moscow; *Career:* grom 1934 assoc, Inst of Organic Chemistry, USSR Acad of Sci; 1946–53 corresp member, USSR Acad of Sci; from 1947 prof, Lomonosov Inst of Fine Chemical Technol, Moscow; did research on acetylene and its derivatives; synthesized numerous vinylethyl carbinols and discovered their conversion into divinyl ketones with subsequent cyclization into cyclopentenones and heterocyclic ketones, which led to the development of the anesthetic "promedol"; developed widely-used carbinol glue; also obtained steroid compounds related to androgenous hormones; *Publ: Khimiya viniletinil-karbinolov* (The Chemistry of Venylethinyl Carbinols) (1945); *Sintez i prevrashcheniya divinilketonov* (The Synthesis and Conversions of Divinyl Ketones) (1949); *O mekhanizme gidratatsii i tsiklizatsii diyeninov* (The Hydration and Cyclation Mechanism of Dienines) (1951); coauthor, *Uspekhi organicheskogo sinteza na osnove atsetilena* (Progress in Acetylene-Base Organic Synthesis) (1955); *Awards:* two Stalin Prizes (1942 and 1946); *Died:* 30 July 1957.

NAZHIVIN, Ivan Fyodorovich (1874–1940) Russian writer; *Born:* 25 Aug 1874 in Moscow, son of a peasant timber merchant; *Career:* early 1890's first work published; supported Stolypin's agrarian reforms; fought for Whites in Civil War; worked for

"Osvaga" Information Agency; from 1920 lived abroad; *Publ:* stories and essays: *Rodnyye kartinki* (Native Pictures) (1900); *Ubogaya Rus'* (Poor Rus) (1901); *Pered rassvetom* (Before Dawn) (1902); *Deshyovyye lyudi* (Cheap People) and *Sredi mogil* (Among the Graves) (1903); *U dverey zhizni* (At the Doors of Life) (1904); *V sumasshedshem dome* (In The Madhouse) (1905); novel "Mene, Tekel, Upharsin" (1907); story "Kikimora" (1917); *Zapiski o revolyutsii* (Notes on the Revolution) (1921); *Nakanune. Iz moikh zapisok* (On the Eve. From My Notes) (1923); novels: "Rasputin" (1923); *Sobach'ya respublika* (The Dogs Republic) (1935); *Glagolyut styagi* (The Banners Speak); *Bes, tvoryashchiy mechtu* (The Demon Who Made a Dream); *Yevangeliye ot Fomy* (The Gospel According to Thomas); *Iudey* (The Israelite), etc; *Died:* 5 Apr 1940 in Brussels.

NAZRULLAYEV, Lutfulla (1903–1962) Uzbek actor; Pop Artiste of Uzbek SSR from 1945; *Born:* 15 July 1903; *Educ:* 1927 grad Kazan' Theater Technicum; studied at Uzbek Studio, Moscow; *Career:* took part in amateur dramatics; 1922–28 actor, Bukhara Theater; from 1928 actor, Khamza Theater; *Roles:* Madazim in "Two Communists" (1929); Polonius in "Hamlet" (1935); Kholmat in Khamza's "The Bey and the Farmhand" (1939); Dzhura in Sultanov's "Flight of the Eagle" (1942); Ladabay in Uygun's "Novbakhor" (1949); Khuseyn in Uygun and Sultanov's "Alisher Navoi" (1949); the Father Superior of the monastery in Wang Shi-fu's "The Spilled Cup" (1957); Kasymaka in Uygun's "Khurriyat" (1958), etc; *Awards:* Stalin Prize (1949); *Died:* 27 Dec 1962.

NEBOL'SIN, Vasiliy Vasil'yevich (1898–1958) Conductor; music teacher; Pop Artiste of RSFSR from 1955; *Born:* 30 May 1898 in Khar'kov; *Educ:* 1920 grad violin and composition classes, Moscow Philharmonic College; *Career:* from 1918 conductor; from 1920 choirmaster; from 1922 conductor, Bolshoy Theater; 1940–45 prof, Moscow Conservatory; *Works:* conducted operas: "Rusalka" (1937); Wagner's "Die Walkuere" (1940); "Khovanshchina" (1941); *Mayskaya noch'* (May Night) (1947); "Mazepa" (1949); "Carmen" (1953, etc; also conducted many symphonies; composed symphonic and chamber works; *Awards:* Stalin Prize (1950); *Died:* 29 Oct 1958 in Moscow.

NECHAYEV, Aleksandr Afanas'yevich (1845–1922) Therapist and hospital organizer; Dr of Med from 1882; hon prof from 1920; *Born:* 1845; *Educ:* 1870 grad Petersburg Med Surgical Acad; *Career:* from 1870 intern, S.P. Botkin's Clinic; 1882 defended doctor's thesis on the inhibitory effect of atropine, morphium and chloral hydrate on the secretion of gastric juices and the excitation of the sensory nerves; 1883–85 senior intern, Alexandrine (now Botkin) Barrack Hospital; 1885–90 chief physician, Obukh Women's Hospital; 1890–1922 chief physician, Obukh Men's Hospital; 9 Jan 1905 ordered the staff of the Obukh Hospital to treat demonstrators injured in the "Bloody Sunday" massacre; made major contribution to the org and development of hospitals in Petersburg, notably the Obukh Hospital, which he directed for 37 years, making it a major center of postgrad med training for physicians from all parts of Russia; introduced the system of asst professorships in hospitals; after 1917 Oct Revol worked on various commissions of Petrograd Health Dept; did research on subjects on the borderline between therapy and surgery and on the treatment of infectious diseases involving damage to the intestinal tract; together with A.A. Tropyanov performed first successful operation in Russia for a ruptured typhoid appendix; from 1921 co-founder and first chm, Botkin Therapeutic Soc; 1922 chm, Congress of Russian Therapists; *Publ:* doctor's thesis *Ob ugnetayushchem vliyanii na otdeleniye zheludochnogo soka atropina, morfiya i khloral-gidrata i razdrazheniya chuvstvitel'nykh nervov* (The Inhibitory Effect of Atropine, Morphium and Chloral Hydrate on the Secretion of Gastric Jiuces and the Excitation of the Sensory Nerves) (1882); *Sluchay perforativnogo petitonita v techeniye bryushnogo tifa* (A Case of Perforated Peritonitis During Typhoid) (1894), etc; *Died:* 1922 in Petrograd.

NECHAYEV, Aleksandr Petrovich (1870–1948) Psychologist; pioneer of experimental pedag psychology in pre-Revol Russia; *Born:* 5 Nov 1870, son o a teacher; *Educ:* grad Petersburg Univ; *Career:* established and directed several psychology laboratories; 1901 founded first Russian laboratory of experimental psychology in Petersburg; 1906–16 organized five All-Russian conferences on psychology and experimental pedag; did research on memory and individual differences in memory power; on the basis of quantitative laboratory data attempted to correlate pedag and psychology; failed in this undertaking because of the then inadequate state of empirical psychology and divided his pupils into critics and supporters; in the face of heavy criticism gained some support for his ideas at the 1906 and 1909 All-Russian Congresses on Pedag Psychology and the 1910, 1913 and 1916 Congresses on Experimental Pedag; expounded his views in his own publ *Knizhki pedagogicheskoy psikhologii* (Booklets in Pedagogic Psychology) (11 issues, 1905–10) and *Yezhegodnik eksperimental'noy pedagogiki* (Yearbook of Experimental Pedagogics) (1909–14); after 1917 Oct Revol worked at various sci establishments in Moscow; Jan 1924 criticized at 2nd Psychoneurological Congress for refusing to accept Marxist philosophy as a basis of psychology and for defending empirical principles; his arguments in favor of the latter were similar to those of Chelpanov; spent last years of life in exile, working at Semipalatinsk Teachers' Training Inst; *Publ: Assotsiatsiya skhodstva* (Association by Similarity) (1905); *Ocherk psikhologii dlya vospitateley i uchiteley* (An Outline of Psychology for Educators and Teachers) (1915); *Trudy po eksperimental'no-pedagogicheskoy psikhologii* (Works on Experimental Pedagogical Psychology); *Uchebnik psikhologii* (A Psychology Textbook); *Rukovodstvo k eksperimentalno-psikhologicheskomu issledovaniyu detey* (A Guide to the Experimental Psychological Study of Children) (1925); *Pamyat' cheleveka i yeyo vospitaniye* (The Human Memory and Its Training) (1930); *Died:* 6 Sept 1948.

NECHAYEV, Yegor Yefimovich (1859–1925) Russian poet; CP member from 1925; *Born:* 13 Apr 1859 in vil Kharitonov, Tver Province; *Career:* from age 9 to age 57 worked at glass factories; began writing in 1880's; from 1885 lived in Moscow; member, "Kuznitsa" (The Smithy) lit assoc; member, All-Russian Assoc of Proletarian Writers; co-founder, Surikov Lit and Music Circle; also wrote under pseudonyms "Uncle Nil," "Someone," "Ya. Dalyokiy," etc; 1891 first work printed; translated Ukr poetry into Russian; *Publ:* verse: "A Winter Picture" (1891); "My Shrine"; "Voice of the Soul"; "Forwards"; verse collections: *Trudovyye pesni* (Labor Songs) (1911); *Vecherniye pesni* (Evening Songs) (1913); *Iz pesen starogo rabochego* (From an Old Worker's Songs) (1922); *Izbrannoye* (Selected Works) (1955); novelettes and stories *Mucheniki guty* (Martyrs of the Glass Furnace), *Bubliki* (Doughnuts), *Glaza* (Eyes), etc; *Died:* 23 Nov 1925 at Pavlovskiy Posad, near Moscow.

NEDELIN, Mitrofan Ivanovich (1902–1960) Mil commander; chief marshal of artillery from 1959; CP member from 1924; *Born:* 9 Nov 1902 in Borisoglebsk, Voronezh Province, son of an office worker; *Educ:* 1923 completed mil polit courses on Turkestani Front; 1929 and 1934 completed Advanced Artillery Commanders Courses; 1941 completed tech tactics courses at Dzerzhinskiy Artillery Acad; *Career:* from 1920 in Red Army; fought in Civil War; 1920–29 polit work in Red Army; 1929–41 commanded artillery battery, then troop; chief of staff, then commander of artillery regt; chief of artillery, infantry div; 1941–43 commanded artillery brigades, then corps; chief of artillery, army; 1943–45 artillery commander, Southwestern Front (20 Oct 1943 renamed 3rd Ukr Front); 1945–48 artillery commander, Southern Forces Group and artillery chief of staff, Sov Army; 1948–50 chief, Main Artillery Bd; 1950–55 artillery commander, Sov Army; from 1952 also USSR Dep War Min (from 1953 Min of Defense); from 1955 USSR Dep Min of Defense; Dec 1959–Oct 1960 first commander, Soviet Rocket Forces and Dep Min of Defense; 1952–60 cand member, CC, CPSU; dep, USSR Supr Sov of 1954 and 1958 convocations; *Awards:* Hero of Sov Union (1945); five Orders of Lenin; four Orders of the Red Star; Order of Suvorov; Order of Bogdan Khmel'nitskiy; Order of the Fatherland War; Badge of Hon; medals; *Died:* 24 Oct 1960 killed in plane crash; buried on Moscow's Red Square.

NEDOGONOV, Aleksey Ivanovich (1914–1948) Russian poet; CP member from 1942; *Born:* 19 Oct 1914 in Grushevsk (now Shakhty), Rostov Oblast; *Educ:* 1935–39 studied at Gorky Lit Inst; *Career:* 1934 first work printed; 1939–46 in Sov Army; fought in WW 2; *Publ:* verse: *Pered grozoy* (Before the Storm); *Doroĝa moyey zemli* (My Life's Path); "Semyon Vdobychenko"; *Ballada o zheleze* (The Ballad of Iron); *Soldatskiy rekviyem* (Soldiers' Requiem); *Vesna na staroy granitse* (Spring on the Old Border) (1944); *Bashmaki* (Shoes) (1945); *Flag nad sel'sovetom* (The Flag Over the Village Soviet) (1947); verse collections: *Prostyye lyudi* (Simple People) (1948); *Izbrannoye* (Selected Verse) (1949); *Lirika* (Lyric Verse) (1964), etc; *Awards:* Stalin Prize (1948); *Died:* 13 Mar 1948 in Moscow.

NEDOLIN (real name: MARKELOV), Ivan Petrovich (1892–1947) Russian writer; *Born:* 17 Oct 1892 in vil Burunovo, Sterlitamak

Uyezd, Ufa Province, son of a worker; *Career:* type-setter; fought in WW 1; during Civil War commanded a partisan detachment in Blyukher's army; worked for newspaper "Krasnaya Bashkiriya"; deleg at 1st All-Union Writers' Congress; 1911 first work printed; 1937 arrested by State Security organs; *Publ:* collected sketches *Reyd Blyukhera* (Blyukher's Raid) (1932); novelette *Pereval* (The Pass) (1934); collected stories *Podvig* (The Feat) (1936), etc; *Died:* 5 Mar 1947 in imprisonment; posthumously rehabilitated.

NEKHODA, Ivan Ivanovich (1910–1963) Ukr poet; CP member from 1942; *Born:* 11 June 1910 in vil Alekseyvka, now Khar'kov Oblast; *Educ:* 1932 grad Khar'kov Inst of Public Educ; 1940 grad Scriptwriting Fac, Moscow Inst of Cinematography; *Career:* worked for Kiev Pioneer newspaper "Na smenu"; 1925 first work published; fought in WW 2 and was seriously wounded; *Publ:* verse tales "Song of Joy" (1935); collected verse: "The Start of a Song" (1937); "Dnieper Country" (1939); "My Booklet" (1940); "I Go to War" (1942); "Forest Dwellings" (1944); "The Road to a Holiday" (1945); "Remembrance of the French Land" (1958); novel in verse "Who Sows the Wind" (1959); "To Thee, My Beloved" (1960), etc; *Died:* 17 Oct 1963 in Kiev.

NEKRASHEVICH, Stepan (1889–1937) Bel linguist; member, Bel Acad of Sci from 1928; *Born:* 20 Dec 1889 in vil Danilovka, now Mogilyov Oblast; *Educ:* grad Ponevezhskaya Teachers' Seminary; grad Vilnius Teachers' Training Inst; *Career:* until 1914 teacher in Vilnius Province; from 1914 in Russian Army on Rumanian Front; 1917-20 in Odessa; from 1921 in Minsk; inspector, Bel Pop Comrt of Educ and head of latter's Sci Terminology Commission; 1922–25 chm, Inst of Bel Culture and head of its Commission to Compile a Dictionary of Spoken Belorussian; 1925–27 chm, Language and Lit Dept, and chm, Dictionary Commission, Inst of Bel Culture; 1927–28 chm, Humanities Dept and head, Chair of Spoken Bel, Inst of Bel Culture; from 1928 vice-pres, Bel Acad of Sci; member, Bel Centr Exec Comt; 1926 attended Acad Conference on the Reform of the Bel Orthography and Alphabet, Minsk; summer 1930 arrested by NKVD; Dec 1930 expelled from Bel Acad of Sci; *Publ:* coauthor, *Belorussko-russkiy slovar'* (A Belorussian-Russian Dictionary) (1926); coauthor, *Russko-belorusskiy slovar'* (A Russian-Belorussian Dictionary) (1928); "The Extension of A-Modulation to Foreign Words"; "The Orthography of Disputed Verb Forms"; "Characteristics of Belorussian Dialects of the Paritsskiy Rayon; "The Language of Kas'yan Rimlyanin the Hermit's Book 'The Monasterial Charter'"; *Died:* 20 Dec 1937 in imprisonment; posthumously rehabilitated.

NEKRASOV, Aleksandr Ivanovich (1883–1957) Mech eng; prof; member, USSR Acad of Sci from 1946; Hon Sci and Tech Worker of RSFSR from 1947; *Born:* 21 Nov 1883 in Moscow; *Educ:* 1906 grad Moscow Univ; *Career:* after grad did postgrad work at Moscow Univ and taught at various higher educ establishments in Moscow; 1930–38 dep dir, Centr Aerohydrodynamics Inst; 1932–46 corresp member, USSR Acad of Sci; from 1937 also prof, Moscow Univ; from 1945 head. Dept of Aerohydromech, Inst of Mech, USSR Acad of Sci; devised new methods of studying steady waves of finite amplitude on the surface of a heavy incompressible liquid; developed basic elements of a non-linear theory of steady wave motion in liquids; solved a number of problems concerning jet flow around a given curvilinear profile in compressible and incompressible liquids; devised new method for determining gas flow on plane contours; also did research on wing flutter and developed non-linear integral equations with a symmetrical core; *Publ: O preryvnom techenii zhidkosti v dvukh izmereniyakh vokrug prepyatstviya v forme dugi kruga* (The Interrupted Flow of a Liquid in Two Dimensions Around an Obstacle in the Form of an Arc of a Circle) (1922); *Diffuziya vikhrya* (Vortex Diffusion) (1931); *Teoriya krana v nestatsionarnom potoke* (The Theory of a Faucet in a Non-Stationary Flow) (1947); *Tochnaya teoriya woln ustanovivshegosya vida na poverkhnosti tyazhyoloy zhidkosti* (A Precise Theory of Steady Waves of the Surface of a Heavy Liquid) (1951), etc; *Awards:* Order of Lenin; Order of the Red Banner of Labor; Stalin Prize (1952); *Died:* 21 May 1957.

NEKRASOV, Vladimir Moiseyevich (1886–1942) Russian writer; CP member from 1940; *Born:* 15 July 1886 in Moscow; *Career:* 1906 printed first work under the pseudonyms of V. Volzhenin, N.Ye. Krasov, etc; in journals "Satirikon" and "Budil'nik"; after 1917 Oct Revol contributed to journals "Begemot," "Smekhach" and "Revizor"; during WW 2 worked in besieged Leningrad; wrote satyrical pieces, feuilletons and pamphlets; *Publ:* collections of satyrical stories *V tochku* (To the Point) (1926); *Beshenaya sobaka* (The Mad Dog) (1927); *Poshchyochina* (The Slap) (1928); *Portretnoye skhodstvo* (Portrait Likeness) (1929); plays on Sov vil life; song lyrics "Fishing by the River", "Oh, Heart, Oh, Girlish Heart," etc; *Died:* 27 Feb 1942 in Yaroslavl.

NEKRASOVA, Kseniya Aleksandrovna (1912–1958) Russian poetess; *Born:* 1912 in vil Irbitskiye Vershiny; Yekaterinburg Province; *Educ:* 1938–41 studied at Gorky Lit Inst; *Publ:* verse *Ukrainka* (The Ukrainian Woman) (1937); *Devushka moyego vremeni* (A Girl of My Time) (1937); *Otdykh* (Rest) (1937); verse collections: *Noch' na bashtane* (Night at the Melonfield) (1955); *A zemlya nasha prekrasna!* (But Our Land Is Beautiful!) (1958), etc; *Died:* 17 Feb 1958 in Moscow.

NEKRASOVA, Ol'ga Vladimirovna (1868–1948) Ballet dancer, choreographer and teacher; *Born:* 20 July 1868; *Educ:* 1886 grad Moscow Ballett College; *Career:* 1886–1924 at Bolshoy Theater; 1924–32 ballet dancer and ballet-master, Children's Ballet Theater, Moscow; from 1918 also taught ballet; 1932–41 founded and taught at School of Stage Dancing and "Dance Island" Choreographic Theater at Moscow's Centr Park of Culture and Rest; one of the eminent methodologists of choreographic educ; *Roles:* the Queen in *Lebedinoye ozero* (Swan Lake); the Countess in "Raymonda"; the Queen in *Spyashchaya krasavitsa* (Sleeping Beauty); the Old Woman in Minkus' *Zolotaya rybka* (The Golden Fish); the Innkeeper in "Don Quixote"; the Mother in "Giselle," etc; *Awards:* Hero of Labor (1922); *Died:* 30 July 1948.

NELEPP, Georgiy Mikhaylovich (1904–1957) Opera singer (lyric dramatic tenor); Pop Artiste of USSR from 1951; CP member from 1940; *Born:* 7 Apr 1904 in vil Bobruyki, Chernigov Province; *Educ:* 1930 grad Leningrad Conservatory; *Career:* 1929–44 soloist, Kirov Opera and Ballet Theater, Leningrad; from 1944 soloist, Bolshoy Theater, Moscow; from 1939 Hon Artiste of RSFSR; *Roles:* Yuriy in Tchaikovsky's *Charodeyka* (The Sorceress); Jenik in "The Bartered Bride"; Sadko in Rimsky-Korsakov's "Sadko"; German and Vakula in Tchaikovsky's *Pikovaya dama* (The Queen of Spades) and *Cherevichki* (The Red Shoes); the Pretender in Moussorgsky's "Boris Godunov"; Gvidon in Rimsky-Korsakov's *Skazka o tsare Saltane* (The Tale of Tsar Saltan); Matyushenko in Chishko's *Bronenosets Potyomkin* (The Battleship Potyomkin); Chapayev in Pashchenko's *Chyornyy yar* (Black Bank); Kakhovskiy in Shaporin's *Dekabristy* (The Decembrists); Jose in Bizet's "Carmen," etc; *Awards:* two Orders of the Red Banner of Labor; Badge of Hon; three Stalin Prizes (1942, 1949 and 1950); *Died:* 18 June 1957 in Moscow.

NELIDOV, Anatoliy Pavlovich (1979–1949) Actor; Hon Artiste of RSFSR from 1940; *Born:* 1879; *Educ:* 1900–03 attended drama courses at Moscow Theatrical College and Musical Drama College of Moscow Philharmonic Soc; *Career:* 1903–04 actor, Meyerhold's New Drama Theater, Kherson; 1905–09 actor, Komissarzhevskaya Theater, Petersburg; 1909–11 with Nikulin's Company in Tiflis; from 1911 actor, Nezlobin Theater, Moscow; in 1920's actor, Moscow Theater of the Revol; 1924–26, 1929–41 and from 1946 actor, Leningrad Acad Drama Theater; also did film work; *Roles:* Prozorov in *Tri sestry* (The Three Sisters); Bessmenov in *Meshchane* (The Philistines); Nikita in *Vlast' t'my* (The Power of Darkness); Zhurden in *Meshchanin vo dvoryanstve* (A Bourgeois Among the Nobility); Khynov in *Goryacheye serdtse* (An Ardent Heart); Kalugin in Belyayev's "Psisha"; Bul'mering in Fayko's *Ozero Lyul'* (Lake Lyul); Muromskiy in Sukhovo-Kobylin's *Delo* (The Case); Lenchitskiy in Romashov's *Boytsy* (The Warriors); Drobnyy in Afinogenov's *Chudak* (The Crank); Zakhar Bardin in *Vragi* (Enemies), etc; *Died:* 1949.

NEMANOV, N.G. (1889–1941) Party and govt official; CP member from 1918; *Born:* 1889; *Career:* 1905–18 member, Jewish Socialist Workers' Party; from 1918 Party and admin work in Gomel', Odessa, Sverdlovsk and Moscow; Gomel' Party org deleg at 11th RCP(B) Congress; from 1929 econ work; chm, Sakhalin Joint-Stock Company; head, All-Union Timber Ind Bd, Moscow; 1920 and 1923 sided with Trotskyism and deviated from CC, RCP(B) line; arrested by State Security organs; *Died:* 1941 in imprisonment.

NEMANSKIY, Yanka (real name: PETROVICH, Ivan Andreyevich) (1890–1940) Bel writer; member, Bel Acad of Sci from 1928; member, Bel Writers' Union from 1934; CP member; *Born:* 31 Mar 1890 in vil Shchorsy, Grodno Oblast; *Educ:* grad Nesvizh Teachers' Seminary; until 1916 studied at Petersburg Univ; *Career:* from 1916 with Tsarist Army at the front; 1918 worked for newspaper "Dzyannitsa," organ of Bel Nat Comrt, RSFSR Council of Pop Comr; 1919–22 in Red Army; in 1920's worked for Inst of

Bel Culture, then Bel Acad of Sci; from 1929 learned secr, Bel Acad of Sci; in 1930's dep chm, Bel Gosplan; simultaneously worked for Bel Acad of Sci; 1920 first work published; 1937 arrested by State Security organs; *Publ:* collected stories *Apavyadanni* (Stories) (1925) and *Na zlome* (The Turning-Point) (1928); novel *Drapezhniki* (Predators) (1928–30), etc; *Died:* 19 Dec 1940 in imprisonment; posthumously rehabilitated.

NEMCHINOV, Vasiliy Sergeyevich (1894–1964) Economist and statistician; member, USSR Acad of Sci from 1946; member, All-Union Lenin Acad of Agric Sci from 1948; member, Bel Acad of Sci from 1940; CP member form 1940; *Born:* 15 Jan 1894; *Educ:* 1917 grad Moscow Business Inst; *Career:* until 1926 directed collation of statistics in Chelyabinsk and Sverdlovsk; 1926–35 worked for centr Sov statistical organs; 1928–40 head, Chair of Statistics, 1940–48 dir, Moscow's Timiryazev Agric Acad; 1953–62 Presidium member, USSR Acad of Sci; 1946–63 chm, Council for the Study of Production Resources, USSR Acad of Sci; from 1947 prof, Chair of Polit Econ, Acad of Soc Sci, CC, CPSU; specialist in agric econ, agrarian relations and statistics; *Publ: Statisticheskoye izucheniye klassovogo rassloyeniya sovetskoy derevni* (Statistical Study of the Class Stratification of the Soviet Village) (1926); *Opyt klassifikatsii krest'yanskikh khozyaystv. Struktura khlebnogo proizvodstva* (Practical Classification of Peasant Farms. The Structure of Grain Production) (1928); textbook *Sel'skokhozyaystvennaya statistika s osnovami obshchey teorii* (Agricultural Statistics with the Principles of General Theory) (1945); *O kriteriyakh razmeshcheniya kul'tur i otrasley zhivotnovodstva* (Criteria for Siting Crops and Branches of Animal Husbandry) (1947); *Osobennosti razvitiya proizvoditel'nykh sil sel'skogo khozyastva* (Features in the Development of Agricultural Production Resources) (1953), etc; *Awards:* three Orders of Lenin; Stalin Prize (1946); Lenin Prize (1965); other orders; *Died:* 5 Nov 1964.

NEMENOV, Mikhail Isayevich (1880–1950) Roentgenologist; Dr of Med from 1916; Hon Sci Worker of RSFSR from 1933; CP member from 1940; *Born:* 28 Jan 1880; *Educ:* 1904 grad Med Fac, Berlin Univ; *Career:* 1907–18 worked at Surgical Clinic, Petersburg (Petrograd) Women's Med Inst; 1913–50 founder-chm, Russian Soc of Roentgenologists and Radiologists; 1916 defended doctor's thesis on the effect of x-ray irradiation of the testicles on the prostate; 1918–50 founder-dir, State Roentgenological and Radiological Inst, Petrograd (Leningrad); 1919–50 founder-ed, journal "Vestnik rentgenologii i radiologii"; from 1930 also head, Chair of Roentgenology, Leningrad Mil Med Acad; supervised development of first Sov field x-ray unit; established that epithelial tumors are more sensitive to radiation than tumors of ectodermal origin and that the greatest resistance to radiation is displayed by entodermal tumors; made roentgenographic study of several renal and ureteric anomalies; devised a pneumoperitoneal method of diagnosing hydatid tapeworm in the abdominal cavity and aneurism of the abdominal aorta; described symptoms permitting differential diagnosis of hydatid tapeworm and metastasis in the lungs; refuted the theory of the insensitivity of nerve cells to x-rays; in the course of research on the functions of the nerve cells by the conditioned reflex method, established that x-ray irradiation of a dog's head reduces conditioned-reflex activity in the cerebral cortex; also demonstrated that x-rays affect the centers of the vegetative nervous system; classified a group of malignant tumors with an embryonal structure which he named "embryocytomas"; hon member, Austrian and Italian Assoc of Roentgenologists; corresp member, Bologna Univ Sci Assoc; member, ed collegia, various for med journals; wrote over 200 works; *Publ:* doctor's thesis *O vliyanii rentgenizatsii yaichek na predstatel'nuyu zhelezu* (The Effect of X-Ray Irradiation of the Texticles on the Prostate) (1916); *Rentgenoterapiya* (X-Ray Therapy) (1920); *Rentgenologiya* (Roentgenology) (1926–36); *Rentgenoterapiya cherez vozdeystviye na nervnuyu sistemu* (X-Ray Therapy Via the Nervous System) (1950); *Awards:* Order of the Red Banner of Labor (1921); three other oders; medals; *Died:* 1950.

NEMILOV, Vladimir Aleksandrovich (1891–1950) Chemist and metallographer; *Born:* 11 July 1891; *Educ:* 1917 grad Petrograd Polytech Inst; *Career:* from 1917 eng, "Northern Cable" Plant; from 1926 assoc, Platinum Inst, USSR Acad of Sci; from 1936 prof, Moscow Univ; from 1934 founder and head, Laboratory of Precious Metal Alloys, Kurnakov Inst of Gen and Inorganic Chemistry, USSR Acad of Sci; studied duplex and triplex metallic systems, particularly alloys of platinum and palladium; discovered new chemical compounds of precious metals with other metals and traced changes in the physical properties of triplex systems depending on their composition; did research on solid metal solutions; *Publ: Obshchaya metallografiya* (General Metallography) (1947); *Awards:* Order of the Red Banner of Labor; Stalin Prize (1948); *Died:* 8 Feb 1950.

NEMIROVA–RAL'F (nee NEMIROVA), Anastasiya Antonovna (1849–1929) Actress; Hon Artiste of RSFSR from 1923; *Born:* 1849; *Career:* in late 1860's began stage work in Nizhniy Novgorod; performed in Vladimir, Nizhniy Novgorod, Kazan', Samara, Khar'kov, Kiev, Odessa, Voronezh, Saratov and Moscow; 1880–81 at Brenko's Pushkin Theater; 1890–91 at Goreva Theater and in Petersburg suburban theaters (in Pavlovsk and Oranienbaum); 1900–29 at Alexandrine Theater; *Roles:* Katerina in *Groza* (The Storm); Tugina in *Poslednyaya zhertva* (The Last Victim); Mar'itsa in Averkiyev's *Kashirskaya starina* (Kashir's Past); Maria Stuart; Margarite Gautier in Dumas-fils' "La Dame aux Camélias," etc; *Died:* 1929.

NEMIROVICH–DANCHENKO, Vasiliy Ivanovich (1845–1936) Russian writer; brother of Vladimir Ivanovich Nemirovich-Danchenko; *Born:* 6 Jan 1845 in Tiflis, son of a Russian officer; *Educ:* studied in Cadet Corps; *Career:* spent his childhood in the Caucasus, living with his father under campaign conditions; toured Russia and much of Europe; later described his travels in numerous fiction works and ethnographical studies; 1877–78 war corresp during Russo-Turkish War; 1904–05 war corresp during Russo-Japanese war; 1914–18 war corresp during WW 1; wrote many novels about the Caucasian and Russo-Turkish War; also wrote stories, novels, collected verse (1882) and his memoirs of Nekrasov; from 1921 lived in Czechoslovakia; *Publ:* over 250 books; *God voyny* (A Year of War) (3 vol, 1872-79;); essays: *Solovki* (1874); *Ocherki Ispanii* (An Outline of Spain) (1889); *Pod afrikanskim nebom* (Under the African Sky) (1896); *Sobraniye sochineniy* (Collected Works) (17 vol, 1910–15); *Novoye sobraniye sochineniy* (New Collected Works) (50 vol, 1916); memoirs *Na kladbishchakh* (In Cemeteries) (1921), etc; *Died:* 8 Sept 1936 in Prague.

NEMIROVICH–DANCHENKO, Vladimir Ivanovich (1858–1943) Impressario, stage dir, writer and playwright; for many years dir, Moscow Acad Arts Theater; Pop Artiste of USSR from 1936; *Born:* 23 Dec 1858 in Ozurgeti, now Makharadze, Geo, son of an officer; *Educ:* 1876–79 studied at Physics and Mathematics Fac, Moscow Univ; *Career:* 1877–98 theater critic and reviewer; until 1901 also writer and playwright; 1891–1901 taught at Drama Dept, Musical Drama College, Moscow Philharmonic Soc; 1898, together with Stanislavskiy, founded Intelligible Arts Theater in Moscow, subsequently reorganized as Moscow Acad Arts Theater; until 1943 artistic mang and dir, above theater; like Stanislavskiy, contributed greatly to development of Russian theater; 1919 founded at Moscow Arts Theater a Music Studio (1926–41 Nemirovich-Danchenko Musical Theater; from 1941 Stanislavskiy and Nemirovich-Danchenko Musical Theater), which was highly experimental and avant-garde; sponsored establishment of Studio School, now named after him, at Moscow Acad Arts Theater; from 1939 first chm, Stalin Prize Comt (for Lit and Art); *Publ:* novels: *Mgla* (Murk) (1896); *Peklo* (Hell) (1898); plays: *Poslednyaya volya* (The Last Will) (1888); *Novoye delo* (A New Case) (1890); *Zoloto* (Gold) (1895); *Tsena zhizni* (The Prize of Life) (1896); *V mechtakh* (In Dreams) (1901); many stories and novelettes; memoirs *Iz proshlogo* (From the Past) (1938); *Teatral'noye naslediye* (Theater Legacy) (2 vol, 1952–54); *P'yesy* (Plays) (1962); *Productions:* Shakespeare's "Julius Caesar" (1903); Chekhov's *Vishnyovyy sad* (The Cherry Orchard) (1904); Griboyedov's *Gore ot uma* (Woe from Wit) (1906); Pushkin's "Boris Godunov" (1907); Gogol's *Revizor* (The Government Inspector) (1908); Ostrovskiy's *Na vsyakogo mudretsa dovol'no prostoty* (There's a Simpleton in Every Sage) (1910); Lev Tolstoy's *Zhivoy trup* (The Living Corpse) (1911); Turgenev's *Nakhlebnik* (The Sponger) (1912); Saltykov-Shchedrin's *Smert' Pazukhina* (The Death of Pazukhin) (1914); Pushkin's *Kamennyy gost'* (The Stone Guest) (1915); Merezhkovskiy's *Budet radost'* (There Shall Be Joy) (1916); Trenyov's *Pugachyovshchina* (The Pugachev Revolt) (1925); Lev Tolstoy's *Voskreseniye* (Resurrection) (1930); Trenyov's "Lyubov' Yarovaya" (1936); Lev Tolstoy's "AnnaKarenina" (1937); Chekhov's *Tri sestry* (The Three Sisters) (1942); Pogodin's *Kremlyovskiye kuranty* (Kremlin Chimes) (1942), etc; *Awards:* Order of Lenin; Order of the Red Banner of Labor; two Stalin Prizes (1942 and 1943); *Died:* 25 Apr 1943 in Moscow.

NEMITTS, Aleksandr Vasil'yevich (1879–1967) Rear-admiral, Russian Navy from 1917; vice-admiral, Sov Navy from 1940; *Born:* 1879; *Educ:* 1902 grad officers' artillery classes; *Career:* from 1902 training work and commands in Russian Navy; 1905 refused to let his company carry out the death sentence on four sailors involved in the mutiny on the "Prut" transport vessel; 1905–06 appeared as defense advocate in the trial of 200 Black Sea Fleet mutineers and managed to achieve the repeal of death sentences; 1917 commanded minelaying brigade, Black Sea Fleet; July–Dec 1917 commander, Black Sea Fleet; sided with Sov regime; 1919–20 chief of staff, Yakir's Southern Forces Group, 12th Army; Feb 1920–Dec 1921 commander, RSFSR Navy; then lectured at Naval Acad and worked for centr organs of Sov Navy; from 1947 retired, but continued to work for Hydrographic Service of Black Sea Fleet; *Awards:* several orders and medals; *Died:* Oct 1967.

NEMTSEV, Iosif Vasil'yevich (1885–1939) Choral conductor and teacher; Hon Artiste of RSFSR from 1932; assoc prof from 1929; *Born:* 1885 in vil Grachevka, Samara Province; *Educ:* 1902–04 studied under A.D. Kastal'skiy and N.M. Danilin at Moscow Synodal College; from 1904 studied under Lyadov at the Court Singing Capella, Petersburg; *Career:* from 1907 taught singing at children's homes and schools in Petersburg; from 1919 instructor, Music Dept, Pop Comrt of Educ; from 1926 instructor, Leningrad Oblast Trade-Union Council; 1925–39 lecturer, in choral work, Leningrad Conservatory; founded workers' choir groups and popularized new choral repertoire and Russian musical classics; sponsored new forms of mass amateur musical activity; 1927 helped stage first Amateur Art Festival in Leningrad; chief conductor and organizer at 10 such festivals, often involving as many as 100,000 participants; *Died:* 14 June 1939 in Leningrad.

NEMTSOV, Nikolay Mikhaylovich (1879–1937) Party and govt official; CP member from 1897; *Born:* 16 Apr 1879 in Tula, son of a worker; *Career:* Party work in Tula, Petersburg and other cities; participated in 1905–07 Revol; 1905 dep, Petersburg Sov; member, Exec Comt, Petersburg Sov; 1906 exiled to Siberia for life; released after 1917 Feb Revol; Apr 1917 member, Factory Comt, Petrograd Metal Plant; elected member, Petrograd RSDRP(B) Comt; member, Centr Council of Plant and Factory Comts; 1917–18 chm, Tyumen' Revol Comt and chm, Tyumen' Party Comt; 1918–19 chm, Tula Sov; 1919–20 secr, Tambov Province RCP(B) Comt; from 1922 in Moscow with RSFSR legal organs; then dep chm, Special Amnesty Commission, USSR Centr Exec Comt; from 1928 secr, Soc of Old Bolsheviks and member, Moscow Control Commission; deleg at 8th–10th and 16 Party Congresses; 1937 arrested by State Security organs; *Died:* 26 Nov 1937 in imprisonment, posthumously rehabilitated.

NEMYTSKIY, Viktor Vladimirovich (1900–1967) Mathematician; Dr of Physics and Mathematics from 1935; prof from 1935; *Born:* 1900 in Smolensk; *Educ:* 1925 grad Moscow Univ; 1939 completed postgrad course at Moscow Univ; *Career:* 1925–35 lecturer, then prof, Mech and Mathematics Fac, Moscow Univ; Studied real variable function theory and topology; did research on qualitative theory of nonlinear equations; *Publ: Teorema sushchestvovaniya i yedinstvennosti dlya nelineynykh integral'nykh uravneniy* (The Theory of the Existence and Unity of Non-Linear Integral Equations) (1934); "Ueber vollstaendig unstabile dynamische Systeme" (1935–36); coauthor, *Kachestvennaya teoriya differentsial'nykh uravneniy* (The Qualitative Theory of Differential Equations) (1949); *O nekotorykh metodakh kachestvennogo issledovaniya "v bol'shom" mnogomernykh avtonomnykh sistem* (Some Methods for the Qualitative Gross Study of Polymetric Autonomous Systems) (1956); *Ob odnom metode razyskaniya vsekh resheniy nelineynykh operatornykh uravneniy* (A Method of Finding all the Solutions to Non-Linear Operator Equations); *K voprosu ob ustanovivshikhsya rezhimakh v sistemakh avtomaticheskogo regulirovaniya* (Established Regimes in Automatic Control Systems) (1960); *Died:* 7 Aug 1967.

NENADKEVICH, Konstantin Avtonomovich (1880–1966) Mineralogist and chemist; corresp member, USSR Acad of Sci from 1946; *Born:* 2 June 1880; *Educ:* 1902 grad Moscow Univ; *Career:* from 1906 worked for various org, Russian (USSR) Acad of Sci, including the Geological and Mineralogical Museums, the Geological Inst and the Inst of the Mineralogy and Geochemistry of Rare Elements; 1916–20 developed techniques for the ind extraction of metallic bismuth from Sov ore; 1926 determined the age of pitchblende by chemical means; *Publ: K voprosu o sodovoy promyshlennosti v SSSR* (The Soviet Soda Indistry) (1924); *Elektroliticheskiy metod razdeleniya nikelya i kobal'ta* (The Electrolytic Method of Extracting Nickel and Cobalt) (1945), etc; *Awards:* two Order of Lenin; Stalin Prize (1948); *Died:* 30 Sept 1966.

NERIS (real name: BACHINSKAYTE–BUCHENE), Salomeya (1904–1945) Lith poetess; Pop Poet of Lith SSR from 1954 (posthumously); *Born:* 17 Nov 1904 in vil Hirshyay, Lith; *Educ:* 1928 grad Kaunas Univ; *Career:* after grad taught at high-school; 1931 member, Lith writers group "Third Front"; 1936–37 lived in Paris; during WW 2 lived in Penza, Ufa and Moscow; after liberation of Lith lived in Kaunas; dep, USSR Supr Sov of 1937 convocation; 1923 first work published; *Publ:* collected verse: "Early in the Morning" (1927); "Tracks in the Sand" (1931); "Over the Breaking Ice" (1935); "Demyadis in Blossom" (1938); poems "Edle, Queen of the Snakes" (1940); "The Bolshevik's Path" (1940); collected verse: "The Nightingale Cannot Sing" (1945); "My Country" (1947), etc; many of the works have been set to music by Lith composers; *Awards:* Stalin Prize (1947, posthumously); *Died:* 7 July 1945 in Moscow.

NERSESYAN, Grachiya Nersesovich (1895–1961) Arm stage and film actor; Pop Artiste of Arm SSR and USSR from 1956; *Born:* 12 Nov 1895 in Nicomedia (now Izmir), Turkey; *Career:* 1915 began stage work in Turkey with Arm operetta and Turkish drama theaters; 1918–22 actor, Arm Drama Soc, Constantinople; from 1920 appeared in Turkish films; 1922 moved to USSR; from 1923 actor, Arm State Drama Theater; from 1925 film work; *Roles:* Hamlet (1924); Macbeth (1933); Falstaff (1939); Othello (1940); King Lear (1953); Zhadov in Ostrovskiy's *Dokhodnoye mesto* (A Lucrative Post); Dikoy in Ostrovskiy's *Groza* (The Storm); Koshkin in "Lyubov' Yarovaya"; (1927); Bersenev in Lavrenev's *Razlom* (Break-Up) (1928); Krechet in Korneychuk's "Platon Krechet" (1935); Safonov in *Russkiye lyudi* (Russian People) (1942); MacGregor in Saroyan's "My Heart's in the Highlands" (1961), etc; film roles in: "Namus" (1925); "Khas-Push" (1927); "Gikor" (1934); "Zangezur" (1938); "David-bek" (1944), etc; *Awards:* Stalin Prize (1941); Order of Lenin; Badge of Hon; *Died:* 6 Nov 1961 in Yerevan.

NESHCHADIMENKO, Rita (Kharitina) Petrovna (1890–1926) Actress; *Born:* 1 Apr 1890 in vil Serdechivtse (now Cherkassy Oblast); *Educ:* 1914–15 studied at Komissarzhevskiy Theater Studio in Moscow; *Career:* 1918 began to act at youth theater; 1919–20 and 1921–22 also at Shevchenko 1st State Drama Theater of Ukr SSR; 1920–21 at Kiev Drama Theater; 1922–26 at Berezil' Theater; *Roles:* Tanya in S. Vasil'chenko's "Prince Zil'ya"; Lyutsilla in Lesya Ukrainka's "Martiyan the Lawyer"; Isabella in Prosper Merimee's "Jacqueries"; Motren'ka in M. Kulish's *Kommuna v stepyakh* (Commune in the Steppe), etc; *Died:* 25 Apr 1926.

NESTEROV, Mikhail Vasil'yevich (1862–1942) Artist; member, Acad of Painting from 1898; member, Petersburg Acad of Arts from 1910; Hon Art Worker of RSFSR from 1942; *Born:* 10 May 1862 in Ufa; *Educ:* 1886 grad Moscow College of Painting, Sculpture and Architecture under V. G. Pirov and I. M. Pryanishnikov; 1884 grad Petersburg Acad of Arts; *Career:* 1883 painted first pictures; from 1889 exhibitor, from 1896 member, Assoc of Itinerant Art Exhibitions; his works are displayed in Moscow's Tret'yakov Gallery, Leningrad's Russian Museum and other art museums; *Works:* sketch "Crushed" (1883); canvases: "House Arrest" (1883); "The Connoisseur" (1884); "Suppliants to the Sovereign" (1886); "The Anchorite" (1889); "The Vision of the Young Varfolomey" (1890); "Sergiy's Youth" (1897); "The Grand Taking of Monastic Vows" (1897); murals in Vladimir Cathedral, Kiev (1900); portraits of: Gorky (1901); O.M. Nesterova (1905); the Polish artist Ja. Stanislawski (1906); "Holy Rus'" (1906); murals in the Martha-Maria Cloister, Moscow (1912); portraits of cultural figures: P.D. and A.D. Korin (1930); I.D. Shadr (1934); I.P. Pavlov (1935); Ye.S. Kruglikova (1938); V.I. Mukhina (1940); landscape "Autumn Was in the Sky" (1942); many other paintings and portraits; *Awards:* Order of the Red Banner of Labor; Stalin Prize (1941); *Died:* 18 Oct 1942 in Moscow.

NESTEROV, Stepan Kuz'mich (1906–1944) Mil commander; col, Russian Army; CP member from 1932; *Born:* 1906 in vil Talitskiy Chamlyk, Voronezh Province, son of a peasant; *Educ:* 1938–41 took courses at correspondence dept, Mil Acad of Armored Troops; *Career:* from 1928 in Red Army; 1941–44 chief of staff, tank regt, then tank brigade; commanded tank brigade, then dep commander, tank corps; 1944 his brigade distinguished itself in liberation of Kaunas and was made a guards unit; *Awards:* Hero of the Sov Union (1945, posthumously); Order of Lenin (1945, posthumously); *Died:* 20 Oct 1944 killed in action; town and railroad station of Shtallupyonen renamed for him; monument erected to him in former Shtallupyonen.

NEUYMIN, Grigoriy Nikolayevich (1886–1946) Astronomer; specialist in astrophotography; *Born:* 3 Jan 1886; *Educ:* 1910 grad Petersburg Univ; *Career:* 1912–41 worked at Simeiz Observatory (now Crimean Astrophysical Observatory); from 1944 dir, Pulkovo Observatory; discovered numerous asteroids and six new comets; made detailed analysis of orbit and motion of a comet he discovered in 1916; *Died:* 1946.

NEVSKIY, Nikolay Aleksandrovich (1892–1945) Orientalist; Dr of Philology; prof from 1922; *Born:* 3 Mar 1892 in Yaroslavl'; *Educ:* 1914 grad Petrograd Univ; *Career:* 1915–29 lived in Japan; from 1922 prof of Russian language, Osaka Inst of For Languages; 1930–38 worked at Inst of Oriental Studies, Leningrad Univ; spezialized in Japanese, Ainu and Tangut; 1938 arrested by NKVD; *Publ: Kul'tovaya poeziya drevney Yaponii VI–VIII vekov* (The Cult Poetry of 6th–8th Century Ancient Japan) (1935); *Aynskiy fol'klor* (Ainu Folklore) (1935); *Tangutskaya filologiya* (Tangut Philology) (1960); *Awards:* Lenin Prize (1960, posthumously); *Died:* 14 Feb 1945 in imprisonment; posthumously rehabilitated.

NEVSKIY (real name: KRIVOBOKOV), Vladimir Ivanovich (1876–1937) Party and govt official; historian; CP member from 1897; *Born:* 14 May 1876 in Rostov-on-Don, son of a merchant; *Educ:* 1897 grad high-school; 1898 and 1900 studied at Moscow Univ; *Career:* 1898 expelled from univ, arrested and exiled to Rostov, where he worked for Don RSDRP Comt; 1900 returned to Moscow Univ and resumed Party propaganda among workers; 1901 exiled to Voronezh, where he founded the "Struggle Fund," an "Iskra"-affiliated Soc-Democratic org; 1904 moved to Geneva and met Lenin; Jan 1905, on orders from Bureau of Bolshevik Comts, returned to Russia and agitated for convocation of 3rd RSDRP Congress; Oct 1905 elected deleg to Tammerfors RSDRP(B) Conference; 1906–08 member, Exec Commission, Petrograd RSDRP(B) Comt; early 1908 arrested and 1909 acquitted in trial of Petersburg Party Comt's Mil Org; 1910 worked in Rostov, then in Khar'kov; summer 1913 co-opted cand member, CC, RSDRP but arrested shortly afterwards and deported to Poltava; 1913 deleg, Poronin RSDRP CC Conference; until 1917 Feb Revol carried out underground Party work in Perm' and Yekaterinburg; 1917 helped direct Mil Org, Petrograd Party Comt and CC, RSDRP(B); member, ed bd, Bolshevik newspapers "Soldatskaya pravda" and "Derevenskaya bednota"; active part in 1917 Oct Revol; member, Petrograd Cheka; after Revol until Mar 1919 Pop Comr of Means of Communication; 1919–20 Presidium member and dep chm, All-Russian Centr Exec Comt; simultaneously head, Dept for Rural Work, CC, RCP(B); for a while sided with workers' opposition; 1921 rector, Sverdlov Communist Univ; from 1922 dep head, Commission for the Study of Party History and the History of the Oct Revol, CC, RCP(B); from 1924 dir, Lenin Library, Moscow; wrote number of works and articles on history of CP, Populism, "Liberation of Labor" group, first workers' orgs in Russia in 1870's and 1905–07 Revol; for a number of years his studies of Party history were used as textbooks; edited and compiled various collections of Party documents; 1935 arrested by State Security organs; *Publ: Ocherki po istorii RKP(b)* (Outline History of the RCP(B)) (1924); *Istoriya RKB(b). Kratkiy ocherk* (The History of the RCP(B). A Short Study) (1926); *Predshestvenniki nashey partii (Severnyy soyuz russkikh rabochikh)* (Our Party's Predecessors. The Northern League of Russian Workers) (1930); *Yuzhno-russkiy rabochiy soyuz v gorode Nikolaeve 1897 goda* (The Southern-Russian Workers' League in Nikolayev in 1897), etc; *Died:* 25 May 1937 in imprisonment; posthumously rehabilitated.

NEVZOROVA-KRZHIZHANOVSKAYA, Zinaida Pavlovna (1870–1948) Revolutionary; *Born:* 1870 in Nizhniy Novgorod, daughter of a teacher; *Career:* from 1894 teacher in Nizhniy Novgorod and member, Soc-Democratic group; 1895 moved to Petersburg; active member, Lenin's League for the Liberation of the Working Class; 1896 arrested; 1897 exiled to Nizhniy Novgorod, 1898 to Siberia; signed Lenin's "Protest of Russian Soc-Democrats," and directed against the Economists; 1901, while with G. M. Krzhizhanovskiy in Samara, represented "Iskra" (The Spark) in Volga and Ural Regions; 1902 secr, Russian "Iskra" org; carried out important assignments for CC, RSDRP; from 1917 worked for Moscow Oblast Sov, then for Pop Comrt of Educ; also taught; *Died:* 24 Apr 1948.

NEYGAUZ, Genrikh Gustavovich (1888–1964) Pianist and music teacher; Dr of Arts; prof from 1919; Hon Art Worker of RSFSR; Pop Artiste of RSFSR from 1956; *Born:* 31 Mar 1888 in Yelizavetgrad; *Educ:* 1914 grad higher technique class, Viennese Musical Acad; 1915 grad Petersburg Conservatory; *Career:* from 1916 taught in Tiflis; 1919–22 prof, Kiev Conservatory; from 1922 prof, Moscow Conservatory; 1935–37 dir, Moscow Conservatory; founded major school of pianists, including: Gilel's, Zak, Malinin and Rikhter, etc; wrote articles on music and edited Chopin's piano works; *Publ: Ob isskusstve fortep'yannoy igry. Zapiski pedagoga* (The Art of Piano Playing. Notes for Instructors) (1958); *Awards:* Order of Lenin; Order of the Red Banner of Labor; medals; *Died:* 10 Oct 1964 in Moscow.

NEZHDANOVA, Antonina Vasil'yevna (1873–1950) Singer (lyric coloratura soprano); Pop Artiste of USSR from 1936; Dr of Arts from 1944; prof, Moscow Conservatory from 1943; *Born:* 17 July 1873 in vil Krivaya Balka, near Odessa; *Educ:* 1902 grad Mazetti's class, Moscow Conservatory; also studied singing under Rubinstein's sister; *Career:* 1902–34 performed with Chaliapine, Sobinov, etc at Moscow Bolshoy Theater; 1912 performed with great success at Paris Grand Opera; also chamber singer; from 1924 singer and musical commentator, Sov radio; 1936 taught at Bolshoy Theater Studio, then at Stanislavskiy's Opera Studio, Odessa Conservatory named after her; *Roles:* Lyudmilla in Glinka's "Ruslan and Lyudmilla"; Tat'yana in Tchaikovsky's "Yevgeniy Onegin"; Gilda in Verdi's "Rigoletto"; also appeared in : Rimsky-Korsakov's *Snegurochka* (The Snow-Maiden), "Sadko" and *Zolotoy petushkok* (The Golden Cockerel); Antonida in Glinka's *Zhizn' za tsarya* (A Life for the Tsar); Marfa in *Tsarskaya nevesta* (Bride of the Tsar); Michaela in "Carmen"; Margarite in "Faust," etc; *Awards:* Order of Lenin; Order of the Red Banner of Labor; Stalin Prize (1943); medals; *Died:* 26 June 1950 in Moscow.

NEZNAMOV, Aleksandr Aleksandrovich (1872–1928) Mil historian and lecturer; maj-gen, Russian Army from 1915; *Born:* 10 Oct 1872, son of a peasant; *Educ:* 1893 grad Nikolay Mil Eng College; 1900 grad Gen Staff Acad; *Career:* fought in Russo-Japanese War; lectured on tactics and strategy at Gen Staff Acad; from 1908 prof, Gen Staff Acad; during WW 1 commanded infantry regt, then quartermaster-gen, 7th Army on Rumanian Front; from July 1918 in Red Army; 1918–22 dept head, Mil Communications Bd; prof, Eng Acad; member, Commission to Study the Experience of World War 1 and the Civil War; from 1922 lectured on strategy at Red Army Mil Acad (now Frunze Mil Acad); senior lecturer, Eng Acad and Eng Tech Acad; also ed, Main Mil Research Ed Bd; member, Higher Acad Mil Pedag Council; *Publ: Sovremennaya voyna. Deystviya polevoy armii* (Modern Warfare. Operations of an Army in the Field) (1912); *Strategicheskiy ocherk voyny 1914–18 godov* (A Strategic Study of the 1914–18 War) (1920); *Sovremennaya voyna* (Modern Warfare) (2 vol, 1921–22); *Boyevyye deystviya soyedinyonnykh rodov voysk* (Combined Military Operations) (1924); *Died:* 28 July 1928.

NEZNAMOV (real name: LEZHANKIN), Pyotr Vasil'yevich (1889–1941) Russian poet; *Born:* 1889 at Novchinsk Plant, now Transbaykal Oblast; *Career:* fought in WW 1; wounded and gassed; 1919 first work printed in journal "Tvorchestvo"; 1922 moved to Moscow; met Mayakovsky, joined "Left Art Front" lit group; helped publish journals "LEF" and "Novyy LEF"; 1929–30 member, "Revol Art Front" lit group; wrote critical articles and polemic reviews of verse and prose; *Publ:* verse collection *Pyat' stoletiy* (Five Centuries) (1923); *Zolotoshit'yo i galuny* (Gold Lace and Embroidery) (1923); *Zveri na svobode* (Animals at Liberty) (1927); *Promakhi i popadaniya* (Misses and Hits) (1927); *Sovetskiy Churkin* (The Soviet Churkin) (1928); *Mimo gazety* (Past and Newspaper) (1928); *O poetakh i ustanovkakh* (Poets and Regulations) (1928); *Na novosel'ye* (At the House-Warming) (1928); *Mayakovskiy v dvadtsatykh godakh* (Mayakovskiy in the 1920's); verse collection *Khorosho na ulitse* (It Is Nice on the Streets) (1929), etc; *Died:* Oct 1941 killed in action in Dorogobuzh, while serving with Moscow Civil Defense.

NICHOLAS II (Nikolay Aleksandrovich ROMANOV) (1868–1918) Last Russian emperor; *Born:* 18 May 1868, elder son of Alexander III; *Educ:* privately tutored; *Career:* 1894 married Princess Alice of Hessen, who took the name Aleksandra Fyodorovna; had four daughters (Ol'ga, Tat'yana, Mariya and Anastasiya) and one son Aleksey, the heir to the throne (1904–1918); 21 Oct 1894 acceded to the throne; ruled in a period of mounting revol unrest; during Nicholas' rule Russia suffered the humiliation of mil defeat in the 1904–05 Russo-Japanese War; 17 Oct 1905, during 1st Russian Revol, issued Manifesto announcing the formation of a legislative Duma and the granting of democratic liberties; 1914 Russia, in alliance with the Anglo-French coalition, began war against Germany; Aug 1915 assumed the duty of supr commander in chief of the army; Mar 1917, in an effort to avert revol and save the monarchy by a change of tsar, Russia's leading democratic parties proposed to the tsar that he abdicate; 15 Mar 1917 abdicated in favor of his brother Mikhail, who declined to accept the throne; 21 Mar 1917 arrested and detained at Tsarskoye Selo, then sent to Tobol'sk and hence to Yekaterinburg (now Sverdlovsk), where on the night of 16/17 July 1918 he and his family were shot on orders from the Ural Oblast Sov; *Died:* 16/17 July 1918.

NIGER (real name: DZHANAYEV, Ivan Vasil'yevich) (1896–1947) Ossetian poet and lit historian; *Born:* 1896 in vil Sindzisar, Ossetia; *Educ:* 1917 grad Ardon Theological Seminary; 1930 grad Lit Fac, North Ossetian Teachers' Training Inst; 1932 completed postgrad course at above inst; *Career:* fought in Civil War in Northern Ossetia; 1920 first work published; wrote studies of K. Khetachurov, Ts. Tadiyev and the Nart epics, etc; wrote poetry mainly on Sov themes, glorifying Oct Revol and new life under Sov regime; *Publ:* verse "I Do Not Fear"; "Ring Out, My Song!"; "The New Era"; "Konchita Malo"; "Gytstsi" (1934); "On the Banks of the Terek" (1939); "The Red Army Man Will Tell" (1945); verse based on folk songs and legends: "Uakhatag's Son, the Brave Guyman" (1935); "Badelyata's Dance" (1935); "Satay Khan" (1940), etc; coauthor, play "Kosta" (1939); *Died:* 3 May 1947 in Ordzhonikidze.

NIGMATI, Galimdzhan (real name: Galimdzhan Amirzhanovich NIGMATULLIN) (1897–1938) Tatar lit historian; CP member from 1919; *Born:* 24 July 1897 in vil Urdyak, now Bash ASSR, son of a peasant; *Educ:* studied at Communist Univ of Workers of the East, then at Moscow Inst of Journalism; *Career:* from 1926 worked in Kazan', editing newspaper "Krasnyy Tatarstan"; 1927–30 chief ed, Tatar Publ House: from 1934 prof, Kazan' Teachers' Training Inst; wrote textbooks and studies on history of Tatar lit; wrote about work of classic Tatar writers G. Kulakhmetov, M. Gafuri, G. Ibragimov, G. Kamal, G. Tukay and about Russian writers Lev Tolstoy, Chekhov, Gorky, etc; arrested by state Security organs; *Publ:* "October and Literature" (1922); "Our Literature Since the Revolution" (1923); "In the World of Literature" (1925); "In the Literary Arena" (1925); "Our Literature in the Years of the Revolution" (1929); "Soviet Tatar Literature" (1930); "Literature and Life" (1931); "Soviet Tatar Literature on the Upsurge" (1934), etc; *Died:* 4 Nov 1938 in imprisonment, posthumously rehabilitated.

NIGMATI, Rashit (real name: Rashit Nigmatullinovich NIGMATULLIN) (1909–1959) Bash poet; Pop Poet of Bash ASSR; CP member from 1944; *Born:* 9 Feb 1909 in vil Dingizbay, now Kuybyshev Oblast, son of a peasant; *Educ:* raised in orphanage; 1930 grad Ufa workers' fac; *Career:* exec secr, bd, Bash Writers' Union; worked as ed for publ house; 1926 first work printed; *Publ:* verse collection "Introduction" (1933); collected verse and poems: "Storm-Born Life" (1938); "Beautiful Are the Valleys of Ak-Idel'" (1940); "In My Garden" (1941); wartime poems: "Kill the Fascist, My Son" (1942); "Letters to Thy Bride" (1943); "The Word of Bashkortstan" (1944); collected verse "Songs of Love and Hatred" (1942); poem "The Bolshevik" (1948); poem "Flame from the Spark" (1958); verse and poem collections: "The Girl from Sakmar" (1952); "A Welcoming Word" (1955); "Selected Works" (1951); plays "Doctor Gimranov" (1939); "On the Bank of the Belaya" (1949–50); children's books: "Answers to My Daughter's Questions" (1944); "A Journey into the Future" (1947); "A Good Journey to You!" (1951); translated into Bash *Slovo o polku Igoreve* (The Lay of the Host of Igor) and works of Pushkin, Lermontov, Mayakovskiy, etc; *Died:* 13 Oct 1959 in Ufa.

NIKANDR, (secular name: VOL'YANIKOV) (1909–1957) Bishop of Omsk and Tyumen'; *Born:* 1909; *Career:* took monastic vows, then appointed archimandrite; until 1949 secr to Bishop of Novosibirsk and vicar of Novosibirsk Eparchy; from 1949 Bishop of Biysk; 1949 signed congratulatory address to Stalin on the occasion of his 70th birthday on behalf of the clergy and parishioners of the Russian Orthodox Church; 1952 appointed Bishof of Omsk and Tyumen'; *Died:* 8 June 1957 in Yalta.

NIKANDROV (real name: SHEVTSOV), Nikolay Nikandrovich (1878–1964) Russian writer; *Born:* 7 Dec 1878 in Petrovsko-Razumovskoye, near Moscow; *Educ:* until 1899 studied at Inst of Railroad Eng and at Forestry Inst; *Career:* 1898 influenced by Lev Tolstoy to become a vil teacher; from 1901 member, Socialist-Revol Party and active in its mil org; 1902 exiled to Nizhniy Novgorod and 1905 to Arkhangel'sk Province for anti-govt propaganda; 1906 went underground and worked in a number of trades; 1910–14 lived abroad in Switzerland, Italy and France; during Civil War in Sebastopol; from 1922 in Moscow; *Publ:* stories: *Chyornaya kost'... belaya kost'* (Ebony ... Ivory) (1903); *Beregovoy veter* (Coast Wind) (1909); novelette *Vo vsyom dvore pervaya* (The First Lady at Court) (1912); story *Vo vremya zatish'ya* (During the Lull) (1914); novelettes: *Diktator Pyotr* (Peter the Dictator) (1923); *Rynok lyubvi* (The Love Market) (1924); *Put' k zhenshchine* (The Path to Woman) (1927); *Krasnaya ryba* (Red Fish) (1930); *Kochevniki morya* (Nomads of the Sea) (1934); *Povesti i rasskazy* (Novelettes and Stories) (1964), etc; *Died:* 18 Nov 1964 in Moscow.

NIKIFOROV, Afinogen Nikiforovich (1891–1967) Party and govt official; CP member from 1911; *Born:* 1891; *Educ:* 1923–30 studied at a workers' fac and at Moscow Univ; *Career:* from age nine worked as a hired farmhand; from 1906 worked at factories in Moscow and Petersburg; 1914 arrested for revol activities, after which he worked at factories in Yenakiyevo and Makeyevka; 1917–18 asst comr, 1st Red Guard Regt; 1918–21 chm, Roslavl' Uyezd Cheka, Smolensk Province; also chm, Roslavl' Uyezd Exec Comt; 1921–22 did Party work; 1931–36 worked for CPSU(B) Centr Control Commission, then for Sov railroads; later held admin posts in Min of Means of Communication; from 1947 penisoner; *Died:* 29 July 1967.

NIKIFOROV, Georgiy Konstantinovich (1884–1939) Russian writer; CP member from 1917; *Born:* 26 May 1884 in Saratov; *Career:* from age 13 apprentice, then lathe-operator, Tambov Railroad Car Workshop; joined RSDRP circle; 1905 arrested for participating in armed uprising in Moscow; 1917 worked at Chelyabinsk Railroad Car Workshops; fought in Civil War; 1918 first work published; member, "Smithy" and "October" lit assoc; arrested by State Security organs: *Publ:* novelette *Ili-ili* (Either ... Or) (1924); story *Natura* (Nature) (1924); novelettes *Sedyye dni* (Grizzled Days) (1925) and *33 okazii* (33 Oddities) (1926–27); novels: *Zhenshchina* (Woman) (1929); *Vstrechnyy veter* (Head-Wind) (1930); *Yedinstvo* (Unity) (1933); historical novel *Mastera* (Masters) (1935–37); plays: *Razval* (Collapse); *Voyna i mir* (War and Peace); children's stories: *Yunyy mashinist* (The Young Engine-Driver); *Savos'kina zhizn'* (Savos'ka's Life), etc; *Died:* 1939 in imprisonment; posthumously rehabilitated.

NIKIFOROV, Pavel Mikhaylovich (1884–1944) Geophysicist; coresp member, USSR Acad of Sci from 1932; CP member from 1932; *Born:* 17 June 1884; *Educ:* 1908 grad Petersburg Univ; *Career:* from 1924 head, Seismic Dept, Physics and Mathematics Inst and head, Seismic System, USSR Acad of Sci; from 1928 dir, Seismological Inst, USSR Acad of Sci; from 1926 head, Chair of Geophysics, Leningrad Univ; from 1933 prof, Leningrad Mining Inst; studied seismic activity in USSR; developed new type of seismograph for recording close-range earth tremors; devised methods for studying deep structure of earth's crust and made first study of elastic waves caused by powerful explosions; designed gravitational variometers; *Publ: Kurskaya gravitatsionnaya anomaliya* (The Kursk Gravitational Anomaly) (1922); *Awards:* Order of Red Banner of Labor; *Died:* 2 Sept 1944.

NIKITIN, Boris Aleksandrovich (1906–1952) Chemist; specialist in radiochemistry; corresp member, USSR Acad of Sci from 1943; CP member from 1941; *Born:* 14 May 1906; *Educ:* 1927 grad Leningrad Univ; *Career:* 1950–52 dir, Radium Inst, USSR Acad of Sci; studied anomalous mixed crystals and molecular compounds of inert gases; devised original method of studying these compounds using isomorphic co-crystallization; discovered and studied various molecular compounds of inert gases and water, phenol, etc; established that the law of the distribution of matter applied to the case of distribution between solid and gas states; studied the diffusion of radium in natural waters; *Publ: Izbrannyye trudy* (Selected Works) (1956); *Awards:* Order of Lenin, Stalin Prize (1943); other orders; *Died:* 20 July 1952.

NIKITIN, Ivan Fyodorovich (1891–1962) Russian writer; CP member from 1926; *Born:* 20 Jan 1891 in Yaroslavl' Province; *Educ:* 1930 grad Philology Fac, Leningrad Univ; *Career:* 1924 first work printed; *Publ:* novelette *Uklon* (Deviation) (1926); novels *Ozorniki*(The Mischief-Makers) (1928); *Gnev* (Wrath) (1930); novelettes: *Budnikov mladshiy* (Budnikov Junior) (1949); *Oni vstupayut v* *zhizn'* (Embarking on Life) (1951); novel *Sozidateli* (The Creators) (1962), etc; *Died:* 5 Feb 1962 in Leningrad.

NIKITIN, Nikolay Akimovich (1887–1963) Circus performer; horse-trainer; Hon Artiste of RSFSR from 1947; *Born:* 5 Dec 1887, son of a circus-dir; *Career:* began performing in father's circus as a boy, with his acts including trampoline acrobatics and juggling on horseback; 1917, after death of father, became dir, Moscow Circus; 1919, after nationalization of Moscow Circus, joined K.I. Bul's Circus in Rostov-on-Don, then toured Italy; 1922 returned to USSR and appeared as a juggler and horse-trainer in various curcuses; *Died:* 28 Nov 1963.

NIKITIN, Nikolay Nikolayevich (1895–1963) Russian writer and playwright; *Born:* 27 July 1895 in Petersburg; *Educ:* 1915–18 studied at Petrograd Univ; *Career:* from 1918 volunteer in Red Army; propaganda work among troops; from 1921 member, "Serapion Brethren" lit assoc; 1922 first work printed; 1923 toured Europe as journalist; 1958 attended 1st Constituent RSFSR Writers' Congress; 1959 member, RSFSR Writers' Union deleg at 3rd All-Union Writers' Congress; *Publ:* novelette *Rvotnyy fort* (Nausea Fort) (1922); collections: *Kamni* (Stones) (1922); *Bunt* (Revolt) (1923); *Seychas na Zapade. Berlin – Rur – London* (The West Nowadays. Berlin – the Ruhr – London) (1924); play *Korona i plashch* (Crown and Raincoat) (1924); *S karandashom v ruke* (With Pencil in Hand) (1926); *Liricheskaya zemlya* (Lyric Land) (1927); novel *Prestupleniye Kirika Rudenko* (The Crime of Kirik Rudenko) (1927); play *Liniya ognya* (Line of Fire) (1931); novelette *Pogovorim o zvyozdakh* (Let's Talk of the Stars) (1934); play *Apsheronskaya noch'* (Apsheron Night) (1937); novels: *Eto nachalos' v Kokande* (It Started in Kokand) (1939); *Severnaya Avrora* (Aurora Borealis) (1950); play *Severnyye zori* (Northern Stars) (1952); *Firsovy* (The Firsovs) (1957), etc; script for films: *Mogila Panburleya* (Panburley's Grave) (1928); *Parizhskiy sapozhnik* (The Parisian Cobbler) (1928); *Awards:* Stalin Prize (1951); *Died:* 26 Mar 1963 in Leningrad.

NIKITIN, Pyotr Vasil'yevich (1909–1959) Govt official; Cand of Tech Sci; CP member from 1930; *Born:* 1909 in vil Sechenka, Vitebsk Oblast, son of a peasant; *Educ:* 1933 grad Leningrad Polytech Inst; 1936 completed postgrad course at above inst; *Career:* 1924 joined Komsomol; from 1933 served in Sov Navy; from 1936 exec work with USSR Gosplan; for a long while member, Gosplan and dep chm, USSR Gosplan; from 1957 head, Main Bd for Econ Relations, USSR Council of Min; then dep chm, State Comt for For Econ Relations, USSR Council of Min; at 19th and 20th Party Congresses elected cand member, CC, CPSU; *Awards:* Order of the Red Banner of Labor; Order of the Red Star; medals; *Died:* 27 Jan 1959.

NIKITIN, Vasiliy Petrovich (1893–1956) Electr eng; specialist in electr mech and electr welding; member, USSR Acad of Sci from 1939; hon member, Turkm Acad of Sci from 1951; Hon Sci and Tech Worker of RSFSR from 1948; CP member from 1938; *Born:* 14 Aug 1893; *Educ:* 1914 grad Petersburg Polytech Inst; *Career:* 1912–18 worked at Baltic Shipbuilding and Mech Plant; then in electr ind; 1925–29 prof, Dnepropetrovsk Mining Inst; 1929–32 prof, Moscow Acad (from 1930 Moscow Steel Inst); from 1933 prof, Moscow Higher Tech College; 1939–42 Presidium member, USSR Acad of Sci and acad secr of its Dept of Tech Sci; 1947–53 Presidium member, USSR Acad of Sci; specialized in physical processes involved in electr arc; developed apparatus for arc welding; designed solid-block regulator-transformer for arc welding, widely used in ind; *Publ: Svoystva vol'tovoy dugi i primennenii k elektricheskoy svarke metallov, obuslovlivayushchiye svoystva istochnika toka, pitayushchego dugu* (The Properties of a Volt Arc Used for the Electrical Welding of Metals Dictating the Properties of the Current Source Feeding the Arc) (1928); *Elektricheskiye mashiny i transformatory dlya dugovoy svarki* (Electrical Machines and Transformers for Arc Welding) (2 vol, 1937); *Russkoye izobreteniye – elektricheskaya dugovaya svarka* (A Russian Invention – Electric Arc Welding) (1952); *Ustoychivost' raboty istochnikov pitaniya elektricheskoy dugi v usloviyakh svarki* (The Functional Stability of Electric Arc Power Sources in Welding) (1947); coauthor, *Dinamicheskoye ravnovesiye magnitnogo sostoyaniya elektricheskikh mashin v sisteme Leonarda* (The Dynamic Balance of the Magnetic State of Electrical Machinery in the Leonard System) (1948); *Awards:* Order of Lenin; Order of the Red Banner of Labor; medals; *Died:* 16 Mar 1956.

NIKITINSKIY, Yakov Yakovlevich (1878–1941) Specialist in sanitary hydrobiology and tech microbiology; prof from 1918; *Born:* 28 Nov 1878, son of well-known chemist Ya.Ya. Nikitinskiy; *Educ:* grad Moscow Univ; *Career:* 1908–18 assoc, from 1918 prof, Moscow Business Inst (now Plekhanov Inst of Nat Econ); from 1912 worked for ad hoc comt to protect water reservoirs in Moscow ind area from pollution with sewage and waste; did microbiological research on the water supply sources of Moscow and various major development projects, including the Magnitogorsk and Dnieper power plants; also did research on food storage and preservation; *Publ: O razlozhenii guminovykh veshchestv mikroorganizmami* (The Microorganic Decomposition of Humic Substances) (1902); *Rol' biologicheskogo issledovaniya v sanitarnoy otsenke vodoyomov pri vybore istochnikov vodosnabzheniya gorodov, syol, fabrik i drugikh posyolkov* (The Role of Biological Analysis in the Sanitary Evalution of Water Reservois for the Choice of Water Supply Sources for Towns, Villages, Factories and Other Settlements) (1914); *Khraneniye pishchevykh produktov v uglekislom gaze* (The Storage of Food Products in Carbon Dioxide Gas) (1933); *Mikrobiologiya skoroportyashchikhsya produktov* (The Microbiology of Perishable Products) (1934), etc; *Died:* 6 May 1941.

NIKOLADZE, Niko (Nikolay) Yakovlevich (1843–1928) Geo publicist; lit critic; Dr of Law; *Born:* 27 Sept 1843 in Kutaisi; *Educ:* 1868 grad Zurich Univ; *Career:* 1860 published first articles in Geo journal "Tsiskari"; from 1861 studied at Petersburg Univ where he made the acquaintance of Chernyshevskiy and contributed to journals "Sovremennik," "Iskra" and newspaper "Narodnoye bogatstvo"; 1861 interned in Peter and Paul Fortress for his part in student polit demonstrations; 1864 in Zurich prepared publ of French-language journal "Left Bank"; 1865 invited to Geneva by Herzen and Ogarev to assist with journal "Kolokol"; late 1865 went to London and met Marx, who asked him to represent 1st International in Transcaucasia; in Geneve together with L. I. Mechnikov, published journal "Sovremennost'"; 1871 in Tiflis founded journal "Krebuli"; 1873 again in Paris, where he published Geo newspaper "Drosha"; 1875 returned to Geo and founded newspaper "Review"; 1880 journal closed down by authorities, who exiled him to Stavropol'; 1881 contributed to "Otechestvennyye zapiski"; 1886 helped lead liberal-bourgeois "Meore dasi" group in Tiflis; from 1886 contributed to newspapers "New Review" and "Caucasus"; from 1894 contributed to journal "Moambe"; 1894–1912 Mayor of Poti; after 1917 Oct Revol became leader of Geo Nationalist–Democrats; member, Geo Constituent Assembly; member, Geo Menshevik Govt; 1921-24 emigre in London; 1924 returned toGeo; 1924 attended 1st Geo Writers' Congress; *Publ:* "The Liberation of the Peasants in Georgia" (1865); "Criticism and Its Importance in Literature" (1871); "The Decadent Press" (1873); articles on poetry of Shota Rustaveli, N. Baratashvili, I.Chavchavadze, Gr. Orbeliani, Pushkin, Gogol, Byron, Nekrasov and Saltykov-Shchedrin; "Hard Labor and Exile" (1927), etc; *Died:* 1 Apr 1928 in Tbilisi.

NIKOLADZE, Yakov Ivanovich (1876–1951) Geo sculptor; prof; member, USSR Acad of Arts from 1947; Hon Artist of Geo SSR from 1946; *Born:* 16 May 1876 in Kutaisi; *Educ:* 1892–94 studied at Stroganov Art College, Moscow; 1894–96 and 1898–99 at Odessa Art College; 1899–1901 studied in Paris; *Career:* prof and head, Chair of Sculpture and co-founder, Tbilisi Acad of Arts; 1904–10 worked at Rodin's studio in Paris, where he was exposed to impressionist influences, trained numerous sculptors, including S.Ya. Kakabadze and K.M. Merabishvili; specialized in realistic busts of Geo writers and artists; *Works:* busts: "Shota Rustaveli" (1897); "Sh.Z. Aragvispireli" (1902); "V.A. Abashidze" (1902); "A.R. Tsereteli" (1914); "V.I. Gaprindashvili" (1915); "P.G. Melkishvili" (1922); "Shota Rustaveli" (1937); "I.G. Chavchavadze" (1937); "G.V. Tabidze" (1939); "I.A. Dzhavakhishvili" (1946), etc; monument to I.G. Chavchavadze (1908–10); *Awards:* Order of Lenin, Badge of Hon; medals; *Died:* 10 Mar 1951.

NIKOLAY (real name: BORETSKIY) (1879–1933) Metropolitan of Kiev and All Ukr, Ukr Autocephalous Orthodox Church; *Born:* 19 Dec 1879 in vil Sarny, Kiev Province, son of a priest; *Educ:* 1901 grad Kiev Theological Seminary; also studied at Khar'kov Higher Teachers' Training Courses; *Career:* 1904 ordained priest and appointed vicar of vil Kokhanovka, Podol'ye; later held vicarages of Zhmerinka and Gaysina and taught the catechism at local schools; 1913 became a widower; 1914 chaplain, 259th Infantry Regt and 65th Div; 1917 dean, Gaysina Cathedral; Apr 1917 advocated autocephality for Ukr Orthodox Church at Congress of Kamenets-Podol'sk and began using the Ukr language in church services in his parish; 1918 forbidden to conduct holy rites but continued his parish work; 1922 ordained Bishop of Gaysina on recommendation of Ecclesiastical Congress held there in previous year; forbidden by Sov authorities to tour his diocese and preach; 1927, after elevation to archbishop, ordained Metropolitan of Kiev and All Ukr at 2nd All-Ukr Synod; 1930 arrested by State Security organs; *Died:* 1933 in Yaroslavl' Prison.

NIKOLAY (secular name: CHERNETSKIY) (1884–1959) Apostolic visitor of Greek-Catholic Church for Volhynia, Kholmshchina and Podles'ye; *Born:* 1884 in Galicia; *Educ:* recieved his educ in Belgium; *Career:* 1909 ordained priest; after returning to Galicia worked at Redemptory Fathers' monastery at Zboiski (near L'vov) and did missionary work; 1931 consecrated bishop and appoined Apostolic visitor for Volhynia, Kholmshchina and Podles'ye, based in Kovel; 1945 arrested by State Security organs for opposing transition to Orthodoxy in accordance with campaign to liquidate Greek-Catholic Church in Western Ukr; sentenced to forced labor and exiled to Siberia; 1953 released and returned to Western Ukr; could not resume his clerical duties since the Greek-Catholic Church was officially abolished; *Died:* 1959.

NIKOLAYEV, A.M. (1887–1938) Govt official; CP member from 1904; *Born:* 1887; *Career:* 1904–07 in revol movement in Saratov Province; 1907–16 lived abroad; after returning to Russia, helped establish Sov regime in Vladimir Province; 1918–24 Collegium member, Pop Comrt of Posts and Telegraphs and chm, Radio Council; then worked with Sov trade missions; dir, Electr Import Bd; from 1931 Presidium member, USSR Gosplan and dep chm, All-Union Soc for Cultural Relations with For Countries; arrested by State Security organs; *Died:* 1938 in imprisonment.

NIKOLAYEV, Aleksandr Panfomirovich (1860–1919) Mil commander; maj-gen, Russian Army from 1916; *Born:* 19 Aug 1860 in Nizhniy Novgorod Province, son of a sergeant; *Educ:* grad Alexandrine Mil College in Moscow; *Career:* fought in 1904–05 Russo-Japanese War; 1914–18 commander, 169th Infantry Regt, infantry div; received Order of St George and gold arms; 1918 joined Red Army; 1918–1919 mil commander, Neva Rayon, Petrograd; commanded special detachment guarding River Neva; from spring 1919 commander, 3rd Brigade, 19th Infantry Div at front near Narva; 13 May 1919 captured by Whitist forces; refused to switch allegiance and serve Whites; sentenced to death; *Awards:* Order of the Red Banner (1922, posthumously); *Died:* late May 1919 publicly hanged in the Marketplace of Yamburg (now Kingisepp); 5 Oct 1919 re-burried in Petrograd.

NIKOLAYEV, Ivan Ivanovich (1893–1964) Transport eng; Dr of Tech Sci; corresp member, USSR Acad of Sci from 1953; Hon Sci and Tech Worker of RSFSR from 1947; prof; assoc, Inst of Comprehensive Transport Problems, USSR Acad of Sci from 1955; CP member from 1942; *Born:* 11 Apr 1893; *Educ:* 1921 grad Moscow Inst of Transport Eng; *Career:* 1921–35 lecturer, 1935–57 prof, Moscow Inst of Transport Eng; 1928–38 lecturer, Moscow Electromech Transport Inst; 1947–51 prof, Acad of Rail Transport; studied dynamics of locomotives and steam distribution in steam locomotives; *Publ: Dinamika i paroraspredeleniye parovoza* (The Dynamics and Steam Distribution of Steam Locomotives) (1953); coauthor, *Opytnoye issledovaniye parovozov* (Experimental Study of Steam Locomotives) (1933); *Voprosy proyektirovaniya parovozov* (Designing Steam Locomotives) (1945); *Teoriya i konstruktsiya parovozov* (The Theory and Design of Steam Locomotives) (1939); coauthor, *Podvizhnoy sostav i tyaga poezdov* (Rolling Stock and Train Traction); coauthor, *Obshchiy kurs zheleznykh dorog* (General Course in Railroads) (1956); *Awards:* Order of Lenin; three other orders; medals; *Died:* 25 Nov 1964.

NIKOLAYEV, Leonid Vasil'yevich (1904–1934) Party official; CP member; *Born:* 1904; *Career:* early 1934 expelled from Party for breach of Party discipline; two months later reinstated after publicly expressing his solidarity with Party policy; 1 Dec 1934, at Smol'nyy near Leningrad, assassinated Kirov; 29 Dec 1934 sentenced to death along with co-defendants by Assizes of Mil Collegium, USSR Supr Court; *Died:* Dec 1934 executed.

NIKOLAYEV, Mikhail Petrovich (1893–1949) Pharmacologist; prof from 1936; corresp member, USSR Acad of Med Sci from 1945; *Born:* 24 Jan 1893; *Educ:* 1914 grad Petrograd Mil Med Acad; *Career:* 1914–22 did mil service; from 1923 asst prof, Chair of pharmacology, Petrograd (Leningrad) Mil Med Acad; from 1927 assoc prof, 1st Leningrad Med Inst; 1936–49 prof and head, Chair of Pharmacology, 1st Moscow Med Inst; specialized in the pharmacology of endocrine drugs, blood circulation and quantitative and pathological pharmacology; wrote 136 works; *Publ: Eksperimental'nyye osnovy farmakologii i toksikologii* (The Experimental Principles of Pharmacology and Toxicology) (1941); *Penitsillin* (Penicillin) (1945); *Biologicheskaya osnova organopreparatov* (The Biological Basis of Organic Drugs) (1948); *Uchebnik farmakologii* (A Textbook on Pharmacology) (1948); *Razvitiye idey N.P. Kravkova v sovetskoy patologicheskoy farmakologii* (The Development of N.P. Krakov's Ideas in Soviet Pathological Pharmacology) (1949), etc; *Awards:* Order of the Red Banner of Labor; *Died:* 1949 in Moscow.

NIKOLAYEV, Viktor Arsen'yevich (1893–1960) Petrographer; corresp member, USSR Acad of Sci from 1946; prof, Leningrad Mining Inst from 1947; Hon Sci Worker of Kir SSR from 1943; *Born:* 6 Dec 1893; *Educ:* 1918 grad Petrograd Mining Inst; *Career:* 1920–47 assoc, Geological Comt (now All-Union Geological Research Inst); 1933–45 prof, Centr Asian Ind Inst; from 1955 pres, All-Union Mineralogical Soc; studied alkaline rocks of Tallass Alatau and some oriferous areas of Centr Asia; explained development of structural-facial zones in shifting belts of the earth's crust; analysed volcanism in Tyan'-Shan'; proposed original theory on the stages of deep-level magmatic activity and analysed the separation of volatile magmatic compounds; *Publ: Vulkanizm v geologicheskoy istorii Tyan'-Shanya* (Volcanism in the Geological History of Tyan'-Shan') (1930); *O vazhneyshey strukturnoy linii Tyan'-Shanya* (The Main Structural Line of the Tyan'-Shan') (1933); *Shcheyolochnyye porody reki Kaindy v Talasskom Alatau* (Alkaline Rocks of the River Kainda in the Talass Alatau) (1935); coauthor, *Osnovnyye problemy v uchenii o magmatogennykh rudnykh mestorozhdeniyakh* (Basic Problems in the Study of Magmatogenic Ore Deposits) (1955); *Fiziko-geograficheskiye rayony del'ty reki Volgi i ikh budushcheye* (The Physical Geographical Zones of the River Volga and Their Future) (1960); *Ob analize struktury stepnykh i polupustynnykh landshaftov po materialem aerofotos'yomki* (Analysis of the Structure of Steppe and Semi-Desert Landscape from Aerial Survey Photos) (1960), etc; *Awards:* Lenin Price (1958); Order of Lenin; other orders; medals; *Died:* 25 Sept 1960.

NIKOLAYEV, Vladimir Vasil'yevich (1871–1950) Pharmacologist; Dr of Med from 1902; prof from 1915; Hon Sci Worker of RSFSR; *Born:* 1871; *Educ:* 1895 grad Med Fac, Kazan' Univ; *Career:* after grad asst to Prof I.M. Dogel'; 1902 defended doctor's thesis on photography of the fundus oculi of animals, in which he described a new method of studying the reaction of the vessels of the retina to various drugs; 1903–06 worked under H. Thoms in Berlin; 1904–15 assoc prof, from 1915 prof, Chair of Pharmacy and Pharmacognostics, Kazan' Univ; 1915 co-founder, Kazan' Women's Med Inst; 1920 co-founder, Kazan' Pharmaceutical Soc; from 1921 prof, Chair of Pharmacology and Drug Prescription, Moscow Univ; 1922 co-founder, Moscow Pharmaceutical Circle; also co-founder, Moscow Assoc of Physiologists, Biochemists, Pharmacologists and Hygienists; from 1925 ed, journal "Vestnik farmatsii"; 1930–50 head, Chair of Pharmacology, 1st Moscow Med Inst; also lecturer, Kazan' and Moscow Pop Univ; founded and held chairs of pharmacology at Smolensk Univ, 3rd Moscow Med Inst and Moscow Stomatological and Pharmaceutical Inst; helped to compile first Sov pharmacopeia and USSR State Pharmacipeia (3rd ed); co-ed, "Tsentral'nyy meditsinskiy zhurnal" and "Bol'shaya meditsinskaya entsiklopediya" (Large Medical Encyclopedia); did research on the physiology and pharmacology of the vegetative nervous system; wrote over 130 works; *Publ:* doctor's thesis *Fotografirovaniye glaznogo dna zhivotnykh* (Photographing the Fundus Oculi of Animals) (1901); *Farmakologiya* (Pharmacology) (1936), etc; *Died:* 1950 in Moscow.

NIKOLAYEVA (real name: VOLYANSKAYA), Galina Yevgen'yevna (1911–1963) Russian writer; physician; *Born:* 5 Feb 1911 in vil Usmanka, Tomsk Province, daughter of a teacher; *Educ:* 1935 grad Gorky Med Inst; *Career:* during WW 2 physician at a hospital; 1939 first work printed; *Publ:* collected verse *Skvoz' ogon'* (Through Fire) (1946); novella *Gibel' komandarma* (The Death of an Army Commander) (1945); *Cherty budushchego* (Traits of the Future) (1949); novel *Zhatva* (Reaping) (1950); novel *Bitva v puti* (The Battle on the Road) (1957); series of novelle *Rasskazy babki Vasilisy pro chudesa* (Grandma Vasilisa's Miracle Stories) (1962); excerpt *Ya lyublyu Neytrino* (I Love a Neutrino) from her unfinished novel *Sil'noye vzaimodeystviye* (Strong Interaction) (1964); blank-verse poem *Nash sad* (Our Garden) (1964); coauthor, play *Vasiliy Bortnikov* (1952); coauthor, play *Pervaya vesna* (The First Spring) (1955); scripts for films: *Vozvrashcheniye Vasiliya Bortnikova* (The Return of Vasiliy Bortnikov) (1953); *V* *stepnoy tishi* (In the Quiet of the Steppe) (1959); "Bitva v Puti" (1961); her works have been translated into many languages; *Awards:* Stalin Prize (1951); *Died:* 18 Oct 1963 in Moscow.

NIKOLAYEVA, Klavdiya Ivanovna (1893–1944) Party and trade-union official; CP member from 1909; *Born:* 13 June 1893 in Petersburg, daughter of a worker; *Educ:* grad municipal high-school; 1926–28 studied at Marxism Courses, Communist Acad; *Career:* after leaving school worked for a bookbinder and joined the revol movement; from 1910 worked for Printers' Trade Union; arrested and exiled to Vologda Province; from 1913 did Party work in Vasiliy Ostrov Rayon, Petrograd; was secr of a workers' hospital fund and contributed to the journal "Rabotnitsa"; after 1917 Oct Revol head, Women's Dept and Dept of Agitation and Propaganda, Petrograd Province RSDRP(B) Comt; from 1922 member, All-Union Centr Exec Comt; 1924–26 head, Women Workers' Dept, CC, CPSU(B); late 1925 sided with Leningrad opposition but recanted at CC plenum in Feb 1927; 1928–30 head, Agitation and Propaganda Dept, North Caucasian Kray CPSU(B) Comt; 1934–36 second secr, Ivanovo Oblast CPSU(B) Comt; 1936–44 secr, All-Union Centr Trade-Union Council; elected cand member, CC at 13th, 17th and 18th CPSU(B) Congresses and full member, CC at 14th, 15th and 16th CPSU(B) Congresses; from 1937 dep, USSR Supr Sov, also Presidium member, USSR Supr Sov; *Awards:* Order of Lenin; *Died:* 28 Dec 1944; buried on Moscow's Red Square.

NIKOLAYEVA, Margarita Fyodorovna (1873–1957) Lit historian and critic; *Born:* 9 May 1873 in vil Bezlesnoye, Saratov Province; *Educ:* 1909 grad Bestuzhev Higher Women's Courses, Petersburg; *Career:* 1896 arrested for involvement with illegal printing press in Lakhta and exiled to Vyatka Province for three years; 1898–1901 corresponded and met with F.E. Dzerzhinskiy; after return from exile worked as a teacher; while attending Bestuzhev Courses joined a Soc-Democratic group and helped to publish and distribute illegal lit, including works by Lenin; while in Petersburg often met with V.G. Korolenko, whose biography she wrote; 1919 moved to Poltava, where she lived with Korolenko's family; during 1930's specialized in the study of Lermontov's life and works and worked for the Lermontov Commission, Inst of Russian Lit, USSR Acad of Sci; from 1939 assoc, Lermontov Museum, Pyatigorsk; *Publ: M. Lermontov. Biograficheskiy ocherk* (M. Lermontov. A Biographical Study) (1940); *M.Yu. Lermontov. Zhizn' i tvorchestvo* (M.Yu. Lermontov. His Life and Works) (1956), etc; *Died:* 20 July 1957 in Pyatigorsk.

NIKOL'SKIY, Aleksandr Mikhaylovich (1858–1942) Zoologist; member, Ukr Acad of Sci from 1919; *Born:* 4 Mar 1858 in Astrakhan', son of mil surgeon; *Educ:* 1881 grad Natural Sci Dept, Physics and Mathematics Fac, Petersburg Univ; *Career:* from 1887 assoc prof; from 1896 zoologist, Zoological Museum, Russian Acad of Sci, Petersburg; 1903–20's prof, Khar'kov Univ; 1921–26 prof, Khar'kov Inst of Educ and Khar'kov Med Inst; from 1926 head, Dept of Zoological Research, Khar'kov Univ; 1881–91 took part in expeditions to Murmansk littoral, Sakhalin, Lake Balkhash, Japan, Transcaspian, Iran and Crimea; 1922–23 consultant, Ochakov Ind Research Station; catalogued some 70 new species of vertebrates; wrote over 120 research works on zoology, zoogeography and comparative anatomy; *Publ:Pozvonochnyye zhivotnyye Kryma* (Vertebrates of the Crimea) (1891); *Geografiya zhivotnykh* (Animal Geography) (1909); *Viznachnyk ryb Ukrainy* (An Index of Ukrainian Fish) (1930); *Died:* 8 Dec 1942.

NIKOL'SKIY, Aleksandr Sergeyevich (1884–1953) Architect; teacher; Dr of Architecture; member, USSR Acad of Architecture from 1939; *Born:* 1884; *Educ:* 1912 grad Petersburg Inst of Civil Eng; *Career:* helped build some sections of Leningrad (Tractor Street, Serafimov section, Kirov Rayon, etc); designed sports installations; bd member, Leningrad Branch, USSR Architects' Union; 1937 attended 1st USSR Congress of Architects and elected bd member, USSR Architects' Union; 1940 seriously criticized in architectural press for his lack of creativity; *Works:* Cooperative Inst, Moscow (1929); co-designed Kirov Stadium, Leningrad (1933–50); designed Victory Park, Leningrad (1953); designed school on Stachki Street and other Schools; *Awards:* Stalin Prize (1951); *Died:* 1953.

NIKOL'SKIY, Dmitriy Petrovich (1855–1918) Hygienist and health service official; Dr of Med from 1897; *Born:* 1855 in Perm', son of a deacon; *Educ:* grad Perm' Theological College and Seminary; 1880 grad Petersburg Med and Surgical Acad; *Career:* 1881–82 zemstvo physician, Yekaterinburg Zemstvo; 1882–88 factory physician, Kishtym Mine Works, after which he moved to Petersburg; until 1909 physician, Neva Factory Hospital, then senior physician, Petersburg Municipal Railroad and, for a while, health officer, Petersburg Municipal Sanitary Commission; taught first courses of occupational hygiene and first aid at various higher educ establishments in Petersburg; from 1897 at Mining Inst; from 1902 at Technol Inst; from 1904 at Polytech Inst; advocated improvement of working and living conditions for labor and the establishment of a factory health inspection system free from employer influence; also advocated the creation of a separate health inspection system for women factory workers; member, Pirogov and various other sci soc (natural sci, anthropological, ethnographical, geographical, etc); 1910 proposed to 11th Pirogov Congress that occupational hygiene be made a compulsory subject at all med fac; from 1910 founder-chm, Labor Welfare Commission, Public Health Soc; chm, various other commissions, including the Commission for the Dissemination of Hygiene Knowledge, Public Health Soc; helped to organize several pop univ and hygiene exhibitions; after 1917 Oct Revol worked for Labor Welfare Dept, Petrograd Oblast Labor Dept; wrote some 250 works; *Publ: Ob issledovanii prichin detskoy smertnosti v Rossii* (Research on the Causes of Child Mortality in Russia) (1901); *O smertnosti detey na fabrikakh* (Child Mortality at Factories) (1904); *Issledovaniye fabrik i zavodov v sanitarnom otnoshenii i vliyaniye ikh na okruzhayushcheye naseleniye* (The Sanitary Inspection of Factories and Plants and Their Influence on the Local Population) (1910); *Neschastnyye sluchai s rabochimi na fabrikakh i zavodakh* (Industrial Accidents) (1910), etc; *Died:* 23 June 1918 of cholera transmitted by a patient.

NIKOL'SKIY, Nikolay Mikhaylovich (1877–1959) Orientalist; Dr of History; member, Bel Acad of Sci from 1931; corresp member, USSR Acad of Sci from 1946; Hon Sci Worker of Bel SSR from 1938; *Born:* 13 Nov 1877, son of a prof; *Educ:* 1900 grad Moscow Univ; *Career:* 1905–06 lecturer for Moscow RSDRP Comt; 1918–21 prof, Smolensk Univ; from 1921 prof, Bel Univ, Minsk; 1937–56 dir, Inst of History, Bel Acad of Sci; 1941–44 served with S. Lazo Partisan Detachment in Bel; classed Sumerian-Accadian soc as feudal and dated the Hammurapi laws from the presumed repeal of feudal law in Babylon; also considered other Ancient Eastern countries feudal (later he termed them semi-patriarchal-semi-feudal); 1938 stopped treating these countries as feudal but stressed the marked contrast in their social forms from those of ancient society; in contrast to most Sov scholars, he considered that all the states of the Ancient East (including the Hittite Kingdom and the Phoenecian cities) were typically despotic societies; postulated the thesis that family and rural communities in the East enjoyed exceptional stability and maintained that from Hammurapi to the time of the Grand Mongols (in India) the structure of oriental soc remained basically unchanged and differed from the structure of slave-owning and feudal Europe; also studied Bel folklore and the history of the Russian Church; *Publ: Drevniy Vavilon* (Ancient Babylon) (1913); *Tsar' David i psalmy* (King David and the Psalms) (1908); *Drevniy Izrail'* (Ancient Israel) (2nd ed, 1922); *Chastnoye zemlevladeniye i zemlepol'zovaniye v drevnem Dvurech'ye* (Private Land Ownership and Land-Tenure in Ancient Mesopotamia) (1948); *Istoriya russkoy tserkvi* (The History of the Russian Church) (2nd ed, 1931); *Proiskhozhdeniye i istoriya belorusskoy svadebnoy obryadnosti* (The Origin and History of Belorussian Marriage Rites) (1956); *Kul'tura drevney Vavilonii* (The Culture of Ancient Babylon) (1959); *Awards:* two Orders of Lenin; Order of the Red Banner of Labor; *Died:* 19 Nov 1959.

NIKOL'SKIY, Pyotr Vasil'yevich (1858–1940) Dermatologist and venereologist; Dr of Med from 1896; prof from 1899; *Born:* 1 Apr 1858 in vil Usman', Tambov Province, son of a priest; *Educ:* 1884 grad Med Fac, Kiev Univ; *Career:* 1884–99 supernumerary intern, grant student and assoc prof, Kiev Clinic of Skin and Venereal Diseases; 1885–99 also intern, then senior intern, Kiev Mil Hospital; 1896 defended doctor's thesis on Pemphigus foliaceus Cazenavi; from 1899 prof, Chair of Skin and Venereal Diseases, Warsaw Univ; 1915–30 founder-head, Chair and Clinic of Venereal and Skin Diseases, Rostov-on-Don Univ; did research on the relation of nervism to dermatology along lines set by S.P. Botkin and A.G. Polotebnov; hypothesized the dependence of dermal processes on the condition of the organism as a whole and higher nervous activity in particular; pioneered injection treatment in Russia and made first examinations of the mercury content in venous and menstrual blood; established how deep gangrene can be caused by the injection of mercury drugs; wrote over 70 works;

Publ: doctor's thesis *Materialy k ucheniyu o Pemphigus foliaceus Cazenavi* (The Theory of Pemphigus foliaceus Cazenavi) (1896); *Prichiny kozhnykh bolezney* (The Causes of Skin Diseases) (1901); *Lektsii o lechenii sifilisa* (Lectures on the Treatment of Syphilis) (1905); *Obshchaya terapiya bolezney kozhi* (The General Therapy of Skin Diseases) (1910); *Bolezni kozhi* (Skin Diseases) (1923–30); *Sifilis i venericheskiye bolezni* (Syphilis and Veneral Diseases) (1924); *Rukovodsvto k issledovaniyu kozhnykh i venericheskikh bol'nykh* (A Guide to the Examination of Skin and Venereal Patients) (1925); *Died:* 17 Mar 1940.

NIKULIN, Lev Veniaminovich (1891–1967) Russian writer; member, Auditing Commission, USSR Writers' Union from 1959; CP member from 1940; *Born:* 1891 in Zhitomir, son of an actor; *Educ:* grad Moscow Business Inst; *Career:* until 1914 contributed to Moscow newspapers and satirical journals; during WW 1 worked for Zemstvo Union; then cultural work with Red Army and Baltic Fleet; 1921–22 with Sov dipl mission in Afghanistan; after WW 2 ed and bibliographer with "Ogonyok" Publ House; 1910 first work published; 1913 visited Germany, Switzerland and Italy; 1921 visited Afghanistan; 1924 toured Turkey and Spain; *Publ:* novels: *Nikakikh sluchaynostey* (No Happenstance) (1924); *Vremya, prostranstvo, dviheniye* (Time, Space, Motion) (1931–33); *Rossii vernyye syny* (Russia's Loyal Sons) (1950); *Dorogi slavy* (The Roads of Glory) (1957); *Trus* (The Coward) (1960); *S novym schast'yem* (Happy New Year) (1963); *Myortvaya zyb'* (Ground Swell) (1965); plays: *Skloka* (The Squabble) (1926); *114–ya stat'ya* (Article 114) (1926); *Inzhener Merts* (Engineer Merts) (1928); "Port Arthur" (1938); travel books: *14 mesyatsev v Afganistane* (Fourteen Months in Afghanistan) (1922); *Pis'ma ob Ispanii* (Letters on Spain) (1930); *Stambul, Ankara, Izmir* (Istanbul, Ankara, Izmir) (1935); book *Lyudi russkogo iskusstva* (Russian Art Figures) (1947); memoirs *Lyudi i stranstvovyniya* (People and Wanderings) (1962); *Velichiye Anatola Fransa* (The Grandeur of Anatole France); documentary novelette *Marshal Tukhachevskiy* (1964); many of his works have been translated into Lat, Kaz, Ukr and German, etc; *Awards:* Badge of Hon; Order of the Red Banner of Labor (1961); Stalin Prize (1952); *Died:* 9 Mar 1967.

NIKULIN, Yuriy Veniaminovich (1907–1958) Russian playwright; *Born:* 7 Aug 1907 in Odessa; *Educ:* studied at Bryusov Higher Lit and Art Inst; *Career:* 1925 first work printed; *Publ:* plays *Lyudi v kozhanykh shlemakh* (People in Leather Helmets) (1925); coauthor, *Magistral'* (Highway) (1931); *Armiya mira* (Army of Peace) (1933); coauthor, "Florida No 306" (1948); *Belyy angel* (White Angel) (1949); *Yego chetvyortoye imya* (His Fourth Name) (1950); *Poslednyaya ispoved'* (The Last Confession) (1952); *Vysokoye napryazheniye* (High Tension) (1954); *Doroga za pereval* (Road Across the Pass) (1955); coauthor, *Vo imya zhizni* (For Life's Sake) (1957), etc; *Died:* 17 Mar 1958 in Moscow.

NIMAN (pseudonym: FYODOROV), Fyodor Avgustovich (1860–1936) Oboist, conductor and composer; Hon Art Worker of RSFSR from 1929; *Born:* 11 Sept 1860 in Nuremberg of German parents; *Career:* from 1880 lived in Russia; 1890–1907 played in orchestra at Maria Theater; 1898–1918 second conductor, from 1918 conductor and artistic dir, Great Russian Orchestra; from 1921 prof, Petrograd (Leningrad) Conservatory; wrote orchestral arrangements of Russian folk songs and an oboe manual; *Died:* 5 Sept 1936 in Leningrad.

NIORADZE, Georgiy Kaplanovich (1886–1951) Geo archeologist; Dr of History; corresp member, Geo Acad of Sci from 1946; Hon Sci Worker of Geo SSR; *Born:* 1886; *Career:* discovered and investigated Paleolithic cave-dwellings in Western Geo (Devis-Khvreli, Sakadzhia) and numerous Geo Neolithic, Bronze, early Iron Age and other ancient monuments at Didube, Mtskheta, Zemo-Avchala, Dmanisi, Samorgi, Kaheti, etc; studied ethnography of Geo and Siberia; founded Chair of Archeology, Tbilisi Univ; also founded Dept of Archeology at Inst of History, Geo Acad of Sci; *Publ:* "Paleolithic Man in the Devis-Khveli Cave-Dwelling" (1933); "The Caucasian Paleolithic" (1937); "Stone-Age Man in the Sakadzhia Cave-Dwelling) (1953), etc; *Died:* 1951.

NISTER, Nistor (real name: KAGANOVICH, Pinkhos Mendelevich) (1884–1950) Jewish writer; *Born:* 1 Nov 1884 in Berdichev; *Educ:* studied Russian language and lit under private tutors; *Career:* 1907 first work published; wrote and gave private lessons; 1922–25 lived in Berlin; arrested by State Security organs; *Publ:* blank verse "Thoughts and Themes" (1907); collected verse: "From My Prossessions" (1929); "Imagination" (1929); collected essays "Three Capitals" (1934); novel "The Mashber Family" (1939); unfinished novel "The Year 1905" published posthumously in 1964; *Died:* 4 June 1950 in imprisonment; posthumously rehabilitated.

NITUSOV, Yevgeniy Vasil'yevich (1895–1961) Electr eng; Dr of Eng and prof from 1940; *Born:* 1895 in Ryazhsk; *Educ:* 1920 grad Fac of Electr Eng, Moscow Higher Tech College; *Career:* 1921–33 assoc, State Inst of Experimental Electr Eng; also taught at Molotov Power Eng Inst, Moscow; 1933–35 dean, Electromech Fac, Molotov Power Eng Inst; from 1940 head, Chair of Electr Machines, Moscow Power Eng Inst; *Publ:* coauthor, *Elektrotekhnika. Obshchiy kurs* (Electrical Engineering. A General Course) (3 vol, 1959–60); *Awards:* Order of Lenin (1951); *Died:* 8 Jan 1961.

NIYAZOV, Ata (1906–1943) Turkmen writer; *Born:* 1906 in vil Bezmeni, near Ashkhabad, son of a peasant; *Educ:* attended boarding school; *Career:* worked as ed; 1927 first work published; translated into Turkmen works of Pushkin, Yanka Kupala and Yakub Kolas; *Publ:* novelette "The Last Night" (1933); verse "The Siren" (1929); poem "Two Orphans" (1929); poem "A Page from History" (1940); 1941–42 verse: "The People's Wrath"; "To the Soviet Army"; "The Red Dzhigit"; "A Son of the Sea"; "250 Days"; "Adamant Fortress"; "Fearless Dare-Devils"; "Ogul'bostan", etc; *Died:* Oct 1943 killed in action.

NIZOVOY (real name: TUPIKOV), Pavel Georgiyevich (1882–1940) Russian writer; *Born:* 1882, Kineshma Uyezd, Kostroma Province, son of a peasant; *Educ:* largely self-educated; attended lectures at Shanyavsky Pop Univ; *Career:* began work at early age: house-painter, glazier, roofer and painter; fought in WW 1; toured Russia; 1907 first verse published; 1911 first story published; 1915–16 wrote pop booklets on history of culture, astronomy and ethnography, published by the Dumnov Press; member, "Kuznitsa" (Smithy) lit assoc; *Publ:* stories: *Fialki* (Violets) (1914); *Golos serdtsa* (The Voice of the Heart) (1914); *Vesenneye tomlen'ye* (Spring Languor) (1916); *Radost'* (Joy) (1918); *Krylo ptitsy* (Bird's Wing) (1921); *V gornykh ushchel'yakh* (In Mountain Ravines) (1924); *Zolotoye ozero* (The Golden Lake) (1924); "Mityakino" (1924); *V lugovykh prostorakh* (The Open Meadows) (1925), etc; novelettes: *Yazychniki* (Pagans) (1922); *Chernozem'ye* (Black Earth) (1923); *Puti dukha moyego* (My Spirit's Paths) (1922); *Povest' o lyubvi* (A Tale of Love) (1927); *U okeana* (At the Ocean) (1926); novels: *Okean* (Ocean) (1920–30); *Stal'* (Steel) (1932); *Nedra* (The Womb) (1934–35); children's works: *V gorakh Altaya* (In the Altay Mountains) (1925); *Sredi vechnykh l'dov* (Among the Eternal Ice) (1927), etc; *Sobraniye sochineniy* (Collected Works) (6 vol, 1928–31); *Rasskazy* (Stories) (1929); *Dve zhizni* (Two Lives) (1933); *Died:* 4 Oct 1940.

NOGIN, Viktor Pavlovich (Party aliases: MAKAR; SAMOVAROV; YABLOCHKOV) (1878–1924) Party and govt official; CP member from 1898; *Born:* 2 Feb 1878 in Moscow, son of a tradesman; *Career:* 1892 errand boy in office, dyer at Bogorodsk-Glukhov Manufacturing Plant; 1896 moved to Petersburg and helped stage strikes at Pal' Factory (1897) and Semennikov Plant (1898); 1897 joined "Workers' Banner" Soc-Democratic group; Dec 1897 arrested and deported to Poltava; 1900 joined Poltava's "Iskra" support group; Aug 1900 emigrated to London and corresponded with Lenin; July 1901 returned to Russia as "Iskra" agent; Sept 1901 arrested and deported to Yeniseysk Province; Apr 1903 fled and went abroad; returned to Russia and worked in Yekaterinoslav for "Iskra"; after 2nd RSDRP Congress sided with Bolsheviks and did Party work in Rostov, Moscow and Nikolayev; Mar 1904 re-arrested and after 17 months' imprisonment deported to Kola Peninsula; Aug 1905 fled abroad; fall 1905 returned to Russia and worked for Petersburg and Baku RSDRP Comt; 1910 worked in Tula; Mar 1911 arrested and exiled to Verkhoyansk; 1914 returned to Moscow, then worked in Saratov, where he helped publish newspaper "Nasha gazeta"; from 1916 in Moscow; member, Moscow Oblast Bureau, CC, RSDRP; engaged in lit and trade-union work; after 1917 Feb Revol helped found Moscow Sov; from Sept 1917 chm, Moscow Sov; member, All-Russian Centr Exec Comt of 1st convocation; after 1917 Oct Revol member Moscow Mil Revol Comt; Pop Comr of Trade and Ind in first Council of Pop Comr; advocated formation of a govt from all socialist parties; 17 Nov 1917 resigned from Council of Pop Comr and publicly stated his disagreement with Party policy; later recanted his error; from 1918 Dep Pop Comr of Labor; Presidium member, Supr Sovnarkhoz; from 1921 chm, All-Russian Union of Cooperative Workers; 1922–24 chm, Bd, All-Russian Textile Workers Union; at 5th–6th Congresses and 7th Conference of RSDRP(B) elected member, CC, RSDRP(B); *Publ: Na polyuse* *kholoda* (At the Cold Pole) (1922); *Died:* 22 May 1924; buried in Moscow's Red Square.

NORIN, Sergey Konstantinovich (1909–1942) Karelian writer; CP member from 1941; *Born:* 1909 in Leningrad, son of a journalist; *Educ:* grad Leningrad Inst of Journalism; *Career:* from age 10 lived in Karelia; wrote in Russian; fought in WW 2; *Publ:* collected essays and stories *Vzorvannyye gody* (Exploded Years) (1932); novel *Na rubezhe* (On the Boundary) (1938); collected stories *Rodnoy bereg* (Native Shore) (1939); *Izbrannoye* (Selected Works) (1949); play *Zastava u Chyornogo ruch'ya* (The Picket on Black Stream) (1940); novelette "Mikko Makkonen" (1947); *Died:* 14 Apr 1942 in Arkhangel'sk hospital after beeing seriously wounded at the front.

NOSENKO, Ivan Isidorovich (1902–1956) Eng; govt official; CP member from 1925; *Born:* 1902, son of a peasant; *Educ:* 1928 grad Nikolayev Shipbuilding Inst; *Career:* from 1914 apprentice, then laborer, Nikolayev Shipbuilding Yards; from 1928 foreman, then chief shipbuilder, Nikolayev Shipbuilding Yards; 1935–37 chief eng at various heavy ind plants in Leningrad; 1928 dir, Ordzhonikidze Baltic Yard; 1939 USSR Dep Pop Comr of Shipbuilding Ind; from May 1940 USSR Pop Comr of Shipbuilding Ind; 1947–51 USSR Pop Comr of Transport Machine-Building; 1951–Mar 1953 USSR Min of Shipbuilding Ind; from Mar 1953 USSR First Dep Min of Transport and Heavy Machine-Building; from June 1953 USSR Min of Transport and Heavy Machine-Building; 1954–56 USSR Min of Shipbuilding Ind; during WW 2, while working at Pop Comrt of Shipbuilding Ind, simultaneously USSR First Dep Min of Tank Ind; at 19th and 20th CPSU Congresses elected cand member, CC, CPSU; dep, USSR Supr Sov of 1954 convocation; *Awards:* three Orders of Lenin; Order of Nakhimov, 1st Class; three Orders of the Red Banner of Labor; Badge of Hon; medals; *Died:* 2 Aug 1956.

NOVACHENKO, Nikolay Petrovich (1898–1966) Orthopedic surgeon and traumatologist; Dr of Med and prof from 1940; corresp member, USSR Acad of Med Sci from 1957; Hon Sci Worker of Ukr SSR from 1952; CP member from 1946; *Born:* 1898 in vil Burin', Kursk Province (now Sumy Oblast); *Educ:* 1922 grad Khar'kov Med Inst; *Career:* 1922–40 intern, head of x-ray section, dept head, clinic head and dep sci and therapy dir, 1940–66 dir, Ukr (M. I. Sitenko) Research Inst of Orthopedics and Traumatology; 1925–34 asst prof, 1934–40 assoc prof, 1941–66 head, Chair of Orthopedics and Traumatology, Khar'kov Inst of Postgrad Med Training; 1937 defended cand thesis; 1940–41 and 1955–56 chief ed, journal "Ortopediya, travmatologiya i protezirovaniye"; 1941–45 chief surgeon, various evacuation hospitals; also chief surgeon, Karaganda Oblast and Volga and Khar'kov Mil Distr; 1945 founded first Ukr Prosthetics Research Inst in Khar'kov; from 1945 chm, Khar'kov Med Soc and Khar'kov Oblast Soc of Traumatologists and Orthopedic Surgeons; also chm, Orthopedics Commission, Learned Med Council, Ukr Min of Health; bd member, All-Union Surgeons' Soc; chm, Ukr and dep chm, All-Union Soc of Traumatologists and Orthopedic Surgeons; 1950 and 1952 deleg, 16th and 17th Congresses of CP Ukr; dep, Ukr Supr Sov of 1955 convocation; devised several original osteoplastic operations and designed new orthopedic equipment; did research on the transplantation and regeneration of bone tissue under experimental conditions; also studied bone fractures and prosthetics; wrote over 100 works; *Publ:* coauthor, *Postoyannoye vytyazheniye* (Permanent Traction) (1940); *Vaskulyarizatsiya peresazhennoy kosti* (The Vascularization of Transplanted Bone) (1946); *Lecheniye kostnosustavnogo tuberkulyoza sanazinom* (The Treatment of Osteoarthritic Tuberculosis with Sanazine) (1951); *Osnovy ortopedii i travmatologii* (The Principles of Orthopedics and Traumatology) (1961); *Awards:* two Orders of Lenin; two Badges of Hon; three medals; *Died:* 16 Oct 1966 in Khar'kov.

NOVIKOV, Ivan Alekseyevich (1877–1959) Russian writer; *Born:* 1 Jan 1877 in vil Il'kovo, Oryol Province; *Educ:* 1901 grad Moscow Agric Inst; *Career:* 1899 first work published; 1901–08 in Kiev; studied history of lit; originally wrote under pseudonym M. Zelenoglazyy; 1904–10 influenced by Symbolism; *Publ: Son Sergeya Ivanovicha* (The Dream of Sergey Ivanovich) (1889); play *V puti* (En Route) (1901); novel *Zolotyye kresty* (Golden Crosses)(1908); novel *Iz zhizni dukha* (The Life of the Spirit) (1906); verse collection *Dukhu Svyatomu* (To the Holy Spirit) (1908); stories *Zhanna d'Ark* (Jeanne d'Arc) (1911); *Chudo sv. Nikolaya* (The Miracle of St Nicholas) (1912); novel *Mezhdu dvukh zor'* (Between Two Dawns) (1915); stories *Gorod, more, derevnya* (City, Sea and Village) (1931); novel *Pushkin v Mikhaylovskom* (Pushkin at Mikhaylovskoye) (1936); play *Pushkin na Yuge* (Pushkin in the South) (1937); study *"Slovo o polku Igoreve" i yego avtor* (The "Lay of the Host of Igor" and Its Author) (1938), including a verse translation of the work; verse translation of *Kraledvorskaya rukopis'* (The Kraledvor Manuscript) (1939); film script *Molodoy Pushkin* (The Young Pushkin) (1949); book *Turgenev – khudozhnik slova* (Turgenev, Artist of the Written Word) (1954); book *Pisatel'i yego tvorchestvo* (The Writter and His Work) (1956), etc; *Died:* 10 Jan 1959 in Moscow.

NOVIKOV, Kuz'ma Nikolayevich (1914–1961) Lawyer; maj-gen, Justice Corps; CP member from 1941; *Born:* 1914; *Educ:* 1941 grad Mil Law Acad; *Career:* from 1941 worked for mil prosecutor's office as investigator, asst mil prosecutor of an army, then div mil prosecutor; after WW 2 worked for Main Mil Prosecutor's Office; from 1952 instructor, CC, CPSU; from 1955 dep chief mil prosecutor, then mil prosecutor, Moscow Mil Distr; *Awards:* Order of the Red Star; medals; *Died:* 1961.

NOVIKOV-PRIBOY (real name: NOVIKOV), Aleksey Silych (1877–1944) Russian writer, specializing in sea stories; *Born:* 24 Mar 1877 in vil Matveyevskoye, Tambov Province, son of a peasant; *Educ:* parish school; *Career:* 1899 drafted into Russian Navy; 1902 and 1903 twice arrested for polit activities; 1904–05 took part in Admiral Z. P. Rozhestvenskiy's squadron's cruise from Kronstadt to the Sea of Japan, leading to naval engagement with Japanese fleet in Tsushima Strait; taken prisoner by Japanese; engaged in anti-govt propaganda among prisoners-of-war; 1906 returned to Russia; 1 Apr 1906 newspaper "Novoye vremya" printed his first lit work, an account of the sinking of the battleship "Borodino" in the Battle of Tsushima; 1907–13 polit emigre in Spain, Italy and North Africa; shipped with merchant ships; 1913 returned to Russia on someone else's passport; from 1917 concentrated on lit work; during WW 2 wrote patriotic articles and essays; *Publ:* stories *Lishniy* (The Extra) (1913); *Porchenyy* (Spoiled) (1917); *Zub za zub* (A Tooth for a Tooth) (1922); *V bukhte "Otrada"* (In Comfort Bay) (1924); *Boynya* (The Massacre) (1925); *Ukhaby* (Potholes) (1927); novelettes *More zovyot* (The Sea Calls) (1919); *Podvodniki* (Submariners) (1923); *Yeralashnyy reys* (The Turbulent Voyage) (1925); *Zhenshchina v more* (Woman at Sea) (1926); novels: *Solyonaya kupel'* (The Salty Font) (1929); "Tsushima" (2 vol, 1932–35); *Kapitan 1-go ranga* (Captain, 1st Class) (2 vol, 1942–44, unfinished); *Awards:* Stalin Prize (1941); *Died:* 29 Apr 1944 in Moscow.

NOVIKOVA-VASHENTSEVA, Yelena Mikhaylovna (1860–1953) Russian writer; CP member from 1920; *Born:* 1 June 1860 in vil Uspenskoye, Moscow Province, daughter of a peasant; *Career:* from age 12 worked in factory; 1905 assisted her son in his revol activities; 1923 moved to Moscow and began to publish notes and stories in journals "Rabotnitsa," "Delegatka" and "Krest'yanka"; from 1925 member, All-Russian Soc of Peasant Writers, which helped her to improve her educ; *Publ:* stories *Kak tyotka Dar'ya uznala o MOPRe* (How Aunt Dar'ya Learnt About the International Organization for Aid to Revolutionary Fighters); *Delegatka Anna* (Anna the Delegate); *Yashka-"Berlin" besprizornik* ("Berlin" Yashka, the Waif), etc, all written in mid 1920's and early 1930's; autobiographical novelette *Marinkina zhizn'* (Marinka's Life) (3 vol, 1930–34); *Tam, gde zhili tsari* (Where the Tsars Lived) (1930); *Kak ya stala pisatel'nitsey* (How I Became a Writer) (1938); *Died:* 19 Dec 1953 in Bogorodsk.

NOVITSKIY, Aleksey Petrovich (1862–1934) Ukr art historian; member, Ukr Acad of Sci from 1922; chm, Archeological Comt, Ukr Acad of Sci; *Born:* 20 Apr 1862 in Simbirsk; *Educ:* 1887 grad Mathematics Fac, Moscow Univ; *Career:* developed an interest in art history as a student; 1911 organized jubilee exhibition of Shevchenko's lit and graphic works in Moscow; compiled account of Rumyantsev Museum and Tret'yakov Gallery; did research on Shevchenko's papers; specialized in history of Ukr art and architecture; *Publ: Peredvizhniki* (The Travelling Art Exhibitors) (1897); *Istoriya russkogo iskusstva s drevneyshikh vremyon* (A History of Russian Art from Ancient Times) (1902–03); *Taras Shevchenko kak khudozhnik* (Taras Shevchenko as an Artist) (1914); *K voprosu o proiskhozhdenii derevyannoy ukrainskoy arkhitektury* (The Origin of Ukrainian Wooden Architecture) (1927); *Proba rekonstruktsii Kiyevskoy Sofii* (The Projected Reconstruction of Kiev's St. Sophia Cathedral) (1930), etc; *Died:* 24 Sept 1934.

NOVITSKIY, Fyodor Fyodorovich (1870–1944) Mil commander and instructor; maj-gen, Russian Army; lt-gen of the Air Force from 1943; *Born:* 2 Aug 1870 in Opatov, Radom Province, brother of V. F. Novitskiy; *Educ:* 1889 grad Paul Mil College; 1895 grad Gen Staff Acad; *Career:* fought in Russo-Japanese War and WW 1; rose in Russian Army to command 43rd Army Corps, 12th Army; from 1918 in Red Army; from Mar 1918 commander, Kaluga Detachment; from June 1918 mil commander, Yaroslavl' Mil Distr; from Dec 1918 chief of staff and asst commander, 4th Army on Eastern Front; 6 Mar–15 Aug 1919 member, Revol Mil Council, 4th Army on Eastern Front; from Aug 1919 assigned to M. V. Frunze; from 1 Nov 1919 dep commander, Turkestani Front; from July 1920 assigned to field staff, RSFSR Revol Mil Council; from Sept 1921 chief of staff, Red Air Force; from Nov 1923 instructor, Air Force Acad; from 1931 duties with Red Army Main Bd; 1933–38 special assignments under commander, Sov Air Force; 1938 dismissed from Red Army; 1943 rejoined Red Army; 1943–44 lecturer, Chair of Mil History, Frunze Mil Acad; *Died:* 6 Apr 1944.

NOVITSKIY, Vasiliy Fyodorovich (1869–1929) Mil commander; gen, Russian Army Gen Staff; Sov mil historian, prof and publicist; *Born:* 18 Mar 1869 in Smolensk Province, son of a nobleman; *Educ:* 1889 grad Mikhail Artillery School; 1895 grad Gen Staff Acad; *Career:* 1901–04 on Mil Training Comt and at Main Headquarters; 1904–05 field officer for special assignments under commander of 2nd Manchurian Army during Russo-Japanese War; after Russo-Japanese War co-ed, newspaper "Voyenny golos," which criticized mil system and especially participation of army in 1905–06 punitive expeditions; 16 July 1906 this newspaper was labelled harmful and was soon closed; 1905–11 on Main Bd, Gen Staff; 1911–14 commanded infantry regt; 1914–17 quartermaster-gen (head, Operations Dept), 1st Army Headquarters; commanded brigade, then div; 1917 Asst Mil Min, Provisional Govt; commanded corps, then 12th Army; commander in chief, Northern Front; Nov 1917 supported 12th Army soldiers' decision to recognize Sov regime; after 1917 Oct Revol prof, Gen Staff Acad; secr, Centr Pedag Museum, Petrograd; dep mil head, Red Army Supr Mil Inspectorate; from Oct 1919 taught at Red Army Mil Acad; concentrated on maneuvers in his theoretical works and underestimated tech factor in war; *Publ: Na puti k usovershenstvovaniyu gosudarstvennoy oborony* (On the Road to Perfecting State Defense) (1909); *Ot Shakhe k Mukdenu (ot nastupleniya k oborone* (From the Shakhe to Mukden – From the Offensive to the Defensive) (1912); *Mirovaya voyna 1914–1918 gg. Kampaniya 1914 v Bel'gii i Frantsii* (The 1914–18 World War. The 1914 Campaign in Belgium and France) (1938); *Died:* 15 Jan 1929 in Moscow.

NOVOKSHONOV, Ivan Mikhaylovich (1895–1943) Russian writer; *Born:* 27 Oct 1895 in vil Gusevo, Tomsk Province, son of a peasant; *Career:* fought in Civil War in Siberia; 1924 first work printed in "Buryat-mongol'skaya pravda"; his works deal mainly with Civil War in Siberia; arrested by State Security organs; *Publ: Velikiy Anym* (Great Anym) (1927); coauthor, *Pamyati pavshikh za Oktyabr'* (In Memory of Those Who Fell for the October Revolution) (1927); novelette *Tayozhnaya zhut'* (The Rigors of the Taiga) (1927); collected stories *Medvezh'ya snorovka* (Bear Lore) (1929); *Partizanskiye byli* (They Were Partisans) (1933); novelette *Potomok Chingis-Khana* (Descendant of Genghis Khan) (1933); coauthor, drama *Nenavist'* (Hatred); children's play *Vesyolyy portnyazhka* (The Merry Tailor); novelette *Zastrel'shchiki* (The Pioneers) (1934); *Lyotchik Fyodorov. Vospominaniya partizana* (Pilot Fyodorov. A Partisan's Reminiscences) (1966), etc; *Died:* May 1943 in imprisonment; posthumously rehabilitated.

NOVOSEL'SKIY, Aleksey Andreyevich (1891–1967) Historian; Dr of History from 1946; prof; *Born:* 16 Oct 1891 in Tambov, son of a teacher; *Educ:* 1915 grad Moscow Univ; *Career:* 1918–30 worked at Antiquities Archives (now Centr State Archives of Ancient Records); from 1919 also lecturer, Moscow Univ; 1922–29 secr, Russian History Section, Inst of History, Russian Assoc of Soc Sci Research Inst; 1930–35 head, Sci Bibliography Section, All-Union Lenin Library; 1935–42 assoc, then dept head, Anthropology Museum, Moscow Univ; 1939–41 also lecturer, Moscow Inst of History, Philosophy and Lit; 1942–53 senior assoc and head, Section of the History of Feudal Russia, then dep dir, Inst of History, USSR Acad of Sci; 1943–46 assoc prof, 1946–56 prof, Moscow Historical Archives Inst; 1953–63 head, Section of Source Research and Auxiliary Historical Disciplines, Inst of History, USSR Acad of Sci; 1963 retired on pension but continued to work at Centr State Archives of Ancient Records; specialized in the socio-econ and polit history of 17th-Century Russia; *Publ:* co-ed, *Pamyatniki istorii krest'yan i kholopov v Moskovskom gosudarstve* (Relics of the History of the Peasants and Serfs of Muscovy) (vol 3–5, 1925); *Votchinnik i yego khozyaystvo v XVII veke* (The Great Landowner and His Patrimonial Estate in the 17th Century) (1929); co-ed, *Akty khozyaystva boyarina Morozova* (The Records of the Estate of Boyar Morozov) (2 vol, 1940–45); *Bor'ba Moskovskogo gosudarstva s tatarami v pervoy polovine XVII veka* (Muscovy's Struggle Against the Tatars in the Early 17th Century) (1948); coauthor, *Istoriya Moskvy* (The History of Moscow) (1952); co-ed, *Vossoyedineniye Ukrainy s Rossiyey* (The Unification of the Ukraine with Russia) (3 vol, 1954); coauthor, *Ocherki istorii SSSR. XVII vek* (Studies in the History of the USSR. The 17th Century) (1955); coauthor, textbook *Istoriya SSSR* (The History of the USSR) (vol 1, 1956); co-ed, *Dokumenty vneshney politiki SSSR* (Documents on the Foreign Policy of the USSR) (4 vol, 1957–60); *Dvortsovyye krest'yane Komaritskoy volosti vo vtoroy polovine XVII veka* (Landed Peasants in Komarichi Volost in the Late 17th Century) (1961); *Vol'nyye i perekhodnyye lyudi v yuzhnykh uyezdakh russkogo gosudarstva v XVII veke* (Freemen and Transients in the Southern Uyezds of the Russian State in the 17th Century) (1962); mang ed, anthologies *Istoricheskiy arkhiv* (Historical Archives), *Materialy po istorii SSSR* (Material on the History of the USSR) and *Problemy istochnikovedeniya* (Problems of Source Research), etc; *Awards:* Order of Lenin; medals; *Died:* 29 Oct 1967.

NOVOSEL'SKIY, Sergey Aleksandrovich (1872–1953) Demographer and health statistician; prof from 1907; member, USSR Acad of Med Sci and Hon Sci Worker of RSFSR from 1945; *Born:* 1872; *Educ:* 1895 grad Petersburg Mil Med Acad; *Career:* 1900–14 head, Health Statistics Section, Main Med Inspection Bd; 1903–14 compiled and published the "Annual Statistical Review of the State of Public Health and the Organization of Medical Aid in Russia"; 1907–24 prof of health and demographic statistics, Statistics Courses, Centr Statistical Comt; 1916–31 assoc prof of health statistics, Petrograd (Leningrad) Inst of Postgrad Med Training; 1916 published first Russian mortality tables, based on the census of 1897; 1918–35 head, Dept of Demographic and Health Statistics, Petrograd (Leningrad) Municipal Statistical Bd; 1918, 1920, 1923 and 1926 supervised population censuses of Leningrad and school censuses in Leningrad Oblast; 1929–30 also worked for the Econ Statistics Section, USSR Gosplan; 1935–50 prof, Leningrad Pediatric Inst; compiled statistics on child mortality, birth-rates, mortality from cancer and tuberculosis, gen health statistics and life-expectancy tables; wrote over 150 works; *Publ: O razlichiyakh v smertnosti gorodskogo i sel'skogo naseleniya* (Differences in Urban and Rural Mortality Rates) (1911); *Smertnost' i prodolzhitel'nost' zhizni v SSSR* (Death Rates and Life-Expectancy in the USSR) (1930); *Osnovy demograficheskoy i sanitarnoy statistiki* (The Principles of Dempgraphic and Health Statistics) (1930) (a revised translation of J. Whipple's book); coauthor, *Poteri v proshlykh voynakh* (Death and Casualty Rates in Past Wars) (1946); *Voprosy demograficheskoy i sanitarnoy statistiki* (Problems of Demograpic and Health Statistics) (1958), etc; *Awards:* Prize of Russian Acad of Sci (1916); *Died:* 1953.

NOZDRIN, Avenir Yevstigneyevich (1862–1938) Russian poet; *Born:* 29 Oct 1862 in vil Ivanovo, Vladimir Province; *Educ:* completed zemstvo primary school; *Career:* in his youth worked as engraver at textile mills; 1905 chm, Ivanovo-Voznesensk Sov of Workers' Dep; 1907–09 exiled in Olonetsk Province; 1890's first work published; wrote many poems on revol themes; arrested by State Security organs; *Publ: Nakanune maya* (On the Eve of May); *Zabastovka* (The Strike); *Na mitinge* (At the Rally); *Nasha Talka* (Our Talka); *Evon kandal'nyy* (Evon of the Chain Gang); verse collections: *Staryy parus* (The Old Sail) (1927); *Izbrannyye stikhotvoreniya* (Selected Verse) (1937); *Died:* 23 Sept 1938 in imprisonment; posthumously rehabilitated.

NUROV, Rabadan (1889–1942) Dag poet and playwright; *Born:* 1889 in vil Sanamakhi, Dag, son of a peasant; *Career:* from age 17 worked in oil fields; drew on Darghinian folk songs for his lit works; revol work in Dag; 1937 arrested by State Security organs; *Publ:* verse: "Awake, Daghestan!" (1919); "Aya-Kaka" (1921); "Is It True? " (1930); "The Dream" (1927); "The Old Woman and the Girl" (1935); plays: "Ayshat in the Clutches of the Adat" (1928); "The Unmasked Sheikh" (1934); *Died:* 1942 in imprisonment; posthumously rehabilitated.

NURUTDINOV, Sirodzh (1911–1966) Party and govt official;

mang, Building Trust No. 6, Uzbek Min of Construction; CP member from 1938; *Born:* 1911; *Educ:* grad Higher Party School, CC, CPSU; *Career:* from 1929 lathe operator, then shop foreman; from 1937 first secr of a city Komsomol comt, then first secr of an oblast Komsomol comt; 1941–45 in Sov Army; from 1945 various Party posts; first secr, Namagan Oblast Party Comt; from 1954 member, CC, CP Uzbek; 1955–56 first secr, Tashkent City Comt, CP Uzbek; 1956–59 first secr, Tashkent Oblast Comt, CP Uzbek; from 1959 chm, Uzbek Republ Trade-Union Council and member, USSR Centr Council of Sports Soc and Org; chm, Uzbek Peace Defense Comt; dep, USSR Supr Sov of 1950, 1954, 1958 and 1962 convocations; *Died:* June 1966.

NUSINOV, Isaak Markovich (1889–1950) Lit critic and historian; Jew; CP member from 1919; *Born:* 2 July 1889 in Chernikhov, Volhynian Province, son of wealthy Jewish parents; *Educ:* 1924 grad Russian Assoc of Soc Sci Research Institutes; *Career:* as a youth took an active part in the workers' movement; 1905 joined Jewish Bund; 1905–17 lived in Switzerland; prof of history of West European lit at Inst of Red Prof; head, Chair of Jewish Lit, Moscow State Teachers' Training Inst; member, Inst of Lit and Art, Communist Acad; member, Inst of Jewish Proletarian Culture, All-Ukr Acad of Sci; from 1929 member, Russian Assoc of Proletarian Writers; charged with erroneous views in his assessment of "petty-bourgeois nationalistic writers" and with underestimating the growth of Jewish proletarian lit; from 1928 on several occasions indulged in self-criticism of his views; 1931 finally recanted his views after a letter from Stalin to the editors of the journal "Proletarskaya revolyutsiya"; 1949 arrested by State Security organs; *Publ: Problema istoricheskogo romana V. Gyugo i A. Fransa* (Victor Hugo and Anatole France's Historical Novels) (1927); "L. N. Tolstoy, M. Gor'kiy, A. P. Chekhov" (1930); "M. Gor'kiy" (1932); "Leonid Leonov" (1935); *Vekovyye obrazy* (Secular Images) (1937); *Pushkin i mirovaya literatura* (Pushkin and World Literature) (1941), etc; numerous articles on for classics and Jewish lit; *Died:* 30 Nov 1950 in imprisonment; posthumously rehabilitated.

NYAGA, Stepan Timofeyevich (1900–1951) Composer; Hon Art Worker of Mold SSR from 1943; bd member, USSR Composers' Union; *Born:* 24 Nov 1900 in Kishinev, son of a musician; *Educ:* 1926 grad Piano and Composition Classes, Bucharest Musical Acad; 1937–39 studied in Paris; *Career:* became a Sov citizen with annexation of Bessarabia; instructor and dep dir, Kishinev Conservatory; dep, Mold Supr Sov of 1947 and 1951 convocations; *Works:* music for Nat Anthem of Mold SSR (1945); three cantatas, including cantata "Twenty-Five Years of the Moldavian SSR" (1949); "Song of Stalin" (1949); oratorio "Song of Resurrection" (1951); two symphonies; "Moldavia" and "Poem of the Dnester" suites; *Awards:* Order of Lenin; Stalin Prize (1950); *Died:* 13 May 1951 in Kishinev.

NYUSTREM, Ragnar Yakovlevich (pen name: RUSKO, Ragnar) (1898–1939) Finnish writer and stage dir; CP member from 1927; *Born:* 20 Sept 1898 in Helsinki, son of a tinsmith; *Educ:* 1932 grad Leningrad Theater Studio; *Career:* worked as turner, ship's stoker; 1914 joined Finnish Soc-Democratic Party; 1917–18 dir, workers' theater; 1918 sentenced to 12 years' penal servitude, escaped; from 1921 lived in USSR; from 1932 stage dir, Petrozavodsk Karelian Drama Theater; early 1920's first work printed; 1937 arrested by State Security organs; *Publ:* polit lyrics: "Red Country"; "People's Front"; plays; articles on theater problems; autobiographical novelette "In Chains" (1930), etc; *Died:* 12 Dec 1939 in imprisonment; posthumously rehabilitated.

O

OBNORSKIY, Sergey Petrovich (1888–1962) Russian linguist; specialist of Russian; Dr of Philology; member, USSR Acad of Sci from 1939; member, RSFSR Acad of Pedag Sci from 1944; member Czech and Bulgarian Acad of Sci; *Born:* 26 June 1888 in Petersburg; *Educ:* 1910 grad History and Philology Fac, Petersburg Univ; *Career:* from 1912 ed work on Russian dictionary at Russian Acad of Sci; 1916–22 lecturer, Perm' Univ; 1922–41 prof, Leningrad Univ and Leningrad Teachers' Training Inst; 1943–46 prof, Moscow State Univ; 1922–41 simultaneously worked for Inst of Language and Thought, USSR Acad of Sci; 1944–50 dir, Inst of Russian Language, USSR Acad of Sci; 1950–52 head, History of Russian Language and Dialects Section, Inst of Linguistics, USSR Acad of Sci; then headed Orthographic Commission, USSR Acad of Sci; studied language of earliest specimens of Russian writing and phonetics and morphology of ancient and modern Russian; at first followed theories of his teacher, A.A. Shakhmatov but differed with him in 1930's and denied Old Slavic origin of Russian literary language; belittling the historical originality of linguistic dualism, typical of the ancient times, he sought original sources for the ancient Russian literary language and claimed that it stemmed from East Slavic folk sources; directed publ of all acad dictionaries of modern Russian and studied orthography, orthoepy and grammatical norms of Russian; *Publ: O yazyke Yefremovskoy Kormchey XII veka* (The Language of the 12th-Century Yefremov Nomokanon" (1912); *Imennoye skloneniye v sovremennom russkom yazyke* (T e Declension of Nouns in Modern Russian) (2 vol, 1927–31); coauthor, *Khrestomatiya po istorii russkogo yazyka* (An Anthology on the History of Russian) (2 vol, 1938–49); *Ocherki po istorii literaturnogo yazyka starshego perioda* (An Outline History of the Old Russian Literary Language) (1946); *Kul'tura russkogo yazyka* (Standard Russian) (1948); *Ocherki po morfologii russkogo glagola* (Outline Morphology of the Russian Verb) (1953); coauthor, *Pravila russkoy orfografii i punktuatsii* (Rules of Russian Orthography and Punctuation) (1956); *Izbrannyye raboty po russkomu yazyku* (Selected Works on the Russian Language) (1960); *Awards:* three Orders of Lenin; Stalin Prize (1947); *Died:* 13 Nov 1962 in Moscow.

OBOLDUYEV, Georgiy Nikolayevich (1898–1954) Russian poet and translator; *Born:* 19 May 1898 in Moscow; *Educ:* 1924 grad V.Ya. Bryusov Higher Inst of Lit and Art; *Career:* 1929 first work published; 1933–39 imprisoned by NKVD; fought in WW 2; after war translated verse by G. Abashidze, G. Emin, I. Grishashvili and A. Kekilov; also translated Mickiewicz's "Grazhina" and Neruda's "Chilean Canto"; published only a small quantity of his own poetry; *Publ:* various poems; libretto for the opera "Vasilisa Prekrasnaya"; libretto for Donizetti's "The Lantern Wedding"; *Died:* 27 Aug 1954 in Golitsyno, Moscow Oblast.

OBORIN, V.P. (1887–1939) Party and govt official; CP member from 1904; *Born:* 1887; *Career:* Party work in Moscow, Petersburg, Kolomna and Yekaterinoslav; after 1917 Oct Revol member, Yekaterinoslav Province Party Comt; then member, Petrograd Province RCP(B) Comt and member, Petrograd Exec Comt; Petersburg Province RCP(B) Comt deleg at 8th RCP(B) Congress; 1927, at 15th CPSU(B) Congress, expelled from the Party for alleged anti-Party activities; arrested by State Security organs; *Died:* 1939 in imprisonment.

OBRADOVICH, Sergey Aleksandrovich (1892–1956) Russian poet; CP member from 1941; *Born:* 2 Sept 1892 in Moscow; *Educ:* studied at Shanyavskiy Univ; *Career:* from age 15 employed at printing works; fought in WW 1; 1917 elected chm, regt comt; 1922–27 dept head, newspaper "Pravda"; member, Proletatian Culture Org, Pop Comrt of Educ; co-founder "Kuznitsa" (The Smithy) lit assoc; bd member, All-Russian Assoc of Proletarian Wirters; *Publ:* verse *K svetu* (To the Light) (1912); verse collections *Vzmakh* (The Stroke) (1921); *Sddvig* (The Shift) (1921); *Oktyabr'* (October) (1922); collections *Novosel'ye* (The House-Warming) (1934), etc; also wrote critical studies and translated poetry of other peoples of the USSR; *Died:* 25 Oct 1956 in Moscow.

OBRAZTSOV, Vasiliy Parmenovich (1851–1920) Clinician; pioneer of Russian school of therapy; Dr of Med from 1880; prof from 1893; pupil of S.P. Botkin and I.P. Pavlov; *Born:* 13 Jan 1851 in Gryazovets, now Vologda Oblast, son of a priest; *Educ:* 1875 grad Petersburg Med Surgical Acad; *Career:* during student years took part in revol activities; after grad zemstvo physician in Vologda Province; 1877–78 mil surgeon in Russo-Turkish War; 1879 worked under Virchow, Volkmann and Gerhardt in Germany; 1880 defended doctor's thesis on "The Morphology of Blood Formation in the Medulla Ossium of Mammals; 1880–88 worked at a mil hospital in Kiev; from 1888 head, Therapy Dept, Kiev City Hospital; 1891–93 assoc prof, 1893–1904 prof, Chair of Special Pathology and Therapy, 1904–18 head, Chair of Fac Therapy Clinic, Kiev Univ; did research on clinical examination methods, cardiovascular and circulatory diseases and diseases of the gastro-intestinal tract; trained numerous outstanding therapists; wrote over 50 works; *Publ:* doctor's thesis *K morfologii obrazovaniya krovi v kostnom mozge u mlekopitayushchikh* (The Morphology of Blood Formation in the Medulla Ossium of Mammals) (1880); *K fizicheskomu issledovaniyu zheludochno-*

kishechnogo kanala i serdtsa (Physical Examination of the Gastro-Intestinal Tract and the Heart) (1915); *Bolezni zheludka, kishok i bryushiny* (Diseases of the Stomach, Intestines and Abdomen) (1924); *Izbrannyye trudy* (Selected Works) (1950), etc; *Died:* 14 Dec 1920.

OBRAZTSOV, Vladimir Nikolayevich (1874–1949) Railroad eng; prof from 1919; member, USSR Acad of Sci from 1939; Hon Sci Worker of RSFSR from 1935; *Born:* 18 June 1874; *Educ:* 1897 grad Petersburg Inst of Trans Eng; *Career:* surveyed and built various railroad lines, from 1901 taught at Moscow Eng College; 1919–22 prof, Inst of Civil Eng; 1923–49 prof, Moscow Inst of Railroad Eng, where he founded a Chair of Stations and Junctions; also taught at other higher educ establishments; 1935–40 also dir, Moscow Railroad Research Inst; 1939–45 Presidium member, USSR Acad of Sci; from 1939 chm, Transport Problems Study Section, from 1946 Presidium member, Council for the Study of Production Resources; helped to standardize and redesign junction systems and to design Moscow Subway system; dep, USSR Supr Sov of 1st and 2nd convocations; *Publ: Entsiklopediya putey soobshcheniya* (A Means of Communication Encyclopedia) (1925); *Osnovnyye dannyye dlya proyektirovaniya zheleznodorozhnykh stantsiy* (Basic Data for the Planning of Railroad Stations) (1929); *Zheleznodorozhnyye uzly* (Railroad Junctions) (1933); coauthor, *O razvitii narodnogo khozyaystva Urala v usloviyakh voyny* (The Economic Development of the Urals in Wartime) (1942); coauthor, *Stantsii i uzly* (Stations and Junctions) (1949); *Awards:* three Orders of Lenin, two Stalin Prizes (1942 and 1943); four other orders; medals; *Died:* 28 Nov 1949.

OBRUCHEV, Sergey Vladimirovich (1891–1965) Geologist; corresp member, USSR Acad of Sci from 1953; *Born:* 1891, son of the geologist and traveler V.A. Obruchev; *Educ:* 1915 grad Moscow Univ; *Career:* 1917–24 made geological study of the Yenisey Basin, leading to the discovery of the Tungus coal basin; 1926–35 studied northeastern Siberia, Indigirka and Kolyma River Basins and also Chukotka Okrug; mapped the orography, geomorphology and the geological structure of northeastern Asia; 1937–54 studied the Eastern Sayans, the Khamar-Dabans and the Eastern Tuva Range; *Publ: V nevedomykh gorakh Yakutii* (In the Unchartered Mountains of Yakutia) (1928); *Na "Perseye" po polyarnym moryam* (In the Polar Seas with the "Perseus") (1929); *Kolymsko-Indigirskiy kray. Geograficheskiy i geologicheskiy ocherk* (The Kolyma-Indigirka Region. Geographical and Geological Studies) (1931); *Na samolyote v Vostochnoy Arktike* (By Plane in the Eastern Arctic) (1934); *V neizvedannykh krayakh* (In Unchartered Regions) (1954); *Novaya orograficheskaya skhema severo-vostochnoy Azii. Ocherk tektoniki severovostochnoy Azii* (A New Orographical Outline of Northeastern Asia. A Study of the Tectonics of Norteastern Asia) (1938); *Osnovnyye cherty tektoniki i stratigrafii Vostochnogo Sayana* (Basic Features of the Tectonics and Stratigraphy of Eastern Sayan) (1942); *Orografiya i geomorfologiya vostochnoy poloviny Vostochnogo Sayana* (The Orography and Geomophology of the Eastern Part of Eastern Sayan) (1946); *Novyye materialy po orografii severo-vostochnoy Tuvy* (New Material on the Orography of Northeastern Tuva) (1955); coordinating ed, *Nizhniy dokembriy* (The Lower Pre-Cambrian) in the 14-vol series *Stratigrafiya SSSR* (The Statigraphy of the USSR) (1963); *Awards:* stalin Prize (1946); Order of the Red Banner of Labor; medals; *Died:* Sept 1965.

OBRUCHEV, Vladimir Afanas'yevich (1863–1956) Geologist and geographer; wirter; explorer of Siberia and Centr Asia; member, USSR Acad of Sci from 1929; Hon Sci Worker of RSFSR from 1927; Hero of Socialist Labor from 1945; *Born:* 10 Oct 1863 in vil Klepenino, now Kalinin Oblast; *Educ:* 1886 grad Petersburg Mining Inst; *Career:* 1901–12 prof, Tomsk Technol Inst; 1919–21 prof, Taurid Univ, Simferopol'; 1921–29 prof, Moscow Mining Acad; 1930–39 chm, Commission (Comt) for the Study of Permafrost, USSR Acad of Sci, from 1939 dir, Inst of Permafrost Studies, USSR Acad of Sci; 1942–46 also acad secr, Geological and Geographical Dept, USSR Acad of Sci; 1886–88 conducted research in Karakum Desert, distinguishing four types of sand relief – dune, ridge, steppe and hillock; 1892–94 took part in G.N. Potainin's expedition; starting from Kyakhta, crossed Mongolia, traversed Northern China, studied Nan Shan Range and ended expedition in Kul'dzha; established that Nan Shan Range consists in fact of a series of ranges running from Northwest to Southeast and divided by valleys of tectonic origin; also established that Eastern and Western Nan Shan contains 9 lateral ranges (and not two or four, as was originally supposed); discovered six new ranges; 1905–06 and 1909 studied Dzungarian Depression and its surrounding ranges (Northwestern China); discovered various oil, gold and ore deposits in Dzungaria; collated research on Eastern Siberia in three-vol monograph *Geologiya Sibiri* (The Geology of Siberia) (1935–38); spezialized in gold deposits; wrote various compilations on auriferous areas of Siberia and Far East; 1892 compiled still valid work on stratigraphy of ancient Paleozoic basin of Upper Lena; also studied genesis of ore deposits; various mountain ranges, peaks, volcanoes, glaciers and a mineral ("obruchevite" – a Dzungarian asphaltite) have been named after him; Inst of Permafrost Studies, USSR Acad of Sci also bears his name; 1938 USSR Acad of Sci instituted an Obruchev Prize for the best works on GSiberian geology; *Publ:* sci works: *Progranichnaya Dzhungariya. Otchyot o puteshestviyakh* (Borderland Dzungaria. A Travel Report) (2 vol, 1912–53); *Tsentral'naya Aziya, Severnyy Kitay i Nan'-Shan* (Central Asia, Northern China and Nan Shan) (2 vol, 1900–01); *Istoriya geologicheskogo issledovaniya Sibiri* (History of the Geological Survey of Siberia) (5 vol, 1931–49); *Geologiya Sibiri* (The Geology of Siberia) (3 vol, 1935–38); *Po goram i pustynyam Sredney Azii* (In the Mountains and Deserts of CentralAsia) (1948); *Moi puteshestviya po Sibiri* (My Travels in Siberia) (1948); *Izbrannyye raboty po geografii* (Selected Works on Geography) (3 vol, 1951); *Ot Kyakhty do Kul'dzhi. Puteshestviye v Tsentral'nuyu Aziyu i Kitay* (From Kyakhta to Kul'dzha. A Journey to Central Asia and China) (1956); *V staroy Sibiri* (In Old Siberia) (1958); *Izbrannyye trudy* (Selected Works) (vol 1, 1958); *Puteshestviya v proshloye i budushcheye* (Journeys into the Past and the Future) (1961), etc; pop sci and sci-fiction works: *Zemlya Sannikova* (Sannikov's Land) (1926); "Plutoniya" (1924); *Zolotoiskateli v pustyne* (Gold-Diggers in the Desert) (1928); *V debryakh Tsentral'noy Azii* (In The Wilds of Central Asia) (1951); *Osnovy geologii* (The Fundamentals of Geology) (1944); *Obrazovaniye gor i rudnykh mestorozhdeniy* (The Formation of Mountains and Ore Deposits) (1932); textbooks *Polevaya geologiya* (Geological Field Work) (1927); *Rudnyye mestorozhdeniya* (Ore Deposits) (1928–29); *Awards:* Przheval'skiy Prize; two Chikhachyov Prizes; Grand Gold Konstantinov Medal; Karpinskiy Gold Medal; Lenin Prize (1926); two Stalin Prizes (1941 and 1950); five Orders of Lenin; *Died:* 19 June 1956 in Zvenigorod, Moscow Oblast.

OBUKH, Varvara Petrovna (1871–1963) Revolutionary; CP member from 1894; *Born:* 1871; *Career:* began revol work as member, Petersburg League for the Liberation of the Working Class; 1898–1916 with Party org in Kiev and Moscow; 1917 member, Bolshevik Faction, Moscow Sov; worked for Moscow educ authorities; 1920–30 with Women's Dept, Moscow CPSU(B) Comt and with Moscow Sov; from 1930 pensioner; *Died:* 29 Mar 1963.

OBUKH, Vladimir Aleksandrovich (1870–1934) Health service official; prof from 1929; revolutionary; personal physician to Lenin, CP member from 1894; *Born:* 6 Apr 1870 in Vitebsk Province, son of an agronomist; *Educ:* 1894 grad Natural Sci Dept, Fac of Physics and Mathematics, Petersburg Univ; 1901 grad Med Fac, Kiev Univ; *Career:* exiled from Petersburg for involvement in Lenin's League for the Liberation of the Working Class; moved to Kiev, where he continued his studies and revol activities; 1901–04 worked as a physician at various Moscow Hospitals; 1901–04 member, Moscow RSDRP Comt; 1904, after several months in prison, exiled to Vitebsk Province; 1905 returned to Moscow illegally and took part in Revol; member, Lit and Lecture Group, Moscow RSDRP comt; 1905–17 worked at 1st Moscow City Hospital; simultaneously member, underground Bolshevik Center; 1917 took active part in Feb and Oct Revol; after advent of Sov rule helped to organize public health service; from 1918 attended Lenin and his family; 1918–29 member and Presidium member, Moscow City Sov and head, Moscow Health Dept; organized public dispensaries (early diagnosis and treatment centers), night sanatoria, dietetic restaurants, etc; 1923 founded Moscow Inst of Labor Hygiene and Occupational Diseases; 1929–31 head, Chair of Soc Hygiene, 2nd Moscow Med Inst; the Moscow street where the Inst of Labor Hygiene and Occupational Diseases is located bears his name; *Publ:* coauthor, *Ozdorovleniye truda i revolyutsiya byta* (Making Working Conditions Healthier and Revolutionizing Living Conditions) (1923); *Dispansernaya sistema zdravookhraneniya i yeyo dostizheniya* (The Early Diagnosis and Treatment [Dispensary] System and Its Achievements) (1926); *Zdravookhraneniye v Moskve k desyatiletiyu Oktyabrya* (The Health Service in Moscow on the Tenth Anniversary of the October Revolution)

(1927); *Konstitutsiya i pogranichnyye oblasti patologii* (The Constitution and the Border Areas of Pathology) (1927); *Died:* 14 June 1934 in Moscow.

OBUKHOVA, Nadezhda Andreyevna (1886–1961) Opera singer (mezzo-soprano); Pop Artiste of USSR from 1937; *Born:* 6 Mar 1886 in Moscow; *Educ:* 1912 grad Moscow Conservatory; *Career:* 1912–16 concert singer; 1916–48 soloist, Bolshoy Theater; *Roles:* Lyubasha in Rimsky-Korsakov's *Tsarskaya nevesta* (The Bride of of the Tsar); Carmen; Hanna, Spring, Lyubava, Kashcheyevna and the Weaver in Rimsky-Korsakov's *Mayskaya noch* (May Night), *Snegurochka* (The Snow Maiden), "Sadko", *Kashchey bessmertnyy* (Kashchey the Immortal) and *Skazka o tsare Saltane* (The Tale of Tsar Saltan); Konchakovna in *Knyaz' Igor* (Prince Igor); Marina in "Boris Godunov"; the Angel in "Demon"; Lyubov' in "Mazepa"; Klariche in Prokof'yev's *Lyubov' k tryom apel'sinam* (Love of Three Oranges); Delilah in Saint-Saens' "Samson and Delilah"; Frick in Wagner's "Das Rheingold" and "Die Walküre," etc; *Publ: Pevets lyubvi i pravdy* (The Bard of Love and Truth) (1954); *Dorogiye serdtsu obrazy* (Images Dear to the Heart) (1958); autobiography *S yunykh let* (From My Youth) (1961); *Awards:* Order of Lenin (1937); Stalin Prize (1943); *Died:* 15 Aug 1961 in Feodosiya.

ODEZHKIN, Nikolay Maksimovich (1900–1964) Ophthalmologist; first Khakas to obtain higher med qualifications; Hon Physician of RSFSR; *Born:* 1900 in vil Uybat, now Kakhass Autonomous Oblast; son of a poor peasant; *Educ:* 1920–23 studied at Non-School Dept, Krasnoyarsk Inst of Public Educ; 1924 studied at Irkutsk Workers' Fac; 1931 grad Tomsk Med Inst; *Career:* from age 12 worked as farmhand; 1923–24 distr librarian, Charkov Volost; from 1931 head, Med Centr in Askiz, where he combatted trachoma and other diseases; also trained numerous oculists, nurses and orderlies; during WW 2 served at front; from 1948 chief physician, Khakass Oblast Trachoma Dispensary, Abakan; *Died:* 21 Oct 1964 suddenly in Abakan.

ODING, Ivan Avgustovich (1896–1964) Mech eng; prof from 1930; corresp member, USSR Acad of Sci from 1946; Hon Sci and Tech Worker of RSFSR from 1956; head, Chair of Metal Sci and Metal Technol, Moscow Power Eng Inst from 1956; dep dir, Inst of Metallurgy, USSR Acad of Sci; CP member from 1942; *Born:* 24 June 1896 in Riga; *Educ:* 1921 grad Mech Fac, Petrograd Technol Inst; *Career:* 1921–23 senior asst prof, Chair of Metallography and Metalworking, Petrograd Technol Inst; 1923–30 at the "Elektrosila" Plant, Petrograd; 1930–32 prof, Chair of Metal Sci, Leningrad Polytech Inst; 1942–47 dir, Centr Research Inst of Technol and Machine-Building; 1947–53 dep dir, Inst of Machine-Building; 1953–56 assoc, Inst of Metallurgy, USSR Acad of Sci; chm, USSR Sci and Tech Council of State Technol; specialized in metal strenght; *Publ: Sovremnennyye metody ispytaniya metallov* (Modern Methods of Metal Testing) (1944); *Prochnost' metallov* (Metal Strength) (1937); *Dopuskayemyye napryazheniya v mashinostroyenii i tsiklicheskaya prochnost' metallov* (Tension Tolerances in Machine-Building and Cyclical Metal Strength) (1947); *Osnovy prochnosti metallov parovykh kotlov, turbin i turbogeneratorov* (The Principles of Metal Strength in Boilers, Turbines and Turbogenerators) (1949); coauthor, *Sverkhprochnyy metall* (Super-Strong Metals) (1962); coauthor, *Mekhanizm ustalostnogo razrusheniya metallov* (The Mechanism of Metal Fatigue) (1963); *Awards:* Stalin Prize (1946); two Orders of Lenin; Badge of Hon; three medals; *Died:* 10 May 1964.

ODINTSOV, Leontiy Yefimovich (1891–1942) Govt official; helped organize Party underground in Minsk during WW 2; CP member from 1918; *Born:* 14 July 1891 in vil Karpilovka, now Minsk Oblast; *Educ:* completed Rudabel'skoye Public College; *Career:* from 1914 in Russian Army; active in revol movement; 1918 member, Rudabel'skoye Underground Party Comt; 1919–20 commanded partisan unit operating against Polish occupation forces; from 1921 worked for Sov establishments in Bobruysk; 1924–30 Bel Dep Pop Comr of Soc Security; 1931–37 chm, Bel Invalids Cooperative Assoc; chm, CC, Peasants' Soc Mutual Aid Org; head, Secretariat, Bel Centr Exec Comt; during WW 2 helped establish Party underground org in Minsk; his apartment was used for meetings of the underground Minsk City Comt, CP(B) Bel; arrested by German occupation authorities; *Died:* Dec 1942 executed by Germans.

ODULOK, Tekki (real name: Nikolay Ivanovich SPIRIDONOV) (1906–1938) Yukagir writer; Cand of Econ; CP member from 1925; *Born:* 22 May 1906 in vil Nelemnoye, Yakutia; *Educ:* 1931 grad Leningrad Univ; *Career:* helped establish Chukotka Nat Okrug; 1927 frist work printed; arrested by State Security organs; *Publ:* collected essays "In the Far North" (1933); articles "The Yukagirs" and "The Yukagir Language" in 1st ed of "Bol'shaya Sovetskaya Entsiklopediya"; novelette "The Life of Imteurgin Senior" (1934), about the life of the Chukchi prior to the Revol; "The Creative Work of the Peoples of the Far North" (1958); *Died:* 1938 in imprisonment. posthumously rehabilitated.

OGNENKO-AVANESOV, Karl Pavlovich (1882–1943) Actor and stage dir; *Born:* 6 Jan 1882; *Career:* from 1900 actor, then stage dir at Ukr and Russian provincial theaters in Rostov, Lugansk, Sukhumi, Baku, Tiflis, Simferopol', Kerch, Smolensk, Kaluga, Chernigov, Vilnius, Khar'kov and Poltava, etc; 1916 moved to Uzbek; founded, directed and acted at soldiers' theater in Tashkent; then worked for Z.A. Malinovskaya's company; 1918 co-founder, Sov Theater, Tashkent; from 1920 head, Theater Dept, Turkestani Pop Comrt of Educ; head, Centr Theaters Bd; dep head, Show Enterprises Bd; 1936 dir, Uzbek State Variety Theater; 1937–41 dir and stagecraft instructor, Tashkent Theatrical College; *Roles:* Bogdan and Mazepa in Staritskiy's "Bogdan Khmel'nitskiy" and "Mazepa"; the Deputy in Kotlyarevskiy's "Natalka-Poltavka"; Gnat in Shevchenko's "Nazar Stodolya"; Yaichnitsa in *Zhenit'ba* (The Wedding); Nekhlyudov in *Voskreseniye* (Resurrection), after Tolstoy; Satin and Teterev in Gorky's *Meshchane* (Philistines); the King in Lunacharskiy's *Korolevskiy bradobrey* (The Trimming of the King's Beard); Dreissiger in Hauptmann's "The Weavers"; Gaspard in Planquette's operetta "The Bells of Corneville"; Agamemnon in Offenbach's "La Belle Helene", etc; *Productions:* Naydyonov's *Deti Vanyushina* (Vanyushin's Children) (1919); *Goryacheye serdtse* (Warm Heart) (1919); *Kovarstvo i lyubov'* (Guile and Love) (1920), etc; *Died:* 13 June 1943.

OGNËV, N. (real name: ROZANOV), Mikhail Grigor'yevich) (1888–1938) Russian writer; *Born:* 14 June 1888 in Moscow; *Career:* active in revol movement; imprisoned for printing illegal journal; went underground; from 1900 lectured for the Soc for the Protection of Schoolchildren, Moscow; from 1912 wrote articles and notes under various pseudonyms in Moscow and provincial neswpapers; 1917–25 lectured at children's colonies, schools and clubs; *Publ:* stories: *Dvenadtsatyy chas* (The Twelfth Hour); *Pavel Velikiy* (Paul the Great); *Sobach'ya radost'* (Canine Joy); *Tyomnaya voda* (Dark Water); collection *Rasskazy* (Stories) (1925); *Dnevnik Kosti Ryabtseva* (the Diary of Kostya Ryabtsev) (1927); novelette *Sledy dinozavra* (Tracks of the Dinosaur) (1928); novel *Tri izmereniya* (Three Dimensions) (1932); *Krusheniye antenny* (The Collapse of the Antenna) (1933); collection *Rasskazy* (Stories) (1933); plays *Zoloto* (Gold) and "Maffiya", etc; *Died:* 22 June 1938 in Moscow.

OGNYOV, Sergey Ivanovich (1886–1951) Zoologist; prof from 1930; Hon Sci Worker of RSFSR from 1947; *Born:* 17 Nov 1886 in Moscow; son of the histologist I.F. Ognyov; *Educ:* 1910 grad Moscow Univ; *Career:* 1914–26 asst prof, 1926–30 assoc prof, from 1930 prof, Moscow Univ; specialized in the taxonomy and faunistics of mammals; wrote numerous popular works and textbooks on vertebrate zoology for secondary schools and higher educ establishments; wrote a complete description of the mammals of the USSR; *Publ: Mlekopitayushchiye Moskovskoy gubernii* (The Mammals of Moscow Province) (1913); *Zveri SSSR i prilezhashchikh stran* (The Wildlife of the USSR and Neighboring Countries) (1928–50); *Ocherki po zoologii* (Studies in Zoology) (1929); *Zoologiya pozvonochnykh* (Vertebrate Zoology) (1945); *Zhizn' lesa* (The Living Forest) (1950); *Ocherki ekologii mlekopitayushchikh* (Studies in Mammalian Ecology) (1951); *Awards:* Order of Lenin; two Stalin Prizes (1942 and 1951); medals; *Died:* 20 Dec 1951 in Moscow.

OGORODNIKOV, Fyodor Yevlampiyevich (1867–1939) Mil commander, instructor and tactician; lt-gen, Russian Army; *Born:* 1867; *Educ:* grad Russian Army's Gen Staff Acad; *Career:* from 1918 in Red Army; after Civil War research and teaching work at mil training establishments; *Publ: Glubokaya operatsiya i yeyo tyl* (Deep Operation and Its Rear) (1933); *Vozdushnaya voyna po zarubezhnym vzglyadam* (Foreign Views on Aerial Warfare) (1934); *Motomekhvoyska v sovremennoy operatsii* (Motorized and Mechanized Troops in Modern Operations) (1935); *Kreposti i pogranichnyye ukrepleniya v budushchey voyne* (Forts and Border Fortifications in Future Warfare) (1936); *Vtorzheniye motomekhanizirovannykh sil i ikh otrazheniye* (Attack by Motorized and Mechanized Forces and Its Repulse) (1937); *Udar po Kolchaku* (The Offensive Against Kolchak) (1938); *Died:* 1939.

OKHLOPKOV, Nikolay Pavlovich (1900–1967) Stage dir, chief stage dir, Moscow's Mayakovskiy Theater from 1943; film actor from 1924; Pop Artiste of USSR from 1948; CP member from 1952; *Born:* 15 May 1900 in Siberia; *Educ:* grad cadets corps; studied at School of Painting, Sculpture and Architecture, Moscow; simultaneously studied cello at Moscow Conservatory; from 1922 studied at Meyerhold State Theatrical Workshops in Moscow; *Career:* 1918 theater debut in Irkutsk; from 1923 actor, Meyerhold Theater, Moscow; 1931–36 dir, State Realistic Theater; 1938–43 stage dir, Vakhtangov Theater; acted in films; member, Arts Council, USSR Min of Culture; taught at Lunacharskiy State Inst of Stagecraft; *Productions:* Mayakovskiy's *Misteriya – buff* Mystery-Buffo) (1922); Gorky's *Mat* (Mother); Serafimovich's *Zheleznyy potok* (The Iron Stream); Pogodin's *Aristokraty* (The Aristocrats) (1935); *Molodaya gvardiya* (The Young Guard), after Fadeyev (1947); Shteyn's *Zakon chesti* (Law of Honor); Leonov's *Sadovnik i ten'* (The Gardener and the Shadow); Ostrovskiy's *Groza* (The Storm) (1953); Shakespeare's "Hamlet" (1954); operas: Meytus' "Molodaya gvardiya" (The Young Guard); Shaporin's *Dekabristy* (The Decembrists); Khrennikov's "Mat" (Mother); *Roles:* film roles in: *Lenin v Oktyabre* (Lenin in October); *Lenin v 1918 godu* (Lenin in 1918); "Aleksandr Nevskiy"; *Povest' o nastoyashchem cheloveke* (The Tale of a Real Man) and *Daleko ot Moskvy* (far from Moscow); *Awards:* Order of Lenin (1960); Order of the Red Banner of Labor (1960); other orders; medals; six Stalin Prizes (1941, 1947, 1949 (twice) and 1951 (twice); *Died:* 8 Jan 1967.

OKINCHITS, Lyudvig Lyudvigovich (1874–1941) Obstetrician and gynecologist; Dr of Med from 1902; prof from 1914; *Born:* 17 July 1874; *Educ:* 1899 grad Petersburg Mil Med Acad; *Career:* from 1899 intern, Gynecological Dept, Obukh Hospital; 1902 defended doctor's thesis on changes of the hymen depending on age; 1906–09 senior asst, from 1909 assoc prof, Obstetrical and Gynecological Clinic, Women's Med Inst; 1911, in a paper delivered at the 4th Congress of Obstetricians and Gynecologists, advocated contraceptives for women to ensure their right of controlled parenthood; 1912–14 head, Gynecological Dept, Petersburg Hospital (now Lenin Hospital); 1914–19 prof, Obstetrical and Gynecological Clinic, from 1920 dir, Psychoneurological Inst (now Inst of Health and Hygiene); from 1922 also dir and sci dir, V.F. Snegirev Maternity Home; bd member, All-Union Inst of Obstetricians and Gynecologists; chm, Leningrad Obstetrical and Gynecological Soc; member, Learned Med Council, RSFSR Pop Comrt of Health; edited various periodicals; did major research on the function of the endocrine glands, internal diseases occuring during pregnancy, postparietal diseases and malignant tumors of the female genital organs; was an outstanding gynecological surgeon; also worked in the field of labor welfare and mother-care; wrote over 50 works; *Publ:* doctor's thesis *Vozrastnyye izmeneniya devstvennoy plevy* (Age-Changes of the Hymen) (1902); *K voprosu o vzaimootnosheniyakh nekotorykh zhelez s vnutrenney sekretsiyey* (The Interrelationship Between Certain Glands and Internal Secretion) (1913); *Ginekologicheskaya klinika* (Gynecological Clinical Practice) (4 vol, 1925–31); *Operativnaya ginekologiya* (Operative Gynecology) (1938), etc; *Died:* 1941.

OKLADSKIY, Ivan Fyodorovich (1859–?) Revolutionary; member, People's Will Party; *Born:* 1859; *Career:* took part in attempted assassination of Tsar Alexander II; 1880 sentenced to death; sentence commuted to hard labor for life; 1880–1917 secret police agent; 1925 sentenced to 10 years' imprisonment; *Died:* date and place of death unknown.

OKNOV, Mikhail Grigor'yevich (1878–1942) Metallurgist; *Born:* 15 Sept 1878; *Educ:* 1904 grad Petersburg Univ; *Career:* worked at Obukhov Steel Foundry and other plants; from 1907 assoc, Petersburg Polytech Inst; from 1930 head, Chair of Metallography, Leningrad Polytech Inst; specialized in conversion processes in aloys with changes in their volume; demonstrated validity of volumetric method in studying phase changes in alloys; 1933 summarized and classified known data on properties and structure of cast iron; wrote several textbooks; *Publ: Izmeneniye udel'nogo obyoma zheleza i stali pri naklyope* (Changes in the Specific Volume of Iron and Steel During Cold Hardening) (1928); *O zalkalke i otpuske evtektoidnykh splavov* (The Templring and Annealing of Entectoid Alloys) (1931); *Toplivo i yego szhiganiye* (Fuel and Its Combustion) (1925); *Metallografiya chuguna* (The Metallography of Cast Iron) (1933), etc; *Died:* 22 Feb 1942.

OKRESTIN, Boris Semyonovich (1923–1944) Fighter-pilot; CP member from 1943; *Born:* 18 Feb 1923 in Moscow; *Career:* from 1942 at the front; Sept 1942–Dec 1943 carried out 381 sorties; 6 July 1944 his plane was hit while attacking a German unit which had broken out of the Minsk "pocket"; he deliberately crashed his flaming plane into the enemy column; *Awards:* Hero of the Sov Union (1944); *Died:* 6 July 1944 in action; buried in Minsk.

OKSYONOV, Innokentiy Aleksandrovich (1897–1942) Russian poet, critic and translator; *Born:* 17 June 1897, son of a teacher; *Educ:* grad 1st Leningrad Med Inst; *Career:* 1915 first work published; typical of his poetry was his contemplative-esthetic approach to reality and his advocacy of life for life's sake; as a critic, polemicized with the Formalists and the Marxists on the grounds that they hampered the organic development of lit; insisted that the writer should maintain an orthodox approach and ideological restraint; 1937–41 acad secr, Pushkin Soc; *Publ:* almanach *Zelyonyy tsvetok* (The Green Flower); collected verse; *Zazhzhyonnaya svecha* (The Lighted Candle) (1917); *Roshcha* (The Grove) (1922); almanachs *Kovsh* (The Ladle), *Sodruzhestvo* (Commonwealth) etc; translated; Stendahl's "Life in Russia", "Notes of a Dilettante" and "Armance" (1936–37); "The Georgian Romantics" (1940), etc; articles; "Modern Russian Criticism" (1925); "Larisa Reysner. A Critical Study" (1927); "Boris Pasternak" (1928); "The Monsters and Naturalia of Yu. Tynyanov" (1931); "Mayakovsky and Pushkin" (1937); "The Life of A.S. Pushkin" (1938), etc; *Died:* 21 Jan 1942 in Leningrad.

OKTYABR'SKAYA, Mariya Vasil'yevna (1902–1944) Tank driver; *Born:* 3 Aug 1902 in vil Kiyat, Tavrida Province; *Career:* from Oct 1943 served at front; donated her savings for building "Battle Friend" tank; 20 Nov 1943 distinguished herself in action at vil Novoye Selo, near Vitebsk; penetrated enemy positions and destroyed anti-tank gun by overrunning it with her tank; gravely wounded; *Awards:* Hero of the Sov Union (1944); *Died:* 15 Mar 1944 in hospital, of her wounds; buried at Smolensk.

OKULOV, Akeksey Ivanovich (1880–1939) Russian writer; CP member from 1903; *Born:* 4 Oct 1880 in vil Karatuz, Yeniseysk Province; *Educ:* 1904 grad Drama School at Moscow Arts Theater; *Career:* did underground revol work and took part in 1905, Feb 1917 and Oct 1917 Revol; after 1917 Feb Revol member, Yeniseysk Province Party Comt and chm, Yeniseysk Province Exec Comt; chm, 1st All-Siberian Writers' Congress; member, All-Russian Centr Exec Comt of four convocations; member, Revol Mil Councils of RSFSR and Southern and Western Fronts; commanded East Siberian troops; then engaged on govt work; from 1924 concentrated in lit work; member, "Pereval" (The Pass) lit group; 1906 first work published; 1937 arrested by State Security organs; *Publ:* collected stories *Na Amyle-reke* (On the Amyl River) (1916); novelettes: *Zametki Ivanova* (Ivanov's Notes) and *Krest'yanskaya voyna* (Peasant War) (1925); stories *V snegakh* (In the Snows) and *Nezhdannaya vstrecha* (Unexpected Encounter) (1928); play *Tam, gde smert'* (Where Death Is) (1919); historical novelettes about the Revol "Kamo" and *Vologodskaya respublika* (Vologda Republic) (1931), etc; *Died:* 1939 in imprisonment; posthumously rehabilitated.

OKULOVA (married name: TEODOROVICH; Party alias: ZAYCHIK), Glafira Ivanovna (1878–1957) Revolutionary and Party official; CP member from 1899; *Born:* 23 Apr 1878 in vil Shoshino, Yeniseysk Province, daughter of a gold-dealer; *Educ:* grad Krasnoyarsk High-School and studied at Moscow Teachers' Training Courses; *Career:* 1896 arrested for involvement in student demonstrations and exiled to Yeniseysk Province; from 1899 did propaganda work for Soc-Democrats in working distr of Kiev; 1900–02 member, Ivanovo-Voznesensk RSDRP Comt; also worked as a distributing agent for the newspaper "Iskra" in Samara and Moscow; 1902 member, Org Comt, 2nd RSDRP Congress; 1902–05 exiled to Yakutsk Province; Nov 1905–08 did Party work in Petersburg; 1908–17 gave up active politics; 1911 accompanied her husband I.A. Teodorovich to Irkutsk Province, where he had been sentenced to hard labor and exile; after 1917 Feb Revol member, Krasnoyarsk Province RSDRP(B) Comt and Presidium member, Krasnoyarsk Province Exec Comt; 1918–20 member, and Presidium member, All-Russian Centr Exec Comt; taught on courses for Party instructors and agitators; head, Polit Dept, Eastern Front and member, Revol Mil Council; 1st, 8th and Reserve Armies; 1920–21 did polit work in Sov trans system; 1921–26 head, Moscow Province Polit Educ Bd; 1926–29 dean, Polit Educ Fac, Communist Training Acad; 1929–30 asst head, Culture and Propaganda Dept, CC, CPSU(B); 1930–37 rector, Higher Communist Agric Schools in Sverdlovsk, Ryazan and Moscow; from 1938 worked for educ authorities, then as assoc,

USSR Museum of the Revol; from 1954 pensioner; *Died:* 19 Oct 1957.

OKUNEVSKIY, Yakov Leont'yevich (1877–1940) Infectionist and health service official; Dr of Med from 1920; Hon Sci Worker of RSFSR; *Born:* 1877; *Educ:* 1904 grad Petersburg Mil Med Acad; *Career:* 1908–12 worked at Odessa Mil Hospital, where he helped to combat plague and cholera epidemics; 1912–14 asst prof and senior lecturer, Chair of Hygiene, Petersburg Mil Med Acad; after 1917 Oct Revol helped to organize Sov health service and to combat typhus epidemics in Petrograd; 1920 defended doctor's thesis on the composition of air in submarines; 1924–40 read course on disinfection at Leningrad Mil Acad; did research on disinfectants and disinfestants (pyridine bases, polychlorides, chloranasol, ammonia, hot air, phenol-cresol preparations, formalin); developed room sterilization techniques and designed a combined stationary disinfection chamber; wrote 120 works; *Publ:* doctor's thesis *K voprosu o sostave vozdukha podvodnykh lodok russkogo flota* (The Composition of Air in the Submarines of the Russian Navy) (1920); *Prakticheskoye rukovodstvo po dezinfektsii* (A Practical Disinfection Manual) (4 vol, 1926–36); coauthor, *Prosteyshiye sposoby ozdorovleniya byta* (The Simplest Methods of Making Living Conditions Healthier) (1939); coauthor *Prakticheskoye rukovodstvo po voyskovoy dezinfektsii* (A Practical Troop Disinfection Manual) (2nd ed, 1940); *Died:* 1940.

OL'DENBURG, Sergey Fyodorovich (1863–1934) Russian Orientologist and Indologist; co-founder, Russian school of Indology; member, Russian (USSR) Acad of Sci from 1900; member, Ukr Acad of Sci from 1925; *Born:* 26 Sept 1863 in vil Byakini, now Chita Oblast; *Educ:* 1885 grad Oriental Languages Fac, Petersburg Univ; attended lectures in England, France and Germany; *Career:* 1889–94 lecturer, from 1894 prof, Petersburg (Leningrad) Univ; 1904–29 secr, Russian (USSR) Acad of Sci; 1930–34 dir, Inst of Oriental Studies, USSR Acad of Sci; 1917 Min of Educ, Provisional Govt; studied culture and religion of ancient and medieval India; 1894 published *Buddiyskiye legendy* (Buddhist Legends), the first of a series of his works on Indian lit and folklore; 1909–10 and 1914–15 directed archeological expecditions in Eastern Turkestan (Sinkiang); deciphered and published East Turkestani texts; deciphered and published the most ancient Pracritic text – "Dhammapady na kharoshthi"; organized sci expeditions to Centr Asia and Tibet; 1897 sponsored in Petersburg publ of int series of Buddhist texts involving the world's major Orientologists – "Bibliotheca buddhica" (32 vol, 1897–1962); *Died:* 28 Feb 1934.

OL'DEROGGE, Vladimir Aleksandrovich (1873–1931) Mil commander; *Born:* 24 July 1873, of noble descent; *Educ:* 1901 grad Gen Staff Acad; *Career:* as maj-gen in command of div fought in Russo-Japanese War and WW 1; from Mar 1918 in Red Army; commanded Novorzhev Sector, div, then chief of staff, Eastern Front; Aug 1919–Jan 1920 commanded Eastern Front; then assigned for special duties to commander, Southern Front; from Oct 1920 inspector of infantry for commander, Ukr and Crimean Armed Forces; from July 1921 chief inspector of mil training establishments, Kiev Mil Distr; inspector, Main Mil Establishments Bd; from Feb 1924 commandant, then asst commandant, Kamenev Joint Services School; mil dir, Polytechn Inst; *Died:* 20 Mar 1931.

OLENICH-GNENENKO, Aleksandr Pavlovich (1893–1963) Writer; CP member from 1918; *Born:* 11 Sept 1893 in vil Kegichevka, Poltava Province; *Educ:* 1916 grad correspondence course at Law Fac, Khar'kov Univ; *Career:* took part in 1917 Oct Revol and Civil War in Eastern Siberia; exec govt and Party work; fought in WW 2; 1951–54 ed, almanach "Don"; 1913 first verse published; wrote children's works and translated from Ukr, Azer and other languages; did one of best translations of Lewis Carroll's "Alice in Wonderland" (1940) and translated verse of Edgar Allan Poe; in his latter years worked on his memoirs and an autobiographical novelette; *Publ:* verse fairy-tales: *Pro medvedya* (The Bear) (1938); *Olen' i yozh* (The Deer and the Hedgehog) (1938), etc; *V gorakh Kavkaza* (In the Mountains of the Caucasus) (1940); poems: *Zubr* (The Aurochs) (1948); *Puteshestviye v Pridon'ye* (A Journey to the Don) (1956); collected verse; *Vesyolyy kray* (Merry Country) (1936); *Lesnaya tropa* (Forest Path) (1940); *Serebryannyay rota* (Silver Company) (1941); *Na lesnoy trope* (On the Forest Path) (1947); *Vesna v gorakh* (Spring in the Mountains) (1949); *Stikhi o prirode* (Verse About Nature) (1952); *Izbrannoye. Proza, Stikhi, Poemy, Skazki, Perevody* (Selected Works, Prose, Verse, Poems, Fairy-Tales, Translations) (1954); *Pro zverey i plits* (Beasts and Birds) (1956); *Chetyre vremeni goda* (The Four Seasons) (1963); *Died:* 13 Mar 1963 in Rostov-on-Don.

OLEVSKIY, Boris Abramovich (1908–1941) Jewish writer; *Born:* 1908 in civil Chernyakhov, Volhynia; *Educ:* 1930 grad Bubnov Teachers' Training Inst, Moscow; *Career:* in his youth Komsomol member; 1926 first work published in Minsk journal "Shtern"; from 1932 asst, Teachers' Training Inst, Moscow; *Publ:* collected verse "Vuks" (1930); poem "Mines" (1933); book of essays "Higher and Higher" (1933); "Osya and His Friends" (1956); "In a Clear Dawn" (1960), etc; *Died:* 1941 killed in action in WW 2.

OLEYNIKOV, Nikolay Makarovich (1898–1942) Russian writer; CP member from 1920; *Born:* 1898 in vil Kamenskaya, Don Oblast; *Career:* fought in Civil War; contributed to Rostov Newspaper "Molot" and Bakhmut (now Artemovsk) newspaper "Vserossiyskaya kochegarka"; member, "Zaboy" Donbass proletarian writers union; 1925 moved to Leningrad and worked for ed staff of Children's Dept, State Publ House; edited children's journals: "Yozh" (1928–29); "Chizh" (1934 and 1937); "Sverchok" (1937); wrote for children under the pseudonyms Makar Svirepyy and S. Kravtsov; 1937 arrested by State Security organs; *Publ:* children's essays and stories: *Boyevyye dni* (Days of Battle) (1926); *Tanki i sanki* (Tanks and Sledges) (1928); *Pervyy sovet* (The First Council) (1926); *Indiyskaya golova* (Indian Head) (1928); *Uchitel' geografii* (Geography Teacher) (1928); *Bloshinyy uchitel'* (The Flea Teacher) (1930); coauthor, scripts for: *Razbudite Lenochku* (Wake Lenochka) (1935); *Lenochka i vinograd* (Lenochka and the Grape) (1936); story *Porokhovoy pogreb* (The Powder-Magazine) (1937); verse *Karas'* (The Carp); *Mukha* (The Fly); *Knizhka s kartinkami* (The Picture Book), etc; *Died:* 5 May 1942; posthumously rehabilitated.

OL'KHON, (real name: PESTYUKHIN), Anatoliy Sergeyevich (1903–1950) Russian poet; *Born:* 24 Mar 1903 in Vologda; *Educ:* grad Herzen Teachers' Training Inst, Leningrad; *Career:* lived and worked in Far North, Centr Asia and Transcaucasia; in 1930's and 1940's toured Eastern Siberia, Buryatia, Yakutia, the Arctic; 1924 first work published; member, "The Pass" lit assoc; 1928–30 dep chm, Moscow Soc of Peasant Writers; from 1931 lived in Irkutsk; translated work of Yakut and Buryat writers; published some 40 collections of verse, translations, fairy-tales and children's books; *Publ:* poems *Sluzhba pogody* (Weather Service) (1948); collections: *Okrainy miloy otchizny* (The Outlying Areas of Our Dear Fatherland) (1948); *Vostochnyy sektor Arktiki* (The Eastern Sector of the Arctic) (1949), etc; poem *Vedomost' o sekretnom prestupnike Chernyshevskom za 1862–1883 gg.* (Report on the Secret Criminal Chernyshevskiy for 1862–1883 (1941); novellas *Ekvator* (The Equator) (1929); verse "Baykal" (1945); play *Vilyuyskiy uznik* (Vilyuysk Prisoner) (1948); *Died:* 13 Nov 1950 in Novaya Ruza, Moscow Oblast.

OL'MINSKIY (real name: ALEKSANDROV), Mikhail Stepanovich (1863–1933) Russian revol; Party official; historian, journalist and lit critic; CP member from 1898, *Born:* 14 Oct 1863 in Voronezh, son of an official of noble descent; *Educ:* 1883 studied at Law Fac, Petersburg Univ; *Career:* as a student joined "People's Will" movement; 1894–98 in solitary confinement in prison; 1898–1903 in Olekminsk, Yakutsk Oblast; in this period switched sympathies to Social-Democrats; 1904 emigrated to Switzerland, met Lenin and joined Bolsheviks; 1905 returned to Petersburg and worked for legal and underground Bolshevik publications ("Vperyod", "Proletariy", "Novaya zhizn'" and "Volna", etc); 1907–09 Party work in Baku; 1909–14 statistician in Petrograd and worked for newspapers "Zvezda" and "Pravda"; 1915 in Saratov, editing legal Bolshevik paper "Nasha gazeta"; from Aug 1916 member, Moscow Oblast RSDRP Bureau and ed, journal "Golos pechatnogo truda"; 1917 active in Bolshevik movement in Petrograd and Moscow; Bureau member, CC, RSDRP(B) and member Moscow RSDRP(B) Comt; contributed to "Pravda"; co-ed, Moscow Bolshevik newspaper "Sotsial-Democrat"; from Dec 1917 Collegium member, Pop Comrt of Finance; 1918–20 member, ed bd, "Pravda"; 1920–24 chm, Commission on the History of the Oct Revol and the RCP(B), CC, RCP(B) and edited its journal "Proletarskaya revolyutsiya"; from 1925 chm, Sov of above Commission and ed, journal "Proletarskaya revolyutsiya"; from 1928 co-dir, Inst of Lenin, CC, CPSU(B); from 1932 chief ed and chm, ed commission for publ of Saltykov-Shchedrin's works; 1922 partly incapacitated by stroke but continued his research on Party history; worked for Russian Assoc of Proletarian Writers and contributed to its organ "Na literaturnom postu"; also helped Stalin in his campaign against Trotsky [collection *Lenin o*

Trotskom i trotzskizme (Lenin on Trotsky and Trotskyism) (1925)] and then against Kamenev, Zinov'yev and Bukharin; *Publ: Tri goda v odinochnoy tyur'me* (Three Years in Solitary) (1923); *Gosudarstvo, byurokratiya i absolyutizm v istorii Rossii* (The State, Bureaucracy and Absolutism in the History of Russia) (1925); *Po voprosam literatury* (Problems of Literature) (1926); *O pechati* (The Press) (1926); "Saltykov-Shchedrin" (1926); *Po literaturnym voprosam* (Literary Problems) (1932); *Bor'ba za partiyu posle II syezda RSDRP* (The Party Struggle After the 2nd RSDRP Congress) (1933); *Sochineniya* (Works) (2 vol, 1935); *Stat'i o Saltykove-Shchedrine* (Articles on Saltykov-Shchedrin) (1959); *Died:* 8 May 1933 in Moscow; buried on Moscow's Red Square.

OL'SHEVSKIY, Anatol' Adamovich (1904–1937) Bel Party official and publicist; CP member from 1919; *Born:* 4 July 1904 in vil Kartuz-Beryoza, now Brest Oblast, son of an office worker; *Educ:* from 1920 studied at Sverdlov communist Univ, Moscow; *Career:* at start of WW 1 evacuated to Russia; lived in Arzamas and studied at non-classical high school; from 1919 in Red Army; after grad Communist Univ worked in Ryazan' and Nizhniy Novgorod; from 1925 underground work in Western Bel; secr, CC, West Bel Communist Youth League; member, CC, Polish Communist Youth League; also member, CC West Bel CP and ed of its centr organs "Bal'shaviki" and "Chyrvony stsyag"; 1927 arrested by Polish authorities; returned to USSR in prisoner exchange; 1928–33 worked for Ed Dept of West Bel CP CC's Mission with CC, CP(B) Bel in Minsk; 1933–37 trade-union work; 1937 arrested by NKVD; *Died:* 1937 in imprisonment.

OLYK, Ipay (real name: STEPANOV, Ipatiy Stepanovich) (1912–1943) Mari poet; Komsomol member, *Born:* 24 Mar 1912 in vil Toymet-Solá, now Mari ASSR; *Educ:* studied at Moscow teachers' training technicum and Film Inst; *Career:* 1928 first work published; translated works of Pushkin, Nekrasov, Mayakovskiy, etc, into Mari; 1937 arrested by State Security organs; *Publ:* coauthor, verse collection "We Are Shock-Workers" (1931); verse collections: "The Young Communard" (1932); "The Time of Burgeoning" (1932); "Song of the Century" (1933); "My Friend" (1933); "We" (1934); "Pioneer Songs" (1935); "Happiness" (1935); "Flourish" (1936); play "Golden Dawn"; short stories; *Died:* 1943 in imprisonment; posthumously rehabilitated.

OLYOSHA, Yuriy Karlovich (1899–1960) Russian writer; *Born:* 19 Feb 1899 in Yelisavetgrad; *Educ:* studied at Novorossiysk Univ, Odessa; *Career:* spent his childhood and youth in Odessa; together with V. Katayev and I. Il'f member, Poets Collective; wrote verse; after establishment of Sov regime in Odessa worked for Ukr Press Bureau; from 1922 worked for railroad newspaper "Gudok" in Moscow, contributing biting verse feuilletons; 1934 berated by Party critics, who even detected "elements of fascism" in his play *Strogiy yunosha* (A Strict Youth); arrested several times during Yezhov Terror; then for 20 years wrote only articles on lit themes, book reviews, reminiscences of writers and the occasional story; not until 1956 was he again mentioned in the Sov press; 1957 saw the republication of his *Izbrannyye sochineniya* (Selected Works); his works have been translated into many for languages; *Publ:* novel *Tri tolstyaka* (Three Fat Men) (1924); novel *Zavist'* (Envy) (1927); play *Zagovor chuvstv* (Conspiracy of the Senses) (1929); collected stories *Vishnyovaya kostochka* (The Cherry Pit) (1931); play *Spisok blagodeyaniy* (A List of Good Deeds) (1931); film script *Strogiy yunosha* (A Strict Youth) (1934); coauthor, film script *Bolotnyye soldaty* (Swamp Soldiers) (1938); stage adaptation of Dostoyevsky's *Idiot* (The Idiot) (1958); *Ni dnya bez strochki* (Not a Day Without a Line) (1961, posthumously); *Died:* 10 May 1960 in Moscow.

OMARSHAYEV, Abdurakhman Gasanovich (1903–1935) Lak poet; *Born:* 1903 in vil Khurukra, now Dagh ASSR; *Educ:* grad Makhachkala Russian Moslem School; *Career:* 1926 first work printed; *Publ:* "Songs in the Lak Language" (1928); "Revolution" (1931); "A New Life" (1931); "Soviet Poems" (1933); "Kasim" (1934); "The Example" (1934); "Garib and Zagir" (1934); "The Cultural Assault" (1934); verse: "The Soviet Plane"; "Youth"; "The Red Army"; "Enthusiasm"; "The Kulak and the Kolkhoznik"; "The Mosque and the Club"; "Fisheries"; "A Summer Morning"; "The Girl at the Factory"; "The Girl Student", "The New Generation"; satirical verse: "The Trader"; "The Mullah's Dreams"; "The Kulak's Experiences", etc; poem "Fifteen Years of My Life" (1935), etc; *Died:* 1935.

OMEL'YANYUK, Vladimir Stepanovich (1917–1942) Partisan; helped organize Party underground in Minsk during WW 2; Hero of the Sov Union from 1965 (posthumously); CP member; *Born:* 1917 at Dno Station, former Pskov Province; *Educ:* at start of WW 2 studied at Communist Inst of Journalism, Minsk; *Career:* from Aug 1941 with underground Party group in Minsk; wrote leaflets, distributed Sov Information Bureau bulletins and maintained liaison with other underground Party groups and partisan units; from May 1942 member, underground Minsk City Comt, CP(B) Bel and head of its Agitation and Propaganda Dept; edited underground publications, particularly newspaper "Zvyazda"; *Died:* 26 May 1942 killed in action.

ONCHUKOV, Nikolay Yevgen'yevich (1872–1942) Russian folklorist; *Born:* 3 Mar 1872; *Career:* 1901–02 and 1907 took part in expeditions to Pechora; in 1920's and 1930's toured Cherdyn and Tavda Krays and Ukr; worked on acad *Slovar' russkogo yazyka* (Dictionary of the Russian Language); arrested by State Security organs; *Publ:* collections: *Pechorskiye byliny* (Pechora Legends) (1904); *Severnyye skazki* (Northern Tales) (1909); *Severnyye narodnyye dramy* (Northern Folk Dramas) (1911); also published stories collected by Acad A.A. Shakhmatov and M.M. Prishvin; *Zapreshchyonnyye pesni o Konstantine i Anne* (Banned Songs About Konstantin and Anna) (1930); *Tri varianta pesni o Kostryuke* (Three Versions of the Song of Kostryuk) (1928); *Pesni i legendy o dekabristakh* (Songs and Legends of the Decembrists) (1935), etc; *Died:* 6 Mar 1942 in imprisonment in Penza; posthumously rehabilitated.

ONUFRIYEV, Yevgeniy Petrovich (1884–1967) Revolutionary and govt official; CP member from 1904; *Born:* 1884; *Career:* helped to organize a Party cell at Obukhov Plant; member, Neva Rayon RSDRP Comt, Petersburg; 1912 deleg at 6th All-Russian RSDRP (B) Conference in Prague, at which he met Lenin; smuggled Party lit from Prague to Petersburg and briefed Petersburg workers on the decisions of the conference; fought in 1917 Oct Revol, after which he worked for the Cheka; later switched to admin work; from 1954 pensioner; *Publ: Vstrechi s Leninym. Vospominaniya delegata Prazhskoy partkonferentsii* (Meetings with Lenin. The Reminiscences of a Delegate to the Prague Party Conference); *Died:* 1 Dec 1967.

OPPEL', Vladimir Andreyevich (1872–1932) Surgeon; pioneer of surgical endocrinology; Dr of Med from 1899; prof from 1908; *Born:* 23 Dec 1872; *Educy:* 1896 grad Petersburg Mil Med Acad; *Career:* 1896–99 did postgrad work at S.P. Fyodorov's Surgical Clinic, Petersburg Mil Med Acad; 1899 defended doctor's thesis on lymphatic angiomas, after which he was sent abroad for further specialist training; worked under Virchow and Mechnikov; 1908–18 head, Chair of Surgical Pathology, Therapy and Clinical Practice, Petersburg (Petrograd) Mil Med Acad; 1918–32 head, Chair of Acad Surgical Clinical Practice, Petrograd (Leningrad) Mil Med Acad; from 1919 hon fellow, British Royal Soc of Surgeons; from 1924 dir, Mechnikov Hospital, Leningrad, where he reorganized the Surgical Dept, enlarging it into a Surgical Clinic, affiliated to the Inst of Postgrad Med Trainung in 1927; 1931 founder-head, Chair of Field Surgery, Leningrad Mil Med Acad; chm, Pirogov Surgical Soc; chm, Endocrinological Soc; chm, various surgical congresses; did major research on surgical endocrinology and collateral blood circulation; wrote first Russian description of "war drainage" and reduced blood circulation; also made major contributions to traumatology, including a prize-winning study on the prevention of frostbite among soldiers in the field; trained numerous outstanding surgeons and wrote over 200 works; *Publ:* doctor's thesis *Limfangiomy* (Lymphatic Angiomas) (1899); "Über Veränderungen des Myokards unter der Einwirkung von Fremdkörpern" (1901); "Über die Regeneration der Deckzellen am Epikard and Endokard" (1901); *Kollateral'noye krovoobrashcheniye* (Collateral Blood Circulation) (1911); *Samoproizvol'naya gangrena* (Spontaneous Gangrene) (1923); *Istoriya russkoy khirurgii* (A History of Russian Surgery) (1923); *Klinika izmeneniy funktsiy epitelial'nykh telets* (Clinical Aspects of Functional Lesions of the Epithelial Bodies); *Samoproizvol'naya gangrena kak giperadrenalinemiya* (Spontaneous Gangrene as Hyperadrenalinemia) (1928); *Travmatizm* (Traumatism) (1929); *Khirurgicheskiy travmatizm i kalecheniye* (Surgical Traumatism and Crippling) (1929); *Khirurgicheskaya patologiya i terapiya dlya vrachey* (Surgical Pathology and Therapy for Physicians) (1929); *Lektsii po klinicheskoy khirurgii i klinicheskoy endokrinologii dlya khirurgov* (Lectures on Clinical Surgery and Clinical Endocrinology for Surgeons) (1929–31); *Ocherki khirurgii voyny* (Studies in War Surgery) (1940); *Awards:* Prize of RSFSR Mil Revol Council (1919); *Died:* 7 Oct 1932 in Leningrad.

ORAKHELASHVILI, Ivan (Mamiya) Dmitriyevich (1881–1937) Party and govt official; CP member from 1903; *Born:* 29 May 1881 in Kutaisi, son of an impoverished nobleman; *Educ:* studied at Med Fac, Khar'kov Univ; 1908 grad Petersburg Mil Med Acad; *Career:* 1903 arrested for involvement in student polit movement; active in 1905–07 Revol in Petersburg; summer 1906 went to Paris and Geneva for med treatment; returned to Russia and arrested for his connection with the Avladar Printing Press case; from 1908 practised med in Transcaspian Oblast; 1914–17 mil surgeon with army in the field; 1917 chm, Vladikavkaz RSDRP(B) Comt and chm, Vladikavkaz Sov of Workers and Soldiers' Dep; Oct 1917–May 1920 member, Caucasian Kray RSDRP(B) Comt; chm, CC, CP Geo and member, Caucasian Bureau, CC, RCP(B); 1921–25, after establishment of Sov regime in Geo, chm, Geo Revol Comt; secr, CC, CP(B) Geo; dep chm, Geo Council of Pop Comr; chm, Transcaucasian SFSR Council of Pop Comr; 1923–25 dep chm, USSR Council of Pop Comr; 1926–29 first secr, Transcaucasian Kray CPSU(B) Comt; also ed-in-chief, newspaper "Zarya Vostoka"; 1930 member, ed bd, newspaper „Pravda", Moscow; from Jan 1931 again chm, Transcaucasian SFSR Council of Pop Comr; then first secr, Transcaucasian Kray CPSU(B) Comt; 1932–37 dep dir, Inst of Marx-Engels-Lenin, CC, CPSU(B); at 12th–14th Party Congresses elected cand member, and at 15th and 16th Congresses elected member, CC, CPSU(B); at 17th Party Congress elected member, Centr Auditing Commission; wrote numerous works on Party history and socialist construction in Geo and Transcaucasia; arrested by State Security organs; *Publ:* "Transcaucasian Bolshevik Organizations in 1917" (1927); "The Victory of the October Socialist Revolution in Georgia" (1935); *Died:* Dec 1937 executed; posthumously rehabilitated.

ORANSKIY (real name: GERSHOV), Viktor Aleksandrovich (1899–1953) Composer and teacher; *Born:* 4 May 1899 in Feodosiya; *Educ:* 1918 grad Moscow Conservatory; *Career:* 1918 began to teach music; 1923–25 musical dir, 2nd Studio, Moscow Arts Theater; 1932–36 musical dir, All-Union Centr Trade-Union Council Theater; 1947–50 musical dir, Yermolova Theater; *Works:* ballets: *Futbolisty* (The Football Players) (1930); *Tri tolstyaka* (Three Fat Men) (1935); *Vindzorskiye prokaznitsy* (The Merry Wives of Windsor) (1942); opera *Bronepoyezd 14–69* (Armored Train 14–69); children's opera *Zvezda radosti* (Star of Joy) (1919); operetta *Nochnyye pauki* (Night Spiders) (1929); music for plays and films: Kal'derons's *Dama-nevidimka* (The Invisible Lady) (1924); *12 mesyatsev* (Twelve Months) (1947); Malyugin's *Staryye druz'ya* (Old Friends) (1945); Globa's "Pushkin" (1950); *Konyok-Gorbunok* (The Little Hunch-Backed Horse), after Yershov; Svetlov's *20 let spustya* (Twenty Years Later), etc; *Died:* 27 Sept 1953 in Moscow.

ORAY, Dmitriy (real name: Dmitriy Fyodorich BOGOSLOVSKIY) (1901–1950) Mari writer; member, USSR Writers' Union; *Born:* 5 Sept 1901; in vil Mari-Pizhay, now Mari ASSR, son of a peasant; *Educ:* completed primary schooling; *Career:* 1929 first work printed; from 1930 newspaper work; fought in WW 2; *Publ:* novelettes: "The Apostate" (1930); "A Steep Rise" (1935); "Olyana" (1935); "The Unblinking Star" (1950); novel "Through the Mists" (1951); *Died:* 22 Jan 1950 in Yoshkar-Ola.

ORBELI, Iosif Abgarovich (1887–1961) Orientalist; member, USSR Acad of Sci from 1935; member, Arm Acad of Sci from 1943; Hon member, London Archeological Soc; hon member, Iranian Acad of Sci from 1957; *Born:* 20 Mar 1887 in Kutaisi; *Educ:* 1911 grad History and Philology Fac and Oriental Fac, Petersburg Univ; *Career:* 1914–31 assoc prof, then prof, Petersburg (Leningrad) Univ; 1919–31 member, State Acad of the History of Material Culture; 1920–34 founder-custodian, Oriental Dept, 1934–51 dir, Hermitage Museum; 1938–43 chm, Arm Branch, USSR Acad of Sci; 1943–47 pres, Arm Acad of Sci; 1955–60 dean, Oriental Fac, Leningrad Univ; 1956–61 head, Leningrad Branch, Inst of Oriental Studies (later Inst of Asian Peoples), USSR Acad of Sci; studied history of Caucasus and medieval culture of Middle East; valuable studies of Sassanid and Seljukian cultures; also studied Arm epigraphy, folk epics and architecture of Geo and Arm and Kurdic language; founded school of Caucasian studies based on combination of material culture and Philology; close assoc of N.Ya. Marr; 1911–12 and 1916 collaborated with Marr in excavation of ancient Arm City of Ani, near Lake Van; *Publ:* *Nadpisi Marmashena* (The Marmashen Inscriptions) (1914); *Raskopki dvukh nish na Vanskoy skale* (The Excavation of Two Bays on the Van Cliff) (1922); *Musul'manskiye izraztsy* (Moslem Tiles) (1923); coauthor, *Sasanidskiy metall* (Sassanid Metal) (1935); *Pamyatniki epokhi Rustaveli* (Monuments of the Rustaveli Period) (1938); *Armyanskiy geroicheskiy narodnyy epos* (The Armenian Heroic Folk Epic) (1939); *Basni srednevekovoy Armenii* (Medieval Armenian Fables) (1956); *Izbrannyye trudy* (Selected Works) (1963); *Awards:* two Orders of Lenin; two Orders of the Red Banner of Labor; medals; *Died:* 2 Feb 1961.

ORDUBADY, Mamed Said (real name: MAMED, Gadzhi-aga ogly) (1872–1950) Azer writer; Hon Art Worker of Azer SSR; CP member from 1918; *Born:* 24 Mar 1872 in Ordubad, now Nachichevan ASSR; *Career:* 1903 first work printed in newspaper "Russkiy Vostok"; from 1906 contributed to revol-democratic journal "Molla Nasreddin"; 1907–11 active in Iranian revol movement; 1913 exiled to Tsaritsyn for revol activities; from 1920 coordinating ed, newspaper "Novyy put'"; member, Azer Assoc of Proletarian Writers; nationalist and pan-Islamist; *Publ:* verse collection "Unconcern" (1906); "Country and Freedom" (1907); novel "The Unfortunate Millionaire, or Rzakuli Francophile" (1914); "The Fighting City" (1938); "Underground Baku" (1940); "The Misty Tavriz" (1933–48); "Sword and Pen" (1946–48); "Ker-ogly" and "Nizami"; translated into Azer: Pushkin's *Bakhchisarayskiy fontan* (The Fountain of Bakhchisaray) and "Boris Godunov"; also works of Lermontov, Dem'yan Bednyy, Akopyan, etc; *Awards:* Order of Lenin; other orders; medals; *Died:* 3 May 1950 in Baku.

ORDZHONIKIDZE, Grigoriy (Sergo) Konstantinovich (1886–1937) Govt and Party official; CP member from 1903; *Born:* 24 Oct 1886 in vil Goresha, Kutaisi Province; *Educ:* grad med orderlies school; *Career:* from 1901 lived in Tiflis, where he took part in a Marxist circle; from 1903 carried out propaganda among workers at Main Railroad Shops; 1905–07 took part in revol in Transcaucasia; Dec 1905 arrested while smuggling arms for revol squads; May 1906 released on bail; Aug 1906 emigrated to Germany; Jan 1907 returned to Russia and did Party work in Baku; from Mar 1907 Party organizer for Balakhan Rayon and member, Baku RSDRP Comt; Nov 1907 re-arrested; Feb 1909 exiled to Yeniseysk Province; Aug 1909 fled and went abroad; 1909–10 worked in Iran for Baku RSDRP Comt; 1910 corresponded with Lenin; spring 1911 studied at Party School, Longjumenau, near Paris; summer 1911 returned to Russia on orders from Lenin and helped prepare 6th RSDRP Conference; as plen of Russian Org Commission, visited numerous Party orgs in main industrial centers; Jan 1912 at 6th All-Russian RSDRP Conference in Prague, elected member, CC, RSDRP and member, Russian Bureau, CC, RSDRP; 14 Apr 1912 rearrested in Petersburg; 9 Oct 1912 sentenced to three years' hard labor, to be followed by exile to Siberia for life; Nov 1912–8 Oct 1915 in irons at Shlissel'burg Convicts Prison, then exiled to Yakutsk Oblast; June 1917 returned to Petrograd and became member, Petrograd RSDRP(B) Comt and member, Exec Comt, Petrograd Sov; from July 1917 hepled arrange for Lenin to go underground; twice visited Lenin at Razliv to brief him on Party developments and receive instructions for Party; at 6th RSDRP(B) Congress explained why Lenin should not face trial arranged by Provisional Govt; fulfilled important CC missions in Petrograd (June–Aug 1917) and Transcaucasia (Sept–Oct 1917); 6 Nov 1917 returned to Petrograd and played active part in Oct Revol; 20 Dec 1917 appointed provisional Extraordinary Comr for Ukr; Pop Comrt of Food's inspector-extraordinary for southern regions; Apr 1918 appointed provisional Extraordinary Comr of Southern Region; 1918–21 during Civil War did senior polit work among Red Army troops and at front; 1918 member, Centr Exec Comt of Don Republ; helped organize defense of Tsaritsyn; chm, North Caucasian Defense Council; 1919, as member, Revol Mil Council of 16th Army, Western Front, and then member, Revol Mil Council of 14th Army, Southern Front, helped rout Denikin's forces at Oryol and liberate Donbass, Khar'kov and Left-Bank Ukr; from Jan 1920 member, Revol Mil Council, Caucasian Front; Feb 1920 chm, Bureau for Restoration of Sov Regime in Northern Caucasus; from Apr 1920 head, Caucasian Bureau, CC, RCP(B); from Feb 1922–Sept 1926 secr, Transcaucasian Kray Party Comt; first secr, North Caucasian Kray CPSU(B) Comt; Nov 1926–Nov 1930 chm, CPSU(B) Centr Control Commission and USSR Pop Comr of Workers and Peasants' Inspection; dep chm, USSR Council of Pop Comr and Labor and Defense Council; Nov 1930 appointed chm, Supr Sovnarkhoz; from Jan 1932 Pop Comr of Heavy Ind; from 1921 member, CC, CPSU(B); from July 1926 cand Politbureau member, from Dec 1930 Politbureau member, CC, CPSU(B); *Awards:* Order of Lenin (1935); Order of the Red Banner (1921); Order of the Red Banner of Labor (1936); *Died:*

18 Feb 1937 committed suicide during Stalinist purges; buried on Moscow's Red Square.

ORDZHONIKIDZE, Zinaida Gavrilovna (1894–1960) Soc worker; G.K. Ordzhonikidze's wife; *Born:* 30 Sept 1894 in Yakutia; *Career:* 1916, while working as teacher, made acquaintance of Bolshevik revolutionaries exiled to Yakutia; participated in 1917 Oct Revol and in Civil War; helped organize aid to waifs and strays; worked for various children's orgs; co-sponsored movement to involve ind managers' wives in soc work; during WW 2 worked in mil hospitals; *Publ:* memoirs about G.K. Ordzhonikidze *Put' bol'shevika* (The Path of a Bolshevik); *Died:* 5 Oct 1960.

OREKHOV, Aleksandr Pavlovich (1881–1939) Chemist; member, USSR Acad of Sci from 1939; *Born:* 7 Nov 1881 in Nizhniy Novgorod; *Educ:* studied at Yekaterinoslav Higher Mining College (expelled for student agitation); 1908 grad Giessen Univ, Germany; *Career:* from 1928 head, Dept of Alkaloid Chemistry, Chemical and Pharmaceutical Research Inst, Moscow; organized research on alkaloid-bearing flora of the USSR; together with his assoc discovered about 100 new alkaloids, some of which he synthesized; supervised development and ind application of methods of obtaining ephedrine, salsoline, anabasine, etc; also abtained medically valuable alkoloids pachycarpine and platiphilline; *Publ: Khimiya alkaloidov* (Alkoloid Chemistry) (1938); *Died:* 19 Oct 1939.

ORESHIN, Pyotr Vasil'yevich (1887–1938) Russian poet; *Born:* 16 July 1887 in Saratov; *Educ:* completed three grades at four-grade municipal school; *Career:* 1911 first work printed; during WW 1 served in Russian Army at the front; 1918 contributed to almanach "Skify" (The Scythians); helped found Peasant Writers Section, Moscow Cultural and Educ Org, Pop Comrt of Educ; 1925 bd member, All-Russian Poets' Union; contributed to newspapers and journals; arrested by State Security organs; *Publ:* verse collections: *Zarevo* (Dawn) (1918); *Rzhanoye solntse* (Rye Sun) (1923); *Solomennaya plakha* (The Straw Beheading Block) (1925); *Rodnik* (The Spring) (1927); novelette *Lyudishki* (Little People) (1927); verse collection *Otkrovennaya lira* (The Frank Lyre) (1928); novelette *Zlaya zhizn'* (The Evil Life) (1931); poems: "Village Correspondent Tsyganok", "Teacher Siskin"; "Policeman Lyuksha"; "Bloodied May"; "Vera Zasulich"; "Rasputin"; "9 January"; "Chapayev", etc; *Died:* 15 Mar 1938 in imprisonment; posthumously rehabilitated.

ORESHNIKOV, Aleksey Vasil'yevich (1855–1933) Historian and numismatist; corresp member, USSR Acad of Sci from 1928; *Born:* 9 Sept 1855 in Moscow; *Educ:* grad Moscow Practical Business Acad; *Career:* 1883–1933 head, Numismatic Dept and senior custodian, State Historical Museum, Moscow; viewed numismatics as an auxiliarly historical discipline, by comparing the history of ancient coins with archeological, epigraphic and other data made numerous broad historical deductions, some of which are still valid; wrote over 130 works; *Publ: Bosfor Kimmeriyskiy v epokhu Spartokidov po nadpisyam i tsarskim monetam* (The Cymerian Bosphorus During the Spartocan Dynasty According to Inscriptions and Imperial Coins) (1884); *Monety Bosporskogo tsarstva i drevnegrecheskikh gorodov* (The Coins of the Kingdom of Bosphorus and the Ancient Greek Cities) (1887); *Russkiye monety do 1547–ogo goda* (Russian Coins Before 1547) (1896); *Materialy k russkoy numizmatike do tsarskogo perioda* (Material on Russian Numismatics Before the Imperial Period) (1901); *Etyudy po numizmatike Chernomorskogo poberezh'ya* (Studies in the Numismatics of the Black Sea Coast) (1921); *Denezhnyye znaki domongol'skoy Rusi* (Money Tokens of Pre-Mongolian Rus) (1936); etc; *Died:* 3 June 1933.

ORLENEV (real name: ORLOV), Pavel Nikolayevich (1869–1932) Actor; Pop Artiste of RSFSR from 1926; *Born:* 6 Mar 1869 in Moscow, son of a merchant; *Educ:* studied at drama courses, Moscow Maly Theater; *Career:* 1881 stage debut with Moscow Artistic Circle; 1886 performed at Maly Theater; 1886–87 worked for Pushkin-Chekrygin Company, Vologda; 1888–93 acted in various towns and performed with dacha theaters such as the "Ozerki" Theater near Petersburg; 1893–95 actor, Korsh Theater, Moscow; 1895–1902 (with intervals) with Theater of Lit and Art Soc, Petersburg; then strolling actor; toured various cities with itinerant drama companies; tried to establish public theaters for peasantry; 1910 organized free shows for peasants at Golitsyn, near Moscow; organized open-air shows at Vostryakov near Moscow; toured abroad: 1904 in Berlin; 1905 in London; 1905–06 and 1911–12 in America; 1908 in Sweden; 1915 in Norway; specialized in comic simpleton, vaudeville and character roles; *Roles:* the Cobbler's Apprentice in Mansfel'd's *S mesta v kar'yer* (Making a Career) (1888); Stepan in Babetskiy's *Shkol' naya para* (The School Couple) (1891); Fyodor Slezkin in Ludvigov-Mayevskiy's *Nevpopad* (Out of Place) (1896); Jacko in Gay's "Trilby" (1896); title role in A.K. Tolstoy's "Tsar' Fyodor Ionnovich" (1898); Raskol'nikov in *Prestupleniye i nakazaniye* (Crime and Punishment) (1899) and Dmitriy Karamazov in *Brat'ya Karamazovy* (The Brothers Karamazov) (1900), after Dostoyevsky; Lorenzaccio in Alfred de Musset's "Lorenzaccio" (1900); Arnold in Hauptmann's "Michael Kramer" (1901); Oswald in Ibsen's "Ghosts" (1903); Brand in Ibsen's "Brand" (1907); Paul I in Merezhkovskiy's *Pavel I* (Paul I) (1902); Rozhnov in Krylov's *Gore-zloschast'ye* (Misfortune) (1902); Nakhnan in Chirikov's *Yevrei* (The Jews) (1904), etc; *Died:* 31 Aug 1932 in Moscow.

ORLOV, Aleksandr Ivanovich (1873–1948) Conductor; Pop Artiste of RSFSR from 1945; *Born:* 18 Aug 1873 in Petersburg; *Educ:* grad Petersburg Conservatory; from 1906 studied conducting under Juon in Berlin; *Career:* 1902 conductor, Kuban' Army Symphony Orchestra; from 1907 symphony and opera conductor in Rostov-on-Don, Odessa, Kiev, Yalta, etc; 1912–17 conductor, Kusevitskiy Symphony Orchestra, Moscow; 1917–25 conductor, Zimin Opera Theater, 1925–29 chief conductor, Shevchenko Opera and Ballet Theater; from 1927 prof, Moscow Conservatory; from 1930 conductor, Grand Symphony Orchestra, All-Union Radio; *Works:* conducted and helped produce operas: Taneyev's "Orestes"; Beethoven's "Fidelio"; Wagner's "Lohengrin"; Nicolai's "Merry Wives of Windsor"; Puccini's "Turandot"; Wolf-Ferrari's "The Madonna's Necklace"; Lysenko's "Taras Bul'ba"; Pashchenko's *Orlinyy bunt* (Eagles Revolt); Prokofiyev's ballet *Shut* (The Jester), etc; *Died:* 10 Oct 1948.

ORLOV, Aleksandr Nikolayevich (1908–1942) Sculptor; *Born:* 1908 in Vitebsk; *Educ:* 1929 grad Vitebsk Art Technicum; *Career:* from 1928 member, Vitebsk Branch, Youth League, Assoc of Artists of the Revol; helped design ornamentation of Govt House in Minsk; 1939 sculpted group "The Border Guard and the Kolkhoz Woman" for All-Union Agric Exhibition in Moscow; *Died:* 1942 in German concentration camp.

ORLOV, Aleksandr Sergeyevich (1871–1947) Lit historian; member, USSR Acad of Sci from 1931; *Born:* 4 Feb 1871 in Moscow; *Educ:* 1906 grad History and Philology Fac, Moscow Univ; defended master's thesis; *Career:* until 1931 taught at Moscow Univ and other higher educ establishments; from 1931 dep dir, Inst of Russian Lit (Pushkin Center) in Leningrad; from 1933 founder-head, Dept of Ancient Russian Lit, Inst of Russian Lit; studied textology and monuments of Ancient Russian lit; tried to influence the study of Ancient Russian lit away from "bibliography" towards the "artistic qualities" and esthetic features of individual lit works; studied Russian chronicles; *Poucheniye Vladimira Monomakha* (The Homily of Vladimir Monomakh); *Domostroy* (The Economicum); *Smutnoye vremya* (The Time of the Troubles); also studied Ancient Russian narrative lit, original and translated; did intensive research on *Slovo o polku Igoreve* (The Lay of the Host of Igor); in 1940's showed an interest in patriotic and heroic themes in Ancient Russian literature; also studied Russian and Kazakh folklore and 18th–19th Century lit, especially Pushkin, Trediakovskiy, Griboyedov, Krylov, Turgenev and Leskov; studied paleography, bibliography and language of Russian writers; *Publ: Ob osobennostyakh formy russkikh voinskikh novostey* (Features of the Form of Russian Military Dispatches) (1902); *O nekotorykh osobennostyakh stilya velikorusskoy istoricheskoy belletristiki 11–16 vv.* (Some Stylistic Features of Great-Russian Historical Belles Lettres of the 11th–16th Centuries) (1909); lecture course *Drevnyaya russkaya literatura 11–16 vv.* (Ancient Russian Literature of the 11th–16th Centuries) (1937); *K izucheniyu srednevekov'ya russkoy literature* (Study of the Middle Ages in Russian Literature) (1931); *Literaturovedeniye russkogo srednevekov'ya* (Literary Studies of the Russian Middle Ages) (1945); *Mysli ob izuchenii literatury russkogo srednevekov'ya* (Thoughts on the Study of Russian Medieval Literature) (1947); *Istoriya russkoy literatury* (The History of Russian Literature) (1948); *Awards:* Order of Lenin; *Died:* 6 Mar 1947 in Leningrad.

ORLOV, Aleksandr Yakovlevich (1880–1954) Astronomer; prof from 1913; corresp member, USSR Acad of Sci from 1927; member, Ukr Acad of Sci from 1939; Hon Sci Worker of Ukr SSR from 1951; *Born:* 25 Mar 1880 in Smolensk; *Educ:* 1902 grad Petersburg Univ; *Career:* 1913–34 dir, Odessa Astronomical

Observatory and prof, Odessa Univ; 1926–34 and 1939–50 dir, Poltava Gravimetric Observatory; 1944–48 and 1950–51 dir, Main Astronomical Observatory, Ukr Acad of Sci; supervised a gravimetric survey of Ukr SSR and led expeditions to Altay and Siberia; did research on tidal and latitudinal fluctuations in the force of gravity; also studied the nutation of the Earth's axis and obtained precise data on the movement of the poles; wrote over 130 works; *Publ: Rezul'taty Yur'yevskikh, Tomskikh i Potdamskikh nablyudeniy nad lunnosolnechnymi deformatsiyami Zemli* (The Results of Observations on Lunar and Solar Deformations of the Earth Made at Yur'yev, Tomsk and Potsdam) (1915); *Teoreticheskaya astronomiya* (Theretical Astronomy) (1920); *Dvizheniye polyusa s 1895 do 1940* (The Motion of the Pole from 1895 to 1940) (1942); *O tryokhosnosti Zemli* (The Triaxiality of the Earth) (1944); *Dvizheniye polyusa Zemli 1939–49* (The Motion of the Earth's Pole, 1939–49) (1951), etc; *Awards:* Order of Lenin; other orders and medals; *Died:* 28 Jan 1954.

ORLOV, Dmitriy Nikolayevich (1892–1955 Actor; Pop Artiste of RSFSR from 1943; *Born:* 8 May 1892 in Spassk, Ryazan' Province: *Educ:* 1916 grad A.I. Il'in's Stagecraft Studio, Khar'kov; *Career:* 1918 joined N.N. Sinel'nikov's Drama Company, Khar'kov; 1920 acted with V.B. Vil'ner and Meyerhold's companies in Novorossiysk; 1922 joined Meyerhold's Higher Theatrical Workshops in Moscow; 1920–21 at Lunacharskiy Theater, Krasnodar; from 1922 actor, Moscow Theater of the Revol; from 1941 at Moscow Drama Theater; from 1944 at Moscow Acad Arts Theater; from 1931 also gave dramatic readings; acted in various films; *Roles:* Rasplyuyev in Sukhovo-Kobylin's *Smert' Tarelkina* (The Death of Tarelkin); Semyon Rak in Romashov's *Vozdushnyy pirog* (The Meringue); Stepan in Pogodin's *Poema o topore* (The Poem of the Axe); Umka in Sel'vinskiy's *Umka – belyy medved'* (Umka the Polar Bear); Tristan and Mengo in Lope de Vega's "Dog in a Manger" and "Fuente Ovejuna"; Globa in Simonov's *Russkiye lyudi* (Russian People); Konyukov in Simonov's *Dni i nochi* (Days and Nights); Luka in Gorky's *Na dne* (The Lower Dephts), etc; *Awards:* Stalin Prize (1947); *Died:* 19 Dec 1955.

ORLOV, Konstantin Khrisanfovich (1875–1952) Ophthalmologist; Dr of Med from 1903; prof from 1912; Hon Sci Worker of RSFSR from 1928; *Born:* 1875; *Educ:* 1898 grad Med Fac, Kazan' Univ; *Career:* 1903 defended doctor's thesis on eye lesions in ergot and ergot-drug poisoning; 1905 joined underground RSDRP org in Kazan'; 1907 imprisoned for revol activities, after which he went first to Pyatigorsk then to Warsaw; from 1912 prof, Chair of Eye Diseases, Warsaw Univ; founder, Warsaw Ophthalmological Soc; 1915 moved with evacuated Univ to Rostov-on-Don, where he founded an eye clinic which he directed until his death and which now bears his name; from 1922 founder and life-chm, Don Ophthalmological Soc; hon member, Odessa, Saratov, Tomsk, Uzbek, Rostov and Gorky Ophthalmological Soc; 1936 co-edited text of Sov Constitution at Extraordinary 8th All-Union Congress of Soviets; wrote over 60 works; *Publ:* doctor's thesis *K ucheniyu ob otravlenii glaza pri khronicheskom otravlenii sporyn'yey i yeyo preparatami* (The Theory of Eye Poisoning in Chronic Poisoning from Ergot and Ergot Drugs) (1903); *K patogenezu simmetricheskikh opukholey glaznits* (The Pathogenesis of Symmetrical Tumors of the Eye-Sockets) (1923); *Plesnevyye gribki kak vozbuditeli keratitov* (Mold Fungi as Keratitis Agents) (1928); *Melitococcia i glaz* (Melitococcia and the Eye) (1928); *K vorprosu o distroficheskikh zabolevaniyakh rogovitsy* (Dystrophic Diseases of the Cornea) (1939); *K patologii i terapii tromboz ven glaznitsy i venoznykh sinusov cherepa* (The Pathology and Therapy of Thrombosis of the Orbital Veins and the Venous Cranial Sinuses) (1939); *K onkologii glaza* (The Oncology of the Eye) (1949); *Died:* 1952 in Rostov-on-Don.

ORLOV (YEGOROV), K. N. (1879–1943) Govt official; CP member from 1903; *Born:* 1879; *Career:* 1917–18 chm, All-Russian Collegium for Arming Red Army; Aug 1918 – Dec 1919 extraordinary polit comr, Tula Munitions Plants and Artillery Depot; 1921 dep chm, Council for Mil Ind; 1922–29 chm, Main Mil Ind Bd; chm, Automobile Trust; chm, State Ind Building Bd, Supr Sovnarkhoz; active in "Workers' Opposition"; expelled from Party and arrested by State Security organs; *Died:* 1943 in imprisonment.

ORLOV, Vladimir Mitrofanovich (1895–1938) Naval commander; fleet flag officer, 1st class; from 1935; CP member from 1918; *Born:* 3 July 1895 in Kherson; *Educ:* studied at Petersburg Univ; 1917 completed midshipman school; 1926 grad Higher Acad Courses, Naval Acad; *Career:* 1916 drafted into Russian Navy; served on cruiser "Oryol"; 1917 elected to ship's comt; 1917–18 watch commander, cruiser "Bogatyr'"; 1919 – Feb 1920 head, Polit Dept, Baltic Fleet; fought against Yudenich; 1920–21 dep head, Main Water Transport Polit Bd; from Dec 1921 asst head, (for naval affairs), Polit Bd, RSFSR Revol Mil Council; head of its Naval Dept; from Mar 1923 head and comr of naval training establishments; from Oct 1926 commander, Sov Naval Forces and member, USSR Revol Mil Council; from Jan 1937 also USSR Dep Pop Comr of Defense; Nov 1937 arrested by State Security organs; *Awards:* Order of the Red Banner; *Died:* 28 July 1938 in imprisonment; posthumously rehabilitated.

ORLOV, Yegor Ivanovich (1865–1944) Chemical eng; prof from 1911; member, Ukr Acad of Sci from 1929; Hon Sci and Tech Worker of RSFSR; *Born:* 2 Feb 1865 in vil Pokrov, now Gorky Oblast; *Educ:* 1894 grad Moscow Univ; *Career:* 1894–1911 teacher, Kostroma College of Chemical Technol; 1902 provided plans for construction of first formalin plant in Russia; 1908 proved the possibility of obtaining higher hydrocarbons from a mixture of carbon monoxide and hydrogen, with which he synthesized etylene; 1911–31 prof, Khar'kov Technol Inst; from 1927 also dir, Kharkov Research Inst of Refractory Materials; from 1931 prof, various higher educ establishments in Moscow; also did research on chemical kinetics, catalysis and other questions of chemical technol; *Publ: Formal'degid, yego dobyvaniye, svoystva i primeneniye* (Formaldehyde, Its Manufacture, Properties and Use) (1935); *Issledovaniya v oblasti kinetiki khimicheskikh reaktsiy i kataliza* (Research on the Kinetics of Chemical Reactions and Catalysis) (1936); *Glazuri emali, keramicheskiye kraski i massy* (Enamel Glazes, Ceramic Paints and Pastes) (1938), etc; *Awards:* Order of the Red Banner of Labor; *Died:* 14 Oct 1944.

ORLOV, Yuriy Aleksandrovich (1893–1966) Paleontologist and histologist; prof from 1933; Dr of Biological Sci; member, USSR Acad of Sci from 1960; Hon Sci Worker of RSFSR from 1946; *Born:* 1893 in vil Tomishovo, Simbirsk Province; *Educ:* 1917 grad Natural Sci Dept, Physics and Mathematics Fac, Petrograd Univ; *Career:* 1917–24 taught histology at Perm' Univ; 1924–37 taught histology at Leningrad Mil Med Acad; 1933–41 prof of paleontology, Leningrad Univ; from 1943 until death prof of paleontology, Moscow State Univ; 1929–45 senior assoc, Inst of Paleontology, USSR Acad of Sci; 1945–66 dir of this inst; from 1959 founder and chief ed, journal "Paleontologicheskiy zhurnal"; 1953–60 corresp member, USSR Acad of Sci; made comparative morphological study of nervous system of invertebrates; studied fauna of Neogene and other vertebrates of Western Siberia, Kaz and Ukr; *Publ: V mire drevnikh zhivotnykh* (In the World of Ancient Animals) (1961); 15-vol *Osnovy paleontologii* (The Principles of Paleontology); *Awards:* Order of Lenin; Lenin Prize (1967, posthumously); other orders; *Died:* 2 Oct 1966.

ORSHANSKIY (real name: BER), Boris Mikhaylovich (1884–1945) Jewish writer and critic; CP member from 1918; *Born:* 30 Nov 1884 in Gorodok, Vitebsk Province, son of a merchant; *Career:* from 1903 member, Jewish Soc-Democratic "Bund"; 1911 began lit work; from 1926 head, Jewish Section, Inst of Bel Culture, Minsk; member, Bel, then Moscow Assoc of Proletarian Writers; 1930–32 assoc, State Acad of Arts; from 1932 edited newspaper in Kamchatka; *Publ:* dramatic poem "Eternal Dream" (1911); plays: "At the Sun's First Rays"; "Anna" (1914); "Together" (1919); "Blood" (1929); coauthor, *Teatral'nyye boi* (Theatrical Battles) (1939); novel "The Potyomkin Mutiny" (1930); *Died:* 15 Dec 1945 in Moscow.

OSADCHIY, Pyotr Semyonovich (1866–1943) Electr eng; *Born:* 1866; *Educ:* 1890 grad Petersburg Electr Eng Inst; *Career:* from 1900 prof, 1918–25 rector, Petersburg Electr Eng Inst, where he founded the Electrophysical Fac; after 1917 Oct Revol member, from 1922 chm, Centr Electr Eng Council, Supr Sovnarkhoz; from 1919 member, Sci and Tech Comt, Pop Comrt of Means of Communication; from 1921 dep chm, Gosplan; prof, Chair of Low-Current Electr Eng, Moscow Higher Tech College; dep chm, All-Union Power Eng Comt; Presidium member, State Learned Council, RSFSR Pop Comrt of Educ; 1931 sentenced to 10 years' imprisonment at Ind Party trial; 1935 released prematurely; 1937 sentence quashed; *Publ: Osnovy teorii telegrafnykh tsepey i primeneniye yeyo k proyektirovaniyu elektricheskikh liniy* (Principles of Telegraph Circuit Theory and Its Application to the Design of Electric Lines (1903); *Pochtovyye, telegrafnyye i telefonnyye soobshcheniya kak element gosudarstvennogo khozyaystva v Yevrope* (Postal, Telegraph and Telephone Communications as an Element of State Economy in Europe) (1908); *Elektrotekhnicheskoye obrazovaniye v SSSR* (Electrotechnical Education in the USSR) (1927), etc; *Died:* 1943.

OSATKIN-VLADIMIRSKIY, Aleksandr Nikolayevich (1885–1937) Party official; CP member from 1904; *Born:* 15 Oct 1885 in vil Voznesenskoye, now Kostroma Oblast, son of a farmhand; *Career:* active in 1905–07 Revol; 1907 deleg at 5th (London) RSDRP Congress; six times imprisoned and twice exiled; 1918–21 Presidium member, All-Russian Centr Trade-Union Council and member, CC, Textile Workers' Union; 1921–22 Turkestani Pop Comr of Econ, dep chm, Turkestani Council of Pop Comr and chm, Turkestani Econ Council; from 1922 instructor, CC, RCP(B); from May 1923 chm, Party and Govt Commission to Consolidate the Bel SSR; from Feb 1924 secr, provisional Bel Bureau, CC, RCP(B); then first secr, CC, CP(B) Bel; from Aug 1924 first dep dept head, CC, CPSU(B); from Feb 1925 first secr, Vladimir Province, CPSU(B) Comt; from Sept 1927 instructor, CC, CPSU(B); from July 1928 chm, All-Union Agric Bank; 1930–31 chm, Far Eastern Kray Exec Comt; from 1932 head, Machine and Tractor Stations Polit Section, Ukr Pop Comrt of Agric; from 1935 head, Ukr Econ Accounting Bd; at 13th RCP(B) Congress elected member, Centr Control Commission; arrested by State Security organs; *Died:* 1937 in imprisonment.

OSHAROV, Mikhail Ivanovich (1894–1943) Russian writer; *Born:* Nov 1894 in vil Lebyazh'ye, Minusinsk Uyezd, Krasnoyarsk Kray, son of a peasant; *Educ:* studied at Shanyavskiy Pop Univ; *Career:* served in Russian Army; 1919 helped disarm Admiral Kolchak's army in Krasnoyarsk; 1919–31 instructor, consumers cooperative system in Northern Region; 1925 began to publish essays, stories; collected and arranged tales and legends of Siberian peoples – Evenki, Kets and Nenets; arrested by State Security organs; *Publ:* novelette *Zveno mogil* (A Group of Graves) (1928); new version entitled *Begut vody Kimchu* (The Running Waters of Kimchu) (1964); novel *Bol'schoy argish* (The Big Argish) (1934), etc; *Died:* 24 June 1943 in imprisonment; posthumously rehabilitated.

OSHKALN, Otomar Petrovich (1904–1947) Govt and Party official; CP member from 1939; *Born:* 12 Apr 1904 in Lat, son of a farmhand; *Educ:* grad Riga Teachers' Training Inst; *Career:* worked as teacher; 1921 joined underground Lat Komsomol; 1934 interned in a concentration camp for revol activities; 1940, after establishment of Sov rule in Lat, elected dep, Pop Sejm; then dep, Lat Supr Sov; second secr, Yekabpils Uyezd Comt, CP(B) Lat; during WW 2 comr, partisan detachment; then comr, "For Sov Lat" Partisan Regt; commanded Lat partisan brigade; member, Operations Group, CC, CP(B) Lat; 1944–46 first secr, Riga Uyezd Party Comt; from 1946 Lat Min of Tech Crops; dep, USSR Supr Sov of 2nd convocation; *Awards:* Hero of the Sov Union (1945): *Died:* 1 Sept 1947.

OSHLEY, Pyotr Matveyevich (1886–1937) Mil commander; CP member from 1917; *Born:* 1886; *Career:* from 1919 in Red Army; during Civil War comr, infantry regt; div comr; member, Revol Mil Council, 6th Army; mil comr, Staff of Ukr and Crimean Forces; after the Civil War secr, USSR Revol Mil Council; mang, USSR Pop Comrt of the Navy; mang, USSR Revol Mil Council; head, Mil Admin Bd, Red Army; arrested by State Security organs; *Died:* 1937 in imprisonment.

OSINSKIY (real name: OBOLENSKIY), Valerian Valerianovich (1887–1938) Govt and Party official; economist; CP member from 1907; *Born:* 6 Apr 1887 in vil Byki, Kursk Province, son of a veterinarian; *Educ:* 1905–07 studied at Moscow, Munich, then Berlin Univ; *Career:* Party work in Moscow, Tver' and Khar'kov; frequently arrested by Tsarist authorities; after 1917 Feb Revol member, Moscow Oblast RSDRP(B) Bureau and member, ed bd, newspaper "Sotsial-demokrat"; deleg at 6th RSDRP(B) Congress; after 1917 Oct Revol mang, RSFSR State Bank; until Mar 1918 first chm, Supr Sovnarkhoz; leading proponent of leftist Communist policy during controversy over 1918 Brest Peace Pact; 1918 worked for ed bd, newspaper "Pravda" and for Sov Propaganda Dept, Supr Sovnarkhoz; 1919-early 1920 All-Russian Centr Exec Comt plen in Penza, Tula, then Vyatka Provinces; 1920 chm, Tula Province Exec Comt and Collegium member, Pop Comrt of Food; 1920–21 active member, opposition "Democratic Centralism" group; 1923 sided with Trotskyist opposition; 1921–23 Dep Pop Comr of Agric and dep chm, Supr Sovnarkhoz; 1923–24 Sov plen in Sweden; 1925 Presidium member, USSR Gosplan; 1926–28 mang, Centr Statistical Bd; from 1929 dir, Inst of Econ; from 1929 dep chm, USSR Supr Sovnarkhoz and chm, All-Union Assoc of the Auto-Tractor Ind; then exec admin and econ work; from 1934 head, Centr Econ Accounting Bd; member, ed bd *Bol'shaya Sovetskaya Entsiklopediya* (Large Soviet Encyclopedia); from 1928 member, Plenum of Communist Acad and member, USSR Acad of Sci; on several occasions elected to USSR Centr Exec Comt; at 10th, 14th, 15th, 16th and 17th Party Congresses elected cand member, CC, CPSU(B); 1937 arrested by State Security organs; Mar 1938, as one of the leaders of the "Leftist Communists", appeared as witness at the trial of the "anti-Sov rightist-Trotskyite Bloc"; *Publ: Mirovoye khozyaystvo v otsenke nashikh ekonomistov* (The World Economy as Assessed by Our Economists) (1923); *Mirovoy krizis sel'skogo khozyaystva* (The World Agricultural Crisis) (1924); *Mirovoye khozyaystvo i krizisy* (The World Economy and Crises) (1925); *Ocherki mirovogo sel'skokhozyaystvennogo rynka* (Studies in the World Agricultural Market) (1925); *Amerikanskoye sel'skoye khozyaystvo po noveyshim issledovaniyam* (American Agriculture According to the Latest Studies) (1925), etc; *Died:* 1 Sept 1938 in imprisonment; posthumously rehabilitated.

OSIPENKO, Polina Denisovna (1907–1939) Aviatrix; mil pilot; maj, Sov Air Force; *Born:* 8 Oct 1907 in vil Novopasovka (now Osipenko), Zaporozhian Oblast; *Educ:* 1932 grad Kachin Flying School; *Career:* pilot, then flight commander with fighter units; set five int women's records, including: 1938 non-stop seaplane flight Sebastopol-Yevpatoriya-Ochakov-Sebastopol-Arkhangel'sk (2,416 km in 10 hours); 24–25 Sept 1938 Moscow-Komsomol'sk-on-the-Amur (6,450 km in 26 hours 29 minutes), together with Grizodubova and Raskova; *Awards:* Hero of the Sov Union (1938); two Orders of Lenin; Order of the Red Banner of Labor; *Died:* 11 May 1939 killed with A. K. Serov in the course of duty; the urn with her ashes is immured in the Kremlin Wall; 7 June 1939 Berdyansk renamed Osipenko in her hon; 1958 former name of Berdyansk restored.

OSIPOV, Aleksandr A. (1911–1967) Anti-religious campaigner; consultant on measures to combat religion from 1959; former archpriest, prof and inspector, Leningrad Theological Acad and Seminary; Master of Divinity; *Born* 1911 in Revel' (now Tallinn, Est); *Educ:* 1934 grad as Cand of Divinity from Orthodox Dept, Theological Fac, Tartu State Univ; *Pos:* 1935 consecrated priest and assigned to missionary work; from 1936 junior priest, then vicar of Russian parish in Tallinn; simultaneously taught divinity at Tallinn Private Russian High-School; 1941 served with eng units in Red Army; from 1942 priest in Perm'; from 1945 priest in his former Tallinn parish; secr, local eparchial bd; from 1946 prof of Old Testament scripture and history of religion, and until 1950 inspector, Leningrad Theological Academy; 1950 renounced his priestly duties but remained a priest, prof and inspector at Leningrad Theological Acad; 1951 entered into a second marriage and resigned from the priesthood; 1955–56 edited a revised ed of the Bible and New Testament, including the Psalms; 1959 renounced religion in an open letter to the rector, staff and students of the Theological Seminary; became a consultant on means of combatting religion; wrote numerous anti-religious pamphlets and articles; 30 Dec 1959 stripped of his priesthood and barred from the Church by a decree of the Moscow Patriarch and Holy Synod; *Career:* while at highschool took an active part in the YMCA-led Boy Scouts movement; from 1928 active member, religious-philosophical Russian Student Christian Movement, directed by Professors Vysheslavtsev, Zander, Zen'kovskiy, Berdyayev, Il'in, etc; 1929 deleg, rapporteur and secr, 2nd Congress of Russian Student Christian Movement; ran Religious Poetry Seminar at 3rd Congress of Russian Student Christian Movement in the Baltic area; contributed to journal "Pravoslavnyy sobesednik"; lectured on religion and philosophy at Russian evening divinity courses in Tallinn; after Sov occupation of Est, wrote plays for Tallinn Theater; *Publ: U rodnykh svyatyn'* (Our Hallowed Places) (1929); account of a journey to Old Valaam (Finland), stories, verse and articles (1926–40); *Put' k dukhovnoy svobode* (The Path to Spiritual Freedom) (1960); *Moy otvet veruyushchim* (My Answer to the Believers) (1960); *Chelovek na lozhnom puti* (Man on the False Path) (1960); *Prodolzhayem razgovor s veruyushchimi* (Continuing Our Conversation with Belivers) (1962); *Katekhizis bez prikras* (Catechism Without the Trimmings) (1963); *Yevangeliye ot iyezuita* (The Gospel According to the Jesuits) (1964); *Zhenshchina pod krestom* (Woman Beneath the Cross) (1966); *Died:* 1967.

OSIPOV, Nikolay Petrovich (1896–1945) Musician; balalaika virtuoso; conductor and music teacher; Hon Artiste of RSFSR; *Born:* 28 Jan 1896 in Petersburg; *Educ:* in his childhood took balalaika lessons from A. M. Dykhov and V. V. Andreyev, a member of the Great Russian Orchestra; also took violin lessons; *Career:* 1928–39 soloist, Moscow Philharmonic Orchestra; 1940–45 conductor and artistic dir, State Rusian Folk Orchestra, which now bears his name; collaborated with various composers in the writing of pieces for solo balalaika, including a concerto by S. N. Vasilenko and M. M. Ippolitov-Ivanov's fantasia "The Sewing Gathering"; *Died:* 9 May 1945 in Moscow.

OSIPOV, Viktor Petrovich (1871–1947) Psychiatrist; pioneer of the pathophysiological school of Sov psychiatry; Dr of Med from 1898; prof from 1906; lt-gen, Med Corps; corresp member, USSR Acad of Sci from 1939; member, USSR Acad of Med Sci from 1944; Hon Sci Worker of RSFSR from 1933; CP member from 1939; *Born:* 12 Nov 1871 in Petersburg; *Educ:* 1895 grad Petersburg Mil Med Acad; *Career:* after grad asst to Prof V. M. Bekhterev, Chair of Nervous and Mental Diseases, Petersburg Mil Med Acad; 1898 defended doctor's thesis on contractions of the stomach, intestines and urinary bladder during epileptic attacks; 1899 sent abroad to work and study under Krepelin, Munch, Nissel, Oppenheim and Mechnikov; 1901–06 assoc prof, from 1906 prof of psychiatry, Kazan' Univ; from 1915 head, Chair of Psychiatry, Petrograd (Leningrad) Mil Med Acad; 1929–47 dir, Bekhterev State Brain Inst; did extensive research on psychiatry, much of which is still valid; correlated Pavlov's theory to psychiatry in gen; refuted the "metasyphilitic" theory of progressive paralysis and interpreted this disease as a late-stage syphilitic psychosis; studied somatic and endocrinal disturbances in manic-depressive psychosis and proved that certain cases of dypsomania are related to this disease; did research on mil psyhiatry during WW 1; during WW 2 studied the clinical aspects of closed brain trauma, traumatic neurosis and mil med expertise; chm, Leningrad Soc of Neuropathologists and Psychiatrists; hon member, various sci soc; founder-chm, Pedological Soc (later banned); chm, Physicians' Trade Union; dep, Leningrad City Soc; member, State Learned Council; member, All-Union Assoc of Sci and Tech Workers for the Advancement of Socialist Construction; member, ed bd, periodical "Vrachebnaya gazeta"; chief ed, "Malaya entsiklopediya prakticheskoy meditsiny" (Small Encyclopedia of Practical Medicine) (4 vol, 1927–30); wrote 190 works; *Publ:* doctor's thesis *O sokrashcheniyakh zheludka, kishek i mochevogo puzyrya v techeniye paduchnykh pristupov* (Contractions of the Stomach, Intestines and the Urinary Bladder During Epileptic Attacks) (1898); *Katatoniya* (Catatonia) (1907); *Kurs ucheniya o dushevnykh boleznyakh* (A Course on Psychopathology) (1917); *Progressivnyy paralich – Pozdniy sifiliticheskiy psikhoz* (Progressive Paralysis – A Late-Stage Syphilitic Psychosis) (1922); *Kurs obshchego ucheniya o dushevnykh boleznyakh* (A General Course on Psychopathology) (1923); *Rukovodstvo po psikhiatrii* (A Psychiatry Manual) (1931); *Granitsy skhizofrenii, yeyo myagkiye formy i ikh legkomyslennoye raspoznavaniye* (The Borders of Schizophrenia, Its Light Forms and Their Careless Diagnosis) (1935); *Znacheniye ucheniya I. P. Pavlova dlya psikhiatrii* (The Importance of Pavlov's Theories for Psychiatry) (1938); *Voprosy psikhiatricheskogo raspoznavaniya i opredeleniya godnosti k voyennoy sluzhbe* (Psychiatric Diagnosis and the Determination of Fitness for Military Service) (1944); *Awards:* two Orders of Lenin; other orders and medals; *Died:* 22 May 1947.

OSMONOV, Alykul (1915–1950) Kir poet; *Born:* Mar 1915 in vil Kaptal-Aryk, Kir, son of a peasant; *Educ:* 1929–33 studied at teachers' training technicum; *Career:* raised in an orphanage; 1930 first work published; 1931 given his own verse column in the newspaper "Leninskaya molodyozh'"; 1937 translated into Kir Pushkin's *Skazka o pope i rabotnike yego Balde* (The Tale of the Priest and His Workman Balda), Krylov's fables, and Lermontov's verse; 1948 translated Pushkin's "Yevgeniy Onegin"; 1949 translated Shakespeare's "Othello"; 1951 translated Shota Rustaveli's "The Knight in the Tiger Skin"; *Publ:* collected verse: "Songs of Dawn" (1935); "Starry Youth" (1937); "Love" (1945); "New Songs" (1949); poems: "Zhenshibek", "Tolubay, the Judge of Horses", "Myrza uul", "Who's That? ", etc; plays: "Kooman, the Horse-Trainer" (1947); "Abylkasym Zhanbolotov" (1948); comedy "We Must Go to Merka" (1949), etc; *Died:* 27 Dez 1950.

OSSOVSKIY, Aleksandr Vyacheslavovich (1871–1957) Russian musicologist and music teacher; Hon Art Workers of RSFSR from 1938; Dr of Arts from 1943; corresp member, USSR Acad of Sci from 1943; CP member from 1945; *Born:* 19 Mar 1871 in Kishinev; *Educ:* 1893 grad Law Fac, Moscow Univ; 1896–98 studied under Rimsky-Korsakov at Petersburg Conservatory; *Career:* 1894 began work as music critic; contributed to "Russkaya muzykal'naya gazeta", newspaper "Slovo" and other periodicals; edited and translated various theoretical works and memoirs; 1915–16 instructor, from 1916 prof, Petrograd (Leningrad) Conservatory; 1943–52 dir, Leningrad Theater and Music Reserach Inst; *Publ:* "A. K. Glazunov" (1907); "N. A. Rimsky-Korsakov" (1944); "B. V. Asaf'yev" (1945); *Mirovoye znacheniye russkoy klassicheskoy muzyki* (The World Significance of Russian Classical Music) (1948); *Izbrannyye stat'i, vospominaniya* (Selected Articles and Memoirs) (1961); *Died:* 31 July 1957 in Leningrad.

OSTROUMOVA-LEBEDEVA, Anna Petrovna (1871–1955) Engraver and painter; Pop Artiste of RSFSR from 1946; member, USSR Acad of Arts from 1949; *Born:* 17 May 1871 in Petersburg; *Educ:* completed classes at Centr College of Tech Drawing; 1900 grad Repin's studio at Acad of Arts; *Career:* 1898–99 worked in Paris; 1899 returned to Russia and worked under Maté in Graphic Studio, Acad of Arts; joined "World of Art" Decadent group; specialized in nature studies, particulary of Petersburg and its environs; 1919–35 taught art; during WW 2 remained in blockaded Leningrad, painting and engaging in soc work; *Works:* engraving "Little Winter" (1900); colored engravings: "The Stock Market Columns and the Fortress" (1908); "The Klyukov Canal" (1910), etc; water color "The Field of Mars" (1922); engraving "Smol'nyy" (1924); water color and colored engraving "The Winter Garden in the Frost" (1929); portraits of S. V. Lebedev, I. V. Yershov, K. F. Bogayevskiy, N. A. Morozov, etc; *Publ: Avtobiograficheskiye zapiski* (Autobiographical Notes) (3 vol, 1935, 1945 and 1951); *Awards:* Order of the Red Banner of Labor; medals: *Died:* 5 May 1955.

OSTROV, Yan Petrovich (1896–1966) Govt official; Lat revol uctionary; CP member from 1917; *Born:* 1896; *Educ:* grad Communist Univ of Western Peoples; *Career:* fought in WW 1; helped organize Red Guard detachments; after establishment of Sov rule in Lat secr, distr Party comt; fought in Civil War; then Party and teaching work in Uzbek SSR; from 1944 in Lat SSR; worked for CC, CP Lat; then with Riga Party Comt; 1947–66 exec govt work in Lat SSR: dep chm, Lat Council of Min; Lat Min of Culture and Foreign Affairs, etc; member, CC, CP, Lat; dep, USSR Supr Sov; *Died:* 7 Sept 1966.

OSTROVSKIY, Nikolay Alekseyevich (1904–1936) Ukr writer; CP member from 1924; *Born:* 29 Nov 1904 in vil Viliya, Volhynian Province, son of a worker; *Educ:* completed vil parish school; studied at higher primary college; *Career:* expelled from college for rowdiness; errand boy in kitchens of station restaurant; asst stoker at electr power plant; 1919 joined Komsomol and volunteered for front; fought in Civil War as private in Kotovskiy's brigade and with Budyonnyy's 1st Cavalry Army; fall 1920 seriously wounded in action at L'vov; 1921–24 worked for local Cheka organs; head, Komsomol Org, Kiev's Main Railroad Workshops; secr, rayon Komsomol comt in Berezdov and Izyaslavl'; 1924 began to suffer progressive arteriosclerosis, then blindness; 1930, though bed-ridden and completely blind, began to dictate his autobiographical novel *Kak zakalyalas' stal'* (How the Steel Was Tempered), about Komsomol members in the 1920's; 1932 this work was serialized in journal "Molodaya gvardiya", was published as a monograph in 1935 and became extremely popular among young people in 1930's; 1934 began work on novel about Civil War in Ukr entitled *Rozhdyonnyye burey* (Born of Storm), but which had less success than his first novel; a few days before his death he managed to complete vol 1 of this novel; his novel "How the Steel Was Tempered" was used as the basis for a film of the same name (1942), for the film "Pavel Korchagin" (1956), for the ballet *Yunost'* (Youth) (1950) and for the opera "Pavel Korchagin" (1961); *Awards:* Order of Lenin (1935); mil title of brigade comr; *Died:* 22 Dec 1936 in Moscow; museums in Sochi (1937), Moscow (1940) and Shepetovka (1946) were opened in his hon.

OSTRYAKOV, Pyotr Alekseyevich (1887–1952) Radio eng; prof from 1949; CP member from 1945; *Born:* 16 Dec 1887; *Educ:* 1909 grad Petersburg Mil Eng College; 1914 grad Officers' Electr Eng School; *Career:* 1918–27 at Nizhniy Novgorod Radio Laboratory; 1929–41 lecturer, Moscow Electr Eng Communications Inst; from 1944 at Communications Research Inst; 1917 together with Bonch-Bruyevich at Tver' Radio Station, organized production of first batches of radio receiving tubes; then studied methods of cooling heavy-duty tubes; 1930 designed ribbed-anode, air-cooled generator tubes; 1921 directed construction of Comintern Radio Station in Moscow; 1923–41 helped design and build several powerful radio stations; wrote works on radio eng and history of its development in USSR; *Publ: Vodookhlazhdayushchiye ustroystva moshchnykh radiostantsiy* (Water-Cooling Equipment for Powerful Radio Stations) (1937); coauthor, *Teplootvodyashchiye ustroystva moshchnykh radiostantsiy* (Heat-Extracting Equipment for Powerful Radio Stations) (1954); *Died:* 24 Feb 1952.

OSTUZHEV (real name: POZHAROV), Aleksandr Alekseyevich (1874–1953) Actor, Pop Artiste of USSR from 1937; *Born:* 28 Apr 1874 in Voronezh, son of a railroad mech; *Educ:* from 1896 studied at Drama School, Moscow Theatrical College; *Career:* 1895 stage debut with A. M. Medvedev's company in Voronezh; from 1898 actor, Maly Theater (1901–02 season acted at Korsh Theater); studied under leading singers, including Chaliapin; continued to act despite progressive deafness (1910 finally lost his hearing) and devised various techniques which enabled him to pick up his cues and continue on the stage; *Roles:* Alyosha in *Deti Vanyushina* (Vanyushin's Children); Romeo in "Romeo and Juliet" (1901); Chatskiy (1902); Theodoro in Lope de Vega's "Dog in a Manger" (1917); Bassanio in "Merchant of Venice" (1923); Mark Antony in Shakespeare's "Julius Caesar" (1924); Quasimodo in "The Hunchback of Notre Dame", after Victor Hugo (1926); Othello (1935); Baron in *Skupoy rytsar'* (The Miserly Knight) (1937); Uriel' in Gutskov's "Uriel' Akosta" (1940), etc; *Awards:* Stalin Prize (1943); *Died:* 1 Mar 1953.

OVANESYAN, Ovanes (1864–1929) Arm poet; *Born:* 26 Apr 1864 in vil Vagarshapat, Arm; *Educ:* 1888 grad Moscow Univ; *Career:* for some 25 years worked as teacher; 1880's first work printed; 1918 worked for Pop Comrt of Educ, Baku; from 1922 active with Arm cultural organs; many of his lyrics have been set to music and have become pop songs; *Publ:* "Prince Syuni"; "The Birth of Vaagn"; "Tsar Artavazd"; "Grain"; "The Village Shrine"; "The Concerto"; "Autumn"; "There Come Moments"; translated into Arm works of Pushkin, Lermontov, Goethe, Mickiewicz, Tychina, etc; *Died:* 29 Sept 1929.

OVEZOV, Dangatar (1911–1966) Composer and conductor; Hon Art Worker of Turkm SSR from 1955; Pop Artiste of Turkm SSR from 1961; *Born:* 1 Jan 1911 in vil Myul'sk-Yusup, now Turkm SSR; *Educ:* from 1940 studied at Leningrad Conservatory; *Career:* 1925–30 active in amateur music circles; 1930–35 teaching and admin work in Tashkent, Ashkhabad and Krasnovodsk; from 1942 conductor, Makhtumkuli Opera and Ballet Theater, Ashkhabad; 1942-48 secr, bd, USSR Composers' Union; 1940–48 chm, 1948–56 dep chm, from 1956 bd member, Turkm Composers' Union; *Works:* coauthor, operas: "Shasenem and Garib" (1944); "Leyli and Medzhnun" (1946); "Ayna" (1957); music for Amanov's play "Soltan Sandzhar" (1945); cantatas "Homeland" (1947) and "The Sounds of the Dutar" (1950); choral works: "Why? ", "The Peach", etc; variety songs: "The Kolkhoz Flower", "The Song of the Merry Fisherman" and "The Girl with the Mole"; oratorio "Lenin" (1964); cantata "The Communist" (1966), etc; *Awards:* Order of the Red Banner of Labor (1955); Badge of Hon (1950); medals; *Died:* 5 May 1966.

OVSYANNIKOV, N. N. (1884–1941) Govt official; CP member from 1903; **Born**: 1884; *Career:* Party work in Serpukhov, Moscow and abroad; participated in Dec 1905 armed uprising in Moscow; repeatedly arrested by Tsarist authorities; after 1917 Feb Revol member, Moscow Okrug RSDRP(B) Comt; ed, newspaper "Sotsial-Demokrat"; deleg at 7th (April) All-Russian RSDRP(B) Conference; after 1917 Oct Revol ed work in Moscow; from 1922 exec work with RSFSR and USSR Supr Courts; then state arbiter, State Arbitration, USSR Council of Pop Comr; from 1938 pensioner; *Died:* 1941.

OYSLENDER, Aleksandr Yefimovich (1908–1963) Poet and translator; *Born:* 1 Dec 1908 in vil Khodorkovo, near Kiev; *Career:* 1926 first work printed; 1926–30 served with Black Sea Fleet; during WW 2 served with Northern Fleet; *Publ:* lyrical verse collections: *Mir svezheyet* (The Freshening World) (1931); *Myortvyy uzel* (Dead Angle) (1933); *Avgust* (August) (1938); *Dalyokiy kray* (A Distant Land) (1942); *Polyarnaya vakhta* (Polar Watch) (1946); *Kostyor na beregu* (The Bonfire on the Shore) (1948); *Vsegda na vakhte* (Always on Watch) (1954); *Dobryy klimat* (A Good Climate) (1956); *More i bereg* (The Sea and the Shore) (1960); *Korabel'naya storona* (Shipside) (1962); *A sneg idyot* (But the Snow Falls) (1965); *Ogni na reyde* (Lights in the Shipping Road) (1965); *Sliyaniye* (The Merging) (1966); *Died:* 6 Dec 1963 in Moscow.

OYSLENDER, Naum Yevseyevich (1893–1962) Jewish writer, lit historian, critic and poet; *Born:* 14 Dec 1893 in vil Khodorkovo, Ukr; *Educ:* 1919 grad Med Fac, Kiev Univ; *Career:* served as surgeon in Red Army; 1917 first work published; after end of the Civil War, settled in Moscow and became co-ed, journal "Strom"; defended nationalist aspirations; 1926–28 head, lit dept, Jewish Section, Inst of Bel Culture, Minsk; 1928–31 head, Lit Section, Inst of Jewish Culture, Ukr Acad of Sci, Kiev; in his latter years head, Criticism Dept, journal "Sovetskaya Rodina"; *Publ:* collected verse: "Lider" (1917); "Batog" (1921); "Front" (1922); *Osnovnyye cherty yevreyskogo realizma* (The Basic Features of Jewish Realism) (1919), about the work of Sholom-Aleykhem, Perests, etc; *Puti i pereput'ya* (Paths and Crossroads) (1924), about the work of the postrevol Jewish writeres Shvartsman, Bergel'son, Markish, etc; *Yevreyskiy teatr* (The Jewish Theater) (1940), an analysis of the work of Jewish playwrights, stage dir and actors between 1887 and 1917; collected stories about the Civil War "Af ladomirer wegn", etc; *Died:* 28 Sept 1962.

OYUNSKIY (real name: SLEPTSOV), Platon Alekseyevich (1893–1939 Yakut writer and politician; CP member from 1917; *Born:* 11 Nov 1893 in what is now Yakut ASSR; *Educ:* 1917 grad Yakutsk Teachers' Seminary; *Career:* 1916 member, illegal Marxist circle run by the exiled Bolsheviks Ye. M. Yaroslavskiy and G. I. Petrovskiy; 1917 Bureau member, Yakutsk Oblast Comt of Public Safety; founded Yakut Laborers' Union; member, Special Commission, Centr Exec Comt of Siberian Soviets; 1918 fought in Red Army against Admiral Kolchak; captured by Kolchak's troops and exiled to Tomsk Oblast; 1921 chm, Yakutsk Province Revol Comt; 1922–25 chm, Yakut Centr Exec Comt; 1927–31 Yakut Pop Comr of Educ; member, USSR Centr Exec Comt of two convocations; bd member, USSR Writers' Union; dep, USSR Supr Sov of 1937 convocation; arrested by State Security organs; *Publ:* verse "Power to the Soviets"; "The Bolshevik Party"; "The Precepts of the Eagle"; poems "The Red Shaman" and "Nyurgun Bootur, the Rash"; verse: "The Iron Horse"; "The Oath"; "To the Chinese People"; "Moscow"; novelette "Out of the Slime" (1936); stories "Kozhemyaka's Dream" and "Solomon the Wise"; plays: "The Bolshevik"; "The Imperial Decree"; studies: "The Yakut Fairy Tale (Olonkho), Its Subject and Content" (1927); "The Yakut Language and its Development" (1937); translated into Yakut the text of "The Internationale" and works by Pushkin and Gorky; *Died:* 21 Oct 1939 in imprisonment; posthumously rehabilitated.

OZAROVSKAYA, Ol'ga Erastovna (1874–1933) Russian folklorist and narrator; *Born:* 13 June 1874 in Nikolayev, daughter of an officer; *Educ:* 1897 grad Mathematics Fac, Higher Women's Courses, Petersburg; *Career:* worked under Mendeleyev at Bd of Weights and Measures; 1906 began artistic career; narrated comic stories and tales at Petersburg "Distorted Mirror" Theater; 1911 founded Studio of the Living Word in Moscow; toured the North, the Trans-Oneg region and Arkhangel'sk in search of folk tales and epics; 1915, during a trip on the River Pinega, met the folk narrator M. D. Krivopolenova and brought her to Moscow; their joint stage appearances proved enormously popular; after Oct Revol ran a Moscow seminar for the narration of Pushkin's works; *Publ: Moy repertuar* (My Repertoire) (1908); *Shkola chtetsa* (Narration Schooling) (1914); *Babushkiny stariny* (Grandmother's Times) (1916); *Moyey studii. Etyudy po khudozhestvennomu chteniyu* (To My Study. Studies in Fiction Narration) (1923); *D. I. Medeleyev. Vospominaniya* (D. I. Mendeleyev. Memoirs) (1929); collected stories *Pyatirechiye* (The Five-Rivers Region) (1931); *Died:* 12 July 1933 in Frunze.

OZERETSKIY, Nikolay Ivanovich (1893–1955) Psychiatrist; prof from 1929; member, USSR Acad of Med Sci from 1948; *Born:* 1893 in Orekhovo-Zuyevo, Moscow Province; *Educ:* 1911–12 studied at Petersburg Mil Med Acad, from which he was expelled for involvement in student strikes; 1917 grad Med Fac, Moscow Univ; *Career:* intern, then asst prof, Inst of Child and Adolescent Welfare; from 1929 prof and head, Chair of Child Psychopathology, Herzen Teachers' Training Inst, Leningrad; from 1933 head, Chair of Child Psychiatry, then 2nd Chair of Psychiatry, 1st Leningrad Med Inst; 1942 worked in Kislovodsk and then founded and directed a med inst in Krasnoyarsk during evacuation from Leningrad; from 1943 until death head, Chair of Psychiatry, 1st Leningrad Med Inst; devised widely-used method of studying the psychomotor system; developed metric scale for the Study of the motor system in children and adolescents which has been translated into most European languages; made valuable contributions to forensic psychiatry with his studies on the effect of epilepsy, schizophrenia, encephalitis, neuroses and psychopathy on the behavior of children and adolescents; also did research on the treatment and rehabilitation of neurotics and psychopaths and studied mental disturbances resulting from alimentary dystrophy and hypertonia; wrote some 70 works; *Publ: K voprosu o shizofrenii u detey* (Schizophrenia in Children) (1924); coauthor, *Psikhomotorika* (The Psychomotor System) (1930); *Psikhopatologia detskogo vozrasta* (Child Psychopathology) (1934); coauthor, *Nevropatologiya detskogo vozrasta* (Child Neuropathology) (1935); coauthor, *Uchebnik psikhiatrii* (A Psychiatry Textbook) (1958); *Died:* 1955 in Leningrad.

OZERNYY, Mark Ostapovich (1890–1957) Kolkhoz worker; CP member from 1940; Hero of Socialist Labor from 1947; *Born:* 3 June 1890 in Yekaterinoslav Province, son of a peasant; *Career:* from age 11 hired farm-hand; from 1933 worked on kolkhoz; from 1936 field-team leader, "Red Partisan" Kolkhoz, Mishchurinoroz; 1936 his field-team harvested 103.6 centners of corn per hectare, 1937 – 108.3, 1939 and 1940 – 120, 1949 – 223.8 centners per hectare for a two-hectare plot and 175 centners a hectare for an 8-hectare plot, thus setting a world corn yield record; developed an new strain of corn which he named "Partizanka"; deleg at 16th–18th Congresses of CP Ukr; dep, Ukr Supr Sov of 2nd–4th convocations; *Publ: Za vysokiy urozhay kukuruzy* (High Corn Yields) (1947); *Moy opyt vyrashchivaniya vysokikh urozhayev kukuruzy* (My Experience in Raising Bumper Corn Crops) (1952); *Kukuruzu – vo vse rayony* (Corn Everywhere) (1955); *Awards:* Stalin Prize (1946); two Orders of Lenin; *Died:* 27 Dec 1957.

OZEROV, Nikolay Nikolayevich (1887–1953) Opera singer (lyric dramatic tenor); Pop Artiste of RSFSR from 1937; *Born:* 3 Apr 1887 in vil Spas-Uteshen'ye Ryazan' Province; *Educ:* 1910 grad Law Fac, Moscow Univ; 1913 grad Opera courses, Russian Music Soc; *Career:* from 1912 with touring opera company; 1918 at Moscow Sov Theater; 1919–24 at Music Studio, Moscow Acad Arts Theater; 1920–46 soloist, Bolshoy Theater; 1947 instructor, from 1948 prof, Moscow Conservatory; *Roles:* Sobinin and Finn in "Ivan Susanin" and "Ruslan and Ludmilla"; Don Juan in Dargomyzhskiy's *Kamennyy gost'* (The Stone Guest); the Pretender, Golitsyn and Gritsko in Moussorgsky's "Boris Godunov," "Khovanshchina" and *Sorochinskaya yarmarka* (Sorochintsy Fair); Andrey in "Mazepa"; Raoul in "The Huguenots"; Samson in Saint Saens' "Samson and Delilah"; German in Tchaikovsky's *Pikovaya dama* (The Queen of Spades); Rhadames in Verdi's "Aida"; Grishka Kuter'ma in Rimsky-Korsakov's *Skazaniye o nevidimom grade Kitezhe i deve Fevronii* (The Legend of the Invisible City of Kitezh and the Maiden Fevronia), etc; *Died:* 4 Dec 1953 in Moscow.

OZERTSKOVSKIY, Aleksey Ivanovich (1851–1928) Psychiatrist; Dr of Med from 1890; Hero of Labor from 1928; Pioneer of Sov mil psychiatry; *Born:* 5 Mar 1851 in Moscow; *Educ:* 1878 grad Med Fac, Moscow Univ; *Career:* after grad enrolled as reserve army surgeon and assigned to Moscow Clinical Mil Hospital; then for two years mil surgeon, 6th Grenadier Tavrida Regt; 1881 sent for two years' postgrad med training to clinics of Med Fac, Moscow Univ and assigned as junior intern, Moscow Mil Hospital, where he worked for 25 years; from 1882 intern, then head, Psychiatric Dept, Moscow Mil Hospital; 1890 co-founder, Soc of Psychiatrists and Neuropathologists, Moscow Univ; 1890 defended doctor's thesis on hysteria among troops; wrote standard work on this subject; 1894–95 worked at Prof Kraepelin's Psychiatric Clinic, Heidelberg; late 1908 appointed chief physician, Tiflis Mil Hospital; 1918 returned to Moscow and worked for first neuropsychiatric organizations, introducing outpatient service; also worked at Mar'inskaya Hospital; then asst chief physician, Dostoyevsky Hospital; specialized in brain paralysis, multiple neuritis, tetany, epilepsy and hysteria; *Publ: Sluchay vrozhdyonnogo myshechnogo spazma* (A Case of Congenital Muscular Spasm) (1883); *K ucheniyu o mnozhestvennom neyrite* (The Theory of Multiple Neuritis) (1883); *O tetanii* (Tetany) (1885); *O rasstroystve obshchey i spetsial'noy chuvstvitel'nosti u epileptikov* (Disorder of General and Specialized Sensitivity in Epileptics) (1886); thesis *Isteriya v voyskakh* (Hysteria in Troops) (1891); coauthor, *O vliyanii razlichnykh yadov na myshechnuyu rabotu* (The Effect of Various Poisons on Muscular Work) (1899); *O dushevnykh zabolevaniyakh v svyazi s russko-yaponskoy voynoy* (Mental Ailments Connected with the Russo-Japanese War) (1905); *Mysli o prirode tak nazyvayemykh fizicheskikh priznakov isterii* (Ideas on the Nature of So-Called Physical Symptoms of Hysteria) (1928), etc; *Died:* 1928 in Moscow.

OZHYOGOV, Sergey Ivanovich (1900–1964) Linguist and lexicographer; *Born:* 23 Sept 1900 in vil Kamennoye, Tver' Province; *Educ:* 1926 grad Leningrad Univ; *Career:* 1927–37 taught at various higher educ establishments in Leningrad, and from 1937 in Moscow; from 1952 head, Speech Standards Section, Inst of Linguistics, then from 1958 Inst of Russian Language, USSR Acad of Sci; helped compile Ushakov's *Tolkovyy slovar' russkogo yazyka* (Explanatory Dictionary of the Russian Language) (4 vol, 1935–40); 1949 compiled standard-setting one-vol *Slovar' russkogo yazyka* (A Dictionary of the Russian Language), containing over 50,000 entries; specialized in 18th–19th Century Russian lit language, historical and modern lexicology, language of individual writers, orthography and orthoepy, linguistic standards, etc; edited *Orfograficheskiy slovar' russkogo yazyka* (Orthographic Dictionary of the Russian Language) (1956; 5th corrected and expanded ed, 1963); edited dictionary-manual *Russkoye literaturnoye proiznosheniye i udareniye* (Russian Literary Pronunciation and Stress) (1955); ed, dictionary-manual *Pravil'nost' russkoy rechi* (Correct Russian Speech) (1962); founder and chief ed, collections *Voprosy kul'tury rechi* (Problems of Linguistic Standards) (6 issues, 1955–65); *Publ: Slovar' russkogo yazyka* (A Russian Dictionary) (6th ed, 1964); *O strukture frazeologii* (The Structure of Phraseology) (1957); *O krylatykh slovakh* (Catchwords) (1957); *O tryokh tipakh tolkovykh slovarey sovremennogo russkogo yazyka* (Three Types of Modern Russian Explanatory Dictionaries) (1952); *Ocherednyye voprosy kul'tury rechi* (Routine Problems of Linguistic Standards) (1955); coauthor, *Russkiy yazyk i sovetskoye obshchestvo* (Russian Language and Soviet Society) (1962); *Died:* 15 Dec 1964 in Moscow.

OZOLIN', Eduard Karlovich (1891–1967) Party official; from 1914 member, Lat Soc-Democratic Party; *Born:* 1891; *Educ:* studied at Communist Univ of Western Peoples; *Career:* textile-worker; 1914 arrested for revol activities and exiled to Narym Kray; 1916 drafted into Russian Army; after 1917 Feb Revol chm, company comt, Lat Reserve Infantry Regt; member, Exec Comt, Val'mier Uyezd Sov; then member, Val'mier Mil Revol Comt; 1919 chm, Exec Comt, Val'mier Uyezd Sov and chm, Val'mier Comt, CP Lat; 1919–22 in Red Army; 1923–28 underground Party work in Lat; 1923 at 7th CP Lat Congress elected CC member; in following years Party and adim work; from Jan 1941 worked for CC, CP Lat; during WW 2 fought with the partisans; from 1944 exec Party and admin work in Lat; from 1956 pensioner; *Died:* 28 Nov 1967.

P

PAGAVA, Akakiy Nestorovich (1887–1962) Stage dir, drama teacher and theater historian; Pop Artiste of Geo SSR from 1962; *Born:* 27 Feb 1887; *Career:* 1908–14 asst stage dir, Moscow Arts Theater; from 1915 stage dir at theaters in Kutaisi, Batumi and Tbilisi; 1920 helped found Geo drama company in Tbilisi (from 1921 Rustaveli Theater); from 1922 founder-dir, first Sov Geo Drama Studio; from 1925 founder-dir, Geo Opera Studio; 1928–34 head, Theatrical Dept, Geo Main Art Bd; 1939–62 prof, Rustaveli Theatrical Inst; 1939–55 head, Chair of Theater History and dep dir, Rustaveli Theatrical Inst; *Publ:* "Lado Meskhishvili" (1938); "Vaso Abashidze" (1954); *Died:* 27 June 1962.

PAKHOMOV, Nikolay Ivanovich (1890– ?) Govt official; CP member from 1912; *Born:* 1890 in Taganrog, son of a worker; *Career:* foundry worker at Taganrog Steel Plant and metallurgical plants in Lugana, Mariupol', etc; from 1910 active in revol movement; took part in 1917 Oct Revol and Civil War; chm, Simferopol' City Exec Comt, then dep chm, Chernigov Province Exec Comt and Bryansk Province Exec Comt; dep secr, USSR Centr Exec Comt; 1928–34 chm, Gorky Kray Exec Comt; Mar 1934–Aug 1938 USSR Pop Comr of Water Transport; at 16th and 17th Party Congresses elected cand member, CC, CPSU(B); member, USSR Centr Exec Comt; arrested by State Security organs; *Died:* date and place of death unknown.

PAL'CHEVSKIY, Yevgeniy Ignat'yevich (1899–1966) Pathoanatomist; Dr of Med and prof from 1944; CP member from 1950; *Born:* 1899; *Educ:* 1925 grad Kiev Med Inst; *Career:* 1925–29 dissector, Bezhitsa Factory Hospital, Bryansk Oblast; 1929–32 asst prof and learned secr, Ukr Pathoanatomical Inst, Khar'kov, senior assoc, Ukr Inst of Experimental Med and head, Pathoanatomical Section, Khar'kov Inst of Roentgenology and Oncology; 1932–52 head, Chair of Pathological Anatomy, Stalino (Donetsk) Med Inst; 1942–45 mil pathoanatomist in Sov Army; 1952–57 head, Chair of Pathological Anatomy and dep dir for sci and training, L'vov Med Inst; 1957–61 head, Chair of Pathological Anatomy and rector, Lugansk Med Inst; 1961–66 again head, Chair of Pathological Anatomy,L'vov Univ; bd member, All-Union and chm, L'vov Soc of Pathoanatomists; member, Higher Certification Commission; wrote over 40 works; *Publ:* doctor's thesis *Morfologiya molochnoy zhelezy pri izmeneniyakh v yaichnikakh i narusheniyakh generativnoy funktsii u zhenshchin* (The Morphology of the Mammary Gland in Lesions of the Ovaries and Disturbances of the Generative Function in Women) (1944), etc; *Awards:* Order of the Red Banner of Labor; medals; *Died:* 27 Sept 1966.

PAL'CHINSKIY, P.I. (? –1930) Eng; *Career:* founder, "Coal Production" Syndicate; maintained close ties with banking circles; after 1917 Feb Revol member, Mil Commission, Provisional Comt, State Duma; then Dep Min of Trade and Ind, Provisional Govt; Aug 1917 governor-gen of Petrograd; 25 Oct 1917 commanded defense of Winter Palace; charged with sabotaging Sov ind; *Died:* 1930 executed.

PALIASHVILI, Ivan Petrovich (1868–1934) Conductor and music teacher; Pop Artiste of Geo SSR from 1924; brother of the composer Z.P. Paliashvili; *Born:* 1 Oct 1868 in Kutaisi; *Educ:* 1888–89 studied composition under Rimsky-Korsakov and conducting under V.I. Suk; *Career:* 1887 choirmaster and concertmaster; from 1889 conductor, opera companies in Perm', Riga, Kiev, Khar'kov, Tiflis, Petersburg, Odessa, etc; 1922 chief conductor, Tiflis Opera Theater; 1922–25 prof, opera class, Tiflis Conservatory; *Works:* conducted: "Daisi" (1923); "Abesalom and Eteri" (1930); *Zolotoy petushok* (The golden Cockerel) and "Ruslan and Ludmilla" (1924); Arakishvili's "Life Is Joy" (1924); Dolidze's "Tsisana" (1924); Z. Paliashvili's "Latavra"; *Died:* 7 Mar 1934 in Tbilisi.

PALIASHVILI, Polikarp Petrovich (1875–1941) Choral conductor; Hon Art Worker of Geo SSR from 1941; brother of the composer Z.P. Paliashvili; *Born:* 20 Juli 1875; *Educ:* 1903 grad M.M. Ippolitov–Ivanov's class, Moscow Conservatory; *Career:* from 1903 worked at Tiflis theaters; 1908 founded Workers' Theater, Pop Center; after establishment of Sov regime in Geo worked as conductor and choirmaster at Tbilisi theaters; from 1933 at Paliashvili Opera and Ballet Theater and Opera Studio, Tbilisi Conservatory; also taught music; *Works:* composed several children's operas and other musical works; conducted operas: "Faust"; "Carmen"; "Demon"; "Rusalka"; "Daisi", etc; *Died:* 12 May 1941.

PALIASHVILI, Zakhariy Petrovich (1871–1933) Composer; conductor; prof from 1919; Pop Artiste of Geo SSR from 1925; *Born:* 4 Aug 1871 in Kutaisi; *Educ:* 1899 grad Tiflis Musical College; 1900–03 studied under S.I. Taneyev at Moscow Conservatory; *Career:* from 1903 conductor, composer, music teacher and folklorist; 1908–17 lecturer and dir, Geo Philharmonic Soc; from 1919 prof, 1919–23 and 1929–32 dir, Tbilisi Conservatory; from 1922 chief conductor, Tbilisi Opera Theater; *Works:* "A Collection of Georgian Folk Songs" (1910); operas: "Abesalom and Eteri" (1919); "Dusk" (1923); "Latavra" (1928); many symphonic and vocal works, including "Solemn Cantata on the 10th Anniversary of the October Revolution" (1927); *Died:* 6 Oct 1933 in Tbilisi; the Tbilisi Opera and Ballet Theater is named after him.

PALIYENKO, Nikolay Ivanovich (1869–1937) Lawyer; Dr of Public Law from 1908; prof from 1903; member, Ukr Acad of Sci from 1930; *Born:* 21 Nov 1869 in Kiev, son of a teacher; *Educ:* 1892 grad Law Fac, Kiev Univ; *Career:* after grad trained for professorship et Kiev Univ and spent two years studying public law abroad; assoc prof and from 1903 prof, Demidov (Yaroslavl') Law Lyceum; from 1906 prof, Chair of Public Law, Khar'kov Univ; prorector, Khar'kov Univ and dean, Law Fac, Khar'kov Higher Women's Courses; after 1917 Oct Revol prof, various Khar'kov higher educ establishments; from 1930 head, Chair of Public Law, Soc and Econ Dept, Ukr Acad of Sci; *Works: Nauka o sushchnosti prava i pravovaya obyazannost' gosudarstva* (The Science of the Nature of Law and the Legal Obligations of the State) (1908); *Pravo grazhdanstva v sovremennykh federatsiyakh i SSSR* (Citizenship Law in Modern Federations and the USSR) (1926); *Problema suvereniteta sovremennogo gosudarstva* (The Problem of the Sovereignty of a Modern State) (1929), etc; *Died:* 11 Nov 1937.

PAMFILOV, Konstantin Dmitriyevich (1901–1943) Govt official; CP member from 1918; *Born:* 1901 in vil Mamonovo, Smolensk Province, son of an office worker; *Educ:* 1923 grad Workers' Fac; 1927 grad Sov Law Fac, Moscow Univ; *Career:* 1918–20 mil, admin and Party work; 1919 commanded special forces detachment; fought against White forces in Smolensk, Vitebsk and Pskov Provinces; 1921 helped crush Kronstadt Mutiny; 1923–27, while a student, did exec work for Moscow Sov; 1932–37 dep head, Housing Dept, Moscow Sov; from Oct 1937 head, Housing Bd, RSFSR Pop Comrt of Communal Econ; from 1938 RSFSR Pop Comr of Communal Econ; from Sept 1940 dep chm, RSFSR Council of Pop comr; from start of WW 2 helped direct transfer of ind enterprises beyond the Urals, evacuating and resettling population; May 1942–43 chm, RSFSR Council of Pop Comr; *Died:* 1943; his ashes are immured in the Kremlin wall on Moscow's Red Square; the Acad of Communal Econ is named after him.

PANFILOV, Aleksey Pavlovich (1898–1966) Mil commander; lt-gen, Armored Forces; CP member from 1918; *Born:* 1898 in Kazan', son of a railroad official; *Educ:* 1938 grad Mil Acad of Armored Forces; *Career:* until 1918 worked on the railroad; 1918 volunteered for Red Army; polit work in Civil War; then comr, cavalry regt, then brigade; 1938 commander, 2nd Mechanized Brigade, Maritime Forces Group in Far East; took part in Lake Khasan counter-offensive; 1938–41 served with unit staffs and Gen Staff; 1941–42 chief, Intelligence Bd, Gen Staff; Gen Staff plen for mustering Anderson's Polish Army in USSR; 1943–45 commander, 6th, then 3rd Guards Tank Corps; 1943 took part in liberation of Kiev; 1944 in Polish campaign; 1945 in East Pomeranian operation; after WW 2various commands and lecturing work at Armored Forces Acad and Gen Staff Acad; *Awards:* Hero of the Sov Union; two Orders of Lenin; five Orders of the Red Banner; Order of Suvorov, 1st and 2nd Class; medals; *Died:* May 1966.

PANFILOV, Fyodor Dmitriyevich (1856–1940) Party official; CP member from 1898; *Born:* June 1856 in vil Cherkasskoye, Yekaterinoslav Province, son of a peasant; *Career:* fitter, miner, stocker, asst mech, then soldier in Russian Army; 1883 first arrested for "disregarding religion"; 1894–1917 served 14 terms of imprisonment and three terms of exile; did Party work in Mariupol', Lugansk and Starobel'sk; took part in 1905–07 Revol; helped establish Sov regime in Starobel'sk; 1919–20 fought in Civil War; then with Workers and Peasants' Inspectorate; deleg at 8th RCP(B) Congress; *Awards:* Order of the Red Banner (1929); *Died:* 1940.

PANFILOV, Ivan Vasil'yevich (1893–1941) Mil commander; maj-gen from 1940; CP member from 1920; *Born:* 1 Jan 1893 in Petrovsk, Saratov Province, son of an official; *Educ:* 1923 grad Kamenev Joint Mil School, Kiev; *Career:* from 1915 Russian Army; nco in WW 1; 1917 member, regt comt, then company commander; Oct 1918 volunteered for Red Army; 1918–21 commanded platoon, then company; from 1924 various commands in Centr Asian Mil Distr; fought against Basmachi; 1932–37 commander, mountain infantry regt; 1937–38 admin work with distr staff; 1938–41 mil comr, Kir SSR; from July 1941 commander, 316th Infantry Div (17 Nov 1941 expanded into 8th Guards Infantry Div); fought in defense of Moscow and on Volokolamsk sector; *Awards:* Hero of the Sov Union (posthumously); Order of Lenin; two Orders of the Red Banner; *Died:* 18 Nov 1941 killed in action; the 8th Guards Infantry Div bears his name; monument erected to him in Frunze.

PANFYOROV, Fyodor Ivanovich (1896–1960) Russian writer and playwright; CP member from 1926; *Born:* 20 Sept 1896 in vil Pavlovka, Saratov Province; *Educ:* studied at Vol'sk Teachers' Seminary; 1923–25 studied at Saratov Univ; *Career:* after 1917 Oct Revolt edited an uyezd newspaper; 1918 first work published; 1934–36 chief ed, journal "Kolkhoznyy teatr"; 1931–60 (with a short interval) chief ed, journal "Oktyabr'"; helped run Russian Assoc of Proletarian Writers; dep, USSR Supr Sov of 1946, 1950 and 1954 convocations; *Publ:* story *Pered rasstrelom* (Before the Execution) (1918); plays: *Deti zemli* (Children of the Land) (1922); *Muzhiki* (The Peasants) and *Urod* (The Freak) (1924); *Bunt zemli* (Revolt of the Land) and *Stal'noy kon'* (The Steel Horse) (1926); trilogy *Bruski* (Beams) (1928–37); plays: *Razval* (The Collapse) (1928); *30-yy god* (The Year 1930) (1939); *Varya Kurbatov* (1959); trilogy *Volga – matushka reka* (Volga – Mother River) (1953–60), etc; *Awards:* Order of the Red Banner of Labor

(1956); two Stalin Prizes (1948 and 1949); *Died:* 10 Sept 1960 in Moscow.

PAN'KIVSKIY, Severin Fyodorovich (1872–1941) Actor and producer; *Born:* 24 Apr 1872 in Galicia, son of a priest; *Educ:* grad high school; *Career:* 1897–99 worked with M.L. Kropivnitskiy's ensemble; 1899–1900 with M.P. Staritskiy's ensemble; from 1900 with "Coryphaei of the Ukr Theater" ensemble; 1905–06 acted at "Russian Conversation" Soc Theater; from 1906 acted at N. K. Sadovskiy's Theater, where he began his career as a producer; 1917 co-founder first Ukr theatrical journal "Teatral'ni visti"; 1918–19 worked at Ukr Pol Theater; 1919–20 at Shevchenko State Drama Theater; in 1920 also did research work for Ukr Acad of Sci; also acted in films and sang; *Roles:* the Witness in Kropivnitskyi's *Po revizii* (The Inspection); Pen'onzhka and Styopochka Kramaryuk in Karpenko-Karyy's "Martyn Borulya" and *Zhiteyskoye more* (The Common Sea); Maksim in *Poka solntse vzoydyot* (Until the Sun Rises); Osip in Gogol's *Revizor* (The Government Inspector); Mikola in Franko's *Ukradennoye schast'ye* (Stolen Happiness); *Died:* 23 Apr 1941.

PANKOV, Nikolay Aleksandrovich (1895–1959) Gipsy writer and translator; *Born:* 19 May 1895 in Petersburg; *Educ:* completed parish primary school; extended his educ through self-study; *Career:* broke with his family at an early age and went to work for Main Telegraph Office; then worked for public notary, as med orderly and as day laborer; from 1931 lit work with Romany Section, Centr Publ House and Pedag Publ House; member, "Kuznitsa" (The Smithy) lit assoc; then member, Romany Section, Moscow Assoc of Proletarian Writers; 1933–38 taught Romany language at Moscow Teachers' Training College; one of first Romany writers; lit ed, first Romany journal "Tsyganskaya zarya" and "Novyy put'"; co-founder, Romany Theater, Moscow; translated into Romany language some works of Lenin, Pushkin and Merimee's novella "Carmen"; edited M.V. Sergiyevskiy and A.P. Barannikov's "Romany-Russian Dictionary" (1938); from 1930 member, British Gipsy Lore Soc; left various unpublished manuscripts: translations from Pushkin and Lermontov; collection of Northern Gipsies fairy-tales, songs and proverbs; "A Gipsy's Notes on Gipsy Choirs"; poem "Kasya"; story *Skripka* (The Violin); "Romany Orthographic Dictionary"; addendum to "Romany-Russian Dictionary," etc; *Died:* 6 Feb 1959 in Moscow.

PANKRATOV, I.I. (Party name: Vanya) (1886–1962) Party and admin official; CP member from 1906; *Born:* 1886; *Career:* laborer by trade; 1905 began revol work; worked at Moscow and Perov Railroad Car Workshops; Dec 1905 participated in armed uprising in Moscow; 1908 arrested and exiled to Vologda Province; 1909 escaped from exile; sent to Party school on the island of Capri; headed Leninist faction at school; late Nov 1909, at Lenin's invitation, attended a lecture course in Paris; after his return to Russia represented Bolshevik Center in Petersburg; early 1910 arrested and exiled for life to Siberia; after 1917 Oct Revol Party, govt and trade-union work in Siberia and the Far East; from 1926 admin work in Moscow; fought in WW 2; *Died:* 1962.

PANKRATOV, Vasiliy Semyonovich (1864–1925) Revolutionary; member, People's Will group; *Born:* 26 Jan 1864; *Career:* 1879 joined revol movement; 1881 joined "People's Will" org and conducted propaganda among workers in Petersburg and Moscow; founder many workers' circles; from 1882 operated in southern Russia; from early 1884 worked for Kiev branch of Young People's Will Party; 4 Mar 1884 arrested in Kiev, despite armed resistance; spent 14 years in Shlisselburg Fortress Prison; 1898 exiled to Yakutia; 1905 fled from exile, joined Socialist-Revolutionary Party; 1905 took part in Dec Revol in Moscow; May 1907 arrested and returned to Yakutia; 1912 returned to Petersburg; until 1917 under secret police surveillance; Juli 1917 attacked Lenin in article in Newspaper "Zhivoye slovo"; Provisional Govt appointed him comr to guard ex-tsar; *Publ:* articles: "Activities Among the Workers in 1880–1884" (1906); "The 1884 Trial of the Twelve Defendants in Kiev" (1907); *Zhizn' v Shlissel'burgskoy kreposti 1884–1898* (Life in Shlisselburg Fortress 1884–1898) (1922); *Vospominaniya* (Memoirs) (1923); *S tsaryom v Tobol'ske* (With the Tsar in Tobolsk) (1925); *Died:* 5 Mar 1925.

PANKRATOVA, Anna Mikhaylovna (1897–1957) Historian; Dr of History from 1935; prof from 1928; member, USSR Acad of Sci from 1953; member, Bel Acad of Sci from 1940; member, RSFSR Acad of Pedag Sci from 1944; Hon Sci Worker of RSFSR and Kaz SSR from 1943; CP member from 1919; *Born:* 9 Feb 1897 in Odessa, daughter of a worker; *Educ:* 1917 grad History Fac, Novorossiysk Univ, Odessa; 1925 grad Inst of Red Prof; *Career:* 1919–20 underground Party work in Odessa; 1920–21 exec Party work in Odessa, Khar'kov and for CC, CP(B) Ukr; 1921–22 exec trade-Union work in the Urals; 1925–26 abroad on research assignment; 1926–27 educ work in Leningrad and assoc, Research Inst for the Study of the Workers' Movement, Leningrad Univ; from 1927 exec research and teaching work at Higher School of Trade-Union Movement, Moscov Univ, Sverdlov Communist Univ and Inst of History, Communist Acad; from 1929 corresp member, Communist Acad; 1939–53 corresp member, USSR Acad of Sci; 1938-57 section head and dep dir, Inst of History, USSR Acad of Sci; 1939–41 also head, Chair of History of the USSR, Moscow and Saratov Univ; 1942–48 head, Chair of History of the USSR, Moscow's Lenin Teachers' Training Inst; 1947–57 head, Chair of History of the USSR, Acad of Soc Sci, CC, CPSU; from 1953 chief ed, journal "Voprosy istorii"; from 1955 chm, Nat Comt of Historians of the USSR; Bureau member, Int Comt of Historical Sci; from 1952 member, CC, CPSU; member, Hungarian Acad of Sci; corresp member, East German and Rumanian Acad of Sci; spezialized in history of Russian workers' movement, 1905–07 Revol and history of Sov soc; chief ed and coauthor, first authoritative textbooks on history of Sov soc; chief ed and coauthor, first authoritative textbooks on history of the USSR for 8th–10th grades; always adhered to Party gen line; at one time sided with Pokrovskiy's historical school but from 1930's actively campaigned against Pokrovskiy's historical teaching; at 20th CPSU Congress unmasked dogmatism and opportunism in Sov historiography of the Stalin era, denounced the Stalin personality cult and the whitewashing of Pokrovskiy; 1957 her journal "Voprosy istorii" was sharply criticized by the Party for liberal trends in the assessment of Sov historiography in the 1930's and 1940's and for revising some essential tenets of Sov and CPSU history; represented Sov historiography at Int Congresseso of Historians in Warsaw (1933–34) and Rome (1955); *Publ: Fabzavkomy Rossii v bor'be za sotsialisticheskuyu fabriku* (Russia's Factory and Plant Committees in the Struggle for the Socialist Factory) (1923); *Fabzavkomy i profsoyuzy v revolyutsii 1917 goda* (The Factory and Plant Committees and Trade Unions in the 1917 Revolution) (1927); *Pervaya russkaya revolyutsiya 1905–1907 godov* (The 1905-07 First Russian Revolution) (1927); *Petersburgskiy "Soyuz bor'by za osvobozhdeniye rabochego klassa"* (The Petersburg "League for the Liberation of the Working Class") (2nd ed, 1940); coauthor, *Istoriya diplomatii* (The History of Diplomacy) (e vol, 1945); ed in chief, *Rabocheye dvizheniye v Rossii v 19-om veku. Sbornik dokumentov i materialov* (The 19th-Century Workers' Movement in Russia. A Collection of Documents and Material) (4 vol, 1950–52); ed in chief, *Revolyutsiya 1905–1907 godov v Rossii. Dokumenty i materialy* (The 1905–07 Revolution in Russia. Documents and Material) (5 vol, 1955); *Formirovaniye proletariata v Rossii v 17–18 vekakh* (The Formation of the Proletariat in Russia in the 17th and 18th Centuries) (1963); *Awards:* Order of Lenin; Stalin Prize (1946); *Died:* 25 May 1957.

PANTELEYEV, Ivan Vasil'yevich (1884–1967) Revolutionary; CP member from 1905; *Born:* 1884; *Career:* 1905 began revol work at Shuya print works; 1905–07 factory Party organizer; rayon Party organizer and member, Shuya RSDRP(B) Comt; 1907 during gen strike elected member and rep, Shuya Sov of Workers' Dep; placed under police surveillance; worked at a printing house and with legal polit educ orgs; 1914–17 in Russian Army; illegal Party work among soldiers; during 1917 Feb Revol member, soldiers' comt; helped establish Sov rule in Shuya; until 1922 in Red Army; 1922–34 with various org in Moscow; from 1934 pensioner; *Died:* Apr 1967.

PANYUNIN, Aleksandr Trifonovich (1882–1965) Revolutionary; govt official; CP member from 1903; *Born:* 1882; *Career:* 1905 took part in Dec revolt in Moscow; chief of staff of an armed workers squad; boilermaker by trade; revol work at plants in Moscow, Petersburg, Revol and Kronstadt; arrested and imprisoned for revol activities; at time of 1917 Oct Revol served as boilerman on cruisers of Baltic Fleet; 1917–18 govt work; 1919–21 boilerman, Moscow-Kursk Railroad and at Locomotive Building Plant; 1921–29 trade-union and cooperative work; from 1929 pensioner; *Died:* 8 June 1965.

PANYUSHKIN, V.L. (1888–1960) Party and govt official; CP member from 1907; *Born:* 1888; *Career:* Party work in Petersburg and with Baltic Fleet; after 1917 Feb Revol member, Kronstadt and Petrograd Sov; fought in Civil war; Apr 1918 appointed Tula Province special mil comr to combat counterrevol; commanded armed workers and sailors squads; fought on Eastern Front, then appointed special mil comr for Volga and Ural region to combat counterrevol; after Civil War did Party work in Tula then in Simbirsk; 1919–20 exec org and instructor, CC, RCP(B); 1921 tried to form "Workers and Peasants' Socialist Party," leading to his expulsion from RCP(B); 1922 reinstated in Communist Party; worked in Donbass, for Supr Sovnarkhoz then for Sov trade mission in Germany; from 1956 pensioner; *Died:* 1960.

PAPALEKSI, Nikolay Dmitriyevich (1880–1947) Physicist; prof; member, USSR Acad of Sci from 1939; *Born:* 2 Dec 1880 in Simferopol'; *Educ:* 1904 grad Strasbourg Univ; *Career:* 1904–14 worked in Strasbourg under the German physicist F. Braun; 1914 returned to Russia and worked as consultant, Russian Wireless Telegraphy and Telephony Company; 1918 helped found Odessa Polytech Inst; 1918–22 assoc prof, from 1922 prof, Odessa Polytech Inst; 1922–35, together with L. I. Mandel'shtam, directed Sci Dept, Centr Radio Laboratories, Leningrad; also did research at State Physical Eng Laboratory (later the Electrophysical Inst) and was a prof at the Leningrad Polytech Inst; from 1935 worked at Physics Inst, from 1938 also at Power Eng Inst, USSR Acad of Sci; from 1944 chm, All-Union Sci Council for Radiophysics and Radio Eng, USSR Acad of Sci; 1914–16 did research on guided radio-telegraphy, radio communications with submarines and remote control; supervised production of first Russian radio tubes; did research on non-linear and parametric oscillation; together with L.I. Mandel'shtam, carried out numerous theoretical and experimental studies of oscillation in non-linear systems; discovered and studied nth-degree resonance, combination resonance, parametric resonance, etc; together with Mandel'shtam, devised the parametric generator for stimulating electr oscillation and studied parametric resonance in complex electrochem circuits; 1930 he and Mandel'shtam invented the interference calibration method and used it to make a detailed study of radio wave propagation over the Earth's surface and to make precise measurements of its speed; these studied led to the development of radio-interference geodesy and navigation; *Publ: Sobraniye trudov* (Collected Works) (1948), etc; *Awards:* Mendeleyev Prize (1936); Stalin Prize (1942); *Died:* 3 Feb 1947.

PAPAZYAN, Vartanes Mesropovich (1866–1920) Arm writer and playwright; *Born:* 13 Apr 1866 in Van, Turkey, son of a priest; *Educ:* 1880 grad Echmiadzin Theological College; 1894 grad Geneva Univ; *Career:* 1883 first work printed; 1889–91 worked for journal "Murch" and newspaper "Mshak"; took part in Arm nat liberation movement in Turkey; *Publ:* novel "Khat Saba" (1890); "Studies in the Life of Turkish Armenians"; "Letters from Turkish Armenia" (1891); stories "Homo homini lupus" (1894); "The Madman" (1897); "The Unsatisfied" (1897); "The Knight" (1898); "A History of Armenian Literature" (1900); story "Vyshan" (1903); novels: "Sovereign of the World" (1904); "The Bearer of Fire" (1904); drama "The Cliff" (1905); "An Outline Armenian History" (1906); stories: "At the Seaside" (1910); "Swan Lake" (1911); historical plays: "For One's Country"; "The Apostate's Mother" (1911), etc; *Died:* 26 Apr 1920 in Yerevan.

PAPIVIN, Nikoley Filippovich (1903–1963) Air Force commander; col-gen, Sov Air Force; CP member from 1919; *Born:* 1903 in Klin, Moscow Province, son of a railroad worker; *Educ:* studied at Air Force College; *Career:* from 1920 in Red Army; during WW 2 commanded large air force unit; 1961 retired on med grounds; member, CC, CP Geo; dep, Geof Supr Sov; *Awards:* Hero of the Sov Union; two Orders of Lenin, three Orders of the Red Banner; Order of Suvorov, 1st Class; Order of Kutuzov, 1st Class; medals; *Died:* 19 Apr 1963 in a car crash.

PAPKOVICH, Pyotr Fyodorovich (1887–1946) Shipbuilding eng; rear-admiral; corresp member, USSR Acad of Sci from 1933; Hon Sci and Tech Worker of RSFSR from 1944; *Born:* 5 Apr 1887; *Educ:* 1911 grad Petersburg Polytech Inst; *Career:* from 1911 helped design and build warships and merchant and passenger vessels; from 1916 lectured on construction mech at Leningrad Polytech Inst; 1925–30 prof, Leningrad Polytech Inst; 1934–40 prof, Leningrad Shipbuilding Inst; from 1934 prof, Naval Acad; developed and perfected methods of calculating the static and dynamic loading of modern ship structures; did important research on elasticity theory; 1932 solved the problem of elasticity theory with displacement in the form of harmonic functions; studied gen theorems of the stability of an elastic system; devised and proved experimental methods of studying ship strength; wrote course on *Stroitel'naya mekhanika korablya* (Construction Ship Machanics); *Publ: Teoriya uprugosti* (Elasticity Theory) (1939); *Stroitel'naya mekhanika korablya* (Construction Ship Mechanics) (2 vol, 1945–47); *Awards:* Stalin Prize (1946); *Died:* 3 Apr 1946.

PARFENOV, Pyotr Semyonovich (1894–1937) Russian poet; CP member from 1917; *Born:* 29 June 1894 in vil Nikol'skoye, Ufa Province; *Career:* fought in WW 1, Oct Revol and Civil War in Siberia and Far East; after demobilization editet journals "Sovetskiy put'" and "Kollektivist"; member, ed bd, "Krest'yanskaya gazeta"; 1925–26 Party CC instructor for Siberia and Far East; 1927–29 dep chm, then chm, RSFSR Gosplan; head, Moscow Writers' Assoc; 1915 first work published; 1935 arrested by State Security organs; *Publ:* verse *Novyy god* (The New Year) (1915); *Ne vsoy to zoloto, chto blestit* (Not All is Gold That Glitters) (1916); *Kuda nas vedut* Whither They Lead Us) (1917); "The Partisan Anthem" (1920); non-fiction works: *Grazhdanskaya voyna v Sibiri, 1918–1920* (The 1918–20 Civil War in Siberia) (1925); *Na soglashatel'skikh frontakh* (On the Conciliation Fronts) (1927); *Bor'ba za Dal'niy Vostok, 1920–1922* (The Struggle for the Far East. 1920–1922) (1931), etc; *Died:* 1937 in imprisonment; posthumously rehabilitated.

PARKHOMENKO, Aleksandr Yakovlevich (1885–1921) Mil commander; CP member from 1904; *Born:* 1885 in vil Makarov-Yar, Yekaterinoslav Province, son of a peasant; *Career:* from age 10 worked as farmhand on an estate, then worked in Lugansk; from 1900 worked at Lugansk Locomotive Plant; from 1903 active in revol movement; organized strike at Locomotive Plant; formed armed workers' squad; summer 1906 directed peasant revolt in Makar-Yar distr; fall 1906 arrested and jailed for four months; then continued revol work in Lugansk; went underground under persecution from tsarist authorities and moved to Sevastopol'; 1909 arrested in Sevastopol' and jailed until 1912; from 1915 worked at Lugansk Ammunition Plant; 1916 helped stage strike at this plant in protest against the war; 1916 re-arrested and drafted into army; assigned to reserve regt at Voronezh, where he conducted Bolshevik propaganda among troops; at time of 1917 Feb Revol served in Moscow with another mil unit; he and his unit took active part in overthrowing tsarist regime, arresting tsarist officials and disarming police; appointed head, Mar'inskiy Rayon, Moscow; Mar 1917 sent to Lugansk to command Red Guards; after 1917 Oct Revol continued to command Lugansk Red Guards; early 1918 appointed dep chm, Lugansk Rayon Staff for Mustering Red Army; summer and fall 1918 active in defense of Tsaritsyn as special plen of 10th Army's Revol Mil Council; from Jan 1919 mil comr, Khar'kov Province; 1919 commanded Yekaterinoslav sector of front and Khar'kov flank; from fall 1919 helped organize 1st Horse Army and appointed special plen of this army's Revol Mil Council; from Apr 1920 commander, 14th Div, 1st Horse Army; led this div 1,000 km from Northern Caucasus to Polish Front, breaching it at Somgorodok; fought at Novograd-Volynsk, Rovno, Dubno and L'vov with great distinction; routed Wrangel's forces at Otrada, Rozhdestvenskiy and Novo-Alekseyevka; *Awards:* two Orders of Red Banner; *Died:* 3 Jan 1921 killed in action.

PARKHOMENKO, Vladimir Aleksandrovich (1880–1942) Historian; *Born:* 1880; *Career:* prof, Dnepropetrovsk Inst of Public Educ and Leningrad Univ; specialized in history of Kievan Rus'; *Publ:* Nachalo khristianstva na Rusi (The Beginning of Christianity in Rus) (1914); *Rus' v IX stoletii* (Rus in the 9th Century) (1917); *U istokov russkoy gosudarstvennosti* (By the Wellsprings of Russian Statehood) (1924); *Kiyevskaya Rus' i khozary* (Kievan Rus and the Khozars) (1927); *Kievskaya Rus' i pechenegi* (Kievan Rus and the Pechenegs) (1929); *K voprosu o normanskom zavoyevanii i proiskhozhdenii Rusi* (The Norman Conquest and Origin of Rus) (1938), etc; *Died:* 1942 during blockade of Leningrad.

PARNAS, Yakub Oskarovich (1884–1949) Biochemist; Dr of Philosophy from 1907; member, USSR, Acad of Sci from 1942; member, USSR Acad of Med Sci from 1944; member, Leopold Acad, Halle; corresp member, Polish Acad of Sci; hon dr of Sorbonne and Athens Univ; *Born:* 28 Jan 1884 in vil Mokryany, now L'vov Oblast; *Educ:* 1904 grad Chemical Dept, Berlin Higher Tech School; 1905–07 specialized training under Hofmeister in Strasburg and Willstetter in Zurich; *Career:* from 1913 assoc prof, Chair of Physiological Chemistry, Strasburg Univ; from 1916 head, Chair of Physiological Chemistry, Warsaw Univ; 1920–42 prof and dir, Inst of Med Chemistry, L'vov Univ; 1943–48 dir, Inst of Biochemistry, USSR Acad of Sci; 1943–49 also head, Laboratory of Physiochemistry, USSR Acad of Sci; studied carbohydrate metabolism of tissues and enzyme processes underlying muscular action; 1935, together with T. Baranovskiy, discovered what he called phosphorolysis, i.e., breakdown of glycogen by phosphoric acid; discovered major reactions connected with intermolecular transfer of phosphate residue involving adenyl nucleotides; theoretically analysed mechanism of glucoside and alcohol fermentation and the links between glycolytic reactions and other changes in the muscles; pioneered use of isotopes in Sov biochemical studies; *Publ: Izbrannyye trudy* (Selected Works) (1960); *Awards:* Stalin Prize (1942); *Died:* 29 Jan 1949.

PARSHIN, Georgiy Mikhaylovich (1916–1956) Test pilot and WW 2 hero; maj; CP member from 1942; *Born:* 23 May 1916 in vil Setukha, now Orel Oblast, son of a peasant; *Educ:* 1949 grad Command Staff Extension Courses, Sov Army; *Career:* 1941 joined Sov Army; during WW 2 fighter pilot, then flight, squadron and wing commander; fought on Western, Southern, Caucasian, Leningrad and 3rd Bel fronts; flew 253 sorties; 1946 retired on med grounds but later returned to active flying duty; from 1949 worked for Aeroflot, then as a test pilot; *Awards:* twice Hero of the Sov Union (1944 and 1945); Order of Lenin; other orders and medals; *Died:* 13 Mar 1956 in an aviation accident.

PARSKIY, Dmitriy Pavlovich (1874–1921) Mil commander; maj-gen, Russian Army; *Born:* 1874; *Career:* during WW 1 commanded 12th Army on Northern Front; Feb 1918 sided with Bolsheviks; commanded troops of Narva Sector; halted, then repulsed German troops in this sector; 26 May – 8 Aug 1918 commanded Northern Sector; 11 Sept – 26 Nov 1918 commanded Northern Front; then chm, Commission to Draft Red Army Regulations; *Died:* 1921 of typhus.

PASHCHENKO, Aleksandr Sofronovich (1906–1963) Graphic artist; Pop Artist of Ukr SSR from 1960; corresp member, USSR Acad of Arts from 1954; prof from 1947; CP member from 1939; *Born:* 14 Sept 1906 in vil Luka, now Vinnitsa Oblast; *Educ::* 1932 grad Kiev Art Inst; *Career:* from 1955 rector, Kiev Art Inst; master of color linocuts and etchings; *Works:* engravings "Kiev Suite" (1936–60); "The Birth of the Kremenchug Hydroelectric Plant" (1958–60); portraits; landscapes, etc; *Died:* 13 June 1963.

PASHENNAYA, Vera Nikolayevna (1887–1962) Actress; Pop Artiste of USSR from 1937; prof from 1941; CP member from 1954; *Born:* 7 Sept 1887 in Moscow; *Educ:* 1907 grad Theatrical College at Maly Theater, Moscow; *Career:* 1907–20 actress, Maly Theater; 1921 actress, Korsh Theater; 1922–23 toured abroad with Moscow Arts Theater; 1924 at Zamoskvorech'ye Theater; from 1925 again at Maly Theater; from 1914 taught drama; directed Studio of Maly Theater; from 1915 head, Chair of Stagecraft, Shchepkin Theatrical College; *Roles:* Kett in Sumbatov's *Dzhentl'men* (The Gentleman) (1907); Mariya Andreyevna in Ostrovskiy's *Bednaya nevesta* (The Poor Bride) (1908); Maria in Schillers *Maria Stuart* (1910); Liza in Griboyedov's *Gore ot uma* (Woe from Wit); Yevgeniya in Ostrovskiy's *Na boykom meste* (A Lively Post); the Maiden in Gorky's *Starik* (The Old Man) (1919); Irina in A. K. Tolstoy's "Tsar' Fyodor Ioannovich"; Vasilisa in Gorky's *Na dne* (The Lower Dephts) (1923–24); Lysistrata in Aristophanes' "Lysistrata" (1924); Lyubov' in Trenyov's "Lyubov' Yarovaya" (1926); Irina in Romashov's *Ognennyy most* (Bridge of Fire) (1929); Varya in Fadeyev's *Razgrom* (Rout) (1932); Polya in Trenyov's *Na beregu Nevy* (On the Banks of the Neva) (1937); Anna Andreyevna in Gogol's *Revizor* (The Government Inspector) (1938); Natal'ya in Korneychuk's *Kalinovaya roshcha* (Viburnum Grove) (1950); Vassa in Gorky's "Vassa Zheleznova" (1952); Kabanikha in Ostrovskiy's *Groza* (The Storm), etc; *Publ:Moya rabota nad rol'yu* (My Work on a Role) (1934); *Iskusstvo aktrisy* (The Actress' Art) (1954), etc; *Awards:* two Orders of Lenin; Order of the Red Banner of Labor; Stalin Prize (1943); Lenin Prize (1961); *Died:* 28 Oct 1962 in Moscow; buried in Novodevich'ye Cemetery.

PASHERSTNIK, Aron Yefimovich (1900–1958) Lawyer; Dr of Law; prof, Moscow Univ; *Born:* 19 Dec 1900; *Career:* specialized in labor law; *Publ: Pravovyye voprosy voznagrazhdeniya za trud rabochikh i sluzhashchikh* (Legal Aspects of Wages and Salaries for Workers and Office Workers) (1949); *Pravovoye regulirovaniye truda v kapitalisticheskikh stranakh* (Labor Regulations in Capitalist Countries) (1955), etc; *Died:* 20 Dec 1958.

PASHKEVICH, Vasiliy Vasil'yevich (1856–1939) Specialist in fruit growing; member, All-Union Lenin Acad of Agric Sci from 1935; Hon Sci and Tech Worker of RSFSR from 1935; *Born:* 1856; *Educ:* 1882 grad Petersburg Univ; *Career:* from 1894 with Dept of Agric, Russian Min of Agric and State Holdings; from 1922 with Agric Comt, later reorganized into All-Union Inst of Plant Growing; from 1922 prof, Leningrad Agric Inst; specialized in pomology and other fruit varieties; did research on biology of blossoming and fructition of fruit trees; studied orchards of USSR and published many monographs on state of Russian fruit growing; also wrote studies on medicinal plants; *Publ: Obshchaya pomologiya ili ucheniye o sortakh plodovykh derev'yev* (General Pomology, or the Study of Fruit Tree Varieties (1930); *Sortoizucheniye i sortovodstvo plodovykh derev'yev* (Fruit Tree Variety Studies and Raising) (1933); *Besplodiye i stepen' urozhaynosti v plodovodstve v zavisimosti ot sorta opylyayushchego* (Infertility and the Degree of Yield in Fruit Growing Depending on the Pollinant Variety) (1931); *Died:* 1939.

PASTERNAK, Boris Leonidovich (1890–1960) Russian writer, poet and translator; Nobel Prize winner for 1958; *Born:* 10 Feb 1890 in Moscow, son of painter Academician L. L. Pasternak; *Educ:* 1913 grad Philosophy Dept, History and Philology Fac, Moscow Univ; 1912 studied at Marburg Univ under Prof Herman Cohen; *Career:* raised in a cultured atmosphere of music (his mother Rozaliya Kaufman-Pasternak was a pianist), painting and lit; at first planned a musical career and took composition lessons from A. N. Skryabin, but later turned to philosophical disciplines; later suddenly broke with philosophy as a basis for a profession and turned to lit, although he always maintained a keen interest in philosophical subjects; first lit works date from 1912, when he joined moderate Futurist group which published its own organ "Tsentrifuga"; soon broke with Futurism, selecting his own, independent creative path unconnected with any of the lit schools or trends fashionable at that time; 1914 published his first verse collection *Bliznets v tuchakh* (A Twin in the Clouds) and in 1917 his verse cycle, contained in the collection *Poverk bar'yerov* (Above Barriers); the Revol and Civil War were scarcely reflected in his works, and the same is true of his verse collection *Sestra moya zhizn'* (Life My Sister), published in 1922; placed art above all else, blending ist with the world of nature and with life as a whole and generally rejecting revol force and violence as a means of achieving any goal, considering that reality has its own imperatives and does not lend itself to forcible reorganization and that artistic creativity is incompatible with soc commissions; 1922–27 sided with Mayakovskiy's "Lef" (Left Art Front) assoc; 1934 attended 1st USSR Writers' Congress; was one of those writeres who were tolerated by Sov regime by dint of their great artistic talent but who were, at the same time, rejected by the Party critics; did a great deal of lit translation, translating works of Goethe, Shakespeare, Kleist, Shelley, Verlaine, Petofi, Hans Sachs and Keats; also translated many Geo poets; particularly effective was his translation of "Faust", published as a monograph in 1955; after WW 2, in addition to a number of poetic works and extensive translations, concentrated on his novel *Doktor Zhivago* (Doctor Zhivago), which he began to write in 1948, although he derived the basic idea from it prior to WW 2; the essential quality of this novel is that it is written from the standpoint of the spirit, not from the standpoint of matter; the novel outlines the principles of human relationships, based on such qualities as genuine feeling, love and purpose as an inner criterion of life; publication of the novel was refused in the USSR, and in 1957 it was published abroad; in 1958 it brought Pasternak the Novel Prize for Lit; Pasternak was then subjected tó a smear campaign in the Party press and expelled from the USSR Writers' Union and its Translators' Section for "polit and moral decadence and treachery toward the Soviet people, the cause of Socialism, peace and progress"; the question of depriving Pasternak of Sov citizenship and expelling him from the USSR was also raised; as a result of this campaign Pasternak was forced to renounce the Nobel Prize and ask Krushchev to let him spend the rest of his life in his native country; deprived of the right to publish his works and to meet friends and visitors, Pasternak spent his declining years in virtual isolation at the vil of Peredelkino, near Moscow; *Publ:* verse collections: *Bliznets v tuchakh* (A Twin in the Clouds) (1914); *Poverkh bar'yerov* (Above Barriers) (1917); *Sestra moya zhizn'* (Life My Sister) (1922); *Vtoroye rozhdeniye* (Second Birth) (1932); *Na rannikh poyezdakh* (On Early Trains) (1943); *Zemnoy prostor* (The Earth's Expanse) (1945); collected stories: *Rasskazy* (Stories) (1925); *Dve knigi* (Two Books) (1927); *Vozdushnyye puti* (Air Ways) (1933); poems: *Vysokaya bolezn'* (High Disease) (1923); *Devyat'sot pyatyy god* (The Year 1905) (1927); *Leytenant Shmidt* (Lieutenant Schmidt) (1927); novel in verse "Spektorskiy" (1931); novel "Doktor Zhivago" (Doktor Zhivago) (1957); *Izbrannyye perevody* (Selected Translations) (1940); *Vil'yam Shekspir v perevode B. Pasternaka* (William Shakespeare as Translated by B. Pasternak) (2 vol, 1949); *Stikhovoreniya i poemy* (Verse and Poems) (1965); *Stikhi* (Verse) (1966), etc; *Died:* 30 May 1960 at Peredelkino; buried at Peredelkino.

PASTERNAK, Leonid Osipovich (1862–1945) Painter and draftsman; prof; father of the writer Boris Pasternak; member, Petersburg Acad of Arts from 1905; *Born:* 22 Mar 1862 in Odessa; *Educ:* studied at Odessa Art School and Munich Acad of Arts; *Career:* late 1880's settled in Moscow and ran his own art school; from 1894 taught at College of Painting, Sculpture and Architecture; from 1921 lived in Germany, then in England, retaining Sov citizenship; *Publ:* canvases; "News from Home" (1889); "To My Kin" (1891); "L. N. Tolstoy's Family at Yasnaya Polyana" (1902); "Portrait of V. O. Klyushevskiy"; lithographs "L. N. Tolstoy at Work"; illustrations for Lev Tolstoy's novel *Voskreseniye* (Resurrection) and for works of Lermontov; after 1917 Oct Revol did a number of portrait sketches of Lenin; while living abroad did portraits of the artist M. Libermann, the physicist Albert Einstein, etc; his works are displayed mainly in Moscow and Leningrad museums; *Died:* 31 May 1945 in London.

PASTUKHOV, Mikhail Dmitriyevich (1882–1964) Party official; CP member from 1908; *Born:* 1882; *Career:* from 1906 revol work among workers of Izhevsk Arms Factory; organized an underground printing house; repeatedly arrested; 1917 member, Exec Comt, Izhevsk Sov of Workers' Dep; during Kolchak's offensive member, Izhevsk Revol Comt; 1920 secr, Vyatka Province RCP(B) Comt; 1922 chm, Kostroma Province Exec Comt; 1927 RSFSR Dep Pop Comr of Workers and Peasants' Inspection; member and Presidium member, Centr Control Commission; member, All-Russian and USSR Centr Exec Comt; in latter years exec econ work in Moscow; from 1943 pensioner; *Died:* 5 Jan 1964.

PATON, Yevgeniy Oskarovich (1870–1953) Eng; specialist in welding and bridge-building; member, Ukr Acad of Sci from 1929; Hon Sci Worker of Ukr SSR from 1940; Hero of Socialist Labor from 1943; CP member from 1944; *Born:* 5 Mar 1870, son of Russian consul in France; *Educ:* 1896 grad Petersburg Inst of Transport Eng; *Career:* 1898–1905 lecturer, Moscow Eng College; 1905–38 lecturer, Kiev Polytech Inst; 1921–32 head, Kiev Bridge-Testing Station; 1930–35 dir, Electrowelding Research Inst, Ukr Acad of Sci; 1946–51 vice-pres, Ukr Acad of Sci; until 1929 concentrated on bridge-building, then turned to electrowelding; did research on automation of welding processes, flux-welding and strength of welded structures; 1941–45 directed research on welding of special steels and adoption of new welding methods in defense ind; designed and supervised construction of first Sov continuous welding lines and developed technol and equipment for automatic on-site welding; developed ind methods for welding pipes, water-mains and storage tanks; 1953 supervised construction of welded bridge over River Dnieper in Kiev; founder-ed, journal "Avtomaticheskaya svarka"; *Publ: Avtomaticheskaya svarka golym elektrodom pod sloyem flyusa* (Bare-Electrode Automatic Flux Welding) (1940); *Izbrannyye trudy* (Selcted Works) (3 vol, 1959–1961); *Awards:* two Orders of Lenin; two Orders of the Red Banner of Labor; Order of the Red Star; Stalin Prize (1941); *Died:* 12 Aug 1953.

PATORZHINSKIY, Ivan Sergeyevich (1896–1960) Opera singer (bass); Pop Artiste of USSR from 1944; CP member from 1946; *Born:* 20 Feb 1896 in vil Petrov-Svistunova, Yekaterinoslav Province; *Educ:* 1922 grad Yekaterinoslav Conservatory; *Career:* 1925–35 soloist, Khar'kov Opera and Ballet Theater; from 1935 soloist, Shevchenko Opera and Ballet Theater, Kiev; chm, Ukr Theatrical Soc; from 1946 prof, Kiev Conservatory; dep, Ukr Supr Sov of 1938, 1947 and 1951 convocations; *Roles:* Karas' in *Zaporozhets za Dunayem* (A Dnieper Cossack Beyond the Danube); the Deputy and Taras' Bul'ba in "Natalka-Poltavka" and "Taras' Bul'ba"; Deacon Gavrila in Dankevich's *Bogdan Khmel'nitskiy*; Val'ko in Meytus' *Molodaya gvardiya* (The Young Guard); Galitskiy in *Knyaz' Igor'* (Prince Igor); Mephistopheles in Gounod's "Faust"; Boris in Moussorgsky's "Boris Godunov", etc; *Awards:* Order of Lenin; three Orders of the Red Banner of Labor; Stalin Prize (1942); *Died:* 22 Feb 1960.

PAUKER, Karl Viktorovich (1893–?) Govt official; *Born:* 1893, son of a worker; *Career:* prior to 1917 worker; took part in 1917 Oct Revol; from 1918 worked for All-Russian Cheka, then State Polit Bd and NKVD; 1935 head, Operations Dept, NKVD; member, All-Russian and USSR Centr Exec Comt; from 1935 ranked as comr of state security, 2nd class; *Awards:* two Orders of the Red Banner; Hon Arms; Cheka Badges of Hon; *Died:* date and place of death unknown.

PAVLENKO, Pyotr Andreyevich (1899–1951) Writer; CP member from 1920; *Born:* 29 June 1899 in Petersburg; *Educ:* 1917 grad Tiflis college; *Career:* 1920 polit officer, then comr in Red Army; after demobilization carried out Party work in Transcaucasia and served on ed staff of newspapers "Krasnyy voin" and "Zarya Vostoka" in Tiflis; 1924–27 secr, Sov trade mission in Turkey and corresp for "Zarya Vostoka" and Odessa "Izvestia"; from 1928 worked for journal "Krasnaya nov'" in Moscow and was member, "Pereval" (The Pass) lit group; 1930 toured Centr Asia with group of writers; in 1930's chief ed, journal "Tridtsat' dney" and almanach "Druzhba narodov"; visited Far East; war corresp in Sov-Finnish War and WW 2 and corresp for "Pravda" and "Krasnaya zvezda"; wounded, contracted tuberculosis and was discharged from army; 1945–51 secr, Crimean Writers' Union; ed, alsmanach "Krym"; from 1947 member, ed bd, journal "Znamya"; 1947 visited America and Europe; dep, USSR Supr Sov of 1950 convocation; *Publ: Lord Bayron* (Lord Byron) (1928); coauthor, anthologies *Aziatskiye rasskazy* (Asian Stories) (1929); *Stambul i Turtsiya* (Istanbul and Turkey) (1930); *Anatoliya* (Anatolia) (1932); novelette *Pustynya* (The Desert) (1931); novelette *Barrikady* (The Barricades) (1932); novel *Na vostoke* (In the East) (1937); wrote or helped write scripts for films: "Aleksandr Nevskiy" (1938); *Russkaya povest'* (A Russian Tale) (1942); *Schast'ye* (Happiness) (1947); *PadeniyeBerlina* (The Fall of Berlin) (1949); non-fiction works: *Amerikanskiye vpechatleniya* (American Impressions) (1949); *Molodaya Germaniya* (Young Germany) (1951), etc; *Awards:* Order of Lenin; other orders; medals; four Stalin Prizes (1941, 1947, 1948 and 1950); *Died:* 16 Apr 1951 in Moscow.

PAVLINOV, Konstantin Mikhaylovich (1845–1933) Therapist; *Born:* 1845; *Educ:* 1868 grad Moscow Univ; *Career:* from 1868 worked at Moscow Univ; later prof, Moscow Univ; supported physiological trend in med; helped introduced artificial pneumothorax for treatment of tuberculosis; proved that uric acid is not formed by the kidneys, but only excreted by them; demonstrated that antipyretics are bad for infectious fevers in that the increased temperature is a defense reaction against the infection; described a particular heart defect – congenital pure mitral stenosis; co-founder, Moscow Therapeutic Soc; *Publ: Chastnaya patologiya i terapiya vnutrennikh bolezney* (Special Pathology and Therapy of Internal Diseases) (1890); *Klinicheskiye lektsii* (Clinical Lectures) (4 vol, 1882–85); *Died:* 1933.

PAVLOV, Aleksandr Vasil'yevich (1880–1937) Mil commander; lt, Russian Army; div commander, Sov Army from 1935; CP member 1917–23; *Born:* 22 Dec 1880; in Odessa, son of a civil servant; *Educ:* grad agric college; 1915 grad ensigns school; *Career:* until 1914 taught agronomy and viticulture; from 1914 in Russian Army; fought in WW 1; 1917 chm, regt comt; member, soldiers' comt, 7th Army on Western Front; commander, Southwestern Front; from Feb 1918 in Red Army; 1918–19 brigade commander, Southern Sector, 233rd Regt, 26th Infantry Div; commander, 27th Infantry Div on Eastern Front; Dec 1919 – July 1920 commander, 10th Army; 1920 commander, Tambov Province troops; helped rout forces of Kolchak and Denikin and crush Antonov revolt; 1921–22 inspector of infantry, Ukr and Crimean Armed Forces; 1922–24 commander and comr, 4th Infantry Corps; 1924–30 asst commander, Western, then Volga Mil Distr; 1930 asst inspector of infantry, Red Army; 1930–37 head, Special Fac (for uneducated Civil War heroes) and asst commandant and lecturer, Frunze Mil Acad; 1937 arrested by NKVD; *Awards:* Order of the Red Banner; engraved sidearm; Scroll of USSR Centr Exec Comt; *Died:* 14 Aug 1937 in imprisonment; posthumously rehabilitated.

PAVLOV, Fyodor Pavlovich (1892–1931) Chuvash composer and playwright; *Educ:* grad Chuvash Teachers' Training School, Simbirsk; 1930–31 studied at Leningrad Conservatory; *Career:* after grad Simbirsk school taught singing and music; 1910 began to compose music and write lit; 1917 founded Chuvash Theater in Akulevo; co-founder and dir, Chuvash State Choir; *Publ:* comedy "In Court" (1919); drama "In the Village" (1922); "The Chuvash and Their Songs and Music" (1926); three collections of folk songs; *Works:* symphonic fantasy "Sornay and Polnay" (1929); 10 choral and orchestral works, etc; *Died:* 2 June 1931 in Sochi.

PAVLOV, Ivan Fomich (1922–1950) Pilot; maj; CP member from 1943; *Born:* 25 June 1922 in vil Boriso-Romanovtsy, Kustanay Oblast, son of a peasant; *Educ:* 1949 grad Frunze Mil Acad; *Career:* from 1940 in Sov Army; during WW 2 pilot, then flight commander; navigator, then commander of an assault air force regt on Kalinin, Centr and 1st Baltic Fronts; flew some 200 missions; *Awards:* twice Hero of the Sov Union; two Orders of Lenin; other orders and medals; *Died:* 12 Oct 1950 killed in the line of duty.

PAVLOV, Ivan Petrovich (1849–1936) Physiologist; prof; Dr of Med; founder of physiological school and study of higher nervous activity in animals and man; member, Russian (USSR) Acad of Sci; Nobel Prize winnder; head, Physiological Dept, Inst of Experimental Med; *Born:* 26 Sept 1849 in Ryazan', son of a priest; *Educ:* grad Ryazan' Theological College and Seminary; 1875 grad Natural Sci Dept, Physics and Mathematics Fac, Petersburg Univ; 1879 grad Petersburg Med Surgical Acad; *Career:* while still a student at Petersburg Univ won Gold Medal; 1876–78, while studying at Med Surgical Acad, also worked as tech, then asst at Prof K. N. Ustimovich's Physiological Laboratory, Petersburg Veterinary Inst; 1877 sent abroad to continue studies at Prof Heidenhain's Physiological Laboratory; after grad stayed on at Med Surgical Acad for postgrad studies and until 1889 headed Physiological Laboratory, Prof S. P. Botkin's Therapeutic Clinic; 1880 received second Gold Star for his research; 1883 defended doctor's thesis on *Tsentrobezhnyye nervy serdtsa* (Efferent Nerves of the Heart); 1884 elected assoc prof, Petersburg Mil Med Acad; 1884–86 worked in Germany at Ludwig and Heidenhain's physiological laboratories; 1890 elected prof-extraordinarius, Chair of Pharmacology, Tomsk Univ; 1890 also elected prof-extraordinarius, Mil Med Acad; 1891–1936 co-founder and head, Physiological Dept, Petersburg (Leningrad) Inst of Experimental Med; 1895 resigned from Chair of Pharmacology and 1895–1925 served as prof of physiology, Mil Med Acad; 1897 confirmed prof-ordinarius; 1901–07 corresp member, from 1907 member, Russian Acad of Sci; 1904 received Nobel Prize for his work *Lektsii o rabote glavnykh pishchevaritel'nykh zhelez* (Lectures on the Work of the Main Digestive Glands); 1913 designed and supervised construction at Inst of Experimental Med of soundproof chambers for studying conditioned reflexes (so-called "silence towers"), subsequently used for int renowed experiments; from 1924 dir, Inst of Physiology, USSR Acad of Sci; and founder-head of its Biological Station at vil Koltusha (now Pavlovo), near Leningrad; 1935 at 15th Int Congress of Physiologists in Leningrad and Moscow awarded hon title "Elder of World Physiologists"; his physiological research extended to several fields; 1874–88 concentrated on physiology of cardiovascular system; demonstrated presence of special nerve fibers which augment or weaken heart activity; on this basis he later constructed his hypothesis of the nervous system's trophic function; another field of study was the physiology of digestion; in this field devised a number of new techniques and research methods, including special operations on the digestive organs which enabled a "chronic experimental" study of the operation of the digestive apparatus in a healthy animal; 1879 first to diagnose chronic fistula of the pancreatic duct and later devised an operation for chronic fistula of the bile duct; 1894 devised a method for observing the activity of the gastric glands by externalising part of the stomach in the form of an isolated ventricle, fully retaining its neural links with the centr nervous system (Pavlov's small ventricle); 1889 he and Ye. O. Shumova–Simonovskaya combined esophagotomy and gastrotomy in dogs to facilitate an experiment with "imaginary feeding"; as a result of these experiments demonstrated the leading role of the nervous system in regulating the digestive process; in addition, studied the dynamics of the gastric, pancreatic and salivary glands' secretory process as well as the operation of the liver using various foodstuffs and proved that they could adapt to the nature of the various secretory agents used; in an effort to combine the interests of physiology and med, he experimented with sci methods of treating experimentally induced pathological states; closely allied with his work on experimantal therapy were his studies of pharmacology; also conducted intensive research into higher nervous activity in animals and man; in this field he did considerable research on the body's connections with its environment via its nervous system; from 1903 gradually developed his theory of conditions and conditioned reflexes; made a detailed study of the laws governing excitation and inhibition processes in the cerebral cortex; established that these processes are closely and even inseparably linked, can irradiate extensively, be concentrated and can mutually affect each other; according to this theory, the entire analyzer and synthesizer activity of the cortex's large hemispheres is based on the complex interplay of these two processes; regarded sleep and hypnosis as processes of inner inhibition radiating widely throughout the cerebral cortex and extending to the subcortical formations; on the basis of his study of conditioned reflex activity of various animals he devised his own classification of types of nervous system; in his latter years specialized in the higher nervous activity of man and advanced a theory of two signal systems of activity: the first – general activity in man and animals, and the second – activity peculiar to man; the second siganl system, inseparably linked with the first, enables man to formulate words and, thanks to these words which enable abstraction and the formation of concepts, make possible higher human abstract thinking; apart from his physiological research, engaged in various soc undertakings; 1900 helped draft a program of physical educ for students at the Mil Med Acad and directed gymnastic exercises; 1902 helped organize courses for health officers and lectured on physiology on these courses; after 1917 Oct Revol he was regarded by the higher Party echelons as a polit conservative; on several occasions he expressed his disbelief in the building of socialism and was opposed to Sov philosophy in gen and to dialectical materialism in particular; until the mid-1930's this led to sharp criticism of his works in the USSR; Sov critics termed him a mechanist and idealist who recognized man's subjective world and "the dark forces embodied in man"; his theories of "purpose reflex", "freedom reflex" and his views on training were termed anti-scientific and injurious, while other of his works were said to need reassesment on the basis of dialectical materialism; nevertheless, his sci authority and reputation were so great throughout the world that even in the early years of Sov rule he was given facilities for his sci work; after Pavlov's death, his physiological teaching was reassessed in the USSR from the viewpoint of dialectical materialism and, with certain corrections and the suppression of a number of chapters, recognized as materialistic and fully "in keeping with the teaching of Marx and Engels"; attempts were even made to take his reflex theories as a basis for shaping a new type of Sov man imbued with socialist psychology and free from "survivals of capitalism"; 1950 a joint sci session of the USSR Acad of Sci and USSR Acad of Med Sci devoted to Pavlov's physiological teaching decided to make this teaching the basis of all Sov med, biology and pedagogics; for an entire decade from this date Pavlov's physiological teaching became in the USSR a dogma circumscribing the creative thinking of scientists engaged in the fields of biology, med and pedagogics; all research in these fields was tied into quotations from Pavlov's works, and no work could be published without mentioning his name; after Stalin's death Sov scientists gradually extricated themselves from the dead-end created in Sov med in 1950, and at present Pavlov's teaching, while still the main ideological basis of med sci, does not play the same oppressive role that it did in the latter years of Stalin's life and the first few years after his death; after Pavlov's death many sci institutes and higher educ establishments in the USSR were named for him; *Publ:* the main body of Pavlov's published works have been issued in a 6-vol ed (2nd ed, 1951–52); *Died:* 27 Feb 1936 in Leningrad; buried at Volkovo Cemetery.

PAVLOV, Ivan Ul'yanovich (1893–1936) Air Force commander; div commander from 1935; Civil War veteran; CP member from 1917; *Born:* 26 Nov 1893 in vil Andreyevka, Kherson Province, son of a peasant; *Educ:* grad agric school; 1915 grad Gatchina Air Force School; 1916 grad French Air Force School at Chartres and higher aerial combat school; *Career:* until 1914 agronomist; from 1914 in Russian Army; 1917–18 fighter-pilot, 1st Air Force Group, Southwestern Front; elected commander of this group; from 1918 in Red Army; 1918–20 commander, 1st Sov Air Force Group on Eastern Front, then composite air force group on Southwestern and Southern Fronts; after Civil War air force commander, Kiev, North Caucasian and Moscow Mil Distr; dep inspector, then chief inspector of Red Army Air Force; *Awards:* three Orders of the Red Banner; *Died:* 11 Apr 1936.

PAVLOV, Mikhail Aleksandrovich (1863–1958) Metallurgist; member, USSR Acad of Sci from 1932; Hero of Socialist Labor from 1945; *Born:* 22 Jan 1863 in Lenkoran', Azer; *Educ:* 1885 grad Petersburg Mining Inst; *Career:* from 1885 eng at steel plants in Vyatka area; from 1896 eng, Sulin Plant near Rostov-on-Don; 1900–04 lecturer, Yekaterinoslav Higher Mining College; 1904–41 prof, Petersburg (Leningrad) Polytech Inst; 1921–30 also prof, Moscow Mining Acad; 1930–41 also prof, Moscow Steel Inst; then head of a laboratory, Inst of Metallurgy, USSR Acad of Sci; specialized in metallurgy of iron; developed theory of blast-furnace processes and proposed method for determining the parameters of blast furnaces; studied parameters of open-hearth furnaces and directed design and development of large blast furnaces in USSR; from 1910 ed, "Zhurnal Russkogo metallurgicheskogo obshchestva"; 1929–38 helped edit journal "Sovetskaya metallurgiya"; 1924 wrote textbook *Metallurgiya chuguna* (Iron Metallurgy); *Publ: Atlas chertezhey po domennomu proizvodstvu* (An Atlas of Blueprints on Blast-Furnace Production) (1902); *Al'bom chertezhey po martenovskomu proizvodstvu* (An Album of Blueprints on Open-Hearth Production) (1904); *Razmery martenovskikh pechey po empiricheskim dannym* (The Parameters of Open-Hearth Furnaces by Empirical Data) (1910); *Raschyot domennykh shikht* (Calculating Blast–Furnace Layers) (1914); *Metallurgiya chuguna* (Iron Metallurgy) (3 vol, 3rd ed, 1948–51); *Vospominaniya metallurga* (Memoirs of a Metallurgist) 2 vol, 2nd ed, 1945); *Awards:* five Orders of Lenin; other orders and medals; two Stalin Prizes (1943 and 1947); *Died:* 10 Jan 1958.

PAVLOV, Pavel Andreyevich (1892–1924) Mil commander and diplomat; junior capt, Russian Army; CP member from 1919; *Born:* 19 Feb 1892 in Tiflis, son of a gen; *Educ:* 1909 grad Cadet Corps; 1909–14 studied at Petersburg Polytech Inst; 1915 grad Oranienbaum Ensigns' School; 1923 grad Higher Acad Courses; *Career:* 1914 expelled from Polytech Inst for revol activities; Sept 1914 drafted into Russian Army; 1915–17 commanded a platoon, then a company on Southwestern Front; 1917 member, regt, div, corps, army then front soldiers' comt; 1918–19 underground work against Hetman Skoropadskiy's govt in Kiev; commanded an insurgent detachment; 1919 Kiev Province comr; commander, Kiev Battle Sector; dep commander, internal front; 1919–22 brigade commander; commander, Perekop Forces Group, 13th Army; commander, composite cadets div; fought against Gen Denikin and Wrangel and against Makhno's forces; 1921 head and comr, Moscow Mil Educ Institutions Bd; as commander, composite cadets unit helped crush Antonov revolt in Tambov Province; 1922 dep commander, Bukhara Forces Group in Centr Asia; fought against Basmachi movement; 1922–23 head, "Vystrel" Tactical Infantry School; 1923–24 commander and comr, 13th Infantry Corps in Centr Asia; Apr 1924 sent to China as Sun Yat-sen's mil counselor; *Awards:* two Orders of the Red Banner; Order of the Bukhara Gold Star, 1st Class; silver sword with the Order of Bukhara Gold Star, 1st Class on the hilt; *Died:* 18 July 1924 drowned in the Sinkiang River while transferring from a launch to a steamer; his ashes are interred at Moscow's Vagan'kov Cemetery.

PAVLOVICH (VOLONTER), Mikhail Pavlovich (real name: Mikhail Lazarevich VEL'TMAN) (1871–1927) Govt official; Orientalist; journalist; CP member from 1918; *Born:* 25 Mar 1871 in Odessa; *Career:* from early 1890's active in revol movement; 1898 joined RSDRP; several times arrested by Tsarist authorities; 1903, after 2nd RSDRP Congress, sided with Mensheviks; 1907 emigrated and lived in Paris, continuing Party, lit and propaganda work; during WW 1 adopted internationalist stand; just prior to 1917 Oct Revol returned to Russia; 1921–23 Collegium member, Pop Comrt of Nationalities; 1919–20 Revol Mil Council plen on Southern Front; 1920, at Congress of Peoples of the East, elected to Action and Propaganda Council; from 1921 head, All-Russian Sci Assoc of Oriental Studies; first rector, Moscow Inst of Oriental Studies; wrote numerous works on imperialism, history of nat-liberation movement in Eastern countries (Chinese and Iranian revol of early 20th Century, nat-liberation movement in Turkey in early 1920's, activities of Turkish CP, etc); *Publ: Sobraniye sochineniy. Imperializm i mirovaya politika poslednikh desyatiletiy* (Collected Works. Imperialism and World Politics in the Last Decades) (vol 1–3, 5, 7 and 9, 1925–27); *Died:* 19 June 1927.

PAVLOVSKIY, Aleksandr Dmitriyevich (1857–1944) Microbiologist and surgeon; *Born:* 13 Oct 1857 in Yaroslavl' Province, son of a priest; *Educ:* 1881 grad Mil Med Acad; *Career:* 1884 defended doctor's thesis on medullary tumors and giant cells; from 1885 assoc prof, Chair of Pathological Anatomy, Mil Med Acad; from 1889 prof, Chair of Surgical Pathology and Therapy, Kiev Univ; 1896–1909 head, Serum Dept, Kiev Bacteriological Inst; specialized in surgical infections, tuberculosis and rhinoscleroma; 1893 prepared anti-cholera serum and 1894 anti-streptococcal serum in the laboratory he established at Kiev Univ; first Kiev physician to use anti-diphtherial serum; addressing 1st Pirogov Congress of Physicians, stressed need for independent chairs of microbiology (bacteriology); co-founder and first dir, Kiev Bacteriological Inst; 1886 carried out first Russian research on microorganism in the air; 1887 postulated idea of bacteriotherapy of infections (treatment of anthrax with Bacterium prodigiosum preparations); instrumental in disseminating bacteriological knowledge in Russia and Ukr; 1894 founded in Kiev soc for combatting infectious diseases; wrote over 100 works; *Publ: Printsipy i zadachi sovremennoy khirurgii* (The Principles and Tasks of Modern Surgery) (1889); *Bor'ba s zaraznymi boleznyami* (Combatting Infectious Diseases) (1897); *K voprosu o khronicheskoy difterii ili diteroide glotki* (Chronic Diphtheria or Diphtheroid of the Pharynx) (1905); *Died:* 18 Oct 1944.

PAVLOVSKIY, Nikolay Osipovich (1903–1960) Mil commander; col-gen; CP member from 1942; *Born:* 9 Feb 1903 in Grodno; son of an office worker; *Educ:* grad Gen Staff Acad; *Career:* 1919 volunteered for Red Army; from 1920 commander ; during WW 2 held various posts, including army chief of staff, head of an operations bd and dep chief of staff, various fronts; helped to plan and implement various front operations against Germans and Japanese; after WW 2 asst to Chief od Gen Staff and dir of a main bd, Sov Army; *Awards:* four Orders of Lenin; four Orders of the Red Banner; Order of Suvorov; three Orders of Kutuzov; Order of Bogdan Khmel'nitskiy; Order of the Fatherland War; numerous for orders and medals; *Died:* 21 Oct 1960 in the line of duty; buried at Novodevich'ye Cemetery, Moscow.

PAVLOVSKIY, Yevgeniy Nikanorovich (1884–1965) Biologist, zoologist and parasitologist; Hon Sci Worker of RSFSR from 1935; Hon Sci Worker of Tadzh SSR from 1943; member, USSR Acad of Sci from 1939; member, USSR Acad of Med Sci from 1944; Hero of Socialist Labor from 1951; lt-gen, Med Corps; CP member from 1940; *Born:* 5 Mar 1884 in Biryuche (now Krasnogvardeyesk, Voronezh Oblast); son of a teacher; *Educ:* 1909 grad Mil Med Acad; *Career:* from 1903 assoc and postgrad student, Chair of Zoology and Comparative Anatomy, Mil Med Acad; 1913 defended doctor's thesis on the structure of the poison glands in arthropods and appointed assoc prof of embryology at Mil Med Acad; 1914 sent to Western Europe, Algeria and Tunisia to study zoological and parasitological service and collect material on poisonous animals; 1917 defended master's thesis on the comparative anatomy and evolution of scorpions; 1921–56 head, Chair of Biology and Parasitology, Mil Med Acad; 1918–30 founder-custodian, Brain Museum, Brain Inst; 1920–22 prof of zoology, Stebutov Agric Inst; 1930–42 senior zoologist and head, Dept of Parasitology, Zoological Museum and Inst, USSR Acad of Sci; 1930–33 head, Dept for the Study of Animal-Husbandry Pests, All-Union Inst of Plant Protection, All-Union Lenin Acad of Agric Sci; 1933–49 founder head, Dept of Parasitology, Gorky All-Union Inst of Experimental Med; from 1946 head, Dept of Parasitology and Microbiology, (later Dept of Natural-Foci Diseases), Gamaleya Inst of Epidemiology and Microbiology, USSR Acad of Med Sci; 1944–62 dir, 1962–65 chief consultant, Zoological Inst, USSR Acad of Sci; 1947–51 dir, Tadzh Base, then Tadzh Branch, USSR Acad of Sci; studied transmissive and parasitic diseases in various parts of the USSR and also in Iran, Iraq and other countries; supervised or headed over 170 expeditions to study tick-borne relapsing typhus, tick-borne and Japanese encephalitis, tick-borne typhus fevers, mosquito fever, skin leishmaniosis, tularemia, helminthoses, pathogenic protozoa of the human intestine, etc; 1960 directed courses on natural-foci diseases, organized in USSR at the request of the World Health Organization and conducted in Moscow, Leningrad and Tbilisi for doctors and biologists from 13 European, Asian and African countries; 1960, at his initiative, the Omsk Inst of Epidemiology was reorganized into the Inst of Natural-Foci Diseases; also sponsored the reorganization of the Dept of Parasitology and Med Zoology into the Dept of Natural-Foci Infections at the Gamaleya Inst of Epidemiology and Microbiology; chem, Ichthyological Commission, USSR Acad of Sci; from 1931 life pres, All-Union Entomological Soc; from 1952 pres, USSR Geographical Soc; 1929–52 founder-chm, Leningrad Parasitological Soc; from 1924 attended numerous int conferences and congresses; hon member, Polish, Czechoslovak and Iranian Acad of Sci; hon dr of Sorbonne and Delhi Univ; hon member of many Sov and for sci soc; the Chair of Biology and Parasitology, Mil Med Acad now bears his name; wrote some 800 research works, including a number of textbooks and monographs on parasitology, methods of studying parasites, etc; *Publ:* master's thesis *Materialy k sravnitel'noy anatomii i istorii razvitiya skorpionov* (Material on the Comparative Anatomy and Developmental History of Scorpions) (1917); "Gifttiere und ihre Giftigkeit" (1927); *Yadovityye zhivot-*

nyye SSSR (Poisonous Animals of the USSR) (1931); *Organizm kak sreda obitaniya* (The Body as a Habitat) (1934); *Metody izucheniya krovososushchikh komarov* (Methods of Studying Bloodsucking Mosquitoes (Culicidae)) (1935); *Praktikum po zoologii* (A practical Zoological Manual) (1938); *Vshi i parazitarnyye tify* (Lice and Parasitic Typhus) (1942); *Yadovityye zhivotnyye Sredney Azii i Irana* (Poisonous Animals of Central Asia and Iran) (1942); *Rukovodstvo po parazitologii cheloveka* (A Manual of Human Parasitology) 2 vol, 1946–48); *Likhoradka pappatachi i yeyo perenoschik* (Pappataci Fever and Its Vector) (1947); *Uchebnik parazitologii cheloveka* (A Textbook of Human Parasitology) (1951); *I. I. Mechnikov i parazitologiya* (I. I. Mechnikov and Parasitology) (1955); *Sovremennoye sostoyaniye ucheniya o prirodnoy ochagovosti bolezney cheloveka* (The Conteporary State of Theory on Natural Foci of Human Diseases) (1960); *Awards:* five Orders of Lenin; other orders; medals; two Stalin Prizes (1941 and 1950); Mechnikov Gold Medal of USSR Acad of Sci (1949); Grand Gold Medal of USSR Geographical Soc (1954); Darwin and Wallace Silver Medal (England), etc; *Died:* 27 May 1965 in Leningrad.

PAVLUNOVSKIY, Ivan Petrovich (1888–?) Party and govt official; CP member from 1905; *Born:* 1888; *Career:* 1903 began revol work with student orgs in Kursk; from 1905 Party organizer and propagandist and member, mil org; arrested; 1906–11 in exile; returned from exile and worked in Petrograd for health insurance fund, Putilov Plant; at start of WW 1 drafted into Russian Army; after 1917 Feb Revol worked in Petrograd; during 1917 Oct Revol member, Mil Revol Comt; during the revolt of the mil cadets, directed the siege of the Vladimir Mil Cadets College; served with Red Army on Eastern Front; then worked for Cheka: 1919–25 chm, Cheka OGPU in Novo-Nikolayevsk; 1926 chm, Transcaucasian Cheka; 1927 Collegium member, OGPU; from Feb 1930 USSR Dep Pop Comr of Workers and Peasants' Inspection; from Nov 1930 dep chm, USSR Supr Sovnarkhoz; member, Centr Control Commission of 15th and 16th convocations; Presidium member, Centr Control Commission; at 17th Party Congress elected cand member, CC, CPSU(B); *Died:* date and place of death unknown.

PAYKES, A.K. (1873–1958) Govt official; CP member from 1918; *Born:* 1873; *Career:* until 1917 (Menshevik; 1918 Pop Comrt of Food plen in Sratov; 1918–20 Collegium member, Pop Comrt of State Control and Siberian Pop Comrt of Workers and Peasants' Inspection; Dep Pop Comr of State Control; member, Siberian Revol Comt; 1921–22 RSFSR plen in China, then in Lith; from 1923 worked for Supr Sovnarkhoz; *Died:* 1958.

PAZHITNOV, Konstantin Alekseyevich (1879–1964) Economist and historian; prof; corresp member, USSR Acad of Sci from 1946; *Born:* 1 Mar 1879; *Educ:* 1907 grad Law Fac, Moscow Univ; *Career:* after 1917 Oct Revol dir, Petrograd Cooperative Inst; then worked for various research and educ establishments; from 1943 senior assoc, Inst of Econ, USSR Acad of Sci; 1943–49 also prof, Moscow Univ; specialized in history of nat econ and working class in Russia; *Publ: Polozheniye rabochego klassa v Rossii* (The Situation of the Working Class in Russia) (3 vol, 1906); *Razvitive sotsialisticheskikh idey v Rossii* (The Development of Socialist Ideas in Russia) (1913); *Gorodskoye i zemskoye samoupravleniye* (Urban and Zemstvo Self-Government) (1912); *Pervyye russkiye sotsialisty* (The First Russian Socialists) (1917); *Osnovy kooperatizma* (The Principles of Cooperativism) (1917); *Istoriya kooperativnoy mysli* (History of the Cooperative Idea) (1918); *Promyshlennyy trud v krepostnuyu epokhu* (Industrial Labor in the Feudal Period) (1924); *Iz istorii rabochikh arteley na Zapade i v Rossii* (The History of Workers' Artels in the West and in Russia) (1924); *Ocherki po istorii bakinskoy neftedobyvayushchey promyshlennosti* (An Outline History of the Baku Oil Industry) (1940); *Ekonomicheskiye vozreniya dekabristov* (The Economic Views of the Decembrists) (1945); *Problema remeslennykh tsekhov v zakonodatel'stve russkogo absolyutizma* (The Problem of Craft Shops in Absolutist Russian Legislation) (1952); *Ocherki istorii tekstil'noy promyshlennosti dorevolyutsionnoy Rossii* (An Outline History of the Pre-Revolutionary Russian Textile Industry) (2 vol, 1955–1958); *Died:* 2 Aug 1964.

PAZOVSKIY, Ariy Moiseyevich (1887–1953) Opera producer; Pop Artiste of USSR from 1940; CP member from 1941; *Born:* 24 Jan 1887 in Perm'; *Educ:* 1904 grad L. Auer's violin class, Petersburg Conservatory; *Career:* until 1908 stage dir at provincial opera theaters in Perm', Yekaterinburg, Saratov, etc; 1908–10 at Zimin Opera Theater, Moscow; 1910–16 at theaters in Khar'kov, Odessa and Kiev; 1916–18 with opera company of Petrograd Pop Center; 1923–24 and 1925–28 stage dir, Bolshoy Theater; 1929–36 directed opera theaters in Baku, Sverdlovsk, Khar'kov and Kiev; 1936–43 artistic dir, Kirov Opera and Ballet Theater; 1943–48 artistic dir, Bolshoy Theater; *Works:* produced operas: "Faust" (1924); "Die Walküre" (1925); "Boris Godunov" (1927); Chishko's *Bronenosets Potyomkin* (The Battleship Potyomkin) (1937); "Carmen" (1938); Tchaikovsky's *Charodeyka* (The Sorceress) (1941); Koval's "Yemel'yan Pugachyov" (1942); "Ivan Susanin" (1945), etc; *Publ: Zapiski dirizhyora* (Notes of a Stage Director); *Awards:* three Stalin Prizes (1941, 1942 and 1943); *Died:* 6 Jan 1953 in Moscow.

PCHILKA, Olena (real name: KOSACH, Ol'ga Petrovna) (1849–1930) Ukr writer; corresp member, Ukr Acad of Sci from 1927; mother of Ukr poetess Lesya Ukrainka; *Born:* 17 July 1849 in Gadyach, Poltava Province; *Educ:* grad Kiev Inst for Young Ladies of the Nobility; *Career:* 1880's first work printed; worked for journal "Zorya" and almanachs "Rada" and "Pershyy vinok"; 1880, under the pseudonym N.G. Volynskiy, published S. Rudanskiy's "Spivomovky"; 1908–14 edited and published newspaper "Ridnyy kray" in Poltava, then Kiev; from 1921 lived and worked in Kiev; translated works of Gogol, Pushkin, Lermontov, Ovid, etc; also wrote for children; *Publ:* ethnographic study "Ukrainian Ornament" (1876); poem "Olena the Cossack Woman" (1884); verse "Hem-Stitched Pillows" (1885); "Autobiography" (1888); play "World Speech"; "Novelettes" (1908); ethnographic study "Ukrainian Decorations" (1912); reminiscences of M. Staritskiy, M. Lysenko and M. Dragomanov; *Died:* 4 Oct 1930.

PECHERSKIY, Lev Filippovich (1885–1937) Govt official; CP member from 1903; *Born:* 1885; *Career:* played active part in 1905 Revol; during Civil War member, Revol Mil Council, 10th Army; after the war member, Revol Mil Council, Turkestani Front; commanded special forces of Turkestani Front; from 1924 exec govt work; arrested by State Security organs; *Died:* 1937 in imprisonment.

PEDANYUK, Ivan Markovich (1917–1965) Journalist; chm, State Press Comt, Ukr Council of Min from 1963; cand member, CC, CP Ukr from 1960; *Born:* 1917 in vil Zherdenevka, now Vinnitsa Oblast; *Educ:* grad Khar'kov Inst of Journalism; *Career:* from 1933 in journalism; from 1937 worked for newspaper "Visti"; 1939–41 worked for Presidium, Ukr Supr Sov; during WW 2 served with Sov Army; from 1953 dep coordinating ed, 1958–63 chief ed, newspaper "Radyans'ka Ukraina"; 1958–63 chm, Bd, Ukr Journalists' Union; 1959–63 secr, Bd, USSR Journalists' Union; 1963 head, Ideological Dept (for agric), CC, CP Ukr; dep and chm, Draft Bills Commission, Ukr Supr Sov of 1959 convocation; dep, Ukr Supr Sov of 1963 convocation; 1950 visited France with group of Sov journalists; *Awards:* Order of Lenin (1962); Order of the Red Star; Order of the Fatherland War, 2nd Class; Badge of Hon; medals; *Died:* 3 Oct 1965.

PEGEL'MAN, Khans Gustavovich (1875–1938) Est revolutionary, journalist and poet; CP member from 1905; *Born:* 30 Dec 1875 in Est, son of a peasant; *Educ:* 1903–05 studied at Leningrad Business Inst; *Career:* worked as vil teacher; from 1898 journalist; Party work in Revel; Feb 1907 directed Conference of Est RSDRP Orgs in Terioki, Finland; then emigrated and lived in France and England; 1908 returned to Russia; May 1909 arrested and exiled to Siberia; 1911 fled from exile and lived in USA, editing Est Soc-Democratic newspaper "Vus ilm"; after 1917 Feb Revol returned to Est; worked in Revel for Bolshevik newspaper "Kiir"; ed, peasants' newspaper "Maatamees"; 1917, member, Exec Comt and head, Land Dept, Est Sov of Workers and Soldiers' Dep; 1918 Collegium member and head, Est Dept, Pop Comrt of Nationalities, Moscow; 1918–19 member, Est Labor Commune govt; then worked in Sov Russia as teacher and ed, Leningrad journal "Klassivoitlus"; member, CC, CP Est; deleg at all Comintern Congresses; member, Comintern Exec Comt; wrote stories, feuilletons and verse; arrested by State Security organs; *Publ:* verse collections: "Rough Sketches" (1910); "Spring Winds" (1926); poem "To Those Who Fell in the Struggle for Their Brothers" (1936); *Died:* 1938 in imprisonment; posthumously rehabilitated.

PEKARSKIY, Eduard Karlovich (1858–1934) Linguist and ethnographer; Hon member, USSR Acad of Sci from 1931; *Born:* 25 Oct 1858 near Smolevich, now Minsk Oblast, son of a nobleman; *Educ:* studied at Khar'kov Veterinary Inst, from which he was expelled in 1881 for participation in Populist movement; *Career:* 1881–1905 lived in Yakutsk Province, collecting folklore material and studying Yakut language; 1894–96 and 1903 took part in Sibiryak and Nel'kano-Ayan expeditions, collecting ethnographic and econ material among the Ayan Tungus (Evenki); later secr, Ethnography Dept, Russian Geographical Soc; contributed to journal "Zhivaya starina"; from 1927 corresp member, USSR Acad of Sci, compiled "Slovar' yakutskogo yazyka" (Dictionary of the Yakut Language); *Publ:* coauthor, *Slovar' yakutskogo yazyka* (Dictionary of the Yakut Language) (13 vol, 1907–30); *Ocherki byta priayanskikh tungusov* (An Account of the Life of the Ayan Tungus) (1913), etc; *Died:* 29 June 1934.

PEL'SHE (KARKLIS), Robert Andreyevich (1880–1955) Lat Party and govt official; Dr of Philology from 1948; member, Lat Acad of Sci from 1951; CP member from 1898; *Born:* 15 Oct 1880 in Matskayshi, Kurlyan Province, Lat, son of a peasant, *Career:* took part in 1905–07 Revol in Lat; member, CC, Lat Soc-Democratic Party; member, Riga, Yalga and Liyepaya Party Comts; attended 5th (London) RSDRP Congress; 1910 began to write lit criticism; 1911–15 in emigration; secr, Paris Section, Lat Soc-Democratic Party; 1917 member, Moscow City RSDRP(B) Comt; deleg at 1918 and 1919 RCP(B) Congresses; from 1924 head, Art Dept, Main Polit Educ Comt, RSFSR Pop Comrt of Educ; ed, journal "Sovetskoye iskusstvo"; 1945–49 prof, Lat Univ; 1946–55 head, Inst of Ethnography and Folklore, Lat Acad of Sci; Hon Cultural Worker of Lat SSR from 1946; wrote numerous works on art theory; *Publ:Problemy sovremennogo iskusstva* (Problems of Modern Art) (1927); *Nravy i iskusstvo frantsuzskoy revolyutsii* (The Mores and Art of the French Revolution) (1919); *Nasha teatral'naya politika* (Our Theater Policy) (1929); *O literaturnom nasledii i sovetskoy dramaturgii* (Literary Heritage and Soviet Drama) (1933); *Dramaturgiya sotsialisticheskoy industrii* (The Dramaturgy of Socialist Industry) (1934); *Latyshsko-russkiye kul'turnyye svyazi* (Latvian-Russian Cultural Ties) (1954), etc; *Died:* 19 June 1955 in Riga.

PEN'KOVSKIY, Oleg Vladimirovich (1919–1963) Sov intelligence officer; col, artillery from 1950; CP member from 1940; *Born:* 23 Apr 1919 in Vladikavkaz (now Ordzhonikidze), son of an eng killed in Civil War while serving with the White forces; *Educ:* 1939 grad 2nd Kiev Artillery School; 1948 grad Frunze Mil Acad; 1953 grad Mil Dipl Acad; 1959 completed sophisticated weaponry courses at Dzerzhinskiy Artillery Eng Acad; *Career:* 1939–40 battery polit officer; took part in West Bel campaign and Sov-Finnish War; 1940–41 asst head, polit dept, Moscow artillery school, in charge of Komsomol work; 1941–42 Komsomol work instructor, Polit Bd, Moscow Mil Distr, 1942–43 adjutant, Mil Council, Moscow Mil Distr; 1943–44 troop commander, anti-tank regt on 1st Ukr Front; 1944–45 adjutant to artillery commander, 1st Ukr Front (S.S. Varentsov, subsequently Marshal of Artillery), 1945 commander, 51st Guards Anti-Tank Artillery Regt on 1st Ukr Front, 1948–49 staff officer, Moscow Mil Distr, then staff officer, Main Ground Forces Command; from 1953 worked for GenStaff's Main Intelligence Bd; 1953–55 with Mideastern Dept, Main Intellegence Bd; 1955–56 dep mil attache and Main Itelligence Bd resident in Ankara, 1956–58 with Near and Middle Eastern Dept, Main Intelligence Bd; 1959–60 with Middle Eastern Dept, Main Intelligence Bd; from 1950 with Special Group, Dept for Southern and Northern America and UK, Main Intelligence Bd; Apr 1961 established contact with British intelligence agency and from then until Spet 1962 transmitted valuable classified information; 22 Oct 1962 arrested by State Security organs; 11 May 1963 sentenced to death by Mil Collegium of USSR Supr Court; *Awards:* two Orders of the Red Banner, Order of the Fatherland War, 1st Class; Order of the Red Star; Order of Aleksandr Nevskiy; eight medals; *Died:* May 1963 executed.

PEREDERIY, Grigoriy Petrovich (1871–1953) Eng; specialist in bridge-building and construction mech; member, USSR Acad of Sci from 1943; Hon Sci and Tech Worker of RSFSR from 1946; CP member from 1939; *Born:* 11 Oct 1871 in Eysk, Krasnodar Kray; *Educ:* 1897 grad Petersburg Inst of Transport Eng; *Career:* from 1902 at Moscow Eng College; from 1907 at Petersburg Inst of Transport Eng; then lecturer at various other inst, 1901 founded journal "Inzhenernoye delo", which introduced new tech ideas in civil eng; specialized in calculation, theory, design and construction of bridges, wrote original courses on bridge-building; designed many viaducts and bridges; developed original structures for prefabricated bridges and use of ind methods and electro-welding in bridge-building; 1932–38 supervised construction of Volodarskiy ferroconcrete bridge over the River Neva in Leningrad and reconstruction of the Shmidt Bridge; *Publ: K teorii bezraskosnykh form* (The Theory of Braceless Forms) (1906); *Kurs mostov* (A Bridges Course) (3 vol, 6th ed, 1944–51); *Awards:* Order of Lenin; five other orders; Stalin Prize (1943); *Died:* 14 Dec 1953.

PEREGONETS, Aleksandra Fyodorovna (1897–1944) Actress; *Born:* 1897; *Educ:* 1915 grad A. P. Petrovskiy's classes at Petrograd Theatrical School; *Career:* made acting debut in Khar'kov in N.N. Sinel'nikov's company; 1922–25 at Petrograd Theater of Miniatures; then at Kazan' Theater, Leningrad Bolshoy Drama Theater and Novosibirsk Theater; 1931 actress, Simferopol' Theater; during WW 2 worked for underground resistance group in Simferopol' until the group's discovery and capture by the Germans in 1944; *Roles:* Desdemona in "Othello"; Mashen'ka in "Mashen'ka"; Valya in *Strakh* (Fear); Dun'ka in "Lyubov' Yarovaya"; Nastya in Gorky's *Na dne* (The Lower Depths); Korinkina and Lidiya in Ostrovskiy's *Bez viny vinovatyye* (The Innocent Guilty); and *Beshenyye den'gi* (Mad Money); Verochka in Turgenev's *Mesyats v derevne* (A Month in the Country), etc; the Martian Ikhoshka in the film "Aelita" (1924); *Died:* 1944 executed by German troops.

PEREMYTOV, Aleksey Makarovich (1888–1938) Mil commander, capt, Russian Army; div Commander, Sov Army from 1935; *Born:* 1888; *Career:* from 1918 in Red Army; during Civil War chief of staff of a div; head of an operations dept, Staff of Southern Front; asst chief of staff, Western Front; chief of staff, North Caucasian Mil Distr; after Civil War chief of staff, 5th Red Banner Army; lecturer, Operations Fac, Frunze Mil Acad; chief of staff, Moscow, Bel and other mil distr, 1937 arrested by NKVD; *Died:* 1938 in imprisonment, posthumously rehabilitated.

PEREPECHKO, Ivan Nikolayevich (1897–1943) Party and trade-union official; CP member from 1914; *Born:* 1897 in Kiev, son of a laborer; *Career:* 1909-Oct 1917 type-setter in various towns; Party work in Moscow; subjected to reprisals by Tsarist authorities; after 1917 Oct Revol trade-union work; secr and dep chm, Southern Bureau, All-Russian Centr Trade-Union Council; 1922 polit work in Red Army; later chm, Bel Centr Trade-Union Council; secr, Far Eastern Kray CPSU(B) Comt; secr, All-Union Centr Trade-Union Council; from 1934 head, Polit Dept, Oct Railroad, 1921–22 sided with "Workers' Opposition" group; 1930 elected cand member, CC, CPSU(B); arrested by State Security organs; *Died:* 1943 in imprisonment.

PEREPELKIN, Dmitriy Ivanovich (1900–1954) Mathematician; specialist in methods of teaching mathematics; Dr of Physics and Mathematics; corresp member, RSFSR Acad of Pedag Sci, from 1950; CP member from 1941; *Born:* 24 June 1900; *Educ:* 1923 grad Physics and Mathematics Fac, Moscow Univ, *Career:* from 1921 taught at Plekhanov Inst of Nat Econ and at Moscow Power Eng Inst; 1935–54 prof, dept head and dean, Physics and Mathematics Fac, Moscow's Lenin State Teachers' Training Inst; specialized in differential geometry of multidimensional space; worked for learned commissions of RSFSR Min of Educ, compiling geometry syllabus and curricula for teachers' training inst and secondary schools; *Publ:* coauthor, *Uchebnyy atlas po nomografii* (A Teaching Atlas on Nomography) (1933); *Osnovaniya geometrii* (The Bases of Geometry) (1945); *Geometricheskiye postroyeniya v sredney shkole* (Geometric Structures in the Secondary School) (1947); *Kurs elementarnoy geometrii* (A course in Elementary Geometry) (2 vol, 1940–49); *Awards:* Order of Lenin; *Died:* 11 Nov 1954.

PERESTIANI, Ivan Nikolayevich (1870–1959) Actor, film dir and script-writer; Pop Artiste of Geo SSR from 1949; *Born:* 1 Apr 1870 in Taganrog; *Career:* helped found Sov Geo film ind; from 1886 actor, Taganrog theater; from 1906 stage dir under pseudonym Nevedomov; from 1916 film actor, from 1917 film dir; 1917–20 worked for Moscow Film Comt; from 1920 film work in Geo, 1927–28 film dir, Odessa Film Studio, 1929–32 in Yerevan; from 1933 actor and film dir, Tbilisi Film Studio, *Works:* directed films: "Two Hussars"; "Sister of a Decembrist"; *Anna na sheye* (Anna on the Neck) (1917), after Chekhov's story; "The Murder of General Gryaznov" (1921); "Suram Fortress" (1922); "The Red Devils" (1923); "Three Lives" (1925); "Anush" (1931), etc, film roles: Baron Rosen in "The Murder of General Gryaznov"; the General in "The Great Dawn"; the Russian Ambassador in "Georgiy Saakadze"; the Jesuit in "David-bek", etc; *Awards:* three orders; medals; *Died:* 14 May 1959.

PERETERSKIY, Ivan Sergeyevich (1889–1956) Lawyer; specialist in int law; dipl with rank of envoy extraordinary and plen, 2nd class; Dr of Law; *Born:* 1889; *Career:* 1943–46 expert consultant,

1946–47 dep head, Legal Dept, USSR Min of For Affairs; dep head, Contractual Law Dept, USSR Min of For Affairs; 1947–53 counsellor, USSR Min of For Affairs; 1953–55 expert consultant, Contractual Law Dept, USSR Min of For Affairs; wrote a number of works on int law; *Died:* 1956.

PERETTS, Vladimir Nikolayevich (1870–1935) Lit historian; specialist in history of Ukr and Russian lit; member, Russian (USSR) Acad of Sci from 1914; member, Ukr Acad of Sci from 1919; *Born:* 31 Jan 1870 in Petersburg, son of a teacher; *Educ:* 1893 grad History and Philology Fac, Petersburg Univ; *Career:* 1903–14 prof, Kiev Univ; then worked for organs of Russian (USSR) and Ukr Acad of Sci; directed seminars on Russian philology in Kiev and Leningrad; at one time head, Philological Section, Ukr Sci Assoc in Kiev and ed of its organ "Zapiski"; studied Russian and Ukr folklore, ancient Russian apocryphal lit, history of Russian, Ukr and Polish theater; also worked on historiography, bibliography and textology of lit; sponsored and directed compilation of collections "Starinyy teatr v Rossii XVII–XVIII vv." (The Old Theater in Russia in the 17th and 18th Centuries) (1923) and "Starinyy spektakl' v Rossii" (Old Plays in Russia) (1928); *Publ: Kukol'nyy teatr na Rusi* (The Puppet Theater in Rus) (1895); *Materialy k istorii apokrifa i legendy* (Material on the History of Apocryphal Literature and Legend) (2 vol, 1899–1901); *Malorusskiye virshi i pesni v zapisyakh XVI–XVIII vekov* (Little-Russian Verse and Songs in the Writings of the 16th–18th Centuries) (1899); *Istoriko-literaturnyye issledovaniya i materialy* (Research) and Materials on the History of Literature) (3 vol, 1900–1902); *Ocherk starinnoy malorusskoy poezii* (An Outline of Old Litte-Russian Poetry) (1903); *Novyye dannyye po istorii starinnoy ukrainskoy liriki* (New Data on the History of Old Ukrainaian Lyrics) (1907); *Issledovaniya i materialy po istorii starinnoy ukrainskoy literatury XVI–XVIII vekov* (Studies and Material on the History of Old Ukrainian Literature in the 16th–18th Centuries) (3 vol, 1926–29); *Issledovaniya i materialy po istorii starinnoy ukrainskoy literatury XVI–XVIII vekov* (Studies and Material on the History of Old Ukrainian Literature of the 16th–18th Centuries) (1962); *Died:* 24 Sept 1935 in Saratov.

PEREVERZEV, Valer'yan Fyodorovich (1882–1968) Lit historian; member, Communist Acad from 1918; *Born:* 18 Oct 1882 in Bobrov, now Voronezh Oblast; *Educ:* 1901–05 studied at Natural Sci Dept, Physics and Mathematics Fac, Khar'kov Univ, from which he was expelled for participation in revol movement; *Career:* 1905–11 exiled in Narym, then imprisoned; from 1911 taught in Moscow; from 1917 taught and did research work; from 1918 member, Socialist (later Communist) Acad; from 1921 prof, Moscow Univ; in 1920's contributed to journals "Pechat' i revolutsiya" and "Literatura i marksizm"; 1929–30 together with Lunacharskiy, edited "Literaturnaya entsiklopediya" (Literary Encyclopedia); in Moscow trained a group of lit historians, subsequently criticized during 1929–30 controversy; Pereverzev and his supporters were accused of revising Marxism in lit history; specialized in Russian realistic prose of the 19th Century; attempted to study the lit process on the basis of historical-materialistic sociology; 1938 arrested and imprisoned in concetration camps for "vulgar sociologism" in lit studies; after rehabilitation in 1956 concentrated primarily on ancient Russian lit; *Publ: Tvorchestvo Gogolya* (The Work of Gogol) (4th ed, 1928); *K voprosu o monisticheskom ponimanii tvorchestva Goncharova voprosu o monisticheskom ponimanii tvorchestva Goncahrova* (The Monistic Interpretation of Goncharov's Work) (1928); *Problemy marksistskogo literaturovedeniya* (Problems of Marxist Literary Studies) (1929); *Bor'ba za istoricheskiy roman v 30-ye gody* (The Campaign for the Historical Novel in the 1930's) (1935); *Shedevr poeticheskogo masterstva drevnerusskoy literatury* (A Masterpiece of Poetic Skill in Ancient Russian Literature) 1959); *U istokov russkogo realisticheskogo romana* (The Sources of the Russian Realistic Novel) (2nd ed, 1965); *Died:* 5 May 1968 in Moscow.

PEREVODCHIKOV, Innokentiy Nikolayevich (1886–1961) Dermatologist and venerologist; Dr of Med from 1926; prof, Hon Sci Worker of RSFSR from 1959; *Born:* 1886 in Blagoveshchensk, now Amur Oblast; *Educ:* 1913 grad Med Fac, Tomsk Univ; *Career:* 1913–21 intern, Skin and Venereal Disease Clinic, Tomsk Univ; 1921–26 asst prof, Skin and Venereal Disease Clinic, Irkutsk Univ; 1926–32 dir, Irkutsk Leprasorium; 1928–32 dep, Irkutsk City Sov; 1932–61 head, Chair of Skin and Venereal Diseases, Astrakhan' State Med INst; 1932–51 dir, Astrakhan' Clincal Leprasorium; 1933–47 dep, Astrakhan' City Sov; 1935–39 also dep, Stalingrad Oblast Sov; 1951–53 dir, 1953–61 sci dir, All-Union Inst for the Study of Leprosy, Astrakhan'; led nine expeditions to study leprosy and skin and veneral diseases; did research on leprosy, skin reactivity, occupational dermatosis, the incidence of skin and venereal diseases and the treatment of syphilis; wrote over 90 works; *Publ: doctor's thesis Matseratsiya kak metod raspoznovaniya kozhnykh bolezney* (Maceration as a Method of Doagnosing Skin Diseases) (1926), etc; *Awards:* various orders and medals; *Died:* 3 Mar 1961.

PEREVYORTKIN, Semyon Nikiforovich (? –1961) Mil commander; col-gen; CP member from 1921; *Career:* 1921 joined Red Army; during WW 2 served on Western, 2nd Baltic and 1st Bel fronts as a div and corps commander; commanded the corps which captured the Reichstag building during the Berlin offensive; after WW 2 worked for USSR Min of Defense and Min of Internal Affairs; in latter years dir, Bd of Army Training Establishments, *Awards:* Hero of the Sov Union; two Orders of Lenin; Order of Suvorov, 2nd Class; Order of Kutuzov, 2nd Class, Order of Bogdan Khmel'nitskiy, 2nd Class; Order of the Red Star; medals, *Died:* 17 May 1961 in a plane crash.

PERIMOV, A. V. (1897–1945) Party official; CP member from 1915; *Born:* 1897; *Career:* after 1917 Oct Revol Party and admin work in Moscow and Kazan'; then polit work in Red Army; chm, Tomsk Province Exec Comt; from 1921 secr, Altay Province RCP(B) Comt, secr, Dag Oblast Party Comt; instructor, Petrograd Province (RCP(B) Comt; chm, Vladivostok Province Sovnarkhoz; deleg at 11th RCP(B) Congress; 1927 signed Trotskyist platform; 1928 expelled from the Party siding Trotsky-Zinov'yevite Bloc; 1928 readmitted to the Party; 1934 again expelled; arrested by State Security organs and sentenced on charges of anti-Sov activities; *Died:* 1945 in imprisonment.

PERINI, Mariya Iosifovna (1873–1939)Ballet dancer and teacher, *Born:* 1873 in Italy; *Educ:* 1890 grad ballet school at Turin's Royal Opera Theater; *Career:* 1888–91 soloist, ballet company of Turin's Royal Opera Theater; 1890–97 toured with Tiflis Opera Theater; 1894 performed at theaters in Tsaritsyn, Saratov, Astrakhan', etc; 1897–1907 leading dancer, Tiflis Opera Theater; 1907–16 specialized in concert work; 1916 founded in Tbilisi first Geo Classical Dance Studio (from 1921 Ballet School of Tbilisi Opera and Ballet Theater); 1921–35 dir of this school; 1935–38 directed the Choreographic Studio School of this theater; trained V. Chabukiani, N. Ramishvili, V. Vronskiy (Nadiradze), Ye. Chivkaidze, etc; *Died:* 1939.

PERKHUROV, Aleksandr Petrovich (1876–1922) Mil commander; col, Russian Army; Civil War veteran; *Born:* 1876 in Tver' Province, son of a nobleman; *Educ:* grad Gen Staff Acad; *Career:* Mar 1918 joined Savinkov's League for the Protection of the Country and Freedom and headed its Centr Staff; directed Local League branches in Yaroslavl', Rybinsk, Murom, Kaluga, etc; planned anti-Sov revolt in Yaroslavl'; 6–21 July 1918 held Yaroslavl'; after defeat of revolt. fled to Kazan' where he helped Czech Legion defend city from Red Army; Sept 1918 – Mar 1920 continued struggle against Sov regime with Pop Army of Constituent Assembly Comt and with Gen Kolchak's Army; commanded separate Kazan' brigade; commanded various partisan detachments operating behind Red Army lines in Siberia; 1921 infiltrated Ural Mil Distr Staff and tried to foment anti-Sov rebellion in Urals; 1922 arrested by State Security organs; July 1922 sentenced to death in Yaroslavl' by Assizes of Supr Tribunal's Mil Collegium; *Died:* 1922 executed.

PEROVSKAYA, Ol'ga Vasil'yevna (1902–1961) Russian children's writer; *Born:* 9 Apr 1902 in vil Vasil'yevka, Tavrida Province; *Educ:* 1923–26 studied at Biology Fac, Moscow Univ; *Publ:* collected stories *Rebyata i zveryata* (Kids and Beasts) (1925); *Moi volchata* (My Wolf Cubs) (1927); "Ishka and Milka" (1928); *Chubaryy* (Speckled) (1929); coauthor novelette *Ostrov v stepi* (The Island in the Steppe) (1934); stories and novelettes about animals: *Neobyknovennyye rasskazy pro obyknovennykh zhivotnykh* (Uncommon Stories About Common Animals) (1939); *Marmotka* (The Marmot) (1939); *Pro porosyat* (About Piglets) (1941); "Vas'ka" (1941); coauthor, novelette *Zolotoye runo* (The Golden Fleece) (1957); *Dzhan – glaza geroya* (Dzhan – the Eyes of a Hero) (1958); *Tigryonok Vas'ka* (Vas'ka the Tiger Cub) (1959); *Died:* 18 Sept 1961 in Moscow.

PERSOV, Samuil Davidovich (1889–1952) Jewish writer, *Born:* 20 Aug 1889 in Oryol Province, son of a teacher; *Career:* 1907–10 lived in USA, where he published his first story in "Die Freie Arbeiterstimme"; 1910 returned to Russia; 1918–19 printed stories in Jewish Communist journals in Moscow and Khar'kov; *Publ:* novelettes and novels: "Skuls" (1922); "Rye Bread" (1928); "A Real Business" (1927); "Counteraction" (1931); "Day and Night" (1933); *Died:* 1952 in imprisonment.

PERTSEV, Vladimir Nikolayevich (1877–1960) Historian; member, Bel Acad of Sci from 1940; Hon Sci worker of Bel SSR from 1944; *Born:* 28 June 1877; *Educ:* 1903 grad History and Philology Fac, Moscow Univ; *Career:* 1899 and 1901 jailed for involvement in student riots; from 1903 taught at secondary educ establishments in Moscow; 1918 prof, Smolensk Univ; 1918–21 prof, Moscow Teachers' Training Inst; 1921–60 prof, Bel State Univ, Minsk; also worked for Inst of History, Bel Acad of Sci; wrote on gen history and history of Bel; *Publ: Uchebnik drevney istorii* (A Textbook of Ancient History) (2vol, 1912–16); *Gogentsollerny* (The Hohenzollerns) (1918); *Ekonomicheskoye razvitiye Anglii v XIX v.* (The Economic Development of England in the 19th Century) (1924); coauthor and and, *Istoriya Belorusskoy SSR* (The History of the Belorussian SSR) (1954); *Germaniya v XVIII veke* (Germany in the 18th Century) (1955); coauthor, *Ocherki istorii istoricheskoy nauki SSSR* (An Outline History of Historiography in the USSR) (vol 1, 1955); coauthor, *Ocherki istorii Germanii XVIII v.* (An Outline History of 18th-Century Germany) (1959); *Died:* 3 June 1960.

PESHEKHONOV, Aleksey Vasil'yevich (1867–1933) Politician; journalist; *Born:* 21 Jan 1867; *Career:* in 1890's statistician for Kaluga, Oryol, Tver' then Poltava zemstvos; published a number of statistical works; 1901 exiled from Poltava and forbidden to engage in zemstvo work, contributed to journal "Russkoye bogatstvo"; from 1904 worked on its ed comt; sided with liberal Populists; also sympathized with Socialist-Revol Party and contributed to its centr organ "Revolyutsionnaya Rossiya"; 8 Jan 1905 member, public deputation which remonstrated with Svyatopolk-Mirskiy, Min of the Interior, and with the chm of the Comt of Min Witte; arrested in connection with this, imprisoned in Peter and Paul Fortress and then exiled to Pskov Province; after the 17 Oct 1905 Manifesto, returned to Petersburg and helped edit newspaper "Syn otechestsva", although without joining the Socialist-Revol Party; co-founder and co-leader, Pop Socialist Party; June 1917, after the merger of this party with the Laborists (Trudoviks), member, CC, Laborist Pop Socialist Party and edited its newspaper "Narodnoye slovo"; member, Main Org Comt, All-Russian Peasant League; May – Aug 1917 Min of Food in Provisional Govt; then asst chm, Pre-Parliament; after 1917 Oct Revol opposed Sov regime; member, League for the Renaissance of Russia, which adopted "Narodnoye slovo" as its press organ; assigned by the League to report on the operations of the Volunteer Army; 1921 worked for Ukr Centr Statistical Bureau; 1922 deported from USSR for anti-Sov activities; lived in Riga, Prague and Berlin; frequently appealed to Sov govt for permission to return to USSR; from 1927 worked as consultant for Sov trade mission in the Baltic area; *Publ: Zemel'nyye nuzhdy derevni* (The Land Needs of the Village); *Agrarnyye problemy v svyazi s krest'yanskim dvizheniyem* (Agrarian Problems in Connection with the Peasant Movement); *Zemel'nyye nuzhdy derevni i osnovnyye zadachi agrarnoy reformy* (The Land Needs of the Village and the Basic Tasks of Agrarian Reform); *Narodno-sotsialisticheskaya (trudovaya) partiya* (The Popular Socialist (Labor) Party) (1917); *Pochemu my togda ushli (K voprosu o politicheskikh gruppirovkakh v narodnichestve* (Why We Quit [Political Factions in the Populist Movement]) (1918), etc; *Died:* 3 Apr 1933 in Riga; buried in Leningrad.

PESHKOV, M. A. (1897–1934) Writer; CP member from 1917; *Born:* 1897, the son of Maxim Gorky; *Career:* after Oct Revol asst commandant, Kremlin; then served in Red Army; worked for Centr Bd of Gen Army Training; from 1 Mar 1921 dipl courier, RSFSR Pop Comrt of For Affairs; from late 1923 personal secr to Maxim Gorky; *Died:* 1934.

PESHKOVA, Yekaterina Pavlovna (1876–1965) Social worker; writer; wife of Maxim Gorky; *Born:* 14 July 1876 in vil Semiren'ki, Khar'kov Province; *Career:* 1895 proof-reader, "Samarskaya gazeta"; active in soc and revol movement; 1904–05 in Crimea; 1907–14 lived abroad; during WW 1 worked for Soc for Aid to War Victims; after 1917 Oct Revol worked for Polit Red Cross; co-founder, Gorky Museum, Moscow; worked for Gorky Archives, Inst of World Lit; edited two-vol ed of Gorky's letters to her *Pis'ma k Ye. P. Peskovoy* (Letters to Ye. P. Peskhova) (2 vol, 1955 and 1966); *Publ:* memoirs of Gorky and his meetings with Lenin, Lev Tolstoy, Chekhov and Chaliapine: "Pamyatnyy vecher" (A Memorable Evening) (1960); *Vstrechi s A. P. Chekhovym* (Meetings with A. P. Chekhov) (1960); *Vstrechi s Shalyapinym* (Meetings with Chaliapine) (1960); *Otryvki iz vospominaniy o Gor'kom* (Excepts from Memories of Gorky) (1963), etc; *Died:* 26 Mar 1965 in Moscow.

PESKOV, Nikolay Petrovich (1880–1940) Chemist; specialist in collodial chemistry; *Born:* 18 Jan 1880, *Educ:* studied at Moscow Higher Tech College; 1912 grad Breslau Univ; *Career:* 1914–17 worked at Moscow Univ; 1917–20 prof, Omsk Polytech Inst; 1920–27 prof, Ivanovo Polytech Inst; 1920–40 prof, Moscow Chemical Technol Inst; defined concepts of colloidal chemistry system and stability of highly-dispersed systems; 1922 demonstrated the difference between kinetic and aggregative stability of colloids; determined stabilizing role of absorptionsolvate films in the coagulation, protection and aging of sols; did research on practical aspects of colloidal chemistry, such as dyeing, tanning, adhesives, etc; *Publ: Rastvor, suspenziya, kolloid. Teoreticheskoye i eksperimental'noye issledovaniye* (Solution, Suspension, Colloid. Theoretical and Experimental Research) (1922); *Fiziko-khimicheskiye osnovy kolloidnoy nauki* (The Physicochemical Principles of Colloidal Science) (2nd ed, 1934); *Kurs kolloidnoy khimii* (A Course in Colloidal Chemistry) (2nd ed, 1948); *Died:* 15 June 1940.

PESTUN, Ye. G. (1889–1939) Party and govt official; CP member from 1918; *Born:* 1889; *Career:* from late 1917 member, food admin, then dep food comr, Mogilev Province; 1919–20 chm, Gomel Province Consumer Cooperative Union; 1920–21 secr, Gomel Province RCP(B) Comt; 1921–22 CC, RCP(B) plen in Bashkiria; from 1922 exec Party and admin work in Rostov Province, Yakut ASSR, Centr Volga Kray, etc; arrested by State Security organs; *Died:* 1939 in imprisonment.

PETCHENKO, Aleksandr Ivanovich (1896–1964) Obstetrician and gynecologist; Dr of Med and prof from 1943; *Born:* 1896; *Educ:* 1921 grad Odessa Med Inst; *Career:* 1921–33 distr physician in Odessa and Podol'sk Oblasts, intern, Odessa 2nd Clinical Hospital, then supervisor of rayon hospitals and obstetrical and gynecological dept of hospitals in Odessa Oblast; 1933–36 head, Obstetrical and Gynecological Dept, Voronezh City Hospital and asst prof, Chair of Obstetrics and Gynecology, Voronezh Med Inst; 1936–37 asst prof, 1937–43 assoc prof, 1943–47 prof, Chair of Obstetrics and Gynecology, 2nd Leningrad Med Inst; 1947–53 head, Chair of Obstetrics and Gynecology, Odessa Inst of Postgrad Med Training; 1953–55 head, Obstetrics Dept and dep sci dir, Leningrad Inst of Obstetrics and Gynecology; USSR Acad of Med Sci; 1955–62 head, Chair of Obstetrics and Gynecology, Leningrad Pediatric Med Inst; 1962–64 head, Chair of Obstetric and Gynecology, Crimean Med Inst, Simferopol'; member, ed council, journal "Akusherstvo i ginekologiya"; wrote over 100 works; *Publ: Fiziologiya i patologiya sokratitel'noy sposobnosti matki* (The Physiology and Pathology of the Contractile Capacity of the Womb) (1948); *Klinika i terapiya slabosti rodovoy deyatel'nosti* (The Clinical Aspects and Treatment of Weak Labor) (1956); *Akusherstvo* (Obstetrics) (1956); *Tekhnika operatsiy i neotlozhnykh manipulyatsiy v akusherstve* (Operation Techniques and Emergency Manipulations in Obstetrics); *Gormonoterapiya nekotorykh rasstroystv sokratitel'noy funktsii matki* (The Hormone Therapy of Certain Disorders of the Contractile Function of the Womb); coauthor, *Fibromy matki* (Uterine Fibromas); *Metodika prakticheskikh zanyatiy po akusherstvu i ginekologii* (Practical Study Methods in Obstetrics and Gynecology) (1958); *Ginekologiya* (Gynecology) (1960); *Died:* 23 June 1964.

PETERS, Yakov Kristoforovich (1886–1938) Party and govt official; CP member from 1904; *Born:* 1886 in Lat, son of a peasant, *Career:* 1905–07 agitation and propaganda among peasantry; Mar 1907 arrested for revol work; Sept 1908 acquitted by Riga Mil Court; 1909 emigrated to London and became a member, European Group of Lat Soc-Democratic Party; Apr 1917 returned to Russia and worked as propagandist for Party's Mil Org; Summer 1917 elected member, CC, Lat Soc-Democratic Party; ed, newspaper "Tsinya"; at time of 1917 Oct Revol member, All-Russian Centr Exec Comt and member, Mil Revol Comt, Petrograd; Collegium member, All-Russian Cheka; 1918, after the suppression of the Leftist Socialist-Revol revolt, for a while actg chm, All-Russian Cheka; then dep chm, All-Russian Cheka and chm, Revol Tribunal; 1919–20 commandant, Petrograd, then Kiev Fortified Area; member, Mil Council, Tula Fortified Area; 1920–22 member, Turkestani Bureau, CC, RCP(B) and All-Russian Cheka plen for Turkestan; from 1925 dep chm, OGPU; also Collegium member

USSR Pop Comrt of Workers and Peasants' Inspection; from June 1930 chm, CPSU(B) Control Commission and head of workers and peasants' inspection for Moscow Oblast; simultaneously first dep chm, Moscow City Sov and Moscow Oblast Exec Comt; 1937 directed light ind group in Bureau of Party Control Commission; at 12th–16th Party Congresses elected member, CPSU(B) Centr Control Commission; at 17th Party Congress elected member, Party Control Commission, arrested by State Security organs; *Awards:* Order of the Red Banner (1927); *Died:* 1938 in imprisonment; posthumously rehabilitated.

PETERSON, Al'bert Davidovich (1895–1941) Govt official and mil commander; CP member from Apr 1917; *Born:* 1895 in Riga, son of a mason; *Career:* agronomist by profession; during WW 1 served with Lat riflemen unit; 1917 member, Lat Riflemen Exec Comt; 1918 secr, Sov Mission in Switzerland; 1919 Collegium secr, Lat Comrt of Mil Affairs; then Lat Dep Comr of Mil Affairs; 1920–21 dep mil comr, Staff, 5th Army on Eastern Front, after Civil War exec econ work; 1932–35 USSR dep trade rep in Germany; 1936–37 dep head, Main Bd of Wood Pulp Chemical Ind; 1937 arrested by State Security organs; *Died:* 1941 in imprisonment, posthumously rehabilitated.

PETERSON, Karl Andreyevich (1877–1926) Party official and mil commander; CP member from 1898; *Born:* 1877 in Lat; *Educ:* grad volost college; *Career:* from 1895 laborer in Riga; then reporter, democratic newspapers in Riga; 1898 organized one of the first Soc-Democratic circles in Riga, 1899 member, Riga RSDRP Comt; from 1900 Party work in Lepaya; 1901 arrested and exiled for three years to Siberia; late 1904 resumed Party work in Riga and Lepaya; headed revol movement of agric workers; 1908 revol work in Moscow; arrested and sentenced to one year fortress confinement; 1911 returned to Riga; ed, Party newspaper "Layka Balss", etc; late 1912 re-arrested and exiled for three years to Arkhangel'sk Province; from late 1915 secr, health insurance org, "Triangle" Factory in Petrograd; from 1916 served with Lat Riflemen reserve regt in Valmier; 1917 member, Lat Riflemen Exec Comt; deleg and Lat Riflemen rep at 2nd All-Russian Congress of Soviets; at 2nd–6th All-Russian Congress of Soviets elected member, All-Russian Centr Exec Comt; during 1917 Oct Revol member, Mil-Revol Comt; Presidium member, All-Russian Centr Exec Comt; member, Revol Tribunal, All-Russian Centr Exec Comt; 1918 comr, Lat div; 1919 member, Sov Lat Govt; Lat Comr of Mil Affairs and member, Revol-Mil Council, Sov Lat Army; 1920 mil comr, Yeniseysk Province; Nov 1920 – Jan 1921 member, Revol-Mil Council, 5th Army on Eastern Front; from 1921 RSFSR Comrt of For Affairs rep in Novorossiysk; *Died:* 17 Jan 1926 of tuberculosis.

PETERSON, R. A. (1897–1940) Mil commander; CP member from 1919; *Born:* 1897; *Career:* during WW 1 railroad worker; then served in Russian Army; fought in Civil War; 1920–35 Kremlin commandant; 1935–37 dep commander, Kiev Mil District; 1937 arrested by State Security organs; *Died:* 1940 in imprisonment.

PETIN, Nikolay Nikolayevich (1876–1937) Mil commander; col, Russian Army Gen Staff; corps commander, Sov Army from 1935; member, Sov Army Gen Staff, CP member from 1932; *Born:* 2 May 1876 in Vologda, son of a nobleman and officer; *Educ:* 1894 grad Nizhniy Novgorod Cadet Corps; 1897 grad Nikolay Eng College; 1907 grad Gen Staff Acad; *Career:* 1897–1905 officer with eng units of Russian Army; 1904 fought in Russo-Japanese War; 1907–14 staff posts in Warsaw Mil Distr; 1914–18 fought in WW 1; 1914–18 asst dept head, Staff of Northwestern Front; senior adjutant, Quartermaster-Gen Dept, 12th Army; dept head, Quartermaster-Gen Bd, Northwestern Front; commander, infantry regt; chief of staff, 8th Siberian Infantry Div; chief of staff, 34th and 50th Army Corps; asst quartermaster-gen and acting quartermaster-gen, Southwestern Front; from 1918 in Red Army; 1918–20 fought in Civil War on Northern and Southern Fronts; helped rout Polish forces at Kiev and Zhitomir; 1918 head, Draft Bd, White Sea Mil Distr; commandant, officers training school, Krasnoborsk; 1918–19 chief of staff, 6th Army; 1919 chief of staff, Western Front; 1919–20 chief of staff, Southern Front; 1920 chief of staff, Southwestern Front; 1920 denounced to the Cheka former army colleagues who tried to persuade him to side with the Whitist forces; 1921 commander, Kiev Mil Distr; 1921–22 asst commander in chief, RSFSR Armed Forces (for Siberia); and member, RSFSR Revol Mil Council; 1922–23 commander, Siberian Mil Distr; 1923–24 commander, West Siberian Mil Distr; 1924–25 chief, Red Army Main Bd; 1925–28 commander, Siberian Mil Distr, 1928–30 attached for special assignments to USSR Revol Mil Council; also dep chief, Red Army Main Bd; 1930–32 inspector, of eng troops, Red Army; 1932–34 chief of eng, Red Army; directed construction of roads, fortified areas, naval bases and coastal defenses along Sov borders; 1934–37 chief, Red Army Eng Bd; member, Mil Council, USSR Pop Comrt of Defense; 1921 member, Kiev City Sov; 1921–24 member, Siberian Revol Comt; 1924 member, Novonikolayevsk Province Exec Comt; 1925 member, Moscow City Sov; 1925 Presidium member, Siberian Kray Exec Comt; cand member, All-Russian Centr Exec Comt of 11th convocation and USSR Centr Exec Comt of 2nd convocation; 1937 arrested by NKVD; *Awards:* Order of Lenin (1936); Order of the Red Banner (1921); *Died:* 7 Oct 1937 in imprisonment; posthumously rehabilitated.

PETLISHENKO, Mark Aleksandrovich (1880–1938) Actor and stage dir; nephew of Ukr playwright M. Kropivnitskiy; *Born:* 30 Dec 1880 near vil Mar'yanovki, now Kirovograd Oblast; *Educ:* 1895 grad Kupyansk Uyezd college; *Career:* from 1895 with M. Kropivnitskiy's drama company; 1900–07 acted with Saksaganskiy and Karpenko-Karyy's company; then at M. Sadovskiy's Theater, with Assoc of Ukr Actors and at Poltava Theater; after 1917 Oct Revol actor and stage dir, Franko Theater, Krasnozavodsk Theater and Khar'kov Komsomol Theater, *Roles:* Voznyy in Kotlyarevskiy's "Natalka Poltavka"; the Bullock in Kropivnitskiy's "The World-Eater, or the Spider"; Gnat Golyy in Karpenko-Karyy's "Sava Chalyy"; the Mayor in Gogol's *Revizor* (The Government Inspector); the Camp Commandant in Pogodin's *Aristokraty* (The Aristocrats), etc; *Died:* 20 Apr 1938.

PETLYAKOV, Vladimir Mikhaylovich (1891–1942) Aircraft designer; *Born:* 17 June 1891 in vil Sambek, now Rostov Oblast, son of an office worker; *Educ:* 1922 grad Moscow Higher Tech College; *Career:* from 1921 worked at Centr Aerohydrodynamic Inst where, under the initial supervision of A. N. Tupolev, he designed aerosleighs and gliders; from 1923 directed design and construction of wings for planes from ANT-1 to ANT-20; from 1932 directed team working on design and series production of heavy multi-engined airplanes; from 1936 chief designer, Experimental Structures Plant, Centr Aerohydrodynamic Inst; from 1940 chief designer, one of Inst's aircraft plants; developed methods of strength calculation and made a great contribution to the design and series production of heavy, all-metal airplanes; *Awards:* Stalin Prize (1941); two Orders of Lenin; Order of the Red Star; *Died:* 6 Jan 1942 in the course of duty.

PETLYURA, Simon Vasil'yevich (1879–1926) Ukr politician; *Born:* 5 May 1879 in Poltava, son of a carrier; *Educ:* studied at theological seminary, from which he was expelled for participation in Ukr nationalist movement; *Career:* after expulsion from the seminary, emigrated to L'vov; from 1900 member, Revol Ukr Party, then Ukr Soc-Democratic Party; returned to Russia and worked as teacher and book-keeper in Kuban'; from 1904 contributed to Kiev newspapers "Hromad'ska dumka" and "Rada"; from 1906 ed, newspaper "Slovo"; 1907, in order to escape police persecution, moved to Petersburg and then to Moscow, where he worked as book-keeper and took part in "Kozbar'" and "Hromada" nationalist circles; from 1912 ed, newspaper "Ukrainskaya zhizn'"; 1914 drafted into Tsarist Army; from 1915 chm, Main Control Commission, All-Russian Zemstvo Union for Western Front; after 1917 Feb Revol founded and headed Ukr Front Comt, May 1917 elected to All-Ukr Army Comt of Centr Rada, Kiev; became its chm, then secr (min), Centr Rada's Gen Secretariat for Mil Affairs; during the Hetmanate chm, Kiev Province Zemstvo and All-Ukr Zemstvo Union; from 14 Nov 1918 member, Ukr Directory and chief mil ataman, Ukr Pop Republ; from 10 Feb 1919 chm, Ukr Directory; after defeat of Director troops, fled to Warsaw and until his death headed the Ukr Pop Govt in exile; 1924 moved to Paris; *Died:* 26 May 1926 assassinated in Paris.

PETRENKO, Yelizaveta Fyodorovna (1880–1951) Singer (mezzo-soprano); singing teacher; prof, Moscow Conservatory from 1935; Hon Art Worker of RSFSR from 1944; *Born:* 23 Nov 1880 in Akhtyrka, Khar'kov Province; *Educ:* 1905 grad N. A. Iretskaya's class, Petersburg Conservatory; *Career:* 1905–15 soloist, Mariinskiy Theater, then at Theater of Pop Center; 1908–14 performed with Chaliapine in "Russian Seasons Abroad" in London, Paris and Rome; 1917–19 at Petrograd Musical Drama Theater, 1921–22 at Moscow Musical Drama Theater; *Roles:* Marfa and Marina in Moussorgsky's "Khovanshchina" and "Boris Godunov"; Spring and Lyubasha in Rimsky-Korsakov's *Snegurochka* (The Snow-Maiden) and *Tsarskaya nevesta* (The Bride of the Tsar);

Delilah in Saint-Saens' "Samson and Delilah"; Amneris in Verdi's "Aida"; Carmen in Bizet's "Carmen"; *Awards:* Order of the Red Banner of Labor; *Died:* 26 Oct 1951 in Moscow.

PETRIKOVSKIY (Party name: PETRENKO), Sergey Ivanovich (1894–1964) Mil commander; maj-gen, Eng and Tech Corps from 1943; CP member from 1911; *Born:* 3 Sept 1894, son of a teacher; *Educ:* 1914–15 studied at Petrograd Univ; 1937 grad Air Force Acad; *Career:* "Pravda" activist; worked for Duma Bolshevik faction; 1914 went on Party assignment to Cracow to contact Lenin and organized the transport of people and lit via Lublin; Mar 1915 arrested and exiled to Eastern Siberia; summer 1916 drafted into Russian Army; helped establish Bolshevik orgs among the troops; as private with 1st Reserve Machine Gun Regt took part in 1917 Feb Revol in Petrograd; member, Vasiliy Ostrov Rayon Party Comt; worked for Mil Org, CC, RSDRP(B); deleg at Petrograd and Apr RSDRP(B) Conferences; took part in 1917 Oct Revol; member, Mil Revol Comt, and commander of revol garrison in Khar'kov; 1918 helped organize partisans in Ukr; 1918–20 chief of staff, 1st Ukr Insurgent Div and 1st Trans-Dnieper Div; commander, Crimean Forces Group; mil comr, 25th Infantry Div; commander, separate cavalry brigade, 44th Infantry Div; commander, 52nd and 40th Infantry Divs; 1921–22 mil comr, Main Mil Mang Bd and dep mil comr, Red Army Main Supply Bd; 1923–25 dep dir, 1st Aircraft Plant; organized series production of first Sov fighter planes; 1926–27 USSR Revol Mil Council plen abroad; then exec admin work; during WW 2 exec posts in mil ind; head, Air Force Centr Aircraft Repair and Experimental Base; *Died:* 28 Jan 1964.

PETROV, Ivan Yefimovich (1896–1958) Mil commander; officer, Russian Army; arm gen, Sov Army from 1944; CP member from 1918; *Born:* 30 Nov 1896 in Trubchevsk, son of an artisan; *Educ:* studied at theological seminary; 1917 grad ensigns' school; 1926 and 1931 grad advanced officer training courses; *Career:* fought in WW 1; 1918 volunteered for Red Army; fought in Civil War; from 1920 served in Centr Asia as brigade comr, 11th Cavalry Div, 1922–26 commander, 1st Turkm Infantry Div; 1931 commander, separate Uzbek brigade; fought against Basmachi; until 1937 commandant, Tashkent Infantry College; removed from this post for "lack of vigilance"; 1941 formed mechanized corps in Centr Asian Mil Distr; with start of Sov-German hostilities commanded 2nd Cavalry Div, then 25th Chapayev Infantry Div; fought in defense of Odessa; from 5 Oct 1941 commanded Separate Maritime Army and supervised its evacuation from Odessa to the Crimea; from 9 Nov 1941, while retaining command of Maritime Army, dep to Admiral Oktyabr'skiy in charge of land defense of Sebastopol, 30 June 1942, upon orders from Supr Command Headquarters, evacuated by submarine from Sebastopol; 26 Aug – 12 Oct 1942 commander, 44th Army on the Transcaucasian Front; 11 Oct 1942 – 16 Mar 1943 commander, Black Sea Forces Group on Transcaucasian and North Caucasian Fronts; 16 Mar – 13 May 1943 1st dep commander and chief of staff, North Caucasian Front; 13 May – 20 Nov 1943 commander, North Caucasian Front; directed operations for liberation of Novorossiysk and Taman Peninsula; from 20 Nov 1943, after liquidation of North Caucasian Front, commanded Separate Maritime Army; prepared operation for liberation of the Crimea but was suddenly replaced as army commander; 14 Apr – 5 June 1944 commander, 2nd Bel Front; removed from this post due to intrigues on the part of Mekhlis; 5 Aug 1944 – Apr 1945 commander, 4th Ukr Front, removed from this post following abortive offensive in the Carpathians; from Apr 1945 chief of staff, 1st Ukr Front; 1945–52 commander, Turkestani Mil Distr; 1952–58 1st dep chief inspector, then head, Main Combat and Physical Training Bd; 1st dep commander in chief of ground forces; chief inspector, Min of Defense; dep, USSR Supr Sov of 1946, 1950 and 1954 convocations, dep, Uzbek Supr Sov; member, CC, CP Uzbek; *Awards:* Hero of the Sov Union (1945); five Orders of Lenin; four Orders of the Red Banner; Order of Suvorov, 1st Class; Order of Kutuzov, 1st Class; Order of the Red Banner of Uzbek SSR; Order of the Red Banner of Turkm SSR; Order of the Red Star; medals; *Died:* 7 Apr 1958 in Moscow.

PETROV, Mikhail Petrovich (1898–1941) Mil commander; maj-gen from 1940; *Born:* 1898 in vil Zalustyuzh'ye, Petersburg Province, son of a stove-maker; *Educ:* 1927 grad Tambov infantry school; 1932 grad Leningrad Tank Commanders Courses, *Career:* until 1917 metalworker at munitions plant in Petrograd; 1917 took part in Feb and Oct Revol; from 1918 in Red Army; fought in Civil War in Ukr, Volga Region, Centr Asia and Transcaucasia; 1932–36 commands with armored troops; 1936–37 volunteer with Spanish Republ tank troops; from 1937 commander, Kalinovskiy Mechanized Corps, then 15th Tank Corps; 1939 took part in Galician campaign; 1941 commander, 50th Army on Bryansk Front; dep, USSR Supr Sov of 1937 convocation; Oct 1941 seriously wounded as the remnants of his army were trying to break out of German encirclement; left with peasants in German-occupied territory; *Awards:* Hero of the Sov Union (1937); Order of Lenin; Order of the Red Star; medals; *Died:* Nov 1941 of gangrene.

PETROV, Nikolay Nikolayevich (1876–1964) Surgeon and oncologist; Dr of Med from 1902; prof from 1912; corresp member, USSR Acad of Sci from 1939; member, USSR Acad of Med Sci from 1944; Hon Sci Worker of RSFSR from 1935; *Born:* 14 Dec 1876 in Petersburg; *Educ:* 1899 grad Petersburg Mil Med Acad; *Career:* after grad did postgrad work at Propaedeutical Surgical Clinic, Petersburg Mil Med Acad; from 1900 member, Pirogov Surgical Soc; 1902 defended doctor's thesis on tuberculosis of the joints after injury; 1903–05 worked at Pasteur Inst, Paris, and at surgical clinis in Austria, France, Switzerland and Germany, from 1905 assoc prof, Petersburg Mil Med Acad; 1908–12 senior asst, surgical clinics in Austria, France, Switzerland and Germany; from Women's Med Inst; from 1912 prof, Hospital Surgery Clinic, Warsaw Univ; 1913–58 head, Chair of Surgical Clinic, Petersburg (Leningrad) Inst of Postgrad Med Training; 1914–17 Red Cross consulting surgeon, Western Front; 1918–20 surgeon, Armavir-Tuapse Railroad Hospital; 1920–21 consulting surgeon, 9th Kuban' Red Army and prof of surgery, Kuban' Univ, Krasnodar; then head, Surgical Dept, Centr Red Army Hospital, Petrograd; 1921–26 prof, Hospital Surgical Clinic, 1st Petrograd (Leningrad) Med Inst; from 1924 chm, Pirogov Surgical Soc; 1926–42 founder-dir, 1942–46 sci dir, Leningrad Oncological Inst, which now bears his name; founder, Experimental Cancer Laboratory, Sukhumi Branch, All-Union Inst of Experimental Med (now the Sukhumi Med-Biological Station); 1930–33 member, CC, German Cancer Soc; 1931–37 chm, Cancer Comt, USSR Pop Comrt of Health; Bureau member, All-Union Surgeons' Soc, from 1935 member, Exec Comt and Admin Council, Int Cancer League; from 1958 hon member, Int Surgical Soc; dep, Leningrad City Sov; ed, journals "Vestnik khirurgii imeni I. I. Grekova", "Voprosy onkologii", etc; co-ed "Surgery" section, "Bol'shaya meditsinskaya entsiklopediya" (Large Medical Encyclopedia); did major research on oncology, surgical tuberculosis, free osteoplasty, etc; trained numerous outstanding surgeons and oncologists; wrote over 300 works; *Publ:* doctor's thesis *Eksperimental'nyye dannyye k voprosu o bugorchatke sustavov v svyazi s povrezhdeniyami* (Experimental Data on Tuberculosis of the Joints After Injury) (1902); *Obshcheye ucheniye ob opukholyakh* (General Oncology) (1910); *Svobodnaya plastika kostey* (Free Osteoplasty) (1913); *Lecheniye infitsirovannykh ran* (The Treatment of Infected Wounds) (1915); *Yazvennaya bolezn' zheludka i dvenadtsatiperstnoy kishki i yeyo khirurgicheskoye lecheniye* (Gastric and Duodenal Ulcers and Their Surgical Treatment) (1941); *Kratkiy ocherk sravnitel'noy patologii opukheley u zhivotnykh i cheloveka* (A Brief Comparative Pathology of Tumors in Animals and Man) (1941); *Lecheniye voyennykh raneniy* (The Treatment of War Wounds) (7th ed, 1945); coauthor, *Dinamika vozniknoveniya i razvitiya zlokachestvennogo rosta v eksperimente na obez'yanakh* (The Appearance Development of a Malignant Growth in an Experiment with Monkeys) (1952); *Voprosy khirurgicheskoy deontologii* (Problems of Surgical Deontology) (1956), etc; *Awards:* three Orders of Lenin; Stalin Prize (1942); I. I. Mechnikov Prize (1953); Hero of Socialist Labor (1957); Lenin Prize (1963); Gold Star; two Orders of the Red Banner of Labor; medals; *Died:* 2 Mar 1964 in Leningrad.

PETROV, Nikolay Vasil'yevich (1890–1964) Stage dir; Pop Artiste of RSFSR from 1945; Dr of Arts; prof; *Born:* 22 June 1890; *Educ:* 1908–10 studied under Nemirovich-Danchenko in Production Class, Moscow Arts Theater; *Career:* 1910–33 asst stage dir, stage, dir, then dir and artistic dir, Alexandrine Theater (now Pushkin Drama Theater) Leningrad; from 1933 stage dir, Khar'kov Russian Drama Theater; from 1937 stage dir, Moscow Theater of the Revol; from 1939 chief stage dir, Centr Transport Theater; from 1948 stage dir, Moscow Satire Theater; from 1956 stage dir, Pushkin Drama Theater, Moscow; also directed Acting Fac and Producing Fac, State Inst of Stagecraft; *Productions:* Lunacharskiy's *Faust i gorod* (Faust and the City) (1921); Oscar Wilde's "An Ideal Husband" (1923); co-producer, Lunacharskiy's *Yad* (Poison)

(1925); Gogol's *Revizor* (The Government Inspector) (1927); Afinogenov's *Chudak* (The Crank) (1930); Chekhov's *Vishnyovyy sad* (Cherry Orchard) (1934); Korneychuk's *Pravda* (The Truth) (1937); Mdivani and Kirov's *Molodoy chelovek* (The Young Man) (1946); co-producer, Romashov's *Velikaya sila* (The Great Force) (1947); *Igrok* (The Gambler), after Dostoyevskiy (1956); *Banya* (The Bath-House) (1958), etc; *Publ: Azbuka teatra* (The Theater ABC) (1927); *Rezhissyor chitayet p'yesu* (The Stage Director Reads a Play) (1934); *Rezhissyor v teatre* (The Stage Director in the Theater) (1961); *Put' k tvorchestvu* (The Path to Creativity) (1963), etc; *Awards:* Order of the Red Banner of Labor, Badge of Hon; medals, Stalin Prize (1948); *Died:* 29 Sept 1964.

PETROV, Pyotr Polikarpovich (1892–1941) Russian writer; *Born:* 13 Jan 1892 in vil Perovskoye, Yeniseysk Province; *Educ:* 1923 grad Krasnoyarsk Inst of Publ Educ; *Career:* fought in the Civil War in Siberia; chm, Joint Council, Badzheysk Steppe Partisan Republ; head, Agitation Dept, Partisan Army; 1919 ed, Minusinsk newspaper "Sokha i molot"; 1927 first work printed; *Publ:* novels: "Borel'" (1928); *Shaytan-pole* (Satan's Field) (1933); *Zoloto* (Gold) (1934); *Polovod'ye* (The Flood) (1936); novelettes: *Sayany shumyat* (Sound of the Sayans) (1932); *Krutyye perevaly* (Steep Passes) (1932), etc; arrested by State Security organs; *Died:* 23 Oct 1941 in imprisonment; posthumously rehabilitated.

PETROV, Sergey Mikhaylovich (1902–1962) Party historian; prof; CP member from 1924; *Born:* 25 Sept 1902 in Kaluga, son of an office worker; *Educ:* 1928 grad Acad of Communist Training; 1932–34 studied at Inst of Red Prof; *Career:* from 1918 volunteer in Red Army, in early 1920's lecturer, Kaluga Province Party School and head, Dept of Propaganda, Kaluga Province Party Comt; from 1928 assoc prof, Chair of Party History, Ural Communist Univ and senior assoc, Commission for the Study of Party History, Ural Oblast CPSU(B) Comt, from 1932 lectured on Party history at Moscow Inst of Sov Construction and Law and at Communist Inst of Journalism; 1934–40 head, Polit Dept, "Uralets" Sovkhoz; then exec Party work; also lectured at Chelyabinsk Teachers' Training Inst; 1940–41 section head, Inst of Marx-Engels-Lenin and lecturer, Higher Party School, CC, CPSU(B); from 1941 volunteer with Sov Army at the front, then polit work; 1949–52 member, ed bd, newspaper "Pravda" and lecturer, Higher Party School and Acad of Soc Sci, CC, CPSU(B); 1952–61 head, Dept of Party History, Higher Party School, CC, CPSU; 1961–62 at Inst of Marxism-Leninism, CC, CPSU; directed team compiling vol 1 of multi-vol "Istoriya KPSS" (History of the CPSU); *Publ: Rabocheye dvizheniye i rasprostraneniye marksizma v Rossii* 1883–1894) (The Workers' Movement and the Spread of Marxism in Russia in 1883–1894); *Nachalo revolyutsionnoy deyatel'nosti V. I. Lenina* (The Start of V. I. Lenin's Revolutionary Work); *Bor'ba za sozdaniye marksistskoy partii v Rossii v 1894–1904 gg.* (The Campaign to Found a Marxist Party in Russia in 1894–1904), etc; *Awards:* two Orders of the Red Star; medals; *Died:* 23 Apr 1962.

PETROV (real name: KATAYEV), Yevgeniy Petrovich (1903–1942) Russian satirical writer; CP member from 1939, *Born:* 13 Dec 1903 in Odessa, son of a teacher; brother of writer V. Katayev; *Educ:* 1920 grad classical high school; *Career:* from 1920 corresp, Ukr News Agency; then criminal investigations inspector, 1923 moved to Moscow and turned to journalism; worked for satirical journal "Krasnyy perets"; 1924–25, under pseudonym "Fyodorov the Foreigner", wrote humorous stories and feuilletons on int topics; printed satirical feuilletons in newspapers "Komsomol'skaya pravda" and "Gudok"; 1925–26 in Red Army; 1926 began to write lit works in collaboration with I. Il'f; 1935 toured USA together with Il'f; at start of WW 2 mil corresp; *Publ: Sbornik yumoristicheskikh rasskazov* (A Collection of Humourous Stories) (1926); coauthor, novel *Dvenadtsat' stul'yev* (The Twelve Chairs) (1928); coauthor, novelette *Svetlaya lichnost'* (A Radiant Personality) (1928); coauthor, cycle of satirical novellas *1001 den', ili Novaya Shakherezada* (The 1,001 Days, or the New Sheherezade) (1929); coauthor, novel *Zolotoy telyonok* (The Golden Calf) (1931); coauthor, collection of humorous stories *Kak sozdavalsya Robinzon* (How Robinson Was Created); coauthor, travel notes *Odnoetazhnaya Amerika* (One-Story America); coauthor, comedy *Bogataya nevesta* (The Rich Bride) (1936); coauthor, play *Nervnyye lyudi* (Nervous People); coauthor, collected stories "Tonya" (1937); comedy *Ostrov mira* (The Island of Peace) (1939); *Frontovoy dnevnik* (Frontline Diary) (1942), etc; *Awards:* Order of Lenin (1939); *Died:* 2 July 1942 killed while returning from besieged Sebastopol.

PETROV-VODKIN, Kuz'ma Sergeyevich (1878–1939) Russian artist and writer; Hon Art Worker of RSFSR from 1930; *Born:* 24 Oct 1878 in Khvalynsk; *Educ:* 1905 grad Moscow College of Painting, Sculpture and Architecture; *Career:* 1901 worked in Ashbe's studio in Munich; made various trips to Western Europe and Africa; member, "World of Art" artists' assoc; from 1913 theater work; from 1917 prof, Petrograd Higher Art College; from 1932 chm, bd, Leningrad Artists' Union; *Works:* paintings: "The Shore" (1908); "Sleep" (1910); "Boys at Play" (1911); "Workers" (1912); "Mother" (1913); sets and costumes for "Orleanskaya deva" (The Maid of Orleans) (1913); paintings: "Girls on the Volga" (1915); "Morning" (1917); "1918 in Petrograd" (1920); sets and costumes for play *Dnevnik satany* (Satan's Diary) (1923); paintings: "The Death of a Commissar" (1928); "1919. Alarm" (1935); sets and costumes for "The Marriage of Figaro" (1935); illustrations for Gorky's stories, children's books, etc; *Publ:* play *Zhertvennyye* (The Sacrificial) (1906); *Poyezdka v Afriku* (A Journey to Africa) (1910); "Aoyya" (1914); *Samarkandiya. Iz putevykh nabroskov* (Samarkand. Travel Notes) (1923); *Moya povest'. Pervaya chast'. Khlynovsk* (My Tale. Part I. Khlynovsk) (1930); *Moya povest'. Vtoraya chast'. Prostranstvo Evklida* (My Tale. Part II. Euclidian Space) (1932), etc; *Died:* 15 Feb 1939 in Leningrad.

PETROVA, Kseniya Semyonovna (1892–1942) Mordovian writer; *Born:* 1892 in Buguruslan, Samara Province, daugher of a peasant; *Educ:* completed teachers' courses; *Career:* after 1917 Oct Revol worked as teacher; 1926 first verse published; *Publ:* plays: "Summer Night" (1932); "In the Old Way" (1933); "Dark Force" (1932); "How they Deafened" (1933); *Died:* 25 Feb 1942.

PETROVA, Mariya Kapitonovna (1874–1948) Physiologist; Dr of Med from 1914; prof from 1935; Hon sci Worker of RSFSR from 1945; pupil of I. P. Pavlov; *Born:* 6 Apr 1874; *Educ:* 1904 grad Bestuzhev Courses; 1908 grad Petersburg Women's Med Inst; *Career:* after grad asst prof, Hospital Therapy Clinic, Petersburg Women's Med Inst, then asst prof, Inst of Experimental Med an Pavlov Physiologial Inst, 1914 defended doctor's thesis on "The Theory of the Irradiation of Excitation and Inhibitory Processes"; from 1935 head, Chair of the Physiology and Pathology of Higher Nervous Activity, Leningrad Inst of Postgrad Med Training; did research on the laws of irradiation of nervous processes, sleep inhibition, protective inhibition, the formation of dynamic stereotypes, types of higher nervous activity, motilic disturbances of nervous processes (pathological inertness and explosivity), etc; established that experimentally induced neuroses lead to premature decrepitude, diseases of the digestive tract and dermodystrophic processes and encourage the development of malignant tumors, defined the protective role of inhibition; made an interesting study of the effect of various doses of bromine and caffeine on different types of nervous systems, during WW 2 studied the effect of close explosions on higher nervous activity during the Leningrad blockade; wrote some 200 works; *Publ:* doctor's thesis *K ucheniyu ob irradiatsii vozbuzhdeniya i tormoznykh protsessov* (The Theory of the Irradiation of Excitation and Inhibitory Processes) (1914); *Sobraniye trudov* (Collected Works) (3 vol, 1953); *O roli funktional'no oslablennoy kory golovnogo mozga v vozniknovenii razlichnykh patologicheskikh protsessov v organizme* (The Role of the Funtionally Delibated Cerebral Cortex in the Emergence of Varios Pathological Processes in the Body) (1955); *Awards:* Pavlov Prize (1940); Stalin Prize (1946), etc; *Died:* 14 May 1948 in Leningrad.

PETROVA, Yevgeniya Nikolayevna (1886–1961) Educationist; specialist in methods of teaching Russian; prof; corresp member, RSFSR Acad of Pedag Sci from 1947; CP member from 1917; *Born:* 20 Apr 1886; *Educ:* 1908 grad Petersburg Teachers' Training Inst; *Career:* 1902 began to teach at zemstsvo school in Tserskosel'ye Uyezd; from 1924 research and educ work in Leningrad at: Inst of Sci Pedagogics; Leningrad Univ; Inst of Advanced Teachers' Training; Herzen Teachers' Training Inst; Pedag Research Inst, RSFSR Acad of Pedag Sci; worked on new teaching aid for schools – "Grammaticheskaya khrestomatiya" (A Grammar Anthology); *Publ: Bor'ba s oshibkami v bezudarnykh glasnykh v sredney shkole* (Countering Errors with Unstressed Vowels in the Secondary School) (1935); *Grammatika v sredney shkole* (Grammar in the Secondary School) (1936); *God raboty* (A Year of Work) (1939); *V. G. Belinskiy o prepodavanii russkogo yazyka v shkole* (V. G. Belinskiy on Teaching Russian in School) (1961); *Elementy morfologii v nachal'nykh klassakh* (Elements of Morphology in the First Grades) (1961); coauthor, *Grammatiches-*

kiye igry dlya nachal'nykh klassov (Grammatical Games for the First Grades) (1963); *Died:* 25 Dec 1961.

PETROVSKIY, Grigoriy Ivanovich (1878–1958) Party and govt official; CP member from 1897; *Born:* 4 Feb 1878 in Khar'kov, son of a craftsman; *Career:* worked at various plants in Yekaterinoslav, Khar'kov and Nikolayev and in the mines of the Donbass; from mid-1890's engaged in underground revol work, printing and distributing proclamations and illegal lit and participating in strikes; joined Soc-Democratic circles in Yekaterinoslav; frequently arrested and imprisoned; 1905–07 organized polit activities of Yekaterinoslav and Yekaterinin railroad workers; 1905 co-founded, Yekaterinoslav Sov of Workers' Dep; member and secr of this Sov, and secr of the Yekaterinoslav Combatant Strike Comt; 1906 emigrated to Germany; 1907 returned to Russia and worked at plants in Mariupol'; 1912 elected member, 4th State Duma, representing Yekaterinoslav Province workers' curia; 1913 attended Cracow and Poronin RSDRP CC conferences with Party workers; Nov 1914, together with other Bolshevik dep, arrested, sentenced to deprivation of rights and settlement in Eastern Siberia; exiled to Turukhan Kray; 1916 arrested in Yeniseysk and exiled to Yakutsk; togesther with Ye. Yaroslavskiy and S. Ordzhonikidze, organized 1917 Feb Revol in Yakutsk; chm, Yakutsk Public Security Comt and Yakutsk Oblast Comr; after 1917 Feb Revol and his return from exile carried out revol work in Petrograd; helped prepare and carry out Oct Revol, Nov 1917 – Mar 1919 RSFSR Pop Comr of Internal Affairs; took part in peace negotiations with Germany and signed 1918 Treaty of Brest-Litovsk; 1919–39 chm, All-Ukr Centr Exec Comt and dep chm, USSR Centr Exec Comt, dep, USSR Supr Sov of 1st convocation; 1938 dep chm, Presidium, USSR Supr Sov; 1920, at 9th Party Congress, elected cand member, CC; 1921–39 member, CC, CPSU(B); 1926–39 cand Politbureau member, CC, CPSU(B); 1939 removed from all polit posts and his sons were arrested; from 1939 dep dir, USSR Revolution Museum; *Awards:* Order of Lenin; Order of the Red Banner; three Orders of the Red Banner of Labor; various medals; 1926 Yekaterinoslav renamed Dnepropetrovsk in his hon; *Died:* 9 Jan 1958; buried on Moscow's Red Square.

PETROVSKIY, Leonid Grigor'yevich (1897–1941) Mil commander; officer, Russian Army; lt-gen, Sov Army from 1941; CP member from 1916; *Born:* 1897 in vil Nelepo-Shcherbinskiy rudnik Donetsk Oblast, son of Ukr Bolshevik G.I. Petrovskiy; *Educ:* during WW 1 grad ensigns' school; 1922 grad Red Army Mil Acad; *Career:* fought in WW 1; from 1918 in Red Army; 1918–20 platoon commander, intelligence chief, then chief of staff of a brigade; regt commander, then chief of staff of a div; fought in Civil War on Northern, Eastern and Southern Fronts; from 1922 commanded battalion, regt, then cavalry div; 1936–37 commanded Proletarian Div in Moscow, then 5th Infantry Corps in Bel Mil Distr, 1937 commander, Centr Asian Mil Distr; 1938 dep commander, Moscow Mil Distr; 1938 expelled from CP, discharged from Red Army and arrested by NKVD; released after a while and 1939 readmitted to CP; 1940 reinstated in Red Army; 1940–41 commander, 63rd Infantry Corps; fought in defense of the Dnieper; June 1941 his corps launched a counter-attack which liberated Rogachev and Zhlobin; *Died:* 17 Aug 1941 killed while extricating his corps from German encirclement; buried in vil Rudenko; 1944 reburied with mil honors in vil Staraya Rudnya.

PETRUSENKO, Oksana Andreyevny (1900–1940) Singer (lyric dramatic soprano); Pop Artiste of Ukr SSR from 1939; *Born:* 5 Feb 1900 in vil Balakleya, Khar'kov Province; *Educ:* studied at Kiev's Lysenko Musical Drama Inst and under P. Saksaganskiy; *Career:* 1917–20 with I. Sagatovskiy's Touring Theater; from 1923 with P. Saksaganskaya's company; 1927–30 at opera theaters in Kazan', Samara, etc; 1934–40 soloist, Shevchenko Opera and Ballet Theater, Kiev; also performed Ukr folk songs at concerts; *Roles:* Natalka in Lysenko's "Natalka-Poltavka"; Odarka in Gulak-Artemovskiy's *Zaporozhets za Dunayem* (A Dnieper Cossack Beyond the Danube); Kupava in Rimsky-Korsakov's *Snegurochka* (The Snow-Maiden); Zemfira in Rachmaninov's "Aleko"; Lushka in Dzerzhinskiy's *Podnyataya tselina* (Virgin Soil Upturned), etc; *Awards:* Badge of Hon; *Died:* 15 July 1940 in Kiev.

PETRUSHEVSKIY, Dmitriy Moiseyevich (1863–1942) Historian, prof from 1897; member, USSR Acad of Sci from 1929; *Born:* 13 Sept 1863 in vil Kobrinovo, now Chernigov Oblast; *Educ:* 1886 grad Kiev Univ; *Career:* 1897–1906 prof, Warsaw Univ; 1906–11 prof, Chair of Gen History, Moscow Univ; 1911 resigned in protest against policies of Educ Min Kasso, 1914–17 prof, Petersburg Univ; 1917–42 prof, Moscow Univ; in 1920's also dir, Inst of History, Russian Assoc of Soc Sci Research Institutes; specialized in Medieval history of Western Europe; followed socio-econ trend in old Russian Medieval studies and was somewhat influenced by historical materialism; after 1907 gradually sided with neo-Kantian idealism of Rikkert and Max Weber in philosophy of history; also sympathized with Austrian historian Dopscha in studying West European feudalism; approached feudalism from a polit-legal stand, regarding it as a polit institution unconnected with specifid forms of econ life, but rather as a purely polit-state system of co-related and subordinated soc strata; in late 1920's this view brought him into conflict with the Marxist historians of M.N. Pokrovskiy's school; from 1934 regained his former prestige following the collapse of the Pokrovskiy school; *Publ: Vosstaniye Uota Taylera* (The Watt Tyler Revolt) (2 vol, 1897–1901); *Ocherki po istorii angliyskogo gosudarstva i obshchestva v sredniye veka* (An Outline History of the English State and English Society in the Middle Ages) (1903); *Ocherki po istorii srednevekovogo obshchestva i gosudarstva* (An Outline History of Medieval Society and Statehood) (1907); *Ocherki iz ekonomicheskoy istorii srednevekovoy Yevropy* (An Outline Economic History of Medieval Europe) (1928), etc; *Died:* 12 Dec 1942.

PEVZNER, Manuil Isaakovich (1872–1952) Therapist and dietologist, prof from 1927; Hon Sci Worker of RSFSR from 1936; *Born:* 1872; *Educ:* 1900 grad Med Fac, Moscow Univ; *Career:* after grad specialized in therapeutics and dietology at Moscow Univ hospital clinics; from 1908 lectured on gastrointestinal diseases at Moscow Univ; 1921 founder, Dept of Diseases of the Digestive Organs and Dietetics (later Dietetic Clinic), Spa Clinic, Health Resort Dept, RSFSR Pop Comrt of Health; 1924–27 assoc prof, 1st Moscow Univ; from 1927 prof, Chair of Diseases of the Digestive Organs and Dietetics, Inst of Balneology; from 1932 head, Chair of Dietetics, Centr Inst of Postgrad Med Training, Moscow; made a major contribution to the development of theoretical and practical dietetics in the USSR; led trend from organotherapy to dietotherapy as a means of influencing the body as a whole and its reactive properties in particular; did research on dietetics for acute and chronic rheumatism, heart diseases and hypertonia and extended his findings to the treatment of other diseases; wrote over 100 works; *Publ: Osnovy dietetiki i dietoterapii* (The Principles of Dietetics and Dietotherapy) (1927); *Ratsional'noye (dieteticheskoye) lechebnoye pitaniya* (Rational [Rational] Therapeutic Nutrition) (1937); *Ratsional'noye i lechebnoye pitaniye* (Rational and Therapeutic Nutrition) (1940); *Yazva zheludka i dvenadtsatiperstnoy kishki* (Ulcers of the the Stomach and Duodenum) (1946), etc; *Died:* 1952 in Moscow.

PFEYFER, Georgiy Vasil'yevich (1872–1946) Mathematician; prof; member, Ukr Acad of Sci from 1920; *Born:* 23 Oct 1872 in vil Sokirintsy, now Chernigov Obl; *Educ:* 1896 grad Kiev Univ; *Career:* 1899–1909 lecturer, Kiev Polytech Inst; 1909–46 prof, Kiev Univ; 1941–44 dir, Joint Inst of Mathematics and Physics, Ukr Acad of Sci; specialized in algebra and integrated differential equations with partial derivatives; wrote over 250 research works; *Publ: Gruppy mnogogrannikov* (Polyhedron Groups) (1903); *Predstavleniye oblastey osobennykh tochek al'gebraicheskikh poverkhnostey ryadami, raspolozhennymi po tselym polozhitel'nym stepenyam dvukh parametrov* (Representing the Areas of Particular Points of Algebraic Surfaces by Series Situated Along the Integral Positive Degress of Two Parameters) (1910), etc; *Died:* 10 Oct 1946.

PICHETA, Vladimir Ivanovich (1878–1947) Historian; Dr of History from 1918; member, Bel Acad of Sci from 1928; member, USSR Acad of Sci from 1946; *Born:* 21 Oct 1878 in Ukr, son of a Croatian emigre from Herzogovina; *Educ:* 1901 grad History and Philology Fac, Moscow Univ; *Career:* 1910–11 assoc prof, Moscow Univ, from which he resigned in protest against policies of Educ Min Kasso; 1918–21 prof of Bel history, Moscow Univ; 1921–30 prof and rector, Bel State Univ, Minsk; from 1922 also worked for Inst of Bel Culture, from late 1928 assoc, Bel Acad of Sci; specialized in history of Bel; summer 1930 arrested for „"Bel nationalism", expelled from Bel Acad of Sci and exiled for five years to Vyatka (now Kirov); mid–1930's released and worked for a time as a teacher at a secondary school; from 1939 corresp member, USSR Acad of Sci; head, Chair of History of Western and Southern Slavs, Moscow State Univ; head, Slavic Studies Section, Inst of History, USSR Acad of Sci; from 1946 full member, USSR Acad of Sci and dep dir of its Inst of Slavic Studies; re-elected member, Bel Acad of Sci; many of his works on Bel history were removed from circulation or remained in manuscript; the latter include: "Istoriya Belorussii s drevneyshikh vremyon do kontsa XIII veka" (The History of Belorussia from Ancient Times Until the Late 18th Century), prepared for the press in 1927; "Istoriya Belorussii" (History of Belorussia) and his two-vol college textbook "Istoriya BSSR" (History of the Belorussian SSR), written in 1939–41; *Publ: Agrarnaya reforma Sigizmunda-Avgusta v Litovskoy-Russkom gosudarstve* (The Agrarian Reform of Sigismund-August in the Lithuanian-Russian State) (2 vol, 1917); *Istoriya Litovskogo gosudarstva do Lyublinskoy unii* (The History of the Lithuanian State Until the Lublin Union) (1921); *Istoriya narodnogo khozyaystva v Rossii XIX–XX vv.* (The History of the National Economy in Russia in the 19th and 20th Centuries) (1922); *Vvedeniye v russkuyu istoriyu* (An Introduction to Russian History) (1922); *Istoriya krest'yanskikh volneniy v Rossii* (The History of Peasant Unrest in Russia) (1923); *Historyya Belarusi* (The History of Belorussia) (vol 1, 1924); *Belaruskaya mova yak faktar natsyyanal'nay kul'tury* (The Belorussian Language as a Factor in National Culture) (1924); *Epokha haradskoy haspadarki u Belarusi* (The Urban Economy Period in Belorussia) (1925); *Belaruskaye adradzhen'ne XVI veku i suchasnaya belaruskaye natsyyanal'na-kul'turnaya adradzhen'ne* (The Belorussian 16th-Century Renaissance and the Modern Belorussian National and Cultural Renaissance) (1925); *Historyya sel'skay haspadarki i zemleuladan'nya u Belarusi* (The History of Agriculture and Land Ownership in Belorussia) (1927); *Osnovnyye momenty istoricheskogo razvitiya Zapadnoy Ukrainy i Zapadnoy Belorussii* (Main Stages in the Historical Development of the Western Ukraine and Western Belorussia) (1940); coauthor, *Ocherki istorii SSSR. Period feodalizma IX–XV vv.* (Outline History of the USSR. The Period of 9th–15th Century Feudalism) (vol 1, 1953); collection *Belorussiya i Litva XV–XVI vekov* (Belorussia and Lithuania in the 15th and 16th Centuries) (1961); *Died:* 23 June 1947 in Moscow.

PIKEL', R.V. (1896–1936) Party official; CP member from 1917; *Born:* 1896; *Career:* originally sided with "Mezhrayontsy" org; after 1917 Oct Revol carried out govt work in Bel and polit work in Red Army; directed secretariat of chm, Comintern Exec Comt; active member, "Trotskyite opposition"; expelled from Party for "anti-Party and anti-state activities"; 1936 arrested by State Security organs; *Died:* 1936 in imprisonment.

PIKSANOV, Nikolay Kir'yakovich (1878–1969) Lit historian; prof; corresp member, USSR Acad of Sci from 1931; Hon Sci Worker of RSFSR from 1957; *Born:* 12 Apr 1878; *Career:* for 50 years prof at higher educ establishments in Moscow, Samara and Tashkent; then prof, Leningrad Univ, where he continued teaching into the 1950's; did research on Griboyedov, Pushkin, Gogol, Goncharov, Turgenev, Gorky, Ostrovskiy, etc; also studied the history of the Russian theater; held seminars on individual writers and whole lit epochs; *Publ: A.S. Griboyedov. Biograficheskiy ocherk* (A.S. Griboyedov. A Biographical Study) (1911); *Griboyedov i Mol'yer* (Griboyedov and Molliere) (1922); *Ostrovskiy. Literaturno-teatral'nyy seminariy* (Ostrovskiy. A Seminar on Theater History) (1923); *Tvorcheskaya istoriya "Gorya ot uma"* (The Creative History of "Woe From Wit") (1928); *Griboyedov. Issledovaniya i kharakteristika* (Griboyedov. Research and Characteristics) (1934); *Gor'kiy i natsional'nyye literatury* (Gorky and the National Literatures) (1946); *Gogol-dramaturg* (Gogol the Playwright) (1952), etc; *Awards:* Order of Lenin; Order of the Red Banner of Labor; medals; *Died:* Feb 1969.

PILATSKAYA, Ol'ga Vladimirovna (1884–1937) Party official; CP member from 1904; *Born:* 30 July 1884 in Moscow; *Career:* took part in 1905 Revol in Moscow; after 1917 Oct Revol govt and Party work in Moscow; 1922–26 head, Agitation and Propaganda Dept, Yekaterinoslav Province Comt, CP(B) Ukr; 1926–30 head, Women's Dept, CC, CP(B) Ukr; 1930–37 dept chm, Ukr Gosplan; at 9th Congress of CP(B) Ukr elected cand member, and at 10th–13th Congresses elected member, CC, CP(B) Ukr; 1927–37 Presidium member, All-Ukr Centr Exec Comt; *Died:* 1937.

PILIPENKO, Sergey Vladimirovich (1891–1943) Ukr writer; CP member from 1919; *Born:* 10 July 1891 in Kiev; *Educ:* studied at Kiev Univ; *Career:* 1913 arrested while studying at univ and drafted into Russian Army; fought for Bolsheviks in Civil War; began to write fables and prose works during Civil War; early 1920's edited newspapers "Kommunist", "Vesti" and "Krest'yanskaya pravda"; 1922–32 co-founder and head, "Plug" (The Plow) lit assoc; 1933 arrested by State Security organs; *Publ:* collections: "A Book of Fables" (1922); "Fables" (1927); "Pigs on the Oak" (1932); collected stories "At Chernigov" (1927); "Simple Stories" (1928); novelette "Dreikreuzen Island" (1930), etc; *Died:* 3 Mar 1943 in imprisonment; posthumously rehabilitated.

PIL'NYAK (real name: VOGAY), Boris Andreyevich (1894–1937) Russian writer; *Born:* 29 Sept 1894 in Mozhaysk; *Educ:* 1920 grad Moscow Business Inst; *Career:* 1915 contributed to journals "Russkaya zhizn'", "Spolokhi" and "Zhatva"; took no part in revol; 1922–23 visited Germany, France, Italy and Britain; later visited Japan and America; arrested by State Security organs; *Publ:* miniature *Vesnoy* (In Spring) (1909); collected stories *S poslednim parokhodom* (With the Last Boat) (1918) and *Byl'yo* (The Past) (1920); novel *Golyy god* (Hungry Year) (1921); novelette *Tret'ya stolitsa* (The Third Capital) (1923); stories; *Nikola-na-Posad'yakh* (Nikola-in-the Suburbs) (1923); *Angliyskiye rasskazy* (English Stories) (1924); *Povest' nepogashennoy luny* (The Tale of the Unextinguished Moon) (1926); *Korni yaponskogo solntsa* (The Roots of the Japanese Sun) (1927); novelette *Krasnoye derevo* (Mahogany) (1929); novel *Volga vpadayet v Kaspiyskoye more* (The Volga Flows into the Caspian Sea) (1930); "O'key" (O. K.) (1933); *Kamni i korni* (Stones and Roots) (1934), etc; *Died:* 1937 in imprisonment; posthumously rehabilitated.

PILYAVSKIY, S.S. (1882–1937) Govt official; CP member from 1903; *Born:* 1882; *Career:* Party work in Petersburg, Lith, Siberia; from Oct 1921 member and rapporteur, Commission for Resolving Practical Problems Connected with Debt Talks, RSFSR Pop Comrt of For Affairs; early 1922 senior secr, Sov deleg at Genoa Conference; in following years held various posts with Pop Comrt of Justice, Centr Council of Consumer Soc, Pop Comrt of Agric, Prosecutor's Office and USSR Supr Court; arrested by State Security organs; *Died:* 1937 in imprisonment.

PINCHEVSKIY, Mikhail Yakovlevich (1894–1955) Jewish poet and playwright; *Born:* 20 Mar 1894 in Teleneshti, now Mold SSR, son of a merchant; *Career:* at age 13 ran away from home and emigrated to Argentina, where he published his book of verse "Flourishing" (1918); 1926 returned to Russia and lived in Moscow, then Khar'kov and Kiev; many of his works have been translated into Russian, Ukr and Czech; *Publ:* poem "Bessarabia" (1929); dramatic fairy-tale poem "Aistenok" (1935); poem "The Monument" (1946); poem "Milking Time" (1947); *Died:* 24 Mar 1955 in Kiev.

PINKEVICH, Al'bert Petrovich (1884–1939) Educationist; specialist in teaching methods; prof; CP member from 1923; *Born:* 5 Jan 1884; *Educ:* 1909 grad Natural Sci Dept, Fac of Physics and Mathematics, Kazan' Univ; *Career:* 1909–14 instructor, Cadet Corps Teachers' Training Seminary, Vol'sk; from 1914 teacher, Tenishev Tech College, Zemstvo Teachers' Training School and Froebel Society Courses, Petrograd; 1919–21 dep chm, then chm, Commission for the Improvement of Living Conditions for Scholars and Sci; 1924–30 prof, Pedag Fac and rector, 2nd Moscow Univ; 1924–26 also dep head, Main Sci Bd, RSFSR Pop Comrt of Educ; from 1926 dir, Research Inst of Sci Pedag; 1930–36 dir, Moscow Teachers' Training Inst; from 1936 worked for All-Union Comt on Higher Educ, USSR Council of Pop Comr; did research on methods of teaching natural sci, the theory and history of pedag, and the org of tuition and educ; helped to draft school reform legislation; 1937 arrested by NKVD; *Publ: Metodika nachal'nogo kursa yestestvoznaniya* (Methods of Teaching a Primary Course on Natural Science) (1914); *Lektsii po metodike shkol'nogo yestestvoznaniya* (Lectures on Methods of Teaching Natural Science in Schools) (1918); *Osnovnyye problemy sovremennoy shkoly* (The Basic Problems of Modern Schools) (1924); *Pedagogika* (Pedagogics) (2 vol, 1924–25); coauthor, *Priroda i trud* (Nature and Labor) (1926); *Sovetskaya pedagogika za desyat' let* (Ten Years of Soviet Pedagogics) (1927), etc; *Died:* 1939 in imprisonment; posthumously rehabilitated.

PIONTKOVSKIY, Sergey Andreyevich (1891–1937) Historian; corresp member, Communist Acad and Bel Acad of Sci; CP member from 1918; *Born:* 8 Oct 1891 in Odessa, son of a law prof; *Educ:* 1914 grad History and Philology Fac, Kazan' Univ; *Career:* from 1917 Kazan' Province Comr of Labor; 1919–20 worked at Higher Inst of Publ Educ, Kazan'; 1921 prof, Sverdlov Communist Univ; simultaneously dep ed, journal "Proletarskaya revolyutsiya"; from 1922 lecturer, then prof, Moscow State Univ; from 1929 member, Section for the Study of Proletarian History, Inst of History, Communist Acad; in 1930's prof, Moscow Inst of Philosophy, Lit and History and Inst of Red Prof; sided with

"Marxist philosophical school" headed by M.N. Prokrovskiy; specialized in history of CP and Russian revolutions; coauthor, 4–vol "istoriya VKP(b)" (The History of the CPSU(B) (1926–29), edited by Yaroslavskiy; compiled many editions of documents on Party history, the history of the working class and the history of revol movements in Russia; 1934, following a resolution of the CC, CPSU(B) and the USSR Council of Pop Comr, helped compile a textbook on Sov history which attacked, inter alia, the conceptions of Pokrovskiy's historical school; 1937 arrested by State Security organs, *Publ:* Kratkiy ocherk istorii rabochego dvizheniya v Rossii s 1870 po 1917 god (A Brief Outline History of the Workers' Movement in Russia from 1870 to 1917) (1925); *Oktyabr'skaya revolyutsiya v Rossii. Yeyo predposylki i khod* (The October Revolution in Russia. Its Premises and Course) (3rd ed, 1926); *Khrestomatiya po istorii Oktyabr'skoy revolyutsii* (An Anthology on the History of the October Revolution) (3rd ed, 1926); *Oktyabr' 1917* (October 1917) (1927); *Ocherki istorii Rossii v XIX–XX vv.* (Studies in 19th–20th Century Russian History) (1928); *Burzhuaznaya istoricheskaya nauka v Rossii* (Bourgeois Historical Science in Russia) (1931); *Ocherki istorii SSSR XIX–XX vv.* (Studies in the History of the USSR in the 19th–20th Centuries) (1935); *Died:* 8 Mar 1937 in imprisonment.

PIOTROVSKIY, Adrian Ivanovich (1898–1938) Russian critic, theater historian and playwright; prof from 1928; Hon Art Worker of RSFSR from 1935; *Born:* 8 Nov 1898 in Vilnius; *Educ:* 1923 grad Philological Fac, Petrograd Univ; *Career:* 1919 head, Theater Dept, Petrograd Polit Educ Comt; organized mass shows and agitation theaters; 1923–29 lit dir, Bolshoy Drama Theater; 1925–32 lit dir, Leningrad Young Workers' Theater; 1933–36 lit dir, Maly Opera Theater; also worked at Kiev Opera and Ballet Theater; 1928–37 artistic dir, Sov Film Studios, Leningrad; from 1918 worked as critic; arrested by State Security organs; *Publ:* plays: *Mech mira* (The Sword of Peace) (1921); *Padeniye Yeleni Ley* (The Downfall of Elena Lee) (1923); *Smert' komandarma* (The Death of an Army Commander) (1925); research work *Antichnyy teatr* (The Ancient Theater) (1931); coauthor, play *Zelyonyy tsekh* (The Green Shop) (1932), etc; translated ancient writers and poets; Theognis' "Elegies" (1922); Catullus' "Book of Lyrics" (1928); Aristophanes' "Comedies" (1933), etc; *Died:* 1938 in imprisonment; posthumously rehabilitated.

PIOTROVSKIY, Lyudvig Marianovich (1886–1959) Electr eng; Dr of Tech Sci from 1938; prof; *Born:* 1886 in Kovno; *Educ:* 1912 grad Electr Eng Dept, Petersburg Polytech Inst; *Career:* from 1914 traveled in France and Switzerland to study latest techniques at electr power plants and electrified railroads; 1916–18 exec work in connection with installing electr equipment at Revel naval fortress; from 1920 lecturer, assoc prof, then prof, Chair of Electr Machinery, Leningrad Polytech Inst; 1919–29 also lectured at Naval Commanders College; 1922–38 lectured at Naval Acad; 1925–26 helped draft "Rules and Standards for Testing Electrical Machinery and Transformers"; 1926–28 worked at physical eng laboratory, in charge of testing electr machinery for the "Elektrik" and "Elektrosila" plants; 1941–45 worked for Uzbek Power System; from 1945 consultant, "Elektro" Plant, Leningrad and prof, Electr Eng Fac, Leningrad Polytech Inst; 1945–47 head, Chair of Electr Eng and Electr Machinery, Dzerzhinskiy Naval Eng College; wrote numerous books and textbooks on testing d.c. electr machinery and on electr equipment and transformers; *Awards:* Order of Lenin; medals; *Died:* 22 May 1959.

PIROGOVSKIY, Aleksandr Sidorovich (1897–1943) Partisan; CP member from 1927; *Born:* 1897 in Podol'sk Province; son of a peasant; *Career:* fought in 1918–20 Civil War; 1924 demobilized from Red Army and worked for Kiev Railroad Depot, then Party work in Kiev; 1941–43 secr, Kiev's underground Railroad Rayon Comt, CP(B) Ukr; organized guerilla actions against German occupation forces; 31 Oct 1943 arrested by German occupation forces; *Awards:* Hero of the Sov Union (1945, posthumously); *Died:* 5 Nov 1943 executed by Germans.

PISAREV, Anatoliy Ivanovich (1886–1963) Revol; CP member from 1905; *Born:* 1886; *Career:* during 1905–07 Revol helped organize armed uprising in Sormovo; member, underground Party comt; 1914 helped organize underground printing house for Sormovo Party Comt; repeatedly arrested; 1916 exiled to Turukhan Kray; during 1917 Oct Revol member, Sormovo and Nizhniy Novgorod Party Comts; commandant, Nizhniy Novgorod garrison; then chm, Nizhniy Novgorod Province Cheka; 1918–21 exec polit work in Red Army; deleg, 8th RCP(B) Congress; 1921–25 secr, Sormovo Rayon Party Comt; secr, okrug Party comt in the Urals; exec instructor, Siberian Kray RCP(B) Comt; 1927–30 admin work in Novorossiysk and Moscow; *Died:* 26 June 1963.

PISARZHEVSKIY, Lev Vladimirovich (1874–1938) Chemist; member, Ukr Acad of Sci from 1925; member, USSR Acad of Sci from 1930; CP member from 1930; *Born:* 13 Feb 1874 in Kishinev; *Educ:* 1896 grad Novorossiysk Univ, Odessa; *Career:* 1904–08 prof, Yur'yev Univ; 1908–11 prof, Kiev Polytech Inst; resigned in protest against policies of Educ Min Kasso; 1911–13 lectured at Bestuzhev Women's Courses and at Psychoneurological Inst, Petersburg; 1913–14 prof, Yekaterinoslav (now Dnepropetrovsk) Mining Inst (from 1918 Univ); from 1927 founder-dir, Ukr Inst of Physiochemistry (now Pisarzhevskiy Inst of Physiochemistry, Ukr Acad of Sci); 1929–34 also worked at Tbilisi Polytech Inst; studied structure and properties of peroxides and per acids, effect of solvent on the chemical balance and free energy of reactions; used electron theory to tackle basic problems of chemistry; postulated now generally accepted ideas on the role of electrons in chemical processes and on redox reactions as electron transfer processes; *Publ: Perekisi i nadkisloty* (Peroxides and Per Acids) (1902); coauthor, *Elektron v khimii rastvorov i v elektrokhimii* (The Electron in Solution Chemistry and in Electrochemistry) (1923); textbook *Vvedeniye v khimiyu* (Introduction to Chemistry) (1926); coauthor, textbook *Neorganicheskaya khimiya* (Inorganic Chemistry) (1930); *Izbrannyye trudy* (Selected Works) (1935); *Izbrannyye trudy v oblasti kataliza* (Selected Works on Catalysis) (1955); *Elektron v khimii. Izbrannyye trudy* (The Electron in Chemistry. Selected Works) (1956); *Awards:* Order of Lenin; Lenin Prize (1930); *Died:* 23 Mar 1938.

PISEMSKIY, Grigoriy Fyodorovich (1862–1937) Obstetrician and gynecologist; Hon Sci Worker of Ukr SSR from 1935; Dr of Med from 1904; *Born:* 7 Feb 1862 in Piryatin, now Poltava Oblast; *Educ:* 1888 grad Med Fac, Koev Univ; *Career:* 1888–1904 intern; from 1905 assoc prof, Chair of Obstetrics and Gynecology, Kiev Univ; 1913–14 prof, Chair of Obstetrics and Gynecology, Moscow Univ; 1915–17 dir, Nadezhdinsk Maternity Home, Petersburg; 1920–30 prof and dir, Obstetrics and Gynecological Clinic, Kiev Med Inst; 1930–34 also sci dir, Kiev Research Inst of Mother and Child Care; 1920–37 also prof and dir, Obstetrics and Gynecological Clinic, Kiev Inst of Postgrad Med Training; sponsored establishment of kolkhoz maternity homes in Ukr; organized Kiev's first consultation service for expectant mothers; chm, Ukr and Kiev Sci Soc of Obstetricians and Gynecologists; 1927 organized and chaired 1st All-Ukr Congress of Obstetricians and Gynecologists; member, Sci Council, Ukr Pop Comrt of Health; ed, journal "Ukrainskiye meditsinskiye vesti"; member, ed bd, journal "Voprosy onkologii", etc; wrote some 70 works; *Publ:* doctor's thesis *K voprosu ob innervatsii matki* (The Innervation of the Womb) (1904); *Ocherk razvitiya khirurgicheskoy ginekologii i yeyo glavneyshiye zadachi* (A Study of the Development of Surgical Gynecology and Its Main Tasks) (1908); *Zabolevaniya matochnykh trub* (Diseases of the Oviducts) (1927); *Zlokachestvennyye novoobrazovaniya matki* (Malignant Neoplasms of the Womb) (1937), etc; *Died:* 25 July 1937 in Kiev.

PISTRAK, Moisey Mikhaylovich (1888–1940) Educationist; Dr of Pedag Sci; prof; CP member from 1924; *Born:* 15 Sept 1888; *Educ:* 1914 grad Physics and Mathematics Fac, Warsaw Univ; *Career:* from 1906 taught at private schools; 1918–31 (with short intervals) worked for RSFSR Pop Comrt of Educ; from 1920 dir, Lepeshinskiy School-Commune; 1931–36 at North Caucasian Teachers' Training Inst, Rostov-on-Don; from July 1936 dir, Centr Educ Research Inst, Higher Communist Inst of Educ; specialized in teaching methods, labor training and polytech training; helped revise gen educ curriculum in Sov schools; wrote first Sov educ textbook for teachers' training institutes; 1937 arrested by State Security organs; *Publ: Materialy po samoupravleniyu uchashchikhsya* (Material on Pupil Self-Management) (1922); ed, *Shkola-Kommuna Narkomprosa* (The Pop Comrt of Education's School-Commune) (1924); *Nasushchnyye problemy sovremennoy sovetskoy shkoly* (Vital Problems of the Modern Soviet School System) (1925); Politekhnizm v shkole (Polytechnism in the School) (1926); *Pedagogika. Uchebnik dlya vysshikh pedagogicheskikh zavedeniy* (Pedagogics. A Textbook for Higher Teachers' Training Establishments) (1934); *Died:* 1940 in imprisonment; posthumously rehabilitated.

PIYP, Boris Ivanovich (1906–1966) Vulcanologist; corresp member, USSR Acad of Sci from 1958; dir, Inst of Vulcanology, Siberian Branch, USSR Acad of Sci from 1963; CP member from 1945; *Born:* 6 Nov 1906; *Educ:* 1931 grad Leningrad Mining Inst;

Career: 1931–34 asst prof, 1934–38 assoc prof, Leningrad Mining Inst; 1931–39 also took part in field trips in Kamchatka and the Urals; 1940–46 and 1950–54 head, Kamchatka Vulcanological Station; 1940–61 assoc, Vulcanology Laboratory, USSR Acad of Sci; 1961–62 dir, Kamchatka Geological and Geophysical Observatory, USSR Acad of Sci; made detailed study of various types of volcanic eruptions; studied volcanoes, hot springs and geological structure of Kamchatka; *Publ: Termal'nyye klyuchi Kamchatki* (The Thermal Springs of Kamchatka) (1937); *Materialy po geologii i petrografii rayona rek Avachi, Rassoshiny, Gavanki i Nalachevy na Kamchatke* (Material on the Geology and Geography in the Area of the Rivers Avacha, Rassoshina, Gavanka and Nalacheva in Kamchatka) (1941); *Klyuchevskaya sopka i yeyo izverzheniya v 1944–1945 godakh i v proshlom (The Klyuchevka Mud Cone and Its Eruption in 1944–45 and in the Past) (1956); Kurilo-Kamchatskaya ekspeditsiya AN SSSR* (The USSR Academy of Sciences' Kurilo-Kamchatka Expedition) (1958), etc; *Awards:* Order of the Red Star; medals; Prize of the USSR Acad of Sci Presidium (1956); *Died:* 10 Mar 1966.

PLAKHIN, Andrey Ivanovich (1904–1957) Diplomat; envoy extraordinary and plen, 2nd class; *Born:* 1904; *Career:* from 1939 head, Dept of Scandinavian Countries, USSR Pop Comrt of For Affairs; 1941 counsellor, USSR mission in Denmark; 1943 USSR Asst Dep Pop Comr of For Affairs; 1944–45 head, Polit Dept, Ukr Pop Comrt of For Affairs; 1945–50 USSR envoy in Denmark; 1954–55 senior posts with USSR High Commission in Austria; 1956–57 dept head, Personnel Bd, USSR Min of For Affairs; *Died:* 1957.

PLAKSIN, Igor' Nikolayevich (1900–1967) Hydrometallurgist; Dr of Tech Sci; corresp member, USSR Acad of Sci from 1946; CP member from 1945; *Born:* 8 Oct 1900; *Educ:* 1926 grad Far Eastern Univ, Vladivostok; *Career:* specialist in theory and technol of hydrometallurgy and concentration and dressing of minerals; 1926–28 worked at Chemical Inst, USSR Acad of Sci; 1928–30 at Moscow Mining Acad; from 1930 prof and head, Chair of Metallurgy of Precious Metals, Moscow (now Krasnoyarsk) Inst of Non-Ferrous Metals and Gold; 1941–43 also dep dir, All-Union Inst for the Mech Processing and Enrichment of Ores; from 1944 also assoc, then dept head, Skochinskiy Inst of Mining; *Publ: Vzaimodeystviye splavoy i samorodnogo zolota s rtut'yu i tsianistymi rastvorami* (The Action of Alloys and Native Gold with Mercury and Cyanide Solutions) (1937); *Metallurgiya blagorodnykh metallov* (The Metallurgy of Precious Metals) (1943); *Oprobovaniye i probirnyy analiz* (Assaying and Sample Analysis) (1947); coauthor, *Gidrometallurgiya* (Hydrometallurgy) (1949); *Rol' gazov i primeneniye kisloroda vo flotatsii* (The Role of Gases and the Use of Oxygen in Flotation) (1952); *Tekhnologicheskoye oborudovaniye obogatitel'nykh fabrik* (The Technological Equipment of Concentration Mills) (1955); *Rezul'taty i perspektivy issledovaniya vzaimodeystviya reagentov s mineralami vo flotatsii* (The Results and Prospects from the Study of the Interaction of Reagents and Minerals in Flotation) (1955); coauthor, *Flotatsionnoye obogashcheniye mysh'yakovo-piritnykh rud* (The Flotation Dressing of Pyrite Arsenate Ores) (1955); *Metallurgiya blagorodnykh metallov* (The Metallurgy of Precious Metals) (1958); coauthor, *Izucheniye poter' smoly, voznikayushchikh v protsesse sorbtsii metallov iz pul'p* (A Study of Pitch Losses Resulting from the Sorption of Metals from Pulps) (1966), etc; *Awards:* Order of Lenin; Order of the Red Banner of Labor; medals; two Stalin Prizes (1951 and 1952); *Died:* 15 Mar 1967.

PLATNER, Ayzik (real name: Isaak Khaymovich) (1895–1961) Jewish poet and writer; member, Bel Writers' Union; *Born:* 17 Nov 1895 in vil Sokolov-Podleskov, Sedlets Province; *Educ:* grad Jewish teachers' training seminary in America; *Career:* in his youth worked in tailor's shops; until 1921 lived in Poland and Lith; 1921 emigrated to America and worked in shirtwaist factories, then taught in schools for workers' children; printed his work in newspaper "Morgen freiheit", organ of CC, US Communist Party; helped found and run lit orgs "Junion skwer" and "Proleten"; 1932 went to USSR; work printed in Sov Jewish journals and newspapers; 1949 arrested by State Security organs; 1956 rehabilitated; *Publ:* book "What the Day Tells" (1930); verse cycle "Creation"; "From Two Countries" (1934); collected verse "The Salt of Life" and poem "Sisters" (1961), etc; *Died:* 26 July 1961 in Minsk.

PLATONOV, Aleksey Nikolayevich (1912–1939) Evenki poet; pioneer of Evenki lit; *Born:* 1912 in Yakutia; *Educ:* studied at Inst of Peoples of the North, Leningrad; *Career:* founded kolkhoz and became its first chm; turned to lit as a student in Leningrad; work printed in collections published in Leningrad in Evenki language; *Publ:* "Before and Now" (1938); "The Joy of the Taiga" (1938); collected verse "Songs of the Evenki" (1938); works translated into Russian: collections *Molodost'* (Youth) (1938) and *Sever poyot* (The North Sings) (1939); also wrote articles about changes in the life of the northern peoples under the Sov regime; *Died:* 7 Nov 1939 in Yakutsk.

PLATONOV (real name: KLIMENTOV), Andrey Platonovich (1899–1951) Russian writer, journalist and critic; *Born:* 20 Aug 1899 in Voronezh; *Educ:* 1924 grad Voronezh Polytech Inst; *Career:* 1918 first work published; worked for newspapers "Voronezhskaya kommuna", "Krasnaya derevnya", "Ogni" and journal "Zheleznyy put'"; fought in Civil War; 1923–26 in charge of provincial land reclamation and directed agric electrification projects; 1927 moved to Moscow; from 1928 worked for journals "Krasnaya nov'", "Novyy mir", "Oktyabr'" and "Molodaya gvardiya"; from 1936, unter the pseudonyms of F. Chelovekov and A. Firsov, contributed to journals "Literaturnyy kritik" and "Literaturnoye obozreniye"; 1942–45 special front-line corresp for newspaper "Krasnaya zvezda"; *Publ: Elektrifikatsiya* (Electrification) (1921); collected verse *Golubaya glubina* (Blue Depth) (1922); satirical novelette *Gorod gorodov* (City of Cities) (1926); collected stories *Yepifanskiye shlyuzy* (The Epiphany Locks) (1927); non-fiction works *Lugovyye mastera* (Masters of the Meadows) and *Sokrovennyy chelovek* (The Innermost Man) (1928); novelette *Proiskhozdeniye mastera* (The Derivation of the Master) (1929); stories *Gosudarstvennyy zhitel'* (The State Inhabitant), *Usomnivshiysya Makar* (Doubting Makar) (1929); *Musornyy veter* (The Garbage Wind); novelettes *Kotlovan* (The Foundation Area) and *Yuvenil'skoye more* (Juvenile Sea); plays *Vysokoye napryazheniye* (High Tension) and *Pushkin v litseye* (Pushkin at the Lyceum); critical studies: "Pushkin, Our Comrade" and "Pushkin and Gorky"; stories *Bessmertiye* (Immortality) and "Fro" (1936); non-fiction work *Reka Potudan'* (Potudan' River) (1937); *Rasskazy o Rodine* (Stories of My Country) (1943); *Cherez reku* (Across the River) (1944); story *Sem'ya Ivanova* (Ivanov's Family) (1946); despite a grave illness, he wrote a great deal in his latter years and left an extensive collection of manuscripts; *Died:* 5 Jan 1951 in Moscow.

PLATONOV, Semyon Pavlovich (1901–1963) Gen Staff officer and mil historian; lt-gen; CP member from 1919; *Born:* 9 Apr 1901 in vil Smolkovo, Samara Province, son of a peasant; *Educ:* 1936 grad Frunze Mil Acad; 1941 grad Gen Staff Acad; *Career:* from 1919 in Red Army; fought in Civil War; 1923–33 various commands; 1936–39 staff posts; head, operations dept, staff of a mil distr; from Aug 1941 dept head, Operations Bd, Gen Staff; responsible for battle reports and operational summary for all fronts submitted daily to Stalin; prepared daily reports for press and radio from Sov Information Bureau; 1945–50 taught at mil acads; 1950–63 head, Mil History Dept, Gen Staff; 1958–63 member, ed bd, "Voyenno-istoricheskiy zhurnal", which he helped to found; for many years member, Expert Commission for Mil Sci and Mil Technique, Higher Certification Commission; co-ed, 6-vol *Istoriya Velikoy Otechestvennoy voyny Sovetskogo Soyuza 1941–1945* (The History of the Soviet Union's 1941–1945 Great Fatherland War); wrote several works on history of Sov mil operations; from Oct 1963 retired; *Awards:* Order of Lenin; three Orders of the Red Banner; Order of Kutuzov, 2nd Class; Order of the Fatherland War; two Orders of the Red Star; six medals; *Died:* 29 Dec 1963 in Moscow.

PLATONOV, Sergey Fyodorovich (1860–1933) Historian; Dr of History from 1899; prof; member, USSR Acad of Sci from 1920; *Born:* 28 June 1860; *Educ:* 1882 grad Petersburg Univ; *Career:* from 1899 prof, Petersburg Univ; 1908–20 corresp member, Russian Acad of Sci; 1918–29 chm, Archeographic Commission; from 1928 chm, Commission for Publ the Works of Pushkin; 1925–29 dir, Pushkin Center, Inst of Russian Lit, USSR Acad of Sci; 1925–28 dir, Library, USSR Acad of Sci; wrote monographs on Russian history in the late 16th and early 17th Centuries; also studied the history of zemstvo assemblies, Peter I's reforms and the colonization of the North; examined soc ferment in various strata of Muscovy population and determined causes of mass movements of population; studied the period of the "troubles" (late 16th and early 17th centuries) and distinguished three periods: dynastic, social and national; sought roots of the "troubles" in Muscovy's soc life of preceding period; explained the "oprichnik" system under Ivan the Terrible as a state reform aimed at breaking the econ and polit power of the princes and boyars in the interests of the nobility and the burghers; regarded the transformation of the peasants into serfs as a state measure in the interests of the nobility and the nation's defense; his views had a great influence on the development of Sov historiography; adhered to old Russian historical school, which brought him into conflict with the Marxist historical school of M. N. Pokrovskiy; 1929, as a result of this, dismissed from his posts with the USSR Acad of Sci and later stripped of his acad title; arrested and exiled to Samara; partially rehabilitated after downfall of Pokrovskiy and his historical school; this is evidenced by the 1937 re-edition of his work *Ocherki po istorii smuty v Moskovskom gosudarstve XVI–XVII vv.* (Outline History of the Troubles in Muscovy in the 16th and 17th Centuries); *Publ: Drevnerusskiye skazaniya i povesti of Smutnom vremeni XVII veka kak istoricheskiy istochnik* (Ancient Russian Tales and Legends About the 17th-Century Troubles as Historical Sources) (1888); *Ocherki po istorii smuty v Moskovskom gosudarstve XVI–XVII vv.* (Outline History of the Troubles in Muscovy in the 16th and 17th Centuries) (1899; 2nd ed, 1939); *Stat'i po russkoy istorii (1883–1912)* (Articles on Russian History [1883–1912]) (1912); *Lektsii po russkoy istorii* (Lectures on Russian History) (10th ed, 1917); "Boris Godunov" (1921); *Ivan Groznyy* (Ivan the Terrible) (1923), etc; *Died:* 10 Jan 1933 in Samara.

PLATTEN, Friedrich (Fritz) (1883–1942) Swiss Communist; professional revol; co-founder, Swiss CP; *Born:* 1883; *Career:* from 1904 Soc-Democratic movement; 1906–07 revol work in Riga; from 1908 secr, Russian emigrés' fund in Switzerland; 1912–18 secr, Swiss Soc-Democratic Party; during WW 1 attended Zimmerwald and Kienthal Conferences; sided with leftist Zimmerwald group; Apr 1917 mainly responsible for organizing Lenin's transfer from Switzerland to Russia; 1919 helped organize 3rd Comintern; Presidium member, 1st Comintern Congress and Bureau member, Comintern; contributed to journal "Kommunisticheskiy Internatsional"; 1921–23 secr, Swiss CP; 1923 moved to USSR; headed Swiss workers' agric commune; then worked at Int Agrarian Inst and Moscow For Language Teachers' Training Inst; *Died:* 1942.

PLEKHANOV, Georgiy Valentinovich (pseudonyms: N. BEL'TOV; N. KAMENSKIY; N. ANDREYEVICH; G. VALENTINOV, etc) (1856–1918) Leading member, Russian and int socialist movement; philosopher, historian and journalist; founder, Marxist movement in Russia; one of leaders, RSDRP(Mensheviks); *Born:* 11 Dec 1856 in vil Gudalovka, now Lipetsk Oblast, son of a nobleman; *Educ:* 1873 completed mil high school in Voronezh; 1873–74 studied at Konstantin Cadets College in Petersburg; 1874–76 at Petersburg Mining Inst; *Career:* 1875 became connected with Populist Revolutionaries and soon became a professional revol, which led to his leaving the Petersburg Mining Inst; 1879, after shism of Populist "Land and Liberty" org into "People's Will" and "Public Redistribution" (Chyornyy peredel) factions, headed the latter which opposed the tactics of polit conspiracy and individual terror as a means of overthrowing autocracy; Jan 1880 emigrated to escape govt persecution and until 1917 lived in Switzerland, Italy, France and other countries; made the acquaintance of leading figures in West European workers' movement and studied socialist lit, including Marx and Engels; also established personal contacts with such socialist leaders as Kautsky, Liebknecht, Bernstein, Lafargue, Bebel, Mering and Engels; broke with Populists and 1883 founded in Geneva first Russian Marxist org – Liberation of Labor Group – which laid the foundation for the spread of Marxism in Russia; in this period wrote his books *Sotsializm i politicheskaya bor'ba* (Socialism and Political Struggle) (1883) and *Nashi raznoglasiya* (Our Differences), criticizing Populism and the views of its ideologists P. L. Lavrov, P. N. Tkachov, M. A. Bakunin and N. K. Mikhaylovskiy; from 1890's one of recognized leaders of 2nd International and attended its congresses in Zurich (1893), Amsterdam (1904) and Copenhagen (1910); from 1898 criticized revionism of Marxism, particularly scathing of Bernsteinism and its Russian version – "economism"; maintained close contacts with Soc-Democrats in Russia and played active part in 2nd RSDRP Congress in 1903; helped draft RSDRP program adopted by 2nd Congress and, together with Lenin and Martov, was elected ed of Party's centr organ, newspaper "Iskra" and a member, RSDRP Council; soon broke with Lenin and his Bolshevik faction and became leader of Menshevik faction; proceeding from Marxist teaching and the principles of historical materialism, considered Russia unprepared for socialist changes and therefore opposed armed revolt and seizure of power by the proletariat; also denfeded principles of democracy both in the Party and in the socialist movement in general and on these grounds differed with the Bolsheviks and, personally, with Lenin whom he termed a polit opportunist and a "demagogue to his fingertips", thirsting for power and personal dictatorship; during WW 1 headed "Unity" Menshevik group, opposed conversion of war into civil war to facilitate seizure of power and insisted on mil defense of Russia; after 1917 Feb Revol returned to Russia, defended so-called "bourgeois revol" and backed Provisional Govt and convening of Constituent Assembly; sharply condemned Lenin's appeals for the proletariat to seize power; denounced 1917 Oct Revol; for this he was later badly treated by the All-Russian Cheka, which subjected him to interrogations and demeaning house searches, despite his grave health; wrote many works on history, econ, sociology, estetics and philosophy; *Publ: K voprosu o razvitii monisticheskogo vzglyada na istoriyu* (The Development of the Monistic View of History) (1895); *Ocherki po istorii materializma* (An Outline History of Materialism) (1897); *K voprosu o roli lichnosti v istorii* (The Role of the Individual in History) (1898); *Istoriya russkoy obshchestvennoy mysli* (A History of Russian Social Thought) (vol 1, 1914); *God na Rodine. Polnoye sobraniye statey i rechey 1917–1918 godov* (A Year in My Country. Complete Collection of Articles and Speeches for 1917–1918) (2 vol, 1921, Paris); "Sochineniya" (Works) (24 vol, 1923–27); *Literaturnoye naslediye G. V. Plekhanova* (The Literary Legacy of G. V. Plekhanov) (8 vol, 1934–40); *Izbrannyye filosofskiye proizvedeniya* (Selected Philosophical Works) (5 vol, 1956–58); *Literatura i i estetika* (Literature and Esthetics) (2 vol, 1958); *Died:* 30 May 1918 at Pitkeyarvi Sanatorium, Finland, of tuberculosis; buried in Leningrad.

PLETNYOV, Dmitriy Dmitriyevich (1872–1938) Therapist; first internist, Kremlin Hospital; Dr of Med from 1906; prof from 1911; Hon Sci Worker of RSFSR; *Born:* 1872; *Educ:* 1896 grad Moscow Univ; *Career:* after grad intern, then asst prof at a clinic; 1906 defended doctor's thesis on cardiac arhythmia; 1906–08 worked abroad, inter alia at the Kraus Clinic, Berlin, and with F. Müller and Naunin; from 1911 prof, Propaedeutic Clinic, Higher Women's Courses; 1917–29 dir, Fac Clinic, then Therapeutic Clinic, 1st Moscow Univ; from 1920 co-founder and exec ed, journal "Klinicheskaya meditsina"; from 1929 prof, Centr Inst of Postgrad Med Training, Moscow, and dir, Research Inst of Functional Diagnostics and Experimental Therapy, Pop Comrt of Health; member, Learned Med Council, RSFSR and Ukr Pop Comrt of Health; bd member, All-Union Therapists' Soc; from 1931 corresp member, Berlin Med Soc; delivered papers at numerous med congresses; chm, 19th Therapists' Congress, Leningrad; trained numerous outstanding therapists, including Klucharyov, Vikhert and Vinogradov; 1938 tried with other members of "rightist Trotskyite bloc" on a charge of complicity in the murder of Gorky and Kuybyshyov; 13 Mar 1938 sentenced to 25 years imprisonment; wrote over 60 works; *Publ:* doctor's thesis *Eksperimental'nyye issledovaniya po voprosu o proiskhozdenii aritmii* (Experimental Research on the Origin of Arhythmia) (1906); *Simptomokompleks Morgan'i-Adams-Stoksa* (The Morgagni-Adams-Stokes Syndrome) (1908); *Sypnoy tif* (Typhus) (2nd ed, 1922); *Russkiye terapevticheskiye shkoly – Zakhar'in, Botkin, Ostroumov* (Russian Schools of Therapy – Zakhar'in, Botkin, Ostroumov) (1923); coauthor, *Osnovy terapii* (The Principles of Therapy) (3 vol, 1925–27); coauthor, *Rentgenodiagnostika* (X-Ray Diagnostics) (2 vol, 1926–28); coauthor, *Chastnaya patologiya i terapiya vnutrennikh bolezney* (The Special Pathology and Therapy of Internal Diseases) (4 vol, 1927–31); coauthor, *Osnovy klinicheskoy diagnostiki* (The Principles of Clincial Diagnostics) (4th ed, 1928); *Osnovy terapii khronicheskoy nedostatochnosti serdtsa* (The Principles of the Therapy of Cardiac Insufficiency) (1932); coauthor, *Kurs infektionnykh zabolevaniy* (A Course on Infectious Diseases) (2 vol, 1932–33), etc; *Died:* 1938 in imprisonment.

PLETNYOV, Valerian Fyodorovich (1886–1942) Russian writer and lit critic; CP member from 1920; *Born:* 3 Sept 1886 in Moscow; *Career:* carpenter by trade; 1904–14 Menshevik; 1915–17 exiled in Siberia for anti-war propaganda; 1918–20 Presidium member, Moscow Province Sovnarkhoz; 1919–20 plen for supply of 1st Turkestani Army; dep plen for Turkestani Front; chm, Turkm Centr Sovnarkhoz; fought in Civil War; 1921–32 head, Proletarian Culture Org, Pop Comrt of Educ; 1936–38 ed work; 1941 volunteer in Civil Defense; 1913 began work as lit critic; 1918 first story published; *Publ:* stories *Na tikhom Plese* (On the Calm Ples) (1919); *Zoloto* (Gold) (1921); *Andriykino gore* (Andrey's Grief) (1921); plays "Lena" (1921); *Uyezdnoye* (The District) (1926); *Nasledstvo Garlanda* (Garland's Inheritance) (1924); comedy *Shlyapa* (The Hat) (1935); articles: "The First Step" (1914); "On the Ideological Front" (1922); "The Paths of Proletarian Poetry" (1923); non-fiction work *Tri tochki zreniya na proletarskuyu kul'turu* (Three Points of View of Proletarian Culture) (1926), etc; *Died:* Apr 1942 killed in action in WW 2.

PLETNYOVA, Nataliya Aleksandrovna (1889–1967) Ophthalmologist; Dr of Med and prof from 1940; *Born:* 1889; *Educ:* 1914 grad Med Fac, Moscow Univ; *Career:* 1914–17 intern, Eye Disease Clinic, Med Fac, Moscow Higher Women's Courses; 1917–26 asst prof, 1926–40 assoc prof, 1940–44 prof, Eye Disease Clinic, 2nd Moscow Med Inst; 1944–67 head, Chair of Eye Diseases, 2nd Moscow Med Inst; chm, Moscow Soc of Ophthalmologists; bd member, All-Union and All-Russian Soc of Ophthalmologists; member, ed collegium, journal "Vestnik oftalmologii"; member, Ophthalmological Problems Comt, USSR Acad of Med Sci; secr, Acad M. I. Averbakh Prize Commission; reviewer, Higher Certifying Commission; member, Learned Council, Moscow City Health Dept; did research on various aspects of ophthalmology, notably on the surgical treatment of glaucoma; wrote some 60 works; *Publ: Rol' mediatora v uchenii o glaukome* (The Role of the Mediator in the Theory of Glaucoma) (1940); *Uchebnik glaznykh bolezney* (A Textbook on Eye Diseases) (published in Russian, Bulgarian and Chinese); coauthor and ed, *Khirurgiya glaza* (Eye Surgery); *Awards:* Order of Lenin; medal "For Outstanding Labor"; medal "In Memory of the 800th Anniversary of the Founding of Moscow"; "Outstanding Health Worker" Badge; *Died:* Feb 1967 in Moscow.

PLUDON, Matis Yanovich (1892–1963) Govt official; CP member from 1917; *Born:* 1892; *Career:* 1914–17 fought in WW 1; 1917–22 fought for Bolsheviks in Civil War; 1922–24 worked for USSR Pop Comrt of the Fishing Ind; 1944–45 USSR Dep Pop Comrt of Fishing Ind; 1945–55 dep chm, Lat Council of Min; 1955–62 first dep chm, Lat Council of Min; member and Bureau member, CC, CP Lat; dep, USSR Supr Sov of 4th and 5th convocations; dep, Lat Supr Sov of 4th–6th convocations; *Awards:* two Orders of Lenin; three Orders of the Red Banner of Labor; medals; *Died:* 13 Dec 1963.

POCHENKOV, Kondrat Ivanovich (1905–1962) Govt official; CP member from 1928; *Born:* 1905; *Educ:* grad Novocherkassk Mining Technicum; *Career:* 1920–27 miner in Donbass; 1927 sent to study at Novocherkassk Mining Technicum; then worked at mines in Donbass; 1938–40 mang, trust; 1940–54 USSR Dep Pop Comr, then Dep Min of Coal Ind; at various times directed Kuzbass, Lugansk, Kizel and Donetsk Coal Combines; from 1954 Ukr Min of Coal Ind; in his latter years dir, Rostov Coal Combine; 1940–55 member, CC, CP Ukr; dep, USSR Supr Sov of 2nd and 5th convocations; dep, Ukr Supr Sov of 3rd convocation; *Awards:* Stalin Prize (1951); *Died:* 6 Aug 1962.

PODBEL'SKIY, Vadim Nikolayevich (1887–1920) Party and govt official; CP member from 1905; *Born:* Nov 1887 in Yakutsk Oblast; *Educ:* studied at Tambov High-School; *Career:* spent childhood in Siberia, where his parents had been exiled for polit activities; 1904 attended illegal student congress in Moscow; 1905 arrested; after release lived abroad, mainly in France; rearrested on return to Tambov; 1908 exiled for three years to Yarensk, Vologda Province; from 1912 ed, newspaper "Tambovskaya zhizn'"; 1915 worked for Zemstvo Union in Moscow and contributed to the newspaper "Russkoye slovo"; after 1917 Feb Revol member, Moscow RSDRP(B) Comt and co-ed, newspaper "Sotsial-demokrat"; helped to prepare and carry out Oct Revol in Moscow; Oct 1917 appointed Moscow City, then Moscow, Okrug Comr of Posts and Telegraphs; from May 1918 RSFSR Pop Comr of Posts and Telegraphs; deleg at 6th and 7th RSDRP(B) Congresses; *Died:* 15 Feb 1920 of a blood infection resulting from a small scratch received while taking part in a "Saturday Work" drive; buried on Red Square, Moscow.

PODLAS, Kuz'ma Petrovich (1893–1942) Mil commander; lt-gen from 1941; CP member from 1918; *Born:* 29 Oct 1893 in vil Dushatino, Bryansk Province, son of a peasant; *Career:* from 1918 in Red Army; fought in Civil War; after Civil War various commands; during Yezhov purges arrested by NKVD and imprisoned; later rehabilitated and released; 1941–42 commander, 40th, then 57th Army, Southwestern Front; 1941 helped defend Kiev and May 1942 participated in the unsuccessful Khar'kov offensive; *Awards:* two Orders of Lenin; other awards; *Died:* 25 May 1942 killed in action at Barvenkovo.

PODVOYSKAYA, Nina Avgustovna (1882–1953) Revolutionary and Party official; CP member from 1902; *Born:* 1882; *Career:* 1897 joined revol Marxist group; did propaganda work in Yaroslavl', Nizhniy Novgorod, Moscow, Kostroma, Perm' and Petersburg; frequently arrested and exiled; 1903–04 did Party work in Yaroslavl' and Nizhniy Novgorod; member, Yaroslavl' RSDRP(B) Comt; 1905 helped to organize armed workers' squads in Kostroma; Dec 1905 helped to organize workers' demonstration in Yaroslavl'; early 1906 exiled to Tobol'sk Province but fled abroad; 1908 returned to Russia and did Party work in Kostroma and Petersburg; from Feb 1917 worked for secretariat, Petrograd RSDRP(B) Comt; during Oct 1917 Revol worked for secretariat, Petrograd Mil Revol Comt; during first years of Sov rule did Party and govt work in Petrograd, Ufa and Moscow; 1920–23 worked for Red Army polit organs and for CC, RCP(B); 1924–53 worked at Marx-Engels-Lenin Inst, CC, CPSU(B); *Awards:* Order of the Red Banner of Labor; medals; *Died:* 1953.

PODVOYSKIY, Nikolay Il'ich (1880–1948) Party official and mil commander; CP member from 1901; *Born:* 28 Feb 1880 in vil Kunashovka, Chernigov Oblast, son of a teacher who later became a vil priest; *Educ:* 1894 grad Nezhin Theological College; 1894–1901 studied at Chernigov Theological Seminary, from which he was expelled for revol activities; from 1901 studied at Demidov Law College, Yaroslavl; *Career:* directed underground RSDRP workers' circle; 1904–05 chm, Bolshevik students' comt and member, Yaroslavl' RSDRP Comt; active in 1905–07 Revol; May–June 1905 helped lead gen textile workers' strike and organize Assembly of Plen Dep (Sov of Workers' Dep) in Ivanovo-Voznesensk; organized workers' combat squads in Yaroslavl'; 20 Oct 1905 seriously wounded in armed clash between workers and police in Yaroslavl'; 1906–07 lived in Germany and Switzerland; 1907 returned to Russia; 1907–08 with Petersburg, 1910–11 with Kostroma and Baku, 1911–17 again with Petersburg RSDRP(B) Comts; frequently arrested; 1908–10 and Nov 1916 – Feb 1917 in prison; 1907–18, together with M. S. Kedrov, directed "Zerno" legal Party publ house in Petersburg; 1910–14 helped found and run newspapers "Zvezda" and "Pravda"; mainly responsible for routing Lenin's correspondence with "Pravda" and with the Bolshevik faction of 4th State Duma; 1915–16 ed, journal "Voprosy strakhovaniya"; member, Finance Commission, Russian Bureau, CC, RSDRP; took part in 1917 Feb Revol in Petrograd; from Mar 1917 member, Petrograd RSDRP(B) Comt; dep, Petrograd Sov; head, Mil Org, CC, RSDRP(B); helped found and edit newspapers "Soldatskaya pravda", "Rabochiy i soldat" and "Soldat"; June 1917 elected chm, All-Russian Bureau of Front and Rear Mil Org, CC, RSDRP(B); deleg at 7th (Apr) Party Conference and 6th Congress, where he presented a report on the Mil Org; helped muster, train and arm Red Guards prior to 1917 Oct Revol; member, Petrograd Mil Revol Comt; Bureau member of latter and member of its Field Staff, Operations Troyka and other organs preparing coup; during 1917 Oct Revol chm, Mil Revol Comt; personally directed storming of Winter Palace; commander, Petrograd Mil Distr; 9 Nov 1917 appointed member, Comt (later Pop Comrt) for Mil and Naval Affairs; Nov 1917 – Mar 1918 RSFSR Pop Comr of Mil Affairs; from Jan 1918 also chm, All-Russian Collegium to Organize and Administer the Red Guards; from Feb 1918 also member, Petrograd Revol Defense Comt; Mar 1918 appointed member, Higher Mil Council, then chm, Higher Mil Inspectorate; Jan – Sept 1919 Ukr Pop Comr of Naval Affairs; 1919–23 chief of gen mil training; 1919–20 member, Mil Revol Council, 7th Army, Western Front and 10th Army, Caucasian Front; fought at Petrograd, on the Volga, in the Urals, on the Don and in the South; 1920–23 chm, Higher Physical Training Council; 1921–23 chm, Sport International (Sportintern); at 13th–15th Congresses elected member, CPSU(B) Centr Control Commission; member, Commission for Collating and Studying Material on the History of the Oct Revol and the CP; from 1935 retired; *Publ: Pervyy Sovet rabochikh deputatov* (The First Soviet Workers' Deputies) (1925); *Kommunary zashchishchayut Krasnyy Petrograd* (The Communards Defend Red Petrograd) (1927); "God 1917" (The Year 1917) (1958); *Lenin v 1917 godu* (Lenin in 1917) (1957); *Krasnaya gvardiya v Oktyabr'skiye dni* (The Red Guards in the Events of October) (1927); *Voennaya organizatsiya Tsk RSDRP(B) i VRK 1917 goda* (The Military Organization of the

RSDRP(B) Central Committee and the Military Revolutionary Committee in 1917) (1923); *Ot Krasnoy gvardii k Krasnoy Armii* (From the Red Guards to the Red Army) (1938); *Awards:* Order of the Red Banner; *Died:* 28 July 1948.

POGODIN (real name: STUKALOV), Nikolay Fyodorovich (1900–1962) Russian playwright; Hon Art Worker of RSFSR from 1949; *Born:* 3 Nov 1900 in vil Gundorovskaya, Don Oblast; *Educ:* 1914 completed primary schooling; *Career:* from 1920 worked as journalist; 1920–22 worked for newspapers "Molot", "Trudovoy Don" and "Trudovaya zhizn'"; 1922–30 corresp and essayist for "Pravda"; 1929 began to write plays; 1947–56 member, ed bd, newspaper "Literaturnaya gazeta"; 1951–60 chief ed, journal "Teatr"; from 1954 bd member, USSR Writers' Union; several times censured by Party critics, but this had no lasting effect on his career; *Publ:* essays *Kumachevoye utro* (Morning at Kumachevo) (1926); stories: *Dom s zolotoy kryshey* (The House with the Golden Roof) (1928); *Stupeni* (Steps) (1928); plays: *Temp* (Tempo) (1929); *Poema o topore* (The Poem of the Axe) (1931); *Sneg* (Snow) (1932); *Moy drug* (My Friend) (1932); *Posle bala* (After the Ball) (1934); *Aristokraty* (The Aristocrats) (1934); *Chelovek s ruzh'yom* (The Man with a Gun) (1937); *Kremlyovskiye kuranty* (Kremlin Chimes) (1941); *Sotvoreniye mira* (The Creation of the World) (1946); *Missuriyskiy val's* (Missouri Waltz) (1949); *Vikhri vrazhdebnyye* (Hostile Whirlwinds) (1953); *Sonet Petrarki* (Petrarch's Sonnet) (1957); *Tret'ya Pateticheskaya* (The Third Pathetique) (1958); *Tsvety zhizni* (Flowers of Life) (1960); *Chyornyye ptitsy* (Black Birds) (1961), etc; scripts for films: *Zaklyuchyonnyye* (The Interned); *Kubanskiye kazaki* (Kuban Cossacks); "Dzerzhinskiy"; *Pervyy eshalon* (The First Echalon), etc; non-fiction works: *Teatr i zhizn'* (Theater and Life) (1953); *Avtobiografiya* (Autobiography) (1959); *Awards:* two Orders of Lenin; Stalin Prize (1941); Lenin Prize (1959); *Died:* 19 Sept 1962 in Moscow.

POKHITONOV, Daniil Il'ich (1878–1957) Conductor; prof, Leningrad Conservatory; Pop Artiste of RSFSR from 1957; *Born:* 27 Mar 1878 in vil Rayvolga, Vyborg Province; *Educ:* 1905 grad Petersburg Conservatory after studying piano under S. F. Tsurmyulen, and composition and instrumentation under Lyadov, Glazunov and Rimsky-Korsakov; *Career:* from 1905 pianist-concertmaster and choirmaster, 1909–56 conductor, Mariinskiy Theater; 1918–32 also conductor, Maly Opera Theater; 1919 and 1938–41 taught at Leningrad Conservatory; worked a great deal with Chaliapine; *Works:* conducted operas: "Khovanshchina" (1912); "The Barber of Seville" (1916); "Eugene Onegin"; Auber's "Fenella"; Boyto's "Mephistopheles" (1918); *Vrazh'ya sila* (The Hostile Force) (1920); "Lohengrin" (1923); Serov's "Judith" (1925); "I Pagliacci" (1929); *Skazka o tsare Saltane* (The Tale of Tsar Saltan) (1930); "Lakme" (1931); *Pskovityanka* (The Woman of Pskov) (1933); Napravnik's "Dubrovskiy" (1947); "Carmen" (1948), etc; *Publ: Iz proshlogo russkoy opery* (The Russian Opera's Past) (1949); *Died:* 31 Dec 1957 in Leningrad.

POKRASS, Daniil Yakovlevich (1905–1954) Composer; *Born:* 30 Nov 1905 in Kiev; *Educ:* studied piano at Kiev Conservatory; *Career:* together with his brother Dmitriy, wrote numerous choral pieces; *Works:* songs: "Cavalry Song" (1936); "Moscow in May" (1937); "Slash Us Not with Sabre Sharp" (1937); "Komsomol Farewell" (1938); "Gather Not, a Thunderclouds" (1938); "If War Breaks Out Tomorrow" (1938); "The Tankmen's March" (1939); "Tankmen Three" (1939); opera "Sady tsvetut" (Gardens in Bloom) (1950), etc; *Awards:* Badge of Hon; medals; *Died:* 16 Apr 1954 in Moscow.

POKROVSKIY, Aleksandr Vasil'yevich (1886–1963) Actor; trade-union official; Hon Art Worker of RSFSR from 1957; CP member from 1919; *Born:* 9 Mar 1886; *Educ:* 1908–11 grad Drama Dept, Moscow Philharmonic College; from 1911 acted at theaters in Tula, Orenburg, Arkhangel'sk, Sebastopol, Kazan', Saratov and Tiflis; 1919–21 head, Theater Club Section, Polit Dept, 10th and 11th Armies; 1930–33 dir, Moscow Comedy Theater; 1933–37 dir, Moscow Operetta Theater; 1939–40 dir, Stanislavskiy Opera Theater; 1947–48 dir, Stanislavsky and Nemirovich-Danchenko Musical Theater; 1948–63 dep chm, Presidium, Council of All-Russian Theatrical Soc; also engaged in trade-union work; 1923–25 dep chm, Geo Art Workers' Union; 1925–28 Presidium member, 1937–39 chm, Moscow Province Art Workers' Union; 1926–52 Presidium member, 1940–47 chm, CC, Art Workers' Union; *Roles:* Neschastlivtsev in Ostrovskiy's comedy *Les* (The Forest); the Mayor and Skalozub in Gogol's *Revizor* (The Government Inspector), etc; *Died:* 4 July 1963.

POKROVSKIY, Aleksey Ivanovich (1880–1958) Ophthalmologist; Hon Sci Worker of RSFSR; *Born:* 1880; *Educ:* 1908 grad Med Fac, Moscow Univ; *Career:* from 1908 intern, A. A. Kryukov's Clinic; 1911–14 asst prof, Eye Clinic, Moscow Higher Women's Courses (now 2nd Moscow Med Inst); 1923–26 asst prof, 1926–29 assoc prof, from 1929 prof, Voronezh Eye Clinic; specialized in pathoanatomy of optic organ; did research on pathogenesis of trachoma, leading to theory of inflammatory genesis of this disease; studied orbital oncology, glaucoma and blindness; made major contribution to org of ophthalmological care in Centr Asia; published fundamental work on blindness in Uzbekistan and Turmenistan, its causes and measures of combatting it; wrote over 100 works: *Publ: K voprosu o geograficheskom rasprostanenii glaukomy i slepoty ot neyo v SSSR* (The Geographical Distribution of Glaucoma and Blindness Stemming from It in the USSR) (1925); *K ucheniyu ob opukholyakh glaznitsy* (The Theory of Tumors of the Eyesocket) (1935); *K voprosu ob operativnom lechenii glaukomy* (The Surgical Treatment of Glaucoma) (1950); *Khirurgiya glaznitsy i pridatochnykh polostey nosa* (Surgery of the Eyesocket and the Nasal Accessory Sinuses) (1959); *Died:* 1958.

POKROVSKIY, Mikhail Nikolayevich (1868–1932) Historan; govt official; member, USSR Acad of Sci from 1929; CP member from 1905; *Born:* 29 Aug 1868 in Moscow; *Educ:* 1891 grad History and Philology Fac, Moscow Univ; *Career:* taught Russian history at women's secondary educ establishments and women's pedag courses in Moscow; 1903–04 active in liberal zemstvo movement; took part in 1905–07 Revol; member, Moscow RSDRP(B) Comt; worked for Bolshevik periodicals; at London RSDRP Congress elected cand member, CC; 1908–17 lived abroad; 1909–11, while in Paris, member of "Vperyod" (Forwards) group; Aug 1917 returned to Russia and helped prepare and carry out Oct Revol; Nov 1917 – Mar 1918 first chm, Moscow Sov of Workers and Soldiers' Dept; May 1918–32 RSFSR Dep Pop Comr of Educ; 1918 sided for a while with "Leftist Communists"; 1923–27 active in anti-Trotsky campaign; attacked "Trotskyist conceptions"; in history; at various times head: Communist Acad; Inst of History, USSR Acad of Sci; Inst of Red Prof; Soc of Marxist Historians; Centr Archives; ed, journals "Istorik-marksist", "Bor'ba klassov" and "Krasnyy arkhiv"; member, Main Ed Staff, 1st ed of "BSE" (Large Soviet Encyclopedia); taught at various higher educ establishments; 1930 elected Presidium member, CPSU(B) Centr Control Commission; member, USSR and All-Russian Centr Exec Comt of various convations; convocations; wrote many works on Sov history, particularly for policy, historiography and 19th–20th-Century revol movement; edited series of archive documents on 17th–18th-Century peasant movements, 1905–07 Revol, and history of Oct Revol and Civil War; although he was a leading Marxist historian, he fell into great disfavor with Stalin; 1934–38 his works and historical views were proclaimed anti-Marxist, pseudo-scientific and injurious; his reputation was not restored until after the 22nd CPSU Congress; *Publ: Russkaya istoriya s drevneyshikh vremyon* (Russian History from the Earliest Times) (4 vol, 1911–12); *Ocherk istorii russkoy kul'tury* (An Outline History of Russian Culture) (2 vol, 1915–18); *Russkaya istoriya v samom szhatom ocherke* (Russian History in Briefest Outline) (1923); *Ocherki russkogo revolyutsionnogo dvisheniya XIX–XX vv.* (Outline of the Russian Revolutionary Movement in the 19th and 20th Centuries) (1924); *Vneshnyaya politika Rossii v XX v.* (The Foreign Policy of Russia in the 20th Century) (1926); collected articles *Imperialisticheskaya voyna* (Imperialist War) (1928); *Istoricheskaya nauka i bor'ba klassov* (Historical Science and Class Struggle) (2 vol, 1933); collected articles *Diplomatiya i voyny tsarskoy Rossii v XIX stoletii* (The Diplomacy and Wars of Tsarist Russia in the 19th Century) (1923); *Izbrannyye prozvedeniya* (Selected Works) (4 vol, 1965–1967), etc; *Died:* 10 Apr 1932; buried on Moscow's Red Square.

POLBIN, Ivan Semyonovich (1905–1945) Air Force commander; maj-gen, Sov Air Force; CP member from 1927; *Born:* 27 Jan 1905 in vil Rtishchevo-Kamenka, Simbirsk Province; *Educ:* 1932 grad flying school; *Career:* from 1927 in Red Army; 1933–38 various posts with air force units; 1938 commanded bomber squadron in Lake Khasan battles; 1941–45 commanded bomber, regt, div, then corps; 1941 fought at Smolensk and Moscow; 1942 at Stalingrad; took part in campaigns for liberation of Ukr and Poland; carried out 157 bomber missions; *Awards:* twice Hero of the Sov Union (1942 and 1945); two Order of Lenin; other orders;

medals; *Died:* 11 Feb 1945 killed in Breslau bombing raid.

POLENOV, Andrey L'vovich (1871–1947) Surgeon, neurosurgeon and traumatologist; Dr of Med from 1901; prof from 1914; member, USSR Acad of Med Sci from 1945; Hon Sci Worker of RSFSR from 1934; *Born:* 19 Apr 1871 in Moscow; *Educ:* 1896 grad Petersburg Mil Med Acad; *Career:* received surgical training at provincial mil hospitals; 1899–1910 surgeon, Kronstadt Naval Hospital; 1901 defended doctor's thesis on the effect of sympathectomy on experimental epilepsy; 1905 studied neurosurgery abroad; from 1914 prof, Chair of Operative Surgery, from 1918 head, Chair of Traumatology and Orthopedics, Petrograd Psychoneurological Inst (now Leningrad Inst of Sanitation and Hygiene); during WW 1 also helped to organize institutions for the treatment and care of war cripples; from 1917 founder-dir, Petrograd Inst of Physical Surgery (from 1924 State Traumatological Inst); founder-head, Chair of Orthopedics and Traumatology, State Inst of Med Knowledge; 1924 founder, Chair of Surgical Neuropathology, State Traumatological Inst; from 1938 founder-dir, Leningrad Neurosurgical Inst, which now bears his name; collegium member, Leningrad Oblast Health Dept; dep, Leningrad City Sov; member, All-Russian Assoc of Sci and Tech Workers for the Promotion of Socialist Construction; chm, Leningrad Soc of Surgeons and Orthopedists; co-chm, Pirogov Surgical Soc; wrote over 120 works; *Publ:* doctor's thesis *Simpatektomiya, vliyaniye yeyo na eksperimental'nuyu epilepsiyu* (Sympathectomy and Its Effect on Experimental Epilepsy) (1901); *Osnovnyye voprosy bor'by s prozvodstvennym travmatizmom i yego posledstviyami* (The Basic Problems in the Campaign Against Industrial Accidents and Their Sequelae) (1931); coauthor, *Troficheskiye zabolevaniya konechnostey* (Trophic Diseases of the Extremities) (1931); coauthor, *Opukholi golovnogo mozga* (Brain Tumors) (1932);; coauthor, *Kratkiy kurs khirurgicheskoy nevropatologii* (A Short Course of Surgical Neuropathology) (1935); coauthor, *Povrezhdeniya i zabolevaniya pokrovov i kostey cherepa, mozgovykh obolochek i golovnogo mozga* (Injuries and Diseases of the Cranial Integuments and Bones, the Meninges and the Brain) (1936); coauthor, *Kratkiy kurs tekhniki operatsiy na perifericheskoy i tsentral'noy nervnoy sistemy* (A Short Course on the Techniques of Operating on the Peripheral and Central Nervous Systems) (1937); coauthor, *Osnovy prakticheskoy nevrokhirurgii* (The Principles of Practical Neurosurgery) (1943); coauthor, *Khirurgiya vegetativnoy nervnoy sistemy* (Surgery of the Vegetative Nervous System) (1947); *Izbrannyye trudy* (Selected Works) (1956); *Awards:* Stalin Prize (1946); Order of Lenin, Order of the Red Banner of Labor; medals; *Died:* 19 July 1947 in Leningrad.

POLETAYEV (pseudonym: POETAN), Fyodor Andrianovich (1909–1945) WW 2 hero; fought with partisans in Italy; *Born:* 1909; in vil Katino, now Ryazan Oblast, son of a peasant; *Career:* worked as a blacksmith; 1941 joined ranks of 28th Guards Artillery Regt, 9th Red Army Guards Infantry Div; summer 1942 captured by Germans and interned in Vyaz'ma cocentration camp; later transferred to concentration camps in Poland, Yugoslavia and, finally, Italy; summer 1944 escaped from camp near Genoa with help of Italian communists and joined Nino Franchi Partisan Brigade; 1945 fell in action near Catalupo; *Awards:* Hero of the Sov Union (1962); Italian Gold Medal of Valor; *Died:* 2 Feb 1945; buried in Genoa.

POLETAYEV, Nikolay Gavrilovich (1889–1935) Russian poet; *Born:* 5 Aug 1889 in Odoyev, Tula Province; *Educ:* grad business school in Moscow; *Career:* railroad clerk; 1918 first work printed; 1918 joined Lit Studio, Moscow Proletarian Culture Org; from 1920 member, "Kuznitsa" (The Smithy) lit assoc; then member, Russian Assoc of Proletarian Writers; printed his works in journals "Gorn", "Gudki," "Tvorchestvo" and "Kuznitsa"; *Publ:* verse collections: *Stikhi* (Verse) (1919); *Pesnya o solov'yakh* (Song of Nightingales) (1921); *Slomannyye zabory* (Broken Fences) (1923); stories *Zhelesznodorozhniki* (Railroad Workers) (1925); verse *Rezkiy svet* (Harsh Light) (1926); *Stikhi* (Verse) (1930); *O solov'yakh, Kotorykh ne slykhal* (Nightingales Unheard) (1932), etc; *Died:* 16 Mar 1935 in Moscow.

POLETAYEV, Nikolay Gur'yevich (1872–1930) Revolutionary; CP member from 1904; *Born:* 15 Apr 1872 in Kostroma Province, son of a peasant; *Career:* from 1891 latheoperator, Putilov Plant; member, Brusnev Group; 1892 deported to his place of birth; 1901 returned to Petersburg and became active in League for the Liberation of the Working Class; Dec 1895 again arrested and exiled; 1898 emigrated to Germany and worked at various plants; 1901–04, after returning to Russia, worked in Ukr; from 1904 again at Putilov Plant; member, Putilov Plant RSDRP Org; 1905 helped organize Putilov strike; Oct 1905 elected member, Petersburg Sov of Workers' Dep; from 1907 dep, 3rd State Duma from Petersburg workers' curia; headed Bolshevik wing of RSDRP faction in Duma; helped publish newspapers "Zvezda" and "Pravda"; from 1913 worked at Petersburg Mech Plant; routed Bolshevik correspondence with Lenin; 1917 directed "Pravda" printing press; 1918–21 publishing and admin work in Moscow; 1921 moved to Tuapse on med grounds and worked for Pop Comrt of For Trade; *Died:* 23 Oct 1930.

POLIDOROV, S.I. (1882–1932) Party and govt official; CP member from 1905; *Born:* 1882; *Career:* did Party work in Moscow, Rybinsk and Yekaterinoslav; 1905 fought in Dec Revol in Moscow; frequently arrested by Tsarist authorities; after 1917 Oct Revol did exec Party and govt work; member, All-Russian Centr Exec Comt; chm, Moscow Province Exec Comt; member, Moscow CPSU(B) Comt; deleg at 8th and 9th RCP(B) Congresses; *Died:* 1932.

POLIKARPOV, Dmitriy Alekseyevich (1905–1965) Party official; Cand of Historical Sci; CP member from 1924; *Born:* 1905; *Educ:* 1948 completed corresp course at Moscow Oblast Teachers' Training Inst; 1948 completed corresp course at Higher Party School, CC, CPSU; 1950 grad Acad of Soc Sci, CC, CPSU; *Career:* 1923–32 instructor, USSR Pop Comrt of Mil Affairs, secr, distr Komsomol comt, then chm, city then rayon sov; 1932–39 head, city, then oblast educ dept; 1939–41 worked for CC, CPSU(B); 1941–44 dep head, Propaganda and Agitation Bd, CC, CPSU(B) and chm, Radio Comt, USSR Council of Pop Comr; 1944–46 and 1954–55 secr, Bd, USSR Writers' Union; 1950–54 dep dir, then dir, Moscow's Lenin Teachers' Training Inst; 1954 secr, Moscow City CPSU Comt; 1955–62 head, 1962–65 dep head, Dept of Culture, CC, CPSU; from 1961 cand member, CC, CPSU; 1956–61 member, CPSU Centr Auditing Commission; dep, RSFSR Supr Sov of 1955 convocation; dep, USSR Supr Sov of 1958 and 1962 convocation; *Died:* Nov 1965.

POLIKARPOV, Nikolay Nikolayevich (1892–1944) Aircraft designer; prof from 1943; *Born:* 8 July 1892; *Educ:* 1916 grad Petrograd Polytech Inst, where he attended aviation and aeronautics courses; *Career:* began working as eng at Aeronautics Dept, Russo-Baltic Works, Petrograd; from 1918 directed various aviation plants; 1923 built his first fighter – the I–1 (IL–400), which was followed by the two-seater 2I–N1, whose performance compared favorably with equivalent for fighters; 1925–30 built the I–3 fighter, the DI–2 two-seater, the R–5 reconnaissance plane, etc; 1927 designed the PO–2 (U–2) trainer, which was still in use in the 1950's; 1933–34 built the highly-maneuverable I–15 fighter biplane and the I–16 monoplane; 1938 designed the I–153 ("Chayka") fighter; 1941–44 worked on high-speed fighters and other mil aircraft; from 1943 prof and head, Chair of Aircraft Design and Planning, Moscow Aviation Inst; *Awards:* prizes at int aviation exhibitions (1930, 1936); Hero of Socialist Labor (1940); two Stalin Prizes (1941 and 1943); two Orders of Lenin; Order of the Red Star; *Died:* 30 July 1944.

POLIKARPOVICH, Konstantin Mikhaylovich (1889–1963) Archeologist; *Born:* 18 Mar 1889 in vil Belaya Dubrova, now Mogilev Oblast, son of a priest; *Educ:* grad Mogilev Theological Seminary; taught himself archeology; *Career:* began archeological research just in prior to WW 1, while working as a teacher; from 1926 worked for Archeological Commission, Inst of Bel Culture; then assoc, Archeological Dept, Inst of History, Bel Acad of Sci; 1932–33 made archeological study of Azov littoral and Southern Bug for Inst of Geology, USSR Acad of Sci; then returned to Bel SSR; 1941–43 field geologist, Kaz Geological Bd and studied Mesolithic and Neolithic sites in various parts of Kazakhstan; from 1943 assoc, from 1944 head, Archeological Section, Inst of History, Bel Acad of Sci; discovered and studied many Paleolithic, Neolithic and Bronce Age sites and Early Iron Age settlements and tumuli in Bel; of particular importance were his studies of the late Paleolithic sites near the settlements of Berdyzh, Yeliseyevichi and Yudinova; developed a method of detecting Paleolithic sites by mapping areas with traces of the bones of large animals from the Quaternary period; *Publ: Dahistarychnyya stayanki syarednyaha Sozha* (Prehistoric Sites of the Central Sozh) (1928); *Paleolit i mezolit BSSR i nekotorykh sosednikh territoriy Verkhnego Pridneprov'ya* (The Paleolithic and Mesolithic in the Belorussian SSR and Some Neighboring Areas of the Upper Dnieper Region) (1934); *Problema palealitu Belarusi* (The Problem of Belorussian Paleolithic) (1949); *Arkheologicheskiye issledovaniya v BSSR v*

1945–1953 godakh (Archeological Research in the Belorussian SSR in 1945–53) (1957), etc; *Died:* 20 Feb 1963.

POLITSEYMAKO, Vitaliy Pavlovich (1906–1967) Actor; Pop Artiste of USSR from 1957; CP member from 1948; *Born:* 5 May 1906; *Educ:* 1927 grad Leningrad Technicum of Stagecraft; *Career:* acted at Leningrad Young Playgoers' Theater; from 1930 actor, Gorky Bolshoy Drama Theater; *Roles:* Yegor Bulychyov, Nil, Redozubov and Dostigayev in Gorky's plays *Yegor Bulychov i drugiye* (Yegor Bulychov and Co), *Meshchane* (The Philistines), *Varvary* (The Barbarians) and *Dostigayev i drugiye* (Dostigayev and Co); Godun in Lavrenyov's *Razlom* (Break-Up); Famusov in Griboyedov's *Gore ot uma* (Woe from Wit); Aesop in Figeiredoux's "The Fox and the Grapes," etc; *Awards:* Stalin Prize (1951); *Died:* 23 Dec 1967.

POLIVANOV, Aleksey Andreyevich(1855–1920) Mil commander; gen of infantry from 1915; *Born:* 1855; *Educ:* 1880 grad Nikolay Eng Acad; 1888 grad Gen Staff Acad; *Career:* fought in 1877–78 Russo-Turkish War; 1899–1904 served with Main Staff and was also asst ed, then chief ed, journal "Voyennyy sbornik" and Min of War rep on newspaper "Russkiy invalid"; 1905–06 chief, Main Staff; 1906–12 asst Min of War; 1912–15 member, State Council; June 1915–Mar 1916 Min of War and chm, Special Defense Council; 1920 member, Special Council under commander in chief of Red Army; 1920 mil expert on Sov deleg negotiating Sov-Polish peace treaty; *Died:* 1920 in Riga of typhus.

POLIVANOV, Yevgeniy Dmitriyevich (1891–1938) Russian philologist and Orientalist; CP member from 1919; *Born:* 12 Mar 1891; *Educ:* 1912 grad Petersburg Univ an Oriental Practical Acad for Japanese Studies; *Career:* from 1912 at Chair of Comparative Philology, Petersburg Univ; 1917–18 head, Dept of Oriental Countries, RSFSR Pop Comrt of For Affairs; 1918–19 founded League of Chinese Workers and edited Chinese Communist newspaper in Petrograd; 1919–21 prof, Petersburg Univ; 1921–26 worked for Comintern in Moscow, then in Tashkent; 1927–29 head, Linguistics Section, Russian Assoc of Soc Sci Research Institutes, Moscow; 1929–37 worked in Samarkand, Tashkent and Frunze; worked on linguistic poetics and poetics of Oriental lit, especially Turkic, Chinese and Japanese; traced migration of subjects and themes from one lit to another and studied folklore, including Kir epic "Manas"; contributed to linguistic theory; planned a major work entitled "Svod poetiki" (Corpus poetricarum) in which he intended to compare the structural features of the world's languages with the poetic traits in their corresponding lit; late 1920's involved in a conflict with N.Ya. Marr and his school and criticized many aspects of his "Japhetic theory"; as a result of this he was forced to quit Moscow and move to Centr Asia; arrested by State Security organs; *Publ: Kratkaya grammatika usbekskogo yazyka* (A Short Uzbek Grammar) (2 vol, 1926); *Vvedeniye v yazykoznaniye dlya vostokovednykh vuzov* (An Introduction to Linguistics for Oriental Study Colleges) (1928); coauthor, *Grammatika yaponskogo razgovornogo yazyka* (A Colloquial Japanese Grammar) (1930); coauthor, *Grammatika sovremennogo kitayskogo yazyka* (A Modern Chinese Grammar) (1930); *Za marksistskoye yazykoznaniye* (For Marxist Linguistics) (1931); *Russkaya grammatika v sopostavlenii s uzbekskim yazykom* (Russian Grammar Compared with Uzbek) (1934); *Opyt chastnoy metodiki prepodavaniya russkogo yazyka uzbekam* (Experience in Special Methods of Teaching Russian to Uzbeks) (1935); *Stat'i po obshchemu yazykoznaniyu* (Articles on General Linguistics) (1968), etc; *Died:* 25 Jan 1938 in Smolensk in imprisonment; posthumously rehabilitated.

POLIYEVKTOV, Mikhail Aleksandrovich (1872–1942) Historian; *Born:* 2 Mar 1872; *Educ:* 1894 grad Petersburg Univ; *Career:* from 1917 prof, Petrograd (Leningrad) Univ; from 1920 lectured on Russian history at Tbilisi Univ; specialized in archeography; did research on Russian for policy in 17th and 18th Centuries; traced, collated and published documents on history of Russian for policy in 13th–18th Centuries and history of Caucasian peoples; *Publ: Baltiyskiy vopros v russkoy politike posle Nishtadtskogo mira (1721–25)* (The Baltic Question in Russian Policy After the Peace of Nystad /1721–25/) (1907); *Nikolay I. Biografiya i obzor tsarstvovaniya* (Nicholas I. A Biography and Review of His Reign) (1918); *Staryy Tiflis v izvestiyakh sovremennikov* (Old Tiflis According to Contemporary Accounts) (1929); *Materialy po istorii gruzinsko-russkikh vzaimootnosheniy, 1615–1640* (Material on the History of Georgian–Russian Relations. 1615–1640) (1937); *Yevropeyskiye puteshestvenniki XIII–XVIII vekov po Kavkazu* (European Travelers in the Caucasus in the 13th–18th Centuries) (1935); *Died:* 21 Dec 1942.

POLKANOV, Aleksandr Alekseyevich (1888–1963) Geologist and petrographer; prof from 1921; member USSR Acad of Sci from 1943; *Born:* 25 May 1888; *Educ:* 1911 grad Petersburg Univ; *Career:* from 1921 prof, Leningrad Univ; from 1950 dir, Laboratory of Pre-Cambrian Geology, USSR Acad of Sci; 1958 chm, 3rd Conference, Int Assoc for the Study of the Lower Regions of the Earth's Crust; specialized in petrology and the structural analysis of instrusive bodies; was an expert on the pre-Cambrian formations and minerals of the Baltic Shield; helped develop the potassium-argon method of determining the absolute age of geological formations; *Publ: Geologo-petrologicheskiy ocherk severozapadnoy chasti Kol'skogo poluostrova* (A Geological and Petrological Study of the Northwestern Kola Peninsula) (1935); *Geologicheskiy ocherk Kol'skogo poluostrova* (A Geological Study of the Kola Peninsula) (1936); coauthor, *Petrologiya plutona Gremyakha-Vyrmes. Kol'skiy poluostrov* (The Petrology of Gremyakh-Vyrmes Pluton. The Kola Peninsula) (1941); *Geologiya khoglyandiya-iotniya Baltiyskogo shchita* (The Geology of Hoglandium-Iotnium in the Baltic Shield) (1956), etc; *Awards:* two orders; medals; Lenin Prize (1962); *Died:* 10 Jan 1963.

POLKOVNIKOV, Georgiy Petrovich (1883–1918) Mil commander; commander, Petrograd Mil Dist Sept–Oct 1917; col, Russian Army; *Born:* 23 Feb 1883 at Kravyanskaya, Don Oblast, son of a Cossack officer; *Educ:* 1904 grad Mikhail Artillery College; 1912 grad Gen Staff Acad; *Career:* fought in 1904–05 Russo-Japanese War; from 1912 commanded a company in 12th Don Cossack Regt; during WW 1 served on staff of 2nd Cavalry Div, 5th Cavalry Corps on Rumanian Front and on Ussuri Cavalry Div; from July 1917 commanded 1st Amur Cossack Regt, 3rd Cavalry Corps and sided with Provisional Govt; 17 Sept 1917 appointed commander, Petrograd Mil Distr; 4–5 Nov 1917 negotiated with Petrograd Mil Revol Comt; 7 Nov 1917 dismissed from his post by Provisional Govt; 1917, commanding army of "Comt for the Salvation of the Country and the Revol," helped organize anti-Sov cadets revolt; fled to Don when this revolt was crushed; Mar 1918 arrested in Don Steppe by Sov authorities and sentenced to death by Revol tribunal; *Died:* Mar 1918 executed.

POLONSKIY, S.M. (1873–1934) Therapist and balneologist; prof; *Born:* 1873; *Career:* from 1901 physician in Kislovodsk; 1920–33 head, Kislovodsk Physiotherapeutic Inst; dir and sci head, Lenin Cardiological Clinic, and consultant, Kislovodsk Resort Bd; *Died:* 1934.

POLONSKIY, Vladimir Ivanovich (1893–1939) Party and govt official; CP member from 1912; *Born:* 1893; *Career:* electr fitter by trade; Party work in Petersburg; arrested by Tsarist authorities; after 1917 Feb Revol secr, Moscow Metalworkers Union; after 1917 Oct Revol polit work in Red Army; then member, Southern Bureau, All-Russian Centr Trade-Union Council and Presidium member, Ukr Council of Pop Comr; from 1921 secr, CC, Miners' Union; then Party work in Moscow; secr, Rogozha-Simonov Rayon Party Comt, Moscow; head, Org Dept, Moscow Party Comt, then secr Moscow Party Comt; May 1929–Aug 1930 secr, All-Union Centr Trade Union Council; then secr, CC, CP(B) Azer; also secr, Transcaucasian Kray CPSU(B) Comt; head, Org Dept, CC, CPSU(B); head, Polit Bd, USSR Pop Comrt of Means of Communication; from 1937 USSR Dep Pop Comr of Communications; at the 15th–17th Party Congresses elected cand member, CC, CPSU(B); arrested by State Security organs; *Died:* 1939 in imprisonment.

POLONSKIY, Vyacheslav (real name: GUSIN, Vyacheslav Pavlovich) (1886–1932) Critic, historian and journalist; *Born:* 5 July 1886 in Petersburg, son of a watchmaker; *Educ:* 1907 passed examinations to qualify as a teacher; entered Psychoneurological Inst; *Career;* 1905 joined Mensheviks; exiled for two years to Olonetsk Province for revol activities; began to write as a student; after 1917 Oct Revol active in journalism, lit, as critic, publicist and historian; from 1919 leading member, Lit Publ Dept, Pop Comrt of Educ; head, Lit Publ Dept, Polit Bd of Revol Mil Council; member, Soc of Marxist Historians; ed or ed staff member, journals and publ "Krasnyy arkhiv," "Istorik-marksist," "BSE" (Large Soviet Encyclopedia), etc; 1921–29 edited first Sov criticism and bibliographical journal "Pechat' i revolyutsiya"; 1925–31 edited lit journal "Novyy mir"; *Publ:* "Maksim Gor'kiy" (1919); *Zhizn' Mikhaila Bakunina* (The Life of Mikhail Bakunin) (1920); *Ukhodyashchaya Rus'* (Vanishing Rus) (1924); *Spor o Bakunine i Dostroyevskom* (The Bankunin-Dostoyevsky Dispute) (1926); *Marksizm i kritika. Iz literaturnykh sporov poslednikh let*

(Marxism and Criticism. From the Literary Disputes of Recent Years) (1927); *Ocherki literaturnogo dvizheniya revolyutsionnoy epokhi (1917–1927)* (Studies in the Literary Movement of the Revolutionary Period /1917–1927/) (1928); *Literatura i obshchestvo* (Literature and Society) (1929); *O Mayakovskom* (Mayakovskiy) (1931); "Magnitostroy" (1932); *Soznaniye i tvorchestvho*(Conscience and Creativity) (1934, posthumously); *Died:* 24 Feb 1932 in Moscow.

POLOSUKHIN, Aleksandr Porfir'yevich (1901–1965) Physiologist; prof; Dr of Med from 1940; member from 1954 and first vice-pres from 1955, Kaz Acad of Sci; CP member from 1944; *Born:* 1901 in Tetyushi, Tat ASSR; *Educ:* 1932 grad Med Fac, Perm' Univ; *Career:* 1919–23 served in Red Army; then studied med at Perm' Univ; 1933–37 asst prof, Chair of Physiology, Sverdlovsk Med Inst; 1937–38 head, physiological laboratory in Sochi; 1938–63 head, Chair of Normal Physiology, Alma-Ata Med Inst; 1944 founded Physiology Section af Kaz Branch, USSR Acad of Sci; subsequently reorganized this into Inst of Physiology, Kaz Acad of Sci and directed this inst until his death in 1965; 1946 elected member, Kaz Acad of Sci; founder-chm, Kaz Branch and Bd member, All-Union Pavlov Physiological Soc; until 1956 dep chm, 1956–60 chm, Kaz Soc for the Dissemination of Polit and Sci Knowledge; dep, Kaz Supr Sov of 1959 and 1963 convocations and chm of its Health and Soc Security Commission; member, ed bd, "Fiziologicheskiy zhurnal SSSR imeni Sechenova"; co-ed, physiology section, 2nd ed of "BSE" (Large Soviet Encyclopedia); specialized in physiology of circulation, respiration and lymph system; also studied metabolism, age physiology, shock, silicosis, etc; developed method of treating shock with his own anti-shock fluid; wrote over 100 works; *Awards:* Order of Lenin; other orders; medals; *Died:* 4 Sept 1965 in Moscow.

POLOVINKIN, Aleksandr Aleksandrovich (1887–1955) Geographer; prof; Dr of Geographical Sci; corresp member, RSFSR Acad of Pedag Sci from 1945; *Born:* 12 Nov 1887; *Educ:* 1912 grad Natural Sci Dept, Physics and Mathematics Fac, Kazan' Univ; *Career:* from 1912 taught at Kazan' Business College; 1920 graduated to high-school teaching; taught geography at Yakutsk Univ, Chita Inst of Public Educ and Far Eastern Univ; 1934–54 prof, dept head, and dean of Geographical Fac, Moscow's Lenin State Teachers' Training Inst; studied physico-geographical characteristics of Siberia; did research on methods of teaching geography in higher and secondary schools; from 1933 helped draft geography syllabi and curricula for higher and secondary educ establishments; helped write 5th-grade textbook "Fizicheskaya geografiya" (Physical Geography); wrote other textbooks and teaching aids for high schools, as well as methodical aids for teachers; *Publ: Osnovy obshchego zemlevedeniya* (The Principles of General Geography) (1958); coauthor, *Metodika geografii* (Geographical Methods) (1939); *Obshchaya fizicheskaya geografiya* (General Physical Geography) (2nd ed, 1952); *Geografiya i rodnaya priroda* (Geography and Nature) (1949); *Geografiya i risovaniye* (Geography and Drawing) (3rd ed, 1955); *Fizicheskaya geografiya* (Physical Geography) (1959); *Metodika prepodavaniya fizicheskoy geografii* (Methods of Teaching Physical Geography) (3rd ed, 1953); *Awards:* Order of Lenin; *Died:* 28 July 1955.

POLOZ, M.N. (1891–1937) Govt official; CP member from 1920; *Born:* 1891; *Career:* 1919–22 Presidium member, All-Russian Centr Exec Comt; 1922–23 member Labor and Defense Council and plen of Ukr SSR; 1923–24 chm, Ukr Gosplan; 1924–26 Dep Pop Comr of Finance, then Pop Comr of Finance; 1927 Presidium member, USSR Centr Exec Comt; then dep chm, Budget Bd, USSR Centr Exec Comt; arrested by State Security organs; *Died:* 1937 in imprisonment.

POLTORATSKIY, Pavel Gerasimovich (1888–1918) Govt and Party official; CP member from 1905; *Born:* 1888 in Novocherkassk, son of a worker; *Career:* type-setter by trade; did revol work in Rostov-on-Don and Baku; 1913 imprisoned; 1917 chm, Novo-Bukhara (Kagan) Sov; deleg at 1st All-Russian Congress of Soviets; helped muster Red Guards in Turkestan; 15 Nov 1917 at 3rd Turkestani Kray Congress of Soviets elected Pop Comr of Labor; then chm, Turkestani Sovnarkhoz; also Presidium member, Turkestani Centr Exec Comt; co-founder and co-ed, Ashkhabad newspaper "Sovetskiy Turkestan"; July 1918 left Ashkhabad for Transcaspian region with detachment of Red Guards to crush an anti-Sov revolt; 22 July 1918 captured by insurgents and executed along with his comrades; 1919–27 the capital of the Turkmen SSR (now Ashkhabad) was named after him; many cultural and public institutions in Turkmen SSR named after him; *Died:* 22 July 1918 executed.

POLUKHIN, Vladimir Fyodorovich (1886–1918) Politican; CP member from 1909; *Born:* 1886; *Career:* from spring 1918 Naval Collegium's comr-extraordinary in Caspian; *Died:* 1918 executed along with 25 other Baku comr.

POLUPANOV, Andrey Vasil'yevich (1888–1956) Party and govt official; CP member from 1912; *Born:* 14 Sept 1888 in the Donbass, son of a miner; *Career:* did mil service with Black Sea Fleet; imprisoned for three years for revol propaganda; during 1917 Feb Revol elected chm, sailors' comt of "Fidonisi" minelayer; during 1917 Oct Revol headed squad of Black Sea sailors; during 1918–20 Civil War commanded armored train, Dnieper Naval Flotilla, then armored units of Red Army; 1920–53 exec Party and govt work; *Died:* 5 Dec 1956.

POLUYAN, D.V. (1886–1937) Party and govt official; CP member from 1918; *Born:* 1886; *Career:* 1904–14 member, RSDRP(B); 1914–18 Menshevik-Defensist; 1919–20 head, Polit Dept, 9th Army and member, Revol Mil Council, 15th Army and 2nd Cavalry Army; 1919 deleg at 8th All-Russian RSDRP(B) Conference; 1921–29 worked for Pop Comrt of Means of Communication, first in Azer, then in Moscow; arrested by State Security organs; *Died:* 1937 in imprisonment.

POLUYAN, Yan Vasil'yevich (1891–1937) Party and govt official; CP member from 1912; *Born:* 9 Oct 1891 of Kuban Cossack descent; *Career:* 1907 joined revol movement; 1915 sentenced to five years at hard labor; 1917 released following Feb Revol; 1917 chm, Exec Comt, Yekaterinodar (Krasnodar) Sov and member, Yekaterinodar RSDRP(B) Comt; 1918–20 chm, Kuban Oblast Revol Comt and Exec Comt; chm, Council of Pop Comr, Kuban-Black Sea SSR; chm, Revol Mil Council, North Caucasian (11th) Army; member, Revol Mil Council, 9th (Kuban) Army; head, Polit Dept, Southwestern Front; 1918–31 member, All-Russian Centr Exec Comt; 1920–22 chm, Kuban Revol Comt and Kuban Oblast Exec Comt; member, Kuban-Black Sea Oblast RCP(B) Comt; member, Caucasian and Southeastern Bureaux, CC, RCP(B); 1921 deleg at 10th RCP(B) Congress; 1922–31 member, USSR Centr Exec Comt; from 1922 chm, Tver' (Kalinin) Province Exec Comt; 1925–29 worked for All–Russian Centr Exec Comt, holding at one time a seat in its Presidium; 1929–30 chm, Far Eastern Kray Exec Comt; 1931–37 chm, Electricity Bd, RSFSR Pop Comrt of Communal Econ; arrested by State Security organs; *Died:* 8 Oct 1937 in imprisonment; posthumously rehabilitated.

POLYAKIN, Miron Borisovich (1895–1941) Violonist; Hon Art Worker of RSFSR; *Born:* 31 Jan 1895 in Cherkassy; *Educ:* 1913 grad L.S. Auer's class, Petersburg Conservatory; *Career:* from 1914, extensive concert work in Russia and abroad; from 1926 prof, Leningrad Conservatory; from 1937 prof, Moscow Conservatory; *Died:* 21 May 1941.

POLYAKOV, Leonid Mikhaylovich (1907–1965) Architect; prof; member, USSR Acad of Building and Architecture; CP member; *Born:* 1907; *Educ:* 1929 grad Leningrad Acad of Arts; *Career:* 1933 joined team designing Palace of Soviets and Sverdlov Square subway station, Moscow; co-designed Leningrad Ind Acad; 1945–55 head of a design studio, Moscow Bd for Planning Housing und Civil Eng Projects "Mosproyekt"; designed apartment blocks on the Arbat, Leningrad Highway and Bryusov Lane, Moscow; also designed Leningrad Hotel and Kaluga, Kursk and new Arbat subway stations; in charge of architectural design of installations on Volga-Don Canal and Tsymlyansk Waterway; designed main gates for All-Union Agric Exhibition and contributed to reconstruction of war-damaged Sebastopol; entered design competitions for buildings to house USSR Council of Pop Comr and "Izvestia" ed offices; 1955 won 2nd prize in design competition for monument commemorating 300th anniversary of incorporation of Ukr in Russia; in same year subjected to scathing Party criticism, stripped of Stalin Prizes and membership of USSR Acad of Building and Architecture and dismissed from "Mosproyekt" by Party and govt decree on "The Elimination of Excesses in Planning and Building"; *Awards:* Order of Lenin; Order of the Red Star; Badge of Hon; two Stalin Prizes (1949 and 1950); medals; *Died:* June 1965.

POLYAKOV, M.Kh.(1884–1938) Govt official; CP member from 1918; *Born:* 1884; *Career:* 1904–18 member, Socialist-Revol Party; 1921 chm, Crimean Revol Comt; from 1922 Collegium member, NKVD; arrested by State Security organs; *Died:* 1938 in imprisonment.

POLYANSKIY, Ivan Vasil'yevich (1898–1956) Govt official; CP member from 1918; *Born:* 1898, son of a worker; *Career:*

1918–21 with partisan detachments and Red Army; helped crush Kronstadt Mutiny; then exec govt work; during WW 2 carried out govt missions during blockade of Leningrad; from 1944 chm, Council for Religious Cults, USSR Council of Min; *Awards:* Order of Lenin; Order of the Red Banner; Badge of Hon; medals: *Died:* 15 Oct 1956.

POLYNOV, Boris Borisovich (1877–1952) Soil scientist, geochemist and geographer; member, USSR Acad of Sci from 1946; CP member from 1951; *Born:* 4 Aug 1877; *Educ:* 1908 grad Petersburg Forestry Inst; 1908 grad Petersburg Univ; *Career:* 1920–23 prof, Don Polytech Inst, Novocherkassk; 1928–46 prof, Leningrad Univ; 1935–36 and 1947 also prof, Moscow Univ; from 1923 worked for USSR Acad of Sci; 1901–07 made soil and geographical study of Chernigov Oblast; 1912–22 studied Don Basin; 1924–26 soil and geographical research in Mongolian Pop Republ; concentrated on origin of soils and weathering of Earth's crust; devised sci standards for classification of geographical landscapes and determination of their geochemical characteristics; *Publ: Peski Donskoy oblasti, ikh pochvy i landshafty* (The Sands of the Don Oblast. Their Soils and Landscapes) (1926); *Kora vyvetrivaniya* (Weathering) (vol 1, 1934); *Geokhimicheskiye landshafty* (Geochemical Landscapes) (1946); *Ucheniye o landshaftakh* (Landscape Theory) (1953); *Awards:* Grand Gold Medal of Russian Geographical Soc (1926); Tyan Shan Semyonov Gold Medal (1928); *Died:* 16 Mar 1952.

POMERANCHUK, Isaak Yakovlevich (1913–1966) Physicist; Dr of Physics and Mathematics; prof; member, USSR Acad of Sci from 1964; *Born:* 20 May 1913; *Educ:* 1936 grad Leningrad Polytech Inst; *Career:* from 1936 worked for institutions of USSR Acad of Sci; from 1946 prof, Moscow Physical Eng Inst; 1953–56 head, Theory Dept, Inst of Theoretical and Experimental Physics, USSR Acad of Sci; also directed theory groups at Kurchatov Inst of Atomic Eng, USSR Acad of Sci; and at Nuclear Problems Laboratory, Joint Inst of Nuclear Research, Dubna; 1953–64 corresp member, USSR Acad of Sci, specialized in elementary particle physics; developed physical principles and methods of calculating nuclear reactors and founded Sov school of reactor theory; studied radiation of high-energy electrons, used in calculating electron accelerators; 1957, in the course of research on quantum theory, formulated theorem according to which at high energies the interaction of particles and of antiparticles is equivalent; *Publ: Nekotoryye voprosy teorii yadra* (Some Aspects of Nuclear Theory) (1950); *K teorii zhidkogo* He^3 (The Theory of Liquid He^3) (1950); *Predely primenimosti teorii tormoznogo izlucheniya elektronov i obrazovaniya par pri bol'shikh energiyakh* (Limits of Applicability of the Electron Bremsstrahlung Theory and Pair Formation at High Energy) (1953); *Ravenstvo nulyu perenormirovannogo zaryada v kvantovoy elektrodinamike* (The Zero Congruence of a Renormed Charge in Quantum Electrodynamics) (1955); *Resheniye uravneniy psevdoskalyarnoy mezonnoy teorii s psevdoskalyarnoy svyaz'yu* (Solving Equations of the Pseudoscalar Meson Theory with a Pseudoscalar Connection) (1955); *O protsessakh, opredelyayemykh fermionnymi polyusami Redzhe* (Processes Governed by Reger's Fermi Poles) (1963); *Awards:* Order of Lenin; Order of the Red Banner of Labor; Stalin Prize (1950); Lenin Prize; *Died:* 14 Dec 1966.

POMERANTSEVA, Aleksandra Vladimirovna (1871–1967) Revolutionary; CP member from 1903; *Born:* 19 Feb 1871; *Career:* 1895 joined Populist movement in Petersburg; 1898 arrested and exiled to Vologda Province; in exile joined "Iskra" group; 1902 revol work in Crimea; from 1905 in Bryansk, then Nizhniy Novgorod; 1908 arrested and exiled to Vologda Province; 1912–13 propagandist in Moscow; 1914 arrested for third time; after 1917 Oct Revol worked for Bolshevik orgs in Achinsk, then Krasnoyarsk; from start of Civil War to late 1919 in imprisonment; 1920 ed, Irkutsk newspaper "Vlast' truda"; member, Irkutsk Province Party Comt; 1921 worked for CC, RCP(B); 1922–23 Party work in Kashira; then worked in Northern Caucasus; deleg at 10th Party Congress; from 1929 pensioner; *Died:* 29 June 1967.

POPOV, Aleksey Dmitriyevich (1892–1961) Stage dir; Pop Artiste of USSR from 1948; prof from 1940; CP member from 1954; *Born:* 24 Mar 1892 in Nikolayevsk, Samara Province; *Career:* 1912–18 actor, Moscow Arts Theater; 1918–23 founder-dir, Kostroma Drama Studio; from 1923 actor and stage dir, 3rd Studio, Moscow Arts Theater (from 1926 Vakhtangov State Theater); 1930–35 artistic dir, Moscow Theater of the Revol; 1935–49 artistic dir, 1949–57 chief stage dir, Centr Theater of the Sov Army; 1949–53 also artistic dir, Lunacharskiy State Inst of Stagecraft; 1955–56 member, Org Comt, All-Union Amateur Art Work Show, All-Union Centr Trade-Union Council; member, Theater Arts Council, USSR Min of Culture; from 1955 dep chm, All-Russian Theatrical Soc, etc; *Productions:* Seyfullina's "Virineya" (1925); Lavrenyov's *Razlom* (Break-Up) (1927); *Poema o topore* (The Poem of the Axe) (1931); *Moy drug* (My Friend) (1932); Pogodin's *Posle bala* (After the Ball) (1934); Shakespeare's "Romeo and Juliet" (1935); "The Taming of the Shrew" (1937); Bakhterev and Razumovskiy's *Polkovodets Suvorov* (General Suvorov) (1939); Chepurin's *Stalingradtsy* (The Stalingraders) (1944); Vinnikov's *Step' shirokaya* (The Broad Steppe) (1949); Shteyn's *Flag admirala* (The Admiral's Flag) (1950); Gogol's *Revizor* (The Government Inspector) (1951); Afinogenov's "Moscow, Kremlin" (1956), etc; *Awards:* Order of Lenin; three Stalin Prizes (1943, 1950 and 1951); *Died:* 1961.

POPOV, Dmitriy Mikhaylovich (1900–1952) Party official; CP member from 1921; *Born:* 7 Nov 1900, son of a peasant; *Educ:* 1930 grad Leningrad Communist Univ; 1933–36 studied at Agrarian Inst; *Career:* 1919–22 in Red Army; fought at Perekop; 1923–27 chm, vil sov; then secr, rayon CPSU(B) comt in Voronezh Oblast; 1930, after grad Leningrad Communist Univ, worked as teacher; from 1936 taught polit econ at higher Propagandists School, CC, CPSU(B); 1939 secr, Krasnodar Kray CPSU(B) Comt; 1940–48 first secr, Smolensk Oblast and City CPSU(B) Comt; during WW 2 member, Mil Council, Western Front; Aug 1942–Sept 1943 chief, Western Partisan Staff; from 1949 dep head, Propaganda and Agitation Dept, CC, CPSU(B); dep, USSR Supr Sov of 2nd and 3rd convocations; *Died:* 7 Jan 1952.

POPOV, Ivan Fyodorovich (1886–1957) Russian writer; *Born:* 16 Sept 1886 in vil Kamenka, Moscow Province; *Educ:* 1913 grad Brussels Univ; *Career:* 1905–14 member, RSDRP(B); 1905 arrested and exiled for his part in the Revol; fled abroad; from 1908 worked under Lenin in the Int Socialist Bureau; German pow during WW 1; 1918 returned to Russia and worked as Sov trade agent in Switzerland; then worked for publ house of Pop Comrt of Workers and Peasants' Inspection; worked for various journals and theatrical orgs; veteran corresp of "Pravda"; *Publ:* in 1930's wrote scripts for films: *Vesenniye dni* (Spring Days); *Kar'yera Ruddi* (Ruddi's Career); *Marionetki* (The Puppets); *Peterburgskaya noch'* (Petersburg Night), etc; novelette *Pod zvezdoyu Moskvy* (Under Moscow's Star) (1942); novel *Poteryannaya i vozvrashchyonnaya Rodina* (Country Lost and Returned) (1941–42); play about the Ul'yanov family *Sem'ya* (The Family) (1949); from this he wrote the script for the film *Sem'ya Ul'yanovykh* (The Ul'yanov Family) (1957); novel *Na iskhode nochi* (At the Break of Night) (1950); memoirs *Odin den' s Leninym* (A Day with Lenin) (1963); *Died:* 10 Dec 1957 in Moscow.

POPOV, Ivan Semyonovich (1888–1964) Zootechnician; prof; member, All-Union Lenin Acad of Agric Sci from 1956; prof, Moscow's Timiryazev Agric Acad from 1937; *Born:* 1888; *Educ:* 1917 grad Moscow Agric Inst; *Career:* until 1919 asst prof at this int; 1919–21 at Saratov Univ; 1921–29 at Moscow Zootech Inst; 1930–37 at All-Union Research Inst of Animal Husbandry; specialized in Sov fodder resources, nutritive value of fodder and methods of feeding agric stock; wrote several works on dairy and meat farming, livestock breeds, etc; *Publ: Metodika zootekhnicheskikh opytov* (Method of Zootechnical Experiments) (1925); *Korma SSSR, sostav i pitatel'nost'* (The Fodder of the USSR, Its Composition and Nutritive Qualities) (1935); *Kormleniye vysokoproduktivnykh korov* (Feeding High-Yield Cows) (1941); *Kormleniye sel'skokhozyaystvennykh zhivotnykh* (Feeding Farm Animals) (1957); *Kormovyye normy i kormovyye tablitsy* (Fodder Norms and Fodder Tables) (1957); *O normakh belkovogo pitaniya doynykh korov* (Protein Feed Norms for Milch Cows) (1959); *Voprosy ratsional'nogo ispol'zovaniya belkovykh kormov v zhivotnovodstve* (The Efficient Use of Protein Fodder in Animal Husbandry) (1960); *Teoriya i praktika primeneniya sinteticheskikh aminokislot v korm sel'skokhozyaystvennym zhivotnym* (The Theory and Practice of Using Synthetic Amino Acids in Livestock Fodder) (1963); *Awards:* Lenin Prize (1959); *Died:* 1964.

POPOV, K.A. (STEPNOY) (1876–1949) Govt official; CP member from 1906; *Born:* 1876; *Career:* Party work in Omsk and Irkutsk; during 1905–07 Revol member, Omsk RSDRP Comt; deleg at 5th RSDRP Congress, arrested by Tsarist authorities; 1917 broke with Bolsheviks and headed Menshevik-Internationalist org in Omsk; chm, Exec Comt, Omsk Sov of Workers and Soldiers' Dep; from

Jan 1920 dep chm, Irkutsk Province Cheka; conducted investigation of Kolchak case; re-joined CP; 1922–28 worked for Agitation and Propaganda Dept, CC, CPSU(B); from 1928 research and teaching work; from 1945 pensioner; *Died:* 1949.

POPOV, Nikolay Aleksandrovich (1871–1949) Stage dir and playwright; Hon Stage Dir from 1927; *Born:* 19 Oct 1871; *Career:* 1894 worked for Art and Lit Soc; 1901–10 (with intervals) chief stage dir, Solovtsov Theater, Kiev; 1902–07 dir, Pop Theater of Vasiliy Ostrov Soc; 1904–06 stage dir, Komissarzhevskaya Theater, Petersburg; 1907–10 stage dir, Maly Theater, Moscow; 1919–20 stage dir, Moscow Bolshoy Theater; also head, Teaching and Theatrical Sections, Theater Dept, Pop Comrt of Educ; 1926–27 stage dir, Moscow Bolshoy Theater; 1929–34 stage dir, Moscow Maly Theater; *Productions:* Chekhov's *Chayka* (The Seagull) and *Dyadya Vanya* (Uncle Vanya); Ostrovskiy's *Dokhodnoye mesto* (A Lucrative Post); Gutskov's "Uriel' Akosta"; Hauptmann's "Elga", etc; *Publ: Mal'chikspal'chik* (Tom Thumb); *Vsem sestram po ser'gam* (Ear-Rings for All Sisters), etc; monograph *Stanislavskiy i yego znacheniye dlya sovremennogo teatra* (Stanislavskiy and His Importance for the Modern Theater) (1909); *Narodnyy teatr i Ostrovskiy* (The Popular Theater and Ostrovskiy) (1911), etc; *Died:* 8 Jan 1949.

POPOV, Nikolay Nikolayevich (1891–1940) Party official; historian; CP member from 1919; *Born:* 9 Jan 1891 in Kutaisi, son of a teacher; *Educ:* 1908 grad Vladikavkaz High-School; 1908-09 studied at Khar'kov, then Moscow Univ; *Career:* 1906–08 conducted revol propaganda in RSDRP high-school and mil orgs in Vladikavkaz; secr, Khar'kov RSDRP Org; 1910 member, Exec Commission, Moscow Okrug RSDRP Org; Dec 1911 arrested and exiled; 1912–17 exiled in Irkutsk Province, where he worked as a teacher; 1917 returned to Khar'kov; 1921–23 secr, Khar'kov Province Comt, CP(B) Ukr; 1924 dep head, Agitation Dept, CC, RCP(B); 1925–26 head, Agitation Dept, CC, CP(B) Ukr; ed, newspaper "Kommunist"; 1929 head, Agitation and Propaganda Dept, Moscow CPSU(B) Comt; member, Moscow Sov; 1930–33 member, ed bd, "Pravda"; 1934–37 secr, CC, CP(B) Ukr; 1927–29 and 1933–37 cand Politbureau member, 1937 Politbureau member, CC, CP(B) Ukr; member, USSR and All-Ukr Centr Exec Comt; deleg at 10th, 11th, 13th–17th Party Congresses and 15th and 16th Party Conferences; at 16th Party Congress elected cand member, CC, CPSU(B); lectured at Khar'kov Univ and Marxism courses of CC, CP(B) Ukr; arrested by State Security organs; *Publ: Ocherk istorii RKP(b)* (Outline History of the RCP(B)) (1926), which served as a textbook for years at higher educ establishments and Party schools, ran through 16 ed and was translated into German, French, English and other languages; *Ocherk istorii KP(b)U* (Outline History of the CP(B) Ukr) (1928); coauthor, *Zhizn' Lenina i leninizm* (The Life of Lenin and Leninism) (1924); *Melkoburzhuaznyye antisovetskiye partii* (Petty Bourgeois Anti-Soviet Parties) (1924); *Natsional'naya politika Sovetskoy vlasti* (The Nationality Policy of the Soviet Regime) (1924); *Oktyabr'skaya revolyutsiya i natsional'nyy vopros* (The October Revolution and the Nationality Question) (1927), etc; *Died:* 12 Mar 1940 in imprisonment; posthumously rehabilitated.

POPOV, Nikolay Vladimirovich (1894–1949) Physician; specialist in forensic med; prof from 1927; *Born:* 1894; *Educ:* 1917 grad Med Fac, Moscow Univ; *Career:* after grad physician, then asst to Prof P. A. Minakov, Chair of Forensic Med, Med Fac, 1st Moscow Univ; from 1927 prof and head, Chair of Forensic Med, Smolensk Med Inst; from 1932 head, Chair of Forensic Med, 1st and 2nd Moscow Med Inst and dir, Research Inst of Forensic Med, USSR Pop Comrt of Health; did research on the forensic med applications of hematology, serology, isoserology, spectral analysis and toxicology; also studied the history of forensic med; considered a pioneer of Sov forensic hematology; introduced techniques of determining hemoglobin and its derivatives and of studying precipitation reaction in forensic med; wrote over 50 works, including several textbooks; *Publ: Reaktsiya izoagglyutinatsii* (Isoagglutination Reaction) (1926); *Individual'noye issledovaniye krovyanykh pyaten pri pomoshchi izoagglyutinatsii* (The Individual Examination of Bloodstains with the Help of Isoagglutination) (1930); *Spektral'nyye issledovaniya krovi* (The Spectro-Analytic Study of Blood) (1932); ed, *Osnovy sudebnoy meditsiny* (The Principles of Forensic Medicine) (1938); textbook *Sudebnaya meditsina* (Forensic Medicine) (1940); *Died:* 1949.

POPOV, Pavel Il'ich (1872–1950) Statistician; CP member from 1924; *Born:* 1872 in Irkutsk; *Educ:* 1904–05 studied at Agronomical Acad, Berlin; *Career:* 1890–94 taught in Ust'-Ude and maintained contact with polit exiles; 1895 moved to Petersburg to pursue his educ and played an active part in revol movement; acted as go-between between League for the Liberation of the Working class and its underground printing press; 1896–97 arrested and imprisoned for his connections with the Lakhtinskiy Printing Press, which printed a pamphlet of Lenin's; 1897 exiled to Ufa Province, where he began to work as statistician; worked for Ufa, Samara, Smolensk, Vologda, Khar'kov and Tula Zemstvos, rising to head of a province statistical dept; after 1917 Feb Revol headed Dept of 1917 Agric Census, Min of Agric; active in drafting "Regulations on State Statistics"; 25 July 1918–1928 mang, Centr Statistical Bd; organized Sov central and provincial statistical system; and helped conduct 1918, 1920, 1923, 1926 and 1939 censuses; supervised publication of statistics on Sov nat econ; published statistical yearbooks, manuals and the journals "Vestnik statistiki" and "Byulleten' TsSU"; from 1921 also Presidium member, USSR Gosplan; 1928–29 Collegium member, Centr Statistical Bd; 1929–49 Presidium member, RSFSR Gosplan and All-Union Lenin Acad of Agric Sci; from 1949 member, Sci Methods Council, USSR Centr Statistical Bd; *Publ: Sel'skoye khozyaystvo Soyuza respublik* (The Agriculture of the Union of Republics) (1924); *Awards:* Order of the Red Banner of Labor; Order of the Fatherland War, 2nd Class; medals; *Died:* 1950.

POPOV, Vasiliy Fyodorovich (1903–1964) Govt official; CP member from 1923; *Born:* 1903; *Educ:* 1937 grad Leningrad Finance Acad; *Career:* 1938 RSFSR Pop Comr of Finance; 1939 USSR First Dep Pop Comr of State Control; 1940–45 acting USSR Pop Comr of State Control; 1946–48 worked for USSR Council of Min; 1948–58 chm, bd, USSR Gosbank; 1958–64 first dep chm, bd, USSR Gosbank; *Died:* Dec 1964.

POPOV, Vladimir Veniaminovich (1902–1960) Entomologist; corresp member, USSR Acad of Sci from 1953; *Born:* 1902; *Educ:* 1927 grad Leningrad Inst of Applied Zoology and Phytopathology; *Career:* from 1927 at Zoological Inst, USSR Acad of Sci; worked on taxonomy, morphology, faunistics, ecology and evolution of Hymenoptera and other arthropoda; studied fauna and ecology of insects of Centr and Southern Urals, Centr Asia, Kaz and Arm; *Publ: Vnutrividovoy i vnutrirodovoy parazitizm i evolyutsiya pereponchatykh nasekomykh /Hymenoptera/* (Intraspecific and Intrageneric Parasitism and Evolution of Hymenoptera) (1948); *O znachenii pchelinykh /Hymenoptera, Apoidea/ v protsese evolyutsii* (The Importance of the Honey Bee Family /Hymenoptera, Apoidea/ in the Evolutionary Process) (1951); *Pchelinyye opyliteli marevykh* (The Honey Bee Family as Pollinators of Chenopodiaceae) (1952); *O paraziticheskom rode Radoszkowskiana /Hymenoptera, Medachilidae/ i yego proiskhozhdenii* (The Parasitic Genus Radoszkowskiana /Hymenoptera, Medachilidae/ and Its Origin) (1955); *Novyye i maloizvestnyye pchelinyye iz Sredney Azii /Hymenoptera, Apoidea/* (New and Little-Known Honey Bees of Central Asia /Hymenoptera, Apoidea/) (1956); *Phelinyye, ikh svyazi s tsvetkovoy rastitel'nost'yu i vopros of opylenii lyutserny* (Honey Bees, Their Connections with Flowers and the Pollination of Lucerne) (1956); *Formicajus Sladen – golarkticheskiy rod pchelinykh* (Formicajus Sladen – a Holarctic Genus of Honey Bee) (1960); *Died:* 3 Nov 1960.

POPOVKIN, Yevgeniy Yefimovich (1907–1968) Russian writer; CP member from 1927; *Born:* 13 Feb 1907 in vil Petroostrov, Kherson Province; *Educ:* 1931 grad Lit Fac, Moscow Univ; *Career:* did Komsomol work; during WW 2 edited an army newspaper; 1957–68 chief ed, journal "Moskva"; 1923 first work published; *Publ: Na boyevom postu* (Battle Stations) (1935); novels: *Sem'ya Rubanyuk* (The Rubanyuk Family) (1947–50); *Bol'shoy razliv* (The Great Flood) (1955); articles and travel notes: *Chekhoslovatskiye vpechatleniya* (Czechoslovakian Impressions) (1956); *Na drevney zemle Ellady* (In the Ancient Land of Hellas) (1957); *Nesentimental'noye puteshestviye* (An Unsentimental Journey) (1963); stories *Kak vybirali Katerinu* (How Catherine Was Chosen), etc; *Awards:* Stalin Prize (1954); *Died:* 15 Feb 1968 in Moscow.

POPUDRENKO, Nikolay Nikitovich (1906–1943) Party official; CP member from 1929; *Born:* 5 June 1906 in Khar'kov Province, son of a peasant; *Career:* 1924–30 worked at metallurgical plant in Dnepropetrovsk; 1930–39 Komsomol and Party work in Dnepropetrovsk, Zhitomir and Chernigov Oblasts; from 1940 secr, Chernigov Oblast Comt, CP(B) Ukr; Aug 1941–July 1943 secr, underground Chernigov Oblast Comt, CP(B) Ukr; also dep commander, Chernigov Oblast partisan unit; *Awards:* Hero of the

Sov Union (1943); *Died:* 6 July 1943 killed in action in the Zlynka forests; buried in Chernigov.

PORAY-KOSHITS, Aleksandr Yevgen'yevich (1877–1949) Chemist; prof from 1918; member, USSR Acad of Sci from 1935; Hon Sci and Tech Worker of RSFSR from 1947; *Born:* 8 Oct 1877 in Kazan'; *Educ:* 1903 grad Petersburg Polytech Inst; *Career:* 1905–18 lecturer, 1918–49 prof, Petersburg (Leningrad) Technol Inst; 1941–44 head, Chair of Organic Dyes, Kazan' Inst of Chemical Technol; from 1941 head, Laboratory of Intermediate Products and Dyes, Inst of Organic Chemistry, USSR Acad of Sci; from 1942 ed, "Zhurnal prikladnoy khimii"; specialized in organic chemistry with special reference to aromatic series; did major research on dye chemistry and technol; synthesized several dyes and studied the chemism of dying processes; devised a method of extracting furfurole from sunflower husks; *Publ: Izbrannyye trudy. Raboty v oblasti organicheskoy khimii, khimii krasyashchikh veshchestv i teorii krasheniya* (Selected Works. Studies in Organic Chemistry, the Chemistry of Dyes and the Theory of Dyeing) (1949), etc; *Awards:* Order of Lenin; three other orders; Stalin Prize (1943); *Died:* 17 Apr 1949.

PORIK, Vasiliy Vasil'yevich (1920–1944) Partisan; lt, Sov Army; member, French Resistance; CP member from 1941; *Born:* 17 Feb 1920 in vil Solomirtsi, Vinnitsa Oblast; son of a peasant; *Educ:* 1941 grad Khar'kov Infantry College; *Career:* from 1938 with Red Army; 1941 platoon commander; fall 1941 taken prisoner by Germans; worked in coal mines in France; 1943 escaped from pow camp and formed partisan squad; then Resistance leader in Northern France; recaptured and imprisoned in Saint Nicaise, whence he again escaped and linked up with Resistançe; July 1944 fell into SS ambush; *Awards:* Hero of the Sov Union (1964, posthumously); *Died:* 22 July 1944 executed in Arras; vil Somomirtsi named after him; memorial plaque in Arras at the site of his execution.

POSKRYOBYSHEV, Aleksandr Nikolayevich (1891–?) Party offical; CP member from 1917; *Born:* 1891, son of a worker; *Career:* 1917–18 chm, Baranchinskiy Sov of Workers' Dep (Sverdlovsk Oblast); 1919 head, Accounting and Information Sections, Polit Dept, Special Turkestani Army; 1919–21 chm, Zlatoust Uyezd Revol Comt, then Exec Comt; 1921–22 dep chm, Ufa Province Exec Comt and head, Org Dept, Ufa Province CPSU(B) Comt; from 1922 instructor, then dep mang, CC, CPSU(B); 1924–28 asst secr, CC, CPSU(B); from 1928 head, Special Section, Secretariat, CC, CPSU(B); Stalin's personal secr; at 17th Party Congress elected cand member, CC, CPSU(B); at 18th and 19th Party Congresses elected member, CC, CPSU(B); dep, USSR Supr Sov of 1st, 2nd and 3rd convocations; chm, Draft Bills Commission, Sov of the Union, USSR Supr Sov of 3rd convocation; *Awards:* Order of Lenin (1939); *Died:* date and place of death unknown.

POSPELOV, Vladimir Petrovich (1872–1949) Entomologist; prof from 1913; member, Ukr Acad of Sci from 1939; *Born:* 22 Mar 1872 in Bogoroditsk, now Tula Oblast, son of a priest; *Educ:* 1896 grad Moscow Univ; *Career:* 1904–13 head, Kiev Entomological Station; 1913–20 prof, Voronezh Agric Inst; 1927–30 prof, Saratov Univ; 1930–40 prof, Leningrad Agric Inst; 1929–40 also worked for All-Union Inst for Plant Protection; 1945–46 prof, Kiev Univ; from 1946 dir, Inst of Entomology and Phytopathology, Ukr Acad of Sci; worked on gen and experimental entomology, particularly anti-pest measures; helped develop biological methods of combatting insect pests; 1904 sponsored org of local establishments for pest control; 1931 sponsored org of Sov plant quarantine service; *Publ: Post-embrional'-noye razvitiye i imaginal'naya diapuza u cheshuyekrylykh* (Postembryonal Development and Imago Diapusa in Lepidoptera) (1911); *Sveklovichnyy dolgonosik i mery bor'by s nim* (The Beet Weevil and How to Combat It) (1913); *Mikrobiologicheskiy metod bor'by s vreditelyami sel'skogo khozyaystva* (The Microbiological Method of Combatting Agricultural Pests) (1944), etc; *Awards:* Badge of Hon; medals; *Died:* 1 Feb 1949.

POSTNIKOV, Aleksandr Mikhaylovich (1886–1937) Govt official; CP member from 1919; *Born:* 1886, son of a peasant; *Career:* 1904 joined RSDRP; 1917 adopted Internationalist stand; 1917 exec secr, Presidium, All-Russian Railroad Union; member, All-Russian Centr Trade-Union Council and member, Supr Sovnarkhoz; 1918 Pop Comrt of Means of Communication inspector on Eastern, Western and Ukr Fronts; from Oct 1919 chief of mil supply, 4th Army and Petersburg Rayon; 1920–21 Ukr Pop Comr of Means of Communication; member, All-Ukr Centr Exec Comt of 5th convocation; 1925–37 exec posts with rail transport in Moscow; USSR Dep Pop Comr of Means of Communication; chief dir of rail transport; dir, Moscow-Bel and Moscow-Kazan' Railroads; Collegium member, Pop Comrt of Means of Communication; head, Main Transport Machine-Building Bd, USSR Pop Comrt of Means of Communication; arrested by State Security organs; *Died:* 1937 in imprisonment.

POSTOLOVSKIY, Dmitriy Simonovich (Party name: MIKHAYLOV; ALEKSANDROV; VADIM) (1876–1948) Party and govt official; CP member; *Born:* 24 Oct 1876; *Career:* 1895 joined revol movement; Party work in Petersburg, Vilnius and Tiflis; 1899 arrested and exiled from Petersburg; 1903 member, Caucasian Joint RSDRP Comt; helped establish underground printing press in Tiflis; from spring 1904 agent for CC, RSDRP; on orders of CC founded in Vilnius Bureau, CC, RSDRP; Apr 1905 appointed CC, RSDRP rep in Party Council; 1905 at 3rd RSDRP Congress elected member, CC, RSDRP; 1905 CC, RSDRP rep in Exec Comt, Petersburg Sov of Workers' Dep; then abandoned politics and in Apr 1917 automatically dropped from RSDRP(B); after 1917 Oct Revol worked for State Draft Bills Commission, USSR Council of Pop Comr; also legal consultant, State Mint; from 1932 pensioner; *Died:* 29 May 1948.

POSTOVSKAYA, Mariya Pavlovna (1865–1953) Specialist in teaching of retarded children; helped found Russia's first auxiliary schools; *Born:* 7 Sept 1865; *Educ:* 1888 grad Lubyanka Higher Women's Courses, Moscow; *Career:* after grad, Women's College, teaching work; from 1896 head, 3rd Kapnitsk Pyatnitskiy Hospital, Moscow; tried to create conditions for all children to finish elementary schooling, regardless of their ability; 1903 petitioned Moscow Municipal Admin to establish auxiliary classes for mentally retarded children at the college; 1908 managed to obtain permission for this, with founding of Russia's first auxiliary class; the class included exercizes to correct speech defects, develop rhythmics, handicrafts and encourage independent work and involve children in class admin; her college became a center for training teachers at auxiliary schools; from early 1918 inspector of special schools for deviant children; from 1930, although retired, continued to sponsor work of auxiliary schools in Moscow; *Publ: Vspomogatel'nyye shkoly za granitsey* (Auxiliary Schools Abroad) (1912); *Novaya shkol'naya organizatsiya s sistemoy vspomogatel'nogo obucheniya* (A New Organization of Schools with an Auxiliary Training System) (1913); *Vospitaniye i obrazovaniye defektivnykh detey* (The Training and Education of Defective Children) (1923); *Obucheniye gramote otstalykh detey* (Teaching Backward Children Reading and Writing) (1930); *Died:* 15 Nov 1953 in Moscow.

POSTYSHEV, Pavel Petrovich (Party name: YERMAK) (1887–1940) Party official; CP member from 1904; *Born:* 18 Sept 1887 in Ivanovo-Voznesensk, son of a weaver; *Career:* electrician by trade; from 1901 active in revol movement; May–July 1905 took part in strike and was elected to Ivanovo-Voznesensk Sov of Workers' Dep; 1906 elected to Bd, Cotton-Printers' Union; 1906 member, Ivanovo City RSDRP Comt; 1907–08 member, Bureau, Ivanovo Okrug RSDRP Comt; Apr 1908 arrested; Feb 1910 sentenced to four years' hard labor; Dec 1912 exiled for life to Irkutsk Province; 1914–17 member, Irkutsk RSDRP Bureau; head, Irkutsk City Metalworkers' Union; from Mar 1917 dep, from Aug 1917 dep chm, Irkutsk City Sov of Workers' Dep, and chm, Centr Bureau of Trade-Union League; helped to establish Sov regime in Eastern Siberia; from Dec 1917 member, Irkutsk Mil Revol Comt; organized Red Guard units; chm, Revol Tribunal and member, Siberian Centr Exec Comt; 1918 represented this Exec Comt on Far Eastern Council of Pop Comr, Khabarovsk; during Civil War did underground work in Far East; commanded partisan units in Amur distr; 1919 comr of a partisan unit; 1920 Khabarovsk distr plen for CC, RCP(B); cand member, Far Eastern Bureau, CC, RCP(B); from Aug 1921 Far Eastern Republ govt plen for the Baykal Oblast; from Oct 1921 member, Provisional Revol Comt, from Dec 1921 member, Mil Council, Eastern Front, Far Eastern Republ; from Apr 1922 oblast comr for Far Eastern Republ govt; Aug 1923 sent by CC, RCP(B) to Ukr to head Org and Instructors Dept, Kiev Province Comt, CP(B) Ukr; Sept 1924 elected secr, Kiev Province, then Kiev Okrug Comt, CP(B) Ukr; Dec 1925 elected member, CC, and cand Politbureau member, CC, CP(B) Ukr; Nov 1926 elected Politbureau and Org Bureau member and secr, CC, CP(B) Ukr; 1926–30 also secr, Khar'kov Okrug and City Comt, CP(B) Ukr; from July 1930 Org Bureau member and Secr, CC, CPSU(B); July 1930–J an 1932 head, Agitation and

Propaganda Dept, and Org Dept, CC, CPSU(B); Mar 1933 again elected secr Politbureau and Org Bureau member and secr, CC, CP(B) Ukr; also secr, CC, CPSU(B) and first secr, Kiev Oblast Comt, CP(B) Ukr (from July 1934); deleg at 9th and 13th–17th Party Congresses; at 14th Congress elected cand member, and at 15th–17th Congresses elected member, CC, CPSU(B); member, USSR and All-Ukr Centr Exec Comt; Presidium member, USSR Centr Exec Comt; from 1934 cand Politbureau member, CC, CPSU(B); dep, USSR Supr Sov of 1937 convocation; 1937 relieved of his post as secr, Kiev Oblast Party Comt and secr, CC, CP(B) Ukr; from Mar 1937 secr, Kuybyshev Kray CPSU(B) Comt; 1938 relieved of duties as cand Politbureau member, CC, CPSU(B); 1938 arrested by State Security organs; *Publ:* posthumously published books: *Grazhdanskaya voyna na Vostoke Sibiri 1917–1922 gg. Vospominaniya* (The 1917–22 Civil War in Eastern Siberia. Memoirs) (1957); stories and essays *Iz proshlogo* (From the Past) (1958); *Awards:* Order of Lenin (1935); Order of the Red Banner; *Died:* 10 Dec 1940 in imprisonment; posthumously rehabilitated.

POTAPOV, Makariy Vasil'yevich (1887–1949) Hydraulic eng; specialist in waterway design and calculation; prof from 1936; corresp member, Bel Acad of Sci from 1940; *Born:* 29 Feb 1887 in Bezhetsk, now Kalinin Oblast; *Educ:* 1915 grad Petersburg Inst of Transport Eng; *Career:* from 1921 dir, Crimean Water Bd; 1925–28 consultant, USSR Gosplan; 1928–30 worked in Centr Asia; 1930–36 lecturer, from 1936 prof, Moscow Inst of Water Management Eng; developed theory of longitudinal-helical flow and a method of artificial lateral circulation; also devised an original system for rearranging flow structure; *Publ: Regulirovaniye stoka* (Flow Control) (2nd ed, 1940); *Regulirovaniye vodnykh potokov metodom iskusstvennoy poperechnoy tsirkulyatsii* (Water Flow Control by the Artificial Lateral Circulation Method) (1947); *Sochineniya* (Works) (3 vol, 1950–51); *Awards:* Stalin Prize (1952, posthumously); *Died:* 9 May 1949.

POTEBNYA, Aleksandr Aleksandrovich (1868–1935) Electr eng; prof from 1902; *Born:* 24 Dec 1868, son of the well-known philologist A. A. Potebnya; *Educ:* 1892 grad Khar'kov Univ; 1900 grad Khar'kov Technol Inst; *Career:* 1902–23 prof, Tomsk Technol Inst; 1923–35 prof, Khar'kov Technol Inst, then Khar'kov Electr Eng Inst; specialized in electr traction motors; *Publ: K teorii parallel'noy raboty al'ternatorov* (The Theory of Alternators Operating in Parallel) (1903); *Elektricheskiye tyagovyye dvigateli na zheleznoy doroge* (Electric Traction Motors on the Railroads) (1930); *Nomogrammy dlya raschyota nagrevaniya tyagovykh motorov* (Nomograms for Calculating Traction-Motor Warm-Up) (1934); *Died:* 16 Nov 1935.

POTEKHIN, Ivan Izosimovich (1903–1964) Ethnographer and historian; Dr of Historical Sci from 1954; dir, Inst of African Inst, USSR Acad of Sci from 1959; CP member from 1922; *Born:* 1 Oct 1903 in vil Krivosheino, now Krasnoyarsk Kray, son of a peasant; *Educ:* 1930–39 grad and postgrad course at Leningrad Oriental Inst; *Career:* until 1930 polit educ work and Party work in Siberia; during WW 2 in Red Army; from 1946 senior assoc, 1949–59 dep dir, Inst of Ethnography, USSR Acad of Sci; 1949–57 also dep chief ed, journal "Sovetskaya etnografiya"; 1959–64, dir, African Inst, USSR Acad of Sci; 1954 and 1960 attended Int Congresses of Orientalists in Cambridge and Moscow; 1956 and 1960 attended Int Congresses of Ethnographers and Anthropologists in Philadelphia and Paris; 1960 attended Int Afro-Asian Solidarity Conference in Conakry; 1962 attended 1st Int Congress of Africanists in Accra; from 1959 chm, Bd, Sov Assoc for Friendship with the Peoples of Africa; from 1962 chm, Commission for Africa, Sov Afro-Asian Solidarity Comt; from 1957 member, Int Soc of Africanists; from 1962 member and Bureau member, Permanent Council, Int Congress of Africanists; studied ethnography and econ of African peoples; concentrated on nat-liberation movements in Africa and development of African countries along "non-capitalist lines"; *Publ: Imperialisticheskaya segregatsiya tuzemtsev Yuzhnoy Afriki* (The Imperialistic Segregation of the Natives of South Africa) (1935); *Naseleniye bantu v gorodakh Yuzhnoy Afriki* (The Bantu Population in the Towns of South Africa) (1947); *Funktsional'naya shkola v etnografii na sluzhbe britanskogo imperializma* (The Functional School in Ethnography in the Service of British Imperialism) (1951); *Britanskaya Vostochnaya Afrika pod gnyotom angliyskogo imperializma* (British East Africa Under the Yoke of British Imperialism) (1953); coauthor and ed, *Narody Afriki* (The Peoples of Africa) (1954); *Formirovaniye natsional'noy obshchnosti yuzhnoafrikanskikh bantu* (The Development of the South African Bantu's National Identity) (1955); ed, *Afrikanskiy etnograficheskiy sbornik* (African Ethnographical Compendium) (2 vol, 1956–58); *Gana segodnya. Dnevnik* (Ghana Today. A Diary) (1959); *Afrika smotrit v budushcheye* (Africa Looks to the Future) (1960); coauthor and chief ed, *Rasovaya diskriminatsiya v Afrike* (Racial Discrimination in Africa) (1960), etc; *Awards:* Order of the Red Banner of Labor (1963); *Died:* 17 Sept 1964.

POTRESOV, Aleksandr Nikolayevich (pen name: STAROVER) (1869–1934) Publicist and critic; *Born:* 1869 in Moscow, son of an officer; *Career:* from 1890's active in workers' movement; member, Petersburg League for the Liberation of the Working Class; 1900 emigrated; worked for "Iskra" org and journal "Zarya"; 1903, after schism in RSDRP, became one of the Menshevik leaders; 1917 co-dir, newspaper "Den'" which opposed Bolsheviks; after 1917 Oct Revol emigrated; *Publ: Zametki zhurnalista* (A Journalist's Notes) (1903); collected articles *Etyudy o russkoy intelligentsii* (Studies on the Russian Intelligentsia) (1906); collection of critical articles *Leytmotivy sovremennogo khaosa* (Leitmotifs of Modern Chaos) (1909); *Kriticheskiye nabroski. I. F. Yakubovich* (Critical Sketches. I. F. Yakubovich) (1911); *O literature bez zhizni i o zhizni bez literatury. Tragediya proletarskoy kul'tury* (Literature Without Life and Life Without Literature. The Tragedy of Proletarian Culture) (1913); *Yeschyo k voprosu o proletarskoy kul'ture* (More About Proletarian Culture) (1914); *N. K. Mikhaylovskiy. K 10-letiyu so dnya smerti* (N. K. Mikhaylovskiy. On the Tenth Anniversary of His Death) (1914); *Zametki publitsista. Odin iz nemnogikh* (A Publicist's Notes. One of the Few) (1917); *Korolenko-grazhdanin* (Korolenko the Citizen) (1918); *Died:* 1934.

POTYOMKIN, Vladimir Petrovich (1878–1946) Govt official; dipl; CP member from 1919; *Born:* 7 Oct 1878 in Tver', son of a physician; *Educ:* 1899 grad History and Philology Fac, Moscow Univ; *Career:* while a student at Moscow Univ arrested by tsarist authorities and imprisoned in Butyrka Prison for revol activities; from 1899 teaching and research work in Moscow, Yekaterinoslav and back in Moscow, whither he returned to evade police search in Yekaterinoslav for his involvement in 1905 Revol; carried out Marxist propaganda in student circles and did propaganda work for Moscow RSDRP(B) Comt; after 1917 Oct Revol worked for educ organs of Moscow Province Sov; 1917 helped found first workers' univ; 1918–19 worked for Dept of School Policy, Pop Comrt of Educ; 1919–20 fought in Civil War; member, Revol Mil Council, 6th Army; head, Polit Dept, Western, then Southern Fronts; after the war head, Odessa Province Educ Dept; also directed Odessa Province Mil-Polit Courses; from 1922 dipl work; 1922 member, Sov Repatriation Commission in France; summer 1923 chm, Sov Repatriation Commission in Turkey; 1924–26 Sov consul-gen in Istanbul; 1927–29 counsellor, USSR mission in Turkey; 1929–32 Sov plen in Greece; 1932–34 Sov plen in Italy; 1933 signed Sov-Italian friendship, non-aggression and neutrality treaty; 1934 member, Sov delegation, League of Nations Assembly; 1934–37 USSR plen in France; helped negotiate and 2 May 1935 signed Franco-Sov mutual aid treaty; 1936 signed agreement prolonging Franco-Sov trade treaty; 1937–40 USSR First Dep Pop Comr of For Affairs; 1939 took part in Moscow negotiations; 1940–46 RSFSR Pop Comr of Educ; 1943–46 founder-dir, Acad of Pedag Sci; 1943 elected member, USSR Acad of Sci; 1939 at 18th Party Congress elected member, CC, CPSU(B); 1937 and 1946 elected dep, USSR Supr Sov; wrote numerous works on history of workers' movement in France and Britain, history of int relations and pedag theory; translated various fundamental works of French historians; chief ed, three-vol *Istoriya diplomatii* (History of Diplomacy) (1941–45); *Awards:* two Stalin Prizes (1942 and 1945); Order of Lenin; Order of the Red Banner; Order of the Red Banner of Labor; *Died:* 23 Feb 1946.

POZDNEYEV, Aleksey Matveyevich (1851–1920) Orientalist; Mongolian specialist; Dr of Philology; prof from 1884; *Born:* 1851; *Educ:* 1876 grad Fac of Oriental Languages, Petersburg Univ; *Career:* from 1884 prof, Petersburg Univ; 1899–1903 co-founder, prof and dir, Vladivostok Oriental Inst; 1903–17 Council member, Min of Public Educ; 1876–78 and 1892–93 toured Mongolia and collected Mongolian and Tibetan books and manuscripts, Buddhist religious objects and ethnographic, econ and geographic data; *Publ: Urginskiye khutukhty. Istoricheskiy ocherk iz proshlogo i sovremennogo byta* (The Hutukhtu of Urga. A Historical Study of Their Past and Present Mores) (1879); *Goroda Severnoy Mongolii* (The Cities of Northern Mongolia) (1880); *Obraztsy* *narodnoy literatury mongol'skikh plemyon* (Samples of the Folk Literature of the Mongolian Tribes) (1881); *Mongol'skiya letopis' "Erdeniyn Erikhe"* (The Mongolian Chronicle "Erdeniyn Erikhe") (1883); *Ocherki byta buddiyskikh monastyrey i buddiyskogo dukhovenstva v Mongolii v svyazi s otnosheniyami sego poslednego k narodu* (Studies in the Everyday Life of the Buddhist Monasteries and Buddhist Clergy of Mongolia with Reference to the Latter's Relations with the People) (1887); unfinished work *Mongoliya i mongoly* (Mongolia and the Mongols) (2 vol, 1896–98); *Died:* 30 Sept 1920.

POZDNEYEV, Dmitriy Matveyevich (1865–1942) Russian Orientalist, philologist, historian and econ; *Born:* 27 Jan 1865; *Educ:* grad Fac of Oriental Languages, Petersburg Univ; *Career:* until 1898 associ prof, then prof, Petersburg Univ; taught Chinese history and econ geography of the Eastern countries; 1900–03 in china; made econ study of Chinese port trade; published reminiscences of Boxer Revolt; 1905–06 dir, Oriental Inst, Vladivostok; 1906–10 in Japan; compiled Russia's first Japanese-Russian hieroglyphic dictionary; returned to Russia and helped found Practical Oriental Acad in Petersburg; 1917–37 taught Japanese history and econ at Leningrad University's Oriental Inst and Moscow's Frunze Mil Acad; wrote numerous textbooks and guides to Japanese language; *Publ: Lektsii po istorii Kitaya* (Lectures on Chinese History) (1898); *Posobiye k izucheniyu kommercheskoy geografii Dal'nego Vostoka* (A Guide to the Study of the Commercial Geography of the Far East) (1898); *Materialy po istorii Severnoy Yaponii i yeyo otnosheniya k materiku Azii i Rossii* (Material on the History of Northern Japan and Its Relations with the Asian Mainland and Russia) (2 vol, 1909); *56 dney pekinskogo siden'ya* (Fifty-Six Days of the Siege of Peking) (1901); *Yaponiya. Strana, naseleniye, istoriya, politika* (Japan. The Country, Its Population, History and Politics) (1925); *Revolyutsiya v izuchenii Dal'nego Vostoka v SSSR za desyatiletiye* (The Revolution in Soviet Studies of the Far East in a Ten-Year Period) (1927); *Died:* 1942.

POZDYUNIN, Valentin L'vovich (1883–1948) Eng; specialist in shipbuilding and mech; member, USSR Acad of Sci from 1939; CP member from 1938; *Born:* 9 Oct 1883; *Educ:* 1908 grad Petersburg Polytech Inst; pursued studies at Kronstadt Naval Eng College; *Career:* 1910–20 lecturer, from 1920 prof, Petrograd (Leningrad) Polytech Inst; from 1924 worked for Tech Council, USSR Registry, contributing expertise on ship design; from 1930 prof, Leningrad Shipbuilding Inst; from 1941 head, Dept of Hydraulics, Inst of Mech, USSR Acad of Sci; worked at various shipyards and research inst; Baltic Shipyard and Mech Plant (1908–14); Admiralty Shipyard (1918–21); Shipbuilding Research Inst, All-Union Shipyard (1930–32), etc; specialized in theory of ship design, theory and calculation of ship structures and systems of high-speed, super-cavitation ship's screws; also studied naval architecture and hydromech; in his gen theory of ship design the task of designing the ship is taken and solved as a single tech and econ problem; devised "method of consecutive approximations" for designing ships; his approximate formulas for determining the relative length of a ship and its stability at a high angle of list have proved very valuable in ship designing; 1939 designed original ship's propeller; wrote textbooks and teaching aids; *Publ: Izbrannyye trudy* (Selected Works) (vol 2–3, 1951); *Novyy metod raschyota truboprovodov ventilyatsionnykh i vodyanykh* (A New Method of Calculating Ventilation and Water Pipes) (1915); *Osnovy proyektirovaniya morskikh kommercheskikh sudov* (The Principles of Designing Merchant Vessels) (2 vol, 1926–27); *Died:* 23 May 1948.

POZERN, Boris Pavlovich (1882–1939) Party and govt official; CP member from 1902; *Born:* 1882 in Nizhniy Novgorod, son of a physician; *Educ:* from 1900 studied at Med Fac, Moscow Univ; *Career:* expelled from univ for revol activities; 1903–17 Party work in Nizhniy Novgorod, Samara, Moscow and Minsk; after 1917 Feb Revol first chm, Minsk Sov; deleg at 1st All-Russian Congress of Soviets; elected member, All-Russian Centr Exec Comt; from July 1917 member, Petrograd RSDRP(B) Comt; deleg at 6th Party Congress; during 1917 Oct Revol helped organize Bolshevik revolt in Pskov; then comr, Northern Front; 1918 comr, Petrograd Mil Distr; May – July 1919 member, Revol Mil Council, Western Front; Aug 1949 member, Revol Mil Council, Eastern Front; Jan – Oct 1920 member, Revol Mil Council, 5th Army; then exec admin and Party work: chm, Main Textile Ind Bd; secr, Southeastern Kray CPSU(B) Comt; rector, Leningrad Communist Univ; secr, Leningrad Oblast CPSU(B) Comt; at 13th–15th CPSU(B) Congresses elected member, CPSU(B) Centr Control Commission; at 16th and 17th Party Congresses elected cand member, CC, CPSU(B); member, All-Russian and USSR Centr Exec Comt of various convocations; arrested by State Security organs; *Died:* 1939 in imprisonment; posthumously rehabilitated.

POZHAROV, Nikolay Arsen'yevich (1895–1925) Revolutionary; CP member from 1910; *Born:* 26 Nov 1895 in vil Zolotkov, Yaroslavl' Province, son of a peasant; *Career:* from 1914 lathe-operator at "Novyy Lessner" Plant, Petrograd; from 1915 ordinary seaman with Baltic Fleet; 1916 arrested for anti-war propaganda; after 1917 Feb Revol released; Mar 1917 elected to Kronstadt Sov from "Aziya" training ship; from June 1917 Kronstadt rep in Centr Fleet Comt; asst chm, CC, All-Russian Navy; member, Kronstadt RSDRP(B) Comt; from Aug 1917 member, Mil Tech Commission, Exec Comt, Kronstadt Sov; helped crush Kornilov revolt; Sept 1917 sent to Sebastopol by CC, RSDRP(B); Oct 1917 elected secr, Sebastopol RSDRP(B) Comt; from Dec 1917 chm, Sebastopol Sov; Jan – May 1918 member, Naval Comrt; from June 1918 chm, Yaroslavl' Uyezd Exec Comt; helped crush Yaroslavl' revolt; early 1919 staff comr, Northern Front; 1919–20 chm, Revol Tribunal, 16th Army and 6th Army; 1921–22 worked for State Polit Bd (State Security organs); from 1923 Party and admin work in Moscow and Leningrad; *Died:* 20 June 1925 for tuberculosis.

POZNANSKIY, Nikolay Fydorovich (1888–1952) Educationist; prof; corresp member, RSFSR Acad of Pedag Sci from 1945; CP member from 1930; *Born:* 19 May 1888; *Educ:* 1913 grad History and Philology Fac, Petersburg Univ; *Career:* 1913 began to teach history and Russian language and lit at a business college and other educ establishments in Petersburg; 1917 organized educ system in Tambov; helped establish Tambov Teachers Training Courses and Tambov Univ; from 1918 prof and head, Chair of Pedag, Tambov Univ; from 1923 prof and head, Chair of Pedag, Saratov Univ; 1931–52 head, Chair of Pedag, Saratov Teachers' Training Inst; specialized in folklore and ethnography; studied history of pedag thought, particulary development of ideas on labor training in pre–Revol Russia and abroad; *Publ: Trudovaya pedagogika Pestalotstsi i sovremennost'* (Pestalozzi Labor Pedagogics and Modern Times) (1925); *K istorii trudovogo vospitaniya v dorevolyutsionnomy Rossii* (The History of Labor Training in Pre-Revolutionary Russia) (1925); *Ideya trudovogo vospitaniya u F. Frebelya* (F. Froebel's Ideas on Labor Training) (1926); *Konstruktivnoye vospitaniye. Pedagogicheskiye idei Ad. Ferr'yera* (Constructive Training. The Pedagogic Ideas of Ad. Ferrier) (1928); *Pedagogicheskiye idei N. G. Chernyshevskogo* (The Pedagogic Ideas of N. G. Chernyshevskiy) (1939); *Pedagogicheskiye idei A. I. Gertsena* (The Pedagogic Ideas of A. I. Herzen) (1946); *V. G. Belinskiy o vospitanii* (V. G. Belinskiy on Training) (1949); *Pedagogicheskiye vzglyady D. I. Pisareva* (The Pedagogic Views of D. I. Pisarev) (1951); *Died:* 13 Feb 1952.

POZNER, V. M. (1877–1957) Philosopher; Dr of Philosophy; prof; CP member from 1917; *Born:* 1877; *Career:* 1897 joined revol movement; Nov 1917 – Nov 1919 Collegium member, RSFSR Pop Comrt of Educ; principal of a combined labor school; 1920–22 did Party and govt work in Turkestan; 1924–25 head, Dnepropetrovsk Propaganda Group, CC, CPSU(B); from 1926 lecturer at higher educ establishments in Saratov and Moscow; 1931–39 worked at Inst of Philosophy, USSR Acad of Sci; from 1939 assoc, Inst of Marx, Engels and Lenin, CC, CPSU(B); deleg, 8th RCP(B) Congress; *Died:* 1957.

PRANSKUS-ZHALYONIS, Bronyus (Anskaytis Vatslovas) (1902–1964) Lith writer; prof from 1934; CP member from 1927; *Born:* 11 Oct 1902; *Educ:* 1926 grad Moscow Univ; *Career:* active in Lith revol movement; helped found Lith Komsomol; 1923 emigrated to USSR; worked for Lith Section, Communist Univ of Nat Minorities of the West; taught Lith language and lit; arrested by State Security organs; 1947 released from imprisonment and returned to Lith; 1956 rehabilitated; *Publ:* poetry collections: "Stirring Forces" (1932); "To a Radiant Future" (1959); "Poems of Struggle" (1961); book "Close Distances" (1962), etc; *Died:* 7 May 1964.

PRASOLOV, Leonid Ivanovich (1875–1954) Soil scientist and geographer; member, USSR Acad of Sci from 1935; *Born:* 13 Apr 1875; *Educ:* 1898 grad Petersburg Univ; *Career:* 1898–1906 head, Soil Dept, Samara Province Zemstvo; 1908–14 directed soil studies on Resettlement Bd's expeditions in Centr Asia, Transbaikal, Semipalatinsk region and Yenisey Province; 1915–18 directed Don soil expedition of Dokuchayev Soil Comt; 1918–25 assoc, Soil Dept, Commission for the Study of Natural Production

Resources, USSR Acad of Sci; 1926–37 assoc, 1937–48 dir, Soil Inst, USSR Acad of Sci; specialized in geography, cartography and classification of soils; made major contribution to compilation of genetic soil classification; developed theory of soil provinces, proposed principle of geographical soil zones, and studied origin and geography of a special type of brown forest soil in the Caucasus and Crimea; by tabulating the soil resources in various countries established the existence of extensive, untapped land reserves; helped compile soil maps of USSR and a soil map of the world; *Publ: Pochvy Turkestana* (The Soils of Turkestan) (1925); *Pochvennaya karta Yevropeyskoy chasti SSSR* (A Soil Map of the European USSR) (1930); *O pochvakh Sredne-Ural'skoy lesostepi* (The Soils of the Central Ural Forest-Steppe) (1934); *Razrabotka yedinoy klassifikatsii i nomenklatury pochv* (Devising a Unified Classification and Nomenclature of Soils) (1936); *Mirovaya pochvennaya karta* (A World Soil Map (1938); coauthor, *Geneticheskiye tipy pochv i pochvennyye oblasti Yevropeyskoy chasti SSSR* (Genetic Types of Soils and Soil Regions in the European USSR) (1939); coauthor, *Raspredeleniye mirovogo zemledeliya po tipam pochv* (The Distribution of World Agriculture by Soil Types) (1947); *Awards:* three Orders of Lenin; Order of the Red Banner of Labor; Stalin Prize (1932); Dokuchayev Gold Medal; (1947); *Died:* 13 Jan 1954.

PRAVDIN, A. G. (1879–1943) Party and govt official; CP member from 1899; *Born:* 1879; *Career:* carried out Party work in Odessa, Petersburg, Lugansk and other Russian cities; took part in 1905–07 Revol; frequently arrested by Tsarist authorities; 1912–14 contributed to "Pravda"; after 1917 Feb Revol Party work in Urals; deleg at 7th (Apr) All-Russian RSDRP(B) Conference; after Oct Revol Dep Pop Comr of Internal Affairs; 1920–22 sided with workers' opposition; from 1923 exec Party and govt work; member, Party Centr Control Commission; Dep Pop Comr of Means of Communication; chm, Bd, Northern Railroads Bd; head, Transport Group, Pop Comrt of Workers and Peasants' Inspection; from 1936 retired; *Died:* 1943.

PRAVDIN, Nikolay Sergeyevich (1882–1954) Toxicologist; founder of a school of ind toxicologists; *Born:* 1882; *Educ:* 1912 grad Natural Sci Dept, then Med Fac, Moscow Univ; *Career:* 1914–18 in Russian Army; from 1918 continued med work in Moscow; 1920 defended doctor's thesis on "Matsesta, matsestinskiye vanny i ikh vliyaniye na krovoobrashcheniye" (Matsesta, Matsesta Baths and Their Effects on the Circulations; from 1927 head, Toxicological Laboratory, Inst of Labor Protection, Pop Comrt of Labor (now a laboratory of the Inst of Labor Hygiene and Occupational Diseases, USSR Acad of Med Sci); from 1943 prof; specialized in experiments on maximum permissible concentration of chemicals in the air of ind premises and the operative mechnism of ind poisons; proposed that the degree of toxicity of chemical substances be judged by the concentration approaching the danger threshhold, and that the hazard of acute poisoning be judged by the toxic action zone; for studying the operative mechanism of toxins stressed the need of studying the dystrophy of biochemical processes within the body, especially dystrophy of the enzyme systems involved in oxidation processes; did valuable research on the operative mechanism of carbon monoxide; demonstrated that in this case a considerable role was played by dystrophy of the enzyme systems, especially the tissue respiration of the brain as a result of carbon monoxide's effects on oxidation enzymes; in his latter years specialized in combined effects of ind poisons and mechanism of chronic poisoning; first to use conditioned reflex methods for toxicological research; made first attempt to classify ind poisons along production lines; wrote over 60 works; *Publ: Rukovodstvo promyshlennoy toksikologii* (A Guide to Industrial Toxicology) (1934); *K toksikologii okisi ugleroda* (The Toxicology of Carbon Monoxide) (1943); *Sovetskaya promyshlennaya toksikologiya k trinadtsatiletiyu Velikoy Oktyabr'skoy sotsialisticheskoy revolyutsii* (Soviet Industrial Toxicology on the 13th Anniversary of the Great October Socialist Revolution) (1947); *Metodika maloy toksikologii promyshlennykh yadov* (Methods of Studying the Petty Toxicological Effects of Industrial Poisons) (1947); *Deystviye yadov na okislitel'nyye protsessy* (The Effects of Poisons on Oxidizing Processes) (1949); *O nekotorykh zadachakh farmakologii i toksikologii v svete idey I. P. Pavlova* (Some Tasks of Pharmacology and Toxicology in the Light of I. P. Pavlov's Ideas) (1952); *Died:* 1954.

PRAVDUKHIN, Valerian Pavlovich (1892–1939) Russian writer and lit critic; *Born:* 21 Jan 1892 in vil Tanalykskaya, Orenburg Province; *Educ:* 1914–17 studied at History and Philology Fac, Shanyavskiy Pop Univ; *Career:* zemstvo lecturer; vil teacher; 1922 ed, journal "Sibirskiye ogni"; 1914 first work published; arrested by State Security organs; *Publ:* play *Novyy uchitel'* (The New Teacher) (1920); *Vissarion Belinskiy – osnovopolozhnik sotsial'noy estetiki* (Vissarion Belinskiy, the Founder of Social Esthetics) (1923); *Tvorets – obshchestvo – iskusstvo* (The Creator, Society and Art) (1923); collected articles *Literaturnaya sovremennost'* (Modern Literature) (1924); plays "Virineya" (1924); coauthor, play *Chyornyy Yar* (1931); novelette *Gugenot iz Teriberki* (The Huguenot from Teriberka) (1931); *Okhotnich'ya yunost'* (Hunting Youth) (1933); collected children's stories *V stepi i gornoy tayge* (In the Steppe and Mountain Taiga) (1933); novel *Yaik ukhodit v more* (Yaik Goes to Sea) (1937), etc; *Died:* 15 July 1939 in imprisonment; posthoumously rehabilitated.

PREOBRAZHENSKAYA, Sof'ya Petrovna (1904–1966) Singer (mezzo-soprano); prof; Pop Artiste of RSFSR from 1939 and of USSR from 1955; *Born:* 27 Sept 1904 in Petersburg; *Educ:* 1928 grad Leningrad Conservatory; *Career:* from 1928 soloist, State Acad Opera and Ballet Theater; 1941–44 performed free for Soviet Army and Navy units; 1949–53 prof, Leningrad Conservatory; *Roles:* Marfa in Moussorgsky's "Khovanshchina"; Jeanne d'Arc in Tchaikovsky's *Orleanskaya deva* (The Maid of Orleans); the Princess in Tchaikovsky's *Charodeyka* (The Sorceress); Yefrosin'ya in Kabalevskiy's *Sem'ya Tarasa* (Taras' Family); Marina Mnishek in Moussorgsky's "Boris Godunov", etc; *Awards:* two Stalin Prizes (1946 and 1951); two orders; medals; *Died:* 21 July 1966.

PREOBRAZHENSKIY, N. F. (1886–1952) Govt official; CP member from 1904; *Born:* 1886; *Career:* took part in 1905–07 Revol in Moscow; during WW 1 did Party propaganda work for Zemstvo and Urban Union; after 1917 Oct Revol elected member, Moscow Sov; chm, Special Commission for Mustering and Supplying Red Army, RSFSR Revol Mil Council; member, Revol Mil Council, 14th Army; from 1920 worked in Siberia: head, Dept for Rural Work, Siberian Bureau, CC, RCP(B); chm, Siberian Control Commission; chm, Siberian State Electrivication Commission; from 1924 worked for Gosplan; mang, Photo-Chemical Trust, USSR Supr Sovnarkhoz; also other admin, cultural and educ posts; *Died:* 1952.

PREOBRAZHENSKIY, Pyotr Fyodorovich (1894–1941) Historian; prof; *Born:* 3 May 1894; *Career:* 1919–21 prof, Samara Univ; 1921–37 prof, Moscow Univ; specialized in history of Ancient Greece and Rome and history of Christianity; in his latter years also studied history of int relations on the eve of WW 1; 1928 and 1933 attended Int Historians' Congresses in Oslo and Warsaw; in early 1930's criticized for "anti-Marxist" distortions in his coverage of ancient history; 1937 arrested by State Security organs; *Publ: Uchreditel'nyye sobraniya na Zapade i Russkoye Uchreditel'noye sobraniye* (Constituent Assemblies in the West and the Russian Constituent Assembly) (1917); *Ocherk istorii sovremennogo imperializma* (An Outline History of Modern Imperialism) (1926); *Tertullian i Rim* (Tertullianus and Rome) (1926); *Kurs etnologii* (An Ethnology Course) (1929); *V mire antichnykh idey i obrazov* (In the World of Ancient Ideas and Images) (1965), a collections of various works published in various journals in the 1920's and 1930's; *Died:* 3 Dec 1941 in imprisonment; posthumously rehabilitated.

PREOBRAZHENSKIY, Yevgeniy Alekseyevich (1886–1937) Economist; Party and govt official; CP member from 1903; *Born:* 1886, son of a priest; *Career:* from 1901 organized Soc-Democratic student circles; 1904–05 Party work in Oryol, Bryansk and Moscow; 1906–08 in the Urals; 1905 attended Tammerfors Conference; repeatedly arrested; 1909–11 in exile; winter 1911 fled from exile; late 1912 arrested and exiled again until 1915; 1915–17 worked in Irkutsk and Chita; participated in 1917 Feb Revol in Chita; Aug 1917 at 6th Party Congress elected cand member, CC, RSDRP(B); during 1917 Oct Revol head, Ural Party Org; during Civil War head, Polit Dept, 3rd Army; member, Commission to Draft Party Program, 8th Party Congress; 1920, at 9th Party Congress elected member, CC, RCP(B); at RCP(B) CC Plenum following 9th Congress elected Politburo and Org Bureau member and secr, CC, RCP(B); 1920–21, during the trade-union controversy, sided with Trotskyist platform and was its chief theorist on the subject of Sov econ; from Mar 1921 chm, Finance Comt, CC and Council of Pop Comr; Collegium member, Pop Comrt of Finance; subsequently chm, Main Professional Educ Bd; co-ed, newspaper "Pravda"; 1922 non-voting deleg at 11th RCP(B) Congress; from 1923 active member, Trotskyist opposition; in this connection 1927 expelled from the Party; summer 1929, together with Radek and Smigla, wrote a letter to the CC, confessing his errors and breaking with Trotskyism; readmitted to the Party; again expelled from the Party and later convicted for alleged anti-Party and anti–Sov activities; *Publ: Bumazhnyye den'gi v epokhu proletarskoy diktatury* (Paper Money in the Age of Proletarian Dictatorship); *Ot nepa k sotsializmu* (From New Economic Policy to Socialism); *O morali i klassovykh normakh* (Morals and Class Norms); *Ekonomika i finansy sovremennoy Frantsii* (The Economy and Finances of Contemporary France); *Ob ekonomicheskikh krizisakh pri nepe* (Economic Crises Under the New Economic Policy); *Novaya ekonomika* (New Economics); coauthor (with Bukharin), *Azbuka kommunizma* (The ABC of Communism), etc; *Died:* 1937 in imprisonment.

PREOBRAZHENSKIY, Yevgeniy Nikolayevich (1909–1963) Mil commander; col-gen, Air Force; CP member from 1940; *Born:* 1909 in Vologda Province, son of a teacher; *Educ:* studied at air force school; *Career:* 1927 drafted into Air Force via Komsomol muster; held various commands with Naval Air Force; during WW 2 commanded large air force unit; chief of staff and commander, air force group; Aug 1941 personally led bomber group on Berlin raid; after WW 2 for many years commanded Naval Air Force; *Awards:* Hero of the Sov Union; three Orders of Lenin; five Orders of the Red Banner; Order of Suvorov, 2nd Class; Order of the Red Star; medals; *Died:* Oct 1963.

PRESNYAKOV, Aleksandr Yevgen'yevich (1870–1929) Russian historian; prof from 1918; corresp member, USSR Acad of Sci from 1920; *Born:* 21 Apr 1870; *Educ:* grad Petersburg Univ; *Career:* 1907–18 assoc prof, from 1918 prof, Petersburg (Leningrad) Univ; from 1919 also prof, Archeological Inst; also taught at Inst of Red Prof; specialized in history of Kiev Rus and Muscowy; made a study of chronicles; adherent of sci materialism school; criticized historical outlines of S. M. Solov'yov and V. O. Klyuchevskiy, especially the theory of "dynastic princely rule" in Kiev Rus and its "mercantile-urban" nature; *Publ: Knyazhoye pravo v Drevney Rusi* (Princely Law in Ancient Rus) (1909); *Moskovskoye tsarstvo* (The Kingdom of Muscowy) (1918); *Obrazovaniye Velikorusskogo gosudarstva* (The Formation of the Great-Russian State) (1918); *14 dekabrya 1825 goda* (14 December 1825) (1925); "Alexander I" (1924); *Apogey samoderzhaviya. Nikolay I* (The Peak of Autocracy. Nicholas I) (1925); *Lektsii po russkoy istorii* (Lectures on Russian History) (2 vol, 1938–39, posthumously); *Died:* 30 Sept 1929.

PREYKSHAS, Kazis Kazevich (1903–1961) Party and govt official; CP member from 1920; *Born:* 14 June 1903, son of a worker on Verbunay Estate, Gruzdzhyay (now Shyanlyay) Volost; *Educ:* 1917–31 studied at Communist Univ of Nat Minorities of the West, then at Int Lenin School, Moscow; 1935 postgrad studies in Moscow; *Career:* during WW 1 evacuated with parents to Moscow; 1917–18 worked at "Provodnik" Plant; 1918 returned to Shyaulyay and worked as farmhand on an estate, then as blacksmith and stevedore; from 1920 active in Shyaulyay trade unions; member, Shyaulyay City and Rayon Comt, CP Lith; 1922–23 arrested for revol activities; 1924 again arrested and sentenced to eight years' imprisonment; released from prison under 28 July 1926 amnesty; from Aug 1931, after completing his schooling, engaged in underground Party work in Kaunas as secr, CC, CP Lith; 28 Dec 1931 re-arrested and sentenced by Kaunas Dist Court to eight years' imprisonment; mil court reviewed the case and sentenced him to 12 years; 1933 sent to Moscow in exchange of polit prisoners between USSR and Lith; sent to Minsk as dep ed, Lith weekly "Raudonasis artoyas"; from fall 1935 postgrad studies in Moscow; went to Spain as volunteer to fight in Spanish Civil War; helped organize int units which fought on Madrid and Catalonian Fronts; after collapse of Spanish Republ interned in camps in France; Apr 1939 released; went to Moscow and helped prepare Lith-language Sov lit for the press; 1940, after establishment of Sov rule in Lith appointed, secr, CC, CP Lith; retained this post until 1948; during WW 2 polit and org work with Lith units of Sov Army; 1948–60 dep chm, Lith Council of Min; from 1961 Lith Min of For Affairs; contributed to underground Lith CP press and Sov Lith press; for many years ed, CC, CP Lith journal "Kommunist"; 1929–31 and 1940–61 member, CC, CP Lith; 1941–54 dep, USSR Supr Sov; 1947–61 dep, Lith Supr Sov; *Awards:* Order of Lenin; Order of the Fatherland War, 2nd Class; three Orders of the Red Banner of Labor; medals; *Died:* 5 Dec 1961.

PRIKLONSKIY, Viktor Aleksandrovich (1899–1959) Hydrogeologist; geological eng; prof from 1950; corresp member, USSR Acad of Sci from 1958; *Born:* 7 Feb 1899; *Educ:* 1920 grad Moscow Univ; 1928 grad Moscow Mining Acad; *Career:* from 1930 lecturer, from 1950 prof, Moscow Geological Surveying Inst; from 1944 also assoc, from 1957 dir, Laboratory of Hydrogeological Problems, USSR Acad of Sci; helped design many major hydraulic structures; established laws for the diffusion of salts in clayey rocks, of importance in the formation of ground water and argillaceous residue; *Publ:Izucheniye fizicheskikh svoystv i khimicheskogo sostava podzemnykh vod* (A Study of the Physical Properties and Chemical Composition of Ground Waters) (1935); *Gruntovedeniye* (Soil Studies) (2 vol, 1952–55); *Awards:* Savarenskiy Prize (1951); Stalin Prize (1952); *Died:* 13 Feb 1959.

PRILEZHAYEV, Nikolay Aleksandrovich (1872–1944) Organic chemist; corresp member, USSR Acad of Sci from 1933; member, Bel Acad of Sci from 1940; *Born:* 27 Sept 1872; *Educ:* grad Warsaw Univ; *Career:* from 1912 prof, Warsaw Univ; from 1915 prof, Kiev Polytech Inst; from 1924 prof, Bel Univ; specialized in reactions involving oxidation of unsaturated compounds; devised gen method of obtain olefin alpha-oxides by direct oxidation of the double bond of benzoil hydroperoxide (Prilezhayev reaction); this method ist also used for the qualitative and quantitative determination of an isolated double band in unsaturated hydrocarbons and in terpenes; *Publ: Organicheskiye perekisi i primeneniye ikh dlya okisleniya nepredel'nykh soyedineniy* (Organic Peroxides and Their Use for Oxidicing Unsaturated Compounds) (1912); *Died:* 26 May 1944.

PRIMAKOV, Vitaliy Markovich (1897–1937) Mil commander; Zaporozhian Cossack; corps commander, Sov Army from 1935; Civil War veteran; CP member from 1914; *Born:* 30 Dec 1897 in vil Semyonovka, Chernigov Province, son of a teacher; *Educ:* 1923 grad Higher Mil Acad Courses; *Career:* while at high-school made the acquaintance of the writer Kotsyubinskiy's son and became a revolutionary; Feb 1915 arrested for distributing anti-war proclamations and sentenced to eight years at hard labor; released after 1917 Feb Revol; Aug 1917 joined 13th Infantry Reserve Regt at Chernigov to conduct Bolshevik propaganda among the troops; elected regt dep to Chernigov Exec Comt and sent as deleg to 2nd All-Russian Congress of Soviets, Petrograd; here elected member, All-Russian Centr Exec Comt; in 1917 Oct Revol played active part in blocking Kerenskiy's troops from Petrograd; Jan 1918 formed Ukr Red Cossack Regt in Khar'kov; led this regt in Partisan operations against the Germans and Hetman Skoropadskiy and Petlyura's troops; 1919, in operations against Denikin, expanded his regt into the 1st Red Cossack Brigade, then into 8th Red Cossack Div; Nov 1919 led this div in rout of White troops at Oryol; from May 1920 commanded 8th Div on Sov-Polish Front and took part in Galician campaign; late 1920 expanded div into 1st Red Cossack Cavalry Corps and commanded this corps until 1924; 1924–25 commandant, Leningrad Higher Cavalry School; 1925–27 head, Kalgan group of Sov mil advisers in China; commanded cavalry in Kalgan fighting; commanded "Revol Gendarmes" Regt in Canton and used it to crush the "Paper Tigers" revolt; 1927–29 Sov mil attache in Kabul; commanded cavalry detachment sent to Afghanistan in order to restore the overthrown Ammanul Khan to his throne; 1930 Sov mil attache in Japan; 1931–33 commander, 13th Infantry Corps in Sverdlovsk; 1933–35 dep commander, North Caucasian Mil Distr; dep inspector of higher mil training establishments; 1935–36 dep commander, Leningrad Mil Distr; deleg at 17th CPS(B) Congress; member, USSR Centr Exec Comt; wrote several books on tactics, Afghanistan and Japan, etc, including his account of his experiences in China *Zapiski leytenanta Allena* (Lieutenant Allen's Notes); Aug 1936 arrested by NKVD; 11 June 1937 sentenced to death together with Marshal Tukhachevskiy and others by Special Tribunal of USSR Supr Court; *Awards:* three Orders of the Red Banner; *Died:* 12 June 1937 executed; posthumously rehabilitated.

PRIOROV, Nikolay Nikolayevich (1885–1961) Orthopedist and traumatologist; Dr of Med from 1940; prof from 1931; member, USSR Acad of Med Sci from 1957; Hon Sci Worker of RSFSR from 1942; CP member from 1946; *Born:* 10 June 1885 in Shenkursk, now Arkhangel'sk Oblast; *Educ:* 1912 grad Med Fac, Tomsk Univ; *Career:* 1910–11 worked as med asst during cholera epidemic; 1911–12 accompanied expeditions to Kara Sea and Baygach Island; 1913–15 and 1919–27 worked at Surgical Dept, Soldatyonkov (now Botkin) Hospital; until 1917 also head, Prosthetic Dept, Orthopedic Hospital; 1917–19 chief physician,

Centr Hospital for Invalid Soldiers, Moscow, then founder-head, Med Dept, Moscow Prosthetic Factory; founder-head, Tech Med Dept, RSFSR Pop Comrt of Soc Security; founder-head, Prosthetic Dept, Therapy Bd, RSFSR Pop Comrt of Health; 1921–61 founder-dir, Therapeutic and Prosthetic Inst (now Centr Inst of Traumatology and Orthopedics, USSR Min of Health), Moscow; 1931–61 also founder-head, Chair of Orthopedics and Traumatology, Centr Inst of Postgrad Med Training, Moscow; from 1932 founder and life-chm, Moscow Soc of Orthopedists and Traumatologists; 1933–38 head, Chair of Traumatology and Orthopedics, 1st Moscow Med Inst; 1938–39 mil surgeon in Russo-Finnish War; 1940 defended doctor's thesis on "Amputation of the Extremities and Prostheses"; 1941–45 chief surgeon of evacuation hospitals, USSR Pop Comrt of Health, then chm, Learned Med Council, USSR Min of Health; 1945–47 USSR Dep Min of Health; from 1947 founder and life-chm, All-Union Soc of Orthopedists and Traumatologists; from 1947 also dep chm, All-Union Surgeons' Soc; attended numerous Sov and for surgical, orthopedic and traumatological congresses; dep ed, journal "Ortopediya, travmatologiya i protezirovaniye"; co-ed, "Surgery" section, "Bol'shaya meditsinskaya entsiklopediya" (Large Medical Encyclopedia) (2nd ed); specialized in prosthetics, the treatment of war-wounded and war cripples and in hospital org; also did research on the treatment of wounds and fractures, osteosynthesis and false joints and the org of the orthopedic and traumatological service; made special studies of treatment of burns, electr shock, the pathology and physiology of the bones and compensatory adaptivity in functional disturbances of the extremities; encouraged the introduction of plastics in Sov med and helped to develop bio-drugs for use in traumatology; also did research on autoplasty, homoplasty and tissue regeneration and developed tissue conservation methods; wrote over 200 works; *Publ:* doctor's thesis *Amputatsii konechnostey i protezy* (Amputation of the Extremities and Prostheses) (1941); *Raneniye taza* (Pelvic Wounds) (1945); *Lozhnyye sustavy i nesrastayuschiyesya perelomy* (False Joints and Non-Healing Fractures) (1948); *Teoriya i praktika osteosinteza pri lechenii perelomov kostey* (The Theory and Practice of Osteosynthesis in the Treatment of Bone Fractures) (1956); *Plastika kostey i sustavov* (Osteoplasty and Arthroplasty) (1959); coauthor, *Primeneniye v travmatologii i ortopedii kostnykh gomotransplantatov, konservirovannykh okhlazhdeniyem* (The Use of Deep-Frozen Bone Homografts in Traumatology and Orthopedics) (1959); *Ozhogi i ikh lecheniye* (Burns and Their Treatment) (1960); *Otkrytyye perelomy kostey, ikh osobennosti i lecheniye* (Open Bone Fractures, Their Characteristics and Treatment) (1960); *Awards:* two Orders of Lenin; Order of the Red Star; Badge of Hon; medals; *Died:* 15 Apr 1961 in Moscow.

PRISHVIN, Mikhail Mikhaylovich (1873–1954) Russian writer; *Born:* 4 Feb 1873 on Khrushchevo Estate, Oryol Province; *Educ:* 1902 grad Leipzig Univ; *Career:* 1897–99 imprisoned for revol activities; then lived abroad; returned to Russia and worked as agronomist; toured much of Northern Russia on foot; 1905 first work printed; member, "Pereval" (The Pass) lit assoc; *Publ:* essays: *V krayu nepugannykh ptits* (In the Land of Unscared Birds) (1905); "Kolobok" (1906); *Chyornyy arab* (The Black Arab) (1912); *Slavnyye bubny* (Glorious Tambourines) (1914); novel *Kashcheyeva tsep'* (Kashchey's Chain) (1924); *Rodniki Berendeya* (The Springs of Berendey) (1925); *Kalendar' prirody* (The Calender of Nature) (1925); *Zhuravlinaya rodina* (Land of the Cranes) (1929); novelette "Zhen'-Shen'" (1933); legendary tale *Kladovaya solntsa* (The Larder of the Sun) (1945); novelette *Korabel'naya chashcha* (The Heart of the Ship) (1954), etc; *Died:* 16 Jan 1954.

PRIVALOV, Ivan Ivanovich (1891–1941) Mathematician; specialist in the theory of the functions of a complex variable; prof from 1918; corresp member, USSR Acad of Sci from 1939; *Born:* 30 Jan 1891; *Educ:* 1913 Moscow Univ; *Career:* from 1918 prof, Saratov Univ; from 1922 prof, Moscow Univ; in the course of his work made regular use of the metric theorem of the functions of a true variable; *Publ: Integral Koshi* (Cauchy's Integral) (1918); *Vvedeniye v teoriyu funktsiy kompleksnogo peremennogo* (An Introduction to the Theory of the Functions of a Complex Variable) (1927); *Analiticheskaya geometriya* (Analytical Geometry) (1927); *Integral'nyye uravneniya* (Integral Equations) (1935); *Subgarmonichnyye funktsii* (Subharmonic Functions) (1937); *Granichnyye svoystva odnoznachnykh analiticheskikh funktsiy* (The Boundary Conditions of Univalent Analytical Functions) (1941), etc; *Died:* 13 July 1941.

PROKHOROVSHCHIKOV, Aleksandr Aleksandrovich (1892–1943) Mil inventor and designer; eng, Red Army; *Born:* 8 July 1892 in Petersburg, son of an architect; *Career:* during WW 1 designed for War Dept the two-seater, dual-control P-4 plane with 50 HP Gnome engine; 19 Jan 1917 the War Dept adopted his design for a half-track cross-country tank; from Aug 1918 in Red Army; qualified as mil pilot and served on Northern, Southern and Western Fronts; 1922–28 plen, Red Army Main Air Force Bd and commander of a special-duty air force group; also designed new planes and improved existing models; 1928 invalided out of Red Army; 1928–41 worked for design bureau; designed high-speed sea sleds, sectional flat-bottomed vessels and a pusher tug; invented specially resistant armor for tanks; designed cotton combine harvester for Centr Asia; 1941 arrested by NKVD; *Died:* 1943 in imprisonment; posthumously rehabilitated.

PROKOF'YEV, Georgiy Alekseyevich (1902–1939) Balloonist; CP member from 1920; *Born:* 17 Aug 1902; *Educ:* studied at Air Force Acad; *Career:* studied aspects of flight in lighter-than-air craft; 1929 performed first independent flight in spherical aerostat; 1933, together with E.K. Birnbaum, and K.D. Godunov, performed record stratospheric flight in "USSR-1" stratostat, reaching an altitude of 19,000 meters; *Awards:* Order of Lenin; medal; *Died:* 23 Apr 1939.

PROKOF'YEV, G. Ye. (1895–?) Govt official; Comr of State Security, 1st Class from 1935; CP member from 1919; *Born:* 1895 in Kiev, son of an office worker; *Career:* early 1917 elected to Kiev Exec Comt of Higher Educ Establishments; 1919 volunteered for Red Army and did polit work in 12th and 1st Cavalry Armies; 1920 polit work in railroad transport; then with All-Russian Cheka, where he was head, Information Dept; 1926 appointed head, OGPU Econ Bd; directed terrorist campaign in ind, agric and financial system; also made use of tech knowledge of sentenced specialists for major ind construction projects; 1929 also appointed Presidium member, Supr Sovnarkhoz; from 1930 head, OGUP Special Dept; 1931 Dep Pop Comr of Workers and Peasants' Inspection; 1932 dep chm, OBPU; 1934 USSR Dep Pop Comr of Internal Affairs; also chm, "Dynamo" Sports Soc; member, All-Russian and USSR Centr Exec Comt; at 17th Party Congress elected member, Sov Control Commission, USSR Council of Pop Comr; *Awards:* Order of the Red Banner; two Cheka Badges of Hon; *Died:* date and place of death unknown.

PROKOF'YEV, Sergey Andreyevich (1874–1944) Construction eng; prof from 1922; *Born:* 7 Dec 1874 in Morshansk, now Tambov Oblast, son of a merchant; *Educ:* 1899 grad Petersburg Inst of Transport Eng; *Career:* worked as road and bridge eng; 1899 built ferroconcrete bridge in the Caucasus; from 1903 lecturer, from 1922 prof, Kiev Polytech Inst, where he read the first course on ferroconcrete in the Ukr in 1905; wrote several works on ferroconcrete and the calculation of arches; *Publ: Teoriya raschyota sploshnykh uprugikh arok i primeneniye yeyo k raschyotu arok parabolicheskikh* (The Theory of the Calculation of Continous Elastic Arches and its Application to the Calculation of Parabolic Arches) (1912), etc; *Died:* 14 Jan 1944.

PROKOF'YEV, Sergey Sergeyevich (1891–1953) Composer, pianist and conductor; Pop Artiste of RSFSR from 1947; *Born:* 11 Apr 1891 in vil Sontsovka, Yekaterinoslav Province; *Educ:* 1909 grad Composition Class, Petersburg Conservatory; 1914 grad piano and conducting classes, Petersburg Conservatory; *Career:* in his early youth displayed outstanding musical talent; from age five studied piano under his mother; 1902–03 took composition lessons from Gliere; 1904–14 pupil of Lyadov, Rimsky-Korsakov and Cherepnin; from 1908 performed as pianist in Petersburg, Moscow and later abroad; 1918 for a short while worked with Chaliapine at the Tragedy Theater, Petrograd; 1918–21 lived in USA; 1921–32 lived in France; performed as pianist and conductor in many countries of the world; late 1932 returned to USSR; frequently in trouble with Party critics, but thanks to his outstanding talent he retained his place in the front rank of Sov musicians; composed over 130 major works, including: 8 operas; 7 symphonies; 7 ballets; 7 cantatas; 14 sonatas; 8 concertos; piano pieces; romances; songs; choral works; music for plays and films, etc; *Works:* "Scythian Suite" (1915); opera *Igrok* (The Gambler), after Dostoyevsky, (1916); fairy-tale opera after K. Gozzi *Lyubov' k tryom apel'sinam* (Love of Three Oranges) (1921); opera *Ognennyy angel* (The Fiery Angel), after V. Ya. Bryusov's novel of the same name (1927); ballets: *Stal'noy skok* (The Steel Leap) (1927); *Bludnyy syn* (The Prodigal Son) (1929); *Na Dnepre* (On the Dnieper) (1932); "Romeo and Juliet" (1933); cantata "Aleksandr

Nevskiy" (1938); opera "Semyon Katko", after Katayev's novelette (1940); opera *Voyna i mir* (War and Peace) (1944); ballet *Zolushka* (Cinderella) (1945); opera *Povest' o nastoyashchem cheloveke* (Tale of a Real Man), after Boris Polevoy's work (1948); ballet *Skazka o kamennom tsvetke* (The Tale of the Stone Flower) (1954), etc; *Awards:* Order of the Red Banner of Labor; five Stalin Prizes (1943, 1946 (two), 1947 and 1951); Lenin Prize (1957); *Died:* 5 Mar 1953 in Moscow.

PROKOF'YEV, Vsevolod Aleksandrovich (1898–1942) Musicologist; *Born:* 12 Apr 1898 in Kaluga; *Educ:* 1923 grad History of Music Fac, Petrograd Inst of Art History; *Career:* from 1922 research work; specialized in history of Russian opera from late 18th Century to early 19th Century; made studies of A. N. Titov, M. A. Matinskiy, O. A. Kozlovskiy, V. A. Pashkevich and other composers of this period; compiled partituras and piano arrangements of old operas and musical vaudevilles; *Publ: Iz istorii russkogo prosveshchyonnogo muzykal'nogo diletantizma. "K materialam o sem'ye Titovykh." Aleksey Nikolayevich Titov (1769–1827)* (From the History of Russian Enlightened Musical Dilettantism. "Material on the Titov Family." Aleksey Nikolayevich Titov [1769–1827]) (1927); *Mikhail Matinskiy i yego opera "Sanktpetersburgskiy Gostinyy Dvor"* (Mikhail Matinskiy and His Opera "The Saint Petersburg Guest Hall") (1927); *Died:* 17 Mar 1942 during the blockade of Leningrad.

PROKOPOVICH, Sergey Nikolayevich (1871–1955) Economist and publicist; politician; *Born:* 1871; *Career:* in 1890's, living in Belgium and Switzerland, joined Union of Russian Soc-Democrats Abroad; 1904 joined Liberation League; 1905 elected member, CC, Constitutional Democratic Party, but resigned from CC shortly afterwards; 1906, together with his wife Ye. D. Kuskova, published in Petersburg journal "Bez zaglaviya" and contributed to newspaper "Tovarishch"; wrote numerous studies of workers' movement; after 1917 Feb Revol Aug – Sept Min of Trade and Ind, and Sept – Oct Min of Food in Provisional Govt; opposed 1917 Oct Revol; 1921, together with Kuskova and N. M. Kishkin, joined Public Famine Relief Comt; 1922 expelled from USSR for anti-Sov activities; lived in Berlin, Prague, Geneva and USA; in 1920's and 1930's published journals "Ekonomicheskiy sbornik", "Russkiy ekonomichesky sbornik" and *Byulleteni Ekonomicheskogo kabineta Professora S. N. Prokopovicha* (Quarterly Bulletins of Soviet-Russian Economics); wrote many books and articles on history of Sov econ, theory and practice of building of socialism , etc; *Publ: Rabocheye dvizheniye na zapade* (The Workers' Movement in the West) (1899); *K kritike Marksa* (A Critique of Marx) (1901); *Rabocheye dvizheniye v Germanii* (The Workers' Movement in Germany) (1905); *Byudzhety petersburgskikh rabochikh* (Petersburg Workers' Budgets) (1909); *Problemy sotsializma. Razvitiye sotsialisticheskoy mysli vo Frantsii* (Problems of Socialism. The Development of Socialist Thought in France) (1911); *Voyna i narodnoye khozyaystvo* (War and the National Economy) (1918); *Ocherki khozyaystva Sovetskoy Rossii* (Studies in the Economy of Soviet Russia) (1923); *Ideya planirovaniya i itogi pyatiletki* (The Idea of Planning and Results of the Five-Year Plan) (1934); *Narodnoye khozyaystvo SSSR* (The National Economy of the USSR) (1952); *Died:* 1955 in Geneva.

PROSH'YAN, Prosh Perchevich (1883–1918) Politician; member, Socialist-Revol Party from 1905; *Born:* 1883 in Ashtarak, Arm; *Educ:* studied at Novorossiysk Univ, Odessa; *Career:* 1905 sentenced to six years' hard labor for attempting to free polit prisoners from Odessa Prison; served sentence in Akatuy and Zerentuy; upon release fled from prescribed place of settlement but was re-arrested and sentenced to a further term at hard labor; 1913 exiled to Siberia, whence he fled abroad; during WW 1 conducted internationalist propaganda; after 1917 Feb Revol returned to Russia; published in Helsingfors newspaper "Sotsialist-revolyutsioner"; sided with left wing of Socialist-Revol Party and sharply attacked defensist views of Party CC, twice leading to his expulsion from party; July 1917 arrested by Provisional Govt; supported idea of active alliance with Bolsheviks; took part in Oct Revol; 1917 at 2nd All-Russian Congress of Soviets elected member, All-Russian Centr Exec Comt; co-founder, Leftist Socialist-Revol Party and member of its CC; Dec 1917 Pop Comr of Posts and Telegraphs; opposed Brest Peace Treaty; and in Mar 1918 resigned from Council of Pop Comr together with gen Socialist-Revol walk-out; 1918 helped plan Leftist Socialist-Revol revolt in Moscow and went underground after this revolt was crushed; Nov 1918 sentenced in absentia by Sov court to three years' imprisonment; *Died:* 16 Dec 1918 in Moscow of typhus.

PROSKURA, Georgiy Fyodorovich (1876–1958) Hydraulic eng; Dr of Eng; prof from 1911; member, Ukr Acad of Sci from 1929; Hon Sci and Tech Worker of Ukr SSR from 1944; *Born:* 28 Apr 1876 in Smela, now Cherkassy Oblast, son of an office worker; *Educ:* 1901 grad Moscow Higher Tech College; *Career:* from 1904 lecturer, from 1911 prof, Khar'kov Technol Inst; 1934 built first Sov hydrodynamic pipe for research on hydrodynamic grids; 1945–54 dir, Laboratory of High-Revolution Machines and Mechanisms, Ukr Acad of Sci; did research on the theory and design of hydroturbines and pumps; also studied cavitation in hydraulic machinery and the use of hydraulic clutches in transport vehicles, etc; designed axial pump for Moskva Canal; *Publ: Vodyanyye turbiny* (Hydroturbines) (2 vol, 1913); *Tsentrobezhnyye i propellernyye nasosy* (Centrifugal and Propeller Pumps) (2nd ed, 1932); *Gidrodinamika turbomashin* (The Hydrodynamics of Turbines) (2nd ed, 1954); *Died:* 30 Oct 1958.

PROSKURYAKOV, Lavr Dmitriyevich (1858–1926) Civil eng; specialist in bridge designing and construction mech; *Born:* 30 Aug 1858; *Educ:* 1884 grad Petersburg Inst of Transport Eng; *Career:* from 1887 lecturer, Petersburg Inst of Transport Eng; from 1896 prof, Moscow Eng College (now Moscow Inst of Rail Transport Eng); designed a number of econ, light bridges with new type of girders (spanning the Rivers Narva, Western Bug, Volkhov, Oka, Amur, Yenisey, Zeya, etc); pioneered design of railroad bridges; his graphic-analytical methods of calculation and his lines of influence theory (covering the influence of mobile loads) provided the basis for late 19th-Century changes in the methods of calculating bridge girders; compiled special "factor tables" for practical calculations; *Publ: K raschyotu skvoznykh ferm* (Calculating Cross-Girders) (1885); *Issledovaniye znacheniy momenta vneshnikh sil ot sosredotochennykh gruzov v pryamykh balkakh* (A Study of the Values of the External Forces Factor from Concentrated Loads in Straight Girders) (1888); *Stroitel'naya mekhanika* (Construction Mechanics) (1925–26); *Awards:* Gold Medal of All-Union Exibition in Paris (1900) for designing a bridge over the Yenisey; *Died:* 14 Sept 1926.

PROTAZANOV, Yakov Aleksandrovich (1881–1945) Film dir; Hon Art worker from 1935; *Born:* 4 Feb 1881 in Moscow; *Career:* 1909–11 script-writer; from 1911 film dir at various studios; 1920–21 worked for Gaumont Firm in Paris and for Ufa Film Studios in Berlin; from 1922 in Sov film ind; *Works:* directed films: *Voyna i mir* (War and Peace) (1915); *Pikovaya dama* (The Queen of Spades) (1916); *Otets Sergiy* (Father Sergiy), after Lev Tolstoy (1918); "Anfisa" after L. Andreyev; *Zakroyshchik iz Torzhka* (The Cutter from Torzhek) (1925); *Protsess o tryokh millionakh* (The Trial of Three Million) (1926); *Sorok pervyy* (The Forty-First) (1927); *Marionetki* (The Puppets) (1934); *Bespridannitsa* (Girl Without a Dowry) (1936); "Salavat Yulayev" (1941), etc; *Awards:* Gold Medal of Paris Exhibition (1937); Badge of Hon (1939); *Died:* 8 Aug 1945.

PROTOPOPOV, Aleksandr Dmitriyevich (1866–1918) Politician; last Tsarist Russian Min of Internal Affairs; maj landowner and industrialist; *Born:* 1866; *Career:* member, Octobrist Party; member, 3rd and 4th State Dumas; from 1914 asst chm, State Duma; member, Progressive Bloc; summer 1916 headed Duma deleg to UK and negotiated in Stockholm with the banker Varburg, an unofficial agent of the German Govt, on the possibility of concluding a separate peace treaty; Sept 1916, with the help of Rasputin and against the wishes of the Octobrist Duma faction and the Progressive Bloc, he became Min of Internal Affairs; close confidant of Tsar and Tsaritsa; Dec 1916 – Oct 1917 founder-ed, newspaper "Russkaya volya"; Feb 1917 tried to crush revol by force; arrested and interned by Provisional Govt in Peter and Paul Fortress; *Died:* 1918 executed by Cheka.

PROTOPOPOV, Viktor Pavlovich (1880–1957) Psychiatrist; Dr of Med from 1909; prof from 1921; member, Ukr Acad of Sci from 1945; Hon Sci Worker of Ukr SSR from 1935; *Born:* 22 Oct 1880 in vil Yurki, now Poltava Oblast; *Educ:* 1906 grad Petersburg Mil Med Acad; *Career:* 1906–21 worked under V. M. Bekhterev at Petersburg (Petrograd) Mil Med Acad; corresponded with I. P. Pavlov; 1921–23 lectured in Perm'; 1923–41 head, Chair of Psachiatry, Khar'kov Med Inst; from 1927 founder-dir, Khar'kov Inst of Clinical Psychiatry and Soc and Mental Hygiene (now Khar'kov Psychoneurological Inst); 1931 founded first Chair of Higher Nervous Activity in USSR; for a while head, Chair of Psychiatry, Khar'kov 2nd Med Inst; 1934–45 corresp member, Ukr Acad of Sci; 1944 founded Dept of Psychiatry, Kiev Inst of Clinical Physiology, Ukr Acad of Sci; also founded Chair of

Psychiatry and Chair of Higher Nervous Activity, Kiev Inst of Postgrad Med Training; member, Learned Med Council and chief psychiatrist, Ukr Min of Health; did major research on psychiatry and the physiology and pathology of higher nervous activity; devised method of inducing conditioned motor reflexes; studied the formation of motor habits in higher animals under natural experimental conditions, the physiological mechanisms of abstract thinking, and the pathophysiology, biochemistry and therapy of schizophrenia and manic-depressive psychosis; was one of first Sov sci to use sleep treatment and detoxication therapy for mental patients; wrote over 110 works; *Publ:* doctor's thesis *O sochetatel'noy dvigatel'noy reaktsii na zvukovyye razdrazheniya* (Combinative Motor Reaction to Sound Stimuli) (1909); *Somaticheskiy sindrom, nablyudayemyy v techeniye maniakal'no-depressivnogo psikhoza* (A Somatic Syndrone Observable in the Course of Manic-Depressive Psychosis) (1920); *Usloviya obrazovaniya motornykh navykov i ikh fiziologicheskaya kharakteristika* (Conditions Governing the Formation of Motor Habits and Their Physiological Characteristics) (1935); *Patofiziologicheskiye osnovy ratsional'noy terapii shizofrenii* (The Pathophysiological Principles of the Efficient Treatment of Schizophrenia) (1946); coauthor, *Issledovaniye vysshey nervnoy deyatel'nosti v yestyestvennom eksperimente* (An experiment on Higher Nervous Activity under Natural Conditions) (1950); *Izbrannyye trudy* (Selected Works) (1961); *Awards:* Grand Silver Medal of Petersburg Mil Med Acad (1906); two Orders of Lenin; Order of the Red Banner of Labor; medals; *Died:* 30 Nov 1957 in Kiev.

PROZOR, V. S. (1884–1962) Government official; CP member from 1905; *Born:* 1884; *Career:* took part in 1905–07 Revol in Petersburg; until 1917 Oct Revol telegraphist, clerk and section tech on railroads; 1918–19 comr for construction of mil strategic railroads; comr, then mang, RSFSR Railroad Construction Bd; 1920–22 head, Railroad Construction Bd; dep chm and Collegium member, Main Comt for State Installations; 1922 left Party; 1922–25 econ admin work at various state institutions and construction projects; *Died:* 1962.

PROZOROV, Leonid Alekseyevich (1877–1941) Psychiatrist; Hon Dr of Med from 1938; *Born:* 1877; *Educ:* 1903 grad Med Fac, Moscow Univ; *Career:* after grad intern, Preobrazhenskoye Psychiatric Hospital, Moscow; helped to organize the house-visit and treatment system in Moscow; was one of first psychiatrists in Russia to practice home-therapy for the mentally-ill; the experience gathered through the home-visit and treatment system served as a basis for the later "outpatient" psychiatric treatment system; after 1917 Oct Revol helped to build up the Sov psychiatric service; did research on the org of in- and outpatient psychiatric treatment, the home-visit system and methods of handling mental patients; also studied problems of legislation on mental illness and questions of forensic and ind psychiatric expertise; compiled statistics on mental disease and its prevention; wrote some 40 works; *Publ: Moskovskiy stolichnyy patronazh dlya dushevno-bol'nykh* (The Moscow Home-Visit and Treatment System for the Mentally-Ill) (1910); *Etapy razvitiya nevro-psikhiatricheskoy organizatsii v RSFSR* (Stages in the Development of the Neuropsychiatric Service in the RSFSR) (1934); *Sostoyaniye nevropsikhiatricheskoy pomoshchi v RSFSR* (The State of the Neuropsychiatric Service in the RSFSR) (1937); *Istoriya vnebol'nichnoy psikhiatricheskoy pomoshchi v Moskve* (The History of the Outpatient Psychiatric Service in Moscow) (1940); *Died:* 1941.

PRUDENSKIY, German Aleksandrovich (1904–1967) Economist; corresp member, USSR Acad of Sci from 1958; dep chm, Sci Council for Specific Soc Studies, USSR Acad of Sci from 1966; CP member from 1931; *Born:* 1904; *Educ:* 1931 grad Moscow Higher Tech College; *Career:* from 1931 eng in Sverdlovsk, then research, teaching and Party work in Sverdlovsk; for many Years, head, Chair of Econ and Org of Machine-Building Production, Ural Polytech Inst; 1951–55 dir of this inst; 1955–58 dep chm, State Comt for Labor and Wages, USSR Council of Min; specialist on econ of socialist ind and org of labor; 1958–66 dir, Inst of Econ and Org of Ind Production, Siberian Branch, USSR Acad of Sci; *Publ: Vnutriproizvodstvennyye rezervy* (Internal Production Reserves) (1954); *Mnogostanochniki* (Multi-Lathe Operators) (1940); *Za nauchnoye obobshcheniye i rasprostraneniye stakhanovskikh metodov truda* (The Scientific Generalization and Dissemination of Stakhanovite Labor Methods) (1951); articles: "There is Scope for Resources and Knowledge" (1959) and "Working and Leisure Time" (1963), etc; *Awards:* Order of the Red Banner of Labor; Order of the Red Star; medals; *Died:* July 1967.

PRUGAVIN, Aleksandr Stepanovich (1850–1920) Specialist on Old Believers and other Russian religious sects; Populist revol; *Born:* 1850; *Educ:* from 1869 studied at Petrov Agric Acad, Moscow; *Career:* 1871 expelled from acad for revol activities and exiled to Arkhangel'sk, then Voronezh Province; from 1877 studied Old Believers sect; after 1917 Oct Revol left Petrograd and settled in Siberia; Mar 1920 arrested by Sov authorities and imprisoned in Krasnoyarsk Jail; *Publ: Religioznyye otshchepentsy* (Religious Schismatics) (1906); *Staroobryadnichestvo vo vtoroy polovine XIX veka* (The Old Believers in the Late 19th Century) (1904); *Staroobryadnicheskiye arkhiyerei v Suzdal'skoy kreposti* (Old Believer Archpriests in the Suzdal' Fortress) (1908); *V kazematakh* (In the Casemates) (1909); *Monastyrskiye tyur'my v bor'be s sektanstvom* (Monastic Prisons in the Struggle Against Sectarianism) (1906); *Nepriyemlyushchiye mira* (Those Who Reject the World) (1918); *Died:* 1920 in Krasnoyarsk Prison.

PRYAMIKOV, Nikolay Nikolayevich (1888–1918) Revolutionary; CP member from 1906; *Born:* 14 Oct 1888; *Career:* from age 12 worked as laborer; took part in 1905–07 strikes; 1907 twice arrested; 1908 exiled for two years to Yaroslavl' Province for distributing Bolshevik pamphlets; 1910–17 worked at Barbed Wire Plant in Syromyatniki and was Party organizer for Moscow RSDRP Comt; July 1917 assigned to revol work in Moscow's Rogozhsko-Simonov Rayon; Aug 1917 elected chm, Exec Comt, Rogozhsko-Simonov Rayon Sov and member, Rayon RSDRP(B) Comt; from 8 Nov 1917 chm, Rogozhskiy Rayon Mil Revol Comt; fought in 1917 Oct Revol; from Feb 1918 chm, Rogozhskiy Rayon Cheka Commission; *Died:* 3 Mar 1918 killed while attempting to crush a revolt; a Moscow square and park are named after him.

PRYANISHNIKOV, Dmitriy Nikolayevich (1865–1948) Agrochemist and plant physiologist; member, USSR Acad of Sci from 1929; member, All-Union Lenin Acad of Agric Sci from 1935; Hero of Socialist Labor from 1945; *Born:* 6 Nov 1865 in Kyakhta, now Buryat-Mongolian ASSR; *Educ:* 1887 grad Moscow Univ, studying under Timiryazev; 1889 grad Petrov Agric Acad; *Career:* 1895–1948 prof, Petrov Agric Acad and Moscow's Timiryazev Agric Acad; 1891–1931 also lectured at Moscow Univ and worked for various inst, uncluding Inst of Fertilizers, All-Union of Fertilizers, Agrotechnics and Agropedology, Centr Sugar Ind Research Ind Research Inst, etc; also worked for Gosplan and Comt for Introducing Chemicals into the USSR Nat Econ; studied plant nutrition and use of artificial fertilizers in agric; valuable research on nitrate nutrition and nitrogen metabolism in plants; plotted conversion of nitrogenous substances in plants and attached great importance to ammonia as a starting substance and derivative in this process; established role of arparagin in plants and refuted existing view that it was a primary product of protein break-down; proved that asparagin is synthesized from ammonia which forms in the plant in the final stage of protein decomposition or enters the plant from outside; drew a parallel between the role of asparagin in plants and urine in animals and considered that asparagin served to neutralize the injurious effects of too high a concentration of ammonia in the plant and animal organism; this enabled him to outline the general process of nitrogen metabolism in flora and fauna and was of great importance in revealing the gen laws of evolution; the research was also of practical use in indicating agric used for ammonia salts and facilitating their large-scale production; assessed value of Russian phosphorites as a direct source of phosphorus for plants and as raw material for the ind production of superphosphates; studied physiological characteristics of Russian potassium salts and various types of nitrogen and phosphorus fertilizers; studied lime-dressing of acid soils and gypsum treatment of solonetz soils; did research on methods of enriching land by planting legume crops (green fertilizer), and the use of peat, dung and other organic fertilizers; studied methods of feeding plants and dressing various types of fertilizer; devised new methods of studying plant nutrition; so-called isolated nutrition method, sterile crop method, fluid solution method; also proposed methods for analysing soils and plants; wrote numerous textbooks which ran through many editions: *Castnoye zemledeliye* (Private Farming) (1st ed, 1898; 8th ed, 1931); *Agrokhimiya* (Agrochemistry) (1st ed, 1934; 3rd ed, 1940); *Publ: Belkovyye veshchestva i ikh prevrashcheniya v rastenii v svyazi s dykhaniyem i assimilyatsiyey* (Protein Substances and Their Conversion in Plants in Connection with Respiration and Assimilation) (1899); *Khimiya rasteniy* (Plant Chemistry) (2 vol, 1907–14); *Ucheniye ob udobrenii* (Fertilizer Theory) (5th ed, 1922); *Sobraniye statey i* *nauchnykh rabot* (Collected Articles and Scientific Works) (2vol, 1927); *Azot v zhizni rasteniy i v zemledelii SSSR* (Nitrogen in Plant Life and Agriculture in the USSR) (1945); *Izbrannyye proizvedeniya* (Selected Works) (3 vol, 1951–52); *Izbrannyye proizvedeniya* (Selected Works) (3 vol, 1952–53); *Moi vospominaniya* (My Memoirs) (1957); *Awards:* two Orders of Lenin; four other orders; Lenin Prize (1926); Stalin Prize (1941); Timiryazev Prize (1946); *Died:* 30 Apr 1948.

PSHENITSYN, Nikolay Konstantinovich (1891–1961) Chemist; prof from 1915; corresp member, USSR Acad of Sci from 1953; *Born:* 15 June 1891; *Educ:* 1915 grad Petrograd Univ; *Career:* 1915–35 prof, Petrograd (Leningrad) Univ; from 1918 worked at various inst, USSR Acad of Sci; did research on complex ammonium and amine chloroplatinites of silver and zinc, sulphur compounds, iridium and the hydrolysis of platinum compounds; developed ind method of obtaining pure iridium; also devised a method of analyzing platinum-bearing sludge and the semiproducts of the refinement of precious metals; wrote works on the chemistry of complex compounds of platinum and other precious metals, their analysis and production control; *Publ: O nekotorykh molekulyarnykh peregruppirovkakh, nablyudayemykh v ryadu kompleksnykh soyedineniy platiny* (Certain Molecular Regroupings Observed in a Number of Complex Platinum Compounds) (1921); coauthor, *Opredeleniye platinovykh metallov metodom potentsiometrii* (The Potentiometric Determination of Platinum Metals) (1950); *Kompleksnyye soyedineniya iridiya (IV) s fosfornoy kisloty* (Complex Compounds of Iririum [IV] With Phosphoric Acid) (1960), etc; *Awards:* Stalin Prize (1946); *Died:* 15 Jan 1961.

PTITSYN, Boris Vladimirovich (1903–1965) Inorganic chemist; corresp member, USSR Acad of Sci; *Born:* 1903; *Career:* from 1960 assoc, Siberian Branch, USSR Acad of Sci; *Publ:* coauthor, *Opredeleniye iodidov v prisutstvii bromidov i khloridov s pomoshch'yu radioaktivnogo ioda* (The Use of Radioactive Iodine to Determine Iodides in the Presence of Bromides and Chlorides) (1960); coauthor, *Ob okislitel'nom potentsiale permanganata* (The Oxidizing Potential of Permanganate) (1960), etc; *Died:* 2 Jan 1965.

PTUKHA, Mikhail Vasil'yevich (1884–1961) Economist and statistician; prof from 1916; member, Ukr Acad of Sci from 1920; corresp member, USSR Acad of Sci from 1943; Hon Sci Worker of Ukr SSR from 1944; *Born:* 7 Nov 1884 in Ostyor, now Chernigov Oblast; *Educ:* 1910 grad Law Fac, Petersburg Univ; *Career:* 1913–16 assoc prof, 1916–18 prof of polit econ and statistics, Perm' Branch, Petrograd Univ;1919–37 dir, Inst of Demography, Ukr Acad of Sci; 1940–50 acad secr, Soc Sci Dept, Ukr Acad of Sci; prof at various Kiev higher educ establishments; specialized in statistical theory and theoretical and applied demography; compiled statistical material for the USSR and Ukr Centr Statistical Bd; helped to organized 1959 All-Union Census; *Publ:Statisticheskaya nauka na Zapade* (The Science of Statistics in the West) (1925); *Smertnost' v Rossii i na Ukraine* (Mortality Rates in Russia and the Ukraine) (1928); *Ocherki po istorii statistiki XVII–XVIII vekov* (Studies in the History of 17th- and 18th-Century Statistics) (1945); "D.P. Zhuravskiy" (1951); *Ocherki po istorii statistiki v SSSR* (Studies in the History of Statistics in the USSR) (2 vol, 1955–59); *Ocherki po statistike naseleniya* (Studies in Population Statistics) (1960), etc; *Awards:* Order of the Red Banner of Labor; other orders; medals; *Died:* 3 Oct 1961.

PTUKHA, Vladimir Vasil'yevich (1894–1942) Party official; CP member from 1917; *Born:* 1894 in Ostyor, now Chernigov Oblast; *Educ:* grad Chernigov secondary school; 1912–17 studied at Petersburg Mining Inst; *Career:* fought in 1917 Oct Revol in Ukr; Sept 1917–Mar 1918 Presidium member, Ostyor Sov of Workers and Soldiers' Dep; during 1917 Oct Revol member, Ostyor Revol Comt; comr, Ostyor partisan unit; comr, 1st Cavalry Regt, 1st Sov Ukr Div; from late 1919 secr, Ostyor Uyezd Comt, CP(B) Ukr; head, Org Dept, Chernigov Province, Comt, CP(B) Ukr; 1923–24 exec posts with CC, CP(B) Ukr; 1924–27 worked for CC, CPSU(B); 1927–34 first secr, Stalingrad Province, Lower Volga, then Stalingrad Kray CPSU(B) Comts; 1935–37 second secr, Far Eastern Kray CPSU(B) Comt; deleg at 12th–17th CPSU(B) Congresses; at 16th and 17th Party Congresses elected cand member, CC, CPSU(B); 1937 arrested by State Security organs; *Died:* 1942 in imprisonment.

PTUKHIN, Yevgeniy Savvich (1900–1941) Air Force lt-gen from 1940; CP member from 1918; *Born:* 1900; *Educ:* 1927 grad Borisoglebsk Flying School; *Career:* 1917–18 in Red Guard; from 1918 in Red Army; fought in Civil War; from 1923 with Sov Air Force; from 1925 fighter-pilot, then various commands; commanded air detachment, Bobuysk Air Brigade; 1937–38 commanded Sov pilots in Republ Spain; shot down several enemy aircraft; carried out history's first fighter raid on an enemy airdrome, destroying some 60 bombers; 1938–40 air force commander, Leningrad Mil Distr; 1939–40 also directed all Sov Air Force operations on Finnish Front; 1940–41 air force commander, Kiev Special Mil Distr; 1941 air force commander, Southwestern Front; June 1941 arrested on orders from Supreme Command Headquarters; *Awards:* Hero of the Sov Union (1940); two Orders of Lenin; Order of the Red Banner; Order of the Red Star; *Died:* June 1941 executed; posthumously rehabilitated.

PUDOVKIN, Vsevolod Illarionovich (1893–1953) Film actor and dir; Pop Artiste of USSR from 1948; CP member from 1939; *Born:* 28 Feb 1893 in Penza; *Educ:* studied at Physics and Mathematics Fac, Moscow Univ and at State School of Cinematography; *Career:* 1914 in Russian Army at the front; wounded and taken prisoner; 1918 returned from captivity; 1920 began film work as actor, then script-writer and from 1925 as film dir; *Roles:* Fedya Protasov in Lev Tolstoy's *Zhivoy trup* (The Living Corpse); the Police Officer in Gorky's *Mat'* (Mother); the God's Fool in *Ioann Groznyy* (Ivan the Terrible), etc; *Productions:* directed Films: *Shakhmatnaya goryachka* (Chess Fever) (1925); Gorky's "Mother" (1926); *Konets Sankt-Petersburga* (The End of Saint Petersburg) (1927); *Potomok Chingis-khana* (Descendant of Genghis Khan) (1928); "Minin i Pozharskiy" (1939); "Suvorov" (1941); "Admiral Nakhimov" (1947); "Zhukovskiy" (1950); *Vozvrashcheniye Vasiliya Bortnikova* (The Return of Vasiliy Bortnikov) (1953), etc; forced to make a new version of "Admiral Nakhimov" after his first version was criticized for "distorting the principles of socialist realism"; *Publ: Kinorezhissyor i kinomaterial* (The Film Director and Film Material) (1926); *Aktyor v fil'me* (The Film Actor) (1934); *Awards:* two Orders of Lenin; three Stalin Prizes (1941, 1947 and 1951); *Died:* 30 June 1953.

PUGACHYOV, Semyon Andreyevich (1889–1943) Mil commander; capt, Russian Army; corps commander, Sov Army from 1935; officer, Red Army Gen Staff; CP member from 1934; *Born:* 25 Feb 1889 in Ryazan', son of a teacher; *Educ:* 1908 grad Aleksey Mil College; 1914 grad Gen Staff Acad; *Career:* served with 6th Siberian Corps in WW 1; suffered from gas poisoning and won various mil orders; served with Operations Bd, Northern Front; from Apr 1918 in Red Army; served on Staff, Ural Mil Distr; from July 1919 head, Operations Dept, Staff of 2nd Army on Eastern Front; from Sept 1919 head, Operations Bd, Staff of Special Group on Southern Front; from Oct 1919 head, Operations Bd, Staff of Southwestern, and from Jan 1920 of Caucasian Fronts; Mar 1920–June 1921 chief of staff, Caucasian Front; from June 1921 chief of staff, Separate Caucasian Army; from June 1922 also Transcaucasian SFSR Asst Pop Comr of Mil and Naval Affairs; from July 1923 commander, Turkestani Front; Apr 1924–Feb 1925 commander, Separate Caucasian Red Banner Army; 1925–28 dep chief of staff, Red Army; 1927 and 1928 attended Geneva Disarmament Conference as mil consultant; 1928–31 chief of staff, Ukr Mil Distr; 1931–32 chief of staff, Centr Asian Mil Distr; Sept 1932–Jan 1939 commandant, Red Army Mil Transport Acad; Jan 1939 arrested by NKVD; *Awards:* Order of the Red Banner; other orders; *Died:* 23 Mar 1943 in imprisonment; posthumously rehabilitated.

PUKHOV, Mikhail Pavlovich (1895–1958) Mil commander; col-gen; CP member from 1941; *Born:* 25 Jan 1895 in vil Grishino, Kaluga Province, son of a teacher; *Educ:* 1952 grad Higher Acad Courses, Gen Staff Acad; *Career:* fought in WW 1 and suffered from gas poisoning; Feb 1918 volunteered for Red Army; fought in Civil War; then staff and teaching posts; 1941 commanded infantry div and took part in defense of Zolotonosha, Kremenchug, Poltava and Khar'kov; Jan 1942–45 commanded 13th Army which fought on the Bryansk, Centr and 1st Ukr Fronts in the battle of Kursk, the forcing of the Dnieper, the liberation of Chernigov, Novograd-Volynskiy and Rovno, took part in the L'vov-Sandomir, Vistula-Oder and Berlin operations and in the final campaign in Czechoslovakia; after WW 2 commanded Odessa, North Caucasian, West Siberian and Siberian Mil Distr; dep, USSR Supr Sov of 1946, 1950 and 1954 convocations; dep, Ukr Supr Sov of 1951 convocation; 1951–53 member, CC, CP Ukr; *Awards:* Hero of the Sov Union; four Orders of Lenin; three Orders of the Red Banner; three Orders of Suvorov, 1st Class; two Orders of Kutuzov, 1st Class; Order of Bogdan Khmel'nitskiy, 1st Class; medals; *Died:* 28

Mar 1958; buried in Moscow's Novodevich'ye Cemetery.

PULATOV–TOLSTOY (real name: P. TOLIS) (1929–1961) Tadzh writer; Bd member, Tadzh Writers' Union; *Born:* 1929 in Leninabad; *Educ:* studied at Tadzh Univ; *Career:* worked as typesetter and linotype-operator; worked for Leninabad Oblast newspaper "Khakikati"; 1946 first work published; exec secr, Tadzh Writers' Union organ "Sharki Surkh"; *Publ:* collected verse "Fires" (1948); collections: "Stories"; "Our Village's Children"; "The Ant-Heap"; novelettes: "Youth" (1950); "Summer" (1957); *Awards:* Badge of Hon (1957); *Died:* Sept 1961.

PURENAS, Antanas Konstantinovich (1881–1962) Organic Chemist; member, Lith Acad of Sci from 1941; prof from 1945; *Born:* 1881; *Educ:* 1910 grad Petersburg Univ; *Career:* 1922–45 lecturer, 1945–51 prof, Kaunas Univ; from 1951 prof, Kaunas Polytech Inst; spezialized in synthesis of bioactive substances and study of local raw materials; *Publ:* "N-aril-β-amino rugšč iu sintez 'e ir ju virtimas i atitinkamus chinolonus" (1955); "N-naftil-β-alanino sinteze ir jo virtimas 4-keto 1,2,3,4-tetra hidro-6, 7-benzochinolinu" (1955); "Aromatiniu chloretilaminu eilés citostatinés medžiagos" (1957); "N-(α-ir-β-antra-chinonil) -β-amino propioniniu rugščiu ir ju dariniu sintezé" (1957(; "β-(β-antrachinonil) -β-amino propionines rugšties ir kai kuriu jos dariniu sintezé ir kitimai" (1957); *Sochetaniye β-aminopiridina s akrilonitrilom i metilakrilatom* (The Combination of β-aminopiridine with Acrylonitryl and Methylacrylate) (1960); *Awards:* Hon Scroll of Lith Supr Sov (1961); *Died:* 1962.

PURISHKEVICH, Vladimir Mitrofanovich (1870–1920) Politician; *Born:* 1870; *Career:* Bessarabian landowner; from 1901 official, Russian Min of Internal Affairs; 1904–06 official for special assignments, Russian Min of Internal Affairs; co-founder, Union of the Russian People; after schism in this org headed Archangel Michael Union; dep, State Duma of 2nd–4th convocations; during WW 1 advocated "strong rule and stern measures" to bring the war to "a successful conclusion"; accomplice in assassination of Rasputin; after 1917 Feb Revol opposed Provisional Govt and advocated restoration of monarchy; Oct 1917 headed counterrevol conspiracy in Petrograd, which was detected in early Nov; 16 Jan 1918 sentenced to four years' forced labor in public trial by Petrograd Revol Tribunal; amnestied under 1 May 1918 Petrograd Sov decree, amnestying polit prisoners; went to Southern Russia and collaborated with White forces; published newspaper "Blagovest" in Rostov-on-Don; *Publ: Dnevnik nepremennogo chlena ministerskoy peredney* (Diary of a Permanent Member of the Ministry Chancelry) (1913); *Ubiystvo Rasputina. Iz dnevnika* (The Assassination of Rasputin. From My Diary) (1923); *Died:* 1920 in Novorossiysk.

PURKAYEV, Maksim Alekseyevich (1894–1953) Mil commander; officer, Russian Army; army gen, Sov Army; CP member from 1918; *Born:* 26 Aug 1894 in vil Nalitovo, now Mordovian ASSR, son of a peasant; *Educ:* 1916 grad Saratov Ensigns School; 1923 grad "Vystrel" Higher Infantry Courses; 1936 grad Frunze Mil Acad; *Career:* from 1915 in Russian Army; 1916–17 nco in reserve regt, then officer in artillery brigade; from July 1918 in Red Army; 1918–21 commanded company, then regt on Eastern and Western Fronts; 1923–33 commander and comr of an infantry regt; asst chief of staff, then chief of staff of a div; head, org and draft dept, mil distr staff; dep chief of staff of a mil distr; 1936–38 commanded infantry div; 1938–39 chief of staff, Bel Mil Distr; 1939 mil attache in Germany; 1939–40 chief of staff, Western Special Mil Distr; 1940–41 chief of staff, Kiev Special Mil Distr; 1941 chief of staff, Southwestern Front; 1941 fought in battle of Moscow; 1941–42 commander, 3rd Shock Army, Western and Northwestern Fronts; 1942–43 commander, Kalinin Front; 1943 his stroops liberated Velikiye Luki; 1943–45 commander, Far Eastern Front; 1945 commander, 2nd Far Eastern Front; Aug 1945 his troops entered Harbin and linked up with the Pacific Fleet to capture Southern Sakhalin and the Kurile Islands; 1945–47 commander, Far Eastern Mil Distr; 1947–52 chief of staff, Far Eastern Mil Distr; 1952 head, Higher Mil Training Establishments Bd; USSR Min of Defense; dep, USSR Supr Sov of 1946 convocation; *Awards:* two Orders of Lenin; four Orders of the Red Banner; Order of Suvorov; Order of Kutuzov; other orders; medals; *Died:* 1 Jan 1953; his native vil Nalitovo now bears his name.

PUSHCHA, Yazep (real name: PLASHCHINSKIY, Iosif Pavlovich) (1902–1964) Bel poet; member, Bel Writers' union from 1958; *Born:* 20 may 1902 in vil Korolishchavichi, now Minsk Oblast, son of a peasant; *Educ:* 1917 grad Minsk Higher Elementary School; early 1920's grad Bel History Courses, Bel Pop Comrt of Educ; 1929 grad Philology Dept, Leningrad Univ; *Career:* in 1920's worked for Mozyr' and Minsk Rayon Educ Dept; taught Bel language and lit in courses and schools; 1923 helped found "Maladnyak" proletarian writers assoc; 1926 helped found "Uzvyshsha" assoc; 1922 first work published; wrote many works on Bel nat and polit themes, demonstrating polit acuity, e.g., verse cycle "Letters to a Dog" (1927) and poem "The Consul's Shadow" (1928) in which the poet urged the Bel people to fight for its polit rights and nat culture; 1930 arrested by NKVD and deported for five years to Shadrinsk, now Kurgan Oblast; then taught in Vladimir Oblast; 1941–45 in Sov Army; from 1945 directed high school in vil Chaadayevo, Murom Rayon, Vladimir Oblast; 1956 rehabilitated; from 1956 lived in Minsk; *Publ:* collected verse and poems "The Morning Roars" (1925); "Vita" (1926); "Spring Days" (1927); "Songs Upon Ruins" (1929); "The Blood-Stained Poster" (1930); "Verse and Poems" (1960); "The Birth of a Legend" (1963); many other works printed in journals "Uzvyshsha" and "Polymya" in late 1920's; *Died:* 14 Sept 1964 in Minsk.

PUSHKIN, Georgiy Maksimovich (1909–1963) Dipl; USSR Dep Min of For Affairs from 1959; cand member, CC, CPSU from 1961; *Born:* 1909; *Educ:* 1931 grad Moscow Planning Inst; 1937 grad Inst of Dipl and Consulate Officials, Moscow; *Career:* 1931 worked for Siberian planning organs; then group head, RSFSR Econ Accounting Bd; 1937–40 with 2nd Western and Centr European Dept, USSR Pop Comrt of For Affairs; 1940–41 assoc, USSR embassies in Slovakia, Germany then Sweden; 1942–44 USSR Consul-gen in Dihua, China's Sinkiang Province; 1945 polit counsellor, Allied Control Commission in Hungary; 1945–49 USSR envoy, then amb in Hungary; 1949–52 head, USSR dipl mission in East Germany; 1952–54 USSR Dep Min of For Affairs; 1954–58 USSR amb in GDR; 1956–61 member, CPSU Centr Auditing Commission; *Awards:* Order of Lenin; Order of the Red Banner of Labor; Order of the Fatherland War, 1st Class; medals; *Died:* Apr 1963.

PUTNA, Vitovt Kazimirovich (1893–1937) Mil commander; Lith; officer, Russian Army; corps commander Sov Army from 1935; Civil War veteran; CP member from 1917; *Born:* 24 Apr 1893 in vil Matskantsy, Vilnius Province, son of a peasant; *Educ:* grad Business and Craft College and art school in Riga; 1917 grad ensigns school; 1923 grad Advanced Mil Acad Courses; *Career:* 1913 arrested for revol activities; 1915 drafted into Russian Army; sustained gas poisoning at the front; promoted officer and given command of battalion; conducted Bolshevik propaganda among troops of 12th Army; Apr 1918 volunteered for Red Army and helped muster Red Army units for Vitebsk Mil Dept; from May 1918 mil comr, Vitebsk Mil Comrt; Sept 1918 – May 1919 comr, 1st Smolensk (later 26th) Infantry Div on Eastern Front; commander, 228th Karelian Regt, 2nd Brigade, 26th Infantry Div; from Dec 1919 commander, 27th Omsk Infantry Div, which played a major role in routing Admiral Kolchak's forces; 1920 fought on Sov-Polish Front; 1921 helped crush Kronstadt Mutiny; 1923, while studying on Higher Mil Acad Courses, sided with Trotskyist opposition; 1923–24 commandant and comr, 2nd Moscow Infantry School; 1924–25 head and comr, Mil Training Bd, Red Army Inspectorate; asst inspector, then inspector of Red Army; 1925 headed Kalgan group of Sov mil advisers in China; 1925–27 head, Red Army Mil Training Establishments Bd; 1927 commander, 6th, then 2nd Infantry Corps; 1927 Sov mil attache in Japan; 1928 Sov mil attache in Finland; 1929–31 Sov mil attache in Germany; 1931–34 commander and comr, 14th Infantry Corps with Maritime Forces Group in Far East; 1934–36 Sov mil attache in Britain; 1936 arrested by NKVD; 11 June 1937 sentenced to death together with Marshal Tukhachevskiy and others by Special Tribunal of USSR Supr Court; *Publ: Vostochnyy front* (The Eastern Front); *K Visle i obratno* (To the Vistula and Back); *Kronshtadt – 16–18 marta 1921 goda* (Kronstadt – 16–18 March 1921); *Died:* 12 June 1937 executed; posthumously rehabilitated.

PUZIKOV, Sergey Timofeyevich (1916–1962) Party and govt official; CP member from 1939; *Born:* 1916; *Educ:* 1935 grad teachers' training college; 1949 grad Higher Party School, CC, CPSU(B); *Career:* from 1935 teacher; then coordinating ed, rayon newspaper; head, polit dept, machine and tractor station; from 1944 Party and govt work; 1954–60 second secr, Rostov Oblast CPSU Comt; 1960 chm, Rostov Oblast Exec Comt; from 1960 first secr, Lipetsk Oblast CPSU Comt; from 1961 cand member,

CC, CPSU; dep, USSR Supr Sov of 1962 convocation; dep, RSFSR Supr Sov of 1955 and 1959 convocations; *Died:* 1962.

PYATAKOV, Georgiy (Yuriy) Leonidovich (1890–1937) Party and govt official; CP member from 1910; *Born:* 1890, son of an eng; *Educ:* studied at Petersburg Univ; *Career:* 1904–05 took part in student revolt circles, originally siding with anarchists; 1910 switched to Marxists and worked with student Soc-Democratic org; late 1910 arrested, expelled from univ and exiled; moved to Kiev and became member, steering group to re-establish the Kiev RSDRP org, then member, Kiev RSDRP Comt; June 1912 arrested; 1913 sentenced to exile; Oct 1914 fled to Japan; attended Bern RSDRP(B) Conference; contributed to journal "Kommunist"; 1915–17 opposed Lenin on nations' right to self-determination; after 1917 Feb Revol chm, Kiev RSDRP(B) Comt; during 1917 Oct Revol chm, Revol Comt; after Revol asst chief comr, then chief comr of Gosbank (State Bank); during controversy over Brest Peace Treaty sided with Leftist Communists; moved to Ukr and engaged in underground Party and insurgent work; Dec 1918 chm, Ukr Provisional Workers and Peasants' Govt; 1919 member, Revol Mil Council of 13th Army; 1920 comr, Mil Acad; 1912 in the Urals with 1st Labor Army; during 1920–21 tradeunion controversy sided with Trotskiy; one of the leaders of the "Mil Opposition"; from May 1920 member, Revol Mil Council, 16th Army on the Polish Front, then 6th Army on the Wrangel Front; 1921 chm, Donbass Centr Coal Ind Bd; from 1923 dep chm, USSR Supr Sovnarkhoz; 1927 Sov trade rep in France; from 1928 dep chm, Bd, State Bank and Collegium member, USSR Pop Comrt of Finance; chm, Main Concessions Comt; from 1929 chm, Bd, State Bank; from 1930 member, Labor and Defense Council; 1931 chm, All-Union Chemical Ind Assoc; 1933–34 USSR Dep Pop Comr of Heavy Ind; at the 10th and 11th Party Congresses elected cand member, at the 12th–14th Congresses elected member, CC, CPSU(B); 1927 at 15th Party Congress expelled from CPSU(B) for Trotskyist sympathies; recanted hir error and was readmitted to the Party on 14 Sept 1929; 1936 again expelled from Party and later sentenced for alleged anti-Party and anti-Sov activities; *Died:* Jan 1937 executed by order of Mil Collegium, USSR Supr Court.

PYATNITSKIY (real name: TARSHIS), Iosif (Osip) Aronovich (Party pseudonyms: PYATNITSA; FREYTAG) (1882–1939) Party official; CP member from 1898; *Born:* 17 Jan 1882 in Vilkomir, Kaunas Province, son of a worker; *Career:* until 1902 tailor in Kaunas and Vilnius; secr, Vilnius Tailors' Union; from 1901 helped smuggle and distribute newspaper "Iskra"; 1902 arrested, escaped from Kiev prison together with other Iskra agents and emigrated to Germany, where he continued to smuggle copies of "Iskra" into Russia; 1905 member, Odessa RSDRP(B) Comt; 1906–08 head of tech problems, Moscow RSDRP(B) Comt; from 1908 in Geneva, directing transport of Bolshevik lit to Russia; 1912 helped organize Prague 6th RSDRP Conference; 1913–14 electr fitter in Vol'sk and Samara; helped found Samara RSDRP(B) Comt; 1914 exiled to Yeniseysk Province; from Apr 1917 member, Moscow RSDRP(B) Comt; during 1917 Oct Revol member, Party Center directing work of Mil Revol Comt; 1917 trade-union work; chm, Railroad Workers' Union; 1918–22 member, Exec Comt, Moscow Sov and member, All-Russian Centr Exec Comt; 1920 secr, Moscow RCP(B) Comt; from 1921 worked for Exec Comt, Comintern; from 1923 secr, Comintern Exec Comt; after 5th Congress member, Comintern Exec Comt; 1935–37 exec work for CC, CPSU(B); deleg at 6th, 7th and 12th–17th Party Congresses; 1924 at 13th and 1925 at 14th Party Congress elected member, CPSU(B) Centr Control Commission; at 9th Congress elected cand member, and at 15th–17th Congresses member, CC, CPSU(B); wrote numerous works on int revol movement; 1937 arrested by NKVD; *Publ:* memoirs *Zapiski bol'shevika* (Notes of a Bolshevik) (1925); *Died:* 30 Oct 1939 in imprisonment; posthumously rehabilitated.

PYATNITSKIY, Mitrofan Yefimovich (1864–1927) Choirmaster; collector of Russian folk songs; dir, Pyatnitskiy Choir; Hon Artiste of RSFSR from 1925; *Born:* 21 June 1864 in vil Aleksandrovka, Voronezh Province; *Educ:* grad theological college; took singing lessons from K. Everardi; *Career:* made a study of peasant life and recorded folk songs; from 1901 member, Musical Ethnography Commission, Moscow Soc of Amateur Natural Scientists, Anthropologists and Ethnographers; 1903 performed Russian songs at "ethnographic concerts" arranged by above soc; 1910 founded from Voronezh peasants the Folk Song Ensemble which subsequently became the Russian Folk Choir (from 1940 the Russian State Pyatnitskiy Folk Choir); *Works: 12 russkikh narodnykh pesen* (Twelve Russian Folk Songs) (1904); *Starinnyye pesni Voronezhskoy gubernii v narodnoy garmonizatsii* (Ancient Songs of the Voronezh Province in Folk Harmonization) (1914); his phonograph recordings of Russian folk songs were partially issued in 1950 in I.K. Zdanovich's collection *Russkiye narodnyye pesni* (Russian Folk Songs); *Died:* 21 Jan 1927 in Moscow.

PYOTR, (secular name: POLYANSKIY, Pyotr Fyodorovich) (1863–1936) Metropolitan of Krutitskiy; Vicar of Patriarchal Throne; Master of Divinity; *Born:* 1863; *Educ:* 1892 grad Moscow Theological Acad as Cand of Divinity; *Career:* after grad, asst inspector, Moscow Theological Acad; then until 1917 Oct Revol successively: supervisor, Zhirovitsy Theological College; head, Training Comt, Most Holy Synod; member, Training Comt and inspector of theological training establishments in European Russia, Siberia and caucasus; 1917–18 attended All-Russian Landed Synod; close aide of Patriarch Tikhon; 1920 took monastic orders and elevated to bishop, patriarchal vicar and then metropolitan; 1924 Patriarch Tikhon named him 3rd cand Vicar of Patriarchal Throne; 1925, after death of Patriarch Tikhon and arrest of first two candidates, became Vicar of Patriarchal Throne; issued message to Russian Orthodox Church categorically rejecting any compromise with either "renovationism" or with Communist regime; prior to his arrest rejected terms of a declaration proposed by government's Church affairs rep Tuchkov; these terms included the removal of bishops opposed to the regime, condemnation of the Foreign Orthodox Church and collaboration with the regime; from 10 Dec 1925 confined under house arrest, then transferred to Lubyanka Prison, Moscow; 1926 places in solitary confinement in Suzdal' Fortress; fall 1926 brought back to Lubyanka and again rejected proposal that he resign Patriarchal Vicarship; Dec 1926 exiled to Tobol'sk; 1927 managed to pass on his famous "Perm' Address to the Public", in which he attempted to organize Church life; 1928 sent to settlement at Zimov'ye, located in the tundra on the Gulf of Ob'; Nov 1928 sent back to Tobol'sk Prison, where Tuchkov offered him his freedom in exchange for resigning the Vicarship; again refused and was returned to Zimov'ye settlement, with his sentence increased by three years; 1930, seriously ill, wrote letter to Metropolitan Sergiy, urging: "If you are powerless to defend the Church, step aside and make way for somebody stronger"; offered his freedom if he would sanction Metropolitan Sergiy's instructions, but again refused; *Died:* Dec 1936 in imprisonment.

PYOTR (secular name: STROD), (1892–1960) Bishop, Roman Catholic Church; Deputy Metropolitan of Riga; Apostolic Administrator of Liepaja Eparchy (Lat SSR); Dr of Philosophy; prof; *Born:* 1892 in vil Bol'shiye Strody, Lat; *Educ:* 1916 grad Petrograd Catholic Seminary; *Career:* 1916–20 priest in various parishes; 1920–23 priest in Rezhitsa, teacher of Divinity and ed, journal "Tsidunis"; 1923–26 studied at Philosophy Fac, Innsbruck and Vienna Univ; from 1938 prof, Catholic Theological Fac, Lat Univ: 1937 appointed prelate; 1947 elevated to bishop and appointed to Libava Eparchy; 1952 attended Zagorsk peace conference of all churches and religious groups in the USSR; *Publ:* wrote over 20 theological works, including: *Pochemu nado verit'* (Why We Must Believe); *Chto takoye mir* (What the World ist); *Svyatoy Avgustin i svyatoy Foma* (Saint Avgustine and Saint Thomas), etc; *Died:* Aug 1960.

PYRERKA (PYRYA), Anton Petrovich (Nenets name: Syarati) (1905–1941) Nenets scholar, writer and translator; CP member from 1930; *Born:* 1905; *Educ:* 1932 grad Communist Univ of Workers of the East; postgrad studies at Inst od Peoples of the North; *Career:* assoc, Inst of Language and Thinking, USSR Acad of Sci; specialized in language and folklore of Nenets people; pioneer of Nenets lit; from 1932 published some dozen textbooks and teaching aids for Nents schools; first to translate Pushkin into Nenets; compiled sveral collections of Nents folklore and first Russian-Nenets dictionary; *Publ:* autobiographical novelette "The Younger Son of Vedo"; *Russko-Nentskiy slovar'* (A Russian-Nenets Dictionary) (1948); *Died:* 1941 killed in action near Leningrad.

R

RABINOVICH, Adolf Iosifovich (1893–1942) Physical chemist;

corresp member, USSR Acad of Sci from 1933; *Born:* 5 Apr 1893; *Educ:* 1915 grad Novorossiysk Univ, Odessa; *Career:* 1915–17 laboratory asst at a plant in Odessa; 1917–23 worked at higher educ establishments in Odessa; from 1923 at L.Ya. Karpov Chemical Inst (later Physicochemical Inst); from 1930 also prof, Moscow Univ; specialized in stability of colloidal systems and photochemistry; studied coagulation of colloids by electrolytes and established a connection between the adsorption of ions and the stability of colloidal systems; devised the adsorption theory of photographic development and explained the effects of adsorption on absorption spectra and the sensitizing effect of dyes; *Publ: O teoriyakh fotograficheskogo proyavleniya* (Theories of Photographic Development) (1935); *Issledovaniya po opticheskoy sensibilizatsii soley serebra* (Studies on the Optical Sensitization of Silver Salts) (1938); *Ustoychivost' kolloidnykh sistem* (The Stability of Colloidal Systems) (1941); *Died:* 19 Sept 1942.

RABINOVICH, F.Ya. (1885–1937) Govt official; CP member from 1919; *Born:* 1885; *Career:* 1919–20 mang, Revol Mil Council, Turkestani Front and mang, Turkestani Council of Pop Comr; 1920–22 man, Secretariat, RSFSR Pop Comrt of For Trade; Labor and Defense Council and Pop Comrt of For Trade dep plen in Transcaucasia; 1922–25 member, then dir, Bd, Anglo-Sov Trading Company, London; Sov dep trade rep in Uk; 1926-30 chm, bd, Ural Oblast Consumers Union; Bd member, Centr Union of Consumer Soc; 1930–37 exec posts, USSR Pop Comrt of For Trade, and Pop Comrt of Forestry Ind; arrested by State Security organs; *Died:* 1937 in imprisonment.

RABINOVICH, Isaak Moiseyevich (1894–1961) Stage designer; Hon Art Worker of RSFSR from 1936; *Born:* 27 Mar 1894 in Kiev; *Educ:* 1905–12 studied at Kiev Art School; *Career:* 1911–20 stage designer in Kiev; from 1920 stage designer in Moscow; from 1955 chief designer, Vakhtangov Theater; *Works:* designed sets for: Oscar Wilde's "Salome" (1918); Chekhov's *Svad'ba"* (The Wedding) (1920); Ash's "Dies Irae" (1921); Prokofiev's *Lyubov'k tryom apel'sinam* (Love of Three Oranges) (1927); Katayev's *Rastratchiki* (The Squanderers) (1928); Aristophanes' "Lisistrata" (1923); Puccini's "Turandot" (1931); "Yevgeniy Onegin" (1933); *Groza* (The Storm) (1934); for ballet *Spyashchaya krasavitsa* (Sleeping Beauty) (1936); "Uriel' Akosta" (1940); Kasumov's *Zarya nad Kaspiyem* (Dawn Over the Caspian) (1951); Balzac's "Quinolle's Dreams" (1954); *Idiot* (The Idiot) (1958), after Dostoyevsky, etc; *Awards:* Order of the Red Banner of Labor (1937); *Died:* 4 Oct 1961 in Moscow.

RADCHENKO, Andrey Fyodorovich (1887–1939) Party and trade-union official; CP member from 1912; *Born:* 1887 in Chernigov Province; *Career:* metalworker by trade; 1904–12 Menshevik; frequently arrested for revol activities; 1917–18 chm, Druzhkovka Sov of Workers and Soldiers' Dep, Donbass; 1918–19 polit work in Red Army; from 1920 exec party, then trade-union work in Donbass; 1924–25 secr, Donetsk Province Comt, CP(B) Ukr; 1925–28 chm, All-Ukr Trade-Union Council; then exec govt work in Vladimir and Ivanovo-Voznesensk; dep, chm, Centr Union of Consumer Soc; Dec 1925–Mar 1928 Politburo member, CC, CP(B) Ukr; deleg at 11th and 12th RCP(B) Congresses; deleg at 4th–8th Conferences and 9th–10th Congresses of CP(B) Ukr; at 7th and 8th Conferences and 9th and 10th Congresses of CP(B) Ukr elected member, CC, CP(B) Ukr; arrested by State Security organs; *Died:* 1939 in imprisonment.

RADCHENKO, Ivan Ivanovich (Party names: ARKADIY; KAS'YAN) (1874–1942) Govt and Party official; CP member from 1898; *Born:* 22 Oct 1874 in Konotop, son of a timber merchant; *Career:* Sept 1898 moved to Petersburg and joined League for the Liberation of the Working Class; to establish contact with the workers, took a job as time-keeper at the Izhora Plant; from 1899 professional revolitionary; 1900 met Lenin in Pskov and 1901–02 served as roving agent for "Iskra"; founded underground "Iskra" presses in Kishinev, and Konotop; visited many Russian towns to establish and maintain "Iskra" contacts with Soc-Democratic groups; 1902 member, Petersburg RSDRP Comt; "Iskra" rep in Org Comt for Convening 2nd RSDRP Congress; 4 Nov 1902 arrested in Pskov and imprisoned in Peter and Paul Fortress; 1903 exiled to Siberia; Aug 1905 fled abroad; Oct 1905 returned to Russia; 1906–07 head, Bolshevik Publ Office, Petrograd; 1908–11 Party work in Baku, Khar'kov and Odessa; 1911 in Petersburg; 1912 worked on construction of peat-fired electr power plant in Moscow area; after 1917 Feb Revol chm, Bogorodsk (now Noginsk) Sov; Nov 1917 commissioned by Lenin to organize Russian peat ind; 1918–31 chm, Main Peat Bd, Supr Sovnarkhoz; 1919–20 dep chm, Main Forestry Comt, Supr Sovnarkhoz; 1921–22 RSFSR Dep Pop Comr of For Trade; 1922 chm, Sugar Trust; 1923–31 Presidium member and dep chm, Supr Sovnarkhoz; 1927–30 and 1934–35 dir, Peat Research Inst; 1936–37 admin work; 1937 arrested by NKVD; *Publ:* numerous articles and *Vospominaniya* (Memoirs) (1960); *Died:* 1 May 1942 in imprisonment; posthumously rehabilitated.

RADEK, Karl Berngardovich (real name: SOBEL'ZON; Party name: PARABELLUM) (1885–1939) Politician; publicist; CP member from 1917; *Born:* 1885 in L'vov; *Career:* from age 14 active in workers' movement in Galicia; from 1901 actice member, Galician Soc-Democratic Party; 1904–08 worked for underground Polish and Lith Soc-Democratic Parties; from 1908 left-wing member, German Soc-Democratic Party; contributed to German Soc-Democratic press on party tactics and int affairs; 1914 adopted internationalist stand; attended Zimmerwald and Kienthal Conferences; after 1917 Oct Revol went to Petrograd; 1918 sided with Leftist Communists in controversy over Brest Peace Treaty; then head, Centr European Dept, Pop Comrt of For Affairs; Nov 1918 illegally entered Germany as member, Sov deleg at Congress of Soviets; helped organize 1st Congress of German CP; Feb 1919 arrested; Dec 1919 released from prison and returned to Russia; 1920–24 secr, Comintern; addressed 2nd and 3rd Comintern Congresses; 1920 addressed Congress of Workers of the East, Baku; 1934 addressed USSR Writers Congress; 1922 member, Comintern deleg at Congress of Three Internationals; 1919–23 member, CC, CPSU(B); 1924 sided with Trotskyist opposition; 1927 expelled from Party and exiled to Siberia; summer 1929, in letter to Party CC, recanted his "erroneous views" and broke with Trotskyism; 1930 readmitted to Party; steady contributor to "Pravda", "Izvestia" and a number of journals; 1934 non-voting deleg at 17th Party Congress; 1936 again expelled from Party for "anti-Party and anti-Sov activities"; Jan 1937 sentenced to 10 years' imprisonment at trial of "anti-Sov Trotskyist Center"; *Publ: Pyat'let Kominterna* (Five Years of the Comintern) (2 vol); *Germanskaya revolyutsiya* (The German Revolution) (3 vol); *Literaturnyye portrety i pamflety* (Literary Portraits and Pamphlets), etc; *Died:* 1939 in imprisonment.

RADIN (real name: KAZANKOV), Nikolay Mariusovich (1872–1935) Actor and stage dir; Hon Artiste of RSFSR from 1925; *Born:* 3 Dec 1872; *Educ:* 1900 grad Law Fac, Petersburg Univ; *Career:* 1902–03 toured with Komissarzhevskaya company; 1903–08 with Korsh Theater, Moscow; 1908–11 acted in Odessa; 1911–14 actor, Solovtsev Theater, Kiev; 1914–18 at Moscow's Sukhodol'skaya Theater; 1918–32 at Moscow City Trade-Union Council Theater, Krasnodar Theater and Korsh Theater (as actor, stage dir and for a while artistic dir); 1932–35 at Maly Theater, Moscow; *Works:* roles: Kessler in Sudermann's "Battle of the Butterflies" Nablotskiy in Baryatinskiy's *Kar'yera Nablotskogo* (Nablotskiy's Career); Muson in Brieux's "The Red Robe"; Astrov in Chekhov's *Dyadya Vanya* (Uncle Vanya); Karenin in Tolstoy's *Zhivoy trup* (The Living Corpse); Tartuffe and Don Juan in Moliere's plays of the same name: Higgins in Shaw's "Pigmalion"; Prince Bel'skiy in A.N. Tolstoy's "The Swallow"; Alceste in Moliere's Misanthrope"; Berlureau in Pagnol and Nivoix's "Merchants of Glory"; Cure in Vauteuil's "The Trade of Monsieur Cure"; Merz in Nikulin's *Inzhener Merts* (Engineer Merts); Bersenev in Lavrenyov's *Razlom* (Break-Up); Zakhar Bardin in Gorky's *Vragi* (The Foes), etc; produced: "Merchants of Glory" (1926); "The Trade of Monsieur Cure" (1927); "Engineer Merts" (1928); *Boloto* (The Swamp) (1929); *Tsianistyy kaliy* (Potassium Cyanide) (1930), etc; *Died:* 24 Aug 1935.

RADIN, Yevgeniy Petrovich (1872–1939) Psychiatrist and health service official; specialist in child and adolescent welfare; *Born:* 1872; *Educ:* 1900 grad Med Fac, Berlin Univ; *Career:* 1882, after two years of study at Natural Sci Fac, Petersburg Univ; exiled to Voronezh for involvement in student polit movement; 1893–95 took part in first Soc-Democratic circles in Voronezh Province and did agitation and propaganda work among students and intellectuals; 1896 moved to Berlin to complete studies; 1902 intern, Kalmovskiy Psychiatric Hospital, Nizhniy Novgorod; 1903–14 intern, Panteleymon Psychiatric Hospital, Petersburg and school health-officer, Lesnoye Business College; 1916–17 physician, Red Cross Psychiatric Hospital; after 1917 Oct Revol assoc, School Health Dept, Pop Comrt of Educ; 1918–28 head, Child and Adolescent Health Dept, RSFSR Pop Comrt of Health; 1929–31 dir, Child and Adolescent Health Research Inst; member, Commission for the Improvement of Children's Living Conditions, and

Presidium member, Supr Council on Physical Educ, All-Russian Centr Exec Comt; wrote over 30 works; *Publ: Okhrana psikhicheskogo zdorov'ya detey* (Mental Health Care for Children) (1918); *Chto delayet Sovetskaya vlast' dlya okhrany zdorov'ya detey?* (What Is the Soviet Regime Doing to Protect Children's Health?) (1921); *Tri perioda sovetskoy fizkul'tury* (Three Periods of Soviet Physical Education) (1927); *Itogi i blizhayshiye perspektivy okhrany zdorov'ya detey i podrostkov* (The Results and Short-Term Prospects of Child and Adolescent Health Care) (1928); *Rabota vracha po okhrane zdorov'ya detey i podrostkov v sovkhozakh i kolkhozakh* (The Physicians Work on Child and Adolescent Health Care at Sovkhozes and Kolkhozes) (1931); *Died:* 1939.

RADISIG, Aleksandr Aleksandrovich (1869–1941) Thermal eng; Dr of Philosophy from 1891; prof from 1900; corresp member, USSR Acad of Sci from 1935; *Born:* 8 Feb 1869; *Educ:* 1891 grad Petersburg Univ; 1891 received degree of Dr of Philosophy at Berlin Univ; *Career:* from 1900 prof, Kiev Polytech Inst; from 1909 prof, Petersburg Polytech Inst; specialized in thermodynamics of vapors, water vapor state equation, seepage theory, steam turbine theory, methods of calculating turbines and condensers, applied mech and history of eng; *Publ: Termodinamika* (Thermodynamics) (1900); *Matematicheskaya teoriya obmena tepla v tsilindrakh parovykh mashin* (The Mathematical Theory of Heat Exchange in the Cylinders of Steam Engines) (1903); *Kurs parovykh turbin* (A Steam Turbines Course) (1926); *Prikladnaya mekhanika* (Applied Mechanics) (3rd ed, 1931); *Formuly, tablitsy i diagrammy dlya vodyanogo para* (Formulas, Tables and Diagrams for Water Vapor) (3rd ed, 1931); *Teoriya i raschyot kondensatsionnykh ustanovok* (The Theory and Calculation of Condenser Assemblies) (2nd ed, 1934); *Istoriya teplotekhniki* (The History of Heat Engineering) (1936), etc; *Died:* 30 Dec 1941.

RADLOV, Sergey Ernestovich (1892–1958) Stage dir; opera and ballet producer; Hon Art Worker of RSFSR from 1940; *Born:* 18 July 1892; *Educ:* 1917 grad Meyerhold's Petersburg Studio; *Career:* 1913–17 worked for journal "Lyubov' k tryom apel'sinam"; 1918–19 with repertoirs section of Petrograd Branch, Theatrical Dept, Pop Comrt of Educ; 1918 founded touring drama company, performing for troops on Civil War fronts; 1918 worked at Drama Theater of State Pop Center, Petrograd; 1920–22 founder-dir, Folk Comedy Theater; 1923–27 at Leningrad State Acad Drama Theater; 1931–34 artistic dir, Leningrad Opera and Ballet Theater; 1936–38 artistic dir, Leningrad's Pushkin Drama Theater; 1922–35 instructor, Leningrad Inst of Stagecraft; 1929–42 dir, Young Theater (from 1939 Leningrad Sov Theater); 1953–58 stage dir, Russian Drama Theater, Daugavpils and stage dir, Riga Russian Drama Theater; *Works:* produced: Toller's "Eugen the Misfortunate" (1923); Aristophanes "Lysistrata" (1924); Schrecker's "Distant Chimes" (1925); Prokofiev's *Lyubov' k tryom apel'sinam* (Love of Three Oranges" (1926); Shakespeare's "Othello" (1927); "Boris Godunov" (1928); Rossini's "William Tell" (1922); ballets: Asaf'yev's *Plamya Parizha* (The Flame of Paris) (1932); *Bakhchisarayskiy fontan* (The Fountain of Bakhchisaray) (1934); plays: Shakespeare's "King Lear" (1935); Afinogenov's *Salyut, Ispaniya* (Salute to Spain) (1936); Trenyov's *Na beregu Nevy* (On the Banks of the Neva) (1937); "Hamlet" (1938); "Romeo and Juliet" (1939), etc; *Publ: Desyat' let v teatre* (Ten Years in the Theater) (1929); *Shekspir i problemy rezhissury* (Shakespeare and Production Problems) (1936); *Nasha rabota nad Shekspirom* (Our Work on Shakespeare) (1939); *Awards:* Order of the Red Banner of Labor; *Died:* 27 Oct 1958.

RADUS-ZEN'KOVICH, Viktor Alekseyevich (1877–1967) Party and govt official; CP member from 1898; *Born:* 31 Dec 1877 in Arkhangel'sk; *Educ:* from 1896 studied at Moscow Univ; *Career:* took part in student polit movement in Moscow; 1902 emigrated and worked for "Iskra" printing press; 1903–08 member, Nikolayev, Baku then Moscow Party Comts; worked for Party Mil Org in Petersburg and Helsingfors; 1905 deleg at Tammerfors RSDRP Conference; took part in 1905–07 Revol; arrested seven times, served six years at hard labor and a number of years in exile; fought in 1917 Oct Revol; 1918 RSFSR Dep Pop Comr of Labor; then chm, Saratov Province Exec Comt; chm, Revol Mil Council, 2nd Volga Labor Army; chm, Kir Council of Pop Comr; secr, Kir Bureau, CC, CRCP(B); from 1923 member, Centr Exec Comt; 1925–30 cand Presidium member, Centr Exec Comt; 1925–27 chm, Bel Centr Control Commission and Bel Pop Comr of Workers and Peasants' Inspection; 1930–33 Dep Pop Comr of Labor; 1933–37 chm, CC, Communications Workers' Union; 1939–56 admin research work at Inst of Marxism-Leninism, CC, CPSU; deleg at 12th–17th and 22nd Party Congresses; at 12th–15th Party Congresses elected member, CPSU(B) Centr Control Commission; from 1956 pensioner; *Awards:* Order of Lenin (1954); *Died:* 4 Oct 1967.

RADZIYEVSKIY, Aleksey Grigor'yevich (1864–1934) Surgeon and urologist; prof; Dr of Med; *Born:* 14 Apr 1864 in Vasil'kovo, Kiev Province; *Educ:* 1890 grad Med Fac, Kiev Univ; *Career:* from 1890 intern, asst prof, then assoc prof, Surgical Clinic, Kiev Univ; 1903–20 prof of surgery, Kiev Higher Women's Courses; 1921–30 prof, Kiev Med Inst; specialized in urology, surgery of the prostate and uremia, and also bacteriology; *Died:* 22 Sept 1934 in Kiev.

RAFAL'SKIY, Mikhail Fyodorovich (1889–1937) Jewish stage dir and drama teacher; *Born:* 1889; *Educ:* studied at Solovtsev Theater Drama School, Kiev, then in Moscow; *Career:* 1917 made stage debut; 1918 co-founder and co-dir, "Unser winkl" Jewish theater, Khar'kov, later turned into Jewish Touring Theater, which played in Kiev, Vitebsk and Minsk; 1921 founded Minsk Jewish Theater Studio; 1922 moved to Moscow with this org and continued his studies; from 1926 dir, Bel State Jewish Theater, Minsk, which developed from this studio; 1937 arrested by State Security organs; *Works:* produced: Perets' stage adaptations of Sholom-Aleykhem's novellas; "Les Caprises de Scapin", after Moliére; Perets' "On a Penitential Chain" (1925); Bev'yurko's "Botvin" (1927); Kushnirov's "Hirsh Lekert" (1928); Bergel'son's "The Deaf-Mute" (1930), etc; *Died:* 1937 in imprisonment; posthumously rehabilitated.

RAGOZA, Nikolay Ivanovich (1883–1956) Infectionist; Hon Sci Worker of RSFSR; maj-gen, Med Corps; *Born:* 1883; *Educ:* 1910 grad Mil Med Acad; *Career:* 1913 defended doctor's thesis on blood lesions with tapeworm; from 1926 prof of propedeutics, Med Fac, Centr Asian Univ; from 1930 head, Chair of Infectious Diseases, Centr Asian Univ; from 1939 headed a chair of infectious diseases in Leningrad; specialized in therapy, resort treatment, early diagnosis and treatment of infectious diseases, and prevention of epidemics among troops; expert on brucellosis and typhus; devised pathogenetic classification of clinical forms of brucellosis and methods of vaccine therapy; trained a great number of specialists, many of whom later headed chairs of infectious diseases; wrote over 80 works; *Publ: Ob izmeneniyakh krovi pri lentochnykh glistakh* (Blood Lesions with Tapeworm) (1913); *Bryushnoy tif* (Typhoid) (1937); *Opyt klassifikatsii klinicheskikh form brutsellyoza* (An Experimental Classification of Clinical Forms of Brucellosis) (1941); *Sypnoy tif* (Typhus) (1946); *Died:* 1956.

RAGOZIN, Vyacheslav Vasil'yevich (1908–1962) Chess Grand Master from 1949; Hon Master of Sport of USSR; Int Chess judge from 1951; CP member; *Born:* 25 Sept 1908; *Educ:* grad Civil Eng Inst; *Career:* 1930 qualified as Chess Master; competed in 1934, 1939 and 1940 USSR Chess Championship; 1940 won Sov Navy Chess Championship; 1945–47 took part in int tournaments between Sov teams and teams from USSR, USA and UK; 1947 placed 2nd in Chigorin Int Tournament in Moscow; this performance was largely responsible for his receiving the title of Int Grand Master in 1949; 1958 won World Correspondence Chess Championship; devised new opening called the Ragozin Defense; civil eng by profession, but for more than 20 years concentrated almost exclusively on chess; after WW 2 held exec posts in Sov chess org; from 1946 coordinating ed, journal "Shakhmaty v SSSR"; from 1947 Sov rep and vice-pres, Int Chess Federation; Presidium member, Chess Section, Comt for Physical Training and Sport, USSR Council of Min; member, ed bd, Int Chess Federation's journal "FIDE"; in 1930's and 1940's was constant chess companion and trainer of World Chess Champion Botvinnik; made many visits abroad, often as Sov rep at Int Chess Federation congresses and at int chess tournaments; wrote many articles on chess; ed, collections *Shakhmaty za 1947–49 gody* (Chess in 1947–49) and *Shakhmaty za 1950 god* (Chess in 1950); *Died:* 11 Mar 1962.

RAKHIMBAYEV, A.R. (1896–1939) Govt official; CP member from 1919; *Born:* 1896; *Career:* secr, Golodnaya Step' Uyezd Party Comt; secr, Samara Oblast Party Comt; chm, Turkestani Centr Exec Comt; Sept 1920–23 secr, CC, CP(B) Turkestan; Mar 1921 Collegium member, Pop Comrt of Nationalities; from late 1923 secr, CC, CP(B) Uzbek; chm, Centr Publ House; Collegium member, RSFSR Pop Comrt of Educ; 1933–37 chm, Tadzh Council of Pop Comr; at 11th and 13th Party Congresses elected cand member, CC, CPSU(B); at 12th Party Congress elected member, CPSU(B) Centr Control Commission; 1937 arrested by State Security organs; *Died:* 1939 in imprisonment.

RAKHMANOV, Guseyn Pasha ogly (1902–?) Party and govt official; CP member from 1923; *Born:* Dec 1902, son of a sailor; *Educ:* completed four grades at Baku high school; 1920 studied at Azer Joint Mil School; 1932–33 at Inst of Red Prof; *Career:* until Sept 1919 messenger, Azer Min of For Affairs; 1919, after establishment of Sov regime in Baku, organized house comts for Baku Soviets's distr food comts; 1920 volunteered for Red Army; 1924 elected 1st secr, CC, Azer Komsomol; from 1926 first secr, Transcaucasian Kray Komsomol Comt; from 1928 second secr, CC All-Union Komsomol; from 1929 third secr, CC, CP(B) Azer; from Apr 1933 secr, CC, CP(B) Azer; then appointed chm, Azer Council of Pop Comr; frequently elected member, CC, CP(B) Azer; Bureau member, Transcaucasian Party Comt; member, Azer, Transcaucasian and USSR Centr Exec Comt; arrested by State Security organs; *Awards:* Order of Lenin (1935); *Died:* in imprisonment; date and place of death unknown; posthumously rehabilitated.

RAKHMANOVA, Ol'ga Vladimirovna (? –1943) Actress, stage dir and drama teacher; *Born:* date and place of birth unknown; *Career:* 1896 stage debut at Nezlobin Theater, Vilnius; then acted at Sukhodol'skaya Drama Theater, Moscow; stage dir and impressario at theaters in Khabarovsk, Odessa, etc; 1905 opened Artistic Reading and Diction Courses in Odessa, later reorganized into School of Stagedraft; after 1917 Oct Revol taught drama in Tula and other cities; also taught diction and stage delivery at State Inst of Stagecraft, Moscow; film work; *Died:* 23 Dec 1943.

RAKH'YA, Eyno Abramovich (1885–1936) Revolutionary; took part in Finnish and Russian revol movement; CP member from 1903; *Born:* 20 June 1885 in Kronstadt, son of a worker; *Career:* 1905–07 fitter on Finnish Railroad; smuggled weapons and illegal lit; 1911–17 Party work in Petersburg; took active part in guarding Lenin and smuggling Lenin to Finland and back; acted as liaison officer between CC, RSDRP(B) and Lenin; 1918, during Finnish Revol, commanded Red Guard detachment; 1919 div comr on Civil War front against Gen Yudenich; until early 1930's mil and polit work in Red Army; helped found Finnish CP; member, CC, Finnish CP; Finnish CP deleg at 1st–3rd Comintern Congress; *Awards:* two Orders of the Red Banner of Labor; *Died:* 26 Apr 1936.

RAKH'YA, Ivan (Yukka) Abramovich (1887–1920) Revolutionary; took part in Russian and Finnish revol movement; CP member from 1902; *Born:* 19 July 1887 in Kronstadt, son of a worker; *Career:* metalworker by trade; member, underground Kronstadt RSDRP(B) Comt; 1905 helped lead Kronstadt uprising; 1905–13 took part in Finnish workers' movement in Kayan, Isalmi and Kuopio; 1913–17 underground Party work in Petrograd; 1917 took part in Feb Revol; member, Petrograd RSDRP(B) Comt; after 1917 Oct Revol Asst High Comr for Finnish Affairs; helped organize Finnish Red Guards; together with his brother, Eyno Rakh'ya, active in Finnish Revol; 1918 co-founder and CC member, Finnish CP; 1919 Finnish CP rep at 1st Comintern Congress and deleg at 2nd Comintern Congress; *Died:* 31 Aug 1920 killed during anti-Sov elements' attack on Petrograd club.

RAKITNY, Sergey (real name: ZAKONNIKOV, Sergey Vasil'yevich) (1909–1942) Bel poet; *Born:* 15 Oct 1909 in vil Litvinovo, now Vitebsk Oblast, son of a peasant; *Educ:* grad Communist Inst of Journalism, Minsk; *Career:* from 1927 member, Orsha Okrug Comt, Bel Komsomol; from 1929 worked for newspaper "Paleskaya prauda", Gomel'; 1932–33 in Red Army; 1933–36 worked for Minsk newspapers, then ed, Bel kolkhoz radio broadcasts; 1925 first work published; praised "socialist changes" in Bel; published only one collection of verse *Ya agituyu za pyatsigodku* (I Agitate for the Five-Year Plan) (1934); 1936 arrested by State Security rgans; *Died:* 23 Mar 1942 in imprisonment.

RAKOV, Aleksandr Semyonovich (1885–1919) Revolutionary; veteran of Oct Revol and Civil War; CP member from Apr 1917; *Born:* 6 Dec 1885 in vil Mal'tsevo, Smolensk Province; *Career:* worked as waiter in Moscow and Petersburg; 1912–13 co-founder and chm, Restaurant Trades Workers Union; 1913 represented union in Steering Commission of RSDRP(B) faction in 4th State Duma; Apr 1914 arrested with other members of this commission and exiled to his native vil; after 1917 Feb Revol Vyborg Sov deleg at 2nd Finnish Oblast Congress of Soviets; chm, Army Comt of 42nd Corps; dep, Petrograd Sov; member, Bolshevik Mil Org in Vyborg; Oct 1917 controlled Vyborg garrison; Feb 1918 took part in revol in Finland; Sept 1918–Jan 1919 mil comr, Spasskiy Rayon and asst chm, Spasskiy Rayon Exec Comt; from Feb 1919 comr, Petrograd Separate Brigade; fought against Yudenich's troops and was surrounded along with regt staff; *Died:* 29 May 1919 committed suicide; buried in Leningrad's Field of Mars; Leningrad street named after him.

RAKOVSKIY (pseudonym: INSAROV), Khristian Georgiyevich (1873–1941) Party and govt official; CP member from 1917; *Born:* 1873; *Career:* from 1889 active in Soc-Democratic movement in Bulgaria; 1890–1903 active in workers' movement in Switzerland, Germany, France, Rumania and Russia; contributed to newspaper "Iskra"; 1904 returned to Russia; 1907 took part in peasant revolt; arrested, deprived of polit rights and deported from Russia; during Balkan War and WW 1 frequently arrested; prior to WW 1 sided with Mensheviks; during war sided with Trotsky; attended Zimmerwald RSDRP Conference; 1917 released from Yassy Prison by Russian troops; worked in Odessa and Petrograd; Jan–Mar 1918 chm, Supr Collegium for Combatting Counter-Revol in Ukr; May–Sept 1918 chm, Sov peace delegation in Kiev; attended 1st Congress of Comintern; 1919–23 chm, Ukr Council of Pop Comr; from 1923 Sov plen in UK; 1925–27 Sov plen in France, then USSR Dep Pop Comr of For Affairs; one of leaders of Trotskyist opposition; 1927 at 15th CPSU(B) Congress expelled from Party; 1934 re-admitted to Party; at 8th–14th Party Congresses elected member, CC, CPSU(B); 1919–21 member, CC, CP(B) Ukr; Jan 1928 exiled to Siberia for involvement with "Trotskyist opposition"; Feb 1934 in statement to CC, CPSU(B) recanted his errors and broke with opposition; summer 1934 re-admitted to Party and returned to Moscow from exile; Sept 1934 headed Sov Red Cross deleg at Int Red Cross Conference in Tokyo; Mar 1938 sentenced to 20 years' imprisonment for membership of the "anti-Sov rightist-Trotskyist bloc"; *Died:* 1941 in imprisonment.

RAMISHVILI, Isidor Ivanovich (1859–1937) Politician; Geo Menshevik; *Born:* 1859; *Career:* teacher by profession; dep, 1st State Duma on behalf of Kutaisi Province; 1906 deleg, 4th (Amalgamative) RSDRP Congress on behalf of Tiflis Party Org; Baku RSDRP Org deleg at 5th RSDRP Congress; 1908 exiled to Astrakhan' Province; 1913 re-arrested and exiled to Samara Province; 1917 Bureau member, Exec Comt, Petrograd Sov; elected member, Constituent Assembly; 1918–20 member, democratic Geo Govt; *Died:* 1937.

RAMISHVILI, N.V. (pseudonyms: BORTSOV; PYOTR; PYOTR TIFLISSKIY) (1881– ?) Geo politician (Menshevik); *Born:* 1881; *Career:* Tiflis RSDRP org deleg at 5th Party Congress; one of leaders of Geo Mensheviks; during WW 1 soc-chauvinist; up to after 1917 Feb Revol member, CC, Geo Menshevik Party; ed, newspaper "Ertoba"; 1918–20 Geo Min of Internal Affairs; opposed Sov regime; 1923, living abroad, directed Menshevik group which attempted to stage a revolt against Sov regime in Geo; *Died:* date and place of death unknown.

RAMZIN, Leonid Konstantinovich (1887–1948) Thermal eng; prof from 1920; *Born:* 26 Oct 1887 in vil Sosnovka, now Tambov Oblast, son of a teacher; *Educ:* 1914 grad Moscow Higher Tech College; *Career:* from 1914 lecturer, from 1920 prof, Moscow Higher Tech College; 1921–22 also member, RSFSR Gosplan; 1921–30 also dir, All-Union Thermal Eng Inst, Moscow; 1930, along with other leading scientists, sentenced to death for alleged membership of "Ind Party"; sentence commuted to 10 years' imprisonment; during this period engaged in valuable research, designing and building a continuously operating coal boiler with a pressure of 140 atmospheres; did thermal calculations for FD locomotive boiler; from 1944 prof, Moscow Thermal Eng Inst and sci dir, All-Union Thermal Eng Inst; specialized in boiler-building, thermal, aerodynamic and hydrodynamic calculations of boiler assemblies, firebox radiation theory, fuel characteristics, etc; *Publ:* *Sovetskoye pryamotochnoye kotlostroyeniye* (Soviet Construction of Continuously Operating Coal Boilers) (1948); *Awards:* Order of Lenin; Stalin Prize (1943); *Died:* 28 June 1948.

RANDVIYR, Aleksandr Augustovich (1895–1953) Actor; Hon Artiste of Est SSR from 1952; *Born:* 1 Mar 1895; *Educ:* studied at Baltic Fleet Theatrical Studio and at Drama Studio Soc's Theatrical College; *Career:* 1924–27 stage dir in Vayvar; 1927–31 actor, Tallin Workers' Theater; 1931–35 actor, Drama Studio Theater, Tallin; 1935–41 actor, Vanemuyne Theater, Tartu; 1949–53 actor, Kingisepp Theater, Tallin; *Roles:* Lepik in Yakobson's "Ghosts"; Per Gynt in Ibsen's "Per Gynt"; Tur'ya Laas in Myalko's "The Flourishing Sea"; Starodum in Fonvizin's *Nedorosl'* (The Ignoramus), etc; also did film work; *Awards:* Stalin

Prize (1952); *Died:* 10 July 1953.

RANOVICH (real name: RABINOVICH), Abram Borisovich (1885–1948) Historian; specialist in Ancient history; Dr of History; prof; *Born:* 15 Dec 1885 in Zhitomir, son of an office worker; *Educ:* 1905–07 studied at Physics and Mathematics Fac, Kiev Univ; 1913 grad History and Philology Fac, Kiev Univ; *Career:* 1907 sentenced to one year's fortress arrest for revol activities; from 1919 taught at teachers' seminary in Kiev and lectured at Kiev Pop Univ; also worked at Inst of Public Educ, Zhitomir; from 1929 worked for Atheist Publ House and State Anti-Religious Publ House; then exec ed, "Moscow Worker" Publ House and Moscow Party State Publ House; also did research at Inst of Philosophy, Sverdlov Communist Acad; 1935–37 member, State Acad of History of Material Culture; 1938–48 senior assoc, Inst of History, USSR Acad of Sci; taught at Moscow Inst of Philosophy, Lit and History; 1937–41 prof, Moscow Univ; 1937–48 dep chief ed, journal "Vestnik drevney istorii"; specialized in Judaism and early Christianity, socio-econ history of Eastern Mediterranean in Ancient times; *Publ: Pervoistochniki po istorii rannego khristianstva* (Sources for the History of Early Christianity) (1933); *Iudeyskaya religiya* (The Judean Religion) (1934); *Antichnyye kritiki khristianstva* (Ancient Critics of Christianity) (1935); *Ocherk istorii drevneyevreyskoy religii* (An Outline History of Ancient Jewish Religion) (1937); *Ocherk istorii rannekhristianskoy tserkvi* (An Outline History of the Early Christian Church) (1941); *Vostochnyye provintsii Rimskoy imerpiiv I-III vekakh* (1949); *Ellinizm i yego istoricheskaya rol'* (Hellinism and Its Historical Role) (1950); *O rannem khristianstve* (Early Christianity) (1959); *Died:* 29 May 1948.

RASKOL'NIKOV (real name: IL'IN), Fyodor Fyodorovich (1892–1939) Writer and journalist; diplomat; CP member from 1910; *Born:* Jan 1892 in Petersburg; *Educ:* studied at Petersburg Polytech Inst; *Career:* 1911 contributed to Bolshevik weekly "Zvezda"; from Apr 1912 secr, newspaper "Pravda"; during WW 1 served with Baltic Fleet; after 1917 Feb Revol contributed to "Pravda", then edited Bolshevik newspaper "Golos pravdy" in Kronstadt; chm, Kronstadt RSDRP(B) Comt; during 1917 July demonstration headed column of Baltic Fleet sailors and was commandant of Kshesinskaya's house, which served as the headquarters of the Centr Comt and the Petrograd RSDRP(B) Comt; July 1917 arrested by Privisional Govt but released three months later; took part in 1917 Oct Revol; 2 Nov 1917 dispatched to Moscow with armored train of Baltic Fleet sailors; late Nov 1917 at All-Russian Naval Congress elected first Red Naval officer; Jan 1918, at meeting of Constituent Assembly, delivered Bolshevik faction's notice of withdrawal from Constituent Assembly; from Nov 1918 comr, Naval Gen Staff; from Jan 1919 Dep Pop Comr for Naval Affairs and Collegium member, Pop Comrt of Naval Affairs; July 1918 appointed member, Revol Mil Council, Eastern Front; from Aug 1918 commanded Volga Naval Flotilla; Sept 1918 member, RSFSR Revol Mil Council; from Dec 1918 asst commander (for naval affairs), 7th Army and member, Revol Mil Council, Baltic Fleet; captured during naval engagement in Baltic; transported to London and in May 1919 exchanged for British officiers held prisoner in Russia; from 1919 commanded Caspian Flotilla; from June 1920 commander Baltic Fleet; from 1921 RSFSR plen in Afghanistan; 1924–30 ed, journals "Molodaya gvardiya" and "Krasnaya nov'"; chief ed, "Moscow Worker" Publ House; chm, Main Comt for Control of Shows and Repertoire, head, Main Art Bd, and Collegium member, RSFSR Pop Comrt of Educ; from 1939 member, USSR Writers' Union; 1930–38 dipl work in Est, Denmark and Bulgaria; July 1939, while in France, published an open letter entitled "How They Made Me an 'Enemy of the People'" defending himself and other prominent Party and govt officials who were falling victim to the Stalinist purges; subsequently deprived of Sov citizenship; wrote numerous articles, books and plays; *Publ:* play "Robespierre" (1930–31); dramatization of Lev Tolstoy's novel *Voskreseniye* (Resurrection); *Afganistan i angliyskiy ul'timatum* (Afghanistan and the British Ultimatum) (1924); *Probudivshiysya Kitay* (An Awakened China) (1925); *Rasskazy michman Il'ina* (The Stories of Midshipman Il'in) (1934); *Rasskazy komflota* (The Stories of a Naval Commander) (1934), etc; *Awards:* two Orders of the Red Banner; an order from the King of Afghanistan; *Died:* 12 Sept 1939 in Nice.

RASKOVA, Marina Mikhaylovna (1912–1943) Russian pilot; maj, Sov Air Force; first Sov woman to become Air Force navigator; *Born:* 28 Mar 1912 in Vyaz'ma, daughter of a singing teacher; *Educ:* 1933 completed two courses at Aerial Navigation Fac, Correspondence Dept of Leningrad Aviation Inst; 1941 studied at Frunze Mil Acad; *Career:* 1928–29 laboratory asst, then analytical chemist at anyline dye plant in Moscow; 1931 draftsman, Aerial Navigation Laboratory, Air Force Acad; as asst to the famous navigator A.V. Belyakov, trained as navigator, at first independently and then under Belyakov's guidance; 1933 served as navigator with expedition pioneering and mapping Odessa-Batumi air route; upon return from expedition took external examinations to qualify as Air Force navigator; from 1934 taught navigation at Air Force Acad; 1934–35 also trained as pilot at Moscow Centr Flying Club; Aug 1935 competed in first women's cross-country flight in sports planes from Leningrad to Moscow; Oct 1937, together with the woman pilot Valentina Grizodubova, established women's world record for non-stop long-distance flight, covering 1,443 km ground distance between Moscow and Aktyubinsk; 2 July 1938, together with the women pilots Polina Osipenko and Vera Lomako, flew non-stop in a sea-plane from Sebastopol to Arkhangel'sk; 24 Sept 1938, set off with Grizodubova and Osipenko to fly non-stop from Moscow to Far East in a "Rodina" plane; before the "Rodina" reached its destination and landed she was forced to bail out and spent 10 days without food or fire in the deserted taiga; from 1942 trained women's air force regiments for front-line duty; from 1938 dep, Moscow City Sov; *Publ: Zapiski shturmana* (Notes of a Navigator) (1939); *Awards:* Hero of the Sov Union (1938); two Orders of Lenin; *Died:* 3 Jan 1943 killed in a plane crash during a night-time front-line flight near Stalingrad; her ashes are immured in the Kremlin Wall, Moscow.

RASPLETIN, Aleksandr Andreyevich (1908–1967) Radio eng; member, USSR Acad of Sci from 1964; Hero of Socialist Labor; CP member from 1954; *Born:* 25 Aug 1908; *Educ:* 1936 grad Leningrad Electr Eng Inst; *Career:* 1958–64 corresp member, USSR Acad of Sci; worked at various research inst; developed new radio equipment; *Awards:* Stalin Prize (1951); Lenin Prize; *Died:* 8 Mar 1967.

RATNER, Lev Moiseyevich (1886–1953) Surgeon, urologist, oncologist and health official; Dr of Med from 1947; prof; *Born:* 29 Aug 1886, son of a physician; *Educ:* 1905 grad Smolensk Boys' High School; 1910 grad Med fac, Moscow Univ; *Career:* after grad specialized at I.Kh. Dzirne's Surgical and Urological Clinic in Moscow; 1912 also trained under Bier, Israel, Krause and Rumpel in Berlin; 1919 moved to Yekaterinburg, where he later became head, Chair of Surgical Propaedeutics, Ural Univ (founded in 1920); 1927 founded a cancer ward at Ural Oblast Surgical Hospital; 1928–30 read numerous papers at Ural Med Soc and med congresses on curability of cancer in early stages and need for establishment of a system of cancer out-patient treatment; founder-dir, Oncological Clinic, Sverdlovsk Inst of Physiotherapy; underwent advanced training at Leningrad Oncological Inst, then directed by N.N. Petrov; 1936 organized and chaired 1st Sverdlovsk Oblast Oncological Conference, which was attended by 60 physicians and sci; subsequently chaired six similar conferences on anti-cancer measures in Ural Oblast, especially in Tyumen', Chelyabinsk and Kurgan Okrugs; wrote 62 works, 24 of which dealt with oncological problems; *Publ: Lecheniye naiboleye rasprostrannyonnykh form zlokachestvennykh novoobrazovaniy* (The Treatment of the Commonest Malignant Neoplasms); *Prekartsinomatozy pishchevaritel'nogo trakta* (Precarcinomatosis of the Digestive Tract); *Diagnosticheskiye oshibki v onkologii* (Diagnostic Errors in Oncology); *Diagnosticheskiye oshibki i diagnostika raka grudnoy zhelezy* (Diagnostic Errors and the Diagnosis of Breast Cancer) (1949), etc; *Awards:* Order of the Red Star (1942); medals "For Victory Over Germany" and "For Labor Valor" (1946); "Outstanding Health Worker" Badge (1947); *Died:* 25 Feb 1953.

RAU, Fyodor Andreyevich (1868–1957) Defectologist; Dr of Pedag; prof from 1925; corresp member, RSFSR Acad of Pedag Sci from 1947; *Born:* 26 Mar 1868 in Germany; *Educ:* 1887 grad teachers' training seminary; *Career:* 1887–1891 taught deaf children at Vatter Inst, Frankfurt-on-Main; 1892 went to Russia after obtaining diploma as teacher of deaf-mutes; 1893–96 private tutor to a deaf boy; 1896 opened a school for the deaf and ran speech correction courses in Moscow; 1899–1928 dir, Arnold-Tret'yakov College for the Deaf, Moscow; 1915 co-founded first Russian kindergarten for deaf-mute children; 1925–48 prof and head, Chair of Surdopedag and Logopedics, Defectological Dept, Pedag Fac, 2nd Moscow Univ; hon member, All-Union Soc of Deaf-Mutes; organized and read papers at conferences on various aspects of defectology; organized lip-reading courses for adults and helped to develop system of educ for deaf-mutes; trained numerous specialists and co-founded present system of advanced training in defectology; schools for deaf mutes in Arkhangel'sk, Kaluga, Tambov and Khar'kov now bear his name; wrote over 50 works; *Publ: Metodika obucheniya glukhonemykh* (Methods of Teaching Deaf-Mutes) (1934); *Bukvar' dlya shkol glukhonemykh* (An ABC-Book for Schools for Deaf-Mutes) (1940); *Metodika obucheniya glukhonemykh proiznosheniyu* (Methods of Teaching Pronounciation to Deaf-Mutes) (1959), etc; *Awards:* Order of Lenin (1951); medal "For Outstanding Labor During the Great Fatherland War"; "Outstanding Educ Worker" Badge; *Died:* 30 May 1957 in Moscow.

RAU, Nataliya Aleksandrovna (1870-1947) Educationist; specialist in methods of teaching deaf-mutes; *Born:* 5 June 1870; *Educ:* 1896 grad Moscow Women's High-School; *Career:* after grad worked as a teacher at a private school for the deaf in Moscow; 1900 founded first Russian nursery for deaf children; 1915 organized courses for the mothers and tutors of deaf preschool children in Moscow; 1915–21 taught at various nurseries for deaf children; 1922, together with her husband F. A. Rau, founded the Moscow Lip-Reading Club; 1925–47 assoc, Defectological Dept, Pedag Fac, 2nd Moscow Univ (now Lenin Teachers' Training Inst); wrote numerous works on the training of deaf children and devised several teaching aids; also did research on teaching lip-reading to adults with acquired deafness; *Publ: Materyam malen'kikh glukhonemykh detey* (For the Mothers of Deaf-Mute Children) (2nd ed, 1928); *Chto mozhet i dolzhna delat' mat' s tol'ko chto oglokhshim rebyonkom?* (What Can and Should the Mother of a Child with Acquired Deafness Do?) (1931); coauthor, *Russkiy yazyk. Uchebnik dlya 2-ogo klassa shkol glukhonemykh* (The Russian Language. A Textbook for the Second Grade of Schools for Deaf-Mutes) (7th ed, 1940); *Doshkol'noye vospitaniye glukhonemykh* (The Preschool Training of Deaf-Mutes) (1947); *Died:* 20 Feb 1947 in Moscow;

RAUER, Aleksandr Eduardovich (1871–1948) Surgeon; specialist in maxillo-facial surgery; *Born:* 1871; *Educ:* 1897 grad Med Fac, Tomsk Univ; *Career:* 1897–1903 worked in Verkhoyansk; then at Tilling Clinic, Petersburg; until 1914 surgeon, Ufa Province Hospital; after 1917 Oct Revol headed Maxillo-Facial Dept, Therapy and Prosthesis Inst, Moscow; from 1932 head, Chair of Maxillo-Facial Surgery, Centr Inst of Postgrad Med Training, Moscow; specialized in jaw fractures and lesions of the soft facial tissues; together with N.M. Mikhel'son, wrote monograph on plastic facial surgery which won a State Prize; devised original operations for dislocation of the lower jaw, anchylosis of the jaw, the formation of an artificial larynx, etc; devised various other restorative operations of the face and jaw; wrote 78 works; *Publ: Perelom chelyustey i povrezhdeniya myagkikh tkaney litsa* (Jaw Fractures and Lesions of the Soft Facial Tissues) (1932); *Died:* 1948.

RAUTIO, Karl Erikovich (1889–1963) Composer and music teacher; Hon Art Worker of Karelian ASSR from 1943; *Born:* 20 Nov 1889 in vil Untamola, Finland; *Career:* wrote songs, arrangements of Karelian folk songs and first Karelian symphonic work – "Karelian Wedding" (1926); dep, Karelo-Finnish Supr Sov of 1947, 1951 and 1955 convocations; *Died:* 15 Dec 1963.

RAVICH, S.N. (Ol'ga) (1879–1957) Party official; CP member from 1903; *Born:* 1879; *Career:* Party work in Khar'kov, Petersburg and abroad; 1917 deleg at Petrograd City and 7th (Apr) All-Russian RSDRP(B) Conferences; Petrograd RSDRP(B) Comt deleg at 6th Party Congress; after 1917 Oct Revol Party and govt work; 1918 opposed conclusion of Brest Peace Treaty; at 14th CPSU(B) Congress sided with "New Opposition"; 1927 at 15th CPSU(B) Congress expelled from Party for siding with "Trotskyist opposition"; 1928 readmitted to Party; 1935 again expelled from Party and later sentenced for alleged anti-Party activities; *Died:* 1957.

RAVICH-SHCHERBO, Vladimir Antonovich (1890–1955) Phthisiatrist; corresp member, USSR Acad of Med Sci; *Born:* 1890; *Educ:* 1916 grad Med Fac, Kazan' Univ; *Career:* 1918 volunteered for Red Army; from 1922 worked at Therapy Clinic, Voronezh Med Inst and at Voronezh Tuberculosis Dispensary; sci dir, Voronezh Inst of Tuberculosis; head, Chairs of Propaedeutics and Tuberculosis, Voronezh Med Inst; then head, Chair of Tuberculosis, Centr Inst of Postgrad Med Training, Moscow; during WW 2 chief therapist at front; bd member, Moscow and All-Union Phthisiatrists' Soc; co-ed, "Opyt Sovetskoy meditsiny v Velikoy Otechestvennoy voyne 1941–45 godov" (The Experience of Soviet Medicine in the 1941–45 Great Fatherland War); did research on pulmonary tuberculosis and pleurisy, allergy and immunity and complex therapy for tuberculosis patients; hypothesized the existence of hypersensitive zones in the pulmonary tissue which are affected by specific and non-specific agents and facilitate the development of infiltrates, lobar pneumonia and pleurisy; together with L. D. Shteynberg, did research on the role of lymphatic concentration in the pathogenesis of tuberculosis and described several neurological symptoms of glandular and mediastinal forms of this disease; on the basis of experimentation and clinical observations he rejected the significance of allergy as an immunity factor and attributed the development of allergy to neuro-reflectional influences; 1925 introduced a bilateral artificial pneumothorax; also advocated the use of blood transfusions to stimulate the body in pulmonary tuberculosis and developed concepts of complex therapy; wrote 108 works, including six monographs; *Publ: Opyt primeneniya dvustoronnego iskusstvennogo pnevmotoraksa pri tuberkulyoze* (Experience in the Use of Bilateral Artificial Pneumothorax in Tuberculosis) (1929); coauthor, *Plevrity (vistseral'nyye i parietal'nyye) i nevrologicheskiye sindromy plevral'nogo proiskhozhdeniya* (Pleurisy [Visceral and Parietal] and Neurological Syndromes of Pleuritic Origin) (1933); coauthor, *Sredosteniye v klinike tuberkulyoza detey i vzroslykh* (The Mediastinum in the Clinical Treatment of Tuberculosis in Children and Adults) (1936); *Iskusstvennyy pnevmotoraks pri lyogochnom tuberkulyoze* (Artificial Pneumothorax in Pulmonary Tuberculosis) (1948); *Tuberkulyoz lyogkikh u vzroslykh* (Pulmonary Tuberculosis in Adults) (1953); *Oshibki v klinike lyogochnogo tuberkulyoza* (Mistakes in the Clinical Treatment of Pulmonary Tuberculosis) (1954); *Died:* 1955 in Moscow.

RAYEVSKIY, Aleksandr Sergeyevich (1872–1924) Eng; locomotive designer; prof; *Born:* 4 Feb 1872 in Khar'kov, son of a teacher; *Educ:* 1895 grad Khar'kov Technol Inst; *Career:* from 1900 designer, Khar'kov Locomotive-Building Plant; from 1910 designer, Putilov (later Kirov) Plant, Petersburg; from 1920 also prof, Petrograd Polytech Inst; designed various locomotives, including underframe of first Sov diesel locomotive SHCH-EL-1; also invented graphoanalytical method of calculating counterweights, method of calculating individual components of locomotivs, etc; *Died:* 23 June 1924.

RAYS, Ignatiy (1899–1937) Party official; CP member from 1927; *Born:* 1 Jan 1899 in Poland, of Jewish parents; *Educ:* studied at Law Fac, Vienna Univ; *Career:* while a student joined revol movement; 1920 sent on underground assignment to Pland as member of Austrian CP; arrested soon afterwards and sentenced to five years imprisonment; released on bail after six months; after his release contacted Comintern in Moscow and carried out its assignments; 1923–26 underground Comintern assignments in the Ruhr, Germany; then returned to Vienna and spent some time in jail; 1927 went to Moscow and then carried out underground work in various Centr and East European countries; 1929–32 worked for centr Party apparatus in Moscow, then sent abroad again; 17 July 1937, while still abroad, sent a letter to the CC, CSPSU(B) notifying his resignation from the CPSU(B); then joined Trotsky's 4th International; *Awards:* Order of the Red Banner (1928), which he returned to the CC, CPSU(B) in 1937; *Died:* 4 Sept 1937 assassinated near Lausanne, Switzerland; at the time he was carrying a Czechoslovakian passport in the name of Herman Eberhard.

RAYSKIY, Mikhail Ivanovich (1873–1956) Specialist in forensic med; *Born:* 13 Sept 1873 in vil Kudryavshchina, Lipetsk Oblast; *Educ:* 1898 grad Med Fac, Tomsk Univ; *Career:* after grad stayed on at Chair of Forensic Med, Tomsk Univ; from 1912 prof, Chair of Forensic Med, Moscow Univ; from 1919 head, Chair of Forensic Med, Saratov Univ; 1941 head, Chair of Forensic Med, Mil Med Acad; from 1949 head, Chair of Forensic Med, Odessa Med Inst; discovered phenomenon of revaccination, important in determining the body's reactivity; provided a sci explanation for the three stages of corpse spots, enabling accurate determination of the time of death; made many contributions to the diagnosis of gunshot injuries ("minus-tissue", pergamentation of the skin at the point of entry of the bullet as evidence of shooting at close range, soot analysis by microscopic study); set forth criteria for establishing the gravity of bodily wounds and contributed to the diagnosis of death from cold; trained many specialists who subsequently headed chairs of forensic med; wrote over 100 works; *Publ: K ucheniyu o raspoznavanii smerti ot kholoda* (The Theory of Diagnosing Death from Cold) (1907); *"Minus-tkani" pri* *ognestrel'nykh povrezhdeniyakh* ("Minus-Tissue" in Gunshot Injuries) (1936); *Sudebnaya meditsina* (Forensic Medicine) (1953); *Died:* 1956.

RAYSKIY, Nazariy Grigor'yevich (1876–1958) Singer (tenor); singing teacher; art historian; Hon Art Worker of RSFSR from 1944; Dr of Arts from 1941; *Born:* 26 Oct 1876 in Lublin; *Educ:* musical training in Warsaw; perfected his singing in Italy; *Career:* from 1900 concert singer; from 1902 opera singer; 1904–09 at Zimin Opera Theater, Moscow; 1908–16 chamber singer; 1919–29 and 1933–49 prof, Moscow Conservatory; 1929–33 prof, Tbilisi Conservatory; *Roles:* Gvidon in *Skazka o tsare Saltane* (The Tale of Tsar Saltan); Enzo in Leoncavallo's "Zaza"; Lenskiy in "Eugene Onegin"; *Publ: Literatura i iskusstvo* (Literature and Art) (1944); *Posledniye dni S.I. Taneyeva* (The Last Days of S.I. Taneyev) (1952), etc; *Died:* 6 Oct 1958 in Moscow.

RAYZER, David Yakovlevich (1904–1962) Eng; govt and Party official; CP member from 1939; *Born:* 1904; *Educ:* grad Odessa Polytech Inst; *Career:* until 1936 dir of works, then chief eng, ind construction trust; from 1936 exec work for USSR Pop Comrt of Heavy Ind and USSR Pop Comrt of Defense Ind and USSR Pop Comrt of Shipbuilding Ind; 1950–53 USSR Min for Construction of Heavy Ind Enterprises; 1953–57 USSR Min for the Construction of Metallurgical and Chemical Ind Enterprises; 1952–61 cand member, CC, CPSU; *Died:* 24 Dec 1962.

RAZDOL'SKIY, Ivan Yakovlevich (1890–1962) Neuropathologist and neurosurgeon; prof from 1933; corresp member, USSR Acad of Med Sci from 1946; Hon Sci Worker of RSFSR from 1946; *Born:* 24 June 1890; *Educ:* 1908 grad Yekaterinodar Med Orderlies' School; 1919 grad Petrograd Mil Med Acad; *Career:* 1908–14 med orderly, Yekaterinodar Hospital; received clinical training from M.I.Astvatsaturov and B.S.Doynikov at Chair of Nervous Diseases, Petrograd Mil Med Acad, where he was a junior instructor; from 1925 assoc prof, Clinic of Nervous Diseases, Leningrad Inst of Postgrad Med Training; 1926–60 also worked at Mechnikov Hospital, Leningrad; from 1933 prof and head, Chair of Nervous Diseases, Mechnikov Teaching Hospital; from 1936 head, Chair of Nervous Diseases, 2nd Leningrad Med Inst; from 1947 head, Chair of Nervous Diseases, Leningrad Inst of Sanitation and Hygiene; bd member, All-Union and Leningrad Soc of Neuropathologists and Psychiatrists and All-Union Soc of Neurosurgeons; member, ed collegium, 10-vol *Rukovodstvo po nevrologii* (Handbook on Neurology); member, ed council, journals "Voprosy neyrokhirurgii" and "Zhurnal nevropatologii i psikhiatrii imeni S.S.Korsakova"; co-ed, neuropathology section, "Bol'shaya meditsinskaya entsiklopediya" (Large Medical Encyclopedia) (2nd ed); wrote over 160 works; *Publ: Evolyutsiya nervnoy sistemy* (The Evolution of the Nervous System) (1926); *Dorzal'no-mostovoy opukholevyy sindrom* (The Dorso-Pontal Tumor Syndrome) (1939); *Opukholi chetvyortogo zheludochka* (Tumors of the Fourth Ventricle) (1940); *Diagnosticheskoye znacheniye i patogenez koreshkovykh boley polozheniya* (The Diagnostic Significance and Pathogenesis of Postural Radicular Pains) (1949); coauthor, Vol 4, 11 and 26, *Opyt sovetskoy meditsiny v Velikoy Otechestvennoy voyne 1941–45* (The Experience of Soviet Medicine in the 1941–45 Great Fatherland War) (1949, 1950, 1952); *Opukholi golovnogo mozga* (Cerebral Tumors) (1954); *Klinika opukholey golovnogo mozga* (The Clinical Aspects of Cerebral Tumors) (1957); *Opukholi spinnogo mozga i pozvonochnika* (Tumors of the Spine and Vertebrae) (1958); coauthor, vol 5, *Rukovodstvo po nevrologii* (Handbook on Neurology) (1961); *Awards:* Motorin Prize; Order of Lenin; Order of the Red Star; Gold Medal of the Mil Med Acad; *Died:* 1962 in Leningrad.

RAZENKOV, Ivan Petrovich (1888–1954) Physiologist; Hon Sci Worker of RSFSR from 1940; member, USSR Acad of Med Sci from 1944; *Born:* 26 Nov 1888; *Educ:* grad Med Fac, Kazan' Univ; *Career:* after grad stayed on at Kazan' Univ to study for professorship; 1915–18 mil surgeon; 1918–22 asst prof, Chair of Physiology, Tomsk Univ and head, Chair of Physiology, Inst of Physical Culture; from 1922 worked at Leningrad Inst of Experimental Med under I.P. Pavlov, conducting important research on higher nervous activity and the physiology of digestion; from 1924 head, Dept of Physiology, Obukh Inst of Labor Hygiene and Occupational Diseases, Moscow; at the same time directed laboratories at the Timiryazev Inst and the Inst of Nutrition; from 1934 head, Dept of Human Physiology and dir, Moscow Branch, All-Union Inst of Experimental Med; from 1944 head, Dept of Vegetative Physiology, 1944–49 dir, Inst of Physiology, USSR Acad of Med Sci; 1948–50 vice-pres, USSR Acad of Med Sci; of particular importance was his work at Pavlov's laboratory on stimulation of the cortex of the cerebral hemispheres in dogs; this led to the discovery of phase conditions in the cerebral cortex; and in turn led to an understanding of the pathophysiological mechanisms of neurotic states; from 1924 specialized in the physiology of digestion; in his latter years hypothesized the circulation of certain substances through the gastro-intestinal tract in the process of intermediate metabolism, with repeated utilization of these substances by the body; made a great contribution to dietology and to the pathogenesis and treatment of gastro-intestinal ailments; headed Chair of Physiology, Liebknecht Ind Pedag Inst; also head, Chairs of Physiology, Lenin Teachers' Training Inst, Centr Inst of Postgrad Med Training and Sechenov 1st Moscow Med Inst; dep chm, then chm, Learned Med Council, USSR Pop Comrt of Health; ed and member, ed bds, "Arkhiv biologicheskikh nauk", "Zhurnal eksperimental'noy meditsiny", "Byulleten' eksperimental'noy biologii i meditsiny" and "Fiziologicheskiy zhurnal SSSR"; for 25 years chm, Moscow Soc of Physiologists; wrote over 100 research works; *Publ: Pishchevareniye na vysotakh* (Digestion at High Altitudes) (1945); *Kachestvo pitaniya i funktsii organizma* (Bodily Functions and the Quality of Nutrition) (1946); *Novyye dannyye po fiziologii i patologii pishchevareniya* (New Data on the Physiology and Pathology of Digestion) (1948); *Rol' zheludochno-kishechnogo trakta v mezhutochnom obmene* (The Role of the Gastrointestinal Tract in Intermediate Metabolism) (1949); *Izbrannyye trudy* (Selected Works) (1959); *Awards:* Pavlov Prize of USSR Acad of Sci (1939); Stalin Prize (1947); Pavlov Gold Medal of USSR Acad of Sci (1952); two Orders of Lenin; medals; "Distinguished Health-Worker" Badge; *Died:* 14 Nov 1954 in Moscow.

RAZUMOVSKIY, Vasiliy Ivanovich (1857–1935) Surgeon; Sov neurosurgery pioneer; Dr of Med from 1884; prof from 1887; Hero of Labor from 1923; *Born:* 1857; *Educ:* 1880 grad Med Fac, Kazan' Univ; *Career:* after grad worked as intern, L.L.Levshin's Surgical Clinic, Kazan'; received specialist training from N.V.Sklifosovskiy, Reyer and S.P.Botkin in Moscow and Petersburg; 1884 defended doctor's thesis on bone atrophy after neurotomy; 1885–86 dissector, 1886–87 assoc prof, from 1887 prof, Chair of Operative Surgery, Kazan' Univ; 1891 transferred to Chair of Hospital Surgery Clinic, 1896 to Chair of Fac Surgery Clinic; first Russian surgeon to perform operation for cortical epilepsy; 1908 devised operation for extirpation of Gasser's nodes by section of posterior nerve-root; from 1909 founder-rector, Saratov Univ; 1912 dismissed from this post by Educ Min Kasso; during WW 1 supervised med care for wounded in Saratov; after 1917 Feb Revol surgeon, Caucasian Army, in which capacity he co-founded Tbilisi and Baku Univ; 1920 resumed clinical work in Saratov; from 1930 devoted himself entirely to org and surgical work; consultant, various health resort org in Mineral'nyye Vody; devised tissue alcoholization method which he used first on nerve columns (instead of neurotomy) and the brain substance (instead of leucotomy), and then on other tissues and organs (for varicose veins, rectal prolapse, etc); also devised original techniques for organopexia, osteoplastic amputation of the foot, etc; trained numerous outstanding surgeons, including Bogolyubov, Opokin and Tikhov; wrote some 150 works; *Publ:* doctor's thesis *K voprosu ob atroficheskikh protsessakh v kostyakh posle pererezki nervov* (Atrophic Bone Processes After Neurotomy) (1884); *Vospalitel'nyye protsessy na sheye* (Inflammatory Processes of the Neck) (1902); *Noveyshiye dannyye po cherepno-mozgovoy khirurgii* (The Latest Data on Craniocerebral Surgery) (1913); *Izbrannyye trudy* (Selected Works) (1959); *Died:* 1935.

RED'KIN, Andrey Mikhaylovich (1900–1963) Mil commander and govt official; eng; rear-admiral; CP member from 1927; *Born:* 14 Feb 1900; *Educ:* 1926 grad Higher Naval Eng College; 1931 grad Naval Acad; *Career:* 1931–37 eng commands in Sov Navy; from 1937 with USSR shipbuilding ind; 1956–59 USSR Min of Shipbuilding Ind; from 1959 retired; *Died:* 19 Apr 1963.

REFORMATSKIY, Sergey Nikolayevich (1860–1934) Chemist; prof from 1891; corresp member, USSR Acad of Sci from 1928; *Born:* 1 Apr 1860; *Educ:* 1882 grad Kazan' Univ; studied under A.M.Zaytsev; *Career:* from 1891 prof, Kiev Univ; did research on metallo-organic synthesis; developed method of synthesizing beta-oxy acids (Reformatskiy's reaction), which also proved important for obtaining saturated and unsaturated straight-chain and branched-chain acids; this reaction found special applications in research on the synthesis of complex natural compounds, notably vitamin A and its derivatives; *Publ: Nachal'nyy kurs organicheskoy *khimii* (A Beginner's Course of Organic Chemistry) (1893); *Predel'nyye mnogoatomnyye alkogoli* (Saturated Polyatomic Alcohols) (1889); *Deystviye smesi tsinka i monokhloruksusnogo efira na ketony i al'degidy. Sintez tretichnykh Beta-oksikislot* (The Reaction of Ketones and Aldehydes to a Mixture of Zinc and Monochloro-acetic Ether. The Synthesis of Tertiary Beta-Oxy Acids) (1890); *Sbornik rabot laboratorii organicheskoy khimii Universiteta svyatogo Vladimira* (Transactions of the Laboratory of Organic Chemistry at Saint Vladimir University) (1907); *Died:* 27 Dec 1934.

REKSTYN', Anna Ivanovna (1894–1967) Revolutionary; CP member from 1917; *Born:* 1894; *Career:* from 1916 in revol movement; 1910–17 worked at factories in Riga and Tushino; during 1917 Oct Revol organized squads of Tushino female workers, then served with Red Guards in Moscow; 1917–18 member, centr and local admin of Rubber Workers Union; during Civil War comr, Moscow Cheka and All-Russian Cheka; 1923–35 asst head, Gen Dept, CC, CPSU(B); 1934–37 worked for CC, CPSU(B); from 1937 exec admin work; then ed, All-Union Radio Comt; from 1954 retired; *Died:* Aug 1967.

REMEYKO, (REMEYKA), Yu. A. (1878–1958) Govt official; CP member from 1905; *Born:*1878; *Career:* Party work in Lith; after 1917 Oct Revol worked for Pop Comrt of Nationalities; 1921 Presidium member, CC, All-Russian Miners' Union; attended Party school run by Moscow RCP(B) Comt; 1922–29 worked for State Polit Bd (OGPU); then admin and govt work; *Died:* 1958.

REMEZOV, Nil Petrovich (1899–1961) Soil scientist; Dr of Geological and Mineralogical Sci from 1941; prof from 1933; CP member from 1957; *Born:* 1899 in Moscow, son of a railroad official; *Educ:* 1923 grad Physics and Mathematics Fac, Moscow Univ; *Career:* 1919–21 in Red Army; 1921–22 at Chair of Meadow Land, Moscow Zootech Inst; 1922–36 at Samoylov Fertilizer Research Inst; 1928 first Sov pedologist to use electrometric method of determining redox factor of soils; 1929–33 supervised detailed study of soils of some 100 experimental fields in European USSR, Siberia, Far East, Centr Asia and Transcaucasia; 1933–38 prof and head, Chair of Soil Sci and Geology, Bryansk Forestry Inst; 1938–42 at All-Union Forest Management Research Inst; 1942–45 dean, Geologist Soil Fac, Moscow Univ; from 1958 head, Chair of Soil Sci and head, Soil Dept, Biological Soil Fac, Moscow Univ; 1956 and 1960 presented papers at 6th and 7th Int Congresses of Soil Sci in Paris; *Publ: Genezis podzolov* (The Genesis of Podzols) (1941); coauthor, *Teoriya i praktika izvestkovaniya pochv* (The Theory and Practice of Liming Soils) (1938); *Uspekhi pochvovedeniya SSSR za posledniye 25 let* (Progress in Soviet Soil Science in the Past 25 Years) (1944); *Pochvennyye kolloidy i poglotil'naya sposobnost' pochv* (Soil Colloids and the Absorptive Potential of Soils) (1957); coauthor, *Potrebleniye i krugovorot azota i zol'nykh elementov v lesakh Yevropeyskoy chasti SSSR* (The Consumption and Circulation of Nitrogen and Ash Elements in the Forests of the European USSR) (1959); *Glavneyshiye svoystva pochv SSSR* (The Main Properties of the Soils of the USSR) (1960); *Awards:* Vil'yams Prize of Timiryazev Agric Acad; *Died:* 25 Mar 1961.

RENTS, Frants Frantsevich (1860–1942) Astronomer; specialist in astrometry; Hon Sci Worker of RSFSR from 1935; *Born:* 17 Feb 1860; *Career:* observed various double stars and comets; studied motion of Jupiter's satellites; established difference in longitude of Pulkovo and Potsdam; supervised compilation of four Pulkovo catalogs of absolute direct ascension of stars; also compiled joint catalog of direct ascension of 1,769 stars, based on observations of eight observatories in various countries; *Publ:* "Telegraphische Laengenbestimmung zwischen Pulkowo und Potsdam" (1903); "Fundamentalkatalog von 1642 Haupt- und 127 Zusatzsternen fuer die Epoche 1925" (1935); *Died:* 1942.

REPIN, Il'ya Yefimovich (1844–1930) Painter; prof and member, Petersburg Acad of Arts from 1893; *Born:* 24 July 1844 in Chuguyev, Khar'kov Province; *Educ:* 1864–73 studied at Petersburg Acad of Arts; *Career:* 1873–76 worked and continued studies in Italy and France on a scholarship from Petersburg Acad of Arts; 1873 displayed works at Vienna Exhibition; from 1877 lived and worked in Chuguyev; 1878 joined Assoc of Hinerant Art Exhibitions; in same year displayed works at Paris Exhibition; 1882 moved to Petersburg after living for a time in Moscow; 1893–1907 prof, Petersburg Acad of Arts; 1900–30 lived in Kuokalla, Finland; *Works:* "Preparing for the Examination" (1865); "Slavic Composers" (1872); "Barge-Haulers on the Volga" (1873); "A Paris Cafe" (1875); "Sadko in the Underwater Kingdom" (1876); "A Hero of the Past War" (1878); "The Seamstress" (1882); "A Religious Procession in Kursk Province" (1883); "They Did Not Wait" (1884); "Ivan the Terrible and His Son Ivan" (1885); "Neva Avenue" (1887); "Dnieper Cossacks Writing a Letter to the Turkish Sultan" (1891); "The Arrest of a Propagandist" (1892); "A Session of the Council of State" (1903); "Breaking Up a Demonstration" (1905); "Gogol's Self-Immolation" (1909); "A Gopak in Ancient Zaporozh'ye", etc; portraits of Moussorgsky, Lev Tolstoy, A.Pisemskiy, V.Serov, N.Pirogov, Franz Liszt, I.Pavlov, Duse, etc; *Died:* 29 Sept 1930 on his estate at Kuokkala.

REPREV, Aleksandr Vasil'yevich (1853–1930) Pathophysiologist; pioneer of Russian endocrinology; *Born:* 26 Aug 1853 near Suzdal', Vladimir Province; *Educ:* 1878 grad Med Surgical Acad; *Career:* 1878 assigned to mil unit serving in Bulgaria; 1880–86 intern, Penza Province Hospital; then worked at Laboratory of Gen and Experimental Pathology, Mil Med Acad; from 1889 assoc prof, from 1890 dissector, Chair of Gen Pathology, Mil Med Acad; from 1891 prof, Chair of Gen Pathology, Tomsk Univ; from 1895 prof, Chair of Gen Pathology, Khar'kov Univ; in Khar'kov soon also headed Chair of Gen Pathology at Women's Med Inst and at Veterinary Inst; from 1912 hon prof; from 1920 prof, Chair of Pathophysiology, Crimean Univ; also dean of its Med Fac; 1922 returned to Chair of Pathophysiology, Khar'kov Univ; in his latter years directed Chair of Experimental Pathology, Ukr Main Bd for Sci, Museum and Artistic Research Establishments; also head, Biological Dept, All-Ukr Roentgenological Inst; head, Dept of Pathology, Ukr Inst of Sci and Practical Veterinary Studies; specialized in metabolism and endocrinology; did research on: metabolism in the case of fever; effects of pregnancy on metabolism; function of sexual organs in relation to nutrition; effects of postnatal period and nursing on bodily functions; also studied internal secretion, effects of x-rays on metabolism, tumors' metabolic effects and links between tumors and disturbances of the endocrine glands; *Publ: O vliyanii beremennosti na obmen veshchestv u zhivotnykh* (The Effects of Pregnancy on Metabolism in Animals) (1888); *Uchebnik obshchey patologii* (A Textbook on General Pathology) (1897); *O vliyanii poslerodovogo perioda pri kormlenii na zhizneproyavleniya* (The Effects of the Postnatal period and Nursing on Bodily Functions) (1906); *Osnovy abshchey i eksperimental'noy patologii* (The Principles of General and Experimental Pathology) (1911); *Kak organizm zashchishchayetsya ot bolezney* (How the Body Protects Itself Against Disease) (1923); *Vnutrennyaya sekretsiya* (Internal Secretion) (1925); *Problema raka* (Cancer) (1929); *Died:* 21 June 1930.

RERBERG, Ivan Ivanovich (1869–1932) Architect; Hon Sci and Tech Worker of RSFSR from 1932; *Born:* 1869; *Educ:* grad Petersburg Eng College and Mil Eng Acad; *Career:* 1898–1912 helped to build Pushkin Fine Arts Museum, Moscow; 1910–11 – Northern Insurance Company building, Moscow; 1911–12 designed and built secondary school on Bol'shaya Kazna Lane, Moscow; 1917 – Kiev Station, Moscow; 1927 Central Telegraph Office, Moscow; designed in classic and late modern style; *Died:* 1932.

RERIKH, Yuriy Nikolayevich (1902–1960) Orientalist; Dr of Philology from 1957; prof; member, Royal Asian Soc, London; member, Asian Soc, Bengal; member, American Archeological and Ethnographical Socs; member, Parisian Geographical Soc; *Born:* 16 Aug 1902 in vil Okulovka, Nizhniy Novgorod Province, son of the painter N.K. Rerikh; *Educ:* studied philology at the world's leading centers of Oriental studies; studied under P. Pelliot, S. Levy, A. Maspero and V.F. Minorskiy; *Career:* 1920 went to USA with his father; 1923–57 lived and worked in India; 1925–29 took part in his father's Centr Asian expedition to Tibet and Sinkiang; then took part in other sci expeditions to China and Mongolia; 1930–42 dir, Inst of Himalayan Studies, Hulu (Himachal-Pradesh); taught Tibetan, Chinese and Sanskrit at higher educ establishments in India; 1957 returned to USSR to head History of Religion and Philosophy Section, Indian Dept, Inst of Oriental Studies, USSR Acad of Sci; (from 1960 Inst of Asian Peoples); supervised Tibetan studies in Moscow, Leningrad and Ulan-Ude and taught Sanskrit, Tibetan and Vedic at higher educ establishments in these cities; specialized in Tibetan studies but was also a leading expert on Indian culture; wrote works on ethnography, material culture of peoples of Centr Asia, Tibetan history and linguistics, iconography, the Geserkhan epic ("Geseriade"), Buddhist philosophy and religion, Indo-Chinese cultural links; translated into Russian the 15th-Century major Tibetan historical work "Blue Tepther" (Blue Annals); spoke Tibetan, Sanskrit, Hindi, Mongolian, Chinese, Iranian and other Oriental languages; *Publ:* "Tibetan Paintings" (1925); "Trails to Innermost Asia" (1931); "Dialects of Tibet. The Tibetan Dialect of Lahul" (1933); "The Epic of King Kesar of Ling" (1942); "The Blue Annals" (2 vol, 1949–53); "A Textbook of Colloquial Tibetan. Dialect of Central Tibet" (1957); "Le parler de l' Amdo. Etude d'un dialècte archaique du Tibet" (1958); *Zverinnyy stil' u kochevnikov Severnogo Tibeta* (The Beast Style among the Nomads of Northern Tibet) (1930); *Tibetskiy yazyk* (Tibetan) (1961), etc; left manuscripts *Istoriya Sredney Azii* (The History of Central Asia) and an extensive Tibetan-English dictionary with Sanskrit equivalents; *Died:* 21 May 1960.

RESHETNIKOV, Il'ya Ivanovich (1872–1936) Fruit-grower and selectionist; *Born:* 1872 in Samara (now Kuybyshev), son of a smallholder; *Educ:* grad Odessa School of Horticulture; also studied horticulture in Germany for several years; *Career:* spent some 30 years studying and cultivating new varieties; 1890 obtained new seed varieties by free pollination; 1900 began work on hybridization; 1912 worked on selection under I.V.Michurin; bred 33 varieties, including 16 apples, 4 pears, 8 plums, Samarets grape, Fortuna raspberry, Avenarius blackberry, Samara alycha (a kind of damson) and Pobeda (Victory) quince; the best strains are Samara Pippin, Samara Beauty, Katusya, Lenya greengage, Liya greengage, black greengage, October Vengerka; also bred a number of strains of musk-melon, water-melon, haricot bean and other vegetables; in latter years headed Fruit and Ornamental Plant Dept, Kuybyshev Botanical Garden; contributed articles to journals "Plodovodstvo", "Progressivnoye sadovodstvo i ogorodnichestvo" and "Sadovodstvo"; *Publ:* catalog *Novinki i novovvedeniya* (Novelties and Innovations) (1910); *Died:* 1936.

REVUTSKIY, Dmitriy Nikolayevich (1881–1941) Ukr folklorist and lit historian; *Born:* 12 Mar 1881 in vil Irzhavets, Poltava Province; brother of the composer L.N.Revutskiy; *Educ:* 1906 grad History and Philology Fac, Kiev Univ; *Career:* 1907–18 taught in Revel' and Kiev; 1918–23 lecturer at Lysenko Musical Drama Inst, Kiev; 1923–34 worked for Ethnographical Commission, Ukr Acad of Sci; from 1938 senior assoc, Inst of Ukr Folklore, Ukr Acad of Sci; *Publ:* "Ukrainian Ballads and Historical Songs" (1919); "Lysenko, the Choral Conductor" (1937); "Shevchenko and Folk Songs" (1939); "The Autobiography of M.V. Lysenko" (1940); collection of Ukr folk songs "Golden Keys" (1926), etc; *Died:* 29 Dec 1941 in Kiev.

REYN, Fyodor Aleksandrovich (1866–1925) Surgeon; *Born:* 3 Mar 1866; *Educ:* 1890 grad Med Fac, Moscow Univ; from 1890 worked at Chair of Topographical Anatomy and Operative Surgery, Moscow Univ; 1894 defended doctor's thesis; 1894–97 at Pavlov Hospital; 1902–11 prof, Chair of Operative Surgery and Topographical Anatomy, Moscow Univ; 1911, with other lecturers and prof, resigned from Moscow Univ in protest against policy of Educ Min Kasso; pioneer of med training for women; founder-member, Moscow Higher Women's Courses; from 1900 taught surgery, from 1907 dean, Med Fac, Moscow Higher Women's Courses; from 1912 chief physician, Pirogov 1st Municipal Hospital; from 1917 also head, Chair of Fac Surgical Clinic; compiled "Kratkoye rukovodstvo po obshchey khirurgii" (A Short Guide to General Surgery), which ran through seven ed; 1901–05, together with P.I. D'yakonov and N.K. Lysenkov, published "Lektsii po operativnoy khirurgii" (Lectures on Operative Surgery); 1908, together with D'yakonov, Lysenkov and N.I. Napalkov, published *Lektsii po topograficheskoy anatomii i operativnoy khirurgii* (Lectures on Topographical Anatomy and Operative Surgery); in these lectures the authors replaced the traditional Greco-Latin terminology and nomenclature with easily intelligible Russian terms; for many years head, Soc of Russian Surgeons; head, Russian Surgical Soc (Moscow); head, Soc of Russian Physicians in Memory of N.I. Pirogov; after 1917 Oct Revol member, Learned Council, Pop Comrt of Health; *Publ: O podkozhnykh povrezhdeniyakh pochki* (Subcutaneous Injuries of the Kidney) (1894); *Prigotovleniye preparatov po topograficheskoy anatomii* (The Preparation of Samples for Topographical Anatomy) (1895); *Borodavchatyye razrastaniya na poverkhnosti sobstvennoy vlagalishchnoy obolochki yaichka* (Papillose Growths on the Surface of the Testicle's Tunica Vaginalis Propria) (1897); *Rezul'taty operativnogo lecheniya Jackson-ovskoy epilepsii i pokazaniya k nemu* (The Results of Operative Treatment of Jacksonian Epilepsy and Indications for It) (1897); *O sochetannom brom-etil-khloroformnom narkoze* (Combined Bromine-Ethyl-Chloroform Narcosis) (1899); coauthor, *Obshchaya operativnaya khirurgiya* (General Operative Surgery) (1903); coauthor, *Russkaya khirurgiya* (Russian Surgery) (1916); *O probodnykh yazvakh zheludka po materialu Moskovskoy 1-oy gorodskoy Pirogovskoy bol'tnitsy* (Perforated Gastric Ulcers According to the Material of Moscow's 1st Pirogov City Hospital) (1925); *Awards:* Hero of Labor; *Died:* 1925.

REYNBERG, Samuil Aronovich (1897–1966) Clinician and roentgenologist; prof from 1927; Hon Sci Worker of RSFSR from 1941; CP member from 1940; *Born:* 10 Apr 1897; *Educ:* 1921 grad 1st Leningrad Med Inst; *Career:* 1921–24 specialized in roentgenology; 1924–27 worked as a roentgenologist in Leningrad; from 1927 founder-head, Chair of Pediatric Roentgenology, Leningrad Pediatric Inst; 1930–41 head, Chair of Roentgenology, Leningrad Inst of Postgrad Med Training; during WW 2 chief roentgenologist, Leningrad Front; from 1943 head, Chair of Roentgenology and Radiology, Centr Inst of Postgrad Med Training, Moscow; also consultant, 1st Clinical Hospital, RSFSR Min of Health and other med establishments; performed first intra vitam human angiography in USSR; co-founder and Presidium member, All-Russian and All-Union Soc of Roentgenologists and Radiologists; hon chm and member, various sci soc in 15 Sov republ; deleg, numerous Sov and for roentgenological and radiological congresses; member, Learned Med Council, USSR Min of Health; member, ed council, journals "Vestnik rentgenologii i radiologii", "Klinicheskaya meditsina", etc; ed, roentgenology section, "Bol'shaya meditsinskaya entsiklopediya" (Large Medical Encyclopedia) (2nd ed); wrote over 350 works; *Publ: Rentgenologicheskiy metod issledovaniya sosudov v teratologii* (An X-Ray Method of Examining Vessels in Teratology) (1922); *K voprosu o deystvii rentgenovykh luchey na rentgenovskiy personal* (The Effect of X-Rays on X-Ray Personnel) (1924); "Roentgenstudien über die normale und pathologische Physiologie des Tracheobronchialbaumes" (1925); *Rentgenodiagnostika zabolevaniy kostey i sustavov* (The X-Ray Diagnosis of Bone and Joint Diseases) (1929); *Tuberkulyoz lyogkikh i yavleniya narusheniya bronkhial'noy prokhodimosti (atelektaz i emfizema* (Pulmonary Tuberculosis and Symptoms of a Disturbance of Bronchial Patency [Lung Collapse and Emphysema]) (1937); *Ocherki voyennoy rentgenologii* (Studies in Military Roentgenology) (1942); *Vyyavleniye lyogochnogo tuberkulyoza pri pomoshchi gruppovykh rentgenologicheskikh issledovaniy* (Detecting Pulmonary Tuberculosis by Group X-Ray Examinations) (1942); *Rentgenologicheskoye raspoznavaniye raka zheludka* (X-Ray Diagnosis of Stomach Cancer) (1952); *Problema bezopasnosti rentgenologicheskikh issledovaniy* (The Safety Problem in X-Ray Research) (1958); *Rentgenodiagnostika zabolevaniy kostey i sustavov* (The X-Ray Diagnosis of Bone and Joint Diseases) (2 vol, 1964), etc; *Awards:* medal "For Labor Valor" (1961); Lenin Prize (1966); other awards; *Died:* 27 Mar 1966 in Moscow.

REYNSHTEYN, B.I. (1866–1947) Trade-union official; CP member from 1918; *Born:* 1866; *Career:* from 1884 active in revol movement; emigrated and worked for American Socialist Workers' Party; represented this party in 2nd International; 1917 returned to Russia and joined Menshevik-internationalists; Apr 1918 joined Bolsheviks; worked for Comintern and Trade-Union International (Profintern); *Died:* 1947.

REYNSON, O.P. (1895–1938) Mil commander; CP member from 1912; *Born:* 1895; *Career:* 8th Volmar Lat Infantry Regt deleg at 6th Party Congress; after 1917 Oct Revol mil, then teaching work; 1921 expelled from Party for violating Party discipline; arrested by State Security organs; *Died:* 1938 in imprisonment.

REYSNER, Igor' Mikhaylovich (1899–1958) Historian; Orientalist; Dr of History from 1953; co-founder, Sov school of Indian and Afghan studies; CP member from 1944; *Born:* 9 Jan 1899 in Tomsk, son of a law prof; *Educ:* 1924 grad Oriental Fac, Red Army Mil Acad; *Career:* 1919–26 worked for Pop Comrt of For Affairs; 1919–21 first secr, Sov embassy in Afghanistan; 1925–35 head, Dept of the East and Colonies, Int Agrarian Inst, Moscow; also prof, Moscow Inst of Oriental Studies; from 1934 prof, from 1956 head, Chair of History of Middle East, Moscow Univ; from 1943 senior assoc, from 1957 head, Section of Indian History, Inst of Oriental Studies, USSR Acad of Sci; specialized in Indian commune, movement of peasants and artisans and Indian nat-liberation movement; did valuable studies of modern Afghan history; *Publ: Afganistan* (Afghanistan) (1929); *Ocherki klassovoy bor'by v Indii* (Studies in the Class Struggle in India) (vol 1, 1932);

chief ed and coauthor, *Novaya istoriya stran zarubezhnogo Vostoka* (The Modern History of Foreign Eastern Countries) (2 vol, 1952); chief ed and coauthor, *Noveyshaya istoriya stran zarubezhnogo Vostoka* (The Recent History of Foreign Eastern Countries) (3 vol, 1954–57); *Razvitiye feodalizma i obrazovaniye gosudarstva u afgantsev* (The Development of Feudalism and Formation of the State Among the Afghans) (1954); chief ed and coauthor, *Narodnoye vosstaniye v Indii 1857–1859 godov* (The 1857–59 National Uprising in India) (1957); *Narodnyye dvizheniya v Indii v XVII-XVIII vekakh* (Popular Movements in India in the 17th and 18th Centuries) (1961); *Died:* 7 Feb 1958.

REYSNER, Larisa Mikhaylovna (1895–1926) Writer and journalist; CP member from 1918; *Born:* 1 May 1895 in Lublin, Poland, daughter of a law prof and polit emigre; *Educ:* grad Psychoneürological Inst, Petersburg; *Career:* 1913 began lit work; 1915–16 formed group of young poets including V. Rozhdestvenskiy, V. Zlobina and L. Nikulina and published journal "Rudin"; wrote under pen-names L. Khrapovitskiy, I. Smirnov, etc; 1916–17 worked for journal "Letopis'" and Gorky's newspaper "Novaya zhizn'"; 1917 comr, Naval Gen Staff; 1918–19 served on Civil War front against Admiral Kolchak as intelligence agent behind the White lines; 1920 with Sov dipl mission in Afghanistan; 1923 visited Germany; 1924 visited Ural and Donets Basin; *Publ:* play "Atlantida" (1913); collected essays: "Front" (1924); *Gamburg na barrikadakh* (Hamburg at the Barricades) (1924); *Ugol', zhelezo i zhivyye lyudi* (Coal, Iron and Living People) (1925); historical studies *Portrety dekabristov* (Portraits of the Decembrists) (1925), etc; *Died:* 9 Feb 1926.

REYSNER, M. A. (1868–1928) Revolutionary; govt official; CP member from 1918; *Born:* 1868; *Career:* until 1905 Populist; 1903 emigrated; formed close ties with German Soc-Democrats and contributed to newspaper "Vorwärts"; 1904 appeared as expert in Koenigsberg trial of Russian Soc-Democrats charged with smuggling Party lit; 1905 sided with Bolsheviks and attended Tammerfors Conference; after 1917 Oct Revol head, Draft Bills Dept, Pop Comrt of Justice; member, Commission to Draft First Constitution; worked for Pop Comrt of Educ; taught at Red Army Mil Acad; *Died:* 1928.

REZANOV, Vladimir Ivanovich (1867–1936) Lit historian; Dr of Philology; prof; corresp member, USSR Acad of Sci from 1923; *Born:* 8 Sept 1867 in vil Lyuboch, now Kursk Oblast; *Educ:* 1890 grad Nezhin History and Philology Inst; *Career:* 1891–99 teacher in Kursk; 1899–1934 lecturer, then prof, Nezhin History and Philology Inst (later turned into Inst of Public Educ, then Teachers' Training Inst); specialized in 17th and 18th-Century Russian and Ukr drama; *Publ: Materialy po etnografii Kurskoy gubernii* (Material on the Ethnography of Kursk Province) (2 vol, 1902–03); *Iz razyskaniy o sochineniyakh V.A. Zhukovskogo* (Research on the Works of V.A. Zhukovskiy) (2 vol, 1906–16); *Ekskurs v oblast' iyezuitskogo teatra* (An Excursion into the Field of the Jesuit Theater) (1910); *Shkol'nyye deystviya XVII-XVIII vv. i teatr iyezuitov* (School Plays of the 17th and 18th Centuries and the Jesuit Theater) (1910); *Shkol'nyye dramy pol'sko-litovskikh iyezuitskikh kollegiy* (School Dramas of the Polish-Lithuanian Jesuit Collegia) (1916); *Ukrainskiy drevniy teatr* (The Ancient Ukrainian Theater) (6 vol, 1925–29), etc; *Died:* 31 Dec 1936.

REZNIK, Lipa Borukhovich (1890–1944) Jewish poet and playwright; *Born:* 15 July 1890 in Chernobil', now Kiev Oblast; *Educ:* studied at Kiev Univ; *Career:* 1914 first work printed; *Publ:* verse collections; "Pale Dawn" (1921); "Velvet" (1922); poem "The Storm" (1925); "Homeland" (1929); "Dawn" (1935); "Fame" (1939); drama "The Revolt" (1927); plays: "The Last Ones" (1931); "The Recruit" (1936); "The Little Daughter" (1938), etc; translated works of Shevchenko, Tychina and Ryl'skiy; *Died:* 5 Apr 1944.

REZNIK, Yakov Borisovich (1892–1952) Educationist; Dr of Pedag Sci; prof; CP member from 1946; *Born:* 23 Apr 1892; *Educ:* 1918 grad Med Fac, Kiev Univ; *Career:* 1919–27 founder-dir, Kiev orphanage; from 1927 lectured on pedag at Odessa Inst of Public Educ, Kiev Univ, Kustanay Teachers' Training Inst, Kiev's Gorky Teachers' Training Inst and Starobel'sk Teachers Inst; from 1924 at Research Inst of Jewish Culture and Ukr Pedag Research Inst; specialized in didactics; wrote methodic teachers' aids; *Publ: Psikhologicheskiye osnovy uchebnogo protsessa* (The Psychological Principles of Tuition) (1940); *Metodika zakrepleniya uchebnogo materiala* (Methods of Consolidating Tuition Material) (1940); *Metody prepodavinya v sovetskoy shkole* (Methods of Teaching in Soviet Schools) (1941); *Poyasnitel'noye chteniye v nachal'noy shkole* (Explanatory Reading in the Elementary School) (1947); *Died:* 17 June 1952.

RIGORIN (real name: LIKHTMAN), Grigoriy Davydovich (1897–1962) Actor; theater dir; Hon Art Worker of Tat ASSR from 1952; CP member from 1943; *Born:* 25 July 1897; *Educ:* studied at Philharmonic Soc's Drama School in Rostov-on-Don; *Career:* from 1918 actor in Mariupol' and other cities; from 1925 actor, until 1932 dir, Red Torch Theater; 1932–34 dir, Marx Theater, Saratov; 1934–62 dir, Kazan' Russian Theater; *Died:* 28 Jan 1962.

RIKHTER, Adol'f Genrikhovich (1884–1963) Govt official; CP member from 1904; *Born:* 10 Jan 1884; *Career:* began revol work in Libava; took part in 1905–07 Revol; arrested; after release, emigrated to England, then lived in Belgium, maintaining links with Lat Section, RSDRP; May 1917 returned to Russia and sent on Party work to Riga; 1918–24 commands and polit work in Red Army; 1924–30 worked for Sov trade missions in Sweden and Norway; 1930–37 exec work for USSR Pop Comrt of For Trade, then eng at plants in Moscow; from 1948 retired; *Died:* 10 Aug 1963.

RIKHTER, Andrey Aleksandrovich (1871–1947) Botanist; specialist in plant physiology; prof from 1917; member, USSR Acad of Sci from 1932; member, Lenin All-Union Acad of Agric Sci from 1935; *Born:* 15 Aug 1871 in vil Kurovskoye, Kaluga Province; *Educ:* 1893 grad Petersburg Univ; *Career:* 1893–1917 worked at Petersburg (Petrograd) Univ; from 1917 prof, Perm Univ; from 1924 prof, Saratov Univ; 1932–34 assoc, Leningrad Laboratory of Biochemistry and Plant Physiology, USSR Acad of Sci; 1934–38 dir, from 1938 assoc, Inst of Plant Physiology, USSR Acad of Sci; did research on photosynthesis; perfected instrument for the exact analysis of small gas exchanges (Povlovtsev-Rikhter apparatus), which is used in many Sov physiological laboratories; made studies of the resistance of plants to drought, cold and salty soils; also made studies of fermentation, the biochemistry of agric crops and the immunity of plants to fungi and other diseases; *Awards:* Order of Lenin; Order of the Red Banner of Labor; *Died:* 9 Apr 1947.

RIKHTER, Georgiy Emil'yevich (1906–1959) Psychiatrist; *Born:* 1906 in Onega, of mixed parentage: father – eng of German origin, mother – a dentist of Chuvash descent; *Educ:* 1929 grad Kiev Med Inst; *Career:* from 1926, while a student, developed an interest in psychiatry; also interested in physical training; after grad asst prof, Prof Ye.K. Krasnushkin's Psychiatric Clinic, 1st Moscow Med Inst; then Prof. V.A. Gilyarovskiy's Psychiatric Clinic, All-Union Inst of Experimental Med; for a while also chief psychiatrist for Moscow, then dep head, Dept of Psychiatric Help, RSFSR Pop Comrt of Health; late 1937 actively campaigned for the release of his mother, arrested in Kiev by NKVD; early 1938 himself arrested for these efforts; 1941, after start of WW 2, evacuated to Far North with other prisoners; escaped en route and joined retreating units of Sov Army, posing as a Dr Petrov, who had managed to escape from German imprisonment; became mil surgeon and gained rapid promotion; appointed head of a frontline hospital; 1945 recognized and reported by a former Kiev acquaintance while in Koenigsburg and re-arrested; stripped of his mil orders and medals and interned for several years in a Moscow prison; some time after Stalin's death, released from prison and rehabilitated, thanks to the strenuous intercession of his wife; recuperated from the effects of his imprisonment, then appointed senior assoc of the Ukr Psychoneurological Research Inst, Khar'kov; 1956–59 head, Org Methods Dept, above inst; helped improve psychoneurological service in Ukr; devised methods of treating schizophrenia and other psychiatric ailments; wrote over 50 research works; *Awards:* various WW 2 orders and medals; *Died:* 7 Nov 1959 in Khar'kov.

RIMSHA, K.I. (1895–1950) Physician; CP member from 1913; *Born:* 1895; *Career:* during WW 1 did revol work in army; deleg, 6th RSDRP(B) Congress; Oct 1917 chm, Yur'yev Mil Revol Comt; 1918 fought against Whitist forces in Crimea and Northern Caucasus; then worked for underground Vilnius Party Org; 1919 member, Vilnius Sov of Workers' Dep; secr, Vilnius Revol Comt; 1919–22 mil polit work; from 1924 worked for public health system; during WW 2 mil surgeon; from 1948 chm, Lith Med Workers' Union; *Died:* 1950.

RIMSKAYA-KORSAKOVA (nee: PURGOL'D), Nadezhda Nikolayevna (1848–1919) Pianist; wife of the composer Rimsky-Korsakov from 1872; *Born:* 1848; *Educ:* studied piano under A.A. Gerke and composition under N.I. Zaremba; *Career:* member,

"Mighty Band" Russian Composers' Club; at club gatherings performed works of Dargomyzhskiy, Rimsky-Korsakov, Borodin and Moussorgsky; arranged for the piano many symphonic and opera works by Dargomyzhskiy, Rimsky-Korsakov, Tchaikovsky and Glazunov; edited "Letopisi moyey muzykal'noy zhizni" (Chronicles of My Musical Life) and other posthumous editions of Rimsky-Korsakov's lit works; *Publ: Moi vospominaniya o A.S. Dargomyzhskom* (My Memories of A.S. Dargomyzhskiy) (1913); *Died:* 1919.

RIMSKY-KORSAKOV, Andrey Nikolayevich (1878–1940) Musicologist; Dr of Philosophy; elder son of the composer N.A. Rimsky-Korsakov; *Born:* 5 Oct 1878 in Petersburg; *Educ:* 1903 grad Strasburg Univ; *Career:* studied music theory under his father and the composer M. Shteynberg; from 1912 wrote on musicology; 1915–17 ed and publisher, journal "Muzykal'nyy sovremennik"; 1918–40 worked for Manuscripts Dept, Saltykov-Shchedrin Public Library; *Publ: K estetike baleta* (The Esthetics of Ballet) (1914); coauthor, *"Boris Godunov" Musorgskogo* (Moussorgsky's "Boris Godunov") (1927); "Maksimilian Shteynberg" (1928); *M.I. Glinka i yego "Zapiski"* (M.I. Glinka and his "Notes") (1930); *N.A. Rimsky-Korsakov. Zhizn' i tvorchestvo* (The Life and Work of N.A. Rimsky-Korsakov) (1933–46); *Gosudarstvennaya Publichnaya biblioteka imeni M.Ye. Saltykova-Shchedrina v Leningrade. Muzykal'nyye sokrovishcha Rukopisnogo otdeleniya* (The Saltykov-Shchedrin State Public Library in Leningrad. Musical Treasures of the Manuscript Department) (1938), etc; *Died:* 23 May 1940 in Leningrad.

RIMSKY-KORSAKOV, Georgiy Mikhaylovich (1901–1965) Composer, musicologist and teacher; assoc prof from 1928; grandson of the composer N.A. Rimsky-Korsakov; *Born:* 13 Dec 1901 in Petersburg; *Educ:* 1927 grad M.O. Shteynberg's composition class, Leningrad Conservatory; 1929 completed postgrad studies at Inst of Theater and Music; *Career:* 1927–62 taught at Leningrad Conservatory; until 1929 asst to B.V. Asaf'yev; wrote articles and several books; *Works:* helped compose music for plays: Kamenskiy's "Stepan Razin" (1924); "Lenin" (1925); symphony (1925); cantata "Revolt", etc; *Publ: Notnaya zapis'* (Notation) (1925); *Rasshifrovka svetovoy stroki Skryabinskogo "Prometeya"* (Deciphering the Light Line of Skryabinskiy's "Prometheus") (1926); *Akusticheskoye obosnovaniye teorii ladovogo ritma* (The Acoustic Foundation of the Harmony Rhythm Theory) (1928); *Died:* 10 Oct 1965 in Leningrad.

RIMSKY-KORSAKOV, Mikhail Nikolayevich (1873–1951) Zoologist; specialist in entomology; prof from 1921; Hon Sci Worker of RSFSR from 1945; *Born:* 1 Sept 1873, son of the famous composer; *Educ:* 1895 grad Petersburg Univ; *Career:* from 1921 prof, Leningrad Timber (now Wood Technol) Inst; specialized in the morphology, anatomy, embryology, taxonomy and biology of various arthropods, especially insects; made major study of forest entomology; *Publ:* coauthor, *Zoologicheskiye ekskursii* (Zoological Excursions) (2 vol, 1924–28); coauthor, *Opredelitel' povrezhdeniy lesnykh i dekorativnykh derev'yev i kustarnikov Yevropeyskoy chasti SSSR* (A Classification Key of Lesions in Forest and Ornamental Trees and Shrubs in the European USSR) (1934); ed and coauthor, *Lesnaya entomologiya* (Forest Entomology) (1935); *Awards:* two Orders of Lenin; medals; *Died:* 11 Mar 1951.

RIVES, Solomon Markovich (1892–1953) Pedagogue; Dr of Pedag; prof; corresp member, RSFSR Acad of Pedag Sci from 1945; *Born:* 15 June 1892; *Educ:* 1924 grad Moscow Higher Sci Teachers' Training Courses; *Career:* from 1924 taught at Krupskaya Acad of Communist Training, at Bel State Univ and other teachers' training establishments; from 1938 lectured on pedag at Lenin Teachers' Training Inst, Moscow; for over 25 years also worked at various research inst, RSFSR Pop Comrt of Educ and RSFSR Acad of Pedag Sci; *Publ:* coauthor, *Opyt kommunisticheskogo vospitaniya. Ot shkoly-kommuny k detskomu gorodku imeni Oktyabr'skoy revolyutsii* (Experience in Communist Training. From the Commune School to the October Revolution Children's Campus) (1924); coauthor, *Preduprezhdeniye neuspevayemosti v shkole* (The Prevention of Poor Progress in School) (1940); *Vospitaniye voli uchashchikhsya v protsesse obucheniya* (Training Pupils' Will-Power During Tuition) (1958); *Awards:* Order of Lenin; *Died:* 6 July 1953.

RODIONOV, Sergey Petrovich (1898–1961) Petrographer; corresp member, Ukr Acad of Sci from 1951; CP member from 1919; *Born:* 8 Oct 1898 in Zagorsk, now Moscow Oblast; *Educ:* 1929 grad Dnepropetrovsk Mining Inst; *Career:* 1929–31 worked at Denpropetrovsk Mining Inst; 1931–35 dir, Krivoy Rog Geological Survey Base and head, Chair of Geology, Krivoy Rog Ore Inst; 1935–38 head, Research Section, Ukr Geological Bd; 1938–61 assoc, Inst of Geology, Ukr Acad of Sci; 1945–52 also head, Chair of Mineralogy and Crystallography, Kiev Univ; did extensive research on Ukr ore deposits; *Died:* 2 May 1961.

RODIONOV, Vladimir Mikhaylovich (1878–1954) Organic chemist; member, USSR Acad of Sci from 1943; *Born:* 28 Oct 1878 in Moscow; *Educ:* 1901 grad Dresden Polytech Inst; 1906 grad Moscow Higher Tech College; *Career:* from 1906 worked as eng at various chemical plants; from 1920 prof, Inst of Chemical Technol and other higher educ establishments in Moscow; 1925–30 tech dir, Aniline Trust; consultant, various inst and plants; 1946–50 vice-pres, from 1950 pres, Mendeleyev All-Union Chemical Soc; devised general amino acid synthesis methods and did research on the properties and conversions of these compounds; developed a number of alkalization methods and a technique for introducing the diase group in phenols; helped to expand the Sov aniline dye, pharmaceutical and perfume ind; *Awards:* Order of Lenin; two other orders; three Stalin Prizes (1946, 1949 and 1950); *Died:* 7 Feb 1954.

RODZYANKO, Mikhail Vladimirovich (1859–1924) Politician; leader, Octobrist Party; landowner in Yekaterinoslav Province; *Born:* 12 Apr 1859; *Career:* 1907–17 dep, State Duma of 3rd and 4th convocations; from 1911 chm, State Duma; prior to this, 1886–96 uyezd marshal of the nobility; 1900–06 chm, Yekaterinoslav Province Zemstvo Admin; 1906–07 member, State Council; at first closely linked with court circles and supported Stolypin's policies; then tried to find common ground with Constitutional Democratic Party; Feb 1917, anticipating revolution begged the Tsar to proclaim a constitution; head, Provisional Comt of State Duma; then head, "Private Consultations" of Duma members; after 1917 Oct Revol fought with Denikin's Volunteer Army in Civil War; 1920 emigrated to Yugoslavia; *Publ:* memoirs about the last years of Tsarist rule *Krusheniye imperii* (The Fall of the Empire) (2nd ed, 1929); *Died:* 19 Jan 1924 in Yugoslavia.

ROGINSKIY, Girsha Zalmonovich (1903–1957) Zoopsychologist; prof; Dr of Pedag Sci; *Born:* 28 Dec 1903; *Educ:* 1927 grad History Fac, Leningrad Univ; 1929 grad Pedag Dept, Leningrad's Herzen Teachers' Training Inst; *Career:* for 10 years teacher; 1930–34 asst to Prof V.A. Vagner, under whom he did research on comparative psychology; helped found Museum of the Evolution of the Nervous System and Comparative Psychology, Bekhterev Brain Inst; 1937–41 lectured at Herzen Teachers' Training Inst in Leningrad, also running Brain Inst Museum; in his latter years prof, Leningrad Univ, then Herzen Teachers' Training Inst; developed materialistic approach to the assessment of existing zoopsychological theories; criticized conceptions of for researchers, especially V. Keller and advanced many new postulates, particularly on the formation of habits in the lower and higher apes; his research findings and theoretical studies shed new light on many aspects of the pre-history of the intellect; *Publ: Psikhika chelovekoobraznykh obez'yan* (The Mentality of the Humanoid Apes) (1945); *Razvitiye mozga i psikhika* (The Development of the Brain and Mentality) (1948); *Navyki i zachatki intellektual'nykh deystviy u antropoidov (shimpanze)* (The Habits and Rudiments of Intellectual Actions and Anthropoids /Chimpanzee/) (1948); *Died:* 19 Oct 1957.

ROMAN (secular name: TANG) (1893–1963) Archbishop of Vilnius and Lith, Russian Orthodox Church from 1963; *Born:* 1893 in Arensburg, Sarema Island; *Career:* 1930 consecrated priest; 1950 took monastic vows and elevated to Bishop of Tallin and Est and vicar of Leningrad Eparchy; 1955 appointed Bishop of Luga and vicar of Luga Eparchy; 1956–58 Bishop of Ivanovo and Kineshma; 1958–59 Bishop of Kursk and Belgorod; 1959–63 Bishop of Vilnius and Lith; *Awards:* right to wear cross on cowl; *Died:* 18 July 1963.

ROMANOV, Boris Aleksandrovich (1889–1957) Historian; Dr of Historical Sci from 1941; prof from 1947; *Born:* 10 Feb 1889; *Educ:* 1912 grad Petersburg Univ; *Career:* 1919–27 and 1944–51 lecturer, then prof, Leningrad Univ; 1918–29 also worked for Centr Archives; from mid 1930's worked for institutes of USSR Acad of Sci; 1944–57 at Leningrad Branch, Inst of History, USSR Acad of Sci; specialized in Ancient Russian history and Russian for policy from late 19th to early 20th Century; also did source research and published historical documents; *Publ: Rossiya v Man'chzhurii, 1892–1906* (Russia in Manchuria, 1892–1906)

(1928); *Ocherki diplomaticheskoy istorii russko-yaponskoy voyny, 1895–1907* (An Outline Diplomatic History of the Russo-Japanese War, 1895–1907) (2nd ed, 1955); *Lyudi i nravy drevney Rusi* (Men and Morals of Ancient Rus) (2nd ed, 1966); *Rabochiy vopros v komissii V.N. Kokovtsova v 1905* (The Question of the Workers in V.N. Kokovtsov's 1905 Commission) (1926); collected documents *Russkiye finansy i yevropeyskaya birzha v 1904–1906 godakh* (Russian Finance and the European Stockmarket in 1904–1906) (1926); *Pravda Russkaya* (Russian Truth) (vol 2, 1947, with commentaries); *Sudebniki XV-XVI vekov* (Legal Codes of the 15th and 16th Centuries) (1952, with commentaries); *Died:* 18 July 1957.

ROMANOV, Mikhail Fyodorovich (1896–1963) Actor and producer; Pop Artiste of USSR from 1951; CP member from 1950; *Born:* 16 Oct 1896 in Petersburg; *Educ:* 1920 completed drama training; *Career:* 1919 volunteer in Red Army, where he directed amateur dramatic productions; 1920 actor, Petrograd Mil Distr Theater; 1921 founded Pop Theater in vil Rozdestvenno, Petrograd Province; 1923–24 at Petrograd's New Drama Theater; 1924–36 at Pushkin Drama Theater, Leningrad; from 1936 actor, 1953–59 artistic dir, Lesya Ukrainka Drama Theater, Kiev; also gave lit readings and did film work; *Roles:* Neznamov in Ostrovskiy's *Bez viny vinovatyye* (Guilty Without Guilt); Nikolay in Ostrovskiy's *Pozdnyaya lyubov'* (Late Love); Pavel Protasov in Gorky's *Deti solntsa* (Children in the Sun); Lavretskiy in *Dvorasnkoye gnezdo* (A Nest of Gentle folk), after Turgenev; the Knight-Commander in Lesya Ukrainka's *Kamennyy vlastelin* (The Stone Sovereign); Telegin in *Khozhdeniye po mukam* (Purgatory), after A.N. Tolstoy; Harry Smith in Simonov's *Russkiy vopros* (The Russian Problem); Fyodor Protasov in Lev Tolstoy's *Zhivoy trup* (The Living Corpse); Molchalin in Griboyedov's *Gore ot uma* (Woe from Wit); Men'shikov in A. Tolstoy's *Pyotr pervyy* (Peter I), etc; *Productions:* Sardoux's "Revolutionary Wedding" (1921); Ostrovskiy's "Late Love" (1921); Yanovskiy's *Doch' prokurora* (The Prosecutor's Daughter) (1954); Arbuzov's *Gody stranstviy* (Years of Wandering) (1955); Sofronov's *Den'gi* (Money) (1956); Romashov's *Ognennyy most* (Bridge of Fire) (1957); Rozov's *V poiskakh radosti* (In Quest of Joy) (1958); "Mashen'ka" (1959); Chekhov's *Dyadya Vanya* (Uncle Vanya) (1960); *Les* (The Forest) (1962), etc; *Awards:* Order of Lenin (1960); *Died:* 4 Sept 1963.

ROMANOV, Sergey Mikhaylovich (1869–1918) Russian Grand Duke; gen of artillery from 1914; *Born:* 25 Sept 1869, son of Grand Duke Mikhail Nikolayevich and nephew of Tsar Alexander II; *Educ:* 1889 grad Mikhail Artillery College; *Career:* from July 1905 inspector-gen of artillery; Jan–June 1915 headed Artillery Distributing Commission which helped increase munitions output; Jan 1916–Apr 1917 field inspector-gen of artillery at Supr Headquarters; *Died:* 18 July 1918, together with other grand dukes, shot by Cheka in Alapayevs.

ROMANOVSKIY, Dmitriy Leonidovich (1861–1921) Therapist, hematologist and specialist in malaria; *Born:* 1861; *Educ:* 1886 grad Mil Med Acad; *Career:* after grad worked as physician at therapeutic depts of mil hospitals, including Petersburg Clinical Mil Hospital; from 1889 senior asst prof, Clinic of Internal Diseases, then prof, Polyclinic, Petersburg Clinical Inst of Postgrad Med Training; specialized in study of infectious diseases, particularly malaria; 1891 defended doctor's thesis, proposing an original method of staining blood samples in order to study the structure of blood cells and the causative agent of malaria and to observe the morphological lesions of plasmodia affected by quinine; using this new method, established the mechanism of quinine's specific action on the causative agent of malaria and preceded Ehrlich in formulating the basic principles of chemotherapy of infectious diseases in gen (etiotropic and organotropic action); his blood staining method has become widely used in med practice; most subsequent methods stem from it; *Publ: K voprosu o stroyenii chuzheyadnykh malyarii* (The Structure of Malarial Parasites) (1890); *K voprosu parazitologii i terapii bolotnoy likhoradki* (The Parasitology and Therapy of Swamp Fever) (1891); *O spetsificheskom deystvii khinina pri bolotnoy likhoradke* (The Specific Action of Quinine in Swamp Fever) (1921); *Died:* 1921.

ROMANOVSKIY, Vladimir Borisovich (1896–1959) Electr eng; Dr of Tech Sci from 1940; prof from 1937; *Born:* 1896 in Orsha; *Educ:* 1928 grad Leningrad Electr Eng Inst; *Career:* from 1928 head, Plant Laboratory, "Elektroapparat" Plant, Leningrad; from 1930 also lecturer, Leningrad Electr Eng Inst; 1932–37 lecturer, from 1937 prof and head, Chair of Theoretical Electr Eng, Leningrad's Bonch-Bruyevich Electr Eng Communications Inst; simultaneously consultant, chief electr eng and permanent member, Tech Council, "Elektroapparat" Plant; pioneered theory of high-tension apparatus; directed design of Heavy-Duty Laboratory, "Elektroapparat" Plant; devised ways of calculating transitional processes in electr circuits; wrote ober 40 research works; *Awards:* Badge of Hon; medals; *Died:* 13 Jan 1959.

ROMANOVSKIY, Vsevolod Ivanovich (1879–1954) Mathematician; member, Uzbek Acad of Sci from 1943; *Born:* 4 Dec 1879; *Educ:* 1906 grad Petersburg Univ; *Career:* 1911–15 assoc prof, then prof, Warsaw Univ; 1915–18 prof, Don Univ, Rostov; from 1918 prof, Centr Asian Univ, Tashkent; specialized in mathematical statistics and theory of propability; derived important results with Markov chains; also worked on mathematical analysis, especially the integration of differential equations with partial derivatives; *Died:* 6 Oct 1954.

ROMASHOV, Boris Sergeyevich (1895–1958) Russian playwright, journalist and drama teacher; Hon Art Worker of RSFSR from 1949; *Born:* 18 June 1895 in Petersburg; *Educ:* studied at Moscow Univ; *Career:* 1896–1916 lived in Kiev; in 1920's actor and stage dir at provincial theaters; 1924 began to write plays; from 1950 prof, Gorky Lit Inst; *Publ: Banket kapitala* (The Capitalist Banquet); *Son grazhdanina Obukhova* (Citizen Obukhov's Dream); drama "Fed'ka-Esaul" (1925); comedies: *Vozdushnyy pirog* (The Meringue) (1925); *Konets Krivoryl'ska* (The End of Krivoryl'sk) (1926); drama *Ognennyy most* (Bridge of Fire) (1929); play *Boytsy* (Warriors) (1934); comedies: *So vsyakim mozhet sluchit'sya* (It Could Happen to Anyone) (1940); *Znatnaya familiya* (A Celebrated Family) (1945); play *Velikaya sila* (The Great Force) (1947); collected articles *Dramaturg i teatr* (The Playwright and the Theater) (1953), etc; *Awards:* Stalin Prize (1948); Order of the Red Banner of Labor (1955); *Died:* 6 May 1958.

ROSHAL', Semyon Grigor'yevich (1896–1917) Politician; CP member from 1914; *Born:* 25 Jan 1896 in Petersburg; *Educ:* studied at Petersburg Psychoneurological Inst; *Career:* from 1910 in revol movement; 1912 arrested and expelled from high-school; 1914–15, while a student, did revol work at Putilov Plant for Petersburg RSDRP(B) Comt; 1915 re-arrested but soon released, drafted into Russian Army and sent to Northern Front; late 1915 returned to Petrograd and conducted anti-war propaganda among soldiers and sailors; Dec 1915 imprisoned; released during 1917 Feb Revol; by order of Party CC sent to Kronstadt; Mar 1917 elected chm, Kronstadt City RSDRP(B) Comt; deleg, 7th (Apr) All-Russian RSDRP(B) Conference; July 1917 arrested by Provisional Govt; released after 1917 Oct Revol; Oct 1917 fought against Kerenskiy and Krasnov's forces near Petrograd; helped liquidate Supr Headquarters in Mogilyov; Nov 1917 Council of Pop Comr appointed him govt comr for Rumanian Front; elected member, Rumania Front Mil-Revol Comt; Dec 1917 arrested by Whitists in Yassy during negotiations between Mil-Revol Council and Gen Shcherbachyov, dep commander of Rumanian Front; *Died:* Dec 1917 executed.

ROSHCHIN, Nikolay Vasil'yevich (1901–1960); Diplomat; amb extraordinary and plen; *Born:* 1901; *Career:* From 1948 in dipl service; 1948–49 Sov amb to Chinese Republ; 1949–52 Sov amb to Chinese Pop Republ; 1952–53 head, Southeast Asian Dept, USSR Min of For Affairs; *Died:* 1960.

ROSKIN, Aleksandr Iosifovich (1898–1941) Russian lit historian, theater historian and critic; *Born:* 7 June 1898; *Career:* 1920 first work printed; from 1930 wrote theater reviews; expert on Chekhov; *Publ: A.P. Chekhov. Stat'i i ocherki* (A.P. Chekhov. Articles and Essays) (1959); *Stat'i o literature i teatre* (Articles on Literature and Theater) (1959); *Died:* Oct 1941 killed at front.

ROSKIN, Grigoriy Iosifovich (1893–1964) Histologist; Dr of Biology; prof; *Born:* 1893; *Educ:* grad Natural Sci Dept, Moscow Univ; *Career:* from 1915 laboratory asst, asst prof, assoc prof, then prof, Chair of Cytology and Histology, Fac of Soil Biology, Moscow Univ; also founder-head, Laboratory of the Cytology and Cytochemistry of Cancer, Moscow Univ; pioneered cell chemistry in the USSR; introduced new concepts to the study of the contractile parts of cells and tissues; identified the contractile function of the interfibrillary plasma of smooth muscle cells and coined the term "myon" for the complex unit of smooth muscle and connective tissue; demonstrated the cytochemical differences between motor and sensory cells and defined the substances which constitute tigroid; developed methods of early cytological diagnosis of malignant tumors; together with M. Ye. Struve, devised a method of diagnosing isolated cancer cells by staining them with methylene blue leucobase; together with N.G. Klyuyeva developed the principles of biotherapy of malignant neoplasms and the cancer drug "crucine", which is manufactured by the Sov pharmaceutical ind; wrote some 180 works for Sov and for journals; *Publ:* coauthor, *Skeletnyy i sokratimyy apparat prosteyshikh* (The Skeletal and Contractile Apparatus of Protozoa) (1930); *Materialy k protofaune SSSR* (Material on the Protofauna of the USSR) (1930); *Terapevticheskoye deystviye protozoynykh endotoksinov na rak* (The Therapeutic Effect of Protozoic Endotoxins on Cancer) (1938); *Problema tsitdiagnostiki zlokachestvennykh kletok* (The Cytological Diagnosis of Malignant Cells) (1938); *Istoriya gistologii v Moskovskom universitete* (The History of Histology at Moscow University) (1940); *Bioterapiya zlokachestvennykh opukholey* (The Biotherapy of Malignant Tumors) (1946); *Mikroskopicheskaya tekhnika. Rukovodstvo* (Microscope Techniques. A Manual) (1946); coauthor, *Mikroskopicheskaya tekhnika* (Microscope Techniques) (1957); coauthor, *Problema protivorakovykh antibiotikov* (Cancer Antibiotics) (1957); *Plasticheskiye i vosstanovitel'nyye protsessy* (Plastic and Regenerative Processes) (1959); *Uzlovyye voprosy tsitologii* (The Crucial Questions of Cytology) (1959), etc; *Awards:* medal "For Valiant Labor" (1961), etc; *Died:* 1964 in Moscow.

ROSSIYSKIY, Dmitriy Mikhaylovich (1887–1955) Clinicist, therapist and med historian; Hon Sci Worker of RSFSR; *Born:* 1887; *Educ:* 1911 grad Med Fac, Moscow Univ; 1920 grad Natural Sci and Biological Dept, Physics and Mathematics Fac, Moscow Univ; *Career:* from 1912 intern, asst prof, assoc prof, prof, and head, Chair of Hospital Therapy Clinic, Med Fac, Moscow Univ; 1922–47 head, Chair of Polyclinic of Internal Diseases, Moscow Univ; 1948 head, Chair of Med History, 1953–55 head, Chair of Pharmacology, 1st Moscow Med Inst; helped compile first Russian manuals "Osnovy endokrinologii" (The Principles of Endocrinology) and "Klinicheskaya endokrinologiya" (Clinical Endocrinology); also studied clinical laboratory methods of research, poisons and antitoxins, balneology and diabetes insipidus; did research on substitutes for scarce med raw materials and use of wild and vitamin plants for needs of army and public; promoted practical use of Chinese Magnolia Vine (Schizandra chinensis); chm, All-Russian Soc of Endocrinologists; chm, All-Union and Moscow Med History and Research Soc; chm, All-Union Anti-Influenza Comt; chm, Comt for the Establishment and Use of Medicinal Substances; ed, journal "Russkaya klinika"; wrote over 350 works, including 150 on history of med; *Publ: O vliyanii ekstrakta iz infundibulyarnoy chasti glandulae pituitariae na obmen veshchestv u zhivotnykh* (The Effects of Infundibular Glandulae Pituitariae Extract on Animal Metabolism) (1914); *Klinicheskiye laboratornyye metody issledovaniya* (Clinical Laboratory Research Methods) (1923); *Lekarstvennyye rasteniya SSSR* (Medicinal Plants of the USSR) (1926); *Gripp* (Influenza) (1942); *Otechestvennyye lekarstvennyye rasteniya i ikh vrachebnoye primeneniye* (Native Medicinal Plants and Their Therapeutic Use) (1944); *200 let meditsinskogo fakul'teta Moskovskogo gosudarstvennogo universiteta – I Moskovskogo ordena Lenina meditsinskogo instituta* (200 Years in the Existence of the Moscow State University's Medical Faculty – the 1st Order of Lenin Moscow Medical Institute) (1955); *Istoriya vseobshchey i otechestvennoy meditsiny i zdravokhraneniya* (The History of General and Russian (Soviet) Medicine and Public Health (1956); *Died:* 1955.

ROSSOLIMO, Grigoriy Ivanovich (1860–1928) Neuropathologist; *Born:* 5 Dec 1860 in Odessa; *Educ:* 1879 grad Odessa High School; 1884 grad Med Fac, Moscow Univ; *Career:* as a med student took an immediate interest in neuropathology; in his second grade performed first independent experimental work under Prof V.Ye. Gliki in Chair of Physiology; 1883 and 1884 wrote new research works; from 1884, after grad, intern at A.Ya. Kozhevnikov's Clinic of Nervous Diseases, Moscow Univ; 1887 defended doctor's thesis on "Eksperimental'noye issledovaniye po voprosu o putyakh, provodyashchikh chuvstvitel'nost' i dvizheniye v spinnom mozgu" (An Experimental Study of the Paths Conducting Sensitivity and Movement in the Spinal Cord); from 1889 assoc prof; from 1890 headed small Clinic of Nervous Diseases, Ostroumov's Clinic of Internal Diseases; 1911 resigned from Moscow Univ along with other prof in protest against policies of Educ Min Kasso; 1911 financed and founded in Moscow Inst of Child Neurology and Psychology; direxted this inst until 1917, when he donated it to Moscow Univ; 1917 elected prof, Chair or Nervous Diseases, 1st Moscow Univ and became dir of clinic and Kozhevnikov Neurological Inst; specialized in anatomy, physiology, and clinical aspects of nervous system, experimental psychology and child defectology; first to trace course of Gower's column toward the cerebrum; first to describe circulatory zones in the afterbrain; described finger reflex, now known as Rossolimo reflex; also described anal and vulvo-anal reflexes; described syndrome of dissociated sensitivity disturbances with injuries of the spinal column; invented new methods of preparing microscopic slides; proposed surgico-toxic method of studying brain functions; contributed to diagnosis of brain tumors, multiple sclerosis and chorea; invented individual dynamometer, a clonograph for registering hyperkinesis; one of first neuropathologists to use surgical methods of treatment, based on topical diagnosis; also one of first to begin using lumbar puncture; laid groundwork for study of child inferiority and collected a mass of data on this subject; founded first European clinic for treatment of nervous diseases in children; after 1917 Oct Revol worked for Pop Comrt of Educ, Pop Comrt of Health, Pop Comrt of Labor, Revol Mil Council and Red Army's Main Mil Health Bd; co-founder and hon member, Moscow Soc of Neuropathologists and Psychiatrists; also member, Rome and Paris Acad, Acad of Philadelphia and German Soc of Neuropathologists; hon member, Est Neurological Soc; member, Pedag Soc, Psychological Soc, Soc of Experimental Psychology and Soc of Amateur Anthropologists and Ethnographists; consultant, Pop Comrt of Health; chm, Commission for the Study of Lethargic Encephalitis; member, Learned Med Council; consultant, Centr Inst for the Study of Occupational Diseases; 1926 Presidium member, Int Psychotechnics Bureau; won recognition of Russian as a nat language of the Int Association of Psychology and Psychotechnics Specialists, on a par with German, French and English; co-founder, "Zhurnal nevropatologii i psikhiatrii im. S.S. Korsakova"; edited this journal until his death in 1928; ed, neuropathology and psychiatry sections in 1st ed, "BME" (Large Medical Encyclopedia); 1960 Moscow street named for him; published 107 works; *Publ: Klinicheskiye lektsii zabolevaniy nervoy sistemy* (Clinical Lectures on Diseases of the Nervous System) (1888); *Obshchaya hkarakteristika psikhologicheskikh profiley bol'nykh nervnymi i dushevnymi boleznyami* (A General Characterization of the Psychological Profiles of Patients with Nervous and Mental Diseases) (1910); *Psikhologicheskiye profili* (Psychological Profiles) (1910); *Uchebnik nervnykh bolezney* (A Textbook on Nervous Diseases) (1923); *Kurs nervnykh bolezney* (A Course on Nervous Diseases) (1927); *Eksperimental'noye issledovaniye psikhomekhaniki po individual'nym i massovym metodam* (An Experimental Study of Psychomechanics by Individual and Mass Methods) (1928); *Awards:* many scrolls of hon and expressions of gratitude, including one expressing special recognition of Revol Mil Council; *Died:* 29 Nov 1928 in Moscow, of a stroke.

ROSTOVTSEV (real name: ROSTOVSKIY), Ivan Alekseyevich (1873–1947) Stage dir; theater organizer; actor; drama teacher; Pop Artiste of RSFSR from 1944; *Born:* 1873; *Career:* from 1892 prompter, then actor, asst stage dir, then second dir, Nizhniy Novgorod Theater; from 1900 stage dir, then chief dir at several leading provincial theaters; also directed drama companies in Vladikavkaz, Nizhniy Novgorod, Novorossiysk, Novocherkassk, Pskov, Rostov-on-Don, Yaroslavl', etc; founded Bauman 1st Moscow Workers' Theater; helped found young people's theatrical studios in Saratov and other cities; artistic dir, Arkhangel'sk, Gorky, Ivanovo, Kuybyshev, Saratov and Smolensk theaters; from 1943 artistic dir, stage dir, then artistic consultant, Yaroslavl' Volkov Theater; noted for his interpretation of Gorky's plays; did extensive drama teaching; *Works:* produced Gorky's plays: *Na dne* (The Lower Depths); *Meshchane* (Philistines); *Varvary* (The Barbarians); *Vragi* (The Foes); *Posledniye* (The Last); *Starik* (The Old Man); "Vassa Zheleznova"; *Chudaki* (The Queer Ones); also produced: "Lyubov' Yarovaya"; *Strakh* (Fear); *Kremlyovskiye kuranty* (The Kremlin Chimes); *Obyknovennyy chelovek* (The Common Man); *Russkiye lyudi* (Russian People); "Front"; "General Brusilov"; produced many plays of Ostrovskiy and Chekhov's; *Died:* 15 June 1947.

ROTSHTEYN, Fyodor Aronovich (1871–1953) Historian and politican; member, USSR Acad of Sci from 1939; CP member from 1901; *Born:* 26 Feb 1871 in Kovno; *Educ:* 1890 grad Poltava High School; *Career:* 1891 emigrated to England; from 1895 member, British Socialist Party and attended Int Socialist Congresses in Paris (1900), Amsterdam (1904) and Stuttgart (1907); from 1911 headed left wing of British Socialist Party; 1919–20 helped found Communist Party of Great Britain and "Hands off Russia" Comt; 1920 also member, Sov peace deleg in talks with British govt; 1920 returned to Russia and became chm, Commission to Revise the Curricula of Soc Sci Fac, RSFSR Council of Pop Comrt; 1921–22 RSFSR plen in Iran; 1923–30 Collegium member, Pop Comrt of For Affairs; also Presidium member, Communist Acad, State Learned Council, Socialist Acad of Soc Sci, Russian Assoc of Soc Sci Research Institutes; Collegium member, Centr Archives; lecturer at Inst of Red Prof and dir, Inst of World Econ and World Politics; chief ed, journal "Mezhdurnarodnaya zhizn'"; from 1930 also member, chief ed bd, "BSE" (Large Soviet Encyclopedia); 1931–41 also member, Commission to Publish Documents from the Archives of the Tsarist and Provisional Govts in the multi-vol *Mezhdunarodnyye otnosheniya v epokhu imperializma* (International Relations in the Age of Imperialism); wrote numerous works on the history of England, and Germany, on colonial policies and int relations; *Publ: Zakhvat i zakabaleniye Yegipta* (The Seizure and Enslavement of Egypt) (1925); *Ocherki po istorii rabochego dvizheniya v Anglii* (An Outline History of the Workers' Movement in England) (1923); *Dve prusskiye voyny* (Two Prussian Wars) (1945); *Iz istorii prussko-germanskoy imperii* (From the History of the Prussian-German Empire) (1948); *Mezhdunarodnyye otnosheniya v kontse XIX veka* (International Relations in the Late 19th Century) (1960); *Awards:* Order of Lenin; Order of the Red Banner of Labor; *Died:* 30 Aug 1953.

ROVIO, G.S. (1887–1938) Party official; CP member from 1905; *Born:* 1887; *Career:* metalworker by trade; from late 1910 lived and worked in Finland; member, Finnish Soc-Democratic Party; 1913–15 secr, CC, Finnish Soc-Democratic Youth League; Apr 1917, in connection with revol events in Finland, appointed Helsingfors police chief by workers' organizations; Aug–Sept 1917 helped conceal Lenin in Finland; 1918 active in workers' revol in Finland, then secr, Finnish Section, Northwestern Bureau, CC, CPSU(B); pro-rector, Leningrad Branch, Communist Univ of Western Nat Minorities; from July 1929 secr, Karelian Oblast CPSU(B) Comt; arrested by State Security organs; *Died:* 1938 in imprisonment.

ROYZENMAN, Boris Anisimovich (Isaak Anshelevich) (1878–1938) Revolutionary; Party and govt official; CP member from 1902; *Born:* 1878; *Career:* stoker by trade; 1899 joined revol movement; active in 1905 Revol in Cherkassy; helped organize Cherkassyggen strike; 1905 arrested and after six months' imprisonment exiled for two years to Kherson Province; went underground and moved to Yekaterinoslav, where he served as Party org and propagandist in workers' circles; 28 Apr 1908 arrested for planning May Day demonstration; after three years' imprisonment exiled to Cherkassy; from 1903 founded health insurance orgs; again exiled, but continued underground Party work in Yekaterinoslav; 1916 drafted into Russian Army, where he continued revol propaganda and agitation among troops; after 1917 Feb Revol Presidium member, Yekaterinoslav Sov of Workers Dep and member, Yekaterinoslav Province Party Comt; member, Yekaterinoslav Party Mil Org; Yekaterinoslav deleg at 6th Party Congress; deleg, Congress of Mil Orgs, Petrograd; 1918–19 RSFSR Council of Pop Comr plen for evacuation of Arkhangel'sk city and port; 1919 RSFSR Council of Pop Comr plen for supply of 8th and 9th Armies on Southern Front; late 1919 RSFSR Defense Council plen in Urals, responsible for export of metal; from 1921 member, Bd, State Assoc of Machine-Building Plants; at the 12th Party Congress elected cand member, CPSU(B) Centr Control Commission; at the 13th–16th Party Congresses elected member, CPSU(B) Centr Control Commission; at the 17th CPSU(B) Congress elected member, Sov Control Commission; from 1924 Presidium member, Centr Control Commission and Collegium member, USSR Pop Comrt of Workers and Peasants' Inspection; also head of latter's Section for the Control and Verification of Fulfillment; 1934–38 dep chm, Sov Control Commission, USSR Council of Pop Comr; arrested by State Security organs; *Awards:* Order of Lenin; *Died:* 1938 in imprisonment.

ROZANOV, Ivan Nikanorovich (1874–1959) Russian lit historian; Dr of Philology from 1939; prof from 1918; *Born:* 22 Aug 1874; *Educ:* 1899 grad Moscow Univ; *Career:* 1900 first work printed; specialized in history of Russian poetry, Russian mass songs and prosody; established authorship of a number of pop mass songs; *Publ: Russkaya lirika* (Russian Lyric Works) (2 vol, 1914–23); *Poety dvadtsatykh godov XIX veka* (Poets of the 1820's) (1925); *Pesni russkikh poetov* (Songs of the Russian Poets) (1936); *Stikhotvornyye razmery v donekrasovskoy poezii i u Nekrasova* (Prosodic Meter in Pre-Nekrasovian Poetry and in Nekrasov) (1939); *Lermontov – master stikha* (Lermontov – Master of Verse) (1942); *Russkiye pesni* (Russian Songs) (1952); *Died:* 22 Nov 1959.

ROZANOV, Vladimir Nikolayevich (1872–1934) Surgeon; Hero of Labor from 1923; *Born:* 15 Feb 1872 in Moscow, son of a physician; *Educ:* 1896 grad Med Fac, Moscow Univ; *Career:* 1896–1910 intern, Staro-Yekaterininskaya Hospital, Moscow; from 1910 founder-head, Surgical Dept, Soldatenkov (now S.P. Botkin) Hospital; simultaneously lecturer, Shanyavskiy Pop Univ; during WW 1 organized med supplies for Moscow and League of Cities; founded Therapeutic Prosthetic Inst and Prosthetics Plant; 1918–20 head, Med Service, Russian Red Cross Soc; from 1919 consultant, Kremlin Sanitary Bd; 24 Apr 1922 performed operation on Lenin at Botkin Hospital for a bullet wound received in assassination attempt; 1927 organized postgrad surgery courses at Botkin Hospital; from 1929 head, Surgical Dept, Kremlin Hospital; 1929–30 dep Moscow City Sov and member; Moscow Oblast Exec Comt; from 1930 collegium member, RSFSR Pop Comrt of Health; from 1931 head, Chair of Surgery, Centr Inst of Postgrad Med Training; founder-ed, journal "Sovremennaya khirurgiya"; member, ed bds, journals "Sovetskiy khirurg" and "Vestnik khirurgii i pogranichnykh oblastey"; member, ed bd, "Bol'shaya meditsinskaya entsiklopediya" (Large Medical Encyclopedia) (1st ed); the 10th Dept at Botkin Hospital now bears his name; *Publ: O perelomakh nadkolennoy chashki* (Fractures of the Kneecap) (1899); *Polnoye udaleniye gortani i rezektsiya pishchevoda* (Total Removal of the Larynx and Resection of the Oesophagus) (1904); *Rezektsia slepoy kishki pri novoobrazovaniyakh* (Resection of the Caecum in the Case of Neoplasm) (1906); *Amputatsiya i protezy* (Amputations and Prosthetics) (1922); *Spazm i nedostatochnost' bauginovoy zaslonki* (Spasma and Insufficiency of Bauhin's Valve) (1923); *Appenditsit* (Appendicitis) (1927); *Awards:* Order of Lenin (1933); *Died:* 16 Oct 1934 in Moscow.

ROZANOV, V.N. (pseudonyms: MARTYN; POPOV) (1876–1939) Politician; *Born:* 1876; *Career:* one of leaders, "Southern Worker" group; helped publish newspaper "Yuzhnyy rabochiy"; late 1890's joined Soc-Democratic movement in Moscow; 1900 joined Southern Worker group in Smolensk; 1901–03 worked in Odessa, Kiev and Khar'kov; vehemently opposed merger of Southern Worker group with "Iskra" org; represented Southern Worker group in Org Comt for Convening 2nd RSDRP Congress; Southern Worker group deleg at 2nd RSDRP Congress, where he adopted a centrist stand; after Congress, sided with Mensheviks; 1904 coopted member, CC, RSDRP; May 1905 at RSDRP (Mensheviks) Conference elected member, Org Commission /Mensheviks' exec organ/; worked in Southern Russia; at 4th (Amalgamative) Party Congress elected member, CC, on behalf of Mensheviks; 1908 emigrated; 1912 in Berlin helped publish Menshevik journal "Russisches Bulletin"; after 1917 Feb Revol member, Menshevik faction, Petrograd Sov; adopted defensist stand; opposed Oct Revol and worked for various counterrevol orgs; sentenced to death in trial of "Tactical Center"; sentence commuted to imprisonment for the duration of the Civil War; after amnesty, abandoned politics and worked for Sov med institutions; arrested by State Security organs; *Died:* 1939 in imprisonment.

ROZEN-SANIN, Mikhail Nikolayevich (1877–1956) Actor; Hon Art Worker of RSFSR from 1947; *Born:* 19 Mar 1877; *Career:* 1893 stage debut; 1898–1914 actor, Pop Center Theater, Petersburg; 1917–18 actor, Volkov Theater, Yaroslavl'; 1920–21 actor, Krasnodar Theater; 1924-56 actor, Moscow City Trade-Union Council (later Moscow City Sov) Theater; *Roles:* Franz Moor; Shylock; Lear; Paganel in "The Children of Captain Grant", after Jules Verne; Kuzovkin in Turgenev's *Nakhlebnik* (The Sponger); Plyuskhin in Gogol's *Myortvyye dushi* (Dead Souls); Boris Godunov in A.K. Tolstoy's *Smert' Ivana Groznogo* (The Death of Ivan the Terrible); Vanyushin in Naydyonov's *Deti Vanyushina* (Vanyushin's Children); Chadov in Bill'-Belotserkovskiy's *Zhizn' zovyot* (Life Is Calling); Tamerlanov in Nikitin's *Apsheronskaya noch'* (Apsheron Night); Gnevyshev in Ostrovskiy's *Bogatyye nevesty* (Rich Brides); Kessler in Simonov's *Russkiy vopros* (The Russian Question); Bek in *Svad'ba Krechinskogo* (Krechinskiy's Wedding); *Died:* 27 Dec 1956.

ROZENBERG,David Iokhelevich (1879–1950) Economist; Dr of Econ from 1934; prof from 1924; corresp member, USSR Acad of Sci from 1939; CP member from 1920; *Born:* 9 Dec 1879 in Lith, son of a poor Jew; *Career:* 1904 joined Jewish Bund; 1914–17 exiled to Narym Kray; from 1917 journalist in Tomsk; from 1920 lecturer in polit econ, Omsk Communist Univ; 1924–31 prof of polit econ, Krupskaya Acad of Communist Training; 1931–37 prof of polit econ, Econ Inst of Red Prof; 1937–41 prof of polit econ, Moscow Univ; from 1936 also assoc, Inst of Econ, USSR Acad of Sci; 1941–43, prof of polit econ, Kazan' Univ; 1945–48 senior assoc, Marx-Engels-Lenin Inst, CC, CPSU(B); *Publ: Kommentarii k Kapitalu Karla Marksa* (Commentaries to Karl Marx's "Capital") (3 vol, 1930–33); *Istoriya politicheskoy ekonomii* (The History of Political Economy) (3 vol, 1934–36); *Ocherki razvitiya ekonomicheskogo ucheniya Marksa i Engel'sa v sorokovyye gody XIX veka* (Studies on the Development of Marx and Engel's Economic Theory in the 1840's) (1954); *Awards:* Order of the Red Banner of Labor; *Died:* 17 Feb 1950.

ROZENBERG, Nikolay Konstantinovich (1876–1933) Infectionist; *Born:* 1876; *Educ:* 1899 grad Mil Med Acad; *Career:* after grad stayed on at Acad for postgrad studies; worked for Chair of Eye Diseases, then Chair of Acute Infectious Diseases; 1901 defended doctor's thesis; from 1902 intern, Tiraspol' Mil Hospital; transferred to Caucasus as a result of his liberal attitude to the troops and only two years later returned to Tiraspol'; from 1911 senior asst prof, Chair of Acute Infectious Diseases, Mil Med Acad; 1915 took part in anti-epidemic campaigns in the Caucasus and Iran, and 1916 in Turkestan; from 1921 prof, Chair of Infectious Diseases, State Inst of Med Knowledge; 1923–29 pro-rector, above inst; from 1924 prof, Chair of Infectious Diseases, Mil Med Acad; studied pathophysiology of various infectious diseases; studied and described clinical treatment of typhus, pathogenesis of tetanus, clinical treatment of influenza, immunity and anaphylaxia; extremely well versed in microbiology, parasitology, physiology, pathoanatomy, etc; wrote over 50 works; *Publ: Eksperimental'nyye materialy k ucheniyu ob otravnykh vospaleniyakh zritel'nogo nerva i setchatki* (Experimental Data on the Theory of Poisonous Inflammations of the Optic Nerve and the Retina) (1901); *Klinika sypnogo tifa* (The Clinical Treatment of Typhus) (1920); *K etiologii ranevogo stolbnyaka* (The Etiology of Wound Tetanus) (1925); *Klinika grippa, vrach i dinamika sepsisov* (The Clinical Treatment of Influenza, the Physician and the Course of Sepsis) (1933); *Infektsionnyye bolezni s osnovami epidemiologii* (Infectious Diseases with the Principles of Epidemiology) (1934); *Died:* 1933.

ROZENGOL'TS, Arkadiy Pavlovich (1889–1938) Economist; Party and govt official; CP member from 1905; *Born:* 1889; *Career:* Party work in Vitebsk, Kiev, Yekaterinoslav, etc; 1907 arrested for revol activities; 1915 banished from Moscow; after 1917 Feb Revol elected Presidium member, Moscow Sov; during 1917 Oct Revol member, Mil-Revol Comt's five-man group to direct the revolt in Moscow; 1918–21 fought in Civil War; member, RSFSR Revol Mil Council; member, Revol Mil Councils of 5th, 8th, 7th, 13th, then 15th Armies; 1918 member, Moscow Oblast Council of Pop Comr and cand Presidium member, All-Russian Centr Exec Comt; 1922 Collegium member, RSFSR Pop Comrt of Finance; 1923–24 member, Revol Mil Council and chief, Main Bd of Air Fleet; 1925–27 counsellor, USSR Mission in Britain and actg Sov plen in Britain; from 1928 Collegium member, USSR Pop Comrt of Workers and Peasants' Inspection, then USSR Dep Pop Comr of Trade; from Nov 1930 USSR Pop Comr of For Trade; at 15th and 16th Party Congresses elected member, CPSU(B) Centr Control Commission and Presidium member, Centr Control Commission; at 17th Party Congress elected cand member, CC, CPSU(B); 1935 elected member, USSR Centr Exec Comt; during 1920–21 trade-union controversy sided with "Trotskyist opposition"; 1923 signed Trotskyist platform; 1937 expelled from Party for alleged anti-Party and anti-Sov activities; Mar 1938 brought to trial for membership in "anti-Sov rightist Trotskyist bloc"; 18 Mar 1938 sentenced to death by Mil Collegium of USSR Supr Court; *Died:* 18 Mar 1938 executed.

ROZENSHTEYN, Lev Markovich (1884–1934) Psychiatrist, psychopathologist and health official; CP member from 1931; *Born:* 1884, son of a physician; *Educ:* 1908 grad Med Fac, Moscow Univ; *Career:* 1906 exiled from Odessa for polit activities; after grad, intern, V.P. Serbskiy's Psychiatric Clinic; 1911–13 asst prof, Psychiatric Clinic, Moscow Higher Women's Courses; 1914 proposed establishment of out-patient centers for treatment of alcoholics; for a number of years worked with P.B. Gannushkin and associated with group of psychiatrists running journal "Sovremennaya psikhiatriya"; 1924–35 founder-dir, first Sov out-patient center for treatment of nervous and mental diseases (Inst of Neuropsychiatric Prophylaxis), RSFSR Pop Comrt of Health; 1930 represented USSR at 1st Int Congress on Mental Health, Washington; 1930 vice-pres, Int Committee on Mental Health; from 1931 head, Chair of Psychiatry, Centr Inst of Postgrad Med Training; Moscow; 1931 elected chm, Commission for the Reconstruction of the Psychiatric Service, RSFSR Pop Comrt of Health; did major research on psychiatric methods; advocated a combined nosological and psychopathological approach to description and interpretation of mental phenomena; made a special study of role of external factors in development of mental disease and investigated development and prevention of occupational mental dieseases; helped to formulate legislation on mental illness; wrote some 100 works; *Publ: K voprosu o lechenii alkogolizma* (The Treatment of Alcoholism) (1917); *O korsakovskoy bolezni i o svoyeobraznoy klinicheskoy forme alkogol'no-arterioskleroticheskogo zabolevaniya melkikh sosudov golovnogo mozga* (Polyneuritic Psychosis and an Unusual Case of Alcohol Arteriosclerosis of the Small Vessels of the Brain) (1921); *Psikhicheskiye faktory v etiologii dushevnykh bolezney* (Mental Factors in the Etiology of Mental Diseases) (1923); *Voprosy psikhiatrii v svete professional'noy patologii* (Problems of Psychiatry in the Light of Occupational Pathology) (1926); *Profilaktika nervnykh i psikhicheskikh bolezney* (The Prevention of Nervous and Mental Diseases) (1927); *Psikhotravmatizm* (Psychotraumatism) (1928); *Raspoznavaniye boleznennykh nervnopsikhicheskikh otkloneniy pri psikhogigiyenicheskikh obsledovaniyakh* (The Detection of Pathological Nervous and Mental Deviations During Mental Health Examinations) (1930); *Died:* 1934 in Moscow.

ROZHANSKIY, Dmitriy Apollinariyevich (1882–1936) Physicist; corresp member, USSR Acad of Sci from 1933; *Born:* 1 Sept 1882 in Kiev; *Educ:* 1904 grad Petersburg Univ; *Career:* 1905–06 worked at Goettingen Univ; 1911–21 prof, Khar'kov Univ; 1911 devised original method of obtaining an oscillogram of the current and electromotive force of a high-voltage spark; 1911–31 did extensive research on the theory and applications of electric oscillations and waves; 1921–23 worked at Nizhniy Novgorod Radio Laboratory; from 1923 assoc, Centr Radio Laboratory, Leningrad; also worked at Leningrad Physiotech and Polytech Inst; helped to develop short-wave transmitters; also did research on frequency stabilization in tube generators and short-wave propagation; in latter years did research on gas discharge and ran a radar research laboratory; *Publ: Elektricheskiye luchi. Ucheniye ob elektromagnitnykh kolebaniyakh i volnakh* (Electric Rays. The Theory of Electromagnetic Oscillations and Waves) (1913); *Kolebaniya i volny. Zvuk. Svet* (Oscillations and Waves. Sound. Light) (1931); *Metod izmereniya dielektricheskikh postoyannykh i absorbtsii pri vysokikh chastotakh* (A Method of Measuring Dialectric Constants and Absorption at High Frequencies) (1933); *Akustika i optika* (Acoustics and Optics) (1935); *Fizicheskiye osnovaniya teorii rasprostraneniya korotkikh voln* (The Physical Bases of Short-Wave Propagation Theory) (1934); *Fizika gazovogo razryada* (The Physics of Gas Discharge) (1937); *Died:* 27 Sept 1936.

ROZHANSKIY, Nikolay Apollinariyevich (1884–1957) Physiologist; Dr of Med from 1913; prof from 1921; member, USSR Acad of Med Sci from 1945; Hon Sci Worker of RSFSR from 1947; *Born:* 28 June 1884; *Educ:* 1909 grad Med Fac, Kiev Univ; *Career:* specialized in physiology under I. P. Pavlov; 1912–16 worked at Chair of Physiology, Moscow Univ; 1913 defended doctor's thesis on the physiology of sleep; 1914–16 gave special course on practical physiology at the Physiological Laboratory, Moscow Univ; 1916–20 assoc prof, from 1921 prof, Chair of Physiology, Rostov Med Inst; founder-chm, Rostov Physiologists' Soc; founded several laboratories and sci inst in Rostov-on-Don; co-ed, physiology section, "Bol'shaya meditsinskaya entsiklopediya" (Large Medical Encyclopedia) (2nd ed); co-ed, various sci journals; did major research on the physiology of digestion; in latter years studied the functions of the subcortical section of the brain; on the basis of Pavlov's structural theory; wrote over 200 works; *Publ:* doctor's thesis *Materialy k fiziologii sna* (Material on the Physiology of Sleep) (1913); *Prakticheskiye zanyatiya po fiziologii zhivotnykh* (Practical Studies in Animal Physiology) (1932); *Ocherki po fiziologii nervnoy sistemy* (Studies in the Physiology of the Nervous System) (1957), etc; *Died:* 25 Nov 1957 in Rostov-on-Don.

ROZHDESTVENSKIY, Dmitriy Sergeyevich (1876–1940) Physicist; Dr of Physics and Mathematics from 1915; prof from 1916; member, USSR Acad of Sci from 1929; *Born:* 7 Apr 1876 in Petersburg; *Educ:* 1900 grad Petersburg Univ; also studied at

Leipzig Univ; *Career:* 1903–07 asst prof, Petersburg Univ; 1907–10 did research at Sorbonne; 1912–16 assoc prof, from 1916 prof, Petersburg (Leningrad) Univ; 1915–18 also, dir, Physics Inst, Petrograd Univ; 1918–32 founder-dir, State Optical Inst; also headed various research laboratories; 1909 devised widely used method of determining anomalous dispersion in the vapors of various metals ("crutch method"); also contributed to the theory and systematics of atomic spectra; hypothesized the magnetic origin of spectral doublets and triplets; also worked on microscope theory; helped to organize Sov optical ind; *Publ: Anomal'naya dispersiya v parakh natriya* (Anomalous Disperion in Sodium Vapors) (1912); *Prostyye sootnosheniya v spektrakh shchelochnykh metallov* (Simple Interrelationships in the Spectra of Alkaline Metals) (1915); *Spektral'nyy analiz i stroyeniye atomov* (Spectral Analysis and Atomic Structure) (1920); *K voprosu ob izobrazhenii prozrachnykh ob'yektov v mikroskopii* (Obtaining Images of Transparent Objects in Microscopy) (1941); *Raboty po anomal'noy dispersii v parakh metallov* (Works on Anomalous Dispersion in Metallic Vapors) (1950); *Died:* 25 June 1940.

ROZHDESTVENSKIY, Sergey Vasil'yevich (1868–1934) Russian historian; Dr of Historical Sci from 1912; corresp member, USSR Acad of Sci from 1920; *Born:* 6 Sept 1868; *Educ:* 1891 grad Petersburg Univ; *Career:* until 1917 prof, Petersburg Women's Teachers Training Inst; from 1917 prof, 1st and 2nd Leningrad Teachers' Training Inst; specialized in socio-econ history of Muscovy in 14th–17th Centuries and history of enlightenment in Russia in 18th–19th Centuries; ran foul of Party authorities during reorg of Russian Acad of Sci and influx of Marxist historians into reorganized USSR Acad of Sci; 1930 arrested on charges of complicity in a "monarchist plot" against the USSR; *Publ: Sluzhiloye zemlevladeniye v Moskovskom gosudarstve XVI veka* (Military Land Tenure in Muscovy in the 16th Century) (1897); *Istoricheskiy obzor deyatel'nosti Ministerstva narodnogo prosveshcheniya* (A Historical Review of the Work of the Ministry of Public Education) (1902); *Ocherki po istorii sistem narodnogo prosveshcheniya v Rossii v XVIII-XIV vekakh* (An Outline History of Public Education Systems in Russia in the 18th and 19th Centuries) (1912); *Pervonachal'noye obrazovaniye Sankt-Peterburgskogo universiteta 8 fevralya 1819 goda i yego blizhayshaya sud'ba* (The Original Founding of Saint Petersburg University on 8 February 1819 and Its Immediate Fate) (1919); *Osnovy sotsial'noy organizatsii pedagogicheskogo truda v XVII-XIX vekakh* (The Principles of the Social Organization of Pedagogic Work in the 18th and 19th Centuries) (1923); *Dvinskiye boyare i dvinskoye khozyaystvo XIV-XVI vekov* (The Dvinsk Boyars and the Dvinsk Economy in the 14th–16th Centuries) (2 vol, 1929); *Died:* 17 June 1934 in imprisonment.

ROZHKOV, Nikolay Aleksandrovich (1868–1927) Historian, journalist and politician; prof from 1922; *Born:* 5 Nov 1868; *Educ:* 1890 grad Fac of History and Philology, Moscow Univ; *Career:* from 1898 assoc prof, Moscow Univ; 1904–05 chm, Moscow Pedag Soc; 1905 ed, Bolshevik newspaper "Bor'ba"; 1906 joined RSDRP and sided with Bolsheviks; 1906 lecturer, Moscow Bolshevik Comt and ed, Bolshevik newspaper "Svetoch"; 1906–07 lecturer, Petersburg Bolshevik Comt; 1906 and 1907 deleg, 4th and 5th RSDRP Congresses; elected member, CC at latter; 1907–08 member, Russian Bureau, CC, RSDRP; Apr 1908 arrested; 1910 exiled to Eastern Siberia; during exile joined Mensheviks, contributed to their journal "Nasha zarya" and edited their newspaper "Novaya Sibir'"; after 1917 Feb Revol returned to Moscow and joined Soc-Democratic group favoring reunion of various factions; appointed Dep Min of Posts and Telegraphs in Provisional Govt; Aug 1917 rejoined Menshevik Party and was elected to CC; opposed Oct Revol; in early 1920's arrested twice on polit grounds; 1922 resigned from Menshevik Party but did not join Bolsheviks; lectured at Leningrad and Moscow Univ, Inst of Red Prof, Inst of History, and Krupskaya Acad of Communist Training; also worked at Historical Museum; 1926–27 co-ed, history section, "BSE" (Large Soviet Encyclopedia); favored the comparative historical method and viewed the historical process as a succession of evolutionary and revol epochs, whereby he treated revol as "accelerated evolution"; considered the Oct Revol as historical accident; *Publ: Sel'skoye khozyaystvo Moskovskoy Rusi v XVI veke* (Agriculture in 16th-Century Muscovite Rus) (1899); *Proiskhozhdeniye samoderzhaviya v Rossii* (The Emergence of Autocracy in Russia) (1900); *Gorod i derevnya v russkoy istorii* (Town and Village in Russian History) (1902); *Obzor russkoy istorii s sotsiologicheskoy tochki zreniya* (A Review of Russian History from the Sociological Viewpoint) (2 vol, 1903–05); *Osnovnyye zakony razvitiya obshchestvennykh yavleniy* (The Basic Laws of the Development of Social Phenomena) (1907); *Russkaya istoriya v sravnitel'no-istoricheskom osveshchenii* (A Comparative View of Russian History) (12 vol, 1918–26); *Iz russkoy istorii* (From Russian History) (2 vol, 1923), etc; *Died:* 2 Feb 1927.

ROZIN', Fritsis Adamovich (1870–1919) Lat Party and soc functionary; co-founder, CP Lat; journalist; *Born:* 7 Mar 1870, son of a peasant; *Educ:* 1891–97 studied at Med and Law Fac, Tartu Univ; *Career:* 1897 arrested and returned to his native vil under police supervision for revol activities; 1899 emigrated to England, where he represented Lat Soc-Democratic movement and edited its journals "Latviesu Stradnieks" and "Socialdemokrats"; Nov 1905 illegally returned to Lat and directed Party press of Lat Kray Soc-Democratic Party; 1907 attended 5th RSDRP Congress and elected member, CC, RSDRP; 1908 arrested and sentenced to four years at hard labor, followed by settlement for life in Siberia; 1913 fled from exile and went to America; 1917 returned to Lat; Dec 1917 as chm, Exec Comt, Sov of Workers, Soldiers and Landless Dep, headed first Sov Lat govt; from Mar 1918 in Moscow; Presidium member and dep chm, All-Russian Centr Exec Comt; Comr for Lat Affairs and RSFSR Dep Pop Comr of Nationalities; from Mar 1919 for a while Comr of Agric in new Sov Lat govt; wrote articles and books on Marxist philosophy, int workers' movement and agrarian relations in Lat; *Died:* 7 May 1919.

ROZMIROVICH, Yelena Fyodorovna (Party pseudonyms: GALINA; TROYANOVSKAYA) (1886–1953) Party and govt official; CP member from 1904; *Born:* 10 Mar 1886 in Petropavlovsk, Kherson Province; *Educ:* 1903 grad Yelizavetgrad high-school; *Career:* from 1904 Party work in Kiev; from 1907 frequently arrested and finally deported from Russia; lived in France and Austria and carried out commissions for For Bureau; CC, RSDRP; 1913 attended Poronin and Cracow Party CC Conferences; sent back to Russia; 1914–15 secr, Bolshevik faction, 4th State Duma; secr, Russian Bureau, CC, RSDRP; member, ed bd, newspaper "Pravda"; 1915 attended conference of foreign RSDRP sections and Socialist Women's Conference in Bern; early 1916 arrested in Russia and exiled to Turukhan' Kray; during 1917 Feb Revol member, Irkutsk Party Comt; deleg at 7th (Apr) All-Russian RSDRP(B) Conference and All-Russian Conference of Front and Rear RSDRP(B) Mil Orgs; member, Centr Bureau, Mil Org, CC, RSDRP(B); during 1917 Oct Revol worked for Mil Revol Comt; 1918–22 chm, Investigating Commission, Supr Tribunal of All-Russian Centr Exec Comt; 1922–30 Collegium member, USSR Pop Comrt of Workers and Peasants' Inspection; 1931–33 Collegium member, USSR Pop Comrt of Means of Communication; 1935–39 dir, Lenin State Public Library; deleg at 13th–15th Party Congresses; from 1924 member, CPSU(B) Centr Control Commission; 1927–30 Presidium member, CPSU(B) Centr Control Commission; member, All-Union Centr Exec Comt of 3rd–5th convocations; *Died:* 30 Aug 1953.

RUBANOV, Stepan Ul'yanovich (1901–1961) Mil commander; col-gen, Air Force; CP member from 1926; *Born:* 28 Oct 1901; *Educ:* 1932 grad mil pilots school; *Career:* from 1919 in in Red Army; fought in Civil War; during WW 2 commanded Air Force div, then corps; after WW 2 various commands in Sov Air Force; from 1959 pensioner; *Died:* 8 Jan 1961.

RUBASHKIN, Vladimir Yakovlevich (1876–1932) Histologist; *Born:* 17 Apr 1876; *Educ:* 1900 grad Mil Med Acad, Petersburg; *Career:* dir, Higher Women's Med Courses, Yur'yev (now Tartu); from 1918 prof, Khar'kov Med Inst; from 1923 also dir, Ukr Protozoal Inst; specialized in histology of nervous system, particularly ependyma and neuroglia in mammals; wrote standand textbook on histology; *Publ: K ucheniyu o stroyenii nevroglii i ependimy* (The Theory of the Structure of the Neuroglia and Ependyma) (1903); *Krovyanyye gruppy* (Blood Groups) (1929); *Osnovy gistologii i gistogeneza cheloveka* (The Principles of Human Histology and Histogenesis) (1931–33); *Died:* 1932.

RUBEL', Arkadiy Nikolayevich (1867–1938) Therapist, phthisiatrist and health service official; Dr of Med from 1909; prof from 1920; *Born:* 22 Aug 1867 in Odessa; *Educ:* 1891 grad Petersburg Mil Med Acad; *Career:* while still a student began specializing in therapy and pathological physiology; spent a year in Vienna, where he worked in Prof Notnagel's Therapeutic Clinik and attended Prof Stricker's lectures on gen pathology; 1893–1900 intern, Therapeutic Dept, Petersburg (now 25 Oct Memorial) Hospital; then intern and asst prof, Therapeutic Clinic, Petersburg Women's (now 1st Leningrad) Med Inst; 1903–04 dir, Andreyevskiy Koumiss Sanatorium; from 1911 assoc prof, Petrograd Women's Med Inst; 1915 founded Sanatorium and Health Resort Commission, League of Cities; 1918–24 co-founder and dir Centr Lung Patients' Station, Petrograd; from 1920 assoc prof, Petrograd Inst of Postgrad Med Training and prof, 2nd Leningrad Med Inst (now Leningrad Inst of Sanitation and Hygiene); a koumiss sanatorium in Bashkir ASSR now bears his name; did major research on the pathology of the lungs and on the clinical aspects and treatment of tuberculosis; wrote over 80 works; *Publ:* doctor's thesis *K ucheniyu o deystvii Bierovskoy zastoynoy giperemii na mestnyy tuberkulyoznyy protsess* (The Theory of the Effect of Bier's Engorged Hyperemia on the Local Tubercular Process) (1909); *Iskusstvennyy pnevmotoraks pri lechenii tuberkulyoza lyogkikh* (Artificial Pneumothorax in the Treatment of Pulmonary Tuberculosis) (1912); *Voprosy patologii i kliniki zabolevaniy lyogkikh* (The Pathology and Clinical Aspects of Lung Diseases) (1925); *Nachal'nyye formy tuberkulyoza lygokikh* (Incipient Forms of Pulmonary Tuberculosis) (1927); coauthor, *Chastnaya patologiya i terapiya vnutrennikh bolezney* (The Special Pathology and Therapy of Internal Diseases) (1931); *Died:* 17 Apr 1938; buried at Bogoslovskoye Cemetery, Leningrad.

RUBIN, Abram Izrailevich (1883–1918) Revolutionary; *Born:* 1883; *Career:* Nov 1917 helped establish Sov regime in Novorossiysk; from Dec 1917 member, from Mar 1918 chm, Black Sea Province Exec Comt; June 1918 elected chm, Centr Exec Comt of Kuban'-Black Sea Sov Republ; from 7 July 1918 chm, Centr Exec Comt of North Caucasian Sov Republ; member, North Caucasian Kray RCP(B) Comt; 1918 arrested in Pyatigorsk by Sov mil commander of Northern Caucasus, Sorokin; *Died:* 21 Oct 1918 executed by Sorokin; Pyatigorsk street named after him.

RUBINSHTEYN, German Rafailovich (1871–1955) Phthisiatrist; Hon Sci Worker of RSFSR; *Born:* 1871; *Educ:* 1896 grad Med Fac, Yur'yev Univ; *Career:* from 1896 asst prof, Chair of Pathoanatomy and Hospital Therapy Clinic, Yur'yev Univ; 1897 defended doctor's thesis; worked at V. P. Obraztsov's Clinic in Kiev; directed "Pushcha-Voditsa" Tuberculosis Sanatorium for children; sci dir, Lenin Tuberculosis Sanatorium of All-Russian Centr Trade-Union Council, Kratovo; also head, Chair of Tuberculosis, Centr Inst of Postgrad Med Training, Moscow; 1941–50 also head, Chair of Tuberculosis, 1st Moscow Med Inst; established that initial form of pulmonary tuberculosis in adults is a focal process; his clinical grouping of forms of tuberculosis provided the basis for the present Sov classification of this disease; wrote manual on differential diagnosis of pulmonary diseases; did research on means of isolating tubercular bacilli in man and animals; stressed need for early active treatment of patients with initial forms of pulmonary and pleural tuberculosis; wrote over 100 works; *Publ: Klinicheskaya gruppirovka lyogochnogo tuberkulyoza* (The Clinical Grouping of Pulmonary Tuberculosis) (1936); *Oshibki v klinike lyogochnogo tuberkulyoza* (Errors in the Clinical Treatment of Pulmonary Tuberculosis) (1941); *Tuberkulyoz lyogkikh* (Tuberculosis of the Lungs) (1948); *Differentsial'naya diagnostika zabolevaniy lyogkikh* (Differential Diagnosis of Pulmonary Diseases) (2 vol, 1949–50); *Problema nasledstvennosti pri tuberkulyoze* (The Problem of Heredity and Tuberculosis) (1951); *Died:* 1955.

RUBINSHTEYN, Sergey Leonidovich (1889–1960) Psychologist and philosopher; corresp member, USSR Acad of Sci from 1943; member, RSFSR Acad of Pedag Sci from 1945; *Born:* 18 June 1889 in Odessa; *Educ:* 1913 grad Novorossiysk Univ, Odessa; *Career:* from 1915 taught psychology and logic at a high-school; from 1919 assoc prof, Chair of Philosophy and Psychology, Odessa Univ; from 1921 also head, Chair of Psychology, Odessa Inst of Educ; 1932–42 head, Chair of Psychology, Leningrad's Herzen Teachers' Training Inst; 1942–50 head, Chair of Psychology, Moscow Univ; 1942–45 also dir, Inst of Psychology, Moscow; from 1945 head, Psychology Section, and dep dir, Inst of Philosophy, USSR Acad of Sci; specialized in theory, philosophical aspects and history of psychology; *Publ: Osnovy psikhologii* (The Principles of Psychology) (1935); *Osnovy obshchey psikhologii* (The Principles of General Psychology) (1940); *Bytiye i soznaniye* (Existence and Consciousness) (1957); *O myshlenii i putyakh yego issledovaniya* (Thinking and Ways of Studying It) (1958); *Printsipy i puti razvitiya psikhologii* (The Principles and Paths of the Development of Psychology) (1959); *Awards:* Stalin Prize (1942); *Died:* 11 Jan 1960.

RUDAKOV, Aleksandr Petrovich (1910–1966) Russian mining eng; secr, CC, CPSU from 1962; member, CC, CPSU from 1962; CP member from 1931; *Born:* 11 Sept 1910 in Pologi, Zaporozhian Oblast; *Educ:* 1937 grad Leningrad Mining Inst; *Career:* 1927–30 miner in Donbass; 1936–37 Komsomol work; 1938–42 and 1944–54 worked for CC, CP Ukr; 1941 plen, Mil Council of Southwestern Front; 1942–44 worked for CC, CPSU(B); 1954–62 head, Dept of Heavy Ind, CC, CPSU; 1962–64 chm, Bureau for Ind and Construction, CC, CPSU; 1954 elected member, CC, CP Ukr; 1956 elected member, CC, CP Lith; deleg at 20th–22nd CPSU Congresses; 1956–62 cand member, CC, CPSU; dep, Ukr Supr Sov and 1947 and 1951 convocations; dep, USSR Supr Sov of 1962 and 1966 convocations; *Awards:* Order of Lenin (1957); *Died:* 10 July 1966; buried on Moscow's Red Square.

RUDAKOV, I. G. (1883–1937) Govt official; CP member from 1905; *Born:* 1883; *Career:* after 1917 Oct Revol exec work in nat econ; 1919 member, Northern Rayon Sovnarkhoz; 1920 head, Petrograd Fuel Dept; later Bel Pop Comr of Forestry Ind; elected member, USSR Centr Exec Comt; arrested by State Security organs; *Died:* 1937 in imprisonment.

RUDIN, Yakov Mikhaylovich (1900–1941) Russian actor, playwright and satirist; *Born:* 30 May 1900; *Educ:* 1918 grad Higher Theatrical College, former Alexandrine Theater; *Career:* 1919–20 Alexandrine Theater; 1921–23 at Mogilev Theater; 1924–41 at Moscow Satire Theater; also did variety work; talented comedian; *Roles:* the Resident in Erdman's *Moskva s tochki zreniya* (Moscow from One Point of View); Bibnev in Ardov and Nikulin's *Tarakanovshchina* (Cockroachism); Pashkovskiy in Ardov's *Melkiye kozyri* (Small Trumps); Pribylev and Semyorkin in Shkvarkin's *Chuzhoy rebyonok* (Another's Child) and *Strashnyy sud* (Doomsday); Lyubin in Finn's *Talanty* (Talents), etc; *Died:* Oct 1941 killed at the front, where he had been performing with a concert team.

RUDNEV, Lev Vladimirovich (1885–1956) Architect; member, USSR Acad of Construction and Architecture from 1956; *Born:* 1 Mar 1885 in Novgorod; *Educ:* 1915 grad Petersburg Acad of Arts; *Career:* after grad worked in Petrograd; for a number of years, prof, All-Russian Acad of Arts; from 1932 lived and worked in Moscow; 1948–52 prof, Moscow Architectural Inst; bd member, USSR Architects' Union; pres, Architecture Section, All-Union Soc for Cultural Relations with For Countries; from 1955 Presidium member, USSR Acad of Architecture; *Works:* "Monument to Fallen Revolutionaries" in Petrograd's Field of Mars (1919); co-designer, Frunze Acad (1937); co-designer admin buildings in Moscow (1937 and 1955); co-designer, Azer Govt House (1952); co-designer, Moscow's Lomonosov Univ (1953); co-designer, Warsaw Palace of Culture and Sci (1955), etc; *Awards:* two Orders of the Red Banner of Labor; Badge of Hon; Stalin Prize (1949); *Died:* 19 Nov 1956.

RUDNEV, Nikolay Aleksandrovich (1894–1918) Mil commander; CP member from 1917; *Born:* 29 Oct 1894 in vil Lyutovichi, Tula Province, son of a priest; *Educ:* studied at History and Philology Fac, Moscow Univ; *Career:* 1916 grad six-month course at Alexandrine Mil College and sent as ensign to 30th Infantry Reserve Regt in Tula; 1917 dep, Tula Sov; Apr 1917 elected member, 30th Infantry Reserve Regt Comt; head, Section Bureau, Tula Garrison RSDRP Mil Org; from June 1917 member, Tula City RSDRP(B) Comt; Aug 1917, after transfer of 30th Regt to Khar'kov, elected member, Exec Comt Khar'kov Sov and member, Revol Staff to Combat Counter-revol; 26 Oct 1917 commanded 30th Regt which, together with Red Guards, occupied main buildings in Khar'kov and handed over power to Mil Revol Comt; Nov 1917 elected commander, 30th Regt; Dec 1917 elected member, Mil Revol Comt; from Feb 1918 dep Pop Comr of Mil Affairs, Donetsk-Krivoy Rog Republ; from Mar 1918 member, Extraordinary Defense Staff; commanded troops on Akhtyrka-Lebedyan' and then Khar'kov sectors; from Apr 1918 chief of staff, 5th Ukr Army which fought a rearguard action from Lugansk to Tsaritsyn; from July 1918 chief of staff, Tsaritsyn Front; from Aug 1918 head, Troops Mustering and Training Dept, North Caucasian Mil Distr; 15 Oct 1918 mortally wounded near vil Beketovka while commanding reserve brigade during Battle of Tsaritsyn; *Died:* 16 Oct 1918 of his wounds.

RUDNEV, Semyon Vasil'yevich (1899–1943) Mil commander; maj-gen; CP member from 1917; *Born:* 28 Feb 1899 in vil Mosivtsi, Kursk Province; *Educ:* 1929 grad Mil Polit Acad; *Career:*

from 1913 worked at Baltic Aeronautic Plant, Petrograd; during 1917 Oct Revolt helped storm Winter Palace; fought in Civil War and wounded in action; instructor, Polit Dept, Donetsk Labor Army, then in Red Army; 1929 comr of regt, then brigade; from 1939 chm, Putivl' rayon council, Soc to Promote the Aviation, Defense and Chemical Ind; during WW 2 co-founder and comr, partisan raiding unit; member, underground CC, CP(B) Ukr; *Awards:* four orders; Hero of the Sov Union (1944, posthumously); *Died:* 5 Aug 1943 killed in action near Delyatin.

RUDNEV, Yevgeniy Ivanovich (1881–1966) Govt official; CP member from 1902; *Born:* 30 Dec 1881; *Career:* while at school joined revol pupils' circle, then engaged in underground revol work in Sormovo, Voronezh and Baku; took part in 1905–07 Revol; frequently arrested; 1908 exiled to Vologda Province; 1910–17 secr, Khar'kov Bolshevik Org; 1919 mil comr, Separate brigade on Southern Front; 1920–24 trade-union and govt work in Moscow; mil comr, Main Gen Mil Training Bd; 1924–28 member, Mil Collegium, USSR Supr Court; 1928–35 dir, Polytech Museum, Lenin All-Union Library; from 1935 worked for All-Union Book Chamber; from 1937 retired; *Died:* 19 July 1956.

RUDZUTAK (Party name: LIBIKH), Yan Ernestovich (1887–1938) Party and govt official; CP member from 1905; *Born:* 3 Mar 1887 in Lat, son of a farmhand; *Career:* farm laborer; from 1904 worked at Riga steel plant; 1906 coopted to Riga RSDRP Comt and to Centr Propaganda Bd; deleg at 5th RSDRP Congress; June 1907 arrested and sentenced by mil tribunal to 10 Years' hard labor, which he served in Riga Centr Prison and Butyrka Jail, Moscow; released after 1917 Feb Revol; 1917 trade-union work in Moscow; Presidium member, Moscow Province Trade-Union Council; after 1917 Oct Revol admin work; Presidium member, Supr Sovnarkhoz; chm, Centr Textile Workers' Union; 1920–21 chm, CC, Transport Workers' Union; chm, Turkestani Commission and Turkestani Bureau, RCP(B); Presidium member and secr-gen, All-Russian Centr Trade-Union Council; member, Sov deleg at 1922 Genoa Conference; 1922 chm, Centr Asian Bureau, CC, RCP(B); 1923–24 secr, CC, RCP(B); cand Politburo member and Org Bureau member, CC, RCP(B); 1924–30 USSR Pop Comr of Means of Communication; 1927–37 dep chm, USSR Council of Pop Comr and Labor and Defense Council; 1926–32 Politburo member, CC, CPSU(B); from 1928 chm, Comt for the Use of Chemicals in the Nat Econ, USSR Council of Pop Comr; Oct 1931 appointed chm, CPSU(B) Centr Control Commission and USSR Pop Comr of Workers and Peasants' Inspection; from 1934 cand Politburo member, CC, CPSU(B); Presidium member, USSR and All-Russian Centr Exec Comt; deleg at 9th–17th Party Congresses; from 1920 member, CC, CPSU(B); 1937 arrested by State Security organs; *Died:* 29 July 1938 in imprisonment; posthumously rehabilitated.

RUFANOV, Ivan Gur'yevich (1884–1956) Surgeon; Dr of Med from 1924; prof; member, USSR Acad of Med Sci from 1944; Hon Sci Worker of RSFSR from 1940; *Born:* 14 Jan 1884; *Educ:* 1911 grad Med Fac, Moscow Univ; *Career:* after grad worked at A. V. Martynov's Surgical Clinic, where he eventually received a professorship; 1924 defended doctor's thesis on pancreatitis stemming from disease of the biliary tract; from 1930 head, Chair of Gen Surgery, dean and dep dir, 2nd Moscow Med Inst; 1938 read paper on theory and treatment of wounds at 24th Congress of Surgeons; from 1939 head, Surgical Dept, All-Union Inst of Work Capacity Expertise, Moscow; from 1942 head, Chair of Gen Surgery, 1st Moscow Med Inst; during WW 2 chief surgeon, various evacuation hospitals; 1943 made study of pathogenesis and treatment of wound sepsis; 1944 co-founded USSR Acad of Med Sci; after WW 2 also head, Laboratory for the Clinical Study of New Antibiotics, USSR Acad of Med Sci; did research on diseases of liver, biliary tract and intestines; proposed an original theory of wound periodization based on changes in the state of tissue colloids; hon member, All-Union Soc of Surgeons; member, ed collegia, journals "Klinicheskaya meditsina", "Meditsinski referativnyy zhurnal", etc; co-ed, surgery section, "Bol'shaya meditsinskaya entsiklopediya" (Large Medical Encyclopedia) (2nd ed); wrote about 100 works; *Publ: Pankreatity v svyazi s vospalitel'nymi protsessami zhyolchnykh putey i puzyrya* (Pancreatitis Related to Inflammatory Processes in the Biliary Tract and Gall Bladder) (1933); *Vrachebnaya ekspertiza trudosposobnosti* (Medical Expertise on Fitness for Work) (1935); *Stolbnyak* (Tetanus) (1940); *Uchebnik obshchey khirurgii* (A Textbook on General Surgery) (1940); coauthor, *Osnovy kompleksnogo lecheniya v gospitalyakh* (The Principles of Comprehensive Hospital Treatment); *Awards:* Order of Lenin; Order of the Red Banner of Labor; medals; *Died:* 1965 in Moscow.

RUKHADZE, Nikolay Pavlovich (1879–1936) Epidemiologist; specialist in malaria; *Born:* 1879; *Educ:* 1902 grad med orderlies' school; 1916 grad Med Fac, Moscow Univ; *Career:* while still a student did research on the morphology of blood and on blood-parasites; 1916–18 intern, Tbilisi Railroad Hospital; 1920–21 asst prof, Chair of Pathological Anatomy, Tbilisi Univ; from 1922 assoc, Sumy Centr Malaria Station; 1925 imported the mosquito-fish (Gambusia affinis) from Italy and used it against anopheles in various regions of the USSR; from 1926 dir and sci dir, Inst of Tropical Diseases, Abkhazian ASSR; wrote some 40 works on malaria; *Publ: K parasitologii i epidemiologii malyarii v Abkhazii* (The Parasitology and Epidemiology of Malaria in Abkhazia) (1925); *Gambusia affinis i yeyo vozmozhnaya rol' v bor'be s malyariyey na poberezh'ye Chyornogo morya i v Zakavkaz'ye* (Gambusia affinis and Its Possible Role in the Campaign Against Malaria on the Black Sea Littoral and in Transcaucasia) (1926); *Sovremennaya profilaktika malyarii* (Modern Malaria Prevention) (1928); *Materialy po izucheniyu malyarii v Abkhazii* (Material on the Study of Malaria in Abkhazia) (1929); *Zooprofilaktika malarii* (The Zooprophylaxis of Malaria) (1936); *Died:* 1936.

RUKHIMOVICH, Moisey L'vovich (1889–1939) Govt official; CP member from 1913; *Born:* 1889 in vil Kaganika, on the Don, son of a locksmith; *Educ:* from 1911 studied at Khar'kov Technol Inst; *Career:* 1904 joined Rostov Bund org; 1906–09 in emigration; 1913 worked in Novorossiysk; 1914–17 in Russian Army; after 1917 Feb Revol member, Khar'kov RSDRP(B) Comt and chm, Mil Section, Khar'kov Sov; during 1917 Oct Revol chm, Khar'kov Mil Revol Comt; helped establish Sov regime in Khar'kov; Dec 1917–Mar 1918 head, Proletarian Detachment; 1918 mil comr, Donetsk-Krivoy Rog Sov Republ; from Dec 1920 chm, Donetsk Exec Province Comt and Bureau member, Donetsk Province Comt, CP(B) Ukr; 1923–25 mang, Don Coal Trust; 1925–26 chm, Ukr Supr Sovnarkhoz; from 1926 dep chm, USSR Supr Sovnarkhoz; 1930 RSFSR Pop Comr of Means of Communication and mang, Kuznets Basin Coal Trust; 1934–36 USSR Dep Pop Comr of Heavy Ind; 1936 USSR Pop Comr of Defense Ind; deleg at 8th and 10th–17th Party Congresses; at the 13th–17th Party Congresses elected member, CC, CPSU(B); at the 6th–18th Conferences and 9th Congress of CP(B) Ukr elected member, CC, CP(B) Ukr; 1925–26 Politburo member, CC, CP(B) Ukr; member, USSR and All-Ukr Centr Exec Comt; arrested by State Security organs; *Died:* 1939 in imprisonment; posthumously rehabilitated.

RUKHLYADEV, Aleksey Mikhaylovich (1882–1946) Architect; CP member from 1944; *Born:* 1882; *Educ:* 1911 grad Petersburg Acad of Arts; *Career:* from 1911 worked in Moscow; from 1922 prof at various Moscow higher educ establishments; from 1930 prof, Moscow Inst of Architecture; 1944–45 prof, Kiev Arts Int; co-founder, Assoc for New Architecture; from 1932 concentrated on forms of classical architecture; helped re-plan Moscow and designed many buildings for Moscow and other cities; 1943–44 directed design team to restore original buildings of Stalingrad; main works: river terminus at Khimki and Karamysh Dam on the Moscow-Volga Canal; *Awards:* Order of Lenin; *Died:* 1946.

RUMYANTSEV, Aleksey Vsevolodovich (1889–1947) Histologist; *Born:* 26 Nov 1889; *Educ:* 1913 grad Moscow Univ; *Career:* 1913–30 worked at Moscow Univ; from 1935 worked at Severtsov Inst of Evolutionary Morphology (now Severtsov Inst of Animal Morphology, USSR Acad of Sci); from 1943 also prof, 3rd Moscow Med Inst; specialized in histology, cytology, tissue culture, hydrobiology, etc; *Publ: Kul'tury tkaney vne organizma i ikh znacheniye v biologii* (Tissue Cultures Outside the Body and Their Importance for Biology) (1932); *Mikrostruktura kozhi i metody yeyo mikroskopicheskogo issledovaniya* (The Microstructure of the Skin and Methods of Its Microscopic Study) (1934); *Kurs gistologii* (A Histology Course) (1946); *Opyt issledovaniya evolyutsii khryashchevoy i kostnoy tkaney* (An Experimental Study of the Evolution of Cartilaginous and Bone Tissue) (1958); *Died:* 1947.

RUMYANTSEV, Ivan Petrovich (1886– ?) Party official; CP member from 1915; *Born:* 1886; *Career:* modeller; until 1917 worked at various plants and carried out revol and trade-union work which led to his dismissal; 1917–18 trade-union work; chm, Ericson Plant Factory Comt and chm, Modellers' Union; 1918 regt comr, Kazan' Front; then commander of a punitive detachment and chm, field tribunal; returned from front and held various exec govt posts; 1919 dep chm, Rybinsk Exec Comt; 1920–21 chm, Yaroslavl' Province Exec Comt; 1921–22 dep chm, Caucasian Province Revol Comt; then switched to Party work; secr, rayon Party comt in Perm'; secr, Zlatoust Okrug Party Comt; secr, Ural Oblast Party Comt; from 1930 secr, Western Oblast Party Comt; from 1947 secr, Vladimir Province Party Comt; at 12th Party Congress elected cand member, at 13th and 17th Party Congresses elected member, CC, CPSU(B); *Died:* date and place of death unknown.

RUMYANTSEV, Pavel Ivanovich (1894–1962) Opera singer (baritone); opera producer; Hon Artiste of RSFSR from 1941; *Born:* 14 Sept 1894; *Educ:* 1918–21 studied singing under Prof A. I. Bartsal at Moscow Conservatory; *Career:* from 1920 soloist, Opera Studio, Bolshoy Theater; 1926–41 soloist, from 1921 also producer, Stanislavskiy Opera Theater; 1941–46 producer, Stanislavskiy and Nemirovich-Danchenko Musical Theater; 1946–47 producer, Sofia Pop Opera Theater; 1947–49 producer, Kiev Opera and Ballet Theater, Leningrad; from 1941 conducted opera class at Leningrad Conservatory; *Roles:* Onegin; Yeletskiy in Tchaikovsky's *Pikovaya dama* (The Queen of Spades); Albert in Massenet's "Werther"; Marcel in "La Boheme"; *Productions:* Smetana's "The Bartered Bride" (1937); Kryukov's *Stantsionnyy smotritel'* (The Stationmaster) (1940); Vasilenko's "Suvorov" (1942); "Carmen" (1948), etc; *Publ: Rabota Stanislavskogo nad operoy "Rigoletto"* (Stanislavskiy's Work on the Opera "Rigoletto") (1955); *Died:* 22 Sept 1962.

RUMYANTSEV, Vladimir Vasil'yevich (1902–1934) Party official; CP member; *Born:* 1902; *Career:* expelled from CP for membership of Zinov'yev bloc but re-admitted to Party after publicly recanting his errors and expressing solidarity with Party and govt policy; Dec 1934 tried for complicity in 1 Feb 1934 assassination of Kirov in Leningrad; 29 Dec 1934 sentenced to death by Assizes of Mil Collegium, USSR Supr Court; *Died:* Dec 1934 executed.

RUSAKOV, Arseniy Vasil'yevich (1885–1953) Pathoanatomist and specialist in forensic med; Dr of Med and prof from 1939; *Born:* 21 July 1885; *Educ:* 1903–06 studied at Med Fac, Moscow Univ; 1909 grad Med Fac, Munich Univ; *Career:* 1906 expelled from Moscow Univ for involvement in student riots and forbidden to live in Russian univ towns; 1909 returned to Russia and obtained med license at Moscow Univ; 1909–20 worked as intern at various Moscow hospitals; for a while worked for State Plague Commission in Transbaykal; 1913 began specializing in pathological anatomy; 1915–18 served in Tsarist Army; 1919–24 asst prof, Chair of Pathological Anatomy, Moscow Higher Med School; from 1920 also head, Pathoanatomical Dept, Sklifosovskiy First Aid Inst, Moscow; 1939 defended doctor's thesis on the pathological physiology of bone tissue; 1940–51 head, Chair of Forensic Med, Med Inst, RSFSR Min of Health, then 1st Moscow Med Inst; chm, Moscow Branch, All-Union Soc of Pathoanatomists; wrote over 60 works; *Publ: Ocherk patologoanatomicheskogo issledovaniya tryokh sluchayev fibroznoy osteodistrofii* (A Pathoanatomical Study of Three Cases of Fibrous Osteodystrophy) (1927); coauthor, *O svyortyvayemosti trupnoy krovi* (The Coagulation of Corpse Blood) (1935); doctor's thesis *Ocherki patologicheskoy fiziologii kostnoy tkani* (A Study in the Pathological Physiology of Bone Tissue) (1939); *K fiziologii i patologii nekotorykh tkaney vnutrenney sredy* (The Physiology and Pathology of Certain Internal Tissues) (1954); *Patologicheskaya anatomiya bolezney kostnoy sistemy* (The Pathological Anatomy of Diseases of the Bone System) (1959); *Awards:* Stalin Prize and Abrikosov Prize (posthumously); *Died:* 23 Apr 1953 in Moscow.

RUSAKOV, Ivan Vasil'yevich (1877–1921) Revolutionary; pediatrician; CP member from 1905; *Born:* 25 Sept 1877; *Educ:* 1900 grad Med Fac, Moscow Univ; *Career:* 1899 joined revol movement; took active part in 1905 Moscow uprising; arrested; 1906–09 exiled in Tobol'sk Province; 1909–17 worked in Moscow; after 1917 Feb Revol member, Sokol'niki Rayon RSDRP(B) Comt and member, Sokol'niki Rayon Exec Comt; during 1917 Oct Revol member, Sokol'niki Rayon Mil Revol Comt; after 1917 Oct Revol member, Med Collegium, Pop Comrt of Internal Affairs; chm, Sokol'niki Rayon Sov; plen, Sanitary Dept, Southern and Southwestern Fronts; head, Moscow Educ Dept; member, Moscow RCP(B) Comt; Presidium member, Moscow Sov; Mar 1921 volunteered to help crush Kronstadt Mutiny; *Died:* 18 Mar 1921 killed in Kronstadt fighting; buried by Kremlin Wall, Moscow; a Moscow street, streetcar depot, children's hospital and club are named after him.

RUSAKOV, Mikhail Petrovich (1892–1963) Geologist; Dr of Geology from 1935; prof from 1936; member, Kaz Acad of Sci from 1946; Hon Sci Worker of Kaz SSR from 1945; *Born:* 21 Nov 1892; *Educ:* 1921 grad Petrograd Mining Inst; *Career:* from 1920 worked in Kazakhstan for Geological Comt, then for Geological Section, Kaz Branch, USSR Acad of Sci; 1925–30 supervised prospecting for copper porphyry deposits; for over 20 years worked for State Resources Commission; also worked at Inst of Geology, Kaz Acad of Sci; discovered Kounrad copper deposit, Semizbugu carunda andalusite deposit and Karagaylinskoye leadbaryte deposit; wrote 150 works and some 300 essay papers; *Publ: Mednoporfirovyye mestorozhdeniya Kazakhstana, SSSR i zarubezhnykh stran* (The Copper-Porphyry Deposits of Kazakhstan, the USSR and Foreign Countries); *Awards:* two Orders of the Red Banner of Labor; Order of the Fatherland War, 1st Class; Lenin Prize; Stalin Prize; *Died:* 25 Oct 1963.

RUSANOV, Andrey Gavrilovich (1874–1949) Surgeon; *Born:* 1874; *Educ:* 1898 grad Med Fac, Moscow Univ; *Career:* after grad worked for three years as intern under L. L. Levshin; from 1907 senior physician and surgeon, Voronezh Province Zemstvo Hospital; 1912 defended doctor's thesis; from 1919 assoc prof and head, Chair of Hospital Surgical Clinic, Voronezh Univ; from 1921 prof, above chair; developed health service in Voronezh Province and centr Black Sea area; specialized in intestinal blockage, ulcers and wound; these observations proved of great use in Sov mil med infection; pioneered non-pledget method of treating wounds; outlined in detail various periods in clinical course of an infected wound; these observarions proved of great use in Sov mil med during WW 2; founder and 1907–49 chm, Voronezh Med Soc; Hospital Surgical Clinic, Voronezh Univ bears his name; wrote over 70 works; *Publ: O prakticheskom i teoreticheskom znachenii nashikh konservativnykh meropriyatiy v probleme lecheniya kishechnoy neprokhodimosti* (The Practical and Theoretical Importance of Our Conservative Measures in the Treatment of Intestinal Obstruction) (1937); *Vospominaniya o L've Nikolayeviche Tolstom* (Memories of Lev Nikolayevich Tolstoy) (1937); *O proiskhozhdenii i znachenii slova ileus* (The Origin and Meaning of the Word Ileus) (1939); *Lecheniye ran* (The Treatment of Wounds) (1940); *Died:* 1949.

RUSANOV, G. A. (1893–1937) Govt official; CP member from 1916; *Born:* 1893; *Career:* Oct 1917–June 1918 comr, 17th Corps and member, Revol Mil Council, Headquarters of Commander in Chief; from June 1918–Feb 1924 worked for All-Russian Cheka; head, Special Dept, 3rd Army, then Caucasian and Turkestani Fronts; All-Russian Cheka and OGPU rep in Transcaucasia, Caucasus and Turkestan; chm, Geo Cheka; 1924–37 worked for Supr Sovnarkhoz and Pop Comrt of Means of Communication; dir, Moscow-White Sea-Baltic and Western Railroads; member, CC, CP(B) Bel; arrested by State Security organs; *Died:* 1937 in imprisonment.

RUSANOV, Nikolay Sergeyevich (1859–1939) Revolutionary; member, Pop Will Party; then Socialist-Revolutionary; *Born:* 1859, son of a rich merchant; *Educ:* studied at Med Surgical Acad, Petersburg; *Career:* from 1877 active in Populist movement; member, People's Will Party; 1882–1905 lived abroad; contributed to periodical "Vestnik narodnoy voli"; in 1890's lived in Paris and helped found Old People's Will Functionaries Group; 1901 helped found Socialist-Revolutionary Party's theoretical organ "Vestnik russkoy revolyutsii"; French corresp for journal "Russkoye bogatstvo", etc; after 1917 Oct Revol emigrated; *Publ: Na rodine. 1859–1882* (In My Country. 1859–1882) (1931); *V emigratsii* (In Emigration) (1929); *Died:* 28 July 1939 in Bern.

RUS'KO, Aleksey Nikitich (1906–1964) Educator; corresp member, RSFSR Acad of Pedag Sci from 1957; CP member from 1925; *Born:* 18 Apr 1906; *Educ:* grad Kiev Chemical Technol Inst; *Career:* worked for Kiev Teachers' Training Inst and Kiev Univ; 1938–44 rector, Kiev Univ; 1944–58 Ukr Dep Min of Educ; 1958–64 dir, Ukr Pedag Research Inst; from 1959 pres, Ukr Pedag Soc; specialized in org of Public educ, teachers' training and methods of chemistry teaching in schools; *Died:* 25 Aug 1964.

RUSSEL'-SUDZILOVSKIY, Nikolay Konstantinovich (1848–1930) Physician; revolutionary; politician; Populist; *Born:* 1848; *Career:* emigrated from Russia and grad med fac in Rumania; developed very pop med practice in Rumania; 1881 arrested and deported from Rumania for revol activities; spent many years in Belgium, Italy, Austria, Spain and Switzerland, working at various chemical, pharmacological and bacteriological clinics and laboratories; specialized in eye diseases; then went to America and campaigned against Orthodox clergy, for which he was excommunicated; became an American citizen; from 1892 settled for many years in Honolulu, Hawaii; here he developed an extensive, pop med practice, learned native language and engaged in soc work; founded and headed native Kanaka Party as counterweight to American influence in Hawaii; when this party won the elections to the House of Representatives and the Senate, Russel'-Zudzilovskiy became pres of the Senate, i.e., virtually head of the Hawaiian Republ; introduced various polit and soc reforms, especially in the field of public health and hygiene legislation; during Russo-Japanese War went to Japan and engaged in educ work and revol propaganda among Russian prisoners-of-war; for this he was deprived of his citizenship by the American govt; after the war he remained in Japan, working on med and chemistry and conducting extensive corresp with specialists in Western Europe and America; also engaged in soc and lit work; spent last nine years of his life in China (Tientsin), practising as oculist among poor peasantry; received pension from Sov govt; *Died:* 1930.

RUTENBERG, Pinkhus (Pyotr) Moiseyevich (1878–1942) Politician; *Born:* 1878 in Poltava, son of a merchant; *Educ:* grad Petersburg Technol Inst; *Career:* 1904 shop foreman, Putilov Plant; made the acquaintance of Father Gapon, who fell under his influence; after 5 Jan 1905 demonstration and massacre helped Gapon flee abroad and tried to persuade him to join Socialist-Revol Party; summer 1905 tried to smuggle weapons to Russia with SS "John Crafton" but was detained; 28 Mar 1906, learning of Gapon's ties with secret police, helped execute him in Ozerki near Petersburg; later switched from Socialist-Revol Party to Zionists; lived in Italy; 1917 returned to Russia and helped establish Zionist org; Oct 1917 asst to Petrograd governor N. M. Kishkin; 1919 in Odessa collaborated with French forces; 1922 emigrated to Palestine, where he held various exec posts in fuel and power companies; *Publ:* memoirs *Delo Gapona* (The Gapon Case) (1917); *Ubiystvo Gapona* (The Assassination of Gapon) (1925); *Died:* 1942.

RUTENBURG, David Mikhaylovich (1899–1961) Otolaryngologist; Dr of Med; prof from 1934; *Born:* 1899 in Nevel', Pskov Oblast; *Educ:* 1914 grad Med Fac, Kiev Univ; *Career:* 1914–17 specialized in otolaryngology at Petrograd Clinical Inst (now Leningrad Inst of Postgrad Med Training); 1918–35 mil surgeon in Red Army; 1921–23 also supernumerary asst prof, asst prof and assoc prof, from 1934 prof, Otolaryngological Clinic, Leningrad Inst of Postgrad Med Training; 1935–61 founder-head, Chair of Ear, Nose and Throat Diseases, Leningrad Pediatric Med Inst; during WW 2 consultant, various hospitals on Leningrad Front; bd member, Leningrad, All-Russian and All-Union Soc of Otolaryngologists; co-ed, "Otolaryngology" section, "Bol'shaya meditsinskaya entsiklopediya" (Large Medical Encyclopedia) (2nd ed); devised "closed" methods of treating mastoiditis in children, and cerebral and cerebellar abscesses; also devised conservative surgical methods of treating laryngal tumors and endonasal operations for tumors of the hypophysis cerebri and labyrinthine fenestration; wrote over 90 works; *Publ: Agranulotsitoz* (Agranulocytosis); *Izmeneniya vestibul'yarnogo apparata pri otravlenii ugarnym gazom* (Lesions of the Vestibular Apparatus in Carbon Monoxide Poisoning); *Labirinty* (The Labyrinths), etc; *Awards:* two Orders of the Red Star; medals; *Died:* 7 Mar 1961 in Leningrad.

RUZHEYNIKOV, Ivan Semyonovich (1878–1929) Mil commander; physician; CP member from 1905; *Born:* 2 June 1878 in Ural'sk, son of a Cossack; *Educ:* from 1894 studied at Orenburg Theological Seminary, but expelled for participating in a revol circle; from 1900 studied at Med Fac, Tomsk Univ; *Career:* student rep in Tomsk RSDRP Comt; arrested for participating in armed demonstration; 1905 member, Omsk RSDRP Comt; collaborated with Kirov and Kuybyshev; Dec 1905 again arrested; 1906 exiled to Minusinsk; fled from exile and worked in Krasnoyarsk, Omsk, Petropavlovsk and Odessa; re-arrested and interned in Krasnoyarsk Fortress; from 1910 physician in Lbishchensk; again arrested; 1914 drafted into Russian Army and sent to front, where he conducted revol propaganda among the Cossacks; 1917 member, Soldiers' Exec Comt, Southwestern Front; 1919 directed defense of Ural'sk; 1920 dep head, Cossack Dept, All-Russian Centr Exec Comt; member, Org Bureau for Convening 1st Congress of Working Cossacks; Presidium member at this congress; together with Kalinin, toured Don Front in propaganda train; from 1921 asst head, Main Sanitary Bd of Red Army; also worked for other Sov institutions; *Died:* 31 Dec 1929.

RUZHITSKIY, Konstantin Ivanovich (1888–1964) Archpriest; rector, Moscow Theological Acad and Seminary from 1951; chm, Training Comt, Holy Synod of Moscow Patriarchy; Master of Divinity from 1960; *Born:* 1888 in vil Mol'chitsy, Volhynian Province; *Educ:* 1912 grad Volynian Theological Seminary; 1916 grad Moscow Theological Acad; *Career:* 1916 ordained priest; 1916–19 taught Scripture and Latin at secondary educ establishments in Slavyansk; 1945–51 dean, St Vladimir Cathedral in Kiev and steward, Patriarchal Exarch of All Ukr; 1948–49 also taught Greek and psychology at Kiev Theological Seminary; 1948 member, Moscow Patriarchy deleg at enthronement of Rumanian Patriarch Justinian; 1951 member, similar deleg at enthronement of Makariy, Metropolitan of Warsaw and All Poland; from 1951 lecturer and head, Chair of Moral Scripture, Moscow Theological Acad and Seminary; 1956 took part in theological discussion with reps of Anglican Church; 1957 attended World Inter-Religious Peace Conference in India; 1958 attended Lambeth Church Conference, London; 1958 went to Syria to attend funeral of Alexander III, Patriarch of Antioch; 1958 visited Yugoslavia; 1959 attended 2nd World Christian Conference in Prague; 1959 also attended celebrations commemorating 600th jubilee of St Gregory of Palama in Greece; 1960 accompanied Patriarch Aleksiy on his visit to the Holy Land; 1961 attended enthronement of Archbishop of Canterbury; regularly received foreign clerics and dignitaries who visited the Moscow Theological Acad and talked with them on the "prosperity and flourishing state of the Russian Orthodox Church in the USSR"; Presidium member, Union of Sov Societies for Friendship and Cultural Relations with For Countries; vice-pres, Soviet-Greek Friendship Soc; *Awards:* medal "For Valiant Labor in the Great Fatherland War"; Patriarchal Cross (1959); Order of St Vladimir (1961); orders of Eastern Orthodox Churches; *Died:* 18 Nov 1964.

RUZSKIY, Nikolay Vladimirovich (1854–1918) Mil surgeon; gen of infantry from 1909; *Born:* 6 Mar 1854; *Educ:* 1870 grad 2nd Konstantin Mil College; 1881 grad Gen Staff Acad; *Career:* fought in 1877–78 Russo-Turkish War; during 1904–05 Russo-Japanese War was for a time chief of Field Staff, 2nd Manchurian Army, 1906–09 commanded corps, then engaged in drafting mil regulations; 1912 drafted Field Regulations; at start of WW 1 commanded 3rd Army; Sept 1914–Mar 1915 commanded Northwestern Front; relieved of command on med grounds and appointed member, State Council; from July 1915 commanded 6th Army; Aug 1915–Apr 1917 (with a break from Dec 1915 to Aug 1916 on med grounds) commanded Northern Front; Feb 1917 advocated abdication of Nicholas II; from Apr 1917 on pension; underwent med treatment in Kislovodsk; Sept 1918 among hostages taken by Caucasian Red Army; *Died:* 19 Oct 1918 executed in Pyatigorsk.

RYABININ, Ye. I. (1892–1941) Party official; CP member from 1917; *Born:* 1892; *Career:* after 1917 Oct Revol govt work in Novgorod and Ryazan'; at time of 11th Party Congress dep head, Org Dept, CC, RCP(B); then secr, Tambov Province Party Comt; chm, Voronezh Oblast Exec Comt, then secr, Voronezh Oblast Party Comt; arrested by State Security organs; *Died:* 1941 in imprisonment.

RYABOV, Aleksey Panteleymonovich (1899–1955) Composer and conductor; Hon Art Worker of Ukr SSR from 1951; *Born:* 17 Mar 1899 in Khar'kov; *Educ:* 1918 grad violin and composition classes, Khar'kov Conservatory; *Career:* 1919–28 concertmaster, choirmaster and conductor at musical theaters in various towns of USSR; from 1929 conductor, first Sov Ukr Musical Comedy Theater, Khar'kov; 1941–55 musical dir, composer and conductor, Kiev Musical Comedy Theater; wrote music for plays, and shows; composed symphonies, etc; *Works:* operettas: "Kolombina" (1924); "Dry Law" (1932); *Sorochinskaya yarmarka* (Sorochintsy Fair), after Gogol (1936); *Svad'ba v Malinovke* (Wedding at Malinovka) (1937); "When Two Err" (1940); "The Blue Stone" (1942); "The Blue Fortress" (1951); "The Wily Lover", after Lope de Vega (1953); "The Red Guelder" (1954); "Shel'menko the Journeyman" (1947); "Miraculous Land" (1949); "The Sound of the Dnieper" (1955); *Died:* 18 Dec 1955.

RYABTSEV, Konstantin Ivanovich (1879–1919) Mil commander; col, Russian Army; commander, Moscow Mil Distr in Oct 1917; *Born:* 14 May 1879 in Kostroma Province, son of a peasant; *Educ:* 1904 grad Tiflis Infantry College; 1912 grad Gen Staff Acad; *Career:* from 1900 in Russian Army; fought in 1904–05 Russo-Japanese War; during WW 1 staff posts with 1st and 10th Armies; from Feb 1917 chief of staff, 31st Infantry Div; 27 July 1917 appointed chief of staff, Moscow Mil Distr; from 2 Sept 1917 commander, Moscow Mil Distr; during 1917 Oct Revol commanded armed forces in Moscow against Bolsheviks; 2 Nov 1917 dismissed by Mil Revol Comt; went to Khar'kov and worked for Menshevik newspaper; late June 1919, after Volunteer Army occupied Khar'kov, arrested on charges of attacking Gen Kornilov and offering only half-hearted resistance to Bolsheviks in Oct 1917; *Died:* 29 July 1919 executed.

RYASTAS, Otto Yur'yevich (1890–1938) Party official; CP member from 1912; *Born:* 5 Mar 1890 in Estland Province, son of a peasant; *Career:* from 1907 worked at plants in Tallin; 1913 moved to Narva and worked for newspaper "Kiyr"; exiled to Yekaterinoslav, then to Khar'kov; 1915 exiled to Tsaritsyn; after 1917 Feb Revol member, 1st Exec Comt, Tsaritsyn Sov; May 1917 returned to Tallin and helped prepare Oct Revol in Est; late 1918–early 1919 member, Estland Workers' Commune; 1920–24 underground Party work in Est; 1920–38 member, CC, CP Est; from 1925 in Moscow; secr, Est Section, CC, RCP(B); from 1929 secr, Est Section, Comintern; from 1936 exec ed, Est newspaper "Edasi" in Leningrad; wrote numerous works and articles on history of Est workers' movement; 1938 arrested by State Security organs; *Died:* 1938 in imprisonment; posthumously rehabilitated.

RYAZANOV (GOL'DENDAKH), David Borisovich (nickname: BUKVOYED) (1870–1938) Party official; CP member from 1917; *Born:* 1870; *Career:* early 1890's began revol work in Odessa as Populist; 1889, while abroad, became a Marxist; 1891 arrested and spent five years in prison, then three years in exile in Kishinev; then went abroad; 1901 began lit work; 1900 founded his own small independent Soc-Democratic group entitled "Struggle"; 1903, after 2nd RSDRP Congress, sided with Mensheviks; 1905–07 worked in Odessa, then Petersburg; active in trade-union work and in Soc-Democratic faction, State Duma; 1907 arrested and detained for a while, then went abroad; did research in libraries abroad and wrote on Marxism, Socialism and history of the workers' movement for Russian and German journals; on behalf of German Soc-Democratic Party, prepared for press an ed of Marx and Engels' works; during WW 1 adopted centrist stand and worked for newspapers "Golos" and "Nashe slovo"; after 1917 Feb Revol returned to Russia and joined Mezhrayontsy (org of revol internationalists); July 1917 joined RSDRP(B) together with other Mezhrayontsy; after 1917 Oct Revol advocated formation of coalition govt comprising Soc-Democrats and Socialist-Revolutionaries; 1918 resigned from Party over Bret Peace Treaty issue, but later reinstated in Party; during trade-union controversy sided with Trotsky; removed from trade-union work; founded Socialist (from 1929 Communist) Acad; 1922 founded Inst of Marx and Engels; member, USSR and All-Russian Centr Exec Comt; from 1929 member, USSR Acad of Sci; Sept 1920–May 1928 member, Commission for Collating and Studying Material on the History of the Oct Revol and the History of the Communist Party; Feb 1931 expelled from CPSU(B) "for directly abetting the Menshevik interventionists and betraying the Party"; also dismissed as dir, Inst of Marx and Engels; 12 Mar 1931 "Pravda" accused him of concealing the original of Marx's letter about Kautzky; in the 23 Feb 1931 "indictment of the counter-revol Menshevik org" RSFSR Public Prosecutor Krylenko had accused him of concealing secret documents of the RSDRP (Mensheviks) For Deleg at the Inst of Marx and Engels; arrested by State Security organs; *Publ: Institut K. Marksa i F. Engel'sa pri TsIK SSSR* (The USSR Centr Executive Committee's Institute of Marx and Engels) (1924); *Died:* 1938 in imprisonment.

RYAZANOV, Vasiliy Georgiyevich (1901–1951) Mil commander; lt-gen, Air Force; CP member from 1920; *Born:* 25 Jan 1901 in vil Velikoye Kozino, now Balakhna, Gorky Oblast, son of a peasant; *Educ:* 1926 grad mil pilots school; 1935 grad Air Force Acad; *Career:* from 1920 in Red Army; until 1941 various commands; during WW 2 commanded large air force units on Southwestern and Western Fronts; after WW 2 various commands in Sov Air Force; dep, Ukr Sov Supr Sov of 3rd convocation; *Awards:* twice Hero of the Sov Union (1944 and 1945); two Orders of Lenin; other orders; medals; *Died:* 8 July 1951.

RYAZHSKIY, Georgiy Georgiyevich (1895–1952) Painter; Hon Art Worker of RSFSR from 1944; member, USSR Acad of Arts from 1949; CP member from 1923; *Born:* 12 Feb 1895 in vil Ignat'yevo, now Moscow Oblast; *Educ:* 1920 grad Higher Tech Art Workshops; *Career:* 1922 co-founder, New Soc of Painters; 1924 joined Assoc of Artists of Revol Russia; 1928–29 visited Italy and Germany; 1932–49 taught at Moscow Art Inst; several of his women's portraits are displayed at the Tret'yakov Gallery, Moscow; *Works:* "The Girl at the Workers' Faculty" (1926); "For a Book" (1927); "The Woman Delegate" (1927); "The Woman Chairman" (1928); "A Chuvash Schoolmistress" (1932); "Political Talk" (1933); "Stakhanov and His Team" (1937); "Into Slavery" (1943), etc; also painted landscapes; *Died:* 20 Oct 1952.

RYBALKO, Pavel Semyonovich (1894–1948) Mil Commander; Ukr; Marshal of Armored Forces from 1945; CP member from 1919; *Born:* 4 Nov 1894 in vil Malyy Istorop, now Sumy Oblast, son of a worker; *Educ:* 1926 and 1930 grad advanced commanders courses; 1934 grad Frunze Mil Acad; *Career:* fought in WW 1; from Dec 1917 in Red Guard; from 1918 in Red Army; soldiering and polit work in Civil War in Ukr; comr of brigade, then asst div commander; 1937–41 mil attache in various countries; 1941–42 mil instructor; summer 1942 commander, 5th Tank Army; from late 1942 commander, 3rd Tank Army (from May 1943 3rd Guards Tank Army); took part in Don, Dnieper, liberation of Ukr and Pland, and Berlin and Prague operations; 1945–47 first dep commander, 1947–48 commander, armored and mechanized troops; dep, USSR Supr Sov of 1946 convocation; *Awards:* twice Hero of the Sov Union (1943 and 1945); two Orders of Lenin; two Orders of the Red Banner; three Orders of Suvorov; Order of Kutuzov; Order of Bogdan Khmel'nitskiy; medals; *Died:* 28 Aug 1948; bronze bust erected in his memory in the vil Malyy Istorop.

RYBKIN, Pyotr Nikolayevich (1864–1948) Radio eng; *Born:* 25 May 1864; *Educ:* 1892 grad Petersburg Univ; *Career:* from 1894 worked at laboratory asst, Mining Officers Class, Kronstadt; then until 1940's trained radio operators at this establishment and then in Popov Communications School, Kronstadt; assisted A. S. Popov in his invention and establishment of radio in Russia; 1899 discovered means of audible reception of telegraphy; *Publ: Telegrafnaya set' i yeyo elementy* (The Telegraph System and Its Elements) (1907); *Izobreteniye radiotelegrafa v Rossii* (The Invention of the Radiotelegraph in Russia) (1919); *Desyat' let s izobretatelem radio* (Ten Years with the Inventor of Radio) (1945); *Awards:* Order of Lenin; Order of the Red Star; medals; *Died:* Jan 1948.

RYBNIKOV, Nikolay Aleksandrovich (1880–1961) Psychologist; Dr of Pedag Sci from 1943; corresp member, RSFSR Acad of Pedag Sci from 1947; *Born:* 29 Oct 1880 in vil Verkhniy Yakimets, now Ryazan' Oblast; *Educ:* 1910 grad History and Philology Fac, Moscow Univ; *Career:* 1913–20 taught at secondary schools; from 1915 also senior asst prof, Inst of Psychology, Moscow; from 1920 lecturer, then prof, Krupskaya Acad of Communist Training, Higher Pedag Courses, 2nd Moscow Univ and Inst of Child Psychology; from 1924 until the end of his working career also worked at Inst of Psychology (later Inst of Psychology, RSFSR Acad of Pedag Sci); also worked at Psychology Laboratory, Mil Acad, at Inst of School Work Methods and at Higher Communist Inst of Educ; wrote numerous works on gen, age-group and pedag psychology; developed biographical method of psychological investigation; collated a vast body of data on child development; *Publ: Opyt eksperimental'nogo issledovaniya uznavaniya i reproduktsii* (The Experimental Study of Learning and Reproduction) (1914); *O logicheskoy i mekhanicheskoy pamyati* (Logical and Mechanical Memory) (1914); *K voprosu o metodike issledovaniya pamyati* (Methods of Studying Memory) (1916); *Detskiye risunki i ikh izucheniye* (Children's Drawings and their Study) (1926); *Yazyk rebyonka* (The Child's Language) (1926); *Detskoye chteniye* (Children's Reading) (1928); *Pamyat', yeyo psikhologiya i pedagogika* (Memory, Its Psychology and Pedagogics) (1930); *Navyki chteniya sovremennogo shkol'nika* (The Modern Schoolchild's Reading Habits) (1936); *Died:* 31 Mar 1961.

RYCHAGOV, Pavel Vasil'yevich (1911–1941) Air force commander; lt-gen, Sov Air Force from 1940; fighter-pilot; CP member from 1938; *Born:* 1911 in Moscow Province, son of a peasant; *Educ:* early 1930's completed Red Army mil pilots school; *Career:* late 1920's enrolled at Red Army mil pilots school; from early 1930's served with fighter air force unit, Ukr Mil Distr; 1936–37 fighter-pilot, flight commander, then squadron leader with Spanish Republ Air Force; shot down 15 enemy aircraft; 1937–38 commanded Sov air force unit in China; 1938 commanded fighter air force in battles at Lake Khasan; 1938 planned mass raid of Japanese air base on Taiwan by Sov bombers stationed in China; 1938–39 air force commander, 1st Separate Red Banner Army in the Far East; 1939–40 air force commander, 9th Army on the Sov-Finnish Front; 1940–41 chief, Red Army Main Air Force Bd and USSR Dep Pop Comr of Defense (for the Air Force); dep,

USSR Supr Sov of 1937 convocation; 1941, shortly before the start of German-Sov hostilities, arrested by State Security organs; *Awards:* Hero of the Sov Union (1936); two Orders of Lenin; three Orders of the Red Banner; *Died:* 1941 in imprisonment; posthumously rehabilitated.

RYKOV, Aleksey Ivanovich (1881–1938) Party and govt official; CP member from 1899; *Born:* 1881; *Educ:* from 1900 studied at Law Fac, Kazan' Univ; *Career:* took part in students and workers' circles in Saratov, then in student revol movement; member, Kazan' RSDRP Comt, supervising workers' circles; Mar 1901 arrested and exiled under police surveillance to Saratov; 1902 went underground, then moved to Geneva, where he first met Lenin; returned to Russia and headed Northern RSDRP Comt; 1905 attended 3rd RSDRP Congress in London and elected member, CC, RSDRP; returned to Russia and headed Petersburg RSDRP Comt; mid-1906 moved to Odessa to develop Bolshevik orgs in the area; returned to Moscow and was exiled for three years to Arkhangel'sk Province, whence he soon fled to continue Party work in Moscow; May 1907 re-arrested; after 17 months' imprisonment in Taganka Jail exiled for two years to Samara; went abroad at Lenin's behest; summer 1909 returned to Russia; Sept 1909 again arrested in Moscow and after three months in jail exiled for three years to Arkhangel'sk Province; Dec 1910 fled to Paris; summer 1911 attended plenary meeting of CC, RSDRP; sided with Bolshevik reconciliationist faction; Aug 1911 returned to Moscow and was again arrested; after nine months' imprisonment exiled for the third time to Arkhangel'sk Province; summer 1913 returned from exile and worked in Petersburg and Moscow, but was shortly arrested and exiled for four years to Narym Kray; Sept 1915 fled to Samara; Oct 1915 re-arrested and returned to Narym, where he lived until the 1917 Feb Revol; returned to Moscow and was elected to Presidium, Moscow Sov; Apr 1917 deleg at 7th All-Russian RSDRP Conference; Oct 1917 helped organize Oct Revol in Petrograd; at 2nd Congress of Soviets appointed Pop Comr of Internal Affairs in first Sov govt; Nov 1917, together with other rightist Bolsheviks, resigned from Council of Pop Comr and from CC, RSDRP(B) in protest against the Bolshevik leadership's refusal to let other socialist parties participate in the govt; Feb 1918 appointed chm, Supr Sovnarkhoz; 1919 also extraordinary plen of Sov defense; summer 1921 dep chm, Council of Pop Comr and Labor and Defense Council; after Lenin's death, 1924–29 chm, RSFSR Council of Pop Comr; 1924–30 chm, USSR Council of Pop Comr; 1931–Sept 1936 USSR Pop Comr of Communications; 1905–34 member, from 1934 cand member, CC, CPSU(B); 1919–29 Politburo member, CC, CPSU(B); 1928, together with Bukharin and Tomsky, led "rightist opposition"; after 1929 Nov plenum of CC, CPSU(B) and after 16th CPSU(B) Congress in 1930 recanted his errors; Mar 1937 expelled from CPSU(B) for alleged anti-Party activities; 18 Mar 1938 sentenced to death in the trial of the "anti-Sov rightist-Trotskyite center" for "active complicity in a conspiratorial group"; *Awards:* Order of the Red Banner of Laber (1928); *Died:* 18 Mar 1938 executed.

RYKUNOV, M. V. (1884–1937) Govt official; CP member from 1903; *Born:* 1884; *Career:* from 1903 revol work in Petersburg, Moscow and Oryol; after 1917 Oct Revol govt, trade-union and admin work; 1921–22 Collegium member, Pop Comrt of For Trade; from 1922 Dep Pop Comr of Agric and head, Turkestani Water Management Bd; then head, Centr Asian Water Management Bd; Labor and Defense Council dep plen for Centr Asia; from 1926 dep chm, All-Union Irrigation Comt, USSR Council of Pop Comr; then head, Capital Construction Section, Automobile Repair and Supply Trust, Moscow; arrested by State Security organs; *Died:* 1937 in imprisonment.

RYLOV, Arkadiy Aleksandrovich (1870–1939) Painter; member, Petersburg Acad of Arts from 1915; prof from 1918; Hon Art Worker of RSFSR from 1935; *Born:* 29 Jan 1870 near Vyatka; *Educ:* 1897 grad A. I. Kuindzhi's class, Petersburg Acad of Arts; *Career:* 1918–29 prof of painting, Leningrad Acad of Arts; painted animals and landscapes; *Works:* "Pecheneg Raid on a Slav Village" (1897); "Waning Camp-Fire" (1898); "Daredevils" (1903); "Sound of Greenery" (1904); "In the Blue Expanse" (1918); "A Hot Day" (1922); "Green Lace" (1928); "Lenin at Razliv" (1934); "A Difficult Journey" (1937), etc; *Died:* 22 June 1939.

RYL'SKIY, Maksim Fadeyevich (1895–1964) Ukr poet; Dr of Philology; member, USSR Acad of Sci from 1958; member, Ukr Acad of Sci from 1943; CP member from 1943; *Born:* 19 Mar 1895 in Kiev; *Educ:* 1918 grad History and Philology Fac, Kiev Univ; *Career:* 1910 first work printed; 1917–29 taught at vil Romanovka, then taught Ukr at Kiev Railroad School and Kiev Inst of Public Educ; from 1939 member, ed bd, journal "Radyans'ka Ukraina"; from 1942 dir, Inst of Folk Creativity and Art, Ukr Acad of Sci (from 1944 Inst of Art History, Folklore and Ethnography), Kiev; Presidium member, USSR and Ukr Writers' Unions; member, ed bd, "Ukrayns'korosyys'kyy slovnyk" (Ukrainian-Russian Dictionary) and "Russko-ukrainskiy slovar' AN USSR" (Russo-Ukrainian Dictionary of the Ukrainian Academy of Sciences); member, ed bd, journal "Vsesvyt"; member, Int Comt of Slavists; chm, Ukr Comt of Slavists; member, Lenin Prize Comt; attended Vienna Peace Congress; in 1920's member, "Neo-Classicists" group; dep, USSR Supr Sov of 1947, 1950, 1954, 1958 and 1962 convocations; wrote lit studies of Shevchenko, Mickiewicz and Pushkin; wrote libretto for opera "Shchors"; translated into Ukr works of Shakespeare, Boileau, Goethe, Moliere, Corneille, Edmond de Rostand, Racine, Victor Hugo, Mickiewicz ("Pan Tadeusz"), Pushkin "Yevgeniy Onegin" and "Mednyy vsadnik" (The Bronze Horseman), Gogol and Krylov; also translated "Slovo o polku Igoreve" (The Lay of the Host of Igor); *Publ:* in Ukrainian: verse collections: "On White Islands" (1910); "The Weighmark" (1932); "Summer" (1936); "The Ukraine" (1938); "Collecting the Grapes" (1940); "World Dawn" (1942); "Bright Weapon" (1942); "Bridges" (1948); "Brotherhood" (1950); "Our Strength" (1952); "The People's Will" (1954); "Roses and Grapes" (1957); "Distant Horizons" (1959); "Evening Talks" (1964); "Art" (1962); in Russian translation: collected articles *Velikaya druzhba* (Great Friendship) (1954); *Izbrannyye proizvedeniya* (Selected Works) (2 vol, 1957); collected articles *Klassiki i sovremenniki* (Classics and Contemporaries) (1958); articles *Literatura i narod* (Literature and the People) (1959); *Awards:* three Orders of Lenin; Order of the Red Banner of Labor; medals; two Stalin Prizes (1943 and 1950); Lenin Prize (1960); *Died:* 24 July 1964.

RYSKULOV, Gurar Ryskulovich (1894–1943) Govt official; CP member from 1917; *Born:* 1894, son of a peasant; *Educ:* grad agric college; *Career:* taught horticulture; after 1917 Oct Revol helped establish Sov regime in Auliye-Ata Uyezd, Syr-Dar'ya Oblast; as chm, Auliye-Ata Uyezd Exec Comt, suppressed several revolts; 1918–mid 1920 Turkestani Republ Pop Comr of Health; also chm, CC, Famine Relief Org and Presidium member, Turkestani Centr Exec Comt; asst chm, then chm, Turkestani Centr Exec Comt; helped found Moslem Bureau, CC, RCP(B); 1920 at Baku Congress of Peoples of the East, elected Council member; 1921–22 Collegium member, RSFSR Pop Comrt of Nationalities, then RSFSR Dep Pop Comr of Nationalities; Nov 1922–1924 again chm, Turkestani Centr Exec Comt; then head, Press Dept, Kaz Kray Party Comt; May 1926–1937 dep chm, RSFSR Council of Pop Comr; at 12th Party Congress elected cand member, CC, CPSU(B); 1937 arrested by State Security organs; *Died:* 1943 in imprisonment.

RYTOV, Andrey Gerasimovich (1907–1967) Air force polit commander; col-gen, Sov Air Force from 1961; CP member from 1929; *Born:* 1907 in Ryazan' Province, son of a farm laborer; *Educ:* 1925 completed seven-year peasant youth school; late 1940's grad Gen Staff Acad; *Career:* from 1939 in Red Army; exec secr, regt Komsomol Bureau; company polit officer; instructor, polit dept of a div; transferred to Sov Air Force; 1937–38 comr, Sov air force unit in China; 1939–40 took part in Sov-Finnish War; 1941–42 comr, 6th Mixed Air Force Div, air force comr of 11th and 57th Armies; comr, 3rd Air Force Strike Group; comr, 244th Air Force Div; comr, 3rd Bomber Corps; 1942–45 dep commander (polit); 3rd Bomber Corps; commander, 8th Air Army; 1950–52 member, Mil Council, Sov Anti-Aircraft Troops; 1952–55 head, Polit Bd, Sov Air Force; from 1955 member, Mil Council, Sov Air Force; deleg at 22nd and 23rd CPSU Congresses; dep, RSFSR Supr Sov of 1963 and 1967 convocations; *Awards:* Order of Lenin; three orders of the Red Banner; Order of Suvorov, 2nd Class; Order of Bogdan Khmel'nitskiy, 1st and 2nd Class; Order of the Fatherland War, 1st Class; two Orders of the Red Star; medals; *Died:* June 1967; buried in Moscow's Novodevich'ye Cemetary.

RYVKIN, Oskar L'vovich (1899–1937) Komsomol and Party official; CP member from 1917; *Born:* 4 Jan 1899 in Petersburg, son of an office worker; *Educ:* 1930–34 studied at Inst of Red Prof; *Career:* apprentice at printing works and pharmacy; 1917 served with Red Guards; helped found and lead Socialist League of

Working Youth, Petrograd; 1918 at 1st Russian Komsomol Congress elected member, CC, Russian Komsomol; chm, CC, Russian Komsomol of 1st convocation; until Oct 1920 first secr, CC, Russian Komsomol; fought in Civil War; from 1924 on Party work; head, Dept of Agitation and Propaganda, and Bureau member, Vyksa Uyezd RCP(B) Comt, Nizhniy Novgorod Province; then head, Dept of Agitation and Propaganda, Nizhniy Novgorod Province CPSU(B) Comt; 1934–37 first secr, Krasnodar City CPSU(B) Comt; deleg at 1st–4th Russian Komsomol Congresses, 2nd Communist Youth International Congress and 9th, 15th, 16th and 17th Party Congresses; at 1st–3rd Komsomol Congresses elected member, CC, Russian Komsomol; at 15th and 16th Party Congresses elected member CPSU(B) Centr Control Commission; arrested by State Security organs; *Died:* 1937 in imprisonment; posthumously rehabilitated.

RYZHOV, Aleksandr Ivanovich (1895–1950) Mil commander; lt-gen; CP member from 1939; *Born:* 23 Nov 1895 in vil Kir'yanis, now Ivanov Oblast, son of a peasant; *Career:* fought in WW 1 and Civil War; from 1918 in Red Army; during WW 2 commanded infantry div, corps and various armies, including 4th Guards Army which in 1944 took part in Korsun'-Shevchenkovo operation on 2nd Ukr Front; after WW 2 various commands in Sov Army; *Awards:* Hero of the Sov Union; four Orders of Lenin; other orders; medals; *Died:* 14 Dec 1950.

RYZHOVA, Varvara Nikolayevna (1871–1963) Actress; Pop Artiste of USSR from 1937; *Born:* 15 Jan 1871 in Moscow; of actor parents; *Educ:* 1893 grad A. Lenskiy's drama class, Moscow Theatrical College; *Career:* 1893–1956 actress, Maly Theater; 1900–03 also performed at Moscow's New Theater; performed some 300 roles; *Roles:* Akulina in Lev Tolstoy's *Vlast' t'my* (The Power of Darkness); Liza in Griboyedov's *Gore ot uma* (Woe from Wit); Ulita, Kupava and Bobylikha in Ostrovskiy's *Les* (The Forest) and *Snegurochka* (The Snow-Maiden); Glumova in Ostrovskiy's *Na vsyakogo mudretsa dovol'no prostoty* (There's a Simpleton in Every Sage); Domna Panteleyevna in Ostrovskiy's *Talanty i poklonniki* (Talents and Admirers); Anfisa Tikhonovna in Ostrovskiy's *Volki i ovtsy* (The Wolves and the Sheep); Emilie in Hauptmann's "The Sisters of Bischofsberg"; Avdot'ya in Uspenskiy's *Rasteryayeva ulitsa* (Rasteryayeva Street); Mar'ya in Trenyov's "Lyubov' Yarovaya"; Motyl'kova in Gusev's *Slava* (Glory); Demid'yevna in Leonov's *Nashestviye* (Invasion), etc; *Publ:* *Avtobiografiya* (Autobiography) (1949); *Awards:* two Orders of Lenin; two Orders of the Red Banner of Labor; medals; Stalin Prize (1943); *Died:* 18 May 1963 in Moscow.

S

SABLIN, Yuriy Vladimirovich (1897–1937) Mil commander; div commander from 1935; CP member from 1919; *Born:* 24 Nov 1897 in Yur'yev (Tartu), son of the Moscow book publisher V.M. Sablin; *Educ:* studied at Moscow Business Inst; 1917 grad ensigns school; grad Mil Acad; 1923 grad Higher Acad Courses; 1925 completed pilots school; 1927 completed Advanced Commanders Courses; *Career:* 1915–17 member, Socialist-Revol Party; 1917–18 member, Leftist Socialist-Revol Party; 1916 volunteered for the front; Mar 1917 elected to Moscow Sov Exec Comt; at 2nd Congress of Soviets elected member, Centr Exec Comt; Oct 1917, during armed uprising in Moscow, member, Revol Comt; commanded battle squad and was wounded; Nov 1917 elected Presidium member, Moscow Sov; Dec 1917 appointed commander, 1st Moscow Revol Detachment; commanding northern sector of Southwestern Front, directed capture of Novocherkassk; 1918 commanded 4th Army on Ukr Front; then comr, Moscow Area of Western Screen; member, All-Russian Centr Exec Comt; 1918 took part in Leftist Socialist-Revol Revolt; sentenced to 12 months' imprisonment, but amnestied by All-Russian Centr Exec Comt, whereupon he broke with Leftist Socialist-Revolutionaries; late 1918–19 commanded insurgent detachment in Ukr; commanded regt and brigade against Gen Denikin; Oct–Nov 1919 commanded forces group of 14th Army, then 41st Infantry Div involved in liberation of Khar'kov; Feb–June 1920 commanded Est and 46th Infantry Div against Gen Wrangel; from June 1920 commanded right-bank group, 13th Army; then commanded Free Cavalry Div and separate cavalry brigade; distinguished by personal valor in battle; from Nov 1920 commanded 16th Cavalry Div; as deleg at 10th Party Congress helped crush Kronstadt Revolt; from 1931 head, 52nd Mil Construction Work Bd and commandant of a fortified area; from 1935 commanded div; arrested by State Security organs; *Died:* 19 June 1937 in imprisonment; posthumously rehabilitated.

SADIKOV, Pyotr Alekseyevich (1891–1942) Historian; *Born:* 1891; *Educ:* 1916 grad History and Philology Fac, Petersburg Univ; *Career:* in 1920's and 1930's worked at Leningrad Univ, Centr Archives and Archeographical Commission, USSR Acad of Sci; then at Inst of History, USSR Acad of Sci; specialized in Russian soc life and lit of 19th and 20th Centuries; studied history of 1905 and 1917 Revol; made a detailed study of Ivan the Terrible's "oprichnina" (secret police) system; *Publ: Ocherki po istorii oprichniny* (An Outline History of Oprichnina) (1950), etc; *Died:* 1942.

SADOVNICHENKO, Dmitriy Gavrilovich (1907–1955) party official; CP member from 1931; *Born:* 26 Oct 1907 in Pavlodar (now Dnepropetrovsk Oblast) son of a worker; *Educ:* grad Higher Party School, CC, CP(B) Ukr; *Career:* Komsomol and Party work; from Aug 1941 dep secr, from Jan 1943 secr, underground Dnepropetrovsk Oblast Comt, CP(B) Ukr; fought with partisans in Ukr during WW 2; from 1950 exec Party work in Khmel'nitskiy Oblast; *Died:* 16 Feb 1955.

SADOVSKAYA, Ol'ga Osipovna (1850–1919) Actress; wife of the actor M.P. Sadovskiy; *Born:* 11 June 1850; *Career:* from 1867 at Moscow Arts Circle Theater; then with Lentovskiy's Company; from 1881 at Maly Theater; performed some 50 roles in plays by Ostrovskiy; *Roles:* Domna Panteleyevna, Nezabudkina, Ulita and Anfusa Tikhonovna in Ostrovskiy's *Talanty i poklonniki* (Talents and Admirers), *Bednaya nevesta* (The Poor Bride), *Les* (The Forest), and *Volki i ovtsy* (The Wolves and the Sheep); the Cook and Matryona in Lev Tolstoy's *Plody prosveshcheniya* (The Fruits of Enlightenment) and *Vlast' t'my* (The Power of Darkness); the Countess in Griboyedov's *Gore ot uma* (Woe from Wit); Poshlyopkina in Gogol's *Revizor* (The Government Inspector); Kabanikha in Ostrovskiy's *Groza* (The Storm); Kukushkina in Ostrovskiy's *Dokhodnoye mesto* (A Lucrative Post); *Died:* 8 Dec 1919.

SADOVSKAYA, Yelizaveta Mikhaylovna (1872–1934) Actress; Hon Artiste of RSFSR from 1927; *Born:* 23 Apr 1872 in Moscow; *Educ:* 1894 grad drama courses, Moscow Theatrical College under O.A. Pravdin and M.P. Sadovskiy; *Career:* 1894–1934 actress, Maly Theater, Moscow; *Roles:* Anna in Ostrovskiy and S. Gedeonov's "Vasilisa Melent'yeva" (1894); Aksyusha in Ostrovskiy's *Les* (The Forest) (1895); title role in *Snegurochka* (The Snow-Maiden) (1900); Glafira in *Volki i ovtsy* (The Wolves and the Sheep) (1904); Ariel in Shakespeare's "The Tempest" (1905); Tanya in *Plody prosveshcheniya* (The Fruits of Enlightenment) (1907); Varvara in Ostrovskiy's *Groza* (The Storm) (1911); the Countess' Grand-Daughter in *Gore ot uma* (Woe from Wit) (1921); Francoise Artikl in Smolin's "Ivan Kozyr' i Tat'yana Russkikh" (1925); the Baroness in "Lyubov' Yarovaya" (1926); Lenchitskaya in Romashov's *Boytsy* (Warriors) (1934), etc; *Died:* 4 June 1934 in Moscow.

SADOVSKIY, Andrey Dmitriyevich (1880–1927) Revolutionary and trade-union official; CP member from 1901; *Born:* 1880 in Simferopol'; *Educ:* grad college in Melitopol'; 1911 grad Petersburg Inst of Transport Eng; *Career:* active in student revol movement; 1905 helped form battle squads at Putilov Plant; 1906–11 transport eng group in RSDRP Joint Student Org; 1914 drafted into Russian Army; active in 1917 Feb Revol; Presidium member, Petrograd Sov, member of its Exec Comt, dep chm of its Soldiers' Section and chm of its Mil Dept; from June 1917 Bureau member, Bolshevik Faction, Petrograd Sov; during 1917 Oct Revol Bureau member, Petrograd Revol Mil Comt, directing supply of arms, communications and transport; then head, Motor Transport Dept, All-Russian Centr Exec Comt; head, Transport Dept, USSR Centr Exec Comt; founder and head, Transport Workers' Union; from Oct 1919 chm, CC, Transport Workers' Union; member, All-Union Centr Trade-Union Council; deleg at 9th-11th Party Congresses; member, All-Russian Centr Exec Comt of all convocations; member, USSR Centr Exec Comt of 1st–3rd convocations; *Died:* 8 July 1927.

SADOVSKIY (real name: TOBILEVICH), Nikolay Karpovich (1856–1933) Actor and stage dir; *Born:* 6 Mar 1956 in vil Kostovatoye, Khar'kov Province; *Educ:* studied at Yelisavetgrad non-classical college; *Career:* 1877–81 volunteer, Russo-Turkish War; won George Cross for valor; 1881 resigned second-lt commission and became an actor with G. Ashkarenko's Ukr company; then acted with Kropovnitskiy and Staritskiy's companies; 1886 with Kropovnitskiy's company on tour in Petersburg; and 1887 in Moscow; 1888 founded theater company in conjunction with his brother and the artiste N. Zankovetskaya; from 1898 head, Assoc of Russian and Little Russian Actors; 1905 dir, drama company of Russian Conversation Soc in L'vov; 1906 founded in Poltava a Ukr theater which shortly afterwards moved to Kiev and operated until 1914; 1918–25 lived abroad, in Uzhgorod and Prague; 1925 returned to Kiev and occasionally acted at clubs with his brother Saksaganskiy; *Roles:* Mykola in Kotlyarevskiy's "Natalka-Poltavka"; Gnat, Taras and Panas in Karpenko-Karyy's *Bestalannaya* (The Ill-Fated Woman), "Bondarivna" and *Burlak* (The Barge-Hauler); Podorozhnyy in Staritskiy's *Zimniy vecher* (A Winter Evening); the Mayor in Gogol's *Revizor* (The Government Inspector); Smirnov in Chekhov's *Medved* (The Bear); Bogdan in Staritskiy's "Bogdan Khmel'nitskiy"; Taras in "Taras Bul'ba" after Gogol; the Commandore in Lesya Ukrainka's *Kamennyy vlastelin* (The Stone Sovereign), etc; *Productions:* de Grazie's "The Old Mine"; Gogol's *Revizor* (The Government Inspector) and *Zhenit'ba* (Marriage); Slovatskiy's "Mazepa"; Sholom Ash's *Bog mesti* (God of Vengeance); Ostrovskiy's *Dokhodnoye mesto* (A Lucrative Post); Lesya Ukrainka's *Kamennyy vlastelin* (The Stone Sovereign), etc; *Publ: Moi teatral'nyye vospominaniya* (My Theater Memories) (1930); *Died:* 7 Feb 1933 in Kiev.

SADOVSKIY, Prov Mikhaylovich (1874–1947) Actor and stage dir; Pop Artiste of USSR from 1937; *Born:* 9 Aug 1874 in Moscow; *Educ:* 1895 grad drama courses at Moscow Theatrical College; *Career:* 1895–1944 actor, 1944–47 actor and stage dir, Maly Theater; *Roles:* Glumov in *Na vsyakogo mudretsa dovol'no prostoty* (There's A Simpleton in Every Sage); Mizgir' in *Snegurochka* (The Snow-Maiden); Dato in Sumbatov's *Izmena* (Treason); the Pretender in *Dmitriy samozvanets i Vasiliy Shuyskiy* (Dmitriy the Pretender and Vasiliy Shuyskiy); Meluzov in *Talanty i poklonniki* (Talents and Admirers); Milovidov in *Na boykom meste* (A Lively Post); Berkutov in *Volki i ovtsy* (The Wolves and the Sheep); Chatskiy in *Gore ot uma* (Woe from Wit); Brutus in Shakespeare's "Julius Caesar"; Alexander I in "Arakcheyevshchina"; Philipp II in "Don Carlos"; Commissar Koshkin in "Lyubov' Yarovaya"; Talanov in *Nashestviye* (Invasion), etc; *Produktions:* "The Snow-Maiden" (1922); "A Lively Post" (1933); "There's A Simpleton in Every Sage" (1938); "The Wolves and the Sheep" (1944); "Ivan the Terrible" (1945), etc; *Awards* two Orders of Lenin; Stalin Prize (1943); *Died:* 4 May 1947 in Moscow.

SAFAROV, G.I. (Party name: YEGOROV) (1891–1942) Party official; CP member from 1908; *Born:* 1891; *Career:* Party work in Petersburg and abroad; during WW 1 sided with Zimmerwald Leftists; worked in France and then from Jan 1916 in Switzerland; after 1917 Feb Revol member, Petrograd RSDRP Comt; after 1917 Oct Revol Party and govt work; 1919 one of leaders of "Mil Opposition", at 8th RCP(B) Congress; from 1921 member, Turkestani Bureau, CC, RCP(B); 1921–22 member, Comintern Exec Comt; head, Eastern Dept, Comintern; at 10th and 12th Party Congresses elected cand member, CC, RCP(B); in the controversy over the Brest Peace Treaty sided with the Leftist Communists; at 14th CPSU(B) Congress sided with "New Opposition", then joined Trotsky-Zinoviev Bloc; 1927 at 15th CPSU(B) Congress expelled from Party as an active member of the Trotskyist opposition; 1928 re-admitted to Party; 1934 again expelled from Party for alleged anti-Party activities and then arrested by State Security organs; *Died:* 1942 in imprisonment.

SAFONOV, Aleksandr Kononovich (1875–1919) Party official; CP member from 1904; *Born:* 1875, son of a peasant; *Career:* house-painter, then teacher; active in 1905 Revol in Yaroslavl'; 1906 arrested and exiled to Arkhangel'sk Province; fled to Petersburg; arrested four times in the course of one year and forced to move to Moscow, where he helped rebuild Party org in Moscow Okrug; 1908 arrested and sentenced to four years' hard labor; 1914 sent to settlement in Verkholensk Uyezd; during 1917 Feb Revol in Irkutsk, where he helped establish Party and trade-union orgs and Irkutsk Sov; Aug 1917 moved to Moscow and worked as touring instructor and agitator for Moscow Okrug Party Comt; organized Party and govt work in Ryazan' and Tambov Provinces; after 1917 Oct Revol Party work and comr of a bank; 1919 went to front; member, Revol Mil Council, 11th Army; *Died:* 1919 killed by explosion on Moscow street.

SAFONOV, Boris Feoktistovich (1915–1942) Pilot, Naval Air Force; lt-col; *Born:* 26 Aug 1915 in vil Sinyavino, now Tula Oblast, son of a worker; *Educ:* 1932 completed glider pilots' school; 1933 completed pilots school; from 1933 in Red Army; 1938–40 asst mil comr of a squadron, in charge of Komsomol work; then squadron commander; during WW 2 flew fighter sorties in Arctic; *Awards:* twice Hero of the Sov Union (1941 and 1942 /posthumously/); two Orders of Lenin; three Orders of the Red Banner; medals; *Died:* 30 May 1942 killed in action.

SAFRONOV, Arseniy Mikhaylovich (1903–1957) Govt official; CP member from 1927; *Born:* 24 June 1903 in Moscow Province, son of a peasant; *Career:* at age 11 began work as apprentice in a factory; 1920–23 admin work, then served in Red Army; from 1925 worked for finance organs as financial agent, head of a distr finance dept, then head, Moscow City Finance Dept; 1939 RSFSR Pop Comr of Finance; 1940–45 dep chm, bd, USSR State Bank; from 1945 RSFSR Min of Finance; 1949–57 first dep chm, RSFSR Council of Min; dep, Moscow City Sov; dep, RSFSR Supr Sov of 1947, 1951 and 1955 convocations; dep, USSR Supr Sov and chm, Budget Commission, Sov of Nationalities of 1954 convocation; *Awards:* Order of the Red Banner of Labor; *Died:* 13 Oct 1957.

SAID-GALIYEV, Sakhibgarey (1894–1939) Party and govt official; CP member from 1917; *Born:* 6 Feb 1894 in Ufa; *Educ:* 1901–04 studied at Tatar primary school; *Career:* began work at age 10 as paper-boy; distributed proclamations and sold revol pamphlets; then laborer on Siberian Railroad; ship's stoker; canvassed subscriptions for "Brockhaus and Efron" Publ House in Saratov, Samara and Orenburg; laborer at Ufa sawmill; 1916 mil service in Yekaterinburg with 126th Infantry Reserve Regt; after 1917 Feb Revol elected member, regt sov; then Presidium member, regt comt; member, Yekaterinburg Sov of Workers and Soldier's Dep; chm, Yekaterinburg Garrison Comt; then chm, Yekaterinburg Province Comt of Moslem Soldiers; agitated among Tatar and Bashkir soldiers in Yekaterinburg and other Ural cities; after 1917 Oct Revol comr for Moslem affairs, 47th Brigade, Yekaterinburg; sponsored mustering of 1st Ural Revol Battalion; early 1918 deleg at 2nd All-Russian Moslem Mil Congress; then deleg at Volga and Cis-Ural (Kazan') Congress of Soviets; Feb 1918 elected comr for nationality Affairs, Kazan' Sov; Nov 1918–Apr 1919 member, Tatar-Bashkir Bureau, Ufa Province RCP(B) Comt; then polit work in Moslem researve battalion and educ work on Moslem Mil Polit Courses in Kazan'; Nov–Dec 1919, at 2nd All-Russian Congress of Communist Orgs of Peoples of the East, in Moscow, elected chm, Centr Bureau of Communist Orgs of Peoples of the East, CC, RCP(B); deleg at 9th, 10th and 12th RCP(B) Congresses; member, All-Russian Centr Exec Comt of several convocations; attended 2nd Comintern Congress; from June 1920 chm, Mil Revol Comt, Tatar Autonomous Republ and Bureau member, Kazan' Province RCP(B) Comt; then chm, Council of Pop Comr, Tatar Autonomous Republ; 1921 elected chm, Council of Pop Comr, Crimean Republ; 1924–26 head, Finance and Econ Inspectorates, Centr Control Commission of Workers and Peasants' Inspection; from 1931 Collegium member, USSR Pop Comrt of Labor; from 1931 head, Polit Dept, Saratov Branch, Ryazan'-Ural Railroad; arrested by State Security organs; *Died:* 1939 in imprisonment; posthumously rehabilitated.

SAKHAROV Vasiliy Vasil'yevich (1889–1932) Party official; CP member from 1910; *Born:* 1889 in Moscow; *Career:* Party work in Moscow, Tashkent and other Russian cities; frequently arrested by Tsarist authorities; after 1917 Feb Revol returned from East Siberian exile; Apr 1917 elected member, Moscow RSDRP(B) Comt and Moscow Sov; secr, Tailors' Union; during 1917 Oct Revol member, Moscow Mil Revol Comt; during Civil War fought on Southern Front; from Feb 1919 head, Polit Dept, Caspian, then Caucasian Fronts; from Fall 1919 mil comr, Ural Infantry Div; from Mar 1920 div commander; after Civil War Party and govt work; member, Moscow Party Comt and Moscow RCP(B) Control Commission; from 1926 dir, 1st Cotton-Printing Mill; from 1928 dir, Three-Mountains Manufacturing Plant; 1930 Sov trade rep in Czechoslovakia; deleg at 11th, 13th and 14th Party Congresses; *Died:* 1932.

SAKSAGANSKIY (real name: TOBILEVICH), Panas Karpovich (1859–1940) Actor and stage dir; Pop Artiste of USSR from 1936; *Born:* 15 May 1859 in vil Kamenno-Kostovatoye, Kherson Province; *Educ:* 1877 grad Yelizavetgrad non-classical high school; 1880 grad Odessa Cadets School; *Career:* from 1883 professional actor; 1885–88 actor, Staritskiy, then Krapivnitskiy Companies; 1886–87 on tour in Petersburg and Moscow; 1888–90 with A. Sadovskiy's Company; 1890 founder-dir, Assoc of Russian and Little-Russian Artistes; from 1889 also worked as stage dir;

1898–1909, together with Sadovskiy, directed Joint Assoc, later Little Russian Company; 1910–15 toured Russia with various companies; 1915 co-founder, Assoc of Ukr Artistes; 1918 founded Pop Theater; 1922 co-founder Zan'kovetskaya Theater, Kiev; 1927–31 at Zan'kovetskaya and Franko Theaters and Khar'kov Pop Theater; *Roles:* Kopach in *Sto tysyach* (The Hundred Thousand); Finogen in Karpenko-Karyy's *Khozyain* (The Proprietor); the Delegate in Kotlyarevskiy's "Natalka Poltavka"; Karas in Gulak-Artemovskiy's *Zaporozhets za Dunayem* (A Dnieper Cossack Beyond the Danube); Ivan in Karpenko-Karyy's *Suyeta* (Fuss); Franz Moor in Schiller's "Die Räuber"; Solopiy Cherevik in *Sorochinskaya yarmarka* (Sorochintsy Fair), after Gogol, etc; *Productions:* "Natalka Poltavka" (1889); *Bestalannaya* (The Ill-Starred Woman) (1890); *Nevol'nik* (The Slave) (1891); "Sorochinskaya yarmarka" (1892); *Dve Sem'i* (Two Families) (1894); "Khozyain" (1901); "Suyeta" (1904); "Uriel' Akosta" (1918); "Die Räuber" (1920); "Othello" (1926), etc; *Publ:* comedies *Litsemery* (The Hyocrites) (1908); *Shantrapa* (Riff-Raff) (1913); *Moya rabota nad rol'yu* (My Work on a Role) (1937); *Iz proshlogo ukrainskogo teatra* (From the Past of the Ukrainian Theater) (1938); *K molodym rezhissyoram* (To Young Stage Directors) (1940), etc; *Awards:* Order of the Red Banner of Labor; *Died:* 17 Sept 1940 in Kiev.

SAKVARELIDZE, P.D. (1882–1937) Politician; *Born:* 1882; *Career:* 1905–10 member, RSDRP(B); Baku Party Org deleg at 4th (Amalgamative) RSDRP Congress; worked for Geo Party orgs in Baku; then became Menshevik; after 1917 Feb Revol and establishment of democratic govt in Geo opposed Bolsheviks and Sov regime; after establishment of Sov rule in Geo concentrated on lit work; worked for Geo State Publ House and other establishments; arrested by State Security organs; *Died:* 1937 in imprisonment.

SAMARIN, Nikolay Nikolayevich (1888–1954) Surgeon; Dr of Med; prof from 1932; corresp member, USSR Acad of Med Sci from 1946; Hon Sci Worker of RSFSR from 1947; *Born:* 1888; *Educ:* 1912 grad Petersburg Mil Med Acad; *Career:* after grad worked as a gen practitioner and at S. S. Girgolav's Clinic; defended doctor's thesis on the healing of spinal injuries; from 1924 senior asst, V. A. Oppel's Clinic, Surgical Dept, Mechnikov Hospital, Leningrad; 1928–32 asst prof, from 1932 prof and head, 2nd Chair of Surgery, Leningrad Inst of Postgrad Med Training; 1950–52 sci dir, Leningrad First Aid Inst; made a major contribution to emergency visceral surgery, especially for acute intestinal blockage and pancreatitis; hypothesized that disturbances of the juice metabolism and loss of disgestive juices constitute a major factor in the lethality of acute intestinal blockage; also specialized in traumatology; organized a model traumatology section of the Surgical Dept, Lenin Hospital; designed several instruments for setting fractures of the shoulder, heel bone and vertebra; wrote over 80 works; *Publ: K khirurgii parashchitovidnykh zhelez* (Surgery of the Parathyroid Gland) (1933); *Patogenez i lecheniye ostroy kishechnoy neprokhodimosti* (The Pathogenesis and Treatment of Acute Intestinal Blockage) (1937); *Raneniya i povrezhdeniya spinnogo mozga* (Wounds and Lesions of the Spine) (1940); ed and coauthor, *Diagnostika "ostrogo zhivota"* (The Diagnosis of "Acute Stomach") (1940) *Ognestrel'nyye raneniya pryamoy kishki, kostey tazy i yagodits* (Gunshot Wounds of the Rectum, Pelvic Bones and Buttock) (1941); *Nablyudeniya nad bol'nymi s ostrymi pankreatitami* (Observations on Acute Pancreatitis Patients) (1953), etc; *Died:* 1954 in Leningrad.

SAMMER, Ivan Adamovich (Party name: LYUBICH; IZMAIL) (1870–1921) Revolutionary; Party official; active in cooperative movement; CP member from 1903; *Born:* 3 Sept 1870 in vil Ocherednoy, Kiev Province; *Educ:* studied at Kiev Univ; *Career:* 1897 joined revol movement in Kiev; as student; then Party work in Petersburg and worked for Free Econ Soc; 1897 arrested and exiled to Samara; 1903 exiled to Velikiy Ustyug, Vologda Province; 1905 returned from exile and helped run Kazan's RSDRP Comt; 1905 deleg at 3rd RSDRP(B) Congress and elected cand member, CC, RSDRP(B); Oct 1905 helped lead armed workers' demonstration in Kazan'; Nov 1906 attended All-Russian Conference of Mil and Militant RSDRP Orgs; 1906–17 exiled in Vologda Province; after 1917 Feb Revol secr, Vologda Sov; after 1917 Oct Revol chm, Vologda Sovnarkhoz; from 1919 Collegium member, Centr Union of Consumer Soc, Moscow; then chm, Ukr Union of Consumer Soc, Khar'kov; *Died:* 21 June 1921.

SAMOKISH, Nikolay Semyonovich (1860–1944) Painter; specialist in battle scenes; graphic artist; art teacher; acad from 1890; Hon Art Worker of RSFSR from 1937; *Born:* 27 Oct 1860 in Nezhin; *Educ:* 1885 grad Petersburg Acad of Arts; *Career:* from 1894 taught art; 1912–17 prof, Battle Studio, Petersburg Acad of Arts; 1936–41 prof, Art Inst, Khar'kov; visited the fronts of the Russo-Japanese War and WW 1 to familiarize himself with mil life; *Works:* paintings: "An Episode in the Battle at Malo-Yaroslavets" (1884); "The Battle of Avilyar in 1887" (1889); album of sketches "From Old Ukrainian Life" (1900); album "1904–1905. The War. From an Artist's Diary"; murals at a house in Poltava Zemstvo (1902–08); "The Defense of the Red Banner" (1920); "Reconnaissance" (1923); "Bogdan Khmel'nitskiy's Entry into Kiev" (1929); "The Battle at Yellow Waters" (1930); "The Battle Between Krivonos and Prince Iyeremiy Vishnevetskiy" (1934); "Fording the Sivash" (1935); "N.Ya. Shchors in Battle at Chernigov" (1938); etc; *Awards:* Order of the Red Banner of Labor; Stalin Prize (1941); *Died:* 18 Jan 1944 in Simferopol'.

SAMOSUD, Samuil Abramovich (1884–1964) Conductor; Pop Artiste of USSR from 1937; *Born:* 2 May 1884; *Educ:* 1906 grad Tiflis Conservatory; *Career:* 1917–25 conductor, Mariinskiy Theater; 1918–36 chief conductor and artistic dir, Leningrad Maly Opera Theater; 1936–43 chief conductor and artistic dir, Bolshoy Theater; 1943–50 chief conductor, Moscow's Stanislavsky and Nemirovich-Danchenko Musical Theater; 1953–57 founder-dir, Symphony Orchestra, Moscow Philharmonic; from 1957 dir, All-Union Radio and Television Opera and Symphony Orchestra; worked with Meyerhold, Eisenstein and Yevreinov; *Works:* produced operas: *Nos* (The Nose) (1930); *Kamarinskiy muzhik* (The Kamarinskiy Peasant) (1933); Shostakovich's *Ledi Makbet Mtsenskogo uyezda* (Lady Macbeth of Mtsensk) (1934); *Tikhiy Don* (Quiet Flows the Don) (1935); *Podnyataya tselina* (Virgin Soil Upturned) (1937); "Ruslan i Lyudmila" (1937); "Ivan Susanin" (1939); "Iolanthe" (1940); *Voyna i mir* (War and Peace) (1947); Kabalevskiy's *Sem'ya Tarasa* (Taras' Family) (1951), etc; *Awards:* Order of Lenin; Badge of Hon; Stalin Prizes (1941, 1947 and 1952); *Died:* 6 Nov 1964.

SAMOYLO, Aleksandr Aleksandrovich (1869–1963) Mil commander; lt-gen, Air Force from 1940; prof from 1940; CP member from 1944; *Born:* 26 Oct 1869 in Moscow, son of a mil surgeon; *Educ:* 1892 grad Moscow Mil College; 1899 grad Gen Staff Acad; *Career:* during WW 1 served with Intelligence Dept, Gen Staff and Headquarters; then chief of staff, 10th Army with rank of maj-gen; after 1917 Oct Revol sided with the Bolsheviks; took part in Brest peace talks; from Feb 1918 dep commander, Western Screen; then chief of staff, White Sea Mil Distr; from May 1918 chief of staff, Northern Front; Nov 1918–Apr 1920 commander, 6th Separate Army (apart from a short interval in May 1919, when he commanded the Eastern Front); 1920–21 asst chief of staff, Red Army; simultaneously chief, All-Russian Main Staff and member, Higher Mil Council; Apr 1920 took part in peace talks with Finland; Mar 1921 took part in peace talks with Turkey; from 1921 taught at mil college; prof, Zhukovskiy Air Force Acad; wrote numerous research works and memoirs; from 1948, although retired, worked for Mil Research Soc, Centr Museum of the Sov Army; *Publ: Dve zhizni* (Two Lives) (1928); *Pouchitel'nyy urok* (A Salutary Lesson) (1962); *Awards:* various orders and medals; *Died:* 8 Nov 1963.

SAMOYLOV, Aleksandr Filippovich (1867–1930) Physiologist; *Born:* 1867; *Educ:* grad Natural Sci Dept, Physics and Mathematics Fac, Novorossiysk Univ, Odessa; grad Med Fac, Yur'yev Univ (Derpt); *Career:* 1892 defended doctor's thesis; 1893–96 worked at I.P. Pavlov's Laboratory, Inst of Experimental Med; from 1896 asst to I.M. Sechenov in Moscow; then assoc prof, Med Fac, Moscow Univ; 1903–30 prof of zoology, comparative anatomy and physiology, Physics and Mathematics Fac, Kazan' Univ; from 1925 also prof of physiology, Veterinary Inst and Physics and Mathematics Fac, 1st Moscow Univ; founder and consultant, Electrocardiographic Centers, Obukh Inst and Botkin Hospital; pioneer of Russian electrophysiology and electrocardiography; collected important physiological data using capillary electrometer and string galvanometer for study of physiological phenomena; introduced electrocardiography into Russia and improved its technique; 1908 published work on practical application of string galvanometer which he himself had improved; one of first physiologists in the world to use string galvanometer for study of skeletal musculature and complex reflex actions; postulated chemical nature of transmission of excitation from somatic nerve to skeletal muscle; also studied humoral nature of centr inhibition; performed basic research on physiology of muscles, nerve fibers, end plates, centr nervous system, cardiac muscle and sensory organs; wrote several studies on history of physiology, including such physiologists as Harvey, Sechenov, Loeb, Pavlov and Magnus; also studied theory of music and connection between physiology of sensory organs and the theory of musical harmony; wrote some 110 works; *Publ: Nekotoyye elektrofiziologicheskiye opyty* (Some Electrophysiological Experiments) (1904); *Elektrokardiogrammy* (Electrocardiograms) (1908); *Teorii myshechnogo sokrashcheniya* (Theories of Muscular Contraction) (1922); *Dialektika prirody i yestestvoznaniye* (The Dialectics of Nature and Natural Sciences) (1926); "Die Rigidität und Plastizität der Muskeln des dezerebrierten Tieres" (1927); *K kharakteristike tsentral'nykh protsessov ugneteniya* (The Characteristics of Central Inhibition Processes) (1927); *Elektrofiziologicheskiy metod v uchenii o refleksakh* (The Electrophysiological Method in Reflex Theory) (1932); *Izbrannyye stat'i i rechi* (Selected Articles and Speeches) (1946); *Awards:* Lenin Prize; *Died:* 1930.

SAMOYLOV, Fyodor Nikitich (1882–1952) Govt and Party official; *Born:* 24 Apr 1882 in Vladimir Province, son of a weaver; CP member from 1903; *Career:* 1905 helped lead Ivanovo-Voznesensk strike; member, Northern RSDRP Comt; member, Sov of Plen – one of first Russian sov of workers' dep; 1906–08 chm, Cotton-Printers' Union; 1912 elected dep, 4th State Duma by workers of Vladimir Province; 1914, together with other Bolshevik Duma dep, arrested and exiled for life to Turukhansk Kray; 1917-18 member, Ivanovo-Voznesensk RSDRP(B) Comt; chm, Ivanovo-Voznesensk Sov of Workers and Soldiers' Dep; 1918 comr of labor, then chm of a tribunal; 1919 Ukr Dep Pop Comr of Labor; then All-Union Centr Exec Comt plen in Bashkir Revol Comt; 1920–22 Ukr Dep Pop Comr of Labor; from 1922 worked for RCP(B) Centr Control Commission; from 1926 dep head, Commission for Collating and Studying Material on the Oct Revol and the History of the Communist Party, CC, RCP(B); from 1928 dep head, Commission for Collating and Studying Material on the Oct Revol and the History of the Communist Party, Moscow CPSU(B) Comt; from 1932 dep chm, All-Union Soc of Old Bolsheviks; from 1937 dir, State Museum of the Revol; deleg at 12th and 14th-17th CPSU(B) Congresses; elected member, All-Russian Centr Exec Comt; from 1941 pensioner; *Publ: Po sledam minuvshego* (In the Tracks of the Past) (1940); *Protsess bol'shevistskoy fraktsii 4-oy Gosudarstvennoy dumy* (The Trial of the Bolshevik Faction of the 4th State Duma), etc; *Died:* 13 Apr 1952.

SAMOYLOVA (nee: GROMOVA), Konkordiya Nikolayevna (1876–1921) Revolutionary; CP member from 1903; *Born:* 1876 in Irkutsk, daughter of a priest; *Educ:* grad Irkutsk high-school; from 1896 studied on Petersburg Higher Women's Courses; *Career:* from 1897 active in revol movement; 1902 sided with "Iskra" group in Paris; 1903 member, Tver', 1905 Odessa, 1906–07 Rostov, Moscow Okrug, then Lugana RSDRP Comt; 1907 deleg at 5th RSDRP Congress; then worked in Baku; 1909–10 member, Petersburg RSDRP Comt; 1912 secr, ed staff, newspaper "Pravda"; helped direct women's proletarian movement; member, ed bd, journal "rabotnitsa"; frequently arrested; after 1917 Feb Revol org and propaganda work among Petrograd workers; after 1917 Oct Revol chm, Commission for Work among Women Workers, Petrograd RSDRP(B) Comt; Nov 1917 directed 1st Conference of Women Workers; Jan 1918 helped organize 1st All-Russian Conference of Women Workers; touring instructor for CC, RCP(B) for propaganda among women workers; contributed to "Pravda" and journal "Kommunistka"; 1919 member, Samara Province and City RCP(B) Comt; then head, Dept for Work Among Women, CC, CP(B) Ukr; 1920–21 head, Polit Dept, "Krasnaya Zvezda" agitation steamer on the Volga; wrote numerous articles and pamphlets; *Died:* 2 June 1921 in Astrakhan' of cholera.

SAMSONOV, Pavel Fyodorovich (1892–1963) Microbiologist; Dr of Med; prof; Hon Sci Worker of Uzbek SSR; *Born:* 1892 in Margelan; *Educ:* 1916 grad Med Fac, Moscow Univ; *Career:* 1916–19 asst dissector, Bacteriological Inst, Moscow Univ; 1919–22 mil surgeon in Turkestan; 1921–32 senior asst prof, Chair of Infectious Diseases, then assoc prof of microbiology, Med Fac, Turkestani State Univ; 1932–35 head, Epidemiological Dept and Dept of Microbiology, Uzbek Inst of Epidemiology and Microbiology; 1935–39 head, Uzbek Republ Brucellosis Station, Tashkent; 1939–63 head, Chair of Microbiology, Tashkent Med Inst and sci consultant, Uzbek Republ Brucellosis Station; first dep chm, Learned Med Council, Uzbek Min of Health; chm, Uzbek Branch, All-Union Soc of Microbiologists, Epidemiologists and Infectionists; member, ed council, "Zhurnal mikrobiologii, epidemiologii i immunologii"; member, Org Comt, 9th Int Microbiology Congress, Moscow; head, Med Section, Tashkent City Dept of Soc for the Dissemination of Polit and Sci Knowledge; devised a variety of methods for the prevention of a number of infections common in Uzbek SSR; wrote over 80 works; *Awards:* Order of Lenin; medal "For Valiant Labor During the Great Fatherland War"; Hon Scrolls of the Uzbek and Karakalpak Supr Sov; *Died:* 1966 in Tashkent.

SANOTSKIY, Vladimir Antonovich (1890–1965) Toxicologist; prof; Dr of Med; member, USSR Acad of Med Sci from 1963; head, Toxicology Laboratory, Inst of Biophysics, USSR Min of Health; *Born:* 1890; *Educ:* 1914 grad Petrograd Mil Med Acad; *Career:* 1914–24 mil surgeon; 1924–34 worked for toxicology laboratories at various research establishments; 1934–52 laboratory head, dep (sci) dir, then dir, Inst of Pathology and Therapy of Intoxication; also head, Toxicology Laboratory, Veterinary Acad; also directed course on toxicology of radioactive substances at Centr Inst of Postgrad Med Training, Moscow; 1953–65 head, Toxicology Laboratory, Inst of Biophysics, USSR Min of Health; 1948–63 corresp member, USSR Acad of Med Sci; then chm, Bureau, Med and Biological Sci Div, USSR Acad of Med Sci; also dep acad secr of this div; member, Centr Council, All-Union Soc of Physiologists; member, Med Section, Plenum of Higher Certification Commission; member, ed bd, journals "Farmakologiya i toksikologiya" and "Byulleten' eksperimental'noy biologii i meditsiny"; from 1950 chm, Pharmacology and Toxicology Section, Moscow Soc of Physiologists, Biochemists and Pharmacologists; studied operative mechanism of toxic substances and did research on methods of treating their effects; did research on pathology and experimental therapy of radioactive lesions; *Publ: coauthor, Patologiya, terapiya i profilaktika otravleniy zhivotnykh boyevymi otravlyayushchimi veshchestvami* (The Pathology, Therapy and Prophylaxis of Poisoning by Military Poisons of Animal Origin) (1940); *Nekotoryye voprosy toksikologii radioaktivnykh veshchestv* (Some Aspects of the Toxicology of Radioactive Substances) (1957); *Obshchiye printsipy terapii porazheniya radioaktivnymi veshchestvami* (General Principles of the Therapy of Lesions by Radioactive Substances) (1957); *Tiolovyye soyedineniya v terapii porazheniy radioaktivnymi veschestvami* (Thiolic Compounds in the Therapy of Lesions from Radioactive Substances) (1959), etc; *Awards:* Order of Lenin; Order of the Red Banner of Labor; medals; Distinguished Health Worker Badge; *Died:* Nov 1965 in Moscow.

SAPOZHKOV (? –1920) Mil commander; member, Leftist Socialist-Revol Party; *Career:* commanded 2nd Turkestani Cavalry Div; July 1920 raised revolt against Sov regime in Buzuluk Uyezd, Samara Province, which then spread to the Samara Uyezd; *Died:* 6 Sept 1920 killed by Bolsheviks suppressing the revolt.

SAPOZHKOV, Konstantin Petrovich (1874–1952) Surgeon; Hon Sci Worker of RSFSR; *Born:* 1874; *Educ:* 1898 grad Med Fac, Warsaw Univ; *Career:* from 1899 dissector, Chair of Descriptive Anatomy; from 1919 asst prof, from 1922 assoc prof, Chair of Operative Surgery, Leningrad Inst of Med Knowledge; from 1927 head, Chair of Fac Surgical Clinic, Yakutsk Med Inst; during WW 2 devised original methods of closing external fecal fistulae by extraperitoneal means and a radical treatment of venous aneurysm; for the last 26 years of his life worked on surgery of the stomach and esophagus; made a precise topographical study of the stomach's ligamentous apparatus and devised new methods for the surgical treatment of ulcers and cancer of the stomach; justified total resection of the stomach for any localization of gastric cancer; wrote over 60 works; *Publ: Novyy ("invaginatsionnyy") sposob nalozheniya gubovidnykh zheludochnykh svishchey (gastrostom)* (A New /Invagionational/Method of Applying Labiate Gastric Fistulae /Gastrostomy/) (1945); *O predel'no radikal'nykh operatsiyakh pri rakakh zheludka* (Maximum Radical Operations for Cancer of the Stomach) (1946); *O svyazochnom apparate zheludka i bryushnogo otdela pishchevoda v osveshchenii khirurgii* (The Ligamentous Apparatus of the Stomach and the Ventral Section of the Esophagus in the Light of Surgery) (1950); *Dva novykh sposoba zakrytiya kul'ti dvenadtsatiperstnoy kishki pri radikal'nykh rezektsiyakh nizko sidyashchikh i penetriruyushchikh yazv etoy kishki* (Two New Methods of Closing the Duodenal Stump in Radical Resection of Low-Seated and Perforated Duodenal Ulcers) (1951); *Ob opredelnii razmerov udalyayemykh uchastkov zheludka* (Determining the Extent of Removable

Portions of the Stomach) (1952); *O nalozhenii pishchevodnokishechnogo soust'ya pri issechenii rakov kardial'noy chasti zheludka i pishchevoda* (Forming an Esophago-Intestinal Anastomosis with Exsection of Cancer of the Cardiac Portion of the Stomach and Esophagus) (1952); *Died:* 1952.

SAPOZHKOV, Pavel Ivanovich (1896–1961) Surgeon; *Born:* 1896; *Educ:* 1925 grad Med Fac, Crimean Univ; *Career:* studied under N.N. Burdenko; from 1936 intern, then prof, 1st Moscow Med Inst; during WW 2 chief surgeon, evacuation hospitals in Chuvash ASSR; studied pathogenesis, clinical aspects, treatment and long-term results of surgical treatment of ulcer patients; did research on neurosurgery; in his latter years specialized in surgical treatment of tumors of the large intestine; helped organize public health service of RSFSR; public health consultant in Hungary and Poland; wrote over 30 works; *Publ: Simptomatologiya i khirurgicheskoye lecheniye pri perforativnykh yazvakh zheludka i dvenadtsatiperstnoy kishki* (The Syndromes and Surgical Treatment of Perforated Gastric and Duodenal Ulcers) (1938); *Otdalyonnyye rezul'taty operatsiy Gil'debrandta* (Long-Term Results of Hildebrandt Operations) (1939); *Klinika i khirurgicheskoye lecheniye travmaticheskikh povrezhdeniy perifericheskikh nervov* (The Clinical Aspects and Surgical Treatment of Traumatic Injuries of the Peripheral Nerves) (1951); *Died:* 1961.

SAPRONOV, Timofey V. (1887–1939) Govt official; CP member from 1912; *Born:* 1887; *Career:* house-painter by trade; 1911 joined revol movement; after 1917 Oct Revol chm, Moscow Province Sov of Workers and Peasants' Dep; 1918, during Brest Peace Treaty controversy, sided with Leftist Communists; 1919–20 chm, Khar'kov Province Revol Comt; 1920–21 chm, CC, Construction Workers' Union; dep chm, Supr Sovnarkhoz; then secr, All-Russian Centr Exec Comt and chm, Small Council of Pop Comr; 1930, during trade-union controversy, headed Democratic Centralist group; 1925–27 member, New Opposition and leader of "The Fifteen" group; Dec 1927 expelled from Party but re-admitted after recanting his errors; Oct 1932 again expelled from Party and banished from Moscow; member, All-Russian Centr Exec Comt; at 11th RCP(B) Congress elected member, CC; member, Sov deleg at Genoa Conference; later sentenced for alleged anti-Sov activities; *Died:* 1939 in imprisonment.

SAPUNOV, Yevgeniy Nikolayevich (1887–1917) Revolutionary; CP member from 1917; *Born:* 6 Feb 1887 in vil Bulantsevo, Kaluga Province, son of a gardener; *Career:* followed his father's example in conducting revol propaganda among peasants; from 1906 worked for local RSDRP org; Nov 1908 arrested; 1914 drafted into Russian Army, where he conducted Bolshevik propaganda among the troops; after 1917 Feb Revol elected member, regt comt; June 1917 arrested and interned in Dvinsk Mil Prison, where he was elected to the prison Party Comt; early Sept, together with other imprisoned "Dvinsk soldiers" of the Northern Front, transferred to Moscow's Butyrka Prison; at the instigation of the Bolsheviks, he and the other "Dvinsk soldiers" were shortly released and recruited to help prepare the Oct uprising; 9 Nov 1917, upon orders from the Moscow Mil Revol Comt, a squad of "Dvinsk soldiers" left Zamoskvorech'ye and headed for the Moscow Sov building; on Red Square they were involved in a battle with officer cadets, in the course of which Sapunov was mortally wounded; *Died:* 9 Nov 1917 killed in action; buried on Moscow's Red Square; Moscow's former Vetoshnyy proyezd has been named after him.

SARGIN, Konstantin Davydovich (1894–1940) Pharmacologist; *Born:* 1894; *Educ:* grad Med Fac, Moscow Univ; *Career:* from 1922 specialized in testing and effects of therapeutic substances in Dept of Pharmacology, Moscow Chemical Pharmaceutical Research Inst; from 1932 head, Pharmacological Dept, State Inst of Experimental Endocrinology; also lectured at Chair of Pharmacology, 2nd Moscow Med Inst; 1938, without defending a thesis, received title of prof and degree of Dr of Med; developed methods for biological standardization of organic drugs; 1938 sponsored foundation of Commission for the State Control of Endocrine Drugs; his monograph on the biological evaluation of medicines is still a valid manual for pharmacological laboratories and so far the sole manual on this field in Russian; *Publ: Biologicheskaya otsenka lekarstvennogo syr'ya i farmatsevticheskikh preparatov* (The Biological Evaluation of Medicinal Raw Material and Pharmaceutical Drugs) (1929); *Farmakologiya endokrinnykh preparatov za 26 let* (The Pharmacology of Endocrine Preparations in the Past 26 Years) (1937); *Biologicheskaya otsenka lekarstvennykh veshchestv* (The Biological Evaluation of Medicines) (1938); *Died:* 1940.

SARKISOV (pseudonym: DANIELYAN), Sarkis Artemovich (1898–1938) Party and govt official; CP member from 1917; *Born:* 1898 in Shusha, now Azer SSR; *Career:* during Civil War carried out Party work in Baku, then exec Party and govt work in Leningrad; 1926–27 sided with Trotskyist opposition; from 1932 member, Procurement Comt, USSR Labor and Defense Council and head, Grain Procurement Bd; 1932–37 secr, Stalino (now Donetsk) Oblast Comt, CP(B) Ukr; for a while head, Donbass Coal Trust; deleg at 11th, 13th, 14th and 17th Party Congresses; at 17th Party Congress elected cand member, CC, CPSU(B); deleg at 12th and 13th Congresses of CP(B) Ukr, at which he was elected to CC; 1937 cand Politburo member, CC, CP(B) Ukr; member, USSR Centr Exec Comt of several convocations; arrested by State Security organs; *Awards:* Order of Lenin; *Died:* 12 Aug 1938 in imprisonment.

SATPAYEV, Kanysh Imantayevich (1899–1964) Geologist; member, USSR and Kaz Acad of Sci from 1946; Hon Sci Worker of Kaz SSR; CP member from 1944; *Born:* 11 Apr 1899 in vil in what is now Semipalatinsk Oblast; *Educ:* 1917 grad teachers' seminary in Semipalatinsk; 1926 grad Tomsk Technol Inst; *Career:* 1926–29 directed surveys in Dzhezkazgan, Uspensk and other mines of Atbasar Metals Trust, Kazakhstan; 1929–41 chief geologist and head, Geological Survey Dept, above trust; 1942–46 chm, Presidium, Kaz Branch, USSR Acad of Sci; 1946–52 and 1955–64 pres, Kaz Acad of Sci; also dir, Inst of Geological Sci, Kaz Acad of Sci; from 1957 Presidium member, USSR Acad of Sci; from 1951 hon member, Tadzh Acad of Sci; voting deleg at 1956 and 1959 CPSU Congresses; from 1956 member, CC, CP Kaz; dep, Kaz Supr Sov of 1954 and USSR Supr Sov 1958 and 1962 convocations; *Publ: Osnovnyye cherty geologii i metallogenii Dzhezkazganskogo mednorudnogo rayona* (The Basic Features of the Geology and Metallogeny of the Dzhezkazgan Copper Ore Area) (1935); *O prognoznykh metallogenicheskikh kartakh Tsentral'nogo Kazakhstana* (Metallogenic Forecast Maps of Central Kazakhstan) (1953); *O metallogenicheskikh epokhak, formatsiyakh i poyasakh Tsentral'nogo Kazakhstana* (The Metallogenic Epochs, Formations and Belts of Central Kazakhstan) (1953); *O nekotorykh spetsificheskikh osobennostyakh geologii medistykh peschanikov Atbasar-Tersakkanskogo rayona* (Some Specific Geological Features of the Copper Sands of the Atbasar-Tsersakkan Area) (1953); *O spetsifike i osnovnykh etapakh razvitiya metallogenii Tsentral'nogo Kazakhstana* (The Specific Features and Main Stages in the Development of the Metallogeny of Central Kazakhstan) (1957); etc; *Awards:* three Orders of Lenin; Order of the Fatherland War, 2nd Class; Stalin Prize (1942); Lenin Prize (1958); *Died:* 31 Jan 1964.

SAUKOV, Aleksandr Aleksandrovich (1902–1964) Geochemist; corresp member, USSR Acad of Sci from 1953; prof, Moscow Univ from 1952; head, Dept of Geochemistry, Inst of Geology, USSR Acad of Sci from 1949; CP member from 1945; *Born:* 1902; *Educ:* 1929 grad Leningrad Polytech Inst; *Career:* did research on geochemistry of rare metals, particularly mercury; devised method of determining small quantities of mercury in various rocks and minerals; *Publ: Geokhimiya rtuti* (The Geochemistry of Mercury) (1946); *Geokhimiya* (Geochemistry) (1951); *Geokhimicheskiye metody poiskov mestorozhdeniy poleznykh iskopayemykh* (Geochemical Methods of Prospecting for Mineral Deposits) (1957); *V.I. Vernadskiy i yestestvennaya radioaktivnost' Zemli* (V.I. Vernadskiy and the Natural Heteroactivity of the Earth) (1963); *Awards:* three orders; medals; two Stalin Prizes (1947 and 1952); *Died:* 23 Oct 1964.

SAVCHENKO, Ivan Grigor'yevich (1862–1932) Pathologist and immunologist; Dr of Med from 1893; prof from 1896; Hon Sci Worker of RSFSR from 1928; *Born:* 2 Mar 1862 in Poltava Province, now Sumy Oblast; *Educ:* 1888 grad Med Fac, Kiev Univ; *Career:* while still a student did research on bone lesions in leprosy patients; after grad dissector, Chair of Gen Pathology, Kiev Univ; 1893 defended doctor's thesis heterotoxic sporozoans in malignant tumors; in same year succesfully tested an oral cholera vaccine on himself and D.K. Zabolotnyy, thus anticipating a method of preventing intestinal infections proposed much later by A.M. Bezredkaya; 1893 also devised an original method of immunizing horses to obtain scarlet fever serum; 1895 worked under I.I. Mechnikov at the Pasteur Inst, Paris; 1896–1919 prof of gen pathology, Kazan' Univ; simultaneously founder-head, Kazan' Bacteriological Inst; 1904–14 did major research on phagocytosis; 1905 discovered scarlet fever toxin; 1907 proposed method of preparing scarlet fever serum which is still used in the USSR and abroad and now bears his name; from 1920 prof, Chair of Pathological Physiology, Kuban' Med Inst and founder-dir, Krasnodar Bacteriological Inst, which now bears his name; read papers at Pirogov Congresses and other sci conferences; wrote over 100 works; *Publ:* coauthor, *Opyt immunizatsii cheloveka protiv kholery* (The Experimental Immunization of Humans Against Cholera) (1893); doctor's thesis *Sporovikovyye chuzheyadenyye v zlokachestvennykh opukholyakh* (Heterotoxic Sporozoans in Malignant Tumors) (1894); coauthor, *K teorii fagotsitoza* (The Theory of Phagocytosis) (1910); coauthor, *O znachenii reaktsii sredy dlya fagotsitoza* (The Importance of the Reaction of the Medium for Phagocytosis) (1911); *Died:* 1932.

SAVEL'YEV, Maksimilian Aleksandrovich (pen name: VETROV) (1884–1939) Writer; Party and govt official; member, USSR Acad of Sci from 1932; Dr of Philosophy; CP member from 1903; *Born:* 1884 in Nizhniy Novgorod, son of a zemstvo official; *Educ:* 1910 grad Leipzig Univ; *Career:* underground Party work in Moscow, Nizhniy Novgorod, Tula and Petersburg; frequently arrested and exiled for revol activities; active in 1905–07 Revol; 1907–10 studied at Leipzig Univ; 1910 returned to Russia; 1911–13 in Petersburg edited journal "Prosveshcheniye" and member, ed staff, newspaper "Pravda"; 1913–17 underground Party work in Voronezh, Khar'kov, Moscow Kiev, etc; 1917 member, Kiev Party Comt; Presidium member and secr, Kiev Sov of Workers and Soldiers' Dep; deleg at 7th (Apr) All-Russian RSDRP(B) Conference and 6th RSDRP(B) Congress; at time of Oct 1917 Revol head, ed bd "Rabochiy put'"; then exec Party and govt work; edited various newspapers, including "Ekonomicheskaya zhizn'" and "Kommunist"; 1921–22 member, USSR Supr Sovnarkhoz and ed, journal "Narodnoye khozyaystvo"; 1921–27 ed, "Torgovo-promyshlennaya gazeta"; 1926–28 dep head, Commission for Party History, CC, CPSU(B) and ed, journal "Narodnoye khozyaystvo"; "Proletarskaya revolyutsiya"; 1928–32 dir, Lenin Inst and member, ed bd, newspaper "Pravda"; member, Chied Ed Bd for Lenin's Works; 1929 ed, newspaper "Izvestiya TsIK SSSR i VTsIK"; 1930 ed, newspaper "Pravda"; from 1931 dep chm, Communist Acad; from 1936 dep dir, Inst of Marx, Engels and Lenin, CC, CPSU(B); at 16th Party Congress elected cand member, CC, CPSU(B); wrote numerous works on Party history; arrested by State Security organs; *Died:* 1939 in imprisonment.

SAVEL'YEVA, Aleksandra Vasil'yeva (1886–1964) Party official; CP member from 1903; *Born:* 23 Apr 1886; *Career:* revol propaganda in Moscow, Petersburg, Yekaterinoslav, Tsaritsyn, Sormovo and Nizhniy Novgorod; several times arrested; 1908–11 lived abroad and helped smuggle party lit into Russia; 1912 returned to Petersburg and worked for "Pravda"; after 1917 Feb Revol member, Nizhniy Novgorod Province RSDRP(B) Comt and Presidium member, Nizhniy Novgorod Sov; edited Nizhniy Novgorod's first Bolshevik newspaper "Internatsional"; at time of 1917 Oct Revol member, Nizhniy Novgorod Mil Revol Comt; from 1921 dipl work; 1923–27 head, Schools Section, Agitation and Propaganda Dept, CC, CPSU(B); 1938–56 worked for State Lit Publ House; from 1956 pensioner; *Died:* 13 Nov 1964.

SAVICH, Aleksandr Antonovich (1890–1957) Historian; Dr of History from 1935; prof from 1926; *Born:* 1890; *Educ:* studied at Moscow and Petersburg Univ; *Career:* from 1921 lectured at univ and teachers' training inst in Minsk, Perm', Yaroslavl' and Moscow; also worked at State Historical Museum, Inst of History, USSR Acad of Sci; did research on the soc and econ history of Russia in the 15th–17th Centuries; also studied the history of soc thought in Russia, Bel and the Ukr and the history of Russia's int relations in the 16th and 17th Centuries; *Publ: Solovetskaya votchina XV-XVII vekov* (The Solovets Patrimonial Estate in the 15th–17th Centuries) (1927); *Pugachyovshchina na Urale* (The Pugachyov Rebellion in the Urals) (1925); *Ocherki po istorii kul'turnykh dvizheniy na Ukraine i v Belorussii v XVI–XVIII vekakh* (An Outline History of Cultural Movements in the Ukraine and Belorussia in the 16th–18th Centuries) (1929); *Ocherki istorii krest'yanskikh volneniy na Urale v XVIII–XX vekakh* (An Outline History of Peasant Unrest in the Urals in the 18th–20th Centuries) (1931); *Deulinskoye peremiriye 1618-ogo goda* (The 1618 Truce of Deulin) (1939), etc; *Died:* Oct 1957.

SAVICH, Vladimir Vasil'yevich (1874–1936) Physiologist and pharmacologist; Dr of Med from 1904; prof from 1921; *Born:* 1874; *Educ:* 1898 grad Petersburg Mil Med Acad; *Career:* after grad worked at I. P. Pavlov's Laboratory, in whose work he became interested while still a student; from 1900 postgrad student under Pavlov at Physiological Dept, Inst of Experimental Med; 1904 defended doctor's thesis on the secretion of intestinal juices; 1904–05 served in Russo-Japanese War; 1907–12 asst prof, Chair of Physiology, Petersburg Mil Med Acad; 1912–18 senior physiologist, Inst of Physiology, Russian Acad of Sci; 1918–26 dissector, Chair of Physiology, Petrograd (1st Leningrad) Med Inst; from 1921 head, Chair of Pharmacology, Petrograd (Leningrad) Veterinary Inst; from 1924 head, Dept of Pharmacology, State Inst of Experimental Med; wrote over 100 works; *Publ: Vozbuditeli sekretsii kishechnogo fermenta* (Stimulants of Intestinal Enzyme Secretion) (1901); doctor's thesis *Otdeleniye kishechnogo soka* (The Secretion of Intestinal Juices) (1904); *O sekretornykh zaderzhivayushchikh nervakh tonkikh kishek* (The Secretory Inhibitory Nerves of the Small Intestines) (1919); *Sekretsiya kishechnogo soka 'par distance'* (The Secretion of Intestinal Juices "Par Distance") (1921); *O roli nervov v sekretsii kishechnogo soka* (The Role of the Nerves in the Secretion of Intestinal Juices) (1922); coauthor, *K voprosu ob innervatsii privratnika* (The Innervation of the Pylorus) (1925); *Okoloshchitovidnyye zhelezy i ikh rol' v organizme* (The Parathyroid Glands and Their Role in the Organism) (1928); *Vodnyy obmen i snotvornyye* (Water Metabolism and Soporifics (1934); *Farmakologicheskiy analiz deystviya sredstv, kupiruyoshchikh eklampticheskiye pripadki* (A Pharmacological Analysis of the Effect of Drugs Which Stop Attacks of Eclampsia) (1935); *Problema obezbolivaniya* (The Problem of Pain Killing) (1936); *Died:* 1936 in Leningrad.

SAVINKOV, Boris Viktorovich (pseudonym: V.ROPSHIN) (1879–1925) Politician; leading member, Socialist-Revol Party; writer; *Born:* 1879; *Career:* in late 1890's joined student polit movement in Petersburg; 1901 joined RSDRP; 1903 joined Socialist-Revol Party, becoming a member of its "militant org"; 15 July 1904 involved in assassination of Interior Min and police chief V.K.Pleve; 4 Feb 1905 involved in assassination of Grand Prince Sergey Aleksandrovich; organized numerous other acts of terror; 1906 sentenced to death but escaped abroad on eve of execution; during WW 1 served as a volunteer in French Army; after Feb 1917 Revol comr, Supr Command Headquarters, comr on Southwestern Front, then Dep Min of War in Provisional Govt; mediated between Kerensky and Gen Kornilov; Sept 1917 expelled from Socialist-Revol Party for "double-dealing"; after Oct 1917 Revol actively opposed Sov regime; helped to organize Volunteer Army and led the League for the Defense of the Homeland and Liberty, which raised revolts against the Sov regime in Yaroslavl', Rybinsk and Muroma in July 1918; subsequently represented Kolchak in Paris; from 1924 lived in Poland; Aug 1924 arrested after crossing Polish-Sov border illegally; during trial, at which he was sentenced to 10 years imprisonement, claimed to recognize Sov regime; *Publ:* novels: *Kon' blednyy* (The Pale Horse) (1909); *To, chego ne bylo* (What Never Was) (1912); *Kon' voronoy* (The Black Horse) (1924); *Died:* 7 May 1925 committed suicide in prison.

SAVINYKH, Andrey Grigor'yevich (1881–1963) Surgeon; Dr of Med from 1938; prof; member, USSR Acad of Med Sci from 1944; Hon Sci Worker of RSFSR from 1943; *Born:* 30 Nov 1881 in vil Mershiny, Vyatka Province; *Educ:* 1913 grad Tobol'sk Theological Seminary; 1917 grad Med Fac, Tomsk Univ; *Career:* 1917–18 mil surgeon on Caucasian Front; 1918–19 zemstvo physician, then dept head, Tobol'sk Province Zemstvo Hospital; 1919–31 intern, then assoc prof, Surgical Clinic, Tomsk Univ; 1931–63 head, Chair of Hospital Surgical Clinic, Tomsk Med Inst; 1952–63 founder-dir, Tomsk Dept, Inst of Experimental Cancer Pathology and Therapy, USSR Acad of Med Sci; founder, Tomsk Blood Transfusion Center; dep, USSR Supr Sov of 1946, 1950, 1954 and 1958 convocations; 1950 toured hospitals in Sweden; from 1958 hon member, Int Soc of Surgeons; member, Int Assoc of Surgeons; hon member, Leningrad, Kuybyshev, Novosibirsk and Krasnoyarsk Surgical Soc; hon member, Tomsk Oblast, All-Russian and All-Union Soc of Surgeons; chm, Tomsk Consulting Bureau, USSR Acad of Med Sci; 1959 attended 18th Congress of Surgeons, Munich; member, ed bd, journal "Khirurgiya"; member, ed council, journal "Klinicheskaya meditsina"; co-ed, "Surgery" section, "Bol'shaya meditsinskaya entsiklopediya" (Large Medical Encyclopedia) (2nd ed); devised methods of removing hydatid tapeworm from unusual locations, of treating alveolar hydatid tapeworm with formalin and of anchoring floating kidneys; developed new techniques of transabdominal mediastinotomy, diaphragmotomy and the radical removal of cardiac cancer; designed several instruments for operations on the cardia and oesophagus and introduced high cerebrospinal sovcain narcosis; wrote over 80 works; *Publ:Radikal'noye i konservativnoye lecheniye raka kardii i nizhnego otdela pishchevoda* (The Radical and Conservative Treatment of Cancer of the Cardia and Lower Oesophagus) (1938); *Chrezbryushinnaya mediastinotomiya* (Transabdominal Mediastinotomy) (1942); *O khirurgii raka kardii i pishchevoda* (The Surgical Treatment of Cancer of the Cardia and Oesophagus) (1951), etc; *Awards:* two Orders of Lenin; Order of the Red Banner of Labor; 1st Prize of USSR Pop Comrt of Health (1938); Hon Scroll of USSR Supr Sov (1942); Stalin Prize (1943); medals; *Died:* 26 Feb 1963.

SAVVIN, Vitt Nikolayevich (1874–1933) Surgeon; *Born:* 1874; *Educ:* grad Med Fac, Moscow Univ; *Career:* after grad worked for Chair of Operative Surgery, Moscow Univ; simultaneously worked at Staro-Yekaterininskaya Hospital; 1903 defended doctor's thesis; from 1908 assoc prof; then senior asst prof, Martynov's Surgical Clinic, Novo-Yekaterininskaya Hospital; from 1909 prof of operative surgery and topographical anatomy, Tomsk Univ; dean, then rector, Tomsk Univ; co-founder and dir, Higher Women's Courses, Tomsk; 1930, attracted by the idea of industrialization of the USSR, moved to Chelyabinsk and directed the construction of a large med complex; *Publ: Operativnyye puti k vnutrigrudnomu otdelu pishchevoda i operatsii na nyom* (Operative Approaches to the Intrathoracic Section of the Oesophagus and Operations on It) (1903); *Kostnaya plastika pri defektakh cherepa* (Osteoplasty for Defects of the Skull) (1917); *K tekhnike polnogo udaleniya okoloushnoy zhelezy* (The Technique of Complete Resection of the Parotid Gland) (1924); *Died:* 1933.

SAZHIN, Ivan Gerasimovich (1885–1964) Trade-union official; CP member from 1903; *Born:* 5 July 1885; *Career:* active in revol movement; during Dec 1905 Revol fought with pop militia and directed erection of barricades in Sormovo; 1908–13 revol work among workers at Motovilikha Plant in the Urals; 1917 food comr, Balakhna and Arzamas Uyezds, Nizhniy Novgorod Province; 1918 Presidium member, Balakhna Sov of Workers and Peasant's Dep; 1921–24 chm, Sormovo Gen Factory Comt, Metalworkers-Union; from 1925 exec trade-union work in Ukr and Moscow; from 1948 pensioner; *Died:* 8 July 1964.

SAZHIN, Mikhail Petrovich (1845–1934) Revolutionary; *Born:* 29 Oct 1845 in Izhevsk, Vyatka Province; *Educ:* studied at Petersburg Technol Inst; *Career:* 1868 expelled from inst for participating in student riots and exiled to Vologda Province; summer 1869 emigrated to America; 1870, in Switzerland, sided with Bakunin's group; 1871 active in Paris Commune; 1875 active in Herzegovina Revolt; 1876 arrived in Russia and was arrested; 1878 tried and sentenced to five years' hard labor, followed by exile in Siberia, where he remained until 1900; 1906–16 econ mang, journal "Russkoye bogatstvo"; *Publ: Vospominaniya. 1860–1880* (Memoirs. 1860–1880) (1925); *Died:* 1934.

SAZONOV, Sergey Dmitriyevich (1860–1927) Russian statesman and diplomat; *Born:* 29 July 1860 in Ryazan' Province, son of a nobleman; *Career:* from 1883 dipl work; from May 1909 Asst Min of For Affairs; Sept 1910–July 1916 Min of For Affairs; pursued policy of rapprochement with Britain and Japan without aggravating relations with Germany and Austro-Hungary; at the same time tried to bind the Balkan states and Turkey into an anti-Austro-Hungarian confederation under Russian aegis; exercized great influence on the Tsar; conducted negotiations with Germany, culminating in the 1911 Potsdam Agreement; concluded 1912 and 1916 agreements with Japan; the deterioration in relations with Austro-Hungary (in the 1912–13 Balkan Wars) and later with Germany led him to strive for consolidation of the Entente; June 1914, during Austro-Serbian conflict, tried to achieve a compromise and avoid open war; however, convinced of Germany and Austro-Hungary's intransigeance, demanded mobilization of the Russian Army, thus precipitating WW 1; 1914–16 negotiated with Britain and France on mil cooperation and future peace terms; 1918–20 member, Denikin and Kolchak govt and their rep in Paris at the peace conference; *Publ: Vospominaniya* (Memoirs) (1927); *Died:* 25 Dec 1927 in emigration.

SEDOY (LITVIN), Zinoviy Yakovlevich (1876–?) Revolutionary and govt official; CP member from 1897; *Born:* 1876; *Career:* metalworker by trade; in emigration worked as automobile mech; from 1893 in revol movement; member, Moscow Workers' Union; 1896 twice arrested; 1897, after release from prison, moved to Petersburg; until 1905 Party work in Petersburg, Nizhniy Novgorod, Moscow and Tiflis; several times arrested and exiled; 1905, during Dec armed revolt in Moscow, chief of staff, battle squads in Presna Rayon; 1906 moved to Finland and served as secr, RSDRP Mil Revol Org; took part in Sveaborg Uprising; late 1906 emigrated after suppression of this revolt; lived in France; twice arrested for anti-war propaganda; 1917 returned to Russia; fought in Cicil War; from 1919 worked for Centr Mil Communications Bd, then for Pop Comrt of Means of Communication; 1921–39 dir, "1905 Dec Armed Uprising" Cotton Technicum; deleg at 4th, 10th, 11th, 13th, 14th and 16th Party Congresses; at 10th Party Congress elected member, Centr Control Commission; *Died:* date and place of death unknown.

SEDYAKIN, Aleksandr Ignat'yevich (1893–1937) Mil commander; CP member from 1917; *Born:* 1893; *Career:* during Civil War comr and commander of a regt, brigade, div; then commandant, Kronstadt Fortress and Petrograd Fortified Distr; after Civil War commander, 5th Red Banner Army; then commander Volga Mil Distr; other commands; held rank of army commander, 2nd class; arrested by State Security organs; *Died:* 1937 in imprisonment.

SEDYKH, Vasiliy Yakovlevich (1887–1963) Chm, Auditing Commission, CP Bel and member, Party Commission, CC, CP Bel from 1954; CP member from 1905; *Born:* 1887; *Career:* dep, Bel Supr Sov of 1955 and 1959 convocations; member, Budget Commission, Bel Supr Sov of 1959 convocation; *Awards:* Order of Lenin (1955); Bel Supr Sov Scroll of Hon (1957, 1962); *Died:* 4 June 1963.

SEGIZBAYEV, Sultan (1899–1938) Party and govt official; journalist; CP member from 1918; *Born:* 1899 in vil Dzhagalbayly, Tashkent Uyezd, son of a peasant; *Educ:* studied at Tashkent high school; 1925–30 studied at Inst of Red Prof; *Career:* member, Marxist circle; participated in 1916 Centr Asian Revolt; from 1918 Party and govt work; 1921 exec secr, Koshchi Union; 1920 deleg, 1st Congress of Peoples of the East, Baku; 1921, as deleg at 10th RCP(B) Congress, helped crush Kronstadt Mutiny; fought against Basmachi; 1923 secr, Fergana Oblast Comt, CP Turkestan; ed, newspaper "Fergana"; 1924 secr, Tashkent Uyezd Party Comt; then dep head, Agitation and Propaganda Dept, CC, CP Turkestan; 1928–30 dean, Evening Communist Univ, Inst of Red Prof; 1932–36 head, Instruction and Org Dept, then Agric Dept, CC, CP Kaz; deleg, 16th and 17th CPSU(B) Congresses; 1937 first secr, North Kaz Oblast CPSU(B) Comt; then chm, Uzbek Council of Pop Comr; 1937–38 dep chm, Sov of the Union, and dep, USSR Supr Sov; arrested by State Security organs; *Died:* 1938 in imprisonment.

SELITSKIY, Sergey Apollinar'yevich (1883–1943) Obstetrician and gynecologist; *Born:* 1883; *Educ:* 1910 grad Med Fac, Moscow Univ; *Career:* 1910–26 intern, then asst prof, R.M. Makeyev, then N.I. Pobedinsky's clinics, Med Fac, Moscow Univ; 1921 defended doctor's thesis on "K voprosu ob eklampsii v klinicheskom otnoshenii" (The Clinical Aspects of Eclampsia), 1926–31 head, Women's Dept, State Research Inst of Mother and Child Care, Moscow; 1931–33 head, Obstetrics and Gynecological Clinic Section, Ivanov Oblast Research Inst; 1933–35 prof, Chair of Obstetrics and Gynecology, 2nd Moscow Med Inst; 1935–38 chief obstetrician and gynecologists, Maloyaroslavets; 1939–43 consultant obstetrician and gynecologist, Med and Health Bd, Pop Comrt of Means of Communication; opposed Stroganov method of treating eclampsia; one of first Russian gynecologists to treat it without drugs; described new form of pregnancy toxicosis (cerebro- et psychopathia toxica gravidarum); classified pregnancy and menstrual dermatosis; schematized correlation of endocrine glands in pregnancy; ed, gynecological section, 1st ed of "BME" (Large Medical Encyclopedia); wrote over 100 works; *Publ: Eklampsia bez sudorog* (Eclampsia Without Convulsions) (1913); *Eklampsiya v klinicheskom otnoshenii* (The Clinical Aspects of Eclampsia) (1926); *Protivozachatochnyye sredstva v istoricheskom otnoshenii* (A History of Contraceptives) (1927); *Protivozachatochnyye sredstva v sovremennom nauchnom osveshchenii* (Contraceptives in the Light of Modern Science) (1927); *Nefropatii, nefrozy i nefrity beremennykh s klinicheskoy tochki zreniya* (Nephropathy, Nephrosis and Nephritis in Pregnancy from a Clinical Point of View) (1936); *Died:* 1943.

SELIVANOVSKIY, Aleksey Pavlovich (1900-1938) Russian lit historian; CP member from 1919; *Born:* 23 Mar 1900 in Ol'gopol', now Vinnitsa Oblast, son of an office worker; *Educ:* 1917 grad non-classical college in Kiev; *Career:* co-founder and first chm, "Zaboy" (Assoc of Donbass Proletarian Writers); ed, journal "Zaboy"; arrested by State Security organs; *Publ: V bor'be protiv shovinizma. Literaturnaya situatsiya na Ukraine* (The Struggle Against Chauvinism. The Literary Situation in the Ukraine)

(1927); *V literaturnykh boyakh* (In Literary Battles) (1930); *Ocherki istorii russkoy sovetskoy poezii* (An Outline History of Soviet Russian History) (1936); *Died:* 21 Apr 1938 in imprisonment.

SEL'TSOVSKIY, Pyotr Lazarevich *(1898–1961) Surgeon; Dr of* Med from 1938; prof from 1945; Hon Sci Worker of RSFSR; *Born:* 1898; *Educ:* 1924 grad Med Fac, Moscow Univ; *Career:* from 1924 worked under S.I. Spasokukotskiy and A.N. Bakulev at surgical clinics, Moscow Univ; 1932–41 worked at Centr Inst of Blood Transfusion; 1941–44 chief surgeon at an evacuation hospital on Western Front, then chief surgeon, North Caucasian Front; 1945–55 chief surgeon, Sov Air Force; from 1945 also head, Chair of Surgical Diseases, Moscow Stomatological Inst; did research on acute intestinal blockage, pathogenesis and treatment of peritonitis, surgical treatment of hypertonia and use of antibiotics; developed glucose-citrate blood conservation method; and an anti-shock solution which was used during WW 2; wrote some 120 works; *Publ: K voprosu o dozirovke krovi pri shoke v svete patogeneza* (Blood Dosage for Shock in the Light of Its Pathogenesis) (1941); *Ostraya kishechnaya neprokhodimost'*(Acute Intestinal Blockage) (1941); *Penitsillin* (Penicillin) (1948); *Krovozamenyayushchiye rastvory i ikh primeneniye v voyenno-lechebnykh uchrezhdeniyakh* (Blood Substitutes and their Use in Military Medical Facilities) (1952); *Uchebnik khirurgicheskikh bolezney* (A Textbook on Surgical Diseases) (1957); coauthor, *Khirurgicheskoye lecheniye gipertonicheskoy bolezni* (The Surgical Treatment of Hypertonia) (1959); *Awards:* Spasokukotskiy Prize; *Died:* 1961.

SEMASHKO, Nikolay Aleksandrovich (1874–1949) Hygienist; Public health official; Hon Sci Worker of RSFSR from 1944; revolutionary; govt official; member and Presidium member, USSR Acad of Med Sci from 1934; member, RSFSR Acad of Pedag Sci from 1945; prof from 1922; CP member from 1893; *Born:* 21 Sept 1874 in vil Livenskoye, Oryol Province, son of a teacher; *Educ:* 1901 grad with distinction, Med Fac, Kazan' Univ; *Career:* 1893, while a student at Moscow Univ, joined Marxist circle; 1893–95 revol propaganda among students and Moscow workers; 1895 arrested and exiled for two years to Yelets; 1898 transferred to Med Fac, Kazan' Univ; 1899–1900, together with A.I. Rykov, founded Soc-Democratic circles in Kazan'; 1901 again arrested for revol activities and banished from Kazan'; 1901 passed state med examination at Kazan' Univ; for some months served as health officer in Novo-Udinsk Uyezd, Samara Province; 1902–03 country dr in Mtsensk Uyezd, Oryol Province; 1904–05 health officer, Nizhniy Novgorod Zemstvo; also conducted underground Party work for Nizhniy Novgorod RSDRP Org; published first socio-hygiene studies on sickness rate in the vil Bogorodskoye and Panino, Nizhniy Novgorod Province; 1905 took part in Revol in Nizhniy Novgorod and Sormovo; arrested and imprisoned for nine months; then emigrated to Switzerland and settled in Geneva, where he assisted Lenin in his Party work; 1907 attended Stuttgart Party Congress; 1907 arrested by Swiss authorities on charges of complicity in the Tiflis expropriation case; 1908, after release from prison, moved with Lenin to Paris and until 1910 was secr, For Bureau, CC, RSDRP(B); 1911–12 published articles in Party press on old-age retirement schemes for workers, agrarian problems, etc; 1912 attended 6th All-Russian RSDRP Conference in Prague; 1912 taught school hygiene at new Russian school near Paris; 1913–17 physician in Serbia and Bulgaria; Sept 1917 moved to Moscow and played active part in Oct Revol; then Bureau member, Council of Rayon Dumas and head of its 9th Med Hygiene Dept; 1918 member, Med Collegium, Pop Comrt of Internal Affairs; then member, Council of Physicians' Collegia and first head, Med Health Dept, Moscow Sov of Workers and Soldiers' Dept; 1918 appointed RSFSR Pop Comrt of Health; 1918 used his authority in this post to order the abolition of the Pirogov Physicians' Soc, the Med Health Council, the Russian Red Cross Soc and other med soc and org; 1918 founded Learned Med Council and Pasteur Sci Inst at Pop Comrt of Health; also nationalized pharmacies and founded Centr Med Library; 1919 nationalized health resort establishments; from 1922 co-founder and chm, Scientists Center, Acad of Sci; founded USSR's first Chair of Soc Hygiene at Med Fac, 1st Moscow Univ (now Sechenov 1st Moscow Med Inst) and worked here as prof; 1923 founded Clinic of Soc and Occupational Diseases, Chair of Soc Hygiene, 1st Moscow Univ; 1928–36 chief ed, "Bol'shaya meditsinskaya entsiklopediya" (Large Medical Encyclopedia); 1929 introduced class principle into med treatment; 1930 CPSU (B) Centr Comt disclosed serious defects in Pop Comrt of Health; despite Semashko's apologies and promise of reforms, he was dismissed as RSFSR Pop Comrt of Health; 1930–36 Presidium member and chm, Children's Commission, All-Russian Centr Exec Comt; 1937–41 with Higher Physical Training Council; 1942–44 dir, Inst of Hygiene, 1st Moscow Med Inst; 1944 helped found USSR Acad of Med Sci and was elected member and Presidium member; 1945–49 dir, Inst of School Hygiene, RSFSR Acad of Pedag Sci; from 1946 founder-head, Commission to Study the Health Consequences of the War, Presidium of USSR Acad of Med Sci; 1947–49 also dir, Inst of Public Health Org and History of Med, USSR Acad of Med Sci; 1948 accused a number of leading Sov sci of idealism; edited many med publ; chm, Bd, All-Union Hygiene Soc; Presidium member, Soc to Promote the USSR Aviation, Defense and Chemical Ind; wrote some 250 works on public health org, history of med, etc; *Publ: Osnovy sovetskoy meditsiny* (The Principles of Soviet Medicine) (1919); *Nauka o zdorov'ye – sotsial'naya gigiyena* (Social Hygiene, the Science of Health) (1922); *Ocherki po teorii organizatsii sovetskogo zdravookhraneniya* (Studies on the Theory of Soviet Public Health Organization) (1947), etc; *Awards:* Order of Lenin; Order of the Red Banner of Labor; medals; *Died:* 18 June 1949 in Moscow; a number of med establishments, factories, etc, now bear his name.

SEMEKA, Sergey Aleksandrovich (1906–1966) Mil surgeon; maj-gen, Med Corps; *Born:* 1906; *Educ:* 1931 grad Leningrad Mil Med Acad; *Career:* 1931–41 mil surgeon in Sov Army; 1941–45 head of a front mil med bd; from 1946 held various exec posts in USSR Min of Defense; for several years dep head, Main Mil Med Bd, USSR Min of Defense; co-ed, "Bol'shaya meditsinskaya entsiklopediya" (Large Medical Encyclopedia) (2nd ed); also helped to compile and edit such med corps manuals as "Entsiklopedicheskiy slovar' voyennoy meditsiny" (An Encyclopedic Dictionary of Military Medicine) and "Entsiklopedicheskiy meditsinskiy spravochnik dlya voyennykh fel'dsherov" (An Encyclopedic Medical Reference Manual for Medical Orderlies); headed chairs of mil med at various inst; *Publ: Meditsina voyennaya* (Military Medicine) (1948); *Meditsinskoye obespecheniye russkoy armii vo vremya Semiletney voyny 1756–63 godov* (Medical Care in the Russian Army During the 1756–63 Seven-Year War) (1951); *Voyennaya meditsina v vooruzhyonnykh silakh Moskovskogo gosudarstva v XVII veke* (Military Medicine in the Armed Forces of Muscovy in the 17th Century) (1952); *Voyenno-meditsinskaya organizatsiya vooruzhyonnykh sil Rossiyskoy dvoryanskoy imperii XVIII veka vo vremya Russko-Turetskoy voyny 1735–39* (The Organization of Military Medicine in the Imperial Russian Armed Forces in the 18th Century During the 1735–39 Russo-Turkish War) (1955), etc; *Awards:* various orders and medals; *Died:* 1966 in Moscow.

SEMENKO, Mikhail Vasil'yevich (1892–1937) Ukr poet; *Born:* 31 Dec 1892 in vil Kibintsy, now Poltava Oblast; *Educ:* for three years studied at Petersburg Psychoneurological Inst; *Career:* 1913 first work printed; major Ukr Futurist; founded Assoc of Pan-Futurists, Assoc of Communist Culture and "New Generation" lit assoc; tried to introduce "Leninism in culture" but his interpretation of Leninism brought him into conflict with Sov regime; criticized for neglecting classical lit and for formalism and forced to recant, e.g., in his verse message "I Begin in the Ranks" (1932); 1935 arrested by State Security organs; *Publ:* verse collections: "Prelude" (1913); "Quero-Futurism" (1914); "Kobzar" (1924); "Modern Verse" (1931); "China on Fire" (1932); "Complete Collected Works" (3 vol, 1929–31); *Died:* 24 Oct 1937 in imprisonment; posthumously rehabilitated.

SEMENNIKOV, Vladimir Petrovich (1885–1936) Historian; lit historian; bibliographer; *Born:* 11 Sept 1885 in Petersburg; *Educ:* 1904 grad Naval Cadet Corps; grad History and Philology Fac, Petersburg Univ; during WW 1 served in Russian Navy at Kronstadt; then research work; compiled "Bibliograficheskiy spisok knig, napechatannykh v provintsii so vremeni vozniknoveniya grazhdanskiy tipografiy po 1807 god" (A Bibliographical List of Books Printed in the Provinces from the Appearance of Civilian Printing Presses to 1807) (1912); edited collection of documents *Monarkhiya pered krusheniyem, 1914–1917 gody* (The Monarchy Before Its Downfall, 1914–1917) (1927); *Publ: Dopolnitel'nyye materialy dlya istorii provintsial'nykh tipografiy XVIII i XIX vekov i dlya bibliografii knig v nikh napechatannykh* (Additional Material on the History of Provincial Printing Presses in the 18th and 19th Centuries and on the Bibliography of Books They Printed) (1913); *Knigoizdatel'skaya deyatel'nost' N.I. Novikova i tipograficheskoy kompanii* (The Book-Publishing of N.I. Novikov and His Printing Company) (1921); *Politika Romanovykh nakanune revolyutsii* (The Policy of the Romanovs on the Eve of the Revolution) (1926); *Revolyutsiya 1905 goda i samoderzhaviye* (The 1905 Revolution and Autocracy) (1928); *Romanovy i germanskiye vliyaniya vo vremya mirovoy voyny* (The Romanovs and German Influences During the World War) (1929); coauthor, *A.I. Radishchev. Materialy i issledovaniya* (A.I. Radishchev. Material and Research) (1936); *Died:* 4 Sept 1936.

SEMEYKO, Nikolay Illarionovich (1923–1945) Mil pilot; capt; CP member from 1943; *Born:* 25 Aug 1923 in Slavyansk, now Donetsk Oblast, son of a worker; *Educ:* 1942 grad Air Force college; *Career:* from 1940 in Sov Army; during WW 2 pilot, flight commander, dep squadron commander, then navigator of regt in Sov Air Force; served on 3rd Bel and 4th Ukr Fronts; *Awards:* twice Hero of the Sov Union (Apr and June 1945); Order of Lenin; other orders; medals; *Died:* 20 Apr 1945 killed in air battle in Eastern Prussia.

SEMKOV, S.M. (Syoma) (1885–1928) Party and trade-union official; CP member from 1903; *Born:* 1885; *Career:* Party work in various Russian towns; during WW 1 lived abroad; after 1917 Oct Revol mil admin work; after Civil War secr, Moscow Trade-Union Council; then chm, Transcaucasian Trade-Union Council; at 14th and 15th Party Congresses elected member, Centr Control Commission; then worked for USSR Pop Comrt of Workers and Peasants' Inspection; *Died:* 1928.

SEMKOVSKIY (real name: BRONSHTEYN), Semyon Yul'yevich (1882–1937) Philosopher; prof; member, Ukr Acad of Sci from 1929; *Born:* 15 Mar 1882 in Mogilev; *Educ:* grad Law Fac, Petersburg Univ; *Career:* 1901 joined Menshevik faction of RSDRP; 1907–17 in emigration, where he contributed to Menshevik and Soc-Democratic publ and worked for Trotsky's "Pravda" in Vienna; 1917 returned to Russia and became member, CC, RSDRP (Mensheviks); from 1918 lived and worked in Ukr; 1920 broke with Mensheviks; from 1921 chm, Sci Comt, Main Bd of Sci Museums and Sci and Art Institutions, Ukr Pop Comrt of Educ; from 1926 head, Chair of Marxism-Leninism, Ukr Acad of Sci; prof of philosophy, Khar'kov Univ and other Ukr higher educ establishments; head, Nature Dialectics Section, All-Russian Assoc of Marxist-Leninist Research Inst; member, Ukr Centr Exec Comt; arrested by State Security organs; *Publ: Dialekticheskiy materializm i printsip otnositel'nosti* (Dialectical Materialism and the Principle of Relativity) (1926), etc; *Died:* 18 Mar 1937 executed by NKVD.

SEMYONOV, Aleksandr Aleksandrovich (1873–1958) Historian; Dr of History from 1942; prof; member, Tadzh Acad of Sci from 1951; corresp member, Uzbek Acad of Sci from 1943; Hon Sci Worker of Uzbek SSR from 1944; hon Sci Worker of Tadzh SSR from 1946; *Born:* 12 Oct 1873 in Tambov Province, son of a peasant; *Educ:* grad Tambov Teachers' Inst; 1900 grad Lazarevskiy Inst of Oriental Languages, Moscow; *Career:* co-founder and prof, Centr Asian Univ, Tashkent; from 1951 dir, Inst of History, Archeology and Ethnography, Tadzh Acad of Sci; member, Bc mbay Sci Soc; studied the history, languages and ethnography of the peoples of Centr Asia; also specialized in the history of Islam; wrote some 230 works; *Died:* 16 Nov 1958.

SEMYONOV, Boris Aleksandrovich (1890–1937) Party official; CP member from 1907; *Born:* 22 Jan 1890 in Petersburg Province, son of a worker; *Career:* worker by trade; from 1907 illegal Party work in Petersburg; 1909 arrested and exiled for life to Irkutsk Province; after 1917 Feb Revol returned to Petrograd; 1917–22 senior Party work in Petrograd, then in Red Army; chm, Petrograd Province Cheka; 1925–27 first secr, Lugansk Okrug Comt, CP(B) Ukr; from 1927 first secr, Dnepropetrovsk Okrug Comt, CP(B) Ukr; 1931–34 second secr, Centr Asian Bureau, CC, CPSU(B); 1934–36 first secr, Crimean, then Stalingrad Oblast CPSU(B) Comt; at 9th, 10th and 11th Congresses of CP(B) Ukr elected member, CC, CP(B) Ukr; from Dec 1925 cand Politburo member, Nov 1927–Mar 1931 Politburo member, CC, CP(B) Ukr; deleg at 9th, 11th, 12th, 14th–17th Party Congresses; at 14th–17th Party Congresses elected cand member, CC, CPSU(B); arrested by State Security organs; *Awards:* Order of Lenin; *Died:* 29 Oct 1937 in imprisonment.

SEMYONOV, G.I. (1891–1937) Politician; member, Socialist-Revol Party; *Born:* 1891; *Career:* 1917 bureau member, Mil Commission, CC, Socialist-Revol Party; organized Centr Mil Detachment for the purpose of assassinating prominent CP and Soviet govt functionaries; took part in many major operations; 1922, while in emigration, published his memoirs *Voennaya i boyevaya rabota partii sotsialistov-revolyutsionerov za 1917–1918 gg.* (The Military and Militant Work of the Socialist-Revolutionary Party in 1917–1918), which divulged the Socialist-Revolutionaries' activities from the time of the Oct Revol; 1922 sentenced to death in trial of Rightist Socialist-Revolutionaries; sentence quashed by tribunal in recognition of his services in revealing the Rightist Socialist-Revolutionaries' activities; 1937 arrested by State Security organs; *Died:* in imprisonment.

SEMYONOV, Grigoriy Mikhaylovich (1890–1946) Mil commander; maj, Russian army; lt-gen, Kolchak's Army from 1919; prominent figure in anti-Sov movement in Far East; *Born:* 13 Sept 1890 in Transbaykal, son of a Cossack; *Educ:* 1911 grad Orenburg Mil College; *Career:* fought in WW 1; from July 1917 comr for mustering volunteer units, Transbaykal Provisional Govt; Dec 1917 with a small group of officers and Cossacks arrested at Manchzhuriya Station local sov of workers and peasants' dep; proclaimed himself ataman, Transbaykal Cossack Army; formed "Special Manchurian Detachment" and with Japanese help established a personal dictatorship in a territory along the Western Line of Chinese-Eastern Railroad, later expanded to include all Transbaykal; Jan 1919 set up a puppet govt in Chita; late 1919 recognized supr authority of Admiral Kolchak; appointed by Kolchak commander, Chita Mil Distr; Jan 1920 Kolchak transferred to him all mil and civil power in Russian Eastern Distr; Nov 1920, under pressure of Sov partisans and Far Eastern Pop Revol Army, retreated with his forces to Maritime Region; Sept 1921 routed and with the rest of his forces retreated to China; 1921–45 lived in Japan and China; headed militarized emigre detachments in Manchuria, operating against USSR; 1945, after the defeat of the Kwantung Army in Manchuria, arrested by Sov counter-intelligence; Aug 1946 sentenced to death by Mil Collegium, USSR Supr Court; *Died:* 30 Aug 1946 hanged.

SEMYONOV, Mikhail Alekseyevich (1892–1967) Party and govt official; CP member from 1912; *Born:* 1892; *Career:* until 1917 carpenter and assembly mech in Moscow and Petersburg; active in 1917 Oct Revol; comr, Finland Railroad Terminus; then worked for Petrograd Sov; 1918–19 member, Moscow's Butyrka Rayon RCP(B) Comt; then plen, Zhitomir Province Mil Comrt; 1920–21 transport comr, Supply Bd, Western Front; 1921–25 Party work; from 1925 econ admin work; from 1947 pensioner; *Died:* Dec 1967.

SEMYONOV of TYAN-SHAN, Andrey Petrovich (1866–1942) Zoologist, entomologist and zoogeographer; *Born:* 21 June 1866; son of P. P. Semyonov of Tyan-Shan; *Educ:* completed higher educ; *Career:* 1888–89 studied the insects of the Transcaspian area and Western Turkestan; 1890–95 custodian, from 1895–97 senior zoologist, Zoological Museum, Russian Acad of Sci; 1897 resigned on political grounds, after which he was active in the Russian Entomological Soc and the Russian Geographical Soc; after 1917 Oct Revol resumed work at Zoological Museum, then worked for Zoological Inst, USSR Acad of Sci; did research on insect taxonomy, zoogeography and fauna; acquired a large collection of Coleoptera; also worked on the theory of species; *Publ: Taksonomicheskiye granitsy vida i yego podrazdeleniy* (The Taxonomic Limits of a Species and Its Subdivisions) (1910); *Predely i zoogeograficheskiye podrazdeleniya Palearkticheskoy oblasti* (The Limits and Zoogeographical Zones of the Paleoarctic Region) (1936), etc; *Died:* 1942.

SEMYONOV of TYAN-SHAN, Veniamin Petrovich (1870–1942) Geographer and statistician; prof from 1919; *Born:* 8 Apr 1870, son of P. P. Semyonov of Tyan-Shan; *Educ:* 1893 grad Petersburg Univ; *Career:* from 1899 member, 1906–18 dep chm, Dept of Physical Geography, 1918–32 chm, Statistics Dept, Russian Geographical Soc; 1895 took part in geological survey of the Salair Ridge in Siberia; also did geological surveys in Ryazan' and Chkalov Oblasts and in Kaz; 1897 and 1926 helped to organize gen censuses; 1919–37 prof, Geographical Inst and Leningrad Univ; simultaneously dir, Centr Geographical Museum, Leningrad; 1921 member, Olonets expedition of the Hydrological Inst; wrote over 200 works; *Publ:* exec ed, *Rossiya. Polnoye geograficheskoye opisaniye nashego otechestva* (Russia. A Complete Geographical Description of Our Fatherland) (19 vol, 1899–1914); *Torgovlya i promyshlennost' Yevropeyskoy Rossii po rayonam* (The Trade and Industry of European Russia by Regions) (12 vol, 1900–11); *Gorod i derevnya v Yevropeyskoy Rossii* (Town and Country in European Russia) (1910); *Tipy mestnostey Yevropeyskoy Rossii i Kavkaza* (The Landscape Types of European Russia and the Caucasus) (1915); *Rayon i strana* (Region and Country) (1928), etc; *Died:* 8 Feb 1942.

SEPP, Yevgeniy Konstantinovich (1878–1957) Neuropathologist; Dr of Med from 1911; prof from 1913; member, USSR Acad of Med Sci from 1944; Hon Sci Worker of RSFSR from 1934; CP member from 1939; *Born:* 17 Sept 1878; *Educ:* 1904 grad Med Fac, Moscow Univ; *Career:* from 1904 intern, asst prof and assoc prof, Clinic of Nervous Diseases, Moscow Univ, where he worked under Prof V.K.Rot; 1911 defended doctor's thesis on the bigeminal bodies in rabbits; from 1913 prof and dir, Clinic of Nervous Diseases, Statkevich and Izachek's Private Med Inst; 1919–24 dir, Clinic of Nervous Diseases, and rector, Higher Med School; 1924–29 head, Chair and Clinic of Nervous Diseases, Med Fac, 2nd Moscow Univ; 1928 devised concept of blood and liquor dynamics; from 1929 until death head, Chair and Clinic of Nervous Diseases, 1st Moscow Med Inst; did research on the normal and pathological morphology of the nervous system, the dynamics of cerebral blood circulation, the history of the development of the nervous system, epilepsy, hysteria, traumata of the nervous system, pathological histology, etc; devised a nerve-tissue staining technique which shows both the nerve cells and fibers; formulated a number of laws governing the spread of an infection through the nervous system; wrote a detailed description of the structure and function of the corpora quadrigemina; 1937 described the quadrigeminal reflex in humans and lesions observed under clinical conditions; devised the "sluice" theory of the function of the sympathetic nervous system; *Publ:* doctor's thesis *O stroyenii i svyazyakh perednego dvukholmiya krolika* (The Structure and Links of the Anterior Bigeminal Bodies in Rabbits) (1911); *Organizatsiya zashchity ot infektsii tsentral'noy nervnoy sistemy cheloveka* (The Organization of the Defense of the Human Central Nervous System Against Infection) (1923); *Shlyuzovaya sistema mozga* (The Brain's Sluice System) (1925); *Klinicheskiy analiz nervnykh bolezney* (The Clinical Analysis of Nervous Diseases) (1927); "Die Dynamik der Blutzirkulation im Gehirn" (1928); coauthor and ed, *Epilepsiya* (Epilepsy) (1937); *Chetverokholmnyy refleks* (The Quadrigeminal Reflex) (1937); *O lokalizatsii funktsiy v kore golovnogo mozga* (The Localization of Functions in the Cerebral Cortex) (1955); *Istoriya razvitiya nervnoy sistemy pozvonochnykh* (The History of the Development of the Nervous System in Vertebrates) (1959); coauthor, *Uchebnik nervnykh bolezney* (A Textbook on Nervous Diseases); *Awards:* Order of Lenin; two other orders; medals; *Died:* 10 Nov 1957 in Moscow.

SEPRE, Oskar Adovich (1900–1965) Economist; Dr of Econ Sci from 1961; corresp member, Est Acad of Sci from 1946; senior assoc, Inst of Econ, Est Acad of Sci from 1949; member, Council for the Study of Production Resources, Est Acad of Sci from 1961; CP member from 1921; *Born:* 20 May 1900; *Educ:* 1939 grad Tartu Univ; *Career:* 1922 helped found Est Communist org Social and Philosophical Student Soc; 1924 sentenced to penal servitude for life for Communist activities; 1940 with a health insurance company in Tallin and member, League of Est Working People; 1941, after Sov occupation of Est, dep chm, Est Council of Pop Comr; member, CC, CP Est; dep, USSR Supr Sov of 1941 by-election; 1944–48 dep chm, Est Council of Min and chm, State Planning Commission, Est Council of Min; 1948 acting acad secr, Dept of Soc Sci, Est Acad of Sci; later head, Transport and Trade Econ Section, Inst of Econ, Est Acad of Sci; *Publ: Osnovnyye cherty ekonomiki burzhuaznoy Estonii* (Basic Traits of Bourgeois Estonia's Economy) (1949); *Zavisimost' promyshlennosti i torgovli burzhuaznoy Estonii ot vneshnikh zaymov* (The Dependence of Bourgeois Estonia's Industry and Trade on Foreign Loans); *Znacheniye remesla i yego udel'nyy ves v burzhuaznoy Estonii* (The Significance of Artisan Trade and Its Extent in Bourgeois Estonia); *Rastsvet sel'skogo khozyaystva burzhuaznoy Estonii* (The Agricultural Boom in Bourgeois Estonia); *Burzhuaznaya Estoniya v sisteme imperializma* (Bourgeois Estonia in the Imperialist System) (1959); *Puti bor'by (o pervom syezde estonskogo komsomola v 1922)* (Paths of Struggle [The First Estonian Komsomol in 1922]) (1962); *Awards:* Order of Lenin; medals "For Valiant Labor in the 1941–45 Great Fatherland War" and "800th Anniversary of Moscow"; Scroll of Hon, Presidium, Est Supr Sov; *Died:* 24 Nov 1965.

SERAFIM (real name: LUK'YANOV, Aleksandr Ivanovich) (1878–1959) Metropolitan, Russian Orthodox Church; Cand of Divinity; *Born:* 1878 in Saratov Province; *Educ:* 1900 grad Saratov Theological Seminary; 1904 grad Kiev Theological Acad; *Career:* 1902 ordained monk with name of Serafim; 1904–07 teacher, Ufa Theological Seminary; 1907 rector, Tavrida Theological Seminary, then rector and archimandrite, Saratov Theological Seminary; from 1914 Bishop of Serdobol' and vicar, Finnish Eparchy; after 1917 Oct Revol Bishop of Finland; removed after proclamation of autonomy of Finnish Church and went to Valaam Monastery; 1926 went to London as Eulogia Metropolitan (Foreign Church) and vicar, West European Metropoly for England; 1927 elevated to full metropolitan and appointed custodian of Russian Orthodox Church parishes in Western Europe with his residence in Paris; after WW 2 came under the jurisdiction of the Moscow Patriarchy; from 1916 Exarch for Western Europe, Moscow Patriarchy; 1947 went to USSR for talks with Patriarchy and Council for Russian Orthodox Church Affairs, USSR Council of Min; 1949 retired on pension; 1954 returned to USSR and lived at Troitse-Sergiy Monastery near Moscow; later moved to Uspenskiy Monastery, Odessa; *Died:* 18 Feb 1959.

SERAFIMOVICH, (real name: POPOV), Aleksandr Serafimovich (1863–1949) Russian writer; CP member from 1918; *Born:* 19 Jan 1863 in vil Nizhne-Kurmoyarskaya, Don Oblast, son of a Cossack; *Educ:* 1883–87 studied at Mathematics Fac, Petersburg Univ; *Career:* while still at high school began to give lessons in order to earn money for his family; 1883 entered Physics and Mathematics Fac, Petersburg Univ, where he met the revolutionary A.I. Ul'yanov, Lenin's elder brother; 1887 wrote revol proclamation in connection with Ul'yanov's attempt to assassinate Alexander III; this led to his arrest and exile to Mezen', Arkhangel'sk Province, where he stayed until 1890; while at univ became acquainted with Marxism; in exile made the acquaintance of P. A. Moiseyenko, who organized the 1885 Morozov Strike; while in exile also began to write, under the encouragement of Korolenko and Uspenskiy; in 1900's member, "Sreda" (Medium) lit and art circle; published his work in Gorky's collections "Znaniye"; during Civil War mil corresp, newspaper "Pravda"; edited journal "Oktyabr'"; Presidium member, Sov Writers Union; during WW 2 made several tours of the front; *Publ:* stories: *Na l'dine* (On the Ice-Floe) (1889); *V buryu* (In the Storm); *Pod zemlyoy* (Under the Earth); *Na zavode* (At the Plant); *Stsepshchik* (The Coupler); *Na Presne* (In Presna); *Pokhoronnyy marsh* (Funeral March); *Sredi nochi* (In the Mid of the Night); novel "Gorod v stepi" (City in the Steppe) (1912); stories; *Serdtse sosyot* (The Sucking Heart); *Vstrecha* (The Meeting); *Na pobyvke* (Home Leave); essays *V Galitsii* (In Galicia); wartime essays *Revolyutsiya. Front i tyl* (Revolution. Front and Rear) (1917–20); novelette *Zheleznyy potok* (The Iron Stream) (1924), etc; *Polnoye sobraniye sochineniy* (Complete Collected Works) (10 vol, 1940–48); *Awards:* Stalin Prize (1943); Order of Lenin; other orders; medals; *Died:* 19 Jan 1949; vil Ust'-Medveditskaya renamed Serafimovich.

SERBICHENKO, Aleksandr Kalistratovich (1890–1938) Party and govt official; CP member from 1907; *Born:* 29 Nov 1890 in Lyubotin, Khar'kov Province, son of a worker; *Educ:* 1903 grad zemstvo college; *Career:* employed at craft workshops; underground Party work in Kremenchug and from 1916 in Khar'kov: after 1917 Feb Revol elected member, Khar'kov Sov of Workers and Soldiers' Dep; member, Khar'kov City RSDRP(B) Comt; after establishment of Sov rule in Khar'kov engaged in Party and govt work; chm, Kremenchug Province Exec Comt; from 1922 chm, Poltava Province Exec Comt; dep chm, Ukr Council of Pop Comr; USSR trade rep in Austria; deleg at 15th and 16th CPSU(B) Congresses; at 9th and 10th Congresses of CP(B) Ukr elected member, CC, CP(B) Ukr; 1930–33 cand Politburo member, CC, CP(B) Ukr; member, All-Ukr Centr Exec Comt of several convocations; arrested by State Security organs; *Died:* 14 Jan 1938 in imprisonment.

SERDICH (SRDIC), Danilo Fyodorovich (1896–1937) Mil commander; CP member from 1918; *Born:* 10 Aug 1896 in vil Verhovina, Croatia; *Educ:* 1919–20 attended Higher Command Courses; 1932 grad Frunze Mil Acad; *Career:* during WW 1 joined Russian Army, then served with Yugoslav Volunteer Corps at Odessa; after 1917 Feb Revol joined anti-military Yugoslav Revol Union; July 1917 took part in storming of Petrograd Winter Palace; from fall 1917 commander, 1st Serbian Sov Detachment, Yekaterinoslav; Feb–Aug 1918 commanded another Serbian detachment; Aug–Nov 1918 commander, 1st Yugoslav Communist Regt near Tsaritsyn; late 1918 commander, Crimean Cavalry Regt; 1919 commander, Special Cavalry Brigade, 14th Army; Oct 1920 commander, 2nd, then 1st Cavalry Brigade, 6th Div, 1st Cavalry Army in battles against Gen Wrangel's troops on Southern Front; also commander, 7th and 12th Cavalry Div; 1934 commander, 4th

Cavalry Corps, 1935–37 commander, 3rd Cavalry Corps, Bel Mil Distr; 1936 elected member, CC, Bel CP and Bel Centr Exec Comt; 1937 arrested by NKVD; *Died:* 28 July 1937 in imprisonment; posthumously rehabilitated.

SERDYUCHENKO, Georgiy Petrovich (1904–1965) Philologist and methodologist; linguist; specialist in Caucasian languages; Dr of Philology; prof; corresp member, RSFSR Acad of Pedag Sci; *Born:* 1904; *Educ:* 1923 grad Novocherkassk Teachers' Training Inst; *Career:* in his latter years head, Dept of Languages, Inst of Asian Peoples, USSR Acad of Sci; helped compile orthography for North Caucasian languages; then worked on written records and transcription of typology and grammar of obscure Oriental languages; founded new sci branch – Oriental linguistics within the framework of Oriental studies; *Publ: Bol'she vnimaniya voprosam yazykovogo stroitel'stva v natsional'nykh oblastyakh* (More Attention to Linguistic Construction in National Regions) (1932); *Unifikatsiya gorskikh (severo-kavkazskikh) alfavitov* (Unification of the Highland [North Caucasian] Alphabets) (1933); *O checheno-ingushskom konsonantizme* (Chechen-Ingush Consonantism) (1935); *Abazinskiy alfavit i orfografiya na russkoy graficheskoy osnove* (The Abazin Alphabet and Orthography Based on the Russian Graphic System) (1938); *Ob abazinskoy pis'mennosti* (The Abazin Written Language) (1939); *Ob abazinskikh dialektakh* (Abazin Dialects) (1939); *Ob izuchenii abazinskikh govorov* (The Study of Abazin Dialects) (1939); *Abaziny i pervyye svedeniya ob ikh yazyke* (The Abazins and the Earliest Data on Their Language) (1940); *Abazinskaya fonetika* (Abazin Phonetics) (1947); *K voprosu o kategorii glagol'nogo vida v yafeticheskikh yazykakh Zapadnogo Kavkaza* (The Category of the Verb Form in the Japhetic Languages of the Western Caucasus) (1947); *Metodika fonetiki rodnogo yazyka v nerusskikh shkolakh Zapadnogo Kavkaza* (Methods of Teaching Native Language Phonetics in Non-Russian Schools of the Western Caucasus) (1952); *Yazyk abazin* (The Abazin Language) (1954); *Fonetika i orfografiya abazinskogo yazyka* (The Phonetics and Orthography of the Abazin Language) (1955); *Osnovnyye grammaticheskiye osobennosti yazykov Zapadnogo Kavkaza* (The Basic Grammatical Features of the West Caucasian Languages) (1955); *Russkaya transkriptsiya dlya yazykov zarubezhnogo Vostoka* (Russian Transcription of Foreign Eastern Languages) (1964); *Died:* 4 July 1965.

SEREBROVSKIY, Aleksandr Pavlovich (1884–1943) Govt and Party official; CP member from 1903; *Born:* 25 Dec 1884 in Ufa, son of a teacher; *Educ:* grad Higher Tech college in Belgium; *Career:* 1905 member, Petersburg Exec Comt; 1907 arrested in Vladivostok for complicity in the mutiny on the minelayer "Dreadnought" and sentenced to 15 years at hard labor; 1908 escaped and fled to Belgium; 1912 returned to Russia and did Party work in Nizhniy Novgorod, Moscow and Rostov; during 1917 Oct Revol commanded Red Guard company; after Revol Collegium member, Pop Comrt of Trade; 1919 dep chm, Extraordinary Commission for the Supply of the Red Army; then Dep Pop Comr of Means of Communication and chief of mil supply for Ukr Front; 1920–26 chm, Azer Oil Trust, Baku; 1924 took part in Sov mil intervention in Geo; from 1926 dep chm, USSR Supr Sovnarkhoz; chm, Bd, All-Russian Petroleum Syndicate; from 1928 chm, Bd, All-Union Gold Trust and Collegium member, USSR Pop Comrt of Finance; 1931–37 USSR Dep Pop Comr of Heavy Ind; at 14th–17th Party Congresses elected cand member, CC, CCPSU(B); 1925–38 member, All-Russian Centr Exec Comt; elected member, USSR Centr Exec Comt; wrote various works on refrigeration, oil ind, metal ind, etc; arrested by State Security organs; *Awards:* Order of the Red Banner; *Died:* 14 Mar 1943 in imprisonment.

SEREBRYAKOV, Leonid Petrovich (1890–1937) Party and govt official; CP member from 1905; *Born:* 1890; *Career:* metalworker by trade; 1904 distributed illegal polit lit in Lugansk; from 1910 professional revol; 1912 attended Prague Party Conference; 1912 arrested in Samara and exiled for three years to Narym, whence he fled in 1914; 1915 arrested in Moscow for organizing May Day demonstration and returned to Narym; 1916 completed term of exile and worked for mil org in Tomsk; after 1917 Feb Revol founded Kostroma Sov, where he worked until mid-1917; 1917–19 Presidium member, Moscow Sov; secr, Moscow Oblast Party Comt; then secr, All-Russian Centr Exec Comt; 1919–20 member and secr, CC, RCP(B); then member, Revol Mil Council, Southern Front and head, Red Army Polit Bd; from late 1921 comr, Main Bd of Means of Communication; from 1922 Dep Pop Comr of Means of Communication; from 1924 dep chm, Chinese Eastern Railroad; 1926 chm, State River Navigation Bd then chm, Commission for Transport Planning; 1928 USSR Pop Comrt of Means of Communication plen in USA; 1921, 1923–24 and 1926–27 one of leaders of Trotskyist opposition; 1921, during trade-union controversy, sided with Bukharin's "buffer group"; Oct 1927 expelled from CPSU(B) for "organizing an illegal printing press"; June 1929 publicly repudiated Trotskyism and recanted his errors; Jan 1930 re-admitted to CPSU(B) and appointed Collegium member, Pop Comrt of Means of Communication; 30 Jan 1937 sentenced to death in trial of "anti-Sov Trotskyist Center"; *Died:* 30 Jan 1937 executed; his wife Galina Serebryakova, was arrested in 1936 and spent 20 years in prisons and camps until her release and rehabilitation in 1956.

SEREBRYAKOV, Mikhail Vasil'yevich (1879– ?) Socio-polit figure; researcher; Dr of Historical Sci; CP member from 1904; *Born:* 1879 in vil Trostyanets, Khar'kov Province, son of a technol eng; *Educ:* 1911 grad Petersburg Univ; *Career:* from 1890's active in revol movement; propaganda among workers in Khar'kov, Rostov-on-Don and Taganrog; 1902 arrested for participating in May Day polit demonstration in Rostov-on-Don, and 1903 exiled to Eastern Siberia; fled from exile and went abroad; 1904 worked with Berlin Group for the Promotion of the RSDRP; 1904 returned to Russia with a transport of illegal propaganda lit and continued party work in Petersburg; from 1914 practised as lawyer; 1918 worked for Petrograd Food Comrt; 1919 with Polit Dept, Baltic Fleet; from 1921 prof, 1927–30 rector, Leningrad Univ; 1930–48 engaged in art and philosophical studies; dir, Inst of Art History, All-Russian Acad of Arts and Econ, Philosophy and Law Inst; wrote 35 research works; *Awards:* Order of Lenin; Order of the Red Banner of Labor; medals; *Died:* date and place of death unknown.

SEREBRYAKOVA, Anna Yegorovna (1857–?)Tsarist security official; *Born:* 1857; *Career:* for 25 years Tsarist security official in Moscow; was responsible for uncovering numerous revol orgs in 1890's and 1900's; 1909 pensioned off; 1925 arrested by NKVD and sentenced to 10 years imprisonment; *Died:* date and place of death unknown.

SEREDA, Semyon Pafnut'yevich (1871–1933) Govt and Party official; CP member from 1903; *Born:* 1 Feb 1871 in vil Setlovo, Chernigov Province, son of a railroad official; *Career:* econ statistician by profession; 1899 arrested for membership of Marxist circle in Smolensk and imprisoned in Petersburg's "Kresty" Jail; subsequently Party work in Kiev, Kaluga and other cities; 1896–1917 statistician in Smolensk and Ryazan'; after 1917 Feb Revol member, Exec Comt, Ryazan' Sov; helped establish Sov regime in Ryazan'; 1918–21 RSFSR Pop Comr of Agric; from 1921 Presidium member, Supr Sovnarkhoz and RSFSR Gosplan; dep mang, then mang, RSFSR Centr Statistical Bd; from 1930 dep chm, RSFSR Gosplan; deleg at 8th, 15th and 16th CPSU(B) Congresses; member, All-Russian Centr Exec Comt; *Publ: Ocherk polozheniya nachal'nogo obrazovaniya v Vyazemskom uyezde v 1897–1898 uchebnom godu* (A Study of the State of Primary Education in the Vyazma Uyezd in the 1897–98 Curricular Year) (1899); *Osnovaniya raskladki gubernskikh sborov s zemel'* (The Principles for the Apportionment of Provincial Land Assemblies) (1904); *Soyuz zemledel'skikh kommun i arteley* (The Union of Agricultural Communes and Artels) (1919); *Osnovnyye zadachi sotsialisticheskogo zemledeliya* (The Basic Tasks of Socialist Agriculture) (1920); *Ob organizatsii sotsialisticheskoy statistiki* (The Organization of Socialist Statistics) (1930), etc; *Died:* 21 May 1933.

SEREYSKIY, Mark Yakovlevich (1885–1957) Psychiatrist; Dr of Med from 1925; prof; *Born:* 1885; *Educ:* 1910 grad Fac of Physics and Mathematics, Petersburg Univ; then studied med at Munich Univ; 1914 grad Med Fac, Moscow Univ; *Career:* after grad intern, asst to Prof P.G. Gannushkin, then dep dir, Psychiatric Clinic, Moscow Univ; 1919–20 worked under A.N. Bakh at Inst of Biochemistry, Russian Acad of Sci; from 1925 head, Chair of Psychiatry, State Inst of Defectology, Moscow; 1930–34 head, Chair of Psychiatry, Rostov Med Inst; 1935–51 head, Chair of Psychiatry, Centr Inst of Postgrad Med Training, Moscow; did research on active therapy of mental diseases; helped develop sleep treatment methods for schizophrenia, etc; helped to improve differential indications and analyzed mechanisms of such active therapy methods as insulin treatment and consulsion therapy; also did research on epilepsy; adopted a unitary approach to pathogenesis, clinical aspects and treatment of mental diseases; wrote some 200 works; *Publ:* coauthor, *Uchebnik psikhiatrii* (A Textbook on Psychiatry) (1928); coauthor, *Primeneniye dlitel'nogo narkoza v psikhiatrii* (The Used of Prolonged Narcosis in Psychiatry) (1936); *Obshchiye voprosy, svyazannyye s problemoy insulinoterapii shizofrenii* (General Problems Concerning the Insulin Treatment of Schizophrenia) (1938); *Stimulyatory nervnoy sistemy* (Nerve Stimulants) (1943); *Novyye puti diagnostiki i lecheniya epilepsii* (New Ways of Diagnosing and Treating Epilepsy) (1945); *Terapiya psikhicheskikh zabolevvaniy* (Mental Therapy) (1948); *Died:* 1957.

SEREZHNIKOV, Vasiliy Konstantinovich (1885–1952) Specialist in the art of reciting; teacher, producer and actor; Hon Artiste of RSFSR from 1934; *Born:* 4 Apr 1885; *Career:* 1913–19 organized, directed and taught Moscow's first courses on diction and recitation; 1915 introduced genre of collective recitation; 1923 founded Moscow Itinerant Recitation Theater; gave public recitation performances and readings; arrested by State Security organs; spent his years in imprisonment in Kazakhstan; *Productions:* Verhaaren's "Wind" and "Revolt"; Nekrasov's *Zelyonyy shum* (Verdant Sound) and excerpts from Nekrasov's poem *Komu na Rusi zhit' khorosho* (Who Lives the Good Life in Russia); "Pushkin"; *Revolyutsionnaya poeziya* (Revolutionary Poetry), etc; *publ: Iskusstva khudozhestvennogo chteniya* (The Art of Recitation) (1923); *Kartavost' i metody yeyo ustraneniya* (Burring and Ways of Overcoming It) (1925); *Kollektivnaya deklamatsiya* (Collective Recitation) (1927); *Masterstvo chtetsa* (The Reader's Art) (1930), etc; *Died:* 20 Sept 1952 in imprisonment; posthumously rehabilitated.

SERGEYEV (PETROV), Andrey Vasil'yevich (1893–1933) Mil commander; CP member from 1911; *Born:* 1893; *Career:* pilot; during WW 1 soldier, Russian Army; 1917–18 chm, All-Russian Air Force Council; first head, RSFSR Air Fleet; during Civil War in charge of Russian Air Force; chief of transport aviation, Civil Air Fleet; *Publ: Strategiya i taktika Krasnogo Vozdushnogo Flota* (The Strategy and Tactics of the Red Air Force) (1925); *Pyat' let stroitel'stva.i bor'by Vozdushnogo flota – 1917–1922 gody* (Five Years in the Formation and Operation of the Air Force – 1917–1922) (1926); *Died:* 1933.

SERGEYEV, Yevgeniy Nikolayevich (1887–1938) Mil commander; *Born:* 1887; *Career:* lt-col, Russian Army; from 1918 in Red Army; during Civil War chief of staff of div, then army; after Civil War chief of staff, various mil distr; lectured at Red Army Mil Acad; arrested by State Security organs; *Died:* 1938 in imprisonment.

SERGEYEV-TSENSKIY, Sergey Nikolayevich (1875–1958) Russian writer; member, USSR Acad of Sci from 1943; *Born:* 30 Sept 1875 in vil Preobrazhenskoye, Tambov Province, son of a teacher; and retired officer; *Educ:* trained as teacher; *Career:* worked as teacher; 1901 first work printed; *Publ:* stories: "Tundra" (1903); *Pogost* (The Grave-Yard) (1904); novelettes: *Pechal' poley* (The Grief of the Fields) (1909); *Nedra* (The Womb) (1913); *Naklonnaya Yelena* (Slanting Yelena) (1914); novel "Babayev" (1907); his epic work *Preobrazheniye Rossii* (The Transformation of Russia), which began in 1914 with the novel "Valya", consists of the novels: *Obrechyonnyye na gibel'* (The Doomed) (1927), *Pushki zagovorili* (The Guns Spoke) (1930), *Iskat', vsegda iskat'!* (Seek, Always Seek!) (1935) and *Brusilovskiy proryv* (The Brusilov Break-Through) (1942–43); novel *Sevastopol'skaya strada* (Sebastopol Toil) (1937–40); *Polnoye sobraniye sochineniy* (Complete Collected Works) (10 vol, 1955–56); *Awards:* Stalin Prize (1941); Order of Lenin; other orders; medals; *Died:* 3 Dec 1958 in Alushta.

SERGIY (secular name: KOSTIN, Viktor) (1885–1959) Bishop of Kostroma and Galich, Russian Orthodox Church; *Born:* 1885 in Vyatka; *Educ:* secondary educ; *Career:* after completing school worked as private secr to Bishop Varsonofiy (Glazovskiy); then parish psalmist; 1910 appointed deacon; from 1920 parish priest in Kirovsk Eparchy; 1949–51 served with Russian Orthodox Mission in Palestine; 1952 dean, Church of the Cross, Moscow Patriarchy, in Berlin; then dean, Tegel Church, Berlin; 1955 returned to USSR and took monastic vows with the name Sergiy; 1955 elevated to archimandrite; shortly afterwards personally consecrated bishop by Patriarch Aleksiy and appointed Bishop of Novorossiysk and vicar of Krasnodar Eparchy; 1956 appointed Bishop of Kostroma and Galich; *Died:* 15 June 1959.

SERGIY (secular name: STAROGORODSKIY, Ivan Nikolayevich) (1867–1944) Patriarch of Moscow and All Russia; chm, Most Holy Synod from 1943; Master of Divinity from 1895; *Born:* 11 Jan 1867 in Arzamas, now Gorky Oblast; *Educ:* 1890 grad Petersburg Theological Acad; *Career:* took monastic vows while still at acad; after grad stayed on at acad for research work; then worked for Orthodox Theological Mission in Japan and taught at a Japanese seminary; 1892 missionary work in Kyoto; 1893 assoc prof, Petersburg Theological Acad; 1894, as archimandrite, chaplain of Russian Embassy Church in Athens; 1897 asst head, Orthodox Theological Mission in Japan; then rector, Petersburg Theological Seminary and inspector, Petersburg Theological Acad; from 1901 rector, Petersburg Theological Acad as Bishop of Yamburg and Vicar of Petersburg Eparchy; from 1905 Archbishop of Finland and Vyborg; from 1911 member, Most Holy Synod and chm, Special Council for Domestic and Foreign Missionary Affairs; 1917, after disbanding of old Synod, headed new Holy Synod and was appointed Archbishop of Vladimir and Shuyskoye; 1918 elevated to metropolitan and appointed to Nizhniy Novgorod Eparchy; was not a close assoc of Patriarch Tikhon; in opposition to patriarchal views, he recognized Renovated Church movement, which was supported by Communist regime; 1924, after collapse of this movement, made public repentance in Moscow; 1925, after death of Patriarch Tikhon and arrest of all his deputies, became debuty vicar of patriarchal throne; 1926, in his address to Sov govt, defended Orthodox Church against regime's attempts to subordinate it to polit goals; 1926–27 in prison; 1927 accepted govt terms for legalization of Church admin and was released from prison; 1927, on behalf of the Synod, signed and published a declaration calling on Russian Orthodox Church to be loyal to the Sov govt; barred clergy who refused to accept this declaration from officiating, which led to the arrest, exile and death of many clergymen; subsequently fully served interests of Sov regime, took an authoritative stand and refused to consider the views of the majority of the episcopate; 1934 took title "Most Blessed Metropolitan of Moscow and Kolomna"; during WW 2 delivered patriotic appeals and organized collection of eparchial donations for the Dmitriy Donskoy Tank Column, for air force squadrons, etc; 1942 published propaganda book "Pravda o religii v Rossii" (The Truth About Religion in Russia), assuring the foreign reader that the Church enjoyed complete freedom in the USSR; 1943, in token of the government's recognition of his services, he was received by Stalin; 1943, in contravention of Orthodox Church canons, he was elected Patriarch of Moscow and All Russia; took stern action against anti-patriarchal factions; 1944 began to receive for delegs and would assure them that there was complete freedom of religion in the USSR; because of their propaganda value, was authorized by Sov regime to open theological training establishments and publish "Zhurnal Moskovskoy Patriarkhii" and other works of a Churchpolit nature; *Awards:* Order of Alexander Nevskiy; diamond cross on cowl; right to wear two panagia; *Died:* 15 May 1944.

SERGIYENKO, Ivan Vasil'yevich (1918–1943) Party official; CP member from 1939; *Born:* 1918 in Kiev Province; *Career:* fought with partisans in Ukr during WW 2; secr, underground Rozvazhev Rayon Comt, CP(B) Ukr; from Sept 1942 secr underground Kiev Oblast Comt, CP(B) Ukr; Jan 1943 arrested by German occupation forces; *Awards:* Hero of the Sov Union (1965, posthumously); *Died:* 1943 in imprisonment.

SEROV, Anatoliy Konstantinovich (1910–1939) Mil pilot; brigade comr; CP member from 1931; *Born:* 1910 in what is now Sverdlovsk Oblast, son of a miner; *Educ:* completed factory and plant school; grad Orenburg Pilots School; 1935–36 studied at Air Force Acad; *Career:* worked as steel founder; from 1929 in Sov Army; served with fighter air force units, then test pilot, State Air Force Test Institute; from 1930 head, Main Flight Inspectorate, Sov Air Force; *Awards:* Hero of Sov Union (1932); Order of Lenin; two Orders of the Red Banner; *Died:* 11 May 1939 killed in a plane crash together with the aviatrix P. D. Osipenko; 7 June 1939 Nadezhdinsk (Sverdlovsk Oblast) was renamed Serov.

SERYSHEV, Stepan Mikhaylovich (1889–1928) Mil commander; CP member from 1917; *Born:* 1889; *Career:* lt, Russian Army; during 1917 Oct Revol commanded Red Guard squad in Centr Siberia; Dec 1917, together with S. G. Lazo, directed suppression of anti-Sov revolt in Irkutsk; then served on staff, Transbaykal Front; from 1918 underground work; arrested; Feb 1920 liberated in Blagoveshchensk by revol forces; helped organize Pop Revol Army of Far Eastern Republ; 1920–22 member, Amur Revol Comt; commander, Amur Oblast Forces; Aug 1920–Mar 1921 commander, Amur Front; Mar–Dec 1921 commander, 2nd Amur Army; Dec 1921–Mar 1922 commander, Eastern Front, Far Eastern Republ; member, Revol Mil Council, Pop Revol Army, Far Eastern

Republ; 1923–24 div commander; 1924–26 asst corps commander; 1926–27 mil attache in Japan; from Oct 1927 manager, Red Army Centr Club; *Died:* 29 Feb 1928.

SEYFULLIN, Saken (1894–1939) Kaz poet and govt official; CP member from 1918; *Born:* 1894; *Educ:* 1916 grad Omsk Teachers' Seminary; *Career:* worked as teacher; in 1920's member, Kaz and All-Russian Centr Exec Comt; chm, Kaz Council of Pop Comr; one of the founders of Sov Kaz lit; 1937 arrested by State Security organs; *Publ:* verse: "The Marseillaise of the Young Kazakhs"; "Come on, Dzhigits!"; "We Mustered for the March"; "Comrades"; verse collections: "Bygone Days" (1915); "The Indomitable Tulpar" (1922); "Dombra" (1924); "Express" (1926); "On the Waves of Life" (1928); "Kokchetau" (1929); "The Albatross" (1933); "The Red Steed" (1934); "Socialistan" (1935); collected stories and novelettes "Aysha" (1935); plays: "The Path to Happiness" (1917); "Red Falcons" (1922); *Died:* 9 Oct 1939 in imprisonment; posthumously rehabilitated.

SEYFULLINA, Lidiya Nikolayevna (1889–1954) Russian writer; *Born:* 3 Apr 1889 in vil Valamva, Orenburg Province, daughter of a priest; *Educ:* 1906 grad high school; *Career:* from 1906 worked as teacher; 1909–14 acted with provincial drama theaters; after 1917 Oct Revol taught in Urals and Siberia; 1921 first work printed; *Publ:* story *Pravonarushiteli* (The Miscreants) (1922); novelette *Peregnoy* (Humus) (1922); *Virineya* (1925); plays: coauthor, "Chyornyy Yar" (1931); *Poputchiki* (Fellow-Travelers) (1932); *Syn* (The Son) (1947); stories: *Aleksandr Makedonskiy* (Alexander of Macedonia) (1922); *Muzhitskiy skaz o Lenine* (A Peasant's Tale of Lenin) (1924); *Sobstvennost* (Property) (1933); "Tanya" (1934); novelette *Na svoyey zemle* (In One's Own Land) (1942); also wrote essays and articles; *Sobraniye sochineniy* (Collected Works) (6 vol, 1928–31); *Izbrannoye* (Selected Works) (1941); *Povesti i rasskazy* (Novelettes and Stories) (1953); *Awards:* Order of the Red Banner of Labor (1939); *Died:* 25 Apr 1954.

SHABALOV, Sergey Maksimovich (1897–1965) Educationist; prof; Dr of Pedag Sci; CP member from 1940; *Born:* 21 Sept 1897; *Educ:* 1919 grad Cherepovets Teachers' Seminary; *Career:* from 1919 taught at school in Cherepovets; from 1924 worked for RSFSR Pop Comrt of Educ in Moscow; from 1927 research and lecturing work at 2nd Moscow Univ, then at Polytech Training Research Inst, Moscow's Potyomkin Teachers' Training Inst and Moscow Univ; specialized in polytech training, production training methods, combination of training with productive work, etc; wrote aids on polytech training methods for secondary schools; *Publ: Na bor'bu za sovetskuyu trudovuyu shkolu* (Into the Struggle for the Soviet Labor School) (1928); *Metodicheskoye rukovodstvo po slesarnomu delu* (Methodological Guide to Metalworking) (1946); *Politekhnicheskoye obucheniye i podgotovka uchashchikhsya k proizvodstvennoy deyatel'nosti* (Polytechnic Education and the Training of Pupils for Production Work) (1955); *Politekhnicheskoye obucheniye* (Polytechnic Training) (1956); *Died:* 19 Nov 1965.

SHADR (real name: IVANOV), Ivan Dmitriyevich (1887–1941) Sculptor; *Born:* 30 Jan 1887 in vil Taktashinskoye, near Shadrinsk, now Kurgan Oblast; *Educ:* 1906 grad Yekaterinburg Ind Art College; 1902–07 studied under sculptor T. Zal'kal in Yekaterinburg; 1907–09 studied at School of Soc for the Promotion of the Arts, Petersburg; 1910–11 studied in Paris and 1911–12 in Rome; *Career:* in his youth learned cabinet-making and stone-cutting, engaging in sculpture in his spare time; 1910–12 went to Paris and Rome to study sculpture on a grant from Shadrinsk Municipal Admin; returned to Russia shortly before Revol; 1920–21 worked for Polit Educ Comt, 5th Army; from 1922 worked in Moscow, reproducing sculptural works on coinage; 1925–32 member, Soc of Russian Sculptors, then Sov Artists' Union; *Works:* statue of Karl Marx, bas-reliefs of Liebknecht, Rosa Luxemburg and Karl Marx (1920–21); busts: "The Worker," "The Peasant" and "The Red Army-Man" (1921); worked on decoration of main facade of All-Union Agric Exhibition, Moscow (1923); statue of Lenin at the Zemo-Avchala Hydroelectr Station (1927); sculpture "The Cobble-Stone is the Weapon of the Proletariat" (1927); portrait of N.A. Kasatkin (1930); memorial for tomb of N.S. Alliluyeva (1933); model of Pushkin Monument (1938); Gorky Monument (1939); memorials for graves of Ye.N. Nemirovich-Danchenko (1939) and V.L. Durov (1940), etc; *Awards:* Stalin Prize (1952); *Died:* 3 Apr 1941.

SHAKHBAZYAN, Yevgeniy Sergeyevich (1902–1966) Surgeon; Dr of Med; prof from 1945; CP member from 1920; *Born:* 1902 in Yerevan, son of a physician; *Educ:* 1926 grad Med Fac, Moscow Univ; *Career:* 1926–39 intern, asst prof, then assoc prof, Chair of Hospital Surgery Clinic, 1st Moscow Med Inst; 1939–40 chief surgeon of a mobile field surgery on Finnish Front; 1941–45 mil surgeon on various fronts; from 1945 head, Chair of Operative Surgery, 1st Moscow Med Inst; member, ed collegium, journal "Klinicheskaya meditsina"; wrote some 50 works; *Publ: Eksperimental'nyye materialy o narushenii venechnogo krovoobrashcheniya v serdtse* (Experimental Material on Disturbances of Venous Circulation in the Heart); "P.I. D'yakonov" (1957); *Kriptorkhizm i yego lecheniye* (Cryptorchism and Its Treatment) (1957), etc; *Awards:* five orders and medals; *Died:* Aug 1966 in Moscow.

SHALYAPIN, (CHALIAPINE), Fyodor Ivanovich (1873–1938) Russian singer (bass); Pop Artiste of RSFSR; *Born:* 13 Feb 1873 in Kazan', son of an office worker; *Educ:* high-school grad; 1892–93 studied singing with Usatov in Tiflis; *Career:* at age ten became a shoemaker's apprentice, then worked for a turner; also worked as clerk and longshoreman; learned to read music while singing with a church choir; 1890 joined S. Ya. Semyonov-Samarskiy's choir in Ufa; 1891–92 toured Russia with G. O. Lyubimov–Derkach's Ukr operetta ensemble; also sang in choir of a French operetta company performing in Baku and with the Klyucharyov ensemble in Batumi and Kutaisi; 1893–94 sang 14 operatic roles in Tiflis under contract to V. L. Forcatti; summer 1894 signed contract with M. V. Lentovskiy to sing at "Arcadia" Theater, Petersburg; fall 1894 performed for Petersburg Opera Soc at Panayevskiy Theater; 1894 joined Mariinskiy Theater, where he sang nine roles; 1896 made guest appearance at Mamontov's private Russian Opera Theater, Moscow, whose ensemble he joined that fall; while here he improved his musical and gen educ and kept company with such artists as V. M. Basnetsov, M. A. Vrubel', K. A. Korovin and V. A. Serov; also befriended by historian V. O. Klyuchevskiy and the Malyy Theater artistes O. O. and M. P. Sadovskiy and G. N. Fedotova; had an especially valuable relationship with S. V. Rachmaninoff, who conducted at Mamontov's theater in the 1897–98 season; 1898 acquired greater fame after a highly-successful guest performance in Petersburg and was patronized by V. V. Stasov, who introduced him to I. Ye. Repin, M. M. Antokol'skiy, N. A. Rimsky-Korsakov, A. K. Glazunov and A. K. Lyadov; 1899 joined Bolshoy Theater but also sang at Mariinskiy Theater and made guest appearances in provinces; 1901 made triumphal guest appearance at La Scala, after which he undertook numerous for tours; in same year befriended Maxim Gorky, who had a strong influence on his artistic views and gained his sympathies for the Soc-Democratic movement; 1905 contributed earnings from a folksong concert to polit funds; 1907–09 and 1913 toured with Diaghilev's "Russian Season Abroad"; from 1914 performed in Moscow and Petersburg under contract to S. I. Zimin and A. R. Aksarin; after 1917 Oct Revol helped to reorganize musical and theatrical performances; 1918 offered artistic directorship of Mariinskiy Theater; 1918–19 sang in some 80 operas and concerts; 1919 appointed dir, Mariinskiy Theater; 1922 refused to return to Russia after a tour abroad; 1928 deprived of title of Pop Artiste of RSFSR by Sov authorities; apart from singing also produced a number of operas; *Roles:* Stol'nik in Moniuszko's "Halka" (1890); Fernando in "The Troubadour" (1891); the Stranger in Verstovskiy's *Askol'dova mogila* (Askold's Grave) (1891); Pyotr in "Natalka-Poltavka" (1892); Orovezo in "Norma" (1892); the Cardianl in Halevy's "The Cardinal's Daughter" (1892); Valentin and Mephestopheles in "Faust" (1893); Ramses in "Aida" (1893); Monterone in "Rigoletto" (1893); Gremin in "Eugene Onegin" (1893); Lord Cockburg in Ober's "Fra Diavolo" (1894); the Miller in "Rusalka" (1894); title role in "Ruslan" (1895); title role in Napravnik's "Dubrovskiy" (1896); Prince Vladimir in Serov's "Rogneda" (1896); the Old Jew in Saint-Saëns' "Samson and Delilah" (1896); Dosifey in "Khovanshchina" (1897); Holofernes in Serov's "Judith" (1898); title role in "Boris Godunov" (1898); Yeryomka in Serov's *Vrazh'ya sila* (Hostile Force) (1902); Philipp II in Verdi's "Don Carlos" (1907); title role in "Don Quixote" (1910); *title role in Ivan Groznyy* (Ivan the Terrible) (1911); Konchak in *Knyaz' Igor'" (Prince Igor) (1914), etc; Died:* 12 Apr 1938 in Paris after a long illness.

SHANIN, Zhumat (1891–1937) Stage dir and playwright; Pop Artiste of Kaz SSR; *Born:* 1891; *Educ:* studied in Omsk; *Career:* after 1917 Oct Revol worked for Party and govt organs in Semipalatinsk and Pavlodar; 1924 founded amateur drama circle in Semipalatinsk; 1926–33 stage dir, first Kaz Nat Theater; from 1933 dir, Kaz Musical Drama Theater; promoted establishment of opera in Kaz; used ancient Kaz folk games, songs and music in his productions; arrested by State Security organs; *Publ:* plays "Arkalyk batyr"; "From Death to Hope"; "Bayan Batyr"; *Productions:* Dzhansugurov's "Vengeance"; Auezov's "For October"; Maylin's "Front"; Seyfullin's "Red Falcons"; "Arkalyk Batyr"; "From Death to Hope"; "Bayan Batyr", etc; *Died:* 1937 in imprisonment; posthumously rehabilitated.

SHAPORIN, Yuriy Aleksandrovich (1887–1966) Composer; prof, Moscow Conservatory from 1940; Hon Art Worker of RSFSR from 1944; Pop Artiste of USSR from 1954; secr, USSR Composers' Union from 1952; *Born:* 27 Oct 1887 in Glukhov, now Sumy Oblast; *Educ:* 1906–08 studied at Philology Fac, Kiev Univ; also studied at Kiev Conservatory; 1913 grad Law Fac, Petersburg Univ; 1918 grad Petersburg Conservatory; *Career:* 1918–19 musical dir, composer and conductor, Maly Drama Theater, Petrograd; 1919–34 at Leningrad Acad Drama Theater (now Pushkin Theater); 1926–30 also dir, "Triton" Music Publ House; 1939–40 instructor, from 1940 prof of composition, Moscow Conservatory; 1926–30 chm, Assoc of Modern Music; 1924–32 bd member, Drama Union; 1932–36 dep chm, Leningrad Sov Composers' Union; 1939–48 member, Org Comt, USSR Composers' Union; 1948–52 bd member, from 1952 secr, USSR Composers' Union; 1948 attended Int Congress of Composers and Musicians, Prague, 1947 Pop Artiste of RSFSR; 1955 member, Sov Comt for the Defense of Peace; *Work:* series of romances to words by Tyutchev (1921), Pushkin and Lermontov (1937), Blok (1940) and Sov poets Rozhdestvenskiy, Shchipachyov, Surkov and Isakovskiy; cycle "As Long as the Kite Circles"; opera *Dekabristy* (The Decembrists); symphony reflecting revol events in Russia (1932); symphony-cantata *Na pole Kulikovom* (On Kulikovo Field); oratorio *Skazaniye o bitve za Russkuye zemlyu* (The Tale of the Battle for the Land of Russia); *Pesnya zhar-ptitsy* (The Song of the Firebird) (1924); choral works to texts from Lermontov and Nekrasov; two piano suites; four cello pieces, etc; music for films: *Dezertir* (The Deserter) (1933); *Minin and Pozharskiy* (1938); "Suvorov" (1940); "Kutuzov" (1944); oratorio *(Dokole korshunu kruzhit'* (As Long as the Kite Circles) (1963); music for theater productions; *Awards:* Order of Lenin; Order of the Red Banner of Labor; Order of the Red Star; medals; three Stalin Prizes (1941, 1946 and 1952); *Died:* 9 Dec 1966.

SHAPOSHNIKOV, Boris Mikhaylovich (1882–1945) Mil commander; col, Russian Army; Marshal of the Sov Union from 1940; CP member from 1930; *Born:* 2 Oct 1882 in Zlatoust, son of a distillery mang and a schoolmistress; *Educ:* 1903 grad Moscow Mil College; 1910 grad Gen Staff Acad; *Career:* 1901 joined Russian Army; 1903–07 officer, 1st Turkestani Infantry Battalion in Centr Asia; 1910–12 company commander; 1912–14 officer, Staff of 14th Cavalry Div; 1914–18 adjutant, Staff of 14th Cavalry Div; staff officer (capt) for special assignments, Quartermaster-Gen Bd, Staff of Commander in Chief, Northwestern Front; chief of staff, Separate Composite Cossack Brigade, 2nd Turkestani Cossack Div; actg chief of staff, 10th Army Corps; commander, 16th Grenadier Mingrel Regt; elected commander, Caucasian Grenadier Div; Mar 1918 demobilized from Russian Army; May 1918 volunteered for Red Army; 1918–21 asst head, Operations Bd, Higher Mil Council; asst chief of staff, Ukr Pop Comrt of Mil and Naval Affairs; head, Intelligence Dept, Operations Bd, Field Staff of RSFSR Revol Mil Council; Feb 1921–May 1925 1st asst chief of staff of Red Army; May 1925–May 1927 commander, Leningrad Mil Distr; May 1927–May 1928 commander, Moscow Mil Distr; May 1928–Apr 1931 chief of staff of Red Army; Apr 1931–Mar 1932 commander, Volga Mil Distr; Mar 1932–Sept 1935 commandant and comr, Frunze Mil Acad; Sept 1935–May 1937 commander, Leningrad Mil Distr; May 1937–Aug 1940 chief of Red Army Gen Staff; after 1939 proposed that main forces of the mil districts be retained within the old state borders behind the fortified-area line, while the newly annexed areas be defended by light covering forces capable of holding off an enemy until the main forces could be deployed; his views were ignored, and this oversight was one of the factors which contributed to the early rout of the Red Army during the early period of WW 2; from 14 Aug 1940 USSR Dep Pop Comr of Defense, in charge of the construction of fortifications; 29 July 1941–26 June 1942 chief, Red Army Gen Staff; from June 1942 USSR Dep Pop Comr of Defense, in charge of revision of mil regulations; June 1943–Mar 1945 commandant, Voroshilov Higher Mil Acad (Gen Staff Acad); 1939–45 cand member, CC, CPSU(B); dep, USSR Supr Sov of 1937 convocation; *Publ:* *Konnitsa* (Cavalry) (1923); *Na Visle* (On the Vistula) (1924); *Mozg armii* (The Brain of the Army) (3 vol, 1927–29); *Varshavskaya operatsiya* (The Warsaw Operation) (1933); *Awards:* three Orders of Lenin; two Orders of the Red Banner; Order of Suvorov, 1st Class; two Orders of the Red Star; *Died:* 26 Mar 1945; his ashes are immured in the Kremlin Wall.

SHAPOVALOV, Aleksandr Sidorovich (1871–1942) Revolutionary; CP member from 1895; *Born:* 1871 in Poltava Province; *Career:* metalworker by trade; 1894 joined People's Will workers' group and helped establish and run People's Will underground Lakhta printing press; did revol propaganda among Petersburg workers; 1895 developed an interest in Marxism, broke with the People's Will Party and became an active member of Petersburg League for the Liberation of the Working Class; 1896 arrested for helping to organize Petersburg textile workers' strike; early 1898 exiled for three years to Eastern Siberia; Dec 1898, while in exile, made the acquaintance of Lenin and 1899 attended 17-member Soc-Democratic Conference; 1901 returned from exile and became agent of Lenin's newspaper "Iskra"; 1901–06 underground organizer and propagandist among workers in Batum, Kineshma, Ivanovo-Voznesensk, Kiev, Tver', Yekaterinoslav, Odessa and Khar'kov; 1905 member, Khar'kov RSDRP(B) Comt; Dec 1905 arrested; June 1906 released on bail and emigrated; lived in Belgium, then France where he worked as a lathe-operator at various plants and took part in various for Bolsheviks org; early July 1917 returned to Petrograd; after 1917 Oct Revol did Party and govt work; 1924, at 13th RCP(B) Congress, elected member, Centr Control Commission; in his latter years pensioner and engaged in lit work; *Publ: Po doroge k marksizmu* (On the Road to Marxism); *Died:* 1942.

SHARIFZADE, Abas Mirza (1892–1937) Actor and stage dir; *Born:* 1892; *Career:* took part in amateur dramatics; 1908 began professional acting career; 1916–17 with Gadzhibekov Opera Company; from 1920 at Azizbekov Theater; also acted in films; arrested by State Security Organs; *Roles:* Iblis, Siyavush and Sheikh Senan in Gusein Dzhavid's "Iblis", "Siyavush" and "Sheikh Senan"; Aydyn, Oktay, El'khan and Eyvaz in Dzhabarly's "Aydyn", "Oktay el' ogly", "Bride of Fire" and "In 1905"; Kadzhar in Adkhverdov's "Aga Mukhammed-shakh Kadzhar"; Nadirshakh in Narimanov's "Nadirshakh"; also played Othello, Hamlet, Karl Moor, Uriel' Akosta, Macbeth, etc; *Died:* 1937 in imprisonment; posthumously rehabilitated.

SHARONOV, Vsevolod Vasil'yevich (1901–1964) Astronomer; prof, Leningrad Univ from 1944; dir, Astronomical Observatory, Leningrad Univ from 1951; CP member from 1949; *Born:* 1901; *Educ:* 1926 grad Leningrad Univ; *Career:* 1936–41 at Main Astronomical Observatory, USSR Acad of Sci, Pulkovo; developed new methods of absolute surface photometry of heavenly bodies; designed various instruments to measure the intensity of natural objects and range of vision; studied planets and atmospheric optics; *Publ: Vidimost' dalyokikh predmetov i ogney* (The Visibility of Distant Objects and Fires) (1944); "Mars" (1947); *Izmereniye raschyot vidimosti dalyokikh predmetov* (Measuring Calculations on the Visibility of Distant Objects) (1947); *Solntse i yego nablyudeniye* (The Sun and Its Observation) (2nd ed, 1953); *Fotometricheskoye issledovaniye prirody planet i sputnikov* (Photometric Study of the Nature of Planets and Satellites) (1954); *Luna i polyoty v Kosmos* (The Moon and Space Flight) (1957); *Nekotoryye rezul'taty nablyudeniy Marsa v protivostoyaniye* (Some Results of Observations of Mars in Opposition) (1958); *Fotometricheskiye i kolorimetricheskiye sravneniya poverkhnosti Marsa s obraztsami limonita i gornykh porod krasnotsvetnykh tolshch* (Photometric and Colorimetric Comparison of the Martian Surface with Samples of Limonite and Red Rocks) (1960); *Pered polyotom na Lunu* (Before Moon Flight) (1963); *Died:* 1964;

SHATELEN, Mikhail Andreyevich (1866–1957) Electr eng; Dr of Tech Sci; corresp member, USSR Acad of Sci from 1931; Hero of Socialist Labor from 1956; Hon Sci and Tech Worker of RSFSR from 1934; Hon Sci and Tech Worker of Uzbek SSR from 1943; *Born:* 13 Jan 1866 in Anapa, Krasnodar Kray; *Educ:* 1888 grad Physics and Mathematics Fac, Petersburg Univ; 1890 grad Paris Higher Electr Eng School; *Career:* from 1891 lecturer, Petersburg Univ and Petersburg Mining Inst; from 1893 prof, Petersburg Electr Eng Inst; 1901–57 prof, Petersburg (Leningrad) Polytech Inst; helped compile and implement Russian State Electrification Plan; from 1921 member, USSR Gosplan; from 1929 pres, USSR Main Chamber of Weights and Measures; for many years chm, Commission for Light Eng, USSR Acad of Sci; specialized in gen electr eng, light eng, metrology and the history of eng; 1929–49 member, Int Weights and Measures Comt; hon member, French Soc of Electr Eng; hon member, British Soc of Electr Eng; hon member, American Inst of Electr Eng; *Publ: Russkiye elektrotekhniki vtoroy poloviny 19-go veka* (Russian Electrical Engineers of the Late 19th Century) (1948), etc; *Awards:* four Orders of Lenin; Order of the Red Banner of Labor; Stalin Prize (1949); *Died:* 31 Jan 1957.

SHATSKIN, L.A. (1902–1937) Party official; CP member from 1917; *Born:* 1902; *Career:* 1917–26 exec official, CC, All-Russian Komsomol and Exec Comt, Communist Youth International; 1918–22 first secr, CC, All-Russian Komsomol; member, ed bd, newspaper "Komsomol'skaya pravda"; then worked for Centr Union of Consumer Soc; and did lecturing work; at 15th and 16th Party Congresses elected member, CPSU(B) Centr Control Commission; 1931 expelled from CPSU(B) Centr Control Commission for siding with Leftist-Rightist Bloc; 1935 expelled from Party for alleged anti-Party and anti-govt activities and later sentenced; *Died:* 1937 in imprisonment.

SHATSKIY, Nikolay Nikolayevich (1899–1934) Eng; *Born:* 1899; *Career:* CP member; 1927 expelled from Party for alleged membership of "anti-Sov Zinoviev group"; Dec 1934 arrested for alleged complicity in assassination of Kirov; defendant in trial of "Leningrad Center", accused of directing an "underground counterrevol terrorist group" and of organizing the assassination of Kirov; sentenced to death by Mil Collegium of USSR Supr Court; *Died:* late Dec 1934 executed.

SHATSKIY, Nikolay Sergeyevich (1895–1960) Geologist; prof; member, USSR Acad of Sci from 1953; *Born:* 28 Aug 1895 in Moscow; *Educ:* 1929 grad Moscow Mining Acad; *Career:* 1932–60 prof, then head, Chair of Historical Geology, Moscow Geological Survey Inst; 1934–35 assoc, 1935–55 head, Tectonics Dept, Inst of Geological Sci, USSR Acad of Sci; 1956–60 dir, Geological Inst, USSR Acad of Sci; created a new trend in tectonics with the study of the development of the tectonic structures of the earth's crust; 1933, together with A.D. Arkhangel'skiy, mapped the gen tectonic structure of the USSR; then mapped the tectonic structure of the Siberian Plateau, the West Siberian Depression and Centr Kazakhstan; established the gen pattern for plateau structure; 1952 and 1956 helped compile tectonic map of the USSR; *Awards:* two Orders of Lenin; Order of the Red Banner of Labor; Stalin Prize (1946); Lenin Prize (1958); *Died:* 1 Aug 1960.

SHAUMYAN, Stepan Georgiyevich (1878–1918) Party and govt official; one of 26 Baku comr; CP member from 1900; *Born:* 1 Oct 1878 in Tiflis; *Educ:* 1900 studied at Riga Polytech Inst; 1902–04 studied at Berlin Univ; *Career:* from 1898 in revol movement; expelled from inst and exiled to Caucasus for revol activities; 1902 co-founder, first Arm Soc-Democratic newspaper "Proletariat"; late 1902 emigrated to Germany; worked with for RSDRP orgs; 1904 returned to Russia; member, Caucasian Joint RSDRP Comt; founder and manager, Bolshevik newspapers "Kavkazskiy rabochiy listok", "Bakinskiy proletariy", etc; wrote works on philosophy, lit and art; deleg, 4th and 5th RSDRP Congresses; summer 1907 assigned to Party work in Baku; 1911 as member, Russian Org Commission, helped prepare 6th All-Russian (Prague) RSDRP Conference but was arrested and exiled to Astrakhan'; at the conference in absentia elected cand member, CC, RSDRP(B); May–July 1914 helped direct gen oil workers' strike in Baku; 1916 again arrested and exiled; released after 1917 Feb Revol; in absentia elected chm, Baku Sov of Workers' Dep; at 6th RSDRP(B) Congress elected CC member; 16 Dec 1917 appointed comr-extraordinary for Caucasian affairs; from Apr 1918 chm, Baku Council of Pop Comr; *Publ: Klassy v sovremennom yevropeyskom obshchestve* (Classes in Contemporary European Society) (1905); *Evolyutsionizm i revolyutsionizm v obshchestvennoy nauke* (The Theories of Evolution and Revolution in Social Science) (1905); *Natsional'-nyy vopros i sotsial-demokratiya* (The Nationality Problem and Social-Democracy) (1906); *Koye-chto o religii L.N. Tolstogo* (A Little about L.N. Tolstoy's Religion) (1911); *O Gor'kom* (Gorky) (1911); *V Papazyan v roli istorika* (V. Papazyan as a Historian) (1912); *O sbornike armyanskoy literatury* (A Collection of Armenian Literature) (1916), etc; *Died:* 20 Sept 1918 executed with other Baku commissars by British troops in Transcaspian steppe.

SHAYDAKOV, Nikolay Alekseyevich (1892–1964) Govt official; CP member from 1917; *Born:* 1892; *Career:* during WW 1 served in Russian Navy; 1917 chm, ship comt; 1918 commanded sailors' squad in battles against Ataman Dutov; 1919 commanded forces group in Centr Asia; War Min of Khorezm Pop Sov Republ; 1925–27 Turkmen Dep Mil Comr, then Mil Comr; 1927–28 dep chm, Ashkhabad City Sov; 1928–29 Transcaucasian SSR rep and USSR trade rep in Iran; from 1934 exec econ work in Moscow; from 1947 pensioner; *Died:* 23 Apr 1964.

SHCHADENKO, Yefim Afanas'yevich (1885–1951) Ukr mil commander; col-gen; CP member from 1905; *Born:* 1885 in Kamensk (now Kamensk-Shakhtinskiy), Rostov Province, son of a worker; *Career:* prior to 1917 Oct Revol tailor's asst; active in revol movement; 1917–18 helped establish Sov regime in Don area; from 1918 in Red Army; 1918–19 commanded cavalry detachment, chief of musters for 10th Army, then inspector of cavalry corps; 1919–20 member, Revol Mil Council, Budyonnyy's 1st Cavalry Army; 1920 member, Revol Mil Council, 2nd Cavalry Army; helped rout Gen Denikin and Wrangel's troops; 1921–22 chm, Taganrog Exec Comt; then commander and comr of div, asst inspector(polit) of cavalry, asst commandant (polit), Frunze Mil Acad; 1937–38 member, Mil Council, Kiev Mil Distr; active part in purging RED Red Army commanders; 1938–41 chief, Main Personnel Bd, Pop Comrt of Defense; 1941–43 chief, Main Musters Bd and Dep Pop Comr of Defense; 1943 member, Mil Council, Southern Front; then inactive due to bad health; *Awards:* four Orders of Lenin; other orders and medals; *Died:* 6 Sept 1951.

SHCHASTNYY, Aleksey Mikhaylovich (? –1918) Capt, Russian Navy; *Career:* Apr–May 1918 commander, Red Baltic Fleet, relieved of this post by Lenin for disobeying Sov regime's orders and for trying to use the Navy against Sov govt; 21 June 1918 sentenced to death by Supr Revol Tribunal; Presidium of Centr Exec Comt of Soviets confirmed the sentence despite remonstrance of Leftist Socialist-Revolutionaries, who were against death penalty; *Died:* 1918 executed.

SHCHEGLOVITOV, Ivan Grigor'yevich (1861–1918) Pre-revol Russian statesman; major landowner in Chernigov Province; *Born:* 1861; *Educ:* 1881 grad law college; *Career:* from 1881 worked for Min of Justice; 1894 prosecutor, Petersburg Okrug Court; 1889–1903 asst senior prosecutor, from 1903 senior prosecutor, Criminal Appeals Dept; Dep Min of Justice, Apr 1906–July 1915 Min of Justice; Aug 1906 helped sponsor introduction of mil field courts; prepared prosecution case in trial of Soc-Democratic factions of 2nd and 4th State Dumas; prosecuted Beylis Case; from Apr 1907 member, from Jan 1917 chm, State Council; arrested during 1917 Feb Revol; *Died:* 1918 executed by State Security organs.

SHCHEPKIN, Nikolay Nikolayevich (1854–1919) Politician; member, CC, Constitutional Democratic Party; *Born:* 1854; *Career:* businessman and realtor; Asst Mayor of Moscow; member, 3rd and 4th State Duma; during WW 1 member, Main Comt, League of Cities; after 1917 Feb Revol founded and supported various counterrevol orgs, including Union of Public Figures; 1918–19 co-founder and dep chm, Renaissance League, Moscow; also asst chm, from early 1919 chm, Nat Center; from Apr 1919 head, Tactical Center; 1919 arrested for counterrevol activities; *Died:* 1919 executed.

SHCHERBAKOV, Aleksandr Sergeyevich (1901–1945) Party official; mil-polit commander; col-gen from 1943; CP member from 1918; *Born:* 10 Oct 1901 in Ruza, Moscow Province, son of a worker; *Educ:* 1921–24 studied at Sverdlov Communist Univ; 1930–32 studied at Inst of Red Prof; *Career:* printer's apprentice in Rybinsk; 1917 joined Red Guards; 1918 co-founded, Rybinsk Komsomol; 1918–21 Komsomol work with Komsomol CC and in Turkestan; 1924–30 Party work in Nizhniy Novgorod Province: dept head, Sormovo Rayon Party Comt; secr, Beregovoy and Balakhnin Rayon Party Comt; ed, newspaper "Nizhegorodskaya kommuna"; head, Agitation and Propaganda Dept, Nizhniy Novgorod Province Party Comt; secr, Murom Okrug Party Comt; from 1932 with CC, CPSU(B); 1934 elected secr, USSR Writers' Union; July 1936–June 1937 secr, Leningrad Oblast CPSU(B) Comt; 1937–38 secr, Irkutsk Oblast CPSU(B) Comt; from Apr 1938 first secr, Donetsk, then Stalino Oblast Comt, CP(B) Ukr; 1938–45 first secr, Moscow City and Oblast CPSU(B) Comt; 1939–45 member, CC, CPSU(B); 1941–45 secr and cand Politburo member, CC, CPSU(B); 1942–45 head, Red Army Main Polit Bd and USSR Dep Pop Comr of Defense; also head, Sov Information Bureau; dep, USSR Supr Sov of 1937 convocation; *Awards:* three Orders of Lenin; Order of Suvorov, 1st Class; Order of Kutuzov, 1st Class; Order of the Fatherland War, 1st Class; *Died:* 10 May 1945 of a heart attack after a long illness; his ashes are immured in Moscow's Kremlin Wall; 1946–57 town of

Rybinsk was named after him.

SHCHETINKIN, Pyotr Yefimovich (1885–1927) Mil commander; CP member from 1918; *Born:* 1885 in vil Chufilovo, Ryazan' Province, son of a peasant; *Career:* carpenter by trade; 1911 entered ensigns' school; during WW 1 won four George Crosses and various medals for valor and rose to the rank of staff – capt; 1917 returned to Achinsk and elected member, Achinsk Sov; also chief, Criminal Investigation Dept; early 1919 organized partisan detachment and fought successfully against White Guards; late Mar 1919 his detachment broke out of encirclement and linked up with A.D. Kravchenko's partisan army; Shchetinkin became Kravchenko's asst; 1919–20 this partisan army (numbering up to 18,000 men) fought against the White Guards in Uryankhay Kray (now Tuva Autonomous Oblast), early Jan 1920 drove White forces from many parts of Yeniseysk Province and finally linked up with units of Red Army; after the rout of Kolchak's forces, Shchetinkin fought against Wrangel's forces in the Crimea and against Ungern in Mongolia; after Civil War worked for Border Troops Bd; 1927 inspector, State Mil Defense in Mongolia; *Died:* 30 Sept 1927.

SHCHORS, Nikolay Aleksandrovich (1895–1919) Ukr revolutionary and mil commander; Civil War veteran; CP member from 1918; *Born:* 6 June 1895 in vil Snovsk, Chernigov Province, son of a railroad machinist; *Educ:* completed mil med orderlies' school; 1915 completed ensigns' school; *Career:* 1914–18 med orderly, then nco in Russian Army at the front; Sept 1918 formed Bogun 1st Ukr Sov Regt from insurgent detachments in Unech' area; led this regt in operations against Petlyura's forces; from Mar 1919 commander, 1st Ukr Sov Div, which operated against Petlyura and on the Sov-Polish Front; 21–30 Aug 1919 commander, 44th Infantry Div; *Awards:* Hon Gold Arms for liberation of Kiev in Feb 1919; *Died:* 30 Aug 1919 killed in action; buried in Samara (now Kuybyshev); his birthplace Snovsk was renamed after him; monuments erected to him in Shchors, Kuybyshev, Kiev, Korosten, Zhitomir, Klintsy and the place where he was killed; in 1939 his popularity prompted the film dir Aleksandr Dovzhenko to make the film "Shchors."

SHCHUKIN, Boris Vasil'yevich (1894–1939) Actor and stage dir; Pop Artiste of USSR from 1936; *Born:* 17 Apr 1894 in Moscow; *Educ:* from 1913 studied at Moscow Higher Tech College; in 1920's grad Vakhtangov's Drama Studio; *Career:* in his youth performed with railroad amateur drama company; during Civil War served with Red Army; co-founder and 1926–39 actor, Vakhtangov State Theater, Moscow; major exponent of Sov realistic style in stagecraft; greatly influenced by esthetic views of Vakhtangov; one of first actors to portray Lenin on stage; also did film work; *Roles:* Curé in Maeterlinck's "The Miracle of Saint Anthony" (1921); Lev Gurych in Lenskiy's "Lev Gurych Sinichkin" (1924); Anton in Leonov's *Barsuki* (The Barsuks) (1927); Malko in Afinogenov's *Dalyokoye* (The Distant Past) (1930); Polonius in Shakespeare's "Hamlet"; (1932); Yegor in Gorky's *Yegor Bulychyov i drugiye* (Yegor Bulychyov and Co) (1932); Lenin in Pogodin's *Chelovek s ruzh'yom* (The Man With a Gun) (1937), etc; film roles: Rogachyov in *Lyotchiki* (The Flyers); Mikhaylov in *Pokoleniye pobediteley* (Generation of Victors); Lenin in *Lenin v Oktyabre* (Lenin in October) and *Lenin v 1918 godu* (Lenin in 1918), etc; *Productions:* helped produce: Pogodin's *Temp* (Tempoo) (1930); "The Human Comedy", after Balzac (1934); Shakespeare's "Measure for Measure" (1939); *Awards:* Order of Lenin; Stalin Prize (1941); *Died:* 7 Oct 1939.

SHCHUKO, Vladimir Alekseyevich (1878–1939) Architect; set designer; member, Acad of Architecture from 1911; *Born:* 5 July 1878 in Tambov; *Educ:* 1904 grad Petersburg Acad of Arts; *Career:* 1901, still a student, took part in Spitzbergen Expedition and expeditions to measure and record monuments of Russian architecture; 1905–07 visited Constantinople, Greece and Italy; from 1906 lectured at School of Soc for the Promotion of the Arts; from 1912 dir, Higher Architectural Courses; 1917–27 prof of architecture, Acad of Arts; 1934 visited Italy, USA, Paris and London; Works: houses on Kamennyy Ostrov Prospekt, Petersburg (1909–11); pavillion at Rome Int Exhibition (1911); Kiev Zemstvo Administration building (1916); Memorial Hall of Acad of Arts (1914); co-designed entrance to Smol'nyy Palace, Leningrad (1922–23); co-designed three substations of Volkhov Construction Project (1924); co-designed architectural details of Lenin Monument outside Finnish Railroad Terminus (1924); designed Rostov-on-Don Drama Theater (1930–35); Main Pavillion of All-Union Agric Exhibition, Moscow (1939); co-designed Grand Stone Bridge over River Moskva (1936–38); designed sets and costumes for many shows at Leningrad theaters and for production of "Boris Godunov" at Maly Theater, Moscow (1937); *Died:* 18 Jan 1939.

SHCHUSEV, Aleksey Viktorovich (1873–1949) Architect; member, Acad of Arts from 1910; Hon Architect of USSR from 1930; member, USSR Acad of Architecture from 1939; member, USSR Acad of Sci from 1943; *Born:* 26 Sept 1873 in Kishinev; *Educ:* 1897 grad Petersburg Acad of Arts; *Career:* after grad studied architecture in Italy, France, England and Tunisia; returned to Russia and began designing buildings; 1910 elected life member, Council, Acad of Arts; from 1918 helped draft Moscow's gen reconstruction plan; 1922–23 chief architect, All-Russian Agric Exhibition, Moscow; 1922–29 chm, Moscow Soc of Architects; 1926–29 dir, Tret'yakov Gallery; from 1932 member, Comt for the Preservation of Revol, Artistic and Cultural Monuments; from 1939 bd member, USSR Architects' Union; from 1946 dir, Museum of Russian Architecture; also taught architecture; prof, Higher Tech Art Inst; *Works:* designed Martha-Maria Cloister in Moscow (1908–09); Trinity Church at Pochayeva Lavra; Memorial Church on Kulikovo Field (1911–13); Kazan' Railroad Terminus, Moscow (1913); Russian Pavillion at Int Exhibition in Venice (1914); Lenin Mausoleum on Moscow's Red Square (1924); Sanatorium at Matsesta (1928); Pop Comrt of Agric building (1928–33); Mil Transport Acad building (1930–34); Moskva Hotel (1935); hotel at Batumi (1938); Navoi Opera and Ballet Theater building, Tashkent (1947); Simeiz Observatory (1948); "Komsomol'skaya-Kol'tsevaya" Metro Station, Moscow; a wing of Pulkovo Observatory, etc; designed gen restoration plans for Novgorod, Pskov, Kishinev, Istra, Tuapse, etc; wrote over 200 works and articles about architecture; *Awards:* Order of Lenin; two Orders of the Red Banner of Labor; four Stalin Prizes (1941, 1946, 1948 and 1952); *Died:* 24 May 1949 in Moscow.

SHEBALIN, Vissarion Yakovlevich (1902–1963) Composer; prof; Dr of Art History from 1941; Pop Artiste of RSFSR from 1947; *Born:* 11 June 1902 in Omsk; *Educ:* 1928 grad Myaskovskiy's composition class, Moscow Conservatory; *Career:* 1923–29 taught at Stasov, Rimsky-Korsakov and Oct Revol Technicums in Moscow; 1928–32 lecturer, 1932–35 assoc prof, from 1935 prof, 1942–48 dir, Moscow Conservatory; 1948–51 senior lecturer, from 1949 head of a chair, Inst of Mil Conductors; from 1958 member, Org Comt, RSFSR Composers' Union; from 1959 bd member, USSR Composers' Union; and dep chm, Moscow Branch, RSFSR Composers' Union; member, Assoc of Modern Music and Russian Assoc of Proletarian Musicians; 1948 accused in CPSU(B) CC resolution of "formalism" and "anti-democratic trends" in his music; 1959 this accusation was quashed by a further CPSU CC resolution; dep, RSFSR Supr Sov of 1947 convocation; *Works:* operas: *Boyevyye druz'ya* (Battle Friends) (1939); *Ukroshcheniye stroptivoy* (The Taming of the Shrew) (1955), after Shakespeare; *Solntse nad step'yu* (The Sun over the Steppe) (1958); comic operetta *Zhenikh iz posol'stva* (The Bridegroom from the Embassy) (1942); four symphonies (1925, 1929, 1934 and 1935); vocal-symphonic poem "Lenin" (1931); two suites (1934 and 1935); ballet suite *Zhavoronok* (The Lark) (1943); *Russkaya uvertyura* (Russian Overture) (1941); cantatas; *Siniy may* (Blue May) (1930) and "Moskva" (1946); seven string quartets (1924, 1934, 1939, 1940, 1942, 1943 and 1947); music for plays: Mayakovskiy's *Banya* (The Bathhouse) (1931); Vishnevskiy's *Posledniy reshitel'nyy* (The Last Decisive Blow) (1932); Alexander Dumas' "La Dame aux Camèlias" (1934); Trenyov's "Lyubov' Yarovaya" (1936); Pushkin's *Skupoy rytsar'* (The Miserly Knight) and *Motsart i Sal'yeri* (Mozart and Salieri) (1937); Lermontov's *Maskarad* (Masquerade) (1939); Shakespeare's "Hamlet" (1944); Oscar Wilde's "Lady Windermere's Fan" (1959), etc; music for films: *Turksib otkryt* (The Turkestani-Siberian Railroad Is Open) (1931); "Pugachyov" (1937); *Semiklassniki* (The Seventh-Graders) (1938); *Frontovyye podrugi* (Frontline Friends) (1940); "Glinka" (1945); "Sadko" (1953), etc; over 50 romances; completed and arranged Moussorgsky's opera *Sorochinskaya yarmarka* (Sorochintsy Fair); completed 2nd Act of Gulak-Artemovskiy's opera *Zaporozhets za Dunayem* (A Dnieper Cossack Beyond the Danube); *Awards:* Order of Lenin (1946); Order of the Red Banner of Labor (1944); Stalin Prizes (1943 and 1947); *Died:* 29 May 1963 in Moscow.

SHEBOLDAYEV, Boris Petrovich (1895–1937) Party official; CP member from 1914; *Born:* 1895; *Educ:* 1921–23 studied on Marxism courses; *Career:* arrested in Petrograd for revol work;

1915 drafted into Russian Army and sent to front; 1917–18 member, Baku RSDRP(B) Comt; Dep Pop Comr of War, Baku Commune; also mil comr, Kizlyar Okrug Div, 12th Army; 1919 arrested by Azer govt in Baku; 1920 secr, Dag Oblast Party Comt and dep chm, Dagh Revol Comt; 1923 head, Org Dept, CC, CP Turkestan; 1924 secr, Tsaritsyn Province RCP(B) Comt; 1925–28 dep head, Org and Distribution Dept, CC, CPSU(B); 1928–30 secr, Ni Lower Volga Kray Party Comt; from 1931 secr, North Caucasian Kray CPSU(B) Comt; at 16th and 17th Party Congresses elected member, CC, CPSU(B); member, USSR Centr Exec Comt; arrested by State Security organs; sentenced to death by USSR Supr Court; *Died:* 16 Dec 1937 executed.

SHEINA (nee: POLDUSHKINA), Pelageya Fyodorovna (1885–1964) Party official; CP member from 1905; *Born:* 11 May 1885; *Career:* took part in 1905–07 Revol, 1917 Oct Revol and Civil War; 1909 arrested and exiled to Saratov for RSDRP activities; 1911–17 worked in Samara, then in Petrograd with Red Cross and on Lesgaft Courses; Party Group organizer for propaganda courses; distributed newspapers "Zvezda" and "Pravda"; after 1917 Oct Revol did Party work among zemstvo intelligentsia in Samara Province; organized first volost sov in Samara Uyezda; 1918 head, Samara Educ Dept; helped found Red Army units; 1920–21 Party work in Samara Province; 1921–29 worked in Leningrad for public health organs and for Leningrad Oblast CPSU(B) Control Commission; from 1931 inspector, Party Commission, Polit Dept of Moscow-Kursk Railroad; then Party investigator, Party Control Commission, CC, CPSU(B); from 1938 pensioner; *Died:* 10 Aug 1964.

SHELEKHES, Il'ya Savel'yevich (1891–1938) Govt and Party official; CP member from 1908; *Born:* 1891 in Moscow; *Career:* did revol work in Moscow; frequently arrested by Tsarist authorities; during Civil War fought in Red Army; head, Polit Dept, 8th Army; late 1919–20 chm, Kursk Province Exec Comt; also Party and govt work in Khar'kov; 1920, during trade-union controversy, sided with Trotsky; from 1921 secr, Nikolayev Province Exec Comt; 1923–24 chm, Yaroslavl' Province Exec Comt and secr, Yaroslavl' Province RCP(B) Comt; 1925 worked in Centr Asia; 1926–28 exec instructor, CC, CPSU(B); secr, Bryansk Province CPSU(B) Comt; from 1929 chm, Western Oblast Exec Comt; from Mar 1933 chm, Khar'kov Oblast Exec Comt and Khar'kov City Sov; 1934–37 first dep chm, Ukr Council of Pop Comr; at 16th and 17th Party Congresses elected member, CPSU(B) Auditing Commission; at 12th and 13th Congresses of CP(B) Ukr elected member, CC, CP(B) Ukr; 1934–36 cand Politburo member, from 1937 Politburo member, CC, CP(B) Ukr; member, All-Ukr and USSR Centr Exec Comt; arrested by State Security organs; *Died:* 4 Oct 1938 in imprisonment.

SHELGUNOV, Vasiliy Andreyevich (1867–1939) Revolutionary; *Born:* 1867 in vil Slavkovichi, Pskov Province, son of a peasant; *Carrer:* 1886 joined revol movement; active in Assoc of Petersburg Factory-Hands and Brusnev's group; 1890–92 served in Russian Army; from 1892 engaged in Marxist propaganda in circles of Obuhhov and Putilov Plant workers; co-founder Petersburg League for the Liberation of the Working Class; Dec 1895 arrested; 1897 exiled for three years to Arkhangel'sk Province; returned from exile and worked for Yekaterinoslav RSDRP Comt; helped found underground "Iskra" printing press in Baku; 1905 active in Petersburg RSDRP(B) org; Dec 1905 arrested; while in prison fell ill and lost his sight; despite this, continued Party work; 1910 helped found newspaper "Zvezda"; 1911 twice arrested as its ed; co-founder and staff member, newspaper "Pravda"; Dec 1912 arrested; 1913 exiled for three years to Northern Caucasus, where he continued Party work; after 1917 Feb Revol did Party work in Petrograd; from 1918 Party work in Moscow; member, Zamoskvorech'ye Rayon Party Comt; member, All-Union Soc of Old Bolsheviks; *Publ: Vospominaniya* (Memoirs) (1921); *Rozhdeniye gazety* (The Birth of a Newspaper) (1937); *Died:* 2 Apr 1939.

SHENGELAYA, Nikolay Mikhaylovich (1903–1943) Film dir; Hon Art Worker of RSFSR from 1935; *Born:* 18 Aug 1903; *Career:* from 1927 worked in film ind; *Works:* "Eliso" (1928); *Dvadtsat' shest' komissarov* (Twenty-Six Commissars) (1935); *Zolotistaya dolina* (The Golden Valley) (1937); *Rodina* (Homeland) (1939); *V chyornykh gorakh* (In the Black Hills) (1941); *On yeshchyo vernyotsya* (He Will Return) (1943); etc; *Awards:* Order of the Red Banner of Labor; Stalin Prize (1941); *Died:* 4 Jan 1943.

SHER, V.V. (1884–1940) Govt official; Menshevik; *Born:* 1884; *Career:* after 1917 Feb Revol secr, Moscow Sov of Soldiers' Dep; after 1917 July riots asst commander, Moscow Mil Distr; then head, Polit Bd, Min of War; after 1917 Oct Revol worked for Centr Union of Consumer Soc, Supr Sovnarkhoz and State Bank; 1931 arrested and sentenced by USSR Supr Court for hostile anti-Sov activities; *Died:* 1940 in imprisonment.

SHERESHEVSKIY, Nikolay Adol'fovich (1885–1961) Endocrinologist; Dr of Med from 1913; prof; Hon Sci Worker of RSFSR from 1936; *Born:* 9 Nov 1885 in Moscow, son of an office worker; *Educ:* 1910 grad Med Fac, Moscow Univ; *Career:* from 1910 intern, Therapeutic Clinic, Moscow Univ; 1913–32 assoc prof, Moscow Univ; 1915–18 head, therapeutic dept of a sanatorium near Moscow; 1918–21 served in Red Army as chief surgeon of various hospitals and chm of a standing med commission; from 1921 lectured on endocrinology at Moscow Women's Med Inst (now 2nd Moscow Med Inst); 1926 wrote first description of endocrine syndrome later formulated by Turner; 1932–61 founder-head, Chair of Endocrinology, Centr Inst of Postgrad Med Training, Moscow; from 1932 also dir, Clinic of Endocrinal Diseases; 1933–61 sci dir, Endocrinological Dept, Botkin Clinical Hospital; 1934–53 also dir, Inst of End ocrinology, RSFSR Pop Comrt of Health; co-founder, secr and chm, Soc of Endocrinologists; founder-ed, journals "Vosprosy endokrinologii" and "Problemy endokrinologii i gormonoterapii"; founder-chm, Centr Goiter Commission, USSR Min of Health; member, Learned Med Council and Biological Commission; USSR Min of Health; chm, Pharmacological Commission, USSR Min of Health; made major contribution to campaign against endemic goiter; developed methods of testing modern hormonal drugs; wrote over 100 works; *Publ:* doctor's thesis *Klinicheskiye nablyudeniya nad vagotoniey* (Clinical Observations on Vagotonia) (1914); *Tireotoksikozy* (Thyreotoxicosis) (1951); *Klinicheskaya endokrinologiya* (Clinical Endocrinology) (1957); *Awards:* two Orders of Lenin; Order of the Red Banner of Labor; medals; *Died:* 1961 in Moscow.

SHERVINSKIY, Vasiliy Dmitriyevich (1850–1941) Therapist; pioneer of Russian endocrinology; Dr of Med from 1879; prof from 1884; Hon Sci Worker of RSRFR from 1928; *Born:* 13 Jan 1850 in Omsk; *Educ:* 1873 grad Med Fac, Moscow Univ; *Career:* after grad dissector, Chair of Anatomy, Moscow Univ; simultaneously intern; Staro-Yekaterinskaya Hospital and postgrad student, Prof Ostroumov's Clinic of Internal Diseases; during 1870's was also active in Pirogov Soc; 1879 defended doctor's thesis on fat embolisms of the lungs; in same year helped to organize quarantine measures to prevent spread of plague into Moscow from Vetlyanka; from 1880 assoc prof, Chair of Pathological Anatomy, Moscow Univ; 1881–82 worked in Germany and France under Cohnheim, Struempel and Charcot; from 1880 extraordinary prof, Chair of Pathological Anatomy, Moscow Univ; 1894–98 prof, Chair of Special Pathology and Therapy, from 1898 dir, Fac Therapy Clinic, Moscow Univ; 1910 and 1912 read papers on endocrinology at session of Moscow Therapeutic Soc and 3rd Congress of Therapists; 1912, together with other prof, resigned from Moscow Univ in protest against policies of Educ Min Kasso; founder-member and chm, from 1913 hon chm, Moscow Therapeutic Soc; from 1918 member, Learned Med Council, RSFSR Pop Comrt of Health; from 1919 dir, Laboratory of Thyroidectomized Goats (later Inst of Organotherapeutic Drugs, then All-Union Inst of Experimental Endocrinology); from 1922 also worked at Student Polyclinic; 1925 founded Moscow Endocrinological Soc; founder, Russian Soc of Therapists; chm, Tuberculosis League; 1929 read paper on treatment of Basedow's disease at 10th Congress of Therapists; *Publ: O vnutrenney sekretsii i yeyo klinicheskom znachenii* (Internal Secretion and Its Clinical Significance) (1910); *Rol' nadpochechnikov v patologii* (The Role of the Suprarenal Glands in Pathology) (1912); *O lechenii bazedovskoy bolezni s terapevticheskoy tochki zreniya* (The Treatment of Basedow's Disease from the Therapeutic Viewpoint) (1929); coauthor, *Osnovy endokrinologii* (The Principles of Endocrinology) (1929); *Died:* 12 Nov 1941.

SHERVUD, Leonid Vladimirovich (1871–1954) Sculptor; prof; Hon Art Worker of RSFSR from 1946; *Born:* 29 Apr 1871 in Moscow; *Educ:* 1892 grad Moscow College of Painting, Sculpture and Architecture; 1898 grad Petersburg Acad of Arts; *Career:* after grad Acad used Acad grant to spend almost a year in Rodin's workshop, Paris; 1901 returned to Russia; from 1918 prof, Acad of Arts; after 1917 Oct Revol helped implement Lenin's "monumental propaganda" plan; in early stages of WW 2 taken ill in Leningrad and evacuated to Ivanovo-Voznesensk; a year later returned to Moscow; displayed his work in exhibitions of Acad of Arts, New Soc and in Rome; *Works:* "The Khan and the Slave Girl" (1898);

bust of Pushkin (1902); monument to the writer Gleb Uspenskiy (1904); monument to Prof S. Vasil'yev in Yur'yev (1906); design for monument to Peter I (1908); monument to Admiral S, Makarov (1914); monumental bust of A. Radishchev (1918); bust of Mendeleyev (1925); bust of Stalin (1928); statue "The Sentry" (1933); design for monument to Kirov (1934); group sculpture "Kirov and Graftio" (1945); group sculpture "Revenge Our People's Sufferings" (1942); designs for monument to Tret'yakov (1945) and Repin (1946), etc; some of his works are on display in the Tret'yakov Gallery and the Russian Museum; *Publ: Put' skul'ptora* (The Sculptor's Path) (1937); *Vospominaniya o monumental'noy propagande v Leningrade* (Reminiscences of Monumental Propaganda in Leningrad) (1939); *Awards:* Order of the Red Banner of Labor (1946); medals; *Died:* 23 Aug 1954.

SHESTAKOV, Andrey Vasil'yevich (1877–1941) Historian and Party official; prof; corresp member, USSR Acad of Sci; CP member from 1903; *Born:* 1877, son of a worker; *Educ:* 1924 grad Inst of Red Prof; *Career:* 1897 joined Soc-Democratic movement; 1905 one of leaders of Dec uprising at Moscow-Kazan' Railroad Terminus in Moscow; 1906–07 worked in textile-workers' trade union; 1908–13 did underground Party work in Crimea and Caucasus; 1913–14 in emigration; 1918–21 newspaper ed and Party official in Voronzh and Ryazan'; from 1925 taught and did research in Moscow; member, Communist Acad; dep dir, Museum of the History of the Revol; co-founder, Soc of Marxist Historians; during 1930's joined in campaign against M.N. Pokrovskiy's school of history; head, Chair of History of USSR, Moscow Teachers' Training Inst; 1937 supervised team of authors who wrote "A Short Course in the History of the USSR for 3rd and 4th Secondary School Grades"; *Publ: Kapitalizatsiya sel'skogo khozyaystva Rossii* (The Capitalization of Soviet Agriculture) (1924); *Oktyabr'skaya stachka 1905–ogo goda* (The Strike of October 1905) (1925); *Krest'yanskaya revolyutsiya 1905–07 godov v Rossii* (The 1905–07 Peasant Revolution in Russia) (1926); *Bor'ba sel'skikh rabochikh v evolyutsii 1905–07 godov* (The Struggle of the Rural Workers in the 1905–07 Revolution) (1930); *Died:* 1941.

SHESTAKOV, Semyon Aleksandrovich (1898–1943) Pilot; col, guards unit; Hon Pilot of Sov Union from 1927; *Born:* 1898 in Bendery, son of a med orderly; *Career:* took part in several long-distance flights, including Moscow-Tokyo-Moscow flight (1927) and "Land of Soviets" flight from Moscow to New York via Siberia and the Pacific (1929); fought in WW 2; *Awards:* Order of the Red Banner (1927); Order of the Red Banner of Labor (1929); *Died:* 1 Aug 1943 killed on mission.

SHESTAKOV, Sergey Petrovich (1864–1940) Philologist and historian; Dr of History from 1898; prof; corresp member, Russian (USSR) Acad of Sci from 1916; *Born:* 1864 in Kazan'; *Educ:* 1886 grad Kazan' Univ; *Career:* 1911–35 prof, Fac of History and Philology, Kazan' Univ; specialized in Ancient Greek philology and history of Byzantium; also studied history of Russo-Byzantine polit and cultural relations; *Publ: O proiskhozhdenii Odissei* (The Origin of the Odyssey) (1892); *O proiskhozhdenii Iliady* (The Origin of the Iliad) (1898); *Ocherki po istorii Khersonesa v VI–X vekakh* (Studies in the History of Chersonesus in the 6th–10th Centuries) (1908); *Vizantiyskiy posol na Rus' Manuil Komnin* (Manuilus Comnenus, the Byzantine Envoy to Rus) (1913), etc; *Died:* 1940.

SHEVKUNENKO, Viktor Nikolayevich (1872–1952) Surgeon and anatomist; Dr of Med from 1898; prof; maj-gen, Med Corps; member, USSR Acad of Med Sci from 1945; Hon Sci Worker of RSFSR from 1935; *Born:* 29 Feb 1872 in Mezen', now Arkhangel'sk Oblast; *Educ:* 1895 grad Petersburg Mil Med Acad; *Career:* after grad intern, Ratimov's Surgical Clinic, Petersburg Mil Med Acad; 1898 defended doctor's thesis on treatment of clubfoot; after touring clinics in England, Austria, Germany, France, Switzerland and USA and acquiring several years clinical experience, specialized in surgical anatomy and operating techniques; from 1912 head, Chair of Operative Surgery and Topographical Anatomy, Petersburg Mil Med Acad; from 1928 also head, Chair of Operative Surgery and Topographical Anatomy, Leningrad Inst of Postgrad Med Training; member, Int Soc of Surgeons; hon member, Pirogov Surgical Soc, Leningrad; member, Moscow, Khar'kov, Tashkent, Irkutsk and Leningrad Urological Soc; bd member, All-Union Soc of Surgeons; did major research on human anatomy on the basis of constitutional and age variations; hypothesized that individual and age characteristics could be classified in a few groups and determined by external features (gen habitus, anthropometric characteristics, etc); trained numerous anatomists and surgeons, including P.A. Kupriyanov, A.N. Maksimenkov, Sozon-Yaroshevich and Val'ker; wrote over 50 works; *Publ:* ed, *Kurs operativnoy khirurgii s anatomo-topograficheskimi dannymi* (A Course of Operative Surgery with Data on Topographical Anatomy) (3 vol, 1927–31); *Tipovaya anatomiya cheloveka* (The Anatomy of Human Types) (1935); ed, *Kurs topograficheskoy anatomii* (A Course of Topographical Anatomy) (1935); ed, *Kratkiy kurs operativnoy khirurgii* (A Short Course of Operative Surgery) (1938); *Atlas perifericheskoy nervnoy i venoznoy sistemy* (An Atlas of the Peripheral Nervous and Venous Systems) (1943); ed, *Kratkiy kurs operativnoy khirurgii s topograficheskoy anatomiyey* (A Short Course of Operative Surgery, Including Topographical Anatomy((1944); *Awards:* three Orders of Lenin; four other orders; Stalin Prize (1943); medals; *Died:* 3 July 1952 in Leningrad.

SHEVTSOVA, Lyubov' Grigor'yevna (1924–1943) Ukr partisan during WW 2; *Born:* 8 Sept 1924 in vil Izvarino, now Voroshilovgrad Oblast, daughter of a miner; *Educ:* 1941 completed secondary school; *Career:* Apr 1942 enrolled in school for partisan scouts; Sept 1942 assigned to Staff of underground Komsomol org "Young Guard"; maintained liason with Ukr Staff of Partisan Movement; active in many partisan operations; Feb 1943 arrested by German mil authorities; *Awards:* Hero of the Sov Union (1943, posthumously); *Died:* 9 Feb 1943 executed at Roven'ki, now Voroshilovgrad Oblast.

SHEYNIN, Lev Romanovich (1906–1967) Lawyer; prosecution and investigation official; writer and playwright; CP member from 1927; *Born:* 25 Mar 1906; *Educ:* studied at Bryusov Higher Inst of Lit and Arts and at Law Dept, Soc Sci Fac, Moscow Univ; *Career:* 1923 assigned by Moscow Komsomol org to Moscow Criminal Investigation Dept; 1923–30 investigator, Moscow Province Court, then Leningrad Oblast Court; 1928 first work printed; 1930–35 investigator for major cases, 1935–50 head, Investigation Dept, USSR Prosecutor's Office; 1946 asst chief prosecutor at Nuremberg Trials; from 1950 confined himself to lit work; his lit works promoted gen espionage mania and mutual suspicion; *Publ:* story *Kar'yera Kirilla Lavrenenko* (Kirill Lavrenenko's Career) (1928); coauthor, plays: *Ochnaya stavka* (The Confrontation) (1936); *General'nyy konsul* (Consul-General) (1939); *Dym otechestva* (The Smoke of the Fatherland) (1942); *Chrezvychaynyy zakon* (Extraordinary Law) (1944); *Gubernator provintsii* (The Governor of the Province) (1947), etc; coauthor, filmscript *Vstrecha na El'be* (Meeting on the Elbe) (1949); collected stories and novelettes *Zapiski sledovatelya* (An Investigator's Notes) (1938); *Staryy znakomyy* (An Old Acquaintance) (1957), etc; *Awards:* Stalin Prize (1950); *Died:* 11 May 1967.

SHIFRES, Aleksandr L'vovich (1898–1937) Red Army polit commander; Jew; army comr, 2nd class from 1935; CP member from 1917; *Born:* 1898 in Grodno; *Educ:* 1916–18 studied at Tomsk Univ; *Career:* 1917 active in Feb Revol in Tomsk; co-founder and first chm, Vitebsk RSDRP(B) Org; agitated for Bolsheviks in Vitebsk Garrison; after 1917 Oct Revol co-ed, Tomsk Province Bolshevik newspaper; comr for combatting counterrevol; member, Tomsk Revol Tribunal; Presidium member, Vitebsk Province RCP(B) Comt; spring 1919 joined Red Army via Party draft; 1919–20. polit officer, 1st Reserve Regt, 5th Army; head, Polit Dept, 126th and 35th Div; 1920–22 chm, Cheremkhovo RCP(B) Comt; head, Polit Dept, then comr, Kuznets Basin Labor Troops Brigade; 1922–24 dep head, Agitation and Propaganda Dept, Red Army Polit Bd; active in campaign against Trotsky opposition; 1924 dep head, Polit Bd, Moscow Mil Distr; 1924–26 asst commandant (polit), Red Army Mil Acad (from 1925 Frunze Acad); 1926–28 head, Press Dept, Red Army Polit Bd; 1928–33 commandant, Mil Polit Acad; 1933 member, Mil Council and head, Polit Bd, Caucasian Red Banner Army; 1934 deleg at 17th CPSU(B) Congress; 1934–35 head, Polit Bd and dep commander, North Caucasian Mil Distr; 1935–37 commandant and comr, Red Army Mil Admin Acad; from 1934 also member, Mil Council, Pop Comrt of Defense; 1937 arrested by NKVD; *Publ: Politicheskaya rabota v territorial'nykh chastyakh* (Political Work in Territorial Units) (1925); *Politicheskoye obespecheniye armeyskoy operatsii* (Political Promotion of Army Operations) (1925); *Politicheskaya rabota na voyennykh igrakh* (Political Work on Maneuvers) (1927); *Awards:* Order of the Red Banner; *Died:* 1937 in imprisonment; posthumously rehabilitated.

SHIFRIN, Nisson Abramovich (1892–1961) Stage designer; Pop Artiste of RSFSR from 1958; CP member from 1944; *Born:* 28

June 1892; *Educ:* 1916 grad Kiev Business Inst; 1912–15 studied at Murashko's Art Studio; 1918–19 at Ekster's Art Studio; *Career:* from 1922 at theaters in Moscow; 1935–61 chief designer, Centr Theater of the Sov Army; 1929–30 taught at Higher State Tech Art Inst; 1934–36 taught at State Inst of Stagecraft; *Works:* designed sets for: Lecoq's "Green Island" (1917) (1919); Ash's *Bog mesti* (God of Vengeance) (1920); Molière's "Le Malade Imaginaire" (1921); "Hiawatha", after Longfellow (1923); Afinogenov's "Chyornyy Yar" (1928); Kirshon's *Khleb* (Bread) (1931); Korneychuk's *Gibel' eskadry* (The End of the Squadron) (1934); Shakespeare's "Taming of the Shrew" (1937); Shakespeare's "Midsummer Night's Dream" (1941); Aliger's *Skazka o pravde* (The Tale of Truth) (1946); Sofronov's *Moskovskiy kharakter* (Moscow Character) (1948); Shteyn's *Flag admirala* (The Admiral's Flag) (1950); Shakespeare's "The Merry Wives of Windsor" (1957); Chekhov's *Chayka* (The Seagull) (1960), etc; *Publ: Khudozhnik v teatre* (The Artist in the Theater) (1964); *Moya rabota v teatre* (My Work in the Theater) (1966); *Awards:* two Stalin Prizes (1949 and 1959); *Died:* 3 Apr 1961.

SHILOVSKIY, Yevgeniy Aleksandrovich (1889–1952) Mil commander; officer, Russian Army; lt-gen, Sov Army from 1940; Dr of Mil Sci; prof; mil theorist and instructor; CP member from 1943; *Born:* 1889 in vil Savinki, Ryazan' Province, son of a nobleman; *Educ:* 1917 grad Gen Staff Acad; *Career:* fought in WW 1; from Aug 1918 in Red Army; 1919–21 chief of staff and 24 Apr–7 May 1921 commander, 16th Army on Western Front; Oct 1928–Feb 1931 chief of staff, Moscow Mil Distr; then research and teaching work at Frunze Mil Acad, Gen Staff Acad and with Gen Staff; studied and summarized experience of Civil War and WW 2; wrote a number or works on operations, tactics, strategy, mil history and training methods; *Publ: Na Berezine. Deystviya XVI armii v 1920 godu* (On the Berezina. The Operations of the 16th Army in 1920) (1928); *Nachal'nyy period voyny* (The Initial Period of War) (1933); *Operatsiya* (Operations) (1937); *Kontrnastupleniye Krasnoy Armii v Belorussii v 1920 godu* (The Red Army's Counteroffensive in Belorussia in 1920) (1940); *Osnova operativnogo proryva* (The Basis of an Operational Break-Through) (1940), etc; *Awards:* Order of Lenin; three Orders of the Red Banner; Order of Suvorov, etc; *Died:* 1952.

SHIMANOV, Aleksey Alekseyevich (1884–1967) Govt official; CP member from 1907; *Born:* 3 Mar 1884; *Career:* from 1900 worked as locksmith in Moscow; took part in 1905 Revol; frequently arrested for revol activities; drafted into Russian Army; 1914–18 prisoner-of-war in Austro-Hungary; from 1918 senior govt and admin work; chm, Tula Uyezd Exec Comt, then chm, Frunze Okrug Exec Comt; from 1953 pensioner; *Died:* 18 Mar 1967.

SHIMANSKIY, Yulian Aleksandrovich (1883–1962) Naval architect; prof from 1938; member, USSR Acad of Sci from 1953; Hon Sci and Tech Worker of RSFSR from 1941; *Born:* 17 Dec 1883 in Tashkent; *Educ:* 1905 grad Kronstadt College of Naval Eng; 1910 grad Petersburg Naval Acad; *Career:* from 1910 design eng at shipbuilding yards in Revel' (now Tallinn), Riga and Petersburg; 1912 in charge of tech modernization of Kronstadt naval repair yard; advisor, Tech Inspectorate, Main Naval Staff; from 1912 instructor, College of Naval Eng; 1927–38 instructor, from 1938 prof, F.S. Dzerzhinskiy Higher College of Naval Eng; from 1932 also worked at Research Inst of the Shipbuilding Ind, Leningrad; from 1945 also prof, Leningrad Shipbuilding Inst; *Publ: Izgib plastin* (Plate Flexure) (1934); *Spravochnik po sudostroyenyiu* (A Reference Manual on Shipbuilding) (1948); *Proyektirovaniye preryvistykh svyazey sudovogo korpusa* (The Design of Discontinuous Hull Connections) (1948); *Sbornik statey po sudostroyeniyu* (A Collection of Articles on Shipbuilding) (1954), etc; *Awards:* Stalin Prize (1941); Order of Lenin; other orders and medals; *Died:* 11 Apr 1962.

SHINGAREV, Andrey Ivanovich (1869–1918) Politician; physician; *Born:* 1869, son of a merchant landowner; *Educ:* grad physics and mathematics fac and med fac of a univ; *Career:* 1895–1903 worked as country physician and zemstvo official; from 1903 head, Health Bureau, Voronezh Province Zemstvo; member, League for the Liberation of the Working Class; from 1905 exec official, Constitutional-Democratic Party; as dep, 2nd, 3rd and 4th State Dumas, was one of chief speakers for Constitutional-Democratic faction; during WW 1 member, Main Comt, League of Cities; from July 1915 chm, Naval Commission, State Duma; 1916 member, Duma deleg which visited UK, France and Italy at the invitation of the Entente; after 1917 Feb Revol mem Min of Agric in Provisional Govt; from 1917 Min of Finance in first coalition govt; 2 July 1917 resigned together with other Constitutional-Democratic ministers; later leader, Constitutional-Democratic faction, Petrograd State Duma; took part in Pre-Parliament; also elected to Constituent Assembly; 27 Nov 1917 arrested by Bolsheviks in Petrograd and interned in Peter and Paul Fortress; 6 Jan 1918 transferred to hospital; *Publ: Vymirayushchaya derevnya* (The Dying Village) (1901); *Died:* in the night of 6/7 Jan 1918 killed (together with F.F. Kokoshkin) by a mob of sailors.

SHIROKOGOROV, Ivan Ivanovich (1869–1946) Pathoanatomist; prof from 1915; Dr of Med from 1907; member, USSR Acad of Med Sci from 1944; member, Azer Acad of Sci; hon Sci Worker of Azer SSR; *Born:* 15 July 1869; *Educ:* 1901 grad Med Fac, Yur'yev Univ; *Career:* 1900, while still a student, appointed asst dissector, Chair of Pathoanatomy, Yur'yev Univ; after grad specialized in pathoanatomy; sent on several for research assignments: 1903 at Wirchow Inst, at Ott and Bend's institutes and under the bacteriologist Ficker in Berlin; 1903 also studied under I.I. Mechnikov in Paris; 1913–14 at Cancer Inst, London, where he discovered mitochondria in nerve cells and reported on this at int med congress; 1908–14 assoc prof, from 1915 prof, Chair of Gen Pathology and Pathological Anatomy, Yur'yev Univ; from 1918 prof of histology and pathoanatomy, Transcaucasian Univ; 1919–46 head, Chair of Pathoanatomy, Med Fac, Azer Univ; for a number of years dean of Med Fac, and rector, Azer Univ; also dir, Microbiological Inst; Baku; chm, Learned Med Council, Azer Pop Comrt of Health; chm, Azer Soc of Pathologists; 1930 chm, Org Comt, and chm, 2nd All-Union Congress of Pathologists, Baku; active in campaigns against various infectious diseases; published over 120 works; *Publ: Adrenalinovyy skleroz arteriy* (Adrenalin Sclerosis of the Arteries) (1907); *Subtropicheskiye bolezni Zakavkaz'ya i v chastnosti Azerbaydzhana* (Subtropical Diseases of Transcaucasia, Particulary Azerbaidzhan) (1932); *Chuma* (Plague) (1933); *Voyenno-polevoy sepsis* (Military Field Sepsis) (1945); *Died:* 1946 in Baku.

SHISHKIN, Boris Konstantinovich (1886–1963) Botanist; Dr of Natural Sci from 1934; prof from 1925; corresp member, USSR Acad of Sci from 1943; *Born:* 19 Apr 1886; *Educ:* 1911 grad Med Fac, Tomsk Univ; *Career:* 1914–18 asst prof, Tomsk Univ; also mil surgeon, Russian Army; 1918–24 assoc, Caucasian Museum; 1925–30 prof, Tomsk Univ; 1931–38 assoc, 1938–49 dir, Botanical Inst, USSR Acad of Sci; studied flora of Uryankhay Kray (1908–09), Semirech'ye Region (1912–14), Yerevan and Novo-Boyazet area (1915), Turkish Arm (1916), Trabzon and Turkish Lazistan (1917) and Eastern Transcaucasia (1918–24); member, ed collegium, "Botanicheskiy zhurnal"; *Publ: Ocherki Uryankhayskogo kraya* (Studies of Uryankhay Kray) (1914); ed, *Flora' zapadnoy Sibiri* (The Flora of Western Siberia) (11 vol, 1927–46); *Botaniko-geograficheskiy ocherk primorskogo sklona Pontiyskogo khrebta* (A Botanical Geographical Study of the Littoral Slopes of the Pontine Range) (1930); *Rastitel'nost' Altaya* (The Vegetation of the Altay) (1937); ed, various vol, *Flora SSSR* (The Flora of the USSR); *Awards:* Order of Lenin; Stalin Prize (1952); medals; *Died:* 21 Mar 1963.

SHKIRYATOV, Matvey Fyodorovich (1883–1954) Govt and Party official; CP member from 1906; *Born:* 1883; *Career:* tailor by trade; 1906 joined RSDRP(B) and did Party work among tailor's assistants in Moscow and Rostov-on-Don; 1911 arrested for third time and exiled for three years to Vologda Province; 1914 returned from exile and engaged in illegal Party work in Moscow; 1915 drafted into Russian Army; during 1917 Feb Revol elected Bolshevik dep, Moscow Sov of Workers and Soldiers' Dep; member, Exec Comt, Soldiers' Section, Moscow Sov; Bureau member, Mil Org, Moscow Sov; prior to 1917 Oct Revol worked in Tula, representing Bolsheviks in Exec Comt, Tula Sov of Workers' Dep; during 1917 Oct Revol member, Tula Mil Revol Comt; 1918 elected secr, Centr Comt, Tailoring Workers' Union; 1920 elected chm, Moscow Province Tailoring Workers' Union and member, Moscow RSDRP(B) Comt; 1921 worked for RCP(B) CC and headed Centr Commission for Verifying and Purging the Party; 1922 at 11th RCP(B) Congress elected member, Centr Control Commission; from 1923 Presidium member, Centr Control Commission; from 1927 Collegium member, USSR Pop Comrt of Workers and Peasants' Inspection; from 1927 also member, Party Collegium and head, Org and Instruction Dept, Centr Control Commission; from 1928 secr, Party Collegium, Centr Control Commission and its rep with Politburo and Org Bureau, CC, CPSU(B); 1934 at 17th Party Congress elected member, Party Control Commission, CC, CPSU(B); then secr, Party Collegium,

Party Control Commission; 1933–36 member, Centr Commission for the Purge of the Party; at 18th and 19th Party Congresses elected member, CC, CPSU(B); 1939–52 dep chm, Party Control Commission, CC, CPSU(B); then chm, Party Control Comt, CC, CPSU; member, All-Russian and USSR Centr Exec Comt of several convocations; dep, USSR and RSFSR Supr Sov; dep, Moscow City Sov; 1937–38 cooperated actively with USSR Pop Comr of Internal Affairs Yezhov in purging Party and govt apparatus; *Awards:* three Orders of Lenin; medals; *Died:* 18 Jan 1954.

SHKLOVSKIY, Grigoriy L'vovich (1875–1937) Party and govt official; CP member from 1898; *Born:* 1875; *Career:* Party work in Bel; several times arrested; 1909 fled from exile and emigrated to Switzerland; continued Party work abroad; 1912 Bolshevik deleg at Basel Congress of 2nd International; Mar 1915 attended Bern Party Conference; after 1917 Feb Revol returned to Russia and worked in Nizhniy Novgorod and Moscow; dep chm, Moscow Council of Rayon Dumas; during 1917 Oct Revol comr, Dorogomylov Rayon; 1918 counsellor, Sov mission in Switzerland; until 1925 worked for Pop Comrt of For Affairs; at 14th Party Congress elected member, CPSU(B) Centr Control Commission; 1927 expelled from Centr Control Commission for siding with Zinov'yev-Trotskyist opposition; from 1928 worked for Chemical Syndicate; 1929–30 bd member, Chemical Import Trust; from 1931 worked for Assoc of Sci and Tech Publ Houses and for Chemical-Pharmaceutical Assoc; arrested by State Security organs; *Died:* 1937 in imprisonment.

SHKLYAR, Boris Solomonovich (1896–1961) Therapist; Dr of Med and prof from 1940; *Born:* 1896 in Borisov, now Bel SSR, son of a joiner; *Educ:* 1914 grad boys' high school in Baku; 1921 grad Med Fac, Kiev Univ; *Career:* 1921–33 intern, then asst prof, Fac Therpeutic Clinic, Kiev Med Inst; head, Therapy Dept, City Hospital and Therapy Section, Berdichev Okrug Health Dept; 1934–41 head, Chair of Propaedeutic Therapy, 1941–61 Chair of Fac Therapy, Vinnitsa Med Inst; 1941–44 head, Chair of Propaedeutic Therapy, Ivanovo Med Inst and head, Med Section, Ivanovo Evacuation Hospital; 1938 deleg, Extraordinary Congress of Ukr Soviets; for several years, dep, Vinnitsa City Sov; bd member, Ukr Soc of Therapists; member, Learned Med Council, Ukr Min of Health; dep chm, Vinnitsa Oblast Soc for the Dissemination of Sci and Polit Knowledge; member, ed council, journals "Klinicheskaya meditsina", "Vrachebnoye delo", etc; co-ed, "Bol'shaya meditsinskaya entsiklopediya" (Large Medical Encyclopedia)(2nd ed); did research on pathology of kidneys, lungs and cardiovascular system; wrote 67 works; *Publ: Pilokarpin i yego otnosheniye k vegetativnoy nervnoy sisteme* (Pylocarpine and Its Relation to the Vegetative Nervous System) (1925); *Klinika i patogenez al'buminurii v svyazi s funktsiyey bol'noy pochki* (The Clinical Aspects and Pathogenesis of Albuminuria in Relation to the Function of the Diseased Kidney) (1940); textbook *Diagnostika vnutrennikh bolezney* (The Diagnosis of Internal Diseases); *Awards:* Order of the Red Banner of Labor (1961); medals "For Valiant Labor" and "For Victory Over Germany"; *Died:* 9 Nov 1961 in Vinnitsa.

SHKODUNOVICH, Nikolay Nikolayevich (1900–1964) Mil commander; lt-gen; CP member from 1919; *Born:* 1900 in Tver' (now Kalinin), son of a worker; *Career:* 1919 volunteered for Red Army and fought in Civil War; 1941–45 commander, 58th Infantry Div, 68th Infantry Corps; after WW 2 lectured at Gen Staff Acad; 1952–64 dep commandant, Frunze Mil Acad; *Awards:* two Orders of Lenin; three Orders of the Red Banner; Order of the Red Banner of Labor; Order of Suvorov, 1st Class; Order of Kutuzov, 1st Class; Order of Bogdan Khmel'nitskiy, 2nd Class; Order of the Red Star; medals; *Died:* 19 Oct 1964 killed in a plane crash en route to Belgrade.

SHKURO, Andrey Grigor'yevich (1886–1947) Mil commander; lt-col, Kuban' Cossack Forces, Russian Army; maj-gen, Armed Forces of Southern Russia; leading Whitist commander; *Born:* 1886; during WW 1 with Russian Expedictionary Corps in Persia; May 1918 mustered and led Kuban' Cossack unit against Sov regime in Northern Caucasus; linked up with Gen Denikin's Volunteer Army; led Cossack brigade in liberation of Stavropol', Kislovodsk and Pyatigorsk; fall 1919, in command of 3rd Cavalry Corps, played major role in Denikin's advance on Voronezh; emigrated after Denikin's defeat at Voronezh; 1942–45 helped muster Cossack units which operated with German Army against Sov regime; 1945 surrendered to British forces, together with Gen Krasnov and others; handed over to Sov authorities; 1947 sentenced to death by Mil Collegium, USSR Supr Court; *Died:* 1947 executed by firing squad.

SHKURUPIY, Geo (Yuriy) Danilovich (1903–1937) Ukr poet and prose writer; *Born:* 20 Apr 1903 in Bendery; *Educ:* grad high-school; studied at Kiev Inst of Int Relations; *Career:* after grad high-school worked as ship's stoker; 1920 first work published in journal "Grono"; co-founded lit groups "Aspanfut", "Komunkul't" (Communist Culture) and "Novaya generatsiya" (New Generation); until 1931 Futurist; *Publ:* collected verse: "Psychotoses" (1922); "The Drum" (1923); collected stories "The Dragon Slayer" (1925); "January Revolt" (1928); novel "Doors to Day" (1929); poem "The Winter of 1930" (1933); novel "Miss Andriyena" (1934); film scripts "The Blue Parcel"; "Spartacus", etc; *Died:* 25 Nov 1937.

SHLAPOBERSKIY, Vasiliy Yakovlevich (1901–1966) Surgeon; Dr of Med from 1938; prof from 1943; CP member; *Born:* 1901 in Lith, son of a physician; *Educ:* 1923 grad Med Fac, 1st Moscow Univ; *Career:* 1923–27 asst dissector and histologist, Moscow Tuberculosis Inst and assoc, Inst of Operative Surgery, 2nd Moscow Univ; 1927–43 intern, postgrad student, asst prof, then assoc prof, 1943–52 prof, Hospital Surgical Clinic, 2nd Moscow Med Inst; 1941–45 also consultant, Moscow and Omsk evacuation hospitals; 1946–48 senior assoc, Inst of Roentgenology and Radiology; 1956–66 dir, Clinic of Adult Osteopathology, Centr Inst of Traumatology and Orthopedics, USSR Min of Health; considered one of best Sov osteopathologist; exec secr, Moscow Soc of Surgeons; bd member, All-Union Soc of Surgeons and All-Union Soc of Traumatologists and Orthopedist; secr and member, ed council, journal "Khirurgiya"; member, ed collegium, journal "Antibiotiki"; hon member, Lith Surgical Soc; discovered that resistance of certain microbes to penicillin is relative and can be overcome by appropriate application and dosage; established role of microbic assoc in treatment with antibiotics; wrote some 140 works; *Publ:* doctor's thesis *Lipogranulematoz – patogenez, patologicheskaya anatomiya i klinicheskoye znacheniye yego* (Lipogranulomatosis – Its Pathogenesis, Pathological Anatomy and Clinical Significance) (1938); coauthor, *Rentgenoterapiya ognestrel'nykh povrezhdeniy* (The X-Ray Therapy of Gunshot Injuries); *Penitsillin v khirurgii* (Penicillin in Surgery); *Khirurgicheskiy sepsis* (Surgical Sepsis); *Ostryye gnoynyya peritonity)* (Acute Suppurative Appendicitis); coauthor, *Diagnostika khirurgicheskikh zabolevaniy* (The Diagnosis of Surgical Diseases) (1959); *Died:* 25 Oct 1966 in Moscow.

SHLIKHTER, Aleksandr Grigor'yevich (Party names: ANAN'IN; APREL'YEV; YEVGEN'YEV; NIKODIM; NESTEROV, etc) (1868–1940) Party and govt official; CP member from 1891; *Born:* 1 Sept 1868 in Lubny, Poltava Province, son of a carpenter; *Educ:* studied at high-school; *Career:* from 1887 in revol movement; 1888 arrested; from 1891 worked for Soc-Democratic circles in Ukr; 1893 he and his wife Yevgeniya Samoylovna were arrested in Kiev and 1895 exiled for five years to Sol'vychegodsk, where they founded a Soc-Democratic circles together with N.Ye. Fedoseyev and others; 1896 transferred to Samara, where he worked for first legal Soc-Democratic newspaper "Samarskiy vestnik" and helped establish an underground printing press in the Urals; 1900 helped found Samara "Iskra" Group; 1903, after 2nd RSDRP Congress, sided with Bolsheviks and campaigned against Legal Marxists, Economists and Mensheviks; 1901 member, Tula, 1902–04 Kiev, 1906 Moscow RSDRP Comt; summer 1903 helped organize and conduct gen strike in Kiev; Feb 1905 led polit strike of Southwestern Railroad and Kiev-Poltava Railroad staff; cofounder, Kiev Bolshevik group "Vperyod" (Forwards), on behalf of which he directed the Oct 1915 gen strike in Kiev; chm, 1st and 2nd Congresses of All-Russian Railroad Workers' Union, Moscow; Oct 1905 helped organize revol demonstrations in Kiev and went underground when these were suppressed; 1906–08 Party work in Petersburg; contributed to Bolshevik centr organ "Proletariy"; 1906 Party CC agent to direct the Sveaborg Revolt; 1907 helped prepare 5th RSDRP Congress, which he attended as one of the Bolshevik faction's secretaries; 1908 arrested and exiled for life to Siberia for his revol activities in Kiev in 1905; 1914 sided with Lenin as regards the war and campaigned against the defensists; during 1917 Feb Revol member, Krasnoyarsk Province Party Comt and Exec Comt, Krasnoyarsk Sov of Workers and Soldiers' Dept; deleg at 6th Party Congress; during 1917 Oct Revol member, Moscow Mil Revol Comt and Moscow Food Comr; 1917–18 Pop Comr of Food; then extraordinary food comr in Siberia, Vyatka and other cities; 1919 Ukr Pop Comr of Food; 1919–27 exec govt work; 1921–22 chm, Joint Russo-Finnish

Commission for Implementation of the Peace Treaty; 1922–23 RSFSR plen and trade rep in Austria; 1923–27 USSR Pop Comrt of For Affairs plen at Ukr Council of Pop Comr; 1924–27 also Collegium member, USSR Pop Comrt of For Affairs; 1923–26 also rector, Artem Communist Univ, Khar'kov; 1927–29 Ukr Pop Comr of Agric; promoted establishment of sovkhoz machine- and tractor columns and machine- and tractor stations; from 1928 member and vice-pres, Ukr Acad of Sci; member, Bel Acad of Sci; chm, Council for the Study of Production Resources, Ukr Acad of Sci; from 1930 dir, Ukr Inst of Marxism-Leninism, then pres, All-Ukr Assoc of Marxist-Leninist Institutes; from 1923 member, CC, CP(B) Ukr; 1923–25 member, Org Bureau, 1925–37 cand Politburo member, CC, CP(B) Ukr; deleg at 5th, 6th and 14th–17th CPSU(B) Congresses; member, All-Russian Centr Exec Comt of various convocations; member, USSR Centr Exec Comt of all convocations; from 1923 Presidium member, Ukr Centr Exec Comt of all convocations; twice elected cand Presidium member, USSR Centr Exec Comt; specialized in agrarian econ problems and wrote some 30 econ, historical and publicistic works; *Publ: Sovremennaya obshchina i agrarnyy vopros* (The Modern Commune and the Agrarian Question) (1906); *Kustarnyye promysly v Yeniseyskoy gubernii* (Craft Enterprises in Yeniseysk Province) (1915); *Ekonomicheskoye polozheniye krest'yan Turukhanskogo kraya* (The Economic Situation of Peasants in Turukhan Kray) (1914–16); *K voprosu o rente usadebnykh i gorodskikh zemel'* (The Ground Rent of Estate and Urban Lands) (1919); *Na barrikadakh proletarskoy revolyutsii* (At the Barricades of the Proletarian Revolution) (1927); *Il'ich, kakim ya yego znal* (Il'ich as I Knew Him) (1928), etc; *Died:* 2 Dec 1940.

SHLIKHTER, Artemiy Aleksandrovich (1902–1962) Economist; Party and govt official; CP member from 1919; *Born:* 2 Mar 1902; *Educ:* 1923 grad Sverdlov Communist Inst (Univ?); 1930 grad Inst of Red Prof; *Career:* co-founder, League of Student Communists, Moscow; fought in Civil War; 1924–27 journalist and Komsomol official; 1930–33 did govt work in Moscow; 1933–39 Party official in Rostov Oblast and Krasnodar Kray; 1939–41 did Party work in Krasnodar; 1941–45 served in Sov Army; from 1946 taught at Moscow Univ; 1957–62 head, Agrarian Problems Section, Inst of World Econ and Int Relations, USSR Acad of Sci; wrote several works on agric; *Died:* 11 Aug 1962.

SHLIKHTER, Yevgeniya Samoylovna (1869–1943) Party and govt official; CP member from 1892; *Born:* 19 Jan 1869 in Kamenets-Podol'sk; *Educ:* 1889–91 studied at Bern Univ; *Career:* did Party work in Ukr; 1893 arrested; 1895 exiled for five years to Sol'vychegodsk; from 1896 continued exile in Samara, where she engaged in underground Party work; 1902–05 worked for Kiev RSDRP Comt; 1906–08 worked for Bolshevik newspapers "Proletariy" and "Vperyod"; 1909 went to Siberia to join her husband in exile; taught and continued revol work; took part in 1917 Oct Revol; from 1919 worked for RSFSR Pop Comrt of Educ; from 1924 with Ukr Pop Comrt of Educ; then dir, Ukr Museum of the Revol; dir, Kiev Oblast Library; *Died:* 5 Dec 1943.

SHLYAPNIKOV, Aleksandr Gavrilovich (1884–1943) Party and govt official; CP member from 1901; *Born:* 1884; *Career:* from 1900 in revol movement; 1903–04 Party work in Murom; Jan 1905 arrested; Oct 1905 released from prison under amnesty; 1906 rearrested and imprisoned until 1908; early 1908 emigrated; Apr 1914 returned to Russia on a French passport and worked at Lessner Plant, Petersburg; carried out missions for Bolshevik faction of State Duma and Petersburg RSDRP(B) Comt; Sept 1914 went abroad to liaise with CC, RSDRP(B); worked in Sweden, Norway, Denmark and England; returned to Russia and established in Petersburg Party CC Bureau to direct revol work in Russia; early 1916 again went abroad on Party assignments; 1915 coopted to CC, RSDRP(B); attended 1st All-Russian Congress of Soviets; after 1917 Feb Revol member, initiating group to establish Sov of Workers' Dep in Petersburg; member, 1st Sov Exec Comt; from Apr 1917 chm, Metalworkers' Union; took part in 1917 Oct Revol in Petrograd; attended 2nd All-Russian Congress of Soviets; Pop Comr of Labor in first Sov govt; 17 Nov 1917 resigned from Council of Pop Comr and CC, RD RSDRP(B) together with Nogin, Rykov, Milyutin, Teodorovich, Ryazanov and others in protest against refusal to allow socialist parties to participate in Sov govt; 1918–20 fought in Civil War; member, Revol Mil Council, Southern and Caspian-Caucasian Fronts; member, Revol Mil Council, 16th Army on Western Front; 1919–22 chm, CC, Metalworkers' Union; 1920–21, during trade-union controversy, headed "Workers' Opposition" which supported syndicalist views; 1924–25 councillor, Sov mission in France; 1926–29 chm, Metal Import Trust; then various econ admin posts; after suppression of "Workers' Opposition" frequently (1923, 1926 and 1927) came out in defense of oppositionist views; expelled from Party in 1933 purge; 1918 at 7th Party Congress elected cand member, CC, RCP(B); 1937 arrested by State Security organs; *Publ:* memoirs *Kanun semnadtsatogo goda* (The Eve of 1917); *Semnadtsatyy god* (1917), etc; *Died:* 1943 in imprisonment.

SHMIDT, Dmitriy Arkad'yevich (1896–1937) Mil commander; ensign, Russian Army; div commander, Sov Army from 1935; CP member from 1915; *Born:* 1896 in Priluki, Poltava Province, son of an office worker; *Career:* until 1914 cinema mechanic in Priluki; fought in WW 1; 1917 head, Priluki RSDRP(B) Org; 1918 commander, Priluki Partisan Detachment; in Neutral Zone stipulated by Brest Peace Treaty mustered insurgent units for mil action in Ukr; from fall 1918 commanded regt, brigade, then div of Red Cossack Army; from 1921 various commands; 1924–36 commandant, 5th Cavalry School in Yelizavetgrad (now Kirovograd); commander, 7th Samara Cavalry Div in Bel Mil Distr; commanded tank brigade in Kiev Mil Distr; 1924–29 member, All-Ukr Centr Exec Comt; 1936 arrested by NKVD; Aug 1936 documents at trial of "Trotsky-Zinov'yevite terrorist center" accused him of plotting the assassination of Voroshilov; *Awards:* two Orders of the Red Banner; Silver Arms; *Died:* 20 May 1937 in imprisonment; posthumously rehabilitated.

SHMIDT, Otto Yul'yevich (1891–1956) Mathematician, astronomer, geophysicist and Arctic explorer; prof; member, USSR Acad of Sci from 1935; CP member from 1918; *Born:* 30 Sept 1891 in Mogilev; *Educ:* 1913 grad Kiev Univ; *Career:* from 1916 assoc prof, Kiev Univ; 1918–20 Collegium member, RSFSR Pop Comrt of Food; 1920–21 Collegium member, RSFSR Pop Comrt of Educ; 1920–23 prof, Moscow Forestry Inst; 1921–24 mang, RSFSR-USSR State Publ House; 1923–26 prof, 2nd Moscow Univ; 1924–41 chief ed, "BSE" (Large Soviet Encyclopedia); also chief ed, journal "Priroda"; 1926–56 prof, Moscow Univ; 1927–30 Collegium member, USSR Pop Comrt of Educ; 1931–32 Presidium member, USSR Gosplan; 1932–39 dir, Main Northern Sea Route Bd; 1938–49 dir, Inst of Theoretical Geophysics (now Geophysical Inst), USSR Acad of Sci; undertook several Arctic expeditions: 1929 in charge of the expedition abroad icebreaker "G.Sedov" which established first sci station on Franz Joseph Land and navigated western coast of Severnaya Zemlya; one of the islands discovered during this trip now bears his name; 1932 led expedition on board the icebreaker "Sibiryakov" which was the first ship to sail non-stop from Arkhangel'sk to the Pacific Ocean; 1933–34 in charge of "Chelyuskin" expedition which attempted a non-stop cruise along the Great Northern Sea Route; May 1937 led expedition to set up "North Pole" drifting station; Feb 1938 led "North Pole" reliefe expedition; did research on theory of groups; devised theorem of the isomorphism of direct expansions of infinite operational groups with a finite main series; founded the Moscow school of algebra; in latter years devised theory that Earth and the other planets were formed from the solid particles in a cloud of gas and cosmic dust which once circled the sun and had a mass approximately the same as the total mass of the planets today; *Publ: Abstraktnaya teoriya grupp* (The Abstract Theory of Groups) (1914); *Beskonechnyye razreshimyye gruppy* (Infinite Solvable Groups) (1945); *Astronomicheskiy vozrast Zemli* (The Astronomical Age of the Earth) (1945); *O zakone planetnykh rasstoyaniy* (The Law of Planetary Distances) (1946); *Vozniknoveniye planet i ikh sputnikov* (The Origin of the Planets and Their Satellites) (1950); *Awards:* Hero of the Sov Union (1937); three Orders of Lenin; other orders and medals; *Died:* 7 Sept 1956.

SHMIDT, Vasiliy Vladimirovich (1886–1940) Party and govt official; CP member from 1905; *Born:* 1886; *Career:* 1907–11 lived abroad; 1912 secr, Petersburg Vyborg Rayon Metalworkers' Union; 1913 arrested; 1914 secr, Petersburg Metalworkers' Union; after his arrest moved to Yekaterinoslav and engaged in professional Party work; summer 1915, to avoid arrest, went into hiding in Petersburg and functioned as secr, Petersburg Party Comt; late 1915 arrested and held until Aug 1916; then again secr, Petersburg Party Comt; late 1916 re-arrested; after 1917 Feb Revol secr, Petersburg Party Comt; from Apr 1917 secr, Petersburg Trade-Union Council; from 1918 secr, All-Russian Centr Trade-Union Council; from late 1918 Pop Comr of Labor; 1928–30 dep chm, USSR Council of Pop Comr and Labor and Defense Council; 1930–31 USSR Dep Pop Comr of Agric; from 1931 chief arbiter,

USSR Council of Pop Comr; at 7th Party Congress elected member, CC, CPSU(B); at 8th, 9th, 10th, 11th and 13th Party Congresses elected cand member, at 14th and 15th Congresses member, and at 16th Congress cand member, CC, CPSU(B); member, USSR Centr Exec Comt; Jan 1933 cautioned by plenary meeting of CC, CPSU(B) and Centr Exec Comt for his links with Eysmont "anti-Party group"; 1933 transferred to admin work; dir, Far Eastern Coal Trust; 1937 expelled from Party and arrested by State Security organs; *Died:* 1940 in imprisonment.

SHNIREL'MAN, Lev Genrikhovich (1905–1938) Mathematician; prof from 1929; corresp member, USSR Acad of Sci from 1933; *Born:* 15 Jan 1905 in Gomel'; *Educ:* 1925 grad Moscow Univ; *Career:* did research on theory of numbers; 1927–29, together with L.A.Lyusternik, developed topological (qualitative) methods of variational calculus; also devised metrical methods for work on the theory of numbers; from 1929 prof, Don Polytech Inst, Novocherkassk; from 1934 prof, Mathematical Inst USSR Acad of Sci; *Died:* 24 Sept 1938.

SHOGAM, Abram Nesanel'yevich (1913–1967) Psychiatrist; Dr of Med from 1967; prof; CP member from 1940; *Born:* 1913 in Odessa; *Educ:* 1936 grad Fac of Psychiatry and Neurology, Khar'kov Med Inst; *Career:* after grad specialized at Chair of Psychiatry, Khar'kov Med Inst; simultaneously asst prof, Dept of Forensic and Labor Expertise, and learned secr, Khar'kov Med Inst; from 1940 asst prof, Chair of Psychiatry, Ukr Research Inst of Psychiatry and Neurology; during WW 2 served in Sov Army; after demobilization dir, Psychiatric Clinic, Khar'kov Psychiatric Hospital and head, Org and Methods Dept, Ukr Research Inst of Psychiatry and Neurology; 1956–60 head, Chair of Psychiatry, Turkm Med Inst; from 1962 head, Dept of Neuroses and Borderline States, Khar'kov Research Inst of Psychiatry and Neurology; did extensive research on the theory, clinical aspects and treatment of mental and nervous diseases with special reference to psychology, neurosurgery, experimental neurophysiology and theoretical biology; studied the functional relationship of the cerebral hemispheres, devised an original classification of states of shock resulting from war traumas and of personality changes during illness, and investigated the clinical aspects of traumatic psychoses; during last 15 years specialized in the physiology and pathology of the brain; wrote over 100 works; *Publ:* doctor's thesis, *Materialy k izucheniyu fiziologii konstruktivnykh deystviy cheloveka* (Study Material on Constructive Human Actions) (1967); *Died:* 5 Dec 1967 in Khar'kov.

SHOKAL'SKIY, Yuliy Mikhaylovich (1856–1940) Oceanographer, cartographer and geographer; prof; hon member, USSR Acad of Sci from 1939; Hon Sci Worker of the RSFSR from 1928; *Born:* 17 Oct 1856 in Petersburg; *Educ:* 1880 grad Hydrographic Dept, Petersburg Naval Acad; *Career:* from 1882 lecturer, Petersburg Naval College; for several years assoc, Main Geophysical Observatory and Main Hydrographic Bd; 1910–30 prof, Petersburg (Leningrad) Naval Acad; 1917–31 pres, Russian (USSR) Geographical Soc; 1923–27 led Black Sea oceanographic expedition; 1925–39 corresp member, USSR Acad of Sci; 1925–40 prof, Leningrad Univ; studied potential of Great Northern Sea Route; supervised compilation of relief map of Russia; did topographical calculations for Asian Russia and measured the length of major rivers; compiled numerous gen and special maps and edited several well-known atlases; corresp or hon member of various for acad and soc; the straits between the islands of Severnaya Zemlya, an island at the entrance of an inlet on the Ob' River, an island in the Straits of Kara and other geographical features now bear his name; *Publ:* "*Okeanografiya* (Oceanography) (1917), etc; *Died:* 26 Mar 1940.

SHOKHIN, Andrey Pavlovich (1901–1941) Educ official; CP member from 1920; *Born:* 1901; *Educ:* 1928 grad History Dept, Inst of Red Prof; *Career:* from 1920 did Komsomol work, first in Nizhniy Novgorod, then in Donbas; 1921–24 worked for CC, Russian Komsomol, for Main Bd of Professional Training and for collegium, RSFSR Pop Comrt of Educ; 1922 attended All-Russian Congress on the Educ of Adolescent Workers; 1923 co-founded Liebknecht Higher Ind Teachers' Training Inst, Moscow; 1929–33 head, Main Bd of Children's Soc Training and Polytech Educ and collegium member, RSFSR Pop Comrt of Educ; 1931–32 ed, journal "Za politekhnicheskuyu shkolu"; 1933 worked for CC, CPSU(B); at 17th Party Congress elected member, Party Control Commission; 1934–37 headed educ group in this commission; organized Komsomol contribution to development of Sov school system; 1937 arrested by NKVD; *Publ: Fabzavuch – leninskaya shkola* (Factory and Plant Training – the Leninist School) (1924); *Komsomol i shkola* (The Komsomol and the Schools) (1926); *Died:* 1941 in imprisonment; posthumously rehabilitated.

SHORIN, Vasiliy Ivanovich (1870–1938) Civil War commander; col, Russian Army; *Born:* 1870 in Kalyazin, Tver' Province; *Educ:* 1892 grad Kazan' Cadet College; *Career:* 1892–1917 junior officer, company commander, battalion commander, then commanded 102nd Vyatka Infantry Regt; fought in WW 1 and won many mil orders; 1917 elected commander; 26th Infantry Div; Sept 1918 volunteered for Red Army; 28 Sept 1918–16 July 1919 commander, 2nd Army on Eastern Front; 1 Aug–27 Sept 1919 commander, Special Forces Group on Southern Front; 27 Sept 1919–16 Jan 1920 commander, Southwestern Front; 16–24 Jan 1920 commander, Caucasian Front; 20 Apr 1920–1 Jan 1922 asst commander in chief of RSFSR Armed Forces in Siberia; 1922–25 asst commander, Leningrad Mil Distr; 1925 transferred to the reserve on med grounds; from 1925 exec posts in Leningrad with All-Union Soc to Promote the Aviation, Chemical and Defense Ind; from 1931 active in Leningrad Group for the Study of Jet Propulsion, which laid the groundwork for the practical design and launching of rockets; 1937 arrested by NKVD; *Awards:* Order of the Red Banner; Golden Arms, with badge of the Order of the Red Banner; Mil Red Order of the Khorezm SSR; *Died:* 29 Apr 1938 in imprisonment; posthumously rehabilitated; a street in Kalyazin bears his name and a monument has been erected to him in Leningrad.

SHORYGIN, Pavel Poliyevktovich (1881–1939) Organic chemist; prof; member, USSR Acad of Sci from 1939; *Born:* 28 Apr 1881; *Educ:* 1906 grad Moscow Higher Tech College; *Career:* from 1906 did research on organic sodium compounds; 1910–18 eng at a Moscow textile factory; 1919–25 prof, Moscow Veterinary Inst and Forestry Inst; 1925–39 prof, Mendeleyev Inst of Chemical Technol, Moscow; from 1931 sci dir, Moscow Artificial Fiber Research Inst; 1932–39 corresp member, USSR Acad of Sci; also did research on chemistry of carbohydrates; *Publ: Kratkiy kurs organicheskoy khimii dlya medikov i biologov* (A Short Course of Organic Chemistry for Physicians and Biologists) (1925); *Khimiya uglevodov* (The Chemistry of Carbohydrates) (3rd ed, 1938); *Kurs organicheskoy khimii* (A Course of Organic Chemistry) (2nd ed, 1940); *Died:* 29 Apr 1939.

SHOTMAN, Aleksandr Vasil'yevich (1880–1939) Govt official; CP member from 1899; *Born:* 1880; *Career:* from age 15 lathe-operator; 1902, while working at Nobel Plant, Vyborg Rayon Party organizer and member, Petersburg RSDRP Comt; 1903 deleg, 2nd RSDRP Congress; from start of RSDRP schism sided with Lenin; underground work in Yaroslavl' and Kostroma as member, Northern Comt; repeatedly arrested; late 1905 banished from Petersburg; went to Odessa; member, Odessa Party Comt; returned to Petersburg and co-opted to Petersburg Party Comt, working in Vyborg Rayon; 1908 member, Centr Bd, Metal-workers' Union; simultaneously member, underground Vasiliy Ostrov Rayon Party Comt; 1910–13 member, Helsingfors Comt, Finnish Soc-Democratic Party; after collapse of Baltic Fleet mil org went abroad; attended Poronin Party Conference; co-opted CC, RSDRP(B) and sent on underground work to Russia; 1913 arrested in Yekaterinoslavl' and exiled for three years to Narym Kray; after 1917 Feb Revol worked in Tomsk, then in Finland; after 1917 July riots arranged Lenin's flight to Helsingfors; after 1917 Oct Revol Collegium member, Pop Comrt of Posts and Telegraphs; 1918–19 Presidium member, Supr Sovnarkhoz; 1920 chm, Ural-Siberian Commission, Labor and Defense Council; then member, Siberian Revol Comt and chm, Siberian Sovnarkhoz; 1921 chm, North Caucasian Econ Council; 1922–23 chm, Karelian Econ Council; 1923–24 chm, Karelian Centr Exec Comt; 1925 chm, Radio Broadcasting Bd; from 1928 Presidium member, USSR Supr Sovnarkhoz; 1930 member, Comt for Kamchatka and Sakhalin Affairs; member, All-Russian and USSR Centr Exec Comt; at 13th, 14th, 15th and 16th Party Congresses elected member, CPSU(B) Centr Control Commission; arrested by State Security organs; *Died:* 1939 in imprisonment.

SHPEKTOROV, N.L. (1890–1937) Mil commander and govt official; CP member from 1920; *Born:* 1890; *Educ:* 1928 grad mil acad; *Career:* from 1918 in Red Army; 1920 head, Mobilization Dept, Krasnoyarsk Province Mil Comrt; 1922–25 head, Mobilization Dept, Polit Bd, RSFSR Revol Mil Council; 1928–37 with Mobilization and Planning Bd, USSR Pop Comrt of Heavy Ind; Mil Chemical Trust; Defense Section of USSR Gosplan and Red Army Gen Staff; 1937 arrested by NKVD; *Died:* 1937 in imprisonment; posthumously rehabilitated.

SHTAKHMAN, Yevgeniy Aleksandrovich (1888–1966) Govt official; CP member from 1904; *Born:* 1888; *Career:* began revol career in Riga with underground Soc-Democratic circles; arrested and sentenced to death for his part in 1905–07 Revol; sentence commuted to hard labor for life; after 1917 Feb Revol returned to Petrograd; took part in 1917 Oct Revol; then exec admin work; fought in Civil War; 1921–34 senior posts with State Security organs and with courts; from 1936 dep chm, then chm, Turkmen Supr Court, also exec posts in Turkmen econ admin; 1941–42 Turkmen Dep Pop Comr of Justice; from 1959 pensioner; *Died:* 26 Aug 1966.

SHTERN, Grigoriy Mikhaylovich (1900–1941) Mil commander; lt-gen from 1940; CP member from 1919; *Born:* 24 July 1900 in Smila, now Cherkassy Oblast; *Educ:* 1927 grad Frunze Mil Acad; *Career:* from 1918 in Red Army; fought in Civil War; then polit work with various units; comr, 7th Samara Cavalry Div; in 1930's mang, USSR Pop Comrt of Defense; commanded cavalry div in Bel Mil Distr; 1934–37 also member, Mil Council, USSR Pop Comrt of Defense; 1937–38, under the pseudonym Grigorovich, commanded all Sov ground-force volunteers in Republ Spain; 1938 chief of staff, Separate Red Banner Far Eastern Army on Far Eastern Front; commanded Sov troops during Lake Khasan fighting; 1938–40 commander, 1st Army in Far East; 1939 also commanded front group formed to direct Far Eastern troops and mil action in the Khalkhin Gol area; 1939–40 commander, 8th Army on Sov-Finnish Front; 1940 commander, Far Eastern Front; from 1939 member, CC, CPSU(B); dep, USSR Supr Sov of 1937 convocation; early 1941 arrested by State Security organs; *Awards:* Hero of the Sov Union (1939); Order of Lenin; Order of the Red Banner; *Died:* 28 Oct 1941 in imprisonment; posthumously rehabilitated.

SHTERNBERG, Pavel Karlovich (1865–1920) Astronomer and Party official; CP member from 1905; *Born:* 3 Apr 1865 in Orel; *Educ:* 1887 grad Fac of Physics and Mathematics, Moscow Univ; *Career:* from 1891 did research at Moscow Univ Observatory and lectured on astronomy and geodesy; 1905, after joining Bolshevik faction of RSDRP, worked for Moscow Party Comt Mil Eng Bureau; 1907–08 made survey of Moscow street system for future use during revol; 1909 gave up active Party work after dissolution of Mil Eng Bureau but maintained contacts with RSDRP and worked in legal org; from 1914 extraordinary prof, from 1917 prof, Moscow Univ; after Feb 1917 Revol helped to organize detachments of armed workers in Moscow; Nov 1917 in charge of revol troops in Zamoskvorech'ye Rayon, then Presidium member, Moscow Province Exec Comt; Sept 1918 sent to Eastern Front as polit comr and member, Revol Mil Council, 2nd Army; 1919 member, Revol Mil Council, Eastern Front; 1919 also head, Dept of Higher Educ Establishments and Collegium member, Pop Comrt of Educ; did research on gravimetry and photoastronomy; established gravimetric link between Pulkovo and Moscow, studied the Moscow gravitational anomaly and determined the exact latitude of Moscow Observatory; led a solar eclipse expedition; the State Astronomical Inst at Moscow Univ now bears his name; *Died:* 1 Feb 1920 of pneumonia.

SHTEYN, Boris Yefimovich (1892–1961) Diplomat; Dr of History from 1943; prof from 1939; *Born:* 1892 in Aleksandrovsk (now Zaporozh'ye, Ukr SSR); *Educ:* 1917 grad Petrograd Polytech Inst; *Career:* from 1920 held a succession of posts in Pop Comrt of For Affairs, including: head, Trade Policy Dept; asst head, Dept of Econ Law; head, Polish and Baltic Dept; head, Centr European Dept; head, Dept of Int Questions; 1922 secr, Sov deleg, Genoa Conference; secr-gen, Sov deleg, Haague Conference; 1927 secr-gen, Sov deleg, Int Econ Conference, Geneva; 1927–33 secr gen, Sov deleg, Preparatory Commission and Arms Limitation Conference; 1932–34 Sov envoy to Finland; 1935–39 amb to Italy; 1934–37 member, Sov deleg, League of Nations Assembly; 1936–37 member, USSR Centr Exec Comt; from 1939 prof, Higher Diplomatic School, USSR Min of For Affairs; 1945–52 counsellor, USSR Min of For Affairs with rank of amb; alternate member, Sov deleg, 1st and 2nd UN Gen Assembly; *Awards:* Order of the Red Banner of Labor; medal "For Valiant Labor During the Great Fatherland War"; *Died:* 1961.

SHTEYNBERG, Maksimilian Oseyevich (1883–1946) Composer; music teacher; Dr of Arts from 1943; Hon Art Worker of RSFSR from 1934; Pop Artiste of Uzbek SSR from 1944; *Born:* 22 June 1883 in Vilnius; *Educ:* 1907 grad Natural Sci Fac, Petersburg Univ; 1908 grad Rimsky-Korsakov's composition class, Petersburg Conservatory; *Career:* 1908–15 lecturer, from 1915 prof of composition theory, Petersburg Conservatory; edited posthumous ed of Rimsky-Korsakov's musical ald lit works; completed his work *Osnovy orkestrovki* (The Principles of Orchestration); trained composers M. Ashrafi, Yu. Shaporin, Shostakovich, etc; *Works:* ballet *Metamorfozy* (Metamorphoses) (1913); oratorio *Nebo i zemlya* (Heaven and Earth) (1918); ballet "Till Eulenspiegel" (1936); caprice "In Armenia" (1940); unfinished opera "Takhir and Zukhra" (1942); violin concerto (1946); five symphonies; two cantatas, etc; *Awards:* Order of the Red Banner of Labor; *Died:* 6 Dec 1946 in Leningrad.

SHTEYNBERG, Sergey Samoylovich (1872–1940) Metallurgist; corresp member, USSR Acad of Sci from 1939; *Born:* 8 Oct 1872; *Career:* 1906–25 at steel plants in Urals; worked on technol of high-quality steels and ferro-alloys; from 1925 prof, Ural Polytech Inst; 1927–40 co-founder and prof, Ural Research Inst of Ferrous Metals; from 1932 assoc, Ural Branch, USSR Acad of Sci; from 1939 dir, Inst of Metallurgy, Metal Sci and Metal Physics, Ural Branch, USSR Acad of Sci; specialized in heat treatment and alloying of steel; studied kinetics and structural mech of phase conversions in the heating and cooling of steel in order to determine the physical aspects of processes which occur in the tempering, annealing and tapping of steel; *Publ: Metallovedeniye* (Metal Science) (vol 1, 3rd ed, 1952; vol 2–3, 1933–35); *Termicheskaya obrabotka stali* (The Heat Treatment of Steel) (1950); *Awards:* Order of the Red Banner of Labor; *Died:* 7 Sept 1940.

SHTEYNGART, Aleksandr Matveyevich (1887– ?) Govt and Party official; CP member from 1913; *Born:* 1887 in Odessa; *Career:* began work as apprentice typesetter at age 14, then worked as typesetter for printing shops in Odessa, Kishinev and Kiev Province; during WW 1 served in Russian Army; imprisoned for agitating among troops; during 1917 Feb Revol fought on Rumanian Front and organized soldiers' comts in eng regts; during 1917 Oct Revol chm, corps RSDRP(B) comt; chm, corps revol comt; 1918 with underground Kiev Party Org; Aug 1919–1921 on Western Front; 1921–25 with Red Army Polit Bd, first as dep chief, then chief, Org Dept; from 1925 exec work in agric cooperative system; 1930–32 Collegium member, RSFSR Pop Comrt of Agric; from 1933 dep head, Polit Bd of Machine-and-Tractor Stations and Sovkhozes, USSR Pop Comrt of Agric; then head, Polit Section of Machine-and-Tractor Stations, and head, North Caucasian Kray Land Admin; from 1934 first secr, Saratov Kray CPSU(B) Comt; at 12th Party Congress elected cand member, CC, CPSU(B); *Awards:* Order of the Red Banner; *Died:* date and place of death unknown.

SHTYKOV, Terentiy Fomich (1907–1964) Party and govt official; col-gen; CP member from 1929; *Born:* 1907 in Vitebsk Province; *Career:* 1925 began work at Proletarian Plant, Leningrad; 1937 elected secr, Vyborg Rayon CPSU(B) Comt, then second secr, Leningrad Oblast CPSU(B) Comt; during WW 2 member, Mil Council, Leningrad, Volkhov, Karelian and Far Eastern Fronts; after the war member, Mil Council, and dep commander (polit), Maritime Mil Distr; 1948 appointed Sov amb in North Korea; 1954–59 first secr, Novgorod Oblast and Maritime Kray CPSU Comts; 1959–60 Sov amb in Hungary; from 1961 chm, State Control Commission, RSFSR Council of Min; then dep chm, Party and State Control Comt, CPSU Centr Comt Bureau for RSFSR and RSFSR Council of Min; at 18th Party Congress elected cand member, at 20th Party Congress elected member, CC, CPSU; dep, USSR Supr Sov of several convocations; *Awards:* three Orders of Lenin; Order of the Red Banner; Order of Suvorov, 1st Class; three Orders of Kutuzov, 1st Class; medals; *Died:* 25 Oct 1964.

SHUL'TS, Eduard Genrikhovich (1881–1941) Otolaryngologist; Dr of Med; *Born:* 23 Dec 1881 in Kiev, son of a brewery-owner; *Educ:* 1900 grad Kiev 2nd Boys' High School; 1907 grad Med Vac, Saint Vladimir Univ, Kiev; *Career:* while still a student prepared specimens for Chair of Anatomy and attended lectures at univ Surgical Clinic; suspended from univ for two years for participation in student strikes; 1907–09 asst dissector, Chair of Anatomy, Kiev Univ; simultaneously, asst to Prof N.P.Trofimov, Ear, Nose and Throat Dept, Kiev Mil Clinical Hospital and asst prof, Chair of Otolaryngology, Kiev Univ; studied surgical techniques at various univ surgical clinics; 1909–10 underwent further training in otolaryngology in Berlin and Lausanne; while abroad wrote doctor's thesis on foreign bodies in otolaryngological practice and developed several instruments for removing them from the ears, nose, larynx and oesophagus; after completion of specialist training toured otolaryngological clinics in Austria, Britain,

France, Germany and Switzerland; after return to Kiev senior intern, Mil Clinical Hospital and asst to Prof Trofimov at Kiev Univ; also maintained a large private practice and provided free treatment for the needy at Pokrovski Monastery Hospital; simultaneously held special courses on otolaryngology at Mil Hopsital and Kiev Clinical Inst (now Inst of Postgrad Med Training); 1909–14 attended all Russian and int otolaryngological congresses and was active in League of Cities and Russian Otolaryngological Soc; 1911 co-founded Saint George Soc of Med Specialists and special hospital and polyclinic in Kiev with the then most modern equipment and facilities; 1915–17 served in army, first as senior surgeon, 147th Voronezh Volunteer Unit, then as a brigade surgeon; 1917 resumed work in Kiev; 1920 ceased work at Prokrovskiy Monastery Hospital and Saint George Hospital after their nationalization; 1923 retired from post at Kiev Mil Hospital and gave up work at Chair of Otolaryngology, Kiev Univ when the Russian-language course was closed; did most of his teaching and clinical work at the Clinical Inst; also worked at Saint George Polyclinic and Red Cross Hospital; until 1937 head, Ear, Nose and Throat Department, Garison Polyclinic, Kiev Oblast Militia; Dec 1939 arrested by NKVD and sentenced to ten years imprisonment in a concentration camp near Karaganda; *Awards:* various WW 1 medas; *Died:* 31 Mar 1941 in imprisonment; posthumously rehabilitated.

SHUMSKIY, Aleksandr Yakovlevich (1890–1946) Party and govt official; CP member from 1920; *Born:* 1890 in Volhynian Province; *Career:* from 1909 active in revol movement with Ukr Socialist-Revolutionaries; 1917, with formation of Ukr Socialist-Revol Party, became one of the leaders of its left wing, the so-called "Left Bankists", (subsequently the "Borotbisty"); also member, Centr Rada, Kiev; from Nov 1917 member, CC, Ukr Socialist'Revol Party; during 1917 Oct Revol took part in plot against Centr Rada aimed at establishing Sov regime in Ukr; also directed underground movement against Skoropadsky Govt; during the Directorate worked to establish Sov regime; 1919 Pop Comr of Educ; during Gen Denikin's rule was chief dir of underground movement in Ukr; 1920 elected member, Politburo member and Org Bureau member, CC, CP(B) Ukr; also Ukr Pop Comr of Internal Affairs; member, Revol Mil Council, 14th Army; then chm, Poltava Province Exec Comt; 1920 took part in talks to negotiate peace treaty with Poland; 1921–23 Ukr amb in Poland; 1923–25 head, Agitation and Propaganda Dept, CC, CP(B) Ukr; 1925–26 Ukr Pop Comr of Educ; 1926 accused of "Nationalist deviation", later termed "Shumskyism"; from 1927 chm, CC, Educ Workers' Union; then rector, Inst of Nat Economy, Leningrad; member, CC, CP(B)U Ukr; member, USSR Centr Exec Comt; from 1926 with CPSU(B) deleg in Comintern; 1933 expelled from Party for nationalism and then arrested by State Security organs; *Died:* 1946 in imprisonment.

SHUMYATSKIY, Boris Zakharovich (pseudonym: CHERVONNYY, Andrey) (1886–1943) Govt official; CP member from 1903; *Born:* 1886; *Career:* 1905 member, Krasnoyarsk Party Comt; member, strike comt; formed Red Guard units and helped organize Dec 1905 revolt at Krasnoyarsk Main Railroad Workshops; after suppression of revolt arrested; escaped from Krasnoyarsk Jail; underground Party work in Omsk and other parts of Siberia; Nov 1907 helped lead Vladivostok revolt, and fled after this was crushed; until 1911 underground work in Harbin and various Siberian towns; 1911–12 abroad; 1912 worked for "Pravda"; then worked in Kiev and Kansk; arrested; 1915 tried for complicity in 1905 armed revolt in Krasnoyarsk and drafted into Russian Army; after 1917 Feb Revol helped found Krasnoyarsk Sov; founder and manager, newspaper "Sibirskaya pravda"; after 1917 July riots worked for Petrograd Bureau of Mil Orgs, CC, RSDRP(B) and with newspaper "Soldat i rabochiy"; deleg, 6th Party Congress; worked for newspapers "Proletariy," "Rabochiy" and "Rabochiy put'"; after 1917 Oct Revol chm, Siberian Centr Exec Comt Sov; fought in Civil War; 1918–19 underground work, then in frontline zone (Tyumen'-Perm'); summer 1919 served with 3rd Army in fighting for Perm' and Tobol'sk; Nov 1919 appointed chm, Tyumen' Province Revol Comt; from early 1920 chm, Tomsk Province Revol Comt; simultaneously dep chm, Siberian Revol Comt and member, Siberian Bureau, CC, RCP(B); summer 1920 member, Far Eastern Bureau, CC, RCP(B) and chm, Council of Min, Far Eastern Republ; 1921–22 member, Revol Mil Council, 5th Army; directed operations against Baron Ungern; NKVD rep for Siberia and Mongolia; 1922–25 USSR plen in Iran; 1926 Party work in Leningrad; late 1926–28 rector, Communist Univ of Workers of the East; 1928–30 member, Centr Asian Bureau, CC, CPSU(B); from late 1930 chm, All-Union Cinematography Bd; from 1932 Collegium member, RSFSR Pop Comrt of Educ and Collegium member, USSR Pop Comrt of Light Ind; from 1933 chm, Cinematography and Photography Ind Bd, USSR Council of Pop Comr; *Awards:* Order of the Red Banner of the Mongolian Republ (1931); *Died:* 1943.

SHUNKOV, Viktor Ivanovich (1900–1967) Historian; Dr of Historical Sci from 1954; prof; corresp member, USSR Acad of Sci from 1962; CP member from 1942; *Born:* 19 Apr 1900 in Kuznetsk, Tomsk Province; *Educ:* 1918–22 studied at History and Philology Fac, Tomsk Univ; 1925 grad Socio-Pedag Dept, Moscow Univ; *Career:* from 1929 taught at higher educ establishments in Moscow: Inst of Advanced Pedag Training, Library Inst of Moscow Univ, Etc; from 1934 also worked for USSR Acad of Sci; from 1936 senior assoc, then learned secr, Inst of History, USSR Acad of Sci; 1941–45 served with Workers' Battalion of Moscow's Kiev Rayon, then in Sov Army at the front; from 1945 dep dir, Inst of History, USSR Acad of Sci; 1949–67 dir, Fundamental Library of Soc Sci, USSR Acad of Sci; from 1959 dep acad secr, Dept of History, USSR Acad of Sci; from 1965 also chm, Archeological Commission, USSR Acad of Sci and ed of the Commission's yearbook; also vice-pres, Int Libraries Fed; chm, Int Commission for Bibliography; chm, Sci Council for Information on Soc Sci, Soc Sci Section, Presidium of USSR Acad of Sci; chm, Council for Library Work, USSR Min of Culture; head, Commission for the History of Agriculture and Peasantry, Inst of History, USSR Acad of Sci; 1954–60 chief ed, journal "Istoricheskiy arkhiv"; then coordinating ed, periodical *Materialy po istorii Sibiri* (Material on the History of Siberia); joint chief ed, 5-vol *Istoriya Sibiri* (The History of Siberia); specialized in Siberian history; *Publ: Ocherki po istorii kolonizatsii Sibiri v XVII - nachale XIII vv.* (An Outline History of Siberian Colonization in the 17th and Early 18th Centuries) (1946); ed, *Istoriya Buryat-Mongol'skoy ASSR* (The History of the Buryat-Mongolian ASSR) (1954); *Ocherki istorii zemledeliya v Sibiri v XVII v.* (An Outline History of Agriculture in Siberia in the 17th Century) (1956); coordinating ed, *Akademiya nauk SSSR. Fundamental'naya biblioteka obshchestvennykh nauk. Iz opyta raboty za 40 let* (The USSR Academy of Sciences. The Fundamental Library of Social Sciences. Experience of 40 Years' Work) (1960); ed, *Sibir' XVII–XVIII vv.* (Siberia in the 17th and 18th Centuries) (1962); *Nekotoryye problemy istorii Sibiri* (Some Problems of Siberian History) (1963); ed, *Ekonomika, upravleniye i kul'tura Sibiri XVI–XIX vv.* (The Economy, Administration and Culture of Siberia from the 16th to the 19th Centuries) (1965); wrote Vol 1 of 5-vol *Istoriya Sibiri* (A History of Siberia); *Awards:* Order of the Red Banner of Labor; two Orders of the Fatherland War; *Died:* 9 Nov 1967.

SHUTKO, K.I. (Mikhail) (1884–1941) Govt official; CP member from 1902; *Born:* 1884; *Career:* Party work in Moscow, Petersburg and other Russian cities; several times arrested; 1916–17 member, Exec Commission, Petrograd RSDRP(B) Comt; after 1917 Feb Revol member, Petrograd RSDRP(B) Comt; member, Exec Comt, Petrograd Sov; dep, Vyborg Rayon Duma; Oct 1917 agitator, Petrograd Mil Revol Comt; after 1917 Oct Revol exec mil-polit, dipl, econ and govt work; *Died:* 1941.

SHUTOV, Stepan Fyodorovich (1902–1963) Mil commander; col; CP member from 1924; *Born:* 30 Jan 1902 in vil Dvorets, Mogilyov Province, son of a farmhand; *Educ:* 1927 grad All-Russian Centr Exec Comt Joint Mil School, Moscow; 1933 grad Leningrad Armored Forces Courses; *Career:* 1917–18 in Red Guards and partisan detachment; fought against German troops; from 1920 in Red Army; fought in Sov-Polish War; 1927–41 commanded cavalry platoon, squadron, tank company, then tank battalion; 1941–43 tank battalion commander; dep commander, tank brigade; commander, 167th Tank Brigade on Western and Volkhov Fronts; 1943–45 commander, 20th Guards Tank Brigade on Voronezh, 2nd Ukr and other fronts; Nov 1943 in campaign to liberate Kiev, his brigade was the first to enter the city; later fought in liberation of Rumania and Hungary; from Sept 1945 in retirement; *Publ:* memoirs *Vsegda v stroyu* (Always in Line) (1950); *Krasnyye strely* (Red Arrows) (1963); *Awards:* twice Hero of the Sov Union (10 Jan and 13 Sept 1944); two Orders of Lenin; two Orders of the Red Banner; other orders and medals; *Died:* 17 Apr 1963.

SHVARTS, Isaak Izrailevich (Party name: SEMYON) (1879–1951) Govt and Party official; CP member from 1899; *Born:* 18 Jan 1879 in Nikolayev; *Career:* from age 13 apprentice in iron foundry, then foundryman at core plant in Nikolayev; twice arrested and exiled to Yakutsk Oblast; fled from exile and went abroad; lived in Geneva, assigned to Party work by Lenin and returned to Russia; helped found Yekaterinoslav Bolshevik Comt; 1905 arrested and exiled to Mezen' in Arkhangel'sk Province; on his way to exile freed under amnesty; worked for a while in Yekaterinoslav, then went to Donbass; arrested immediately on arrival in Lugansk and exiled to Tobol'sk Province, whence he fled to Urals; settled in Yekaterinburg; helped restore Yekaterinburg Oblast Party Comt; 1907 helped prepare elections to 2nd State Duma; 1907 Ural Party Org deleg at 5th (London) Party Congress; 1908 visited Lenin in Kuokkala and commissioned to restore Party orgs in Urals; 1910 again fled from exile and went to Paris; attended Lenin's Party school, training for further revol work in Russia; as a member of For Org Commission, sent to Russia to restore Bolshevik orgs; Aug 1911 founded Russian Org Commission to convene Party gen conference; directed Russian preparations for 6th (Prague) All-Russian Party Conference; Oct 1911 arrested in Petersburg and exiled for life to Yeniseysk Province, where he remained until 1917 Feb Revol; in the course of his revol work arrested and exiled seven times; six times fled from exile; after 1917 Feb Revol did Party work in Odessa and Nikolayev, preparing for 7th (Apr) Party Conference; then exec Party and govt work in Ukr; 1918 at 1st Congress of CP(B) Ukr elected member, CC, CP(B) Ukr; 1919–20 chm, All-Ukr Cheka; then Labor and Defense Council plen in Odessa and Nikolayev; helped restore Donbass; at 11th and 12th Party Congresses elected member, Centr Control Commission; at 13th–17th Party Congresses elected member, CC, CPSU(B); from 1921 chm, CC, Miners' Union; Plenary member, All-Russian Centr Trade-Union Council; from 1925 Presidium member, All-Russian Centr Trade-Union Council; from 1930 econ admin work; chm, Coal Union; then mang, All-Union Shale Trust; 1938–51 founder-head, All-Union Research Laboratory for Dispersive Drugs; *Died:* 26 Oct 1951.

SHVARTS, Nikolay Nikolayevich (1882– ?) Mil commander, officer, Russian Army; maj-gen from 1940; *Born:* 1882; *Career:* during Civil War chief of staff, Tukhachevskiy's Western Front; after Civil War taught tactics and warfare at Frunze Mil Acad and Gen Staff Acad; *Publ: Ustroystvo voyennogo upravleniya* (The Organization of Military Adminstration) (1927); *Podgotovka i provedeniye komandovaniyem i shtabom frontovoy i armeyskoy operatsii* (The Preparation and Implementation of a Front or Army Operation by Command and Staff) (1936); *Material'noye obespecheniye nastupleniya Zapadnogo fronta v iyule–avguste 1920* (The Logistics of the Western Front's July–August 1920 Offensive) (1936); *Awards:* Order of the Red Banner; Order of the Red Star; *Died:* date and place of death unknown.

SHVARTS, Yevgeniy L'vovich (1896–1958) Russian writer and playwright; *Born:* 21 Oct 1896 in Rostov-on-Don, son of a physician; *Educ:* studied at Moscow Univ; *Career:* worked as actor; 1923 began to write; wrote essays for newspapers and feuilletons for periodicals in Donbass; *Publ:* play ("Underwood") (1929); *Snezhnaya koroleva* (The Snow Queen) (1930), after Andersen's tale; children's play *Klad* (The Treasure) (1931); fairy-tale plays for adults *Ten'* (The Shadow) (1941); satirical comedy on themes from Andersen's fairy-tales *Obyknovennoye chudo* (An Ordinary Miracle) (1942–43); children's plays *Dva klada* (Two Treasures) (1953); film comedy *Zolushka* (Cinderella); *Izbrannyye proizvedeniya* (Selected Works) (1956); collection of plays for puppet theaters *Kukol'nyy gorod* (Puppet Town) (1959); selected works *Skazki, povesti i p'yesy* (Stories, Tales and Plays) (1960); fairy-tale *Dva Brata* (The Two Brothers) (1962); collection *P'yesy* (Plays) (1962); book in Hungarian translation "The First-Grader" (1963); *Died:* 17 Jan 1958.

SHVETSOV, Arkadiy Dmitriyevich (1892–1953) Aviation engine designer; lt-gen, Eng Corps; Hero of Socialist Labor from 1942; *Born:* 25 Jan 1892; *Educ:* 1921 grad Moscow Higher Tech College; *Career:* from 1923 designed aviaton engines such as the M-8-RAM and the M-11; from 1934 chief designer at an aviation engine-building plant; supervised the design and construction of the high-performance ASh family of piston-driven, water-cooled radial engines; founded school of water-cooled aviation engine designers; dep, USSR Supr Sov of 2nd and 3rd convocations; *Awards:* five Orders of Lenin; three other orders; four Stalin Prizes (1942, 1943, 1946 and 1948); *Died:* 1953.

SIBIRTSEV, Vsevolod Mikhaylovich (1893–1920) Revolutionary; CP member from 1913; *Born:* 18 July 1893 in Petersburg, son of an intellectual and member of the "Narodnaya volya" (People's Will) Party; *Educ:* from 1911 studied at Petersburg Polytech Inst; during WW 1 attended cadet college; *Career:* from 1917 in 12th Army on Western Front; attended 1st and 2nd All-Russian Congresses of Soviets; active in 1917 Oct Revol; Jan 1918 sent by Party to Vladivostok to become secr, Exec Comt, Vladivostok Sov; June 1918 arrested by Czech Legion and interned in concentration camp; Aug 1919 escaped from camp; edited illegal Bolshevik newspaper "Kommunist" and engaged in party polit work with partisan units; 1919 mil comr, Vladivostok Garrison; 1920 member, Mil Council, Maritime Oblast Zemstvo Admin; captured by Japanese occupation forces; *Died:* May 1920 burned alive together with S.G. Lazo and A.N. Lutskiy in the firebox of a locomotive at Murav'yevo-Amurskaya Railroad Station (now Lazo Station).

SIBIRTSEV, Yustin Mikhaylovich (1853–1933) Local historian; corresp member, USSR Acad of Sci from 1928; *Born:* 28 May 1853; *Career:* collated, processed and evaluated material on the history of the Arkhangel'sk Kray in the 15th–18th Centuries; 1909, together with A.A. Shakhmatov, published several of 15th-Centruy Dvinsk scrolls; *Died:* 1933.

SIDOROV, Arkadiy Lavrovich (1900–1966) Historian; Dr of History from 1943; prof; CP member from 1920; *Born:* 8 Feb 1900 in Pochinki, Nizhniy Novgorod Province, son of a peasant; *Educ:* 1923 grad Sverdlov Communist Univ; 1928 grad Inst of Red Prof; *Career:* 1929–36 did Party work in Nizhniy Novgorod (Gorky), Vladivostok and Khabarovsk; from 1937 taught and did research at Inst of History, USSR Acad of Sci, at Moscow Univ, at Inst of Int Relations and at Acad of Soc Sci, CC, CPSU; during 1930's played a major role in the campaign against M.N.Pokrovskiy's school of history, the glorification of Stalin and the dogmatization of Sov historical sci; 1948–52 prorector, Moscow Univ; from 1952 head, Chair of the History of the USSR, Moscow Univ; 1953–59 dir, Inst of History, USSR Acad of Sci; from 1954 also chief ed, periodical "Istoricheskiye zapiski"; member, Main Ed Bd, "BSE" (Large Soviet Encyclopedia), "Sovetskaya istoricheskaya entsiklopediya" (Soviet Historical Encyclopedia), "Istoriya SSSR" (The History of the USSR), and "Vsemirnaya istoriya" (World History); co-founder and ed of an 18-vol series of documents on the 1905–07 Revol and 10-vol series *Dokumenty po istorii Velikoy Oktyabr'skoy sotsialisticheskoy revolyutsii* (Documents on the History of the Great October Socialist Revolution) (1957–63); from 1962 chm, Section on the Gen Laws and Features of the Development of Russia in the Age of Imperialism, Sci Council for the History of the Great October Socialist Revol, USSR Acad of Sci; attended 10th and 11th Int Congresses of Historical Sci; specialized in 19th- and early 20th-century Russian history; *Publ:* coauthor and ed, *Protiv antimarksistskoy kontseptsii M.N.Pokrovskogo* (Contra the Anti-Marxist Conception of M.N.Pokrovskiy) (vol 1, 1939); *Russko-yaponskaya voyna 1904–05 godov* (The Russo-Japanese War of 1904–05 (1946); exec ed, *Ekonomicheskoye polozheniye Rossii nakanune Oktyabr'skoy sotsialisticheskoy revolyutsii* (The Economic Condition of Russia on the Eve of the October Socialist Revolution) (2 vol, 1957); *Finansovoye polozheniye Rossii v gody pervoy mirovoy 1914–17* (The Financial Position of Russia During the 1914–17 First World War) (1960); co-author and ed, *Ob osobennostyakh imperializma v Rossii* (The Features of Imperialism in Russia) (1963); *Materialy a sverzhenii tsarizma v fonde Chrezvychaynoy sledstvennoy komissii Vremennogo pravitel'stva* (Material on the Overthrow of Tsarist Rule in the Files of the Provisional Government's Extraordinary Investigative Commission) (1964), etc; *Awards:* Order of Lenin; Order of the Red Banner of Labor; medals; *Died:* 11 Mar 1966.

SIDOROVA, Nina Aleksandrovna (1910–1961) Medievalist; Dr of History from 1949; prof; CP member from 1939; *Born:* 26 May 1910 in vil Kraskovo, now Moscow Oblast, daughter of a teacher; *Educ:* grad Moscow Teachers' Training Inst; *Career:* from 1934 worked at Museum of the Inst of Marxism-Leninism, CC, CPSU(B) and at Lenin Centr Museum; 1936–42 also taught at Moscow City Teachers' Training Inst and Moscow Inst of Philosophy, Lit and History, then at Kazan' Teachers' Training Inst; from 1942 senior assoc, from 1952 head, Medieval History Section, Inst of History, USSR Acad of Sci; from 1943 also taught at Moscow Univ; did research on the medieval history of Western Europe with special reference to France; bd member, Sov-French Friendship Soc; *Publ:* coauthor, *Istoriya srednikh vekov* (Medieval History) (vol 1, 1952); *Ocherki po istorii ranney gorodskoy kul'tury vo Fransii* (Studies in the History of Early Urban Civilization in France)

(1953); coauthor and ed, *Vsemirnaya istoriya* (World History) (vol 3, 1957); ed, *Pyotr Abelyar. Istoriya moikh bedstviy* (Pierre Abelard. The Story of my Misadventures) (1959); *Antifeodal'nyye dvizheniya v gorodakh Frantsii vo vtoroy polovine XIV-nachale XV veka* (Antifeudal Movements in the Towns of France in the Late 14th and Early 15th Century) (1960), etc; *Awards:* Order of the Red Banner of Labor; medals; *Died:* 30 Nov 1961.

SIKORSKIY, Sergey Ivanovich (1907–1960) Govt and Party official; Bel Min of Internal Affairs; CP member from 1930; Hero of the Sov Union; *Born:* 1907 in Bobruysk; *Educ:* 1937 grad Minsk Higher Communist Agric School; 1950 grad Higher Party School, CC, CPSU(B); *Career:* 1929–31 in Red Army; 1931–35 chm of a kolkhoz, then of a vil sov; secr, vil Party org in Bobruysk Rayon; 1937–39 worked for CC, CP(B) Bel; 1939–41 secr, Brest Oblast Comt, CP(B) Bel; 1941–43 in Red Army; 1943–44 secr, underground Brest Oblast Party Comt and partisan organizer in Brest Oblast; 1944–46 chm, Brest Oblast Exec Comt; from 1950 first secr, Mogilev Oblast Comt, CP(B) Bel; then Bel Min of Internal Affairs; 1954–60 member, CC, CP Bel; *Awards:* Order of Lenin; Order of the Red Banner of Labor; Order of the Red Banner; Order of Suvorov, 2nd Class; Order of the Fatherland War, 1st Class; medals; *Died:* Apr 1960.

SIL'VIN, Mikhail Aleksandrovich (Party names: BEM; BRODYAGA; BRODYAGIN; TAGANSKIY) (1874–1955) Govt official; *Born:* 20 Nov 1874 in Nizhniy Novgorod, son of an official; *Educ:* studied at Law Fac, Petersburg Univ; *Career:* 1891 helped found Nizhniy Novgorod's first Marxist circle; from 1893 in Petersburg, where he was a member of a Soc-Democratic circle; Sept 1893 made the acquaintance of Lenin and joined Centr Group, Petersburg League for the Liberation of the Working Class; 1896 arrested and 1898 exiled for three years to vil Yermakovskoye, Yeniseysk Province; in exile again met Lenin; summer 1899 signed Lenin's "Protest of the Russian Social–Democrats Against the Economists' 'Credo'"; from 1901 "Iskra" agent; 1902 arrested; 1904 exiled to Irkutsk Province; Auf 1904 fled from exile and went abroad; coopted to CC, RSDRP; late 1904 sided for a while with the Mensheviks, but then rejoined Bolsheviks; 1905 returned to Russia; 1905–08 contributed to Bolsheviks newspapers; 1908 abandoned politics and left the Party; after 1917 Oct Revol worked for various Sov organs; worked for RSFSR Pop Comrt of Educ; 1923–31 insurance agent with USSR trade mission in England; from 1931 taught for languages at higher educ establishments in Leningrad; from 1932 retired on pension; *Publ:* articles on history of Petersburg League for the Liberation of the Working Class; book *Lenin v period zarozhdeniya partii* (Lenin in the Period of the Party's Inception) (1958); *Died:* 28 May 1955.

SIMONI, Pavel Konstantinovich (1859–1939) Historian, lit critic and bibliographer; corresp member, USSR Acad of Sci from 1929; *Born:* 1 Dec 1859 in Petersburg, son of a civil servant; *Educ:* 1896 grad Petersburg Univ; *Career:* did research on various aspects of the history of Russian lit, folklore, bibliography, etc; *Publ: Russkiy yazyk v yego narechiyakh i govorakh* (The Russian Language in Its Dialects and Patois) (1899); *Starinnyye sborniki russkikh poslovits, pogovorok, zagadok i prochikh XVII–XIX stoletiy* (Old Anthologies of Russian Proverbs, Sayings, Riddles, Etcetera from the 17th–19th Centuries) (1899); *K istorii obikhoda knigopistsa, pereplyotchika i ikonnogo pistsa pri knizhnom i ikonnom stroyenii* (The History of the Working Techniques of Scribes, Bookbinders and Ikon Painters) (1906); *Mstislavskoye Yevangeliye nachala XII stoletiya v arkheologicheskikh i paleograficheskikh otnosheniyakh* (The Archeological and Paleographic Aspects of the Early 12th-Century Mstislav Gospel) (1910); *Skazaniye o kievskikh bogatyryakh kak khodili vo Tsar'grad i kak pobili tsaregradskikh bogatyrey, uchinili sebe chest'* (The Tale of How the Heroes of Kiev Marched into Tsar'grad, Defeated the Heroes of Tsar'grad and Increased Their Honor) (1922); *Knizhnaya torvovlya v Moskve XVIII–XIX stoletiy* (The Moscow Book Trade in the 18th and 19th Century) (1927); *Died:* 17 Mar 1939.

SIMOV, Viktor Andreyevich (1858–1935) Set designer; Hon Art Worker of RSFSR from 1932; *Born:* 2 Apr 1858; *Educ:* 1882 grad Moscow College of Painting, Sculpture and Architecture; *Career:* 1885–86 set designer with private Russian opera company in Moscow; 1898–1912 set designer, Moscow Arts Theater; 1913–25 designed sets and costumes for Free Theater, Maly Theater and Stanislavsky Opera Theater–Studio; 1925–35 again set designer, Moscow Arts Theater; 1925 head, Experimental Design Workshop, Moscow Arts Theater; *Works:* designed sets and costumes for: Hauptmann's "The Sunken Bell" (1897); *Snegurochka* (The Snow-Maiden) (1900); *Na dne* (The Lower Depths) (1902); "Julius Caesar" (1903); *Chayka* (The Seagull) (1904); *Vishnyovyy sad* (The Cherry Orchard) (1904); *Zhivoy trup* (The Living Corpse) (1911); *Shutniki* (The Jokers) (1917); *Tsarskaya nevesta* (The Bride of the Tsar) (1926); *Bronepoyezd 14-69* (Armored Train 14-69) (1927); *Myortvyye dushi* (Dead Souls) (1932), etc; *Publ:* memoirs *Moya rabota s rezhissyorami* (My Work with Stage Directors); *Moya vstrecha s Gor'kim* (My Meeting with Gorky) (1937); *Moya rabota nad "Zhivym trupom"* (My Work on "The Living Corpse") (1935), etc; *Died:* 21 Aug 1935.

SIPOVSKIY, Pyotr Vasil'yevich (1906–1963) Pathoanatomist; Dr of Med from 1937; prof from 1939; *Born:* 1906; *Educ:* 1927 grad 1st Leningrad Med Inst; 1930 completed postgrad studies at Chair of Pathological Anatomy, 2nd Leningrad Med Inst (now Inst of Sanitation and Hygiene); *Career:* 1930–32 assoc, Leningrad Inst of Roentgenology and Radiology; 1933–39 asst prof, Chair of Pathological Anatomy, 3rd Leningrad Med Inst; 1939–45 head, Chair of Pathological Anatomy and dep sci dir, Stalinabad Med Inst; 1945–50 prof of pathological anatomy and head, Pathoanatomical Laboratory, Leningrad Stomatological Inst; 1950–63 head, Chair of Pathological Anatomy, Leningrad Inst of Postgrad Med Training; senior assoc, Leningrad Traumatological and Orthopedic Research Inst; sci dir, Pathoanatomical Dept, Leningrad Blood Transfusion Research Inst; consultant, Pathoanatomical Laboratory, Children's Orthopedic Research Inst; dep chm, Leningrad Soc of Pathoanatomists; bd member, All-Union Soc of Pathoanatomists; did research on the role of the nervous system in various pathological processes, hematology, the effect of various drugs on wound healing, the regional pathology of Tadzh, goiter, the pathology of the structural and motor system, etc; wrote over 100 works; *Publ: Morfologicheskaya kharakteristika prisposobitel'nykh (kompensatornykh) i reparativnykh reaktsiy kostnoy tkani, a takzhe nekotorykh form ikh narusheniy i iskhodov* (The Morphological Characteristics of the Adaptive [Compensatory] and Restorative Reactions of Bone Tissue and Certain Forms of Disturbances and Results) (1961), etc; *Awards:* various orders and medals; *Died:* 15 Feb 1963 in Leningrad.

SISAKYAN, Norayr Martirosovich (1907–1966) Biochemist; prof; Dr of Biological Sci from 1940; member, USSR Acad of Sci from 1960 and Arm Acad of Sci from 1965; CP member from 1937; *Born:* 25 Jan 1907; *Educ:* 1932 grad Timiryazev Agric Acad, Moscow; *Career:* 1932–36 worked at Timiryazev Agric Acad, Moscow; from 1960 Presidium member, from 1963 chief learned secr, USSR Acad of Sci; from 1936 head, Laboratory of Enzymology, Bakh Inst of Biochemistry, USSR Acad of Sci; 1960–63 acad secr, Biological Sci Div, USSR Acad of Sci; also prof, Moscow Univ; 1953–60 corresp member, USSR Acad of Sci; 1945–65 corresp member, Arm Acad of Sci; co-ed, chemistry dept, 2nd ed of "BME" (Large Medical Encyclopedia); from 1965 chief ed, journal "Vestnik AN SSSR"; Sov rep on UNESCO Exec Council; member of many Sov and for sci soc; 1960 attended session of UN Exec Comt and 11th session of UNESCO Gen Conference, Paris; 1961 attended All-Union Meeting of Sci Workers and 4th Int Congress of Biochemists, Moscow; 1962 attended joint session of Biological Sci Div, USSR Acad of Sci and USSR Acad of Med Sci; developed tech biochemical processes and efficient technol for viniculture and for drying and dehydration of produce; wrote more than 400 sci works on action of enzymes in metabolism and problems of space biology; *Publ: Biokhimicheskaya kharakteristika zasukhostoychivykh rasteniy* (The Biochemical Characteristics of Drought-Resistant Plants) (1940); *Fermentativnaya aktivnost' protoplazmennykh struktur* (The Enzymatic Activity of Protoplasmic Structures) (1951); *Biokhimiya obmena veshchestv* (The Biochemistry of Metabolism) (1954); *Biokhimiya plastid* (The Biochemistry of Plastids) (1954); *Khimicheskaya priroda i biokhimicheskiye funktsii plastid* (The Chemical Nature and Biochemical Functions of Plastids) (1956); coauthor and ed, *Biokhimiya i vinodeliye* (Biochemistry and Viniculture) (1947–57 and 1960); *Awards:* two Orders of the Red Banner of Labor; medals; Bakh Prize (1949); Mechnikov Prize (1950); Stalin Prize (1952); *Died:* 12 Mar 1966.

SITENKO, Mikhail Ivanovich (1885–1940) Surgeon; corresp member, Ukr Acad of Sci; Hon Sci Worker of Ukr SSR from 1936; *Born:* 12 Nov 1885 in vil Ryabushki, Khar'kov Province, son of a priest; *Educ:* 1904 grad Sumy Boys' High-School; 1910 grad Med Fac, Khar'kov Univ; *Career:* asst prof, Chair of Operative Surgery and Topographical Anatomy, Khar'kov Univ; simultaneously specialized in clinical surgery under L. V. Orlov at Fac Surgical

Clinic, then at Surgical Dept, Khar'kov Province Zemstvo Hospital; 1914–18 mil surgeon; 1918–21 dissector, Chair of Operative Surgery and Topographical Anatomy, Khar'kov Univ; from 1921 asst prof from 1926 dir, Khar'kov Inst of Med Mech (now Sitenko Inst of Traumatology and Orthopedics); 1927–28 toured clinics in Germany, Italy and Austria; created new therapeutic institutions, including a children's orthopedic "prophylactorium" and a "labor prophylactorium", which were subsequently established in a number of Sov cities; founded first Ukr Chair of Orthopedics and Traumatology at Inst of Postgrad Med Training; 1927–40 founder-ed, journal "Ortopediya i travmatologiya"; from 1930 Presidium member, Surgical Section, Khar'kov Physicians' Assoc; from 1928 dep chm, Orthopedic Section, Khar'kov Med Soc; chm, Orthopedic Section, Learned Med Council, Ukr Pop Comrt of Health; member, Sci Prosthetics Council, RSFSR Pop Comrt of Soc Security; from 1931 Presidium member, Khar'kov Med Soc; from 1932 Presidium member, CC, Ukr Red Cross; from 1936 Presidium chm, Ukr Soc of Orthopedists and Traumatologists; member, All-Union Surgical Soc; member, Learned Med Council, USSR Pop Comrt of Health; hon member, Leningrad, Khar'kov, Tbilisi, Baku, Odessa, and Dnepropetrovsk orthopedic soc; hon member, Moscow Soc of Surgeons and Orthopedists; *Died:* 13 Jan 1940 of cancer of the liver.

SIVERS, Rudol'f Ferdinandovich (1892–1918) Mil commander; CP member from 1917; *Born:* 23 Nov 1892 in Petersburg, son of a Bavarian immigrant office worker; *Career:* during WW 1 drafted into Civil Defense unit; from Nov 1915 ensign, 436th Novoladozhsk Infantry Regt; after 1917 Feb Revol elected member, regt comt; co-founder and co-ed, 12th Army Bolshevik newspaper "Okopnaya pravda"; July 1917 arrested by Provisional Govt; during 1917 Oct Revol released from prison; commanded Red Guard and sailors detachment which fought at Pulkovo against Kerenskiy and Gen Krasnov's troops; Nov 1917 transferred with his detachment to the Ukr; 24 Feb 1918 his troops took Rostov-on-Don; Mar–Apr 1918 commanded 5th Sov Army (later renamed the 2nd Special Army); from Summer 1918 commanded special brigade (from Sept 1918 1st Special Ukr Brigade) as part of 9th Army on Southern Front; 15 Nov 1918 seriously wounded in action near vil Zhelnovka; *Died:* 8 Dec 1918 in Moscow; 1919 buried on Field of Mars, Petrograd.

SKACHKOV, Pyotr Yemel'yanovich (1892–1964) Historian and sinologist; *Born:* 13 Feb 1892; *Educ:* 1925 grad Leningrad Inst of Living Oriental Languages; *Career:* specialized in Chinese bibliography, historiography and the publ of historical documents; 1925–27 worked with group of mil advisers in China; from 1930 senior assoc, Inst of Oriental Studies (from 1960 Inst of the Peoples of Asia), USSR Acad of Sci; 1932 completed compilation of bibliography of Russian-language books and articles on China beginning from 1730; 1960 enlarged bibliography to include publ up to 1957; also wrote an unpublished history of sinology in Russia up to 1917; *Died:* 8 Nov 1964.

SKIPIN, Georgiy Vasil'yevich (1900–1964) Physiologist; Dr of Med; prof; corresp member, RSFSR Acad of Pedag Sci from 1953; CP member from 1946; *Born:* 22 Mar 1900; *Educ:* 1926 grad Leningrad Mil Med Acad; *Career:* 1923 began research work under I. P. Pavlov, in whose laboratories he worked until 1934; from 1934 taught at various higher educ establishments in Donetsk, Vinnitsa, Alma-Ata and Ivanovo; from 1952 head, Laboratory of Motor Reflexes, Moscow Inst of Higher Nervous Activity, USSR Acad of Sci; did research on the physiology of higher nervous activity and conditioned reflexes; made a major study of the motor (kinesthetic) analyzer; contributed to knowledge of the physiology of voluntary movements and developed the sci basis of various aspects of physical educ; *Publ: O vzaimodeystvii protsessov vneshnego i vnutrennego tormozheniya* (The Interaction of the External and Internal Inhibition Processes) (1918); *O sistemnosti v rabote bol'shikh polushariy* (Systematism in the Function of the Large Hemispheres) (1938); *Analiz vysshey nervnoy deyatel'nosti sobaki po uslozhnennoy sekretorno-dvigatel'noy metodike* (An Analysis of Canine Higher Nervous Activity by the Compound Secretory Motoric Method) (1941); *Vyrabotka uslovnykh dvigatel'nykh refleksov na zritel'nyy razdrazhitel' u obez'yan gamadril* (The Development of Conditioned Reflexes to a Visual Stimulus in Hamadryads) (1933); *K izucheniyu fiziologicheskogo mekhanizma tak nazyvayemykh proizvol'nykh dvizheniy* (The Physiological Mechanism of So-Called Voluntary Movements) (1951); *K voprosu o lokalizatsii protsessov uslovnogo (vnutrennego) tormozheniya u sobak* (The Localization of the Process of Conditioned [Internal] Inhibition in Dogs) (1956); *O vzaimodeystvii razlichnykh form dvigatel'ykh oboronitel'nykh uslovnykh refleksov u zhivotnykh* (The Interaction of Various Forms of Conditioned Motoric Defense Reflexes in Animals) (1959); *Died:* 6 June 1964.

SKITALETS (real name: PETROV), Stepan Gavrilovich (1869–1941) Russian writer; *Born:* 28 Oct 1869 in Samara Province, son of a peasant; *Educ:* studied at teachers' seminary; *Career:* in 1890's began to write; from 1900 member, "Medium" lit assoc; 1922–34 lived abroad, mainly in Harbin; 1934 returned to USSR; *Publ:* stories *Polevoy sud* (The Field Court) (1905); verse *Tikho stalo krugom* (And All Around Was Still) (1906); autobiographical novelette *Etapy* (Stages) (1908); novel *Dom Chernovykh* (The Chernovs' House) (1929); reminiscences of Lev Tolstoy, Gorky, Chekhov, etc (1937); *Died:* 25 June 1941.

SKLYANSKIY, Efraim Markovich (1892–1925) Govt and Party official; mil commander; physician; CP member from 1913; *Born:* 31 July 1892 in Fastov, of middle-class parents; *Educ:* 1911–16 studied at Med Fac, Kiev Univ; *Career:* propaganda work for Kiev RSDRP Comt; from 1916 soldier, then physician, Russian Army; after 1917 Feb Revol member, soldiers' comts; member, soldiers' comt, 19th Corps; chm, soldiers' comt, 5th Army; member, Dvinsk RSDRP(B) Comt; deleg and Presidium member, 2nd All-Russian Congress of Soviets; member, Petrograd Mil Revol Comt; mustered artillery to fight Kerenskiy's troops; comr, Main Staff and Headquarters of Supr Commander in Chief at Mogilev; 1917–18 Collegium member, and Dep Pop Comr of the Navy; from Mar 1918 member, RSFSR Higher Mil Council; from Oct 1918 dep chm, RSFSR Revol Mil Council; member, Defense Council; 1920–21 member, Labor and Defense Council and Collegium member, Pop Comrt of Health; deleg at 10th Party Congress; Apr 1924 assigned to Supr Sovnarkhoz; chm, Moscow Cloth Trust; *Died:* 27 Aug 1925 drowned while on assignment in America.

SKOBELEV, Matvey Ivanovich (1885–1939) Politician; Menshevik from 1903; CP member from 1922; *Born:* 1885 in Baku, son of a peasant; *Career:* from 1903 Party organizer and propagandist in Baku; 1907–12 lived abroad and worked for newspaper "Pravda" in Vienna; from 1912 Transcaucasian dep, 4th State Duma and one of the leaders of the Soc-Democratic faction; 1914 helped direct Baku gen strike; after 1917 Feb Revol member, Exec Comt and dep chm, Petrograd Sov; dep chm, Centr Exec Comt of 1st convocation; May–Aug 1917 Min of Labor in Provisional Govt; after 1917 Oct Revol worked for cooperative movement; late 1918 moved to Transcaucasia; late 1920 emigrated; 1921–late 1923 worked in France, establishing trade relations between Sov Russia and France; from 1924 member, Sov trade deleg in London; 1925 helped found Sov mission and trade mission in Paris; Centr Union of Consumer Soc rep in Paris and Brussels; 1925–26 chm, For Trade Section, USSR Gosplan; 1926–30 member, Main Concessions Comt and chm, RSFSR Concessions Comt; from 1930 worked for Magnitostroy Trust; 1936–37 worked for All-Union Radio Comt; 1937 arrested by State Security organs; *Died:* 1939 in imprisonment; posthumously rehabilitated.

SKOCHINSKIY, Aleksandr Aleksandrovich (1874–1960) Mining specialist; member, USSR Acad of Sci from 1935; Hon Sci and Tech Worker of RSFSR from 1934; Hero of Socialist Labor from 1954; *Born:* 13 July 1874 in Olekminsk, now Yakut ASSR; *Educ:* 1900 grad Petersburg Mining Inst; *Career:* 1906–30 prof, Petersburg Mining Inst; from 1930 prof, Moscow Mining Inst; simultaneously 1935–38 head, Mining Group, Dept of Tech Sci, USSR Acad of Sci; from 1938 dir, Mining Inst, USSR Acad of Sci; 1944–51 simultaneously chm, Presidium, West-Siberian Branch, USSR Acad of Sci; specialized in ventilation, gas conditions and fire-fighting in mines; *Publ: Rudnichnyy vozdukh i osnovnoy zakon dvizheniya yego po vyrabotkam* (Air in Mines and the Basic Law of Its Motion in Mine Workings) (1904); *Rudnichnaya atmosfera* (Mine Atmosphere) (2nd ed, 1933); coauthor, *Issledovaniya v oblasti primeneniya antipirogenov pri bor'be s rudnichnymi pozharami endogennogo proiskhozhdeniya* (Research on the Use of Antipyrogenes for Extinguishing Mine Fires of Edogenous Origin) (1947); coauthor, *Rudnichnaya ventilyatsiya* (Ventilation of Mines) (2nd ed, 1951); coauthor, *Rudnichnyye pozhary* (Mine Fires) (2nd ed, 1954); *Awards:* five Orders of Lenin; two Orders of the Red Banner of Labor; "Hammer and Sickle" gold medal; two Stalin Prizes (1950 and 1951); *Died:* 6 Oct 1960.

SKORODUMOV, Nikolay Vladimirovich (1887–1947) Russian stage dir; *Born:* 1887; *Educ:* studied at Moscow Business College and

Natural Sci Dept, Physics and Mathematics Fac, Moscow Univ; *Career:* 1906, while a student, founded in vil Burmakino, Yaroslavl' Province, a folk theater which existed until 1912; together with the young actor B.V. Gotovtsev, staged here: "Boris Godunov"; Lev Tolstoy's *Vlast' t'my* (The Power of Darkness); Ostrovskiy's *Ne vsyo kotu maslenitsa* (All Good Things Come to an End); *Publ: Novyy metod uproshchyonnykh postanovok* (A New Method of Simplified Productions) (1914); *Ustroystvo stseny i dekoratsiy v narodnom teatre* (Arranging the Stage and Sets in a Folk Theater) (1920); *Died:* 1947.

SKOROPADSKIY, Pavel Petrovich (1873–1945) Russian gen, politician and landowner; *Born:* 1873, son of a nobleman; *Career:* owned large estates in Chernigov and Poltava Province; aide-de-campe to Nicholas II; During WW 1 commanded a cavalry div; Oct 1917 appointed commander of Ukr Centr Rada mil formations at Chigrina Congress of Free Cossacks; 29 Apr 1918–14 Dec 1918 Hetman of Ukr; Dec 1918 fled to Germany, where he continued to oppose Sov system until his death; *Died:* 1945.

SKOVNO, A.A. (Abram) (1888–1938) Party official; CP member from 1903; *Born:* 1888; *Career:* 1908 fled from exile and went abroad; from 1910 lived in France; member, Paris RSDRP Section; from 1914 lived in Switzerland; returned to Russia together with Lenin; after 1917 Oct Revol Party and admin work in Moscow; arrested by State Security organs; *Died:* 1938 in imprisonment.

SKRYPNIK, Nikolay Alekseyevich (Party names: SHCHUR; SHCHENSKIY; STEPAN VASIL'YEVICH; NIKOLAY; PETERBURZHETS; VALER'YAN; IVAN VASIL'YEVICH) (1872–1933) Govt and Party official; CP member from 1897; *Born:* 25 Jan 1872 in vil Yasnovatyy, Yekaterinoslav Province, son of a railroad official; *Educ:* studied at Petersburg Technol Inst; *Career:* 1901 arrested for 4 Mar demonstration on Petersburg's Kazan' Square and exiled to Yekaterinoslav; sided with Lenin's "Iskra" group; early 1902 arrested and exiled to Yakutsk Province; fled from exile and worked for Party orgs in Tsaritsyn, Samara, Yekaterinoslav, Yaroslavl' and Odessa; 1905 deleg at 3rd RSDRP Congress; 1905–07 secr, Petersburg RSDRP Comt; then worked in Riga and Krasnoyarsk for CC, RSDRP; exiled to Turukhansk Kray but again fled and in 1907 worked for Petersburg RSDRP Comt; Party work in Ukr, Volga area, Moscow and in Urals; 1908 met Lenin in Geneva; 1908–13 exiled in Yakutsk Province; 1913 ed, Petersburg journal "Voprosy strakhovaniya"; 1914 member, ed bd, newspaper "Pravda"; after 1917 Feb Revol worked in Petrograd as chm and secr, Centr Council of Factory and Plant Comts; member, All-Russian Centr Exec Comt of 1st and 2nd convocations; 1917 at 6th Party Congress elected cand member, CC, RSDRP(B); played active part in 1917 Oct Revol; member, Petrograd Mil Revol Comt; from Dec 1917 Ukr Pop Comr of Labor and Ind; from Mar 1918 chm, Ukr Sov Govt and Ukr Pop Comr of For Affairs; co-founder, CP(B) Ukr; from Jan 1919 Ukr Pop Comr of State Control; from Jan 1920 Pop Comr of State Control; from 1920 Pop Comr of Workers and Peasants' Inspection; fought in Civil War; head, Special Dept, Southwestern Front; from July 1921 Ukr Pop Comr of Internal Affairs; 1922–27 Ukr Pop Comr of Justice; and Ukr Prosecutor-Gen; 1927–33 Ukr Pop Comr of Educ; from Feb 1933 dep chm, Ukr Council of Pop Comr and chm, Ukr Gosplan; deleg at 9th–16th Party Congresses; at 12th–14th Party Congresses elected cand member, CC, CPSU(B); at 15th and 16th Party Congresses elected member, CC, CPSU(B); 1920–33 member, CC, CP(B) Ukr; 1923–25 cand Politburo member, CC, CP(B) Ukr; 1925–33 Politburo member, CC, CP(B) Ukr; deleg at all Comintern Congresses; at 6th Comintern Congress elected member, Comintern Exec Comt; member, USSR Centr Exec Comt of 3rd, 4th and 6th Convocations; from 1927 chm, Sov of Nationalities, USSR Supr Sov; wrote over 270 works on sci, culture, Party history, art, lit and the nationality problem; member, USSR Communist Acad; member, Ukr and Bel Acad of Sci; accused of nationalist deviation; *Awards:* Order of the Red Banner (1922); Order of the Ukr Red Banner of Labor (1928); *Died:* 7 Apr 1933 committed suicide as the result of a polit smear campaign; buried in Khar'kov; posthumously rehabilitated.

SKVERI, Mikhail Petrovich (1856–1924) Revolutionary; *Born:* 8 Nov 1856 in Odessa, son of an Italian and a Russian peasant-woman; *Educ:* studied at Odessa non-classical high-school; *Career:* worked at Odessa plant; met Ye. O. Zaslavskiy and became active member, South Russian Workers' League; attended meetings, distributed pamphlets and acted as cashier and dep, League group at Blanshard Plant; Jan 1876 arrested; 1877 tried in case of South Russian Workers' League and exiled to Tobol'sk Province; from 1884 lived in Odessa under secret police surveillance; organized sunday schools, health insurance schemes, factory libraries and reading rooms; 1907 helped organize All-Russian Teachers' Congress, for which he was again arrested; 1917 active in establishing public libraries; dept head, Odessa Public Library; worked for Odessa Archives of the Revol; contributed to "Katorga i ssylka" and other journals; *Died:* 13 Oct 1924.

SKVIRSKIY, Boris Yevseyevich (1887–1941) Diplomat; *Born:* 1887; *Career:* from 1920 in dipl service; 1920 worked for Min of For Affairs, Far Eastern Republ; 1921–22 member, Far Eastern Republ deleg in USA; 1922–23 Pop Comrt of For Affairs dipl agent in USA; 1933–36 counsellor and Sov charge d'affaires in USA; 1936–37 USSR plen repl in Afghanistan; arrested by State Security organs; *Died:* 1941 in imprisonment.

SKVORTSOV, Mikhail Aleksandrovich (1876–1963) Pathoanatomist; specialist in the pathological anatomy of children; prof from 1939; member, USSR Acad of Med Sci from 1945; Hon Sci Worker of RSFSR from 1942; *Born:* 2 Oct 1876 in Moscow; *Educ:* 1899 grad Med Fac, Moscow Univ; *Career:* after grad worked as zemstvo physician in Kaluga Province; 1902–19 asst prof, Chair of Pathological Anatomy, Med Fac, Moscow Univ; 1911–53 dissector, Morozovskaya Hospital (now 1st Clinican Children's Hospital), where he specialized in child pathology and established a 1,500-exhibit museum on this subject and a histological museum containing 1,500 specimens; 1920–39 assoc prof, from 1939 prof, Chair of Pathology, 2nd Moscow Med Inst; 1942–47 prof, 1st Moscow Med Inst; from 1945 assoc Inst of Normal and Pathological Morphology and Inst of Pediatrics, USSR Acad of Med Sci; wrote 104 works; *Publ: Ocherki patologicheskoy anatomii detskikh infektsionnykh bolezney* (Studies in the Pathological Anatomy of Infectious Children's Diseases) (1925); coauthor, *Kostno-sustavnoy tuberkulyoz u detey* (Osteoarticular Tuberculosis in Children) (1928); *Gistomorfologiya revmaticheskogo miokardita i yeyo klinicheskoye znacheniye* (The Histomorphology of Rheumatic Myocarditis and Its Clinical Significance) (1938); *Morfologiya i patogenez pupochnogo sepsisa* (The Morphology and Pathogenesis of Omphalic Sepsis) (1945); *Patologicheskaya anatomiya vazhneyshikh zabolevaniy detskogo vozrasta* (The Pathological Anatomy of the Most Important Childhood Diseases) (1946); co-ed and coauthor, *Patologicheskaya anatomiya zabolevaniy detskogo vozrasta i novorozhdyonnykh* (The Pathological Anatomy of Children's and Babies' Diseases) (1960), etc; *Awards:* Order of Lenin; Order of the Red Banner of Labor; medals; *Died:* 8 Mar 1963 in Moscow.

SKVORTSOV-STEPANOV (real name: SKVORTSOV), Ivan Ivanovich (pen name: I. STEPANOV) (1870–1928) Party and govt official; writer; historian; economist; CP member from 1896; *Born:* 8 Mar 1870, son of a worker; *Educ:* 1890 grad Moscow Teachers' Inst; *Career:* after grad worked as schoolteacher in Moscow; 1891 joined revol movement; 1895 arrested for revol propaganda among workers and exiled to Tula; 1901 re-arrested and exiled for three years to Eastern Siberia; 1905 worked in Moscow; member, Lit-Lecturers' Group, Moscow Party Comt; 1906 deleg at 4th (Amalgamative) RSDRP Congress; at the Congress sided with Lenin; 1907 Bolshevik cand in elections to 3rd State Duma; 1911 again Bolshevik cand in elections to State Duma; arrested and exiled for three years to Astrakhan'; after 1917 Feb Revol headed ed bd, newspaper "Izvestia Moskovskogo soveta rabochikh i soldatskikh deputatov"; then member, ed bd, newspaper "Sotsial-demokrat"; active in 1917 Oct Revol; member, Moscow Mil Revol Comt; at 2nd All-Russian Congress of Soviets appointed Pop Comr of Finance; then returned to lit work and journalism; 1919–20 asst chm, All-Russian Council of Workers' Cooperatives; Bd member, Centr Union of Consumer Soc; dep chm, ed bd, State Publ House; from 1925 coordinating ed, newspaper "Izvestia TsIK SSSR i VTsIK"; from 1926 dir, Lenin Inst, CC, CPSU(B); co-ed, "Bol'shaya Sovetskaya Entsiklopediya" (Large Soviet Encyclopedia); 1921–24 member, RCP(B) Centr Auditing Commission; from 1925 member, CC, CPSU(B); elected member, All-Russian and USSR Centr Exec Comt; from 1927 also dep mang ed, newspaper "Pravda"; Presidium member, Communist Acad; 1926–28 head, ed bd, newspaper "Leningradskaya pravda"; wrote numerous articles and major works on econ, history, natural sci, atheism, etc; translated from German into Russian three vol of Marx's "Kapital" and many other works by Marx and Engels; *Publ: Parizhskaya kommuna 1871 goda i voprosy taktiki v proletarskoy revolyutsii* (The 1871 Paris Commune and Tactics in the Proletarian Revolution) (1921); *Elektrifi-*

katsiya RSFSR v svyazi s perekhodnoy fazoy mirovogo khozyaystva (The Electrification of the RSFSR in Connection with the Transitional State of the World Economy) (1922); *Died:* 8 Oct 1928 of typhoid; buried on Moscow's Red Square.

SLASHCHEV, Yakov Aleksandrovich (1885–1928) White Army gen; *Born:* 1885; *Career:* fought against Red Army during Civil War in Crimea; 1920 returned to Russia after a period abroad and worked at Higher Infantry School; *Died:* 1928; killed by relative of a man he shot in Crimea.

SLAVIN, Iosif Yeremeyevich (1893–1938) Mil commander; army comr, 2nd class; CP member from 1917; *Born:* 11 Apr 1893 in Belaya Tserkov'; *Career:* took part in 1917 Oct Revol in Kiev Province; 1918 worked for underground Kiev RSDRP(B) Org; during Civil War head, brigade, then div polit dept; 1920–23 head, Polit Bd, Kiev Mil Distr; then member, Mil Council, Leningrad Mil Distr; dep head, Red Army Polit Bd; member, Revol Mil Council; 1935–38 head, Red Army Mil Training Establishments Bd; member, Mil Council, Pop Comrt of Defense; arrested by State Security organs; *Publ: Voprosy voyennogo dela v svete materialisticheskoy dialektiki* (Military Affairs in the Light of Materialist Dialectics) (1935); *Died:* 15 Mar 1938 in imprisonment.

SLAVIN, Nikolay Vasil'yevich (1903–1958) Mil commander; diplomat; CP member from 1927; *Born:* 16 May 1903 in Bryansk Province; *Career:* 1917, at age 14, began work; from 1921 in Red Army, where he rose from the ranks to lt-gen; 1946–50 senior posts with Gen Staff; 1950–53 mil training commands; from 1953 head, 2nd European Dept, USSR Min of For Affairs; 1955–58 USSR amb in Denmark; *Awards:* Order of Lenin; three Orders of the Red Banner; Order of Kutuzov, 1st and 2nd Class; Order of the Fatherland War, 1st Class; Order of the Red Star; medals; *Died:* 9 Sept 1958.

SLAVINSKIY, Karl Ernestovich (1892–1967) Party and govt official; CP member from 1911; *Born:* 8 Mar 1892; *Educ:* 1929 grad Mil Polit Acad; *Career:* 1911 arrested and exiled to Arkhangel'sk Province; Oct 1917 took part in Bolshevik coup in Petrograd; during Civil War comr of mil units on Northern and Southern Fronts; during WW 2 admin work in Gorky Oblast; from 1945 worked in Lat SSR; from 1952 assoc, then dir, Raynis State Lit Museum; from 1962 pensioner; *Died:* 19 Dec 1967.

SLEPNYOV, Mavrikiy Trofimovich (1896–1965) Explorer and pilot; col; CP member from 1934; *Born:* 1896 in Petersburg; *Educ:* grad Gatchina Aviation School; 1935 grad Air Force Eng Acad; *Career:* from age 16 worked at a factory; during WW 1 served as an aerial observer; fought in Civil War; 1922–25 worked at Moscow Aviation School; from 1925 flew for Centr Asian airline; 1929 worked in Yakutia; in same year searched for crew of missing American plane and accompanied bodies back to US; explored northern USSR, undertaking a footmarch from the mouth of the Anabara River to Dudinka during which he mapped the shoreline and discovered new islands; 1934 helped to rescue crew of SS "Chelyuskin" after it was crushed in an ice-floe in the Bering Straits; from 1935 member, USSR Centr Exec Comt; wrote several books and articles; *Awards:* Hero of the Sov Union (1934); two Orders of Lenin; Order of the Red Banner; medals; *Died:* Dec 1965.

SLUTSKIY, Abram Aronovich (1898–1938) Govt official; comr of State Security, 2nd Class; dept head, Main State Security Bd, NKVD; CP member from 1917; *Born:* 1898, son of a railroad official; *Career:* from age 16 worked at a factory; then private, Russian Army; after 1917 Oct Revol in Centr Asia; led Red Army unit against the Basmachi; *Awards:* various orders; *Died:* 17 Feb 1938 killed in the course of duty.

SLUTSKIY, Anton Iosifovich (? –1918) Party and govt official; CP member; *Born:* date and place of birth unknown; *Career:* 1905 joined revol movement; after 1917 Feb Revol Party org at Obukhov Plant, Petrograd; member, Exec Commission, Petrograd RSDRP(B) Comt; Petrograd RSDRP(B) Comt deleg at 6th RSDRP(B) Congress; Oct 1917 took part in Bolshevik coup in Petrograd; at 2nd All-Russian Congress of Soviets elected member, All-Russian Centr Exec Comt; Mar 1918 appointed chm, Council of Pop Comr of the Tavrida (Crimean) Sov Republ; *Died:* 22 Apr 1918 executed by White troops in Alushta.

SLYN'KO, Pyotr Fyodorovich (1895–1919) Party official; CP member from 1918; *Born:* 25 Jan 1895 in vil Orzhitsa, now Poltava Oblast, son of a peasant; *Career:* 1915 joined revol movement; 1915 arrested and exiled to Siberia; after 1917 Feb Revol worked in Lubny; sided with Soc-Democrats and Socialist-Revolutionaries; 1918 attended 1st Congress of CP(B) Ukr, at which he was elected cand member, CC, CP(B) Ukr; underground Party work in Kiev and Poltava; member, Kiev Oblast Comt, CP(B) Ukr; at 4th (Sept) Plenum of CC, CP(B) Ukr coopted member, CC; at 2nd Congress of CP(B) Ukr elected member, CC, CP(B) Ukr; late 1918–early 1919 underground Party work as member, Kiev Province Comt, CP(B) Ukr, member, Kiev Province Revol Comt, Presidium member, Kiev Province Exec Comt and chm, Kiev Revol Tribunal; at 3rd All-Ukr Congress of Soviets elected member, All-Ukr Centr Exec Comt; summer 1919 assigned by CC, CP(B) Ukr to run Khar'kov Party org; arrested by mil authorities of Volunteer Army; *Died:* 30 Nov 1919 executed.

SMIDOVICH, Pyotr Germogenovich (1874–1935) Govt official; CP member from 1898; *Born:* 7 May 1874 in Rogachev, Mogilev Province; *Educ:* 1892–94 studied at Moscow Univ; grad Electr Eng High School, Paris; *Career:* active in student polit movement at Moscow Univ; 1894 expelled from Univ and exiled to Tula for revol work; 1895 arrested for founding illegal Soc-Democratic circles; late 1895 went abroad; after studies in Paris worked at factories in France and Belgium; 1898 returned to Russia with the passport of a Belgian worker and was hired as electrician at Bryansk Steel Plant; then worked in Yekaterinoslav, Moscow and Petersburg; late 1900 arrested for membership of Petersburg RSDRP Comt, spent one year in investigative custody and then, as a foreigner, was deported from Russia without right of return; shortly afterwards returned to Russia with another passport; 1901–02 worked as "Iskra" agent, delivering newspapers from Marseilles to Batum; 1902 worked for underground printing press in Uman', which was then printing "Iskra"; after 2nd RSDRP Congress sided with Bolsheviks; 1905 propaganda work in Baku and Tula; Dec 1905 played active part in armed uprising in Moscow; 1905–08 member, Moscow Okrug RSDRP Comt, then member, Moscow RSDRP Comt; founded in Moscow illegal trade-union bureau; 1906 deleg at Stockholm RSDRP Congress; until 1912 worked at Moscow Streetcar Depot; from 1912 electr eng at Moscow "1886" Power Plant (renamed after him following the Oct Revol); member, Petersburg, Moscow, Baku, Ural and Northern RSDRP(B) Comts; during WW 1 sided with Bolsheviks' defeatist stand; 1916 member, Moscow Bureau, CC, RSDRP(B); after 1917 Feb Revol elected member and Presidium member, Moscow Sov of Workers and Soldiers' Dept; after 1917 Oct Revol Presidium member, Supr Sovnarkhoz; 1918 chm, Moscow Sov; simultaneously head, Power Dept, Supr Sovnarkhoz; late 1918–1919 chm, Moscow Province Sovnarkhoz; 1920 head, Moscow Educ Dept; 1920–22 dep chm, Commission for Famine Relief; 1920 member, Sov deleg at peace talks with Poland; from 1917 Presidium member, All-Russian, then USSR Centr Exec Comt; 1921 at 10th RCP(B) Congress elected member, RCP(B) Centr Control Commission; from 1924 chm, Commission for Apportioning Land to Jewish Workers, Presidium, Sov of Nationalities, USSR Centr Exec Comt; chm, Comt for Assistance to the Peoples of the Outlying North; from 1927 also chm, Centr Bureau of Regional Studies; *Awards:* Order of Lenin; *Died:* 16 Apr 1935 in Moscow.

SMIDOVICH, Sof'ya Nikolayevna (1872–1934) Party official; CP member from 1898; *Born:* 20 Mar 1872 in Tula, daughter of a lawyer; *Career:* teacher by profession; Party propaganda work in Moscow, Tula, Kiev and Kaluga; frequently arrested and exiled; from 1914 member, from Feb 1917 secr, Moscow Oblast Bureau, CC, RSDRP(B); after 1917 Oct Revol secr, Presidium, Moscow Sov; 1918–19 Collegium member, Moscow Educ Dept; 1919–22 head, Women's Dept, Moscow RCP(B) Comt; 1922–24 head, Dept of Women Workers and Peasants, CC, RCP(B); ed, journals "Rabotnitsa" and "Kommunistka"; at 14th and 15th Party Congresses elected member, CPSU(B) Centr Control Commission; also member, Party Collegium, Centr Control Commission; from 1931 dep chm, Comt for Improving the Working and Living Conditions of Women, USSR Centr Exec Comt; Presidium member, and dep chm, All-Union Soc of Old Bolshevik; *Awards:* Order of Lenin; *Died:* 26 Nov 1934.

SMILGA, Ivar Tenisovich (1892–1938) Economist; Party and govt official; CP member from 1907; *Born:* 1892, son of a peasant; *Career:* 1906 his father was executed by a punitive squad for his active part in the 1905 Revol; worked as propagandist and agitator in Lat, Moscow and Petersburg; several times arrested and twice exiled; after 1917 Feb Revol returned from exile; at 1917 Apr Party Conference elected member, CC, RSDRP(B); during 1917 Oct Revol chm, oblast comt of Russian soviets in Finland; took part in 1917 Oct and 1918 Finnish Revol; 1918–21, during Civil

War, on mil work: member, Revol Mil Council, 3rd Army and Eastern, Southwestern, Western, Southern and Caucasian Fronts; from 1921 admin econ work; 1921–23 dep chm, Supr Sovnarkhoz and head, Main Fuel Bd; 1924–26 dep chm, USSR Gosplan; 1925–27 rector and prof, Plekhanov Inst of Nat Econ; from 1927 chm, Far Eastern Bank; from 1930 dep head, Draft Bd, USSR Supr Sovnarkhoz; 1920–21, during trade-union controversy, sided with Trotsky; after 14th Party Congress joined Trotskyist opposition; 1927, at 15th Congress, expelled from Party; summer 1929 recanted his errors and dissociated himself from Trotskyist opposition; Jan 1930 readmitted to Party; at 6th, 7th, 8th and 13th Party Congresses elected member, and at 9th–12th Party Congresses elected cand member, CC, CPSU(B); again expelled from Party for alleged anti-Party activities and brought to trial; *Publ: Voyennyye ocherki* (Military Studies); *Vosstanovitel'nyy protsess* (The Process of Restoration); *Died:* 1938 in imprisonment.

SMIRNOV, Aleksandr Petrovich (party names: FOMA; TSVETKOV) (1877–1938) Party and govt official; CP member from 1896; *Born:* 1877, son of a peasant; *Career:* in his youth worked as shepherd; at age 16 began work at Tver' textile mill; 1895 moved to Petersburg and became involved in revol movement; 1897 joined Petersburg League for the Liberation of the Working Class; 1898 arrested and exiled; shortly afterwards began work at Tver' factory; 1900 again exiled to Novgorod; 1901 returned to Tver', where he worked as a weaver and founded a workers' circle; 1903 arrested; 1904 released from prison, returned to Tver' and continued revol work, joining Tver' RSDRP Comt and helping to run an underground printing press; during 1905 Revol elected asst chm, Tver' Sov and head of battle squads; moved to Petersburg after suppression of revol in Tver'; lived in Petersburg illegally, elected member, Petersburg RSDRP(B) Comt; deleg, Stockholm Party Congress; 1907 deleg, London Party Congress; returned to Russia, was arrested and a year later exiled to Ust'-Sysol'sk; 1908 fled from exile and returned to Petersburg, but was soon arrested and returned to Ust'-Sysol'sk; completed term of exile and moved to Moscow, but was shortly arrested and exiled for three years to Narym; during this period elected member, CC, RSDRP(B); with start of WW I drafted into Russian Army and sent to Persia as a driver; after 1917 Feb Revol worked in Moscow Province; Presidium member, Moscow Province Sov; after 1917 Oct Revol Collegium member, NKVD and Dep Pop Comr of Internal Affairs; from 1919 Collegium member, Pop Comrt of Food; 1923 appointed Pop Comr of Agric; fall 1923–spring 1928 secr-gen, Peasants International (Krestintern); 1927–29 dep chm, RSFSR Council of Pop Comr; 1928–30 secr, CC, CPSU(B); from 1930 Presidium member, USSR Supr Sovnarkhoz and chm, All-Union Forestry Ind Trust; then chm, All-Union Council for Communal Utilities, USSR Centr Exec Comt; at 13th–16th Party Congresses elected member, CC, CPSU(B); 1934 expelled from Party for alleged anti-Party activities; arrested by State Security organs; *Died:* 1938 in imprisonment.

SMIRNOV, Ivan Ivanovich (1909–1965) Historian; Dr of History; prof; CP member from 1941; *Born:* 1909; *Educ:* 1930 grad Vyatka Teachers' Training Inst; did postgrad studies at USSR Acad of Sci; *Career:* senior assoc, Leningrad Section, Inst of History, USSR Acad of Sci; prof, Leningrad Univ; specialized in soc and polit history of medieval Russia and history of feudalism and peasant movements; made a special study of age of Ivan the Terrible; *Publ: Ivan Groznyy* (Ivan the Terrible) (1944); *Vosstaniye Bolotnikova 1606–07* (The 1606–07 Bolotnikov Uprising) (1949); *Ocherki politicheskoy istorii Russkogo gosudarstva 30-50-ykh godov XVI veka* (An Outline Political History of the Russian State in the 1530's – 1550's) (1958); *Zametki o feodal'noy Rusi* (Notes on Feudal Rus) (1962); *Maksim Grek i mitropolit Makariy* Maxim Grek and Metropolitan Makariy) (1963); *Ocherki sotsial'no-ekonomicheskikh otnosheniy Rusi XII–XIII vekov* (Studies in the Social and Economic Relations of Rus in the 12th–13th Century) (1963); *Awards:* two Badges of Hon; Stalin Prize (1950); medals; *Died:* 14 May 1965.

SMIRNOV, Ivan Nikitich (1881–1936) Party and govt official; CP member from 1899; *Born:* 1881, son of a peasant; *Career:* railroad, then factory worker; 1899 arrested and exiled to Irkutsk Province; 1903 fled from exile and did Party propaganda and org work in Tver' and Vyshniy-Volochok; 1904 arrested; 1905 Party org, Moscow's Lefortov Rayon; during 1905 Revol Party org, Blagushin Sub-Rayon, then Railroad Rayon, Moscow; 1909 exiled from Moscow and moved to Petersburg, where he worked as Party organizer; 1910 arrested and exiled to Narym; 1912 fled from exile and worked in Rostov and Khar'kov; 1913 arrested in Khar'kov and returned to Narym; by an oversight released en route from prison and returned to Moscow; 1914 re-arrested and installed in Narym, where he remained until 1916; 1916 drafted into Russian Army; served in Tomsk, where he conducted revol propaganda among troops; after 1917 Feb Revol member, Exec Comt, Tomsk Sov of Soldiers' Dep; Aug 1917 moved to Moscow and founded "Volna" Party publ house; fought in Civil War; member, Revol Mil Council, Eastern Front; commanded 5th Army; after defeat of Kolchak's forces, in charge of all Sov and Party work in Siberia as chm, Siberian Revol Comt; 1922 secr, Petrograd CPSU(B) Comt and secr, Northwestern Bureau, CC, CPSU(B); then Presidium member, Supr Sovnarkhoz; 1923–late 1927 USSR Pop Comr of Posts and Telegraphs; at 8th and 10th Party Congresses elected cand member, and at 9th Congress member, CC, RCP(B); after 14th CPSU(B) Congress sided with "Leftist Opposition"; 1927 at 15th Party Congress expelled from CPSU(B); fall 1929 broke with Leftist Opposition and recanted his errors; 1930 re-admitted to Party; admin work; 1931 went to Germany on party assignment; Jan 1933 again expelled from Party for alleged "anti-Party activities" and sentenced to 10 years' imprisonment; Aug 1936 tried in connection with Trotsky-Zinoviev bloc; 24 Aug 1936 sentenced to death by Mil Collegium of USSR Supr Court; *Died:* 1936 executed.

SMIRNOV, Nikolay Ivanovich (1906–1962) Shipbuilding eng; chm, Exec Comt, Leningrad City Sov of Workers' Dep from 1955; cand member, CC, CPSU from 1956; CP member from 1931; *Born:* 1906; *Educ:* 1941 grad Leningrad Shipbuilding Inst; *Career:* 1921–35 consecutively blacksmith's apprentice, blacksmith, private in the Red Army; then foreman, dept head, various Leningrad plants; 1941–43 dept head, Rybinsk Shipyard; 1944–45 factory dir in Perm'; 1946–48 dir, Kiev's "Leninskaya kuznitsa" (Lenin Forge) Plant; 1949 dir, Gorky's "Krasnoye Sormovo" Plant; 1950–54 dir, Leningrad Kirov Plant; dep and Presidium member, RSFSR Supr Sov of 1955 covocation; dep, USSR Supr Sov of 1954, 1958 and 1962 convocations; from 1956 member, from 1960 Bureau member, Leningrad City CPSU Comt; 1959 visited Indonesia with USSR Supr Sov deleg; *Awards:* two Orders of Lenin (1955 and 1957); *Died:* 1962.

SMIRNOV, Pyotr Ivanovich (1897–1940) Naval commander; squadron commander, 2nd class; CP member from 1919; *Born:* 1897; *Career:* took part in 1917 Oct Revol in Petrograd; 1919–20 commanded Dnepropetrovsk Naval Flotilla; then senior commands in Sov Navy; arrested by State Security organs; *Died:* 17 Mar 1940 in imprisonment.

SMIRNOV, Sergey Sergeyevich (1895–1947) Geologist and mineralogist; prof; member, USSR Acad of Sci from 1943; *Born:* 16 Sept 1895 in Ivanovo; *Educ:* 1919 grad Petrograd Mining Inst; *Career:* 1919-30 lecturer, from 1930 prof, Petrograd (Leningrad) Mining Inst; simultaneously worked for Geological Comt (now All-Union Geological Research Inst); from 1924 member, from 1945 pres, All-Union Mineralogical Soc; from 1945 also head, Ore Dept, Inst of Geological Sci, USSR Acad of Sci; consultant, various govt establishments in the ore-mining and mineral ind; did research on ore deposits and ore-bearing regions in the Baykal and Transbaykal regions, the Northeastern USSR and the Maritime region; studied and described various iron, non-ferrous and rare metal deposits; contributed to the theory of ore-deposit formation; *Publ: Materialy k geologii i mineralogii Yuzhnogo Pribaykal'ya* (Material on the Geology and Mineralogy of the Southern Baykal) (1928); *K mineralogii Srednesibirskoy platformy* (The Mineralogy of the Central Siberian Platform) (1933); *O tikhookeanskom rudnom poyase* (The Pacific Ore Belt) (1946); *Nekotoryye obshchiye voprosy izucheniya rudnykh mestorozhdeniy* (Some General Problems of the Study of Ore Deposits) (1946); *O sovremennom sostoyanii teorii obrazovaniya magmatogennykh rudnykh mestorozhdeniy* (The Present State of the Theory of the Formation of Magmatogenous Ore Deposits) (1947); *Zona okisleniya sulfidnykh mestorozhdeniy* (The Oxidation Zone of Sulfide Deposits) (1951); *Awards:* three Orders of Lenin; Order of the Red Banner of Labor; Stalin Prize (1946); *Died:* 20 Aug 1947.

SMIRNOV, V.M. (1887–1937) Party and govt official; CP member from 1907; *Born:* 1887; *Career:* economist by profession; after 1917 Feb Revol worked in Moscow and helped edit "Sotsial-demokrat"; during 1917 Oct Revol member, Mil Revol Comt, Moscow Sov; after 1917 Oct Revol Presidium member, Supr

Sovnarkhoz; 1917 member, Commission to Revise the Party Program; his articles on this subject were published in the collection *Materialy po peresmotru partiynoy programmy* (Material on the Revision of the Party Program); fought in Civil War; member, Revol Mil Council, 5th and 16th Armies; then worked for econ organs; 1921–22 Presidium member, Gosplan; member, Commission to Utilize the Material Resources of the RSFSR; during the Brest Peace Treaty controversy sided with Leftist Communists and worked for ed staff, newspaper "Kommunist"; 24 Feb 1918 resigned his Party and govt posts in protest against Brest Peace Treaty; 1919 leading member of "Mil Opposition" at 8th Party Congress; 1920–21 sided with Democratic Centralism group; from 1923 member, Trotskyist opposition; 1926 broke with Trotskyism and joined with Sapronov to form a new opposition group which published the so-called "Fifteen-Signatory Anti-Revol Platform"; 1926 expelled from the Party for factionalist activities; 1926 re-admitted to Party; Dec 1927 again expelled from Party at 15th CPSU(B) Congress; subsequently sentenced for alleged anti-Sov activities; *Died:* 1937 in imprisonment.

SMIRNOV, Vasiliy Zakharovich (1899–1962) Pedag and historian; Dr of Pedag Sci from 1947; prof; corresp member, RSFSR Acad of Pedag Sci from 1955; CP member from 1940; *Born:* 9 Jan 1899; *Educ:* 1920 grad Moscow Inst of Public Educ; *Career:* 1931–37 assoc prof, then head, Chair of Pedag, Kuybyshev Teachers' Training Inst; from 1943 prof and head, Section for the History of Pedag and Schools, Moscow Inst of Pedag, RSFSR Acad of Pedag Sci; *Publ: Ya. A. Komenskiy o naglyadnosti v obuchenii* (Comenius on Visual Methods of Instruction) (1940); *Pedagogicheskiye vzglyady A. N. Radishcheva* (The Pedagogic Views of A. N. Radishchev) (1952); *N. F. Bunakov i yego pedagogicheskiye proizvedeniya* (N. F. Bunakov and His Works on Pedagogics) (1953); *Reforma nachal'noy i sredney shkoly v 60-ykh godakh XIX veka* (The Primary and Secondary School Reform of the 1860's) (1954); *Khrestomatiya po istorii pedagogiki* (A Primer on the History of Pedagogics) (1957); *Pedagogicheskiye idei N. G. Chernyshevskogo i N. A. Dobrolyubova* (The Pedagogic Ideas of N. G. Chernishevskiy and N. A. Dobrolyubov) (1957); *Ocherki po istorii progressivnoy russkoy pedagogiki XIX veka* (Studies in the History of Progressive Russian Pedagogics in the 19th Century) (1963); coauthor, *Istoriya pedagogiki. Uchebnik dlya pedagogicheskikh uchilishch* (The History of Pedagogics. A Textbook for Teachers' Training Colleges) (3rd ed, 1965); *Died:* 29 Oct 1962.

SMIRNOVA (Party name: SHELOMOVICH), Valentina Andrianovna (1902–1965) Party official; CP member from 1917; *Born:* 21 May 1902; *Career:* fought against Denikin's forces in Tula Province; from 1919 Party and Komsomol work; 1921–24 instructor, Women Workers Dept, CC, RCP(B); 1934–35 ed, newspaper "Bol'shevistskiy put'"; 1937–38 Party work in Moscow; deleg at 18th Party Congress; for a number of years worked at Inst of Marxism-Leninism, at Higher Party School, CC, CPSU(B) and at Moscow Univ; did research work at Inst of Slavic Studies, USSR Acad of Sci; 1947–50 dep dir, above inst; from 1950 pensioner; *Died:* 24 Aug 1965.

SMIRNOVA-ZAMKOVA, Aleksandra Ivanovna (1880–1962) Pathologist and microbiologist; Dr of Med from 1906; prof from 1934; corresp member, Ukr Acad of Sci from 1939; *Born:* 31 May 1880 in Pereyaslav (now Pereyaslav-Khmel'nitskiy), Ukr, daughter of a physician; *Educ:* studied at Med Fac, Montpelier Univ, France; 1906 grad Med Fac, Kiev Univ; *Career:* 1907–08 asst prof, Kiev Bacteriological Inst; 1908–30 asst prof, Chair of Pathological Anatomy, Kiev Women's Inst; 1930–38 co-founder and senior assoc, Pathological Research Laboratory, Ukr Acad of Sci; 1933–41 prof and head, Chair of Pathological Anatomy, 2nd Kiev Med Inst; 1945–60 head, Dissection Dept, Ukr Inst of Clinical Med; 1953–62 head, Morphological Laboratory, Bogomolets Inst of Physiology, Ukr Acad of Sci; *Publ:* doctor's thesis "Les recherches sur les lésions et le parasite de l'actinomycose" (1906); "Zur pathologischen Anatomie des Scharlachs" (1926); "Zum Studium der Genese von Geweben in embryonalen Geschwülsten" (1935); *Osnovnoye agritofil'noye veshchestvo i yego funktsional'noye znacheniye* (The Basic Agrirophilic Substance and Its Functional Significance) (1955); *Problema osnovnogo mezhutochnogo veshchestva* (The Problem of the Basic Intermediate Substance) (1957), etc; *Awards:* Order of Lenin; Badge of Hon; medal "For Valiant Labor During the Great Fatherland War"; *Died:* 22 Oct 1962 in Kiev.

SMITTEN, Ye.G. (1883–1942) Party official; CP member from 1904; *Born:* 1883; *Career:* Party work in Vitebsk and Petersburg; after 1917 Oct Revol dep secr, Centr Council of Factory and Plant Comts, Petrograd; then worked for All-Russian Cheka; from 1921 exec work for CC, RCP(B); from 1932 research, ed and publ work; *Died:* 1942.

SMOL'YANINOV, Vadim Aleksandrovich (1890–1962) Govt and Party official; CP member from 1908; *Born:* 1890; *Career:* 1917–22 head, Smolensk Province Party Comt; 1917–21 member, Smolensk Sov; deleg at 2nd All-Russian Congress of Soviets; 1917–22 member, All-Russian Centr Exec Comt; Mar 1921–July 1924 dep mang, Council of Pop Comr and Labor and Defense Council, in charge of econ matters; July 1924–July 1929 mang, RSFSR Council of Pop Comr and chm, Small Council of Pop Comr; from 1927 chm, Econ Consutative Bd, RSFSR Council of Pop Comr; 1929–32 head, Magnitostroy Construction Trust; 1932–33 dep head, Eastern Steel Trust; 1933–38 dir, Leningrad Inst for Designing Metallurgical Plants; late 1938–1941 head, Tech Dept, and shift mang, Moscow's "Red Pipe" Pipe Plant; deleg at 7th–10th Party Congresses; from 1956 pensioner; *Died:* 1962.

SMUSHKEVICH, Yakov Vladimirovich (1902–41) Mil commander; lt-gen, Sov Air Force from 1940; CP member from 1918; *Born:* 15 Apr 1902 in Rokishkis, now Lith SSR, son of a tailor; *Educ:* 1932 grad mil pilots' school; *Career:* from 1918 served in Red Army; from 1932 held command posts; 1936–39 fought in Spanish Civil War; 1939 fought in battle of Khalkhin-Gol; 1939–40 served in Sov-Finnish war; from Nov 1939 commander, Red Army Air Force; from 1940 dep commander in charge of aviation, Red Army Gen Staff; from 1939 cand member, CC, CPSU(B); dep, USSR Supr Sov of 1st convocation; 1941 arrested by NKVD; *Awards:* twice Hero of the Sov Union (1937, 1939); two Orders of Lenin; *Died:* 28 Oct 1941 in imprisonment; posthumously rehabilitated.

SNESAREV, Andrey Yevgen'yevich (1865–1937) Mil commander; lt-gen, Russian Army; army commander, Red Army; prof; Orientalist; Hero of Labor; *Born:* 13 Dec 1865 in vil Staraya Kalitva, Voronezh Province; *Career:* in his youth singer, Bolshoy Theater; also concert singer; joined Russian Army; from May 1918 in Red Army as mil leader, North Caucasian Mil Distr and commander, 16th Army; organized defense of Tsaritsyn; Aug 1919–21 commandant, Gen Staff Acad; from 1921 prof and chief dir for mil geography and statistics, also head, Oriental Fac, Red Army Gen Staff Acad; member, Higher Mil Ed Council and head, Statistical Dept, USSR Mil Revol Council; 1937 arrested by NKVD in connection with the Marshal Tukhachevskiy case; *Publ: Severoindiyskiy teatr (voyenno-geograficheskoye opisaniye)* (The North Indian Theater (A Military Geopgraphical Account) (1903); *Indiya, kak glavnyy faktor v sredneaziatskom voprose* (India as the Chief Factor in the Central Asian Problem) (1906); *Voyennaya geografiya Rossii. Chast' obshchaya* (Military Geography of Russia. General Section) (1909); *Afganistan* (Afghanistan) (1921); *Vvedeniye v voyennuyu geografiyu* (An Introduction to Military Geography) (1924); *Died:* 4 Dec 1937 in imprisonment.

SOBINOV, Leonid Vital'yevich (1872–1934) Russian singer (lyric tenor); Pop Artiste of RSFSR from 1923; *Born:* 7 June 1872 in Yaroslavl', son of a sales clerk; *Educ:* 1894 grad Law Fac, Moscow Univ; 1897 grad Musical Drama College, Moscow Philharmonic Soc; *Career:* while a student, sang in the univ choir and choir of Ukr company which performed in Moscow; 1895–99 asst public notary; while studying at Musical Drama College, sang with Italian Opera Company; from 1897 soloist, Opera Company, Bolshoy Theater; 1905–11 performed at Scala and other West European opera theaters; 1917–18 dir, Bolshoy Theater; 1918–19 artistic dir, Kiev Opera Theater; in his latter years dir and artistic dir, Stanislavsky Opera Theater; *Roles:* Bayan in Glinka's *Ruslan i Lyudmila* (Ruslan and Ludmilla); Vladimir Igor'yevich in Borodin's *Knyaz' Igor'* (Prince Igor); Berendey and Levko in Rimsky-Korsakov's *Snegurochka* (The Snow-Maiden) and *Mayskaya noch'* (May Night); Lohengrin in Wagner's "Lohengrin"; Romeo in Gounod's "Romeo and Juliet", etc; *Awards:* Order of the Red Banner of Labor; *Died:* 14 Oct 1934 in Riga; the Saratov Conservatory and the Yaroslavl' Musical College are named after him.

SOBOLEV, Arkadiy Aleksandrovich (1903–1964) Diplomat; USSR Dep Min of For Affairs from 1960; Collegium member, USSR Min of For Affairs; eng; *Born:* 1903; *Educ:* grad Leningrad Electr Eng Inst; *Career:* 1930–39 engaged in research on machine-building; 1939–42 secr-gen, USSR Pop Comrt of For Affairs; 1942–45 counsellor, Sov embassy in London; 1945 attended Potsdam

Conference; 1945–46 polit counsellor to Marshal Zhukov at Allied Council, Berlin; 1946–49 Sov rep in UN, then dep secr-gen, UN; 1949–51 head, American Dept, USSR Min of For Affairs; 1951–53 Sov amb in Poland; 1953–54 head, American Dept, USSR Min of For Affairs; 1954 attended Berlin For Min Conference; 1954–55 USSR dep permanent rep, Mar 1955–Sept 1960 USSR permanent rep in UN; *Awards:* Order of the Red Banner of Labor (1963); *Died:* 1 Dec 1964.

SOBOL'SHCHIKOV-SAMARIN (real name: SOBOL'SHCHIKOV), Nikolay Ivanovich (1868–1945) Russian actor, stage dir and drama teacher; Pop Artiste of RSFSR from 1934; *Born:* 9 Apr 1868 in Petersburg, son of a peasant; *Career:* until 1883 studied at mil topographical school; performed at clubs in Petersburg and Petersburg suburbs; became provincial actor; 1892 actor and stage dir, Vasiliy Ostrov Workers' Theater, Petersburg; 1892–99 actor and stage dir, Nizhniy Novgorod Theater; 1924–44 dir, Nizhniy Novgorod (now Gorky) Drama Theater; *Productions:* Gorky's *Meshchane* (The Philistines) (1903, 1926 and 1934); Gogol's *Revizor* (The Government Inspector) (1930); Shakespeare's "Hamlet" (1936); Ostrovskiy's *Son na Volge* (Dream of the Volga) (1941); *Roles:* Neschastlivtsev and Ivan the Terrible in Ostrovskiy's *Les* (The Forest) and "Vasilisa Melent'yeva"; Teterev in Gorky's "Meshchane"; Lear in Shakespeare's "King Lear", etc; *Publ: Zapiski* (Notes) (1940); *Died:* 20 July 1945 in Gorky.

SOKOL'NIKOV, Grigoriy Yakovlevich (1888–1939) Party and govt official; lawyer; Dr of Econ; CP member from 1905; *Born:* 1888; *Educ:* completed higher educ; *Career:* 1905–07 agitator and propagandist in Moscow; 1907–09 in prison, then in exile in Siberia, whence he fled; 1909–17 lived abroad; from Apr 1917 member, Moscow Oblast RSDRP(B) Bureau; then member, ed bd, "Pravda"; attended 6th RSDRP(B) Congress and elected member, CC, RSDRP(B); after 1917 Oct Revol directed nationalization of banks; 1918–20 member, Revol Mil Council, 2nd, 9th, 13th and 8th Armies; Aug 1920–Mar 1921 chm, Turkestani Commission, All-Russian Centr Exec Comt and RSFSR Council of Pop Comr; member, Revol Mil Council and commander, Turkestani Front; from 1921 USSR Dep Pop Comr, 1922–26 Pop Comr of Finance; 1926 dep chm, USSR Gosplan; from 1928 chm, Oil Syndicate; 1929–34 USSR plen in UK and Dep Pop Comr of For Affairs; from May 1934 USSR Dep Pop Comr of Forestry Ind; 1917–19 and 1922–30 member, CC, CPSU(B); from 1930 cand member, CC, CPSU(B); 1936 expelled from Party and arrested for alleged anti-Party and anti-govt activities; 1937 sentenced to 10 years' imprisonment in trial of "anti-Sov Trotskyist center"; *Died:* 1939 in imprisonment.

SOKOLOV, Georgiy Vasil'yevich (1904–1934) Party official; student; CP member; *Born:* 1904; *Educ:* studied at higher educ establishment; *Career:* Dec 1934 tried for complicity in assassination of Kirov; 29 Dec 1934 sentenced to death with co-defendants by Assizes of Mil Collegium, USSR Supr Court; *Died:* Dec 1934 executed.

SOKOLOV, Nikolay Vladimirovich (1882–1963) Surgeon; Dr of Med from 1924; prof from 1926; Hon Sci Worker of RSFSR and Tatar ASSR; *Born:* 22 Feb 1882 in Shuran, Kazan' Province; *Educ:* 1908 grad Med Fac, Kazan' Univ; *Career:* 1909–13 intern, Fac Surgical Clinic, Kazan' Univ; 1913 surgeon, Mamyk Zemstvo Hospital, Vyatka Province; 1914–17 mil surgeon in Tsarist Army; 1918–21 surgeon at Red Army hospitals in Kazan' and head, Surgical Department, Admiralty Hospital; 1920–21 simultaneously asst dissector, Chair of Operative Surgery, Kazan' Univ; from 1921 asst prof, Hospital Surgical Clinic, Kazan' Univ; 1925 assoc prof, 1926–40 prof and head, Chair of Operative Surgery, Kazan' Inst of Postgrad Med Training; 1931–33 head, Chair of Operative Surgery, 1933–35 – Chair of Gen Surgery, 1940–63 – Chair of Hospital Surgery, Kazan' Med Inst; 1933–36 and 1938–42 also dean, Therapy Fac, Kazan' Med Inst; 1937–39 chm, Sci Workers' Section, 1938–51 member, Qualifications Commission, 1945–46 dep sci dir, Kazan' Med Inst; member, ed bd, "Kazanskiy meditsinskiy zhurnal"; dep, Kazan' City Sov; hon bd member, All-Russian and Tatar Soc of Surgeons; attended All-Union and All-Russian Surgical Congresses; trained numerous outstanding surgeons and wrote some 50 works on topographical anatomy, immunology, field surgery, anaesthesiology, history of surgery in Kazan', etc; *Awards:* Order of Lenin; Order of the Red Banner of Labor; Badge of Hon; medals; *Died:* 22 Sept 1963 in Kazan'.

SOKOLOV-SKALYA, Pavel Petrovich (1889–1961) Painter and graphic artist; prof from 1949; member, USSR Acad of Arts from 1949; Pop Artist of RSFSR from 1956; CP member from 1952; *Born:* 2 July 1889 in Strel'na, Petersburg Province; *Educ:* 1914–18 studied at I.I. Mashkov's private studio in Moscow; 1922 grad Higher Tech Art Workshops; *Career:* from 1921 displayed his work in the "World of Art" and "Existence" exhibitions; from 1922 illustrator and cartoonist for newspaper "Batrak" and other periodicals; 1922–25 member, "Existence" Assoc; from 1946 member, Assoc of Artists of Revol Russia; during WW 2 painted some 100 polit posters for and helped direct "Tass Windows" org; 1957 dir, Exhibition of Fine and Applied Art, Moscow; *Works:* "Paris Before a Storm" (1925); "The Taman Campaign" (1928); "The Path from Gorki" (1929); "Brothers" (1932); diorama "The 1st Cavalry Army in Wrangel's Rear" (1937); triptych "Shchors" (1938); "Stalin at Tsaritsyn" (1939); "The Storming of the Winter Palace" (1940); "Ivan the Terrible at Kokengauzen" (1943); "The Liberation of Kaluga" (1947); "The Red Don Soldiers" (1948); supervised erection of F.A. Rubo's panorama "The Defense of Sebastopol" (1954); designed sets and costumes for: A.N. Tolstoy's *Ivan Groznyy* (Ivan the Terrible) (1945); *Narod bessmerten* (The People Is Immortal) (1946), after Grossmann's novel, etc; *Awards:* two Stalin Prizes (1942 and 1949); *Died:* 3 Aug 1961.

SOKOLOVSKAYA, Sof'ya Ivanovna (Party name: Yelena Kirillovna) (1894–1938) Party official; CP member from 1915; *Born:* 1894 in Odessa; *Educ:* studied at Bestuzhev Courses, Petersburg; *Career:* from 1903 lived in Chernigov and took part in student revol activities; from 1917 Party work in Chernigov; after 1917 Oct Revol chm, Chernigov Sov of Workers and Soldiers' Dep; 1918 member, underground Chernigov Province Party Comt; then member, underground Kiev Oblast Comt, CP(B) Ukr and secr, Kiev Province Revol Comt; from Oct 1918 secr, underground Odessa Oblast Comt, CP(B) Ukr; helped organize For Collegium, Odessa Oblast Comt, CP(B) Ukr; 1919 Party and govt work in Odessa, then in Moscow; 1930–34 worked for Centr Control Commission of Workers and Peasants' Inspection; at 16th Party Congress elected member, CPSU(B) Centr Control Commission; deleg at 17th CPSU(B) Congress; *Died:* 26 Aug 1938.

SOKOLOVSKIY, Nestor Fyodorovich (1902–1950) Bel composer; CP member from 1944; *Born:* 9 Nov 1902 in vil Veshki, Minsk Province; *Educ:* 1931 grad Bel State Music Technicum; 1932–35 and 1947–50 studied at Bel State Conservatory; *Career:* from 1918 with Teravskiy's "Bel Hut" Choir, Minsk; 1921–23 chorist with Ukr touring company; also performed at Tumanov Theater; from 1926 choirmaster, Vladislav Golubka's Bel touring drama theater; 1937–41 choirmaster, Bel State Song and Dance Ensemble; 1941–44 for a while worked at a factory in Chuvash ASSR, then served in Sov Army with guards units; wounded and demobilized; artistic dir, Bel State Song and Dance Ensemble; from 1944 head, Dept of Amateur Artistic Activities, Bel Arts Bd and artistic dir, Bel Folk Art Center; from 1946 ed, Musical Dept, Bel State Publ House; in late 1940's criticized by Party, especially for his "Song of Neman" (1942) and for "nationalistic deviations" in other works; expelled from Bel Composers' Union; later reinstated in union; 1944 composed State Anthem of Bel SSR – "We Are Belorussians"; *Works:* romances: "Cradle Song"; "Kupala Festival Evening"; "Eagles Spring"; "Ballads", etc; three suites on Bel folk themes; piano pieces on Bel folk song themes; songs to words by Bel poets; many arrangements of Bel folk songs; *Awards:* Badge of Hon; *Died:* 16 Nov 1950 in Minsk.

SOLLOGUB, N. V. (1883–1937) Mil commander; *Born:* 1883; *Career:* col, Russian Army; from 1918 in Red Army; chief of staff, Eastern Front; member, Higher Mil Inspectorate; head, operations bd, staff of an army on Western Front; commander, 16th Army; 1920 chief of staff, Southern Front; chief of staff, Ukr and Crimean Armed Forces; from 1923 senior posts in mil training establishments; arrested by State Security organs; *Died:* 1937 in imprisonment.

SOLOV'YOV, Aleksandr Aleksandrovich (1893–1967) Pathomorphologist; Dr of Med; prof; corresp member, USSR Acad of Med Sci; *Born:* 1893; *Educ:* 1917 grad Med Fac, Moscow Univ; *Career:* 1917–20 mil surgeon; 1921–32 asst prof, Dept of Pathological Anatomy, 1932–35 head, Pathomorphology Laboratory, Leningrad Inst of Experimental Med; 1935–67 head, Pathomorphology Laboratory, All-Union Inst of Experimental Med, Moscow; also head, Morphology Laboratory, Moscow Inst of Normal and Pathological Physiology, USSR Acad of Med Sci; bd member, All-Union Soc of Oncologists; member, ed collegium, journal "Byulleten' eksperimental'noy meditsiny"; did research on the intermediate substance in the vessel walls and its role in arterial lesions due to the aging process and arteriosclerosis; also studied the role of the neurotrophic element in the genesis and metastasis of tumors; wrote over 40 works; *Publ: O nekotorykh voprosakh patogeneza i gistopatologii tuberkulyoznogo meningita* (Some Questions of the Pathogenesis and Histopathology of Tubercular Meningitis) (1936); *Materialy k gistopatologii eksperimental'nogo brutsellyoza ovets* (Material on the Histopathology of Experimental Brucellosis in Sheep) (1937); coauthor, *O nekotorykh voprosakh patogeneza eksperimental'noy difteriynoy intoksikatsii* (Some Questions of the Pathogenesis of Experimental Diptheric Intoxication) (1957); *Rol' nervnoy sistemy v patogeneze opukholey i osnovnyye perspektivy razvitiya etogo voprosa* (The Role of the Nervous System in the Pathogenesis of Tumors and the Basic Prospects of Developing This Subject) (1960); *Died:* Dec 1967 in Moscow.

SOLOV'YOV, Vasiliy Ivanovich (1890–1939) Govt official; CP member from 1913; *Born:* 1890; *Career:* dir, Moscow newspaper "Nash put'"; secr, health insurance fund in Moscow; 1913–14 proof-reader, newspaper "Pravda"; 1915 worked at a sawmill; 1916 worked for Land League; also did Party work; 1917 helped organize newspaper "Sotsial-demokrat"; until 1918 Bureau member, Moscow Party Comt; also worked for Moscow Sov; 1920 member, Commission to Draft the Reorganization of the Pop Comrt of Educ; 1921 dep chm, Main Bd for Lit and Educ; then Collegium member, Agitation and Propaganda Dept, CC, RCP(B); 1924 USSR counsellor and charge d'affaires in Afghanistan; dep head, Press, Dept, CC, CPSU(B); 1925 counsellor, USSR mission in China; member, Comintern Eastern Secretariat; USSR Pop Comrt of For Affairs plen in Uzbekistan; member, ed bd, journal "Novyy mir"; chm, and plen, Main Bd for Lit and Publ Houses; dir, State Book Chamber, etc; member, All-Russian Centr Exec Comt of several convocations; arrested by State Security organs; *Died:* 1939 in imprisonment.

SOLOV'YOV, Zinoviy Petrovich (1876–1928) Public health official; CP member from 1898; *Born:* 22 Nov 1876 in Grodno, son of a surveyor; *Educ:* 1904 grad Med Fac, Kazan' Univ; *Career:* 1899 arrested for revol work at Kazan' ind enterprises; worked as public health dr in Simbirsk and Saratov Zemstvos; 1909 re-arrested for underground Party work and exiled to Ust'-Sysol'sk; while in exile engaged in journalism; 1912 completed term of exile and moved to Moscow, where he worked for the Bd of the Pirogov Soc of Russian Physicians; co-ed, journal "Obshchestvennyy vrach"; ed, journal "Vrachebnaya zhizn'"; secr, Anti-Tuberculosis League; played active part in 1917 Oct Revol in Moscow; 1918 appointed med dir, Pop Comrt of Internal Affairs and member, Council of Physicians' Collegia; 1918–28 Dep Pop Comr of Health; head, Dept of Civil Med, from 1920 head, Main Mil Health Bd; co-founder and head, Russian Red Cross Soc; specialized in child health care; 1925 sponsored foundation of "Artek" Pioneer Camp-Sanatorium in the Crimea; from 1923 prof, Chair of Soc Hygiene, Med Fac, 2nd Moscow Univ; made major contributions to development of Sov health service, particularly outpatient treatment, org of mil health facilities, etc; opposed "eugenic" theories in med; *Publ: Voprósy zdravookhraneniya. Izbrannyye stat'i i rechi* (Public Health Problems. Selected Articles and Speeches) (1940); *Died:* 6 Nov 1928 in Moscow.

SOL'TS, Aaron Aleksandrovich (1872–1945) Party and govt official; CP member from 1898; *Born:* 1872; *Educ:* studied at univ; *Career:* 1895 joined revol movement; member, "Workers' Banner" group; 1899 expelled from univ for participating in student riots; became professional revolutionary; 1901 arrested in Vilnius for connection with Soc-Democratic Workers' Library; after his released sided with "Iskra" group; late 1901 again arrested; May 1902 exiled to Irkutsk Province; Nov 1902 fled from exile and settled in Yekaterinoslav, running an underground printing press; May 1903 arrested and imprisoned for 2 1/2 years; 1905–May 1906 worked in Vilnius; member, Vilnius Party Comt; July 1906 arrested in Petersburg; imprisoned until Feb 1907, then exiled for three years to Turinsk, Tobol'sk Province; moved to Tyumen', set up underground printing press and served on Tyumen' Party Comt; 1909 re-arrested after collapse of Tyumen' Party org; Feb 1910 ended term of exile and worked for six months in Baku; late 1910–Feb 1913 lived illegally in Petersburg and served as member, Petersburg Party Comt; arrested and exiled to Narym; 1914 fled from exile and went to Moscow; July 1914 arrested and sentenced to two years fortress arrest; from Oct 1916 worked in Moscow; after 1917 Feb Revol member, ed staff, newspapers "Sotsialdemokrat" then "Pravda"; fought in 1917 Oct Revol in Moscow; 1918, during Brest Peace Treaty controversy, sided with Leftist Communists; worked for Pop Comrt of Justice; from 1920 member, Party Centr Control Commission; 1921–34 Presidium member, CPSU(B) Centr Control Commission; 1921 member, Centr Verification Commission; from 1921 member, Supr Court; member, Int Control Commission; worked for USSR Public Prosecutor's office; deleg at 17th and 9th–17th CPSU(B) Congresses; at 9th–15th Congresses elected member, CPSU(B) Centr Control Commission; *Died:* 1945.

SORIN, Vladimir Gordeyevich (1893–1944) Party official; CP member from 1917; *Born:* 1893 in Ukr, son of an office worker; *Educ:* grad Odessa high-school; from 1912 studied at Moscow Univ; *Career:* 1917–early 1918 secr, ed bd, newspaper "Sotsial-demokrat"; then secr, ed bd, newspaper "Pravda"; 1918 sided with Leftist Communists and opposed Brest Peace Treaty; 1918 secr, Serpukhov City Party Comt; Sept 1918–Feb 1919 chm, Eastern Front Mil Tribunal; upon return from Eastern Front worked for Moscow Province Party Comt; then Bureau member and head, Agitation and Propaganda Dept, Moscow Province Party Comt; simultaneously member, Moscow Province Exec Comt and member, Moscow Province Mil Revol Comt; from May 1920 member, Bureau member and head, Agitation and Propaganda Dept, Moscow City Party Comt; 1924 dep head, Press Dept, CC, RCP(B); 1924 appointed asst dir, Lenin Inst; 1936–39 dep dir, Inst of Marxism-Leninism; 1939 arrested by State Security organs; *Publ: Ucheniye Lenina o partii* (Lenin's Teaching about the Party) (1924); *Rabochaya gruppa* (The Workers' Group) (1924); *Partiya i oppozitsiya* (The Party and the Opposition) (1925); *V.I. Lenin. Kratkaya biografiya* (V.I. Lenin. A Short Biography) (1932); *Pervyye shagi Lenina po sozdaniyu partii* (Lenin's First Steps in Forming the Party) (1934); *Lenin v dni Bresta* (Lenin at the Time of Brest) (1936); *Died:* late 1944 in imprisonment; posthumously rehabilitated.

SOSITSKIY, Lev Il'ich (1899–1934) Party official; CP member; *Born:* 1899; *Career:* expelled from CP for membership of Zinov'ev bloc but re-admitted after publicly recanting his errors and expressing solidarity with Party and govt policy; Dec 1934 tried for complicity in assassination of Kirov; 29 Dec 1934 sentenced to death with co-defendants by Assizes of Mil Collegium, USSR Supr Court; *Died:* Dec 1934 executed.

SOSNOVSKIY, Lev Semyonovich (1886–1937) Journalist; Party and govt official; CP member from 1904; *Born:* 1886; *Career:* from 1903 in revol movement; active in 1905 Revol; 1906–12 organized trade unions in Tashkent, Baku and Moscow; 1912 worked for newspaper "Pravda" then for journal "Voprosy strakhovaniya"; fall 1913 arrested and exiled to Chelyabinsk; after 1917 Feb Revol worked in Urals; after 1917 Oct Revol chm, Yekaterinoslav Province Exec Comt; Presidium member, All-Russian Centr Exec Comt; chm, Khar'kov Province RCP(B) Comt; head, Agitation and Propaganda Dept, CC, RCP(B); 1918–25, with intervals, edited newspaper "Bednota"; during 1920–21 trade-union controversy sided with Trotsky; 1925–26 Collegium member, RSFSR Pop Comrt of Agric; 1923 sided with Trotskyist opposition; 1927 expelled from Party at 15th CPSU(B) Congress; 1935 reinstated in Party; 1936 expelled again for alleged anti-Party activities and later sentenced; *Died:* 1937 in imprisonment.

SOSYURA, Vladimir Nikolayevich (1898–1965) Ukr poet and translator; bd member, USSR Writers' Union from 1959; Presidium member, Ukr Writers' Union; CP member from 1920; *Born:* 6 Jan 1898 in Debal'tsevo, now Donetsk Oblast; *Educ:* completed two-grade college, then studied at agric school; 1922–23 studied at Khar'kov Communist Univ; 1923–25 studied at Workers' Fac, Khar'kov Inst of Public Educ; *Career:* telephonist with mine admin; laborer at soda plant; 1917 first work printed; 1918–19 private, then officer cadet, Ukr Nat Army; during Civil War contributed to frontline press, writing mainly in Russian; from 1920 private, then polit officer, eng company, Red Army; 1933–38 editing work; during WW 2 mil corresp for frontline and republ newspapers; successively member, "Plow", "Gart", "Vaplite" and VUSSP lit orgs; the artificial famine in the Ukr in 1933, the suicide of Skripnik and Khvilyovyy and the constant threat of his own arrest and execution brought Sosyura to a nervous breakdown, and he spent some time in a mental hospital; subjected to constant persecution and pressure by Sov authorities; several times "recanted his errors" and promised to reform his ways; in early 1930's, after the appearance of his poem "The Ukraine", he fell into official disfavor and his works were not printed; during WW 2, when it was again possible to write of Ukr patriotism, Sosyura wrote his famous poem "Love the Ukraine",

(1944); 1951, several years after the war ended, he was roundly criticized for this same poem by the centr press in Moscow; his poetic style was strongly influenced by folk songs; translated into Ukr works of Pushkin, Lermontov, Krylov, Nekrasov and some Sov Russian poets; his own works have been translated into many of the languages of the peoples of the USSR and into other for languages; *Publ:* collected verse: "Verse" (1921); "Red Winter" (1921); poem "1871" (1923); poem "Oksana" (1923); poem "1917" (1921), about Lenin; verse "Funeral March" (1924); poems "None Has Loved So" (1922); "Swallows in the Sun" (1922); "I Recall the Glowing, Tossing Cherries" (1923); pamphlets: "To the Neo-Classicists" (1926); "An Answer" (1927); ballad "The Komsomol Member" (1927); poem "The State Political Board" (1928); verse collections: "New Verse" (1937); "I Love" (1939); poem "A Letter to My Countrymen"; poem "Oleg Koshevoy" (1945); collection "Let the Gardens Rustle" (1947); *Awards:* two Orders of Lenin; Order of the Red Banner; Badge of Hon; medals; Stalin Prize (1948); Shevchenko Prize (1963); *Died:* 8 Jan 1965; buried in Kiev.

SPASOKUKOTSKIY, Sergey Ivanovich (1870–1943) Surgeon; Dr of Med from 1898; prof from 1912; member, USSR Acad of Sci from 1942; Hon Sci Worker of RSFSR from 1934; *Born:* 10 June 1870 in Kostroma, son of a physician; *Educ:* 1893 grad Med Fac, Moscow Univ; *Career:* after grad worked at L.L.Levshin's Surgical Clinic; 1897 served in Greco-Turkish War; 1898 defended doctor's thesis on osteoplasty in amputation of the extremities; 1898–1909 head, Surgical Dept, Smolensk Province Hospital; 1909–11 head, Surgical Dept, Smolensk City Hospital; from 1912 prof, Chair of Topographical Anatomy and Operative Surgery, then Chair of Hospital Surgery Clinic, Saratov Univ; after 1917 Oct Revol founded a traumatological inst for treatment of Red Army soldiers in Saratov; from 1926 head, Chair of Fac Surgery Clinic, 2nd Moscow Univ (later 2nd Moscow Med Inst); from 1927 also head, Surgical Section, Blood Transfusion Inst and chief surgeon, Kremlin Hospital; pioneered modern gastrointestinal surgery in Russia; did valuable research on intestinal blockage, gastroenterostomy, resection of the stomach, postoperative diets, etc; designed several instruments for stomach operations; was first Russian surgeon to use "blind" sutures for gunshot wounds of the cranium and abdominal cavity with organ damage; developed subsequently improved method of disinfecting the surgeon's hands which is now generally used in the USSR; devised a number of original urological operations; made major contribution to methods of treating suppurative trauma of the lungs; 1938 performed one of first successful operations for removal of lobe of the lung; helped to organize Sov blood transfusion service; trained numerous outstanding surgeons, including A.N. Bakulev, V.I. Kazanskiy, I.G.Kochergin, V.S.Levit and B.E.Linberg; wrote 143 works; *Publ:* doctor's thesis *Kostnaya plastika pri amputatsiyakh konechnostey* (Osteoplasty in Amputation of the Extremities) (1898); *Khirurgiya gnoynykh zabolevaniy lyogkikh i plevry* (The Surgery of Suppurative Pulmonary and Pleural Diseases) (1938); *Aktinomikoz lyogkikh* (Pulmonary Actinomycosis) (1940); *Trudy* (Works) (2 vol, 1947–48), etc; *Awards:* Order of Lenin; Order of the Red Banner of Labor; Stalin Prize (1942); medals; *Died:* 17 Nov 1943 in Moscow.

SPERANSKIY, Aleksey Dmitriyevich (1888–1961) Pathologist and physiologist; maj-gen, Med Corps; Dr of Med from 1913; prof from 1920; member, USSR Acad of Sci from 1939; member, USSR Acad of Med Sci from 1944; Hon Sci Worker of RSFSR from 1934; CP member from 1943; *Born:* 11 Jan 1888 in Urzhum, now Kirov Oblast; *Educ:* 1911 grad Med Fac, Kazan' Univ; 1923–27 received specialist training in physiology at Acad I.P. Pavlov's laboratories, Leningrad Inst of Experimental Med; *Career:* 1911–13 dissector, Chair of Anatomy, Kazan' Univ; simultaneously specialized in surgery at Surgical Clinic, Kazan' Univ; 1914–19 mil surgeon; 1920–23 prof of operative surgery and topographical anatomy, Med Fac, Irkutsk Univ; 1923–27 specialist training under Pavlov; 1928–33 head, Dept of Pathological Physiology, Leningrad Inst of Experimental Med; from 1934 head, Dept of Gen Pathology, All-Union Inst of Experimental Med, Moscow; during WW 2 worked for Main Health Bd, Sov Army; 1945–54 dir, Inst of Gen and Experimental Pathology, USSR Acad of Sci, Moscow; 1954–61 head, Dept of Gen Pathology, Inst of Normal and Pathological Physiology, USSR Acad of Med Sci; championed the theory of "nervism"; trained numerous pathophysiologists in the theories of I.P.Pavlov, N.V.Vvedenskiy and A.A.Ukhtomskiy; member, ed council, journal "Patologicheskaya fiziologiya i eksperimental'naya terapiya"; *Publ: Nervnaya sistema v patologii* (The Nervous System in Pathology) (1930); *Epilepticheskiy pristup* (The Epileptic Attack) (1932); *Elementy postroyeniya teorii meditsiny* (The Building-Blocks of the Theory of Medicine) (1935); *Sovremennyye voprosy obshchey patologii i meditsiny* (Contemporary Problems of General Pathology and Medicine) (1950); *Zabolevaniye, lecheniye i vyzdorovleniye* (Disease, Treatment and Recovery) (1952); *Problemy reaktivnosti v patologii* (The Problem of Reactivity in Pathology) (1954); *Refleksy s lyogkogo v terapii tuberkulyoza i nekotorykh drugikh zabolevaniy* (Pulmonary Reflexes in the Treatment of Tuberculosis and Some Other Diseases) (1957); *Izbrannyye trudy* (Selected Works) (1955); *Awards:* Pavlov Prize (1937); two Orders of Lenin; Stalin Prize (1943); two Orders of the Red Banner of Labor; medals; *Died:* 23 July 1961.

SPERANSKIY, Georgiy Nestorovich (1873–1969) Pediatrician; Dr of Med; prof; corresp member, USSR Acad of Sci from 1943; member, USSR Acad of Med Sci from 1944; Hon Sci Worker of RSFSR from 1937; Hero of Socialist Labor from 1957; *Born:* 19 Feb 1873; *Educ:* 1898 grad Med Fac, Moscow Univ; *Career:* 1898–1909 intern, 1909–11 asst prof, Clinic of Children's Diseases, Moscow Univ; 1907–10 physician, Dept for New-Born Babies, Abrikosova Maternity Home, where he established a childcare advice section; 1910 founded first med establishment in Moscow combining a polyclinic, advice-center and milk-kitchen for babies; from 1912 founder-ed, periodical "Materialy po izucheniyu grudnogo vozrasta"; 1915–18 asst prof, Children's Clinic, Moscow Higher Women's Courses; 1918–19 worked at Prof V. V. Voronin's Laboratory; 1919–20 founder-head, Chair of Children's Diseases, Kuban' Univ, Krasnodar; 1921–22 founder-dir, Moscow Child Welfare Home; 1922 founded periodical "Zhurnal po izucheniyu rannego detskogo vozrasta"; from 1922 ed, journal "Pediatriya"; 1922–30 dir, 1930–48 sci dir, Centr Inst of Child and Mother Care (now Inst of Pediatrics, USSR Acad of Med Sci); 1931–61 head, Chair of Infant Pediatrics, Centr Inst of Postgrad Med Training; 1948–51 dir, 1951–69 senior assoc and consultant, Inst of Pediatrics, USSR Acad of Med Sci; from 1952 member, Home-Care Comt, Int Child Welfare Conference; from 1959 member, Pediatrics Prize Comt, USSR Acad of Med Sci; did research on acute and chronic nutritional and digestive diseases and acute gastro-intestinal diseases in infants; also studied the pathology of older children with special reference to rheumatism; tested various therapeutic drugs to determine efficacy and dosage in relation to age; wrote over 160 works; *Publ: K izucheniyu sepsisa u detey rannego vozrasta* (The Study of Infantile Sepsis) (1947); *Dizenteriya u detey rannego vozrasta* (Infantile Dysentery) (1952); coauthor, *Khronicheskiye rasstroystva pitaniya v rannem detskom vozraste* (Chronic Infantile Feeding Disorders) (1953); *Azbuka materi* (The Mother's ABC); *Zdorovyy rebyonok* (The Healthy Baby); *Mat' i ditya* (Mother and Child); *Uchebnik bolezney rannego detskogo vozrasta* (A Textbook of Infantile Diseases) (1934); chief ed, *Pediatriya* (Pediatrics) (5 vol; Vol 1, 1956) coauthor, *Zakalivaniye rebyonka rannego i doshkol'nogo vozrasta* (Increasing the Resistance of Infants and Preschool Children (1964), etc; *Awards:* four Orders of Lenin; two Orders of the Red Banner of Labor; medals; *Died:* 14 Jan 1969 in Moscow.

SPERANSKIY, Ivan Ivanovich (1894–1962) Therapist; Dr of Med from 1940; corresp member, USSR Acad of Med Sci from 1953; *Born:* 1894; *Educ:* 1916 grad Med Fac, Moscow Univ; *Career:* after grad mil surgeon in Tsarist Army; after 1917 Oct Revol asst prof, then assoc prof, Med Fac, Moscow Univ; from 1946 head, Clinical Dept, from 1946 dep sci dir, Inst of Therapy, USSR Acad of Med Sci; member, Int Soc of Internal Med; did research on infectious and occupational pathology, rheumatism and avitaminosis; wrote over 50 works; *Publ: Differentsirovannaya sedativnaya terapiya bol'nykh gipertonicheskoy bolezn'yu* (Differential Sedation Therapy for Hypertonia Patients) (1952); *Sedativnaya terapiya yazvennoy bolezni v zavisimosti ot kharaktera vysshey nervnoy deyatel'nosti bol'nykh* (Sedation Therapy for Ulcers in Accordance with the Nature of the Patients' Higher Nervous Activity) (1953); *Otsenka sostoyaniya vysshey nervnoy deyatel'nosti v klinike vnutrenney bolezney* (Evaluating the State of Higher Nervous Activity in the Clinical Diagnosis of Internal Diseases) (1957); *Nasledstvenno-semeynyye dannyye u bol'nykh gipertonicheskoy bolezni* (The Hereditary and Family Background of Hypertonia Patients) (1959); *Rol' nervnogo faktora v proiskhozhdenii gipertonicheskoy bolezni* (The Role of the Nervous Factor in the Development of Hypertonia) (1961), etc; *Awards:*

Order of Lenin; Order of the Red Banner of Labor; Order of the Red Star; medals; *Died:* 22 Feb 1962 in Moscow.

SPIRIDONOVA, Mariya Aleksandrovna (1884–1941) Politician; member, Socialist-Revol Party; *Born:* 1884; *Career:* Jan 1906 assassinated Vice-Governor of Tambov Luzhenovskiy in Kozlov; arrested and sentenced to hard labor; served sentence in Akatuy until 1917 Feb Revol; sided with Leftist Socialist-Revolutionaries and became member, Party CC; differed with Bolsheviks over Brest Peace Treaty and helped prepare July 1918 revolt in Moscow; Nov 1918 sentenced to 12 months' imprisonment by Revol Tribunal but amnestied a few days later; abandoned politics; *Died:* 1941.

SPIRIN, Ivan Timofeyevich (1898–1960) Sov aviation pioneer; maj-gen, Soviet Air Force; Dr of Geography; prof; CP member from 1920; *Born:* 28 Aug 1898 in Kolomna, son of a dairy-worker; *Career:* worked as railroad repair-man; 1918 volunteered for Red Army; 1919 qualified as pilot; pioneered flight navigation systems in USSR; 1927 flew in Great European Air Race; 1929 helped to find missing American aircrew in Arctic; 1930 took part in several recordbreaking long-distance flights in USSR; 1931 took part in Moscow-Ankara-Teheran-Kabul-Moscow flight; in same year, together with Gromov, set up endurance flight record of 75 hours during which he covered 12,411 kilometers without landing; 1937 was navigator on Moscow-North Pole flight; during WW 2 commanded an air force unit on active duty; 1955 retired on pension; also taught and did research work and held a chair at a higher educ establishment; *Publ: Navigatsiya odinochnogo samolyota* (Navigating a Single-Seater Plane); *Polyoty v oblakakh* (Flying in Cloud), etc; *Awards:* Hero of the Sov Union (1937); three Orders of Lenin; two Orders of the Red Banner; Order of the Fatherland War, 1st Class; two Orders of the Red Star; medals; *Died:* Nov 1960.

SPONTI, Ye.I. (pseudonym: "Teacher of Life") (1866–1931) Govt official; Soc-Democrat; *Born:* 1866; *Career:* early 1890's began revol work; 1894–95 active in Moscow Workers' League; spring 1895 went abroad with Lenin to establish contacts with Liberation of Labor group; Dec 1895 arrested; 1897 exiled to Arkhangel'sk Province; Dec 1905 took part in rail strike, was arrested and imprisoned; 1918–23 worked for Nizhniy Novgorod Province Land Admin; 1923–25 with Minsk Province Land Admin; *Died:* 1931.

SPUNDE, Aleksandr Petrovich (1892–1962) Govt official; CP member from 1909; *Born:* 1892; *Career:* Party work in the Urals, Perm' and Vyatka Province; frequently arrested by Tsarist authorities; deleg at 2nd All-Russian Congress of Soviets and Bureau member, Communist faction at the congress; member, Constituent Assembly, elected on Bolshevik ticket for Vyatka Province; 1918 underground revol propaganda among troops of German occupation forces in Ukr; late Apr 1918 mang, State Bank; helped establish Sov regime in Urals and Siberia; 1918–19 member, Ural Oblast Party Comt; chm, Chelyabinsk and Omsk Province Party Comt; chm, Krasnoyarsk Revol Comt; 1920–21 All-Russian Centr Exec Comt plen for organizing famine relief in Kaluga Province; 1921–22 chm, Vyatka Province Party Comt and chm, Vyatka Province Exec Comt; 1922–24 econ and Party work in Khar'kov and Chita; 1924–31 econ work in Moscow; 1926–31 Bd member, State Bank; Collegium member, Pop Comrt of Finance and Pop Comrt of Means of Communication; from 1935 pensioner; late 1930's expelled from Party; 1956 rehabilitated and reinstated in Party; *Died:* 19 Sept 1962.

STAL' (ZASLAVSKAYA), Lyudmila Nikolayevna (pseudonyms: YELENA; MARIYA; IVANOVNA) (1872–1939) Party official; CP member from 1899; *Born:* Mar 1872 in Yekaterinoslav, daughter of an industrialist; *Career:* 1900 arrested while returning from abroad with a batch of copies of the newspaper "Iskra" and exiled to Siberia; fled from exile and did Party work in Petersburg, Odessa, Nikolayev and Moscow; frequently arrested and exiled; 1905 member, Moscow Party Comt; 1906 member, Petersburg RSDRP(B) Comt; 1907–17 lived abroad, where she was active in Paris Bolshevik Section and in French Socialist Party; after 1917 Feb Revol returned to Russia; deleg at 7th RSDRP(B) Conference; member, Kronstadt RSDRP(B) Comt; edited newspaper "Kronshtadtskaya pravda"; took part in 1917 Oct Revol; agitator for Petrograd RSDRP(B) Comt; then with Dept of Women Workers, CC, RSDRP(B); deleg at 8th RCP(B) Congress; during Civil War did polit work in Red Army; member, ed staff, journal "Rabotnitsa"; from 1926 head, Mass Lit Dept, State Publ House; from 1928 dep chm, "Down With Illiteracy" Soc; 1928–39 research work at USSR State Museum of the Revol; *Awards:* Order of Lenin; *Died:* 23 Apr 1939.

STALIN (real name: DZHUGASHVILI), Iosif Vissarionovich (Party names: I. BESOSHVILI: DAVID: K. KATO: K. KO: KOBA: KOBA IVANOVICH: NIZHERADZE: CHIZHIKOV: IVANOVICH: VASIL'YEV: K. SALIN: K. STALIN: K. STEFIN) (1879–1953) Revolutionary; Party and govt official; Hero of Socialist Labor; Hero of the Sov Union; secr-gen, CC, CPSU; chm, USSR Council of Min; CP member from 1898; *Born:* 21 Dec 1879 in Gori, Tiflis Province, son of a shoemaker; *Educ:* grad Gori Theological College; 1893 entered Tiflis Orthodox Theological Seminary; *Career:* 1898 joined Tiflis RSDRP Org and was expelled from seminary for unreliability; 1900 elected member, Tiflis RSDRP Comt; 1901 went underground after May Day demonstration; late 1901 moved to Batum and worked for Batum Party Comt; Feb 1902 helped organize strike and polit demonstration; arrested and late 1902 exiled; 1904 fled to Tiflis from Siberian exile and served as member, Transcaucasian Joint Party Comt; directed illegal organ "Bor'ba proletariata"; late 1905 attended Tammerfors Party Conference; 1906 deleg at 4th Stockholm RSDRP Congress; 1907 deleg at 5th London RSDRP Congress; 1906 directed illegal Baku organ "Bakinskiy rabochiy"; Mar 1908 arrested and exiled to Vologda Province; fled and returned to Baku; 1910 rearrested and returned to exile; late 1911 again fled and engaged in underground Party work in Petersburg, where he directed Duma faction and newspapers "Zvezda" and "Pravda"; spring 1913 arrested and exiled to Turukhansk Kray, where he remained until 1917 Feb Revol; after 1917 Feb Revol returned to Petersburg and became member, CC, RSDRP(B); at one time advocated support of Provisional Govt, only abandoning this stand after Lenin's return; 1917 at 6th RSDRP(B) Congress presented CC polit report; at time of 1917 Oct Revol member, group which directed the coup; after 1917 Oct Revol until 1922 Pop Comr of Nationalities in first Council of Pop Comr; 1919–22 also Pop Comr of Peasants' Inspection; 1922, at Lenin's suggestion, elected secr-gen, CC; from 1925 Presidium member, Comintern Exec Comt; from 1917 member, All-Russian Centr Exec Comt; from 1922 member, USSR Centr Exec Comt; from 1937 dep, USSR Supr Sov and supr soviets of all union-republics; 1918–20 member, Revol Mil Council, Southern Front, RSFSR and Western and Southwestern Fronts; defended Lenin's stand in trade-union controversy; late 1923 launched his campaign against Trotsky; 1925 at 14th Party Congress proclaimed program for industrialization of country; at 15th Congress announced collectivization and socialist offensive against capitalist elements in cities and country; 1927 at 15th CPSU(B) Congress expelled Trotskist-Zinov'yevite block from Party; 1929–32 carried out purge of Party and govt apparatus; 1934–38 purged his main opponents, including Bukharin, Zinov'yev, Rykov and Pyatakov; 1939 entitled Hero of Socialist Labor; from 1940 chm, USSR Council of Pop Comr; from 1941 supr commander in chief, Soviet Armed Forces; Feb 1943 entitled generalissimus; many cities, districts, streets and squares in the USSR named for him; Stalin Prizes initiated for outstanding services in sci, culture and art; as secr-gen, CC, CPSU(B) concentrated all power in his own hands and made skillful use of Party apparatus, differences of opinion in leadership and terrorist means to establish his personal, unlimited dictatorship in USSR; at one time Lenin warned the Party against such an eventuality; he wrote that Stalin, after becoming secr-gen of the Party, had ". . . concentrated tremendous power in his hands, and I am not sure that he is always capable of using this power with due caution . . . Stalin is too crude, and this defect, while quite tolerable in the milieu and relations of us Communists, becomes intolerable in the post of secretary-general. I therefore propose, Comrades, that we think of a way of removing Stalin from this post and replacing him with someone else"; 1924 this document, known as Lenin's Testament, was brought to the attention of the delegates at the 13th Party Congress which, after discussing the letter, decided to leave Stalin in this post; as Party and state leader he committed numerous crimes; introduced term "enemy of the people" which automatically precluded the necessity of proof that a person was guilty of ideological errors; this concept enabled ruthless reprisals to be taken against any person suspected – often without the least grounds – of intending to commit a hostile act; justified individual and mass reprisals with the thesis that the class struggle would intensify as the USSR moved nearer to socialism; responsible for millions of victims among the peoples of the Sov Union; a specially appointed Party commission established that of the 139

CC members and cand members elected at the 17th Party Congress, some 70 percent were arrested and executed; Academician A.D. Sakharov maintains that: "... in 1936–39 alone more than 1.2 million CPSU(B) members – or half the Party – were arrested; only 50,000 saw freedom again; the rest were tortured to death during interrogation, executed (600,000) or perished in the concentration camps"; 1956 CPSU CC statement claimed that Stalin "immeasurably overestimated his own merits, laid claim to infallibility, committed a number of grave crimes ... and applied unworthy methods"; fathered three children, including son Yakov from his first marriage with Mariya; wrote numerous works, collected in "Voprosy leninizma" (Problems of Leninism) and "Sochineniya" (Works); his role in journalism, theoretical works and publ was greatly exaggerated in his lifetime; *Died:* 5 Mar 1953 in Kuntsevo, near Moscow; interred in Lenin Mausoleum; Oct 1961, by decision of 22nd CPSU Congress, his body was removed from the Mausoleum and buried by the Kremlin Wall on Moscow's Red Square.

STALIN, Vasiliy Iosifovich (1921–1962) Air Force lt-gen; son of I.V. Stalin and Nadezhda Alliluyeva; *Born:* 1921 in Moscow; *Educ:* 1941 grad Lipetsk Mil Pilots College; *Career:* 1941–43 chief of inspection, Red Army Air Force; spring 1943 arrested on Stalin's orders on charges of "moral degeneracy", held for 10 days in custody and sent to the front; 1943–45 commanded air force regt, div, then corps; 1945–47 commanded air force corps with Sov Occupation Forces in East Germany; 1947–52 air force commander, Moscow Mil Distr; May 1952 removed from his post on Stalin's orders for disobeying command instructions and assigned for course of study at Gen Staff Acad; prevented from studying by chronic alcoholism; Mar 1953, after his father's death, raised a great fuss and accused govt of killing off Stalin; as a result of this Min of Defense Bulganin ordered him out of Moscow and assigned him to duty in a mil distr; refused to comply with this order; discharged from USSR Armed Forces and 28 Apr 1953 arrested by State Security organs; sentenced to eight years' imprisonment for abusing his position and intrigues; Jan 1960 released by Khrushchev before completing his sentence; Apr 1960, arrested for drunkenness and returned to prison to serve out the rest of his original sentence; spring 1961 released from prison in connection with his deteriorating health and barred from residence in Moscow; *Died:* 19 Mar 1962 in Kazan', completely debilitated by alcoholism; buried in Kazan' in the Dzhugashvili family grave.

STAL'SKIY, Suleyman (real name: GASANBEKOV) (1869–1937) Poet; Pop Poet of Dag ASSR; *Born:* 18 May 1869 in vil Ashaga-Stal', Dag; son of a Lezghin peasant; *Career:* from age 13 farmhand in Ashaga'Stal', then worked in Baku oilfields and on construction of bridge over Amu-Dar'ya River; again farmhand in Ashaga-Stal'; member, Kirov Kolkhoz, Ashaga-Stal'; illiterate, but composed songs in Dag oral tradition; member, Dag Centr Exec Comt; 1934 deleg, 1st USSR Writers' Congress; member, USSR Writers' Union; *Works:* poems: "The Mullahs" (1912); "The Rich Merchants" and "The Judges" (1913); "February" (1917); "Friends, Free Is Out Lot!" (1917); "Daghestan" (1917); "Friends, Our Path Is Ill-Fated!" (1918–19); "In Kyure the Game is Legion" (1918–19); "The Caucasus" (1918–19); "On the Death of the Best Stalinist, Comrade Kirov"; "For the Bolsheviks There Is No Obstacle"; "Our Strength"; "To October"; "The Teacher"; "On the Crash of the 'Maxim Gorky' Aircraft" (1935); "Speech at the Ceremony to Mark the 15th Anniversary of the Daghestani ASSR" (1935); "Song of Vigilance" (1936); "Red Army" (1936); "To the 8th Extraordinary USSR Congress of Soviets Which Approved the Stalin Constitution" (1936); a series of poems about Stalin: "Song of Comrade Stalin" (1935); "To Beloved Stalin, Light of the World" (1935); "I Shall Sing of the Bolsheviks" (1936); poem "Daghestan" (1935–37); "Poem of Sergo Ordzhonikidze, Beloved Fellow-Champion and Friend of the Great Stalin" (1936), to mark Ordzhonikidze's 50th birthday; *Awards:* Order of Lenin (1936); *Died:* 23 Nov 1937 in his native vil Ashaga-Stal'; buried in Makhachkala.

STANISLAVSKIY (real name: ALEKSEYEV), Konstantin Sergeyevich (1863–1938) Actor, stage dir and drama teacher; founder of Moscow Arts Theater; Pop Artiste of USSR from 1936; *Born:* 5 Jan 1863 in Moscow; *Educ:* 1878–81 studied at Lazarev Inst of Oriental Languages, Moscow; *Career:* from 1877 actor, from 1882 stage dir, for Alekseyev Circle's amateur productions; from 1885 performed at Paradise Theater, German Club and Moscow-area theaters; 1888, together with stage dir and playwright A. Fedotov, stage designer F. Sologub and singer F. Komissarzhevskiy, founded Art and Lit Soc; 1888–98 actor and stage dir for this soc; 1898, together with Nemirovich-Danchenko, founded Pop Arts Theater (later Moscow Acad Arts Theater), where he performed as actor and stage dir until his death; 1912 founded at Moscow Arts theater 1st Studio, and 1916 2nd Studio; 1918 founded Opera Studio at Bolshoy Theater; 1920 founded 3rd studio and 1922 – 4th Studio at Moscow Arts Theater; 1922–24 directed Moscow Acad Arts Theater tours of Europe and USA; 1935 founded and directed Opera Drama Studio (now Moscow's Stanislavskiy Drama Theater); Moscow Musical Theater and Museum-Center also named for him; *Roles:* Trigorin in Chekhov's *Chayka* (The Seagull); Astrov in Chekhov's *Dyadya Vanya* (Uncle Vanya); Gayev in Chekhov's *Vishnyovyy sad* (The Cherry Orchard); Vershinin in Chekhov's *Tri sestry* (The Three Sisters); Shabel'skiy in Chekhov's "Ivanov"; Ivan Shuyshkiy in "Tsar' Fyodor Ioannovich"; Ivan in A.K. Tolstoy's *Smert' Ioanna Groznogo* (The Death of Ivan the Terrible); Famusov in Griboyedov's *Gore ot uma* (Woe from Wit); Abrezkov in Lev Tolstoy's *Zhivoy trup* (The Living Corpse); Argand in Moliere's "Le Malade Imaginaire"; Satin in Gorky's *Na dne* (The Lower Depths); Stockman in Ibsen's "Doctor Stockman"; Rakitin in Turgenev's *Mesyats v derevne* (A Month in the Country), etc; *Productions:* A.K. Tolstoy's "Tsar' Fyodor Ioannovich" (1898); Chekhov's "Chayka" (1898); Chekhov's "Dyadya Vanya" (1899); Gorky's *Meshchane* (The Philistines) and "Na dne" (1902); Lev Tolstoy's *Vlast' t'my* (The Powers of Darkness) (1902); Chekhov's "Vishnyovyy sad" (1904); Griboyedov's "Gore ot uma" (1906); Gogol's *Revizor* (The Government Inspector) (1908); Shakespeare's "Hamlet" (1911); Moliere's "Le Malade Imaginaire"; (1913); Bulgakov's *Dni Turbinykh* (The Days of the Turbins) (1926); Ivanov's *Bronepoyezd 14-69* (Armored Train 14-69) (1927); Leonov's "Uptilovsk" (1928); operas: Tchaikovskiy's *Yevgeniy Onegin* (Eugene Onegin) (1922); Rimsky-Korsakov's *Tsarskaya nevesta* (A Bride for the Tsar) (1926); Moussorgsky's "Boris Godunov" (1929); Rossini's "The Barber of Seville" (1933); Bizet's "Carmen" (1935), etc; *Publ: Moya zhizn' v iskusstve* (My Life in Art) (1926); *Rabota aktyora nad soboy* (An Actor's Work on Himself) (1938), etc; *Awards:* Order of Lenin; Order of the Red Banner of Labor; *Died:* 7 Aug 1938 in Moscow.

STARCHENKO, Vasiliy Fyorodovich (1904–1948) Govt official; corresp member, Ukr Acad of Sci from 1945; CP member from 1928; *Born:* 20 Mar 1904 in vil Temryuk-Ukrainskiy, now Donetsk Oblast; *Educ:* 1929 grad Kiev Agric Inst; *Career:* 1934–38 dir and sci dir, Mironov Selection Research Station; 1938 chm, Kiev Oblast Exec Comt; from Dec 1938 dep chm, Ukr Council of Pop Comr; from 1946 dep chm, Ukr Council of Min; at 18th Party Congress elected cand member, CC, CPSU(B); 1938–40 cand member, from 1940 member, CC, CP(B) Ukr; dep, USSR and Ukr Supr Sov of 1st and 2nd convocations; *Awards:* two Orders of Lenin; other orders; medals; *Died:* 17 July 1948.

STARITSKAYA, Mariya Mikhaylovna (1865–1930) Actress, stage dir and drama teacher; *Born:* 1865; *Educ:* grad Petersburg Theatrical College; *Career:* while still at high-school performed with Kiev amateur dramatic group; from 1885 acted with her father, M.P. Staritskiy's, drama company; worked for Russian companies in Petersburg and Moscow; from 1898 stage dir and instructor for various drama groups and for Lit and Arts Soc, Kiev; 1904–27 head, Drama Dept, Lysenko Music and Drama School (from 1918 Inst), Kiev; *Roles:* Anna Petrovna, Limerikha, the Mother, and Hanna in Staritskiy's plays *Ne suzhdeno* (It Is Not Fated), *Za dvumya zaytsami* (After Two Hares), "Marusya Boguslavka" and "Bogdan Khmel'nitskiy"; Vasilisa and Kabanikha in Ostrovskiy's "Vasilisa Melent'yeva" and *Groza* (The Storm); *Productions:* Karpenko-Karyy's *Burlak* (The Barge Hauler) and *Naymichka* (The Hireling); Griboyedov's *Gore ot uma* (Woe from Wit); Staritskiy's *Oborona Bushi* (The Defense of Busha); Lesya Ukrainka's "Joanna, Wife of Hus", "Mohammed and Aysha" and "The Stone Sovereign" (1914), etc; *Died:* 20 Dec 1930 in Kiev.

STARITSKAYA-CHERNYAKHOVSKAYA, Lyudmila (1868–1941) Ukr writer; *Born:* 1868 in Poltava Province, daughter of a landowner; *Career:* in her youth began to write and take an active part in Ukr nat movement; joined group of writers centered around Lesya Ukrainka; influenced by Populism and Modernism; embodied ideals of Ukr nat liberation movement in her work; translated for lit works into Ukr; 1930 sentenced to death in Khar'kov in trial of Ukr Liberation League; sentence commuted to eight years' exile; *Publ:* plays "Claudius Appius" and "Hetman Doroshenko", etc; lit criticism "Twenty-Five Years of Ukrainian

Theater"; "Yanoskayas Human Happiness"; "Ganna Barvinok"; *Died:* 1941 in imprisonment.

STARK (real name: RYABOVSKIY), Leonid Nikolayevich (1889–1937) Diplomat; CP member from 1905; *Born:* 1889; *Career:* 1912 deported from Russia; joined Trotsky's group and lived for a while in Vienna, then on Capri; contributed to Bolshevik publications "Zvezda", "Pravda" and "Prosveshcheniye" and Menshevik journal "Sovremennik"; 1915–16 member, Exec Commission, Petersburg RSDRP(B) Comt; contributed to "Pravda" and journal "Letopis'"; secr, "Ogni" (Fires) Publ House; after 1917 Oct Revol worked for Petrograd News Agency and Russian News Agency; 1919–20 mil work; May 1920–37 dipl work; 1920–22 counsellor, RSFSR mission in Geo; 1922–23 counsellor, RSFSR mission in Est; 1923–24 RSFSR plen in Est; 1924–36 USSR plen in Afghanistan; 1936–37 USSR Pop Comrt of For Affairs plen in Geo SSR; arrested by State Security organs; *Died:* 1937 in imprisonment.

STASHEVSKIY, Vasiliy Petrovich (1895–1938) Bel writer; member, Bel Writers' Union from 1934; *Born:* 1895 in vil Svinka, Minsk Oblast, son of a peasant; *Educ:* 1914 grad Nesvizh Seminary; 1924 grad Minsk Teachers' Inst; 1918–20 studied at Minsk Teachers' Training Inst; studied at opera and drama studio, Moscow and on Higher Bel Study Courses, Minsk; *Career:* from 1914 with Russian Army at the front; 1920 in partisan unit and mil comr, Nesvizh Uyezd Mil Revol Comt; from 1921 with Bel Pop Comrt of Educ; from 1922 teacher, Uzda Seven-Grade School; 1924–26 taught history and lit at Orsh Workers' Fac; from 1926 exec secr, "Maladnyak" Lit Assoc; from 1929 exec secr, "Polymya" Lit Assoc, Minsk; 1925 first work published; 1937 arrested by State Security organs; *Publ:* plays "Father and Son" (1927); "In Darkness' (1927); "Katsyaryna" (1928); "Sing, Spring!" (1928); "Oath in the Forest" (1930); collected stories and novelettes: "Under a Local Sun" (1931); "The Rustling Birch Wood" (1933); selected works "The Rustling Birch Wood" (1963); *Died:* 8 Sept 1938 in imprisonment; posthumously rehabilitated.

STASHKOV, Nikolay Ivanovich (1907–1943) Party Official; CP member from 1931; *Born:* 2 Apr 1907 in Odessa, son of a worker; *Career:* prior to WW 2 Party work in Dnepropetrovsk; from 1941 secr, underground Dnepropetrovsk Oblast Comt, CP(B) Ukr; July 1942 arrested by German occupation authorities; *Awards:* Hero of the Sov Union (1945, posthumously); *Died:* Jan 1943 executed.

STASOVA, Yelena Dmitriyevna (1873–1966) Party official; CP member from 1898; *Born:* 3 Oct 1873 in Petersburg, daughter of a lawyer; *Educ:* grad high-school; *Career:* worked with Krupskaya in Sunday workers' schools; until 1905 underground revol work in Petersburg, Oryol, Moscow and other Russian cities; secr, Petersburg RSDRP Comt; secr, Northern Bureau, CC, RSDRP; Aug 1905–Jan 1906 worked in Geneva for Party CC; 1907–12 Party work in Tiflis; 1911 worked for Russian Org Commission; 1917 at 6th (Prague) All-Russian RSDRP Conference elected member, CC, RSDRP(B); frequently arrested and imprisoned for revol activities; 1913–16 exiled in Yeniseysk Province; helped carry out 1917 Oct Revol; Feb 1917–Mar 1920 secr, CC, RSDRP(B) /RCP(B)/ in Petrograd, then in Moscow; 1917 at 6th RSDRP(B) congress elected cand member, at 7th and 8th RCP(B) Congresses elected member, CC, Party; 1920–21 exec Party work in Petrograd, then in Baku; 1920 helped organize 1st Congress of Peoples of the East; elected secr, Propaganda and Action Council of Peoples of the East; also worked for Caucasian Bureau, CC, RCP(B); 1921–26 worked for Comintern; 1927–38 chm, CC, Int Org for Aid to Revol Fighters and dep chm of its Exec Comt; 1930–34 member and Party Collegium member, CPSU(B) Centr Control Commission; 1935–43 member, Int Control Commission; 1932 at Amsterdam Anti-War Congress elected member, World Anti-War and Anti-Fascist Comt; 1934 helped found World Anti-War and Anti-Fascist Women's Comt; 1938–46 ed, journal "International Literature" (in French and English); from 1946 engaged in soc and lit work; member, All-Russian Centr Exec Comt of several convocations; from 1935 member, USSR Centr Exec Comt; *Awards:* three Orders of Lenin; Hero of the Sov Union (1960); medal; *Died:* 31 Dec 1966 in Moscow; buried on Moscow's Red Square.

STEFAN (secular name: NIKITIN, Sergey Alekseyevich) (1895–1963) Bishop of Mozhaysk; Vicar of Moscow Eparchy from 1960; *Born:* 1895 in Moscow; *Educ:* 1922 grad Med Fac, Moscow Univ; *Career:* from 1922 intern, nervous diseases clinic and neuropathologist at various Moscow med establishments; then worked at hospitals in Vladimir Oblast; 1927 ordained priest and served in parishes of Tashkent Eparchy, then at Tikhva Cloister, Ukr; 1959 took monastic vows and served in Minsk Metropolitan Church; 1960 elevated to bishop; *Died:* 28 Apr 1963.

STEFAN (secular name: PROTSENKO) (1889–1960) Metropolitan of Khar'kov and Bogodukhov, Russian Orthodox Church from 1959; *Born:* 2 Aug 1889 in vil Paleyevka, now Sumy Oblast; *Educ:* 1922 grad History Dept, Nezhin History and Philology Inst; grad three courses at Kiev Theological Acad; *Career:* 1922 Father Superior, Holy Trinity Monastery in vil Nosovki, Chernigov Oblast; took monastic orders and elevated to archimandrite; from 1926 Bishop of Kozelets; from 1934 Bishop of Chernigov and Nosovka; from 1942 Archbishop of Ufa; from 1944 Archbishop of Poltava and Kremenchug; from 1945 Archbishop of Khar'kov and Bogodukhov; 1950 spoke at All-Union Conference of Peace-Fighters, Moscow; *Awards:* right to wear cross on cowl (1945); medal "For Valiant Labor in the 1941–45 Great Fatherland War"; *Died:* 6 Oct 1960 in Khar'kov.

STEPANISHCHEV, Mikhail Tikhonovich (1917–1946) Mil pilot; lt-col; CP member from 1944; *Born:* 12 Dec 1917 in vil Kolosovo, now Lipetsk Oblast, son of a peasant; *Educ:* 1938 grad mil pilots school; *Career:* during WW 2 mil pilot, flight commander, navigator of air force regt, dep commander of air force regt; fought on Southern, 4th Ukr and 3rd Bel Fronts; flew 222 sorties; *Awards:* twice Hero of the Sov Union (1944 and 1945); Order of Lenin; other orders; medals; *Died:* 8 Sept 1946.

STEPANOV (Party name: BRAUN), Sergey Ivanovich (1876–1935) Party official; CP member from 1897; *Born:* 1876; *Career:* metalworker by trade; 1895 began revol work at Tula Munitions Plant; frequently arrested; 1903 deleg at 2nd RSDRP Congress; after 2nd Congress sided with Bolsheviks; worked in Tula, Petersburg, Moscow and Lugansk; 1915 exiled to Irkutsk Province; after 1917 Feb Revol returned from exile to Tula; after 1917 Oct Revol directed nationalization of Tula Ammunition Plant; from 1919 dir of this plant; 1925–30 chm, Tula Province Exec Comt, then chm, Tula Okrug Exec Comt; from 1930 dep chm, Moscow Oblast Exec Comt; secr, Party Collegium, Moscow Oblast Control Commission; 1933–35 chm, Moscow Oblast Court; at 13th Party Congress elected member, CPSU(B) Centr Control Commission; at 14th and 15th Party Congresses elected member, Auditing Commission, CC, CPSU(B); *Died:* 14 Aug 1935.

STEPANOV, Vyacheslav Vasil'yevich (1889–1950) Mathematician; prof from 1928; corresp member, USSR Acad of Sci from 1946; *Born:* 4 Sept 1889; *Educ:* univ grad; *Career:* from 1928 prof, Moscow Univ; 1943–49 vice-pres, from 1949 hon member, Moscow Mathematical Soc; did research on the theory of functions; also studied the theory of differential equations and their application to celestial mech and other subjects; investigated the properties of Stepanov's "almost periodic" functions and the conditions determining the existence of a gen and generalized differential for the function of two variables; 1947, together with V.V.Nemytskiy, wrote first systematic Russian exposition of qualitative methods in the theory of differential equations; *Publ:* *Kurs differentsial'nykh uravneniy* (A Course on Differential Equations) (1937); coauthor, *Kachestvennaya teoriya differentsial'nykh uravneniy* (The Qualitative Theory of Differential Equations) (1947); *Awards:* Stalin Prize (1951); *Died:* 22 July 1950.

STEPANYAN, Nel'son Georgiyevich (1913–1944) Mil pilot; col; CP member from 1932; *Born:* 28 Mar 1913 in Shusha, Azer; *Educ:* 1935 grad mil pilots school; *Career:* from 1941 in Red Army; during WW 2 commanded flight, squadron, then regt with Baltic Fleet Air Force; *Awards:* twice Hero of the Sov Union (1942 and 1945 /posthumously/); two Orders of Lenin; other orders; medals; *Died:* 14 Dec 1944 killed in action.

STETSKIY, Aleksey Ivanovich (1896–1938) Party official; CP member from 1915; *Born:* 1896, son of an official; *Career:* office worker; 1911 began revol work in Chernigov; during WW 1 worked for Petrograd Party org; after 1917 Feb Revol leading member, Syzran' Party Org; deleg at 6th RSDRP(B) Congress; helped muster Red Guard units in Volga area; 1918–21 fought in Civil War; 1918 with Polit Dept, Eastern Front; 1919 commanded brigade of 42nd Div; after Civil War Party work; head, Dept of Agitation and Propaganda, CC, CPSU(B); deleg at 13th–17th CPSU(B) Congresses; at 13th and 14th Congresses elected member, Centr Control Commission; at 16th and 17th Congresses elected member, CC, CPSU(B); arrested by State Security organs; *Died:* 1938 in imprisonment.

STOMONYAKOV, Boris Spiridonovich (1882–1941) Diplomat;

Bulgarian; CP member from 1902; *Born:* 1882; *Educ:* studied at mining inst; *Career:* 1902 expelled from inst for participation in student revol movement; 1904 deported from Russia; lived in Liege and worked for For Bureau, CC, RSDRP, smuggling lit and weapons into Russia; 1906 lived in Bulgaria, then returned to Russia but was soon arrested; released upon the representations of the Bulgarian Govt and moved to Liege, then to Bulgaria; 1909 moved to Paris and engaged in Party work; 1910 moved to Berlin and abandoned Party work; 1915 returned to Bulgaria and served in Bulgarian Army; 1917 served in Bulgarian embassy in Holland; resigned after end of WW 1; 1920–35 Sov trade plen in Berlin; from 1926 Collegium member, USSR Pop Comrt of For Affairs; 1934–38 USSR Dep Pop Comr of For Affairs; arrested by State Security organs; *Died:* 1941 in imprisonment.

STOPANI, Aleksandr Mitrofanovich (1871–1932) Govt official; CP member from 1893; *Born:* 9 Oct 1871 in vil Usol'ye, Irkutsk Province, son of mil surgeon; *Career:* 1892 joined revol movement; worked for Soc-Democratic circles in Kazan' and Yaroslavl'; 1896 arrested and placed under public police surveillance; 1900 attended Pskov meeting arranged by Lenin to discuss founding of newspaper "Iskra"; 1901 worked for Northern Workers' League; 1902–03 member, Org Comt for Convening 2nd RSDRP Congress; deleg at 2nd RSDRP Congress; 1903–04 worked for Yaroslavl' and Baku RSDRP(B) Comt; 1905–07 secr, Kostroma RSDRP(B) Comt; 1907 deleg at 5th (London) RSDRP Congress; from 1908 worked in Baku for Petroleum Ind Workers' Union; secr, ed bd, publication "Gudok"; member, Baku RSDRP(B) Comt; arrested in Baku for complicity in 1905–07 revol events in Kostroma and sent to Kostroma; later returned to Baku; 1913–14 helped stage Baku gen strike; 1917 chm, Baku Food Comt; from 1918 Collegium member, Pop Comrt of Labor; 1919 member, Higher Mil Inspectorate; 1920 member, North Caucasian Revol Comt; 1921–22 member, Revol Mil Council, Labor Army; from 1922 member, RSFSR Supr Court; 1924–29 RSFSR prosecutor for labor cases; 1930–32 dep chm, All-Union Soc of Old Bolsheviks; member, Moscow CPSU(B) Comt; member, Moscow Control Commission and Bureau member, Moscow's Zamoskvorech'ye Rayon CPSU(B) Comt; *Died:* 23 Oct 1932.

STRASHUN, Il'ya Davidovich (1892–1967) Hygienist and med historian; prof from 1940; member, USSR Acad of Med Sci from 1944; CP member from 1920; *Born:* 1892; *Educ:* 1915 grad Med Fac, Moscow Univ; *Career:* 1915–17 mil surgeon in Russian Army; 1918–21 mil surgeon in Red Army; 1921–30 dir, Sanitary Educ Publ House; 1923–30 also asst prof, Chair of Soc Hygiene, Med Fac, 2nd Moscow Univ; from 1929 founder-dean, Fac of Sanitation and Hygiene, 1st Moscow Med Inst; 1930, together with A. V. Mol'kov, founder Soc Hygiene Museum and organized a health exhibition; 1930 organized Sov pavilion at the Dresden Int Exhibition; 1930–35 assoc prof of med history, 1935–40 head, Chair of Med History, 1st Moscow Med Inst; 1934–39 also head, Dept of Higher Med Educ Establishments, RSFSR Pop Comrt of Health; 1940–41 prof of soc hygiene, 1941–45 dir, 1st Leningrad Med Inst; 1945–47 acting dir, 1947–49 senior assoc, Inst of Health Service Org and N. A. Semashko Inst of Med History; 1945–48 also head, Chair of Med History, 1st Moscow Med Inst; 1949–67 consultant, Centr Inst of Sanitary Educ, USSR Min of Health; member, Ed Comt for the Publ of Classic For and Russian Med Works; Presidium member and hon member, All-Russian Soc of Med Historians; hon member, Moscow, Kiev and other municipal soc of med historians; member, Council of Sanitary Educ, USSR Min of Health; *Publ:* *Russkiy vrach na voyne* (A Russian Doctor at War) (1947); *Osnovnyye etapy razvitiya instituta za polveka. O pervom Leningradskom meditsinskom institute* (The Main Stages in the Development of the Leningrad Medical Institute in the Last Fifty Years. The First Leningrad Institute) (1947); coauthor, *Okhrana zdorov'ya trudyashchikhsya v Sovetskom Soyuze* (Workers' Health Care in the Soviet Union) (1947); *Obshchebiologicheskiye vzglyady vrachey drevnego Kitaya* (The General Biological Views of Doctors in Ancient China) (1955), etc; *Died:* Feb 1967 in Leningrad.

STRAZHESKO, Nikolay Dmitriyevich (1876–1952) Clinician and therapist; Dr of Med from 1904; prof from 1907; member, Ukr Acad of Sci from 1934; member, USSR Acad of Sci from 1943; member, USSR Acad of Med Sci from 1944; Hon Sci Worker of Ukr SSR from 1934; Hero of Socialist Labor from 1947; *Born:* 29 Dec 1876 in Odessa, son of a lawyer; *Educ:* 1899 grad Med Fac, Saint Vladimir Univ, Kiev; *Career:* after grad trained and worked under V.P.Obraztsov; 1902–04 prepared doctor's thesis on physiology of intestines at Pavlov's Laboratory, Petersburg Mil Med Acad; 1907–19 prof, Chair of Special Pathology and Therapy, Kiev Women's Med Inst; from 1919 head, Chair of Therapy, Novorossiysk Univ; from 1922 dir, Propaedeutic Clinic, then Hospital Clinic, 1929–52 dir, Fac Clinic, Kiev Med Inst; from 1934 also worked at Inst of Clinical Physiology, Ukr Acad of Sci; during WW 2 hospital consultant, USSR Min of Health and prof, Chair of Therapy, Bashkir Med Inst and 1st Moscow Med Inst; from 1943 dir, Ukr Inst of Clinical Med, which he founded in 1936 and which now bears his name; bd member, All-union and All-Ukr Soc of Therapists; member, Learned Council, Ukr Pop Comrt of Health; member, Rheumatism Comt; ed, various med journals; did research on pathology of circulatory system and described several cardiovascular syndromes; together with V.P. Obraztsov, made first intra vitam study of coronary occlusion; devised theory and classification of circulatory insufficiency; hypothesized that rheumatism is an infectious-allergic disease with a streptococcic etiology; studied relationship between sepsis, endocarditis and rheumatism; wrote over 100 works; *Publ:* doctor's thesis *K fiziologii kishok* (The Physiology of the Intestines) (1904); *K voprosu o bolezni Adams-Stoksa* (Adam Stokes' Disease) (1906); coauthor, *K simptomatologii i diagnostike tromboza venechnykh arteriy serdtsa* (The symptomatology and Diagnostics of Coronary Thrombosis) (1910); *Strofantin kak serdechnoye sredstvo* (Strophantine as a Cardiac Drug) (1910); *Osnovy fizicheskoy diagnostiki zabolevaniy bryushnoy polosti* (The Principles of the Physical Diagnosis of Diseases of the Abdominal Cavity) (1924); coauthor, *Atlas klinicheskoy gematologii* (An Atlas of Clinical Hematology) (1940); *Gematoparenkhimatoznyy bar'yer vo vnutrenney patologii* (The Hematoparenchymatous Barrier in Internal Pathology) (1943); *Revmatizm i yego otnosheniye k streptokokkovoy infektsii* (Rheumatism and Its Relation to Streptococcic Infection) (1950); coauthor, *Punktaty limfaticheskikh uzlov. Atlas* (Puncture Specimens of Lymph Nodes. An Atlas) (1953); *Neposredstvennoye vyslushivaniye serdtsa i sosudov s tsel'yu diagnostiki izmeneniy v nikh* (Direct Auscultation of the Heart and Vessels for the Diagnosis of Lesions) (1954); *Izbrannyye trudy* (Selected Works) (2 vol, 1955–56); *Awards:* two Orders of Lenin; other orders and medals; *Died:* 27 June 1952 in Kiev.

STREL'TSOV, Vladimir Vladimirovich (1902–1947) Physician; specialist in aeromed; *Born:* 1902; *Educ:* 1926 grad Leningrad Mil Med Acad; *Career:* after grad specialized in physiology; from 1930 head, Aeromed Section, Sanitary Research Inst; from 1935 head, Centr Psychophysiological Laboratory, USSR Civil Air Fleet; from 1939 head, Chair of Aeromed, 2nd Moscow Med Inst and Centr Inst of Postgrad Med Training; 1934–35 supervised the development of a physical training program for pilots aimed at improving resistance to disturbances of the vestibular apparatus and to g-load during flight; was an adherent of L. A. Orbeli's views on physiological evolution; his research provided valuable material for the subsequent development of Sov space med; wrote over 100 works; *Publ:* co-ed, *Psikhonevrologiya, psikhogigiyena i psikhologiya v grazhdanskom vozdushnom flote* (Psychoneurology, Mental Hygiene and Psychology in Civil Aviation) (1937); *Vysotnyye polyoty i vliyaniye ikh na organizm cheloveka* (High-Altitude Flights and Their Effect on the Human Body) (1939); ed, *Voprosy aviatsionnoy meditsiny* (Problems of Aeromedicine) (1939); *Vliyaniye vysoty i uskoreniy na organizma lyotchika* (The Effect of Altitude and Acceleration the Pilot's Body) (1945); *Died:* 1947.

STRIYEVSKIY, Konstantin Konstantinovich (1885–1939) Govt official; CP member from 1902; *Born:* 1885 in Vilnius Province, son of a peasant; *Career:* from age 11 worked at a Riga yeast plant; 1900–09 locksmith, then asst machinist, Riga Railroad Workshops; 1902–08 Party organizer and propagandist in Riga; member, Riga Party Comt; 1905 member, armed workers' squad; Dec 1905 arrested; from 1906 bd member, Railroad Workers' Union; 1909–11 exiled in Vologda Province; member, Velikiy Ustyug Party Comt; from 1911 worked at Moscow Electr Power Plant; 1911–13 propaganda work in Moscow; 1913 arrested and exiled to Olonetsk Province, then worked at a plant in Astrakhan'; took part in 1917 Oct Revol; 1918–19 food comr in Petrograd; 1919 Collegium member, Ukr Pop Comrt of Food; 1919–22 chief of mil food supply for Southwestern, Caucasian, Western and Petrograd Fronts; 1923–27 chm, Moscow Province Metalworkers' Union; member, Plenum, All-Russian Centr Trade-Union Council; 1927–29 chm, Moscow Sovnarkhoz; 1929 chm, Moscow Province

Trade-Union Council; from 1930 dep chm, then chm, RSFSR Supr Sovnarkhoz; then econ and govt work; at 13th, 14th and 17th Party Congresses elected cand member, at 15th and 16th Party Congresses elected member, CC, CPSU(B); arrested by State Security organs; *Died:* 1939 in imprisonment.

STROGANOV, Vasiliy Andreyevich (1888–1938) Party and govt official; CP member from 1905; *Born:* 1888 in Yeniseysk Province, son of a leather craftsman; *Career:* machinist by trade; 1905–17 revol work in Krasnoyarsk, Irkutsk and Kansk; frequently arrested; after 1917 Oct Revol exec Party work in Kansk, Nizhneudinsk, Irkutsk and Sormovo; 1925–27 secr, Yaroslavl' Province Party Comt; 1927–30 secr, Donetsk Okrug Party Comt; 1930–32 second secr, CC, CP(B) Ukr; 1932–33 secr, Dnepropetrovsk Party Comt; 1933–35 second secr, Sverdlovsk Oblast CPSU(B) Comt; from 1935 chm, Northern Kray, then Northern Oblast Exec Comt; deleg at 4th and 11th–17th Party Congresses; at 15th and 16th Congresses elected cand member, CC, CPSU(B); deleg at 10th and 11th Congresses of CP(B) Ukr; 1930–33 Politburo member, CC, CP(B) Urk; arrested by State Security organs; *Died:* 22 Apr 1938 in imprisonment.

STROKACH, Timofey Amvrosiyevich (1903–1963) Mil commander; lt-gen; CP member from 1927; *Born:* 4 Mar 1903 in vil Astrakhantsy, now Maritime Kray, son of a peasant; *Career:* 1919–22 fought with partisans in Far East; 1923–40 served with border troops; from Oct 1941 USSR Dep Pop Comr of Internal Affairs; with start of WW 2 directed mustering of raider battalions and partisan units; fought in defense of Kiev and Moscow; June 1942–May 1945 chief of staff, Ukr partisan units; 1945–46 Ukr Dep Pop Comr of Internal Affairs; 1946–56 Ukr Min of Internal Affairs; 1956–57 chief, Main Bd of Border Troops and USSR Dep Min of Internal Affairs; deleg at 18th CPSU(B) Congress; at 14th–19th Congresses of CP(B) Ukr elected member, CC, CP(B) Ukr; dep, USSR Supr Sov of 1st–4th convocations; dep, Ukr Supr Sov of 2nd convocation; *Awards:* three Orders of Lenin; Order of Suvorov, 1st Class; other orders and medals of USSR and other countries; *Died:* 15 Aug 1963.

STRUVE, Pyotr Berngardovich (1870–1944) Econ; philosopher; politician; prof; *Born:* 1870; *Educ:* 1893 grad Law Fac, Petersburg Univ; *Career:* criticized Populist interpretation of development of capitalism in Russia; also criticized some tenets of Marxism; 1896 attended Int Socialist Congress, London; 1898 wrote "Manifest RSDRP" (Manifesto of the RSDRP); 1902–05 theorist and organizer, liberal wing of League for the Liberation of the Working Class; edited its illegal for organ "Osvobozhdeniye"; from 1905 member, CC, Constitutional Democratic Party; 1905–07 edited its journal "Polyarnaya Zvezda"; also edited its newspaper "Duma"; 1907–17 prof, Petersburg Polytech Inst; from 1917 member, Russian Acad of Sci; during Civil War member, Denikin and Wrangel anti-Sov govts; from 1920 lived in Prague, then Paris, where he edited Constitutional-Democratic journal "Russkaya mysl'" and newspaper "Vozrozhdeniye"; *Publ: Kriticheskiye zametki k voprosu ob ekonomicheskom razvitii Rossii* (Critical Notes on the Economic Development of Russia) (1894); *Khozyaystvo i tsena* (The Economy and Prices) (2 vol, 1913–16); *Sotsial'naya i ekonomicheskaya istoriya Rossii* (The Social and Economic History of Russia) (1952), etc; *Died:* 1944 in Paris.

STRUVE, Vasiliy Vasil'yevich (1889–1965) Orientalist; Dr of History from 1928; prof from 1916; member, USSR Acad of Sci from 1935; corresp member, Prague Acad of Sci from 1937; Hon Sci Worker of Uzbek SSR from 1943; *Born:* 2 Feb 1889 in Petersburg; *Educ:* 1911 grad History and Philology Fac, Petersburg Univ; *Career:* 1916–65 prof and from 1945 head, Chair of the History of the Ancient East, Petrograd (Leningrad) Univ; 1918–33 head, Egyptian Dept, Leningrad Hermitage; 1935–50 dir, Inst of Anthropology and Ethnography, USSR Acad of Sci; 1941–50 also dir, Inst of Oriental Studies, USSR Acad of Sci; from 1955 chm, Oriental Commission, USSR Geographical Soc; from 1959 head, Dept of the Ancient East, Inst of Oriental Studies (from 1960 Inst of the Peoples of Asia), USSR Acad of Sci; bureau member, Dept of Historical Sci (from 1963 Dept of History), USSR Acad of Sci; specialized in the ancient history of the Middle East with special reference to Egypt, Babylon, Persia and Israel; studied ancient Sumerian documents, which he made available to numerous students of Assyrian history; deciphered numerous ancient writings, including Egyptian papyruses; wrote Egyptian hieroglyphs and demotic script, as well as Sumerian, Babylonian, Assyrian, Hittite, Urart and Persian cuneiform; also learned Ancient Hebrew, Aramaic and Arabic; chief ed, journal "Vestnik drevney istorii"; member, Main Ed Bd, "Sovetskaya istoricheskaya entsiklopediya" and "Vsemirnaya istoriya"; *Publ: Petersburgskiye sfinsky* (The Sphinxes of Petersburg) (1912); *Izrail' i Yegipet* (Israel and Egypt) (1920); *Proiskhozhdeniye alfavita* (The Origin of the Alphabet) (1923); *Manefon i yego vremy* (Manephones and His Times) (1928); *Problema zarozhdeniya, razvitiya i razlozheniya rabovladel'cheskogo obhchestva drevnego Vostoka* (The Birth, Development and Decay of the Slave-Owning Society of the Ancient East) (1934); *Ocherki sotsial'no-ekonomicheskoy istorii drevnego Vostoka* (An Outline Socio-Economic History of the Ancient East) (1934); *Istoriya drevnego Vostoka* (The History of the Ancient East) (1935); *Fashistskiy antisemitizm* (Fascist Antisemitism) (1942); *Gorod Lagash* (The City of Lagash) (1961); exec ed, *Korpus bosporskikh nadposey* (The Body of Bosphoran Inscriptions) (1965); *Awards:* Order of Lenin (1945); Order of the Red Banner of Labor) (1959); *Died:* 15 Sept 1965.

STUCHKA, Pyotr Ivanovich (pseudonym: VETERAN) (1865–1932) Party and govt official; lawyer; prof; chm, USSR Supr Court from 1923; CP member from 1903; *Born:* 14 July 1865; *Educ:* 1888 grad Law Fac, Petersburg Univ; *Career:* 1888–97 ed, Lat democratic newspapers "Denas Lapa" and "Yauna-Strava"; 1897–1902 exiled in Vyatka Province; from 1903 chm, CC, Lat Soc-Democratic Party; worked for RSDRP orgs in Vitebsk Province and Riga; from 1907 in Petersburg, where he contributed to Lat Soc-Democratic periodicals and to Bolshevik organ "Prosveshcheniye"; after 1917 Feb Revol member, Bolshevik Faction, Petrograd Sov; after 1917 Oct Revol Pop Comr of Justice; then Collegium member, Pop Comrt of For Affairs; 1918–19 chm, Lat Sov govt; 1921–23 RSFSR (USSR) Dep Pop Comr of Justice; 1923–32 chm, USSR Supr Court; cand member, then member, CC, RCP(B); also member, CC, CP Lat and its rep in the Comintern; *Publ: Revolyutsionnaya rol' prava i gosudarstva* (The Revolutionary Role of Law and the State) (1921); *Ucheniye o gosudarstva i konstitutsii RSFSR* (The Theory of State and Constitution in the RSFSR) (6th ed, 1922); *Klassovoye gosudarstvo i grazhdanskoye pravo* (The Class State and Civil Law) (1942); *Kurs sovetskogo grazhdanskogo prava* (A Course in Soviet Civil Law) (3 vol, 1927–31); *Ucheniye o sovetskom gosudarstve i yego konstitutsii – SSSR i RSFSR* (The Theory of the Soviet State and Its Constitutions – USSR and RSFSR) (1929); *Awards:* Order of the Red Banner of Labor; *Died:* 25 Jan 1932.

STUKOV, Innokentiy Nikolayevich (1887–1937) Party and govt official; CP member from 1905; *Born:* 1887, son of a priest; *Career:* 1915 exiled for revol activities; early 1916 exiled to Verkholensk Uyezd, where he remained until 1917 Feb Revol; 1917 member, Petrograd Party Comt; went to Siberia to help arrange 1917 Apr Party Conference; after 1917 July riots member, Moscow Oblast Party Bureau; during 1917 Oct Revol member, Moscow Mil Revol Comt and member, Party Center; during Brest Peace Treaty controversy sided with Leftist Communists; from 1918 asst commander, Moscow Mil Distr; fought on Western and Eastern Fronts; member, Mil Revol Council, 5th Army; 1919, as chm, Ufa Revol Comt, conducted negotiations with members of Samara Constituent Assembly on behalf of Party CC; 1920 worked for Siberian Burea, Party CC; ed, periodical "Sovetskaya Sibir'"; 1920–21 sided with "Democratic Centralists"; 1921–24 Bureau member, Moscow Party Comt and head of its Agitation and Propaganda Dept; coordinating ed, "Moscow Worker" Publ House; from 1924 chm, Centr Ind Oblast Planning Bd; from 1926 learned secr, RSFSR Gosplan; 1927 sided with Trotskyist opposition and signed Trotskyist platform; 1927–28 dep chm, bd, State Tech Publ House; from 1930 cand Presidium member, USSR Gosplan; arrested by State Security organs; *Died:* 1937 in imprisonment.

SUKHOMEL, Georgiy Iosifovich (1888–1966) Eng; specialist in hydraulics and hydromech; prof from 1927; member, Ukr Acad of Sci from 1951; Hon Sci and Tech Worker of Ukr SSR from 1957; CP member from 1952; *Born:* 11 Sept 1888 in vil Mikolaivka, now Vinnitsa Oblast, son of a peasant; *Educ:* 1913 grad Kiev Polytech Inst; *Career:* 1914–27 lecturer, 1927–48 prof, Kiev Polytech Inst; from 1916 also taught at Kiev Hydro-Melioration Inst; 1940–58 dir, Inst of Hydrology and Hydraulic Eng, Ukr Acad of Sci; 1939–51 corresp member, Ukr Acad of Sci; *Publ: Neravnomernoye dvizheniye zhidkosti otkrytkykh ruslakh gidrotekhnicheskikh sooruzheniyakh* (The Irregular Motion of a Liquid in Open Channels and Hydrotechnical Structures) (1940); *Voprosy gidravliki otkrytykh rusel i sooruzheniy* (The Hydraulics of Open

Channels and Structures) (1949); *Issledovaniye dvizheniya sudov po ogranichennym farvateram* (An Investigation on the Motion of Vessels Along Limited Fairways) (1956); *Awards:* Stalin Prize (1951); Order of Lenin; other orders and medals; *Died:* 18 July 1966.

SUKHOMLIN, Kirill Vasil'yevich (1886–1938) Party and govt official; CP member from 1905; *Born:* 23 May 1886 in Krasnopol'ye, now Chernigov Oblast, son of a worker; *Career:* locksmith by trade: from 1904 worked at depots of Borzya, Manchuria and Zabaykal'ye Railroad Stations; conducted revol propaganda among railroad workers; during 1917 Oct Revol helped to establish Sov regime in Irkutsk, at the Manchuria Station and at other stations of the Trans-Baykal Railroad; member, Mil Revol Comt, East Siberian Okrug Bureau of Soviets; during Civil War fought with partisans in Far East; from 1920 trade-union work; member, CC, Railroad Workers' Union; also worked in Khar'kov as chm, Southern Bureau, CC, Railroad Workers' Union; from Feb 1925 Ukr Dep Pop Comr of Workers and Peasants' Inspection; from late 1925 Ukr Pop Comr of Labor; from Apr 1927 chm and Presidium member, USSR Supr Sovnarkhoz; Feb 1932 appointed dep chm, Ukr Council of Pop Comr; from 1933 chm, Centr Control Comission, CP(B) Ukr and Ukr Pop Comr of Workers and Peasants' Inspection; 1935–38 Ukr Pop Comr of Local Ind; Chm, Ukr Gosplan; also dep chm, Ukr Council of Pop Comr; deleg at 14th–17th CPSU(B) Congresses; at 15th and 16th Congresses elected cand member, CC, CPSU(B); at 17th Congress elected member, CPSU(B) Centr Auditing Commission; deleg at 6th–8th Conferences and 9th–13th Congresses of CP(B) Ukr; at 8th Conference elected member, Centr Control Commission, CP(B) Ukr; at 9th–13th Congresses elected member, CC, CP(B) Ukr; 1926–29 cand Politburo member, 1930–37 Politburo member, CC, CP(B) Ukr; member, and Presidium member, All-Ukr Centr Exec Comt of several convocations; arrested by State Security organs; *Awards:* Order of Lenin; *Died:* 26 Aug 1938 in imprisonment.

SUKHOV, Ivan Prokof'yevich (1895–1962) Mil commander; lt-gen, Armored Troops; *Born:* 1895; *Educ:* studied at "Vystrel" Higher Mil Courses; *Career:* from 1918 in Red Army; after Civil War commanded infantry brigade; after attending "Vystrel" Courses taught on Advanced Commanders Courses in Moscow; 1933–35 senior lecturer, 1938–40 head, Chair of Major Unit Tactics, Mil Acad for the Motorization and Mechanization of the Red Army; during WW 2 commanded major armored units; after WW 2 senior posts with USSR Min of Defense; *Publ: Tanki v sovremennoy voyne* (Tanks in Modern Warfare) (1940); *Died:* 1962.

SULEYMAN, Nikolay Aleksandrovich (1878–1938) Mil commander; *Born:* 1878; *Career:* gen, Russian Army; from 1918 in Red Army; research and teaching work at mil acads; arrested by State Security organs; *Publ: Tyl i snabzheniye deystvuyushchey armii* (The Rear and Supply of the Army in the Field) (1927); *Died:* 1938 in imprisonment.

SULTAN-GALIYEV, M. (1892–1939) Party official; CP member from 1917; *Born:* 1892; *Career:* 1919 appointed Comr for Moslems of Inner Russia; 1927 expelled from Party and sentenced for alleged anti-Party, anti-govt nationalistic activities; *Died:* 1939 in imprisonment.

SUPRUN, Stepan Pavlovich (1907-1941) Mil pilot; lt-col; CP member from 1930; *Born:* 2 Aug 1907 in vil Rechnki, now Sumy Oblast, son of a peasant; *Educ:* 1930 grad mil pilots school; *Career:* served at Khalkhin Gol and in 1939–40 Sov-Finnish War; during WW 2 commanded air force regt on Western Front; dep, USSR Supr Sov of 1st convocation; *Awards:* twice Hero of the Sov Union (1940 and 1941); Order of Lenin; other orders; medals; *Died:* 4 July 1941 killed in action over Bel; buried at Moscow's Novodevich'ye Cemetery.

SURITS, Yakov Zakharovich (1882–1952) Diplomat; CP member from 1917; *Born:* 1882 in Dvinsk; *Educ:* studied at Polit and Soc Sci Dept, Philosophy Fac, Berlin Univ; *Career:* 1902–03 member, Bund; 1903–14 member, RSDRP (Mensheviks); from 1902 active in revol movement; several times arrested and imprisoned by Tsarist authorities; 1907–10 exiled in Tobol'sk Province; 1918–47 dipl work; 1918–19 head, Sov mission in Denmark; 1919–21 Sov plen in Afghanistan, where he concluded the 1921 Sov-Afghan Treaty; 1921–22 member, Turkestani Commission, All-Russian Centr Exec Comt and RSFSR Pop Comrt of For Affairs plen for Turkestan and Centr Asia; 1922–23 Sov plen in Norway; 1923–34 Sov plen in Turkey; 1925 concluded Sov-Turkish Friendship and Neutrality Treaty; signed additional protocol to this treaty and an agreement extending term of treaty; 1934 negotiated establishment of dipl relations between USSR and Bulgaria; 1934–37 Sov plen in Germany; 1937–40 Sov plen in France; 1937–39 member, Sov deleg at all sessions of League of Nations; 1940–46 counsellor (with amb rank), USSR Pop Comrt of For Affairs; 1946–47 USSR amb in Brazil; *Awards:* Order of Lenin; Order of the Red Banner of Labor; *Died:* 1952.

SUSAYKOV, Ivan Zakharovich (1903–1962) Mil commander; lt-gen, Armored Troops; CP member from 1925; *Born:* 12 Sept 1903; *Educ:* 1937 grad Mil Acad of Armored Troops; *Career:* from 1924 in Red Army; during WW 2 member, mil council of various fronts; after WW 2 senior commands in Sov Army; dep, USSR Supr Sov of 4th convocation; from 1960 retired; *Died:* 12 July 1962.

SUSHKEVICH, Boris Mikhaylovich (1887–1946) Stage dir, actor and drama teacher; Pop Artiste of RSFSR from 1944; pupil and assoc of Stanislavsky and Vakhtangov; *Born:* 7 Feb 1887 in Petersburg; *Educ:* studied at History Fac, Moscow Univ; *Career:* as a student, took part in amateur dramatics; 1908–12 with Moscow Arts Theather; 1912 helped found 1st Studio, Moscow Arts Theater; 1912–33 Bd member, 1st Studio (from 1924 2nd Moscow Arts Acad Theater); 1933–36 artistic dir, Leningrad Acad Drama Theater; 1937–46 dir, Leningrad New Theater; 1933–41 prof, from 1936 dir, Leningrad Theatrical Inst; *Roles:* Suslov in *Dachniki* (The Dacha-Dwellers) (1906); the Investigator in *Brat'ya Karamazovy* (The Brothers Karamazov) (1910), after Dostoyevsky; Stratton in Berger's *Potok* (The Flood) (1915); Person in Strindberg's "Erik XIV" (1921); Matthias Klausen in Hauptmann's "Before Sunset" (1940); Kutuzov in Solov'yov's *Fel'dmarshal Kutuzov* (Fieldmarshal Kutuzov) (1941); Famusov in Grigoyedov's *Gore ot uma* (Woe from Wit), etc; Productions: Dickens' "The Cricket on the Hearth" (1914); Strindberg's "Erik XIV" (1921); *Rastochitel'* (The Spendthrift) (1924), after Leskov; Sukhovo-Kobylin's *Delo* (The Case) (1927); A. Tolstoy's *Pyotr I* (Peter I) (1930); Pushkin's "Boris Godunov" (1934); Gorky's "Platon Krechet" (1935); Gogol's *Revizor* (The Government Inspector) (1936); Molière's "Le Misanthrope" (1938); Hauptmann's "Before Sunset" (1940); Solov'yov's "Fieldmarshal Kutuzov" (1941); *Russkiye lyudi* (Russian People) (1942), etc; *Publ: Sem' momentov raboty nad rol'yu* (Seven Factors in Working up a Role) (1933); *Molodyozh' v teatre* (Youth in the Theater) (1937); *Osnovnyye momenty vospitaniya aktyora* (Basic Factors in Training an Actor) (1941); *Awards:* Order of the Red Banner of Labor; *Died:* 10 July 1946.

SUS, Nikolay Ivanovich (1880–1967) Reforestation expert; Dr of Agric; prof from 1924; hon member, Lenin All-Union Acad of Agric Sci; Hon Sci Worker of RSFSR from 1947; *Born:* 1880 in vil Volochisk, now Khmel'nitskiy Oblast; *Educ:* 1907 grad Petersburg Forestry Inst; *Career:* from 1907 worked on the Kamyshin River with a sandy-ravine team from the Forestry Dept; 1914 founded Kamyshin Reforestation Center; 1916 in charge of reforestation work in Saratov, Samara, then Orenburg Province; 1918–31 responsible for reforestation in Saratov Province, then in Lower Volga Kray; from 1920 also lecturer, Saratov Univ; from 1924 prof and head, Chair of Reforestation, Saratov Agric Inst; co-founder and 1931–38 dep sci dir, All-Union Research Inst for Land Improvement, Moscow; *Publ: Agromeliorativnoye delo* (Land Improvement) (1938); *Zashchitnoye lesorazvedeniye* (Protective Afforestation) (1948); *Eroziya pochvy i bor'ba s neyu. Lesomeliorativnyye meropriyatiya* (Soil Erosion and Countermeasures. Reforestation) (1949); textbook *Agromelioratsiya* (Land Improvement); *Awards:* Order of Lenin; two Orders of the Red Banner of Labor; Badge of Hon; medals; *Died:* 26 Aug 1967.

SVANIDZE, Aleksandr Semyonovich (1886–1942) Govt official; historian; CP member from 1903; *Born:* 1884 in vil Badzhi, Kutaisi Province; *Educ:* studied at History and Philology Fac, Jena Univ; *Career:* underground revol work in Transcaucasia; returned to Russia and took part in 1918–20 Civil War; 1921–24 Geo Pop Comr of Educ, Pop Comr of Finance and Pop Comr of For Affairs; 1924–37 Sov trade rep in Germany; chm, bd, USSR For Trade Bank; dep chm, bd, USSR State Bank; studied history of Ancient Orient; from Assyrian and Urart source material prepared outline history of ancient Transcaucasia; co-founder and first ed, journal "Vestnik drevney istorii"; brother of Stalin's first wife; 1937 arrested by State Security organs; *Publ: Materialy po istorii alarodiyskikh plemyon* (Material on the History of the Alarodian Tribes) (1936); *Nazvaniya drevnevostochnykh bogov v gruzinskikh pesnyakh* (The Names of the Ancient Oriental Gods in Georgian

Songs) (1937), etc; *Died:* 14 Nov 1942 in imprisonment; posthumously rehabilitated.

SVECHIN, Aleksandr Andreyevich (1878–1938) Mil historian and theorist; maj-gen from 1916; *Born:* 29 Aug 1878 in Yekaterinoslav, son of a gen; *Educ:* 1897 grad Mikhail Artillery College; 1903 grad Gen Staff Acad; *Career:* fought in 1904–05 Russo-Japanese War; company commander and staff officer, 3rd Army; during WW 1 attached for special assignments to chief of staff, Supr Commander in Chief; from July 1915 commanded 6th Finnish Infantry Regt; from Jan 1917 commanded separate naval div; from July 1917 chief of staff, 5th Army; 1918 joined Red Army; 1918 chief, All-Russian Main Staff; chm, Commission to Study and Utilize the Experience of the 1914–18 War; prof, Frunze Mil Acad and Gen Staff Acad; wrote numerous works on strategy, tactics and mil history; arrested by State Security organs; *Publ: Voyna v gorakh* (Mountain Warfare) (1907); *Russko-yaponskaya voyna 1904–05 godov po dokumental'nym dannym truda Voyenno-istoricheskoy komissii i drugim istochnikam* (The 1904–05 Russo Japanese War from the Documentary Data of the Military History Commission and Other Sources) (1910); *Takticheskiye uroki Russko-yaponskoy voyny* (The Tactical Lessons of the Russo-Japanese War) (1912); *Istoriya voyennogo isskusstva* (The History of Warfare) (3 vol, 1922–23); *Strategiya* (Strategy) (2nd ed, 1927); *Evolyutsiya voyennogo iskusstva* (The Evolution of Warfare) (2 vol, 1927–28); *Died:* 29 July 1938 in imprisonment; posthumously rehabilitated.

SVECHNIKOV, Anatoliy Grigor'yevich (1908–1962) Composer; Hon Art Worker of Ukr SSR from 1954; *Born:* 2 June 1908 in Kiev; *Educ:* 1932 grad Lysenko Musical Drama Inst, Kiev; 1936–38 postgrad studies at Kiev Conservatory; *Career:* 1932–33 musical dir and composer, Donbass Drama Theater; 1933–36 at theaters in Kiev; 1936–41 and 1944–51 musical dir, Ukr Radio; 1945–56 taught composition at Kiev Conservatory; *Works:* two etudes and prelude for piano (1928); "Variations on a Ukrainian Theme" (1930); "Suite on Themes of the Eastern Peoples" (1939); poems: "Karmelyuk" (1945); "Shchors" (1949); music for the ballet "Marus'ya Boguslavka" (1951); "My Beloved Kiev" (1959); "My Native Party" (1959); "Fishermen's Lyric" (1959); "The Komsomol Card" (1960); "Song of the Young Tourists" (1963); "Hey, Pioneers, Line Up!" (1963); music for films; arrangements of songs, etc; *Awards:* Stalin Prize (1950); medal "For Labor Valor" (1960); *Died:* 12 Mar 1962.

SVERDLOV, V.M. (1886–1940) Govt official; *Born:* 1886; *Career:* 1902–09 member, RSDRP; 1909 abandoned polit work; 1918 comr, Operations Bd, Pop Comrt of Means of Communication; 1919–20 Dep Pop Comr of Means of Communication and chm, Higher Transport Council; Collegium member, Supr Sovnarkhoz; worked for Mining Dept and Sci and Tech Dept, Supr Sovnarkhoz; dir, road research inst; arrested by State Security organs; *Died:* 1940 in imprisonment.

SVERDLOV, Yakov Mikhaylovich (Party names: ANDREY; MAKS) (1885–1919) Party and govt official; CP member from 1901; *Born:* 4 June 1885 in Nizhniy Novgorod (now Gorky), son of an engraver craftsman; *Career:* while at high school established contacts with local Soc-Democratic org; from age 15 worked at a pharmacy; engaged in propaganda among workers; set up illegal printing press; 7 Nov 1901 arrested for taking part in demonstration against Gorky's banishment from Nizhniy Novgorod; became professional revolutionary; 1902–03 several times arrested and exiled; Nov 1904–Sept 1905 Party work in Yaroslavl', Kostroma, Kazan' and other cities; Sept 1905 assigned by Party CC to Party work in Yekaterinburg (now Sverdlovsk); coordinated work of Yekaterinburg, Ufa and Perm' Party orgs; Nov–Dec 1905 headed Yekaterinburg RSDRP Comt; Jan 1906 moved to Perm' and restored local Party orgs, smashed by police; Feb 1906 directed in Yekaterinburg 2nd Ural Oblast Party Conference; elected to Ural Oblast Party Comt; June 1906 arrested; 23 Sept 1907 sentenced to two years' fortress detention, served in Yekaterinburg and Perm'; Sept 1909, after completing term of imprisonment, went to Finland, then to Moscow; helped restore Moscow Party Comt; 13 Dec 1909 arrested during expanded session of Moscow RSDRP Comt; Mar 1910 exiled for three years to Narym Kray; 27 July 1910 fled from exile and returned to Petersburg; as RSDRP CC plen worked with Petersburg Party Org; 14 Nov 1910 re-arrested; Apr 1911 exiled for four years to Narym Kray; continued revol work in exile; after abortive bid to flee from exile was deported to remote settlement of Maksimkin Yar; 1912 after 6th (Prague) Party Conference coopted to CC, RSDRP and Russian Bureau, CC; 6 Dec 1912 fled from exile and made his way to Petersburg; helped run newspaper "Pravda" and Bolshevik faction of 4th State Duma; 10 Feb 1913 arrested; May 1913 exiled to Turukhan Kray, to settlement Kureyku (beyond Arctic Circle); then transferred to vil Monastyrskoye in centr Turukhansk Kray; late July 1915 in Monatsyrskoye took part in meeting of CC and Russian Bureau members with members of 4th Duma's Bolshevik faction and exiled Bolsheviks; after 1917 Feb Revol returned to Petrograd and engaged in active revol work; sent by Party CC to Yekaterinburg; 14–15 Apr 1917 directed Ural Oblast Party Conference; 24–29 Apr 1917, as Yekaterinburg Party Comt deleg, attended 7th (Apr) Party Conference, at which he first met Lenin; elected member, CC, RSDRP(B); after the conference elected secr, CC, RSDRP(B) and delegated to All-Russian Centr Exec Comt; directed Org Bureau to convene 6th RSDRP(B) Congress; presented CC's org report at this congress; helped prepare 1917 Oct Revol; 23 Oct 1917 attended meeting of CC, RSDRP(B) at which it was decided to attempt armed coup; 29 Oct 1917 at meeting of CC, RSDRP(B) elected member, Mil Revol Party Center to direct the uprising; one of Bolshevik leaders at 2nd All-Russian Congress of Soviets; 8 Nov 1917 elected chm, All-Russian Centr Exec Comt; chm, Commission to draft first RSFSR Constitution; 1918 presented Party CC's org report at 7th RCP(B) Congress; July 1918 founded school for agitators and instructors under All-Russian Centr Exec Comt; this later developed into Sverdlov Communist Univ; helped prepare 1st Comintern Congress, held in Moscow in Mar 1919; Jan-Feb 1919 attented 1st Lat Congress of Soviets and 1st Bel Congress of Soviets; early Mar 1919 went to Khar'kov to attend 3rd Congress of CP(B) Ukr and 3rd All-Ukr Congress of Soviets, at which he delivered a speech on a Ukr constitution; during his return journey from Khar'kov to Moscow held whistle-stop talks with local Party and govt officials and addressed rallies; caught a chill at one of these rallies and arrived in Moscow seriously ill; *Died:* 16 Mar 1919; buried on Moscow's Red Square.

SVERDLOVA (nee NOVGORODTSEVA), Klavdiya Timofeyevna (Party name: OL'GA) (1876–1960) Politician; wife of Ya.M. Sverdlov; CP member from 1904; *Born:* 22 Mar 1876 in Yekaterinburg (now Sverdlovsk), daughter of a merchant; *Educ:* 1897–99 studied at Lesgaft Physical Training Teachers' Courses, Petersburg; *Career:* 1894–97 taught at school of Sysert Plant, Urals; 1899 took part in illegal Marxist circles in the Urals; 1904 elected member, Yekaterinburg RSDRP Comt; 1906 elected member, Perm RSDRP Comt; 1906 deleg at 4th (Amalgamative) RSDRP Congress; several times arrested and exiled; 1906–08 under fortress arrest; 1915–17 with Sverdlov in exile in Turukhansk Kray; from 1917 in Petrograd directed "Priboy" book publ house of CC, RSDRP(B); 1918–20 asst secr, CC, RCP(B) and head of the CC Secretariat; 1920–25 worked for educ organs; 1925–31 head, Children's Lit Dept and Textbooks Dept, Assoc of State Publ Houses; 1941–44 worked for Main Bad for the Protection of Mil and State Secrets in the Press (Sov censorship); 1918 member, All-Russian Centr Exec Comt; from 1924 member, Moscow Sov; *Publ:* several books about Sverdlov, including "Yakov Mikhaylovich Sverdlov" (1960); *Awards:* Order of the Red Banner of Labor (1954); *Died:* 23 Mar 1960.

SVETLOV, Mikhail Arkad'yevich (1903–1964) Russian poet and playwright; *Born:* 4 June 1903 in Yekaterinoslav; *Educ:* from 1922 studied at a workers' fac; 1928–29 studied at Lit Fac, Moscow Univ and at Bryusov Lit and Art Inst; *Career:* 1919 head, Press Dept, Yekaterinoslav Province Komsomol Comt; 1920–22 in Red Army; 1920 worked for Press Dept, CC, Ukr Komsomol; during WW 2 corresp for newspaper "Krasnaya zvezda" in Leningrad, then on Northwestern and 1st Bel Fronts; also corresp, Army and corps newspapers; 1923 joined "Perval" lit group; 1917 first work published; *Publ:* poem *Materi* (To a Mother) (1917); verse collection *Rel'sy* (Rails) (1923); collection *Stikhi* (Verse) (1924); poem "Grenada" (1926); *Stikhi o Moskve* (Moscow Verse) (1924); *Pesnya o Kakhovke* (The Song of Kakhovka) (1935); plays: *Glubokaya provintsiya* (The Depths of the Provinces) (1935); *Skazka* (The Tale) (1939); poem *Dvadtsat' vosem'* (Twenty-Eight) (1943); play *Brandenburgskiye vorota* (The Brandenburg Gate) (1946); *Stikhi o Lize Chaykinoy* (Verse About Liza Chaykina) (1948); play *Dvadtsat' let spustya* (Twenty Years Later) (1955); collection *Gorizont* (Horizon) (1956); dramatic poem *S novym schast'yem* (A Happy New Year) (1957); *Zametki o moyey zhizni* (Notes on My Life) (1959); collection *Stikhotvoreniya* (Poems) (1959); collection "Stikhotvoreniya" (1963); coauthor, collection of grotesques and epigrams *Muzey vremeni* (The Museum of Time)

(1963), etc; *Awards:* Hon Scroll of Tadzh Supr Sov Presidium (1960); *Died:* 28 Sept 1964.

SVIDERSKIY, Aleksey Ivanovich (1878–1933) Govt official; diplomat; CP member from 1899; *Born:* 20 Mar 1878 in Chernigov Province, son of a civil servant and landowner; *Educ:* from 1897 studied at Petersburg Univ; *Career:* active in student polit movement; 1898 connected with Petersburg League for the Liberation of the Working Class; ran workers' Marxist circles; 1899 arrested for these activities and exiled for three years to Ufa Province; subsequently several times arrested in Petersburg, Samara, Tula, Kiev and Riga for his Party work; 1905 sentenced to five years' exile in Olonets Province; but went underground to evade his sentence; contributed to Bolshevik newspapers "Novaya zhizn'", "Volan", "Vperyod", "Ekho" and "Vestnik zhizni"; Mar–Oct 1917 ed, Bolshevik newspaper "Vperyod"; from June 1917 chm, Ufa Sov; from Feb 1918 Collegium member, RSFSR Pop Comrt of Food, from May 1921 Collegium member, RSFSR Pop Comrt of Workers and Peasants' Inspection; frequently elected member, All-Russian and USSR Centr Exec Comt; 1923–28 RSFSR Dep Pop Comr of Agric; from 1928 Collegium member, Pop Comrt of Educ and head, Main Arts Bd; Sept 1929 appointed Sov plen in Lat; *Died:* 10 May 1933 in Riga.

SVIREZHEV, Mikhail Vasil'yevich (1917–1967) Surgeon and phthisiatrist; Dr of Med from 1963; prof from 1964; Hon Physician of RSFSR; CP member from 1941; *Born:* 1917; *Educ:* 1938 grad Gorky Med Inst; *Career:* after grad, mil surgeon in Sov Army; during WW 2 served with a med battalion, then ran a field surgery; July 1944 demobilized after being seriously wounded; from Aug 1944 chief physician, and surgeon at a rayon hospital; from 1948 chief physician, Vladimir Oblast Bone Tuberculosis Sanatorium; dep, Vladimir Oblast Sov; from 1953 postgrad student, Inst of Tuberculosis, USSR acad of Med Sci; 1957 defended cand thesis; Apr 1960–67 dir, Novosibirsk Tuberculosis Research Inst; chm, Novosibirsk Soc of Phthisiatrists; 1963 defended doctor's thesis on surgical methods of restoring damaged functions of tubercular arthritis patients; from Jan 1966 head, Main Bd of Tuberculosis Service and Special Sanatoria, RSFSR Min of Health, where he established a sci methods council; member, ed council, journal "Sovetskaya meditsina"; bd member, All-Russian Soc of Phthisiatrists; wrote over 80 works; *Publ:* doctor's thesis *Operativnoye lecheniye tuberkulyoza kostnogo sustava s vostanovleniyem funktsiy* (The Operative Treatment of Tuberculosis of the Joints with the Restoration of Function) (1963), ect; *Awards:* Order of the Red Star; Order of the Fatherland War, 2nd Class; Badge of Hon (1967); medals; *Died:* 27 Dec 1967.

SVYATLOVSKIY, Vladimir Vladimirovich (1869–1927) Historian; Dr of Historical Sci from 1897; *Born:* 1869 in Moscow, son of an office worker; *Educ:* 1896 grad Munich Univ; *Career:* while living in Petersburg joined Brusnev Group; 1892 emigrated to Germany; from 1898 again in Petersburg; sided with Mensheviks; 1905–06 member, Centr Bureau of Petersburg Trade Unions; ed of its journal "Professional'ynyy soyuz"; after arrest of members of Petersburg Exec Comt, served in new Exec Comt; 1902–24 taught at Petersburg Univ, Psychoneurological Inst and Naval Acad; specialized in agrarian and housing problems and trade-union movement; one of first to systematize history of Russian econ thought; *Publ: Gosudarstvennoye strakhovaniye rabochikh v Germanii (State Insurance of Workers in Germany) (1895); Kvartirnyy vopros* (Housing) (1898); *K istorii politicheskoy ekonomii i statistiki v Rossii* (The History of Political Economy and Statistics in Russia) (1906); *Periodicheskaya pressa proletarskikh soyuzov, 1905–1919* (The Periodical Press of the Proletarian Unions, 1905–1919) (1919); *Istoriya ekonomicheskikh idey v Rossii* (The History of Economic Ideas in Russia) (1923); *Proiskhozhdeniye deneg i denezhnykh znakov* (The Origin of Money and Currency) (1923); *Istoriya profsoyuznogo dvizheniya v Rossii ot vozniknoveniya rabochego klassa do kontsa 1917 goda* (The History of the Trade-Union Movement in Russia from the Emergence of the Working Class to the End of 1917) (2nd ed, 1925); *Died:* 22 Nov 1927.

SYRTSOV, Sergey Ivanovich (1893–1938) Party and govt official; CP member from 1913; *Born:* 1893 in Yekaterinoslav Province; *Educ:* 1912–16 studied at Petrograd Polytech Inst; *Career:* participated in illegal student organizations; from 1914 revol propaganda among Petrograd workers; 1916 exiled to Irkutsk Province; after 1917 Feb Revol returned to Petrograd and worked as propagandist; then chm, Rostov Sov and Rostov Mil Revol Comt; 1918–19 mil comr of a div at the front; 1920 chm, Odessa Province Party Comt; 1921–23 head, Accounting and Distribution Dept, Party CC; from 1924 head, Agitation and Propaganda Dept, Party CC; Presidium member, Communist Acad; ed, journal "Kommunisticheskaya revolyutsiya"; from 1926 secr, Siberian Kray Party Comt; from 1929 chm, RSFSR Council of Pop Comr; Apr 1930 headed opposition bloc; late 1930 replaced as chm, RSFSR Council of Pop Comr, then worked as dir, Nogin Mil Chemical Plant; 1924–27 cand member, 1927–30 member, CC, CPSU(B); 1918 sided with Leftist Communists and opposed Brest Peace Treaty; 1920–21, during the trade-union controversy, sided with Trotsky; arrested by State Security organs; *Died:* 1938 in imprisonment.

SYSIN, Aleksey Nikolayevich (1879–1956) Hygienist; prof from 1922; member, USSR Acad of Med Sci from 1944; *Born:* 4 Oct 1879 in Nizhniy Novgorod, son of a land surveyor; *Educ:* 1897 grad Nizhniy Novgorod Boys' Classical High-School; 1908 grad Med Fac, Moscow Univ; *Career:* arrested several times during student years for involvement with Soc-Democrats; served two prison terms and was exiled to Siberia; 1905 received amnesty; 1908–13 distr physician and health officer in Vologda, Saratov, Yekaterinoslav and Nizhniy Novgorod Provinces; 1911–13 mang, Zemstvo Sanatoria Bureau, Nizhniy Novgorod Province; in same period also made study tours of France, England, Germany and Austro-Hungary; 1911 and 1913 helped to organize hygiene exhibitions in Dresden and Petersburg; from 1913 health officer in Moscow, where he also lectured on univ hygiene courses; 1914–17 supernumerary asst prof, Chair of Hygiene, Med Fac, Moscow Univ; during same period in charge of evacuation hospital affairs and anti-epidemic measures organized by Moscow City Admin; 1915–18 head, Sanitary Bureau, Main Comt, All-Russian League of Cities; helped to organize Sov health service; 1918–32 head, Sanitary and Epidemic Dept, RSFSR Pop Comrt of Health; helped to formulate health legislation and organize hygiene and anti-epidemic measures; from 1919 asst prof, Chair of Soc Hygiene, from 1922 prof, Chair of Hygiene, 1st Moscow Univ; 1922 wrote decree on "The Sanitary Organs of the Republic", which provided the basis for the development of sanitary org in the USSR; established numerous training courses for health officers and founded the journal "Gigiyena i epidemologiya"; 1926 attended the Int Sanitary Conference, Paris, which formulated the Int Sanitary Convention; thereafter he represented the USSR at all annual sessions of the Int Soc Hygiene Bureau; 1931–51 head, Chair of Communal Hygiene, from 1944 dir, Centr Inst of Postgrad Med Training, Moscow; 1932 attended Russo-Polish and European Sanitary Conferences; Presidium member and bd chm, All-Union Soc of Hygienists; cm, Water Supply and Sanitary Technol Soc; member, Learned Council, USSR, RSFSR, Ukr and other Min of Health; dep chm, Learned Med Council, USSR Min of Health; member, Centr Bureau, Sci Workers' Section; from 1950 acad secr, Dept of Hygiene, Microbiology and Epidemiology, USSR Acad of Med Sci; member, ed collegium, various journals; dep chief ed, journal "Gigiyena i sanitariya"; asst chief ed, "Bol'shaya meditsinskaya entsiklopediya" (Large Medical Encyclopedia) (1st ed); wrote ober 250 works; *Publ: Sanitarnoye sostoyaniye Rossii i SSSR* (Sanitary Conditions in Russia and the USSR) (1927); *Zhilishche* (Housing) (1927); *Spravochnik sanitarnogo vracha* (The Health Officer's Reference Book) (1926); coauthor, *Kurs dezinfektsii, deinsektsii i deratizatsii* (A Course on Disinfection, Anti-Insectation and Anti-Rodent Measures) (1932); ed and coauthor, *Uchebnik gigiyeny* (A Hygiene Textbook) (1933), etc; *Awards:* Order of Lenin; Order of the Red Banner of Labor; medal "For Valiant Labor During the Great Fatherland War"; medal "For the Defense of Moscow"; memorial medal "800th Anniversary of Moscow" ; *Died:* 25 June 1956 in Moscow.

SYSOYEV, Ivan Grigor'yevich (1903–1957) Diplomat; envoy ectraordinary and plen, 2nd class; *Born:* 1903; *Career:* from 1938 in dipl service; 1948–50 counsellor, Sov mission in Finland; 1950–52 counsellor, USSR embassy in Sweden; 1952–54 counsellor, USSR mission in Iceland; 1954–55 USSR envoy in Denmark; *Died:* Mar 1957.

SYTIN, P. P. (1870–1938) Mil commander; *Born:* 1870; *Career:* gen, Russian Army; after 1917 Oct Revol joined Red Army; 1918 mil commander, Bryansk Forces Group; then commanded Southern Front; head, Mil Admin Dept, RSFSR Revol Mil Council; from 1920 RSFSR Mil rep in Geo; then teaching and research work at Red Army Mil Acad; arrested by State Security organs; *Died:* 1938 in imprisonment.

T

TABIDZE, Galaktion Vasil'yevich (1892–1959) Geo poet; Pop Poet of Geo SSR from 1933; member, Geo Acad of Sci from 1944; *Born:* 6 Sept 1892 in vil Chkviisi, Geo; *Educ:* from 1908 studied at Tiflis Theological Seminary; *Career:* 1908 became connected with Geo revol circles; 1908 first work printed; 1916 met Russian Symbolist poets in Moscow; 1922 founded "Zhurnal Galaktiona Tabidze"; 1935 attended 1st World Anti-Fascist Congress in Paris; *Publ:* verse "First of May" (1908); "Sun, Rise!" (1910); "Book of Verse" (1914); "The SS 'Doland'" (1918); "We Are the Poets of Georgia" (1925); "Renewed Peaks" (1929); verse cycles: "Pacifism" (1930); "The Epoch" (1930); "Revolutionary Georgia" (1931); collected verse: "Fatherland, My Life" (1941); "Moscow" (1947); "Red Square"; "For Peace"; "Memories of Europe"; "Selected Works" (1953); "Verse and Poems" (1958), etc; *Awards:* Order of Lenin; *Died:* 17 Mar 1959.

TABIDZE, Titsian Yustinovich (1895–1937) Geo poet; *Born:* 2 Apr 1895 in vil Shuamta, near Orpiri, Geo; *Educ:* grad Philology Fac, Moscow Univ; *Career:* 1915 helped found Geo symbolists school "Blue Horns" in Kutaisi; for a number of years edited newspaper "Barrikady"; after the reestablishment of Sov rule in Geo gradually turned from Symbolism and Surrealism and sympathized with Sov regime; helped found Geo Writers' Union; *Publ:* "Selected Works" (1957); "Anthology of Georgian Poetry" (1958); "Verse" (1960) in Geo and Russian; *Died:* 16 Dec 1937.

TAGANTSEV, V.N. (1890–1921) Prof; *Born:* 1890; *Career:* 1921 helped lead an Anti-Sov plot; 24 Aug 1921 sentenced to death by Petrograd Cheka; *Died:* executed 1921.

TAGIROV, Afzal Mukhutdinovich (1890–1937) Bash playwright; Presidium member, USSR Centr Exec Comt; chm, Bash Centr Exec Comt from 1931; Bureau member, Bash Oblast Party Comt; CP member from 1913; *Born:* 13 Oct 1890 in vil Abdurakhmanovo, now Bash ASSR; *Educ:* 1925–27 studied at Communist Acad, Moscow; arrested by State Security organs; *Publ:* comedy "Bichura" (1907); play "Yanchura" (1912), drama "The Forkers" (1921); *plays:* "In the Transitional Period" (1923); "17–30" (1929); "Gil'man the Siberian" (1930); "Ala-Tau" (1932); "The Plant" (1932); comedy "From Jest to Earnest"; children's play "The Story of Little Akhat" (1934), etc; *Died:* 1937 in imprisonment; posthumously rehabilitated.

TAGIZADE, Ali (1883–1966) Govt official; CP member from 1906; *Born:* Apr 1883; *Career:* dyer by trade; from 1903 in revol movement; worked for illegal Marxist circles, distributed illegal lit; repeatedly arrested and imprisoned; connected with Persian revol movement; helped found Sov regime in the Caucasus; 1922–29 exec Party and econ work in Geo; from 1929 govt and Party work in Arm; 1959–63 chm, Azer Supr Sov; Presidium member, Azer Supr Sov; member, CC, CP Azer; member, Geo Centr Exec Comt and Transcaucasian SFSR Centr Exec Comt of several convocations; member, CC, CP(B) Azer; member, Arm Centr Exec Comt; *Died:* 3 Feb 1966.

TAIROV (real name: KORNBLIT), Aleksandr Yakovlevich (1885–1950) Stage dir; Pop Artiste of RSFSR from 1935; *Born:* 24 June 1885 in Rovno; *Educ:* 1913 grad Law Fac, Petersburg Univ; *Career:* 1905 actor with M. Boroday's company in Kiev; 1906–07 actor, Komissarzhevskaya Theater, Petersburg; until 1913 acted at theaters in Petersburg, Riga and Simbirsk; spent three years with P.P. Gaydeburov's Mobile Theater, where he took up stage directing; 1913 stage dir, Free Theater, Moscow; 1914 co-founder, Moscow Chamber Theater; 1914–49 dir, above theater; 1917 first chm, Moscow Artistes' Union; 1919–36 Presidium member, CC, Art Workers' Union; from 1944 vice-pres, Theater Section, All-Union Soc for Cultural Relations with For Countries; claimed to be the founder of what he called "neo-realism" in stagecraft, opposed to naturalism and the principles of Meyerhold's "conditioned" theater; *Productions:* "Hamlet" (1908); Chekhov's *Dyadya Vanya* (Uncle Vanya) (1908); "The Marriage of Figaro" (1915); Oscar Wilde's "Salome" (1917); Lothar's "King Harlequin" (1917); Scribe's "Adrienne Lecouvrère" (1919); Claudel's "Benediction" (1920); Shakespeare's "Romeo and Juliet" (1921); Racine's "Phedre" (1922); Ostrovskiy's *Groza* (The Storm) (1924); O'Neill's "The Hairy Ape") (1926); operetta "Sirocco")1928); "Egyptian Nights" (1934); comic opera *Bogatyri* (The Epic Warriors), after Dem'yan Bednyy (1936); "Madame Bauvary" after Flaubert (1940); Gorky's *Starik* (The Old Man) (1946); *U sten Leningrada* (At the Walls of Leningrad) (1945); Grin's *Veter s yuga* (The Wind from the South) (1948), etc; *Publ: Proklamatsii khudozhnika* (Proclamations of an Artist) (1917); *Zapiski rezhissyora* (A Stage Director's Notes) (1921); *V poiskakh stilya* (In Search of Style) (1936); *Teatr i dramaturg* (Theater and Playwright) (1947), etc; *Awards:* Order of Lenin; Order of the Red Banner of Labor; *Died:* 25 Sept 1950 in Moscow.

TAIROV, Vasiliy Yegorovich (1859–1938) Viticulturist and viniculturist; *Born:* 1 Nov 1859 in vil Velikiy Karaklis, now Arm SSR; *Educ:* 1884 grad Moscow's Petrine Acad of Agric and Forestry; *Career:* helped organize campaign against phylloxera, and introduced immune vine stocks in Russia; studied methods of growing vines on sandy soils and zoning of viticulture in the USSR, etc; 1905, from public subscriptions, founded in Odessa first Russian viticulture research institution – the Viniculture Station of Russian Viticulturists and Viniculturists (now Ukr Tairov Research Inst of Viticulture and Viniculture); 1892 founded, 1892–1918 and 1927–32 edited first journal on wine-growing and wine-making "Vestnik vinodeliya"; *Died:* 23 Apr 1938.

TAKAISHVILI, Aleksandr Aleksandrovich (1895–1959) Stage dir; Pop Artiste of Geo SSR from 1941; *Born:* 29 Sept 1895; *Educ:* studied at Law Fac, Kiev and Moscow Univ; studied at Studio of Tbilisi Russian Theater; *Career:* from 1925 at Rustaveli Theater; 1928 co-founded Geo Young Playgoers' Theater; 1928–45 dir, Young Playgoers' Theater; 1945–56 artistic dir, Griboyedov Theater; produced shows at Paliashvili Opera and Ballet Theater and Mardzhanishvili Theater; *Productions:* "Suram Fortress" (1934), after Chonkadze; Gamrekeli and Nakhutsrishvili's "Natsarkekiya" (1935); "Romeo and Juliet" (1942); *Dokhodnoye mesto* (A Lucrative Post) (1945); *Revizor* (The Government Inspector) (1951), etc; *Died:* 1959.

TAKAYSHVILI, Yevfimiy Semyonovich (1863–1953) Geo historian and archeologist; prof; member, Geo Acad of Sci from 1946; *Born:* 1863; *Educ:* 1890 grad Petersburg Univ; *Career:* from 1890 teacher, secondary educ establishments in Tiflis; member, Russian Archeological Soc; helped found Caucasian Branch, Moscow Archeological Soc and Caucasian Inst of History and Archeology in Tiflis; 1907–21 founder-head, Geo History and Ethnography Soc; edited the society's collections "Drevnosti Gruzii" (Georgian Antiquities) (3 vol, 1899–1910) and "Drevnyaya Gruziya" (Ancient Georgia) (4 vol, 1909–15); 1918–21 co-founder and prof, Geo Univ, Tiflis; 1921–45 lived and worked in Paris; 1945 returned to Geo; wrote over 250 works in Geo, Russian, French and English; *Publ: Istochniki gruzinskikh letopisey. Tri khroniki* (Origins of the Georgian Annals. Three Chronicles) (1900); *Materialy po arkheologii Kavkaza* (Material on Caucasian Archeology) (1909); ed, *Rasporyadok gosudareva dvora* (Regulations of His Majesty's Court) (1920), etc; *Died:* 1953.

TAKHTAREV, Konstantin Mikhaylovich (1871–1925) Historian; specialist in history of primitive soc; *Born:* 1871; *Educ:* until 1897 studied at Mil Med Acad; *Career:* in 1890's and 1900's active in revol movement in Russia; 1898 attended Zurich Congress of League of Russian Soc-Democrats Abroad; 1900 edited newspaper "Rabochaya mysl'"; attended Paris Congress of 2nd International; deleg at 2nd RSDRP Congress in London; did agitation and propaganda work for Party; 1896 arrested; from 1897 lived abroad and studied sociology; from 1903 concentrated on research and teaching; 1903–05 read sociology course at Russian Higher School of Soc Sci, Paris; 1907 returned to Russia and worked for a numer of higher educ establishments; from 1917 at Petrograd Univ; 1924 assoc, Inst of Marx and Engels; specialized in study of primitive culture, especially religion, and backward peoples of the present; *Publ: Ocherki po istorii pervobytnoy kul'tury* (An Outline History of Primitive Culture) (1907); *Sravnitel'naya istoriya razvitiya chelovecheskogo obshchestva i obshchestvennykh form* (A Comparative History of the Development of Human Society and Social Forms) (2 vol, 1924); *Died: 1925.*

TAKHTI (real name: Il'ya Yefimovich YEFIMOV) (1889–1938) Chuvash writer; *Born:* 1889; *Educ:* grad Moscow Lit Inst and Ethnography Fac, Moscow Univ; *Career:* at first wrote in Russian, then turned to Chuvash; after 1917 Oct Revol wrote essays and feuilletons for newspaper "Chavash kreschene", "Kommunar", "Kanash" and journal "Suntal" etc; *Publ:* stories "Khuras'" (1911); novelette "Temme" (1915–16); collection of Chuvash folk songs (1911); *Died:* 1938.

TAKTAKISHVILI, Shalva Mikhaylovich (1900–1965) Geo composer and conductor; Hon Art Worker of Geo SSR from 1941; *Born:* 27 Aug 1900 in vil Kvemo-Khviti, Geo; *Educ:* 1928 grad Tbilisi Conservatory; *Career:* 1937–39 directed, opera class, from 1941 prof, from 1951 conductor, Opera Studio, Tbilisi Conservatory; *Works:* operas "The Deputy" (1940); "Otar's Widow" (1942); children's operas: "World of Flowers" (1922); "1st of May" (1924); "Autumn" (1925); "Dawn" (1926); ballet "Maltakva" (1937); symphonic and chamber music; arrangements of folk songs; *Died:* 18 July 1965 in Tbilisi.

TALALAYEV, Vladimir Timofeyevich (1886–1947) Pathoanatomist; Hon Sci Worker of RSFSR from 1942; CP member from 1946; *Born:* 10 June 1886; *Educ:* 1912 grad Med Fac, Moscow Univ; *Career:* 1912–15 senior asst dissector, 1915–26 senior asst prof, from 1926 assoc prof, Chair of Pathoanatomy, 1st Moscow Med Inst; from 1912 also dissector, Staro-Yekaterininskaya Hospital, Moscow; from 1918 head, Pathomorphological Dept, Moscow Oblast Clinical Research Inst; 1930–41 head, from 1941 prof, Chair of Pathoanatomy, Centr Inst of Postgrad Med Training; 1932–44 head, Chair of Pathoanatomy, 4th Moscow Med Inst; from 1944 head, Chair of Pathoanatomy, Med Inst of RSFSR Pop Comrt of Health; specialist in rheumatism; wrote over 70 research works; *Publ: Patologicheskaya anatomiya sifilisa tsentral'noy nervnoy sistemy* (The Pathoanatomy of Siphilis of the Central Nervous System) (1927); *Ostryy revmatizm (istinnyy revmatizm)* (Acute Rheumatism /Genuine Rheumatism/) (1932); *Patogenez i patologicheskaya anatomiya zhelchno-kamennoy bolezni* (The Pathogenesis and Pathoanatomy of Gallstone Disease) (1936); *Izbrannyye trudy* (Selected Works) (1953); *Awards:* Badge of Hon; medals; *Died:* 1947 in Moscow.

TALALIKHIN, Viktor Vasil'yevich (1918–1941) Fighter-pilot; lt; Komsomol member; *Born:* 18 Sept 1918 in vil Teplovka, Saratov Oblast; *Educ:* 1938 grad pilots' school; *Career:* fought in 1939–40 Sov-Finnish War; during WW 2 in the night of 7 Aug 1941 carried out first ramming action in a night-time air battle, downing an enemy bomber approaching Moscow; in subsequent sorties shot down five more enemy planes; *Awards:* Order of Lenin; Order of the Red Star; Hero of the Sov Union (1941); *Died:* 27 Oct 1941 killed in air battle; his name is permanently inscribed in the rolls of the 1st Squadron of the fighter regt in which he served.

TALASH, Vasiliy Isaakovich (alias: Grandfather TALASH) (1844–1946) Bel partisan of Civil War (1918–20) and WW 2 (1941–45); *Born:* 1844; *Career:* 1918 headed partisan detachment operating in Poles'ye; later chm, Novosyolki Vil Sov, Gomel' Oblast; fought with partisans during WW 2; leading character of Yakub Kolas' work *Drygva* (Quagmire) (1934); *Awards:* Order of the Red Banner (for Civil War); Order of the Fatherland War, 1st Class; *Died:* 1946.

TALENSKIY, Nikolay Aleksandrovich (1901–1967) Mil historian; Dr of History; prof; maj-gen; *Born:* 1901; *Career:* until WW 2 head, Research Dept, Frunze Mil Acad; during WW 2 head, Historical Dept, Gen Staff and prof, Gen Staff Acad and Frunze Mil Acad; exec ed, newspaper, "Krasnaya zvezda"; 1959–60 read papers on int security at conferences in Baden (Austria) and Moscow; *Publ: Somma 1916–ogo goda* (The Somme 1916) (1937); *Pervaya mirovaya imperialisticheskaya voyna 1914–18–ogo godov. Kampaniya 1917–ogo goda* (The 1914–18 First Imperialist World War. The Campaign of 1917) (1938); *Dva sokrushitel'nykh udara* (Two Crushing Blows) (1941); *Porazheniye nemetskikh fashistov na yuge* (The Defeat of the German Fascists in the South) (1945); *K voprosu o kharaktere zakonov v voyennoy nauke* (The Nature of Laws in Military Science) (1953); *O kharaktere 2–oy mirovoy voyny* (The Nature of the Second World War) (1961), etc; *Died'* July 1967.

TALLAT-KELPSHA, Iosif Antonovich (TALLAT-KYALPSHA, Yuozas Antano) (1888–1949) Composer, conductor and teacher; Hon Art Worker of Lith SSR from 1945; *Born:* 20 Dec 1888 in vil Kalnuyay, Kovno Province; *Educ:* 1916 grad composition class, Petrograd Conservatory; *Career:* from 1908 organized and produced Lith opera shows; 1919 co-founder and conductor, Kaunas Opera and Ballet Theater; from 1920 taught music; from 1933 instructor, from 1948 prof, Kaunas Conservatory; chm, Lith Composers' Union; bd member, USSR Composers' Union; *Works:* opera "The Sargeant-Major's Daughter" (1938); cantata (1946); symphonic overture; wind quartet; piano pieces; over 700 recordings of Lith and Bel folk-songs, etc; *Awards:* Stalin Prize (1948); *Died:* 5 Feb 1949.

TAL'YAN, Shara Mkrtychevich (1893–1965) Opera singer (tenor and baritone); Pop Artiste of Arm SSR from 1939; *Born:* 16 July 1893; *Educ:* 1916–17 studied at Petrograd Conservatory under S.I. Gabel'; *Career:* 1924 founded opera ensemble in Leninakan; later founded various operetta ensembles, which toured Centr Asia; 1942 helped found Arm Theater of Musical Comedy; 1933–53 soloist, Spendiarov Opera and Ballet Theater; also gave concerts; *Roles:* Saro in Tigranyan's "Anush"; Sos in Kazaryan's "Sos and Varditer"; Shaumyan in Tigranyan's "David Bek"; title role in Chukhadzhyan's "Arshak II", etc; *Died:* 7 Nov 1965.

TALYBZADE, Abdulla Shaik Mustafa ogly (1881–1959) Azer writer and playwright; Hon Art Worker of Azer SSR from 1938; *Born:* 25 Feb 1881 in Tiflis; *Career:* from 1900 teacher in Baku; artistic and training dir, Azer Young Playgoers' Theater; dep, USSR Supr Sov of 1946 convocation; *Publ:* children's plays: "A Fine Spring" (1910); "Who Is Right? " (1912); "The Talking Doll" (1913); plays: "Il'dyrym"(1927); "Khasay" (1937); "El' Ogly" (1939); novel "Ariz" (1940); plays: "Homeland" (1943); "Mother" (1944); "Nushebe" (1945); "Khalif for an Hour", etc; translated into Azer works of Nizami, Shakespeare, Pushkin, Nekrasov, etc; *Awards:* Order of Lenin; Order of the Red Banner of Labor; medals; *Died:* 24 July 1959.

TAMANYAN (TAMANOV), Aleksandr Oganesovich (1878–1936) Architect; prof; member, Acad of Architecture from 1914; Pop Architect of Arm SSR from 1924; *Born:* 14 Mar 1878 in Yekaterinodar; *Educ:* 1904 grad Petersburg Acad of Arts; *Career:* from 1904 worked in Petersburg; 1913–17 lecturer; 1917–18 prof and vice-pres, Petrograd Acad of Arts; member, Soc of Architects and Artists and ed of its journal; from 1923 worked in Arm; chief eng, Arm Council of Pop Comr; 1925–36 member, Arm Centr Exec Comt; for several years chm, Arm Comt for the Protection of Historical Monuments; *Works:* the Kochubey house at Tsarskoye Selo (1912); the Shcherbatov house in Moscow (1913); Kratov TB Sanatorium near Moscow (1923); Yerevan gen reconstruction plan (1924); Yerevan hydroelectr plant (1926); Yerevan Opera and Ballet Theater (1926–39); Arm Govt House (1936–41); sets and costumes for plays: Blok's *Roza i krest* (The Rose and the Cross); Shakespeare's "Macbeth", etc; *Awards:* Stalin Prize (1942); *Died:* 20 Feb 1936.

TANANAYEV, Nikolay Aleksandrovich (1878–1959) Chemist; CP member from 1948; *Born:* 18 May 1878 in vil Serpovo, Tambov Province; *Educ:* 1908 grad Yur'yev (now Tartu) Univ; *Career:* 1921–37 prof, Kief Polytech Inst; from 1938 prof, Ural Polytech Inst; specialized in analytical chemistry; developed drop analysis, fractional analysis and non-chip method of analysis; *Publ: Analiticheskaya khimiya* (Analytical Chemistry) (1934); *Kurs obiyomnogo analiza* (A Course of Volumetric Analysis) (1913); *Vesovoy analiz* (Weidht Analysis) (1931); *Besstruzhkovyy metod analiza chyornykh, tsvetnykh i dragotsennykh splavov* (The Non-Chip Method of Analysing Ferrous, Non-Ferrous and Precious Alloys) (1948); *Issledovaniye ryada napryazheniy s tochki zreniya pravila ryadov* (Studying an Electrochemical Series from the Viewpoint of Series Law) (1943); *Drobnyy analiz. Kachestvennyye reaktsii i analiz neorganicheskikh soyedineniy drobnym metodom* (Fractional Analysis. Qualitative Reactions and the Analysis of Inorganic Compounds by the Fractional Method) (1950); *Kapel'nyy metod. Kachestvennyy analiz neorganicheskih soyedineniy kapel'nym metodom* (The Drop Method. Qualitative Analysis of Inorganic Compounds by the Drop Method) (1954); *O nekotorykh anomaliyakh okislitel'no-vosstanovitel'nykh reaktsiy* (Some Anomalies of Redox Reactions) (1956); *Awards:* Order of Lenin; Badge of Hon; medal; Stalin Prize (1949); *Died:* 7 June 1959.

TANGIYEVA–BIRZNIYEK (real name: BEK–MELIK TANGIYEVA), Yelena Aleksandrovna (1907–1965) Ballet-dancer, ballet-master and ballet teacher; Pop Artiste of Lat SSR from 1956; *Born:* 13 Apr 1907; *Educ:* 1924 grad O.I. Preobrazhenskaya and A.Ya. Vaganova's class, Petrograd Choreographic College; *Career:* 1924–27 soloist, Ballet Company, Leningrad Opera and Ballet Theater; 1925–27 instructor, Leningrad Choreographic College; 1927–37 soloist, Ballet Company, Lat Opera Theater, Riga; 1932–37 instructor, Ballet Studio, Lat Operat Theater; 1945–51 ballet-master, Lat Opera and Ballet Theater; 1951–56 ballet-master, Lat Musical Comedy Theater; 1945–65 instructor, Ballet Studio, Lat Opera Theater; 1956–65 chief ballet-master, Lat Opera and Ballet Theater; *Roles:* Manu in Minkus' "Bailadeira"; the Cat in *Spyashchaya krasavitsa* (Sleeping Beauty); Gulnar in Adam's "The Corsair"; Ayna in Ya. Medyn's *Pobeda lubvi* (The Victory of Love); *Productions:* "The Corsair" (1935); "Don Quixote" (1945); *Bakhchisarayskiy fontan* (The Fountain of Bakhchisaray) (1946); "Sleeping Beauty" (1948); *Krasnyy tsvetok* (The Red Flower) (1949); Chulaki's *Yunost* (Youth) (1950); *Lebedinoye ozero* (Swan Lake) (1951); "Raymonda" (1954); "The Blue Danube," to music by Strauss (1957); *Volshebnyye kukly* (The Magic Dolls), to music by Rossini (1958); Grinblat's "Rigonda" (1959); Chulaki's *Skazka o pope i o rabotnike yego Balda* (The Tale of the Priest and His Workman Balda) (1962); Balasanyan's "Shakuntala" (1963), etc; *Died:* 31 July 1965.

TAPALTSYAN, Khristofor Knyazevich (1911–1967) Arm writer; Presidium member, Arm Writers' Union from 1959; CP member from 1943; *Born:* 1911 in Arm; *Educ:* 1930 grad Leninakan Teachers' Training Inst; 1938 grad Philology Fac, Yerevan Univ; *Career:* worked as school teacher, principal and inspector; until WW 2 also worked for Arm newspaper; during WW 2 war corresp; from 1946 worked for "Literaturnaya gazeta"; criticized for deviating from principles of "socialist realism"; 1963 attended session of CC, CP Arm on development of Arm lit; *Publ:* novel "Victoria" (1938); novel "The Dawn of Life" (1939); collection of short stories "The Homeland" (1942); novel "War" (2 vol, 1946, 1949); novel "The Golden Valley" (1956); novel "For Thee, Moscow" (1956); novel "Ayrenashen" (1963); *Awards:* Order of the Red Star; medals; *Died:* 1967.

TARASEVICH, Lev Aleksandrovich (1868–1927) Microbiologist and health service official; Dr of Med; *Born:* 14 Feb 1868 in Tiraspol', now Mold SSR; *Educ:* 1891 grad Natural Sci Fac, Novorossiysk Univ, Odessa; 1891 studied at Petersburg Mil Med Acad; 1897 completed med training in Paris; *Career:* 1899–1902, after a spell of work under V.V.Podvysotskiy at Chair of Gen Pathology, Kiev Univ, joined Mechnikov in Paris, where he defended his doctor's thesis; from 1902 dissector, then assoc prof, Chair of Gen Pathology, Novorossiysk Univ, Odessa; 1907–11 assoc prof, Moscow Univ; 1908–24 taught bacteriology at Moscow Higher Women's Courses; during WW 2 helped to organize mass vaccinations against cholera and typhoid in Russian Army; after 1917 Oct Revol worked for Pop Comrt of Health; Aug 1918 founded first Sov Bacterial Drug Control Unit (now Tarasevich Med Biological Drug Control Inst); founder-dir, State Inst of Public Health; from 1918 also chm, Learned Med Council, Pop Comrt of Health; organized and chaired congresses of bacteriologists, epidemiologists and health workers; helped to re-establish sci contacts with for countries after Oct Revol; founder, ed, "Zhurnal mikrobiologii, patologii i infektsionnykh bolezney" (now "Zhurnal mikrobiologii, epidemiologii i immunobiologii") and journal "Gigiyena i epidemiologiya"; wrote over 70 works; *Publ:* "Contagiosité syphilitique tardive, contagiosité tertiaire" (1897); *K ucheniyu o gemolizinakh* (The Theory of Hemolysins) (1902); *O golodanii* (Starvation) (1907); *Obshchaya patologiya* (General Pathology) (1908); *O predokhranitel'nykh privivkakh protiv bryushnogo tifa i kholery* (Preventive Typhoid and Cholera Innoculations) (1915); ed and coauthor, *Meditsinskaya mikrobiologiya* (Medical Microbiology) (3 vol, 1912–15); *Kurs obshchey patologii* (A Course of General Pathology) (1917); "Les édpidémies en Russie depuis 1914" (1922); *Died:* 12 June 1927; committed suicide during a trip abroad.

TARASHKEVICH, Bronislav Adamovich (1892–1937) Bel linguist and socio-polit figure; member, Bel Acad of Sci from 1928; member, Communist Party of Western Bel; *Born:* 20 Jan 1892 in vil Matsyulishki, Vilnius Province; *Educ:* 1916 grad History and Philology Fac, Peterburg Univ; *Career:* 1916–18 junior asst, Chair of Russian Language and Lit, then assoc prof, Chair of Greek and Latin Languages, Petersburg Univ; from 1919 dir, Bel High-School and member, Bel Sci Assoc in Vilnius; from 1922 chm, Bel Embasy Club, Polish Sejm; 1925–27 headed West Berl Bel socio-polit org – Bel Peasants and Workers' Assoc; also chm of its Deputies Club; active in organizing Bel schools in Western Bel; for a while head, Bel School Soc; 1927 arrested after Polish authorities suppressed the Bel Peasants and Workers' Assoc and sentenced to 12 years' imprisonment; July 1930 released; Feb 1931 re-arrested; fall 1933 deported to Bel SSR in exchange of polit prisoners; became member, Bel Acad of Sci; late 1933 moved to Moscow; 1934–37 head, Poland and Baltic Dept, Int Agrarian Inst; did research on Bel language and lit and translated Homer into Bel; 7 May 1937 arrested by NKVD; *Publ;:* "Belorussian Grammar for Schools" (1918); "Belorussian Syntax" (1923, in manuscript); "Western Belorussia – a Bridgehead of Imperialist Intervention" (1931); "How Peasants in Other Countries Live" (1935); "Differentiation of the Peasantry in Poland During the Crisis" (1935); *Died:* 1937 in imprisonment; in early 1960's posthumously rehabilitated.

TARASOV, Aleksandr Pavlovich (1904–1958) Mil commander; col-gen; CP member from 1924; *Born:* 1904 in Irkutsk; *Educ:* grad Frunze Mil Acad; *Career:* bookbinder in a printing house; from 1920 in Sov Army; during WW 2 senior staff posts on several fronts; after WW 2 senior commands in various mil distr; dep, RSFSR and Geo Supr Sov; member, CC, CP Geo; *Awards:* Order of Lenin; three Orders of the Red Banner; Order of Kutuzov, 1st and 2nd Class; Order of Suvorov, 2nd Class; Order of Bogdan Khmel'nitskiy, 2nd Class; two Orders of the Fatherland War, 1st Class; medals; *Died:* 19 May 1958.

TARASOV, Nikolay Grigor'yevich (1866–1942) Historian; art critic; local historian; *Born:* 1866; *Educ:* grad Dept of History and Philology, Moscow Univ; attended lectures on history of arts at Sorbonne and Berlin Univ; *Career:* from 1891 history teacher, Moscow High-School Nr. 5; 1897 founded first model methodological history group and an auditorium for curricular and extra-curricular studies at this school; also worked as inspector of same school; 1903–09 chief ed, periodical "Pedagogicheskiy muzey pedagogicheskogo obshchestva pri Moskovskom universitete"; prof of history and history methods, Tikhomirov Teachers' Training Courses, Shelaputin Higher Teachers' Training Courses, etc; from 1934 head, Chair of History Teaching Methods, Moscow's Lenin Teachers' Training Inst; advocated extensive individual study, use of visual aids and excursions in teaching of history; *Publ: Iz istorii russkoy kul'tury* (From the History of Russian Culture) (14 issues, 1908–13); *Naglyadnyye posobiya v otsenke pedagogicheskogo muzeya byvshego pedagogicheskogo obshchestva* (Visual Aids in the Estimation of the Pedagogic Museum of the Former Pedagogic Society) (1910); *Mestnyye ekskursii. Trudy komissii po organizatsii ekskursiy dlya uchashchikh i uchashchikhsya srednikh uchebnykh zavedeniy Moskovskogo okruga* (Local Excursions. The Work of the Commission for Organizing Excursions of Secondary-School Teachers and Pupils in the Moscow Region) (1911); coauthor, *Kul'turno-istoricheskiye kartiny iz zhizni Zapadnoy Yevropy IV–XVIII vv.* (Pictures of West-European Cultural and Historical Life in the 4th–18th Centuries) (1924); *Massovyye obshchestvovedcheskiye ekskursii i obshchestvenno poleznyy trud. Teoriya i prakticheskoye oformleniye* (Social Science Mass Excursions and Socially Useful Labor. Theory and Practical Arrangement) (1927); *Died:* 1942.

TARKHANOV (real name: MOSKVIN), Mikhail Mikhaylovich (1877–1948) Actor, stage dir and drama teacher; Pop Artiste of USSR from 1937; Dr of Arts; prof from 1939; brother of the actor I.M. Moskvin; CP member from 1947; *Born:* 7 Sept 1877 in Moscow; *Career:* 1898 theater debut with I. Shuvalov's company in Ryazan'as prompter, asst stage dir, then actor; then acted at provincial theaters; 1914–19 at Sinel'nikov Theater, Kiev; and Khar'kov; from 1922 actor, Moscow Arts Theater; 1925–27 artistic dir, 4th Studio, Moscow Arts Theater; 1942–48 artistic dir, State Inst of Stagecraft; *Roles:* Zemlyanika and Osip in Gogol's *Revizor* (The Government Inspector); Orgon in Moliere's "Tartuffe"; Polonius in "Shakespeare's "Hamlet"; Robinzon in Ostrovskiy's *Bespridannitsa* (Girl Without a Dowry); Bogdan Kuryukov in A.K. Tolstoy's "Tsar' Fyodor Ioannovich" (1923); Gradoboyev in Ostrovskiy's *Goryacheye serdtse* (A Warm Heart) (1926); Firs in Chekhov's *Vishnyovyy sad* (The Cherry Orchard) (1928); Semyon Semyonych in Ivanov's *Bronepoyezd 14–69* (Armored Train 14–69) (1929); Sobakevich in *Myortvyye dushi* (Dead Souls), after Gogol; (1932); Dikiy in Ostrovskiy's *Groza* (The Storm) (1934); Furnachev in Saltykov-Shchedrin's *Smert Pazukhina* (The Death of Pazukhin) (1939); Bogomazov in Bulgakov's *Posledniye dni* (The Last Days) (1943), etc; *film roles:* Modest Alekseyevich in *Chiny i lyudi* (Titles and People); Derunov in "Iudushka Golovlev"; Spitsyn in "Dubrovskiy"; Sheremetev in *Pyotr I* (Peter I); Polivanov in *Yunost' Maksima* (Maksim's Youth), etc; *Productions:* "Goryacheye serdtse" (1926); Ostrovskiy's *Ne bylo ni grosha, da vdrug altyn* (From Rags to Riches); Moliere's "Tartuffe"; Nizovoy's *Na zemle* (On Earth); *Tsement* (Cement), after Gladkov, etc; *Publ: Kak ya stal aktyorom* (How I Became an Actor) (1938); *Awards:* two Orders of Lenin; Order of the Red Banner of Labor; Stalin Prize (1943); *Died:* 18 Mar 1948.

TARLE, Yevgeniy Viktorovich (1875–1955) Historian; Dr of Historical Sci from 1909; prof from 1913; member, USSR Acad of Sci from 1927; *Born:* 8 Nov 1875 in Kiev, son of an office Worker; *Educ:* 1896 grad History and Philology Fac, Kiev Univ;

Career: 1903–17 assoc prof, from 1917 prof, Petersburg (Leningrad) Univ; 1913–18 also prof, Yur'yev Univ; 1921–27 corresp member, USSR Acad of Sci; also prof, Moscow Univ; specialized in modern and recent history of Western Europe and Russia; wrote noteworthy study of French Revol and reign of Napoleon; belonged to so-called progressive materialist historians but refused to incorporate historical events into the framework of historical materialism; 1929 critized by the M.N. Pokrovskiy historical school for tenets expressed in his work *Yevropa v epokhu imperializma, 1871–1919* (Europe in the Age of Imperialism, 1871–1919) (1927); in this work he denied that there was aggravation of the class struggle on the eve of WW 1 and laid the main blame for the war on Germany; this contradicted both the postulates of the Marxist historians and Sov policy toward Germany at that time; 1931 arrested on charges of complicity in alleged "monarchist plot" involving historians S.F. Platonov, S.V. Rozhdestvenskiy, Ye. V. Tarle, etc, and supposedly aimed at overthrowing the Sov regime and restoring monarchy; returned from exile and resumed his leading place in Sov historiography after official criticism of the Pokrovskiy historical school and a swing in Sov policy toward Germany; member, Oslo Acad of Sci; corresp member, British Acad for the Advancement of Historical, Philosophical and Philological Sci; Hon Dr of the Sorbonne and Brno, Oslo and Algiers Univ; member, Sov Peace Comt; *Publ: Istoriya Italii v sredniye veka* (Italian History in the Middle Ages) (1901); *Istoriya Italii v novoye vremya* (Modern Italian History) (1901); *Rabochiy klass vo Frantsii v epokhu revolyutsii* (The Working Class in France at the Time of the Revolution) (2 vol, 1909–11); *Kontinental'naya blokada* (The Continental Blockade) (2 vol, 1913–16); *Rabochiy klass vo Frantsii v pervyye vremena mashinnogo proizvodstva* (The Working Class in France in the Early Times of Industrial Production) (1928); *Napoleon* (1936); *Nashestviye Napoleona na Rossiyu. 1812 god* (Napoleon's Invasion of Russia. The Year 1812) (1938); *Taleyran* (Talleyrand) (1939); *Krymskaya voyna* (The Crimean War) (2 vol, 1941–43); *Gorod russkoy slavy. Sevastopol' v 1854–1855 gg* (City of Russian Fame. Sebastopol in 1854–1855) (1954); *Tri ekspeditsii russkogo flota* (Three Expeditions of the Russian Navy) (1956); *Ocherki istorii zapadnoyevropeyskikh gosudarstv. Konets XV – nachalo XIX vekov* (An Outline History of the West European States. Late 15th – Early 19th Centuries) (1965); *Sochineniya* (Works) (12 vol, 1957–62); *Awards:* three Orders of Lenin; two Orders of the Red Banner of Labor; three Stalin Prizes (1942, 1943 and 1946); *Died:* 5 Jan 1955.

TARNOGORODSKIY, Nikolay Pavlovich (1894–1938) Party and govt official; CP member from 1915; *Born:* 1894 in Podol'ye Province; *Educ:* from 1914 studied at Med Fac, Kiev Univ; *Career:* 1915–16 worked for underground Bolshevik org in Kiev; Apr 1916 arrested; Apr 1917 moved to Vinnitsa to head Vinnitsa City RSDRP(B) Comt; member, Western–Eastern Kray RSDRP(B) Comt; Oct 1917 chm, Vinnitsa Revol Comt; then underground work; 1919 chm, Podol'ye Province Exec Comt and member, Podol'ye Province Comt, CP(B) Ukr; worked for CC, CP(B) Ukr as head, Dept for Rural Work; from Oct 1920 chm, Podol'ye Province Revol Comt; from 1921 secr, Poltava Province Comt, CP(B) Ukr; then exec Party work in Ukr, Northern Caucasus and Far East; for a number of years senior posts with Comintern Exec Comt; deleg at 16th CPSU(B) Congress; member, All-Russian and All-Ukr Centr Exec Comt of several convocations; arrested by State Security organs; *Died:* 1938 in imprisonment.

TASHKENBAYEV, Ingaberdy (1886–1963) Circus artiste; rope-walker; Pop Artiste of RSFSR from 1939; Pop Artiste of Uzbek SSR; CP member from 1941; *Born:* 1886; *Career:* developed the art of Uzbek "dorbozes" (slack-wire dancers at fairs, public festivals, etc); at age ten began appearing with his father, also a rope-walker; from age 15 performed independently; founder-dir Uzbek rope-walkers ensemble; performed with this ensemble in Moscow, Kiev, Khar'kov, Odessa, Yerevan, Tbilisi, Kharbarovsk, Vladivostok, Minsk and other Sov cities; trained a large number of rope-walkers; *Awards:* Hero of Labor of Uzbek SSR; *Died:* 1963.

TASHKIN, A. M. (1892–1942) Government and trade-union offi-official; CP member from 1917; *Born:* 1892; *Career:* after 1917 Oct Revol trade-union work in Urals and Siberia; then instructor, CC, Metalworkers' Union; exec posts with Pop Comrt of Heavy Ind in the Urals and in Leningrad; 1921–22 sided with "Workers' Opposition"; 1922 subscribed to 22-signatory address to Comintern; 1937 expelled from Party for alleged anti-Party activities; arrested by State Security organs; *Died:* 1942 in imprisonment.

TASHMATOV, Orifdzhan (1887–1944) Actor; musician; Pop Artiste of Uzbek SSR from 1937; *Born:* 1887; *Educ:* grad Moslem school; *Career:* from 1905 actor and musician with itinerant companies; 1918–19 musician and comedy actor, Turkestani Kray Touring Polit Company; 1920–25 at Andizhan Theater; 1926–33 at Asakinskiy Kolkhoz-Sovkhoz Theater; 1933–44 dir, musical ensemble in Andizhan; *Died:* 1944.

TATARINOV, Vladimir Vasil'yevich (1878–1941) Radio eng; *Born:* 20 Sept 1878; *Educ:* 1904 grad Moscow Univ; *Career:* from 1904 teacher, Nizhniy-Novgorod (now Gorky) secondary schools; 1919–29 at Nizhniy-Novgorod Radio Laboratory; from 1929 worked for Leningrad Centr Radio Laboratory; 1918–29 simultaneously teacher, Nizhniy-Novgorod Univ; 1932–35 teacher, Leningrad Inst of Communication Eng; spezialized in shortwave communications; together with M. A. Bonch-Bruyevich established principle of using different wave lengths for day and night work, which in 1927 led to successful operation of the first Moscow-Tashkent shortwave telegraph; 1925–26 designed new directional shortwave antennas consisting of parallel half-wave bars; studied antenna metering and feeding of shortwave antennas; developed method of calculating complex resistances for compound antennas with active and passive reflectors; developed antennas for meter and decimeter bands; one of the first to use ultra high-frequency current in med; *Publ: Korotkovolnovyye napravlennyye antenny* (Directional Shortwave Antennas) (1936); *Issledovaniye sdviga faz v pryamolineynykh vibratore i rezonatore* (Research on Phase Shift in Rectilinear Vibrators and Resonators) (1925); *Moshchnaya nenapravlennaya korotkovolnovaya antenna* (Powerful Non-Directional Shortwave Antennas) (1929); *O pitanii begushchey volnoy korotkovolnovykh antenn i ob opredelenii ikh soprotivleniya* (The Progressive Wave Feeding of Shortwave Antennas and the Determination of Their Resistance) (1931); *O raschyote soprotivleniya antenn s aktivnymi i passivnymi zerkalami* (Calculating the Resistance of Antennas with Active and Passive Reflectors) (1932); *Died:* 1941.

TAUSON, Vladimir Ottonovich (1894–1946) Microbiologist and phytophysiologist; *Born:* 17 Feb 1894; *Educ:* 1924 grad Moscow Univ; *Career:* from 1929 at Grain Inst, from 1930 at Microbiology Inst, from 1938 at Inst of Plant Physiology, USSR Acad of Sci; studied geological activity of microbes and role of microorganisms in the break-down if chemically stable compounds (natural petroleums, pitches, and terpenes, etc); his studies of the bioenergentic processes in microorganisms a special branch of biology – bioenergetics; presented a new approach to study of the energetic aspects of respiration and synthetic processes in cells and shed new light on the nutritive value of various compounds and of metabolism in heterotrophic organisms; *Publ: Osnovnyye polozheniya rastitel'noy bioenergetiki* (The Basic Tenets of Plant Bioenergetics) (1950); *Izmeneniya napravleniya i biokhimizma nekotorykh protsessov v rastitel'noy kletke v khode evolyutsii* (Changes in the Trend and Biochemism of Certain Processes in the Plant Cell in the Course of Evolution) (1941); *Awards:* Badge of Hon; medals; *Died:* 24 Oct 1946.

TAUTIYEV, Solomon Kirillovich (1910–1946) Actor; Pop Artiste of North-Ossetian ASSR from 1940; CP member from 1938; *Born:* 1910, son of a peasant; *Educ:* 1926 entered Vladikavkaz (now Ordzhonikidze) Sov Party School; 1935 grad Ossetian Studio, Moscow's State Inst of Stagecraft; *Career:* Helped found Ossetian professional theater; until 1931 amateur actor; from 1935 with the newly foundet North Ossetian Drama Theater in Ordzhonikidze; also taught drama; *Roles:* Platon in Korneychuk's "Platon Krechet"; Oleko in Kats and Rzheshevskiy's "Oleko Dundich"; Kltsyko in Britayev's *Dve sestry* (Two Sisters); title role in Mamsurov's "Afkhardty Khasan"; Kosta Khetagurov in Yepkhiyev and Dzhanayev's "Kosta"; Don Juan in Pushkin's *Kamennyy gost* (The Stone Guest); Neznamov in Ostrovskiy's *Bez viny vinovatyye* (Guilty Without Guilt), etc; *Awards:* Order of Lenin; *Died:* 1946.

TAVBIN, Yuliy Abramovich (1911–1940) Bel poet; *Born:* 1911 in Mstislavl', now Mogilev Oblast, son of a pharmacist; *Educ:* grad Mstislavl' Teachers' Training Technicum; 1931–33 studied at Lit Fac, Gorky Teachers' Training Inst, Minsk; *Career:* member, "Maladnyak" lit assoc, then Bel Assoc of Proletarian Writers; 1926 first work printed; 1931–32 subjected to Party criticism; his collection "Lyrics. Epos" scheduled for the press in 1932, was not published; 1933 arrested and exiled to Tyumen'; from 1936 in exile in Tobol'sk; 1937–39 contributed to "Ogonyok" and helped publish *Antologiya novoy angliyskoy poezii* (Anthology of New English Poetry) (Leningrad, 1937); 1940 re-arrested; *Publ:* collected verse and poems "Fires" (1930); "Live, Sing and Stay Young" (1931); "Three Poems" (1931); "My Secound Book" (1932); "Selected Verse"; poem "Tavrida" (1932); *Died:* 1940 in imprisonment; posthoumusly rehabilitated.

TAVLAY, Valentin Pavlovich (1914–1947) Bel poet; *Born:* 8 Feb 1914 in Baranovichi, son of a railroad worker; *Educ:* studied at Bel high-school in Vilnius; 1929 expelled from school for participating in underground Komsomol org; *Career:* 1930–32 lived in Bel SSR and worked for newspaper "Zvyazda"; later returned to West Bel and resumed underground Communist activities: worked for newspaper "Chyrvony stsyah" and edited illegal newspaper "Belaruskaya hazeta"; soon arrested by Polish authorities and until 1939 imprisoned in Grodno jail; during WW 2 fought with partisans; after WW 2 senior assoc, Yanka Kupala Museum, Minsk; *Publ:* "Selected Works" (1947); "Selected Works" (1951); "Verse and Poems" (1955); "Selected Works" (1958); *Died:* 27 Apr 1947.

TAVRIZIAN, Mikhail Arsen'yevich (1907–1957)Conductor; Pop Artiste of USSR from 1956; *Born:* 14 May 1907 in Baku; *Educ:* 1932 grad viola class, 1934 grad Gauk's conducting class, Leningrad Conservatory; *Career:* from 1925 viola player, Leningrad opera and symphony orchestras; 1934–35 conductor, Tbilisi's Paliashvili Opera and Ballet Theater; 1935–38 conductor, from 1938 chief conductor, Yerevan's Spendiarov Opera and Ballet Theater; dep, USSR Supr Sov of 1954 convocation; *Works:* conducted and staged operas: "Lusabatsin" (1938); Chukhadzhyan's "Arshak II" (1945); *Geroinya* (The Heroine) (1950); Tigranyan's "David-bek" (1956); Babayev's "Artsvaberd" (1957); Glinka's "Ivan Susanin"; Meyerbeer's "The Huguenots," etc; also conducted symphony orchestras; *Awards:* two Stalin Prizes (1946 and 1951); *Died:* 17 Oct 1957 in Yerevan.

TAVZISHVILI, Georgiy Yasonovich (1902–1963) Pedag; prof; Dr of Pedag Sci; Hon Sci Worker of Geo SSR from 1960; *Born:* 6 Apr 1902; *Educ:* 1926 grad Moscow Univ; *Career:* from 1926 lecturer, Chair of Pedag, 2nd Moscow Univ; 1930–63 teaching and research work at Tbilisi Univ; 1938–58 also taught at Tbilisi's Pushkin Teachers Training Inst; lectured at Kutaisi, Sukhumi and Batumi Teachers' Training Institutes; dep dir (for research), Inst of Pedag, Geo Pop Comrt of Educ; specialized in history of public educ and history of pedag thought in Geo; also worked as lit critic; member, Geo Writers' Union; *Publ:* "The Purpose of Man and the Ideas of Education in 'The Man in the Tiger Skin'" (1937); "The History of Higher Eduction in Georgia" (1938); "International Training in the Soviet School" (1940); "Ushinskiy. On the 75th Anniversary of His Death" (1945); "The History ob Public Education and Pedagogic Thought in Georgia" (1948); "Ya. Gogebashvili's Literary Work" (1949); "Il'ya Chavchavadze. Pedagogic Ideas" (1957); "Yakov Gogebashvili" (1959); *Died:* 5 Oct 1963.

TAZHDAROVA, Nagima Akhmadullovna (1888–1948) Actress; Pop Artiste of Tatar ASSR from 1939; Hon Artiste of RSFSR from 1940; *Born:* 1888; *Career:* 1915 stage debut with Sayyar Company; from 1917 with Shirkat Company, Orenburg; during Civil War acted with frontline drama company; 1922–26 at Bashkir Drama Theater; from 1926 actress, Kamal Theater; *Roles:* Mariya Antonovna in *Revizor* (The Government Inspector); Korinkina in *Bez viny vinovatyye* (Guilty Without Guilt); Yulin'ka in *Dokhodnoye mesto* (A Lucrative Post); Louise in "Kabale und Liebe"; Amalie in "The Robbers"; Tat'yana in *Razlom* (The Break-Up); Oksana n *Gibel' eskadry* (Death of a Squadron); Gul'nisa in Gizzat's "Streams"; Sazhida in Abliyev's "Shamsikamar"; Nafiga in Amirov's "Minnikamal," etc; *Died:* 1948.

TAZHIBAYEV, Tulegen Tazhibayevich (1910–1964) Psychologist and pedag; Dr of Pedag Sci from 1963; prof from 1949; member, Kaz Acad of Sci from 1954; envoy extraordinary and plen, 1st class; CP member from 1939; *Born:* 1910; *Educ:* 1935 grad, 1938 completed postgrad studies, Krupskaya Acad of Communist Educ; *Career:* 1938–40 assoc prof and head, Chair of Pedag and Psychology, Abay Kaz Teachers' Training Inst; 1940 Kaz Pop Comr of Educ; 1941–56 dep chm, Kaz Council of Pop Comr (Council of Min); Kaz Min of For Affairs and Kaz Min of Culture; 1957–60 counselor-envoy, USSR embassy in India; 1947–54 rector, Kaz State Univ; 1961–64 prof and head, Chair of Pedag, Kaz State Univ; did research on history of schools and pedag thought in Kaz; works deal with K. D. Ushinskiy's psychological views, Kaz poet and educator Abay Kunanbayev's psychological and pedag views; rote research studies, sci-pop articles and booklets on various aspects of psychology and pedag; *Publ:* in Russian translation: *Psikhologiya i pedagogicheskaya psikhologiya K. D. Ushinskogo* (K. D. Ushinskiy's Psychology and Pedagogic Psychology) (1948); *Abay Kunanbayev o vospitanii molodyozhi* (Abay Kunanbayev's Views on the Training of Youth) (1954); *O kommunisticheskoy morali* (Communist Morals) (1956); *Filosofskiye, pedagogicheskiye i psikhologicheskiye vzglyady Abaya Kunanbayeva* (Abay Kunanbayev's Philosophic, Pedagogic and Psychological Views) (1957); *Razvitiye prosveshcheniya i pedagogicheskoy mysli v Kazakhstane vo vtoroy polovine 19-go veka* (The Development of Education and Pedagogic Thought in Kazakhstan in the Late 19th Century) (1958); *Kazakhskaya shkola pri Orenburgskoy pogranichnoy komissii (1850–1869)* (The Kazakh School of the Orenburg Frontier Commission [1850–1869]) (1961); *Prosveshcheniye i shkoly Kazakhstana vo vtoroy polovine 19-go veka* (Education and Schools in Kazakhstan in the Late 19th Century) (1962); *Died:* 14 June 1964.

TAZHIYEV, Ibragim Tausiyevich (1904–1960) Kaz govt official; Cand of Tech Sci; CP member from 1930; *Born:* 1904; *Educ:* grad Leningrad Polytech Inst; *Career:* from 1931 eng and mang of trusts; dep chm, Kaz Council of Pop Comr; Kaz Pop Comr of Municipal Econ; directed construction of Karaganda Electr Power Plant; from 1943 dep chm, Kaz Council of Min; from 1954 secr, CC, CP KA Kaz; from 1959 permanent rep of Kaz Council of Min in USSR Council of Min; dep, USSR Supr Sov of 1954 convocations; member, CC, CP Kaz; *Died:* 28 Sept 1960.

TELESHEVA, Yelizaveta Sergeyevna (1892–1943) Actress, stage dir and drama teacher; Hon Artiste of RSFSR from 1933; *Born:* 26 Jan 1892 in Moscow; *Educ:* grad A.I. Adashev's Drama School; *Career:* 1916–24 actress, 2nd Studio, Moscow Acad Arts Theater; also worked as stage dir; from 1916 taught Stanislavsky methods at Theatrical School; 2nd Studio of Moscow Acad Arts Theater, at N. Khmelyov's Studio, at State Inst of Stagecraft and at All-Union State Inst of Cinematography; *Roles:* Lebedeva in Gippius' *Zelyonoye kol'tso* (The Green Ring); Igumen'ya in Leskov's *Nekuda* (Nowhere to Go); Beatrice in Calderon's "The Invisible Lady"; Catherine I in Smolin's "Yelizaveta Petrovna"; *Productions:* "The Robbers"; *Groza* (The Storm); "Marriage of Figaro" (1927); *Myortvyye dushi* (Dead Souls) (1932); *Gore ot uma* (Woe from Wit) (1938); *Poslednyaya zhertva* (The Last Sacrifice) (1944); *Bespridannitsa* (Girl Without a Dowry) (1932); *Meshchane* (The Philistines) (1935); "Vassa Zheleznova" (1936); *Publ: Rezhissyorskiye kommentarii* (A Producer's Commentaries) (1935); *V.V. Luzhskiy, pedagog* (The Teacher V.V. Luzhskiy) (1946), etc; *Awards:* Badge of Hon; *Died:* 9 July 1943.

TELESHOV, Nikolay Dmitriyevich (1867–1957) Writer; Hon Art Worker of RSFSR from 1938; *Born:* 10 Nov 1867; *Educ:* studied at Moscow Practical Acad; *Career:* 1884 first work published; toured Urals and Siberia; from 1926 dir, Moscow Arts Theater Museum; wrote stories and novels about peasant life, mining and revol; *Publ: Na tropikakh* (In the Tropics) (1895); *Povesti i rasskazy* (Stories and Tales) (1896); *Za Ural* (For the Urals); *S Bogom* (Go with God); *Nuzhda* (Need); *Shakhty* (The Pits); *Sukhaya beda* (Drought); *Chyornoy noch'yu* (In the Black of Night); *Kramola* (Sedition); *Nachalo kontsa* (The Beginning of the End) (1933); *Zapiski pisatelya* (A Writers' Notes) (1943); children's stories: *Yolka Mitricha* (Mitrich's Fir Tree); *Domoy* (Home); *Belaya tsaplya* (The White Heron), etc; *Awards:* two Orders of the Red Banner of Labor; *Died:* 14 Mar 1957 in Moscow.

TEL'MAN, Solomoniya Fyodorovna (1898–1967) Party and govt official; CP member from 1917; *Born:* 25 July 1898; *Educ:* 1943–44 studied at Moscow Statistical Inst; *Career:* participated in revol movement in Est; from 1918 illegal Party work; 1922, on Party orders, hid Est CP leader V. Kingisepp; for this sentenced to penal servitude for life; 1938 released and resumed revol work; participated in June 1940 coup and helped reestablish Sov rule in Est; after the liberation of Est from German troops dep head, Est Statistical Bd; 1947–59 with Kreytsval'd State Public Library; 1947–58 dep, Tallin Sov; from 1959 pensioner; *Died:* 21 July 1967.

TELYAKOVSKIY, Vladimir Arkad'yevich (1861–1924) Theatrical impressario; *Born:* 1861; *Educ:* grad Gen Staff Acad; *Career:* served in cavalry; 1898–1901 dir, Moscow Bd of Imperial Theaters; 1901–17 dir of Imperial Theaters; raised artistic level of Moscow and Petersburg's official theaters by recruiting such young and talented actors and stage dir as Chaliapine, Sobinov, Meyerhold, etc, and set designers linked with the "World of Art" assoc – K.A. Korovin, A.Ya. Golovin, etc; 1898–1917 kept a diary which runs to 50 vol and contains valuable data for theater historians (displayed at Bakhrushin Theater Museum); *Publ: Imperatorskiye teatry i 1905 god* (The Imperial Theaters and 1905) (1926); *Moy sosluzhivets Shalyapin* (My Colleague Chaliapine) (1927); *Vospominaniya* (Memoirs) (1965); *Died:* 1924.

TENNER, Grigoriy Samoylovich (1889–1943) Sculptor; *Born:* 13 Oct 1889 in Akkerman, now Belgorod-Dnestrovskiy, Odessa Oblast; *Educ:* studied at Petersburg and Munich Acads of Arts; *Career:* from 1932 taught at Odessa Art Inst; *Works:* statues: "Lenin on the Armored Car" (1930); "A.S. Pushkin" (1935); "Karl Marx" (1935–36); portraits of Herzen and Plekhanov (1930); designed monuments to Shevchenko (1925) and Lenin (1927), etc; *Died:* 31 Oct 1943.

TEODOROVICH, Ivan Adol'fovich (1876–1940) Govt offivial; CP member from 1895; *Born:* 1876, of noble parentage; *Educ:* 1894 studied at Natural Sci Fac, Moscow Univ; *Career:* arrested for involvement in student riots; 1895 joined Moscow League for the Liberation of the Working Class; founded first Soc-Democratic circle in Smolensk; 1901 member, Moscow Party Comt; sided with "Iskra" group; ran workers' circles; 1902 arrested and after a long period of custody exiled for six years to Yakutsk Oblast; after 2nd RSDRP Congress sided with Bolsheviks; summer 1905 fled from exile; made his way to Geneva and became acquainted with Lenin; secr, ed staff, periodical "Proletariy"; Oct 1905 returned to Russia and became member, Petersburg RSDRP Comt and member, CC, RSDRP; attented Stockholm and London Party Congresses; Feb 1908 arrested in Urals and sentenced to four years' hard Labor; from 1914 enforced settlement in Yakutsk Province; after 1917 Feb Revol asst chm, Petrograd City Duma; member, CC, RSDRP (B); after 1917 Oct Revol Pop Comr of Food; Nov 1917 resigned from govt in protest against Bolshevik leadership's refusal to establish a coalition govt including members of other polit parties; 1919–20 Kansk Revol Comt plen for instructing Sov and Party orgs; 1920–28 Collegium member, Pop Comrt of Agric; from 1922 Dep Pop Comr of Agric; from 1925 dir, Int Agrarian Inst; from 1928 secr-gen, Peasants' International; member, All-Russian Centr Exec Comt; charged with "rightist-opportunist errors" in his work at the Pop Comrt of Agric in 1928–29; later chief ed, Soc of Polit Convicts; exed ed, journal "Katorga i ssylka"; wrote articles on agric policy and history of revol movement; arrested by State Security organs; *Publ: Istoricheskoye znacheniye partii Narodnoy voli* (The Historical Importance of the People's Will Party) (1930); *Died:* 1940 in imprisonment.

TEPLOV, Boris Mikhaylovich (1896–1965) Psychologist; Dr of Pedag Sci from 1947; Member, RSFSR Acad of Pedag Sci from 1945; Hon Sci Worker of RSFSR from 1957; *Born:* 21 Oct 1896; *Educ:* 1921 grad History and Philology Fac, Moscow Univ; *Career:* 1921–23 worked for Red Army research establishments; 1929–33 assoc, from 1933 laboratory head, dept head, then dep dir for research, Moscow Inst of Psychology; 1946–53 also head, Chair of Logic and Psychology, Acad of Soc Sci, CC, CPSU; for many years also taught psychology at Moscow Univ; 1958–65 chief ed, journal "Voprosy psikhologii"; 1959–65 Presidium member, Centr Council, Psychologists Soc; founded Laboratory of Individual Psychological Differences at Inst of Psychology, RSFSR Acad of Pedag Sci; continued Pavlov's research on higher nervous activity in man; did first Sov research on visual sensation and perception; studied effects of light in mil camouflage and in architecture; did research on psychology of art and psychology of musical ability; established theoretical principles of ability and talent, connected with individual psychological differences; studied history of psychology, especially views of Russian revol democrats and history of Sov psychology; did research on practical intellectual quotient; in 1950's studied basic (typological) properties of human nervous system; devised original methods for determining the properties of the nervous system, made a statistical check of these methods and discovered some new properties of higher nervous activity; began a study of the psychological manifestations of these properties in educ and in the labor process; 1954 attended 14th Int Psychology Congress in Montreal and read a paper on "The Theory of Types of Nervous Activity and Psychology"; 1956 also spoke on this topic in Paris; coauthor and ed, five-vol *Tipologicheskiye osobennosti vysshey nervnoy deyatel'nosti cheloveka* (The Typological Features of Human Higher Nervous Activity) (1959–66); wrote secondary-school psychology textbook; wrote and edited various textbooks for higher educ establishments; *Publ: Tsvetovedeniye dlya arkhitektorov* (Light Studies for Architects) (1938); *Psikhologiya muzykal'nykh sposobnostey* (The Psychology of Musical Ability) (1947); *K voprosu o prakticheskom myshlenii* (The Problem of Practical Thinking); textbook *Psikhologiya* (Psychology); *O ponyatiyakh slabosti i inertnosti nervnoy sistemy* (The Concepts of Weakness and Inertness of the Nervous System) (1955); *Ob izuchenii tipologicheskikh svoystv nervnoy sistemy i ikh psikhologicheskikh yavleniy* (The Study of Typological Properties of the Nervous System and Their Psychological Manifestations) (1957); *Problemy individual'nykh razlichiy* (Problems of Individual Differences) (1961); *Novyye dannyye po izhucheniyu svoystv nervnoy sistemy cheloveka* (New Date on the Study of the Properties of the Human Nervous System) (1963); *Awards:* two First Prizes of the RSFSR Acad of Pedag Sci; 1947 and 1956; *Died:* 28 Sept 1965 in Moscow.

TER-ABRAMYAN, Armenak Yefremovich (1898–1957) Opera and operetta artist (tenor); Pop Artiste of Arm SSR from 1954; *Born:* 15 Sept 1898; *Educ:* 1920 grad Tbilissi Conservatory; *Career:* 1937–41 soloist, Spendiarov Opera and Ballet Theater, Yerevan; from 1942 co-founder and artiste, Arm Musical Comedy Theater, Yerevan; *Roles:* Saro in Tigranyan's "Anush"; Seto in Stepanyan's "Lusabatsin", etc; *Died:* 1957.

TER-ARUTYUNYANTS, Mikhail Karpovich (1894–1961) Govt official; CP member from 1917; *Born:* 1894; *Career:* 1917 member, Comt of Mil Orgs, Petrograd Comt; during 1917 Oct Revol comr, Armory, Petropavlovsk Fortress; helped crush Petrograd cadet revolt and defeat Kerenskiy and Krasnov's troops approaching the city; comr, Pulkovo detachment; then head, revol field staff of commander in chief N. V. Krylensko's Headquarters; during Civil War fought in Red Army as mil commander, then head, Revol Field Staff Against Counterrevol; often carried out special mil missions for Lenin; after the Civil War for many years with Centr Control Commission and Workers and Peasants' Inspection; in latter years taught at Moscow's higher educ institutions and Higher Party School; *Died:* 25 Aug 1961.

TER-ASTVATSATURYAN, Iosif Andreyevich (1886–1938) Hydraulic power eng; *Born:* 1 May 1886; *Educ:* 1912 grad Petersburg Inst of Transport Eng; *Career:* from 1912 worked on various civil eng projects, including bridges, a wharf in Saratov, etc; 1922–25 dep head, Arm Supr Sovnarkhoz; and dir of construction, Shirak Irrigation Canal; 1928–33 directed construction of Dzora Hydroelectr Plant, Armenia's first major hydroelectr plant; from 1932 head, Arm Branch, Hydropower Design Org; 1931 drafted plan for utilizing the waters of the high-altitude Lake Sevan; directed construction of Sevan-Razdan barrage of hydroelectr power plants; member, USSR Centr Exec Comt of three convocations; *Died:* 19 July 1938.

TER-DAVTYAN, Gevork Zakhar'yevich (1850–1934) Actor; Pop Artiste of Arm SSR from 1923; *Born:* 25 Aug 1850; *Career:* 1872 began acting; one of the greatest Arm realist comedy actors; *Roles:* 1st gravedigger in "Hamlet" (1880); Belogubov in *Dokhodnoye mesto* (A Lucrative Post) (1880); Molchalin in *Gore ot uma* (Woe from Wit) (1881); Dobchinskiy in *Revizor* (The Government Inspector) (1882); Zhevakin in *Zhenit'ba* (The Marriage) (1882); Sprich in "Masquerade" (1882); the Fool in "King Lear" (1887), etc; *Died:* 13 Nov 1934.

TER-GABRIELYAN, Saak Mirzoyevich (1886–1937) Govt and Party official; CP member from 1902; *Born:* 10 Mar 1886; *Career:* from 1900 engaged in revol movement among Baku proletariat; member, underground Baku RSDRP Comt; after 1917 Feb Revol Presidium member, Bolshevik faction, Baku Sov of Workers' Dep; attented 7th (April) RSDRP(B) Conference; during the Baku Commune chm, Cheka; after the fall of Baku Commune worked in Moscow as Comr for transport of all kinds of fuel; Collegium member, Main Oil Comt; worked for Cheka; helped establish Sov rule in Arm; member, Arm Revol Comt; 1921–23 Arm permanent rep in Moscow; from 1923 Transcaucasian SFSR permanent rep in Moscow; 1928–35 chm, Arm Council of Pop Comr; Bureau member, CC, CP(B) Arm; member, Arm Centr Exec Comt; Bureau member, Transcaucasian Kray Party Comt and member, Transcaucasian Centr Exec Comt; from 1921 member, All-Russian Centr Exec Comt and cand Presidium member, All- Russian Centr Exec Comt; member, USSR Centr Exec Comt of six convocations; elected cand Presidium member, USSR Centr Exec Comt; arrested by State Security organs; *Died:* 19 Aug 1937 in imprisonment.

TER-GAZARYAN (pseudonym: LERR), G.G. (1874–1958) Politician; *Born:* 1874; *Career:* 1903 helped found Arm Soc-Democratic ("Specifists") Party, which held the same views on organizational problems as the Jewish Bund; represented this party at the 2 Apr

1905 Geneva Conference, convened by Gapon; 1907–17 worked in Baku; represented "Specifists" at 5th RSDRP Congress; after 1917 Oct Revol worked with Geo Menshevik-Internationalists; after the establishment of Sov rule in Transcaucasia worked for Transcaucasian Gosplan; 1923–28 with Transcaucasian Sovnarkhoz; simultaneously taught at higher educ institutions; from 1934 teacher in Arm; from 1955 pensioner; *Died:* 1958.

TER-GEVONDYAN, Anushavan Grigor'yevich (1887–1961) Composer and musicologist; Pop Artiste of Arm SSR from 1953; *Born:* 24 Feb 1887 in Tiflis; *Educ:* 1915 grad Lyadov and Glazunov's class, Petersburg Conservatory; *Career:* 1918–25 instructur, Tbilisi Conservatory; 1926–30 dir, 1930–34 instructor, Yerevan Conservatory; 1934–38 dir, Baku Conservatory; from 1938 prof, from 1949 head, Chair of Composition Theory, Yerevan Conservatory; *Works:* "Shiraz Etudes" (1917); opera "Seda" (1921); symphonic poem "Vaagn's Birth" (1922); ballet "Bride of Fire" (1934); rhapsody "Rast" (1935); ballet "Anait" (1940); opera "In the Rays of the Sun" (1949); symphonic poem "In Memory of Lenin" (1958); music for plays and films; *Died:* 6 June 1961 in Yerevan.

TER-GRIGORYAN, Emin Ovakimovich (1855–1939) Arm playwright; *Born:* 1855; *Educ:* grad Lazarev Inst, Moscow; *Career:* wrote dramas and vaudeville pieces; his work has been translated into Azer, Geo and Turkish; 1908–13 the Tiflis journal "Usharar" carried his recollections of Yerevan theater life in the 1870's; *Publ:* plays: "Inzhir Khecho" (1869); "Victim of Deprivation"; "Love or Death"; "Under the Guise of Benevolence" (1892); "The Damocles Sword"; "Sword and Fire"; comedies: "Fashion"; "The Savage Woman"; "The Domestic"; "Two in Love"; "I Was the Cause of Dissension"; *Died:* 26 Dec 1939.

TER-VAGANYAN, Vagarshak Arutyunovich (1893–1936) Office worker; *Born:* 1893; *Career:* Aug 1936 charged with membership of "Trotsky-Zinov'yevite Center," accused of organizing a terrorist group for assassinating Sov govt and Party leaders; sentenced to death by Mil Collegium, USSR Supr Cour; *Died:* 1936 executed.

TER-YEGIAZAR'YAN, Mikhail Andreyevich (? –1934) Govt official; *Educ:* grad higher institution; *Career:* 1917–18 worked for Moscow Party org; then chm, Oryol Province Exec Comt; 1921–24 chm, Nizhniy Novgorod Province Exec Comt; from 1924 exec work in various oblasts: dep chm, Ural Oblast Exec Comt; chm, Centr Asian Econ Council; chm, Ivanovo-Voznesensk Exec Comt; dep chm, Transcaucasian Council of Pop Comr; member, Commodity Funds Comt, Labor and Defense Council; in his latter years dep chm, Moscow Oblast Exec Comt; member, USSR Centr Exec Comt; *Died:* 28 Jan 1934 during an operation at the Kremlin Hospital.

TEREBINSKIY, Nikolay Naumovich (1880–1959) Surgeon; Dr of Med from 1907; prof from 1920; Hon Sci Worker of RSFSR; *Born:* 1880; *Educ:* 1904 grad Med Fac, Moscow Univ; *Career:* after grad intern, Prof. P. I. D'yakonov's Hospital Surgical Clinic; 1907 defended doctor's thesis on the operative treatment of cancer of the larynx; from 1909 co-ed, journal "Khirurgiya"; 1911 assoc prof, Moscow Univ; from 1912 head, Children's Surgical Dept, Saint Vladimir Children's Hospital (now Rusakov Children's Hospital); 1919 founded Surgical Dept, Moscow Junction Hospital (now Centr Roentgenological and Radiological Hospital, USSR Min of Means of Communication); from 1920 prof, Surgical Clinic, Moscow Higher Med School; from 1924 head, Hospital Surgical Clinic, 2nd Moscow Univ (now 2nd Moscow Med Inst); 1930 in the course of research at S. S. Bryukhonenko's Laboratory proved the feasibility of open-heart surgery with a heart-lung machine; during WW 2 consultant, various evacuation hospitals and chief surgeon, 4th Bd, USSR Min of Health; specialized in heart surgery; chm, Moscow Surgical Soc; hon member, All-Union Soc of Surgeons; chm, 24th Congress of Surgeons; *Publ:* doctor's thesis *Nekotoryye dannyye k voprosu o zlokachestvennykh novoobrazovaniyakh gortani i operativnom lechenii ikh* (Some Data on Malignant Neoplasms of the Larynx and Their Operative Treatment) (1907); *Obzor deyatel'nosti khirurgicheskogo otdeleniya Moskovskoy gorodskoy detskoy bol'nitsy Svyatogo Vladimira* (A Review of the Work of the Surgical Department of the Saint Vladimir Municipal Children's Hospital in Moscow) (1914); *Ob eksperimental'nom vosproizvedenii porokov klapanov serdtsa* (The Experimental Reproduction of Disorders of the Cardiac Valves) (1930); *Materialy po izucheniyu otkrytogo dostupa k atrioventrikulyarnym klapanam serdtsa* (Study Material on Open Acces to the Atrioventricular Valves of the Heart) (1940): *K istorii rossiyskikh i vsesoyuznykh s'yezdov khirurgov* (The History of the Russian and All-Union Congresses of Surgeons) (1946); *Died:* 1959 in Moscow.

TEREGULOV, Mamed Khanifa Gasanovich (1877–1942) Azer Actor; CP member from 1905; Hero ob Labor; *Born:* 27 Nov 1877; *Educ:* 1899 grad Transcaucasian Teachers' Seminary, Gori; *Career:* taught in Yerevan Province, then in Baku; 1910 co-founder, Azer Nat Music Theater; performed at theater as baritone and helped found its Opera Chorus; *Roles:* Nofel' in "Leyli and Medzhnun"; Mastavar in "Shakh Abbas and Khurshid banu"; the Priest Arsen in "Asli and Kerem": Shakh-Aslan in "Shakh Ismail", etc; *Awards:* Hero of Labor; *Died:* 18 Dec 1942.

TERENIN, Aleksandr Nikolayevich (1896–1967) Physiochemist; prof and dept head, Leningrad Univ from 1932; member, USSR Acad of Sci from 1939; dep dir, State Optics Inst; *Born:* 8 May 1896 in Kaluga; *Educ:* 1921 grad Physics and Mathematics Fac, Petrograd Univ; *Career:* from 1919 worked for State Optics Inst; specialist in nature of chemical and physical processes occuring in substances under the effect of light; first to record infra-red spectra of gases under extreme pressure; specialized in photosynthesis; 1932–39 corresp member, USSR Acad of Sci; founder-dir, Catalysis Laboratory, Leningrad Univ; founder-dir, Photobiochemistry Laboratory, Inst of Biochemistry, USSR Acad of Sci; 1960–63 Bureau member, Dept of Chemical Sci, USSR Acad of Sci; 1965 reported on kinetics of fast reactions at 6th European Congress on Molecular Spectroscopy, Copenhagen; chm, Sci Council on Photosynthesis, USSR Acad of Sci; *Publ: Vvedeniye v spektroskopiyu* (An Introduction to Spectroscopy) (1933); *Fotokhimiya soley* (The Photochemistry of Salts) (1934); *Fotokhimicheskiye protsessy v aromaticheskikh soyedineniyakh* (Photochemical Processes in Aromatic Compounds) (1944); *Fotokhimiya krasiteley i rodstvennykh organicheskikh soyedineniy* (The Photochemistry od Dyes and Allied Organic Compounds) (1947); coauthor, *Vozbuzhdeniye svobodnykh radikalov pri rasshcheplenii mnogoatomnykh molekul fotonami vakuumnoy ul'trafioletovoy oblasti* (The Excitation of Free Radicals in the Break-Down of Polyatomic Molecules by Photons of the Vacuum Ultraviolet Band) (1963); *Awards:* Hero of Socialist Labor; (1966); Stalin Prize (1946); three Orders of Lenin; Order of the Red Banner; Order of the Red Star; medals; *Died:* 18 Jan 1967.

TERENT'YEV, Valentin Aleksandrovich (1910–1965) Govt official; cand member, CC, CP Ukr from 1960; *Born:* 1910; *Educ:* 1931 grad Dneprodzerzhinsk Metallurgical Inst; *Career:* from 1931 worked on construction of factories and directed various construction trust and bds; from 1954 USSR Dep Min for the Construction of Metallurgical and Chemical Ind Enterprises; 1956–57 Ukr Min for the Construction of Metallurgical Ind Enterprises; 1958 dept head, Ukr Gosplan; 1958–62 Ukr Min of Construction; 1963–65 Ukr Min of Assembly and Special Construction Works; dep, Ukr Supr Sov of 1959 and 1963 convocations; *Awards:* two Orders of Lenin; Order of the Red Banner of Labor; medals *Died:* 15 Jan 1965.

TERESHKOVICH, Maks Abramovich (1897–1939) Actor, stage dir and drama teacher; *Born:* 17 Nov 1897; *Career:* 1914 actor, Moscow's Komissarzhevskaya Theater; 1920–22 at 1st RSFSR Theater; 1922–23 at Moscow's Revol Theater; from 1927 stage dir; 1929 organized Lunacharskiy Theater Studio; 1933–36 artistic dir, Yermolova Theater Studio; *Roles:* the Intellectual in Mayakovskiy's "Mystery-Buffo" (1921); Tarelkin in Sukhovo-Kobylin's *Smert' Tarelkina* (Tarelkin's Death) (1922); Kron in *Ozero Lyul* (Lake Lyul') (1923); Koromyslov in Romashov's *Vozdushnyy pirog* (The Meringue) (1925); Sevast'yanov in Romashov's *Konets Krivoryl'ska* (The End of Krivoryl'sk) (1926); Granatov in Fayko's *Chelovek s portfelem* (The Man with a Briefcase) (1928); Yermakov in Glebov's "Inga", etc; *Productions:* Zola's "Rabourdin's Inheritance" (1927); *Gorod Glupov* (The City of Glupov) (1932), after Saltykov-Shchedrin; *Bednost' ne porok* (Poverty Is No Vice) (1933); *Poslednyaya zhertva* (The Last Victim) (1934); Skrib's *Iskusstvo intrigi* (The Art of Intrigue) (1935); Balzac's "Stepmother" (1936, co-dir), etc; *Died:* 24 Feb 1939.

TERLEMEZYAN, Panos (Fanos) Pogosovich (Pavlovich) (1865–1941) Landscape painter; Pop Artist of Arm SSR from 1935; *Born:* 11 Mar 1865 in Van, Turkey; *Educ:* 1895–97 studied at Petersburg School of Soc for the Promotion of the Arts; 1904 grad Julien Acad, Paris: *Career:* 1893, after participating in Arm nat liberation movement, emigrated to Russia; 1897 at the request of the Turkish govt; imprisoned for a year, then deported to Persia; 1899–1928 lived in France, Constantinople, USA and various European countries; 1928 moved to Arm SSR; member, Assoc of

Artists of Revol Russia; *Works:* "A Lori Shepherd" (1905); "Working District of Paris" (1910); "Portrait of the Composer Komitas" (1913); "View of Mount Sipan from Ktuts Island" (1915); "The Breton Coast" (1921); ind landscapes: "The Dzora Hydroelectric Plant" and "The River Debed" (1930), etc; *Awards:* Order of the Red Banner of Labor; *Died:* 30 Apr 1941.

TERLETSKIY, Sidor Ivanovich (1892–1953) Actor and stage dir; *Born:* 7 June 1892 in Chernovtsy, son of a worker; *Career:* 1910–14 actor, "Russian Conversation" Theater, L'vov; 1919–28 dir, Drama Theater, Chernovtsy Pop Center; 1928–39 actor, Ukr Drama Theater; also performed with amateur drama companies; fought in WW 2, captured and interned in Buchenwald; *Roles:* the Delegate in Lysenko's "Natalka-Poltavka"; Karas' in Gulak-Artemovskiy's *Zaporozhets za Dunayem* (A Dnieper Cossack Beyond the Danube); Gryts' in Staritskiy's "Oh, Don't Go, Gryts'"; Fyodor Protasov in Lev Tolstoy's *Zhivoy trup* (The Living Corpse), etc; *Died:* 7 Feb 1953.

TERNOVSKIY, Sergey Dmitriyevich (1896–1960) Surgeon; corresp member, USSR Acad of Med Sci; Hon Sci Worker of RSFSR; *Born:* 1896; *Educ:* 1919 grad Med Fac, Moscow Univ; *Career:* 1919–24 served in Red Army and took part in defense of Tsaritsyn; 1924–25 intern, Surgical Clinic, 1st Moscow Univ; 1925 asst prof, Inst of Mother and Child Care, where he helped found the Surgical Dept; 1927–43 worked at 1st Model Children's Hospital; 1936 became cand of med; 1938 defended doctor's thesis on the treatment of suppurative pleuritis in children; from 1941 head, Children's Surgical Clinic, Centr Pediatric Inst, RSFSR Pop Comrt of Health; from 1942 prof of children's surgery; from 1943 head, Chair of Children's Surgery, 2nd Moscow Med Inst; specialized in surgical treatment of congenital and developmental defects in children, surgery of bone and joint tuberculosis, traumatology and orthopedics, children's thoracic surgery, etc; wrote standard textbook on children's surgery, which was translated into many for languages; founded Russian school of newborn infant surgery; devised surgical methods of treating cleft upper gum and palate and anterior cranial hernia, congenital raised scapula, etc; 1946 performed first Sov operation for ethmoid skin flap graft in children; 1953 described original symptom for specific ailment of the coxofemoral joint in children; Bd member, All-Union Soc of Surgeons, All-Union Soc of Orthopedists and Traumatologists; member, ed bd, journal "Pediatriya"; dep, Moscow City Sov; 1952 founded Children's Surgery Section, Moscow City and Oblast Surgical Soc; published some 70 research works; *Publ: Diagnostika khirurgicheskikh zabolevyniy detskogo vozrasta* (The Diagnosis of Children's Surgical Ailments). (1943); *Diagnostika nekotorykh khirurgicheskikh zabolevaniy detskogo vozrasta* (The Diagnosis of Some Children's Surgical Ailments) (1948); *Nezarashcheniye verkhney guby (zayach'ya guba) u detey i yego operativnoye lecheniye* (Cleft Upper Gum (Harelip) in Children and Its Surgical Treatment) (1952); *Khirurgiya detskogo vozrasta* (Children's Surgery) (1949); *Nekotoryye voprosy detskoy travmatologii* (Some Aspects of Child Traumatology) (1955); *O vnutricherepnom khirurgicheskom podstupe pri operatsiyakh po povodu peredney mozgovoy grizhy u detey* (Intracranial Surgical Access in Operations for Anterior Cerebral Hernia in Children) (1957); *Khirurgiya novorozhdyonnykh* (Surgery of the Newborn) (1959); *Awards:* Order of Lenin; "Distinguished Public Health Worker" Badge; medals; *Died:* 1960 in Moscow.

TERPIGOREV, Aleksandr Mitrofanovich (1873–1959) Mining eng; Dr of Tech Sci; member, USSR Acad of Sci from 1935; prof; Hon Sci and Tech Worker of RSFSR from 1934; *Born:* 21 Nov 1873 in Tambov; *Educ:* 1897 grad Petersburg Mining Inst; *Career:* directed mines in Donbas; 1900 switched to research and teaching work at Yekaterinoslav Higher Mining College (now Dnepropetrovsk Mining Inst); Dec 1905 arrested for revol activities and exiled to Ryazan' under police surveillance; Sept 1906 returned to Yekaterinoslav after representations by the Mining Inst; from 1906 prof, then head, Chair of Mining Technique; 1922–28 prof, Chair of Mining Technique and pro-rector of studies, Moscow Mining Acad; 1929, after reorganization of this acad, dep dir, then dir, Moscow Mining Inst; instigated establishment of chairs of mining machinery at Sov mining institutes; 1937–47 head, Chair of Mining Machinery, from 1948 head, Chair of Seam Working, Moscow Mining Inst; head, Dept of Deposit Working Methods, Inst of Mining, USSR Acad of Sci; supervised drafting of gen plan for restoration of Donets Basin after WW 2; from 1937 member, Org Bureau, All-Union Mining and Sci-Tech Soc; from 1941 Bureau member, Dept of Tech Sci, USSR Acad of Sci; from 1943 chm, Tech Terminology Comt, USSR Acad of Sci; chm, Commission for Underground Gasification, USSR Acad of Sci; wrote numerous research works and textbooks on all aspects of mining; compiled first Sov textbook on mining machinery; *Publ: Razbor sistem razrabotok kamennogo uglya, primenyayemykh na rudnikakh Yuga Rossii v svyazi s bodgotovkoy mestrorozhdeniya k chistoy dobyche* (A Study of Coal-Working Systems Used in Southern Russian Mines in Connection with Preparing a Deposit for Cleared Working); *Opisaniye Donetskogo basseyna* (An Account of the Donetsk Basin); *Awards:*Stalin Prize (1943); three Orders of Lenin; two Orders of the Red Banner of Labor; medals; *Died:* 8 Nov 1959.

TERYAN (real name: TER-GRIGORYAN), Vaan (1885–1920) Arm poet and politician; CP member from 1917; *Born:* 9 Feb 1885 in vil Gandza, Geo, son of a priest; *Educ:* 1906 grad Lazarev Inst of Oriental Languages, Moscow; grad History and Philology Fac, Moscow Univ; 1913–17 studied at Oriental Fac, Petersburg Univ; *Career:* 1918–20 head, Comrt for Arm Affairs, Pop Comrt of Nationalities; member, All-Russian Centr Exec Comt; as consultant for Eastern problems, took part in Brest Peace Talks; for a considerable time influenced by Symbolism, then switched to revol optimism; his verse is imbued with a profound lyricism; *Publ:* verse "Day-Dreams of Anticipation" (1908); "Verse" (1912); "Collected Works" (4 vol, 1923); pamphlet "What Lenin Is Telling the Peasants" (1919); *Died:* 7 Jan 1920.

TERYOKHIN, Nestor Yakovlevich (1895–1966) Party and govt official; CP member from 1912; *Born:* 1895; *Career:* active in revol movement; metalworker by trade;collected subscriptions for workers' newspaper "Pravda"; 1916 drafted into Tsarist Army; worked at Ural munitions plants; after 1917 Feb Revol helped found Metalworkers and Woodworkers'Unionsin Ufa; bd member, Ufa Trad-Union Council; after 1917 Oct Revol member, Ufa Sov of Workers and Soldiers' Dep; fought in the Civil War in the Urals; 1921–25 in agric cooperative system; 1925–38 with State Bank organs in Sverdlovsk, the Crimea and Western Siberia; during WW 2 polit officer in Sov Army; 1946–50 with Alma-Ata Communal Bank; from 1950 pensioner; *Died:* 27 Apr 1966.

TERZIBASHYAN, Vagram Vaganovich (1898–1964) Theater critic and lit historian; Dr of Philological Sci from 1962; Hon Art Worker of Arm SSR from 1961; *Born:* 6 Jan 1898; *Educ:* 1916 grad Arm Seminary, Tiflis; *Career:* 1924 began lit work; 1946–49 taught history of Arm theater at Yerevan Theatrical Inst; from 1958 senior assoc, Inst of Arts, Arm Acad of Sci; *Publ: Shekspir* (Shakespeare) (1956); *Istoriya armyanskoy dramaturgy* (A History of Armenian Dramaturgy) (2 vol, 1959 and 1964);"Petros Duryan" (1959); articles on Arm theater and lit's links with Russian, Italian and French culture; *Died:* 16 May 1964.

TETEL'BAUM, Semyon Isaakovich (1910–1958) Radio eng; prof from 1940; corresp member, Ukr Acad of Sci from 1948; *Born:* 7 July 1910 in Kiev, son of a physician; *Educ:* 1932 grad Kiev Polytech Inst; 1932–40 lecturer, from 1940 prof, Kiev Polytech Inst; 1941–44 dean, Radio Eng Fac, Centr Asian Ind Instr; 1945–58 head, High-Frequency Current Laboratory, Inst of Electr Eng, Ukr Acad of Sci; also head, Chair of Radio Transmission Devices, Kiev Polytech Inst; wrote more than 120 works; specialized in wireless long-distance power transmission; devised new, efficient modulation methods; did research on television and radar; designed vhf generators, etc; *Died:* 1958.

TETYAYEV, Mikhail Mikhaylovich (1882–1956) Geologist; *Born:* 23 Sept 1882; *Educ:* 1912 grad Liege Univ, Belgium; *Career:* from 1912 worked for Geological Comt; did research in Baykal Region, Transbaykal Region, Irkutsk Basin, etc; 1920–30 also lecturer, from 1930 prof, Leningrad Univ; main works deal with geotectonics; devised theory of the forms of tectonic movements; introduced the principle of vertical movements connected with assumed compression and expansion of the Earth's matter; proved the importance of oscillatory movements in the formation of the Earth's structure; explained stratification and revised theory of geosynclines; wrote regional studies on the connection of minerals with tectonic structures; one of the first to map geotectonic zones of the USSR; *Publ: Osnovy geotektoniki* (The Principles of Geotectonics) (1941); *Geotektonika SSSR* (Geotectonics of the USSR) (1938); *Awards:* Order of Lenin; two other orders; medals; *Died:* 11 Oct 1956.

TEVOSYAN, Ivan Fyodorovich (1902–1958) Govt official; CP member from 1918; *Born:* 1902 in Shusha, Azer, son of a tailor; *Educ:* grad Moscow Mining Acad; *Career:* helped establish Sov regime in Azer; 1919 secr, underground rayon Party Comt in

Baku; after establishment of Sov regime secr, Baku City Party Comt; 1920 deleg, 10th RCP(B) Congress; helped crush Kronstadt Mutiny; after grad Mining Acad worked at "Elektrostal'" Plant, Moscow Oblast as foreman, shop mang, then chief eng; 1931–36 directed "Spetsstal'" Assoc of quality-steel and ferro-alloy plants, Pop Comrt of Heavy Ind; 1936–39 head, Main Bd, Pop Comrt of Defense Ind; then USSR First Dep Pop Comr of Defense Ind; 1939–40 USSR Pop Comr of Shipbuilding Ind; 1940–49 USSR Pop Comr of Ferrous Metallurgy; 1949–56 dep chm, USSR Council of Min; from Dec 1956 USSR amb to Japan; at 16th Party Congress elected member, Central Control Commission; at 18th–20th Party Congresses elected member, CC, CPSU; dep, USSR Supr Sov of 1st–5th convocations; *Awards:* Hero of Socialist Labor; five Orders of Lenin; three Orders of the Red Banner of Labor; medals; *Died:* 30 Mar 1958 after a long illness.

TEZAVROVSKIY, Vladimir Vasil'yevich (1880–1955) Actor and stage dir; Hon Artiste of RSFSR from 1945; *Born:* 1880; *Career:* 1905–18 actor, Moscow Arts Theater; 1918 founded Odessa Arts Studio; then stage dir, Mass Drama Theater, Odessa; 1941–46 chief stage dir, Moscow Oblast Young Playgoers' Theater; *Roles:* the Cat in Maeterlinck's "Blue Bird"; Osrick in "Hamlet"; Shaaf in Turgenev's *Mesyats v derevne* (A Month in the Country); *Productions:* Kirshon's *Rel'sy gudyat* (The Roar of the Rails); Ostrovskiy's *Ne bylo ni grosha, da vdrug altyn* (From Rags to Riches); Pogodin's *Aristokraty* (The Aristocrats); Yakovlev's *Pioner Pavel Morozov* (The Pioneer Pavel Morozov); Pavlenko and Radzinskiy's "Il'ya Muromets"; Malyarevskiy's *Mech Kitaya* (The Sword of China). etc; *Died:* 1955.

TEZYAKOV, Nikolay Ivanovich (1859–1925) Health official; *Born:* 1859; *Educ:* 1884 grad Med Fac, Kazan' Univ; *Career:* 1884–89 distr physician, Perm' Province; 1889–96 distr health officer, Kherson Province; 1893–1903 head, Health Dept, Voronezh Province Zemstvo Admin; 1903–15 head, Public Health Dept, Saratov Zemstvo Admin; organized zemstvo public health service; studied health conditions and med and health facilities for rural areas of Russia; specialist in incidence of disease, movement of population, infantile mortality, spread of epidemics, soc diseases, health conditions in schools, physical development of schoolchildren, working and living conditions of agric laborers; sponsored and organized med and health service for agric workers in Kherson Province, then in other provinces; his works on this branch of med were used by Lenin in his work *Razvitiye kapitalizma v Rossii* (The Development of Capitalism in Russia); 1918–20 worked in Saratov; then head, Sanatoria Dept, Pop Comrt of Health; wrote over 200 research works; *Publ: Sel'skokhozyaystvennyye rabochiye i organizatsii za nimi sanitarnogo nadzora v Khersonskoy gubernii* (Agricultural Workers and the Organization of Health Facilities for Them in Kherson Province) (1896); *Besedy po gigiyene v primenenii yeyo k narodnoy shkole* (Talks on Hygiene as Applied to the Public School) (1899); *O rasprostranenii difteriynykh epidemiy v Rossii za 25 let, s 1886 po 1910 g.* (The Spread of Diphteria Epidemics in Russia in the 25-Year Period from 1886 to 1910) (1914); *Sypnoy tif kak narodnoye bedstviye i bor'ba s nim* (Typhus as a Public Calamity and Means of Combatting It) (1920); *Died:* 1925 in Moscow in the course of his duties at the Pop Comrt of Health.

TIGRANYAN, Armen Tigranovich (1879–1950) Arm composer and choir conductor; Hon Art Worker of Arm SSR from 1935 and Geo SSR from 1936; *Born:* 26 Dec 1879 in Aleksandropol (now Leninakan); *Educ:* 1902 grad Tiflis musical college; studied composition theory under M. Yekmalyan; *Career:* 1902 founded choir in Aleksandropol' and toured Transcaucasia with it; recorded and arranged Arm folk songs; from 1913 lived in Tiflis and taught at musical college; *Works:* first Arm opera on everyday life "Anush", after O. Tumanyan's poem (1912); opera "David-bek" (1949); "Cantata on the 15th Anniversary of Soviet Armenia" (1936); instrumental works; a number of songs, piano pieces and music for several plays; etc; *Awards:* Order of Lenin (1939); *medals; Died:* 10 Feb 1950.

TIGRANYAN (TIGRANOV), Nikogayos (Nikolay Faddeyevich) (1856–1951) Arm musicologist and folklorist; Pop Composer of Arm SSR from 1933; Hero of Labor from 1936; *Born:* 31 Aug 1856 in Aleksandropol (now Leninakan); *Educ:* studied music in Vienna and Petersburg; *Career:* at the age of nine lost eyesight; specialized in collection and study of Arm, Azer, Geo, Iranian and Kurdish folk songs; collected and arranged "mugams" (folk classical music); wrote a number of works for piano, orchestra and string quartet based on folk song and dance melodies; one of the founders of Arm piano music; *Awards:* Order of the Red Banner of Labor (1939); medals; *Died:* 17 Feb 1951 in Yerevan.

TIKHANE, Anatoliy Georgiyevich (1900–1967) Est Min of Finance from 1955; member, CC, CP Est from 1961; *Born:* 1900; *Career:* 1954–61 cand member, CC, CP Est; dep, Est Supr Sov of 1955 and 1963 convocations; *Awards:* Order of Lenin (1959); Est Supr Sov Hon Scroll (1960); *Died:* 26 Jan 1967.

TIKHOMIRNOV, German Aleksandrovich (1899–1955) Govt official; CP member from 1917; *Born:* 1899 in Kazan'; *Career:* from 1916 active in revol movement; organized Bolshevik student groups; during 1917 Oct Revol staff member, Red Guard squad in Kazan; 1918–21 in Red Army; 1921–25 exec work for Party CC; 1925–37 head, Centr Party Archives, Marx-Engels-Lenin Inst, CC, CPSU(B); 1937–38 worked for Secretariat of chm, USSR Council of Pop Comr; 1938–40 comr of Sov section, New York Int Exhibition; from 1947 research and teaching work, Inst of Marxism-Leninism, CC, CPSU(B); *Awards:* Badge of Hon; *Died:* 1955.

TIKHOMIRNOV, Viktor Aleksandrovich (pseudonym: VIKTOR) (1889–1919) Govt official; CP member from 1905; *Born:* 1889 in Kazan'; *Educ:* studied at Kazan' non-classical high-school; from 1911 studied at Moscow Business College; *Career:* while still at school joined revol movement in Kazan'"; 1909 arrested and exiled to Arkhangel'sk Province, then went abroad; returned to Russia and 1912 exiled to Olonets Province; 1914 again emigrated; contributed to and helped publish newspaper "Pravda" during WW 1 Party work in Petrograd and abroad; smuggled in Bolshevik lit, etc; active in 1917 Feb Revol; deleg at 6th RSDRP(B) Congress; then sent to Moscow, where he played an active part in 1917 Oct Revol; subsequently Collegium member, NKVD; *Died:* 1919 in Kazan.

TIKHOMIROV, Aleksandr Andreyevich (1850–1931) Zoologist; *Born:* 1 Oct 1850; *Educ:* 1872 grad Petersburg Univ; 1876 grad Moscow Univ; *Career:* from 1888 prof, 1896–1904 dir, Zoological Museum, Moscow Univ; 1911–17 trustee, Moscow Educ Distr; studied anatomy, embryology and physiology of silkworm; 1886 discovered artficial parthenogenesis in silkworm eggs; also did research on zoology, anthropology and gen biology, in which he took an anti-Darwinist stand; *Publ: Istoriya razvitiya tutovogo shelkopryada (Bombyx mori L.) v yaytse* (The History of the Development of the Silkworm (Bombyx mori L.) in the Egg) (1882); "Die künstliche Parthenogenes bei Insekten" (1886); *Osnovy prakticheskogo shelkovodstva* (The Principles of Practical Silk Production) (1914); *Atlas po shelkovodstvu* (An Atlas of Silk Production) (1896); *Died:* 23 Oct 1931.

TIKHOMIROV, Lev Aleksandrovich (1852–1923) Politician; leading member, "People's Will" Party; *Born:* 1852; *Educ:* grad Kerch High-School; from 1870 studied at Med Fac, Moscow Univ; *Career:* did revol propaganda among Moscow workers; 1873 arrested and interned for four years in Peter and Paul Fortress; late 1878 joined "Land and Liberty" Party and helped edit its organ; from 1879 member, Exec Comt, "People's Will" Party; 1883, after suppression of "People's Will" Party, emigrated; ed, periodical "Vestnik Narodnoy voli"; 1888 renounced his former convictions and printed in Paris a pamphlet entitled *Pochemu ya perestal byt' revolyutsionerom* (Why I Have Ceasend to Be a Revolutionary); 1889, after writing a letter to the tsar, granted permission to return to Russia; became leading monarchist; contributed to periodicals "Moskovskiye vedomosti", "Novoye vremya" and "Russkoye obozreniye"; 1917 settled in Zagorsk and abandoned politics; *Publ:* pamphlet *Gde luchshe? Skazka o chetyryokh brat'yakh i ob ikh priklyucheniyakh* (Where Is Best? A Tale of Four Brothers and Their Adventures) (1868); *Yemel'yan Ivanovich Pugachyov, ili bunt 1773 goda* (Yemel'yan Ivanovich Pugachyov, or the 1773 Revolt) (1869); *Died:* 1923.

TIKHOMIROV, Mikhail Nikolayevich (1893–1965) Historian; Dr of History; prof from 1934; member, USSR Acad of Sci from 1953; member, Polish Acad of Sci from 1959; *Born:* 1 June 1893; *Educ:* 1917 grad Fac of History and Philology, Moscow Univ; *Career:* specialized in history of Russia and Slavic countries, source study, historiography, archeography, historical geography and history of civilization; 1919–23 asst prof, Samarkand Univ; 1923–34 taught at a secondary school, then worked for Soc for the Study of Moscow Oblast and for State Historical Museum; from 1934 prof, 1945–47 dean, History Fac, from 1952 head, Chair for the Study of Soviet Historical Sources, Moscow Univ; from 1935 also senior assoc, Inst of History, USSR Acad of Sci; 1946–53 corresp member, USSR Acad of Sci; 1953–57 acad secr, Dept of History, USSR Acad of Sci; from

1955 member, Main Ed Bd, "Vsemirnaya istoriya"; from 1957 Bureau member, Dept of History, USSR Acad of Sci; from 1959 in charge of group of historians at Inst of History, USSR Acad of Sci for publ of complete ed of Russian chronicles; from 1960 member, Main Ed Bd, "Sovetskaya istoricheskaya entsiklopedia"; 1960 attended 11th Int History Congress, Stockholm; *Publ: Pskovskoye vosstaniye 1650–ogo goda* (The Pskov Uprising of 1650) (1935); *Istochnikovedeniye istorii SSSR. S Drevneyshikh vremyon do kontsa 18–ogo veka* (Source Research on the History of the USSR. From Earliest Times to the End of the 18th Century) (vol 1, 1940; enlarged ed, 1962); *Issledovaniye o "Russkoy Pravde"* (A Study of "Russian Truth") (1941); *Drevnerusskiye goroda* (Ancient Russian Towns) (1946); *Istoricheskiye svyazi russkogo naroda s yuzhnymi slavyanami s drevneyshikh vremyon do poloviny 17–ogo veka* (The Russian People's Historical Links with the Southern Slavs from Earliest Times to the Mid-17th Century) (1947); *Posobiye dlya izucheniya "Russkoy Pravdy"* (An Aid to the Study of "Russian Truth") (1953); *Krest'yanskiye i gorodskiye vosstaniya na Rusi c 11–13 vekakh* (Peasant and Urban Uprisings in Rus in the 11th–13th Centuries) (1955); Chief ed, *Istoriya istoricheskoy nauki v SSSR* (The History of Historical Science in the USSR) (vol 1, 1955); *Srednevekovaya Moskva v 14–15 vekakh* (Medieval Moscow in the 14th–15th Centuries) (1957); *Prisoyedineniye Merva k Rossii* (The Annexation of Merv by Russia) (1960); coauthor, *Sobornoye ulozheniye 1649–ogo goda* (The Synodal Code of 1649) (1961); *Merilo Pravednoye po rukopisi 14–ogo veka* ("The Just Measure" According to a 14th–Century Manuscript) (1961); *Zakon sudnyy lyudem prostrannoy i svodnoy redaktsii* (The Law of Civil Jurisdiction, Complete and Abridged Texts) (1961); *Zakon sudnyy lyudem. Spisok kratkoy redaktsii i vosproizvedeniye spiskov* (The Law of Civil Jurisdiction. Abridged and Reproduced Rolls) (1961); *Kratkiye zametki o letopisnykh proizvedeniyakh v rukopisnykh sobraniyakh Moskvy* (Short Notes on the Chronicles in the Moscow Manuscript Collections) (1962); *Rossiya v 16–om veke* (Russia in the 16th Century) (1962), etc; *Awards:* Order of Lenin; two Orders of the Red Banner of Labor; medals; *Died:* 2 Sept 1965.

TIKHOMIROV, Pavel Yefremovich (1895–1964) Ophthalmologist; Hon Sci Worker of RSFSR from 1962; *Born:* 1895; *Educ:* 1919 grad Med Fac, 1st Moscow Univ; *Career:* from 1919 worked at Helmholz Eye Diseases Research Inst, Moscow; 1945–64 head, Chair of Eye Diseases, 2nd Leningrad Med Inst (now Health and Hygiene Med Inst); also chm, Leningrad, and bd member, All-Union Sci Soc of Ophthalmologists; co-ed, "Ophthalmology" section, 2nd ed of "Bol'shaya meditsinskaya entsiklopediya" (Large Medical Encyclopedia); member, ed council, journal "Vestnik oftal'mologii"; devised methods for early diagnosis of glaucoma, so-called campimetric drinking-water test; specialized in injuries, especially war injuries of eye; wrote over 90 sci works; *Publ:* Vliyaniye nagruzki vodoy na razmery slepogo pyatna v glaukomatoznykh i zdorovykh glazakh (The Effects of Water Loading in the Size of the Blind Spot in Glaucomatous and Healthy Eyes) (1941); *Klinika i terapiya boyevykh travm glaza* (The Clinical Aspects and Therapy of Eye War Injuries) (1943); *Raneniya i bolezni glaz v Velikuyu Otechestvennuyu voynu i lecheniye ikh t tylovykh evakogospitalyakh* (Injuries and Diseases of the Eye in the Great Fatherland War and Their Treatment in Rear Evacuation Hospitals) (1947); *Patologiya i terapiya slezootvodyashchikh putey* (The Pathology and Therapy of the Tear Ducts) (1949); *Nashi nablyudeniya nad operatsiyey iridenkleyza* (Our Observations on the Operation for Iridenclasis) (1960); *Novoye v lechenii i profilaktike glaukomy* (New Developments in the Treatment and Prevention of Glaucoma) (1960), etc; *Awards:* Averbakh Prize (1950); USSR Acad of Med Sci Presidium Prize, etc; *Died:* 1964 in Leningrad.

TIKHOMIROV, Vasiliy Dmitriyevich (1876–1956) Ballet dancer, ballet-master and ballet teacher; Pop Artiste of RSFSR from 1934; *Born:* 17 Mar 1876 in Moscow; *Educ:* 1894 grad I.A. Yermolov's class, Moscow Theatrical College; *Career:* 1893 debut at Mariinskiy Theater; 1893–1935 ballet-dancer, 1900–35 ballet-master, 1924–30 ballet dir, Bolshoy Theater, Moscow; 1920–31 taught at Moscow Theatrical College; *Roles:* Conrad in Adam's "The Corsair"; Jan de Brien in "Raimonda"; Basil in "Don Quixote"; Solor in Minkus' "Bayadyorka"; *Productions:* ballets: "Les Sylphides" (1925); "Esmeralda" (1926); *Krasnyy mak* (Red Poppy) (1927); *Died:* 20 June 1956.

TIKHON (secular name: BELLAVIN, Vasily Ivanovich) (1865–1925) Patriarch of Moscow and All Russia from 1917; *Born:* 19 Jan 1865 in Toropets, Pskov Province; *Educ:* 1888 grad Petersburg Theological Acad; *Career:* after grad taught at Pskov Theological Seminary; 1891 took monastic vows name Tikhon and was appointed arch-monk and inspector of Kholm Theological Seminary; soon elevated to archimandrite and appointed rector, above seminary; 1898 consecrated Bishop of Lyublin; and vicar of Kholm Eparchy; 1899 appointed Bishop of Aleutia and Alaska; 1905 elevated to archbishop; 1907 appointed Archbishop of Yaroslavl', but shortly transferred to Vilnius Eparchy; his simplicity and sociability soon made him very popular, and upon his transfer he was made an hon citizen of Yaroslavl'; 1914, with the start of WW 1, he was evacuated with the relics of the Vilnius martyrs to Moscow, then settled in Disna, on the periphery of his eparchy, whence he ministered to the troops, visited the front and attended meetings of the Synod; after 1917 Feb Revol removed from Synod; 1917 appointed Archbishop of Moscow; 15 Aug 1917 All-Russian Orthodox Assembly met in Moscow, elevated him to metropolitan and elected him chm of Assembly; 5 Feb 1917 elected by the Assembly Patriarch of Moscow and All Russia; despite Communist terror following Oct Revol, he preached in defense of the faith and denounced Communist atrocities; 19 Jan 1918, in address to ministers of the church and the laity, termed the Bolsheviks' bloody reprisals the work of Satan and excommunicated them from the Church; 26 Oct 1918, in address to Council of Pop Comr, accused Sov regime of deceiving the public, of unprecedented terrorism and of meddling in the Church's internal affairs; when the wholesale arrest of members of the Assembly began, he rejected the idea of of emigrating, thereby dooming himself to martyrdom; 1919, after the Bolshevik regime began to persecute the Church in earnest, he forbade the clergy and laity to make any public attacks on the regime; 1921, during the Volga famine, appealed to the laity to organize famine relief and authorized for this purpose the donation of Church valuables not needed for divine service; Sov autorities rejected this offer, coupled as it was the demand that the Church supervise the destination of the funds, and the Patriarch was accused of trying to incite public resistance to the regime; he was proclaimed an enemy of the people and placed under house arrest; the forcible expropriation of Church valuables and various acts of blashphemy provoked widescale protests and resistance on the part of religious believers, leading to some 2,000 trials and executions and the summary liquidation of some 10,000 clergy and believers; Apr 1922 the Patriarch appeared as a witness in the trial of a group of clergy charged with resisting the expropriation of Church valuables and testified that he alone was to blame, since the defendants were merely fulfilling the will of their superior, sent by God; in an effort to save the Church from the "renovationist" schism and spare arrested clergy from execution, the Patriarch made some compromises with the Sov regime; however, this did not satisfy the Bolsheviks, who wanted a person more subservient to their orders on the Patriarchal Throne; fall 1922 the Patriarch was arrested and incarcerated, at first in a monastery and then at Moscow Main Polit Bd (OGPU) headquarters; prior to his arrest the Patriarch had appointed Metropolitan Agafangel his provisional deputy; the arrest of the head of the Russian Orthodox Church triggered int protests: an appeal by Pope Pius XI to the Genoa Conference, a speech by the Archbishop of Canterbury, a protest by the French clergy and appeals by various govts; all this induced the Bolsheviks to free the Patriarch on 26 June 1923; upon his release the Patriarch was in a deplorable physical and spiritual state, none of his concessions had satisfied the Communist govt, since he had steadfastly refused to sacrifice the Church's spiritual freedom or serve the interests of the regime, as his successors were shortly to do; 9 Dec 1923 his private secr was murdered in the Patriarch's presence; Jan 1925 the Patriarch's health was so undermined by his imprisonment, constant interrogation and spiritual distress that he had to be hospitalized; *Died:* 25 Mar 1925 at the age of 60; in the opinion of Prof Zhizhilenko, Bishop Maksim of the Catacomb Church, the Patriarch was in fact poisoned.

TIKHONOV, Pavel Il'ich (1877–1944) Opera singer (bass); singing teacher; Hon Art Worker of Bel SSR from 1940; *Born:* 15 Feb 1877; *Educ:* 1900 grad Law Fac, Petersburg Univ; 1918 grad Odessa Conservatory; *Career:* from 1905 soloist, Opera Company of Pop Center, Petersburg; 1907–11 at opera theaters in Kiev and Odessa; 1911–17 soloist, Bolshoy Theater, Moscow; 1917–19 opera singer in Odessa; 1920–28 soloist, Bolshoy Theater;

1923–24 at Stanislavskiy's Opera Studio; 1928–33 assoc prof, Vocal Fac, Moscow Conservatory; from 1933 prof, Bel Conservatory, Minsk; during WW 2 in Saratov directing Vocal Fac, joint Saratov and Moscow Conservatories; chm, first corporation of soloist artists; co-founder, Vocal Music Studio, Bolshoy Theater; *Roles:* Lothario in "Mignon"; Susanin in *Zhizn' za tsarya* (A Life for the Tsar); Mephistopheles in "Faust"; Dodon in *Zolotoy petushok* (The Golden Cockerel); Bartholo in "The Barber of Seville"; Wotan in Wagner's "Walküre", etc; *Died:* 23 Mar 1944.

TIKHONOVICH, Nikolay Nikolayevich (1872–1952) Geologist; Hon Sci Worker of RSFSR from 1947; *Born:* 1872; *Educ:* 1897 grad Khar'kov Univ; *Career:* from 1904 worked for Geological Comt (later All-Union Geological Survey Inst); 1943–52 prof, Moscow Oil Inst; specialized in geology of oil; studioed geomorphology and geological structure of Sakhalin, stratigraphy, tectonics and oil-bearing qualities of Emba region; mapped Groznyy oil-bearing region; did geotectonic and paleographic studies of Timan-Pechora oil-bearing province; studied abyssal tectonics and oil-bearing properties of Devonian rocks of Russian Plateau; made hydrogeological study of southern Cis-Ural region and studied phosphorites of eastern Russian Plateau and coal-bearing properties of eastern slope of Urals; *Publ: Devonskiye otlozheniya Russkoy platformy i Priural'ya* (The Devonian Deposits of the Russian Plateau and the Cis-Ural Region) (1951); *Awards:* Order of theRed Banner of Labor; *Died:* 1952.

TIKHOV, Gavriil Adrianovich (1875–1960) Astronomer; corresp member, USSR Acad of Sci from 1927; member, Kaz Acad of Sci from 1946; *Born:* 1 May 1875 in vil Smolevichi, now Minsk Oblast; *Educ:* 1897 grad Moscow Univ; 1906–41 worked at Pulkovo Observatory; from 1947 head, Astrobotanics Section, Kaz Acad of Sci; spezialized in astrometry and spectrophotometry; developed photometric observation methods, particularly filter colorimetry method, longitudinalspectrography method for determining the color of stars, etc; his parallel study of the spectrophotometric properties of the Martian surface and terrestrial flora laid the basis for a new branch of astrophysics – astrobotanics; did research on atmospheric optics and aerial photo-survey; designed serveral astronomical instruments; *Publ: Astrobotanica* (Astrobotanics) (1949); *Osnovy vizual'noy i fotograficheskoy fotometrii* (The Principles of Visual and Photographic Photometry) (1950); *Gipoteza o paleobotanike Marsa i Venery* (A Hypothesis on the Paleobotanics of Mars and Venus) (1953); *Osnovnyye trudy. Tom. 1. Astrofizika (1897–1919)* (Basic Works. Volume 1. Astrophysics /1897–1919/) (1954); *Awards:* Order of Lenin; Order of the Red Banner of Labor; medal; *Died:* 25 Jan 1960.

TIKHVINSKIY, M. M. (1868–1921) Chemical eng; prof; *Born:* 1868; *Career:* 1899–1911 worked at Kiev Polytech Inst; sympathized with Bolsheviks; from 1912 chief chemist, Nobel Brothers' Soc; after 1917 Oct Revol prof, Petrograd Technol Inst and Mining Inst; laboratory head, Main Oil Comt, Supr Sovnarkhoz; 1921 sentenced to death by Petrograd Cheka for alleged complicity in plot against State; *Died:* 24 Aug 1921 executed by firing squad.

TIMANOVA, Vera Viktorovna (1855–1942) Pianist; *Born:* 6 Feb 1855 in Ufa; *Educ:* studied under K. Tauzig and F. Liszt; *Career:* 1865 first public performance; 1870's–1880's concert tours in Russia and abroad; from late 1880's teacher, Ye. Rapgof's Music Courses and concertmaster in Petersburg; her playing was highly rated by Liszt and by Tchaikovsky, who dedicated his "Humorous Scherzo" to her; *Died:* 1942 in Leningrad.

TIMCHENKO, Iosif Andreyevich (1852–1924) Inventor; *Born:* 15 Apr 1852 in Khar'kov Province, son of a serf; *Career:* 1873 moved to Odessa; from 1880 mech, Novorossiysk Univ, in Odessa, where he established a firstclass precision instruments workshop; designed various automatic meteorological instruments, including an anemorhumbograph, a pluviograph and a recording mercury barometer; 1893, together with the Russian physicist N. A. Lyubimov, invented a constant frame-shift gate mechanism; using this, together with the Russian inventor M. F. Freydenberg, he designed the first Russian film camera, termed a "kinetoskop"; 1894 publicly demonstrated this device; helped Freydenberg build the first modeal automatic telephone exchange; also designed a number of astronomical and physical instruments; *Died:* 20 May 1924.

TIMIRYAZEV, Arkadiy Klement'yevich (1880–1955) Prof; Dr of Physics and Mathematics; CP member from 1921; *Born:* 1880, son of K. A. Timiryazev; *Career:* until 1917 Oct Revol asst prof, assoc prof, then prof, Chair of Physics, Moscow Univ and other higher educ establishments; after 1917 Oct Revol prof of physics, Moscow Univ and Sverdlov Communist Univ; member, then Presidium member, Communist Acad; wrote over 100 works on theoretical physics, history and methodology of physics; until Jan 1955 headed Chair of History of Physics, Moscow Univ; *Publ: Kineticheskaya teoriya materii* (The Kinetic Theory of Matter); *Fizika* (Physics); collected articles *Yestestvoznaniye i dialekticheskiy materializm* (Natural Science and Dialectical Materialism); *Died:* 1955.

TIMIRYAZEV, Kliment Arkad'yevich (1843–1920) Naturalist, botanist and physiologist; Dr of Botany from 1875; prof from 1871; corresp member, Russian Acad of Sci from 1890; *Born:* 3 June 1843 in Petersburg, son of a nobleman; *Educ:* 1861 began studying at Fac of Law, 1866 grad Natural Sci Dept, Petersburg Univ; *Career:* 1868–70 worked and studied at laboratories in France and Germany; from 1869 lecturer in botany, Petrine Acad of Arable Farming and Forestry (now Moscow Agric Acad), 1871 defended master's thesis on spectral analysis of chlorophyll; from 1871 extraordinary prof, Petrine Acad; 1875 defended doctor's thesis on light absorption in plants; from 1877 prof, Chair of Plant Anatomy and Physiology, Moscow Univ; 1892 dismissed from Petrine Acad for polit activities; 1898 lost professorship at Moscow Univ "on expiration of contract"; 1902 banned from lecturing but continued work in Botanical Section; 1911 resigned from Moscow Univ with other fac members in protest against policies of Educ Minister Kasso; 1917 reinstated as prof, Moscow Univ but was unable to resume work immediately for health reasons; 1920 dep, Moscow City Sov; hon dr, Cambridge, Glasgow and Geneva Univ; member, British Royal Soc and Edinburgh and Manchester Botanical Soc; considered by Sov sci to be one of foremost Darwinists; after his death a memorial and museum to him were opened in Moscow; a distr in Moscow, the Moscow Agric Acad and the Inst of Plant Physiology, USSR Acad of Sci now bear his name; a Timiryazev Prize for the best works on plant physiology is awarded annually; *Publ: Garibaldi na Kaprere* (Garibaldi on Caprera) (1862); *Golod v Lankashire* (The Lancashire Famine) (1863); *Kniga Darvina, yeyo kritiki i kommentatory* (Darwin's Book, Its Critics and Commentators) (1864); *Stoletniye itogi fiziologii rasteniy* (A Hundred Years of Plant Physiology) (1901); *Osnovnyye cherty istorii razvitiya biologii v XIX stoletii* (The Basic Aspects of the Development of Biology in the 19th Century) (1907); *Probuzhdeniye yestestvoznaniya v tret'yey chetverti veka* (The Awakening of Natural Science in the Third Quarter of the Century) (1907); *Uspekhi botaniki v XX veke* (The Progress of Botany in the 20th Century) (1917); *Nauka i demokratiya* (Science and Democracy) (1920); *Istoricheskiy metod v biologii* (The Historical Method in Biology) (1922); *Solntse, zhizn' i khlorofill* (Sun, Life and Chlorophyll) (1923); *Sochineniya* (Works) (10 vol, 1937–40); *Died:* 28 Apr 1920.

TIMOFEYEV, Vladimir Maksimilianovich (1884–1935) Geologist and Petrographer; *Born:* 20 July 1884; *Educ:* 1909 grad Petersburg Univ; *Career:* Prof at various higher educ institutions in Leningrad; from 1918 taught at Petrograd Univ; from 1917 with Geological Comt; 1917–29 did geological survey of Karelia; did research on diabasic rock, Karelian marble, quartzite and shungite; discovered lava streams on Suisari Island; studied globular lava; 1930–35 directed compilation of geological map of the Karelian ASSR; *Publ: Petrografiya Karelii* (The Petrography of Karelia) (1935); *Died:* 3 Aug 1935.

TIMOFEYEV, Ye. M. (1885–1941) Politician; *Born:* 1885; *Career:* member, CC, Socialist-Revol Party; organized battle groups and revolts against Sov rule; 1922 sentenced to death in trial of Rightist Socialist-Revolutionaries; by order of All-Russian Centr Exec Comt the execution was postponed; *Died:* 1941 executed.

TIMOFEYEVSKIY, Pavel Il'ich (1878–1943) Mil med officer; brigade surgeon; Dr of Med; *Born:* 1878; *Educ:* 1903 grad Mil Med Acad; *Career:* mil surgeon in 1904–05 Russo-Japanese War; 1914–18 served with disinfection squad; then head, casualty clearing station; head, Petrograd Mil Health Bd; dep head, Red Army Main Mil Health Bd; 1923 began teaching; organized course on mil med admin and mil health tactics; ran a study circle on health tactics for Mil Med Acad students; thus initiating the teaching of these disciplines at the Mil Med Acad; 1914 did research on establishment and equipment of hospitals and casualty transports in war time; studied med service for troops during operations, in overcoming enemy defenses and during joint operations with naval and river fleet units; also studied med services for mechanized troops and med service in the anti-aircraft system; this research work laid the foundation for further development of the mil med service and established his own school in this field; his handbook *Sanitarnaya taktika* (Sanitary Tactics) ran through four ed (1925–31) and was the first to cover med aid to gas casualties; published over 30 research works; *Publ: Sanitarnaya taktika peredovykh perevyazochnykh punktov: dnevnoy, oboronitel'nyy boy* (Sanitary Tactics of Frontline Aid Stations: Defensive Daylight Action) (1908); *Skhema sanitarnoy sluzhby v period operativnykh deystviy* (System of Medical Aid During Military Operations) (1909); *Ustroystvo i oborudovaniye lechebnykh zavedeniy i sanitarnykh transportov v voyennoye vremya* (Organizing and Equipping Hospitals and Casualty Transports in War Time) (1914); *Sanitarnoye obespecheniye voysk pri preodolenii polosy zagrazhdeniy i razrusheniy* (Medical Aid for Troops Overcoming Obstacle and Demolition Zones) (1932); coauthor, *Sanitarno-evakuatsionnoye obespecheniye boyevykh deystviy rechnykh flotiliy* (Medical Aid and Casualty Clearing Service in Military Operations of River Fleet Units) (1936); *Lechebno-evakuatsionnoye obespecheniye polka pri forsirovanii rechnoy pregrady* (Medical Aid and Casualty Clearing Service for a Regiment Forcing a River Obstacle) (1937); *Died:* 1943.

TINCHURIN, Karim (1887–1947) Tatar playwright, actor and stage dir; Hon Artiste of Tatar ASSR from 1926; *Born:* 15 Sept 1887 in vil Tarakanovka, now Penza Oblast; *Career:* 1900–05 studied at medressah; expelled for particiapating in student polit movement; 1906 wrote first comedy; from 1910 actor, then stage dir, Sayyar Company, Kazan'; from 1918 dir, Sayyar Company; 1922 co-founded State Theater, Kazan'; 1922–37 artistic dir, actor and stage dir, Tatar State Acad Theater; 1937 arrested by State Security organs; *Works:* plays "The Discussion" (1906); plays: "First Flowers" (1913); "A Dangerous Step" (1914); "The Capricious Bridegroom" (1915); "The Hungry Lover" (1915); "The Last Greeting" (1916); " A Flighty Creature" (1916); comedies: "Yusuf and Zuleykha" (1918); "The Parrot" (1919); "The American" (1924); musical plays: "The Blue Shawl" (1926); "The Swarm" (1929); plays: "On the River Kandra" (1930); "The Lark" (1932); "Grandad Bulat's Family" (1932); "They Were Three" (1935), etc; *Roles:* Tagir in Burnash's "Tagir and Zyugra"; Gali in Kulakhmetov's "Young Life"; Khestakov in Gogol's *Revizor* (The Government Inspector); Maguzm in "Extinct Stars"; Batyrkhan in "Without Sails"; Zhantimir in "The Swarm"; Iskander in "The American"; Bulat in "The Blue Shawl", etc; *Productions:* "The Blue Shawl" (1926); Gorky's *Na dne* (The Lower Depths) (1932); "On the River Kandra" (1933); "The Government Inspector" (1932); G. Kamal's "Bankrupt" (1932); Sayfi;Kazanla's "Foes" (1934), etc; *Died:* 7 May 1947 in imprisonment; posthumously rehabilitated.

TIPOT, Viktor Yakovlevich (1893–1960) Russian playwright and stage dir; *Born:* 16 Mar 1893; *Career:* member, "Blue Blouse" group; co-founder, Moscow Satire Theater; wrote in collaboration with A. M. Argo, V. Ye. Ardov, D. G. Gutman, etc; produced shows at Review Theater of Moscow Press Center and at Centr Theater of Red Army; *Works:* reviews: *Moskva s tochki zreniya* (Moscow from One Point of View) (1924); *Spokoyno, snimayu* (Watch the Birdie) (1925); *Naschyot lyubvi* (As for Love); *Mishka, verti* (Spin, Mishka) and *Lyubov' i vsyo ostal'noye* (Love and All That) (1926); *Vecherniy vypusk* (Evering Edition) and *Igra* (The Game) (1927); *Univermag i volshebnik* (The Department Store and the Magician) (1928); helped write libretto for musical comedies and operettas: *Svad'ba v Malinovke* (Wedding at Malinovka) (1937); *Na beregu Amura* (On the Banks of the Amur) (1939); *Bespokoynoye schast'ye* (Troubled Fortune) (1947); *Vol'nyy veter* (Free Wind) (1947); *Devichiy perepolokh* (Girlish Confusion) (1950); *Syn klouna* (The Clown's Son) (1950), etc; also produced: *Prigotov'te bilety* (Have Your Tickets Ready) (1929); *Ya vas lyublyu* (I Love You) (1935); *God 1919* (The Year 1919) (1963), etc; *Died:* 12 Oct 1960.

TIRASPOL'SKAYA, Nadezhda L'vovna (1867–1962) Actress; Hon Art Worker of RSFSR from 1931; *Born:* 9 May 1867; *Educ:* 1892 grad Musical Drama College, Moscow Philharmonic Soc; *Career:* 1892 began acting in provicial theaters; 1895–1902 actress, Maly Theater; 1903–56 at Aleksandrinskiy Theater (now Leningrad's Pushkin Theater); *Roles:* Juliet in "Romeo and Juliet"; Yudif in Gutskov's "Uriel' Akosta"; Margarite Gauthier in Dumas fils' "Le Dame aux Camélias"; Yelana Karmina in *Zhenit'ba Belugina* (Belugin's Marriage); Varvara in *Groza* (The Storm); Ranevskaya in Chekhov's *Vishnyovyy sad* (The Cherry Orchard); Murzavetskaya in *Volki i ovtsy* (The Wolves and the Sheep); Mrs Higgins in Shaw's "Pygmalion"; *Publ:* memoirs *Iz proshlogo Russkoy stseny* (From the Past of the Russian Stage) (1950); *Zhizn' aktrisy* (An Actress' Life) (1962); *Died:* 30 May 1962.

TISHCHENKO, Sergey Illarionovich (1903–1967) Govt official; dep chm, Ukr Gosplan from 1960; *Born:* 1903 in Donetsk; *Educ:* 1930 grad Khar'kov Technol Inst; *Career:* from 1920 apprentice fitter; from 1930 shift foreman, chief eng of a plant, then dir of various metallurgical plants; until 1954 dir, metallurgical plant in Ukr; 1954–57 Ukr Min of Ferrous Metallurgy; 1957–60 Ukr Min of Metallurgical Ind and head, Dept of Metallurgical Ind, Ukr Gosplan; 1954–60 member, 1960–61 cand member, CC, CP Ukr; dep, USSR Supr Sov of 1954 convocation; *Awards:* three Orders of Lenin; three Orders of the Red Banner of Labor; Badge of Hon; medals; *Died:* 20 Nov 1967.

TISHCHENKO, Vyacheslav Yevgen'yevich (1861–1941) Chemist; member, USSR Acad of Sci from 1935; prof; *Born:* 19 Aug 1861 in Petersburg; *Educ:* 1884 grad Petersburg Univ; *Career:* asst to D. I. Mendeleyev; 1900–15 prof, Women's Med Inst; 1907–41 prof, Leningrad Univ; 1928–35 corresp member, USSR Acad of Sci; demonstrated that fatty aldehydes may take part in the Cannizzaro reaction (Tishchenko-Cannizzaro reaction); specialized in wood chemistry; composition of terpentine, soft resin and other wood products; devised a new ind method of synthesizing camphor from terpentine; developed a presciption for a new kind of chemical laboratory glassware; invented a new type of flask for washing and drying gases (Tishchenko flask); during WW 1 directed research on technol of synthesizing iodine from seaweed and techniques for producing chemically pure reagents; *Publ: Sbornik izbrannykh trudov* (A Collection of Selected Works) (1934); *Awards:* Stalin Prize (1941); *Died:* 25 Feb 1941.

TISSE, Eduard Kazimirovich (1897–1961) Cameraman and teacher; Hon Art Worker of RSFSR from 1935; CP member from 1940; *Born:* 13 Apr 1897; *Educ:* 1914 grad Studio of Painting and Photography; *Career:* from 1914 worked in Russian film ind, starting as a newsreel cameraman in WW 1, then turning to feature films; worked for Eisenstein and Aleksandrov; *Films: Serp i molot* (Hammer and Sickle) (1921); *Stachka* (Strike); *Bronenosets Potyomkin* (The Battleship "Potemkin") (1925); *Oktyabr* (October) (1927); *Aleksandr Nevskiy* (1938); *Ivan Grozny* (Ivan the Terrible) (part 1, 1945); *Vstrecha na El'be* (The Meeting on the Elbe) (1949); *Kompozitor Glinka* (The Composer Glinka) (1952), etc; *Awards:* two Orders of the Red Banner of Labor; three Stalin Prizes (1946, 1949 and 1950); *Died:* 18 Nov 1961.

TITOV, (real name: STEPANOV), Ivan Ivanovich (1876–1941) Stage manager; *Born:* 1876; *Career:* from age 16 stage-hand at Hermitage Theater, Private Russian Opera Theater and other Moscow theaters; worked under Bolshoy Theater set-designer K. V. Wal'ts; implemented ideas and designs of such set designers as K. A. Korovin, V. D. Polyonov, A. Ya. Golovin, M. A. Vrublyov, V. V. Dmitriyev, P. V. Vil'yams and V. F. Ryndin; from 1897 worked under Stanislavsky and set designer V. A. Simov at Lit and Art Soc; from 1898 stage-hand, Moscow Arts Theater; 1906–41 stage technician and stage manager at this theater; directed assembly of almost all sets for Moscow Arts Theater productions in this period; improved set assembly and change equipment and methods; *Awards:* Hero of Labor (1938); Order of the Red Banner of Labor; *Died:* 1941.

TKACHENKO, Mikhail Yelevfer'yevich (1878–1950) Forestry expert; *Born:* 14 Nov 1878; *Educ:* 1904 grad Forestry Inst, Petersburg; *Career:* 1919–50 prof, Petrograd Forestry Inst (later Forestry Tech Acad); 1944–46 also worked at Forestry Inst, USSR Acad of Sci; headed various forestry research expeditions; traced connection between forests and local environment; studied taxation, econ and org of forestry, soil sci, etc; helped map forests of USSR; specialized in forests of the North; *Publ: Lesa Severa* (The Forests of the North) (vol 1, 1911); *Kontsentrirovannyye rubki, ekspluatatsiya i vozobnovleniye lesa* (The Concentrated Felling, Exploitation and Renewal of Forests) (1931); *Obshcheye lesovodstvo* (General Forestry) (1939); *Awards:* Order of the Red Banner of Labor; medals; *Died:* 1950.

TOBILEVICH, Sofiya Vital'yevna (1860–1953) Ukr writer and actress; *Born:* 15 Oct 1860 in vil Novoselitsy, now Vinnitsa Oblast; niece of the Polish revolutionary Z. Serakowski; wife of playwright and impressario I. K. Karpenko-Karyy; *Career:* 1880 appeared with Lysenko and Staritskiy's amateur choirs in Kiev; professional stage debut with Sadovskiy Theater, Kiev; after 1917 Oct Revol acted at Franko Theater, Kiev; collected and wrote folk songs, tales and proverbs; wrote memoirs of pre-revol Ukr theater and a biography of Karpenko-Karyy; translated Polish and French plays into Ukr; together with Karpenko–Karyy, wrote drama *Chertova skala* (Devil's Rock); *Roles:* Terpilikha in Lysenko's "Natalka Poltavka"; Old Bushlya and Tat'yana in Karpenko–Karyy's "Chumaki" and *Suyeta* (Fuss); Limerikha in Mirnyy's "Limarivna"; *Died:* 7 Oct 1953.

TOCHISSKIY, Pavel Varfolomeyevich (1864–1918) Politican; *Born:* 16 Apr 1864 in Yekaterinburg, son of an officer; *Educ:* studied at high school, grad trade school; *Career:* 1884 came to Petersburg; 1885 founded Assoc of St Petersburg Artisans; early 1888 arrested and exiled; revol work in Moscow, Yekaterinoslav and other cities; 1894 emigrated to Bulgaria; involved Bulgarian revol movement; 1898 member, Moscow Intellectual Propagandists Circle; arrested and exiled; participated in 1905–07 Revol, particularly in Dec 1905 armed revolt in Moscow; during 1917 Oct Revol member, Beloretsk RSDRP(B) Comt; chm, revol comt; mil comr; *Died:* July 1918 killed during anti-Sov revolt.

TODORSKIY, Aleksandr Ivanovich (1894–1965) Mil commander; lt-gen; CP member from 1918; *Born:* 13 Sept 1894 in vil Deledino, Tver' Province; *Educ:* 1927 grad Mil Acad; *Career:* from 1914 in Russian Army; fought in WW 1 in the ranks, and then as officer; 1918–19 helped establish Sov regime and restore econ in Ves'yegonsk Uyezd; 1919 volunteered for Red Army; commanded brigade, then div against Denikin, insurgent troops in Dag, Azer and Arm, Ferghana and Bukhara; 1927 appointed commander and comr, of infantry corps, then asst commander Bel Mil Distr; from 1930 head, Red Army Mil Training Establishments Bd; from 1934 commandant, Zhukovskiy Air Force Acad; from 1936 head, Red Army Higher Mil Training Establishments Bd; 1955 pensioned; *Publ: God s vintovkoy i plugom* (A Year with Rifle and Plow) (1918); *Krasnaya Armiya v gorakh. Deystviya v Dagestane* (The Red Army in the Mountains. Operations in Daghestan) (1924); *Awards:* four Orders of the Red Banner; *Died:* 31 Sept 1965.

TODRIYA, Sil'vestr Yaseyevich (1880–1936) Govt official; writer; CP member from 1901; *Born:* 1880 in vil Yanauli, Kutaisi Province, son of a peasant; *Career:* from 1897 typesetter in Batumi; 1901 participated in printers' strike; 1902 helped equip and establish illegal Soc-Democratic printing house in Batumi; late 1902–fall 1905 worked for illegal printing houses in Baku; late 1905 left for Moscow; 11 Dec 1905, during the armed revolt, arrested and imprisoned in Butyrka Jail; after his release worked for CC, RSDRP's underground printing house in Moscow; early 1907 arrived in Petersburg and later worked at illegal printing house in Vyborg, Finland; 1908–15 at various Petersburg printing houses; revol work in Printers' Union; late 1915 went to Tiflis, where he headed printers' union and Party wort; 1917 member, Tiflis and Caucasian Kray Party Comt; Feb 1917 founded illegal printing house in Tiflis; early 1918 moved to Vladikavkaz with other members of Caucasian Kray Party Comt; engaged in polit and lit work; helped establish Terek Republ; after establishment of Sov rule in Geo on 25 Feb 1921 held various exec posts: chm, Tiflis Revol Comt; Pop Comr of Soc Security; 1921–24 Pop Comr of Agric; 1924–27 secr, Geo Centr Exec Comt; 1927–29 Pop Comr of Labor; 1928–33 secr, Geo Exec Comt; 1933–36 secr, Transcaucasian SFSR Centr Exec Comt; member, CC, CP Geo and member, Transcaucasian Kray CPSU(B) Comt; member, Geo Centr Exec Comt; member, Transcaucasian SFSR Centr Exec Comt and member, USSR Centr Exec Comt; helped found and direct Geo Assoc of proletarian Writers; 1917 began lit work; wrote mainly humorous and satirical works; *Publ:* books *Smekh skvoz' slyozy* (Laughter Through Tears) (1922); *Krivoye zerkalo* (Distorting Mirror) (1927); *Satira i yumor* (Satire and Humor) (1934); *Vetkhiy i novyy zavety* (The Old and the New Testaments) (1934); *Zhitiye Gruzii* (Georgian Life) (1936), etc; *Died:* 8 July 1936.

TOIDZE, Mose Ivanovich (1871–1953) Geo painter; member, USSR Acad of Arts from 1947; Pop Artist of USSR from 1953; *Born:* 21 Jan 1871 in Tbilisi, son of an artisan; *Educ:* 1896–99 studied at Repin's workshop, Petersburg Acad of Arts: *Career:* 1899 expelled from Acad and exiled to Tiflis for participating in student demonstrations; 1922–29 founder-dir, Pop Art Studio, Tbilisi; 1930–53 prof and head, Chair of Painting, Tbilisi Acad of Arts; in his early period toyed with Classicism and Impressionism, then switched to realism and socialist realism; Works: "Mtskhetoba", "Portrait of a Mother," "Laundry", "The Craftsman" and "A Moonlit Night" (1900–10); "Bazaskhana" and "Revolution" (1910–18); "Industry" (1930); "Chiatura Studies" and "A Happy Life" (1934); "Woman of Georgia Prepare Gifts for the Front" (1945); "Song of Victory" (1948), etc; *Died:* 17 June 1953.

TOKAREVA, Mariya Aleksandrovna (1894–1964) Actress; Pop Artiste of RSFSR from 1950; *Born:* 25 Mar 1894; *Career:* 1912 began work as professional actor in Simferopol'; later acted in Tiflis, Mogilyov, Nikolayev, Bryansk and Yaroslavl'; from 1931 with Sverdlovsk Theater; *Roles:* Marina Mnished in Pushkin's "Boris Godunov"; Katerina in *Groza* (Thunderstorm); Nastya in *Na dne* (The Lower Depths); Reagan in "King Lear"; title role in Capek's "Mother"; Shura in *Yegor Bulychov i drugiye* (Yegor Bulychov and Co); Polina Bardina in *Vragi* (Enemies); Anna Somova in *Somov i drugiye* (Somov and Co); Natal'ya Kovshik in Korneychuk's *Kalinovaya roshcha* (Viburnum Grove); Ol'–Ol' in Andreyev's *Dni nashey zhizni* (Days of Our Life); Irina in A.K. Tolstoy's "Tsar' Fyodor Ioannovich"; Verochka in Surguchyov's *Osenniye skripki* (Autumn Violins); Liza in Griboyedov's *Gore ot uma* (Woe from Wit), etc; *Died:* 27 Jan 1964.

TOKMAKOV, Yevgeniy Alekseyevich (1884–1964) Stage dir and actor; Pop Artiste of Chuvash ASSR from 1947; *Born:* 10 Feb 1884; *Educ:* 1908 grad College of Music and Drama, Philharmonic Soc; 1918 grad Studio, Komissarzhevskaya Theater; *Career:* 1918 actor, Komissarzhevskaya Theater; 1919–20 at Moscow Pedag Theater; 1920–22 at Omsk Theater; 1922 again at Pedag Theater; 1923–25 at Komissarzhevskaya Theater; 1930–36 at 2nd Moscow Acad Arts Theater; 1934–37 simultaneously artistic dir, Balashov Kolkhoz-Sovkhoz Theater; from 1937 artistic dir, Chuvash Theater and Russian Drama Theater of Chuvash ASSR; also acted in films; *Roles:* Chichikov in *Myortvyye dushi* (Dead Souls); Kuligin in *Groza* (The Storm); Malyuta in Ostrovskiy and Gedeonov's "Vasilisa Melent'yeva", etc; *Productions:* staged plays: *Na dne* (The Lower Depths) (1937); "Groza" (1938); *Deti solntsa* (Children of the Sun); *Vragi* (Enemies) (1939); Trenyov's *Na beregu Nevy* (On the Banks of the Neva) (1941); *Kremlyovskiye kuranty* (The Kremlin Chimes) (1943); *Yegor Bulychov i drugiye* (Yegor Bulychov and Co) (1947); *Tri sestry* (Three Sisters) (1954), etc; *Died:* 1964.

TOKTOGUL, Satylganov (1864–1933) Kir akyn (bard); composer and virtuoso musician; *Born:* Apr 1864 in vil Sasyk-Zhiyde, near Ferghana, Kir; *Career:* 1898 arrested and sentenced to death for his polit songs directed against feudal system and Tsarist officials; sentence commuted to hard labor in Siberia; 1910 excaped and fled to Kir; one of the founders of Kir poetry; left many songs and folk melodies, recorded by musicologists directly from him and his pupils; *Publ: Izbrannyye stikhi i pesni* (Selected Verse and Songs) (2 vol, 1940); "Toktogul" (1950); "Chygarmalarynyn" (2 vol, 1964); *Izbrannoye* (Selected Works) (1964); *Died:* 29 Dec 1933.

TOLBUKHIN, Fyodor Ivanovich (1894–1949) Mil commander; capt, Russian Army; Marshal of the Sov Union from 1944; CP member from 1938; *Born:* 16 June 1894 in vil Andronniki, Yaroslavl' Province, son of an artisan-peasant; *Educ:* 1914 grad Petersburg Business College; 1915 grad Oranienbaum Ensigns' School; 1934 grad Operations Fac, Frunze Mil Acad; *Career:* 1911–15 bookkeeper; from 1915 in Russian Army; dispatch rider, junior officer, company commander, then battalion commander on Northwestern and Southwestern Fronts; from 1918 in Red Army; 1918–19 volost mil commander; 1919–20 div dep chief of staff, then chief of staff; chief, Operations Dept, Staff, 3rd Army; 1920–30 chief of staff, 56th Infantry Div; 1929 acting regt commander; 1930–37 chief of staff, 1st then 19th Infantry Corps, Leningrad Mil Distr; 1937–38 commander, 72nd Infantry Div; 1938–41 chief of staff, Transcausasian Mil Distr; 1941–42 chief of staff, Transcaucasian then Caucasian and Crimean Fronts; 1942–43 commander, 57th Army; fought at Stalingrad; 1943 commander, 68th Army on Northwestern Front; participated in abortive operation to rout German forces in Dem'yansk region; May–20 Oct 1943 commander, Southern Front; directed liberation of Donets Basin; 20 Oct 1943–May 1944 commander, 4th Ukr Front; played an important role in liberation of the Crimea; May 1944 until end of war commander, 3rd Ukr Front; Aug 1944 his troops joined with forces of 2nd Ukr Front in major Yassy-Kishinev operation; later his troops participated in the Budapest, Belgrade and Vienna operations; 1945–46 supr commander, Southern Forces Group stationed in Bulgaria and Rumania; 1946–49 commander, Transcaucasian Mil Distr; dep, USSR Supr Sov of 1946 convocation; *Awards:* Hero of the Sov Union; two Orders of Lenin; Order of Victory; two Orders of the Red Banner; other orders and medals; *Died:* 17 Oct 1949; buried on Moscow's Red Square; the Bulgarian town Dobric was renamed for him and a monument to him erected in Moscow.

TOLMACHEV, Nikolay Gur'yevich (1896–1919) Polit comr, Red Army; Civil War veteran; CP member from 1913; *Born:* 1896 in Rostov-on-Don; *Educ:* 1912 grad high-school and entered Petersburg Polytech Inst; *Career:* 1913 arrested for participation in May Day demonstration; after his release headed workers' circles in Vyborg Rayon; from Mar 1916 member, Exec Commission, Petrograd Party Comt; ed, newspaper "Proletarskiy golos"; summer 1916 Party work at Verkh-Isetsk Plant in the Urals; 1917 Party work among Petrograd streetcar workers; from May 1917 touring agitator in Ural Oblast; after 1917 Oct Revol secr, Vyborg Rayon Sov of Workers' Dep; sent to Perm'; elected to Constituent Assembly from Perm' Province; worked for Perm' Oblast Sov and Perm' Oblast RSDRP(B) Comt; appointed detachment commander and fought against Dutov's troops; in Yekaterinburg appointed dep commander, Siberian and Ural Front; then polit comr in Red Army; 1919 head, Cultural and Educ Dept, Petrograd Okrug Mil Comrt; during Yudenich's offensive organized defense of Luga; surrounded near Krasnaya Gorka by Yudenich's troops; *Died:* 1919 committed suicide near Krasnaya Gorka.

TOLMACHEV, Vladimir Nikolayevich (1886–?) Party and govt official; CP member from 1904; *Born:* 1886; *Career:* 1905 member, Kostroma Party Comt; 1906 arrested and exiled to Vologda Province; 1910 returned from exile and went to Black Sea coast; at start of WW 1 drafted into Russian Army; after 1917 Feb Revol organized soviets of soldiers' dep on Turkish Front; Dec 1917 chm, Novorossiysk Party Comt and Novorossiysk Okrug Mil Comt; 1919 member, Crimean Repul Mil Council; 1920 chm, Novorossiysk Revol Comt; 1921–22 secr, Kuban'-Black Sea Oblast Party Comt; 1922–24 chm, Kuban'-Black Sea Exec Comt; 1924–28 dep chm, North Caucasian Kray Exec Comt; from 1928 RSFSR Pop Comr of Internal Affairs; member, All-Russian and USSR Centr Exec Comts; *Died:* date and place of death unknown.

TOLMAZOV, Andrey Il'ich (1899–1934) CP member; *Born:* 1899; *Educ:* studied in Leningrad; *Career:* 1934 arrested by State Security organs on charges of conspiracy in 1 Dec 1934 assassination of Kirov in Leningrad; 29 Dec 1934 sentenced to death, with co-defendants, by Assizes of Mil Collegium, USSR Supr Court; *Died:* Dec 1934 executed.

TOLOKONTSEV, Aleksandr Fyodorovich (1889–1937) Govt official; CP member from 1914; *Born:* 1889, son of a peasant; *Career:* metalworker by trade; after 1917 Oct Revol govt, trade-union and econ admin work; member, CC, Metalworkers Union; Presidium member, All-Russian Centr Exec Comt and USSR Supr Sovnarkhoz; 1921–22 sided with Workers' Opposition and subscribed to 22-signatory address to Comintern; then head, Main Bd of Machine-Building and Metalworking Ind; mang, All-Union Assoc of Heavy Machine-Building; Collegium member, USSR Pop Comrt of Heavy Ind; dir, of a plant; at 13th Party Congress elected cand member, and at 14th–16th Congresses elected member, CC, CPSU(B); arrested by State Security organs; *Died:* 1937 in imprisonment.

TOL'SKIY, Andrey Petrovich (1874–1942) Forestry expert; *Born:* 13 Aug 1874; *Educ:* 1897 grad Petersburg Forestry Inst; *Career:* 1903–17 did experimental forestry work at Buzulukskiy bor; 1917–20 prof, Novo-Aleksandriyskiy Inst, Khar'kov; 1920–22 prof, Higher Agric Courses, Moscow; 1925–30 prof, Kazan' Inst of Agric and Forestry; 1930–32 prof, Kazan' Forestry Tech Inst; from 1932 prof, Volga Forestry Tech Inst, Yoshkar-Ola; did research on physiology and ecology of trees and shrubs, water conservation properties of forests and forestry meteorology; *Publ: Chastnoye lesovodstvo* (Special Forestry) (4 vol, 1927–31); *Lesnoye semenovodstvo* (Forestry Seed-Growing) (1932); *Died:* 1942.

TOLSTOY, Aleksey Nikolayevich (1882–1945) Russian writer and playwright; member, USSR Acad of Sci from 1939; *Born:* 10 Jan 1883 in Nikolayevsk, Samara Province (now Pugachyov, Saratov Oblast); *Educ:* 1901 studied at Petersburg Technol Inst; *Career:* 1905 first work printed; 1914–16 mil corresp, newspaper "Russkiye vedomosti"; 1918–23 emigre in Paris and Berlin; 1921–22 contributed to "Change of Landmarks" movement's organ "Nakanune"; 1923 returned to USSR and sided with Bolsheviks; 1935–37 deleg at Int Anti-Fascist Congresses in Paris, London and Madrid; at end of WW 2 member, commission to investigate Katyn Woods massacre of Polish officers; dep, USSR Supr Sov of 1937 convocation; the Nobel Prize winner Bunin, who knew him well, has described him as a man who combined rare personal amorality with rare talent and artistic gifts; *Publ:* collected verse *Lirika* (Lyric Verse) (1907); story *Staraya bashnya* (The Old Tower) (1908); collection *Soroch' i skazki* (Magpie Tales) (1910); novels: *Chudaki* (The Cranks) (1911) and *Khromoy barin* (The Lame Gentleman) (1912); comedies *Nechistaya sila* (The Evil Force) (1916) and *Mrakobesy* (The Obscurantists) (1917); *Detstvo Nikity* (Nikita's Childhood) (1920); historical stories: *Den' Petra* (Peter's Day); *Graf Cagliostro* (Countr Cagliostro); *Smert' Dantona* (The Death of Danton) (1920–23); sci fiction novels: "Aelita" (1923); *Giperboloid inzhenera Garina* (Engineer Garin's Hyperboloid) (1926); play *Na dybe* (On the Rack) (1929); novels: *Chyornoye zoloto* (Black Gold) (1931); *Pyotr I* (Peter I) (1934); children's book *Zolotoy klyuchik, ili priklyucheniye Buratino* (The Golden Key, or the Buratino Adventure) (1936); trilogy *Khozhdeniye po mukam* (The Road to Calvary), consisting of the novels: *Syostry* (Sisters) (1921); *Vosemnadtsatyy god* (Nineteen-Eighteen) (1928) and *Khuroye utro* (A Dull Morning) (1941); series of two plays *Ivan Groznyy* (Ivan the Terrible), consisting of *Oryol i orlitsa* (The Eagle and the She-Eagle) (1942) and *Trudnyye gody* (Difficult Years) (1943); *Rasskazy Ivana Sudaryova* (The Stories of Ivan Sudaryov) (1944); *Polnoye sobraniye sochineniy* (Complete Collected Works) (15 vol, 1946–53); *Izbrannyye sochineniya* (Selected Works) (6 vol, 1950–53); many of his works have been translated into foreign languages; some of his works have formed the basis for operas, including: *Khozhdeniye po mukam* (The Road to Calvary); *Russkiy kharakter* (The Russian Character); *Ivan Groznyy* (Ivan the Terrible); *Awards:* Order of Lenin; Order of the Red Banner of Labor; Badge of Hon; three Stalin Prizes (1941, 1943 and 1946); *Died:* 23 Feb 1945 in Moscow.

TOLSTOY, Sergey L'vovich (1863–1947) Composer; *Born:* 16 June 1863 in Yasnaya Polyana, Tula Province, the son of Lev Tolstoy; *Career:* 1921–32 assoc, State Inst of Musical Sci, Moscow; *Works:* romances; arrangements of Indian songs and dances; collection of Scottish songs, etc; *Publ:* "Sputnik etnografa" (The Ethnographer's Companion) (1929); "Ocherki bylogo" (Studies of the Past) (1929); *Died:* 23 Dec 1947 in Moscow.

TOLSTYAKOV, Pavel Nilovich (1880–1938) Composer and choirmaster; *Born:* 28 Dec 1880 in Moscow; *Educ:* grad Petersburg Conservatory; *Career:* dir, Court Choir; from 1912 chief choirmaster, Mariinskiy Theater, Petrograd Petersburg; 1921–23 choirmaster, Khar'kov Opera Theater; from 1933 choirmaster, Odessa Opera Theater; *Works:* arranged some 20 Ukr folk songs; music for film "Koliivshchyna"; piano works; choral works: "Socialism"; "The Song of the Smith"; "In Memory of Lenin"; *Died:* 25 May 1938.

TOMASHEVSKIY (pseudonym: LEON), A.F. (1868–1937) Politician; *Born:* 1868; *Career:* from 1889 member, Polish Workers' Union; from 1900 member, Soc-Democratic Party of Poland and Lith; participated in 1905–07 Revol; deleg, 5th RSDRP Congress; during WW 1 with Warsaw Comt, Soc-Democratic Party of Poland and Lith; 1918 joined Polish CP; arrested by Polish authorities; 1932 emigrated to USSR; worked for Polish Section, Exec Comt, Comintern; from 1936 pensioner; *Died:* 1937.

TOMASHEVSKIY, Boris Viktorovich (1890–1957) Lit historian and textologist; *Born:* 17 Nov 1890; *Educ:* completed higher tech educ at Liege Univ, Belgium; *Career:* in 1930's read courses on higher mathematics; from 1915 engaged in lit research; 1917 first work printed; 1919 joined Soc for Studying the Theory of Poesy; edited and did textological research for definitive editions of works of Pushkin, Batyushkov, Del'vig, Dostoyevsky, etc; *Publ:* study of Pushkin's "Gavriliad" (1922); *Russkoye stikhoslozheniye. Metrika* (Russian Prosody. Metrics) (1923); *Teoriya literatury* (The Theory of Literature) (1925); *O stikhe* (Verse) (1929); studies of Pushkin's lyric verse and poems (1941); articles: "Pushkin and Populism" (1941); "Pushkin and the Southern Slavs" (1946); "Pushkin and the Russian Theater of His Time" (1952); "The Problem of Language in Pushkin's Work" (1953); *Pushkin. Opyt izucheniya tvorcheskogo razvitiya* (Pushkin. A Study of Creative Development) (1956); *Died:* 24 Mar 1957.

TOMIN, Nikolay Dmitriyevich (1877–1924) Mil commander; Civil War veteran; CP member from 1924; *Born:* 1887 in vil Kurtamysh, Orenburg Province; *Educ:* 1924 grad Higher Mil Acad Courses; *Career:* during WW 1 private, 1st Orenburg Cossack Div; 1918 organized Red Guard squad in Troitsk; Sept 1918 his squad, operatin in Southern Urals in the rear of Kolchak's forces, linked up with units of the 3rd Army, Eastern Front and was reorganized into a brigade under Tomin's command; 1920 commander, 10th Cavalry Div on Western Front; 1921 helped rout White forces in Kuban' and crush Antonov Revolt in Tambov Province; from late

1921 commanded Trans-Baykal Forces Group; May 1924 commanded Separate Altay Cavalry Brigade in campaign against Basmachi movement in eastern Bukhara; *Died:* 12 Aug 1924 killed in action.

TOMSKIY (real name: YEFREMOV), Mikhail Pavlovich (1880–1936) Party and trade-union official; CP member from 1904; *Born:* 1880; *Career:* printing worker by trade; 1904 joined RSDRP and played active part in revol movement; 1905 dep, Revel' Sov; 1906 arrested; fled from exile; 1907 deleg, London RSDRP Congress; July 1907 deleg, All-Russian Party Conference, Helsingfors; late 1907 rearrested and imprisoned until Apr 1909; Dec 1909, after some months of underground Party work, rearrested and after two years' investigatory custody sentenced to five years' imprisonment; 1916 released from prison but restricted to life settlement in Siberia; after 1917 Feb Revol returned to Petrograd and became member, Exec Commission, Petersburg RSDRP(B) Comt; after July 1917 Bolshevik riots moved to Moscow and worked for Metalworkers' Union and for journal "Metallist"; from Dec 1917 chm, Moscow Trade-Union Council and ed, All-Russian Centr Trade-Union Council journal "Profsoyuznyy vestnik"; from 14th Trade-Union Conference in 1918 Presidium member, All-Russian Centr Trade-Union Council; from 2nd Trade-Union Congress chm, All-Russian Centr Trade-Union Council; from 2nd Trade-Union Congress chm, All-Russian Centr Trade-Union Council; 1920 helped found Trade-Union International (Profintern) and Anglo-Russian Comt; 1921 chm, Turkestani Commission, All-Russian Centr Exec Comt and RSFSR Council of Pop Comr; also Presidium member, USSR Supr Sovnarkhoz and chm, All-Union Chemical Ind Trust; in his latter hears years headed Joint State Publ House, Moscow; member, All-Russian and USSR Centr Exec Comt of several convocations; from 8th Party Congress member, from 17th Party Congress cand member, CC, CPSU(B); Apr 1922–29 Politburo member, CC, CPSU(B); 1921, during trade-union controversy prior to 10th Party Congress, he defended Lenin's views and helped draft resolution on trade unions which was adopted by 10th Congress; 1928 headed "rightist opposition" in Party; 1929 Nov Plenum of CC, CPSU(B) took up the matter of the leaders of the "rightist opposition", and Tomskiy confessed his "errors" and dissociated himself from them; 1934 at 17th Party Congress he again recanted his past "oppositionary errors" and dissociated himself once and for all from opposition factions; despite such statements and his 22 Aug 1936 statement along the same lines, at a meeting of the Party Comt, Joint State Publ House, he was slated for arrest together with other opposition leaders; *Died:* Aug 1936 committed suicide upon learning of his impending arrest.

TONKOV, Vladimir Nikolayevich (1872–1954) Anatomist; Dr of Med from 1898; prof from 1900; lt-gen, Med Corps; member, USSR Acad of Med Sci from 1944; Hon Sci Worker of RSFSR from 1934; CP member from 1932; *Born:* 14 Jan 1872 in vil Kosa, now Perm' Oblast; *Educ:* 1895 grad Petersburg Mil Med Acad; *Career:* after grad trained for professorship at Chair of Normal Anatomy, Petersburg Mil Med Acad; 1898 defended doctor's thesis on arteries feeding intervertebral ganglia and cerebrospinal nerves, after which he underwent further specialist training abroad; from 1900 prof, Chair of Anatomy, Women's Med Inst; from 1905 head, Chair of Normal Anatomy, Kazan' Univ; 1915–50 head, Chair of Normal Anatomy, 1915–17 learned secr, 1917–25 dir, 1950–54 consulting prof, Leningrad Mil Med Acad; did research on normal and comparative anatomy, histology and embryology with special reference to vascular system; was one of first sci to use x-rays for anatomical research; made valuable contributions to morphology of blood circulation and research on regulator mechanisms of circulatory system; was first Russian sci to approach anatomy from ontophilogenetic viewpoint; helped to organize anatomical museums for training purposes and developed a system of combined instruction including practical, theoretical, experimental and functional elements; founder-chm, Soc of Pop Univ; co-founder, Comt for Improvement of Scientists' Living Conditions; member, Leningrad City Sov and Vyborg Rayon Sov; member or hon member, numerous Sov and for med soc; trained many outstanding anatomists, including B.A. Dolgo-Saburov, G.F. Ivanov and A.N. Maksimenko; wrote over 100 works; *Publ:* doctor's thesis, *Arterii, pitayushchiye mezhpozvonochnyye uzly i spinno-mozgovyye nervy cheloveka* (The Arteries Feeding the Human Intervertebral Ganglia and Cerebrospinal Nerves) (1898); *Posobiye k prakticheskomu izucheniyu sosudov i nervov cheloveka* (An Aid to the Practical Study of Human Vessels and Nerves) (1956); *Izbrannyye trudy* (Selected Works) (1959); *Uchebnik normal'noy anatomii cheloveka* (A Textbook of Normal Human Anatomy); (1962); *Awards:* two Orders of Lenin; two Orders of the Red Banner; Order of the Red Banner of Labor; Order of the Red Star; medals; *Died:* 6 Oct 1954 in Leningrad.

TOPANOV, Aleksandr Mikhaylovich (1903–1959) Khakas playwright; one of the founders of Khakas lit; *Born:* 1903; *Career:* 1920 began lit work; took part in amateur lit and dramatic circles; founded "Blue Blouse" circle in Abakan; 1931 artistic dir and actor, Khakas Nat Theater, which he helped found; *Works:* plays: "Scroll Without Need" (1928); "The Thistle" (1932); "From Gun to Tractor" (1933); "Class Enemies" (1933); "Woman's Gain" (1938); coauthor, musical comedy "Khorkhlo Befooled" (1942); plays: "Blood for Blood"; "Steel Hearts"; "Vengeance", all written during WW 2; *Died:* 1959.

TOPCHIYEV, Aleksandr Vasil'yevich (1907–1962) Organic chemist; prof from 1938; member from 1949 and vice-pres from 1958, USSR Acad of Sci; CP member from 1932; *Born:* 9 Aug 1907; *Educ:* 1930 grad Moscow Chemical Technol Inst; *Career:* 1932–38 lecturer, Moscow Chemical Technol Inst and Moscow Technol Inst of Food Ind; 1938–40 prof, Technol Inst of Food Ind; 1940–43 prof, 1943–47 dir, Moscow Oil Inst; 1947–49 USSR Dep Min of Higher Educ; 1949–58 chief learned secr, Presidium, USSR Acad of Sci; from 1952 simultaneously head, Dept of Oil Chemistry and Technol, and head, Laboratory of Oil and Gas Chemistry, Oil Inst, USSR Acad of Sci; from 1958 also dir, Inst of Petrochemical Synthesis, USSR Acad of Sci; hon member, various for acad; dep, RSFSR Supr Sov of 4th and 5th convocations; from 1950 member, Sov Peace Comt; chm, Moscow City Dept, All-Union Soc for the Dissemination of Polit and Sci Knowledge; bd member, USSR Assoc for the Promotion of the UN; 1960 headed Sov deleg at 6th Pugwash Conference; did research on catalytic processes of nitration, halogenation, polymerization and alkalization of various hydrocarbons; *Publ: Nitrovaniye uglevodorodov i drugikh organicheskikh soyedineniy* (The Nitration of Hydrocarbons and Other Organic Compounds) (1949); *Soyedineniya ftoristogo bora, kak katalizatora v reaktsiyakh alkilirovaniya, polimerizatsii i kondensatsii* (Boron Fluoride Compounds as Catalysts in Alkalization, Polymerization and Condensation Reactions) (1949); *Nad chem rabotayut sovetskiye uchyonyye* (What Soviet Scientists Are Working Upon) (1959); *Ne byvat' voyne* (To Prevent War) (1960), etc; *Awards:* Lenin Prize; Stalin Prize (1949); two Orders of Lenin; other orders; medals; *Died:* 27 Dec 1962.

TOPURIDZE, D.A. (pseudonyms: ISAY; ISARI; KARSKIY) (1871–1942) Geo politician; Menshevik; *Born:* 1871; *Career:* member, "Mesame dasi", Georgia's first Soc-Democratic org; Tiflis RSDRP Comt deleg at 2nd RSDRP Congress; started out as "Iskra" Bolshevik but reconsidered his views and by the end of the Congress was voting with the "Iskra" Mensheviks; after the Congress joined Mensheviks and protested against the centr Party organs elected at the Congress; early Oct 1903 the Caucasian Joint RSDRP Comt relieved him of all Party work because of these objections; 1918–21 held various senior posts during period of democratic govt in Geo; after establishment of Sov regime in Geo worked for Comrt of Finance, did research and engaged in journalism; *Died:* 1942.

TORAMANYAN, Toros (1864–1934) Architect and archeologist; Hon Sci Worker of Arm SSR from 1933; *Born:* 18 Mar 1864 in Turkey, son of a landowner; *Educ:* 1893 grad Constantinople Acad of Arts; *Career:* 1894–1900 worked as architect in Constantinople and Bulgaria; 1903 moved to Arm and spent the rest of his life studying and protecting ancient Arm architectural monuments; 1904–12 took part in excavation and study of Ani monuments; reconstructed Ani churches of Grigoriy, Bakhtageka, Pastoral Church; reconstructed bridge over River Akhuryan; reconstructed Zvartnots Church; traced connections between Arm architectural monuments and architecture of neighboring countries; *Publ:* "An Outline History of Armenian Architecture" (2 vol, 1942–48); *Died:* 1 March 1934.

TORCHINSKIY, G.B. (1886–1951) Party and govt official; CP member from 1917; *Born:* 1886; *Career:* deleg from Jewish Section, CP(B) Ukr at 8th RCP(B) Congress; after 1917 Oct Revol admin, Party and dipl work; 1917–18 Collegium member, Ukr Pop Comrt of Labor; head, Jewish Section, CC, CP(B) Ukr; Ukr Dep Pop Comr of Justice; then ed, journal "Zhizn' natsional'nostey"; secr, USSR embassy in Iran; from 1923 research and teaching work at higher educ institutions; *Died:* 1951.

TOTROV, Boris Ivanovich (1882–1964) Actor and drama teacher; Hon Art Worker of North Ossetian ASSR from 1940; *Born:* 10 Jan 1882; *Educ:* grad private musical drama college in Moscow; *Career:* 1904 founded drama group in settlement Ol'ginskoye; 1908 organized amateur dramatic company in Vladikavkaz and staged Britayev's plays; 1913–14 at Aleksandrinskiy Theater; from 1915 again with drama company in Vladikavkaz; after 1917 Oct Revol head, Drama Section, Vladikavkaz Educ Dept; 1926 founded "Children of the Mountains" song and dance ensemble; 1931 with Ossetian Studio, State Inst of Stagecraft, Moscow; from 1935 actor, North Ossetian Theater and taught stagecraft at the theater's Studio; *Roles:* Kambolat and Isiam in Britayev's "Two Sisters" and "Khazbi"; Bata in Mamsurov's "The Bata Brothers"; Brabanzio in "Othello"; Bartolo in "Marriage of Figaro"; Zheleznov in "Vassa Zheleznova", etc; *Productions:* Britayev's drama "Death Dishonor"; Britayev's comedy "The Man Who Had Lived in Russia, etc; *Died:* 26 June 1964.

TOTSKIY, Ivan Kornilovich (1896–1957) Opera singer (bass); Pop Artiste of Ukr SSR from 1948; *Born:* 12 Apr 1896; *Educ:* 1925 grad Kiev Conservatory; *Career:* 1925–27 soloist, Khar'kov Opera and Ballet Theater; 1927–42 soloist, Odessa Opera and Ballet Theater; 1943–45 soloist, Kirov Opera and Ballet Theater, Leningrad; 1946-57 again at Odessa Opera and Ballet Theater; *Roles:* Taras in Lysenko's "Taras Bul'ba"; Karas' in *Zaporozhets za Dunayem* (A Dnieper Cossack Beyond the Danube); Pimen in "Boris Godunov"; Dosifey in "Khovanshchina"; Ivan the Terrible in *Pskovityanka* (The Woman of Pskov); Chub in *Noch' pered Rozhdestvom* (The Night Before Christmas); Sobakin in *Tsarskaya nevesta* (The Bride of the Tsar); Don Basilio in "The Barber of Seville"; Taras in Kabalevskiy's *Sem'ya Tarasa* (Taras' Family), etc; *Died:* 16 Dec 1957.

TOVIYA (secular name: OSTROUKHOV, Aleksandr Il'ich) (1884-1957) Archbishop Molotovsk and Solikamsk; archeologist; *Born:* 1884; *Educ:* 1900 grad Moscow Theological Seminary; 1915 grad Moscow Archeological Inst; *Career:* from 1919 priest, then archpriest in Vladimir Eparchy; 1944 took monastic vows as Toviya and appointed Bishop of Sverdlovsk and Chelyabinsk; 1945 appointed Bishop of Sverdlovsk and Irbit; until 1947 also administered Chelyabinsk Eparchy; from 1953 archbishop; 1955 one of seven selected hierarchs who signed address to Patriarch of Moscow on the occasion of the 10th anniversary of his patriarchal rule; from 1957 Arbhishop of Molotovsk and Solikamsk; *Died:* 5 May 1957.

TOVSTOLIS, Dimitriy Ivanovich (1877–1939) Forestry expert; *Born:* 8 Sept 1877 in Chernigov, son of an office worker; *Educ:* 1902 grad Petersburg Inst of Forestry; *Career:* from 1912 prof, Petersburg Women's Agric Courses; from 1923 prof, Bel Agric Inst; from 1925 head, Chair of Forest Taxation, Kiev Agric Inst, then Kiev Forest Management Inst; did research on theory of tree growth; helped develop method for sustained terpentining of pines connected with supervisory felling; also developed system of forest-park econ; *Died:* 28 July 1939.

TOVSTUKHA, Ivan Pavlovich (1889–1935) Govt and Party official; CP member from 1913; *Born:* 22 Feb 1889 in Berezna, now Chernigov Oblast; *Career:* from 1905 in revol movement; 1909–12 in exile in Siberia; 1912 fled from exile; 1912–17 lived abroad; 1917–18 worked for Red Army Centr Staff, Moscow; 1918–21 secr and Collegium member, Pop Comrt of Nationalities; then exec work for CC, CPSU(B); 1924–26 asst dir, Lenin Inst; 1926–30 worked for CC, CPSU(B) and for Lenin Inst; 1930 dep dir Lenin Inst; from 1931 dep dir, Inst of Marx-Engels-Lenin; at 17th Party Congress elected cand member, CC, CPSU(B); member, USSR Centr Exec Comt; *Died:* 8 Aug 1935.

TRAKHTENBERG, Iosif Adol'fovich (1883–1960) Economist; prof from 1914; member, USSR Acad of Sci from 1939; *Born:* 28 Jan 1883; *Educ:* 1912 grad Law Fac, Tomsk Univ; *Career:* 1909–11 statistician, Tomsk Resettlement Bd; 1914–17 prof, Khar'kov Business Inst; 1917–21 prof, Khar'kov Univ; 1921–49 prof, Inst of Red Prof, Sverdlov Communist Univ and other higher educ establishments; 1921–25 head, Econ Dept, then dep head, Econ Bd, Supr Sovnarkhoz in Moscow; 1925–26 Collegium member, RSFSR Gosplan, dep mang, Centr Statistical Bd and Presidium member, USSR Gosplan; 1931–59 at Inst of World Econ and World Politics (from 1947 Inst of Econ), USSR Acad of Sci; 1932–36 Collegium member, Centr Public Econ Accounting Bd; specialist on circulation of money. credit and theory and history of econ crises; *Publ: Bumazhnyye den'gi* (Paper Money) (1918); *Sovremennyy kreditnyy krizis* (The Modern Credit Crisis) (1932); *Denezhnyye krizisy. 1821–1938* (Money Crises. 1821–1938) (1939); *Kapitalisticheskoye vosproizvodstvo i ekonomicheskiye krizisy* (Capitalist Reproduction and Economic Crises) (1947); *Kreditno-denezhnaya sistema kapitalisma posle vtoroy mirovoy voyny* (The Credit and Money System of Capitalism After the Second World War) (1954), etc; *Awards:* Order of Lenin; Order of the Red Banner of Labor; *Died:* 5 Sept 1960.

TRAKHTENBERG, Orest Vladimirovich (1889–1959) Philosopher; Dr of Philosophy; prof; member, RSFSR Acad of Pedag Sci from 1947; CP member from 1952; *Born:* 30 Aug 1889; *Educ:* 1915 grad Law Fac, Petrograd Univ; *Career:* from 1921 in Moscow; at Krupskaya Acad of Communist Educ; Centr Inst of Educ Org and Planning; Inst of Marxist-Leninist Pedag; Moscow Oblast Teachers' Training Inst, etc; from 1933 research work at Inst of Philosophy, USSR Acad of Sci; from 1943 simultaneously directed a lecture course at Moscow State Univ; specialized in dialectical and historical materialism and history of philosophy; *Publ: Besedy s uchitelem po istoricheskomu materializmu* (Discussions with a Teacher on Historical Materialism) (1925); *Besedy s uchitelem po dialekticheskomu materializmu* (Discussions with a Teacher on Dialectical Materialism) (1928); *Dialekticheskiy materializm* (Dialectical Materialism) (1931–32); coauthor, *Fazy obshchestvennogo razvitiya* (Stages of Social Development) (1929); coauthor, *Kratkiy uchebnik po istorii razvitiya obshchestvennykh form* (A Short Textbook on the History of the Development of Social Forms) (1928); *Istoricheskiy materializm* (Historical Materialism) (1929); coauthor, *Rabochaya kniga po istorii* (A History Workbook) (1931); coauthor, *Istoriya. Epokha feodalizma* (History. The Age of Feudalism) (1933); *Razvitiye materializma i yego bor'ba protiv idealizma v period pervykh burzhuaznykh revolyutsiy (konets 16 - nachalo 18 v.)* (The Development of Materialism and Its Struggle Against Idealism in the Period of the First Bourgeois Revolutions [Late 16th – Early 18th Centuries] (1956); *Ocherki po istorii zapadno-yevropeyskoy srednevekovoy filosofii* (Outline History of West European Medieval Philosophy) (1957); *Ocherki po istorii filosofii i sotsiologii Anglii 19 v.* (Outline History of Philosophy and Sociology in 19th-Century England) (1959); *Awards:* Order of Lenin, Stalin Prize (1943); *Died:* 23 May 1959.

TRANSHEL', Vladimir Andreyevich (Vol'demar Genrikhovich) (1868–1942) Botanist and mycologist; prof; *Born:* 16 Jan 1869; *Educ:* 1889 grad Petersburg Univ; *Career:* from 1900 assoc, Botanical Museum; subsequently until 1942 head, Mycology Section, Botanical Inst, USSR Acad of Sci; 1909–23 also prof, Women Teachers' Training Inst, Petersburg; 1923–30 also prof, Inst of Applied Zoology and Phytopathology, Leningrad; *Publ: Obzor rzhavchinnykh gribov SSSR* (A Review of the Rust Fungi of the USSR) (1939); *Died:* 21 Jan 1942.

TRAVNIKOV, Aleksey Stepanovich (1911–1961) Mining eng; CP member from 1959; *Born:* 25 Dec 1911; *Educ:* 1937 grad Irkutsk Mining Inst; *Career:* 1954–55 eng, from 1955 chief eng and dep dir, Zyryan Lead Combine; helped develop and introduce forced block felling in mines of the Leninogorsk Polymetallic Combine; *Awards:* Lenin Prize (1961); *Died:* 8 June 1961.

TRAYNIN, Aron Naumovich (1883–1957) Criminal lawyer; corresp member, USSR Acad of Sci from 1946; Hon Sci Worker of RSFSR; *Born:* 9 July 1883; *Educ:* 1908 grad Law Fac, Moscow Univ; *Career:* 1905 participated in students' movement; after grad stayed at univ to train for professorship; 1911 resigned from univ in protest against the policy of Min of Educ Kasso; after 1917 Oct Revol prof of criminal law, Moscow Univ; 1945 Sov rep at London Four-Power Conference (USSR, USA, UK and France) which established the statutes of the Nuremberg War Crimes Tribunal; Sov prosecution consultant at Nuremberg Trials; 1947 and 1948 elected vice-pres, Int Assoc of Democratic Lawyers; *Publ: Zashchita mira i ugolovnyy zakon* (The Defense of Peace and the Criminal Law) (1937); *Ucheniye o souchastii* (The Theory of Complicity) (1941); *Ugolovnaya otvetstvennost' gitlerovtsev* (Criminal Responsibility of the Nazis) (1944); *Sostav prestupleniya po sovetskomu ugolovnomu pravu* (Corpus Delicti in Soviet Criminal Law) (1951); *Awards:* two Orders of the Red Banner of Labor; *Died:* 7 Feb 1957.

TRAYNIN, Il'ya Pavlovich (1887–1949) Lawyer; member, USSR Acad of Sci from 1939; CP member from 1904; *Born:* 7 Jan 1887 in Riga; *Career:* 1922–24 ed, journal "Zhizn' natsional'nostey"; 1924–30 head, Main Repertoire Comt, RSFSR Pop Comrt of Educ; 1931–42 senior assoc, 1942–47 dir, Inst of Law, USSR Acad of Sci; 1946–49 also acad secr, Dept of Econ and Law and

Presidium member, USSR Acad of Sci; specialized in state law and nationality questions; *Publ: Gosudarstvo i kommunizm* (State and Communism) (1940); *Voprosy territorii v gosudarstvennom prave* (Territorial Questions in State Law) (1947), etc; *Died:* 27 June 1949.

TREGUBENKO, Aleksandr Fyodorovich (1904–1963) Electrometallurgical eng; CP member from 1924; *Born:* 14 Apr 1904; *Educ:* 1934 grad Dnepropetrovsk Metallurgical Inst; *Career:* from 1920 lathe operator at Rostov-on-Don Railroad Workshops; 1924–30 exec Komsomol work; 1934–39 worked at "Zaporothstal'" Steel Combine; 1939–62 dir, "Dneprospetsstal'" Special Steels Plant; improved technol for producing special steels and alloys, especially the electro-slag resmelting of used electrodes in a metallic, water-cooled crystallizer pan; *Awards:* Lenin Prize (1963); *Died:* 20 June 1963.

TRENYOV, Konstantin Andreyevich (1876–1945) Russian author and playwright; *Born:* 21 May 1876 in vil Romashovo, Khar'kov Province, son of a serf; *Educ:* 1903 grad Petersburg Archeological Inst and Theological Acad; 1921 grad Agronomy Fac, Tavrida Univ; *Career:* 1898 began writing; 1903–18 worked as a teacher in Khar'kov Province; 1907 wrote first play; *Publ:* stories- *Omel'ko-pastukh* (Omel'ko the Shepherd) (1899); "Olesya" (1901); *Gore Ivana Taya* (Ivan Tay's Grief) (1902); Zateryannaya konnitsa (The Lost Cavalry) (1909); *Na bazare* (At the Market) (1912); *Mokryy ovrag* (The Wet Ravine) (1913); essays *Na Ukraine* (In the Ukraine) (1916); plays- *Doroginy* (The Dorogins) (1912); *Pugachyovshchina* (The Pugachev Rebellion) (1924); *Lyubov' Yarovaya* (1926); *Zhena* (The Wife) (1928); *Yasnyy log* (The Bright Ravine) (1931); *Opyt* (Experiment) (1934); *Gimnazisty* (The High-Schoolers) (1935); *Na beregu Nevy* (On the Banks of the Neva) (1937); "Anna Luchinina" (1941); *Navstrechu* (Encounter) (1942); *Polkovodets* (The General) (1945); *Izbrannyye proizvedeniya* (Selected Works) (2 vol, 1955); *Awards: Stalin Prize (1941);* Died: *19 May 1945.*

TREPLEV, Avraam Davydovich (1891–1955) Stage dir; *Born:* 1 July 1891; *Educ:* 1921 grad Odessa Theater School; *Career:* 1924–25 with Odessa Russian Theater; 1925–26 with Moscow's Revol Theater; 1926 co-founder, Reciter's Theater; 1932 artistic dir, Smolensk Theater, 1933–35 in Odessa; 1935–36 in Sverdlovsk; 1939–41 in Odessa; 1942 in Penza; 1945–46 in Kuybyshev; 1947–48 in Perm'; 1954–55 in Dnepropetrovsk; helped organize Kazan's Bolshoy Drama Theater; *Productions: Chudak* (The Crank) (1929); *Pervaya Konnaya* (1st Mounted Army) (1930); *Strakh* (Fear) (1931); *Portret* (Portrait) (1934); *Dalyokoye* (Things Far Away) (1935); Vishnevskiy's *Optimisticheskaya tragediya* (An Optimistic Tragedy) (1936); Capek's "Mother" (1939); "Mashen'ka" (1941); *Nakanune* (On the Eve) (1942); Aliger's *Skazka o pravde* (The Tale of Truth) (1947), etc; *Died:* 26 Aug 1955.

TRET'YAKEVICH, Viktor Iosifovich (1924–1943) Komsomol official; Komsomol member from 1939; *Born:* 9 Sept 1924 in vil Yasenki, Voronezh Oblast, son of an office worker; *Educ:* studied at Voroshilovgrad; *Career:* 1932 moved to Krasnodon with his parents; from 1941 studied in Voroshilovgrad; secr, Komsomol Comt, Voroshilov School; when Germanss occupied the city, he was a member, Voroshilovgrad City Komsomol Comt and scout for partisan detachment; then staff member and comr, "Young Guard" underground Komsomol org in Krasnodon; 1 Jan 1943 arrested by German mil authorities; *Died:* 15 Jan 1943 in German imprisonment.

TRET'YAKOV, Andrey Fyodorovich (1905–1966) Health official; *Born:* 1905; *Educ:* 1929 grad Voronezh Med Inst; *Career:* 1929–35 headed Publ Health Depts in Tambov and Kursk Oblasts; 1935–39 head, Kalinin Oblast Health Dept; 1939 head, Main Resorts and Sanatoria Bd, USSR Pop Comrt of Health; 1940–46 RSFSR Pop Comr, then Min of Health; 1941–45 founded evacuation hospitals and organized blood supply for front areas; 1946–48 USSR Min of Med Ind; 1948–53 dir, Centr Research Inst of Resort Treatment, USSR Min of Health; 1953–54 USSR Min of Health; from 1954 Collegium member, RSFSR Min of Soc Security and head, Med Labor Expertise Bd; published over 100 works on health org, resort treatment, radiology and med labor expertise; *Publ: Okhrana narodnogo zdorov'ya v RSFSR* (Public Health Care in the RSFSR) (1944) *Ocherednyye zadachi medikosanitarnogo obsluzhivaniya naseleniya* (Routine Tasks of the Public Medical and Health Service) (1944); *Sroki lecheniya ranenykh v evakogospitalyakh* (Wounded Treatment Periods in Evacuation Hospitals) (1944); *Nauchno-metodicheskiye i organizatsionnyye osnovy vrachebnotrudovoy ekspertizy* (The Scientific Methods and Principles of Organizing Medical-Labor Expertise) (1960); *Died:* 22 May 1966.

TRET'YAKOV, Dmitriy Konstantinovich (1878–1950) Histologist and zoologist; member, Ukr Acad of Sci from 1929; Hon Sci Worker of Ukr SSR from 1940; CP member from 1945; *Born:* 6 Nov 1878 in vil Shumarova, Yaroslavl, Province; *Educ:* 1901 grad Petersburg Univ; *Career:* 1901-11 at Petersburg Univ; 1912–41 prof, Novorossiysk Univ, Odessa; from 1944 prof, Kiev Univ; 1944–48 dir, Zoological Inst, Ukr Acad of Sci; specialized in histology of bone tissue, nervous system and sense organs of lower vertebrates and the organs of the lateral line in fish, which he termed the seismosensory system; *Publ: Mozg peskoroyki* (The Brain of Ammocoetes br. Cuv) (1910); *Organy chuvstv rechnoy minogi* (The Sense Organs of the River Lamprey) (1915); *Ocherki po filogenii ryb* (Studies on the Philogeny of Fish) (1944), etc; *Awards:* Order of the Red Banner of Labor; medals; *Died:* 26 Sept 1950.

TRET'YAKOV, Konstantin Nikolayevich (1892–1956) Neuropathologist; Dr of Med from 1919; prof from 1932; corresp member, USSR Acad of Med Sci from 1945; *Born:* 1892; Educ: 1919 grad Med Fac, Sorbonne Univ; *Career:* 1916–23 worked under P. Mari in Paris; 1919 defended doctor's thesis on pathological anatomy and clinical aspects of Parkinson's disease; 1926 returned to Russia; from 1932 head, Chair of Nervous Diseases, Saratov Med Inst; did research on histopathology of nervous system; devised "niger" theory of Parkinsonism; wrote some 100 works; *Publ:* doctor's thesis "Contribution à l'étude de l'anatomié pathologique du locus niger de Soemmering avec quelques déductions rélatives à la pathogenie des troubles du tonus musculaire et la maladie de Parkinson" (1919); ed and coauthor, *Trudy kafedry nervnykh bolezney Saratovskogo meditsinskogo instituta* (Transactions of the Chair of Nervous Diseases at Saratov Medical Institute) (1948); coauthor, *Nevralgii i ikh lecheniya* (Neuralgia and Its Treatment) (1949), etc; *Died:* 1956.

TRET'YAKOV, Sergey Mikhaylovich (1892–1939) Russian poet and publicist; *Born:* 8 June 1892 in Riga, *Educ:* 1915 grad Moscow Univ; *Career:* 1913 first work printed; Futurist poet, then active member, "LEF" lit group (so named after journal"Levyy front," edited by Mayakovskiy); from 1928 chief ed, journal "Novyy LEF," which advocated "lit of facts" and the "soc commission" theory in lit; *Publ:* verse collections *Itog* (The Sum Total) (1923); "Rechevik" (1929); historical novelette *Den'-Shi-Khua* (Teng Shi-hua) (1930); play *Rychi, Kitay* (Growl, China) (1932); essays *Lyudi odnogo kostrishcha* (People of One Campfire) (1936); *Strana-perekrest'ya* (The Crossroads Country) (1937), etc; *Died:* 9 Aug 1939.

TRIANDAFILLOV, Vladimir Kiriakovich (1894–1931) Mil commander and theorist; CP member from 1919; *Born:* 1894 in vil Magaradzhi, Kars Oblast (now Turkey), son of a peasant; *Educ:* 1924 grad Red Army Mil Acad; *Career:* capt, Russian Army; from July 1918 in Red Army; during 1918–20 Civil War commanded regt, then brigade on Eastern, Southern and Southwestern Fronts; 1923 grad Red Army Mil Acad; 1923–31 dept head, then chief, Operations Bd, Red Army Staff; commander and comr, infantry corps; dep chief of staff of Red Army; wrote several works on mil history and mil theory; *Publ: Razmakh operatsiy sovremennykh armiy* (The Scale of Operations of Modern Armies) (1925); *Kharakter operatsiy sovremennykh armiy* (The Nature of the Operations of Modern Armies) (1929), etc; *Awards:* Order of the Red Banner; *Died:* 1931 killed in plane crash.

TRIFONOV, Roman Maksimovich (1896–1966) Opera singer (bass); opera teacher; Pop Artiste of Uzbek SSSR from 1945; Pop Artiste of Azer SSR from 1958; *Born:* 24 July 1896; *Educ:* 1927 grad Saratov Conservatory; *Career:* 1928–30 soloist, Kiev State Opera Theater; 1931–36 at opera theaters in Saratov, Odessa and Sverdlovsk; 1936–40 at Kirov Opera and Ballet Theater, Leningrad; 1940–47 at Navoi Opera and Ballet Theater, Tashkent; from 1948 at Akhundov Opera and Ballet Theater, Baku; from 1940 taught at Tashkent Conservatory; from 1948 taught at Azer Conservatory; *Roles:* Suvorov in Vasilenko's "Suvorov"; Aleksandr Nevskiy in Taranov's *Ledovoye poboishche* (The Battle of the Ice); Boris and Varlaam in "Boris Godunov"; Dosifey in "Khovanshchina"; Kochubey in Tchaikovsky's "Mazepa"; Ibragim-khan in Gadzhibekov's "Ker-ogly", etc; *Died:* 5 Apr 1966.

TRIFONOV, V. A. (1888–1938) Govt and Party official; CP member from 1904; *Born:* 1888; *Career:* active in 1905–07 Revol; during 1917 Feb Revol secr, Bolshevik faction, Petrograd

Sov; comr for Vasiliy Ostrov, Petrograd Sov; helped prepare and carry out 1917 Oct Revol; Nov 1917-May 1919 member, Commission to Combat Counterrevol; member, All Russian Cheka; member, All-Russian Collegium for Organizing the Red Army; Collegium member, Pop Comrt of Mil Affairs; commander, Kama Naval Flotilla; member, Revol Mil Council, 3rd Army; from summer 1919 comr, Special Expeditionary Corps; member, Revol Mil Council, Southeastern and Caucasian Fronts; from June 1921 dep head, Main Fuel Bd; chm, Petroleum Syndicate; chm, Mil Collegium, Supr Court; from 1926 worked abroad, then chm, Main Concessions Comt, USSR Council of Pop Comr; arrested by State Security organs; *Died:* 1938 in imprisonment.

TRILISSER, Meyer Abramovich (1883– ?) Govt and Party official; CP member from 1901; *Born:* 1883; *Career:* from 1901 revol work in Odessa; 1902 arrested; member, Astrakhan', Samara, Kazan', Ural and Petersburg Party Comt; member, Centr Group of Mil Orgs in Finland; 1907 sentenced to five years at hard labor, which he served at Shlisselburg Fortress; 1914 exiled to Siberia; after 1917 Feb Revol secr, Irkutsk Sov; 1918 dep chm, Siberian Mil Comrt; member, Centr Siberian Comt; 1918–20 fought in Civil War in Siberia; 1920 member, underground centr operations staff in Blagoveshchensk; chm, Blagoveshchensk Oblast Revol Comt; 1921-26 head, For Dept, OGPU; from 1926 dep chm, OGPU; from Feb 1930 RSFSR Dep Pop Comr of Workers and Peasants' Inspection; at 15th and 16th Party Congresses elected member, CPSU(B) Centr Control Commission; from 1930 Presidium member, CPSU(B) Centr Control Commission; at 17th CPSU(B) Congress elected member, Sov Control Commission, USSR Council of Pop Comr; *Died:* date and place of death unknown.

TRINKLER Gustav Vasil'yevich (1876–1957) Inventor; specialist in internal-combustion engines; *Born:* 24 Apr 1876; *Educ:* 1894 entered Petersburg Technol Inst; *Career:* 1898, while still a student, devised a high-compression compressorless self-ignition internal-combustion engine; 1899 claimed and 1904 received patent license Nr 8766 for this engine; although the engine had been built and tested at the Putilov Plant (now Leningrad's Kirov Plant), he was not able to manufacture it in Russia; 1905 went to Germany, where his Trinkler engine was manufactured by the Kerting Plant; 1907–28 worked at Sormovo (now Red Sormovo) Plant; from 1934 prof, Gorky Inst of Water Transport Eng; *Publ: Dvigatelestroyeniye za polustoletiye* (Half a Century of Engine Building) (1958); *Died:* 4 Feb 1957.

TRIUMFOV, Aleksandr Viktorovich (1897–1963) Neuropathologist; prof; maj gen, Med Corps; corresp member, USSR Acad of Med Sci from 1951; *Born:* 1897; *Educ:* 1917 grad Petrograd Mil Med Acad; *Career:* after grad specialized in neuropathology at Chair of NervousDiseases, Petrograd Mil Med Acad; 1919–22 asst to V. M. Bekhterev; from 1923 asst to M. I. Astvatsaturova; 1931–38 head, Chair of Neuropathology, Novosibirsk Inst of Postgrad Med Training; during this period helped to organize neuropathological facilities in Kuznets Basin and West Siberian Kray; 1938–40 head, Chair of Nervous Diseases, 3rd Leningrad Med Inst; from 1940 head, Chair of Nervous Diseases, Leningrad Naval Med Acad, during WW 2 chief neuropathologist, Sov Navy; did research on typhic psychosis, deep abdominal reflexes and architectonics of peripheral nervous system; described sensation of "electr discharge" accompanying cerebral traumas; also studied neurological and morphological aspects of agranulocytic angina, morphological lesions of sympathetic ganglia and war trauma of nervous system; bd member, Leningrad Soc of Neuropathologists and Psychiatrists; member, ed council, State Med Publ House and "Zhurnal nevropatologii i psikhiatrii imeni S. S. Korsakova"; co-ed, neurology section, "Bol'schaya meditsinskaya entsiklopediya" (2nd ed); dep, Leningrad City Sov; wrote some 100 works; *Publ: Topicheskaya diagnostika zabolevaniy tsentral'noy nervnoy sistemy* (The Topic Diagnosis of Diseases of the Central Nervous System) (1943); *Nauchno-issledovatel'skaya rabota kafedry nervnykh bolezney za pyat' let, 1940–45* (The Research Work of the Chair of Nervous Diseases from 1940 to 1945) (1946); *Metastaticheskiye abstsessy mozga pri gnoynykh oslozhneniyakh raneniy lyogkikh* (Metastatic Brain Abscesses in Suppurative Complications of Lung Wounds) (1946); *Nekotoryye porazheniya nervnoy sistemy, soputstvuyushchiye ognestrel'nym raneniyam grudnoy kletki* (Injuries of the Nervous System Concomitant to Gunshot Wounds of the Thorax) (1946); Epilepsiya (Epilepsy) (1949); *Nekotoryye itogi opyta izucheniya boyevoy travmy i zabolevaniy nervnoy sistemy v period Velikoy Otechestvennoy voyny* (A Resumé of Experience in the Study of Battle Trauma and Diseases During the Great Fatherland War) (1950); *Ognestrel'nyye porazheniya mezhryobernykh nervov i grundibryushnogo nerva* (Gunshot Injuries of the Intercostal Nerves and the Phrenic Nerve) (1952); *Topicheskaya diagnostika zabolevaniy nervnoy systemy* (The Topic Diagnosis of Diseases of the Nervous System) (1959); *Awards:* Order of Lenin; Order of the Red Banner of Labor; Order of the Fatherland War; Order of the Red Star; medals; *Died:* July 1963 in Leningrad.

TROFIMENKO, Sergey Georgiyevich (1899–1953) Mil commander; col-gen; Hero of the Sov Union from 1944; CP member from 1918; *Born:* 5 Oct 1899 in Bryansk Oblast, son of an office worker; *Educ:* 1932 grad Frunze Mil Acad; 1937 grad Gen Staff Acad; *Career:* 1914–18 worker at Bryansk Station Locomotive Depot; from 1919 in Sov Army; fought in 1919–21 Civil War; 1939 took part in seizure of Western Ukr; fought in 1939–40 Sov-Finnish War; after 33 WW 2 senior sommands in Sov Army; dep, USSR Supr Sov of 2nd and 3rd convocations; *Awards:* three Orders of Lenin; other orders; madals; *Died:s, 16 Oct 1953.*

TROFIMOV, Vasiliy Mikhaylovich (1865–1926) Artillery and ordinance specialist; *Born:* 1865 in Kerch, son of a mil serviceman; *Educ:* 1892 grad Mikhail Artillery Acad, Petersburg; *Career:* from 1892 worked for Main Artillery Range and for Artillery, Comt, Main Artillery Bd; 1910 appointed chief, Main Artillery Range; from 1917 helped improve existing and develop new artillery pieses; 1919–24 worked on several important artillery theory works, including a study of external and internal ballistics and the design of new artellery systems; *Publ: O teoreticheskom opredelenii veroyatnykh otkloneniy otdel'nykh trayektoriy snaryadov ot sredney* (The Theoretical Determination of Individual Shell Trajectories' Probable Deviation from the Mean) (1895); *Deystviye shrapneli pri strel'be iz 3-dyuymovoy polevoy pushki* (The Effects of Shrapnel when Firing from a Three-Inch Field Gun) (1903); *Awards:* Gen Rasskazov Prize; Minor Mikhail Prize (1895); Grand Mikhail Prize (1903); *Died:* 1926.

TROITSKIY, Aleksey Alekseyevich (1866–1942) Chess master for composition studies; Hon Art Worker of RSFSR from 1928; *Born:* 1866; *Career:* forester by profession; from 1895 devised over 750 chess studies; founded the theory of modern chess studies; *Publ: Osnovnyye polozheniya iskusstva sostavleniya skakhmatnykh etyudov* (The Basic Principles of the Art of Compiling Chess Studies) (1910); *Sbornik shakhmatnykh etyudov* (A Collection of Chess Studies) (1934); *Died:* 1942.

TROTSKIY (real name: BRONSHTEYN), Lev Davidovich (1879–1940) Revolutionary; Party and govt official; opponent of Stalin; CP member from 1917; *Born:* 7 Nov 1879 in vil Yanovka, Kherson Province, son of a Jewish colonist; *Educ:* 1896 grad nonclassical college in Nikolayev; completed his educ by self-study; *Career:* 1897 co-founded and directed in Nikolayev Southern Russian Workers' Union; Jan 1898 arrested with other members of this group and exiled for four years to Verkholensk, Siberia; 1902 fled from exile and made his way to London, where he helped publish newspaper "Iskra", founded by Lenin together with Plekhanov and Martov; 1903 attended 2nd RSDRP Congress and sided with Menshevik faction, from which he soon dissociated himself, adopting a centrist stand in the RSDRP; Feb 1905 returned to Russia and lived in Kiev, then Petersburg; in Petersburg began to publish "Rabochaya gazeta" and then, together with Parvus, "Russkaya gazeta"; also collaborated with the Mensheviks and helped publish a joint organ, the newspaper "Nachalo"; instrumental in organizing Oct 1905 strike in Petersburg; member, then chm, Petersburg Sov of Workers' Dep; together with Parvus, developed theory of so-called permanent revolution, to which he subsequently also adhered; this theory foresaw the immediate and forcible development of a bourgeois-democratic revolution into a socialist revol and constant expansion of the latter on a global scale; Dec 1905, together with other members of Petrograd Sov, arrested and again exiled to Siberia; fled at Beryozovo, en route to Obdorsk, and again made his way abroad – this time to Vienna; 1908–12, together with A. Ioffe, published in Vienna newspaper "Pravda" and 1912 founded anti-Bolshevik "Aug Bloc"; 1912–13 mil corresp in Balkans for newspaper "Kiyevskaya mysl'"; with start of WW 1 lived in Switzerland, then in France; 1914 founded in France journal "Bor'ba"; 1915 attended Zimmerwald Conference, adopting centrist stand; as regards WW 1, rejected idea of defeatism and transition of this conflict into a civil war; 1916 deported from France to Spain, then made his way to America; after 1917 Feb

Revol returned to Petersburg and sided with "Mezhrayontsy" faction of RSDRP, midway between Bolsheviks and Mensheviks; at 6th RSDRP(B) Congress joined Bolshevik faction and was elected to CC, RSDRP(B); after Bolsheviks' July 1917 attempt to seize power, he was arrested by Provisional Govt but shortly released and was elected chm, Petrograd Sov of Workers and Soldiers' Dep; in this capacity, and as member, CC, RSDRP(B) and member, then chm, Mil Revol Comt, he played a key role in preparing and carrying out Oct 1917 Bolshevik coup; entered new Sov govt as Pop Comr of For Affairs but in connection with his stand at Brest peace talks of "neither war nor peace" he resigned from this post and in Feb 1918 appointed Pop Comr of Mil Affairs; later also appointed chm, Revol Mil Council; from 1922 Pop Comr of Mil and Naval Affairs and chm, Revol Mil Council; 1920–21 also ran Pop Comrt of Means of Communication; instrumental in organizing Red Army and in restoring navy, thus facilitating Bolsheviks' victory in Civil War; throughout this period Politburo member, CC, RCP(B) (CPSU/B/) and member, Comintern Exec Comt; throughout Lenin's illness and particularly after his death, in the course of the power struggle, came into conflict with Stalin, which led to the so-called opposition trend of "Trotskyism"; Jan 1925 dismissed as Pop Comr of Mil and Naval Affairs; fall 1926, as a further step in Stalin's campaign against the "Trotskyist Bloc," he was expelled from Politburo and Oct 1927 from CC, CPSU(B) and Comintern Exec Comt; Nov 1927 expelled from CPSU(B); Apr 1928 also expelled from USSR Centr Exec Comt; Jan 1928 exiled from Moscow to Alma-Ata; Feb 1929 deported from USSR to Turkey; 20 Feb 1932 USSR Centr Exec Comt decree deprived him of USSR citizenship; living abroad, Trotsky continued to campaign against Stalin and against Stalinism in the USSR and the int Communist movement; as a counterweight to the Comintern, he founded the independent 4th International; like Stalin, in this campaign he proceeded from Lenin's theoretical and practical legacy; ignoring his disagreements with Lenin in 1903–17; *Publ: Nasha revolyutsiya* (Our Revolution) (1906); *Perspektivy russkoy revolyutsii* (The Prospects of Russian Revolution) (1917); *Voprosy byta. Epokha "kul'turnichestva" i yeyo zadachi* (Problems of Living. The Age of "Culturalism" and Its Tasks) (1923); *1917 god. Uroki Oktyabrya* (The Year 1917. The Lessons of October) (1924); "Russland in der Revolution" (1909); "The Bolsheviks and World Peace" (1918); "The Real Situation in Russia" (1928); "Terrorismus und Kommunismus" (1929); "Main Leben. Versuch einer Autobiographie" (1930); "The History of the Russian Revolution" (3 vol, 1932); "Die permanente Revolution" (1930); "The Revolution Betrayed" (1937); "Stalins Verbrechen" (1937); "Stalin. Eine Biographie" (1952); "L' Internationale Communiste après Lénine, ou grand organisateur des défaites" (2 vol, 1969), etc; *Died:* 20 Aug 1940 killed in Mexico by a Stalinist agent.

TROTSKIY, Noy Abramovich (1895–1940) Architect; prof; *Born:* 1895; *Educ:* 1920 grad Architectural Fac, All-Russian Acad of Arts; later grad Petrograd's 2nd Polytech Inst; *Career:* after grad inst, worked for Monument Protection Dept; lived and worked mainly in Leningrad; participated in competitions for designing Leningrad Crematorium, apartment houses on Stachek Street, workers' settlements for Groznyy Oil Combine in Groznyy, Palace of Labor in Moscow (1923); designed a number of ind enterprises, designed House of Soviets in Leningrad's Kirov Rayon; co-designed House of Culture on Vasil'iy Island in Leningrad (1932); co-designed Kirov Monument on Kirov Square in Leningrad; submitted competition designs for the Murmansk House of Culture; House of Shock-Workers (1934); theater building in Minsk (1934); gen store in Leningrad (1934); Kuybyshev House of Culture; also participated in the closed competition for the USSR Acad of Sci building in Moscow (1934); together with M. V. Tomskiy, designed Lenin Lighthouse Monument for Leningrad Merchant Port and the Kirov Monument for the Leningrad Meat Combine; also directed construction of apartment houses and schools; his most outstanding work is the House of Soviets in Leningrad; also taught architecture; *Died:* 1940 in Leningrad.

TROYANKER, Benedikt Ustinovich (1900– ?) Sov Air Force polit commander; corps comr from 1935; CP member from 1917; *Born:* 1900; *Career:* 1917 took part in Oct Revol in Uman'; 1918 underground Party work in Ukr during German occupation; 1918–19 head, Agitation and Propaganda Dept, Vasiliy Ostrov Rayon RCP(B) Comt, Petrograd; secr, Vasiliy Ostrov Sov; 1919–21 regt Party organizer in campaign against Gen Yudenich; 1921 polit officer, Caucasian Red Banner Army; 1922–23 head, Polit Dept, Dag Brigade; comr, 13th Dag Infantry Div; 1923–29 worked for polit Bd, North Caucasian Mil Distr; 1929–32 dep head, Polit Bd, Bel Mil Distr; member, CC, CP(B) Bel; 1932–37 head, Culture and Propaganda Dept, Red Army Polit Bd; asst chief (polit), Red Army Air Force; head, Dept of Exec Polit Organs, Red Army Polit Bd; head; Polit Bd, Main Civil Aviation Bd; dep head, Main Civil Aviation Bd; 1937 member, Mil Council, Moscow Mil Distr; deleg at 15th and 16th CPSU(B) Congresses; 1937 arrested by NKVD; *Awards:* Order of the Red Star; *Died:* in imprisonment; posthumously rehabilitated.

TROYANOVSKIY, Aleksandr Antonovich (1882–1955) Diplomat; CP member 1904–17 and from 1923; *Born:* 1882 in Tula, son of an officer; *Educ:* completed mil educ; *Career:* from 1903 mil service; 1902 joined revol movement; 1907–08 twice arrested by Tsarist authorities; 1909 exiled to vil Bel'skoye, Yeniseysk Province; 1910 fled abroad, joined Bolshevik for org; 1912 RSDRP CC deleg member at Basel Congress; attended 1912 Cracow Conference of CC, RSDRP and State Duma members; 1913 attended Poronin Conference; 1917 returned to Russia; 1917–21 member, RSDRP (Mensheviks); 1918–21 in Red Army; simultaneously worked for Main Records Bd; 1921–24 with Workers and Peasants' Inspection; 1924 appointed chm, State Trade Comt and Collegium member, Pop Comrt of For Trade; 1927–33 USSR amb to Japan; took part in Sov-Japanese negotiations on the sale of the Chinese-Eastern Railroad, conclusion of an non-aggression treaty, etc; early 1933 appointed dep chm, USSR Gosplan; Nov 1933, after reestablishment of US-Sov dipl relations; appointed USSR amb to Washington; held this post until 1939; then returned to USSR and engaged in lit and teaching work; taught at Higher Dipl School, Min of For Affairs; from 1941 worked for Sov Information Bureau; wrote a number of works on for policy; *Died:* 23 June 1955.

TROYANOVSKIY, Boris Sergeyevich (1883–1951) Balalaika virtuoso; composer; *Born:* 3 Apr 1883 in vil Rugodevo, Pskov Province; *Career:* 1904–11 soloist, V. V. Andreyev's orchestra; 1908–15 gave concerts in England, Germany, USA, France, Sweden, etc; 1919 together with P. I. Alekseyev founded concert ensemble in Moscow (now Osipov State Pop Orchestra); his concerts helped popularize instrumental folklore; *Works:* arranged for balalaika and piano Liszt's 2nd Rhapsody, Rimsky-Korsakov's "Spanish Capriccio", and Sarasate's fantasia on themes of Bizet's "Carmen"; wrote a suite for balalaika on Russian themes; arrangements of Russian folk songs, etc; *Died:* 2 June 1951 in Leningrad.

TRUBLAINI (real name: TRUBLAYEVSKIY), Nikolay Petrovich (1907–1941) Ukr writer; *Born:* 25 Apr 1907 in vil Vil'shantsy, now Vinnitsa Oblast, son of a lumberjack; *Educ:* studied on All–Ukr Journalism Courses, run by CC, CP(B) Ukr in Khar.kov; *Career:* member, "Molodnyak" lit org; corresp for various newspapers and journals; traveled extensively, particularly in the Arctic; sponsored various children's and youth organizations; 1924 first work printed; *Publ:* incorporated his experiences in various travel notes: *Do Arktyky cherez tropiky* (To the Arctic Via the Tropics) (1931); *Lyudyna pospishaye na pivnich* (Man Hastens North) (1931); *Na pivnochi* (In the North) (1933); *Litke-peremozhets' kryhy* (Litke, Conqueror of the Ice) (1933); *Kursom nord-ost* (Course Northeast) (1933); *Radyans'kyy prapor nad polyusom* (The Soviet Flag at the Pole) (1937); stories: *Volod'ka - rybalka* (Volod'ka the Fisherman); *Bereh nevydomoho ostrova* (The Shore of an Unknown Island); *Lovy biloho vedmedya* (Hunting the Polar Bear); *Volokha* (The Moldavian); *Vovky honyat'sya za olenyamy* (Wolves Chasing Deer); *Pohonych blakitnoho kyta* (Hunting the Blue Whale); *Morem plyv tyulen'* (The Seal Sails the Seas); *Khata na kryzi* (The House on the Ice); *Malyy poslanets'* (The Little Messenger); *Kryla rozhevoi chayky* (The Wings of the Pink Seagull); novelettes: "Lakhtak" (1935); *Mandrivnyky* (The Travelers) (1938); *Shkhuna* (Schooner); *Kolumb* (Columbus) (1940); sci fiction novel *Hlybynnyy shlyakh* (The Deep Road); unifinished novelette *Orlyni hnizda* (Eagle's Eyries) (1941); *Died:* 5 Oct 1941 in action in WW 2.

TRUSEVICH, Boris Ippolitovich (1892–1961) Therapist; member, Bel Acad of Sci from 1956; prof from 1934; Hon Sci Workers of Bel SSR from 1946; *Born:* 5 Aug 1892; *Educ:* 1916 grad Med Fac, Kiev Univ; *Career:* 1918–20 intern, Clinic of Internal Diseases, Kiev Univ; 1920–28 physician at various Rostov-on-Don med establishments; 1928–34 asst prof, then assoc prof, Minsk Med Inst; 1934–61 also head, Chair of Fac Therapy, Minsk Med Inst; co-ed, internal diseases section, 2nd ed of "Bol'shaya meditsinskaya entsiklopediya" (Large Medical Encyclopedia); member, ed council, journals "Klinicheskaya meditsina" and "Terapevticheskiy arkhiv"; member, ed bd, Bel journal "Zdravookhraneniya"; devised methods of palpating the lesser curvature of the stomach and the pancreas and a new technique for palpating the kidneys; invented continuous percussion of the thorax; devised method of determining diastolic murmur in the cases of insuffiency of the aorta valves at the so-called sixth point; proposed methods of diagnosing dry and moist rales and for detecting the sound of pleural and pericardial friction; wrote works on clinical and experimental med, internal pathology and infections and improvements in physical methods of treating patients; *Publ: Vliyaniye khinina na razlichnyye uzly serdtsa* (The Effects of Quinine on Various Cardiac Nodes) (1933); *Vliyaniye vagotropnykh yadov na iskusstvennuyu zheludochkovuyu ekstrasistoliyu* (The Effects of Vagotropic Poisons on Artificial Ventricular Extrasystolia) (1934); *Materialy k probleme ostroy sosudistoy nedostatochnosti (Ostryy zastoy v vorotnoy sisteme)* (Material on the Problem of Acute Vascular Insufficiency /Acute Infacction of the Portal System/) (1950); coauthor, *Sbornik klinicheskikh retseptov* (A Compendium of Clinical Prescriptions) (2nd ed, 1954); coauthor, *Vliyaniye nervnoy sistemy na sakharnuyu krivuyu* (The Effects of the Nervous System on the Sugar Graph) (1957); *Awards:* Order of the Red Banner of Labor (1961); other orders; medals; *Died:* 14 Nov 1961 in Minsk.

TRUSH, Ivan Ivanovich (1869–1941) Painter and art critic; *Born:* 17 Jan 1869 in vil Vysotskoye, now L'vov Oblast, son of a peasant; *Educ:* 1891–97 studied under Ya. Stanislavskiy at Cracow Acad of Arts; *Career:* began as landscape painter, then turned to portraiture; portrayed leading Ukr cultural figures; 1898 founded Assoc for the Development of Russian Art; 1905 founded Assoc of Devotees of Ukr Lit, Sci and Art; 1899 founded journal "Buduchnist'"; 1905 founded journal "Artystychnyy vistnyk"; 1939 founded "L'vov Branch, Ukr Artists' Union; 1905 sponsored in L'vov first All-Ukr art exhibition at which works from both Western and Eastern Ukr were displayed; taught at Murashko Art School, Kiev; *Works:* portraits: Ivan Franko (1897); V. Stefanyk (1897); Lesya Ukrainka (1900); N. Lysenko (1900); landscapes of Dnieper area, Carpathians, Crimea, Italy, Egypt and Palestine; many genre paintings depicting the life of the Hutsuls; wrote lit and lit critical studies; "Vasyl' Stefanyk" (1899); "Can We Have Art? " (1899); "The Exhibition of Ukrainian Artists" (1905) "Ivan Franko and Our Society" (1912); "The Art and Life of Shevchenko" (1914); *Died:* 22 Mar 1941.

TRUSHKOV, Nikolay Il'ich (1876–1947) Mining eng; specialist in working and assaying of ore deposits; Hon Sci and Tech Worker of RSFSR from 1945; *Born:* 28 Apr 1876; *Educ:* 1900 grad Petersburg Mining Inst; *Career:* 1900–02 at Donets Basin mines; from 1902 at Ural mines; 1918–20 and 1925–47 prof, Leningrad Mining Inst; in the Ural mines used square-frame timbering for shoring and devised an original method of ore storage; instituted valuable courses on working and assaying ore deposits; *Publ: Ekspertiza rudnykh mestorozhdeniy* (Assaying Ore Deposits) (1934–35); *Bureniye pri razrabotke rudnykh mestorozhdeniy* (Drilling in Working Ore Deposits) (1937); *Razrabotka rudnykh mestorozhdeniy* (Working Ore Deposits) (1946–47); *Awards:* Order of Lenin, Order of the Red Banner of Labor; medals; *Died:* 26 May 1947.

TRUTNEV, Vasiliy Kuz'mich (1892–1960) Otolaryngologist; Hon Sci Worker of RSFSR; *Born:* 1892; *Educ:* 1916 grad Med Fac, Saratov Univ; *Career:* after grad remained at univ and worked for M.F. Tsytovich's Chair of Otolaryngology; 1924 defended doctor's thesis on "Simptom Kerniga pri zabolevaniyakh nosa, gorla i ushey" (Koernig's Symptom in Diseases of the Ear, Nose and Throat); from 1925 head, Chair of Ear, Nose and Throat Diseases, Kazan Univ; from 1926 also head, Chair of Ear, Nose and Throat Diseases, Inst of Postgrad Med Training; from 1940 head, Chair of Otolaryngology, Centr Inst of Postgrad Med Training; from 1943 dir, Moscow Ear, Nose and Throat Diseases Research Inst; head, Chair of Otolaryngology, Moscow Stomatological Inst; devised methods of tracheobronchoscopy; studied pathology of the mastoid process and the clinical aspects of latent and other atypical forms of mastoiditis; made a detailed study of mastoiditis of fusospirillum etiology; for many years chief otolaryngologist of RSFSR Min of Health; bd member, Moscow Sci Soc of Otolaryngologists; member, Learned Med Council, RSFSR Min of Health; member, ed bd, journal "Vestnik otorinolaringologii"; hon member, All-Union, Kazan, Saratov and Perm Sci Soc of Otolaryngologists; wrote over 80 research works; *Publ: Trakheobronkhoskopiya* (Tracheobronchoscopy) (1952); *Trakheotomiya* (Tracheotomy) (1954); *Awards:* two Orders of Lenin; medals; *Died:* Dec 1960 in Moscow.

TSAGOLOV, Georgiy Aleksandrovich (1897–1919) Party official; CP member from 1916; *Born:* 1897 in settlement Digora (former Vol'no-Khristianskoye), North-Ossetian ASSR (former Terek Oblast), son of a priest; *Educ:* 1916 grad Vladikavkaz high school; studied at Law Fac, Moscow Univ; *Career:* Feb-Mar 1917 revol activities in Moscow; Apr 1917 returned to Vladikavkaz; polit propaganda among workers at Alagir Plant, railroad car repair shops, etc; directed Bolshevik take-over of Ossetian Revol Workers' Parth "Kermen"; late 1917 elected chm, Kermen CC; Dec 1917 deleg, Caucasian Kray Congress in Tiflis; chm, Caucasian Front Revol Mil Council in Sarakamysh; then Party work in Baku; sent to Northern Caucasus to figth counterrevol elements; directed formation of Kermen mil detachments; member, Terek Oblast Pop Sov; chm, Ossetian Revol Mil Council; helped organize defense of Vladikavkaz; *Died:* 29 Apri 1919 killed by White Army forces; streets in Ordzhonikidze (former Vladikavkaz) and Digora have been named for him; novels, novelettes, verse and studies were written about him.

TSANDER, Fridrikh Arturovich (1887–1933) Rocket eng; *Born:* 23 Aug 1887 in Riga, son of a physician; *Educ:* 1914 grad Riga Polytech Inst; *Career:* 1914–19 with Riga "Provodnik" Plant; from 1919 with Moscow "Motor" Plant; designed airplane jet engines, liquid fuel rocket engines, rockets and rocket planes; his rocket engine was tested 1930–32; wrote a number of works on theory of jet engines and space rockets; *Died:* 28 Mar 1933.

TSAREVSKIY, Mikhail Mikhaylovich (1898–1963) Mil commander; maj-gen, Eng and Tech Corps; CP member from 1917; *Born:* 19 Mar 1898; *Career:* from 1918 in Sov Army; from 1925 engaged in civil eng; directed construction of Gorky Automobile Plant, Nizhniy Tagil Steel Plant and other major ind projects in the Urals and Siberia; *Awards:* Hero of Socialist Labor; *Died:* 29 July 1963.

TSERETELI, Irakliy Georgiyevich (1882–1959) Politician; Menshevik; *Born:* 1882; *Career:* 1902 exiled to Eastern Siberia for involvement in student polit movement; 1903 returned from exile to Tiflis and edited Geo journal "Kvali"; member, 2nd State Duma; leader, Soc-Democratic faction; after dissolution of Duma on 3 June 1907 he was brought to trial together with entire faction and sentenced to penal servitude in Siberia; 1912 released for Siberian settlement; finally freed by 1917 Feb Revol; returned to Petrograd to head RSDRP (Mensheviks); member, Exec Comt, All-Russian Centr Exec Comt of 1st convocation; Min of Posts and Telegraphs in first coalition Provisional Govt; after 1917 Oct Revol led anti-Sov bloc in Cinstituent Assembly; leader, Geo Mensheviks and member, Geo Govt; 1921 emigrated; represented Geo Soc-Democratic Party in Int Socialist Bureau; member, Exec Comt, 2nd International; in his latter years lived in USA; *Died:* 1959.

TSEREVITINOV, Fyodor Vasil'yevich (1874–1947) Organic chemist; specialist in chemistry and technol of food products; Hon Sci and Tech Worker of RSFSR from 1935; *Born:* 24 July 1874; *Educ:* grad Moscow Higher Tech College; *Career:* 1899–1930 prof, Moscow Higher Tech College; 1908–47 simultaneously prof, Moscow Business Inst (then Plekhanov Inst of Nat Econ); 1921–37 prof, Moscow's Timiryazev Agric Acad; developed organic magnesium method of determining mobile hydrogen atoms in organic compounds (Tserevitinov-Chugayev method); did research on chemical composition of fruits and vegetables and chemical processes during ripening and storing of fruits and vegetables; developed methods of processing fruits and vegetables; devised ind method of obtaining pectin; *Publ: Osnovy plodovogo i yagodnogo vinodeliya* (The Principles of Wine-Making from Fruits and Berries) (1906); *Khimiya i tovarovedeniye svezhikh plodov i ovoshchey* (Chemistry and the Storage of Fresh Fruits and Vegetables) (3rd ed, 1949); *Awards:* Order of Lenin; *Died:* 10 June 1947.

TSINTSADZE, K.M. (1887–1930) Govt official; CP member 1904–27; *Born:* 1887; *Career:* Party work in Tiflis, Kutaisi, Batumi and Baku; after establishment of Sov regime in Geo chm, Geo Cheka; member, CC, CP(B) Geo; member, Geo Centr Exec Comt; *Died:* 1930.

TSINZERLING, Vsevolod Dmitriyevich (1891–1960) Pathoanatomist; corresp member, USSR Acad of Med Sci; *Born:* 1891 in Petersburg; *Educ:* studied at Mil Med Acad but expelled for participation in student riots; grad Med Fac, Yur'yev (Tartu) Univ;

Career: 1914–17 mil surgeon in Russian Army; from 1920 asst prof, then assoc prof, Chair of Pathoanatomy, 1st Leningrad Med Inst; 1921–37 assoc, Dept of Pathoanatomy, then laboratory head, Inst of Experimental Med; 1941–45 chief pathoanatomist of Leningrad Front; from 1943 head, Dept of Pathoanatomy, Leningrad Health and Hygiene Med Inst; member, Leningrad Sci Soc of Pathoanatomists; also secr, bd member and chm of this soc; specialized in atherosclerosis, infectious diseases and wartime pathology; *Publ: O nachal'nykh stadiyakh eksperimental'nogo kholesterin-esterovogo ozhireniya* (The Initial Stages of Experimental Cholesterin Ester Obesity) (1922); *Patologicheskaya anatomiya i etiologiya ateroskleroza na osnovanii issledovaniya detskikh aort* (The Pathological Anatomy and Etiology of Atherosclerosis on the Basis of a Study of Children's Aortas) (1922); *K ucheniyu o skarlatine* (The Theory of Scarlatina) (1935); *Sravnitel'no-morfologicheskiye issledovaniya po patologii arteriy* (Comparative Morphological Research on the Pathology of Arteries) (1935); *Voprosy patologicheskoy anatomii pnevmoniy* (The Pathological Anatomy of Pneumonia) (1951); coauthor and ed, *Pnevmonii* (Pneumonia) (1958); coauthor, *Angionevroz konechnostey (tak nazyvayemyy "obliteriruyushchiy endarterit") i mesto yego sredi drugikh bolezney sosudistoy sistemy* (Angioneurosis of the Extremities [So-Called "Obliterating Endarteritis"] and Its Place Among Other Diseases of the Vascular System) (1959); coauthor, *Patologicheskaya anatomiya ostrykh pnevmoniy raznoy etiologii* (The Pathoanatomy of Acute Pneumonia of Various Etiology) (1963); *Died:* 16 Feb 1960 in Leningrad.

TSIOLKOVSKIY, Konstantin Eduardovich (1857–1935) Sci and inventor; *Born:* 17 Sept 1857 in vil Izhevskoye, now Ryazan' Oblast, son of a forester; *Educ:* self-taught; *Career:* almost completely lost hearing as a result of a serious childhood illness; 1879 passed teachers' examinations after correspondence study course; 1880–92 taught arithmetic; geometry and physics at Borovsk Uyezd College, Kaluga Province; from 1892 taught at Kaluga High-School and Kaluga Eparchial College; did research on three basic problems: sci principles for designing an all-metal dirigible airship (1885–92); design of a streamlined airplane (research published 1894); interplanetary rockets (from 1896); developed jet flight theory; 1883 mooted possibility of using jet-propulsion for aviation; 1903 in the article *Issledovaniye mirovykh prostranstv reaktivnymi priborami* (Exploring Cosmic Space by Jet-Propelled Instruments) advanced theory of rocket flight, calculating the changes in the rocket's mass during its motion; substantiated the feasibility of using jet-propulsion devices for interplanetary flight; here and in his subsequent articles described theoretical principles of a liquid-fueled jet engine and explained its basic design; 1929 advanced a theory of multi-stage rockets or rocket trains; solved the problem of rocket motion in a homogeneous gravitational field and calculated the fuel needed to overcome the Earth's gravity; his studies on interplanetary flight gave sci proof of the possibility of achieving cosmic speed; examined the problem of launching a rocket into orbit as an artificial Earth satellite; raised the idea of setting up extraterrestrial way stations as staging bases for interplanetary travel, etc; also did research on aerodynamics, philosophy, linguistics; wrote works on soc system of a people living on artificial islands orbiting the Sun between Mars and Earth; in the USSR he is venerated as the founder of interplanetary flight theory, rocketry and modern space flight; *Publ: Izbrannyye trudy* (Selected Works) (2 vol, 1934); *Trudy po raketnoy tekhnike* (Works on Rocketry Engineering) (1947); *Izbrannyye trudy* (Selected Works) (1962); *Awards:* Order of the Red Banner of Labor (1932); *Died:* 19 Sept 1935 in Kaluga.

TSITOVICH, Ivan Sergeyevich (1876–1955) Physiologist and pharmacologist; Hon Sci Worker of RSFSR from 1940; *Born:* 1876; *Educ:* 1903 grad Mil Med Acad; *Career:* 1903–07 surgeon in Warsaw Mil Distr; from 1908 asst prof, Chair of Physiology, Petersburg Women's Med Inst; 1911 defended doctor's thesis; from 1917 prof of physiology, Tiflis Med Inst; 1919–55 head, Chair of Pharmacology, Rostov Med Inst; from 1928 also dept head, Rostov of Inst of Labor Protection; began research in Pavlov's laboratory; 1902 studied effects of pylocarpine on the secretion of the gastric glands; 1902 studied effects of alcohol on gastric secretion, a research work which won a Mil Med Acad prize; founded a new trend in pharmacology – age-group pharmacology; established a relation between age groups and pharmacodynamics of narcotics, analeptics, gastro-intestinal drugs, cardiac glucosides, etc; studied balneological factors and pharmacological plants of Northern Caucasus; wrote over 140 research works; *Publ: Proiskhozhdeniye i obrazovaniya natural'nykh uslovnykh refleksov* (The Derivation and Formation of Natural Conditioned Reflexes) (1911); *Sbornik zadach po fiziologii (A Compendium of Physiological Problems) (1913); Vliyaniye atsetona na tsentral'nuyu nervnuyu sistemu* (The Effect of Acetone on the Central Nervous System) (1935); coauthor, *Fiziologiya v opytakh* (Physiology in Experiments) (1952); *Died:* 1955 in Rostov-on-Don.

TSIVTSIVADZE, Il'ya Venediktovich (1881–1941) Party and govt official; CP member from 1903; *Born:* 1881; *Career:* Founded illegal printing houses in Batumi and Tiflis; late 1904 arrested; Oct 1905 released under amnesty; worked for Imeretiya-Guriya Party Comt; 1906–08 ed, Bolshevik newspaper "Dor"; held various posts with Transcaucasian Party org; late 1911 active in the so-called Tver' Bolshevik Group in Moscow; 1915 arrested and exiled to Irkutsk Province; Mar 1917 returned to Moscow; Party work in Moscow's Zamoskvorech'ye Rayon; during 1917 Oct Revol one of staff chiefs for Zamoskvorech'ye Rayon; chm, Investigating Commission; dep chm, Moscow Revol Tribunal; Presidium member and mang, Moscow Sov; member, All-Russian Centr Exec Comt of several convocations; at 8th Party Congress elected member, Centr Auditing Commission; 1921–22 mang, Geo Council of Pop Compr; dep chm, Tiflis Exec Comt; 1922–29 dep head, Moscow Communal Econ Dept; 1929 dep chm, Moscow Oblast Workers and Peasants' Inspection; 1930–31 chm, Moscow Meat Ind Comt; 1931–34 head, Moscow Oblast Road Transport Commission; from 1934 dir, Special Tech Bureau; *Died:* 1941.

TSKHAKAYA, Mikhail Grigor'yevich (Party names: MIKHA; BARSOV; LEONOV; GURGEN) (1865–1950) Professional revolutionary; govt official; CP member from 1898; *Born:* 4 May 1865 in vil Khuntsi, now Geo SSR; *Educ:* studied at secondary school; *Career:* from 1880 in revol movement; while still at secondary school conducted revol propaganda and organized Marxist circles among urban workers, farm laborers and poor peasants; 1888 propaganda work in Tiflis, Baku, Batum and Kutaisi; 1897 expelled from Caucasus for five years; 1898–1900 Party work in Khar'kov and Yekaterinoslav; 1900 arrested in Yekaterinoslav and in 1902 exiled to his place of birth under police suveillance; fled ent went underground; helped lead, Caucasian Joint RSDRP Comt; 1903 helped prepare 2nd RSDRP Congress but could not attend congress since he was engaged in organizing gen strike in Caucasus; 1905 helped prepare and attended 3rd RSDRP Congress; as the senior ranking deleg, opened first meeting of 3rd RSDRP Congress; 1906 arrested and interned in Metekhi Prison, Tiflis; 1907 deleg at 5th (London) Party Congress; 1907–17 lived in Geneva; after 1917 Feb Revol returned to Russian together with Lenin; then went to Caucasus to strengthen Bolshevik comts; 1917–20 member, Tiflis Party Comt; June 1919 arrested and jailed in Kutaisi Prison; May 1920 released; from Feb 1921, after establishment of Sov regime in Geo, exec Sov and Party posts; 1921–22 Geo SSR plen in RSFSR; chm, Transcaucasian SFSR Centr Exec Comt; chm, Geo Centr Exec Comt; member, CC, CP(B) Geo; deleg at11th;13th, 15th and 16th Party Congresses; attended all Comintern Congresses (except 1st); member, Comintern Exec Comt; from 1931 Presidium member, International Control Commission; dep, USSR Supr Sov of 1st-3rd convocations; *Awards:* Order of Lenin (1944); *Died:* 19 Mar 1950; buried in Tbilisi.

TSULUKIDZE, Aleksandr Petrovich (1888–1967) Urologist; Dr of Med from 1925; prof from 1930; corresp member, USSR Acad of Med Sci from 1945; member, Geo Acad of Sci from 1955; Hon Sci worker of Geo SSR from 1941; CP member from 1946; *Born:* 1888 in Geo; *Educ:* 1913 grad Med Fac, Khar'kov Univ; *Career:* 1913–14 health officer in Gunib, Dag; 1914–15 chief surgeon on a field surgery train, Southwestern Front; 1916–18 intern, Surgical Dept, Tiflis Field Hospital, League of Cities; 1919–20 senior asst, Chair of Gen Surgery, Tiflis Univ; 1921–26 senior asst, 1926–27 lecturer, Chair of Hospital Surgery, Tiflis Univ; 1923–24 and 1926 underwent specialist training in Austria, Germany and France; 1927–30 head Urological Dept, Tiflis 1st City Hospital; 1928–30 assoc prof and head, Chair of Operative Surgery, Tbilisi Med Inst and Inst of Postgrad Med Training, where he also read a course on urology; 1930–35 head Chair of Surgery, Stomatological Fac and Fac of Child and Mother Care, Tbilisi Med Inst; 1935 attended 16th German Congress of Urologists, Hamburg; 1935–53 heas, Chair of Surgery and dir, Tbilisi Inst of Postgrad Med Training; 1941–45 member, Evacuation Hospital Bd, Geo Pop Comrt of Health. 1953–59 founder-head,Chair of

Urology, Tbilisi Inst of Postgrad Med Training; from 1959 founder-dir, Urological Research Inst; Geo Acad of Sci; hon member and bd member, All-Union and Geo Soc of Urologists; hon chm, Tbilisi Soc of Urologists; bd member, All-Union Soc of Surgeons; co-ed, urology section, "Bol'shaya meditsinskaya entsiklopediya" (2nd ed); wrote over 130 works; *Publ: Urologiya. Kratkoye rukovodstvo. Obshchaya chast'* (Urology. A Short Manual. General Section) (1936); *Vrachi-gruziny XIX stoletiya* (Georgian Physicians of the 19th Century) (1948); "Urology" (in Geo, 1952); *Khirurgicheskiye zabolevaniya mochevykh i polovykh organov* (Surgical Diseases of the Urinary and Genital Organs) (1955); *Ocherki operativnoy urologii* (Studies in Operative Urology) (1955); coauthor, *Vyklyucheniye i udeleniye mochevogo puzyrya* (Bypassing and Removing the Urinary Bladder) (1957); *Klinicheskiye materialy mochekamennoy bolezni* (Clinical Material on Bladderstones) (1958); coauthor, *Rukovodstvo po khirurgii* (A Surgery Manual) (vol 10, 1959); *Osnovy urologicheskoy khirurgii* (The Principles of Urological Surgery) (1962), etc; *Awards:* Order of Lenin, two Orders of the Red Banner of Labor; two Orders of the Red Star; three medals; *Died:* Sept 1967.

TSVETYAEV, Vyacheslav Dmitriyevich (1893–1950) Mil commander; col-gen; CP member from 1943; *Born:* 5 Jan 1893 in Maloarkhangel'sk, now Orel Oblest, son of an office worker; *Educ:* 1916 grad ensigns' school; *Career:* fought in WW 1 and Civil War; during WW 2 commanded army operations group; dep commander, 1st Bel Front; then commanded various armies; from 1945 dep commander in chief, then commander in chief, Southern Forces Group; from 1948 commandant, Frunze Mil Acad; *Awards:* Hero of the Sov Union; two Orders of Lenin; other orders; medals; *Died:* 11 Aug 1950.

TSVETAYEVA, Marina Ivanovna (1892–1941) Russian writer and poetess; *Born:* 26 Sept 1892 in Moscow, daughter of a prof of philology; *Career:* 1910 first work printed; turned to playwriting after joining a circle of young people which was later developed into the 3rd Studio, Moscow Arts Theater under the direction of Ye. B. Vakhtangov; 1922–39 lived abroad; 1939 returned to USSR; under Stalin her works were not published in the USSR; it was only after Stalin's death that her poems and some of her prose were published; some of her verse and prose works have never been published in the USSR; translated works of Slavic poets, including Ivan Franko, Lesya Ukrainka, etc; *Publ:* verse collection *Vecherniy al'bom* (Evening Album) (1910); verse plays: "Fortuna" (1919); *Kamennyy angel* (The Stone Angel) (1919); trilogy on Casanova – *Metel* (The Blizzard) (1918); *Priklyucheniye* (The Adventure) (1919); *Feniks (Konets Kazanovy)* (Phoenix /The End of Casanova/) (1919); *Versty* (Milestones) (1922); "Ariadna" (1924); *Fedra* (Phedra) (1927); collection *Svetovoy liven'* (Downpour of Light); *Iskusstvo pri svete sovesti* (Art in the Light of Conscience); *Toska za rodinoy* (Homesickness); *Stikhi k synu* (Poems to My Son) (1932); cycle of anti-fascist verse *Sentyabr* (September) and *Mart* (March) (1938–39); *Died:* 31 Aug 1941 committed suicide.

TSVILLING, Samuil Moiseyevich (1891–1918) Party official; CP member from 1905; *Born:* 1891 in Tobol'sk; *Career:* spent his childhood in Omsk, where at the age of 15 he joined the revol movement; spring 1906 arrested for distributing leaflets and collecting funds for RSDRP; exiled to Tomsk, where he led a battle squad for local RSDRP comt; Oct 1907 rearrested and sentenced to four years' imprisonment; served this term in Tomsk and Tobol'sk prisons, then sent by Party to Southern Urals, where he helped direct Chelyabinsk, then Orenburg RSDRP(B) org; deleg at 6th RSDRP(B) Congress; after 1917 Ovt Revol was first chm, Orenburg Mil Revol Comt; *Died:* 2 Apr 1918 killed in battle at vil Izobil'naya, Orenburg Province.

TSYURUPA, Aleksandr Dmitriyevich (1870–1928) Party and govt official; CP member from 1898; *Born:* 1 Oct 1870 in Aleshki (now Tsyurupinsk), Tavrida Province, son of a city admin official; *Educ:* grad Aleshki Municipal College; from 1886 studied at agric college in Kherson; *Career:* from 1890 active in revol circles; 1893 arrested and spent six months in prison, followed by four years' police surveillance; after release from prison carried out revol propaganda and helped found new revol circle in Kherson; 1895 re-arrested; from 1896 worked for zemstvo statistical dept in Simbirsk and Ufa; 1897–1901 in Ufa directed group of Iskra supporters, then Bolsheviks, including Sviderskiy, Popov, the Boykovs, Velichkina, etc; also made the acquaintance of Lenin and Krupskaya; 1901 moved to Khar'kov and joined Khar'kov Party Comt; late 1901 moved to Tula to evade police pursuit and continued Party work until his arrest in 1902; 1903, after five months' imprisonment, exiled to Olonets Province; 1905 returned from exile to Ufa Province and worked as agronomist; during 1905–07 Revol active in Ufa RSDRP(B) Org; after 1917 Feb Revol member, Ufa Joint RSDRP Comt, then member, Ufa RSDRP(B) Comt; member, Ufa Sov of Workers and Peasants' Dep; chm, Ufa Province Food Comt; spokesman for Ufa Province and Uyezd Zemstvo; chm, reorganized Ufa City Duma; during 1917 Oct Revol member, Ufa Mil Revol Comt; Nov 1917 summoned by Party CC to Petrograd; Nov 1917 appointed Dep Pop Comr of Food; from early 1918 Pop Comr of Food; during Civil War directed food supply to Red Army; late 1921–1928 dep chm, Council of Pop Comr and Labor and Defense Council; 1922, after abolition of Pop Comrt of Food, appointed Pop Comr of Workers and Peasants' Inspection; 1923 chm, USSR Gosplan; 1925 appointed Pop Comr of Domestic and For Trade; from 1922 also Presidium member, All-Russian Centr Exec Comt; from 1923 Presidium member, USSR Centr Exec Comt; at 12th–15th Party Congresses elected member, CC, CPSU(B); *Died:* 8 May 1928 in Crimea.

TSYURUPA, G.D. (1885–1940) Electr eng; *Born:* 1885; *Career:* 1919–26 chief eng at construction of Kashira State Distr Electr Power Plant; from May 1921 dep chm, Main Comt of State Structures; 1925–29 chm, Bd, Electr Construction Trust and Bd member, Power Construction Trust, All-Russian Sovnarkhoz; then exec admin work; *Died:* 1940.

TUAYEV, David Afanas'yevich (1903–1964) Ossetian playwright; Hon Art Worker of North Ossetian ASSR from 1955; *Born:* 15 Oct 1903; *Career:* electr eng in Rostov-on-Don at Sadon mines; from 1941 playwright; his plays staged at Geo, Tatar and Kabardian theaters; *Publ:* plays "The Mother of Orphans" (1941); "The Crazy Shepherd" (1941); comedy "The Memorialists" (1942); plays based on Ossetian epic themes: "Tatarkhan's Family" and "Nart Syrdon" (1943); musical comedy "The Heart's Desire" (1944); children's play "The Fairy-Tale" (1945); plays: "Fatima Kharzoyeva" and "By the White Mountain" (1945); "Kosta" (1959); "Your Acquaintances" (1963); "Two Sons" (1964), etc; *Died:* 3 Aug 1964.

TUBEL'SKIY, Leonid Davydovich (1905–1961) Russian playwright; *Born:* 11 Apr 1905; *Career:* journalist; 1923 began lit work in cooperation with P. L. Ryzhei under the pseudonym "Tur Brothers"; also wrote in coauthorship with L. Sheynin; *Publ:* coauthor of plays: *Neft'* (Oil) (1930); *Zemlya i nebo* (Earth and Sky) (1932); *Vostochnyy batal'on* (Eastern Battalion) (1935); *General'nyy konsul* (Consul-General) (1939); *Ochnaya stavka* (Confrontation) (1938); *Neravnyy brak* (Mesalliance) (1941); *Poyedinok* (The Duel) (1944); *Komu podchinyayetsya vremya* (Whom Time Obeys) (1946); *Gubernator provintsii* (Governor of the Province) (1947); *Osobnyak v pereulke* (The Mansion in the Alley) (1949); *Tret'ya molodost'* (Third Youth) (1952); *Koleso schast'ya* (Wheel of Fortune) (1955); *Pobeg iz nochi* (Escape from the Night) (1958); *Severnaya madonna* (The Northern Madonna) (1961), etc; *Died:* 14 Feb 1961.

TUCHAPSKIY (MIKHAYLOVICH), P.L. (1869–1922) Politician; *Born:* 1869; *Career:* from 1893 in revol movement; did lit work; worked for Kiev newspaper "Rabochaya gazeta" and various illegal Soc-Democratic periodicals; member, Kiev League for the Liberation of the Working Class; 1898 attended 1st RSDRP Congress; 1903, after the schism in the RSDRP, sided with Bolsheviks; attended 4th (Amalgamative) RSDRP Congress; in 1910's broke with Bolsheviks and abandoned active polit work; during 1917 Revol member, RSDRP (Mensheviks); 1917 ed, Odessa Menshevik newspaper "Yuzhnyy rabochiy"; 1918–19 worked for Odessa Province Union, 1921–22 chm, Council of Old Revolutionaries, Commission for the Study of Revol Archives, Odessa Province Law Dept; 1921 invited by Ukr Acad of Sci to Kiev where he worked as librarian, Ukr Acad of Sci; also did lit work; *Died:* 1922.

TUGAN–BARANOVSKIY, Mikhail Ivanovich (1865–1919) Economist; *Born:* 1865 in Ukr; *Educ:* grad Physics and Mathematics Fac and Law Fac, Khar'kov Univ; *Career:* teaching and research work; prominent rep of "Legal Marxism," then a "critic" of Marxism; during 1905–07 Revol joined Constitutional-Democratic Party; 1917–18 Min of Finance, Ukr Centr Rada; then abandoned politics and concentrated on teaching and research work at Kiev Univ and Ukr Acad of Sci; rated a leading expert on history of Russian econ; in his books and articles on polit econ attacked Marxist theories and proceeded from standpoint of so-called

"Austrian school"; *Publ: Zh. Prudon. Yego zhizn'i obshchestvennaya deyatel'nost'* (Pierre Joseph Proudhon. His Life and Social Work) (1891); *D.S. Mill', yego zhizn' i uchyono-literaturnaya deyatel'nost'* (John-Stuart Mill. His Life, Teaching and Writings) (1892); *Promyshlennyye krizisy v sovremennoy Anglii, ikh prichiny i vliyaniye na narodnuyu zhizn* (The Industrial Crises of Modern England, Their Causes and Effects an Public Life) (1894); *Russkaya fabrika v proshlom i nastoyashchem* (The Russian Factory Past and Present) (vol 1, 1898); *Zemel'naya reforma* (Land Reform) (1905); *Teoreticheskiye osnovy marksizma* (The Theoretical Principles of Marxism) (1905); *Sovremennyy sotsializm v svoyom istoricheskom razvitii* (Modern Socialism in Its Historical Development) (1906); *Osnovy politicheskoy ekonomii* (The Principles of Political Economy) (1909); *Sotsial'naya teoriya raspredeleniya* (The Social Theory of Distribution) (1913); *Ocherki iz noveyshey istorii politicheskoy ekonomii i sotsializma* (An Outline Modern History of Political Economy and Socialism) (7th ed, 1919); *V poiskakh novogo mira* (In Search of a New World) (2nd ed, 1919); *Bumazhnyye den'gi i metall* (Paper Money and Metal) (1919); *Sotsializm, kak polozhitel'noye ucheniye* (Socialism as a Positive Teaching) (1918); *Politicheskaya ekonomiya* (Political Economy) (1919); *Died:* 1919.

TUGANOV, Aleksandr Aleksandrovich (1871–1960) Actor, stage dir and drama teacher; Pop Artiste of Azer SSR from 1936; *Born:* 19 Mar 1871; *Career:* 1878 acted with amateur dramatic company in Moscow; for 10 years worked at Korsh Theater in Moscow and at theaters throughout European Russia and Siberia; from 1915 dir, Tiflis Theater of Assoc of Artists of the Russian Theater Soc; from 1924 dir and chief stage dir, Azizbekov Theater and Gorky Young Playgoers' Theater, Baku; from 1945 head, from 1947 prof, Chair of Acting, M. A. Aliyev Azer Theatrical Inst; *Roles:* Chatskiy; Hamlet; Petruccio in "Taming of the Shrew"; *Productions: Revizor* (The Government Inspector) (1924); *Na dne* (The Lower Depths) (1925); Schiller's "Wilhelm Tell" (1925); Moliére's "Don Juan" (1926); "Seville" (1928); "Almas" (1931); *Nevesta ognya* (Bride of Fire) (1928); Glebov's "Zagmuk" (1929); "Macbeth" (1936); "Romeo and Juliet" (1937); *Ne bylo ni grosha, da vdrug altyn* (From Rags to Riches) (1941), etc; *Died:* 6 Mar 1960.

TUGARINOV, Ivan Ivanovich (1905–1966) Dipl; amb extraordinary and plen; *Born:* 1905; *Educ:* 1948 grad Higher Party School, CC, CPSU; *Career:* from 1948 in dipl service; 1948–60 dep head, then head, Bd, USSR Min of For Affairs; 1960–63 head, Far Eastern Dept and Collegium member, USSR Min of For Affairs; 1963–66 USSR amb to the Netherlands; *Died:* 1966.

TUKHACHEVSKIY, Mikhail Nikolayevich (1893–1937) Mil commander; lt, Russian army; Marshal of the Sov Union from 1935; CP member from 1918; *Born:* 3 Feb 1893 on Aleksandrovskoye Estate, son of a nobleman and a peasant woman; *Educ:* 1914 grad Alexandrine Mil College; *Career:* 1914–15 as officer, Semyonov Guards Regt fought in WW 1; decorated with six mil orders, 1915 taken prisoner by Germans; three times attempted to escape and for this confined in Ingolstadt Fortress; 1917 escaped and returned to Russia; 1917–18 elected company commander, Semyonov Guards Regt; from 5 Apr 1918 in Red Army; 1918 instructor, Mil Dept, All-Russian Centr Exec Comt; mil comr for defense of Moscow Distr, Western Flank; 26 June 1918 appointed commander, 1st Revol army on Eastern Front which he reorganized into a regular army; for the first time in Soc Republ drafted former officers into Red Army; Aug 1918 his army launched an offensive and drove White and Czechoslovak troops from Simbirsk, Syzran', Samara and Belebey; Dec 1918-Jan 1919 dep commander, Southern Front; Jan-Mar 1919 commander, 8th Army on Southern Front; 23 Mar 1919 appointed commander, 5th Army on Eastern Front; his army drove Admiral Kolchak's troops from Buguruslan, Bugul'ma, Zlatoust and Omsk; 22 Dec 1919 appointed commander, 13th Army on Southern Front; 31 Jan 1920, before he could assume this command, appointed commander, Caucasian Front; his troops attacked and routed Gen Denikin's forces in Tikhoretsk sector; 29 Apr 1920 appointed commander, Western Front; 4 July 1920 began Igumensk–Minsk offensive against Polish troops, which developed later into Warsaw offensive; 12 Aug 1920 his forces reached Warsaw but then for various objective reasons (troop fatigue, over-extension of communication and supply lincs, Stalin's disastrous transfer of 1st Mounted Army to the Western Front to reinforce its flank) were routed and had to retreat to Sov territory; 5 Mar 1921 appointed acting commander, 7th Army simultaneously retaining command of Western Front; 17 Mar 1921 units of this army took by assault Kronstadt naval fortress which had rebelled under the slogan "Soviet Rule Without the Communists"; Apr 1921 appointed commander, Tambov Province forces, still retaining command of Western Front; May 1921 his forces defeated the main force of Antonov's rebel armies; 5 Aug 1921–24 Jan 1922 commandant, Red Army Mil Acad; 24 Jan 1922–1 Apr 1924 again commander, Western Front; member, Bel Centr Exec Comt and member, CC, CP(B) Bel; 1 Apr 1924–17 Feb 1925 dep chief of staff, Red Army; 17 Feb–13 Nov 1925 commander, Western Mil Distr; 1924–34 member, USSR Revol Mil Council; 13 Nov 1925–5 May 1928 chief of Red Army Gen Staff; Dec 1927 wrote to Stalin stressing necessity of rearming Red Army with modern planes, armor and automatic weapons; 5 May 1928–19 June 1931 commander, Leningrad Mil Distr; from 19 June 1931 dep chm, USSR Revol Mil Council and Red Army chief of munitions; from 21 June 1934 USSR Second Dep Pop Comr of Defense; Feb 1936 visited England and France; 9 Apr 1936–11 May 1937 USSR First Dep Pop Comr of Defense and head, Mil Training Bd, Red Army; 11 May 1937 appointed commander, Volga Mil Distr; 1934–37 cand member, CC, CPSU(B); 26 May 1937 arrested in Kuybyshev by State Security; 11 June 1937, together with I. E. Yakir, I. P. Uborevich and other mil commanders, sentenced to death by Special Session of USSR Supr Court; his wife, mother, sisters and brothers were then also arrested; his mother, sister Sof'ya and brothers Nikolay and Aleksandr were executed; three sisters survived concentration camps; his daugher, who was put in a concentration camp after reaching maturity, also survived; *Publ: Strategiya natsional'naya i klassovaya* (National and Class Strategy) (1920); *Pokhod za Vislu* (The Vistula Campaign) (1923); *Voprosy vysshego komandovaniya* (Problems of the Supreme Command) (1924); *Voprosy sovremennoy strategii* (Problems of the Modern Strategy) (1926); *Voyna kak problema vooruzhonnoy voyny* (War as a Problem of Armed Conflict) (1928); *Novyye voprosy voyny* (New Problems of Warfare) (1932); *Voyennyye plany nyneshney Germanii* (The Military Plans of Contemporary (Germany) (1935), etc; *Awards:* Order of Lenin; Order of the Red Banner, hon golden arms; *Died:* executed in the night of 11/12 June 1937; posthumously rehabilitated.

TULAYKOV, Nikolay Maksimovich (1875–1938) Agronomist; prof from 1920; member, USSR Acad of Sci from 1932; member, All-Union Acad of Agric from 1935; CP member from 1930; *Born:* 7 Aug 1875 in vil Akshut, now Ul'yanovsk Oblast, son of a peasant; *Educ:* 1901 grad Moscow Agric Inst; *Career:* 1910–16 dir, Bezenchuk Agric Experimental Station; 1920–25 assoc, from 1925 dir, Saratov Agric Experimental Station; from 1929 dir, All-Union Agric Research Inst; studied pedology, agronomy, plant-growing, tillage systems and plant physiology; opposed Acad Vil'yams' grass-arable system and advocated reclamation of Virgin Lands; *Awards:* Lenin Prize (1929); *Died:* 20 Jan 1938.

TULEBAYEV, Mukan Tulebayevich (1913–1960) Composer; music teacher; Hon Art Worker of Kaz SSR from 1945; Pop Artiste of USSR from 1959; CP member from 1956; *Born:* 28 Feb 1913 in vil Karachigan, now Kaz SSR; *Educ:* 1951 grad N. Myaskovskiy and V. Fere's composition class, Moscow Conservatory; *Career:* from 1953 taught at Alma Ata Conservatory; 1956–60 chm, Kaz Composers' Union; dep, Kaz Supr Sov of 1955 and 1959 convocations; *Works:* symphonic ocerture (1943); coauthor, opera "Amangel'di" (1944); helped compose music for State Anthem of Kaz SSR (1945); opera "Birzhan and Sara" (1946); cantata "The Fires of Communism" (1951); poem for violin and piano; fantasia on Kaz folk themes; choral works; songs; romances, etc; *Awards:* Order of the Fatherland War, 2nd Class; Stalin Prize (1949); *Died:* 2 Apr 1960 in Alma Ata.

TULUB, Zinaida Pavlovna (1890–1964) Ukr writer; *Born:* 28 Nov 1890 in Kiev; *Educ:* 1913 grad Kiev Higher Women's Courses; *Career:* wrote in Ukr and Russian; 1910 first work published; wrote novels, plays, filmscripts and translations from Russian into Ukr and vice versa; *Works:* novelette *Na rasput'ye* (At the Crossroads) (1916); novels – *Lyudolovy* (Manhunters) (1934–37); *Za bortom* (Overboard) (1962); "Sagaydachnyy" (1962); *V stepi beskonechnoy za Uralom* (In the Endless Steppe Beyond the Urals) (1964); *Died:* 26 Sept 1964.

TULUPOV, Aleksandr Vasil'yevich (1886–1967) Govt official; CP member from 1905; *Born:* 29 Aug 1886; *Career:* active in revol movement; began work at age 14 as laborer in Kursk factories; 1917–54 worked for rail transport system; frequently arrested for revol activities; 1917–18 Presidium member and chm, Kursk Mil Revol Comt; 1918–19 comr, Kursk Railroad Depot and chm,

Kursk Transport Section Cheka; 1919–20 head, Southern Front Cheka; then admin work with rail transport; from 1944 pensioner; *Died:* Apr 1967.

TUMANOV, N.G. (1887–1936) Govt official; CP member from 1917; *Born:* 1887; *Career:* 1922–23 Collegium member, RSFSR Pop Comrt of Finance; then Transcaucasian SFSR Pop Comr of Finance and member, Transcaucasian SFSR Centr Exec Comt; in his latter years chm, Bd, USSR State Bank; Presidium member, Gosplan and Spur Sovnarkhoz; USSR trade rep in France; head, USSR Ind Bank; *Died:* 1936.

TUMANYAN, Mikhail Galustovich (1886–1950) Plant breeder, geneticist and selectionist; member, Arm Acad of Sci from 1943; Hon Sci Worker of Arm SSR from 1935; CP member from 1945; *Born:* 28 Feb 1886; *Educ:* 1911 grad Moscow Univ; 1914 grad Moscow Agric Inst; *Career:* from 1923 head, from 1926 prof, Chair of Phytoculture, Yerevan Univ (then Arm Agric Inst); 1943–49 dir, Inst of Agric, Arm Acad of Sci; 1943–45 acad secr, Dept of Agric Sci, Arm Acad of Sci; specialized in field crops, especially Arm and Transcaucasian wheats; devised principle of zoning local ancient varieties of wheat and studied patterns of formation development in wheat; *Publ: Karlikovyye pshenitsy Armenii* (The Dwarf Wh ats of Armenia) (1928); *Botanicheskiy sostav dikikh pshenits Armenii i usloviya ikh proizrastaniya v prirode* (The Botanical Properties of Armenian Wild Wheats and the Conditions of Their Natural Growth) (1934); *Rol' pyl'noy golovni v formoobrazovanii pshenits i yeyo znacheniye dlya selektsii* (The Role of the Pollen Head in the Formation of Wheat and Its Importance in Selection) (1941); *Proiskhozhdeniye pshenitsy Persicum* (The Origin of Persicum Wheat) (1944); *Opredelitel' khlebnykh zlakov (kolosovyye)* (A Key to Cereals) (1933); *Awards:* two orders; medals; *Died:* 1950.

TUMUNOV, Zhamso Tumunovich (1916–1955) Buryat writer; CP member from 1939; *Born:* 5 Feb 1916 in vil Tabtanay, now Chita Oblast, son of a cattle-breeder; *Educ:* 1951 grad Higher Party School, CC, CPSU(B); *Career:* late 1930's began lit work; works deal with Civil War in Transbaykal Region, socialist changes in Mongolia and deeds of the Buryat people during WW 2; *Publ:* play "Sesegma" (1938); collected poetry, poems and stories "Eagle of the Steppes" (1945); poem "Sukhe-Bator" (1946); novels "The Wide Steppes" (1949); "Golden Rain" (1955), etc; *Died:* 12 Jan 1955.

TUNKEL', David Vladimirovich (1905–1966) Stage dir; Hon Art Worker of RSFSR from 1954; *Born:* 29 Mar 1905; *Educ:* 1927 grad Theater School at Revol Theater; *Career:* 1936–66 at Centr Red (now Sov) Army Theater; also worked at Moscow Variety and Miniatures Theater and Moscow Satirical Theater; specialized in modern plays; *Works:* co-directed plays: Sukhovo-Kobylin's *Delo* (The Case) (1940); Trenyov's *Polkovodets* (The Commander) (1945); staged plays: *Na vsyakogo mudretsa dovol'no prostoty* (There's a Simpleton in Every Sage) (1941); Lavrenyov's *Za tekh, kto v more!* (For Those at Sea!) (1947); Prut's *Tikhiy okean* (The Pacific Ocean) (1949); *Varvary* (The Barbarians) (1955); Dürrenmatt's "Die Physiker" (1965); Sobko's *Za vtorym frontom* (Behind the Second Front) (1949); Baratashvili's *Strekoza* (The Dragon-Fly) (1953); Makayonka's *Izvinite, pozhaluysta* (Excuse Me, Please) (1954); Smirnov's *Krepost' nad Bugom* (Fprtress Over the Bug) (1956); Shtok's *Karavan* (The Caravan) (1957); Shtok's *Yakornaya ploshchad'* (The Anchorage) (1960); V. Tur's *Boy s ten'yu* (Fight with a Shadow) (1966); Dykhovichnyy and Slobodskoy's *Klyaksy* (Blots) (1959); Dykhovichnyy, Slobodskiy and Chervinskiy's "Guriy L'vovich Sinichkin" (1963); Larin's *Chetvyortyy pozvonok* (The Fourth Vertebra) (1961), etc; *Died:* 18 June 1966.

TUNKEL', Vul'f Isaakovich (1884–1940) Actor, stage dir and impressario; CP member from 1920; *Born:* 1884; *Career:* 1907–19 actor, stage dir and impressario in Khar'kov, Simferopol, Lugansk, Vladikavkaz and Stavropol', etc; 1920–39 with CC, Art Workers' Union; mustered companies for provincial theaters; 1939 dir, Centr Theatrical Library, Moscow; *Died:* 4 Aug 1940.

TUNTUL, I.Ya. (1892–1938) Party official; CP member from 1907; *Born:* 1892; *Career:* Party Work in Lat and Urals; deleg at 6th RSDRP(B) Congress; after 1917 Oct Revol exec Party and govt work; 1921, at 10th RCP(B) Congress, elected member, CC, RCP(B); at 14th CPSU(B) Congress sided with "New Opposition"; 1928 expelled from Party for membership of Trotskyist opposition; later reinstated; 1935 again expelled from Party for alleged anti-Party activities; arrested by State Security organs; *Died:* 1938 in imprisonment.

TURCHANINOVA, Yevdokiya Dmitriyevna (1870–1963) Actress; Pop Artiste of USSR from 1943; *Born:* 14 Mar 1870 in Moscow; *Educ:* 1891 grad Moscow Theatrical College; *Career:* from 1891 with Maly Theater; *Roles:* Tanya in Lev Tolstoy's *Plody prosveshcheniya* (The Fruits of Englightenment); Ul'yana, Poliksena and Barabosheva, and Lel' in Ostrovskiy's *Voyevoda* (The Provincial Governor), *Pravda khorosho, a schast'ye luchshe* (Truth Is Good, But Happiness Is Better) and *Snegurochka* (The Snow Maiden); Mariya Antonovna and the Matchmaker in Gogol's *Revizor* (The Government Inspector) and *Zhenit'ba* (Marriage); Gornostayeva in Trenyov's *Lyubov' Yarovaya*; Motilkova in Gusev's *Slava* (Glory); Bogayevskaya in Gorky's *Varvary* (The Barbarians); Madame Grandet in "Eugene Grandet", after Balzac, etc; *Awards:* two Stalin Prizes (1943 and 1948); two Orders of Lenin; Order of the Red Banner of Labor; *Died:* 27 Dec 1963.

TURENKOV, Aleksey Yevlampiyevich (1886–1958) Composer; Hon Art Worker of Bel SSR from 1939; *Born:* 21 Jan 1886 in Petersburg; *Educ:* 1914 grad A.K. Lyadov and N.A. Sokolov's Composition Class, Petersburg Conservatory; *Career:* 1919–34 teacher in Mogilyov and Gomel'; then composer in Minsk; works are based on Bel folklore and folk songs; *Works:* operas "Flower of Happiness" (1940); "Clear Dawn" (1958); ballet "A Forest Tale" (1952); „Belorussian Suite" (1933); cantatas; choral works; romances; arrangements of Bel folk songs; *Died:* 27 Sept 1958 in Minsk.

TURNER, Genrikh Ivanovich (1858–1941) Orthopedic surgeon; Hon Sci Worker of RSFSR from 1927; founder of first Russian orthopedic school and pioneer of children's orthopedics service in Russia; *Born:* 29 Oct 1858 in Petersburg; *Educ:* 1881 grad Petersburg Acad of Med and Surgery; *Career:* after grad worked at K.K. Reyyer's Surgical Clinic, then in Surgical Dept, Obukh Hospital; 1892 defended doctor's thesis on "The Anatomy of the Caecum and the Vermiform Appendix in Relation to the Pathology of Peritiphlitis"; 1894 assoc prof, from 1895 prof, of clinical surgery, Chair of Desmurgy and Mechanurgy, Mil Med Acad; 1900 reorganized this chair into Russia's first Chair and Clinic of Orthopedics, which he directed until his death; campaigned for regular state aid for crippled children; sponsored foundation of Leningrad Children's Orthopedics Inst; did valuable research on the orthopedic treatment of the sequelae of infantile paralysis and tuberculosis of the bones and joints; the Clinic of Orthopedics now bears his name; Hon member, Pirogov Surgical Soc, Russian Surgical Soc in Moscow and a number of for sci soc; founded Leningrad Soc of Orthopedic Surgeons and was elected its first chm; wrote some 400 sci works; *Publ: o lechenii rubtsovykh suzheniy pishchevoda* (The Treatment of Scar Stricture of the Oesophagus) (1890); doctor's thesis *K anatomii slepoy kishki i chervebraznogo otrostka v otnoshenii k patologii peritiflita* (The Anatomy of the Caecum and the Vermiform Appendix in Relation to the Pathology of Peritiphlitis) (1892); *Rukovodstvo k nalozheniyu povyazok* (A Bandaging Manual) (1899); *O lechenii neoslozhnennykh perelomov kostey konechnostey* (Treating Simple Fractures of the Extremities) (1907); *Mysli o lechenii perelomov* (Ideas for the Treatment of Fractures) (1927); *Izbrannyye proizvedeniya* (Selected Works) (1958); *Died:* 1941 in Leningrad.

TURSUN, Parda (1909–1957) Uzbek writer; CP member from 1946; *Born:* 1909 in vil Charkisar, now Ferghana Oblast, son of a peasant; *Educ:* studied at Centr Asian Econ Planning Inst; *Career:* worked as teacher; 1932 first work printed; *Publ:* collected stories "Violence" (1932); novelettes "The True Road" (1945–47); "The Teachers' Path" (1949); novel "The Teacher" (1952); *Died:* 20 Sept 1957.

TURSUNKULOV, Khamrakul (1892–1965) Uzbek Kolkhoz official; chm, "Shark yulduzi" Kolkhoz, Yangiyul' Rayon, Tashkent Oblast from 1935; hon member, Uzbek Acad of Agric from 1957; member, CC, CP Uzbek from 1954; CP member from 1946; *Born:* 1892 in vil Vuadil', now Fergana Oblast; *Educ:* grad elementary school; *Career:* until 1917 hired farm hand; from 1917 fought with partisans in Fergana Oblast; from 1921 chm, Vuadil' Vil Sov; from 1922 chm, volost exec comt; 1927–29 water management tech, Alty-Arak Rayon, Fergana Oblast; 1931–35 dir ected, sovkhoz in Tadzh; dep, USSR Supr Sov of 1946, 1950, 1954, 1958 and 1962 convocations; 1958–62 Presidium member, USSR Supr Sov; *Awards:* thrice Hero of Socialist Labor (1948, 1951 and 1957); seven Orders of Lenin; two Orders of the Red Banner of Labor; medals; *Died:* 9 Aug 1965.

TURUSBEKOV, Dzhusup (1910–1944) Kir playwright and poet; CP member from 1930; *Born:* 24 Dec 1910 in vil Kum-Batysh, now Kir SSR; *Publ:* collection "Dzhusup's Verse" (1932); musical drama "Not Death, But Life" (1934); drama "The Besh-Moypok Case" (1937); coauthor, libretto for opera "Aychurek" (1939); his lyric verse "The Red Kerchief" and "The Black-Eyed Girl" were turned into pop songs; during WW 2 wrote patriotic verse "Lenin's Path", "My Beloved", etc; translated Pushkin's *Kamennyy gost'* (The Stone Guest) into Kir; *Died:* Apr 1944 killed in action during WW 2.

TURZHANSKIY, Leonid Viktorovich (1875–1945) Landscape painter; *Born:* 30 Sept 1875; *Educ:* 1909 grad Moscow College of Painting, Sculpture and Architecture; studied under K. Korovin and V. Serov; *Career:* 1904–11 exhibitor, from 1911 member, Assoc of Itinerant Art Exhibitions; member, Russian Painters' Union; member, Russian Painters' Assoc; many of his works are displayed at Moscow's Tret'yakov Gallery; *Works:* paintings: "The North. A Quiet Evening" (1905); "Gulls. Kama" (1909); "Early Spring in the Urals" (1914); "Under the Barn" (1916); "Quiet Evening" (1925); "Spring" (1928); "New Sverdlovsk" (1937), etc; *Died:* 31 Mar 1945.

TUSHINSKIY, Mikhail Dmitriyevich (1882–1962) Therapist, clinician, hematologist and infectionist; Dr of Med from 1922; prof from 1930; member, USSR Acad of Med Sci from 1945; CP member from 1945; *Born:* 1882 in Petersburg; *Educ:* 1907 grad Petersburg Mil Med Acad; *Career:* 1907–24 therapist and infectionist, then head, Therapeutic Dept, Obukh Hospital, Petersburg; 1914–17 mil surgeon at various hospitals; 1922–24 asst prof, 1924–30 assoc prof, Therapeutic Clinic, Leningrad Med Inst; 1930–62 head, Chair of the Propaedeutics of Internal Diseases, Leningrad Med Inst; 1934–41 consultant at mil hospitals; 1942–50 chief therapist, Leningrad City; together with G.A. Ivashentsov and M.A. Zhitkov devised method of intravenous injection of saline solutions as part of cholera treatment; first Sov therapist to treat lung gangrene with neosalvarsan; from 1934 studied influenza and influenzal pneumonia, formulating their clinical description and classification; proved experimentally that influenza is infectious; together with A.A. Smorodintsev studied active and passive influenza immunization; described the Bittof-Tushiniskiy phenomenon, the "granulous smear" symptom and blood pictures of various internal and infectious diseases; first Sov therapist to apply antidotes against poisoning by heavy metals; co-ed, "Internal Diseases" section, "Bol'shaya meditsinskaya entsiklopediya", 2nd ed; member, ed council, journal "Terapevticheskiy arkhiv"; consultant, Leningrad City Health Bd; hon member, All-Union Therapists Soc; wrote over 100 sci works, dealing with clinical aspects and bacteriology of cholera, typhus, dysentery, Botkin's disease, study of blood picture and hematogenic organs in the case of infection; *Publ:* doctor's thesis *Nablyudeniya nad svoystvami spinomozgovoy zhidkosti i krovi u sypnotifoznykh bol'nykh* (Observations on the Properties of the Spinal Fluid and Blood of Typhus Patients) (1922); *Pervaya pomoshch' pri ostrykh otravleniyakh* (First Aid in Cases of Acute Poisoning) (1939); *Boleznis organov dykhaniya* (Diseases of the Respiratory Organs) (1940); *Bolezni sredosteniya* (Mediastinum Diseases) (1940); *Bolezni sistemy krovi* (Diseases ot the Blood System) (1940); coauthor, *(A Course on Acute Infectious Diseases) (1951);* coauthor, *Bolezni sistemy krovi* (Diseases of the Blood System) (1959); coauthor, *Bolezni sistemy dykhaniya* (Diseases of the Respiratory System) (1960); *Died:* 6 Jan 1962.

TUSHNOV, Mikhail Pavlovich (1879–1935) Microbiologist and pathophysiologist; member, All-Union Lenin Acad of Agric Sci from 1935; *Born:* 24 May 1879; *Educ:* 1902 grad Kazan' Veterinary Inst; *Career:* after grad served in Russian Army and took part in Russo-Japanese War; 1905–11 lecturer, from 1911 prof, Chair of Microbiology, Kazan' Veterinary Inst; 1923–28 prof, Kazan' Physicians Inst; 1929–35 head, Laboratory for the Study of Lysates, All-Union Inst of Experimental Med, Leningrad; 1932–35 also prof, Moscow Zooveterinary Inst; then prof, Chair of Microbiology and Pathophysiology, Moscow Veterinary Acad; specialized in methods of preparing organic drugs (histolysates) and the indications and counter-indications for their use in treating diseases of farm animals; 1926–28 developed the theory of the action of histolysates (the products of the artificial break-down of tissue) on animals and man; hyothesized that animal histolysates could be used for treating various diseases on the grounds that such treatment would restore normal metabolism; did valuable research on spermotoxins, which contributed to the knowledge of cytotoxins and cytotoxic stimulation; wrote some 50 research works; *Publ:* thesis *Deystviye spermotoksinov na organizm samki i yaytso* (The Effects of Spermotoxins on the Female and on the Egg) (1911); *K ucheniyu o spermotoksinakh* (The Theory of Spermotoxins) (1911); *Natural'nyye kletochnyye yady* (Natural Cellular Toxins) (1931); *Problemy spermotoksinov i lizatov* (Problems of Spermotoxins and Lysates) (1938); *Died:* 19 Sept 1935.

TUSKIYA, Iona Irakliyevich (1901–1963) Composer; music teacher; Pop Artiste of Geo SSR from 1962; CP member from 1949; *Born:* 11 Dec 1901 in Ozurgeti; *Educ:* 1926 grad M.M. Ippolitov-Ivanov's composition class and M. Vasil'yev's violin class, Tiflis Conservatory; 1931 grad Leningrad Conservatory; *Career:* 1922 co-founder, Geo Young Musicians Soc; from 1932 instructor, from 1947 prof, 1952–61 rector, Tbilisi Conservatory; 1935–37 chm, Geo Composers' Union; *Works:* music for films and shows: "Lamara" (1926), after Vazha Pshavela; *Razlom* (Break-Up) (1928); Dadiani's "Tetnul'd" (1931); Kldiashvili's "Autumn Nobility" (1936); "Othello" (1937); *Chelovek s ruzh'yom* (The Man with a Gun) (1939); opera *Rodina* (Homeland) (1941); music for films: V. Solov'yov's *Velikiy gosudar'* (Grand Sovereign) (1945); Dolidze's "Eagles' Nest" (1948); symphonic pictures; string quartet; violin sonata; romances, songs, etc; *Died:* 8 Oct 1963 in Paris.

TUTKOVSKIY, Pavel Apollonovich (1858–1930) Geologist and geographer; member, Ukr Acad of Sci from 1918; member, Bel Acad of Sci from 1928; *Born:* 1 Mar 1858 in vil Lipovtsy, Vinnitsa Oblast; *Educ:* 1882 grad Kiev Univ; *Career:* 1884–95 custodian, Mineralogical and Geological Study Centers, Kiev Univ; from 1904 taught at secondary schools in Kiev; inspector and dir of public colleges in Ukr; from 1914 prof, Kiev Univ; from 1919 chm, Physics and Mathematics Dept, Ukr Acad of Sci; from 1924 head, Chair of Geological Research, Ukr Acad of Sci (later reorganized into Inst of Geological Sci, Ukr Acad of Sci); founded Geological Museum at this inst; specialized in mineralogy, petrography, dynamic and historical geology and paleontology; did noteworthy research on Quaternary geology and geomorphology; advanced theory of sol origin of loess; pioneered micropaleontological method of studying sedimentary rocks; 1895 proposed project for artesian water supply of Kiev, later put into effect; *Publ: K voprosu o mekhanizme obrazovaniya sloistikh vulkanov* (The Mechanism for the Formation of Stratified Volcanoes) (1893); *K voprosu o sposobe obrazovaniya lyossa* (The Mechanism for the Formation of Loess) (1899); *"Polesskaya bezvalunnaya oblast". – Yeyo osobennosti i prichiny yeyo vozniknoveniya* (The "Polessian Boulderless Region", Its Features and the Causes of Its Formation) (1900); *Piramidal'nyye valuny na Yuzhnom Poles'ye* (Pyramidal Boulders of Southern Polessie) (1903); *Iskopayemyye pustyni Severnogo Polushariya* (Desert Fossils of the Northern Hemisphere) (1909), etc; also wrote textbooks on mineralogy and geography; *Died:* 3 June 1930.

TVALCHRELIDZE, Aleksandr Antonovich (1881–1957) Mineralogist; member, Geo Acad of Sci from 1941; CP member from 1941; *Born:* 30 Nov 1881; *Educ:* 1912 grad Moscow Univ; *Career:* from 1919 prof, Tbilisi Univ; from 1929 head, Geo Branch, All-Union Inst of Mineral Raw Materials (now Caucasian Inst of Mineral Raw Materials); from 1941 chm, Council for the Study of Production Resources), Geo Acad of Sci; specialist in mineralogy and petrography of Geo; 1916 discovered Gumbrin deposits, then studied Gumbrin, Askana and other deposits of bleaching clays and helped develop ind exploitation of these clays; wrote a number of textbooks in Russian and Geo; *Publ: K mineralogii Batumskogo kraya* (The Mineralogy of Batum Kray) (1912); *Floridinovyye i bentonitovyye gliny zapadnoy Gruzii* (The Floridine and Bentonite Clays of Western Georgia) (1933); "Introduction to Crystal Optics" (1938); *Gliny otbelivayuhchiye* (Bleaching Clays) (1941); "The Petrography of Magnetic Rocks" (1950); *Awards:* two Orders of Lenin; three other orders; medals; *Died:* 29 July 1957.

TVERETSKIY, Pyotr Vasil'yevich (1900–1963) Opera producer; Hon Art Worker of Azer SSR from 1940; *Born:* 29 June 1900; *Career:* from 1918 at Saratov Pop Opera Studio, then with Opera Company, Polit Dept, North Caucasian Mil Distr; from 1922 with Tiflis Opera Theater, then with Paliashvili Opera and Ballet Theater; 1925–59 producer, Akhundov Opera and Ballet theater, Baku; from 1938 taught at Opera Studio, Akhundov Opera and Ballet Theater, then at Azer Conservatory; *Productions:* operas: *Pikovaya dama* (The Queen of Spades) (1941); *Tsarskaya nevesta*

(Bride of the Tsar) (1944); Dzerzhinskiy's "Nadezhda Svetlova" (1945); Seidmann's "Masquerade" (1945); Smetana's "Bartered Bride" (1951), etc; *Died:* 20 May 1963.

TVERSKOY (real name: KUZ'MIN-KARAVAYEV), Konstantin Konstantinovich (1890–1944) Russian stage dir, drama teacher and theater critic; Hon Artiste of RSFSR; *Born:* 17 Mar 1890; *Career:* worked with Meyerhold; began stage dir work in Petrograd; 1918 stage dir, Kolomna Rayon Commune Theater; 1919 stage dir, Bolshoy Drama Theater; then at various Leningrad theaters: at State Pop Center, Liga Drama Theater, Red Theater, etc; 1927–29 stage dir, 1929–35 chief stage dir and artistic dir, Bolshoy Drama Theater; from 1922 taught drama; from 1936 worked at Karl Marx Theater and Chernyshevskiy Opera and Ballet Theater, Saratov; arrested by State Security organs; *Productions:* Cervantes' "Theater of Miracles" (1918); Loewberg's "Danton" (1919); *Razlom* (Break-Up) (1927); Fayko's *Chelovek s portfelem* (Man with a Briefcase) (1928); Kirshon's *Gorod vetrov* (City of Winds) (1929); Olesha's *Zagovor chuvstv* (Conspiracy of the Senses) (1929) and *Tri tolstyaka* (Three Fat Men) (1930); *Yegor Bulychyov i drugiye* (Yegor Bulychyov and Co) (1932); "Richard III" (1935); *Pikovaya dama* (The Queen of Spades); *Tikhiy Don* (Quiet Flows the Don), etc; *Died:* 1944 in imprisonment; posthumously rehabilitated.

TYAGNO, Boris Fomich (1904–1964) Stage dir; Pop Artiste of Ukr SSR from 1954; CP member from 1949; *Born:* 23 Aug 1904 in Khar'kov; *Educ:* 1923 grad Producing Dept, Kiev's Lysenko Musical Drama Inst; *Career:* 1922–29 actor and stage dir, Berezil' Theater; 1932–37 artistic dir, Khar'kov Working Youth Theater; 1938–40 dir, Dnepropetrovsk's Shevchenko Theater; 1940–44 dir, Dneprodzerzhinsk Russian Drama Theater; 1944–47 dir, Odessa Theater of the Oct Revol; 1948–62 chief stage dir, Zan'kovetskaya Theater, L'vov; also did film work and taught drama at the Studio of the Zan'kovetskaya Theater; *Productions:* "Jacquerie", after Mérimée; *Bronepoyezd 14–69* (Armored Train 14–69); *Aristokraty* (The Aristocrats); Brushteyn's *Prodolzheniye sleduyet* (To Be Continued); *Gibel' eskadry* (The Death of a Squadron); Korneychuk's "Makar Dubrava" (1948); *Meshchane* (The Philistines) (1950); Franko's Son *knyazya Svyatoslava* (Prince Svyatoslav's Dream) (1954); "Hamlett" (1957), etc; *Died:* 18 Jan 1964.

TYCHINA, Pavlo Grigor'yevich (1891–1967) Ukr poet and govt official; Dr of Biology; member, Ukr Acad of Sci from 1929; corresp member, Bulgarian Acad of Sci from 1947; dep chm, USSR, Supr Sov from 1954; member, CC, CP Ukr from 1954; CP member from 1944; *Born:* 27 Jan 1891 in vil Peski, now Chernigov Oblast; *Educ:* 1913 grad Chernigov Theological Seminary; studied at Kiev Business Inst; *Career:* 1916–23 lived in Kiev and toured Ukr with K. Stetsenko's choir; 1917–19 worked for journal "Mystetstvo revolyutsii" and for All-Union State Publ House; 1920 head, Cooperative Art Museum, Dnieper Consumers' Union, then Kiev Province Consumers' Union; 1920 also chrincler for the composer M.L. Stetsenko's choir in its tour of Right-Bank Ukr; 1920–23 lit dir, Shevchenko State Theater, Kiev; 1922 co-founder, Ukr Music School; 1923–34 worked for Khar'kov Journal "Chervonyy shlyakh"; 1936–38 and 1941–43 directed Inst of Lit, Ukr Acad of Sci; from 1941 dir, Inst of Lit and Language, Ukr Acad of Sci, Ufa then Moscow; 1943–48 Ukr Pop Comr (then Min) of Educ; from 1949 dep chm, Ukr Peace Comt; 1953–59 chm, Ukr Supr Sov; 1956 and 1959 voting deleg at 20th and 21st CPSU Congresses; dep, USSR Supr Sov of 1946, 1950, 1954 and 1958 convocations; dep, Ukr Supr Sov of all convocations; chm, Ukr Supr Sov of 1955 and 1959 convocations; dep chm, Sov of Nationalities, USSR Supr Sov of 1954 and 1958 convocations; 1929 member, Sov Orientalists deleg in Istanbul and Ankara; 1935 attended Int Anti-Fascist Congres, Paris; 1945 attended Pan-Slavic Congress, Sofia; 1947 member, Sov writers' deleg in Warsaw; 1949 visited England and Scotland for 25th anniversary of British Soc for Cultural Relations with the USSR; member, ed bd, journal "Slavyane" and "Vitchyzna"; member, Sov Inst of Lit and council member, Soc Sci Div, Ukr Acad of Sci; translated works of Pushkin, Krylov, Arm poet Tumanyan and Jewish poets Shvartsman and Hofstein, etc; *Publ: Pam'yaty trydtsyaty* (In Memory of the Thirty) (1918); collected verse: *Sonyashni klarnety* (Sunny Clarinets) (1918); *Pluh* (The Plow) (1920); *Zamist' sonetiv i oktav* (Instead of Sonets and Octaves) (1920); *Viter s Ukrainy* (Wind from the Ukraine) (1924); "Chernigov" (1930); *Partiya vede* (The Party Leads) (1933); *Chuttya yedynoi rodyny* (The Feeling of a United Family) (1938); *Mahistralyamy zhyttya* (By the Highways of Life) (1941); *Pokhorony druha* (Burial of a Friend) (1943); *Virshi y poemy* (Verse and Poems) (1950); *Vybrani poezii* (Selected Poetry) (1951); *Srybnoy nochi* (On a Silvery Night) (1964); coauthor, text of Ukr Nat Anthem; wrote books and articles on lit history: *Hryhoriy Skovoroda* (1939); *Patriotizm v tvorchestve M. Gafuri* (Patriotism in the Work of M. Gafuri) (1942); *Tvorcha syla narodu* (The Creative Force of the People) (1943); *V armii velykoho strateha* (In the Army of the Great Strategist) (1952); *Syla "Kobzarya"* (The Force of "Kobzar"') (1961); children's verse: "Ivasyk Telesyk" (1929); "Ku-Ku" (1934); "Lidka" (1940); *Svite nashe sontse* (Our Sun Shines) (1947); *Sade zelenyy* (The Green Garden) (1949); *Dudaryk* (The Piper) (1950); *Slava Bat'kivshchyni* (Glory to the Fatherland) (1951); *Muzykal'nyy ranok v konservatorii* (A Musical Matinée at the Conservatory) (1955); *Khor lisovykh dzvynochkiv* (The Choir of Forest Bellringers) (1958); *Awards:* Hero of Socialist Labor (1967); three Orders of Lenin; two Orders of the Red Banner of Labor; medals; Stalin Prize (1941); Shevchenko Prize (1962); Ukr Supr Sov Scroll of Hon (1961); *Died:* 16 Sept 1967.

TYNYANOV, Yuriy Nikolayevich (1894–1943) Russian writer; *Born:* 8 Oct 1894 in Rezhitsa, Vitebsk Province, son of a physician; *Educ:* 1918 grad History and Philology Fac, Petrograd Univ; *Career:* 1921–30 lecturer on the history of Russian poetry, Leningrad Inst of History of Arts; from 1921 art critic; sided with Formalism; wrote critical studies of V. K. Kyukhel'beker, Pushkin, Griboyedov, etc; translated Heine's works into Russian; his works combined historical and biographical research and painstaking documentary accuracy with profound psychological penetration; *Publ:* papers: *Dostoyevskiy and Gogol* (1921); *Problema stikhotvornogo yazyka* (The Problem of Poetic Language) (1924); "Kyukhlya" (1925); novel *Smert' Vazir-Mukhtara* (Vazir-Mukhtar's Death) (1927–28); story *Podporuchik Kizhe* (Lieutnant Kije) (1928); collected articles *Arkhaisty i novatory* (Archaists and Innovators) (1929); *Sobraniye sochineniy* (Collected Works) (1931); story *Maloletniy Vitushishnikov* (Young Vitushishnikov) (1933); *Rasskazy* (Stories) (1935); novel *Pushkin* (1936); *Died:* 20 Dec 1943.

TYULENIN, Sergey Gavrilovich (1925–1943) Partisan; one of the leaders of "Young Guard" underground org; Hero of the Sov Union from 1943; *Born:* 12 Aug 1925 in vil Kiselevo, Orel Oblast, son of a sovkhoz worker; *Career:* at start of WW 2 began work as miner in Krasnodon; then drafted to help build fortifications; after German occupation of Ukr joined "Young Guard" org; led battle group, then staff member, "Young Guard" org; Jan 1943 arrested by Gestapo; *Died:* 31 Jan 1943 in German imprisonment.

TYUMENBAYEV, Shamshi (1909–1964) Actor; Pop Artiste of Kir SSR from 1958; CP member from 1946; *Born:* 24 Dec 1909; *Educ:* grad Kir Musical Drama Studio, Frunze; *Career:* 1930–64 actor, Kir Drama Theater; also did film work; *Roles:* Khlestakov in *Revizor* (The Government Inspector); Trufaldino in Goldoni's "A Servant to Two Masters"; Robinzon in *Bespridannitsa* (The Girl Without a Dowry); Trubach in *Yegor Bulychev i drugiye* (Yegor Bulychev and Co); Dzhapalak in Shupurbekov's "Dzapalak Dzhatpasov"; Alankoz in Malykov and Kutubayev's "We Are Not What We Were", etc; *Died:* 18 Mar 1964.

TYUMENEV, Aleksandr Il'ich (1880–1959) Historian; specialist in ancient history; member, USSR Acad of Sci from 1932; *Born:* 5 Sept 1880 in Petersburg; *Educ:* 1904 grad Philology and History Fac, Petersburg Univ; *Career:* from 1921 prof, Leningrad Univ; 1928–31 at Inst of Marxist Methodology; 1931–38 at State Acad of the History of Material Culture; his research led him to the conclusion that ancient Eastern and Western civilizations were not two consecutive stages of historical development, but two different types of a slave-holding society, whereby Oriental soc had its own specific features and only superficially resembled the slave-owning system; *Publ: Teoriya istoricheskogo materializma* (The Theory of Historical Materialism) (1907); *Ocherki ekonomicheskoy i sotsial'noy istorii Drevney Gretsii* (Outline Economic and Social History of Ancient Greece) (3 vol, 1920–22); *Sushchestvoval li kapitalizm v Drevney Gretsii?* (Did Capitalism Exist in Ancient Greece?) (1923); *Razlozheniye rodovogo stroya i revolyutsiya v VII–VI vv. v Gretsii* (The Decay of the Tribal System and the Greek Revolution in the 7th–6th Centuries) (1934); *Istoriya antichnykh rabovladel'cheskikh obshchestv* (History of the Ancient Slave-Owning Societies) (1935); *Gosudarstvennoye khozyaystvo Drevnego Shumera* (The State Economy of Ancient Sumer) (1956), etc; *Awards:* Order of the Red Banner of Labor;

Died: 1 June 1959.

TYURIN, Ivan Vladimirovich (1892–1962) Soil scientist; prof from 1928; member, USSR Acad of Sci from 1953; Bureau member, Biological Sci Div, USSR Acad of Sci; dir, Soil Inst, USSR Acad of Sci from 1949; chief ed, journal "Pochvovedeniye" from 1953; *Born:* 2 Nov 1892 in Menzelinsk, now Tatar ASSR; *Educ:* 1919 grad Petrine Agric Acad (now Timiryazev Agric Acad); *Career:* 1919–28 asst, then assoc prof, 1928–30 prof, Kazan' Univ and Kazan' Inst of Agric and Forestry; 1944–51 prof, Forest Eng Acad, Leningrad; 1944–52 prof, Leningrad, Univ; 1930–49 prof, from 1949 dir, Soil Inst, USSR Acad of Sci; 1946–53 corresp member, USSR Acad of Sci; wrote some 100 works on soil sci, particularly humus; devised original methods of analysing the composition of humus and established geographical pattern for the formation of humus in the soils of the USSR; also devised new methods for the chemical analysis of soils; *Publ: Kurs pochvovedeniya dlya lesnykh vtuzov* (A Pedology Course for Forestry Technical Colleges) (1933); *Organicheskoye veshchestvo pochv i yego rol' v pochvoobrazovanii i plodorodii* (The Organic Matter of Soils and Its Role in Soil Formation and Fertility); *Ucheniye o pochvennom gumuse* (The Theory of Soil Humus) (1937); *Pochvy lesostepi* (The Soils of the Forest-Steppe) (1939); *Geograficheskiye zakonomernosti gumusoobrazovaniya* (The Geographical Laws Governing Humus Formation) (1949); *Opyt klassifikatsii lesnykh ploshchadey vodookhrannoy zony po ikh vodookhrannoy i zashchitnoy roli* (A Practical Classification of the Forest Areas of a Water-Protection Zone According to their Water-Protection and Conservationist Role) (1953), etc; *Awards:* Dokuchayev Gold Medal; Order of Lenin; Red Banner of Labor; medals; *Died:* 12 May 1962.

TYURK, Eduard Yukhanovich (1888–1966) Actor and stage dir; *Born:* 11 Apr 1888; *Career:* began stage work with Uganiya Amateur Dramatic Company in Tartu; 1907–12 at Vanemuyne Theater; 1912–13 at Endla Theater; 1913–16 at Vanemuyne Theater; 1916–17 at Drama Theater; 1917–18 at Estonia Theater; 1918–24 at Drama Theater; 1925–35 at Endla Theater; 1935–41 again at Drama Theater; 1944–48 artistic dir, 1948–51 dir, Endla Theater, Pyarnu; *Roles:* Abram Sikk in Kunder's "The Soldier"; Per Gynt in Ibsen's "Per Gynt"; Katku Villu in Tammsaare's "Kyrboy's Master"; Maurus in Tammsaare's "Maurus' School"; Bessmenov in *Meshchane* (The Philistines); Oedipus in Sophocles' "Oedipus Rex" *Productions:* Rutov's "Against the Current" (1916); Gorky's *Na dne* (The Lower Depths) (1917); Sophocles' "Oedipus Rex" (1923); Tagore's "The Sacrifice" (1923); Kitzberg's "Match-Making" (1926); "Maurus' School" (1945), etc; *Died:* 14 Mar 1966.

TYUTCHEV, Nikolay Sergeyevich (1856–1924) Politician; Populist, then from 1904 Socialist-Revolutionary; *Born:* 1856 in Moscow, son of a nobleman; *Educ:* 1875–77 studied at Petersburg Med Surgical Acad; *Career:* late 1876 joined "Land and Liberty" Soc; conducted revol propaganda among workers; 1878 arrested and exiled to Eastern Siberia; 1892 settled in Novgorod; played leading part in organizing "Pop Right" liberal populist party; 1894 re-arrested; 1895 exiled for eight years to Eastern Siberia; 1904 returned to European Russia; 1905 accomplice in plot to assassinate Petersburg Governor-Gen Trepov; 1905 emigrated; from 1918 worked for History of the Revol Archives, Petrograd; from 1923 contributed to journal "Katorga i ssylka"; *Died:* 1924.

TYUTYUNNIK, Vasiliy Savvich (1860–1924) Opera singer (bass); opera producer; teacher; *Born:* 12 Mar 1860; *Educ:* 1886 grad L.F. Kazati and F.P. Komissarzhevskiy's class, Moscow Conservatory; *Career:* 1886–88 soloist, Mariinskiy Theater, Petersburg; 1888–1912 soloist, Bolshoy Theater, Moscow; 1903–10 chief producer, Bolshoy Theater; in 1910's taught at Musical Drama College, Moscow Philharmonic Soc; 1920–24 prof, Moscow Conservatory; *Roles:* Leporello in "Don Juan"; Papageno in "The Magic Flute"; Bartholo in "The Marriage of Figaro"; Giacomo in "Fra Diavolo"; Farlas in "Ruslan and Ludmilla"; Mephistopheles in "Faust"; Varlaam in "Boris Godunov"; Skula in "Prince Igor"; Mamyrov in Tchaikovsky's *Charodeyka* (The Sorceress); Yeletskiy and Tomskiy in *Pikovaya dama* (The Queen of Spades), etc; *Died:* 24 May 1924.

TYZHNOV, Vsevolod Ivanovich (1870–1949) Metallurgist; *Born:* 1 May 1870; *Educ:* 1895 grad Petersburg Univ; *Career:* 1899–1902 at Petersburg's Putilov Plant (now Leningrad's Kirov Plant); 1902–06 at bryansk Plant in Bezhitsa; 1908–37, with intervals, at Motovilikha's Perm' Artillery Plant; introduced ind production of high-quality acid alloyed Martin steel by silicon reduction process; 1926 developed method of producing technically pure iron in electr and open-hearth furnaces; 1939 at Research Inst of High-Quality Steels and Ferroalloys; then with Centr Research Inst of Ferrous Metallurgy; *Publ: Malouglerodistoye martenovskoye i elektro-VIT-zhelezo* (Low-Carbon Technically Pure Iron Produced in Electric and Open-Hearth Furnaces) (1934); *Kremnevosstanovitel'nyy martenovskiy protsess* (The Silicon Reduction Open-Hearth Process) (1947); *Died:* 1949.

U

UBOREVICH (UBORYAVICHUS), Iyeronim Petrovich (1896–1937) Mil commander; Lith; 2nd lt, Russian Army; army commander, lst class from 1935; Civil War Veteran; CP member from 1917; *Born:* 14 Jan 1896 in vil Antandriya, Kaunas Province, son of a peasant; *Educ:* 1915 studied at Petersburg Polytech Inst; 1916 grad Konstantin Artillery College; 1927–28 attended courses at Higher Mil Acad, German Gen Staff; *Career:* 1915 volunteered for Russian Army; 1916–17 battery commander, then senior battery officer, heavy artillery battalion; commanded revol company on Rumanian Front; 1917–18 elected commander, revol workers and peasants' regt; fought against Austro-German occupation troops; 1918 taken prisoner but managed to escape; from 1918 in Red Army; 1918–19 artillery instructor; then commander, heavy howitzer battery, Lower Dvina Brigade; commander, 18th Infantry Div on Northern Front; fought against Anglo-American intervention forces; 1919–20 commander, 14th Army on Southern Front; 1920 commander, 9th (Kuban') Army on Caucasian Front; then commanded 14th and 13th Armies on Southwestern Front; fought against Denikin, Wrangel and Polish troops; 1920–21 commander, 14th Army; participated in final operations against Petlyura's forces; 1921 dep commander, Ukr and Crimean Armed Forces; dep commander, Tambov Province Armed Forces; Commander, Minsk Province Armed Forces; directed rout of Makhno's troops; helped suppress Antonov revolt and headed liquidation of Bulak-Bulakhovich's insurgent detachments; 1921–22 commander, 5th Army and East Siberian Mil Distr; from 17 Aug 1922 Min of War, buffer Far Eastern Republ and supr commander of its Pop Revol Army; member, Far Eastern Bureau, CC, RCP(B); headed the assault of Spassk fortress and liberation of the Far East from occupation troops; 1922–23 commander, 5th Red Banner Army; 1923–25 dep commander, Western Front; commander, 5th Red Banner Army; attached for special assignments to RSFSR Revol Mil Council; dep commander, Ukr and Crimean Armed Forces; chief of staff, Ukr Mil Distr; 1925–27 commander, Northcaucasian Mil Distr; 1928–30 commander, Moscow Mil Distr; 1930–31 USSR Dep Pop Comr of Mil and Naval Affairs and dep chm, USSR Revol Mil Council; 1931–37 commander, Bel Mil Distr; 1926–34 member, USSR Revol Mil Council; 1934–37 member, Mil Council, USSR Pop Comrt of Defense; 1930–37 cand member, CC, CPSU(B); from 1922 permanent member, USSR Centr Exec Comt; 29 May 1937 arrested by NKVD upon arriving from Smolensk in Moscow; 11 June 1937 sentenced to death by special session of USSR Supr Court together with Tukhachevskiy, Yakir and other army commanders; a short time later his wife and daughter were also arrested; his wife died in imprisonment in 1941; *Publ: Printsipy vedeniya boya i znacheniye ikh v dele vospitaniya i obucheniya Krasnoy Armii (po opytu mirovoy i grazhdanskoy voyn)* (The Principles of Warfare and Their Importance in Training and Drilling the Red Army /Based on the Experience of World War I and the Civil War/) (1922); *Podgotovka komsostava RKKA (starshego i vysshego). Polevyye poyezdki, uskorennyye voyennyye igry i vykhody v pole* (Training Red Army Commanding Staff /Senior and Supreme Commanders/. Field Trips, Forced Maneuvers and Field Exercises) (1928); *Operativno-takticheskiye i aviatsionnyye voyennye igry* (Tactical Operation and Air Force Maneuvers) (1929); *Awards:* three Orders of the Red Banner; *Died:* 12 June 1937 executed; posthumously rehabilitated.

UDAL'TSOV, Aleksandr Dmitriyevich (1883–1958) Historian; Dr of Historical Sci; prof; corresp member, USSR Acad of Sci from 1939; CP member from 1928; *Born:* 14 May 1883; *Career:* from 1919 prof, Moscow Univ; 1946–56 also dir, Inst of the History of Material Culture (later Inst of Archeology), USSR Acad of Sci; 1946–50 head, Chair of Medieval History, Acad of Soc Sci, CC,

CPSU(B); 1949–50 chief ed, journal "Voprosy istorii"; specialized in medieval history of Western Europe; also studied ethnogenesis of Eastern Slavs; proceeding from N.Ya. Marr's Japhetic theory, he regarded the formation of the Eastern Slavs as the result of a protracted and uneven process of mutual penetration and acculturation of various tribes; 1950 criticized for these views and dismissed from his post as head, Commission for the Ethnogenesis of the Peoples of the USSR; also dismissed as head, Chair of Medieval History, Acad of Soc, Sci, CC CPSU(B) and relieved of his post as chief ed, "Voprosy istorii"; subsequently revised his views on the ethnogenesis of the Eastern Slavs; *Publ: Svobodnaya derevnya Zapadnoy Neystrii v epokhu Merovingov and Karolingov* (The Free Villages of Western Neustria in the Merovingian and Carolingian Era) (1912); *Iz agrarnoy istorii karolingskoy Flandrii* (The Agrarian History of Carolingian Flanders) (1935); *Nachal'nyy period vostochnoslavyanskogo etnogeneza* (The Initial Period of East Slav Ethnogenesis) (1934); *Plemena Yevropeyskoy Sarmatii II veka n.e.* (The Tribes of European Sarmatia in the 2nd Century A.D.) (1946), etc; *Awards:* Order of Lenin; other orders; *Died:* 25 Sept 1958.

UDAL'TSOV, Ivan Dmitriyevich (1885–1958) Economist; prof; CP member from 1905; *Born:* 20 Mar 1885; *Educ:* grad Moscow Univ; *Career:* 1905–07 head, Bolshevik Comt of Moscow Univ; arrested and exiled; 1921–22 head, Propaganda Sub-Dept, Agitation and Propaganda Dept, CC, RCP(B); 1921–58 prof, 1928–30 rector, from 1928 head, Chair of the History of Econ Theories and Nat Econ, Moscow Univ; from 1947 also prof, Acad of Soc Sci, CC, CPSU(B); *Died:* 30 Jan 1958.

UDINTSEV, Fyodor Aristarkhovich (1877–1956) Internist; Dr of Med; prof; Hon Sci Worker of Ukr SSR from 1943; CP member from 1942; *Born:* 19 Sept 1877 in Irbit, now Sverdlovsk Oblast; *Educ:* 1903 grad Med Fac, Kiev Univ; *Career:* specialized in internal med at Kiev Univ clinics, then worked as asst prof and, later, assoc prof; 1921–56 head, Chair of Gen Therapy, Kiev Med Inst; for many years chm, Kiev Soc of Therapists; wrote several works on diseases of the liver, gall-bladder, ulcers, koumiss treatment, etc; *Died:* 18 Apr 1956 in Kiev.

UGAROV, Fyodor Yakovlevich (1885–1940) Party official; CP member from 1905; *Born:* 1885 in Tver' Province, son of a peasant; *Career:* locksmith by trade; active in Petersburg strikes; ran an underground printing press; 1906 arrested and exiled to Astrakhan' Province, whence he fled to Baku; 1909–12 underground work in Petersburg; 1912 arrested for participation in strikes and demonstrations and exiled to Tobol'sk Province, whence he soon fled; early 1914 worked for textile union, after start of WW 1 worked at "Vulkan" Plant and elected bd member, plant's sick fund; 1917 member, Petrograd Sov; helped organize Red Guard; during 1917 Oct Revol tock part in storming of the Winter Palace and action at Pulkovo; worked for Pop Comrt of Labor; during Civil War fought on Denikin and Polish Fronts; from 1920 chm, Kiev Province Trade-Union Council; 1923–25 chm, All-Ukr Trade-Union Council; 1926–29 chm, Leningrad Oblast Trade-Union Council; 1928–29 sided with Bukharin; from 1930 chm, Moscow State Trust of Medium and Small-Scala Industry; deleg at 10th, 12th, 13th, 14th, 15th and 16th CPSU(B) Congresses; at 14th Congress elected cand member, at 15th Congress elected member, CC, CPSU(B); at 5th–8th Conferences and 9th Congress of CP(B) Ukr elected member, CC, CP(B) Ukr; 1923–25 Politburo member, CC, CP(B) Ukr; member, All-Ukr and USSR Centr Exec Comt of several convocations; arrested by State Security organs; *Died:* 1940 in imprisonment.

UGLANOV, Nikolay Aleksandrovich (1886–1940) Govt and Party official; CP member 1907; *Born:* 1886 son of a peasant; *Career:* from 1903 in revol movement; 1905 bd member, 1913 chm, Petersburg Trade and Ind Employes' Union; took part in 1917 Feb and Oct Revol; member, Petrograd Sov; after Oct Revol with Red Guard; 1918 chm, Centr Commission to Organize Armed Food Squads; from May 1919 Collegium member, Petrograd Comrt of Food; 1919 secr, Petrograd Province Trade-Union Council; 1919–21 fought on Civil War fronts and helped crush Kronstadt Mutiny; 1921–22 secr, Petrograd Party Comt; 1922–24 secr, Nizhniy Novgorod Province Party Comt; 1924–28 secr, Moscow Party Comt; 1928–Jan 1931 USSR Pop Comr of Labor; sided with Bukharin, Rykov and Tomskiy; at 10th CPSU(B) Congress elected cand member, at 12th-15th Congress elected member, CC, CPSU(B); from Dec 1927 cand Politburo, Org Bureau and Secretariat member, CC, CPSU(B); Oct 1932 expelled from Party for connections with Ryutin "counterrevol group", but later reinstated in Party; 1936 again expelled from Party and sentenced; *Died:* 1940 in imprisonment.

UGLOV, Vladimir Aleksandrovich (1874–1942) Hygienist; Dr of Med from 1934; prof from 1935; *Born:* 1874; *Educ:* 1898 grad Petersburg Mil Med Acad; pupil of G.B. Khlopin; *Career:* 1901–11 head, Chemical and Bacteriological Laboratory, Khabarovsk Mil Hospital; 1912 helped to combat plague in Don area; 1913 specialized in hygiene in France, Switzerland and Germany; until 1918 worked at various mil med establishments; from 1918 junior, then senior lecturer, Chair of Hygiene, Petrograd Mil Med Acad; from 1923 head, Chair of Hygiene, Fac of Chemistry and Pharmaceutics, Petrograd Univ; from 1927 head, Chair of Gen Hygiene, Khar'kov Med Inst; from 1930 head, Chair of Gen and Mil Hygiene, Leningrad Mil Med Acad; simultaneously head, Chair of Gen Hygiene, Leningrad Med Inst; did major research on mil hygiene, food hygiene, sanitation and epidemiology; made special study of water purification methods; *Publ: O zerne pshenitsy i rzhi Ussuriyskogo kraya i Amurskoy oblasti v svyazi s khimicheskim sostavom i analizom zerna voobshche* (The Wheat and Rye Grain of the Ussuri Kray and Amur Oblast in Relation to the Chemical Composition and Analysis of Grain in General) (1913); *Teoriya i praktika khlorirovaniya vody* (The Theory and Practice of Water Chlorination) (1930); *Sanitarnoye izucheniye istochnikov vodosnabzheniya na meste i ikh kharakteristika* (On-the-Spot Sanitary Analysis of Water Sources and Their Characteristics) (1931); *Died:* 1942.

UFIMTSEV, Anatoliy Georgiyevich (1880–1936) Inventor and aircraft designer; *Born:* 24 Mar 1880 in Kursk; *Educ:* 1890–98 studied at Kursk High School; *Career:* 1900 imprisoned in Peter-and-Paul Fortress and then exiled to Siberia for revol activities and for helping to blow up a "miraculous" icon in Kursk; after return from exile worked on aircraft design; 1909–10 built "spheroplane"; designed birotary aircraft engines with cylinders arranged X–wise around the crankshaft; 1911 took out Patent 19997 on a four-cylinder birotary engine, for which he won Grand Silver Medal at 1912 Int Aviation Exhibition, Moscow; did research on wind-powered devices; 1918 invented an inertion accumulator; together with V.P.Vetchinkin, designed a wind-motor which was used successfully in wind-driven power stations; his other inventions included a high-speed printing machine and cartridges for muzzle-loaders; *Died:* 10 July 1936.

UFIMTSEV, N.I. (1888–1938) Party and govt official; CP member from 1906; *Born:* 1888; *Career:* 1917 touring instructor for Ural Oblast Party Comt; 1918–19 fought in Civil War; polit work in Red Army; then Party and econ admin work; secr, Yekaterinburg, then Simferopol' Province RCP(B) Comt; chm, Northern Chemical Trust; USSR trade rep in Austria; dep head, Main Chemical Bd; USSR Supr Sovnarkhoz; Collegium member, USSR Pop Comrt of Heavy Ind; 1928 expelled from Party for active membership of Trotskyist opposition; 1930 readmitted to Party; 1933 again expelled for alleged anti-Party activities; arrested by State Security organs; *Died:* 1938 in imprisonment.

UKHANOV, Konstantin Vasil'yevich (1891–1939) Govt official; CP member from 1907; *Born:* 1891 in Kazan'; *Educ:* studied at preparatory college in Nizhniy Novgorod; from 1904 studied at Maydak Craft Workshop, Kostroma Province; *Career:* began work at age 15; locksmith at various factories and plants; active in revol movement; from 1907 propaganda among workers and helped set up trade-union and cultural orgs; worked for Rodniki Party Org (now Ivanovo Oblast); 1912–13 helped organize Ivanovo-Voznesensk and Kostroma Textile Rayon Party Conference; subsequently arrested and imprisoned; upon his release went to Petersburg and continued underground revol work; after 1917 Feb Revol member, Moscow Sov; also chm, Simonov Sov, Simonov Admin and Rogozha-Simonov Sov; member and Presidium member, Moscow Province Exec Comt of several convocations; Mar 1921, together with other delegates at 10th Party Congress, helped crush Kronstadt Mutiny; 1921 dir, "Dinamo" Plant; 1922 appointed chm, Electr Eng Trust; 1925, with amalgamation of two trusts, appointed chm, Joint State Electr Eng Trust; May 1926 elected chm, Moscow Sov; from 1929 chm, Moscow Oblast Exec Comt; member and Bureau member, Moscow Party Comt; at 12th–17th Party Congresses elected member, CC, CPSU(B); Presidium member, All-Russian and USSR Centr Exec Comt of several convocations; from Feb 1932 USSR Dep Pop Comr of Supply; from 1934 RSFSR Pop Comr of Local Ind; from Oct 1936 RSFSR Pop Comr of Light Ind; 1937 arrested by State Security organs; *Died:* 1939 in imprisonment.

UKHTOMSKIY, Aleksey Alekseyevich (1875–1942) Physiologist; member, USSR Acad of Sci from 1935; *Born:* 25 June 1875 in vil Vesloma, now Yaroslavl' Oblast; *Educ:* 1906 grad Natural Sci Dept, Fac of Physics and Mathematics, Petersburg Univ; *Career:* after grad worked under N. Ye. Vvedenskiy, Chair of Animal Physiology, Petersburg Univ; 1911 defended master's thesis on dependence of cortical motor effects on secondary centr influences; 1919 co-founded Workers' Fac, Petrograd Univ; from 1920 head, Physiological Laboratory, Peterhof Inst of Natural Sci; 1922–42 held chair vacated by Vvedenskiy's death; 1930 co-founded Chair of Labor Physiology, Leningrad Univ; 1930–38 pres, Leningrad Soc of Natural Scientists; 1932–35 corresp member, USSR Acad of Sci; 1935 founded Physiological Inst, Leningrad Univ; 1937 founded Electrophysiological Laboratory, USSR Acad of Sci; in the course of research along lines begun by I.M.Sechenov and N.Ye.Vvedenskiy discovered one of basic principles of nervous activity which he called the "dominant"; also did research on lability, fatigue, excitation and inhibition; approached physiology from materialistic viewpoint and opposed idealistic treatment of certain physiological phenomena; *Publ: Dominant kak rabochiy printsip nervnykh tsentrov* (The Dominant as the Working Principle of the Nerve Centers) (1923); *Usvoyeniye ritma v svete ucheniya o parabioze* (The Acquisition of Rhythm in the Light of the Theory of Parabiosis) (1926); *Fiziologiya dvigatel'nogo apparata* (The Physiology of the Motor Apparatus) (1927); *Parabioz i dominanta* (Parabiosis and the Dominant) (1927); *O pokazatele labil'nosti (funktional'noy podvizhnosti) fiziologicheskikh priborov* (The Lability Index [Functional Motility] of Physiological Equipment) (1934); *Fiziologicheskiy pokoy i labil'nost' kak biologicheskiye faktory* (Physiological Dormancy and Lability as Biological Factors) (1937); coauthor, *Parametr fiziologicheskoy labil'nosti i nelineynaya teoriya kolebaniy* (The Parameter of Physiological Lability and the Non-Linear Theory of Oscillations) (1940); *Ocherki fiziologii nervnoy sistemy* (Studies in the Physiology of the Nervous System) (1945); *Sobraniye sochineniy* (Collected works) (4 vol, 1945–51; 6 vol, 1950–62); *Awards:* Lenin Prize (1931); *Died:* 31 Aug 1942 in Leningrad.

ULEZKO-STROGANOVA, Klavdiya Petrovna (1858–1943) Obstetrician and gynecologist; Dr of Med from 1921; prof from 1928; Hon Sci Worker of RSFSR from 1936; *Born:* 1858; *Educ:* 1885 grad Women's Med Courses, Nikolay Mil Hospital; *Career:* after grad health officer; from 1890 worked at Petersburg Clinical Inst of Postgrad Med Training; simultaneously asst prof, Chair of Histology, Petersburg Women's Med Inst; 1903 transferred to Petersburg Inst of Midwifery (now Inst of Obstetrics and Gynecology, USSR Acad of Sci), where she founded a laboratory and chair of normal and pathological anatomy and histology of the female sexual organs; 1921 defended doctor's thesis on uterine fribroma; during WW 2 did research on wound infection; spezialized in histogenesis of tumors (especially cancerous) of female genital organs; also did research on reticuloendethelial system; during blockade of Leningrad helped to organize and run hospital service; hon member, Leningrad Soc of Obstetrics and Gynecology; wrote 125 works; *Publ: O stroyenii podzheludochnoy zhelezy pri usloviyakh yeyo pokoya i deyatel'nosti* (The Structure of the Dormant and Active Pancreas) (1883); *Kratkiy kurs mikroskopicheskoy diagnostiki v ginekologii* (A Short Course of Microscope Diagnostics in Gynecology) (1912); *Mikroskopicheskaya diagnostika v ginekologii* (Microscope Diagnostics in Gynecology) (1926); *Normal'naya i patologicheskaya anatomiya i gistologiya zhenskikh polovykh organov* (The Normal and Pathological Anatomy and Histology of the Female Genital Organs) (1939); *Problema raka i aktivnaya mezenkhima* (The Problem of Cancer and Active Mesenchyme) (1940); *Awards:* Order of the Red Banner of Labor; medals; *Died:* 11 Dec 1943 in Leningrad.

ULITOVSKIY, Aleksey Vasil'yevich (1893–1957) Eng; specialist in instrument-building, metallurgy and electronics; prof and Dr of Physics and Mathematics from 1935; *Born:* 16 Mar 1893; *Educ:* 1915 grad Petrograd Univ; *Career:* from 1915 teaching and research work; from 1938 worked for various ind enterprises and research insts; developed methods for the molten drawing of fine and super-fine metal wire; *Awards:* Stalin Prize (1951); Lenin Prize (1960, posthumously); *Died:* 6 Nov 1957.

UL'VI, Radzhab (1903–1937) Actor and stage dir; *Born:* 1903; *Career:* 1922 at Tbilisi Azer Theater; from 1925 leading actor, Baku's Azizbekov Theater; staged plays by Schiller, Shakespeare, G. Dzhavid and D. Dzhabarly; arrested by State Security organs; *Roles:* Othello, Hamlet and Romeo; Franz Moor; Guinplain in Hugo's "The Man Who Laughs"; Akshin in *Nevesta ognya* (The Bride of Fire); Yashar in "Yashar Dzhabarly"; Yarov in "Lyubov' Yarovaya", etc; *Died:* 1937 in imprisonment; posthumously rehabilitated.

UL'YANOV, Andrey Vladimirovich (1900–1957) Geologist; Dr of Geology and Mineralogy from 1941; prof from 1945; CP member from 1952; *Born:* 21 May 1900; *Educ:* 1925 grad Leningrad Mining Inst; *Career:* 1925–29 geologist at Baku Oil Fields; 1929–46 directed study groups and expeditions for Oil Research and Geological Survey Inst; 1946–51 with Oil Inst, USSR Acad of Sci; from 1951 dep dir (for sci), All-Union Oil and Geological Survey Sesearch Inst; 1950–56 also prof, Acad of Oil Ind; helped discover and survey major gas condensate deposits in Krasnodar Kray; *Awards:* Lenin Prize (1961, posthumously); *Died:* 25 June 1957.

UL'YANOV, Dmitriy Il'ich (1874–1943) Health service official; brother of Lenin; CP member from 1896; *Born:* 16 Aug 1874; *Educ:* 1893 entered Moscow Univ; 1901 grad Med Fac, Yur'yev (Tartu) Univ; *Career:* 1897 imprisoned for almost a year for revol activities, after which he was kept under police surveillance; 1901–14 health officer in Kherson Province, Kiev, Yekaterinoslav Province, Genichesk, Tula, Simbirsk Province, then Serpukhov Uyezd; while in Genichesk studied properties of curative muds; during WW 2 mil hospital intern, Rumanian Front; frequently arrested for polit activities in period before Oct Revol; after 1917 Oct Revol member, Tavrida (Crimean) Oblast RSDRP(B) Comt and member, ed collegium, newspaper "Tavricheskaya pravda"; 1918 head, Syzran' City Health Dept; led partisan movement during occupation of Crimea by White Army; after establishment of Sov rule in Crimea, dep chm, Crimean Council of Pop Comr and Comr of Health and Soc Security; then plen for Crimean health resorts, RSFSR Pop Comrt of Health; founder, Centr Bd of Crimean Health Resorts; 1921–23 held admin posts in RSFSR Pop Comrt of Health; 1925–30 worked at Sverdlov Communist Univ; from 1933 assoc, Polyclinic Sci Section, Kremlin Therapy and Health Bd; assoc, Lenin Museum, Moscow; *Died:* 16 June 1943.

UL'YANOV, I.I. (1884–1946) Govt official; CP member from 1911; *Born:* 1884; *Career:* Party work in Ural'sk and Saratov; after 1917 Oct Revol member, All-Russian Centr Exec Comt of several convocations; until May 1919 chm, Ural Oblast Revol Comt; later exec admin and econ work: Main Fishing Ind Bd plen in Kerch' and Ivanovo-Voznesensk; State Trade Comt plen in Petrozavodsk and Saratov; *Died:* 1946.

UL'YANOV, Nikolay Pavlovich (1875–1949) Painter and set designer; corresp member, USSR Acad of Arts from 1949; Hon Art Worker of RSFSR from 1932; *Born:* 19 Apr 1875; *Educ:* 1900 V. Serov's class, Moscow College of Painting, Sculpture and Architecture; *Career:* 1904–05 set designer, Moscow Arts Theater; later sympathized with "Blue Rose" Symbolists assoc and with the "World of Art" assoc; after 1917 member, "Four Arts" Soc; his works are displayed in Tret'yakov Gallery and in the Russian Museum; as set designer worked at Maly Theater, Moscow Arts Theater, Meyerhold Theater and Stanislavsky Opera Theater; *Works:* paintings: "Portrait of A. P. Chekhov" (1904); "Portrait of A. N. Tolstoy" (1912); "A. S. Pushkin"(1937); "A. S. and N. N. Pushkin at a Court Ball" (1937); "Loriston at Kutuzov's Headquarters" (1945); K. S. Stanislavsky at Work" (1947), etc; designed sets and costumes for plays: "Scapin's Pranks"; "Days of the Turbiny"; "Molière"; "Carmen"; *Gore umu* (Woe to Wit). etc; *Publ: Moi vstrechi. Vospominaniya* (My Encounters. Memoirs) (1952); *Awards:* Order of the Red Banner of Labor; Stalin Prize (1948); *Died:* 5 May 1949.

UL'YANOVA, Mariya Il'inichna (1878–1937) Journalist; revol; younger sister of Lenin; CP member from 1898; *Born:* 18 Feb 1878; *Educ:* 1896 completed Moscow high school; attended Higher Women's Courses in Moscow and New Univ in Brussels; *Career:* joined revol movement as a student; member, illegal student circles; several times arrested; spent a total of two years in prison and five years in exile; did Party work in Petersburg, Moscow, Saratov and other cities; from 1900 corresp, Lenin's newspaper "Iskra"; from 1903 worked for secretariat, CC, RSDRP; 1904–05 and 1908–09 lived abroad; 1910 worked for Saratov newspaper "Privolzhskaya gazeta" and for Bolshevik org; 1917–29 member, ed bd and exec secr, newspaper "Pravda"; helped organize workers and rural correspondents movement; ed, journal "Raboche-krest'yanskiy korrespondent"; member, Moscow Party Control Commission; from 1925 member, Party Centr Control Commission; from 1932 Presidium member, Centr Control Commission; from 1934 member and Bureau member, Sov Control Commission and head of its Complaints Bureau; from 1935 member, USSR Centr Exec Comt; *Awards:* Order of Lenin (1933); *Died:* 12 June 1937; buried on Moscow's Red Square.

UMANSKIY, Konstantin Aleksandrovich (1902–1945) Journalist; diplomat; *Born:* 1902; *Educ:* studied at Moscow Univ and Inst of Red Prof; *Career:* 1918–22 worked for various newspapers and journals; edited newspaper "Iskusstvo"; Russian News Agency corresp in Vienna; 1923–28 worked for TASS; 1925–26 TASS corresp in Rome; 1928–30 head, Paris and Geneva TASS Bureaux; from 1931 dipl work; dep head, then head, Press Dept, USSR Pop Comrt of For Affairs; 1936–39 counsellor, then charge d'affaires, USSR embassy in Washington; May 1939 appointed USSR amb in USA; 1941 returned from USA and appointed Collegium member, USSR Pop Comrt of For Affairs; from June 1943 USSR amb in Mexico; from June 1944 also USSR envoy to Republ of Costa Rica; *Awards:* Order of the Red Banner of Labor; *Died:* 25 Jan 1945 killed in plane crash in Mexico while en route to Costa Rica to present his credentials.

UMANSKIY, Morits Borisovich (1907–1948) Set designer; *Born:* 8 Mar 1907 in Zhitomir; *Educ:* 1930 grad Kiev Art Inst; *Career:* 1923 began theater work; in 1930's and 1940's designed sets at Franko Theater, Lesya Ukrainka Theater and other theaters; also did film work; *Works:* designed sets and costumes for plays: *Gibel' eskadry* (Death of a Squadron) (1933); "Shchors" (1939); Franko's *Ukradyonnoye schast'ye* (Stolen Happines) (1940); *Russkiye lyudi* (Russian People) (1943); A. Tolstoy's *Khozhdeniye po mukam* (Purgatory) (1947); Lesya Ukrainka's *Kamennyy vlastelin* (The Stone Sovereign) (1947); "Twelfth Night" (1948), etc; *Awards:* Stalin Prize (1948); *Died:* 19 Dec 1948.

UMAROV, Sultan Umarovich (1908–1964) Tadzh physicist; prof from 1949; pres, Tadzh Acad of Sci from 1957; member, Uzbek Acad of Sci from 1943; chm, Terminology Comt, Tadzh Acad of Sci; member, Comt for Lenin Prizes for Sci and Technol, USSR Council of Min from 1960; Hon Sci Worker of Tadzh SSR; member, CC, CP Tadzh from 1958; CP member from 1943; *Born:* 24 Aug 1908 in Khodzhent, now Leninabad; *Educ:* 1930 grad Uzbek Teachers' Training Acad, Samarkand; *Career:* 1930–33 asst prof, Chair of Physics, Samarkand Teachers' Training Acad; 1933–36 worked for USSR Acad of Sci; 1936–42 lecturer and head, Chair of Physics, Uzbek Univ, Samarkand; 1942–49 lecturer, 1949–56 prof, Centr Asian Univ, Tashkent; 1942–43 and 1945–50 also rector, Centr Asian Univ; 1943–45 dep chm, Uzbek Council of Min; 1950–56 dir, Uzbek Physical Eng Inst; specialized in kinetic theory, electronics and theory of semiconductor equipment; 1951–52 developed theory of water absorption in cotton fibers and theory of electr conductivity of fibers; head, Dept of Soc and Natural Sci, Tadzh Acad of Sci; lectured on modern physics in India, Pakistan and Iran; dep, USSR Supr Sov of 1958 and 1962 convocations; member, Econ Commission, Sov of Nationalities, USSR Supr Sov of 1962 convocation; chm, Tadzh Republ Branch, Sino-Sov Friendship Soc from 1960; *Publ: Raspredeleniye energii po dlinam infrakrasnoy chasti spektra* (Energy Distribtuion Among the Wave-Lengths of the Infra-Red Spectrum) (1931); *Teoriya brounovskogo dvizheniya nekotorykh sistem, sovershayushchikh malyye kolebaniya* (The Theory of Brownian Movement in Some Low-Oscillation Systems) (1937); *O fazovom prostranstve, ne privedyonnom k normal'nym usloviyam* (Phase Space Unrelated to Normal Conditions) (1949); *O probege vtorichnykh elektronov v metalle i dielektrike* (The Path of Secondary Electrons in Metal and Dielectrics) (1952); *O probege vtorichnykh elektronov v metalle i dielektrike, svyazannom s elektronnymi soudareniyami* (The Path of Secondary Electrons in Metal and Dielectrics Connected with Electron Collisions) (1953); coauther, *K teorii kontakta metall-poluprovodnik* (Metal-Semiconductor Contact Theory) (1956); *Awards:* Order of Lenin; two Orders of the Red Banner of Labor; *Died:* 6 May 1964.

UNDRITS, Vil'gel'm Fomich (1891–1963) Otolaryngologist; prof; Dr of Med from 1935; corresp member, USSR Acad of Med Sci from 1946; Hon Sci Worker of RSFSR from 1962; *Born:* 1891; *Educ:* 1914 grad Petrograd Mil Med Acad; *Career:* 1914–18 mil surgeon in Russian Army; 1918–40 intern, junior lecturer, senior asst prof, then prof and dep head, Chair of Otolaryngology, Petrograd (Leningrad) Mil Med Acad; also consultant, Leningrad Deaf and Dumb Inst; from 1930 also head, Experimental Biology Dept, Leningrad Sci Practical Inst for Ear, Nose and Throat Diseases; 1940–63 head, Chair of Otolaryngology, lst Leningrad Med Inst; 1941–45 chief otolaryngologist of Leningrad Front and consultant for Leningrad evacuation hospitals; for many years bd member, All-Union Sci Soc of Otolaryngologists and chm of its Leningrad Branch; co-ed, "Otolaryngology" section, 2nd ed of "Bol'shaya meditsinskaya entsiklopediya"; member, ed council, journal "Vestnik otorinolaringologiya"; emphasized physiological and clinico-physiological trend in otolaryngology; designed instruments and new methods of studying and treating ear, nose and throat diseases; first to describe symptom of cortical deafness – an imbalance in the perception of simple and complex sounds (1923); devised method of using electro-acoustic apparatus for studying and speech-training deaf mutes; first Sov sci to study functions of the inner ear by recording cochlear currents; devised methods of recording the nystagment reaction of the eye muscles; established working pattern of the vestibular apparatus; traced central paths of the nystagma reflex; experimentallay studied the limits of absolute and relative acoustic injury; studied the factor of cooling and role of cold in the etiology of acute inflammation of the upper respiratory tract; studied allergy and vasomotor dysfunction of the nasal mucous membrane; wrote thesis on new clinical form of lymphadenitis – alimentary lymphadenitis; devised original means of removing foreign bodies from awkward corners of the epipharynx and with intracranial wounds; wrote chapter on injuries of the middle and inner ear for the multi-vol publication *Opyt sovetskoy meditsiny v Velikoy Otechestvennoy voyne 1941–1945 gg* (The Experience of Soviet Medicine in the 1941–45 Great Fatherland War); wrote over 100 research works; *Publ:* thesis *Alimentarynyy limfadenit* (Alimentary Lymphadenitis) (1935); *Atlas ognestrel'nykh raneniy ukha, gorla i nosa* (An Atlas of Gunshot Wounds of the Ear, Nose and Throat); coauthor, *Ognestre'nyye raneniya litsa, LOR-organov i shei* (Gunshot Wounds of the Face, the ENT Organs and the Neck) (1949); *Ostryye stenozi gortani* (Acute Stenosis of the Larynx) (1950); coauthor and ed, *Voprosy klinicheskoy fiziologii v otorinolaringologii* (Problems of Clinical Physiology in Otolaryngology) (1955); coauthor, *Bolezni ukha, nosa i gorla* (Ear, Nose and Throat Diseases) (1960); *Fiziologiya ukha i metodika fiziologicheskogo eksperimenta na ukhe* (The Physiology of the Ear and Methods of Physiological Experiments on the Ear) (1960); coauthor, *Rukovodstvo po klinicheskoy audiologii* (A Manual on Clinical Audiology) (1962); *Awards:* two Orders of Lenin; Order of the Fatherland War, lst Class; medals; *Died:* 1963 in Leningrad.

UNSHLIKHT (Party alias: YUROVSKIY), Iosif Stanislavovich (1879–1937) Party and govt official; Pole; CP member from 1900; *Born:* 19 Dec 1879 in Mlava, Plotsk Province, Poland; *Educ:* Completed secondary and specialized tech training in Warsaw; *Career:* from his youth in revol movement; 1900 joined Soc-Democratic Party of Poland and Lith and was deleg of its 5th and 6th Congresses; attended 5th (London) RSDRP Congress; member, Warsaw, Lodz and Interregional Comt, Soc-Democratic Party of Poland and Lith; repeatedly arrested and exiled; 1916 exiled to vil Tungurka, Irkutsk Province; after 1917 Feb Revol with Irkutsk Exec Comt and with Irkutsk RSDRP(B) Comt; from Apr 1917 member, Petrograd Sov; member, Centr Exec Comt, Soc-Democratic Party of Poland and Lith groups in Russia; worked for Polish newspaper "Tribuna"; elected to Constituent Assembly on Petrograd Bolshevik list; July 1917 arrested by Provisional Govt; participated in 1917 Oct Revol; member, Petrograd Mil Revol Comt; Collegium member, NKVD; late 1918 sent to Western Front; elected member, CC, CP Bel and Lith; Bel and Lith Pop Comr of Mil Affairs; from Apr 1919 in Red Army; member, Revol Mil Council, 16th Army; then member, Revol Mil Council, Western Front; from Apr 1921 dep chm, All-Russian Cheka (OGPU); late 1923 appointed member, USSR Revol Mil Council and Red Army chief of supply; from Feb 1925 USSR Dep Pop Comr of Mil and Naval Affairs; 1927 elected dep chm, USSR Soc to Promote the Aviation, Chemical and Defense Ind; 1930 Presidium member, Supr Sovnarkhoz; 1930–33 dep chm, USSR Gosplan; 1933 chief arbiter, USSR Council of Pop Comr; 1933–35 head, Main Civil Aviation Bd; Feb 1935 at 7th Congress of Soviets elected secr, Union Council, USSR Centr Exec Comt; member, Centr Exec Comt of all convocations; at 13th Party Congress elected member, CPSU(B) Centr Auditing Commission; at 14th, 15th and 17th Party Congresses elected cand member, CC, CPSU(B); arrested by State Security organs; *Publ: Voyennoye* *delo – na rel'sy leninizma* (Military Affairs on Leninist Lives) (1925); *Na osnove leninskogo yedinstva ukrepim boyevuyu moshch' Krasnoy Armii* (We Shall Strengthen the Striking Power of the Red Army on the Basis of Leninist Unity) (1929); *Novoye v stroitel'stve Krasnoy Armii* (New Developments in the Building of the Red Army) (1930); *Awards:* Order of the Red Banner; *Died:* 1937 in imprisonment; posthumously rehabilitated.

URATADZE, G. I. (1879–?) Menshevik Party official; *Born:* 1879; *Career:* before 1917 Oct Revol did Party work in Batumi and Tiflis; member, Caucasian Oblast RSDRP Comt; 1917 leading figure in Geo SDRP; 1918 member, Transcaucausian Sejm; 1919 member, Geo Constituent Assembly; ed, Geo SDRP newspaper "Ertoba"; 1920 Geo govt rep at signing of peace treaty with RSFSR; after establishment of Sov rule in Geo went into emigration; in latter years ed, Paris journal "Chveni Drosha"; member, Exec Comt, Geo Nat Council and member Foreign Bureau, Geo Soc-Democratic Party; *Died:* date and place of death unknown.

URAYEV, Pyotr Vasil'yevich (1910–1967) Party official; Russian; first secr, Mari Oblast CPSU Comt from 1963; cand member, CC, CPSU from 1966; CP member from 1939; *Born:* 1910; *Educ:* 1933 grad Timiryazev Agric Technicum; 1949 grad Higher Party School, CC, CPSU; *Career:* 1933–35 in Sov Army; 1935–42 senior agronomist, then dir, Bogorodsk Machine-and-Tractor Station, Perm' Oblast; from 1942 secr, rayon Party comt, then dept head, oblast Party comt; 1949–56 dept instructor, then dep sub-dept head, Agric Dept, CC, CPSU; 1956–57 second secr, Tatar Oblast CPSU Comt; 1957–63 second secr, Bashkir Oblast CPSU Comt; dep, USSR Supr Sov of 1958, 1962, and 1966 convocations; 1958–66 member, Draft Bills Commissions, Sov of Nationalities, USSR Supr Sov; from 1966 member, Draft Bills Commission, Sov of the Union, USSR Supr Sov; *Awards:* Order of Lenin (1965); Order of the Red Banner of Labor (1957); *Died:* July 1967.

URAZBAYEVA, Alma Din'mukhammedovna (1898–1943) Party official; CP member from 1919; *Born:* 28 Dec 1898 in vil Urda, Ural Oblast, Kaz SSR, daughter of a farmhand; *Educ:* 1916 grad teachers' training courses; 1919 studied at Communist Univ; *Career:* 1917 propaganda in vils of Bukey Steppe; during Civil War mustered Kaz nat units in Red Army; fall 1918 appointed agitator, lst Sov Model Kaz Cavalry Regt; from 1919 plen, Kir (Kaz) Oblast RCP(B) Bureau and Mil Revol Comt; 1920 elected to first Kazakhstani govt; member, Moslem Section, Orenburg Province Party Comt; worked for Kir Oblast RCP(B) Bureau; 1921 assigned to Bukey Province Party Comt, where she became a Presidium member and directed work among women; June 1921 deleg at lst Kaz Oblast Party Conference; then coopted to Kaz Oblast Party Comt; subsequently frequently elected to Kaz Oblast (then Kray) Party Comt; from Mar 1922 head, Dept for Work Among Women, Kir (Kaz) Oblast Party Comt; Mar 1925 delivered report at All-Union Conference of Workers Among Eastern Women; from 1926 head, Kaz Polit Educ Comt; from June 1928 head, Dept for Work Among Women, Lower Volga Kray CPSU(B) Comt; deleg at 12–4th Congresses and 16th Conference of CPSU(B); cand member, USSR and All-Russian Centr Exec Comt; 1924 member, Sov deleg at 3rd Int Conference of Communist Women, Berlin; 1930 retired on med grounds; *Died:* spring 1943.

URAZOV, Georgiy Grigor'yevich (1884–1957) Chemist and metallurgist; member, USSR Acad of Sci from 1946; *Born:* 18 Jan 1884; *Educ:* 1909 grad Petersburg Polytech Inst; *Career:* 1909–21 lecturer, from 1921 prof, Petersburg Polytech Inst; from 1934 dept head, Inst of Gen and Inorganic Chemistry; USSR Acad of Sci; from 1938 also prof, Moscow Inst of Fine Chemical Technol; 1939–46 corresp member, USSR Acad of Sci; from 1943 also prof, Moscow Inst of Non-Ferrous Metals and Gold; did research on metallic alloys, metal systems, sulfides and chlorides, metallic ores and ore refining, hydrated salt balance and natural salts; compiled diagrams showing the state of numerous metallic systems and discovered a number of new intermetallic compounds; 1911 discovered solid-state conversions in a magnesium-cadmium system; 1914, together with N.S. Kurnakov, discovered Berthollide phase in an iron-silicon system; 1919 discovered AlSb compound in aluminum-antimony system; studied properties of triple alloys of aluminum: aluminium-silicon-copper (1929); aluminum-silicon-magnesium (1936); aluminum-magnesium-copper (1946), etc; this provided the sci base for selecting the materials and conditions for the heat working of light, high-tensile alloys; 1915 began extensive research into metals' interaction with sulfur and metal sulfides and chlorides; also studied chemical equilibrium in chloride and sulfide systems; this provided the theoretical base for such complex non-ferrous metallurgical processes as precipitation alloying, chlorination, etc; studied chemical composition and physicochemical nature of Tikhva bauxites (1920–24); 1928 devised original methods for processing them into pure alumina; did research on technol for processing natural salts in USSR; invented a method for extracting iodine from raw materials available in USSR; 1930 advanced physicochemical hypothesis for genesis of Solikamsk potassium salt deposits; from 1934 organized expeditions to study the salt deposits of the Caspian and the Kara-Bogaz-Gol Gulf; *Awards:* two Orders of Lenin; three other orders; medals; *Died:* 27 Apr 1957.

URBANSKIY, Yevgeniy Yakovlevich (1932–1965) Actor; Hon Artiste of RSFSR from 1962; CP member from 1962; *Born:* 1932; *Educ:* 1957 grad Nemirovich-Danchenko Studio; *Career:* from 1957 with Moscow's Stanislavskiy Drama Theater; also acted in films; *Roles:* stage roles: Richard Duggan in Shaw's "The Devil's Apprentice"; Pyotr in Kogout's *Takaya lyubov'* (Such Love); Mart Tuysk in Rannet's *Bludnyy syn* (The Prodigal Son); John Proctor in Miller's "The Crucible"; Kirill in Braginskiy's *Raskrytoye okno* (The Open Window); Adam in Ebralidze's *Sovremennaya tragediya* (A Modern Tragedy); Latsis in Shatrov's *Shestoye iyulya* (The Sixth of July), etc; film roles: Vasiliy Gubanov in "Communism"; Astakhov in *Chistoye nebo* (Clear Sky), etc; *Died:* 5 Nov 1965.

URITSKIY, Moysey Solomonovich (1873–1918) Revolutionary; chm, Petrograd Cheka; cand member, CC, RCP(B); CP member from 1917; *Born:* 14 Jan 1873 in Cherkassy, Ukr; *Educ:* 1897 grad Law Fac, Kiev Univ; *Career:* 1897 arrested for revol propaganda and exiled for five years to Yakutsk Province; 1903, after 2nd RSDRP Congress, sided with Mensheviks; 1905 revol work in Petersburg; again arrested and exiled to Siberia; Sept-Oct 1905 played active part in revol events in Krasnoyarsk, leading to armed revolt and temporary seizure of power (Dec–early Jan 1906) by so-called Revol Govt of Krasnoyarsk Republ; prior to WW 1 emigrated; worked with Trotsky on the Paris newspaper "Nashe slovo"; after 1917 Feb Revol returned to Petrograd and sided with Revol Internationalists; together with this group, joined Bolshevik Party; at 6th Party Congress elected member, CC, RSDRP(B); Oct 1917 member, Party Center to Direct Oct Revol; member, Mil Revol Comt; then comr, Constituent Assembly; opposed Brest Peace Treaty, urged revol war and sided with Leftist Communists, contributing to their journal "Kommunist"; together with Pyatakov, Lomov and others resigned from Party and govt posts in protests against Brest Peace Treaty; Dec 1917 appointed chm, Petrograd Cheka; Mar 1918, at 7th RCP(B) Congress, elected cand member, CC; *Died:* 30 Aug 1918 assassinated in Petrograd by the Socialist-Revol student Kanegiser; streets, squares and various settlements bear his name.

URNOV, Konstantin Vasil'yevich (1907–1964) Electr eng; Cand of Tech Sci from 1947; *Born:* 1907; *Career:* 1932 lecturer, Kalinin Inst of Agric Machine-Building; 1935–39 lecturer, from 1939 assoc prof, Moscow Power Eng Inst; dept head, Moscow Polygraphic Inst; developed and introduced electr drive for first machine tools, printing machinery and newsprint assemblies including electr drive for asynchronous rotary press for printing of newspaper "Pravda"; *Publ: Elektroprivod poligraficheskikh mashin. Uchebnoye posobiye* (Electric Drives for Printing Machines. A Handbook) (1950), etc; *Died:* 11 Dec 1964.

URUNKHODZHAYEV, Sayd-Khodzha (1901–1967) Kolkhoz official; CP member from 1929; *Born:* 1901; *Career:* 1918 began work; fought against Basmachi movement and helped establish Sov rule in Tadzh; chm, farmhands' comt and chm, assoc for org of kolkhozes; dep dir, cotton mill; from 1933 life chm, "Moskva" Kolkhoz, Khodzhent Rayon, Tadzh SSR; deleg, 20th–23rd CPSU Congresses; dep, USSR Supr Sov of 5th–7th convocations; *Awards:* twice Hero of Socialist Labor (1948 and 1957); *Died:* 14 Sept 1967.

USACHYOV, Aleksandr Artem'yevich (1863–1937) Actor; Hon Artiste of RSFR from 1934; *Born:* 6 Aug 1863; *Educ:* 1891 grad Sazynov's class, Drama Courses, Petersburg Theatrical College; *Career:* 1891–1937 at Petersburg Alexandrine Theater (later Leningrad's Pushkin Drama Theater) *Roles:* Molchalin in *Gore ot uma* (Woe from Wit); Wurm in "Kabale und Liebe"; Dobchinskiy and Khlestakov in *Revizor* (The Government Inspector); Sprich in "Masquerade"; Yaka in *Vishnyovyy sad* (The Cherry-Orchard); Sing Bing-wu in *Bronepoyezd 14–69* (Armored Train 14–69); Petrishchev in *Plody prosveshcheniya* (The Fruits of Enlightenment); Kostyuk in *Yarost'* (Fury); Pechenegov in *Vragi* (Enemies), etc; *Publ:* memoirs *Povest' ob odnom aktyore* (Tale of an Actor) (1935); *Died:* 21 Jan 1937.

USENBAYEV, Alymkul (1894–1963) Kir bard; Pop Artiste of Kir SSR from 1936; CP member from 1944; *Born:* 16 May 1894 in vil Kara Archa, now Kir SSR; *Career:* in his youth worked as shepherd and composed his own songs; 1923 met the famous Kir bard Toktogul and learned from him the art of poetic improvisation; from 1936 soloist, Kir State Philharmonic; dep, Kir Supr Sov of 1938, 1947, 1951, 1955, 1959 and 1963 convocations; *Works:* songs: "Preparation for Spring"; "Views of Talas"; "My Kirghiz People"; "Our Festival"; "To a Heroic People"; "The City of Lenin"; "For Peace"; song collections: *Stepnyye poemy* (Poems of the Steppe); "Komuz"; *Stikhi o mire i trude* (Poems of Peace and Labor); *Schastlivyye deti* (Happy Children), etc; recorded many folk poems and the tale *Chelovek verkhom na tigre* (The Man on the Tiger); *Died:* 2 Aug 1963.

USHAKOV, Dmitriy Nikolayevich (1873–1942) Linguist; specialist in Russian linguistics; prof; Dr of Philology from 1918; corresp member, USSR Acad of Sci from 1939; *Born:* 24 Jan 1873 in Moscow, son of a physician; *Educ:* 1895 grad History and Philology Fac, Moscow Univ; *Career:* 1895–1913 taught at Moscow high-schools; 1909–19 taught at Higher Women's Courses; after 1917 Oct Revol taught at Prechistenskiy Courses and Higher Mil Teachers' Training School; in 1920's and 1930's taught at Bryusov Higher Inst of Lit and Arts, State Inst of Speech, and Inst of Philosophy, Lit and History, etc; 1907–42 prof, Moscow Univ; 1915–31 chm, Moscow Dialectological Commission, USSR Acad of Sci; member, Acad Commission for Preparing 1917 Reform of Russian Orthography; wrote numerous research and educ works on gen linguistics, history of Russian language, lexicography, dialectology, orthography and orthoëpy; in the field of gen linguistics and Russian grammar popularized ideas of his teacher, F. F. Fortunatov; one of the founders of Russian orthoëpy; his works on Russian dialectology (in coauthorship with N. N. Durnovo and N. N. Sokolov) played an important part in its development; campaigned for systematic improvement in speech standards and literacy of gen public; helped compile curricula and Russian language textbooks for elementary, secondary and higher schools; coauthor, *Orfograficheskiy slovar* (Orthographic Dictionary) for schools; wrote teachers' manuals; *Publ: Ocherk russkoy dialektologii. Prilozheniye k karte. "Dialektologicheskaya karta russkogo yazyka v Yevrope"* (Outline of Russian Dialectology. Supplement to Map. Dialectological Map of the Russian Language in Europe) (1915); *Russkoye pravopisaniye* (Russian Orthography) (1917); *Russkaya orfoepiya i yeyo zadachi* (Russian Orthoepy and Its Tasks) (1928); *Kratkoye vvedeniye v nauku o yazyke* (A Short Introduction to Linguistics) (9th ed, 1929); *Russkiy yazyk. Kratkoye sistematicheskoye shkol'noye rukovodstvo po grammatike, pravopisaniyu i proiznosheniyu* (The Russian Language. A Short Systematic School Manual on Grammar, Spelling and Pronunciation) (6th ed, 1929); coauthor and ed, *Tolkovyy slovar' russkogo yazyka" (Explanatory Dictionary of the Russian Language) (4 vol, 1947–48); coauthor, Orfograficheskiy slovar' dlya nachal'noy i sredney shkoly* (Orthographic Dictionary for Elementary and High Schools) (21st ed, 1966); *Died:* 17 Apr 1942.

USHAKOV, Georgiy Alekseyevich (1901–1963) Polar explorer; Dr of Geography from 1950; CP member from 1924; *Born:* 30 Jan 1901 in vil Lazarevo, Amur Oblast, son of an Amur Cossack; *Educ:* studied at Far Eastern Univ; *Career:* 1919–20 fought with partisans in the Far East; 1926–29 headed expedition to secure Wrangel and Geral'd Islands for the USSR; 1930–32 headed a four-man expedition, which discovered and mapped Severnaya Zemlya archipelago; 1934 directed rescue of members of ill-fated Chelyuskin expedition; 1935 headed ice-breaker "Sadko" lst Arctic expedition, which explored the northern Kara Sea and discovered an island; 1932–36 dep head, Main Northern Seaway Bd; 1936–40 head, Main Hydrometeorological Service Bd; 1940–43 and 1945–58 worked for various USSR Acad of Sci institutions; 1943–45 dep dir, Inst of Applied Geophysics, Min of Oil Ind; from 1957 pensioner; an island in the Kara Sea, a cape and a settlement on Wrangel Island, a glacier and a river on Severnaya Zemlya and a mountain in the Antarctic have been named after him; *Awards:* Order of Lenin; Order of the Red Star; Order of the Red Banner of Labor; *Died:* 3 Dec 1963.

USHAKOV, Ivan Mikhaylovich (1910–1966) Stage designer; Hon Art Worker of Bel SSR from 1949; *Born:* 19 Jan 1910; *Educ:* 1933 grad Vitebsk Art College; *Career:* from 1933 stage designer, 1939–52 chief stage designer, lst Bel State Theater (now Yanka Kupala Drama Theater); *Works:* designed sets and costumes for: Klimkovich's *Katerina Zhernosek* (1938); Samuylenok's *Gibel' volka* (The Death of the Wolf) (1939); "Front" (1942); Romanovich's *Poleshchuki* (1944); Movzon's "Konstantin Zaslonov" (1947); Gubarevich's *Tsitadel' slavy* (Citadel of Glory) (1950); Chekhov's *Vishnyovyy sad* (The Cherry-Orchard) (1951); Korneychuk's "Makar Dubrava" (1952); Makayenok's *Izvinite, pozhaluysta* (Excuse Me, Please!) (1954), etc; *Died:* 26 Aug 1966.

USHAKOV, Sergey Nikolayevich (1893–1964) Organic chemist and technologist; corresp member, USSR Acad of Sci from 1943; prof from 1930; Hon Sci and Tech Worker of RSFSR from 1943; CP member from 1943; *Born:* 16 Sept 1893; *Educ:* 1921 grad Petrograd Polytech Inst; *Career:* from 1930 prof, Leningrad Technol Inst; 1931–38 assoc, 1938–41 dir, Plastics Research Inst; 1945–49 dir, Research Inst of Polymeric Plastics; 1948–53 dir, Inst of Polymolecular Compounds, USSR Acad of Sci; did research on phenolaldehyde condensation, synthesis and study of polymers of unsaturated compounds, particularly vinyl derivatives, elementary cellulose esters, etc; *Publ: Iskusstvennyye smoly i ikh primeneniye v lakovoy promyshlennosti* (Artificial Resins and Their Use in the Varnish Industry) (1929); *Plasticheskiye massy iz efirov tsellyulozy* (Plastics from Cellulose Esters) (1932); *Efiry tsellyulozy i plasticheskiye massy na ikh osnove* (Cellulose Esters and Plastics Based on Them) (1941); *O poluchenii plyonok, nitey, poroplastov i tiksotropnykh geley iz yodnykh kompleksov polivinilovogo spirta i yego sopolimerov* (Producing Films, Fibers, Poroplasts and Tixotropic Gels from Iodine Complexes of Polyvinyl Alcohol and Its Co-Polymers) (1960); *O sinteze kremnevykh proizvodnykh polivinilovogo spirta* (The Synthesis of Silicon Products of Polyvinyl Alcohol) (1960); *Khimiya – meditsine* (Chemistry in Medicine) (1963); *Awards:* three Orders of Lenin; three other orders; medals; two Stalin Prizes (1942 and 1950); *Died:* 16 Sept 1964.

USHINSKIY, Nikolay Grigor'yevich (1863–1934) Pathologist and bacteriologist; Dr of Med from 1891; prof; *Born:* 1863; *Career:* pupil of V.V. Pashutin; 1895–1907 head, Chair of Gen Pathology, Warsaw Univ; 1922–34 head, Chair of Gen Pathology, Odessa, Leningrad, then Baku Univ; did research on mineral springs in Azer and Dag; discovered anaerobic flora in hot oil springs over a kilometer below the Earth's surface; wrote about 100 works on pathological physiology, microbiology and balneology; *Publ:* doctor's thesis *Gazoobmen i teploproduktivnost' pri floridizinovoy glyukozurii* (Gas Metablism and Calorific Value in Floridizinic Glucosuria) (1891); *Lektsii po obshchey i eksperimental'noy patologii* (Lectures on General and Experimental Pathology) (1906); *Died:* 1934.

USIYEVICH, Grigoriy Aleksandrovich (1891–1918) Revolutionary; CP member from 1908; *Born:* 1891 in Tambov, son of a merchant; *Educ:* 1907 studied at Petersburg Univ; *Career:* Party work among students and workers while still at high-school; 1908 joined Petersburg RSDRP(B) Comt; 1909 arrested and imprisoned for two years; 1911 exiled to Yeniseysk Province; where he continued revol work and contributed to Bolshevik journal "Prosveshcheniye"; 1914 fled from exile, went to Petersburg, then emigrated; arrested in Austria immediately on his arrival and interned in concentration camp until early 1916; then moved to Switzerland, where he had frequent contacts with Lenin; after 1917 Feb Revol returned to Russia with Lenin and worked for Moscow RSDRP(B) Comt; during 1917 Oct Revol member, Moscow Mil Revol Comt; Mar 1918 sent to Western Siberia to organize food supplies for Moscow; member, Omsk Mil Revol Staff; June 1918 elected chm, Tyumen' Revol Staff; *Died:* 3 Aug 1918 killed in battle with White forces at Kamyshlov.

USOV, Mikhail Antonovich (1883–1939) Geologist; prof from 1913; member, USSR Acad of Sci from 1939; *Born:* 20 Feb 1883; *Educ:* 1908 grad Tomsk Technol Inst; *Career:* 1906–09 member, V.A. Obruchyov's expeditions to Dzhungaria; after grad remained at Tomsk Technol Inst to train for professorship, which he gained in 1913; from 1917 did major research on the geological structure and tectonics of the Kuzbas coalbearing regions; 1921–30 head, Siberian Branch, Geological Comt; 1932–39 corresp member, USSR Acad of Sci; until 1938 sci dir, West Siberian Geological Survey Trust; apart from Siberia also studied the geology of the neighboring areas of China and Mongolia; *Publ:Fazy effuzivov* (The Phases of Effusive Rock Formation) (1924); *Fatsii i fazy intruzivov* (The Facies and Phases of Intrusive Rock Formation)

(1925); *Elementy tektoniki Kuzbassa i stratigrafii uglenosnykh otlozheniy Kuzbassa* (The Elements of the Tectonics of the Kuzbas and the Stratigraphy of Coal-Bearing Deposits in the Kuzbas) (1934); *Fazy i tsikly tektogeneza Zapadno-Sibirskogo kraya* (The Phases and Cycles of the Tectogenesis of the West Siberian Kray) (1936), etc; *Died:* 26 July 1939.

USOVA, Aleksandra Platonovna (1898–1965) Educ theorist; specialist in pre-school educ; Dr of Pedag Sci; corresp member, RSFSR Acad of Pedag Sci from 1950; CP member from 1928; *Born:* 11 Nov 1898; *Educ:* 1926 grad Pre-School Educ Fac, Herzen State Teachers' Training Inst, Leningrad; *Career:* 1921 began teaching work in Irkutsk; 1928–37 taught at Herzen State Teachers' Training Inst, Leningrad; 1937–41 lectured at Krupskaya Teachers' Training Inst; 1942–45 dir, Centr Office of Sci Methods of Pre-School Educ, RSFSR Min of Educ; from 1945 did research work at institutes of RSFSR Acad of Pedag Sci; 1960–65 studied theory and history of pedag and pre-school educ; developed theoretical principles of teaching pre-school-age children in kindergarten and at home; studied ways of improving their preparedness for school; *Publ: Igra i igrushka* (Play and Toys) (1940); coauthor, *Doshkol'naya pedagogika* (Pre-School Pedagogics) (1946); ed, collection *Voprosy obucheniya v detskom sadu* (Kindergarten-Training) (2nd ed, 1955); *Obucheniye v detskom sadu* (Training in Kindergarten) (1961); *Died:* 16 July 1965.

USPENSKIY, Fyodor Ivanovich (1845–1928) Byzantine historian; prof; member, Russian (USSR) Acad of Sci from 1900; pioneer of Byzantine studies in Russia; *Born:* 19 Feb 1845 in Kostroma Province; *Educ:* grad Petersburg Univ; *Career:* 1879–94 prof, Novorossiysk Univ, Odessa; 1894–1914 founder-dir, Russian Archeological Inst, Constantinople; from 1914 in Petrograd; 1915–28 ed, periodical "Vizantiyskiy vremennik"; chm, Commission for Byzantine Studies, Russian Acad of Sci; 1922–27 prof, Leningrad Univ; 1894–1914 headed archeological expeditions in Syria, Palestine, etc; also carried out archeological excavations in Bulgaria; wrote some 200 research works; *Publ: Pervyye slavyanskiye monarkhii na severo-zapade* (The First Slav Monarchies in the Northwest) (1872); *Obrazovaniye Vtorogo bolgarskogo tsarstva* (The Formation of the Second Bulgarian Kingdom) (1879); *Ocherki po istorii vizantiyskoy obrazovannosti* (An Outline History of Byzantine Learning) (1891); *Istoriya Krestovykh pokhodov* (A History of the Crusades) (1900); *Istoriya Vizantiyskoy imperii* (A History of the Byzantine Empire) (3 vol, 1913, 1926 and 1948); *Ocherki po istorii Trapezundskoy imperii* (An Outline History of the Trapezund Empire) (1929); *Died:* 10 Sept 1928.

USPENSKIY, Vasiliy Vasil'yevich (1881–1952) Surgeon; Hon Physician of RSFSR from 1944; *Born:* 1881; *Educ:* 1910 completed med training; *Career:* after grad worked as zemstvo physician in Kostroma, Tambov and Ufa Provinces; 1912–14 specialized in surgery at Petersburg Inst of Postgrad Med Training and Staro-Yekaterininskaya Hospital, Moscow; 1914 directed hospital in Kologriva; 1918 moved to Tver' and until his death headed the Surgical Dept, Tver' (now Kalinin) Joint Municipal Hospital; 1935 entitled Dr of Med, Honoris Causau; for a number of years head, Chair of Anatomy and Physiology, Kalinin Teachers' Training Inst; from 1937 prof of anatomy and physiology; wrote works on surgical treatment of gastric and duodenal ulcers; *Publ:* coauthor, *Na "yazvennoy epidemii"* (The "Ulcer Epidemic") (1929); *Otdalyonnyye rezul'taty khirurgicheskogo lecheniya krugloy yazvy i povtornyye operatsii na zheludke* (The Long-Term Results of Surgical Treatment of Round Ulcers and Repeated Operations on the Stomach) (1935); *Died:* 1952.

USPENSKIY, Viktor Aleksandrovich (1879–1949) Music ethnographer; composer; Dr of Arts; prof; Pop Artiste of Turkm SSR from 1929 and Uzbek SSR from 1937; *Born:* 19 Aug 1879 in Kaluga; *Educ:* 1913 grad Lyadov's Composition Class, Petersburg Conservatory; *Career:* in his childhood lived in Osh and Tashkent, Centr Asia; from 1918 worked in Tashkent; participated in three folk-lore expeditions; 1918–22 teacher, Pop Concervatory; 1928–34 at Tashkent Musical College; 1932–49 researcher, then head, Inst of Art Criticism; 1936–49 prof, Tashkent Conservatory; reconstructed Uzbek folk music instruments; *Works:* recordings of six "makoms" (folk classical music) "Shash-Makom" (1924); musical drama "Farkhad and Shirin" (1934; 1940 rewritten into an opera); suite "Mukanna" (1944); "Lyric Poem in Memory of Navoi" (1947); etc; *Publ: Klassicheskaya muzyka uzbekov* (Uzbek Classical Music) (1927); coauthor, *Turkmenskaya muzyka* (Turkmenian Music) (1928); *Awards:* Badge of Hon; *Died:* 9 Oct 1949 in Tashkent.

USTINOV, Aleksey Mikhaylovich (1879–1937) Govt official; CP member from 1920; *Born:* 1879; *Career:* from 1901 in revol movement; 1906–17 member, Socialist-Revol Party; 1908–17 lived in Switzerland and France; 1917 member, Exec Comt for Repatriation of Russian Polit Emigrés from Switzerland; 1917–18 member, Leftist, Socialist-Revol Party; 1917–20 member, All-Russian Centr Exec Comt; from 1921 dipl work; 1924–29 USSR plen in Greece; 1929–33, USSR Pop Comrt of For Affairs plen in Transcaucasian Federation; 1934–37 USSR plen in Est; arrested by State Security organs; *Died:* 1937 in imprisonment.

USTRYALOV, Nikolay Vasil'yevich (1890–?) Lawyer; journalist; leading member, Constitutional-Democratic Party; *Born:* 1890; *Educ:* grad univ; *Career:* from 1913, after grad, assoc prof, Moscow and Perm' Univ; 1916–18 worked for newspaper "Utro Rossii"; 1918, while in Siberia, chm, Eastern Dept, CC, Constitutional-Democratic Party; published Omsk newspaper "Russkoye delo" and headed Press Bureau in Kolchak govt; after end of Civil War in Siberia emigrated to Harbin; 1921–22 worked for collection and journal "Smena vekh", published in Prague and Paris; one of ideologists of "Change of Landmarks" movement; sided with those emigres who considered further armed struggle against the Bolshevik regime pointless after the end of the Civil War and urged Russian intellectuals to return home and collaborate with the Soviet authorities; 1920–34 prof, Harbin Univ; from 1928 dir, Centr Library, Chinese-Eastern Railroad; 1935 returned to USSR; from 1935 prof of geographical econ, Moscow Inst of Trans Eng; 1937 arrested and sentenced for alleged anti-Sov activities by Mil Collegium, USSR Supr Court; *Died:* date and place of death unknown.

USYSKIN, Il'ya D. (1910–1934) Balloonist; Komsomol member from 1927; *Born:* 1910 in Yaroslavl', son of a worker; *Educ:* 1925–28 studied at Electr Eng Dept, Moscow Higher Tech College; 1931 grad Physics and Mathematics Fac, Leningrad Polytech Inst; *Career:* from 1931 postgrad student, Leningrad Polytech Inst; simultaneously junior asst, then assoc, Leningrad Inst of Physics Eng; during his postgrad studies accomplished two important research projects on the diffraction of fast electrons; Mar 1933 appointed to adapt the Wilson camera for the study of cosmic radiation in the stratosphere, also assigned to stratispheric balloon flights; did research on cosmic radiation; designed an improved version of the Wilson camera; 30 Jan 1934 ascended to 20,600 meters with a balloon of the Soc to Promote the USSR Aviation, Chemical and Defense Ind; balloon encountered bad weather and crashed, killing all crew members; *Died:* 30 Jan 1934 killed in balloon crash; his ashes are immured in the Kremlin wall on Moscow's Red Square.

UTKIN, Iosif Pavlovich (1903–1944) Russian poet; Jew; *Born:* 15 May 1903 in settlement Hinkang, China; *Educ:* 1927 grad Moscow Inst of Journalism; *Career:* 1920 left Irkutsk high-school and volunteered for Red Army; 1923 first work printed; 1929–30 publicly criticized his own poetry; during WW 2 worked for army newspapers; *Publ:* verse "A Soldier's Tale" (1924); poem "Tale of the Redheaded Motel" (1926); *Pervaya kniga stikhov* (A First Book of Poetry) (1927); *Miloye detstvo* (Dear Childhood) (1933); *Frontovyye stikhi* (Frontline Poetry) (1942); *O rodine. O druzhbe. O lyubvi* (Fatherland. Friendship. Love) (1944), etc; *Died:* 13 Nov 1944 killed in a plane crash.

UYGUR real name: MADZHIDOV), Mannon (1897–1955) Uzbek playwright, actor and stage dir; Pop Artiste of Uzbek SSR from 1932; *Born:* 11 Oct 1897; Educ: *1927 grad Drama Studio, Uzbek Educ Center, Moscow; Career:* 1916 amateur actor with "Turon" Company, Tashkent; 1919 founder-dir, professional Karl Marx Company, Tashkent; from 1927 actor, stage dir and artistic dir, Khamza Theater; taught at Tashkent Theatrical Art Inst; *Roles:* Eshimkul in "The Turkestani Healer"; Gafur in Khamza's "The Bey and the Farmhand"; Rakhim in Zafari's "Khalima", etc; *Productions:* "The Bey and the Farmhand" (1919); "Khalima" (1920); Yashen's "Two Communists" (1929); Fatkhullin's "The Mask Removed" (1932); "Hamlet" (1935); Sheykh-zade's "Dzhalaletdin" (1944); Uygun's "Song of Life" (1947), etc; *Works:* comedy "The Turkestani Healer" (1918); one-act plays; translated plays from Azer and Tatar; *Awards:* Stalin Prize (1949); *Died:* 16 Oct 1955.

UZNADZE, Dmitriy Nikolayevich (1887–1950) Psychologist; member, Geo Acad of Sci from 1941; *Born:* 1 Jan 1887; *Educ:* 1909 grad Philosophy Inst, Leipzig Univ; *Career:* 1910 began to teach; 1915 founded Georgia's first girls' secondary school where

Geo was the language of tuition; 1918 co-founder, Tbilisi Univ; where he established the Dept of Psychology, the Chair of Psychology and the Laboratory of Experimental Psychology; from 1941 co-founder and dir, Inst of Psychology (since 1950 Uznadze Inst of Psychology), Geo Acad of Sci; devised original theory of orientation, regarding orientation as a factor in the individual's expedient and adaptive behavior; studied the formation of orientation and developed an experimental method for studying it; wrote a number of works on the psychology of thinking, speech, perception, activity, etc; wrote first psychology textbooks and systematic courses in Georgian: *Publ:* "An Introduction to Experimental Pedagogics" (1912); "Impersonalia" (1923); "Principles of Experimental Psychology" (1925); "General Psychology" (1940); "Die metaphysische Weltanschauung W. Solowjows, mit orientierendem Überblick seiner Erkenntnistheorie" (1909); "Ein experimenteller Beitrag zum Problem der psychologischen Grundlagen der Namengebung" (1924); "Über die Gewichtstäuschung und ihre Analoga" (1931); "Zum Problem der Bedeutungserfassung (Inhalt und Gegenstand)" (1927); "Die Gruppenbildungsversuche der vorschulpflichtigen Kinder" (1929); "Die Begriffsbildung im vorschulpflichtigen Alter" (1929); "Untersuchungen zur Psychologie der Einstellung" (1939); in Russian translation: *K voprosu ob osnovnom zakone smeny ustanovki* (The Basic Law of Substitute Orientation) (1930); *Eksperimental'nyye osnovy psikhologii ustanovki* (The Experimental Principles of the Psychology of Orientation) (1961); *Psikhologicheskiye issledovaniya* (Psychological Research) (1966); *Died:* 12 Oct 1950.

V

VACHNADZE, Nato (real name: Nataliya Georgiyevna) (1904–1953) Actress; Pop Artiste of Geo SSR; Hon Artiste of RSFSR; CP member from 1943; *Born:* 14 June 1904 in Warsaw; *Film Roles:* Nino in "Arsen the Bandit" (1924); Nunu in "The Pillar of Shame" (1924); Esme in "Three Lives" (1925); Despine in "The Tariel Mklavadze Case" (1925); the Unknown Woman in "Law and Duty" after Stefan Zweig's novella "Amok" (1928); Dzhemma in *Ovod* (The Gadfly), after Voynich (1928); Tamara in *Posledniy maskarad* (The Last Masquerade) (1934); Nani in *Zolotistaya dolina* (The Golden Valley) (1937); Mano in *Kolybel' poeta* (The Cradle of a Poet) (1947), etc; *Publ: Vstrechi i vpechatleniya* (Meetings and Impressions) (1953); *Awards:* three Orders of the Red Banner of Labor; Badge of Hon; Stalin Prize (1941); *Died:* 14 June 1953.

VADETSKIY, Boris Aleksandrovich (1907–1962) Russian writer; CP member from 1927; *Born:* 16 Dec 1907 in Petersburg; *Career:* 1928 first work printed; wrote mainly on historical subjects; *Publ:* poem "The Harbor" (1931); novelette *Vozvrashcheniye* (The Return) (1939); novelette *V moryakh tvoya doroga* (Thy Way Lies in the Seas) (1945); stories *Shtorm* (The Storm) (1945); *Povest' voyennykh let* (A Tale of Wartime) (1947); historical novelette "Fyodor Matyushkin" (1949); *novels: Prostoy smertnyy* (An Ordinary Mortal) (1950); "Glinka" (1954); novelette *Obreteniye schast'ya* (The Acquisition of Happiness) (1956); novel "Akyn Terezi" (1956); novelette *Skazaniye o flotovodtse* (The Tale of an Admiral) (1958); stories *Tvorimaya legenda* (Legend in the Making) (1959), etc; *Died:* 29 Mar 1962 in Moscow.

VAGA, August Yanovich (1893–1960) Botanist; prof; member, Est Acad of Sci from 1954; *Born:* 3 Mar 1893; *Educ:* 1923 grad Tartu Univ; *Career:* 1923–31 taught at Est secondary schools; 1931–46 asst prof and assoc prof, from 1946 prof, Tartu Univ; until 1954 corresp member, Est Acad of Sci; 1947–52 also dep dir, Inst of Biology, Est Acad of Sci; specialized in theory of phytocenology and plant taxonomy and phylogeny; *Publ:* "Futotsonologia pohikusimusi" (1940); "Eostaimede susteemi kujunemiskaik ja praegused probleemid" (1946); *Filema organicheskogo mira* (The Phylema of the Organic World) (1952); "Hoimkond sonajalgtaimed" (1953); textbook *Anatomiya kornya* (Root Anatomy); *Botanicheskiye issledovaniya v Estonskoy SSR* (Botanical Research in the Estonian SSR); *Flora Estonskoy SSR* (The Flora of the Estonian SSR) (1960), etc; *Died:* 1960.

VAGANOVA, Agrippina Yakovlevna (1879–1951) Ballet dancer; ballet teacher and choreographer; Pop Artiste of RSFSR from 1934; *Born:* 24 June 1879; *Educ:* 1897 grad Petersburg Theatrical College; *Career:* 1897 debut at Mariinskiy Theater; won popularity as virtuoso classical dancer; 1916 abandoned stage work; from 1917 taught ballet; 1921–46 instructor, 1946–51 prof, Leningrad Choreographic College; 1931–37 artistic dir, Ballet Company, Leningrad Opera and Ballet Theater; then concentrated on teaching; 1946–51 head, Chair of Choreography, Leningrad Conservatory; trained such outstanding dancers as G.S. Ul'yanova, M.T. Semyonova, O.G. Iordan, N.A. Anisimova, T.M. Vecheslova, N.M. Dudinskaya, F.I. Balabina, A.Ya. Shelest, etc; *Roles:* Odette-Odile; the Tsar-Maiden in Pugny's *Konyok-gorbunok* (The Little Hunchback-Horse); main role in "Chopiniana", etc; *Productions: Lebedinoye ozero* (Swan Lake) (1933); "Esmeralda" (1935), etc; *Publ: Osnovy klassicheskogo tantsa* (The Principles of Classic Dance) (1934); *Awards:* Stalin Prize (1946); Order of the Red Banner of Labor; medals; *Died:* 5 Nov 1951.

VAGARSHYAN, Vagarsh Bogdanovich (1894–1959) Actor, stage dir and playwright; Pop Artiste of USSR from 1954; CP member from 1944; *Born:* 14 Feb 1894 in Shusha, son of a baker; *Educ:* grad Tiflis Business College; *Career:* from 1915 with Arm Touring Company; performed with and managed companies in Krasnodar, Rostov and other North Caucasian towns; from 1923 actor and stage dir, 1st Arm State Theater, Yerevan (now Sundukyan Theater); 1941–44 artistic dir of a theater; instructor, from 1946 prof, Yerevan Theatrical Inst; dep, USSR Supr Sov of 1st convocation; dep, Arm Supr Sov of 2nd–4th convocations; theater in Goris named for him; *Roles:* Belogubov in Ostrovskiy's *Dokhodnoye mesto* (A Lucrative Post) (1929); Aslan-ami in Vagarshyan's "In the Ring" (1930); Figaro (1933); Yegor in Gorky's *Yegor Bulychov i drugiye* (Yegor Bulychov and Co) (1933); Tikhon in Ostrovskiy's *Groza* (The Storm) (1935); Polezhayev in Rakhmanov's *Bespokoynaya starost,* (Restless Old Age) (1938); Lenin in Pogodin's *Chelovek s ruzh'yom* (The Man with a Gun) (1938); Suren in Shirvanzade's *Iz-za chesti* (For Honor's Sake) (1939); Suren Spandaryan in Gulakyan's "Great Friendship" (1939); Gagik in Demirchan's "My Native Land" (1940); Miron in "Front" (1942); Hamlet (1942); Smith in Simonov's *Russkiy vopros* (The Russian Question) (1947); Lavrov in Romashov's *Velikaya sila* (The Great Force) (1948); Firs in Chekhov's *Vishnyovyy sad* (The Cherry Orchard) (1951), etc; *Productions: Dostigayev i drugiye* (Dostigayev and Co) (1934); "Vassa Zheleznova" (1937); "Kabale und Liebe" (1938); Ovchinnikov's *Derzaniye* (Daring) (1950), etc; *Works:* plays: *V kol'tse* (In the Ring) (1930); *Neft'* (Oil) (1932); *Ministr finansov* (Minister of Finance) (1935); "David Sasunskiy" (1940); *Monastyrskoye ushchel'ye* (Monastery Canyon) (1945); *Den' v Salonike* (A Day in Salonika), etc; *Awards:* two Stalin Prizes (1941 and 1952); *Died:* 6 May 1959 in Moscow.

VAGNER, Vladimir Aleksandrovich (1849–1934) Biologist (Darwinist) and psychologist; pioneer of comparative psychology in Russia; *Born:* 17 Mar 1849; *Educ:* 1874 grad Law Fac, 1882 grad Natural Sci Dept, Fac of Physics and Mathematics, Moscow Univ; *Career:* 1895–1905 assoc prof, Moscow Univ; 1906–31 prof, Petersburg (Leningrad) Univ; contributed to the journals "Priroda" and "Yestestvoznaniye v shkole"; founder, Museum of the Evolution of the Nervous System and Psyche, Brain Inst; co-founder, Psychoneurological Inst; *Publ: Metody yestestvoznaniya v nauke i shkole* (Natural Science Methods in Science and School) (1893); *Biologicheskiy metod v zoopsikhologii* (The Biological Method in Zoopsychology) (1902); *Biologicheskiye osnovaniya sravnitel'noy psikhologii* (The Biological Basis of Comparative Psychology) (2 vol, 1910–13); coauthor, *Yestestvoznaniye v shkole* (Natural Science in School) (1912); *Biopsikhologiya i smezhnyye nauki* (Biopsychology and Related Sciences) (1923); *Vozniknoveniye i razvitiye psikhicheskikh sposobnostey* (The Emergence and Development of Mental Abilities) (1924–29); *Metodika nablyudeniy nad zhivotnymi* (Methods of Observing Animals) (1926); *Priroda i shkol'nik* (Nature and the Schoolboy) (1926); *Died:* 8 Mar 1934.

VAGZHANOV, Aleksandr Petrovich (1877–1919) Party official; CP member from 1896; *Born:* 24 Aug 1877 in vil Yamskaya Sloboda, near Tver', son of a laborer; *Career:* from age 13 worked in Tver' and Petersburg factories; during 1904–05 Russo-Japanese War served in Manchuria and did revol work among soldiers; arrested and exiled; 1906 member, Tver' RSDRP Comt; 1907 Tver' Province dep, 2nd State Duma; member, Soc-Democratic faction; after dispersal of 2nd State Duma arrested and sentenced to four years hard labor; then exiled to Siberia; May 1917 returned to Tver' and elected member, Exec Comt, Tver' Sov; deleg, 1st All-Russian Congress of Soviets; member, All-Russian Centr Exec

Comt of 1st convocation; from Oct 1917 member, Tver' RSDRP (B) Comt; chm, Exec Comt, Tver' Sov of Workers' Dep; chm, Tver' Revol Comt; from Dec 1917 chm, Tver' Province Exec Comt; from Apr 1918 worked in Siberia and the Far East; headed underground Baykal RCP(B) Comt; member, underground Siberian Oblast RCP(B) Comt; *Died:* June 1919 executed by White forces in Chita; Berg Factory in Kalinin (former Tver) and the street where he was born were renamed after him.

VAKAR, V. V. (PRAVDIN, V.) (1878–1926) Politician and soc worker; *Born:* 1878; *Career:* early 1890's began revol work; 1899 arrested for involvement in Kiev Univ student movement; 1902 member, Kiev RSDRP Comt; after 2nd RSDRP Congress sided with Bolsheviks; 1906 sentenced to one year fortress confinement; after his release abandoned Party work; after 1917 Oct Revol trade-union, legal, cultural and educ work outside the Party; *Died:* 1926.

VAKHITOV, Mulla-Nur (1885–1918) Tatar revol; Civil War veteran; journalist; *Born:* 10 Aug 1885 in vil Kazayevo, Perm' Province; *Educ:* 1907 studied at Petersburg Polytech Inst, then at Neurological Inst; *Career:* twice expelled from inst for revol activities; from 1910 worked for railroad in Kazan'; Apr 1917 helped found in Kazan' Moslem Socialist Comt, which worked under the direction of the Kazan' RSDRP(B) Comt; ed, newspaper "Krasnoye znamya"; Oct 1917 member, Kazan' Mil Revol Comt; 1918 Centr Moslem Comrt comr with RSFSR Council of Pop Comr; also chm, Centr Mil Moslem Collegium, Pop Comrt of the Navy; directed mustering of Moslem units for Red Army; Aug 1918 led 2nd Tatar-Bash Battalion in defense of Kazan' against Whitist troops; Aug 1918 captured by Whitist forces; *Died:* 19 Aug 1918 executed by Whitist troops.

VAKHRUSHEV, Vasiliy Vasil'yevich (1902–1947) Econ and govt official; CP member from 1918; *Born:* 28 Feb 1902 in Tula, son of a worker; *Career:* early 1918 volunteered for Red Army; after Civil War exec Party and admin work in Tula; later dir, Kosorog Metallurgical Plant; dir, Kalinin Railroad Car Plant; dir, Kashira State Electr Plant; head, Moscow Distr Power Bd; 1937 RSFSR Pop Comr of Local Ind; from 1938 dep chm, then chm, RSFSR Council of Pop Comr; from 1939 USSR Pop Comr of Coal Ind; at 18th CPSU(B) Congress elected member, CC, CPSU(B); dep, USSR Supr Sov of 1st and 2nd convocations; dep, RSFSR Supr Sov; from 1946 USSR Min of Coal Ind for Eastern Regions; *Awards:* two Orders of Lenin; Order of the Red Banner of Labor; "Hammer and Sickle" gold medal; Hero of Socialist Labor (1943); *Died:* 13 Jan 1947; buried on Moscow's Red Square.

VAKHTANGOV, Yevgeniy Bagrationovich (1883–1922) Stage dir, actor and impresario; *Born:* 13 Feb 1833 in Vladikavkaz, the son of Russian-Arm parents; *Educ:* studied at Moscow Univ; from 1909 at A.I. Adashev's Acting School, Moscow Arts Theater; from 1911 actor, Moscow Arts Theater; studied under Stanislavskiy; from 1911 taught Stanislavskiy method at various Moscow schools and studios; from 1912 actor and stage dir, 1st Studio, Moscow Arts Theater; after 1917 Oct Revol worked for Stage Dir Section, Theater Dept, Pop Comrt of Educ; 1918 founded short-lived Pop Arts Theater; from 1920 head, 3rd Studio, Moscow Arts Theater (1926 reorganized into Vakhtangov State Theater); *Roles:* Tackleton in "The Cricket on the Hearth", after Dickens; Frazier in Berger's *Potop* (The Flood); *Productions:* Hauptmann's "The Festival of the World" (1913); Berger's "The Flood" (1915); Maeterlinck's "St Anthony's Miracle" (1916–18); Ibsen's "Rosmersholm" (1918); Chekhov's *Svad'ba* (The Wedding) (1920); Strindberg's "Eric XIV"; "Princess Turandot"; (1922); *Publ: Zapiski. Pis'ma, stat'i* (Notes, Letters and Articles) (1939, posthumously); *Died:* 29 May 1922 in Moscow.

VAKHTEROV, Vasiliy Porfir'yevich (1853–1924) Educationist; specialist in elementary school teaching methods; *Born:* 25 Jan 1853, son of a consistory watchman; *Educ:* studied at Arzamas Theological College, then Nizhniy Novgorod Theological Seminary; *Career:* from 1872 taught at municipal public college in Vasil'sursk, then at uyezd college in Ardatov; 1881–96 inspector of public colleges; campaigned for expansion of elementary and secondary school syllabus; criticized parish schools; worked for Moscow Literacy Comt; campaigned for gen obligatory elementary educ; sponsored foundation of schools for workers and establishment of various extracurricular institutions; his work antagonized some elements in the Moscow Educ Distr; 1896 forced to resign, but continued educ and cultural work; 1898–1902 lectured on teachers' training courses in Khorol, Dubny, Kursk, Saratov, etc; helped organize 1st All-Russian Congress of Students' Mutual Aid Societies; 1893–1903 worked at school run by Morozova Plant, Tver'; 1903 arrested and exiled to Novgorod Province; returned to Moscow and resumed lit, teaching and social work, during 1905–07 Revol helped organize Teachers' Union; 1913–14 helped organize All-Russian Congress on Public Educ; 1916 helped organize 1st All-Russian Congress of Russian Language Teachers; after 1917 Oct Revol taught on courses for invalids, Red Army literacy courses, teachers' training courses, etc; 1923–24 lecturer, Teachers' Training Fac, 2nd Moscow Univ; *Publ: Russkiy bukvar'* (A Russian Primer) (1898); *Sel'skiye voskresnyye shkoly* (Rural Sunday Schools) (1896); *Narodnyye chteniya* (Folk Readings) (1897); coauthor, *Mir v rasskazakh dlya detey* (The World in Children's Stories) (3 vol, 1902–08); *Spornyye voprosy obrazovaniya* (Moot Education Problems) (1907); *Predmetnyy metod obucheniya* (The Subject Teaching Method) (1907); *Osnovy novoy pedagogiki* (The Principles of the New Pedagogics) (1913); *Vsenarodnoye shkol'noye i vneshkol'noye obrazovaniye* (General Public School and Extracurricular Education) (1917); *Died:* 3 Apr 1924.

VAKULICH, Pavel Ivanovich (1890–1937) Mil commander; CP member from 1919; *Born:* 1890; *Career:* officer in Russian Army; during Civil War directed 1st Saratov Courses; after Civil War head, 1st Dept and dep head, 1st Bd, Red Army Staff; head, Operations Fac, Red Army Mil Acad; dept head, Gen Staff Acad; arrested by State Security organs; *Died:* 1937 in imprisonment.

VALAYEV, A.A. (1877–1928) Economist; *Born:* 1877; *Career:* 1903–17 worked in cooperative credit system; joined Menshevik faction of RSDRP; during 1917 Feb Revol switched allegiance to Constitutional Democratic Party; after 1917 Oct Revol withdrew from politics; worked in Purchasing Dept, Pop Comrt of Food; Sept 1921–Jan 1922 member, Extraordinary Export Commission, Labor and Defense Council; 1922 head, Purchasing Dept, Pop Comrt of For Trade; in latter years worked for Agric Union and Grain Center; *Died:* 1928.

VALEDINSKIY, Ivan Aleksandrovich (1874–1954) Therapist and balneologist; Hon Sci Worker of RSFSR; *Born:* 1874; *Educ:* 1901 grad Med Fac, Tomsk Univ; *Career:* from 1906 senior asst prof of hospital therapeutic clinique, Tomsk Univ; from 1908 Dr of Med; from 1920 prof and head, Chair of Special Pathology and Therapy, Tomsk Univ; 1920–23 directed research at Siberian health resort of Karachi; from 1924 head, Therapy Dept, Health Resort Clinic of Pop Comrt of Health, Moscow (later Centr Inst of Resort Treatment); 1924 and 1925 founded resort clinics for Pop Comrt of Health covering all groups of Caucasian mineral waters; dir, Lenin Cardiological Clinic, Kislovodsk; for a number of years directed Centr Inst of Resort Treatment's comprehensive expedition to study the curative factors of the Sochi-Matsesta health resort; 1936 helped in its reconstruction and founded Balneological Inst in Sochi; 1932 headed comprehensive expedition to study the curative factors of the Tskhaltubo health resort, whose recommendations were then used for developing and expanding this resort; 1941–45 sci dir and consultant at evacuation hospitals in Caucasian mineral water resorts and in Siberia; directed research on resort treatment for war wounded; studied innervation of the heart, hematology, diagnosis of gastric cancer and treatment of rheumatism; popularized use of artificial sulfur baths (of the Matsesta type) according to a method developed under his supervision at the Centr Inst of Resort Treatment; Presidium member, Centr Sci Resort Council; member of many sci soc; member, ed bd, journal "Voprosy kurortologii"; member, ed bd, multi-vol manual *Osnovy kurortologii* (The Principles of Resort Treatment); published some 100 research works; *Publ:* thesis *Materialy po voprosu o prisutstvii i mestoraspolozhenii nervnykh uzlov zheludochkov serdtsa nekotorykh mlekopitayushchikh* (Material on the Presence and Location of the Nerve Ganglions of the Cardiac Ventricles in Some Mammals) (1908); *Ob izmeneniyakh krovi pri achylia gastrica simplex* (Blood Lesions in the Case of Achylia gastrica simplex) (1911); *O lechenii serdechnososudistykh zabolevaniy serovodorodnymi vannami* (Treating Cardiovascular Ailments with Sulfur Baths) (1929); *K voprosu o sushchnosti revmatizma* (The Nature of Rheumatism) (1932); *Kurortoterapiya zabolevaniy serdtsa i sosudov* (Resort Therapy of Cardiac and Vascular Diseases) (1936); *Klinicheskiye formy i stepeni khronicheskoy nedostatochnosti krovoobrashcheniya* (Clinical Forms and Degrees of Chronic Circulatory Insufficiency) (1940); *Died:* 1954 in Moscow.

VALETSKIY (WALECKI), Genrik (real name: KHORVITS [HORWITZ] Maksimilian) (1877–1938) Polish revol; *Born:* 6 Sept 1877 in Warsaw; *Educ:* 1898 grad Gent Univ; *Career:* 1895 joined Polish Socialist Party (PSP); 1904—05 left wing leader, PSP; 1905 member, Centr Workers' Comt, PSP; 1906, after PSP schism, elected member, Centr Exec Comt, Leftist PSP; supported amalgamation of Leftist PSP and Soc-Democratic Party of Poland and Lith into the CP Poland; attended Zimmerwald Conference; after 1917 Oct Revol ed, Zurich newspaper "Narodnoye pravo"; 1918—19 and 1923—25 member, CC, CP Poland; repeatedly arrested for revol activities; first by Tsarist Secret Polit Police and then by Polish authorities; 1921—25 CP Poland rep in Comintern; 1925 transferred from CP Poland to CPSU(B) with Party membership back dated from 1905; 1935, at 7th Comintern Congress, elected member, Int Control Commission; 1935 ed, journal "Kommunisticheskiy Internatsional"; 1937 arrested by State Security organs; *Died:* 1938 in imprisonment; posthumously rehabilitated.

VAL'TER, Anton Karlovich (1905—1965) Physicist; prof; member, Ukr Acad of Sci from 1951; Hon Sci Worker of Ukr SSR from 1953; CP member from 1941; *Born:* 24 Dec 1905 in Petersburg; *Educ:* 1926 grad Leningrad Polytech Inst; *Career:* 1924—30 assoc, Physical Eng Inst, Leningrad; from 1930 assoc, Physical Eng Inst, Ukr Acad of Sci; from 1940 prof, Khar'kov Univ; specialized in physics of dielectrics, semiconductors and atomic nucleus; developed methods of generating super-high voltages; did research on vacuum eng and design of electrostatic charged particle accelerators; *Publ: Ataka atomnogo yadra* (Attacking the Atomic Nucleus) (1935); coauthor, *Izucheniye reaktsii* He^3 *s deytronami* (Studying He^3 Reaction with Deutrons) (1956); coauthor, *Izmereniye effektivnykh poperechnykh secheniy reaktsiy* C^{12} */p, y/ i* C^{12} */d,n/ v oblasti malykh energiy bombardiruyushchikh chastits* (Measuring the Effective Cross Sections of C^{12} /p, y/ and C^{12} /d,n/ Reactions to Low-Energy Bombarding Particles) (1957); coauthor, *Vertikal'nyy elektrostaticheskiy generator FTI AN USSR na 4 Mv* (The Ukrainian Academy of Sciences FTI 4 Mv Vertical Electrostatic Generator) (1957); *Uprugoye rasseivaniye deytronov na izotopakh khroma i tsinka* (The Flexible Scattering of Deutrons on Chrome and Zinc Isotopes) (1963), etc; *Awards:* two Orders of Lenin; Order of the Red Banner of Labor; *Died:* 13 July 1965.

VANIN, Vasiliy Vasil'yevich (1898—1951) Actor and stage dir; Pop Artiste of USSR from 1949; *Born:* 13 Jan 1898 in Tambov, son of a railroad clerk; *Educ:* 1920 grad drama studio in Tambov; *Career:* from 1915 stagehand, extra, then actor, Tambov Theater; 1920—21 in Sov Army; 1921—24 at theaters in Tambov and Petrograd; 1924—49 at Moscow Province Trade-Union Council Theater (from 1930 Moscow Oblast Trade-Union Council Theater); 1950—51 chief stage dir, Moscow's Pushkin Theater; from 1927 film work; also taught stagecraft; from 1930 taught at Drama School, Moscow Oblast Trade-Union Council Theater; from 1944 taught at All-Union State Inst of Cinematography; from 1949 prof; *Roles:* stage roles: Gaston in Brisbar and New's "The Beggars of Paris"; Janson in *Rasskaz o semi poveshennykh* (The Tale of the Seven Hanged Men), after Andreyev; Kostylev in Gorky's *Na dne* (The Lower Depths); Vilenchuk and Patsyuk in Bill'-Belotserkovskiy's *Shtorm* (The Storm) and *Golos nedr* (The Voice of the Depths) (1929); Chapayev in Furmanov's "Chapayev"; (1930); Kadeyev in Afinogenov's "Mashen'ka" (1941); Fayunin in *Nashestviye* (Invasion) (1943); Nikon Kamen' in Surov's *Obida* (The Insult) (1948), etc; film roles: Matveyev in *Lenin v Oktyabre* (Lenin in October) and *Lenin v 1918 godu* (Lenin in 1918); Yefim Sokolov in *Chlen pravitel'stva* (A Member of the Government); Kochet in *Sekretar' raykoma* (The Secretary of the District Committee); Fayunin in "Nashestviye", etc; *Productions:* Surov's "Obida" (1948); *Svad'ba Krechinskogo* (Krechinskiy's Marriage) (1949), etc; *Awards:* Order of Lenini two Orders of the Red Banner of Labor; three Stalin Prizes (1943, 1946 and 1949); *Died:* 12 May 1951 in Moscow.

VANNIKOV, Boris L'vovich (1897—1962) Govt official and mil commander; col-gen, Artillery Eng Corps; CP member from 1919; *Born:* 7 July 1897 in Baku; *Educ:* studied at Moscow Higher Tech College; *Career:* from 1918 in Red Army; 1920—26 exec work with USSR Pop Comrt of Workers and Peasants' Inspection; simultaneously studied at Moscow Higher Tech College; dir, Lyuboretsk, Tula then Perm' machine-building plants; 1937 appointed USSR Dep Pop Comr of Defense Ind; 1939 USSR Pop Comr of Armament; during WW 2 USSR Pop Comr of Munitions; after WW 2 exec posts in defense and machine-building ind; at 17th, 19th and 20th CPSU Congresses elected member, CC, CPSU; dep, USSR Supr Sov of 2nd and RSFSR Supr Sov of 3rd convocations; from 1958 retired; *Awards:* thrice Hero of Socialist Labor; two Stalin Prizes; six Orders of Lenin; Order of Suvorov, 1st Class; Order of Kutuzov, 1st Class; *Died:* 22 Feb 1962; buried on Moscow's Red Square by the Kremlin Wall.

VARDANYAN, Anushavan (1879—1954) Arm writer; CP member from 1907; *Born:* 2 Apr 1879 in vil Tskhna, Azer; *Career:* in his youth moved to Tiflis and worked at footwear factory; from 1900 active in workers' orgs and Marxist circles; in this period began lit wirk; *Publ:* plays: "The Strike" (1906); "Ghosts, or in Sundukyan Gabo's House" (1913); "The Signal" (1931); "Red Partisans" (1937); "In Position" (1931); "On the Banks of the Araks"(1940); "At the Gates of the Caucasus" (1947), etc; *Died:* 4 Aug 1954 in Yerevan.

VARDIN (MGELADZE), I. V. (1890—1943) Party official; CP member from 1907; *Born:* 1890; *Career:* after 1917 Feb Revol member, Saratov Province RSDRP(B) Comt and member, Saratov Exec Comt; ed, Saratov newspaper "Sotsial-demokrat"; after 1917 Oct Revol Party work: member, Saratov Province Party Comt; head, Polit Dept, 1st Mounted Army; head, Press Sub-dept, CC, RCP(B); 1918 during Brest peace talks sided with "Leftist Communists"; 1925 sided with "New Opposition"; then member, "Trotsky-Zinov'yevite Bloc"; 1927, at 15th CPSU(B) Congress, expelled from the Party for membership of Trotskyist opposition; 1930 readmitted to the Party; 1935 again expelled for alleged anti-Party and anti-Sov activities and convicted; *Died:* 1943 in imprisonment.

VARENTSOVA, Ol'ga Afanas'yevna (1862—1950) Party official; CP member from 1893; *Born:* 26 June 1862 in Ivanovo-Voznesensk, daughter of a weaver; *Career:* 1880's joined "Narodnaya volya" (People's Will) Party; early 1890's switched to Soc-Democrats; engaged in revol propaganda among Ivanovo-Voznesensk workers; from 1895 head, Ivanovo-Voznesensk Soc-Democratic org; then Party work in Ufa, Voronezh, Yaroslavl', Vladimir and Vologda; 1901 founder-leader, Northern Workers' Union; exec secr, CC, above union; also member, Yaroslavl's RSDRP Comt and secr, Vologda RSDRP Group; 1905—07 took part in revol assemblies in Yaroslavl', Petersburg, Ivanovo-Voznesensk and Moscow; member, Ivanovo-Voznesensk RSDRP Committee's Exec Bureau to coordinate and direct local Party orgs in Ivanovo-Voznesensk and Shuya and surrounding area; several times arrested, imprisoned and exiled; 1910—16 underground work in Moscow; during 1917 Feb Revol member, Moscow Party Comt; secr, Mil Bureau, Moscow Party Comt; during 1917 Oct Revol member, Battle Triumvirate of Moscow's Municipal Rayon, liaising with Mil Revol Comt; directed reconnaissance and mil operations connected with the revolt; set up underground printing presses and distributed Party propaganda; active "Iskra" agent and propagandist; 1913 helped prepare publication of newspaper "Nash put'";late 1916 member, Lit Group, Moscow Oblast Party Bureau; 1917 contributed to journal "Rabotnitsa"; after 1917 Oct Revol Party work in Caucasus; then Party, govt and research work with various establishments; 1919—21 secr, Ivanovo-Voznesensk Province RCP (B) Comt; 1921—28 Council member, Commission to Collate and Study Material on the History of the Oct Revol and the History of the Communist Party; then worked for Inst of Marx-Engels-Lenin, CC, CPSU(B); at 11th Party Congress elected member, RCP(B) Centr Control Commission; published numerous works on history of Party and revol movement; published her memoirs; *Publ: Severnyy rabochiy soyuz, 1900—1903* (The Northern Workers' Union. 1900—1903) (1925); *Vozniknoveniye "Iskry" i yeyo rabota* (The Emergence of "Iskra" and Its Work) (1926); *Raznoglasiya v redaktsii "Iskry"* (Differences of Opinion in the "Iskra" Editorial Office) (1933), etc; *Awards:* Order of Lenin; *Died:* 24 Mar 1950.

VARES, Iokhannes Yakovich (pen name: BARBARUS) (1890—1946) Est govt official and poet; Hon Writer of Est SSR; *Born:* 1890 in Southern Est, son of a peasant; *Educ:* 1914 grad Med Fac, Kiev Univ; *Career:* during WW 1 drafted into Russian Army; 1918 returned from Army and for 20 years worked in Pyarnu as physician for a health insurance agency; headed revol movement against Est Govt; 1928 and 1935 visited USSR; 1936 organized Spanish Republ aid movement; under constant police surveillance; June 1940 became prime min of first Est Pop Democratic Govt; July 1940, with establishment of Sov regime in Est, elected chm, Presidium, Est Supr Sov; also dep chm, Presidium, USSR Supr Sov; during WW 2 helped muster Est nat units in Sov Army; 1910 began writing career; visited France,

Spain, Hungary, Albania and Greece; as a result of these journeys wrote his collection "Over the Threshhold", containing a verse cycle "Classics" about the art of Ancient Greece; after establishment of Sov regime in Est was elected chm, Est Writers' Union and ed of polit and lit-art almanach "The Battle Horn"; *Publ:* verse collections: "Correlations" (1922); "The Geometrical Man" (1924); "The Multiplied Man" (1927); "The World Is Open" (1930); "Fire Concentration" (1934); "Fish Out of Water" (1937); "Over the Threshhold" (1939); *Awards:* Order of Lenin (1946); *Died:* 1946.

VAREYKIS, Iosif Mikhaylovich (1894–1939) Govt and Party official; CP member from 1913; *Born:* 18 Sept 1894 in Kovno Province, son of a Lith worker; *Educ:* grad trade school; *Career:* Party work at towns in Moscow Province; arrested; after 1917 Feb Revol Presidium member, Podol'sk Sov; early 1918 secr, Khar'kov Oblast RCP(B) Comt and Pop Comr of Soc Security, Donetsk-Krivoy Rog Republ; June 1918–Aug 1920 chm, Simbirsk Province RCP(B) Comt and member, Revol Mil Council; during revolt of Czech Legion extraordinary comr of defense for Simbirsk; helped crush anti-Sov revolt led by Eastern Front commander Murav'yov; 1921–23 dep chm, Baku Sov; from 1923 secr, Kiev Province RCP(B) Comt; then secr, Centr Asian Bureau, CC, CPSU(B); head, Press Dept, CC, CPSU(B); secr, Saratov Province CPSU(B) Comt; secr, Voronezh Oblast CPSU(B) Comt; secr, Far Eastern Kray CPSU(B) Comt; at 13th–15th Party Congresses elected cand member, CC, CPSU(B); at 16th and 17th Party Congresses elected member, CC, CPSU(B); member, All-Russian and USSR Centr Exec Comt; 9 Oct 1937 arrested by State Security organs; *Awards:* Order of Lenin (1934); *Died:* 1939 in imprisonment; posthumously rehabilitated.

VARFOLOMEYEV, Nikolay Yefimovich (1890–1941) Mil commander; junior capt, Russian Army; *Born:* 1890; *Career:* from 1918 in Red Army; head, operations bd, then chief of staff of an army; dep chief of staff of a front; dep chief of strategy studies, Frunze Mil Acad; chief of staff of a mil distr; arrested by NKVD; *Publ: Strategicheskoye narastaniye i istoshcheniye v grazhdanskoy voyne* (Strategic Build-Up and Exhaustion in the Civil War) (1928); *Udarnaya armiya* (The Assault Army) (1933); *Nastupatel'naya operatsiya* (Offensive Operations) (1937); *Strategiya v akademicheskoy postanovke* (The Academic Approach to Strategy) (1928); *Operativnoye iskusstvo na sovremennom etape* (The Modern Art of Operations) (1932), etc; *Died:* 1941 in imprisonment.

VARFOLOMEY (secular name: GORODTSEV, Sergey Dmitriyevich) (1866–1956) Metropolitan of Novosibirsk and Barnaul from 1949; Hon Dr of Divinity; *Born:* 1866 in Ryazan' Province; *Educ:* 1890 grad Petersburg Theological Acad as Cand of Divinity; *Career:* 1890 asst inspector, Mogilev Theological Seminary; 1892 consecrated priest; 1892–1917 dean in Tiflis; built churches and shrines and was chm, Geo Eparchial Council; chm, Missionary Brotherhood Council; dean of Russian Orthodox churches in Geo; after 1917 Oct Revol left Tiflis and, to escape the terror and persecution of the clergy, constantly changed his place of residence, living in Azer, Ufa and Voronezh Province; 1935 settled in Klin, Moscow Oblast and was assigned a parish in Klin area; 1942 took monastic vows and was elevated to bishop, then archbishop and given the Eparchy of Novosibirsk and Barnaul; frequently used his sermons for propaganda against the Korean War; *Publ: Mysli pastyrya o nekotorykh izrecheniyakh apostola Petra* (A Pastor's Thoughts on Some of Peter the Apostle's Sayings); *Pastyr'-propovednik po Ioannu Zlatoustu* (The Pastor — the Preacher According to John Chrystostom); *Kak nuzhno ponimat' vozglas svyashchennika na utreney "Slava Tebe, pokazavshemu nam svet"* (How to Interpret the Priest's Morning Service Call "Glory to Thee, Who Has Shown Us the Light"); *Kniga Iova — opyt bibleyskopsikhologicheskogo obozreniya* (The Book of Job, a Biblical-Psychological Review), etc; *Awards:* right to wear two panagia (1952); *Died:* 1 June 1956.

VARGA, Yevgeniy Samoylovich (1879–1964) Economist; Party official; politician; member, USSR and Ukr Acad of Sci from 1939; CP member from 1920; *Born:* 6 Nov 1879 in Hungary; *Career:* from 1906 member, Hungarian Soc-Democratic Party; worked for its press organs; from 1918 prof of polit econ, Budapest Univ; 1919 helped establish Sov rule in Hungary; Hungarian Pop Comr of Finance; then chm, Sov Hungary's Supr Sovnarkhoz; 1920 emigrated to USSR and worked for Comintern; deleg at Comintern congresses; attended plenary sessions, Comintern Exec Comt; simultaneously ed, "Yezhegodnik" and other Comintern publ; 1927–47 chm, Inst of World Econ, Communist Acad; then dir, Inst of World Econ and World Politics, USSR Acad of Sci; chief ed, inst journal "Mirovoye khozyaystvo i mirovaya politika"; late 1940's critized for his work *Izmeneniya v ekonomike kapitalizma v itoge vtoroy mirovoy voyny* (Changes in Capitalist Economy as a Result of World War II) (1946), which allegedly contained "serious bourgeois-reformist errors"; 1947 relieved of his posts as dir, Inst of World Econ and World Politics, USSR Acad of Sci and chief ed, journal "Mirovoye khozyaystvo i mirovaya politika"; 1949 forced to recant his errors; later worked for Inst of Econ, USSR Acad of Sci and on ed staff, journal "Mirovaya ekonomika i mezhdunarodnyye otnosheniya"; *Publ: Problemy ekonomicheskoy politiki pri proletarskoy diktature* (Problems of Economic Policy Under the Dictatorship of the Proletariat) (1922); *Krizis mirovogo kapitalisticheskogo khozyaystva* (The Crisis of World Capitalist Economy) (1923); *Zakat kapitalizma* (The Decline of Capitalism) (1923); *Novyye yavleniya v mirovom ekonomicheskom krizise* (New Phenomena in the World Economic Crisis) (1934); *Kapitalizm i sotsializm za 20 let* (Twenty Years of Capitalism and Socialism) (1938); *Izmeneniya v ekonomike kapitalizma v itoge vtoroy mirovoy voyny* (Changes in Capitalist Economy as a Result of World War II) (1946); *Osnovnyye voprosy ekonomiki i politiki imperializma posle vtoroy mirovoy voyny* (The Main Problems of Imperialist Economy and Policy After World War II) (1953); *Kapitalizm 20-go veka* (Twentieth Century Capitalism) (1961); *Sovremennyy kapitalizm i ekonomicheskiye krizisy (Modern Capitalism and Economic Crises)* (1962), etc; *Awards:* two Orders of Lenin (1954 and 1959); Stalin Prize (1954); Lenin Prize (1963); *Died:* 7 Oct 1964.

VARLAKOV, Mikhail Nikolayevich (1906–1945) Pharmacist; physician; specialist in medicinal plants; *Born:* 1906 in vil Voskresenskoye, Orenburg Province; *Educ:* 1929 grad Med Fac, Irkutsk Univ; *Career:* carried out expeditions to Trans-Baikal and Eastern Sayan on behalf of Chemical Pharmaceutical Research Inst to study medicinal herbs used in Tibetan and Siberian medicine; co-founder, Siberian Branch, Chemical Pharmaceutical Research Inst; did research on Siberian valerian adonis, and Thermopsis Lanceolata R. Br. as a source of ipecacuana; also studied other varieties of Siberian plants of value in pharmaceutics; donated his collections to the Herbarium of Tomsk Univ; on the basis of his collections L.A. Sergiyevskaya named a poisonous plant used in Tibetan med as Oxytropis Varlakovi; wrote several dozen research works on medicinal plants; *Publ: Lekarstvennyye sredstya tibetskoy meditsiny* (Medicinal Drugs of Tibetan Medicine) (1931); *Farmatsiya i retseptura tibetskoy meditsiny* (The Pharmacy and Prescriptions of Tibetan Medicine) (1931); *Ekspeditsiya nauchno-issledovatel'skogo khimiko-farmatsevticheskogo instituta v Zabaykal'ye* (The Chemical Pharmaceutical Research Institute's Expedtion to Trans-Baikal) (1931); *Vostochnaya belladona* (Eastern Belladona) (1932); *Lekarstvennyye rasteniya vostochnogo Zabaykal'ya* (The Medicinal Plants of Eastern Trans-Baikal) (1932); *Sibirskiye valeriany* (Siberian Valerian) (1932); *Sibirskiy goritsvet* (Siberian Adonis) (1932); *Sibirskiy filial NIKhFI* (The Siberian Branch of the Chemical Pharmaceutical Research Institute) (1932); Atragene sibirica L. (1933); *Vostochno-Sayanskaya ekspeditsiya NIKhFI* (The Chemical Pharmaceutical Research Institute's Eastern Sayan Expedition) (1933); "Patrinia scabiosaefolia" (1933); "Sophora flavescens" (1933); "Thermopsis lanceolata R. Br." (1933); coauthor, *Izucheniye narodnoy meditsiny neobkhodimo dlya razvitiya lekarstvennoy terapii* (The Study of Folk Medicine Is Essential to the Development of Medicinal Therapy) (1941); *Zamena importnoy senegi kornyami Polemonium coerulium* (Replacing Imported Senega with the Roots of Polemonium coerulium) (1943); *O rastitel'nykh krovoostanavlivayushchikh sredstvakh* (Plant Hemostatic Substances) (1943); *Novyye vidy lekarstvennykh rasteniy s sosudoraschiryayushchim deystviyem* (New Species of Medicinal Plants with Vascular Dilating Properties) (1944); *O stimuliruyushchem deystvii kitayskogo limonnika* (The Stimulating Action of Chinese Melissa) (1944); coauthor, *Problema izucheniya lekarstvennykh rasteniy otechestvennoy flory* (Studying the Medicinal Plants of Our Native Flora) (1944); coauthor, *Tysyachelistnik* (Milfoil) (1944); *O novykh rastitel'nykh protivovospalitel'nykh sredstvakh* (New Plant Antiphlogistics) (1946); *Died:* 6 Feb 1945 in Moscow.

VARLAMOV, Leonid Vasil'yevich (1907–1962) Chronicle and documentary film dir; Hon Art Worker of RSFSR from 1950; CP member from 1952; *Born:* 13 July 1907; *Educ:* 1931 grad Directing Fac, State Inst of Cinematography, Moscow; *Career:*

from 1929 worked at "Kul'turfil'm" Studios, Moscow; from 1932 directed documentary films; from 1935 directed "Pioneriya", "Union Film Journal" and "Daily News" film chronicles; 1941–45 worked for various frontline film groups; after WW 2 traveled abroad, making documentaries on the life of other peoples; *Productions:* films: *Komsomoliya* (Komsomol Life) (1929); *Zemlya i klimaticheskiye poyasa* (The Earth and Climatic Belts) (1933); *Boy kitov* (Whaling) (1935); *Nash Sergo* (Our Sergo) (1936); *Lyotchiki* (Pilots) (1938); *Arkticheskiy reys* (An Arctic Voyage) (1940); co-dir, *Razgrom nemetskikh voysk pod Moskvoy* (The Rout of the German Troops at Moscow) (1942); "Stalingrad" (1943); *Yugoslavtsy* (The Yugoslavs) (1946); co-dir, *Pobeda kitayskogo naroda* (The Chinese People's Victory) (1950); *Po Indii* (Around India) (1952); *Sto dney v Birme* (A Hundred Days in Burma) (1957); *Vstrechi v Amerike* (Meetings in America) (1960); *Protsess nad Pauersom* (The Powers Trial) (1960); *Suetskiy kanal* (The Suez Canal) (1961), etc; *Awards:* Badge of Hon; five Stalin Prizes (1942, 1943, 1947, 1949 and 1951); *Died:* 3 Sept 1962.

VARSKIY (real name), WARSZAWSKI-WARSKI), Adol'f Yezhi (1868–1937) Polish Party official and journalist; *Born:* 20 Apr 1868, son of a tradesman; *Career:* 1889 co-founded Polish Workers' Union; 1893 helped found Soc-Democratic Party of the Kingdom of Poland, then Soc-Democratic Party of the Kingdom of Poland and Lith (SDPKPL); member of its Main Bd; edited Party organs "Sprawa robotnicza" then "Przeglad socjal-demokratyczny"; 1905–07 active in revol movement in Poland; SDKPL deleg at 2nd and 4th RSDRP Congresses; 1906, after SDKPL was amalgamated in RSDRP, he represented SDKPL on CC, RSDRP; several times arrested and exiled; 1918 helped merge SDKPL with Polish (Leftist) Socialist Party into Communist Workers' Party of Poland – Polish CP; 1919–29 member, CC, Polish CP; 1923 elected Politburo member, CC, Polish CP; 1926 Polish CP dep in Sejm; 1921, 1922, 1924 and 1928 attended 3rd, 4th, 5th and 6th Comintern Congresses; Mar 1929 forced to emigrate to USSR; worked on history of Polish workers' movement at Inst of Marx-Engels-Lenin; 1937 arrested by State Security organs; *Died:* 21 Aug 1937 in imprisonment; posthumously rehabilitated.

VARSONOFIY (secular name: GRINEVICH, Konstantin Diomidovich) (1875–1958) Archbishop of Kalinin and Kashin, Russian Orthodox Church; Cand of Divinity; *Born:* 1875; *Educ:* grad Kazan' Theological Acad; *Career:* priest, then archpriest; 1945 took monastic vows with name Varsonofiy and elevated to Bishop of Grodno and Baranovichi; organized month-long pastoral divinity courses, including lectures on Sov Constitution; 1949 appointed Bishop of Semipalatinsk and Pavlodar; 1950 appointed Bishop of Chkalov and Buzuluki; 1953 retired; 1954 appointed Bishop of Kalinin and Kashin; until 1956 also managed Velikiye Luki Eparchy; 1956 elevated to archbishop; known for his patriotic sermons on "peace, love of one's country and the wisdom of the authorities"; *Died:* 13 Mar 1958.

VARTANYAN, Ruzana Tigranovna (1896–1957) Arm actress; Pop Artiste of Arm SSR from 1945; *Born:* 27 May 1896; *Career:* worked as secondary-school teacher; 1927 stage debut; helped run Russian and Arm amateur dramatic groups in Northern Caucasus; from 1927 with Arm 1st State Theater, Yerevan' (now Sundukyan Theater); from 1944 taught at Yerevan' Theatrical Inst; *Roles:* Polina in Ostrovskiy's *Dokhodnoye mesto* (A Lucrative Post) (1929); Rosina in "The Marriage of Figaro" (1933); Shurka in *Yegor Bulychyov i drugiye* (Yegor Bulychyov and Co) (1933); Lida in "Platon Krechet" (1935); Susan and Margarit in Shirvanzade's "Namus" (1936) and "For Honor" (1939); Eriknaz in Proshyan's "For Bread" (1937); Areg in Bulakyan's "At Dawn" (1937); Donna Anna in Pushkin's *Kamennyy gost'* (The Stone Guest) (1937); Luise in "Kabale und Liebe" (1938); Desdemona in "Othello" (1940); Ophelia in "Hamlet" (1942); Larisa in Ostrovskiy's *Bespridannitsa* (Girl Without a Dowry) (1946); Ganna Likhta in Virta's *Zagovor obrechyonnykh* (Conspiracy of the Doomed) (1949); Ranevskaya in Chekhov's *Vishnyovyy sad* (The Cherry Orchard) (1951); Arusyak in Boryan's "Under One Roof" (1957); *Died:* 9 Dec 1957.

VARZAR, Vasiliy Yegorovich (1851–1940) Statistician; pioneer of ind statistics in Russia; *Born:* 1851, son of an office worker; *Educ:* 1875 grad Petersburg Technol Inst; *Career:* while a student connected with Revol Populists; his pamphlet "Khitraya mekhanika" (Cunning Mechanics), exposing the workings of the Tsarist tax system, was widely used for revol propaganda and frequently published illegally in Russia; for some 20 years engaged in zemstvo statistics; 1894–1917 worked for Min of Finance and Min of Trade and Ind; 1900 and 1908 initiated and supervised two major statistical censuses of Russian ind ("Varzar Censuses"), on which Lenin drew extensively for his works; his statistical surveys of labor (strikes statistics) provide valuable material on the workers' revol movement in Russia in 1895–1908; after 1917 Oct Revol worked for Supr Sovnarkhoz and Centr Statistical Bd; also taught at higher educ establishments; *Publ: Khitraya mekhanika* (Cunning Mechanics) (1874); *Statisticheskiye svedeniya o fabrikakh i zavodakh po proizvodstvam, ne oblozhennym aktsizom za 1900 god* (Statistical Data on Factories and Plants for Products Not Excised for 1900) (1903); *Statisticheskiye svedeniya o stachkakh rabochikh na fabrikakh i zavodakh za desyatiletiye 1895–1904* (Statistical Data on Workers' Strikes at Factories and Plants for the Decade 1895–1904) (1905); similar study for 1905 (1908); another study for 1906–08 (1910); *Statisticheskiye svedeniya po obrabatyvayushchey fabrichnozavodskoy promyshlennosti Rossii za 1908 god* (Statistical Data on the Russian Factory and Plant Processing Industry for 1908) (1912); *Vospominaniya starogo statistika* (The Memoirs of an Old Statistician) (1924); *Novyy sposob postroyeniya pokazatel'nykh diagramm* (A New Method of Drafting Demonstration Diagrams) (1926); *Ocherki osnov promyshlennoy statistiki* (Studies in the Principles of Industrial Statistics) (1925–27), etc; *Died:* 29 Sept 1940.

VASENKO, A.B. (1899–1934) Airship designer and test-pilot; *Born:* 1899 in Petersburg, son of an eng; *Educ:* 1927 grad Leningrad Inst of Transport Eng; *Career:* 1919–22 served in Red Army; while still a student worked at the Inst of Aerology and gained practical experience at Inst of Actinometry, Inst of Magnetism and Inst of Meteorology; 1927–31 head, Research Section and asst dir, Inst of Aerology, then assoc, Aerial Photography Inst and Civil Aviation Research Inst; active member, Soc for the Promotion of the Sov Aviation, Defense and Chemical Ind; 1927 designed airship for high-altitude research; 1930–32 designed and tested balloons for high-altitude research and aerial photography; did research on various aspects of high-altitude ballooning, especially the problem of icing; 30–31 Jan 1934, together with Fedoseyenko and Usyskin, reached a height of 20,600 meters with the balloon "Osoaviakhim-1"; the balloon crashed as a result of icing, killing the whole crew; *Died:* 31 Jan 1934; his ashes are immured in the Kremlin Wall, Moscow.

VASIL'CHENKO, Semyon Filippovich (1884–1937) Party official; writer; CP member from 1901; *Born:* 1884 in Don Oblast, son of a railroad worker; *Career:* as a youth began work in Rostov railroad workshops; soon joined one of the first illegal Soc-Democratic circles; 1902 for the first time arrested, released after six months; 1903 arrested again helping to stage a major demonstration in Rostov; summer 1905, after his release from Akatuy Jail, participated in Rostov's Temernik Rayon revolt; July 1905 arrested and until 1913 exiled; 1913 released and ordered to settle in Verkholensk Uyezd, Irkutsk Province; fled and lived illegally in various Siberian towns; 1914–15 founded in Irkutsk pro-Bolshevik Siberian Workers' Union; summer 1915, after suppression of the union, re-arrested and imprisoned; after 1917 Feb Revol returned to Rostov; chm, Rostov-Nakhichevan RSDRP(B) Comt; 1918–19 held various posts on Southern Front: in Kozlov, Donbass, Khar'kov, Kazan' (Reserve Army), Krasnodar, etc; early 1918 member, Donetsk-Krivoy Rog Oblast Bolshevik Comt; admin comr, Govt of Donetsk-Krivoy Rog Republ; 1920 moved to Moscow and worked for Moscow Party Comt; founded "Moskovskiy rabochiy" Publ House; wrote numerous works, mainly of an autobiographical character; arrested by State Security organs; *Publ:* scenes for reading and performance *Dve sestry* (Two Sisters) (1921); novelettes *Kar'yera podpol'shchika* (The Career of an Underground Man) (1924); *Priklyucheniya podpol'shchika* (Adventures of an Underground Agent) (1925); *Posle dekabrya* (After December), etc; *Died:* 1937 in imprisonment.

VASIL'CHENKO (real name: PANASENKO), Stepan Vasil'yevich (1878–1932) Ukr writer; *Born:* 27 Dec 1878 in vil Ichna, now Chernigov Oblast; *Educ:* 1898 grad Korostyshev Teachers' Seminary; 1904 studied for a while at Glukhov Teachers' Inst; *Career:* 1900 began writing; taught in Donbass; 1906 arrested for revol propaganda among peasantry; 1908 released from prison, gave private lessons and wrote; 1910 first work printed; during WW 1 served in Russian Army at the front; after 1917 Oct Revol taught in Kiev; in his latter years worked on biography of Shevchenko (uncompleted); his works are imbued with a subtle lyricism and humor; *Publ:* collection "Sketches" (1911); collection "Stories" (1915); "Vova" (1910); "With the Centry" (1910); "Peasant Arithmetic" (1911); "Right from the Start" (1911); "Sin" (1912); "On the First Walk" (1911); "Ossetian Tales" (1912); "The Juvenile" (1913); "Autumn Sketch" (1915); "At the Farmstead" (1915); "Basurman" (1919); "Talent" (1924); "The Flying Club" (1925); "The Pewter Thimble" (1927); "The Carmelite" (1927), etc; novelette "In the Tall Weeds" (1938); "Complete Collected Works" (4 vol, 1928–30); *Died:* 11 Aug 1932 in Kiev.

VASILEK, Mikhas' (real name: KOSTEVICH, Mikhail Osipovich) (1905–1960) Bel poet; member, Bel Writers' Union; *Born:* 14 Nov 1905 in vil Bobrovnya, now Grodno Oblast, son of a peasant; *Career:* 1925 first work printed; active in Bel nat and soc-revol movement in Western Bel (until 1939 part of Poland); several times arrested and imprisoned; his first verse collection "The Rustling Pine Woods" (1929) was confiscated by the Polish police; the same fate befell his second collection in 1934; 1939 taken prisoner by Germans while serving with Polish Army; 1941 escaped and joined Bel partisans; 1950's worked for Grodno oblast newspaper "Grodnenskaya pravda"; *Publ:* verse collections: "From Peasant Cornfields" (1937); "Selected Verse" (1950); "Selected Works" (1955); in Russian translation *Zori nad Nemanom* (Dawns over the Neman) (1958); *Died:* 3 Sept 1960 in Grodno.

VASILENKO, Matvey Ivanovich (1888–1937) Mil commander; *Born:* 1888; *Career:* officer in Russian army; from 1918 in Red Army; during Civil War commanded, 11th, 9th then 14th Armies; after Civil War commander, 45th Infantry Div and 9th, then 17th Infantry Corps; Red Army Infantry inspector; dep commander, Ural Mil Distr; arrested by State Security organs; *Died:* 1937 in imprisonment.

VASILENKO, Nikolay Prokof'yevich (1866–1935) Historian and politician; specialist in legal history; prof; member, Ukr Acad of Sci from 1920; *Born:* 1866 near Chernigov; *Educ:* completed higher educ; *Career:* from early 1890's worked as teacher and journalist in Kiev; member, polit org "Soc of Ukr Progressivists" and ed, Progressivist newspaper "Kievskiye otkliki"; contributed to journal "Kievskaya starina"; also worked for Ancient Documents Archives; from 1908 member, Ukr Sci Soc, Kiev, and ed of its journal "Zapiski"; 1908 arrested and imprisoned for polit activities; 1910 appointed assoc prof, Kiev Univ but forbidden to teach by Tsarist authorities; 1917 curator, Kiev School Distr; 1918 Collegium Member, Ukr Gen Court; Min of Educ in Hetman Skoropadskiy's cabinet, then chm, State Senate; 1919 chm, Historical Soc of Nestor the Chronicler; 1920–29 head, Soc and Econ Dept, Ukr Acad of Sci; 1921 elected pres, Ukr Acad of Sci but was denied approbation by Sov Ukr govt; 1924 sentenced to ten years imprisonment in trial of "counterrevol Kiev Oblast Action Center" but subsequently amnestied; 1929 deprived of right to hold high office in Ukr Acad of Sci; *Publ: O.M. Bodyagskiy i yego zaslugi po izucheniyu Malorossii* (O.M. Bodyagskiy and His Services to the Study of Russia Minor) (1904); *Materialy dlya istorii ekonomicheskogo, yuridicheskogo i obshchestvennogo byta staroy Malorossii* (Material on the History of Economic, Legal and Social Life in Ancient Russia Minor) (3 vol, 1901–08); *Ocherki po istorii zapadnoy Rusi i Ukrainy* (Studies in the History of Western Rus and the Ukraine) (1916); *Kak byl uprazdnyon Litovskiy Statut* (How the Lithuanian Statute Was Repealed) (1926); "O.M. Lazarevich" (1927); *Territoriya Ukrainy XVII veka* (The Territory of the Ukraine in the 17th Century) (1927); *Materialy po istorii ukrainskogo prava* (Material on the History of Ukrainian Law) (1929); *Died:* 1935.

VASILENKO, Sergey Nikiforovich (1872–1956) Composer and conductor; Dr of Arts; Pop Artiste of RSFSR from 1940; Pop Artiste of Uzbek SSR from 1939; *Born:* 30 Mar 1872 in Moscow; *Educ:* 1895 grad Law Fac, Moscow Univ; 1901 grad Moscow Conservatory; *Career:* from 1907 prof, Moscow Conservatory, composed music for theater and cinema; did arrangements and instrumentations; *Works:* opera-cantata *Skazaniye o grade velikom Kitezhe i tikhom ozere Svetoyare* (The Tale of the Great City of Kitezh and the Calm Lake Svetoyar) (1901); operas: *Syn solntsa* (Son of the Sun) (1929); "Christopher Columbus" (1933, in Spanish); "Suvorov" (1941); coauthor, operas *Buran* (The Snow Storm) (1938) and *Velikiy kanal* (The Grand Canal) (1940); ballets: "Noya" (1923); "Iosif Prekrasnyy" (1925); *V solnechnykh luchakh (In Sunbeams) (1926); "Lola" (1926);* 2nd version *(1943); Treugolka* (The Cocked Hat) (1935); *Tsygany* (Gypsies) (1936); "Akbilyak" (1942); "Mirandolina" (1946); two operettas; cantata on the 20th Anniversary of the Oct Revol (1937); several symphonies, including his 3rd Italian Symphony (for balalaika and dombra orchestra with wind instruments) (1934) and his 4th Arctic Symphony (1934); symphonic suites, including "Turkmenian Pictures" (1931); "Soviet East" (1932), ballet suite "Mirandolina" (1946); poems and rhapsodies; four concertoes, including one for balalaika (1931); over 60 romances; *Publ: Instrumentovka dlya simfonicheskogo orkestra* (Instrumentation for the Symphonic Orchestra) (vol 1, 1952; vol 2, 1959); *Stranitsy vospominaniy* (Pages of Reminiscences) (1948); *Awards:* two Orders of th Red Banner of Labor; medals; Stalin Prize (1947); *Died:* 11 Mar 1956 in Moscow.

VASILEVSKAYA, Vanda L'vovna (1905–1964) Polish writer; wife of Ukr writer A. Korneychuk; Dr of Philosophy; bd member, USSR and Ukr Writers' Unions; CP member from 1941; *Born:* 21 Jan 1905 in Krakow, daughter of an ethnographer and journalist; *Educ:* 1927 grad Philology Fac, Krakow Univ; *Career:* 1921 first work published; joined Polish socialist movement at an early age; from 1928 secondary-school teacher and ed of a children's magazine; during 1930's contributed to Polish leftist newspapers and journals; bd member, Human and Civil Rights Defense League; 1939 moved to L'vov and assumed Sov citizenship; 1939–41 lit dir, L'vov Polish Theater; during WW 2 polit comr, Southwestern Front, then col-propagandist, Main Polit Bd, Sov Army; 1943 led "League of Polish Patriots in the USSR" and helped to form the Kosciuszko Div; 1944 dep chm, Polish Nat Liberation Comt; simultaneously ed, Ukr newspaper "Za Radyans'ku Ukrainu" and Polish newspaper "Free Poland"; also contributed to "Pravda", "Izvestia" and "Krasnaya zvezda"; after WW 2 settled in Kiev; member, World Peace Council; dep, USSR Supr Sov of 1st–6th convocations; 1961 visited Cuba; *Publ* (in Polish): novels "Homeland" (1935); "Subjugated Land" (1938); trilogy "Canto on the Waters" (1940–51); novelettes: "The Day's Countenance" (1934); "The Rainbow" (1942); "Simply Love" (1944); "When the Light Goes On" (1947); "In Mortal Struggle" (1958); coauthor, libretto for the opera "Bogdan Khmel'nitskiy"; "Collected Works" (6 vol, 1954–55); *Awards:* two Orders of Lenin; Order of the Polish Democratic Republ; three Stalin Prizes (1943, 1946 and 1952); *Died:* 29 July 1964 in Kiev.

VASILIY (secular name: LIPKOVSKIY, Vasiliy) (1864–1938) Metropolitan of Kiev and All the Ukr, Ukr Autocephalous Orthodox Church; *Born:* 30 Mar 1864 in vil Popudne, Kiev Province; *Educ:* 1889 grad Kiev Theological Acad; *Career:* 1891 consecrated priest; 1892 appointed dean and inspector of church schools in Lipovets; from 1903 dir, Kiev Church Teachers' School; 1904 dismissed for "Ukrainophilism" and appointed dean, St Pokrovskiy Church, Kiev; 1905 chm, Kiev Clergy's Congress to discuss ukrainianization of Church; placed under police surveillance, but remained vicar of his parish; 1918, now archpriest, sponsored 1st All-Ukr Church Synod; 1919 organized Ukr parishes and translated liturgical books into Ukr; appointed dean of Sofia Cathedral, Kiev; 1920 supervised work of preparatory commission to convene All-Ukr Church Synod in Kiev; 1921 at this synod elevated to Metropolitan of Kiev and All the Ukr; 1926 arrested, but soon released; banned from preaching; 1927 at 2nd All-Ukr Church Synod relieved of his metropolitanship on orders from State Polit Bd; 1928 barred from carrying out Divine Service; 1938 arrested by NKVD; *Died:* 1938 in imprisonment.

VASILYAUSKAS, Kazimir Iosifovich (1879–1957) Eng; specialist in construction mech; member, USSR Acad of Construction and Architecture from 1957; corresp member, Lith Acad of Sci from 1946; Hon Sci Worker of Lith SSR from 1947; *Born:* 5 Mar 1879, *Educ:* 1907 grad Riga Polytech Inst, *Career:* worked for various construction orgs; 1922–25 lecturer, from 1925 prof, Kaunas Univ; from 1951 prof, Kaunas Polytech Inst; specialized in calculation of pivotal systems, construction of effect lines, etc; *Publ:* "The Circumference Method in Structural Statics" (1929); textbook "The Resistance of Materials" (1941); *Died:* 24 Nov 1957.

VASIL'YEV, Georgiy Nikolayevich (1899–1946) Film dir and scriptwriter; Hon Art Worker of RSFSR from 1940; *Born:* 25 Feb 1899; *Educ:* studied at Warsaw Polytech Inst; then under I. Pevtsov at the "Young Masters" Theater Studio, Moscow; *Career:* from 1923 journalist; worked for newspaper "Rabochaya gazeta" and journal "'Zhizn' iskusstva"; wrote a number of articles on the cinema; from 1924 cutter for foreign films at State Film Studio; after merger of Northwestern Film Studio with State Film Studio and Sov Film Studio he began to work with his brother S.D.

Vasil'yev in a team known as the "Vasil'yev Brothers"; worked with and greatly influenced by Eisenstein; *Works:* documentary film *Podvig vo l'dakh* (Exploit Among the Ice) (1928); *Spyashchaya krasavitsa* (Sleeping Beauty) (1930); *Lichnoye delo* (A Private Affair) (1932); scripted and directed films: "Chapayev" (1934); *Volochayevskiye dni* (Volochayevka Days) (1937); *Oborona Tsaritsyna* (The Defense of Tsaritsyn) (part 1, 1942); "Front" (1943); *Awards:* two Stalin Prizes (1941 and 1942); Order of Lenin; Order of the Star; *Died:* 18 June 1946.

VASIL'YEV, Leonid Leonidovich (1891–1955) Physiologist; prof; from 1943; Dr of Biological Sci; corresp member, USSR Acad of Med Sci; *Born:* 1891 in Pskov; *Educ:* 1914 grad Petersburg Univ; *Career:* 1915–20 taught biology at Ufa high schools; 1921–48 head, Physiology Dept, Bekhterev Brain Inst, Leningrad; co-ed, physiology section, 2nd ed of "BME" (Large Medical Encyclopedia); member, ed council, journal "Fiziologicheskiy zhurnal SSSR im. I.M. Sechenova"; 1925–37 developed theory of two types of inhibition which emerge consecutively in the course of parabiosis; 1925 established basic quantitative law of treshhold parabiosis; 1937 studied phenomenon of restoring nerve and muscular functions (including the heart) by electr current; 1937–41 demonstrated parabiotic nature of electro-sleep and local and gen anaphylaxia; 1954 detected parabiosis-eliminating influences emanating from centr nervous system; popularized therapeutic use of ionized air treatment; wrote over 100 works; *Publ:* coauthor, *Elektricheskoye vosstanovleniye fiziologicheskikh funktsiy* (The Electrical Restoration of Physiological Functions) (1937); *Teoriya i praktika lecheniya ionizirovannym vozdukhom* (The Theory and Practice of Ionized Air Treatment) (1953); *Znacheniye fiziologicheskogo ucheniya N.Ye. Vvedenskogo dlya nevropatologii* (The Importance of N.Ye. Vvedenskiy's Physiological Theories for Neuropathology) (1953); *Eksperimental'nyye issledovaniya myslennogo vnusheniya* (Experimental Studies of the Inspiration of Ideas) (1963), etc; *Died:* 1955.

VASIL'YEV, Nikolay Grigor'yevich (1908–1943) Mil commander; CP member from 1929; *Born:* 27 July 1908; *Career:* from 1930 polit work in Red Army; from July 1941 commander, 2nd Partisan Brigade in Leningrad Oblast; by late 1941 his brigade had driven German troops from a territory of about 11,000 square kilometers and establihed the so-called "Partisan Kray" which existed until Sept 1942; *Awards:* Hero of Sov Union (1944, posthumously); *Died:* 25 Mar 1943; buried in Valday.

VASIL'YEV, Sergey Dmitriyevich (1900–1959) Film dir and scriptwriter; Pop Artiste of USSR from 1948; *Born:* 4 Feb 1900; *Educ:* 1924 grad Acting and Directing Dept, Inst of Screen Art, Leningrad; *Career:* took part in 1917 Oct Revol in Petrograd; until 1922 in Red Army; from 1924 ed, then cutter, Moscow Dept, Northwestern Film Studio; after merger of Northwestern Film Studio with State Film Studio and Sov Film Studio he began to work with G.N. Vasil'yev in a team called the "Vasil'yev Brothers"; worked with and greatly influenced by Eisenstein; 1944–46 artistic dir, 1955–57 dir, Lenin Film Studio; chm, Org Bureau, Leningrad Dept, USSR Cinematographic Workers' Union; *Works:* documentary: *Podvig vo l'dakh* (Exploit Among the Ice) (1928); *Spyashchaya krasavitsa* (Sleeping Beauty) (1930); *Lichnoye delo* (A Private Affair) (1932); scripted and directed films: "Chapayev" (1934); *Volochayevskiye dni* (Volochayevka Days) (1937); *Oborona Tsaritsyna* (The Defense of Tsaritsyn) (part 1, 1942); "Front" (1943); *Geroi Shipki* (Heroes of Shipka) (1955); *V dni Oktyabrya* (The Days of October) (1958); *Awards:* two Stalin Prizes (1941 and 1942); Order of Lenin; Order of the Red Banner of Labor; Order of the Red Star; *Died:* 16 Dec 1959.

VASIL'YEV, Valerian Mikhaylovich (1883–1961) Mari philologist; *Born:* 1 Jan 1883 in vil Susady-Ebalak, Ufa Province, son of a peasant; *Educ:* 1906 grad Kazan' Theological Seminary; from 1913 studied at Fac of History and Philology, Kazan' Univ; *Career:* did research on Mari philology, compiled a definitive grammar of this language and collected Mari folk-songs and poems; *Publ: O kharaktere i stroye cheremisskikh pesen* (The Character and Structure of Cheremis Songs) (1909); *Mari muro. Pesni naroda mari* (Mari Muro. Songs of the Mari People) (1919); *Zapiski po grammatike yazyka naroda mari* (Notes on Mari Grammar) (2nd ed, 1919); *Nekotoryye voprosy mariyskogo yazykoznaniya* (Some Problems of Mari Linguistics) (1948); *Died:* 3 May 1961 in Yoshkar-Ola.

VASIL'YEV, Vasiliy Yefimovich (1890–1956) Metallurgist; prof from 1926; corresp member, Ukr Acad of Sci from 1939; *Born:* 20 Mar 1890 in Yelisavetgrad (now Kirovograd), son of an office worker; *Career:* from 1926 head, Chair of Metallurgy and the Theory of Metallurgical Processes, Kiev Polytech Inst; 1939–49 head, Metallurgy Section, from 1949 head, Tech Dept, Inst of Machine Sci and Agric Mech, Ukr Acad of Sci; *Publ: Domennaya plavka na ustoychivykh shlakakh* (Blast-Furnace Smelting with Stable Slags) (1956), etc; *Died:* 14 Aug 1956.

VASIL'YEV-BUGLAY, Dmitriy Stepanovich (1888–1956) Composer; Hon Art Worker of RSFSR from 1947; *Born:* 9 Aug 1888 in Moscow; *Educ:* 1898–1906 studied at Moscow Synodal College; *Career:* toured Russia as precentor and choral accompanist; after 1917 Oct Revol worked in Tambov as musical organizer for Red Army frontline units; composed some of first Sov revol songs; *Works:* songs: "Horse and Master", "The Harvest" and romance "The Red Flower" (1918); agitation variety slogan songs (to words by Dem'yan Bednyy): "In the Monastery", "Tit the Loafer", "Wondrous Wonder", "Priests Are Drones and Live By Tricks", etc; "The Ballad of the Slain Red Army Man"; songs: "How My Mother Saw Me Off", "The Testament", "The Red Engineer" and "Red Youth"; opera *Rodina zovyot* (The Homeland Calls) (1937); children's opera "Kolobok" (1941); choral works of 1940's: choral suite "Moscow"; cantata "Borodino", to words by Lermontov; oratorio "Poltava", to words by Pushkin and A.K. Tolstoy; cycle of four songs to words by Gorky: "Let Us Sing the Fame of Brave Men's Madness", "Vas'ka Buslayev's Monologue", "Lyric Song" and "The Stormy Petrel"; choral suite "Stepan Razin", to words by Pushkin; songs: "Fly to Moscow, Little Nightingale", "In the Wastes of the Barents Sea", "Mountain Eagle", "The Death of Chapayev" and "Harvest Dance"; *Awards:* Stalin Prize (1951); *Died:* 15 Oct 1956 in Moscow.

VASIL'YEVSKIY (pen name: V. VOKHINSKIY), Vladimir Nikolayevich (1893–1957) Party official; CP member from 1912; *Born:* 1893; *Career:* 1914–17 illegal Party work in Russian Army; participated in 1917 Oct Revol; 1917 member, Mil Bureau, Moscow Party Comt; comr, Mil-Revol Comt for Petrograd Ammunition Depots; 1914 asst secr, then secr, newspaper "Pravda"; dir, journal "Voprosy strakhovaniya"; after 1917 Oct Revol held various exec posts; 1926 worked for CC, CPSU(B); also film work; 1929–31 member, ed bd, newspaper "Izvestia"; from 1931 member, ed bd, newspaper "Pravda"; 1918–21 ed and member, ed bd, "Petrogradskaya pravda"; co-publisher and ed, newspaper "Boyevaya pravda"; head, Press Dept, Petrograd Sov and 7th Army; *Publ: Pravdistskoye povetriye* (Pravdist Infection) (1926); *Tribuna rabochego vosstaniya* (The Tribune of the Workers' Revolt) (1962), etc; *Died:* 1957.

VASNETSOV, Apollinariy Mikhaylovich (1856–1933) Landscape painter and stage designer; member, Petersburg Acad of Arts from 1900; *Born:* 26 June 1856 in vil Ryabovo, Vyatka Province; *Educ:* studied painting from his brother, the artist V.M. Vasnetsov; *Career:* in 1870's vil teacher; 1880 did illustrations for journals "Zhivopisnoye obozreniye" and "Vsemirnaya illyustratsiya" in Petersburg; from 1883 exhibitor, from 1899 member, Assoc of Itinerant Art Exhibitions; from 1890 lived and worked mainly in Moscow; toured Urals, Siberia and Ukr; 1898 visited Spain and Paris; from 1890's concentrated on historical landscapes and reconstructed many architectural landscapes of Ancient Moscow; 1901–18 ran landscape class at Moscow College of Painting, Sculpture and Architecture; from 1918 chm, Commission for the Study of Old Moscow; many of his works are displayed at the Tret'yakov Gallery, Russian Museum and other major sov museums; *Works:* paintings: "Homeland" (1886); "Dusk" (1889); "Taiga in the Urals. Blue Mountain" (1891); "Siberia" (1894); "Kama" (1895); "Northern Country. Siberian River" (1898); "Late 17th-Century Moscow. Dawn at the Voskresenskiye Gates" (1900), etc; designed sets and costumes for: *Zhizn' za tsarya* (A Life for the Tsar) (1885); *Snegurochka* (The Snow-Maiden) (1896); "Khovanshchina" (1897); "Sadko" (1900); *Skazaniye o nevidimom grade Kitezhe i deve Fevronii*(The Tale of the Invisible City of Kitezh and the Maiden Fevroniya) (1906); "Oprichnik" (1911), etc; *Publ: Khudozhestvo. Opyt analiza ponyatiy, opredelyayushchikh iskusstvo zhivopisi* (Art. An Analysis of the Concepts Underlying the Art of Painting) (1908); *Died:* 23 Jan 1933.

VASNETSOV, Viktor Mikhaylovich (1848–1926) Painter; member, Petersburg Acad of Arts form 1893; *Born:* 15 May 1848 in vil Lop'yal, Vyatka Province; *Educ:* completed school of Soc for the Promotion of the Arts; 1868–75 studied at Petersburg Acad of Arts; *Career:* took up painting and drawing as a student in Vyatka; 1867 moved to Petersburg to study art and began to do illustrations for journals and publ houses; 1876–77 lived and worked in Paris; from 1874 exhibitor, from 1878 member, Assoc of Itinerant Art Exhibitions; from 1878 lived in Moscow; 1885–91 worked in Kiev, decorating Vladimir Cathedral; prior to this visited Italy to study ancient Byzantine monuments; many of his paintings are displayed at the Tret'yakov Gallery, Moscow; *Works:* paintings: "From Apartment to Apartment" (1876); "The Book Stall" (1876); "Paris Booths" (1877); "Military Telegram" (1878); "Preference" (1879); "After Igor Svyatoslavich's Battle with the Polovtsians" (1880); "Alyonushka" (1881); panel "The Stone Age" (1883–85); "Tsarevich Ivan on the Grey Wolf" (1883); decorations of Vladimir Cathedral, Kiev (1885–96); paintings "Sirin and Alkonost" (1896); "Tsar Ivan Vasilevich the Terrible" (1897); "The Bogatyrs" (1881–98); numerous portraits; designed sets for production of Ostrovskiy's *Snegurochka* (The Snow-Maiden); designed church and fairy-tale "Hut on Chicken's Legs" at Abramtsevo, near Moscow; designed facade of Tret'yakov Gallery, etc; *Died:* 23 July 1926 in Moscow.

VATAGIN, Aleksey Ivanovich (1881–1947) Artist; specialist in Palekhian miniatures; *Born:* 1881; *Career:* decorated boxes, caskets, etc, with subjects drawn from folk epics and fiction; adopted some techniques of ancient Russian painting, particulary the 16th-Century Moscow school; specialized in historical themes; also did frescoes, murals and book illustrations; *Works:* murals in Sverdlovsk Pioneers Center; "Russian Cities in the Struggle for Independence" (1942); "Hail to Russian Arms" (1944); "The Campaign of Minin and Pozharskiy" (1944), etc; *Died:* 1947.

VATIN (real name: BYSTRYANSKIY), Vadim Aleksandrovich (1886–1940) Russian revol; Party publicist; CP member from 1907; *Born:* 1886 in Petersburg, son of a railroad eng; *Educ:* studied at Petersburg and Zurich Univ; *Career:* 1907 member, Petersburg RSDRP Comt; 1909–16 in exile; from late 1916 member, Kiev RSDRP(B) Comt; after 1917 Oct Revol ed, newspaper "Golos sotsial-demokrata"; co-ed, Yekaterinoslav newspaper "Zvezda"; from late 1917 ed, Khar'kov newspaper "Donetskiy proletariy"; 1918–20 ed, various Petrograd newspapers; 1920–30 teaching and research work; deleg, 8th and 16th Party Congresses; wrote a number of works on Marxist-Leninist philosophy, atheism, Party Org, ect; *Died:* 1940.

VATSETIS, Ioakim Ioakimovich (1873–1938) Mil commander; commander, 2nd class; *Born:* 23 Nov 1873 in Kurland Province, son of a farmhand; *Educ:* 1897 grad Vilnius Mil College; *Career:* 1914–17 fought in Russian Army, where his last rank was col; during Oct 1917 Revol transferred allegience to Red Army; Jan 1918 put down anti-Sov mutiny in Gen Dowbor Musicki's Polish Corps; spring 1918 commanded Lat Infantry Div; in same year led suppression of "Leftist" Socialist-Revol uprising in Moscow; from July 1918 commander, Eastern Front; 4 Sept 1918 – 8 July 1919 commander in chief, RSFSR Armed Forces; Aug 1919–1921 worked for RSFSR Revol Mil Council; from 1922 prof, (Frunze) Mil Acad; 1938 arrested by NKVD; *Publ: O voennoy doktrine budushchego* (Future Military Doctrine) (1923); *Boyevyye deystviya v Vostochnoy Prussii v iyule, avguste i nachale sentyabrya 1914-ogo goda. Strategicheskiy ocherk* (Military Operations in Eastern Prussia in July, August and Early September 1914. A Study in Stragegy) (1923); *Died:* 28 July 1938 in imprisonment; posthumously rehabilitated.

VATULYA, Aleksey Mikhaylovich (1891–1955) Ukr actor; Pop Artiste of Ukr SSR from 1940; *Born:* 2 Aug 1891 in vil Novo-Nikolayevka, now Poltava Oblast; *Educ:* 1913–16 studied at Lysenko Musical Drama School, Kiev; *Career:* 1916 joined Young Theater, Kiev; 1920 founder-actor, Franko Theater, Kiev; in his latter years specialized in character parts; *Roles:* Oedipus in Sophocles' "Oedipus Rex" (1921); Mikhail in Karpenko-Karyy's *Suyeta* (Fuss) (1923); Uriel' in Gutskov's "Uriel' Akosta" (1921); Krizhen' in Mikitenko's *Kadry* (Cadres) (1923); Gayday, Berest, Krivonos and Gorlov in Korneychuk's *Gibel' eskadry* (Death of a Squadron) (1933); "Platon Krechet" (1934); "Bogdan Khmel'nitskiy" (1939) and *Front* (The Front) (1942); Yakov in Gorky's *Posledniye* (The Last Ones) (1937); Pribytkov in *Poslednyaya zhertva* (The Last Victim) (1939); Stessel' in Stepanov and Popov's "Port Arthur" (1953); *Died:* 20 May 1955.

VATUTIN, Nikolay Fyodorovich (1901–1944) Mil commander; gen; CP member from 1921; *Born:* 16 Dec 1901; in vil Chepukhino, now Kursk Oblast, son of a peasant; *Educ:* 1922 grad Poltava Infantry School; grad advanced extension courses in Kiev; 1929 grad Frunze Mil Acad; 1937 grad Operations Fac, Frunze Mil Acad and Gen Staff Acad; *Career:* Apr 1920 joined Sov Army, rising quickly from private to platoon commander; later chief of staff, Kiev Mil Distr; headed Gen Staff Operations Bd; later First Dep Chief of Gen Staff; during WW 2 chief of staff, Northwestern, Bryansk, Voronezh, Southwestern and 1st Ukr fronts; also commander, Voronezh, Southwestern and 1st Ukr fronts; *Awards:* Order of Lenin; Order of the Red Star; Order of Suvorov, 1st Class; Order of Kutuzov, 1st Class; *Died:* 15 Apr 1944 of war wounds; buried in Kiev.

VAVILOV, Nikolay Ivanovich (1887–1943) Botanist and geneticist; prof; member, USSR and Ukr Acad of Sci; member, All-Union Lenin Acad of Agric Sci from 1929; *Born:* 13 Nov 1887 in Moscow; *Educ:* 1911 grad Moscow Agric Inst; *Career:* stayed on at Moscow Agric Inst to train for professorship; 1917–21 prof, Saratov Univ; 1923–29 dir, State Inst of Experimental Agronomy, Leningrad; 1929–35 pres, 1935–37 vice-pres, All-Union Lenin Acad of Agric Sci; 1924–40 dir, All-Union Inst of Applied Botany and New Crops; 1930–40 dir, Inst of Genetics, USSR Acad of Sci; 1931–40 pres, All-Union Geographical Soc; organized and took part in expeditions to Mediterranean, Ethiopia, Japan, Korea and Northern, Centr and South America, accumulating a worldwide collection of cultivated plants; established the main for ci of the origin of cultivated plants; devised original classification of plant immunity phenomena; member, Royal Soc, London and many other for sci and learned soc; adopted independent stand on genetic theory and research, diametrically opposed to that officially endorsed by the CP and practised by Lysenko, at that time pres of All-Union Lenin Acad of Agric Sci; 1940 arrested and expelled from Acad; *Publ:Immunitet rasteniy k infektsionnym zabolevaniyam* (Plant Immunity to Infectious Diseases) (1919); *Polevyye kul'tury Yugo-Vostoka* (Field Crops of the Southeast) (1922); *Tsentry proiskhozhdeniya kul'turnykh rasteniy* (The Centers of Origin of Cultivated Plants) (1926); *Linneyevskiy vid kak sistema* (The Linnaean Species as a System) (1931); *Selektsiya kak nauka* (Selection as a Science) (1934); *Problema novykh kul'tur* (The Problem of New Crops) (1932); *Botaniko-geograficheskiye osnovy selektsii* (The Botanico-Geographical Principles of Selection) (1935); *Zakon gemologicheskikh ryadov v nasledstvennoy izmenchivosti* (The Law of Hemological Series in Hereditary Mutability) (1935); *Ucheniye ob immunitete rasteniy k infektsionnym zabolevaniyam* (The Theory of Plant Immunity to Infectious Diseases) (1935); *Ucheniye o proiskhozhdenii kul'turnykh rasteniy posle Darvina* (The Theory of the Origin of Cultivated Plants After Darwin) (1939), etc; *Awards:* Lenin Prize (1926); Przheval'skiy Gold Medal; *Died:* 26 Jan 1943 in imprisonment; in Magadan camp.

VAVILOV, Sergey Ivanovich (1891–1951) Physicist; govt official; member, USSR Acad of Sci from 1932; *Born:* 24 Mar 1891 in Moscow; *Educ:* 1914 grad Physics and Mathematics Fac, Moscow Univ; *Career:* worked at P.N. Lebedev's Laboratory, where he carried out his first research work "Teplovoye vytsvetaniye krasok" (The Thermal Bleaching of Dyes); 1915 received for this work Gold Prize of Soc of Natural Scientists, Anthropologists and Ethnographers, Moscow Univ; 1914–18 with eng and radio communication units, Russian Army; conducted important radio research; devised a new method of radio direction finding; 1919 published his study "Chastata kolebaniy nagruzhennoy antenny" (The Oscillating Frequency of a Loaded Antenna); 1918–29 assoc prof, 1929–32 prof of physics, Moscow Univ; 1920–30 prof, Moscow Higher Zootech Inst; 1918–30 also head, Dept of Physical Optics, Inst of Physics and Biophysics, Pop Comrt of Health; from 1932 dir, Physics Inst, USSR Acad of Sci; 1932–45 sci dir, State Optical Inst; 1945 elected pres, USSR Acad of Sci; chm, Council to Coordinate the Work of the Union-Republ Academies of Sci; from 1945 chm, Ed and Publ Council, USSR Acad of Sci; edited journals: "Uspekhi fizicheskikh nauk"; "Zhurnal eksperimental'noy i teoreticheskoy fiziki"; "Priroda", etc; edited physics sections in "Tekhnicheskaya entsiklopediya" and 1st and 2nd ed, "BSE" (Large Soviet Encyclopedia); from 1949 chief ed, 2nd ed, "BSE"; from 1933 head, Commission for the Publ of Pop Sci Lit and the series *Itogi i problemy sovremennoy nauki* (The Results and Problems of Modern Science), USSR Acad fo Sci; co-founder, All-Union Soc for the Dissemination of Polit and Sci Knowledge; first chm, above soc; specialized in physical optics; for some 30 years studied nature of photoluminescence, particularly luminescence of solutions; directed research on luminescence of crystallic phosphorus and practical applications of luminescence; invented a new, econ lighting source based on converting invisible ultraviolet radiation of a light source into visible light by covering lamps with luminofors; directed work on technol for producing luminescent lamps pf the "daylight" or "cold light" type; pioneered development of luminescent analysis techniques; did research on visual method of observing quantum fluctuations of light; 1934 supervised P.A. Cherenkov in his research leading to the discovery that pure liquids luminesce under the action of gamma- and beta-radiation; immediatedly pointed out that this luminescence was not normal luminescence but was connected with the motion of free electrons (so-called Vavilov-Cherenkov effect); in his book *Mikrostruktura sveta* (The Microstructure of Light) (1950) he summarized the results of his research on physical optics; this laid the basis for a new research field which he called microoptics; also studied philosophy of natural sci and history of sci; collated, published and popularized sci legacy of M.V. Lomonosov and V.V. Petrov; wrote a study of the works of L. Euler; headed Commission for the History of the USSR Acad of Sci; wrote studies assessing the sci work of Lucretius, Galileo and Newton; studied history of atomism; dep, RSFSR Supr Sov of 1938 and USSR Supr Sov of 1946 and 1950 convocations; during WW 2 worked for USSR State Defense Comt; developed new instruments for Sov Armed Forces; Inst of Physical Problems, USSR Acad of Sci in Moscow and State Optical Inst in Leningrad are named for him; USSR Acad of Sci instituted the Vavilov Gold Medal, awarded annually for outstanding works in physics; *Publ:* "Die Fluoreszenzausbeute von Farbstofflösungen" (1924); "Die Auslöschung der Fluoreszenz von Farbstofflösungen bei großen Konzentrationen" (1925); "Die Beziehungen zwischen Fluoreszenz und Phosphoreszenz in festen und flüssigen Medien" (1926); "Die Fluoreszenzausbeute von Farbstofflösungen als Funktion der Wellenlänge des anregenden Lichtes" (1927); "Studien zur Kenntnis der Natur der Photolumineszenz von Uranylsalzen" (1928); *Novyye svoystva polyarizatsii fluorestsentsii zhidkostey* (New Fluorescence Polarization Properties of Liquids) (1929); coauthor, "Visuelle Messungen der statischen Photonenschwankungen" (1933); "Über die Eigenschaften der Interferenz von weitgeöffneten Lichtbündeln" (1933); *O vozmozhnykh prichinakh sinego gamma-svecheniya zhidkostey* (The Possible Causes of Blue Gamma-Luminescence of Liquids) (1934); *Priroda elementarnykh izluchateley i yavleniya interferentsii* (The Nature of Elementary Emitters and Interference Phenomena) (1937); *Lyuminestsentnyye istochniki sveta* (Luminescent Light Sources) (1941); *O fotolyuminestsentsii rastvorov* (The Photoluminescence of Solutions) (1945); *Lyuminestsentsiya i yeyo dlitel'nost'* (Luminescence and Its Duration) (1947); *Lomonosov i russkaya nauka* (Lomonosov and Russian Science) (1947); *Eksperimental'nyye issledovaniya migratsii energii vo fluorestsiruyushchikh rastvorakh* (Experimental Research on Energy Migration in Fluorescent Solutions) (1949); *Lenin i filosofskiye problemy sovremennoy fiziki* (Lenin and Philosophical Problems of Modern Physics) (1950) *Sobraniye sochineniy* (Collected Works) (3 vol, 1952–56); *Awards:* two Orders of Lenin; Order of the Red Banner of Labor; three Stalin Prizes (1943, 1946 and 1951 [posthumously]); *Died:* 25 Jan 1951 in Moscow.

VAYCHYUNAS, Pyatras (1890–1959) Lith playwright and poet; Hon Art Worker of Lith SSR from 1954; *Born:* 29 June 1890 in vil Pilyakal'nyay, Lith, son of a peasant; *Educ:* studied at Petrograd Psychoneurological Inst; *Career:* wrote over 20 plays; translated into Lith several plays by Schiller, Slovacky, Hauptmann, Ibsen, etc; *Publ:* verse collections: "Dewy Rays" (1923); "Sunny Treasure" (1935), etc; comedies: "Vain Efforts" (1926); "Patriots" (1927); "Sunday" (1927), etc; *Died:* 7 June 1959 in Vilnius.

VAYNSHTEYN (Party name: RAKHMILEVICH), Aron Isaakovich (1877–1938) Govt official; CP member from 1921; *Born:* 1877; *Educ:* grad Vilnius Jewish Teachers' Training Inst; *Career:* from 1893 in revol movement; from 1897 member, Bund; 1901–21 member, 1917–21 also chm, CC, Bund; repeatedly arrested; 1914–17 in exile; attended 5th RSDRP Congress and the Paris, Tammerfors and Helsingfors Party Conferences; early 1912 organized conference of nat Soc-Democratic groups and orgs; organized voting bloc, Bund and Polish Soc-Democratic Party for 4th State Duma; during WW 1 adopted centrist, then defensist stand; 1917 worked in Bel; member, Exec Comt, Minsk City Sov and chm, Minsk City Duma; during 1917 Oct Revol supported All-Russian Exec Comt of Railroad Union's demand for a "united socialist govt" ranging from populist socialists to Bolsheviks; 1919, after German revol, supported socialist revol and Sov rule; 1920 member, Bel Mil Revol Comt; 1921, after Bund's incorporation in the RCP(B), Presidium member, Centr Exec Comt; dep chm, Bel Council of Pop Comr; member, Centr Bureau, CP Bel; then member and Bureau member, CC Kir Oblast Party Comt; 1922 chm, Kir Labor and Defense Council; from 1923 Collegium member, USSR Pop Comrt of Finance; simultaneously member, Comt for the Allotment of Land to Jews, USSR Centr Exec Comt; then exec admin and econ work; arrested by State Security organs; *Died:* 1938 in imprisonment.

VECHESLOV (YUR'YEV), M. G. (1869–1934) Revolutionary and physician; CP member from 1918; *Born:* 1869; *Career:* 1900 organized Berlin group of "Iskra" supporters and helped to smuggle the newspaper into Russia over the Western border; member, For League of Russian Revol Soc-Democrats; after 2nd RSDRP Congress joined Menshevik faction; 1908–17 worked as physician and bacteriologist in Russia; after Oct 1917 Revol took charge of Health Section, RSFSR Pop Comrt of Means of Communication; from 1919 Collegium member, RSFSR Pop Comrt of Health; during Civil War Centr Health Council comr on various fronts; physician, Soc of Old Bolsheviks; *Died:* 1934.

VEDENEYEV, Boris Yevgen'yevich (1885–1946) Hydropower eng; member, USSR Acad of Sci from 1932; member, USSR Acad of Architecture from 1941; *Born:* 2 Jan 1885 in Tiflis; *Educ:* 1909 grad Petersburg Inst of Trans Eng; 1909–10 attended lectures at Darmstadt Polytech; *Career:* 1910–11 eng, Tech Dept, Bd of Vladikavkaz Railroad; 1911–12 taught electr eng and hydraulics at Moscow Secondary Mech-Tech College; 1912–14 eng with special prospecting party along the coast of the Sea of Japan; 1914–16 senior works mang for expansion of Vladivostok Merchant Port; 1916–17 directed construction of piers in Kola Bay and Murmansk Port; 1918–19 eng, irrigation bd in Turkestan; 1919–20 worked on construction of irrigation system in Chu Basin and for Moscow Nizhniy Novgorod Distr Water Mang Bd; 1920 helped compile plan of State Commission for the Electrification of Russia; 1920–22 lecturer, Chair of Electr Eng, Leningrad Inst of Trans Eng; 1920–27 also head, Hydrotech Dept; then head, Tech Dept and chief eng, Volkhov Construction Trust; 1922–27 also head, Chair of Hydroelectr Power Assemblies, Leningrad Inst of Trans Eng; from 1926 helped build Dnieper Hydroelectr Power Plant; 1927–34asst chief eng, then first dep head and chief eng, Joint Dnieper Construction Trust; 1932–34 also dep head, Centr Volga Construction Trust; during this period also worked on construction of hydroelectr plants on the Volga and Kama Rivers; 1934–40 chief eng and dep head, Main Hydropower Construction Trust, USSR Pop Comrt of Heavy Ind; 1940–41 member, Fuel and Electr Mang Council, USSR Council of Pop Comr; from 1941 also state councillor, USSR Council of Pop Comr; 1942–46 chm, Tech Council, USSR Min of Electr Power Plants, with rank of dep min; 1943–45 also worked for USSR State Defense Comt and was member, Council for Sci and Tech Expertise, USSR Gosplan; from 1945 also chm, USSR Min of Electr Power Plants Comt on USSR participation in int power eng associations; head, All-Union Council of Sci Eng and Tech Soc; ed, journal "Elektrichestvo"; dep, USSR Supr Sov of 1st and 2nd convocations; member, Extraordinary State Commission to Investigate the Misdeeds of the German Fascist Usurpers; *Publ:* textbook *Gidroelektricheskiye silovyye ustanovki* (Hydroelectric Power Assemblies) (2nd ed, 1926); articles: "Dams on the Volga" (1934); "A Simple Objective Method of Determining the Cost of Hydropower Complexes and Its Use in Designing" (1936); "The Methodology of Determining Power Costs in Designing Hydroelectric Plants" (1945); "Molotov Oblast – the Power Base of the Urals" (1946), etc; *Awards:* three Orders of Lenin; Order of the Fatherland War, 1st Class; medals; Stalin Prize (1943); *Died:* 25 Sept 1946.

VEDENISOV, Boris Nikolayevich (1869–1952) Railroad eng; Dir-Gen of Track and Construction, 2nd Class; corresp member, USSR Acad of Sci from 1943; Hon Sci and Tech Worker of RSFSR from 1942; *Born:* 24 July 1869; *Educ:* 1891 grad Moscow Univ; 1900 grad Moscow Eng College, Dept of Means of Communication; *Career:* 1905–06 in prison for revol activities; from 1920 taught at Moscow Higher Tech College; from 1921 at Moscow Inst of Rail Trans Eng; also worked for Section for Sci Study of Trans Problems, USSR Acad of Sci; 1902 produced original designs and work methods for construction of installations at Vindava Port; 1908 first to use slag blocks, later used extensively neutralize whirlpools; first to use horizontal drilling in order to tap underground water and reinforce hillsides; pioneered mechanization of track work; 1913 first to use pneumatic packing of sleepers on Russian railroads. devised formulas and simple techniques for determining the shortest distance between two points; designed and helped build major rail bridges and stations; wrote several textbooks and sponsored introduction of a gen course on railroads at trans eng institutes; *Publ: Mekhanizatsiya puteveykh rabot i, v chastnosti, podbivki shpal ballastom* (The Mechanization of Track Work and, in Particular, the Packing of Sleepers with Ballast) (1923); *O perekhodnykh krivykh pro bol'shikh skorostyakh dvizheniya* (Transition Curves for High Operating Speeds) (1936); *Issledovaniye o provedenii zheleznodorozhnykh liniy mezhdu dvumya otdalyonnymi punktami* (A Study of the Laying of Railroad Lines Between Two Distant Points) (1936); *Ustroystvo puti i sposoby yego lecheniya* (Track Laying and Means of Track Correction) (2 vol, 1937); *Proyektirovaniye i soderzhaniye podkosov zemlyanogo polotna s uchyotom ikh raspolozheniya po stranam sveta* (The Design and Maintentance of Earthern Road Bed Embankments in Relation to Their Situation in the Various Countries of the World) (1950); *Awards:* Order of Lenin; two Orders of the Red Banner of Labor; Stalin Prize (1943); *Died:* 11 July 1952.

VEDENYAPIN, Mikhail Aleksandrovich (1879–?) Politician; member, Socialist-Revol Party; *Born:* 1879, *Career:* 1901, while a student, distributed proclamations; arrested and exiled for two years to Tashkent under police surveillance; 1903 went abroad and joined Socialist-Revol Party; late 1905 directed Samara Group, Socialist-Revol Party; 4 Dec 1906 sentenced in Saratov to Siberian settlement; 1907 fled from exile; 1908 arrested in Moscow and sentenced to four years at hard labor; after 1917 Feb Revol elected member, CC, Socialist-Revol Party; sided with Rightist Socialist-Revolutionaries; after 1917 Oct Revol opposed Sov regime; June 1918 went to Samara to organize revolt and established contacts with Czechoslovakian command; headed Dept of For Affairs in Constituent Assembly Comt (govt); 1922 tried in Moscow in grand trial of Rightist Socialist-Revolutionaries; sentenced to 10 years' imprisonment in strict isolation; this term of imprisonment was reduced under a subsequent amnesty; *Died:* date and place of death unknown.

VEDERNIKOV (SIBIRYAK), Aleksey Stepanovich (1880–1919) Party official; CP member from 1897; *Born:* Oct 1880 in Siberia, son of an office worker; *Career:* from eight years of age apprentice at a plant; at age 16 joined revol movement; participated in 1905–07 Revol; Oct 1905 member, Tomsk three-men Party Commission; headed battle squads; during 1905 Dec revolt member, Moscow Party Comt; fought at barricades of Moscow's Presnya Rayon; after the sollapse of 1905–07 Revol Party work in the Urals and Perm'; 1907 deleg, 5th (London) Party Congress; shortly after his return from the Congress arrested and sentenced to penal servitude; after 1917 Feb Revol returned to Moscow; deleg, 7th (April) All-Russian RSDRP(B) Conference; May 1917 member, Centr Commission for Formation of Red Guard Units; member, Operations Staff, Red Guards Centr Staff; during 1917 Oct Revol member, Mil-Revol Comt; co-founder and head, Moscow Red Guards Headquarters; 25 Oct 1917 directed seizure of Moscow's major strategic objectives by revol forces: telegraph, telephone and post offices; after 1917 Oct Revol comr, Vyksun and Kulebaka Plants, Nizhniy Novgorod Province; 1918 commanded detachment sent to crush anti-Sov revolt in Murom; *Died:* 12 Jan 1919 of heart failure.

VEDROV, Nikolay Simonovich (1891–1949) Dermatologist and venereologist; corresp member, USSR Acad of Med Sci; *Born:* 1891; *Educ:* 1914 grad Med Fac, Moscow Univ; *Career:* from 1925 worked at Obukh Inst of Occupational Diseases; 1938–41 assoc prof, Chair of Skin and Venereal Diseases, 2nd Moscow Med Inst; 1942 defended doctor's thesis; 1943–49 head, Chair of Skin and Venereal Diseases, Moscow Med Inst, RSFSR Min of Health; did valuable research on occupational dermatosis and treatment of syphilis; published some 50 research works; *Publ: K voprosu o dermatozakh ot dinitrokhlorbenzola* (Dermatoses from Dinitrochlorbenzole) (1928); *Materialy k voprosu o sensibilizatsii kozhi* (Material on Skin Sensitization) (1931); *Kapel'naya metodika ispytaniya povyshennoy chuvstvitel'nosti kozhi k khimicheskim veshchestvam* (The Drop Method of Testing Heightened Skin Sensitivity to Chemical Substances) (1933); *Professional'nyye bolezni kozhi* (Occupational Skin Diseases) (1936); *Lecheniye sifilisa vismutom v svete dannykh po yego absorbtsii i vydeleniyu* (The Bismuth Treatment of Syphilis in the Light of Data on Its Absorption and Excretion) (1941); *Sifilis* (Syphilis) (1950); *Died:* 1949 in Moscow.

VEGER, Yevgeniy Il'ich (1899–1938) Party and govt official; cand member, CC, CPSU(B) from 1934; CP member from 1917; *Born:* 1899 in Odessa, son of an office worker; *Career:* during Civil War in Red Army; 4th Army deleg at 10th RCP(B) Congress; then exec Party work in Sverdlovsk, Bryansk and Crimea; exec instructor, CC, CPSU(B); 1933–37 first secr, Odessa Oblast Comt, CP(B) Ukr; deleg at 14th, 15th and 17th CPSU(B) Congresses; deleg at 12th and 13th Congresses of CP(B) Ukr; 1933–37 cand Politburo member, CC, CP(B) Ukr; member, USSR Centr Exec Comt; 1937 arrested by State Security organs; *Died:* 10 July 1938 in imprisonment.

VEKSLER, Ivan Ivanovich (1885–1954) Russian lit historian; *Born:* 8 Sept 1885 in Vitebsk; *Educ:* 1912 grad Vilnius Teachers' Training Inst; 1932 completed postgrad studies at USSR Acad of Sci; *Career:* assoc, Inst of Russian Lit (Pushkin Center); in 1930's one of first to study work of F.M. Reshyotnikov; 1936–48 edited six-vol ed *Polnoye sobraniye sochineniy Reshyotnikova* (Complete Collected Works of Reshyotnikov); in 1940's studied works and biography of A.N. Tolstoy and published a monograph about him; 1946–49 helped edit complete 15-vol collection of A.N. Tolstoy's works; *Publ: K istorii gornozavodskikh romanov F.M. Reshyotnikova* (The History of F.M. Reshyotnikov's Mining Novels) (1932); *F.M. Reshyotnikov v kritike* (The Critics on F.M. Reshyotnikov) (1932); *Dobrolyubov i pisateli-raznochintsy* (Dobrolyubov and the Non-Gentry Writers) (1936); *P.Zh. Beranzhe i V.S. Kurochkin* (P.G. Beranger and V.S. Kurochkin) (1932); *I.S. Turgenev i politicheskaya bor'ba shestidesyatykhh godov* (I.S. Turgenev and the Political Campaign of the Sixties) (1934); *Permskiy period zhihni i tvorchestva F.M. Reshyotnikova* (The Perm' Period of F.M. Reshyotnikov's Life and Work) (1936); *K probleme satiricheskogo obraza u Shchedrina* (Shchedrin's Satirical Image) (1946); *Aleksey Nikolayevich Tolstoy. Zhiznennyy i tvorcheskiy put'* (Aleksey Nikolayevich Tolstoy. His Life and Career) (1948); *Died:* 24 Apr 1954 in Leningrad.

VEKSLER, Vladimir Iosifovich (1907–1966) Physicist; prof; member, USSR Acad of Sci from 1958; CP member from 1937; *Born:* 4 Mar 1907; *Educ:* 1931 grad Moscow Inst of Power Eng; *Career:* began work as fitter at a factory; 1930–36 assoc, All-Union Inst of Power Eng; 1936–56 assoc, Inst of Physics, USSR Acad of Sci; 1946–58 corresp member, USSR Acad of Sci; from 1956 head, High Energy Laboratory, Joint Nuclear Research Inst, Dubna; simultaneously head of a chair, Moscow Univ; 1956 member, Geneva Nuclear Research Conference; 1959 led Sov sci deleg to USA; 1962 head, Sov deleg at Int Conference on High-Energy Physics, Geneva; from 1963 acad secr, Dept of Nuclear Physics, USSR Acad of Sci; did research on cosmic rays and accelereator theory; proposed phase-stability hypothesis which contributed to development of synchrotrons and phasotrons; *Publ:* coauthor, *Eksperimental'nyye metody yedernoy fiziki* (The Experimental Methods of Nuclear Physics) (1940); *Novyy metod uskoreniya relyativistskikh chastits* (A New Method of Accelerating Relativistic Particles) (1944); coauthor, *Elektronno-yadernyye livni kosmicheskikh luchey i yaderno-kaskadnyy protsess* (Nuclear Electron Cosmic Showers and the Nuclear Cascade Process) (1949); coauthor, *Ionizatsionnyye metody issledovaniya izlucheniy* (Ionization Methods of Radiation Study) (2nd ed, 1950); coauthor, *Mezhdunarodnaya konferentsiya po fizike vysokikh energiy i apparature* (The International Conference on High-Energy Physics and Equipment) (1962); etc; *Awards:* Lenin Prize (1959); State Prize; "Atoms for Peace" Prize (1963); *Died:* 22 Sept 1966.

VELICHKINA (BONCH-BRUYEVICH), Vera Mikhaylovna (1868–1918) Party official; writer and publicist; CP member from 1903; *Born:* 1868; *Career:* physician by profession; from 1890's worked for Soc-Democratic org in Russia and abroad; 1899 emigrated to Canada with Dukhobors religious sect; 1900 returned to Russia, arrested and deported; in London joined For League of Soc-Democratic Org; after RSDRP schism joined Bolsheviks; helped smuggle illegal lit into Russia; co-ed, Soc-Democratic journal "Rassvet"; contributed to Bolshevik newspapers "Vperyod", "Proletariy", etc; 1906 returned to Russia, helped organize workers' clubs; from 1908 helped run "Zhizn' i znaniye" (Life and Knowledge) Publishing House; during 1917 Feb Revol founded Revol Red Cross org; for some time secr, Petrograd newspaper "Izvestiya Soveta Rabochikh Deputatov"; during 1917 Oct Revol organized med aid for battle squads; until Sept 1918 head, Children's Health Dept, Pop Comrt of Educ; helped organize Pop Comrt of Health; Collegium member, Pop Comrt of Health;

translated a number of books from German, French and English; *Publ: Dukhobory v Kanade* (The Dukhobors in Canada) (1900); *Istoriya inkvizitsii* (A History of the Inquisition) (1904); *V golodnom godu* (The Hungry Year) (1910); a biography of Pestalozzi entitled *Drug detey* (The Children's Friend) (1922); *Shveytsariya, opisaniye strany* (Switzerland, a Description of the Country) (1923); Blanka's biography *Vechnyyy uznik* (The Eternal Prisoner) (1927), etc; *Died:* 1918.

VELICHKO, Konstantin Ivanovich (1856–1927) Mil eng; fortifications specialist; lt-gen; prof; *Born:* 20 May 1856; *Career:*1877–78 fought in war against Turkey; during Russo- Japanese War in charge of fortification work in Manchuria; during WW 1 chief mil eng, Southwestern Front; then field eng inspector, Command Headquarters; did research on principles of fortification and camouflage; founder, Inst of Mil Eng; build forts at Kovno and Novogeorgiyevsk and designed forts for Port Arthur and Vladivostok; permanent member, Russian State Commission for Defense Eng; 1918 in charge of eng works during German advance on Petrograd; from May 1918 chm, Russian Defense Eng Collegium; from 1919 in charge of fortification of Moscow region; until 1923 morked for Main Eng Bd; 1923–27 prof of fortifications, Mil Tech Acad; *Publ: Issledovaniye noveyshykh sredstv osady i oborony sukhoputnykh krepostey* (A Study of the Latest Means of Besieging and Defending Inland Forts) (1890); *Oboronitel'nyye sredstva krepostey protiv uskorennykh atak* (Means of Defending Forts against Sudden Attack) (1892); *Inzhenernaya oborona gosudarstv i ustroystvo krepostey. Chast' 1- Sukhoputnyye kreposti* (State Defense Engineering and Fortification. Part 1 – Inland Forts) (1903); *Ukreplyonnye pozitsii i inzhenernnaya podgotovka ikh ataki* (Fortified Positions and Their Engineering Preparation for Attack) (1919); *Russkiye kreposti v svyazi s operatsiyami polevykh armiy v mirovuyu voynu* (Russian Forts and the Operations of the Field Armies in the World War) (1926), etc; *Died:* 15 May 1927.

VELIKANOV, Mikhail Dmitriyevich (1895–1938) Mil commander; army commander, 2nd class; CP member from 1924; *Born:* 27 Dec 1895 in vil Nikol'skoye, Ryazan' Oblast, son of an office worker; *Educ:* 1915 grad ensigns' school; *Career:* from 1918 in Red Army; brigade commander, 24th Iron Div; fought in battle of Simbirsk, then commanded special army group in defense of Orenburg; commanded shock forces group, 10th Army which routed White Army cavalry units at Yegorlykskaya and Ataman; after Civil War held exec posts in Sov army; corps commander; 1930–33 dep commander, North-Caucasian Mil Distr; 1933–37 commander, Centr Asian Mil Distr; from June 1937 commander, Transbaykal Mil Distr; arrested by State Security organs; *Awards:* three Orders of the Red Banner; *Died:* 27 July 1938 in imprisonment; posthumously rehabilited.

VELIKHOV, Lev Aleksandrovich (1875–?) Lawyer; publisher; functionary and CC member, Constitutional-Democratic Party; *Born:* 1875; *Educ:* grad Law Fac, Petersburg Univ; *Career:* member and councillor, Petersburg City Council; owner of a publ house in Petersburg and co-publisher and co-ed, journals "Zemskoye delo" and "Gorodskoye delo" and newspaper "Russkaya Molva"; active member, Free-Econ Soc, Tech Soc, etc; Petersburg dep, 4th State Duma; 1917 member, Provisional Comt, State Duma; then Provisional Govt comr in Odessa; in 1920's prof of polit econ, North Caucasian Univ; *Publ: Istinnyye vyvody istoricheskogo materializma* (True Inferences of Historical Materialism) (1907); *Teoriya i praktika proportsional'nogo predstavitel'stva* (Theory and Practice of Proportional Representation) (1908); *Sravnitel'nyye tablitsy russkikh politicheskikh partiy* (Comparative Tables of Russian Political Parties) (1908–17; *Tablitsy blagoustroystva gorodov Rossiyskoy imperii* (Diagrams on the Planning and Organization of Public Services in the Towns of the Russian Empire) (1917); *Opyt munitsipal'noy programmy* (Municipal Program Experience) (1926); *Osnovy gorodskogo khozyaystva* (The Principles of Urban Economy) (1928), etc; *Died:* date, place and cause of death unknown.

VEL'TMAN, Mikhail Lazarevich (pen name: M.P. PAVLOVICH) (1871–1927) Revolutionary; publicist; economist; historian; CP member from 1917; *Born:* 1871 in Odessa, son of a Jewish office worker; *Educ:* studied at high school; *Career:* while a student joined revol movement; founded several self-educ circles; 1892 arrested with some 50 other circle members and a large group of workers and sailors; charged with propaganda among Odessa proletariat and Voluntary Fleet sailors; for 18 months in solitary confinement, then exiled for five years to Eastern Siberia; after his release moved to Kishinev, engaged for two years in underground work, then emigratet to Paris; 1903, after RSFRP schism, joined Mensheviks; under the pen name "Volontyor" contributed to "Iskra"; 1905 moved to Petersburg; ed, illegal army newspaper "Kazarma"; welcomed Dec 1905 revolt in Moscow; Nov 1906 attended All-Russian Conference of Mil and Battle Groups; soon afterwards arrested and imprisoned; after his release continued work in mil org; re-arrested but managed to escape and flee abroad; studied Oriental countries and consorted with Turkish, Iranian and Indian revol emigrés; edited their proclamations and contributed to their periodicals; published a number of articles on Oriental problems in Russian and for journals: "Nasha zarya", "Sovremennik", "Neue Zeit", "Zukunft", "Mouvement socialiste", "Revue du monde musulman", etc; during WW 1 took Internationalist stand; contributed to Paris newspaper "Nashe Slovo"; after 1917 Feb Revol elected secr, Org for Repatriation of Russian Emigrés; helped study documents of the so-called "Black Cabinet" of the Russian Embassy, then returned to Russia; worked for Pop Comrt of For Affairs; attended Brest-Litovsk peace talks as an expert; for some years headed Main Comt for State Construction Projects; 1919–20 Revol Mil Comt rep for construction problems on the Southern Front; 1920, at the Congress of Peoples of the East, elected member, Council for Action and Propaganda; from 1921 Collegium member, Pop Comrt of Nationalities; from 1921 head, Assoc for Oriental Studies; co-founder and until 1927 rector, Moscow Inst of Oriental Studies; co-founder, Moscow Inst of Modern Oriental Languages; lectured at higher institutions for Oriental studies and at Red Army Mil Acad; simultaneously headed Russian-Eastern Chamber of Commerce and edited journal "Novyy Vostok"; *Publ: Chto dokazala Anglo-burskaya voyna?" (What Did the Anglo-Boer War Prove?) (1901); God voyny* (A Year of War) (1904); *Regulyarnaya armiya ili militsiya* (Regular Army or Militia) (1904); "La derniére bataille (la Revolution en Perse)" (1914); "Zélin Khan et le brigandage au Caucase" (1914); Aziya i yeyo rol' v mirovoy voyne (Asia and Its Role in the World War) (1918); *Internatsional smerti i razrusheniya (voyennaya industriya v Anglii, Frantsii i Germanii)* (International of Death and Destruction [The Military Industry of England, France and Germany]) (1918); *Mirovaya voyna i bor'ba za razdel Chyornogo kontinenta (monopolisticheskiy kapitalizm)* (The World War and the Struggle for the Partition of the Black Continent [Monopolistic Capitalism]) (1918); *Voprosy natsional'noy i kolonial'noy politiki i III Internatsional* (Problems of National and Colonial Policy and the Third International) (1920); "The Foundation of Imperialist Policy" (1922); *Mirovaya voyna i gryadushchiye voyny* (The World War and Wars to Come) (1923); *Russkiy vopros v angliyskoy vneshney politike 1922–24* (The Russian Problem in 1922–24 English Foreign Policy) (1924); *Gibel' turetskikh kommunistov* (The End of the Turkish Communists) (1924); *Lenin. Materialy k izucheniyu leninizma* (Lenin. Material for the Study of Leninism) (1924); *Itogi mirovoy voyny* (Results of the World War) (1924); coauthor, *Lenin i Vostok* (Lenin and the Orient) (1924); *Frantsuzskiy imperializm v posleversal'skiy period* (French Imperialism in the Post-Versailles Period) (1925); coauthor, *Turtsiya v bor'be za nezavisimost'* (Turkey and Its Fight for Independence) (1925); coauthor, *Kitay v bor'be za nezavisimost'* (China and Its Fight for Independence) (1925); coauthor, *Persiya v bor'be za nezavisimost'* (Iran and Its Fight for Independence) (1925); *Revolyutsionnaya Turtsiya* (Revolutionary Turkey) (1927); *RSFSR v imperialisticheskom okruzhenii* (The RSFSR in Imperialist Encirclement), etc; *Died:* 1927.

VEL'YAMINOV, Nikolay Aleksandrovich (1855–1920) Surgeon and clinicist; prof, Mil Med Acad; writer; hon member, Royal College of Surgeons from 1900; hon member, Pirogov Soc; member, USSR Acad of Sci from 1913; *Born:* 27 Feb 1855 in Petersburg; *Educ:* 1877 grad Med Fac, Moscow Univ; *Career:* after grad mil surgeon and asst, Prof K.K. Reyer's Surgical Clinic; until 1884 served on Caucasian Front; from 1885 physician with Red Cross Krestovozdvizhenskaya Community; 1889 defended doctor's thesis; 1895 appointed prof, Acad Clinic, Mil Med Acad; 1910–12 head, Mil Med Acad; wrote many works which have become classics of their kind: a study of the effects of light; studies of the effects of ultraviolet radiation on bacteria, lupus exudens, epitheliomas and connective tissue; pioneered techniques of light therapy in Russia; did research on tuberculosis surgery and popularized modern tuberculosis surgery techniques at congresses and in the med press; founded at Vindava a seaside sanatorium for the treatment of bone tuberculosis; one of first to study how arthritis is affected by removal of the thyroid gland; described thyrotoxic effects of thyroid gland on some forms of joint ailments and isolated a particular form which he called "polyarthritis progressiva chronica thyreotoxica"; studied care, training and assistance of people crippled by injuries or as a result of bone tuberculosis and rickets; to this end founded an asylum-school at the Maksimilian Clinic, as well as the first First-Aid Comt in Petersburg; made major contributions to the study of ind injuries; 1907 founded Workers' Expertise Bureau; also worked for Red Cross; organized supplies and med aid in Chinese War, Russo-Japanese War and WW 1; from Apr 1917 chief field sanitary inspector; after WW 1 concentrated on writing; founder, Petersburg Med Surgical Soc; founded first surgical journal "Khirurgicheskiy vestnik"; (1885–1894), which was later merged with the "Letopis' russkoy khirurgii" (1896–1901) and was then called the "Russkiy khirurgicheskiy arkhiv" (1902–09) and from 1910 until it ceased publication in 1917 the "Khirurgicheskiy arkhiv Vel'yaminova"; *Publ:* doctor's thesis *O vylushchenii pryamoy kishki s predvaritel'noy kolotomiyey po Magelungu* (Enucleation of the Rectum with Preliminary Magelung Colotomy) (1899); *Sifilis sustavov* (Syphilis of the Joints) (1903); *Ucheniye o boleznyakh sustavov* (The Theory of Diseases of the Joints) (1924, posthumously); *Died:* 9 Apr 1920.

VENDEROVICH, Yevgeniy Leonidovich (1881–1954) Neuropathologist; *Born:* 1881; *Educ:* 1906 grad Med Fac, Moscow Univ; *Career:* 1910 asst prof, Prof V.M. Bekhterev's Clinic of Nervous Diseases, Petersburg Womens's Med Inst; 1933 assoc prof, 1935 qualified as Doctor of Med; from 1938 prof, Chair of Nervous Diseases, 1st Leningrad Med Inst; specialized in neuromorphology; devised an original method of preparing constant series of smear slides from sections of the entire human brain; the method enabled researchers to locate the prod projection centers in the brain; also studied the pathogenesis, diagnosis and therapy of several nervous diseases; shed new light on the pathogenesis of choreic convulsions, narcolepsy and Tay-Sachs disease; drafted excellent classification of closed brain lesions; proposed original hypothesis of the nature and pathogenesis of subarachnoid hemorrhage; described so-called ulnar defect with lesion of the pyramidal fascicle; 1942–45 reactivated and directed Leningrad Neuropathologists Soc; *Publ: Ob etiopatogeneze intrakranial'nykh subarakhnoidal'nykh gemorragiy* (The Ethiopathogenesis of Intracranial Subarachnoid Hemorrhage) (1935); *Etiologiya narkolepticheskogo sindroma Zhelino* (The Etiology of Zhelino's Narcoleptic Syndrome) (1936); *O lissentsefalicheskom (pakhi-agiricheskom) idiotizme* (Lissencephalic /Pachi-Agirici) Idiocy) (1939); *O fibulyarnom sensitivnom defekte* (Fibulary Sensitive Defect) (1953); *Died:* 1954.

VENEDIKTOV, Anatoliy Vasil'yevich (1887–1959) Lawyer; Dr of Law; prof from 1922; member, USSR Acad of Sci from 1958; Hon Sci Worker of RSFSR from 1942; *Born:* 30 June 1887 in vil Zirgani, now Bashkir ASSR; *Educ:* 1910 grad Petersburg Polytech Inst; 1910 grad Petersburg Univ; *Career:* 1910–17 taught at higher educ establishments in Petersburg (Petrograd); from 1922 prof, Petrograd (Leningrad) Polytech Inst; from 1929 prof, Law Fac, Leningrad Univ; 1947–54 senior assoc, Inst of Law, USSR Acad of Sci; specialized in Sov civil law but also dealt with econ questions; *Publ: Sliyaniye aktsionernykh kompaniy* (Mergers of Shareholding Companies) (1914); *Dogovornaya distsiplina v promyshlennosti* (Contractual Discipline in Industry) (1935); *Zashchita fakticheskogo vladeniya v usloviyakh mirnogo i voyennogo vremeni* (The Defense of De Facto Possession in Conditions of Peace and War) (1947); *Gosudarstvennaya sotsialisticheskaya sobstvennost'* (Socialist State Ownership) (1948); *Voprosy sotsialisticheskoy sobstvennosti v trudakh I.V. Stalina* (Questions of Socialist Ownership in the Works of J.V. Stalin) (1949); *Awards:* Order of Lenin; Stalin Prize (1948); *Died:* 9 Aug 1959.

VENGEROV, Semyon Afanas'yevich (1855–1920) Lit historian and bibliographer; prof; *Born:* 17 Apr 1855 in Lubny; *Educ:* 1879 grad Law Fac, Petersburg Univ; 1880 grad History and Philology Fac, Yur'yev Univ; *Career:* from 1891 ed, Lit Dept, "Brockhaus and Efron Encyclopedic Dictionary"; from 1897 prof, Petersburg Univ and other higher educ establishments; 1899–1905 barred from teaching as polit unreliable; 1906 returned to Petersburg Univ; dir, Lit Bibliography Inst; from 1917 founder-dir, Russian Book Bd, Petrograd; then dir, Inst of Bibliography; represented cultural historical school in lit history and sided with Populists; from 1901 directed publication of *Biblioteka velikikh pisateley* (The Library of Great Writers); *Publ: Kritiko-biograficheskiy slovar' russkikh pisateley i uchyonykh* (A Critical Biographical Dictionary of Russian Writers and Scholars) (6 vol, 1899–1904); *Russkaya poeziya* (Russian Poetry) 2 vol, 1893–1901); *Russkiye knigi* (Russian Books) (3 vol, 1897–99); *Istochniki slovarya russkikh pisateley* (The Sources of the Dictionary of Russian Writers) (4 vol, 1900–17); *Osnovnyye cherty istorii noveyshey russkoy literatury* (The Basic Features of the History of Recent Russian Literature) (1899); *Ocherki po istorii russkoy literatury* (An Outline History of Russian Literature) (1907); *Geroicheskiy kharakter russkoy literatury* (The Heroic Nature of Russian Literature) (1911); *V chyom ocharovaniye russkoy literatury XIX veka* (The Charm of Russian 19th-Century Literature) (1912); *Sobraniye sochineniy* (Collected Works) (5 vol, 1911–19); *Died:* 14 Sept 1920.

VENUOLIS (real name: ZHUKAUSKAS), Antanas Yulianovich (1882–1957) Lith writer and playwright; Pop Writer of Lith SSR from 1957; *Born:* 7 Apr 1882, son of a peasant; *Career:* for many years worked as a pharmacist in Russia; active in 1905 Revol; from 1918 lived in Lith; after establishment of Sov regime in Lith in 1940 member, Lith Writers' Union; dep, Lith Supr Sov of 2nd–4th convocation; *Publ:* essays' "Prison Impressions" (1908); "Crimean Impressions" (1913); stories "The Drowned Woman" (1913); "The Last Place" (1912); novel "Before Day" (1925); novelettes: "Cancer" (1922); "The Chamber of Intellectuals" (1920); collected stories "To Brazil" (1926); novel "At the Crossroads" (1932); plays: "1831" (1931); "The Fortress" (1936); "At Dusk" (1940); novelette "The Stepdaughter" (1948); novel "Puodzhyunas Court" (1942), etc; *Died:* 17 Aug 1957.

VEPRINTSEV, P.A. (1883–1941) Govt official; CP member from 1920; *Born:* 1883; *Career:* 1917–20 superintended ind plants in Zlatoust Okrug; member, Zlatoust Sov of Workers, Peasants and Soldiers' Dep; 1920–22 with CC, Metalworkers' Union; 1922–32 with All-Russian Sovnarkhoz, Agric Machinery Syndicate, Pop Comrt of Trade, All-Union Power Comt, etc; *Died:* 1941.

VERBITSKIY, Vsevolod Alekseyevich (1896–1951) Actor; Pop Artiste of RSFSR from 1948; *Born:* 29 Feb 1896; *Career:* from 1916 with Moscow Acad Arts Theater; co-founder and dir, 2nd Studio, Moscow Arts Theater; *Roles:* Tal'berg and Shervinskiy in Bulgakov's *Dni Turbinykh* (The Days of the Turbins); Benkendorf in Bulgakov's *Posledniye dni* (The Last Days); Prince Dulebov in Ostrovskiy's *Talanty i poklonniki* (Talents and Admirers); Biron in Smolin's "Yelizaveta Petrovna"; Kurchayev in Ostrovskiy's *Na vsyakogo mudretsa dovol'no prostoty* (There's a Simpleton in Every Sage); the Baron in Gorky's *Na dne* (The Lower Depths); Nikolay Skrobotov in *Vragi* (The Enemy); Lord Caversham in Oscar Wilde's "An Ideal Husband"; Sir Oliver Surface in Sheridan's "A School for Scandal", etc; *Died:* 11 Aug 1951.

VERESAYEV (real name: SMIDOVICH), Vikentiy Vikent'yevich (1867–1945) Russian writer; *Born:* 16 Jan 1867 in Tula, son of a physician; *Educ:* 1875–84 studied at Tula High School; 1888 grad History and Philology Fac, Petersburg Univ; 1894 grad Med Fac, Derpt Univ; *Career:* 1894 returned to Tula and set up in med practice; shortly afterwards moved to Petersburg; 1885 first work printed; in 1890's sided with Legal Marxists and printed his work in Marxist journals "Novoye slovo", "Nachalo", "Zhizn'", etc; in 1900's member, "Sreda" (Medium) lit circle; contributed to Gorky's collections "Znaniye"; served as physician in 1904–05 Russo-Japanese War; 1911–18 co-founder, and dir, Writers Book Publ House, Moscow; also worked as lit historian and critic; 1914 again drafted as mil surgeon into Russian Army and until 1917 headed Mil Health Dept, Moscow Railroad Depot; 1917, chm, Artistic Educ Commission, Moscow Sov; 1919 member, Public Educ Collegium, Feodosiya (Crimea); from 1921 lived in Moscow; chm, All-Russian Writers' Union; member, State Larned Council; consultant, "Nedra" Press; *Publ: story Zagadka* (The Puzzle) (1887); novelette *Bez dorogi* (Without a Road) (1895); story *Povetriye* (The Craze) (1898); novelette *Na povorote* (At the Turning Point) (1902); *Zapiski vracha* (A Physician's Notes) (1901); *Rasskazy o voyne* (War Stories) (1906); *Na voyne* (At War) (1907–08); novelette *K zhizni* (Toward Life) (1909); critical and philosophical works: *Zhivaya zhizn'* (Vital Life) (1910); *Apollon i Dionis* (Apollo and Dionysius) (1915); novel *V tupike* (Deadlocked) (1922); novel *Syostry* (The Sisters) (1933); memoirs *V yunyye gody* (In the Days of My Youth) (1927); *V studencheskiye gody* (In My Student Years) (1929); books: *Pushkin v zhizni* (Pushkin in Life) (1926–27); *Gogol' v zhizni* (Gogol in Life) (1933); *Sputniki Pushkina* (Pushkin's Companions) (1934–36); *Nevydumannyye rasskazy o proshlom* (True Tales of the Past)

(1940); translated such ancient works as: Homer's "Hymns"; "Sappho"; "Archiloches", etc; late 1930's began work on his translation of the "Iliad" (published posthumously 1949) and the "Odyssey" (published posthumously 1953); *Sochineniya* (Works) (5 vol, 1898–1910); *Polnoye sobraniye sochineniy* (Complete Collected Works) 16 vol, 1928–29); *Sochineniya* (Works) (4 vol, 1946–48); *Sobraniye sochineniy* (Collected Works) (5 vol, 1961); *Awards:* Stalin Prize (1943); *Died:* 3 June 1945 in Moscow.

VERETENNIKOV, N.I. (1871–1955) Teacher and govt official; first cousin to Lenin; *Born:* 1871; *Educ:* 1896 grad Kazan' Univ; *Career:* from 1896 physics and mathematics teacher; after 1917 Oct Revol dept head, Pop Comrt of Finance; 1924–28 worked for Statistical Dept, CC, CPSU(B); subsequently returned to teaching; *Died:* 1955.

VEREYSKIY, Georgiy Semyonovich (1886–1962) Graphic artist; member, USSR Acad of Arts from 1949; Pop Artiste of RSFSR from 1962; *Born:* 30 July 1886 in Proskurov; *Educ:* studied privately under Ye. Shreder in Khar'kov; *Career:* 1905, after taking part in revol movement, emigrated to Italy and Germany; 1907 returned to Russia; 1913–16 worked at Ostroumova-Lebedeva, Lansere and Kustodiyev's studio in Petersburg; 1918–30 head, Drawings and Engravings Dept, State Hermitage; lectured on the history of engravings at Acad of Arts, Leningrad; *Works:* "Portraits of Russian Artists" (1922 and 1927); landscape "The Garden of the Russian Museum" (1925); "Portraits of Russian Writers" (1928); landscape "Wharf at Romny" (1930); "Portrait of My Mother" (1930); etchings: "Portrait of M.M. Gerasimova" (1936); "Marienburg near Gatchina"; lithographic portraits of Lenin, Stalin and other Party leaders; some 250 portraits of Sov pilots; many portraits of scientists, cultural figures, artists and Heroes of the Sov Union; *Awards:* Order of the Red Banner of Labor; Stalin Prize (1946); medals; *Died:* 19 Dec 1962.

VERIKOVSKIY, Mikhail Ivanovich (1896–1962) Composer and conductor; prof; Hon Art Worker of Ukr SSR from 1944; *Born:* 21 Nov 1896 in Kremenets, Ternopol' Province; *Educ:* 1923 grad B. Yavorskiy's composition class, Kiev Conservatory; *Career:* from 1919 conducted workers' choirs; from 1921 member, Leonrovich Assoc; 1928–35 member, All-Ukr Assoc of Revol Musicians; 1926–28 conductor, Kiev then Khar'kov Opera Theater; 1934–35 head, Opera Studio, Khar'kov Musical Drama Inst and Khar'kov Opera Theater; conducted symphony concerts in Kiev, Khar'kov, Moscow, Slavyansk, Ufa, etc; taught special conducting at Kiev Musical Drama Inst and Kiev Conservatory; from 1946 prof, conducting class, Kiev Conservatory; *Works:* operas "Heavenly Deeds" (1932); "The Centurion" (1938); "The Woman Farmhand" (1939–40); "Viy" (1946); "The Refugees" (1948); ballet "Pan Kanevskiy" (1930); oratorio "The Ballad of the Prisoner Girl" (1923); revised, orchestral version (1955); cantatas: "October Cantata" (1936); "On the 25th Anniversary of the Ukr Acad of Sci" (1944); "Finale of a Collective Cantata for the 16th CP(B) Ukr Congress)" (1949); choral-symphony work "The Wrath of the Slavs" (1941); quartet (1923); piano works: "Dance" and "Militant March" (1920); three preludes (1928), etc; for violin and piano: "Ukrainian Suite" (1947); "Ukrainian Melody" (1924); some 40 choral works, including: fantasia "The Haydemaki" (1919); "Requiem in Memory of Lysenko" (1922); cantatas: "Joy"(1924); "Mykola Lysenko" (1942); over 60 romances and songs; music for shows and films, etc; *Died:* 14 June 1962 in Kiev.

VERKHOVINETS (KOSTIV), Vasiliy Nikolayevich (1880–1938) Composer; choral conductor; music teacher; folklorist; *Born:* 5 Jan 1880 in vil Myzuni, now Stanislav Oblast; *Educ:* 1899 grad L'vov Teachers' Seminary; studied music under Lyubomirskiy and Lysenko; *Career:* 1906–19 musician, Choirmaster and conductor, Sadovskiy Theater; 1919–32 singing instructor on Lysenko conducting courses, Poltava Teachers' Training Inst; also taught singing at Kiev Musical Drama Inst; 1927–28 dir, Khar'kov Okrug "Chumak" Capella; 1929–30 organized "Zhinkhorans" Women's Choir; wrote many songs, romances, choral works and arrangements of Ukr folk songs; *Publ:* Teoriya ukrainskogo narodnogo tantsa (Ukrainian Folk Dance Theory) (1919–20); *Ukrainskaya svad'ba* (Ukrainian Wedding) (1912); *Died:* 11 Apr 1938.

VERKHOVSKIY, Aleksandr Ivanovich (1886–1941) Mil commander; corps commander; prof from 1927; *Born:* 27 Feb 1886 of noble parentage; *Educ:* 1911 grad Gen Staff Acad; *Career:* fought in Russo-Japanese War and WW 1; 16 July–15 Sept 1917 commanded Moscow Mil Distr; 16 Sept 1917 promoted maj-gen and appointed Min of War, Provisional Govt; advocated partial demobilization of army and Russian withdrawal from WW 1; these proposals were rejected by the Pre-Parliament and 3 Nov 1917 he was dismissed from his post; 17 Nov 1917 went to Headquarters and tried to establish a "Democratic Anti-Bolshevik Govt"; 1918 arrested by All–Union Cheka, but was soon released; 1919 joined Red Army and served with rear units and on Eastern Front; 1921–30 lectured at Red Army Mil Acad; 1922 mil expert with Sov deleg at Genoa Conference; 1930–32 chief of staff, North Caucasian Mil Distr; then lectured on "Vystrel" Courses and at Gen Staff Acad and served on Gen Staff; 1937 arrested by State Security organs; *Publ: Rossiya na Golgofe* (Russia at Golgotha) (1918); *Ocherk po istorii voyennogo iskusstva v Rossii XVIII i vekov* (An Outline History of Military Art in Russia in the 18th and 19th Centuries) (1921); *Obshchaya taktika* (General Tactics) (35d ed, 1927), etc; *Died:* 1941 in imprisonment.

VERKHOVSKIY, Vadim Nikandrovich (1873–1947) Chemist and teacher; Dr of Pedag; prof from 1918; member, RSFSR Acad of Pedag Sci from 1944; Hon Sci Worker of RSFSR from 1940; *Born:* 30 Oct 1873; *Educ:* grad Fac of Physics and Mathematics, Petersburg Univ; *Career:* from 1899 assoc, Sci and Tech Laboratory, Naval Dept; 1905–18 lecturer, Petersburg Women's Teachers' Training Inst; 1918–47 prof, Chair of Inorganic Chemistry, Herzen Teachers' Training Inst, Petrograd (Leningrad); did research on the interaction of metals with acids and hydrogen salts under pressure; also studied the mechanisms of hydrolytic reactions and the formation conditions of basic salts; *Publ:* coauthor, *Pervyye raboty po khimii* (First Projects in Chemistry) (1907); coauthor, *Elementarnyy kurs khimii* (An Elementary Chemistry Course) (1911); *Tekhnika i metodika eksperimenta v shkole* (The Techniques and Methods of Chemical Experiments in School) (1933); coauthor, *Metodika prepodavaniya khimii v sredney shkole* (Methods of Teaching Chemistry in Secondary Schools) (1936); *Neorganicheskaya khimiya (Inorganic Chemistry) (1948); coauthor, Organicheskaya khimiya* (Organic Chemistry) (1948), etc; *Died:* 6 Jan 1947.

VERKHOSKIY, Yuriy Nikandrovich (1878–1956) Russian poet, translator and lit historian; *Born:* 4 June 1878 in vil Grishnevo, now Smolensk Oblast; *Educ:* 1902 grad history and Philology Fac, Petersburg Univ; *Career:* 1899 first work printed; as a poet, sided with "classical wing" of Symbolist movement; translated Renaissance poets, Mickiewicz, Geo lyric poets, etc; wrote studies on the poetry of the Pushkin period; from 1917 lectured on Russian and Western lit in Petersburg, Tiflis, Perm', Tomsk, Moscow and Smolensk; during WW 2 published collection of patriotic verse "Budet tak" (So Be It) (1943); *Publ: Raznyye stikhotvoreniya* (Various Poems) (1908); *Idillii i elegii* (Idylls and Elegies) (1910); *Ye.A. Boratynskiy. Materialy k yego biografii* (Ye.A. Boratynskiy. Biographical Material) (1916); *Stikhotvoreniya* (Verse) (1917); *Poety pushkinskoy pory* (The Poets of Pushkin's Time) (1919); *Baron Del'vig. Materialy biograficheskiye i literaturnyye* (Baron Del'vig. Biographical and Literary Material) (1922); *Solntse v zatochenii. Stikhotvoreniya* (The Incarcerated Sun. Verse) (1922); *Poety dekabristy* (The Decembrist Poets) (1926); *Died:* 23 Sept 1956 in Moscow.

VERMEL', Samuil Borisovich (1868–1926) Physiotherapist and roentgenologist; Dr of Med from 1898; *Born:* 1868; *Educ:* 1893 grad Med Fac, Moscow Univ; *Career:* from 1918 assoc prof of physiotherapy, 1st Moscow Univ; from 1921 head, Chair of Gen and Physical Therapy, 1st Moscow Univ; from 1920 founder-dir, State Inst of Physiotherapy and Orthopedics; pioneered many trends of Sov physiotherapy and did research on the operating mechanisms of such physical factors as x-rays, light rays, mineral baths and galvanic current; hypothesized that the whole spectrum of radiant energy causes biological changes; tried to develop a classification of physical agents; helped to organize Sov physiotherapy service; from 1923 chm, Moscow Physiotherapy Soc; from 1925 dep chm, All-Russian Assoc of Physiotherapists; *Publ:* doctor's thesis, *Zheltukha novorozhdyonnykh (Jaundice in New-Born Babies) (1898); Rukovodstvo k lecheniyu svetom dlya vrachey i studentov* (A Doctors' and Students' Guide to Light Treatment) (1910); "Über den Mechanismus der Wirkung der kohlensauren Mineralbäder" (1926); ed, *Meditsinskoye svetoucheniye (biologicheskoye i lechebnoye deytsviye sveta)* (The Medical Theory of Light [The Biological and Therapeutic Effects of Light]) (1928); *Died:* 1926.

VERMYSHEV, Aleksandr Aleksandrovich (1879–1919) Russian writer; CP member from 1903; *Born:* 29 Aug 1879 in vil Zugdidi, Kutaisi Province, son of a Forestry Dept official; *Educ:* 1902 entered Law Fac, Petersburg Univ; 1910 grad Yur'yev, then

Petersburg Univ; *Career:* while a student, several times arrested for revol activities; served a prison term; 1905 first work printed; wrote essays and verse; 1917 took part in storming of Winter Palace; after 1917 Oct Revol worked for Petrograd Oblast Comrt of Labor; then worked for Centr Criminal Investigation Commission; head, Trans Dept, Petrograd Comrt of Food; fought in Civil War; 1919 polit comr on Southern Front; *Publ:* plays: *Za pravdoy* (For the Truth) (1908); *Gontsy* (The Racers) and *Bankroty* (The Bankrupts) (1910); *Krasnaya pravda* (Red Truth) (1919), etc; *Died:* 31 Aug 1919 killed in action at Yelets.

VERNADSKIY, Vladimir Ivanovich (1863–1945) Mineralogist and geochemist; prof; Dr of Geology and Geognosy from 1897; member, USSR Acad of Sci from 1912; member, Czechoslovakian Acad of Sci from 1926; member, Parisian Acad of Sci from 1928; *Born:* 28 Feb 1863 in Petersburg, son of the economist Prof I. Vernadskiy; *Educ:* 1885 grad Petersburg Univ; *Career:* from 1886 custodian, Mineralogical Museum, Petersburg Univ; 1888–90 sci studies abroad; 1885–90 took part in soil and geological expeditions and field trips; from 1890 assoc prof of mineralogy, Moscow Univ; from 1891 Master of Geology and Geognosy; from 1898 prof of mineralogy and crystallography, Moscow Univ; 1906 prof extraordinarius, Petersburg Acad of Sci; from 1909 acad extraordinarius, Petersburg Acad of Sci; from 1914 dir, Geological and Mineralogical Museum, Acad of Sci; 1915 co-founder and chm, Commission to Study the Natural Production Resources of Russia; 1917 lived in Ukr and helped plan Ukr Acad of Sci; 1919 pres, Ukr Acad of Sci; 1920–21 prof, Tavrida Univ, Simferopol'; 1921 founded Meteorite Dept, Mineralogical Museum, Petrograd Acad of Sci; 1922 founder-dir, Radium Inst, Petrograd; 1923–26 worked in France, Czechoslovakia and Poland; 1926 founder-chm, Commission for the History of Knowledge, USSR Acad of Sci; 1926–30 chm, Commission to Study Natural Production Resources, USSR Acad of Sci; 1927–29 research in France, Holland, Czechoslovakia, Norway and Germany; from 1929 founder-dir, Biogeochemical Laboratory, USSR Acad of Sci; 1930 founded Commission for Permafrost Studies; 1937 founder and vice-pres, Int Commission to Determine the Absolute Age of Geological Rocks by Radioactive Methods; co-founder and from 1940 chm, Isotopes Commission; advanced hypothesis of connection between crystallic form and physicochemical structure of matter; proposed evolutionary theory of minerals; established that isomorphic series are not constant but shift and change under the influence of temperature and pressure; developed his theory of the structure of alumosilicates; founded new sci geochemistry; from 1910 conducted first surveys to prospect for radium and uranium in Russia; 1922 wrote that "the time is not far away when man will have atomic energy in his hands"; *Publ: O gruppe sillimanita i roli glinozema v silikatakh* (The Sillimanite Group and the Role of Alumina in Silicates) (1891); *Opyt opisatel'noy mineralogii* (Pracital Descriptive Mineralogy) (1908); *Ocherki i rechi* (Studies and Speeches) (1922); "La Géochimie" (1924); *Biosfera* (The Biosphere) (1926); *Ocherki po geokhimii* (Studies in Geochemistry) (1934); *Problemy biokhimii* (Problems of Biochemistry) (1935); *Radioaktivnost' i novyye problemy geologii* (Radioactivity and New Problems of Geology (1935); *Istoriya mineralov zemnoy kory* (The History of the Minerals in the Earth's Crust) (1936); coauthor, *Zemnyye silikaty, alyumosilikaty i ikh analogi* (Telluric Silicates, Alumosilicates and Their Analogues) (1937); *Biogeokhimicheskiye ocherki* (Biogeochemical Studies) (1940); *Izbrannyye sochineniya* (Selected Works) (1955), etc; *Awards:* Stalin Prize (1943); *Died:* 6 Jan 1945 in Moscow; buried in Novodevich'ye Cemetery.

VERSHIGORA, Pyotr Petrovich (1905–1963) Russian writer; maj-gen; CP-member from 1943; *Born:* 16 May 1905 in vil Severinovtsy, now Mold SSR, son of a teacher; *Educ:* 1930 grad Odessa Conservatory; 1938 grad Moscow Cinematographic Acad; *Career:* from 1925 head, volost reading-room; from 1926 in Red Army; from 1930 actor and stage dir in Izhevsk, Gorky, Donets Basin, Rostov, Kiev, Odessa; 1938–44 at Kiev Film Studio; during WW2 dep platoon commander, battalion commander, then commander, partisan formation in 1st Ukr Kovpak Partisan Div; *Publ: Lyudi s chistoy sovest'yu* (People with a Clean Conscience) (1946); *Karpatskiy reyd* (Carpathian Raid) (1950); *Reyd na San i Vislu* (The San and the Vistula Raids) (1959); stories *Dorogoy bessmertiya* (The Immortal Road); novelette *Pereprava* (The Crossing); novel *Dom rodnoy* (Native Home) (1962); historical study *Voyennoye tvorchestvo narodnykh mass* (Military Art of the Public Masses) (1961); etc; *Awards:* Hero of the Soviet Union (1944); Stalin Prize (1946); two Orders of Lenin; Order of the Red Banner; Order of Bogdan Khmel'nitskiy, 1st Class; eight medals; *Died:* 27 Mar 1963.

VERSHININ, Nikolay Vasil'yevich (1867–1951) Pharmacologist; member, USSR Acad of Sci; Hon Sci Worker of RSFSR; *Born:* 1867; *Educ:* 1894 grad Med Fac, Tomsk Univ; *Career:* from 1904 Doctor of Med; during Russo-Japanese War served as chief chemist and bacteriologist of Harbin hospitals; 1908–51 head, Chair of Pharmacology, Tomsk Univ (from 1930 Tomsk Med Inst); specialized in pharmacology of cardiovascular drugs, gen pharmacology, toxicology and balneology; studied and introduced into med practice Siberian levorotatory camphor, which from 1936 freed the USSR of the necessity of importing camphor; organized comprehensive study of new Siberian medicinal plants, recruiting for this purpose botanists, pharmacologists, chemists and clinicians at Tomsk higher educ establishments, the All-Union Inst of Experimental Med and the West Siberian Branch of the USSR Acad of Sci; co-founder, Chair of Pharmacology, Omsk Med Inst and Omsk Veterinary Inst; published 78 research works: *Publ: Materialy k ucheniyu o yadovitosti normal'noy mochi cheloveka* (Material on the Study of the Toxicity of Normal Human Urine) (1904); *Nauchno-issledovatel'skaya rabota kafedry farmakologii Tomskogo medinstituta za 30 let* (Thirty Years of Research Work at the Tomsk Medical Institute's Chair of Pharmacology) (1952); *Died:* 1951.

VERSHININ, Semyon Petrovich (1900–1967) Eng; CP member from 1917; *Born:* 8 Sept 1900; *Educ:* 1923–27 studied at Moscow Higher Tech College; *Career:* 1917–18 post officer comr in Kokand; 1918–20 commanded a special detachment of Turkestan troops; communications chief of a cavalry army; head, Staff Operations Section, Turkestani Front; 1922–23 secr, Turkestani Republ Council of Pop Comr; 1927–34 worked as Gosplan eng on construction projects in Ashkhabad and Tashkent; 1934–38 worked as eng for USSR Main Hydropower Plant Construction Bd; arrested by State Security organs; 1939–48 worked on building projects as a prisoner in Komi ASSR; 1949–56 construction site supervisor in Karaganda; 1956 chief power plants construction specialist, Inst for the Planning and Org of Power Plant Construction; from 1957 pensioner; *Died:* 26 Mar 1967.

VERTINSKIY, Aleksandr Nikolayevich (1889–1957) Variety artist, poet and composer; *Born:* 21 Mar 1889 in Kiev; *Educ:* completed high school; *Career:* after completing high school active at Alator Theater, Moscow; 1915 made variety debut, performing his own songs in Pierrot make-up and costume; 1914–18 film work; 1919 emigrated; 1920–43 gave variety concerts in Poland, Rumania, Germany, France, Italy, England, China and USA; also did film work; from 1943 lived and worked in USSR; invented his own special genre – the musical novella; *Works:* songs: "Alien Towns"; "Another's Song"; "Farewell Supper"; "Face to Face with One's Country"; "Arabian Song"; composed songs to words by Blok, Yesenin, Inber, ect; song cycle to texts by Sov poets – Antokol'skiy's *Yunost mira* (The Youth of the World), Shubin's *Kust rakitovyy* (The Broom Bush), etc, (1943); *Roles:* in films: *Korol' bez ventsa* (King without a Crown); *Ot rabstva k vole* (From Slavery to Freedom); *Zagovor obrechyonnykh* (Conspiracy of the Doomed) (1950); *Velikiy voin Albanii Skandeberg* (Albania's Great Warrior Skandeberg); *Anna na sheye* (Anna on the Neck), etc; *Awards:* Stalin Prize (1951); *Died:* 21 May 1957 in Leningrad.

VERTOV, Dziga (real name: KAUFMAN, Denis Arkad'yevich) (1896–1954) Film dir, scriptwriter and theorist; *Born:* 2 Jan 1896 in Belostok, now Poland; *Educ:* studied at Psychoneurological Inst and Moscow Univ; *Career:* after 1917 Oct Revol worked for Film Chronicle Dept, Moscow Film Comt; directed work of frontline film teams and toured with All-Russian Centr Exec Comt agitation trains; then ed and cutter, journal "Kinonedelya"; *Works:* films: *Godovshchina revolyutsii* (The Anniversary of the Revolution) (1919); *Agitpoyezd VTsIK* (The All-Russian Central Executive Committee Agitation Train) (1921); *Istoriya grazhdanskoy voyny* (The History of the Cicil War) (1922); ed, film journals *Kino-pravda* (Cinema Truth) (1922–24); *Kino-glaz* (The Cinema Eye) (1924); *Odinnadtsatyy* (The Eleventh) (1928); *Chelovek s kinoapparatom* (The Man with a Cinecamera) (1929); *Leninskaya kinopravda* (Lenin Cinema Truth) (1924); *V serdtse krest'yanina Lenin zhiv* (Lenin Lives in the Peasant's Heart) (1925); *Shagay, Sovet!* (Stride, Soviet!) (1926); *Shestaya chast' mira* (The Sixth Continent) (1926); *Simfoniya Donbassa* (Donbass Symphony) (1930); *Tri pesni o Lenine* (Three Songs of Lenin) (1934); other films: *Protsess Mironova* (The Mironov Trial) (1919); *Protsess eserov* (The Socialist-Revolutionaries Trial) (1922); *Vchera, segodnya, zavtra!* (Yesterday, Today and Tomorrow!) (1923); *Vesennyaya pravda* (Spring Truth) (1923); coauthor, *Sergo Ordzhonikidze* (1937); *Kolybel'naya* (Cradle Song) (1937); *Slava sovetskim geroinyam* (Glory to the Soviet Heroines) (1938); *Tri geroini* (Three Heroines) (1938); *Krov' za krov', smert' za smert'* (Blood for Blood, Death for Death) (1941); *V gorakh Ala-Tau* (In the Ala-Tau Mountains) (1944); *Klyatva molodykh* (The Vow of the Young) (1944); *Publ: Ikh nastoyashcheye* (Their Present) (1927); aritcles: "We. A Manifesto Version" (1922); "He and I" (1922); "The Cinema Eye" (1924); "Paths of the Documentary Film" (1930); "Cinema Truth" (1934); "More about Mayakovskiy" (1957), etc; *Died:* 12 Feb 1954.

VERYOVKA, Grigoriy Gur'yevich (1895–1964) Composer and conductor; prof, Kiev Conservatory from 1947; dir, Ukr State Folk Choir from 1943; Bd member, Ukr Composers' Union; Hon Art Worker of Ukr SSR from 1946; Pop Artiste of Ukr SSR from 1961; CP member from 1946; *Born:* 1895 in vil Beryozdino, now Chernigov Oblast; *Educ:* 1933 grad Kiev Musical Drama Inst; 1910–16 studied at Chernigov Theological Seminary; *Career:* 1919–23 taught music theory and directed choir of Pop Conservatory; 1949–44 founded and directed civilian and army amateur music groups; 1923–27 taught choral conducting and elementary music theory at Kiev Musical Drama Inst; 1925–31 instructor and dir, Musical Trade School; 1931–44 taught theoretical disciplines at Musical Drama Technicum; 1934–41 and 1943–47 lecturer, from 1947 prof, Chair of Conducting, Kiev Conservatory; 1941–45 senior assoc, Inst of Folklore, Ukr Acad of Sci; also lecturer, Bash Dept, Moscow Conservatory; 1948–52 chm, bd, Ukr Composers' Union; 1948–57 bd member, USSR Composers' Union; *Works:* "Suite of Five Folk Songs" (1927); "Pieces" (1928–31); "Sonata" (1933); "Pieces" (1934); Ukr clapping folk dance (1935); songs to lyrics by Tychina, Shevchenko and Franko; arrangements of folk and revol songs, etc; song for voice and piano "Oh, Don't Drink the Beer and Mead" (1963); *Awards:* Order of Lenin; (1951); Order of the Red Banner of Labor (1948); Badge of Hon (1953); medals; Stalin Prize (1948); *Died:* 21 Oct 1964 in Kiev.

VESELOVSKIY, Boris Borisovich (1880–1954) Historian; specialist in zemstvo movement, agrarian relations and municipal econ; prof from 1927; *Born:* 22 June 1880; *Educ:* studied at Moscow Higher Tech College; *Career:* while a student, joined Soc-Democratic movement; 1902 arrested and exiled to Olonets Province; 1905 returned from exile and engaged in research, teaching and journalism; worked for newspaper "Nachalo" then journals "Obrazovaniye" and "Sovremennyy mir"; 1907–12 worked for Soc-Democratic faction, 3rd State Duma; 1914–15 chm, Econ Dept, 1915–17 learned secr, Free Econ Soc; from 1915 ed, this society's periodical "Trudy"; 1915–18 also ed, journal "Zemskoye delo"; after 1917 Feb Revol joined Plekhanov's "Yedinstvo" (Unity) group and was head, Dept of Agric, Provisional Government's Min of Internal Affairs; from 1921 worked for Centr Records Office and USSR Gosplan; lecturer, from 1927 prof, Moscow Univ; also taught at Moscow's Ordzhonikidze Econ Eng Inst; from 1925 head, Moscow Agric Soc; pioneered new branch of econ – municial econ; *Publ: K voprosu o klassovykh interesakh v zemstve* (Class Interests in the Zemstvo) (1905); *Krest'yanskiy vopros i krest'yanskoye dvizheniye v Rossii (1902–06)* (The Peasant Question and the Peasant Movement in Russia in 1902–06) (1907); *Istoriya zemstva za sorok let* (Forty Years in the History of the Zemstvo) (4 vol, 1909–11); *Istoricheskiy ocherk deyatel'nosti zemskikh uchrezhdeniy Tverskoy gubernii (1864–1913)* (A Historical Outline of the Work of Zemstvo Establishments in Tver' Province in 1864–1913) (1914); *Istoricheskiy obzor deyatel'nosti zemskikh uchrezhdeniy v Sankt-Petersburgskoy gubernii (1865–1915)* (A Historical Review of the Work of Zemstvo Establishments in the Saint-Petersburg Province from 1865 to 1915) (1917); *Kurs ekonomiki i organizatsii gorodskogo khozyaystva* (A Course in the Economics and Organization of Municipal Management) (1951); *Died:* 28 May 1954.

VESELOVSKIY, Stepan Borisovich (1876–1952) Historian; Dr of History; prof from 1917; member, USSR Acad of Sci from 1946; *Born:* 16 Sept 1876 in Moscow, son of an agronomist; *Educ:* 1902 grad Law Fac, Moscow Univ; *Career:* from 1907 member, Soc of History and Russian Antiquities, Moscow Univ; 1917–25 prof, Moscow Univ; 1929–46 corresp member, USSR Acad of Sci; from 1936 senior assoc, Inst of History, USSR Acad of Sci; 1938–41 prof, Historical Archives Inst; also taught at Inst of History, Russian Assoc of Soc Sci Research Institutes and at Communist Univ of Workers of the East; specialized in the soc, econ and polit history of 14th–17th century Russia; compiled numerous anthologies of archive records on these subjects; in late 1940's was criticized by Party for alleged methodical errors and for underestimating the national factor in the formation of the Russian state; *Publ: Novyye akty o smutnom vremeni* (New Records of the Time of the Troubles) (1912); *Akty pistsovogo dela Moskovskogo gosudarstva dlya istorii zemleustroystva i pryamogo oblozheniya v Moskovskom gosudarstve* (The Muscovite Cadaster Records for the History of the Organziation of Land Exploitation and Direct Taxation in Muscovy) (2 vol, 1913–17); *Arzamasskiye pomestnyye akty 1578–1618 godov* (The Records of the Arzamas Estate, 1578–1618) (1915); *Soshnoye pis'mo. Issledovaniye po istorii kadastra i pososhnogo oblozheniya Moskovskogo gosudarstva* (The Plowshare Letter. A Study of the History of the Cadaster and Plowshare Tax in Muscovy) (2 vol, 1915–16); *K voprosu o proiskhozhdenii votchinnogo rezhima* (The Emergence of the Patrimonial System) (1926); *Pamyatniki sotsial'no-ekonomicheskoy istorii Moskovskogo gosudarstva XIV–XVII vekov* (Relics of the Social and Economic History of Muscovy in the 14th–15th Centuries) (1929); *Selo i derevnya v Severo-Vostochnoy Rusi XIV–XVII vekov* (Village and Countryside in Northeastern Rus in the 14th–17th Centuries) (1936); *Feodal'noye zemlevladeniye Severo-Vostochnoy Rusi* (Feudal Land Ownership in Northeastern Rus) (1947); *Akty sotsial'no-ekonomicheskoy istorii Severo-Vostochnoy Rusi XIV–XVII vekov* (Records of the Social and Economic History of Northeastern Rus in the 14th–17th Centuries) (2 vol, 1952–59); *Awards:* Order of the Red Banner of Labor (1945); Order of Lenin (1950); *Died:* 23 Jan 1952.

VESNIN, Aleksandr Aleksandrovich (1883–1959) Architect and set designer; prof; Hon Member, USSR Acad of Construction and Architecture from 1956; *Born:* 15 May 1883 in Yur'yevets, now Ivanovo Oblast; *Educ:* 1912 grad Petersburg Inst of Civil Eng; *Career:* 1919–25 set designer; 1926–35 prof of architectural design, Moscow Architectural Inst and Higher Tech Art Workshops; from 1935 directed an architectural design workshop; as an architect worked mainly with his brothers Viktor and Leonid; *Works:* designed sets and costumes for: Gogol's *Revizor* (The Government Inspector) (1919); "The Marriage of Figaro" (1920); Topelius' "The Pearl of Aldamina" (1921); Racine's "Phedre" (1922); Skrib's "Paths to Glory" (1922); Chesterton's "The Man Who Was Thursday" (1923); Claudel's "The Annunciation" (1920); together with his brothers designed: Palace of Labor, Moscow (1923); Moscow Palace of Soviets (1932); Khar'kov Mass Shows Theater (1931); second building of Council of Pop Comr, Moscow (1940), etc; *Awards:* Hon Diploma at Paris Exhibition of Decorative Arts (1925); *Died:* 7 Nov 1959.

VESNIN, Leonid Aleksandrovich (1880–1933) Architect; prof; *Born:* 10 Dec 1880 in Yur'yevets, now Ivanovo Oblast; *Educ:* 1909 grad Inst of Civil Eng; *Career:* worked mainly with his brothers Viktor and Aleksandr; after 1917 Oct Revol prof of architectural design, Moscow Higher Tech College and Higher Tech Art Workshops; *Works:* designs for Shatura Electr Power Plant (1919–20); various designs for workers' apartment blocks and settlements; helped draft urban development plan for Tuapse (1927); urban development plan for Kuznetsk (1930), etc; together with his brothers designed: Palace of Soviets, Moscow (1932); Palace of Culture for Stalin Automobile Plant, Moscow (1930–34); Moscow Metro station (1939), etc; *Awards:* Order of the Red Banner of Labor; top award at Paris Exhibition of Decorative Arts (1925); *Died:* 8 Oct 1933.

VESNIN, Viktor Aleksandrovich (1882–1950) Architect; prof; member, USSR Acad of Sci from 1943; member, USSR Acad of Architecture; *Born:* 9 Apr 1882 in Yur'yevets, now Ivanovo Oblast; *Educ:* 1912 grad Petersburg Inst of Civil Eng; *Career:* worked mainly in collaboration with his brothers Leonid and Aleksandr; 1932–34 directed "Centr Volga Construction" design org; from 1937 Presidium member and exec secr, USSR Architects' Union; 1938–49 pres, USSR Acad of Architecture; 1934–50 dir, Architectural Design Workshop, Pop Comrt of Heavy Ind; dept head, Moscow Higher Tech College; dep, USSR Supr Sov of 1937 and 1946 convocations; *Works:* Stables of Moscow Hippodrome (1912); co-designer, Sirotkin House in Nizhniy Novgorod (1913); chemical plants at Kineshma, Tambov Province, and Zhilyova, near Moscow; buildings of Kineshma Manufacturing Plant (1914–16); Chernorech'ye Superfosfate

Plant (1918–19); Colophony and Turpentine Plant at Vakhtang, (1923); co-designer, Palaca of Labor, Moscow (1923); co-designers, Dnieper Hydroelectr Plant (1927–30); Zaporozh'ye City Distr (1928–30); co-designer, Palace of Culture, Moscow Automobile Plant (1930–34); co-designer, 2nd building of Council of Pop Comr, Moscow (1940), etc; *Publ:* articles: "A Creative Account" (1935) and "The Training of Young Architects" (1938); *Awards:* Order of Lenin; two Order of the Red Banner of Labor; Badge of Hon; *Died:* 17 Sept 1950.

VESOLOVSKIY, Bronislav Euzebiush (VESELOVSKIY, B. A.) (1870–1919) Party and govt official; leading functionary, Soc Democratic Party of Poland and Lith; CP member from 1893; *Born:* 1870; *Career:* member, Main Bd, Soc-Democratic Party of Poland and Lith; during 1905–07 Revol secr, Warsaw Comt, above party; represented party at 5th (London) RSDRP Congress; repeatedly arrested and exiled; served terms of solitary confinement and hard labor; deleg. 6th Party Congress; 1906 worked for journals "Vestnik zhizni", "Volna" and "Nasha mysl'"; 1912–14 with newspapers "Zvezda", "Nevskaya zvezda" and "Pravda"; 1917 worked for "Izvestiya Petrogradskogo Soveta rabochikh i soldatskikh deputatov" and contributed to "Pravda"; 1917 member, Petrograd Sov of Workers and Soldiers' Dep and member, Sov Centr Exec Comt; worked for Secretariat, CC, RSDRP(B); after 1917 Oct Revol secr, All-Russian Centr Exec Comt; chm, Supr Tribunal; active in Polish and Lith Soc-Democratic Group and Polish Bureau, CC, RCP(B); 1919 headed Russian Red Cross deleg to Warsaw; *Died:* 1919, together with other deleg members, killed in Warsaw by Polish police under unexplained circumstances.

VESTER, Rudol'f Yegorovich (1909–1963) Govt official; Est Min of Trade from 1950; Cand member, CC, CP Est from 1960; *Born:* 1909; *Career:* 1927–37 in forestry ind; from 1937 exec posts with USSR State Bank; dep, Est Supr Sov of 1963 convocation; *Awards:* Order of the Red Banner of Labor; Hon Scroll of USSR Supr Sov Presidium (1959); *Died:* 5 Aug 1963.

VESYOLYY, Artem (real name: KOCHKUROV, Nikolay Ivanovich) (1899–1939) Russian writer; CP member from 1917; *Born* 29 Sept 1899 in Samara, son of a stevedore; *Educ:* 1922 began to study at Bryusov Higher Lit and Art Inst, then at Moscow Univ; *Career:* from age 14 worked as hired hand; took part in 1917 Oct Revol; 1918 wounded; 1919 volunteer in fighting against Denikin's troops; 1922 with Black Sea Fleet; then worked for Cheka; from 1917 worked for Bolshevik newspapers; until 1926 member, "Pereval" (The Pass) lit group; then joined Russian Assoc of Proletarian Writers; 1937 arrested by State Security organs; *Publ:* play *Razryv-trava* (Picklock Grass) (1919); play *My* (We) (1921); novelettes: *Reki ognennyye* (Rivers of Fire) (1924); *Strana rodnaya* (Native Land) (1926); stories *Maslenitsa* (Shrovetide) (1921); *Dikoye serdtse* (The Savage Heart) (1925); etc; novel *Rossiya, krov'yu umytaya* (Russia Washed in Blood) (1932); historical novel *Gulyay Volga!* (Up the Volga!) (1932); *Died:* 2 Dec 1939 in imprisonment; posthumously rehabilitated.

VETCHINKIN, Vladimir Petrovich (1888–1950) Eng; specialist in aerodynamics; prof from 1928; Hon Sci and Tech Worker of RSFSR from 1946; *Born:* 29 June 1888: *Educ:* 1915 grad Moscow Higher Tech College; *Career:* while still a student began working on propeller theory with N. Ye. Zhukovskiy; 1913 refined propeller theory by including the factor of the change in the circulation of longitudinal blade speed; after grad taught at Moscow Higher Tech College, Mil Aviation Eng Acad and Moscow Aviation Inst; 1916 founded an experimental calculation bureau at Moscow Higher Tech College, where he calculated aircraft reliability factors and designed airscrews; from 1918 assoc, Centr Aerodynamics Inst; from 1928 prof, Moscow Aviation Inst; did research on the curvilinear and continuous motion of aircraft on and near the ground and in regular flight; conducted experiments to determine the stresses on aircraft performing aerobatics; did major research on aircraft reliability; also worked on navigational astronomy, ballistics, jet flight and computation techniques; made a study of wind power, wind motors and fans; helped edit N. E. Zhukovskiy's works; member, Acad of Artillery Sci; *Publ: Dinamika polyotov* (Flight Dynamics) (1927); *Metody priblizhyonnogo i chislennogo integrirovaniya obyknovennykh differentsial'nykh uravneniy* (Methods of Approximate and Numerical Integration of Common Differential Equations) (1932–35); *Dinamika samolyota* (Aircraft Dynamics) (1933); coauthor, *Reaktivnoye dvizheniye* (Set Propulsion) (1935); coauthor, *Teoriya i raschyot vozdushnogo grebnogo vinta* (The Theory and Calculation of Airscrews) (1940); coauthor, *Novyye formuly chislennykh kvadratur* (New Formulas for Numerical Squaring) (1949); *Izbrannyye trudy* (Selected Works) (Vol 1, 1956); *Awards:* Stalin Prize (1943); *Died:* 6 Mar 1950.

VETOSHKIN, Mikhail Kuz'mich (1884–1958) Party and govt official; Dr of Historical Sci; prof from 1953; CP member from 1904; *Born:* 17 Nov 1884 in vil Usol'ye, former Irkutsk Province, son of a worker; *Educ:* 1903 grad Irkutsk Teachers' Training Seminary; 1917 grad Petersburg Univ; *Career:* 1905–07 with Siberian RSDRP Union and member, Krasnoyarsk, Tomsk, Chita and Harbin Party Comts; 1908–12 worked for illegal Bolshevik orgs in Pskov and Vologda Provinces; from Apr 1917 member, Vologda and Velikiy Ustyog Sov; from Dec 1917 member, Vologda Province RSDRP(B) Comt; Mar 1918–early 1920 chm, Vologda Province Exec Comt and chm, Vologda Province RCP(B) Comt; simultaneously member, Revol Mil Comt, 6th Army, Northern Front; 1918 and 1919 attended 7th and 8th RCP(B) Congresses; elected member, All-Russian Centr Exec Comt; 1920 member, Crimean Revol Comt and member, Crimean Oblast Comt, CP(B) Ukr; later chm, Kiev Province Revol Comt and member, Kiev Oblast Comt, CP(B) Ukr; from late 1920 Collegium member, Pop Comrt of Workers and Peasants' Inspection and member, Small Council of Pop Comr; from Jan 1922 Ukr Pop Comr of Justice, then Ukr Pop Comr of Workers and Peasants' Inspection; 1925–41 exec secr, Budget Commission, USSR Centr Exec Comt; from 1944 research and teaching work; 1949–53 assoc prof, Moscow Univ; from 1953 prof, Chair of CPSU History, Inst of Extension Courses for Soc Sci Teachers, Moscow State Univ; *Publ: Sibirskiye bol'sheviki v period pervoy russkoy revolyutsii* (The Siberian Bolsheviks in the Period of the First Russian Revolution (1939); *Zabaykal'skiye bol'sheviki i chitinskoye vooruzhyonnoye vosstaniye 1905–1906 gg* (The Transbaykal Bolsheviks and the 1905–06 Chita Armed Revolt) (1949); *Ocherki po istorii bol'shevistskikh organizatsiy i revolyutsionnogo dvizheniya v Sibiri* (An Outline History of Bolshevik Organizations and the Revolutionary Movement in Siberia) (1953); *Bol'sheviki Dal'nego Vostoka v pervoy russkoy revolyutsii* (Far Eastern Bolsheviks in the First Russian Revolution) (1956), etc; *Awards:* Order of Lenin; *Died:* 2 Feb 1958.

VEVER, E.Ya. (1882–1937) Party official; CP member from 1917; *Born:* 1882; *Career:* during 1917 Oct Revol worker and Red Guards man; 1918–24 dir, "Gorki" Sanatorium; later Party and admin work; arrested by State Security organs; *Died:* 1937 in imprisonment.

VEYNBAUM, Grigoriy Spiridonovich (Party name: VALENTIN) (1891–1918) Mold govt official; CP member; helped establish Sov regime in Siberia; *Born:* 1891, son of a Petersburg high official; *Educ:* studied at Petersburg Univ; *Career:* while at high-school joined Soc-Democratic movement; 1909–10 propaganda work; Apr 1910 arrested and exiled to Yeniseysk Province; after 1917 Feb Revol helped organize Minusinsk Sov; newspaper "Izvestiya Minusinskogo soveta" and Bolshevik newspaper "Iovarishch"; from May 1917 Party work in Krasnoyarsk; ed, newspaper "Krasnoyarskiy rabochiy"; from July 1917 chm, Krasnoyarsk Sov; after 1917 Oct Revol chm, Siberian Province Exec Comt and member, Siberian Centr Exec Comt; early 1918 Pop Comrt of For Affairs rep in Siberia; *Died:* 25 Oct 1918 executed in Krasnoyarsk after the collapse of Sov regime in Siberia during the so-called Czechoslovak Legion revolt.

VEYNBERG, Boris Petrovich (1871–1942) Physicist; Dr of Physics from 1906; prof from 1909; *Born:* 1 Aug 1871; *Educ:* 1893 grad Petersburg Univ; *Career:* 1906 defended doctor's thesis on the internal friction of ice, in which he formulated the theory of the movement of ice in an inclined bed; also did research on the movement of Arctic ice and on the physical and mech properties of ice in gen; 1909–24 prof, Tomsk Technol Inst; 1909–14 organized 23 expeditions to study magnetic phenomena; from 1924 dir, then fellow, Main Geophysical Observatory, Leningrad; 1927 designed an instrument to measure the intensity of a magnetic field and devised methods of observing and compiling data on the Earth's magnetic field; from 1927 supervised the org of solar research in the USSR; 1931 developed eng principles of solar-powered equipment; designed solar steam boilers, water desalination equipment, etc; together with his son V. B. Veynberg, designed an efficient solar-powered motor; from 1940 head, Theoretical Research Dept, Earth Magnetism Research Inst; *Publ:* doctor's thesis *O vnutrennem trenii l'da* (The Internal Friction of Ice) (1906); *Zadachi fiziki tvyordogo tela* (The Tasks of Solid-State Physics) (1907); *Opyt metodiki nauchnoy raboty i podgo-*

tovki k ney (Experience in Preparing and Conducting Scientific Projects) (1928); *Solnechnyye opresniteli* (Solar Water Desalination Installations) (1933); *Lyod* (Ice) (1941); *Died:* 1942 killed during Leningrad blockade.

VEYNBERG, Gavriil Davydovich (1881–1946) Trade-union official; CP member from 1906; *Born:* 1881; *Career:* metalworker; from age 14 participated in strikes; worked for Mogilyov, Odessa and Kiev Party org; twice arrested for revol activities; exiled to Yeniseysk Province; after 1917 Feb Revol worked at Petrograd's "Promyot" Plant; Apr 1917 elected chm, Bd, Metalworkers' Union; 1918 Party work in Petrograd; then Presidium member, Supr Sovarkhoz and head, Econ Dept, CC, Metalworkers' Union; 1928 chm, CC, Food Ind Workers' Union; then Presidium member and dept head, All-Union Centr Trade-Union Council; simultaneously Presidium member, Supr Sovarkhoz; at 14th and 15th CPSU(B) Congresses elected member, CC, CPSU(B); at 16th, 17th and 18th Congresses elected cand member, CC, CPSU(B); Feb 1941 at 18th All-Russian Conference relieved of cand membership of CC, CPSU(B); arrested by State Security organs; *Died:* 1946 in imprisonment.

VEYSBERG, Yuliya Lazarevna (1880–1942) Composer; wife of the musicologist A.N. Rimsky-Korsakov; *Born:* 6 Jan 1880 in Orenburg; *Educ:* musical training in Berlin; *Career:* contributed to journal "Muzykal'nyy sovremennik"; *Works:* operas *Rusalochka* (The Little Water-Nymph) (1923); "Gyul'nara" (1935); children's opera to a libretto by S. Marshak *Gusi-lebedi* (The Swan-Geese) (1937); radio opera *Myortvaya tsarevna* (The Dead Princess) (1937); choral work "The Twelve" (1938); symphonies, chamber works, works for voice and orchestra, instrumental pieces, etc; romances and children's songs; arrangements of folk songs, including Mordovian songs; *Died:* 4 Mar 1942 in Leningrad.

VEYSBROD, Boris Solomonovich (1874–1942) Surgeon and soc worker; prof; CP member from 1904; *Born:* 1874; *Educ:* 1899 grad Khar'kov Univ; *Career:* while a student engaged in illegal polit work; exiled to Kovno Province; then worked as zemstvo distr physician in Saratov, then Khar'kov Province; 1903, to escape arrest, emigrated to Germany and worked at Bergmann, Israel and Czerny's clinics; 1906 returned to Russia and worked as intern, 1st Moscow Municipal Hospital; after 1917 Oct Revol headed Public Health Dept, Zamoskvorech'ye Sov and was comr of theapeutic establishments; 1919–20 appointed chm, Extraordinary Commission to Combat Epidemics on Turkestani and Southwestern Fronts; from 1922 chief physician, 2nd Moscow Municipal Hospital (now named for him) and prof, 2nd Moscow Med Inst; studied clinical syndromes of disease and its pathological features; contributed to org of Sov health service; co-founder, Moscow First Aid Inst; helped organize system of med home care for patients; member, Sci and Tech Section, State Learned Council, Pop Comrt of Educ; bd member, Moscow Surgical Soc and All-Union Assoc of Surgeons; from 1924 chm, Centr Bureau, Physicians Section, Union of Med and Health Workers; wrote numerous works on pathoanatomy and surgery; helped treat Lenin; *Awards:* Order of Lenin; *Died:* 1942.

VEYTS, Veniamin Isaakovich (1905–1961) Power eng; prof; corresp member, USSR Acad of Sci from 1933; *Born:* 5 Jan 1905; *Educ:* 1924 grad 1st Moscow Univ; 1925 grad Moscow Higher Tech College; *Career:* from 1925 lecturer, various higher educ establishments; 1932–41 assoc, then head of a chair, Moscow Power Eng Inst; during WW 2 helped to organize power resources in Eastern USSR; after WW 2 in charge of various research and development projects, including Moscow combined power system, Sov European grid, Siberian grid, etc; attended several int conferences on power eng; 1960 read paper on fuel and power balance of USSR at Worls Power Conference, Madrid; *Publ: Struktura energeticheskogo balansa i osnovy elektrifikatsii, gazifikatsii i teplofikatsii promyhlennosti* (The Power Balance Structure and the Principles of Developing Power, Gas and Heating Grids for Industry) (1947); *Energotekhnologicheskoye kombinirovaniye i energeticheskiy koeffitsiyent poleznogo deystviya promyshlennogo proizvodstva* (The Combination of Power Systems and the Power Efficiency in Industrial Production) (1948); *Elektrifikatsiya narodnogo khoyaystva SSSR* (The Electrification of the Soviet National Economy) (1948); *Tekhnicheskiy progress sovetskoy energetiki* (The Technical Progress of Soviet Power Engineering) (1950); *Yedinaya energeticheskaya sistema SSSR* (The Standardized Power System of the USSR) (1954), etc; *Awards:* Order of the Red Banner of Labor; Stalin Prize 1st Class (1942); medals; *Died:* 31 Jan 1961.

VEZIROV, Nadzhafbek Fatalibek ogly (1854–1926) Azer playwright, journalist and impresario; *Born:* 15 Feb 1854 in Shusha, son of an impoverished nobleman; *Educ:* studied in Shusha, then at Baku non-classical high school; 1878 grad Petrine Agric Acad, Moscow; *Career:* studied Russian and West European lit and soc thought; specialized in Ostrovskiy's plays; made the acquaintance of Korolenko; published his work in frist Azer newspaper "Ekinchi", contributing feuilletons and articles; 1873–1912 staged and produced shows in Baku; wrote some 15 plays; *Works:* comedies: "The Meat for You, the Bones for Me" (1873); "A Picture of Domestic Upbringing" (1875); play "Only the Name Remained" (1891); comedies: "Out of the Rain and Into the Downpour" (1895); "Fakhreddin's Grief" (1896); "A Hero of Our Day" (1898); play "The Start of a New Age" (1924); *Died:* 9 Feb 1926 in Baku.

VIGILEV, Boris Dmitriyevich (1883–1924) Diplomat; CP member from 1921; *Born:* 28 May 1883 in Moscow; *Educ:* studied at Moscow Univ; *Career:* from 1902 in revol movement; 1905–06 member, Vilnius RSDRP Comt; member, oblast comt, Northwestern RSDRP Union; at 4th (Amalgamative) RSDRP Congress sided with Mensheviks; from 1909 lived in Zakopane, Galicia; worked for Zakopane Natural History Soc, Ethnographical Soc, Geological Soc and Meteorological Soc; active member, Cracow League for Aid to Polit Prisoners; maintained contacts with Soc-Democratic Party of Poland and Lith; from 1921 secr, Russo-Ukr-Polish Repatriation Commission; then until 1923 Sov consul in Warsaw; helped to trace and collect Lenin's library and archives which had been left in Poland; *Died:* late 1924 in Zakopane.

VIGNERE-GRINBERGA, Malvina (1873–1949) Lat opera and concert singer; Hon Art Worker of Lat SSR from 1945; *Born:* 12 Oct 1873 in Riga; *Educ:* studied singing in Riga, Moscow, Petersburg and Berlin; *Career:* from 1891 gave concerts of Lat folk songs; sang with German opera company in Liepaya and Riga; from 1913 with Riga Opera Theater; 1944 founder-dir, Lat Folk Song Ensemble; *Roles:* the Countess in Tchaikovsky's *Pikovaya dama* (The Queen of Spades); the Angel in "Demon"; Carmen; Martha in Gounod's "Faust", etc; *Died:* 6 June 1949 in Riga.

VIKHLYAYEV, P.A. (1869–1928) Statistician and agronomist; member, Socialist-Revol Party; *Born:* 1869; *Career:* 1896–98 head, Econ Dept, Tver' Zemstvo Admin; 1907–17 head, Statistics Dept, Moscow Zemstvo Admin; Asst Min of Agric in Provisional Govt; after 1917 Oct Revol worked for Centr Statistical Bd; also prof, higher educ establishments in Moscow; *Publ: Krest'yanskoye khozyaystvo* (Peasant Economy) (1897); *Ocherki iz russkoy sel'skokhozyaystvennoy deystvitel'nosti* (Studies in Russian Agricultural Reality) (1901); *Ocherki teoreticheskoy statistiki* (Studies in Theoretical Statistics) (1924), etc; *Died:* 1928.

VIKSNE, Paul' (1894–1941) Lat critic and journalist; *Born:* 1894; *Educ:* 1912 grad Val'miyer Teachers' Seminary; 1924 grad Philology Fac, Moscow Univ; *Career:* from 1912 active in revol movement; fought in WW 1; active in 1917 Oct Revol; fought in Civil War against Denikin, Wrangel, etc; 1929–37 ed, Lat journal "Tseltne" in Moscow; published lit and critical essays in this and other Lat periodicals; *Publ:* monograph "The Life and Work of Sudrabu Edzhus" (1935); *Died:* 1941.

VIKTOR, (secular name: SVYATIN, Leonid) (1893–1966) Metropolitan of Krasnodar and Kuban', Russian Orthodox Church from 1961; *Born:* 1893 in Verkhneural'sk, Orenburg Province; *Educ:* grad Orenburg Theological Seminary; studied at Kazan' Theological Acad; *Career:* during WW 1 junior capt, Russian Army; after defeat of Volunteer Army emigrated to China and worked for Russian Orthodox Mission in Peking; took monastic vows with name Viktor and was appointed arch-monk; 1921 served in Vladivostok; 1922 vicar, Orthodox parish in Tientsin, where he built a church and founded a hospital, a Russian school and a hostelry for foreigners; 1928 elevated to archimandrite; 1929 founded in Tsientsin Serafim Sarovskiy House of Charity; 1932 appointed Bishop of Shanghai and vicar to Archbishop of China and Peking; 1933 head, Russian Orthodox Mission in China; then Archbishop of China and Peking; after WW 2 came under jurisdiction of Moscow Patriarchy; 1950 attended Peace Conference of Heads of Russian, Geo and Arm Churches; from 1952 Exarch of Moscow Patriarchy in Eastern Asia; 1952 in pastoral letter denounced Americans as aggressors allegedly engaging in bacteriological warfare in Korea and China; 1954 repatriated to USSR; 1956–61 Archbishop of Krasnodar and Kuban'; *Awards:* Moscow Patriarchy Order of St Vladimir, 1st Class (1963); *Died:* 18 Aug 1966.

VIKTOROV, Mikhail Vladimirovich (1893–1938) Mil commander; naval squadron commander, 1st class from 1935; *Born:* 1893 in Yaroslavl', son of an officer; *Educ:* 1913 grad Navy Corps; 1924 grad Advanced Courses at Naval Acad; *Career:* during WW 1 served with Baltic Fleet; after 1917 Oct Revol in Sov Navy; 1919 senior navigator, cruiser "Oleg", then commanded destroyer "Vsadnik", battleship "Andrey Pervozvannyy" and then "Gangut"; 1921 helped crush Kronstadt Mutiny and was later appointed senior naval commander, Kronstadt Base; from May 1921 commander, Baltic Naval Forces; 1924 commander, Black Sea Naval Forces; from 1925 again commander, Baltic Fleet; from 1932 commanded newly-formed Pacific Fleet; arrested by State Security organs; *Died:* 1 Aug 1938 in imprisonment; posthumously rehabilitated.

VILENSKIY, Dmitriy Germogenovich (1892–1961) Spol scientist; geobotanist; specialist in floristics; Dr of Geological and Mineralogical Sci; *Born:* 18 June 1892 in Shepetovka, Volhynian Province; *Educ:* grad Kiev Polytech Inst; *Career:* 1916–21 studied Lower Volga, mainly at Saratov Agric Experimental Station; from 1921 at Agric Fac, Tiflis Polytech Inst; 1924–30 prof of botany, Khar'kov Agric Inst, then prof of soil sci, Soil Improvement Inst; then prof of soil sci and head Chair of Soil Geography, Moscow Univ; pres, Int Commission for the Classification, Cartography and Geography of Soils; vice-pres, Solonetz Subcommission, Int Soc of Soil Scientists; member, Org Bureau, All-Union Soc of Soil Scientists; co-ed, journal "Pochvovedeniye"; attended Int Congress of Soil Scientists in USA; also visited Germany, Austria, Czechoslovakia and Hungary; contributed articles to journals "Pochvovedeniye", "Vestnik MGU", "Vestnik AN SSR", etc; *Publ: O kul'ture lekarstvennykh rasteniy v Novouzenskom uyezde* (The Cultivation of Medicinal Plants in the Novouzensk Uyezd) (1916); *Seno, yego prigotovleniye, sostav i sposoby opredeleniya kormovogo dostoinstva* (Hay, Its Preparation, Composition and Means of Rating Its Feed Value) (1918); *Analogichnyye ryady v pochvoobrazovanii i ikh znacheniye dlya postroyeniya geneticheskoy klassifikatsii pochv* (Analogous Rows in Soil Formation and Their Importance in the Genetic Classification of Soils) (1924); *Zasolennyye pochvy, ikh proiskhozhdeniye, sostav i sposoby uluchsheniya* (Salty Soils, Their Origin, Composition and Means of Improving Them) (1924); college courses textbook *Botanika* (Botany) (1928); *Russkaya pochvenno-kartograficheskaya shkola i yeyo vliyaniye na razvitiye mirovoy kartografii pochv* (The Russian Soil Cartography School and Its Influence on the Development of World Soil Cartography) (1945); *Died:* 14 June 1961.

VILENSKIY, L. S. (pseudonym: LENSKIY) (1880–1950) Govt official; *Born:* 1880; *Career:* 1899 joined Soc-Democratic movement in Kiev; from 1902 worked in Yekaterinoslav; Yekaterinoslav Party Comt deleg at 2nd RSDRP Congress; majority Iskraist; from 2nd Congress until 1905 Bolshevik; 1905 left RSDRP and joined Communist Anarchists; 1912 abandoned polit work; after 1917 Oct Revol worked for various econ and financial establishments; from 1949 pensioner; *Died:* 1950.

VILLUAN, Vasiliy Yul'yevich (1850–1922) Russian violinist, composer and conductor; *Born:* 16 Oct 1850 in Moscow; *Career:* 1873–1918 founder-dir, Music Classes, Nizhniy Novgorod Dept, Russian Music Soc (1907–18 College, then Conservatory, from 1921 Technicum); taught violin, piano and music theory; *Works:* three operas for young people, including "Lelio" (1902); four string quartets; piano pieces; romances, etc; wrote textbook on elementary music theory (1878); *Awards:* Hero of Labor (1918); *Died:* 15 Sept 1922 in Nizhniy Novgorod.

VILUMSON, Eduard Fridrikhovich (1893–1931) Mil commander; *Born:* 1893; *Educ:* grad Mil Acad Courses for Red Army Higher Command Staff; *Career:* 1th in Russian Army; from 1918 in Red Army; during Civil War div, then corps chief of staff; after Civil War dep chief, then chief of staff, 4th Infantry Corps; then asst chief of supply, Bel Mil Distr; *Died:* 1931.

VIL'NER, Vladimir Bertol'dovich (1885–1952) Stage dir; Pop Artiste of Ukr SSR from 1940; *Born:* 9 Mar 1885 in Grodno; *Educ:* 1910 grad drama courses; 1912 grad Petersburg Univ; *Career:* 1911–12 actor, New Drama Theater, Petersburg; 1918–20 stage dir, Khar'kov Theater under N.N. Sinel'nikov; then stage dir at theaters in Krasnodar and Novorossiysk, at Khar'kov Young Playgoers' Theater and Moscow Comedy Theater; 1928–38 stage dir, Kiev, Rostov and Leningrad theaters; 1938–41 chief stage dir, Franko Theater; 1942–44 artistic dir, Kuybyshev Theater; 1944–47 artistic dir, Directorate of (touring) Frontline Theaters, Moscow; 1947–50 chief stage dir, Kiev Musical Comedy Theater; 1927–52 taught drama; prof from 1947; also did film work: *Productions:* Griboyedov's *Gore ot uma* (Woe from Wit); Yanovskiy's *Yarost* (Fury); Fayko's *Chelovek s portfelem* (The Man with a Briefcase) (1928–29); Vishnevskiy's *Pervaya Konnaya* (The 1st Cavalry) (1930); Gogol's *Revizor* (The Government Inspector) (1938); *Poslednyaya zhertva* (The Last Victim) (1939); "Much Ado About Nothing" (1941); Strauss' "Die Fledermaus" (1948); Dunayevskiy's *Vol'nyy veter* (Free Wind) (1947); Milyutin's "Trembita" (1950), etc; *Died:* 9 Aug 1952.

VIL'YAMS, Pyotr Vladimirovich (1902–1947) Stage designer; prof; Hon Art Worker of RSFSR from 1944; *Born:* 17 Apr 1902 in Moscow; *Educ:* studied in V.N. Meshkov's workshop; 1924 grad Higher Tech Art Workshops; *Career:* 1924 painting assignments in Italy, France and Germany; from 1925 member, Lathe Artists Soc; from 1929 theater set designer; 1941–47 chief artist, Bolshoy Theater, Moscow; also taught; from 1947 prof, Moscow Inst of Applied and Decorative Art; designed sets and costumes at Moscow Acad Arts Theater, Nemirovich-Danchenko Musical Theater and Bolshoy Theater; *Works:* sets and costumes for: Watkins' "The Advertisement"; "Pickwick Papers", after Dickens (1934); "La Traviata" (1934); Dzerzhinskiy's *Podnyataya tselina* (Virgin Soil Upturned) (1937); Asaf'yev's *Kavkazskiy plennik* (Prisoner of the Caucasus) (1938); "Ivan Susanin" (1939); "Tartuffe" (1939); Prokofiev's "Romeo and Juliet" (1940); Rossini's "William Tell" (1942); Bulgakov's *Posledniye dni* (The Last Days) (1943); A.K. Tolstoy's "Ivan the Terrible" (1946); *Kak zakalyalas' stal'* (How the Steel Was Tempered) (1947), etc; *Awards:* three Stalin Prizes (1943, 1946 and 1947); *Died:* 4 Dec 1947 in Moscow.

VIL'YAMS, Vasiliy Robertovich (1863–1939) Soil scientist; member, USSR Acad of Sci from 1931; prof and rector, Moscow's Timiryazev Agric Acad; member, All-Union Lenin Acad of Agric Sci from 1935; member, Bel Acad of Sci from 1929; CP member from 1928; *Born:* 27 Sept 1863 in Moscow; *Educ:* 1887 grad Petrine Agric and Forestry Acad (now Timiryazev Agric Acad, Moscow); *Career:* 1888 went abroad to complete his studies; met Pasteur in France and studied microbiology at Pasteur's Laboratory; in Munich worked at German agronomist E. Volny's laboratory; 1891 returned to Russia; 1892 began to lecture on agric at Petrine Acad; 1894 defended master's thesis on "Opyt issledovaniya v oblasti mekhanicheskogo analiza pochv" (Practical Research in the Mechnical Analysis of Soils); from 1894 head, Chair of Agric and Agric Machinery, Petrine Acad; also headed Experimental Field and Seed Control Station; from 1899 lectured on soil sci; led a number of soil field study trips in Lyubertsy, Lyublino, Kara-Kum Steppe, Chakva, Azer, etc; during 1905–06 Revol rector, Moscow Agric Inst; forced to resign after considerable friction with the authorities; 1922–25 rector, Moscow's Timiryazev Agric Acad; worked for State Learned Council, Pop Comrt of Educ; also worked for Gosplan and Pop Comrt of Agric; outlined his theory of a single, cohesive soil formation process in his work *Pochvovedeniye* (Soil Science) (1914–24); 1919 published Part 1 and 1922 – Part 2 of his work *Obshcheye zemledeliye* (General Farming), outlining the principles of his so-called grass-arable system; 1927 published his work *Obshcheye zemledeliye s osnovami pochvovedeniya* (General Farmin with the Principles of Soil Science); member, USSR Centr Exec Comt; dep, USSR Supr Sov from 1937; *Awards:* various orders; *Died:* 11 Nov 1939; monument erected to him at Timiryazev Agric Acad.

VINAVER, Maksim Moiseyevich (1863–1926) Politician; co-founder and CC member, Constitutional-Democratic Party; *Born:* 1863; *Career:* lawyer by profession; Petersburg dep in 1st State Duma; opposed Sov regime; 1919 Min of For Affairs, Crimean Kray Govt; 1919 emigrated to Paris; contributed to White emigre journal "Yevropeyskaya tribuna" and newspaper "Posledniye novosti"; *Publ: Issledovaniye pamyatnika pol'skogo obychnogo prava 13-go veka* (Study of a 13th-Century Polish Common Law Document) (1888); *Ocherki ob advokature* (An Outline of the Legal Profession) (1902); *Iz oblasti tsivilistiki* (From the Civil Law) (1908); *Konflikty v pervoy Dume* (Conflicts in the First Duma) (1907); *Istoriya Vyborgskogo vozzvaniya* (The History of the Vyborg Proclamation) (1917); *Nedavneye. Vospominaniya i kharakteristiki* (The Recent Past. Memoirs and Characteristics) (1917); *Died:* 1926.

VINER, Meyer (1893–1941) Jewish writer; lit historian; CP member; *Born:* 31 Dec 1893 in Cracow; *Educ:* during WW 1 studied philosophy in Zurich; *Career:* after WW 1 moved to Vienna to write poetry and do translations; 1922–25 lived in Berlin and joined CP; 1927 went to USSR; fought in WW 2; wrote articles on modern Russian and Jewish writers (P. Markish, ect); *Publ:*

novelette "The Death of Eli Falek" (1929); "Folklorism and Folklore Studies" (1932); coauthor, "Problems of Criticism" (1933); historical novelette "Kolev Askenazi" (1934); coauthor, "The Socialist Content and Nationalist Form of Soviet Literature" (1940); "The History of 19th-Century Jewish Literature" (1940); unfinished historical novel "By the Mediterranean"; *Died:* 1941 killed in action in WW 2.

VINNICHENKO, Vladimir Kirillovich (1880–1951) Ukr writer and politician; *Born:* 26 July 1880 in Kherson Province, son of a hired shepherd; *Educ:* studied at Kiev Univ; *Career:* studied at Yelisavetgrad high school; quit 7th grade and set out to roam the Ukr, earning his living by day-laboring; 1901 entered Kiev Univ, joined Revol Ukr Party circles and engaged in propaganda among workers; 1902 arrested and imprisoned for a while in Kiev; released but barred from resuming univ studies; became active Revol Ukr party agent and engaged in propaganda among peasantry; as an expelled student, drafted into Russian Army but soon deserted and went to Galicia, where he worked for socialist periodicals and organized the dispatch of revol lit to the Ukr; arrested in the course of one of these smuggling expeditions and again imprisoned in Kiev; then transferred to Kiev Fortress and placed in solitary confinement; 1904 released from fortress arrest under an amnesty but assigned to disciplinary battalion; 1904 again went abroad and worked for Soc-Democratic organ "Selyanin"; 1905 returned illegally to Ukr and moved from one area to another, hiring out as a farm laborer and organizing farmhands' strikes, which played an important role in the 1905 Revol in the Ukr; addresed workers' rallies in Poltava; after schism in Revol Ukr Party he became one of the leaders of its majority faction, reorganized into the Ukr Soc-Democratic Workers' Party (Ukr SDRP); after suppression of 1905–07 Revol again arrested and interned for third time in Luk'yanovka Prison; released on bail pending trial; 1907 emigrated; attended Stockholm Congress of Ukr SDRP and elected to its CC; until 1914 lived in several European countries; during this period gained recognition as a writer in the Ukr and Russia; his novels and novelettes were translated into Russian and his plays were staged in major Russian cities; 1914 returned illegally to Ukr to establish liaison with local Ukr SDRP orgs; with start of WW 1 lived illegally in Yekaterinoslav and Moscow and published anti-war pamphlets; after suppression of Ukr press, he collaborated with Prof Grushevskiy and others in Moscow to publish sole legal Ukr journal "Promin'"; after 1917 Feb Revol left Moscow for Kiev, where he established Centr Ukr SDRP organ "Robitnnycha hazeta"; end helped found Ukr Centr Rada; June 1917 elected chm, Secretariat-Gen, Centr Rada Govt; then on behalf of Centr Rada negotiated with Russian Provisional Govt and signed an agreement with it on the basis of its declaration recognizing Ukr autonomy; drafted 3rd and 4th Universals, proclaiming an independent Ukr Pop Republ; headed its govt and also conducted unofficial talks with Rakovskiy and Manuil'skiy, leaders of the Sov peace deleg; Nov 1918 – Feb 1919 headed Ukr Directory; 1919–20 in emigration, organized Foreign Group, Ukr CP and on its behalf published newspaper "Nova doba"; summer 1920 went to Moscow, then to Ukr and negotiated admission to CP(B) Ukr and Sov Ukr Govt; for a few days he was a member of Sov Ukr Govt as Pop Comr for Foreign Affairs fand dep chm, Ukr Council of Pop Comr; also member, CC, CP(B) Ukr; refused admission to Politburo, CC, CP(B) Ukr, he resigned all his posts and returned abroad; from 1920 lived in France, where he concentrated on lit work; wrote numerous stories, novelettes and novels; *Publ: Rasskazy* (Stories) (3 vol, 1911–13); stories *Pobeditel'* (The Victor) (1926); stories *Radost'* (Joy) (1926); novels *Na vesakh zhihni* (On the Scales of Life) (1912); *Zapiski kurnosogo mefistofelya* (The Notes of a Snub-Nosed Mephistopheles) (1917); *Solnechnaya mashina* (The Sun Machine) (1928); *Novaya zapoved'* (The New Commandment) (1949), etc; *Vozrozhdeniye natsii* (The Rebirth of a Nation) (3 vol, 1920); *Revolyutsiya v nebezpetsi* (Revolution in Danger) (1921); *Died:* 6 May 1951 at Mougins, France.

VINOGRADOV, Anatoliy Korneliyevich (1888–1946) Russian writer; *Born:* 9 Apr 1888 in vil Polotnyanyye Zavody, Smolensk Province, son of a teacher; *Educ:* 1912 grad History and Philology Fac, Moscow Univ; *Career:* dir, Rumyantsev Museum; 1921–25 dir, Lenin State Library; worked with Gorky, publishing foreign lit classics; edited series "Istoriya molodogo cheloveka 19-go stoletiya" (The History of a Young Man of the 19th Century); *Publ: Merime v pis'makh k Sobolevskomu* (Mérimée in His Letters to Sobolevskiy) (1928); *Merime v pis'makh k Dubenskoy; Pis'ma sem'i Lagrene* (Mérimée in His Letters to Dubenskaya. Letters of the Lagrenet Family) (1937); biographical works: *Tri tsveta vremeni* (Three Colors of the Time) (1931); *Poteryannaya perchatka. Stendal' v Moskve* (The Lost Glove. Stendhal in Moscow) (1931); *Povest' o brat'yakh Turgenevykh* (The Story of the Turgenev Brothers) (1932); *Chyornyy konsul* (The Black Consul) (1932); *Osuzhdeniye Paganini* (The Condemnation of Paganini) (1936); *Bayron* (Byron) (1936); *Stendal' i yego vremya* (Stendhal and His Time) (1938); novel *Khronika Malevinskikh* (The Malevinskiy Chronicle) (1941); *Died:* 26 Nov 1946 in Moscow.

VINOGRADOV, A. K. (1876–1938) Politician; *Born:* 1876; *Career:* Soc-Democratic faction of 2nd State Duma deleg at 5th RSDRP Congress; Bolshevik; 1906 joined Soc-Democratic movement; worked in Siberia; Akmolinsk Oblast dep, 2nd State Duma; arrested and tried with other members of Soc-Democratic faction, 2nd State Duma; after 1917 Feb Revol sided with Menshevik-Internationalists; 1918–19 member, Soc-Democratic Internationalist Party; worked for public health system; *Died:* 1938.

VINOGRADOV, Pavlin Fyodorovich (1890–1918) Govt official; Civil war veteran; *Born:* Jan 1890 near Petersburg, son of a tobacco factory salesman; *Career:* from age ten worked at Sestroretsk Arms Plant; later at semyannikov Shipyard; from 1905 in revol movement; 1912 arrested and drafted into Russian Army; for his refusal to take the oath and for revol propaganda sentenced to eight years' hard labor; confined at Shlissel'burg Fortress and Alexandrine Centr Jail; after 1917 Feb Revol returned to Petrograd; helped storm Winter Palace; Feb 1918 sent by Pop Comrt of Food to Arkhangel'sk to organize food supply for Petrograd; arranged dispatch of over 160 tons of grain to Petrograd; dep chm, Arkhangel'sk Oblast Exec Comt; July 1918 directed suppression of anti-Sov revolt in Shenkur Uyezd; Aug 1918 founder and commander, Northern Dvina Flotilla; 10 Aug 1918 commanded battle against enemy ships near Bereznik; *Died:* 8 Sept 1918 killed in action while defending Kotlas near vil Shidrovo.

VINOGRADOV, Sergey Arsen'yevich (1869–1938) Landscape painter; member, Acad of Arts from 1912; *Born:* 1869; *Educ:* grad Moscow College of Painting, Sculpture and Architecture; *Career:* from 1892 displayed his work in exhibitions of Assoc of Itinerant Artists; then joined Russian Artist's Union; contributed to "World of Art" exhibitions; *Works:* in 19th Century peasant genre paintings; in early 20th Century specialized in landscapes and interiors, including "The Workers' Dinner" (1890); "Women" (1893), etc; *Died:* 1938 in emigration.

VINOGRADOV, Vasiliy Ivanovich (1895–1967) Mil commander; col-gen; *Born:* 1895; *Educ:* 1923 grad Red Army Acad, Moscow; *Career:* 1918–20 fought in Civil War; 1939–40 fought in Sov-Finnish War; during WW 2 dept head, then dep head, Sov Army Main Rear Bd; 1945 head, Operations Group, Red Army Rear Bd, attached to Far Eastern Main Command; from early 1950's head, Sov Army Main Rear Bd; dep, RSFSR Supr Sov of 1955 convocation; *Awards:* Order of Lenin; Order of the Red Star; other orders; medals; *Died:* May 1967.

VINOGRADOV, Vladimir Nikitich (1882–1964) Therapist; prof from 1929; Dr of Med from 1924; member, USSR Acad of Med Sci from 1944; Hon Sci Worker of RSFSR from 1940; Hero of Socialist Labor from 1957; *Born:* 11 Mar 1882 in Yelets, Oryol Province; *Educ:* 1907 grad Med Fac, Moscow Univ; *Career:* 1907–10 extern, 1910–12 intern, Fac Therapy Clinic, Moscow Univ; 1912–21 asst prof, Propedeutic Therapy Clinic, Moscow Higher Women's Courses; 1921–24 asst prof, 1924–28 senior asst prof, Fac Therapy Clinic, Moscow Univ; 1925–28 head, Occupational Diseases Clinic, Moscow Univ; 1928 head, Fac Therapy Clinic, Moscow Univ; 1929–35 head, Chair of Propedeutic Therapy Clinic, 2nd Moscow Univ; 1935–43 head, Chair of Fac Therapy, 2nd Moscow Med Inst; 1943–64 head, Chair of Fac Therapy, 1st Moscow Med Inst; hon member, All-Union and Sverdlovsk Soc of Therapists; 1938–45 dep chm, from 1945 chm, Moscow Therapeutic Soc; 1947–49 dep chm, from 1949 chm, All-Union Soc of Therapists; from 1958 bd member, All-Russian Soc of Therapists; from 1934 consultant, 4th Main Bd, USSR Pop Comrt of Health (former Kremlin Therapy and Health Bd); Dec 1952 arrested on charge of Spying for UK and of deliberately administering wrong med treatment to Sov Party and Govt officials; after Stalin's death in 1953 released and rehabilitated; from 1943 ed, journal "Terapevticheskiyi arkhiv"; co-ed, therapy section, multi-vol "Opyt sovetskoy meditsiny v Velikoy Otechestvennoy voyne 1941–45 godov" (The Experience of Soviet Medicine in the 1941–45 Great Fatherland War); introduced new drugs and methods of diagnosis and treatment (pneumothorax, intestinal probe, angiocardiography, cardiac catheterization, bronchoscopy, gastroscopy, the use of radioactive isotopes, etc); wrote some 70 works on tuberculosis, sepsis, infectious heaptitis, kidney ailments, vegetative nervous system, rheumatism, influenza, hypertony, arteriosclerosis, occupational pathology and chemotherapy; *Publ: Ob izmeneniyakh pochek pri tuberkulyoze lyogkikh* (Kidney Lesions with Tuberculosis of the Lungs); *Skhema klinicheskogo issledovaniya bol'nogo* (The System of the Clinical Examination of Patients) (1929); *Priobretyonnyy sifilis pecheni u vzroslykh* (Acquired Syphilis of the Liver in Adults) (1928); *O medikamentoznom lecheni apepsii* (The Medicinal Treatment of Apepsia) (1925); ed and coauthor, *Materialy po eksperimental'noklinicheskoy elektro-kardiografii* (Material on Experimental-Clinical Cardiography) (1953); *Lecheniye antibiotikami bol'nykh pnevmoniyami* (The Antibiotic Treatment of Pneumonia Patients) (1956); *Awards:* Hero of Socialist Labor (1957); four Orders of Lenin; Order of the Red Banner of Labor; "Hammer and Sickle" Gold Medal; four other medals; *Died:* 29 July 1964 in Moscow.

VINOKUR, Grigoriy Osipovich (1896–1947) Russian linguist and lit historian; prof; *Born:* 17 Nov 1896 in Warsaw; *Educ:* 1922 grad Moscow Univ; *Career:* prof, Moscow Univ, Moscow Inst of History, Philosophy and Lit and Moscow Teachers' Training Inst; from 1933 member, Pushkin Commission, USSR Acad of Sci; from 1935 senior assoc, USSR Acad of Sci; 1935–40 helped to compile Ushakov's famous 4-vol *Tolkovyy slovar' russkogo yazyka* (Explanatory Dictionary of the Russian Language); coedited and annotated various ed of Pushkin's works published by the USSR Acad of Sci; supervised the compilation of a "Dictionary of Pushkin's Language"; *Publ: Biografiya i kul'tura* (Biography and Culture) (1927); *Kritika poeticheskogo teksta* (The Criticism of Poetry Texts) (1927); *Kul'tura yazyka* (Standards of Speech) (1929); commentaries to "Boris Godunov" in 7-vol ed of Pushkin's works (1937); *O nekotorykh yavleniyakh slovoobrazovaniya v russkoy tekhnicheskoy terminologii* (Some Word Formation Phenomena in Russian Technical Terminology) (1939); *Slovo i stikh v "Yevgenii Onegine"* (Word and Verse in "Eugene Onegin") (1941); *Orfografiya i yazyk Pushkina v akademicheskom izdanii yego sochineniy* (The Orthography and Language of Pushkin in the Academy of Science Edition of His Works) (1941); *Nasledstvo XVIII veka v stikhotvornom yazyke Pushkina* (The Heritage of the 18th Century in Pushkin's Poetic Language) (1941); *O zadachakh istorii yazyka* (The Tasks of the History of Language) (1941); *Mayakovskiy – novator yazyka* (Mayakovskiy – The Word-Coiner) (1943); *Russkiy yazyk. Istoricheskiy ocherk* (The Russian Language. A Historical Study) (1945). *Zametki po russkomu slovoobrazovaniyu* (Notes on Russian Word Formation) (1946); *O slavyanizmakh v sovremennom russkom literaturnom yazyke* (Slavisms in Modern Literary Russian) (1947); *Russkoye stsenicheskoye proiznosheniye* (Russian Stage Pronunciation) (1948); *"Gore ot uma" kak pamyatnik russkoy khudozhestvennoy rechi* ("Woe from Wit" as a Monument of Artificial Russian Speech) (1948); *Izbrannyye raboty po russkomu yazyku* (Selected Papers on the Russian Language) (1959); *Died:* 17 Apr 1947 in Moscow.

VINOKUROV, Aleksandr Nikolayevich (1869–1944) Physician; Party, govt and health service official; CP member from 1893; *Born:* 31 Aug 1869 in Yekaterinoslav, son of a civil servant; *Educ:* 1888 grad high-school; 1894 grad Med Fac, Moscow Univ; *Career:* joined revol movement while still a student; together with S. I. Mitskevich, organized Marxist group in Moscow; provided apartment for meetings attended by Lenin; frequently arrested and exiled to Siberia; 1905–07 did revol work in Yekaterinoslav, Moscow and Petersburg; while working as a health officer maintained contacts with Bilshevik faction in 4th Duma, took part in Workers' Insurance Movement and spoke at congresses held by factory physicians; using the pseudonyms "Viv" and "Vrach", helped to write Bolshevik leaflets and pamphlets demanding state insurance for workers; on Lenin's instructions, used hospital funds for polit work; ed, Bolshevik journal "Voprosy strakhovaniya"; after 1917 Feb Revol continued insurance work; opposed Mensheviks at 1st and 2nd Insurance Conferences and critized insurance law proclaimed by Provisional Govt; after 1917 Oct Revol helped to organize Sov health service; member, Med Collegium, Main Mil Health Bd; chm, Council of Physicians' Collegia; 1918–21 RSFSR Pop Comr of Soc Security; 1921–24 worked on Famine Commission; 1922–24 chm, RSFSR Supr Count; 1924–38 chm, USSR Supr Court; from 1939 until death head, Sanitary Educ Dept, USSR Pop Comrt of Health; during WW 2 did ed and polit work in Med Publ House; wrote numerous articles on the Oct Revol and soc insurance; *Publ: Trud i zdorov'ye rabochikh* (Labor and the Workers' Health) (1916); etc; *Died:* 9 Nov 1944.

VINOKUROV-CHAGYLGAN, Il'ya Dorofeyevich (1914–1952) Yakut poet; *Born:* 31 July 1914 in vil Konta-Krest, Yakutia; *Educ:* 1932 grad Xakutsk Teachers' Training Technicum; *Career:* 1931 first work printed; *Publ:* collected verse "Happy Land" (1944); songs: "Our Hearts" (1942); "Song of a Hero" (1945); "Ski Song" (1942); "The Song of the Hunter" (1945); collections: "On a Distant Journey" (1948); "Verse" (1948); "Songs of Our Days" (1952), etc; *Died:* 9 Sept 1952.

VINTER, A.V. (1878–1958) Power eng; member, USSR Acad of Sci from 1932; *Born:* 10 Oct 1878 in vil Starosel'tsy, Grodno Province, son of a worker; *Educ:* 1899 studied at Kiev Polytech Inst; 1912 grad Petersburg Polytech Inst; *Career:* worked at electr power plant in Baku; after grad asst chief, then chief of construction of Russia's first peat-fired distr electr power plant; after 1917 Oct Revol directed construction of peat-fired Shatura Power Plant; 1927–32 directed construction of Dnieper Hydro-electr Plant and Dnieper Ind Combine; 1932–34 head, Main Power Ind Bd and Dep Pop Comr of Heavy Ind; then exec work for Min of Electr Power Plants; from 1946 dep dir, Krzhizhanovskiy Power Eng Inst; 1930–37 cand member, then member, USSR Centr Exec Comt; also member, Ukr Centr Exec Comt of 5th and 7th convocations; *Awards:* Order of Lenin; Order of the Red Banner of Labor; medals; *Died:* 9 Mar 1958.

VIPPER, Robert Yur'yevich (1859–1954) Historian; Dr of History and prof from 1894; member, USSR Acad of Sci from 1943; *Born:* 26 July 1859; *Educ:* 1880 grad Moscow Univ; *Career:* 1880–85 taught at a girls' high-school; 1887–94 teacher, Moscow College of Painting, Sculpture and Architecture; 1894–97 prof, Novorossiysk Univ, Odessa; 1897–99 assoc prof, 1899–1922 prof, Moscow Univ; 1924 emigrated to Lat; 1927–40 prof, Riga Univ; after Sov occupation of Lat returned to Moscow; 1941–48 prof, Moscow Univ; also prof, Moscow Inst of Philosophy, Lit and History; 1941–43 prof, Centr Asian Univ, Tashkent; from 1943 senior assoc, Inst of History, USSR Acad of Sci; dealt with various aspects of ancient, medieval and modern history; at one time criticized the theoretical principles of historical materialism; after his return to the USSR had difficulty in adapting his eclectic approach to history to the requirements of Sov historiography, although his earlier work on Ivan the Terrible found sufficient official favor to merit republication in 1944; *Publ: Obshchestvennye ucheniya i istoricheskiye teorii* (Social and Historical Theories) (1899); *Lektsii po istorii Gretsii* (Lectures on the History of Greece) (1905); *Ocherki istorii Rimskoy imperii* (Studies on the History of the Roman Empire) (1908); *Ocherki teorii istoricheskogo poznaniya* (Studies on the Theory of Historical Perception) (1911); *Istoriya Gretsii v klassicheskuyu epokhu* (The History of Greece in the Classical Age) (1916); *Drevniy Vostok i egeyskaya kul'tura* (The Ancient East and the Aegean Civilization) (2nd ed, 1916); *Vozniknoveniye khristianstva* (The Emergence of Christianity) (1918); *Ivan Groznyy* (Ivan the Terrible) (1922, 1944); *Vozniknoveniye khristianskoy literatury* (The Emergence of Christian Literature) (1946); *Istoriya srednikh vekov* (Medieval History) (1947); *Rim i ranee khristianstvo* (Rome and Early Christianity) (1954); *Died:* 30 Dec 1954.

VIRSALADZE, Spiridon Semyonovich (1868–1930) Therapist and Geo health service official; Dr of Med from 1909; prof from 1919; *Born:* 1868; *Educ:* 1896 grad Tomsk Univ; *Career:* after grad distr physician in Dag Oblast; then worked under A. A. Nechayev, V. M. Bekhterev and I. P. Pavlov in Petersburg; 1901 ascertained the part played by excitation of the cerebral cortex in bile production; 1909 defended doctor's thesis at Petersburg Mil Med Acad on premature thickening of the peripheral arteries; 1912 underwent specialist training at clinics in Rome, Berlin and Hamburg; from 1913 asst chief physician and head, Therapeutic Dept, Mikhail Hospital, Tiflis; from 1916 founder-member; Geo Soc of Physicians and Natural Scientists; 1918 co-founder, Med Fac, Tbilisi Univ; 1918 helped to organize campaign against malaria and other tropical diseases in Geo; 1919–30 head, Chair of Special Pathology and Therapy, then head, Chair of Hospital Therapy, Tbilisi Univ; from 1919 ed, first Geo med journal "Ekimi" (The Physician); 1924–30 founder-dir, Inst of Tropical Diseases, Geo Comrt of Health, which now bears his name: from

1924 ed, "Bulletin of the Institute of Tropical Diseases"; 1927 organized expedition to study and combat malaria in the Alazan Valley; member, Caucasian Med Soc; from 1928 considered to be the father of the Geo school of tropical med; trained numerous specialists, including Prof M. D. Kandelaki, Prof N. A. Kipshidze, Prof G. V. Kvitashvili and Prof T. Ye. Mamaladze; co-ed, 1st ed, "Bol'shaya meditsinskaya entsiklopediya" (Large Medical Encyclopedia); *Publ: O vliyanii razdrazheniya kory mozga na otdeleniya zhyolchi* (The Effect of Stimulation of the Cerebral Cortex on Bile Secretion) (1901); *Nauchnyye printsipy bol'nichnogo stroya i deystvuyushchee bol'nichnoye zakonodatel'stvo v Rossii* (The Scientific Principles of the Hospital System and Hospital Legislation in Effect in Russia) (1902); doctor's thesis *K voprosu o prezhdevremennoy plotnosti perifericheskikh arteriy i ob yeyo otnoshenii k tak nazyvayemoy gipoplazii* (The Premature Thickening of the Peripheral Arteries and Its Relation to Aortal Hypoplasia) (1910); "Zur Diagnose der Leber- und Subdiaphragmalabszesse" (1927); *Tropicheskaya meditsina, yeyo ob'yom i zadachi* (Tropical Medicine, Its Scope and Tasks) (1929), etc; *Died:* 1930 in Tbilisi.

VIRTANEN, Yalmari Erikovich (1889–1939) Karelian poet; CP member from 1920; *Born:* 8 Jan 1889 in vil Mayniyeme, Finland; *Career:* took part in 1905 Revol; 1906 first work printed; founder of Sov Karelian lit; *Publ:* "Shepherd's Songs" (1906); "The Call" (1907); "The Wish" (1910); "A Prometheus of Work" (1918); "Song of Karelia"; The Old Man and the Kolkhoz"; "The North", etc; verse collection "Verse" (1933); *Died:* 2 Apr 1939.

VISHNEVSKIY (real name: VISHNEVETSKIY), Aleksandr Leonidovich (1861–1943) Actor; Hon Art Worker of RSFSR; Hero of Labor from 1933; *Born:* 20 Jan 1861 in Taganrog; *Educ:* studied with Chekhov at Taganrog high school; *Career:* from 1883 appeared in schows of Taganrog Musical Drama Soc; became professional actor and appeared at theaters in Khar'kov, Yekaterinoslav, Odessa, Saratov, etc; from 1898 with Moscow Arts Theater; *Roles:* Boris Godunov in A.K. Tolstoy's "Tsar' Fyodor Ioannovich" (1898), A.K. Tolstoy's *Smert' Ionna Groznogo* (The Death of Ivan the Terrible) (1899) and Pushkin's "Boris Godunov" (1907); Mark Antony in Shakespeare's "Julius Caesar" (1903); Antonio in Shakespeare's "The Merchant of Venice" (1898); Hofstad in Ibsen's "Dr Stockman" (1900); Tatrin in Gorky's *Na dne* (The Lower Depths) (1902); Prince Tugoukhovskiy in Griboyedov's *Gore ot uma* (Woe from Wit) (1906); David Leyzer in Andreyev's "Anathema" (1909); Pan Wrublewski in *Brat'ya Karamazovy* (The Brothers Karamazov) (1910); the Chairman of the Court in *Voskreseniye* (Resurrection) (1930); the Policeman in *Myortvyye dushi* (Dead Souls), after Gogol (1932); Dorn in Chekhov's *Chayka* (The Seagull) (1898); Voynitskiy in Chekhov's *Dyadya Vanya* (Uncle Vanya) (1899); Kulygin in Chekhov's *Tri sestry* (The Three Sisters) (1901); *Publ: Klochki vospominaniy* (Scraps of Memories) (1928); *Died:* 27 Feb 1943.

VISHNEVSKIY, Aleksandr Vasil'yevich (1874–1948) Surgeon; member, USSR Acad of Med Sci from 1947; Hon Sci Worker of RSFSR from 1934; *Born:* 3 Sept 1874 in vil Chir-Yurt, Dag; *Educ:* 1894 grad Astrakhan' boys' high school; 1899 grad Med Fac, Kazan' Univ; *Career:* from 1899 dissector, Chair of Anatomy and Operative Surgery, Kazan' Univ; from 1912 prof, Surgical Clinic, Kazan' Univ (now named for him); from 1934 dir, Surgical Clinic, Centr Inst of Postgrad Med Training and All-Union Inst of Experimental Med; from 1946 dir, Inst of Surgery, USSR Acad of Med Sci (which now bears his name); did clinical research on the surgery ρf the bile tract, the urinary system, the thoracic cavity, neurosurgery and the surgery of war wounds and suppurative processes; advanced hypothesis on the role of the nervous trophic system in the inflammatory process; proceeding from this, devised new methods of treating inflammations suppurative wounds and traumatic shock (with novocain block, vagosympathic block, balsam oil poultices, etc); improved techniques for surgical treatment of mammary and rectal cancer; 1930 devised original method using creeping novocain infiltrate for local anesthesia in surgery; this technique has been widely used in the USSR and abroad; his research on the effects of novocain on the course of pathological processes led him to study the entire problem of the nervous trophic system and nervism; one of first scientists to use Sechenov-Pavlov nervism idea in clinical practice; established that novocain not only anesthetizes but also affects the nervous system and thereby the trophic system of the tissues; as a slight irritant, a novocain solution has a positive effeckt on inflammations and the healing of wounds; his second method – a balsam oil poultice – has also proved efficacious in treating wounds; the poultice acts not only as an antiseptic medium but also, via the nervous system, has a beneficial effect on the tissues in the focus of inflammation; a combination of novocain and balsam oil poultice furnished a new method of treating inflammatory processes used in spontaneous gangrene of the legs, trophic ulcers, thrombophlebitis, abscesses, carbuncles, and other ailments; his new analgesic methods of treating wounds were used by the sov Army in WW 2; 1937 performed first lung resection under local anesthesia on a patient suffering from bronchiectasis; chm, Tatar Surgical Soc; chm, Moscow Soc of Surgeons; bd member, All-Union Surgical Soc; *Publ: Obezbolivaniye v khirurgii* (Anesthesia in Surgery) (1929); *Mestnoye obezbolivaniye po metodu polzuchego infiltrata* (Local Anesthesia by the Creeping Infiltrate Method) (1932); *Novokainovyy blok nervnoy sistemy, kak metod vozdeystviya na troficheskiye rasstroystva tkaney* (Novocain Block of the Nervous System as a Method of Treating Trophic Disturbances of the Tissues) (1936); *Pokazaniya k primeneniyu novokainovogo bloka i maslyanykh antiseptikov* (Indications for the Use of Novocain Block and Oil Antiseptics) (1946); coauthor, *Novokainovaya blokada i maslyano-bal'zamicheskiye antiseptiki, kak osobyy vid patogeneticheskoy terapii* (Novocain Blockade and Balsam Oil Antiseptics as a Special Form of Pathogenetic Therapy) (1948); *Sobraniye trudov* (Collected Works) (5 vol, 1950–52); *Awards:* Stalin Prize (1942); other awards; *Died:* 13 Nov 1948 in Moscow.

VISHNEVSKIY, Vsevolod Vital'yevich (1900–1951) Russian writer and playwright; dep secr-gen, USSR Writers' Union; CP member from 1937: *Born:* 21 Dec 1900 in Petersburg, son of a surveyor; *Educ:* studied at Petersburg High School; *Career:* at age 14 volunteered for Russian Army and served at front during WW 1; took part in 1917 Oct Revol; 1918–20 machine-gunner, 1st Cavalry Army; then commander and polit work, Baltic and Black Sea Fleets; 1920 first work published; edited journal "Krasnoflotets"; 1937 went to Spain to attend anti-fascist writers' congress; 1939–40 war corresp for "Pravda" on Sov-Finnish Front; 1941–42 fought in defense of Leningrad, then served as war corresp; from 1944 ed, journal "Znamya"; wrote plays and film scripts on war and patriotic themes; *Works:* plays: *Pervaya Konnaya* (The First Cavalry Army) (1929); *Posledniy reshitel'nyy* (The Last Decisive Battle) (1931); *Na Zapade boy* (Fighting in the West) (1931); *Optimisticheskaya tragediya* (An Optimistic Tragedy) (1933); *U sten Leningrada* (At the Walls of Leningrad) (1944); *Nezabyvayemyy 1919-y* (Unforgettable 1919) (1949); scripts for films: *My iz Kronshtadta* (We Are from Kronstadt) (1933); *My – russkiy narod* (We Are the Russian People) (1937; screened 1965); "Optimisticheskaya tragediya" (screened 1963); *Publ: Stat'i dnevniki, pis'ma o literature i iskusstve* (Articles, Diaries and Letters on Literature and Art) (1961); *Sobraniye sochineniy* (Collected Works) (5 vol, 1954–60); *Awards:* two Orders of Lenin; three Orders of the Red Banner; other orders and medals; Stalin Prize (1950); *Died:* 28 Feb 1951 in Moscow.

VISHNYA, Ostap (real name: GUBENKO, Pavel Mikhaylovich) (1889–1956) Ukr writer, satirist and humorist; *Born:* 11 Nov 1889 in vil Grun', now Sumy Oblast, son of a peasant; *Educ:* 1907 grad Kiev Med Orderlies' School; studied at but did not grad Kiev Univ; *Career:* 1907–17 worked as med orderly; 1919 first work printed; late 1920's and early 1930's worked for newspapers "Visti" and "Selyanska pravda" and for various satirical journals; a master of the short pamphlet, satirical feuilleton and humoresques; drew extensively on Ukr folk humor and folk speech; early 1930's attacked by Party critics for his ironic attitude to Sov Life, especially the system of so-called writers brigades formed for the "lit servicing" of kolkhozes, construction projects, etc; 1933 arrested by State Security organs and exiled for ten years to Solovki, then to a concentration camp in the Far North; 1943 released from imprisonment but remained in the North until 1945, working for an Arkhangel'sk newspaper; after 1945 wrote a great deal about Ukr "bourgeois nationalists" and Ukr polit emigres; *Publ:* collections: *Usmishky* (Grind) (4 vol, 1928); *Samostiyna dirka* (The Independent Hole) (1945); *Vesna-krasna)* (Beautiful Spring) (1949); *Vyshnevi usmishky* (Vishnya's Smiles) (1950); *Vybrane* (Selected Works) (1954); *Tvory* (Works) (2 vol, 1956); *Pryvit! Pryvit!* (Greetings! Greetings!) (1957); in Russian translation: *Izbrannoye* (Selected Works) (1958); *Dumy moi, dumy moi* (My Thoughts, My Thoughts) (1959); *Died:* 28 Sept 1956.

VISHNYAK, Ya. I. (1886–1948) Electr eng; govt official; CP member from 1917; *Born:* 1886; *Career:* 1906 joined RSDRP; 1907–17 lived in France; from 1910 member, French Socialist

Party; 1913 joined "Mezhrayontsy" group which merged with the RSDRP(B) at 6th party Congress in Aug 1917; during Civil War fought in Siberia and Crimea; 1921–24 and 1928–30 worked at Sov trade missions abroad; in latter years held exec eng and govt posts; *Died:* 1948.

VISHNYAKOVA, Praskov'ya Ivanovna (1887–1967) Party official; CP member from 1903; *Born:* 25 Oct 1887; *Career:* 1905–06 member, Dubno RSDRP Comt; 1907 worked with illegal printing house; 1914–16 working at a Petrograd plant, collected funds for "Pravda"; 1916 exiled to Yakutsk Province; 1917–22 member, Kuban' Oblast RCP(B) Comt and member, Krasnodar RCP(B) Comt; fought in Civil War; 1922–28 with Party control organs in Don Oblast; at 13th Party Congress elected member, RCP(B) Centr Control Commission; until 1930 worked for Centr Control Commission and Pop Comrt of Workers and Peasants' Inspection; from 1932 Presidium member, CC, Woodworkers' Union; from 1935 pensioner; *Died:* 10 Jan 1967.

VISKOVSKIY, Stefan Valerianovich (1892–1953) Infectionist and epidemiologist; Hon Sci Worker of RSFSR; *Born:* 1892; *Educ:* 1914 grad Mil Med Acad; *Career:* 1918–23 and 1927–31 lecturer, 1934–51 head, chair of Infectious Diseases, Leningrad Health and Hygiene Med Inst; also chief physician, Botkin Infectious Clinical Hospital; during WW 2 chief epidemiologist of Leningrad Front; 1945–52 dept head, Mil Med Museum; during his latter years head, Chair of Infectious Diseases, Kirov Mil Med Acad, Leningrad; 1924 first to detect presence of mosquito fever in Centr Asia; deliberately infected himself to determine the role of Ornithodorus ticks in the transmission of relapsing typhus; made an extensive treatment of the clinical aspects and epidemiology of dysentery; member, Leningrad Branch, Soc of Microbiologists, Epidemiologists and Infectionists; ed, 2 vol of *Opyt Sovetskoy meditsiny v Velikoy Otechestvennoy voyne 1941–1945* (Soviet Medical Experience in the 1941–45 Great Fatherland War); wrote some 50 research works; *Publ:* coauthor, *Pervyye opyty vaktsinoterapii batsillyarnoy dizenterii* (The Frist Experiments in Vaccine Therapy of Bacillary Dyssentery) (1921); *K voprosu o mekhanizme kollyapsa pri batsillyarnoy dizenterii* (The Mechanism of Collapse in Bacillary Dysentery) (1926); coauthor, *Epidemiologicheskiye i klinicheskiye nablyudeniya nad likhoradkoy pappatasi v Sredney Azii* (Epidemological and Clinical Observations of Pappataci Fever in Central Asia) (1927); *Rannyaya diagnostika osnovnykh infektsionnykh bolezney* (The Early Diagnosis of the Main Infectious Diseases) (1943); *Osnovnyye voprosy epidemiologii infektsionnoy zheltukhi* (Basic Aspects of the Epidemiology of Infectious Jaundice) (1944); *Iz kliniko-epidemiologicheskikh nablyudeniy nad dinamikoy batsillyarnoy dizenterii v Leningrade za posledniye 25 let* (Clinical and Epidemiological Observations of the Course of Bacillary Dysentery in Leningrad in the Past 25 Years) (1945); *Dizenteriya* (Dysentery) (1955); *Died:* 1953 in Leningrad.

VISKOVSKIY, Vyacheslav Kazimirovich (1881–1933) Film dir and actor; *Born:* 1881; *Career:* from 1915 in film work; worked for many pre-revol Russian film companies and for private film companies in USSR up to nationalization of film ind: 1917–18 with "Russian Golden Series" film company; 1917–18 with "Biofil'm" company; 1917–19 with "D. Kharitonov" company; 1918–19 with Taldykina's "Screen" Company, etc; 1920 emigrated and worked for American film studio; mid-1920's returned tu USSR and worked as film dir for Northwestern Film Studios; in his latter years played film roles; screened many classical lit works and modern lit and dramatic works; also covered historical and revol themes; *Productions:* directed films: *Durakam schast'ye* (Fools' Happiness) (1915); *Otsy i deti* (Fathers and Sons) (1915); *Pervaya lyubov'* (First Love) (1915); *Sil'neye smerti* (Stronger than Death) (1915); *Vrazh'ya sila* (Enemy Force) (1916); "Vasilisa" (1916); *Yego glaza* (His Eyes) (1916); *Zhretsy Molokha* (Priests of Moloch) (1917); *Semnadtsatiletniye* (The Seventeen-Year-Olds) (1917); *Rassudit tol'ko bog* (Only God Can Judge) (1918); "Masquerade" (1919); *Pod oblomkami samoderzhaviya* (Under the Debris of Autocracy) (1917); *Otrechyomsya ot starogo mira* (Renounce the Old World) (1917); *Skreshchyonnyye mechi* (Crossed Swords) (1918); *Zvezda Olimpii* (The Star of Olympia) (1918); *My segodnya rasstalis' s toboy* (Wa Parted Today) (1919); *Chayka* (The Seagull) (1924); *Krasnyye partizany* (Red Partisans) (1924); *Devyatoye yanvarya* (The Ninth of January) (1925); *Minaret smerti* (Minaret of Death) (1925); *Tret'ya zhena mully* (The Mullah's Third Wife) (1928); "Khabu" (1928), etc; *Roles:* the Factory Owner in *Oblomok imperii* (A Fragment of Empire) (1929); the Police Chief in *Beglets* (The Fugitive) (1932), etc; *Died:* 1933.

VITACHEK, Yevgeniy Frantsevich (1880–1946) Specialist in bowed instruments; Hon Art Worker of RSFSR from 1932; *Born:* 29 Apr 1880 in Sklenarica, Czechoslovakia; *Career:* from 1895 lived in Russia; from 1898 in Moscow; 1918 co-founder 1st State School of Violin Masters and Masters of Bowed Instruments, Moscow Conservatory; from 1919 custodian and restorer, State Collection of Unique Musical Instruments, Moscow; built over 400 bowed instruments, remarkable for their excellent tone and finish; *Publ: Ocherki po istorii postroyeniya smychkovykh instrumentov* (An Outline History of Bowed Instrument Building) (1952); *Awards:* top awards at All-Russian Competition of String Instruments (1913 and 1926); *Died:* 16 Feb 1946 in Moscow.

VITAS, Yuozas Tomovich (real name: VALUNAS, Ionas Tomovich) (1899–1943) Party official; CP member from 1919; *Born:* 1899 in vil Varanauskas, now Lith SSR; *Career:* participated in 1917 Oct Revol and fought in Civil War; early 1919 commanded partisan detachment in Lith; 1920 arrested near Daugavpils and drafted into White Army; while serving in Ukmerg organized underground Lith CP org; arrested again but escaped and 1921 moved to Sov Russia; studied and worked as eng; 1940 after annexation of Lith, chm, Vilnius City Exec Comt; in WW 2 founded underground "League for the Liberation of Lith"; from early 1943 secr, underground Vilnius City Comt, CP Lith; 19 June 1943 arrested by Gestapo; *Died:* 1943 in German imprisonment.

VITKOVSKIY, Vasiliy Vasil'yevich (1856–1924) Geodesist; emeritus prof, Gen Staff Acad; *Born:* 13 Nov 1856; *Educ:* 1885 grad Geodetic Dept, Gen Staff Acad; *Career:* 1885 mil geodesist, Topographic Corps; 1885–89 did geodetic survey and triangulation work in Finland and Petersburg Province; from 1889 lectured at various mil and civilian educ establishments; 1897–1905 chm, Dept of Mathematical Cartography, Russian Geographical Soc; *Publ: Prakticheskaya geodeziya* (Practical Geodesy) (1898); *Topografiya* (Topography) (1904); *Kartografiya* (Cartography) (1907); *Died:* 20 Mar 1924.

VITOLIN, P.Ya. (1892–1938) Party official; CP member from 1908; *Born:* 1892; *Career:* Party work in various Lat towns; after 1917 Feb Revol chm, Kaluga Province RSDRP(B) Comt; after 1917 Oct Revol chm, Kaluga Province Party Comt and chm, Kaluga Province Exec Comt; member, Tambov Province Party Comt and chm, Kozlovo Uyezd RCP(B) Comt; deleg, 8th RCP(B) Congress; during Civil War polit officer in Red Army on Southern Front; in latter years Party and Sov work; arrested by State Security organs; *Died:* 1938 in imprisonment.

VITTORF, Nikolay Mikhaylovich (1869–1929) Inorganic chemist and metallographer; prof, Mikhail Artillery Acad; *Born:* 25 Apr 1869; *Career:* 1904, in the course of thermal analysis of the nitrogen oxide-nitrogen dioxide system, demonstrated that NO and N_2O_4 form only one compound – nitrogen anhydride N_2O_3; 1909, on the basis of the theory of thermodynamic potential, provided conclusions to all types of diagrams for binary systems; hypothesized the existence of carbides with the probable composition Fe_4C, FeC and FeC_2; despite for eign criticism of this hypothesis, it was never refuted experimentally; *Publ: Teoriya splavov v primenenii k metalicheskim sistemam* (The Theory of Alloys Applied to Metallic Systems) (1909); *Predvaritel'noye issledovaniye pervichnoy kristallizatsii i posleduyushcikh fiziko-khimicheskikh prevrashcheniy v zhelezouglerodnykh splavakh, soderzhashchikh bolee 4% ugleroda* (A Preliminary Investigation of Primary Crystallization and Subsequent Physiochemical Conversions in Ferro-Carbon Alloys Containing More Than 4% Carbon) (1911); *Ucheniye o splavakh* (The Theory of Alloys) (1927), etc; *Died:* 1929.

VITVER, Ivan Aleksandrovich (1891–1966) Geographer; specialist in econ geography; prof from 1934; *Born:* 1891; *Educ:* 1921 grad Moscow Univ; *Career:* head, Chair of Econ-Polit Geography, Moscow Univ; from 1934 prof, State Inst of Int Relations; wrote works on econ geography of for countries, including Caribbean area, Latin America, Britain, Germany, etc; compiled econ geography maps; *Publ: Yuzhnaya Amerika* (South America) (1930); *Karaibskiye strany* (The Caribbean Countries) (1931); *Germaniya. Kratkiy ekonomiko-geograficheskiy ocherk* (Germany. A Short Economic-Geographical Study) (1945); *Frantsuzskaya shkola geografii cheloveka* (The French School of Human Geography) (1940); *Ekonomicheskaya geografiya Germanii* (The Economic Geography of Germany) (1939); *Istoriko-geograficheskoye vvedeniye v ekonomicheskuyu i politicheskuyu geogra-*

fiyu kapitalisticheskogo mira (A Historical-Geographical Introduction to the Economic and Political Geography of the Capitalist World) (1945); *Velikobritaniya. Ekonomiko-geograficheskiy ocherk* (Great Britain. An Economic-Geographical Study) (1947); *Ekonomicheskaya geografiya zarubezhnykh stran* (The Economic Geography of Foreign Countries) (1955); *Frantsiya. Ekonomicheskaya geografiya* (France. An Economic Geography) (1958); *Istoriko-geograficheskoye vvedeniye v ekonomicheskuyu geografiyu zarubezhnogo mira* (A Historic-Geographical Introduction to the Economic Geography of the Outside World) (1963); *Awards:* Stalin Prize (1951); *Died:* 17 Aug 1966.

VIV'YEN, Leonid Sergeyevich (1887–1966) Russian actor; chief stage dir, Pushkin State Acad Drama Theater, Leningrad from 1940; prof, Leningrad Theatrical Institute from 1940; Pop Artiste of USSR from 1954; CP member from 1945; *Born:* 29 Apr 1887; *Educ:* 1910 grad Petersburg Polytech Inst; 1913 grad Petersburg Theatrical College; *Career:* 1911–24 actor, 1924–38 stage dir, 1938–49 artistic dir, former Alexandrine Theater (now Leningrad State Acad Drama Theater); 1917–18 member, Provisional Comt to Manage the Moscow Acad Arts Theater; 1922 taught at Leningrad Theaterical Inst and ran Theater of Acting; 1929 dir, Red Army Theater, Leningrad; member, Theater Art Council, USSR Min of Culture; *Roles:* Yakov Bardin in Gorky's *Vragi* (The Enemy); Repetilov in Griboyedov's *Gore ot uma* (Woe from Wit); Zhadov and Karandyshev in Ostrovskiy's *Dokhodnoye mesto* (A Lucrative Post) and *Bespridannitsa* (Girl Without a Dowry); the Baron and Pyotr in Gorky's *Na dne* (The Lower Depths) and *Meshchane* (The Philistines); Prof Higgins in Shaw's "Pygmalion"; *Productions:* Gorky's *Deti solntsa* (Children of the Sun) and "Meshchane"; Leonov's *Nashestviye* (Invasion); Ostrovskiy's "Dokhodnoye mesto"; Gogol's *Revizor* (The Government Inspector); Shteyn's *Personal'noye delo* (A Personal Affair); Chekhov's *Chayka* (The Seagull); Alyoshin's *Vsyo ostayotsya lyudyam* (It's All Up to People), etc; *Publ: Vospominaniya o narodnoy artistke SSSR Ye.P. Korchaginoy-Aleksandrovskoy* (Reminiscences of the People's Artiste of the USSR Ye.P. Korchagina-Aleksandrovskaya); *Tvorcheskiy opyt actyora, rezhissyora i pedagoga* (The Creative Experience of an Actor, Stage Director and Teacher); *Awards:* Stalin Prize (1951); Order of Lenin (1957); *Died:* 1 Aug 1966.

VIZE, Vladimir Yul'yevich (1886–1954) Polar explorer and scientist; corresp member, USSR Acad of Sci from 1933; prof; *Born:* 21 Feb 1886; *Career:* 1912–14 took part in G.Ya. Sedov's Polar Expedition; 1921–22 took part in "Taymir" Arctic Expedition; 1924-28 and 1931 took part in "Malygin" Arctic Expedition; from 1928 assoc, Arctic Inst; took part in and helped direct following expeditions; 1929 and 1930 on the "Sedov"; 1932 on the "Sibiryakov"; 1934 on the "Litke"; 1936 and 1937 on the "Sadko"; 1930, during the "Sedov" Expedition, discovered an unknown island in the Kara Sea, now called Vize Island; predicted the existence of this island back in 1924 in his work "O poverkhnostnykh techeniyakh v Karskom more" (Surface Currents in the Kara Sea), based on an analysis of the drift of G.L. Brusilov's expeditionary ship, caught in the pack ice; 1932; during the "Sibiryakov" Expedition, performed the first non-stop passage of the Northern Sea Route, from 1945 prof, Leningrad Univ; wrote over 200 works, mainly on oceanology, meteorology, glaciology and history of Arctic research; studied patterns of atmospheric circulation and its role in the formation of the Arctic seas' ice cover and hydrological regime; *Publ: Nablyudeniya nad prilivami, proizvedyonnyye v 1912–13 godakh polyarnoy ekspeditsiyey G.Ya. Sedova v bukhte Svyatoy Foki na Novoy Zemle* (Tidal Observations Carried Out in 1912–13 by G.Ya. Sedov's Polar Expedition in Saint Phoca Bay on Novaya Zemlya) (1918); *Morya Sovetskoy Arktiki. Ocherki po istorii issledovaniya* (The Seas of the Soviet Arctic. An Outline History of Research) (3rd ed, 1948); *Uspekhi russkikh v issledovanii Arktiki* (The Achievements of Russians in the Study of the Arctic) (1948); *Russkiye polyarnyye morekhody iz promyshlennykh, torgovykh i sluzhilykh lyudey XVII–XIX vekov* (Russian Polar Mariners from the Industrial, Mercantile and Military Classes in the 17th–19th Centuries) (1948); *Na "Sibiryakove" i "Litke" cherez Ledovityye morya. Dva istoricheskikh plavaniya 1932 i 1934 godov* (On the "Sibiryakov" and the "Litke" Across the Arctic Seas. Two Historic Voyages of 1932 and 1934) (1946); *Awards:* Stalin Prize (1946); Order of Lenin; Grand Gold Medal of All-Union Geological Soc (1950); *Died:* 19 Feb 1954.

VLADIMIROV, Ivan Alekseyevich (1869–1947) Painter and graphic artist; Hon Art Worker of RSFSR from 1946; *Born:* 19 Dec 1869 in Vilnius; *Educ:* 1897 grad battle class, Petersburg Acad of Arts; *Career:* artist and correspondent for Russian illustrated journals in Russo-Japanese War, Balkan War and WW 1; portrayed many of his own experiences in Civil War; *Works:* paintings; "At the Fire" (1894); "The Benefactor" (1897); "Grief" (1902); "The Inventor and the Capitalist" (1905); "Artillery Battle" (1905); "The Battle of the Presna" (1906); "On Watch in Manchuria" (1912); "Cold in the Trenches" (1914); "Down with the Eagles" (1917); "The Landing of the "Aurora" Unit" (1923); "The Slaughter of Striking Workers" (1925); "Capturing Tanks at Kakhovka" (1927); "Liquidation of the Wrangel Front" (1932), etc; *Publ:* memoirs *Iz Port-Arturskogo bloknota* (From a Port Arthur Notebook) (1945); *Awards:* Orders of the Red Banner of Labor; medals; *Died:* 14 Dec 1947.

VLADIMIROV (real name: ITSEGSON), Mikhail Vladimirovich (1870–1932) Composer and conductor; *Born:* 16 Jan 1870 in Perkhov, Pskov Province; *Educ:* 1899 grad Petersburg Conservatory; *Career:* from 1897 conducted brass band; 1900–10 conducted Count A.D. Sheremetev's symphony orchestra in Petersburg; early 1900's founded Baltic Fleet music school; from 1905 head, Org Comt, Petersburg Soc for Orchestral Musician's Mutual Aid; 1920 founded Land Forces Mil Music School in Petrograd; taught brass band orchestration at Leningrad Conservatory and mil educ establishments; *Work:* original works and arrangements for brass bands, choral works, romances, etc; *Publ: Voyennaya muzyka v Rossii* (Martial Music in Russia) (1899); *Avtobiograficheskiye zametki* (Autobiographical Notes) (1914); *Muzyka v Krasnoy Armii* (Music in the Red Army) (1926); *Prakticheskoye rukovodstvo po instrumentovke dlya dukhovykh orkestrov* (A Practical Manual on Instrumentation for Brass Bands) (1930); *Died:* 13 Oct 1932 in Leningrad.

VLADIMIROV (real name: SHEYNFINKEL'), Miron Konstantinovich (Party name: LYOVA) (1879–1925) Party and govt official; CP member from 1917; *Born:* 15 Nov 1879; *Career:* 1903 joined RSDRP; did Party work in Gomel'; member, Polessian RSDRP Comt; deleg at 3rd RSDRP Congress; 1905–07 Party work in Petersburg, Odessa, Lugansk and Yekaterinoslav; Aug 1907 exiled to Siberia; May 1907 fled from exile and Lived in Vienna and Paris; 1911 lectured on nationality problems at Lenin's Party School at Longjumeau, near Paris; then sided with "reconciliationists"; Aug 1917 admitted to RSDRP(B) together with "Mezhrayontsy" group; at time of 1917 Oct Revol headed Petrograd Food Bd; then Collegium member, Pop Comrt of Food; 1919 member, Revol Mil Council and chm, Special Food Commission, Southern Front; 1921 Ukr Pop Comr of Food, then Ukr Pop Comr of Agric; 1922–24 RSFSR Pop Comr of Finance; then USSR Dep Pop Comr of Finance; from 1 Nov 1924 dep chm, USSR Supr Sovnarkhoz; 1925 cand member, CC, CPSU(B); 1925 member, USSR and All-Russian Centr Exec Comt; *Publ: Stat'i, rechi, pis'ma (1920–25)* (Articles, Speeches and Letters /1920–25/) (1925); *Ocherednyye zadachi khozyaystvennogo stroitel'stva* (Present Tasks in the Building of the Economy) (1925); *Died:* 20 Mar 1925 of a lung hemorrhage; his ashes were immured in the Kremlin Wall on Moscow's Red Square.

VLADIMIROV, Pyotr Parfenovich (1905–1953) Dipl with rank of amb extraordinary and plen; CP member from 1927; *Born:* 1905; *Educ:* grad Moscow Inst of Oriental Studies; *Career:* began work as locksmith's apprentice at Voronezh Locomotive Maintenance Plant; from 1931 in Red Army; from 1935 student; 1941–48 TASS correspondent in China; 1948–51 USSR consul-gen in Shanghai; 1952–53 USSR amb in Burma; *Awards:* Order of Lenin; Order of the Red Banner; Order of the Fatherland War; Order of the Red Star; medals; *Died:* Sept 1953 in Moscow.

VLADIMIROV (real name: BERLE), Vladimir Konstantinovich (1886–1953) Theater manager; *Born:* 1886; *Educ:* grad Moscow Univ; *Career:* 1906 stage debut in Moscow; 1910–14 acted in provinces; 1921–22 worked in Simferopol'; Collegium member, Crimean Council of Pop Comr; chm, Crimean Art Workers' Bd; dir, Simferopol' Drama Theater; 1923–24 head, Art Dept, Pop Comrt of Educ; ed, Moscow Journal "Khudozhnik i zritel'"; from 1924 rector, State Inst of Stagecraft and dir, Maly Theater; 1934–38 artistic dir, State Music, Variety and Circus Assoc; 1939–48 head, Creative Workshop, Bolshoy Theater; 1948–53 consultant, Presidium, All-Russian Theatrical Soc; *Died:* 1953.

VLADIMIROVA, Mariya Vladimirovna (1879–1965) Chamber singer and singing teacher; Hon Art Worker of RSFSR from 1945; Hon Art Worker of Bash ASSR from 1946; *Born:* 17 Jan 1879 in

Astrakhan'; *Educ:* 1908 grad Moscow Conservatory; *Career:* as concert singer performed in many Russian cities; from 1906 taught singing; from 1939 prof, Moscow Conservatory; trained singers from Tatar and Bash ASSR and other republ; *Died:* 8 Nov 1965 in Moscow.

VLADIMIRSKIY, Mikhail Fyodorovich (1874–1951) Party and govt official; CP member from 1895; *Born:* 20 Feb 1874 in Arzamas; *Educ:* grad Med Fac, Moscow Univ; *Career:* in 1890's took part in Marxist circles in Nizhniy Novgorod, then as a student in Moscow; 1896 arrested and exiled until 1898 for helping to found Moscow Workers' Union; 1898–99 worked for Moscow RSDRP Org; spring 1899 again exiled, then went abroad; worked for "Iskra" group; 1903–05 Party work in Nizhniy Novgorod; from fall 1905 Party work in Moscow; member, Moscow RSDRP(B) Comt; took part in Dec 1905 armed uprising in Moscow; 1906 rearrested but emigrated to France before he could be brought to trial; worked for Parish Bolshevik Group and for Comt of For Party Orgs; from July 1917 Bureau member, Moscow RSDRP(B) Comt; during 1917 Oct Revol member, Party battle center directing uprising in Moscow; after 1917 Oct Revol worked for Presidium, Moscow Sov; 1918 at 7th RCP(B) Congress elected member, CC, RCP(B); 1919–21 Presidium member, All-Russian Centr Exec Comt; RSFSR Dep Pop Comr of Internal Affairs; 1922–25 secr, CC, CP(B) Ukr; chm, Centr Control Commission, CP(B) Ukr; Ukr Pop Comr of Workers and Peasants' Inspection; dep chm, Ukr Council of Pop Comr; 1925 at 14th Party Congress elected member, CPSU(B) Centr Control Commission; 1926–27 dep chm, USSR Gosplan; 1927–51 chm, CPSU(B) Centr Auditing Commission; 1930–34 RSFSR Pop Comr of Health; dep, USSR Supr Sov; contributed articles to journal "Vlast' Sovetov"; wrote a number of works on the building of socialism in the USSR; *Publ: organizatsiya sovetskoy vlasti na mestakh* (The Local-Level Organization of Soviet Rule) (1919), etc; *Awards:* two Orders of Lenin; *Died:* 2 Apr 1951; buried on Moscow's Red Square.

VLADIMIRTSOV, Boris Yakovlevich (1884–1931) Orientalist; specialist in Mongolian language and history; prof from 1921; member, USSR Acad of Sci from 1929; *Born:* 20 July 1884 in Kamenets-Podol'skiy; *Educ:* 1909 grad Fac of Oriental Languages, Petersburg Univ; *Career:* 1911 toured Western Mongolia to collect linguistic, folkloristic and ethnographic material; 1912 sent for further studies to Paris and London; while in Paris compiled a catalog of Mongolian books and manuscripts in the Nat Library and attended lectures by leading French Orientalists; while in London did research at British Museum; after completion of studies in Western Europe spent over two years in Mongolia recording epic lit; kept detailed journals which were subsequently lost; also evaluated the collection of Mongolian documents at the Asian Museum, USSR Acad of Sci; *Publ: Turetskiye elementy v mongol'skom yazyke* (Turkish Elements in the Mongolian Language) (1911); *Mongol'skiy sbornik rasskazov iz "Pancatantra"* (A Mongolian Anthology of Stories from the "Pancatanthra") (1921); *Chingiskhan* (Genghis Khan) (1922); annotated translation *Mongolo-oyratskiy geroicheskiy epos* (The Mongol-Oirat Heroic Epic) (1923); *Sravitel'naya grammatika mongol'skogo pis'mennogo yazyka i khalkhaskogo narechiya.* (A Comparative Grammar of Written Mongolian and the Khalkha Dialect) (1929); *Mongol'skiy literaturnyy yazyk* (Literary Mongolian) (1931), etc; *Died:* 17 Aug 1931 in Leningrad.

VLASENKO, Stepan Numovich (1888–1963) Govt official; CP member from 1913; *Born:* 1888; *Career:* at age ten began work in Donbass mines, then factory worker in Southern Russia; 1916 arrested and exiled to Irkutsk Province for revol activities; during 1917 Oct Revol comr, Yekaterinoslav Railroad; fought in Civil War in Ukr and Turkestan; 1921–27 govt work in Ukr; 1927–29 secr, All-Ukr Centr Exec Comt; 1930–54 exec econ work; from 1954 pensioner; *Died:* Mar 1963.

VLASOV, Aleksandr Vasil'yevich (1900–1962) Architect; member, USSR and Ukr Acad of Architecture; CP member from 1949; *Born:* 1 Feb 1900 in vil Koshi, now Kalinin Oblast; *Educ:* 1928 grad Architectural Dept, Moscow Higher Tech College; 1936 grad Postgrad Fac, USSR Acad of Architecture; *Career:* 1944–50 chief architect of Kiev; 1950–55 chief architect of Moscow; 1955–56 directed construction of Luzhniki Sports Complex in Moscow; 1955–56 pres, USSR Acad of Architecture; 1956–61 vice-pres, USSR Acad of Construction and Architecture; from 1931 taught at Moscow Architectural Inst, USSR Acad of Architecture, etc; 1932–41 helped draft Moscow gen plan; 1941–44 designed plans for extension of communities in Eastern USSR; *Works:* designs for: All-Union Centr Trade-Union Council building, Moscow (1931–39); parts of Centr Park of Culture and Rest, Moscow; interior of Moscow Pioneers Center (1936); Sov Square, Moscow (1939); interiors of Centr Architects' Club, Moscow (1940); architectural details of Crimean Bridge, Moscow (1936–38); coauthor, Kiev gen reconstruction plan; *Awards:* Stalin Prize (1950); Lenin Prize (1959); Order of Lenin; Order of the Red Banner of Labor; medals; *Died:* 25 Sept 1962.

VLASOV, Andrey Andreyevich (1900–1946) Mil commander, lt-gen; founder and leader of anti-Sov Russian Liberation Movement and commander in Chief, Russian Liberation Army during WW 2; CP member from 1930; *Born:* 1900 in Vladimir Province, now Ivanovo Oblast; *Educ:* grad mil college, then Frunze Mil Acad; *Career:* from 1918 in Red Army; rose from private to commander of a front; from 1938 Sov mil adviser in China; late 1938 recalled from China and appointed commander of infantry regt, then div with forces of Ukr Mil Distr; 1940 led his div in the occupation of Western Ukr; 1940 Vlasov's 99th Div was rated the best trained after an inspection by Pop Comr of Defense Timoshevnko; with start of WW 2 commandered motor-mechanized corps, with which he retreated from Western Ukr to Kiev area; Aug–Sept 1941 commanded army in battle of Kiev and commanded Kiev Fortified Area on Southwestern Front; after the Sov forces group at Kiev was routed, Vlasov broke out of German encirclement with the remains of his army and joined up with main body of Sov troops; Dec 1941–Jan 1942 in battle of Moscow commanded 20th Sov Army on Zhukov's Western Front and in winter counter-offensive near Moscow achieved first major Sov success, taking Solnechnogorsk and smashing the Germans' 2nd Tank Div and two infantry div; winter 1942 appointed dep commander of chief, Volkhov Front; Feb–Apr 1942 in the operation to lift the blockade of Leningrad, when two Sov armies were surrounded on the western bank of the Volkhov, he coordinated the operations of the surrounded armies which, for a long time, the Sov command would not allow to break out of encirclement; summer 1942, after these armies were routed, retreated to the forests with the remnants of the Sov units and was finaly captured by the Germans; he later testified that it was at this time that he underwent a crisis in his Communist outlook, caused by his realization that the Sov high command was mismanaging mil operations, the contradiction between the interests of the people and the regime, dawning nationalist feelings and his awareness that the Sov regime was incapable of polit evolution; this explains the fact that, while in German captivity, he agreed to head an anti-Sov Russian nationalist movement; fall 1942 published his "Smolensk Appeal", urging Russians to fight the Communist regime and headed the Russian Nat Comt; however, the German polit authorities' decision to use his name for propaganda purposes virtually prevented development of this liberation movement; from 1942 to fall 1944 he did everything he could to try and overcome the German Nazi regime's opposition to development of the "Liberation Movement", but it was not until the fall of 1944 that the Nazis removed some of their obstacles; Nov 1944 the Comt for the Liberation of the Peoples of Russia published in Prague a manifest outlining the Liberation Movements' polit program and Vlasov was authorized to form two divs of the Russian Liberation Army from the various Russian battalions scattered throughout the German Army; May 1945, with the occupation of Czechoslovakia by the American and Sov forces, he surrendered with his two divs to the Americans but was handed over to Sov authorities together with his closest aides; *Awards:* Order of Lenin; Order of the Red Banner; medal "Twenty Years of the Red Army"; *Died:* Aug 1946 hanged in Moscow together with 11 of his closest aides.

VLASOV, Vasiliy Zakharovich (1906–1958) Civil eng; Dr of Tech Sci from 1936; prof; corresp member, USSR Acad of Sci from 1956; *Born:* 24 Feb 1906 in vil Karevo, now Kaluga Oblast; *Educ:* 1924–26 studied at Geodesy Fac, Moscow Surveying Inst; 1930 grad Civil Eng Fac, Moscow Higher Tech College; *Career:* 1930–42 lectured at Chair of Construction Mech, Higher Construction Eng College; 1930–51 also at Centr Research Inst of Ind Structures; from 1931 also prof, Moscow's Kuybyshev Construction Eng Inst; specialized in calculation and design of thin-walled spatial shell-type systems for ind and mil objects (ind buildings, hangars and covered slips); ran seminar on construction mech, elasticity theory and theory of plasticity at Inst of Mech, USSR Acad of Sci; chm, Theory of Structures Section, Commission for Construction Problems, USSR Acad of Sci; *Publ: Stroitel'naya* *mekhanika obolochek* (Shell Construction Mechanics) (1936); *Tonkostennyye uprugiye sterzhni* (Thin-Walled Elastic Beams) (1940); *Obshchaya teoriya obolochek* (General Shell Theory) (1949); *Stroitel'naya mekhanika tonkostennykh prostranstvennykh sistem* (The Construction Mechanics of Thin-Walled Spatial Systems) (1949), etc; *Awards:* two Stalin Prizes (1941 and 1951); *Died:* 7 Aug 1958.

VLYZ'KO, Aleksey Fyodorovich (1908–1934) Ukr poet; *Born:* 17 Feb 1908 in vil Korosten', now Novgorod Oblast, son of a psalmist; *Educ:* studied at Lit Fac, Kiev Inst of Public Educ; *Career:* at age 14 or 15 lost his speech and hearing; 1925 first work printed; member, "Molodnyak" lit assoc and All-Ukr Assoc of Proletarian Writers; influenced by Ukr Futurists; his works are marked by zest for life and rich lyricism; welcomed romantic aspects of the building of socialism but criticized Sov encroachment of nat rights; Dec 1934 accused as "White Guard terrorist" and sentenced to death by Mil Collegium, USSR Supr Court; *Publ:* verse collections: "I Shall Speak for All" (1927); "The Journey" (1930); "Book of Ballads" (1930); "Ordinance March" (1931); "The Drunken Ship" (1933); "My Friend Don Juan" (1934), etc; *Died:* 16 Dec 1934 executed; posthumously rehabilitated.

VOBLYY, Konstantin Grigor'yevich (1876–1947) Ukr economist, geographer and statistician; member and vice-pres, Ukr Acad of Sci; *Born:* 7 May 1876 in Chary-Tsanty, now Poltava Oblast, son of a priest; *Educ:* 1904 grad Law Fac, Warsaw Univ; *Career;* from 1906 assoc prof, then prof, Kiev Univ and Kiev Business Inst; 1928–30 vice-res, Ukr Acad of Sci; 1943–47 dir, Inst of Econ, Ukr Acad of Sci, from 1945 member, Ukr Gosplan; wrote numerous works on econ and statistics containing a wealth of factual material; wrote several textbooks on econ geography; *Publ: Ocherki po istorii pol'skoy fabrichnoy promyshlennosti* (An Outline History of the Polish Manufacturing Industry) (1909); *Tret'ya professional'no-promyslovaya perepis' v Germanii. Opyt analitiko-metodologicheskogo issledovaniya* (The Third Trades and Crafts Census in Germany. An Analytical and Methodological Study) (1911); *Osnovy ekonomii strakhovaniya* (The Principles of Insurance Economics) (1923); *Opyt istorii sveklosakharnoy promyshlennosti SSR* (A History of the USSR Sugar Beet Industry) (1928); *Ekonomicheskaya geografiya Ukrainy* (The Economic Geography of the Ukraine) (1930); *Ocherki iz istorii russko-ukrainskoy sakharnoy promyshlennosti* (An Outline History of the Russian and Ukrainian Sugar Industry) (1930–31); *Problema bol'shogo Dnepra* (The Problem of the Greater Dnieper) (1933); *Organizatsiya truda nauchnogo rabotnika* (Labor Organization for Scientific Personnel) (1949); *Awards:* Order of Lenin; Order of the Red Banner of Labor; *Died:* 12 Sept 1947.

VOINOV, A. I. (1880–1964) Admin official; CP member from 1919; *Born:* 1880; *Career:* fought in Civil War; from Dec 1919 comr of track maintenance, Omsk Railroad, 1920-21 chief comr and dir, Tomsk Railroad, then with Pop Comrt of Means of Communication: comr, then dep chief comr, Learned Tech Comt; comr, Tech Bd; 1922–29 dep dir, Oct Railroad; 1929–35 chm, Centr Eng and Tech Section and Presidium member, CC, Railroad Workers' Union; from 1935 exec work with Pop Comrt (later Min) of Communications; *Died:* 1964.

VOLGIN, Vyacheslav Petrovich (1879–1962) Historian; Party official; prof from 1919; member, USSR Acad of Sci from 1930; CP member from 1920; *Born:* 14 June 1879; *Educ:* 1908 grad History and Philology Fac, Moscow Univ; *Career:* from 1899 active in revol movement; arrested and exiled to Eastern Siberia; 1911–17 worked for Gorky's journal "Letopis'" also taught at Shanyavskiy Pop Univ and on Prechistenka Workers' Courses; 1917 co-ed, periodical "Izvestiya Moskovskogo Soveta"; 1918 co-founder, Socialist (later Communist) Acad; from 1919 prof and dean, Soc Sci Fac, 1921–25 rector and 1925–30 prof and dean, History and Philosophy Fac, Moscow Univ; 1919–29 also member, State Learned Council; 1921–22 dep chm, Main Trade and Tech Training Comt; 1921–23 chm, High School Council, USSR Pop Comrt of Educ; in 1920's, together with M.N. Pokrovskiy, founded and directed Inst of Red Prof, Inst of History, Russian Assoc of Soc Sci Research Institutes, Communist Acad, and Soc of Marxist Historians; 1930–35 secr, 1942–46 acad secr, Dept of History and Philosophy, 1942–53 vice-pres, USSR Acad of Sci; 1945–48 chief ed, journal "Voprosy istorii"; 1946–49 chm, Commission for the History of Historiography; from 1956 chm, French History Study Group, Inst of History, USSR Acad of Sci; also headed Socialist Ideas Study Group; founded and ran series *Predshestvenniki nauchnogo sotsializma* (The Precursors of Scientific Socialism); chief ed, 30-vol collection of Herzen's works; 1928, 1933 and 1960 attended Int Congress of Historical Sci in Oslo, Warsaw and Stockholm; 1947 headed Sov deleg at All-Ind Sci Congress; 1958 head, Sov deleg at Franco-Sov historians conference, Paris; 1949–50 member, Int Peace Comt; 1949 and 1950 attended 1st and 2nd World Peace Congresses; from 1947 hon dr of history, Delhi Univ; specialized in history of socialist ideas; founded new branches of historiography – history of socialist and Communist ideas; in 1920's, together with M.N. Pokrovskiy, directed Soc of Marxist Historians and campaigned against non-Marxist historians; in 1930's and 1940's turned against his former colleague and campaigned against Pokrovskiy's Marxist historical school; *Publ: Ocherki po istorii sotsializma* (An Outline History of Socialism) (1923); *Sen-Simon i sensimonizm* (Saint-Simon and Saint-Simonism) (1925); *Istoriya sotsialisticheskikh idey* (The History of Socialist Ideas) (2 vol, 1928–31); *Sotsial'nyye i politicheskiye idei vo Frantsii pered revolyutsiyey (1748–1789)* (Social and Political Ideas in France Prior to the Revolution /1748–1789/) (1940); *Razvitiye obshchestvennoy mysli vo Frantsii v XVIII veke* (The Development of Social Thought in France in the 18th Century) (1958); *Frantsuzskiy utopicheskiy kommunizm* (French Utopian Communism) (1960), etc; *Awards:* three orders of Lenin; Order of the Red Banner of Labor; medals, Stalin Prize (1961); *Died:* 3 July 1962.

VOLIN, Abram Grigor'yevich (1895–1967) Party and govt official; CP member from 1917; *Born:* 1895; *Educ:* 1928 grad Moscow Higher Tech College; *Career:* 1913–18 teacher; 1918–19 chm, Ruzhin Revol Comt, Kiev Province; 14th Army's Revol-Mil Council plen for establishment of Sov rule; 1928–55 exec work with Pop Comrt of Heavy Ind and Pop Comrt of For Trade; from 1955 pensioner; *Died:* 31 May 1967.

VOLIN, (real name: FRADKIN), Boris Mikhaylovich (1886–1957) Govt official and journalist; CP member from 1904; *Born:* 1 June 1886; *Educ:* 1913 grad Moscow Univ; *Career:* 1905 member, Yekaterinoslav Marty Comt; 1906–07 Party work in Bryansk and in the Urals; ed, underground Bolshevik newspaper "Ufimskiy rabochiy"; frequently arrested; 1910 emigrated; in Paris studied at law fac; 1913 returned to Russia and resumed Marty work; 1917 member, Moscow RSDRP(B) Comt; during 1917 Oct Revol chm, Zamoskvorech'yev Mil Revol Comt; 1918 co-ed, newspaper "Pravda"; 1918–21 chm, Orel, Kostroma, then Khar'kov Province Exec Comt; Ukr Dep Pop Comr of Internal Affairs; 1921–24 ed, newspaper "Rabochaya Moskva" and journal "Perets"; 1924–25 secr, Sov mission in France; 1925–26 dep ed, newspaper "Izvestiya TsIK"; 1926–27 head, Tass Bureau in Vienna; 1927–29 head, Press Dept, Pop Comrt of For Affairs; 1931–32 Collegium member, Pop Comrt of Educ and head, Main Bd for Lit and Publ Houses; from 1932 dir, Inst of Red Prof and ed, journal "Bor'ba klassov"; 1934–35 head, Schools Dept, CC, CPSU(B); during WW 2 served with partisans; from 1945 assoc, Inst of Marx-Engels-Lenin, CC, CPSU; wrote numerous works on Party history and gen politics; *Publ: Vsenarodnaya partizanskaya voyna* (Popular Partisan Warfare) (1942); *Statistika i politika* (Statistics and Politics) (1947); *Lenin v Povolzh'ye. 1870–93* (Lenin in the Volga Area. 1870–93) (1955), etc; *Awards:* Order of Lenin; two Orders of the Fatherlands War, 1st Class; Order of the Red Banner of Labor; medals; *Died:* 16 Feb 1957.

VOLKONSKAYA, Sof'ya Nikolayevna (1889–1942) Health educ official and theorist; *Born:* 1889; *Educ:* 1915 grad Moscow Higher Women's Courses; *Career:* 1916–17 worked at a private mental asylum and Savelovskiy Hospital; simultaneously did underground work for RSDRP(B); during Oct 1917 helped to organize med aid for victims of street fighting in Moscow; 1921–29 in charge of a health educ org, Moscow Health Dept; 1929–39 founder-dir, Moscow Oblast Inst of Health Training (now Central Health Educ Research Inst, USSR Min of Health); 1936 read paper at 1st All-Union Conference of Health Educ Workers; from 1939 assoc prof, Chair of Med History, Centr Inst of Postgrad Med Training, Moscow; during WW 2 did research on sci health educ methods; *Publ: Opyt Moskovskogo sanprosveta* (The Experience of the Health Education Service in Moscow) (1924); *Sanitarnoye prosveshcheniye i dispanserizatsiya* (Health Education and the Outpatient System) (1926); coauthor, *Sanitarnoye prosveshcheniye v rekonstruktivnyy periodj* (Health Education in the Period of Reconstruction) (1930), etc; *Died:* 1942.

VOLKONSKIY (real name: MURAV'YOV), Nikolay Osipovich (1890–1948) Stage dir; Hon Artiste of RSFSR from 1928; *Born:*

1890; *Educ:* 1910–13 studied at K.V. Bravich, F.F. Komissarzhevskiy and M.P. Yartsev's drama school, Moscow; *Career:* 1914–18 at Komissarzhevskaya Theater; 1919–31 at Maly Theater; 1932 at Music Hall; 1920–21 and 1926–27 stage dir, Korsh Theater; 1922–26 stage dir, Komissarzhevskaya Theater; 1927–30 co-founder and dir, Trade-Union Club Workshop; also staged plays at Moscow Drama and Comedy Theater; produced a number of radio shows and variety shows; *Productions: Nedorosl'* (The Ignoramus) (1923); Sukhovo-Kobylin's *Otzhitoye vremya* (Used Time) (1923); Shakespeare's "Comedy of Errors" (1923); Ostrovskiy's *Dokhodnoye mesto* (A Lucrative Post) (1926); Glebov's "Zagmuk" (1925); Ostrovskiy's *Na vsyakogo mudretsa dovol'no prostoty* (There's a Simpleton in Every Sage) (1928); Averkiyev's *Kashirskaya starina* (Life in Old Kashira) (1946); *Died:* 1948.

VOLKOV, Ivan Mikhaylovich (1899–1964) Party historian; col; prof from 1938; CP member from 1920; *Born:* 1899, son of a worker; *Educ:* 1924 grad Higher Mil Teachers' Training School; 1934 grad Inst of Red Prof; *Career:* 1919–49 in Red Army; rose from private to col and head, army polit dept; fought in Civil War; taught in various mil educ establishments; head, Chair of Marxist-Leninist Principles, Kuybyshev Mil Eng Acad and Frunze Mil Acad; fought in WW 2; 1946–64 prof and dep head, Chair of Party History, Acad of Soc Sci, CC, CPSU; member, ed bd, journal "Voprosy istorii"; *Publ:* coauthor, *Istoriya Kommunisticheskoy partii Sovetskogo Soyuza* (History of the Communist Party of the Soviet Union) (1959), etc; *Awards:* Order of Lenin; Order of the Red Banner; Order of the Fatherland War, 1st and 2nd Class; medals; *Died:* 14 Jan 1964.

VOLKOV, Konstantin Vasil'yevich (1871–1938) Surgeon; hon Dr of Med from 1935; *Born:* 1871; *Educ:* 1893 grad Natural Sci Dept, Fac of Physics and Mathematics, Kazan' Univ; 1897 grad Med Fac, Moscow Univ; *Career:* after grad worked as a physician in Bogorodsk, Moscow Province; 1901–07 worked in Yalta Uyezd; during Russo-Japanese War worked at a hospital in Manchuria; 1905–07 took active part in Revol, for which he was arrested; 1907 exiled to Yadrin; 1908–11 worked as a physician at a sugar refinery in Brailova, Podol'sk Province; 1911–38 worked in Yadrin, Chuvash ASSR, where he performed a total of 30,000 surgical, gynecological, eye and other operations; did research on use of dialectic method in med; championed application of Marxist-Leninist principles in med in a series of polemical articles published by journal "Khirurgiya na rasput'i"; lectured on med dialectics at Leningrad and Kazan' Inst of Postgrad Med Training; also did research on health service org, med statistics, med training and clinical observation techniques; devised several new operations; attended several Russian and All-Union surgeons' congresses; chaired four congresses of Tatar physicians; chm, 3rd Congress of Volga Physicians; 1932–38 bd member, All-Union Soc of Surgeons; from 1927 member, Chuvash Centr Exec Comt; also member, Yadrin City Sov and Yadrin City CPSU(B) Comt; wrote 84 works; *Publ: Nabroski i vospominaniya o L. N. Tolstom* (Sketches and Reminiscences of L. N. Tolstoy) (1920); *Khirurgicheskoye lecheniye yazvy zheludka* (The Surgical Treatment of Stomach Ulcers) (1923); *Khirurgiya v puti* (Surgery under Way) (1927); *Ob odnom iz novykh putey v khirurgii* (A New Way in Surgery) (1930); *Dialektika v khirurgii* (Dialectics in Surgery) (1930); *Khirurgiya vne opasnosti* (Surgery Out of Danger) (1931), etc; *Awards:* Hero of Labor; *Died:* 1938.

VOLKOV, Nikolay Dmitriyevich (1894–1965) Theater critic and historian; playwright; *Born:* 22 Dec 1894 in Penza; *Works:* libretto for ballets: *Plamya Parizha* (The Flame of Paris); *Bakhchisarayskiy fontan* (The Fountain of Bakhchisaray); *Kavkazskiy plennik* (Prisoner of the Caucasus); *Serdtse gor* (Heart of the Mountains); *Zolushka* (Cinderella); *Spartak* (Spartacus), etc; *Publ:* monographs: *Aleksandr Blok i teatr* (Aleksandr Blok and the Theater) (1926); *Russkiy teatr i Meyyerkhol'd* (The Russian Theater and Meyerhold) (1928), etc; *Died:* 3 Apr 1965 in Moscow.

VOLKOV, Roman Mikhaylovich (1885–1959) Lit historian; prof; *Born:* 1 Oct 1885 in Novgorod–Severskiy; *Educ:* 1912 grad Nezhin History and Philology Inst; *Career:* 1918–20 assoc prof, 1920-41 prof, Odessa Univ; then prof, L'vov and Chernovtsy Univs; specialized in Russian and Ukr folklore folk drama and folk tales; pioneered study of style and composition of Russian folk tales; *Publ: Skazka. Razyskaniya po syuzhetoslozheniyu narodnoy skazki. Skazka velikorusskaya, ukrainskaya i belorusskaya* (The Folk Tale. Research on the Theamatics of Folk Tales. Great Russian, Ukrainian and Belorussian Folk Tales) (vol 1, 1924); *Narodnyye istoki tvorchestva A.S. Pushkina* (The Folk Sources of A.S. Pushkin's Work) (1960); *Narodnyye istoki "Pesni pro tsarya Ivana Vasil'yevicha" Lermontova* (The Folk Sources of Lermontov's "The Ballad of Tsar Ivan Vasil'yevich") (1960); *Died:* 6 May 1959 at Chernovtsy.

VOLKOV, Yefim Yefimovich (1844–1920) Landscape painter; prof; member, Petersburg Acad of Arts from 1899; *Born:* 1844; *Educ:* 1867–69 studied at Petersburg Acad of Arts; *Career:* 1870 received artist's diploma; from 1872 member, Soc for the Promotion of the Arts; from 1880 member, Assoc of Itinerant Art Exhibitions; 1878–1918 contributed to these exhibitions; his works are displayed at the Tret'yakov Gallery in Moscow and at the Russian Museum in Leningrad; *Works:* paintings: "Swamp in Autumn" (1871); "A Trip to Market" (1874); "The Forest in Spring" (1876); "Winter Landscape" (1876); "October" (1883); "Early Snow" (1883); "At Night-Time" (1884); "Morning on the Volga" (1899); "Late Evening" (1901); "Above the River" (1901); "Spring Morning" (1905); "Silence" (1912); "Spring", "Two Pines", "The Windmill", etc (post 1917); *Died:* 1920.

VOLKOVICH, Daniil Ivanovich (1900–1943) Bel Party official; second secr, CC, CP Bel from 1934; CP member from 1919; *Born:* 1900 in vil Zanemansk, Grodno Province, son of a Peasant; *Educ:* 1915 completed primary school in Zanemansk; 1924 grad workers' fac, Minsk; *Career:* 1915 evacuated with his family to Vyatka Province; from 1918 in Red Army, first at front against Kolchak, then with All-Russian Cheka; 1920 secr, Malmyzh Uyezd RCP(B) Comt, Vyatka Province; from Aug 1920 head, Special Mil Dept, Polish Front in Bel; then commanded Komsomol platoon which helped crush anti-Sov revolts in Mozyr' Uyezd; 1921–24 member, CC, Bel Komsomol; head, Dept of Rural Affairs, then instructor, CC, CP(B) Bel; 1924–26 secr, Koydan Rayon Party Comt; 1926–28 secr, Lyakhovichi Rayon Party Comt, Minsk; 1928–30 worked for CC, CP(B) Bel; then head, Org Dept, Mogilev Okrug Party Comt; 1930–34 first secr, Klimovichi Rayon Party Comt; then first secr, Bobruysk City Party Comt; 1934 Bel Dep Pop Comr of Agric; Aug 1934–May 1937 second secr, CC, CP(B) Bel; from June 1937 chm, Bel Council of Pop Comr; 9 Sept 1937 arrested by NKVD; *Died:* 17 Apr 1943 in imprisonment;

VOLKOVICH, Nikolay Markianovich (1858–1928) Surgeon; member, Ukr Acad of Sci from 1928; *Born:* 8 Dec 1858 in Gorodnya, Chernigov Province; *Educ:* 1882 grad Kiev Univ; *Career:* 1882–85 intern, Prof Borngaunt's Hospital Surgical Clinic, Kiev; 1888 defended doctor's thesis; 1893–1903 head, Surgical Dept, Kiev City Alexandrine Hospital; from 1903 head, Hospital Surgical Clinic, Kiev Univ; 1911–22 head, Chair of Fac Surgical Clinic, from 1923 head, Chair of Med Research, Kiev Branch, Main Bd for Sci, Museum and Artistic Research Establishments; described new symptoms of chronic appendicitis ("Volkovich-muscular symptom"); 1906 designed new apparatus and splint for treating fractures of the extremities (Volkovich splint); invented new operations: extracapullar exsection of the knee joint for tuberculosis; formation of a nose from a finger; (1910); osteoplastic trepanning of the mastoid process; plastic closure of colpocystosyrinxes (1904); 1898, independently of the American surgeon MacBurney, began to use an oblique physiological incision of the abdominal wall for appendectomy, known as the "MacBurney Incision"; 1908 founded Kiev Surgical Soc; wrote over 80 works: *Publ: K khirurgii i patologii zhyolchno-kamennoy bolezni* (The Surgery and Pathology of Cholelithiasis) (1909); *Appenditsit, zhyolchno-kamennaya bolezn', turberkulyoznyy peritonit* (Appendicitis, Cholelithiasis and Tubercular Peritonitis) (1926); *Povrezhdeniya kostey i sustavov* (Injuries of the Bones and Joints) (1928); *Died:* 11 July 1928 in Kiev.

VOL'NOV (real name: VLADIMIROV), Ivan Yegorovich (1885–1931) Russian writer; *Born:* 1885 in vil Bogorodskoye, Oryol Province; *Educ:* grad Kursk Teachers' Seminary; *Career:* taught at vil schools in Oryol Province; from 1903 member, Socialist-Revol Party; 1908 exiled to Siberia for attempted assassination of Mtsensk Distr police officer; 1910 fled from exile and made his way abroad; met Gorky on Capri; 1917 returned to Russia and fought in Civil War; 1920's settled in his native vil; 1912 first work printed; *Publ:* stories *Tri gryozy* (Three Day-Dreams) and *Kak eto bylo* (How It Was); autobiographical *Povest' o dnyakh moyey zhizni* (A Tale of the Days of My Life), including: *Detstvo* (Childhood), *Otrochestvo* (Adolescence) (1912) and *Yunost'* (Youth) (1913); novelettes: *Na rubezhe* (On the Border) (1926); *Vstrecha* (Encounter) (1927); *Vozvrashcheniye* (The Return) (1928); *Sobraniye sochineniy* (Collected Works) (1928); *Died:* 9 Jan 1931.

VOLNUKHIN, Sergey Mikhaylovich (1859–1921) Sculptor; member, Petersburg Acad of Arts from 1910; *Born:* 8 Nov 1859; *Educ:* 1880 grad Moscow College of Painting, Sculpture and Architecture; *Career:* 1895–1917 taught at Moscow College of Painting, Sculpture and Architecture, from 1918 at Free Art Workshops; *Works:* busts of M.S. Shchepkin (1893), P.M. Tret'yakov (1901) and S.A. Ivanov (1901); monument to "I.Fyodorov, the Printing Pioneer" (1910) 1909); Shevchenko Monument (1918); design for K.D. Ushinskiy Monument (1919), etc; *Died:* 11 June 1921.

VOLOBUYEV, Mikhail (1900– ?) Ukr economist; *Born:* 1900; *Career:* lectured at Khar'kov Inst of Nat Econ; also assoc, All-Ukr Pedag Research Inst; 1928 theoretical organ of CP(B) Ukr, journal "Bil'shovyk Ukrainy" published his work "On the Problems of the Ukrainian Economy", rejecting the dogma of the unity of the Imperialist Russian econ prior to the revol and demonstrating that the Ukr was "a historically formed, economic organism" which had its own paths of development and needed independence of existence even in the "socialist stage of development"; also demonstrated Ukraine's colonial dependence on Sov Russia and stressed the need to ensure "Ukr econ centers their rights and opportunities to effectively manage the entire national economy"; urged abolition of the system whereby ind was managed by All-Union trusts in Moscow and stressed that the Ukr govt alone should approve the Ukr SSR's budget and control the Ukr econ; staunchly advocated econ independence of Sov Ukr; his arguments were termed "nationalistic" and a massiv campaign was launched against him; was accused of furnishing econ justification for "nationalist deviationism" in the CP(B) Ukr ("Shumskyism" was regarded as the polit embodiment, and "Khvylyovyism" as the cultural embodiment of "nationalist deviation"); although he had no connection with either Shumskiy or Khvylyovyy, he was nevertheless lumped together with them, 1928, after scathing criticism by Sov and Party authorities, he published in "Bil'shovyk Ukrainy" a letter recanting his views; 1930 published in this periodical the article "Against the Economic Platform of Nationalism", borrowing official arguments to attack his own views, now known as "Volobuyevism"; with the suppression of Ukr nat Communism, he was arrested and exiled to Kazakhstan; further fate unknown; *Died:* date and place of death unknown.

VOLODARSKIY, V. (real name: GOL'DSHTEYN, Moisey Markovich) (1891–1918) Party official; Jew; CP member from 1917; *Born:* 1891 in vil Ostropole, Volhynian Province, son of an artisan; *Educ:* studied at high-school; *Career:* from 1905 in revol movement, in early years Bund member, later Menshevik; expelled from 6th grade of high-school as politically suspect; repeatedly arrested for revol activities; 1911 exiled to Arkhangel'sk Province; after his release 1913 emigrated to USA; joined American Socialist Party and Int Tailors' Union; continued revol work; during WW 1 took internationalist stand; May 1917 returned to Petrograd; 1917 attended 6th RSDRP(B) Congress; member, Petrograd RSDRP(B) Comt; Party propaganda among workers and soldiers; fought against Mesheviks and Socialist-Revolutionaries; Sept 1917 elected Presidium member, Petrograd Sov; deleg at 2nd, 3rd and 4th Congresses of Soviets; member and Presidium member, All-Russian Centr Exec Comt; after 1917 Oct Revol Petrograd comr of press, propaganda and agitation; ed, newspaper "Krasnaya gazeta"; *Died:* 20 June 1918 assassinated by Socialist-Revolutionary Sergeyev; buried in Petrograd's Field of Mars.

VOLODIN (real name: IVANOV), Vladimir Sergeyevich (1891–1958) Operetta singer; Pop Artiste of RSFSR from 1947; *Born:* 20 July 1891; *Educ:* studied at private drama school in Moscow; *Career:* 1906 stage debut in Moscow; 1912–14 at Zon Theater; 1914–18 at theaters in the Ukr; 1921–23 at Moscow Hermitage Theater; 1923–26 at theaters in the Far East; 1927–28 at Moscow Al'kazar Theater; from 1929 at Moscow Operetta Theater; performed in comedies, dramas, revues, miniatures and operettas; also did film work; *Roles:* stage roles: Louis Philippe in Kalman's "Bayadera"; Eisenstein in Strauss' "Fledermaus"; Piastro in Suppe's "Boccaccio"; Lorio in Hervé's "Mademoiselle Nitouche", etc; film roles: Mudretsov in *Kubanskiye kazaki* (Kuban' Cossacks); senior navigator in "Volga-Volga"; Commandant Taldykin *Svetlyy put'* (The Radiant Path), etc; *Awards:* Stalin Prize (1951); *Died:* 13 Feb 1958.

VOLOGDIN, Sergey Petrovich (1874–1926) Metallurgist; *Born:* 12 Aug 1874; *Educ:* 1897 grad Petersburg Technol Inst; *Career:* from 1899 asst head, then head, copper rolling shop at a plant of the Franco-Russian Plants Co, Petersburg; late 1905 arrested and sentenced to exile in Siberia; sentence commuted to three years exile abroad; 1906–09 worked at Le Chatelier's Laboratory in Paris; from 1909 prof of metallurgy, Don Polytech Inst (now Novocherkassk Polytech Inst); founded metallographic laboratory in Petersburg; 1905, together with M.G. Yevangullov, published first Russian metallographic textbook *Metallografiya* (Metallography); studied properties of refractory materials and reported his findings in 1909 at the Int Congress on Applied Chemistry; did research on the crystallization of iron and alloys; studied corrosion of boiler iron; determined formation point of silicates, manganese sulfide, calcium ferrates and other compunds in metallurgical slag; *Publ: Izucheniye napryazheniy v myagkom zheleze po metodu otzhiga* (Tension Studies in Soft Iron by the Tempering Method) (1925); *Obrazovaniye treshchin razyedaniya v zheleze vo vremya raboty parovogo kotla* (Corrosion Cracking in Iron During the Operation of a Steam Boiler) (1916); *Died:* 6 June 1926.

VOLOGDIN, Valentin Petrovich (1881–1953) Electr eng; specialist in high-frequency eng; prof from 1921; corresp member, USSR Acad of Sci from 1939; Hon Sci Worker of RSFSR from 1942; *Born:* 10 Mar 1881; *Educ:* 1907 grad Petersburg Technol Inst; *Career:* 1918 co-founder, Nizhniy Novgorod Radio Laboratory; from 1921 prof, Nizhniy Novgorod Univ; from 1923 dir, Low-Voltage Factory Trust; from 1947 dir, Research Inst for the Ind Application o f High–Frequency Current; also head, Laboratory of High-Frequency Thermal Eng, USSR Acad of Sci and prof, Leningrad Inst of Electr Eng; *Publ:* coauthor, *Generatory vysokoy chastoty* (High-Frequency Generators) (1935); *Vypryamiteli* (Rectifiers) (1936); *Poverkhnostnaya zakalka s tokami vysokoy i povyshennoy chastoty* (Casehardening with High-Frequency and Stepped-Up Current) (1940); *Poverkhnostnaya induktsionnaya zakalka* (Induction Casehardening) (1947); *Awards:* two Stalin Prizes (1943 and 1952); Popov Gold Prize (1948); *Died:* 23 Apr 1953.

VOLOKIDIN, Pavel Gavrilovich (1877–1936) Painter; prof; *Born:* 10 Dec 1877 in vil Arkhorovo, Oryol Province; *Educ:* 1905 grad Odessa Art School; 1906 grad Petersburg Acad of Arts; *Career:* from 1907 member, Assoc of Southern Russian Artists; contributed to its exhibitions; 1918–34 taught at Odessa Art Inst; 1934–36 taught at Kiev Art Inst; *Works:* "The Model" (1906); "Kherson Wharf" (1914); "Portrait of a Student" (1918); "Self-Portrait" (1921); "Portrait of a Woman" (1924); "Portrait of Z. Gayday" (1935); views of Odessa Harbor, etc; *Died:* 16 Mar 1936.

VOLONENKO, Anatoliy Nikonovich (1902–1965) Stage designer; Hon Art Worker of Ukr SSR from 1958; *Born:* 20 Sept 1902 in Khar'kov; *Educ:* 1929 grad Khar'kov Art Inst; *Career:* 1925–35 at Khar'kov Opera and Ballet Theater; from 1951 at Kiev Opera and Ballet Theater; *Works:* designed sets and costumes for operas: Moussorgsky's "Boris Godunov"; Tchaikovsky's *Yevgeniy Onegin* (Eugene Onegin); Verdi's "Aidda"; Gulak-Artemovskiy's *Zaporozhets za Dunayem* (A Dniepper Cossack Beyond the Don); Arkas' "Katerina"; Skorul'skiy's *Lesnaya pesn'* (Forest Song); Svechnikov's "Marusya Boguslavka", etc; *Died:* 21 Aug 1965.

VOLOSHIN, (real name: KIRPENKO-VOLOSHIN), Maksimilian Aleksandrovich (1878–1932) Russian poet; *Born:* 28 May 1878 in Kiev, of noble descent; *Educ:* completed Feodosiya High School; studied at Law Fac, Moscow Univ; *Career:* expelled from univ for taking part in student riots; 1900 first work printed; sided with Symbolists; worked for journals "Vesy", "Zolotoye runo" and Acmeist organ "Apollon"; lived for many years in Paris and was strongly influenced by French poets Verlaine and Renier and by Impressionist painters; studied painting and produced some well-known Crimean water colors; opposed 1917 Oct Revol; from 1917 lived at Koktebel', Crimea; during Oct Revol and Civil War adopted the stand of being "above the conflict", urging people to "be a man, and not a citizen"; translated French poetry into Russian; wrote articles on many aspects of culture and art, partially collected in the book *Liki tvorchestva* (The Faces of Art); (1914); *Publ: Stikhotvoreniya* (Poetry) (1910); "Anno mundi ardentis" (1916); *Izbrannyye stikhotvoreniya* (Selected Poetry) (1918); *Demony glukhonemyye* (Deaf-and-Dumb Demons) (1919); *Stikhi* (Verse) (1922); *Died:* 11 Aug 1932 in Koktebel.

VOLOSHINOV, Viktor Vladimirovich (1905–1963) Composer; Cand of Arts from 1947; prof from 1953; *Born:* 1905 in Kiev; *Educ:* 1924 grad Musical Drama Inst in Kiev; 1929 grad composition class, Leningrad Conservatory; 1932 completed post-grad studies at Leningrad Conservatory; *Career:* 1925–29 taught music at a labor school; 1927–32 taught musical theory at 2nd and 1st Musical Technicums; 1931–33 taught composition at Workers' Fac, Leningrad Conservatory; 1932–35 instructor,

1935–53 assoc prof, from 1948 head, Chair of Composition, from 1953 prof of composition, Leningrad Conservatory; 1943–44 studied Uzbek folklore in Tashkent; 1948–51 bd member, Leningrad Branch, USSR Composers' Union; *Works:* operas: *Slava* (Glory) (1939); *Sil'neye smerti* (Stronger Than Death) (1942); "Uzbek Suite" (1944); "Khorezm Suite" (1944); violin concerto (1954); quartet (1929); violin and piano sonata (1950); some 30 romances and 20 songs; vocal cycle to texts by Sov poets "The Russian Man" (1949); *Awards:* Badga of Hon (1954); medal; *Died:* 1963.

VOL'PE, Abram Mironovich (1893–1937) Mil commander; CP member from 1917; *Born:* 1893; *Educ:* 1922 grad Red Army Mil Acad; *Career:* fought in Civil War; taught at Frunze Mil Acad; exec posts with Pop Comrt of Defense; in early 1930's div commander; then chief of staff, Moscow Mil Distr; bd head, Red Army Main Bd; arrested by State Security organs; *Publ: Frontal'nyy udar* (Frontal Thrust) (1931), etc; *Died:* 1937 in imprisonment.

VOL'SKIY, Anton Nikolayevich (1897–1966) Metallurgist; Dr of Tech Sci; prof from 1934; member, USSR Acad of Sci from 1960; *Born:* 1897; *Educ:* 1924 grad Moscow Inst of Public Educ; *Career:* 1928–48 assoc, State Research Inst of Non-Ferrous Metals; 1929–34 lecturer, from 1934 prof, Moscow Inst of Non-Ferrous Metals; prof and dept head Krasnoyarsk Inst of Non-Ferrous Metals; 1953–60 corresp member, USSR Acad of Sci; specialized in chemical equilibrium of non-ferrous alloys; *Publ: Izvlecheniye tsinka i svintsa iz otkhodov metallurgicheskikh zavodov* (The Extraction of Zinc and Lead from Steel Plant Waste) (1934); *Teoriya metallurgicheskikh protsessov* (The Theory of Metallurgical Processes) (1935); *Osnovy teorii metallurgicheskikh plavok* (Principles of the Theory of Metallurgical Smelting) (1943); *Vzaimodeystviya mezhdu sul'fidami i okislyami pri plavkakh rud i bessemerovanii shteynov* (The Interaction of Sulfides and Oxides in Smelting Ores and Bessemerizing Mattes) (194); coauthor, *Ognennyye rudniki – Chyornaya metallurgiya* (Igneous Mines. Ferrous Metallurgy) (1963) *Awards:* two Stalin Prizes (1949 and 1953); Lenin Prize; *Died:* 9 Jan 1966.

VOLYNSKIY, A. (real name: FLEKSER, Akim L'vovich) (1863–1926) Lit critic and historian; *Born:* 3 May 1863 in Zhitomir; *Educ:* grad Law Fac, Petersburg Univ; *Career:* from 1889 worked for and then virtually directed journal "Severnyy vestnik", where he presided as the ideologist of the Decadence movement and an advocated of idealistic esthetics; 1898, after the journal closed down, concentrated on the history of painting, theater and music; 1911 edited memoirs and letters of Richard Wagner; after 1917 Oct Revol studied ballet, directed a choreographic technicum and published a study of dance *Kniga likovaniy* (The Book of Exultation) (1925); 1920–24 chm, Leningrad Branch, Sov Writers' Union; *Publ:* "Leonardo da Vinchi" (Leonardo da Vinci) (1900); *Russkiye kritiki* (Russian Critics) (2nd ed, 1907); collected articles *Bor'ba za idealizm* (The Struggle for Idealism) (1900); *Tsarstvo Karamazovykh* (The Kingdom of the Karamazovs) (1901); *Kniga velikogo gneva* (The Book of Grand Wrath) (2nd ed, 1904); "Dostoyevskiy" (2nd ed, 1909), etc; *Died:* 6 July 1926.

VORNOSKOV, Vasiliy Petrovich (1871 /or 1876/ –1940) Woodcarver; master of Abramtsevo-Krudrinskoye woodcarving school; *Born:* 1871 (or 1876); *Educ:* 1887–90 trained in Ye.D. Polenova's workshop in Abramtsevo; *Career:* developed original version of bas-relief carving as a decoration for household objects, incorporating a plastically represented detailed floral pattern; founded his own school of woodcarvers, including his own sons; *Works:* portal "Guarding the Borders of the USSR" (1937); decorations for the Chita Hall, Far East Pavilion at All-Union Agric Exhibition (1939); *Died:* 4 Feb 1940.

VOROB'YOV, Anatoliy Markovich (1900–1955) Ukr physiologist; corresp member, Ukr Acad of Sci from 1951; CP member from 1947; *Born:* 30 Nov 1900 in vil Mitrofanovka, now Crimean Oblast, son of an office worker; *Educ:* 1926 grad Khar'kov Med Inst; *Career:* from 1936 prof, Khar'kov Stomatological Inst; from 1945 prof, L'vov Med Inst; from 1952 dir, Inst of Physiology, Ukr Acad of Sci; specialized in physiology of digestion and higher nervous activity in animals; *Awards:* Order of the Red Banner of Labor; *Died:* 26 Oct 1955.

VOROB'YOV, Klementiy Yakovlevich (1866–1930) Statistician; *Born:* 1866; *Career:* worked as a teacher but was dismissed for polit activities and sentenced to a year in prison; 1889–1917 worked for statistical bureaux in Tver', Yaroslavl' and Simbir' zemstvos; 1905–07 exiled to Vologda, where he also did statistical work; after 1917 Oct Revol, head, Omsk and Ulyanovsk Statistical Bureaux; from 1925 worked for USSR Centr Statistical Bd; supervised compilation of statistics on domestic ind in Yaroslavl' Province which Lenin quoted in his book "The Development of Capitalism in Russia"; while working in Simbir' Province conducted first-ever short-term zemstvo household census with the help of voluntary workers; in latter years worked on questions of agr-c zoning; *Publ: Otkhoziye promysly krest'yanskogo naseleniya Yaroslavskoy gubernii* (Seasonal Occupations of the Peasant Population of Yaroslavl' Province) (1903); *Kustarnyye promysly* (Domestic Crafts); *Statistiko-ekonomicheskoye issledovaniye gruntovykh dorog Tverskoy gubernii* (A Statistical and Economic Study of Unpaved Roads in Tver' Province) (1911); *Kustarno-remeslennyye promysly Simbirskoy gubernii* (Domestic Industry and Handicrafts in Simbirsk Province) (1916); *Metodologiya sel'skokhozyaystvennogo rayonirovaniya* (The Methodology of Agricultural Zoning), etc; *Died:* 1930.

VOROB'YOV, Mikhail Petrovich (1896–1957) Mil commander; marshal of Eng Troops from 1944; CP member from 1919; *Born:* 29 Dec 1896 in Khasavyurt, Dag ASSR, son of an office worker; *Educ:* studied at mining Inst; 1917 grad ensigns' school; 1929 grad Mil Eng Acad; *Career:* 1916 drafted into Russian Army as private; Oct 1917 elected chm, regt comt; from 1918 in Red Army; commanded a road- and bridge-building company; then brigade and div eng in operations on Southern, Western and Caucasian Fronts; from 1940 inspector-gen of Eng Troops, Sov Army; from July 1941 head, Eng Bd, then chief of Eng Troops on Western Front; 1941 directed construction of defenses on approaches to Moscow; from Apr 1942 chief of Eng Troops, Sov Army; after WW 2 chief of Eng Troops, Kiev and Baltic Mil Distr; from 1953 directed various mil construction projects and quartering of troops; dep, RSFSR Supr Sov of 2nd convocation; *Died:* 12 June 1957.

VOROB'YOV, Vasiliy Petrovich (1887–1954) Composer; Hon Art Worker of Chuvash ASSR from 1940; CP member from 1940; *Born:* 20 Mar 1887 in vil Aldnarovo, Chuvashia; *Career:* 1917–40 founded and directed choir (from 1924 Chuvash State Choir); taught singing at schools and directed amateur choirs in Cheboksary; *Works:* over 100 songs and choral works, including "The White Dove" and "We Visited Cheboksary"; song-cantate "The October Path"; some 60 children's songs; recorded some 800 Chuvash folk songs, including "On Kolkhoz Fields" and "The Bay Horse"; *Awards:* Order of the Red Banner of Labor; medal; *Died:* 10 Dec 1954 in Cheboksary.

VOROB'YOV, Viktor Aleksandrovich (1864–1941) Phthisiatrist; Dr of Med from 1892; prof from 1901; Hon Sci Worker of RSFSR; *Born:* 1864; *Educ:* 1888 grad Med Fac, Moscow Univ; *Career:* from 1888 intern, then assoc prof, A.A. Ostroumov's Clinic; 1892 defended doctor's thesis on the effect of Koch's tuberkoulin on nitrogen metabolism and tissue matter; 1901–09 prof, Chair of Special Pathology and Therapy, Moscow Univ; from 1911 lectured on clinical aspects and pathogenesis of tuberculosis; 1921 prof, Chair of Tuberculosis, Med Fac, Moscow Univ; from 1921 founder-dir, State Tuberculosis Inst (now Inst of Tuberculosis, USSR Acad of Med Sci); contributed new insights on development and treatment of tuberculosis; co-founder and life chm, All-Russian Tuberculosis League; consultant, Tuberculosis Dept and member, Learned Med Council, RSFSR Pop Comrt of Health; attented numerous int conferences on tuberculosis; member, Int TuberculosisAssoc;member, edcollegium,variousmedjournals;wrote 68 works; *Publ:* doctor's thesis *K voprosu o vliyanii tuberkulina Kokha na azotistyy obmen* (The Effect of Koch's Tuberculin on Nitrogen Metabolism) (1892); *Klinika lyogochnogo tuberkulyoza vzroslykh* (The Clinical Aspects of Adult Pulmonary Tuberculosis) (1932); *Lyogochnyye formy tuberkulyoza vzroslykh, ikh patologicheskaya differentsirovka i gruppirovka* (Adult Forms of Pulmonary Tuberculosis, Their Pathological Differentiation and Grouping) (1932); *Vegetativnaya zhizn' organizma i yeyo rol' v patogeneze tuberkulyoza* (The Body's Vegetative Life and Its Role in the Pathogenesis of Tuberculosis) (1936), etc; *Died:* 1951.

VOROB'YOV, V. A. (1896–1937) Party official; CP member from 1914; *Born:* 1896; *Career:* after 1917 Feb Revol secr, Nev'yansk RSDRP(B) Comt and secr, Nev'yansk Sov of Workers and Peasants' Dep; ed, newspaper "Derevenskiy kommunist"; Vyatka Province deleg at 8th RCP(B) Congress; during 1920–21 trade-union controversy sided with Trotsky; 1927 at 15th CPSU(B) Congress expelled from the Party for siding with Trotskyist opposition; 1928 readmitted to the Party; later again expelled and then convicted for alleged anti-Party and anti-Sov activities; *Died:* 1937 in imprisonment.

VOROB'YOV, Vladimir Petrovich (1876–1937) Anatomist; member, Ukr Acad of Sci from 1934; *Born:* 27 June 1876 in Odessa; *Educ:* 1903 grad Med Fac, Khar'kov Univ; *Career:* from 1903 asst prof, Chair of Anatomy, Khar'kov Univ; then studied anatomy under Prof Stied in Königsberg; 1908 defended doctor's thesis; from 1910 assoc prof and head, Chair of Anatomy, Khar'kov Women's Med Inst; 1913 elected prof, Yur'yev Med Inst, but Min of Educ Kasso refused to confirm his appointment; the same occured when he was elected prof of Warsaw Univ; 1917–37 prof, Khar'kov Med Inst; pioneer of functional anatomy; considered every anatomical object an integral part of a single entity – the living human body – formed as a result of ontophylogenesis and modified under environmental conditions; devised macro-microscopic method of studying human tissues; studied his specimens stereometrically, in three dimensions; using his method, organs and tissues could be studied in relation to the body as a whole; in effect, discovered a new field of morphology which he called the "border area of macro-microscopic vision"; studied vegetative nervous ganglia and plexi of internal organs; drew up an exhaustive picture of the distribution of nerve ganglia and plexi of the heart, larynx, lungs, esophagus, stomach, intestines, liver, pancreas, kidneys, bladder, womb and spleen; devised original method of preparing anatomical museum specimens; also developed a method of sutured electrodes and effective methods for prolonged preservation of dead tissue and the restoration of their in vitam coloring; founded in Khar'kov unique Museum of Man's Development; compiled original *Atlas anatomii cheloveka* (An Atlas of Human Anatomy) (5 vol, 1938–42); together with B.I. Zbarskiy, devised a new method of preserving corpses; helped embalm Lenin's body; co-ed, 1st ed of "BME" (Large Medical Encyclopedia); member, All-Ukr Centr Exec Comt from 1935; *Publ: Vynikhi kostey zapyast'ya* (Dislocations of the Carpal Bones) (1908); "Die Methode der Durchleuchtung und ihre Anwendung bei Untersuchung der Magennerven" (1910); *Nervy zheludka sobak* (The Gastric Nerves of Dogs) (1913); *K topografii uzlov i stvolov na serdtse cheloveka* (The Topography of Ganglia and Trunks of the Human Heart) (1917); "Methodik der Untersuchungen von Nervenelementen des Makro- und Mikroskopischen Gebietes" (1927); *Differentsial'naya okraska spinnomozgvykh i simpaticheskikh nervov* (Differential Staining of the Cerebrospinal and Sympathetic Nerves) (1935); *Gipoteza V.P. Vorob'yova o roli limfoidnoy tkani v pishchevaritel'noy trubke cheloveka i zhivotnykh* (V.P. Vorob'yov's Hypothesis on the Role of the Lymphoid Tissue in the Digestive Tract of Man and Animals) (1937); *Awards:* two gold medals for student works; Prof Alekseyenko Prize; Lenin Prize (1927); Order of Lenin; other orders; *Died:* 31 Sept 1937 in Khar'kov.

VORONIKHIN, Nikolay Nikolayevich (1882–1956) Botanist; *Born:* 17 June 1882; *Educ:* 1907 grad Petersburg Univ; *Career:* 1907–15 asst to prof V. L. Komarov, Petersburg (Petrograd) Higher Women's Courses; 1908–10 studied the taxonomy of brown, red and green benthic plants in the Black Sea; from 1922 worked at Petrograd (Leningrad) Botanical Garden, then at Botanical Inst, USSR Acad of Sci; did research on mycology with special reference to floristics and taxonomy; named 75 new species and six new genera of fungi; described several then unknown crop parasites; 1949, together with Ye. V. Shlyapina, completed first classification key to fresh-water algae in the USSR; *Publ: Gribnyye i bakterial'nyye bolezni sel'skokhozyaystvennykh rasteniy* (Fungus and Bacterial Diseases of Agricultural Plants) (1922); *Materialy k flore gribov Kavkaza* (Material on Fungus Flora in the Caucasus) (1927); *Gribnyye i bakterial'nyye bolezni tsitrusov* (Fungus and Bacterial Diseases of Citrus Plants) (1937); *Rastitel'nyy mir okeana* (The Vegetable Kongdom of the Ocean) (1945); coauthor, *Vodorosli* (Algae) (1949); *Died:* 18 Mar 1956.

VORONIN, Vladimir Ivanovich (1890–1952) Seaman; capt of an icebreaker fleet; *Born:* 1890; *Educ:* 1916 grad Arkhangel'sk Nautical College; *Career:* 1916–18 navigation officer, Murmansk Line ships; from 1918 Capt on oceanic voyages; 1928 with icebreaker "G. Sedov" took part in search for U. Nobile's expedition; 1929–30 on Franz-Josef-Land and Severnaya Zemlya; 1932 with the SS "Sibiryakov" made first non-stop traverse of the Northern Sea Route; 1933–34 took part in "Chelyuskin" expedition; 1934–38 capt, icebreaker "Yermak"; late 1938 with icebreaker "I. Stalin" made a trip to high Arctic latitudes to rescue the drifting "G. Sedov"; during WW 2 capt, icebreaker "I. Stalin"; 1946–47 commanded Antarctic Whaling Flotilla; from 1947 again capt, icebreaker "I. Stalin"; dep, USSR Supr Sov of 2nd convocation; an island in the Kara Sea is named for him; *Awards:* Order of Lenin; six other orders; medals; *Died:* 18 Oct 1952.

VORONSKIY, Aleksandr Konstantinovich (1884–1943) Russian lit critic, journalist and writer; CP member from 1904; *Born:* 31 Aug 1884 in vil Dobrinka, Tambov Province, son of a priest; *Educ:* studied at Tambov Theological Seminary; *Career:* expelled from seminary for polit unreliabilitiy; did Party work in Tambov, Petersburg, Vladimir, Nikolayev, etc; attended Prague Party Conference; arrested, imprisoned, then exiled; after 1917 Oct Revol worked in Odessa and Ivanovo-Voznesensk, editing newspaper "Rabochiy kray"; 1921–27 ed, journal "Krasnaya nov'" which united writers of various generations such as Gorky, Veresayev, Ivanov and Seyfullin; also directed *Krug* (Circle) Publ House; 1923–27 ed, journal "Prozhektor"; 1925–28 sided with "Trotskyist opposition" and in connection with this expelled from CPSU(B); later broke with opposition and was reinstated in Party; worked fro State Fiction Publ House; 1911 first work printed; published many articles and reviews on theory of art, lit movements of 1920's and work of individual writers; polemicized with other lit critics and historians; 1937 arrested by State Security organs; *Publ:* collections of lit critical articles: *Na styke* (At the Junction) (1923); *Iskusstvo i zhizn'* (Art and Life) (1924); *Literaturnyye tipy* (Literary Types) (1925); *Literaturnyye zapisi* (Literary Notes) (1926); *Mister Britling p'yot chashu do dna* (Mister Britling Drains His Cup) (1927); *Iskusstvo videt' mir* (The Art of Seeing the World) (1928); *Literaturnyye portrety* (Literary Portraits) (1928–29); stories "Bursa". *Glaz uragana* (The Eye of the Hurricane), etc; book "Zhelyabov" (1934), etc; *Died:* 13 Oct 1943 in imprisonment.

VORONTSOV, Daniil Semyonovich (1886–1965) Physiologist; prof from 1922; Dr of Biological Sci; member, Ukr Acad of Sci from 1957; *Born:* 1886; *Educ:* 1912 grad Natural Sci Dept, Physics and Mathematics Fac, Petersburg Univ; *Career:* 1912–16 worked for Physiological Laboratory, Chair of Physiology, Petersburg Univ; 1914–16 asst prof, Chair of Physiology, Bestuzhev Higher Women's Courses, Petrograd; 1916–22 asst prof, then assoc prof, Chair of Physiology, Novorossiysk Univ, Odessa; 1922–30 prof, Chair of Physiology, Smolensk Univ; 1930–35 prof, Chair of Physiology, Kazan' Univ and Kazan' Med Inst; 1935–41 prof, Chair of Physiology, Kiev Med Inst; 1939–57 corresp member, Ukr Acad of Sci; 1944–65 prof, of physiology, Kiev Univ; 1956–65 head, Electrophysiology Laboratory, Inst of Physiology, Ukr Acad of Sci; 1922 founded Chair of Physiology at Smolensk Univ; co-ed, physiology section, 2nd ed of "BME" (Large Medical Encyclopedia); member, ed council, journal "Fiziologicheskiy zhurnal SSSR imeni I.M. Sechenova"; specialized in physiology of nervous System and electrophysiology; wrote over 100 works' *Publ: Ob elektrogramme predserdiy* (Electrocardiograms of the Atria) (1917); *Vliyaniye postoyannogo toka na nerv, obrabotannyy vodoy* (The Effects of Direct Current on a Nerve Treated with Water) (1924); *Elektrotonicheskaya reaktsiya spinnomozgovykh koreshkov* (The Electrotonic Reaction of the Spinocerebral Radicles) (1947); coauthor, *Fiziolohiya tvaryn i cholovika* (The Physiology of Animals and Man) (1952); *Summatsiya elektrotonicheskikh reaktsiy spinnomozgovykh koreskhkov* (A Summary of the Electrotonic Reactions of the Spinocerebral Radicles) (1952); *Obshchaya elektrofiziologiya* (General Electrophysiology) (1961); *Vliyaniye strikhnina, gamma-aminomaslyannoy kisloty, atsetil kholina i khinina na razvitiye fizicheskogo elektrona v nerve* (The Effects of Strychnine, Gamma-Aminobutyric Acid, Cholin Acetyl and Quinine on the Development of the Physical Electron in the Nerve) (1963), etc; *Died:* 12 July 1965.

VORONYY, Mikolay Kondrat'yevich (1871–1942) Ukr poet, theater historian and translator; *Born:* 7 Dec 1871 in Ukr; *Educ:* studied at L'vov Univ; *Career:* rep of Ukr Modernism; 1893 first work printed; in 1900's member, Revol Ukr Party; worked as journalist and stage dir; 1920–26 in emigration; returned to Ukr to teach and study theater history; translated into Ukr the "Internationale", the "Marseillaise", the "Varshavyanka" and Russian and West European classics; *Publ:* "From the Clouds and from the Valleys" (1903); "Lyrical Poetry" (1911); "Poetry" (1929); "Selected Poetry" (1959); *Died:* 1942.

VOROVSKIY, Vatslav Vatslavovich (1871–1923) Party and govt official; dipl; publicist; lit critic; CP member from 1894; *Born:* 27 Oct 1871 in Moscow, son of a Polish eng; *Educ:* 1801–97 studied at Moscow Higher Tech College; *Career:* from 1893 active in revol student circles; 1897–99 imprisoned for revol activities, then exiled to Vyatka Province; 1902 emigrated; 1903, after 2nd RSDRP Congress, joined Bolsheviks; collaborated with Lenin's "Iskra"; 1905, together with Lenin, M. S. Ol'minskiy and A. V. Lunacharskiy, edited newspapers "Vperyod" and "Proletariy"; 1905 and 1906 helped prepare and attented 3rd and 4th Party Congresses; Nov 1905 returned to Russia; Party and lit work in Petersburg and Odessa; repeatedly arrested; in his publicistic and critical articles promoted Marxism; from 1915 revol work abroad; 1917 member, For Bureau, CC, RSDRP(B); 1917–19 Sov plen in Scandinavian countries; 1921–23 Sov plen in Italy; 1922 attended Genoa and 1922–23 Lausanne Conference; *Publ:* articles "Superfluous People (1905); "The Night After the Battle" (1908); "D. I. Pisarev" (1908; "The Bourgeoisie of the Modernists" (1908); "Bazarov and Samin. Two Nikilisms" (1909); "Leonid Andreyev" (1910); "Maksiim Gorky" (1910); "V.G. Belinskiy" (1911), etc; *Died:* 10 May 1923 assassinated in Lausanne by White emigré Konradi.

VOROZHTSOV, Nikolay Nikolayevich (1881–1941) Organic chemist; prof from 1916; *Born:* 16 Apr 1881 in Tomsk; *Educ:* 1904 grad Khar'kov Technol Inst; *Career:* 1904–09 senior laboratory technician, Tomsk Technol Inst; 1909–11 continued studies abroad; 1912 synthesized first four samples of thioindigo dyes in the naphthalene series; 1913–16 assoc, 1916–20 prof, Warsaw Polytech Inst; 1920–22 prof, 1922–24 rector, Ivanovo-Voznesensk Polytech Inst; from 1924 worked ad Moscow Inst of Chemical Technol; 1925–30 sci dir, Aniline Dye Trust; from 1932 consultant, Research Inst of Organic Semiproducts and dyes; devised method of manufacturing photographic paper without silver for daylight printing; formulated "Vorozhtsov's rule" to describe the relation between the structure of naphthalene derivatives and their capacity for reaction with sodium bisulfite; described the catalytic mechanism of sulfates in mutual conversion reactiongs of oxy- and amino-derivates in the naphthalene series; developed a gen theory of alkali floatation reactions; *Publ: Osnovy sinteza krasiteley* (The Principles of Dye Synthesis) (1925); *Stupeni v sinteze krasiteley* (Stages of Dye-Synthesis) (1926); coauthor, *K voprosu o deystvii kislogo sernistokislogo natriya na nitrozo-naftoly* (The Action of Acid Sodium Bisulfite on Nitrosonaphthols (1929); coauthor, *O svetochuvstvitel'nykh nitrosoyedineniyakh* (Photosensitive Nitro Compunds) (1932); *Problema polucheniya khloroproizvodnykh aromaticheskogo ryada* (The Problem of Obtaining Aromatic Series Chlorine Derivatives) (1936); *K teorii shchyolochnikh plavov* (The Theory of Alkali Floatation) (1940); *Osnovy sinteza promezhutochnykh produktov i krasniteley* (The Principles of Intermediary Product and Dye Synthesis) (1955); *Awards:* Stalin Prize (1952); *Died:* 9 Aug 1941.

VORVULEV, Nikolay Dmitriyevich (1917–1967) Opera singer (baritone); Pop Artiste of USSR from 1956; *Born:* 22 Jan 1917; *Educ:* 1954 grad Ye. Viting's class, Minsk Conservatory; *Career:* from 1939 with Red Army Song and Dance Ensemble of Bel Mil Distr; from 1946 soloist, Bel Opera and Ballet Theater, Minsk; from 1957 soloist, Shevchenko Opera and Ballet Theater, Kiev; *Roles:* Kastus Kalinovskiy in Lukas' "Kastus Kalinovskiy"; Opanas in Tikotskiy's "The Grandfather from Polessie"; Maksim in Mayboroda's "Arsenal"; Petruccio in Shebalin's "The Taming of the Shrew"; the Demon in Rubinstein's "Demon"; Rigoletto in Verdi's Rigoletto", etc; *Died:* 29 Aug 1967.

VOSKANOV, Gaspar Karapetovich (1886–1937) Arm mil commander; lt-col in Russian Army; corps commander from 1935; Civil War veteran; CP member from 1919; *Born:* 1886; *Pos:* fought in WW 1; 1917 elected regt commander; from 1918 in Red Army; 1918–21 commanded 25th and 49th Infantry Div and 4th and 12th Armies; after Civil War commanded 47th Infantry Div, then 6th Infantry Corps; asst commander, Turkestani Front; head, Mil Section, All-Union Standardization Comt; mil attaché in Turkey, Finland and Italy; dep chm, Soc for Furthering the Defense, Aviation and Chemical Ind of the USSR; *Career:* Jan 1919 his 25th Infantry Div captured Ural'sk; Oct 1919 his 49th Infantry Div played important role in defeating White troops near Aktyubinsk; Jan 1920 his 4th Army occupied Gur'yev and smashed the Whites' Ural Front; 1937 arrested by NKVD; *Awards:* two Orders of Red Banner; *Died:* 1937 in imprisonment; posthumously rehabilitated.

VOSKANYAN, Arus Tigranovna (1889–1943) Actress; Pop Artiste of Arm SSR from 1935; *Born:* 10 May 1889 in Constantinople; *Career:* 1908 stage debut in Constantinople; 1910 moved to Transcacasia and joined Arm company in Baku; from 1917 acted in Tiflis; 1921 joined 1st Arm State Theater, Yerevan and became one of its leading actresses; during WW 2 also gave dramatic readings at factories and hospitals; *Roles:* Ophelia (1912); Desdemona (1913); Susdan in Shirvanzade's "Namus" (1913); Sona in Shirvanzade's "The Evil Spirit" (1914); Antigone in Sophocles' "Antigone" (1922); Margarite in Shirvanzade's "For Honor's Sake" (1923); Catherine in "The Taming of the Shrew" (1923); Rima in Lunacharskiy's *Yad* (Poison) (1926); Panova in Trenyov's "Lyubov' Yarovaya" (1927); Anu sh in Paronyan's "Uncle Bagdasar" (1927); Kseniya in *Razlom* (Break-Up) (1928); Nastya in Gorky's *Na dne* (The Lower Depths) (1932); Lady Macbeth in Shakespeare's "Macbeth" (1933); Susanna in "The Marriage of Figaro" (1933); Manya in Shkvarkin's *Chuzhoy rebyonok* (Another's Child) (1934); Katerina in Ostrovskiy's *Groza* (The Storm) (1935); Rshel' in Gorky's "Vassa Zheleznova" (1937); Kruchinina in Ostrovskiy's *Bez viny vinovatyye* (Guilty Without Guilt) (1939); the Empress in Demirchan's "Native Land" (1940); Zeynab in Subatov:s "Treason" (1941); Mariya Nikolayevna in Simonov's *Russkiye lyudi (Russian People)* (1942), etc; *Died:* 20 July 1943 in Yerevan.

VOSKANYAN, Ovsep Atanasovich (1883–1939) Actor; Hon Artiste of Azer SSR from 1931; *Born:* 21 Feb 1883; *Educ:* from 1905 studied in Prof Durasova's opera class, Musical Drama College, Moscow Philharmonic Soc; also attended drama courses at Moscow Arts Theater; *Career:* 1902 stage debut; in 1910's toured Turkey and Persia with O.A. Abelyan's company; helped establish Arm musical theater in Transcaucasia; 1910 founded a musical drama company which performed throughout the Caucasus; after establishment of Sov regime worked at Baku Arm Theater; *Roles:* Arbenin in *Maskerad* (Masquerade); Krechinskiy in *Svad'ba Krechinskogo* (Krechinskiy's Wedding); Othello; Tokeramo in Lendel's *Tayfun* (Typhoon); Andrey Belugin in Ostrovskiy and Solov'yov'y *Zhenit'ba Belugina* (The Marriage of Belugin); Sagatel, Voskan and Mintoyev in Shirvanzade's "For Honor", "The Evil Spirit" and "Morgan's Godfather"; Ayrapet aga in Tarayan's "Azrail'"; Nazar in Demirchan's "Brave Nazar", etc; *Publ:* plays "Tatos Ivanych" (1918); "Ashug Garib" (1918); "Leyli and Medzhnun" (1919); "Sos and Varditer" (1919), etc; *Died:* 29 Nov 1939.

VOSKOV, Semyon Petrovich (1889–1920) Party official; CP member from 1917; *Born:* 1889 in Poltava Province; *Career:* at age 16 arrested for distributing revol lit; during 1905 Revol member, battle squad; repeatedly arrested; 1906 emigrated; after 1917 Feb Revol returned to Petrograd and joined RSDRP(B); Apr 1917 Party work for CC, RSDRP(B) at Sestroretsk Arms Factory; after 1917 Oct Revol food comr in Northern Region; member, Petrograd Exec Comt; member, All-Russian Centr Exec Comt; from Nov 1918 commands and polit work in Red Army: commander, 7th Army; comr, 10th Div; 1919 comr, 7th Div; member, army revol mil council; comr, 9th Div; fought at Oryol and Kursk; *Awards:* Order of the Red Banner; *Died:* 14 Mar 1920 of typhus; buried on Petrograd's Square of Victims of the Revol.

VOSKRESENSKIY, Pavel Ivanovich (1868–1925) Public health official; *Born:* 13 Sept 1869 in Kishinev, now Mold SSR; *Educ:* grad Natural Sci Dept, Physic and Mathematics Fac, Novorossiysk Univ, Odessa; grad Med Fac, Moscow Univ; *Career:* worked as factory doctor; then for 15 years health officer at construction of Eastern-Chinese Railroad in Manchuria; 1912 health officer, Akkerman Uyezd Zemstvo; during WW 1 corps physician; from 1917 head, Moscow City Health Center; tested various disinfectants and insecticides; during Civil War founded Expert Commission on Bread Surrogates; 1918 founded first Russian experiimental food center and bakery; compiled extensive herbarium of plants which could be used as additional sources of nutrition; 1921 reorganized Health Center into Moscow Health Inst; dir, above inst; learned secr, Sci Food Council, *Narpit* (Public Nutrition) joint-stock company; consultant, Sanitary Food Section, Moscow Health Dept and Public Nutrition Council, USSR Pop Comrt of Health; 1921 sponsored Health Inst's first conference on food standards, arranged by USSR Pop Comrt of Health; established standards for food products and compiled USSR Food Code; co-founder and member, ed bd, journal "Gigiyena i epidemiologiya"; taught at health officers courses and campaigned for improvement of gen public's hygiene standards: *Publ: O kombinirovannykh privivkakh protiv bryushnogo tifa i kholery* (Combined Vaccination Against Typhoid and Cholera) (1916); *Moloko i molochnyye produkty Moskovskogo rynka v*

1923 godu (Milk and Dairy Produce on the Moscow Market in 1923); (1924); *Died:* 1925 in Moscow.

VOSTORGOV, Ioann Ioannovich (1867–1918) Protopriest: *Born:* 1867; *Career:* worked as a priest in Geo; 1906 moved to Moscow, where he organized the "Union of the Russian People" and published the monarchist newspaper "Russkaya zemlya", the journals "Poteshnyy" and "Vernost" and numerous pamphlets; had considerable influence in the Synod and was involved in all major polit developments; took part in Duma election campaign; 1908 attended 4th Missionaries Congress in Kiev, where he called the struggle against socialism the basic task of the clergy; after 1917 Oct Revol arrested as active supporter of old regime; *Died:* 1918; executed by Moscow Cheka.

VOSTRETSOV, Stepan Sergeyevich (1883–1932) Mil commander; Civil War veteran; CP member from 1920; *Born:* 17 July 1883 in vil Kazantsevo, Ufa Province, son of a peasant; *Educ:* 1927 grad mil acad courses; *Career:* blacksmith by trade; 1906–09 private, Russian Army; 1909 sentenced to three years' imprisonment for revol propaganda among soldiers; 1905–18 Menshevik; fought in WW 1; 1916 for bravery promoted ensign; from 1918 in Red Army; 1919–20 commanded 242nd Volga Regt on Eastern and Western Fronts; distinguished himself during the capture of Chelyabinsk and Minsk; from 1921 head, All-Russian Cheka Bd for Guarding the Siberian Borders; late 1922 commanded, forces group of Far Eastern Republ Pop Revol Army in capture of Spassk and rout of White Army in the Far East; 1923 headed expeditionary detachment which routed Gen Pepelyayev's White Army units in the Okhotsk–Ayansk area; 1927–29 div commander; from 1929 corps commander; *Awards:* four Orders of the Red Banner; *Died:* 2 May 1932.

VOTCHAL, Yevgeniy Filippovich (1864–1937) Plant physiologist; member, Ukr Acad of Sci from 1921; prof, Kiev Agric Inst; Dr of Botany from 1897; *Born:* 1864; *Educ:* 1889 grad Kazan' Univ; *Career:* from 1889 at Moscow Univ and Petrine Agric Acad; from 1898 prof, Agric Fac, Kiev Polytech Inst; in 1920's head, Chair of Biology, Kiev Med Inst; 1929–30 co-founder and prof, Sci Inst of Selection (then Ukr Sugar Ind Research Inst); from 1932 engaged exclusively in research; *Publ: K voprosu o dvizhenii vody v rastenii* (The Movement of Water in a Plant) (1892); *Ucheniye o mikroorganizmakh (mikrobiologiya)* (The Theory of Microorganism [Microbiology]) (vol 1, 1896); *O dvizhenii pasoki v rastenii* (The Movement of Bleeding Sap in a Plant) (1897); *K vorprosu o stotave i roli pasoki* (The Composition and Role of Bleeding Sap) (1916); *K postanovke voprosa o bor'be rasteniy s zasukhoy (Plants' Struggle Against Drought) (1922); coauthor, Dnevnoy khod ispareniya i geograficheskiye faktory* (The Daily Course of Evaporation and Geographical Factors) (1928); *Ionizatsiya vozdukha list'yami* (Ionization of the Air by Foliage) (1928); *Novy dani pro budovu da rozvytok tsukrovoho buryaku* (New Data on the Structure and Development of Sugar Beet) (1935); *Died:* 1 Apr 1937.

VOVSI, Miron Semyonovich (1897–1960) Therapist and clinician; Dr of Med from 1938; prof from 1936; maj-gen, Med Corps; member, USSR Acad of Med Sci from 1948; Hon Sci Worker of RSFSR from 1944; *Born:* 13 May 1897; *Educ:* 1919 grad Med Fac, Moscow Univ; *Career:* 1919–22 senior regt surgeon, 6th Proletarian Div, Red Army; 1922–25 intern, then asst prof and assoc prof, Fac Therapy Clinic, 1st Moscow Univ; 1925–34 senior assoc, Med and Biological Inst, Moscow Univ; 1933 also sci dir, Therapeutic Dept, Basmanov Hospital; 1934 head, Therapeutic Dept, S.P. Botkin Hospital, Moscow, which housed the 3rd Chair of Therapy, Centr Inst of Postgrad Med Training from 1935; head, 2nd, then 3rd Chair of Therapy, Centr Inst of Postgrad Med Training; 1938, with other physicians, campaigned for execution of Moscow physicians Pletnyov, Levin, Vinogradov and Kazakov who had been charged with sabotage; 1941–49 chief therapist, Sov Army and consultant, Kremlin Therapy and Health Bd; from 1950 in charge of a team of researchers at Inst of Therapy, USSR Acad of Med Sci; 1952 arrested together with other physicians on charges of espionage and of premeditated incorrect treatment of Party and mil leaders; after Stalin's death rehabilitated and reinstated; pioneered field therapy, then a new branch of mil med; devised a new classification of angina pectoris; member, Learned Med Council, USSR Min of Health; dep, Moscow Distr Sov; member, ed collegium, journal "Terapevticheskiy arkhiv"; member, ed council, journal "Klinicheskaya meditsina"; co-ed, therapy section, *Bol'shaya meditsinkaya entsiklopediya* (Large Medical Encyclopedia) (1st and 2nd ed); ed, therapy section, *Opt sovetskoy meditsiny v Velikoy Otechestvennoy voyne 1941–45* (The Experience of Soviet Medicine in the 1941–45 Great Fatherland War); wrote over 60 works; *Publ: Syvorotochnoye lecheniye krupoznoy pnevmonii* (The Seriotherapy of Croupous Pneumonia) (1934); *Nekotoryye voprosy patogeneza i kliniki krupoznoy pnevmonii* (Some Questions of the Pathogenesis and Clinical Aspects of Croupous Pneumonia) (1940); *S.P. Botkin kak terapevt gospitaley russkoy armii* (S.P. Botkin as a Therapist in the Hospitals of the Russian Army) (1944); *Ostriy nefrit* (Acute Nephritis) (1946); *Vnutrennyaya meditsina v period Velikoy Otechestvennoy voyny* (Internal Medicine During the Great Fatherland War) (1949); coauthor, *Nefrity i nefrozy* (Forms of Nephritis and Nephrosis) (1955); *K klinike i patogenezu infarkta miokarda* (The Clinical Aspects and Pathogenesis of Myocardic Infarct) (1956); *Klinika i patogenez ostroy koronarnoy nedostatochnosti* (The Clinical Aspects and Pathogenesis of Acute Coronary Insufficiency) (1957); *Awards:* Order of Lenin; Order of the Red Banner of Labor; Order of the Red Star; 1st Prize, USSR Pop Comrt of Health (1936); medals; *Died:* 6 June 1960 in Moscow.

VOYEVODIN, Pyotr Ivanovich (1884–1964) Revolutionary; Party official; CP member from 1899; *Born:* 12 July 1884; *Career:* worked at Yekaternoslav plants and joined a Marxist circle there; repeatedly arrested for revol activities; participated in 1905–07 Revol, heading fighting squad; member, Samara RSDRP Comt; then Party work in Chita, Omsk and Zlatoust; 1912 emigrated to USA; joined Russian Group, American Socialist Party; 1913 returned to Russia illegally; arrested in Baku and exiled to Narym Kray; 1917 elected chm, West Siberian and Ural Kray Comt; then chm, West Siberian Sovnarkhoz; from 1919 member, All-Russian Centr Exec Comt and CC, RSP(B) plen on Civil War fronts; dep chm, Sci and Tech Soc for the Electrification of the USSR; 1932–35 in New York with American Trade Bd; 1935–40 cultural work; from 1940 pensioner; deleg at 22nd CPSU Congress; *Awards:* Hero of Socialist Labor (1964); *Died:* 25 Nov 1964.

VOYKOV, Pyotr Lazarevich (1888–1927) Diplomat; CP member from 1917; *Born:* 1888 in Kerch', son of a teacher; *Educ:* completed high school; *Career:* while at school active in Soc-Democratic circles; expelled from 6th grade for polit unreliability; 1903 joined RSDRP; 1905 attended Congress of Southern Soc-Democratic Orgs in Melitopol'; went underground to avoid arrest by Tsarist police; 1907–17 lived in Switzerland; May 1917 returned to Russia; Oct 1917 secr, Yekaterinburg Oblast Trade-Union Bureau; then chm, Yekaterinburg City Duma; after 1917 Oct Revol chm, Ural Plants Council; then Ural Oblast Food Comr; 1919 appointed Council of Pop Comr rep on bd of Centr Union of Consumer Soc; 1920 Collegium member, Pop Comrt of For Trade; 1921 chm, Sov-Polish Commission to Implement 1921 Riga Treaty; from Oct 1924 Sov rep in Poland; *Died:* 7 June 1927 killed in Warsaw by emigre Kaverda; buried by Kremlin Wall on Moscow's Red Square.

VOYTKEVICH, Anton Feliksovich (LESHIN) (1876–1951) Bacteriologist; prof from 1919; *Born:* 1876; *Career:* from 1896 in revol movement; arrested and exiled; 1900 worked for Nizhniy Novgorod Soc-Democratic Org; 1903–04 with Baku RSDRP Comt; 1904–06 with Petersburg, then Moscow RSDRP Comt; deleg at 4th (Amalgamative) RSDRP Congress; 1905–06 senior battle organizer for Lefortov, then Zamoskvorech'ye Rayons of Moscow; 1917–18 with Moscow RSDRP(B) Comt; then abandoned politics; teaching and research in the field of agric bacteriology; from 1918 dir, Bacteriological Agronomical Station, Pop Comrt of Agric, Moscow; 1919–22 prof, Golitsyn Agric Courses; from 1922 prof, Moscow Zootech Inst; wrote major studies of microbiology of milk, fermentation of milk products, etc; *Publ: Propionovokisloye brozheniye v shveytsarskom syre* (Propionic Acid Fermentation in Swiss Cheese) (1925), etc; *Died:* 1951.

VOYTOLOVSKIY, Lev Naumovich (1876–1941) Physician, writer and critic; *Born:* 3 Mar 1876 in Lubny, Poltava Province; *Educ:* 1901 grad Med Fac, Khar'kov Univ; *Career:* 1901 first work printed; from 1904 contributed regularly to Marxist periodicals, including "Pravda"; wrote about Gogol', Chekhov and Andreyev; 1904 drafted into army as physician during Russo-Japanese War; his mil impressions were published in the newspaper "Kiyevskaya mysl'"; 1908–09 contributed to collection *Literaturnyy raspad* (Literary Decay); 1914 again drafted into army and serbed at front until the end of WW 1; fought in Civil War; during Polish War served with 12th Army; continued to write despite increasing blindness; *Publ: Po sledam voyny. Pokhodnyye zapiski. 1914–1917* (In the Footsteps of War. Campaign Notes. 1914–1917) (1925–27); *Ocherki istorii russkoy literatury 19 i 20 vekov* (An Outline History of 19th- and 20th-Century Russian Literature) (1927–28), etc; *Died:* 7 Nov 1941 during the blockade of Leningrad.

VOZDVIZHENSKIY, Nikodim Dmitriyevich (1893–1966) Party and govt official; CP member from 1914; *Born:* 13 Nov 1893; *Educ:* 1923–28 studied at Moscow Land-Survey Inst; *Career:* 1912–14 helped found Syzran' RSDRP(B) org; during WW 1 anti-war propaganda work; 1916 member, provisional bureau, Syzran' Bolshevik group and member, Syzran' Soc-Democratic Initiative Group; then member, Syzran' RSDRP Comt; Mar 1917 attended All-Russian Party Workers' Conference; 1917–18 secr, Syzran' Province Woodworkers' Union and secr, Syzran' Party Comt; Oct 1917 deleg, Syzran' Oblast and All-Russian Congresses of Soviets; chem, Syzran' Exec Comt, Sov Workers and Soldiers' Dep; until May 1919 investigator, Special Dept, All-Russian Cheka and Moscow Cheka; 1919–22 member, Prosecutors Collegium, Kiev Mil Distr Tribunal; 1923 secr, Moscow's Bauman Rayon Party Comt; 1928–37 exec communal econ work in Moscow; 1937–40 arrested and detained by State Security organs; 1940 rehabilitated; 1940–54 tech and eng work in Oryol Oblast and Mordovian and Dagestani ASSR; from 1954 pensioner; *Died:* 4 June 1966.

VOZNESENSKIY, Ivan Nikolayevich (1887–1946) Eng; specialist in hydraulic machinery and automatic control; corresp member, USSR Acad of Sci from 1939; *Born:* 5 Jan 1887; *Educ:* grad Petersburg Technol Inst; *Career:* from 1921 taught at various higher educ establishments, including the Leningrad Polytech Inst; during 1920 criticized prevalent methods of calculation for hydraulic machinery and advocated the use of hydrodynamic methods; during 1930's, after solving the problem of two-dimensional hydromech and developing the basis for the solution of three-dimensional hydromech, devised a new theory of hydroturbines along with methods of calculation; 1935, together with a team of eng, designed and built powerful and economical propeller pumps; extended the classical theory of machine-speed regulation to the regulation of any other unitary parameters; developed a theory of linked autonomous control for turbines in distr heating plants, which he subsequently generalized for any machine and any quantity of regulable parameters; co-founder, I.I. Polzunov Boiler and Turbine Inst; *Publ: Koeffitsiyent poleznogo deystiya vodyanykh turbin po uravneniyam gidrodinakimi* (The Efficiency of Hydroturbines According to the Equations of Hydrodynamics); *Tryokhrazmernaya teoriya turbin* (Three-Dimensional Turbine Theory); *K voprosu o vybore skhemy regulirovaniya tyoplofikatsionnykh turbin* (The Selection of a Control Circuit for Turbines in District Heating Plants); *O regulirovanii mashin s bol'shim chislom reguliruyemykh parametrov* (The Control of Machines with a Large Number of Regulable Parameters); *Uravneniya gidrodinamiki i konstruksiya vodyanykh mashin* (Hydrodynamic Equations and the Design of Hydraulic Machines) (1948), etc; *Awards:* Order of Lenin; Order of the Red Banner of Labor; Stalin Prize (1946); *Died:* 28 June 1946.

VOZNESENSKIY, Nikolay Alekseyevich (1903–1950) Party and govt official; dep chm, USSR Council of Pop Comr from 1939; Dr of Econ from 1935; member, USSR Acad of Sci from 1943; CP member from 1919; *Born:* 1 Dec 1903 in vil Tyoploye, now Tula Oblast, son of an officer worker; *Educ:* 1924 grad Svardlov Communist Univ; 1931 grad Inst of Red Prof; *Career:* 1919–21 Komsomol exec in Chern' and Tula; 1924–28 Party exec in Donbas; from 1931 lecturer, Inst of Red Prof; 1932–35 worked for Centr Control Commission, Workers and Peasants' Inspection; from 1934 member, Sov Control Commission; from 1935 chm, Leningrad City Planning Commission and dep chm, Exec Comt, Leningrad City Sov; from Dec 1937 chm, USSR Gosplan and Bureau member, Sov Control Commission; from 1939 also dep chm, USSR Council of Pop Comr (USSR Council of Min); from Mar 1939 simultaneously member, CC, CPSU(B); from Feb 1941 cand Politburo member, from 1947 Politburo member, CC, CPSU(B); during WW 2 member, State Defense Comt; from 1943 also member, Comt for Econ Reconstruction in Former German-Occupied Areas, USSR Council of Pop Comr; dep, RSFSR Supr Sov of 1st convacation; dep, USSR Supr Sov of 2nd convocation; early 1949 fell in disfavor and was removed from all Party and govt posts, losing his seat in the Politburo and the CC; subsequently arrested on charges of involvement in "Leningrad affair" and sentenced to death; his popular book "The War Economy of the USSR During the Fatherland War" incurred Stalin's wrath and was declared "anti-Marxist" and "anti-sci"; *Publ: Voyennaya ekonomika SSSR v period Otechestvennoy voyny* (The War Economy of the USSR During the Fatherland War) (1947); unfinished book *Politicheskaya ekonomiya kommunizma* (The Political Economy of Communism) (written 1948–49); *Awards:* two Orders of Lenin; *Died:* 30 Sept 1950; executed by firing squad.

VOZNYAK, Mikhail Stepanovich (1881–1954) Ukr lit historian; member, Ukr Acad of Sci from 1929; CP member from 1951; *Born:* 3 Oct 1881 in vil Volytsya, L'vov Oblast; *Educ:* 1908 grad Philosophy Fac, L'vov Univ; *Career:* 1902 first work printed; wrote some 600 studies, monographs, articles, reviews, etc; wrote studies of late 19th- and early 20th-Century Ukr writers: I.P. Kotlyarevskiy, T.G. Shevchenko, M.S. Shashkevich, Markov Vovchok, I.S. Nechuye-Levitskiy, Lesya Ukrainka, etc; specialized in work of Ivan Franko; *Publ: filologicheskiye trudy I. Mogil'nitskogo* (The Philological Works of I. Mogil'nitskiy) (1910); *Galitsiyskiye grammatiki ukrainskogo yazyka* (Galician Grammars of Ukrainian) (1911); *Materialy k istorii ukrainskoy pesni i stikhi* (Material on the History of Ukrainian Song and Verse) (1913–25); *Istoriya ukrainskoy literatury* (The History of Ukrainian Literature) (1920–24); *Ukrainskiye narodnyye skazki* (Ukrainian Folk Tales) (1946–48); *Pisatel'skaya deyatel'nost' Ivana Boretskogo na Volyne i vo L'vove* (Ivan Boretskiy's Writing Work in Volhynia and L'vov) (1954); *Iz zhizni i tvorchestva Ivana Franko* (From the Life and Work of Ivan Franko) (1955); *Ocherki o mirovozrenii Ivana Franko* (Studies in the Philosophical Outlook of Ivan Franko) (1955); *Gigant mysli i truda. Put' zhizni i bor'by Ivana Franko* (A Giant of Thought and Labor. The Career and Campaign of Ivan Franko) (1958), etc; *Died:* 20 Nov 1954.

VRANGEL', Pyotr Nikolayvich (1878–1928) Mil commander; lt-gen, Russian Army; baron; *Born:* 1878; *Educ:* grad Petersburg Mining Inst; 1907 grad Gen Staff Acad; *Career:* from 1904 on mil service; toward end of WW 1 commanded cavalry corps; during Civil War served with Gen Denikin's forces and commanded 1st Cavalry Div, then Cavalry Corps; spring 1919 commanded Caucasian Volunteer Army; Dec 1919 appointed commander, main forces of Volunteer Army in Khar'kov Sector; Apr 1920, at Mil Council in Sebastopol, elected commander in chief of Southern Russian Armed Forces in place of Gen Denikin; after Red Army's victory in Crimea he was evacuated to Constantinople with the remnants of his forces; *Publ: Zapiski ("Beloye delo")* (Notes /The Whitist Cause/), (vol 5 and 6, 1928); *Died:* 1928 in Burssels; burried in Belgrade.

VREDEN, Roman Romanovich (1867–1934) Surgeon; pioneer of Russian orthopedics; *Born:* 22 Mar 1867; *Educ:* 1890 grad Mil Med Acad; *Career:* from 1890 postgrad work at V.A. Ratimov's Hospital Surgical Clinic; 1893 defended doctor's thesis and worked as intern, Kiev Mil Hospital; 1896 senior asst, Prof Ratimov's Chair of Surgery; 1898 assoc prof, Mil Med Acad; 1900–02 replaced Ratimov during his illness; 1902–04 worked for Main Health Bd; during 1904–05 Russo-Japanese War chief surgeon, Manchurian Army; 1906–34 founder-dir, Russia's first orthopedics inst at Petersburg; from 1911 prof of orthopedics, Psychoneurological Inst; also lectured on mil field surgery at Mil Med Acad; from 1918 prof of orthopedics, 1st Petrograd Med Inst; and head of orthopedics course, Petrograd Inst of Postgrad Med Training; devised new orthopedic operations and improved existing techniques; wrote first Russian-language orthopedics textbook; contributed to treatment of bone tuberculosis, skeletal deformation, poliomyelitis sequelae and mil field surgery; chm and hon member, Pirogov Surgical Soc and Leningrad Soc of Orthopedic Surgeons; chm, All-Union and republ congresses of surgeons; member, Int Soc of Surgeons; 1903 attended Int Congress of Mil Surgeons; 1908 member, Commission to Revise Red Cross Geneva Convention; 1912 and 1913 member, Red Cross Int Conventions; member, American Soc of Mil Physicians; wrote some 80 works; *Publ:* doctor's thesis *K etiologii tsistita* (The Etiology of Cystitis) (1893); *Prakticheskoye rukovodstvo po voyenno-polevoy khirurgii* (A Practical Manual on Military Field Surgery) (1911); *Prakticheskoyw rukovodstvo po ortopedii* (A Practical Manual on Orthopedics) (1925), etc; *Died:* 7 Feb 1934 in Leningrad.

VREVSKIY, Mikhail Stepanovich (1871–1929) Physiochemist; corresp member, USSR Acad of Sci; prof; *Born:* 15 Feb 1871; *Educ:* 1895 grad Petersburg Univ; *Career:* from 1898 asst to Prof Konovalov at Petersburg Univ; from 1913 prof, Petersburg Univ, where he founded a separate Physical Chemistry Laboratory; from

1921 also head, Chemical Dept, Lesgaft Sci Soc; from 1924 worked for Commission to Reform Russian Alcoholimetry, Main Bd of Weights and Measures; studied solution theory, thermodynamic theory of binary liquid systems of all concentrations; established connection between temperature and composition of liquid vapor and the partial tensions of its components; also established conection between temperature and composition of the vapor of azeotropic mixtures; developed a gen theory covering all cases in the equilibrium of interchangeable phases; made a systematic study of the relation between temperature and the properties of binary liquid systems; 1927 he and B.P. Nikol'skiy published their new method for determining the latent evaporation point of solutions at a constant temperature; 1927 also devised new method for determining partial vapor tension and degree of dissociation in solution vapors containing molecules of the associated component; 1929 proposed a theory for the evaporation of solutions and an equation for determining the evaporation point of binary solutions; his methods and findlings have been incorporated in physicochemical manuals and reference books; ***Publ:*** ***Ob uprugosti para vodnospirtovykh rastvorov soley*** (The Vapor Tension of Water-Alcohol Salt Solutions) (1900); master's thesis, *O sostave i uprugosti para rastvorov* (The Composition and Vapor Tension of Solutions) (1911); doctor's thesis *Izucheniye rastvorov pri razlichnykh temperaturakh* (A Study of Solutions at Various Temperatures) (1916); *Uprugost' para i teplovyye effekty obrazovaniya gazovakh rastvorov* (The Vapor Tension and Thermal Effects of the Formation of Gaseous Solutions) (1924); *Metod opredeleniya skrytoy ispareniya chistykh zhidkostey i rastvorov* (A Method of Determining the Latent Evaporation Point of Pure Liquids and Solutions) (1927); "Theoretische und experimentelle Untersuchung über Verdampfung binärer Gemische" (1929), etc; *Awards:* Zinin and Voskresenskiy Prize (1916); Lenin Prize (1924); *Died:* 29 May 1929.

VSEVOLODSKIY-GERNGROSS, Vsevolod Nikolayevich (1882–1962) Theater historian; Dr of Arts from 1933; prof from 1921; *Born:* 25 Sept 1882; *Educ:* 1908 grad Higher Drama Courses, Petersburg; 1909 grad Petersburg Mining Inst; *Career:* 1909–19 actor, Alexandrine Theater and other Petersburg theaters; 1910–49 taught at Inst of Stagecraft, Leningrad and Lunacharskiy State Inst of Stagecraft, Moscow, etc; also did research on history of the Russian theater and folk art; 1923 founded Experimental Theater, Petrograd; 1930 founded Ethnographic Theater, Russian Museum, Leningrad; *Publ: Teatr Rossii v epokhu Otechestvennoy voyny* (The Russian Theater in the Period of the Fatherland War) (1912); *Istoriya teatral'nogo obrazovaniya v Rossii* (The History of Theatrical Training in Russia) (1913); *Teoriya russkoy rechevoy intonatsii* (The Theory of Russian Intonation) (1922); *Iskusstvo deklamatsii* (The Art of Delivery) (1925); *Istoriya russkogo teatra* (The History of the Russian Theater) (2 vol, 1929); "I.A. Dmitriyevskiy" (1945); *Russkiy teatr. Ot istokov do serediny XVIII veka* (The Russian Theater, From Its Origins to the Mid-18th Century) (1957); *Russkaya ustnaya narodnaya drama* (Russian Oral Folk Drama) (1959); *Russkiy teatr vtoroy poloviny XVIII veka* (The Russian Theater of the Late 18th Century) (1960); *Fonvizin-dramaturg* (Fonvizin the Playwright) (1960), etc; *Died:* 26 Oct 1962.

VUKOLOV, Semyon Petrovich (1863–1940) Chemist; specialist in explosives and gunpowders; *Born:* 4 Sept 1863; *Educ:* 1887 grad Petersburg Univ; *Career:* from 1889 worked at Mendeleyev's Laboratory, Petersburg Univ; from 1891 Mendeleyev's asst in his Sci and Tech Laboratory, Dept of the Navy; 1893 Mendeleyev developed in this laboratory his smokeless powder (pyrocollodion powder); during 1904–05 Russo-Japanese War developed at this laboratory technol for production and sampling of trotyl and later tetryl; developed original percussion-operated mercury fulminate-tetryl capsule detonator; during WW 1 supervised research on production and properties of various new explosives; also studied effects of underwater explosions and reulting pressure waves; organized supplies of raw material for production of explosives; 1919–23 asst chm, Special Tech Commission for the Inspection of Powders and Explosives; 1919–27 worked for State Inst of Applied Chemistry; from 1926 prof, Naval Acad; also prof, Leningrad Univ; from 1932 again worked for Sci and Tech Naval Laboratory and for Leningrad Technol Inst; *Died:* 9 Oct 1940.

VUL'F, Aleksandr Viktorovich (1867–1923) Electr eng; specialist in electr traction engines; *Born:* 24 July 1867; *Educ:* 1889 grad Petersburg Univ; *Career:* from 1891 instructor, Petersburg Eng Acad and Eng College; from 1900 extraord prof, Warsaw Polytech Inst; 1904 began research on electr traction; 1907–12 lecturer, from 1912 prof, Petersburg (Petrograd) Polytech Inst; influenced the development of research on electr traction in USSR; helped to draft and realize plan for the electrification of Russia; proposed combined electrification of railroads and adjacent areas and argued that the former should be run on high-voltage direct current (up to 5,000 volts); these proposals were subsequently implemented; *Publ: Nagrevaniye tyagovogo elektrodvigatelya i yego opredeleniye* (The Warmingup of an Electric Traction Engine and Its Definition) (1909); *Elektricheskaya tyaga* (Electric Traction) (2nd ed, 1926); *Died:* 1923.

VUL'F, Georgiy Viktorovich (1863–1925) Crystallographer; corresp member, USSR Acad of Sci from 1921; *Born:* 22 June 1863 in Chernigov; *Educ:* 1885 grad Warsaw Univ; *Career:* 1885–97 asst prof, then assoc prof, Warsaw Univ; 1897–98 prof, Kazan' Univ; 1899–1906 prof, Warsaw Univ; 1906–07 lived in Geneva; from 1908 assoc prof, Moscow Univ; 1911 resigned from Moscow Univ in protest against policies of Educ Kasso; from 1911 head, Chair of Mineralogy and Crystallography, Moscow Higher Women's Courses; also did experimental work at newly-opened Shanyavskiy Pop Univ; from 1918 prof, Moscow Univ; in geometrical crystallography devised a simple graphic method of processing the results of measuring crystals; this method was linked to the stereographic diffuser he invented in 1897 and which is named for him; used least squares method for precise calculation of crystal constants; made his main contribution on internal structure of crystals; 1913 (at the same time as Bragg in England) devised a formula now known as the Vul'f-Bragg formula, underlying x-ray structural analysis; 1913 carried out first x-ray structural research in Russia; during WW 1 developed a new method of preparing x-ray screens used in med practice; *Publ: Izbrannyye raboty po kristallofizike i kristallografii* (Selected Works on Crystal Physics and Crystallogdraphy) (1952); *Died:* 25 Dec 1925.

VUL'F, Pavla Leont'yevna (1878–1961) Actress, stage dir and drama teacher; Hon Artiste of RSFSR from 1927; *Born:* 19 July 1878; *Educ:* 1900 grad Petersburg Theatrical College; *Career:* prior to 1917 Oct Revol worked at Korsh Theater and Nezlobin Theater in Moscow; also worked at theaters in Odessa, Kiev, Khar'kov, Irkutsk, Saratov, etc; after 1917 Oct Revol helped found first Sov theater in the Crimea; performed at theaters in Simferopol', Yalta, Sebastopol, Kazan', Baku, Smolensk and Dnepropetrovsk; 1935 at Centr Theater of the Red Army; 1936–38 Gorky Theater, Rostov; 1938 at Leningrad Sov Theater; from 1929 also stage dir; taught F.G. Ranevskaya; taught drama at Baku Young Workers' Theater; State Inst of Stagecraft and Studio of Chamber Theater, etc; wrote her reminiscences of pre revol theatrical life in Moscow and the provinces and Sov theatrical life and figures in the 1920's and 1930's; *Roles:* Liza Kalitina in *Dvoryanskoye gnezdo* (A Nest of Gentlefolk), after Turgenev; Anya in Chekhov's *Vishnyovyy sad* (The Cheryy Orchard); Irina in Chekhov's *Tri sestry* (Three Sisters); Margarite Gauthier in Dumas-fils' "La Dame aux Camelias"; Marie Chardin in Kosorotov's *Mechta lyubvi* (A Dream of Love); Motyl'kova in Gusev's *Slava* (Glory); Katerina in Ostrovskiy's *Groza* (The Storm); Nastya in Gorky's *Na dne* (The Lower Depths); Hedvig in Ibsen's "The Wild Duck"; Lyubov' in "Lyubov' Yarovaya"; Mamasha in Andreyev's *Dni nashey zhizni* (The Days of Our Life), etc; *Productions:* Olyosha's *Zagovor chuvstv* (Conspiracy of the Senses) (1929), etc; *Publ: V starom i novom teatre* (In the Old and New Theater) (1962); *Died:* 8 June 1961.

VUL'F, Yevgeniy Vladimirovich (1885–1941) Botanist and geographer; Dr of Biology from 1936; prof from 1921; *Born:* 25 May 1885 in Simferopol'; *Educ:* 1906 grad Moscow Univ; 1909 grad Vienna Univ; *Career:* 1914–16 worked at Nikita Botanical Garden; 1921–26 prof, Crimean Univ; later sci specialist, All-Union Inst of Plant-Breeding, Leningrad; *Publ: Rastitel'nost' vostochnykh yayl Kryma* (The Vegetation of the Eastern Crimean Mountain Pastures) (1925); *Flora Kryma* (The Flora of the Crimea) (1927–30); *Vvedeniye v istoricheskuyu geografiyu rasteniy* (An Introduction to the Historical Geography of Plants) (1933); *Istoricheskaya geografiya rasteniy* (The Historical Geography of Plants) (1936); *Istoricheskaya geografiya rasteniy. Istoriya flor zemnogo shara* (The Historical Geography of Plants. The History of the World's Flora) (1944); *Died:* 21 Dec 1941 in Leningrad.

VUL'FSON (DAVYDOV), S.D. (1879–1932) Govt official; CP member from 1902; *Born:* 1879; *Career:* Party work in Yekaterinsolav, Lugansk, Caucasus, Baku, Samara, etc; repeatedly arrested; during Civil War with Red Army supply organs; member, Crimean Council of Pop Comr; after the Civil War econ work; 1921–24 dep chm, then chm, Moscow Consumer Soc; member, Moscow Party Comt; Presidium member, Moscow Sov; from 1924 worked for Pop Comrt of For Trade; Sov trade rep in Italy and Austria; Sov trade mission official in Paris and Berlin; from 1927 exec work connected with grain exports; *Died:* 1932.

VURGUN, Samed (real name: VEKILOV, Samed Vurgun Yusif ogly) (1906–1956) Azer poet, playwright and soc worker; Pop Poet and Hon Art Worker of Azer SSR; member, Azer Acad of Sci from 1945; CP member from 1940; *Born:* 21 Mar 1906 in vil Yukhari Salauli, Azer, son of a peasant; *Educ:* 1924 grad Kazakh Teachers' Seminary; 1929–31 studied at 2nd Moscow Univ; then postgrad studies in Baku; *Career:* from 1924 taught at schools in Kazakh, Kuba and Kirovabad; 1924 first work printed; founded new school of poetics in Azer; dep, USSR Supr Sov of 1st–4th convocations; wrote articles on Pushkin, Mayakovskiy, Nizami, Gorky, etc; translated into Azer: Pushkin's *Yevgeniy Onegin* (Eugene Onegin); part of Shota Rustaveli's "The Hero in the Tiger Skin"; Nizami's poem "Leyli and Medzhnun"; Gorky's *Devushka i smert.* (The Firl and Death); Shevchenko's "Katerina"; verse of Chavchavadze, Dzhambul, etc; *Publ:* collected verse "A Poet's Curse" (1930); collection "The Lantern" (1932); "Komsomol Poem" (part 1, 1933); "Chair of Death" (1934); "The Twenty-Six" (1935); "Basti" (1937); "Talystan" (1938); verse dramas: "Varif" (1937); "Khanlar" (1939); "Farkhad and Shirin" (1941); verse: "A Mother's Word" (1941); "The Nurse" (1941); "Guarding the Homeland" (1941); "To the Partisans of the Ukraine" (1942); "So They Told Me" (1943); poems: "Burning Books" (1947); "A Negro Talks" (1948); "Mugan'" (1949); "Old Friends" (1949); "Reading Lenin" (1950); "Aygyun" (1951); "Standard-Bearer of the Age" (1954); verse cycle "Recollection of Europe" (1947–50), etc; *Awards:* two Stalin Prizes (1941 and 1942); two Orders of Lenin; other orders; medals; *Died:* 27 May 1956 in Baku.

VVEDENSKIY, Aleksandr Ivanovich (1856–1925) Kantian philosopher; prof; *Born:* 1856; *Career:* from 1888 prof of logic and psychology, Petersburg Univ; also taught at other higher educ establishments in Petersburg; 1899–1921 chm, Petersburg (Petrograd) Philosophical Soc; an opponent of materialism, he propounded a form of Kantian agnosticism, maintaining that human perception is merely a form of psychic activity with no objective content; championed the idealist concept of logical forms and laws; laid special stress on the role of faith, religion and divine revelation; *Publ: Opyt postroyeniya teorii materii na printsipakh kriticheskoy filosofii* (An Attempt to Construct a Theory of Matter on the Principles of Critical Philosophy) (1888); *Kritiko-filosofskiy analiz massy i svyaz' vysshykh zakonov materii v zakone proportsional'nosti* (A Critical Philosophical Analysis of Mass and the Relation of the Higher Laws of Matter to the Law of Proportionality) (1889); *O predelakh i priznakakh odushevleniya. Novyy psikhofiziologicheskiy zakon v svyazi s voprosom o vozmozhnosti metafiziki* (The Limits and Characteristics of Animation. A New Psychophysiological Law in Cennection with the Possibility of Metaphysics) (1892); *Psikhologiya bez vsyakoy metafiziki* (Psychology Without Metaphysics) (1914); *Sud'ba very v Boga v bor'be s ateizmom* (The Fate of Belief in God in the Struggle Against Atheism) (1922); *Filosofskiye ocherki* (Philosophical Essays) (1924), etc; *Died:* 1925.

VVEDENSKIY, Ivan Nikolayevich (1875–1960) Psychiatrist; Dr of Med and prof from 1935; *Born:* 1875; *Educ:* 1900 grad Med Fac, Moscow Univ; *Career:* specialized in psychiatry at Moscow Mental Sanatorium; 1903–06 intern, Psychiatric Clinic, Moscow Univ, where he worked under Prof V.P. Serbskiy; 1906–18 dir, Moscow Alcoholics' Sanatorium; after 1917 Oct Revol specialized in forensic psychiatry; 1924–60 senior assoc, V.P. Serbskiy Centr Research Inst of Forensic Psychiatry; 1934–41 also head, Chair of Psychiatry, Smolensk Med Inst; for over 50 years member, Moscow Soc of Neuropathologists and Psychiatrists; member, various other sci soc and org; exec ed, journal "Sovremennaya psikhiatriya"; wrote some 70 works on alcoholism, reactive states, forensic psychiatry, the clinical aspects and diagnosis of states of withdrawal, etc; coauthored several textbooks on forensic psychiatry; *Awards:* Order of Lenin; Badge of Honor; medals; *Died:* Oct 1960.

VVEDENSKIY, Nikolay Yevgen'yevich (1852–1922) Physiologist; Dr of Med from 1886; pioneer of materialistic approach to natural history; prof from 1889; *Born:* 28 Apr 1852 in vil Kochkovo, Vologda Province, son of a priest; *Educ:* 1872 grad Vologda Theological Seminary; 1879 grad Natural Sci Dept, Fac of Physics and Mathematics, Petersburg Univ; *Career:* during student years became involved with Populist movement; 1874–77 imprisoned for spreading revol ideas among peasants; 1884 defended master's thesis on "Telephonic Studies of Electrical Phenomena in the Muscular and Nerve Apparatus"; pioneered research on the laws governing the reaction of stimulated systems; 1886 defended doctor's thesis on "The Interrelationship of Excitation and Stimulation in Tetanus"; from 1889 prof, Petersburg Univ; 1900 hon pres, Paris Med Congress; member, Nat Health Soc and Soc of Psychiatrists and Neuropathologists; taught at Higher Women's Courses and, from 1907, at Psychoneurological Inst; co-founder, Soc of Physiologists; 1917 co-organized 1st Russian Physiological Congress; Sov rep, Org Bureau for Int Physiological Congresses; member, Petersburg Soc of Natural Scientists; wrote numerous works; edited various publications of Petersburg Soc of Natural Scientists and Physiological Laboratory, Petersburg Univ; *Publ: Vozbuzhdeniye, tormozheniye i narkoz* (Stimulation, Inhibition and Narcosis) (1901); *Sobraniye sochineniy* (Collected Works) (6 vol, 1951–56); *Died:* 16 Sept 1922 in Petrograd.

VYATKIN, Leonid Yakovlevich (? –1967) Govt official; cand member, CC, CP Kaz from 1966; *Born:* date and place of birth unknown; *Career:* 1961–62 first secr, Ust'-Kamenogorsk City Comt, CP Kaz; 1963–64 secr, East Kaz Oblast Comt (Ind), CP Kaz; 1965–67 head, Construction Dept, CC, CP Kaz; 1967 Kaz Dep Min for the Construction of Heavy Ind Enterprises; 1961–65 member, CC, CP Kaz; 1961 deleg at 22nd CPSU Congress; *Died:* 12 Aug 1967.

VYATKIN, Mikhail Porfir'yevich (1895–1967) Historian; Dr of Historical Sci from 1944; prof from 1946; corresp member, Kir Acad of Sci from 1954; Hon Sci Worker of RSFSR from 1965; *Born:* 9 Aug 1895; *Educ:* 1913–17 studied at History and Philology Fac, Petersburg Univ; 1921 grad History and Philology Fac, Tomsk Univ; *Career:* 1921–22 taught at Chair of Russian History, Tomsk Univ; from 1922 taught at secondary school, then colleges in Leningrad; from 1934 senior assoc, from 1957 chm, Leningrad Branch, Inst of History, USSR Acad of Sci; for many years head, Chair of USSR History, Leningrad's Pokrovskiy Teachers' Training Inst; after this was amalgamated with Leningrad's Herzen State Teachers' Training Inst in the late 1950's, he worked as prof at the latter; specialized in the history of the peoples of Centr Asia and econ history of Russia; from 1957 member, ed bd, journal "Istoricheskiye zapiski"; *Publ: Torgovy y kapitalizm v Rossii* (Mercantile Capitalism in Russia) (1927); *Ocherki po istorii Kazakhskoy SSR* (An Outline History of the Kazakh SSR) (1941); "Batyr Srym" (1947); coauthor and ed, *Istoriya Kazakhskoy SSR* (The History of the Kazakh SSR) (2 vol, 1949); coauthor and exec ed, *Ocherki istorii Leningrada* (An Outline History of Leningrad) (vol 1, 1955); coauthor and ed, *Istoriya Kirgizii* (The History of Kirghizia); coauthor, *Ocherki istorii SSSR. Period feodalizma. XVIII vek* (An Outline History of the USSR. The Period of Feudalism The 18th Century) (1956); *Monopolisticheskiy kapital v Sredney Azii* (Monopolistic Capital in Central Asia) (1962); coauthor and ed, *Kratkaya istoriya SSSR* (A Brief History of the USSR) (vol 1, 1963); *Gornozavodskoy Ural v 1900–1917 godakh* (The Mining Urals in 1900–1917) (1965), etc; *Awards:* Order of the Red Banner of Labor; Badge of Hon; Stalin Prize; *Died:* 7 Dec 1967.

VYATKIN, Vasiliy Lavrent'yevich (1869–1932) Archeologist; *Born:* 1869; *Career:* from 1896 founder-dir, Samarkand Museum; initiated excavations in Eastern Medieval section of Samarkand; discovered 15th-Century astronominal abservatory of Ulugbek near Samarkand; also did research on the 14th-Century architecture of Samarkand; *Publ: Afrasnab. Gorodishche bylogo Samarkanda* (Afrasnab. The Ancient Settlement of Samarkand) (1927); booklets on the architecture of Samarkand, etc; *Died:* 1932.

VYAZEMSKAYA, Lyubov' Orestovna (1869–1958) Educationist; specialist in methods of teaching English; Dr of Pedag Sci; prof; *Born:* 3 Nov 1869; *Educ:* 1901 grad Cambridge Univ; then grad 2nd Moscow Univ; *Career:* from 1902 taught English at a girl's high school in Moscow; from 1924 teaching and research work at Moscow Inst of Rail Trans Eng; 1938–57 head, Chair of For Languages, above inst; specialized in methods of teaching English at tech schools and tech colleges; *Publ: Angliyskiy yazyk dlya russkikh tekhnicheskikh shkol* (English for Russian Technical Schools) (2nd ed, 1930); *Angliyskiy yazyk dlya vzroslykh.*

Tekhnika ustnoy i pis'mennoy rechi (English for Adults. The Technique of Speaking and Writing) (1930); coauthor, *Angliyskaya khrestomatiya po dorozhnym mashinam* (An English Reader on Road Machinery) (1932); *Died:* 1958.

VYGODSKIY, Nikolay Yakovlevich (1900–1939) Organist, pianist and composer; *Born:* 3 Apr 1900 in Petersburg; *Educ:* grad piano class, Baku Conservatory and organ and composition classes, Moscow Conservatory; *Career:* taught at Moscow Conservatory; gave organ performances and tried to popularize the organ among the gen public; composed and arranged works for organ and piano; arranged for organ romances and songs of Schubert, Liszt and Wolf and excerpts from Wagner's operas "Tannhäuser" and "Lohengrin"; 1935 arrested by State Security organs; *Died:* 1939 in imprisonment; posthumously rehabilitated.

VYOTSKIY, Nikolay Konstantinovich (1864–1932) Geologist; mining eng; *Born:* 23 Apr 1864; *Educ:* 1891 grad Petersburg Mining Inst; *Career:* studied geological structure of Western Siberia and Urals; compiled detailed account of Tertiary and Quaternary deposits of Western Siberia; studied main ind areas of Urals; also made several regional studies and a geological map of the Urals (1931); *Died:* 7 Aug 1932.

VYSHELESSKIY, Sergey Nikolayevich (1874–1958) Epizoologist; member, Bel Acad of Sci from 1928; Hon member, All-UNion Lenin Acad of Agric Sci from 1956; Hon Sci Worker of RSFSR from 1941; Hon Sci Worker of Bel SSR from 1940; *Born:* 20 Oct 1874; *Educ:* 1899 grad Warsaw Veterinary Inst; *Career:* 1922–24 assoc, 1924–30prof, Veterinary insts in Vitebsk; 1933–34 prof, Kaz Veterinary Research Inst; from 1934 prof, Moscow Veterinary Inst (now Moscow Veterinary Acad); developed method of producing L.S. Sen Tsenkovskiy's anthrax vaccines on agar; did theoretical and practical research on methods of combined vaccinations against anthrax; developed methods of vaccinating northern reindeer against this disease; discovered the nature of plague in reindeer, facilitating its prevention and treatment; *Publ: Opyt kul'tivitovaniya sibireyazvennykh vaktsin na agare i prakticheskogo ikh primeneniya* (Experience in the Cultivation of Anthrax Vaccines on Agar and Their Practical Application) (1910); *O rezul'tatakh sibireyazvennykh privikok vaktsinami* (The Results of Anthrax Vaccinations) (1908); *Padezh oleney v tundre v 1913 godu* (Reindeer Murrain in the Tundra in 1913); (1915); Opyty izucheniya immuniteta pri stade iskusstvennogo i yestestvennogo zarasheniya (Experiments in the Study of Immunity in the Course of Artificial and Natural Infection) (1926); *Allergicheskaya reaktsiya v diagnostike brutsellyoza u domashnikh zhivotnykh* (The Allergic Reaction in Diagnosing Brucellosis in Domestic Animals) (1934); *Infektsionnyy entsefalomiyelit loshadey* (Infectious Encephalomyelitis of Horses) (1944); co-ed, *Chastnaya epozootologiya* (Special Epizoology) (3rd ed, 1954); *Awards:* Stalin Prize (1941); *Died:* 14 Jan 1958.

VYSHINSKIY, Andrey Yanuar'yevich (1883–1954) Lawyer and diplomat; Dr of State and Soc Sci from 1935; prof from 1923; member, USSR Acad of Sci from 1939; CP member from 1920; *Born:* 28 Nov 1883 in Odessa; *Educ:* 1913 grad Law Fac, Kiev Univ; *Career:* 1903 joined RSDRP and worked for Baku Menshevik org; 1905 organized Soc-Democratic battle squads in Caucasus and served as secr, Baku Sov; several times arrested and exiled; 1906 served one year in prison for his connection with the 1905 rail strike; 1907 wounded together with his wife in an assassination bid by a Russian Pop Union terrorist group; 1913 after grad Kiev Univ, stayed on at univ to prepare for professorship but was later expelled on polit grounds; 1913–17 lit and teaching work; 1915–17 also asst barrister in Moscow; after 1917 Oct Revol held various exec posts at Pop Comrt of Food and Public Prosecutor's Office; 1919 volunteer in Red Army; 1921–22 lectured at Moscow Univ; also dean, Econ Fac, Plekhanov Inst of Nat Econ; 1923–25 prosecutor, Criminal Collegium, USSR Supr Court; also prof, Chair of Criminal Law, 1st Moscow Univ; 1925–28 rector, 1st Moscow Univ; 1928–31 Collegium member, RSFSR Pop Comrt of Educ; head, Main Professional Training Bd; dep chm, State Learned Council; from 1928 chm, Special Office of USSR Supr Court for so-called "Shakhtinskiy Case"; 1930, chm, Special Office of USSR Supr Court to try Prof Ramzin's "Ind Party" case; 1931–33 RSFSR Prosecutor and Dep Pop Comr of Justice; 1933–35 USSR Dep Pop Prosecutor; 1935–39 USSR Public Prosecutor; 1933–38 appeared as state prosecutor at many major trials: 1933 in Metro-Vickers trial; 1936 in "Joint Trotskyist-Zinov'yevite Terrorist Center" trial; 1937 in "Parallel Trotskyist Center" trial; 1938 in "Joint Anti-Sov Rightist-Trotskyist Bloc" trial; obediently carried out Stalin's will, trampling all principles of justice and morality in these trials; 1935–37 member, USSR Centr Exec Comt; 1936 member, Commission to Draft USSR Constitution; 1937–41 dir, Inst of Law, USSR Acad of Sci; also ec, journal "Sovetskoye gosudarstvo i pravo' from 1937 dep, USSR Supr Sov; at 18th and 19th Party Congresses elected member, CC, CPSU(B); June 1939–1944 dep chm, USSR Council of Pop Comr; 1940–46 also USSR First Dep Pop Comr of For Affairs; 1946–49 USSR Dep Min of For Affairs, in charge of gen matters; also chm, Juridical Commission, USSR Council of Min; 1949–53 USSR Min of For Affairs; 1953–54 USSR First Dep Min of For Affairs; attended major int conferences and meetings: represented Sov govt an Consultative Council for Italy; Sov rep on Allied Control Commission in Rumania; member, Sov deleg at Crimean and Berlin summit conferences, involving USSR, USA and UK; member, Sov deleg at 1943 and 1945 Moscow meetings of USSR, US and UK for mins; 8 May 1945 represented USSR Pop Comrt of For Affairs at signing of unconditional surrender of Germany; member, "Triumvirate" (Viyshinskiy, Kerr and Harriman) to settle Rumanian question; 1946 headed Sov deleg in first stage of 1st UNGA Session in London; member, Sov deleg at Paris Peace Conference and in second stage of 1st UNGA Session in New York; also member, Sov deleg at for min conference in New York; 1947 member, Sov deleg at USSR, US, UK and French for min meeting in Moscow; from 1947 head, Sov deleg at UN; *Publ: Kurs ugolovnogo protsessa* (A Course in Criminal Prosecution) (1927); *Sudoustroystvo v SSSR* (The Judicial System of the USSR) (1939); *Teoriya sudebnykh dokazatel'stv v sovetskom prave* (The Theory of Judicial Proof in Soviet Law) (1941); *Voprosy teorii gosudarstva i prava* (Problems of State and Law Theory) (1949); *Voprosy mezhdunarodnogo prava i mezhdunarodnoy politiki* (Problems of International Law and International Politics) (1951), etc; *Awards:* six Orders of Lenin; Order of the Red Banner of Labor; medals; Stalin Prize (1947); *Died:* 22 Nov 1954 in New York; his ashes are immured in the Kremlin Wall on Moscow's Red Square.

VYSOTSKIY, Georgiy Nikolayevich (1865–1940) Pedologist, geobotanist and dendrologist; prof; member, Ukr Acad of Sci and Lenin All-Union Acad of Agric Sci from 1935; *Born:* 7 Feb 1865 in vil Nikitovka, now Chernigov Oblast; *Educ:* 1890 grad Petrovsk Agric Acad; *Career:* accompanied Veliko-Anadol'sk expedition organized by Yekaterinoslav Province Forestry Dept; from 1904 member, Permanent Commission on Experimental Forestry; 1920–22 prof, Crimean Univ; 1923 prof, Bel Agric Inst; from 1926 prof, Khar'kov Inst of Agric and Forestry; from 1930 consultant, Khar'kov Research Inst of Forestry and Agric Melioration; did research on the effect of hydrological conditions on forests, the selection of trees for steppe afforestation programs, etc; wrote some 40 works; *Publ: O vybore naibolee podkhodyashchikh dlya kul'tury v stepyakh form drevesnoy rastitel'nosti* (The Selection of the Forms of Timber Vegetation Most Suitable for Steppe Cultivation) (1894); *Biologicheskiye, pochvennyye i fenologicheskiye nablyudeniya i issledovaniya v Veliko-Anadol'skom lesnichestve* (Biological, Pedological and Phenological Observations and Research in the Veliko-Anadol'sk Forest Region) (1901); *O nauchnykh issledovaniyakh, kasayushchikh stepnogo lesorazvedeniya* (Scientific Research on Steppe Afforestation) (1901); *O v zaimootnoshenii mezhdu stepnoy rastitel'nost'yu i vlagoy* (The Relationship Between Steppe Vegetation and Moisture) (1904); *Yergeniya* (Ergenia) (1915); *Lesa Ukrainy i usloviya ikh proizrastaniya i vozobnovleniya* (The Forests of the Ukraine and the Conditions for Their Growth and Regeneration) (1916); *Pokrovovedeniye* (Cover-Cropping) (1925); *O gidrologicheskom i meteorologicheskom vliyanii lesov* (The Hydrological and Meteorological Influence of Forests) (1938); *Died:* 6 Apr 1940.

VYSOTSKIY, Mikhail Konstantinovich (1885–1950) Actor; Pop Artiste of Ukr SSR from 1943; *Born:* 1885; *Educ:* 1914 grad Mochalov Theatrical School, Odessa; *Career:* for many years performed under his teacher N.I. Sobol'shchikov-Samarin in Kiev and other Volga cities; from 1930 at Kiev Russian Theater; specialized in comedy and character roles; *Roles:* Kutuzov in Solov'yov's *Fel'dmarshal Kutuzov* (Fieldmarshal Kutuzov); Rasplyuyev in *Svad'ba Krechinskogo* (Krechinskiy's Marriage); Vanyushin in Naydyonov's *Deti Vanyushina* (Vanyushin's Children); Sganarelle in Lesya Ukrainka's *Kamennyy vlastelin* (The Stone Sovereign); McPherson in Simonov's *Russkiy vopros* (The Russian Question), etc; *Died:* 1950.

Y

YABLOCHKINA, Aleksandra Aleksandrovna (1866–1964) Actress; Pop Artiste of USSR from 1937; *Born:* 15 Nov 1866 in Petersburg, daughter of an actor and stage dir; *Career:* 1885–86 at Tiflis theater; 1886–88 at Korsh Theater, Moscow; from 1888 at Maly Theater, Moscow; from 1915 member, All-Russian Theatrical Soc; 1946–62 chm, Council Presidium, All-Russian Theatrical Soc; *Roles:* Lidiya in Ostrovskiy's *Beshenyye den'gi* (Mad Money); Mamyeva and Turusina in Ostrovskiy's *Na vsyakogo mudretsa dovol'no prostoty* (There's a simpleton in Every Sage); Vasilisa in Ostrovskiy's "Vasilisa Melent'yeva"; Gurmyzhskaya in Ostrovskiy's *Les* (The Forest); Murzavetskaya in Ostrovskiy's *Volki i ovtsy* (The Wolves and the Sheep); Khlestova in Griboyedov's *Gore ot uma* (Woe from Wit); Zvezdintseva and Karenina in Lev Tolstoy's *Plody prosveshcheniya* (The Fruits of Enlightenment) and *Zhivoy trup* (The Living Corpse); Bogayevskaya in Gorky's *Varvary* (The Barbarians); Queen Elizabeth in Schiller's "Maria Stuart"; Cordelia in Shakespeare's "King Lear"; Lady Anne in Shakespeare's "Richard III"; Kseniya in Romashov's *Ognennyy most* (Bridge of Fire); Gornostayeva in Trenyov's "Lyubov' Yarovaya"; Skutarevskaya in Leonov's "Skutarevskiy"; Varvara in Korneychuk's "Bogdan Khmel'nitskiy"; Goritsvet in Korneychuk's *Kryl'ya* (Wings); Miss Crowley in "Vanity Fair", after Thackeray; *Publ:* Vospominaniyas, (Memoirs) (1937); *Zhizn' v teatre* (Life in Theater) (1953); *Awards:* Stalin Prize (1943); three Orders of Lenin; two Orders of the Red Banner of Labor; medals; *Died:* 20 Mar 1964.

YACHEVSKIY, Artur Arturovich (1863–1932) Botanist, mycologist and phytopathologist; corresp member, USSR Acad of Sci from 1923; *Born:* 27 Jan 1863; *Educ:* studied in Switzerland; *Career:* for a while lived and worked in Switzerland; 1894 returned to Russia; studied mycoflora of Smolensk and Moscow Provinces; from 1896 assoc, Petersburg Botanical Garden; 1901–06 head, Phytopathological Station; from 1907 head, Mycology and Phytopathology Bureau, Learned Comt, Main Land Exploitation and Agric Bd; from 1909 also prof at various higher educ establishments in Peterburg; 1904–17 edited various journals and compiled *Yezhegodnik svedeniy o boleznyakh i povrezhdeniyakh kul'turnykh i dikorastushchikh poleznykh rasteniy* (Almanac on Diseases and Injuries of Cultivated and Wild Useful Plants); specialized in taxonomy and phylogenetics, viral and bacterial diseases of plants, phytotoxicology, fungicides, etc; *Publ: Opredelitel' gribov* (A Classification Key to Funghi) (1897); *Golosumchatyye griby* (Gymnoasci) (1926); *Muchnistorosechnyye griby* (Perisporiales) (1927); coauthor, *Fikomitsety* (Phycomycetes) (1931); *Osnovy mikologii* (The Principles of Mycology) (1933); *Bakteriozy rasteniy* (Plant Bacteriosis) (1935), etc; *Died:* 12 Feb 1932.

YAGLOM, Ya. K. (1898–1939) Trade-union and govt official; CP member from 1918; ex-member, Bund; *Born:* 1898; *Career:* at time of 11th Party Congress member, Ural Bureau, All-Union Centr Trade-Union Council; from 1929 chm, Siberian Kray Planning Commission; member, West Siberian Kray CPSU(B) Comt; dep chm, West Siberian Kray Exec Comt; 1930 expelled from Party for alleged "rightist-opportunist activities" in trade-union work; recanted his errors and reinstated in Party; head, Main Canning Ind Bd; arrested by State Security organs; *Died:* 1939 in imprisonment.

YAGODA, Genrikh Grigor'yevich (1891–1938) Govt official; CP member from 1907; USSR Pop Comr of Internal Affairs from 1934; CP member from 1907; *Born:* 1891; *Career:* statistician by profession; 1904–05 worked for underground printing press; 1913 worked for Putilov Plant's sick insurance fund, Petersburg; twice exiled; 1915 drafted into Russian Army; Feb 1917 member, RSDRP(B) Mil Org; helped organize Red Guard in Petrograd; for a while ed, newspaper "Soldatskaya pravda"; Dec 1917 appointed ed, newspaper "Derevenskaya bednota"; during Civil War served with Higher Mil Inspectorate on Southern and Eastern Fronts; 1919 Collegium member, Pop Comrt of For Trade; from 1920 Presidium member, All-Russian Cheka; from 1924 dep chm, Joint State Polit Bd (OGPU); from July 1934 USSR Pop Comr of Internal Affairs; as NKVD chief arranged for use of prison camp labor for construction of White Sea and Volga-Moscow Canals and for building of railroads, resulting in the death of hundreds of thousands of workers; Nov 1935 promoted Comr-Gen of State Security; Sept 1936 replaced and appointed USSR Pop Comr of Communications; Apr 1937 dismissed from this post; Mar 1938 sentenced to death in trial of "rightist-Trotskyist center"; member, USSR Centr Exec Comt of several convocations; 1930 at 16th Party Congress elected cand member, 1934 at 17th Party Congress elected member, CC, CPSU(B); *Awards:* Order of Lenin; Order of the Red Banner; *Died:* 1938 executed.

YAKHONTOV, Valerian Ivanovich (1878–1926) Party and govt official; CP member from 1917; *Born:* 1907 in Nizhniy Novgorod, son of a peasant; *Educ:* 1907 grad Moscow Univ; *Career:* expelled from high-school for "free-thinking", passed external matriculation examinations and entered Moscow Univ; 1902 active in student polit movement; 9 Feb 1902 arrested at student assembly; spent six months in prison; 1903 resumed univ studies and began to work for Moscow RSDRP(B) org; after Dec 1905 uprising moved to Nizhniy Novgorod and worked for Nizhniy Novgorod Party Comt; from 1907 active in trade-union and workers' insurance movement; 1914, together with I.I. Skvortsov and I.G. Smidovich, directed Moscow RSDRP(B) Org; 1916 worked for Minsk Land and City Unions and organized RSDRP(B) group; 1917 Minsk RSDRP(B) Org deleg at Apr Party Conference; spring 1917 broke with Bolsheviks, joined Moscow "Amalgamated" Org and elected to Amalgamationist CC; early 1920 readmitted to CP; from 1922 Collegium member, Pop Comrt of Justice; subsequently RSFSR Asst Prosecutor; head, Draft Bills Dept and member, Small Council of Pop Comr; *Died:* 1926.

YAKHONTOV, Vladimir Nikolayevihch (1899–1945) Actor; specialist in dramatic readings; *Born:* 1899 in Siedlce, Warsaw Voevodstvo, son of an official; *Educ:* from 1918 studied at 2nd, then 3rd Studio, Moscow Arts Theater; *Career:* 1924–26 at Meyerhold Theater; from 1925 concentrated on variety work; 1927, together with his regular producer Ye. Ye. Popova, founded Contemporary Theater, a monodrama theater which existed until 1935; gave straight lit readings and also compiled his own shows, involving readings of verse and fiction, journalistic and sci works, memoirs, letters and even excerpts from newspapers; his shows of this type included *Torzhestvennoye obeshchaniye* (Solemn Pledge) (1929), about Stalin's first five-year plan and *Novyye gody* (New Years) (1935); 1937, for the anniversary of Pushkin's death, gave four special programs; in the first of these he devoted two evenings to a complete reading of *Yevgeniy Onegin* (Eugene Onegin); 1940 presented a "Yesenin Evening" and "Blok Evening"; *Roles:* Baron Feyervari in Fayko's *Uchitel' Bubus* (Bubus the Teacher), etc; *Productions:* lit readings: *Na smert' Lenina* (On the Death of Lenin) (1924); *Oktyabr'* (October) (1924); "Lenin" (1925); "Pushkin" (1926); "Petersburg" (1927); *Voyna* (War) (1929); "Yevgeniy Onegin" (1930); *Vechera Mayakovskogo* (Mayakovskiy Evenings) (1931); "Nastas'ya Filippovna" (1933); *Novyye plody* (New Fruits) (1935); *Torzhestvennoye obeshchaniye* (Solemn Pledge) (1929); trilogy *Vsegda s Leninym* (Always with Lenin) (1939); *Vecher Yesenina* (Yesenin Evening) (1940); *Vecher Bloka* (Blok Evening) (1940); *Za Rodinu, za Stalina* (For One's Country, for Stalin) (1941);; *Vozvrashcheniye Mayakovskogo* (The Return of Mayakovskiy) (1943); *Tost za zhizn'* (A Toast to Life) (1944); *Gore ot uma* (Woe from Wit) (1945), etc; *Awards:* 1st Prize, All-Union Competition of Lit Narrators (1937); *Died:* 1945.

YAKHNOVSKIY, Ivan Timofeyevich (1881–1966) Govt official; CP member from 1901; *Born:* 1881; *Career:* 1902–03 revol work among sailors of Black Sea Fleet; chm, RSDRP Naval Comt and chief Naval Comt; May 1904 arrested for revol work; escaped from Sebastopol Prison and went abroad; continued Party Work in Switzerland and France; 1905 returned to Russia and did Party work in Krasnodar and Rostov-on-Don; then revol propaganda among sailors of Baltic Fleet; several times arrested; exiled to Irkutsk Province; fought in Civil War in Siberia; 1920 Presidium member, Irkutsk City and Uyezd RCP(B) Comt; 1922–23 exec work with State Polit Bd in Moscow; from 1924 exec admin econom work; from 1943 pensioner; *Died:* 8 Nov 1966.

YAKHSHIBAYEV, Sabit (1890–1930) Bash stage designer; *Born:* 1890; *Career:* from 1912 worked with "Sayyar" Drama Company; during Civil War worked with army drama companies and first Bash drama company in Sterlitamak; 1920–30 stage designer, Bash Drama Theater, Ufa; *Works:* designed sets and costumes for: Kamal's "Bankruptcy" and "Our Town's Secret" (1912); Amirkhan's "The Unequal" (1915), etc; *Died:* 16 June 1930.

YAKIMOVA, (pseudonym: DIKOVSKAYA), Anna Vasil'yevna (1856–1942) Russian revolutionary; Populist; *Born:* 1856 in Vyatka Province, daughter of a priest; *Career:* 1873–75 vil teacher; propaganda among peasantry; 1875 arrested and brought to trial for revol activities; acquitted; member, Land and Liberty Soc; 1879, after the schism in this soc, member, Exec Comt, People's Will Party; 1879, together with A.I. Zhelyabov, and 1880, together with Yu.N. Bogdanovich, plotted to assassinate Alexander II; 1882 tried and sentenced to death; sentence commuted to indefinite hard labor in Siberia; 1899 released to post-penal settlement in Chita; after 1917 Oct Revol lived in Moscow and worked for cooperative orgs; member, Soc of Polit Convicts; *Died:* 1942.

YAKIMYCHEV, Aleksandr Mikhaylovich (1897–1938) Mil commander; *Born:* 1897; *Educ:* 1917 grad naval pilots school; 1926 grad Naval Fac, Naval Acad; *Career:* 1928–31 asst prof and lecturer, Naval Acad; 1934 asst naval attache in USA; arrested by State Security organs; *Publ: Voyna "malym /slabym/ flotom" i "Malaya voyna" v epokhu parovogo flota* ("Small /Weak/ Fleet" Warfare and the "Little War" in the Steam Navy Era) (1928); *Ugroza bazam flota po opytu voyny 1914–1918 godov* (The Threat to Naval Bases from the Experience of the 1914–1918 War) (1932); *Died:* 1938 in imprisonment.

YAKIR, Iona Emmanuilovich (1896–1937) Mil commander; Jew; arm commander, 1st class from 1935; CP member from 1917; *Born:* 15 Aug 1896 in Kishinev, son of a pharmacist; *Educ:* 1913 completed private college in Kishinev; 1913–14 studied at Basel Univ; 1914–15 at Khar'kov Technol Inst; 1928–29 at German Higher Mil Acad; *Career:* 1915–16 deferred from mil service while working as machinist at Odessa munitions plant; from 1915 active in Revol movement; 1917 agitated among troops of Kishinev Garrison; member, Exec Comt, Bessarabian Sov of Workers and Soldiers' Dep; after 1917 Oct Revol fought against Rumanian troops; 1917–18 with Red Guards; commanded Red Guard detachment in Bessarabia; 1918 commanded composite detachment, then commandant Tiraspol' Fortress and secr, Mil Council, Tiraspol' Detachment; comr, Voronezh Distr, Southern Screen; commander and comr, Povorino Distr, Southern Screen; member, Revol Mil Council, 8th Army on Southern Front; 1918 frequently distinguished himself in action against Gen Krasnov's troops; May–July 1918 member, Bessarabian Govt and CC, CP Bessarabia, formed in Odessa in preparation for the Sov take-over of Bessarabia; 1919–20 commanded 45th Infantry Div; Aug–Sept 1919 his Southern Forces Group sallied from Odessa and broke through Gen Denikin's rear echelons to Zhitomir, where it linked up with 12th Army; 1920–21 acting commander, 14th Army; May–June 1920 his Fastov Forces Group launched an offensive against Pilsudski's Polish forces and occupied Fastov, Brusilov, Rodomysl' and Kazatin; Aug 1920 his 45th Infantry Div, operationg as part of Budyonny's 1st Cavalry Army, fought its way to L'vov and then operated against Pelyura's Ukr Pop Republ forces and Gen Wrangel's White Army; 1921 commander and comr, 3rd Kazan' Div, Crimea; Nov 1921 finally routed remnants of Petlyura's Ukr nationalist troops at Bazar; 1921–22 commanded Kiev Mil Distr; 1922–23 commanded Kiev Mil Area (renamed distr); 1923 commander and comr, 14th Infantry Corps; 1923–24 asst to M.V. Frunze, commander of Ukr and Crimean Forces; 1924–25 head, Red Army Main Mil Training Establishments Bd; also exec ed, journal "Voyennyy vestnik"; 1925–35 commander, Ukr Mil Distr; from 1926 organized improved defenses of Polish and Rumanian border areas (radiocontrolled minefields, provisions to blow up railroad bridges, etc); 1928–29 lectured to German Reichswehr Gen Staff on Civil War in Russia and received a personal gift from Pres Hindenburg; 1930–36 member, USSR Revol Mil Council; from 1930 directed establishment of fortified areas along Western border of USSR and supervised training of partisans and establishment of bases for the event of an invasion of the USSR; 1931 negotiated the release of a group of distr staff officers, former officers to the Russian Army, arrested by the State Security organs on charges of anti-Sov conspiracy; 1931–32 supervised design and construction of first, fast Sov BT tanks; 1932 formed in his mil distr the Red Army's first mechanized corps; 1933, in connection with the famine in the Ukr, together with several Ukr Party officials and mil commanders, signed a letter to the Politburo, CC, CPSU(B) asking for a stop to grain procurements in the Ukr and seeking permission to organize famine relief from the mil district's reserves; the letter had its effect, but Stalin never forgave the military's interference in state affairs; 1935–37 commander, Kiev Mil Distr; 1935 directed maneuvers of Kiev and Khar'kov Mil Districts which demonstrated for the first time the combined operations of large air force, mechanized and paratroop units; from 1936 member, Mil Council, Pop Comrt of Defense; 1936–37, with the mass arrest of mil commanders, tried to protect individual commanders in his distr from unwarranted arrest; from 1925 member, CC, CP(B) Ukr; from 1926 member, Ukr and USSR Centr Exec Comt; from 1927 Politburo member, CC, CP(B) Ukr; from 1930 cand member, CC, CPSU(B); 1 Jan 1937 arrested while traveling by train from Kiev to Moscow; from prison wrote a letter to Stalin, assuring him of his loyalty to the Party and to Stalin personally; Stalin scrawled on it: "A villain and a prostitute"; 11 June 1937 sentenced to death together with Marshal Tukhachevskiy and others on charges espionage and treason; *Awards:* three Orders of the Red Banner; *Died:* June 1937 executed by firing squad.

YAKOBSON, August Mikhkelevich (1904–1963) Est writer and playwright; Pop Writer of Est SSR from 1950; CP member from 1942; *Born:* 2 Sept 1904; *Educ:* 1929 entered Tartu Univ, where he studied econ before transferring to Med Fac; *Career:* late 1920's began lit career; dep, USSR Supr Sov of 1st, 3rd and 4th convocations; 1950–58 chm, Presidium, Est Supr Sov and dep chm, Presidium, USSR Supr Sov; *Publ:* novels: "The Settlement of Poor Sinners" (1927); "A Predator's Path" (1936); plays: "Ghosts" (1938); "Life in the Citadel" (1946); "Struggle Without Front Lines" (1947); "Rust" (1947); "Two Camps" (1948); "Our Life" (1949); "The Builders" (1950); "Jackals" (1951); "The Guardian Angel of Nebraska" (1953); "Dying" (1954); "The Old Oak" (1955); dramatic chronicle of five plays "Storm Knots" (1957–58); *Awards:* two Stalin Prizes (1947 and 1948); two Orders of Lenin; other orders and medals; *Died:* 23 May 1963.

YAKOVENKO, Vasiliy Grigore'yevich (1889–1938) Govt official; CP member from 1917; *Born:* 1889 in vil Taseyevo, Yeniseysk Province, son of a peasant; *Career:* until the age of 18 hired agric laborer; 1914–17 in Russian Army at the front; during Civil War helped partisan units in Siberia; chm, Council, Northern Kana Partisan Front; from 1920–22 chm, Kana Revol Comt and Kana Uyezd Exec Comt; then dep chm, Krasnoyarsk Province Exec Comt; 1922–23 RSFSR POP Comr of Agric; 1923–26 Pop Comr of Sov Security; 1927 subscribed to Trotskyist platform; 1928–32 worked for Kalinin as chm, Land and Electoral Commission; 1932–35 with USSR Gosplan; Presidium member and chm, Nat Bureau, USSR Gosplan; from 1935 member, Council, then dir, Research Inst of New Fiber Crops, USSR Pop Comrt of Agric; arrested by State Security organs; *Died:* 1938 in imprisonment.

YAKOVKIN, Aleksandr Aleksandrovich (1860–1936) Chemist; prof from 1896; Dr of Chemistry from 1898; corresp member, USSR Acad of Sci from 1925; Hon Sci Worker of RSFSR from 1928; *Born:* 1860; *Educ:* 1884 grad Moscow Univ; *Career:* from 1884 chemist at private print works; from 1890 at Moscow Univ; from 1896 prof, Petersburg Technol Inst; from 1919 also co-founder and assoc, State Inst of Applied Chemistry; chm, Chemistry Dept, Russian Physicochemical Soc; continued and expanded Mendeleyev's research on solutions and ind chemistry; *Publ:* master's thesis *Raspredeleniye veshchestv mezhdu dvumya rastvoritelyami* (The Distribution of Matter Between Two Solvents) (1895); doctor's thesis *O gidrolize khlora* (The Hydrolysis of Chlorine) (1898); *Osnovnyye zakony i ponyatiya khimii* (The Basic Laws and Concepts of Chemistry) (1907); *Uchebnik obshchey khimii /teoreticheskoy i prokladnoy/* (A Textbook of General Chemistry [Theoretical and Applied]) (1935), etc; *Awards:* Order of the Red Banner of Labor; *Died:* 22 Nov 1936.

YAKOVLEV, Aleksandr Ivanovich (1900–?) Party official; CP member from 1917; *Born:* 1900; *Educ:* 1922–23 attented a course on Marxism; *Career:* office worker; 1917–18 agitator, Odessa RSDRP(B) City Comt; 1918–19 secr, North Caucasian RSDRP(B) Comt; 1919–20 held polit posts in various Red Army commands; 1920–21 dep chm, Baku Exec Comt; 1924–26 bd member, Village Union and cand bd member, Butter Distribution Bd; 1928 instructor, CC, CPSU(B), then dep chm, Dept for Work in Rural Areas; 1929 worked for Pop Comrt of Workers and Peasants' Inspection; then chm, Ural Oblast Control Commission of Workers and Peasants' Inspection; chm, Transcaucasian Kray Control Commission and Party Comt, Transcaucasian SFSR Workers and Peasants' Inspection; from 1931 secr, Transcaucasian Kray CPSU(B) Comt; member, Centr Control Commission of 15th and 16th convocations; cand Presidium member, Centr Control Commission; at 17th Party Congress elected member, Party Control Commission, CC, CPSU(B); *Died:* date and place of death unknown.

YAKOVLEV, Aleksandr Stepanovich (1886–1953) Russian writer; *Born:* 1886 in Vol'sk, Saratov Province, son of a housepainter;

Educ: studied at Petersburg Univ; *Career:* worked as postal clerk; 1905, as Maximalist Socialist-Revolutionary, took part in terrorist acts; several times arrested and exiled; began lit work by writing newspaper essays; *Publ:* novelette *Povol'niki* (The Libertines) (1923); *Oktyabr'* (October) (1923); *Oshibka* (The Error) (1923); novels: *Chelovek i pustynya* (Man and Desert) (1926); *Pobeditel'* (The Victor) (1927); *Ogni v pole* (Fires in the Field) (1927); *Stupeni* (Steps) (1946); children's books: *Pioner Pavel Morozov* (Pavel Morozov the Pioneer) (1938); *Zhizn' i priklyucheniya Roal'da Amundsena* (The Life and Adventures of Roald Amundsen) (1932); *Tayna Saratovskoy zemli* (The Secret of the Saratov Region) (1946), etc; *Polnoye sobraniye sochineniy* (Complete Collected Works) (4 vol, 1926); *Polnoye sobraniye sochineniy* (Complete Collected Works) (7 vol, 1928–29); *Rasskazy* (Stories) (1929); *Izbrannoye. Povesti i rasskazy* (Selected Works. Novelletes and Stories) (1955); *Died:* 1953.

YAKOVLEV, Aleksey Ivanovich (1878–1951) Historian; corresp member, USSR Acad of Sci from 1929; son of the Chuvash educationist I.Ya. Yakovlev; *Born:* 1878; *Career:* teaching and research at Moscow Univ, Higher Women's Courses, Library Inst, Inst of History, USSR Acad of Sci and Lenin All-Union Library; specialized in socio-econ history of Russia in 17th Century, history of Russian peasants and serfs and organization of Russian armed forces; *Publ: Zasechnaya cherta Moskovskogo gosudarstva v XVII veke* (The Blaze Marks of Muscovy in the 17th Century) (1916); *Prikaz sbora ratnykh lyudey 1637–1653)* (The Order for Mustering Men-at-Arms, 1637–1653) (1917); *Kholopstvo i kholopy v Moskovskom gosudarstve XVII veka* (Serfdom and Serfs in 17th-Century Muscovy) (1943); *Novgorodskiye zapisnyye kabal'nyye knigi 100–104 i 111 godov* (The 100–104 and 111 Novgorod Kabal Notebooks) (1938); *Akty khozyaystva boyarina B.I. Morozva* (The Boyar V.I. Morozov's Management Records) (1940); *Tamozhennyye knigi Moskovskogo gosudarstva XVII veka* (The 17th-Century Muscovy Customs Books) (3 vol, 1950–52); *Dokumenty i materialy po istorii Mordovskoy ASSR* (Documents and Material on the History of the Mordovian ASSR) (4 vol, 1939–1952); *Awards:* Order of the Red Banner of Labor; medals; *Died:* 1951.

YAKOVLEV, Ivan Yakovlevich (1848–1930) Chuvash writer, translator and teacher; *Born:* 30 April 1848; *Educ:* 1868 grad high school; 1875 grad Kazan' Univ; *Career:* 1868 opened first Chuvash teachers' training school in Simbirsk, where he taught pedag, logic and mathematics for over 50 years; 1875–1903 inspector of Chuvash schools, Kazan' Teaching Distr; instructed Mordavian, Mari and Udmurt teachers in modern teaching methods; devised Chuvash alphabet and wrote first Chuvash ABC primer and readers; translated into Chuvash all L. N. Tolstoy's "Books for Reading" and numerous works by Pushkin, Lermontov and Nekrasov; several schools now bear his name; *Publ: Bukvar' dlya chuvash s prisoyedineniyem russkoy azbuki* (A Chuvash ABC Book with a Russian Alphabet Appendix) (1873); *O shkol'nom obrazovanii chuvash* (Chuvash School Education) (1896); *Bukvar' dlya chuvash, chast' 2 – Russkiye razgovornyye uroki* (A Chuvash ABC Book, Part 2 – Russian Conversation Lessons) (16th ed, 1904); *Kratkiy ocherk Simbirskoy uchitel'skoy skholy* (A Short Survey of the Simbirsk Teachers' Training School) (1908); *Vospominaniya o Lenine* (Reminiscences of Lenin) (1925), etc; *Died:* 23 Oct 1930.

YAKOVLEV, Vasiliy Nikolayevich (1893–1953) Painter, restorer and art teacher; Dr of Arts; Pop Artiste of RSFSR from 1943; member, USSR Acad of Arts from 1947; *Born:* 13 Jan 1893 in Moscow; *Educ:* 1917 grad College of Painting, Sculpture and Architecture in Moscow; *Career:* from 1922 member, Assoc of Artists of Revol Russia; 1924–27 restorer at Centr State Restoration Workshops; 1927–32 at State Museum of the Fine Arts; 1935–38 taught at Acad of Arts; from 1948 at Moscow Art Inst; *Works:* paintings: "A Newspaper at the Front" (1923); "Red Commanders" (1927); "Prospectors Write a Letter to I.V. Stalin" (1937); portraits of Gorky (1933) and Maj-Gen I.V. Panfilov (1942); painting "Kolkhoz Herd" (1948); landscapes, still lifes and numerous drawings; *Publ: O zhivopisi* (Painting) (1951); *O velikikh russkikh khudozhnikakh* (Great Russian Artists) (1952); *Awards:* Order of Lenin; two Stalin Prizes (1943 and 1949); *Died:* 26 Sept 1953.

YAKOVLEV, Vasiliy Vasil'yevich (1880–1957) Musicologist; Dr of Arts from 1944; *Born:* 19 Sept 1880 in Moscow; *Educ:* 1908 grad Mil Eng Acad; studied music under A.A. Il'inskiy in Moscow and N.A. Sokolov in Petersburg; *Career:* 1905 began musical and lit career; worked for: State Theaters Bd, Pop Comrt of Educ; Bolshoy Theater; State Acad of Arts; Moscow Conservatory; Tchaikovsky Museum Center, etc; wrote several works on history of Russian music, especially musical theater; did studies of Tchaikovsky, Moussorgsky, Taneyev and Rachmaninov; traced connections between music and lit in works of Pushkin and Ostrovskiy and wrote studies of such older composers as S.N. Vasilenko, and A.F. Gedike; *Publ: Opera v Bol'shom teatre za sto let, 1825–1925* (Opera at the Bolshoy Theater in the Hundred Years from 1825–1925) (1925); *Pushkin i russkiy opernyy teatr* (Pushkin and the Russian Opera Theater) (1937); *A.N. Ostrovskiy v perepiske s russkimi kompozitorami* (A.N. Ostrovskiy in his Correspondence with Russian Composers) (1937); *Pushkin i muzyka* (Pushkin and Music) (1949); *Proshloye russkoy muzyki. Materialy i issledovaniya* (The Russian Musical Past. Material and Research) (1920); *M.P. Musorgskiy. K pyatidesyatiletiyu so dnya smerti, 1881–1931* (M.P. Moussorgsky. On the Fiftieth Anniversary of His Death. 1881–1931) (1932); ed, *Dni i gody P.I. Chaykovskogo. Letopis' zhizni i tvorchestva* (The Days and Years of P.I. Tchaikovsky. A Chronicle of His Life and Work) (1940); *Died:* 8 Aug 1957 in Moscow.

YAKOVLEV, Viktor Vasil'yevich (1871–1945) Mil eng; fortifications specialist, Dr of Eng; lt-gen, Eng Corps; Hon Sci and Tech Worker of RSFSR from 1929; *Born:* 30 Oct 1871; *Career:* until 1917 prof, Nikolay Eng Acad; from 1918 served in Sov Army; worked at Kuybyshev Mil Eng Acad; *Publ: Oborona sovremennykh dolgovremennykh fortov v period blizhney ataki* (The Defense of Modern Permanent Forts During Close Attack) (1910); *Ataka i oborona dolgovremenno-ukreplyonnykh pozitsiy* (The Attack and Defense of Long-Term Fortified Positions) (vol 1, 1929); *Evolyutsiya dolgovremennoy fortifikatsii* (The Evolution of Long-Term Fortification) (1931), etc; *Awards:* Stalin Prize (1943); *Died:* 7 Sept 1945.

YAKOVLEV (real name: EPSHTEYN), Yakov Arkad'yevich (1896–1939) Politician; CP member from 1913; *Born:* 1896; *Career:* member of student circle at Petersburg Polytech Inst; from 1914 active in workers' circles in Nevskaya Zastava distr; Feb 1917 arrested; after 1917 Feb Revol helped organize workers' militia and soldiers' comts; then until spring 1918 secr, Yekaterinoslav Party Comt; during most of Civil War engaged in underground Party work in Ukr; chm, Kiev and Khar'kov underground revol comt; helped lead revolt against Petlyura; 1918–20 member, Yekaterinoslav Province Party Comt and head, Polit Dept, 14th Army; 1919, during evacuation of Ukr, chm, Vladimir Province Exec Comt; 1920 member, Polit and Org Bureau, CC, CP(B) Ukr and chm, Khar'kov Province Party Comt; helped found comts of poor peasants; 1921 exec post with Main Polit Educ Comt, RSFSR Pop Comrt of Educ, Moscow; 1922–23 dep head, Agitation and Propaganda Dept, CC, RCP(B); 1923–24 head, Press Dept, CC, RCP(B), then ed, newspaper "Bednota"; from late 1923 founder-ed, newspaper "Krest'yanskaya gazeta"; also chm, All-Union Kolhoz Council and member of various commissions dealing with rural affairs; from 1926 USSR Dep Pop Comr of Workers and Peasants' Inspection; from 1929 USSR Pop Comr of Agric; as such, responsible for collectivization of agric; deleg at 8th–17th CPSU(B) Congresses; at 16th and 17th Party Congresses elected member, CC, CPSU(B); member, USSR Centr Exec Comt; from 1934 head, Agric Dept, CC, CPSU(B); 1937 arrested by State Security organs; *Publ: Derevnya kak ona yest'* (The Country as It Is); *Nasha derevnya* (Our Village); *Ob oshibkakh khlebo-furazhnogo balansa TsSU i yego istolkovatelyakh* (Errors in the Central Statistical Board's Grain and Forage Balance and Its Interpreters) (directed against Kamenev's "errors"); *K voprosu o sotsialisticheskom pereustroystve sel'skogo khozyaystva* (The Socialist Reorganization of Agriculture); co-ed, *Rabocheye dvizheniye v 1917* (The Workers' Movement in 1917), *1917 v derevne* (Nineteen-Seventeen in the Country) and *Razlozheniye armii v 1917* (The Break-Up of the Army in 1917), etc; *Died:* 14 Mar 1939 in imprisonment.

YAKOVLEVA, Varvara Nikolayevna (1885–1944) Govt official; CP member from 1904; *Born:* 1885; *Career:* began Party Work in student circles in Moscow; from early 1905 propagandist in workers' circles; after 1905 Dec Revolt Party work in Moscow; 1906 arrested; 1908 re-arrested; between these arrests legal and illegal Party work in Moscow; 1910 helped re-establish Moscow Party org; arrested and exiled for four years to Narym; fled abroad; 1912 illegally returned to Russia; CC agent for Moscow Oblast and member, CC's Moscow Oblast Bureau; early 1913 arrested and returned to Narym but fled again; on her arrival in Petersburg at once arrested and exiled to Astrakhan' Province; after release in early 1916 joined CC's Moscow Oblast Bureau; from Jan 1917 secr, Moscow Oblast Bureau, CC, RSDRP(B); during 1917 Oct Revol member of five-man bd directing Moscow revolt; 1917 Collegium member, NKVD; from Jan 1918 business manager, Supr Sovnarkhoz; from July 1918 Collegium member, All-Russian Cheka; 1919–20 Collegium member, Pop Comrt of Food; from summer 1920 member, Siberian Bureau, CC, RCP(B) and head, Siberian Polit Communications Bd; from Dec 1920 secr, Moscow RCP(B) Comt; from early 1921 secr, Siberian Bureau, CC, RCP(B); from 1922 head, Main Vocational Training Bd; then RSFSR Dep Pop Comr of Educ; from 1930 RSFSR Pop Comr of Finance; member, All-Russian and USSR Centr Exec Comt; 1918 sided with Leftist Communists; during 1920–21 trade-union controversy sided with "buffer" group which later joined Trotsky; 1923 signed 46-signature Trotskyist declaration; 1924–26 org work in Trotskyist Center, then withdrew from opposition; arrested by State Security organs; *Died:* 1944 in imprisonment.

YAKUBOV, Nor (1914–1965) Party and govt official; member, CC CP Uzbek from 1954; CP member from 1942; *Born:* 1914; *Educ:* 1938 grad Samarkand Inst of Public Educ; 1946 grad Tashkent Law Inst; *Career:* 1939–48 worked for justice organs; from 1952 chm, Samarkand Oblast Exec Comt; 1954–57 first secr, Samarkand Oblast Comt, CP Uzbek; 1957–64 Uzbek Public Prosecutor; from 1965 head, Dept of Trade Admin Organs, Samarkand Oblast Comt, CP Uzbek; dep, USSR Supr Sov of 1954 convocation; dep, Uzbek Supr Sov of 1959 and 1963 convocations; voting deleg at 20th CPSU Congress; *Awards:* Order of the Red Banner of Labor; *Died:* 18 July 1965.

YAKUBOVSKIY, Aleksandr Yur'yevich (1886–1953) Orientalist and historian; prof; corresp member, USSR Acad of Sci from 1943; Hon Sci Worker of Uzbek and Tadzh SSR; *Born:* 1 Feb 1886; *Educ:* 1913 grad Fac of History and Philology, 1924 Oriental Fac, Petersburg Univ; *Career:* from 1925 worked at State Acad of the History of Civilization; from 1928 also worked at Hermitage Museum; from 1935 prof, Leningrad Univ; from 1937 assoc, Inst of the History of Civilization (now Inst of Archeology), USSR Acad of Sci; from 1945 directed Sogdiana-Tadzh (now Tadzh) archeological expedition; specialized in history of Centr Asia and Middle East; *Publ: Samarkand pri Timure i timuridakh* (Samarkand Under Timur and the Timurites) (1933); *Makhmud Gaznevi. K voprosu o proiskhozhdenii i kharaktere Gaznevidskogo gosudarstva* (Mohammed Gaznevi. The Origin and Character of the Gaznevi State) (1934); *Vosstaniye Tarabi v 1238-om godu* (The Tarabi Revolt of 1238) (1936); *Irak na grani VIII–IX vekov* (Iraq on the Threshhold of the 9th Century) (1937); coauthor, *Zolotaya Orda i yeyo padeniye* (The Golden Horde and Its Downfall) (1937); *Vosstaniye Mukanny. Dvizheniye lyudey v "belykh odezhdakh"* (The Mukanna Revolt. The Movement of the "White-Robed" People) (1948), etc; *Awards:* Stalin Prize (1948); *Died:* 21 Mar 1953.

YAKUSHKIN, Ivan Vyacheslavovich (1885–1960) Agronomist; member, All-Union Lenin Acad of Agric Sci from 1935; Hon Sci Worker of USSR; prof; CP member from 1945; *Born:* 1885 in Moscow; *Educ:* 1909 grad Petrine-Razumovskiy Agric Acad; *Career:* 1909–12 distr, then uyezd agronomist in Poltava Province; 1912–17 at Moscow Agric Inst; 1917–20 and 1922–32 prof, Voronezh Agric Inst; 1922–32 also dir, Romanovskaya Sugar Beet Experimental Station; chm, State Qualifications Commission, Voronezh Inst; from 1932 head, Chair of Plant-Growing, Moscow's Timiryazev Agric Acad; until 1956 chm, Tech Crops Section, All-Union Acad of Agric Sci; ed, journal "Izvestiya Timiryazevskoy sel'skokhozyaystvennoy akademii"; specialized in improvement of sowing qualities of seed for agric crops; developed methods for laboratory determination of the germinating force of seeds and proposed various specific crop rotation systems; directed research on comprehensive agrotech measures for the cultivation of various field crops; also studied the agrotechnics of bread grains, potatoes, fodder root crops and grasses; studied optimum irrigation of field crops; devised methods for growing such southern crops as maize, Sudan-grass and soya in northern areas; revised and published Pryanishnikov's textbook for higher agric colleges; *Publ: Rasteniyevodstvo* (Plant-Growing) (1947), etc; *Awards:* two Orders of Lenin; two other orders; two Stalin Prizes (1943 and 1948); *Died: 19 July 1960.*

YALAVA, G.E. (1874–1950) Revolutionary; CP member from 1925; *Born:* 1874; *Career:* 1917 drove locomotive in which Lenin, then operating in the underground, was twice smuggled across the Finnish border; active in 1905–07 Revol; after 1917 Oct Revol taught apprentice locomotive drivers; worked for Karelian ASSR Centr Exec Comt; 1941–45 complaints inspector, Admin of Sverdlovsk Railroad; *Died:* 1950.

YAMPOL'SKIY, Abram Il'ich (1890–1956) Violin teacher; Hon Art Worker of RSFSR from 1937; Dr of Arts from 1940; *Born:* 11 Oct 1890 in Yekaterinoslav, now Dnepropetrovsk; *Educ:* 1912 grad Petersburg Conservatory; *Career:* 1913–20 taught at Yekaterinoslav Music College; also performed as solo violinist, in chamber groups and as conductor; from 1920 asst concertmaster, Bolshoy Theater Orchestra, Moscow; from 1922 head orchestra and violin classes, Moscow Conservatory; from 1926 prof, Moscow Conservatory; 1922–32 artistic co-dir, 1st Symphony Ensemble of Moscow City Sov; founded leading Sov violin school; *Publ: O metode raboty s uchenikami* (Methods of Working with Pupils) (1959); *Podgotovka pal'tsev i ostavleniye ikh na strunakh* (Training Fingers and Leaving Them on the Strings) (1960); *Died:* 17 Aug 1956 in Moscow.

YAMPOL'SKIY, Mark Il'ich (1879–1951) Cellist; prof; *Born:* 24 Jan 1879 in Yekaterinoslav; *Educ:* studied under F. Mulert and E. Gerbek; *Career:* prof, Moscow Conservatory; taught L. Ginzburg, B. Dobrokhotov, V. Simon, Ya Slobodkin, A. Stogorskiy, I. Turich, etc; *Publ: Violonchel'naya tekhnika. Gammy i arpedzhio* (Cello Technique. Scales and Arpeggios) (1939); *Died:* 18 Feb 1951 in Moscow.

YAMPOL'SKIY, Vladimir Yefimovich (1905–1965) Pianist; *Born:* 1905 in Cherkass, Kiev Province; *Educ:* studied under L. Nikolayev; *Career:* from 1920's performed with M. Polyakin; from 1940's performed with David Oistrakh; *Died:* 2 June 1965 in Kemerovo.

YAN, V. (real name: YANCHEVETSKIY, Vasiliy Grigor'yevich) *(1875–1954) Russian writer; Born:* 1875 in Kiev, son of a teacher; *Educ:* 1898 grad History and Philology Fac, Petersburg Univ; *Career:* 1890 first verse printed; also contributed essays and feuilletons to periodicals in Revel' (Tallin); *Publ:* historical novels: *Chingiz-khan* (Genghis Khan) (1939); "Baty" (1942); historical novelettes: *Finikiyskiy korabl'* (The Phoenician Ship) (1931); *Yunost' polkovodtsa* (The General's Youth) (1952); *Awards:* Stalin Prize (1942); *Died:* 1954.

YANISHEVSKIY, Mikhail Erastovich (1871–1949) Geologist and paleontologist; prof from 1902; Hon Sci Worker of RSFSR from 1945; *Born:* 14 Dec 1871; *Educ:* 1893 grad Kazan' Univ; *Career:* 1895–1902 worked at Kazan' Univ; 1902–11 prof, Tomsk Technol Inst; 1912–32 worked for Geological Comt; from 1916 prof, Petrograd Higher Women's Courses; 1919–49 prof, Petrograd (Leningrad) Univ; made surveys of Volga area, Urals and Western Siberia; studied mineral deposits of northwestern Russian Plateau; surveyed Carboniferous strate of northwestern Moscow coal basin; also did research on Paleozoic Baltic; made a study of paleozoic fossils with special reference to invertebrates; *Publ: Fauna kamennougol'nogo izvestnyaka, vystupayushchego po reke Shartymke na vostochnom sklone Urala* (The Fauna of the Carboniferous Limestone Outcrops Along the Shartymka River on the Eastern Slopes of the Urals) (1900); *Fauna brakhiopod nizhnego karbona Leningradskoy oblasti* (The Brachiopod Fauna of the Lower Carboniferous in the Leningrad Oblast) (1954), etc; *Died:* 4 Dec 1949.

YANOVSKIY, Anton Kirillovich (1865–1942) Roentgenologist; prof from 1919; *Born:* 1865; *Educ:* 1889 grad Natural Sci Fac, Petersburg Univ; 1893 grad Med Fac, Moscow Univ; *Career:* 1896, together with N.V. Sklifosovskiy, began research on practical applications of x-rays three months after their discovery by Roentgen; from 1907 taught course on x-ray methods at Petersburg Inst of Postgrad Med Training; from 1911 assoc prof, Chair of Surgery; 1919–30 prof, Petrograd Inst of Postgrad Med Training; first Sov roentgenologist to hold a chair in this subject; made major contribution to development of x-ray techniques; *Publ: O nastoyashchem polozhenii rentgenovskoy tekhniki v Rossii* (The Present State of X-Ray Techniques in Russia) (1916); *Rentgenoterapiya khronicheskikh porazheniy kostey i sustavov* (The X-Ray Therapy of Chronic Bone and Joint Ailments) (1924); coauthor, *Itogi rentgenoterapii bazedovoy bolezni za 20 let, 1909–29* (The Results of X-Ray Therapy of Basedow's Disease in the Last 20 Years, 1909–29) (1929); coauthor, *Rentgenoterapiya vospalitel'nykh khirurgicheskikh zabolevaniy* (The X-Ray Treatment of Inflammatory Surgical Diseases) (1929); *Died:* 1942.

YANOVSKIY, Boris Karlovich (1875–1933) Composer, conductor and music critic; *Born:* 31 Dec 1875 in Moscow; *Educ:* grad Kiev Univ; *Career:* until 1910 conductor and music critic in Kiev; 1910–18 conductor and music critic in Petersburg and Moscow; from 1918 taught history of music at Music Technicum and Muscial Drama Inst, Khar'kov; *Works:* 10 operas, including: *Dva P'yero ili Kolombina* (Two Pierrots or Colombine) (1907); *V 1812 godu* (In the Year 1812) (1912); *Florentiyskaya tragediya* (A Florentine Tragedy) (1913); *Ved'ma* (The Witch) (1916); *Vzryv* (Explosion) (1927); *Duma Chernomorskaya* (Black Sea Ballad) (1929); ballets: *Araviyskaya noch'* (An Arabian Night) (1916); *Ferendzhi* (Ferengi) (1930); orchestral works: "Eastern Suite"; poems: "Viy" and "The Faun and the Shepherdess"; "The Tale of the Dead Princess and the Seven Heroes"; string quartet; piano and cello pieces; choral works; romances; arrangements of Ukr folk songs; music for plays; *Died:* 19 Jan 1933 in Khar'kov.

YANOVSKIY, Feofil Gavrilovich (1860–1928) Therapist; member, Ukr Acad of Sci from 1927; *Born:* 24 June 1860 in vil Min'kovtsky, now Khmel'nitskiy Oblast, son of an official; *Educ:* 1884 grad Med Fac, Kiev Univ; form 1884 stayed on at Kiev Univ to train for professorship; 1889 defended doctor's thesis on *K biologii tifoznykh batsill* (The Biology of Typhus Bacilli); from 1904 prof of hospital therapy clinic, Novorossiysk Univ, Odessa; from 1905 prof of med diagnosis, Kiev Univ; 1914 transferred to Chair of Hospital Therapy Clinic; described new physical syndromes of pulmonary and pleural diseases; studied immunity in pulmonary tuberculosis and diagnosis and clinical treatment of this disease; founded his own school of internists; Ukr Tuberculosis and Thoracic Surgery Research Inst in Kiev is named for him; co-ed, 1st ed, "Bolshaya meditsinskaya entsiklopediya"; wrote some 40 works; *Publ: Tuberkulyoz lyogkikh* (Pulmonary Tuberculosis) (1923); *Diagnostika zabolevaniy pochek v svyazi s ikh patologiyey* The Diagnosis of Kidney Ailments in Connection with Their Pathology) (1927); *Died:* 8 July 1928 in Kiev.

YANOVSKIY, Mikhail Iosifovich (1888–1949) Rear-admiral; eng; specialist in steam and gas ship's turbines; corresp member, USSR Acad of Sci from 1943; *Born:* 8 June 1888; *Educ:* 1909 grad Naval Eng College, Kronstadt; 1923 grad Naval Acad; *Career:* from 1935 prof, Naval Acad, Leningrad; devised original methods for calculating high-speed disks, support and thrust bearings, gear transmissions and other turbine parts; *Publ: Morskiye parovyye turbiny* (Marine Steam Turbines) (1925); *Teoriya i teplovyye raschyoty morskikh parovykh turbin* (The Theory and Thermal Calculations of Marine Steam Turbines) (1941); *Sudovyye kondensatsionnyye ustanovki* (Ship's Condensation Plant) (1943); *Konstruirovaniye i raschyot na prochnost' detaley parovykh turbin* (The Design and Strength Calculation of Steam Turbine Parts) (1947), etc; *Awards:* Order of Lenin; other orders and medals; Stalin Prize (1949); *Died:* 15 July 1949.

YANOVSKIY, Mikhail Vladimirovich (1854–1927) Therapist; Dr of Med from 1884; prof; *Born:* 1854; *Educ:* 1877 grad Natural Sci Fac, Petersburg Univ; 1880 grad Med Surgical Acad; *Career:* from 1881 asst to Prof S. P. Botkin; 1884 defended doctor's thesis on the effect of butyric acid on the kidneys and nervous system; 1896–1925 head, Chair of Diagnostics and Gen Therapy, Petersburg (Leningrad) Mil Med Acad; did research on clinical aspects of cardiovascular diseases; hypothesized that blood circulation is assisted by rythmic contraction and expansion of the blood vessels; devised clinical methods of examining osmotic stability of erythrocytes; laid particular emphasis on physiotherapy within the framework of gen therapy and established a physiotherapy section at Petersburg Clinical Mil Hospital; wrote 35 works; *Publ:* doctor's thesis *O vliyanii maslyanoy kisloty na pochki i ob ugnetayushchem yeyo deytsvii na nervnuyu sistemu* (The Influence of Butyric Acid on the Kidneys and Its Inhibitory Effect on the Nervous System) (1884); *Kurs obshchey terapii* (A General Therapy Course) (1900); *Kurs obshchey terapii vnutrennikh bolezney* (A Course on the General Therapy of Internal Diseases) (1923); *Znacheniye pokoya i dvizheniya dlya zheludochnogo pishchevareniya* (The Importance of Rest and Movement for Gastric Digestion) (1905); *Kurs diagnostiki vnutrennikh bolezney* (A Course on the Diagnostics of Internal Diseases) (1908); *Died:* 1927 in Leningrad.

YANOVSKIY, Yevgeniy Grigor'yevich (1889–1950) Russian playwright; CP member from 1941; *Born:* 3 Jan 1889 in Uman', Kiev Province; *Career:* 1909 began lit work; also stage dir at theaters in Kiev and Dnepropetrovsk; wrote sketches, one-act plays and variety shows; *Works:* plays: *Nashestviye Napoleona* (Napoleon's Invasion) (1912); *Khalat* (The Dressing Gown) (1929); *Yarost'* (Fury) (1929); *Zhenshchina* (Woman) (1932); *Stolitsa* (The Capital) (1935); *Gde-to v Podmoskov'ye* (Somewhere in the Sub-Moscow Area); one-act plays: *Rodnoy rebyonok* (One's Own Child), *Svoy dom* (One's Own House) and *Talanty iz glubiny* (Talent from the Depths) (1941–45); *Died:* 12 June 1950.

YANOVSKIY, Yuriy Ivanovich (1902–1954) Ukr writer and playwright; *Born:* 14 Aug 1902 in Yelizavetgrad (now Kirovograd); *Career:* 1924 first work printed; worked as statistician at an oblast statistical bureau; inspector for Workers and Peasants' Inspection; his works have been translated into many Sov and for languages; *Publ:* collected novellas *Mamontovy bivni* (Mammoth Tusks) (1925); *Krov' zemli* (The Blood of the Earth) (1927); novels: *Master Korablya* (Master of the Ship) (1927); *Chetyre sabli* (The Four Sabres) (1931); *Vsadniki* (The Horsemen) (1935); tragedy *Duma pro Britanku* (The Ballad of Britanka) (1938); drama *Potomki* (Descendants) (1940); play *Doch' prokurora* (The Prosecutor's Daughter) (1954); collection *Kiyevskiye rasskazy* (Kiev Stories) (1948); collected stories *Novaya kniga* (The New Book) (1954); novel *Mir* (Peace) (1956), etc; *Awards:* Stalin Prize (1949); *Died:* 25 Feb 1954.

YAN'SHINOV, Aleksey Ivanovich (1871–1943) Violinist and music teacher; *Born:* 28 Mar 1871 in Moscow; *Educ:* studied under V. Bezekirskiy; *Career:* taught at musical establishments in Moscow; compiled exercises, studies and pieces for violin; *Publ: Tekhniki smychka* (Bowing Technique) (1930); *Died:* 4 Feb 1943 in vil Babushkino, Moscow Oblast.

YANSON, Nikolay Mikhaylovich (1882– ?) Party and govt official; CP member from 1905; *Born:* 1882, son of a worker; *Career:* metalworker by trade; 1905–06 worked in Poland and Estland; arrested in Revel' and 1906 exiled to Tobol'sk Province; 1906 fled from exile; 1907 emigrated to USA and took part in American workers' movement; June 1917 returned to Revel'; elected asst chm, Revel' Municipal Admin; 1918, after German occupation of Revel', arrested and sent to RSFSR; 1918–21 worked in Samara as dir of a plant and chm, Samara Province Trade-Union Council; 1921–23 secr, CC, and chm, Moscow Rayon Dept, Metalworkers' Union; from 1923 secr, CPSU(B) Centr Control Commission; from 1925 USSR Dep Pop Comr of Workers and Peasants' Inspection; 1927 chm, Main Disciplinary Court; 1928–31 RSFSR Pop Comr of Justice; from 1930 also dep chm, RSFSR Council of Pop Comr; 1931–35 USSR Pop Comr of Water Trans; 1923–34 member, and Presidium member, CPSU(B) Centr Control Commission; 1934 elected member, CPSU(B) Centr Auditing Commission; *Died:* date and place of death unknown.

YANSON, Ye.D. (BUNTOVITS) (1886–1939) Govt official; CP member from 1904; *Born:* 1886; *Career:* Party work in Riga and Yelgava; Riga deleg at 5th RSDRP Congress; repeatedly arrested by Tsarist authorities; 1914 exiled to Irkutsk Province; after 1917 Feb Revol member, Irkutsk RSDRP Comt; during 1917 Oct Revol member, Irkutsk Revol Comt and member, Irkutsk Sov of Workers and Soldiers' Dep; from 1918 NKVD chm for Centr Siberia and Far East; Min of For Affairs, Far Eastern Republ; later exec admin work; from 1935 with Moscow's "Akademiya" Publ House; arrested by State Security organs; *Died:* 1939 in imprisonment.

YANUSHEVSKIY, P.S. (1870– ?) Technol eng; *Born:* 1870; *Career:* 1895–1917 worked on railroads; 1917–20 chief of traction service and dep head, Vladikavkaz Railroad; head, Azer Railroad; then chm, Caucasian Okrug Freight Comt; 1921–28 Council member and dep chm, Higher Tech Comt and Council member, Sci and Tech Comt, Pop Comrt of Means of Communication; also worked for Gosplan; *Died:* Date and place of death unknown.

YANYSHEV, Mikhail Petrovich (1873–1920) Party and govt official; *Born:* 1873; *Career:* textile worker in Ivanovo-Voznesensk area; active in revol movement; took part in 1905–07 Revol; 1906 went underground to escape police search, then emigrated and lived in Germany and in USA; in USA worked at steel plant and engaged in propaganda among Russian workers; active in American Socialist Party; after 1917 Feb Revol returned to Russia and worked for Moscow Oblast RSDRP(B) Bureau; Oct 1917 active in Oct 1917 Revol in Moscow; member, Moscow Exec Comt; member, All-Russian Centr Exec Comt; chm, Moscow Revol Tribunal; Collegium member, Moscow Cheka; 1919 commanded Moscow unit which helped to repulse Yudenich's assault on Petrograd; early 1920 mil comr, 15th Div on Southern Front; *Died:* 1920 killed in action; buried by the Kremlin Wall in Moscow's Red Square.

YAREMICH, Stepan Petrovich (1869–1939) Landscape painter and art historian; *Born:* 3 Aug 1869 in vil Galayki, now Kiev Oblast; *Educ:* studied at N.I. Murashko's Art School, Kiev; *Career:* spent several years abroad, mainly in Paris, where he was strongly influenced by Impressionism; contributed to journal "Mir iskusstva", etc; leading specialist on West European painting; made major contribution to organization of Russian art training; in 1930's in charge of restoration work at the Hermitage Museum; his paintings and water colors are displayed at the Tret'yakov Gallery, the Shevchenko Museum in Kiev and the Arm State Museum, Yerevan; wrote studies of the work of M. Vrubel', V. Serov and articles about Ukr art; *Works:* helped decorate Vladimir Cathedral, Kiev; paintings: "Mount Knyazha near Kanevo"; "View of the Dnieper"; "A Ukrainian Girl"; "The Field", etc; *Died:* 14 Oct 1939.

YARILOV, Arseniy Arsen'yevich (1868– ?) Soil scientist; CP member from 1930; *Born:* 1868; *Educ:* grad Yur'yev Univ; *Career:* 1904–05 active in revol movement; emigrated and lived abroad until 1913; upon his return headed chairs at various higher agric training establishments; dir, Inst of Colonization and Resettlement; from 1921 worked for Sci and Tech Soc, Supr Sovnarkhoz, for Gosplan, State Learned Council, etc; co-founder, All-Union Assoc of Sci and Tech Workers for the Promotion of the Building of Socialism; studied history and methodology of soil sci, regional studies and agric geography; active in Int Soc of Soil Scientists, of which he was asst chm; *Publ: Pedologiya kak samostoyatel'naya yestestvenno-nauchnaya distsiplina o zemle* (Pedology as an Independent Natural Scientific Discipline of the Earth) (1904–05); *Plodorodiye pochvy i bonitirovka* (Soil Fertility and Grading) (1930); *Pochvennoye plodorodiye i bonitirovka pochv* (Soil Fertility and the Grading of Soils) (1930); *Died:* date and place of death unknown.

YARKHO, Arkadiy Isaakovich (1902–1935) Anthropologist; *Born:* 1902; *Career:* specialized in racial characteristics and methods of racial analysis and anthropological structure of peoples of the Altay, Sayan and Centr Asia; also did research on physical development of man; *Publ: O vzaimootnoshenii rosta, vesa i okruzhnosti grudnoy kletki i ikh znacheniye dlya otsenki fizicheskogo razvitiya cheloveka* (The Relationship Between Height, Weight and Circumference of the Thorax and Its Importance in Assessing the Physical Development of Man) (1924); *O nekotorykh voprosakh rasovogo analiza* (Some Aspects of Racial Analysis) (1934); "Die Altersveränderungen der Rassenmerkmale bei den Erwachsenen" (1935); *Altaye-sayanskiye tyurki. Antropologicheskiy ocherk* (The Altay-Sayan Turks. An Anthropological Study) (1947, posthumously), etc; *Died:* 1935.

YARKOV, Pyotr Glebovich (1875–1945) Russian folk singer; connoisseur and collector of Russian folk songs; *Born:* 15 Aug 1875 in vil Sel'tso, Moscow Province; *Career:* from 1919 founder-dir, peasant choir which won first place at 1930 All-Russian Song Olympiad; toured USSR with this choir; *Died:* 18 Dec 1945 in Moscow.

YARON, Grigoriy Markovich (1893–1963) Operetta singer and dir; Pop Artiste of RSFSR from 1940; drama critic; *Born:* 25 Feb 1893 in Petersburg; *Educ:* 1912 grad drama school in Petersburg; *Career:* 1912–26 worked at theaters in Petersburg, Tambov, Kiev, Odessa, Khar'kov etc; 1927 founded Moscow Operetta Theater; 1927–39 and 1942–45 artistic dir, Moscow Operetta Theater; *Roles:* Menelaus in Offenbach's "Die schöne Helene"; Volyapyuk in Kalman's "Silva"; Popandopulo in Aleksandrov's "Svad'ba v Malinovke" (Wedding at Malinovka), etc; *Productions:* operettas: Ryabov's *Sorochinskaya yarmarka* (Sorochintsy Fair) (1937); Blanter's *Na beregu Amura* (On the Banks of the Amur) (1939); Kalman's "Silva" (1941), "Maritza" (1943) and "The Violet of Montmartre" (1945), etc; *Publ: O lyubimom zhanre* (My Favorite Genre) (1960); wrote many articles and radio and tv broadcasts about operetta; *Died:* 31 Dec 1963.

YAROSHENKO (pen name: VOLYAR), Vladimir Moiseyevich (1898–1937) Ukr poet and prose writer; *Born:* 1898 in vil Yakhniki, now Poltava Oblast; *Educ:* studied at Kiev Business Inst; *Career:* 1917 began to write in Russian; fought in Civil War; 1920 member, Ukr CP ("Borotbisty"); then teacher; from 1923 ed work; member, "Mars" lit group; *Publ: Stikhi* (Verse) (1917); collected verse *Svetoten'* (Chiaroscura) (1918); play *Kooperativnaya mobilizatsiya* (Cooperative Mobilization) (1924); *Skazki* (Tales) (1925); collected stories *Kriminal'naya khronika* (Criminal Chronicle) (1927); novelette *Grobovishche* (The Graveyard) (1928); children's story *Zamarashka* (The Sloven), etc; *Died:* 13 July 1937.

YAROSLAVENKO (real name: VINTSKOVSKIY), Yaroslav Dmitriyevich (1880–1958) Composer; *Born:* 30 Mar 1880 in L'vov; *Educ:* 1896–98 studied at L'vov Music School; 1904 grad L'vov Polytech Inst; *Career:* 1905–18 eng; 1905 co-founder, "Torban" Ukr Musical Publ House; *Works:* opera *Ved'ma* (The Witch) (1922), based on Gogol's *Poteryannaya gramota* (The Lost Scroll); operetta *Babiy bunt* (Revolt of the Women) (1921); march for brass band; songs, etc; *Died:* 26 June 1958.

YAROSLAVSKIY, Yemel'yan Mikhaylovich (real name: GUBEL'MAN, Miney Izrailevich; other pseudonyms: YEMEL'YAN; IL'YAN) (1878–1943) Party official; member, USSR Acad of Sci from 1939; CP member from 1898; *Born:* 19 Feb 1878, son of an exiled settler; *Educ:* grad three-grade municipal college; passed examinations for 4th grade at high school; *Career:* worked as book-binder and pharmacist's asst; 1898 organized first Soc-Democratic circle for workers of Transbaykal Railroad, as well as a student polit circle; 1901 went abroad and returned with a shipment of illegal lit; member, Chita RSDRP Comt; 1903 arrested; released, placed under police surveillance and went underground; moved to Petersburg; member, Petersburg RSDRP Comt; propagandist and organizer at enterprises in Narvskaya Zastava distr; Apr 1904 arrested while preparing May Day demonstration and imprisoned until mid-Dec 1904; released on bail and resumed Party work; after 9 Jan 1905 riots forced to leave Petersburg; exec Party work in Tver', Nizhniy Novgorod, Kiev and Odessa; 13 Feb 1905 rearrested in Odessa and held in prison until June 1905; released after a 10-day hunger strike and returned to Party work in Odessa, then Tula; Oct-Dec 1905 helped lead revol movement in Yaroslavl'; Dec 1905 attended Tammerfors RSDRP(B) Conference, then moved to Moscow and became a member, Moscow Party Comt; worked for mil org, Moscow Party Comt and helped publish journal "Zhizn' soldata"; spring 1906 arrested at Conference of Moscow Bolshevik Mil Org; escaped from Suchchyovo Police Headquarters; sent by Yaroslavl' Party Org to 4th RSDRP Congress in Stockholm; then Party work in Yekaterinoslav, Moscow and Petersburg; in Petersburg edited underground mil newspaper "Kazarma"; late 1906 attended 1st RSDRP Mil-Battle Conference in Tammerfors, which appointed the Provisional Bureau of Mil and Battle Orgs; spring 1907 attended 5th RSDRP Congress in London as deleg from Mil Orgs of Petersburg and Kronstadt; returned from the congress to Petersburg, was arrested and held in Kresty Jail for 18 months; tried but acquitted for connections with printing of newspaper "Rabochiy"; for connections with Mil-Battle Org sentenced to seven years hard labor, reduced to five years upon appeal; served two years of the sentence in Petersburg Transient Prison, then at Butyrka Prison in Moscow and from 1912 at Gornyy Zerentuy; then until 1917 Feb Revol lived at a settlement in Yakutsk Oblast; 1915–17 custodian, Yakutsk Oblast Museum; July 1917 returned to Moscow and worked for Moscow Mil Org; ran Bolshevik newspaper "Sotsial-demokrat"; fall 1917 edited Bolshevik newspaper "Derevenskaya pravda"; Aug 1917 attended 6th RSDRP(B) Congress; during 1917 Oct Revol member, Moscow Mil Revol Comt; helped direct armed coup in Moscow; Moscow Bolshevik deleg, Constituent Assembly; from 1918 asst comr, then comr, Moscow Mil Distr; polit educ work in Red Army; sided with Leftist Communists over Brest Peace Treaty; 1920 worked in Perm', then Omsk for Siberian Oblast Bureau and Omsk Party Comt; at 8th and 9th Party Congresses elected cand member, and at 10th and 11th Congresses member, CC, RCP(B); 1921 secr, CC, RCP(B); fall 1921–late 1922 worked in Siberia as member, Siberian Oblast Party Comt; at 12th–16th Party Congresses elected member, CPSU(B) Centr Control Commission; from 1923 secr, Party Collegium, CPSUB(B) Centr Control Commission; member, USSR Centr Exec Comt; head, Soc of Exiles and Polit Prisoners; bd member, Inst of Lenin; member, ed bd, newspaper "Pravda" and journals "Bol'shevik" and "Istorik-Marksist"; from 1925 chm, USSR Union of Atheists; 1922–41 ed, newspaper "Bezbozhnik"; 1926–32 ed, journal "Bezbozhnik"; 1926–41 ed, journal "Anti-religioznik"; from 1931 ed, ed bd, journal "Voinstvuyushchiy ateist"; from 1931 chm, Soc of "Old Bolsheviks"; head, Chair of CPSU(B) History, Higher Party School, CC, CPSU(B); head, Lecturers Group, CC, CPSU(B); at 17th Party Congress elected member, Party Control Commission, CC, CPSU(B); at 18th Party Congress elected member, CC, CPSU(B); from 1937 dep, USSR Supr Sov; *Publ: Bibliya dlya veruyushchikh i neveruyushchikh* (The Bible for Believers and Non-Believers) (1923–25); ed, *Istoriya VKP(b)* (The History of the CPSU(B)) (4 vol, 1926–31); *Kratkiye ocherki po istorii VKP(b)* (A Brief

Outline History of the CPSU(B)) (2 vol, 1926–28); *Kratkaya istoriya VKP(b)* (A Short History of the CPSU(B)) (1930); *Istoriya VKP(b)* (The History of the CPSU(B)) (2 vol, 1933); *Ocherki po istorii VKP(b)* (An Outline History of the CPSU(B)) (1936); *Kurs istorii VKP(b)* (A Course in the History of the CPSU(B)) (1940–44), etc; *Awards:* Order of Lenin; *Died:* 4 Dec 1943; buried by the Kremlin Wall on Moscow's Red Square.

YAROTSKIY, Aleksandr Ivanovich (1866–1944) Therapist; Dr of Med from 1898; prof from 1904; *Born:* 1866; *Educ:* 1889 grad Petersburg Mil Med Acad; *Career:* after grad worked as zemstvo physician; from 1894 physician, Obukh City Hospital, then Peter and Paul Hospital, Petersburg; 1898 defended doctor's thesis on reaction of pancreas to starvation; 1899–1901 asst prof, Women's Med Inst Clinic; 1901 exiled from Petersburg for involvement in demonstration on Kazan' Square; 1901–02 worked under I.I. Mechnikov in Paris; 1903 returned to Russia; 1904–18 prof of therapy, Yur'yev Univ; 1910 devised special diet for gastric and duodenal ulcers; 1919–24 prof of therapy, Crimean Univ; from 1924 prof of therapy, 1st Moscow Univ; then prof of therapy, Moscow Oblast Clinical Inst; together with A.M.Levin, designed an oscillograph for measuring mean arterial pressure; 1931 devised method of treating diphtheria with antitoxic serum; also studied psychotherapy of internal diseases; contributed to non-med journals "Novoye slovo", "Nachalo" and "Severnyy kur'yer"; member, Free Econ Soc; *Publ:* doctor's thesis *Ob izmeneniyakh velichiny i stroyeniya kletok podzheludochnoy zhelezy pri nekotorykh vidakh golodovaniya* (Changes in the Size and Structure of the Cells of the Pancreas in Certain Forms of Starvation) (1898); *Lecheniye krugloy yazvy zheludka* (The Treatment of Round Stomach Ulcers) (1918); *Dieticheskoye lecheniye krugloy yazvy zheludka i dvenadtsatiperstnoy kishki* (The Dietetic Treatment of Round Gastric and Duodenal Ulcers) (1928); *Novyy metod lecheniya difterii spetsificheskoy syvorotkoy* (A New Method of Treating Diphtheria with a Specific Serum) (1931); *Died:* 1944.

YAROVOY, Pavel (real name: KOMAROV, Fedot Yemel'yanovich) (1887– ?) Russian writer; *Born:* 1887, son of a peasant; *Career:* 1913 first work published; member, Neverov Writers' Circle; member, All-Russian Union of Proletarian Writers' Associations; wrote mainly on revol and rural themes; *Publ:* "Mark Mikolaychev" (1926); novel *Zhizn' tsvetyot* (Life Flourishes); novel *Na ostriyo nozha* (On the Edge of the Knife), etc; *Died:* date and place of death unknown.

YAROVYY, Mikhail Mikhaylovich (1864–1940) Artist; *Born:* 1864 in vil Moshny, now Cherkassy Oblast; *Educ:* grad Moscow College of Painting, Sculpture and Architecture; *Works:* painting "Odessa Harbor" (1886); portrait of O. Korin (1893); painting "Two Generations" (1894); illustrations for Chekhov's works (1903–09); portrait of the violinist M. Yerdenko, (1912), etc; some of his works are displayed at the Ukr Art Museum, Kiev; *Died:* 1940.

YASENSKIY, Bruno (1901–1941) Polish and Russian writer; *Born:* 17 July 1901 in vil Klimontuvo, Radoma Province (Poland), son of a physician; *Educ:* studied at Cracow Univ; *Career:* 1918 began lit career as Futurist; sided with Polish pro-Communist orgs; from 1924 worked for Communist newspaper "Rabochaya tribuna"; 1925 emigrated to Paris and joined French CP; with the help of Polish emigres founded and wrote plays for Proletarian Touring Theater; 1929 deported from France for his novel "I Burn Paris"; 1931 moved to USSR; worked with writers' teams which visited the major construction projects; at 2nd Int Conference of Writers elected secr, Int Assoc of Revol Writers and appointed ed of its centr organ "Literatura mirovoy revolyutsii"; 1937 arrested by State Security organs on charges of espionage; all his books were confiscated; *Publ:* collected verse *Sapog v petlitse* (The Shoe in a Noose) (1921); poem *Pesnya o golode* (The Song of Famine) (1922); collected verse *Zemlya vlevo* (The Earth to the Left); play *Slovo o Yakove Shele* (The Lay of Yakov Shel'); novel *Ya zhgu Parish* (I Burn Paris) (1929); essay "Jimmy Clark on Top of the World) (1932); novel *Chelovek menyayet kozhu* (Man Changes His Skin) (1932–33); satirical play *Bal manekenov* (The Mannequins' Ball) (1931); unfinished novel *Zagovor ravnodushnykh* (Conspiracy of the Indifferent) (1956), etc; *Died:* 20 Oct 1941 in imprisonment; posthumously rehabilitated.

YASHEK, Nikolay Fyodorovich (1883–1966) Bibliographer; *Born:* 23 Sept 1883 in vil Panyutino, now Khar'kov Oblast; *Publ:* bibliographic indexes: *Lenin pro literaturu ta mystetstvo* (Lenin on Literature and Art); coauthor, *Desyat' rokiv ukrainskoy literatury, 1917–27* (Ten Years of Ukrainian Literature, 1917–27) (1928); *Materialy dlya bibliografii T.G.Shevchenko* (Bibliographic Material on T.G.Shevchenko), etc; *Died:* 17 Aug 1966.

YASHVILI, Paolo (Pavle) Dzhibrayelovich (1895–1937) Geo poet and translator; *Born:* 29 June 1895 in vil Argveti, now Geo SSR; *Educ:* studied at Inst of Arts, Paris; *Career:* wrote and published verse while still at school; 1914–16 lived and studied in Paris; 1916 co-founder "Blue Horns" group of Geo Symbolist poets; 1918–21, prior to establishment of Sov rule in Geo, wrote verse mainly on Geo nat themes; translated into Geo works of Pushkin, Lermontov and Mayakovskiy; *Publ:* verse: "Peacocks in Town"; "The Red Bull"; "To New Georgia"; "Lenin" (1924); "To a Heroic People" (1924); "Morning"; "Blessed Agitation"; "Argveti Nights"; unfinished poem "Happy Paths"; "Selected Verse" (1958); *Died:* 22 July 1937.

YASINSKIY, Anton Nikitich (1864–1933) Russian historian and Slavist; specialist in agrarian history of Medieval Bohemia; *Born:* 1864; *Career:* prof, Kiev, Yur'yev, then Smolensk Univ; first to draw extensively on Czech land inventories ("ubaria"); wrote a study of agrarian relations in Bohemia from 10th to 14th Centuries; criticized hypothesis that foreign colonization played a decisive role in history of Czech people; *Publ: Padeniye zemskogo stroya v Cheshskom gosudarstve (X–XIII veki)* (The Collapse of the Zemstvo Structure in the Czech State /X–XIII Centuries/) (1895); *Ocherki i issledovaniya po sotsial'noy i ekonomicheskoy istorii Chekhii v sredniye veka* (Studies and Research on the Social and Economic History of Bohemia in the Middle Ages) (1901); *Osnovnyye cherty razvitiya prava v Chekhii, XIII–XV veka. Istoriko-yuridicheskiy ocherk* (The Basic Features of the Development of Law in Bohemia. XIII–XV Centuries. A Historico-Legal Study)(1902); *Sochineniya knyazya Kurbskogo, kak istoricheskiy material* (Prince Kurbskiy's Works as Historical Material) (1889); *Died:* 1933.

YASINSKIY, Iyeronim Iyeronimovich (pen name: Maksim BELINSKIY) (1850–1931) Russian writer and journalist; CP member; *Born:* 1850 in Khar'kov, of noble descent; *Educ:* studied at Kiev, then Petersburg Univ; *Career:* in 1870's began to publish verse, novelettes, stories, plays, feuilletons and reviews in the journals "Slovo," "Otechestvennyye zapiski," etc; from 1878 member, ed staff, journal "Slovo"; 1898–1902 edited periodical "Birzhevyye vedomosti"; contributed to this periodical under the pseudonym "Nezavisimyy" (Independent); 1900–02 published journal "Yezhemesyachnyye sochineniya" and other periodicals; after 1917 Oct Revol worked for "Proletkul't" org; joined RCP(B); *Publ: Na chistotu* (Outspoken) (1880); *Vskhody* (Shoots) (1882); *Bolotnyy tsvetok* (Swamp Flower) (1883); *Polnoye sobraniye povestey i rasskazov* (Complete Collection of Novelettes and Stories) (4 vol, 1888); verse collection *Voskresnuvshiye sny* (Resurrected Dreams) (1919); play *Posledniy boy* (The Last Battle) (1920); memoirs *Roman moyey zhizni* (The Novel of My Life) (1926), etc; *Died:* 1931.

YASNOPOL'SKIY, Leonid Mikhaylovich (1873–1957) Econ; prof; member, Ukr Acad of Sci from 1925; *Born:* 1 Feb 1873 in Kiev; *Educ:* 1895 grad Petersburg Univ; *Career:* from 1895 lecturer, Chair of Polit Econ, Petersburg Univ; from 1902 lecturer, Khar'kov, then Kiev Univ; 1905 dismissed from Kiev Univ for criticizing Russo-Japanese War in a lecture; 1906–10 lectured on budget law and statistics at Petersburg Polytech Inst; from 1910 prof, Kiev Univ; from 1917 also taught at Inst of Nat Econ; 1926–30 chm, Permanent Commission for Study of Ukr Production Resources Ukr Acad of Sci, from 1931 assoc, various research inst in Moscow; from 1943 assoc, Inst of Econ, Ukr Acad of Sci; also worked for Dnieper Reconstruction Commission, USSR Gosplan; *Publ: Kamennougol'naya promyshlennost' Donetskogo basseyna* (The Donbass Coal Industry) (1957), etc; *Died:* 23 May 1957.

YASTREBTSOV, (YASTREBTSEV), Vasiliy Vasil'yevich (1866–1934) Russian writer and composer; *Born:* 18 Aug 1866 in Mogilev; *Educ:* 1890–91 studied at Peterburg Conservatory; *Career:* biographer and researcher of N.A. Rimsky-Korsakov; composed various musical works; *Publ: Nikolay Andreyevich Rimskiy-Korsakov. Ocherk yego zhizni i deyatel'nosti* (Nikolay Andreyevich Rimsky-Korsakov. A Study of His Life and Work) (1908); *Moi vospominaniya o Nikolaye Andreyeviche Rimskom-Korsakove* (My Memories of Nikolay Andreyevich Rimsky-Korsakov) (1917); *Died:* 25 Sept 1934 in Leningrad.

YASTREYSKIY, Boris Sergeyevich (1877– ?) Statistician; *Born:* 1877; *Educ:* grad Physics and Mathematics Fac, Khar'kov Univ; *Career:* from 1909 secr, Mathematics Section, then secr-gen,

Insurance Knowledge Soc; 1911–15 directed compilation of mortality actuarial tables; after 1917 Oct Revol head, Statistics Dept, Pop Comrt for Insurance; after this was closed down worked for Centr Statistical Bd; with merger of Centr Statistical Bd with Gosplan worked for Nat Econ Accounting Section, USSR Gosplan; *Publ: Zakon dostatochno bol'shikh chisel* (The Law of Sufficiently Large Numbers) (1914); *Teoriya dispersii, kak teoriya izmenyayemosti statisticheskikh ryadov* (The Therory of Dispersion as the Theory of the Changeability of Statistical Series) (1915); *Zakon malykh chisel v svete teorii izmenyayemosti statisticheskikh ryadov* (The Law of Small Numbers in the Light of the Theory of the Changeability of Statistical Series) (1922); *Kolichestvennoye vyrazheniye subyektivnoy kharakteristiki urozhaya* (The Quantitative Expression of the Subjective Characteristics of Harvest); *Statika i dinamika v matematiko-statisticheskom issledovanii* (Statics and Dynamics in Mathematical-Statistical Research) (1923); *Peremennaya Korrelyastiya* (Variable Correlation) (1924); *O svyaznom analize statisticheskikh ryadov* (The Connective Analysis of Statistical Series) (1925); *Golyy empirizm i krivyye raspredeleniya Pirsona* (Bare Empirism and Pearson's Distribution Curves) (1927); *Chastost', veroyatnost' i zakon bol'shikh chisel* (Frequency, Probability and the Law of Large Numbers) (1928); *Nekotoryye zamechaniya po povodu vyborochnykh perepisey* (Some Comments on Election Censuses) (1929); coauthor and ed, *Teoriya matematicheskoy statistiki* (The Theory of Mathematical Statistics) (1930); *Died:* Date and place of death unknown.

YATSENKO, Grigoriy Fyodorovich (1910–1942) Party official; CP member; *Born:* 1910 in Nikolayev, son of a railroad worker; *Educ:* grad one-year Marxism-Leninism courses run by Kiev Oblast Comt, CP Ukr; *Career:* until 1929 farmhand; 1929–30 kolkhoz bookkeeper; 1931–39 Komsomol and journalist work in Kiev and Poltava Oblast; 1939–40 dep ed, newspaper "Zarya Poltavshchiny"; 1940–41 dep head, Propaganda Dept, Poltava Oblast Comt, CP(B) Ukr; from 1941 secr, then second secr, underground Poltava Oblast Comt, CP(B) Ukr; *Died:* 17 Jan 1942 killed in action near Gadyach.

YATSINEVICH, Yakov Mikhaylovich (1869–1945) Composer and choral conductor; *Born:* 27 Oct 1869 in Belaya Tserkov', now Kiev Oblast; *Educ:* studied music under M. Lysenko; *Career:* 1891–1904, together with Lysenko, helped found Ukr choirs; 1899–1912 directed Choir of Kiev Univ; 1906–1917 musical dir at Ukr theaters; 1925–30 dir, Odessa City Choir; 1930–40 taught music in Zaporozh'ye; 1942–45 dir, Adyge Song and Dance Ensemble, Maykop; *Works:* symphony "1905"; oratorio *Pechal'naya mat'*(The Sad Mother); choral works; arrangements of Ukr folk songs, including "The Neighbor"; *Died:* 24 Apr 1945.

YATSKIV, Mikhail Yur'yevich (1873–1961) Ukr writer; *Born:* 5 Oct 1873 in vil Lesivka (now Ivano-Frankovsk Oblast); *Educ:* completed high school; *Career:* worked at a theater, then as bookkeeper; 1899 first work printed; from 1939 worked as librarian; wrote his memoirs of Ivan Franko; *Publ:* collected stories "In the Realm of Satan" (1900); collected stories and novelettes "The Fires Burn" (1902); "Lightning" (1913); novelettes "Dance of the Shadows" (1916–17); new version of this entiled "In the Clutches" (1956), etc; *Died:* 9 Dec 1961.

YATSUNSKIY, Viktor Kornelyevich (1893–1966) Historian; Dr of Historical Sci from 1950; prof from 1950; *Born:* 20 Jan 1893 in Moscow; *Educ:* 1911–16 studied at History and Philology Fac, Moscow Univ; 1911–15 also studied at Econ Dept, Moscow Business Inst; studied 11 foreign languages; *Career:* after grad Moscow Univ worked for zemstvo statistical dept, cooperative system and Main Polit Educ Bd; from 1921 taught at Sverdlov Communist Univ, then at Moscow Univ, Moscow Oblast and City Teachers' Training Institutes, Moscow Historical Archives Inst and other higher educ establishments; from 1946 at Inst of History, USSR Acad of Sci; from 1962 head, Historical Geography Group, Inst of History, USSR Acad of Sci, working on a historical atlas of the USSR; 1958 co-founder, Inter-Republ Symposium for Agrarian History of Eastern Europe; dep chm, Sci Council on the Genesis of Capitalism, Dept of Historical Sci, USSR Acad of Sci; dep chm, Commission of the History of Agric and Peasantry, Inst of History, USSR Acad of Sci; chm, Dept of the History of Geographical Knowledge and Historical Geography, Moscow Branch, USSR Geographical Soc; member, ed bd, journal "Istoriya SSSR"; attended numerous int history congresses and conferences; helped compile maps, diagrams and tables showing trends in the econ geography and econ history of the USSR; *Publ: Istoricheskaya geografiya. Istoriya yeyo vozniknoveniya i razvitiya v XIV–XVIII vekakh* (Historical Geography. The History of Its Emergence and Development in the 14th–18th Centuries) (1955); *Osnovnyye etapy genezisa kapitalizma v Rossii* (The Main Stages in the Genesis of Capitalism in Russia) (1958); *Genezis kapitalizma v sel'skom khozyaystve Rossii* (The Genesis of Capitalism in Russian Agriculture) (1961); *Promyshlennyy perevorot v Rossii* (The Industrial Revolution in Russia) (1962); *Geografiya rynka zheleza v dorevolyutsionnoy Rossii* (The Geography of the Iron Market in Pre-Revolutionary Russia); *Pomeshchich'i sakharnyye zavody v Rossii v pervoy polovine XIX veka* (Estate Sugar Refineries in Russia in the First Half of the 19th Century), etc; *Died:* 13 Oct 1966.

YAUSHEV, Illarion Maksimovich (1902–1961) Singer (bass); Pop Artiste of Mordovian ASSR from 1945; Hon Artiste of RSFSR from 1960; *Born:* 26 Feb 1902; *Career:* 1923 began singing career; soloist with Mordovian and Moscow Philharmonic; performed at Mordovian Musical Drama Theater; also concert singer; *Roles:* Varlaam in "Boris Godunov"; Gremin in "Yevgeniy Onegin" (Eugene Onegin); Pumraz in Kiryukov's "Nesmeyan and Lamzur'," etc; *Died:* 31 May 1961.

YAVLINSKIY, Natan Aronovich (1912–1962) Electr eng; Cand of Eng from 1947; assoc prof from 1957; CP member from 1932; *Born:* 1912 in Kanev, now Kiev Oblast; *Educ:* 1936 grad Kiev Inst of Electr Eng; *Career:* until 1948 worked at Corresp Inst of Power Eng; from 1948 senior assoc, Inst of Atomic Energy, USSR Acad of Sci; did research on high-temperature plasma obtained with powerful pulse dischages in a gaseous medium; *Publ: Bystrodeystvuyushchiye vychislitel'nyye mashiny i avtomatizatsiya proizvodstvennykh protsessov* (High-Speed Computers and the Automation of Production Processes) (1956), etc; *Awards:* Stalin Prize (1949); Lenin Prize (1958); *Died:* 1962.

YAVORSKIY, Boleslav Leopol'dovich (1877–1942) Musicalogist; musical theorist; teacher, pianist and composer; *Born:* 22 June 1877 in Khar'kov; *Educ:* 1903 grad S.I. Taneyev's composition class, Moscow Conservatory; *Career:* 1906–16 co-founder and instructor, Pop Conservatory Moscow; 1916–21 co-founder and instructor, Pop Conservatory Kiev; founded theory of harmony rhythm; from 1930 member, Arts Council, Bolshoy Theater; 1938–42 prof, Moscow Conservatory; from 1940 Dr of Arts; *Works:* operas "Peleas and Melisanda" (uncompleted, 1904); *Vyshka Oktyabrya* (The October Tower) (1930); ballets "John Wilmore" (1910); libretto for ballets: *Okameneloye tsarstvo* (The Petrified Kingdom) (1905); *Publ: Stroyeniye muzykal'noy rechi* (The Structure of Musical Speech) (3 vol, 1908); *Osnovnyye elementy muzyki* (The Basic Elements of Music) (1923); *Uprazhneniya v obrazovanii skhem ladovogo ritma* (Exercises in the Formation of Harmony Rhythm Schemes) (2nd ed, 1928); *Died:* 26 Nov 1942 in Saratov.

YAVORSKIY, Vladimir Polikarpovich (1876–1942) Organic chemist; prof from 1926; member, Ukr Acad of Sci from 1934; *Born:* 27 July 1876; *Educ:* 1901 grad Kiev Univ; *Career:* until 1924 lecturer, Kiev Univ; from 1926 prof, Kiev Polytech Inst; from 1935 prof, Kiev Univ; did research on application of S. N. Reformatskiy's reaction to synthesis of highly unsaturated acids in the sorbin and hydrosorbin series; devised method of synthesis involving unsaturated organic magnesium halide compounds; studied organic derivatives of hydrozoate; sythesized numerous new alcohols with complex unsaturated and cyclic structures; *Died:* 24 Sept 1942.

YEFIMOV, Aleksey Sergeyevich (1887–1965) Govt official; CP member from 1904; *Born:* 1887; *Career:* textile worker; 1904 joined local Czenstochowa org, Soc-Democratic Party of Poland and Lith; 1912 deleg, Czestochowa Okrug Party Conference; 1912–17 in Tsarist jail; 1917–19 founder and chm, Pavlovskiy Posad Exec Comt; member, Moscow Province Party Comt; co-founder, Pavlovskiy Posad Party Comt; deleg, 2nd All-Russian Congress of Soviets; 1919–53 exec econ work; from 1953 pensioner; *Died:* June 1965.

YEFIMOV, Il'ya Yefimovich (pen name: TKHTI) (1889–1938) Chuvash writer; *Born:* 4 Sept 1889; *Educ:* grad Bryusov Higher Lit-Art Inst, Moscow; *Career:* prior to 1917 Oct Revol worked as teacher; *Publ:* cautionary tales "Lazy Khuras" (1912); poem "Kolchak" (1919); stories and novellas "Sherkulla" (1926); "Vas'ka, Van'ka and Akhmet" (1926); "Vitamins" (1928); "Odd and Even" (1927), etc; *Died:* 22 Feb 1938.

YEFREMOV, Aleksandr Illarionovich (1904–1951) Govt official; CP member from 1924; *Born:* 1904 in Moscow, son of a worker;

Educ: 1935 grad Moscow Machine-Tool Inst; *Career:* 1918–23 Komsomol work; 1923–26 in Sov Navy; 1929–30 toolmaker and Party org secr, Appliances and Dies Plant "Metalorg" Trust; 1935–38 foreman, shop mang, then dir, Ordzhonikidze Machine-Tool Plant; 1938–39 dep chm, Moscow Sov; chm, Moscow Province Exec Comt and chm, Moscow Sov; Mar 1939–Apr 1940 USSR First Dep Pop Comr of Heavy Machine-Building; Apr 1940–June 1941 USSR Pop Comr of Heavy Machine-Building; 1941–49 USSR Pop Comr (Min) of Machine-Tool Building; from Mar 1949 dep chm, USSR Council of Min; 1939 at 18th CPSU(B) Congress elected member, CC, (CPSU(B); 1938–47 dep, RSFSR Supr Sov; from 1946 Presidium member, RSFSR Supr Sov; dep, USSR Supr Sov; *Awards:* two Orders of Lenin; Order of the Red Banner of Labor; Order of Kutuzov, 2nd Class; medals; *Died:* 1951.

YEFREMOV, D.I. (SHTEYMAN, M.Ye.) (1881–1925) Govt official; CP member from 1902; *Born:* 1881; *Career:* Party work in Petersburg; May-Sept 1918 secr, Moscow Party Comt; Sept 1918–Oct 1919 member, Revol–Mil Council, 10th Army; then head, Yekaterina Railroad and comr, Donets Railroad; from 1921 chm, USSR Main State Insurance Bd; *Died:* 1925.

YEFREMOV, Dmitriy Vasil'yevich (1900–1960) Govt official; power plant specialist; *Born:* 1900; *Educ:* 1924 grad Leningrad Polytech Inst; *Career:* 1924–47 worked at "Elektrosila" Plant; 1947 USSR Dep Min of Electr Power Ind; 1948–51 USSR First Dep Min of Electr Power Ind; 1951–53 USSR Min of Electr Power Ind; 1953–54 USSR First Dep Min of Electr Power Plants and Electr Ind; 1954–56 dep chm, Bureau for Chemistry and Electr Power Eng, USSR Council of Min, 1956–60 dep head, Main Bd for the Use of Atomic Energy, USSR Council of Min; *Awards:* five Stalin Prizes (1946, 1948, 1952, 1953 und 1959); *Died:* Nov 1960.

YEFREMOV, Ivan Semyonovich (1898–1959) Actor and stage dir; Hon Art Worker of RSFSR from 1943; CP member from 1945; *Born:* 25 June 1898; *Educ:* studied at Moscow College of Painting, Sculpture and Architecture and at F.A. Ukhov's drama studio; *Career:* from 1918 with Red Army; amateur dramatics instructor; acted with army theater; after demobilization headed Theater Section, Donetsk Province Educ Dept; then actor and stage dir, Krasnozavodsk Theater, Khar'kov; 1927 moved to far East with this theater; from 1931 actor and stage dir, then artistic dir, Sverdlovsk Theater; directed theater in Kirov, Perm', Rostov-on-Don and Vladivostok; 1950–52 chief stage dir, Leningrad Bolshoy Drama Theater; from 1952 with Culture Bd, Leningrad City Sov; *Productions:* "Lyubov' Yarovaya" (1934); *Gibel' eskadry* (Death of a Squadron) (1935); Trenyov's *Na beregu Nevy* (On the Banks of the Neva) (1937); A.K. Tolstoy's "Tsar' Fyodor Ioannovich" (1938); *Chelovek s ruzh'yom* (The Man with a Gun) (1938); Capek's "Mother" (1939); Lope de Vega's "Dog in a Manger" (1939), etc; *Died:* 11 June 1959.

YEFREMOV, Mikhail Grigor'yevich (1897–1942) Mil commander; lt-gen; CP member from 1919; *Born:* 27 Feb 1897 in Tarusa; *Educ:* 1933 grad Mil Acad; *Career:* from 1917 with Red Guards, then with Red Army; fought in Civil War; after the end of the Civil War commanded div, then corps; commanded Volga, Trans-baykal, Orel and Transcaucasian Mil distr; 1st dep inspector-gen of infantry; 1941–42 commanded 21st, then 33rd Army; member, All-Russian Centr Exec Comt; dep, USSR Supr Sov of 1st convocation; Apr 1942, during Smolensk fighting, surrounded by Germans and seriously wounded; *Awards:* Order of Lenin; three Orders of the Red Banner, *Died:* 19 Apr 1942 shot himself to avoid falling into German hands; a monument to him was erected in Vyaz'ma.

YEFREMOV, Nikolay Nikolayevich (1886–1947) Chemist; Hon Sci Tech Worker of RSFSR from 1947; *Born:* 6 Mar 1886; *Educ:* 1911 grad Petersburg Polytech Inst; *Career:* from 1911 taught at Petersburg Polytech Inst; from 1919 prof, Petrograd Pharmaceutical Inst; from 1924 prof, Sverdlovsk Polytech Inst; from 1926 dir, Centr Chemical Laboratory, Sverdlovsk; 1927–29 sci dir, above laboratory; 1929–30 head, Potassium Dept, Ural Sci Chemical Inst; 1932 prof, Perm' Chemical Technol Inst; 1933 prof, Berezniki Chemical Technol Inst; from 1936 founder-head, Laboratory for Physicochemical Analysis of Organic Systems, Inst of Gen and Inorganic Chemistry, USSR Acad of Sci; 1936–39 prof, Moscow Inst of Chemical Machine-Building; 1936–40 prof, Moscow Polygraphic Inst; founded physicochemical analysis of systems formed by organic compounds; devised simple method of studying microstructure of organic fluxes; proposed method of microcinematography in polarized light; *Publ: Kamfora in fenoly* (Camphor and Phenols) (1913); *O soyedineniyakh pikrinovoy kisloty s uglevodorodami* (Compounds of Picric Acid and Hydrocarbons) (1919); coauthor, *Tvyordyye rastvory vysshikh zhirnykh kislot i triglitseridov* (Solid Solutions of Higher Fatty Acids and Triglycerides) (1948), etc; *Awards:* Order of the Red Banner of Labor; medals; *Died:* 26 Feb 1947.

YEFREMOV, Sergey Aleksandrovich (1876–?) Politician, journalist and lit historian; *Born:* 1876, son of a priest; *Educ:* studied at Kiev Theological Seminary; grad Law Fac, Kiev Univ; *Career:* from 1890's worked for Ukr newspapers and journals and for some Russian periodicals; 1905 co-founder, Ukr Radical Party, which soon merged with the Democrat Party into the Ukr Radical Democratic Party; helped lead this party and edited its organs "Nova hromada," "Hromad'ska dumka" and "Rada"; during WW 1 supported Tsarist govt; after 1917 Feb Revol helped found Ukr Socialist-Federalist Party, which advocated an agreement with the Provisional Govt based on Ukr autonomy; as ed, newspaper "Nova rada" conducted a fierce campaign against the Bolsheviks; from 1917 asst chm, Centr Ukr Rada and Min for Nationalities, Ukr Pop Republ; 1920, after establishment of Sov regime in Ukr, went underground; from 1921 vice-pres, All-Ukr Acad of Sci; wrote many publicistic and lit critical articles, as well as monographs on Ukr writers, 1930 arrested and sentenced to 10 years' imprisonment in trail of "Ukr Liberation League"; *Publ:* "The History of Ukrainian Literature" (1911), etc; *Died:* date and place of death unknown.

YEGOLIN, Aleksandr Mikhaylovich (1896–1959) Lit historian; corresp member, USSR Acad of Sci from 1946; member, RSFSR Acad of Pedag Sci from 1945; CP member from 1925; *Born:* 4 Sept 1896 in Samara, son of a worker; *Educ:* 1933 grad Inst of Red Prof; *Career:* from 1914 taught at zemstvo elementary school; from 1930 high school teacher; 1937–41 prof and dept head, Moscow Inst of Philosophy, Lit and Art; 1948–52 dir, Gorky Inst of World Lit; 1953–55 dep acad secr, Dept of Lit and Language, USSR Acad of Sci; 1955–57 senior assoc, 1957–59 section head, Inst of World Lit, USSR Acad of Sci; ed, journal "Zvezda"; specialized in life and work of Nekrasov and poets of Nekrasov school; *Publ: Nekrasov – poet krest'yanskoy demokratii* (Nekrasov, the Poet of Peasant Democracy) (1935); "A.I. Herzen" (1940); *Nekrasov. Kritiko-biograficheskiy ocherk* (Nekrasov. A Critical and Biographical Study) (1941); *Osvobitel'nyye i patrioticheskiye idei literatury XIX veka* (The Liberation and Patriotic Ideas of 19th-Century Russian Literature) (1946); *Gor'kiy i russkaya literatura* (Gorky and Russian Literature) (1949); *Nekrasov i poety-demokraty 60–80-kh godov XIX veka* (Nekrasov and the Democrat-Poets of the 1860's–1880's) (1960); *Died:* 6 May 1959 in Moscow.

YEGOROV, Aleksandr Il'ich (1883–1939) Mil commander; Marshal of the Sov Union from 1935; CP member from 1918; *Born:* 22 Oct 1883 in Buzuluk, Samara Province, son of a worker; *Educ:* 1905 grad Kazan' Infantry College; *Career:* in his youth worked as laborer and smith; also studied and passed external examinations for high-school certificate; from 1904 in revol movemant; member, Socialist-Revol Party; served in Russian Army, at first as volunteer; soon quit army and turned to acting; 1914 redrafted and fought in WW 1; five times wounded; distinguished himself in battle; 1917 commanded regt as lt-col; 1917 sided with Leftist Socialist-Revolutionaries, breaking with them in the summer of 1918; 1 May 1917 relieved of his command for anti-war statements, court-martialed and sentenced to fortress arrest; deleg at 2nd All-Russian Congress of Soviets; member, All-Russian Centr Exec Comt; 1918 comr, All-Russian Main Staff and chm, Higher Certification Commission to Select Officers for the Red Army; from Aug 1918 commanded 9th Army which beat off Krasnov's offensive in the Balashov-Novokhopersk-Kamyshin sector; from Dec 1918 commanded 10th Army in defense of Tsaritsyn; sponsored formation of Budyonnyy's Cavalry Div, then Cavalry Corps; from Aug 1919 commanded 14th Army on Kiev and Bryansk fronts; Oct 1919 appointed commander, Southern Front; Jan–Dec 1920 commanded Southwestern Front; after Civil War commanded Kiev and Petrograd Mil Distr, Caucasian Army, Ukr and Crimean Armed Forces and from 1927 Bel Mil Distr; 1925–26 mil attache in China; 1931–37 Rd chief of Red Army Gen Staff; from 1937 USSR First Dep Pop Comr of Defense; arrested by State Security organs; *Publ: L'vov-Varshava* (L'vov-Warsaw) (1920); *Vzaimodeystviye frontov* (The Cooperation of Fronts) (1929); *Razgrom Denikina, 1919* (The 1919 Rout of

Denikin) (1931); *Awards:* four Orders of the Red Banner; *Died:* 22 Feb 1939 in imprisonment; posthumously rehabilitated.

YEGOROV, Dmitriy Fyodorovich (1869–1931) Mathematician; hon member, USSR Acad of Sci from 1929; corresp member, USSR Acad of Sci from 1924: *Born:* 22 Dec 1869 in Moscow; *Career:* from 1903 prof, Moscow Univ; 1922–30 prof, Moscow Mathematical Soc; opposed Sov efforts to reorganize high schools and sci insts; 1929 dismissed from his post as dir, Inst of Mathematics and Mech; 1930 expelled from Moscow Mathematical Soc; specialized in differential geometry, the theory of integral equations, variation calculus and the theory of real variable functions; *Publ: Ob odnom klasse ortogonal'nykh sistem* (A Class of Orthogonal Systems) (1901); *Uravneniya s chastnymi proizvodnymi 2-go poryadka po dvum nezavisimym peremennym. Obshchaya teoriya integralov, kharakteristiki* (Equations with Second-Order Partial Derivatives for Two Independent Variables. The General Theory of Integrals, Characteristics) (1898); "Sur les Suites des Fonctions Mesurables" (1911); *Died:* 10 Sept 1931.

YEGOROV, Dmitriy Nikolayevich (1878–1931) Historian; Dr of Historical Sci from 1915, prof; pupil of P.G. Vinogradov; *Born:* 26 Oct 1878; *Educ:* 1901 grad Moscow Univ; *Career:* prof of gen history on Moscow Higher Women's Courses; and at Shanyavskiy Pop Univ; from 1917 prof, Moscow Univ; in 1920's also worked for Inst of History, Russian Assoc of Soc Sci Research Institutes, Assoc of Oriental Studies and Lenin Library, directing bibliographical work on gen history; maintained idealistic views on methods of historiography; 1928 passed over for selection to full membership of USSR Acad of Sci; persecuted for "adherence to counterrevol circle of bourgeois intelligentsia"; 1930 arrested and exiled; *Publ: Slavyano-germanskiye otnosheniya v sredniye veka. Kolonizatsiya Meklenburga v XIII veke* (Slavo-German Relations in the Middle Ages. The 13th-Century Colonization of Mecklenburg) (2 vol, 1915); *Srednevekov'ye v yego pamyatnikakh* (The Middle Ages in its Monuments) (1913); *Imperializm kul'turnyy, ekonomicheskiy i politicheskiy* (Cultural, Economic and Political Imperialism) (2 vol, 1911); *Chto takoye istoriya kul'tury* (What the History of Culture Is) (1920); *Genrikh Shliman* (Heinrich Schliemann) (1923); *Died:* 24 Nov 1931 in imprisonment.

YEGOROV, Pyotr Ivanovich (1899–1967) Therapist; Dr of Med from 1936; prof; maj-gen, Med Corps; corresp member, USSR Acad of Med Sci from 1948; CP member from 1940; *Born:* 1899, son of a peasant; *Educ:* 1918 grad boys' high-school in Petersburg; 1923 grad Mil Med Acad; *Career:* 1923–24 intern, Communist Hospital, Moscow; 1924–29 assoc, Pavlov Inst of Aviation Med; 1929–41 intern, asst prof, assoc prof, then prof, Chair of Special Pathology, Therapy and Diagnostics, then Chair of Fac Therapy, Leningrad Mil Med Acad; 1932 designed first Sov pressure chamber for the training of flight personnel; 1929–30 studied the biomed effects of long-duration flights; 1941–45 chief therapist, Western, then Leningrad Front; 1945–47 dep head, Chair of Fac Therapy, Kirov Mil Med Acad; 1945 attented Int Congress of Mil Surgeons, Belgrade; 1947–52 head, Kremlin Therapy and Health Bd; 1952 accused in "doctors' plot" of espionage for UK and of intentionally giving Sov leaders incorrect med treatment; 1953 arrested by State Security organs but rehabilitated after Stalin's death; 1954–64 head, 4th Chair of Therapy, Centr Inst of Postgrad Med Training, Moscow; 1957–67 head, Lung Pathology Dept, Inst of Therapy, USSR Acad of Med Sci; 1964–67 section head, Inst of Biomed Problems, USSR Min of Health; bd member, All-Union, All-Russian and Moscow Soc of Therapists; dep chm, Gastroenterological Section, Moscow Therapeutic Soc; member, ed collegium, journal "Terapevticheskiy arkhiv"; dep, Moscow City and Distr Sov; Bureau member, Leningrad Distr CPSU Comt; co-ed, *Opyt sovetskoy meditsiny v Velikoy Otechestvennoy voyne 1941–45 godov* (The Experience of Soviet Medicine in the 1941–45 Great Fatherland War); co-ed, *Entsiklopedicheskiy slovar' voyennoy meditsiny* (An Encyclopedic Dictionary of Military Medicine); co-ed, *Spravochnik dlya prakticheskogo vracha* (The General Practitioner's Reference Manual); apart from aviation and mil med also did major research on the clinical aspects and therapy of internal diseases, hematology and the pathology of the lungs and cardiovasular system; wrote over 80 works; *Publ: Differentsial'nyy flebomanometr* (A Differential Blood-Pressure Gauge); *Sfigmografiya pri sypnom tife i perifericheskoye serdtse pro nadpochechnikovoy gangrene* (Sphygmography in Typhus and the Peripheral Heart in Suprarenal Gangrene) (1922–23); *Potolok lyotchika* (The Pilot's Ceiling) (1931); doctor's thesis *Kislorodnoye golodaniye i bor'ba s nim* (Oxygen Starvation and Countermeasures) (1936); *Vliyaniye vysotnykh polyotov na organizm lyotchika* (The Effect of High-Altitude Flights on the Pilot's Body) (1937); *Voyenno-polevaya terapiya* (Field Therapy) (1945); *Organizatsiya terapevticheskoy sluzhby i opyt izucheniya zabolevayemosti po materialam Otechestvennoy voyny* (The Organization of the Therapeutic Services and Experience in the Study of Sick-Rates in the Records of the Fatherland War) (1945), etc; *Awards:* Order of Lenin; Order of the Great Fatherland War, 1st Class; Order of the Red Star; two Orders of the Red Banner; medal "For the Defense of Leningrad"; medal "For the Defense of Moscow"; medal "For Victory over Germany"; medal "For 30 Years of the Sov Army"; *Died:* 13 Jan 1967 in Moscow.

YEGOROV, Vladimir Yevgen'yevich (1878–1960) Stage and film designer; prof; Pop Artiste of RSFSR from 1944; *Born:* 19 Mar 1878; *Educ:* 1900 grad Moscow's Stroganov College; studied under the artists K. Korovin, S. Ivanov and F. Shekhtel'; *Career:* did book illustrations; 1906–12 stage designer, Moscow Arts Theater; 1911–17 instructor, Stroganov College, Moscow; from 1915 film designer; from 1945 instructor, Moscow Higher Ind Art College; *Works:* designed sets for stage shows: Hamsun's "The Drama of Life"; Andreyev's *Zhizn' chelovka* (The Life of Man) (1907); Maeterlinck's "The Blue Bird" (1908); Yushkevich's "Miserere" (1910); Rebikov's *Yolka* (The Christmas Tree) (1912); *Sobor Parizhskoy Bogomaterii* (The Cathedral of Notre Dame), after Victor Hugo's "The Hunchback of Notre Dame" (1926); Gorky's *Meshchane* (The Philistines) (1946), etc; sets for films: "The Portrait of Dorian Grey" (1915); Gorky's *Mat'* (Mother) (1920); *Prizrak brodit po Yevrope* (A Ghost Stalks Europe) (1923); *Slesar' i kantsler* (Carpenter and Chancellor) (1924); *Zakroyshchik iz Torzhka* (The Cutter from Torzhok) (1925); *Kryl'ya kholopa* (The Wings of a Serf) (1926); *Anna na sheye* (Anna on the Neck) (1929); *Konveyyer smerti* (The Death Conveyor) (1933); "Iudushka Golovlev" (1936); "Dubrovskiy" (1936); "Suvorov" (1941); "Kutuzov" (1944); Ostrovskiy's *Bez viny vinovatyye* (Guilty Without Guilt) (1945); "Admiral Nakhimov" (1947); *Schastlivyy reys* (The Happy Voyage) (1949); "Dzhambul" (1953), etc; *Publ: Khudozhnik v kino* (The Artist in the Cinema) (1950); *Awards:* Order of the Red Banner of Labor; Stalin (1946); *Died:* 8 Oct 1960.

YEGOROV, Yegor Yegorovich (1877–1949) Opera singer (bass); singing teacher; Hon Art Worker of RSFSR from 1948; Dr of Arts from 1944; *Born:* 22 July 1877 in Moscow; *Educ:* 1902 grad Moscow Conservatory; *Career:* 1902–04 with Moscow Private Russian Opera Company; 1904–06 with Kiev Opera Theater; 1906–08 with Bolshoy Theater, Moscow; 1908–10 at opera theaters in Odessa, Tiflis, etc; from 1910 taught singing; 1924–39 prof, Moscow Conservatory; from 1939 prof, Sverdlovsk Conservatory; *Died:* 15 Feb 1949 in Sverdlovsk.

YEGOROVA, Ye.N. (1892–1938) Trade-union official; CP member from 1911; *Born:* 1892; *Career:* Party work in Riga and Moscow; after 1917 Feb Revol secr, Petrograd's Vyborg Distr RSDRP(B) Comt; then head, Agitation Dept, Petrograd Province RCP(B) Comt; 1919 secr, Saratov RCP(B) Comt; deleg, 8th RCP(B) Congress; in following years exec trade-union work; chm, CC, Sewing Ind Workers' Union; Presidium member, All-Union Centr Trade-Union Council; from 1934 chm, CC, Rubber and Synthetic Rubber Ind Workers' Union; then secr, All-Union Centr Trade-Union Council; arrested by State Security organs; *Died:* 1938 in imprisonment.

YEGOR'YEV, Vladimir Nikolayevich (1869–?) Mil commander; *Born:* 1869 in Moscow, son of an official; *Educ:* mil training; *Career:* served in Russian Army; 1910, in view of his polit views and activities but officially in connection with manpower cuts, sent to Montenegro as an instructor to the Montenegran Army; during WW 1 held various staff posts and commands, ranging from command of a regt to command of an army; 1917 dep chm, Mil Revol Comt, Special Army; with formation of Red Army commanded Western Sector of Defensive Screen; Sept 1918 Sov mil agent in Ukr; 1919, prior to Red Army's offensive against Denikin, commanded Southern Front; mil expert at talks to conclude peace treaty with Finland and Poland; from 1922 mil training work; *Died:* date and place of death unknown.

YELANSKIY, Nikolay Nikolayevich (1894–1964) Surgeon; lt-gen, Med Corps; prof from 1932; Dr of Med from 1924; Hon Sci Worker of RSFSR from 1942; *Born:* 1894; *Educ:* 1917 grad Mil Med Acad; *Career:* 1917–18 regt physician with Russian Army on Southwestern Front; 1918–21 physician, Makarovo Distr

Hospital, Voronezh Oblast; 1921–34 intern, S. P. Fyodorov's Fac Surgical Clinic, Mil Med Acad; also intern, Pavlov Laboratory and other med establishments; 1934–46 head, Chair of Fac Surgery, Leningrad Pediatric Med Inst; 1937–38 head, Chair of Gen Surgery, 1938–39 Chair of Mil Field Surgery, Mil Med Acad; during Sov-Japanese War, Sov-Finnish War and WW 1 supervised surgical work on various fronts; 1946–47 again head, Chair of Gen Surgery, Mil Med Acad; 1947–64 head, Chair of Fac Surgery, 1st Moscow Med Inst; chief surgeon, Sov Army; co-ed, surgery section, 2nd ed of "BME" (Large Medical Encyclopedia); co-ed, journals "Khirurgiya" and "Voyenno-meditsinskiy zhurnal"; member, ed council, journal "Antibiotiki"; edited vol 14 and 15 of *Opyt sovetskoy meditsiny v Velikoy Otechestvennoy voyne 1941–45 godov* (The Experience of Soviet Medicine in the 1941–45 Great Fatherland War); did research on gen and mil field surgery, blood transfusion, urology, etc; 1960 attended Int Congress of Phlebologists at Chamery, France; 1962 attended 8th Int Cancer Congress, Moscow; wrote over 100 works; *Publ:* thesis *O vzaimootnosheniyakh mezhdu yazvoy i rakom zheludka* (The Relationship Between Stomach Ulcer and Cancer) (1924); *O zlokachestvennom pererozhdenii yazv zheludka* (The Malignant Degeneration of Gastric Ulcers) (1923); *Perelivaniye krovi* (Blood Transfusion) (1926); *O travmaticheskom toksikoze pri massivnykh zakrytykh povrezhdeniyakh myagkikh tkaney* (Traumatic Toxicosis in the Case of Massive Closed Damage of the Soft Tissue) (1950); *Voyenno-polevaya khirurgiya* (Military Field Surgery) (1952); *Vnutrikostnyy metallicheskiy osteosintez pri otkrytykh infitsirovannykh perelomakh* (Intraosseous Metallic Osteosynthesis with Compound Infected Fractures) (1953).; *Fiziologicheskiye osnovy sovremennoy khirurgii* (The Physiological Principles of Modern Surgery) (1956); *O mnozhestvennykh opukholyakh zheludka* (Multiple Gastric Tumors) (1963), ect; *Awards:* Stalin Prize (1952); 15 orders and medals; *Died:* 1964.

YELENKIN, Aleksandr Aleksandrovich (1873–1942) Botanist; *Born:* 16 Sept 1873 in Warsaw; *Educ:* 1897 grad Warsaw Univ; *Career:* 1898–1942 worked at Petersburg Botanical Gardens (later Botanical Inst, USSR Acad of Sci); 1898 founded Spores Herbarium (now Dept of Spore Plants, Botanical Inst); pioneered lichenology in Russia; proposed theory of endoparasitosaprophytism, explaining the relations between fungus and algae in a lichen symbiosis, whereby the fungus lives as a parasite on the living algae and feeds saprophytically on dying algae contained in the body of the lichen; devised a new classification of lichens which he called combinative and pointed out that this was no phylogenetic system but enabled corrections to be made to the structure of the natural system; wrote unique monograph *Sinezelyonyye vodorosli SSSR* (The Blue-Green Algae of the USSR) (2 vol, 1936–49); also published unique *Flora mkhov Sredney Rossii* (The Moss Flora of Central Russia) (1909); *Died:* 19 Sept 1942 in Kazan'.

YELEONSKAYA, Yelena Nikolayevna (1873–1951) Ethnographer and folklorist; *Born:* 25 July 1873 in Moscow; *Career:* specialized in folklore and ethnography under V.F. Miller; worked for journals "Etnograficheskoye obozreniye", "Russkiy arkhiv", etc, in which she published some 100 articles, reviews and summaries on folklore and ethnography; together with Miller, prepared for the press the collections *Byliny novoy i nedavney zapisi iz raznykh mestnostey Rossii* (Folk Epics from Different Localities of Russia, Recently and Formerly Recorded) (1908) and *Istoricheskiye pesni russkogo naroda 16-17 vekov* (Historical Songs of the Russian People from the 16th and 17th Centuries) (1915); *Publ: Nekotoryye zamechaniya o perezhitkakh pervobytnoy kul'tury v russkikh narodnykh skazkakh* (Some Notes on Survivals of Primitive Culture in Russian Folk Tales) (1906); *Nekotoryye zamechaniya o roli zagadok v skazke* (Some Notes on the Role of Conundrums in Tales) (1907); *Nekotoryye zamechaniya po povodu slozheniya skazok. Zagovornaya formula v skazke* (Some Notes on the Composition of Tales. The Charm Formula in Tales) (1912); *Material dlya zanyatiy v seminarii po narodnoy slovesnosti* (Material for Seminary Lessons on Folklore) (1912); *Velikorusskiye skazki Permskoy gubernii* (Great-Russian Tales from Perm Province) (1915); *K izucheniyu koldovstva i zagovora v Rossii* (The Study of Magic and Charms in Russia) (1917), etc; *Died:* 3 Oct 1951 in Moscow.

YELICHEV, Aleksey Ivanovich (1909–1959) Party official; CP member from 1931; *Born:* 1909 in Leningrad, son of a worker; *Educ:* grad Mil Eng Acad; *Career:* 1925–33 trade-union and govt work in Kalinin Oblast and Leningrad; from 1933 studied at Mil Eng Acad; after grad served with Main Mil Eng Bd of Sov Army; 1942–47 and from 1951 exec posts with CC, CPSU; *Awards:* Order of the Red Banner of Labor; Order of the Red Banner; Order of the Fatherland War, 2nd Class; two Orders of the Red Star; medals; *Died:* 13 July 1959.

YELISEYEV, Nikolay Aleksandrovich (1897–1966) Geologist and petrographer; prof from 1938; corresp member, USSR Acad of Sci from 1953; *Born:* 19 Dec 1897; *Educ:* 1924 grad Leningrad Univ; *Career:* 1939–47 prof, Leningrad Mining Inst; from 1947 prof, Leningrad Univ; from 1949 also at Laboratory of Precambrian Geology, USSR Acad of Sci; specialized in petrography of Altay, Kola Pensinsula and methods of petrographic research; *Publ: Petrografiya Rudnogo Altaya i Kalby* (The Petrography of the Oriferous Altay and Kalba) (1938); coauthor, *Petrologiya plutona Gremyakha-Vyrmes. Kol'skiy poluostrov* (The Petrology of the Gremyakha-Vyrmes Pluton. The Kola Pensinsula) (1941); *Strukturnaya petrologiya* (Structural Petrology) (1953); *Metody petrograficheskikh issledovaniy* (Methods of Petrographical Research) (1956); *Metamorfizm* (Metamorphism) (1960), etc; *Awards:* Order of Lenin; *Died:* 24 June 1966.

YELISEYEV, Vladimir Grigor'yevich (1899–1966) Histologist; prof from 1934; Dr of Med from 1938; CP member from 1932; *Born:* 25 July 1899 in Krasnoyarsk, son of an office worker; *Educ:* 1926 grad Med Fac, Tomsk Univ; *Career:* 1926–34 postgrad student, asst prof, then assoc prof, Chair of Histology and Embryology, Tomsk Univ; 1934–52 head, Chair of Histology and Embryology, Omsk Med Inst; during WW 2 helped organize evacuation hospitals in Omsk; directed an evacuation hospital; dep dir, Omsk Med Inst; 1952–66 head, Chair of Histology and Embryology, Sechenov 1st Moscow Med Inst; also dep chm, All-Union Sci Soc of Anatomists, Histologists and Embryologists; chm, bd, Moscow Soc of Anatomists, Histologists and Embryologists; chm, Morphology Problem Commission, Learned Med Council, RSFSR Min of Health; member, Expert Commission, Higher Qualifications Commission; member, ed bd, journal "Arkhiv anatomii, gistologii i embriologii"; Presidium member, Learned Med Council, RSFSR Min of Health; member, Party Bureau, 1st Moscow Med Inst; presented papers at 1947 Histological in Leningrad and at 1949 and 1958 Congresses of Anatomists, Histologists and Embryologists; wrote over 50 works on histology, methods of teaching histology, studies of connective tissue, inflammatory processes, vitamin deficiency, reactivity of cell elements, regeneration, etc; *Publ: Metodicheskiye ukazaniya k prakticheskim zanyatiyam po gistologii* (Methodic Instructions for Practical Histology Studies) (1956); *Mikroskopicheskaya tekhnika* (Microscopic Technique) (1956); *Soyedinitel'naya tkan' / gistofiziologicheskiye ocherki/* (Connective Tissue [Histophysiological Studies]) (1959); *Awards:* various govt awards; *Died:* 1966.

YELIZAROV, Mark Timofeyevich (1863–1919) Govt official; CP member from 1893; *Born:* 22 Mar 1863, son of a peasant; *Educ:* 1886 grad Physics and Mathematics Fac, Petersburg Univ; *Career:* close friend of Lenin's brother, A.I. Ul'yanov and married to his sister Anna (A.I. Yelizarova-Ul'yanova); worked for Petersburg Treasury, then in Samara and as bookkeeper for Railroad Admin in Moscow and Petersburg; Aug 1901 arrested for assisting Moscow RSDRP Comt and exiled for two years to Syzran'; 1905, in Petersburg, served on Org Bureau for 1st All-Russian Congress of Railroad Officials and headed Junction Railroad Strike Comt; arrested and again exiled to Syzran' for three years; here, under the pseudonym "Scorpion", he contributed to newspapers "Syzran'" and "Syzranskoye utro"; 1906 moved to Samara and joined Samara RSDRP Comt; 1908 went abroad and met Lenin; 1909–17 insurance agent for Salamandra Co; also worked for Saratov RSDRP Org; after 1917 Oct Revol Pop Comr of Means of Communication; from 23 Mar 1918 chief comr for insurance, from 22 Jan 1919 Collegium member, Pop Comrt of Trade and Ind; *Died:* 10 Mar 1919 of typhus.

YELIZAROVA-UL'YANOVA, Anna Il'inichna (1864–1935) Party official; CP member from 1898; *Born:* Aug 1864 in Nizhniy Novgorod, V. I. Lenin's sister; *Educ:* 1880 grad Simbirsk Girls High-School; 1883 studied at Bestuzhev Higher Women's Courses; *Career:* teacher; 1887 arrested in connection with A. I. Ul'yanov's attempted assassination of Alexander III and exiled to Kazan' Province where she was kept under police surveillance; later tranferred to vil Alakayevka, Samara Province, then to Samara; late 1893 moved to Moscow and worked for Soc-Democratic circles; 1896 member, Petersburg League for the Liberation of the Working Clas; wrote workers' proclamations; 1897 established connection with Liberation of Labor group; 1898 member,

Moscow RSDRP Comt; Lenin, who at that time was in Siberian exile, entrusted her with various commissions; 1900 went abroad and for two years worked for Lenin's "Iskra"; 1902 Party work in Tomsk, Samara and Kiev; Jan 1904 arrested in connection with the case of Party CC and Kiev Party Comt; 1904–06 with Petersburg Bolshevik Comt; smuggled to Moscow and other Russian towns Bolshevik newspapers "Vperyod" and "Proletariy"; late 1908–09 arranged Moscow publ of Lenin's book "Materializm i empiriokrititsizm" (Materialism and Empirical Criticism); from late 1905 worked for "Proletariy"; 1910 with Saratov Party Comt; arrested; 1912–14 worked for newspapers "Pravda" and "Prosveshcheniye"; during WW 1 maintained liaison between Russian Party org and Party center abroad; 1916 re-arrested and exiled to Astrakhan' Province; after 1917 Feb Revol secr, "Pravda"; ed, journal "Tkach"; helped prepare and carry out 1917 Oct Revol; 1918–21 head, Dept for Mother and Child Care, Pop Comrt of Educ; also Party work; from 1921 with Commission to Collect and Study Material on Party History and Oct Revol; member, ed bd, journal "Proletarskaya revolyutsiya"; then assoc, Marx-Engels-Lenin Inst; *Publ: Detskiye i shkol'nyye gody Il'icha* (Il'ich's Childhood and School Years) (1925); *Vospominaniya ob Il'iche* (Recollections of Il'ich) (1926); *Aleksandr Il'ich Ul'yanov i delo 1 marta 1887 goda* (Aleksandr Il'ich Ul'yanov and the 1 March 1887 Case) (1927), etc; *Died:* 19 Oct 1935; buried at Leningrad's Volkov Cemetery next to the graves of her mother, her sister Ol'ga and her husband M. T. Yelizarov.

YELPAT'YEVSKIY, Sergey Yakovlevich (1854–1933) Physician, writer and journalist; *Born:* 3 Nov 1854 in vil Novoselok Kudrino, Vladimir Province, son of a priest; *Educ:* grad Med Fac, Moscow Univ; *Career:* 1872–78, while at Moscow Univ, sided with Revol Populists and became one of the leaders of the Moscow student movement; after grad univ served as zemstvo physician; 1880 imprisoned for six months for harboring revolutionaries and then exiled; worked as physician in Ufa, where he was placed under admin exile after distributing illegal lit on his way to spend three years in Eastern Siberia; 1887–96, after completing his term of exile, engaged in cultural, educ and lit work and practised as physician in Nizhniy Novgorod; from late 1890's lived in Yalta, where he founded a sanatorium for poor tuberculosis patients; from late 1890's member, ed staff, journal "Russkoye bogatstvo"; 1906 member, Org Comt, Pop Socialist Party; wrote several polit articles and pamphlets; brought to trial for his 1906 pamphlet "Land and Liberty"; 1910–11 imprisoned in Peter and Paul Fortress; after 1917 Oct Revol lived in Moscow; 1922–28 physician, Outpatients' Dept, Kremlin Hospital; *Publ:* novelette *Ozim'* (Winter Crop) (1880); *Ocherki Sibiri* (Studies of Siberia) (1893); *Rasskazy o proshlom* (Stories of the Past) (1900–01); travel notes: *Za granitsey* (Abroad) (1910); *Yegipet* (Egypt) (1911); *Krymskiye ocherki* (Crimean Notes) (1913); *Vospominaniya za 50 let* (Memoirs of Fifty Years) (1929); other works: *Rasskazy* (Stories) (3 vol, 1904); *Sobraniye sochineniy* (Collected Works) (4 vol, 1912); *Rasskazy* (Stories) (4 vol, 1914); *Blizkiye teni* (Near Shadows) (1909); *Literaturnyye vospominaniya* (Literary Memoirs) (2 vol, 1916); *Krutyye gory. Rasskazy o proshlom* (Steep Mountains. Tales of the Past) (1929); *V Sibiri* (In Siberia) (1938); *Died:* 9 Jan 1933 in Moscow.

YELSUKOV, Mikhail Petrovich (1902–1965) Agronomist; specialist in plant-growing; prof; corresp member, All-Union Lenin Acad of Agric Sci from 1956; CP member from 1931; *Born:* 1902; *Educ:* 1931 grad Leningrad Agric Inst; 1934 completed postgrad courses at above inst; *Career:* 1931–37 asst prof, 1937–41 assoc prof, Pushkino Agric Inst; 1935–39 head, Bureau of High-Mountain Agric and dir, Centr Asian Dept, All-Union Inst of Plant-Growing; 1939–41 dir, All-Union Research Inst of Plant Protection; from 1945 dir, Vil'yams All-Union Fodder Research Inst; then head, Dept of Field Grass-Sowing, above inst; carried out various expeditions to study soils in connection with plant-growing and farming: 1932 to Leningrad Oblast; 1933 to Northern Dvina Delta; 1936 to Southern Altay; 1937 to Altay Valley and Pamirs; 1938 to Kyzyl-Kums; 1956 Sov rep at Int Congress of Meadow Culture, Palmerston (New Zealand); *Publ: Uluchsheniye lugov i vygonov v Avtonomnoy Karel'skoy SSR* (The Improvement of Meadows and Pastures in the Autonomous Karelian SSR) (1935); *Silosnyye rasteniya i silosovaniye* (Silage Plants and Ensilaging) (1936); *Odnoletniye kormovyye kul'tury v smeshannykh posevakh* (Annual Fodder Crops in Mixed Sowings) exec ed, *Kormoproizvodstvo. Uchebnoye posobiye* (Fodder Production. A Teaching Manual) (1960), etc; *Awards:* two Orders of the Red Banner of Labor; Order of the Fatherland War, 2nd Class; two Orders of the Red Star; *Died:* 23 Oct 1965.

YEMCHENKO, Andrey Ivanovich (1893–1964) Phyiologist; prof from 1933; Dr of Med; corresp member, Ukr Acad of Sci from 1957; *Born:* 28 Oct 1893 in vil Mikhaylovka, now Cherkassy Oblast; *Educ:* 1925 grad Kiev Med Inst; *Career:* 1925–32 asst prof, then assoc prof, Chair of Physiology, Kiev Med Inst and Kiev Univ; member, ed council, periodical "Zhurnal vyshey nervnoy deyatel'nosti imeni I.P. Pavlova"; edited several Ukr-language eds of Pavlov's works; 1933–64 head, Chair of Physiology, Kiev Univ; specialized in physiology of cardiac activity and digestion and higher nervous activity of animals and man; *Publ:* coauthor, *Uchebnik fiziologii zhivotnykh i cheloveka* (A Textbook of the Physiology of Animals and Man) (1952); *Died:* 18 Nov 1964.

YEMEL'YANENKO, Pavel Terent'yevich (1905–1947) Pipe-rolling specialist; prof; corresp member, Ukr Acad of Sci from 1939; CP member from 1926; *Born:* 5 July 1905 in vil Bobrikovo-Petrovskoye, Yekaterinoslav Province; *Educ:* 1931 grad Dnepropetrovsk Metallurgical Inst; *Career:* 1934–41 instructur, 1941–47 prof, Dnepropetrovsk Metallurgical Inst; 1946 supervised design of original pipe-welding mill; *Publ: Pil'gerstany* (Pilger Mills) (1937); coauthor, *Truboprokatnoye proizvodstvo* (Pipe-Rolling Production) (1940); *Zakhvat metalla pri prokatke trub v avtomaticheskom stane Shtifeiya* (Metal Catchment in Pipe-Rolling in an Automatic Stiefel Mill (1949); *Teoriya kosoy i piligrimovoy prokatki* (The Theory of Bias and Pilgrim Rolling) (1949), etc; *Awards:* Stalin Prize (1943); *Died:* 13 Nov 1947.

YEMEL'YANOV, Nikolay Aleksandrovich (1871–1958) Govt official; CP member from 1904; *Born:* 1871 in Sestroretsk; son of a worker; *Career:* worked at Sestroretsk Arms Factory; 1899 joined Soc-Democratic org; 1905 organized a factory fighting squad; helped smuggle weapons and revol lit from Finland; late 1905 met Lenin; Dec 1905 arrested and exiled for five years to Novgorod Province; from 1910 again at Setroretsk Arms Factory; after 1917 Feb Revol dep, Petrograd Sov; July–Aug 1917 harbored Lenin at Razliv Station after his arrest was ordered by the Provisional Govt; during 1917 Oct Revol helped guard Smol'nyy and storm the Winter Palace; 1918 mil comr; 1919 chm, Exec Comt, Sestroretsk Sov; 1921 helped crush Kronstadt Mutiny; Sept 1921–23 with RSFSR trade mission in Est; then admin work; *Publ: Vospominaniya o V. I. Lenine* (Memories of V. I. Lenin) (1956); *Died:* 13 Aug 1958.

YEMSHANOV, A. I. (1891–1941) Govt official; CP member from 1917; *Born:* 1891; *Career:* railroad worker; 1917–20 chm, Track Comt, Perm' Railroad Bd; then dir, Perm' Railroad; 1920–21 Pop Comr of Means of Communication; 1921–22 Dep Pop Comr of Means of Communication; then worked for Pop Comrt of Means of Communication; arrested by State Security organs; *Died:* 1941 in imprisonment.

YENUKIDZE, Avel' Safronovich (Party name: AVEL'; ABDUL; GOLDFISH) (1877–1937) Govt and Party official; CP member from 1898; *Born:* 19 May 1877 in vil Tskhadisi, Kutaisi Province, son of a peasant; *Educ:* secondary tech educ in Tiflis; Career: 1897–1900 worker, Transcaucasian Railroad Main Workshops, then asst locomotive driver in Baku, where he founded workers' circles and helped found Baku Soc-Democratic Org; co-founder and until 1906 assoc, "Nina" underground printing press; 1906–14 Party work in Transcaucasia, Rostov, Moscow and Petersburg; Oct 1914 exiled to Yeniseysk Province; late 1916 drafted into Russian Army; during 1917 Feb Revol played an active part in troops' revol actions in Petrograd; at 1st Congress of Soviets elected Bolshevik member, All-Russian Centr Exec Comt; from June 1917 member, Petrograd Sov and Exec Comt; took part in 1917 Oct Revol and attented 2nd All-Russian Congress of Soviets; Nov 1917 – fall 1918 head, Mil Dept, All-Russian Centr Exec Comt; fall 1918–1923 Presidium member and secr, All-Russian Centr Exec Comt; 1923 – Mar 1935 Presidium member and secr, USSR Centr Exec Comt; 1936 dir, Khar'kov Oblast Automobile and Horse Trans Trust; deleg at 6th, 8th, 9th and 11th–17th CPSU(B) Congresses; 1924–34 member, CPSU(B) Centr Control Commission; 1934 at 17th Party Congress elected member, CC, CPSU(B); 1935 expelled from Party for polit abuses and private immorality; 1937 arrested and sentenced to death; *Awards:* Order of Lenin; *Died:* 16 Dec 1937 executed; 1959 rehabilitated.

YENUKIDZE, Trifon Teymurazovich (1877–1937) Govt official; CP member from 1899; *Born:* 1877 in Geo; *Career:* from age 15 worked at Tiflis mech plants; from 1899 revol work in Balakhany;

1902 helped found and 1903–05 worked at Baku illegal printing house; after 1905 Revol moved to Moscow; in Lesnaya Street established underground printing press to print journal "Rabochiy"; 1906 arrested in Petersburg and exiled to Arkhangel'sk Province, but soon escaped; 1907 worked in Vyborg and helped publish newspaper "Proletariy"; 1908 worked in Berezin's printing house in Petersburg, then moved to Baku; 1912 exiled; 1914–17 Oct Revol worked at Petrograd's Siemens-Schuckert Plant; 1918 directed All-Russian Centr Exec Comt's printing houses; from 1919 dir, State Admin for the Issue of Bank-Notes; arrested by State Security organs; *Died:* 1937 in imprisonment.

YEPKHIYEV, Tatari (1911–1958) Ossetian poet and lit historian; *Born:* 22 Nov 1911 in vil Ardon, Northern Ossetia; *Educ:* 1937 grad Philosophy Fac, Moscow Inst of Philosophy, Lit and History; *Career:* 1927 first work printed; contributed to Ossetian periodicals; also taught; wrote studies of Ossetian lit; *Publ:* verse collections: "Seething Epoch" (1931); "Ossetia on Fire" (1941–45); poems: "Two Hearts" (1936); "The Nameless Tumulus" (1938); "The Ear of Grain Fills" (1950); coauthor, *Osetinskaya literatura* (Ossetian Literature) (1952); novel "The Tsorayev Family" (1956), etc; *Died:* 2 Apr 1958.

YERBANOV, Mikhey Nikolayevich (1889–1937) Party and govt official; CP member from 1917; *Born:* 1889, son of a Buryat peasant; *Career:* printer by profession; 1917–18 member, Buryat Nat Revol Comt; 1918–19 worked for underground Irkutsk RCP(B) org; founded partisan detachments in Buryat regions; 1919 organized illegal Buryat Communist group attached to Irkutsk Province RCP(B) Comt; 1920–21 member, Irkutsk Province RCP(B) Comt and head, Irkutsk Province Land Dept; 1921–22 chm, Centr Exec Comt, Buryat-Mongolian Autonomous Oblast, Eastern Siberia and chm, Revol Comt, Buryat-Mongolian Autonomous Oblast, RSFSR; 1923–27 chm, Buryat-Mongolian ASSR Council of Pop Comr; 1927 chm, Buryat-Mongolian ASSR Centr Exec Comt; 1929–37 first secr, Buryat-Mongolian Oblast CPSU(B) Comt and member, Siberian Kray CPSU(B) Comt; from 1922 member, All-Russian, then USSR Centr Exec Comt; arrested by State Security organs; *Died:* 1937 in imprisonment; posthumously rehabilitated.

YEREMEYEV, Konstantin Stepanovich (1874–1931) Party official and mil commander; journalist; CP member from 1896; *Born:* 1874 in Olonetsk Province; *Career:* during his army service 1894–95 joined revol movement; 1897 arrested, for two years imprisoned in Warsaw Fortress, then exiled; after his release worked at a Petersburg plant; again arrested and exiled; 1904 fled from exile and emigrated; 1906 returned to Russia; from 1910 with ed bd, newspapers "Zvezda" and "Pravda"; during WW 1 headed mil org, North Baltic RSDRP(B) Comt; late 1917 Party work on Northern Front; worked with Petrograd Mil-Revol Comt; during 1917 Oct Revol member, field staff, Mil-Revol Comt; commanded squads storming Winter Palace from the Field of Mars; commanded unit sent to Moscow to help workers' revolt; from Dec 1917 commander, Petrograd Mil Distr; 1918 helped defend Petrograd and crush Moscow mutiny; 1919–22 exec govt, mil and Party work; All-Russian Centr Exec Comt and CC, RCP(B) plen for drafting recruits into Red Army; founder and dep head, State Publ House; ed, newspaper "Rabochaya gazeta", etc; 1923–25 member, Revol Mil Council, Baltic Fleet; from 1925 head, Polit Bd, Baltic Fleet and fleet rep on USSR Revol-Mil Council; 1923 at 12th Party Congress elected member, RCP(B) Centr Control Commission; 1926–29 Sov merchant fleet rep in France; 1929–31 ed, journal "Krasnaya niva"; wrote a number of works on 1917 Oct Revol and Civil War; member, USSR Writers' Union; *Died:* 28 Jan 1931; buried on Field of Mars in Leningrad.

YERMANSKIY, O. A. (other pseudonym: GUSHKO, A. O.; real name: KOGAN, Osip Arkad'yevich) (1866–1941) Revolutionary; Party official; *Born:* 1866, son of an artisan; *Career:* from late 1880's in revol movement; 1899–1902 in Southern Russia; worked for newspaper "Yuzhnyy rabochiy"; 1902 arrested and exiled to Siberia, but soon fled and went abroad; after 2nd Party Congress sided with Mensheviks; in 1910's took liquidationist stand; during WW 1 member, "Initiativist Group"; 1917 Menshevik-Internationalist; 1918 member, CC, RSDRP (Mensheviks); co-ed, journal "Rabochiy Internatsional"; 1921 broke with Mensheviks; research and publ work in Moscow; member, Communist Acad; 1930 expelled from acad for his unorthodox views; from 1934 pensioner; *Publ: Nauchnaya ratsionalizatsiya i sistema Teylora* (Scientific Rationalization and the Taylor System) (1922), later re-printed under the title *Teoriya i praktika ratsionalizatsii* (The Theory and Practice of Rationalization); *Died:* 1941.

YERMILOV, Vladimir Vladimirovich (1904–1965) Russian critic and lit historian; CP member from 1927; *Born:* 29 Oct 1904; *Educ:* 1924 grad Moscow Univ; *Career:* 1920 first work printed; 1920–21 ed, newspaper "Yunosheskaya pravda"; 1926–29 ed, journal "Molodaya gvardiya"; from 1928 co-secr, Russian Assoc of Proletarian Writers; 1932–38 chief ed, journal "Krasnaya nov'"; 1946–50 chief ed, newspaper "Literaturnaya gazeta"; *Publ: O gumanizme Gor'kogo* (Gorky's Humanism) (1941); "A.P. Chekov" (revised ed, 1949); "N. V. Gogol'" (1953); *Dramaturgiya A. P. Chekova* (A. P. Chekhov's Plays) (1954); *O traditsiyakh sovetskoy literatury. Tvorchestvo A. Malyshkina, A. Makarenko, Yu. Krymova* (The Traditions of Soviet Literature. The Work of A. Malyshkin, A. Makarenko and Yu. Krymov) (1955); "F. M. Dostoyevskiy" (1956); *Geniy Gogolyeva* (Gogol's Genius) (1959); *Tolstoy-khudozhnik i roman "Voyna i mir"* (Tolstoy the Artist and the Novel "War and Peace") (1961); *Roman L. N. Tolstogo "Anna Karenina"* (L. N. Tolstoy's Novel "Anna Karenina") (1963), etc; *Awards:* Order of the Red Banner of Labor (1955); Stalin Prize (1950); *Died:* 18 Nov 1965.

YERMOLOVA, Mariya Nikolayevna (1853–1928) Actress; Pop Artiste of RSFSR from 1920; *Born:* 15 July 1853 in Moscow; *Educ:* from age nine trained at theater school; 1871 grad Theatrical College; *Career:* 1870 made stage debut; May 1871 enrolled at Maly Theater, with which she performed until 1921; *Roles:* Katerina in Ostrovskiy's *Groza* (The Storm) (1873); Tugina in Ostrovskiy's *Poslednyaya zhertva* (The Last Victim) (1877); Yevlaliya in *Nevol'nitsa* (The Prisoner) (1880); Negina in Ostrovskiy's *Talanty i poklonniki* (Talents and Admirers) (1881); Lyudmila in Ostrovskiy's *Pozdnyaya lyubov'* (Late Love) (1896); Kruchinina in Ostrovskiy's *Bez viny vinovatyye* (Guilty Withouts Guilt (1908); Laurenzia in Lope de Vega's "The Sheep's Spring" (1876); Joan in Schiller's "The Maid of Orleans" (1884); Yudif' in Gutskov's "Uriel' Akosta" (1879); Maria in Schiller's "Maria Stuart" (1886); Queen Margaret in Shakespeare's "Richard III"; Princess Plavutina-Plavuntsova in Gnedich's *Kholopy* (The Serfs); *Awards:* Hero of Labor (1924); *Died:* 12 Mar 1928 in Moscow.

YERNSHTEDT, Pyotr Viktorovich 1890–1966) Philologist; specialist in Greek and Coptic; prof, Leningrad Univ; corresp member, USSR Acad of Sci from 1946; *Born:* 1890; *Career:* published and annotated many previously unpublished Greek and Greco-Egyptian papyri relating to the late Roman, Byzantine and Arabic periods; wrote accounts of two collections of Coptic papyri; studied ancient links between Greek and Egyptian languages; *Publ:* "Spätrömische und byzantische Texte" (1929); "Die Kome-Aphrodito Papyri der Sammlung Lichcov" (1927); *Yegipetskiye zaimstvovaniya v grecheskom yazyke* (Egyptian Loan Words in Greek) (1953); *Grecheskiye yegiptizmy vremeni sushchestvovaniya grecheskikh faktoriy v Yegipte* (Greek Egyptianisms from the Period of the Existence of the Greek Manufacturies in Egypt) (1956); *Died:* 28 Dec 1966.

YEROFEYEV, Vladimir Alekseyevich (1898–1940) Film dir; CP member from 1917; *Born:* 1 Apr 1898; *Career:* 1922 began work with cinema press as ed, newspaper' "Kinogazeta" and head, "Kino-Moskva" Publ House; 1925–26 head, Photographic and Cinema Dept, Sov Trade Mission in Germany; from 1927 film dir, Sov Film Studio, Leningrad; made one of first Sov synchronous sound documentary films – *Olimpiada iskusstv* (The Arts Olypmics) (1930); organized first Sov sound film expedition to shoot the film *Daleko v Azii* (Far Off in Asia) (1931); *Productions:* films: *Za Polyarnym krugom* (Beyond the Polar Circle) (1927); *Krysha mira* (The Roof of the World) (1928); *Serdtse Azii* (The Heart of Asia) (1929); *K schastlivoy gavani* (Toward a Happy Harbor) (1930); "Persia" (1935); *K sobytiyam v Ispanii* (On the Events in Spain) (20 parts, 1936–37); *Put' otkryt* (The Path is Open) (1937); *Geroicheskiy perelyot* (A Heroic Flight) (1938); *Lyudi morya* (Men of the Sea) (1938); *V Ussuriyskoy tayge* (In the Ussuri Taiga) (1938); "S.M. Kirov" (1939); *VSKhV* (The All-Union Agricultural Exhibition) (1940); *Biblioteka imeni Lenina* (The Lenin Library) (1940), etc; *Publ:Kino-industriya Germanii* (The German Film Industry) (1926); *Po "Kryshe mira" s kino-apparatom* (In the "Roof of the World" with a Cinecamera) (1929); *Died:* 14 July 1940.

YEROSHENKO, Vasiliy Yakovlevich (1890–1952) Russian writer; *Born:* 12 Jan 1890 in vil Obukhovka, Belgorod Oblast; *Educ:* studied at Moscow school for the blind; *Career:* wrote in Japanese and Esperanto; in his early youth went blind; played with a blind orchestra in Moscow restaurants; studied Esperanto and then, with the aid of European Esperantists, went to London and entered the Royal College for the Blind; 1914 went to Tokyo; mastered Japanese and from 1916 published his Japanese-language stories and tales; 1919 deported to Vladivostok as a "Bolshevik agent"; thence moved to Peking; lectured on Russian Lit at Peking Univ; 1923 returned to USSR; in Moscow translated Marxist classics into Japanese; *Publ:* in Esperanto: "A Page from My School Life" (1923); "The Groan of a Lonely Soul" (1923); stories: "A Day of Worldwide Pacification", "Man", "The Rainbow Land", "Rain", "The Tower Doomed to Collapse" (1923–27); in Japanese: "The Tiger's Cage", "Desperate Heart", "Near the Swamp", etc; verse in Esperanto: "Cradle Song"; verse play in Japanese "The Peach-Colored Cloud"; tales in Japanese: "The Tale of the Paper Lantern", "The Fish's Grief", "The Heart of the Lion", "Dream on an Spring Night", etc; in Esperanto "The Story of the Withered Leaf", etc; *Died:* 23 Dec 1952.

YERSHOV, Il'ya Semyonovich (1929–1967) Mech eng; CP member from 1964; *Born:* 29 Apr 1929; *Educ:* 1952 grad Mining Fac, Moscow Peat Inst; *Career:* 1952–54 worked at an enterprise of USSR Min of Construction Materials Ind; 1954 at Ural State Inst for the Design of Metallurgical Plants; from 1961 chief designer, Rolling Dept; helped develop technol and put into production the heat treatment of railroad rails; *Awards:* State Prize (1967); *Died:* 4 Jan 1967.

YERSHOV, Ivan Vasil'yevich (1867–1943) Opera singer (dramatic tenor); Pop Artiste of USSR from 1938; Dr of Arts from 1941; *Born:* 20 Nov 1867 in Malyy Nesvetay, near Novocherkassk; *Educ:* 1888 entered Petersburg Conservatory, graduating in 1893; *Career:* 1893 stage debut at Mariinskiy Theater; fall 1893 went to Milan; 1894 performed at Reggio nell' Emilia Municipal Theater and at Alfieri Theater, Turin; 1894–95 worked at Khar'kov Opera Theater; 1895–1929 at Mariinskiy Theater; from 1916 taught singing; prof, Leningrad Conservatory; famous for his exposition of Wagnerian roles, including Tannhäuser, Lohengrin and Tristan; *Roles:* Sobinin and Finn in "Ivan Susanin" and "Ruslan and Ludmilla"; Berendey, Mikhayla Tucha, Sadko and Grishka Kuter'ma in Rimsky-Korsakov's *Snegurochka* (The Snow Maiden), *Pskovityanka* (The Woman of Pskov), "Sadko" and *Skazaniye of nevidimom grade Kitezhe i deve Fevronii* (The Tale of the Invisible City of Kitezh and the Maiden Fevronia); Orestes in Taneyev's "Oresteia"; Florestan in Beethoven's "Fidelio"; Othello in Verdi's "Othello"; *Awards:* Order of Lenin; *Died:* 21 Nov 1943 in Tashkent.

YERUSALIMSKIY, Arkadiy Samsonovich (1901–1965) Historian; Dr of Historical Sci from 1948; prof; CP member from 1938; *Born:* 1 June 1901; *Educ:* studied at Samara and Moscow Univ; *Career:* specialized in modern and recent history of West European countries, particularly Germany; 1925–41 senior assoc, Inst of World Econ and World Politics, USSR Acad of Sci; from early 1930's taught at Inst of Red Prof, Moscow Inst of History, Philosophy and Lit and at Higher Dipl School; 1939–41 head, Chair of Dipl Sci, Higher Dipl School; 1941–45 in Sov Army; headed For Dept, newspaper "Krasnaya zvezda"; 1945–65 senior assoc, Inst of History, USSR Acad of Sci; 1944–56 prof, History Fac, Moscow Univ; 1948–50 head, Chair of Modern and Recent History, Moscow Univ; from 1956 head, Group to Study the History of Germany, Inst of History, USSR Acad of Sci; also chm, Sov Section, Sov-GDR Historians Commission: *Publ: Voyennaya trevoga 1875 goda* (The Military Alert of 1875) (1928); *Problemy vneshney politiki Bismarka v poslevoyennoy germanskoy diplomatii* (Bismarck's Foreign Policy Problems in Post-War German Diplomacy) (1929); *Bismark, kak diplomat* (Bismarck as a Diplomat) (1940); *Veneshnyaya politika germanskogo imperializma v kontse 19-go veka* (The Foreign Policy of German Imperialism in the Late 19th Century) (1948); *Legenda i pravda o pervoy mirovoy voyne* (Legend and Truth About the First World War) (1954); *Germanskiy imperializm: istoriya i sovremennost'* (German Imperialism: History and Present) (1964), etc; *Awards:* Stalin Prize (1950); *Died:* 30 Nov 1965.

YERYOMIN, Igor' Petrovich (1904–1963) Russian lit historian; *Born:* 18 Apr 1904 in Tallin; *Educ:* 1924 grad Leningrad Univ; *Career:* 1926 first work published; worked at Acad V.M. Peretts' Russian Philology Seminary; from 1938 prof, Leningrad Univ; studied genre features of Ancient Russian lit, their stylistics and artistic method; also studied 16th–17th-Century Ukr journalism and history of folk theater; prepared annotated eds of ancient writers: Simeon Polotskiy (1953), Feofan Prokopovich (1961), Ivan Vishenskiy (1955), etc; *Publ: Poeticheskiy stil' Simeona Polotskogo* (Simeon Polotskiy's Poetic Style) (1948); *Kiyevskaya letopis' kak pamyatnik literatury* (The Kiev Chronicle as a Literary Monument) (1949); coauthor, *Slovo o polku Igoreve. Sbornik issledovaniy i statey* (The Lay of the Host of Igor. Collected Studies and Articles) (1950); "I.P. Kotlyarevskiy" (1952); *Khudozhestvennaya proza Kiyevskoy Rusi XI–XIII vekov* (The Artistic Prose of Kievan Rus in the 11th–13th Centuries) (1957); coauthor, *Nachal'nyy etap formirovaniya russkogo natsional'nogo yazyka* (The Initial Stage in the Formation of the Russian National Language) (1961), etc; *Died:* 17 Sept 1963 in Leningrad.

YESENIN, Sergey Aleksandrovich (1895–1925) Russian poet; *Born:* 3 Oct 1895 in vil Konstantinovo, Ryazan' Province (now vil Yesenino, Ryazan' Oblast), son of a peasant; *Educ:* 1909 grad Konstantinovo Zemstvo College; 1912 completed teachers' training school at Spas-Klepiki; *Career:* 1912 went to Moscow and worked at a merchant's office, then as a proof-reader at a printing shop; took part in Surikov Lit and Music Circle; from early 1914 contributed verse to Moscow journals; Mar 1915 moved to Petrograd; met Blok, who immediately realized his talent; also made the acquaintance of S. Gorodetskiy and N. Klyuyev; 1916 first verse collection *Radonitsa* (Remembrance of the Dead) published; welcomed to major lit and soc saloons and to Merezhkovskiy and Gippius circle; 1916 drafted into Russian Army; after 1917 Feb Revol quit the army and joined a battle squad of the Leftist Socialist-Revol Party; welcomed 1917 Oct Revol, but in his own individual manner, with a "peasant deviation", as he himself put it; toured Russia and lived in Murmansk, Arkhangel'sk, Kir Steppe, Ukr and Crimea; made friends with *Skify* (Scythians) group writers – Ivanov-Razumnikov and A. Belyy; from 1919 also sided with "Imaginists" but then gradually dissociated himself from both the "Scythians" and the "Imaginist" movement; 1922–23 made an extensive tour of Germany, France, Belgium and Italy with the dancer Isadora Duncan; spent four months in USA; 1924–25 toured Transcaucasia; wrote verse from age 14; *Publ:* verse collections: "Radonitsa" (1916); *Tovarishch* (Comrade) (1917); *Nebesnyy barabanshchik* (The Heavenly Drummer) (1918); *Iordanskaya golubitsa* (The Jordanian Dove) (1918); *Ionii* (To Ionia) (1918); verse cycle *Moskva kabatskaya* (Moscow Taverns) (1921–24) verse collections *Moskva kabatskaya* (1924); *Stikhi* (Verse (1924); *O Rossii i Revolyutsii* (Russia and the Revolution) (1925); *Rus' Sovetskaya* (Soviet Rus) (1925); *Vozrashcheniye na rodinu* (Return Home); *Rus' ukhodyashchaya* (Fading Rus); *Pis'mo k zhenshchine* (Letter to a Woman); *Pis'mo k materi* (A Letter to One's Mother); *Otvet* (The Answer); *Stansy* (Stanzas); *Ballada o dvadtsati shesti* (The Ballad of the Twenty-Six) (1924); poem "Anna Snegina" (1925); dramatic poem "Pugachyov" (1921); *Pesn' o velikom pokhode* (The Song of the Great Campaign) (1924); *Persidskiye motivy* (Persian Motifs) (1924–25); poem *Chyornyy chelovek* (The Black Man) (1925); novelette *Yar* (The Ravine) (1916); story "Bobyl' i Druzhok" (1917); essay *Zheleznyy Mirgorod* (Iron Mirgorod) (1923), etc; *Died:* 28 Dec 1925 committed suicide in Leningrad.

YESIPOV, Boris Petrovich (1894–1967) Educationist; Dr of Pedag Sci; corresp member, RSFSR Acad of Pedag Sci; CP member from 1948; *Born:* 1894; *Educ:* 1918 grad Petersburg Univ; *Career:* from 1918 taught at secondary school in Glazov, Udmurt ASSR; from 1928 taught at higher educ establishments; member, Learned Council, Research Inst of the Theory and History of Pedag, USSR Acad of Pedag Sci; head, Didactics Section, Research Inst of the Theory and History of Pedag, USSR Acad of Pedag Sci; head, Pedag Section, All-Union, Soc for the Dissemination of Polit and Sci Knowledge; member ed bd, journal "Sovetskaya pedagogika"; specialized in methods of inculcating Communist outlook in schoolchildren; *Publ: Urok v nachal'noy shkole* (Lessons in the Elementary School) (1944); coauthor, *Pedagogika* (Pedagogics) (1950); *Vospitatel'naya rabota v shkole sovmestnogo obucheniya* (Training Work in the Joint Education School) (1954); *Sistema vospotatel'noy raboty v shkole* (The Training Work System in School) (1955); *Organizatsiya i vospitaniye kollektiva shkol'nikov v svete ucheniya A. Makarenko* (Theo Organization and Training of the Pupils Collective in the Light of A. Makarenko's Teaching) (1956); coauthor, *Didaktika* (Didactics) (1957); *Samostoyatel'naya rabota uchashchikhsya na urokakh* (Pupils' Independent Work During Lessons) (1961), etc; *Awards:* Ushinskiy Medal; *Died:* 21 Feb 1967.

YES'MAN, Iosif Gavrilovich (1868–1955) Hydraulic eng; Hon Sci Worker of Azer SSR from 1927; member, Azer Acad of Sci fom

1945; *Born:* 13 Dec 1868; *Educ:* 1892 grad Petersburg Technol Inst; *Career:* after grad taught at colleges in Petersburg; from 1922 head, Chair of Hydraulics, Azer Ind Inst, Baku; specialized in construction of hydraulic machinery; did research on the motion of viscous liquids through local obstructions; worked on theory and calculation of piston and centrifugal pumps; helped elaborate V.Ye. Grum-Grzhimaylo's hydraulic theory of the motion of gases in metallurgical furnaces; helped design major oil and water pipelines and pumping stations; *Publ: Vodyanyye dvigateli* (Hydraulic Motors) (1928); *Tsentrobezhnyye nasosy* (Centrifugal Pumps) (1931); *Porshnevyye nasosy* (Piston Pumps) (1931); *Nasosy* (Pumps) (1939); *Gidravlika* (Hydraulics) (1947), etc; *Died:* 30 June 1955.

YEVDOKIMOV, Grigoriy Yeremeyevich (1884–1936) Party official; CP member from 1903; *Born:* 1884; *Career:* from age 15 sailor; 1908–13 Party work in Omsk and Pavlodar; from 1913 worked in Petersburg and took part in strikes, three times arrested; on one occasion exiled for four years; after 1917 Feb Revol agitator, Petrograd Comt; after 1917 Oct Revol worked in the provinces organizing Sov rule; during Civil War head, Polit Dept, 7th Army in Campaign against Gen Yudenich; from 1922 chm, Petrograd Trade-Union Council; dep chm, Petrograd Sov; dep chm, Econ Conference, Labor and Defense Council; from 1925 secr, Leningrad RCP(B) Comt; at 8th, 12th, 13th and 14th Party Congresses elected member, CC, CPSU(B); at 14th CPSU(B) Congress sided with Trotskyist opposition; for this expelled from CC, and in Dec 1927 expelled from Party; 1928 recanted his errors and readmitted to Party; 1931 Bd member, Centr Grain and Cattle Raising Bd; Jan 1935, after Kirov's assassination, arrested and sentenced to eight year's imprisonment for "active membership of Moscow Center counterrevol group"; Aug 1936 re-tried for membership of "Trotsky-Zinov'yevite Terrorist Center"; *Died:* 1936 executed together with Zinov'yev, Kamenev and others.

YEVDOKIMOV, Ivan Vasil'yevich (1887–1941) Russian writer; *Born:* 3 Feb 1887 in Kronstadt; *Educ:* 1911–15 studied at History and Philology Fac, Petersburg Univ; *Career:* telegraphist on railroad; 1905–08 worked for underground Vologda Bolshevik Org; after 1917 Oct Revol worked as teacher, lecturer and ed for publ house; 1915 first work printed; *Publ:* novels *Kolokola* (The Bells) (1926); *Chistyye prudy* (Clean Ponds) (1927); "Zaozer'ye" (1928); *Sever v istorii russkogo iskusstva* (The North in the History of Russian Art) (1921); *Vologodskiye stennyye rospisi* (Vologda Murals) (1922); *Russkaya igrushka* (Russian Toys) (1925); "Borisov-Musatov" (1924); "M.A. Vrubel'" (1925); "V.I. Surikov" (1933); "Repin" (1940); "Levitan" (1940); *Sobraniye sochineniy* (Collected Works) (1928–31); *Died:* 28 Aug 1941 in Moscow.

YEVDOKIMOV, Nikolay Nikolayevich (1868–1940) Astronomer; specialist in astrometry; Hon Sci Worker of Ukr SSR from 1935; *Born:* 7 Apr 1868 in Khar'kov; *Educ:* 1890 grad Khar'kov Univ; *Career:* from 1893 astronomer, Khar'kov Astronomical Observatory; from 1914 prof, Khar'kov Univ; 1917–37 dir, Khar'kov Observatory; from a meridian observed zodiacal and faint stars; determined star parallaxes; carried out extensive observations of position of large planets; took part in expeditions to observe solar eclipses; *Publ: Opredeleniye parallaksov nepodvizhnykh zvyozd po nablyudeniyam meridiannym krugom astronomicheskoy observatorii Khar'kovskogo universiteta* (Determining the Parallaxes of Stationary Stars by Meridian Circle Observations at Khar'kov University's Astronomical Observatory) (1912); *Opredeleniye polozheniy planet meridiannym krugom Khar'kovskoy astronomicheskoy observatorii/1 seriya: skloneniya 1924–1927 /* (Determining the Positions of Planets from the Meridian Circle at Khar'kov Astronomical Observatory /1st Series: 1924–27 Declinations) (1941), etc; *Died:* 5 Apr 1940.

YEVGEN'YEV-MAKSIMOV (real name: MAKSIMOV), Vladislav Yevgen'yevich (1883–1955) Russian lit historian; *Born:* 18 Sept 1883 in vil Demidovka, Kursk Province; *Educ:* grad Petersburg Univ; *Career:* after grad univ until 1917 taught at secondary educ establishments and "pop univs"; from 1920 lecturer, then prof, Leningrad Univ; 1902 began journalistic work; 1908 published a student work "Literaturnyye debyuty N.A. Nekrasova" (N.A. Nekrasov's Literary Debuts); wrote numerous articles, studies, pop works on Nekrasov, etc; also books and papers on Saltykov-Shchedrin, Chernyshevskiy, Dobrolyubov, Pisarev, Goncharov and Korolenko; sponsored establishment of memorial museums to Nekrasov in Leningrad and Karabikh, Yaroslavl' Oblast; wrote one of first textbooks on 20th-Century Russian lit *Ocherk istorii noveyshey russkoy literatury* (An Outline History of Modern Russian Literature) (1925); *Publ: Nekrasov kak chelovek, zhurnalist i poet* (Nekrasov as Man, Journalist and Poet) (1928); *Nekrasov i yego sovremenniki* (Nekrasov and His Contemporaries) (1930); *Nekrasov v krugu sovremennikov* (Nekrasov in the Circle of His Contemporaries) (1938); *Zhizn' i deyatel'nost' N.A. Nekrasova* (The Life and Work of N.A. Nekrasov) (3 vol, 1947–52); *Tvorcheskiy put' N.A. Nekrasova* (The Career of N.A. Nekrasov) (1953); co-ed, *Polnoye sobraniye sochineniy Nekrasova* (The Complete Collected Works of Nekrasov) (1948–53); *Ocherki po istorii sotsialisticheskoy zhurnalistiki v Rossii XIX veka* (An Outline History of Socialist Journalism in 19th-Century Russia) (1927); *Iz proshlogo russkoy zhurnalistiki* (Russian Journalism's Past) (1930); *"Sovremennik" v 40-50-kh godakh ot Belinskogo do Chernyshevskogo* (The "Sovremennik" in the 1840's and 1850's from Belinskiy to Chernyshevskiy) (1934); *"Sovremennik" pri Chernyshevskom i Dobrolyubove* (The "Sovremennik" Under Chernyshevskiy and Dobrolyubov) (1936); *Posledniye gody "Sovremennika", 1863–1866* (The Last Years of the "Sovremennik", 1863–1866) (1939); *Died:* 1 Jan 1955 in Leningrad.

YEVREINOV, Nikolay Nikolayevich (1879–1953) Russian playwright; stage dir and theater historian and theorist; *Born:* 26 Feb 1879; *Career:* co-founder and 1907–08 and 1911–12 dir, Petersburg Ancient Theater; 1908–09 produced plays at Komissarzhevskaya Theater; 1921 stage dir, Petersburg's Distorted Mirror Theater; early 1920 emigrated to France; *Publ:* plays: *Krasivyy despot* (The Handsome Despot) (1907); *Takaya zhenshchina* (Such a Woman) (1908); *Samoye glavnoye* (The Main Thing) (1921); studies: *Vvedeniye v monodramu* (An Introduction to Monodrama) (1909); *Ispanskiy aktyor XVI–XVII vekov* (The Spanish Actor of the 16th and 17th Centuries) (1911); *Proiskhozhdeniye dramy* (The Origin of Drama) (1921); *Pervobytnaya drama germantsev* (Original German Drama) (1922); *Teatral'nyye inventsii* (Theatrical Inventions) (1922); *Azazel i Dionis. O Proiskhozhdenii stseny v svyazi s zachatkami dramy u semitov* (Azazel and Dionysius. The Origin of the Stage in Connection with the Source of Drama Among the Semites) (1924); *Krepostnyye aktyory* (Serf Actors) (1911); *Dramaticheskiye sochineniya* (Dramatic Works) (3 vol, 1908–23); *Teatr v Rossii do 1946 goda* (The Theater in Russia Prior to 1946); (1946); *Istoriya russkogo teatra* (The History of the Russian Theater) (1947); *Died:* 7 Feb 1953 in France.

YEVREINOV, Nikolay Nikolayevich (1892–?) Trade-union official; CP member from 1912; *Born:* 1892, son of an office worker; *Educ:* from 1911 studied at Petersburg Univ; *Career:* 1908–11 organized revol circles at his high school and then helped run Kostroma student org; 1911 entered Petersburg Polytech Inst; 1912 Party work in Petersburg; 1913 arrested; 1917 member and agitator, Petrograd RSDRP(B) Comt; June 1917 sent to Kineshma, coopted to rayon Party comt and elected member, Kineshma Exec Comt; Oct 1917 helped to establish Sov rule in Kineshma; from 1918 mainly trade-union work; chm, Ivano-Voznesensk and Tula trade-Union Councils; from 1926 Presidium member, All-Russian Centr Trade-Union Council; wrote various articles and pamphlets on trade-union movement and labor affairs; May 1929 elected secr, All-Union Centr Trade-Union Council; Feb 1930 elected chm, CC, USSR Textile Workers' Union; from 1921 member, All-Russian Centr Exec Comt, then USSR Centr Exec Comt; at 15th and 16th Party Congresses elected member, CPSU(B) Centr Control Commission; *Died:* date and place of death unknown.

YEVSEV'YEV, Makar Yevsev'yevich (1864–1931) Mordovian linguist and ethnographer; *Born:* 30 Jan 1864 in vil Malyye Karmaly, Chuvashia, son of a peasant; *Educ:* 1883 grad Kazan' Seminary for Non-Russians; *Career:* until 1898 taught at elementary school; 1898–1920 taught at Seminary for Non-Russians, Kazan'; 1906–12 head, pupils'workshops at this seminary; after 1917 Oct Revol lectured on Mordovian language, history and ethnography at Kazan' Eastern Acad, Kazan' Eastern Teachers' Training Inst and Kazan' Communist Univ; wrote a "Grammar" which helped shape Erzya-Mordovian and Moksha-Mordovian lit languages; *Publ:* "Mordovian Dictionary" (1886); "Samples of Mordovian Folk Lore" (1892); "The Principles of Mordovian Grammar" (1928); "Erzya Tales" (1928); "Erzya Songs" (1928); "The Mordovian Wedding" (1892); *Erzyansko-russkiy slovar'* (Erzya-Russian Dictionary) (1931); "Selected Works" (5 vol, 1961–64); *Awards:* Gold and Silver Medals of Russian Geographical Soc; Hero of Labor; *Died:* 10 May 1931 in Kazan'.

YEZHOV, Nikolay Ivanovich (1895–?) Govt and Party official; CP member from 1917; *Born:* 1895 in Petersburg; *Career:* took part in 1917 Oct Revol; until 1921 mil comr of various units in Red Army; from 1922 exec Party work; secr, Semipalatinsk Province, then Kaz Kray CPSU(B) Comt; 1927–28 worked for CC, CPSU(B); 1929–30 USSR Dep Pop Comr of Agric; 1930–34 head, Assignment Dept and Personnel Dept, CC, CPSU(B); Apr 1933 at joint plenum of CC, CPSU(B) and CC, CPSU(B) appointed to Centr Commission to Purge the Party; 1934 at 17th CPSU(B) Congress elected member, CC and member, Party Control Commission, CC, CPSU(B); also appointed member, Org Bureau, CC, CPSU(B) and dep chm, Party Control Commission, CC, CPSU(B); Mar 1935 appointed secr, CC, CPSU(B) and chm, Party Control Commission; 1935 elected member, USSR and All-Russian Centr Exec Comt; also member, Comintern Exec Comt; Sept 1936 appointed USSR Pop Comr of Internal Affairs; Jan 1937 promoted Comr-Gen of State Security; at Oct 1937 Party CC Plenum elected cand Politburo member, CC, CPSU(B); Dec 1937 elected dep, USSR Supr Sov of 1st convocation; Mar 1938 also appointed Pop Comr of Water Trans; Dec 1938 dismissed as USSR Pop Comr of Internal Affairs and then as Pop Comr of Water Trans; 1937–38, in accordance with Stalin's instructions, carried out massive purges to liquidate or isolate the maximum number of "socially-alien elements" in the USSR – in other words, anybody at all opposed to the Soviet-Stalinist system; the purge extended at first to the Party and govt apparatus but then included the gen public; this period of the mass liquidation of so-called "enemies of the people" has come to be known as the "Yezhov Terror"; arrested by State Security organs; *Awards:* Order of Lenin (1937); *Died:* date and place of death unknown.

YOGANSEN, Mikhail (Mayk) Gervasiyevich (1895–1937) Ukr writer; *Born:* 28 Feb 1895 in Khar'kov, son of a teacher; *Educ:* grad Khar'kov Univ; *Career:* began to write verse in Russian; from 1919 wrote in Ukr; member, "Gart", "Vaplite" and "Group A" writers' orgs; also linguist and lit historian; from 1925 concentrated on prose works; his book "How a Story Is Built" was sharply attacked by Party critics; subjected to reprisals by State Security organs; *Publ:* collected verse *V goru* (To the Mountain) (1921); verse collections: *Revolyutsiya* (Revolution) (1923); *Prolog k kommune* (Prologue to the Commune) (1924); "Ballads of War and Restoration" (1933); various collected stories and adventure novelettes; children's stories; non-fiction work "How A Story Is Built"; "Creation" (1924); "The Ash-Tree" (1930); "Poetry" (1933); "17 Minutes" (1925); "Stories" (1932); "A Journey to Daghestan" (1933); "Kos Chagil in Yemba. Sketches" (1936); "Dzhan and Other Stories" (1937); *Died:* 27 Oct 1937 in imprisonment; posthumously rehabilitated.

YOKUM, Konrad Yanovich (1894–1941) Lat writer; CP member from 1918; *Born:* 23 Apr 1894 in Luban Volost; *Educ:* grad Luban City School; *Career:* 1913-16 worked in Riga and Moscow; served in Russian Army; 1918–21 served in Red Army; brigade comr, Lat Rifle Div; edited a peasants' newspaper; member, ed bd, journal "Tseltne"; secr, Bureau of Lat Writers; 1921–37 lived in Moscow and worked as a writer and journalist; wrote mainly on Civil War themes; also wrote humorous, critical and historical articles; 1937 subjected to reprisals by State Security organs; *Publ:* short stories and novellae: "Order Nr 325" (1929); "Bread" (1931); "Riflemen and Grenades" (1936); sketches "The Sun on the Wheat" (1935); plays "The Man Without a Shirt" (1929); "Alarm in the Cornfields" (1930); coauthor, "Adventure" (1935); *Died:* 1941 in imprisonment; posthumously rehabilitated.

YORISH, Vladimir Yakovlevich (1899–1945) Ukr conductor and composer; Hon Artiste of Ukr SSR from 1933; *Born:* 25 Feb 1899 in Yekaterinoslav; *Educ:* studied music at Yekaterinoslav Music College and Music Technicum; *Career:* 1920 began working as a conductor; musical dir and conductor; drama and opera theaters in Dnepropetrovsk, Khar'kov and other Ukr towns; 1934–43 conductor, from 1943 chief conductor, Shevchenko Theater of Opera and Ballet; wrote new arrangements of and added scenes to the operas *Zaporozhets za Dunayem* (A Dnieper Cossack Beyond the Danube) and "Natalka-Poltavka"; *Works:* operas "Karmelyuk", about the Ukr folk hero (1929); *Poema pro stal'* (The Poem of Steel) after Pogodin's play *Poema o topore* (The Poem of the Axe) (1932); *Boguntsy (Shchors)* (Bogun's Partisans [Shchors]) (1936); *Poetova dolya (Shevchenko)* (The Poet's Fate [Shevchenko]) (1940); ballet *Chortova noch'* (The Night of the Devil) (1944), etc; *Died:* 21 June 1945.

YUDENICH, Nikolay Nikolayevich (1862–1933) Mil commander; gen, Russian Army; *Born:* 1862; *Educ:* 1887 grad Gene Staff Acad; *Career:* fought in 1904–05 Russo-Japanese War; 1905–06 command in Caucasus; from 1913 chief of staff, Caucasian Mil Distr; 1915–17 commander, Caucasian Army; from Mar 1917 commander, Caucasian Front; after 1917 Oct Revol went to Finland; 1919 appointed commander in chief, Northwestern Army, which in May and Aug launched first campaign against Petrograd; member, Northwestern Govt; Oct–Nov 1919 launched attack on Petrograd which was beaten off by Red Army; Nov 1919 retreated to Est with the remnants of his troops; Jan 1920 his army was demobilized; emigrated to England; *Died:* 1933.

YUDIN, Mikhail Alekseyevich (1893–1948) Composer; prof from 1939; Hon Art Worker of Tatar ASSR from 1945; *Born:* 1893 in Petersburg; *Career:* from 1926 lecturer, 1939–41 prof, Leningrad Conservatory; from 1941 prof, from 1945 dean of Conducting and Choral Fac, Kazan' Conservatory; *Works:* opera-poem "Farida" (1943); cantata *Pesnya o vesne i radosti* (The Song of Spring and Joy) (1936); *Geroicheskaya oratoriya* (Heroic Oratorio) (1937); solo suites; symphonic poems; concertos; quartets; choral works; romances; songs; arrangements of folk songs; *Died:* 8 Feb 1948 in Kazan'.

YUDIN, Pavel Fyodorovich (1899–1968) Philosopher; govt official; diplomat; member, USSR Acad of Sci from 1953; CP member from 1918; *Born:* 1899 in vil Apraksino, Nizniy Novgorod Province (now Gorky Oblast), son of a peasant; *Educ:* 1924 grad Leningrad Business Inst; 1931 grad Inst of Red Prof; *Career:* 1917–19 machinist in locomotive workshops; 1919–21 regt comr, Red Army; from 1924 edited provincial newspaper and headed Agitation Dept, Novgorod Province Party Comt; 1932–38 dir, Red Prof Inst of Philosophy; also edited various centr periodicals, taught philosophy and Party history and engaged in Party work; 1937–46 head, RSFSR Assoc of State Publ Houses; 1938–44 dir, Inst of Philosphy, USSR Acad of Sci; 1939–53 corresp member, USSR Acad of Sci; 1943–48 head, Chair of Marxism-Leninism, Moscow Univ; 1946–53 chief ed, journal "Sovetskaya kniga"; 1947 chief ed, newspaper "Trud"; 1953 polit adviser to chm, Sov Control Commission, and also USSR Dep High Commissioner in Germany; 1953–59 USSR amb to China; dep, USSR Supr Sov of 1950 and 1954 convocations; 1952 and 1956 at 19th and 20th CPSU Congresses elected member, CC, CPSU; wrote works on historical materialism and polit econ; *Awards:* Order of Lenin; Order of the Red Banner of Labor; medals; Stalin Prize (1943); *Died:* 10 Apr 1968.

YUDIN, Sergey Sergeyevich (1891–1954) Surgeon; member, USSR Acad of Med Sci from 1944; Hon Sci Worker of RSFSR; hon member, Priogov Surgical Soc; hon member, Gorky Surgical Soc, Geo Surgical Soc, British Royal Soc of Surgeons, Paris Soc of Surgeons, American Soc of Surgeons, Czechoslovakian Soc of Surgeons, Catalonian Soc of Surgeons and Assoc of Surgeons of Great Britain and Ireland; hon dr of the Sorbonne and Paris Acad; *Born:* 9 Oct 1891 in Moscow; *Educ:* 1915 grad Med Fac, Moscow Univ; *Career:* from 1915 served as regt physician at the front in WW 1; then intern, evacuation hospital in Tula; then at Zakhar'ino Sanatorium; 1922–28 headed a surgical dept at a factory hospital in Serpukhov, where he began his research work; 1928–54 chief surgeon, Sklifosovskiy First Aid Inst; Moscow; pioneered radical surgery for gastric ulcers; devised many gastric and duodenal operations; introduced and popularized drip blood transfusion; 1930 first to use for transfusion purposes the blood from the corpses of people who had met a sudden death; in time the transfusion of corpse blood became standard med practice; speciali zed in restorative surgery for esophagal blockage resulting from chemical burns and performed over 600 operations of this kind; devised new methods for forming an artificial esophagus; contributed to mil field surgery; pioneered and organized anesthesiological service in USSR; 1931–54 head, Chair of Urgent Surgery, Centr Inst of Postgrad Med Training; apllied results of Pavlovian Experiments with animals to humans, opening up new vistas in clinical physiology; wrote over 120 works; *Publ: Spinnomozgovaya anesteziya* (Cerebrospinal Anesthesia) (1925); *Nekotoryye vpechatleniya i razmyshleniya o 80-i sluchayakh operatsiy iskusstvennogo pishchevoda* (Some Impressions and Ideas from 80 Artificial Esophagus Operations) (1941); *Vosstanovitel'naya khirurgiya pri neprokhodimosti pishchevoda* (Restorative Surgery for Esophagal Blockage) (1954); *Etyudy zheludochnoy khirurgii* (Studies in Gastric Surgery) (1955); *Izbrannyye proizvedeniya* (Selected Works) (3 vol, 1960–63); *Awards:* S.P. Fyodorov Prize; F.A. Reyn Prize (1925); two Stalin Prizes (1924 and 1948); Lenin Prize (1962, posthumpusly); Order of Lenin; three other orders; medals; *Died:* 12 June 1954 in Moscow.

YUDIN, Tikhon Ivanovich (1879–1949) Psychiatrist; Hon Sci Worker of Ukr SSR from 1941; *Born:* 14 June 1879 in Tula Province; *Educ:* 1903 grad Med Fac, Moscow Univ; *Career:* 1904–07 intern, Moscow Psychiatric Clinic; 1907–14 intern, Khar'kov Psychiatric Hospital at Saburov Dacha and Moscow Psychiatric Hospital at Kanatchikov Dacha; 1914 drafted into Russian Army; 1915–18 German pow; 1918 returned to Russia and worked in Prof Gannushkin's Clinic, 1st Moscow Univ; 1924–32 prof of psychiatry in Kazan'; from 1 Nov 1932 prof of psychiatry, 2nd Khar'kov Med Inst; dir, Clinical Inst, All-Ukr Psychoneurological Acad; also prof, Psychoneurological Inst, above acad; from 1943 head, Chair of Psychiatry, Moscow Med Inst, RSFSR Pop Comrt of Health; prior to Oct 1917 Revol helped reorganize hospital at Saburov Dacha, developing it into a model psychiatric establishment; 1919–24 Presidium member, Med Fac, 1922 bd member, 1st Moscow Univ; 1929–32 dean, Therapy Fac, Kazan' Med Inst; chm, Kazan' Soc of Neuropathologists and Psychiatrists; then vice-pres, All-Ukr Psychoneurological Acad; helped edit various journals; 1930–33 ed, from 1933 dep ed, psychoneurology section, *Bol'shaya meditsinskaya entsiklopediya* (Large Medical Encyclopedia); from 1933 member, Learned Med Council, Ukr Pop Comrt of Health; wrote over 70 works on the role of exogenic factors in the genesis of various mental disturbances, problems of heredity in psychiatry, schizophrenia, progressive paralysis, epilepsy, traumatic psychoses, history of psychiatry, etc; *Publ: Psikhopaaticheskiye konstitutsii* (Psychopathic Constitutions) (1926); *Yevgenika* (Eugenics) (1928); *Died:* 19 Oct 1949.

YUDOVSKIY, Vladimir Grigor'yevich (1880–1949) Revolutionary; physician; CP member from 1903; *Born:* 1880 in Voronezh; *Career:* Party work in Voronezh Province, Tula, Serpukhov and Petrograd; several times arrested; after 1917 Feb Revol member, Vasiliy Ostrov Rayon Party Comt; member, Petrograd Sov; after 1917 Oct Revol chm, Centr Exec Comt of Soviets of Rumanian Front, Odessa Oblast and Black Sea Fleet; member, Odessa Party Comt; 1918 chm, Revol Comt directing struggle against Haydemaks and White Forces; then chm, Odessa Council of Pop Comr; 1918 also govt and Party work in Moscow; 1919 Party work in the Ukr; then secr, Syr-Dar'ya Oblast Party Comt and member, CC, CP(B) Turkestan; 1922 deleg at 11th Party Congress; 1923–49 teaching work; *Died:* 1949.

YUKNYAVICHYUS, Romual'das Mikolo (1906–1963) Lith stage dir, actor and drama teacher; Hon Art Worker of Lith SSR from 1956; *Born:* 1906; *Career:* acted with amateur drama groups at Kaunas Business College and Kaunas Univ; 1930 helped found "Stedra" Soc Student Theater, producing and acting in its plays; from 1931 actor, Kaunas State Theater; 1933–34 with Young People's Theater; 1936–39 with Klaypeda Theater; from 1939 stage dir, Kaunas Theater; from 1940 dir and artistic dir, Vilnius Drama Theater; 1949–53 at Tel'shyay, Klaypeda and Kaunas theaters; from 1953 stage dir, Lith Drama Theater, Vilnius; taught at Vilnius Conservatory and Vilnius Univ; *Productions:* Hauptmann's "Before Sunset" (1940); Pagnol's "Topaze" (1940); *Bronepoyezd 14-69* (Armored Train 14-69) (1941); Dauguvetis' "Battle Mission" (1946); Chekhov's *Dyadya Vanya* (Uncle Vanya) (1954); Lev Tolstoy's *Plody prosveshcheniya* (The Fruits of Enlightenment) (1955); Pogodin's *Tret'ya pateticheskaya* (The Third Pathethique) (1961); *Mesyats v derevne* (A Month in the Country), after Turgenev (1962), etc; *Roles:* Podkolyosin in *Zhenit'ba* (The Wedding); Yepikhodov in Chekov's *Vishnyovyy sad* (The Cherry Orchard); Shmaga in Ostrovskiy's *Bez viny vinovatyye* (Guilty Without Guilt); Kibilda in Gritsyus' "On the Eve", etc; *Died:* 13 Apr 1963.

YULTYY, Daut Iskhakovich (1893–1938) Bash writer; CP member from 1919; *Born:* 18 Apr 1893 in vil Yultiyevo, now Orenburg Oblast; *Career:* worked as teacher; helped establish Sov regime in Ukr; 1917 first work printed; 1920–29 edited various Bash newspapers and artistic journals; wrote at first in Tatar; *Publ:* verse "At the Arsenal" (1917); collected verse "Ural Melodies" (1931); "Poem of Today" (1932); poems "Maysara" (1930) and "Aykhlu" (1933); autobiographical novel "Blood" (1934); play "Karagul" (1920), etc; *Died:* 18 Apr 1938.

YUMAGULOV, Kh. Yu. (1891–1937) Govt official; *Born:* 1891; *Career:* 1918–22 member, CP; 1922 expelled for alleged nationalistic activities; 1927 reinstated cand member, 1931 member, CPSU(B); 1919–20 chm, Bashkir Republ Revol Comt; then admin and govt work; arrested by State Security organs; *Died:* 1937 in imprisonment.

YUNG (real name: SHPIKOLITSER), Klara Markovna (1883–1952) Operetta and variety singer; *Born:* 10 Dec 1883; *Career:* lived in North America and performed with touring Jewish groups; from 1903 acted in Boston, New York, Piladelphia and Toronto; from 1910 concentrated on operetta and variety roles; toured in Britain, France, Italy and Russia; 1934 assumed Sov citizenship; directed Jewish variety company which toured USSR; *Roles:* appeared in Yungvits' operettas: "Jeikele Blofer", "Leibele Odessit", "Berele Tremp", "A Man and His Wife", "Mlle Goplya" and "Alma, Where Do You Live? "; musical comedy roles in: Rakov and Rushinskiy's "Khanche in America"; Katnel'son's "Anna Blaib", etc; *Died:* 27 Apr 1952.

YUNOSOV, K. A. (1884–1938) Party official; CP member from 1905; *Born:* 1884; *Career:* active in 1905–07 Revol; Party work in Petersburg, Kronstadt, etc; arrested by Tsarist authorities; 1912–17 lived abroad; after 1917 Feb Revol secr, Sestroretsk Rayon RSDRP(B) Comt; deleg at 8th All-Russian RSDRP(B) Conference; after 1917 Oct Revol member, Petrograd Province RSDRP(B) Comt and member, Petrograd Province Sov of Workers and Soldiers' Dep; 1922 chm, Pskov Province Exec Comt; 1925 member, Leningrad Province CPSU(B) Comt; dep chm, Control Commission; member, All-Russian and USSR Centr Exec Comt; 1927 elected member, CPSU(B) Centr Control Commission; 1937 expelled from Party; arrested by State Security organs; *Died:* 1938 in imprisonment.

YUNOV (pseudonym: NOVOGRUDSKIY), Yu. M. (1895–1937) Trade-Union and admin official; *Born:* 1895; *Career:* 1917–18 member, Jewish Bund; 1919 joined RSDRP(B); 1920–23 worked for miners' trade-union; dep chm, Yuzov Rayon Comt; from Jan 1921 member, CC; member, Southern Bureau, CC; member; Donetsk Province Dept, Miners' Union; exec secr, Donetsk Province Trade-Union Council; during 1920–21 trade-union controversy sided with Trotsky; Sept 1923–1937 head, Chistyakovo Mine Bd; dep dir, Karaganda Coal Trust; senior section eng, Donbass and Main Coal Trusts; dir of construction, Bureya Construction Trust; dir, Kuznetsk Coal Combine; arrested by State Security organs; *Died:* 1937 in imprisonment.

YUON, Konstantin Fyodorovich (1875–1958) Painter; graphic artist; stage designer; Pop Artiste of USSR from 1950; member USSR Acad of Arts from 1947; CP member from 1951; *Born:* 24 Oct 1875; *Educ:* 1894–98 studied at Moscow College of Painting, Sculpture and Architecture; 1899–1900 studied at V. A. Serov's Workshop; *Career:* from 1903 member, Russian Artists Union; from 1917 taught art; from 1925 member, Acad of Arts; 1957–58 first secr, USSR Artists Union; many of his works are displayed at the Tret'yakov Gallery; *Works:* landscapes: "A Sunny Spring Day" (1910); "March Sun" (1915); "Spaciousness" (1917), ect; old town views of Sergiyev Posad, Pskov, Uglich, Torzhok, Nizhniy Novgorod, Moscow, etc; "Cupola and Swallows" (1921); "The End of Winter. Noon" (1929); "Red Square Parade in Moscow on 7 November 1941" (1942); "The Open Window" (1947); "An August Evening. The Last Ray" (1948); "Morning in Industrial Moscow." (1949); designed sets and costumes for: Gorky's *Yegor Bulychov i drugiye* (Yegor Bulychov and Co (1934); Ostrovskiy's *Serdtse ne kamen'* (The Heart Is Not a Stone) (1923); Ostrovskiy's *Bez viny vinovatyye* (Guilty Without Guilt) (1940), etc; Gorky's "Foma Gordeyev" (1955–56), at the Vakhtangov Theater; Moussorgsky's "Khovanshchina" (1939), at the Bolshoy Theater, etc; *Awards:* Stalin Prize (1943); *Died:* 11 Apr 1958.

YURA, Gnat (Ignatiy) Petrovich (1888–1966) Actor and stage dir; Pop Artiste of USSR from 1940; CP member from 1938; *Born:* 8 Jan 1888 in vil Fedvar, now Kirovograd Oblast; *Career:* began acting with amateur groups in Yelisavetgrad; 1907 stage debut; actor and stage dir with S. Maksimovich's troupe, then from 1913 with "Russian Conversation" Soc Theater, L'vov; 1917–19 at Kiev Young Theater; 1919 directed New Theater in Vinnitsa (from 1920 Franko Theater); actor, stage dir and dir, above theater; from 1938 taught stagecraft at Kiev Inst of Stagecraft; also did film work; *Roles:* Kopystka in Kulish's "97"; Maloshtan in Mikitenko's "Dictatorship"; Schweik in "The Adventures of the Good Soldier Schweik". after Hašek; Figaro in "The Marriage of Figaro"; *Productions:* "97" (1924; Kulish's "Commune in the Steppes" (1925); *Myatezh* (Revolt), after Furmanov (1928); *Bornepoyezd 14-69* (Armored Train 14-69) (1928); Mikitenko's "Dictatorship" (1929), "Personnel" (1930), "An Affair of Honor" (1931), "The Girls of Our Country" (1932), "The Bastille of the Mother of God" (1934) and "Flute Solo" (1935); A. Ye. Korneychuk's *Kamennyy ostrov* (Stone Island) (1930), *Gibel' eskadry* (The End of a Squadron) (1933), *Bankir* (The Banker)

(1937), *Pravda* (Truth) (1937), "Bogdan Khmel'nitskiy" (1939), *V stepyakh Ukrainy* (In the Ukrainian Steppe) (1940), *Priyezzhayte v Zvonkovoye* (Come to Zvonkovoye) (1945), "Makar Dubrava" (1948), *Kalinovaya roshcha* (Viburnum Grove) (1950) and *Kryl'ya* (Wings) (1954); Kocherga's *Mastera vremeni* (Masters of Time) (1934) and *Svad'ba Svichki* (Svichka's Marriage) (1960); Yu. I. Yanovskiy's *Potomki* (Descendants) (1940); Karpenko-Karyy's *Suyeta* (Fuss) (1920); *Sto tysyach* (The Hundred Thousand) (1945); Franko's *Ukradennoye schast'ye* (Stolen Happiness) (1940); Gorky's *Na dne* (The Lower Depths) (1920); "Midsummer Night's Dream" (1927); "Don Carlos" (1936), etc; *Publ:* Zhizn' i stsena (Life and the Stage) (1965); *Awards:* two Stalin Prizes (1949 and 1951); Order of Lenin; three other orders; medals *Died:* 18 Jan 1966.

YURASOVSKIY, Aleksandr Ivanovich (1890–1922) Composer and conductor; *Born:* 27 June 1890, son of the singer M. V. Salina; *Educ:* grad Law Fac, Moscow Univ and Moscow Conservatory; *Career:* until 1921 conducted symphony concerts in Smolensk; from 1921 head, Museum Dept, Main Polit Educ Comt, RSFSR Pop Comrt of Educ; *Works:* opera "Trilby", to his own libretto based on the novel by Du Mau rier (1919), etc; *Died:* 31 Jan 1922.

YURENEV, Konstantin Konstantinovich (1888–1938) Diplomat; CP member from 1917; *Born:* 1888, son of a railroad worker; *Career:* from 1904 active in revol movement; 1906 member, Dvinsk RSDRP Comt; 1908 member, Northwestern Oblast Party Bureau; 1909 arrested and exiled for three years to Arkhangel'sk Province; 1911 worked für Petersburg Party Org and in Narva Rayon; 1913 helped found Petersburg *Mezhrayon* (Inter-Distr) Comt; 1915 arrested and brought before court-martial, but acquitted; after 1917 Feb Revol member, Petrograd Exec Comt, then member, Centr Exec Comt; Aug 1917 joined Bolshevik Party together with other "mezhrayontsy"; Sept 1917 chm, Main Red Guard Staff; 1918–20 Collegium member, Pop Comrt of Naval Affairs and All-Russian Collegium for Mustering the Red Army; also chm, All-Russian Bureau of Mil Comr; 1919 member, Revol Mil Council, Eastern, then Western Fronts; 1920 member, Moscow Party Comt; then chm and Presidium member, Kursk Province Exec Comt; 1921 Sov plen in Bukhara; 1922 Sov plen in Lat; 1923 Sov plen in Czechoslovakia; 1924 Sov plen in Italy; 1925 Sov plen in Persia; from 1927 Sov plen in Austria; from 1929 Collegium member, USSR Pop Comrt of For Affairs; 1933–37 Sov plen in Japan; 1937–38 plen in Germany; arrested by State Security organs; *Died:* 1938 in imprisonment.

YURENEVA, Vera Leonidovna (1876–1962) Actress; Hon Artiste of RSFSR from 1935; *Born:* 22 Apr 1876; *Educ:* 1902 grad drama courses at Alexandrine Theater; *Career:* from 1902 played one season at above theater; then acted at theaters in Odessa, Kiev, Novocherkassk, Rostov-on-Don, etc; 1911–17 actress, Nezlobin Theater, Moscow and Petersburg; 1918–19 acted in Kiev; 1919–20 at Korsh Theater, Moscow; 1922–24 with Leningrad Acad Drama Theater; 1930–36 at 2nd Moscow Acad Arts Theater; 1936–39 again at Leningrad Acad Drama Theater; 1939–47 gave dramatic readings; 1947–55 with Lit Drama Theater of All-Russian Theatrical Soc; did film work and wrote books and articles; *Roles:* Margarite in "Faust", after Goethe; Victoria in "The History of a Love Affair" after Hamsun; Violanta in Fletcher's "The Spanish Priest"; Ose in Ibsen's "Peer Gynt", etc; *Publ: Zapiski aktrisy* (An Actress' Notes) (1946); *Moi zapiski o kitayskom teatre* (My Notes on the Chinese Theater) (1928); *Aktrisy* (Actresses) (1925); *Zhenshchiny teatra* (Women in the Theater) (1923); "Vladimir Yakhontov" (1932); *Died:* 19 Jan 1962.

YUREVICH, Aleksandr Donatovich (1895–1966) Party official; CP member from 1917; *Born:* 14 Jan 1895; *Career:* during WW 1 served with Lat Riflemen unit; active in 1917 Oct Revol; 1919–44 exec Party work in Pskov Province and Voronezh; during WW 2 polit work in Sov Army; then worked for Lat Union of Consumer Societies and Lat Min of Educ; from 1954 pensioner; *Died:* 12 Dec 1966.

YUREZANSKIY, Vladimir (real name: NOS, Vladimir Timofeyevich) (1888–?) Writer; *Born:* 1888, son of a peasant; *Educ:* wrote short stories and novelettes about the Revol, the Civil War and everyday life in the USSR; *Publ:* collection of stories *Rzhi tsvetut* (The Rye's in Ear) (1924); novelettes *Znoy* (Burning Heat) (1926); novelette *Zarevo nad polyami* (Glow Above the Fields) (1926); *Died:* date and place of death unknown.

YUROVSKIY, Ya. M. (1878–1938) Party and govt official; CP member from 1905; *Born:* 1878; *Career:* after 1917 Oct Revol member, Mil Dept and chm, Investigation Commission, Ural Oblast Revol Tribunal; asst comr of justice, Ural Oblast; Collegium member, Ural Oblast Cheka; from late 1918 head Moscow rayon Cheka depts; Collegium member, Moscow Cheka; 1919–20 member, Yekaterinburg Province Exec Comt; chm, Yekaterinburg Province Cheka; head, Yekaterinburg Province Soc Security Dept; then worked for Pop Comrt of Workers and Peasants' Inspection; 1921–23 with State Depositary of Valuables; then various party, econ and admin work; arrested by State Security organs; *Died:* 1938 in imprisonment.

YUROVSKIY (real name: SARUKHANOV), Yuriy Il'ich (1894–1959) Actor and stage dir; Pop Artiste of USSR from 1956; *Born:* 3 May 1894 in Tiflis; *Career:* 1914 stage debut with Tiflis Arts Soc; worked at theaters in Tiflis, Yekaterinburg, Penza, Rostov, Odessa and Khar'kov; while in emigration performed at Bulgarian, Czechoslovakian and German theaters; 1924 joined Russian Drama Theater, Riga; 1924 helped found and run Riga Workers' Theater (closed in 1934); taught at Lat Theatrical Inst; *Roles:* Macbeth and Lear; Lynyayev and Karandyshev in Ostrovskiy's *Volki i ovtsy* (The Wolves and the Sheep) and *Bespridannitsa* (The Bride Without a Dowry); Astrov in Chekov's "Dyadya Vanya"; Vas'ka Pepel and Somov in Gorky's *Na dne* (The Lower Depths) and *Somov i drugiye* (Somov and Co); Godun in Lavrenyov's *Razlom* (Break-Up); Polezhayev in Rakhmanov's "Professor Polezhayev"; the Commissar in Prut's *Mstislav Udaloy* (Mstislav the Bold); Kleberg in Upit's "Susannah's Bath"; Zabelin in Pogodin's *Kremlyovskiye kuranty* (The Kremlin Chimes); Makar in Korneychuk's "Makar Dubrava"; *Productions:* Afinogenov's "Mashen'ka"; Kron's *Kandidat partii* (Party Candidate); Latsis' "The Beacon on the Island"; Raynis' "Love Is Stronger than Death"; Lavrenyov's "Razlom"; Blauman's *V ogne* (In the Fire), etc; film roles: Otto Dietrich in *Vstrecha na El'be* (Meeting on the Elbe); Zhukovskiy in "Zhukovskiy"; Prince Viel'gorskiy in *Kompozitor Glinka* (Glinka the Composer), etc; *Awards:* two Stalin Prizes (1950 and 1951); Lat State Prize (1959); Order of the Red Banner of Labor; Badge of Hon; medals; *Died:* 30 Dec 1959.

YUR'YAN, Pavul Andreyevich (1866–1948) Lat conductor and composer; Hon Art Worker of Lat SSR from 1945; *Born:* 22 Feb 1866; *Educ:* 1890 grad French horn class, Khar'kov Music College; 1898 grad singing class, Petersburg Conservatory; *Career:* 1913–15 founder, dir and conductor, first Lat opera theater – Lat Opera Theater, Riga, later expanded into Lat Opera and Ballet Theater; also organized first Lat symphony concerts; arranged Lat folk songs; from 1904 taught at Riga Music College; 1919–27 lecturer, 1927–40 prof, Lat Conservatory; *Died:* 6 Oct 1948.

YUR'YEV, Boris Nikolayevich (1889–1957) Eng; specialist in aerodynamics; prof; member, USSR Acad of Sci from 1943; lt-gen, Eng and Tech Corps; Hon Sci and Tech Worker of RSFSR from 1940; *Born:* 1889; *Educ:* 1919 grad Moscow Higher Tech College; *Career:* 1919–25 lecturer, from 1925 prof, Moscow Higher Tech College; 1920–49 also founder-head, Chair of Experimental Aerodynamics, Zhukovskiy Air Force Eng Acad and Moscow Aviation Inst; helped found Centr Aerohydrodynamic Inst, Moscow Aviation Inst and Air Force Eng Acad; supervised design and construction of aerodynamic laboratories at these establishments; 1944–50 chm, Commission for the History of Eng, USSR Acad of Sci; from 1950 at Inst of Mech, USSR Acad of Sci; 1910–11, together with Sabinin, developed airscrew theory; did research on theory and design of helicopters; from 1925 supervised preliminary experiments and helped design EA-1 helicopter, built at Centr Aerohydrodynamic Inst; 1941, together with I. P. Brakhutin, designed twin-screw "Omega" helicopter; helped standardize aerodynamic terminology; helped publish manual for aircraft designers; *Publ:* coauthor, *Aerodinamicheskiya issledovaniya* (Aerodynamic Research) (1928); *Vozdushnyye vinty* (Airscrews) (1933); *Eksperimental'naya aerodinamika* (Experimental Aerodynamics) (1936–38); *Issledovaniye letnykh svoystv gelikopterov* (A Study of the Flying Characteristics of Helicopters) (1939); *Impul'snaya teoriya vozdushnykh vintov* (The Pulse Theory of Airscrews) (1948); *Vikhrevaya teoriya vintov* (Vortical Screw Theory) (1947), etc; *Awards:* Gold Metal at Int Exhibition of Aeronautics (1912); two Orders of Lenin; two other orders; medals; two Stalin Prizes (1943 and 1946); *Died:* 14 Mar 1957.

YUR'YEV, Vasiliy Yakovlevich (1879–1962) Plant selectionist; member, Ukr Acad of Sci from 1945; hon member, All-Union Lenin Acad of Agric Sci from 1956; Hon Sci Worker of Ukr SSR from 1949; CP member from 1956; *Born:* 1879 in vil Virga, now Penza Oblast; *Educ:* 1905 grad Novo-Aleksandriyski Inst of Agric and Forestry; *Career:* 1905–09 uyezd agronomist in Penza

Province; 1909–44 assoc, from 1944 dir, Khar'kov Selection Station; from 1937 prof, Khar'kov Agric Inst; from 1946 dir, Inst of Genetics and Selection, Ukr Acad of Sci (now Inst of Plant-Growing, Selection and Genetics, Ukr Min of Agric); 1956–62 member, Ukr Acad of Sci; studied theoretical and practical aspects of selection and seed-growing for agric crops; bred new varieties of winter and spring wheat, rye, barley, millet and maize which were then extensively used in the USSR; coauthor and ed, textbook *Obshchaya selektsiya i semenovodstvo polevykh kul'tur* (The General Selection and Seed-Growing of Field Crops) (1940); *Publ: Sortoispytaniye yarovoy pshenitsy za 1911–1925 gody* (The Variety Testing of Spring Wheat for 1911–1925) (1928); *Metodika selektsii pshenitsy na Khar'kovskoy stantsii* (Methods of Wheat Selection at the Khar'kov Station) (1939); *Raboty po selektsii i semenovodstvu* (Selection and Seed-Growing Works) (1947), etc; *Awards:* twice Hero of Socialist Labor (1954 and 1956); four Orders of Lenin; three other orders; medals; Stalin Prize (1947); *Died:* 8 Feb 1962.

YUR'YEV, Yuriy Mikhaylovich (1872–1948) Actor; Pop Artiste of USSR from 1939; *Born:* 15 Jan 1872 in Moscow; *Educ:* 1889–1893 studied in Moscow at Philharmonic College and on Drama Courses at Maly Theater; *Career:* while still a student played parts in shows of Moscow Philharmonic Soc and Maly Theater; 1893–1948 (with intervals) actor at Alexandrine Theater (now Pushkin Acad Drama Theater, Leningrad); from 1898 taught acting at Petersburg Drama Courses and Leningrad Theatrical Inst; 1918 helped found Tragedy Theater in Petrograd; 1919 helped found Bolshoy Drama Theater; 1922–28 artistic dir, Leningrad Acad Theater; *Roles:* Ferdinand in Schiller's "Kabale und Liebe"; Akosta in Gutskov's "Uriel' Akosta"; Ruy Blas and Carl in Victor Hugo's "Ruy Blas" and "Ernani"; Hippolitus in Euripides' "Hippolitus"; Don Juan in Moliére's "Don Juan"; Molchalin and Chatskiy in Griboyedov's *Gore ot uma* (Woe from Wit); Mizgir' in Ostrovskiy's *Snegurochka* (The Snow Maiden); Arbenin in Lermontov's "Masquerade"; Don Carlos in Schiller's "Don Carlos"; Mark Antony in Shakespeare's "Antony and Cleopatra"; Berkutov in Ostrovskiy's *Volki i ovtsy* (The Wolves and the Sheep); Neschastlivtsev in Ostrovskiy's *Les* (The Forest); Velikatov in Ostrovskiy's *Talanty i poklonniki* (Talents and Admirers); Batov in Lunacharskiy's *Yad* (Poison); Dante in Kamenskiy's *Pushkin i Dantes* (Pushkin and Dante); Bryzgalov in Trenyov's *Na beregu Nevy* (On the Banks of the Neva), etc; also gave public readings, including Goethe's "Egmont"; *Publ: Tvorcheskaya beseda s molodymi aktyorami* (A Creative Talk with Young Actors) (1939); *Besedy aktyora* (Talks of an Actor) (1946); *Zapiski . . . 1872–1893* (Notes . . . 1872–1893) (1939); *Zapiski . . . 1893–1917* (Notes . . . 1893–1917) (1945); *Awards:* Stalin Prize (1943); Order of Lenin; Order of the Red Banner of Labor; Badge of Hon; medals; *Died:* 13 Mar 1948.

YUSHCHENKO, Aleksandr Ivanovich (1869–1936) Psychiatrist; Hon Sci Worker of Ukr SSR; member, Ukr Acad of Sci from 1934; *Born:* 2 Dec 1869 in vil Vodo-Techa, now Sumy Oblast, son of a peasant; *Educ:* 1893 grad Med Fac, Khar'kov Univ; *Career:* 1893–96 specialized in psychiatry under Prof. P. I. Kovalevskiy in Khar'kov; 1896 defended doctor's thes . on the structure of the sympathetic ganglia in mammals and man; 1896–97 worked at V. M. Bekhterev and I. P. Pavlov's laboratories; 1901–15 at Biochemical Laboratory, Inst of Experimental Med; from 1918 prof of psychiatry, Tartu, Voronezh then Rostov-on-Don Univ; from 1929 assoc, Ukr Inst of Psychiatry, Khar'kov; from 1932 assoc, Psychoneurological Acad; helped found biochemical trend in psychiatry; established enzymatic and oxidation changes in mental diseases and experimental endocrinopathy; studied clinical aspects of progressive paralysis, particularly congenital paralysis, psychopathy and neuroses; wrote over 120 works; *Publ: Yunosheskiy progressivnyy paralich* (Progressive Juvenile Paralysis) (1895); *Sushchnost' dushevnykh bolezney i biologo-khimicheskiye issledovaniya ikh* (The Nature of Mental Diseases and Their Biochemical Study) (1912); *Lektsii po psikhiatrii* (Lectures on Psychiatry) (1923); *Voprosy klassifikatsii, profilaktiki i lecheniya taknazyvayemykh travmaticheskikh nevrozov* (The Classification, Prophylaxis and Treatment of So-Called Traumatic Neuroses) (1935); *Died:* 13 June 1936.

YUSHKEVICH, Semyon Solomonovich (1868–1927) Russian writer and playwright; *Born:* 25 Sept 1868 in Odessa, son of Jewish parents; *Educ:* grad med fac, Paris; *Career:* 1897 first work printed; contributed to Gorky's collections "Znaniye"; wrote several plays on life of Jews; 1920 emigrated; *Publ:* plays: *Korol'* (The King) (1906); *Golod* (Famine) (1907); *Komediya braka* (The Comedy of Marriage) (1910); "Miserere" (1910); "Mendel' Spivak" (1914); *Povest' o gospodine Son'kine* (The Tale of Mister Son'kin) (1917); *Bes* (The Demon) (1913); novel *Epizody* (Episodes) (1923), etc; *Died:* 12 Feb 1927.

YUSHKOV, Serafim Vladimirovich (1888–1952) Historian; specialist in history of state and law; prof; corresp member, Ukr Acad of Sci from 1939; member, Kaz Acad of Sci from 1946; *Born:* 1888 in vil Trofimovka, Penza Province; *Educ:* 1912 grad Law Fac and History and Philology Fac, Petersburg Univ; *Career:* 1916–19 assoc prof, 1919–52 prof of law history, Saratov, then Leningrad and Moscow Univ; wrote numerous works on history of state and law; *Publ: Feodal'nyye otnosheniya i Kiyevskaya Rus'* (Feudal Relations and Kievan Rus) (1924); *Ocherki po istorii feodalizma v Kiyevskoy Rusi* (An Outline History of Feudalism in Kievan Rus) (1939); *Obshchestvenno-politicheskiy stroy i pravo v Kiyevskoy Rusi* (Socio-Political System and Law in Kievan Rus) (1949); textbook *Istoriya gosudarstva i prava SSR* (State and Law History of the USSR) (1950), etc; *Died:* 14 Aug 1952.

YUSHMANOV, Nikolay Vladimirovich (1896–1946) Linguist; *Born:* 24 Feb 1896; *Career:* specialized in Semitic and African languages; contributed to unification of orthographies and terminology; *Publ: Grammatika literaturnogo arabskogo yazyka* (The Grammar of Literary Arabic) (1928); *Stroy amkharskogo yazyka* (The Structure of Amkhar) (1936); *Stroy yazyka khausa* (The Structure of the Hausa Language) (1937); *Stroy arabskogo yazyka* (The Structure of Arabic) (1938); *Died:* 2 Apr 1946.

YUSKIN, Ignatiy Grigor'yevich (1898–1934) Office worker; CP member; *Born:* 1898; *Career:* Dec 1934 charged with complicity in assassination of S. M. Kirov; 29 Dec 1934 sentenced to death along with co-defendants by Assizes of Mil Collegium, USSR Supr Court; *Died:* Dec 1934 executed.

YUSUPOVA, Saradzhan Mikhaylovna (1910–1966) Geochemist; prof from 1949; member, Tadzh Acad of Sci from 1951; *Born:* 18 May 1910; *Educ:* 1935 grad Uzbek Univ, Samarkand; *Career:* 1948–49 lecturer, from 1949 prof, Tadzh Univ; did x-ray structural research on colloid minerals with special reference to argillaceous group; also studied geochemistry of celestine and mineral resources of Tadzh SSR; *Publ: Koloidno-khimicheskiye svoystva glin Uzbekistana* (The Colloidal Properties of the Clays of Uzbekistan) (1941); *Mineralogicheskiye osobennosti lyossov Sredney Azii* (The Mineralogical Features of the Loess of Central Asia) (1951); *Mikroelementy i zhizn'* (The Microelements and Life) (1960); *O zakonomernostyakh raspredeleniya redkikh elementov v nekotorykh osadochnykh otlozheniyakh Yuzhnogo Tadzhikistana* (The Distribution Pattern of Rare Elements in Some Sediment Deposits of Southern Tadzhikistan) (1962); *Died::* 17 May 1966.

YUZEFOVICH, Iosif Sigizmundovich (1890–?) Trade-union official; CP member from 1919; *Born:* 1890, son of a worker; *Career:* 1905 joined Bund in Poland; 1912 sentenced for revol activities to four years' imprisonment, which he served in Warsaw and Lomzha; after his release settled illegally in Moscow and worked for underground orgs; 1917 member, Moscow Centr Trade-Union Bureau; co-founder, then secr, Moscow Leatherworkers' Union; 1918 sided with Internationalists; late 1919 joined RCP(B) together with Internationalists; until 1928 chm, CC, Leatherworkers' Union; also head, Int Leatherworkers' Propaganda and Action Comt; Presidium member, All-Russian Centr Trade-Union Council; 1928, at 4th Profintern (Trade-Union International) Congress, elected member, Centr Council, Profintern; from 1928 member, Exec Bureau, Profintern; Aug 1930 reelected and subsequently delegated to Centr Council, Profintern; attended various int congresses, conferences and councils of revol trade unions in the USSR and abroad; wrote pamphlets on history of trade-unionism; *Died:* date and place of death unknown.

YUZHIN (real name: SUMBATOV), Aleksandr Ivanovich (1857–1927) Actor, playwright and impresario; Hon Academician from 1917; Pop Artiste of RSFSR from 1922; *Born:* 4 Seot 1857 in vil Kukuyevka, Tula Province, son of a Geo prince; *Educ:* 1878–81 studied at Law Fac, Petersburg Univ; *Career:* while still at school acted in amateur productions; 1876 professional stage debut; 1877 began to write plays; 1878–79 acted at clubs in Petersburg; 1881 at Moscow's Brenko Theater; 1882–1909 actor, 1909–18 co-manager, 1918 Council chm, 1919–23 chm of directorate, 1923–26 dir, from 1926 hon dir, Maly Theater; after 1917 Oct Revol worked for Theatrical Dept, Pop Comrt of Educ and for Centr Theater Bd, etc; lectured and wrote articles on theater, advocating realistic art and classic dramaturgy; *Roles:* Dunois in Schiller's "The Maid of Orleans" (1884); Don Carlos in Hugo's "Ernani" (1889); Ruy in Hugo's "Ruy Blas" (1891); Marquis Posa in Schiller's "Don Carlos" (1894); Macbeth (1890, 1895 and 1914); Richard III (1897); Figaro (1910); Repetilov in Griboyedov's *Gore ot uma* (Woe from Wit) (1911); Bolingbroke in Scribe's "The Glass of Water" (1915); Telyatev in Ostrovskiy's *Beshenyye den'gi* (Mad Money) (1917); Monrichard in Scribe's "The Ladies' War" (1924); Tamernitsyn in his own play *Vozhdi* (The Leaders) (1909); Lidman in Sederberg's *Lyubov' – vsoy* (Love Is All) (1910); Gleb Mironovich in A. K. Tolstoy's *Posadnik* (The Steward) (1918); Cromwell in Lunacharskiy's "Oliver Cromwell" (1921); King August XIII in Ryndy-Alekseyev's *Zheleznaya stena* (The Iron Wall) (1923), etc; *Works:* plays: *List'ya shelestyat* (The Rustling Foliage) (1881); coauthor, *Sokoly i vorony* (Falcons and Ravens)) (1885); *Tsepi* (Chains) (1888); comedies: *Dzhentl'men* (The Gentleman) (1897); *Zakat* (The Sunset) (1899); *Nevod* (The Sweep-Net) (1905); plays: *Staryy zakal* (The Old Stock) (1895); *Izmena* (Treason) (1903); *Nochnoy tuman* (Night Mist) (1916); *Vozhdi* (The Leaders) (1909), etc; *Died:* 17 Sept 1927 in Nice; buried in Moscow.

YUZHIN (real name: VASIL'YEV), Mikhail Ivanovich (1876–1937) Party and govt official; CP member; *Born:* 1876 in Pyatigorsk, son of a worker:*Educ:* studied at Pyatigorsk and Vladikavkaz high-schools; from 1895–96 studied at Moscow Univ; *Career:* from 1896 involved with Marxist circles; 1899 arrested and exiled from Moscow; for several years engaged in revol work in southern Russia, Crimea and Caucasus; 1905 went abroad; met Lenin in Geneva and at his suggestion began to work for Bolshevik organs "Vperyod" and "Proletary"; summer 1905 sent by Lenin to Odessa for mil revol work in southern Russia; then worked in Moscow; coopted to Moscow Party Comt; member, Exec Commission, Moscow Party Comt; 1905 helped found Moscow Sov of Workers' Dep; edited Moscow Party Committee's legal newspaper "Vperyod"; helped organize Dec 1905 armed uprising in Moscow and was a member of its executive staff, arrested shortly after the start of the revolt; 1906–17 Party work in various towns of southern Russia and Volga area; imprisoned 11 times and exiled twice; Mar 1917 helped establish Saratov Sov of Workers and Soldiers' Dep; chm, Saratov Province RSDRP(B) Comt; Oct 1917 directed Bolshevik revolt in Saratov; Jan 1919 – Jan 1921 Collegium member, Pop Comrt of Internal Affairs (NKVD); helped organize Sov police force; summer 1919 member, Revol Mil Council, 15th Army; late 1921 – Mar 1924 asst prosecutor, RSFSR Supr Court; 1924–37 dep chm, USSR Supr Court; *Publ: Moskovskiy Sovet Rabochikh Deputatov v 1905 godu i podgotovka im vooruzhyonnogo vosstaniya* (The Moscow Soviet of Workers' Deputies in 1905 and Its Preparation of the Armed Uprising) (1925); *V ogne pervoy revolyutsii* (In the Fire of the First Revolution) (1931); *Died:* 1937.

YUZOVSKIY, Iosif Il'ich (1902–1964) Theater and lit critic; lit historian; *Born:* 18 Dec 1902; *Educ:* 1924 grad Soc Sci Fac, Don Univ, Rostov-on-Don; 1925 grad Dept of Art History, Don Archeological Inst; *Career:* 1925 first work printed; from 1930 lived in Moscow; from 1930's functioned mainly as critic; studied work of such stage dir as Meyerhold, Okhlopkov, Tairov, Nemirovich-Danchenko and Stanislavskiy and plays of Gorky, Pogodin, etc; wrote on drama theater, ballet, opera, music, operetta, circus, variety shows, painting, etc; specialized in plays of Gorky; 1946–48 senior assoc, Inst of World Lit; translated plays from Polish, German and Czech, including Jurandot's "Such Were the Times", Brecht's "The Good Man from Szechuan" and Askenazy's "A Guest from the Night"; *Publ: Voprosy sotsialisticheskoy dramaturgii* (Problems of Socialist Dramaturgy) (1934); *Spektakli i p'yesy* (Shows and Plays) (1935); *Gor'kiy na stsene MKhAT* (Gorky at the Moscow Acadmic Arts Theater) (1939); *Dramaturgiya Gor'kogo* (Gorky's Plays) (1940); *Obraz i epokha* (Image and Age) (1947); *M. Gorkiy i yego dramaturgiya* (M. Gorky and His Plays) (1959); *Zachem lyudi khodyat v teatr* (Why People Go to the Theater) (1964); *Sovetskiye aktyory v gor'kovskikh rolyakh* (Soviet Actors in Gorky's Roles) (1964); *Razgovor zatyanulsya za polnoch'* (The Conversation Lasted Past Midnight) (1966); *Died:* 15 Dec 1964.

YYVAN, Kyrlya (IVANOV, Kirill Ivanovich) (1909–1943) Mari poet and film actor; *Born:* 4 Mar 1909 in vil Kup-Sola, Sernurskiy Rayon, now Mari ASSR; *Educ:* studied at Moscow Cinematography Technicum; *Career:* after his father was killed during collectivization of agric, worked as shepherd and begged for a living; 1929 first verse published; from 1936 actor, Mari Theater; played role of Mustafa in the first Sov sound film *Putyovka v zhizn'* (A Start in Life) (1931); arrested by State Security organs; *Publ:* coauthor, verse anthology "We the Shockworkers" (1931); collected verse: "I Sing with the Voice of Revolution" (1932); "Birthday" (1935); *Died:* 1943 in imprisonment; posthumously rehabilitated.

Z

ZABLUDOVSKIY, Anton Martynovich (1881–1953) Surgeon and med historian; Dr of Med from 1911; prof; Hon Sci Worker of RSFSR; *Born:* 1881; *Educ:* 1908 grad Moscow Univ; *Career:* 1911 defended doctor's thesis in methods of sterilizing the hands and the operating area: 1914–17 served on German Front; 1918–20 worked in Moscow hospitals; 1920–28 asst prof, senior asst prof and assoc prof, Gen Surgery Clinic, 1st Moscow Univ; 1928–53 head, Chair of Gen Surgery, 1st Leningrad Med Inst; 1948–51 also head, Chair of the History of Med; wrote over 120 works; *Publ:* doctor's thesis *O nekotorykh novykh metodakh obezzarazhivanniya ruk i operatsionnogo polya* (Some New Methods of Sterilizing the Hands and the Operating Area) (1911); *Vnedreniye v khirurgicheskuyu kliniku* (An Introduction to Surgical Clinical Practice) (1922); *Uchebnik chastnoy khirurgii* (A Textbook on Special Surgery) (1933); *Kurs obshchey khirurgii* (A Course on General Surgery) (1935); *Iz istorii russkikh khirurgicheskikh s'yezdov* (The History of Russian Surgical Congresses) (1941); *Died:* 1953.

ZABOLOTNYY, Daniil Kirillovich (1866–1929) Microbiologist and epidemiologist; pioneer of Russian epidemiology member, USSR Acad of Sci from 1929; member from 1928, Ukr Acad of Sci; *Born:* 28 Dec 1866 in vil Chebotartsy, Podol'ya Province (now vil Zabolotnoye, Vinnitsa Oblast), son of a peasant and former serf; *Educ:* 1891 grad Natural Sci Dept, Physics and Mathematics Fac, Novorossiysk Univ, Odessa; 1894 grad Med Fac, Kiev Univ; *Career:* began research work while a student in Odessa; expelled from univ for student polit activities; admitted to Russia's first Bacteriological Station, founded by Mechnikov in 1866; here he detected the phenomenon of the autosterilization of soil as a result of bacterial antagonism and carried out experiments on the infection and immunization of marmots with cholera vibrion via the intestine; 1893, together with I.G. Savchenko, immunized himself with killes cholera vibrion cultures and then checked the efficacy of immunization by taking live cholera cultures; thereby proved that healthy persons can act as carriers of cholera and laid the basis for enteral cholera immunization; 1897 took part in Russian expedition to study plague in India, then Arabia; proved the identical etiology of bubonic and pneumonic plague and the therapeutic effect of plague antiserum; 1898 undertook expedition through the Gobi Desert and China to Eastern Mongolia to study endemic plague in Weichan; then combatted plague in Mesopotamia, Persia and various parts of Russia; 1910–11 directed expedition to study pneumonic in Manchuria and Eastern Mongolia; proved that wild rodents help spread plague among people, developed methods of vaccination and opened a number of anti-plague laboratories; also took part in expeditions to combat cholera, malaria and typhus; 1903 succeeded in inducing in baboons; observed Spyrochaeta pallida for two years prior to its official discovery in 1905 by Chaudin and Hofmann; 1898 established Russia's first Chair of Bacteriology at Petersburg Univ; until 1928 headed this chair; also founded USSR's first Chair of Epidemiology at Odessa Med Inst; founder and hon member, Microbiological Soc, Leningrad; founded Int Soc of Microbiologists; attended many int conferences and congresses; member, Learned Council, Pop Comrt if Health; organized courses for epidemiologists; from 1921 founder-rector, Odessa Med Inst; founded Kiev Inst of Microbiology and Epidemiology, now named for him; member, Petrograd, then Kiev City Sov; 1921 elected member, All-Russian and All-Ukr Centr Exec Comt; wrote some 100 works; *Publ: Chuma. Epidemiologiya, patogenez i profilaktika* (Plague. Epidemiology, Pathogenesis and Prophylaxis) (1907); *Chastnaya bakteriologiya* (Special Bacteriology) (1908); thesis *Sifilis, yego patogenez i etiologiya* (Syphilis, Its Pathogenesis and Etiology) (1909); *Obshchaya bakteriologiya* (General Bacteriology) (1909); *Kholernaya epidemiya 1908–1909 godov v Petersburge* (The 1908–1909 Cholera Epidemic in Petersburg) (1910);

Chuma na yugo-vostoke SSSR (Plague in the Southeastern USSR) (1926); *Osnovy epidemiologii* (The Principles of Epidemiology) (1927); *Died:* 15 Dec 1929 in Kiev.

ZABOLOTNYY, Vladimir Ignat'yevich (1898–1962) Architect; prof from 1940; member, USSR and Ukr Acad of Construction and Architecture from 1956; CP member from 1944; *Born:* 11 Sept 1898 in vil Karan', Kiev Province; *Educ:* 1927 grad Kiev Art Inst; *Career:* 1945–56 pres, Ukr Acad of Architecture; from 1957 head, Dept of History of Ukr Art, Presidium, Ukr Acad of Construction and Architecture; wrote a number of research studies on Ukr architecture and building; *Works:* Ukr Supr Sov building in Kiev (1936–39); Dneprodzerzhinsk Palace of Culture (1932); co-designed Palace of Pioneers in Kiev (1936–37); "Constructor" Steel Settlement in Dnepropetrovsk (1948–50); Ukr Cooperative Union Building in Kiev (1955–57), etc; *Awards:* Stalin Prize (1941); *Died:* 3 Aug 1962.

ZABOLOTSKIY, Nikolay Alekseyevich (1903–1958) Russian poet and translator; *Born:* 7 May 1903 in Kazan'; son of an agronomist; *Educ:* 1920 studied at Moscow Med Inst; 1925 grad Leningrad Teachers' Training Inst; *Career:* 1910 moved to vil Sernur, Vyatka Province with his familiy; contributed to children's magazines "Yozh" and "Chizh"; 1938 arrested by NKVD; subsequently held jobs as construction worker and draughtsman in Sov Far East, Altay Kray and Karaganda; 1946 returned to Moscow; translated Goethe, Schiller, Lesya Ukrainka, Shota Rustaveli, David Guramishvili, etc into Russian; *Publ:* children's stories: *Krasnyye i siniye* (The Reds and the Blues), *Rezinovyye golovy* (The Rubberheads) (1928–29); verse collections: *Stolbtsy* (Columns) (1929); *Vtoraya kniga* (The Second Book) (1937); poem *Torzhestvo zemledeliya* (The Triumph of Farming) (1933); verse cycle: *Venchaniye plodami* (Crowned with Fruit) (1932); *Sever* (The North) (1936); "Sedov" (1937); *Tvortsy dorog* (The Trail-Blazers) (1947); *Ya ishchu garmonii v prirode* (I Seek Harmony in Nature) (1947); *Skvoz' volshebnyy pribor Levenguka* (Through Levenguk's Magic Device) (1948); *Khodoki* (The Messengers) (1954); *Nekrasivaya devochka* (The Ugly Girl) (1955); *Staraya aktrisa* (The Old Actress) (1956); *Protivostoyaniye Marsa* (Mars in Opposition) (1956); *Smert' vracha* (The Death of a Physician) (1957); poem *Rubruk v Mongolii* (Rubruk in Mongolia) (1948); *Died:* 14 Oct 1958 in Moscow.

ZABUDSKIY, Grigoriy Aleksandrovich (1854–1930) Technol chemist; Hon Sci and Tech Worker of RSFSR; *Born:* 21 July 1854; *Educ:* 1874 grad Mikhail Artillery College; 1879 grad Mikhail Artillery Acad, Petersburg; *Career:* from 1879 asst, from 1891 head, Chemical Laboratory, Mikhail Artillery Acad; from 1893 prof, above Acad; 1914 co-founder and dir, Centr Sci and Tech Laboratory, War Dept (1928 reorganized into Leningrad Inst of Metals); helped re-equip army with small arms; introduced smokeless powders and produced high explosives for shells; wrote basic courses in explosives and shells; *Publ: O porokhakh, upotreblyayemykh v russkoy i inostrannoy artillgriyakh dlya pushek raznykh kalibrov* (Powders Used in the Russian and Foreign Artillery for Guns of Various Caliber) (1887); *Prigotovleniye i svoystva razlichnykh malodymnykh i bezdymnykh porokhov* (The Preparation and Properties of Various Low-Smoke and Smokeless Powders) (1893); *Vzryvchatyye veshchestva* (Explosives) (1898); *Prigotovleniye porokhov* (The Preparation of Powders) (1901), etc; *Died:* 1930.

ZAGAROV (real name: FESSING), Aleksandr Leonidovich (1877–1941) Actor and stage dir; Hon Art Worker of RSFSR from 1940; *Born:* 17 Jan 1877 in Yelizavetgrad, now Kirovograd; *Educ:* 1898 grad Nemirovich-Danchenko's class at Drama Dept, Musical Drama College, Moscow Philharmonic Soc; *Career:* 1898–1906 (with intervals) worked for Moscow Arts Theater; 1901 began stage dir work in Yaroslavl; actor and stage dir at theaters in Tiflis, Riga, Kherson and Kiev; 1909–10 chief stage dir, Korsh Theater, Moscow; 1911–16 actor and stage dir, Alexandrine Theater, Petrograd; after 1917 Oct Revol worked for over 10 years in Ukr; directed Shevchenko Theater in Kiev, then Khar'kov Krasnozavodskiy Theater; then actor and stage dir at theaters in Penza, Vladivostok, Khabarovsk, Kovrov, etc; 1939–41 at Saratov Young Playgoers' Theater and Saratov's Marx Theater; from 1901 taught stagecraft at S.V. Khalyutina's Studio, Moscow Arts Theater School, Sukhodol'skaya Theater Studio, etc; from 1920 prof, Kiev Musical Drama Inst; wrote many articles on the theater; *Roles:* Kleshch in Gorky's *Na dne* (The Lower Depths); Sorin in Chekhov's *Chayka* (The Seagull); Publius and Pindar in Shakespeare's "Julius Caesar"; Stockman in Ibsen's "Doctor Stockman"; Orgonne in "Tartuffe"; Yegor in *Yegor Bulychov i drugiye* (Yegor Bulychyov and Co), after Gorky; Mal'ko in Afinogenov's *Strakh* (Fear) and *Dalyokoye* (The Distant Past); *Productions* "Tartuffe"; "The Marriage of Figaro"; *Vragi* (The Enemies); *Aristokraty* (The Aristocrats); Ostrovskiy's *Besprodannitsa* (Girl Without a Dowry); Rakhmanov's *Bespokoynaya starost'* (Restless Old Age), etc; *Publ: Iskusstvo aktyora* (The Actor's Art) (1920); *Died:* 12 Dec 1941.

ZAGORSKIY, Mikhail Borisovich (1885–1951) Russian theater critic and historian; *Born:* 1 Jan 1885; *Career:* 1904 first work printed; wrote under the pen names "Knizhnik," "Momus," "Rey-Mey" and "M. Charskiy"; 1919–21 head, ed staff, journal "Vestnik teatra"; worked for periodicals "Novyy zritel'," Zhizn Isskusstva," "Teatr" and "Sovetskoye iskusstvo"; wrote over 2,000 articles and revues dealing with individual shows, history of Russian theater and criticism of various research works; *Publ: Stepan Kuznetsov. Zhizn' i tvorchestvo* (Stepan Kuznetsov. Life and Work) (1927); *Shchepkin v otsenke sovremennoy yemu kritike* (Shchepkin as Rated by His Contemporary Critics) (1938); *Polemicheskiye zametki* (Polemic Notes) (1939); *Pushkin i teatr* (Pushkin and the Theater) (1940); "M.M. Tarkhanov" (1946); *Krylov – dramaturg* (Krylov as Playwright) (1944); *Shekspir v Rossii* (Shakespeare in Russia) (1947); *Problemy teatra Pushkina* (Problems of Pushkin's Theater) (1949); *Gogol' i teatr* (Gogol and the Theater) (1952), etc; *Died:* 23 Aug 1951.

ZAGORSKIY (LUBOTSKIY), Vladimir Mikhaylovich (1883–1919) Party official; CP member from 1903; *Born:* 1883 in Nizhniy Novgorod; *Career:* together with Ya. M. Sverdlov attended first illegal Soc-Democratic circles in Nizhniy Novgorod and Sormovo; 1902 exiled to Yeniseysk Province for organizing Nizhniy Novgorod and Sormovo workers' May Day demonstration; after 2nd RSDRP Congress joined Bolsheviks; 1904 fled from exile to Geneva; Jan 1905 sent by Lenin to Moscow, where he prepared Dec revolt; after suppression of this revolt continued illegal Party work in Moscow; 1908 went to London; 1910 re-entered Russia illegally; Party work in Saratov; again left Russia and lived in Leipzig; while in Germany worked for Bolshevik Center; during WW 1 interned in a German concentration camp; after 1917 Oct Revol returned to Russia; after conclusion of 1918 Brest-Litovsk Peace Treaty counsellor, RSFSR Embassy in Berlin; 1918, after returning to Moscow, elected secr, Moscow Party Comt; *Died:* 25 Sept 1919 killed by a bomb tossed into the premises of the Moscow Party Comt on Leont'yev Alley; buried on Moscow's Red Square; 1930 the town of Sergiyev, Moscow Oblast, was renamed Zagorsk.

ZAGRODSKIY, Andrey Aleksandrovich (1886–1948) Linguist; specialist in methods of teaching languages; *Born:* 2 Dec 1886 in vil Zelen'kovo, now Kiev Oblast; *Educ:* 1912 grad Philology Fac, Warsaw Univ; *Career:* from 1923 taught at Kiev Higher Educ Establishments; from 1943 at Ukr Pedag Research Inst; wrote several works on methods of teaching languages; also wrote 5th–6th grade secondary-school Ukr language textbooks; *Died:* 30 Nov 1948.

ZAGUL, Dmitriy Yur'yevich (1890–1938) Ukr poet; *Born:* 28 Aug 1890 in vil Miliyevo, Chernovtsy Oblast, son of a peasant; *Educ:* studied at Chernovtsy Univ; *Career:* 1912 first work printed; used various pen names, such as Maydan, Suchansnyy, Yuras', Tyverets and Sulamit; during WW 1 moved to Russia, then lived in Kiev; 1923 member, Assoc of Sov Writers; early 1925 member, "Western Ukraine" lit group; then member, All-Ukr Assoc of Proletarian Writers; translated into Ukr Blok's *Dvenadtsat'* (The Twelve) and works of Schiller, Goethe and Heine; arrested by State Security organs; *Publ:* verse collections: "Hem-Stitch" (1913); "From the Green Hills" (1918); "On the Verge" (1919); "Our Day" (1925); "Motifs" (1927); lit theory course "Poetics" (1923), etc; *Died:* 1938 in imprisonment; posthumously rehabilitated.

ZAIKIN, Ivan Mikhaylovich (1880–1949) Wrestler and circus artiste; *Born:* 5 Nov 1880, son of a peasant; *Career:* from 1902 engaged in heavy athletics; 1904 won All-Russian Weightlifting Contest; 1908 placed 2nd in Int Weightlifting Championship, Paris; 1920 emigrated and performed as athlete and wrestler in Japan, USA, France, Italy and Rumania; 1940 returned to USSR and lived in Kishinev; *Died:* 1949.

ZAKHAROV, Georgiy Fyodorovich (1897–1957) Mil commander; gen of the army from 1944; CP member from 1919; *Born:* 5 May 1897 in vil Shilovo, Saratov Province, son of a peasant; *Educ:* 1916 grad Chistopol' Ensigns School; 1932 grad FRunze Mil

Acad; 1939 grad Gen Staff Acad; *Career:* fought in WW 1; from 1919 in Red Army; fought in Civil War as company commander; by start of WW 2 chief of staff, 22nd Army; Aug 1941 – Feb 1943 chief of staff and dep commander, Bryansk, Western and other Fronts (Oct-early Dec 1941 commanded Bryansk Front); from Feb 1943 commanded 51st, then 2nd Guards Army which broke through German defenses on River Mius and River Molochnaya to liberate the Crimea; from June 1944 commander, 2nd Bel Front in liberation of Bel; from Nov 1944 commander, 4th Guards Army which forced the Danube and helped storm Budapest; from Feb 1945 dep commander, 1st Bel, then 4th Ukr Front; after WW 2 commanded Southern Ural and East Siberian Mil Distr; from Sept 1950 commandant, "Vystrel" Higher Tactical Courses; from Sept 1954 dep head, Main Mil Training Bd for Ground Forces; *Awards:* Order of Lenin; four Orders of the Red Banner; three Orders of Suvorov; Order of Kutuzov; Order of Bogdan Khmel'nitskiy; medals; *Died:* 26 Jan 1957.

ZAKHAROV, Ivan Nikolayevich (1885–1930) Mil commander; *Born:* 1885; *Career:* lt-col, Russian Army; from 1918 in Red Army; during Civil War chief of staff and inspector of infantry, 1st Army on Eastern Front; asst commander, Caucasian and Western Fronts; after Civil War exec posts with centr apparatus administering Red Army; *Died:* 1930.

ZAKHAROV, Sergey Aleksandrovich (1878–1949) Soil scientist and geographer; Dr of Agric Sci from 1935; prof; *Born:* 29 Aug 1878 in Tiflis; *Educ:* 1900 grad Natural Sci Dept, Physics and Mathematics Fac, Moscow Univ; *Career:* after grad took part in V.V. Dokuchayevs's expedition to study the soils of the Caucasus; 1915 qualified as Master of Agronomy at Moscow Univ; until 1935 prof, Petrograd Forestry Inst, Tiflis Polytech Inst and Kuban' Agric Inst in Krasnodar; 1935–49 prof and head, Chair of Soil Sci, Rostov Univ; studied soils of the Caucasus, their origin and geography, vertical zoning and interaction of forest and steppe in the Caucasus; did research on intial stages of soil formation, salting of steppe soils, etc; *Publ: Pochvennyye rastvory, rol' ikh v pochvoobrazovanii, priyomy ikh issledovaniya i znacheniye ikh dlya kharakteristiki pochvennykh tipov* (Soil Solutions, Their Role in Soil Formation, Means of Studying Them and Their Importance for the Classification of Soil Types) (1906); *K kharakteristike vysokogornykh pochv Kavkaza* (The Characteristics of Caucasian Mountain Soils) (1914); *Kurs pochvovedeniya* (A Soil Science Course) (1927); "Soil of the Black Sea Coast Near Batum" (1930); *Pochvy gornykh rayonov SSSR* (The Soils of the USSR's Mountainous Areas) (1937); *Ob obshchey klassifikatsii pochv SSSR* (The General Classification of the Soils of the USSR) (1943); *K probleme Bol'shoy Amur-Dar'i* (The Problem of the Great Amur-Dar'ya) (1947); *Ucheniye o zonal'nosti pochv v proshlom i nastoyashchem* (Past and Present Soil Zonality Theory) (1948), etc; *Awards:* Badge of Hon; Dokuchayev Gold Medal; *Died:* 2 Jan 1949 in Rostov-on-Don.

ZAKHAROV, Stepan Stepanovich (1890–1965) Party and govt official; CP member from 1907; *Born:* 4 Aug 1890; *Career:* in 1905 Revol fought at barricades in Moscow; 1909–12 org and propaganda work at Moscow and Moscow region enterprises; repeatedly arrested and exiled; during 1917 Oct Revol chief of staff, Moscow's Butyrka Rayon Red Guard units; during Civil War polit work in Red Army; 1921–34 Party work; 1936–44 admin work in Moscow and Moscow Oblast; 1944–53 admin work in Lat; deleg at 12th–15th Party Congresses; member, All-Russian and USSR Centr Exec Comt; from 1953 pensioner; *Died:* 4 Sept 1965.

ZAKHAROV, Vladimir Grigor'yevich (1901–1956) Composer; Pop Artiste of USSR from 1944; CP member from 1944; *Born:* 18 Oct 1901 at Bogodukhovskiye Rudniki, Donbass; *Educ:* 1927 grad Don Conservatory, Rostov-on-Don; *Career:* late 1929, after completing mil service, moved to Moscow and did radio work, conducted a local orchestra and wrote music for radio shows; from 1931 artistic dir (together with I.M. Kaz'min), Pyatnitskiy Russian Folk Choir; wrote many works and folk song arrangements for this choir; *Works:* songs: "Hail to the Soviet State"; "Song of Russia"; "Two Falcons", "Trough the Countryside"; "The Infantry"; "Katyusha"; "Our Strength in a Just Cause"; "Russian Beauty", etc; *Awards:* three Stalin Prizes (1942, 1946 and 1952); Order of Lenin; Order of the Red Banner of Labor; medals; *Died:* 13 July 1956 in Moscow.

ZAKHVATAYEV, Nikanor Dmitriyevich (? –1963) Mil commander; col-gen; *Educ:* grad Frunze Mil Acad; *Career:* 1918–20 fought in Civil War on side of Red Army; 1939–40 took part in Finno-Sov War as div commander; 1941–45 successively commanded div, Guards corps and 4th Guards Army, which took part in the Vienna offensive; fought against Japanese in Manchuria as army commander; 1945–55 served in Bel Mil Distr; from 1955 dep commander, Frunze Mil Acad; dep, USSR Supr Sov of 1955 convocation; *Awards:* Order of Lenin; Order of Suvorov, 1st Class; Order of Kutuzov, 1st Class; Order of the Red Star; Hero of the Sov Union; other orders and medals; *Died:* Feb 1963.

ZAKS, G.D. (1882–1937) Politician and govt official; CP member from 1918; *Born:* 1882; *Career:* member, Socialist-Revol Party; 1917 co-founder, Leftist Socialist-Revol Party; during 1917 Oct Revol member, Mil-Revol Comt and member, Extraordinary Investigation Commission; then dep chm, Petrograd City Duma; from Dec 1917 dep Pop Comr of Educ; dep chm, All-Russian Cheka; after 1918 July revolt of Leftist Socialist-Revol and suppression of Leftist Socialist-Revol Party co-founder, Communist Populist Party; Nov 1918 joined Bolshevik Party; fought in Civil War; then mil and govt work; arrested by State Security organs; *Died:* 1937 in imprisonment.

ZAKS (GLADNEV), Samuil Markovich (1884–1937) Writer; CP member from 1906; *Born:* 1884; *Career:* 1904, while in Germany, joined German Soc-Democratic movement; joined RSDRP and sided with Mensheviks; 1906 returned to Russia, switched to Bolsheviks and worked for Petersburg Okrug Party Org; from spring 1911 worked for periodical "Zvezda"; 1912–13 with newspaper "Pravda" and "Priboy" Publ House; 1913 arrested for his connections with an illegal workers' sick fund; 1915 sentenced to 12 months' fortress arrest for his connections with the "Priboy" Publ House; 1917 worked in Ukr; chm, Nikolayev Party Comt and ed, Nikolayev Party newspaper; 1918–20 worked for German CP; then worked for various govt and Party publ houses; ed, newspapers "Proletariy," "Krasnaya gazeta" and "Leningradskaya pravda"; prior to 14th Party Congress sided with "New Opposition" but dissociated himself from it after 15th Party Congress; from 1928 head, For Dept, TASS; 1930–31 worked for ed bd, "Malaya Sovetskaya Entsiklopediya" (Small Soviet Encyclopedia); from 1932 econ admin work; 1935 expelled from Party for alleged anti-Party activities and arrested by State Security organs; *Died:* 1937 in imprisonment.

ZAKUSHNYAK, Aleksandr Yakovlevich (1879–1930) Variety artiste, narrator and dramatic actor; *Born:* 1 Mar 1879 in Odessa; *Educ:* 1906 grad Philological Fac, Kiev Univ; *Career:* while still a student performed in dramatic and operetta shows and read Chekhov's humorous stories in variety programs; 1906 professional stage debut; with New Drama Assoc in Poltava and Tiflis; 1907–10 at Komissarzhevskaya Theater, Petersburg; 1908 toured abroad with Komissarzhevskaya; 1910 gave in Odessa his first 30 concerts – "Intimate Reading Evenings"; 1910–14 gave concerts in Odessa, Kiev, Kishinev, Kherson, Riga, Yaroslavl', Kostroma and Moscow; 1914–18 at the front; after demobilization performed in Moscow at New Theater, 1st RSFSR Theater, Chamber Theater and children's theaters; 1924 resumed his narration evenings; *Roles:* Prince Myshkin in *Idiot* (The Idiot), after Dostoyevsky; Raskol'nikov in *Prestupleniye i nakazaniye* (Crime and Punishment), after Dostoyevsky; Peleas in "Peleas and Melesandra"; Belidor in Maeterlinck's "Sister Beatrice"; Figaro in "The Marriage of Figaro"; the Fool in Shakespeare's "Tempest"; *Productions:* stage narrations: Mark Twain's "The Banknote"; Anatole France's "Revolt of the Angels" (1923–24); Maupassant's "In Port" (1925); Pushkin's *Yegipetskiye nochi* (Egyptian Nights) (1925–26); Gogol's "Taras Bul'ba" (1926–27); "Katyusha Maslova," after Lev Tolstoy (1928); Blok's *Dvenadtsat'* (The Twelve) (1929); stories by Chekhov, Maupassant, Jack London, Babel', Mark Twain, Sholom Aleichem, Korolenko, etc; *Publ: Vechera rasskaza* (Narration Evenings) (1926); *Vechera rasskaza. Vospominaniya, Teksty* (Narration Evenings. Memoirs. Texts) (1940); *Died:* 21 Apr 1930 in Leningrad.

ZALESSKIY, Grigoriy Denisovich (1902–1967) Internist; Dr of Med and prof from 1945; Hon Sci Worker of RSFSR from 1958; CP member from 1920; *Born:* 1902; *Educ:* 1926 grad Med Fac, Tomsk Univ; *Career:* 1928–31 asst prof, Chair of Physiotherapy and Balneology, Tomsk Univ; 1931–45 assoc prof, 1945–47 head, Chair of Fac Therapy, Omsk Med Inst; 1947 dir, Novosibirsk Inst of Postgrad Med Training; 1947–67 head, Chair of Fac Therapy, 1947–64 rector, Novosibirsk Med Inst; did research on Siberian health resorts, the permeability of blood capillaries, the role of viruses in the etiology and pathogenesis of rheumatism; organized med training at Novosibirsk Med Inst, where he also sponsored 25 cand and five doctor's theses; chm, Novosibirsk Med Soc; bd member, All-Union and All-Russian Soc of Therapists; chm, Novosibirsk Oblast Rheumatism Comt; member, All-Union Rheumatism Comt; member, ed council, journals "Terapevticheskiy arkhiv" and "Sovetskaya meditsina"; member, ed collegium, journal "Voprosy revmatizma"; member, Learned Council, RSFSR Min of Health; 1953 and 1959 attended Int Rheumatism Congresses in Geneva and Istanbul; dep, Novosibirsk City and Oblast Sov; member, Novosibirsk Oblast CPSU Comt; deleg, 22nd CPSU Congress; wrote over 50 works; *Publ: Pronitsayemost' stenki krovenosnykh kapillyarov pri revmatizme* (The Permeability of the Walls of Blood Capillaries in Rheumatism) (1949); *Awards:* Order of Lenin; Order of the Red Banner of Labor; Badge of Honor; *Died:* 1967 in Novosibirsk.

ZALESSKIY, Mikhail Dmitriyevich (1877–1946) Paleobotanist and geologist; prof from 1918; corresp member, USSR Acad of Sci from 1929; *Born:* 15 Sept 1877 in Oryol; *Educ:* 1900 grad Physics and Mathematics Fac, Petersburg Univ; *Career:* 1903–40 worked for Geological Comt and for research institutes which were formed from this in 1930; 1918–22 co-founder and prof, also dean, Physics and Mathematics Fac, Oryol Univ; specialized in paleozoic flora; described many new species and genera and made a basic study of fossil plants in many areas; established Permian age of Kuznets Basin's main coal seams; member of many sci soc, including Russian Paleontological Soc, All-Union Mineralogical Soc, London Geological Soc and Belgian Geological Soc; *Publ: Materialy po kamennougol'noy flore Donetskogo basseyna* (Material on the Carboniferous Flora of the Donets Basin) (1907); *Ocherk po voprosu obrazovaniya uglya* (A Study on the Formation of Coal) (1914); *Yestestvennaya istoriya odnogo uglya* (The Natural History of a Coal) (1915); *Paleozoyskaya flora Angarskoy serii* (The Paleozoic Flora of the Angara Series) (1918); *Permskaya flora ural'skikh predelov Angaridy* (The Permian Flora of the Angarida's Ural Ranges) (1927); *Kamennougol'naya flora Severnogo Kavkaza* (The Carboniferous Flora of the Northern Caucasus) (1934); coauthor, *Iskopayemaya flora srednego otdela kamennougol'nykh otlozheniy Donetskogo basseyna* (The Fossil Flora of the Donets Basin Coal Deposits' Mesosoma) (1938); coauthor, *Permskaya flora Pecherskogo Urala i khrebta Pay-Khoya* (The Permian Flora of the Pecheran Ural and the Pay-Khoy Peak) (1938), etc; *Awards:* Lomonosov Prize of the Russian Acad of Sci (1915); *Died:* 22 Dec 1946 in Leningrad.

ZALESSKIY, Viktor Feofanovich (1901–1963) Theater historian and critic; CP member from 1927; *Born:* 24 Sept 1901; *Educ:* 1922 grad Novorossiysk Univ, Odessa; *Career:* 1921 first work printed; 1931–32 dep ed, newspaper "Literaturnaya gazeta"; 1937–41 and 1946–51 dep chief ed, journal "Teatr"; 1932–36 dep dir, 2nd Moscow Arts Theater; *Publ: A.V. Polyakov. Ocherk o tvorchestve* (A.V. Polyakov. A Study of His Work) (1940); "A.K. Tarasova" (1949); "S.V. Giatsintova" (1949); "I.M. Tolchanov" (1952); "Suren Akimovich Kocharyan" (1955); *Iskusstvo aktyora* (The Actor's Art) (1959), etc; *Died:* 22 Nov 1963.

ZALESSKIY, Vyacheslav Konstantinovich (1871–1936) Plant physiologist and biochemist; corresp member, Ukr Acad of Sci from 1925; Hon Sci Worker of Ukr SSR from 1935; *Born:* 22 Aug 1871 in Khar'kov; *Educ:* 1893 grad Khar'kov Univ; *Career:* from 1895 trained for professorship at Khar'kov Univ; 1897 qualified as a Master of Botany; from 1900 junior prof, Novo-Aleksandriya Inst of Agric and Forestry; from 1903 prof, Chair of Plant Physiology, Khar'kov Univ; studied protein synthesis in living plant organism and role of carbohydrates in this process; proved that proteins could be formed by the higher plants from potassium nitrate and carbohydrates in darkness, without the participation of solar energy; studied the conversion and role of phosphorus and iron compounds in plants; *Publ: Usloviya obrazovaniya belkovykh veshchestv v rasteniyakh* (The Conditions for the Formation of Proteins in Plants) (1900); *Prevrashcheniye i rol' soyedineniy fosfora v rasteniyakh* (The Conversion and Role of Phosphorus Compounds in Plants) (1912); *Usloviya usvoyeniya ammiaka i aminokislot plesnevymi gribami* (The Conditions for Mould Fungi's Assimilation of Ammonia and Amino Acids) (1914); *K mikrobiologii pochvy* (The Microbiology of Soil (1922); *Metod anaerobioza dlya bor'by s pyl'noy golovnyoy pshenitsy* (The Anaerobiosis Method of Combatting Wheat Smut (1935), etc; *Died:* 10 Nov 1936.

ZALEZHSKIY, Vladimir Nikolayevich (Party names: YURIY; VLADIMIR) (1880–1957) Govt and Party official; lecturer; CP member from 1902; *Born:* 1880; *Career:* from 1899 active in revol movement; Party work in Volga area, Yekaterinoslav and Petersburg; 1911 helped smuggle Party lit; several times arrested by Tsarist authorities; 1912 exiled to Narym Kray; 1915 fled from exile; 1916 rearrested in Petersburg and tried by court martial; after 1917 Feb Revol member, Exec Commission, Petrograd RSDRP(B) Comt; then worked for Helsingfors Bolshevik Org; deleg at 6th RSDRP(B) Congress; after 1917 Oct Revol mil polit and admin work; Collegium member, Pop Comrt of Posts and Telegraphs; polit comr, Mil Acad; polit comr, 1st Cavalry Army; worked for CC, RCP(B); from 1922 research and teaching work; dept head, Moscow Physical Eng Inst; *Awards:* Order of Lenin; Order of the Red Banner of Labor; medals; *Died:* 2 Feb 1957.

ZALITE, Elina Augustovna (1898–1955) Lat writer and playwright; Hon Cultural Worker of Lat SSR from 1954; *Born:* 7 Oct 1898 in Gauen, Lat; *Career:* 1922 first work printed – translations of Est lyric verse; 1928–34 lit dir, Lat Arts Theater, Riga; *Publ:* comedy "A Dangerous Age" (1927); verse collection "Forest Flowers" (1930); drama "Purchased Happiness" (1932); collected essays "Sunny Egypt" (1937); plays: "Autumn Dews" (1939); "The Song of the Oriole" (1940); drama "Country Returned" (1948); musical comedy "In the Land of Blue Lakes" (1953), etc; *Died:* 7 Apr 1955.

ZALKA, Mate Mikhaylovich (Mate ZALKA) (1896–1937) Hungarian writer and revolutionary; CP member from 1920; *Born:* 23 Apr 1896 in vil Matolcz, Hungary, son of an innkeeper; *Educ:* completed business college; *Career:* during WW 1 nco in Austro-Hungarian Army; 1916 taken prisoner by Russians; 1918 organized Hungarian Red Guard unit in Khabarovsk and then operated with Kravchenko and Shchetinkin's partisan army; from 1920 in Red Army; commanded battalion on Polish Front and at Perekop; 1921–23 worked for All-Russian Cheka and State Polit Bd; from 1923 dipl courier; then directed a sculpture factory in Moscow; from 1925 dir, Theater of the Revol, Moscow; from 1928 worked for CC, CPSU(B); member, All–Russian Assoc of Proletarian Writers and secretariat member, Moscow Assoc of Proletarian Writers; 1924 first work printed; from 1936 fought in Spanish Civil War under the name of Gen Lukacs; commanded 12th Int Brigade; wrote in Hungarian; *Publ:* "The Story of a Hungarian Soldier" (1925); "Revolt" (1925); "The Death of a Communard" (1926); "Marching" (1927); "A Hero of Great 1914" (1929); "On the Blue Danube" (1930); novel "Doberdo" (1937), etc; *Died:* 11 June 1937 killed in action in Spain.

ZALKIND, I.A. (1885–1928) Diplomat; CP member from 1903; *Born:* 1885; *Career:* Party work in Petersburg, Yaroslavl' and Odessa; took part in 1905–07 Revol; 1908–17 in emigration; from late Nov 1917 worked for RSFSR Pop Comrt of For Affairs; May–Nov 1918 with Sov mission in Switzerland; 1920–21 member, Nizhniy Novgorod Province Party Comt; then worked for Pop Comrt of For Affairs; *Died:* 1928.

ZAL'KIND, Yuliy Sigizmundovich (1875–1948) Organic chemist; Hon Sci and Tech Worker of RSFSR from 1947; *Born:* 1875; *Educ:* 1898 grad Petersburg Univ; *Career:* from 1903 read course on chemistry of aromatic hydrocarbons at Petersburg Technol Inst; from 1930 prof, from 1934 head, Chair of Organic Chemistry, Leningrad Technol Inst; studied catalytic hydration of acetylene derivatives in the presence of colloidal palladium and platinum black; 1933 studied unsaturated compounds with chains similar to Vitamin A; also studied aromatic polynuclear derivatives; 1927 first to synthesize iodine phenanthrene; devised original method of synthesizing phenanthroamines from phenanthroles; also worked on the synthesis of various solvents, plasticizers and plastics; his methods were used for the ind production of camphor (from terpentine), tetrachlorphthalic acid, styrene, etc; *Publ: O deystvii magniya na efiry galoidozameshchyonnykh karbonovykh kislot* (The Action of Magnesium on Haloid-Substituted Carbonic Acid Esters) (1913); *Atsetilen i yego primeneniye* (Acetylene and Its Uses) (1925); coauthor, *Khimiya organicheskikh soyedineniy s otkrytoy tsep'yu* (The Chemistry of Open-Chain Organic Compounds) (4th ed, 1937); *Awards:* Order of the Red Banner of Labor; *Died:* 1948.

ZALOMOV, Pyotr Andreyevich (1877–1955) Politician; CP member from 1905; *Born:* 3 May 1877 in Nizhniy Novgorod, son of a worker; *Career:* metalworker; 1901–02 founded in Sormovo Soc-Democratic org; May 1901 member, Nizhniy Novgorod RSDRP Comt; helped organize 1902 May Day demonstration in Sormovo; carried red banner with the slogan "Down with Autocracy"; arrested and sentenced to exile for life to Eastern Siberia; with the aid of Gorky, who sent 300 rubles to arrange his escape, fled to Kiev, then lived illegally in Petersburg and Moscow; joined Bolsheviks; 1905 active in armed revolt in Moscow; organized battle squads; after 1917 Feb Revol helped organize soviets in Kursk Province; elected member, Sudzhan Exec Comt; fought in Civil War; founded "Krasnyy Oktyabr'" kolkhoz; prototype of Pavel Vlasov, the hero in Gorky's novel "Mat'" (Mother); *Publ: Vospominaniya* (Memoirs) (1939); *Died:* 18 Mar 1955.

ZALUTSKIY, Pyotr Antonovich (1887–1937) Party and govt official; CP member from 1907; *Born:* 1887; *Career:* from 1904 in revol movement; 1905 worked at Petersburg plants and joined Socialist-Revol Party; after 1905 Oct strike went to Siberia and worked on a railroad; 1906 left Socialist-Revol Party and 1907 joined Harbin RSDRP(B) org; 1909 moved to Vladivostok; member, Vladivostok RSDRP(B) Comt; repeatedly arrested; 1911 moved to Petersburg; worked at Franco-Russian Plant; helped found newspapers "Zvezda" and "Pravda"; attended Prague Party Conference; 1912 arrested and exiled for three years to Vologda Province; 1914 fled, returned to Petersburg and resumed Party work; member; Petrograd RSDRP(B) Comt; 1915 arrested and exiled for three years to Eastern Siberia; late 1916 fled to Petrograd; member, Exec Commission, Petrograd Party Comt and member, Russian Bureau, CC, RSDRP(B); after 1917 Feb Revol member, Petrograd Sov and founded its Soldiers' Section; member, Petrograd Party Comt; during 1917 Oct Revol member, Petrograd Mil-Revol Comt; during Civil War exec posts on Eastern, Southern and Western Fronts; member, All-Russian Centr Exec Comt of most convocations; 1921 Presidium member and secr, All-Russian Centr Exec Comt; member, Centr Commission for Purging the Party; secr, Ural and Northwestern Bureau, CC and secr, Leningrad Party Comt; member, CC, CPSU(B) of several convocations; at 14th and 15th Party Congresses sided with "New Opposition"; then member, Trotsky-Zinov'yevite Bloc; at 15th Congress expelled from the Party; 1928 readmitted to CPSU(B) after recanting his errors; 1929–32 chm, Lower Volga Kray Sovnarkhoz; then directed construction of electr plant in Kashira; 1934 again expelled from the Party for alleged anti-Party and anti-Sov activities and then arrested; *Died:* 1937 in imprisonment.

ZAMARIN, Yevgeniy Alekseyevich (1884–1962) Hydraulic eng; prof; member, All-Union Lenin Acad of Agric Sci from 1948; Hon Sci and Tech Worker of RSFSR from 1943; CP member from 1945; *Born:* 10 Dec 1884; *Educ:* 1916 grad Petrograd Polytech Inst; *Career:* 1916–25 eng engaged in surveying, designing and construction of hydrotech installations; 1925–29 lectured at Tashkent Water Mang Technicum; from 1932 prof, Moscow Inst of Water Trans Eng; developed theory of the movement of underground water in closed and open spillways; developed theory of hydrodynamic networks and its use for calculating and designing hydrotech installations; also studied theoretical principles of the calculation and design of water-storage irrigation installations, their reservoirs and through-put capacity; *Publ: Gidrotekhnicheskiye sooruzheniya* (Hydrotechnical Installations) (1933); *Dvizheniye gruntovykh vod pod gidrotekhnicheskimi sooruzheniyami* (The Movement of Ground Water Under Hydrotechnical Installations) (1934); *Gidrotekhnicheskiye seti dvizheniya* (Hydrotechnical Traffic Networks) (1937); *Proyektirovaniye gidrotekhnicheskikh sooruzheniy* (The Design of Hydrotechnical Installations) (1949); coauthor, *Gidrotekhnicheskiye sooruzheniya* (Hydrotechnical Installations) (1954), etc; *Awards:* Order of Lenin; other orders and medals; *Died:* 1962.

ZAMOSHKIN, Nikolay Ivanovich (1896–1960) Russian lit critic; *Born:* 6 Apr 1896 in Moscow; *Educ:* 1926 grad Ethnology Fac, Moscow Univ; *Career:* 1923 first work printed; until 1932 member, "Pereval" (The Pass) lit assoc; from 1944 directed creative prose writing seminar at Gorky Lit Inst; *Publ:* articles: "M. Prishvin's Work" (1928); "Literary Boundaries" (1930); "Stronger Than Death" (1936); "Gorky, Founder of the Journal 'Kolkhoznik'" (1937); "In Memory of Gorky" (1938); "Aleksey Tolstoy's 'Bread'" (1938); "The Search for Happiness. Notes on M. Prishvin's Children's Stories) (1940); "Sergeyev-Senskiy" (1940); "Mikhail Mikhaylovich Prishvin" (1958), etc; *Died:* 6 Oct 1960 in Moscow.

ZAMOTIN, Ivan Ivanovich (1873–1942) Lit historian; prof; member, Bel Acad of Sci from 1928; *Born:* 20 Oct 1873 in Bezhitsa Uyzed, Tver' Province; *Educ:* grad Petersburg History and Philology Inst; *Career:* after grad assoc prof, Petersburg Univ; from 1908 prof, Warsaw Univ; from 1922 prof of Bel universities; proponent of cultural history method in lit history; also did research on methods of teaching lit; wrote studies on work of Pushkin, Turgenev, Nekrasov, Serafimovich, Yanka Kupala, Yakub Kolas, etc; *Publ: Ranniye romanticheskiye veyaniya v russkoy literature* (Early Romantic Trends in Russian Literature) (1900); *Predaniye o Vadime Novgorodskom v russkoy literature* (The Vadim of Novgorod Tradition in Russian Literature) (1901); *Romantizm dvadtsatykh godov 19–go stoletiya v russkoy literature* (The Romanticism of the 1820's in Russian Literature) (1903); *Literaturnyye techeniya i literaturnaya kritika tridtsatykh godov* (The Literary Trends and Literary Criticism of the 'Thirties) (1908); *Ocherk istorii zhurnalistiki za pervuyu polovinu 19–go veka* (An Outline History of Journalism in the First Half of the 19th Century) (1909); *F.M. Dostoyevskiy v russkoy kritike* (F.M. Dostoyevsky in Russian Criticism) (1913); "M.Yu. Lermontov" (1914); *Na perelome. Skhema literaturnykh iskaniy 19–20–go verkov* (At the Turning Point. An Outline of the Literary Questing of the 19th and 20th Centuries) (1927); A.S. Pushkin. *Narys zhytstsya i tvorchastsi* (A.S. Pushkin. A Study of His Life and Work) (1937), etc; *Died:* 1942.

ZAMOYSKIY (real name: ZEVAL'SKIY), Pyotr Ivanovich (1896–1958) Russian writer; CP member from 1918; *Born:* 25 June 1896 in vil Sobolevka, Penza Province; *Educ:* studied at Higher Lit and Art Inst; 1928 grad Moscow Univ; *Career:* worked as herder, then waiter in an inn; revol work in rural areas; 1921 first work printed; helped organize the first kolkhozes; 1924–29 chm, All-Union Soc of Peasant Writers; *Publ:* collected stories: *Barskaya plyotka* (The Whip of the Gentry) (1925); *V derevne* (In the Country) (1925); *V uyezdnykh sugrobakh* (In Uyezd Snowdrifts) (1927); *Kanitel'* (Long-Winded Proceedings) (1929); *Dve pravdy* (Two Truths) (1932); *Sosedi* (Neighbors) (1934); *Utro* (Morning) (1937); novel *Lapti* (Bast Shoes) (4 vol, 1929–36); autobiographical trilogy, comprising the novelettes *Podpasok* (The Herdsboy) (1939), *Molodost'* (Youth) (1946) and *Voskhod* (Sunrise) (1957); story *Vladyki mira* (The Rulers of the World) (1956); children's stories *derevne* (In the Country), *Podpasok* (The Herdsboy), etc; *Died:* 21 July 1958 in Moscow.

ZAMYATIN, Yevgeniy Ivanovich (1884–1937) Russian writer; *Born:* 20 Jan 1884 in Lebedyan', now Lipetsk Oblast; *Educ:* 1908 grad Shipbuilding Dept, Petersburg Polytech Inst; *Career:* active in 1905–07 Revol; member, RSDRP; arrested and imprisoned; 1906–11 underground work; prior to WW 1 visited Constantinople, Alexandria and Jerusalem; 1916 emigrated to England; 1917 returned to Russia; lectured at Arts Center Studio; member, ed bd, "World Lit" Publ House; contributed to journals "Sovremennyy zapad", "Russkiy sovremennik" and "Zapiski mechtateley"; cofounder, "Serapion Brethren" lit group; sharply criticized in Sov press for publishing in England in English his novel "We," in effect a pamphlet criticizing Sov socialist soc; All-Russian Writers' Union took him to task for this work but he refused to give any explanation and demonstratively resigned from the Writers' Union; following this, his works were no longer printed in the USSR; 1932, after writing a letter to Stalin, managed to receive permission to emigrate; *Publ:* novelettes: *Uyezdnoye* (Uyezd Life) (1913); *Na kulichkakh* (In the Back of Beyond) (1909); *Ostrovityane* (The Islanders) (1918); story *Lovets chelovekov* (Catcher of Men) (1918); *Peshchera* (The Cave) (1920); "Mamay" (1920); novel "We" (published 1924 in England); *Narodnoye shutochnoye predstavleniye "Blokha"* (The Farcical Folk Presentation of "The Bed Bug") (1925); *Nechestivyye rasskazy* (Profane Stories) (1927); "Attila" (1928); *Sobraniye sochineniy* (Collected Works) (1929); *Navodneniye* (Flooding) (1930), etc; *Died:* 10 Mar 1937 in Paris.

ZAN'KOVETSKAYA (real name: ADASOVSKAYA), Mariya Konstantinovna (1860–1934) Actress and impressario; Pop Artiste of Ukr SSR from 1922; *Born:* 3 Aug in vil Zan'ki, Chernigov Province, daughter of an impoverished landowner; *Educ:* completed private girls boarding school in Chernigov; studied singing at Helsingfors Branch, Petersburg Conservatory; *Career:* while at boarding school frequently performed in amateur productions; 1882 professional debut in Yelizavetgrad with M.L. Kropivnitskiy's company; then performed with Ukr companies of M. Staritskiy, M. Sadovskiy, P. Saksaganskiy, I. Karpenko-Karyy and I. Mar'yanenko; performed in Petersburg, Moscow and many Russian cities; 1905 in Galicia; 1912–15 in Caucasus and Volga area; 1907, together with Sadovskiy, founded 1st Ukr Stationary Theater, Kiev; 1917 directed Pop Theater, Nezhin; 1918, together with Saksaganskiy, founded Pop Theater in Kiev (from 1922 Zan'kovetskaya Theater); until 1921 performed at this theater;

abandoned active stage work and taught drama at Zan'kovetskaya Studio; at 1st All-Russian Congress of Stage Workers demanded greater freedom for Ukr theater; her talent was highly rated by Stanislavskiy, Tchaikovsky, Lev Tolstoy and Chekhov; *Roles:* Natalka in Kotlyarevskiy's "Natalka Poltavka"; Kharitina in Karpenko-Karyy's *Naymichka* (The Hired Girl); Natal'ya in Mirskiy's "Limerivna"; Galya in Shevchenko's "Nazar Stodolya"; Olena and Zinka in Kropivnitskiy's *Miroyed, ili Pauk* (The World Eater, or the Spider) and *Dve sem'i* (Two Families); Aza in Staritskiy's *Tsyganka Aza* (Aza the Gypsy); Sof'ya in Karpenko-Karyy's *Goremychnaya* (The Wretched Women); Aksyusha in Ostrovskiy's *Les* (The Forest), etc; film roles in: "Natalka Poltavka"; *Batrachka* (The Hired Farm Girl); "Ostap Bandura"; *Died:* 4 Oct 1934 in Kiev.

ZARDALISHVILI, Yuza Frantsevich (1883–1943) Geo actor; Pop Artiste of Geo SSR from 1940; *Born:* 20 Nov 1883; *Career:* 1907 made stage debut; worked at Geo theaters in Kutaisi and Tiflis; after establishment of Sov rule in Geo appointed comr of all Tbilisi theaters, then comr, Rustaveli Theater; *Roles:* Levan Khimshiashvili in Eristavi's "Homeland"; Soleyman in Subatov-Yuzhin's "Treason"; Kvabulidze in Tsereteli's "Patara Kakhi"; Hamlet; Uriel' in Gutskov's "Uriel' Akosta"; Franz Moor in Schiller's "The Robbers", etc; *Died:* 13 May 1943.

ZARETSKIY, Mikhas' (KOSENKOV, Mikhail Yefimovich) (1902–1941) Bel writer; member, Bel Writers' Union from 1934; *Born:* 12 Jan 1902 in vil Vysokiy Gorodets, now Vitebsk Oblast, son of a vil deacon; *Educ:* prior to 1917 studied at Mogilev Theological Seminary; late 1920's and early 1930's studied in Lit Dept, Teachers' Training Fac, Bel Univ, Minsk; *Career:* 1919–20 schoolteacher; chm, volost' teachers' assoc; head, volost' educ dept; then member, Mogilev Educ and Socialist Culture Workers' Bd; attended 2nd All-Russian Congress of Educ Workers and was elected cand member, CC, Educ Workers' Union; 1920–27 in Sov Army; 1930–31 dep ed, newspaper "Savetskaya Belarus'"; from 1931 with Bel Acad of Sci; from 1924 member, "Maladnyak" proletarian writers' assoc; from 1927 co-founder and member, "Polymya" lit assoc; 1921 first work published; criticized for his novels "Paths and Roads" and "The Hypocrites" for his ironic attitude to Sov nationality policy in Bel and for criticizing Party opportunism and the collectivization policy; accused of preparing "a revolt of Bel nat democrats against the Sov regime"; 1936 arrested by NKVD and sentenced; *Publ:* collected stories and essays: "In the Depth of Life" (1925); "The Spring Sang" (1925); "Under the Sun" (1926); "Forty-Two Documents" (1926); "On the Railroad" (1928); "Journey to a New Land" (1929); "Shell Millstone" (1930); "Letters to an Acquaintance" (1930–31); "Spring 1930" (1931); "His Father's Son" (1932); novelette "The Naked Beast" (1926); plays: "Whirlwind in the Swamp" (1928); "White Roses" (1929); novel "Paths and Roads" (1928); his novel "The Hypocrites" was banned by the censors, but individual chapters were printed in the journal "Uzvyshsha" in 1929; *Died:* 13 June 1941 in imprisonment; posthumously rehabilitated.

ZARIN'SH (ZARIN), Yanis Petrovich (1886–1965) Party and govt official; CP member from 1911; *Born:* 1886; *Career:* construction worker; participated in 1905–07 Revol in Riga; his apartment was used to house underground printing house of Riga Party Comt; at the start of WW 1 member, Lat Northern RSDRP Group in Moscow; 1916–17 in exile and emigration; after 1917 Feb Revol helped organize and lead Lat Red Guard detachments in Moscow; participated in 1917 Oct Revol; 1917–22 exec Party and admin work in Red Army; 1922–44 econ admin work; June–Nov 1941 militiaman, 5th Div, Moscow's Frunze Rayon; from 1944 dir, Lat Museum of the Revol; *Died:* 27 Mar 1965.

ZARKHI, Natan Abramovich (1900–1935) Playwright; Hon Art Worker of RSFSR from 1935; *Born:* 1900; *Career:* wrote plays and film scripts; *Works:* scripts for films: *Osobnyak Golubinykh* (The Golubin House) (1925); *Mat'* (Mother), after Gorky (1926); *Konets Sankt-Petersburga* (The End of St Petersburg) (1927); *Pobeda zhenshchiny* (A Woman's Victory), after Leskov (1927); coauthor, "Bulat-batyr" (1928); coauthor, *Goroda i gody* (Cities and Years) (1930); coauthor, *Samyy schastlivyy* (The Happiest Man) (1935); *Pobeda* (Victory) (1938); play *Ulitsa radosti* (The Street of Joy) (1932); unfinished and partially published book *Kinodramaturgiya* (Cinema Drama); *Died:* 17 July 1935.

ZARUBIN, Georgiy Nikolayevich (1900–1958) Dipl with rank of amb extraordinary and plen; Party official; CP member from 1919; *Born:* 1900 in vil Golitsyno, Penza Province; *Educ:* 1928–30 studied at Stalin Ind Acad; *Career:* from 1913 messenger boy; 1918–24 in Red Army; 1931–35 dir, Molotov Ind Acad; 1935–38 head, Main Educ Institutions Bd, USSR Pop Comrt of Light Ind; 1938–40 comr-gen, Sov Section, New York Int Exhibition; 1940–41 head, Consular Dept, USSR Pop Comrt of For Affairs; 1941–44 head, Dept for USA, USSR Pop Comrt of For Affairs; 1944–46 USSR amb to Canada; 1946–52 USSR amb to Great Britain; from 1952 cand member, CC, CPSU; 1952–57 USSR amb to USA; 1958 USSR Dep Min of For Affairs; attended various int conferences and talks; *Died:* 24 Nov 1958.

ZARUDIN, Nikolay Nikolayevich (1899–1937) Russian writer and poet; *Born:* 1 Oct 1899 in Pyatigorsk; *Career:* 1921 first work printed; 1924–32 chm, "Pereval" (The Pass) lit assoc; 1930 criticized for "reactionary attitudes," including the idealization of everything Russian, down to patriarchal rural life; arrested by State Security organs; *Publ:* verse collection *Sneg vishennyy* (The Cherry Snow) (1923); selected verse *Polem-yunost'yu* (By the Field of Youth) (1928); documentary novel *Tridtsat' nochey na vinogradnike* (Thirty Nights in the Vineyard) (1933); collected stories *Strana smysla* (The Land of Sense) (1934); coauthor, *Nash drug Ovakim Petrosyan. Rasskazy ob Armenii* (Our Friend Ovakim Petrosyan. Stories of Armenia) (1935), etc; *Died:* 1937 in imprisonment; posthumously rehabilitated.

ZARUDNAYA, Varvara Mikhaylovna (1857–1939) Singer (lyric soprano); singing teacher; *Born:* 17 Dec 1857 in Yekaterinoslav; *Educ:* 1882 grad Petersburg Conservatory; *Career:* took part in Balakirev, Borodin and Rimsky-Korsakov's musical soirees; performed at opera theaters in Kiev and Tiflis; together with the composer M.M. Ippolitov-Ivanov (her husband from 1883), helped found Tiflis Musical College; 1893–1924 prof, Moscow Conservatory; *Roles:* Ruf' and Zorayya in Ippolitov-Ivanov's "Ruf'" and "Azra"; Mariya in Tchaikovsky's "Mazepa"; the Godmother in Tchaikovsky's *Charodeyka* (The Sorceress), etc; *Died:* 14 Mar 1939 in Moscow.

ZARUDNYY, Aleksandr Sergeyevich (1863–?) Lawyer; defense counsel in polit cases; *Born:* 1863; *Educ:* grad Law College in Petersburg; *Career:* court official; 1901 began lawyer's career and specialized in defending polit cases; defense counsel in trial of: "Romanovites"; 1905 1st Sov of Workers' Dep; Peasants' Union CC; Lt Shmidt; "Memory of Azov" case; attempt on life of Nicholas II; partisans; Beylis case; 1917 joined Pop Socialist Party and was Provisional Govt's Dep Min of Justice; May 1917 resigned; 24 July 1917 appointed Min of Justice, 3rd Provisional Govt; late Aug 1917, after Kerenskiy established the Directorate, left Provisional Govt; while Min of Justice appointed commission for release of July 1917 demonstrators; 1918 left Pop Socialist Party; from 1933 pensioner; *Died:* date and place of death unknown.

ZASLAVSKIY, David Iosifovich (1880–1965) Satirist, feuilletonist and lit critic; CP member from 1934; *Born:* 13 Jan 1880 in Yelizavetgrad, now Kirovograd; *Educ:* 1910 grad Kiev Univ; *Career:* joined Mensheviks in Kiev, then member of Bund; prior to 1917 Oct Revol worked for newspapers "Kiyevskaya mysl'," "Kiyevskiye otkliki," "Den'," "Severnyye zapiski," "Novaya zhizn'," "Sovremennyy mir" and "Nasha zarya" under various pseudonyms; edited several Bund and Menshevik periodicals; 1907 attended 5th (London) RSDRP Congress; several times arrested and imprisoned; during Civil War in the Ukr; 1919, after establishment of Bolshevik rule in Kiev, wrote a letter to newspaper "Kommunist" confessing his former "errors" and renouncing politics; 1924 wrote letter to newspaper "Pravda" further recanting his Menshevik views; 1925 resumed press work as feuilletonist for Leningrad "Krasnaya gazeta" then for "Leningradskaya pravda"; 1926–28 worked for ed staff, newspaper "Izvestiya"; from 1928 contributed to newspaper "Pravda"; 1934 admitted to CP on Stalin's personal recommendation; *Publ:* "G. V. Plekhanov" (1923); *Lassal'* (Lassales) (1925); "Saltykov-Shchedrin" (1939); *Fel'yetony* (Feuilletons) (1949); "F.M. Dostoyevskiy" (1956); *Den' za dnyom. Izbrannyye proizvedeniya* (Day by Day. Selected Works) (1960), etc; *Awards:* Order of Lenin, two Orders ot the Red Banner of Labor (1955 and 1962); *Died:* 27 Mar 1965.

ZASLAVSKIY, Pyotr Savel'yevich (1890–1967) Party official; CP member from 1905; *Born:* 14 July 1890; *Career:* from age 12 messenger boy for a coal dealer and in a printing house in Nikolayev; 1909, 1912 and 1914 arrested; exiled to Vologda Province and Narym Kray; helped establish Sov rule in Odessa region; 1917–18 secr, Odessa Province RSDRP(B) Comt; 1918 secr, Petrograd Party Comt; 1919–29 exec Party work: secr,

Ivanovo-Voznesensk Province Party Comt; with Moscow Party Comt; member, Siberian Bureau, CC, RCP(B); secr, Novonikolayevsk Province Party Comt; with CC, RCP(B); secr,Gomel', then Kostroma Province Party Comt; from 1931 chm, CC, Finance and Bank Workers' Union; 1938–40 dep chief ed, "BSE" large Soviet Endyclopedia);1940–56 state arbitrator; deleg, 11th – 15th Party Congresses; from 1956 pensioner; *Died:* 22 Feb 1967.

ZASLONOV, Konstantin Sergeyevich (partisan alias: Uncle Kostya) (1910–1942) Railroad worker; Bel partisan leader during WW 2; CP member from 1942; *Born:* 7 Jan 1910 in Ostashkov, Tver' Province; *Career:* metalworker by trade; from 1937 head, Roslavl' Locomotive Depot; from 1939 head, Orsha Locomotive Depot; 1941 after occupation of Orsha by German troops turned partisan and organized a detachment; on orders of Partisan Staff registered at Orsha Labor Exchange; the Germans, in sore need of railroad specialists, appointed him head, Orsha Locomotive Depot; late 1941 a partisan group under his command skilfully sabotaged the whole locomotive park and Orsha railroad junction; when his underground activities were discovered by German mil authorities, hid in Bel forests; unified small partisan groups and became commander, Orsha Partisan Brigade; *Awards:* Hero of Sov Union (1943, posthumously); *Died:* 14 Nov 1942 killed in action, in Orsha a monument was erected to him; a film and a play entitled "Konstantin Zaslonov" were written in his hon.

ZASULICH, Vera Ivanovna (1849–1919) Revolutionary; journalist and critic; *Born:* 8 Aug 1849 in vil Mikhaylovka, Smolensk Province, daughter of a nobleman; *Educ:* completed private girls boarding school in Moscow; *Career:* 1867 passed examinations to qualify as private tutor; for a year worked as clerk to a rural magistrate in Serpukhov; then worked at a book-binding workshop; late 1868 met the revol Nechayev and served as his go-between to transmit correspondence; 1869–71 imprisoned for her connections with Nechayev; from 1875 went underground and worked for Kiev Populist circle; 24 Jan 1878 shot Mayor of Petersburg Trepov; her assassination bid and subsequent acquittal by a jury brought her considerable renown; 1879 joined "Chyornyy peredel" (Land Redistribution) Populist org; from early 1880 in emigration; 1883, together with Plekhanov, founded first Russian Marxist group – Liberation of Labor; corresponded with Marx and Engels; on friendly terms with Engels; winter 1889–1900 illegally resided in Petersburg, where she met Lenin; member, ed staff, newspaper "Iskra" and journal "Zarya"; 1903, after 2nd RSDRP Congress, sided with Mensheviks; 1905 returned to Russia; helped lead Liquidationists; during WW 1 sided with Social Chauvinists; 1917 member, "Unity" Defensist group; opposed to 1917 Oct Revol; translated Marx's "The Poverty of Philosophy" and Engels' "The Development of Socialism from Utopia to Science" and "Social Relations in Russia"; published journalistic and lit-critical articles in the collection "Sotsial-demokrat," in the German journals "Die Neue Zeit" and "Gleichheit" and in the Legal Marxist publications "Novoye slovo," "Nauchnoye obozreniye," "Zarya," "Iskra," etc; *Publ: Vol'ter*(Voltaire) (1893); *Zhan–Zhak Russo* (Jean-Jacques Rousseau) (1898); *Sbornik statey* (Collected Articles) (1907); various polemical articles, including: "Our Modern Literary Contradictions" (1890); "The Feudal Lining of 'Progressive Speeches'" (1900); "N. A. Dobrolyubov" (1901); "A Nihilist's Career" (1892); "Sergey Mikhaylovich Kravchinskiy /Stepnyak/" (1896), etc; *Died:* 8 May 1919 in Petrograd.

ZASYAD'KO, Aleksandr Fyodorovich (1910–1963) Govt official; CP member from 1931; *Born:* 7 Sept 1910 in Gorlovka; *Educ:* 1935 grad Donetsk Mining Inst; *Career:* 1935–43 exec eng and tech work in Donets Basin; 1943–47 USSR Dep Pop Comr of Coal Ind; USSR Dep Min for Construction of Fuel Enterprises; 1947–56 USSR Min of Coal Ind for Western Regions, then USSR Min of Coal Ind; 1956–57 Ukr Min of Coal Ind; 1957 member, then dep chm, USSR Gosplan; from 1958 dep chm, USSR Council of Min; 1960–62 chm, State Sci Econ Council, USSR Council of Min; from 1952 member, CC, CPSU; dep, USSR Supr Sov of 2nd, 4th, 5th and 6th convocations; *Publ: Toplivno-energeticheskaya promyshlennost' SSSR* (USSR Fuel and Power Industry); *Awards:* Hero of Socialist Labor (1957); Order of Lenin; other orders and medals; *Died:* 5 Sept 1963.

ZATONSKIY, Vladimir Petrovich (1888–1940) Govt and Party official; CP member from 1917; *Born:* 8 Aug 1888 in vil Lysets, Podol'ya Province, son of a volost clerk; *Educ:* 1912 grad Kiev Univ; *Career:* from 1912 taught physics at Kiev Polytech Inst; 1905 joined RSDRP and sided with Mensheviks; several times arrested for revol activities; after 1917 Feb Revol broke with Mensheviks and Mar 1917 joined RSDRP(B); from May 1917 member, Kiev RSDRP(B) Comt; helped lead 1917 Oct revolt in Kiev; member, Kiev Revol Comt; Nov 1917 chm, Kiev RSDRP(B) Comt; Dec 1917 at 1st All-Ukr Congress of Soviets elected to Pop Secretariat of Ukr SSR (Ukr govt); head, Secretariat (Pop Comrt) of Educ; Mar 1918 at 2nd All-Ukr Sov Congress of Soviets elected chm, Ukr Centr Exec Comt; headed Ukr Centr Comt deleg at 4th Extraordinary All-Russian Congress of Soviets and supported Lenin's stand on the necessity of concluding the 1918 Brest Peace Treaty; member, Org Bureau to convene the 1st Congress of CP(B) Ukr, at which he was elected to the CC; helped direct underground Ukr Party orgs; from Mar 1919 Ukr Pop Comr of Educ; 1919–20 member, Revol Mil Council, 12th, 13th then 14th Armies and Revol Mil Council, Southern Front; member, All-Ukr Revol Comt; deleg at 10th RCP(B) Congress; member, Commission for the Nationality Problem at this congress; helped crush Kronstadt Mutiny; 1923 Ukr Pop Comr of Educ; 1924–26 mil work; 1927–33 chm, Centr Control Commission, CP(B) Ukr and Ukr Pop Comr of Workers and Peasants' Inspection; 1933–38 Ukr Pop Comr of Educ; member and Politburo member, CC, CP(B) Ukr; member, Centr Control Commission, CP(B) Ukr; deleg at 10th–17th CPSU(B) Congresses; at 17th Party Congress elected cand member, CC, CPSU(B); Presidium member, USSR Centr Exec Comt; Presidium member, All-Ukr Centr Exec Comt; member, Ukr Acad of Sci from 1929; arrested by state Security organs; *Awards:* Order of the Red Banner; *Died:* Nov 1940 in imprisonment; posthumously rehabilitated.

ZATYRKEVICH–KARPINSKAYA, Anna Petrovna (1856–1921) Actress; *Born:* 22 Jan 1856 in vil Sribno, near Poltava, daughter of a landowner; *Career:* 1882 performed with amateur drama company in Romny; 1883–92 with M. L. Kropivnitskiy's Company; 1892–97 with N. K. Sadovskiy's Company, then O. Z. Suslov and T. P. Kolesnichenko's companies; 1919–20 at Kiev Pop Theater; performed for Red Army units; *Roles:* Tat'yana in Kotlyarevskiy's *Soldat-charodey* (The Sorcerer-Soldier); Ryndychka in Kropivnitskiy's *Po revizii* (After the Audit); Fyokla in Kropivnitskiy's *Poka solntse vzoydyot, rosa ochi vyyest*(Before the Sun Rises, the Dew Will Dissolve Your Eyes); Stekha in Kropivnitskiy's *Miroyed, ili Pauk* (The World Eater, or the Spider); Anna in Karpenko-Karyy's *Bestalannaya* (The Luckless Woman); Limerivna in Mirnyy's "Limerivna"; Sekleta in Staritskiy's *Za dvumya zaytsami* (After Two Hares); Stekha in Shevchenko's "Nazar Stodolya," etc; *Died:* 19 Sept 1921 in Romny.

ZAVALISHIN, Aleksandr Ivanovich (1891–1939) Writer; CP member from 1920; *Born:* 30 June 1891 in Kulevchinskiy Settlement, Nikolayevskaya vil, Orenburg Region; *Career:* as a child worked as hired farmhand; then clerk and statistician; took part in Revol and civil War in Moscow, Southern Urals ans Siberia; after 1917 Oct Revol public, lit and ed work; from 1922 lived in Moscow and worked for newspaper "Bednota"; 1925 first work printed; wrote short humorous stories and one-act plays for rural amateur drama groups; arrested by State Security organs; *Publ:* stories: *Pervyy blin* (The First Pancake) (1927); *Pepel* (Ash) (1928); plays: *Chastnoye delo* (A Private Affair) (1929); *Partbilet* (Party Card) (1927); *Fal'shivaya bumazhka* (The Forged Banknote) (1929); *Stroyfront* (The Construction Front) (1932); collected essays *Sveszhaya borozda* (The Fresh Furrow) (1934) and *Khata Budyonnogo* (Budyonnyy's Hut) (1938); *Died:* 1939 in imprisonment; posthumously rehabilitated.

ZAVARIN, Aleksandr Pavlovich (1903–1959) Designer of cinematographic equipment; assoc prof; CP member from 1946; *Born:* 1903; *Educ:* 1930 grad Nizhniy Novgorod Univ; *Career:* 1930–45 taught at Leningrad Inst of Film Eng and Inst of Fine Mech; from 1946 at Inst of Nat Econ, Samarkand; 1933 helped design "Gekord" mobile cinecamera; *Publ: Uchebnoye posobiye po proyektsionno-zvukovosproizvodyashchey apparature* (A Training Manual on Projection and Sound Reproduction Apparatus) (1940); coauthor, *Zvukovaya kinoperedvizhka "Gekord"* (The "Gekord" Mobile Sound Cinecamera) (1941); *Died:* 1959.

ZAVARITSKIY, Aleksandr Nikolayevich (1884–1952) Geologist and petrographer; member, USSR Acad of Sci from 1939; prof; *Born:* 14 July 1884 in Ufa; *Educ:* 1909 grad Petersburg Mining Inst; *Career:* 1921–40 prof, Leningrad Mining Inst; from 1933 worked for USSR Acad of Sci; carried out geological and petrographical surveys in the Urals, Kaz and the Caucasus; from 1931 studied active volcanoes in Kamchatka and extinct volcanoes in Arm; 1932 studied ultrabasic eruptive rocks on Mount Ray-Iz in the Polar Urals; 1937 studied alkaline rocks in Berdyaush Pluton; 1939 studied alkaline rocks in Ilmen' Mountains; developed geometrical method of analysing composition of rocks with the aid of diagrams, thereby laying the basis for a new branch of sci – petrochemistry; improved universal-optic method using thin microsections; *Publ: Fiziko-khimicheskiye osnovy petrografii izverzhennykh porod* (The Physicochemical Principles of the Petrography of Eruptive Rocks) (1926); *Gora Magnitnaya i yeyo mestorozhdeniya zheleznykh rud* (Mount Magnitnaya and Its Iron Ore Deposits) (1922–27); *Geologicheskiy ocherk mestorozhdeniy mednykh rud na Urale* (A Geological Study of Copper Ore Deposits in the Urals) (1927–29); *Periodotitovyy massiv Ray-Iz v Polyarnom Urale* (The Ray-Iz Peridotite Massif in the Polar Urals) (1932); *Petrografiya Berdyaushskogo plutona* (The Petrography of Berdyaush Pluton) (1937); *Nekotoryye osnovynyye voprosy geologii Urala* (Some Basic Aspects of the Geology of the Urals) (1941); *Vvedeniye v petrokhimiyu* (An Introduction to Petrochemistry) (1944); *Vvedeniye v petrokhimiyu izverzhennykh gornykh porod* (An Introduction to the Petrochemistry of Eruptive Rocks) (1950), etc; *Awards:* two Orders of Lenin; two Stalin Prizes (1943 and 1946); Lenin Prize (1958); *Died:* 23 July 1952.

ZAVARZIN, Aleksey Alekseyevich (1886–1945) Histologist; Dr of Med from 1913; prof from 1916; member, USSR Acad of Sci from 1943; member, USSR Acad of Med Sci from 1944; *Born:* 25 Mar 1886; *Educ:* 1907 grad Natural Sci Dept, Fac of Physics and Mathematics, Petersburg Univ; *Career:* after grad asst to prof A. S. Dogel', Chair of Histology, Petersburg Univ; 1913 defended doctor's thesis on the sensory nerve system and optic ganglia of insects; from 1916 prof, Chair of Histology, Perm' Branch, Petrograd Univ; from 1922 prof, Chair of Histology, Petrograd (Leningrad) Mil Med Acad; 1932 founded Dept of Gen Morphology, All-Union Inst of Experimental Med; from 1944 also dir, Moscow Inst of Cytology, Histology and Embryology, USSR Acad of Sci; did research on the comparative histology of blood, connective tissue, the epithelium and the nervous system; also studied tissue evolution, the morphological concept of histological structure, etc; devised theory of parallelisms, according to which tissues subject to the same forms of interrelationship between organism and environment display similar structural and evolutionary features in different types of animals; this theory came under heavy criticism during Stalin's rule; founder, Leningrad Soc of Anatomists, Histologists and Embryologists; ed, journal "Arkhiv anatomii, gistologii i embriologii"; *Publ:* doctor's thesis, *Gistologicheskoye issledovaniye chuvstvitel'noy nervnoy sistemy i opticheskikh gangliyev nasekomykh* (A Histological Investigation of the Sensory Nervous System and Optic Ganglia of Insects) (1913); *Kurs gistologii i mikroskopicheskoy anatomii* (A Course on Histology and Microscopic Anatomy) (5th ed, 1939); *Kratkoye rukovodstvo po embriologii cheloveka i pozvonochnykh zhivotnykh* (A Short Guide to the Embryology of Man and Vertebrate Animals) (4th ed, 1939); *Ocherki po evolyutsionnoy gistologii nervnoy sistemy* (Studies in the Evolutionary Histology of the Nervous System) (1941); *Ocherki evolyutsionnoy gistologii krovi i soyedinitel'noy tkani* (Studies in the Evolutionary Histology of Blood and Connective Tissue) (2 vol, 1945–47), etc; *Awards:* Stalin Prize (1942); *Died:* 25 July 1945 in Moscow.

ZAVENYAGIN, Avraamiy Pavlovich (1901–1956) Govt official; CP member from 1917; *Born:* 14 Apr 1901 in Uzlovaya, Moscow Oblast, son of a laborer; *Educ:* 1930 grad Moscow Mining Acad; *Career:* 1917–23 Party and govt work: secr, Uzlovaya Uyezd Party Comt; head , div polit dept; secr, Yuzovka Okrug Party Comt, etc; after grad acad dir, Leningrad State Inst for Designing Metallurgical Plants; 1931–32 with Supr Sovnarkhoz; then dir, Dzerzhinskiy Plant and dir, Magnitogorsk Metallurgical Combine; 1937–38 Dep Pop Comr of Heavy Ind; from 1938 dir, Noril'sk Metallurgical Combine; during and after WW 2 USSR Dep Pop Comr (Min) of Internal Affairs; directed construction of major enterprises; also worked for USSR Council of Min; 1953–55 USSR Dep Min of Medium Machine-Building; from 1955 dep chm, USSR Council of Min and USSR Min of Medium Machine-Building; at 17th (1934) and 19th (1952) Party Congress elected cand member, CC, CPSU; at 20th (1956) Party Congress elected member, CC, CPSU; dep, USSR Supr Sov; *Awards:* twice Hero of Socialist Labor; Stalin Prize; six Orders of Lenin; medals; *Died:* 31 Dec 1956; buried on Moscow's Red Square.

ZAV'YALOVA, Yelizaveta Nikolayevna (1888–1952) Educationist; specialist in training of defective children; *Born:* 8 Apr 1888; *Career:* until 1916 worked at elementary schools; in this period began to cooperate with the psychiatrist G. Rossolimo, studying mentally retarded children; from 1916 concentrated on the study and training of mentally backward children and directed an auxiliary school in Moscow; after 1917 Oct Revol helped organize state system of auxiliary training for retarded children; lectured at 2nd Moscow Univ and then taught future defectologists at Lenin Teachers' Training 1st; from 1931 methodological research at Inst of Defectology; did research on methods of teaching reading and writing to children with severe speech defects, such as alexia and agraphia; studied individual characteristics of mentally retarded children; *Publ: Opyt obucheniya gramote detey s lokal'nymi narusheniyami* (Experience in Teaching Reading and Writing to Children with Local Disturbances) (1941); *Sostoyaniye orfograficheskikh navykov u uchenikov vspomogatel'noy shkoly* (The Condition of Orthographic Habits in Auxiliary School Pupils) (1947); *Individual'nyy podkhod k uchashchimsya vspomogatel'noy shkoly v protsesse obucheniya ikh gramote* (The Individual Approach to Auxiliary School Pupils in the Process of Teaching Them Reading and Writing) (1952); *Died:* 23 Sept 1952.

ZAYDSHNUR, Isaak Arkad'yevich (? –1967) Hygienist; specialist in labor hygiene; *Born:* date and place of birth unknown; *Career:* for several decades assoc, Centr Inst of Labor Protection, All-Union Centr Trade-Union Council; member, ed council, journal "Gigiyena truda i professional'nyye zabolevaniya"; contributed to study of ind microclimate; did research on physiology of vision, analysis of effects of infra-red radiation on workers, etc; studied ways of improving sanitary working conditions in synthetic materials ind; drew up standards for labor protextion; helped revise sanitary standards for design of ind premises; trained many ind-sanitation specialists; *Died:* 1967.

ZAYONCHKOVSKIY, Andrey Medardovich (1862–1926) Mil historian; infantry gen; *Born:* 8 Dec 1862 in Orel Province, of noble descent; *Educ:* completed Orel Mil High School, grad Nikolay Eng Collge; 1888 grad Nikolay Gen Staff Acad; *Career:* during Russo-Japanese War commanded infantry regt and brigade; from 1912 commander, 37th Infantry Div; from Mar 1915 commanded 30th Corps; July–Oct 1916 commander, 47th Corps and Dobrudzha Army; Oct 1916–Apr 1917 commander, 18th Corps; May 1917 appointed chief of staff, 13th Army; 1922–26 prof, Red Army Mil Acad and senior instructor on the history of wars; *Publ: Uchebnik prikladnoy taktiki* (A Textbook of Applied Tactics) (2 vol, 1889–1900); *Vostochnaya voyna 1853–1856 v svyazi s sovremennoy politicheskoy obstanovkoy* (The 1853–1856 Eastern War in Connection with the Contemporary Political Situation) (2 vol, 1908–13); *Oborona Sevastopolya* (The Defense of Sebastopol) (2nd ed, 1904); *Strategicheskiy ocherk voyny 1914–1918* (A Strategic Study of the 1914–1918 War) (vol 6–7, 1923); *Podgotovka Rossii k imperialisticheskoy voyne* (Russia's Preparation for the Imperialistic War) (1926); *Podgotovka Rossii k mirovoy voyne v mezhdunarodnom otnoshenii* (The International Aspects of Russia's Preparations for the World War) (1926); *Mirovaya voyna 1914–1918* (The 1914–1918 World War) (3rd ed, 3 vol, 1938–39); *Died:* 1926.

ZAYTSEV, Filipp Adamovich (1877–1957) Zoologist; member, Geo Acad of Sci from 1941; Hon Sci Worker of Geo SSR from 1946; *Born:* 13 Mar 1877; *Educ:* 1900 grad Petersburg Univ; *Career:* from 1901 worked at Woman's Med Inst; from 1911 co-founder and head, Entomological Study Center, Tiflis Botanical Garden and Dept of Entomology, Caucasian Museum; from 1927 prof and rector, Tiflis Polytech Inst; from 1941 dir, Inst of Zoology, Geo Acad of Sci; specialized in taxonomy, fauna and biology of insects and other arthropods of the Caucasus; *Publ: Zametki o zhyostkokrylykh Kavkaza i sopredel'nykh stran* (Notes on the Coleopters of the Caucasus and Contiguous Countries) (1916); *Materialy o faune zhyostkokrylykh Kavkaza* (Material on the Coleopter Fauna of the Caucasus) (1915–16); *Vodyanyye zhuki kollektsii Mochul'skogo* (Water Beetles of the Mochul'skiy Collection) (1916); *Khlopkovaya sovka i yeyo gusenitsa-"korovochnyy cherv"* (The Cotton-Ball Worm and Its Larva - the "Box Worm") (1924); *Kak borot'sya s tlyoy na khlopchatnike* (How to Combat Aphids on Cotton Plants) (1925), etc; *Died:* 10 June 1957.

ZAYTSEV, Fyodor Ivanovich (1894–1960) Party official; CP member from 1915; *Born:* 1894 in vil Kolpni, now Orel Oblast, son of a worker; *Career:* from age 12 worked at Yuzovka Metallurgical Plant, Donbass; 1917–21 secr, Yuzovka Party Comt; 1918 also asst chm, Yuzovka Exec Comt; 1919 chm, underground revol comt; 1922–23 chm, Bakhmut Province Control Commission; 1924–29 with Workers and Peasants' Inspection and CP(B)

Ukr Centr Control Commission; then Presidium member and secr, CP(B) Ukr Centr Control Commission; 1929–30 secr, Lugansk Okrug, then City Party Comt; 1931 secr, Dnepropetrovsk City Party Comt; from Feb 1932 secr, CC, CP(B) Ukr, then secr, Smolensk Oblast CPSU(B) Comt; plen for Tatar ASSR, Party Control Commission, CC, CPSU(B); from 1939 govt work; fought in WW 2; then pensioner; at 15th and 16th Party Congresses elected member, CC, CPSU(B) Centr Control Commission; at 17th Party Congress elected member, Party Control Commission, CC, CPSU(B); member, All-Russian Centr Exec Comt; *Died:* 1 Sept 1960.

ZAYTSEV, (TAL–MARZA), Georgiy Vasil'yevich (1895–1921) Chuvash writer, playwright, actor and stage dir; *Born:* 27 Sept 1895 in vil Ubeyevo, Simbirsk Province; *Educ:* 1909–14 studied at Chuvash Teachers' Training School, Simbirsk; from 1917 studied at Northeastern Archeological and Ethnographical Inst, Kazan'; *Career:* from 1916 teacher; from 1919 acted with Chuvash Touring Theater, Kazan'; from 1920 with Chuvash Company, Polit Dept, Transcaspian Army; *Roles:* Vanyuk in his own play "Who Is to Blame? "; Potap Maksimovich in *V lesakh* (In the Forests), after Mel'nikov-Pecherskiy; Akhov in Ostrovskiy's *Ne vsyo kotu maslenitsa* (All Good Things Come to an End); the Judge in Pavlov's *Na Sude* (On Trial), etc; *Works:* plays: "Who Is to Blame? "; "The Guilt of the Strong"; "Ukhater"; "Sil'bi" (1927); "The Dawn of a New Life"; translated into Chuvash: "Les Caprices de Scapin"; Schiller's "Die Räuber"; Pisemskiy's *Gor'kaya sud'bina* (A Bitter Fate); Lunacharskiy's *Korolevskiy bradobrey* (The King's Barber), etc; *Died:* 8 Dec 1921.

ZAYTSEV, Ivan Afinogenovich (1863–1936) Puppet-master; Hon Artiste of RSFSR from 1935; *Born:* 1863; *Career:* 1870 tumbler with Ginne Circus, Moscow; then acrobat, sword-swallower and ventriloquist at various circuses; from 1890's gave puppet shows in show-booths, country fairs and town squares; made his own puppets, including some mechanical ones; 1932, together with his partner A. D. Triganova, began to perform at Centr Puppet Theater, but here too he used only his own puppets and staged such traditional shows as "The Comedy of Petrushka" and "The Circus"; *Died:* 1936.

ZAYTSEV, Nikolay Aleksandrovich (1902–1965) Mining eng; corresp member, Ukr Acad of Sci from 1951; CP member from 1945; *Born:* 29 Dec 1902 in vil Lyubnitsy, Novgorod Province; *Educ:* 1929 grad Leningrad Mining Inst; *Career:* 1929–41 chief eng at mines of a Donbass trust; 1941–45 chief eng at mines in the Urals; 1946–53 head, Stalin Coal Combine and Artem Coal Combine; 1953–54 dir, Donetsk Coal Research Inst; 1955–57 USSR Dep Min of the Construction of Coal Ind Enterprises; 1957–60 head, Dept of Coal, Peat and Shale Ind, RSFSR Gosplan; dep, Ukr Supr Sov of 1947 and 1951 convocations; *Awards:* Hero of Socialist Labor (1948); *Died:* 21 Sept 1965.

ZAYTSEV, Vasiliy Aleksandrovich (1911–1961) WW 2 fighter pilot; col; CP member from 1932; *Born:* 10 Jan 1911 in Kolomna, Moscow Province; *Career:* 1932 joined Sov Army; during WW 2 squadron, regt, then brigade commander, Sov Air Force; 1946 retired on med reasons; *Awards:* twice Hero of the Sov Union; two Orders of Lenin; other orders and medals; *Died:* 19 May 1961.

ZAYTSEV, Vladimir Mikhaylovich (1885–1967) Govt official; CP member from 1905; *Born:* 1885; *Career:* sailor, Black Sea Fleet; summer 1905 arrested; escaped and worked at Kazan' powder factory; 1911–13 sailed on Volga merchant ships and engaged in propaganda work; 1915–17 in the army; during 1917 Feb Revol member, Kronstadt Bolshevik Comt; Baltic Fleet rep on Exec Comt, Petrograd Sov; during 1917 Oct Revol commanded a sailors' squad in storming of the Winter Palace; comr, sailors' squad and comr, Putilov Plant's battle squads; then comr, Petrograd printing houses; 1918 comr, Internal Waterways Bd; then chm, Tatar-Bash Republ Sov; Tatar-Bash Comr of Waterways; fought in Civil War; 1920–21 member, Tatar Republ Centr Exec Comt; 1921–33 exec posts in trade and vocational training; from 1933 pensioner; *Died:* 1 Mar 1967.

ZAZUBRIN (real name: ZUBTSOV), Vladimir Yakovlevich (1895–1938) Russian writer; *Born:* 6 June 1895 in Penza; *Career:* 1916 arrested for revol propaganda; during Civil War drafted into Kolchak's Army; Nov 1918 defected and joined Red Army; 1923–28 secr, ed staff, journal "Sibirskiye ogni"; 1926–28 co-founder and leading member, Sibirian Writers' Union; 1928 invited to Moscow by Gorky to work for State Publ House and journal "Kolkhoznik"; arrested by State Security organs; *Publ:* chronicle novel *Dva mira* (Two Worlds) (1921); novelettes *Blednaya pravda* (Pale Truth) (1923); *Obshchezhitiye* (The Hostel) (1923); film scripts: *Krasnyy gaz* (The Red Gas) (1924); *Izbushka na Baykale* (The Hut on the Baykal) (1926); novel *Gory* (The Hills) (1933); memoirs of Gorky *Posledniye dni* (The Last Days) (1936); edited Altay epic "Kogutey" (1935); unfinished play *Chelovecheskiye obyazannosti* (Human Obligations); *Died:* 6 July 1938 in imprisonment; posthumoussly rehabilitated.

ZBARSKIY, Boris Il'ich (1885–1954) Biochemist; member, USSR Acad of Med Sci from 1944; Hon Sci Worker of RSFSR; Hero of Socialist Labor from 1945; CP member from 1930; *Born:* 26 July 1885; *Educ:* 1911 grad Geneva Univ; *Career:* 1911 defended doctor's thesis on the effects of acids and alkalis on phenolase and peroxidase; did research on biochemistry at Prof V. S. Gulevich's Laboratory, Moscow Univ; 1918, together with A. N. Bakh, founded Karpov Chemical Inst; 1920 founded Biochemical Inst, RSFSR Pop Comrt of Health (now Biochemical Inst, USSR Acad of Sci), where he engaged in research work until 1930; from 1930 founder-dir, Inst of Nutrition, subsequently incorporated in the USSR Acad of Med Sci; 1945–52 head, Laboratory of Cancer Biochemistry, USSR Acad of Med Sci; from 1923 head, Chair of Biochemistry at Pedological Inst, then 2nd Moscow Med Inst; 1934–54 head, Chair of Biochemistry, 1st Moscow Med Inst; first dir, Laboratory at Lenin Mausoleum; studied role of erythrocytes in protein metabolism, particularly in the mechanism of the transportation of amino acids; proposed theory whereby erythrocytes act as a physiological depot of amino acids and control their content in the blood plasma; studied the chemism of immunity; established that some amino acids neutralize the effects of diphteria and tetanus toxins and hypothesized that amino acids and the products of protein decomposition could be used for therapeutic purposes; determined the amino acid content of proteins in food products and the organs of the human body, research which proved of considerable importance to comparative biochemistry, to clinical practice and for estimating the body's nutrient amino acid requirement; his research on cancer biochemistry showed that tumor proteins have an amino acid composition which differs from the proteins of normal organs and tissues; hypothesized that tumors contain a special tumor protein formed by distortion of protein synthesis under the effects of carcinogenic factors; contributed to the produktion technol of methyl alcohol, acetone and the dry distillation of wood; devised an original means of producing chloroform; synthesized an antiseptic preparation called "Zbarskiy's bactericide" and a hydrolysis preparation called "Parentit" for parenteral protein nutrition, widely used in clinical practice; together with V. P. Vorob'yov, embalmed Lenin's body; 1949 directed team which embalmed body of Bulgarian Communist leader Georgiy Dimitrov; 1917 elected chm, Yelabuk Uyezd Sov of Workers' and Soldiers' Dept; 1926 and 1931 founded respectively journals "Eksperimental'naya biologiya i meditsina" and "Voprosy pitaniya"; published some 70 works; *Publ: K ucheniyu o yavleniyakh immuniteta* (The Theory of Immunity Phenomena) (1925); coauthor, "Zur Kenntnis des Mechanismus der Immunitätserscheinungen" (1926–27); *Rol' eritrotsitov v obmene belkov* (The Role of Erythrocytes in Protein Metabolism) (1934); *Mavzoley V. I. Lenina* (The V. I. Lenin Mausoleum) (1946); *Belki i zlokachestvennyye opukholi* (Protein and Malignant Tumors) (1947); coauthor, *Rol' eritrotsitov v obmene belkov* (The Role of Erythrocytes in Protein Metabolism) (1949); coauthor, *Praktikum po biologicheskoy khimii* (Practical Studies in Biological Chemistry) (1949); coauthor, *Biologicheskaya khimiya* (Biological Chemistry) (1954); *Awards:* Stalin Prize (1944), etc; *Died:* 7 Oct 1954.

ZDOBNOV, Nikolay Vasil'yevich (1888–1942) Bibliographer; *Born:* 21 Oct 1888 in Shadrinsk, now Kurgan Oblast; *Educ:* 1915 grad Shanyavskiy Pop Univ, Moscow; *Career:* 1922–30 with Russian Bibliographical Soc, Moscow Univ; 1924–36 worked for Centr Bureau of Regional Studies; 1925–32 with Soc for the Study of the Urals, Siberia and the Far East and with State Centr Book Chamber; trained bibliographers at higher educ establishments and technicums; spezialized in regional bibliography of the Urals, Siberia and the Far East and the history of bibliography; 1941 arrested by State security organs; *Publ: Osnovy krayevoy bibliografii* (The Principles of Regional Bibliography) (1926); *Ukazatel' bibliograficheskikh posobiy po Uralu* (An Index of Bibliographical Works on the Urals) (1927); *Bibliografiya Dal'nevostochnogo kraya, 1890–1931* (The Bibliography of the Far Eastern Kray, 1890–1931) (2 vol, 1935); *Bibliografiya Buryat-Mongolii za 1890–1936* (The Bibliography of Buryat-Mongolia for 1890–

1936) (4 vol, 1939–46); *Istoriya russkoy bibliografii do nachala XX veka* (The History of Russian Bibliography up to the Start of the 20th Century) (2 vol, 1944–47); *Russkaya knizhnaya statistika* (Russian Book Statistics) (1959); *Sinkhronicheskiye tablitsy russkoy bibliografii 1700–1928* (Synchronous Tables of Russian Bibliography for 1700–1928) (1962); *Bibliografiya i krayevedeniye* (Bibliography and Regional Studies) (1963); *Died:* 15 May 1942 in imprisonment; posthumously rehabilitated.

ZDRAVOSMYSLOV, Vladimir Mikhaylovich (1871–1942) Microbiologist and health official; prof; *Born:* 1871; *Educ:* 1895 grad Med Fac, Kazan' Univ; *Career:* 1888–1930 founder-dir, Perm' Zemstvo Bacteriological Laboratory (from 1912 Bacteriological Inst), which began producing diphtheria vaccine in 1900 and scarlet fever, cholera and tuberculosis vaccine in 1908; after Oct 1917 Revol organized numerous courses for physicians, nurses and orderlies; 1916–29 head, Chair of Bacteriology, Perm' Univ; 1931–34 worked in Sverdlovsk; from 1934 worked in Rostov-on-Don; did research on the chemical aspects of immunity and tried to obtain antibodies in vitro with the help of enzymes; studied techniques of microbiological examination and the preparation of bacterial brugs; wrote ober 20 works; *Publ:* "Rapport de bactérologie du zemstwo de Perm pour la periode du 15 mai 1898 au 31 octobre 1901" (1903); coauthor, *Polucheniye iskusstvennykh gemolizinov in vitro fermentativnym putyom* (Obtaining Artificial Hemolysines in Vitro by the Enzyme Method) (1926); coauthor, "Über die fermentative Methode der Diphtherieantitoxinerhaltung in vitro" (1927); *Died:* 1942.

ZELENEV, Nikolay Andreyevich (1885–1939) Mil health official; *Born:* 1885; *Educ:* 1913 grad Med Fac, Moscow Univ; *Career:* while still a student arrested and exiled for revol activities; during WW 1 served with Red Cross mobile units; 1918 joined Sov Army; Feb 1919–29 dep chm, Main Mil Health Bd; organized mil med and health services; read papers on this subject at various All-Union Med Congresses; *Publ: Bor'ba s tuberkulyozom v Krasnoy Armii i flote* (The Campaign Against Tuberculosis in the Red Army and Navy) (1923); *Voyennaya gigiyena* (Military Hygiene) (1928); *Voyenno-sanitarnoye delo* (The Military Health Service) (1928); *Gigiyena pokhoda* (Campaign Hygiene) (1930); *Printsipy i metody protivoepidemieheskoy bor'by v voyskakh v voyennoye vremya* (The Principles and Methods of Combatting Epidemics Among Troops in Wartime) (1930), etc; *Awards:* Hero of the Sov Health Service; *Died:* 1939.

ZELENIN, Dmitriy Konstantinovich (1878–1954) Folklorist; dialectologist and ethnographer; corresp member, USSR Acad of Sci from 1925; member, Bulgarian Acad of Sci from 1946; *Born:* 2 Nov 1878 in vil Lyuk, Vyatka Province; *Educ:* 1904 grad History and Philology Fac, Yur'yev (Tartu) Univ; *Career:* from 1916 prof, Khar'kov Univ; from 1925 prof, Leningrad Univ; 1926–49 also worked at Inst of Ethnography, USSR Acad of Sci; *Publ: Pesni derevenskoy molodyozhi* (The Songs of Rural Youth) (1903); *Iz byta i poezii krest'yan Novgorodskoy gubernii* (From the Life and Poetry of the Peasants of Novgorod Province) (1905); *Velikorusskiye govory* (Great Russian Dialects) (1913); *Bibliograficheskiy ukazatel' russkoy etnograficheskoy literatury o vneshnem byte narodov Rossii, 1700–1910* (A Bibliographical Index to Russian Ethnographic Literature on the Outward Life of the Peoples of Russia, 1700–1910) (1913); *Opisaniye rukopisey Uchyonogo arkhiva Russkogo geograficheskogo obshchestva* (An Account of the Manuscripts in the Learned Archives of the Russian Geographical Society) (3 vol, 1914–16); *Velikorusskiye skazki Permskoy gubernii* (Great Russian Tales of Perm' Province) (1914); *Velikorusskiye skazki Vyatskoy gubernii* (Great Russian Tales of Vyatka Province) (1915); *Problema pervonachal'noy religii* (The Problem of Primordial Religion) (1937); *Ob istoricheskoy obshchnosti kul'tur russkogo i ukrainskogo narodov* (The Historical Community of the Cultures of the Russian and Ukrainian Peoples) (1940); *O kiyevskom proiskhozhdenii karpatskikh ukraintsev-gutsulov* (The Kievan Origin of the Carpathian Ukrainian Hutsuls) (1953); *Died:* 31 Aug 1954 in Leningrad.

ZELENKO, Aleksandr Ustinovich (1871–1953) Educationist; architect; *Born:* 11 Oct 1871; *Educ:* 1892 grad Petersburg Inst of Civil Eng; *Career:* 1900–03 taught drawing at a Moscow high school; 1903–04 studied child training and educ system in America; 1905 helped found children's summer labor colony at Shchyolkovo, near Moscow and Russia's first children's club; 1906 organized courses for adolescents at this club; 1906, together with Shatskiy, founded "Settlement" Soc, which opened workshops with the help of a subsidy from the Min of Educ; 1905–09 taught on Prechistenka Workers' Courses and at Sunday workers' schools; 1909, after closure of "Settlement" Soc and a period unter arrest, went to America; 1910 returned to Russia and worked for "Children's Labor and Recreation" Soc; also worked for journals "Svobodnoye vospitaniye" and "Dlya narodnogo uchitelya"; 1911–17 lecturer, Shanyavskiy Pop Univ, Moscow; after 1917 Oct Revol research and teaching work at Inst of Methods of Extracurricular Work and various teachers' training establishments; worked for journal "Svobodnoye vospitaniye"; 1921–23 member, Sci Pedag Section, State Studies Council, RSFSR Pop Comrt of Educ; 1947–53 assoc, Inst of Art Training, RSFSR Acad of Pedag Sci; *Publ:* coauthor, *Plan zanyatiy v nachal'noy shkole* (The Elementary School Studies Plan) (1911); *Sovremennyye reformatory vospitaniya i obrazovaniya* (Modern Training and Education Reformers) (1911–14); coauthor *Kak postroit' narodnyy dom* (How to Build a Public Center) (1918); *Detskiye muzei v Severnoy Amerike* (Children's Museums in North America) (1925); *Amerikanskiye sel'skiye kluby molodyozhi i metod domashnikh proyektov* (American Rural Youth Clubs and the Home Projects Method) (1926); *Amerikantsy v svoikh klubakh i obshchestvennykh tsentrakh* (The Americans in Their Clubs and Social Centers) (1927); *Voprosy politekhnicheskogo vospitaniya v amerikanskoy pedagogicheskoy presse* (Polytechnic Training in the American Pedagogic Press) (1929); *Shkol'noye professional'noye obucheniye v Severnoy Amerike* (School Trade Training in North America) (1931); *Detskiye parki* (Children's Parks) (1938), etc; *Died:* 21 July 1953.

ZELENSKIY, Isaak Abramovich (1890–1938) Party official; CP member from 1906; *Born:* 1890; *Educ:* grad Saratov Elementary College; *Career:* 1906–07 Party and trade-union work; 1908 arrested and exiled to Orenburg Province; 1909 fled from exile; worked in Astrakhan' and Penza, then returned to Orenburg, where he worked for railroad; 1910 arrested and exiled again; settled in Samara, established contact with Party org and did extensive Party work; 1912 rearrested and exiled for three years to Narym; 1913 fled from exile but was shortly arrested and returned to Narym; 1914 again fled from exile; worked in Samara, then Moscow, 1915 moved to Sormovo and worked as secr of a sick insurance fund; within a few weeks arrested and exiled to Verkholensk Uyezd, Yakutsk Province; late 1916 fled to Moscow; after 1917 Feb Revol organizer, Moscow's Basmannyy Rayon Party Org; then chm, Basmannyy Rayon Sov; 1918–20 exec Party work in Moscow; 1920 secr, Moscow Party Comt, then Collegium member, Pop Comrt of Food; 1921–24 again secr, Moscow Party Comt; 1924 secr, CC, CPSU(B); 1924–31 secr, Centr Asian Bureau, CC, CPSU(B); from 1931 chm, Centr Union of Consumer Soc; at 10th Party Congress elected cand member, at 11th Party Congress – member, CC, CPSU(B); member, USSR Centr Exec Comt; arrested by State Security organs; Mar 1938 sentenced to death by Mil Collegium, USSR Supr Court; *Died:* Mar 1938 executed.

ZELENSKIY, Vladimir Iosifovich (pseudonyms: Leontiy KOTOMKA; Comrade LEONID) (1890–1965) Journalist; CP member from 1906; *Born:* 26 July 1890; *Educ:* 1912–16 studied on Higher Agric Courses, Petrograd; *Career:* active in revol movement; 1912–16, while still a student, contributed to newspaper "Pravda"; revol work among students; during 1917 Oct Revol agitator, Moscow Party Comt; helped found Komsomol; worked for Moscow newspaper "Sotsial-demokrat"; during Civil War edited army newspapers; 1921–25 ed, periodical "Saratovskiye izvestiya"; 1925–36 ed work for "Izvestiya VTsIK" and state Lit Publ House; then pensioner; *Died:* 22 Nov 1965.

ZELINSKIY, Nikolay Dmitriyevich (1861–1953) Chemist; Dr of Chemistry from 1891; prof from 1893; member, USSR Acad of Sci from 1929; Hon Sci Worker of RSFSR from 1926; Hero of Socialist Labor from 1945; *Born:* 6 Feb 1861 in Tiraspol'; *Educ:* 1884 grad Novorossiysk Univ, Odessa; *Career:* 1885 worked in Göttingen, Germany; 1886 obtained first sample dichlorodiethyl sulfide (mustard gas); from 1888 assoc prof, Novorossiysk Univ; from 1893 head, Chair of Analitic Chemistry, Moscow Univ; 1895–1907 synthesized homologs of cyclopenthane and cyclohexane; did major research on organic synthesis; 1911 resigned from Moscow Univ in protest against policies of Educ Min Kasso and became head, Petersburg Centr Laboratory, Min of Finance; in same year discovered dehydrogenation catalysis reaction subsequently used on an ind scale to obtain aromatic hydrocarbons from oil for the manufacture of drugs, dyes, synthetic rubber, explosives, etc; 1915–24 did research on the regeneration of coked catalysts with air, achieving results providing the basis for ind catalytic cracking and dehydrogenation 20–25 years later; 1915 also developed coal gasmask for universal use; 1917 returned to Moscow Univ, where he worked until his death; 1918 benzinized heavy oil carbons; trained numerous outstanding chemists, many of whom now hold professorships; co-founder, Mendeleyev All-Union Chemical Soc; also founded chemistry facs at various univ; founded Chair of Organic Catalysis and Oil Chemistry, Moscow Univ; co-founder, Inst of Organic Chemistry, USSR Acad of Sci, which now bears his name; wrote over 500 works; *Publ:* master's thesis *K voprosu ob izomerii v tiofenovom ryadu* (Isomerism in the Thiophene Series) (1889); doctor's thesis *Issledovaniye yavleniy stereoizomerii sredi nasyshchennykh uglerodistykh soyedineniy* (An Investigation of Stereoisomeric Phenomena in Saturated Carbon Compounds) (1891), etc; *Awards:* four Orders of Lenin; three Stalin Prizes (1942, 1946 and 1948); two Orders of the Red Banner of Labor; medals; *Died:* 31 July 1953 in Moscow.

ZELYONYY, Georgiy Pavlovich (1878–1951) Physiologist; Dr of Med from 1907; prof; *Born:* 1878; *Educ:* 1901 grad Med Fac, Kiev Univ; *Career:* while still a student began research on gen pathology and clinical aspects of internal diseases; 1905 joined Petersburg (Leningrad) Inst of Experimental Med, where he wrote his doctor's thesis under the supervision of I. P. Pavlov; the thesis, which dealt with conditioned reactions to sonic stimuli, established several laws governung the operation of the upper section of the canine cerebrum and provided material for further research at Pavlov's laboratories; demonstrated that dogs deprived of the cortex of their cerebral hemispheres retain complex unconditioned reflexes but are incapable of forming conditioned reflexes; in further research at Petrograd Veterianry Inst came to the conclusion that animals without cerebral hemispheres can form simple conditioned reflexes; devised original methods of inducing conditioned motor reflexes; also studied physiology of digestion and physiology of labor; made special studies of human higher nervous activity; 1921–51 head, Chair of Physiology, Leningrad Veterinary Inst; *Publ:* doctor's thesis *Materialy k voprosu o reaktsii sobak na zvukovyye razdrazheniya* (Material on the Reaction of Dogs to Sonic Stimuli) (1907); *Sobaka bez polushariy bol'shogo mozga* (A Dog Without Large Cerebral Hemispheres) (1911–12); *Rezul'taty poslednikh opytov nad sobakami bez mozgovykh polushariy* (The Results of the Latest Experiments on Dogs Without Cerebral Hemispheres) (1930); *Died:* 1951.

ZEMLYACHKA (SAMOYLOVA), Rozaliya Samoylovna (Party names: DEMON; OSIPOV) (1876–1947) Govt and Party official; CP member from 1896; *Born:* 1 Apr 1876 in Kiev; *Educ:* completed high school; *Career:* from 1890's in revol movement; from 1901 "Iskra" agent in Odessa and Yekaterinoslav; 1903 Odessa Party Org deleg at 2nd RSDRP Congress; 1903 coopted to CC, RSDRP; 1904 member, Bureau of Bolshevik Comts; 1905 Petersburg Party Org deleg at 3rd RSDRP Congress; 1905 secr, Moscow RSDRP Comt; Party organizer for Rogozhsko–Simonov Rayon; worked for Party's Mil Org; several times arrested; Oct 1917 imprisoned in Petersburg's Lith Castle; 1909, after release from prison, sent to Baku as secr, Baku Party Org; then went abroad; 1914 returned illegally to Moscow; 1915–16 member, Moscow Bureau, CC, RSDRP; 1917 first secr, Moscow RSDRP(B) Comt; deleg at 7th (Apr) All-Russian Party Conference and 6th RSDRP(B) Congress; during 1917 Oct Revol directed revolt in Rogozhsko-Siminovskiy Rayon; 1918 head, Polit Dept, 8th and 13th Armies; Nov 1920, after liberation of Crimea, secr, Crimean Oblast RCP(B) Comt; 1922–23 secr, Moscow's Zamoskvorech'ye Rayon RCP(B) Comt; 1924–25 member, Southeastern Bureau, CC, RCP(B); then secr, Motovilikha Rayon RCP(B) Comt, Urals; 1926–31 Collegium member, Pop Comrt of Workers and Peasants' Inspection; 1932–33 Collegium member, Pop Comrt of Means of Communication; from 13th RCP(B) Congress in 1924 member, Centr Control Commission; 1934, at 17th CPSU(B) Congress, elected member, Sov Control Commission; dep chm, then chm, Sov Control Commission; 1939, at 19th Party Congress, elected member, CC, CPSU(B); 1939–43 dep chm, USSR Council of Pop Comr; then dep chm, Party Control Commission, CC, CPSU(B); dep, USSR Supr Sov of 1937 convocation; wrote reminiscences of Lenin; *Awards:* two Orders of Lenin; Order of the Red Banner; *Died:* 21 Jan 1947; buried on Moscow's Red Square.

ZEMLYANSKIY, Dmitriy Semyonovich (1912–1963) Party official; Cand of Historical Sci; CP member from 1931; *Born:* 1912; *Educ:* 1955 grad Acad of Soc Sci, CC, CPSU; *Career:* from 1929 Komsomol work; 1934–37 secr, Korotoyak, then Mordva Rayon Komsomol Comt in Voronezh Oblast; later worked for CC, Kaz Komsomol; 1941–52 secr, Kustanay Oblast Comt, CP Kaz; secr, Komi Oblast Party Comt; then secr, Oryol Oblast CPSU Comt; 1955–61 secr, Alma-Ata Oblast Party Comt; dir, Party School, CC, CP Kaz; secr, Kuybyshev Oblast CPSU Comt; 1961–62 with CC, CPSU; 1962–Sept 1963 second secr, CC, CP Geo; dep, Geo Supr Sov; *Died:* 23 Sept 1963.

ZEMNUKHOV, Ivan Aleksandrovich (1923–1943) Komsomol official; *Born:* 8 Sept 1923 in vil Illarionovka, Ryazan' Province; *Educ:* 1941 completed secondary school; *Career:* from 1932 lived with his family in Krasnodon, Lugansk Oblast; after completing school worked as Pioneer leader; fall 1942, after German occupation of Krasnodon, formed an underground youth group which later became the nucleus of the "Young Guard" underground org; staff member, Young Guard; took part in its operations against German occupation troops; organized underground printing press and wrote a number of leaflets; arrested by German mil authorities; *Awards:* Hero of the Sov Union; *Died:* 15 Jan 1943 in German imprisonment.

ZEMYATCHENSKIY, Pyotr Andreyevich (1856–1942) Geologist and soil sci; corresp member, USSR Acad of Sci from 1928; assoc of V. V. Dokuchayev; *Born:* 26 Nov 1856; *Educ:* 1882 grad Petersburg Univ; *Career:* 1887–98 assoc prof, from 1898 prof, Chair of Mineralogy, Petersburg Univ; took part in Dokuchayev's expeditions to study the soil, geology and hydrogeology of the Nizhniy Novgorod, then Poltava Provinces; 1899–1907 soil and geological research in various areas of Centr Russia; studied iron ores of centr zone and clays of southern zone of Russian Plain; 1922–, on the basis of a study of the processes accompanying the initial stages of soil formation, published a work on the weathering of feldspars; his soil studies proved of practical value to road-building and civil eng; *Publ: Kaolinitovyye obrazovaniya yuzhnoy Rossii* (The Kaolinite Formations of Southern Russia) (1896); *Gliny SSSR. Obshchaya chast'* (The Clays of the USSR. General Section) (1935); *Died:* 27 Feb 1942.

ZENZINOV, Vladimir Mikhaylovich (1881– ?) Politician; *Born:* 1881; *Career:* from 1903 active in revol movement; 1905 member, Moscow Socialist-Revol Comt; Dec 1905 took part in armed uprising in Moscow, during WW 1 adopted defensist stand; 1917 member, Exec Comt, Petrograd Sov; co-ed, Socialist-Revol organ "Delo naroda"; after 1917 Oct Revol opposed Sov regime; 1918 worked with Comt of Members of the Constituent Assembly, Samara; cand member, Ufa Directorate; emigrated to France; 1920 joined Foreign Deleg of Socialist-Revol Party; *Died:* date and place of death unknown.

ZERNOV, Pavel Mikhaylovich (1905–1964) Mil commander; lt-gen, Eng Corps; Cand of Tech Sci from 1937; CP member from 1925; *Born:* 19 Jan 1905; *Educ:* 1933 grad Moscow Higher Tech College; *Career:* from 1938 dep head, Main Tractor Ind Bd, USSR Pop Comrt of Machine-Building; during WW 2 Dep Pop Comr of Tank Ind; from 1946 directed a research center; from 1951 USSR Dep Min of Medium Machine-Building; then dep chm, USSR State Production Comt for Medium Machine-Building; *Awards:* twice Hero of Socialist Labor; Lenin Prize; two Stalin Prizes; *Died:* 7 Feb 1964.

ZERNOV, Sergey Alekseyevich (1871–1945) Zoologist and hydrobiologist; founder of Russian hydrobiology; member, USSR Acad of Sci from 1931; CP member from 1930; *Born:* 10 June 1871; *Educ:* 1895 grad Physics and Mathematics Fac, Moscow Univ; *Career:* 1897 arrested for revol propaganda among Moscow workers and exiled for two years to Vyatka Province; then worked in Crimea; founded nat sci museum in Simferopol'; studied the fishing ind of Tavrida Province; 1902–14 directed Sebastopol Biological Station, Acad of Sci, 1913 published monograph *K voprosu ob izuchenii zhizni Chyornogo morya* (Studying the Life of the Black Sea), for which Moscow Univ made him a Master of Zoology; in this work he described the ecology, fauna and biocenoses of the Black Sea and laid down the laws governing their distribution; in the northwestern sector of the Black Sea discovered beds of red seaweed which enabled him to organize the ind production of iodine; 1914 founded first Chair of Hydrobiology at Moscow Agric Inst (now Timiryazev Agric Acad); 1924 founded Chair of Hydrobiology at Moscow Univ; 1914–30 prof, Timiryazev Agric Acad; 1924–30 prof, Moscow Univ; from 1917 first dean, Workers' Fac, Petrine Agric Acad; helped found Main Fishery Bd and Floatng Marine Inst; 1931–42 dir, Zoological Inst,

USSR Acad of Sci, Leningrad; Sov rep at 1921, 1925 and 1927 Int Hydrobiological Congresses; Presidium member, Int Assoc of Limnologists; *Publ: Izucheniye donnoy proizvoditel'nosti morey SSSR* (A Study of the Deep-Level Productivity of the Seas of the USSR) (1933); *Obshchaya gidrobiologiya* (General Hydrogiology) (2nd ed, 1949); *Korennyye i prishlyye elementy fauny SSSR i prilegayushchikh morey* (The Indigenous and Alien Elements of the Fauna of the USSR and the Surrounding Seas) (1938); *O predelakh zhizni pri otritsatel'nykh temperaturakh v nezamerzshey vode v prirodnykh uslovivakh* (The Limits of Life at Negative Temperatures in Unfrozen Water Unter Natural Conditions) (1944); *Awards:* Order of Lenin; *Died:* 22 Feb 1945.

ZEROV, Nikolay Konstantinovich (1890–1941) Ukr poet, lit historian, critic and translator; *Born:* 26 Apr 1890 in vil Zin'kovo, Poltava Province, son of a teacher; *Educ:* 1912 grad Kiev Univ; *Career:* from 1923 prof, Kiev Inst of Public Educ; from 1933 prof of Ukr lit, Kiev Univ; 1912 first work printed; contributed reviews to pedag journal "Svet"; 1919–20 ed, bibliographical journal "Knigar'"; 1921 member, ed staff, journal "Golos pechati"; contributed to journals "Literaturno-nauchnyy vestnik," "Krasnyy put'" and "Zhizn' i revolyutsiya"; in 1920's member, Ukr Neoclassicists; during 1925–27 lit controversy supported Khvylyovyy, who opposed the socialist principles of Sov Ukr lit; 1930 recanted his views and criticized his "ideological errors"; wrote articles on Lesya Ukrainka, A. Svidnitsky, I. Franko, A. Shchogolev, Marko Cheremshin, V. Samoylenko, P. Tychina, M. Ryl'skiy and V. Sosyura; also wrote studies of Ukr fables and proverbs and modern Ukr poetry; translated into Ukr Latin poet , Russian, French and Polish writers and Lat verse of G. Skovoroda; arrested by State Security organs; *Publ: Antologiya rimskoy poezii* (An Anthology of Roman Poetry) (1920); *Novaya ukrainskaya pis'mennost'* (New Ukrainian Writing) (1924); "Lesya Ukrainka" (1924); *K istochnikam. Literaturno-kriticheskiye stat'i* (To the Sources. Literary-Critical Articles) (1926), etc; *Died:* 13 Oct 1941 in imprisonment; posthumously rehabilitated.

ZEVIN, Yakov Davydovich (Savka) (1888–1918) Party official; CP member from 1904; *Born:* 1884 in vil Krasnopol'ye, Mogilev Province; *Career:* Party work in Kamenskoye, Yekaterinoslav, Baku and other towns in southern Russia; several times arrested by Tsarist authorities; in 1910's sided with Plekhanov's Menshevik group; attended Lenin's Party School at Longjumeau, near Paris; Yekaterinoslav Party Comt deleg at 6th (Prague) RSDRP Conference; after this conference sided with Bolsheviks; from 1915 member, Baku RSDRP Comt; after 1917 Feb Revol worked for Moscow Sov and carried out assignments for Moscow Oblast RSDRP(B) Comt; from Auf 1917 exec work in Baku; helped lead struggle to establish Sov regime in Azer; from Apr 1918 Comr of Labor, Baku Council of Pop Comr; *Died:* 20 Sept 1918 executed with 25 other Baku comr after collapse of Baku Commune.

ZEYLIGER, Dmitriy Nikolayevich (1864–1936) Geometrist and mech specialist; Hon Sci Worker of RSFSR from 1927; *Born:* 24 May 1864; *Educ:* 1887 grad Novorossiysk Univ, Odessa; *Career:* 1895–1914 and 1917–29 prof, Kazan' Univ; specialist in linear geometry; *Publ: Teoriya dvizheniya podobno-izmenyayemogo tela* (The Theory of the Motion of a Similarly-Variable Body) (1892); *Kompleksnaya lineychataya geometriya. Poverkhnosti i kongruentsii* (Comprehensive Linear Geometry. Surfaces and Congruences) (1934), etc; *Died:* 25 June 1936.

ZEYNALLY KHANAFI (1896–1937) Azer lit historian, critic and folklorist; *Born:* 1896; *Career:* head, Lit Studies Dept, Azer Publ House; collected folklore; classified typical themes in Azer folklore; arrested by State Security organs; *Publ:* articles "October and Our Literature" about Guseyn Dzhavid's dramas "Sheykh-Sanan" and "Sheida"; "Azerbaidzhani Proverbs," etc; *Died:* 1937 in imprisonment; posthumously rehabilitated.

ZHAKOV, M.P. (1893–1936) Party official; CP member from 1911; *Born:* 1893; *Career:* Party work in Kazan' and Siberia; arrested by Tsarist authorities; after 1917 Oct Revol Party work; early 1918 member, Govt of Donetsk-Krivoy Rog Republ and member, Donetsk-Krivoy Rog Oblast RSDRP(B) Comt; 1921–22 member and secr, Donetsk RCP(B) Comt; deleg at 9th RCP(B) Congress; 1923 signed 46-signature Trotskyist platform; 1928 expelled from Party for siding with "Trotskyist Opposition"; 1929 readmitted to Party; from 1929 teaching and research work at Transcaucasian Communist Univ, Communist Acad and Acad of Material Culture; from 1935 pensioner; *Died:* 1936.

ZHAKOVA, Vera Nikolayevna (1914–1937) Russian writer; *Born:* 19 Aug 1914 in vil Nikulino, Simbirsk Province; *Career:* 1918 began to correspond with Gorky, who helped her to become a writer; Gorky suggested topics, corrected her manuscripts and helped to get her work published; wrote on historical themes; in her latter years, at Gorky's suggestion, wrote a book on the history of Nizniy Novgorod; most of her writings remain in manuscript, preserved at Gorky Archives in Moscow and Gorky Oblast Archives; *Publ:* novelettes and stories: *O mastere Aristotele Fioroventi* (Master Aristotle Fioroventi) (1934); *O chyornom cheloveke Fyodore Kone* (Fyodor Kon, the Black Man) (1934); *Gorestnaya zhizn' arkhitektora V.I. Bazhenova* (The Sad Life of the Architect V.I. Bazhenov) (1934); *Zhizn' i chudesa yurodivoy Yeleny Yagunovoy, podvizhnitsy Troitskogo monastyrya* (The Life and Miracles of God's Fool Yelena Yagunova, Hermit of Troitsa Monastery) (1937); *Shkola Stupina* (Stupin's School) (1937), etc; *Died:* 13 Mar 1937 in Gorky.

ZHAMTSARANO, Tsyben Zhamtsaranovich (1881–1937) Buryat scholar, educationist, translator and politician; Dr. of Philology; *Born:* 26 Apr 1881; *Educ:* 1901 grad Irkutsk Teachers' Training Seminary; 1902 attended lectures at Petersburg Univ; *Career:* 1901 teacher at a parish school; 1903–06 commissioned by Acad of Sci to collect ethnographical and linguistic material in Yakutsk Province and Transbaikal; some of this material was published by the Acad of Sci in several parts of "Obraztsy narodnoy slovestnosti mongol'skikh plemyon" (Samples of the Mogolian Tribes' Folk Literature); 1906 founded a union called the "Banner of the Buryat People" which united some 60 teachers at Buryat schools in Yakutsk Province; went underground; Jan 1907 – summer 1908 lectured on Mongolian language at Petersburg Univ; 1918 at 3rd Congress of the Peasants, Workers, Kazaks and Buryats of Transbaikal Oblast, elected member, Transbaikal Oblast Exec Comt of Soviets; after the congress appointed Comr of Nationality Affairs; from 1920 active in Mongolian people's revol movement; 1921 appointed Asst Min of Internal Affairs, Mongolian Pop Republ; upon his initiative, the Mongolian Min of For Affairs opened its first Sov school; published first Mongolian newspaper "Capital Gazette" and the journal "New Mirror"; 1932–37 worked at Inst of Oriental Studies, USSR Acad of Sci, Leningrad; translated into Mongolian works of Lev Tolstoy, Jack London, Jules Verne, etc; 1926 published a textbook on Mongolian geography; 1937 arrested by State Security organs; *Died:* 1937 in imprisonment; posthumously rehabilitated.

ZHANTO, Viktor Aleksandrovich (1879–1957) Circus artist; Hon Artiste of RSFSR from 1939; CP member from 1924; *Born:* 31 Jan 1879, son of a circus artist; *Career:* from age eight performed in circus; juggler, tumbler, balancer, solo clown and musical eccentric; scored great success with his juggling number "Lisette and Zhanto" and also in his piece "The Mexican Girl and the Indian"; 1939–41 founder-dir, Assoc of Kolkhoz Circuses; 1943–47 dir and artistic dir, circus art college; also producer, staging individual numbers and entire shows; *Died:* 27 Apr 1957.

ZHARKO, A.M. (1889–1939) Govt official; CP member from 1904; *Born:* 1889; *Career:* 1907–17 Party work at locomotive repair plant in Poltava; 1917 member, Poltava Sov; 1918 member, Centr Exec Comt, All-Russian Railroad Union; 1919 Ukr Pop Comr of Means of Communication; then exec admin work; arrested by State Security organs; *Died:* 1939 in imprisonment.

ZHARKO, Yakov Vasil'yevich (1861–1933) Ukr writer and actor; *Born:* 25 Febr 1861 in Poltava; *Educ:* 1880 grad med orderlies school; *Career:* 1886–1896 performed with Staritskiy, Kropivnitskiy and Saksaganskiy companies; after 1917 Oct Revol worked for Krasnodar educ authorities; 1884 first work printed; translated Russian poets into Ukr; contributed to journal "Zhizn' i revolyutsiya" *Publ:* verse collection "First Lyric Works" (1884); "Fables" (1889); "Stories" (1899); "Songs" (1905); "Fables" (1912); "Ballads and Legends" (1913), etc; *Died:* 25 May 1933.

ZHAROKOV, Tair Zharokovich (1908–1965) Kazakh poet; CP member from 1939; *Born:* 22 Sept 1908 in vil Zhatibay, now West Kaz Oblast; *Educ:* 1931 grad Alma-Ata Teachers' Training Inst; 1934–36 postgrad studies at Leningrad Inst of Lit and Language; *Career:* 1926 first work printed; translated into Kaz Russian Classics and Sov writers; from 1959 member, Centr Auditing Commission, USSR Writers' Union; *Publ:* collected verse: "The Radiance of the Stars" (1932); poems "Neftestan" (1933); "At the Dawn of Communism" (1933); "The Sun Spake" (1934); collected verse "Stalin's Falcons" (1941); poem "The Tale of Zoy" (1944); verse collection "The Generation"; poems "The Steel Founder" (1949); "The Forest Rustles in the Desert" (1949); "Steel Born of the Steppe" (1954); Russian-language collection of verse and poems *Burya v peskakh* (Storm in the Sands) (1960); verse *Blizost'* (Nearness), *Chaban v gorakh* (The Boar in the Hills) and *Gory poyut* (The Hills Sing) (1963), etc; *Awards:* Order of the Red Banner of Labor (1959); *Died:* 11 Mar 1965.

ZHAVORONKOV, Semyon Fyodorovich (1899–1967) Marshal of the Air Force from 1944; specialist in org and use of fleet air arm; CP member from 1917; *Born:* 23 Apr 1899 in vil Sidorovskaya, Ivanovo Oblast, son of a peasant; *Educ:* 1918 grad Moscow Party School; 1926 grad Mil Polit Acad; 1932 grad Red Army Advanced Command Courses, Zhukovskiy Air Force Acad; 1934 grad Kachin Mil Pilots' School; 1936 grad Operations Fac, Zhukovskiy Air Force Acad; *Career:* 1910–18 textile worker; participated in 1917 Oct Revol in Vichug; 1918 dep secr, Vichug Rayon RSDRP(B) Comt; 1918 helped crush anti-Sov revolt in Yaroslavl'; 1918–21 private, then battalion comr in Red Army; fought in Civil War on Eastern, Southern and Polish Fronts; 1926–29 dep head (polit), Air Force Mil Eng Acad; dep commander (polit), air force brigade; 1929–31 comr and head, Polit Dept, Black Sea Fleet Air Force; 1932–33 commander, and comr, 66th Air Squadron, 34th Air Group, Black Sea Fleet Air Force; 1934 qualified as pilot; 1934–35 commanded, air brigade, Black Sea Fleet Air Force; 1937–39 commander, 5th Heavy Bomber Corps; air force commander, Pacific Fleet; 1939–45 commander, Sov Naval Air Force; 1941 initiated and directed Sov Naval Air Force bombing raids on Berlin; 1945 arranged the flight of Yalta Conference delegates to USSR; 1945–59 dep head, then head, Main Bd, Civil Air Fleet, USSR Council of Min; from 1959 retired; *Awards:* two Orders of Lenin; four Orders of the Red Banner; Order of Nakhimov, 1st Class; two Orders of Ushakov, 1st Class; Order of Kutuzov, 2nd Class; other orders and medals; *Died:* 8 June 1967.

ZHAVRUK, Ales' (real name: SINICHKIN, Aleksandr Dmitriyevich (1910–1942) Bel poet; *Born:* 19 Aug 1910 in Roslavl', son of an office worker; *Educ:* 1934 grad Rogachev Teachers' Training Technicum; 1939 grad Moscow Inst of Philosophy, Lit and History; *Career:* 1926 first work printed; from 1939 postgrad studies at Bel Acad of Sci; then in Red Army; during WW 2 served at front; 1942 worked for newspaper of Polit Dept, 62nd Army; *Publ:* verse collections: "Streams" (1936); "The Dnieper Floods Its Banks" (1938); children's poems; libretto for opera *Zarechny bor* (The Riverside Wood); *Died:* 1942 killed in action in defense of Stalingrad.

ZHDANKO, Mikhail Yefimovich (1855–1921) Hydrographer and geodesist; *Born:* 1855; *Educ:* grad Physics and Mathematics Fac, Moscow Univ; *Career:* served in Russian Navy; 1884–86 studied at Naval Acad; 1891–98 directed hydrographical survey of White Sea; 1898–1913 head, Pacific Hydrographical Expedition; 1914–17 head, Main Hydrographical Bd; after 1917 Oct Revol worked for Permanent Polar Commission, Commission to Study the Natural Production Resources of Russia, Commission for the Study and Practical Utilization of the Russian North, etc; helped to equip first Sov Polar expeditions; head, High Seas Dept, Russian Hydrological Inst; carried out hydrographic and hydrological research and magnetic observations in Novaya Zemlya, Pechora, etc; compiled maps showing magnetic deviation of various seas; 1890 drew up meridional tables for compiling Mercator-projection maps; 1900 compiled tables of true solar azimuth north of 60°; a Cape in Novaya Zemlya's Schubert Bay and a peak on Sakhalin Island are named for him; *Died:* 1921.

ZHDANOV, Andrey Aleksandrovich (1896–1948) Govt and Party official; col-gen from 1944; CP member from 1915; *Born:* 14 Feb 1896 in Mariupol' (now Zhdanov), son of a public school inspector; *Career:* from 1912 in revol movement; from Mar 1916 member, Tver' RSDRP(B) Comt; 1917 in Russian Army, serving in 139th Reserve Regt at Shadrinsk; engaged in Bolshevik propaganda among troops; from Aug 1917 chm, Shadrinsk RSDRP(B) Comt; after 1917 Feb Revol elected to regt comt, then chm, sov of soldiers' dep; after establishment of Sov rule in Shadrinsk in Jan 1918 appointed Comr of Agric, Shadrinsk Uyezd Sov; 1918–20 polit work in Red Army in Urals and Tver'; ed, newspaper "Tverskaya pravda"; from 1922 chm, Tver' Province Exec Comt; 1924–34 secr, Nizhniy Novgorod Province Party Comt; secr, Gorky Kray CPSU(B) Comt; 1925 and 1927 at 14th and 15th Party Congresses elected cand member, CC, CPSU(B); from 16th Party Congress in 1930 member, CC, CPSU(B); from 3rd All-Union Congress of Soviets member, USSR Centr Exec Comt; after 17th Party Congress in 1934 secr, CC, CPSU(B); from Dec 1934 also secr, Leningrad Oblast and City CPSU(B) Comt; from Feb 1935 cand Politburo member, from Mar 1939 Politburo member, CC, CPSU(B); dep, USSR Supr Sov of 1st and 2nd convocations; during WW 2 member, Mil Council, Leningrad Front; from 1944 worked for CC, CPSU(B), drafting and implementing measures concerning ideology and culture, particularly music and lit; *Publ:* pamphlets: *Sovetskaya literatura – samaya ideynaya, samaya peredovaya literatura v mire* (Soviet Literature Is the Most Principled and Most Advanced Literature in the World) (1934); *Doklad o zhurnalakh "Zvezda" i "Leningrad"* (A Report on the Journals "Zvezda" and "Leningrad") (1946); *Vystupleniye na diskussii po knige G.F. Aleksandrova "Istoriya zapadnoyevropeyskoy filosofii"* (A Speech in the Debate of G. F. Aleksandrov's Book "The History of West European Philosophy") (1947); *Vstupitel'naya rech' i vystupleniye na soveshchanii deyateley sovetskoy muzyki v TsK VKP(b)* (Introduction and Speech at the Meeting of Soviet Musical Figures at the CPSU(B) Central Committee) (1948); *O mezhdunarodnom polozhenii. Doklad, sdelannyy na informatsionnom soveshchanii predstaviteley nekotorykh kompartiy v Pol'she v kontse sentyabrya 1947 goda* (The International Situtation. A Report at the Informative Meeting of Representatives of Some Communist Parties in Poland in Late September 1947) (1947), etc; *Awards:* two Orders of Lenin; Order of the Red Banner; Order of the Red Banner of Labor; Order of Suvorov, 1st Class; Order of Kutuzov, 1st Class; *Died:* 31 Aug 1948.

ZHDANOV, Pyotr Segeyevich (1903–1949) Electr eng; prof; *Born:* 19 July 1903; *Educ:* 1933 grad Moscow Power Eng Inst; *Career:* 1927–42 worked for All-Union Electr Eng Inst; from 1941 prof, Moscow Power Eng Inst; specialized in static stability of electr systems, using the least oscillation method and establishing the degree of approximation to reality of previously known practical stability criteria; also studied long-range a.c. electr power transmission; 1938–39 and 1949 helped design Kuybyshev-Moscow electr power transmission lines; *Publ:* coauthor, *Ustoychivost' parallel'noy raboty elektricheskikh sistem* (The Stability of the Parallel Operation of Electrical Systems) (1934); *Ustoychivost' elektricheskikh sistem* (The Stability of Electrical Systems) (1948), etc; *Awards:* Stalin Prize (1947); *Died:* 30 Dec 1949.

ZHDANOV, Vladimir Ivanovich (1902–1964) Mil commander; col-gen, Tank Corps; CP member from 1941; *Born:* 29 Apr 1902 in Kiev; *Educ:* grad infantry school; after WW 2 grad Gen Staff Acad; *Career:* fought in Civil War; during WW 2 chief of staff and commander of a mechanized corps; fought in the Battle of the Volga and in south Ukr; took part in the Yassy-Kishinev operation and the liberation of Bulgaria, Yugoslavia and Hungary; after WW 2 dir, Armored Forces' Mil Acad; *Awards:* Hero of the Sov Union; Pop Hero of Yugoslavia; two Orders of Lenin; three Orders of the Red Banner; Order of Suvorov, 1st Class; two Order of Suvorov 2nd Class; Order of Kutuzov, 2nd Class; Order of the Red Star; various for orders and medals; *Died:* 19 Oct 1964 in a plane crash near Belgrade.

ZHDANOVICH, Florian Pavlovich (1884–1937) Actor and stage dir; *Born:* 1884; *Career:* from 1902 with Polish and Russian touring companies; acted with Bel drama companies; from 1911 in Bel professional theater; co-founder 1st Bel Drama and Comedy Assoc; co-founder, stage dir and actor, Yanka Kupala Theater; *Roles:* Rys' in Ozhesko's "On a Winter Evening" (1917); Symon in Yanka Kupala's "The Ruined Nest" (1917); Karayayev in *Myatezh* (Mutiny) (1927); Peklevanov in *Bronepoyezd 14–69* (Armored Train 14–69) (1928); *Productions:* Yanka Kupala's "Pavlinka" (1913); Ozheshko's "On a Winter Evening" (1920); "The Ruined Nest" (1921); Golubka's "Ganka" (1921); *Les shumit* (The Rustling Forest), after Korolenko (1922); *Died:* 1937.

ZHEBELYOV, Sergey Aleksandrovich (1867–1941) Ancient historian and archeologist; prof; member, USSR Acad of Sci from 1927; Hon Sci Worker of RSFSR; *Born:* 10 Sept 1867 in Petersburg; *Educ:* 1890 grad History and Philology Fac, Petersburg Univ; *Career:* 1899–1904 assoc prof, 1904–27 prof, Petersburg (Leningrad) Univ; for many years directed research on ancient history of northern Black Sea littoral at State Acad for the History of Material Culture, then at Inst for the History of Material Culture, USSR Acad of Sci; 1941 directed all USSR Acad of Sci establishments in besieged Leningrad; studied polit history of Greece, ancient history of northern Black Sea littoral, classic archeology and ancient religions; *Publ: Iz istorii Afin* (From the History of Athens) (1889); *Akhaika* (Acheon Studies) (1903); *Drevnyaya Gretsiya* (Ancient Greece) (1922); *Drevniy Rim*

(Ancient Rome) (1923); *Vvedeniye v arkheologiyu* (An Introduction to Archeology) (1923); *Vozniknoveniye Bosporskogo gosudarstva* (The Emergence of the Bosphorus State) (1930); *Osnovnyye linii ekonomicheskogo razvitiya Bosporskogo gosudarstva* (The Main Lines in the Economic Development of the Bosphorus State) (1934); *Bosporskiya etyudy* (Bosphorus Studies) (1935); *Posledniy Perisad i skifskoye vosstaniye na Bospore* (The Last Perisad and the Sythian Revolt in the Bosphorus) (1938); published translations of Aristotle's "Politics," Plato's works, etc; *Died:* 28 Dec 1941 in Leningrad.

ZHEBRAK, Anton Romanovich (1901–1965) Geneticist, cytologist and selectionist; Dr of Biology; prof; member, Bel Acad of Sci from 1940; Hon Sci Worker of Bel SSR from 1944; CP member from 1918; *Born:* 1901; *Educ:* 1925 grad Timiryazev Agric Acad, Moscow; *Career:* 1934–48 head, Chair of Genetics and Cytology, Timiryazev Agric Acad; 1948–49 prof, Moscow Forestry Inst; from 1949 prof, Moscow Pharmaceutical Inst and head, Laboratory of Experimental Polyploidy, Inst of Biology, Bel Acad of Sci; did research on prepotency in hybrid plants, gramineous grafts and the development of polyploid and amphidiploid crop forms; *Publ: Sintez novykh vidov pshenits* (The Synthesis of New Wheat Species) (1944); *Priroda vidoizmeneniya dominirovaniya* (The Nature of Prepotency Mutation) (1946); *Izmenchivost' mezhsortovykh amfidiploidov grechikhi* (The Mutability of Interspecific Buckwheat Amphidiploids) (1955); *Priroda privivok v vysshykh rasteniyakh* (The Nature of Grafting in Higher Plants) (1956); *Otdalyonnaya gibridizatsiya i eksperimental'naya poliploidiya v rode Triticum* (Remote Hybridization and Experimental Polyploidy in the Genus Triticum) (1963); *Died:* 1965.

ZHEGALKIN, Ivan Ivanovich (1869–1947) Mathematician; prof; Hon Sci Worker of RSFSR from 1945; *Born:* 3 Aug 1869; *Educ:* grad Moscow Univ; *Career:* from 1902 assoc prof, then prof, Moscow Univ; also taught at other higher educ establishments in Moscow; 1911 resigned from Moscow Univ with other colleagues in protest against policies of Educ Min Kasso; 1917–47 again prof, Moscow Univ; wrote works on algorithmic solution of so-called solvability theory; coauthor, textbooks on mathematical analyses; *Publ: Stroka Teylora dlya neyavnoy funktsii* (Taylor's Theorem for an Implicit Function) (1902); master's thesis *Transfinitnyye chisla* (Transfinite Numbers) (1907); *Ob odnom primenenii ostatka Shlomil'kha* (An Application of the Schloemilch Remainder) (1914), etc; *Awards:* Order of the Red Banner of Labor; *Died:* 1947.

ZHEGALOV, Sergey Ivanovich (1881–1927) Geneticist; selectionist and plant breeder; prof; *Born:* 2 Oct 1881 in vil Vasil'kovo, Smolensk Province; *Educ:* 1906 grad Moscow Agric Inst; *Career:* from 1906 asst head, Shatilov Experimental Station, Orel Province; 1909–27 worked at Selection Station, Moscow Agric Inst (later Timiryazev Agric Acad); 1910 sci research in Germany, Austria and Sweden; from 1920 prof, Timiryazev Agric Acad, where he founded the Griboyedov Selection Station; from 1924 prof, Moscow Univ; head, Selection Dept, Moscow Oblast Agric Station; by cross-breeding and analytical selection produced several high-yield varieties of horticultural, grain and other crops; bred "Inexhaustible" and "Zhegalov" varieties of sugarpod garden pea, "Northern Pioneer" maize, "Kolkhoznitsa" cabbage, etc; *Publ: K voprosu o dostovernosti srednikh velichin* (The Reliability of Mean Values) (1910); *Genetika v sovremennom osveshchenii* (Genetics in the Light of Modern Knowledge) (1911); *Yavleniye gigantizatsii ovsa* (The Phenomenon of Oat Gigantism) (1914); *Novaya dlya Rossii forma ovsa* (A Form of Oats New to Russia) (1920); *Vvedeniye v selektsiyu sel'skokhozyaystvennykh rasteniy* (An Introduction to the Selection of Agricultural Plants) (1924); *Geterozis i yego znacheniye* (Heterosis and Its Importance) (1926); *Vyvedeniye novykh sortov sel'skokhozyaystvennykh rasteniy [selektsiya]* (The Breeding of New Agricultural Plant Varieties [Selection]) (1926); *Stimulirovaniye semyan po metodu professora M. Popova* (Seed Stimulation by Professor M. Popov's Method) (1927), etc; *Died:* 20 Sept 1927 in Moscow.

ZHELEZNOV, Vladimir Yakovlevich (1869–1933) Economist; *Born:* 1869; *Educ:* 1892 grad Law Fac, Kiev Univ; *Career:* taught polit econ and statistics at Kiev Univ, Moscow Agric Acad, Shanyavskiy Pop Univ and other higher educ establishments; after 1917 Oct Revol worked for USSR Pop Comrt of Finance; wrote several books on the circulation of currency, finance, business situation, market and other econ problems; the 1st ed of his book *Ocherki politicheskoy ekonomii* (Studies in Political Economy) (1902) was banned by the Tsarist censorship; *Publ: Glavnyye napravleniya v razrabotke teoriy zarabotnoy platy* (Main Trends in Developing Wage Theories) (1904); *Ekonomicheskoye mirovozzreniye drevnikh grekov* (The Economic Philosophy of the Ancient Greeks) (1916); *Ekonomicheskaya nauka v Rossii v kontse 19-go stoletiya* (Economic Science in Russia in the Late 19th Century) (1927), etc; *Died:* 1933.

ZHELEZNYAKOV (ZHELEZNYAK), Anatoliy Grigor'yevich (1895–1919) Mil commander; Civil War veteran; *Born:* 20 Apr 1895 in vil Fedoskin, Moscow Province; *Career:* laborer, then stoker on Black Sea merchant ships; from late 1915 served in Baltic Fleet; 1916 deserted to avoid arrest for revol activities; Mar 1917 returned to Petrograd; June and July 1917 twice arrested for activities against Provisional Govt; escaped from jail and fled to Helsingfors; Oct 1917 arrived in Petrograd with a sailors squad; deleg, 2nd All-Russian Congress of Soviets; although basically an anarchist, supported Bolsheviks; helped storm the Winter Palace, then fought counterrevol forces in Ukr; Jan 1918 as commander of the guard at the Tavrida Palace, ordered Constituent Assembly dep to leave the palace; Jan 1918 appointed member, Supr Collegium for Rumanian and Russian Affairs and comr, Danube Flotilla; Mar 1918 commanded Birzul fortified region and fought in southern Ukr; summer 1918 regt commander, 16th Infantry Div; early 1919 underground work in Odessa; Apr 1919 chm, Merchant Sailor's Union; from May 1919 armored train commander; *Died:* 26 July 1919 killed near vil Verkhovtsevo; buried at Vagan'kovo Cemetery.

ZHELYABUZHSKIY, Yuriy Andreyevich (1888–1955) Film dir, cameraman and scriptwriter; CP member; *Born:* 1888; *Career:* 1915 began film work as asst cutter; during 1917 Feb Revol worked as cameraman for a newsreel team, filming workers' demonstration organized by Moscow Sov; 1918 filmed Lenin; film dir and cameraman at private film studios; helped create first Sov cartoon films; prof, Chair of Camera Operating, All-Union State Inst of Cinematography; *Works:* wrote scripts, directed or filmed: "Tsarevich Aleksey" (1918); *Novoye plat'ye korolya* (The King's New Clothes) (1919); *Voyna voyne* (War on War) (1920); "Polikushka" (1922); *Deti – tsvety zhizni* (Children Are the Flowers of Life) (1919); *Gidrotorf* (The Hydropeat Trust) (1920); fairy-tale film "Morozko" (1924); satirical comedy *Papirosnitsa ot Mossel'proma* (The Cigarette Girl from the Moscow Rural Industry Trust) (1924); drama *V gorod vkhodit'nel'zya* (You Can't Enter Town) (1929); directed and shot film *Kollezhskiy registrator* (Collegium Registrar) (1925); cartoon films; *Priklyucheniya Bolvashki* (Blockhead's Adventures) (1927); art films *Zhivopis' Repina* (Repin's Painting) and "Vasiliy Ivanovich Surikov" (1946–47), etc; *Publ: Isskusstvo operatora* (The Cameraman's Art) (1932); *Vopros, reshyonnyy pri pomoshchi kino / ob ispol'zovanii kino pri reshenii V.I. Leninym voprosa o Gidrotorfe. Vospominaniya/* (A Problem Resolved with the Help of Filming [The Use of Filming in V.I. Lenin's Decision Regarding the Hydropeat Question. Reminiscences]) (1932); *Shkola realisticheskogo masterstva* (A School of Realistic Craftsmanship) (1938); *Izobrazitel'naya kompozitsiya fil'ma* (The Fine Composition of a Film) (1960), etc; *Died:* 1955.

ZHEMCHUZHNIKOV, Yuriy Apollonovich (1885–1957) Geologist; specialist in geology and petrography of coal; corresp member, USSR Acad of Sci from 1946; prof; *Born:* 8 May 1885; *Educ:* 1915 grad Petrograd Mining Inst; *Career:* 1920–30 lecturer, from 1930 prof, Leningrad Mining Inst; 1920–41 assoc, All-Union Geological Research Inst; studied geology of coal basins; developed principles for classifying coal according to the species of spores they contain; supervised research on methods of studying the coal fossils of the USSR; supervised compilation of *Atlas mikrostruktury ugley SSSR* (An Atlas of the Microstructure of the Coals of the USSR) (1937) and collection *Kosaya sloistost' i yeyo geologicheskaya interpretatsiya* (Oblique Bedding and Its Geological Interpretation) (1940); *Publ: Vvedeniye v petrografiyu ugley* (An Introduction to the Petrography of Coals) (1934); *Obshchaya geologiya iskopayemykh ugley* (The General Geology of Coal Fossils) (1948); *Uglenosnaya tolshcha i metodika yeyo izucheniya* (Coal-Bearing Seams and Methods of Studying Them) (1951); *Uglenosnyye tolshchi kak formatsii* (Coal-Bearing Seams as Formations) (1955); etc; *Died:* 9 Jan 1957.

ZHEMCHUZHNYY, Sergey Fyodorovich (1873–1929) Inorganic chemist and metallographer; *Born:* 5 July 1873 in Kerch'; *Educ:* 1895 grad Moscow Univ; 1900 grad Petersburg Mining Inst; *Career:* from 1901 close assoc of N. Kurnakov at Mining Inst and Polytech Inst, Kiev; from 1915 senior chemist, Chemical Laboratory, Acad of Sci; his joint research with Kurnakov laid the basis of physicochemical analysis; 1905 studied zinc-antimony and magnesium-silver binary metallic systems; 1913 studied cadmium-arsenic binary metallic system; 1917 discovered plasticity of manganese containing small additions of copper; together with his pupils, studied electrically resistant alloys and laid the basis for their production in the USSR; 1916 discovered a means of obtaining pure platinum and established its properties; devised a method of studying the microstructure of salt alloys in reflected light; studied means of using the USSR's natural salt deposits in the Caspian's Kara-Bogaz-Gol Gulf and the salt lakes of the Crimea; *Publ: Polucheniye chistoy platiny i yeyo svoystva. Elektroprovodnost' splavov platiny s metallami platinovoy gruppy* (The Production of Pure Platinum and Its Properties. The Electrical Conductivity of Platinum Alloys with Metals of the Platinum Group) (1916); *Elektroprovodnost' i tvyordost' margantsevo-mednykh spavov* (The Electrical Conductivity and Hardness of Manganese-Copper Alloys) (1917); coauthor, *Splavy dlya elektricheskikh izmeritel'nykh i nagrevatel'nykh priborov* (Alloys for Electrical Measuring and Heating Apparatus) (1928), etc; *Died:* 27 Sept 1929.

ZHEMOCHKIN, Boris Nikolayevich (1887–1961) Civil eng; maj-gen, Eng and Tech Corps; prof; Dr of Tech Sci; member, Acad of Architecture and Construction from 1956; Hon Sci and Tech Worker of RSFSR; *Born:* 1887; *Educ:* 1909 grad Moscow Eng College, Dept of Means of Communication; *Career:* from 1909 worked on construction of various projects in Moscow, then on railroad; 1913–34 taught at Moscow Eng College, Dept of Means of Communication (now Moscow Inst of Trans Eng); from 1932 prof, Kuybyshev Mil Eng Acad; from 1934 also prof, Moscow Architectural Inst; 1950–56 member, Acad of Architecture; worked on calculation of statically indefinite systems and flexibly-based beams by the elasticity theory method; also specialized in calculation of hydraulic installations; *Publ: Raschyot odezhd otkosov* (The Calculation of Embankment Cladding) (1928); *Raschyot ram. Kratkiy kurs* (Frame Calculation. A Short Course) (1933); *Raschyot kruglykh plit na uprugom osnovanii na simmetrichnuyu nagruzku* (The Calculation of Round Plates on a Flexible Base for Symmetrical Loading) (1938); *Teoriya uprugosti. Kratkiy kurs dlya inzhenerov-stroiteley* (Elasticity Theory. A Short Course for Civil Engineers) (1948); *Kurs stroitel'noy mekhaniki.* (A Construction Mechanics Course) (1950); *Teoriya uprugosti* (Elasticity Theory) (1957); *Raschyot randbalok i peremychek* (The Calculation of Edge Beams and Tie Plates) (1960), etc; *Awards:* Order of the Red Banner; Order of the Red Star; Stalin Prize (1951); *Died:* Oct 1961.

ZHERVE, Boris Borisovich (1879–1937) Mil commander; *Born:* 1879; *Educ:* 1898 grad Naval Corps; 1901 completed mine courses; *Career:* from 1918 lectured at Mil Tech Acad; also worked for Historical Commission to Study the Experience of Naval Warfare; 1922–23 chm of this commission; 1914 began lit research work; edited collection *Operatsiya flota protiv berega* (Fleet Anti-Coastal Operations); arrested by State Security organs; *Publ: Osnovy voyenno-morskoy strategii* (The Principles of Naval Strategy) (1919–21); *Znacheniye morskoy sily dlya gosudarstva* (The Importance of Naval Power to a State) (1923); *Morskaya strategiya Napoleona* (Napoleon's Naval Strategy) (1926); *Desantnaya operatsiya* (Landing Operations) (1931), etc; *Died:* 1937 in imprisonment.

ZHGENTI, Tengiz Gigoyevich (1887–1937) Party and govt official; CP member 1903; *Born:* 1887; *Career:* Took part in Geo peasant revol movement; did Party work in Batumi, Chiatura and Kutaisi; 1918–20 did underground work in Tbilisi and Baku; from 1921 held various Party and govt posts; chm, Batumi Sov Workers' Dep; 1st secr, Adzhar Oblast CPSU(B) Comt; chm, Commission for the Collection and Study of Material on the History of the Oct Revol and the History of the CP, CC, CP Geo; secr, Geo Centr Exec Comt; member, CC, CP Geo; 1937 arrested by NKVD; *Died:* 1937 in imprisonment; posthumously rehabiltated.

ZHIGA (real name: SMIRNOV), Ivan Fyodorovich (1895–1949) Russian writer and essayist; CP member from 1917; *Born:* 10 Feb 1895 in vil Ivanovskoye, Smolensk Province; *Educ:* completed parish school; studied at Higher Lit and Art Inst and at Moscow Univ; *Career:* from age 18 worked at a plant; 1915 drafted into Russian Army; active in Bolshevik underground; fought in 1917 Oct Revol and Civil War; 1917 deleg, 2nd All-Russian Congress of Soviets; 1918–22 worked for Cheka; 1914 first work printed; 1922–25 worked for newspaper "Pravda"; edited uyezd newspapers; member, "Kuznitsa" (The Smithy) lit assoc; during WW 2 worked for frontline periodicals; *Publ:* collected essays: *Dumy rabochikh, zaboty, dela* (Workers' Thoughts, Cares and Affairs) (1927); *Novyye rabochiye* (New Workers) (1928); *Na Krasnom putilovtse* (At Red Putilov); *Podzemnaya gazifikatsiya* (Underground Gasification); *Noch' Oktyabrya* (The Night of October) (1935); *Pervyy boy* (The First Battle) (1948); articles on the theory of essay writing *Za vysokoye iskusstvo* (For High Art), etc; *Gor'kiy. Vospominaniya* (Gorky. Reminiscences) (1955) *Died:* 9 Nov 1949 in Moscow.

ZHIGARYOV, Pavel Fyodorovich (1900–1963) Mil commander; Air Force Chief Marshal from 1955; CP member from 1920; *Born:* 19 Nov 1900 in vil Brikovo, Tver' Province, son of a peasant; *Educ:* 1922 grad 4th Tver' Cavalry School; 1927 grad pilots' school; 1937 grad commanders Fac, Zhukovskiy Air Force Acad; *Career:* from 1919 in Sov Army; fought in Civil War; Nov 1937 – Sept 1938 asst mil attaché in China; then worked for Pop Comrt of Defense; during WW 2 dep commander, Sov Air Force; then commander, Air Force of Far Eastern Front; during operations against Japan commanded 19th Air Army; from 1946 first dep commander, Sov Air Force; from 1949 USSR Dep Min of Defense; from 1957 head, Main Civil Air Fleet Bd; from 1959 commandant, Anti-Aircraft Defense System Mil Command Acad; 1952–61 cand member, CC, CPSU; dep, USSR Supr Sov of 3rd–5th convocations; *Awards:* two Orders of Lenin; three Orders of the Red Banner; Order of Kutuzov, 1st Class; Order of the Red Star; medals; *Died:* 2 Oct 1963.

ZHIGUR, Yan Matisovich (1895–1937) Mil commander; *Born:* 1895; *Career:* senior posts with Red Army Staff; senior instructor, Frunze Mil Acad, then Gen Staff Acad; dep chief, Mil Chemical Bd; 1937 arrested by State Security organs; *Publ: Vliyaniye sovremennoy voyennoy tekhniki na kharakter budushchikh voyn* (The Effects of Modern Military Equipment on the Nature of Future Wars) (1927); *Budushchaya voyna i zadachi oborony SSSR* (Future Warfare and the USSR's Defense Tasks) (1928); *Razmakh budushchey imperialisticheskoy voyny* (The Scope of Future Imperialist War) (1930); *Khimicheskoye oruzhiye v sovremennoy voyne* (Chemical Weapons in Modern Warfare) (1933); *Proryv oboronitel'noy sistemy po opytu mirovoy voyny* (Breaching Defense Systems from the Experience of the World War) (1935); *Proryv i yego razvitiye* (Break-Through and Its Development) (1937), etc; *Died:* 1937 in imprisonment.

ZHILINA, Yelena Yefimovna (1890–1963) Actress; Pop Artiste of USSR from 1957; *Born:* 9 May 1890; *Educ:* 1922 grad Kazan' Theatrical Studio; *Career:* performed in amateur productions; from 1922 actress, Kazan' Bolshoy Drama Theater; 1936–42 at Arkhangel'sk Theater; from 1942 again at Kazan' Theater; *Roles:* Felitsata in Ostrovskiy's *Pravda khorosho, a schast'ye luchshe* (Truth is Good, But Happiness is Better); Domna Panteleyevna in Ostrovskiy's *Talanty i poklonniki* (Talents and Admirers); Korobochka in Gogol's *Myortvyye dushi* (Dead Souls); Talanova in Leonov's *Nashestviye* (Invasion), etc; *Died:* 29 Jan 1963.

ZHILKA, Vladimir Adamovich (1900–1933) Bel poet; *Born:* 27 May 1900 in vil Makashy, now Minsk Oblast, son of a peasant; *Educ:* 1926 grad Fac of History and Philology, Prague Univ; *Career:* lived in Vilnius, then emigrated to Czechoslovakia; 1926 took part in Acad Conference for the Reform of Bel Orthography, Minsk, after which he stayed in Bel SSR; 1927 joined "Maladnyak" proletarian writers' assoc, from which he was expelled in the following year; from 1927 member, "Uzvyshsha" lit assoc; criticized for "bourgeois aesthticism" and support of Bel national and cultural heritage; 1930 arrested as "national democrat" but released during pretrial investigation when he contracted tuberculosis; 1931 exiled to Urzhum, now Kirov Oblast; before death wrote a poetic "testament" on his love for Bel and hatred of her suppressors; *Publ:* verse collection *Uyaulen'ne* (Imagination) (1923); *Na rostani* (At the Crossroads) (1924); *Z palyou Zakhodnyay Belarusi* (From the Fields of Western Belorussia) (1927); *Died:* 1 Mar 1933 in Urzhum of tuberculosis; buried at Urzhum Cemetery.

ZHILYAYEV, Nikolay Sergeyevich (1881–1938) Composer, music theorist, critic and textologist; *Born:* 18 Oct 1881 in Kursk; *Educ:* 1905 grad Moscow Conservatory; *Career:* from 1926 lecturer, then prof, Moscow Conservatory; friend and teacher of M. Tukhachevskiy; wrote piano romances; 1937 arrested by NKVD; *Died:* 28 Jan 1938 in imprisonment; posthumously rehabilitated.

ZHIRKOV, Mark Nikolayevich (1892–1951) Yakut composer; Hon Art Worker of RSFSR from 1947; *Born:* 13 Mar 1892 in Vilyuysk; *Educ:* 1936 grad Moscow Conservatory; *Career:* 1936–

40 musical dir, Yakutsk Drama Theater; dep, Yakut Supr Sov of 2nd and 3rd convocations; *Works:* on the basis of the "Olonkho" (a Yakut heroic folk epic) composed first Yakut musical drama "D'uluruyar N'yurgun Bootur" to a libretto by D. Sivtsev-Omollon (1940); together with G.I. Litinskiy composed opera "N'yurgun Bootur" (1945–47); also with Litinskiy, composed opera "Sygryy Kyrynaastyyr" (1946) and first Yakut ballets "Field Flower" (1947) and "The Crimson Kerchief" (1948); music for plays: Sivtsev-Omollon's "Kyukyur the Smith" (1936); Mordinov's "Man"; Sapronov's *Lyubov'* (Love) (1943), etc; *Died:* 15 Apr 1951 in Yakutsk.

ZHISLIN, Samuil Grigor'yevich (1898–1967) Psychiatrist; Dr of Med; prof; *Born:* 1898; *Educ:* 1924 grad Med Fac, Moscow Univ; *Career:* 1924–30 assoc, Narcotics Dispensary and assoc prof, Chair of Psychiatry, Bel Univ, Minsk; 1930–32 asst prof, Chair of Psychiatry, 1st Moscow Med Inst; 1932–50 head, Chair of Psychiatry, Voronezh Med Inst; 1950–52 head, Chair of Psychiatry, Perm' Med Inst; from 1952 senior assoc, Inst of Neuropsychiatric Prophylaxis and Gannushkin Inst of Psychiatry, Moscow; 1952–67 also dir, Clinic of Adult Psychoses, State Inst of Psychiatry, RSFSR Min of Health; co-ed, psychiatry section, "Bol'shaya meditsinskaya entsiklopediya" (Large Medical Encyclopedia) (2nd ed) and "Malaya meditsinskaya entsiklopediya" (Small Medical Encyclopedia); *Publ: Rol' vozrastnogo somatogennogo faktora v vozniknovenii i techenii nekotorykh form psikhoza* (The Role of the Somatogenic Age Factor in the Development and Course of Certain Forms of Psychosis) (1956); *Ocherki klinicheskoy psikhiatrii* (Studies in Clinical Psychiatry) (1965); *Alkogol' – vrag nervnoy sistemy* (Alcohol – the Enemy of the Nervous System) (1966); *Died:* 1967.

ZHITKOV, Boris Stepanovich (1882–1938) Russian children's writer; *Born:* 11 Sept 1882 in Novgorod, son of a mathematics teacher; *Educ:* 1906 grad Natural Sci Dept, Novorossiysk Univ, Odessa; 1916 grad Shipbuilding Dept, Petrograd Polytech Inst; *Career:* worked as an ichthyologist, naval architect, navigator, captain of a research vessel, teacher of mathematics and drawing and principal of a tech college; 1924 first work published; contributed to the children's magazines and newspapers "Novyy Robinzon," "Yozh," "Pioner," etc; *Publ:* story collections: *Zloye more* (The Cruel Sea) (1924); *Morskiye istorii* (Tales of the Sea) (1925–37); novelette "Elchan-Kaya" (1926); stories: *Pro slona* (The Elephant) (1926); *Grivennik* (The Ten-Copeck Piece) (1937); *Pro obez'yanku* (The Monkey) (1928); novelette *Shkval* (The Tornado) (1929); pop books: *Pro etu knigu* (About This Book) (1927); *Svet bez ognya* (Light Without Fire) (1927); *Parokhod* (The Steamer) (1935); *Rasskazy o zhivotnykh* (Animal Stories) (1935); encyclopedic novelette *Chto ya videl* (What I Have Seen) (1939); *Rasskazy* (Stories) (1940); *Rasskazy o tekhnike* (Tales of Technology) (1947), etc; *Died:* 19 Oct 1938 in Moscow.

ZHIVAGO, Pyotr Ivanovich (1883–1948) Cytologist; *Born:* 8 Sept 1883; *Educ:* 1911 grad Moscow Univ; *Career:* from 1911 at Chair of Zoology, Moscow Univ; 1943–48 head, Karyology Laboratory, Inst of Cytology, Histology and Embryology, USSR Acad of Sci; studied fine structure of cell nucleus; contributed new data to dynamics of cell mitosis; *Publ: O primenenii metoda V.I. Favorskogo k prizhiznennomu issledovaniyu yadernykh struktur* (The Application of V.I. Favorskiy's Method to the Intravitam Study of Nuclear Structures) (1928); *K probleme izmenyayemosti kariotipa v individual'nom razvitii organizma* (The Changeability of the Karyotype in the Individual Development of the Organism) (1940); *Died:* 1948.

ZHLOBA, Dmitriy Petrovich (1887–1944) Mil commander; Civil War veteran; CP member from 1917; *Born:* 3 June 1887 in Kiev; *Career:* worker by trade; 1905 member, workers' battle squad in Nikolayev; May 1916 drafted into Russian Army for taking part in a strike at Gorlovka Mines and sent to Moscow; 1917 elected member, Moscow Sov; took part in 1917 Oct Revol in Moscow; late 1917 mil comr in Donbass; musterd miners' Red Guard unit and fought against Kaledin's forces, at Kiev and in Northern Caucasus; 1918 commanded regt, brigade, then 1st Steel Div which marched 800 km from Nevinnomysskaya to Tsaritsyn and on 15 Oct 1918 struck Krasnov's forces in the rear; 1919–20 commanded separate partisan unit, then forces group on Caspian-Caucasian Front; commanded 1st Cavalry Corps and Cavalry Forces Group in operations against Gen Wrangel; Mar 1921 commanded 18th Cavalry Div; after Civil War senior econ and govt work in Northern Caucasus; 10 June 1938 arrested by State Security organs; *Awards:* two Orders of the Red Banner; golden arms; *Died:* 23 May 1944 in imprisonment; posthumously rehabilitated.

ZHMACHENKO, Filipp Feodosiyevich (1895–1966) Mil commander; col-gen; chm, Ukr DOSAAF from 1955; Presidium member, USSR DOSAAF from 1958; CP member from 1917; *Born:* 1895 in vil Mogel'ni, now Zhitomir Oblast; *Educ:* 1922 grad Higher Tactics School; 1925 grad "Vystrel" Higher Tactics Courses; 1947 grad Higher Acad Courses, Voroshilov Higher Mil Acad; *Career:* fought in WW 1; 1917 with Red Guards; from 1918 in Red Army; 1925–41 rose from command of battalion to command of infantry corps; 1941–45 commander, 3rd Army on Bryansk Front, then 47th and 40th Armies on 1st Ukr Front; 1947 asst commander in chief of Occupation Forces in Austria and dep commander, Bel and Ciscarpathian Mil Distr; deleg at 1958 and 1960 CP Ukr Congresses; *Awards:* Hero of the Sov Union; *Died:* 19 June 1966.

ZHOLTOV, I.I. (1890–1939) Govt and admin official; CP member from 1917; *Born:* 1890; *Career:* took part in 1917 Revol in Moscow; after 1917 Oct Revol chm, Moscow's Bauman Rayon Sov; directed plant at Bezhitsa, near Bryansk; chm, Moscow Province Trade-Union Council; dep chm, Uzbek Council of Pop Comr; Collegium member, USSR Pop Comrt of Labor; from 1931 directed construction of plants at Chelyabinsk, Ufa, etc; arrested by State Security organs; *Died:* 1939 in imprisonment.

ZHOLTOVSKIY, Ivan Vladislavovich (1867–1959) Architect; Hon Sci and Art Worker of RSFSR from 1962 member, USSR Acad of Architecture from 1939; hon member, Bel Acad of Sci from 1947; member, USSR Acad of Construction and Architecture from 1956; *Born:* 27 Nov 1867 in Pinsk; *Educ:* 1896 grad Petersburg Acad of Arts; *Career:* prior to 1917 Oct Revol designed buildings and lectured at Stroganov College, Moscow; after 1917 Oct Revol taught at Higher State Tech Art Workshops, then Higher State Tech Art Inst; 1924–26 lived abroad; 1932–37 directed Design Workshop, Moscow Sov; from 1937 bd member, USSR Architects' Union; from 1940 dir, Moscow Architectural Inst; from 1953 directed a workshop school and was consultant to many construction orgs; *Works:* Skakov Soc building (1900); dwelling house on Spiridonovka, Moscow (1905–06); prior to WW 1 built factories, country mansions and town houses; 1918–23 helped draft Moscow's first reconstruction plan; 1923 architectural designs for All-Russian Agric Axhibition in Moscow; drew up gen plan of this exhibition and designed a number of its pavilions; 1926 his design was used for the construction of the Sov Pavilion at the Int Exhibition, Milan; 1926–31 State Bank building in Moscow; Daghestani ASSR House of Soviets in Makhachkala, etc; 1933–34 apartment house on Moscow's Mokhovaya Street; 1935–36 house of USSR Council of Ministers' rep in Sochi, bridge over River Sochi, etc; 1949 apartment houses on Smolensk Square and Bol'shaya Kaluzhskaya Street, Moscow; 1957 apartment house on Peace Prospect, etc; *Publ: Proyekty i postroyki* (Designs and Buildings) (1955); translated A. Palladio's treatise on architecture; *Awards:* Order of Lenin; three Orders of the Red Banner of Labor; Stalin Prize (1950); *Died:* 16 July 1959.

ZHORDANIYA, Noy Nikolayevich (alias: KOSTROV, An.) (1870–1953) Journalist and Menshevik politician; *Born:* 1870; *Educ:* grad Tiflis Theological Seminary; then studied at Warsaw Veterinary Inst; *Career:* from 1894 in revol movement; several times arrested and exiled; attended 2nd RSDRP Congress; Tiflis dep, 1st State Duma, led Duma's Soc-Democratic faction; from 1905 edited Geo-language newspaper "Social-Democrat"; at 5th (London) Party Congress elected Menshevik member, CC, RSDRP; after 1917 Feb Revol chm, Tiflis Sov; 1918–Feb 1921 chm, Geo Govt; from 1921, after establishment of Sov regime in Geo, lived abroad; *Died:* 1953.

ZHUK, Sergey Yakovlevich (1892–1957) Hydraulic eng; member, USSR Acad of Sci from 1953; Hero of Socialist Labor from 1952; CP member from 1942; *Born:* 4 Apr 1892; *Educ:* 1917 grad Petrograd Inst of Trans Eng; *Career:* from 1917 worked for various orgs, designing and building hydraulic eng structures; 1930–32 asst chief eng for design of White Sea-Baltic Canal; 1933–37 eng on construction of Moscow Canal, then chief eng for design and construction of Uglich and Rybinsk Hydroelectr Plants; 1937–41 chief eng for construction of Kuybyshev Hydropower Complex and Main Bd for Construction of Volga-Baltic Waterway; from 1942 dir and chief eng, Design, Prospecting and Research Bd for Construction of Hydraulic Eng Installations, USSR Min of Electr Power Plants; 1948–52 also chief eng for construction of Volga-Don Shipping Canal, etc; from 1953 also chm, Section for

Water Mang Problems, USSR Acad of Sci; dep, USSR Supr Sov of 1937 and 1954 convocations; *Awards:* two Stalin Prizes (1950 and 1951); three Orders of Lenin; Order of the Red Banner; Order of the Red Banner of Labor; two Orders of the Red Star; *Died:* 1 Mar 1957.

ZHUKOV, Ivan Ivanovich (1880–1949) Chemist; corresp member, USSR Acad of Sci from 1946; Hon Sci and Tech Worker of RSFSR from 1943; *Born:* 2 Dec 1880; *Educ:* 1903 grad Petersburg Univ; *Career:* 1903–49 worked at Petersburg (Leningrad) Univ; 1919–25 lectured at Higher Inst of Photography and Photographic Eng; 1926–30 at Leningrad Med Inst; 1903–26 did research on nitrogen and hydrogen interaction with metals; studied colloidal chemistry, particularly electrokinetic phenomena in dispersed systems for the purpose of water purification; developed theory and means of measuring electrokinetic potential, coagulation of hydrophobic colloids by electrolytes, etc; established the importance of the surface conductivity of dispersed and, particularly, capilaary-porous systems in electroosmotic phenomena; made detailed physicochemical study of Sov synthetic rubbers; *Publ: Kolloidnaya khimiya* (Colloidal Chemistry) (1949); *Awards:* Mendeleyev Prize of Russian Physicochemical Soc; (1912); two orders; *Died:* 3 Aug 1949.

ZHUKOV, Leonid Alekseyevich (1890–1951) Ballet dancer; Hon Artiste of RSFSR from 1933; *Born:* 20 Apr 1890; *Educ:* 1909 grad Ballet Dept, Moscow Theatrical College; *Career:* 1933–46 (with intervals) with ballet company of Bolshoy Theater; also worked as choreographer; 1925 and 1933–35 ballet teacher and choreographer in Ukr; 1938 ballet teacher and choreographer in Kaz SSR; 1945 ballet teacher and choreographer in Tatar ASSR; 1948 ballet teacher and choreographer in Kir SSR; *Roles:* Dezire in Tchaikovsky's *Spyashchaya krasavitsa* (Sleeping Beauty); Franz in "Coppelia," etc; *Productions:* ballets: "Spanish Caprice" (1923) and "Sheherezade" to music by Rimsky-Korsakov; Tchaikovsky's *Lebedinoye ozero* (Swan Lake) (1949); *Bakhchisarayskiy fontan* (The Fountain of Bakhchisaray) (1948); *Krasnyy mak* (The Red Poppy) (1950), etc; *Died:* 3 Nov 1951.

ZHUKOV, Mikhail Nikolayevich (1901–1960) Conductor; Hon Artiste of RSFSR from 1941; Hon Art Worker of Lat SSR from 1949; *Born:* 1901; *Educ:* grad M.S. Golovanov's composition class, Moscow Synodal College; *Career:* 1918 concert-master, 1919–25 and 1926–33 musical dir and conductor, Stanislavsky Opera Studio (from 1924 Opera Studio, Bolshoy Theater; from 1928 Stanislavsky Opera Theater); 1935–41 conductor, Stanislavsky Opera Theater; 1933–34 conductor, Kirov Opera and Ballet Theater; 1944–46 conductor, Moscow Operetta Theater; 1946–49 conductor, from 1949 chief conductor, Lat Opera and Ballet Theater, Riga; from 1951 conductor, Bolshoy Theater; *Works:* produced operas: *Tsarskaya nevesta* (Bride of the Tsar) (1926); *Zolotoy petushok* (The Golden Cockerel) (1932); Donizetti's "Don Pasquale" (1936); Prokofiev's "Semyon Kotko" (1940); "Boris Godunov" (1949); Rimsky-Korsakov's *Skazaniye o nevidimom grade Kitezhe i o deve Fevronii* (The Tale of the Invisible City of Kitezh and the Maid Fevronia) (1949); Moussorgsky's *Sorochinskaya yarmarka* (Sorochintsy Fair) (1952), etc; wrote operas: *Triumf* (The Triumph) (1924); *Ovod* (The Gadfly) (1928); *Groza* (The Storm) (1941); *Died:* 8 Nov 1960.

ZHUKOVICH, Anna Vasil'yevna (1905–1966) Otolaryngologist and otoneurologist; Dr of Med from 1958; prof from 1965; *Born:* 1905; *Educ:* 1930 grad Odessa Med Inst; *Career:* 1930–37 otolaryngologist, Mariupol' Therapy Assoc; 1937–44 intern, Ear, Nose and Throat Clinic, 1st Leningrad Med Inst and consultant, Uritskiy Hospital; 1944–51 assoc, Leningrad Ear, Nose, Throat and Speech Research Inst; 1945 defended candidate's thesis; 1951–62 permanent consultant, A.L. Polenov Neurosurgical Inst, Leningrad; 1962–66 head, Otolaryngological Dept, 1964–66 dep sci dir, Leningrad Neurosurgical Inst; trained numerous physicians in otoneurology; wrote over 60 works; *Publ:* candidate's thesis *O vestibulo-vegetativnoy adaptatsii* (Vestibular Vegetative Adaptation) (1945); doctor's thesis *O roli tsentral'noy nervnoy sistemy v vestibulyarnoy funktsii* (The Role of the Central Nervous System in the Vestibular Function) (1958), etc; *Died:* 9 May 1966 in Leningrad.

ZHUKOVSKIY, Grigoriy Yul'yevich (1878–1939) Technol chemist; specialist in glass-making; *Born:* 1878; *Educ:* 1902 grad Petersburg Univ; *Career:* from 1912 asst prof, Petersburg Polytech Inst; from 1912 prof, Warsaw Polytech Inst; from 1916 worked on production of optical glass; from 1921 prof, Khar'kov Technol Inst; from 1929 at various higher educ establishments in Moscow and Gorky; studied physicochemical properties of optical glass and technol properties of refractory clays and kavlins; *Publ: Proizvodstvo opticheskikh styokol* (The Production of Optical Glass) (1918); *Obezzhelezivaniye peskov mekhanicheskim sposobom* (The Mechanical Extraction of Iron from Sands) (1936); *Died:* 1939.

ZHUKOVSKIY, Nikolay Yegorovich (1847–1921) Hydromech and aeromech eng; Dr of Applied Mech from 1882; prof from 1879; corresp member, Russian Acad of Sci from 1894; *Born:* 17 Jan 1847 in vil Orekhovo, now Vladimir Oblast, son of a railroad eng; *Educ:* 1868 grad Physics and Mathematics Fac, Moscow Univ; *Career:* from 1872 mathematics lecturer, 1874–79 assoc prof, from 1879 prof and from 1887 head, Chair of Mech, Moscow Higher Tech College; from 1885 also assoc prof, from 1886 prof extraordinarius, Chair of Mech, Moscow Univ; 1872–1920 also taught mech at Practical Acad of Business Sci; from 1918 sci dir, Centr Aerohydrodynamic Inst; from 1918 also worked at Experimental Inst of Means of Communication, where he founded an Aerodynamics Dept and planned research on air resistance to the movement of trains and automobiles; 1904 sponsored foundation in vil Kuchin, near Moscow of Europe's first Aerodynamics Inst; 1910 founded Aerodynamics Laboratory at Moscow Higher Tech College; during WW 1 and Civil War directed Aviation Calculation and Testing Bureau, Moscow Higher Tech College, which developed methods for aerodynamic and strength calculation of airframes; organized at Moscow Higher Tech College theoretical courses for mil pilots, later reorganized into the Moscow Aviation Technicum and subsequently into the Inst of Aviation Eng, and then in 1922 into the Zhukovskiy Air Force Eng Acad; did research on aerodynamics and aviation, hydraulics and hydrodynamics, mech of invariable systems and mathematics and astronomy; 1891 published his major study *O paradokse Dyubuya* (The Dubois Paradox) in which he demonstrated that the reason for the great resistance of a static body in a moving liquid compared with the resistance of the same body moving in a static liquid is the formation of vortices in the liquid stream; 1904 discovered the law governing the lift of a plane's wing; 1910–11 established the best profiles for wings and plane airscrews; 1912–18 developed airscrew vortical theory; founded the sci of experimental aerodynamics; 1902 supervised establishment of one of the world's first wind tunnels and invented a device for testing airscrews; in the field of hydraulics and hydrodynamics devised methods for determining the effects on a vessel of an inflowing or outflowing liquid, of use in solving the tech problem of designing jet-powered vessels; carried out various research on the theory of the pitching and tossing of marine vessels; 1898 founded the theory of so-called hydraulic impact; also studied the theory of the motion of a heavy, solid body around a fixed point, the stability of motion, theoretical astronomy, etc; from 1876 member, from 1905 pres, Moscow Mathematics Soc; also member, Moscow Soc of Experimental Scientists and Soc of Natural Scientists, Anthropologists and Ethnographers; 1920 RSFSR govt appointed a Zhukovskiy Prize for the best works on mathematics and mech; often termed "The Father of Russian Aviation"; *Publ: Polnoye sobraniye sochineniy* (Complete Collected Works) (9 vol, 1935–37); *Sobraniye sochineniy* (Collected Works) (7 vol, 1948–50); *Died:* 17 Mar 1921 in Moscow.

ZHUKOVSKIY, Valentin Alekseyevich (1858–1918) Orientalist; specialist in Persian studies; corresp member, Russian Acad of Sci from 1899; *Born:* 23 Apr 1858; *Career:* prof, Petersburg Univ; specialized in Persian language, lit, folklore and ethnography; *Publ: Materialy dlya izucheniya persidskikh narechiy* (Material on the Study of Persian Dialects) (3 vol, 1888–1922); coauthor, *Kratkaya grammatika novopersidskogo yazyka* (A Short Grammar of New Persian) (1890); *Drevnosti Zakaspiyskogo kraya* (Antiquities of Transcaspia) (1894); *Obraztsy persidskogo narodnogo tvorchestva* (Samples of Persian Folklore) (1902); *Died:* 1918.

ZHURAKOVSKIY, Gennadiy Yevgen'yevich (1894–1955) Educationist; Dr of Pegag Sci; prof; corresp member, RSFSR Acad of Pedag Sci from 1945; *Born:* 23 Aug 1894; *Educ:* grad Dept of History of Arts and Philosophy Dept, Kiev Univ; *Career:* from 1917 taught humanities at a secondary school; from 1922 teaching and research work at Kiev higher educ establishments; from 1934 in Moscow; in his latter years prof, Chair of Pedag, Krupskaya Teachers' Training Inst, Moscow; specialized in history of pedag, particularly of Ancient World, Middle Ages and Renaissance; also studied pedag legacy of Lev Tolstoy, Pirogov and Makarenko; compiled visual aids for teaching history of pedag; *Publ: K voprosu ob osnovakh psikhologii otrochestva* (The Principles of the

Psychology of Adolescence) (1922); *Ocherki po istorii pedagogiki v svyazi s istoriyey klassovoy bor'by* (An Outline History of Pedagogics in Connection with the History of the Class Struggle) (1926); *Stronin i Poltavskaya gimnaziya v kontse 50-kh godov 19–go veka* (Stronin and the Poltava High School in the Late 1850's) (1943); *K voprosu o vozniknovenii pervykh voskresnykh shkol v Kiyeve* (The Emergence of the First Sunday Schools in Kiev) (1944); *Problema gumanizma i obshchego obrazovaniya v pedagogicheskoy sisteme N.I. Pirogova* (Humanism and General Education in N.I. Pirogov's Educational System) (1946); *Komsomol v zhizni i rabote uchrezhdeniy A.S. Makarenko* (The Komsomol in the Life and Work of A.S. Makarenko Institutions) (1953); *Ucheniye A.S. Makarenko o distsipline* (A.S. Makarenko's Theory of Discipline) (1957); *Pedagogicheskiy talant i pedagogicheskaya tekhnika v oblasti istorii pedagogiki obshchey, khudozhestvennoy, muzykal'noy i teatral'noy* (Pedagogic Talent and Pedagogic Technique in the History of General, Artistic, Musical and Theatrical Pedagogics) (1958); *Pedagogicheskiye idei A.S. Makarenko* (A.S. Makarenko's Pedagogic Ideas) (1963); *Ocherki po istorii antichnoy pedagogiki* (An Outline History of Ancient Pedagogics) (1963), etc; *Died:* 10 Mar 1955.

ZHURAVLENKO, Pavel Maksimovich (1887–1948) Opera singer (bass); Pop Artiste of RSFSR from 1938; *Born:* 11 July 1887 in the Ukr; *Educ:* studied singing at a music school; from 1906 studied under A.V. Sekar-Rozhanskiy in Moscow; *Career:* 1911 opera debut in Kazan'; 1912–18 at Petersburg Musical Drama Theater; from 1918 at Mariinsky Theater and Maly Opera Theater; 1918–21 partnered Chaliapine during his performances in Petrograd; *Roles:* Dodon, Saltan and Mayor in Rimsky-Korsakov's *Zolotoy petushok* (The Golden Cockerel), *Skazka o tsare Saltane* (The Tale of Tsar Saltan) and *Mayskaya noch'* (May Night); Varlaam and Cherevik in Moussorgsky's "Boris Godunov" and *Sorochinskaya yarmarka* (Sorochintsy Fair); Leporello in Dargomyzhskiy's *Kamennyy gost'* (The Stone Guest); Skula in Borodin's *Knyaz' Igor'* (Prince Igor); Leporello in "Don Juan"; Yeryomka in Serov's *Vrazh'ya sila* (Enemy Power), etc; also performed in operetta; *Died:* 28 June 1948 in Leningrad.

ZHURAVLYOV, Pyotr Mironovich (1903–1943) Mil health official; maj-gen, Med Corps; *Born:* 1903; *Educ:* 1923 grad infantry commanders school; 1929 grad Leningrad Mil Med Acad; *Career:* after grad junior and senior regt surgeon, then div surgeon; from 1939 dep chm, Red Army Health Bd; helped to improve supply system for troop med centers, field hospitals, etc; from 1941 head, Med and Health Supply Bd, Main Mil Health Bd; *Publ: Profilaktika i lecheniye gazovoy gangreny pri pomoshchi novykh biologicheskikh antiseptikov anaerobnykh bakteriofagov* (The Prevention and Treatment of Gas Gangrene with New Biological Antiseptics – Anaerobic Bacteriophages) (1943); coauthor, *Fagoprofilaktika i fagoterapiya gazovoy gangreny* (The Prevention and Treatment of Gas Gangrene with Bacteriophages) (1943); co-ed, *Posobiye po meditsinskomu snabzheniyu Krasnoy armii* (The Red Army Medical Supply Manual) (1944); *Died:* 1943 on active service.

ZIFEL'DT (SIMUMYASH), A.R. (1889–1938) Party and govt official; CP member from 1915; *Born:* 1889; *Career:* from 1906 in revol movement; member, Socialist-Revol Party; later member, Labor Pop Socialist Party; 1908–10 anarcho-syndicalist; from 1913 lived in Switzerland; for some time sided with Plekhanovites, then with "Nashe slovo" (Our Word) group in RSDRP; from 1915 Bolshevik; Odessa Party org deleg at 6th RSDRP(B) Congress; after 1917 Oct Revol mil, Party, admin and research work in the Caucasus; arrested by State Security organs; *Died:* 1938 in imprisonment.

ZIL'BER, Lev Aleksandrovich (1894–1966) Microbiologist, immunologist and virologist; prof from 1929; Dr of Med; member, USSR Acad of Med Sci from 1945; *Born:* 27 Mar 1894; *Educ:* 1917 grad Natural Sci Dept, Physics and Mathematics Fac, Petrograd Univ; 1919 grad Med Fac, Moscow Univ; *Career:* 1919–20 health officer in Zvenigorod, now Moscow Oblast; 1920–21 mil surgeon in Red Army; 1921–29 assoc, Inst of Microbiology, RSFSR Pop Comrt of Health; 1929–30 head, Chair of Microbiology, Baku Med Inst; then dir, Azer Inst of Microbiology, Baku; 1930–40 head, Chair of Microbiology, Centr Inst of Postgrad Med Training, Moscow; 1939–45 head, Virology Dept, Gamalea Inst of Epidemiology and Microbiology, USSR Acad of Med Sci; 1945–66 head, Dept of Virology and Immunology of Malignant Tumors, above inst; sci consultant, Virology Laboratory, Herzen State Oncological Inst and consultant, Burdenko Inst of Neurosurgery, USSR Acad of Med Sci; 1921, under the direction of V.A. Barykin, studied immunity and mutability of microorganisms; 1935 founded Centr Virological Laboratory, later combined with Dept of Virology, Centr Inst of Experimental Med and then reorganized into Inst of Virology, USSR Acad of Med Sci; 1939 founded Dept of Virology, Inst of Microbiology, USSR Acad of Sci; sponsored 1st All-Union Conference on Ultramicrobiology and Filtrable Viruses; 1937 headed expedition to study etiology of encephalitis in Far East, discovered its causative agent and together with Acad Ye. M. Pavlovskiy established its epidemiology, described clinial aspects and hypothesized that encephalitis was spread by ticks; established presence of Scottish encephalitis in USSR; from 1945 worked in viral theory of the pathogenesis of cancer; supervised preparation of over 20 doctor's and cand thesis; bd member, All-Union Soc of Microbiologists, Epidemiologists and Infectionists; bd member, All-Union Soc of Oncologists; member, Cancer Council, Presidium of USSR Acad of Med Sci; ed, microbiology section, 2nd ed of "BME" (Large Medical Encyclopedia); member, ed bd, journal "Voprosy virusologii"; member, ed council, journals "Voprosy onkologii," "Zhurnal mikrobiologii, epidemiologii i immunologii," etc; 1958 attended conference on tissue grafts in Czechoslovakia; 1960 presented paper on paths of transmission of carcinogenic viruses at Int Epidemiological Symposium, Prague; attended UNESCO consultants' conference on "Cell Biology"; attended "Cell Beiology and Growth Inhibition" symposium at Louvain, Belgium; attended Sov-American Cancer Session in New York; member, comt to convene 8th Int Cancer Congress, held in Moscow in 1962; wrote over 200 works, including nine monographs; *Publ: Paraimmunitet* (Paraimmunity) (1928); *Epidemicheskiye entsefality* (Epidemic Encephalitis) (1945); *Osnovy immuniteta* (The Principles of Immunity) (1948); *O spetsificheskom komponente zlokachestvennykh opukholey* (The Specific Component of Malginant Tumors) (1950); *Ucheniye o virusakh* (Virus Theory) (1956); *Osnovy immunologii* (The Principles of Immunology) (1958), etc; *Awards:* Stalin Prize (1967, posthumously); Order of Lenin (1961); other orders and medals; Gamalea Prize (1958); *Died:* 10 Nov 1966 in Moscow.

ZIMIN, Sergey Ivanovich (1875–1942) Theater impressario; *Born:* 3 July 1875 in Orekhovo-Zuyevo; *Educ:* studied singing under N.M. Kedrov, A.I. Bartsal and M.I. Miller; *Career:* 1903 organized student concerts; 1904 organized Bolshoy Theater opera shows in the "Gay" Gardens at Kuskovo, near Moscow; 1904 founded Private Opera Theater in Moscow, later known as the Zimin Opera Theater; engaged for this theater many of the members of Ippolitov-Ivanov's Assoc of Moscow Private Opera Artistes, closed in 1904; from 1917 member, Directorate, Zimin State Opera Theater; 1918 and 1921–22 artistic consultant, Moscow Acad Arts Theater; 1919–20 member, Directorate, State Malaya Opera Theater; 1922–24 chm, Zimin Free Opera Theater; 1924–42 artistic consultant, Bolshoy Theater branch; *Died:* 26 Aug 1942 in Moscow.

ZINOV'YEV, Georgiy Vasil'yevich (1887–1934) Mil commander; CP member from 1917; *Born:* 20 Nov 1887 in Petersburg, son of a mil official; *Educ:* 1917 grad Sebastopol Pilots School; *Career:* during WW 1 drove an armored car; from Oct 1917 chm, Mil Revol Comt, 3rd Siberian Corps; mustered first Socialist Detachment, Western Front and fought against Germans and Dovbor-Musnitskiy's Corps; then directed campaign against White Cossacks at Orenburg; from Mar 1919 commanded Turkestani Army; then Assault Group of Southern Forces Group on Eastern Front in the campaign against Kolchak; from Aug 1919 commanded 1st Army at Orsk, Aktyubinsk and in Transcaspia; 1920 commanded forces group in Bukhara operation, then Ferghana Forces Group against insurgents; after Civil War head, Air Forces Training Establishments Bd; commander, Air Force of Leningrad Mil Distr; commandant, Mil Eng Adac; *Died:* 26 Apr 1934.

ZINOV'YEV (real name: RADOMYSL'SKIY), Grigoriy Yevseyevich (1883–1936) Party official; CP member from 1903; *Born:* 1883 in Kherson Province; *Educ:* studied at Bern Univ; *Career:* 1901 joined RSDRP; 1903 at 2nd RSDRP Congress sided with Bolsheviks; 1902 emigrated to Switzerland; 1905 returned to Russia; member, Petersburg RSDRP Comt; from 1907 member, CC, RSDRP; 1907 attended 5th (London) RSDRP Congress; spring 1908 again emigrated; 1909 co-ed, periodical "Sotsialdemokrat"; then worked for "Zvezda," "Mysli" and "Pravda"; during WW 1 adopted Internationalist stand; 1916, together with Lenin, attended Kienthal Conference; after 1917 Feb Revol returned to Russia with Lenin and other Bolsheviks; after 1917 July revolt went underground and hid with Lenin at Razliv Station; during preparations for 1917 Oct Revol opposed idea of immediate armed coup; after 1917 Oct Revol elected chm, Petrograd Sov; advocated formation of coalition govt; 16 Nov 1917 resigned from Party CC in protest against CC resolution barring other polit parties from the govt; within a few days rejoined Party CC; 1919–26 chm, Comintern Exec Comt; 1922–23, together with Stalin and Kamenev, constituted the so-called „troyka" which wielded virtually all power during Lenin's illness and particularly after Lenin's death; 1923–24, with the aid of the Party apparatus, the troyka prepared and carried out the campaign against Trotsky and his supporters; at CC Plenum elected at 14th Party Congress in 1925, he was elected Politburo member, CC, CPSU(B); 1925, as chm of Leningrad Sov, headed so-called "Leningrad Opposition"; 1926 joined forces with Trotsky; June 1926 expelled from Politburo and Nov 1927 from CPSU(B); 1928 recanted his "errors" and was readmitted to Party; from fall 1928 Presidium member, Centr Union of Consumer Soc; then Collegium member, Pop Comrt of Food; Oct 1932 again expelled from Party and exiled from Moscow as an accomplice of the "Ryutin counterrevol group"; Mar 1933 wrote a letter confessing his "errors and anti-Party actions" and was reinstated in the Party; Jan 1935 sentenced to 10 years' imprisonment as "one of the leaders of the Moscow Center, underground counterrevol group"; Aug 1936, in trial of Trotskyite-Zinov'yevite "Terrorist Center" sentenced to death for "organizing the joint Trotskyite-Zinov'yevite Terrorist Center for the assassination of Soviet government and CPSU(B) leaders"; *Publ: Voyna i krizis sotsializma* (War and the Crisis of Socialism) (1920); coauthor, *Protiv techeniya* (Against the Current) (1923); coauthor, *Za tretiy Internatsional* (For the Third International (1924); *Sobraniye sochineniy* (Collected Works) (9 vol); *Died:* Aug 1936 executed.

ZLATOGOROV, Semyon Ivanovich (1873–1931) Microbiologist and epidemiologist; prof from 1920; corresp member, USSR Acad of Sci from 1929; *Born:* 2 May 1873; *Educ:* 1897 grad Petersburg Mil Med Acad; *Career:* after grad specialized at Chair of Infectious Diseases, Petersburg Mil Med Acad; organized and accompanied following expeditions to combat plague, cholera and other epidemics: 1899 to Astrakhan' Province; 1902 to the Don; 1904 to Persia; 1911 to China; did research on the biology of the plague microbe; from 1920 prof of this chair and Chair of Microbiology, Petrograd (Leningrad) Med Inst; from 1920 also helped to organize anti-epidemic measures in Red Army; from 1924 prof of bacteriology, Khar'kov Med Inst; and dir, Mechnikov Sanitary Bacteriological Inst; did major research on the etiology and prevention of measles and scarlet fever; proved that the scarlet fever streptococcus is activated by a filtrable virus; criticized for his attempts to apply Mendel's laws of heredity to bacterial reproduction processes; *Publ: Ucheniye o mikroorganizmakh* (The Theory of Microorganisms) (3 vol, 1916–18); *O vaktsine, predokhranyayushchey odnovremenno protiv dizenterii i letnikh kishechnykh infektsiy* (A Vaccine Providing Simultaneous Protection Against Dysentery and Summer Intestinal Infections) (1924); *Etiologiya, epidemiologiya, profilaktika i seroterapiya skarlatiny* (The Etiology, Epidemiology, Prevention and Serum Treatment of Scarlet Fever) (1927); *Ucheniye ob infektsii i immunitete* (The Theory of Infection and Immunity) (2nd ed, 1928); coauthor, *Kor'. Epidemiologiya, etiologiya, klinika i profilaktika* (Measles. Its Epidemiology, Etiology, Clinical Aspects and Prevention) (1930); *Died:* 17 Mar 1931.

ZLOBIN, Stepan Pavlovich (1903–1965) Russian writer; *Born:* 24 Nov 1903; *Educ:* 1924 grad Higher Lit Art Inst; *Career:* 1924 first work published; wrote historical novels on pop revolts; *Publ:* historical novel on Pugachyov rebellion "Salavat Yulayev" (1929); novels: *Ostrov Buyan* (Buyan Island) (1949); "Stepan Razin" (1951); *Propavshiye bez vesti* (Reported Missing) (1956); articles "The Cream of Chekhov" (1960); "Life is the Source of Creativity" (1963), etc; *Awards:* Stalin Prize (1952); *Died:* 15 Sept 1965.

ZNAMENSKIY, Andrey Aleksandrovich (1886–1943) Dipl; mil commander; CP member; *Born:* 1886 in Don Oblast; *Educ:* from 1911 studied at Law Fac, Shanyavskiy Pop Univ, Moscow; studied English, French, Italian, Spanish and Latin; *Career:* spent his childhood in Irkutsk, where his father worked on the Siberian Railroad; from 1902 in revol movement; 1905 member, Irkutsk RSDRP Comt; arrested by Tsarist police; from 1915 worked for Moscow Union of Consumer Soc; edited journal "Soyuz potrebiteley"; 1917 member, Moscow RSDRP(B) Comt; from Nov 1917 commanded Moscow Special Assignments Unit; fought in Civil War; Min of Internal Affairs, Far Eastern Republ; 1922 commanded Air Force; from late 1923 CC, RCP(B) and RSFSR rep in Bukhara Pop Republ; then USSR amb in Manchuria; from 1930 USSR amb in China; *Died:* 1943.

ZOF, Vyacheslav Ivanovich (1889–1940) Lat mil commander and govt official; CP member from 1913; *Born:* Dec 1889; *Educ:* grad elementary school and gen educ courses; *Career:* metalworker; from 1910 in revol movement; during WW 1, while at Sestroretsk Arms Factory, did underground work; 1917–18 member, Council of Transport Factory and Plant Comts; 1918–19 brigade and div comr; chief of supply, 3rd Army; 1919–20 member, Revol-Mil Council, Baltic Fleet; 1921–24 comr to Naval supr commander; 1924–26 Naval commander in chief and member, Russian Revol-Mil Council; 1926 bd chm, potassium trust; after 14th CPSU(B) Congress joined Leningrad opposition, then Trotsky-Zinov'yevite Bloc; in letter of 27 Aug 1927 admitted his errors and left opposition; 1927–29 Collegium member, Pop Comrt of Means of Communication and chm, Sov Merchant Fleet; 1930–31 Dep Pop Comr of Water Trans; arrested by State Security organs; *Died:* 29 Oct 1940 in imprisonment; posthumously rehabilitated.

ZOGRAF, Aleksandr Nikolayevich (1889–1942) Numismatist; Dr of Historical Sci; *Born:* 26 Feb 1889; *Career:* from 1912 worked at Museum of Fine Arts, Moscow; from 1922 assoc, from 1935 head, Dept of Numismatics, State Hermitage, Leningrad; specialist in ancient numismatics, especially the coinage of the northern Black Sea littoral; dated and made the first full classification of the coins of ancient cities along the northern Black Sea littoral; *Publ: Reforma denezhnogo obrashcheniya v Bosparskom tsarstve pri Savromate II* (The Currency Reform in the Kingdom of Bospar under Savromat II) (1938); *Rasprostraneniye nakhodok antichnykh monet na Kavkaze* (The Distribution of Ancient Coin Finds in the Caucasus) (1945); *Antichnyye monety* (Ancient Coins) (1951); *Monety Tiry* (The Coins of Tyre) (1957); *Died:* 17 Jan 1942.

ZOLOTARYOV, Vasiliy Andreyevich (1873–1964) Composer and music teacher; prof from 1908; Hon Artiste of RSFSR from 1932; Pop Artiste of Bel SSR from 1949; *Born:* 7 Mar 1873 in Taganrog; *Educ:* 1892 grad Petersburg Singing Capella, where he studied under M.A. Balakirev and A.K. Lyadov; 1900 grad Rimsky-Korsakov's composition class, Petersburg Conservatory; *Career:* 1906–08 instructor, Rostov-on-Don Music College; 1909–18 prof, Moscow Conservatory; 1918–24 taught at Don and Kuban' Conservatories; 1924–26 at Odessa Musical Drama Inst; 1926–31 at Kiev Musical Drama Inst; 1933–41 prof, Minsk Conservatory; 1931–33 taught at Sverdlovsk Music Technicum; from 1941 lived and worked in Moscow; *Works:* operas: *Dekabristy* (The Decembrists) (1924); new version of this entitled "Kondratiy Ryleyev" (1957); "Khves'ko Andiber" (1928); "Akgyul'" (1942); ballet *Knyaz'ozero* (The Prince Lake) (1948); symphonies: "Wrath Symphony" (1902); "1905" (1929); "The Chelyuskinites" (1935); "Belorussia" (1936); "1941" (1942); "My Homeland" (1964); "7th Symphony" (1962); "Moldavian Suite" (1928); "Uzbek Suite" (1931); "Tadzhik Suite" (1932); "Belorussian Dance Suite" (1936); six quartets; cantatas, rhapsodies, choral works, romances and arrangements of folk songs; *Awards:* Order of the Red Banner of Labor (1940); Order of Lenin (1955); Stalin Prize (1950); *Died:* 25 May 1964 in Moscow.

ZORGE, Rikhard (Richard SORGE) (1895–1944) Spy; journalist; Dr of Soc Sci; CP member from 1925; *Born:* 8 Oct 1895 in Baku, a relative of F. Zorge; *Educ:* studied in Germany; *Career:* at age three moved to Berlin with his parents; raised, educated and influenced by revol events in Germany; during WW 1 drafted into German Army; wounded; 1919 joined German CP, worked in mines, taught on Party courses and edited a newspaper; 1924 "Proletariy" Publ House published his pop ed of Rosa Luxemburg's book "The Accumulation of Capital"; 1924 moved to Moscow and took Sov citizenship; assoc, Inst of Marx and Engels, Moscow; then worked for Sov Intelligence; 1929 went to Shanghai on intelligence mission; 1933 recalled to Moscow and then sent to Berlin; Sept 1933 sent to Japan, where he officially represented a German newspaper; set up an excellent, ramified intelligence org, became Press Attache at German Embassy and a confidant of the German amb; this enabled him to gather and pass on vital information to Sov Intelligence; 15 May 1941 reported precise date of German invasion of USSR; July 1941 reported that Japan did not plan to join the war against USSR; Oct 1941 reported Japan's intention to launch Pacific war against USA; 1941 arrested by Japanese Counter-Intelligence; for over three years held in Sugamo Prison, Tokyo; *Awards:* Hero of the Sov Union (1964, posthumously); *Died:* 7 Nov 1944 executed in Tokyo.

ZORGENFREY, Vil'gel'm Aleksandrovich (1882–1938) Russian poet and translator; *Born:* 30 Aug 1882 in Akkerman; *Career:* 1905 first work printed; similar to Blok in his choice of themes and imagery; 1922 wrote his reminiscences of Blok; translated Goethe, Herder, Grillparzer, Hebbel, Claudel, Renier and Heine; edited translations of Kleist, Novard and Thomas Mann; arrested by State Security organs; *Publ:* verse collection *Strastnaya subbota* (Good Saturday) (1922), etc; *Died:* 21 Sept 1938 in imprisonment; posthumously rehabilitated.

ZORICH (real name: CHERNOBRIVETS), Stefaniya Petrovna (1893–1954) Opera singer (soprano); Hon Artiste of RSFSR from 1937; *Born:* 1893; *Educ:* from 1918 studied at Moscow Conservatory Studio; *Career:* from 1908 chorist, Kolesnichenko's Kremenchug Ukr Company, with which she performed in the Ukr, Voronezh and Tula; from 1914 soloist, Gaydamaka's Ukr Company, which performed at that time in Moscow; in Moscow studied under Levitskaya-Amfiteatrova; 1919 with Opera Company, Sergiyevsky Pop Center, Moscow; from 1920 soloist, Bolshoy Theater; *Roles:* Mariya in Tchaikovskiy's "Mazepa"; Tosca; Mimi; Trilby, etc; *Died:* 17 Feb 1954.

ZORIN–GOMBERG, S.S. (1890–1937) Party official; CP member from 1917; *Born:* 1890; *Career:* 1911–17 lived abroad; worked for American Socialist Party; after 1917 Oct Revol Party and govt work in Petrograd and Ivanovo-Voznesensk; 1925 sided with "New Opposition," then Trotsky-Zinov'yevite Bloc; 1927 at 15th CPSU(B) Congress expelled from Party as active member of Trotskyite opposition; 1930 re-admitted to the Party; 1935 for alleged anti-Party and anti-Sov activities again expelled from the Party and arrested; *Died:* 1937 in imprisonment.

ZOR'YAN (real name: RARAKEL'YAN), Stefan Yegnayevich (1890–1967) Arm writer; member Arm Acad of Sci; *Born:* 4 Sept 1890 in vil Karaklis (now Kirovakan, Arm SSR); *Career:* 1906 moved to Tiflis; 1909 began lit work; from 1910 worked for Tbilisi and Yerevan newspapers; from 1922 secr, Arm State Publ House, bd member, Arm Writers' Union; dep, USSR Supr Sov of 1954, 1958 and 1966 convocations; dep, Arm Supr Sov of 1963 convocation; translated into Arm works of Lev Tolstoy, Turgenev, etc; *Publ:* collected stories and novellas "Gloomy People", (1918); stories "The Apple Orchard" (1920); "The Girl from the library" (1926); "Chairman of the Revolutionary Committee" (1926); novel "The White City" (1930); autobiographical novel "The History of a Life" (1938); historical novel "Tsar Pap" (1944); "The Amiryanov Family"; "The Armenian Fortress" (1958–59); "Collected Works" (1961–63); story "High Post, Deep Secret" (1966), etc; *Awards:* Order of Lenin (1956); *Died:* 1967.

ZOSHCHENKO, Mikhail Mikhaylovich (1895–1958) Russian satirical writer; *Born:* 10 Aug 1895 in Poltava, son of an itinerant artist and member of the Ukr hereditary nobility; *Educ:* 1913 completed Petersburg High School; 1913–14 studied at Law Fac, Petersburg Univ; *Career:* 1915 left univ and volunteered for the front; early 1917 demobilized as junior capt after being wounded and sustaining gas poisoning; after 1917 Feb Revol head of posts and telegraphs and commandant, Petrograd Main Post Office; from Sept 1917 adjutant, Arkhangel'sk armed workers detachment and secr, regt court; from Juli 1918 with border troops in Strel'nya and Kronstadt; from Sept 1918 with Red Army at the front as adjutant, 1st Model Regt of Rural Poor; from Apr 1919, after demobilization, tried various trades, including:criminal investigation agent and inspector, Ligovo-Oranienbaum Criminal Inspection Dept; clerk, Petrograd Mil Port; then cobbler; 1921 first work printed; from 1921 member, Serapion Brethren lit group; then member, USSR Writers' Union; after start of WW 2 worked for Leningrad newspapers, radio and journal "Krokodil"; Oct 1941–Mar 1943 lived in Alma-Ata and worked for Moscow Film Studio's Sets Dept; from 1 Mar 1943 member, ed bd, journal "Krokodil"; specialized in short comic novellas, whose comic element often verge on the tragic; also wrote feuilletons and comedies; mainly portrayed the man-in-the-street trying to come to terms with the new Sov regime; his typical characters often abuse their false impression of their own worth, political slogans, and ideological arguments; his biting satire often verged on mockery of Sov reality; 1943–44 sharply attacked for this by Party critics, particularly incensed at his novelette *Pered vskhodom solntsa* (Before Sunrise), printed in 1943 in the journal "Oktyabr'"; he was dismissed from the journal "Krokodil" and concentrated on theater work; 14 Aug 1946 again attacked in CC, CPSU(B) resolution on the journals "Zvezda" and "Leningrad"; the resolution charged that in his "base" and "apolitical" works Zoshchenko "depicted Soviet manners and Soviet people in a hideously caricatured form, libellously presenting Soviet people as primitive, uncultured fools with common tastes and manners"; Aug 1946 expelled from USSR Writers' Union and thus deprived of the right to print his work; 1946–52 engaged exclusively in translating; June 1953 readmitted to USSR Writers' Union; 1954 published in "Krokodil" an article stressing the importance of criticism stemming from writers themselves; for this "Pravda" again relegated him to the "proponents of apolitical, unprincipled views"; his works were not printed again until after the 20th CPSU Congress; *Publ: Rasskazy* (Stories) (1923); *Sobraniye sochineniy* (Collected Works) (6 vol, 1929–31); *Vozvrashchyonnaya molodost* (Returned Youth) (1933); *Golubaya kniga* (The Blue Book) (1935); *Fel'yetony, rasskazy, povesti. 1940–1945* (Feuilletons, Stories and Novelettes. 1940–1945) (1946); *Izbrannyye rasskazy i povesti. 1923–1956* (Selected Stories and Novelettes. 1923–1956) (1956); *Rasskazy, fel'yetony, povesti* (Stories, Feuilletons and Novelettes) (1958); *Rasskazy i povesti. 1923–1956* (Stories and Novelettes. 1923–1956) (1960); *Fel'yetony, komedii, neizdannyye proizvedeniya* (Feuilletons, Comedies and Unpublished Works) (1963); *Died:* 22 July 1958 in Leningrad.

ZOTOV, Stepan Andreyevich (1882–1938) Mil commander; CP member from 1919; *Born:* 23 Nov 1882 in vil Golubinskaya, Don Army Oblast, son of a poor Cossack; *Educ:* 1910 grad sub-ensigns' school; 1917 grad Tiflis Mil College; 1923 grad Mil Acad; 1930 grad Preparatory Courses for Higher Commanders, Mil-Polit Acad; *Career:* from 1904 in Russian Army; fought in WW 1; 1918 organized a partisan detachment and fought against White Cossacks on the Don and at Tsaritsyn; 1918–20 brigade commander; dep chief of staff, 4th Cavalry Div; head, Staff Operation Dept, Budyonnyy's 1st Mounted Corps; chief, Field Staff, 1st Mounted Army; commanded cavalry div and corps; 1932–34 head, Red Army Horse-Stocks Bd; 1934–38 asst, then dep cavalry inspector, Red Army; arrested by State Security organs; *Awards:* two Order of the Red Banner, golden weapon; *Died:* 29 Sept 1938 in imprisonment.

ZRAZHEVSKIY, Aleksandr Ivanovich (1886–1950) Actor; Pop Artiste of USSR from 1949; CP member from 1940; *Born:* 6 Sept 1886 in Nikolayev; *Career:* from 1905 acted in amateur shows, then in Ukr theaters; from 1925 actor, Leningrad Acad Drama Theater; 1927–33 actor, Korsh Theater; 1933–35 at Moscow Oblast Trade-Union Council Theater; from 1935 at Moscow Maly Theater; from 1937 film work; *Roles:* Lynyayev in Ostrovskiy's *Volki i ovtsy* (The Wolves and the Sheep); Varlaam in Pushkin's "Boris Godunov"; Sir Toby Belch in Shakespeare's "Twelfth Night"; Galushka in *V stepyakh Ukrainy* (In the Ukrainian Steppes); Budkov in Lavrenyov's *Za tekh, kto v more* (For Those at Sea); film roles: Yerofeyev in *Vozvrashcheniye Maksima* (Maksim's Return) (1937); Bishof in *Bolotnyye soldaty* (Swamp Soldiers) (1938); Sokolov in *Noch' v sentyabre* (A Night in September) (1939); Semyon Dement'yevich in *Lyubimaya devushka* (A Beloved Girl) (1940); Dubok in *Velikiy grazhdanin* (Great Citizen) (1938–39); Mertts in *Bor'ba prodolzhayetsya* (The Struggle Continues); Gen Panteleyev in *Velikiy perelom* (The Great Turning Point) (1945); Belyayev in *Kreyser "Varyag"* (The Cruiser "Varyag") (1946); Poloznev in *Vo imya zhizni* (On Behalf of Life) (1947); Ryabushkin in *Mal'chik s okrainy* (The Boy from the Outskirts) (1948), etc; *Awards:* four Stalin Prizes (1941, 1942, 1946 and 1947); *Died:* 14 Dec 1950.

ZUBOK, Lev Izrailevich (1894–1967) Historian; Dr of Historical Sci from 1940; prof from 1938; CP member from 1925; *Born:* 28 Dec 1894 in Odessa, son of a worker; *Educ:* grad univ in USA; *Career:* specialized in gen modern history, history of USA and history of int Communist movement; 1913–24 emigre in USA; 1924 returned to Russia and worked for Trade-Union International (Profintern); 1930–49 lectured at Higher Propagandists Courses and Higher Party School, CC, CPSU(B); 1921–41 at Moscow Inst of History, Philosophy and Lit; 1942–49 at History Fac, Moscow Univ; 1948–61 at Inst of Int Relations; 1938–49 and 1957–67 senior assoc, Inst of History, USSR Acad of Sci; exec ed, 9-vol "Vsemirnaya istoriya" (World History) (1962); *Publ: Imperialisticheskaya politika SShA v stranakh Karibskogo basseyna, 1900–1939* (The Imperialistic Policy of the USA in the Caribbean Countries in 1900–1939) (1948); *Noveyshaya istoriya* (Recent

History) (3rd ed, 1948); *Ocherki istorii SShA, 1877–1918* (An Outline History of the USA, 1877–1918) (1956); coauthor, secondary-school textbook *Novaya istoriya* (Modern History) (1959); *Ocherki istorii rabochego dvizheniya v SShA, 1865–1918* (An Outline History of the Workers' Movement in the USA, 1865–1918) (1962); coauthor, *SShA posle vtoroy mirovoy voyny* (The USA After the Second World War) (1963), etc; *Died:* 13 May 1967.

ZUBOV, Konstantin Aleksandrovich (1888–1956) Actor, stage dir and drama teacher; Pop Artiste of USSR from 1949; CP member from 1942; *Born:* 20 Sept 1888 in vil Bazarynyy Sizgan, now Kuybyshev Oblast, son of a teacher; *Educ:* studied at Nancy Tech College and History and Philology Fac, Paris Univ; from 1906 studied at History and Philology Fac, Petersburg Univ; also studied under V.N. Davydov at Petersburg Theatrical College; 1908–10 studied at Sanin and Petrovskiy's School of Stagecraft; *Career:* 1908 professional stage debut with Davydov's Summer Touring Company; 1910–12 and 1914–15 with N.N. Sinel'nikov's Company in Khar'kov and Kiev; 1913–14 in Samara; 1915–17 at Moscow Korsh Theater; 1917–18 head, Actors' Assoc, Irkutsk Drama Theater; began work as stage dir at Irkutsk Drama Theater; 1921–24 at 1st Far Eastern Mil Revol Theater; 1925–31 actor, stage dir and head, Moscow's Theater of the Revol; 1932–38 artistic dir, Leningrad Sov Theater in Moscow; 1936–46 actor and stage dir, from 1947 chief stage dir, Maly Theater; from 1920 taught stagecraft; from 1946 prof, Shchepkin Theatrical College; dep, RSFSR Supr Sov of 4th convocation; *Roles:* Alyosha in Naydyonov's *Deti Vanyushina* (Vanyushin's Children); Hamlet; Korzinkin in Romashov's *Konets Krivoryl'ska* (The End of Krivoryl'sk); Semyon Rak in Romashov's *Vozdusnyy pirog* (The Meringue); Min Kal'man in Toller's *Gop-lya, my zhivyom* (Hop-La, We Live On); Platon in "Platon Krechet"; Higgins in Shaw's "Pygmalion"; Stessel' in Stepanov and Popov's "Port Arthur"; Famusov and Repetilov in Griboyedov's *Gore at uma* (Woe from Wit); Rastyogin in Trenyov's *Na beregu Nevy* (On the Banks of the Neva); Telyatev in Ostrovskiy's *Beshenyye den' gi* (Mad Money); Gorodulin in Ostrovskiy's *Na vsyakogo mudretsa dovol'no prostoty* (There's a Simpleton in Every Sage), etc; *Productions:* Chekhov's *Vishnyovyy sad* (The Cherry Orchard); Gorky's *Meshchane* (The Philistines); Gorky's *Na dne* (The Lower Depths); *Razgrom* (Rout), after Fadeyev; "Platon Krechet"; "Eugene Grandet," after Balzac (1939); *Varvary* (The Barbarians) (1941); helped produce: Shaw's "Pygmalion" (1943); Lavrenyov's "For Those at Sea" (1946); Romashov's *Velikaya sila* (The Great Force) (1947); "Vassa Zheleznova" (1952); "Port Arthur" (1953), etc; *Publ: Realisticheskoye iskusstvo sovetskogo teatra* (The Realistic Art of the Soviet Theater) (1956); *Awards:* four Stalin Prizes (1946, 1947, 1948 and 1951); *Died:* 22 Nov 1956.

ZUBRILIN, Aleksey Alekseyevich (1906–1966) Agronomist, zootech and biochemist; prof from 1940; Dr of Agric Sci from 1939; *Born:* 23 Mar 1906 in Moscow Province; *Educ:* 1928 grad Agronomy Fac, Moscow's Timiryazev Agric Acad; *Career:* from 1931 assoc, Vil'yams All-Union Fodder Research Inst; 1932–1942 founded Vitamin Laboratory; from 1948 founder-head, Dept of Fodder Technol; 1950–56 dir, All-Union Research Inst for the Feeding of Agric Animals; from 1956 dept head, All-Union Stock-Raising Research Inst, Moscow; *Publ: Kartofel'* (Potatoes) (1933); *Teoreticheskiye osnovy silosovaniya kormov* (The Theoretical Principles of Silaging Fodder) (1934); coauthor, *Silosovaniye kormov* (The Silaging of Fodder) (1935); *Konservirovaniye zelyonykh kormov* (Preserving Green Fodder) (1938); *Nauchnyye osnovy konservirovaniya zelyonykh kormov* (The Scientific Principles of Preserving Green Fodder) (1947); *O kachestve silosa i prakticheskikh priyomakh yego otsenki* (Silage Quality and Practical Means of Assessing It) (1960); *Iz rabot professora A.A. Zubrilina* (From the Works of Professor A.A. Zubrilin) (1962), etc; *Awards:* two Stalin Prizes (1947 and 1950); *Died:* Oct 1966.

ZUSKIN, Veniamin L'vovich (1899–1952) Jewish actor and stage dir; Pop Artiste of RSFSR from 1939; *Born:* 1899; *Career:* 1921 joined Studio and three months later admitted to Company of State Jewish Chamber Theater; from 1935 taught at Theatrical College, Moscow Jewish Theater; from 1948 artistic dir, State Jewish Theater; also film work; *Roles:* the First Jew in Sholom Aleichem's "Saliyene" (1921); main role in Gol'dfaden's "The Witch" (1922); Soloveychik in Sholom Aleichem's "200,000" (1923); Dr Bobritskiy in Bergel'son's "Measure of Severity" (1933); the Fool in Shakespeare's "King Lear" (1935); Gotsmakh in "Wandering Stars," after Sholom Aleichem (1940); Badkhen in "Freylekhs" (1945); Lyakhovich in Lin'kov's "The Noise of the Forests" (1947), etc; *Died:* 1952.

ZUTIS, Yan Yakovlevich (1893–1962) Historian; prof; member, Lat Acad of Sci from 1951; corresp member, USSR Acad of Sci from 1953; head, Medieval Lat History Section, Inst of History and Material Culture, Lat Acad of Sci from 1946; Hon Sci Worker of Lat SSR from 1953; *Born:* 16 Aug 1893; *Educ:* 1924 grad Moscow Univ; *Career:* specialized in the history of the Baltic peoples; supported concept of Baltic peoples' "historical unity" with the other peoples of the USSR; 1929–37 lecturer, Voronezh Univ and Voronezh Teachers' Training Inst; 1937–41 lecturer, Moscow Inst of History, Philosophy and Lit; 1937–46 assoc, Inst of History, USSR Acad of Sci; 1946–62 head, Chair of Gen History, Riga Univ; attended 1955 and 1960 Int Congresses of Historical Sci; dep, Lat Supr Sov of 1951, 1955 and 1959 convocations; *Publ: Politika tsarizma v Pribaltike v pervoy polovine XVIII veka* (Tsarist Policy in the Baltic in the Early 18th Century) (1937); *Ostzeyskiy vopros v XVIII veke* (The Ostsee Question in the 18th Century) (1946); *Ocherki po istorii Latvii* (An Outline History of Latvia) (vol 1, 1949); *Osnovnyye napravleniya v istoriografii narodov Vostochnoy Pribaltiki. XIX-XX vv.* (Basic Trends in the Historiography of the Eastern Baltic Peoples in the 19th and 20th Centuries) (1955), etc; *Awards:* Order of Lenin; two Orders of the Red Banner of Labor; Stalin Prize (1950); *Died:* 28 June 1962.

ZUYEV, Aleksandr Yuvenal'yevich (1856–1924) Naval surgeon; Dr of Med from 1889; *Born:* 1856; *Career:* 1889 defended doctor's thesis on the effect of ligature of the ductus thoracici on nitrogen exchange in dogs; 1908–21 in charge of Naval Med Service; abolished vodka ration on naval vessels, campaigned against venereal disease, designed a shipboard steam sterilizer and published a 3-vol report on the Russian Navy during the 1904–05 war with Japan; 1918 joined Red Navy; organized incorporation of Naval Med Service into RSFSR Pop Comrt of Health; 1918–20 head, Venerological Section, RSFSR Pop Comrt of Health; *Died:* 1924.

ZVAVICH, Isaak Semyonovich (1904–1950) Historian; specialist on English history; prof from 1938; CP member from 1945; *Born:* 17 May 1904; *Educ:* 1926 grad London School of Economics; *Career:* 1922–27 consultant with Sov trade mission in England; 1932–37 senior assoc, Inst of World Econ and World Politics, USSR Acad of Sci; from 1928 taught at higher educ establishments; 1930–34 lecturer, Moscow State For Language Teachers' Training Inst; 1934–41 lecturer, Lenin Teachers' Training Inst, Moscow; 1940–49 lecturer, History Fac, Moscow Univ; 1944–49 lecturer, Higher Dipl School; 1946–49 taught at Acad of Soc Sci, CC, CPSU(B); among first Sov historians to study English historiography; *Publ:* coauthor, *Obnishchaniye proletariata v kapitalisticheskikh stranakh* (The Impoverishment of the Proletariat in the Capitalist Countries) (1936); *Istoriografiya vneshney politiki Velikobritanii v yeyo noveyshikh predstavitelyakh* (The Historiography of British Foreign Policy in Its Latest Representatives) (1947); *Istoriya angliyskogo rabochego dvizheniya v trudakh Vebbov i ikh shkoly* (The History of the British Workers' Movement in the Works of the Webbs and Their School) (1947); *Died:* 15 May 1950.

ZVEREV, Daniil Yevdokimovich (1894–1941) Mil commander; CP member from 1917; *Born:* 21 Nov 1894 in vil Borisovka, Samara Province, son of a peasant; *Educ:* as external student completed two grades at Moscow Construction Inst; *Career:* in his youth worked as hired framhand; 1912 drafted into Russian Army; during WW 1 promoted lt and awarded four George Crosses for bravery in action; sided with Bolsheviks and engaged in revol propaganda among troops; after 1917 Oct Revol returned home and helped to establish Sov regime; 1918 joined Red Army; taken prisoner by Kolchak's troops at Samara; Dec 1918 joined Kolchak militia with other troops, then switched allegiance to Bolsheviks and remained in Siberia with his detachment, which was incorporated in the Siberian Red Partisans Front; early 1920 appointed commander, East Siberian Sov Army; after reestablishment of Sov rule in East Siberia recalled to Moscow to work with Gen Staff, then sent to Orenburg to Higher Mil School, shortly relocated in Tashkent; fought against remnants of Emir of Bukhara's forces; from 1921 asst comr, Higher Mil School; from Sept 1924 comr, Lenin Mil School, Tashkent; Apr 1925 appointed comr, Staff of 13th Infantry Corps, which fought against the Basmachi in Tadzh; 1926 transferred to Moscow as mil comr, Main Mil Store Depots;

1928 appointed head of communal mang at construction of Dnieper Hydroelectr Plant; then works mang for State Dnieper Construction Trust; from 1930 dir, East Siberian Kray Kolkhoz Construction Agency; early 1933 chm, East Siberian Kray Council, Soc for the Promotion of the USSR Defense, Aviation and Chemical Ind; from 1934 chm, Vinnitsa Oblast Council, above soc; *Died:* Nov 1941 killed in action.

ZVEZDOV, Vasiliy Ivanovich (1902–1934) CP member; *Born:* 1902; *Educ:* univ student; *Career:* Dec 1934 charged with complicity in the 1 Dec 1934 assassination of Kirov in Leningrad; 29 Dec 1934 sentenced to death along with co-defendants by Assizes of Mil Collegium, USSR Supr Court; *Died:* Dec 1934 executed.

ZVONKOV, Vasiliy Vasil'yevich (1890–1965) Trans eng; prof from 1933; Dr of Tech Sci; corresp member, USSR Acad of Sci from 1939; Hon Sci and Tech Worker of RSFSR from 1948; CP member from 1956; *Born:* 25 Dec 1890 in Borovichi, Novgorod Province; *Educ:* 1917 grad Moscow Inst of Trans Eng; *Career:* until 1929 worked for various trans orgs; 1929–32 at Moscow Inst of Trans Eng; 1933–50 prof, Mil Trans Acad; 1939–55 with Section for the Sci Study of Trans Problems, USSR Acad of Sci; from 1955 assoc, Inst of Comprehensive Trans Problems, USSR Acad of Sci; from 1922 worked on restoration, planning and development of water trans system and comprehensive use of various types of trans; chm, Sci and Tech Council, USSR Min of Merchant Marine; chm, Water Mang Council, USSR Acad of Sci; member, Gosplan Commission for Long-Term Planning; Tech Dept member, ed bd, periodical "Izvestiya AN SSSR"; *Publ: Organizatsiya sudokhodnogo predpriyatiya. Raschyoty* (The Organization of a Shipping Enterprise. Calculations) (1929); *Sudovyye torgovyye raschyoty s primerami prakticheskikh resheniy* (Shipping Trade Calculations and Examples of Practical Solutions) (1932); *Dispetcherkskaya sistema na vodnom transporte* (Water Transport *Dispetcherskaya sistema na vodnom transporte* (Water Transport *nicheskikh sredstv vnutrennego transporta* (The Comprehensive Standardization of Technical Means of Internal Transport) (1948), etc; *Awards:* four Orders of Lenin; Order of the Red Star; Badge of Hon; six medals; *Died:* 13 Nov 1965.

ZYUKOV, Anatoliy Matveyevich (1886–1953) Therapist and infectionist; prof; *Born:* 1 Dec 1886 in Poltava, son of an office worker; *Educ:* 1911 grad Med Fac, Kiev Univ; *Career:* after grad specialized in internal and infectious diseases at Kiev Univ; intern, then asst to prof F.G. Yanovskiy, first at Chair of Med Diagnostics, then at Hospital Therapy Clinic; senior assoc, Inst of Clinical Therapy, Ukr Acad of Sci; 1927–53 head, Chair of Infectious Diseases, Kiev Med Inst; did research on water metabolism, kidney functions, reactivity, infectious allergies, etc; wrote numerous works, including manuals and textbooks on infectious diseases and helminthiasis; *Died:* 13 Dec 1953.

Index by Career and Profession

COMMUNIST PARTY

1. Members and Candidate Members of CC Politbureau, Presidium, Bureau and Members of CC Secretariat

Akhundov, R.A. ogly
Akulov, I.A.
Aliyev, A.M.
Ammosov, M.K.
Angaretis (Aleksa), Z.I.
Antikaynen, T.
Asatkin-Vladimirskiy, A.N.
Asfendiarov, S.Dzh.
Bagirov, M.Dzh.A.
Balitskiy, V.A.
Baltagulov, T.B.
Baran, M.L.
Batyrov, Sh.B.
Bauman, K.Ya.
Belyayev, N.I.
Beriya, L.P.
Broydo, G.I.
Bubnov, A.S.
Bukharin, N.I.
Burmistrenko, M.A.
Chagin (Boldovkin), P.I.
Chernyavskiy, V.I.
Chervyakov, A.G.
Chubar, V.Ya.
Chuvyrin, M.Ye.
Demchenko, N.N.
Dzerzhinskiy, F.E.
Dzhafarov, S.M. ogly
Epshteyn, M.S.
Eykhe, R.I.
Frunze, M.V.
Gadzhiyev, N.M. ogly
Gayevoy, A.I.
Gikalo, N.F.
Gladkiy, D.S.
Gogoberidze, L.D.
Goloded, N.M.
Gribkov, M.P.
Grishko, G.Ye.
Guseynov, M.D.B. ogly
Ignatov, N.G.
Igantovskiy, V.M.
Ikramov, A.
Iskenderov, M.S.
Ivanov, A.V.
Ivanov, V.I.
Kakhiani, M.I.
Kalinin, M.I.
Kamenev, L.B.
Kaminskiy, G.N.
Karayev, D.D.
Karibzhanov, F.
Kartvelishvili, L.I.
Khandzhyan, A.G.
Khatayevich, M.M.
Kirkizh, K.O.
Kirov, S.M.
Klimenko, I.Ye.
Knorin, V.G.
Komyakhov, V.G.
Kon, B.
Kornyushin, F.D.
Kosior, S.V.
Kozlov, F.R.
Kozlov, V.I.
Krestinskiy, N.N.
Krinitskiy, A.I.
Krumin, Ya.M.
Kubyak, N.A.
Kurbanov, Sh.K.
Kuusinen, O.V.
Kviring, E.I.
Kuybyshev, V.V.
Kuznetsov, A.A.
Lebed, D.Z.
Lenin, V.I.
Loginov, F.G.
Lomov-Oppokov, G.I.
Lyubchenko, P.P.
Manuil'skiy, D.Z.
Mayorov, M.M.
Mazayev, A.V.
Mdivani, P.G.
Medvedev, A.V.
Mezhlauk, I.I.
Mikhaylov, V.M.
Mirzoyan, L.I.
Moskovin, I.M.
Muradov, A.
Musabekov, G.M. ogly
Narimanov, N.K.N. ogly
Naymushin, G.F.
Nazaretyan, A.M.
Orakhelashvili, I.D.
Ordzhonikidze, G.K.
Osatkin-Vladimirskiy, A.N.
Petrovskiy, G.I.
Pludon, M.Ya.
Polonskiy, V.I.
Popov, N.N.
Postyshev, P.P.
Preobrazhenskiy, Ye.A.
Preykshas, K.K.
Radchenko, A.F.
Rakhimbayev, A.R.
Rakhmanov, G.P. ogly
Rudakov, A.P.
Rudzutak, Ya.E.
Rukhimovich, M.L.
Rykov, A.I.
Sarkisov, S.A.
Semyonov, B.A.
Serbichenko, A.K.
Serebryakov, L.P.
Shcherbakov, A.S.
Shelekhes, I.S.
Shlikhter, A.G.
Shumskiy, A.Ya.
Skrypnik, N.A.
Stalin, I.V.
Stroganov, V.A.
Sukhomlin, K.V.
Sverdlov, Ya.M.
Tazhiyev, I.T.
Ter-Gabrielyan, S.M.
Tomskiy, M.P.
Trotskiy, L.D.
Ugarov, F.Ya.
Uglanov, N.A.
Vaynshteyn, A.I.
Veger, Ye.I.
Volkovich, D.I.
Voznesenskiy, N.A.
Yakir, I.E.
Yaroslavskiy, Ye.M.
Yezhov, N.I.
Zatonskiy, V.P.
Zaytsev, F.I.
Zelenskiy, I.A.
Zemlyanskiy, D.S.
Zhdanov, A.A.
Zinov'yev, G.Ye.

2. Members and Candidate Members of CC and Members of Central Auditing Commission, Central Control Commission, Party Control Commission, etc.

Abbasov, Kh.M.
Abdullayev, Kh.M.
Afanas'yev, S.I.
Agranov, Ya.S.
Akhmedov, A.M.-ogly
Akulov, I.A.
Alabyan, K.S.
Aladzhalova, N.N.
Aleksandrovich, A.I.
Aliyev, M.I.
Ambartsumyan, S.
Amosov, A.M.
Amosov, P.N.
Angelina, P.N.
Antipov, N.K.
Antonov, V.I.
Antselovich, N.M.
Anvel't, Ya.Ya.
Apin, E.P.
Apse, M.Ya.
Armand, Ye.F.
Aronshtam, L.N.
Artyom (Sergeyev), F.A.
Arzumanyan, A.A.
Atarbekov, G.A.
Averin, V.K.
Avilov, N.P.
Badayev, A.Ye.
Bagirova, B.M.-kyzy
Bakayev, I.P.
Balitskiy, V.A.
Banaytis, Yu.A.
Baranov, P.I.
Barshauskas, K.M.
Begma, V.A.
Beloborodov, A.G.
Belov, S.A.
Berezhnov, P.A.
Berzin, Ya.A.
Biniyatov, B.N.A.O.
Biryuzov, S.S.
Blakitnyy (Yellinskiy), V.M.

Bliznichenko, A.Ye.
Blyukher, V.K.
Bogdanov (Malinovskiy), A.A.
Bogdanov, I.A.
Bogdanov, S.I.
Bokiy, G.I.
Bondarenko, A.D.
Boychenko, A.M.
Boytsov, V.I.
Brykov, A.P.
Bryukhanov, N.P.
Budzyn'skiy, S.
Bulatov, D.A.
Bulin, A.S.
Buniat-zade, D.Kh.
Butsenko, A.I.
Chaplin, N.P.
Chekin, P.O.
Chentsov, I.D.
Chicherin, G.V.
Chodrishvili, M.I.
Chudov, M.S.
Chutskayev, S.Ye.
Danishevskiy (German), K.-Yu.Kh.
Dashtoyan, R.P.
Dekanosov, V.G.
Deribas, T.D.
Didzhyulis, K.
Dimanshteyn, S.M.
Dogadov, A.I.
Drobnis, Ya.N.
Dubkovetskiy, F.I.
Dudnik, A.M.
Dvornikov, P.I.
Dygay, N.A.
Dzhafarov, S.M. ogly
Dzhaparidze, P.A.
Efendiyev, S.M.
Eliava, Sh.Z.
Fabritsius, Ya.F.
Fadeyev (Bulyga), A.A.
Fedaravichyus, P.
Fed'ko, I.F.
Fenigshteyn, Ya.G.
Figatner, Yu.P.
Filatov, N.A.
Fokin, V.A.
Fomin, V.V.
Gamarnik, Ya.B.
Gaza, I.I.
Gel'dyyev, A.
Gey, K.V.
Goloshchyokin, F.I.
Gol'tsman, A.Z.
Gopner, S.I.
Gorbachyov, Ye.G.
Gorshkov, I.I.
Govorov, L.A.
Grin'ko, G.F.
Gulyam, G.G.
Gusev, S.I.
Guseyn, M.
Ibragimov, U.I.
Ignatov, N.F.
Il'in, N.I.
Isametdinov, M.I.
Isayev, U.D.
Ivannikov, G.I.
Ivanov, S.V.
Izotov, N.A.
Kabakov, I.D.
Kadatskiy, I.F.
Kadyrli, M.N.-ogly
Kaganovich, M.M.
Kaktyn, A.M.
Kalizhnyuk, S.K.
Kalmanovich, M.I.
Kalmykov, M.V.
Karavayev, P.N.
Kasumov, M.B.F. ogly
Kaz'min, N.D.
Khloplyankin, M.I.
Khodzhayev, F.A.
Khokhol, Ye N.
Khrunichev, M.V.
Kidin, A.N.
Kingisepp, S.V.
Kirkhenshteyn, A.M.
Kirponos, M.P.
Kiselyov, A.S.
Kochar, R.
Kochubey, A.D.
Kogan, Ye.S.
Kokovikhin, M.N.
Kolas, Ya.
Kolesnikova, N.N.
Kollontay, A.M.
Kolotilov, N.N.
Komarov, N.P.
Korneyev, I.I.
Korostelev, A.A.
Korostelev, G.A.
Korotkov, I.I.
Kosarev, A.V.
Kosarev, V.M.
Kosior, I.V.
Kotsyubinskiy, Yu.M.
Kovpak, S.A.
Krasin, L.B.
Kreysberg, I.M.
Krivov, T.S.
Krumin, G.I.
Krupskaya, N.K.
Krylenko, N.V.
Krzhizhanovskiy, G.M.
Kucherenko, V.A.
Kulik, I.Yu.
Kul'kov, M.M.
Kurashov, S.V.
Kurskiy, D.I.
Lashevich, M.M.
Latsis, V.T.
Lengnik, F.V.
Leonov, F.G.
Lepse, I.I.
Lezhava, A.M.
Likhachyov, I.A.
Litvinov, M.M.
Lizarev, F.S.
Lobov, S.S.
Loginov, S.P.
Lozovskiy, S.A.
Lukin, A.M.
Lyubimov, I.Ye
Malinin, M.S.
Malinovskiy, R.Ya.
Malyshev, V.A.
Mamedaliyev, Yu.G.
Martikyan, S.N.
Mekhlis, L.Z.
Mel'nichanskiy, G.N.
Menzhinskiy, V.R.
Merkulov, F.A.
Meshcheryakov, V.N.
Messing, S.A.
Mezhlauk, V.I.
Milyutin, V.P.
Minin, S.K.
Minkov, I.I.
Mironov, N.R.
Moroz, G.S.
Morozov, D.G.
Muranov, M.K.
Murysev, A.S.
Myasnikov, A.F.
Nedelin, M.I.
Nikitin, P.V.
Nikolayeva, K.I.
Nogin, V.P.
Nosenko, I.I.
Nurutdinov, S.
Osinskiy, N.
Ostrov, Ya.P.
Pakhomov, N.I.
Pankratova, A.M.
Papivin, N.F.
Pastukhov, M.D.
Pavlunovskiy, I.P.
Pedanyuk, I.M.
Pegel'man, Kh.G.
Perepechko, I.N.
Peters, Ya.Kh.
Petrov, I.Ye.
Pilatskaya, O.V.
Pochenkov, K.I.
Podvoyskiy, N.I.
Pokrovskiy, M.N.
Polikarpov, D.A.
Poskryobyshev, A.N.
Potyomkin, V.P.
Pozern, B.P.
Pravdin, A.G.
Ptukha, V.V.
Pukhov, M.P.
Pushkin, G.M.
Puzikov, S.T.
Pyatakov, G.L.
Pyatnitskiy, I.A.
Radek, K.B.
Radus-Zen'kovich, V.A.
Rakovskiy, Kh.G.
Rayzer, D.Ya.
Royzenman, B.A.
Rozengol'ts, A.P.
Rozmirovich, Ye.F.
Rumyantsev, I.P.
Rusanov, G.A.
Ryskulov, G.R.
Ryvkin, O.L.
Safarov, G.I.
Sapronov, T.V.
Satpayev, K.I.
Savel'yev, M.A.
Sedoy, Z.Ya.
Sedykh, V.Ya.
Semkov, S.M.
Sepre, O.A.
Serdich, D.F.
Serebrovskiy, A.P.
Shaposhnikov, B.M.
Shapovalov, A.S.
Shatskin, L.A.
Shaumyan, S.G.

Sheboldayev, B.P.
Shkiryatov, M.F.
Shklovskiy, G.L.
Shlyapnikov, A.G.
Shmidt, V.V.
Shokhin, A.P.
Shotman, A.V.
Shtern, G.M.
Shteyngart, A.M.
Shtykov, T.F.
Shvarts, I.I.
Sikorskiy, S.I.
Skvortsov-Stepanov, I.I.
Slyn'ko, P.F.
Smidovich, P.G.
Smidovich, S.N.
Smilga, I.T.
Smirnov, A.P.
Smirnov, N.I.
Smushkevich, Ya.V.
Sokol'nikov, G.Ya.
Sokolovskaya, S.I.
Sol'ts, A.A.
Starchenko, V.F.
Stasova, Ye.D.
Stepanov, S.I.
Stetskiy, A.I.
Striyevskiy, K.K.
Strokach, T.A.
Stuchka, P.I.
Syrtsov, S.I.
Tagizade, A.
Teodorovich, I.A.
Terent'yev, V.A.
Tevosyan, I.F.
Tikhane, A.G.
Tishchenko, S.I.
Todriya, S.Ya.
Tolokontsev, A.F.
Tovstukha, I.P.
Trilisser, M.A.
Troyanker, B.U.
Tsintsadze, K.M.
Tsivtsivadze, I.V.
Tskhakaya, M.G.
Tsyurupa, A.D.
Tukhachevskiy, M.N.
Tuntul, I.Ya.
Tursunkulov, Kh.
Tychina, P.G.
Uborevich, I.P.
Ukhanov, K.V.
Ul'yanova, M.I.
Umarov, S.U.
Unshlikht, I.S.
Urayev, P.V.
Uritskiy, M.S.
Vakhrushev, V.V.
Vannikov, B.L.
Varentsova, O.A.
Vareykis, I.M.
Vester, R.Ye.
Veynberg, G.D.
Vinnichenko, V.K.
Vishnyakova, P.I.
Vladimirov, M.K.
Vladimirskiy, M.F.
Vyatkin, L.Ya.
Vyshinskiy, A.Ya.
Yagoda, G.G.
Yakovlev, A.I.
Yakovlev, Ya. A.
Yakubov, N.
Yanson, N. M.
Yefremov, A. I.
Yenukidze, A. S.
Yeremeyev, K. S.
Yevdokimov, G. Ye.
Yevreinov, N. N.
Yudin, P. F.
Yudovskiy, V.G.
Yunosov, K. A.
Zalutskiy, P. A.
Zarubin, G. N.
Zasyad'ko, A. F.
Zavenyagin, A. P.
Zemlyachka, R. S.
Zhgenti, T. G.
Zhigaryov, P. F.

3. Other Party Leading Officials

Abolin, A.K.
Adamovich, Ye.N.
Adoratskiy, V.V.
Agasiyev, K.-M.
Aggeyev, S.P.
Aleksandrov, A.S.
Alekseyev, M.N.
Alekseyev, N.A.
Alekseyeva, Ye.P.
Alliluyev, P.S.
Alliluyev, S.Ya.
Alliluyeva-Stalina, N.S.
Alyutin, A.P.
Amelin, M.P.
Anan'yev (Kutuzov), V.Ye.
Andreyeva (Yurkovskaya), M.F.
Angarskiy (Klestov), N.S.
Anisimov, V.A.
Anskiy (Rapoport), S.A.
Antonov (Saratovskiy), V.P.
Antonov-Ovseyenko, V.A.
Aristarkhov, A.A.
Armand, F.A.
Arosev, A.Ya.
Arveladze, P.Ya.
Avdeyev, N.N.
Avilova, M.A.
Avramov (Abramov), R.P.
Azizbekov, M.A.-bek-ogly
Babkin, I.P.
Babushkin, Ye.A.
Bagdat'yev, S.Ya.
Bakulin, I.I.
Balashov, S.I.
Baranov, K.A.
Barisova, R.B.
Barkhatova, L.N.
Baturin (Zamyatin), N.N.
Bayar, Ye.M.
Beburishvili, M.Ye.
Bednyakov, K.N.
Bekzadyan, A.A.
Belen'kiy, G.Ya.
Bobinskiy, S.Ya.
Bobrovskaya (Zelikson), Ts.S.
Bobrovskiy, V.S.
Bogachyov, P.M.
Bonch-Bruyevich, V.D.
Borchaninov, A.L.
Borisov, P.S.
Borodin (Gruzenberg), M.M.
Bosh, M.P.
Bosh, Ye.B.
Brichkina, S.B.
Brodskaya, S.A.
Bronskiy, M.G.
Brusnyov, M.I.
Buachidze, S.G.
Bukharina-Lukina, N.M.
Burovtsev, M.V.
Butkevich, A.Ya.
Buyko, A.M.
Buyko, M.S.
Buynakskiy, U.D.
Charot, M. (Kudel'ka), M.S.
Chebotaryov, I.N.
Chepurov, M.N.
Chernyak (Todorskaya), R.I.
Chuchin, F.G.
Chudovskiy, N.M.
Chugurin, I.D.
Dakhadayev, M.-A.
Danilov, S.S.
Danilova-Dobryakova, A.P.
Dashkevich, P.V.
Dauge, P.G.
Dauman, A.E.
Davydov, I.A.
Degtyaryova-Boksberg, A.Ya.
Derbyshev, N.I.
Dermanis, V.
Deryabina, S.I.
Dik, I.O.
Dikovskaya (Yakimova), A.V.
Dimitrov, G.M.
Dobrodzhanu-Gerya (Dobrogeanu-Gherea), A.
Dodonova, A.A.
Dok (Blyum), P.O.
Dorokhov, R.A.
Dosser, Z.N.
Drabkina, F.I.
Dubrovinskiy, Ya.F.
Dunayev, Ye.A.
Dyogot, V.A.
Dzerzhinskaya, S.S.
Dzerzhinskiy, Ya.F.
Endrup (Vidin), R.Ya.
Epshteyn Sh. (Ben-Yakir)
Essen, A.M.
Essen, M.M.
Etingof, B.Ye.
Fioletov, I.T.
Fisher, G.M.
Fokin, I.I.
Fridolin, V.Yu.
Frumkina, M.Ya.
Fyodorov, G.F.
Gamburg, I.K.

Gartnyy, T.
Gavrilov, N.A.
Gavrilyuk, A.A.
Gedris, K.Yu.
German, I.E.
Gessen, S.M.
Glushchenko, A.P.
Glyasser, M.I.
Gorchilin, A.I.
Grasis, K.Ya.
Gubel'man, M.I.
Gukasyan, G.O.
Gukovskiy, I.E.
Gurvich, Ye.A.
Gzhel'shchak (Grzelszczak), F.Ya.
Ibragimov, A.
Il'in-Zhenevskiy, A.F.
Ingulov, S.B.
Ionov, N.I.
Ivanov, S.M.
Ivanov, S.N.
Kabakchiyev, Kh.S.
Kalnin, T.P.
Katanyan, R.P.
Katenina, L.M.
Kauchukovskiy, G.D.
Kazakov, A.A.
Kharechko, T.I.
Kharitonov, M.M.
Khodorovskiy, I.I.
Khrushchyova-Yelagina, A.A.
Khudayberdin, Sh.A.
Khvesin, T.S.
Kirsanova, K.I.
Kobetskiy, M.V.
Komlev, V.T.
Kondratenko, S.F.
Konstantinovich, A.S.
Kopylov, N.V.
Korganov, G.N.
Korolyov-Batyshev, I.G.
Korzinov, G.N.
Kosior, V.V.
Kotsko, V.F.
Kozhevnikov, S.N.
Kozhin, M.V.
Kozlov, I.A.
Kozlovskiy, M.Yu.
Krylov, S.N.
Krzhizhanovskaya-Nevzorova, Z.P.
Kulyabko, P.I.
Kun, B.
Kurayev, V.V.
Kyaspert, I.Yu.
Landa, M.M.
Latsis, M.I.
Lazurkin, M.S.
Leder, V.L.
Lentsman, Ya.D.
Lepeshinskiy, P.N.
Leyteyzen, G.D.
Liberman, L.A.
Likhachyov, V.M.
Lisinova, L.
Lobova, V.N.
Losev, V.N.
Lunacharskiy, A.V.
Mambetaliyev, M.
Mandel'shtam, A.V.
Mandel'shtam, N.N.
Markhlevskiy (Marchlewski), Yu.Yu.
Markov, A.T.
Markovich, V.
Maurer, Zh.A.
Meyerzon, Zh.I.
Mikhaylov, A.F.
Mikhaylov, L.M.
Minkin, A.Ye.
Mitrofanov, A.Kh.
Mitskevich, V.S.
Mitskyavichyus-Kapsukas, V.S.
Moiseyenko, P.A.
Moiseyev, S.N.
Morozov, N.A.
Mostovenko, P.N.
Moyrova, V.A.
Muralov, A.I.
Naneyshvili, V.I.
Nemanov, N.G.
Nemtsov, N.M.
Nevskiy, V.I.
Nikiforov, A.N.
Oborin, V.P.
Obukh, V.P.
Okulova, G.I.
Ol'minskiy, M.S.
Ol'shevskiy, A.A.
Ordzhonikidze, Z.G.
Oshkaln, O.P.
Ozolin, E.K.
Panfilov, F.D.
Pankratov, I.I.
Panteleyev, I.V.
Panyushkin, V.L.
Pel'she, R.A.
Pestun, Ye G.
Peterson, K.A.
Petrov, S.N.
Pisarev, A.I.
Platten, F.
Podbel'skiy, V.N.
Podvoyskaya, N.A.
Poletayev, N.G.
Polidorov, S.I.
Polukhin, V.F.
Polupanov, A.V.
Poluyan, D.V.
Poluyan, Ya.V.
Pomerantseva, A.V.
Popov, D.M.
Popov, K.A.
Popudrenko, N.N.
Postolovskiy, D.S.
Pryamikov, N.N.
Radchenko, I.I.
Rakh'ya, E.A.
Rakh'ya, I.A.
Rays, I.
Rekstyn, A.I.
Reynshteyn, B.I.
Rotshteyn, F.A.
Rovio, G.S.
Rozin, F.A.
Ryabinin, Ye.I.
Ryastas, O.Yu.
Ryazanov, D.B.
Sadovnichenko, D.G.
Safonov, A.K.
Said-Galiyev, S.
Sakharov, V.V.
Samoylov, F.N.
Samoylova, K.N.
Savel'yeva, A.N.
Segizbayev, S.
Semashko, N.A.
Semyonov, M.A.
Sheina, P.F.
Shelgunov, V.A.
Shestakov, A.V.
Shlikhter, Ye.S.
Shternberg, P.K.
Shumyatskiy, B.Z.
Sil'vin, M.A.
Skovno, A.A.
Slavinskiy, K.E.
Slutskiy, A.I.
Smirnov, I.N.
Smirnova, V.A.
Smitten, Ye.G.
Smol'yaninov, V.A.
Sorin, V.G.
Sosnovskiy, L.S.
Stal, L.N.
Stashkov, N.I.
Stopani, A.M.
Stukov, I.N.
Sverdlova, K.T.
Tarnogorodskiy, N.P.
Tel'man, S.F.
Ter-Arutyunyan, M.K.
Tikhomirnov, G.A.
Tikhomirnov, V.A.
Tochisskiy, P.V.
Tomashevskiy, A.F.
Torchinskiy, G.B.
Tsagolov, G.A.
Tsviling, S.M.
Tuchapskiy, P.L.
Ufimtsev, N.I.
Urazbayeva, A.D.
Vagzhanov, A.P.
Vakar, V.V.
Vakhitov, M.-N.
Valetskiy (Walecki), G.
Vardin, I.V.
Varskiy, A.Ye.
Vasil'chenko, S.F.
Vasil'yevskiy, V.N.
Vatin, V.A.
Vedyornikov, A.S.
Velichkina, V.M.
Veretennikov, N.I.
Vesolovskiy, B.E.
Vetoshkin, M.K.
Vever, E.Ya.
Veynbaum, G.S.
Vinokurov, A.N.
Vitolin, P.Ya.
Volodarskiy, V.
Vorovskiy, V.V.
Voskov, S.P.
Voyevodin, P.I.
Vozdvizhenskiy, N.D.
Yaglom, Ya.K.
Yakhontov, V.I.
Yakovleva, V.N.
Yalava, G.E.
Yanyshev, M.P.
Yatsenko, G.F.
Yelichyov, A.I.
Yelizarova-Ul'yanova, A.I.
Yerbanov, M.N.
Yurevich, A.D.
Yuzhin, M.I.
Zagorskiy, V.M.
Zakharov, S.S.

Zarin'sh, Ya.P.
Zaslavskiy, P.S.
Zevin, Ya.D.
Zhakov, M.P.
Zifel'dt, A.R.
Zorin-Gomberg, S.S.

GOVERNMENT

1. Chairmen and Deputy Chairmen of Central Executive Committee, Supreme Soviet, Presidium of Supreme Soviet and of Supreme Court

Adamovich, I.A.
Agamaly-Ogly, S.-A.
Akhunbabayev, Yu.
Ambartsumyan, S.
Apin, E.P.
Atabayev, K.S.
Badayev, A.Ye.
Barbarus (Vares), I.Ya.
Bezdonnyy (Pelekhatyy), K.N.
Burmistrenko, M.A.
Chanba, S.Ya.
Chelyshev, M.I.
Chervyakov, A.G.
Didzhyulis, K.
Dobrokhotov, M.S.
Dzhafarov, S.M. ogly
Dzhangil'din, A.T.
Efendiyev, S.M.
Ibragimov, U.I.
Ignatov, N.G.
Ivanov, S.V.
Kalinin, M.I.
Kamenev, L.B.
Karibzhanov, F.
Kasumov, M.B.F. ogly
Kas'yan, S.I.
Khodzhayev, F.A.
Khudayberdin, Sh.A.
Kirkhenshteyn, A.M.
Kovpak, S.A.
Kozlov, V.I.
Krasikov, P.A.
Kuusinen, O.V.
Makharadze, F.I.
Mantsev, V.N.
Martikyan, S.N.
Minkin, A.Ye.
Musabekov, G.M. ogly
Myasnikov, A.F.
Narimanov, N.K.N.-ogly
Nevskiy, V.I.
Orakhelashvili, I.D.
Ordzhonikidze, G.K.
Oyunskiy, P.A.
Petrovskiy, G.I.
Ryskulov, G.R.
Shotman, A.V.
Shtakhman, Ye.A.
Stuchka, P.I.
Sverdlov, Ya.M.
Tagirov, A.M.
Tagizade, A.
Tskhakaya, M.G.
Tychina, P.G.
Vares, I.Ya.
Vinokurov, A.N.
Yakobson, A.M.
Yerbanov, M.N.
Yuzhin, M.I.
Zatonskiy, V.P.

2. Chairmen and Deputy Chairmen of Council of People's Commissars and Council of Ministers

Abdullayev, Kh.M.
Adamovich, I.A.
Aliyev, A.M.
Ambartsumyan, S.
Antipov, N.K.
Antonov-Ovseyenko, V.A.
Artyom (Sergeyev), F.A.
Babkin, I.P.
Bagirov, M.Dzh.A.
Barbarus (Vares), I.Ya.
Bekzadyan, A.A.
Belyayev, I.S.
Beriya, L.P.
Boguslavskiy, M.S.
Buniat-zade, D.Kh.
Chervyakov, A.G.
Chubar, V.Ya.
Dekanosov, V.G.
Drobnis, Ya.N.
Dudnik, A.M.
Dygay, N.A.
Eliava, Sh.Z.
Fenigshteyn, Ya.G.
Gegechkori, A.A.
Gogoberidze, L.D.
Goloded, N.M.
Grin'ko, G.F.
Guseynov, M.D.B. ogly
Gyulling, E.O.V.
Ignatov, N.G.
Isayev, U.D.
Ivannikov, G.I.
Kaktyn, A.M.
Kamenev, L.B.
Karayev, D.D.
Kartvelishvili, L.I.
Khodzhayev, F.A.
Khrunichev, M.V.
Khudayberdin, Sh.A.
Kochubey, A.D.
Kosior, S.V.
Kotsyubinskiy, Yu.M.
Kozlov, F.R.
Kozlov, V.I.
Kucherenko, V.A.
Kuybyshev, V.V.
Latsis, V.T.
Lebed, D.Z.
Lenin, V.I.
Lezhava, A.M.
Lyubchenko, P.P.
Lyubovich, A.M.
Makharadze, F.I.
Malyshev, V.A.
Mambetaliyev, M.
Manuil'skiy, D.Z.
Mazayev, A.V.
Mdivani, P.G.
Mezhlauk, V.I.
Musabekov, G.M. ogly
Myasnikov, A.F.
Narimanov, N.K.N.-ogly
Ostrov, Ya.P.
Pamfilov, K.D.
Pludon, M.Ya.
Preykshas, K.K.
Rakhimbayev, A.R.
Rakhmanov, G.P. ogly
Rakovskiy, Kh.G.
Rudzutak, Ya.E.
Rykov, A.I.
Safronov, A.M.
Segizbayev, S.
Sepre, O.A.
Serbichenko, A.K.
Seyfullin, S.
Shaumyan, S.G.
Shelekhes, I.S.
Shmidt, V.V.
Skrypnik, N.A.
Smirnov, A.P.
Stalin, I.V.
Starchenko, V.F.
Sukhomlin, K.V.
Syrtsov, S.I.
Tazhibayev, T.T.
Tazhiyev, I.T.
Ter-Gabrielyan, S.M.
Ter-Yegiazar'yan, M.A.
Tevosyan, I.F.
Tsyurupa, A.D.
Umarov, S.U.
Vakhrushev, V.V.
Vaynshteyn, A.I.
Vinnichenko, V.K.
Vladimirskiy, M.F.
Volkovich, D.I.
Voznesenskiy, N.A.
Vyshinskiy, A.Ya.
Yanson, N.M.
Yerbanov, M.N.
Zasyad'ko, A.F.
Zavenyagin, A.P.
Zemlyachka, R.S.
Zheltov, I.I.

3. People's Commissars, Ministers and their Deputies

Abakumov, V.S.
Aggeyev, S.P.
Agranov, Ya.S.
Akhmedov, A.M. ogly
Akhundov, R.A. ogly
Akopov, S.A.
Akulov, I.A.
Aliyev, M.I.
Alksnis (Astrov), Ya.I.
Al'skiy, A.O.
Amir'yan (Amirov), A.
Amosov, A.M.
Angaretis (Aleksa), Z.I.
Anikst, A.M.
Antonov (Saratovskiy), V.P.
Antselovich, N.M.
Anvel't, Ya.Ya.
Ashurkov, Ye.D.
Atarbekov, G.A.
Avanesov, V.A.
Avilov, N.P.
Azizbekov, M.A.-bek-ogly
Balabanova, A.I.
Balitskiy, V.A.
Banaytis, S.I.
Banaytis, Yu.A.
Baranov, M.I.
Baranov, P.I.
Bardin, I.P.
Beloborodov, A.G.
Berezhnov, P.A.
Berzin, Ya.K.
Biryuzov, S.S.
Blagonravov, G.I.
Bliznichenko, A.Ye.
Bogdanov, P.A.
Bogolepov, D.P.
Borisov, I.N.
Borisov, S.A.
Borodin (Gruzenberg), M.M.
Bosh, Ye.B.
Bronskiy, M.G.
Broydo, G.I.
Bryukhanov, N.P.
Bubnov, A.S.
Buyko, A.M.
Chicherin. G.V.
Chutskayev, S.Ye.
Danishevskiy (German), K.-Yu.Kh.
Demchenko, N.N.
Derbyshev, N.I.
Dimanshteyn, S.M.
Dovgalevskiy, V.S.
Dvornikov, P.I.
Dyogot, V.A.
Dzerzhinskiy, F.E.
Dzhafarov, S.M. ogly
Dzhaparidze, P.A.
Epshteyn, M.S.
Eykhe, R.I.
Eysmont, N.B.
Fedaravichyus, P.
Fed'ko, I.F.
Fomin, V.V.
Fridrikhson, L.Kh.
Frumkin, M.I.
Frunze, M.V.
Gabiyev, S.I.
Galler, L.M.
Gamarnik, Ya.B.
Gay, G.D.
Golovko, A.G.
Gopner, D.Yu.
Gopner, S.I.
Gorbachyov, Ye.G.
Govorov, L.A.
Grashchenkov, N.I.
Gromadin, M.S.
Gukovskiy, I.E.
Ignatov, N.F.
Ignatovskiy, V.M.
Il'in, N.I.
Isakov, I.S.
Isametdinov, M.I.
Ivanov, V.I.
Ivanov, V.I.
Kaganovich, M.M.
Kalashnikov, A.G.
Kalashnikov, V.D.
Kalmanovich, M.I.
Kamenev, S.S.
Kaminskiy, G.N.
Karakhan, L.M.
Karelin, V.A.
Karibzhanov, F.
Kasumov, M.B.F. ogly
Khalepskiy, I.A.
Khinchuk, L.M.
Khloplyankin, I.I.
Khloplyankin, M.I.
Khodorovskiy, I.I.
Khrulyov, A.V.
Khvesin, T.S.
Kikodze, G.D.
Kirkizh, K.O.
Kiselyov, A.S.
Klimenko, I.Ye.
Kobozev, P.A.
Kokovikhin, M.N.
Kollontay, A.M.
Komarov, N.P.
Kononenko, P.P.
Korganov, G.N.
Korneyev, I.I.
Korobov, A.V.
Korobov, P.I.
Kosior, I.V.
Kost, N.A.
Krasin, L.B.
Krasnoshchyokov, A.M.
Krestinskiy, N.N.
Krivov, T.S.
Krupskaya, N.K.
Krylenko, N.V.
Krzhizhanovskiy, G.M.
Kubyak, N.A.
Kuchaidze, G.L.
Kuliyev, M.Z. ogly
Kurashov, S.V.
Kviring, E.I.
Lakhuti, A.A.
Lander, K.I.
Lengnik, F.V.
Likhachyov, I.A.
Lisitsyn, N.V.
Litvinov, M.M.
Lobachyov, I.S.
Lobov, S.S.
Loginov, F.G.
Lomov-Oppokov, G.I.
Lozovskiy, S.A.
Lukashkin, N.I.
Lunacharskiy, A.V.
Lyubimov, I.Ye.
Maksimov, K.G.
Maksimovskiy, V.N.
Malinovskiy, R.Ya.
Mamed'yarov, M.
Mantsev, V.N.
Mayorov, M.M.
Mekhlis, L.Z.
Melikov, F.A. ogly
Merkulov, F.A.
Milyutin, N.A.
Milyutin, V.P.
Miroshnikov, I.I.
Moyrova, V.A.
Muklevich, R.A.
Muradov, A.
Muralov, A.I.
Nadtochiy, M.F.
Nedelin, M.I.
Nevskiy, V.I.
Nogin, V.P.
Nosenko, I.I.
Odintsov, L.Ye.
Ordzhonikidze, G.K.
Orlov, V.M.
Oshkaln, O.P.
Osinskiy, N.
Oyunskiy, P.A.
Pakhomov, N.I.
Pasthukov, M.D.
Pavlunovskiy, I.P.
Paykes, A.K.
Pochenkov, K.I.
Podbel'skiy, V.N.
Podvoyskiy, N.I.
Pokrovskiy, M.N.
Polonskiy, V.I.
Poloz, M.N.
Popov, V.F.
Postnikov, A.M.
Potyomkin, V.P.
Pravdin, A.G.
Priorov, N.N.
Prokof'yev, G.Ye.
Pushkin, G.M.
Pyatakov, G.L.
Radchenko, I.I.
Radus-Zen'kovich, V.A.
Raskol'nikov, F.F.
Rayzer, D.Ya.
Red'kin, A.M.
Rozengol'ts, A.P.
Rozin, F.A.
Rudakov, I.G.
Rukhimovich, M.L.
Rus'ko, A.N.
Rychagov, P.V.
Rykunov, M.V.
Ryskulov, G.R.
Samoylov, F.N.
Semashko, N.A.
Serebrovskiy, A.P.
Serebryakov, L.P.
Sereda, S.P.
Shaposhnikov, B.M.
Shchadenko, Ye.A.
Shcherbakov, A.S.

Shlikhter, A.G.
Shlyapnikov, A.G.
Shtakhman, Ye.A.
Shumskiy, A.Ya.
Sikorskiy, S.I.
Sklyanskiy, E.M.
Skvortsov-Stepanov, I.I.
Smirnov, I.N.
Sobolev, A.A.
Sokol'nikov, G.Ya.
Solov'yov, Z.P.
Stomonyakov, B.S.
Strokach, T.A.
Stuchka, P.I.
Svanidze, A.S.
Sverdlov, V.M.
Sviderskiy, A.I.
Teodorovich, I.A.
Terent'yev, V.A.
Tikhane, A.G.
Tishchenko, S.I.
Todriya, S.Ya.
Tolmachyov, V.N.
Topchiyev, A.V.
Torchinskiy, G.B.
Tret'yakov, A.F.
Trilisser, M.A.
Trotskiy, L.D.
Tukhachevskiy, M.N.
Tumanov, N.G.
Tychina, P.G.
Uborevich, I.P.
Uglanov, N.A.
Ukhanov, K.V.
Unshlikht, I.S.
Vannikov, B.L.
Vedeneyev, B.Ye.
Vester, R.Ye.
Vetoshkin, M.K.
Vinokurov, A.N.
Vinter, A.V.
Vladimirov, M.K.
Volin, B.M.
Vyatkin, L.Ya.
Yagoda, G.G.
Yakovenko, V.G.
Yakovlev, Ya.A.
Yakovleva, V.N.
Yefremov, A.I.
Yefremov, D.V.
Yegorov, A.I.
Yelizarov, M.T.
Yemshanov, A.I.
Yezhov, N.I.
Zaks, G.D.
Zarubin, G.N.
Zatonskiy, V.P.
Zaytsev, N.A.
Zernov, P.M.
Zharko, A.M.
Zhigaryov, P.F.
Zof, V.I.

4. Other Government Key Officials

Abolin, A.K.
Achkanov, F.P.
Achkanov, G.P.
Akopyan, A.
Alabyan, K.S.
Aleksandrovich, A.I.
Alekseyev, N.A.
Alibekov, A.K. ogly
Alonov, Ye.F.
Alyutin, A.P.
Ammosov, M.K.
Amosov, P.N.
Angarskiy (Klestov), N.S.
Armand, Ye.F.
Asatkin-Vladimirskiy, A.N.
Asfendiarov, S.Dzh.
Averin, V.K.
Babushkin, Ye.A.
Bakayev, I.P.
Bakh, A.N.
Balashov, S.I.
Baltagulov, T.B.
Baran, M.L.
Baryshnikov, V.A.
Batyrov, Sh.B.
Bauman, K.Ya.
Beburishvili, M.Ye.
Bednyakov, K.N.
Begma, V.A.
Belen'kiy, G.Ya.
Belov, I.P.
Belyayev, N.I.
Berg, P.S.
Berzin, Ya.A.
Binasik, M.S.
Biniyatov, B.N.A.O.
Birkenfel'd, Ya.Kh.
Bitsenko, A.A.
Blakitnyy (Yellanskiy), V.M.
Blazhevich, I.F.
Bobrov, A.N.
Bogdanov, I.A.
Bokiy, G.I.
Bonch-Bruyevich, V.D.
Borchaninov, A.L.
Bosh, M.P.
Boychenko, A.M.
Brichkina, S.B.
Brykov, A.P.
Bukharin, N.I.
Bulatov, D.A.
Burovtsev, M.V.
Butkevich, A.Ya.
Butsenko, A.I.
Chaplin, N.P.
Charot, M. (Kudel'ka, M.S.)
Chernyavskiy, V.I.
Cheyshvili, N.S.
Chirkin, V.G.
Chodrishvili, M.I.
Chudov, M.S.
Chudovskiy, N.N.
Dashkevich, P.V.
Dashtoyan, R.P.
Demirchyan, D.K.
Deribas, T.D.
Deryabina, S.I.
Dizhbit, A.M.
Dogadov, A.I.
Dorokhov, R.A.
Dreyman, R.A.
Dzerzhinskaya, S.S.
Eydeman, R.P.
Eyduk, A.V.
Fabritsius, Ya.F.
Figatner, Yu.P.
Filatov, N.A.
Fioletov, I.T.
Fridberg, V.I.
Fyodorov, G.F.
Galagan, N.I.
Gamburg, I.K.
Gandurin, K.D.
Gavenis, Yu.P.
Gegechkori, Ye.P.
Gindin, Ya.I.
Glukhachenkov, I.K.
Glyasser, M.I.
Gol'dberg, B.I.
Gol'dman, L.I.
Gol'tsman, A.Z.
Goloshchyokin, F.I.
Golubev, I.M.
Golubeva-Yasneva, M.P.
Golyakov, I.T.
Gorbunov, N.P.
Gorbunov, P.P.
Gorin-Galkin, V.F.
Gorvits, A.B.
Goykhbarg, A.G.
Gozhanskiy, S.N.
Gribkov, M.P.
Gridasov, N.S.
Grinberg, Z.G.
Ibragimov, A.
Ibragimov, Yu.I.
Ignatov, Ye.N.
Il'in, F.N.
Inar, G.
Ivanov, A.V.
Ivanov, B.I.
Ivanov, N.I.
Kadatskiy, I.F.
Kadyrli, M.N. ogly
Kalinina, Ye.I.
Kalmykov, B.E.
Kalmykova, A.M.
Kalnin, T.P.
Kamenskiy, A.Z.
Katanyan, R.P.
Kazakov, A.A.
Khalatov, A.B.
Kirov, S.M.
Kirsanov, P.N.
Kolesnikova, N.N.
Kolotilov, N.N.
Kon, F.Ya.
Kornyushin, F.D.
Korostelev, A.A.
Korostelev, G.A.
Kosarev, V.M.
Kosior, V.V.
Kostyayev, F.V.
Kozhin, M.V.
Kristi, M.P.
Krylov, S.N.
Krzhizhanovskaya-Nevzorova, Z.P.
Kuklev, I.A.

Kurskiy, D.I.
Kutuzov, I.I.
Kyaspert, I.Yu.
Landa, M.M.
Lashevich, M.M.
Levin, R.Ya.
Lopukhin, A.A.
Lunacharskaya, A.A.
Lur'ye, G.N.
Makharadze, G.F.
Malinovskiy, P.P.
Malyshev, S.V.
Markov, A.T.
Markov, S.D.
Marshev, M.L.
Maslov, I.N.
Mekhonoshin, K.A.
Mel'nichanskiy G.N.
Menzhinskaya, L.R.
Menzhinskaya, V.R.
Meranvil, L.A.
Meshcheryakov, V.N.
Meshcheryakova, A.I.
Mesyatsev, P.A.
Metelev, A.D.
Mezhlauk, I.I.
Mikhaylov, L.M.
Minin, S.K.
Mironov, I.F.
Mitskyavichyus-Kapsukas, V.S.
Model, M.I.
Moiseyev, S.I.
Mostovenko, P.N.
Mrochkovskiy, S.I.
Murysev, A.S.
Natsarenus, S.P.
Nazaretyan, A.M.
Nemtsov, N.M.
Nikiforov, A.N.
Oborin, V.P.
Ovsyannikov, N.N.
Ozolin, E.K.
Pankratov, I.I.
Panyushkin, V.L.
Pecherskiy, L.F.
Pilyavskiy, S.S.
Polidorov, S.I.
Polupanov, A.V.
Poluyan, D.V.
Poluyan, Ya.V.
Polyanskiy, I.V.
Postolovskiy, D.S.
Pozern, B.P.
Preobrazhenskiy, Ye.A.
Prozor, V.S.
Reysner, M.A.
Rikhter, A.G.
Royzenman, B.A.
Rozmirovich, Ye.F.
Rudnev, Ye.I.
Said-Galiyev, S.
Sapronov, T.V.
Semyonov, M.A.
Shaydakov, N.A.
Sheynin, L.R.
Shimanov, A.A.
Shlikhter, Ye.S.
Shumyatskiy, B.Z.
Shutko, K.I.
Skobelev, M.I.
Slavinskiy, K.E.
Smidovich, P.G.
Smol'yaninov, V.A.
Sol'ts, A.A.
Sosnovskiy, L.S.
Sponti, Ye.I.
Stopani, A.M.
Stroganov, V.A.
Tarnogorodskiy, N.P.
Tel'man, S.F.
Ter-Arutyunyan, M.K.
Teryan, V.
Tikhomirnov, G.A.
Tikhomirnov, V.A.
Topuridze, D.A.
Tovstukha, I.P.
Trifonov, V.A.
Tsivtsivadze, I.V.
Urayev, P.V.
Vareykis, I.M.
Vavilov, I.M.
Vecheslov, M.G.
Velichkina, V.M.
Veretannikov, N.I.
Vesolovskiy, B.E.
Veynbaum, G.S.
Vlasenko, S.N.
Volin, A.G.
Voyevodin, P.I.
Vozdvizhenskiy, N.D.
Yaglom, Ya.K.
Yakhontov, V.I.
Yakubov, N.
Yanson, Ye.D.
Yenukidze, A.S.
Yenukidze, T.T.
Yumagulov, Kh.Yu.
Yurevich, A.D.
Zakharov, S.S.
Zalomov, P.A.
Zarin'sh, Ya.P.
Zarudnyy, A.S.
Zaslavskiy, P.S.
Zaytsev, V.M.
Zelenskiy, I.A.
Zevin, Ya.D.
Zhdanov, A.A.
Zhgenti, T.G.
Zifel'dt, A.R.

5. Ambassadors and Other Diplomatic Functionaries

Aleksandrovskiy, S.S.
Antonov-Ovseyenko, V.A.
Aralov, S.I.
Arosev, A.Ya.
Aussem (Gromov), O.Kh.
Aussem, V.Kh.
Bazykin, V.I.
Bekzadyan, A.A.
Bel'gov, V.P.
Belyayev, V.A.
Berens, Ye.A.
Berzin, Ya.A.
Chernyshyov, I.S.
Dekanosov, V.G.
Dovgalevskiy, V.S.
Durdenevskiy, V.N.
Etingof, B.Ye.
Ganetskiy, Ya.S.
Golunskiy, S.A.
Grabar, V.E.
Gukovskiy, I.E.
Ignat'yev, A.A.
Il'in-Zhenevskiy, A.F.
Ioffe, A.A.
Iordanskiy, N.I.
Ivannikov, G.I.
Ivanov, I.A.
Kamenev, L.B.
Karakhan, L.M.
Khassis, A.I.
Khinchuk, L.M.
Kirsanov, S.P.
Kiselyov, Ye.D.
Klyshko, N.K.
Kobetskiy, M.V.
Kollontay, A.M.
Kopp, V.L.
Koptelov, M.Ye.
Korovin, Ye.A.
Kotsyubinskiy, Yu.M.
Kozlovskiy, M.Yu.
Krasin, L.B.
Krestinskiy, N.M.
Krylov, S.B.
Kulik, I.Yu.
Kurskiy, D.I.
Lapinskiy, P.L.
Lentsman, Ya.D.
Leplevskiy, G.M.
Litvinov, M.M.
Lomakin, Ya.M.
Lorents, I.L.
Lunacharskiy, A.V.
Lyubarskiy, N.M.
Manuil'skiy, D.Z.
Markhlevskiy (Marchlewski), Yu.Yu.
Martens, L.K.
Mikhaylov, L.M.
Minkin, A.Ye.
Mostovenko, P.N.
Natsarenus, S.P.
Osinskiy, N.
Paykes, A.K.
Peretyorskiy, I.S.
Plakhin, A.I.
Potyomkin, V.P.
Pushkin, G.M.
Rakovskiy, Kh.G.
Raskol'nikov, F.F.
Roshchin, N.V.
Rotshteyn, F.A.
Rozengol'ts, A.P.
Shteyn, B.Ye.
Shtykov, T.F.
Shumyatskiy, B.Z.
Skvirskiy, B.Ye.
Slavin, N.V.
Sobolev, A.A.
Solov'yov, V.I.
Stark, L.N.
Surits, Ya.Z.

Sviderskiy, A.I.
Sysoyev, I.G.
Tazhibayev, T.T.
Troyanovskiy, A.A.
Tugarinov, I.I.
Umanskiy, K.A.
Ustinov, A.M.
Vigilev, B.D.
Vladimirov, P.P.
Vorovskiy, V.V.
Voykov, P.L.
Vyshinskiy, A.Ya.
Yudin, P.F.
Yurenev, K.K.
Zalkind, I.A.
Zarubin, G.N.
Znamenskiy, A.A.

STATE SECURITY

Abakumov, V.S.
Agranov, Ya.S.
Akulov, I.A.
Aleksandrovich (Dmitriyevskiy), V.A.
Amosov, P.N.
Andrianov. N.G.
Antipov, N.K.
Antonov (Saratovskiy), V.P.
Atarbekov, G.A.
Avanesov, V.A.
Averin, V.K.
Bagirov, M.Dzh.A.
Bakayev, I.P.
Balitskiy, V.A.
Belen'kiy, A.Ya.
Beriya, L.P.
Berzin, R.I.
Blagonravov, G.I.
Blyumkin, Ya.G.
Bogorodskiy, F.S.
Bokiy, G.I.
Borchaninov, A.L.
Bulatov, D.A.
Chugurin, I.D.
Deribas, T.D.
Dizhbit, A.M.
Dukis, K.Ya.
Dzerzhinskiy, F.E.
Eyduk, A.V.
Fomin, V.V.
Galagan, N.I.
Gegechkori, A.A.
Gerson, V.L.
Glukhachenkov, I.K.
Kadomtsev, E.S.
Kashirin, I.D.
Kedrov, M.S.
Kingisepp, S.V.
Kolesnikov, A.K.
Krapivyanskiy, N.G.
Krusser, A.S.
Kyaspert, I.Yu.
Latsis, M.I.
Lobov, S.S.
Lyakhin, N.Ye.
Mantsev, V.N.
Menzhinskiy, V.R.
Messing, S.A.
Mironov, N.R.
Mogilyovskiy, S.G.
Moroz, G.S.
Morozov, D.G.
Myasnikov, A.F.
Naymushin, G.F.
Nikiforov, A.N.
Onufriyev, Ye.P.
Pauker, K.V.
Pavlunovskiy, I.P.
Peters, Ya.Kh.
Polyakov, M.Kh.
Popov, K.A.
Pozharov, N.A.
Prokof'yev, G.Ye.
Rekstyn, A.I.
Remeyko, Yu.A.
Rusanov, G.A.
Shvarts, I.I.
Sikorskiy, S.I.
Slutskiy, A.A.
Strokach, T.A.
Trifonov, V.A.
Trilisser, M.A.
Tsintsadze, K.M.
Tulupov, A.V.
Unshlikht, I.S.
Uritskiy, M.S.
Vostretsov, S.S.
Vozdvizhenskiy, N.D.
Yagoda, G.G.
Yakhnovskiy, I.T.
Yakovleva, V.N.
Yezhov, N.I.
Yurovskiy, Ya.M.
Zaks, G.D.
Zalka, M.M.

ARMED FORCES

1. Commanders in Chief, Members of General Staff, Revolutionary-Military Council, Military Council, Committee for Defense and Higher Military Council

Alksnis (Astrov), Ya.I.
Al'tfater, V.M.
Amelin, M.P.
Antonov, A.I.
Antonov-Ovseyenko, V.A.
Appoga, E.F.
Aralov, S.I.
Aronshtam, L.N.
Arzhanov, M.M.
Atabayev, K.S.
Baranov, P.I.
Barskiy, B.Ye.
Belov, I.P.
Beriya, L.P.
Berzin, Ya.K.
Biryuzov, S.S.
Bitte, A.M.
Blyukher, V.K.
Bonch-Bruyevich, M.D.
Bosh, Ye.B.
Brusilov, A.A.
Bubnov, A.S.
Bulin, A.S.
Danilov, S.S.
Danishevskiy (German), K.-Yu.Kh.
Dauman, A.E.
Dubovoy, I.N.
Dybenko, P.Ye.
Eydeman, R.P.
Fed'ko, I.F.
Fel'dman, B.M.
Fishman, Ya.M.
Fokin, V.A.
Frunze, M.V.
Gamarnik, Ya.B.
Gar'kavyy, I.I.
Gaylit, Ya.P.
Germanovich, M.Ya.
Golovko, A.G.
Govorov, L.A.
Gribov, S.Ye.
Gromadin, M.S.
Gryaznov, I.K.
Isakov, I.S.
Kamenev, S.S.
Kashirin, N.D.
Kazanskiy, Ye.S.
Khalepskiy, I.A.
Khripin, V.V.
Khrulyov, A.V.
Kork, A.I.
Kozhanov, I.K.
Krylenko, N.V.
Kuchinskiy, D.A.
Lebedev, P.P.
Levandovskiy, M.K.
Levichev, V.N.
Malandin, G.K.
Malinin, M.S.
Malinovskiy, R.Ya.

Mekhonoshin, K.A.
Mezheninov, S.A.
Muklevich, R.A.
Myasnikov, A.F.
Nedelin, M.I.
Orlov, V.M.
Oshley, P.M.
Petin, N.N.
Raskol'nikov, F.F.
Shaposhnikov, B.M.
Shifres, A.L.
Shtern, G.M.
Sklyanskiy, E.M.
Slavin, I.Ye.
Stalin, I.V.
Trotskiy, L.D.
Tukhachevskiy, M.N.
Uborevich, I.P.
Unshlikht, I.S.
Vatsetis, I.I.
Yakir, I.E.
Yegorov, A.I.
Yeremeyev, K.S.
Zof, V.I.

2. Marshals of the Soviet Union, Chief Marshals of Branches of Arms and Admirals of the Fleet, Generals, Admirals and Other Higher Commanding Staff

Akhutin, M.N.
Alafuzov, V.A.
Aleksandrov, A.V.
Aleksandrov, A.P.
Alksnis, Ya.Ya.
Andreyev, F.F.
Apanasenko, I.R.
Astakhov, F.A.
Avksent'yevskiy, K.A.
Banaytis, S.I.
Barabanov, A.Ye.
Bazilevich, G.D.
Begma, V.A.
Belov, P.A.
Belokoskov, V.Ye.
Berkalov, Ye.A.
Berzarin, N.E.
Berzin, R.I.
Blagonravov, A.I.
Blazhevich, I.F.
Bobrov, B.I.
Bocharov, L.P.
Bogdanov, S.I.
Bokis, G.G.
Borisenko, A.N.
Borisoglebskiy, V.V.
Borzilov, S.V.
Burdenko, N.N.
Byalokoz, Ye.L.
Bykov, K.M.
Charnyavskiy, B.B.
Chernetskiy, S.A.
Chernyakhovskiy, I.D.
Dashichev, I.F.
Demichev, M.A.
Dmokhovskiy, V.K.
Dovator, L.M.
Doynikov, B.S.
Drozd, V.P.
Drozdov, N.F.
Dukhov, N.L.
Dushenov, K.I.
Dzhanelidze, Yu.Yu.
Entin, D.A.
Falaleyev, F.Ya.
Fedorenko, Ya.N.
Figurnov, K.M.
Frolov, V.A.
Fyodorov, V.G.
Galaktionov, M.R.
Galanin, I.V.
Galler, L.M.
Galling, A.K.
Gapich, N.I.
Gavro, L.M.
Gay, G.D.
Gekker, A.I.
Gerasimenko, V.F.
Geveling, N.V.
Giroglav, S.S.
Gittis, V.M.
Glagolev, V.P.
Goffe, V.I.
Golikov, A.G.
Gorbachyov, G.S.
Gordov, V.N.
Gorodovikov, O.I.
Grave, I.P.
Grendel, V.D.
Grigorovich, I.K.
Grishko, G.Ye.
Gusev, D.N.
Gusev, N.I.
Ignat'yev, A.A.
Ivanov, I.I.
Kakurin, N.Ye.
Kalashnikov, V.P.
Kalinovskiy, K.B.
Kalmykov, M.V.
Karbyshev, D.M.
Kavrayskiy, V.V.
Keldysh, V.M.
Khakhan'yan, G.D.
Khlopin, N.G.
Khol'zunov, V.S.
Khrunichev, M.V.
Khryukin, T.T.
Kireyev, G.P.
Kirpichyov, N.L.
Kirponos, M.P.
Kiselyov, I.A.
Klimov, V.Ya.
Klyuss, I.A.
Klyuyev, L.L.
Kniga, V.I.
Kolenkovskiy, A.K.
Kolpakchi, V.Ya.
Koroteyev, V.A.
Korsun, N.G.
Kosich, D.I.
Kosmodem'yanskiy, N.P.
Kostenko, F.Ya.
Kostikov, A.G.
Kostyayev, F.V.
Kovalenkov, V.I.
Kovpak, S.A.
Kovtyukh, Ye.I.
Kozak, S.A.
Kozlov, V.I.
Kravchenko, A.G.
Kravchenko, G.P.
Kravtsov, I.K.
Krivoruchko, N.N.
Kulikovskiy, G.G.
Kupriyanov, P.A.
Kutyakov, I.S.
Kuybyshev, N.V.
Kuznetsov, A.A.
Kuznetsov, F.I.
Kuznetsov, V.I.
Kvyatek (Kwiatek), K.F.
Lapchinskiy, A.N.
Lapin, A.Ya.
Latsis, Ya.Ya.
Lavochkin, S.A.
Levit, V.S.
Loktionov, A.D.
Longva, R.V.
Ludri, I.M.
Mal'kov, P.D.
Malyshev, V.A.
Maslov, M.S.
Matusevich, N.N.
Medvedev, M.Ye.
Mekhlis, L.Z.
Melikov, V.A.
Mel'nikov, A.V.
Mironov, N.R.
Morozov, A.P.
Muralov, N.I.
Naymushin, G.F.
Nemitts, A.V.
Nesterov, S.K.
Neznamov, A.A.
Novikov, K.N.
Novitskiy, F.F.
Ol'derogge, V.A.
Osipov, V.P.
Panfilov, A.P.
Panfilov, I.V.
Papivin, N.F.
Papkovich, P.F.
Parskiy, D.P.
Pavlov, A.V.
Pavlov, I.U.
Pavlov, P.A.
Pavlovskiy, N.O.
Pavlovskiy, Ye.N.
Peremytov, A.M.
Perevyortkin, S.N.
Petrikovskiy, S.I.
Petrov, I.Ye.
Petrov, M.P.
Petrovskiy, L.G.
Platonov, S.P.
Podlas, K.P.
Polbin, I.S.
Preobrazhenskiy, Ye.N.
Primakov, V.M.
Ptukhin, Ye.S.
Pugachyov, S.A.

Pukhov, M.P.
Purkayev, M.A.
Putna, V.K.
Ragoza, N.I.
Rubanov, S.U.
Rudnev, S.V.
Ryazanov, V.G.
Rybalko, P.S.
Rychagov, P.V.
Rytov, A.G.
Ryzhov, A.I.
Sablin, Yu.V.
Samoylo, A.A.
Sedyakin, A.I.
Semeka, S.A.
Serdich, D.F.
Sergeyev, A.V.
Sergeyev, Ye.N.
Serov, A.K.
Seryshev, S.M.
Shchadenko, Ye.A.
Shcherbakov, A.S.
Shevkunenko, V.N.
Shilovskiy, Ye.A.
Shkodunovich, N.N.
Shmidt, D.A.
Shorin, V.I.
Shtykov, T.F.
Shutov, S.F.
Shvarts, N.N.
Svetsov, A.D.
Slavin, N.V.
Smirnov, P.I.
Smushkevich, Ya.V.
Snesarev, A.Ye.
Speranskiy, A.D.
Spirin, I.T.
Stalin, V.I.
Strokach, T.A.
Sukhov, I.P.
Susaykov, I.Z.
Svechin, A.A.
Talenskiy, N.A.
Tarasov, A.P.
Todorskiy, A.I.
Tolbukhin, F.I.
Tonkov, V.N.
Triandafillov, V K.
Triumfov, A.V.
Trofimenko, S.G.
Troyanker, B.U.
Tsarevskiy, M.M.
Tsvetayev, V.D.
Vannikov, B.L.
Varfolomeyev, N.Ye.
Vasilenko, M.I.
Vatutin, N.F.
Velichko, K.I.
Velikanov, M.D.
Verkhovskiy, A.I.
Vershigora, P.P.
Viktorov, M.V.
Vinogradov, V.I.
Vlasov, A.A.
Vol'pe, A.M.
Vorob'yov, M.P.
Voskanov, G.K.
Vostretsov, S.S.
Vovsi, M.S.
Yakovlev, V.V.
Yanovskiy, M.I.
Yefremov, M.G.
Yegorov, P.I.
Yegor'yev, V.N.
Yelanskiy, N.N.
Yur'yev, B.N.
Zakharov, G.F.
Zakhvatayev, N.D.
Zernov, P.M.
Zhavoronkov, S.F.
Zhdanov, A.A.
Zhdanov, V.I.
Zhemochkin, B.N.
Zhigaryov, P.F.
Zhmachenko, F.F.
Zhuravlyov, P.M.
Zinov'yev, G.V.
Znamenskiy, A.A.
Zotov, S.A.

3. Other Military Functionaries, Politruks, Civil War and WW II Veterans and Partisans, Persons Engaged in Military ans Space Research

Achkanov, F.P.
Achkanov, G.P.
Afanas'yev, F.M.
Afanas'yev, V.A.
Aksyonov, A.M.
Alekseyev, M.N.
Alekseyev, V.P.
Algazin, A.S.
Alliluyev, P.S.
Amangel'dy Imanov
Amirov, T.M.
Ammosov, S.N.
Anisimov, N.A.
Antikainen, T.
Antonov, A.A.
Anvel't, Ya.Ya.
Apanasenko, I.R.
Apinis, R.A.
Apse, M.Ya.
Arenson, I.A.
Armand, F.A.
Arskiy, P.A.
Arvatov, Yu.I.
Arveladze, P.Ya.
Askol'dov, Ya.L.
Aussem (Gromov), O.Kh.
Aussem, V.Kh.
Averin, V.K.
Avetisyan, U.M.
Avinovitskiy, Ya.L.
Avrov, D.N.
Azin, V.M.
Babushkin, M.S.
Badin, A.L.
Bagirov, M.Dzh.A.
Bakayev, I.P.
Bakhrushin, A.M.
Bakhturov, P.N.
Balakhonov, Ya.F.
Baryshnikov, V.A.
Batyuk, Ya.P.
Bekauri, V.I.
Belitskiy, S.M.
Belotskiy, M.L.
Berends, K.G.
Berens, Ye.A.
Blagonravov, A.I.
Blagonravov, G.I.
Blinov, M.F.
Blumental, F.L.
Bondarenko, A.D.
Bondarenko, M.Z.
Bozhenko, V.N.
Bubenets, I.K.
Bubnov, I.G.
Budnitskiy, Ya.G.
Bumazhkov, T.P.
Butyrskiy, V.P.
Buyko, P.M.
Byuler, V.A.
Chapayev, V.I.
Chaykina, Ye.I.
Chekalin, A.P.
Chernyak (Todorskaya), R.I.
Cheveryov, A.M.
Cheyshvili, N.S.
Chkalov, V.P.
Chudnovskiy, G.I.
Chudovskaya, M.Kh.
Dakhadayev, M.-A.
Dashichev, I.F.
Degtyaryov, V.A.
De-Lazari, A.N.
Dik, I.O.
Dobrynin, P.G.
Dolgov, P.I.
Dozitis, K.M.
Dundich, O. (Cholich, M.)
D'yachenko, D.G.
Dzarakhokhov, Kh.-M.U.
Dzerzhinskiy, F.E.
Dzevaltovskiy, I.L.
Dzhangil'din, A.T.
Epshteyn, M.S.
Essen, A.M.
Essen, E.E.
Eykhe, G.Kh.
Fabritsius, Ya.F.
Favitskiy, V.V.
Fedoseyenko, P.F.
Fenigshteyn, Ya.G.
Filatov, N.A.
Filatov, N.M.
Fioletov, I.T.
Fishman, Ya.M.
Fokin, I.I.
Frunze, T.M.
Furmanov, D.A.
Gabiyev, S.I.
Gabyshev, I.Ya.
Gastello, N.F.
Gavrilov, N.A.
Gaza, I.I.
Ge, A.
Golenkin, F.I.
Golubenko, N.V.
Golubev, A.V.
Golubev, V.M.
Grigorovich, D.P.
Gritsevets, S.I.
Gromova, U.M.

Gruzman, Sh.A.
Ignatov, G.P.
Ignatov, Ye.P.
Il'mer, K.P.
Ioffe, A.A.
Ivanov, I.I.
Ivanov, I.I.
Kadomtsev, E.S.
Kalandarishvili, N.A.
Kalinin, K.A.
Kalmykov, B.E.
Kalnin, O.Yu.
Kalnyn, F.K.
Kamo
Kapustin, N.Ya.
Karpov, A.T.
Khikhlovskiy, V.V.
Khokhryakov, S.V.
Khomenko, V.K.
Khoruzhaya, V.Z.
Kikvidze, V.I.
Klembovskiy, V.N.
Klimov, V.Ya.
Klubov, A.F.
Kober, A.P.
Kochubey, I.A.
Kolbas'yev, Ye.V.
Kolyada, N.Z.
Komarov, V.M.
Kondratenko, S.F.
Kondrat'yev, A.A.
Kondratyuk, Yu.V.
Kopenkin, I.I.
Korobko, V.I.
Korobkov, V.M.
Korolyov, S.P.
Koshevoy, O.V.
Kosmodem'yanskaya, Z.A.
Kostikov, A.G.
Kotel'nikov, G.Ye.
Kotik, V.A.
Kotovskiy, G.I.
Kotsko, V.F.
Kravchenko, A.D.
Krusser, A.S.
Krylov, A.N.
Kryzhanovskiy, V.P.
Kudryashov, V.S.
Kuk, A.I.
Kuklev, I.A.
Kulishenko, G.Ya.
Kunikov, Ts.L.
Kuybyshev, V.V.
Kuz'min, G.P.
Kuz'min, N.N.
Kuznetsov, N.I.
Latsis, V.T.
Lavochkin, S.A.
Lazimir, P.Ye.
Lazo, S.G.
Lebedinskiy, A.V.
Lekhin, I.V.
Leshchenko, D.I.
Levanevskiy, S.A.
Lifshits, B.S.
Lin'kov, G.M.
Lipatov, T.I.
Liskonozhenko, N.G.
Luks, K.Ya.
Lutskiy, A.N.
Makarov, S.I.
Malakhovskiy, V.F.
Malenkov, Ye.M.
Maletskiy, A.M.
Malygin, I.V.
Mamontov, Ye.M.
Markin, N.G.
Matiyasevich, M.S.
Matrosov, A.M.
Mavrinskiy, I.L.
Mel'nikayte, M.Yu.
Mendeleyev, V.D.
Mironov, F.K.
Mokrousov, A.V.
Morgunenko, V.S.
Movchin, N.N.
Mukhin, F.N.
Murav'yov, M.A.
Nakhimson, S.M.
Nalyotov, M.P.
Nazarbekyan, A.Z.
Nevzorova-Krzhizhanovskaya, Z.P.
Nikolayev, A.P.
Novitskiy, V.F.
Odintsov, L.Ye.
Ogorodnikov, F.Ye.
Okrestin, B.S.
Oktyabr'skaya, M.V.
Omel'yanyuk, V.S.
Onufriyev, Ye.P.
Osipenko, P.D.
Ostrovskiy, N.A.
Parkhomenko, A.Ya.
Parshin, G.M.
Pavlov, I.F.
Pen'kovskiy, O.V.
Peregonets, A.F.
Peterson, A.D.
Peterson, K.A.
Peterson, R.A.
Petlyakov, V.M.
Pirogovskiy, A.S.
Poletayev, F.A.
Polikarpov, N.N.
Polivanov, A.A.
Poltoratskiy, P.G.
Popov, V.D.
Popudrenko, N.N.
Porik, V.V.
Pozharov, N.A.
Krokhorovshchikov, A.A.
Prokof'yev, G.A.
Rakov, A.S.
Raskova, M.M.
Red'kin, A.M.
Reynson, O.P.
Roshal, S.G.
Rubin, A.I.
Rudnev, N.A.
Rusakov, I.V.
Ruzheynikov, I.S.
Sadovnichenko, D.G.
Safonov, B.F.
Said-Galiyev, S.
Sapunov, Ye.N.
Semeyko, N.I.
Sergiyenko, I.V.
Shchetinkin, P.Ye.
Shchors, N.A.
Shestakov, S.A.
Shevtsova, L.G.
Shpektorov, N.L.
Shvetsov, A.D.
Sibirtsev, V.M.
Sivers, R.F.
Slepnyov, M.T.
Sollogub, N.V.
Stepanishchev, M.T.
Stepanyan, N.G.
Suleyman, N.A.
Suprun, S.T.
Sytin, P.P.
Talalaykhin, V.V.
Talash, V.I.
Tolmachyov, N.G.
Tomin, N.D.
Tret'yakevich, V.I.
Trofimov, V.M.
Tsagolov, G.A.
Tsander, F.A.
Tsiolkovskiy, K.E.
Tsviling, S.M.
Tyulenin, S.G.
Ufimtsev, A.G.
Usiyevich, G.A.
Usyskin, I.D.
Vakhitov, M.-N.
Vakulich, P.I.
Vasenko, A.B.
Vasil'chenko, S.F.
Vasilevskaya, V.L.
Vasil'yev, N.G.
Vedyornikov, A.S.
Vermishev, A.A.
Vershinin, S.P.
Vilumson, E.F.
Vinogradov, P.F.
Vitas, Yu.T.
Voskov, S.P.
Vukolov, S.P.
Yakimychev, A.M.
Yanyshev, M.P.
Yemel'yanov, N.A.
Yudovskiy, V.G.
Zakharov, I.N.
Zalka, M.M.
Zaslonov, K.S.
Zayonchkovskiy, A.M.
Zaytsev, V.A.
Zelenev, N.A.
Zemlyachka, R.S.
Zemnukhov, I.A.
Zheleznyakov, A.G.
Zherve, B.B.
Zhigur, Ya.M.
Zhloba, D.P.
Zorge (Sorge), R.
Zverev, D.Ye.

NATIONAL ECONOMY

Abdullayev, Kh.M.
Abrosimov, P.V.
Achkanov, G.P.
Afanas'yev, S.I.
Agabal'yants, G.G.
Agranovskiy, L.S.
Aldabergenov, N.
Aleksandrov, A.S.
Aleksandrov, I.G.
Al'skiy, A.O.
Amosov, P.N.
Angelina, P.N.
Anikst, A.M.
Antipin, P.F.
Antipov, N.K.
Aralov, S.I.
Arenson, I.A.
Aristarkhov, A.A.
Artyom'yev, N.A.
Arzhanov, M.M.
Aussem, V.Kh.
Avanesov, V.A.
Avilov, B.V.
Avramov (Abramov), R.P.
Babkin, I.P.
Badayev, A.Ye.
Bagayev, M.A.
Bagdat'yev, S.Ya.
Bagirova, B.M.-kyzy
Bakulin, I.V.
Baranov, P.I.
Bazarov, V. (Rudnev, V.A.)
Bazhanov, V.M.
Belyakov, A.A.
Berezin, M.Ye.
Berkengeym, A.M.
Berlin, P.A.
Bitsenko, A.A.
Bliznichenko, A.Ye.
Bogdanov (Malinovskiy), A.A.
Bogdanov, P.A.
Bogolepov, D.P.
Bogolepov, M.I.
Borisov, I.N.
Borisov, P.S.
Bortkevich, V.M.
Britske, E.V.
Bronskiy, M.G.
Bruno, G.I.
Brutskus, B.D.
Brykov, A.P.
Bryukhanov, N.P.
Budnikov, M.S.
Budnitskiy, Ya.G.
Bukharin, N.I.
Buniat-zade, D.Kh.
Butkevich, A.Ya.
Chaplin, N.P.
Chaplin, V.M.
Chasovennyy, S.I.
Chayanov, A.V.
Chekunov, I.A.
Chelintsev, A.N.
Cherdantsev, G.N.
Cherlyunchakevich, N.A.
Chirkin, V.G.
Chubar, V.Ya.
Chugurin, I.D.
Danishevskiy (German), K.-Yu.Kh.
Den, V.E.
Derbyshev, N.I.
Dimo, N.A.
Dmitriyev, A.M.
Dmitriyev, V.V.
Dobrokhotov, A.N.
Dominikovskiy, F.N.
Dosser, Z.N.
Dreyman, R.A.
Dubelir, G.D.
Dubkovetskiy, F.I.
Dudnik, A.M.
Duka, S.Kh.
Dul'chevskiy, D.A.
Dushechkin, A.I.
Dvornikov, P.I.
D'yakov, M.I.
Dyla, I.L.
Eykhe, G.Kh.
Eysmont, N.B.
Fal'kner, S.A.
Fel'dman (Pavlovets), G.K.
Filyanskiy, K.D.
Fridrikhson, L.Kh.
Frolov, A.M.
Frolov, A.N.
Frumkin, M.I.
Gakkel, Ya.M.
Generalov, F.S.
Getsov, S.A.
Ginzburg, V.G.
Gobi, L.Kh.
Golovatyy, F.P.
Gorev, A.A.
Graftio, G.O.
Grinberg, M.I.
Grinevetskiy, V.I.
Grin'ko, G.F.
Groman, V.G.
Gubkin, I.M.
Gurariy, M.S.
Il'inskiy, M.A.
Ioffe, A.A.
Ipat'yev, V.N.
Ivanov, I.I.
Ivanov, M.F.
Ivanov, N.P.
Ivanov, S.V.
Izotov, N.A.
Kablukov, N.A.
Kagan, N.I.
Kaganovich, M.M.
Kaktyn, A.M.
Kalinin, K.A.
Kalinin, S.I.
Kalizhnyuk, S.K.
Kalmanovich, M.I.
Kamenev, L.B.
Kapelyushnikov, M.A.
Karpov, L.N.
Kazakov, A.A.
Kazantsev, F.P.
Kedrov, M.S.
Keldysh, V.M.
Kertselli, S.V.
Khalatov, A.B.
Khobta, Ye.S.
Khotinskiy, V.I.
Khrunichev, M.V.
Kirpichnikov, V.D.
Kirpichyov, N.L.
Klasson, R.E.
Klimenko, I.Ye.
Klyshko, N.K.
Kochubey, A.D.
Komar, A.N.
Komarov, N.P.
Kondakov, N.A.
Kondrat'yev, N.D.
Kononenko, P.P.
Kopylov, N.V.
Korneyev, I.I.
Korobov, A.V.
Korobov, I.G.
Korobov, P.I.
Korolyov, S.I.
Korzinov, G.N.
Koshova, A.D.
Kosior, I.V.
Kovylkin, S.T.
Krasnoshchyokov, A.M.
Kravtsov, P.V.
Kritsman, L.N.
Krivchenko, G.A.
Krzhizhanovskiy, G.M.
Krumin, G.I.
Kubyak, N.A.
Kucherenko, V.A.
Kurako, M.K.
Kurayev, V.V.
Kuybyshev, V.V.
Kviring, E.I.
Larin, Yu.
Latsis, M.I.
Levin, R.Ya.
Lezhava, A.M.
Likhachyov, V.M.
Lobachyov, I.S.
Lobov, S.S.
Loginov, F.G.
Lomov-Oppokov, G.I.
Lozhechkin, M.P.
Luganovskiy, E.V.
Lukashyov, A.M.
Lukin, A.M.
Lyakhin, N.Ye
Lyubimov, I.Ye.
Lyubovich, A.M.
Makhlin, L.D.
Maksimov, K.G.
Malakhovskiy, B.S.
Malyshev, I.S.
Mamin, Ya.V.
Markov, A.T.
Martens, L.K.
Maslov, A.M.
Maslov, P.P.
Mavrinskiy, I.L.
Mazay, M.N.
Mazayev, A.V.
Mdivani, P.G.
Mel'nichanskiy, G.N.
Merkulov, F.A.
Meysner, V.I.
Mezhlauk, V.I.
Michurin, I.V.
Mikhalevskiy, F.I.
Milyutin, V.P.
Mityushin, N.T.
Morozov, P.T.
Moskovin, I.M.

Muralov, A.I.
Myaskov, K.G.
Nemanov, N.G.
Nemanskiy, Ya.
Nemchinov, V.S.
Nikitin, P.V.
Nikolayev, A.M.
Orlov, K.N.
Osadchiy, P.S.
Osinskiy, N.
Ozyornyy, M.O.
Pankratov, I.I.
Pavlunovskiy, I.P.
Paykes, A.K.
Pestun, Ye.G.
Peterson, A.D.
Pilatskaya, O.V.
Pludon, M.Ya.
Pochenkov, K.I.
Popov, P.I.
Popov, V.F.
Postnikov, A.M.
Preobrazhenskiy, N.F.
Preobrazhenskiy, Ye.A.
Prudenskiy, G.A.
Pryanishnikov, D.N.
Ptukha, M.V.
Pyatakov, G.L.
Rabinovich, F.Ya.
Radchenko, I.I.
Ramzin, L.K.
Rayevskiy, A.S.
Reshetnikov, I.I.
Rukhimovich, M.L.
Rusanov, G.A.
Rykunov, M.V.
Sakharov, V.V.
Sammer, I.A.
Sepre, O.A.
Serebrovskiy, A.P.
Sereda, S.P.
Shatelen, M.A.
Sher, V.V.
Shotman, A.V.
Shteyngart, A.M.
Shvarts, I.I.
Smilga, I.T.
Smirnov, A.P.
Smirnov, N.I.
Smirnov, V.M.
Sokol'nikov, G.Ya.
Spunde, A.P.
Striyevskiy, K.K.
Stukov, I.N.
Sukhomlin, K.V.
Sus, N.I.
Sverdlov, V.M.
Tairov, V.Ye.
Tashkin, A.M.
Ter-Astvatsaturyan, I.A.
Ter-Gazaryan, G.G.
Teryokhin, N.Ya.
Tishchenko, S.I.
Tolokontsev, A.F.
Trakhtenberg, I.A.
Travnikov, A.S.
Tregubenko, A.F.
Trifonov, V.A.
Trushkov, N.I.
Tsyurupa, A.D.
Tsyurupa, G.D.
Tulaykov, N.M.
Tulupov, A.V.
Tumanov, N.G.
Tursunkulov, Kh.
Tyzhnov, V.I.
Ufimtsev, N.I.
Ul'yanov, A.V.
Ul'yanov, I.I.
Urunkhodzhayev, S.-Kh.
Vakhrushev, V.V.
Valayev, A.A.
Varzar, V.Ye.
Vedeneyev, B.Ye.
Vedenisov, B.N.
Veprintsev, P.A.
Vershinin, S.P.
Veynberg, G.D.
Veyts, V.I.
Vikhlyayev, P.A.
Vilenskiy, L.S.
Vinter, A.V.
Vishnyak, Ya.I.
Vladimirov, M.K.
Voblyy, K.G.
Voinov, A.I.
Vorob'yov, K.Ya.
Voronin, V.I.
Voznesenskiy, N.A.
Vul'fson, S.D.
Yaglom, Ya.K.
Yakovenko, V.G.
Yanushevskiy, P.S.
Yarilov, A.A.
Yasnopol'skiy, L.M.
Yastreyskiy, B.S.
Yefimov, A.S.
Yefremov, D.I.
Yershov, I.S.
Yevdokimov, G.Ye.
Yunov, Yu.M.
Zasyad'ko, A.F.
Zavenyagin, A.P.
Zaytsev, N.A.
Zernov, P.M.
Zharko, A.M.
Zhegalov, S.I.
Zheleznov, V.Ya.
Zheltov, I.I.
Zverev, D.Ye.
Zvonkov, V.V.

SCIENCE AND EDUCATION

1. Presidents, Vice-Presidents, Full and Corresponding Members of the USSR Academy of Sciences, Union-Republik Academies of Sciences and Other Academies

Abakumov, S.I.
Abdullayev, Kh.M.
Abegyan, M.Kh.
Abramovich, D.I.
Abrikosov, A.I.
Abrosimov, P.V.
Acharyan, R.A.
Adoratskiy, V.V.
Akhutin, M.N.
Akimov, G.V.
Alabyan, K.S.
Aleksandrov, G.F.
Aleksandrov, I.G.
Aleksandrovich, A.I.
Alekseyev, V.M.
Alimdzhan Khamid
Al'shvang, A.A.
Alymov, A.Ya.
Amirslanov, A.A.-ogly
Andreyev, M.S.
Andronov, A.A.
Anichkov, N.N.
Anisimov, I.I.
Antipov, P.F.
Antons, R.I.
Anuchin, D.N.
Arakishvili (Arakchiyev), D.I.
Arinkin, M.I.
Aristovskiy, V.M.
Arkad'yev, V.K.
Arkhangel'skiy, A.D.
Arkhangel'skiy, A.S.
Arkhangel'skiy, B.A.
Arkhangel'skiy, S.I.
Arkhipov, A.Ye.
Arkin, D.Ye.
Arkin, Ye.A.
Arnol'd, I.V.
Arzhanov, M.A.
Arzumanyan, A.A.
Asaf'yev, B.V.
Ashmarin, N.I.
Atakhanov, E.I.
Auezov, M.O.
Averbakh, M.I.
Avilov, M.I.
Aynalov, D.V.
Ayni (Sadriddin, S.)
Azbukin, D.N.
Babayants, R.A.
Bagaley, D.I.
Bagdasarov, A.A.
Bakh, A.N.
Bakh, R.R.
Bakhrushin, S.V.
Bakhurin, I.M.
Baksheyev, V.N.
Bakulov, A.N.
Balandin, A.A.
Balukhatyy, S.D.

Banaytis, S.I.
Barannikov, A.P.
Baranov, P.A.
Baranskiy, N.N.
Bardin, I.P.
Barkov, A.S.
Barshauskas, K.M.
Bartol'd, V.V.
Batkis, G.A.
Batyrov, Sh.B.
Baykov, A.A.
Beketov, A.N.
Beklemishev, V.A.
Beklemishev, V.N.
Beletskiy, A.I.
Belopol'skiy, A.A.
Belyankin, D.S.
Belyavskiy, S.I.
Belyayev, N.M.
Belyayev, Ye.A.
Benua, L.N.
Berg, L.S.
Berkalov, Ye.A.
Bernshteyn, N.A.
Bertel's, Ye.E.
Betekhtin, A.G.
Bilibin, Yu.A.
Bilyashevskiy, N.F.
Blazhko, S.N.
Blumbakh, F.I.
Bogolepov, M.I.
Bogomolets, A.A.
Bogoroditskiy, V.A.
Bogoslovskiy, M.M.
Bogoyavlenskiy, S.K.
Bonch-Bruyevich, M.A.
Boris (Vik, B.I.)
Borisyak, A.A.
Borovkov, A.K.
Borukayev, R.A.
Boruta, K.
Braytsev, V.R.
Britske, E.V.
Brodskiy, N.L.
Brounov, P.I.
Bubnov, A.P.
Bubrikh, D.V.
Budnikov, M.S.
Bulakhovskiy, L.A.
Bulankin, I.N.
Bunin, I.A.
Burdenko, N.N.
Bush, N.A.
Butkevich, V.S.
Buzeskul, V.P.
Bykov, K.M.
Chagovets, V.Yu.
Chaplygin, S.A.
Chavdarov, S.Kh.
Chebotaryov, N.G.
Chekhov, N.V.
Chelintsev, V.V.
Cherdantsev, G.N.
Cheremnykh, M.M.
Chernorutskiy, M.V.
Chernyayev, I.I.
Chernyshyov, A.A.
Chernyshyov, A.B.
Chernyshyov, B.I.
Chernyshyov, S.Ye.
Chetayev, N.G.
Chichibabin, A.Ye.
Chizhevskiy, N.P.
Chudakov, Ye.A.
Dadashev, S.A.-ogly
Danilevskiy, A.Ya.
Danilevskiy, V.V.
Danilevskiy, V.Ya.
Danilov, V.I.
Davidenkov, N.N.
Davidenkov, S.N.
Deborin (Ioffe), A.M.
Demchuk, P.I.
Demidenko, T.T.
Demirchyan, D.K.
Dem'yanov, N.Ya.
Derzhavin, K.N.
Derzhavin, N.S.
Dimo, N.A.
Dinnik, A.N.
Dmitriyev, A.I.
Dmitriyev, N.K.
Dobiash-Rozhdestvenskaya, O.A.
Dobrokhotov, N.N.
Dobrokhotova, A.I.
Dobroklonskiy, M.V.
Dobrovol'skiy, V.V.
Dogel, V.A.
Dolgo-Saburov, B.A.
Dosmukhamedov, Kh.D.
Doynikov, B.S.
Drozhzhin, S.D.
Dubinskiy, D.A.
Dudinov, O.A.
Duka, S.Kh.
Dukhov, N.L.
Dumanskiy, A.V.
Dushechkin, A.I.
Dvornikov, P.I.
Dyachenko, V.Ye.
D'yakov, M.I.
Dzhanashia, S.N.
Dzhanelidze, Yu.Yu.
Dzhavakhishvili, I.A.
Dzhivelegov, A.K.
Effendiyev, F.A.-ogly
Endzelin, Ya.
Evarnitskiy (Yavornitskiy), D.I.
Farmakovskiy, B.V.
Favorskiy, A.Ye.
Favorskiy, V.A.
Faydysh, A.P.
Fazlullin, M.A.
Fedot'yev, P.P.
Fersman, A.Ye.
Fialkov (Naftulovich), Ya.A.
Figurnov, K.M.
Filatov, V.P.
Filippovich, A.N.
Firsov, G.P.
Florin, V.A.
Flyorina, Ye.A.
Fol'bort, G.V.
Fomin, I.A.
Frenkel' Ya.I.
Friche, V.M.
Frolov, A.M.
Fronshteyn, R.M.
Fyodorov, L.N.
Fyodorov, M.M.
Fyodorov, Ye.Ye.
Fyodorovskiy, F.F.
Fyodorovskiy, N.M.
Gafur-Gulyam
Galyorkin, B.G.
Gamaleya, N.F.
Gamburtsev, G.A.
Ganshina, K.A.
Garshin, V.G.
Gartnyy, T.
Gedroyts, K.K.
Gel'freykh, V.G.
Gerasimov, A.M.
Gerasimov, S.V.
German, A.P.
Gersevanov, N.M.
Gilyarov, A.N.
Gilyarovskiy, V.A.
Gintsburg, I.Ya.
Ginzburg, M.Ya.
Gira, L.K.
Giroglav, S.S.
Glazenap, S.P.
Glazunov, M.F.
Glinka, K.D.
Godin, Yu.N.
Golovin, N.M.
Golubev, V.V.
Golunskiy, S.A.
Goncharov, V.L.
Gorbunov, B.N.
Gorbunov, N.P.
Gordlevskiy, V.A.
Gordyagin, A.Ya.
Gorelov, G.N.
Gorodetskiy, A.A.
Gorshkov, I.S.
Goryachkin, V.P.
Got'ye, Yu.V.
Govorov, L.A.
Grabar, I.E.
Grabar, V.E.
Graftio, G.O.
Grashchenkov, N.I.
Grave, D.A.
Grave, I.P.
Grebenshchikov, I.V.
Grekov, B.D.
Grinberg, A.A.
Grinshteyn, A.M.
Grishashvili, I.G.
Grossgeym, A.A.
Grozin, B.D.
Grum-Grzhimaylo, V.Ye.
Grushevskiy, M.S.
Gubergrits, M.M.
Gubkin, I.M.
Gudtsov, N.T.
Gudziy, N.K.
Gulevich, V.S.
Gulyam, G.G.
Gurevich, M.O.
Guseynov, G.N. ogly
Gutorov, I.V.
Gvozdyov, A.N.
Gyunter, N.M.
Igantov, N.K.
Igantovskiy, V.M.
Il'ichyov, A.S.
Il'in, A.A.
Il'in, L.A.
Il'inskiy, M.A.
Ioffe, A.F.
Ipat'yev, V.N.
Isachenko, B.L.
Isakov, I.S.

Ismailov, Ye.S.
Istrina, Ye.S.
Ivanov, A.A.
Ivanov, A.A.
Ivanov, I.I.
Ivanov, I.I.
Ivanov, L.A.
Ivanov, L.N.
Ivanov, M.F.
Ivanov, V.N.
Iyerusalimskiy, N.D.
Izgaryshev, N.A.
Izmailov, N.A.
Kablukov, I.A.
Kachalov, N.N.
Kalashnikov, A.G.
Kalinovich, M.Ya.
Kammari, M.D.
Kapantsyan, G.A.
Kapelyushnikov, M.A.
Kardovskiy, D.N.
Kareyev, N.I.
Karinskiy, N.M.
Karnaukhov, M.M.
Karpinskiy, A.P.
Karskiy, Ye.F.
Kas'yanov, A.M.
Kedrov-Zikhman, O.P.
Kekcheyev, K.Kh.
Keldysh, V.M.
Kell, N.G.
Keller, B.A.
Kharkevich, A.A.
Khinchin, A.Ya.
Khlopin, N.G.
Khlopin, V.G.
Khodukhin, N.I.
Khokhol, Ye.N.
Kholodnyy, N.G.
Khoroshko, V.K.
Khrushchov, G.K.
Khrushchov, V.M.
Khvol'son, O.D.
Kinshidze, N.A.
Kirichenko, I.N.
Kirpichyov, M.V.
Kiselyov, S.V.
Kistyakovskiy, V.A.
Kizhner, N.M.
Klimov, V.Ya.
Knipovich, N.M.
Kochin, N.Ye.
Kogan, P.S.
Kokovtsev, P.K.
Kolas, Ya.
Kolesnik, I.D.
Kolessa, F.M.
Komar, A.N.
Komarov, V.L.
Kondakov, V.A.
Koni, A.F.
Konovalov, D.P.
Konovalov, N.V.
Konstantinov, N.A.
Konstantinov, P.N.
Korchak-Chepurkovskiy, A.V.
Korin, P.D.
Kornilov, K.N.
Kornoukhov, N.V.
Korobchanskiy, I.Ye.
Korolyov, S.P.
Korotkov, A.A.
Korovin, Ye.A.
Korzhenevskiy, N.L.
Koshlyakov, N.S.
Koshtoyants, Kh.S.
Kosminskiy, Ye.A.
Kosonogov, I.I.
Kostikov, A.G.
Kostinskiy, S.K.
Kostyakov, A.N.
Kostychyov, S.P.
Kotov, P.I.
Kovalenkov, V.I.
Kozlov, P.K.
Kozo-Polyanskiy, B.M.
Krachkovskiy, I.Yu.
Kramarenko, L.P.
Krasnobayev, T.P.
Krasovskiy, F.N.
Krasuskiy, K.A.
Kravchuk, M.F.
Kravets, T.P.
Kravkov, N.P.
Kravkov, S.V.
Krechetovich, L.M.
Krestovnikov, A.N.
Kripyakevich, I.P.
Krishtofovich, A.N.
Krol, M.B.
Kropachyova, M.V.
Krug, K.A.
Kuprskaya, N.K.
Krylov, A.N.
Krylov, N.M.
Krymov, A.P.
Krymov, N.P.
Krymskiy, A.Ye.
Kryukov, A.N.
Krzhizhanovskiy, G.M.
Kucherenko, V.A.
Kuftin, B.A.
Kuleshov, P.N.
Kupala, Ya.
Kupalov, P.S.
Kupriyanov, P.A.
Kurashov, S.V.
Kurchatov, I.V.
Kurnakov, N.S.
Kustodiyev, B.M.
Kuusinen, O.V.
Kuvshinnikov, P.A.
Kuznetsov, N.I.
Kuznetsov, V.D.
Kvaratskheliya, T.K.
Landsberg, G.S.
Lang, G.F.
Lansere, Ye.Ye.
Lappo-Danilevskiy, I.A.
Larichev, P.A.
Larin, B.A.
Lashas, V.L.
Latyshev, N.I.
Lavochkin, S.A.
Lavrent'yev, B.I.
Lazarev, P.P.
Lazarenko, F.M.
Lebedev, A.B.
Lebedev, P.I.
Lebedev, S.V.
Lebedev, V.V.
Lebedev-Polyanskiy, P.I.
Lebedeva, S.D.
Lebedinskiy, A.V.
Lebedinskiy, V.V.
Lein'sh, P.Ya.
Leontovich, A.V.
Lepeshinskaya, O.B.
Leporskiy, N.I.
Levina, R.S.
Levinson-Lessing, F.Yu.
Levitskiy, O.D.
Leybenzon, L.S.
Lipin, V.N.
Lishev, V.V.
Liskun, Ye.F.
Loboda, A.M.
Lugovtsev, M.V.
Luka (Voyno-Yesenetskiy, V.F.)
Lukashkin, N.I.
Lukha, A.Kh.
Lukin, N.M.
Lunacharskiy, A.V.
Luppol, I.K.
Luzin, N.N.
L'vov, S.D.
Lyapunov, B.M.
Lyashchenko, P.I.
Lyubavskiy, M.K.
Lyubimenko, V.N.
Maddison, O.A.
Maksimov, N.A.
Maksutov, D.D.
Malov, S.Ye.
Mal'tsev, A.I.
Mamandyan, Ya.A.
Mamedeliyev, Yu.G.
Mandel'shtam, L.I.
Manizer, M.G.
Man'kovskiy, B.N.
Manuil'skiy, D.Z.
Markelov, G I.
Markov, V.N.
Marr, N.Ya.
Martens, L.K.
Marzeyev, A.N.
Maslov, M.S.
Maslov, P.P.
Maslov, S.I.
Maysuryan, N.A.
Medynskiy, Ye.N.
Melikov, F.A. ogly
Mel'nikov, A.V.
Mel'nikov-Razvedenkov, N.F.
Merkurov, S.D.
Meshchaninov, I.I.
Meshcheryakov, N.L.
Meshkov, V.V.
Michurin, I.V.
Mikenas, Yu.I.
Mikhalevskiy, F.I.
Mir-Kasimov, M.A.M.A. ogly
Mirchink, G.F.
Mironov, S.I.
Mirotvortsev, S.R.
Mislavskiy, N.A.
Mitkevich, V.F.
Modorov, F.A.
Modzalevskiy, B.L.
Mogil'nitskiy, B.N.
Molchanov, V.I.
Moravov, A.V.
Mordvinov, A.G.
Morozkin, N.I.
Morozov, M.A.
Morozov, M.V.

Morozov, N.A.
Mosolov, V.P.
Movchan, V.A.
Mukhadze, G.M.
Mukhina, V.I.
Mul'tanovskiy, B.P.
Muradov, Sh.
Muralov, A.I.
Muromtsev, S.N.
Musin, A.Ch.
Myasnikov, A.L.
Mysh, V.M.
Namyotkin, S.S.
Nasonov, D.N.
Nasonov, N.V.
Natadze, G.M.
Natali, V.F.
Natishvili, A.N.
Naumov, N.A.
Navashin, S.G.
Nazarov, I.N.
Nekrashevich, S.
Nekrasov, A.I.
Nemanskiy, Ya.
Nemchinov, V.S.
Nenadkevich, K.A.
Nesterov, M.V.
Nikiforov, P.M.
Nikitin, B.A.
Nikitin, V.P.
Nikoladze, Ya.I.
Nikolayev, I.I.
Nikolayev, M.P.
Nikolayev, V.A.
Nikol'skiy, A.M.
Nikol'skiy, A.S.
Nikol'skiy, N.M.
Nioradze, G.K.
Novachenko, N.P.
Novitskiy, A.P.
Novosel'skiy, S.A.
Obnorskiy, S.P.
Obraztsov, V.N.
Obruchev, S.V.
Obruchev, V.A.
Oding, I.A.
Ol'denburg, S.F.
Orbeli, I.A.
Orekhov, A.P.
Oreshnikov, A.V.
Orlov, A.S.
Orlov, A.Ya.
Orlov, Ye.I.
Orlov, Yu.A.
Osinskiy, N.
Osipov, V.P.
Ossovskiy, A.V.
Ostroumova-Lebedeva, A.P.
Ozeretskiy, N.I.
Paliyenko, N.I.
Pankratova, A.M.
Papaleksi, N.D.
Papkovich, P.F.
Parnas, Ya.O.
Pashchenko, A.S.
Pashkevich, V.V.
Paton, Ye.O.
Pavlov, I.P.
Pavlov, M.A.
Pavlovskiy, Ye.N.
Pazhitnov, K.A.
Pchilka, O.
Pekarskiy, E.K.
Pel'she, R.A.
Perederiy, G.P.
Perepyolkin, D.I.
Peretts, V.N.
Pertsev, V.N.
Petrov, N.N.
Petrova, Ye.N.
Petrushevskiy, D.M.
Pfeyfer, G.V.
Picheta, V.I.
Piksanov, N.K.
Pisarzhevskiy, L.V.
Plaksin, I.N.
Platonov, S.F.
Pokrovskiy, M.N.
Polenov, A.L.
Polkanov, A.A.
Polosukhin, A.P.
Polovinkin, A.A.
Polyakov, L.M.
Polynov, B.B.
Pomeranchuk, I.Ya.
Popov, I.S.
Popov, V.V.
Poray-Koshits, A.Ye.
Pospelov, V.P.
Potapov, M.V.
Potyomkin, V.P.
Pozdyunin, V.L.
Poznanskiy, N.F.
Prasolov, L.I.
Presnyakov, A.Ye.
Priklonskiy, V.A.
Prilezhayev, N.A.
Priorov, N.N.
Privalov, I.I.
Proskura, G.F.
Protopopov, V.P.
Prudenskiy, G.A.
Pryanishnikov, D.N.
Pshenitsyn, N.K.
Ptitsyn, B.V.
Ptukha, M.V.
Purenas, A.K.
Rabinovich, A.I.
Radtsig, A.A.
Ranovich, A.B.
Raspletin, A.A.
Rau, F.A.
Ravich-Shcherbo, V.A.
Razdol'skiy, I.Ya.
Razenkov, I.P.
Reformatskiy, S.N.
Repin, I.Ye.
Rezanov, V.I.
Rikhter, A.A.
Rives, S.M.
Rodionov, S.P.
Rodionov, V.M.
Romanovskiy, V.I.
Rotshteyn, F.A.
Rozenberg, D.I.
Rozhanskiy, D.A.
Rozhanskiy, N.A.
Rozhdestvenskiy, D.S.
Rozhdestvenskiy, S.V.
Rubinshteyn, S.L.
Rudnev, L.V.
Rufanov, I.G.
Rusakov, M.P.
Rus'ko, A.N.
Ryazanov, D.B.
Ryazhskiy, G.G.
Rybnikov, N.A.
Rylov, A.A.
Ryl'skiy, M.F.
Samarin, N.N.
Samokish, N.S.
Samotskiy, V.A.
Satpayev, K.I.
Saukov, A.A.
Savel'yev, M.A.
Savinykh, A.G.
Semkovskiy, S.Yu.
Semyonov, A.A.
Sepp, Ye.K.
Sepre, O.A.
Serdyuchenko, G.P.
Sergeyev-Tsenskiy, S.N.
Shatelen, M.A.
Shatskiy, N.S.
Shchuko, V.A.
Shchusev A.V.
Shestakov, A.V.
Shestakov, S.P.
Shevkunenko, V.N.
Shimanskiy, Yu.A.
Shirokogorov, I.I.
Shishkin, B.K.
Shlikhter, A.G.
Shmidt, O.Yu.
Shnirel'man, L.G.
Shokal'skiy, Yu.M.
Shorygin, P.P.
Shteynberg, S.S.
Shunkov, V.I.
Sibirtsev, Yu.M.
Simoni, P.K.
Sisakyan, N.M.
Sitenko, M.I.
Skochinskiy, A.A.
Skrypnik, N.A.
Skvortsov, M.A.
Smirnov, S.S.
Smirnov, V.Z.
Smirnova-Zamkova, A.I.
Sokolov-Skalya, P.P.
Solov'yov, A.A.
Spasokukotskiy, S.I.
Speranskiy, A.D.
Speranskiy, G.N.
Speranskiy, I.I.
Starchenko, V.F.
Stepanov, V.V.
Strashun, I.D.
Strazhesko, N.D.
Struve, P.B.
Struve, V.V.
Sukhomel, G.I.
Sus, N.I.
Svanidze, A.S.
Sysin, A.N.
Tabidze, G.V.
Takayshvili, Ye.S.
Tamanyan, A.O.
Tarashkevich, B.A.
Tarle, Ye.V.
Tazhibayev, T.T.
Teplov, B.M.
Terenin, A.N.
Ternovskiy, S.D.
Terpigorov, A.M.
Tertel'baum, S.I.

Tikhomirov, M.N.
Tikhov, G.A.
Timiryazev, A.A.
Timiryazev, K.A.
Tishchenko, V.Ye.
Toidze, M.I.
Tolstoy, A.N.
Tonkov, V.N.
Topchiyev, A.V.
Trakhtenberg, I.A.
Trakhtenberg, O.V.
Traynin, A.N.
Traynin, I.P.
Tret'yakov, D.K.
Tret'yakov, K.N.
Triumfov, A.V.
Trusevich, B.I.
Tsinzerling, V.D.
Tsulukidze, A.P.
Tulyakov, N.M.
Tumanyan, M.G.
Tursunkulov, Kh.
Tushinskiy, M.D.
Tushnov, M.P.
Tutkovskiy, P.A.
Tvalchrelidze, A.A.
Tychina, P.G.
Tyumenev, A.I.
Tyurin, I.V.
Udal'tsov, A.D.
Ukhtomskiy, A.A.
Ul'yanov, N.P.
Umarov, S.U.
Undrits, V.F.
Urazov, G.G.
Ushakov, D.N.
Ushakov, S.N.
Usov, M.A.
Usova, A.P.
Uspenskiy, F.I.
Uznadze, D.N.
Vaga, A.Ya.
Val'ter, A.K.
Varga, Ye.S.
Vasilenko, N.P.
Vasilyauskas, K.I.
Vasil'yev, L.L.
Vasil'yev, V.Ye.
Vasnetsov, A.M.
Vasnetsov, V.M.
Vavilov, N.I.
Vavilov, S.I.
Vedeneyev, B.Ye.
Vedenisov, B.N.
Vedrov, N.S.
Veksler, V.I.
Venediktov, A.V.
Vereyskiy, G.S.
Verkhovskiy, V.N.
Vernadskiy, V.I.
Veselovskiy, S.B.
Vesnin, A.A.
Vesnin, V.A.
Veyts, V.I.
Vil'yams, V.R.
Vinogradov, S.A.
Vinogradov, V.N.
Vinter, A.V.
Vipper, R.Yu.
Vishnevskiy, A.V.
Vize, V.Yu.
Vladimirtsov, B.Ya.
Vlasov, A.V.
Vlasov, V.Z.
Voblyy, K.G.
Volgin, V.P.
Volkov, Ye.Ye.
Volkovich, N.M.
Volnukhin, S.M.
Vologdin, V.P.
Vol'skiy, A.N.
Vorob'yov, A.M.
Vorob'yov, V.P.
Vorontsov, D.S.
Votchal, Ye.F.
Vovsi, M.S.
Voznesenskiy, I.N.
Voznesenskiy, N.A.
Voznyak, M.S.
Vrevskiy, M.S.
Vul'f, G.V.
Vurgun, S.
Vyatkin, M.P.
Vyshelesskiy, S.N.
Vyshinskiy, A.Ya.
Vysotskiy, G.N.
Yachevskiy, A.A.
Yakovkin, A.A.
Yakovlev, A.I.
Yakovlev, V.N.
Yakubovskiy, A.Yu.
Yakushkin, I.V.
Yanovskiy, F.G.
Yanovskiy, M.I.
Yaroslavskiy, Ye.M.
Yasnopol'skiy, L.M.
Yavorskiy, V.P.
Yefremov, S.A.
Yegolin, A.M.
Yegorov, D.F.
Yegorov, P.I.
Yeliseyev, N.A.
Yelsukov, M.P.
Yemchenko, A.I.
Yemel'yanenko, P.T.
Yernshtedt, P.V.
Yesipov, B.P.
Yes'man, I.G.
Yudin, P.F.
Yudin, S.S.
Yuon, K.F.
Yur'yev, B.N.
Yur'yev, V.Ya.
Yushchenko, A.I.
Yushkov, S.V.
Yusupova, S.M.
Yuzhin, A.I.
Zabolotnyy, D.K.
Zabolotnyy, V.I.
Zalesskiy, M.D.
Zalesskiy, V.K.
Zamarin, Ye.A.
Zamotin, I.I.
Zatonskiy, V.P.
Zavaritskiy, A.N.
Zavarzin, A.A.
Zaytsev, F.A.
Zaytsev, N.A.
Zbarskiy, B.I.
Zelenin, D.K.
Zelinskiy, N.D.
Zemyatchenskiy, P.A.
Zernov, S.A.
Zhebelyov, S.A.
Zhebrak, A.P.
Zhemchuzhnikov, Yu.A.
Zhemochkin, B.N.
Zholtovskiy, I.V.
Zhuk, S.Ya.
Zhukov, I.I.
Zhukovskiy, N.Ye.
Zhukovskiy, V.A.
Zhurakovskiy, G.Ye.
Zil'ber, L.A.
Zlatogorov, S.I.
Zor'yan, S.Ye.
Zutis, Ya.Ya.
Zvonkov, V.V.

2. Associates of Research Institutes and Pedagogic Staff of Higher Educational Institutions

Abashidze, E.K.
Afanas'yev, P.O.
Agabal'yants, G.G.
Agarkov, M.M.
Akhmanov, A.S.
Akhmatov, V.V.
Akimenko, I.P.
Alchevskaya, Kh.D.
Aleksandrenko, G.V.
Al'medingen-Tumim (Tumim-Al'medingen), N.A.
Alpatov, N.I.
Alyokhin, V.V.
Andrushchenko, A.I.
Anson, K.K.
Antonov, A.A.
Arnol'di, V.M.
Arsen'yev, V.K.
Artsikhovskiy, V.M.
Artyom'yev, N.A.
Aryamov, I.A.
Asknaziy, A.I.
Assur, L.V.
Atabekov, G.I.
Avdeyev, N.N.
Avenarius, G.A.
Baal-Dim'yon (Shtif, N.)
Babenko, A.K.
Bachinskiy, A.I.
Bakhmet'yev, B.A. (Nikol'skiy, N.)
Bakhmutskiy, A.I.
Balabanov, M.S.
Barbashev, N.I.
Bari, N.K.
Baronenkov, A.V.
Barsova (Vladimirova), V.V.
Basov, M.Ya.
Baturin, V.P.
Bauman, V.I.
Bazilevich, K.V.
Bedro, I.P.

Begichev (Bigichev), N.A.
Bekhteryov, V.M.
Belyayev, M.F.
Berdyayev, N.I.
Berezhkov, N.G.
Berkengeym, A.M.
Bernshtam, A.N.
Bernshteyn, A.N.
Beryozkin, V.A.
Bilanovskiy, I.D.
Bizov, B.V.
Bliznyak, Ye.V.
Blokh, M.A.
Blokhin, A.A.
Blonskiy, P.P.
Bobynin, V.V.
Bochvar, A.M.
Bogayevskiy, B.L.
Bogdan, V.S.
Bogdanov (Malinovskiy), A.A.
Bogdanov, Ye.A.
Bogolepov, M.A.
Bogoraz-Tan, V.G.
Bogoroditskiy, N.P.
Bogorodskiy, A.Ya.
Boguslavskiy, S.A.
Boklevskiy, K.P.
Boldyryov, A.K.
Boltunov, A.P.
Borodin, I.P.
Bortkevich, V.M.
Borzov, A.A.
Brauner, A.A.
Breyterman, A.D.
Bubnov, I.G.
Bukreyev, B.Ya.
Buturlin, S.A.
Buzuk, P.A.
Byalokoz, Ye.L.
Byalynitskiy-Birulya, A.A.
Bykov, N.A.
Byzov, B.V.
Chaplin, V.M.
Charnoluskiy, V.I.
Chayanov, A.V.
Chelpanov, G.P.
Chelyapov, N.I.
Chicherov, V.I.
Chirvinsky, P.N.
Chistyakov, V.M.
Chugayev, L.A.
Chumburidze, T.S.
Chuvashyov, I.V.
Dadenkov, N.F.
Dauge, P.G.
Davydov, B.V.
Davydov, I.A.
Delone, N.B.
De-Mets, G.G.
Demkov, M.I.
Den, V.E.
Depp, G.F.
Deratani, N.F.
Dermanis, V.
Deryugin, K.M.
Desnitskiy, V.A.
Dichenko, M.P.
Divayev, A.A.
Dmitriyev, A.M.
Dmitriyev, N.I.
Dmitriyev, V.V.
Dmokhovskiy, V.K.
Dobrotvor (Aleksandrov), N.M.
Dobrovol'skiy, V.A.
Dobrynin, B.F.
Dokturovskiy, V.S.
Dominikovskiy, F.N.
Dovnar-Zapol'skiy, M.V.
Doynikova, Ye.D.
Dravert, P.L.
Drizhenko, F.K.
Druzyakina, S.I.
Dubelir, G.D.
Dubina, K.K.
Dubinskiy, S.A.
Dubrovskiy, K.K.
Dubrovskiy-Eshke, B.V.
Durdenevskiy, V.N.
Durylin, S.N.
D'yakonov, M.M.
Dyla, I.L.
Edel'shteyn, Ya.S.
Epimakh-Shipila, B.I.
Essen, E.E.
Fadeyev, A.V.
Fal'kner, S.A.
Fedchenko, B.A.
Feynberg, S.Ye.
Figurnov, P.K.
Filipchenko, Yu.A.
Fitrat (Rashidov, A.)
Flyorov, V.A.
Fortunatov, A.A.
Frank, S.L.
Freydenberg, M.F.
Freyman, I.G.
Frolov, A.N.
Frolov, M.P.
Gabashvili, G.
Gadzhibekov, U.A.G. ogly
Gakkel, Ya.M.
Gal'perin, A.L.
Gander, V.A.
Gapeyev, A.A.
Gastev, A.K.
Gauk, A.V.
Gaysinovich, S.Ye.
Gedike, A.F.
Gerasimenko, M.P.
Gerasimov, A.P.
Gerbil'skiy, N.L.
Gernet, M.N.
Gershun, A.A.
Geveling, N.V.
Ginzburg, G.R.
Glagolev, N.A.
Glagoleva-Arkad'yeva, A.A.
Glazunov, A.K.
Glushkov, V.G.
Gnesina, Ye.F.
Gol'dberg, N.M.
Gil'denveyzer, A.B.
Gol'ts, G.P.
Golubtsov, I.A.
Golubyatnikob, D.V.
Goluzin, G.M.
Golyakov, I.T.
Gopner, S.I.
Gorbov, A.I.
Gorchakov, N.M.
Gorev, A.A.
Gorev, B.I.
Gorodtsov, V.A.
Gratsianskiy, N.P.
Grdina, Yu.V.
Grigor'yev, S.G.
Grinberg, M.I.
Grinevetskiy, V.I.
Grum-Grzhimaylo, G.Ye.
Gruzinskiy, A.S.
Gubaydullin, G.S.
Gurko-Kryazhin, V.A.
Gurvich, L.G.
Gusev, V.N.
Idel'son, N.I.
Ignatov, K.M.
Ignatov, S.S.
Ignatovich, N.K.
Ignat'yev, A.M.
Igumnov, K.N.
Il'in, S.I.
Il'in, V.S.
Ilovayskiy, A.S.
Ilovayskiy, D.I.
Iordanskiy, N.N.
Ippolitov-Ivanov, M.M.
Iskenderov, M.S.
Itkis, M.B.
Ivanov, A.N.
Ivanov, I.I.
Ivanov, N.N.
Ivanov, S.M.
Ivanovskiy, D.I.
Izvekov, N.P.
Kagan, V.F.
Kalandarishvili, G.M.
Kalitin, N.N.
Kalitskiy, K.P.
Kalnyn, A.Ya.
Kanchaveli, Z.A.
Kartashov, N.I.
Kashkarov, D.N.
Katul'skaya, Ye.K.
Kaverin, F.N.
Kavrayskiy, V.V.
Kaydanova, O.V.
Kazanli, D.N.
Kechek'yan, S.F.
Kezma, T.G.
Kharik, I.
Kharuzina, V.N.
Khudyakov, N.N.
Khudyakov, P.K.
Kirsanov, A.T.
Kiselyov, A.P.
Kizevetter, A.A.
Klimov, A.F.
Kobozev, P.A.
Kocherin, D.I.
Kolesnikov, V.P.
Korobeynikova, Yu.I.
Korolyov, S.I.
Korovin, M.K.
Korshikov, A.A.
Kotel'nikov, A.P.
Kovalyov, S.I.
Kozhukhova, M.A.
Krainskiy, S.V.
Kramol'nikov, G.I.
Krasheninnikov, F.N.
Krasnosel'skaya, T.A.
Krasyuk, A.A.
Kravkov, S.P.
Krishtafovich, N.I.
Krivchenko, G.A.
Krupenina, M.V.

Krylov, S.B.
Kukushkin, S.M.
Kulik, L.A.
Kurbangaliyev, M.Kh.
Kuznetsov, V.V.
Kyuner, N.V.
Lalayan, E.A.
Lapirov-Skoblo, M.Ya.
Lebedev, A.N.
Lebedinsky, V.K.
Levchenko, M.V.
Longinov, V.V.
Lozovskiy, S.A.
Lur'ye, S.Ya.
Lyadov, M.N.
Lyavdanskiy, A.N.
Lyubomirov, P.G.
Makarenko, A.S.
Makarenko, N.Ye.
Makovskiy, V.M.
Maksimov, A.N.
Maksimovich, N.I.
Maksimovich, S.O.
Malakhovskiy, V.F.
Malyarov, D.Ye.
Martynov, A.V.
Mashkin, N.A.
Matusevich, N.N.
Mazing, Ye.K.
Mershin, P.M.
Mertsalov, N.I.
Mesyatsev, I.I.
Mikhaylov, M.M.
Mikhel'son, V.A.
Mikhin, N.A.
Miller, B.V.
Minkevich, N.A.
Minorskiy, V.F.
Mishulin, A.V.
Mityushin, N.T.
Moiseyev, N.D.
Morokhovets, Ye.A.
Muzychenko, A.F.
Nasonov, A.N.
Nastyukov, A.M.
Nemilov, V.A.
Nemytskiy, V.V.
Neuymin, G.N.
Nevskiy, N.A.
Nevskiy, V.I.
Nitusov, Ye.V.
Novosel'skiy, A.A.
Ognyov, S.I.
Oknov, M.G.
Ostryakov, P.A.
Ozhyogov, S.I.
Parkhomenko, V.A.
Pasherstnik, A.Ye.
Pavlovich, M.P.
Peskov, N.P.
Petrov, S.M.
Pinkevich, A.P.
Piontkovskiy, S.A.
Piotrovskiy, L.M.
Pistrak, M.M.
Polikarpovich, K.M.
Polivanov, Ye.D.
Poliyevktov, M.A.
Popov, N.N.
Potebnya, A.A.
Potyokhin, I.I.
Pozdneyev, A.M.
Pozdneyev, D.M.
Pozner, V.M.
Preobrazhenskiy, P.F.
Prokof'yev, S.A.
Proskuryakov, L.D.
Prugavin, A.S.
Ramzin, L.K.
Rau, N.A.
Rayevskiy, A.S.
Remezov, N.P.
Rents, F.F.
Rerikh, Yu.N.
Reysner, I.M.
Reznik, Ya.B.
Rimskiy-Korsakov, M.N.
Roginskiy, G.Z.
Romanov, B.A.
Romanovskiy, V.B.
Rozhkov, N.A.
Rybkin, P.N.
Sadikov, P.A.
Savich, A.A.
Semennikov, V.P.
Semyonov-Tyan-Shanskiy, A.P.
Semyonov-Tyan-Shanskiy, V.P.
Serebryakov, M.V.
Shabalov, S.M.
Sharonov, V.V.
Shlikhter, A.A.
Shokhin, A.P.
Shternberg, P.K.
Sidorov, A.L.
Sidorova, N.A.
Skachkov, P.Ye.
Smirnov, I.I.
Spirin, I.T.
Svyatlovskiy, V.V.
Takhtarev, K.M.
Tananayev, N.A.
Tarasov, N.G.
Tatarinov, V.V.
Tauson, V.O.
Tavzishvili, G.Ya.
Tetyayev, M.M.
Tikhomirov, A.A.
Tikhonov, P.I.
Tikhonovich, N.N.
Timchenko, I.A.
Timofeyev, V.M.
Tkachenko, M.Ye.
Tol'skiy, A.P.
Tovstolis, D.I.
Transhel, V.A.
Trinkler, G.V.
Trushkov, N.I.
Tserevitinov, F.V.
Tugan-Baranovskiy, M.I.
Tyzhnov, V.I.
Udal'tsov, I.D.
Ulitovskiy, A.V.
Ul'yanov, A.V.
Urnov, K.V.
Ushakov, G.A.
Ustryalov, N.V.
Vagner, V.A.
Vakhterov, V.P.
Vasil'yev, V.M.
Vel'tman, M.L.
Vengerov, S.A.
Veryovka, G.G.
Veselovskiy, B.B.
Vetchinkin, V.P.
Vetoshkin, M.K.
Veynberg, B.P.
Vilenskiy, D.G.
Vitkovskiy, V.V.
Vittorf, N.M.
Vitver, I.A.
Volin, B.M.
Volkov, I.M.
Volobuyev, M.
Vologdin, S.P.
Voronikhin, N.N.
Vorozhtsov, N.N.
Vsevolodskiy-Gerngross, V.N.
Vul'f, A.V.
Vul'f, Ye.V.
Vvedenskiy, A.I.
Vyatkin, V.L.
Vyazemskaya, L.O.
Vysotskiy, N.K.
Yanishevskiy, M.E.
Yarkho, A.I.
Yasinskiy, A.N.
Yatsunskiy, V.K.
Yavłenskiy, N.A.
Yefremov, N.N.
Yegorov, D.N.
Yelenkin, A.A.
Yerusalimskiy, A.S.
Yevdokimov, N.N.
Yevsev'yev, M.Ye.
Yushmanov, N.V.
Zabudskiy, G.A.
Zagrodskiy, A.A.
Zakharov, S.A.
Zalezhskiy, V.N.
Zal'kind, Yu.S.
Zavarin, A.P.
Zav'yalova, Ye.N.
Zelenko, A.U.
Zeyliger, D.N.
Zhakov, M.P.
Zhamtsarano, Ts.Zh.
Zhdanko, M.Ye.
Zhdanov, P.S.
Zhegalkin, I.I.
Zhegalov, S.I.
Zhemchuzhnyy, S.F.
Zhivago, P.I.
Zhukovskiy, G.Yu.
Zograf, A.N.
Zubok, L.I.
Zubrilin, A.A.
Zvavich, I.S.

LITERATURE AND ART

1. Writers and Poets, Literary Critics, Journalists and Editors, etc.

Abaginskiy (Kudrin-Abaginskiy), A.G.
Abasheli (Chochiya), A.V.
Abasov, E.Dzh.-ogly
Abegyan, M.Kh.
Abramovich, D.I.
Adamov, G. (Gibs, G.B.)
Adaryukov, V.Ya.
Adzhzi (Siddiki, Kh.S.-A.-kh.)
Afinogenov, A.N.
Agamaly-Ogly, S.A.
Aganbekyan, A.A.
Agranenko (Yerukhimovich), Z.M.
Agumaa, K.K.
Akhmadiyev, Sh.
Akhmatova (Gorenko), A.A.
Akhmed Dzhavad (Akhunzade, Dzh.M.-ogly)
Akhospireli (Beglaridze), B.B.
Akhundov, S.S.
Akhverdov, A.-bek A.-ogly
Akopyan, A.
Aksel'rod (Ortodoks), L.I.
Aksel'rod, Z.M.
Akyyev, K.
Alamyshev, A.-D.
Alazan (Garbuzyan, V.M.)
Al'berton, M.I.
Alchevskaya, Kh.A.
Aldanov, M. (Landau, M.A.)
Aleksandrov (Keller), V.B.
Aleksandrovich, A.I.
Aleksandrovskiy, V.D.
Alimdzhan Khamid
Alish, A. (Alishev, A.B.)
Altauzen, Ya.M.
Altayev, A. (Yamshchikova, M.V.)
Alymov, S.Ya.
Al'tman, I.L.
Amantay, A.G.
Amanzholov, K.R.
Amfiteatrov, A.V.
Amirkhan, F.Z.
Andreyev, N.P.
Angarskiy (Klestov), N.S.
Anisimov, I.I.
Anskiy (Rapoport), S.A.
Antonov, I.Z.
Antonovskaya, A.A.
Antsiferov, N.P.
Anvel't, Ya.Ya.
Appakova, D.S.
Aristov, F.F.
Arkhangel'skiy, A.G.
Arkhangel'skiy, A.S.
Arkin, D.Ye.
Arosev, A.Ya.
Arsen'yev, V.K.
Arskiy, P.A.
Arvatov, B.I.
Asaf'yev, B.V.
Asatiani, L.N.
Asayev, N.N.
Ashkhamat, D.A.
Astapenka, D.Ye.
Astreyka, S.A.
Ata Salikh
Auezov, M.O.
Avdeyev, A.D.
Avenarius, G.A.
Averchenko, A.T.
Av.ov, G.A.
Ayanbergen Musayev
Aydyn (Manzura Sabirova)
Aynalov, D.V.
Ayni (Sadriddin, S.)
Baal-Dim'yon (Shtif, N.)
Baazov, G.D.
Babarenka, A.A.
Babel, I.E.
Baduyev, S.S.
Bagatur, Ye.B.
Bagrayev, S.K.
Bagritskiy (Dzyubin), E.G.
Bagun, M. (Bloshkin, M.F.)
Bakhmet'yev, V.M.
Bakunts, A.
Bal'mont, K.D.
Balukhatyy, S.D.
Baranovykh, S. (Baranov, S.Ya.)
Barbarus (Vares), I.Ya.
Barnovi, V.Z.
Baryshnikova, A.K.
Basangov, B.B.
Batyrmurzayev, Z.N.
Bayan, N.G.
Bayganin, N.
Baykulov, D.P.
Bayram Shakhir (Mamedov)
Baytursunov, A.
Bazhov, P.P.
Bednyy, D. (Pridvorov, Ye.A.)
Begimov, A.I.
Begizov, Ch.D.
Bekov, T.D.
Beletskiy, A I.
Beliashvili, A.I.
Belousov, I.A.
Belyayev, A.R.
Belyayev, S.M.
Belyy, A. (Bugayov, B.N.)
Bernikov, Ya.P.
Berezovskiy, F.A.
Bergel'son, D.R.
Bespalov, I.M.
Bessal'ko, P.K.
Bezborodov, M.I.
Bezdonnyy (Pelekhatyy), K.N.
Bianki, V.V.
Biryukov, N.Z.
Biryukov, P.I.
Birzniyek-Upit (Birznieks-Upitis), E.T.
Blagov, A.N.
Blakitnyy (Yellanskiy), V.M.
Blok, A.A.
Blyakhin, P.A.
Bobinskiy, V.P.
Bogdanova, M.I.
Bogoraz-Tan, V.G.
Bokonbayev, Dzh.
Bol'shintsov, M.V.
Bondin, A.P.
Boruta, K.
Botsiyev, B.T.
Boychenko, A.M.
Bozhko, S.Z.
Brik, O.M.
Britayev, Ye.Ts.
Brodskiy, N.L.
Bryusov, V.Ya.
Budyak, Yu. (Pokos, Yu.Ya.)
Bugoslavskiy, S.A.
Bulakhovskiy, L.A.
Bulgakov, M.A.
Bunin, I.A.
Burnash, F. (Burnashev, F.Z.)
Burunov, K.
Bush, V.V.
Buz'ko, D.I.
Buzuk, P.A.
Byadulya, Z. (Plavnik, S.Ye.)
Bychkov, I.A.
Bykov, A.V.
Bykov, P.V.
Byvalov, Ye.S.
Chanba, S.Ya.
Chapygin, A.P.
Charents (Sogomonyan), Ye.
Charot, M. (Kudel'ka, M.S.)
Chavayn (Grigor'yev), S.G.
Chechvyanskiy (Gubenko), V.M.
Chekhov, M.P.
Chekhova, M.P.
Chemenzeminli, Yu.V.
Chertkov, V.G.
Chervinskiy, M.A.
Chikovani, S.I.
Chirikov, Ye.N.
Chornyy, K. (Romanovskiy, N.K.)
Chukovskiy, N.K.
Chulpan, Kh.
Chumandrin, M.F.
Chuprynka, G.A.
Chyurlenene-Kimantayte, S.
Dadau Magometov
Dadiani, Sh.N.
Daletskiy, P.L.
Dal'nya, S.(Derman, S.Ya.)
Danelia, S.I.
Daniel, M.N. (Meyerovich, D.)
Daniel'son, N.F.
Danilov, S.S.
Danilov-Chaldun, M.N.
Dan'ko, Ye.Ya.
Danovskaya, Z.N.
Daraseli, V.A.
Dauguvetis, B.F.
Davkarayev, N.
Davletshin, F.D.
Davletshin, G.K.
Davletshina, Kh.L.
Davtyan, M.D.
Davydov, Z.S.
Dayredzhiyev, B.L.
Dekhoti, A.P.
Dement'yev, N.I.
Demidov, A.A.
Demirchyan, D.K.
Derman, A.B.
Dermanis, V.
Derunov, K.N.
Derzhavin, K.N.
Derzhavin, N.S.
Desnitskiy, V.A.
Desnyak, A. (Rudenko, A.I.)

Deyev-Khomyakovskiy, G.D.
Dikovskiy, S.V.
Dinamov, S.S.
Dinmagomayev, R.D.
Dmitriyev, A.M.
Dmitriyev, T.P.
Dmitriyeva, V.I.
Dniprovskiy, I. (Shevchenko, I.D.)
Dobrovol'skiy, L.M.
Dobrushin, I.M.
Dobrzhinskiy, G.V.
Dol'd-Mikhaylyk, Yu.
Don, Ts. (Dondubon, Ts.D.)
Donchenko, O.V.
Donentayev, S.
Dorofeyev, Z.F.
Dorogoychenko, A.Ya.
Dorokhov, P.N.
Doroshkevich, A.K.
Dorozhnyy, S. (Sevada, S.M.)
Dosvitnyy, O. (Skripal, A.F.)
Dovzhenko, A.P.
Dravert, P.L.
Dray-Khmara, M.A.
Dudar, A. (Daylidovich, A.A.)
Dumavi (Takhtamyshev), N.
Durylin, S.N.
Dyadynkov, I.T.
Dykhovichnyy, V.A.
Dyla, I.L.
Dyshechkov, M.P.
Dzhabarly, Dzh.
Dzhalil (Dzhalilov), M.M.
Dzhambul Dzhabayev
Dzhansugurov, I.
Dzhavakhisvili, M. (Adamashvili, M.S.)
Dzhavid, G. (Rasi-zade)
Dzhimiyev, G.S.
Dzhivelegov, A.K.
Dzhura Sultan
Efendiyev, R.-bek I.-ogly
Efros, A.M.
Efros, N.Ye.
Epimakh-Shipila, B.I.
Erenburg, I.G.
Eristavi-Khoshtariya, A.G.
Ermans, V.K.
Evarnitskiy (Yavornitskiy), D.I.
Eydeman, R.P.
Eykhenbaum, B.M.
Fadeyev (Bulyga), A.A.
Fal'kivskiy, D.N.
Fat'yanov, A.I.
Fayzi, A.S.
Fayzi, M.
Fefer, I.S.
Filippov, V.A.
Fininberg, E.I.
Fitrat (Rashidov, A.)
Fomin, S.F.
Forsh, O.D.
Franko, O.F.
Franko, P.I.
Friche, V.M.
Furmanov, D.A.
Gabbe, T.G.
Gabiyev, S.I.
Gabriyelyan, G.B.
Gadiyev, Ts.S.
Gadzhibekov, U.A.G. ogly
Gafur-Gulyam
Gafuri, M.
Gafurov, A.G.
Galaktionov, M.R.
Galan, Ya.A.
Galeyev, M.V.
Galkin, S.Z.
Gaprindashvili, V.I.
Garri, A.N.
Gartnyy, T.
Gartsman. M.D.
Gastev, A.K.
Gauzner, G.O.
Gauzner, Zh.V.
Gavrilyuk, A.A.
Gaydar, A.P.
Gekht, S.G.
Gerasimenko, K.M.
Gerasimov, M.P.
Gereyev, Yu.
German, Yu.P.
Germano, A.V.
Gershenzon, M.O.
Gessen, Yu.I.
Getman, D.G.
Gilyarovskiy, V.A.
Gippius, Z.N.
Gira, L.K.
Gizzat, T.
Gladkoborodova, A.I.
Gladkov, F.V.
Glebov, A.G.
Glivenko, I.I.
Globa, A.P.
Godiner, Sh.D.
Gofman, M.L.
Gol'dberg, I.G.
Gollerbakh, E.F.
Golodnyy, M.
Golovach, P.R.
Golovchiner, V.Ya.
Golovenchenko, F.M.
Gol'tsev, V.V.
Golubkova, M.R.
Golubok, V.I.
Golubov, S.N.
Gorbachyov, G.Ye.
Gorbatov, B.L.
Gorbunov-Posadov, I.I.
Goretskiy, M.I.
Gorky, M.
Gornfel'd, A.G.
Goyda, Yu.A.
Grebner, G.E.
Grigorenko, G.
Grigor'yev, S.T.
Grin, A.
Grinchenko, M.N.
Grishashvili, I.G.
Grossman, L.P.
Grossman, V.S.
Gruzdev, I.A.
Gruzinov, I.V.
Gruzinskiy, A.Ye.
Gubaydullin, G.S.
Guber, B.A.
Guber, P.K.
Gudkov, V.P.
Gudziy, N.K.
Gukovskiy, G.A.
Gulia, D.I.
Gulyam, G.G.
Gumilyov, N.S.
Gurevich, E.L.
Gurevich, L.Ya.
Gurlo, A.
Gurshteyn, A.Sh.
Gusev, V.M.
Guseyn, D.
Guseyn, M.
Guseynov, G.N. ogly
Gutorov, I.V.
Guttari, T.O.
Gut'yar, N.M.
Gvetadze, R.M.
Gvozdyov, A.A.
Ibragimov, G.
Ibragimov, Kh.K.
Ignatiyenko, V.A.
Ignatov, S.S.
Ignat'yev, N.V.
Il'f, I.
Il'in, M.
Il'in, Ya.N.
Il'ina, Ye.
Illarionov, I.I.
Imanzhanov, M.
Iminagiyev, A.
Ioannisyan, I.M.
Ioganson (Johansson), O.E.
Ionov, V.M.
Irchan, M.
Isaakyan, A.S.
Isakov, I.S.
Isayev, D.Ye.
Ishanov, K.
Ishemgulov, B.Z.
Ismailov, Kh.
Ismailov, Ye.S.
Istomin, K.K.
Istrin, V.M.
Ivanov, A.A.
Ivanov, I.I.
Ivanov, V.I.
Ivanov, V.V.
Ivanov-Razumnik, R.V.
Ivanter, B.A.
Ivashchenko, A.F.
Ivchenko, M.Ye.
Iving, V.P.
Ivnik, I.N.
Iyezuitov, N.M.
Kabak, N.P.
Kadyri, A.
Kagan, A.Ya.
Kalinin, F.I.
Kalinovich, M.Ya.
Kalyuga, L.
Kamal, G.G.
Kamal, Sh.
Kamenskiy, A.P.
Kapiyev, E.M.
Karimi, F.
Karnaukhova, I.V.
Karpov, M.Ya.
Kashkin, I.A.
Kastorskiy, S.V.
Kas'yanov, V.P.
Katayev, I.I.
Kaval, V.
Kazakevich, E.G.
Kekilov, Sh.
Kel'in, F.V.
Keul'kut, V.G.
Khadyka, V.M.
Khamza, Kh. zade

Nikiforov, G.K.
Nikitin, I.F.
Nikitin, N.N.
Nikoladze, N.Ya.
Nikolayeva, G.Ye.
Nikoleva, M.F.
Nikulin, L.V.
Nikulin, Yu.V.
Nister
Niyazov, A.
Nizovoy, P.G.
Norin, S.K.
Novikov, I.A.
Novikov-Priboy, A.S.
Novikova-Vashentseva, Ye.M.
Novokshonov, I.M.
Nozdrin, A.Ye.
Nurov, R.
Nusinov, I.M.
Nyustrem (Nyström), R.Ya.
Obolduyev, G.N.
Obradovich, S.A.
Obruchev, V.A.
Odulok, T.
Ognyov, N.
Oksyonov, I.A.
Okulov, A.I.
Olenich-Gnenenko, A.P.
Olevskiy, B.A.
Oleynikov, N.M.
Ol'khon, A.S.
Ol'minskiy, M.S.
Olyosha, Yu.K.
Olyk, I.
Omarshayev, A.G.
Onchukov, N.Ye.
Oray, D.
Ordubady, M.S.
Oreshin, P.V.
Orlov, A.S.
Orshanskiy, B.M.
Osharov, M.I.
Osmonov, A.
Ostrovskiy, N.A.
Ovanesyan, O.
Oyslender, A.Ye.
Oyslender, N.Ye.
Oyunskiy. P.A.
Panfyorov, F.I.
Pankov, N.A.
Papazyan, V.M.
Parfenov, P.S.
Pasternak, B.L.
Pavlenko, P.A.
Pavlov, F.P.
Pchilka, O.
Pegel'man, Kh.G.
Pereverzev, V.F.
Perovskaya, O.V.
Persov, S.D.
Peshkov, M.A.
Peshkova, Ye.P.
Petrov, P.P.
Petrov, Ye.P.
Petrov-Vodkin, K.S.
Petrova, K.S.
Piksanov, N.K.
Pilipenko, S.V.
Pil'nyak, B.A.
Pinchevskiy, M.Ya.
Piotrovskiy, A.I.
Platner, A.
Platonov, A.N.
Platonov, A.P.
Pletnyov, V.F.
Pogodin, N.F.
Poletayev, N.G.
Polonskiy, V.
Popov, I.F.
Popovkin, Ye.Ye.
Pranskus-Zhalyonis, B.
Pravdukhin, V.P.
Prishvin, M.M.
Pulatov-Tolstoy
Pushcha, Ya.
Pyrerka, A.P.
Rakitnyy, S.
Raskol'nikov, F.F.
Revutskiy, D.N.
Reysner, L.M.
Rezanov, V.I.
Reznik, L.B.
Romashov, B.S.
Roskin, A.I.
Rozanov, I.N.
Rozin, F.A.
Rudin, Ya.M.
Ryl'skiy, M.F.
Savinkov, B.V.
Selivanovskiy, A.P.
Semenko, M.V.
Serafimovich, A.S.
Sergeyev-Tsenskiy, S.N.
Seyfullin, S.
Seyfullina, L.N.
Sheynin, L.R.
Shkurupiy, G.D.
Shvarts, Ye.L.
Skitalets, S.G.
Sosyura, V.N.
Stal'skiy, S.
Staritskaya-Chernyakhovskaya, L.
Stashevskiy, V.P.
Svetlov, M.A.
Tabidze, G.V.
Tabidze, T.Yu.
Tagirov, A.M.
Takhti
Talenskiy, N.A.
Talybzade, A.Sh.M. ogly
Tapaltsyan, Kh.K.
Tavbin, Yu.A.
Tavlay, V.P.
Teleshov, N.D.
Ter-Grigoryan, E.O.
Teryan, V.
Terzibashyan, V.V.
Tipot, V.Ya.
Tobilevich, S.V.
Todriya, S.Ya.
Tolstoy, A.N.
Tomashevskiy, B.V.
Topanov, A.M.
Trenyov, K.A.
Tret'yakov, S.M.
Trublaini, N.P.
Tsvetayava, M.I.
Tuayev, D.A.
Tubel'skiy, L.D.
Tulub, Z.P.
Tumunov, Zh.T.
Tursun, P.
Turusbekov, D.
Tychina, P.G.
Tynyanov, Yu.N.
Utkin, I.P.
Uygur, M.
Vadetskiy, B.A.
Vardanyan, A.
Vares, I.Ya.
Vasil'chenko, S.F.
Vasil'chenko, S.V.
Vasilevskaya, V.L.
Vasil'yev, G.N.
Vasil'yev, S.D.
Vasilyok, M.
Vaychyunas, P.
Veksler, I.I.
Venuolis, A.Yu.
Verbitskiy, V.A.
Veresayev, V.V.
Verkhovskiy, Yu.N.
Vermishev, A.A.
Vershigora, P.P.
Vertinskiy, A.N.
Vertinskiy, A.N.
Vesyolyy, A.
Vezirov, N.F. ogly
Viksne, P.
Viner, M.
Vinnichenko, V.K.
Vinogradov, A.K.
Vinokur, G.O.
Vinokurov-Chagylyan, I.D.
Virtanen, Ya.Ye.
Vishnevskiy, V.V.
Vishnya, O.
Vlyz'ko, A.F.
Volkov, N.D.
Volkov, R.M.
Vol'nov, I.Ye.
Volodin, V.S.
Voloshin, M.A.
Volynskiy, A.
Voronskiy, A.K.
Voronyy, M.K.
Vorovskiy, V.V.
Voytolovskiy, L.N.
Voznyak, M.S.
Vurgun, S.
Yakobson, A.M.
Yakovlev, A.S.
Yakovlev, I.Ya.
Yan, V.
Yanovskiy, Ye.G.
Yanovskiy, Yu.I.
Yaroshenko, V.M.
Yarovoy, P.
Yasenskiy, B.
Yashek, N.F.
Yashvili, P.D.
Yasinskiy, I.I.
Yastrebtsov, V.V.
Yatskiv, M.Yu.
Yefimov, I.Ye.
Yefremov, S.A.
Yegolin, A.M.
Yeleonskaya, Ye.N.
Yelpat'yevskiy, S.Ya.
Yepkhiyev, T.
Yermilov, V.V.
Yeroshenko, V.Ya.
Yeryomin, I.P.
Yesenin, S.A.
Yevdokimov, I.V.
Yevgen'yev-Maksimov, V.Ye.

Yevreinov, N.N.
Yogansen, M.G.
Yokum, K.Ya.
Yultyy, D.I.
Yurezanskiy, V.
Yushkevich, S.S.
Yuzhin, A.I.
Yuzovskiy, I.I.
Yyvan, K.
Zabolotskiy, N.A.
Zagorskiy, M.B.
Zagul, D.Yu.
Zalesskiy, V.F.
Zalite, E.A.
Zalka, M.M.
Zamoshkin, N.I.
Zamotin, I.I.
Zamoyskiy, P.I.
Zamyatin, Ye.I.
Zaretskiy, M.
Zarkhi, N.A.
Zarudin, N.N.
Zaslavskiy, D.I.
Zavalishin, A.I.
Zaytsev, G.V.
Zdobnov, N.V.
Zelenin, D.K.
Zelenskiy, V.I.
Zerov, N.K.
Zeynally Khanafi
Zhakova, V.N.
Zhamtsarano, Ts.Zh.
Zharko, Ya.V.
Zharokov, T.Zh.
Zhavruk, A.
Zhelyabuzhskiy, Yu.A.
Zhiga, I.F.
Zhilka, V.A.
Zhitkov, B.S.
Zlobin, S.P.
Zorge (Sorge), R.
Zorgenfrey, V.A.
Zor'yan, S.Ye.
Zoshchenko, M.M.

2. Painters, Sculptors and Architects

Abrasimov, P.V.
Aden, V.B.
Akhikyan, V.G.
Alabyan, K.S.
Alyoshin, S.S.
Andreyev, N.A.
Andreyev, V.A.
Arkhipov, A.Ye.
Arutchyan, M.A.
Avilov, M.I.
Bakanov, I.M.
Bakh, R.R.
Baksheyev, V.N.
Bakushinskiy, A.V.
Bartram, N.D.
Bashindzhagyan, G.Z.
Bazhenov, P.D.
Beglyarov, S.N.
Beketov, A.N.
Beklemishev, V.A.
Belokur, Ye.V.
Belostotskiy, Ye.I.
Ben'kov, P.P.
Benua, A.N.
Benua, L.N.
Beringov, M.M.
Bershadskiy, Yu.R.
Bilibin, I.Ya.
Bogayevskiy, K.F.
Bogdanov, I.P.
Bogolyubov, V.Ya.
Bogorodskiy, F.S.
Borisov, A.A.
Brodskiy, I.I.
Bryagin, A.I.
Bublikov, N.Ye.
Bubnov, A.P.
Bukovetskiy, Ye.I.
Burachek, N.G.
Bushkin, A.I.
Cheptsov, Ye.M.
Cheremnykh, M.M.
Chernyshyov, S.Ye.
Dadashev, S.A.-ogly
Dan'ko, N.Ya.
Davydova, N.Ya.
Dayts, I.A.
Deni (Denisov), V.N.
Denisov, V.I.
Dmitriyev, A.I.
Dobroklonskiy, M.V.
Domogatskiy, V.N.
Dovgal, A.M.
Dubinskiy, D.A.
Durnov, M.A.
Erzya (Nefyodov), S.D.
Favorskiy, V.A.
Faydysh, A.P.
Fomin, I.A.
Gabashvili, G.
Gel'freykh, V.G.
Gerasimov, A.M.
Gerasimov, S.V.
Gintsburg, I.Ya.
Ginzburg, M.Ya.
Golikov, I.I.
Golosov, I.A.
Golosov, P.A.
Gol'ts, G.P.
Golubkina, A.S.
Gonchar, I.T.
Gorelov, G.N.
Grabar, I.E.
Grekov, M.B.
Il'in, L.A.
Ingal, V.I.
Ivanov, D.D.
Avanov, D.D.
Izhakevich, I.I.
Kardovskiy, D.N.
Kasatkin, N.A.
Kas'yanov, A.M.
Klykov, N.P.
Kodzhoyan, A.K.
Konchalovskiy, P.P.
Korin, P.D.
Kotov, P.I.
Kotyagin, A.F.
Kozlovskiy, S.V.
Krasitskiy, F.S.
Kravchenko, A.I.
Krichevskiy, F.G.
Krichevskiy, V.G.
Krymov, N.P.
Kuklinskiy, S.I.
Kupreyanov, N.N.
Kustodiyev, B.M.
Lansere, Ye.Ye.
Lebedev, V.V.
Lebedeva, S.D.
Levandovskiy, V.V.
Lishev, V.V.
Makushenko, I.S.
Malevich, K.S.
Malyutin, S.V.
Manizer, M.G.
Merkurov, S.D.
Meshkov, V.N.
Meshkov, V.V.
Mikenas, Yu.I.
Modorov, F.A.
Moor, D.S.
Moravov, A.V.
Mordvinov, A.G.
Mukhina, V.I.
Muradov, Sh.
Nesterov, M.V.
Nikoladze, Ya.I.
Nikol'skiy, A.S.
Orlov, A.N.
Ostroumova-Lebedeva, A.P.
Pashchenko, A.S.
Pasternak, L.O.
Petrov-Vodkin, K.S.
Polyakov, L.M.
Rabinovich, I.M.
Repin, I.Ye.
Rerberg, I.I.
Rudnev, L.V.
Rukhlyadov, A.M.
Ryazhskiy, G.G.
Rylov, A.A.
Samokish, N.S.
Shadr, I.D.
Shchuko, V.A.
Shchusev, A.V.
Shervud, L.V.
Sokolov-Skalya, P.P.
Tamanyan, A.O.
Tenner, G.S.
Terlemezyan, P.P.
Toidze, M.I.
Toramanyan, T.
Trotskiy, N.A.
Trush, I.I.
Turzhanskiy, L.V.
Ul'yanov, N.P.
Vasnetsov, A.M.
Vasnetsov, V.M.
Vatagin, A.I.
Vereyskiy, G.S.
Vesnin, A.A.
Vesnin, L.A.
Vesnin, V.A.
Vinogradov, S.A.
Vladimirov, I.A.

Vlasov, A.V.
Volkov, Ye.Ye.
Volnukhin, S.M.
Volokidin, P.G.
Vornoskov, V.P.
Yakovlev, V.N.
Yaremich, S.P.
Yarovyy, M.M.
Yuon, K.F.
Zabolotnyy, V.I.
Zelenko, A.U.
Zholtovskiy, I.V.

3. Composers, Conductors, Performing Musicians, etc.

Aleksandrov, A.V.
Al'shvang, A.A.
Andreyev, V.V.
Arakishvili (Arakchiyev), D.I.
Arends, A.F.
Arenkov, K.M.
Arkad'yev, I.P.
Arkhangel'skiy, A.A.
Asaf'yev, B.V.
Avraamov, A.M.
Avranek, U.I.
Azmayparashvili, Sh.I.
Babayev, A.A.
Bagadurov, V.A.
Balanchivadze, M.A.
Balkashin, Yu.A.
Baramishvili, O.I.
Barvinskiy, V.A.
Bayetov, M.
Bikhter, M.A.
Blazhevich, V.M.
Blok, D.S.
Blumenfel'd, F.M.
Bogatyryov, S.S.
Boguslavskiy, K.Ye.
Braudo, Ye.M.
Bryusova, N.Ya.
Bugoslavskiy, S.A.
Buksha, M.M.
Bulychyov, V.A.
Chelyapov, N.I.
Cherkasskiy, E.D.
Chernetskiy, S.A.
Chernomordikov, D.A.
Chernov, M.M.
Chkhikvadze, Z.I.
Churkin, N.N.
Danilin, N.M.
Davidenko, A.A.
Davidovskiy, G.M.
Demutskiy, P.D.
Dem'yanov, N.I.
Dmitrevskiy, G.A.
Dobroveyn (Barabeychik), I.A.
Dogadin, A.A.
Dolidze, V.I.
Dolivo, A.L.
Dorliak, K.N.
Dranishnikov, V.A.
Dunayevskiy, I.O.
Dyoshevov, V.M.
Dzbanivskiy, A.T.
Ekkert, F.F.
Erdenko (Yardenko), M.G.
Eshpay (Ishpaykin), Ya.A.
Eykhenval'd, A.A.
Fel'dt, P.E.
Feynberg, S.Ye.
Fomin, N.P.
Frolov, M.P.
Fuks-Martin, G.S.
Gachev, D.I.
Gadzhibekov, U.A.G. ogly
Gadzhibekov, Z.A.G. ogly
Galynin, G.G.
Gasanov, G.A.
Gauk, A.V.
Gayday, Z.M.
Gaygerova, V.A.
Gedike, A.F.
Ginzburg, G.R.
Glazunov, A.K.
Glier, R.M.
Gnesin, M.F.
Gnesina, Ye.F.
Gol'denveyzer, A.B.
Golovanov, N.S.
Grigoryan, G.A.
Gruodis, Yu.M.
Gudkov, V.P.
Gulomaliyev, G.
Igumnov, K.N.
Ippolitov-Ivanov, M.M.
Ivanov-Boretskiy, M.V.
Ivanov-Radkevich, N.P.
Kalnyn, A.Ya.
Kapp, A.I.
Kastal'skiy, A.D.
Kaz'min, P.M.
Khamza, Kh. zade
Khessin, A.B.
Khodzha-Eynatov, L.A.
Khotkevich, G.M.
Kiladze, G.V.
Klimov, M.G.
Knushevitskiy, S.N.
Kochetov, N.R.
Kochurov, Yu.V.
Kolessa, F.M.
Kolotilova, A.Ya.
Konyus, G.E.
Korchmaryov, K.A.
Kosenko, V.S.
Kovalyova, O.V.
Kozolupov, S.M.
Krasev, M.I.
Kreyn, A.A.
Kreytner, G.G.
Krivonosov, V.M.
Kroshner, M.Ye.
Kruchinin, N.N.
Kuchugura-Kucherenko, I.Yo.
Kuper, E.A.
Kushnerik, F.D.
Kvitka, K.V.
Lamm, P.A.
Leontovich, N.D.
Litvinenko-Vol'gemut, M.I.
Magomayev, M.M.
Maksimov, S.M.
Margulyan, A.E.
Melik-Pashayev, A.Sh.
Metallov, V.M.
Metner, N.K.
Mil'ner, M.A.
Minayev, K.A.
Mostras, K.G.
Myaskovskiy, N.Ya.
Nebol'sin, V.V.
Nemtsev, I.V.
Neygauz, G.G.
Nezhdanova, A.V.
Niman, F.A.
Nyaga, S.T.
Oranskiy, V.A.
Orlov, A.I.
Osipov, N.P.
Ossovskiy, A.V.
Ovezov, D.
Paliashvili, I.P.
Paliashvili, P.P.
Paliashvili, Z.P.
Pavlov, F.P.
Pokhitonov, D.I.
Pokrass, D.Ya.
Polyakin, M.B.
Prokofiev, S.S.
Prokof'yev, V.A.
Pyatnitskiy, M.Ye.
Rautio, K.E.
Rayskiy, N.G.
Rimskaya-Korsakova, N.N.
Rimskiy-Korsakov, A.N.
Rimskiy-Korsakov, G.M.
Ryabov, A.P.
Shalyapin, F.I.
Shaporin, Yu.A.
Shebalin, V.Ya.
Shteynberg, M.O.
Sokolovskiy, N.F.
Svechin, A.G.
Taktakishvili, Sh.M.
Tallat-Kelpsha, I.A.
Tashmatov, O.
Tavrizian, M.A.
Ter-Gevondyan, A.G.
Tigranyan, A.T.
Tigranyan, N.
Timanova, V.V.
Toktogul, S.
Tolstoy, S.L.
Tolstyakov, P.N.
Troyanovskiy, B.S.
Tulebayev, M.T.
Turenkov, A.Ye.
Tuskiya, I.I.
Usenbayev, A.
Uspenskiy, V.A.
Vasilenko, S.N.
Vasil'yev-Buglay, D.S.
Verikovskiy, M.I.
Verkhovinets, V.N.
Vertinskiy, A.N.
Veryovka, G.G.
Veysberg, Yu.L.
Villuan, V.Yu.
Vitachek, Ye.F.
Vladimirov, M.V.
Vladimirova, M.V.

Voloshinov, V.V.
Vorob'yov, V.P.
Vygodskiy, N.Ya.
Yakovlev, V.V.
Yampol'skiy, A.I.
Yampol'skiy, M.I.
Yampol'skiy, V.Ye.
Yanovskiy, B.K.
Yan'shinov, A.I.
Yarkov, P.G.
Yaroslavenko, Ya.D.
Yastrebtsov, V.V.
Yatsinevich, Ya.M.
Yaushev, I.M.
Yavorskiy, B.L.
Yorish, V.Ya.
Yudin, M.A.
Yurasovskiy, A.I.
Yur'yan, P.A.
Zakharov, V.G.
Zarudnaya, V.M.
Zhilyayev, N.S.
Zhirkov, M.N.
Zhukov, M.N.
Zolotaryov, V.A.

4. Stage and Film Directors, Artists and Stage Designers

Abashidze, A.V.
Abashidze, V.A.
Abbasov, M.A.
Abdulov, O.N.
Abelyan, O.A.
Absalyamov, M.Sh.
Abzhalilov, Kh.G.
Afonin, G.I.
Aganbekyan, A.A.
Agdamskiy (Badalbeyli, A.B.)
Agranenko (Yerukhimovich), Z.M.
Akhmeteli, A.V.
Akhundov, S.R.F. ogly
Aksyonov, V.N.
Alekperov, A.G.A. ogly
Aleksandrov, N.G.
Alekseyev, V.S.
Aleksi-Meshishvili, V.S. (Alekseyev-Meskhiyev; Meskhishvili, L.)
Aleksyutovich, K.A.
Aleynikov, M.N.
Alikhanyan, I.S.
Aliyev, M.A.A. ogly
Al'medingen, B.A.
Amaglobeli, S.I.
Amtman, T.
Amtman-Briyedit (Amtmanis), A.F.
Andreyev, N.A.
Andreyev, P.Z.
Andreyeva (Yurkovskaya), M.F.
Andronikashvili, K.I.
Annenkova-Bernar, N.P.
Antonov, A.P.
Apollonskiy, R.B.
Arablinskiy (Khalafov), G.M.-ogly
Arapov, A.A.
Arbatov, I.I.
Arbatov (Arkhipov), N.N.
Ardarov (Bogdanovich), G.P.
Aristov, V.M.
Arkadin, I.I.
Armand, P.N.
Arsenko, A.D.
Arutyunyan, Kh.O.
Askochenskiy, A.K.
Aslanov, N.P.
Asmik (Akopyan), T.S.
Astangov (Ruzhnikov), M.F.
Avdeyev, A.D.
Avetyan, G.K.
Avlov, G.A.
Aydarov, S.Kh.
Aydarov (Vishnevskiy), S.V.
Aykazyan, V.N.
Ayvazyan, T.N.
Azarin (Messerer), A.N.
Babadzhanov, Ya.
Babiy, A.M.
Bakhrushin, A.A.
Bakhutashvili-Shul'gina, O.A.
Balaban, B.A.
Balanovskaya, L.N.
Ballyuzek, V.V.
Bantsan, R.F.
Barantsevich, Z.F.
Baratov, L.V.
Barkhudaryan, P.A.
Barnet, B.V.
Barskaya (Chardynina), M.A.
Barskiy, V.G.
Barsova (Vladimirova), V.V.
Baryshev, N.A.
Basov, O.N.
Basov, V.S.
Batalov, N.P.
Bayseitova, K.
Bek-Nazarov (Ambartsum), A.I.
Bek-Nazaryan, G.I.
Belinskiy, M.L.
Belousov, M.M.
Belov, G.A.
Bel'skaya, S.A.
Belyayev, S.A.
Benua, A.N.
Beresnev, N.Ya.
Berishvili, Z.I.
Bernotas, N.I.
Beroyan, M.G.
Bersenev (Pavlishchev), I.N.
Berzin, R.Ya.
Betskiy (Kobetskiy), M.A.
Beyer, V.I.
Bilibin, I.Ya.
Blagoobrazov, V.S.
Blinov, B.V.
Bliokh, Ya.M.
Blyumental'-Tamarina, M.M.
Bocharov, A.I.
Bogdankevich, V.I.
Bogdanovich, A.V.
Bol'shakov, N.A.
Bol'shintsov, M.V.
Bol'ska (Skompskaya), A.Yu.
Boltyanskiy, G.M.
Bonachich, A.P.
Bondarenko, F.P.
Bondi, Yu.M.
Borin-Shvartsman, B.A.
Borisevich, O.M.
Borisoglebskaya, A.I.
Borisov (Gurovich), B.S.
Boronikhin, Ye.A.
Bravin (Vasyatkin), N.M.
Brenko, A.A.
Brill' Ye.A.
Bryantsev, A.A.
Bubrik, S.D.
Buchma, A.M.
Bugayskiy, B.N.
Bulgakov, A.D.
Bulgakov, A.S.
Burdzhalov (Burdzhalyan), G.S.
Burdzhalyan, A.S.
Bure (Nebel'sen), V.A.
Bushkin, A.I.
Butorin, N.N.
Bykov, A.V.
Bykov, N.V.
Byul-Byul (Mamedov), R.-ogly
Chaplygin, N.N.
Cheban (Chebanov), A.I.
Chekhov, M.A.
Chekrygin, A.I.
Cherkasov, N.K.
Chernyshyova, L.S.
Chkheidze, N.P.
Chkheidze, U.V.
Dal'skaya, Ye.K.
Danielyan, A.B.
Danilevskaya, R.G.
Darskiy (Shavrov), M.Ye.
Dashkovskiy, N.A.
Dauguvetis, B.F.
Davidovskiy, K.A.
Davitashvili, N.Sh.
Davudova, M.Yu.-kyzy
Davydov (Levenson), A.M.
Davydov, V.N. (Gorelov, I.N.)
Demidenko, A.M.
Demutskiy, D.P.
Derzhavin, M.S.
Derzhinskaya, K.G.
Devlet, V.P.
Digmelov, A.D.
Dikiy, A.D.
Dmitriyev, I.I.
Dmitriyev, V.V.
Dneprov, M.I.
Dneprov, S.I.
Dobkevich, A.I.
Dobromyslov, D.K.
Dobronitskiy, V.V.
Dobronravov, B.G.
Dobuzhinskiy, M.V.
Dobzhinskiy, K.A.
Dolina (Gorenko), M.I.
Dolina (Popikov), P.T.
Doller, M.I.
Domashyova, M.P.
Donauri (Mardzhanishvili), Ye.I.
Donets, M.I.
Dorokhin, N.I.
Doroshevich, A.M.

Dovbishchenko, V.S.
Dovzhenko, A.P.
Dranishnikov, V.A.
Drozzhin, M.M.
Druzyakina, S.I.
Dubov, N.I.
Dubovik, L.F.
Dubrovskiy-Eshke, B.V.
Dudarev, D.A.
Durov, A.A.
Durov, V.L.
Dvorishchin, I.G.
Dybcho, S.A.
Dzhalilov, A.
Dzhanan (Dzhananyan), M.M.
Dzhavakhishvili, N.G.
Dzidzariya, K.F.
Ekskuzovich, I.V.
Engel'kron (Filippov), V.M.
Erdman, B.R.
Ermler, F.M.
Eyzenshteyn, S.M.
Fenster, B.A.
Feona, A.N.
Fetisova, L.M.
Figner, M.I.
Fride, N.A.
Fyodorovskiy, F.F.
Gabovich, M.M.
Gabriyelyan, G.B.
Gambashidze, Sh.K.
Gamrekeli, I.I.
Gamsakhurdiya, R.S.
Ganiyev, N.
Gardin, V.R.
Gavrilova, A.I.
Gaydeburov, P.P.
Gelovani, M.G.
Gel'tser, Ye.V.
Georgiyevskiy, A.G.
Gerasimchuk, L.P.
Getman, D.G.
Geyrot, A.A.
Giatsintov, A.M.
Giber, G.V.
Gikov, R.B.
Gizzat, T.
Glebov, G.P.
Glovatskiy, G.V.
Golovchiner, V.Ya.
Golubinskiy, D.M.
Gorchakov, N.M.
Gordon, K.V.
Gorskiy, A.A.
Goryunov, A.I.
Granovskiy, A.M.
Grekov, K.D.
Gribkov, V.V.
Gulakyan, A.K.
Gulomaliyev, G.
Gzovskaya, O.V.
Idayatzade, I.G. ogly
Il'inskiy, A.K.
Il'inskiy, A.V.
Ilovayskiy, S.D.
Imashev, T.-B.G.
Imedashvili, A.S.
Imedashvili, I.Z.
Isetskiy, L.N.
Ismailov, A.A. ogly
Ivanov, A.V.
Ivanov, L.G.
Ivanov-Barkov, Ye.A.
Ivanovskiy, N.P.
Kachalov, V.I.
Kalantar, L.A.
Kalinina, O.P.
Kanin, A.I.
Kardovskiy, D.N.
Karelina-Raich, R.A.
Kari-Yakubov, M.
Kariyev, A.
Kashakashvili, V.S.
Kastorskiy, V.I.
Kas'yanov, V.P.
Katul'skaya, Ye.K.
Kaverin, F.N.
Kavsadze, V.L.
Kazanskiy, G.
Khalyutina, S.V.
Khanson, B.B.
Khanzhonkov, A.A.
Kharazyan, A.G.
Khidoyatov, A.
Khmelyov, N.P.
Khokhlov, A.Ye.
Khokhlov, K.P.
Khovanskiy, A.P.
Khurshid, Sh.
Klimov, M.M.
Knipper-Chekhova, O.L.
Kolesnikov, N.N.
Komarov, S.P.
Komissarov, N.V.
Kondyryov, L.A.
Konstantinov, V.D.
Korchagina-Aleksandrovskaya, Ye.P.
Korf, R.G.
Korel'chuk, A.I.
Kostromskiy, N.F.
Kotlubay, K.I.
Koval-Samborskiy, I.I.
Kozhukhova, M.A.
Kozlovskiy, N.F.
Kramov, A.G.
Krasovskiy, I.F.
Krushel'nitskaya, S.A.
Krushel'nitskiy, M.M.
Kuchiyak, P.V.
Kurbas, A.S.
Kushitashvili, V.P.
Kustodiyev, B.M.
Kuznetsov, S.L.
Kuznetsov, Ye.M.
Lapitskiy, I.M.
Lavrovskiy, L.M.
Lazarenko, V.V.
Lazarenko, V.Ye.
Lebedev, V.N.
Leonidov, L.M.
Leont'yev, Ya.L.
Levandovskiy, V.V.
Libert, Ya.G.
Lilina, M.P.
Litovtseva, N.N.
Losskiy, V.A.
Loyter, E.B.
Luk'yanov, S.V.
Mardzhanishvili, K.A.
Marshak, N.Ya.
Mar'yanenko, I.A.
Maslovskaya, S.D.
Massalitinova, V.O.
Matsiyevskaya, L.V.
Maysuryan, O.M.
Mel'nikov, P.I.
Meshcherskaya, A.Ye.
Mestnikov, V.V.
Meyerkhol'd, V.E.
Michurina-Samoylova, V.A.
Mikhoels, S.M.
Mirovich, Ye.A.
Mirskiy, D.P.
Mordvinov, N.D.
Mosin, A.G.
Moskvin, I.M.
Muradyan, B.G.
Nardov, V.L.
Narokov, M.S.
Naydyonova, Ye.I.
Nazrullayev, L.
Nekrasova, O.V.
Nelepp, G.M.
Nelidov, A.P.
Nemirova-Ral'f, A.A.
Nemirovich-Danchenko, V.I.
Nersesyan, G.N.
Neshchadimenko, R.P.
Nikitin, N.A.
Obukhova, N.A.
Ognenko-Avanesov, K.P.
Okhlopkov, N.P.
Orlenev, P.N.
Orlov, D.N.
Ostuzhev, A.A.
Ozarovskaya, O.E.
Ozyorov, N.N.
Pagava, A.N.
Pan'kivskiy, S.F.
Pashennaya, V.N.
Patorzhinskiy, I.S.
Pazovskiy, A.M.
Peregonets, A.F.
Perestiani, I.N.
Perini, M.I.
Petlishenko, M.A.
Petrenko, Ye.F.
Petrov, N.V.
Petrusenko, O.A.
Pokrovskiy, A.V.
Politseymako, V.P.
Popov, A.D.
Popov, N.A.
Preobrazhenskaya, S.P.
Protazanov, Ya.A.
Pudovkin, V.I.
Radin, N.M.
Radlov, S.E.
Rafal'skiy, M.F.
Rakhmanova, O.V.
Randviyr, A.A.
Rigorin, G.D.
Romanov, M.F.
Rostovtsev, I.A.
Rozen-Sanin, M.N.
Rudin, Ya.M.
Rumyantsev, P.I.
Ryzhova, V.N.
Sadovskaya, O.O.
Sadovskaya, Ye.M.
Sadovskiy, N.K.
Sadovskiy, P.M.
Saksaganskiy, P.K.
Samosud, S.A.
Seryozhnikov, V.K.
Shalyapin, F.I.

Shanin, Zh.
Sharifzade, A.M.
Shchukin, B.V.
Shchuko, V.A.
Shengelaya, N.M.
Shifrin, N.A.
Simov, V.A.
Skorodumov, N.V.
Sobinov, L.V.
Sobol'shchikov-Samarin, N.I.
Stanislavskiy, K.S.
Staritskaya, M.M.
Sushkevich, B.M.
Tairov, A.Ya.
Takaishvili, A.A.
Tal'yan, Sh.M.
Tangiyeva-Birzniyek, Ye.A.
Tarkhanov, M.M.
Tashkenbayev, I.
Tashmatov, O.
Tautiyev, S.K.
Tazhdarova, N.A.
Telesheva, Ye.S.
Telyakovskiy, V.A.
Ter-Abramyan, A.Ye.
Ter-Davtyan, G.Z.
Teregulov, M.Kh.G.
Tereshkovich, M.A.
Terletskiy, S.I.
Tezavrovskiy, V.V.
Tikhomirov, V.D.
Tikhonov, P.I.
Tinchurin, K.
Tipot, V.Ya.
Tiraspol'skaya, N.L.
Tisse, E.K.
Titov, I.I.
Tobilevich, S.V.
Tokareva, M.A.
Tokmakov, Ye.A.
Totrov, B.I.
Totskiy, I.K.
Treplev, A.D.
Trifonov, R.M.
Tuganov, A.A.
Tunkel, D.V.
Tunkel, V.I.
Turchaninova, Ye.D.
Tveretsskiy, P.V.
Tverskoy, K.K.
Tyagno, B.F.
Tyumenbayev, Sh.
Tyurk, E.Yu.
Tyutyunnik, V.S.
Ul'vi, R.
Ul'yanov, N.P.
Umanskiy, M.B.
Urbanskiy, Ye.Ya.
Usachyov, A.A.
Ushakov, I.M.
Uygur, M.
Vachnadze, N.
Vaganova, A.Ya.
Vagarshyan, V.B.
Vakhtangov, Ye.B.
Vanin, V.V.
Varlamov, L.V.
Vartanyan, R.T.
Vasil'yev, G.N.
Vasil'yev, S.D.
Vatulya, A.M.
Vertinskiy, A.N.
Vertov, D.
Vesnin, A.A.
Vigner-Grindberg, M.
Vil'ner, V.B.
Vil'yams, P.V.
Vishnevskiy, A.L.
Viskovskiy, V.K.
Viv'yen, L.S.
Vladimirov, V.K.
Volkonskiy, N.O.
Volonenko, A.N.
Vorvulev, N.D.
Voskanyan, A.T.
Voskanyan, O.A.
Vul'f, P.L.
Vysotskiy, M.K.
Yablochkina, A.A.
Yakhontov, V.N.
Yakhshybayev, S.
Yaron, G.M.
Yefremov, I.S.
Yegorov, V.Ye.
Yegorov, Ye.Ye.
Yermolova, M.N.
Yerofeyev, V.A.
Yershov, I.V.
Yevreinov, N.N.
Yuknyavichyus, R.M.
Yung, K.M.
Yuon, K.F.
Yura, G.P.
Yureneva, V.L.
Yurovskiy, Yu.I.
Yur'yev, Yu.M.
Yuzhin, A.I.
Yyvan, K.
Zagarov, A.L.
Zakushnyak, A.Ya.
Zan'kovetskaya, M.K.
Zardalishvili, Yu.F.
Zatyrkevich-Karpinskaya, A.P.
Zaytsev, G.V.
Zaytsev, I.A.
Zhanto, V.A.
Zharko, Ya.V.
Zhdanovich, F.P.
Zhelyabuzhskiy, Yu.A.
Zhilina, Ye.Ye.
Zhukov, L.A.
Zhuravlenko, P.M.
Zimin, S.I.
Zorich, S.P.
Zrazhevskiy, A.I.
Zubov, K.A.
Zuskin, V.L.

JOURNALISTS, CORRESPONDENTS, EDITORS

Akhundov, R.A. ogly
Aksel'rod, T.L.
Antonov, V.G.
Baturin (Zamyatin), N.N.
Bazarov, V. (Rudnev, V.A.)
Belyakov, A.A.
Berdnikov, A.I.
Berlin, P.A.
Bespalov, I.M.
Bezdomnyy (Pelekhatov), K.N.
Blakitnyy (Yellanskiy), V.M.
Bonch-Bruyevich, V.D.
Borodin (Gruzenberg), M.M.
Brichkina, S.B.
Bubnov, A.S.
Bukharin, N.I.
Bulgakov, S.N.
Bystryanskiy, V.A.
Chagin (Boldovkin), P.I.
Chernyshyov, I.S.
Dauge, P.G.
Divil'kovskiy, A.A.
Donentayev, S.
Drabkina, F.I.
Endrup (Vidin), R.Ya.
Erenburg, I.G.
Fenigshteyn, Ya.G.
Gel'dyyev, A.
Grunt, Ya.Ya.
Il'in-Zhenevskiy, A.F.
Ingulov, S.B.
Iordanskiy, N.I.
Irchan, M.
Ivanov, S.N.
Ivanov, V.V.
Kabakchiyev, Kh.S.
Kamal, Sh.
Kanatchikov, S.I.
Karimi, F.
Karpinskiy, V.A.
Kolosov, A.I.
Kol'tsov, M.Ye.
Kon, F.Ya.
Kostrov, T.
Krumin, G.I.
Kutuzov, A.V.
Ladyzhnikov, I.P.
Landa, M.M.
Malkin, B.F.
Mikhaylov, L.M.
Mikhel's, V.A.
Minin, S.K.
Mordvinkin, V.Yu.
Nikoladze, N.Ya.
Pedanyuk, I.M.
Polikarpov, D.A.
Preykshas, K.K.
Radek, K.B.
Rakitny, S.
Raskol'nikov, F.F.
Savel'yev, M.A.
Shcherbakov, A.S.
Shotman, A.V.
Skvortsov-Stepanov, I.I.
Ul'yanova, M.I.
Umanskiy, K.A.

Vasilevskaya, V.L.
Vasil'yevskiy, V.N.
Vatin, V.A.
Vel'tman, M.L.
Volin, B.M.
Yakovlev, Ya.A.
Yaroslavskiy, Ye.M.
Yudin, P.F.
Zaks, S.M.
Zasulich, V.I.

PUBLIC HEALTH

Abashidze, E.K.
Abramovich, F.V.
Abrazhanov, A.A.
Abrikosov, A.I.
Adzhi-Mollayev, A.A.
Afanas'yev, V.A.
Akhutin, M.N.
Akimenko, I.P.
Al'bitskiy, P.M.
Aleksandrov, V.A.
Alekseyev, A.G.
Alibekov, A.K. ogly
Alibekov, S.Yu.
Aliyev, A.M.
Aliyev, M.I.
Alonov, Ye.F.
Alyakritskiy, V.V.
Alymov, A.Ya.
Andreyev, F.A.
Andreyev, F.F.
Andreyev, L.A.
Andreyev, P.N.
Andreyev, V.A.
Anichkov, N.N.
Anserov, N.I.
Arinkin, M.I.
Aristovskiy, V.M.
Arkhangel'skiy, B.A.
Arkin, Ye.A.
Asatiani, M.M.
Ashurkov, Ye.D.
Astakhov, N.A.
Astvatsaturov, M.I.
Atakhanov, E.I.
Averbakh, M.I.
Avtokratov, D.M.
Azbukin, D.I.
Babayants, R.A.
Bagdasarov, A.A.
Bagotskiy, S.Yu.
Bakulev, A.N.
Balodis, K.Ya.
Banaytis, S.I.
Barabanov, A.Ya.
Baranov, M.I.
Bardakh, Ya.Yu.
Barykin, V.A.
Batkis, G.A.
Bazhenov, N.N.
Bekaryukov, D.D.
Beklemishev, V.N.
Bekritskiy, A.A.
Belitser, A.V.
Bellyarminov, L.G.
Bereznegovskiy, N.I.
Bernshteyn, A.N.
Bernshteyn, N.A.
Beryozov, Ye.L.
Blumenau, L.V.
Bobrovskiy, V.S.
Bogayevskiy, A.T.
Bogdanov (Malinovskiy), A.A.
Bogdanov, N.N.
Bogolepov, A.A.
Bogomolets, A.A.
Bogoraz, N.A.
Bogoslovskiy, S.M.
Bokarius, N.S.
Bol, B.K.
Bol, K.G.
Bonch-Bruyevich (Velichkina), V.M.
Borovskiy, P.F.
Braytsev, V.R.
Brushteyn, S.A.
Brusilovskiy, L.Ya.
Brusilovskiy, Ye.M.
Bryukhonenko, S.S.
Brzhozovskiy, A.G.
Bublichenko, L.I.
Burdenko, N.N.
Burlachenko, G.A.
Butomo, V.G.
Butyagin, P.V.
Buyko, P.M.
Bykhovskiy, G.B.
Bykov, K.M.
Chagovets, V.Yu.
Charnyy, A.M.
Chentsov, V.V.
Chernomordik, S.I.
Chernorutskiy, M.V.
Chernyak, V.Z.
Chistovich, F.Ya.
Damskiy, A.Ya.
Danilevskiy, A.Ya.
Danilevskiy, V.Ya.
Danyushevskiy, I.I.
Darkshevich, L.O.
Dauge, P.G.
Davidenkov, S.N.
Dem'yanov, G.S.
Dem'yanovich, M.P.
Diatroptov, P.N.
Didrik, K.G.
Dillon, Ya.G.
Diterikhs, M.M.
Dmitrenko, L.F.
Dobrokhotov, M.S.
Dobrokhotova, A.I.
Dobromyl'skiy, F.I.
Dogel, A.S.
Dogel, V.A.
Dolgopolov, N.I.
Dolgo-Saburov, B.A.
Domrachyov, I.V.
Dosmukhamedov, Kh.D.
Dovgyallo, N.D.
Doynikov, B.S.
Drennova, K.A.
Drobot'ko, V.G.
Dudin, O.A.
Dvizhkov, P.P.
Dykhno, A.M.
Dyoshin, A.A.
Dzhanelidze, Yu.Yu.
Effendiyev, F.A.-ogly
Eliava, G.G.
Emdin, P.I.
Entin, D.A.
Epshteyn, G.V.
Favorskiy, A.V.
Faynshmidt, I.I.
Fedotov, N.P.
Fialkov (Naftulovich), Ya.A.
Figurnov, K.M.
Filatov, V.P.
Filippovich, A.N.
Fokht, A.B.
Fol'bort, G.V.
Frenkel, S.R.
Freyberg, N.G.
Fromgol'd, Ye.Ye.
Fronshteyn, R.M.
Frumina, A.Ye.
Frumkin, A.P.
Fyodorov, L.N.
Fyodorov, S.P.
Gal'pern, Ya.O.
Gamaleya, N.F.
Gannushkin, P.B.
Garshin, V.G.
Gel'shteyn, E.M.
Genter, G.G.
German, V.A.
Gertsen, P.A.
Get'ye, F.A.
Geymanovich, A.I.
Geymanovich, Z.I.
Gilyarovskiy, V.A.
Ginetsinskiy, A.G.
Giroglav, S.S.
Glavche, Ye.S.
Glazunov, M.F.
Glushkov, P.A.
Gnezdilov, V.G.
Gofung, Ye.M.
Golant, R.Ya.
Gol'dshteyn, D.Ye.
Golovin, S.S.
Gol'st, L.L.
Golubkov, A.P.
Gorash, V.A.
Gorinevskaya, V.V.
Gorinevskiy, V.V.
Gorodetskiy, A.A.
Gotlib, Ya.G.
Grachyova, Ye.K.
Gran, M.M.
Grashchenkov, N.I.
Grauerman, G.L.
Grechishchev, K.M.
Grekov, I.I.
Grigor'yev, P.S.

Grinberg, G.I.
Grinshteyn, A.M.
Gruzdev, V.S.
Gubarev, A.P.
Guber-Grits, D.S.
Gubergrits, M.M.
Gurevich, M.O.
Gurevich, N.I.
Gurvich, A.G.
Gusakov, G.V.
Ignatov, N.K.
Ignatovskiy, A.F.
Ignat'yev, V.Ye.
Il'chenko, P.Ya.
Il'in, F.N.
Il'in, L.F.
Ilovayskiy, S.A.
Imamaliyev, S.A.
Ioff, I.G.
Iordan, A.P.
Iosifov, G.M.
Iost, V.I.
Itsenko, N.M.
Ivakhnenko, G.S.
Ivanov, A.F.
Ivanov, G.F.
Ivanov, V.N.
Ivanov, V.V.
Ivanov, V.V.
Ivanov-Neznamov, V.I.
Ivanovskiy, B.A.
Ivanovskiy, D.I.
Ivanovskiy, P.M.
Ivashentsov, G.A.
Iyerusalimskiy, N.D.
Kadyrli, M.N.-ogly
Kalashnikov, V.P.
Kannabikh, Yu.V.
Kaplanskiy, S.Ya.
Kaplun, S.I.
Karuzin, P.I.
Kashchenko, V.P.
Katin-Yartsev, V.N.
Kats, Ya.Yu.
Katts, A.Ya.
Kedrovskiy, V.I.
Kekcheyev, K.Kh.
Khalatov, S.S.
Kharmandar'yan, G.I.
Khatenever, L.M.
Khlopin, G.V.
Khlopin, N.G.
Khmel'nitskiy, B.M.
Khodukin, N.I.
Khokhol, Ye.N.
Khol'tsov, B.N.
Khoroshko, V.K.
Khrisanfov, N.Ye.
Kinshidze, N.A.
Kireyev, M.P.
Kisel, A.A.
Klimov, N.N.
Klumov, Ye.V.
Klyuss, I.A.
Kogan, B.B.
Kogan-Yasnyy, V.M.
Kolokolov, V.G.
Kolosov, A.A.
Kolosov, M.A.
Koltypin, A.A.
Komendantov, L.Ye.
Konchalovskiy, M.P.
Konovalov, N.V.
Kopel'man, S.L.
Kopp, I.F.
Korchak-Chepurkovskiy, A.V.
Korshun, S.V.
Koshtoyants, Kh.S.
Kost, N.A.
Krainskiy, N.V.
Kramer, V.V.
Krasnobayev, T.P.
Krasnushkin, Ye.K.
Kravkov, N.P.
Kravkov, S.V.
Krestovnikov, A.N.
Krichevskiy, A.M.
Krogius, A.A.
Krol, M.B.
Krontovskiy, A.A.
Krymov, A.P.
Kryukov, A.N.
Kuchaidze, G.L.
Kucherenko, P.A.
Kulikovskiy, G.G.
Kulyabko, A.A.
Kupalov, P.S.
Kupriyanov, P.A.
Kurashov, S.V.
Kurkin, P.I.
Kurlov, M.G.
Kurlyandskaya, E.B.
Kuvshinnikov, P.A.
Ladygina-Kots, N.N.
Lampert, F.M.
Lang, G.F.
Lashas, V.L.
Latyshev, N.I.
Lavrent'yev, B.I.
Lazarenko, F.M.
Lebedev, N.Ye.
Lebedev, V.N.
Lebedevskiy, B.N.
Lebedinskiy, A.V.
Lemberskiy, B.A.
Leontovich, A.V.
Lepeshinskaya, O.B.
Leporskiy, N.I.
Levin, L.G.
Levit, V.S.
Likhachyov, A.A.
Lisovskaya, S.N.
Lubotskiy, D.N.
Luka (Voyno-Yasenetskiy, V.F.)
Lukomskiy, I.G.
Lunin, N.I.
Lur'ye, A.Yu.
Lur'ye, M.S.
Lysenkov, N.K.
Mamaladze, G.P.
Man'kovskiy, B.N.
Marzeyev, A.N.
Markaryan, M.G.
Markelov, G.I.
Martsinovskiy, Ye.I.
Martynov, A.V.
Maslov, M.S.
Maslov, P.N.
Medovikov, P.S.
Melkikh, S.M.
Mel'nikov, A.V.
Mel'nikov-Razvedenkov, N.F.
Meshchaninov, A.I.
Meshcherskiy, G.I.
Metallikov, M.S.
Mikhaylovskiy, S.V.
Miloslavskiy, V.V.
Minor, L.S.
Mir-Kasimov, M.A.M.A. ogly
Mirotvortsev, S.R.
Mirza-Avakyan, U.G.
Mislavskiy, A.A.
Mislavskiy, A.N.
Mislavskiy, N.A.
Mitskevich, S.I.
Mogil'nitskiy, B.N.
Molchanov, V.I.
Mol'kov, A.V.
Molokhov, A.N.
Morozkin, N.I.
Morozov, M.A.
Morzon, V.O.
Mukhadze, G.M.
Murashyov, G.V.
Muromtsev, S.N.
Musabekov, G.M. ogly
Myasnikov, A.L.
Mysh, V.M.
Napalkov, N.I.
Nasonov, D.N.
Natadze, G.M.
Natishvili, A.N.
Nechayev, A.A.
Nechayev, A.P.
Nemenov, M.I.
Nikitinskiy, Ya.Ya.
Nikolayev, M.P.
Nikolayev, V.V.
Nikol'skiy, D.P.
Nikol'skiy, P.V.
Novachenko, N.P.
Novosel'skiy, S.A.
Obraztsov, V.P.
Obukh, V.A.
Odyozhkin, N.M.
Okinchits, L.L.
Okunevskiy, Ya.L.
Oppel, V.A.
Orlov, K.Kh.
Osipov, V.P.
Ozeretskiy, N.I.
Ozertskovskiy, A.I.
Pal'chevskiy, Ye.I.
Pavlinov, K.M.
Pavlov, I.P.
Pavlovskiy, A.D.
Pavlovskiy, Ye.N.
Perevodchikov, I.N.
Petchenko, A.I.
Petrov, N.N.
Petrova, M.K.
Pevzner, M.I.
Pisemskiy, G.F.
Pletnyov, D.D.
Pletnyova, N.A.
Pokrovskiy, A.I.
Polenov, A.L.
Polonskiy, S.M.
Polosukhin, A.P.
Popov, N.V.
Postovskaya, M.P.
Pravdin, N.S.
Priorov, N.N.
Protopopov, V.P.
Prozorov, L.A.
Radin, Ye.P.

Radziyevskiy, A.G.
Ragoza, N.I.
Ratner, L.M.
Rauer, A.E.
Ravich-Shcherbo, V.A.
Rayskiy, M.I.
Razdol'skiy, I.Ya.
Razenkov, I.P.
Razumovskiy, V.I.
Reprev, A.V.
Reyn, F.A.
Reynberg, S.A.
Rikhter, G.E.
Rimsha, K.I.
Romanovskiy, D.L.
Roskin, G.I.
Rossiyskiy, D.M.
Rossolimo, G.I.
Rozanov, V.N.
Rozenberg, N.K.
Rozenshteyn, L.M.
Rozhanskiy, N.A.
Rubashkin, V.Ya.
Rubel, A.N.
Rubinshteyn, G.R.
Rufanov, I.G.
Rukhadze, N.P.
Rumyantsev, A.V.
Rusakov, A.V.
Rusanov, A.G.
Russel-Sudzilovskiy, N.K.
Rutenburg, D.M.
Samarin, N.N.
Samoylov, A.F.
Samsonov, P.F.
Sanotskiy, V.A.
Sapozhkov, K.P.
Sapozhkov, P.I.
Sargin, K.D.
Savchenko, I.G.
Savich, V.V.
Savinykh, A.G.
Savvin, V.N.
Selitskiy, S.A.
Sel'tsovskiy, P.L.
Semashko, N.A.
Semeka, S.A.
Sepp, Ye.K.
Sereyskiy, M.Ya.
Shakhbazyan, Ye.S.
Shereshevskiy, N.A.
Shervinskiy, V.D.
Shevkunenko, V.N.
Shirokogorov, I.I.
Shklyar, B.S.
Shlapoberskiy, V.Ya.
Shogam, A.N.
Shul'ts, E.G.
Sipovskiy, P.V.
Sitenko, M.I.
Skinin, G.V.
Skvortsov, M.A.
Smirnova-Zamkova, A.I.
Sokolov, N.V.
Solov'yov, A.A.
Solov'yov, Z.P.
Spasokukotskiy, S.I.
Speranskiy, A.D.
Speranskiy, G.N.
Speranskiy, I.I.
Strashun, I.D.
Strazhesko, N.D.
Strel'tsov, V.V.
Svirezhev, M.V.
Sysin, A.N.
Talalayev, V.T.
Tarasevich, L.A.
Terebinskiy, N.N.
Ternovskiy, S.D.
Tezyakov, N.I.
Tikhomirov, P.Ye.
Timofeyevskiy, P.I.
Tonkov, V.N.
Tret'yakov, A.F.
Tret'yakov, K.N.
Triumfov, A.V.
Trusevich, B.I.
Trutnev, V.K.
Tsinzerling, V.D.
Tsitovich, I.S.
Tsulukidze, A.P.
Turner, G.I.
Tushinskiy, M.D.
Udintsev, F.A.
Uglov, V.A.
Ulezko-Stroganova, K.P.
Ul'yanov, D.I.
Undrits, V.F.
Ushinskiy, N.G.
Uspenskiy, V.V.
Valedinskiy, I.A.
Varlakov, M.N.
Vasil'yev, L.L.
Vedrov, N.S.
Vel'yaminov, N.A.
Venderovich, Ye.L.
Vermel, S.B.
Vershinin, N.V.
Veysbrod, B.S.
Vinogradov, V.N.
Vinokurov, A.N.
Virsaladze, S.S.
Vishnevskiy, A.V.
Viskovskiy, S.V.
Volkonskaya, S.N.
Volkov, K.V.
Volkovich, N.M.
Vorob'yov, A.M.
Vorob'yov, V.A.
Vorob'yov, V.P.
Vorontsov, D.S.
Voskresenskiy, P.I.
Vovsi, M.S.
Voytkevich, A.F.
Vreden, R.R.
Vvedenskiy, I.N.
Vvedenskiy, N.Ye.
Yanovskiy, A.K.
Yanovskiy, F.G.
Yanovskiy, M.V.
Yarotskiy, A.I.
Yegorov, P.I.
Yelanskiy, N.N.
Yeliseyev, V.G.
Yemchenko, A.I.
Yudin, S.S.
Yudin, T.I.
Yushchenko, A.I.
Zabludovskiy, A.M.
Zabolotnyy, D.K.
Zalesskiy, G.D.
Zavarzin, A.A.
Zaydshnur, I.A.
Zbarskiy, B.I.
Zdravomyslov, V.M.
Zelenev, N.A.
Zelyonyy, G.P.
Zhislin, S.G.
Zhukovich, A.V.
Zhuravlyov, P.M.
Zil'ber, L.A.
Zlatogorov, S.I.
Zuyev, A.Yu.
Zyukov, A.M.

YOUTH AND MASS ORGANIZATIONS

1. Executive Officials of Komsomol and of Other Youth Organizations

Alekseyev, V.P.
Boychenko, A.M.
Chaplin, N.P.
Golovach, P.R.
Il'in, Ya.N.
Khitarov, R.M.
Khoruzhaya, V.Z.
Kosarev, A.V.
Krupskaya, N.K.
Rakhmanov, G.P. ogly
Ryvkin, O.L.
Shatskin, L.A.
Tregubenko, A.F.
Tret'yakevich, V.I.
Volkovich, D.I.
Zemlyanskiy, D.S.
Zemnukhov, I.A.

2. Outstanding Sportsmen

Alyokhin, A.A.
Dolgov, P.I.
Ragozin, V.V.
Troitskiy, A.A.
Zaikin, I.M.

3. Executive Officials of the Trade Union

Abolin, A.K.
Agranovskiy, L.S.
Akulov, I.A.
Amosov, A.M.
Anikst, A.M.
Antipov, N.K.
Antselovich, N.M.
Artyom (Sergeyev), F.A.
Avilov, N.P.
Bagayev, M.A.
Baltagulov, T.B.
Blyakhin, P.A.
Boguslavskiy, M.S.
Bosh, Ye.B.
Boyarskiy, Ya.O.
Chirkin, V.G.
Chubar, V.Ya.
Chuvyrin, M.Ye.
Derbyshev, N.I.
Dogadov, A.I.
Figatner, Yu.P.
Fyodorov, G.F.
Gladkiy, D.S.
Gol'tsman, A.Z.
Gorbachyov, Ye.G.
Ignatov, Ye.N.
Ivanov, B.I.
Ivanov, N.I.
Kaminskiy, G.N.
Kirkizh, K.O.
Kiselyov, A.S.
Kornyushin, F.D.
Korostelev, A.A.
Kubyak, N.A.
Kutuzov, I.I.
Kuybyshev, V.V.
Lepse, I.I.
Lozovskiy, S.A.
Lutovinov, Yu.Kh.
Lyubovich, A.M.
Makhlin, L.D.
Markov, A.T.
Marshev, M.L.
Medvedev, S.P.
Mel'nichanskiy, G.N.
Mikhaylov, V.M.
Mirzoyan, L.I.
Moroz, G.S.
Nikolayeva, K.I.
Nurutdinov, S.
Panyunin, A.T.
Perepechko, I.N.
Pokrovskiy, A.V.
Polonskiy, V.I.
Pyatnitskiy, I.A.
Radchenko, A.F.
Radus-Zen'kovich, V.A.
Reynshteyn, B.I.
Rimsha, K.I.
Rudzutak, Ya.E.
Sadovskiy, A.D.
Sapronov, T.V.
Sazhin, I.G.
Semkov, S.M.
Shkiryatov, M.F.
Shlyapnikov, A.G.
Shmidt, V.V.
Shumskiy, A.Ya.
Shvarts, I.I.
Striyevskiy, K.K.
Sukhomlin, K.V.
Tairov, A.Ya.
Tashkin, A.M.
Tolokontsev, A.F.
Tomskiy, M.P.
Tunkel, V.I.
Ugarov, F.Ya.
Vakar, V.V.
Veprintsev, P.A.
Veynberg, P.A.
Vishnyakova, P.I.
Voinov, A.I.
Yaglom, Ya.K.
Yegorova, Ye.I.
Yevreinov, N.N.
Yunov, Yu.M.
Yuzefovich, I.S.
Zaslavskiy, P.S.
Zheltov, I.I.

4. Officials of Other Mass Organizations

Aladzhalova, N.N.
Alibekov, S.Yu.
Arosev, A.Ya.
Arzumanyan, A.A.
Barsova (Vladimirova), V.V.
Bednyakov, K.N.
Belitskiy, S.M.
Belotskiy, M.L.
Belov, P.A.
Cherkasov, N.K.
Chernomordik, S.I.
Dinamov, S.S.
Dobrodzhanu-Gerya (Dobrogeanu-Gherea), A.
Drabkina, F.I.
Eydeman, R.P.
Fadeyev (Bulyga), A.A.
Gedris, K.Yu.
Grekov, B.D.
Grishashvili, I.G.
Kost, N.A.
Kuznetsov, V.I.Kuznetsov, V.I.
Lepeshinskiy, P.N.
Mamed'yarov, M.
Markhlevskiy (Marchlewski), Yu.Yu.
Min'kov, M.I.
Mitskyavichyus-Kapsukas, V.S.
Moyrova, V.A.
Natishvili, A.N.
Nikolayev, A.M.
Nurutdinov, S.
Rudnev, L.V.
Ruzhitskiy, K.I.
Sitenko, M.I.
Solov'yov, Z.P.
Stasova, Ye.D.
Tairov, A.Ya.
Tychina, P.G.
Zhmachenko, F.F.

RELIGION

1. Clergy

Agafangel (Preobrazhenskiy, A.L.)
Amvrosiy (Khelaiya)
Andrey (Sheptitskiy, R.-M.)
Antoniy (Pel'vetskiy)
Boris (Vik, B.I.)
Budkevich, K.
Chekhovskoy, V.M.
Dorzhiyev, A.
Flavian (Ivanov, V.L.)
Germogen (Kozhin, V.V.)
Grigoriy (Chukov, N.K.)
Guriy (Yegorov, V.M.)
Innokentiy (Sokal', I.I.)
Ioann (Ivanov, I.S.)
Ioann-Baptist (Tseplyak)
Ioasaf (Zhurmanov, A.Ye.)
Iosafat (Kozilovskiy, I.)
Iosif (Orekhov, I.S.)
Isaiya (Kovalyov, V.D.)
Kolchitskiy, N.F.
Kostel'nik, G.

Luka (Voyno-Yasenetskiy, V.F.)
Makariy (Dayev, S.)
Makariy (Oksiyuk, M.F.)
Mazhelis, P.
Melkhisedek (Payevskiy, M.)
Melkhisedek (Pkhaladze, M.)
Mitrofan (Gutkovskiy)
Nikandr (Vol'yanikov)
Nikolay (Boretskiy)
Nikolay (Chernetskiy)
Pyotr (Polyanskiy, P.F.)
Pyotr (Strod)
Roman (Tang)
Ruzhitskiy, K.I.
Serafim (Luk'yanov, A.I.)
Sergiy (Kostin, V.)
Sergiy (Starogorodskiy, I.N.)
Stefan (Nikitin, S.A.)
Stefan (Protsenko)
Tikhon (Bellavon, V.I.)
Toviya (Ostroukhov, A.I.)
Varfolomey (Gorodtsev, S.D.)
Varsonofiy (Grinevich, K.D.)
Vasiliy (Lipkovskiy, V.)
Viktor (Svyatin, L.)
Vostorgov, I.I.

2. Anti-Religious Functionaries

Bonch-Bruyevich, V.D.
Krasikov, P.A.
Osipov, A.A.
Yaroslavskiy, Ye.M.

RESISTANCE

1. Politicians of Opposition and Other Parties, Factions and Alliances

Abramovich (Reyn), R.A.
Aksel'rod (Ortodoks), L.I.
Aksel'rod, P.B.
Aleksandra Fyodorovna
Aleksandrova, Ye.M.
Aptekman, O.V.
Argunov (Voronovich), A.A.
Ashenbrenner, M.Yu.
Avilov, B.V.
Avksent'yev, N.D.
Ayzenshtadt (Yudin), I.L.
Azanchevskaya, S.V.
Bakhmet'yev, B.A. (Nikol'skiy, N.)
Balabanov, M.S.
Balabanova, A.I.
Bekrenev, V.P.
Belen'kiy, G.Ya.
Berkengeym, A.M.
Bicherakhov, G.F.
Binasik, M.S.
Bitsenko, A.A.
Bobrishchev-Pushkin, A.V.
Bogayevskiy, A.P.
Bogayevskiy, M.P.
Boguslavskiy, M.S.
Bramson, L.M.
Breshko-Breshkovskaya, Ye.K.
Brutskus, B.D.
Bukharin, N.I.
Bulgakov, S.N.
Burtsev, V.L.
Bychkov, A.I.
Chaykovskiy, N.V.
Chekhovskoy, V.M.
Chernov, V.M.
Chichinadze, N.G.
Chkheidze, N.S.
Dalin (Levin), D.Yu.
Dan (Gurvich), F.I.
Dan, L.O.
Daniel'son, N.F.
Deych (Yevgen'yev), L.G.
Dobruskina (Mikhaylova), G.N.
Dolgorukov, P.D.
Donskoy, D.D.
Drey, M.I.
Dukhonin, N.N.
Dzyubinskiy, V.I.
Figner (Filippova), V.N.
Finn-Yenotayevskiy, A.Yu.
Frederiks, V.B.
Frolenko, M.F.
Gal'bershtadt, R.S.
Gedeonovskiy, A.V.
Gegechkori, Ye.P.
Gekker, N.L.
Gessen, I.V.
Ginzburg, B.A.
Gol'denberg, I.P.
Golitsyn, N.D.
Golubovich, V.A.
Gomarteli, I.G.
Gorev, B.I.
Gots, A.R.
Grushevskiy, M.S.
Guchkov, A.I.
Igant'yev, V.I
Ikov, V.K.
Ionov, F.M.
Kamenev, L.B.
Kamkov, B.D.
Karelin, V.A.
Kishkin, N.M.
Kizevetter, A.A.
Klyuchnikov, Yu.V.
Kolegeyev, A.L.
Korzinov, G.N.
Kosior, V.V.
Koval'skaya, Ye.N.
Kozhevnikov, V.V.
Krokhmal, V.N.
Kropotkin, P.A.
Kuskova, Ye.D.
Kutler, N.N.
Kuz'min-Karavayev, V.D.
Liber, M.I.
Lobanov, M.I.
Lokerman, A.S.
Lordkipanidze, G.S.
Lutovinov, Yu.Kh.
L'vov, N.N.
L'vov, V.N.
Makhayskiy, Ya.-V.K.
Maksimovskiy, V.N.
Martov, L.
Martynov, A.S.
Medvedev, S.P.
Melenevskiy, M.I.
Mel'gunov, S.P.
Mgeladze, I.V.
Milyukov, P.N.
Min'kov, M.I.
Mogilyanskiy, M.
Mrachkovskiy, S.V.
Muralov, N.I.
Murav'yov, M.A.
Myasnikov, G.I.
Nabokov, V.D.
Naumov, I.K.
Nicholas II (Romanov, N.A.)
Nikoladze, N.Ya.
Okladskiy, I.F.
Orlov, K.N.
Osinskiy, N.
Pankratov, V.S.
Perimov, A.V.
Pikel, R.V.
Plekhanov, G.V.
Potresov, A.N.
Preobrazhenskiy, Ye.A.
Prokopovich, S.N.
Protopopov, A.D.
Prugavin, A.S.
Pyatakov, G.L.
Radek, K.B.
Rakovskiy, Kh.G.
Ramishvili, I.I.
Ramishvili, N.V.
Ravich, S.N.
Rays, I.
Rozanov, V.N.
Rozengol'ts, A.P.
Rozhkov, N.A.
Romanov, S.M.
Rumyantsev, V.V.
Rusanov, N.S.
Rutenberg, P.M.
Ruzskiy, N.V.
Rykov, A.I.
Safarov, G.I.
Sakvarelidze, P.D.

Sapronov, T.V.
Sazhin, M.P.
Serebryakov, L.P.
Serebryakova, A.Ye.
Shatskin, L.A.
Shatskiy, N.N.
Shchastnyy, A.M.
Shcheglovitov, I.G.
Shchepkin, N.N.
Shingaryov, A.I.
Shlyapnikov, A.G.
Skveri, M.P.
Smilga, I.T.
Smirnov, I.N.
Smirnov, V.M.
Sokolov, G.V.
Sositskiy, L.I.
Spiridonova, M.A.
Struve, P.B.
Stukov, I.N.
Sultan-Galiyev, M.
Ter-Gazaryan, G.G.
Ter-Vaganyan, V.A.
Tikhomirov, L.A.
Tolmazov, A.I.
Tomskiy, M.P.
Topuridze, D.A.
Trotskiy, L.D.
Tsereteli, I.G.
Tuchapskiy, P.L.
Tugan-Baranovskiy, M.I.
Tuntul, I.Ya.
Ufimtsev, N.I.
Uglanov, N.A.
Uratadze, G.I.
Ustryalov, N.V.
Vardin, I.V.
Velikhov, L.A.
Vikhlyayev, P.A.
Vinaver, M.M.
Vinogradov, A.K.
Volobuyev, M.
Vorob'yov, V.A.
Yakimova, A.V.
Yakovleva, V.N.
Yefremov, S.A.
Yermanskiy, O.A.
Yevdokimov, G.Ye.
Yuskin, I.G.
Zaks, G.D.
Zalutskiy, P.A.
Zasulich, V.I.
Zenzinov, V.M.
Zhakov, M.P.
Zhordaniya, N.N.
Zinov'yev, G.Ye.
Zorin-Gomberg, S.S.
Zvezdov, V.I.

2. Leading Figures in the Armed Resistance to the Soviet Regime

Aleksandrovich (Dmitriyevskiy), V.A.
Alekseyev, M.V.
Annenkov, B.V.
Antonov, A.S.
Antonov, N.S.
Bicherakhov, L.F.
Boldyryov, V.G.
Bulak-Balakhovich, S.N.
Chekhovskoy, V.M.
Chernov, V.M.
Chuprynka, G.A.
Denikin, A.I.
Diteriks, M.K.
Dreytser, Ye.A.
Drozdovskiy, M.G.
Dubrovin, A.I.
Dutov, A.I.
Funtikov, F.A.
Fyodorov, M.M.
Gendel'man, M.Ya.
Glazenap, P.V.
Gotsinskiy, N.
Grigor'yev, N.A.
Grishin-Almazov, A.N.
Ignat'yev, V.I.
Isuv, I.A.
Kaledin, A.M.
Kappel, V.O.
Karelin, V.A.
Khanik, L.O.
Kolchak, A.V.
Konopleva, L.V.
Kornilov, L.G.
Kotolynov, I.I.
Kraskov, P.N.
Krivoshein, A.V.
Kutepov, A.P.
Kuz'min-Karavayev, V.D.
Levin, V.S.
Levitskiy-Tsederbaum, V.O.
Lianozov, S.G.
Lukomskiy, A.S.
Lyakhov, V.P.
Makhno, N.I.
Malinovskiy, R.V.
Mamontov, K.K.
Mandel'shtam, S.O.
May-Mayevskiy, V.Z.
Miller, Ye.K.
Myasnikov, N.P.
Nikolayev, L.V.
Pal'chinskiy, P.I.
Perkhurov, A.P.
Peshekhonov, A.V.
Petlyura, S.V.
Polkovnikov, G.P.
Prosh'yan, P.P.
Purishkevich, V.M.
Rodzyanko, M.V.
Ryabtsev, K.I.
Sapozhkov
Savinkov, B.V.
Sazonov, S.D.
Semyonov, G.I.
Semyonov, G.M.
Shkuro, A.G.
Skoropadskiy, P.P.
Slashchyov, Ya.A.
Tagantsev, V.N.
Tikhvinskiy, M.M.
Timofeyev, Ye.M.
Vedenyapin, M.A.
Vlasov, A.A.
Vrangel, P.N.
Yudenich, N.N.